RAND McNALLY

Houston
street guide

TELL US WHAT YOU THINK
comment card on last page

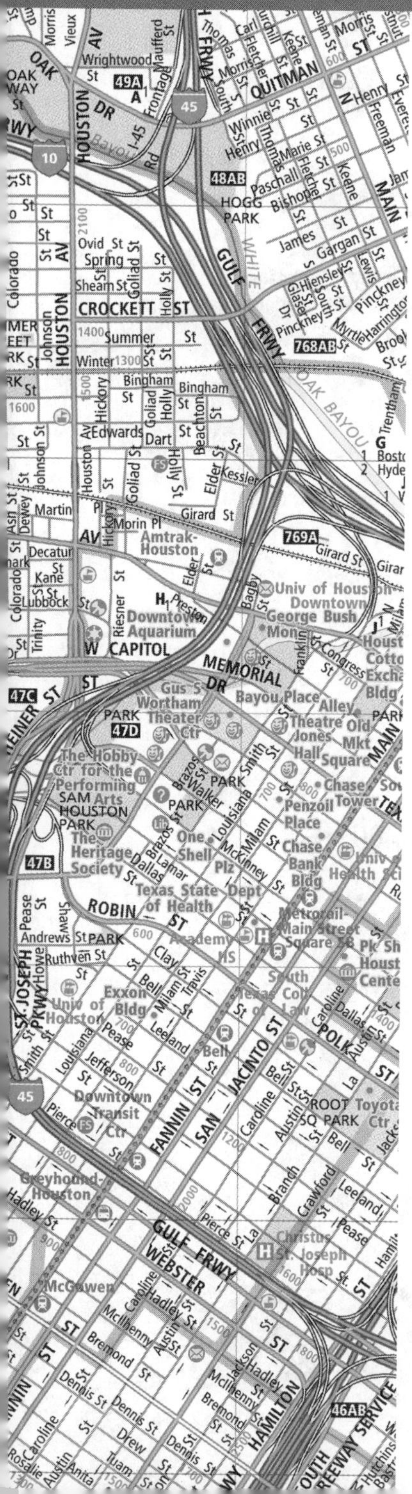

HOUSTON AV
Wrightwood St
49A
45
10
I-45
QUITMAN
48AB
HOGG PARK
GULF FRWY
WHITE OAK BAYOU
CROCKETT ST
Summer St
Winter St
Bingham
Edwards
Dart St
Girard St
Kessler
Martin
AV
Morin Pl
Amtrak-Houston
769A
768AB
Decatur
Kane
Lubbock St
Downtown Aquarium
W CAPITOL
Univ of Houston Downtown
George Bush Mon
MEMORIAL DR
Bayou Place
Gus S Wortham Theater Ctr
PARK
47D
47C
47B
Jones Hall
Alley Theatre
Old Mkt Square
The Hobby Ctr for the Performing Arts
SAM HOUSTON PARK
The Heritage Society
Penzoil Place
Chase Tower
One Shell Plz
Chase Bank Bldg
Texas State Dept of Health
Metrorail-Main Street Square
ROBIN ST
Academy HS
Exxon Bldg
Univ of Houston
Downtown Transit Ctr
FANNIN ST
SAN JACINTO ST
POLK ST
ROOT SQ PARK
Toyota Ctr
Greyhound-Houston
GULF FRWY
WEBSTER ST
Christus St. Joseph Hosp
HAMILTON
46AB

Contents

Introduction

Using Your Street Guide A

PageFinder™ Map B

Legend D

We've Got You Covered E

Maps

Downtown Map F

Street Guide Detail Maps 2236–5654

Vicinity Map Inside back cover

Lists and Indexes

Cities & Communities Index 1

List of Abbreviations 2

Street Index and Points of Interest Index 3

Comment Card Last page

D1206590

PageFinder™ Map U.S. Patent No. 5,419,586
Canadian Patent No. 2,116,425
Patente Mexicana No. 188186

RAND McNALLY
Rand McNally Consumer Affairs
P.O. Box 7600
Chicago, IL 60680-9915
randmcnally.com

For comments or suggestions, please call
(800) 777-MAPS (-6277)
or email us at:
consumeraffairs@randmcnally.com

NAVTEQ ON BOARD™

Legend

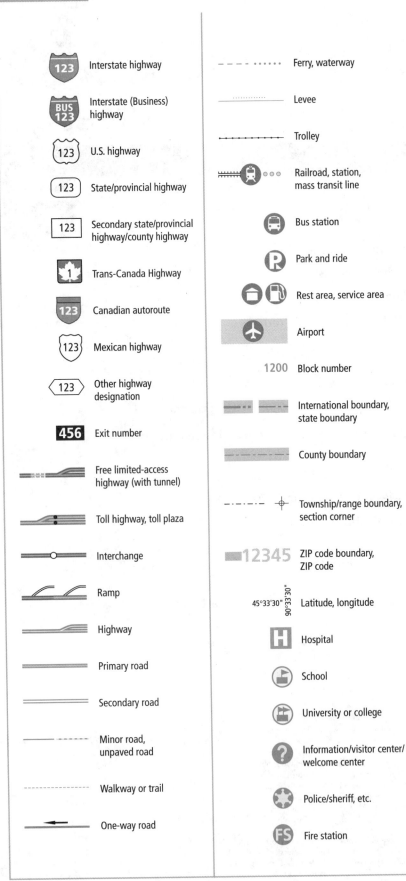

- 123 Interstate highway
- BUS 123 Interstate (Business) highway
- 123 U.S. highway
- 123 State/provincial highway
- 123 Secondary state/provincial highway/county highway
- 1 Trans-Canada Highway
- 123 Canadian autoroute
- 123 Mexican highway
- 123 Other highway designation
- 456 Exit number
- Free limited-access highway (with tunnel)
- Toll highway, toll plaza
- Interchange
- Ramp
- Highway
- Primary road
- Secondary road
- Minor road, unpaved road
- Walkway or trail
- One-way road

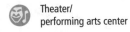

- Ferry, waterway
- Levee
- Trolley
- Railroad, station, mass transit line
- Bus station
- Park and ride
- Rest area, service area
- Airport
- 1200 Block number
- International boundary, state boundary
- County boundary
- Township/range boundary, section corner
- 12345 ZIP code boundary, ZIP code
- 45°33'30" 90°33'30" Latitude, longitude
- Hospital
- School
- University or college
- Information/visitor center/welcome center
- Police/sheriff, etc.
- FS Fire station

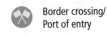

- City/town/village hall and other government buildings
- Courthouse
- Post office
- Lib Library
- Museum
- Border crossing/Port of entry
- Theater/performing arts center
- Golf course
- Other point of interest

we've got you COVERED

Rand McNally's broad selection of products is perfect for your every need. Whether you're looking for the convenience of write-on wipe-off laminated maps, extra maps for every car, or a Road Atlas to plan your next vacation or to use as a reference, Rand McNally has you covered.

Street Guides

Get Around® Houston Street Atlas
Houston
Montgomery County

Folded Maps

EasyFinder® Laminated Maps
Houston
Houston & Vicinity
Texas

Paper Maps
Conroe & Lake Conroe
Galveston/Texas City
Houston
Houston & Vicinity
North Suburban Houston/The Woodlands
Northeast Suburban Houston
Northwest Suburban Houston
Pasadena/Baytown
South Suburban Houston/Pearland & Friendswood
Southwest Suburban Houston/Missouri City & Sugar Land
Texas

Road Atlases

Texas Road Atlas
Road Atlas
Road Atlas & Travel Guide
Large Scale Road Atlas
Midsize Road Atlas
Deluxe Midsize Road Atlas
Pocket Road Atlas

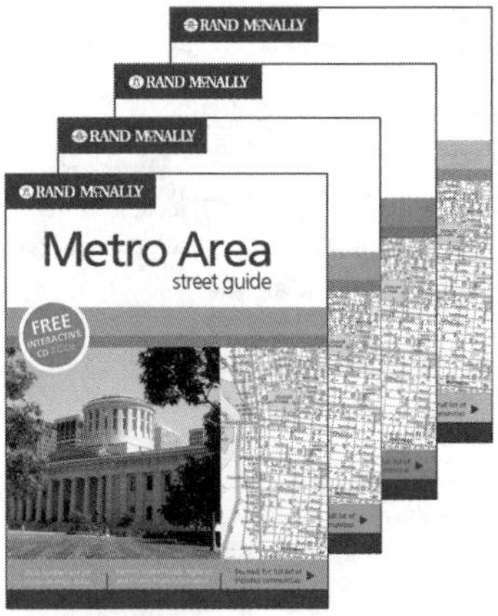
RAND McNALLY
Metro Area
street guide
FREE

Metro Area

Downtown Houston

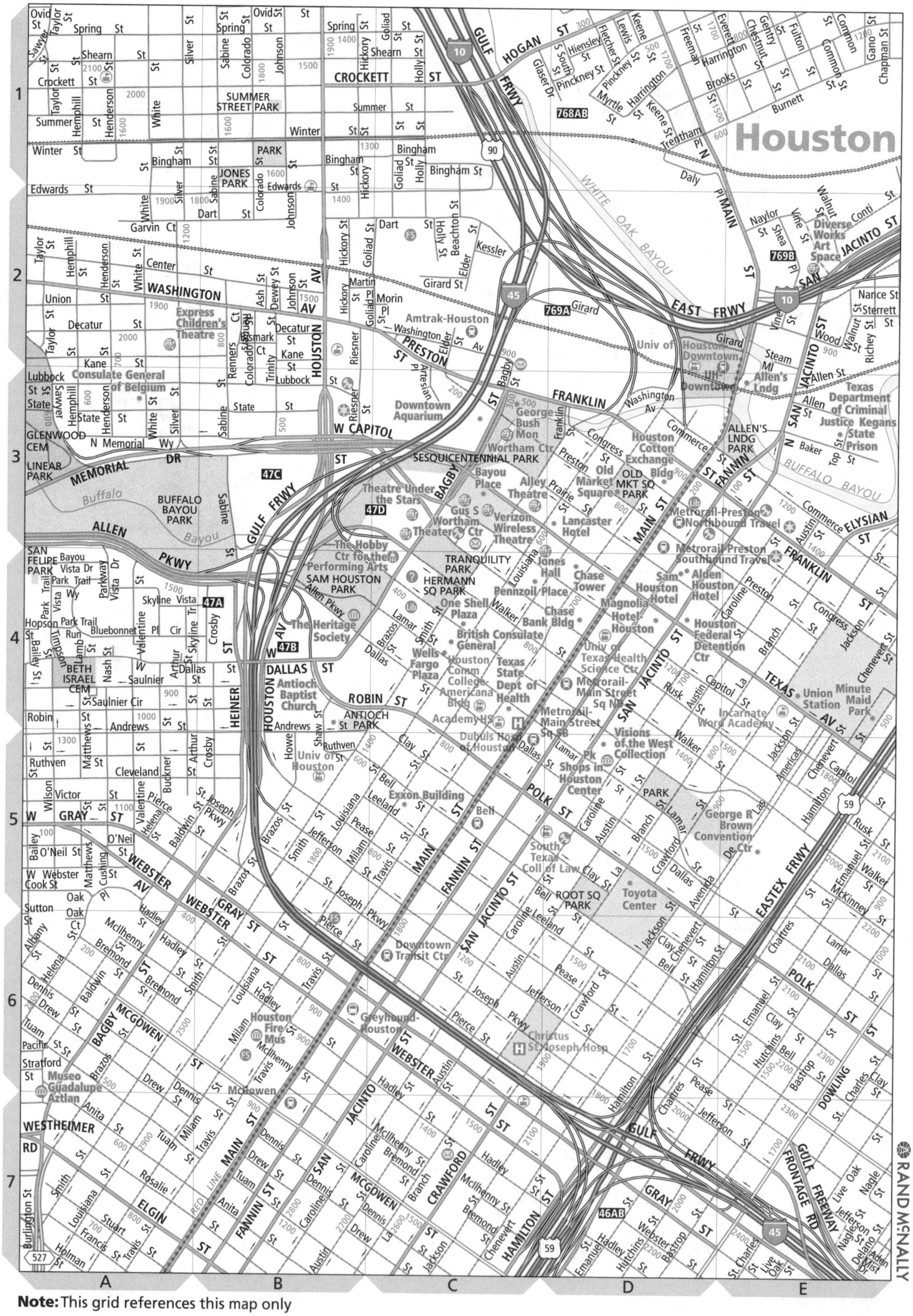
Houston
GULF FRWY
EAST FRWY
EASTEX FRWY
MEMORIAL DR
ALLEN PKWY
WASHINGTON AV
W CAPITOL ST
FRANKLIN
PRESTON
MAIN ST
FANNIN ST
SAN JACINTO ST
HOUSTON AV
WEBSTER ST
GRAY ST
W GRAY ST
WESTHEIMER RD
ELGIN
MCGOWEN ST
HAMILTON ST
CRAWFORD
BAGBY ST
HEINER
CROCKETT ST
HOGAN ST
POLK ST
DALLAS ST
ROBIN ST
TEXAS AV
DOWLING ST
ELYSIAN ST
GULF FREEWAY FRONTAGE RD
SUMMER STREET PARK
JONES PARK
BUFFALO BAYOU PARK
GLENWOOD CEM
LINEAR PARK
Buffalo Bayou
WHITE OAK BAYOU
SESQUICENTENNIAL PARK
TRANQUILITY PARK
HERMANN SQ PARK
SAM HOUSTON PARK
ANTIOCH PARK
BETH ISRAEL CEM
OLD MKT SQ PARK
ROOT SQ PARK
ALLEN'S LNDG PARK
Minute Maid Park
George R Brown Convention Ctr
Toyota Center
Downtown Aquarium
Express Children's Theatre
Consulate General of Belgium
Amtrak-Houston
Univ of Houston-Downtown
Allen's Lndg
Texas Department of Criminal Justice Kegans State Prison
Diverse Works Art Space
Houston Cotton Exchange
Old Market Square
Alley Theatre
Bayou Place
Theatre Under the Stars
Wortham Ctr
Gus S Wortham Theater Ctr
Verizon Wireless Theatre
The Hobby Ctr for the Performing Arts
The Heritage Society
Pennzoil Place
Jones Hall
Chase Tower
Chase Bank Bldg
Lancaster Hotel
Magnolia Hotel-Houston
Sam Houston Hotel
Alden Houston Hotel
Houston Federal Detention Ctr
Union Station
Incarnate Word Academy
British Consulate General
One Shell Plaza
Wells Fargo Plaza
Houston Comm College-Americana Bldg
Texas State Dept of Health
Metrorail-Main Street Sq NB
Metrorail-Main Street Sq SB
Metrorail-Preston Northbound Travel
Metrorail-Preston Southbound Travel
Visions of the West Collection
Shops in Houston Center
Antioch Baptist Church
Academy HS
Dubuis Hosp of Houston
Exxon Building
Univ of Texas Health Science Ctr
South Texas Coll of Law
Downtown Transit Ctr
Greyhound-Houston
Houston Fire Mus
Museo Guadalupe Aztlan
Christus St Joseph Hosp
George Bush Mon
768AB
769A
769B
47A
47B
47C
47D
46AB
10
45
59
90
527
RED LINE
1
2
3
4
5
6
7
A
B
C
D
E
RAND McNALLY

Note: This grid references this map only

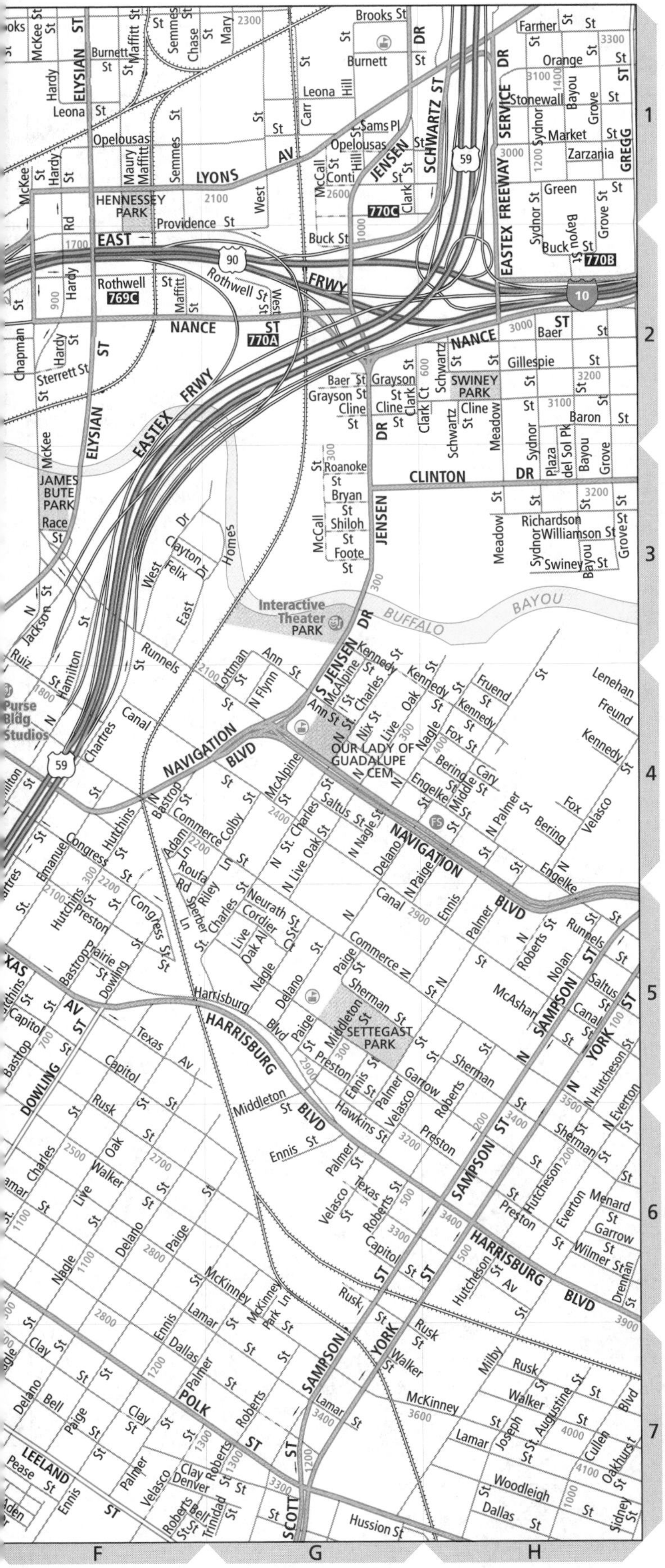
EAST FRWY
EASTEX FRWY
EASTEX FREEWAY SERVICE DR
LYONS AV
NANCE ST
CLINTON DR
JENSEN DR
NAVIGATION BLVD
HARRISBURG BLVD
SAMPSON ST
YORK ST
DOWLING ST
POLK ST
LEELAND ST
SCOTT ST
ELYSIAN ST
GREGG ST
SCHWARTZ ST
HENNESSEY PARK
JAMES BUTE PARK
SWINEY PARK
SETTEGAST PARK
Interactive Theater PARK
OUR LADY OF GUADALUPE CEM
BUFFALO BAYOU
Purse Bldg Studios
769C
770A
770B
770C
1
2
3
4
5
6
7
F
G
H

Points of Interest

Allen's Landing	E3
Allen's Landing Park	E3
Alley Theatre	C3
Amtrak-Houston	C2
Bayou Place	C3
Buffalo Bayou Park	A3
Chase Bank Building	D4
Chase Tower	D4
Christus St. Joseph Hospital	C6
Civic Center Station Post Office	C3
Criminal Justice Center	E3
Downtown Aquarium	C3
Express Children's Theatre	A2
Exxon Building	C5
George Bush Monument	C3
George R Brown Convention Center	D5
Greater Houston Convention & Visitors Bureau	C4
Greyhound-Houston	B6
Gus S Wortham Theater Center	C3
Harris County Civil Courts	D3
Harris County Law Library	D3
Harris County Municipal Court	B3
Harris County Sheriff's Department	E4
Hennessey Park	F1
Hermann Square Park	C4
Highlands Police Department	E3
Houston City Hall	C4
Houston Community College-Americana Building	C4
Houston Cotton Exchange Building	D3
Houston Federal Detention Center	D4
Houston Fire Museum	B6
Houston Main Post Office	C2
Houston Police Department	B3
Houston Public Library-Central	C4
James Bute Park	F3
Jones Hall	C4
Jones Park	B1
Lancaster Hotel	D3
Magnolia Hotel-Houston	D4
Metrorail-Bell	C5
Metrorail-Downtown Transit Center	C6
Metrorail-Main St Square Northbound	D4
Metrorail-Main St Square Southbound	C5
Metrorail-McGowen	B7
Metrorail-Preston Northbound Travel	D3
Metrorail-Preston Southbound Travel	D3
Metrorail-UH-Downtown	D2
Minute Maid Park	E4
Museo Guadalupe Aztlan	A6
Old Market Square	D3
Old Market Square Park	D3
One Shell Plaza	C4
Park Shops in Houston Center	D5
Pennzoil Place	C4
Root Square Park	D5
Sam Houston Carrier Station Post Office	C7
Sam Houston Hotel	D4
Sam Houston Park	B4
Sesquicentennial Park	C3
Settegast Park	G5
South Texas College of Law	C5
Summer Street Park	B1
Swiney Park	H2
Texas State Department of Health	C4
The Heritage Society	B4
The Hobby Center for the Performing Arts	B3
Toyota Center	D5
Tranquility Park	C4
Union Station	E4
United States Bankruptcy Court	C3
University of Houston	B5
University of Houston-Downtown	D2
University of Texas-Health Science Center	D4
Verizon Wireless Theatre	C3
Wells Fargo Plaza	C4

1 in. = 1400 ft.

0 0.25 0.5

miles

1:24,000
1 in. = 2000 ft.
0 0.25 0.5
miles

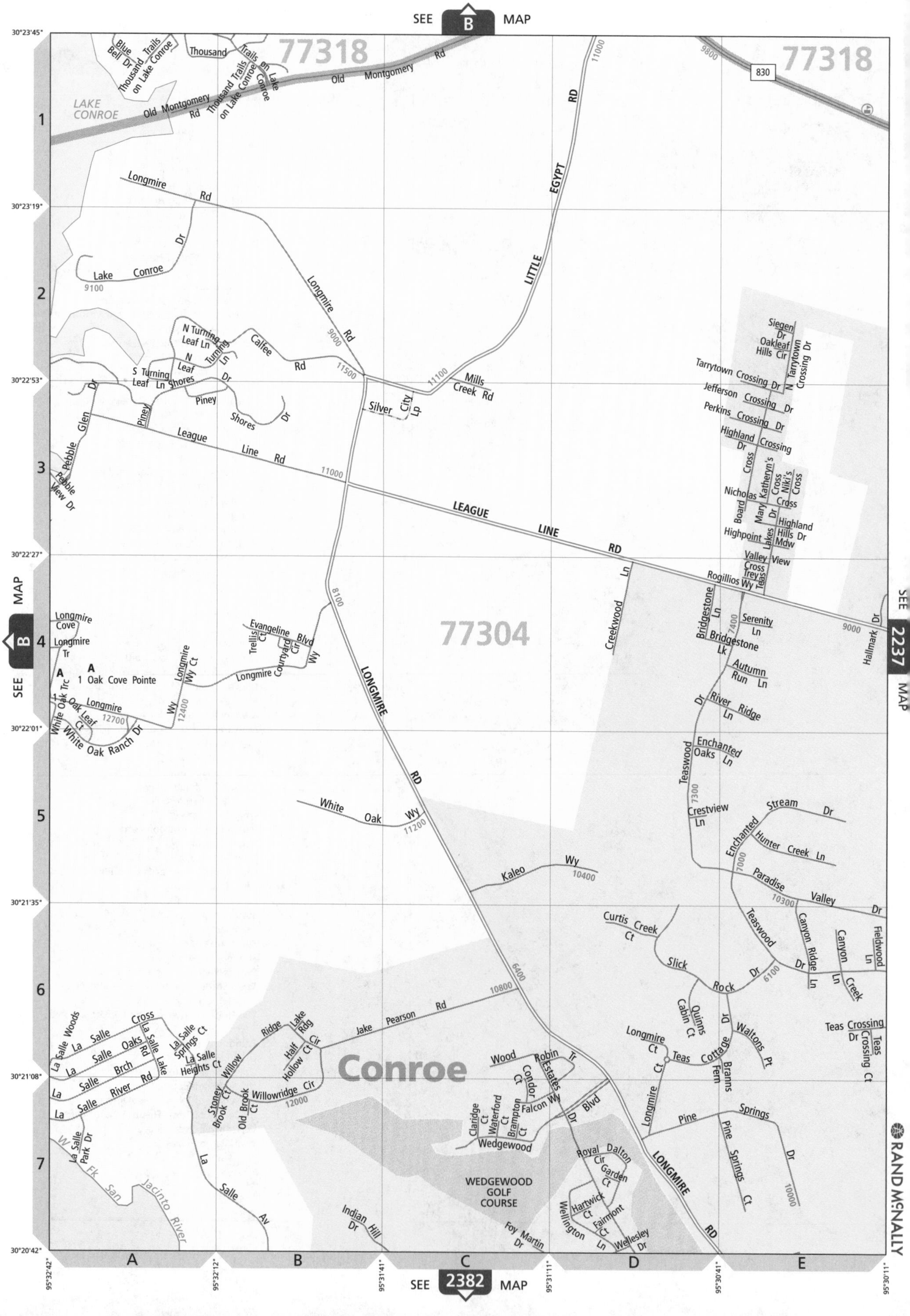
SEE B MAP
SEE 2382 MAP
SEE B MAP
SEE 2237 MAP
77318
77318
77304
Conroe
LAKE CONROE
WEDGEWOOD GOLF COURSE
Old Montgomery Rd
Blue Bell Dr
Thousand Trails on Lake Conroe
Longmire Rd
Lake Conroe Dr
LITTLE EGYPT RD
N Turning Leaf Ln
N Leaf Turning Ln
S Turning Leaf Ln
Shores
Piney Shores Dr
Calfee Rd
Mills Creek Rd
Silver City Lp
Pebble Glen Dr
Pebble View Dr
League Line Rd
LEAGUE LINE RD
LONGMIRE RD
Longmire Cove
Longmire Tr
1 Oak Cove Pointe
White Oak Trc
Oak Leaf Ct
White Oak Ranch Dr
Longmire Wy
Longmire Wy Ct
Evangeline Blvd
Trellis Ct
Courtyard Cir
White Oak Wy
Kaleo Wy
Creekwood Ln
Siegen Dr
Oakleaf Hills Cir
Tarrytown Crossing Dr
N Tarrytown Crossing Dr
Jefferson Crossing Dr
Perkins Crossing Dr
Highland Crossing Dr
Nicholas Cross
Katheryn's Cross
Niki's Cross
Mary Lakes Dr
Highland Hills Dr
Highpoint Mdw
Valley View
Trey's Cross
Rogillios Wy
Bridgestone Ln
Bridgestone Lk
Serenity Ln
Autumn Run Ln
River Ridge Ln
Enchanted Oaks Ln
Teaswood Dr
Crestview Ln
Stream Dr
Enchanted Hunter Creek Ln
Paradise Valley Dr
Canyon Ridge Ln
Canyon Creek Ln
Fieldwood Ln
Hallmark Dr
Curtis Creek Ct
Slick Rock Dr
Quins Cabin Ct
Waltons Pt
Longmire Ct
Teas Cottage
Branns Fern
Teas Crossing Dr
Teas Crossing Ct
Pine Springs Dr
Pine Springs Ct
Jake Pearson Rd
Lake Ridge Cir
Half Hollow Ct
Willowridge Cir
Stoney Brook Ct
Old Brook Ct
La Salle Woods
La Salle Oaks
La Salle Brch
La Salle River Rd
La Salle Cross
La Salle Lake Rd
La Salle Springs Ct
La Salle Heights Ct
La Salle Park Dr
La Salle Av
W Fk San Jacinto River
Indian Hill Dr
Foy Martin Dr
Wood Robin Tr
Condor Ct
Estates Dr
Falcon Wy
Blvd
Claridge Ct
Waterford Ct
Brampton Ct
Wedgewood
Royal Dalton Cir
Garden Ct
Hartwick Ct
Fairmont Ct
Wellington Ln
Wellesley Dr
830
1 2 3 4 5 6 7
A B C D E
RAND McNALLY

1:24,000
1 in. = 2000 ft.
0 0.25 0.5
miles

SEE B MAP

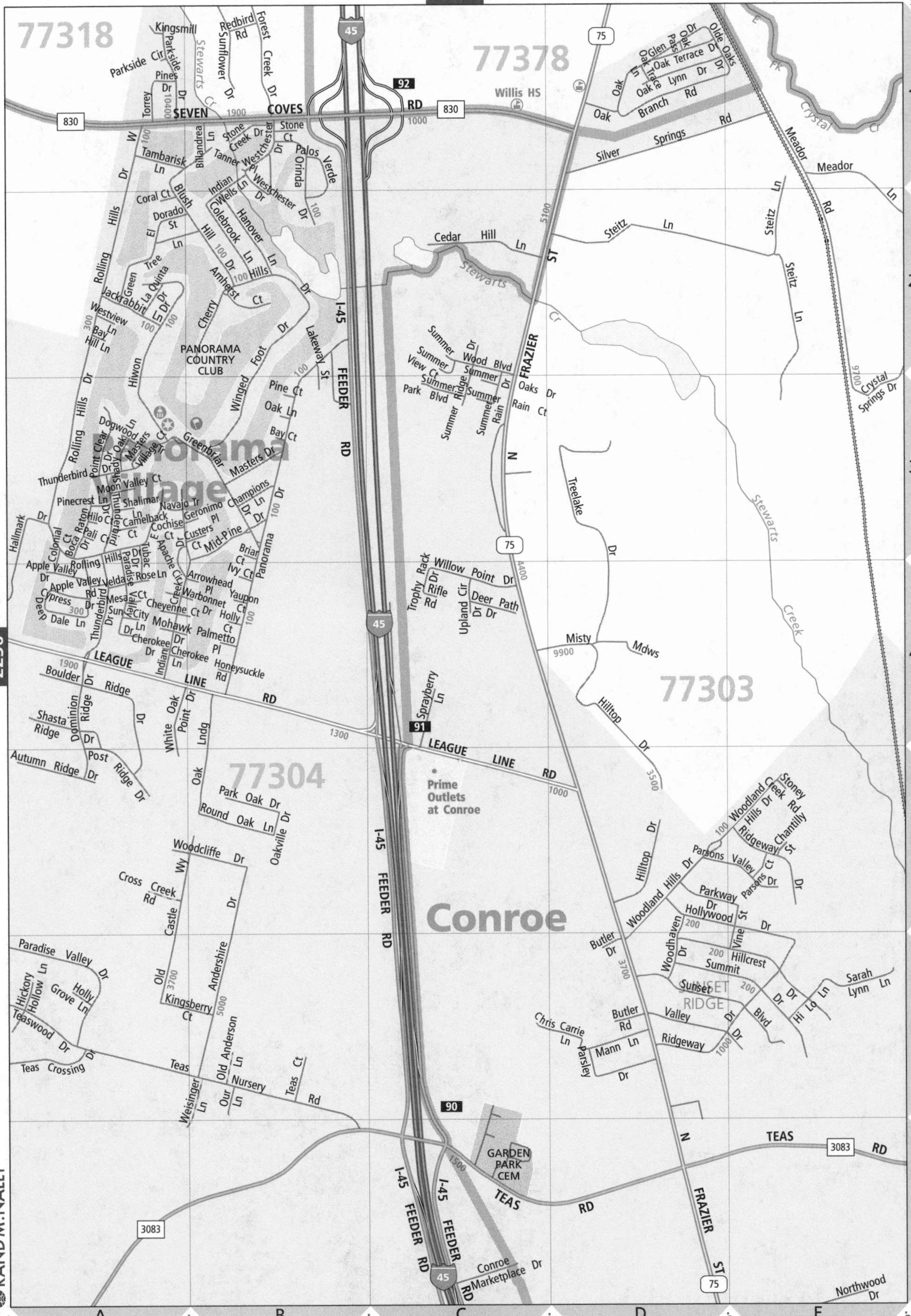
77318
77378
77303
77304
Panorama Village
PANORAMA COUNTRY CLUB
Conroe
Willis HS
Prime Outlets at Conroe
GARDEN PARK CEM
SUNSET RIDGE
SEVEN COVES RD
LEAGUE LINE RD
TEAS RD
N FRAZIER ST
I-45 FEEDER RD
Stewarts Cr
Stewarts Creek
Crystal Cr
Silver Springs Rd
Meador Rd
Steitz Ln
Cedar Hill Ln
Treelake Dr
Misty Mdws
Hilltop Dr
Woodland Hills Dr
Paradise Valley Dr
Teas Crossing Dr
Teas Nursery Rd
Conroe Marketplace Dr
Northwood Dr
Rolling Hills Dr
Champions Dr
Panorama Dr
Andershire Dr
Woodcliffe Dr
Oakville Dr
Round Oak Ln
Park Oak Dr
Willow Point Dr
Summer Wood Blvd
Crystal Springs Dr
30°23'43"
30°23'17"
30°22'51"
30°22'25"
30°21'59"
30°21'33"
30°21'06"
30°20'40"
95°30'11"
95°29'41"
95°29'11"
95°28'41"
95°28'10"
95°27'40"
A
B
C
D
E
1
2
3
4
5
6
7

SEE 2236 MAP
SEE 2238 MAP
SEE 2383 MAP

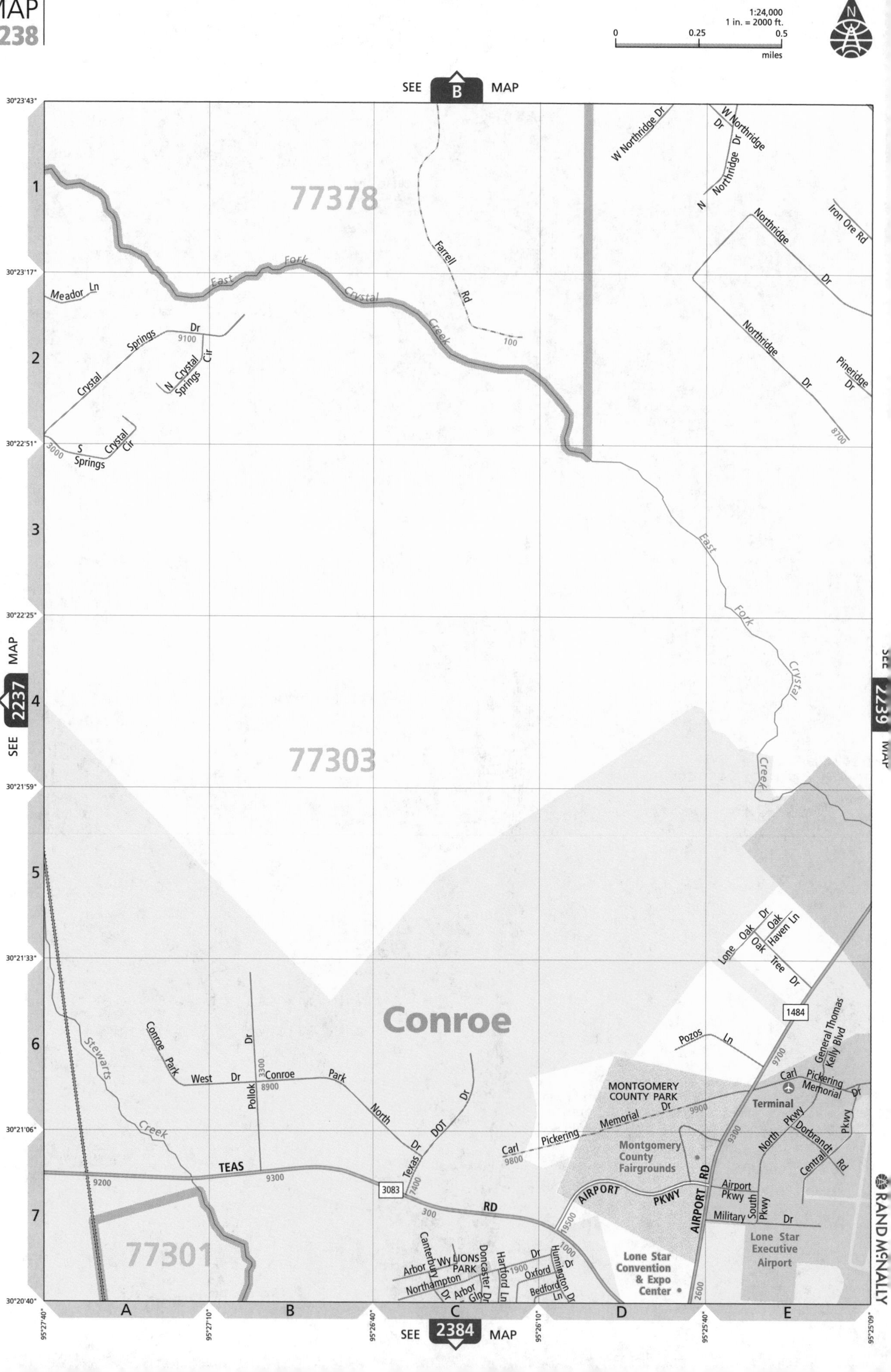
1:24,000
1 in. = 2000 ft.
0 0.25 0.5
miles
SEE B MAP
SEE 2237 MAP
SEE 2239 MAP
SEE 2384 MAP
77378
77303
77301
Conroe
East Fork Crystal Creek
Stewarts Creek
Meador Ln
Crystal Springs Dr
9100
N Crystal Springs Cir
S Crystal Springs Cir
3000
Farrell Rd
100
W Northridge Dr
W Northridge Dr
N Northridge Dr
Northridge Dr
Iron Ore Rd
Pineridge Dr
8700
Lone Oak Dr
Oak Haven Ln
Oak Tree Dr
1484
Pozos Ln
9700
General Thomas Kelly Blvd
Carl Pickering Memorial Dr
Terminal
MONTGOMERY COUNTY PARK
Carl Pickering Memorial Dr
9900
9800
Montgomery County Fairgrounds
North Pkwy
Dorbrandt Rd
Central
Pkwy
9300
Airport Pkwy
AIRPORT PKWY
AIRPORT RD
South Pkwy
Military Dr
Lone Star Executive Airport
Lone Star Convention & Expo Center
2600
19500
1000
Conroe Park West Dr
Pollok Dr
3300
8900
Conroe Park North Dr
DOT Dr
Texas
7400
TEAS RD
9200
9300
3083
300
Canterbury Dr
Arbor Wy
LIONS PARK
Northampton
Arbor Gln
Doncaster Dr
Hartford Ln
1900
Oxford Dr
Huntington Dr
Bedford Ln
30°23'43"
30°23'17"
30°22'51"
30°22'25"
30°21'59"
30°21'33"
30°21'06"
30°20'40"
95°27'40"
95°27'10"
95°26'40"
95°26'10"
95°25'40"
95°25'05"
1
2
3
4
5
6
7
A
B
C
D
E
RAND McNALLY

1:24,000
1 in. = 2000 ft.
0 0.25 0.5
miles

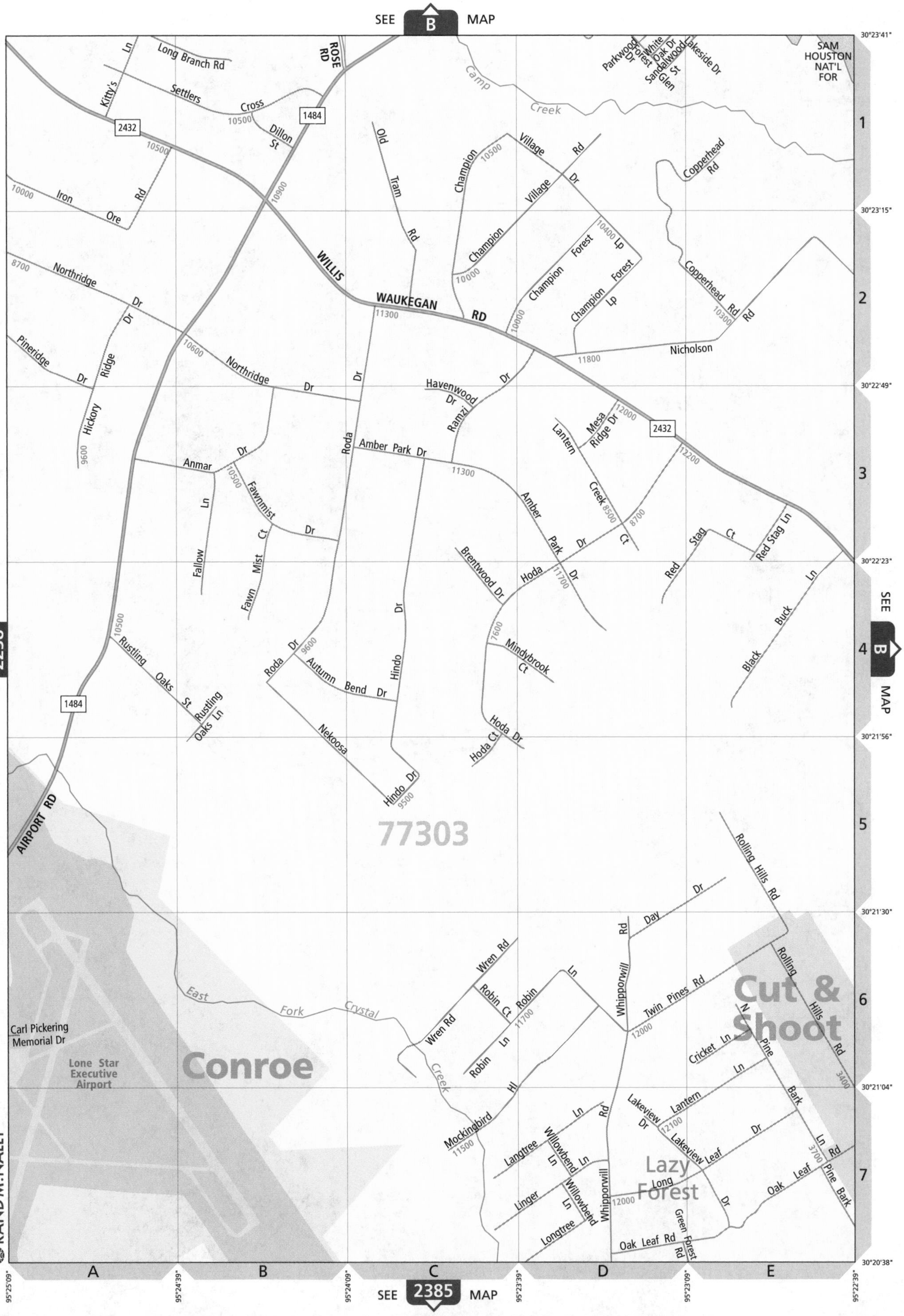
SEE B MAP
SEE 2238 MAP
SEE B MAP
SEE 2385 MAP
Long Branch Rd
Kitty's Ln
Settlers Cross
Dillon St
ROSE RD
1484
2432
Iron Ore Rd
Old Tram Rd
Camp Creek
Parkwood Dr
White Forest
Oak Dr
Sandalwood Glen St
Lakeside Dr
SAM HOUSTON NAT'L FOR
Copperhead Rd
Champion Village Rd
Village Dr
Champion Forest Lp
Northridge Dr
WILLIS WAUKEGAN RD
Nicholson
Pineridge Dr
Hickory Ridge Dr
Havenwood Dr
Ramzi Dr
Mesa Ridge Dr
Lantern Creek Ct
Roda Dr
Amber Park Dr
Anmar Dr
Fawnmist Dr
Fallow Ln
Fawn Mist Ct
Hindo Dr
Red Stag Ct
Red Stag Ln
Black Buck Ln
Brentwood Dr
Hoda Dr
Mindybrook Ct
Hoda Ct
Rustling Oaks St
Rustling Oaks Ln
Autumn Bend Dr
Nekoosa
AIRPORT RD
77303
Rolling Hills Rd
Day Dr
Whipporwill Rd
Wren Rd
Robin Ct
Robin Ln
Twin Pines Rd
East Fork Crystal Creek
Carl Pickering Memorial Dr
Lone Star Executive Airport
Conroe
Cut & Shoot
Cricket Ln
N Pine Bark Ln
Mockingbird Hl
Lakeview Dr
Lantern Ln
Langtree Ln
Willowbend Ln
Lakeview Leaf Dr
Lazy Forest
Long Forest Dr
Linger Ln
Longtree Ln
Oak Leaf Rd
Green Forest Rd
Pine Bark Rd
A B C D E
1 2 3 4 5 6 7
30°23'41" 30°23'15" 30°22'49" 30°22'23" 30°21'56" 30°21'30" 30°21'04" 30°20'38"
95°25'09" 95°24'39" 95°24'09" 95°23'39" 95°23'09" 95°22'39"

1:24,000
1 in. = 2000 ft.

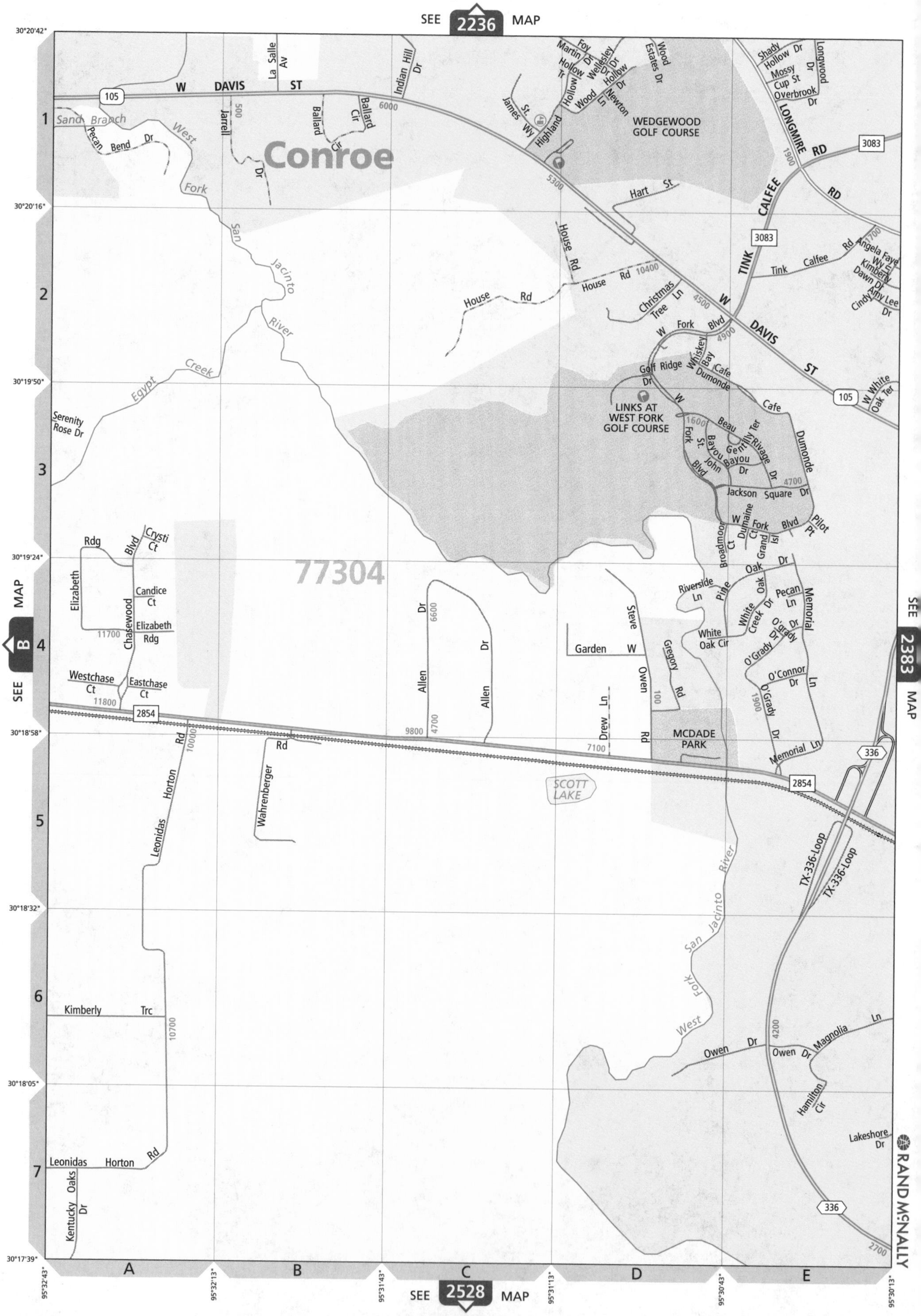
SEE 2236 MAP
SEE 2528 MAP
SEE B MAP
SEE 2383 MAP
Conroe
77304
W DAVIS ST
105
La Salle Av
Indian Hill Dr
Jarrell
Ballard Cir
Ballard Dr
Sand Branch
Pecan Bend Dr
West Fork San Jacinto River
Egypt Creek
Serenity Rose Dr
WEDGEWOOD GOLF COURSE
LINKS AT WEST FORK GOLF COURSE
LONGMIRE RD
3083
TINK CALFEE RD
Tink Calfee Rd
Hart St
House Rd
Christmas Tree Ln
W Fork Blvd
Golf Ridge Dr
Whiskey Bay
Cafe Dumonde
Jackson Square Dr
Beau Rivage Dr
Gentilly Ter
Bayou Dr
St. John
Dumaine Ct
Grand Isl
Broadmoor Ct
Pilot Pt
Riverside Ln
Pine Oak Dr
White Oak Cir
White Oak Creek Dr
Pecan Ln
O'Grady Dr
O'Connor Dr
Memorial Ln
MCDADE PARK
SCOTT LAKE
Steve Owen Rd
Gregory Rd
Garden W
Drew Ln
Allen Dr
2854
336
TX-336-Loop
Elizabeth Rdg
Chasewood Blvd
Crysti Ct
Candice Ct
Westchase Ct
Eastchase Ct
Leonidas Horton Rd
Wahrenberger Rd
Kimberly Trc
Kentucky Oaks Dr
Owen Dr
Magnolia Ln
Hamilton Cir
Lakeshore Dr
Shady Hollow Dr
Mossy Cup St
Overbrook Dr
Longwood Dr
Angela Faye Wy
Kimberly Dawn Dr
Amy Lee Dr
Cindy
W White Oak Ter
Wood Estates Dr
James Wy
Highland
Martin Hollow Tr
Foy Dr
Wellesley Dr
Newton
Hollow Wood Ln
A B C D E
1 2 3 4 5 6 7

1:24,000
1 in. = 2000 ft.
0 0.25 0.5
miles

SEE 2237 MAP

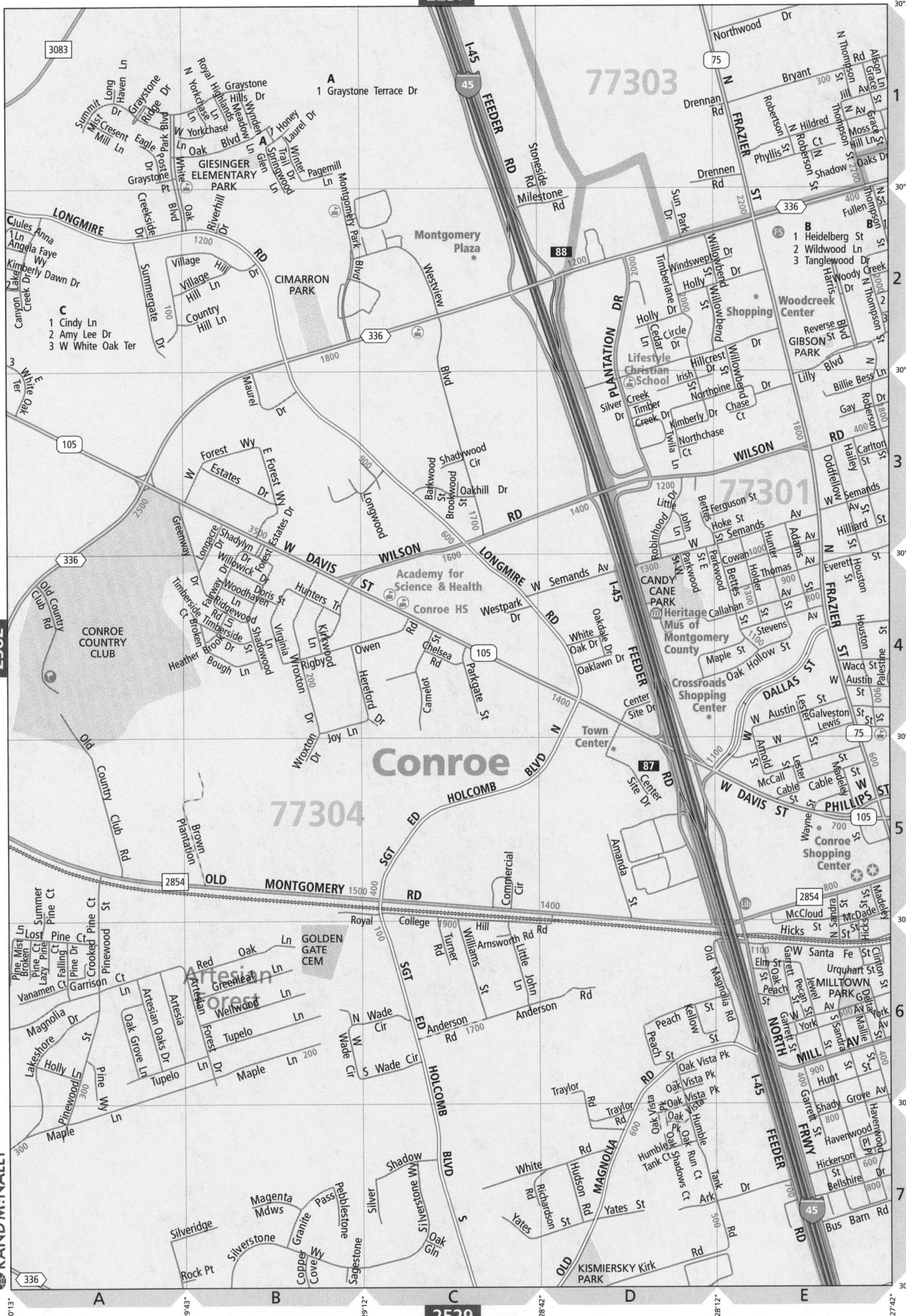
77303
77301
77304
Conroe
I-45
FEEDER RD
N FRAZIER ST
PLANTATION DR
LONGMIRE RD
W DAVIS ST
WILSON RD
OLD MONTGOMERY RD
SGT ED HOLCOMB BLVD N
SGT ED HOLCOMB BLVD S
NORTH FRWY
MILL AV
OLD MAGNOLIA RD
PHILLIPS ST
DALLAS ST
Montgomery Plaza
CIMARRON PARK
GIESINGER ELEMENTARY PARK
CONROE COUNTRY CLUB
Academy for Science & Health
Conroe HS
Lifestyle Christian School
Shopping Center
Woodcreek Center
GIBSON PARK
CANDY CANE PARK
Heritage Mus of Montgomery County
Crossroads Shopping Center
Town Center
Conroe Shopping Center
GOLDEN GATE CEM
Artesian Forest
MILLTOWN PARK
KISMIERSKY KIRK PARK
A
1 Graystone Terrace Dr
B
1 Heidelberg St
2 Wildwood Ln
3 Tanglewood Dr
C
1 Cindy Ln
2 Amy Lee Dr
3 W White Oak Ter
30°20'40"
30°20'14"
30°19'48"
30°19'22"
30°18'56"
30°18'29"
30°18'03"
30°17'37"
95°30'13"
95°29'43"
95°29'12"
95°28'42"
95°28'12"
95°27'42"
A
B
C
D
E
1
2
3
4
5
6
7

SEE 2382 MAP

SEE 2384 MAP

SEE 2529 MAP

1:24,000
1 in. = 2000 ft.
0 0.25 0.5
miles

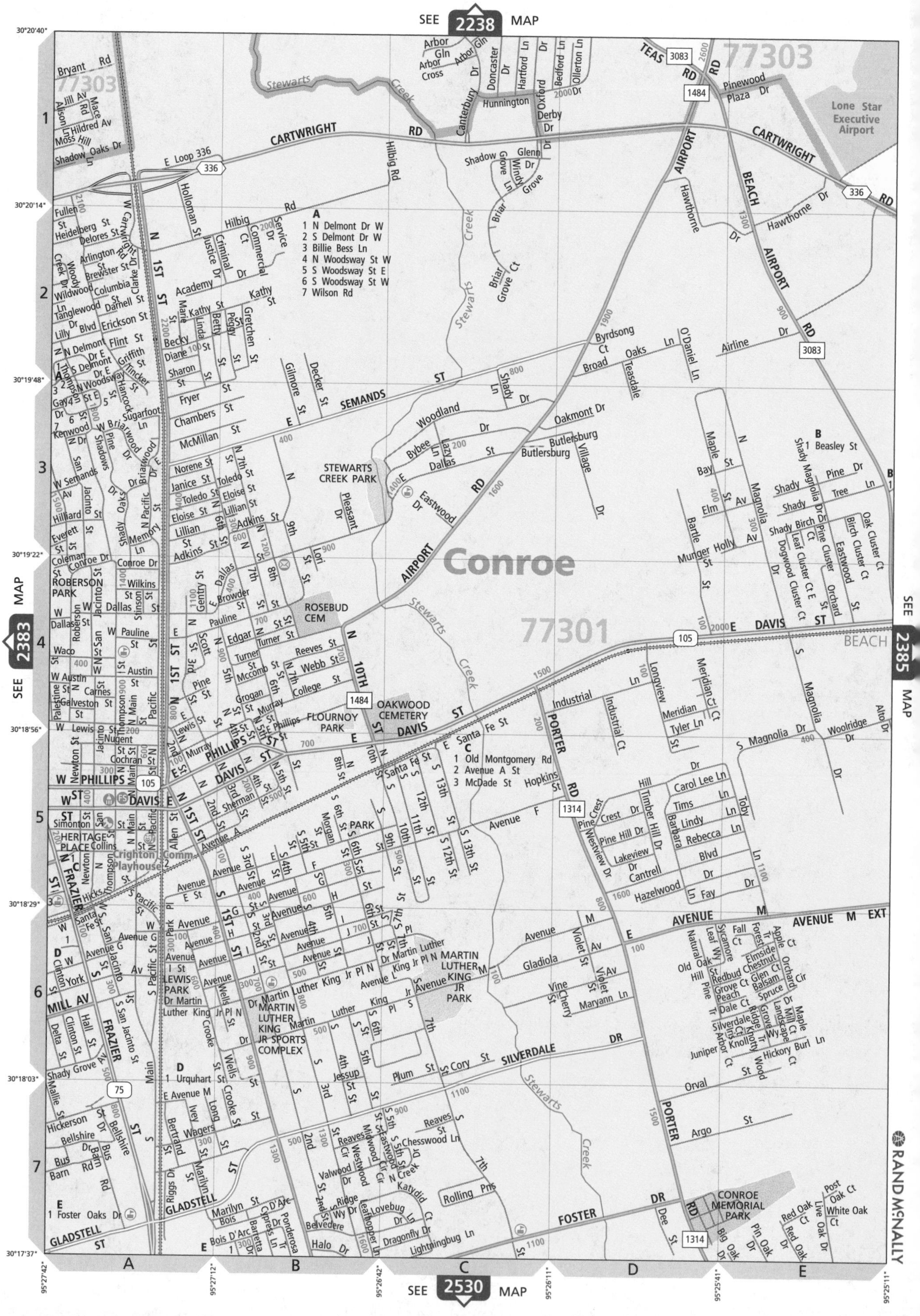
SEE 2238 MAP
SEE 2383 MAP
SEE 2385 MAP
SEE 2530 MAP
Conroe
77303
77301
Lone Star Executive Airport
STEWARTS CREEK PARK
ROSEBUD CEM
OAKWOOD CEMETERY
FLOURNOY PARK
ROBERSON PARK
HERITAGE PLACE
Crighton Comm. Playhouse
LEWIS PARK
MARTIN LUTHER KING JR PARK
MARTIN LUTHER KING JR SPORTS COMPLEX
CONROE MEMORIAL PARK
CARTWRIGHT RD
E Loop 336
SEMANDS ST
AIRPORT RD
BEACH AIRPORT RD
E DAVIS ST
W DAVIS ST
W PHILLIPS ST
PHILLIPS ST
N FRAZIER ST
FRAZIER
N 1ST ST
S 1ST ST
N 10TH ST
PORTER RD
AVENUE M
AVENUE M EXT
SILVERDALE DR
FOSTER DR
GLADSTELL ST
MILL AV
TEAS RD
Stewarts Creek
A
1 N Delmont Dr W
2 S Delmont Dr W
3 Billie Bess Ln
4 N Woodsway St W
5 S Woodsway St E
6 S Woodsway St W
7 Wilson Rd
B
1 Beasley St
C
1 Old Montgomery Rd
2 Avenue A St
3 McDade St
D
1 Urquhart St
E
1 Foster Oaks Dr
30°20'40"
30°20'14"
30°19'48"
30°19'22"
30°18'56"
30°18'29"
30°18'03"
30°17'37"
95°27'42"
95°27'12"
95°26'42"
95°26'11"
95°25'41"
95°25'11"
A B C D E
1 2 3 4 5 6 7
RAND McNALLY

1:24,000
1 in. = 2000 ft.
0 0.25 0.5
miles

SEE 2239 MAP

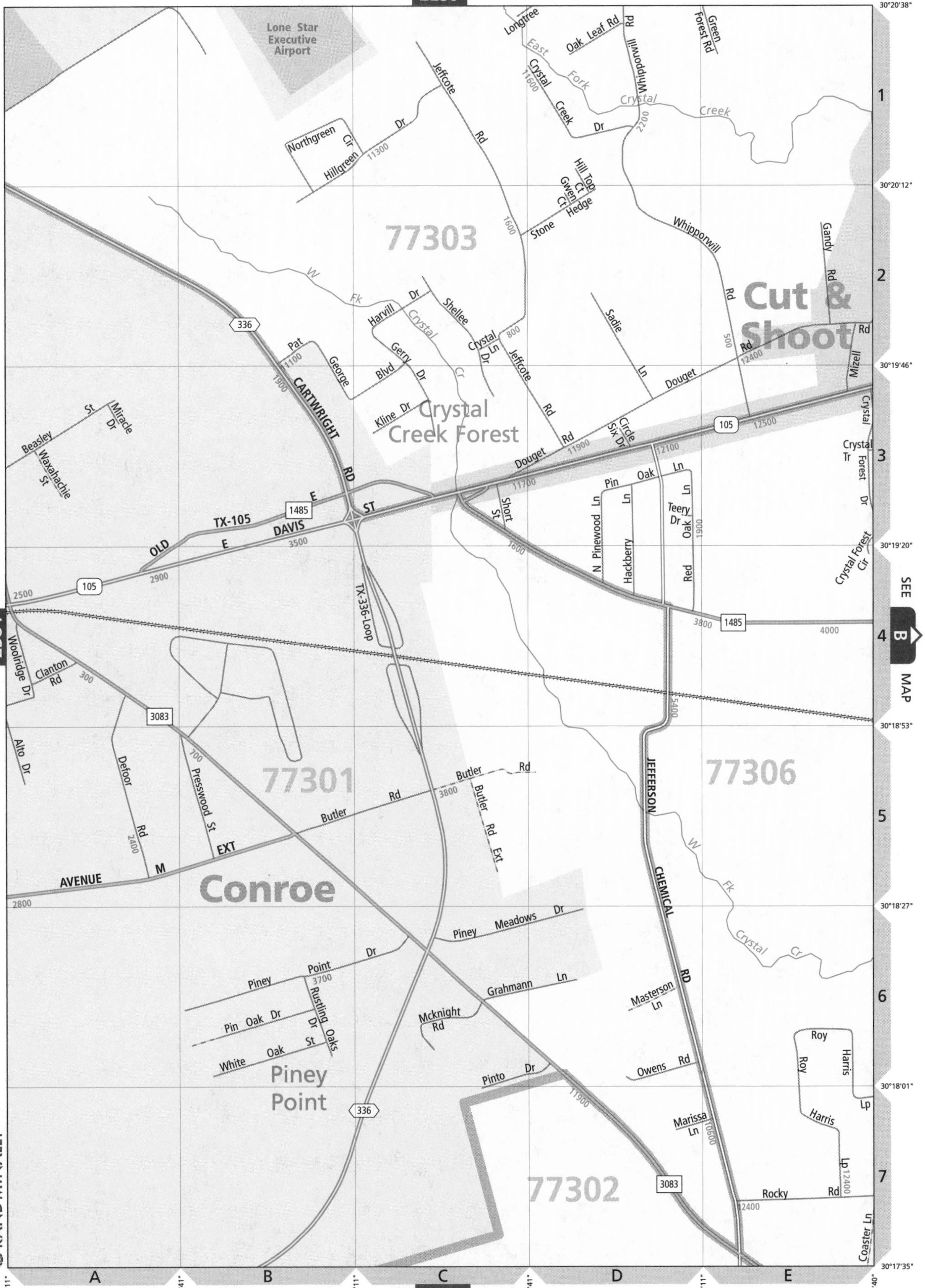
Lone Star Executive Airport
77303
77301
77306
77302
Cut & Shoot
Crystal Creek Forest
Conroe
Piney Point
Longtree
Oak Leaf Rd
Whippoorwill Rd
Green Forest Rd
East Fork Crystal Creek
Crystal Creek Dr
Jeffcote Rd
Northgreen Cir
Hillgreen Dr
Hill Top Ct
Gwen Ct
Hedge
Stone
Whippoorwill Rd
Gandy Rd
Mizell Rd
W Fk Crystal Cr
Harvill Dr
Shellee
Crystal Ln
Jeffcote Rd
Sadie Ln
Dougets Rd
Pat George
Gerry Blvd
Kline Dr
CARTWRIGHT RD
Beasley St
Miracle Dr
Waxahachie St
Circle Six Dr
Crystal Tr
Crystal Forest Dr
Crystal Forest Cir
Pin Oak Ln
N Pinewood Ln
Hackberry Ln
Teery Oak Dr
Red Oak Ln
Short St
TX-105
OLD E DAVIS ST
E DAVIS ST
TX-336-Loop
Woolridge Dr
Clanton Rd
Alto Dr
Defoor Rd
Presswood St
Butler Rd
Butler Rd Ext
AVENUE M EXT
JEFFERSON
CHEMICAL RD
W Fk Crystal Cr
Piney Meadows Dr
Piney Point Dr
Rustling Oaks Dr
Pin Oak Dr
White Oak St
Grahmann Ln
Mcknight Rd
Pinto Dr
Masterson Ln
Owens Rd
Marissa Ln
Roy Harris Lp
Rocky Rd
Coaster Ln
105
336
1485
3083
1
2
3
4
5
6
7
A
B
C
D
E
30°20'38"
30°20'12"
30°19'46"
30°19'20"
30°18'53"
30°18'27"
30°18'01"
30°17'35"
95°25'11"
95°24'41"
95°24'11"
95°23'41"
95°23'11"
95°22'40"

SEE 2384 MAP

SEE B MAP

SEE 2531 MAP

SEE 2382 MAP

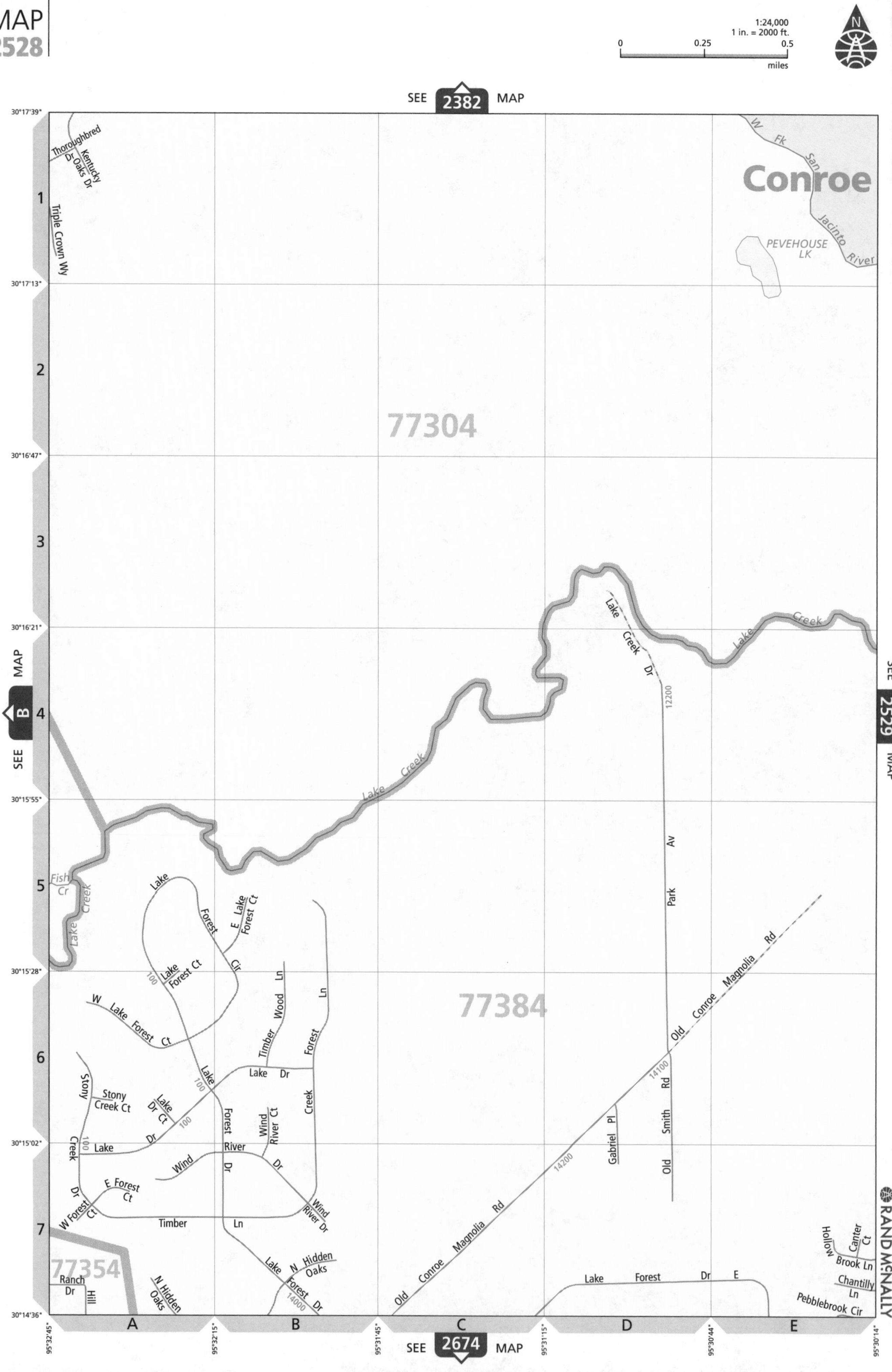
1:24,000
1 in. = 2000 ft.
0
0.25
0.5
miles
N
Conroe
W Fk San Jacinto River
PEVEHOUSE LK
77304
77384
77354
Thoroughbred Dr
Kentucky Oaks Dr
Triple Crown Wy
Lake Creek
Lake Creek Dr
Fish Cr
12200
Park Av
Old Conroe Magnolia Rd
14100
14200
Old Smith Rd
Gabriel Pl
Lake Forest Cir
E Lake Forest Ct
Lake Forest Ct
W Lake Forest Ct
Timber Wood Ln
Forest Creek Ln
Lake Dr
Stony Creek Dr
Stony Creek Ct
Lake Dr Ct
Lake Dr
Forest River Dr
Wind River Ct
Wind River Dr
E Forest Ct
W Forest Ct
Timber Ln
100
Lake Forest Dr
N Hidden Oaks
14000
Ranch Dr
Hill
Lake Forest Dr E
Hollow Brook Ln
Canter Ct
Chantilly Ln
Pebblebrook Cir
1
2
3
4
5
6
7
A
B
C
D
E
30°17'39"
30°17'13"
30°16'47"
30°16'21"
30°15'55"
30°15'28"
30°15'02"
30°14'36"
95°32'45"
95°32'15"
95°31'45"
95°31'15"
95°30'44"
95°30'14"

SEE B MAP

SEE 2529 MAP

SEE 2674 MAP

1:24,000
1 in. = 2000 ft.
0 0.25 0.5
miles

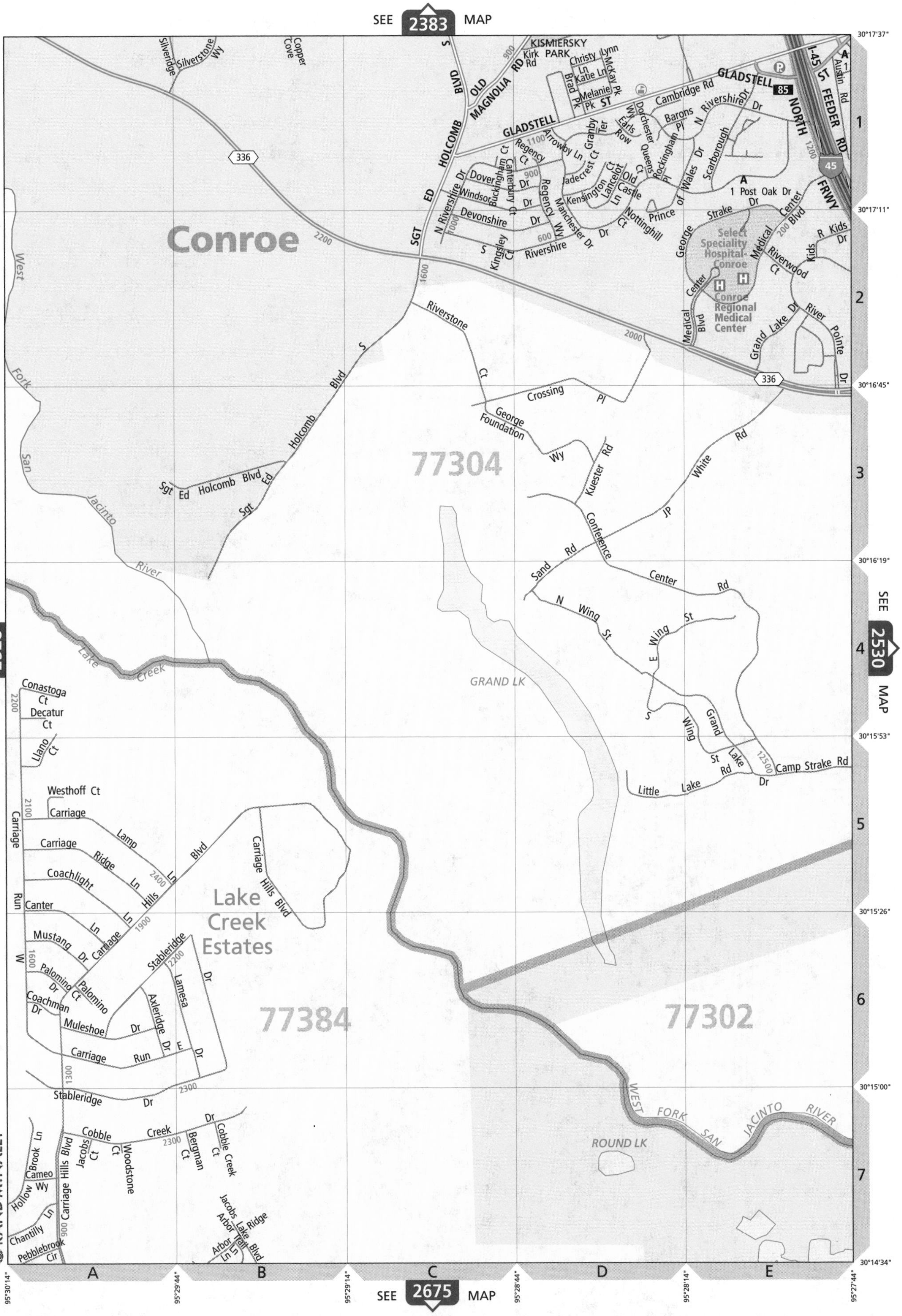
SEE 2383 MAP
SEE 2675 MAP
SEE 2528 MAP
SEE 2530 MAP
Conroe
77304
77384
77302
Lake Creek Estates
GRAND LK
ROUND LK
KISMIERSKY PARK
Select Speciality Hospital-Conroe
Conroe Regional Medical Center
GLADSTELL ST
SGT ED HOLCOMB BLVD S
OLD MAGNOLIA RD
I-45 NORTH FRWY
I-45 ST FEEDER RD
Austin Rd
Cambridge Rd
N Rivershire Dr
Barons Pl
Scarborough
Prince of Wales Dr
Rockingham Pl
Queens Ct
Dorchester Ct
Earls Row
Granby Ter
Jadecrest Ct
Arrowby Ln
Regency Ct
Regency Wy
Dover Dr
Windsor Dr
Devonshire Dr
Buckingham Ct
Canterbury Ct
Kensington Ct
Lancelot Ln
Old Castle Ct
Nottinghill Ct
Manchester Dr
Riverhire
Kingsley Ct
Christy Ln
Katie Ln
Lynn McKay Pk
Brad Pk
Melanie Pk
Kirk Rd
1 Post Oak Dr
George Strake Dr
Medical Center Blvd
Riverwood Ct
Kids R Kids Dr
River Pointe Dr
Grand Lake Dr
Riverstone Ct
Crossing Pl
George Foundation Wy
Kuester Rd
White Rd
JP Conference
Sand Rd
Center Rd
N Wing St
E Wing St
S Wing St
Grand Lake St
Little Lake Rd
Camp Strake Rd
Silverstone Wy
Silverridge
Copper Cove
West Fork San Jacinto River
Lake Creek
Conastoga Ct
Decatur Ct
Llano Ct
Westhoff Ct
Carriage Lamp Ln
Carriage Ridge Ln
Coachlight Ln
Canter Ln
Mustang Dr
Carriage Hills Blvd
W Carriage Run
Palomino Dr
Palomino Ct
Coachman Dr
Muleshoe Dr
Carriage Run Dr
Stableridge Dr
Axleridge Dr E
Lamesa Dr
Cobble Creek Dr
Jacobs Ct
Woodstone Ct
Bergman Ct
Cobble Creek Ct
Brook Ln
Cameo Wy
Hollow Ln
Chantilly Ln
Pebblebrook Cir
Jacobs Lake Ridge Blvd
Arbor Trail Ln
Arbor Ln
336
45
85
A B C D E
1 2 3 4 5 6 7
30°17'37"
30°17'11"
30°16'45"
30°16'19"
30°15'53"
30°15'26"
30°15'00"
30°14'34"
95°30'14"
95°29'44"
95°29'14"
95°28'44"
95°28'14"
95°27'44"

1:24,000
1 in. = 2000 ft.
0 0.25 0.5
miles

SEE 2384 MAP

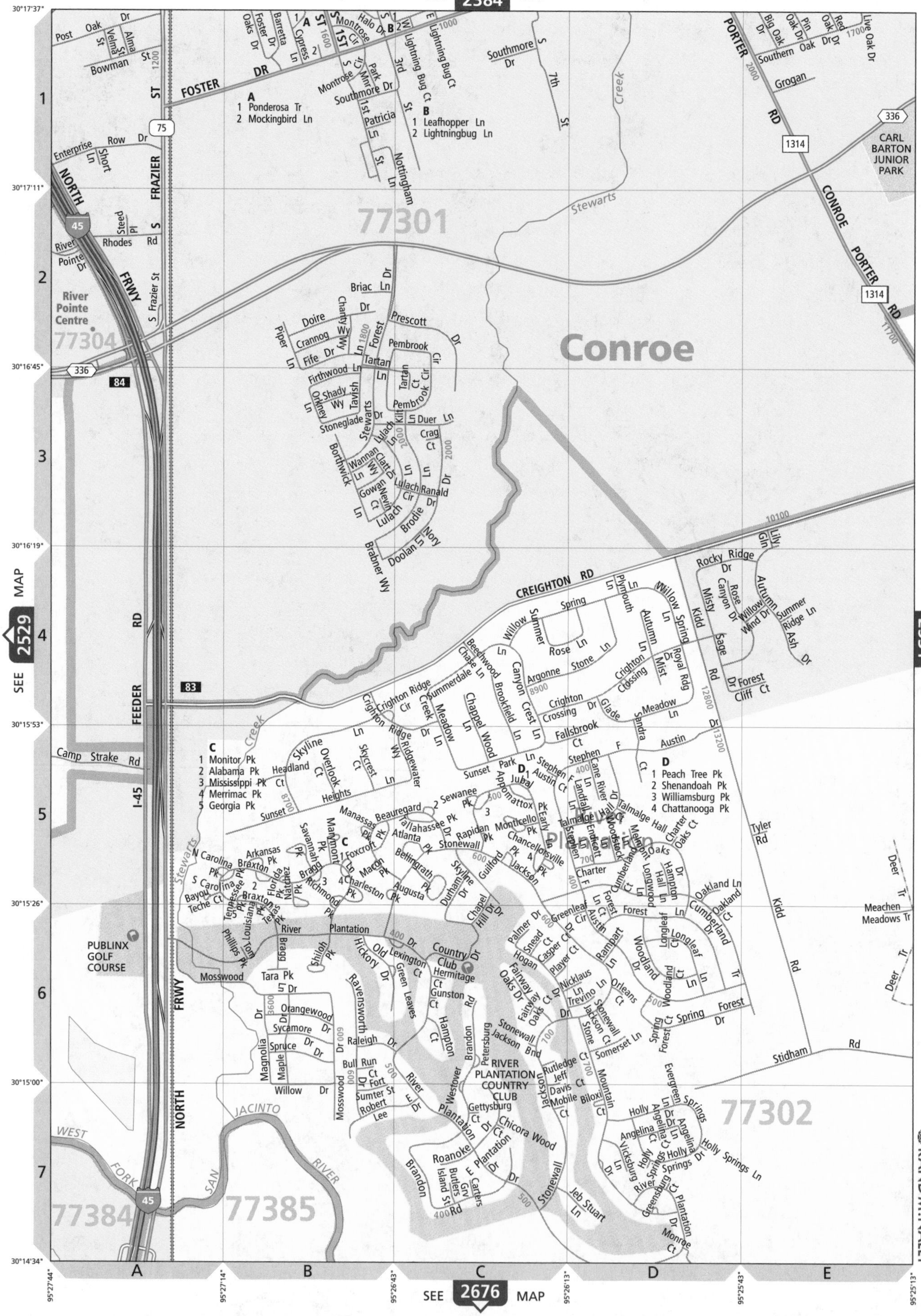
30°17'37"
30°17'11"
30°16'45"
30°16'19"
30°15'53"
30°15'26"
30°15'00"
30°14'34"
95°27'44"
95°27'14"
95°26'43"
95°26'13"
95°25'43"
95°25'13"
1
2
3
4
5
6
7
A
B
C
D
E
77301
77304
77302
77384
77385
Conroe
A
1 Ponderosa Tr
2 Mockingbird Ln
B
1 Leafhopper Ln
2 Lightningbug Ln
C
1 Monitor Pk
2 Alabama Pk
3 Mississippi Pk
4 Merrimac Pk
5 Georgia Pk
D
1 Peach Tree Pk
2 Shenandoah Pk
3 Williamsburg Pk
4 Chattanooga Pk
FOSTER DR
NORTH FRAZIER ST
S FRAZIER ST
NORTH FRWY
FEEDER RD
I-45
CREIGHTON RD
PORTER RD
CONROE PORTER RD
River Pointe Centre
CARL BARTON JUNIOR PARK
PUBLINX GOLF COURSE
RIVER PLANTATION COUNTRY CLUB
River Plantation
Stewarts Creek
WEST FORK SAN JACINTO RIVER
Camp Strake Rd
Stidham Rd
Kidd Rd
Tyler Rd
Meachen Meadows Tr
Deer Tr
Southern Oak Dr
Grogan
Southmore Dr
Enterprise Row Dr
Rhodes Rd
Post Oak Dr
Bowman St
Prescott Dr
Pembrook Cir
Briac Ln
Doire Dr
Stoneglade Dr
Brabner Wy
Doolan Ln
Rocky Ridge Dr
Summer Ridge Ln
Forest Cliff Ct
Willow Spring Ln
Crighton Crossing Dr
Fallsbrook Ct
Austin Dr
Sunset Park Ln
Skyline Ln
Headland Ct
Stonewall Jackson Bnd
Country Club Dr
Mosswood
Tara Pk
Orangewood Dr
Sycamore Dr
Spruce Dr
Willow Dr
Raleigh Dr
River Plantation Dr
Chicora Wood Dr
Roanoke Rd
Jeb Stuart Ln
Holly Springs Ln
Evergreen Springs
Spring Forest Dr
Oakland Ln
Cumberland Tr
Longleaf Ln
Woodland Dr
Hampton Ct
Gettysburg Ct
Brandon Rd
Greensburg Ct
Monroe Ct
Vicksburg Ln
Angelina Dr
75
336
1314
45
83
84

SEE 2529 MAP

SEE 2531 MAP

SEE 2676 MAP

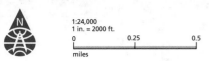

1:24,000
1 in. = 2000 ft.
0 0.25 0.5
miles

SEE 2385 MAP

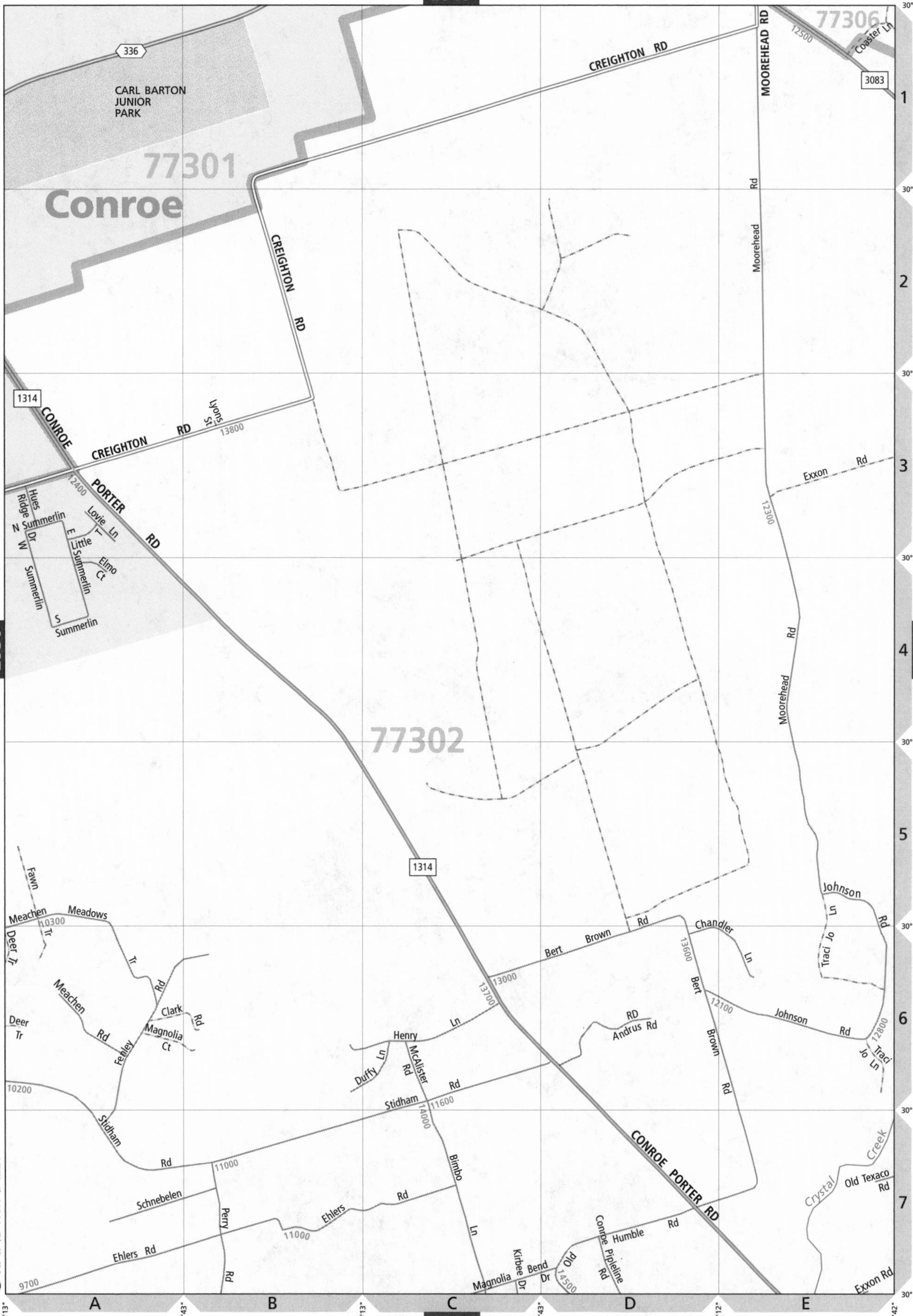
336
CARL BARTON
JUNIOR
PARK
77301
Conroe
CREIGHTON RD
MOOREHEAD RD
77306
12500
Coaster Ln
3083
Moorehead Rd
CREIGHTON RD
1314
CONROE
CREIGHTON RD
Lyons St
13800
12400
PORTER RD
Hues Ridge Dr
N Summerlin
Lovie Ln
E Little Summerlin
Elmo Ct
W Summerlin
S Summerlin
Exxon Rd
12300
Moorehead Rd
77302
1314
Fawn
Meachen
Meadows
10300
Tr
Deer Tr
Tr
Rd
Meachen Rd
Clark Rd
Magnolia Ct
Fenley
Deer Tr
Johnson
Ln
Traci Jo
Rd
Bert Brown Rd
Chandler Ln
13600
13000
13700
Bert Brown Rd
12100
Johnson Rd
12800
Jo Traci Ln
Henry Ln
Duffy Ln
McAlister Rd
RD
Andrus Rd
10200
Stidham Rd
11600
14000
Stidham Rd
11000
Bimbo Ln
CONROE PORTER RD
Crystal Creek
Old Texaco Rd
Schnebelen
Perry Rd
Ehlers Rd
11000
Ehlers Rd
9700
Kirbee Dr
Magnolia Bend Dr
Old 14500
Conroe Pipeline Rd
Humble Rd
Exxon Rd
1 2 3 4 5 6 7
A B C D E
30°17'35" 30°17'09" 30°16'43" 30°16'16" 30°15'50" 30°15'24" 30°14'58" 30°14'32"
95°25'13" 95°24'43" 95°24'13" 95°23'43" 95°23'12" 95°22'42"

SEE 2530 MAP

SEE 2532 MAP

SEE 2677 MAP

1:24,000
1 in. = 2000 ft.
0 0.25 0.5
miles

SEE B MAP

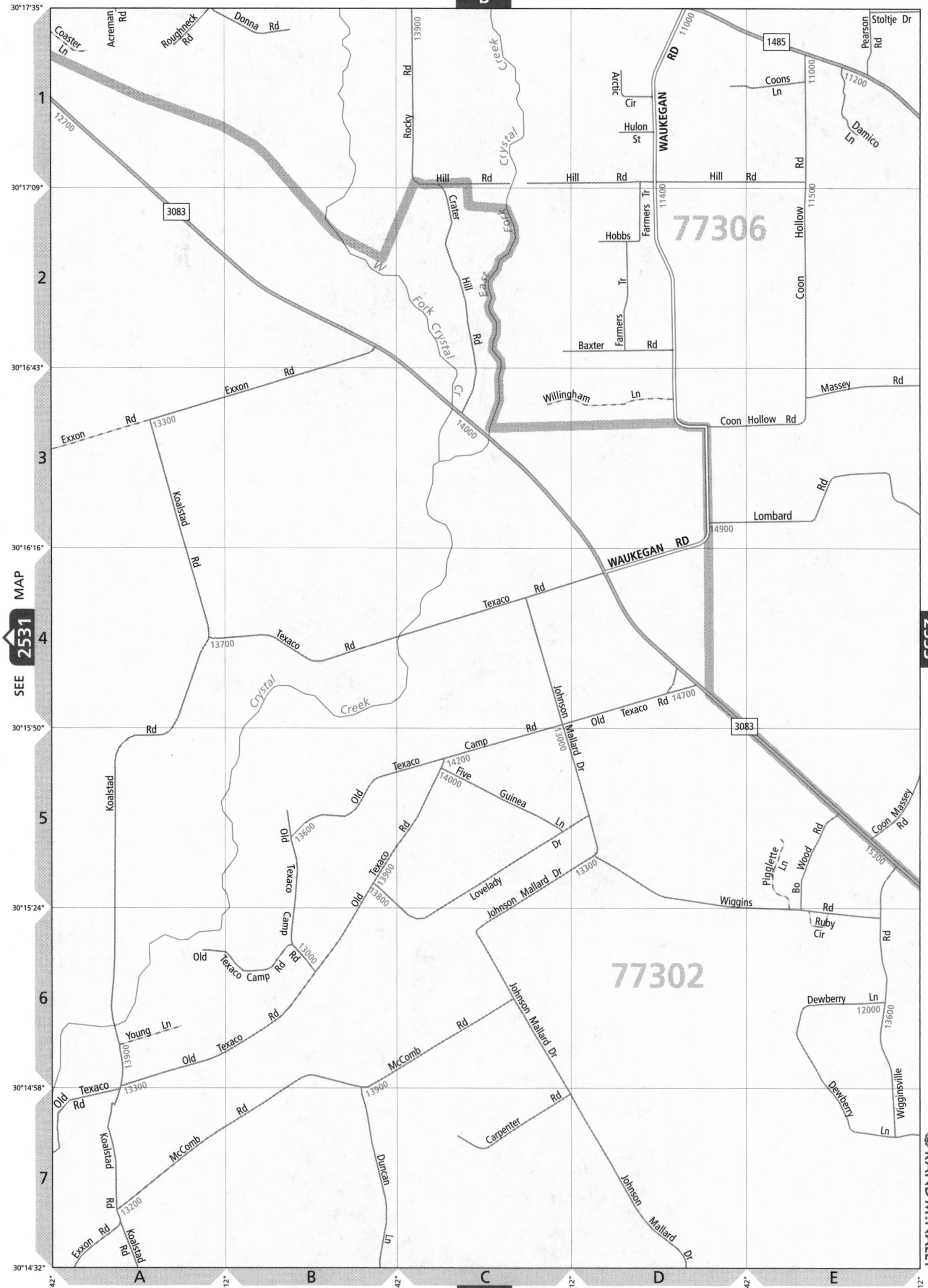
Coaster Ln
Acreman Rd
Roughneck Rd
Donna Rd
Rocky Rd
13900
East Crystal Creek
Fork
WAUKEGAN RD
11000
1485
Pearson Rd
Stoltje Dr
Arctic Cir
Coons Ln
11200
Damico Ln
Hulon St
12700
3083
Hill Rd
Crater
Hill Rd
Farmers Tr
11400
11500
Hobbs
77306
Coon Hollow Rd
W Fork Crystal Cr
Baxter Rd
Willingham Ln
Massey Rd
Exxon Rd
13300
14000
Coon Hollow Rd
Koalstad Rd
Lombard Rd
14900
WAUKEGAN RD
Texaco Rd
13700
Texaco Rd
Crystal Creek
Johnson Mallard Dr
13000
Old Texaco Rd
14700
3083
Texaco Camp Rd
14200
14000
Five Guinea Ln
Old
Old Texaco Camp
13600
Rd
Koalstad
Coon Massey Rd
Bo Wood Rd
Pigglette Ln
15300
Lovelady Dr
Old Texaco
13900
13800
Johnson Mallard Dr
13300
Wiggins Rd
Ruby Cir
Rd
Old Texaco Camp Rd
13000
77302
Dewberry Ln
12000
13600
Young Ln
13900
Old Texaco Rd
Johnson Mallard Dr
McComb Rd
Old Texaco
Old Rd
13300
13900
Dewberry Ln
Wigginsville
Carpenter Rd
Koalstad Rd
McComb Rd
Duncan Ln
13200
Johnson Mallard Dr
Exxon Rd
Koalstad Rd
30°17'35"
30°17'09"
30°16'43"
30°16'16"
30°15'50"
30°15'24"
30°14'58"
30°14'32"
95°22'42"
95°22'12"
95°21'42"
95°21'12"
95°20'42"
95°20'12"
A B C D E
1 2 3 4 5 6 7

SEE 2531 MAP

SEE 2533 MAP

SEE 2678 MAP

1:24,000
1 in. = 2000 ft.
0 0.25 0.5
miles

SEE B MAP

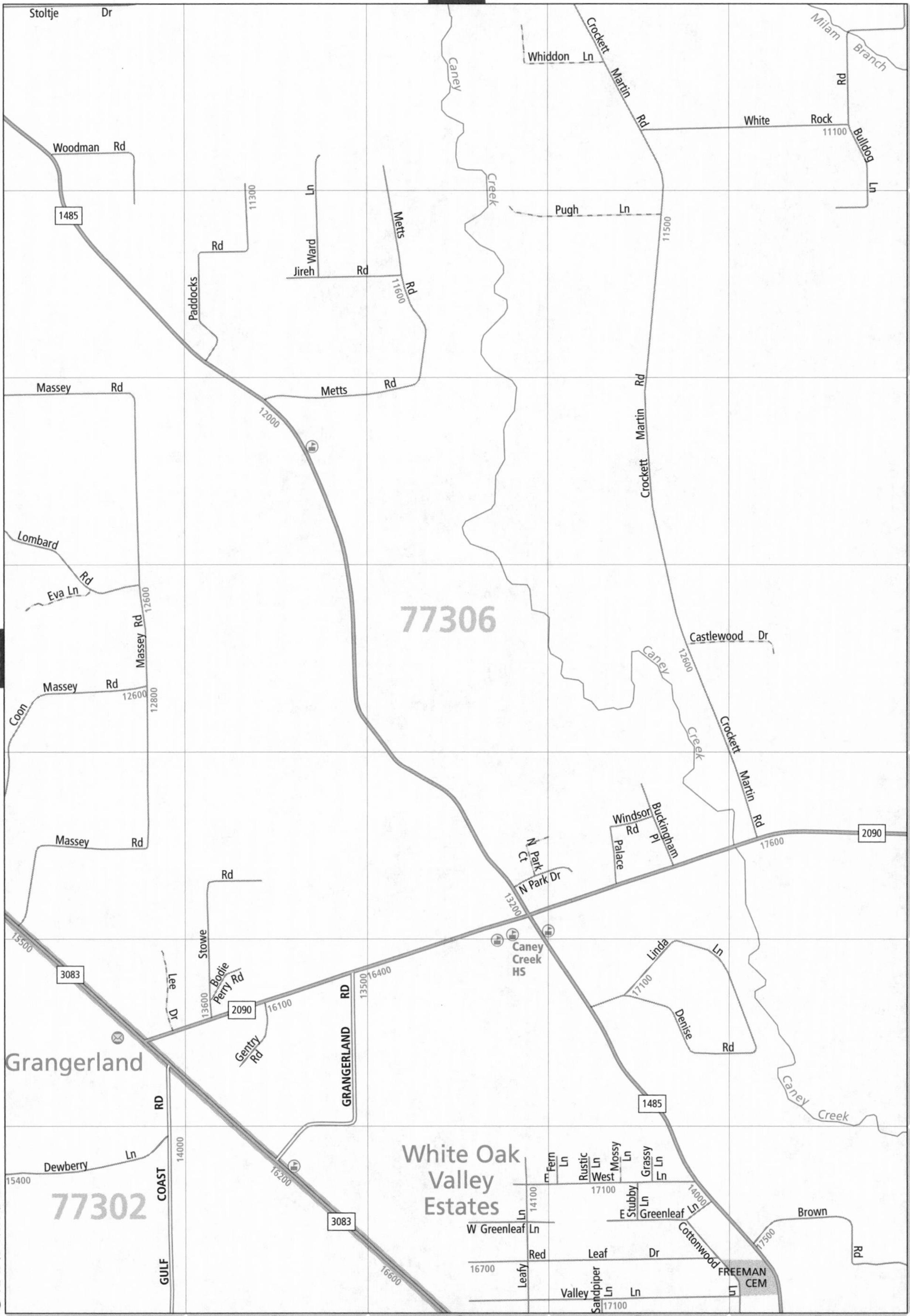

Stoltje Dr
Woodman Rd
1485
Paddocks Rd
11300
Ward Ln
Jireh Rd
Metts Rd
11600
Caney Creek
Whiddon Ln
Crockett Martin Rd
White Rock
11100
Bulldog Ln
Rd
Milam Branch
Pugh Ln
11500
Massey Rd
Metts Rd
12000
Lombard Rd
Eva Ln
12600
Massey Rd
Massey Rd
12600
12800
Coon
77306
Castlewood Dr
12600
Caney Creek
Crockett Martin Rd
Massey Rd
Windsor Rd
Buckingham Pl
Palace
2090
17600
N Park Ct
N Park Dr
13200
Rd
Stowe
Caney Creek HS
13500
3083
Lee Dr
Bodie Perry Rd
13600
2090
16100
16400
13500
RD
GRANGERLAND
Linda Ln
17100
Denise Rd
Gentry Rd
Grangerland
RD
COAST
GULF
14000
1485
Caney Creek
Dewberry Ln
15400
77302
16200
3083
White Oak Valley Estates
Fern Ln
E
Rustic Ln
West
Mossy Ln
Grassy Ln
17100
14100
Ln
W Greenleaf Ln
E Stubby Ln
Greenleaf Ln
14000
Cottonwood Ln
Brown Rd
17500
Red Leaf Dr
16700
Leafy
Sandpiper Ln
Valley Ln
17100
Ln
FREEMAN CEM
16600

30°17'32"
30°17'06"
30°16'40"
30°16'14"
30°15'48"
30°15'22"
30°14'55"
30°14'29"

1 2 3 4 5 6 7

A B C D E

95°20'12" 95°19'42" 95°19'11" 95°18'41" 95°18'11" 95°17'41"

SEE 2534 MAP

SEE 2532 MAP

SEE 2679 MAP

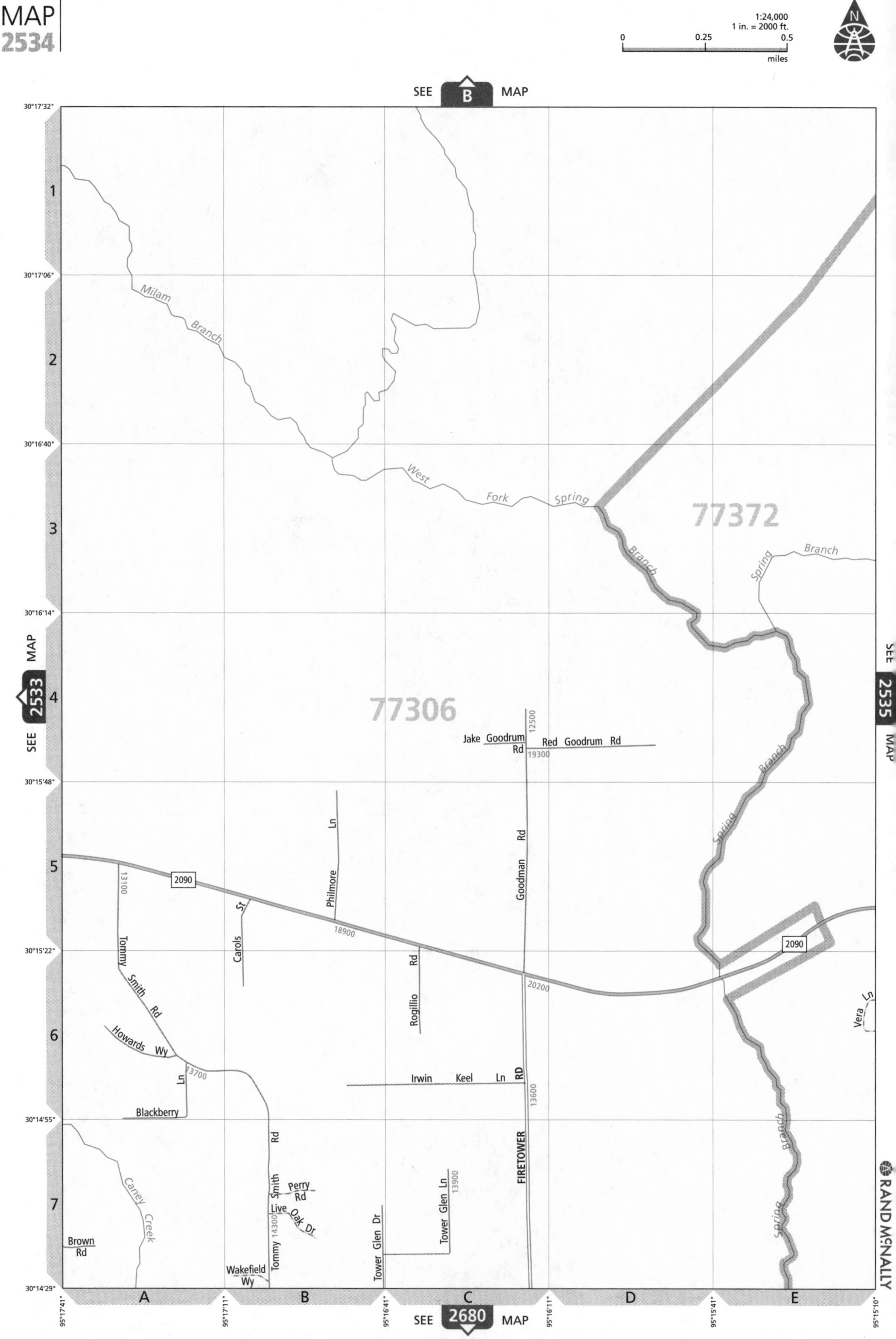
1:24,000
1 in. = 2000 ft.
0
0.25
0.5
miles
SEE B MAP
SEE 2533 MAP
SEE 2535 MAP
SEE 2680 MAP
30°17'32"
30°17'06"
30°16'40"
30°16'14"
30°15'48"
30°15'22"
30°14'55"
30°14'29"
95°17'41"
95°17'11"
95°16'41"
95°16'11"
95°15'41"
95°15'10"
1
2
3
4
5
6
7
A
B
C
D
E
Milam Branch
West Fork Spring Branch
Spring Branch
77372
77306
Jake Goodrum Rd
Red Goodrum Rd
12500
19300
Philmore Ln
Goodman Rd
2090
13100
Carols St
18900
Tommy Smith Rd
Rogillio Rd
20200
Howards Wy
13700
Ln
Blackberry
Irwin Keel Ln
FIRETOWER RD
13600
Vera Ln
Caney Creek
Brown Rd
Smith Rd
Perry Rd
Live Oak Dr
14300
Tommy
Wakefield Wy
Tower Glen Dr
Tower Glen Ln
13900
RAND McNALLY

1:24,000
1 in. = 2000 ft.
0 0.25 0.5
miles

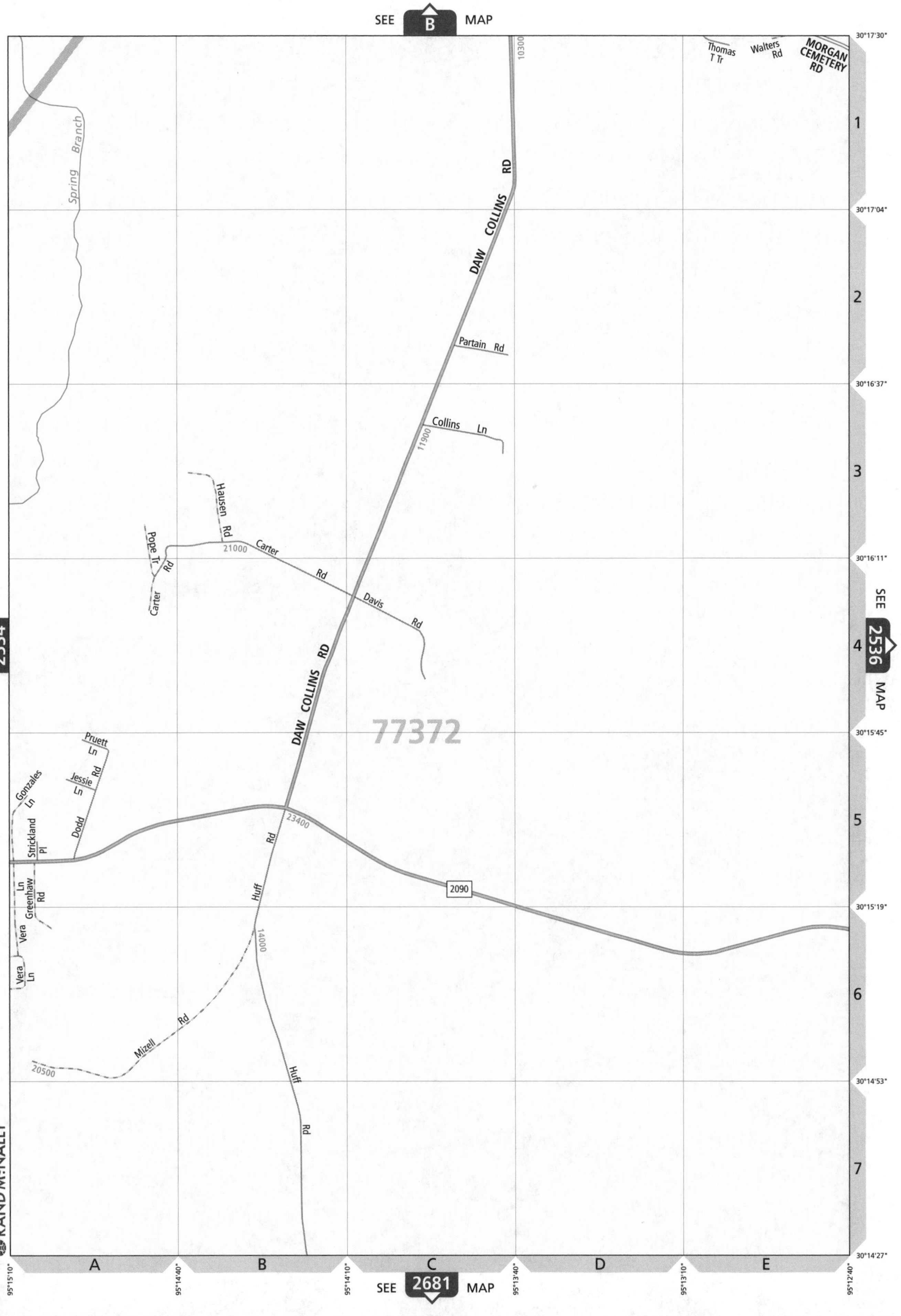
SEE B MAP
SEE 2681 MAP
SEE 2534 MAP
SEE 2536 MAP
DAW COLLINS RD
Spring Branch
Thomas T Tr
Walters Rd
MORGAN CEMETERY RD
Partain Rd
Collins Ln
11900
10300
Hausen Rd
Pope Tr
Carter Rd
21000
Carter
Davis Rd
77372
Pruett Ln
Jessie Ln
Rd
Dodd
Gonzales Ln
Strickland Pl
Greenhaw Rd
Ln
Vera
Vera Ln
Huff Rd
23400
2090
14000
Mizell Rd
20500
Huff Rd
1
2
3
4
5
6
7
A
B
C
D
E
30°17'30"
30°17'04"
30°16'37"
30°16'11"
30°15'45"
30°15'19"
30°14'53"
30°14'27"
95°15'10"
95°14'40"
95°14'10"
95°13'40"
95°13'10"
95°12'40"

1:24,000
1 in. = 2000 ft.
0 0.25 0.5
miles

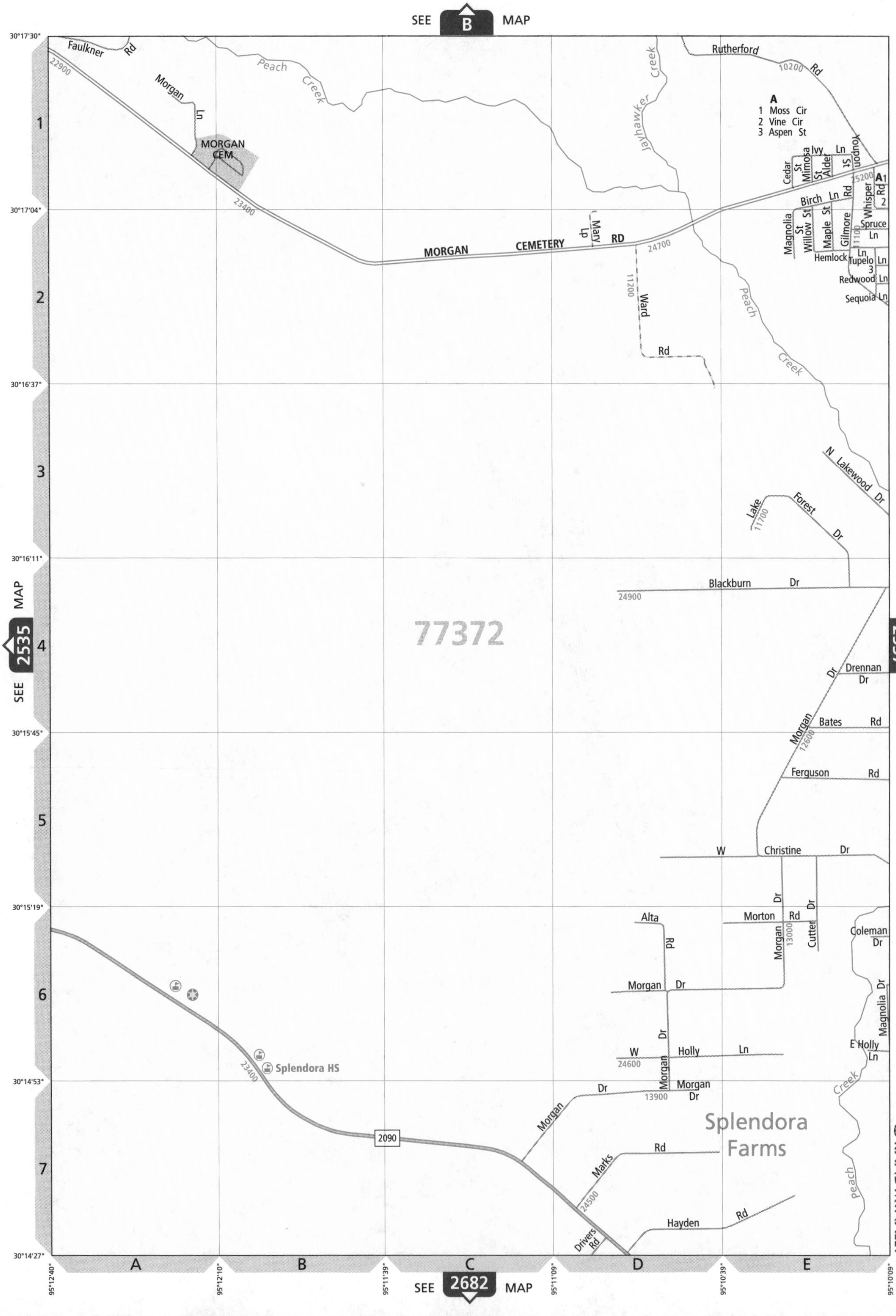
SEE B MAP
SEE 2535 MAP
SEE 2537 MAP
SEE 2682 MAP
30°17'30"
30°17'04"
30°16'37"
30°16'11"
30°15'45"
30°15'19"
30°14'53"
30°14'27"
95°12'40"
95°12'10"
95°11'39"
95°11'09"
95°10'39"
95°10'09"
1
2
3
4
5
6
7
A
B
C
D
E
Faulkner Rd
22900
Morgan Ln
Peach Creek
MORGAN CEM
23400
MORGAN CEMETERY RD
Mary Lp
24700
11200
Ward Rd
Jayhawker Creek
Rutherford Rd
10200
A
1 Moss Cir
2 Vine Cir
3 Aspen St
Ivy Ln
Cedar St
Mimosa St
Alder St
Juniper
Birch Ln
Rd
Whisper
Magnolia St
Willow St
Maple St
Gilmore
Spruce Ln
Hemlock
Tupelo Ln
Redwood Ln
Sequoia Ln
N Lakewood Dr
Lake
11700
Forest Dr
Blackburn Dr
24900
77372
Drennan Dr
Morgan Dr
12600
Bates Rd
Ferguson Rd
W Christine Dr
Alta Rd
Morton Rd
Dr
Cutter Dr
13000
Coleman Dr
Morgan Dr
Magnolia Dr
W Holly Ln
24600
E Holly Ln
Splendora HS
23400
Morgan Dr
13900
Splendora Farms
2090
Marks Rd
24500
Drivers Rd
Hayden Rd
Peach Creek

1:24,000
1 in. = 2000 ft.
0 0.25 0.5
miles

SEE B MAP

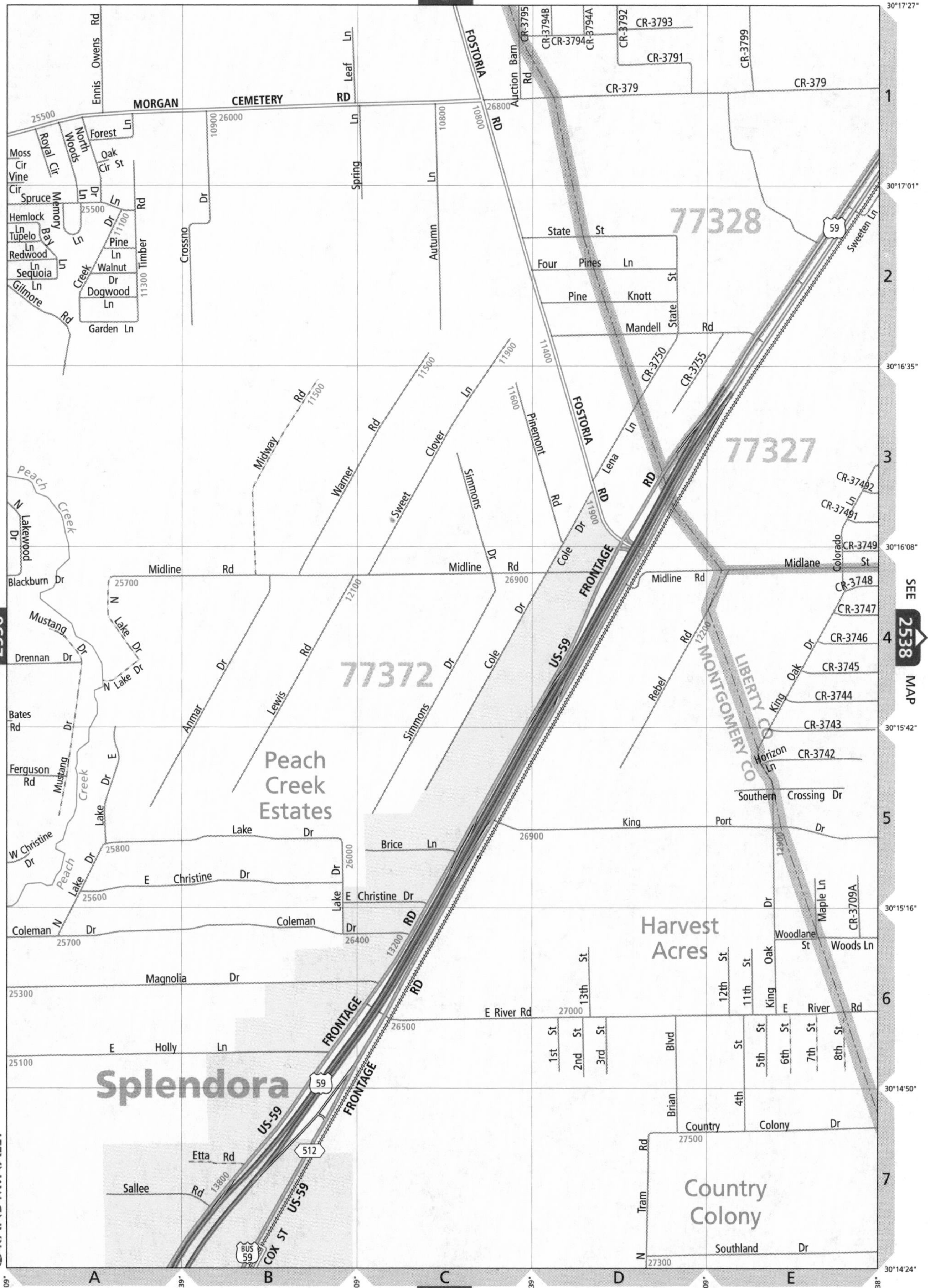
MORGAN CEMETERY RD
Ennis Owens Rd
Leaf Ln
FOSTORIA RD
CR-3795
CR-3794B
CR-3794A
CR-3794
CR-3792
CR-3793
CR-3791
CR-3799
CR-379
Auction Barn Rd
Forest Ln
Moss Cir
Royal Cir
North Woods
Oak Cir
St
Vine Cir
Spruce
Memory Ln
Dr
Ln
Rd
Hemlock Ln
Tupelo Ln
Redwood Ln
Sequoia Ln
Gilmore Rd
Bay Ln
Creek
Pine Ln
Walnut Dr
Dogwood Ln
Garden Ln
Timber
Crossno Dr
Spring Ln
Autumn Ln
77328
59
Sweeten Ln
State St
Four Pines Ln
Pine Knott St
Mandell State Rd
CR-3750
CR-3755
Midway Rd
Warner Rd
Clover Ln
Pinemont Rd
Simmons Dr
Sweet
Lena Ln
77327
CR-37492
CR-37491
Peach Creek
N Lakewood Dr
Blackburn Dr
Midline Rd
Midlane St
Colorado
CR-3749
CR-3748
CR-3747
CR-3746
CR-3745
CR-3744
CR-3743
CR-3742
Cole Dr
FRONTAGE RD
US-59
Rebel Rd
MONTGOMERY CO
LIBERTY CO
King Oak Dr
Mustang Dr
Drennan Dr
N Lake Dr
Anmar Dr
Lewis Rd
77372
Simmons Dr
Bates Rd
Ferguson Rd
Mustang
E Lake Dr
Peach Creek Estates
Horizon Ln
Southern Crossing Dr
King Port Dr
Lake Dr
W Christine Dr
Brice Ln
E Christine Dr
Lake Dr
Maple Ln
CR-3709A
Coleman Dr
Harvest Acres
Woodlane St
Woods Ln
Magnolia Dr
13th St
12th St
11th St
King Oak
E River Rd
1st St
2nd St
3rd St
Brian Blvd
4th St
5th St
6th St
7th St
8th St
E Holly Ln
Splendora
59
Country Colony Dr
512
Etta Rd
Sallee Rd
Tram Rd
Country Colony
Southland Dr
BUS 59
COX ST
1
2
3
4
5
6
7
A
B
C
D
E

SEE 2536 MAP

SEE 2538 MAP

SEE 2683 MAP

1:24,000
1 in. = 2000 ft.
0 0.25 0.5
miles

SEE B MAP

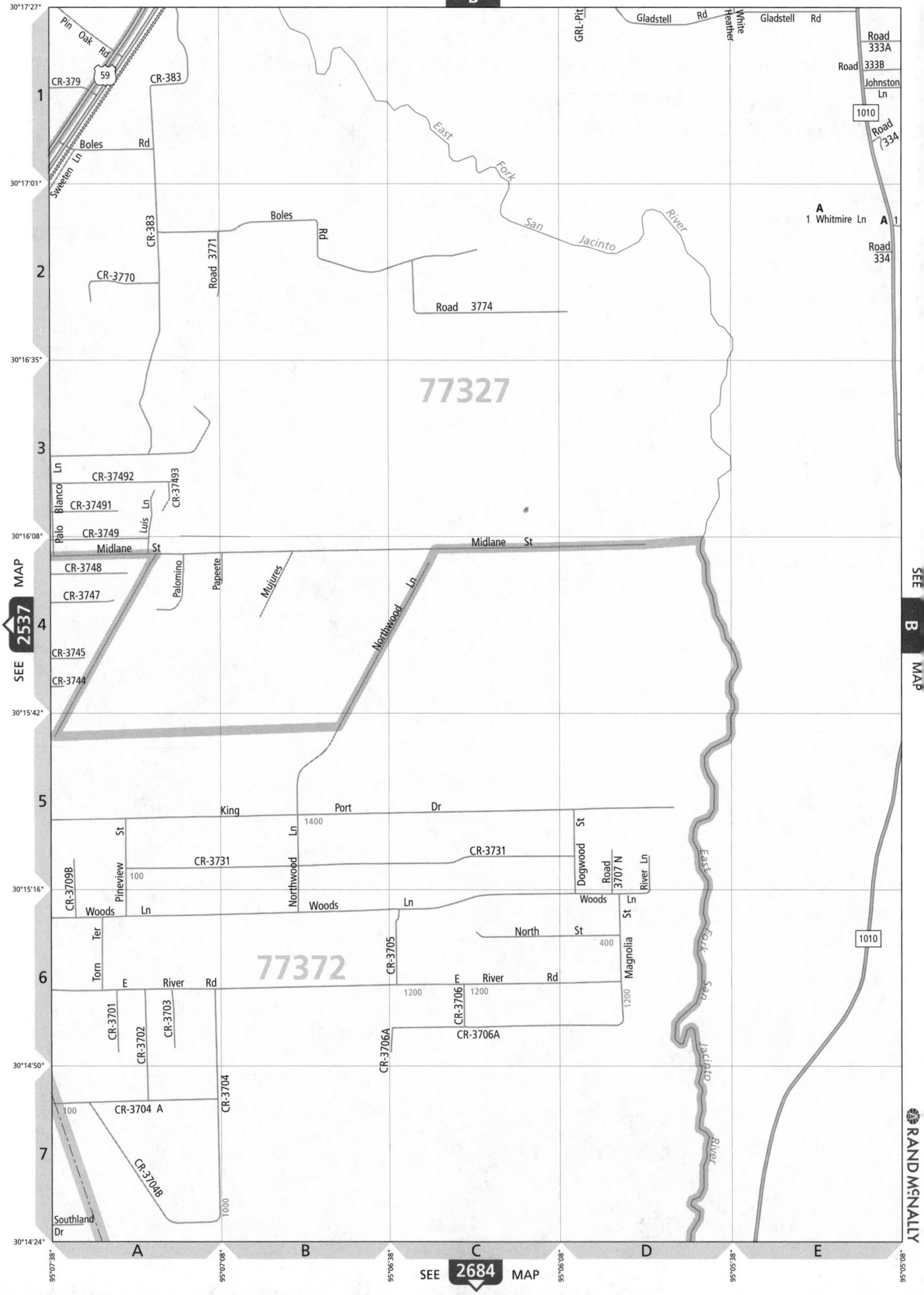
Pin Oak Rd
59
CR-379
CR-383
Boles Rd
Sweeten Ln
Boles Rd
Road 3771
CR-3770
Road 3774
East Fork San Jacinto River
GRL-Pit
Gladstell Rd
White Heather
Gladstell Rd
Road 333A
Road 333B
Johnston Ln
1010
Road 334
A
1 Whitmire Ln
A 1
Road 334
77327
Ln
CR-37492
CR-37493
Palo Blanco
CR-37491
Luis Ln
CR-3749
Midlane St
Midlane St
CR-3748
Palomino
Papeete
Mujures
Northwood Ln
CR-3747
CR-3745
CR-3744
King Port Dr
1400
Pineview St
CR-3709B
100
CR-3731
Northwood Ln
CR-3731
Dogwood St
Road 3707 N
River Ln
Woods Ln
Woods Ln
Woods Ln
North St
400
Torn Ter
77372
CR-3705
Magnolia St
1010
E River Rd
E River Rd
1200
1200
1200
CR-3701
CR-3702
CR-3703
CR-3706
CR-3706A
CR-3706A
East Fork San Jacinto River
CR-3704
100
CR-3704 A
CR-3704B
1000
Southland Dr
30°17'27"
30°17'01"
30°16'35"
30°16'08"
30°15'42"
30°15'16"
30°14'50"
30°14'24"
95°07'38"
95°07'08"
95°06'38"
95°06'08"
95°05'38"
95°05'08"
1
2
3
4
5
6
7
A
B
C
D
E

SEE 2537 MAP

SEE B MAP

SEE 2684 MAP

1:24,000
1 in. = 2000 ft.
0 0.25 0.5
miles

SEE B MAP

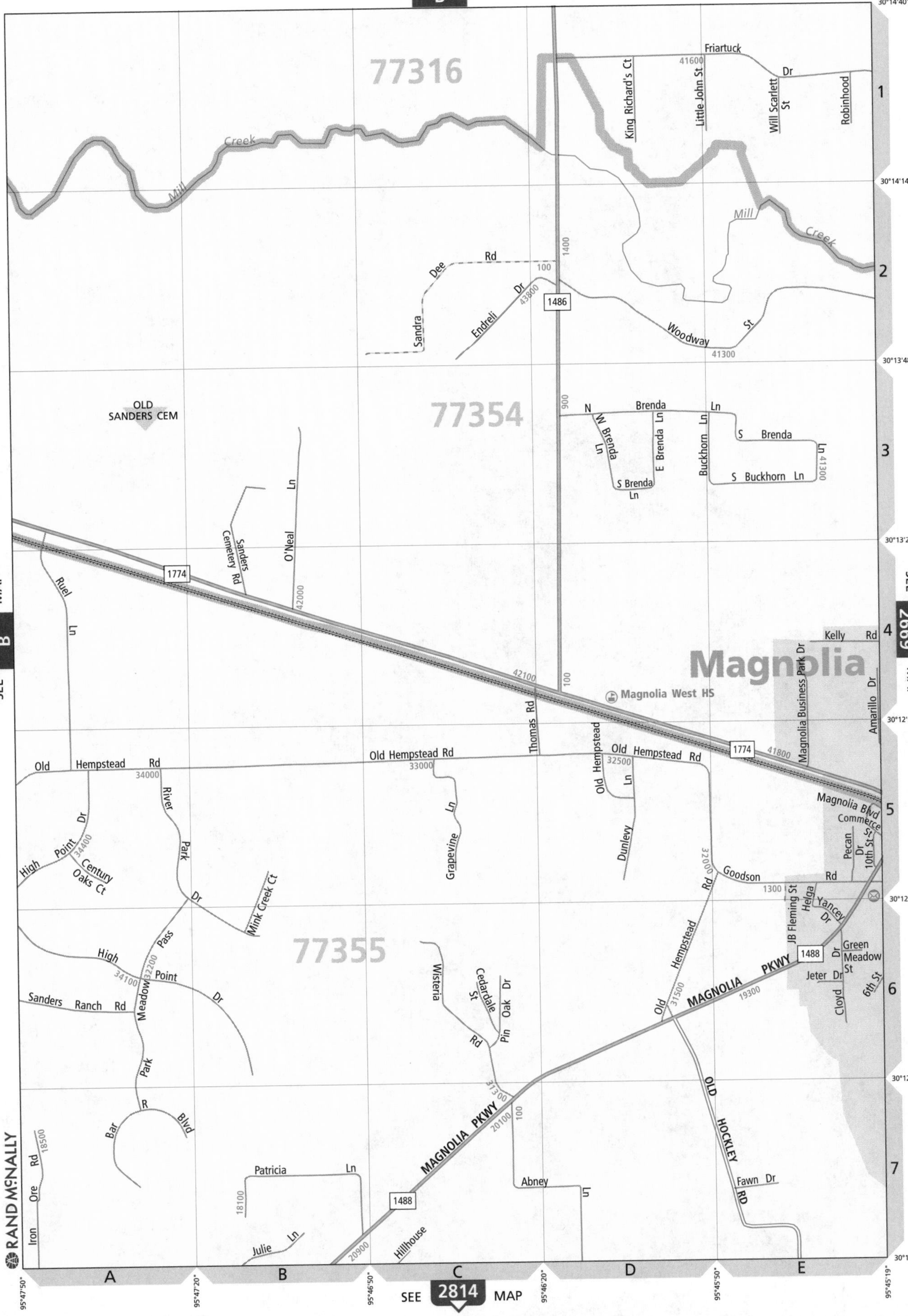
77316
77354
77355
Magnolia
Mill Creek
Friartuck
King Richard's Ct
Little John St
Will Scarlett St
Dr
Robinhood
41600
Dee Rd
Sandra
Endreli Dr
43800
100
1400
1486
Woodway St
41300
OLD SANDERS CEM
900
N Brenda Ln
W Brenda Ln
E Brenda Ln
Buckhorn Ln
S Brenda
S Brenda Ln
S Buckhorn Ln
Ln 41300
O'Neal Ln
Sanders Cemetery Rd
42000
1774
Ruel Ln
Kelly Rd
Magnolia Business Park Dr
Amarillo Dr
42100
100
Magnolia West HS
Thomas Rd
Old Hempstead Rd
34000
33000
32500
Old Hempstead Ln
41800
Magnolia Blvd
Commerce St
Pecan Dr
10th St
River Park Dr
High Point Dr
34400
Century Oaks Ct
Mink Creek Ct
Grapevine Ln
Dunlevy
32000
Goodson Rd
1300
JB Fleming St
Helga
Yancey Dr
Green Meadow Dr
Green Meadow St
Jeter Dr
Cloyd
6th St
1488
High Point Dr
34100
32200
Meadow Pass
Sanders Ranch Rd
Meadow Park
Wisteria
Cedardale St
Pin Oak Dr
Rd
Old Hempstead Rd
31500
MAGNOLIA PKWY
19300
31300
20100
100
OLD HOCKLEY RD
Bar R Blvd
Iron Ore Rd
18500
Patricia Ln
18100
Julie Ln
20900
Hillhouse
Abney Ln
Fawn Dr
1
2
3
4
5
6
7
A
B
C
D
E
30°14'40"
30°14'14"
30°13'48"
30°13'22"
30°12'56"
30°12'29"
30°12'03"
30°11'37"
95°47'50"
95°47'20"
95°46'50"
95°46'20"
95°45'50"
95°45'19"

SEE B MAP

SEE 2669 MAP

SEE 2814 MAP

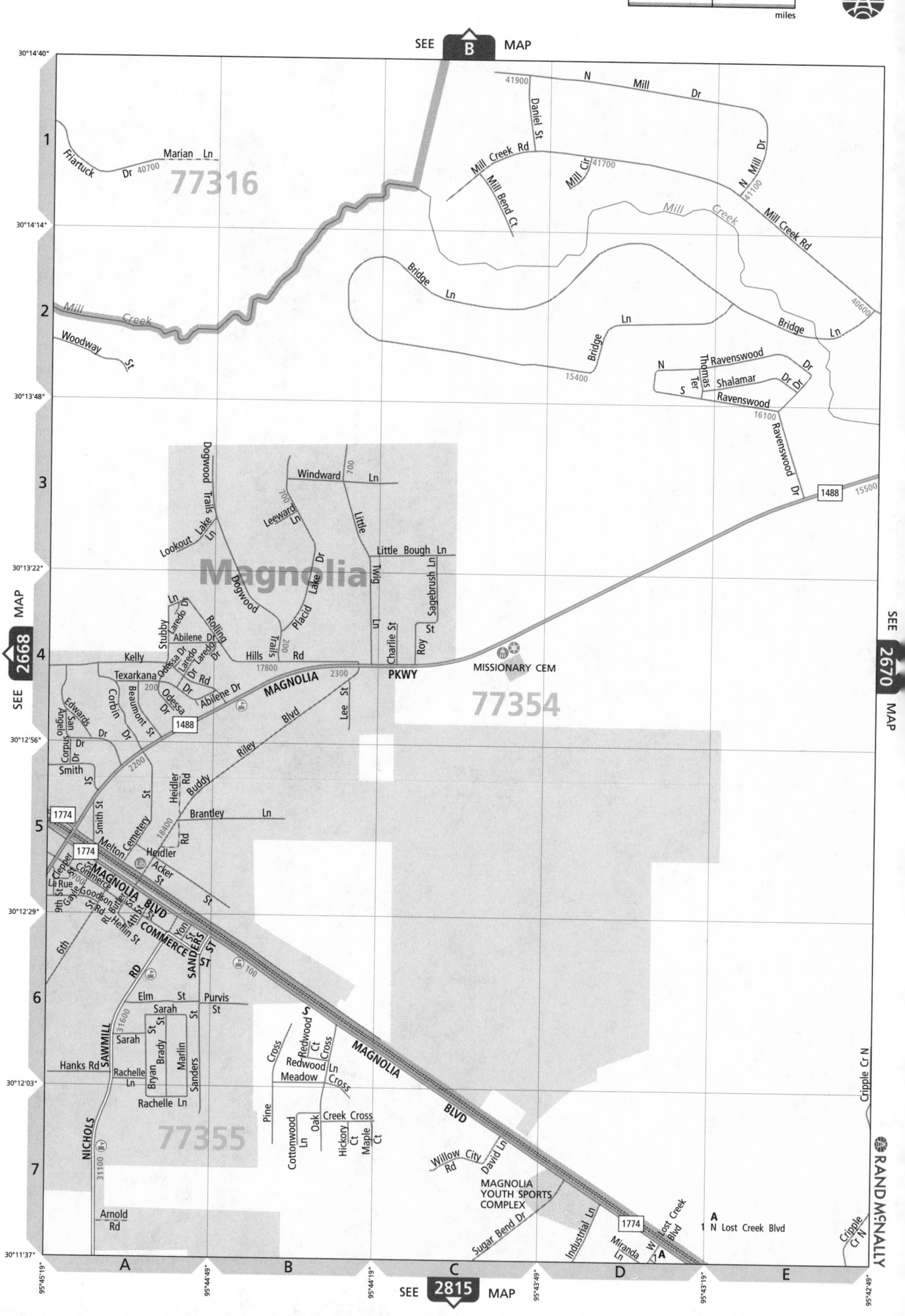
1:24,000
1 in. = 2000 ft.
0
0.25
0.5
miles
N
SEE B MAP
SEE 2668 MAP
SEE 2670 MAP
SEE 2815 MAP
Magnolia
77316
77354
77355
N Mill Dr
Daniel St
Mill Creek Rd
Mill Bend Ct
Mill Cir
N Mill Dr
Mill Creek
Mill Creek Rd
Friartuck Dr
Marian Ln
Woodway St
Bridge Ln
Bridge Ln
N Ravenswood Dr
Thomas Ter
Shalamar Dr
S Ravenswood Dr
Ravenswood Dr
Windward Ln
Leeward Ln
Little Twig Ln
Little Bough Ln
Sagebrush Ln
Dogwood Trails
Lookout Lake Ln
Dogwood Trails
Placid Lake Dr
Rolling Hills Rd
Stubby Ln
Laredo Dr
Abilene Dr
Odessa Dr
Kelly
Texarkana
Charlie St
Roy St
Lee St
MAGNOLIA PKWY
MISSIONARY CEM
Edwards Dr
San Angelo Dr
Corbin Dr
Beaumont St
Corpus Dr
Smith St
Riley Blvd
Buddy Rd
Heidler Rd
Brantley Ln
Smith St
Cemetery St
Melton St
Heidler
Acker St
Clepper St
9th St
La Rue
Gayle
Goodson Rd
Commerce
MAGNOLIA BLVD
Butler
4th St
Heflin St
6th
COMMERCE ST
Von St
SANDERS ST
SAWMILL RD
Elm St
Purvis St
Sarah
Sarah
Brady St
Marlin
Sanders
Hanks Rd
Rachelle Ln
Bryan
Rachelle Ln
NICHOLS
Arnold Rd
Pine Cross
S Redwood Ct
Cross
Redwood Ln
Meadow Cross
Cottonwood Ln
Oak Ct
Creek Cross
Hickory Ct
Maple Ct
MAGNOLIA BLVD
Willow City Rd
David Ln
MAGNOLIA YOUTH SPORTS COMPLEX
Sugar Bend Dr
Industrial Ln
Miranda Ln
W Lost Creek Blvd
A
1 N Lost Creek Blvd
Cripple Cr N
Cripple Cr N
1488
1774
RAND McNALLY
A
B
C
D
E
1
2
3
4
5
6
7

1:24,000
1 in. = 2000 ft.
0 0.25 0.5
miles

SEE B MAP

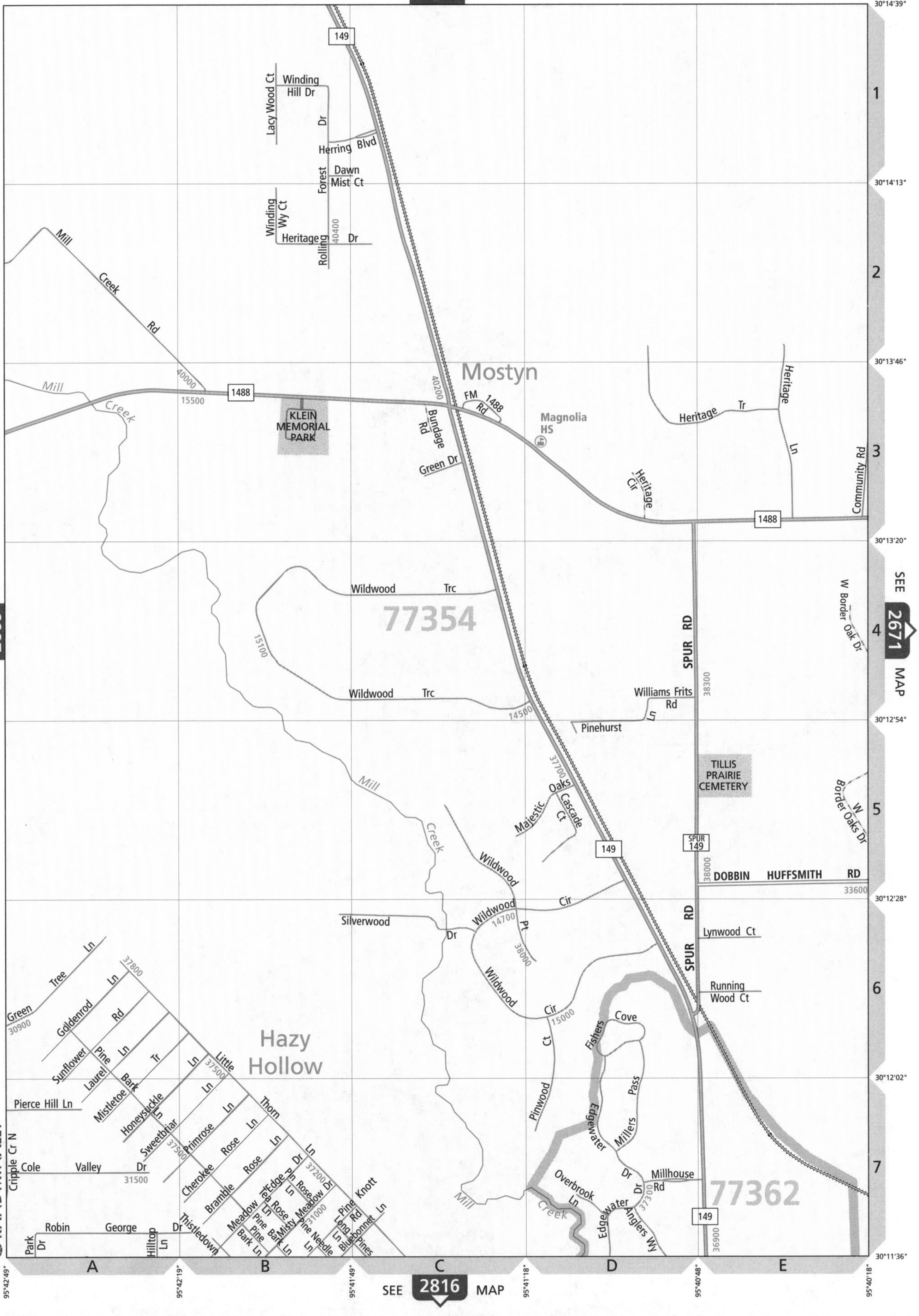
30°14'39"
30°14'13"
30°13'46"
30°13'20"
30°12'54"
30°12'28"
30°12'02"
30°11'36"
1
2
3
4
5
6
7
A
B
C
D
E
149
Winding
Hill Dr
Lacy Wood Ct
Dr
Herring Blvd
Forest
Dawn
Mist Ct
Winding
Wy Ct
Heritage
Dr
Rolling
40400
Mill
Creek
Rd
40000
15500
1488
KLEIN
MEMORIAL
PARK
Mostyn
40200
Bundage
Rd
FM 1488
Rd
Magnolia
HS
Green Dr
Heritage
Cir
Heritage
Tr
Heritage
Ln
Community Rd
1488
Wildwood
Trc
77354
15100
Wildwood
Trc
14500
SPUR RD
38300
Williams Frits
Rd
Ln
Pinehurst
W Border Oak Dr
37700
Oaks
Majestic
Cascade
Ct
TILLIS
PRAIRIE
CEMETERY
W Border Oaks Dr
149
SPUR
149
Wildwood
38000
DOBBIN HUFFSMITH RD
33600
Cir
Silverwood
Dr
Wildwood
14700
Pt
38000
Lynwood Ct
SPUR RD
Running
Wood Ct
Wildwood
Cir
15000
Ct
Cove
Fishers
Pass
Hazy
Hollow
Pinwood
Edgewater
Millers
Dr
Millhouse
Rd
Overbrook
Ln
Edgewater
Dr
37300
Anglers Wy
Creek
Mill
77362
149
36900
Green
30900
Tree
Ln
37800
Goldenrod
Ln
Rd
Sunflower
Pine
Ln
Tr
Laurel
Bark
Ln
Little
37500
Ln
Mistletoe
Honeysuckle
Ln
Pierce Hill Ln
Sweetbriar
Primrose
Ln
Thorn
37500
Ln
Cripple Cr N
Cole
Valley
Dr
31500
Cherokee
Rose
Rose
Dr
Ln
37200
Bramble
Edge
Pin Rose
Meadow
Tea Rose
Misty Meadow Dr
31000
Pine Knott
Rd
Ln
Ln
Robin
George
Dr
Park
Dr
Hilltop
Ln
Thistledown
Pine
Bark Ln
Pine
Bark Ln
Pine Needle
Ln
Long Leaf
Ln
Bluebonnet
Pines
Ln
95°42'49"
95°42'19"
95°41'49"
95°41'18"
95°40'48"
95°40'18"

SEE 2669 MAP

SEE 2671 MAP

SEE 2816 MAP

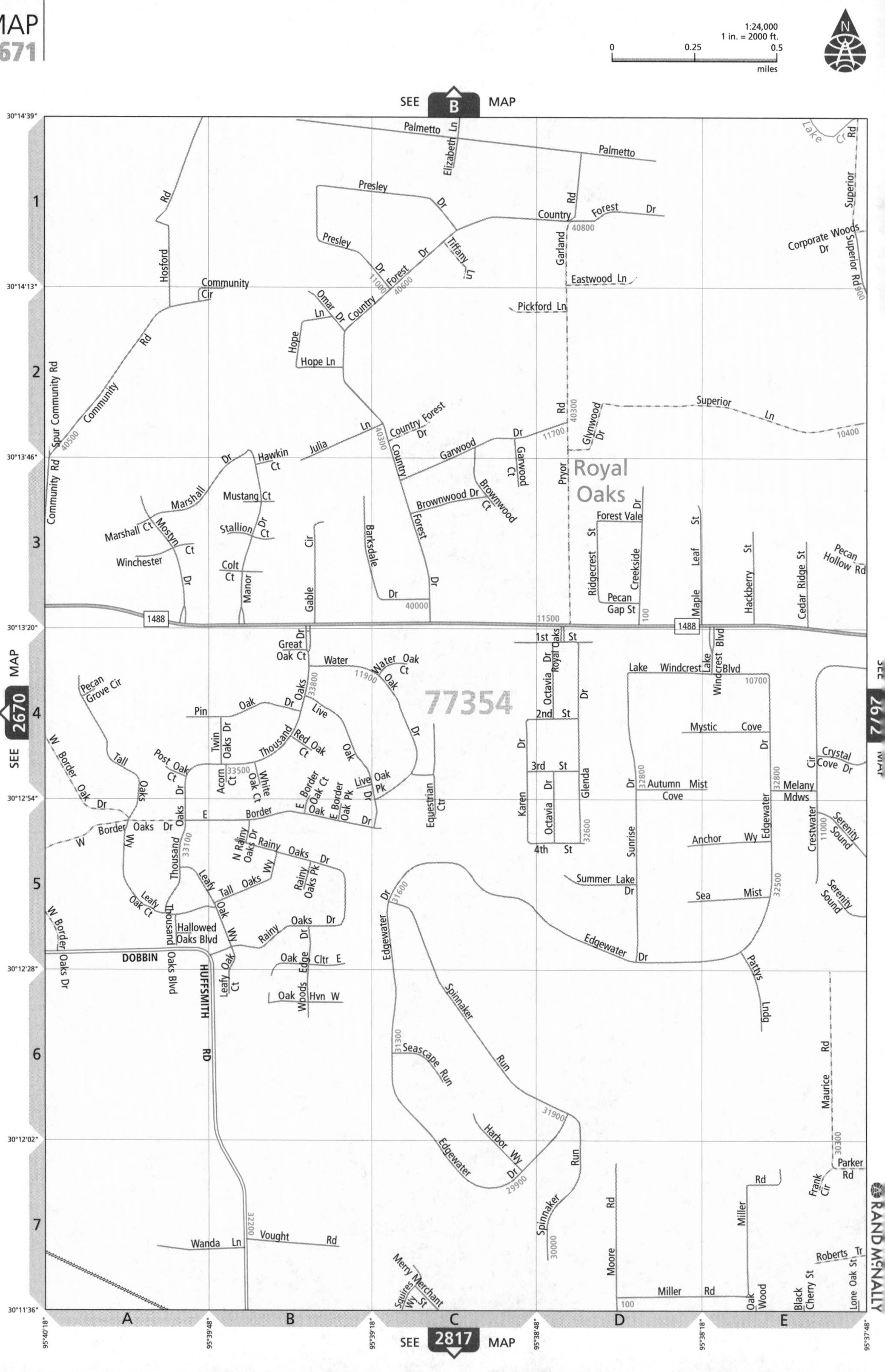
1:24,000
1 in. = 2000 ft.
0
0.25
0.5
miles
N
SEE B MAP
SEE 2817 MAP
SEE 2670 MAP
SEE 2672 MAP
30°14'39"
30°14'13"
30°13'46"
30°13'20"
30°12'54"
30°12'28"
30°12'02"
30°11'36"
95°40'18"
95°39'48"
95°39'18"
95°38'48"
95°38'18"
95°37'48"
A
B
C
D
E
1
2
3
4
5
6
7
Palmetto
Elizabeth Ln
Presley Dr
Country Forest Dr
Tiffany Ln
Garland Rd
40800
Eastwood Ln
Pickford Ln
Hosford Rd
Community Cir
Community Rd
Spur Community Rd
40500
Omar Dr
Hope Ln
Julia Ln
40300
11000
40600
Country Forest Dr
Garwood Dr
Garwood Ct
Brownwood Dr
Brownwood Ct
11700
Glynwood Dr
Superior Ln
10400
Corporate Woods Dr
Superior Rd
Lake Cir
Royal Oaks
Pryor
Community Rd
Marshall Dr
Marshall Ct
Hawkin Ct
Mustang Ct
Stallion Ct
Mostyn Dr
Winchester Ct
Colt Ct
Manor Dr
Gable Cir
Barksdale Dr
40000
Forest Vale Dr
Ridgecrest St
Creekside
Pecan Gap St
100
Maple Leaf St
Hackberry St
Cedar Ridge St
Pecan Hollow Rd
1488
11500
Great Oak Dr
Great Oak Ct
Water Oak Dr
Water Oak Ct
11900
33800
1st St
Royal Oaks
Octavia Dr
2nd St
3rd St
4th St
Karen Dr
Glenda Dr
32600
77354
Lake Windcrest Blvd
Windcrest Blvd
10700
Mystic Cove Dr
Crystal Cove Dr
Cir
Autumn Mist Cove
32800
Melany Mdws
Crestwater
11000
Serenity Sound
Pecan Grove Cir
Pin Oak Dr
Live Oak Dr
Twin Oaks Dr
Thousand Oaks Dr
Red Oak Ct
Post Oak Ct
Acorn Ct
33500
White Oak Ct
E Border Oak Ct
E Border Oak Pk
Live Oak Pk
Equestrian Ctr
W Border Oak Dr
Tall Oaks Wy
E Border Oaks Dr
W Border Oaks Dr
33100
N Rainy Oaks Dr
Rainy Oaks Dr
Rainy Oaks Pk
Leafy Tall Oak Wy
Leafy Oak Ct
Hallowed Oaks Blvd
Thousand Oaks Blvd
Oak Edge Cltr E
Oak Hvn W
Woods Edge Dr
DOBBIN
HUFFSMITH RD
Sunrise Dr
Anchor Wy
Edgewater Dr
Summer Lake Dr
Sea Mist
32500
Pattys Lndg
31600
Spinnaker Run
31300
Seascape Run
31900
Harbor Wy
29900
30000
Maurice Rd
30300
Parker Rd
Frank Cir
Moore Rd
Miller Rd
Oak Wood
Black Cherry St
Roberts Tr
Lone Oak St
Wanda Ln
Vought Rd
32200
Merry Merchant St
Squires Wy
RAND McNALLY

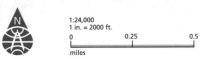

1:24,000
1 in. = 2000 ft.
0 0.25 0.5
miles

SEE B MAP

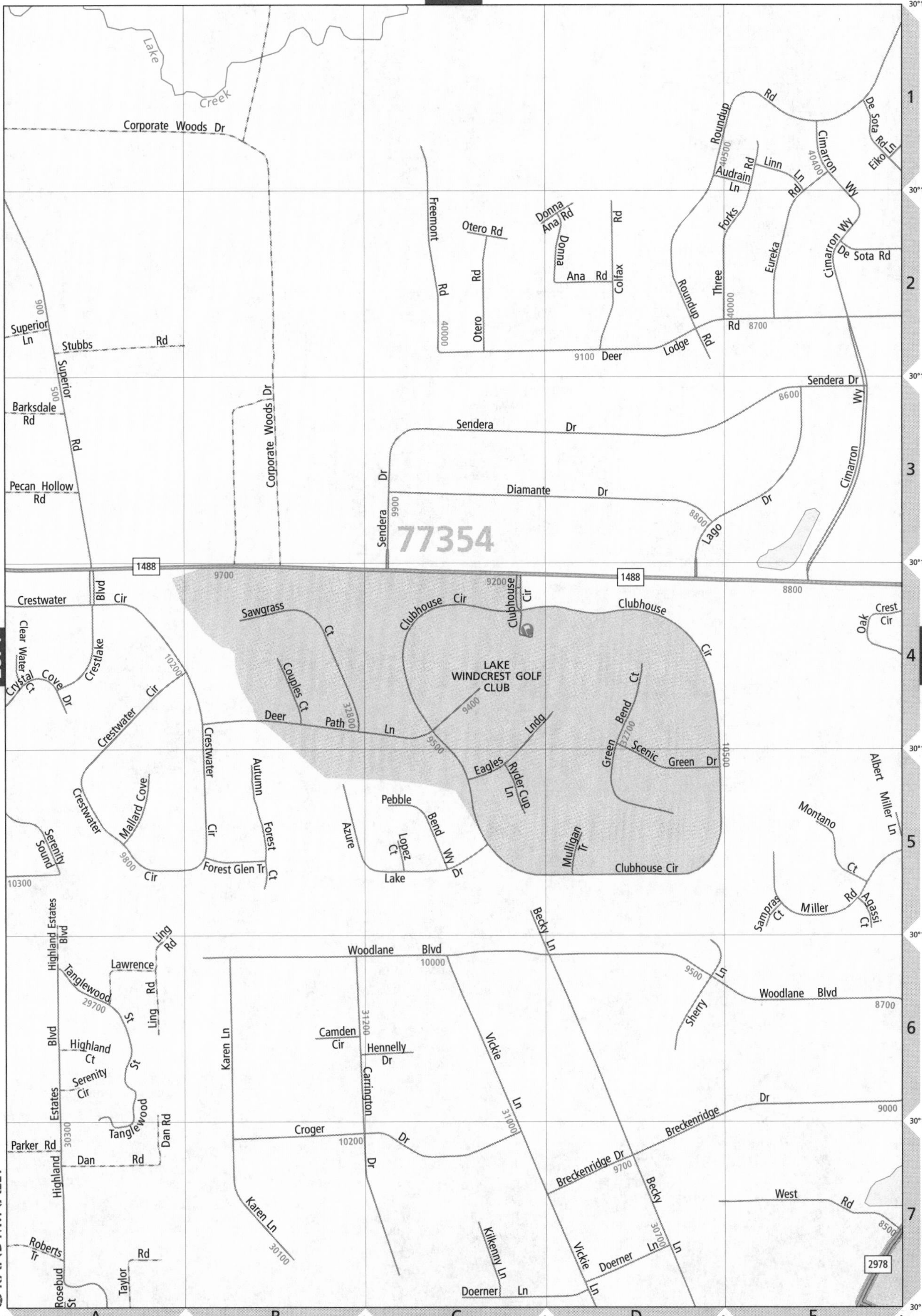
Lake Creek
Corporate Woods Dr
Corporate Woods Dr
Superior Ln
Stubbs Rd
Superior Rd
Barksdale Rd
Pecan Hollow Rd
Freemont Rd
Otero Rd
Otero Rd
Donna Ana Rd
Donna Ana Rd
Colfax Rd
Deer Lodge Rd
Roundup Rd
Audrain Ln
Linn Ln
Forks Rd
Three Forks Rd
Eureka Rd
Cimarron Wy
De Sota Rd
De Sota Rd Ln
Eiko Ln
Sendera Dr
Diamante Dr
Lago Dr
77354
1488
Crestwater Blvd Cir
Clear Water Ct
Crystal Cove Dr
Crestlake
Crestwater Cir
Sawgrass Ct
Couples Ct
Deer Path Ln
Clubhouse Cir
LAKE WINDCREST GOLF CLUB
Eagles Lndg
Ryder Cup Ln
Green Bend Ct
Scenic Green Dr
Mulligan Tr
Clubhouse Cir
Oak Crest Cir
Albert Miller Ln
Montano Ct
Miller Rd
Agassi Ct
Sampras Ct
Mallard Cove
Serenity Sound
Autumn Forest Ct
Forest Glen Tr
Azure
Pebble Bend Wy
Lopez Ct
Lake Dr
Becky Ln
Woodlane Blvd
Sherry Ln
Highland Estates Blvd
Tanglewood St
Lawrence Rd
Ling Rd
Highland Ct
Serenity Cir
Karen Ln
Camden Cir
Hennelly Dr
Carrington Dr
Vickie Ln
Croger Dr
Breckenridge Dr
Parker Rd
Dan Rd
Dan Rd
West Rd
2978
Kilkenny Ln
Doerner Ln
Roberts Tr
Taylor Rd
Rosebud St
A
B
C
D
E
1
2
3
4
5
6
7

SEE 2673 MAP

SEE 2818 MAP

1:24,000
1 in. = 2000 ft.
0 0.25 0.5
miles

SEE B MAP

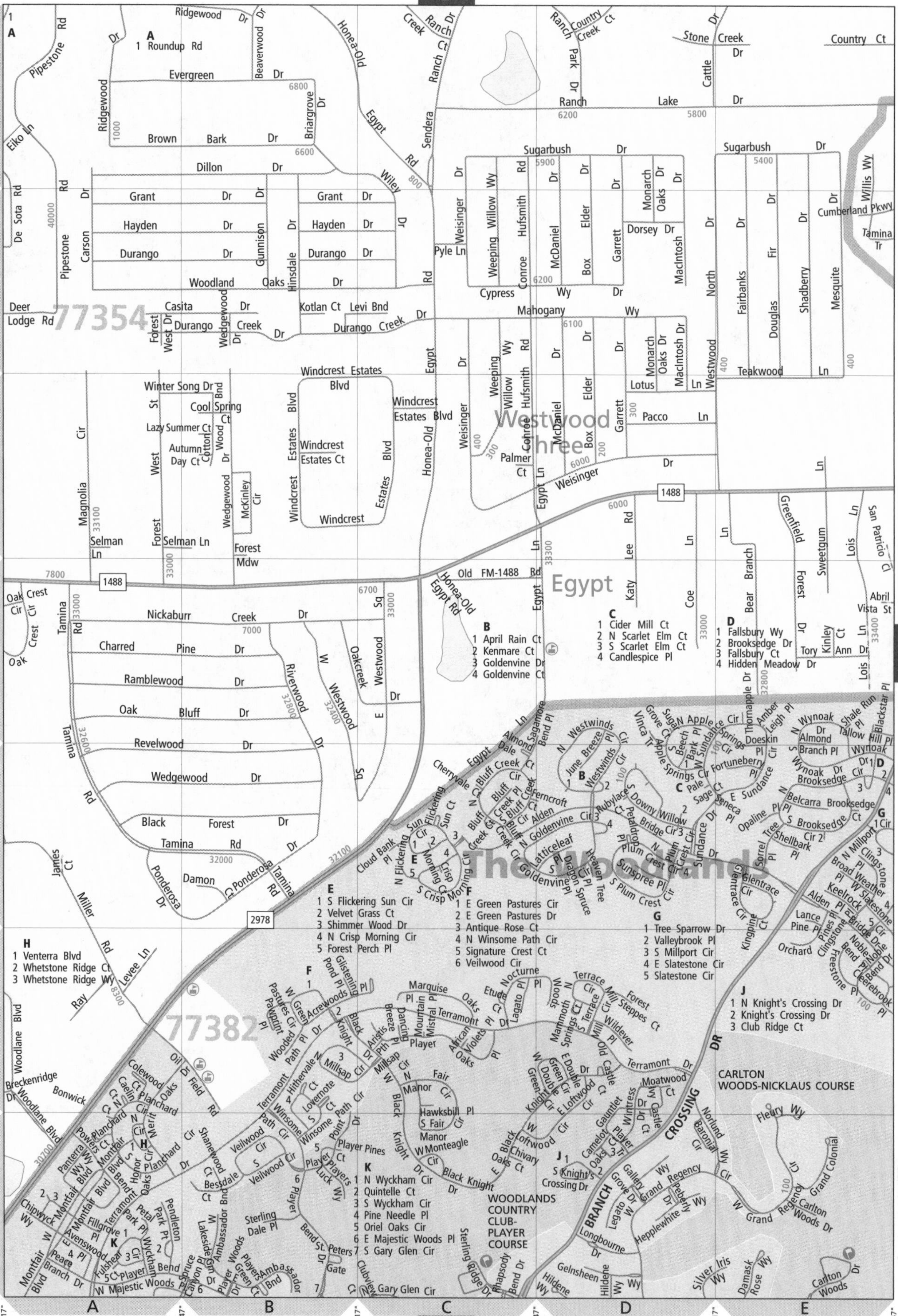
1 Roundup Rd
Ridgewood Dr
Evergreen Dr
Brown Bark Dr
Dillon Dr
Grant Dr
Hayden Dr
Durango Dr
Woodland Oaks Dr
Honea-Egypt Rd
Ranch Lake Dr
Sugarbush Dr
Mahogany Wy
Cypress Wy
Teakwood Ln
Windcrest Estates Blvd
Westwood Three
Weisinger Dr
1488
Old FM-1488 Rd
Egypt
Nickaburr Creek Dr
Charred Pine Dr
Ramblewood Dr
Oak Bluff Dr
Revelwood Dr
Wedgewood Dr
Black Forest Dr
Tamina Rd
2978
77354
77382
The Woodlands
WOODLANDS COUNTRY CLUB-PLAYER COURSE
CARLTON WOODS-NICKLAUS COURSE
Branch Crossing Dr
B
1 April Rain Ct
2 Kenmare Ct
3 Goldenvine Dr
4 Goldenvine Ct
C
1 Cider Mill Ct
2 N Scarlet Elm Ct
3 S Scarlet Elm Ct
4 Candlespice Pl
D
1 Fallsbury Wy
2 Brooksedge Dr
3 Fallsbury Ct
4 Hidden Meadow Dr
E
1 S Flickering Sun Cir
2 Velvet Grass Ct
3 Shimmer Wood Dr
4 N Crisp Morning Cir
5 Forest Perch Pl
F
1 E Green Pastures Cir
2 E Green Pastures Dr
3 Antique Rose Ct
4 N Winsome Path Cir
5 Signature Crest Ct
6 Veilwood Cir
G
1 Tree Sparrow Dr
2 Valleybrook Pl
3 S Millport Cir
4 E Slatestone Cir
5 Slatestone Cir
H
1 Venterra Blvd
2 Whetstone Ridge Ct
3 Whetstone Ridge Wy
J
1 N Knight's Crossing Dr
2 Knight's Crossing Dr
3 Club Ridge Ct
K
1 N Wyckham Cir
2 Quintelle Ct
3 S Wyckham Cir
4 Pine Needle Pl
5 Oriel Oaks Cir
6 E Majestic Woods Pl
7 S Gary Glen Cir
A B C D E
1 2 3 4 5 6 7
30°14'37"
30°14'11"
30°13'45"
30°13'19"
30°12'52"
30°12'26"
30°12'00"
30°11'34"
95°35'17"
95°34'47"
95°34'17"
95°33'47"
95°33'17"
95°32'47"

SEE 2672 MAP

SEE 2819 MAP

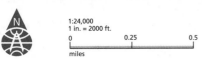

1:24,000
1 in. = 2000 ft.
0 0.25 0.5
miles

SEE 2528 MAP

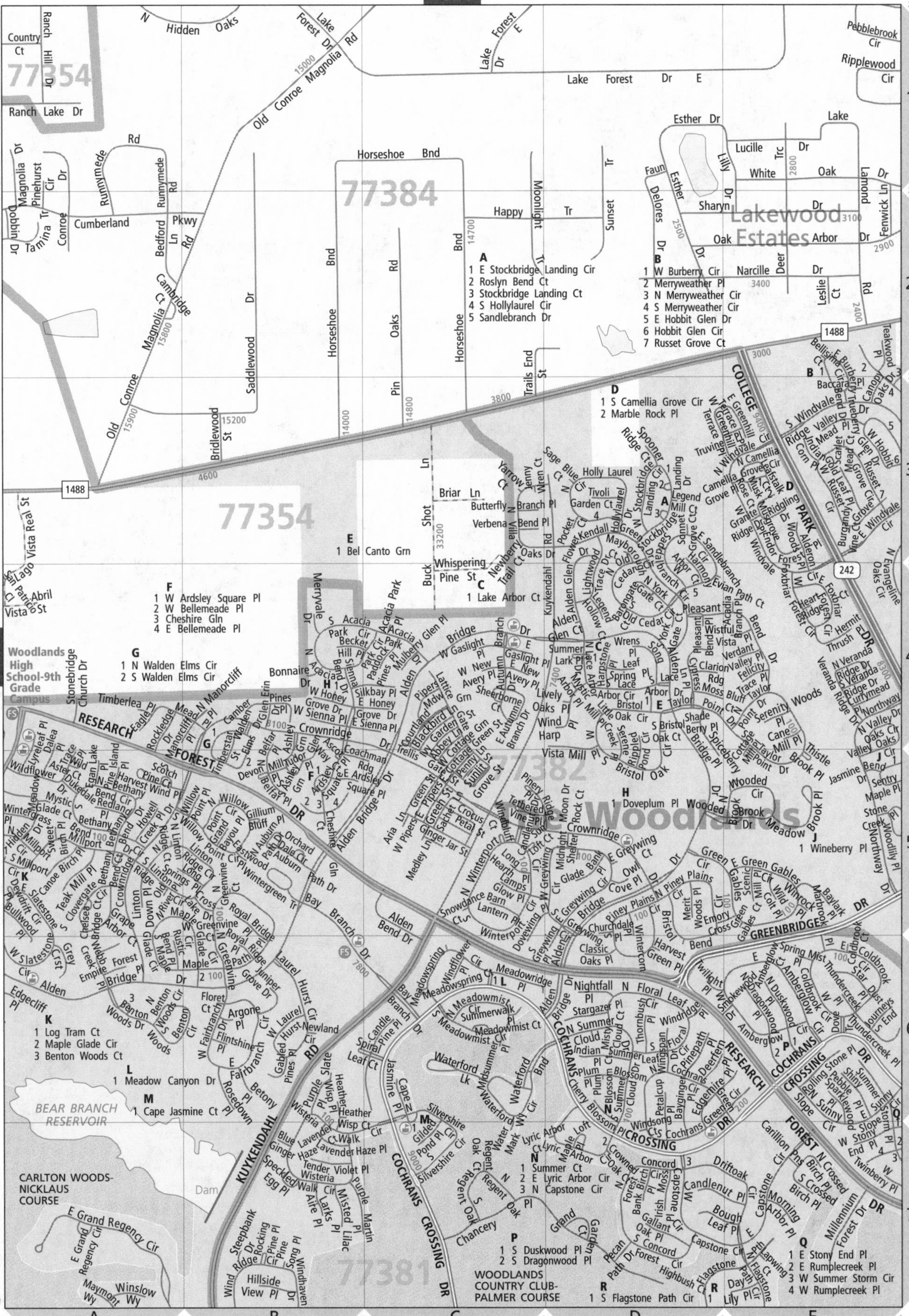

77354
77384
77382
77381
Lakewood Estates
The Woodlands
Woodlands High School-9th Grade Campus
BEAR BRANCH RESERVOIR
CARLTON WOODS-NICKLAUS COURSE
WOODLANDS COUNTRY CLUB-PALMER COURSE
RESEARCH FOREST DR
KUYKENDAHL RD
COCHRANS CROSSING DR
GROGANS MILL RD
COLLEGE PARK DR
GREENBRIDGE DR
Lake Forest Dr E
Old Conroe Magnolia Rd
1488
242
A
1 E Stockbridge Landing Cir
2 Roslyn Bend Ct
3 Stockbridge Landing Ct
4 S Hollylaurel Cir
5 Sandlebranch Dr
B
1 W Burberry Cir
2 Merryweather Pl
3 N Merryweather Cir
4 S Merryweather Cir
5 E Hobbit Glen Dr
6 Hobbit Glen Cir
7 Russet Grove Ct
C
1 Lake Arbor Ct
D
1 S Camellia Grove Cir
2 Marble Rock Pl
E
1 Bel Canto Grn
F
1 W Ardsley Square Pl
2 W Bellemeade Pl
3 Cheshire Gln
4 E Bellemeade Pl
G
1 N Walden Elms Cir
2 S Walden Elms Cir
H
1 Doveplum Pl
J
1 Wineberry Pl
K
1 Log Tram Ct
2 Maple Glade Cir
3 Benton Woods Ct
L
1 Meadow Canyon Dr
M
1 Cape Jasmine Ct
N
1 Summer Ct
2 E Lyric Arbor Cir
3 N Capstone Cir
P
1 S Duskwood Pl
2 S Dragonwood Pl
Q
1 E Stony End Pl
2 E Rumplecreek Pl
3 W Summer Storm Cir
4 W Rumplecreek Pl
R
1 S Flagstone Path Cir
30°14'35"
30°14'09"
30°13'43"
30°13'17"
30°12'50"
30°12'24"
30°11'58"
30°11'32"
95°32'47"
95°32'16"
95°31'46"
95°31'16"
95°30'46"
95°30'16"

A B C D E
1 2 3 4 5 6 7

SEE 2675 MAP

SEE 2673 MAP

SEE 2820 MAP

1:24,000
1 in. = 2000 ft.
0 0.25 0.5
miles

SEE 2529 MAP

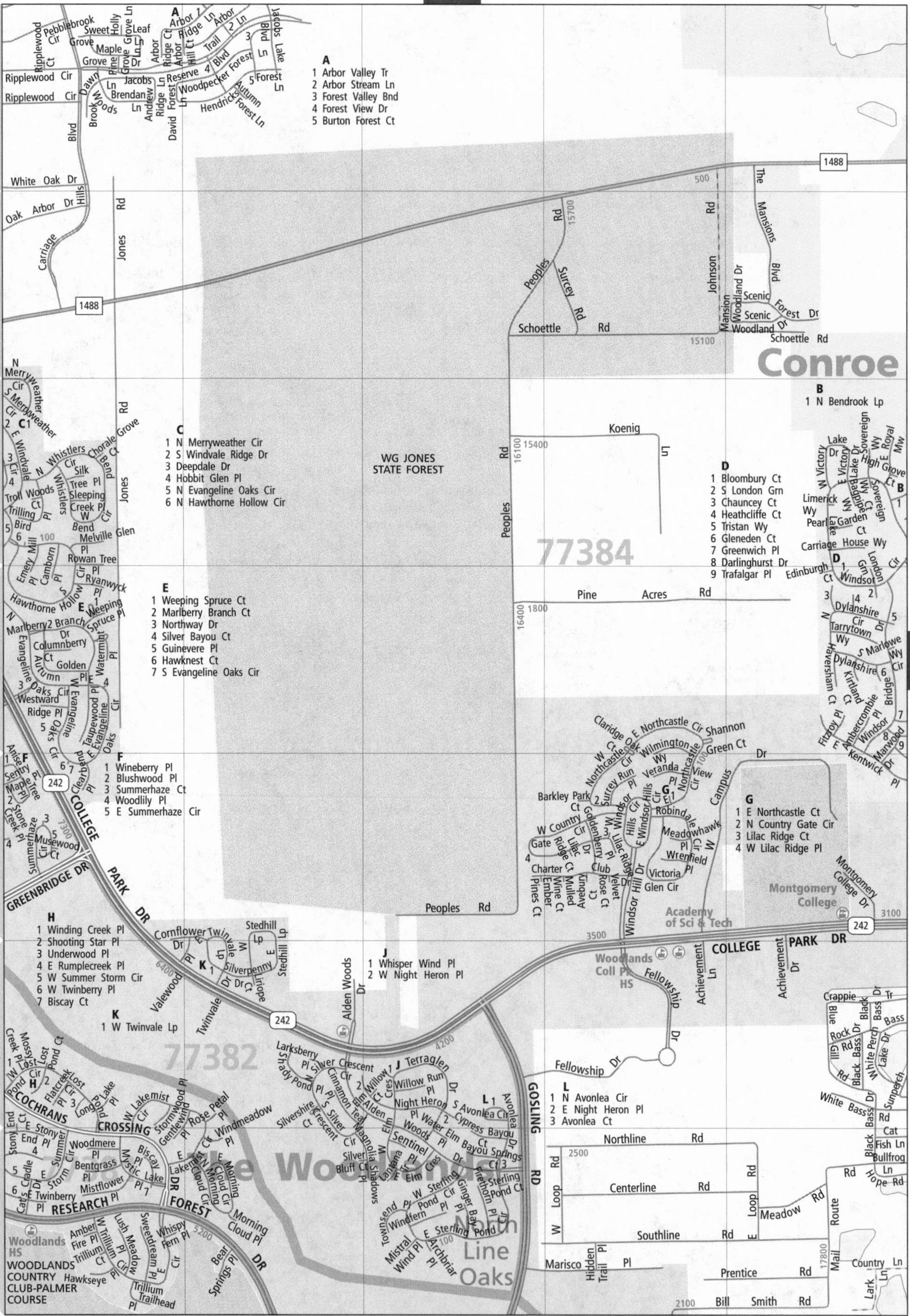
A
1 Arbor Valley Tr
2 Arbor Stream Ln
3 Forest Valley Bnd
4 Forest View Dr
5 Burton Forest Ct
B
1 N Bendrook Lp
C
1 N Merryweather Cir
2 S Windvale Ridge Dr
3 Deepdale Dr
4 Hobbit Glen Pl
5 N Evangeline Oaks Cir
6 N Hawthorne Hollow Cir
D
1 Bloombury Ct
2 S London Grn
3 Chauncey Ct
4 Heathcliffe Ct
5 Tristan Wy
6 Gleneden Ct
7 Greenwich Pl
8 Darlinghurst Dr
9 Trafalgar Pl
E
1 Weeping Spruce Ct
2 Marlberry Branch Ct
3 Northway Dr
4 Silver Bayou Ct
5 Guinevere Pl
6 Hawknest Ct
7 S Evangeline Oaks Cir
F
1 Wineberry Pl
2 Blushwood Pl
3 Summerhaze Ct
4 Woodlily Pl
5 E Summerhaze Cir
G
1 E Northcastle Ct
2 N Country Gate Cir
3 Lilac Ridge Ct
4 W Lilac Ridge Pl
H
1 Winding Creek Pl
2 Shooting Star Pl
3 Underwood Pl
4 E Rumplecreek Pl
5 W Summer Storm Cir
6 W Twinberry Pl
7 Biscay Ct
J
1 Whisper Wind Pl
2 W Night Heron Pl
K
1 W Twinvale Lp
L
1 N Avonlea Cir
2 E Night Heron Pl
3 Avonlea Ct
WG JONES
STATE FOREST
Conroe
77384
77382
The Woodlands
North Line Oaks
1488
242
COLLEGE PARK DR
GOSLING RD
RESEARCH FOREST DR
COCHRANS CROSSING DR
GREENBRIDGE DR
Jones Rd
Peoples Rd
Schoettle Rd
Johnson Rd
Koenig Ln
Pine Acres Rd
Northline Rd
Centerline Rd
Southline Rd
Meadow Rd
Prentice Rd
Bill Smith Rd
Marisco Pl
Mail Route Rd
Montgomery College
Academy of Sci & Tech
Woodlands Coll Pk HS
Woodlands HS
WOODLANDS COUNTRY CLUB-PALMER COURSE
30°14'35"
30°14'09"
30°13'43"
30°13'17"
30°12'50"
30°12'24"
30°11'58"
30°11'32"
95°30'16"
95°29'46"
95°29'16"
95°28'46"
95°28'15"
95°27'45"
A B C D E
1 2 3 4 5 6 7

SEE 2674 MAP

SEE 2676 MAP

SEE 2821 MAP

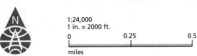

1:24,000
1 in. = 2000 ft.
0 0.25 0.5
miles

SEE 2530 MAP

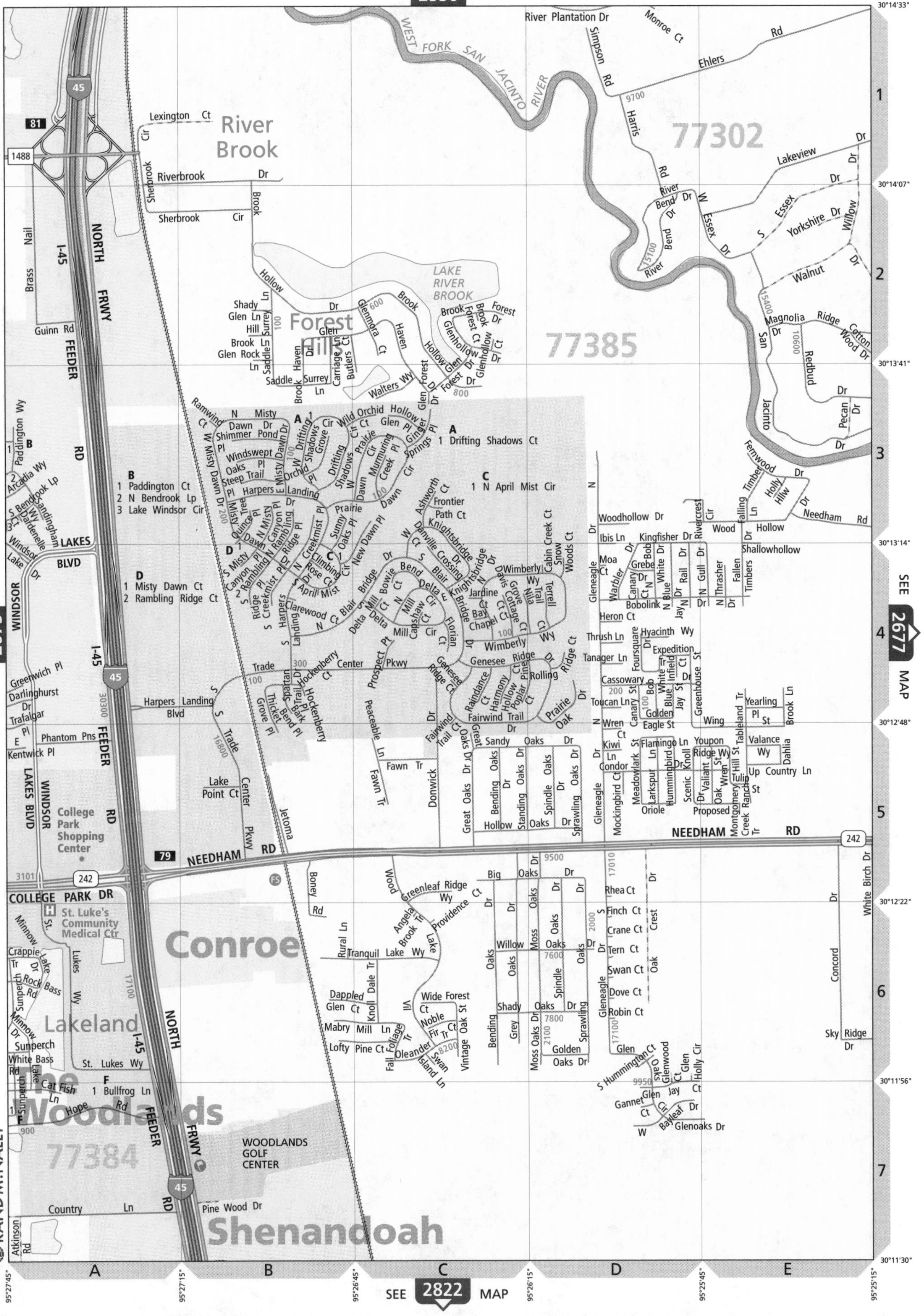
River Brook
Forest Hill
Lake River Brook
77302
77385
77384
Conroe
Lakeland
The Woodlands
Shenandoah
West Fork San Jacinto River
North Frwy
I-45
Needham Rd
Lakes Blvd
Windsor Lakes Blvd
College Park Dr
College Park Shopping Center
St. Luke's Community Medical Ctr
Woodlands Golf Center
River Plantation Dr
Simpson Rd
Ehlers Rd
Harris Rd
Lakeview Dr
Yorkshire Dr
Walnut Dr
Magnolia Ridge Dr
Fernwood Dr
Needham Rd
Lexington Ct
Riverbrook Dr
Sherbrook Cir
Brass Nail
Guinn Rd
Harpers Landing Blvd
Trade Center Pkwy
Lake Point Ct
Jetoma
Genesee Ridge Dr
Wimberly Wy
Great Oaks Dr
Sandy Oaks Dr
Gleneagle
Big Oaks Dr
Greenleaf Ridge Wy
Tranquil Lake Wy
Wide Forest Ct
Concord Dr
White Birch Dr
Sky Ridge Dr
Country Ln
Pine Wood Dr
Atkinson Rd
St. Lukes Wy
A
1 Drifting Shadows Ct
B
1 Paddington Ct
2 N Bendrook Lp
3 Lake Windsor Cir
C
1 N April Mist Cir
D
1 Misty Dawn Ct
2 Rambling Ridge Ct
F
1 Bullfrog Ln
30°14'33"
30°14'07"
30°13'41"
30°13'14"
30°12'48"
30°12'22"
30°11'56"
30°11'30"
95°27'45"
95°27'15"
95°26'45"
95°26'15"
95°25'45"
95°25'15"
A B C D E
1 2 3 4 5 6 7
SEE 2677 MAP

SEE 2822 MAP

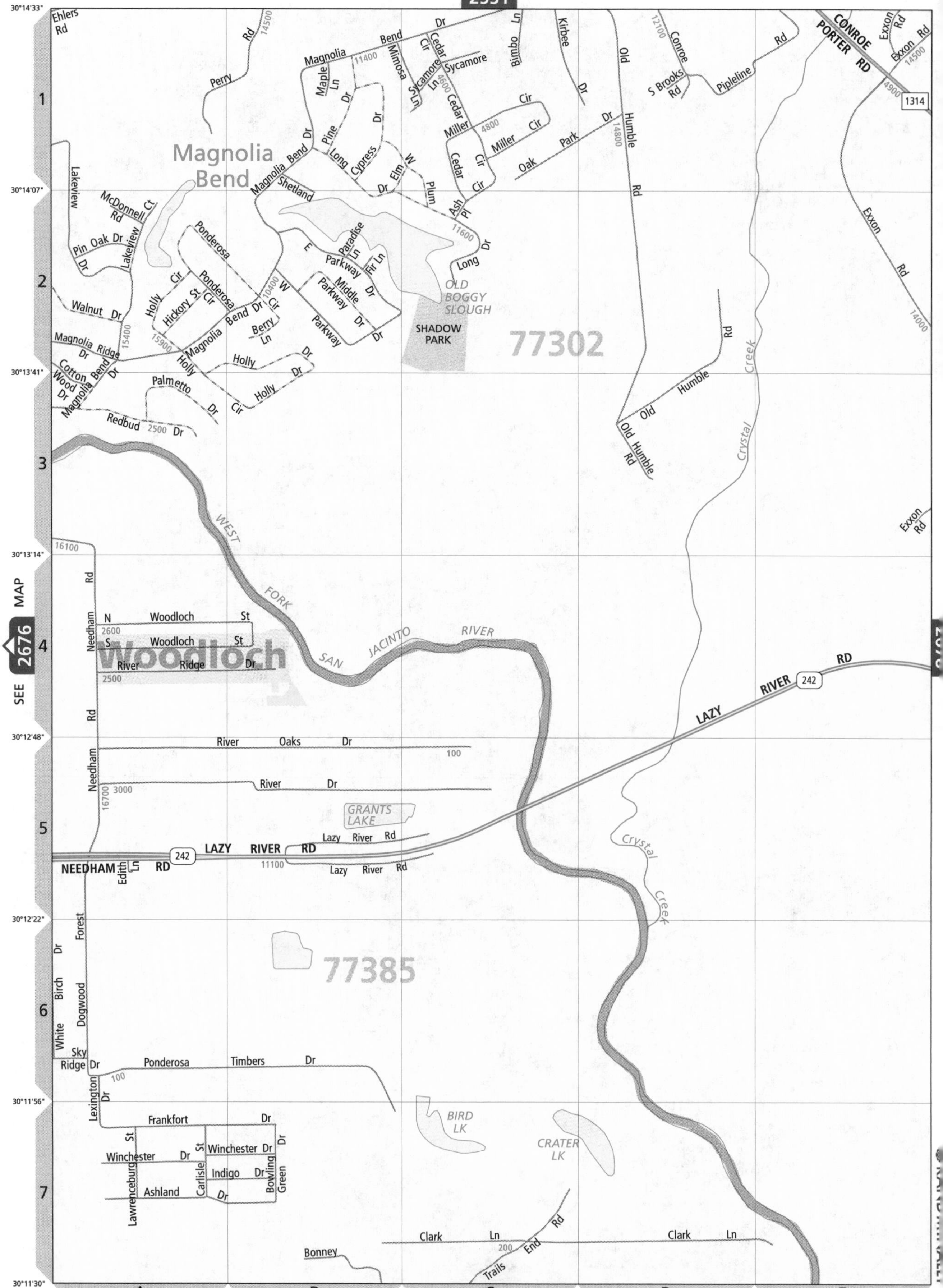
1:24,000
1 in. = 2000 ft.
0 0.25 0.5 miles
Magnolia Bend
Woodloch
77302
77385
SHADOW PARK
OLD BOGGY SLOUGH
GRANTS LAKE
BIRD LK
CRATER LK
WEST FORK SAN JACINTO RIVER
Crystal Creek
LAZY RIVER RD
NEEDHAM RD
CONROE PORTER RD
Old Humble Rd
Exxon Rd
Pipleline Rd
Clark Ln
Ponderosa Timbers Dr
River Oaks Dr
Magnolia Bend Dr
242
1314

SEE 2531 MAP

SEE 2676 MAP

SEE 2823 MAP

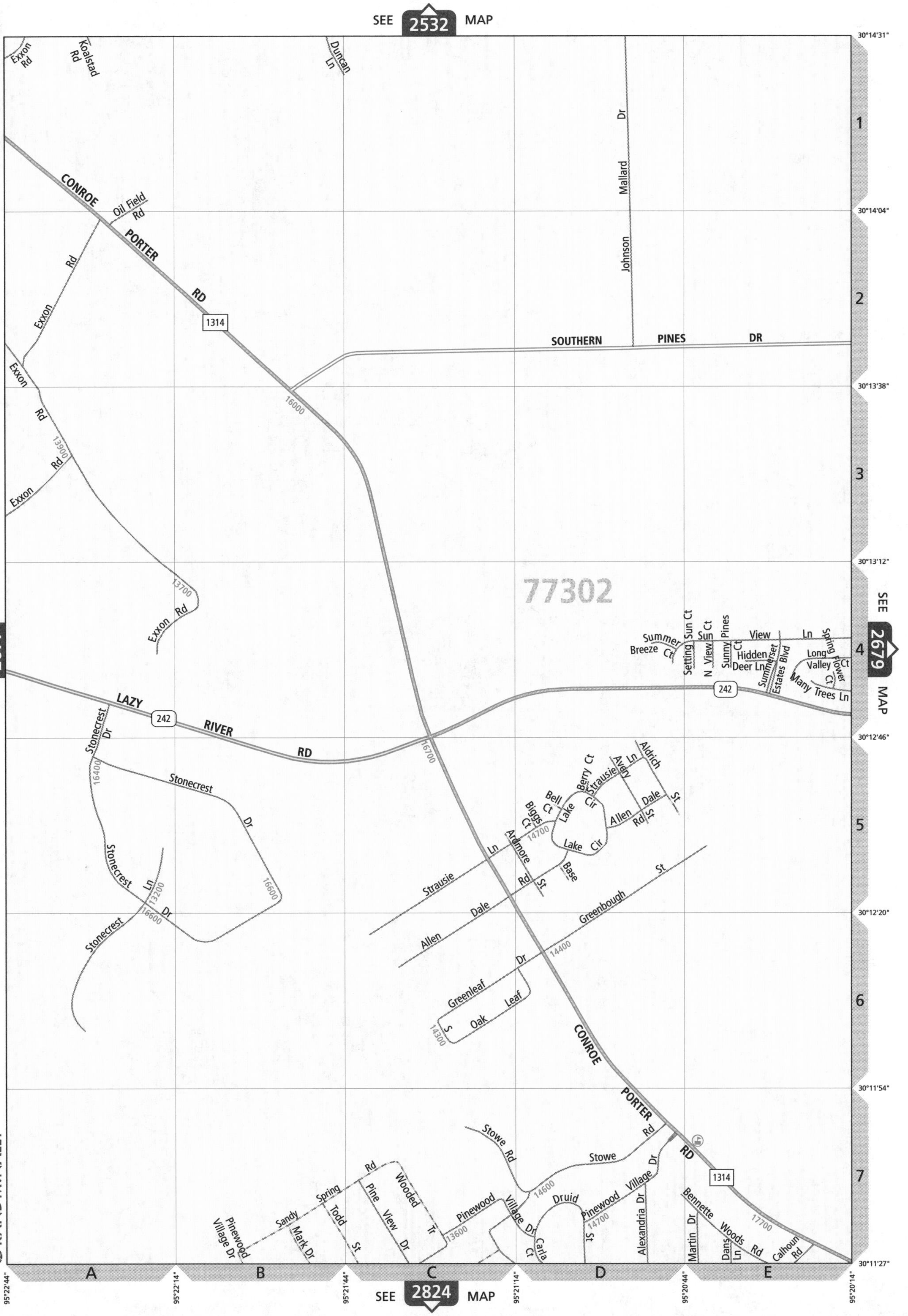
1:24,000
1 in. = 2000 ft.
0 0.25 0.5
miles
SEE 2532 MAP
SEE 2679 MAP
SEE 2824 MAP
77302
CONROE PORTER RD
1314
SOUTHERN PINES DR
LAZY RIVER RD
242
Exxon Rd
Koalstad Rd
Duncan Ln
Mallard Dr
Johnson
Oil Field Rd
Stonecrest Dr
Stonecrest Ln
Strausie Ln
Allen Dale Rd
Greenbough St
Greenleaf Dr
S Oak Leaf
Ardmore St
Biggs Ct
Bell Ct
Berry Ct
Lake Cir
Strausie Cir
Avery Ln
Aldrich St
Allen Dale Rd
Base
Summer Breeze Ct
Setting Sun Ct
N View Sun Ct
Sunny Pines Ct
View Ln
Hidden Deer Ln
Summerset Estates Blvd
Long Valley Ct
Spring Flower Ct
Many Trees Ln
Stowe Rd
Pinewood Village Dr
Sandy
Spring
Todd St
Mark Dr
Pine View Dr
Wooded Tr
Druid St
Carla Ct
Alexandria Dr
Martin Dr
Bennette Woods Rd
Dans Ln
Calhoun Rd
16000
13900
13700
16700
16400
16600
13200
14700
14400
14300
14600
13600
17700
1
2
3
4
5
6
7
A
B
C
D
E
30°14'31"
30°14'04"
30°13'38"
30°13'12"
30°12'46"
30°12'20"
30°11'54"
30°11'27"
95°22'44"
95°22'14"
95°21'44"
95°21'14"
95°20'44"
95°20'14"

1:24,000
1 in. = 2000 ft.
0 0.25 0.5
miles

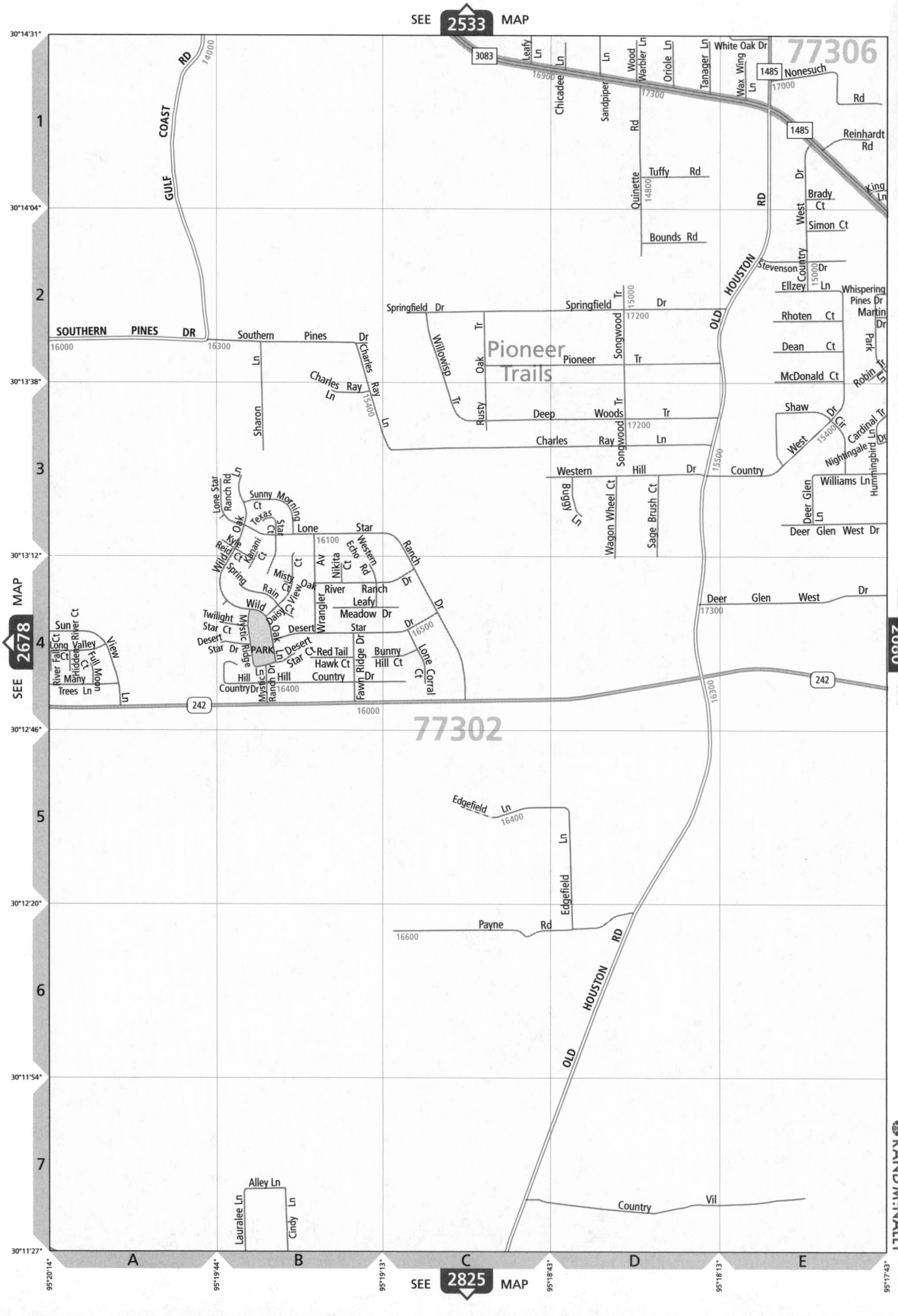
SEE 2533 MAP
SEE 2825 MAP
SEE 2678 MAP
2680
30°14'31"
30°14'04"
30°13'38"
30°13'12"
30°12'46"
30°12'20"
30°11'54"
30°11'27"
95°20'14"
95°19'44"
95°19'13"
95°18'43"
95°18'13"
95°17'43"
A
B
C
D
E
1
2
3
4
5
6
7
77306
77302
Pioneer Trails
GULF COAST RD
14000
SOUTHERN PINES DR
16000
16300
Southern Pines Dr
Sharon Ln
Charles Ray Ln
15400
Springfield Dr
Willowisp Tr
Rusty Oak Tr
Pioneer Tr
Deep Woods Tr
Songwood Tr
15000
17200
Charles Ray Ln
Western Hill Dr
Country
Buggy Ln
Wagon Wheel Ct
Sage Brush Ct
OLD HOUSTON RD
15500
16300
3083
Leafy Ln
Chicadee Ln
16900
Sandpiper Ln
Wood Warbler Ln
Oriole Ln
Tanager Ln
17300
White Oak Dr
Wax Wing Ln
1485
Nonesuch Rd
17000
Reinhardt Rd
Quinette Rd
14800
Tuffy Rd
Bounds Rd
West Dr
Brady Ct
Simon Ct
King Ln
Stevenson Dr
Country
Ellzey Ln
Whispering Pines Dr
Martin Dr
Rhoten Ct
Park
Dean Ct
McDonald Ct
Robin Tr
Shaw Dr
West Cir
Cardinal Tr
Nightingale Ln
Hummingbird Dr
Williams Ln
Deer Glen Ln
Deer Glen West Dr
Deer Glen West Dr
17300
Lone Star Ranch Rd
Ln
Sunny Morning Ct
Texas Star Ct
Lone Star Western Ranch Dr
16100
Wild Oak
Kyle
Reid Ct
Kanani Ct
Wild Spring
Misty Rain Ct
Oak View Ct
Ct
Av
Nikita Ct
Echo Rd
Wrangler
River Ranch Dr
Leafy Meadow Dr
Wild Daisy Ct
Twilight Star Ct
Mystic Ridge
Desert Star Dr
Oak Ln
PARK
Desert Star Ct
Desert Star Dr
16500
Red Tail Hawk Ct
Fawn Ridge Dr
Bunny Hill Ct
Lone Corral Ct
Hill Country Dr
Mystic Ln
Ranch Dr
16400
Hill Country Dr
16000
242
Sun River Ct
Long Valley
River Falls Ct
Hidden Ct
Full Moon Ct
Many Trees Ln
View Ln
Edgefield Ln
16400
Edgefield Ln
Payne Rd
16600
Alley Ln
Lauralee Ln
Cindy Ln
Country Vil
RAND McNALLY

1:24,000
1 in. = 2000 ft.
0 0.25 0.5
miles

SEE 2534 MAP

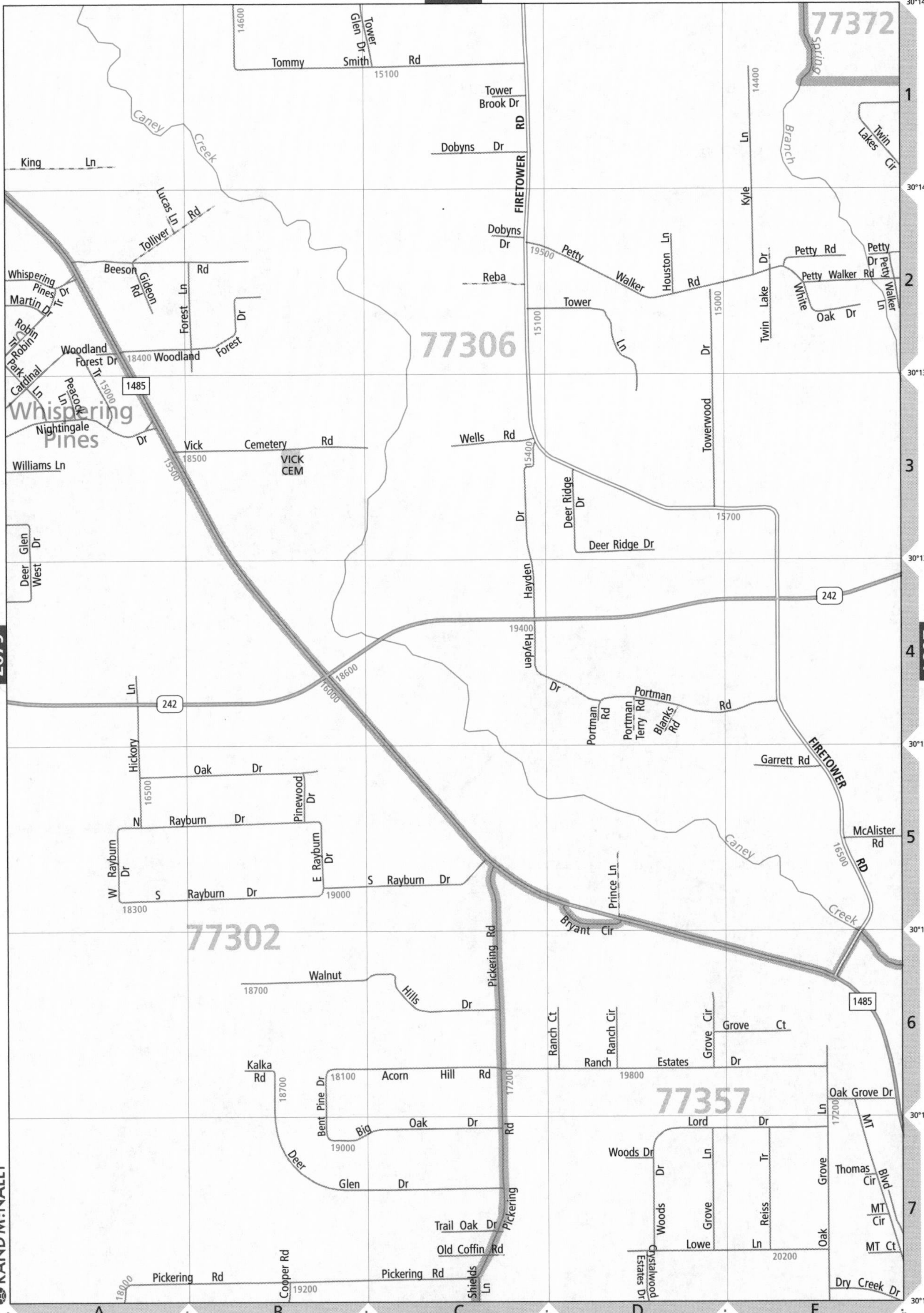
Tommy Smith Rd
Tower Glen Dr
14600
15100
Tower Brook Dr
Caney Creek
King Ln
Dobyns Dr
FIRETOWER RD
77372
Spring Branch
14400
Kyle Ln
Twin Lakes Cir
Lucas Ln
Tolliver Rd
Dobyns Dr
19500
Petty Walker Rd
Houston Ln
Petty Rd
Petty Dr
Petty Walker Rd
Petty Walker Ln
White Oak Dr
Twin Lake Dr
Whispering Pines Dr
Beeson Rd
Gideon Rd
Forest Ln
Martin Dr
Tr
Reba
Tower Ln
15000
15100
77306
Robin Tr
Robin
Park
Cardinal Ln
Woodland Forest Dr
18400
Woodland Forest Dr
Peacock Ln
15000
1485
Whispering Pines
Nightingale Dr
Vick Cemetery Rd
18500
VICK CEM
Wells Rd
15400
Towerwood Dr
Williams Ln
15500
Deer Ridge Dr
15700
Deer Ridge Dr
Hayden Dr
Deer Glen West Dr
242
19400
Hayden Dr
18600
16000
Ln
242
Portman Rd
Portman Terry Rd
Blanks Rd
Garrett Rd
FIRETOWER RD
Hickory
Oak Dr
Pinewood Dr
16500
N Rayburn Dr
McAlister Rd
Caney Creek
16500
W Rayburn Dr
E Rayburn Dr
S Rayburn Dr
S Rayburn Dr
18300
19000
Prince Ln
Bryant Cir
77302
Caney Creek
Pickering Rd
Walnut Hills Dr
18700
1485
Ranch Ct
Ranch Cir
Grove Cir
Grove Ct
Ranch Estates Dr
19800
Kalka Rd
18700
Acorn Hill Rd
18100
Bent Pine Dr
17200
77357
Oak Grove Dr
Big Oak Dr
19000
Rd
Lord Dr
17200
Ln
MT
Woods Dr
Ln
Tr
Grove
Thomas Cir
Blvd
Deer Glen Dr
MT Cir
Pickering
Woods
Grove
Reiss
Trail Oak Dr
Old Coffin Rd
Lowe Ln
20200
Oak
MT Ct
Crystalwood
Estates Dr
18000
Pickering Rd
Cooper Rd
19200
Pickering Rd
Shields Ln
Dry Creek Dr
1
2
3
4
5
6
7
A
B
C
D
E
30°14'28"
30°14'02"
30°13'36"
30°13'10"
30°12'43"
30°12'17"
30°11'51"
30°11'25"
95°17'43"
95°17'13"
95°16'43"
95°16'13"
95°15'43"
95°15'13"

SEE 2679 MAP
SEE 2681 MAP
SEE 2826 MAP

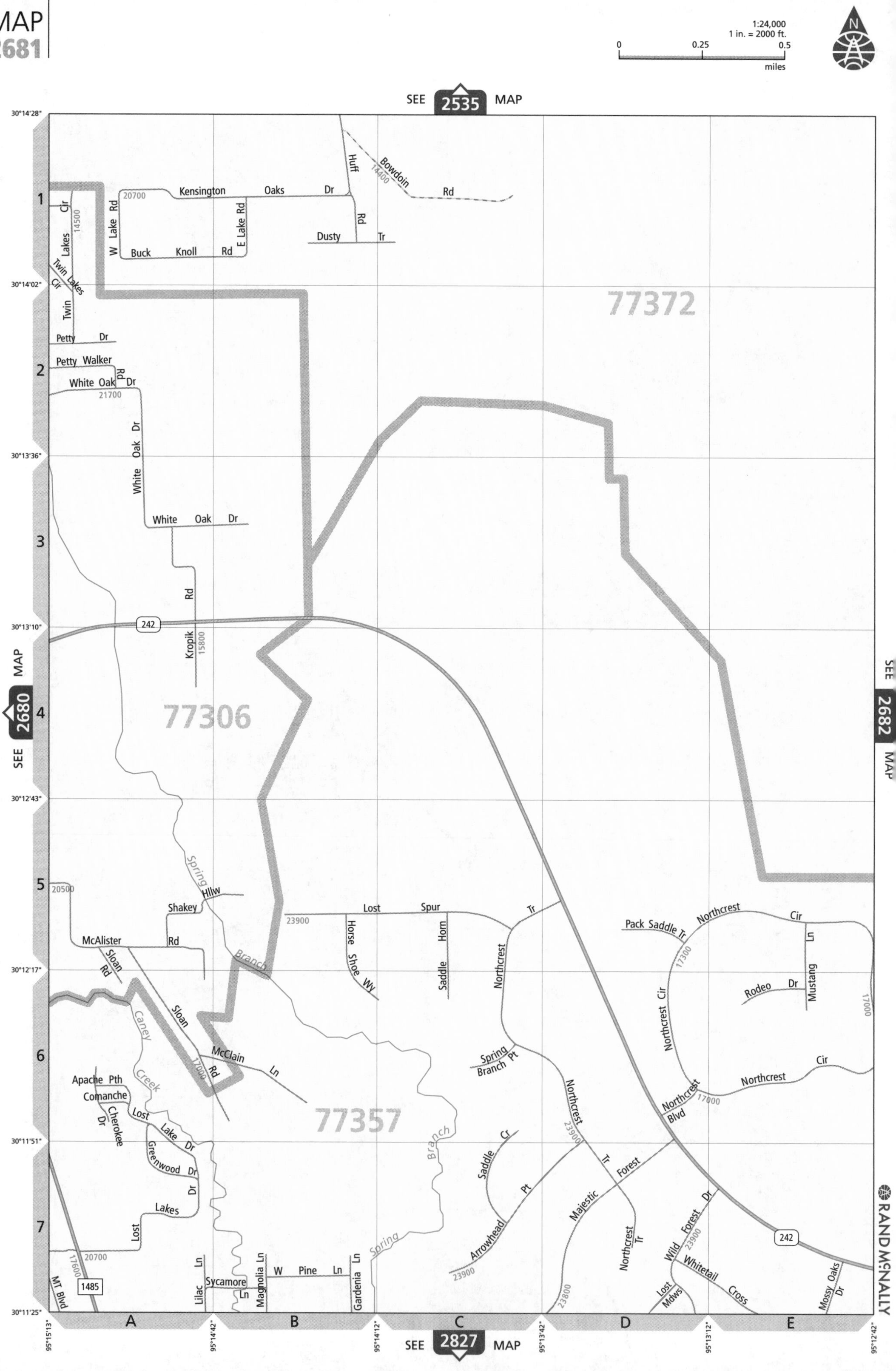
1:24,000
1 in. = 2000 ft.
0 0.25 0.5
miles
N
SEE 2535 MAP
SEE 2680 MAP
SEE 2682 MAP
SEE 2827 MAP
77372
77306
77357
Kensington Oaks Dr
20700
W Lake Rd
E Lake Rd
Buck Knoll Rd
Huff Rd
Bowdoin Rd
14400
Dusty Tr
Lakes Cir
14500
Twin Lakes Cir
Twin
Petty Dr
Petty Walker Rd
White Oak Dr
21700
White Oak Dr
White Oak Dr
Kropik Rd
15800
242
Spring Hllw
Shakey
20500
McAlister Rd
Sloan Rd
Sloan
Branch
Caney Creek
McClain Rd
17000
McClain Ln
Lost Spur Tr
23900
Horse Shoe Wy
Saddle Horn
Northcrest
Spring Branch Pt
Pack Saddle Tr
Northcrest Cir
17300
Ln
Mustang
Rodeo Dr
Northcrest Cir
17000
Northcrest Cir
Northcrest Blvd
17000
Northcrest Tr
23900
Apache Pth
Comanche Dr
Cherokee
Lost Lake Dr
Greenwood Dr
Dr
Lakes
Lost
Branch
Saddle Cr
Arrowhead Pt
23900
Forest
Majestic
Northcrest Tr
Wild Forest Dr
23900
Whitetail Cross
Lost Mdws
23800
Mossy Oaks Dr
242
Spring
20700
17600
MT Blvd
1485
Lilac Ln
Sycamore Ln
Magnolia Ln
W Pine Ln
Gardenia Ln
1
2
3
4
5
6
7
A
B
C
D
E
30°14'28"
30°14'02"
30°13'36"
30°13'10"
30°12'43"
30°12'17"
30°11'51"
30°11'25"
95°15'13"
95°14'42"
95°14'12"
95°13'42"
95°13'12"
95°12'42"
RAND McNALLY

1:24,000
1 in. = 2000 ft.
0 0.25 0.5
miles

SEE 2536 MAP

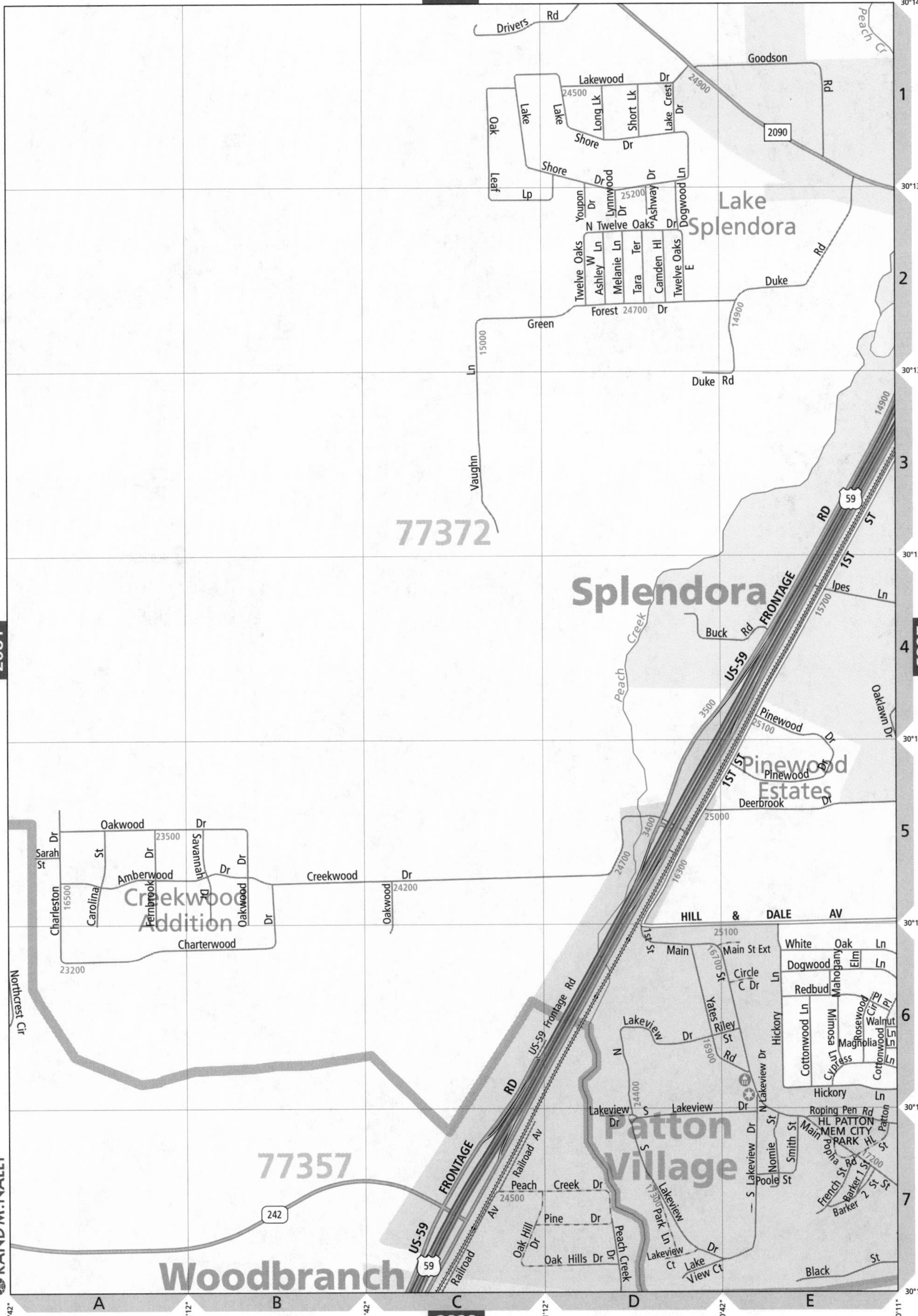

Drivers Rd
Goodson Rd
Lakewood Dr
24500
24900
2090
Oak Leaf Lp
Lake Shore Dr
Long Lk
Short Lk
Lake Crest Dr
Youpon Dr
Lynnwood Dr
25200
Ashway Dr
Dogwood Ln
N Twelve Oaks Dr
Lake Splendora
Twelve Oaks W
Ashley Ln
Melanie Ln
Tara Ter
Camden Hl
Twelve Oaks E
Forest 24700 Dr
Green
Duke
Duke Rd
14900
15000
Vaughn Ln
77372
Splendora
Peach Creek
Peach Cr
Ipes Ln
15700
Buck Rd
FRONTAGE RD
US-59
1ST ST
59
3500
Pinewood Dr
25100
Pinewood Estates
Deerbrook Dr
25000
Oaklawn Dr
Oakwood Dr
23500
Sarah St
Carolina St
Charleston
16500
Amberwood Dr
Fernbrook Dr
Savannah Dr
Oakwood Dr
Creekwood Addition
Creekwood Dr
24200
Charterwood
23200
3400
24700
16300
HILL & DALE AV
25100
1st St
Main
Main St Ext
16700
Circle C Dr
Yates St
Riley St
Rd
16900
Lakeview Dr
White Oak Ln
Dogwood Ln
Redbud Ln
Mahogany
Elm
Cottonwood Ln
Hickory
Mimosa Ln
Rosewood Cir
Walnut Ln
Magnolia Ln
Cypress
Cottonwood Ln
Hickory Ln
Roping Pen Rd
HL PATTON MEM CITY PARK
Main
Popha
Patton
Northcrest Cir
US-59 Frontage Rd
FRONTAGE RD
24400
Lakeview Dr
S Lakeview Dr
N Lakeview Dr
Patton Village
Nomie St
Smith St
Poole St
French St
Barker 1 St
Barker 2 St
17200
77357
242
Railroad Av
Peach Creek Dr
24500
Pine Dr
Oak Hill Dr
Oak Hills Dr
Peach Creek
Lakeview Park Ln
Lakeview Ct
Lake View Ct
Black St
Woodbranch
US-59
59
30°14'25"
30°13'59"
30°13'33"
30°13'07"
30°12'41"
30°12'14"
30°11'48"
30°11'22"
95°12'42"
95°12'12"
95°11'42"
95°11'12"
95°10'42"
95°10'11"
1
2
3
4
5
6
7
A
B
C
D
E

SEE 2681 MAP

SEE 2683 MAP

SEE 2828 MAP

1:24,000
1 in. = 2000 ft.
0 0.25 0.5
miles

SEE 2537 MAP

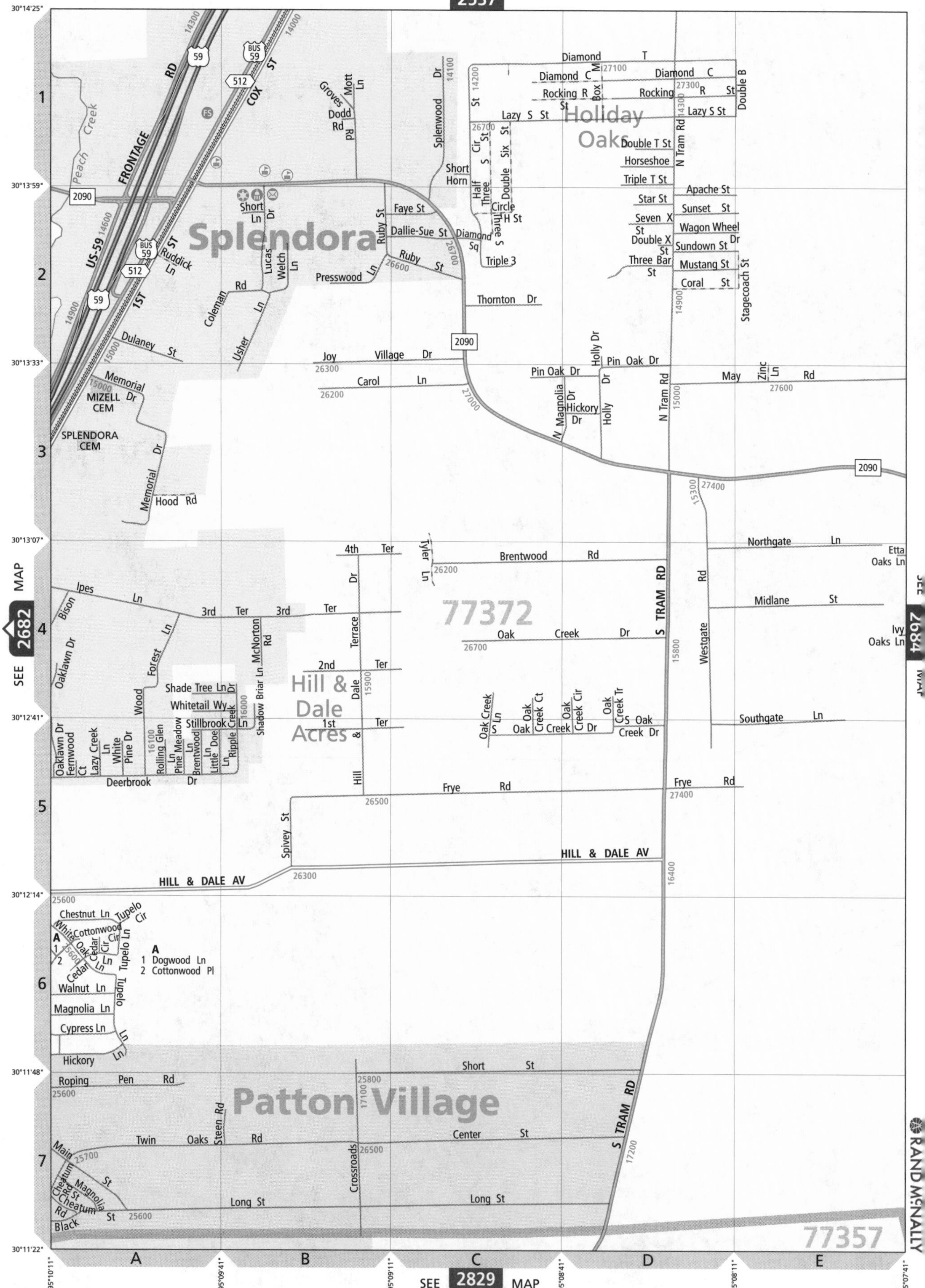
Splendora
Holiday Oaks
Hill & Dale Acres
Patton Village
77372
77357
US-59
FRONTAGE RD
COX ST
1ST ST
2090
512
59
BUS 59
Peach Creek
Ruddick Ln
Dulaney St
Memorial Dr
MIZELL CEM
SPLENDORA CEM
Hood Rd
Coleman Rd
Usher Ln
Lucas Welch Ln
Presswood Ln
Ruby St
Faye St
Dallie-Sue St
Diamond Sq
Splenwood Dr
Short Horn
Groves Mott Ln
Dodd Rd
Short Ln
Thornton Dr
Joy Village Dr
Carol Ln
Pin Oak Dr
Holly Dr
N Magnolia Dr
Hickory Dr
N Tram Rd
May Rd
Zinc Ln
Diamond T
Diamond C
Rocking R
Lazy S St
Double T St
Horseshoe
Triple T St
Star St
Seven X St
Double X St
Three Bar St
Apache St
Sunset St
Wagon Wheel Dr
Sundown St
Mustang St
Coral St
Stagecoach St
Double B
Triple 3
Half Three Cir
Double Six St
Three S Circle
H St
Box M St
Northgate Ln
Etta Oaks Ln
Brentwood Rd
Tyler Ln
Midlane St
Ivy Oaks Ln
Westgate Rd
Oak Creek Dr
S TRAM RD
Southgate Ln
Ipes Ln
Bison
3rd Ter
4th Ter
2nd Ter
1st Ter
Terrace Dr
Hill & Dale
Oaklawn Dr
Forest Ln
Wood
Shade Tree Ln
Whitetail Wy
Stillbrook
Shadow Briar Ln
McNorton Rd
Ripple Creek Ln
Little Doe Ln
Brentwood Ln
Pine Meadow Ln
Rolling Glen
Pine Dr
White
Lazy Creek Ln
Fernwood Ct
Deerbrook Dr
Oak Creek Ln
S Oak Creek Dr
Oak Creek Ct
Oak Creek Cir
Oak Creek Tr
Frye Rd
Spivey St
HILL & DALE AV
Chestnut Ln
Tupelo Cir
Tupelo Ln
White Oak Ln
Cedar Cir
Cottonwood
Cedar Ln
Walnut Ln
Magnolia Ln
Cypress Ln
Hickory Ln
A
1 Dogwood Ln
2 Cottonwood Pl
Roping Pen Rd
Short St
Steen Rd
Twin Oaks Rd
Center St
Crossroads
Main
Cheatum Rd
Magnolia St
Long St
Black

SEE 2682 MAP

SEE 2684 MAP

SEE 2829 MAP

1:24,000
1 in. = 2000 ft.
0 0.25 0.5
miles

SEE 2538 MAP

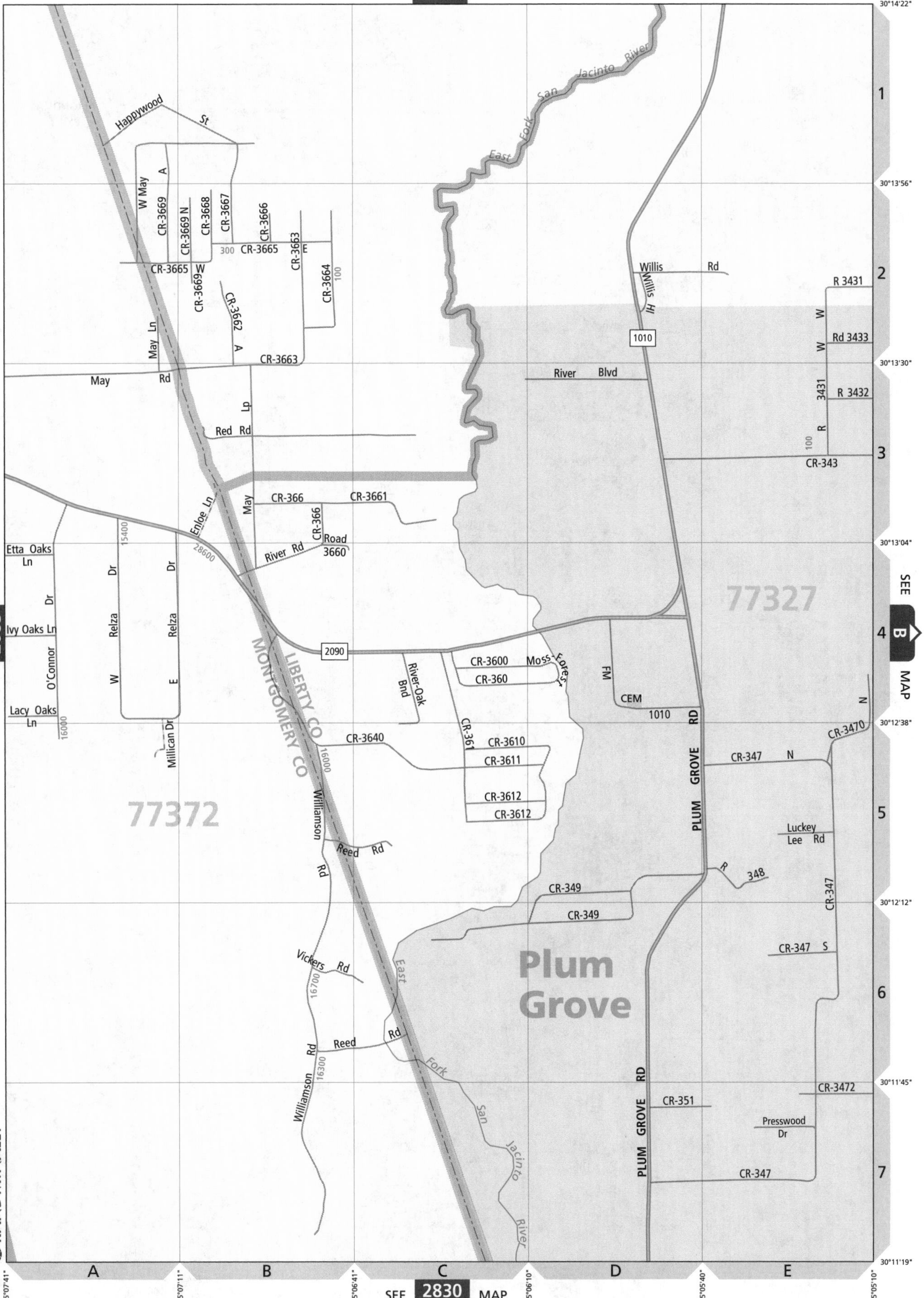
30°14'22"
30°13'56"
30°13'30"
30°13'04"
30°12'38"
30°12'12"
30°11'45"
30°11'19"
1
2
3
4
5
6
7
A
B
C
D
E
95°07'41"
95°07'11"
95°06'41"
95°06'10"
95°05'40"
95°05'10"
East Fork San Jacinto River
Happywood St
W May A
CR-3669
CR-3669 N
CR-3668
CR-3667
CR-3666
300 CR-3665
CR-3663 E
CR-3665 W
CR-3669
CR-3664
100
CR-3662 A
May Ln
CR-3663
May Rd
Lp
Red Rd
Willis Rd
Willis H
1010
River Blvd
R 3431
W
Rd 3433
W
3431
R 3432
R
100
CR-343
77327
Enloe Ln
May
CR-366
CR-3661
CR-366
Road 3660
River Rd
28600
15400
Etta Oaks Ln
Dr
Ivy Oaks Ln
O'Connor
Lacy Oaks Ln
16000
W Relza Dr
E Relza Dr
Millican Dr
LIBERTY CO
MONTGOMERY CO
2090
River-Oak Bnd
CR-3600
Moss Forest
CR-360
FM
CEM
1010
RD
N
CR-3470
CR-3640
16000
CR-361
CR-3610
CR-3611
CR-347 N
CR-3612
CR-3612
PLUM GROVE
77372
Williamson Rd
Reed Rd
Luckey Lee Rd
R 348
CR-349
CR-349
CR-347
CR-347 S
Plum Grove
Vickers Rd
16700
East
Reed Rd
Rd
Fork
San
Jacinto
River
Williamson Rd
16300
PLUM GROVE RD
CR-351
CR-3472
Presswood Dr
CR-347
SEE B MAP

SEE 2830 MAP

2683

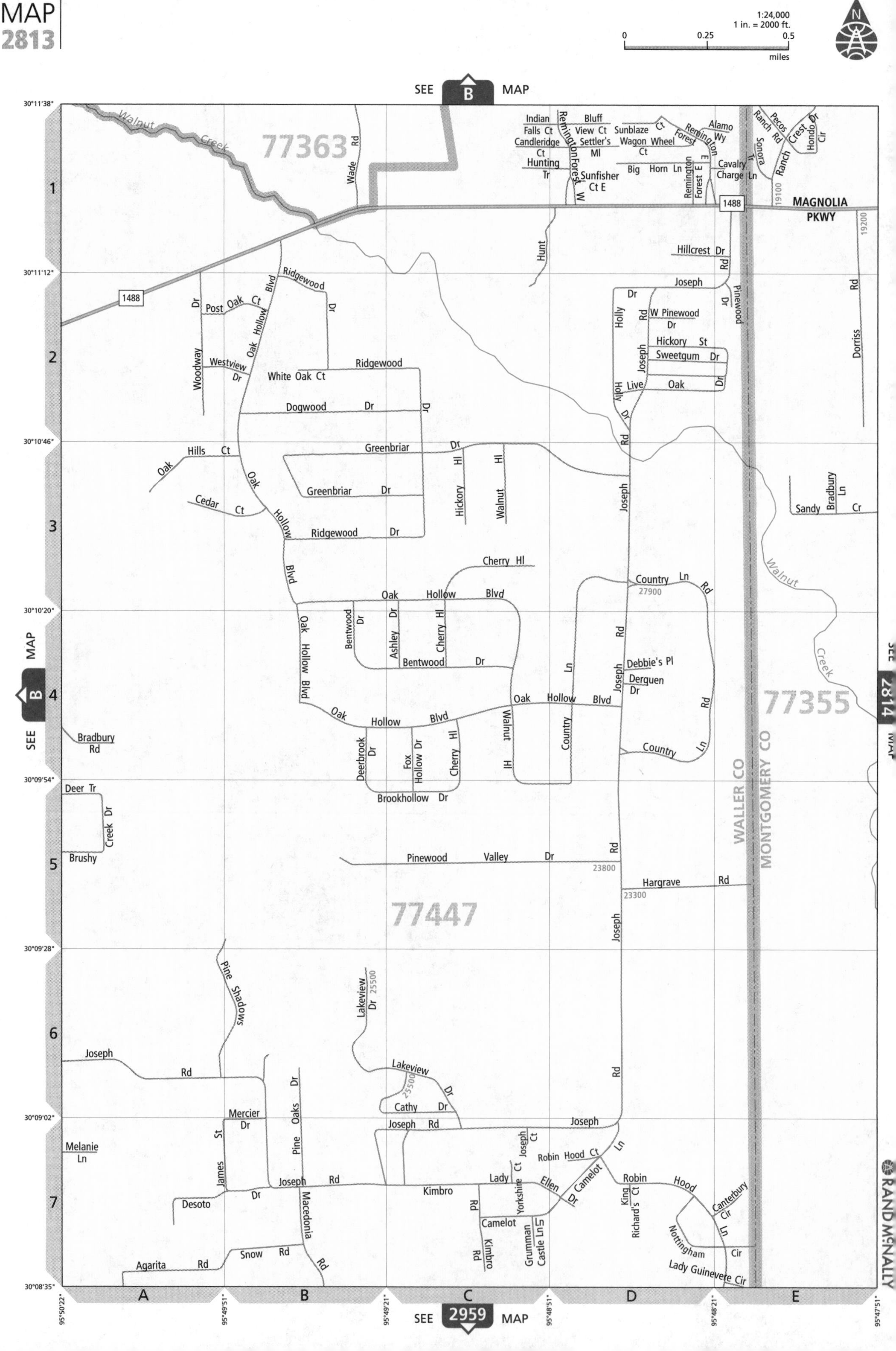
1:24,000
1 in. = 2000 ft.
0 0.25 0.5
miles
SEE B MAP
SEE 2959 MAP
SEE B MAP
SEE 2814 MAP
77363
77447
77355
WALLER CO
MONTGOMERY CO
MAGNOLIA PKWY
1488
Walnut Creek
Wade Rd
Indian Falls Ct
Bluff View Ct
Candleridge Ct
Settler's Ml
Hunting Tr
Remington Forest W
Sunfisher Ct E
Sunblaze Ct
Wagon Wheel Ct
Remington Forest
Alamo Wy
Big Horn Ln
Remington Forest E
Cavalry Ln
Charge Ln
Pecos Ranch Rd
Sonora Tr
Ranch Crest Dr
Hondo Cir
19100
19200
Hunt
Hillcrest Dr
Joseph Rd
Pinewood Dr
Dorriss Rd
Holly Dr
W Pinewood Dr
Hickory St
Sweetgum Dr
Live Oak Dr
Ridgewood Dr
Post Oak Ct
Woodway Dr
Westview Dr
Oak Hollow Blvd
White Oak Ct
Dogwood Dr
Greenbriar Dr
Oak Hills Ct
Cedar Ct
Hickory Hl
Walnut Hl
Sandy Bradbury Ln Cr
Cherry Hl
Country Ln Rd
27900
Bentwood Dr
Ashley Dr
Debbie's Pl
Derquen Dr
Country Ln
Bradbury Rd
Deerbrook Dr
Fox Hollow Dr
Brookhollow Dr
Deer Tr
Creek Dr
Brushy
Pinewood Valley Dr
23800
Hargrave Rd
23300
Pine Shadows
Lakeview Dr
25500
Joseph Rd
Cathy Dr
Mercier Dr
Pine Oaks Dr
James St
Melanie Ln
Desoto Dr
Macedonia Rd
Kimbro Rd
Joseph Ct
Robin Hood Ct
Robin Hood Ln
Lady Yorkshire Ct
Ellen Dr
Camelot Dr
Camelot
Grumman Ln
Castle Ln
King Richard's Ct
Canterbury Cir
Nottingham Ln
Cir
Lady Guinevere Cir
Snow Rd
Agarita Rd
1 2 3 4 5 6 7
A B C D E
30°11'38" 30°11'12" 30°10'46" 30°10'20" 30°09'54" 30°09'28" 30°09'02" 30°08'35"
95°50'22" 95°49'51" 95°49'21" 95°48'51" 95°48'21" 95°47'51"
RAND McNALLY

1:24,000
1 in. = 2000 ft.
0 0.25 0.5
miles

SEE 2668 MAP

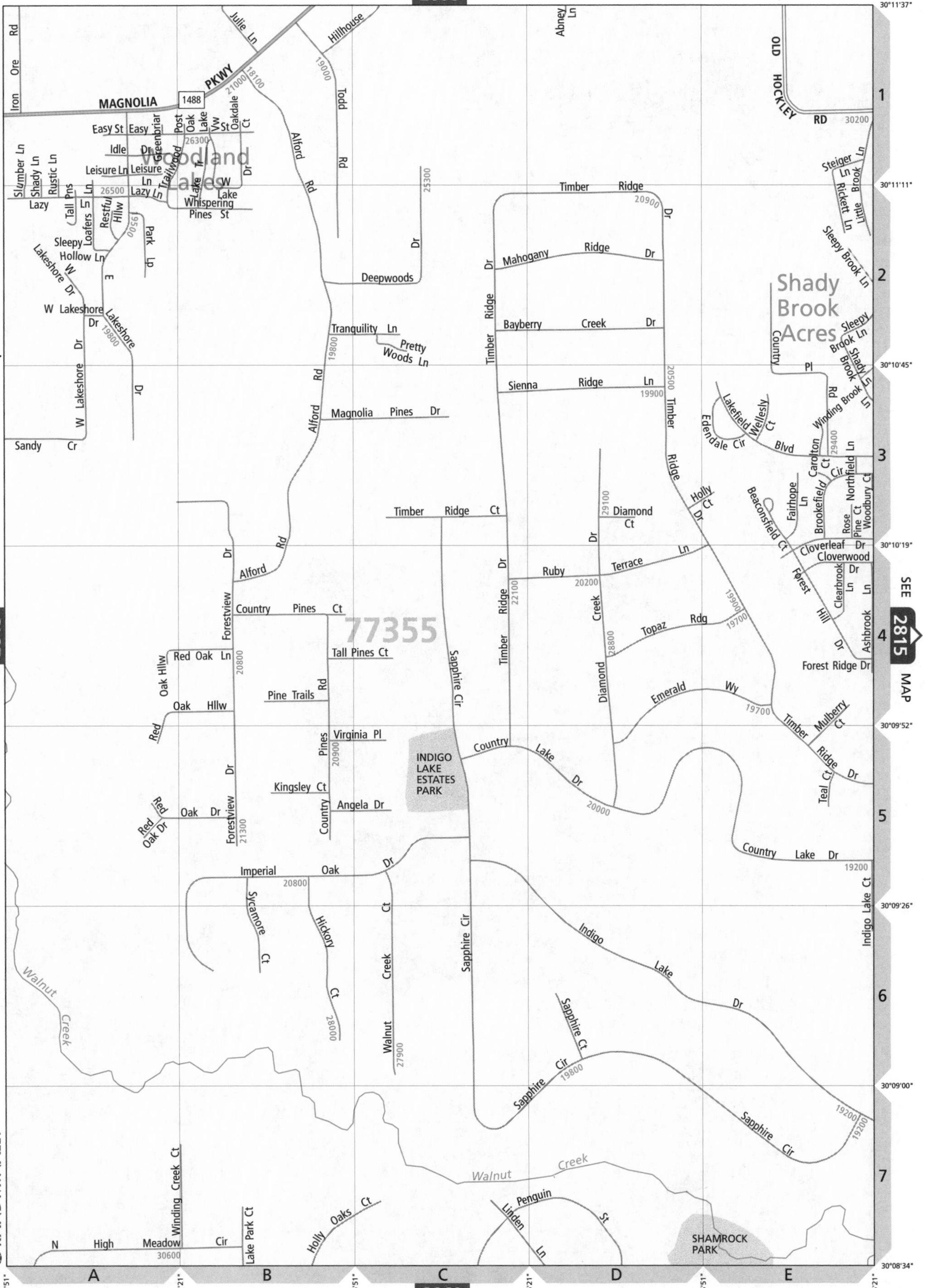
Iron Ore Rd
MAGNOLIA PKWY
1488
Julie Ln
Hillhouse
Abney Ln
OLD HOCKLEY RD
30200
Easy St
Easy
Idle Dr
Greenbriar
Post Oak
Lake Vw
St
Oakdale Ct
26300
Woodland Lakes
Slumber Ln
Shady Ln
Rustic Ln
Leisure Ln
Leisure Ln
Trailwood
Lake Tr
Lazy Ln
W Lake
Whispering Pines St
26500
Lazy
Tall Pns
Loafers Ln
Restful Hllw
19500
Park Lp
Sleepy Hollow Ln
W Lakeshore Dr
E Lakeshore Dr
W Lakeshore Dr
19800
Dr
Sandy Cr
Alford Rd
19000
Todd Rd
25300
Deepwoods Dr
Tranquility Ln
Pretty Woods Ln
19800
Alford Rd
Magnolia Pines Dr
Timber Ridge Dr
20900
Mahogany Ridge Dr
Bayberry Creek Dr
Sienna Ridge Ln
19900
20500
Timber Ridge
Timber Ridge Dr
Steiger Ln
Rickett Ln
Little Brook
Sleepy Brook Ln
Shady Brook Acres
Country Pl
Sleepy Brook Ln
Shady Brook Ln
Winding Brook Rd
Lakefield
Wellesly Ct
Edendale Cir
Blvd
29400
Carolton Ct
Northfield Ln
Cir
Brookefield
Woodbury Ct
Rose Pine Ct
Fairhope Ln
Beaconsfield Ct
Cloverleaf Dr
Cloverwood Dr
Forest Hill Dr
Clearbrook Ln
Ln
Ashbrook
Forest Ridge Dr
Holly Ct
Dr
Timber Ridge Ct
29100
Diamond Ct
Diamond Creek Dr
Ruby
Terrace Ln
20200
22100
Timber Ridge Dr
19900
19700
Topaz Rdg
28800
Emerald Wy
19700
Timber Ridge Dr
Mulberry Ct
Teal Ct
Alford Rd
Forestview Dr
Country Pines Ct
77355
Tall Pines Ct
Red Oak Ln
Oak Hllw
20800
Pine Trails Rd
Sapphire Cir
Red Oak Hllw
Virginia Pl
Country Pines
20900
INDIGO LAKE ESTATES PARK
Country Lake Dr
20000
Kingsley Ct
Angela Dr
Red Oak Dr
Red Oak Dr
Forestview
21300
Country Lake Dr
19200
Imperial Oak Dr
20800
Sycamore Ct
Hickory Ct
28000
Walnut Creek Ct
27900
Sapphire Cir
Indigo Lake Dr
Indigo Lake Ct
Walnut Creek
Sapphire Ct
Sapphire Cir
19800
Sapphire Cir
19200
19200
Walnut Creek
Winding Creek Ct
Holly Oaks Ct
Penguin St
Linden Ln
SHAMROCK PARK
N High Meadow Cir
30600
Lake Park Ct
A
B
C
D
E
1
2
3
4
5
6
7
30°11'37"
30°11'11"
30°10'45"
30°10'19"
30°09'52"
30°09'26"
30°09'00"
30°08'34"
95°47'51"
95°47'21"
95°46'51"
95°46'21"
95°45'51"
95°45'21"

SEE 2813 MAP

SEE 2815 MAP

SEE 2960 MAP

1:24,000
1 in. = 2000 ft.
0 0.25 0.5
miles

SEE 2669 MAP

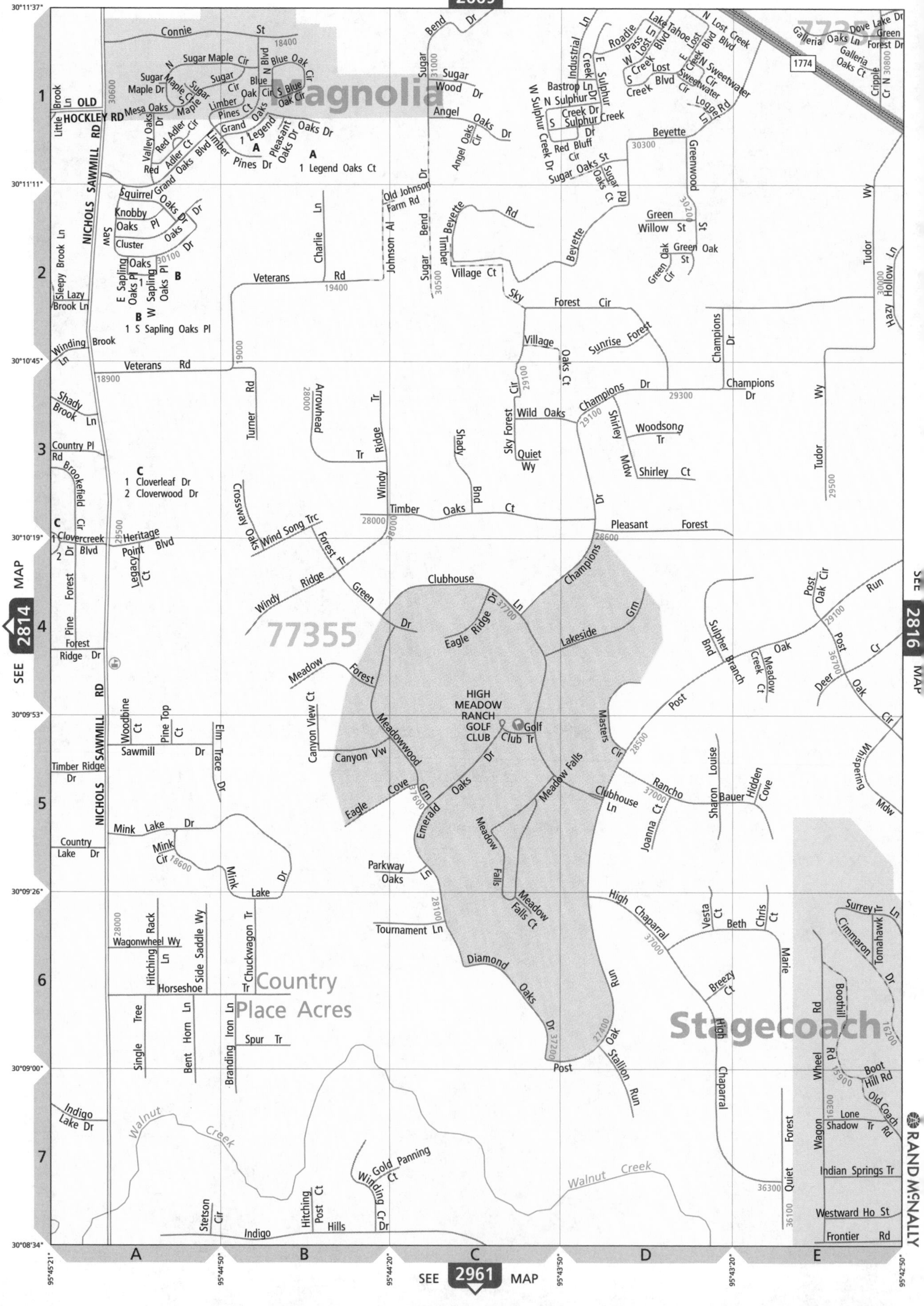
Magnolia
77355
Stagecoach
Country Place Acres
HIGH MEADOW RANCH GOLF CLUB
NICHOLS SAWMILL RD
OLD HOCKLEY RD
Connie St
Sugar Maple Cir
Veterans Rd
Johnson Al
Sugar Bend Dr
Old Johnson Farm Rd
Beyette Rd
Greenwood St
Tudor Wy
Hazy Hollow Ln
Champions Dr
Pleasant Forest
Clubhouse Dr
Lakeside Grn
Meadowwood
Emerald Oaks Dr
Meadow Falls
Masters Cir
Rancho
Post Oak
Sulpher Branch Bnd
High Chaparral
Diamond Oaks Dr
Stallion Run
Walnut Creek
Indigo Hills Dr
Indigo Lake Dr
Mink Lake Dr
Sawmill Dr
Timber Oaks Ct
Windy Ridge Tr
Arrowhead
Turner Rd
Sky Forest Cir
Wild Oaks
Forest Cir
Quiet Forest
Wagon Wheel Rd
Boothill Rd
Indian Springs Tr
Westward Ho St
Frontier Rd
1774
A 1 Legend Oaks Ct
B 1 S Sapling Oaks Pl
C 1 Cloverleaf Dr 2 Cloverwood Dr
30°11'37"
30°11'11"
30°10'45"
30°10'19"
30°09'53"
30°09'26"
30°09'00"
30°08'34"
95°45'21"
95°44'50"
95°44'20"
95°43'50"
95°43'20"
95°42'50"
A
B
C
D
E
1
2
3
4
5
6
7
SEE 2814 MAP
SEE 2816 MAP
RAND McNALLY

SEE 2961 MAP

1:24,000
1 in. = 2000 ft.
0 0.25 0.5
miles

SEE 2670 MAP

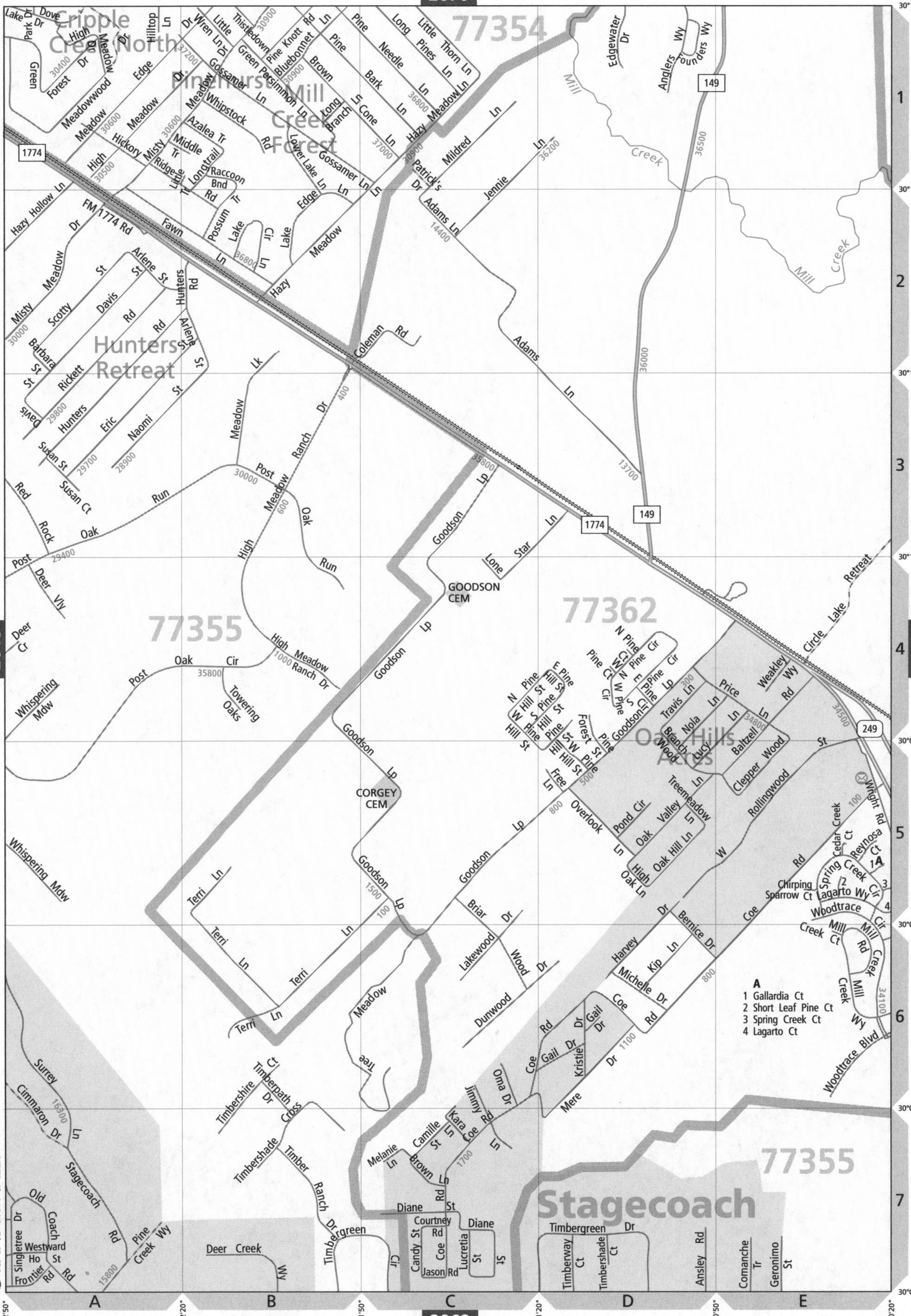
77354
77355
77362
77355
Cripple Creek North
Pinehurst
Mill Creek Forest
Hunters Retreat
Oak Hills Acres
Stagecoach
GOODSON CEM
CORGEY CEM
1774
FM 1774 Rd
149
249
Mill Creek
Lake Dr
Dove
Park Dr
High Meadow Dr
Hilltop Ln
Green Forest Dr
Meadowwood
Meadow Edge
Wren Ln
Little Thistledown
Gossamer
Green Persimmon
Pine Knott Rd
Bluebonnet
Pine Needle
Long Pines
Little Thorn Ln
Brown
Bark
Cone
Hazy Meadow Ln
Whipstock Rd
Azalea Tr
Middle
Longtrail
Raccoon Bnd
Long Branch
Lower Lake Ln
Gossamer Ln
Hickory Ridge
Misty
Mildred
Jennie Ln
Patrick's Dr
Adams Ln
Edgewater Dr
Anglers Wy
Founders Wy
Hazy Hollow Ln
Fawn Ln
Possum Tr
Lake Cir Ln
Lake Meadow
Hazy
Arlene St
Hunters Rd
Misty Meadow Dr
Scotty St
Davis St
Barbara St
Rickett Rd
Hunters Rd
Eric St
Naomi St
Susan St
Susan Ct
Coleman Rd
Meadow Lk
Ranch Dr
Post Oak Run
Red Rock
Post
Deer Vly
Deer Cr
High Meadow
Oak Run
Goodson Lp
Lone Star Ln
Adams Ln
Circle Lake Retreat
Weakley Wy
Price Rd
Travis Ln
Nola Ln
Baltzell Ln
Clepper Wood
Rollingwood St
Lucy
Branch Wood
Pine Hill St
Forest St
Free Ln
Overlook Ln
Pond Cir
Oak Valley
Treemeadow Ln
Oak Hill Ln
High Oak Ln
W Coe Rd
Wright Rd
Cedar Creek Ct
Reynosa Ct
Spring Creek Cir
Lagarto Wy
Chirping Sparrow Ct
Woodtrace Cir
Mill Creek Ct
Mill Creek Rd
Mill Creek Wy
Woodtrace Blvd
High Meadow Ranch Dr
Post Oak Cir
Towering Oaks
Whispering Mdw
Terri Ln
Briar Dr
Lakewood Dr
Wood Dr
Dunwood
Meadow Tree
Harvey Dr
Bernice Dr
Kip Ln
Michelle Dr
Coe Rd
Gail Dr
Kristie Dr
Mere Dr
Oma Dr
Jimmy Rd
Camille St
Kara Ln
Melanie Ln
Brown Ln
Timbershire Ct
Timberpath Dr
Cross
Timbershade Timber
Ranch Dr
Timbergreen
Surrey Ln
Cimmaron Dr
Stagecoach Rd
Old Coach Dr
Singletree Dr
Westward Ho St
Frontier Rd
Pine Creek Wy
Deer Creek Wy
Diane St
Courtney Rd
Candy St
Coe Rd
Lucretia St
Jason Rd
Timbergreen Dr
Timberway Ct
Timbershade Ct
Ansley Rd
Comanche Tr
Geronimo St
A
1 Gallardia Ct
2 Short Leaf Pine Ct
3 Spring Creek Ct
4 Lagarto Ct
30°11'36"
30°11'09"
30°10'43"
30°10'17"
30°09'51"
30°09'25"
30°08'59"
30°08'32"
95°42'50"
95°42'20"
95°41'50"
95°41'20"
95°40'50"
95°40'20"
A B C D E
1 2 3 4 5 6 7

SEE 2817 MAP

SEE 2962 MAP

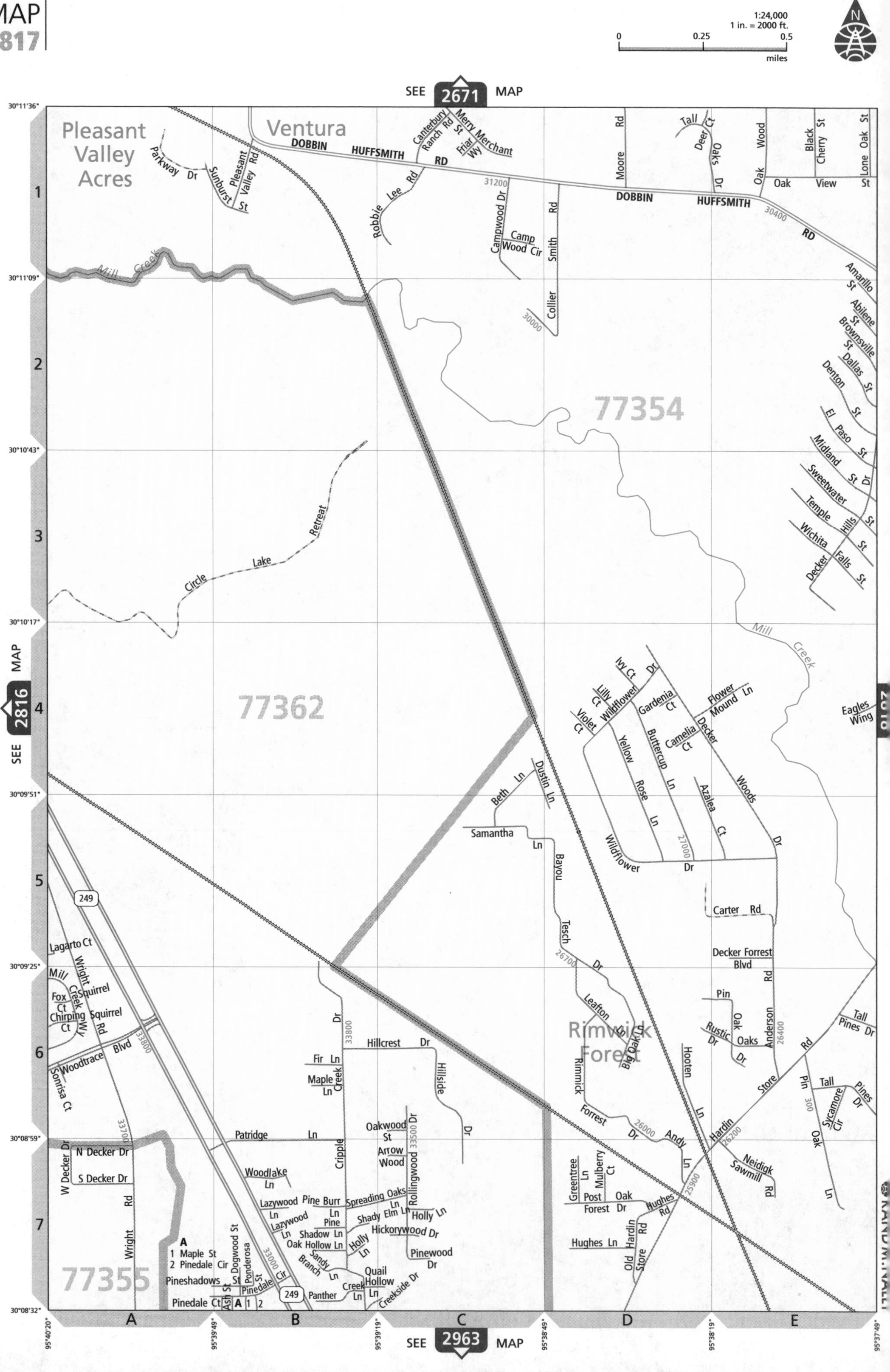
1:24,000
1 in. = 2000 ft.
0
0.25
0.5
miles
N
SEE 2671 MAP
SEE 2816 MAP
SEE 2963 MAP
30°11'36"
30°11'09"
30°10'43"
30°10'17"
30°09'51"
30°09'25"
30°08'59"
30°08'32"
95°40'20"
95°39'49"
95°39'19"
95°38'49"
95°38'19"
95°37'49"
A
B
C
D
E
1
2
3
4
5
6
7
Pleasant Valley Acres
Ventura
Rimwick Forest
77354
77362
77355
DOBBIN HUFFSMITH RD
Parkway Dr
Sunburst St
Pleasant Valley Rd
Canterbury Ranch Rd
Merry Merchant St
Friar Wy
Robbie Lee Rd
31200
Campwood Dr
Camp Wood Cir
Smith Rd
Collier
30000
Moore Rd
Tall Deer Ct
Oaks Dr
Oak Wood
Black Cherry St
Lone Oak St
Oak View St
30400
Amarillo St
Abilene St
Brownsville St
Dallas St
Denton St
El Paso St
Midland St
Sweetwater Dr
Temple Hills St
Wichita Falls St
Decker
Mill Creek
Circle Lake Retreat
Eagles Wing
Ivy Ct
Lilly Ct
Wildflower Dr
Violet Ct
Gardenia Ct
Flower Mound Ln
Camelia Ct
Decker Woods Dr
Yellow Rose Ln
Buttercup Ln
Azalea Ct
27000
Beth Ln
Dustin Ln
Samantha Ln
Bayou Tesch Dr
26700
Carter Rd
Decker Forrest Blvd
Anderson Rd
26400
Pin Oak Dr
Rustic Oaks Dr
Tall Pines Dr
Store Rd
Leafton Ln
Big Oak Ln
Rimmick Forrest Dr
26000
Hooten Ln
Andy Ln
Hardin Store Rd
26200
Neidigk Sawmill Rd
Pin Oak Ln
300
Tall Pines Dr
Sycamore Cir
25900
Greentree Ln
Mulberry Ct
Post Oak Forest Dr
Hughes Rd
Hughes Ln
Old Hardin Store Rd
249
33800
Lagarto Ct
Wright Rd
Mill Creek Wy
Fox Ct
Squirrel Chirping Ct
Squirrel
Woodtrace Blvd
Sonrisa Ct
33700
N Decker Dr
S Decker Dr
W Decker Dr
Hillcrest Dr
Hillside Dr
Fir Ln
Maple Ln
Cripple Creek Dr
Patridge Ln
Oakwood St
Arrow Wood
33500
Rollingwood Dr
Woodlake Ln
Lazywood Ln
Pine Burr Ln
Pine
Spreading Oaks Ln
Shady Elm Ln
Holly Ln
Shadow Ln
Oak Hollow Ln
Hickorywood Dr
Pinewood Dr
Sandy Branch Ln
Quail Hollow Ln
Creek Ln
Creekside Dr
Panther
Dogwood St
Ponderosa St
33000
Pinedale Cir
Pineshadows St
Pinedale Ct
Ash St
A
1 Maple St
2 Pinedale Cir
RAND McNALLY

1:24,000
1 in. = 2000 ft.
0 0.25 0.5
miles

SEE 2672 MAP

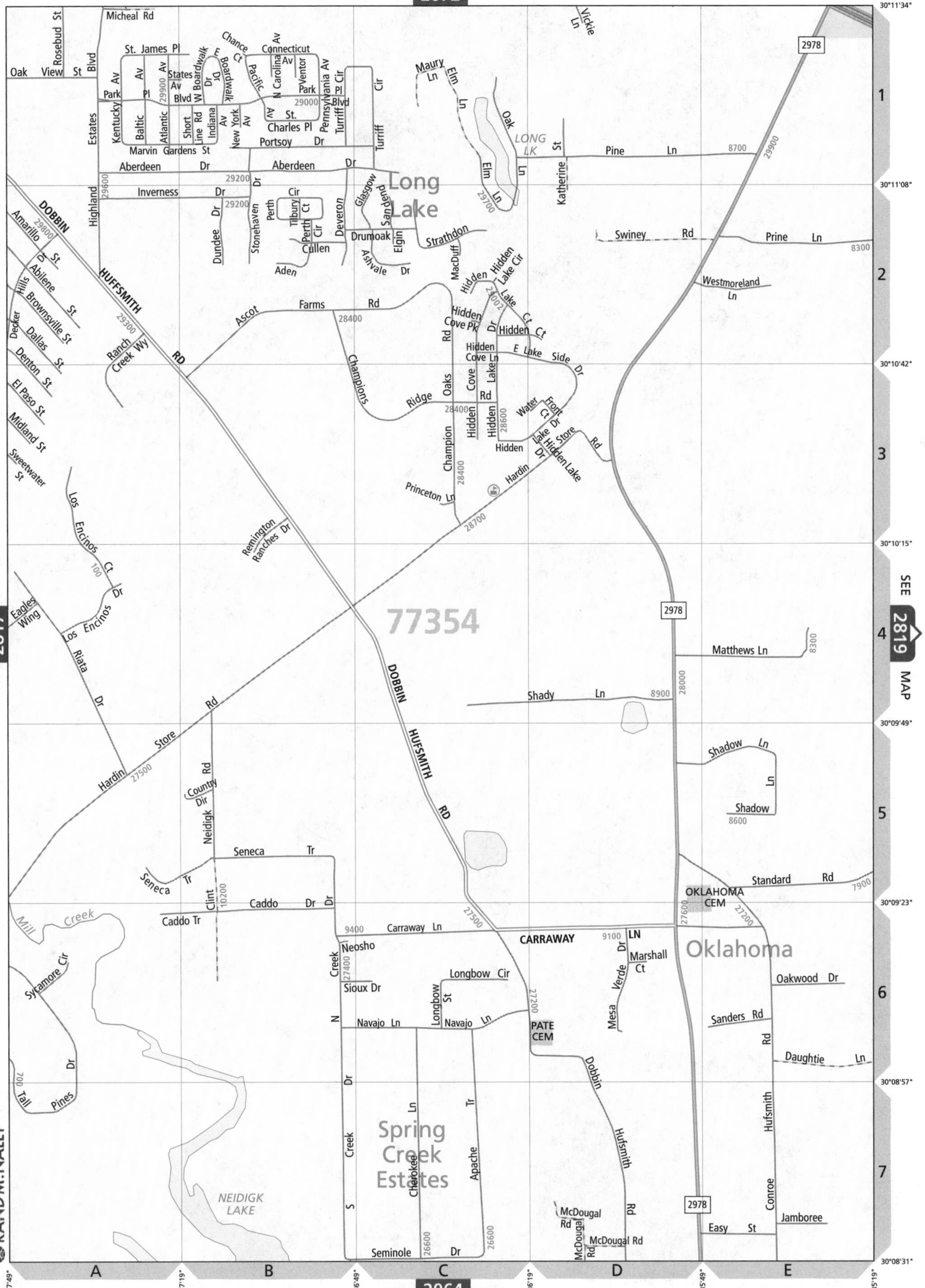
Long Lake
LONG LK
77354
Oklahoma
Spring Creek Estates
OKLAHOMA CEM
PATE CEM
NEIDIGK LAKE
Mill Creek
DOBBIN HUFFSMITH RD
CARRAWAY LN
Hardin Store Rd
2978
Micheal Rd
Oak View St
Rosebud St
Estates Blvd
St. James Pl
Chance Ct
Connecticut Av
Boardwalk
Pacific Av
N Carolina Av
Ventor Av
Pennsylvania Av
Park Pl
Turriff Cir
Kentucky Av
Baltic Av
Atlantic Av
States Av
Short Line Rd
Indiana Av
New York Av
St. Charles Pl
Marvin Gardens St
Portsoy Dr
Aberdeen Dr
Inverness Dr
Highland
Dundee Dr
Stonehaven Dr
Perth Cir
Tilbury Ct
Cullen
Aden
Deveron
Glasgow
Sandend
Drumoak
Elgin
Ashvale Dr
Strathdon
Maury Ln
Elm Ln
Oak Ln
Katherine St
Pine Ln
Vickie Ln
Swiney Rd
Prine Ln
Westmoreland Ln
MacDuff
Hidden Lake Cir
Hidden Lake Ct
Hidden Cove Pk
Hidden Cove Ln
E Lake Side Dr
Ascot Farms Rd
Champions
Ridge Oaks Rd
Water Front Ct
Hidden Lake Dr
Champion
Princeton Ln
Remington Ranches Dr
Ranch Creek Wy
Amarillo St
Abilene St
Hills
Brownsville St
Decker
Dallas St
Denton St
El Paso St
Midland St
Sweetwater St
Los Encinos Ct
Los Encinos Dr
Eagles Wing
Los Riata Dr
Matthews Ln
Shady Ln
Shadow Ln
Standard Rd
Country Dir
Neidigk Rd
Seneca Tr
Clint
Caddo Dr
Caddo Tr
Sycamore Cir
Tall Pines Dr
Neosho
N Creek
Sioux Dr
Longbow Cir
Longbow St
Navajo Ln
S Creek Dr
Cherokee Ln
Apache Tr
Seminole Dr
Mesa Verde Dr
Marshall Ct
Dobbin Hufsmith Rd
McDougal Rd
Oakwood Dr
Sanders Rd
Daughtie Ln
Hufsmith Rd
Conroe
Jamboree
Easy St
A B C D E
1 2 3 4 5 6 7
30°11'34"
30°11'08"
30°10'42"
30°10'15"
30°09'49"
30°09'23"
30°08'57"
30°08'31"
95°37'49"
95°37'19"
95°36'49"
95°36'19"
95°35'49"
95°35'19"

SEE 2819 MAP

SEE 2964 MAP

1:24,000
1 in. = 2000 ft.
0 0.25 0.5
miles

SEE 2673 MAP

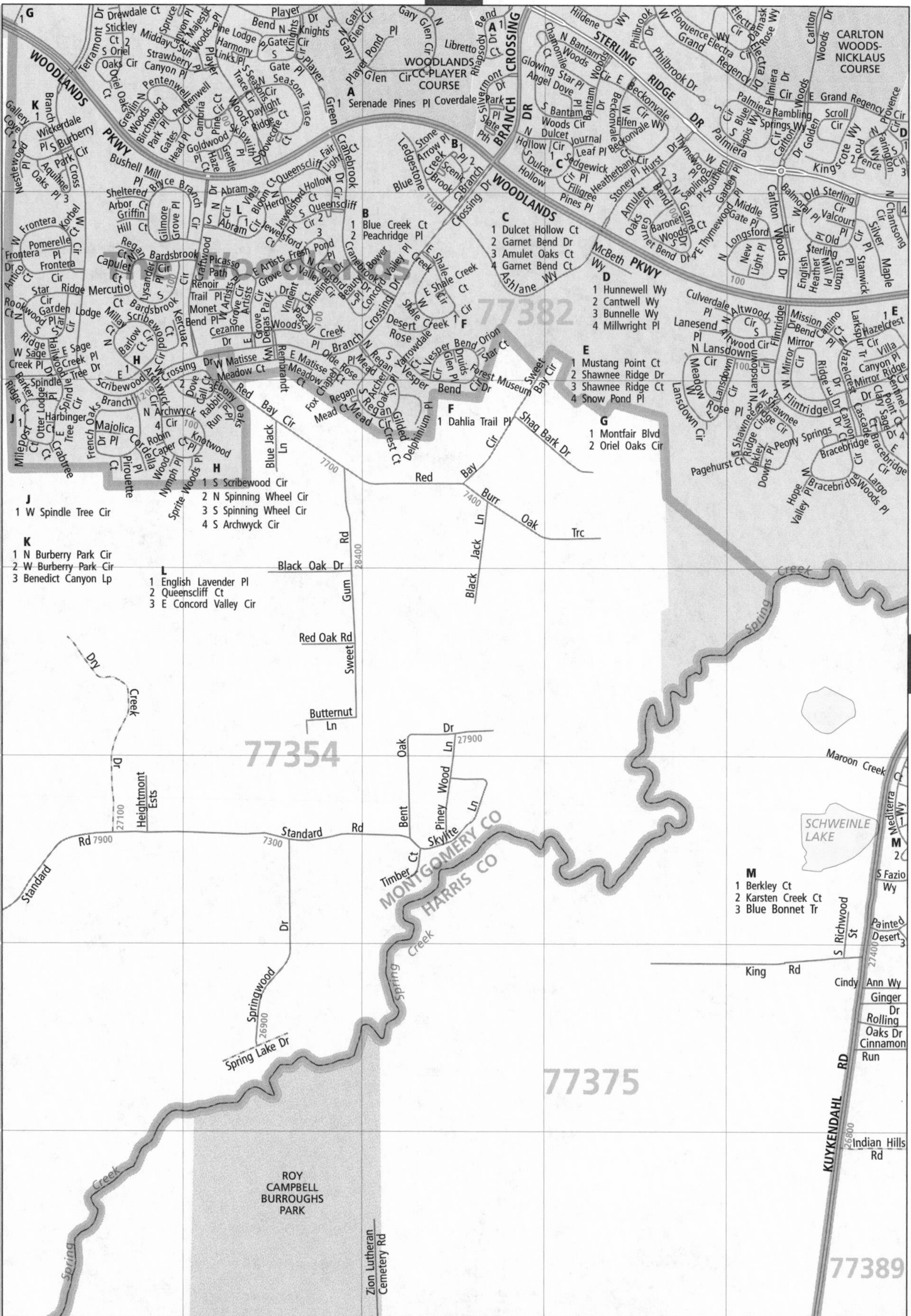
WOODLANDS PKWY
WOODLANDS CC-PLAYER COURSE
CARLTON WOODS-NICKLAUS COURSE
STERLING RIDGE DR
BRANCH CROSSING DR
McBeth PKWY
The Woodlands
77382
77354
77375
77389
MONTGOMERY CO
HARRIS CO
SCHWEINLE LAKE
ROY CAMPBELL BURROUGHS PARK
KUYKENDAHL RD
Spring Creek
Dry Creek Dr
Standard Rd
Sweet Gum Rd
Red Bay Cir
Burr Oak Trc
Black Jack Ln
Black Oak Dr
Red Oak Rd
Butternut Ln
Oak Dr
Bent Oak Dr
Piney Wood Ln
Skylite Ln
Timber Ct
Heightmont Ests
Springwood Dr
Spring Lake Dr
Zion Lutheran Cemetery Rd
King Rd
S Richwood St
Maroon Creek
Indian Hills Rd
Cindy Ann Wy
Ginger Dr
Rolling Oaks Dr
Cinnamon Run
Painted Desert
S Fazio Wy
Mediterra Wy
Shag Bark Dr
A
1 Serenade Pines Pl
B
1 Blue Creek Ct
2 Peachridge Pl
C
1 Dulcet Hollow Ct
2 Garnet Bend Dr
3 Amulet Oaks Ct
4 Garnet Bend Ct
D
1 Hunnewell Wy
2 Cantwell Wy
3 Bunnelle Wy
4 Millwright Pl
E
1 Mustang Point Ct
2 Shawnee Ridge Dr
3 Shawnee Ridge Ct
4 Snow Pond Pl
F
1 Dahlia Trail Pl
G
1 Montfair Blvd
2 Oriel Oaks Cir
H
1 S Scribewood Cir
2 N Spinning Wheel Cir
3 S Spinning Wheel Cir
4 S Archwyck Cir
J
1 W Spindle Tree Cir
K
1 N Burberry Park Cir
2 W Burberry Park Cir
3 Benedict Canyon Lp
L
1 English Lavender Pl
2 Queenscliff Ct
3 E Concord Valley Cir
M
1 Berkley Ct
2 Karsten Creek Ct
3 Blue Bonnet Tr
30°11'34"
30°11'08"
30°10'42"
30°10'15"
30°09'49"
30°09'23"
30°08'57"
30°08'31"
95°35'19"
95°34'48"
95°34'18"
95°33'48"
95°33'18"
95°32'48"
A B C D E
1 2 3 4 5 6 7

SEE 2818 MAP

SEE 2965 MAP

1:24,000
1 in. = 2000 ft.
0 0.25 0.5
miles

SEE 2674 MAP

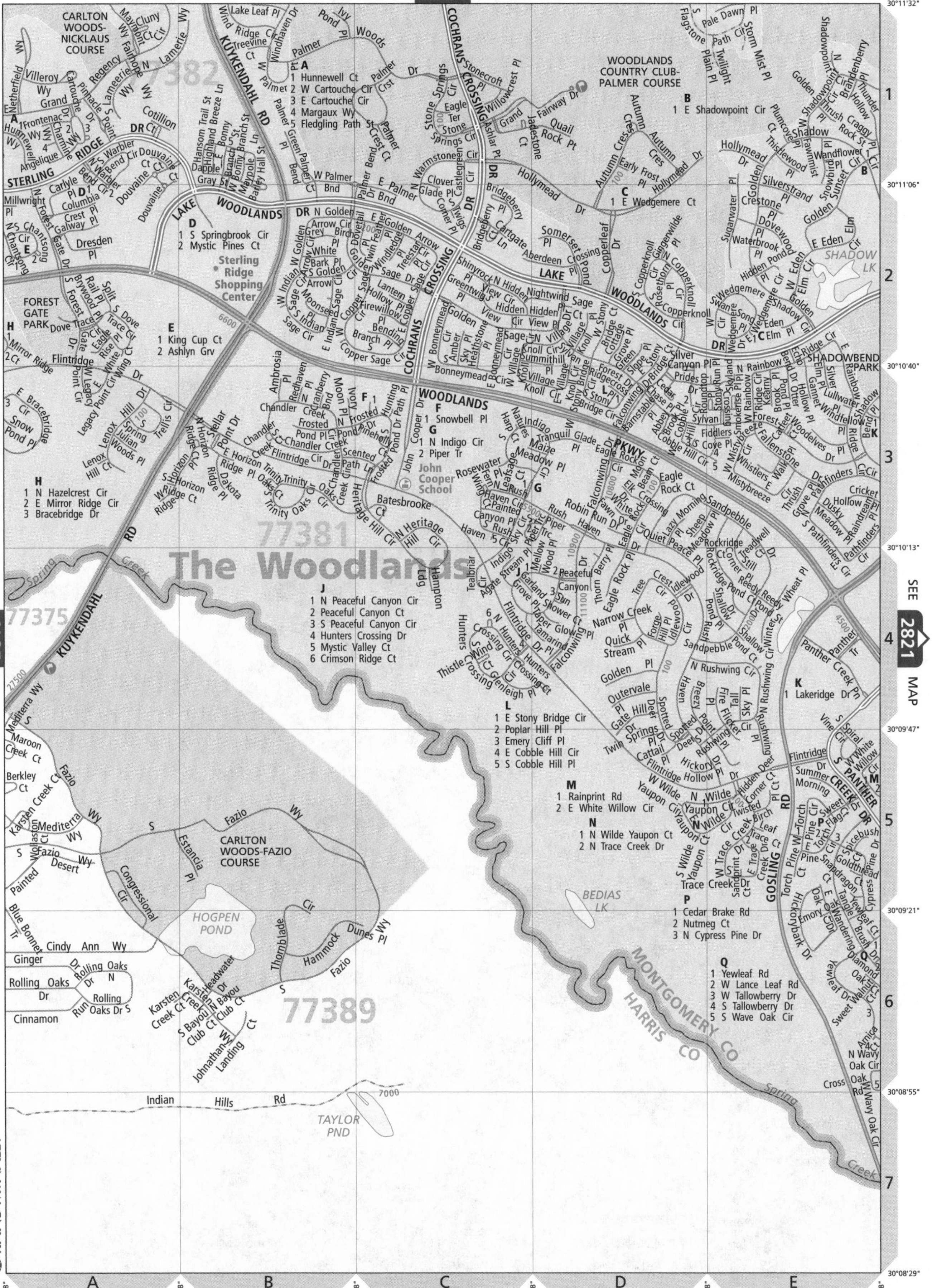
The Woodlands
77382
77381
77375
77389
CARLTON WOODS-NICKLAUS COURSE
WOODLANDS COUNTRY CLUB-PALMER COURSE
CARLTON WOODS-FAZIO COURSE
FOREST GATE PARK
SHADOWBEND PARK
Sterling Ridge Shopping Center
John Cooper School
HOGPEN POND
BEDIAS LK
TAYLOR PND
SHADOW LK
MONTGOMERY CO
HARRIS CO
Spring Creek
KUYKENDAHL RD
COCHRANS CROSSING DR
LAKE WOODLANDS DR
WOODLANDS PKWY
STERLING RIDGE DR
GOSLING RD
PANTHER CREEK DR
Indian Hills Rd
A
1 Hunnewell Ct
2 W Cartouche Cir
3 E Cartouche Cir
4 Margaux Wy
5 Fledgling Path St
B
1 E Shadowpoint Cir
C
1 E Wedgemere Ct
D
1 S Springbrook Cir
2 Mystic Pines Ct
E
1 King Cup Ct
2 Ashlyn Grv
F
1 Snowbell Pl
G
1 N Indigo Cir
2 Piper Tr
H
1 N Hazelcrest Cir
2 E Mirror Ridge Cir
3 Bracebridge Dr
J
1 N Peaceful Canyon Cir
2 Peaceful Canyon Ct
3 S Peaceful Canyon Cir
4 Hunters Crossing Dr
5 Mystic Valley Ct
6 Crimson Ridge Ct
K
1 Lakeridge Dr
L
1 E Stony Bridge Cir
2 Poplar Hill Pl
3 Emery Cliff Pl
4 E Cobble Hill Cir
5 S Cobble Hill Pl
M
1 Rainprint Rd
2 E White Willow Cir
N
1 N Wilde Yaupon Ct
2 N Trace Creek Dr
P
1 Cedar Brake Rd
2 Nutmeg Ct
3 N Cypress Pine Dr
Q
1 Yewleaf Rd
2 W Lance Leaf Rd
3 W Tallowberry Dr
4 S Tallowberry Dr
5 S Wave Oak Cir
SEE 2821 MAP
SEE 2819 MAP
30°11'32"
30°11'06"
30°10'40"
30°10'13"
30°09'47"
30°09'21"
30°08'55"
30°08'29"
95°32'48"
95°32'18"
95°31'48"
95°31'18"
95°30'48"
95°30'18"
A B C D E
1 2 3 4 5 6 7

SEE 2966 MAP

1:24,000
1 in. = 2000 ft.
0 0.25 0.5
miles

SEE 2675 MAP

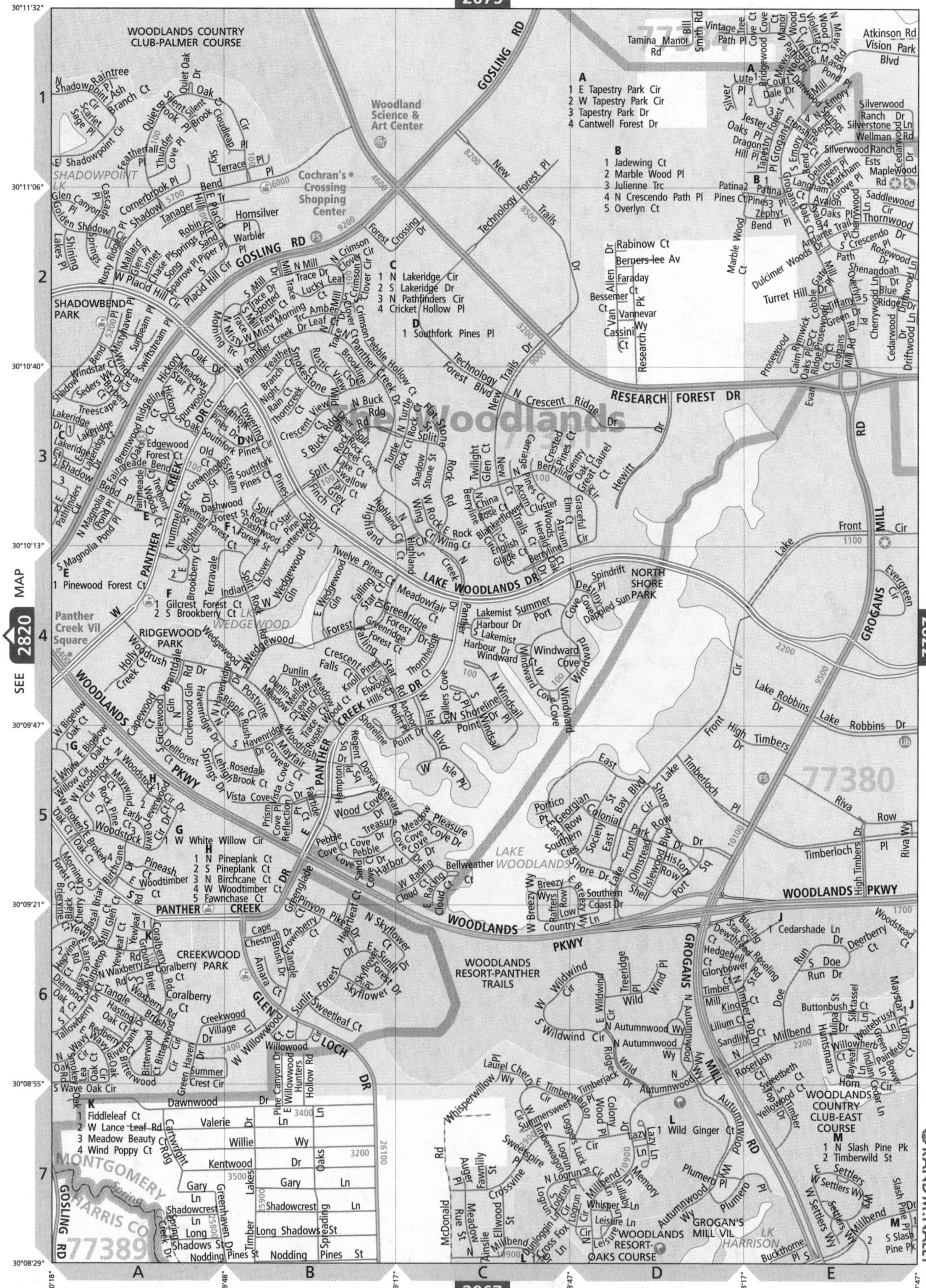
WOODLANDS COUNTRY CLUB-PALMER COURSE
Woodland Science & Art Center
Cochran's Crossing Shopping Center
SHADOWPOINT LK
SHADOWBEND PARK
GOSLING RD
RESEARCH FOREST DR
The Woodlands
77381
77384
77380
77389
LAKE WOODLANDS DR
NORTH SHORE PARK
Panther Creek Vil Square
RIDGEWOOD PARK
LK WEDGEWOOD
WOODLANDS PKWY
PANTHER CREEK DR
LAKE WOODLANDS
CREEKWOOD PARK
WOODLANDS RESORT-PANTHER TRAILS
GROGANS MILL RD
WOODLANDS COUNTRY CLUB-EAST COURSE
WOODLANDS RESORT-OAKS COURSE
GROGAN'S MILL VIL
LK HARRISON
MONTGOMERY CO
HARRIS CO
Spring Creek
A
1 E Tapestry Park Cir
2 W Tapestry Park Cir
3 Tapestry Park Dr
4 Cantwell Forest Dr
B
1 Jadewing Ct
2 Marble Wood Pl
3 Julienne Trc
4 N Crescendo Path Pl
5 Overlyn Ct
C
1 N Lakeridge Cir
2 S Lakeridge Dr
3 N Pathfinders Cir
4 Cricket Hollow Pl
D
1 Southfork Pines Pl
E
1 Pinewood Forest Ct
F
1 Gilcrest Forest Ct
2 S Brookberry Ct
G
1 W White Willow Cir
H
1 N Pineplank Ct
2 S Pineplank Ct
3 N Birchcane Ct
4 W Woodtimber Ct
5 Fawnchase Ct
J
1 Cedarshade Ln
K
1 Fiddleleaf Ct
2 W Lance Leaf Rd
3 Meadow Beauty Ct
4 Wind Poppy Ct
L
1 Wild Ginger Ct
M
1 N Slash Pine Pk
2 Timberwild St
SEE 2820 MAP
SEE 2822 MAP
A B C D E
1 2 3 4 5 6 7
30°11'32" 30°11'06" 30°10'40" 30°10'13" 30°09'47" 30°09'21" 30°08'55" 30°08'29"
95°30'18" 95°29'48" 95°29'17" 95°28'47" 95°28'17" 95°27'47"

SEE 2967 MAP

1:24,000
1 in. = 2000 ft.
0 0.25 0.5
miles

SEE 2676 MAP

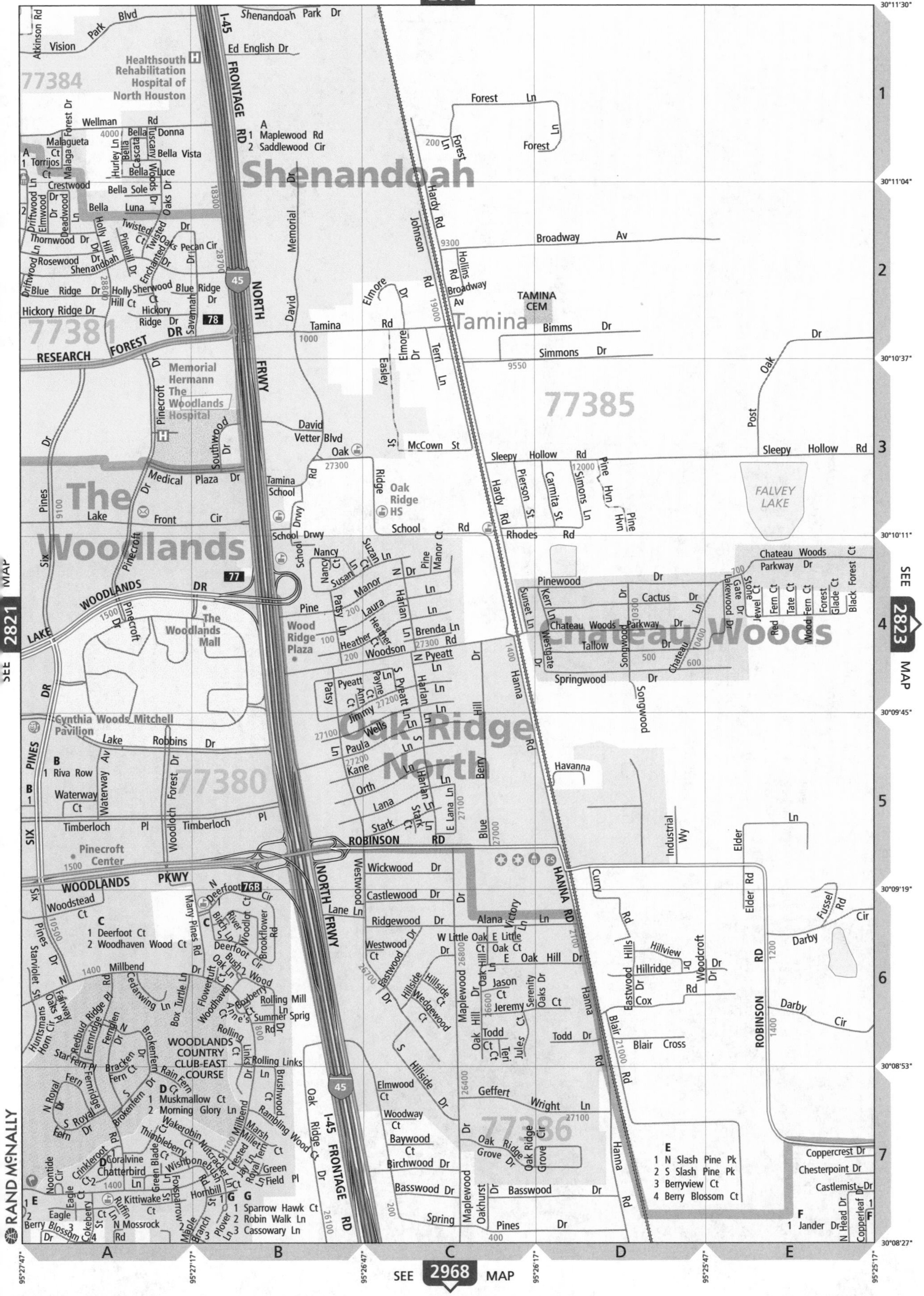
Shenandoah
The Woodlands
Tamina
Oak Ridge North
Chateau Woods
77384
77381
77385
77380
77386
Healthsouth Rehabilitation Hospital of North Houston
Memorial Hermann The Woodlands Hospital
TAMINA CEM
FALVEY LAKE
Oak Ridge HS
Tamina School
The Woodlands Mall
Wood Ridge Plaza
Cynthia Woods Mitchell Pavilion
Pinecroft Center
WOODLANDS COUNTRY CLUB-EAST COURSE
I-45 FRONTAGE RD
NORTH FRWY
RESEARCH FOREST DR
WOODLANDS DR
WOODLANDS PKWY
LAKE WOODLANDS DR
SIX PINES DR
ROBINSON RD
HANNA RD
Shenandoah Park Dr
Ed English Dr
Vision Park Blvd
Atkinson Rd
Wellman Rd
Forest Ln
Hardy Rd
Johnson Rd
Broadway Av
Tamina Rd
Bimms Dr
Simmons Dr
Sleepy Hollow Rd
Post Oak Dr
David Memorial Dr
David Vetter Blvd
McCown St
School Rd
Rhodes Rd
Pinewood Dr
Cactus Dr
Chateau Woods Parkway Dr
Tallow Dr
Springwood Dr
Songwood Dr
Medical Plaza Dr
Lake Front Cir
Lake Robbins Dr
Timberloch Pl
Wickwood Dr
Castlewood Dr
Ridgewood Dr
Oak Hill Dr
Blair Cross
Geffert Wright Ln
Basswood Dr
Spring Pines Dr
Industrial Wy
Elder Rd
Darby Cir
Fussel Rd
Curry Rd
Millbend Dr
A 1 Maplewood Rd 2 Saddlewood Cir
B 1 Riva Row
C 1 Deerfoot Ct 2 Woodhaven Wood Ct
D 1 Muskmallow Ct 2 Morning Glory Ln
E 1 N Slash Pine Pk 2 S Slash Pine Pk 3 Berryview Ct 4 Berry Blossom Ct
F 1 Jander Dr
G 1 Sparrow Hawk Ct 2 Robin Walk Ln 3 Cassowary Ln
SEE 2821 MAP
SEE 2823 MAP
RAND McNALLY

SEE 2968 MAP

1:24,000
1 in. = 2000 ft.
0 0.25 0.5
miles

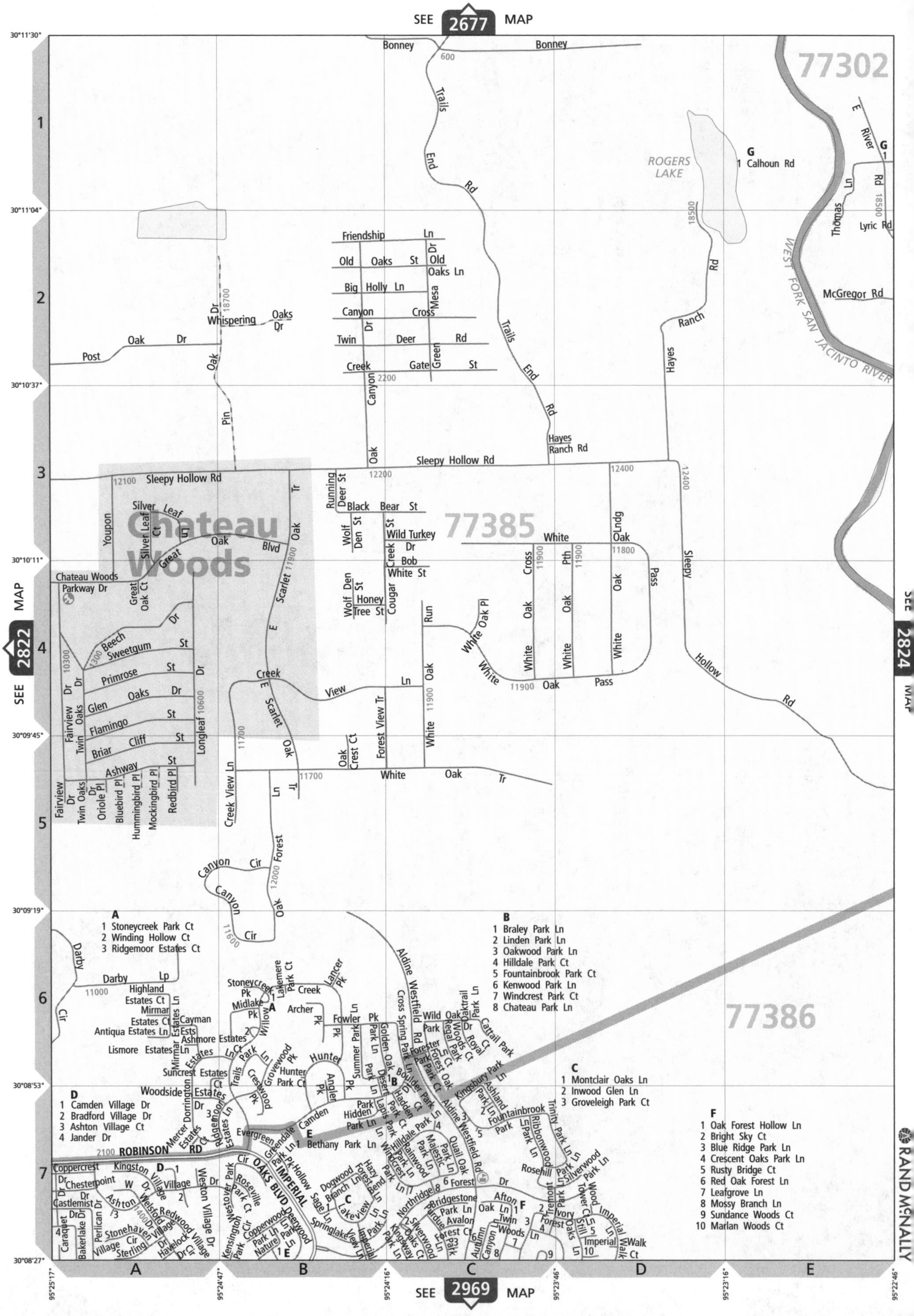
SEE 2677 MAP
SEE 2822 MAP
SEE 2824 MAP
SEE 2969 MAP
77302
77385
77386
Chateau Woods
ROGERS LAKE
WEST FORK SAN JACINTO RIVER
Bonney
Trails End Rd
Hayes Ranch Rd
Sleepy Hollow Rd
Post Oak Dr
Whispering Oaks Dr
Pin Oak Dr
Friendship Ln
Old Oaks St
Old Oaks Ln
Big Holly Ln
Canyon Cross
Twin Deer Rd
Creek Gate St
Canyon Oak Dr
Mesa Dr
Green
Running Deer St
Black Bear St
Wolf Den St
Wild Turkey Dr
Bob White St
Cougar Creek St
Honey Tree St
White Oak Lndg
White Oak Pass
White Oak Pth
White Oak Pl
White Oak Run
White Oak Tr
Creek View Ln
Forest View Tr
Oak Crest Ct
Scarlet Oak Tr
E Scarlet Oak Tr
Great Oak Blvd
Great Oak Ct
Silver Leaf Ln
Silver Leaf Ct
Youpon
Chateau Woods Parkway Dr
Beech Dr
Sweetgum St
Primrose St
Glen Oaks Dr
Flamingo St
Briar Cliff St
Ashway St
Longleaf Dr
Fairview Dr
Twin Oaks Dr
Oriole Pl
Bluebird Pl
Hummingbird Pl
Mockingbird Pl
Redbird Pl
Forest Oak Ln
Canyon Cir
Darby Lp
Darby Cir
Calhoun Rd
Thomas Ln
E River Rd
Lyric Rd
McGregor Rd
Aldine Westfield Rd
Kingsbury Park
Robinson Rd
Oaks Blvd
Imperial Oaks Blvd
A
1 Stoneycreek Park Ct
2 Winding Hollow Ct
3 Ridgemoor Estates Ct
B
1 Braley Park Ln
2 Linden Park Ln
3 Oakwood Park Ln
4 Hilldale Park Ct
5 Fountainbrook Park Ct
6 Kenwood Park Ln
7 Windcrest Park Ct
8 Chateau Park Ln
C
1 Montclair Oaks Ln
2 Inwood Glen Ln
3 Groveleigh Park Ct
D
1 Camden Village Dr
2 Bradford Village Dr
3 Ashton Village Ct
4 Jander Dr
E
1 Bethany Park Ln
F
1 Oak Forest Hollow Ln
2 Bright Sky Ct
3 Blue Ridge Park Ln
4 Crescent Oaks Park Ln
5 Rusty Bridge Ct
6 Red Oak Forest Ln
7 Leafgrove Ln
8 Mossy Branch Ln
9 Sundance Woods Ct
10 Marlan Woods Ct
G
1 Calhoun Rd

SEE 2678 MAP

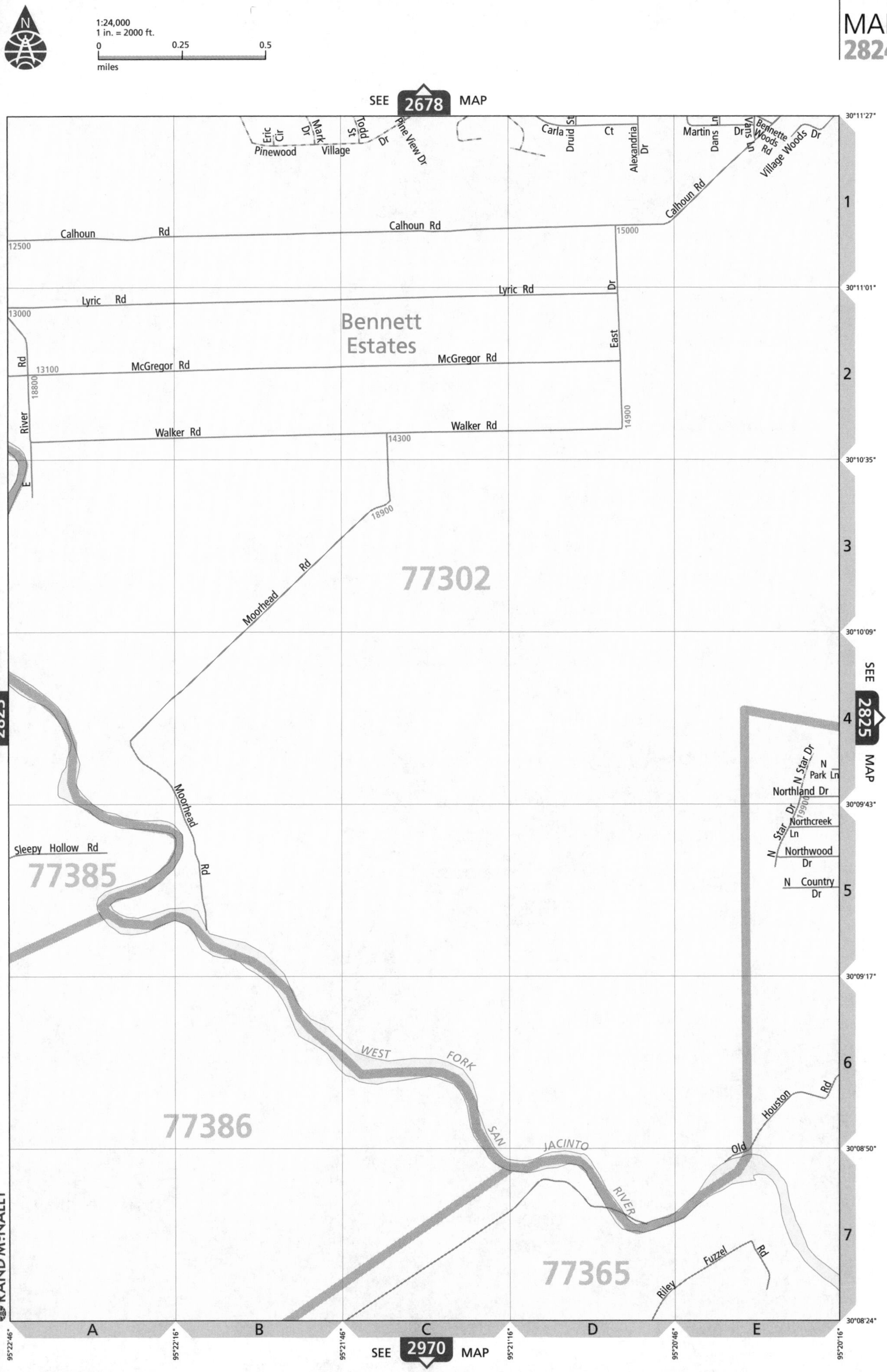
N
1:24,000
1 in. = 2000 ft.
0 0.25 0.5
miles
Eric Cir
Mark Dr
Todd St
Pinewood Village Dr
Pine View Dr
Carla
Druid St
Ct
Alexandria Dr
Martin
Dans Ln
Dr
Vans Ln
Bennette Woods Rd
Village Woods Dr
Calhoun Rd
Calhoun Rd
Calhoun Rd
12500
15000
Lyric Rd
Lyric Rd
13000
Bennett Estates
McGregor Rd
McGregor Rd
13100
18800
East Dr
14900
River Rd
Walker Rd
Walker Rd
14300
E
18900
Moorhead Rd
77302
Moorhead Rd
N Star Dr
N Park Ln
Northland Dr
19900
N Star Dr
Northcreek Ln
Northwood Dr
N Country Dr
Sleepy Hollow Rd
77385
WEST FORK SAN JACINTO RIVER
77386
Old Houston Rd
77365
Riley Fuzzel Rd
1
2
3
4
5
6
7
A
B
C
D
E
30°11'27"
30°11'01"
30°10'35"
30°10'09"
30°09'43"
30°09'17"
30°08'50"
30°08'24"
95°22'46"
95°22'16"
95°21'46"
95°21'16"
95°20'46"
95°20'16"

SEE 2825 MAP

SEE 2970 MAP

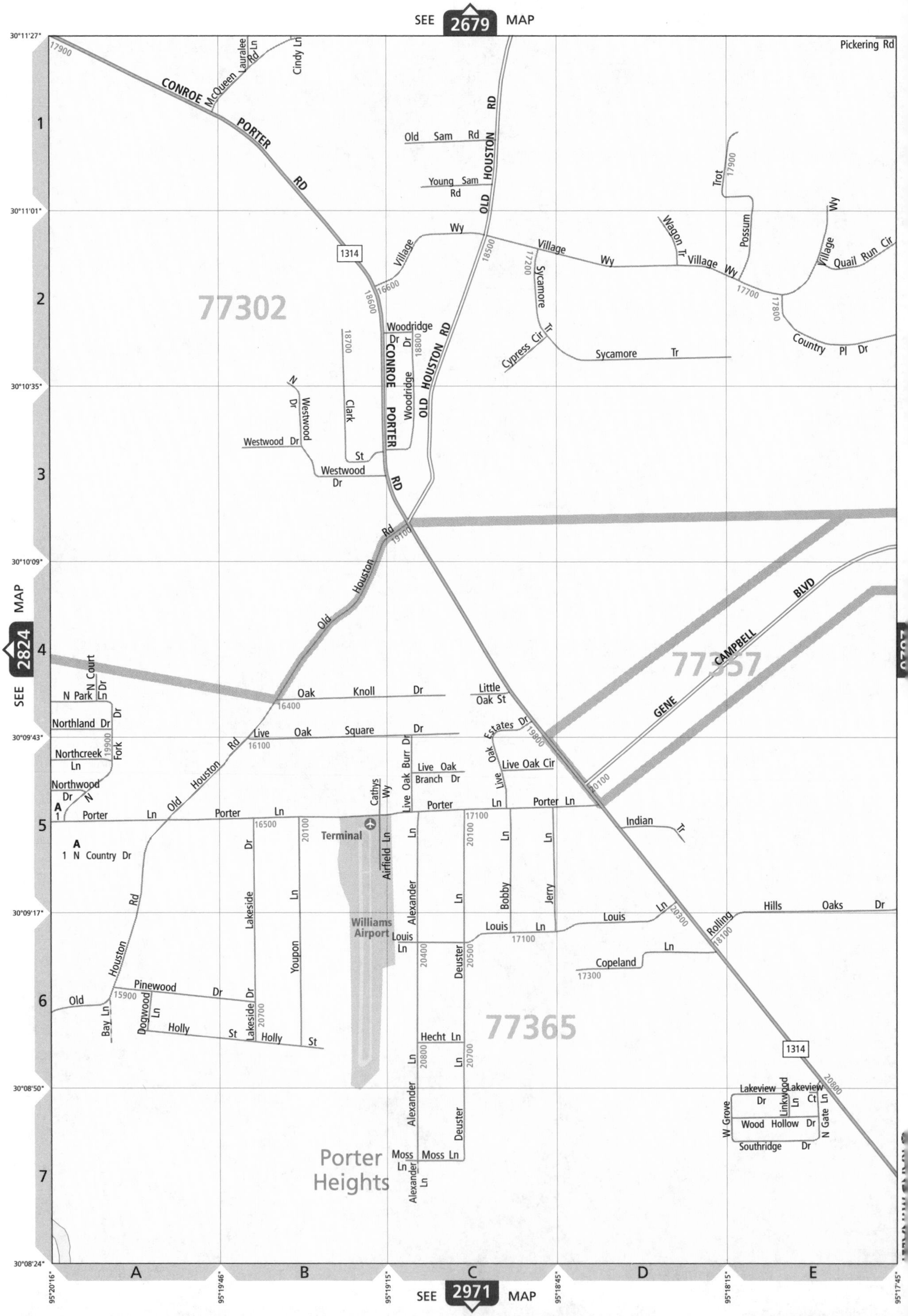
1:24,000
1 in. = 2000 ft.
0 0.25 0.5
miles
SEE 2679 MAP
SEE 2824 MAP
SEE 2971 MAP
CONROE PORTER RD
OLD HOUSTON RD
1314
77302
77357
77365
GENE CAMPBELL BLVD
Village Wy
Old Sam Rd
Young Sam Rd
Sycamore Tr
Cypress Cir
Country Pl Dr
Quail Run Cir
Pickering Rd
Wagon Tr
Possum Trot
Woodridge Dr
Clark St
Westwood Dr
N Westwood Dr
McQueen Rd
Lauralee Ln
Cindy Ln
Old Houston Rd
Oak Knoll Dr
Live Oak Square Dr
Little Oak St
Oak Estates Dr
Live Oak Cir
Live Oak Branch Dr
Live Oak Burr Dr
Porter Ln
Indian Tr
Cathys Wy
Airfield Ln
Terminal
Williams Airport
Alexander Ln
Deuster Ln
Bobby Ln
Jerry Ln
Louis Ln
Rolling Hills Oaks Dr
Copeland Ln
Hecht Ln
Moss Ln
Porter Heights
Lakeside Dr
Youpon Ln
Pinewood Dr
Holly St
Dogwood Ln
Bay Ln
N Park Ln
N Court Dr
Northland Dr
Fork Dr
Northcreek Ln
Northwood Dr
N Country Dr
Lakeview Dr
Lakeview Ct
Linkwood Ln
Wood Hollow Dr
W Grove
N Gate Ln
Southridge Dr
A B C D E
1 2 3 4 5 6 7

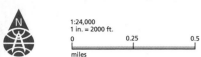

1:24,000
1 in. = 2000 ft.
0 0.25 0.5
miles

SEE 2680 MAP

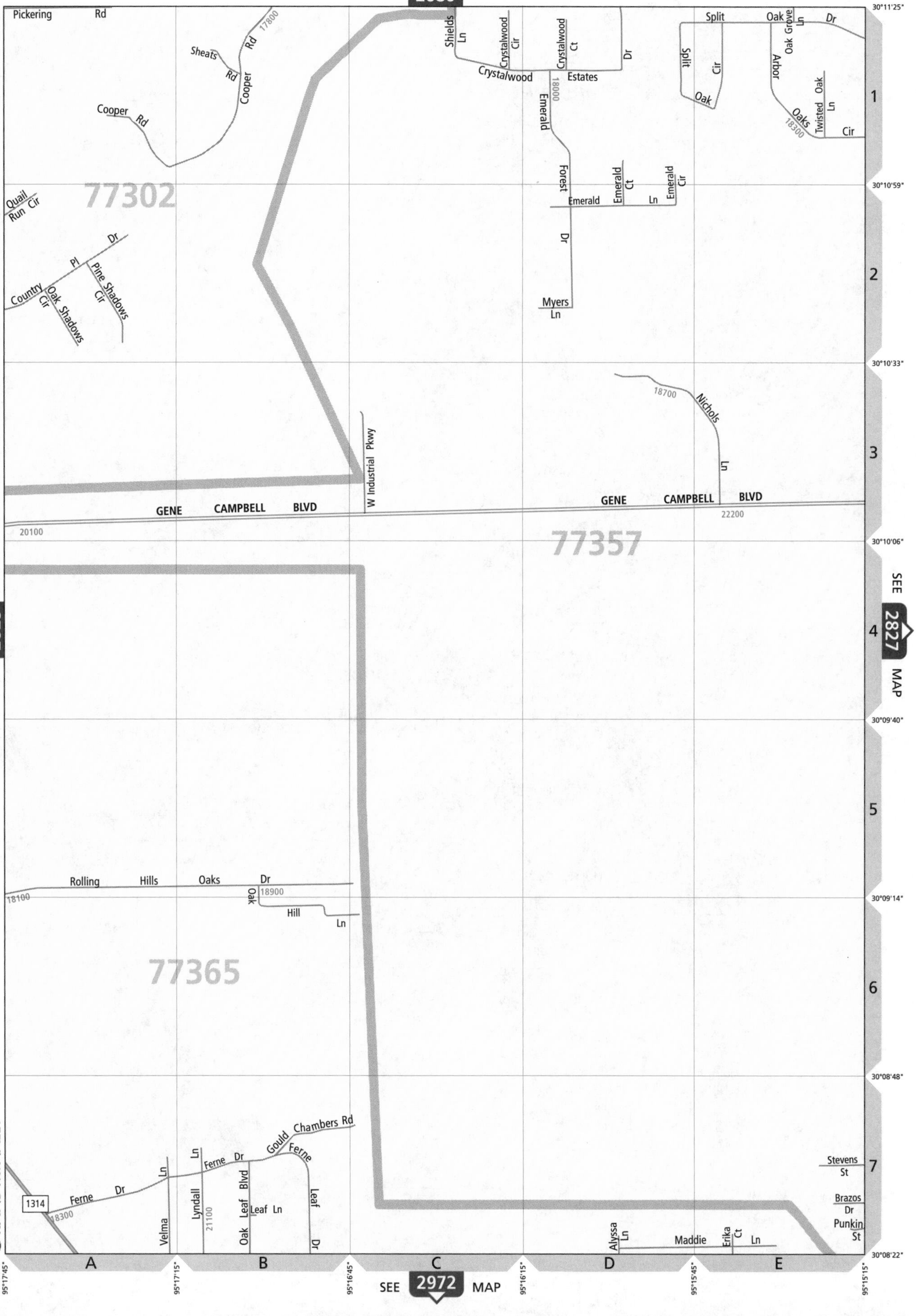
Pickering Rd
Sheats Rd
Cooper Rd
17800
Cooper Rd
Shields Ln
Crystalwood Cir
Crystalwood Ct
Crystalwood Estates Dr
18000
Emerald Forest Dr
Emerald Ln
Emerald Ct
Emerald Cir
Myers Ln
Split Oak Cir
Oak Grove Ln
Arbor Oaks Dr
18300
Twisted Oak Ln
Cir
77302
Quail Run Cir
Country Pl
Dr
Pine Shadows Cir
Oak Shadows Cir
18700
Nichols Ln
W Industrial Pkwy
GENE CAMPBELL BLVD
20100
22200
77357
Rolling Hills Oaks Dr
18100
18900
Oak Hill Ln
77365
Gould Chambers Rd
Ferne Dr
1314
18300
Velma Ln
Lyndall Ln
21100
Oak Leaf Blvd
Leaf Ln
Leaf Dr
Ferne
Stevens St
Brazos Dr
Punkin St
Alyssa Ln
Maddie Ln
Erika Ct
1
2
3
4
5
6
7
A
B
C
D
E
30°11'25"
30°10'59"
30°10'33"
30°10'06"
30°09'40"
30°09'14"
30°08'48"
30°08'22"
95°17'45"
95°17'15"
95°16'45"
95°16'15"
95°15'45"
95°15'15"

SEE 2827 MAP

SEE 2972 MAP

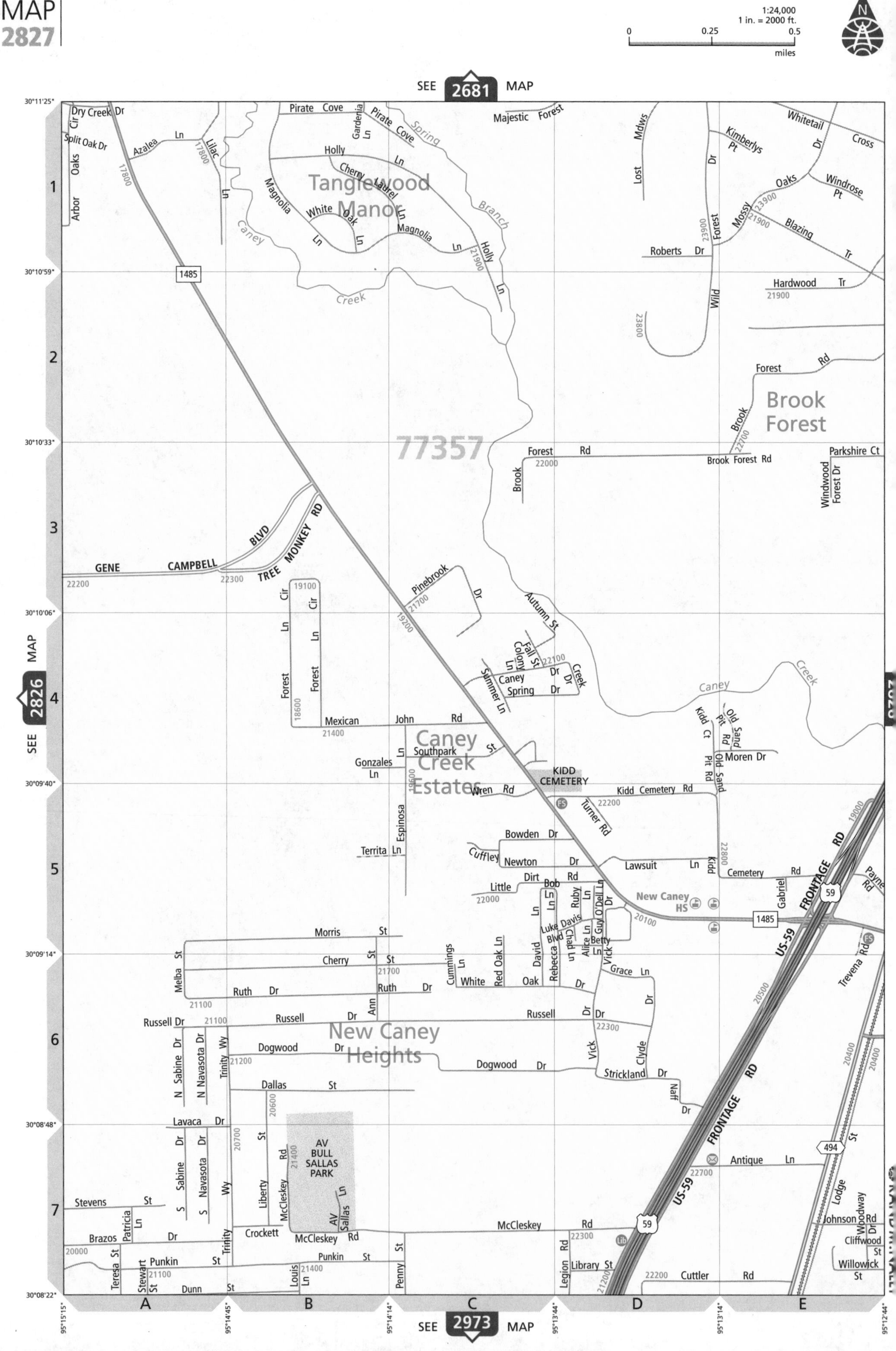
1:24,000
1 in. = 2000 ft.
0
0.25
0.5
miles
N
SEE 2681 MAP
SEE 2973 MAP
SEE 2826 MAP
30°11'25"
30°10'59"
30°10'33"
30°10'06"
30°09'40"
30°09'14"
30°08'48"
30°08'22"
95°15'15"
95°14'45"
95°14'14"
95°13'44"
95°13'14"
95°12'44"
A
B
C
D
E
1
2
3
4
5
6
7
Tanglewood Manor
77357
Brook Forest
Caney Creek Estates
New Caney Heights
KIDD CEMETERY
AV BULL SALLAS PARK
New Caney HS
Dry Creek Dr
Cir
Split Oak Dr
Arbor Oaks
Azalea Ln
Lilac Ln
17800
Pirate Cove
Gardenia Ln
Pirate Cove
Spring Branch
Majestic Forest
Holly Ln
Cherry Laurel Ln
Magnolia Ln
White Oak Ln
Magnolia Ln
Holly Ln
21900
Caney Creek
1485
Lost Mdws
Wild Forest Dr
23900
23800
Kimberlys Pt
Whitetail Dr
Cross
Windrose Pt
Mossy Oaks
23900
21900
Blazing Tr
Roberts Dr
Hardwood Tr
21900
Forest Rd
Brook Forest
22700
Forest Rd
22000
Brook
Brook Forest Rd
Parkshire Ct
Windwood Forest Dr
GENE CAMPBELL BLVD
TREE MONKEY RD
22200
22300
19100
Forest Cir Ln
Forest Cir Ln
18600
Pinebrook Dr
21700
19200
Autumn St
Fall St
Colony Ln
22100
Caney Creek Dr
Caney Spring Dr
Summer Ln
Caney Creek
Kidd Ct
Old Sand Pit Rd
Moren Dr
Mexican John Rd
21400
Southpark St
Gonzales Ln
19600
Wren Rd
Kidd Cemetery Rd
22200
Turner Rd
Espinosa
Territa Ln
Bowden Dr
Cuffley
Newton Dr
Lawsuit Ln
22800
Kidd
Cemetery Rd
Gabriel
FRONTAGE RD
19000
Payne Rd
59
Dirt Rd
Bob Ln
Little
22000
Ln
Ruby Ln
O'Dell Ln
Dr
Luke Davis Blvd
Chad Ln
Guy Ln
Alice Ln
Betty Ln
Vick
20100
1485
US-59
Trevena Rd
Morris St
Cherry St
21700
Melba St
Cummings Ln
White Oak Dr
Red Oak Ln
David
Rebecca
Grace Ln
Dr
Ruth Dr
Ruth Dr
21100
Ann
Russell Dr
21100
Russell Dr
Russell Dr
Dr
22300
20500
Dogwood Dr
21200
Dogwood Dr
Vick
Clyde
Strickland Dr
Naff Dr
N Sabine Dr
N Navasota Dr
Trinity Wy
Dallas St
20600
FRONTAGE RD
20400
20400
Lavaca Dr
S Sabine Dr
S Navasota Dr
20700
Wy
St
Liberty
McCleskey Rd
21400
AV Sallas Ln
494
St
Antique Ln
22700
US-59
Lodge
Stevens St
Patricia Ln
Brazos Dr
Crockett
McCleskey Rd
McCleskey Rd
22300
Lib
59
Johnson Rd
Woodway Dr
Cliffwood St
20000
Teresa St
Stewart St
Punkin St
21100
Trinity
Punkin St
21400
Penny St
Legion Rd
Library St
21200
Willowick St
Dunn St
Louis Ln
22200
Cuttler Rd

1:24,000
1 in. = 2000 ft.
0 0.25 0.5
miles

SEE 2682 MAP

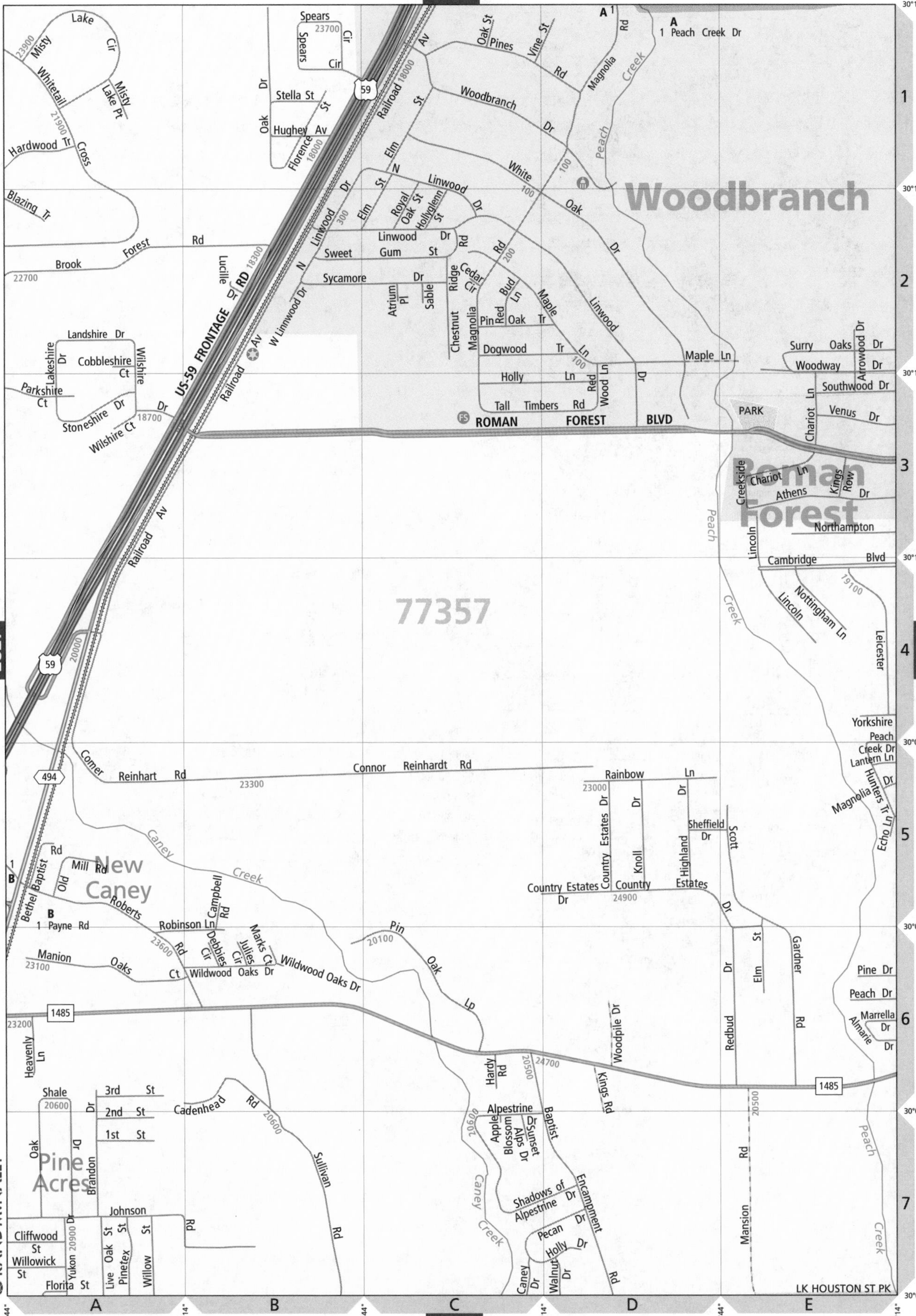
Woodbranch
Roman Forest
New Caney
Pine Acres
77357
US-59 FRONTAGE RD
59
494
1485
ROMAN FOREST BLVD
Railroad Av
W Linwood Dr
N Linwood Dr
N Elm St
Woodbranch Dr
White Oak Dr
Linwood Dr
Sweet Gum St
Sycamore Dr
Royal Oak St
Hollyglenn St
Linwood Ridge Rd
Cedar Cir
Bud Ln
Maple Ln
Magnolia Rd
Chestnut Rd
Atrium Pl
Sable
Red Oak Tr
Pin Oak Tr
Dogwood Tr
Holly Ln
Tall Timbers Rd
Red Wood Ln
Oak St
Pines Rd
Vine St
Peach Creek
1 Peach Creek Dr
Spears Cir
Stella St
Hughey Av
Oak Dr
Florence St
Lucille Dr
Misty Lake Cir
Misty Lake Pt
Whitetail Cross
Hardwood Tr
Blazing Tr
Brook Forest Rd
Landshire Dr
Lakeshire Dr
Cobbleshire Ct
Wilshire Dr
Parkshire Ct
Stoneshire Dr
Wilshire Ct
PARK
Surry Oaks Dr
Woodway Dr
Arrowood Dr
Southwood Dr
Venus Dr
Chariot Ln
Creekside
Athens Dr
Kings Row
Northampton
Lincoln
Cambridge Blvd
Nottingham Ln
Leicester
Yorkshire
Peach Creek Dr
Lantern Ln
Hunters Tr Dr
Magnolia
Echo Ln
Comer
Reinhart Rd
Connor Reinhardt Rd
Rainbow Ln
Country Estates Dr
Knoll Dr
Highland Estates Dr
Sheffield Dr
Scott Dr
Country Estates Dr
Caney Creek
Bethel Baptist Rd
Old Mill Rd
Roberts Rd
1 Payne Rd
Robinson Ln
Campbell Rd
Debbies Cir
Julies Cir
Marks Ct
Wildwood Oaks Dr
Manion Oaks Ct
Pin Oak Lp
Redbud Dr
Elm St
Gardner Rd
Pine Dr
Peach Dr
Marrella Dr
Almarie Dr
Heavenly Ln
Woodpile Dr
Hardy Rd
Kings Rd
Shale
3rd St
2nd St
1st St
Oak Dr
Brandon
Cadenhead Rd
Sullivan Rd
Alpestrine Dr
Apple Blossom
Alps Dr
Sunset Dr
Baptist Encampment Rd
Shadows of Alpestrine Dr
Pecan Dr
Holly Dr
Caney Dr
Walnut Dr
Mansion Rd
Johnson Rd
Cliffwood St
Willowick St
Yukon Dr
Florita St
Live Oak St
Pinetex St
Willow St
LK HOUSTON ST PK
A B C D E
1 2 3 4 5 6 7
30°11'22" 30°10'56" 30°10'30" 30°10'04" 30°09'38" 30°09'11" 30°08'45" 30°08'19"
95°12'44" 95°12'14" 95°11'44" 95°11'14" 95°10'44" 95°10'14"

SEE 2829 MAP

SEE 2974 MAP

1:24,000
1 in. = 2000 ft.
0 0.25 0.5
miles

SEE 2683 MAP

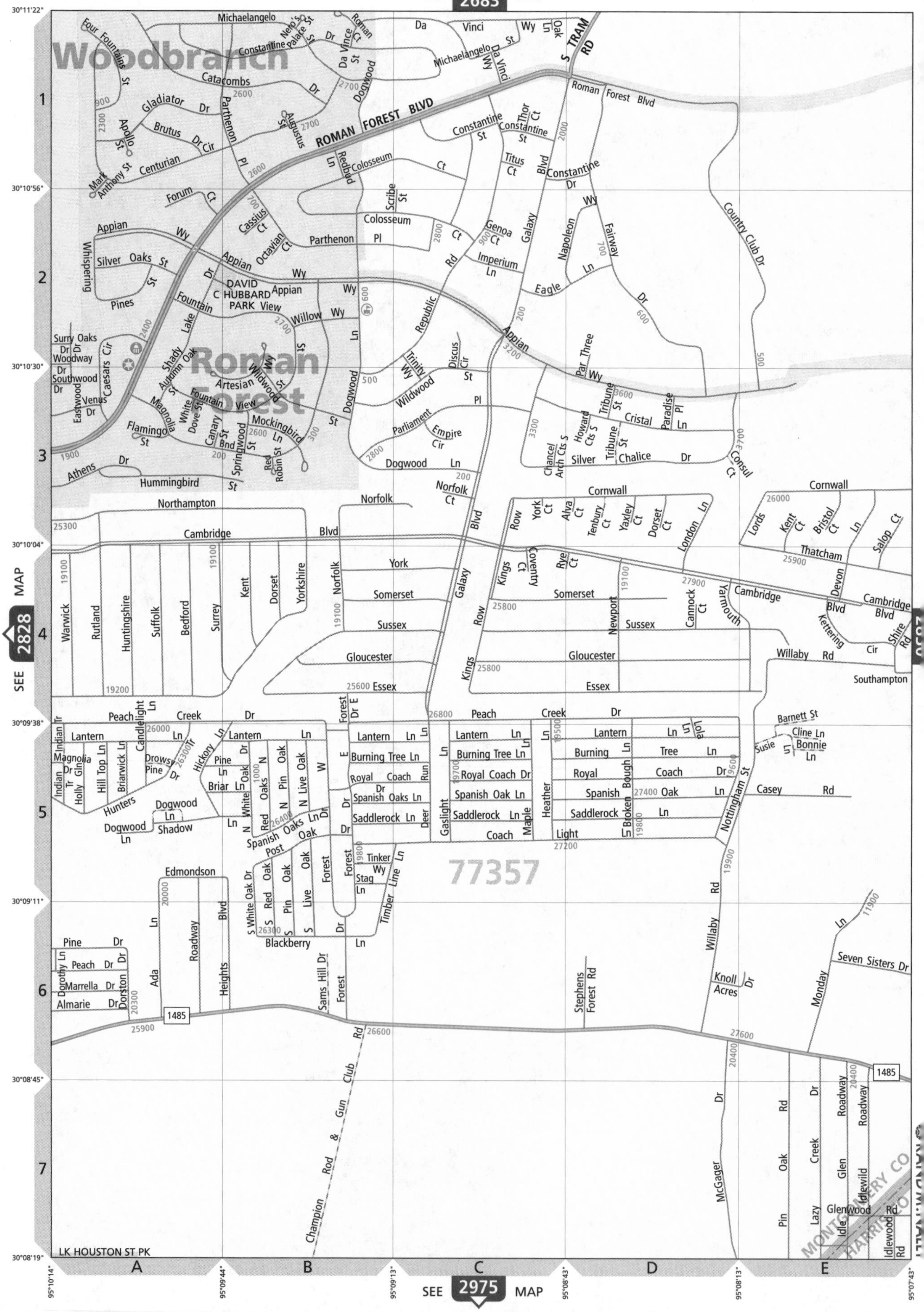
Woodbranch
Roman Forest
77357
ROMAN FOREST BLVD
Roman Forest Blvd
S TRAM RD
Michaelangelo
Constantine
Catacombs
Parthenon Pl
Gladiator Dr
Apollo St
Brutus Dr Cir
Centurian
Mark Anthony St
Augustus St
Four Fountains St
Da Vinci Wy
Dogwood
Redbud Ln
Colosseum Ct
Scribe St
Forum Ct
Cassius Ct
Octavian Ct
Appian Wy
Whispering Pines
Silver Oaks St
DAVID C HUBBARD PARK
Fountain View
Willow Wy
Lake Dr
Surry Oaks Dr
Woodway Dr
Southwood Dr
Eastwood Dr
Venus Dr
Caesars Cir
Shady Autumn Oak St
Artesian Wy
Wildwood St
Magnolia St
White Dove St
Canary Bnd
Springwood St
Mockingbird Ln
Red Robin St
Flamingo St
Athens Dr
Hummingbird St
Genoa Ct
Imperium Ln
Republic Rd
Galaxy Blvd
Titus Ct
Thor Ct
Constantine St
Constantine Dr
Napoleon Wy
Fairway Dr
Eagle Ln
Country Club Dr
Trinity Wy
Discus Cir
Parliament Pl
Empire Cir
Par Three Wy
Tribune St
Cristal Ln
Paradise Pl
Chancel Arch Cts S
Howard Cts S
Silver
Chalice Dr
Consul Ct
Norfolk Ct
Northampton
Norfolk
Cambridge Blvd
Cornwall
Row
York Ct
Alva Ct
Tenbury Ct
Yaxley Ct
Dorset Ct
London Ln
Lords
Kent Ct
Bristol Ct
Salop Ct
Thatcham
Devon
Kettering Cir
Shire Rd
Warwick
Rutland
Huntingshire
Suffolk
Bedford
Surrey
Kent
Dorset
Yorkshire
York
Somerset
Sussex
Gloucester
Essex
Kings Row
Coventry Ct
Rye Ct
Newport
Cannock Ct
Yarmouth
Willaby Rd
Southampton
Peach Creek Dr
Lantern Ln
Candlelight Ln
Indian Tr
Magnolia Dr
Holly Tr
Hill Top Ln
Briarwick Ln
Drowsy Pine Dr
Hickory Ln
Pine Ln
Briar Ln
White Oak Dr
Red Oaks
Pin Oak
Live Oak
Burning Tree Ln
Royal Coach Dr
Spanish Oaks Ln
Saddlerock Ln
Deer Run
Gaslight Ln
Heather
Maple
Broken Bough Ln
Coach Light
Lola Ln
Barnett St
Cline Ln
Bonnie Ln
Susie Ln
Nottingham St
Casey Rd
Hunters Dr
Dogwood Ln
Shadow
Spanish Oaks Ln
Post Oak
Tinker Ln
Stag Wy
Timber Line Ln
Forest Dr
Edmondson
Ada Ln
Roadway
Heights Blvd
Blackberry Ln
S White Oak Dr
Pine Dr
Peach Dr
Marrella Dr
Almarie Dr
Dorothy Ln
Dorston
1485
Sams Hill Dr
Champion Rod & Gun Club Rd
Stephens Forest Rd
Knoll Acres Dr
Seven Sisters Dr
Monday
McGager Dr
Pin Oak Rd
Lazy Creek Dr
Glen Roadway
Idlewild
Glenwood Rd
MONTGOMERY CO
HARRIS CO
LK HOUSTON ST PK
A B C D E
1 2 3 4 5 6 7

SEE 2828 MAP

SEE 2975 MAP

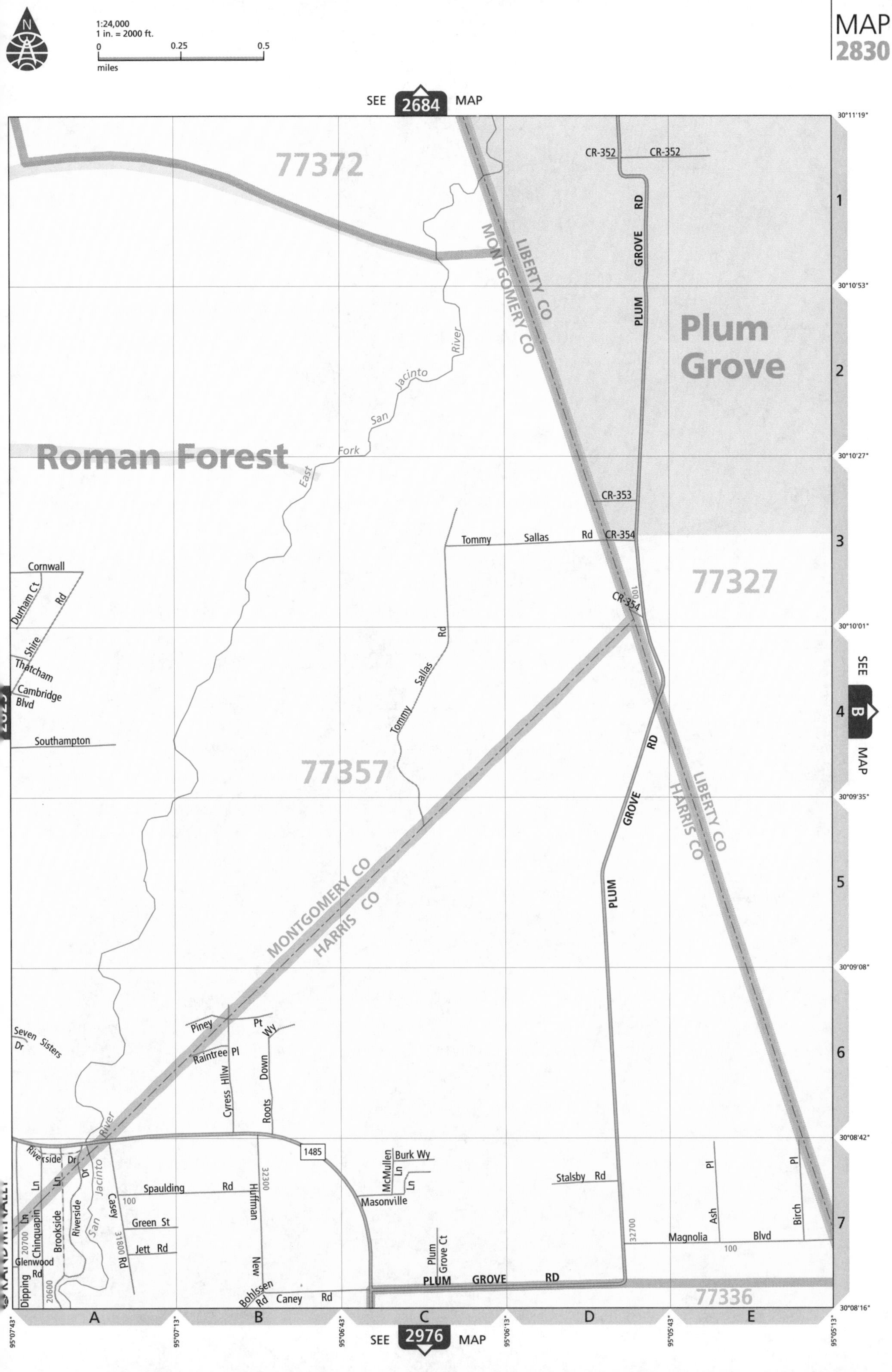
1:24,000
1 in. = 2000 ft.
0 0.25 0.5
miles
SEE 2684 MAP
SEE 2976 MAP
SEE B MAP
77372
77357
77327
77336
Roman Forest
Plum Grove
MONTGOMERY CO
LIBERTY CO
HARRIS CO
PLUM GROVE RD
CR-352
CR-353
CR-354
Tommy Sallas Rd
East Fork San Jacinto River
Cornwall Rd
Durham Ct
Shire
Thatcham
Cambridge Blvd
Southampton
Seven Sisters Dr
Piney Pt
Wy
Raintree Pl
Cyress Hllw
Down Roots
1485
Riverside Dr
Dipping Ln
Chinquapin Ln
Brookside Ln
Riverside Dr
San Jacinto River
Casey Rd
Spaulding Rd
Huffman
Green St
Jett Rd
Glenwood Rd
New Bohlssen Rd
Caney Rd
Burk Wy
McMullen Ln
Masonville
Plum Grove Ct
Stalsby Rd
Ash Pl
Birch Pl
Magnolia Blvd
32300
32700
31800
20700
20600
100
1001
A
B
C
D
E
1
2
3
4
5
6
7
30°11'19"
30°10'53"
30°10'27"
30°10'01"
30°09'35"
30°09'08"
30°08'42"
30°08'16"
95°07'43"
95°07'13"
95°06'43"
95°06'13"
95°05'43"
95°05'13"

1:24,000
1 in. = 2000 ft.
0 0.25 0.5
miles

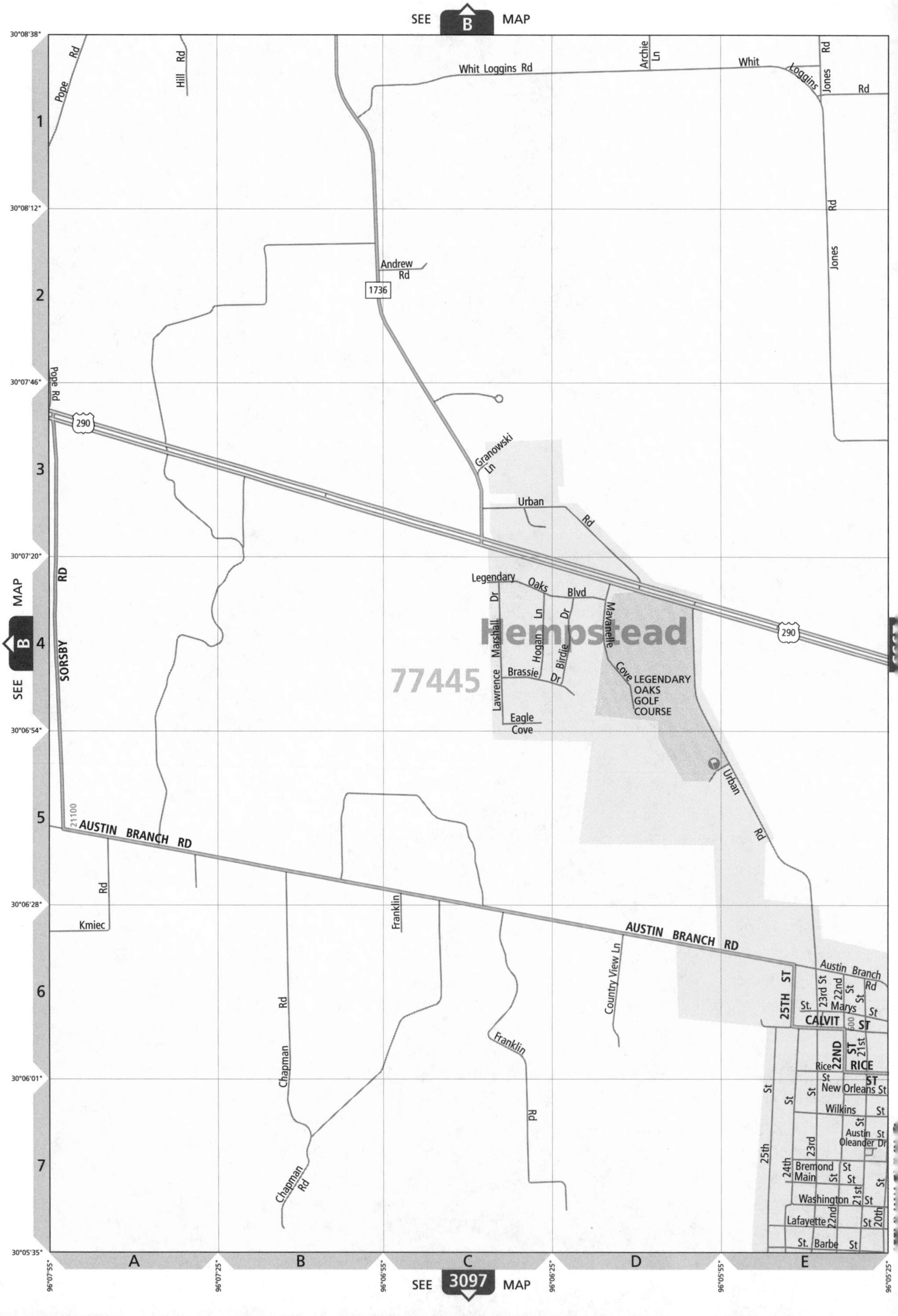
SEE B MAP
SEE B MAP
SEE 3097 MAP
30°08'38"
30°08'12"
30°07'46"
30°07'20"
30°06'54"
30°06'28"
30°06'01"
30°05'35"
96°07'55"
96°07'25"
96°06'55"
96°06'25"
96°05'55"
96°05'25"
1
2
3
4
5
6
7
A
B
C
D
E
Pope Rd
Hill Rd
Whit Loggins Rd
Archie Ln
Whit Loggins
Jones Rd
Rd
Jones Rd
Andrew Rd
1736
Pope Rd
290
Granowski Ln
Urban Rd
Legendary Oaks Blvd
Dr
Marshall
Lawrence
Hogan Ln
Birdie Dr
Brassie Dr
Mavanelle Cove
Eagle Cove
Hempstead
77445
LEGENDARY OAKS GOLF COURSE
Urban Rd
SORSBY RD
21100
AUSTIN BRANCH RD
Kmiec Rd
Franklin
Chapman Rd
Franklin Rd
Country View Ln
AUSTIN BRANCH RD
Austin Branch Rd
25TH ST
St. Marys St
23rd St
22nd St
St
CALVIT ST
600
22ND ST
21st
Rice St
RICE ST
New Orleans St
Wilkins St
Austin St
Oleander Dr
25th St
24th
23rd St
Bremond St
Main St
St
Washington St
21st
Lafayette St
22nd
20th
St. Barbe St

1:24,000
1 in. = 2000 ft.
0 0.25 0.5
miles

SEE B MAP

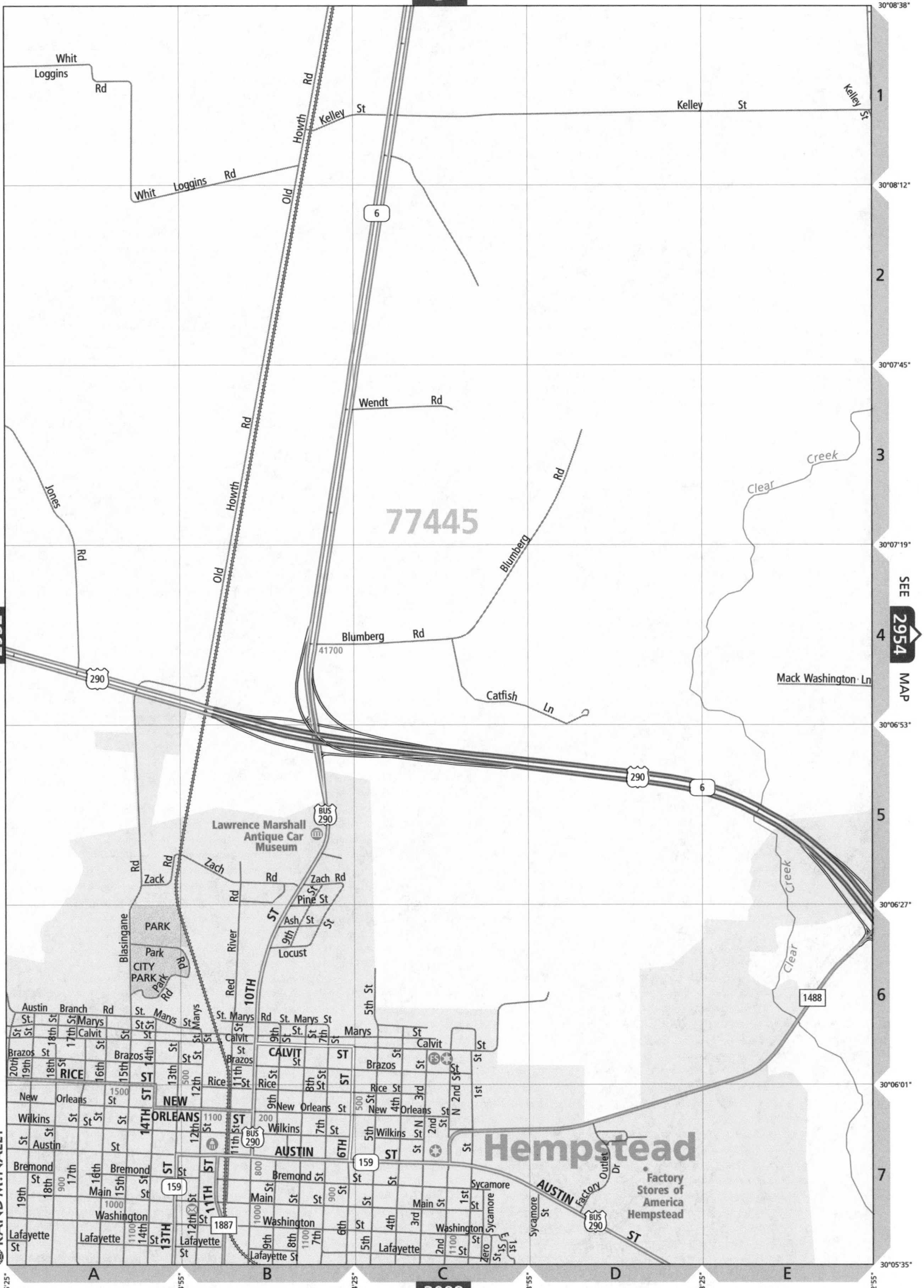
Whit Loggins Rd
Kelley St
Old Howth Rd
6
Wendt Rd
Jones Rd
Clear Creek
77445
Blumberg Rd
41700
290
Catfish Ln
Mack Washington Ln
Lawrence Marshall Antique Car Museum
BUS 290
Zack Rd
Zach Rd
Pine St
Ash St
9th St
Locust
River Rd
10TH ST
PARK
Blasingane
Park Rd
CITY PARK
1488
Austin Branch Rd
St. Marys St
Calvit St
Brazos St
RICE ST
Rice St
NEW ORLEANS ST
New Orleans St
Wilkins St
AUSTIN ST
Bremond St
Main St
Washington St
Lafayette St
Sycamore St
159
1887
Hempstead
Factory Outlet Dr
Factory Stores of America Hempstead
1
2
3
4
5
6
7
A
B
C
D
E
30°08'38"
30°08'12"
30°07'45"
30°07'19"
30°06'53"
30°06'27"
30°06'01"
30°05'35"
96°05'25"
96°04'55"
96°04'25"
96°03'55"
96°03'25"
96°02'55"

SEE 2952 MAP

SEE 2954 MAP

SEE 3098 MAP

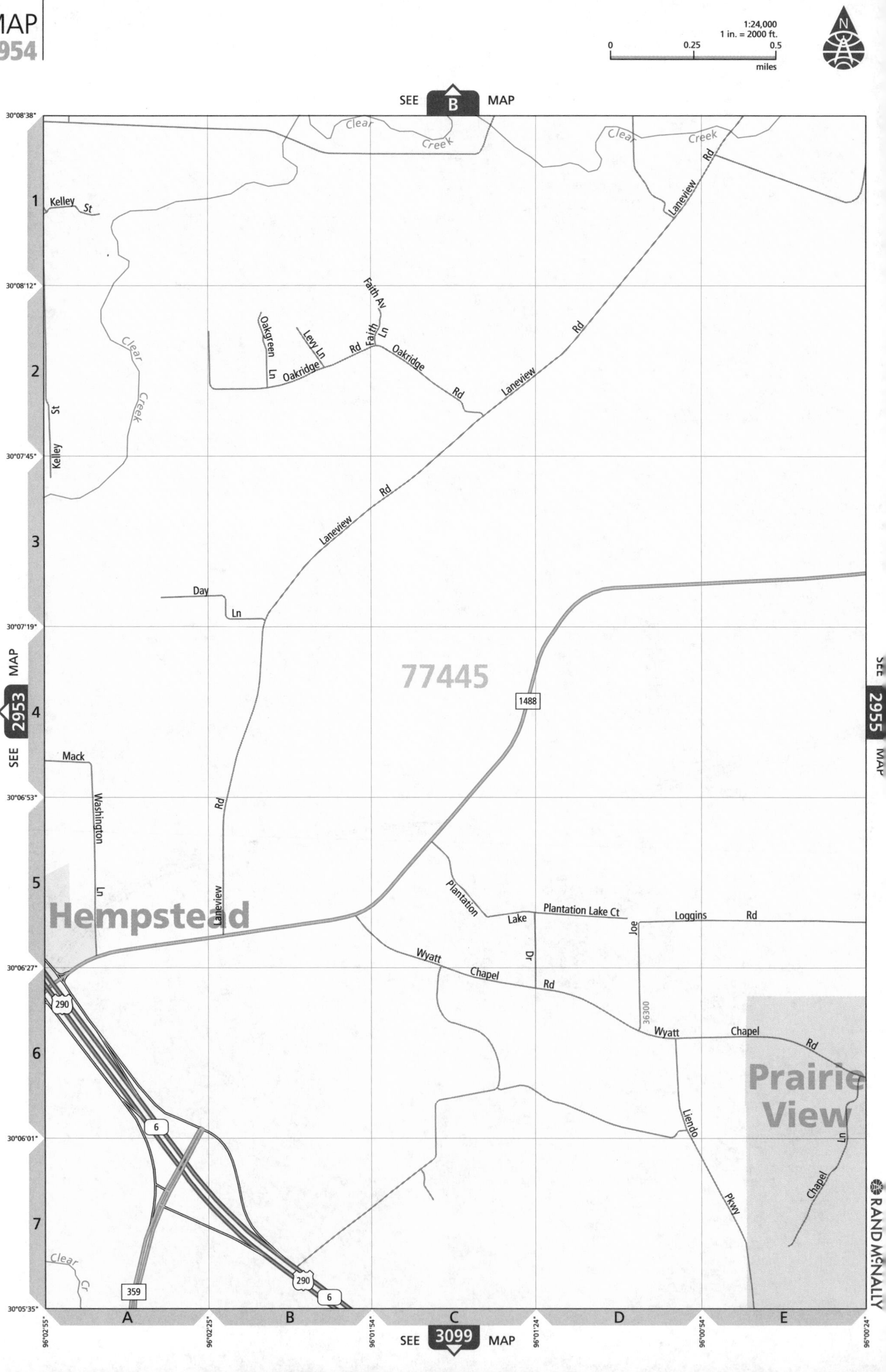
1:24,000
1 in. = 2000 ft.
0 0.25 0.5
miles
N
SEE B MAP
SEE 2953 MAP
SEE 2955 MAP
SEE 3099 MAP
Clear Creek
Clear Cr
Kelley St
Faith Av
Faith Ln
Oakgreen Ln
Levy Ln
Oakridge Rd
Laneview Rd
Day Ln
77445
1488
Mack
Washington Ln
Hempstead
Plantation Lake
Plantation Lake Ct
Joe Dr
Loggins Rd
Wyatt Chapel Rd
36300
Liendo Pkwy
Chapel Ln
Prairie View
290
6
359
RAND McNALLY
30°08'38"
30°08'12"
30°07'45"
30°07'19"
30°06'53"
30°06'27"
30°06'01"
30°05'35"
96°02'55"
96°02'25"
96°01'54"
96°01'24"
96°00'54"
96°00'24"
1
2
3
4
5
6
7
A
B
C
D
E

1:24,000
1 in. = 2000 ft.
0 0.25 0.5
miles

SEE B MAP

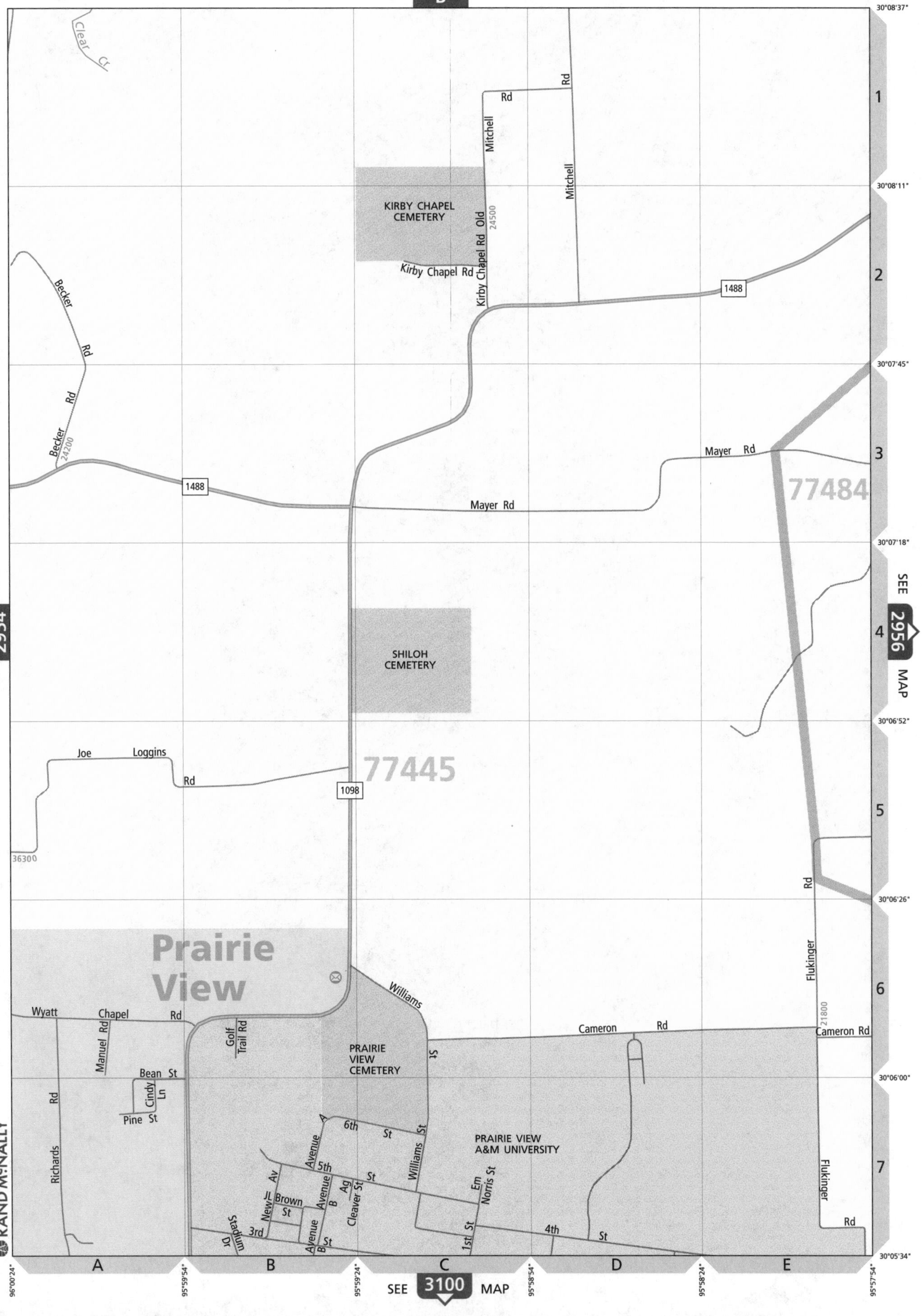
Clear Cr
Mitchell Rd
Mitchell
KIRBY CHAPEL CEMETERY
Kirby Chapel Rd Old
24500
Kirby Chapel Rd
1488
Becker Rd
Becker Rd
24200
1488
Mayer Rd
Mayer Rd
77484
SHILOH CEMETERY
Joe Loggins Rd
77445
1098
36300
Rd
Flukinger
21800
Prairie View
Wyatt Chapel Rd
Manuel Rd
Golf Trail Rd
Williams St
PRAIRIE VIEW CEMETERY
Cameron Rd
Cameron Rd
Bean St
Cindy Ln
Pine St
Richards Rd
Avenue A
6th St
Williams St
PRAIRIE VIEW A&M UNIVERSITY
5th St
Av
JL Brown St
New
Avenue B
Ag Cleaver St
Em Norris St
Flukinger Rd
3rd
Stadium Dr
Avenue B St
1st St
4th St
1 2 3 4 5 6 7
A B C D E
30°08'37" 30°08'11" 30°07'45" 30°07'18" 30°06'52" 30°06'26" 30°06'00" 30°05'34"
96°00'24" 95°59'54" 95°59'24" 95°58'54" 95°58'24" 95°57'54"

SEE 2954 MAP

SEE 2956 MAP

SEE 3100 MAP

1:24,000
1 in. = 2000 ft.
0 0.25 0.5
miles

SEE B MAP

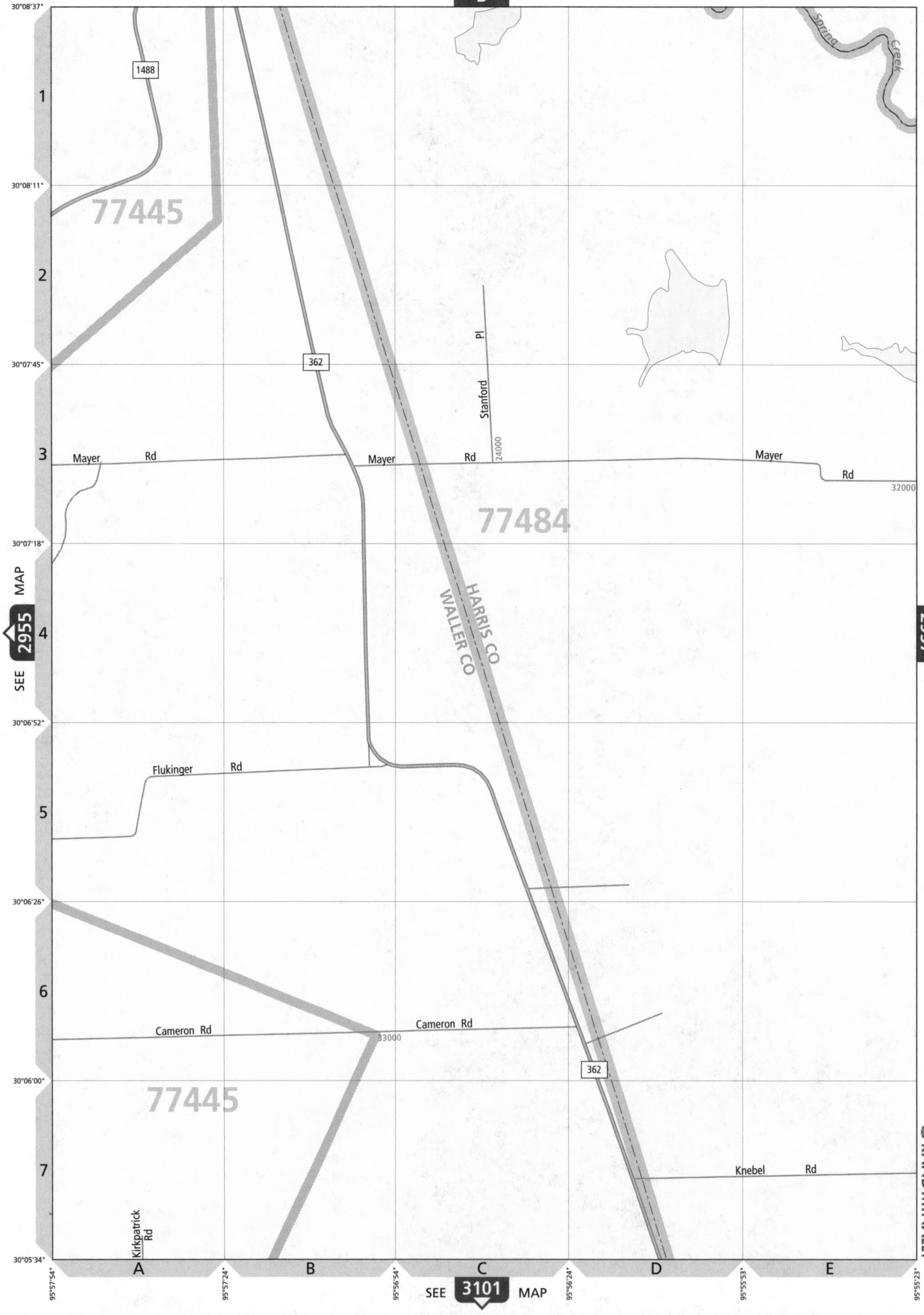
30°08'37"
30°08'11"
30°07'45"
30°07'18"
30°06'52"
30°06'26"
30°06'00"
30°05'34"
95°57'54"
95°57'24"
95°56'54"
95°56'24"
95°55'53"
95°55'23"
1
2
3
4
5
6
7
A
B
C
D
E
1488
77445
Spring Creek
362
Stanford Pl
24000
Mayer Rd
Mayer Rd
Mayer Rd
32000
77484
HARRIS CO
WALLER CO
Flukinger Rd
Cameron Rd
33000
Cameron Rd
362
77445
Knebel Rd
Kirkpatrick Rd

SEE 2955 MAP

SEE 2957 MAP

SEE 3101 MAP

1:24,000
1 in. = 2000 ft.
0 0.25 0.5
miles

SEE B MAP

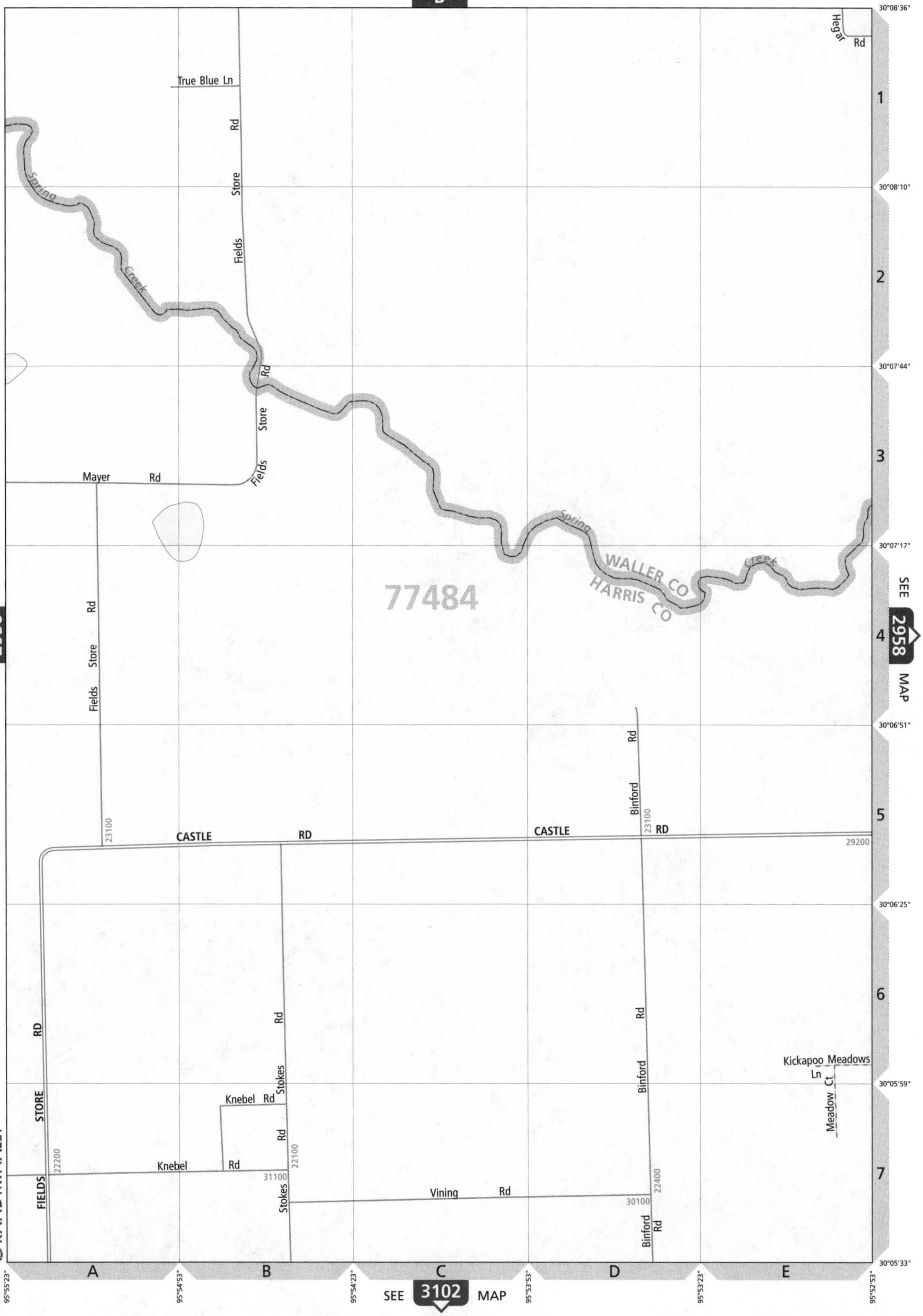
True Blue Ln
Fields Store Rd
Spring Creek
Mayer Rd
77484
WALLER CO
HARRIS CO
Hegar Rd
CASTLE RD
23100
29200
Binford Rd
Stokes Rd
Knebel Rd
FIELDS STORE RD
22200
31100
22100
Vining Rd
30100
22400
Kickapoo Meadows Ln
Meadow Ct
1
2
3
4
5
6
7
A
B
C
D
E
30°08'36"
30°08'10"
30°07'44"
30°07'17"
30°06'51"
30°06'25"
30°05'59"
30°05'33"
95°55'23"
95°54'53"
95°54'23"
95°53'53"
95°53'23"
95°52'53"

SEE 2958 MAP

SEE 3102 MAP

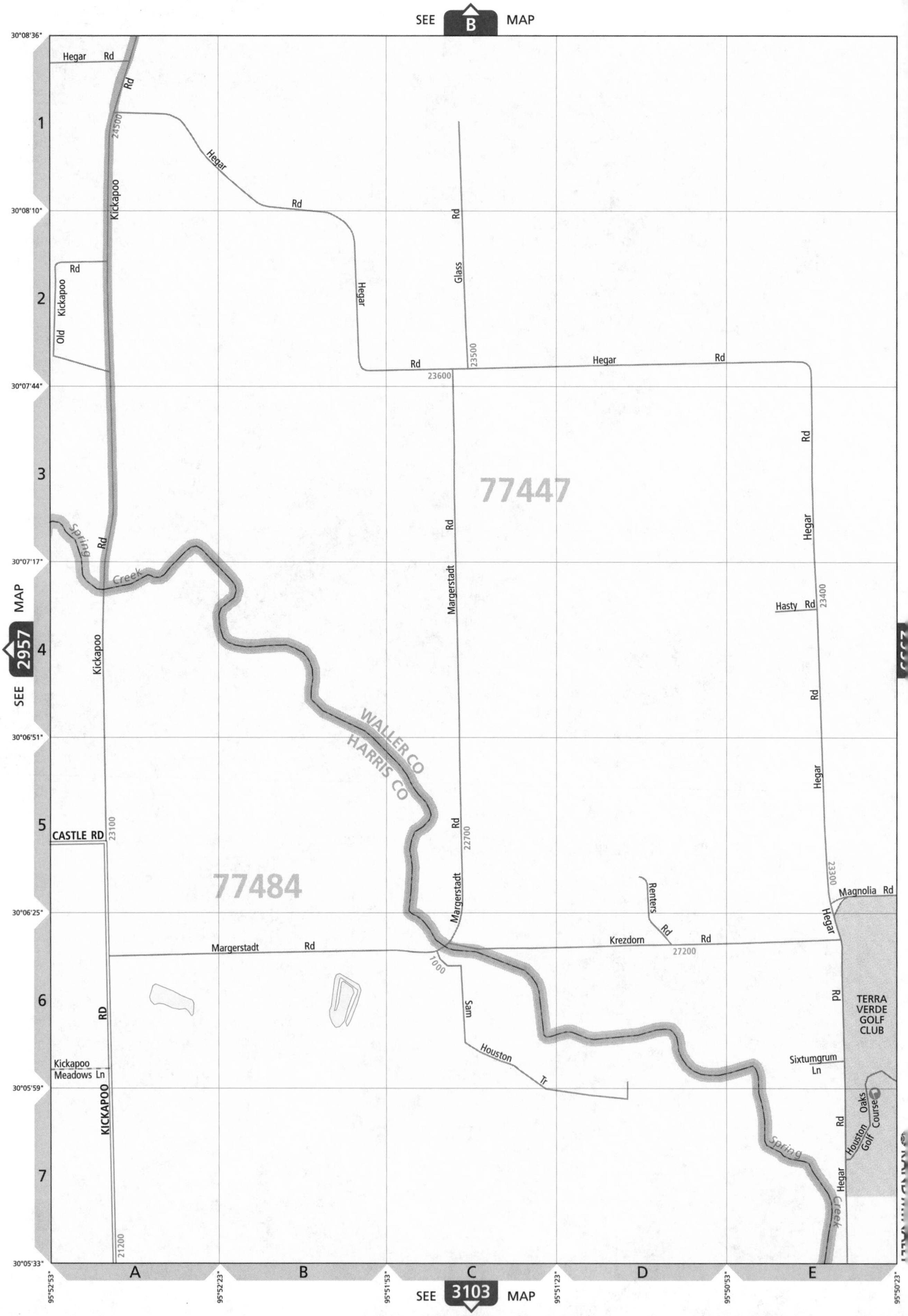
1:24,000
1 in. = 2000 ft.
0 0.25 0.5
miles
N
SEE B MAP
SEE 2957 MAP
SEE 3103 MAP
30°08'36"
30°08'10"
30°07'44"
30°07'17"
30°06'51"
30°06'25"
30°05'59"
30°05'33"
95°52'53"
95°52'23"
95°51'53"
95°51'23"
95°50'53"
95°50'23"
1
2
3
4
5
6
7
A
B
C
D
E
Hegar Rd
Kickapoo Rd
24500
Hegar Rd
Glass Rd
Hegar
Old Kickapoo Rd
23500
Rd
23600
Hegar
Rd
77447
Rd
Hegar
Spring Creek
Rd
Hasty Rd
23400
Margerstadt Rd
Kickapoo
Rd
WALLER CO
HARRIS CO
Hegar
CASTLE RD
23100
Rd
22700
77484
Margerstadt
Renters Rd
23300
Magnolia Rd
Hegar
Margerstadt Rd
Krezdorn Rd
27200
1000
Sam Houston Tr
Rd
TERRA VERDE GOLF CLUB
KICKAPOO RD
Kickapoo Meadows Ln
Sixtumgrum Ln
Houston Oaks Golf Course
Rd
Hegar
Spring Creek
21200

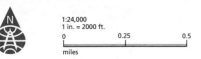

1:24,000
1 in. = 2000 ft.
0 0.25 0.5
miles

SEE 2813 MAP

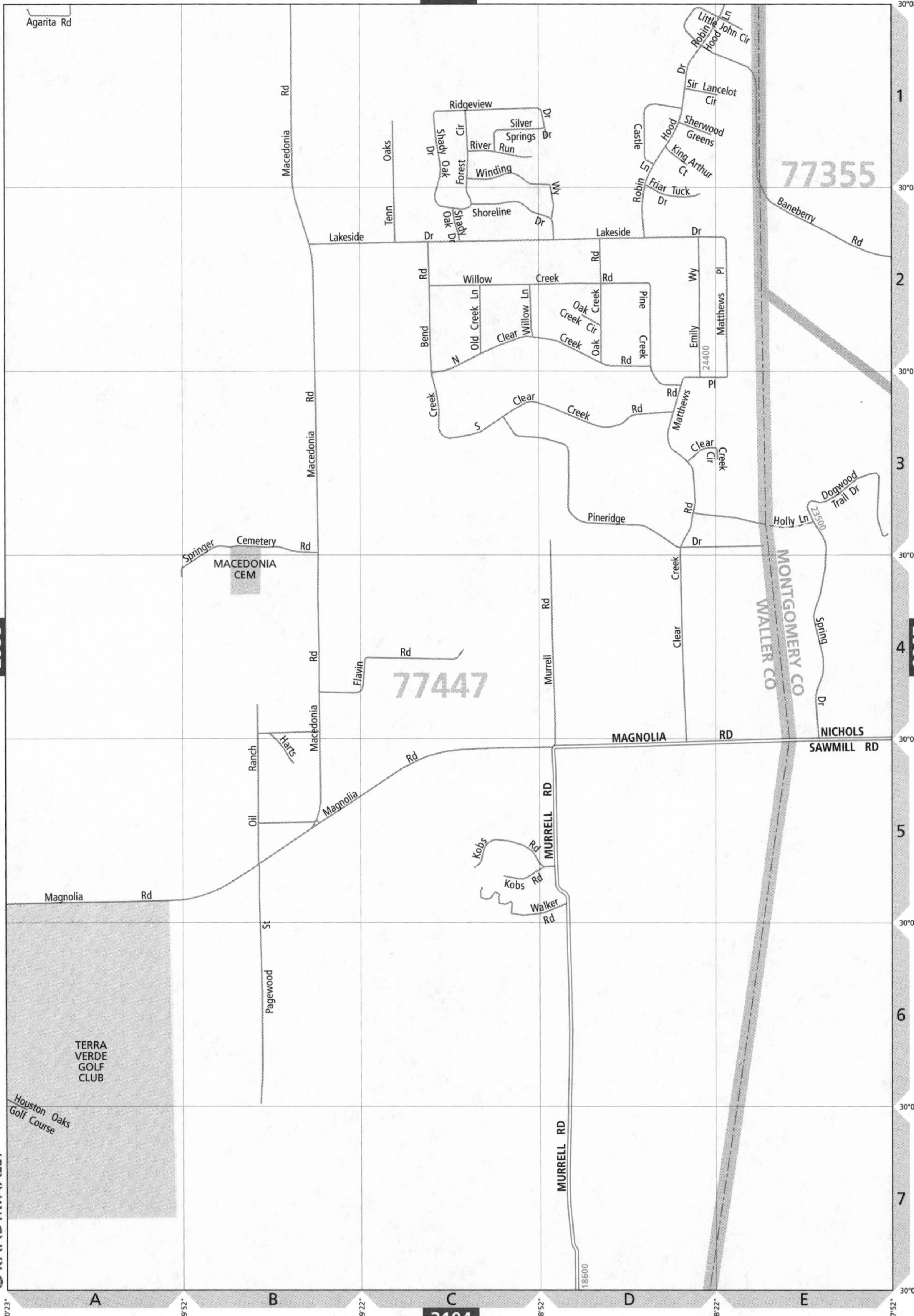
Agarita Rd
Macedonia Rd
Ridgeview
Silver Springs Dr
River Run
Shady Oak Dr
Forest Cir
Winding Wy
Shoreline Dr
Oaks
Tenn
Lakeside Dr
Lakeside Dr
Little John Cir
Robin Hood Ln
Sir Lancelot Cir
Sherwood Greens
Castle Hood
King Arthur Ct
Friar Tuck Dr
77355
Baneberry Rd
Willow Creek Rd
Bend Rd
Old Creek Ln
Willow Ln
Oak Creek Cir
N Clear Creek Rd
Pine Creek Rd
Oak Creek
Emily Wy
Matthews Pl
24400
S Clear Creek Rd
Matthews Rd
Clear Creek Cir
Pineridge Dr
Holly Ln
Dogwood Trail Dr
23500
Springer Cemetery Rd
MACEDONIA CEM
Clear Creek
Murrell Rd
Spring Dr
MONTGOMERY CO
WALLER CO
Flavin Rd
77447
Ranch Rd
Harts
MAGNOLIA RD
NICHOLS SAWMILL RD
Magnolia Rd
Oil
MURRELL RD
Kobs Rd
Walker Rd
Pagewood St
TERRA VERDE GOLF CLUB
Houston Oaks Golf Course
18600
A
B
C
D
E
1
2
3
4
5
6
7
30°08'35"
30°08'09"
30°07'42"
30°07'16"
30°06'50"
30°06'24"
30°05'58"
30°05'32"
95°50'23"
95°49'52"
95°49'22"
95°48'52"
95°48'22"
95°47'52"

SEE 2960 MAP

SEE 3104 MAP

1:24,000
1 in. = 2000 ft.
0 0.25 0.5
miles

SEE 2814 MAP

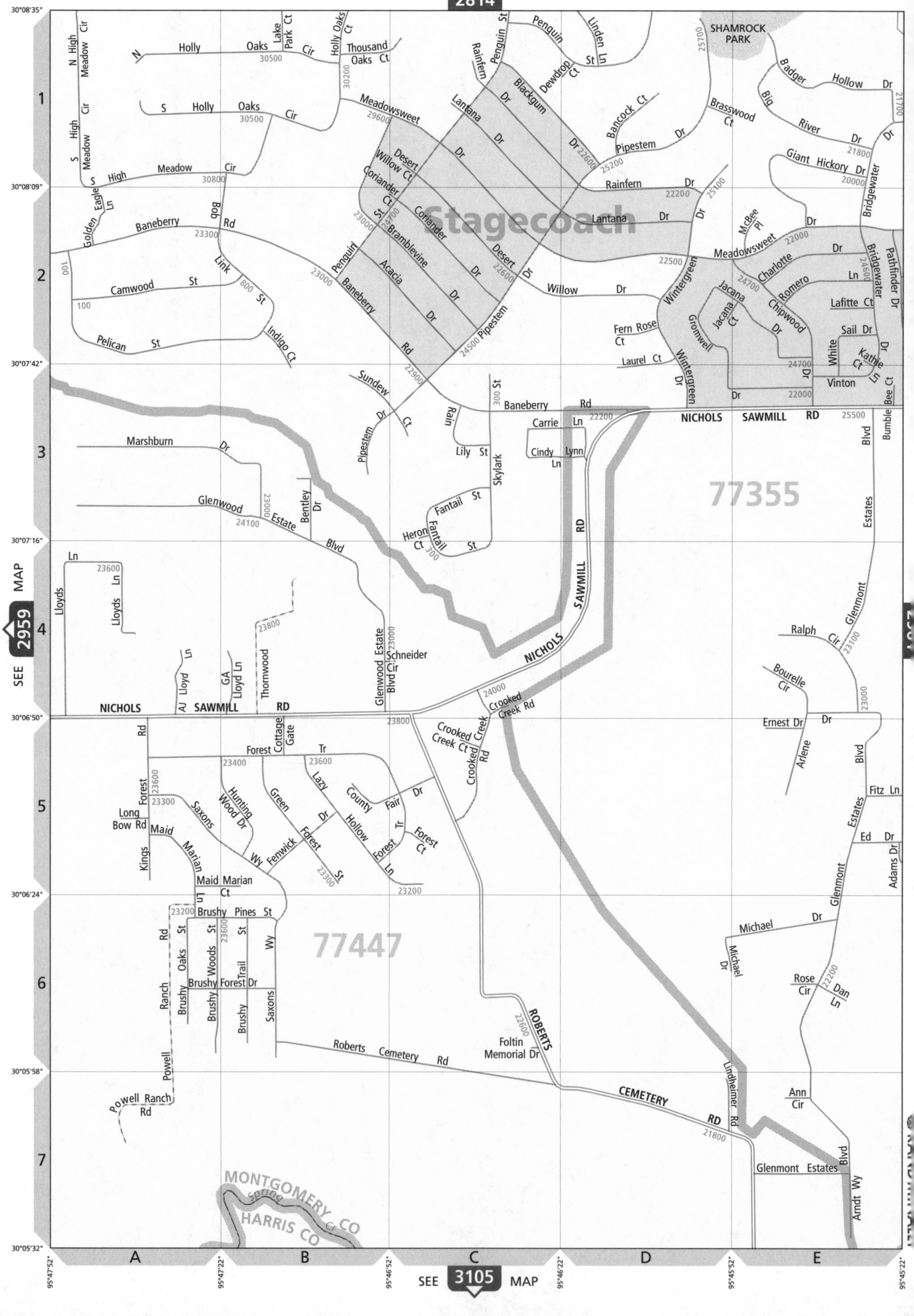

Stagecoach
SHAMROCK PARK
77355
77447
MONTGOMERY CO
HARRIS CO
Spring Cr
NICHOLS SAWMILL RD
ROBERTS CEMETERY RD
Roberts Cemetery Rd
N Holly Oaks Cir
S Holly Oaks Cir
Lake Park Ct
Holly Oaks Ct
Thousand Oaks Ct
N High Meadow Cir
S High Meadow Cir
S High Meadow Cir
Golden Eagle Ln
Baneberry Rd
Bob Link
Camwood St
Pelican St
Indigo Ct
Meadowsweet
Desert Willow Ct
Coriander Ct
Coriander Dr
Bramblevine Dr
Acacia Dr
Desert Dr
Penguin St
Penguin Baneberry Rd
Rainfern
Lantana Dr
Blackgum Dr
Dewdrop Ct
Linden Ln
Bancock Ct
Pipestem Dr
Brasswood Ct
Rainfern Dr
Lantana Dr
Willow Dr
Fern Rose Ct
Laurel Ct
Wintergreen Dr
Gromwell
Jacana Ct
Charlotte
Romero
Chipwood Dr
McBee Pl
Badger Hollow Dr
Big River Dr
Giant Hickory Dr
Bridgewater
Pathfinder Dr
Lafitte Ct
Sail Dr
White Dr
Kathie Ln
Vinton
Bee Ct
Bumble
Sundew Ct
Pipestem Dr
Rain
Lily St
Skylark
Carrie Ln
Cindy Ln
Lynn
Fantail St
Heron Ct
Marshburn Dr
Glenwood Estate Blvd
Bentley Dr
Lloyds Ln
AJ Lloyd Ln
GA Lloyd Ln
Thornwood
Schneider Cir
Crooked Creek Rd
Crooked Creek Ct
Estates Blvd
Glenmont
Ralph Cir
Bourelle Cir
Ernest Dr
Arlene
Fitz Ln
Ed Dr
Adams Dr
Michael Dr
Rose Cir
Dan Ln
Ann Cir
Lindheimer Rd
Glenmont Estates Blvd
Arndt Wy
Forest Tr
Cottage Gate
Forest Rd
Long Bow Rd
Kings
Maid Marian Ln
Maid Marian Ct
Saxons Wy
Hunting Wood Dr
Green Forest Dr
Lazy Hollow Dr
County Fair Dr
Forest Ct
Forest Ln
Fenwick
Brushy Pines St
Brushy Oaks St
Brushy Woods St
Brushy Trail St
Brushy Forest Dr
Ranch Rd
Powell Ranch Rd
Foltin Memorial Dr
A B C D E
1 2 3 4 5 6 7
30°08'35" 30°08'09" 30°07'42" 30°07'16" 30°06'50" 30°06'24" 30°05'58" 30°05'32"
95°47'52" 95°47'22" 95°46'52" 95°46'22" 95°45'52" 95°45'22"

SEE 2959 MAP

SEE 3105 MAP

1:24,000
1 in. = 2000 ft.
0 0.25 0.5
miles

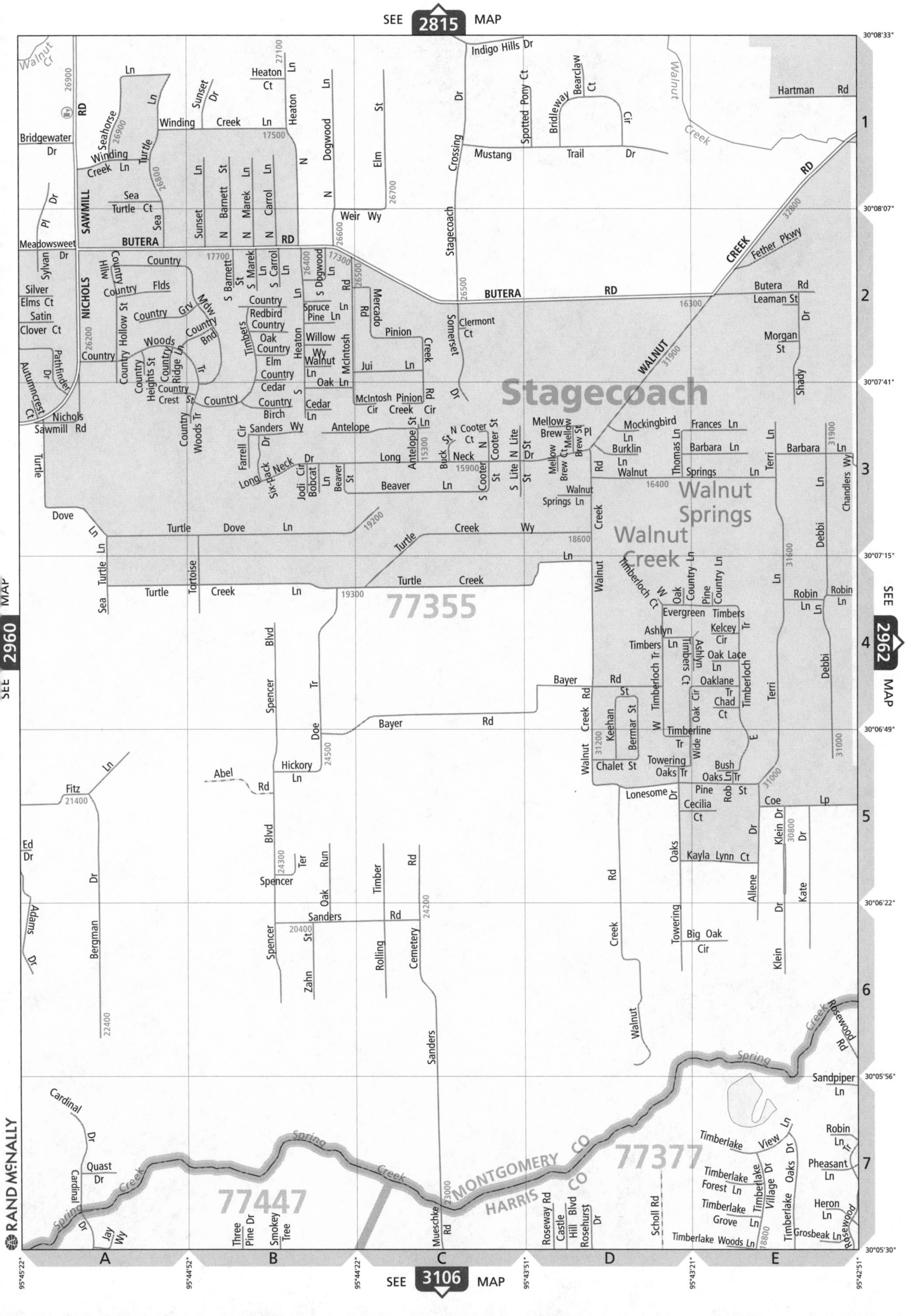
SEE 2815 MAP
SEE 3106 MAP
SEE 2960 MAP
SEE 2962 MAP
Stagecoach
Walnut Springs
Walnut Creek
77355
77377
77447
MONTGOMERY CO
HARRIS CO
Spring Creek
Walnut Cr
Walnut Creek
BUTERA RD
NICHOLS RD
SAWMILL RD
WALNUT CREEK RD
Indigo Hills Dr
Hartman Rd
Heaton Ct
Heaton Ln
Sunset Dr
Winding Creek Ln
Seahorse Ln
Turtle Ln
Bridgewater Dr
Dogwood Ln
Elm St
Crossing Dr
Spotted Pony Ct
Bridleway
Bearclaw Ct
Mustang Trail Dr
Sea Turtle Ct
Meadowsweet Dr
Sylvan Pl
Silver Elms Ct
Satin Clover Ct
Weir Wy
Stagecoach Dr
Fether Pkwy
Butera Rd
Leaman St
Morgan St
Shady Dr
Country Hllw
Country Flds
Country Grv
Country Mdw
Country Bnd
Country Hollow St
Country Woods Tr
Country Ridge Ln
Country Heights St
Country Crest St
Autumncrest Ct
Pathfinder Dr
Nichols Sawmill Rd
Redbird Country
Oak Country
Elm Country
Cedar Country
Birch Country
Timbers Ln
S Barnett St
S Marek St
S Carrol Ln
S Dogwood Ln
Spruce Pine Ln
Willow Wy
Walnut Ln
Oak Ln
Cedar Ln
McIntosh Rd
McIntosh Cir
Mercado Rd
Pinion Creek Rd
Pinion Creek Cir
Jui Ln
Somerset Dr
Clermont Ct
Sanders Wy
Farrell Cir
Antelope Ln
Antelope St
Long Neck Dr
Six-pack Neck Dr
Jodi Cir
Bobcat Ln
Beaver St
Beaver Ln
Buck St
N Cooter Ct
Cooter St
S Cooter St
N Lite St
S Lite St
Mellow Brew Pl
Mellow Brew Ct
Mellow Brew St
Mockingbird Ln
Burklin Ln
Walnut Springs Ln
Thomas Ln
Frances Ln
Barbara Ln
Springs Ln
Terri Ln
Chandlers Wy
Debbi Ln
Turtle Dove Ln
Turtle Creek Wy
Turtle Creek Ln
Sea Turtle Ln
Tortoise
Dove
Timberloch Ct
W Oak Country Ln
Pine Country Ln
Evergreen Timbers Tr
Kelcey Cir
Ashlyn Ln
Ashlyn Ct
Timbers Ct
Oak Lace Ln
Oaklane Tr
Chad Ct
Timberloch Tr
Timberloch
Timberline Tr
Wide Oak Cir
Bayer Rd
Bayer St
Keehan St
Bermar St
Chalet St
Towering Oaks Tr
Bush Oaks Tr
Robin Ln
Robin Ln
Walnut Creek Rd
Lonesome Dr
Pine Rob St
Cecilia Ct
Coe Lp
Klein Dr
Kate Dr
Allene Dr
Kayla Lynn Ct
Oaks
Towering
Big Oak Cir
Spencer Blvd
Spencer Ter
Doe Tr
Hickory Ln
Abel Rd
Fitz Ln
Ed Dr
Adams Dr
Bergman Dr
Sanders Rd
Zahn St
Oak Run
Rolling Timber Rd
Cemetery Rd
Sanders
Walnut
Creek
Rosewood Rd
Sandpiper Ln
Cardinal Dr
Quast Dr
Jay Wy
Three Pine Dr
Smokey Tree
Mueschke Rd
Roseway Rd
Castle Hill Blvd
Rosehurst Dr
Scholl Rd
Timberlake View Ln
Timberlake Forest Ln
Timberlake Grove Ln
Timberlake Village Dr
Timberlake Oaks Dr
Timberlake Woods Ln
Robin Ln
Pheasant Ln
Heron Ln
Grosbeak Ln
Rosewood Tr
A
B
C
D
E
1
2
3
4
5
6
7
30°08'33"
30°08'07"
30°07'41"
30°07'15"
30°06'49"
30°06'22"
30°05'56"
30°05'30"
95°45'22"
95°44'52"
95°44'22"
95°43'51"
95°43'21"
95°42'51"

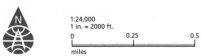

1:24,000
1 in. = 2000 ft.
0 0.25 0.5
miles

SEE 2816 MAP

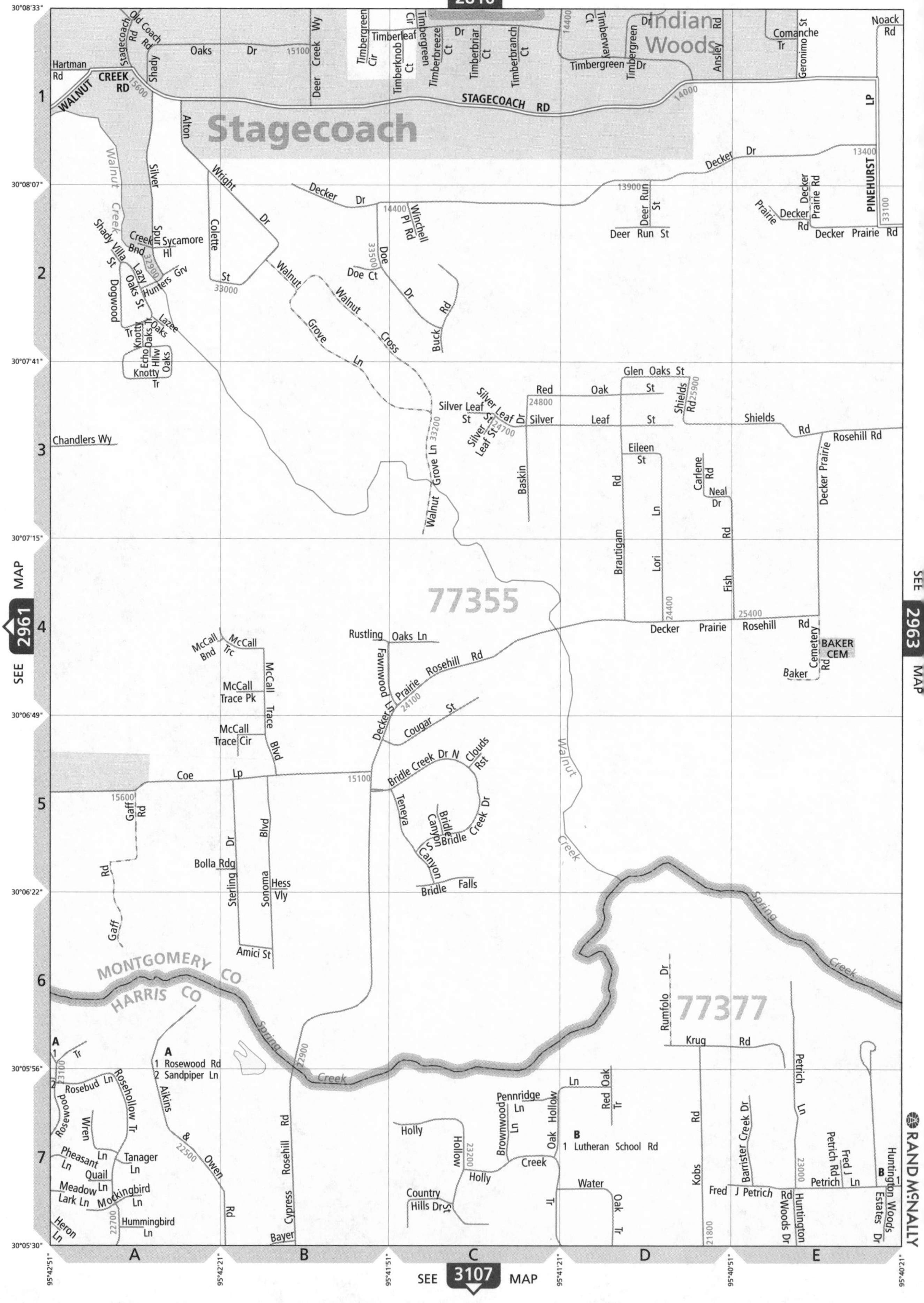
Stagecoach
Indian Woods
77355
77377
STAGECOACH RD
WALNUT CREEK RD
Hartman Rd
Stagecoach Rd
Old Coach Rd
Shady
Oaks Dr
Deer Creek Wy
Timbergreen Cir
Timberleaf
Timberknob Ct
Timbergreen Cir
Timberbreeze Ct
Timberbriar Ct
Timberbranch Ct
Timberway Ct
Timbergreen Dr
Ansley Rd
Comanche Tr
Geronimo St
Noack Rd
PINEHURST LP
Alton
Wright Dr
Colette St
Silver Spur
Walnut Creek
Creek Bnd
Sycamore Hl
Shady Villa St
Lazy Oaks St
Hunters Grv
Dogwood Tr
Knotty Oaks
Echo Hllw
Knotty Oaks Tr
Lazee Oaks
Decker Dr
Winchell Pl Rd
Doe Dr
Doe Ct
Buck Rd
Walnut Grove Ln
Walnut Cross
Deer Run St
Decker Prairie Rd
Prairie
Glen Oaks St
Red Oak St
Silver Leaf St
Silver Leaf Dr
Shields Rd
Rosehill Rd
Chandlers Wy
Eileen St
Brautigam Rd
Lori Ln
Baskin
Carlene Rd
Neal Dr
Fish Rd
Decker Prairie
Decker Prairie Rosehill Rd
BAKER CEM
Cemetery Rd
Baker
Rustling Oaks Ln
Fawnwood
Prairie Rosehill Rd
Decker Ln
Cougar St
McCall Bnd
McCall Trc
McCall Trace Blvd
McCall Trace Pk
McCall Trace Cir
Coe Lp
Gaff Rd
Bridle Creek Dr N
Clouds Rst
Teneya
Bridle Creek Dr
Bridle Canyon
Canyon
Bridle Falls
Sterling Dr
Sonoma Blvd
Bolla Rdg
Hess Vly
Amici St
MONTGOMERY CO
HARRIS CO
Spring Creek
Walnut Creek
Rumfolo Dr
Krug Rd
Petrich Ln
A 1 Rosewood Rd 2 Sandpiper Ln
Rosebud Ln
Rosehollow Tr
Rosewood
Wren
Pheasant Ln
Quail Ln
Tanager Ln
Meadow Ln
Lark Ln
Mockingbird Ln
Hummingbird Ln
Heron Ln
Aikins
Owen Rd
Rosehill Rd
Cypress Rosehill Rd
Bayer
Pennridge Ln
Brownwood Ln
Oak Hollow Ln
Red Oak Tr
B 1 Lutheran School Rd
Holly
Holly Hollow
Holly Creek
Country Hills Dr St
Water Oak Tr
Kobs Rd
Barrister Creek Dr
Fred J Petrich Rd
Petrich Rd
Fred J Ln
Huntington Woods Dr
Huntington Woods Estates Dr
RAND McNALLY

SEE 2961 MAP

SEE 2963 MAP

SEE 3107 MAP

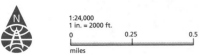

1:24,000
1 in. = 2000 ft.
0 0.25 0.5
miles

SEE 2817 MAP

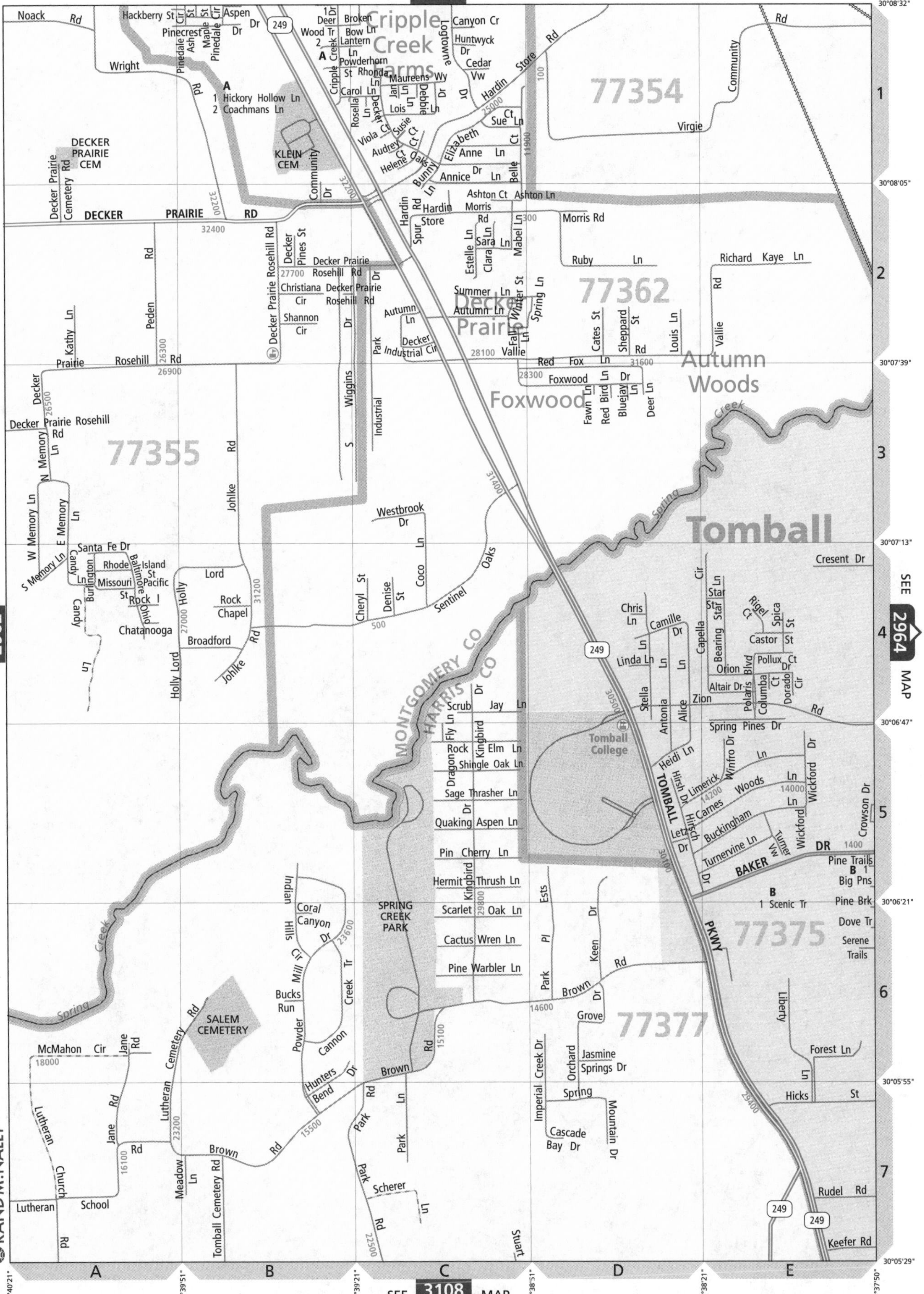
Cripple Creek Farms
Decker Prairie
Autumn Woods
Foxwood
Tomball
77354
77362
77355
77375
77377
DECKER PRAIRIE CEM
KLEIN CEM
SALEM CEMETERY
SPRING CREEK PARK
Tomball College
MONTGOMERY CO
HARRIS CO
DECKER PRAIRIE RD
TOMBALL PKWY
BAKER DR
Noack Rd
Wright Rd
Hardin Store Rd
Community Rd
Virgie
Morris Rd
Ruby Ln
Richard Kaye Ln
Vallie Rd
Red Fox Ln
Foxwood Dr
Zion Rd
Spring Pines Dr
Brown Rd
Lutheran Cemetery Rd
Tomball Cemetery Rd
Lutheran School Rd
Lutheran Church Rd
Jane Rd
McMahon Cir
Park Rd
Scherer Ln
Hicks St
Rudel Rd
Keefer Rd
Forest Ln
Liberty
Crowson Dr
Cresent Dr
Johlke Rd
Peden Rd
Rosehill Rd
Holly Lord
Broadford
Rock Chapel
Lord
Sentinel Oaks
Westbrook Dr
S Wiggins Dr
Industrial Park Dr
Spring Creek
A
1 Hickory Hollow Ln
2 Coachmans Ln
B
1 Scenic Tr
Pine Trails
Big Pns
Pine Brk
Dove Tr
Serene Trails
249
1
2
3
4
5
6
7
A
B
C
D
E
30°08'32"
30°08'05"
30°07'39"
30°07'13"
30°06'47"
30°06'21"
30°05'55"
30°05'29"
95°40'21"
95°39'51"
95°39'21"
95°38'51"
95°38'21"
95°37'50"

SEE 2964 MAP
SEE 2962 MAP
SEE 3108 MAP

1:24,000
1 in. = 2000 ft.
0 0.25 0.5
miles

SEE 2818 MAP

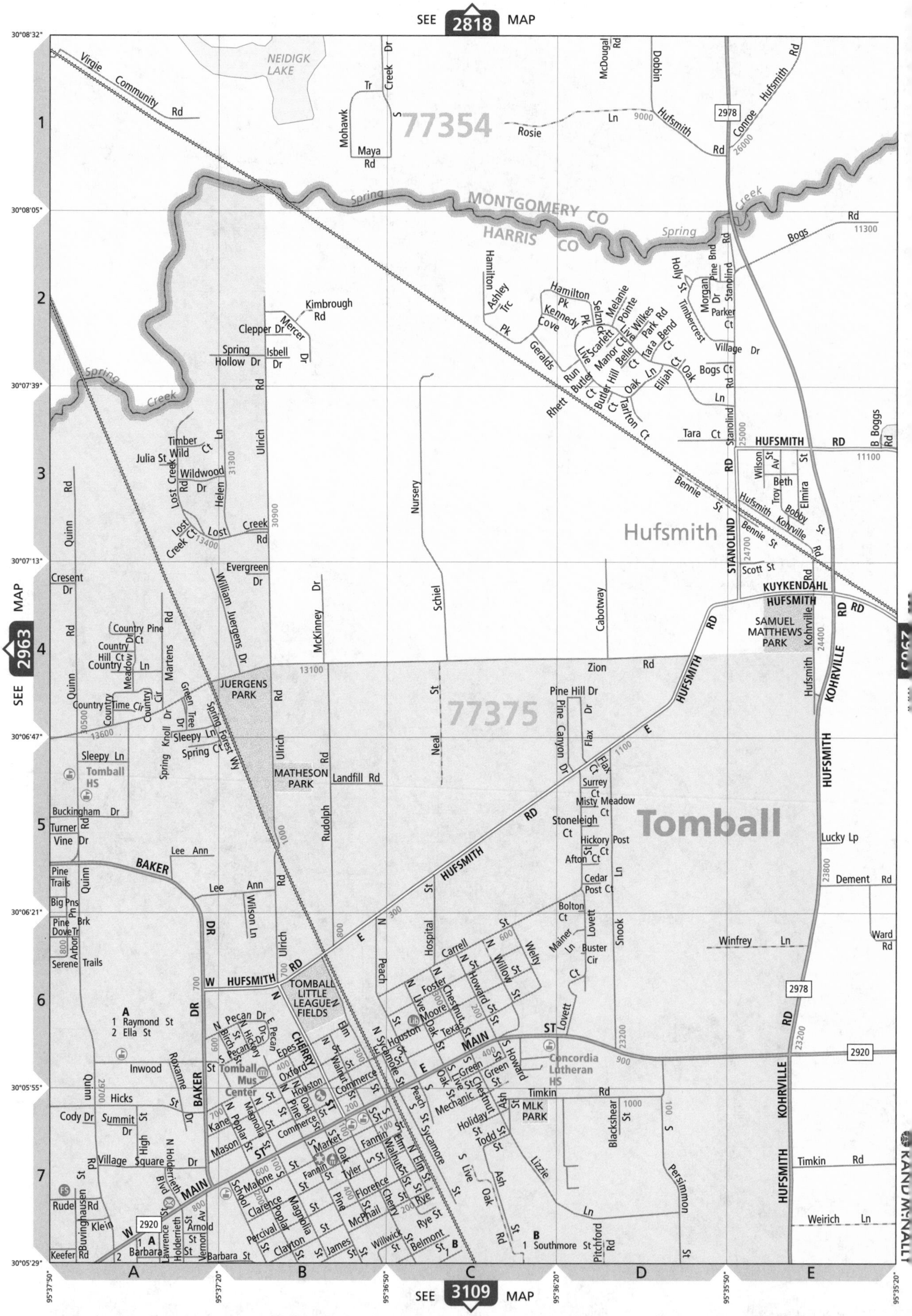
NEIDIGK LAKE
77354
77375
MONTGOMERY CO
HARRIS CO
Spring Creek
Hufsmith
Tomball
Virgie Community Rd
Mohawk
Maya Rd
Creek Dr
Tr
Rosie Ln
McDougal Rd
Dobbin Hufsmith Rd
Conroe Hufsmith Rd
2978
Bogs Rd
Kimbrough Rd
Clepper Dr
Mercer Dr
Spring Hollow Dr
Isbell Dr
Ulrich Rd
Hamilton Pk
Ashley Trc
Kennedy Cove
Gerailds
Rhett Run
Butler Ct
Scarlett
Live Oak Ln
Manor Ct
Belle Ct
Tara Bend Ct
Elijah Ct
Tarlton Ct
Holly St
Timbercrest
Morgan Dr
Pine Bnd
Stanolind Rd
Parker Ct
Village Dr
Bogs Ct
Tara Ct
HUFSMITH RD
B Boggs Rd
Wilson Av
Beth
Troy
Bobby
Elmira St
Bennie St
Hufsmith Kohrville Rd
Scott St
KUYKENDAHL RD
SAMUEL MATTHEWS PARK
Timber Wild Ct
Julia St
Wildwood Dr
Lost Creek Rd
Helen
Lost Creek Ct
Quinn Rd
Cresent Dr
Evergreen Dr
William Juergens Dr
McKinney Dr
Nursery
Schiel
Cabotway
Country Pine Dr
Country Hill Ct
Country Meadow Ln
Martens Rd
Country Time Cir
JUERGENS PARK
Green Tree Dr
Spring Knoll Dr
Sleepy Ln
Spring Ct
Spring Forest Wy
Zion Rd
Pine Hill Dr
Pine Canyon Dr
Flax Dr
Neal St
Tomball HS
Buckingham Dr
Turner Rd
Vine Dr
MATHESON PARK
Landfill Rd
Rudolph Rd
Surrey Ct
Misty Meadow Ct
Stoneleigh Ct
Hickory Post Ct
Afton Ct
Cedar Post Ct
Lucky Lp
Dement Rd
BAKER DR
Lee Ann Dr
Wilson Ln
Pine Trails
Big Pns
Pine Dove Tr
Arbor
Serene Trails
Bolton Ct
Lovett Ct
Mainer Ln
Buster Cir
Snook Ln
Winfrey Ln
Ward Rd
W HUFSMITH RD
E HUFSMITH RD
TOMBALL LITTLE LEAGUE FIELDS
Hospital St
Carrell St
Peach
Welty
Willow St
N Cherry St
Raymond St
Ella St
Inwood
Roxanne Dr
Hicks St
Tomball Mus Center
Concordia Lutheran HS
MAIN ST
Timkin Rd
MLK PARK
Blackshear St
Persimmon St
KOHRVILLE RD
HUFSMITH KOHRVILLE
2920
Cody Dr
Summit Dr
High Square Dr
Village
N Holderrieth Blvd
Buvinghausen Rd
Rude Rd
Klein
Keefer Rd
Barbara St
Lawrence St
Arnold St
Vernon Av
Malone St
Clarence St
Magnolia St
Percival St
Clayton St
James St
Willwick St
Belmont St
Rye St
McPhail St
Florence St
Tyler St
Fannin St
Market St
Commerce St
Oxford St
Houston St
Epes St
Kane St
Mason St
Sycamore St
Mechanic St
Holiday St
Todd St
Lizzie Ln
Pitchford Rd
Southmore St
Timkin Rd
Weirich Ln
A B C D E
1 2 3 4 5 6 7

SEE 2963 MAP

SEE 3109 MAP

1:24,000
1 in. = 2000 ft.
0 0.25 0.5
miles

SEE 2819 MAP

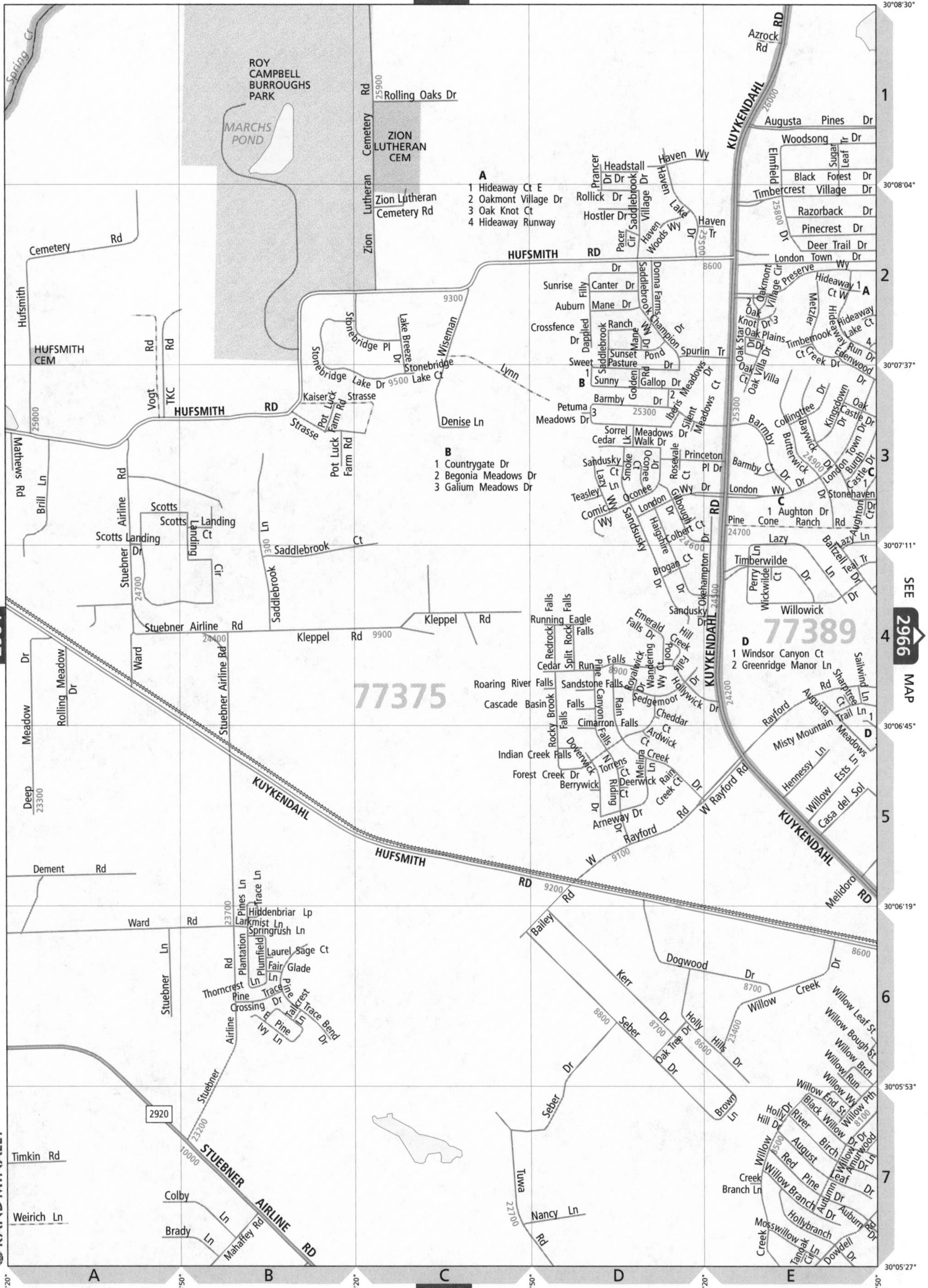
ROY CAMPBELL BURROUGHS PARK
MARCHS POND
ZION LUTHERAN CEM
HUFSMITH CEM
Spring Cr
Rolling Oaks Dr
Zion Lutheran Cemetery Rd
Cemetery Rd
Hufsmith
HUFSMITH RD
Vogt Rd
TKC Rd
Stonebridge Pl
Stonebridge Lake Dr
Lake Breeze Dr
Stonebridge Lake Ct
Wiseman
Lynn
Kaiser Strasse
Pot Luck Farm Rd
Denise Ln
Mathews Rd
Brill Ln
Airline Rd
Scotts Landing Dr
Scotts Landing Ct
Scotts Landing Cir
Saddlebrook Ct
Saddlebrook Ln
Stuebner Airline Rd
Kleppel Rd
Ward Rd
Rolling Meadow Dr
Deep Meadow Dr
77375
77389
KUYKENDAHL RD
Azrock Rd
Augusta Pines Dr
Woodsong Dr
Sugar Leaf Tr
Elmfield Dr
Black Forest Dr
Timbercrest Village Dr
Razorback Dr
Pinecrest Dr
Deer Trail Dr
London Town Dr
Headstall Dr
Prancer Dr
Rollick Dr
Hostler Dr
Haven Wy
Haven Lake Dr
Haven Woods Wy
Haven Tr
Pacer Cir
Saddlebrook Village Dr
A
1 Hideaway Ct E
2 Oakmont Village Dr
3 Oak Knot Ct
4 Hideaway Runway
B
1 Countrygate Dr
2 Begonia Meadows Dr
3 Galium Meadows Dr
C
1 Aughton Dr
D
1 Windsor Canyon Ct
2 Greenridge Manor Ln
Sunrise Filly Dr
Canter Dr
Auburn Mane Dr
Crossfence Dr
Dappled
Ranch
Saddlebrook Dr
Donna Farms Champion Dr
Sweet Pasture
Sunset Pond
Spurlin Tr
Sunny Gallop Dr
Golden Rod
Barmby Dr
Petuma Meadows Dr
Iberis Meadows Ct
Silent Meadows
Sorrel Meadows Dr
Cedar Walk Dr
Sandusky
Smoke
Oconee
Lazy Ln
Teasley Wy
Comic Wy
Rosevale Ct
Princeton Pl Dr
London Wy
Sandusky
Galbough
Haigshire
Colbert Ct
Brogan Ct
Okehampton Dr
Oak Star Dr
Oak Villa
Oak Plains
Oakmont Village Cir
Preserve
Hideaway Ct W
Metzler
Hideaway Lake Ct
Timbernook Ct
Creek Run
Edenwood
Collingtree
Kingsdown
Baywick
Castle Dr
Butterwick
London Town Dr
Stonehaven
Pine Cone
Ranch Rd
Lazy Ln
Timberwilde
Perry Wickwilde Ct
Balzell
Teal Tr
Willowick
Running Eagle Falls
Redrock Falls
Split Rock Falls
Cedar Run
Emerald Falls Dr
Hill Creek Dr
Pool Falls
Wandering Wy
Royalwick
Hollywick Dr
Roaring River Falls
Sandstone Falls
Pine Canyon
Cascade Basin Falls
Rain Falls
Sedgemoor
Cheddar Ct
Cimarron Falls
Ardwick Ct
Rocky Brook
Indian Creek Falls
Doverwick
Torrens Ct
Melina Ln
Creek Rain
Forest Creek Dr
Berrywick
Deerwick Ct
Riding
Arneway Dr
W Rayford Rd
Rayford Rd
Sailwind Ln
Shamtree Ct
Augusta Trail Ln
Misty Mountain Meadows Ln
Hennessy Ln
Willow Ests
Casa del Sol
Meliodoro
Dement Rd
Ward Rd
Pines Ln
Trace Ln
Hiddenbriar Lp
Larkmist Ln
Springrush Ln
Plantation Rd
Plumfield Ln
Laurel Sage Ct
Fair Glade Ln
Thorncrest Pine Crossing
Trace Pine Dr
Hallcrest Ln
Trace Bend Dr
Ivy Pine Ln
Stuebner Ln
Stuebner Airline
2920
STUEBNER AIRLINE RD
Timkin Rd
Colby Ln
Brady Ln
Mahaffey Rd
Weirich Ln
Bailey Rd
Kerr Dr
Dogwood Dr
Willow Creek
Holly Hills Dr
Oak Tree Dr
Seber Dr
Brown Ln
Tuwa Rd
Nancy Ln
Willow Leaf St
Willow Bough St
Willow Brch
Willow Run
Willow Wy
Willow End St
Black Willow Pth
Holly Hill Dr
River Birch
Willow Dr
Amurwood
August Leaf
Red Pine
Willow Branch Dr
Autumn
Auburn Dr
Hollybranch
Creek Branch Ln
Mosswillow Ln
Tangak Cir
Dowdell Dr
Creek

SEE 2966 MAP

SEE 3110 MAP

1:24,000
1 in. = 2000 ft.
0 0.25 0.5
miles

SEE 2820 MAP

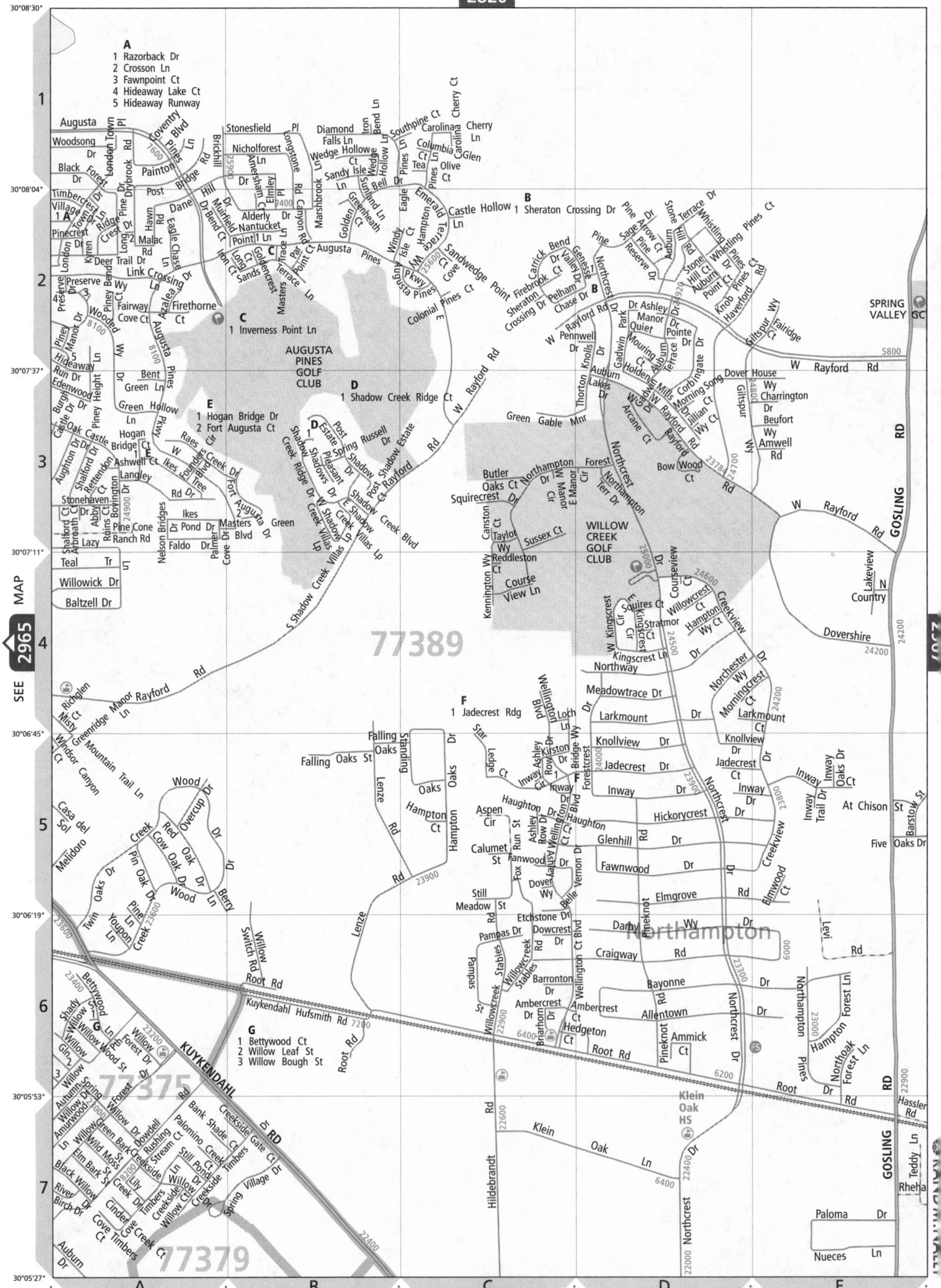
A
1 Razorback Dr
2 Crosson Ln
3 Fawnpoint Ct
4 Hideaway Lake Ct
5 Hideaway Runway
B
1 Sheraton Crossing Dr
C
1 Inverness Point Ln
D
1 Shadow Creek Ridge Ct
E
1 Hogan Bridge Dr
2 Fort Augusta Ct
F
1 Jadecrest Rdg
G
1 Bettywood Ct
2 Willow Leaf St
3 Willow Bough St
AUGUSTA PINES GOLF CLUB
WILLOW CREEK GOLF CLUB
SPRING VALLEY GC
77389
77375
77379
Northampton
Klein Oak HS
W Rayford Rd
Rayford Rd
GOSLING RD
KUYKENDAHL RD
Kuykendahl Hufsmith Rd
Root Rd
Northcrest Dr
Hildebrandt Rd
Klein Oak Ln
Lenze Rd
Augusta Pines Pkwy
S Shadow Creek Villas Lp
Shadow Creek Blvd
Willow Switch Rd
Pineknot Rd
Creekview Dr
Craigway Rd
Bayonne Dr
Allentown Dr
Northampton Pines
Paloma Dr
Nueces Ln
30°08'30"
30°08'04"
30°07'37"
30°07'11"
30°06'45"
30°06'19"
30°05'53"
30°05'27"
95°32'50"
95°32'20"
95°31'49"
95°31'19"
95°30'49"
95°30'19"
1
2
3
4
5
6
7
A
B
C
D
E

SEE 2965 MAP

SEE 3111 MAP

1:24,000
1 in. = 2000 ft.
0 0.25 0.5
miles

SEE 2821 MAP

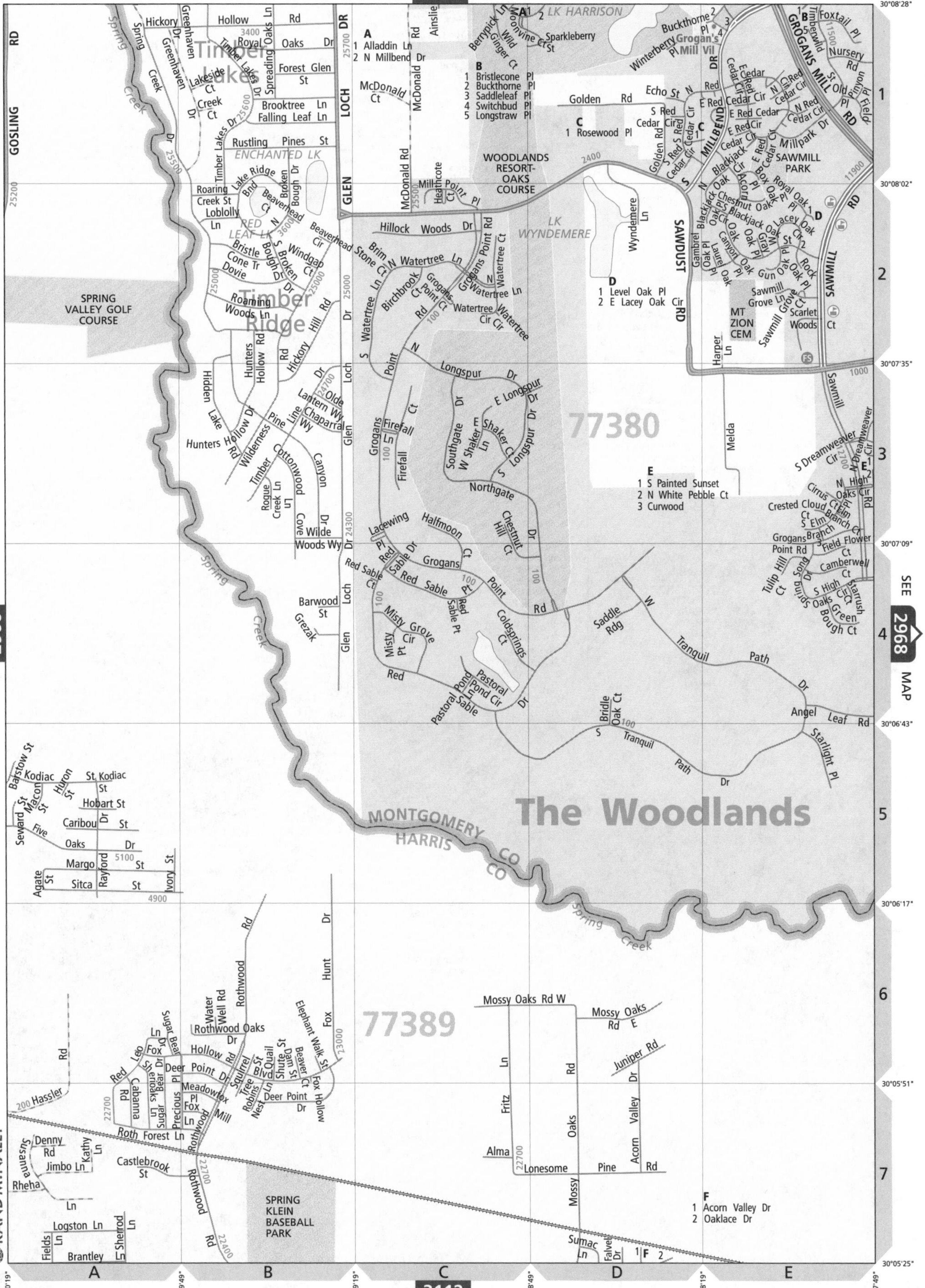
Timber Lakes
Timber Ridge
The Woodlands
77380
77389
SPRING VALLEY GOLF COURSE
WOODLANDS RESORT-OAKS COURSE
LK WYNDEMERE
LK HARRISON
ENCHANTED LK
RED LEAF LK
SAWMILL PARK
MT ZION CEM
SPRING KLEIN BASEBALL PARK
MONTGOMERY CO
HARRIS CO
Spring Creek
GOSLING RD
LOCH GLEN DR
SAWDUST RD
MILLBEND DR
GROGANS MILL RD
SAWMILL RD
Grogan's Mill Vil
A
1 Alladdin Ln
2 N Millbend Dr
B
1 Bristlecone Pl
2 Buckthorne Pl
3 Saddleleaf Pl
4 Switchbud Pl
5 Longstraw Pl
C
1 Rosewood Pl
D
1 Level Oak Pl
2 E Lacey Oak Cir
E
1 S Painted Sunset
2 N White Pebble Ct
3 Curwood
F
1 Acorn Valley Dr
2 Oaklace Dr
30°08'28"
30°08'02"
30°07'35"
30°07'09"
30°06'43"
30°06'17"
30°05'51"
30°05'25"
95°30'19"
95°29'49"
95°29'19"
95°28'49"
95°28'19"
95°27'49"
SEE 2968 MAP
2966
RAND McNALLY

SEE 3112 MAP

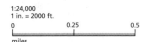

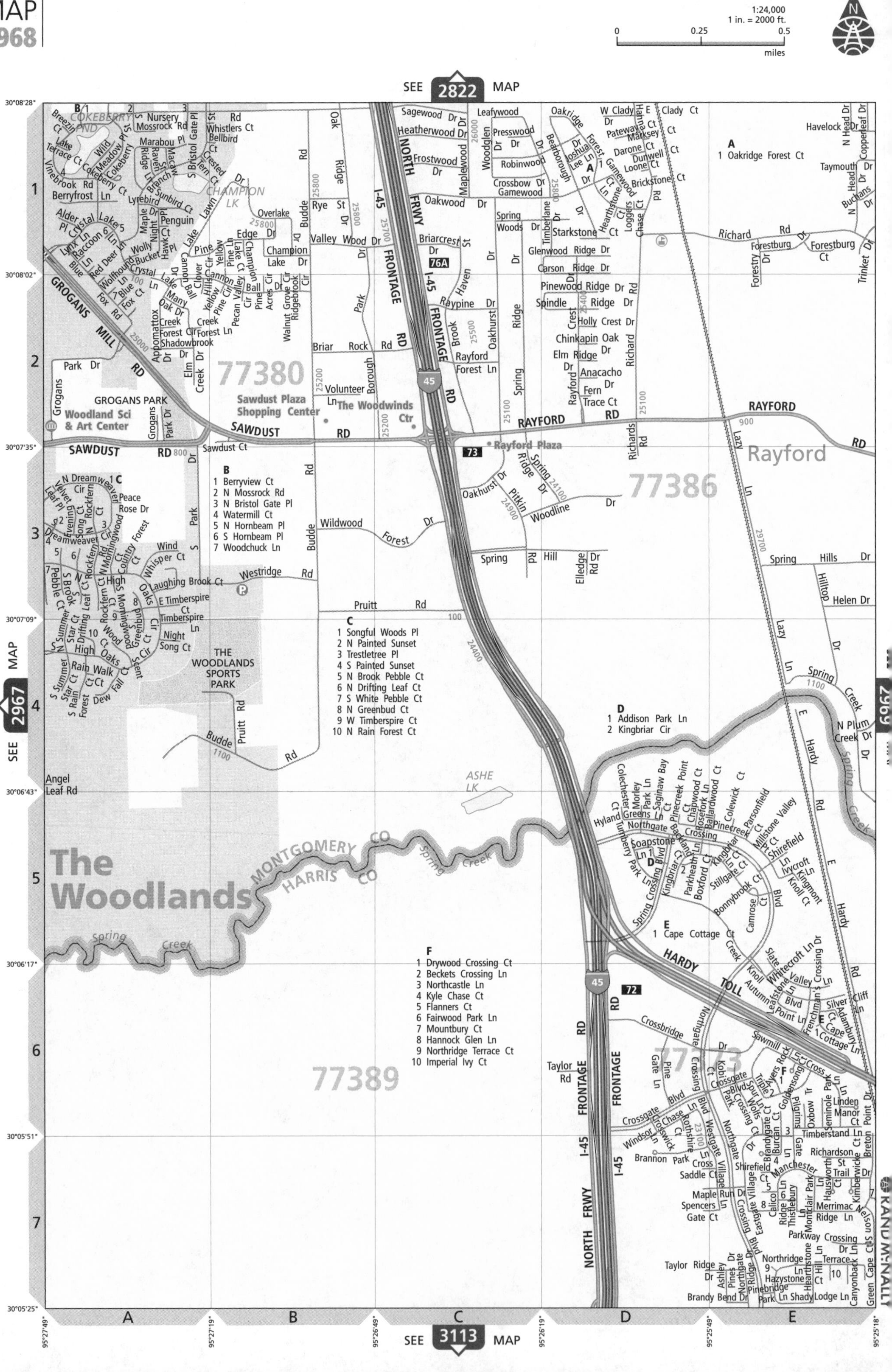
1:24,000
1 in. = 2000 ft.
0 0.25 0.5
miles
SEE 2822 MAP
SEE 3113 MAP
SEE 2967 MAP
77380
77386
77389
77373
Rayford
The Woodlands
GROGANS PARK
Woodland Sci & Art Center
Sawdust Plaza Shopping Center
The Woodwinds Ctr
Rayford Plaza
THE WOODLANDS SPORTS PARK
MONTGOMERY CO
HARRIS CO
Spring Creek
ASHE LK
CHAMPION LK
COKEBERRY POND
I-45
NORTH FRWY
FRONTAGE RD
SAWDUST RD
RAYFORD RD
GROGANS MILL RD
HARDY TOLL RD
Budde Rd
Pruitt Rd
Lazy Ln
Richard Rd
Spring Hills Dr
Wildwood Forest Dr
Westridge Rd
Angel Leaf Rd
Taylor Rd
A
1 Oakridge Forest Ct
B
1 Berryview Ct
2 N Mossrock Rd
3 N Bristol Gate Pl
4 Watermill Ct
5 N Hornbeam Pl
6 S Hornbeam Pl
7 Woodchuck Ln
C
1 Songful Woods Pl
2 N Painted Sunset
3 Trestletree Pl
4 S Painted Sunset
5 N Brook Pebble Ct
6 N Drifting Leaf Ct
7 S White Pebble Ct
8 N Greenbud Ct
9 W Timberspire Ct
10 N Rain Forest Ct
D
1 Addison Park Ln
2 Kingbriar Cir
E
1 Cape Cottage Ct
F
1 Drywood Crossing Ct
2 Beckets Crossing Ln
3 Northcastle Ln
4 Kyle Chase Ct
5 Flanners Ct
6 Fairwood Park Ln
7 Mountbury Ct
8 Hannock Glen Ln
9 Northridge Terrace Ct
10 Imperial Ivy Ct
A B C D E
1 2 3 4 5 6 7
30°08'28" 30°08'02" 30°07'35" 30°07'09" 30°06'43" 30°06'17" 30°05'51" 30°05'25"
95°27'49" 95°27'19" 95°26'49" 95°26'19" 95°25'49" 95°25'18"
RAND McNALLY

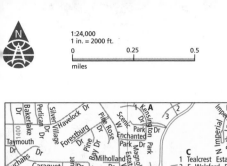

1:24,000
1 in. = 2000 ft.
0 0.25 0.5
miles

SEE 2823 MAP

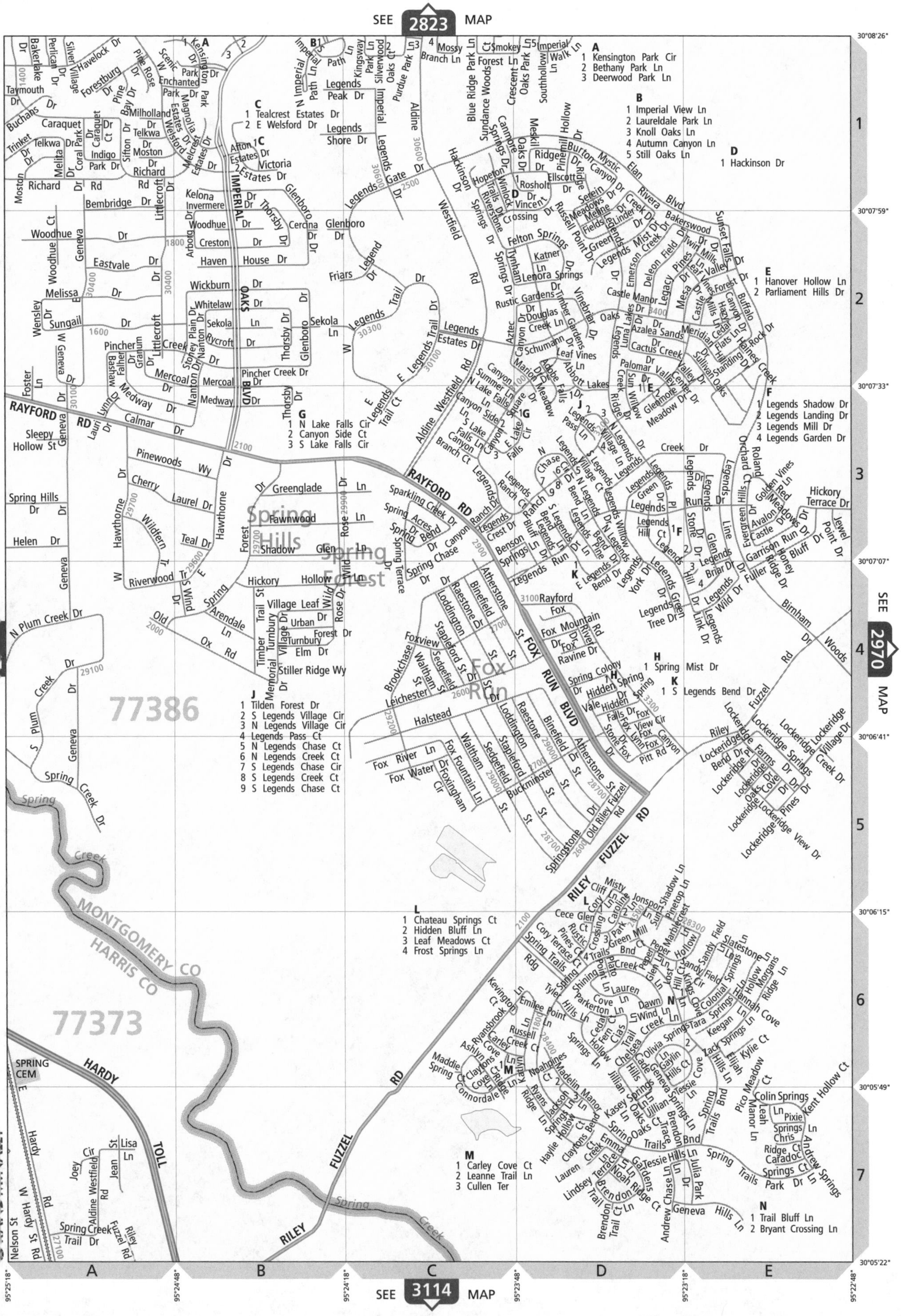
A
1 Kensington Park Cir
2 Bethany Park Ln
3 Deerwood Park Ln
B
1 Imperial View Ln
2 Laureldale Park Ln
3 Knoll Oaks Ln
4 Autumn Canyon Ln
5 Still Oaks Ln
C
1 Tealcrest Estates Dr
2 E Welsford Dr
D
1 Hackinson Dr
E
1 Hanover Hollow Ln
2 Parliament Hills Dr
F
1 Legends Shadow Dr
2 Legends Landing Dr
3 Legends Mill Dr
4 Legends Garden Dr
G
1 N Lake Falls Cir
2 Canyon Side Ct
3 S Lake Falls Cir
H
1 Spring Mist Dr
J
1 Tilden Forest Dr
2 S Legends Village Cir
3 N Legends Village Cir
4 Legends Pass Ct
5 N Legends Chase Ct
6 N Legends Creek Ct
7 S Legends Chase Cir
8 S Legends Creek Ct
9 S Legends Chase Ct
K
1 S Legends Bend Dr
L
1 Chateau Springs Ct
2 Hidden Bluff Ln
3 Leaf Meadows Ct
4 Frost Springs Ln
M
1 Carley Cove Ct
2 Leanne Trail Ln
3 Cullen Ter
N
1 Trail Bluff Ln
2 Bryant Crossing Ln
RAYFORD RD
IMPERIAL OAKS BLVD
FOX RUN BLVD
RILEY FUZZEL RD
HARDY TOLL
Spring Hills
Spring Forest
Fox Run
77386
77373
MONTGOMERY CO
HARRIS CO
SPRING CEM
Spring Creek
SEE 2970 MAP
30°08'26"
30°07'59"
30°07'33"
30°07'07"
30°06'41"
30°06'15"
30°05'49"
30°05'22"
95°25'18"
95°24'48"
95°24'18"
95°23'48"
95°23'18"
95°22'48"
A B C D E
1 2 3 4 5 6 7

SEE 3114 MAP

1:24,000
1 in. = 2000 ft.
0 0.25 0.5
miles

SEE 2824 MAP

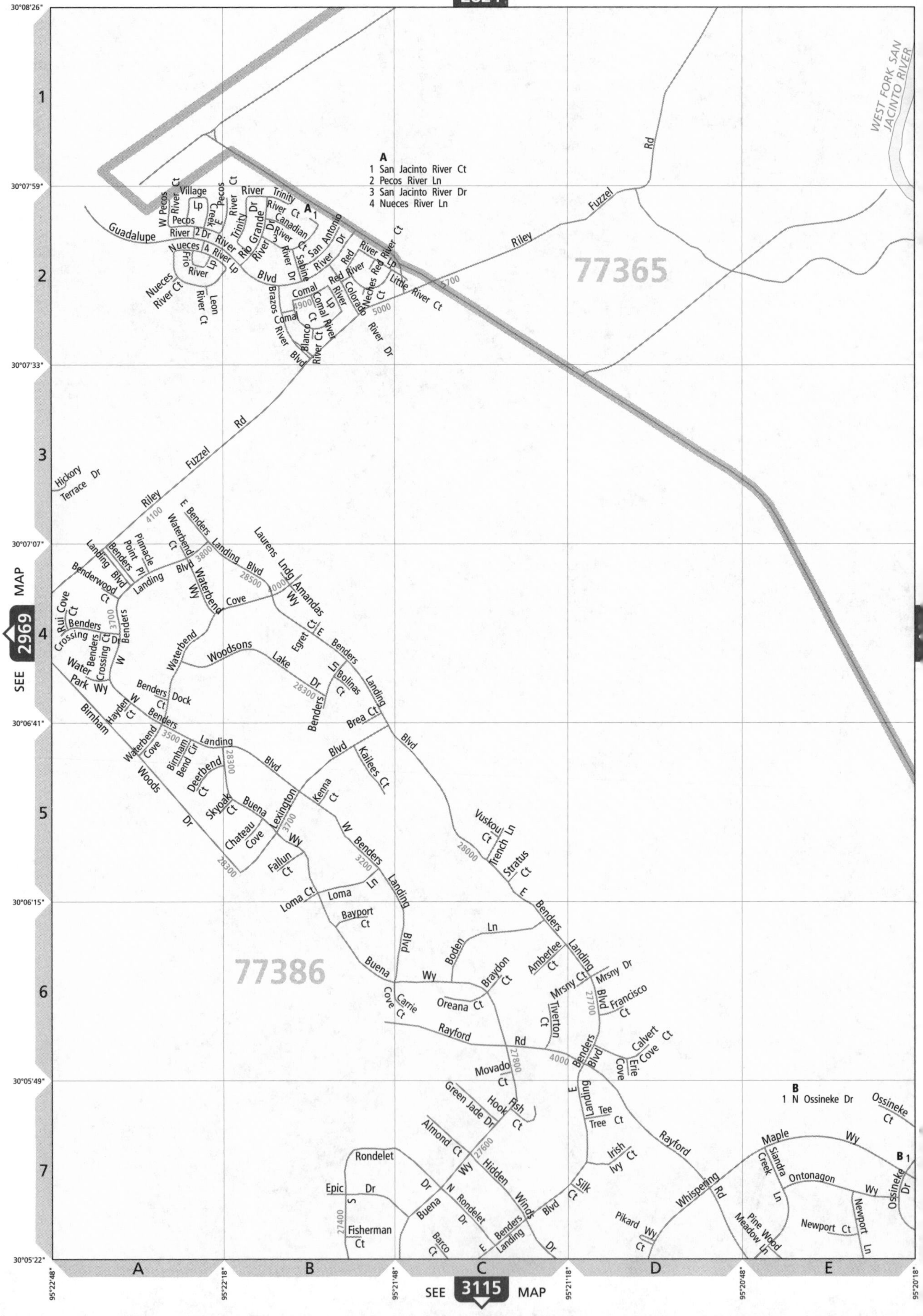
30°08'26"
30°07'59"
30°07'33"
30°07'07"
30°06'41"
30°06'15"
30°05'49"
30°05'22"
95°22'48"
95°22'18"
95°21'48"
95°21'18"
95°20'48"
95°20'18"
1
2
3
4
5
6
7
A
B
C
D
E
77365
77386
WEST FORK SAN JACINTO RIVER
A
1 San Jacinto River Ct
2 Pecos River Ln
3 San Jacinto River Dr
4 Nueces River Ln
B
1 N Ossineke Dr
Riley Fuzzel Rd
Guadalupe River Dr
W Pecos River Ct
Village Lp
Pecos Creek Ct
Pecos River Ct
Trinity River Ct
Rio Grande River Dr
Canadian River Ct
San Antonio River Dr
Sabine River Dr
Nueces River Lp
Frio River
Leon River Ct
Nueces River Ct
Brazos River Blvd
Comal River Ct
Blanco River Ct
Red River Lp
Colorado River Dr
Neches River Ct
Red River Ct
Little River Ct
4900
5000
5700
Hickory Terrace Dr
4100
E Benders Landing Blvd
Laurens Lndg
Amandas Wy
Waterbend Ct
Waterbend Wy
Waterbend Cove
3800
28500
4000
Pinnacle Point Pl
Benders Landing
Landing Blvd
Benderwood Ct
Rui Cove Ct
Benders Crossing Ct
Benders Crossing Dr
W Benders
3700
Water Park Wy
Woodsons Lake Dr
28300
Egret Ct
Bolinas Ct
Benders Ct
Brea Ct
Benders Dock Ct
Hayden Ct
Birnham Woods Dr
Waterbend Cove
Birnham Bend Cir
3500
Landing Blvd
Deerbend Ct
Skyoak Ct
Buena Cove
Chateau Cove
Lexington Wy
Kenna Ct
Kailees Ct
Fallun Ct
W Benders Landing Blvd
3200
Loma Ct
Loma Ln
Bayport Ct
Vuskou Ct
Trench Ln
Stratus Ct
28000
E Benders Landing Blvd
Boden Ln
Braydon Ct
Amberlee Ct
Mrsny Ct
Mrsny Dr
Buena Wy
Carrie Cove Ct
Oreana Ct
Tiverton Ct
27700
Francisco Ct
Rayford Rd
Calvert Cove Ct
Erie Cove
Movado Ct
27800
4000
Green Jade Dr
Fish Hook Ct
Tee Tree Ct
Almond Ct
Irish Ivy Ct
27600
Hidden Winds Dr
Rondelet
Epic Dr
S
27400
Fisherman Ct
Buena Wy
N Rondelet Dr
Barco Ct
Benders Landing
Silk Blvd
Silk Ct
Pikard Wy Ct
Whispering Rd
Maple Wy
Siandra Creek Ln
Ontonagon Wy
Pine Wood Meadow Ln
Newport Ct
Newport Ln
Ossineke Ct
Ossineke Dr

SEE 2969 MAP

SEE 3115 MAP

1:24,000
1 in. = 2000 ft.
0 0.25 0.5
miles

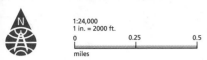

SEE 2825 MAP

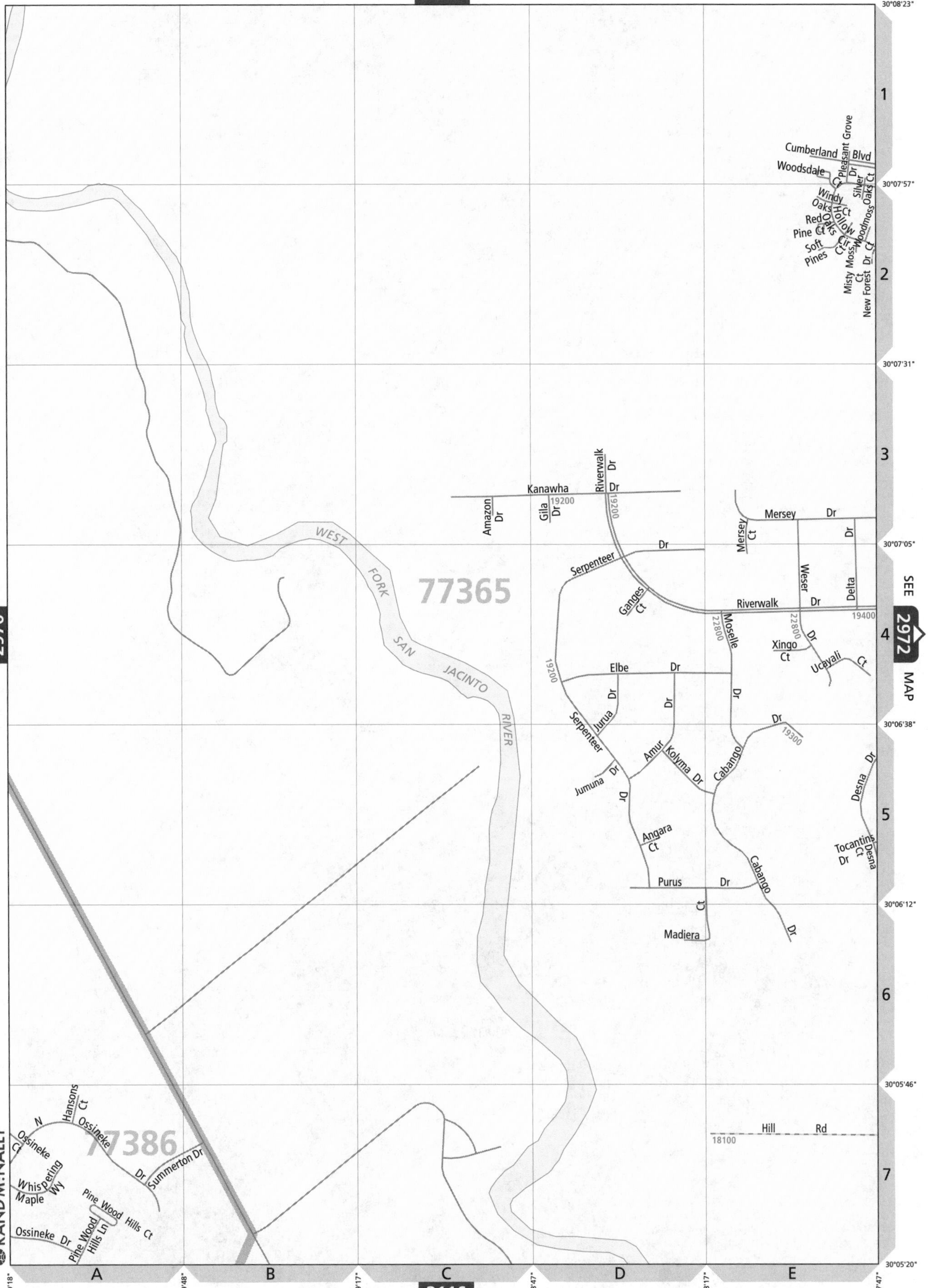
77365
77386
WEST FORK SAN JACINTO RIVER
Cumberland Blvd
Pleasant Grove Dr
Woodsdale Ct
Silver Oaks Ct
Windy Oaks Ct
Hollow
Red Oaks Cir
Pine Ct
Woodmoss
Soft Pines Ct
Misty Moss Ct
New Forest Dr
Kanawha Dr
Riverwalk Dr
Amazon Dr
Gila Dr
19200
Serpenteer Dr
Ganges Ct
Riverwalk Dr
19400
Mersey Dr
Mersey Ct
Weser Dr
Delta Dr
Moselle Dr
22800
Xingo Ct
Ucayali Ct
Elbe Dr
Jurua Dr
Serpenteer Dr
Amur Dr
Kolyma Dr
Cabango Dr
19300
Jumuna Dr
Desna Dr
Tocantins Dr
Desna Ct
Angara Ct
Purus Dr
Madiera Ct
Hill Rd
18100
N Hansons Ct
Ossineke Ct
Ossineke Dr
Summerton Dr
Whispering Wy
Maple
Pine Wood Hills Ct
Pine Wood Hills Ln
1
2
3
4
5
6
7
A
B
C
D
E
30°08'23"
30°07'57"
30°07'31"
30°07'05"
30°06'38"
30°06'12"
30°05'46"
30°05'20"
95°20'18"
95°19'48"
95°19'17"
95°18'47"
95°18'17"
95°17'47"

SEE 2972 MAP

2970

SEE 3116 MAP

SEE 2826 MAP

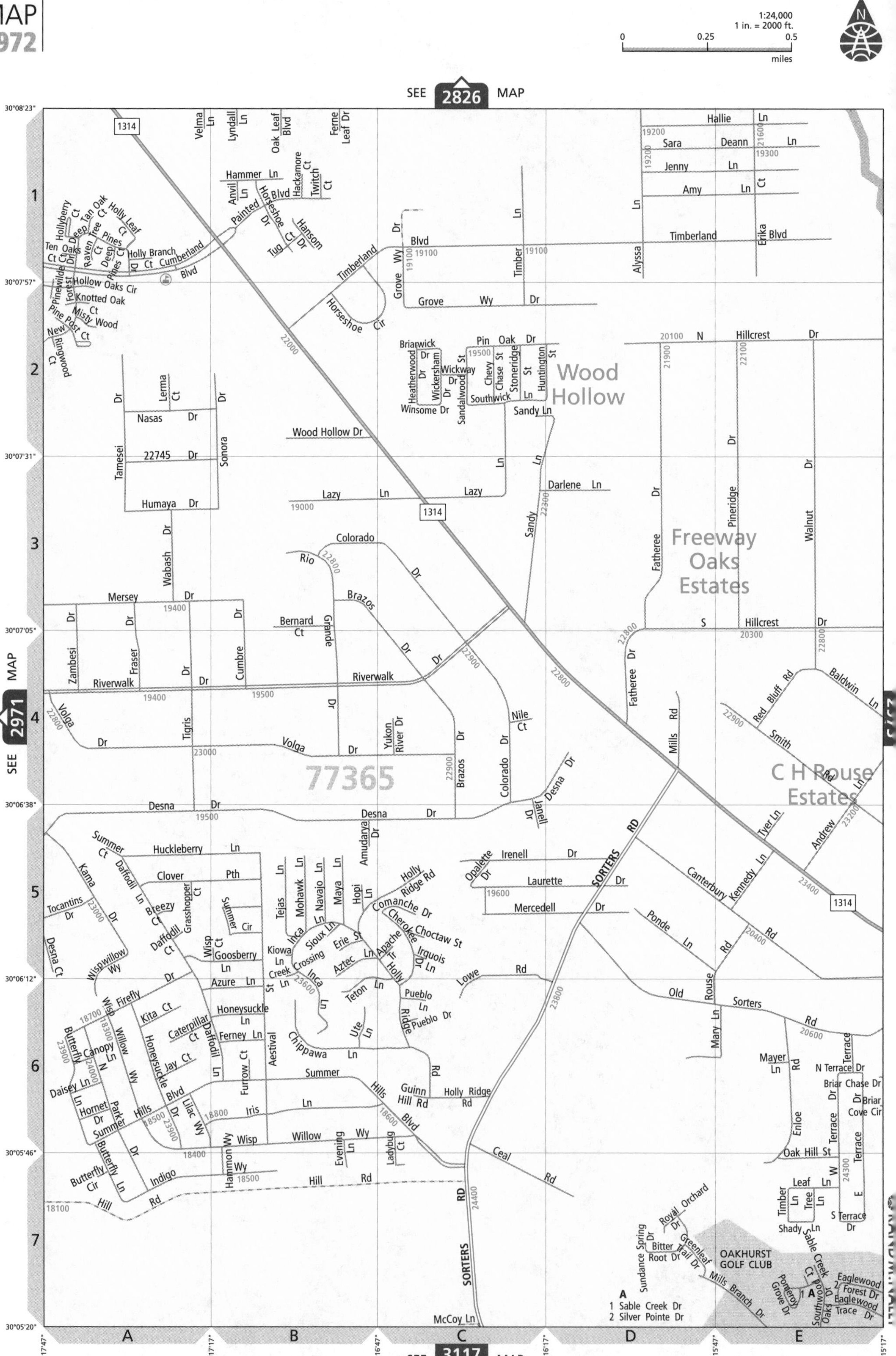
1:24,000
1 in. = 2000 ft.
0 0.25 0.5
miles
N
Wood Hollow
Freeway Oaks Estates
C H Rouse Estates
77365
OAKHURST GOLF CLUB
1314
SORTERS RD
Old Sorters Rd
Hillcrest Dr
Timberland Blvd
Grove Wy Dr
Riverwalk Dr
Desna Dr
Volga Dr
Mills Rd
Rouse Rd
Sandy Ln
Lazy Ln
Wood Hollow Dr
Colorado Dr
Brazos Dr
Rio Grande Dr
Mersey Dr
Tigris Dr
Fatheree Dr
Pineridge Dr
Walnut Dr
Canterbury Rd
Kennedy Ln
Ceal Rd
Hill Rd
Summer Hills Blvd
Chippawa Ln
Holly Ridge Rd
Hollow Oaks Cir
Cumberland Blvd
Wisp Wy
Willow Wy
Butterfly Cir
McCoy Ln
A
1 Sable Creek Dr
2 Silver Pointe Dr
A B C D E
1 2 3 4 5 6 7
30°08'23" 30°07'57" 30°07'31" 30°07'05" 30°06'38" 30°06'12" 30°05'46" 30°05'20"
95°17'47" 95°17'17" 95°16'47" 95°16'17" 95°15'47" 95°15'17"

SEE 2971 MAP

SEE 3117 MAP

1:24,000
1 in. = 2000 ft.
0 0.25 0.5
miles

SEE 2827 MAP

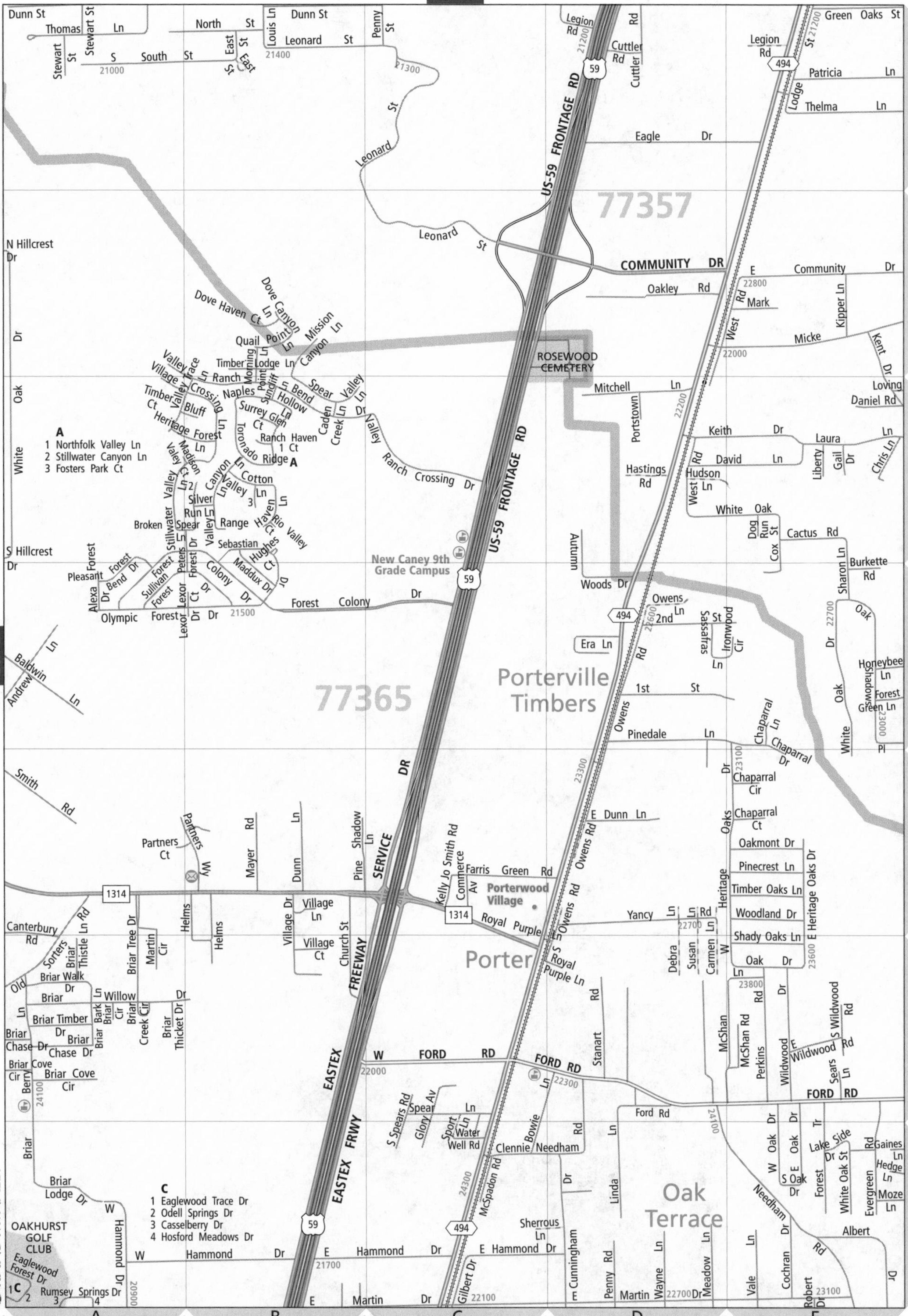
77357
77365
Porterville Timbers
Porter
Porterwood Village
Oak Terrace
ROSEWOOD CEMETERY
New Caney 9th Grade Campus
OAKHURST GOLF CLUB
US-59 FRONTAGE RD
EASTEX FRWY
EASTEX FREEWAY SERVICE DR
COMMUNITY DR
W FORD RD
FORD RD
Dunn St
Thomas Ln
Stewart St
South St
North St
Leonard St
Penny St
Green Oaks St
Legion Rd
Cuttler Rd
Patricia Ln
Thelma Ln
Eagle Dr
E Community Dr
Oakley Rd
Mark
Kipper Ln
Micke
Kent Dr
Loving Daniel Rd
Mitchell Ln
Portstown
Keith Dr
Laura
David Ln
Hudson Ln
Hastings Rd
White Oak
Cactus Rd
Burkette Rd
Sharon Ln
Autumn Woods Dr
Owens Ln
2nd St
Sassafras
Ironwood Cir
Era Ln
1st St
Pinedale Ln
Chaparral Ln
Chaparral Dr
Chaparral Cir
Chaparral Ct
E Dunn Ln
Oakmont Dr
Pinecrest Ln
Timber Oaks Ln
Woodland Dr
Shady Oaks Ln
E Heritage Oaks Dr
Yancy
Forest Colony Dr
Valley Ranch Crossing Dr
N Hillcrest Dr
S Hillcrest Dr
White Oak Dr
Baldwin Ln
Andrew Ln
Smith Rd
Partners Ct
Partners Wy
Mayer Rd
Dunn Ln
Pine Shadow Ln
Village Dr
Village Ln
Village Ct
Church St
Helms
Kelly Jo Smith Rd
Commerce Av
Farris Green Rd
Royal Purple Ln
Canterbury Rd
Briar Walk Dr
Briar Timber Dr
Briar Cove Cir
Briar Lodge Dr
W Hammond Dr
E Hammond Dr
Martin Dr
Clennie Needham
McShan Rd
Wildwood Rd
Needham Rd
Albert
A
1 Northfolk Valley Ln
2 Stillwater Canyon Ln
3 Fosters Park Ct
C
1 Eaglewood Trace Dr
2 Odell Springs Dr
3 Casselberry Dr
4 Hosford Meadows Dr
59
494
1314
21000
21400
21300
21200
22800
22000
22200
21500
22600
22700
23000
23100
23300
23600
23800
24100
22300
24300
21700
20900
22100
23100
30°08'20"
30°07'54"
30°07'28"
30°07'02"
30°06'36"
30°06'10"
30°05'43"
30°05'17"
95°15'17"
95°14'47"
95°14'17"
95°13'47"
95°13'16"
95°12'46"
A B C D E
1 2 3 4 5 6 7

SEE 2974 MAP

SEE 3118 MAP

1:24,000
1 in. = 2000 ft.
0 0.25 0.5
miles

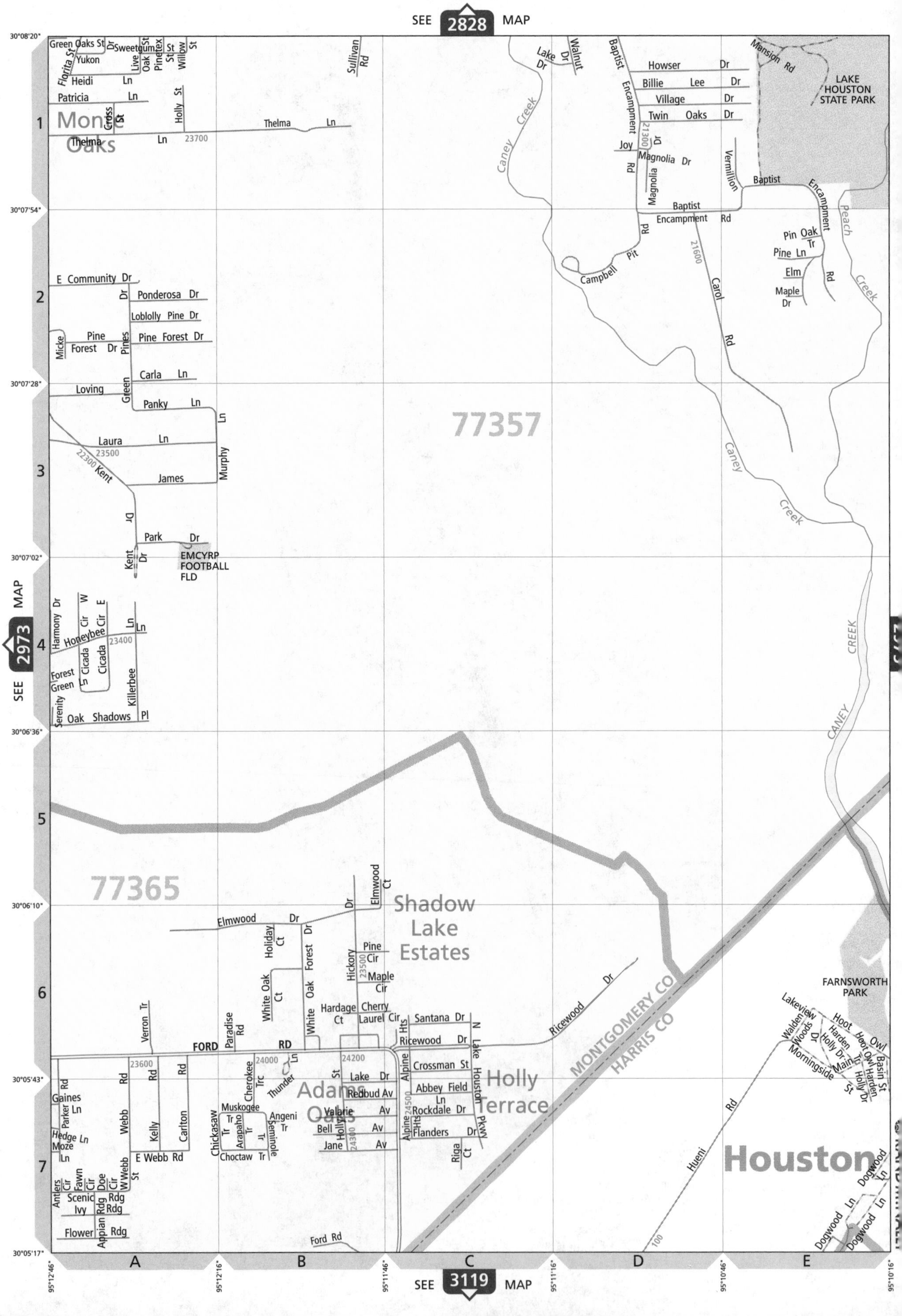
SEE 2828 MAP
SEE 2973 MAP
SEE 3119 MAP
30°08'20"
30°07'54"
30°07'28"
30°07'02"
30°06'36"
30°06'10"
30°05'43"
30°05'17"
95°12'46"
95°12'16"
95°11'46"
95°11'16"
95°10'46"
95°10'16"
A
B
C
D
E
1
2
3
4
5
6
7
Monte Oaks
77357
77365
Shadow Lake Estates
Adams Oaks
Holly Terrace
Houston
LAKE HOUSTON STATE PARK
FARNSWORTH PARK
EMCYRP FOOTBALL FLD
MONTGOMERY CO
HARRIS CO
Caney Creek
Peach Creek
Green Oaks St
Florita St
Yukon
Sweetgum
Live Oak St
Pinetex St
Willow St
Heidi Ln
Patricia Ln
Cross St
Holly St
Thelma Ln
23700
Sullivan Rd
Lake Dr
Walnut Dr
Baptist Encampment Rd
Mansion Rd
Howser Dr
Billie Lee Dr
Village Dr
Twin Oaks Dr
21300
Joy Dr
Magnolia Dr
Vermillion
Baptist Encampment Rd
Pin Oak Tr
Pine Ln
Elm
Maple Dr
Campbell Pit Rd
21600
Carol Rd
E Community Dr
Ponderosa Dr
Loblolly Pine Dr
Pine Forest Dr
Micke
Pines
Carla Ln
Loving
Green
Panky Ln
Laura Ln
23500
22300
Kent Dr
James
Murphy
Park Dr
Harmony Dr
Honeybee Cir
Cicada Cir
23400
Killerbee Ln
Forest Green Ln
Serenity
Oak Shadows Pl
Elmwood Dr
Elmwood Ct
Holiday Ct
Forest Dr
Hickory
23500
Pine Cir
Maple Cir
White Oak Ct
White Oak
Hardage Ct
Cherry Laurel Cir
Santana Dr
Ricewood Dr
N Lake Houston Pkwy
Verron Tr
Paradise Rd
FORD RD
23600
24000
24200
Gaines Rd
Parker Ln
Hedge Ln
Moze Ln
Webb Rd
Kelly Rd
Carlton Rd
E Webb Rd
W Webb St
Muskogee Tr
Chickasaw Tr
Arapaho Tr
Cherokee Trc
Thunder Ln
Seminole Tr
Angeni Tr
Choctaw Tr
Lake Dr
Redbud Av
Valarie Av
Bell Av
Jane Av
Holly St
24300
24500
Alpine Hts
Crossman St
Abbey Field Ln
Rockdale Dr
Flanders Dr
Riga Ct
Antlers Cir
Fawn Cir
Doe Cir
Scenic Rdg
Ivy Rdg
Appian
Flower Rdg
Ford Rd
Hueni Rd
100
Lakeview
Walden Woods Dr
Hoot Owl
Harden
Holly Dr
Morningside
Main St
Basin St
Dogwood Ln

1:24,000
1 in. = 2000 ft.
0 0.25 0.5
miles

SEE 2829 MAP

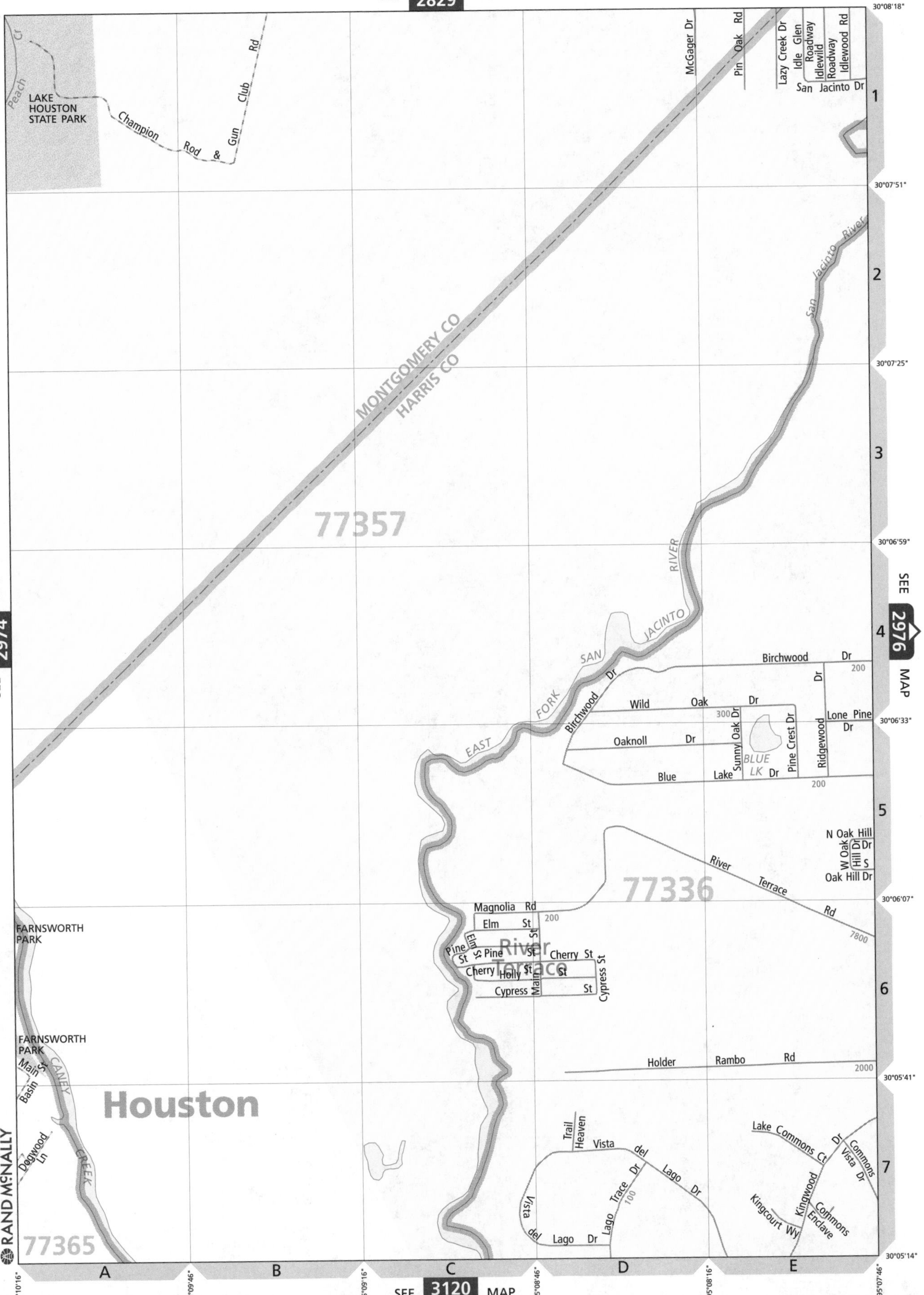
LAKE HOUSTON STATE PARK
Peach Cr
Champion Rod & Gun Club Rd
McGager Dr
Pin Oak Rd
Lazy Creek Dr
Idle Glen
Roadway
Idlewild
Roadway
Idlewood Rd
San Jacinto Dr
MONTGOMERY CO
HARRIS CO
San Jacinto River
77357
RIVER
EAST FORK SAN JACINTO
Birchwood Dr
Birchwood Dr
200
Wild Oak Dr
300
Sunny Oak Dr
Lone Pine Dr
Oaknoll Dr
Pine Crest Dr
Ridgewood Dr
Blue Lake Dr
BLUE LK
200
N Oak Hill Dr
W Oak Hill Dr
S Oak Hill Dr
River Terrace Rd
77336
7800
Magnolia Rd
Elm St
200
Elm St
Pine St
Pine St
Main St
River Terrace
Cherry St
Cherry St
Holly St
St
Cypress St
Cypress St
St
FARNSWORTH PARK
FARNSWORTH PARK
Main St
Basin St
CANEY CREEK
Houston
Dogwood Ln
Holder Rambo Rd
2000
Trail Heaven
Vista del Lago Dr
Lago Trace Dr
100
Vista del Lago Dr
Lake Commons Ct
Commons Vista Dr
Dr
Kingwood Commons Enclave
Kingcourt Wy
77365
30°08'18"
30°07'51"
30°07'25"
30°06'59"
30°06'33"
30°06'07"
30°05'41"
30°05'14"
1
2
3
4
5
6
7
A
B
C
D
E
95°10'16"
95°09'46"
95°09'16"
95°08'46"
95°08'16"
95°07'46"

SEE 2974 MAP

SEE 2976 MAP

SEE 3120 MAP

1:24,000
1 in. = 2000 ft.
0 0.25 0.5
miles

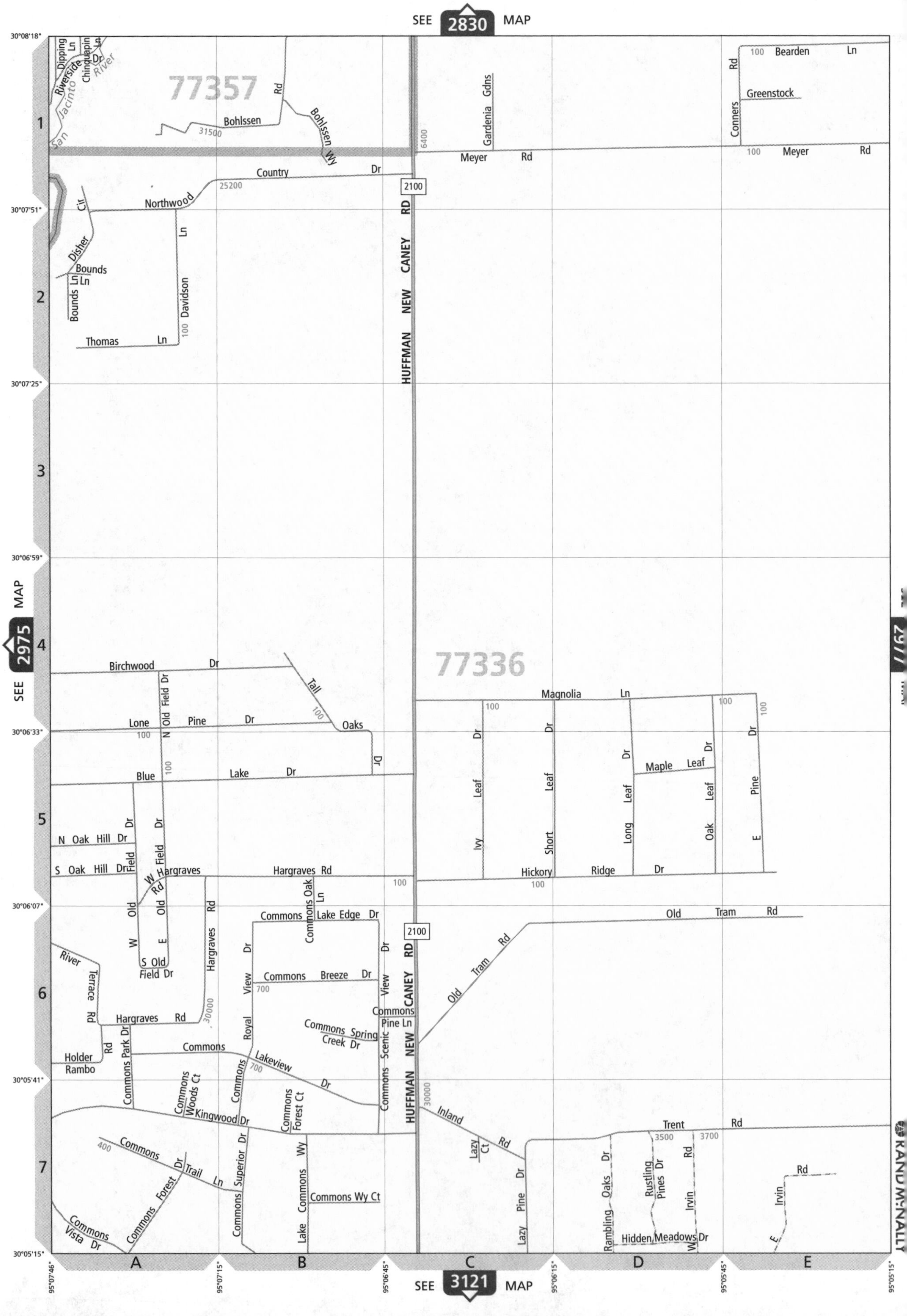
SEE 2830 MAP
SEE 2975 MAP
SEE 2977 MAP
SEE 3121 MAP
77357
77336
San Jacinto River
Dipping Ln
Riverside
Chinquapin Dr
Bohlssen Rd
Bohlssen Wy
31500
Meyer Rd
6400
Gardenia Gdns
Bearden Ln
Greenstock
Conners Rd
100
Country Dr
25200
2100
Northwood Cir
Northwood
Davidson Ln
Disher
Bounds Ln
Bounds Ln
Thomas Ln
HUFFMAN NEW CANEY RD
Birchwood Dr
Tall Oaks Dr
Lone Pine Dr
N Old Field Dr
Blue Lake Dr
Magnolia Ln
Ivy Leaf Dr
Short Leaf Dr
Long Leaf Dr
Maple Leaf Dr
Oak Leaf Dr
E Pine Dr
Hickory Ridge Dr
N Oak Hill Dr
S Oak Hill Dr
W Old Field Dr
E Old Field Dr
W Hargraves Rd
Hargraves Rd
S Old Field Dr
Commons Oak Ln
Commons Lake Edge Dr
Old Tram Rd
River Terrace Rd
Commons Breeze Dr
Royal View Dr
Commons View Dr
Commons Pine Ln
Commons Spring Creek Dr
700
30000
Hargraves Rd
Holder Rd
Rambo
Commons Park Dr
Commons
Lakeview Dr
Commons Woods Ct
Commons Scenic Dr
Kingwood Dr
Commons Forest Ct
Inland Rd
Lazy Ct
Trent Rd
3500
3700
Commons Trail Ln
400
Commons Forest Dr
Commons Superior Dr
Commons Wy
Lake Commons Wy
Commons Wy Ct
Lazy Pine Dr
Rambling Oaks Dr
Rustling Pines Dr
W Irvin Rd
Hidden Meadows Dr
E Irvin Rd
Commons Vista Dr
A B C D E
1 2 3 4 5 6 7
30°08'18"
30°07'51"
30°07'25"
30°06'59"
30°06'33"
30°06'07"
30°05'41"
30°05'15"
95°07'46"
95°07'15"
95°06'45"
95°06'15"
95°05'45"
95°05'15"
RAND McNALLY

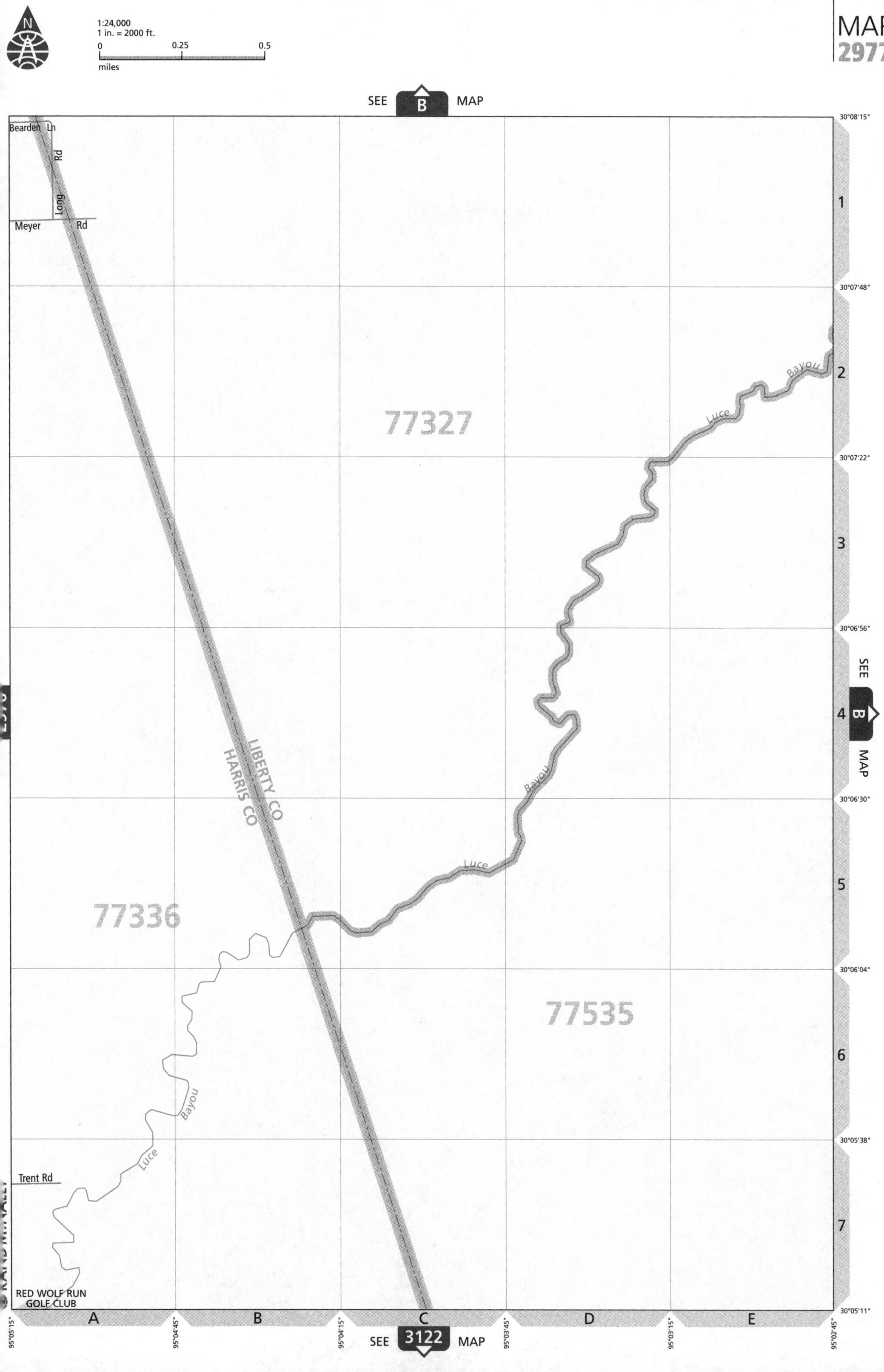
N
1:24,000
1 in. = 2000 ft.
0
0.25
0.5
miles
SEE B MAP
Bearden Ln
Long Rd
Meyer Rd
77327
77336
77535
Luce Bayou
LIBERTY CO
HARRIS CO
Trent Rd
RED WOLF RUN GOLF CLUB
SEE 3122 MAP
A
B
C
D
E
1
2
3
4
5
6
7
30°08'15"
30°07'48"
30°07'22"
30°06'56"
30°06'30"
30°06'04"
30°05'38"
30°05'11"
95°05'15"
95°04'45"
95°04'15"
95°03'45"
95°03'15"
95°02'45"

1:24,000
1 in. = 2000 ft.
0 0.25 0.5
miles

SEE 2952 MAP

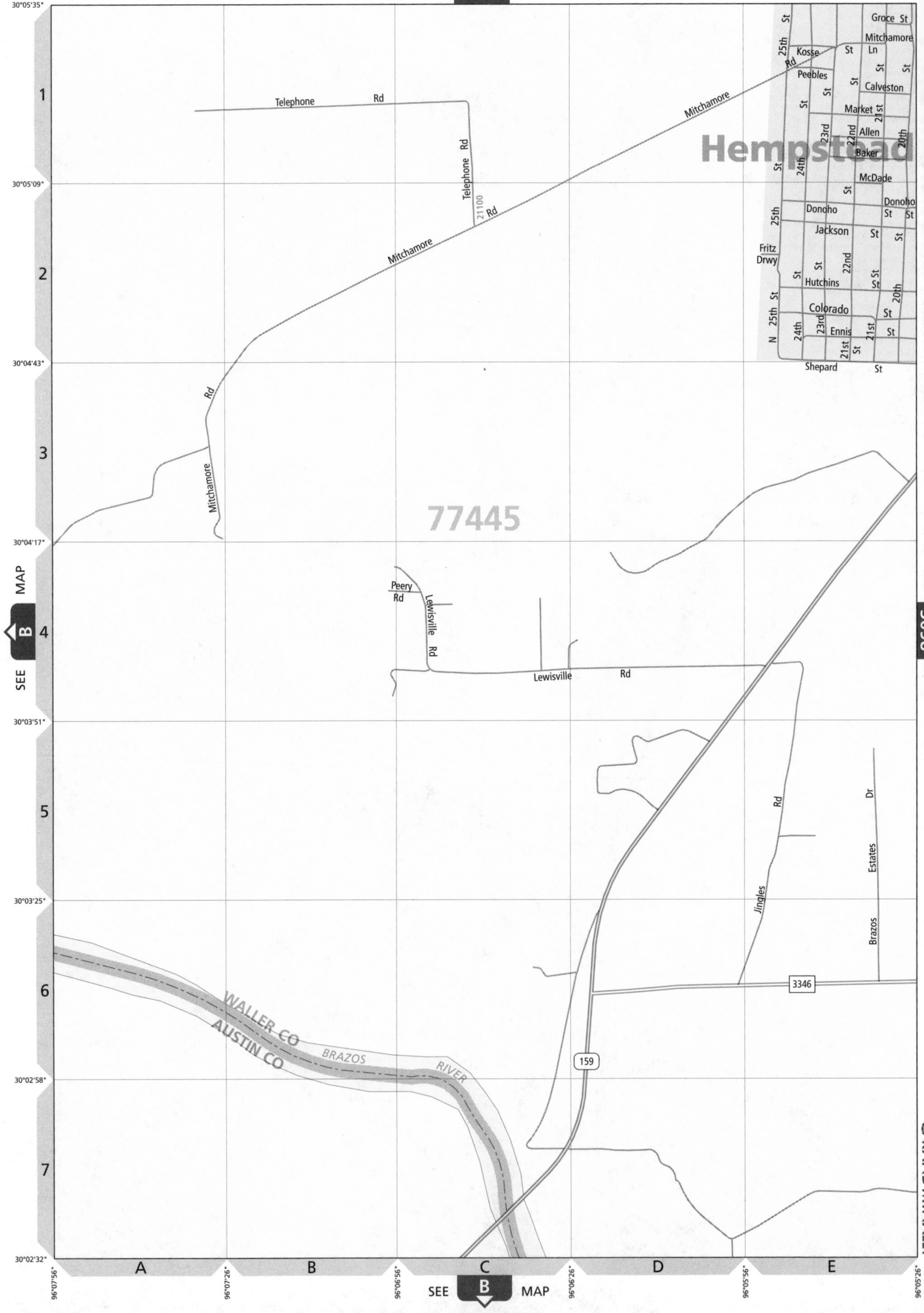
Hempstead
77445
Telephone Rd
Mitchamore Rd
21100
Peery Rd
Lewisville Rd
Jingles Rd
Brazos Estates Dr
3346
159
WALLER CO
AUSTIN CO
BRAZOS RIVER
Groce St
Mitchamore
Kosse St
Peebles St
Calveston
Market St
Allen
Baker
McDade
Donoho St
Jackson St
Hutchins St
Colorado St
Ennis St
Shepard St
Fritz Drwy
25th St
24th
23rd
22nd
21st
20th
N 25th St
30°05'35"
30°05'09"
30°04'43"
30°04'17"
30°03'51"
30°03'25"
30°02'58"
30°02'32"
96°07'56"
96°07'26"
96°06'56"
96°06'26"
96°05'56"
96°05'26"
1
2
3
4
5
6
7
A
B
C
D
E

SEE B MAP

SEE B MAP

1:24,000
1 in. = 2000 ft.
0 0.25 0.5
miles

SEE 2953 MAP

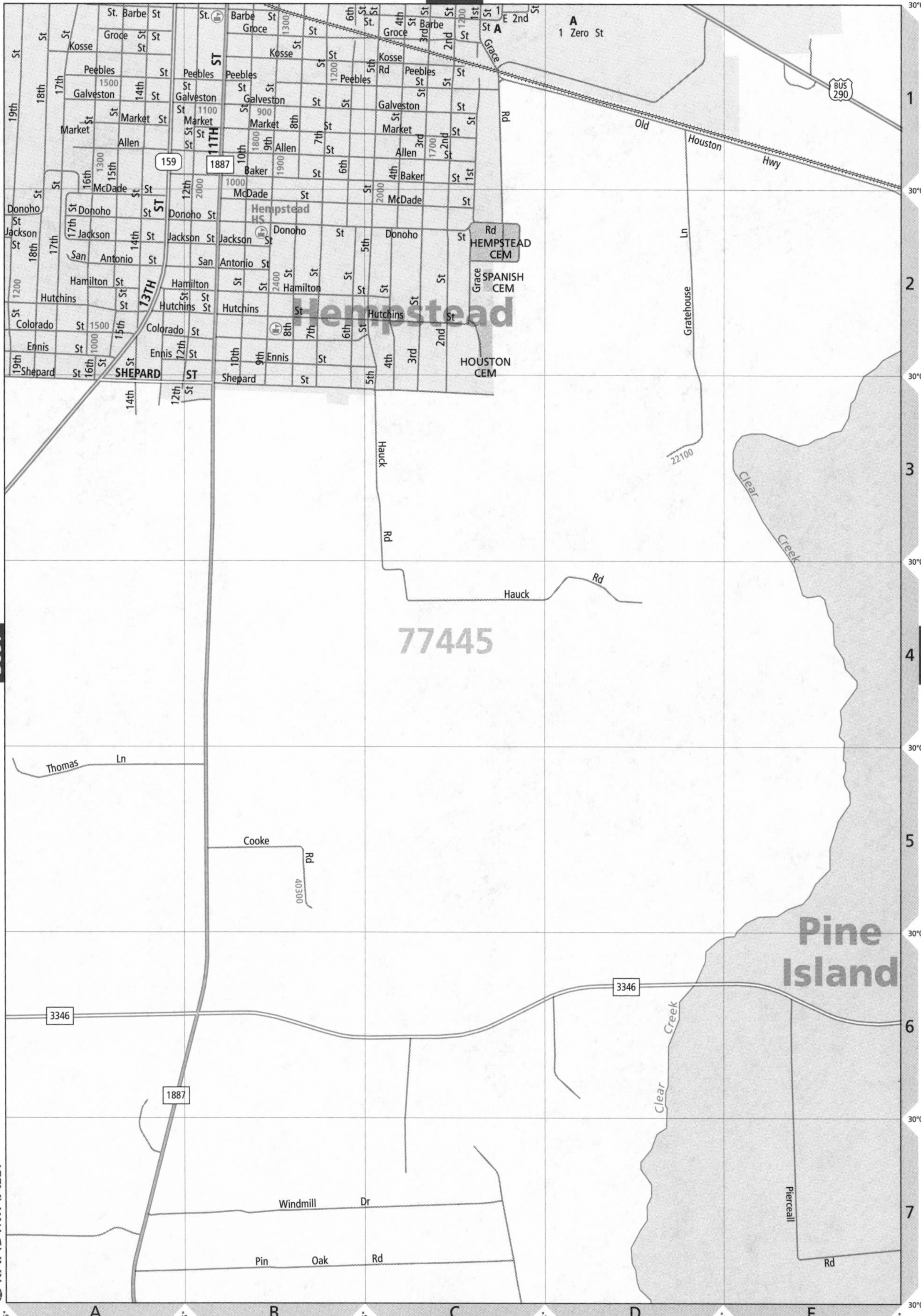
Hempstead
77445
Pine Island
HEMPSTEAD CEM
SPANISH CEM
HOUSTON CEM
Hempstead HS
Old Houston Hwy
Gratehouse Ln
Hauck Rd
Thomas Ln
Cooke Rd
Windmill Dr
Pin Oak Rd
Pierceall Rd
Clear Creek
Grace Rd
Zero St
Barbe St
Groce St
Kosse St
Peebles St
Galveston St
Market St
Allen St
Baker St
McDade St
Donoho St
Jackson St
San Antonio St
Hamilton St
Hutchins St
Colorado St
Ennis St
Shepard St
SHEPARD ST
11TH ST
13TH ST
159
1887
3346
BUS 290
22100
40300
1
2
3
4
5
6
7
A
B
C
D
E
30°05'35"
30°05'09"
30°04'42"
30°04'16"
30°03'50"
30°03'24"
30°02'58"
30°02'32"
96°05'26"
96°04'55"
96°04'25"
96°03'55"
96°03'25"
96°02'55"

SEE 3099 MAP

SEE 3097 MAP

SEE 3243 MAP

1:24,000
1 in. = 2000 ft.
0 0.25 0.5
miles

SEE 2954 MAP

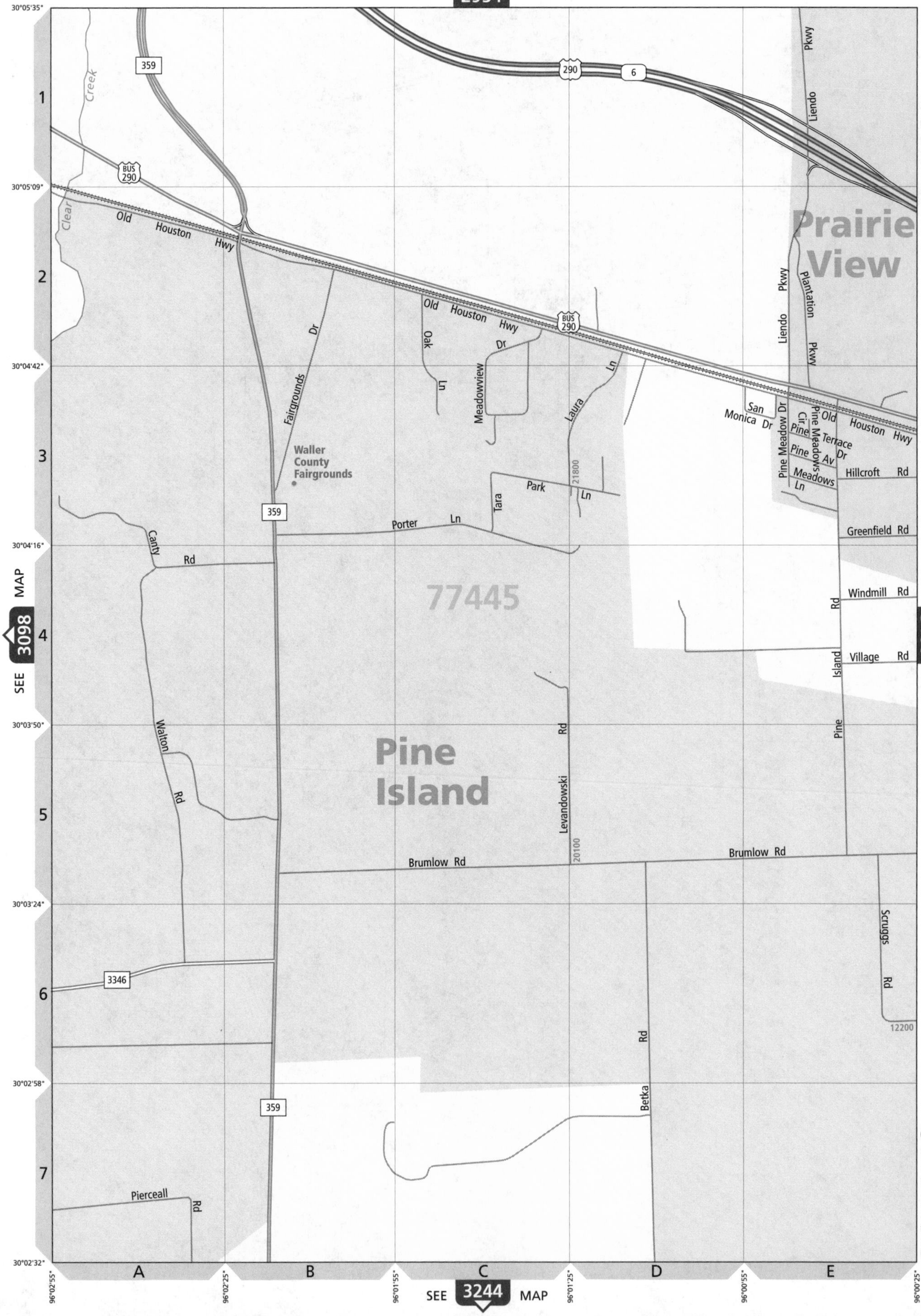
Prairie View
Pine Island
77445
Waller County Fairgrounds
Clear Creek
Old Houston Hwy
359
290
6
BUS 290
3346
Liendo Pkwy
Plantation Pkwy
Fairgrounds Dr
Oak Ln
Meadowview Dr
Laura Ln
Tara Park Ln
21800
Porter Ln
Canty Rd
Walton Rd
Levandowski Rd
20100
Brumlow Rd
Betka Rd
Pierceall Rd
Scruggs Rd
12200
San Monica Dr
Pine Meadow Dr
Pine Cir
Pine Meadows Dr
Pine Av
Pine Meadows Ln
Pine Terrace
Old Houston Hwy
Hillcroft Rd
Greenfield Rd
Windmill Rd
Village Rd
Pine Island Rd
1
2
3
4
5
6
7
A
B
C
D
E
30°05'35"
30°05'09"
30°04'42"
30°04'16"
30°03'50"
30°03'24"
30°02'58"
30°02'32"
96°02'55"
96°02'25"
96°01'55"
96°01'25"
96°00'55"
96°00'25"

SEE 3098 MAP

SEE 3100 MAP

SEE 3244 MAP

SEE 2955 MAP

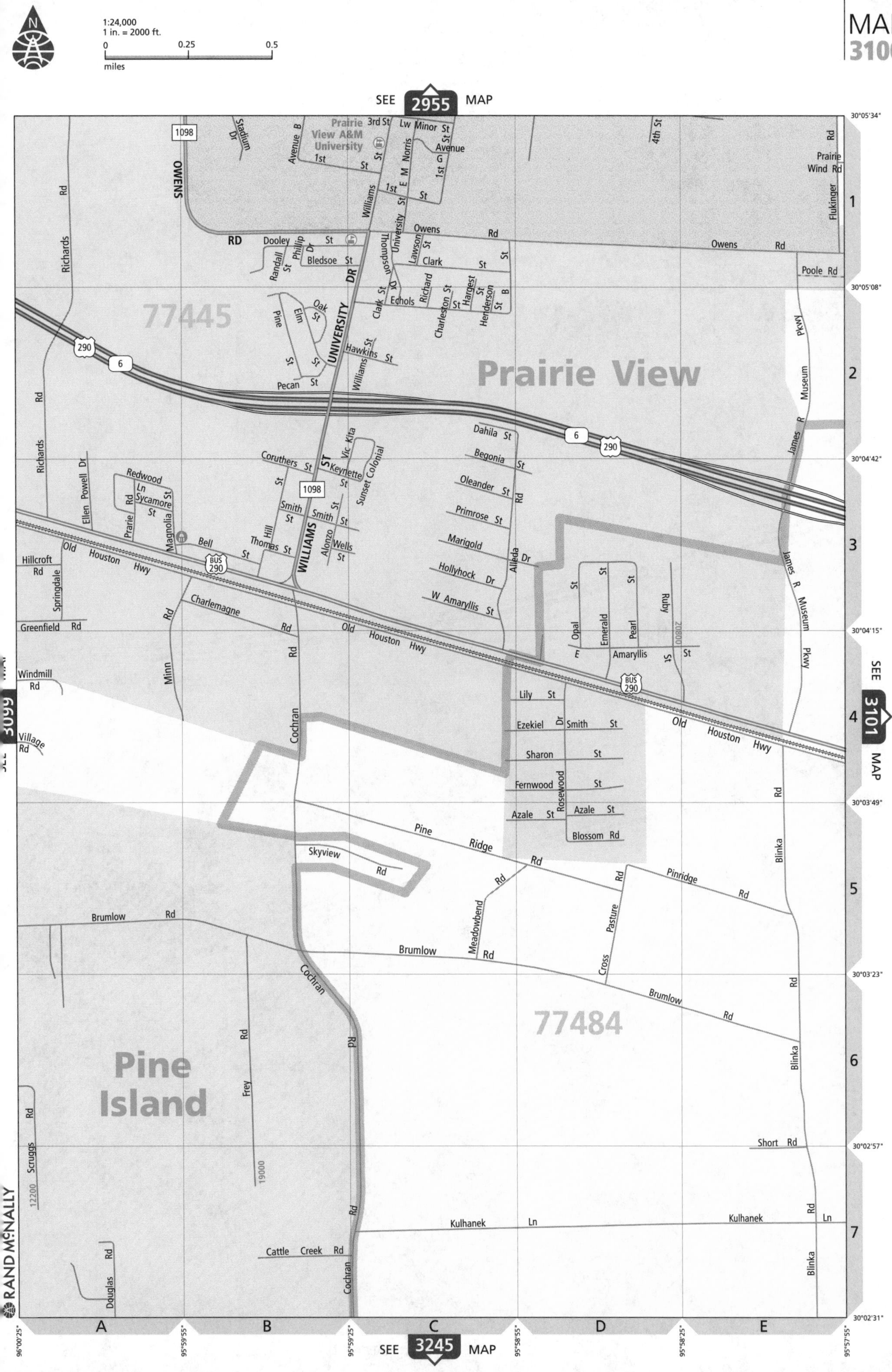
1:24,000
1 in. = 2000 ft.
0 0.25 0.5
miles
Prairie View A&M University
Prairie View
77445
77484
Pine Island
OWENS RD
Owens Rd
UNIVERSITY DR
WILLIAMS ST
Richards Rd
Stadium Dr
Avenue B
3rd St
Lw Minor St
Avenue G
1st St
E M Norris St
Williams St
University St
Dooley St
Phillip Dr
Randall St
Bledsoe St
Thompson Dr
Lawson St
Clark St
Clark St
Echols
Richard
Charleston St
Hargest St
Henderson St
B
Oak St
Elm St
Pine St
Hawkins St
Pecan St
4th St
Prairie Wind Rd
Flukinger Rd
Poole Rd
James R Museum Pkwy
Dahila St
Begonia St
Oleander St
Primrose St
Marigold
Hollyhock Dr
W Amaryllis St
Alleda Dr
Coruthers St
Vic Kita
Keynette St
Sunset Colonial
Smith St
Wells St
Alonzo
Hill
Thomas St
Redwood Ln
Sycamore St
Prairie Rd
Magnolia St
Ellen Powell Dr
Bell St
Old Houston Hwy
Hillcroft Rd
Springdale
Greenfield Rd
Charlemagne Rd
Minn Rd
Windmill Rd
Village Rd
Cochran Rd
Opal St
Emerald St
Pearl St
Ruby
20800
E Amaryllis St
Lily St
Ezekiel Dr
Smith St
Sharon St
Fernwood St
Rosewood
Azale St
Azale St
Blossom Rd
Pine Ridge Rd
Skyview Rd
Meadowbend Rd
Pinridge Rd
Cross Pasture Rd
Blinka Rd
Brumlow Rd
Frey Rd
19000
Scruggs Rd
12200
Short Rd
Kulhanek Ln
Cattle Creek Rd
Douglas Rd
1098
290
6
BUS 290
30°05'34"
30°05'08"
30°04'42"
30°04'15"
30°03'49"
30°03'23"
30°02'57"
30°02'31"
96°00'25"
95°59'55"
95°59'25"
95°58'55"
95°58'25"
95°57'55"
A B C D E
1 2 3 4 5 6 7

SEE 3101 MAP

SEE 3099 MAP

SEE 3245 MAP

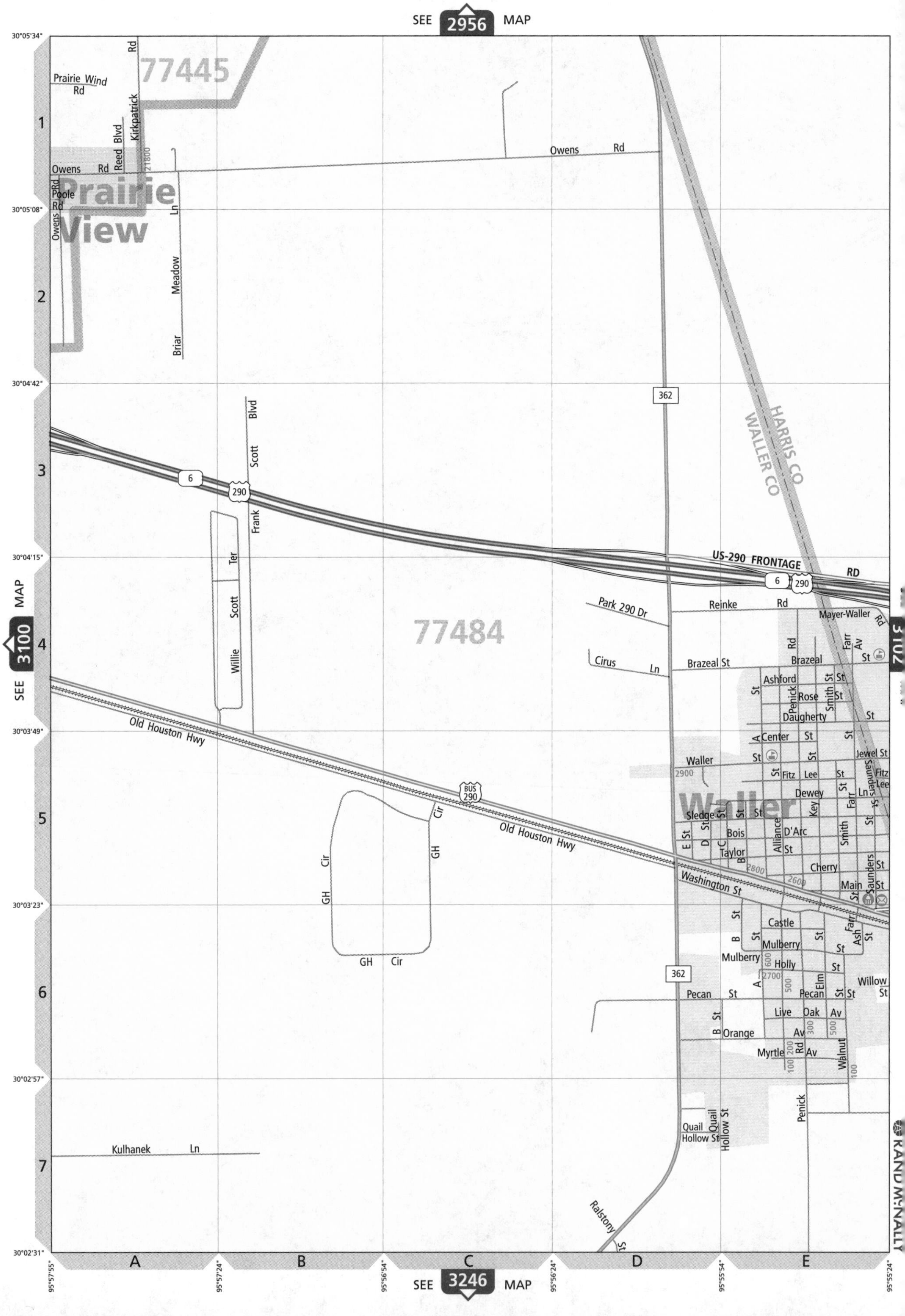
1:24,000
1 in. = 2000 ft.
0 0.25 0.5
miles
SEE 2956 MAP
77445
Prairie Wind Rd
Kirkpatrick Rd
Reed Blvd
Owens Rd
Poole Rd
Owens Rd
Prairie View
Meadow Ln
Briar
Owens Rd
Scott Blvd
Frank
Scott Ter
Willie
6
290
362
HARRIS CO
WALLER CO
US-290 FRONTAGE RD
77484
Park 290 Dr
Reinke Rd
Mayer-Waller Rd
Cirus Ln
Brazeal St
Old Houston Hwy
BUS 290
GH Cir
Old Houston Hwy
Washington St
Waller
Pecan St
Orange
Myrtle
Quail Hollow St
Penick
Kulhanek Ln
Ralston St
SEE 3100 MAP
A
B
C
D
E
1
2
3
4
5
6
7
30°05'34"
30°05'08"
30°04'42"
30°04'15"
30°03'49"
30°03'23"
30°02'57"
30°02'31"
95°57'55"
95°57'24"
95°56'54"
95°56'24"
95°55'54"
95°55'24"
SEE 3246 MAP
RAND McNALLY

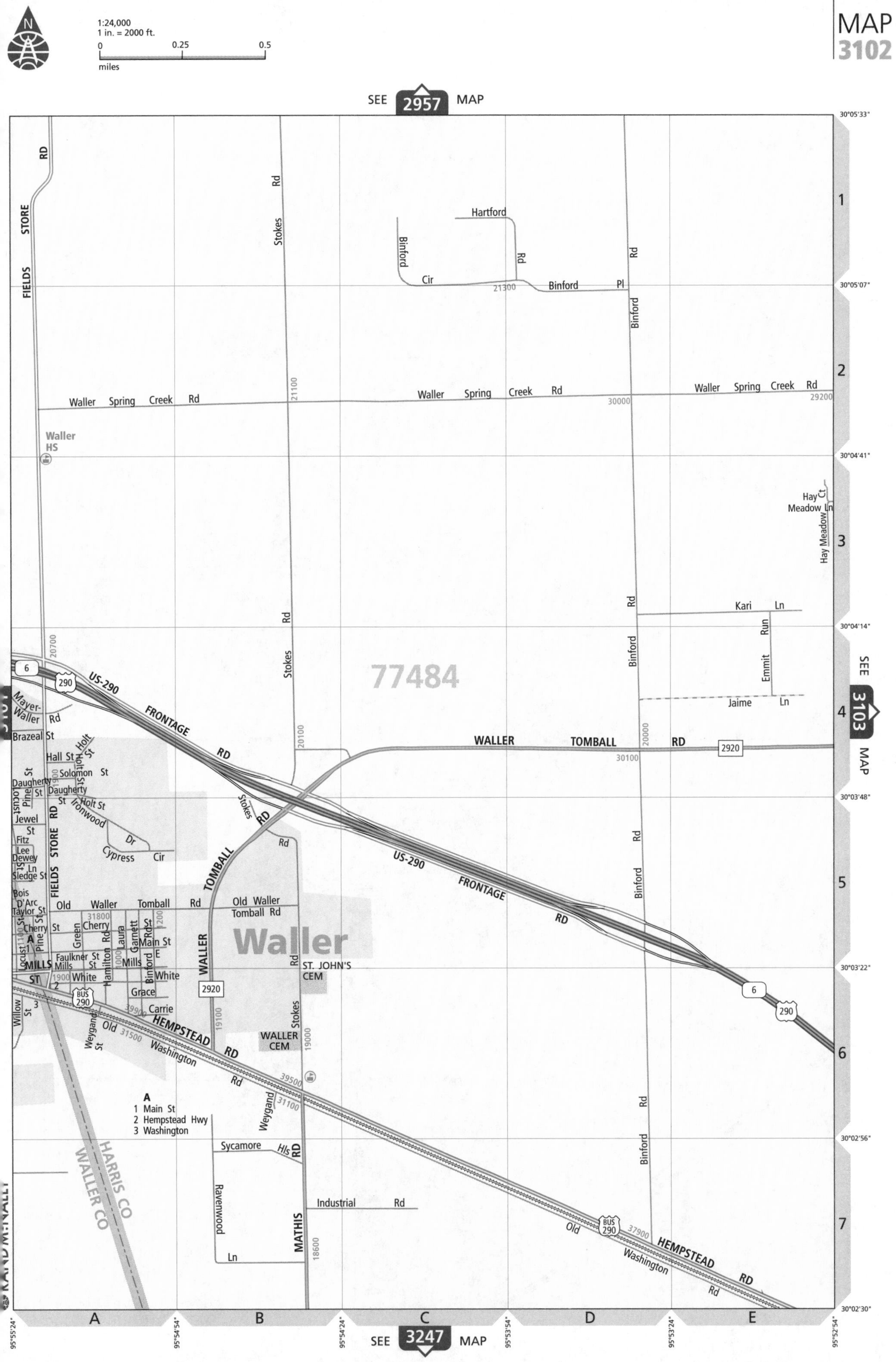
1:24,000
1 in. = 2000 ft.
0 0.25 0.5
miles
SEE 2957 MAP
SEE 3103 MAP
SEE 3247 MAP
FIELDS STORE RD
Stokes Rd
Hartford
Binford Cir
Rd
Binford Pl
Binford Rd
Waller Spring Creek Rd
Waller HS
Hay Meadow Ct
Hay Meadow Ln
Kari Ln
Emmit Run
Jaime Ln
77484
US-290 FRONTAGE RD
WALLER TOMBALL RD
2920
Mayer-Waller Rd
Brazeal St
Hall St
Holt St
Solomon St
Daugherty St
Pine St
Locust St
Ironwood Dr
Cypress Cir
Jewel St
Fitz St
Lee Ln
Dewey St
Sledge St
Bois D'Arc St
Taylor St
Old Waller Tomball Rd
Cherry St
Green St
Hamilton Rd
Laura St
Garnett Rd
Main St
Binford St
Faulkner St
Mills St
MILLS ST
White St
Grace St
Carrie St
Willow St
Weygand St
Old Washington Rd
HEMPSTEAD RD
Waller
ST. JOHN'S CEM
WALLER CEM
Stokes Rd
Weygand Rd
A
1 Main St
2 Hempstead Hwy
3 Washington
Sycamore Hls RD
Ravenwood Ln
MATHIS RD
Industrial Rd
HARRIS CO
WALLER CO
6
290
BUS 290
A B C D E
1 2 3 4 5 6 7

1:24,000
1 in. = 2000 ft.
0 0.25 0.5
miles

SEE 2958 MAP

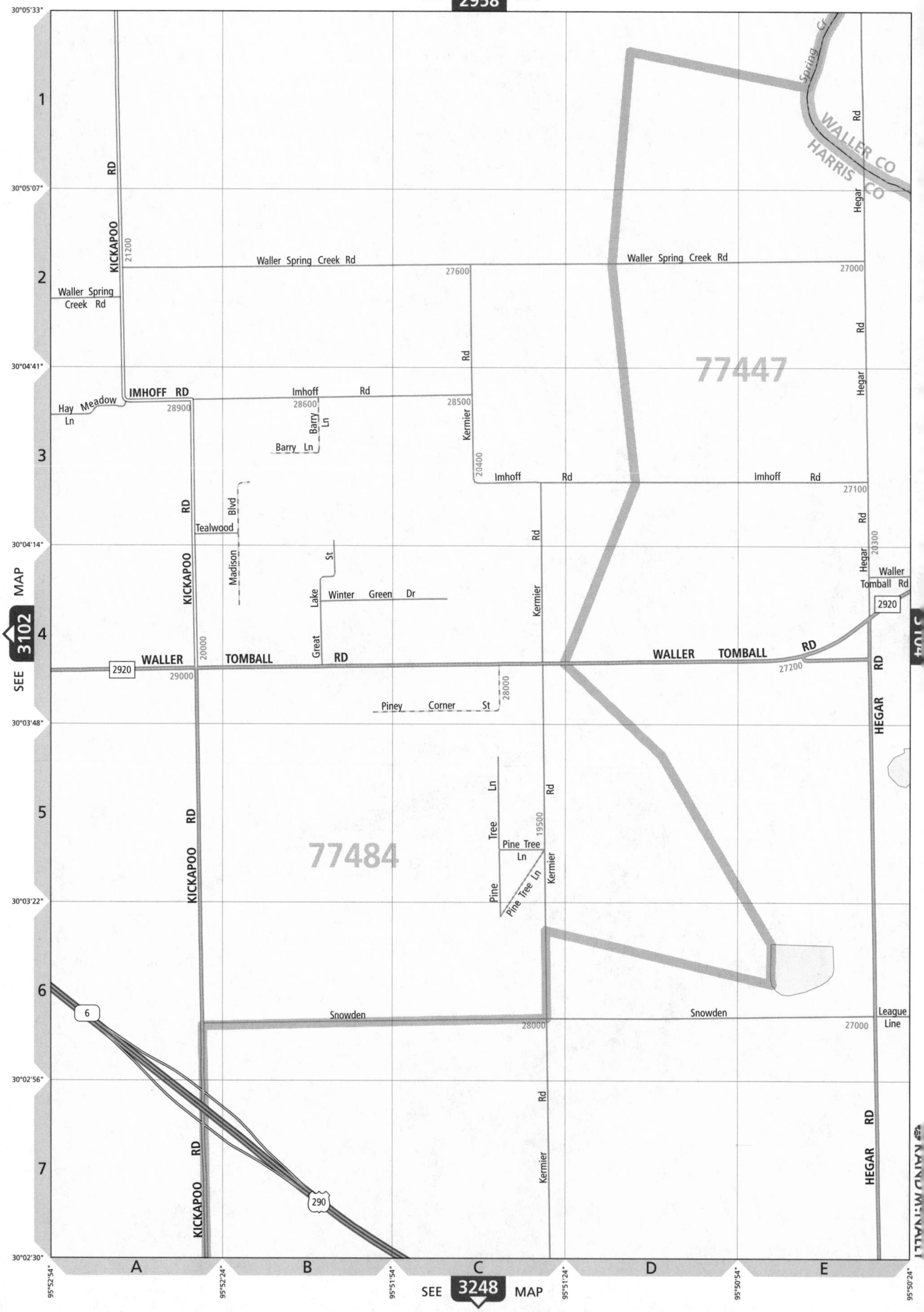
Waller Spring Creek Rd
KICKAPOO RD
21200
27600
27000
Hegar Rd
Spring Cr
WALLER CO
HARRIS CO
77447
Kermier Rd
Hay Meadow Ln
IMHOFF RD
Imhoff Rd
28900
28600
28500
Barry Ln
20400
27100
Tealwood
Madison Blvd
Lake St
Winter Green Dr
Great
20300
Waller Tomball Rd
2920
WALLER TOMBALL RD
20000
29000
27200
HEGAR RD
Piney Corner St
28000
77484
Pine Tree Ln
19500
6
Snowden
League Line
290
1
2
3
4
5
6
7
A
B
C
D
E
30°05'33"
30°05'07"
30°04'41"
30°04'14"
30°03'48"
30°03'22"
30°02'56"
30°02'30"
95°52'54"
95°52'24"
95°51'54"
95°51'24"
95°50'54"
95°50'24"

SEE 3102 MAP

SEE 3248 MAP

1:24,000
1 in. = 2000 ft.
0 0.25 0.5
miles

SEE 2959 MAP

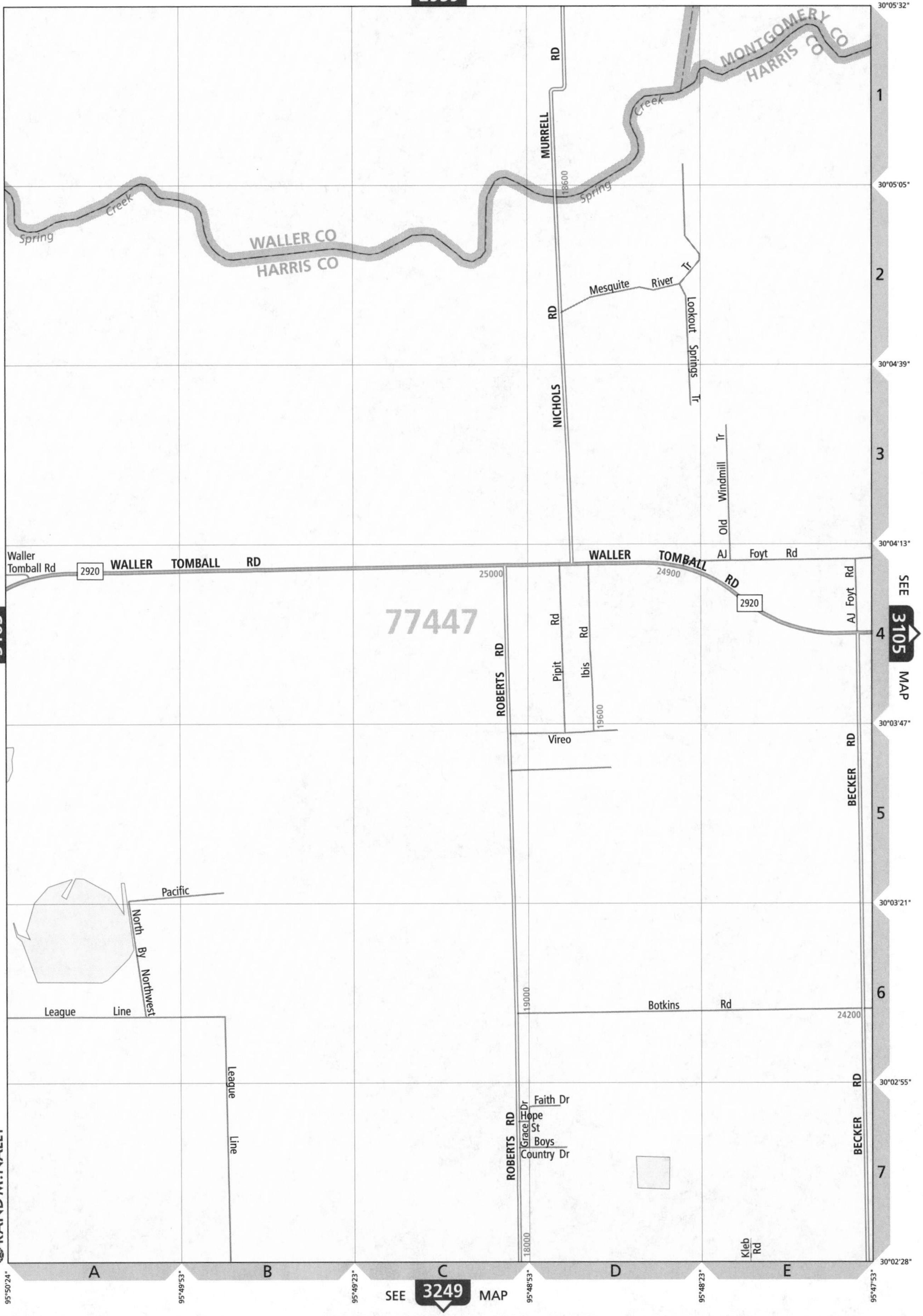
MURRELL RD
MONTGOMERY CO
HARRIS CO
Spring Creek
WALLER CO
HARRIS CO
18600
Mesquite River Tr
NICHOLS RD
Lookout Springs Tr
Old Windmill Tr
Waller Tomball Rd
2920
WALLER TOMBALL RD
25000
24900
AJ Foyt Rd
77447
ROBERTS RD
Pipit Rd
Ibis Rd
19600
Vireo
BECKER RD
Pacific
North By Northwest
League Line
19000
Botkins Rd
24200
Faith Dr
Grace Dr
Hope St
Boys Country Dr
18000
Kleb Rd
30°05'32"
30°05'05"
30°04'39"
30°04'13"
30°03'47"
30°03'21"
30°02'55"
30°02'28"
1
2
3
4
5
6
7
A
B
C
D
E
95°50'24"
95°49'53"
95°49'23"
95°48'53"
95°48'23"
95°47'53"

SEE 3105 MAP

SEE 3249 MAP

1:24,000
1 in. = 2000 ft.
0 0.25 0.5
miles

SEE 2960 MAP

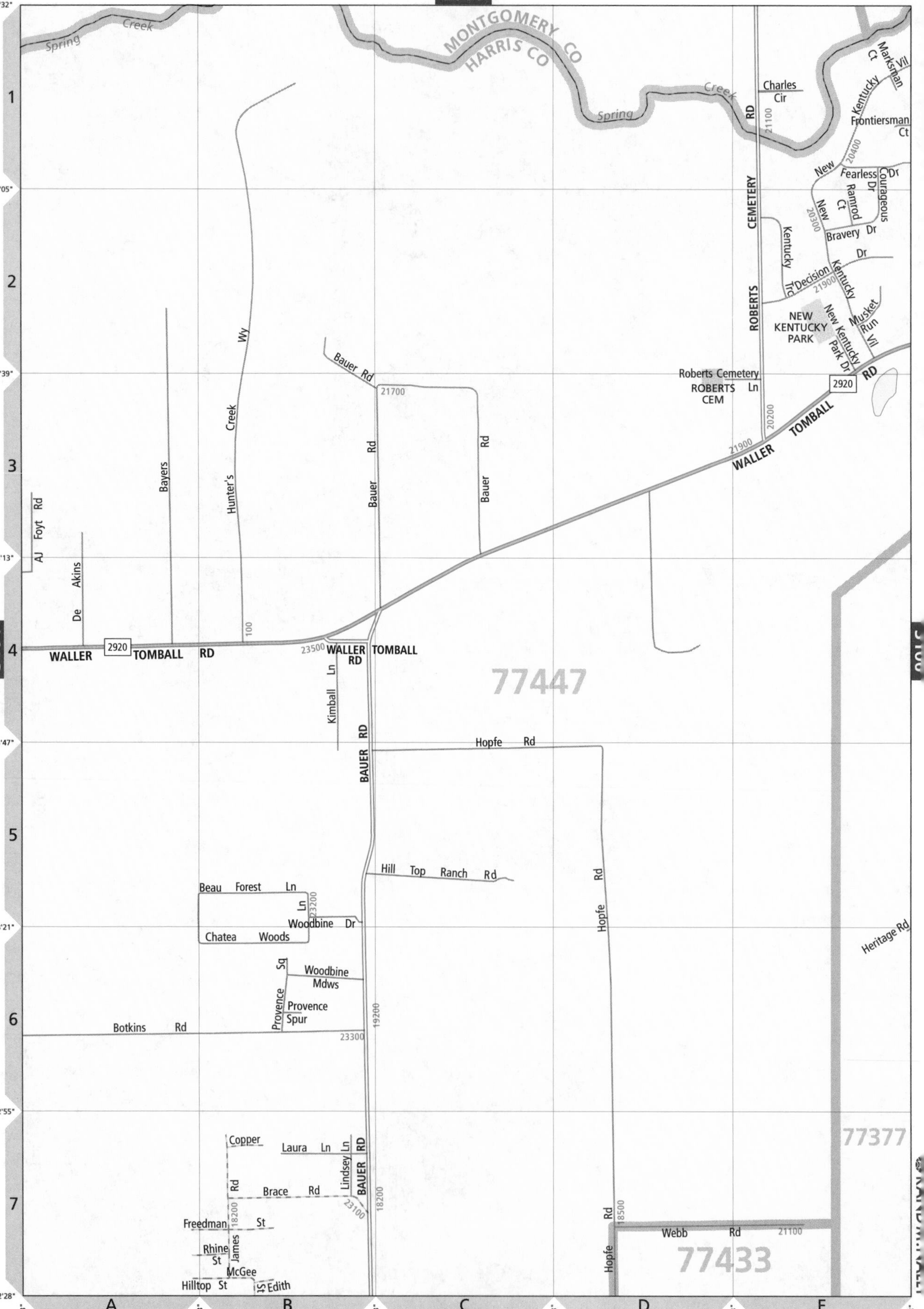
Spring Creek
MONTGOMERY CO
HARRIS CO
Charles Cir
ROBERTS CEMETERY RD
21100
Marksman Ct
Vil
Kentucky
Frontiersman Ct
20400
New
Fearless Dr
Courageous
Ramrod Ct
New
20300
Bravery Dr
Kentucky Trc
Decision Dr
21900
Kentucky
NEW KENTUCKY PARK
New Kentucky Park Dr
Musket Run Vil
Roberts Cemetery Ln
ROBERTS CEM
2920
RD
TOMBALL
WALLER
21900
20200
Bauer Rd
21700
Bauer Rd
Bauer Rd
Hunter's Creek Wy
Bayers
AJ Foyt Rd
De Akins
100
WALLER 2920 TOMBALL RD
23500
WALLER TOMBALL RD
Kimball Ln
77447
BAUER RD
Hopfe Rd
Hill Top Ranch Rd
Hopfe Rd
Beau Forest Ln
Ln
23200
Woodbine Dr
Chatea Woods
Heritage Rd
Sq
Woodbine Mdws
Provence
Provence Spur
Botkins Rd
19200
23300
77377
Copper
Laura Ln
Ln
Lindsey
BAUER RD
Rd
Brace Rd
23100
18200
18200
Freedman St
Rhine St
James
McGee
Hilltop St
St Edith
Rd
Hopfe
18500
Webb Rd
21100
77433
A B C D E
1 2 3 4 5 6 7
30°05'32" 30°05'05" 30°04'39" 30°04'13" 30°03'47" 30°03'21" 30°02'55" 30°02'28"
95°47'53" 95°47'23" 95°46'53" 95°46'23" 95°45'53" 95°45'23"

SEE 3104 MAP

SEE 3250 MAP

1:24,000
1 in. = 2000 ft.
0 0.25 0.5
miles

SEE 2961 MAP

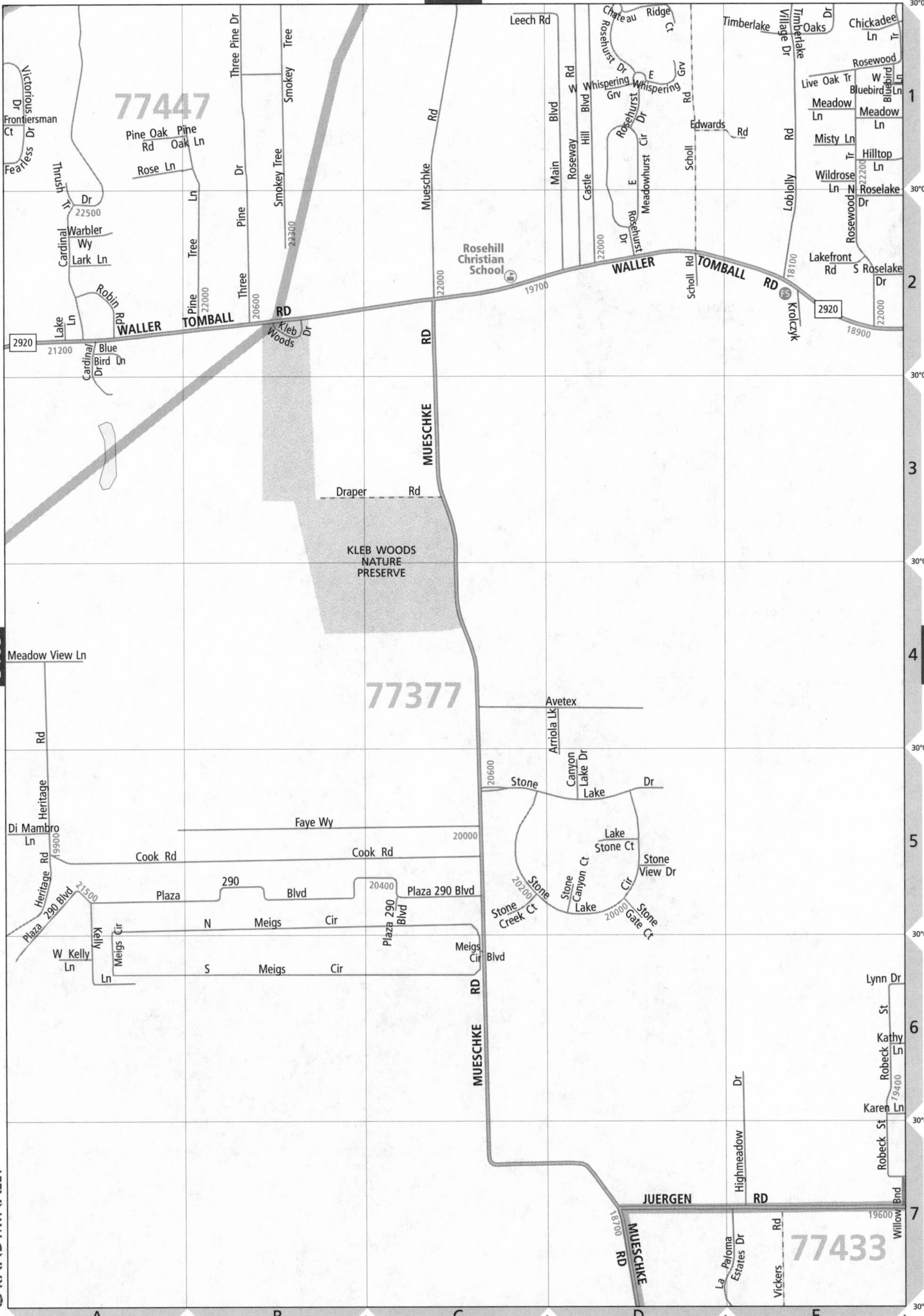

77447
77377
77433
Victorious Dr
Frontiersman Ct
Fearless Dr
Thrush Tr
Dr
22500
Cardinal
Warbler Wy
Lark Ln
Robin Rd
Lake Ln
Cardinal Dr
Blue Bird Ln
2920
21200
WALLER TOMBALL RD
Kleb Woods Dr
Pine Oak Rd
Pine Oak Ln
Rose Ln
Pine Tree Ln
22000
Three Pine Dr
20600
Smokey Tree
22300
Mueschke Rd
22000
MUESCHKE RD
Rosehill Christian School
19700
Leech Rd
Main Blvd
Roseway Hill Blvd
Castle
Chateau Ridge Ct
Rosehurst Dr
W Whispering Grv
E Whispering Grv
Rd
Rosehurst Cir
E Meadowhurst Dr
22000
Edwards Rd
Scholl Rd
Timberlake
Village Dr
Timberlake Oaks Dr
Loblolly Rd
18100
Krolczyk
Chickadee Ln
Tr
Rosewood
Live Oak Tr
W Bluebird Ln
Bluebird
Meadow Ln
Meadow Ln
Misty Ln
Hilltop Ln
Tr
Wildrose Ln
N Roselake Dr
Rosewood
22200
Lakefront Rd
S Roselake Dr
22000
18900
Draper Rd
KLEB WOODS NATURE PRESERVE
Meadow View Ln
Heritage Rd
Di Mambro Ln
19900
Heritage Rd
Plaza 290 Blvd
21500
Cook Rd
Cook Rd
Faye Wy
20000
Plaza 290 Blvd
20400
Plaza 290 Blvd
Plaza 290 Blvd
N Meigs Cir
S Meigs Cir
Kelly Ln
W Kelly Ln
Meigs Cir
Meigs Cir Blvd
Avetex
Arriola Lk
Canyon Lake Dr
20600
Stone Lake Dr
Lake Stone Ct
Stone View Dr
Stone Canyon Ct
Stone Lake Cir
20200
Stone Creek Ct
20000
Stone Gate Ct
MUESCHKE RD
Lynn Dr
Robeck St
Kathy Ln
19400
Karen Ln
Robeck St
Highmeadow Dr
JUERGEN RD
19600
Willow Bnd
18700
MUESCHKE RD
La Paloma Estates Dr
Vickers Rd
1
2
3
4
5
6
7
A
B
C
D
E
30°05'30"
30°05'04"
30°04'38"
30°04'12"
30°03'46"
30°03'19"
30°02'53"
30°02'27"
95°45'23"
95°44'53"
95°44'23"
95°43'53"
95°43'23"
95°42'53"

SEE 3107 MAP

SEE 3251 MAP

1:24,000
1 in. = 2000 ft.
0 0.25 0.5
miles

SEE 2962 MAP

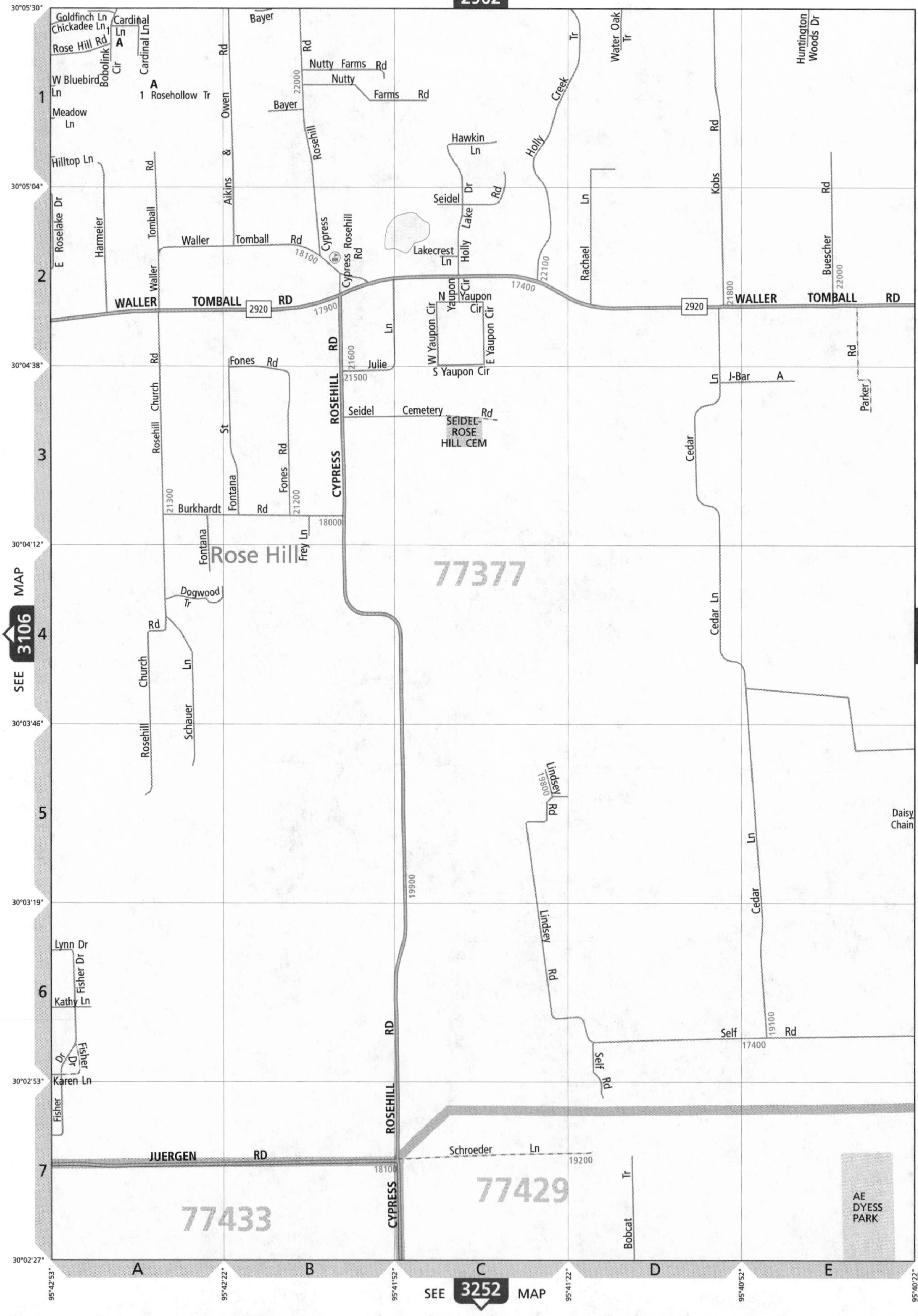
WALLER TOMBALL RD
2920
ROSEHILL RD
CYPRESS ROSEHILL RD
JUERGEN RD
Rose Hill
77377
77429
77433
SEIDEL-ROSE HILL CEM
AE DYESS PARK
Goldfinch Ln
Chickadee Ln
Cardinal Ln
Rose Hill Rd
Bobolink Cir
W Bluebird Ln
1 Rosehollow Tr
Meadow Ln
Hilltop Ln
E Roselake Dr
Harmeier
Tomball Rd
Waller
Aikins & Owen Rd
Bayer
Nutty Farms Rd
Rosehill Rd
Cypress Rosehill Rd
Hawkin Ln
Seidel
Holly Lake Dr
Lakecrest Ln
Holly Creek Tr
N Yaupon Cir
W Yaupon Cir
E Yaupon Cir
S Yaupon Cir
Julie Ln
Water Oak Tr
Rachael Ln
Kobs Rd
Huntington Woods Dr
Buescher Rd
Parker Rd
J-Bar Ln
Cedar Ln
Fones Rd
Fontana St
Burkhardt Rd
Frey Ln
Seidel Cemetery Rd
Rosehill Church Rd
Dogwood Tr
Schauer Ln
Lindsey Rd
Self Rd
Daisy Chain
Lynn Dr
Fisher Dr
Kathy Ln
Karen Ln
Schroeder Ln
Bobcat Tr
A
B
C
D
E
1
2
3
4
5
6
7
30°05'30"
30°05'04"
30°04'38"
30°04'12"
30°03'46"
30°03'19"
30°02'53"
30°02'27"
95°42'53"
95°42'22"
95°41'52"
95°41'22"
95°40'52"
95°40'22"

SEE 3106 MAP

SEE 3252 MAP

1:24,000
1 in. = 2000 ft.
0 0.25 0.5
miles

SEE 2963 MAP

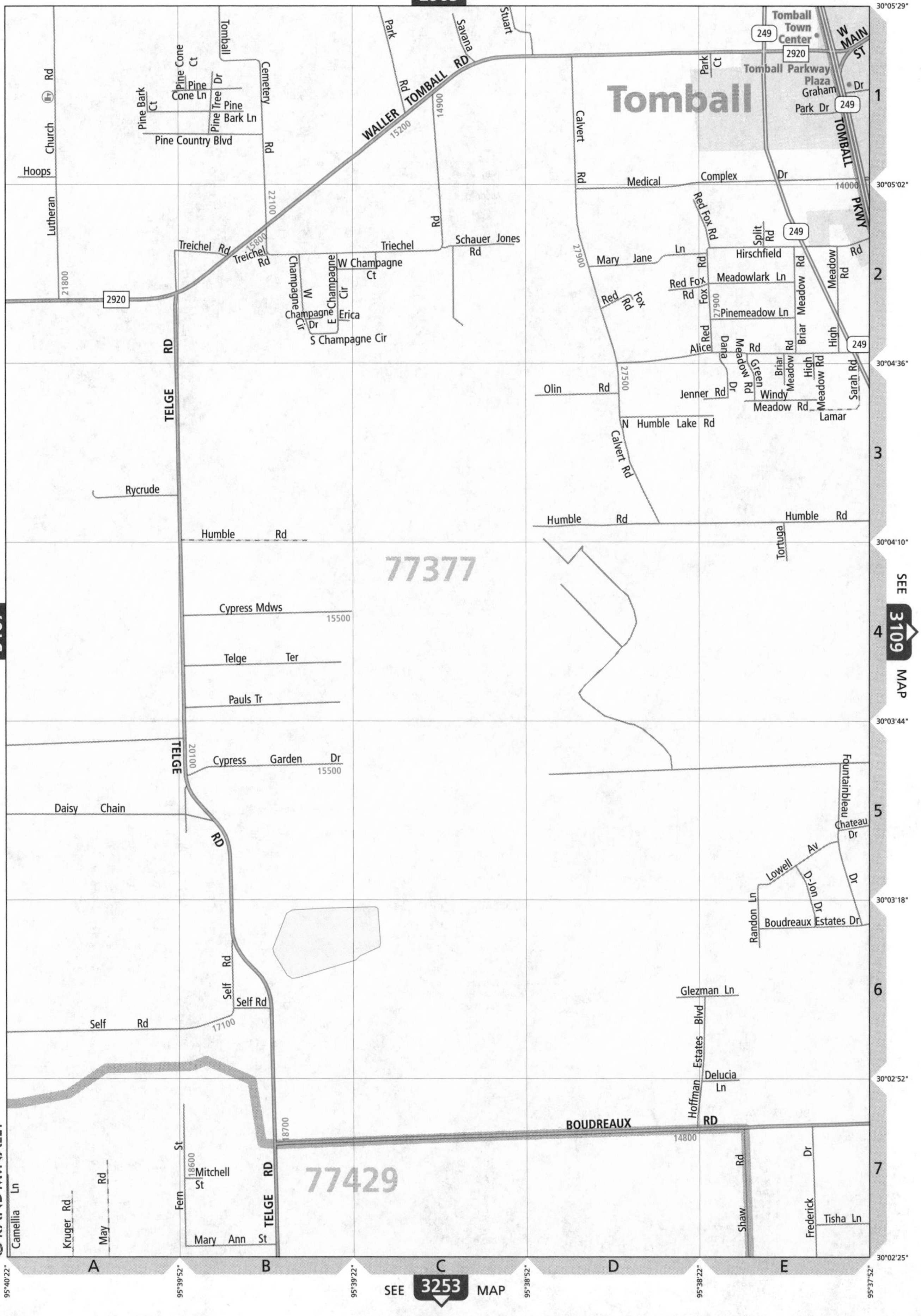
Tomball
Tomball Town Center
249
2920
W MAIN ST
Tomball Parkway Plaza
Graham Dr
Park Dr
TOMBALL PKWY
Park Ct
Stuart
Savana
Park Rd
WALLER TOMBALL RD
15200
14900
Tomball Cemetery Rd
Pine Cone Ct
Pine Cone Ln
Pine Tree Dr
Pine Bark Ln
Pine Bark Ct
Pine Country Blvd
Church Rd
Hoops
Lutheran
21800
22100
Treichel Rd
15800
Triechel
W Champagne Ct
W Champagne Cir
E Champagne Cir
Champagne Dr
Erica
S Champagne Cir
Schauer Jones Rd
Calvert Rd
Medical Complex Dr
14000
Red Fox Rd
Split Rd
Hirschfield
Mary Jane Ln
27900
Meadowlark Ln
Pinemeadow Ln
Meadow Rd
Briar Meadow Rd
High Meadow Rd
Alice
Dana Dr
Green Meadow Rd
Windy Meadow Rd
Briar Meadow
Sarah Rd
Lamar
Jenner Rd
Olin Rd
27500
N Humble Lake Rd
Calvert Rd
TELGE RD
Rycrude
Humble Rd
Tortuga
77377
Cypress Mdws
15500
Telge Ter
Pauls Tr
Cypress Garden Dr
20100
Daisy Chain
Fountainbleau
Chateau Dr
Lowell Av
D-Jon Dr
Randon Ln
Boudreaux Estates Dr
Self Rd
17100
Glezman Ln
Hoffman Estates Blvd
Delucia Ln
BOUDREAUX RD
14800
18700
77429
Shaw Rd
Frederick Dr
Tisha Ln
Fern St
18600
Mitchell St
Mary Ann St
Camellia Ln
Kruger Rd
May Rd
30°05'29"
30°05'02"
30°04'36"
30°04'10"
30°03'44"
30°03'18"
30°02'52"
30°02'25"
95°40'22"
95°39'52"
95°39'22"
95°38'52"
95°38'22"
95°37'52"
A
B
C
D
E
1
2
3
4
5
6
7
3107
RAND McNALLY

SEE 3109 MAP

SEE 3253 MAP

1:24,000
1 in. = 2000 ft.
0 0.25 0.5
miles

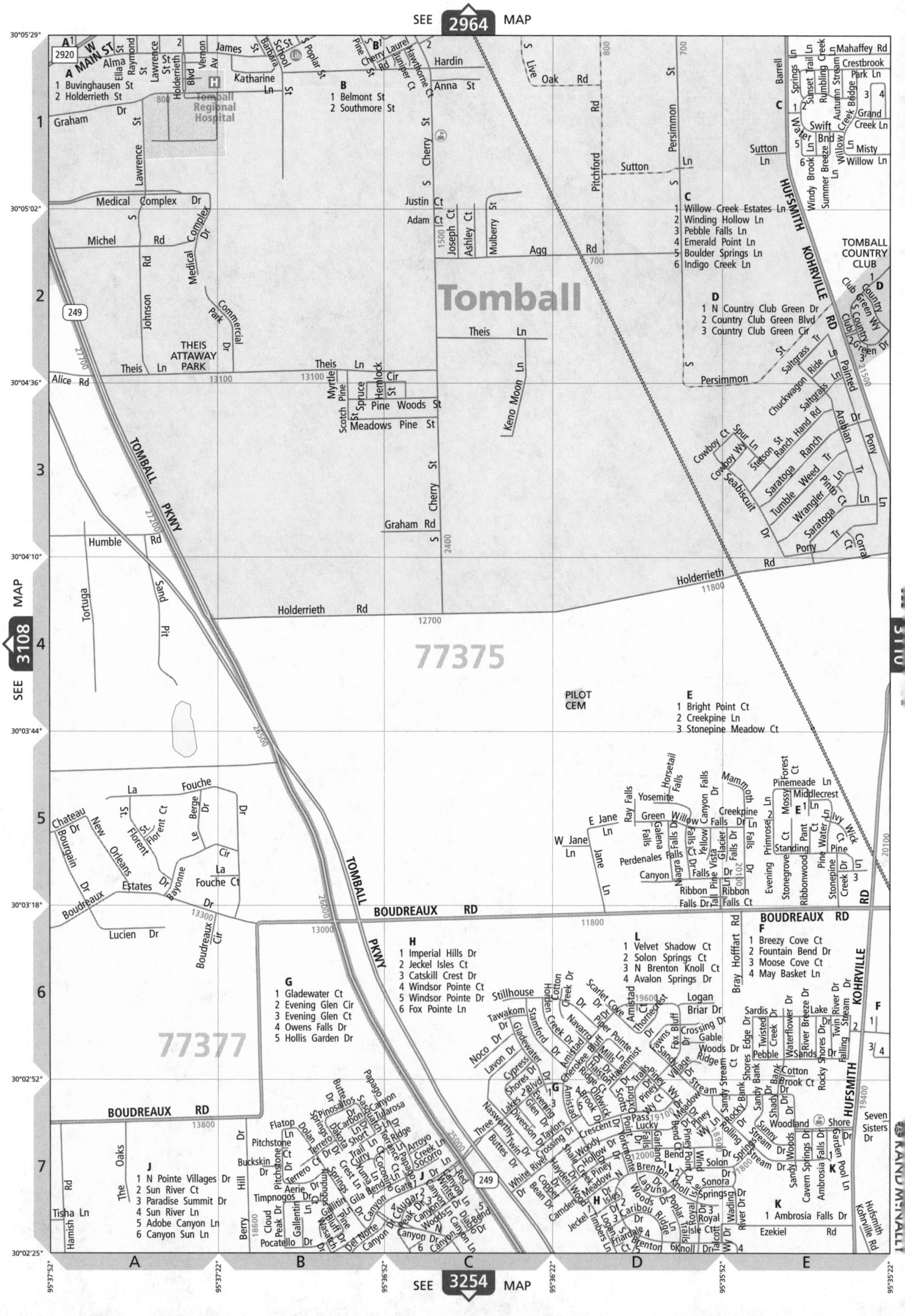
SEE 2964 MAP
SEE 3254 MAP
SEE 3108 MAP
Tomball
77375
77377
TOMBALL REGIONAL HOSPITAL
THEIS ATTAWAY PARK
TOMBALL COUNTRY CLUB
PILOT CEM
TOMBALL PKWY
BOUDREAUX RD
HUFSMITH KOHRVILLE RD
Holderrieth Rd
Humble Rd
Alice Rd
Theis Ln
Medical Complex Dr
Michel Rd
Johnson Rd
Commercial Park Dr
Cherry St
Graham Rd
Graham Dr
Agg Rd
Pitchford Rd
Persimmon St
Sutton Ln
Live Oak Rd
Hardin
Anna St
James St
Katharine Ln
W MAIN ST
Keno Moon Ln
Sand Pit
Tortuga
Lucien Dr
Boudreaux Cir
Fouche Dr
La Fouche Ct
New Orleans Estates Dr
Chateau Bourgain Dr
Bray Hoffart Rd
The Oaks
Hill Dr
Berry
Hamish Rd
Tisha Ln
Ezekiel Rd
Stillhouse
Logan Briar Dr
A
1 Buvinghausen St
2 Holderrieth St
B
1 Belmont St
2 Southmore St
C
1 Willow Creek Estates Ln
2 Winding Hollow Ln
3 Pebble Falls Ln
4 Emerald Point Ln
5 Boulder Springs Ln
6 Indigo Creek Ln
D
1 N Country Club Green Dr
2 Country Club Green Blvd
3 Country Club Green Cir
E
1 Bright Point Ct
2 Creekpine Ln
3 Stonepine Meadow Ct
F
1 Breezy Cove Ct
2 Fountain Bend Dr
3 Moose Cove Ct
4 May Basket Ln
G
1 Gladewater Ct
2 Evening Glen Cir
3 Evening Glen Ct
4 Owens Falls Dr
5 Hollis Garden Dr
H
1 Imperial Hills Dr
2 Jeckel Isles Ct
3 Catskill Crest Dr
4 Windsor Pointe Ct
5 Windsor Pointe Dr
6 Fox Pointe Ln
J
1 N Pointe Villages Dr
2 Sun River Ct
3 Paradise Summit Dr
4 Sun River Ln
5 Adobe Canyon Ln
6 Canyon Sun Ln
K
1 Ambrosia Falls Dr
L
1 Velvet Shadow Ct
2 Solon Springs Ct
3 N Brenton Knoll Ct
4 Avalon Springs Dr
30°05'29"
30°05'02"
30°04'36"
30°04'10"
30°03'44"
30°03'18"
30°02'52"
30°02'25"
95°37'52"
95°37'22"
95°36'52"
95°36'22"
95°35'52"
95°35'22"

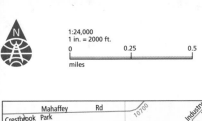

1:24,000
1 in. = 2000 ft.
0 0.25 0.5
miles

SEE 2965 MAP

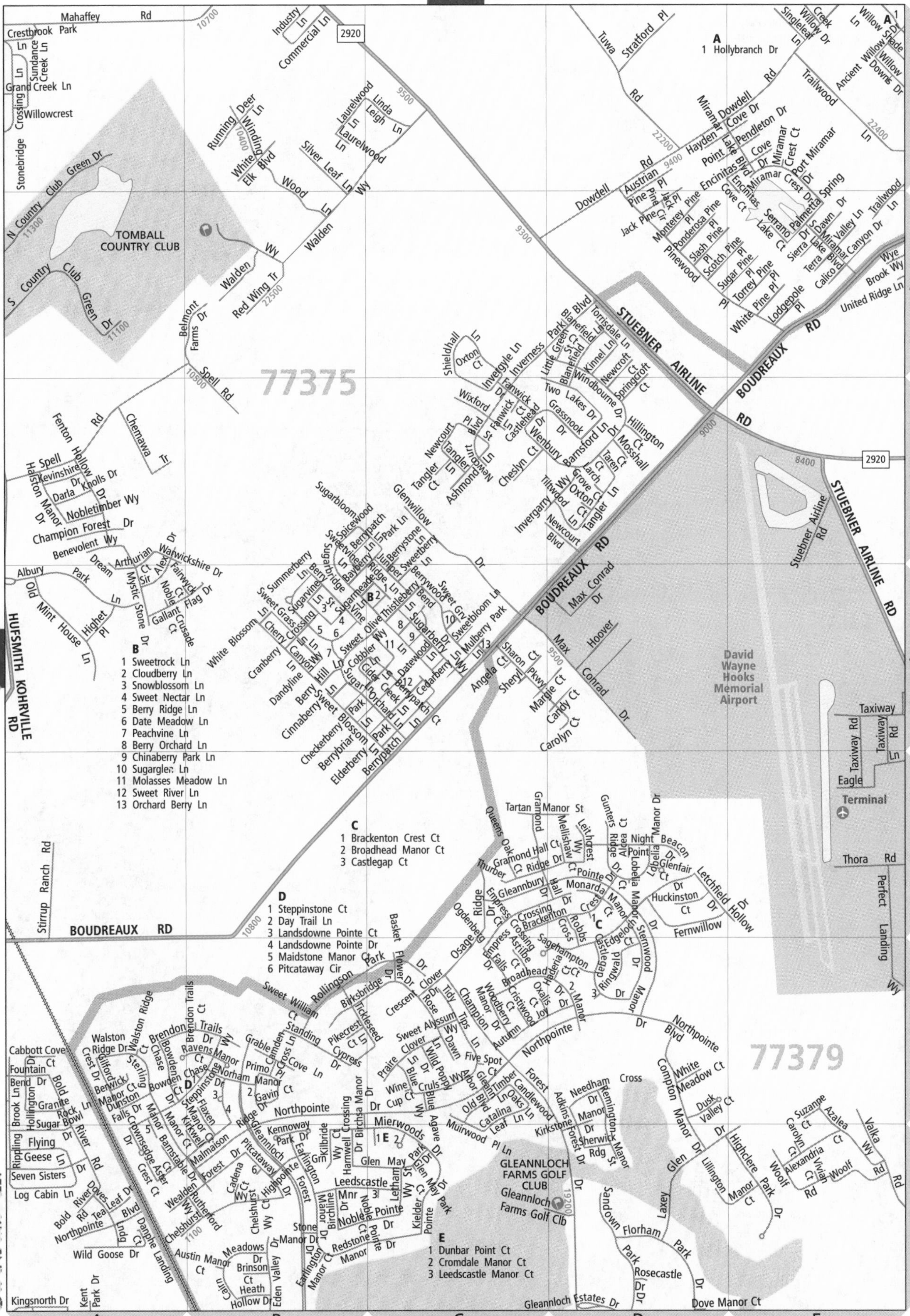
30°05'27"
30°05'01"
30°04'34"
30°04'08"
30°03'42"
30°03'16"
30°02'50"
30°02'24"
95°35'22"
95°34'51"
95°34'21"
95°33'51"
95°33'21"
95°32'51"
A
B
C
D
E
1
2
3
4
5
6
7
77375
77379
TOMBALL COUNTRY CLUB
David Wayne Hooks Memorial Airport
Terminal
GLEANNLOCH FARMS GOLF CLUB
2920
STUEBNER AIRLINE RD
BOUDREAUX RD
HUFSMITH KOHRVILLE RD
Mahaffey Rd
Spell Rd
Max Conrad Dr
Northpointe Blvd
A
1 Hollybranch Dr
B
1 Sweetrock Ln
2 Cloudberry Ln
3 Snowblossom Ln
4 Sweet Nectar Ln
5 Berry Ridge Ln
6 Date Meadow Ln
7 Peachvine Ln
8 Berry Orchard Ln
9 Chinaberry Park Ln
10 Sugarglen Ln
11 Molasses Meadow Ln
12 Sweet River Ln
13 Orchard Berry Ln
C
1 Brackenton Crest Ct
2 Broadhead Manor Ct
3 Castlegap Ct
D
1 Steppinstone Ct
2 Day Trail Ln
3 Landsdowne Pointe Ct
4 Landsdowne Pointe Dr
5 Maidstone Manor Ct
6 Pitcataway Cir
E
1 Dunbar Point Ct
2 Cromdale Manor Ct
3 Leedscastle Manor Ct

SEE 3111 MAP

SEE 3255 MAP

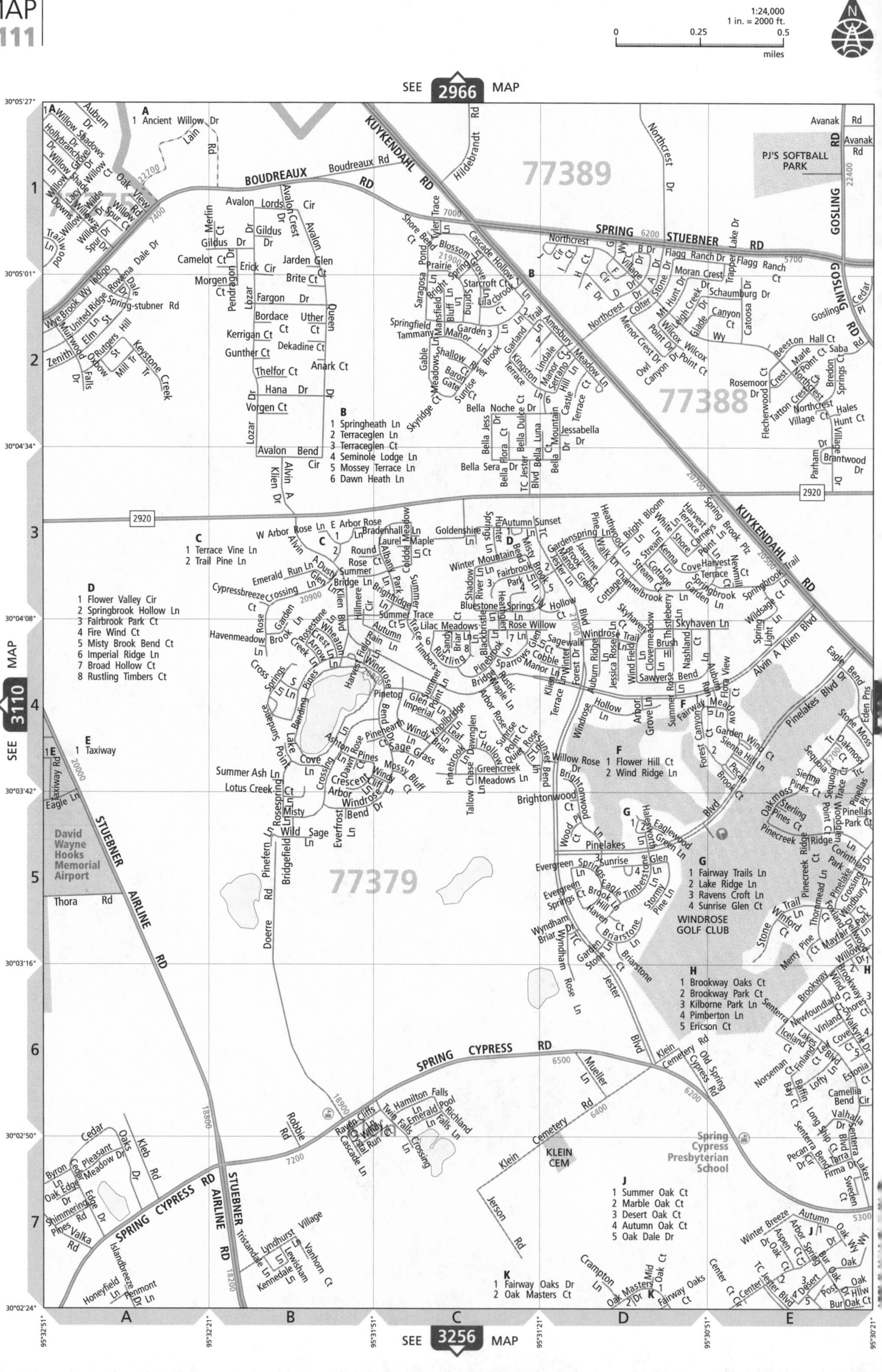
1:24,000
1 in. = 2000 ft.
0 0.25 0.5
miles
N
SEE 2966 MAP
SEE 3256 MAP
SEE 3110 MAP
77389
77388
77379
KUYKENDAHL RD
SPRING STUEBNER RD
BOUDREAUX RD
GOSLING RD
SPRING CYPRESS RD
STUEBNER AIRLINE RD
2920
PJ'S SOFTBALL PARK
David Wayne Hooks Memorial Airport
WINDROSE GOLF CLUB
KLEIN CEM
Spring Cypress Presbyterian School
A
1 Ancient Willow Dr
B
1 Springheath Ln
2 Terraceglen Ln
3 Terraceglen Ct
4 Seminole Lodge Ln
5 Mossey Terrace Ln
6 Dawn Heath Ln
C
1 Terrace Vine Ln
2 Trail Pine Ln
D
1 Flower Valley Cir
2 Springbrook Hollow Ln
3 Fairbrook Park Ct
4 Fire Wind Ct
5 Misty Brook Bend Ct
6 Imperial Ridge Ln
7 Broad Hollow Ct
8 Rustling Timbers Ct
E
1 Taxiway
F
1 Flower Hill Ct
2 Wind Ridge Ln
G
1 Fairway Trails Ln
2 Lake Ridge Ln
3 Ravens Croft Ln
4 Sunrise Glen Ct
H
1 Brookway Oaks Ct
2 Brookway Park Ct
3 Kilborne Park Ln
4 Pimberton Ln
5 Ericson Ct
J
1 Summer Oak Ct
2 Marble Oak Ct
3 Desert Oak Ct
4 Autumn Oak Ct
5 Oak Dale Dr
K
1 Fairway Oaks Dr
2 Oak Masters Ct
30°05'27"
30°05'01"
30°04'34"
30°04'08"
30°03'42"
30°03'16"
30°02'50"
30°02'24"
95°32'51"
95°32'21"
95°31'51"
95°31'21"
95°30'51"
95°30'21"

1:24,000
1 in. = 2000 ft.
0 0.25 0.5
miles

SEE 2967 MAP

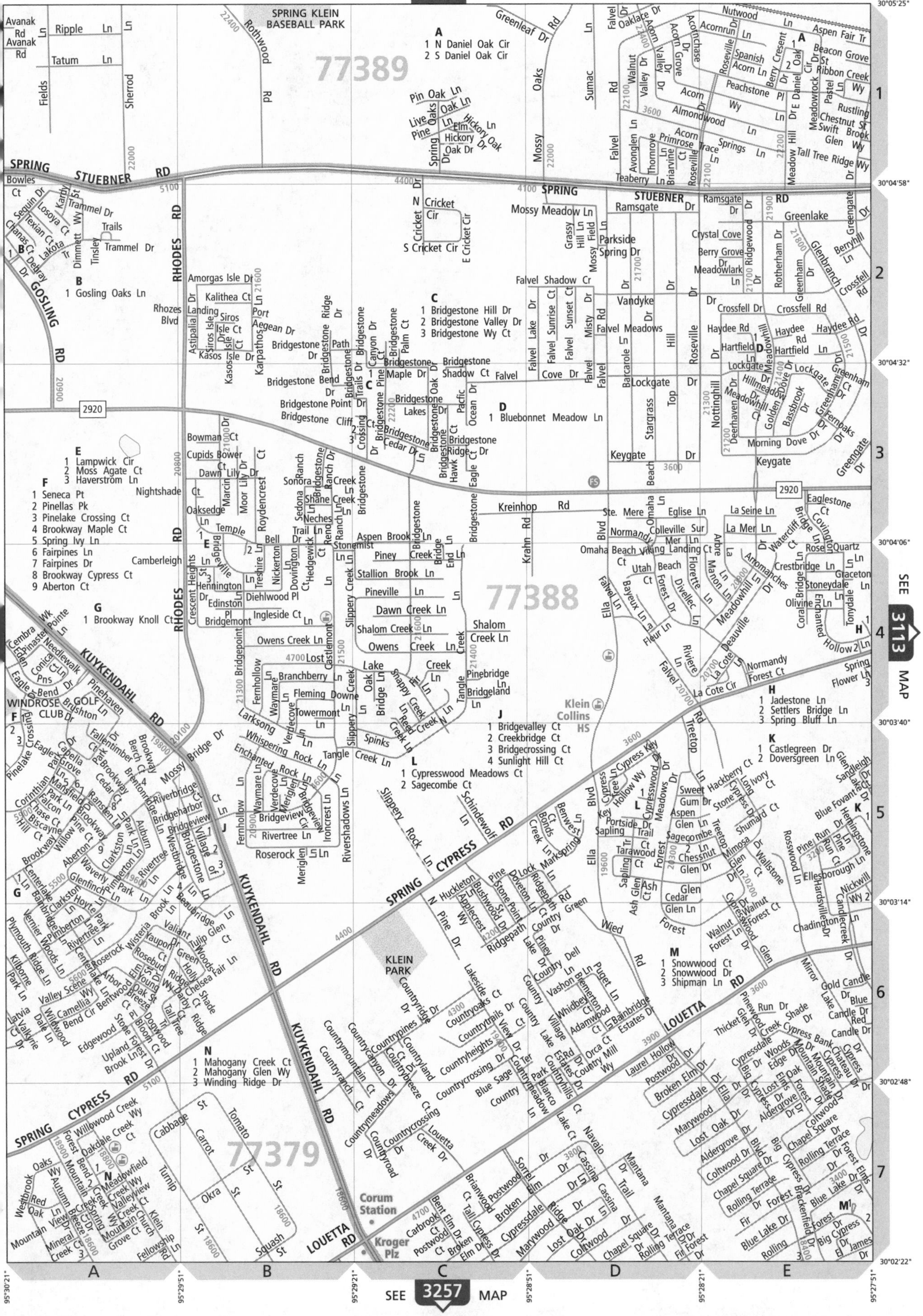
SPRING KLEIN BASEBALL PARK
77389
77388
77379
SPRING STUEBNER RD
RHODES RD
GOSLING RD
KUYKENDAHL RD
SPRING CYPRESS RD
LOUETTA RD
2920
WINDROSE GOLF CLUB
KLEIN PARK
Klein Collins HS
Corum Station
Kroger Plz
A
1 N Daniel Oak Cir
2 S Daniel Oak Cir
B
1 Gosling Oaks Ln
C
1 Bridgestone Hill Dr
2 Bridgestone Valley Dr
3 Bridgestone Wy Ct
D
1 Bluebonnet Meadow Ln
E
1 Lampwick Cir
2 Moss Agate Ct
3 Haverstrom Ln
F
1 Seneca Pt
2 Pinellas Pk
3 Pinelake Crossing Ct
4 Brookway Maple Ct
5 Spring Ivy Ln
6 Fairpines Ln
7 Fairpines Dr
8 Brookway Cypress Ct
9 Aberton Ct
G
1 Brookway Knoll Ct
H
1 Jadestone Ln
2 Settlers Bridge Ln
3 Spring Bluff Ln
J
1 Bridgevalley Ct
2 Creekbridge Ct
3 Bridgecrossing Ct
4 Sunlight Hill Ct
K
1 Castlegreen Dr
2 Doversgreen Ln
L
1 Cypresswood Meadows Ct
2 Sagecombe Ct
M
1 Snowwood Ct
2 Snowwood Dr
3 Shipman Ln
N
1 Mahogany Creek Ct
2 Mahogany Glen Wy
3 Winding Ridge Dr
30°05'25"
30°04'58"
30°04'32"
30°04'06"
30°03'40"
30°03'14"
30°02'48"
30°02'22"
95°30'21"
95°29'51"
95°29'21"
95°28'51"
95°28'21"
95°27'51"
A
B
C
D
E
1
2
3
4
5
6
7

SEE 3113 MAP

SEE 3257 MAP

1:24,000
1 in. = 2000 ft.
0 0.25 0.5
miles

SEE 2968 MAP

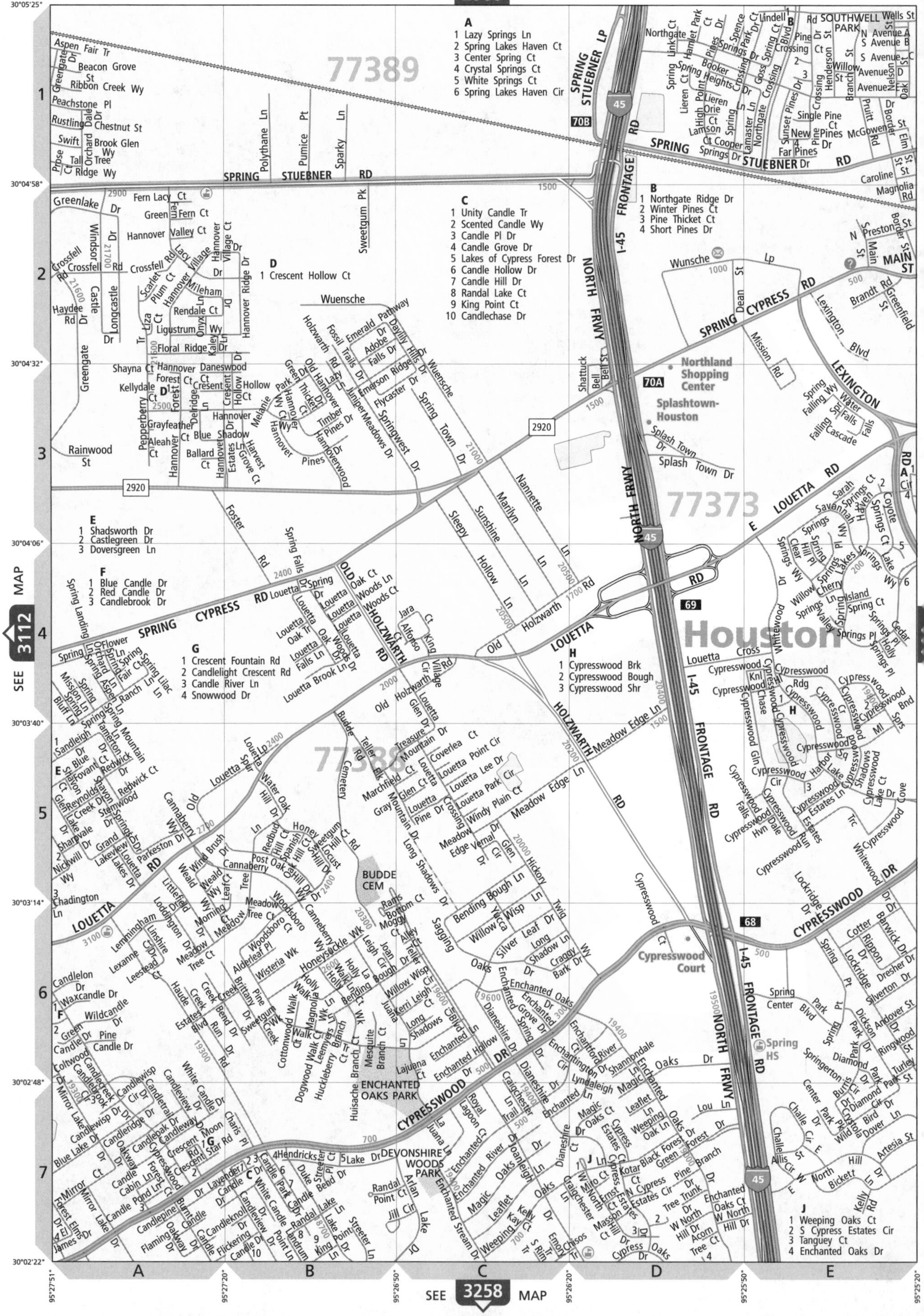

A
1 Lazy Springs Ln
2 Spring Lakes Haven Ct
3 Center Spring Ct
4 Crystal Springs Ct
5 White Springs Ct
6 Spring Lakes Haven Cir
B
1 Northgate Ridge Dr
2 Winter Pines Ct
3 Pine Thicket Ct
4 Short Pines Dr
C
1 Unity Candle Tr
2 Scented Candle Wy
3 Candle Pl Dr
4 Candle Grove Dr
5 Lakes of Cypress Forest Dr
6 Candle Hollow Dr
7 Candle Hill Dr
8 Randal Lake Ct
9 King Point Ct
10 Candlechase Dr
D
1 Crescent Hollow Ct
E
1 Shadsworth Dr
2 Castlegreen Dr
3 Doversgreen Ln
F
1 Blue Candle Dr
2 Red Candle Dr
3 Candlebrook Dr
G
1 Crescent Fountain Rd
2 Candlelight Crescent Rd
3 Candle River Ln
4 Snowwood Dr
H
1 Cypresswood Brk
2 Cypresswood Bough
3 Cypresswood Shr
J
1 Weeping Oaks Ct
2 S Cypress Estates Cir
3 Tanguey Ct
4 Enchanted Oaks Dr
77389
77373
77388
Houston
SPRING STUEBNER RD
SPRING CYPRESS RD
LOUETTA RD
CYPRESSWOOD DR
NORTH FRWY
FRONTAGE RD
I-45
HOLZWARTH RD
LEXINGTON BLVD
SOUTHWELL PARK
Northland Shopping Center
Splashtown-Houston
Cypresswood Court
BUDDE CEM
ENCHANTED OAKS PARK
DEVONSHIRE WOODS PARK
Spring HS
70B
70A
69
68
2920
30°05'25"
30°04'58"
30°04'32"
30°04'06"
30°03'40"
30°03'14"
30°02'48"
30°02'22"
95°27'51"
95°27'20"
95°26'50"
95°26'20"
95°25'50"
95°25'20"
A B C D E
1 2 3 4 5 6 7

SEE 3112 MAP

SEE 3258 MAP

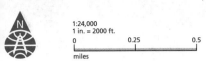

1:24,000
1 in. = 2000 ft.
0 0.25 0.5
miles

SEE 2969 MAP

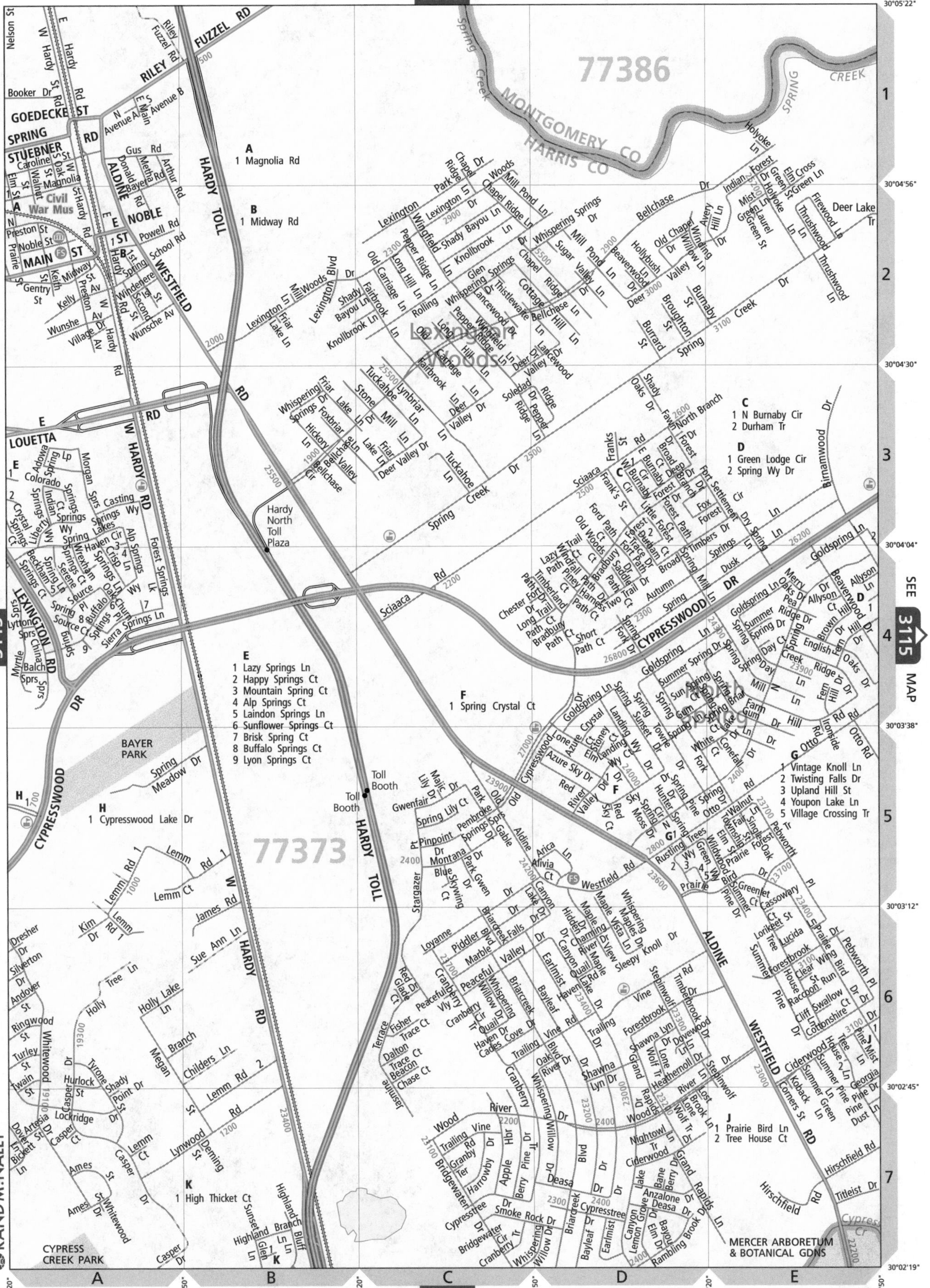
77386
77373
MONTGOMERY CO
HARRIS CO
Spring Creek
Lexington Woods
North Spring
BAYER PARK
CYPRESS CREEK PARK
MERCER ARBORETUM & BOTANICAL GDNS
Civil War Mus
Hardy North Toll Plaza
Toll Booth
HARDY TOLL
W HARDY RD
CYPRESSWOOD DR
LOUETTA RD
WESTFIELD RD
ALDINE WESTFIELD RD
RILEY FUZZEL RD
SPRING STUEBNER RD
GOEDECKE ST
MAIN ST
NOBLE ST
LEXINGTON RD
Sciaaca Rd
A
1 Magnolia Rd
B
1 Midway Rd
C
1 N Burnaby Cir
2 Durham Tr
D
1 Green Lodge Cir
2 Spring Wy Dr
E
1 Lazy Springs Ln
2 Happy Springs Ct
3 Mountain Spring Ct
4 Alp Springs Ct
5 Laindon Springs Ln
6 Sunflower Springs Ct
7 Brisk Spring Ct
8 Buffalo Springs Ct
9 Lyon Springs Ct
F
1 Spring Crystal Ct
G
1 Vintage Knoll Ln
2 Twisting Falls Dr
3 Upland Hill St
4 Youpon Lake Ln
5 Village Crossing Tr
H
1 Cypresswood Lake Dr
J
1 Prairie Bird Ln
2 Tree House Ct
K
1 High Thicket Ct
30°05'22"
30°04'56"
30°04'30"
30°04'04"
30°03'38"
30°03'12"
30°02'45"
30°02'19"
95°25'20"
95°24'50"
95°24'20"
95°23'50"
95°23'20"
95°22'50"
A B C D E
1 2 3 4 5 6 7

SEE 3115 MAP

SEE 3259 MAP

1:24,000
1 in. = 2000 ft.
0 0.25 0.5
miles

SEE 2970 MAP

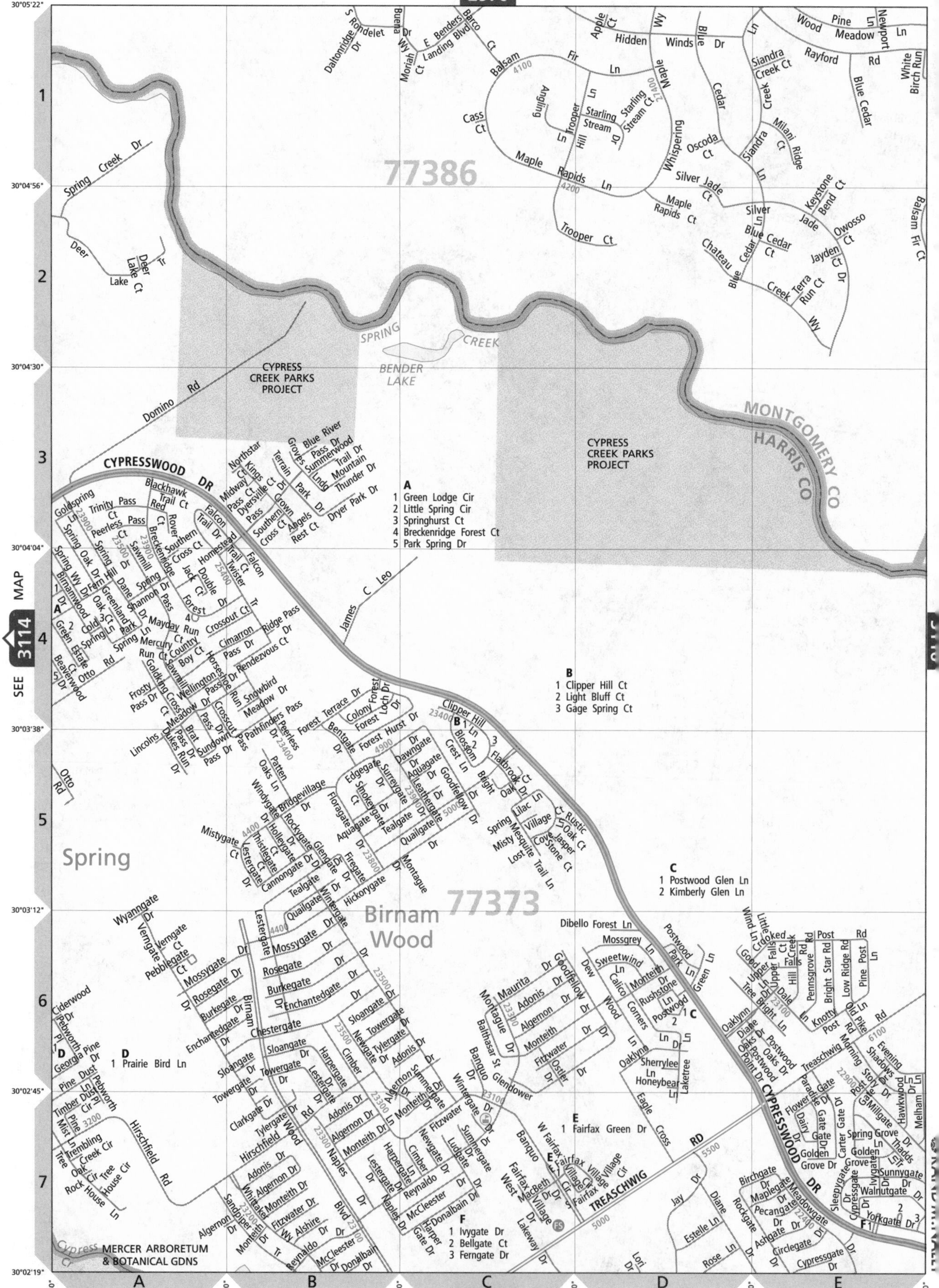
77386
77373
SPRING CREEK
BENDER LAKE
CYPRESS CREEK PARKS PROJECT
CYPRESS CREEK PARKS PROJECT
MONTGOMERY CO
HARRIS CO
Spring
Birnam Wood
CYPRESSWOOD DR
TREASCHWIG RD
Domino Rd
James C Leo
Spring Creek Dr
Deer Lake Ct
Maple Rapids Ln
Whispering Cedar
Hirschfield Rd
Birnam Wood Blvd
Naples Blvd
Eagle Cross Dr
MERCER ARBORETUM & BOTANICAL GDNS
A
1 Green Lodge Cir
2 Little Spring Cir
3 Springhurst Ct
4 Breckenridge Forest Ct
5 Park Spring Dr
B
1 Clipper Hill Ct
2 Light Bluff Ct
3 Gage Spring Ct
C
1 Postwood Glen Ln
2 Kimberly Glen Ln
D
1 Prairie Bird Ln
E
1 Fairfax Green Dr
F
1 Ivygate Dr
2 Bellgate Ct
3 Ferngate Dr
30°05'22"
30°04'56"
30°04'30"
30°04'04"
30°03'38"
30°03'12"
30°02'45"
30°02'19"
95°22'50"
95°22'20"
95°21'50"
95°21'20"
95°20'50"
95°20'20"
1
2
3
4
5
6
7
A
B
C
D
E

SEE 3114 MAP

SEE 3260 MAP

1:24,000
1 in. = 2000 ft.
0 0.25 0.5
miles

SEE 2971 MAP

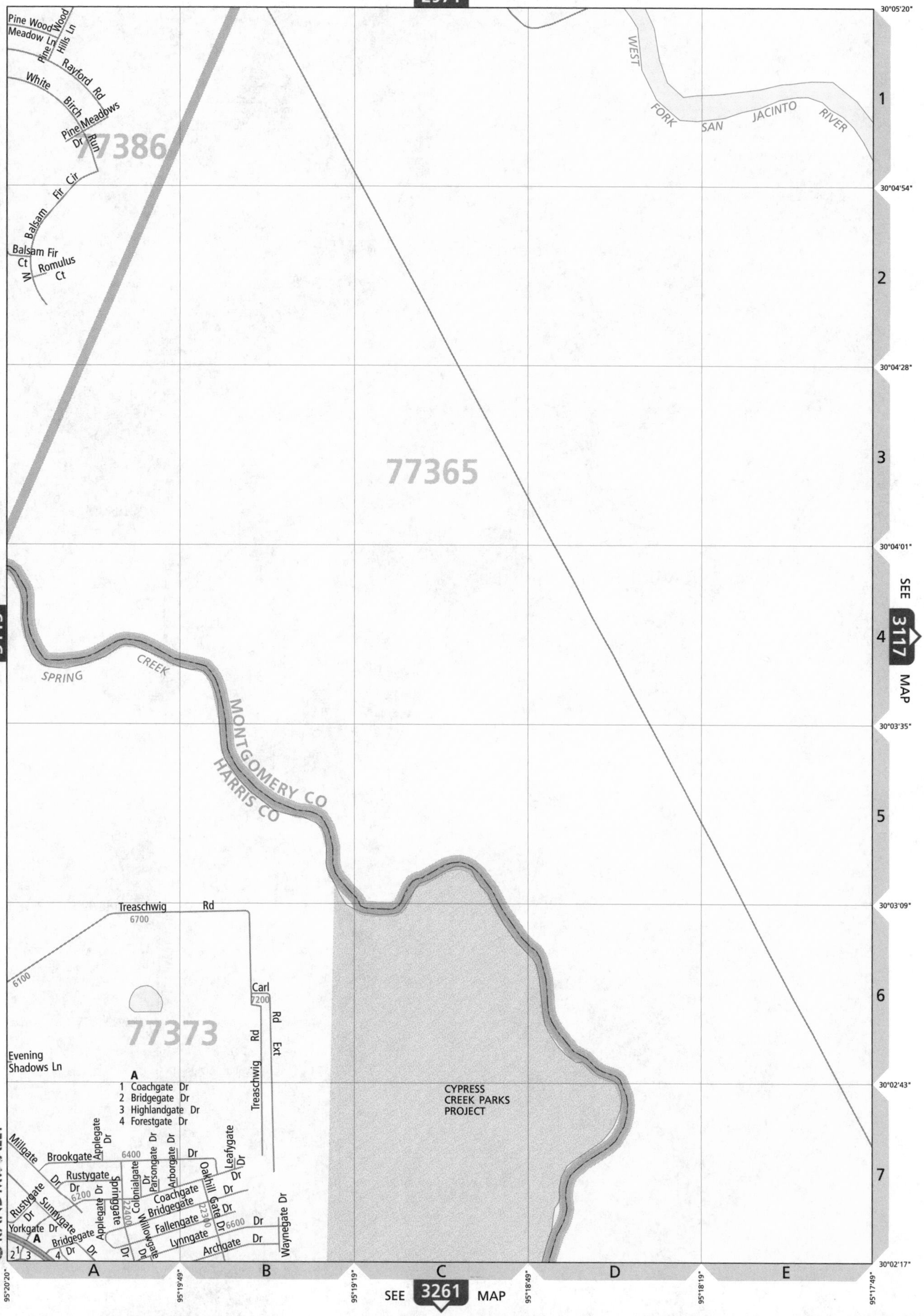
Pine Wood
Meadow Ln
Pine Ln
Wood Hills Ln
Rayford Rd
White Birch Run
Pine Meadows Dr
77386
Balsam Fir Cir
Balsam Fir Ct
W Romulus Ct
WEST FORK SAN JACINTO RIVER
77365
SPRING CREEK
MONTGOMERY CO
HARRIS CO
Treaschwig Rd
6700
6100
Carl Rd
7200
Carl Rd Ext
Treaschwig Rd
77373
Evening Shadows Ln
A
1 Coachgate Dr
2 Bridgegate Dr
3 Highlandgate Dr
4 Forestgate Dr
CYPRESS CREEK PARKS PROJECT
Millgate Dr
Brookgate Dr
Applegate Dr
6400
Rustygate Dr
6200
Rustygate Dr
Sunnygate
Yorkgate Dr
Bridgegate Dr
Springgate
Applegate Dr
Colonialgate Dr
Parsongate Dr
Arborgate Dr
Willowgate Dr
Coachgate Dr
Bridgegate
Fallengate Dr
Lynngate
Oakhill Gate Dr
Leafygate Dr
22400
22300
6600
Archgate Dr
Waynegate Dr
1 2 3 4
30°05'20"
30°04'54"
30°04'28"
30°04'01"
30°03'35"
30°03'09"
30°02'43"
30°02'17"
95°20'20"
95°19'49"
95°19'19"
95°18'49"
95°18'19"
95°17'49"
A B C D E
1 2 3 4 5 6 7

SEE 3117 MAP

SEE 3261 MAP

1:24,000
1 in. = 2000 ft.
0 0.25 0.5
miles

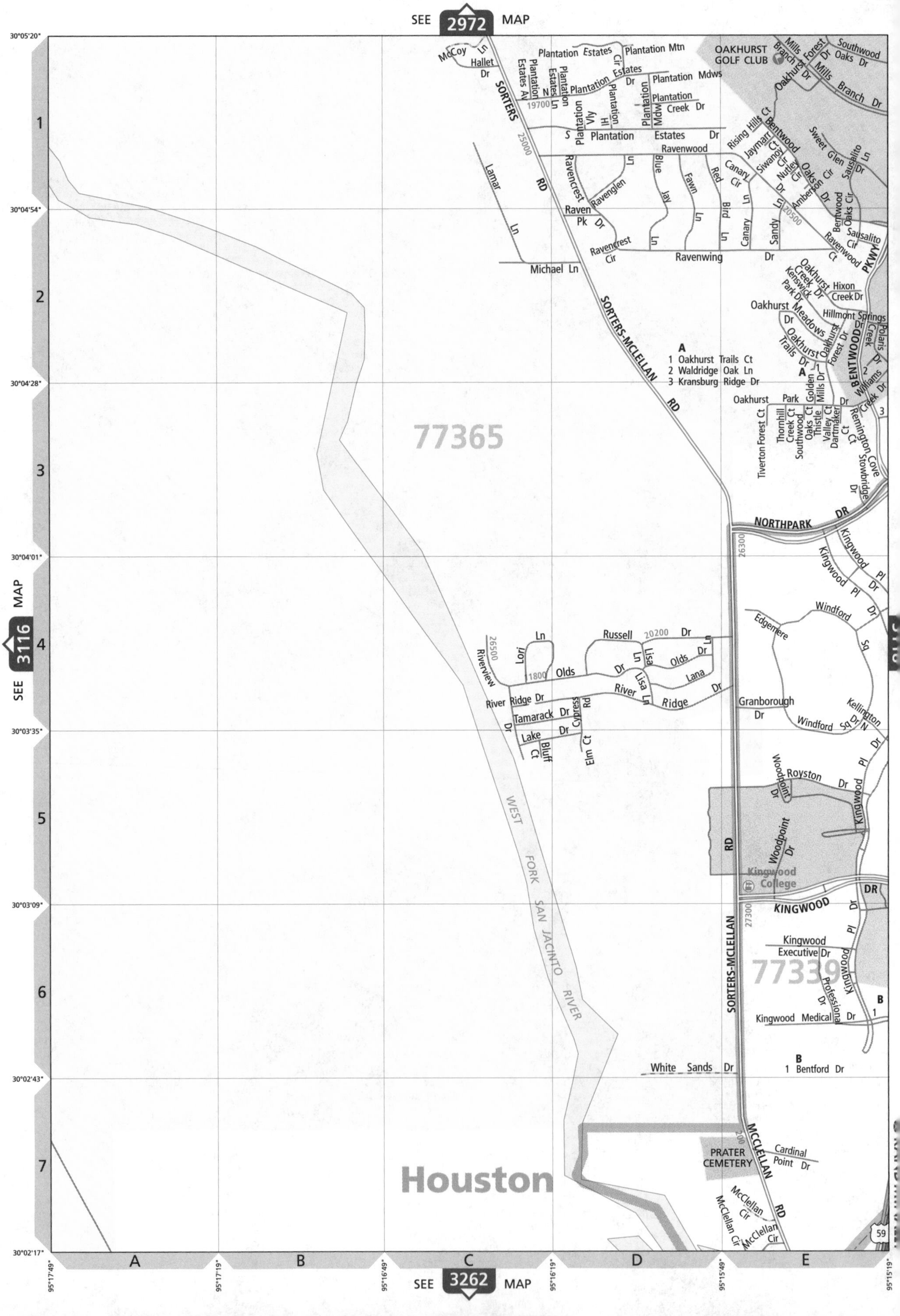
SEE 2972 MAP
SEE 3116 MAP
SEE 3262 MAP
30°05'20"
30°04'54"
30°04'28"
30°04'01"
30°03'35"
30°03'09"
30°02'43"
30°02'17"
95°17'49"
95°17'19"
95°16'49"
95°16'19"
95°15'49"
95°15'19"
A
B
C
D
E
1
2
3
4
5
6
7
77365
77339
Houston
OAKHURST GOLF CLUB
SORTERS RD
SORTERS-MCCLELLAN RD
MCCLELLAN RD
NORTHPARK DR
KINGWOOD DR
BENTWOOD PKWY
WEST FORK SAN JACINTO RIVER
Kingwood College
PRATER CEMETERY
McCoy Ln
Hallet Dr
Plantation Estates Cir
Plantation Mtn
Plantation Estates Dr
Plantation Mdws
Plantation Creek Dr
Ravenwood
Ravencrest
Ravenglen
Raven Pk Dr
Ravencrest Cir
Ravenwing Dr
Lamar Ln
Michael Ln
Blue Jay Ln
Fawn Ln
Red Bird Ln
Canary Ln
Sandy Ln
Rising Hills Ct
Mills Branch Dr
Southwood Oaks Dr
Sweet Glen Ln
Sausalito Dr
Oakhurst Meadows Dr
Hixon Creek Dr
Hillmont Springs
Oakhurst Park Dr
A
1 Oakhurst Trails Ct
2 Waldridge Oak Ln
3 Kransburg Ridge Dr
Tiverton Forest Ct
Thornhill Creek Ct
Remington Cove
Stowbridge Dr
Kingwood Pl Dr
Windford Dr
Edgemere
Granborough Dr
Windford Sq
Kellington Dr N
Russell Dr
Lori Ln
Olds Dr
Lisa Ln
Lana
River Ridge Dr
Riverview Dr
Tamarack Dr
Cypress Rd
Lake Dr
Bluff Ct
Elm Ct
Royston Dr
Woodpoint Dr
Kingwood Executive Dr
Professional Dr
Kingwood Medical Dr
B
1 Bentford Dr
White Sands Dr
Cardinal Point Dr
McClellan Cir
59

1:24,000
1 in. = 2000 ft.
0 0.25 0.5
miles

SEE 2973 MAP

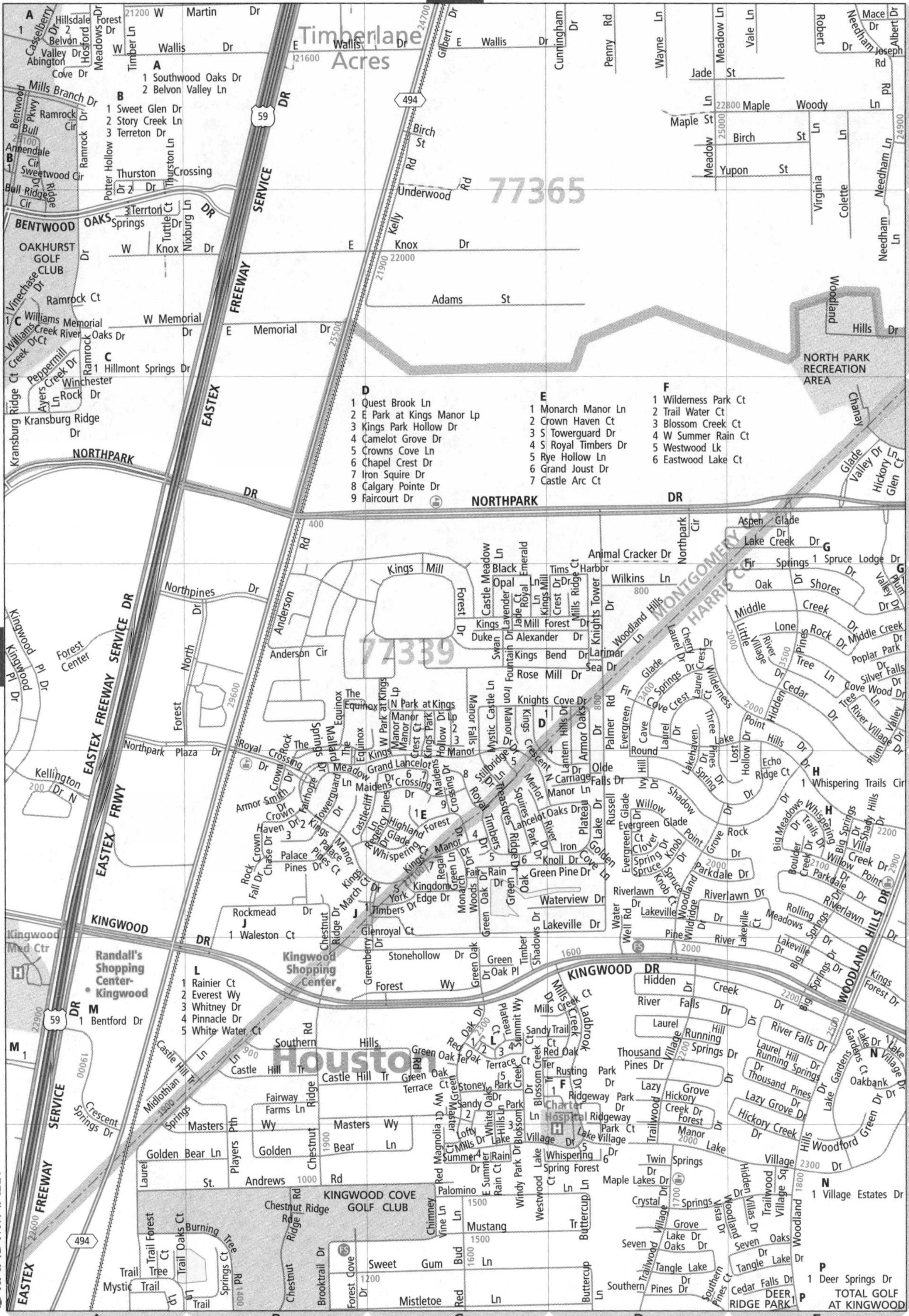
Timberlane Acres
77365
77339
Houston
EASTEX FREEWAY
EASTEX FRWY
SERVICE DR
NORTHPARK DR
KINGWOOD DR
BENTWOOD OAKS DR
MONTGOMERY CO
HARRIS CO
WOODLAND HILLS DR
OAKHURST GOLF CLUB
NORTH PARK RECREATION AREA
KINGWOOD COVE GOLF CLUB
Kingwood Med Ctr
Randall's Shopping Center-Kingwood
Kingwood Shopping Center
Charter Hospital
Forest Center
TOTAL GOLF AT KINGWOOD
DEER RIDGE PARK
W Martin Dr
Wallis Dr
E Wallis Dr
Knox Dr
Adams St
Memorial Dr
W Memorial Dr
Kelly Rd
Birch St
Underwood Rd
Gilbert Dr
Cunningham Dr
Penny Rd
Wayne Ln
Meadow Ln
Vale Ln
Jade St
Maple St
Woody Ln
Yupon St
Virginia
Colette
Robert Dr
Needham Ln
Mace Dr
Albert Dr
Joseph Rd
Woodland Hills Dr
Chanay
Anderson Rd
Anderson Cir
Northpines Dr
North Forest Dr
Northpark Plaza Dr
Kings Mill
Kellington Dr N
Kingwood Pl Dr
Rockmead Dr
Chestnut Ridge Dr
Stonehollow Dr
Forest Wy
Southern Hills
Castle Hill Tr
Masters Wy
Golden Bear Ln
St. Andrews Rd
Sweet Gum Ln
Mistletoe Ln
Mustang Tr
Palomino Ln
Buttercup Ln
Lake Village Dr
Twin Springs Dr
Crystal Springs
Hidden Falls Dr
River Falls Dr
Creek Dr
Rolling Meadows
Riverlawn Dr
Lakeville Dr
Waterview Dr
Aspen Glade Dr
Lake Creek Dr
Middle Creek Dr
Whispering Trails Cir
A
1 Southwood Oaks Dr
2 Belvon Valley Ln
B
1 Sweet Glen Dr
2 Story Creek Ln
3 Terreton Dr
C
1 Hillmont Springs Dr
D
1 Quest Brook Ln
2 E Park at Kings Manor Lp
3 Kings Park Hollow Dr
4 Camelot Grove Dr
5 Crowns Cove Ln
6 Chapel Crest Dr
7 Iron Squire Dr
8 Calgary Pointe Dr
9 Faircourt Dr
E
1 Monarch Manor Ln
2 Crown Haven Ct
3 S Towerguard Dr
4 S Royal Timbers Dr
5 Rye Hollow Ln
6 Grand Joust Dr
7 Castle Arc Ct
F
1 Wilderness Park Ct
2 Trail Water Ct
3 Blossom Creek Ct
4 W Summer Rain Ct
5 Westwood Lk
6 Eastwood Lake Ct
G
1 Spruce Lodge Dr
H
1 Whispering Trails Cir
J
1 Waleston Ct
L
1 Rainier Ct
2 Everest Wy
3 Whitney Dr
4 Pinnacle Dr
5 White Water Ct
M
1 Bentford Dr
N
1 Village Estates Dr
P
1 Deer Springs Dr
30°05'17"
30°04'51"
30°04'25"
30°03'59"
30°03'33"
30°03'07"
30°02'40"
30°02'14"
95°15'19"
95°14'49"
95°14'19"
95°13'49"
95°13'19"
95°12'49"
A B C D E
1 2 3 4 5 6 7

SEE 3119 MAP

SEE 3263 MAP

1:24,000
1 in. = 2000 ft.
0 0.25 0.5
miles

SEE 2974 MAP

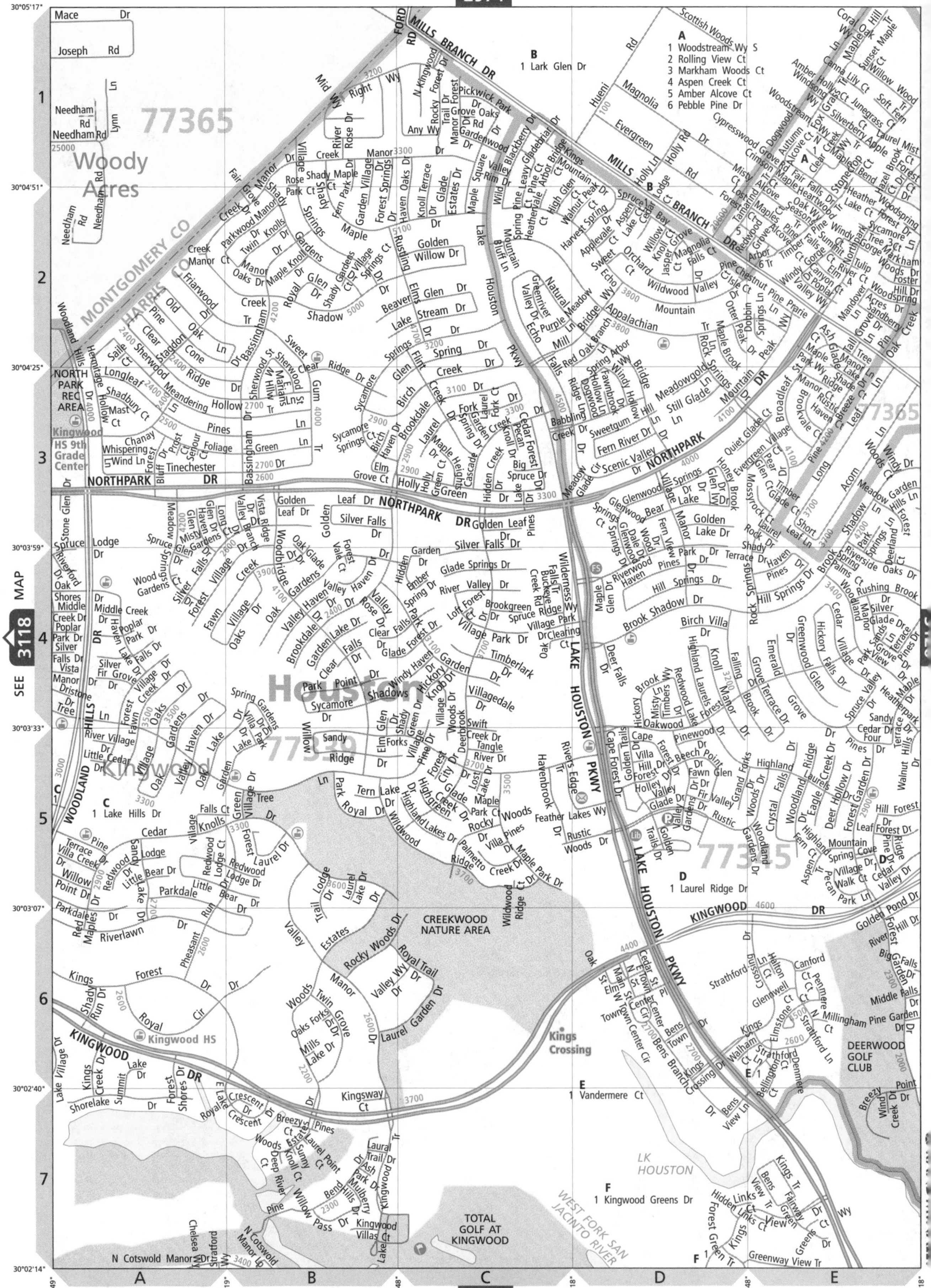
77365
Woody Acres
MONTGOMERY CO
HARRIS CO
NORTHPARK DR
MILLS BRANCH DR
LAKE HOUSTON PKWY
WOODLAND HILLS DR
KINGWOOD DR
Houston
77339
77345
NORTH PARK REC AREA
Kingwood HS 9th Grade Center
CREEKWOOD NATURE AREA
Kingwood HS
Kings Crossing
DEERWOOD GOLF CLUB
LK HOUSTON
WEST FORK SAN JACINTO RIVER
TOTAL GOLF AT KINGWOOD
Kingwood
A
1 Woodstream Wy S
2 Rolling View Ct
3 Markham Woods Ct
4 Aspen Creek Ct
5 Amber Alcove Ct
6 Pebble Pine Dr
B
1 Lark Glen Dr
C
1 Lake Hills Dr
D
1 Laurel Ridge Dr
E
1 Vandermere Ct
F
1 Kingwood Greens Dr
30°05'17"
30°04'51"
30°04'25"
30°03'59"
30°03'33"
30°03'07"
30°02'40"
30°02'14"
95°12'49"
95°12'19"
95°11'48"
95°11'18"
95°10'48"
95°10'18"

SEE 3118 MAP

SEE 3264 MAP

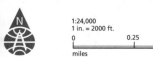

1:24,000
1 in. = 2000 ft.
0 0.25 0.5
miles

SEE 2975 MAP

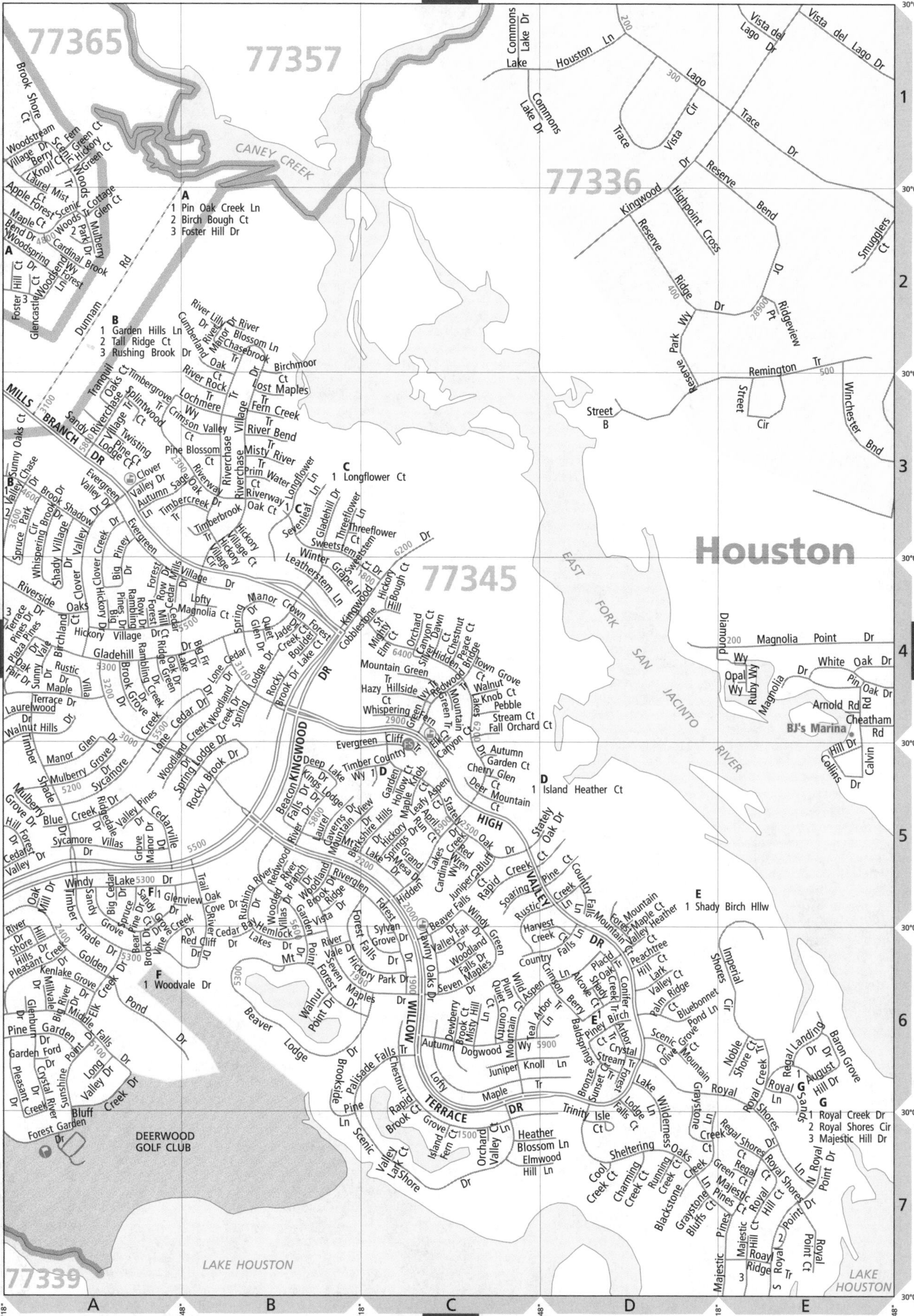
77365
77357
77336
77345
77339
Houston
CANEY CREEK
EAST FORK SAN JACINTO RIVER
LAKE HOUSTON
DEERWOOD GOLF CLUB
BJ's Marina
MILLS BRANCH DR
KINGWOOD DR
WILLOW TERRACE DR
HIGH VALLEY DR
A
1 Pin Oak Creek Ln
2 Birch Bough Ct
3 Foster Hill Dr
B
1 Garden Hills Ln
2 Tall Ridge Ct
3 Rushing Brook Dr
C
1 Longflower Ct
D
1 Island Heather Ct
E
1 Shady Birch Hllw
F
1 Woodvale Dr
G
1 Royal Creek Dr
2 Royal Shores Cir
3 Majestic Hill Dr
30°05'14"
30°04'48"
30°04'22"
30°03'56"
30°03'30"
30°03'04"
30°02'38"
30°02'11"
95°10'18"
95°09'48"
95°09'18"
95°08'48"
95°08'18"
95°07'48"
1
2
3
4
5
6
7
A
B
C
D
E

SEE 3121 MAP

SEE 3265 MAP

1:24,000
1 in. = 2000 ft.
0 0.25 0.5
miles

SEE 2976 MAP

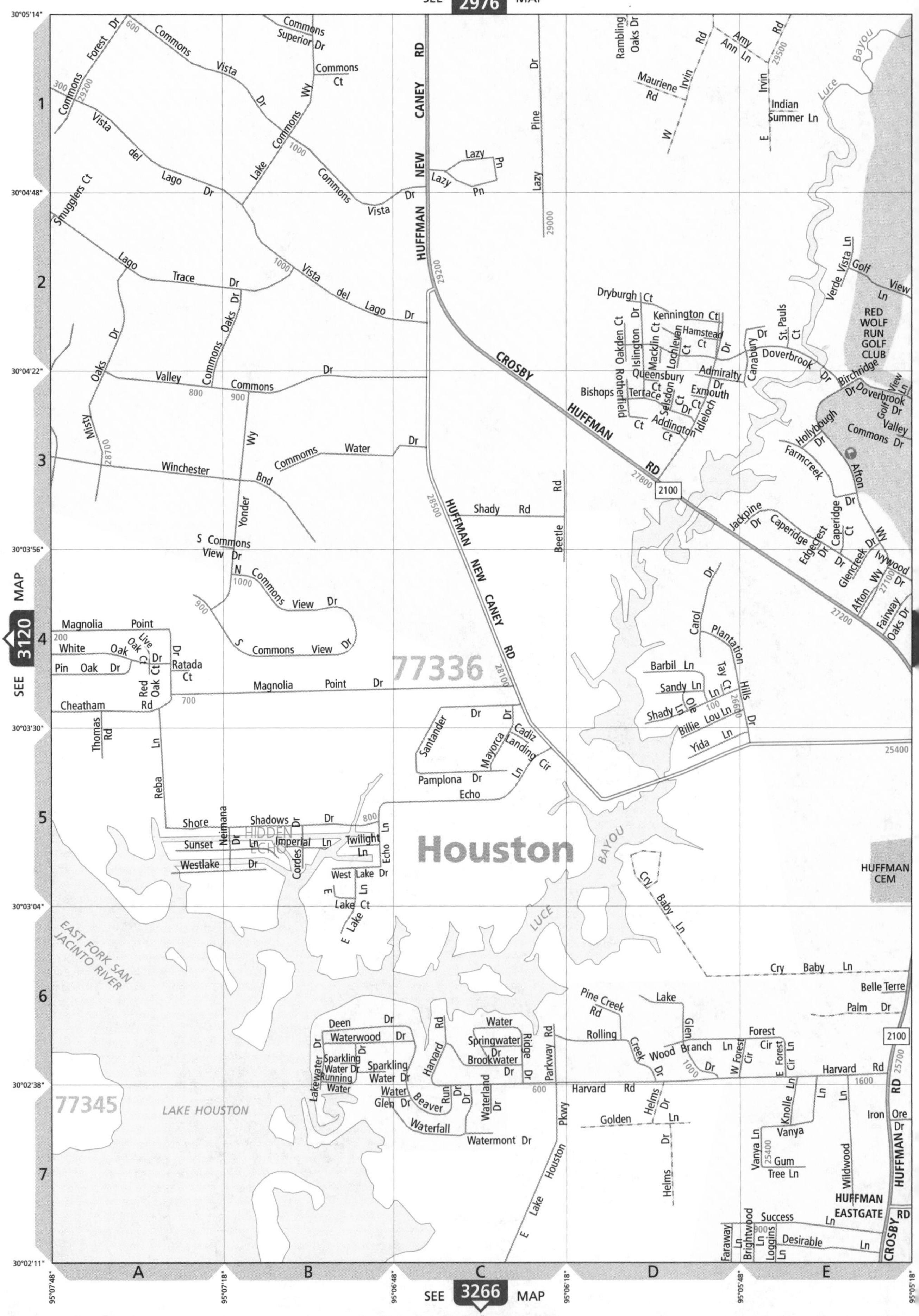

HUFFMAN NEW CANEY RD
CROSBY HUFFMAN RD
Houston
77336
77345
LAKE HOUSTON
EAST FORK SAN JACINTO RIVER
LUCE BAYOU
RED WOLF RUN GOLF CLUB
HUFFMAN CEM
HUFFMAN EASTGATE
HIDDEN ECHO
2100
Commons Forest Dr
Commons Vista Dr
Commons Superior Dr
Commons Ct
Lake Commons Wy
Vista del Lago Dr
Smugglers Ct
Lago Trace Dr
Commons Oaks Dr
Misty Oaks Dr
Valley Commons Dr
Winchester Bnd
Commons Water Dr
Yonder Wy
S Commons View Dr
N Commons View Dr
Magnolia Point Dr
White Oak Dr
Pin Oak Dr
Live Oak Ct
Ratada Ct
Red Oak Ct
Cheatham Rd
Thomas Rd
Reba Ln
Shore Shadows Dr
Sunset Dr
Neimana Ln
Imperial Ln
Twilight Ln
Westlake Dr
Cordes Ln
Echo Ln
West Lake Dr
E Lake Ct
E Lake Ln
Lazy Pn
Pine Dr
Shady Rd
Beetle Rd
Santander Dr
Mayorca Dr
Cadiz Landing Cir
Pamplona Dr
Echo Ln
Rambling Oaks Dr
Mauriene Rd
W Irvin Rd
Amy Ann Ln
E Irvin Rd
Indian Summer Ln
Dryburgh Ct
Kennington Ct
Hamstead Ct
Oakden Ct
Islington Dr
Macklin Ct
Lochleven Ct
Admiralty Dr
Canabury Dr
St. Pauls Ct
Doverbrook Dr
Queensbury Ct
Rotherfield Ct
Bishops Terrace Ct
Selsdon Dr
Exmouth Ct
Idleloch Dr
Addington Ct
Verde Vista Ln
Golf View Ln
Birchridge Dr
Golf Commons Dr
Valley Dr
Hollybough Dr
Farmcreek Dr
Afton Wy
Jackpine Dr
Caperidge Dr
Edgecrest Dr
Glencreek Dr
Ivywood Dr
Fairway Oaks Dr
Carol Dr
Plantation Hills Dr
Barbil Ln
Tay Ct
Sandy Ln
Shady Ln
Ole Ln
Billie Lou Ln
Yida Ln
Cry Baby Ln
Belle Terre
Palm Dr
Deen Dr
Waterwood Dr
Lakewater Dr
Sparkling Water Dr
Running Water
Water Glen Dr
Beaver Run Dr
Harvard Rd
Waterfall
Waterland Dr
Watermont Dr
Water Ridge Dr
Springwater Dr
Brookwater Dr
Parkway Rd
Pine Creek Rd
Rolling Creek Dr
Lake Glen Dr
Wood Branch Ln
Forest Cir
W Forest Cir
E Forest Cir Ln
Helms Dr
Golden Ln
Lake Houston Pkwy
Knolle Ln
Iron Ore Dr
Vanya Ln
Gum Tree Ln
Wildwood Ln
Success Ln
Desirable Ln
Faraway Ln
Brightwood Ln
Loggins Ln

SEE 3120 MAP

SEE 3266 MAP

1:24,000
1 in. = 2000 ft.
0 0.25 0.5
miles

SEE 2977 MAP

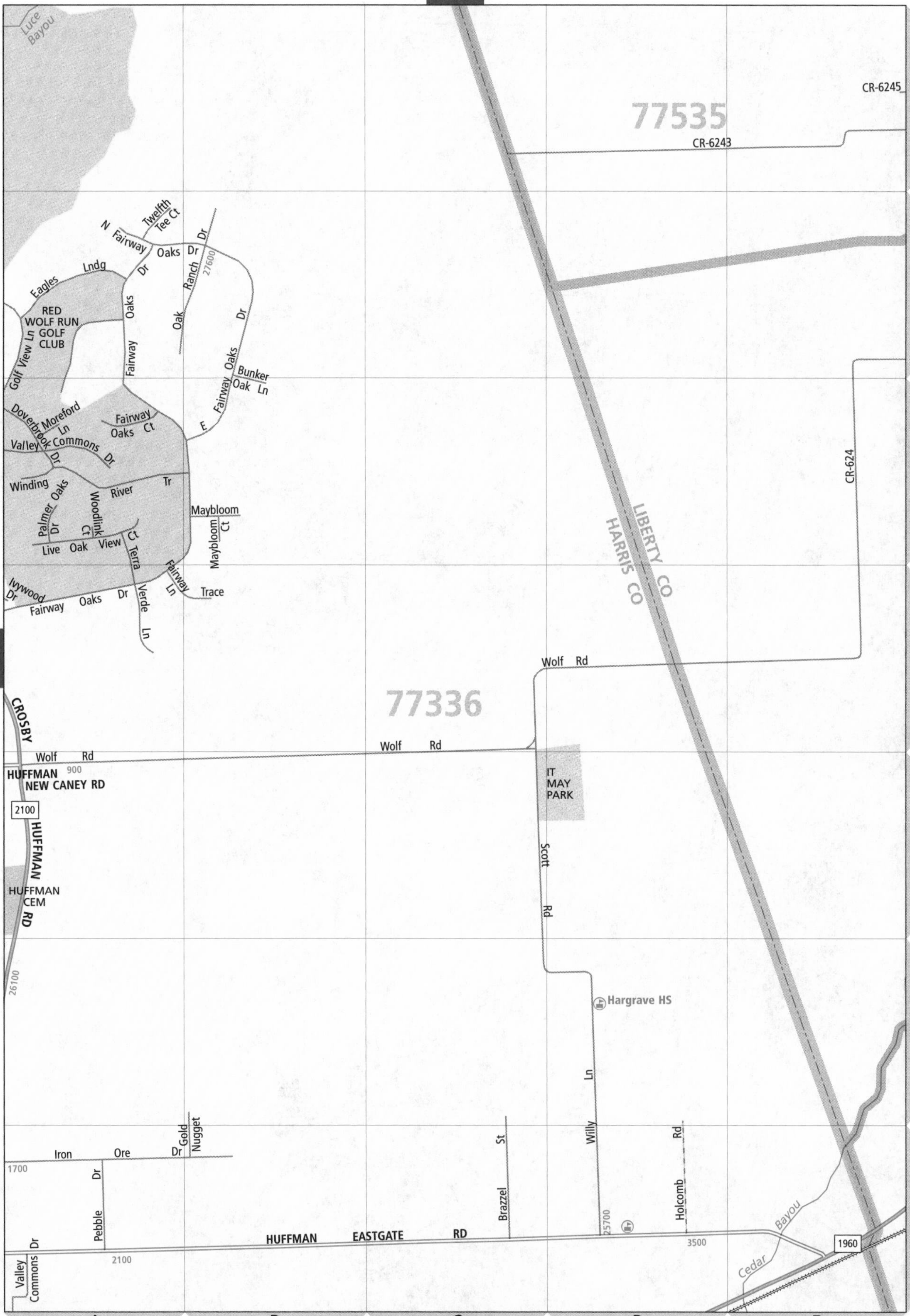
Luce Bayou
CR-6245
77535
CR-6243
N Fairway Dr
Twelfth Tee Ct
Oaks Dr
Ranch Dr
27600
Eagles Lndg
Oak
RED WOLF RUN GOLF CLUB
Golf View Ln
Fairway Oaks
Dr
Bunker Oak Ln
E Fairway Oaks
Doverbrook Dr
Moreford Ln
Fairway Oaks Ct
Valley Commons Dr
Winding River Tr
Palmer Oaks Dr
Woodlink Ct
Maybloom
Maybloom Ct
Live Oak View Ct
Terra Verde Ln
Fairway Ln
Trace
Ivywood Dr
Fairway Oaks Dr
LIBERTY CO
HARRIS CO
CR-624
Wolf Rd
77336
CROSBY
Wolf Rd
900
HUFFMAN
NEW CANEY RD
2100
HUFFMAN RD
IT MAY PARK
Scott Rd
HUFFMAN CEM
26100
Hargrave HS
Willy Ln
Gold Nugget Dr
Iron Ore Dr
1700
Pebble Dr
Brazzel St
Holcomb Rd
2500
HUFFMAN EASTGATE RD
2100
3500
1960
Bayou
Cedar
Valley Commons Dr
A B C D E
1 2 3 4 5 6 7
30°05'11" 30°04'45" 30°04'19" 30°03'53" 30°03'27" 30°03'01" 30°02'34" 30°02'08"
95°05'18" 95°04'48" 95°04'17" 95°03'47" 95°03'17" 95°02'47"

SEE B MAP

SEE 3121 MAP

SEE 3267 MAP

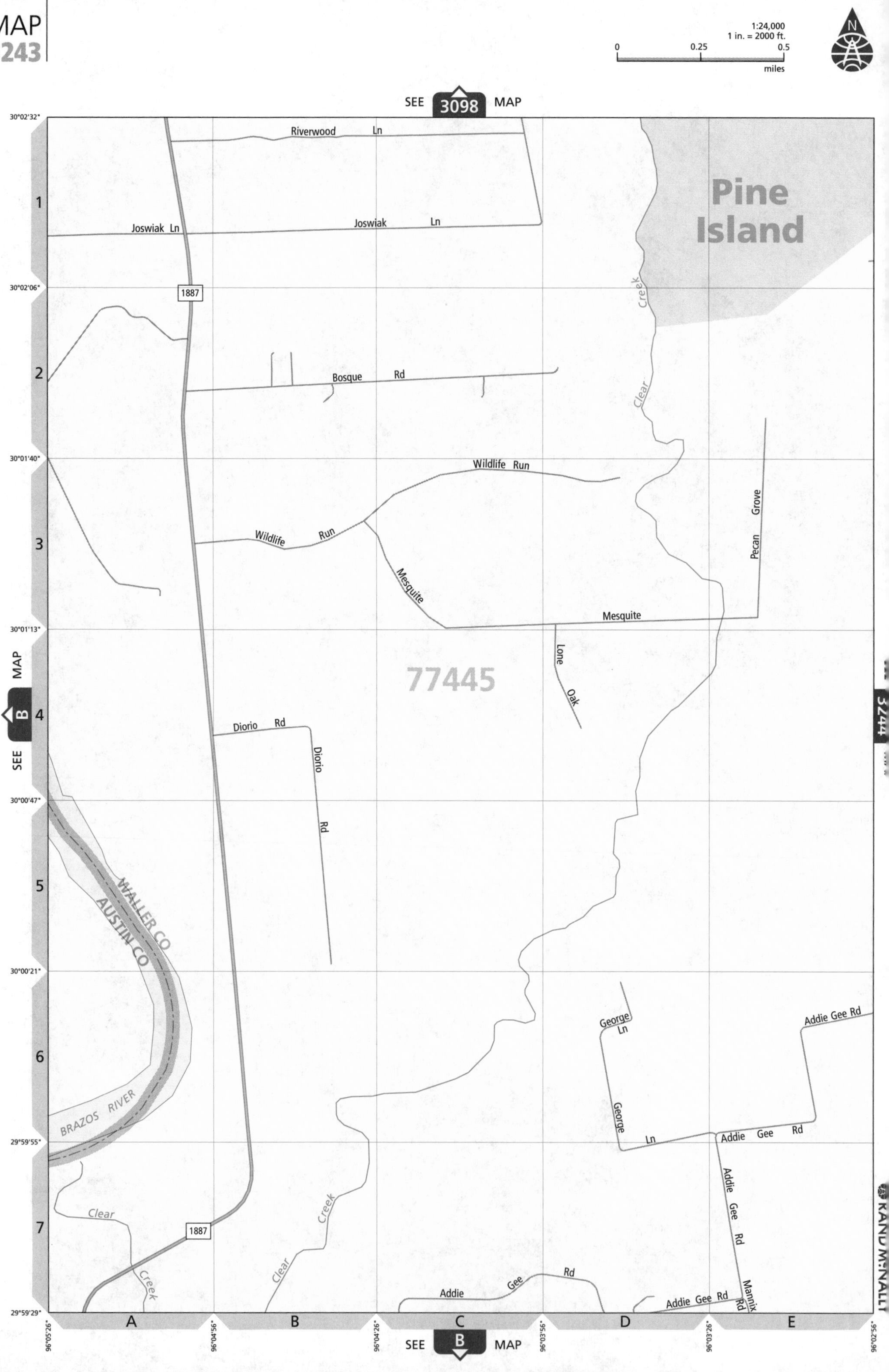
1:24,000
1 in. = 2000 ft.
0
0.25
0.5
miles
N
SEE 3098 MAP
SEE B MAP
SEE B MAP
3244
Pine Island
77445
Riverwood Ln
Joswiak Ln
Joswiak Ln
1887
Bosque Rd
Wildlife Run
Wildlife Run
Mesquite
Mesquite
Pecan Grove
Lone Oak
Diorio Rd
Diorio Rd
Clear Creek
Clear Creek
Clear Creek
WALLER CO
AUSTIN CO
BRAZOS RIVER
George Ln
George Ln
Addie Gee Rd
Addie Gee Rd
Addie Gee Rd
Addie Gee Rd
Addie Gee Rd
Mannix Rd
1
2
3
4
5
6
7
A
B
C
D
E
30°02'32"
30°02'06"
30°01'40"
30°01'13"
30°00'47"
30°00'21"
29°59'55"
29°59'29"
96°05'26"
96°04'56"
96°04'26"
96°03'56"
96°03'26"
96°02'56"
RAND McNALLY

1:24,000
1 in. = 2000 ft.
0 0.25 0.5
miles

SEE 3099 MAP

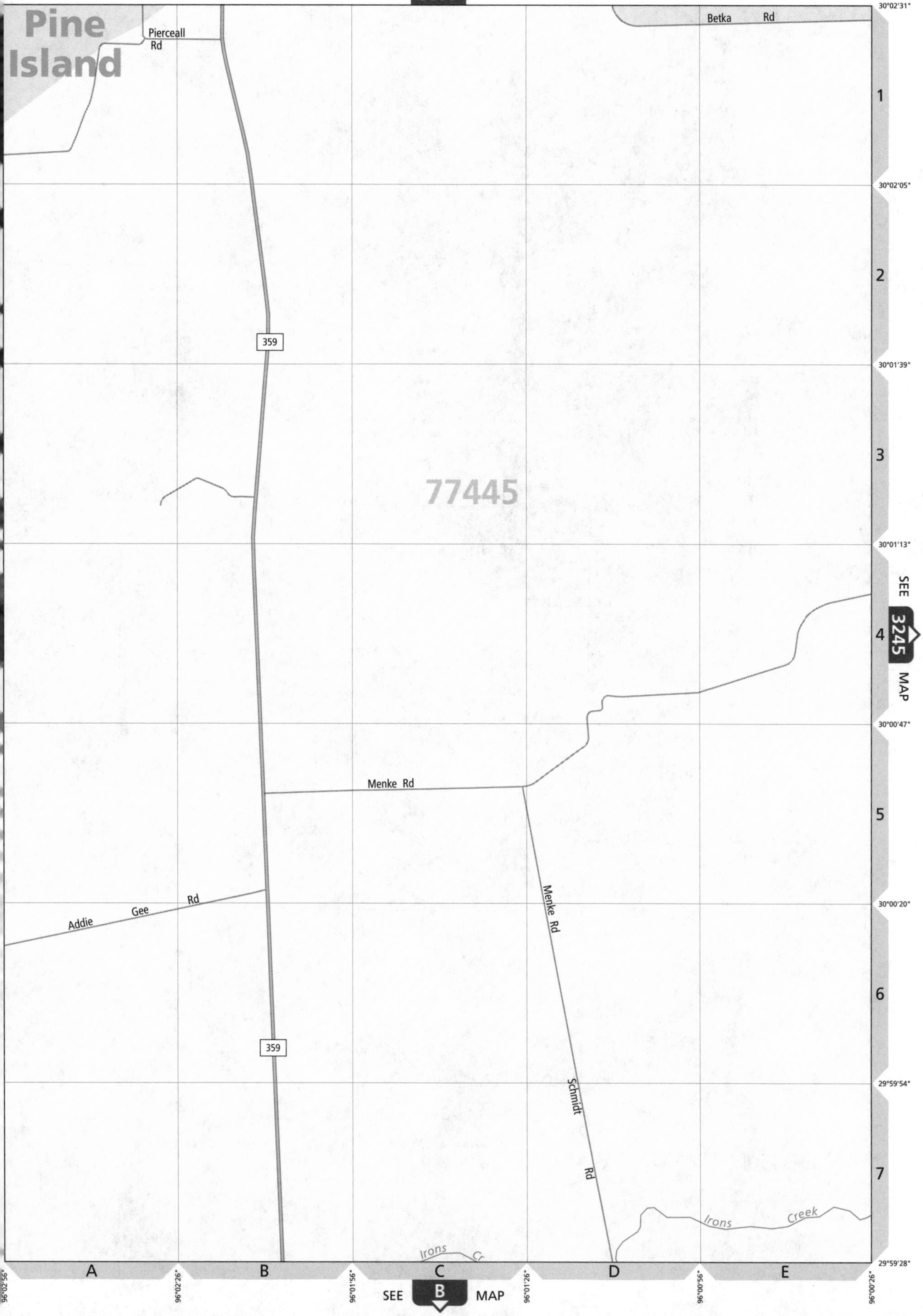
Pine Island
Pierceall Rd
Betka Rd
359
77445
Menke Rd
Addie Gee Rd
Menke Rd
Schmidt Rd
Irons Creek
Irons Cr
1
2
3
4
5
6
7
A
B
C
D
E
30°02'31"
30°02'05"
30°01'39"
30°01'13"
30°00'47"
30°00'20"
29°59'54"
29°59'28"
96°02'56"
96°02'26"
96°01'56"
96°01'26"
96°00'56"
96°00'26"

SEE 3245 MAP

SEE B MAP

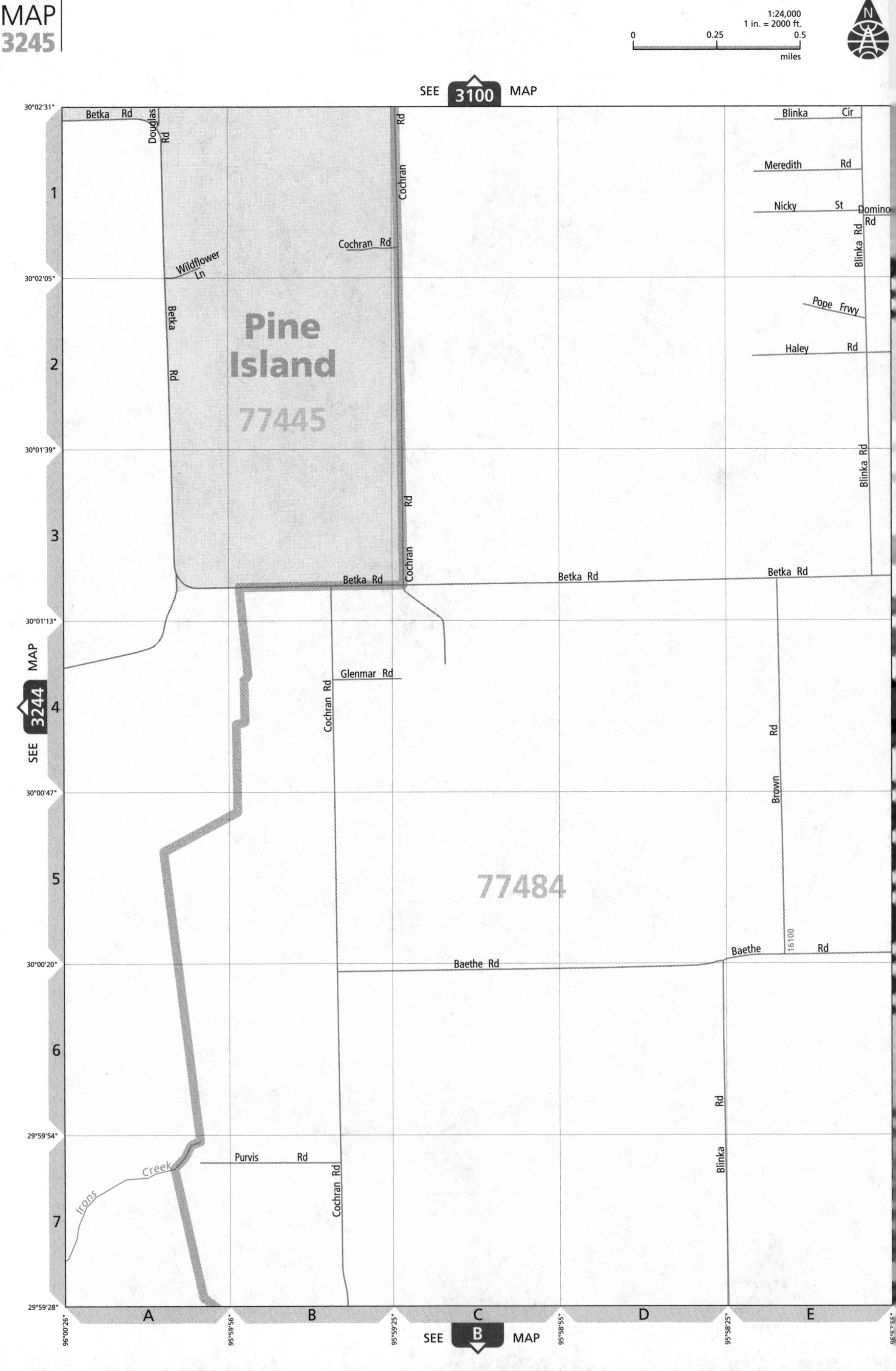
1:24,000
1 in. = 2000 ft.
0
0.25
0.5
miles
N
SEE 3100 MAP
SEE 3244 MAP
SEE B MAP
30°02'31"
30°02'05"
30°01'39"
30°01'13"
30°00'47"
30°00'20"
29°59'54"
29°59'28"
96°00'26"
95°59'56"
95°59'25"
95°58'55"
95°58'25"
1
2
3
4
5
6
7
A
B
C
D
E
Pine Island
77445
77484
Betka Rd
Douglas Rd
Cochran Rd
Wildflower Ln
Betka Rd
Blinka Cir
Meredith Rd
Nicky St
Domino Rd
Blinka Rd
Pope Frwy
Haley Rd
Glenmar Rd
Brown Rd
16100
Baethe Rd
Purvis Rd
Irons Creek

1:24,000
1 in. = 2000 ft.
0 0.25 0.5
miles

SEE 3101 MAP

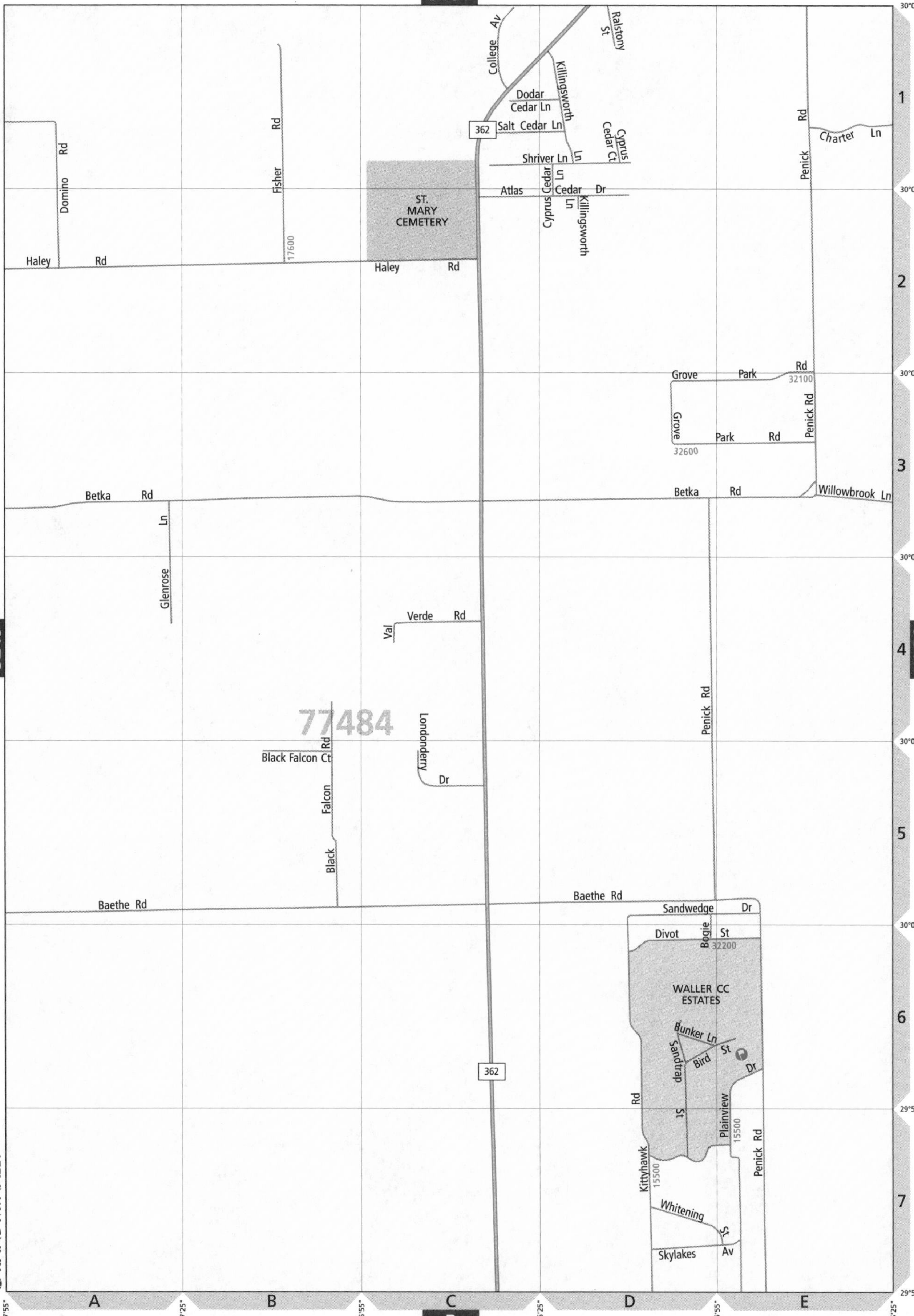
College Av
Ralstony St
Killingsworth Ln
Dodar Cedar Ln
362
Salt Cedar Ln
Cyprus Cedar Ct
Shriver Ln
Atlas
Cedar Dr
Cyprus Cedar Ln
Killingsworth Ln
Penick Rd
Charter Ln
Domino Rd
Fisher Rd
17600
ST. MARY CEMETERY
Haley Rd
Haley Rd
Grove Park Rd
32100
Grove Park Rd
Penick Rd
32600
Betka Rd
Betka Rd
Willowbrook Ln
Glenrose Ln
Val Verde Rd
77484
Black Falcon Ct
Black Falcon Rd
Londonderry Dr
Penick Rd
Baethe Rd
Baethe Rd
Sandwedge Dr
Divot St
Bogie
32200
WALLER CC ESTATES
Bunker Ln
Sandtrap St
Bird St
Dr
362
Kittyhawk Rd
15500
Plainview
15500
Penick Rd
Whitening St
Skylakes Av
1
2
3
4
5
6
7
A
B
C
D
E
30°02'30"
30°02'04"
30°01'38"
30°01'12"
30°00'46"
30°00'19"
29°59'53"
29°59'27"
95°57'55"
95°57'25"
95°56'55"
95°56'25"
95°55'55"
95°55'25"

SEE 3247 MAP

SEE B MAP

3245

1:24,000
1 in. = 2000 ft.
0 0.25 0.5
miles

SEE 3102 MAP

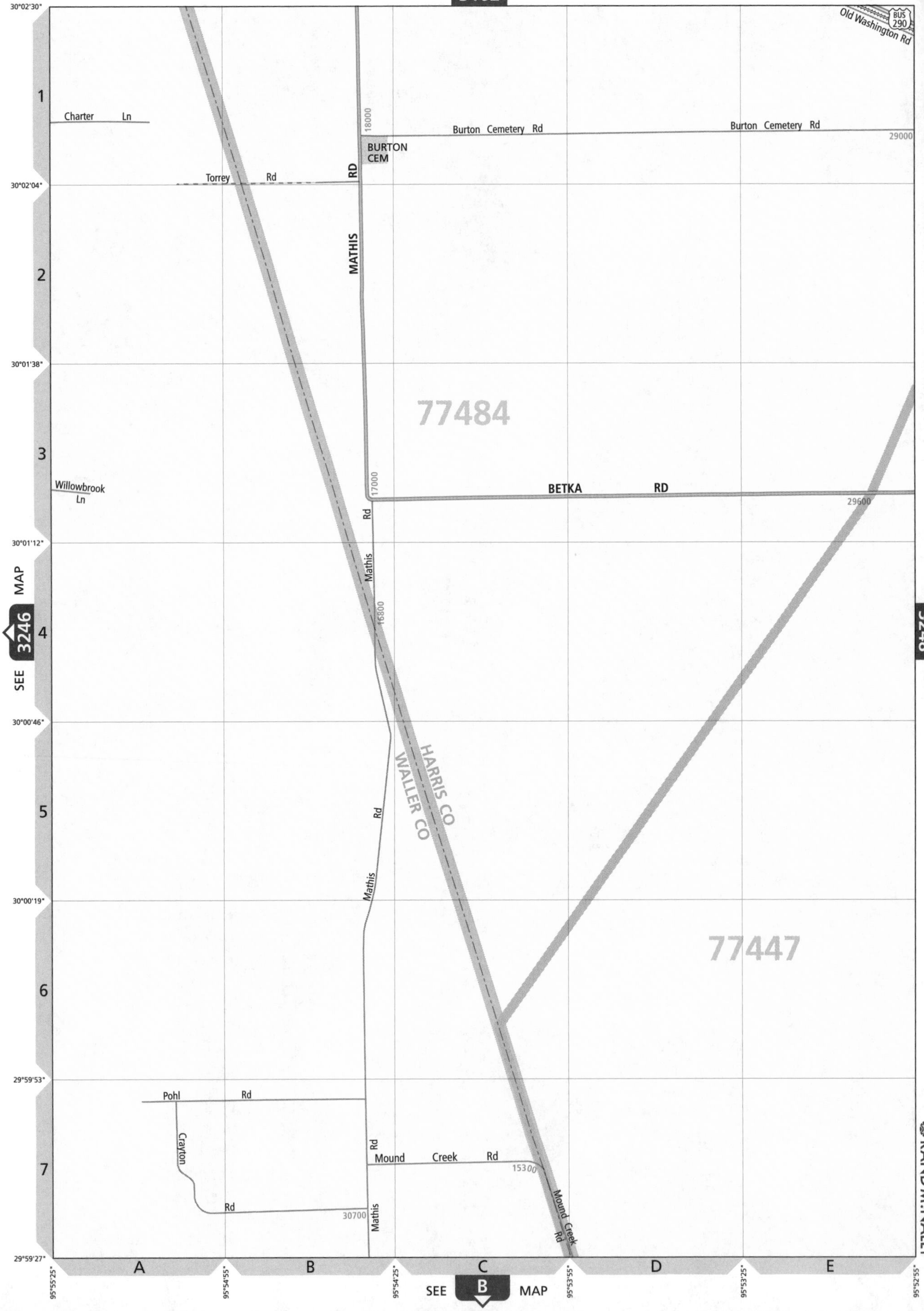
30°02'30"
Old Washington Rd
BUS 290
Charter Ln
18000
Burton Cemetery Rd
Burton Cemetery Rd
29000
BURTON
CEM
Torrey Rd
RD
30°02'04"
MATHIS
30°01'38"
77484
Willowbrook Ln
17000
BETKA RD
29600
Rd
Mathis
30°01'12"
16800
30°00'46"
HARRIS CO
WALLER CO
Rd
Mathis
30°00'19"
77447
29°59'53"
Pohl Rd
Crayton
Rd
Mound Creek Rd
15300
Rd
30700
Mathis
Mound Creek Rd
29°59'27"
1
2
3
4
5
6
7
A
B
C
D
E
95°55'25"
95°54'55"
95°54'25"
95°53'55"
95°53'25"
95°52'55"

SEE 3246 MAP

SEE B MAP

1:24,000
1 in. = 2000 ft.
0 0.25 0.5
miles

SEE 3103 MAP

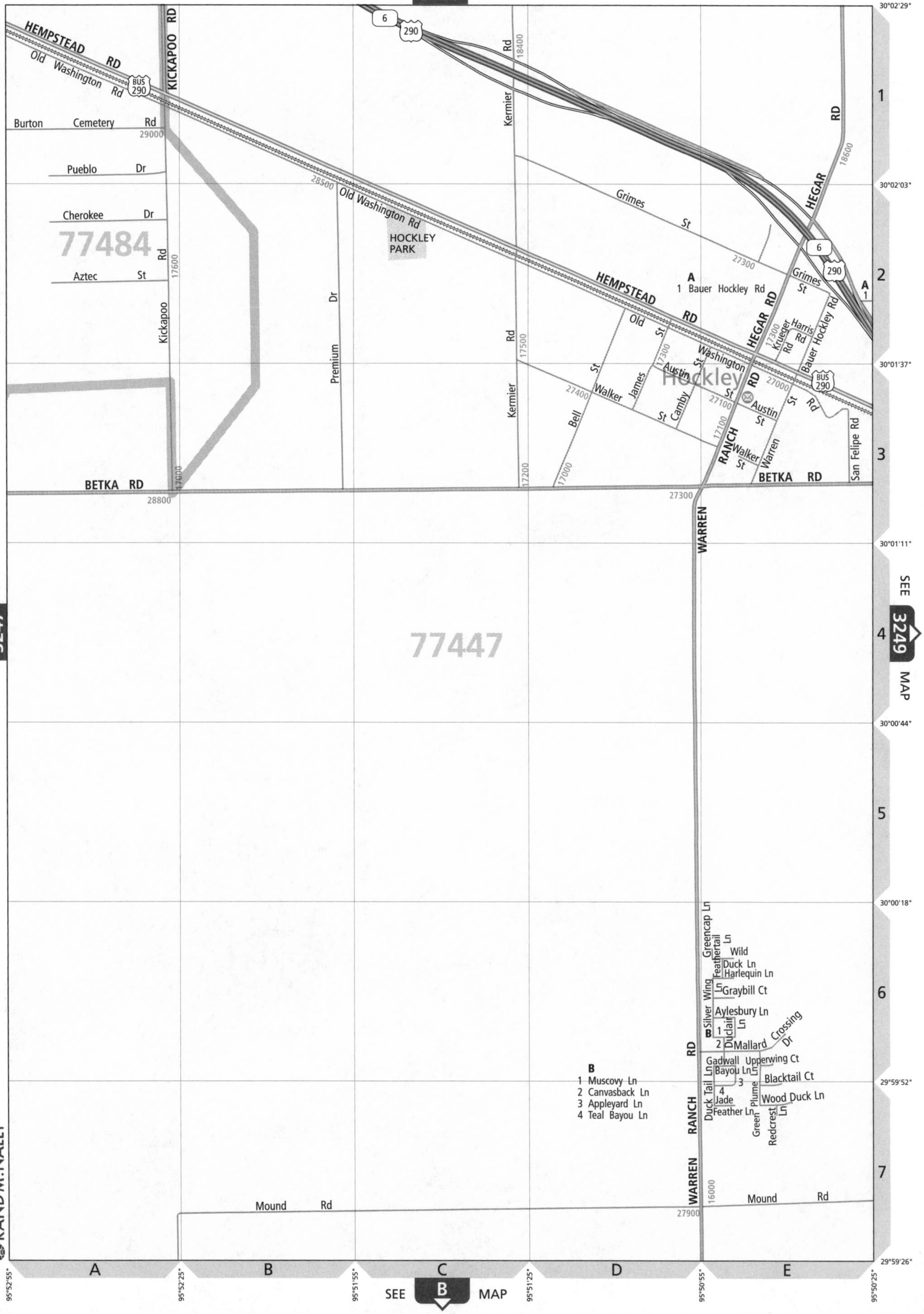
HEMPSTEAD RD
Old Washington Rd
BUS 290
KICKAPOO RD
Burton Cemetery Rd
29000
Pueblo Dr
Cherokee Dr
77484
Aztec St
Kickapoo Rd
17600
6
290
Kermier Rd
18400
HEGAR RD
18600
28500
Old Washington Rd
HOCKLEY PARK
Grimes St
27300
Premium Dr
A
1 Bauer Hockley Rd
HEMPSTEAD RD
Old St
Washington St
HEGAR RD
Krueger Rd
Harris Rd
Bauer Hockley Rd
17300
17500
Kermier Rd
27400
Walker
James
Austin
Hockley
Camby
Bell St
27100
27000
Austin St
Grimes
San Felipe Rd
RANCH
Walker St
Warren
17100
17000
17200
17000
BETKA RD
28800
27300
BETKA RD
WARREN
77447
Greencap Ln
Feathertail Ln
Wild Duck Ln
Harlequin Ln
Silver Wing Ln
Graybill Ct
Aylesbury Ln
Duclair Ln
Mallard Crossing Dr
Gadwall Ln
Upperwing Ct
Bayou Ln
Blacktail Ct
Duck Tail Ln
Jade
Feather Ln
Green Plume Ln
Wood Duck Ln
Redcrest Ln
B
1 Muscovy Ln
2 Canvasback Ln
3 Appleyard Ln
4 Teal Bayou Ln
WARREN RANCH RD
16000
Mound Rd
27900
Mound Rd
1
2
3
4
5
6
7
A
B
C
D
E
30°02'29"
30°02'03"
30°01'37"
30°01'11"
30°00'44"
30°00'18"
29°59'52"
29°59'26"
95°52'55"
95°52'25"
95°51'55"
95°51'25"
95°50'55"
95°50'25"

SEE 3249 MAP

SEE B MAP

1:24,000
1 in. = 2000 ft.
0 0.25 0.5
miles

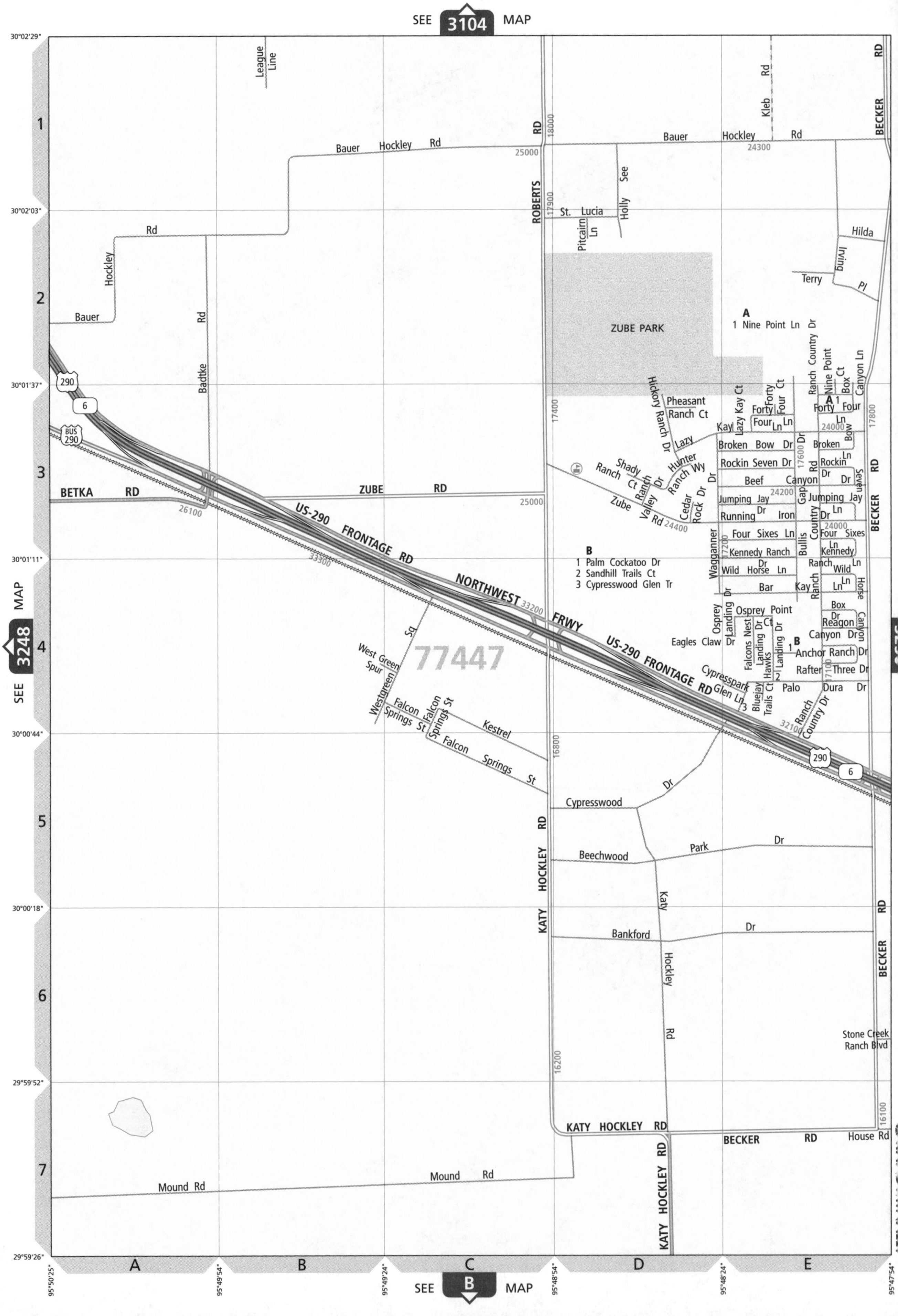
SEE 3104 MAP
SEE 3248 MAP
SEE B MAP
A
B
C
D
E
1
2
3
4
5
6
7
30°02'29"
30°02'03"
30°01'37"
30°01'11"
30°00'44"
30°00'18"
29°59'52"
29°59'26"
95°50'25"
95°49'54"
95°49'24"
95°48'54"
95°48'24"
95°47'54"
League Line
Bauer Hockley Rd
Bauer Hockley Rd
24300
25000
18000
Kleb Rd
BECKER RD
ROBERTS RD
17900
St. Lucia
Pitcairn Ln
Holly See
Hilda
Irving
Terry
Pl
Hockley
Rd
Bauer
Badtke
Rd
ZUBE PARK
A
1 Nine Point Ln Dr
290
6
BUS 290
Pheasant Ranch Ct
Hickory Ranch Dr
Lazy Kay Ct
Forty Four Ct
Forty Four Ln
Ranch Country Dr
Nine Point Ct
Box
Canyon Ln
Forty Four
24000
17800
17400
Lazy
Kay
Broken Bow Dr
Broken Bow
Rockin Seven Dr
Rockin Ln
Hunter Ranch Wy
Shady Ranch Ct
17600
Gap Rd
Beef Canyon Dr
Dr
Seven
BECKER RD
Valley Ranch Dr
Cedar Rock Dr
Jumping Jay
24200
Jumping Jay
Running Dr
Iron
Ln
Dr
Zube Rd
24400
BETKA RD
26100
ZUBE RD
25000
US-290 FRONTAGE RD
33300
Four Sixes Ln
Four Sixes
24000
Wagganner
17200
Kennedy Ranch Dr
Kennedy Ln
Bullis Ranch Country
Wild Horse Ln
Ranch Wild Ln
Bar Kay Ranch
Ln Horse
B
1 Palm Cockatoo Dr
2 Sandhill Trails Ct
3 Cypresswood Glen Tr
NORTHWEST
33200
FRWY
Osprey Landing Dr
Osprey Point Ct
Box Dr
Reagon Canyon Dr
Eagles Claw Dr
Falcons Nest Landing Dr
Hawks Landing Dr
B
1
2
Anchor Ranch Dr
Rafter Three Dr
17100
Palo Dura Dr
US-290 FRONTAGE RD
Cypresspark Glen Ln
3
Bluejay Trails Ct
Ranch Country Dr
32100
West Green Spur
Sq
Westgreen
77447
Falcon Springs St
Falcon Springs St
Kestrel
Falcon Springs St
16800
Cypresswood Dr
KATY HOCKLEY RD
Beechwood Park Dr
Katy Hockley Rd
Bankford Dr
BECKER RD
16200
Stone Creek Ranch Blvd
16100
KATY HOCKLEY RD
BECKER RD
House Rd
Mound Rd
Mound Rd
KATY HOCKLEY RD

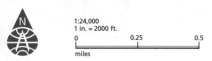

1:24,000
1 in. = 2000 ft.
0 0.25 0.5
miles

SEE 3105 MAP

30°02'28" 30°02'02" 30°01'35" 30°01'09" 30°00'43" 30°00'17" 29°59'51" 29°59'25"

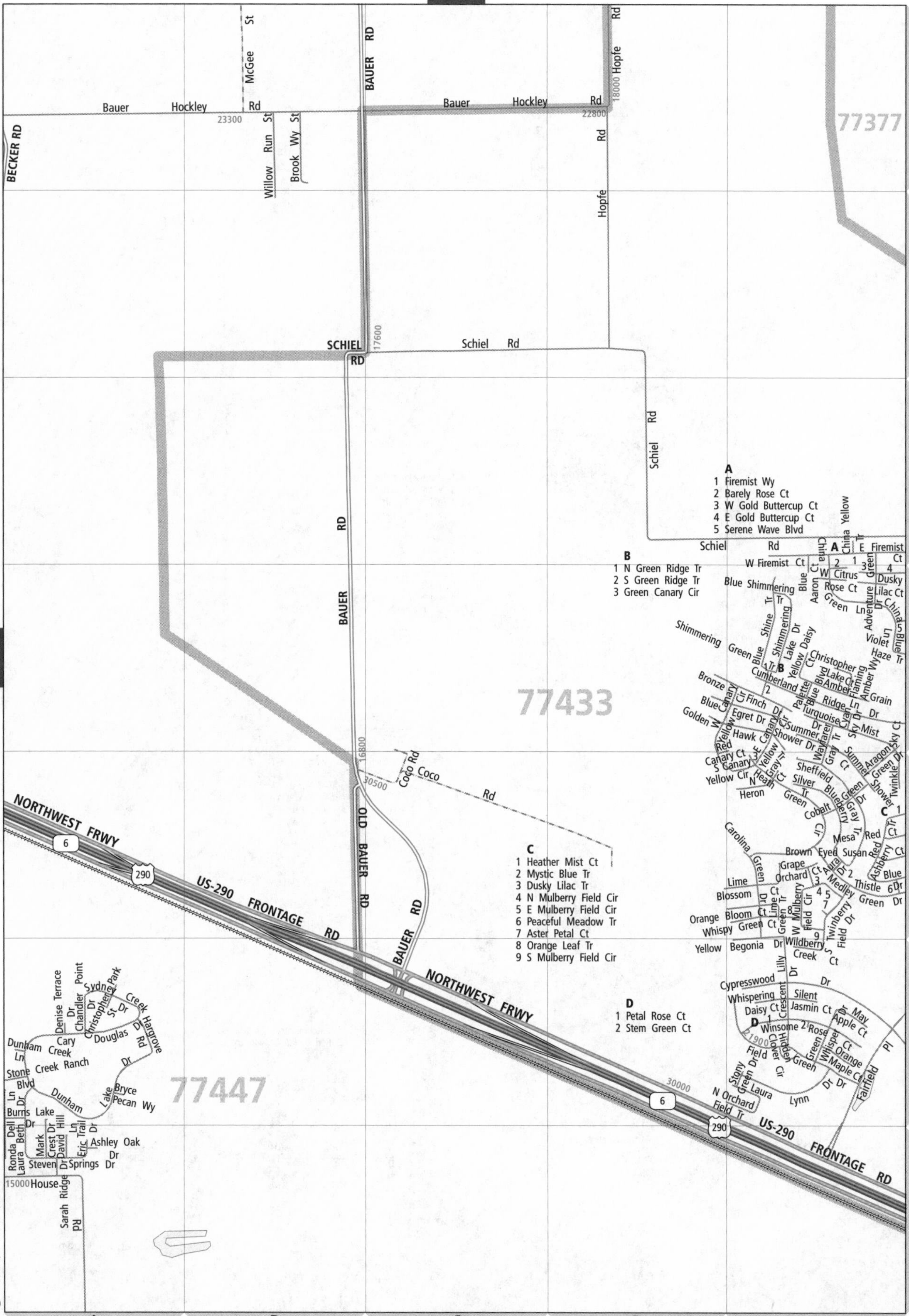
Bauer
Hockley
Rd
23300
22800
McGee St
BAUER RD
Hopfe Rd
18000
Willow Run St
Brook Wy St
BECKER RD
77377
SCHIEL RD
Schiel Rd
17600
BAUER RD
77433
16800
30500
Coco Rd
OLD BAUER RD
BAUER RD
NORTHWEST FRWY
6
290
US-290 FRONTAGE RD
30000
77447
A
1 Firemist Wy
2 Barely Rose Ct
3 W Gold Buttercup Ct
4 E Gold Buttercup Ct
5 Serene Wave Blvd
B
1 N Green Ridge Tr
2 S Green Ridge Tr
3 Green Canary Cir
C
1 Heather Mist Ct
2 Mystic Blue Tr
3 Dusky Lilac Tr
4 N Mulberry Field Cir
5 E Mulberry Field Cir
6 Peaceful Meadow Tr
7 Aster Petal Ct
8 Orange Leaf Tr
9 S Mulberry Field Cir
D
1 Petal Rose Ct
2 Stem Green Ct
15000 House
Sarah Ridge Rd

1 2 3 4 5 6 7

SEE 3251 MAP

A B C D E

95°47'54" 95°47'24" 95°46'54" 95°46'24" 95°45'54" 95°45'24"

SEE B MAP

1:24,000
1 in. = 2000 ft.
0 0.25 0.5
miles

SEE 3106 MAP

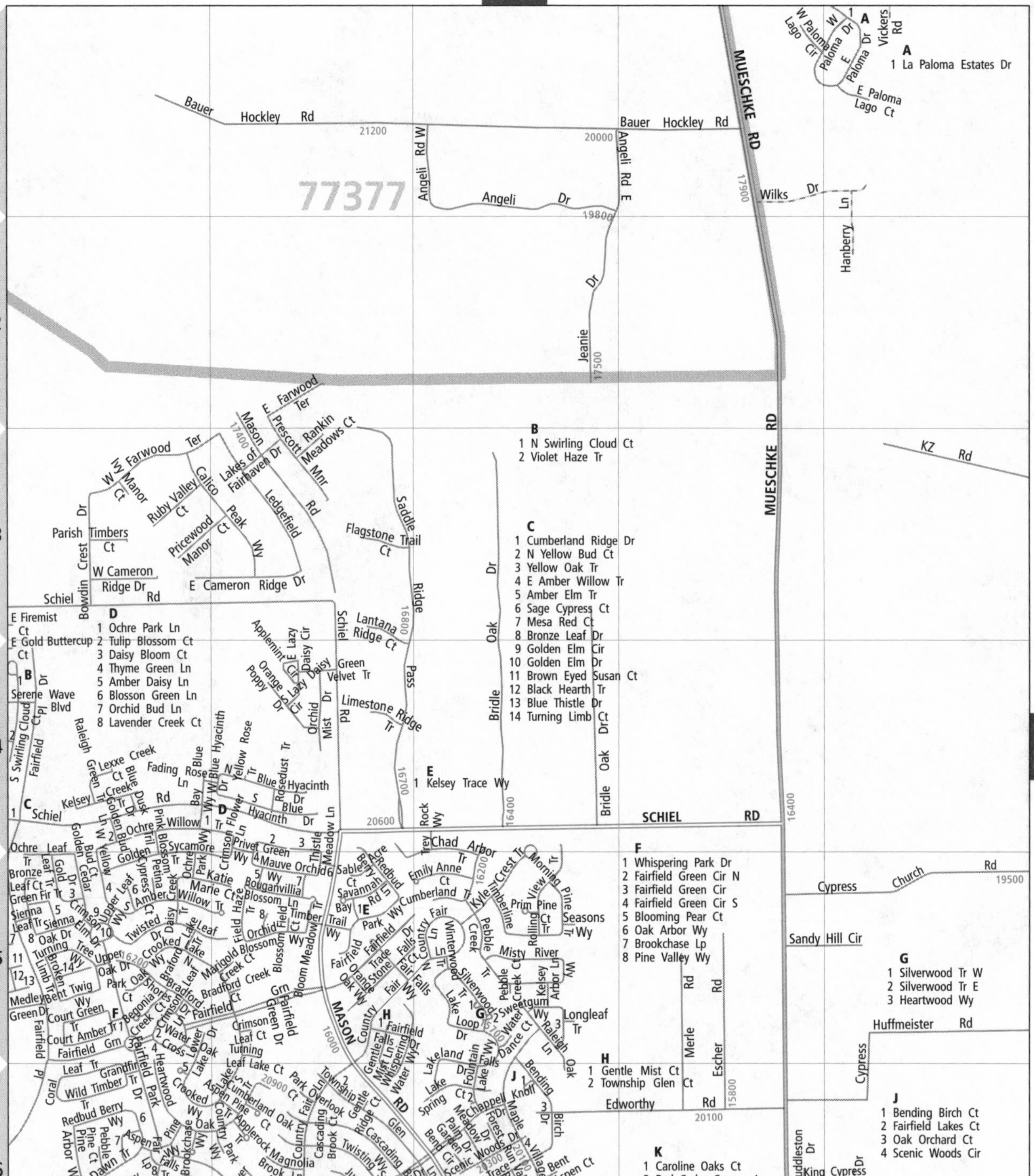
77377
77433
77447
MUESCHKE RD
SCHIEL RD
MASON RD
Bauer Hockley Rd
Angeli Rd W
Angeli Rd E
Angeli Dr
Jeanie Dr
Wilks Dr
Hanberry Ln
KZ Rd
Cypress Church Rd
Sandy Hill Cir
Huffmeister Rd
Edworthy Rd
Bridle Oak Dr
Merle Rd
Escher Rd
Saddle Ridge Pass
Flagstone Trail Ct
Lantana Ridge Ct
Limestone Ridge Tr
Chappell
NORTHWEST FRWY US-290 FRONTAGE RD
Cypresswood Dr
CYPRESS LAKES GC
A
1 La Paloma Estates Dr
B
1 N Swirling Cloud Ct
2 Violet Haze Tr
C
1 Cumberland Ridge Dr
2 N Yellow Bud Ct
3 Yellow Oak Tr
4 E Amber Willow Tr
5 Amber Elm Tr
6 Sage Cypress Ct
7 Mesa Red Ct
8 Bronze Leaf Dr
9 Golden Elm Cir
10 Golden Elm Dr
11 Brown Eyed Susan Ct
12 Black Hearth Tr
13 Blue Thistle Dr
14 Turning Limb Ct
D
1 Ochre Park Ln
2 Tulip Blossom Ct
3 Daisy Bloom Ct
4 Thyme Green Ln
5 Amber Daisy Ln
6 Blosson Green Ln
7 Orchid Bud Ln
8 Lavender Creek Ct
E
1 Kelsey Trace Wy
F
1 Whispering Park Dr
2 Fairfield Green Cir N
3 Fairfield Green Cir
4 Fairfield Green Cir S
5 Blooming Pear Ct
6 Oak Arbor Wy
7 Brookchase Lp
8 Pine Valley Wy
G
1 Silverwood Tr W
2 Silverwood Tr E
3 Heartwood Wy
H
1 Gentle Mist Ct
2 Township Glen Ct
J
1 Bending Birch Ct
2 Fairfield Lakes Ct
3 Oak Orchard Ct
4 Scenic Woods Cir
K
1 Caroline Oaks Ct
2 Red Cedar Canyon Ln
A B C D E
1 2 3 4 5 6 7

SEE 3250 MAP

SEE 3395 MAP

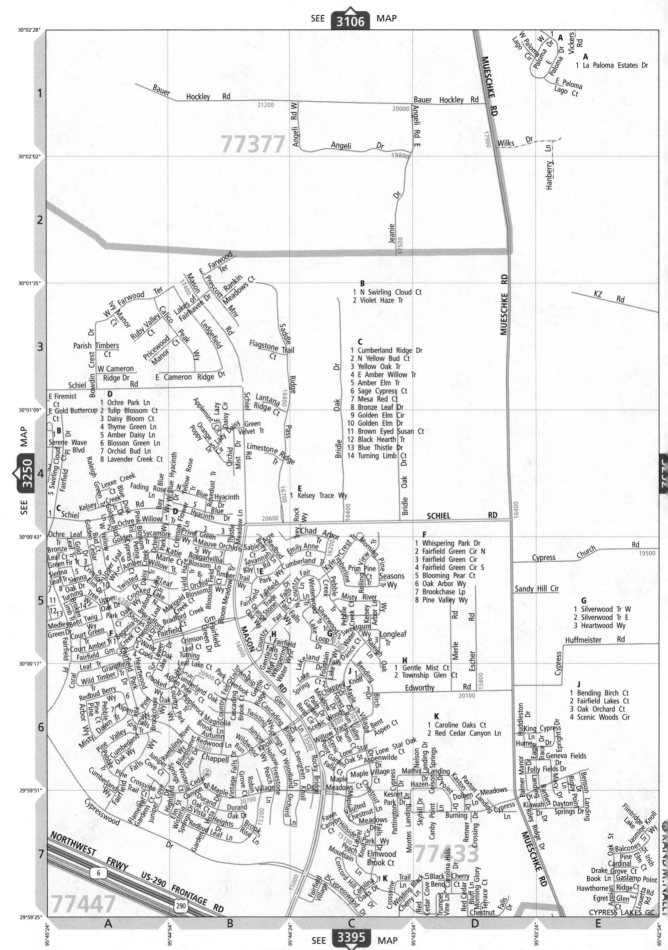

1:24,000
1 in. = 2000 ft.
0 0.25 0.5
miles

SEE 3107 MAP

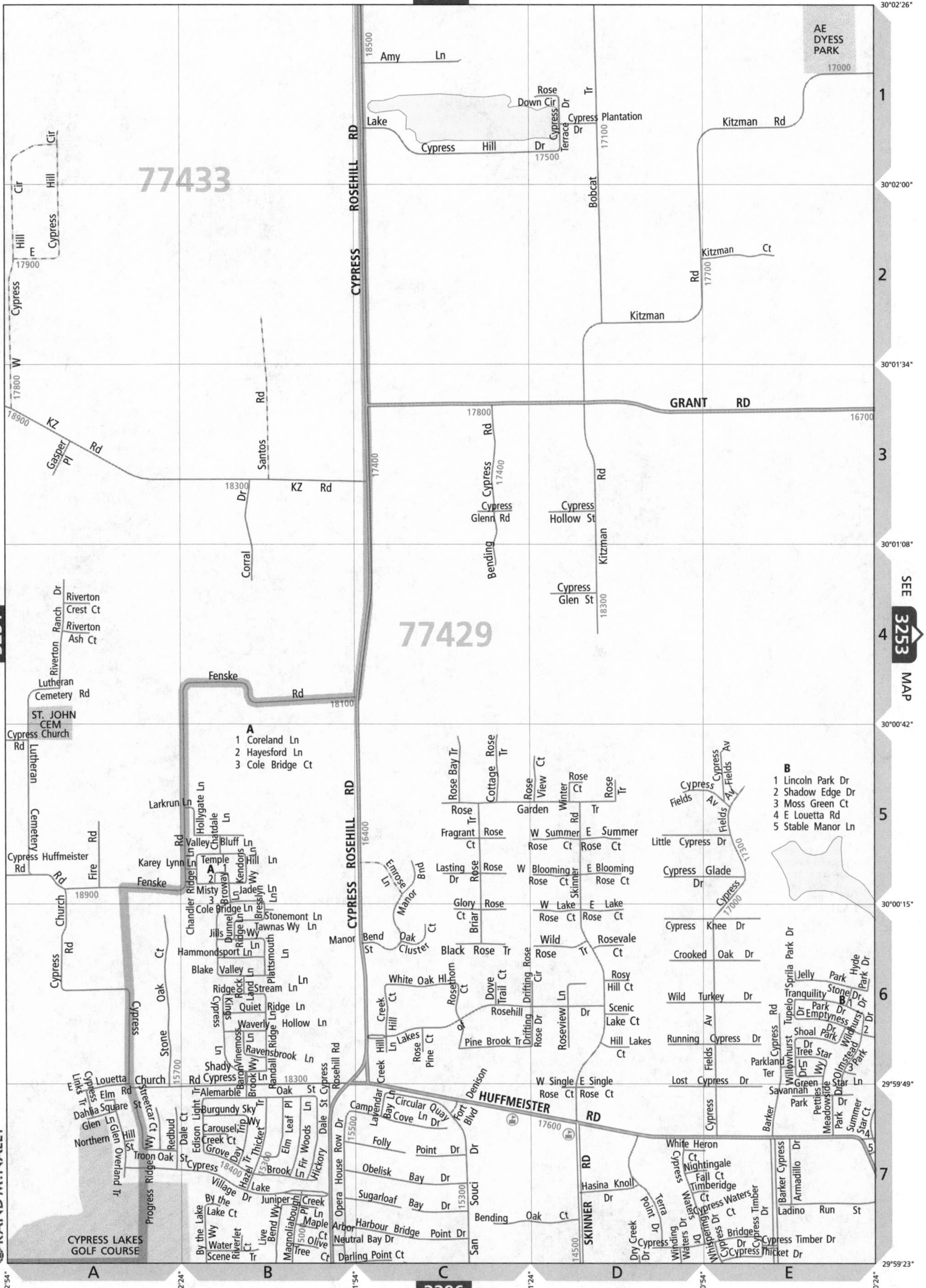
77433
77429
AE DYESS PARK
Amy Ln
Lake
Cypress Hill Dr
Rose Down Cir
Cypress Terrace Dr
Cypress Plantation Dr
Bobcat Tr
Kitzman Rd
Kitzman Ct
Kitzman
GRANT RD
CYPRESS ROSEHILL RD
KZ Rd
Gasper Pl
Santos Rd
Corral Dr
Cypress Hill Cir
E Cypress Hill Cir
W Cypress Rd
Cypress Glenn Rd
Bending Cypress Rd
Cypress Hollow St
Cypress Glen St
Kitzman Rd
Riverton Ranch Dr
Riverton Crest Ct
Riverton Ash Ct
Lutheran Cemetery Rd
ST. JOHN CEM
Cypress Church Rd
Fenske Rd
A
1 Coreland Ln
2 Hayesford Ln
3 Cole Bridge Ct
B
1 Lincoln Park Dr
2 Shadow Edge Dr
3 Moss Green Ct
4 E Louetta Rd
5 Stable Manor Ln
Larkrun Ln
Hollygate Ln
Chatdale Ln
Valley Bluff Ln
Karey Lynn Ln
Temple Hill Ln
Misty Jade Ln
Cole Bridge Ln
Stonemont Ln
Tawnas Wy
Jills Wy
Hammondsport Ln
Blake Valley Ln
Plattsmouth Ln
Ridge Stream Ln
Quiet Ridge Ln
Waverly Hollow Ln
Ravensbrook Ln
Shady Cypress
Cypress Huffmeister Rd
Cypress Church Rd
Fire Rd
Oak Ct
Stone Oak
Louetta Church Rd
Elm Rd
Dahlia Square St
Glen Ln
Northern Hill
Glen Overland Tr
Troon Oak St
Progress Ridge
Streetcar Ct
Redbud Wy
Dale Ct
Edison Light Tr
Alemarble Brook
Burgundy Sky Tr
Carousel Trip
Creek Ct
Grove Day
Hazel Tr
Thicket
Elm Leaf Pl
Fir Woods
Hickory
Cypress Lake Village Dr
Juniper Creek
By the Lake Ct
By the Lake Wy
Water Scene Riverlet Ct Tr
Live Bend Wy
Magnoliabough Pl
Maple Ln
Olive Ct
Tree Ct
Rosehill Rd
Opera House Row Dr
Arbor Neutral Bay Dr
Darling Point Ct
Harbour Bridge Point Dr
Sugarloaf Bay Dr
Obelisk Bay Dr
Folly Point Dr
Camp Lavendar Bay Ln
Circular Quay Cove Ln Dr
Fort Denison Blvd
San Souci Dr
Bending Oak Ct
HUFFMEISTER RD
CYPRESS LAKES GOLF COURSE
Rose Bay Tr
Cottage Rose Tr
Rose View Ct
Winter Rose Ct
Rose Garden Rd
Rose Tr
Fragrant Rose Ct
W Summer Rose Ct
E Summer Rose Ct
Lasting Rose Dr
W Blooming Rose Ct
E Blooming Rose Ct
Skinner
Glory Rose Ct
Briar Rose
W Lake Rose Ct
E Lake Rose Ct
Wild Rose Tr
Rosevale Ct
Black Rose Tr
Emrose Ln
Manor Bnd
Manor Bend St
Oak Cluster Ct
White Oak Hl
Rosehorn Ct
Dove Trail Ct
Drifting Rose Cir
Roseview Ln
Rosy Hill Ct
Scenic Lake Ct
Rosehill Dr
Pine Brook Tr
Drifting Rose Dr
Hill Lakes Ct
Creek Hill Ct
Lakes of Rosehill
Rose Pine Ct
W Single Rose Ct
E Single Rose Ct
Cypress Fields Av
Little Cypress Dr
Cypress Glade Dr
Cypress Knee Dr
Crooked Oak Dr
Wild Turkey Dr
Running Cypress Dr
Lost Cypress Dr
Fields Av
Cypress Rd
Sprila Park Dr
Jelly Park Dr
Hyde Park Dr
Tranquility Park Dr
Stone Dr
Tupelo Dr
Emptyness Dr
Shoal Park Dr
Wildhurst Dr
Tree Star
Olmstead Park
Willowhurst
Parkland Ter
Savannah Green Park
Star Ln
Pettiet Dr
Meadowside Park Dr
Summer Star Ct
Barker Cypress Rd
Armadillo Dr
Ladino Run St
White Heron Ct
Nightingale Ct
Fall Ct
Timberidge Ct
Cypress Waters Ct
Cypress Timber Dr
Cypress Bridge Dr
Cypress Thicket Dr
Cypress Timber Dr
Whispering Cypress Dr
Winding Waters Dr
Dry Creek Dr
Cypress Terra Point Dr
Hasina Knoll Dr
SKINNER RD
18500
17500
17100
17000
17900
17700
17800
18900
18300
17400
16700
18100
16400
17300
18900
15700
18300
18400
15300
15500
15300
17600
14500
1
2
3
4
5
6
7
A
B
C
D
E
30°02'26"
30°02'00"
30°01'34"
30°01'08"
30°00'42"
30°00'15"
29°59'49"
29°59'23"
95°42'54"
95°42'24"
95°41'54"
95°41'24"
95°40'54"
95°40'24"
SEE 3253 MAP
3251

SEE 3396 MAP

1:24,000
1 in. = 2000 ft.
0 0.25 0.5
miles

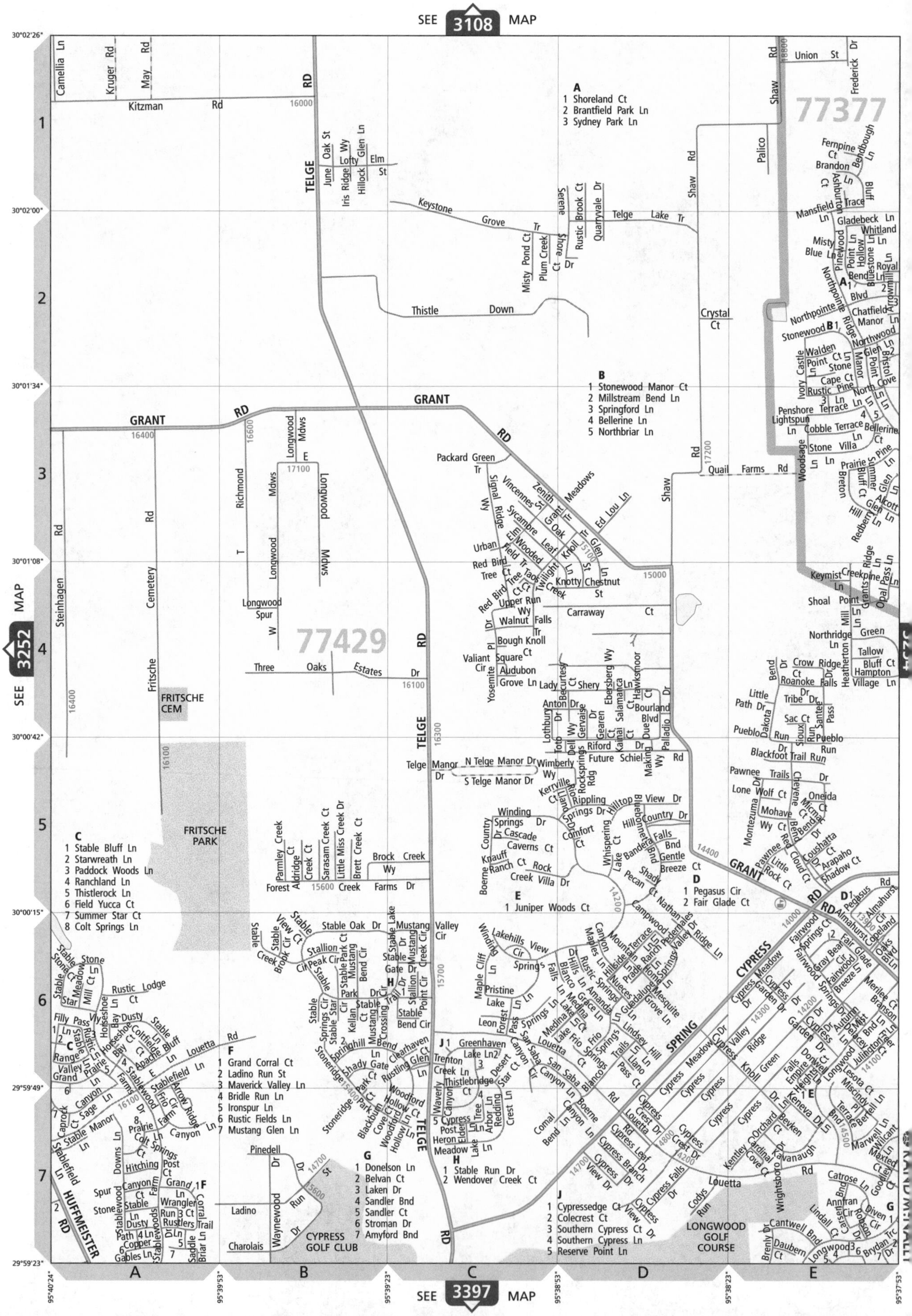
SEE 3108 MAP
SEE 3397 MAP
SEE 3252 MAP
77377
77429
GRANT RD
TELGE RD
CYPRESS
SPRING
HUFFMEISTER RD
Kitzman Rd
Shaw Rd
Cemetery Rd
Steinhagen Rd
Fritsche
FRITSCHE CEM
FRITSCHE PARK
Longwood Mdws
Richmond
Three Oaks Estates Dr
Keystone Grove Tr
Thistle Down
Telge Lake Tr
Crystal Ct
Quail Farms Rd
Carraway Ct
Louetta Rd
Telge Manor Dr
N Telge Manor Dr
S Telge Manor Dr
Brock Creek Wy
Forest Creek Farms Dr
Stable Oak Dr
Mustang Valley Cir
Pinedell Dr
Ladino
Charolais
Waynewood Dr
CYPRESS GOLF CLUB
LONGWOOD GOLF COURSE
Union St
Frederick Dr
Palico
Camellia Ln
Kruger Rd
May Rd
A
1 Shoreland Ct
2 Brantfield Park Ln
3 Sydney Park Ln
B
1 Stonewood Manor Ct
2 Millstream Bend Ln
3 Springford Ln
4 Bellerine Ln
5 Northbriar Ln
C
1 Stable Bluff Ln
2 Starwreath Ln
3 Paddock Woods Ln
4 Ranchland Ln
5 Thistlerock Ln
6 Field Yucca Ct
7 Summer Star Ct
8 Colt Springs Ln
D
1 Pegasus Cir
2 Fair Glade Ct
E
1 Juniper Woods Ct
F
1 Grand Corral Ct
2 Ladino Run St
3 Maverick Valley Ln
4 Bridle Run Ln
5 Ironspur Ln
6 Rustic Fields Ln
7 Mustang Glen Ln
G
1 Donelson Ln
2 Belvan Ct
3 Laken Dr
4 Sandler Bnd
5 Sandler Ct
6 Stroman Dr
7 Amyford Bnd
H
1 Stable Run Dr
2 Wendover Creek Ct
J
1 Cypressedge Ct
2 Colecrest Ct
3 Southern Cypress Ct
4 Southern Cypress Ln
5 Reserve Point Ln
30°02'26"
30°02'00"
30°01'34"
30°01'08"
30°00'42"
30°00'15"
29°59'49"
29°59'23"
95°40'24"
95°39'53"
95°39'23"
95°38'53"
95°38'23"
95°37'53"
A B C D E
1 2 3 4 5 6 7

1:24,000
1 in. = 2000 ft.
0 0.25 0.5
miles

SEE 3109 MAP

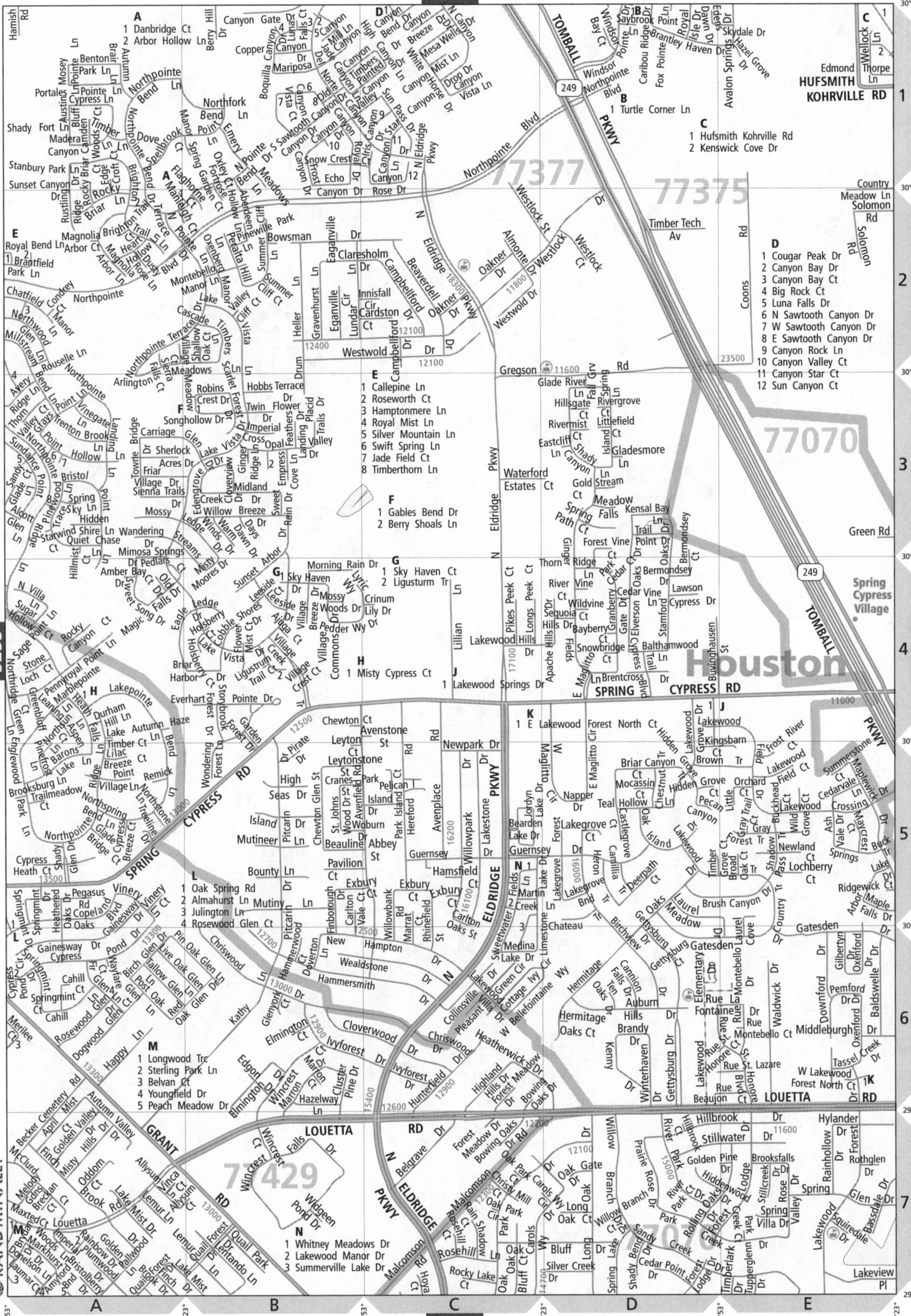
30°02'25"
30°01'58"
30°01'32"
30°01'06"
30°00'40"
30°00'14"
29°59'48"
29°59'21"
1
2
3
4
5
6
7
A
B
C
D
E
95°37'53"
95°37'23"
95°36'53"
95°36'23"
95°35'53"
95°35'23"
A
1 Danbridge Ct
2 Arbor Hollow Ln
B
1 Turtle Corner Ln
C
1 Hufsmith Kohrville Rd
2 Kenswick Cove Dr
D
1 Cougar Peak Dr
2 Canyon Bay Dr
3 Canyon Bay Ct
4 Big Rock Ct
5 Luna Falls Dr
6 N Sawtooth Canyon Dr
7 W Sawtooth Canyon Dr
8 E Sawtooth Canyon Dr
9 Canyon Rock Ln
10 Canyon Valley Ct
11 Canyon Star Ct
12 Sun Canyon Ct
E
1 Callepine Ln
2 Roseworth Ct
3 Hamptonmere Ln
4 Royal Mist Ln
5 Silver Mountain Ln
6 Swift Spring Ln
7 Jade Field Ct
8 Timberthorn Ln
F
1 Gables Bend Dr
2 Berry Shoals Ln
G
1 Sky Haven Ct
2 Ligusturm Tr
H
1 Misty Cypress Ct
J
1 Lakewood Springs Dr
K
1 E Lakewood Forest North Ct
L
1 Oak Spring Rd
2 Almahurst Ln
3 Julington Ln
4 Rosewood Glen Ct
M
1 Longwood Trc
2 Sterling Park Ln
3 Belvan Ct
4 Youngfield Dr
5 Peach Meadow Dr
N
1 Whitney Meadows Dr
2 Lakewood Manor Dr
3 Summerville Lake Dr
TOMBALL PKWY
249
HUFSMITH KOHRVILLE RD
Northpointe Blvd
77377
77375
77070
77429
Timber Tech Av
Coons Rd
Solomon Rd
Green Rd
Gregson Rd
Westwold Dr
Eldridge Pkwy
N Eldridge Pkwy
Spring Cypress Village
Houston
SPRING CYPRESS RD
LOUETTA RD
GRANT RD
Gatesden Dr
Lakewood Forest North Ct
Bowsman Dr
Waterford Estates Ct
Lakeview Pl
RAND McNALLY

SEE 3255 MAP

SEE 3253 MAP

SEE 3398 MAP

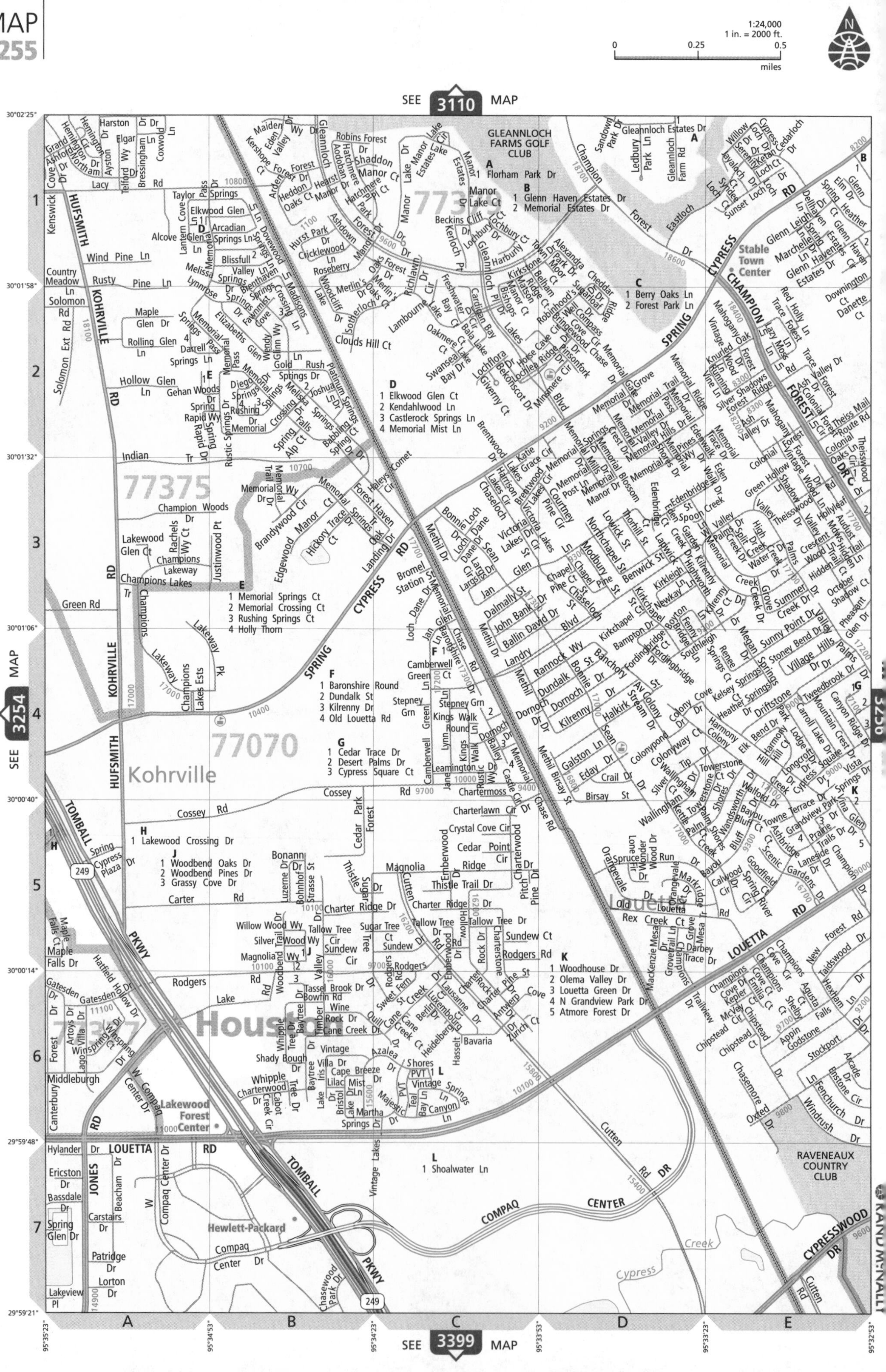
1:24,000
1 in. = 2000 ft.
0 0.25 0.5
miles
N
SEE 3110 MAP
SEE 3254 MAP
SEE 3399 MAP
3256
GLEANNLOCH FARMS GOLF CLUB
RAVENEAUX COUNTRY CLUB
Stable Town Center
Lakewood Forest Center
Hewlett-Packard
Kohrville
Houston
Louetta
77379
77375
77070
77377
HUFSMITH KOHRVILLE RD
SPRING CYPRESS RD
CHAMPION FOREST DR
TOMBALL PKWY
LOUETTA RD
COMPAQ CENTER DR
CYPRESSWOOD DR
JONES RD
Cypress Creek
A
1 Florham Park Dr
B
1 Glenn Haven Estates Dr
2 Memorial Estates Dr
C
1 Berry Oaks Ln
2 Forest Park Ln
D
1 Elkwood Glen Ct
2 Kendahlwood Ln
3 Castlerock Springs Ln
4 Memorial Mist Ln
E
1 Memorial Springs Ct
2 Memorial Crossing Ct
3 Rushing Springs Ct
4 Holly Thorn
F
1 Baronshire Round
2 Dundalk St
3 Kilrenny Dr
4 Old Louetta Rd
G
1 Cedar Trace Dr
2 Desert Palms Dr
3 Cypress Square Ct
H
1 Lakewood Crossing Dr
J
1 Woodbend Oaks Dr
2 Woodbend Pines Dr
3 Grassy Cove Dr
K
1 Woodhouse Dr
2 Olema Valley Dr
3 Louetta Green Dr
4 N Grandview Park Dr
5 Atmore Forest Dr
L
1 Shoalwater Ln
30°02'25"
30°01'58"
30°01'32"
30°01'06"
30°00'40"
30°00'14"
29°59'48"
29°59'21"
95°35'23"
95°34'53"
95°34'23"
95°33'53"
95°33'23"
95°32'53"
RAND McNALLY

1:24,000
1 in. = 2000 ft.
0 0.25 0.5
miles

SEE 3111 MAP

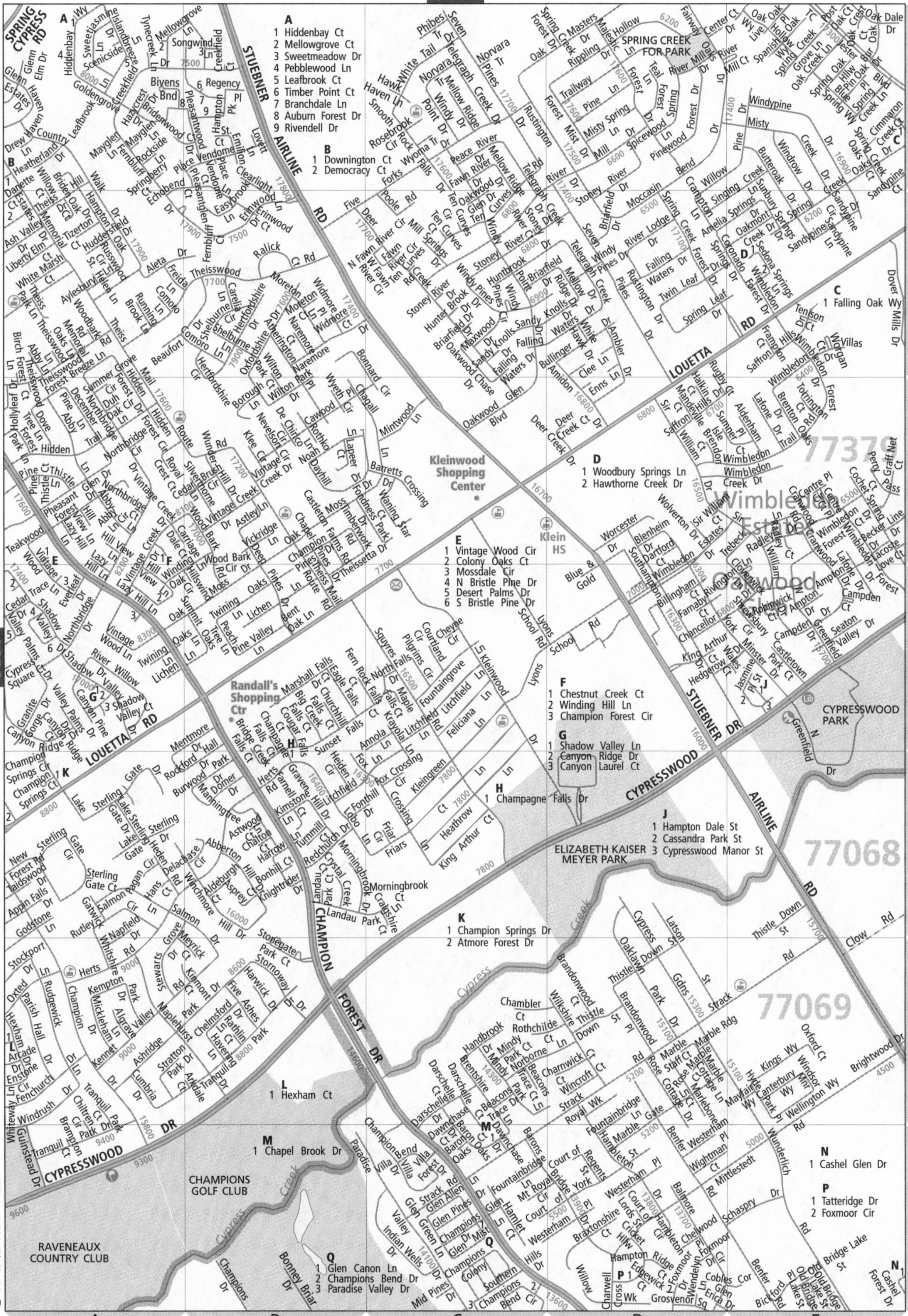
A
1 Hiddenbay Ct
2 Mellowgrove Ct
3 Sweetmeadow Dr
4 Pebblewood Ln
5 Leafbrook Ct
6 Timber Point Ct
7 Branchdale Ln
8 Auburn Forest Dr
9 Rivendell Dr
B
1 Downington Ct
2 Democracy Ct
C
1 Falling Oak Wy
D
1 Woodbury Springs Ln
2 Hawthorne Creek Dr
E
1 Vintage Wood Cir
2 Colony Oaks Ct
3 Mossdale Cir
4 N Bristle Pine Dr
5 Desert Palms Dr
6 S Bristle Pine Dr
F
1 Chestnut Creek Ct
2 Winding Hill Ln
3 Champion Forest Cir
G
1 Shadow Valley Ln
2 Canyon Ridge Dr
3 Canyon Laurel Ct
H
1 Champagne Falls Dr
J
1 Hampton Dale St
2 Cassandra Park St
3 Cypresswood Manor St
K
1 Champion Springs Dr
2 Atmore Forest Dr
L
1 Hexham Ct
M
1 Chapel Brook Dr
N
1 Cashel Glen Dr
P
1 Tatteridge Dr
2 Foxmoor Cir
Q
1 Glen Canon Ln
2 Champions Bend Dr
3 Paradise Valley Dr
SPRING CREEK FOR PARK
Kleinwood Shopping Center
Klein HS
Randall's Shopping Ctr
CYPRESSWOOD PARK
ELIZABETH KAISER MEYER PARK
CHAMPIONS GOLF CLUB
RAVENEAUX COUNTRY CLUB
Wimbledon Estates
Oakwood Glen
77379
77068
77069
STUEBNER AIRLINE RD
LOUETTA RD
CYPRESSWOOD DR
CHAMPION FOREST DR
AIRLINE RD
SPRING CYPRESS RD
Cypress Creek
30°02'23"
30°01'56"
30°01'30"
30°01'04"
30°00'38"
30°00'12"
29°59'46"
29°59'19"
95°32'53"
95°32'23"
95°31'53"
95°31'23"
95°30'53"
95°30'23"
A B C D E
1 2 3 4 5 6 7

SEE 3257 MAP

SEE 3400 MAP

1:24,000
1 in. = 2000 ft.
0 0.25 0.5
miles

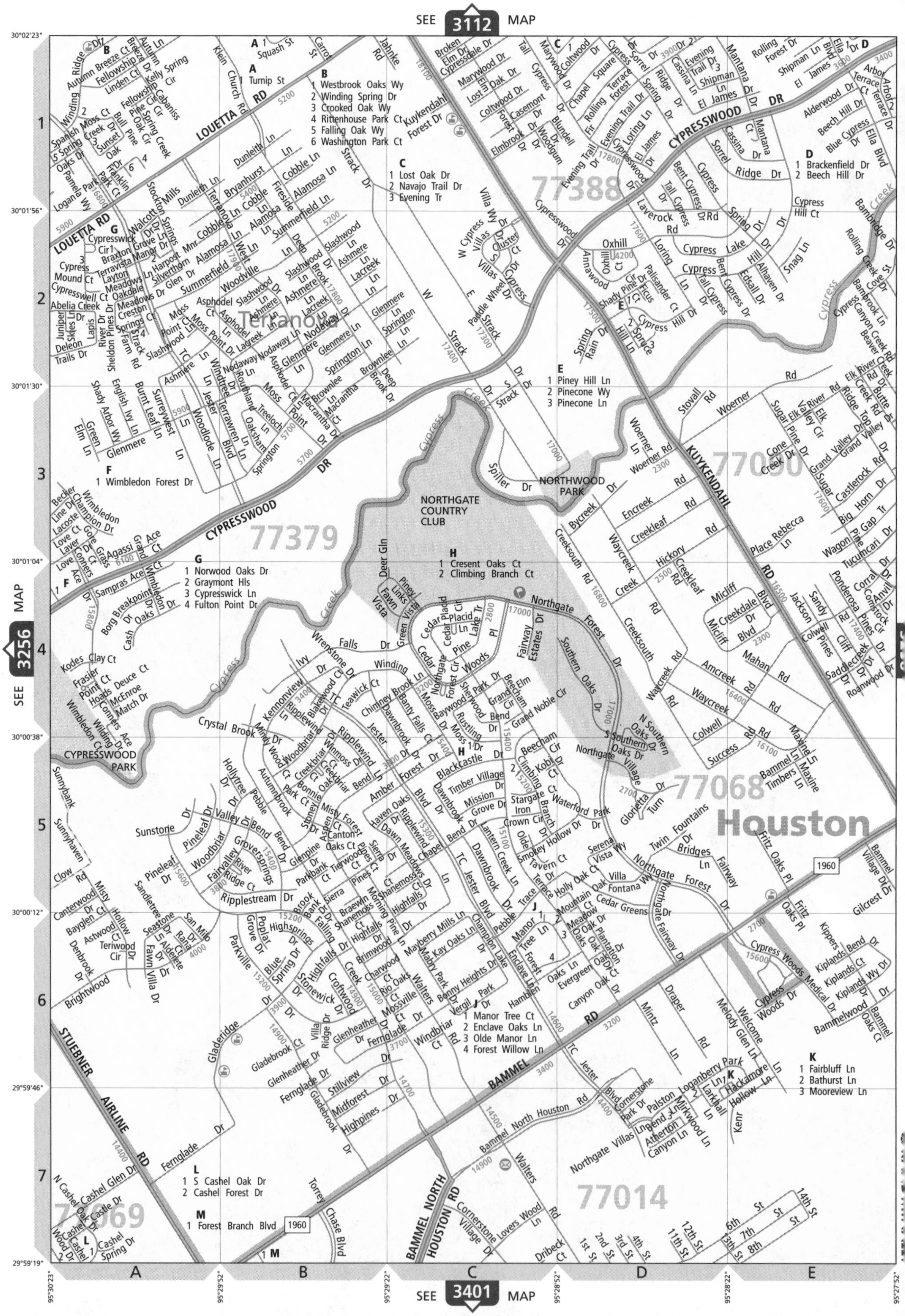
SEE 3112 MAP
SEE 3256 MAP
SEE 3401 MAP
A 1 Squash St
A 1 Turnip St
B
1 Westbrook Oaks Wy
2 Winding Spring Dr
3 Crooked Oak Wy
4 Rittenhouse Park Ct
5 Falling Oak Wy
6 Washington Park Ct
C
1 Lost Oak Dr
2 Navajo Trail Dr
3 Evening Tr
D
1 Brackenfield Dr
2 Beech Hill Dr
E
1 Piney Hill Ln
2 Pinecone Wy
3 Pinecone Ln
F
1 Wimbledon Forest Dr
G
1 Norwood Oaks Dr
2 Graymont Hls
3 Cypresswick Ln
4 Fulton Point Dr
H
1 Cresent Oaks Ct
2 Climbing Branch Ct
J
1 Manor Tree Ct
2 Enclave Oaks Ln
3 Olde Manor Ln
4 Forest Willow Ln
K
1 Fairbluff Ln
2 Bathurst Ln
3 Mooreview Ln
L
1 S Cashel Oak Dr
2 Cashel Forest Dr
M
1 Forest Branch Blvd
LOUETTA RD
CYPRESSWOOD DR
KUYKENDAHL RD
BAMMEL RD
STUEBNER AIRLINE RD
BAMMEL NORTH HOUSTON RD
1960
77388
77379
77090
77068
77014
77069
Houston
Terranova
NORTHGATE COUNTRY CLUB
NORTHWOOD PARK
CYPRESSWOOD PARK
Cypress Creek
30°02'23"
30°01'56"
30°01'30"
30°01'04"
30°00'38"
30°00'12"
29°59'46"
29°59'19"
95°30'23"
95°29'52"
95°29'22"
95°28'52"
95°28'22"
95°27'52"
A
B
C
D
E
1
2
3
4
5
6
7

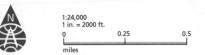

1:24,000
1 in. = 2000 ft.
0 0.25 0.5
miles

SEE 3113 MAP

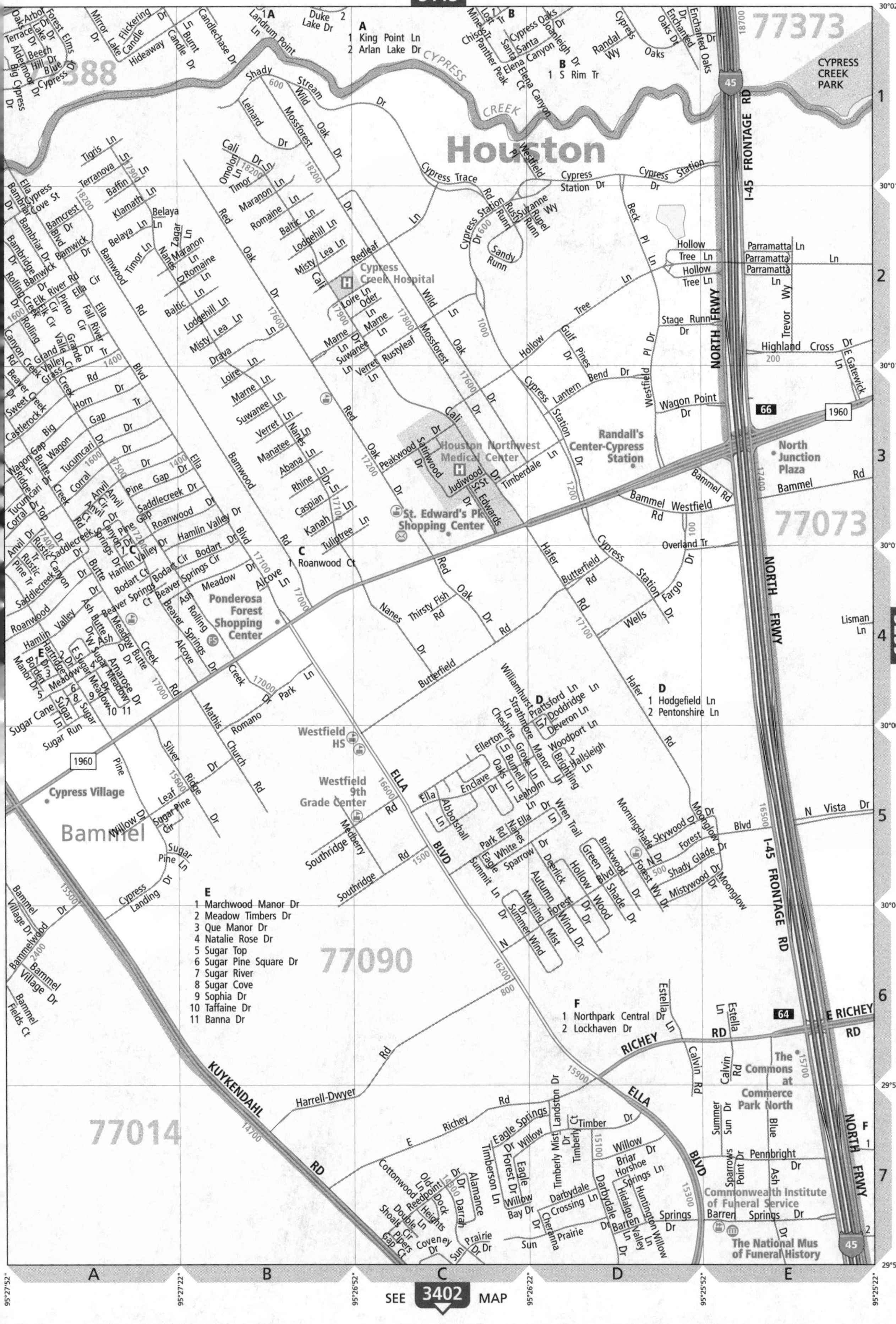
Houston
77373
77388
77073
77090
77014
Bammel
CYPRESS CREEK PARK
CYPRESS CREEK
Cypress Creek Hospital
Houston Northwest Medical Center
St. Edward's Pk Shopping Center
Randall's Center-Cypress Station
North Junction Plaza
Ponderosa Forest Shopping Center
Westfield HS
Westfield 9th Grade Center
Cypress Village
The Commons at Commerce Park North
Commonwealth Institute of Funeral Service
The National Mus of Funeral History
I-45 FRONTAGE RD
NORTH FRWY
KUYKENDAHL RD
ELLA BLVD
RICHEY RD
E RICHEY RD
1960
45
66
64
A
1 King Point Ln
2 Arlan Lake Dr
B
1 S Rim Tr
C
1 Roanwood Ct
D
1 Hodgefield Ln
2 Pentonshire Ln
E
1 Marchwood Manor Dr
2 Meadow Timbers Dr
3 Que Manor Dr
4 Natalie Rose Dr
5 Sugar Top
6 Sugar Pine Square Dr
7 Sugar River
8 Sugar Cove
9 Sophia Dr
10 Taffaine Dr
11 Banna Dr
F
1 Northpark Central Dr
2 Lockhaven Dr
30°02'20"
30°01'54"
30°01'28"
30°01'02"
30°00'36"
30°00'10"
29°59'43"
29°59'17"
95°27'52"
95°27'22"
95°26'52"
95°26'22"
95°25'52"
95°25'22"
A B C D E
1 2 3 4 5 6 7

SEE 3259 MAP

SEE 3402 MAP

1:24,000
1 in. = 2000 ft.
0 0.25 0.5
miles

SEE 3114 MAP

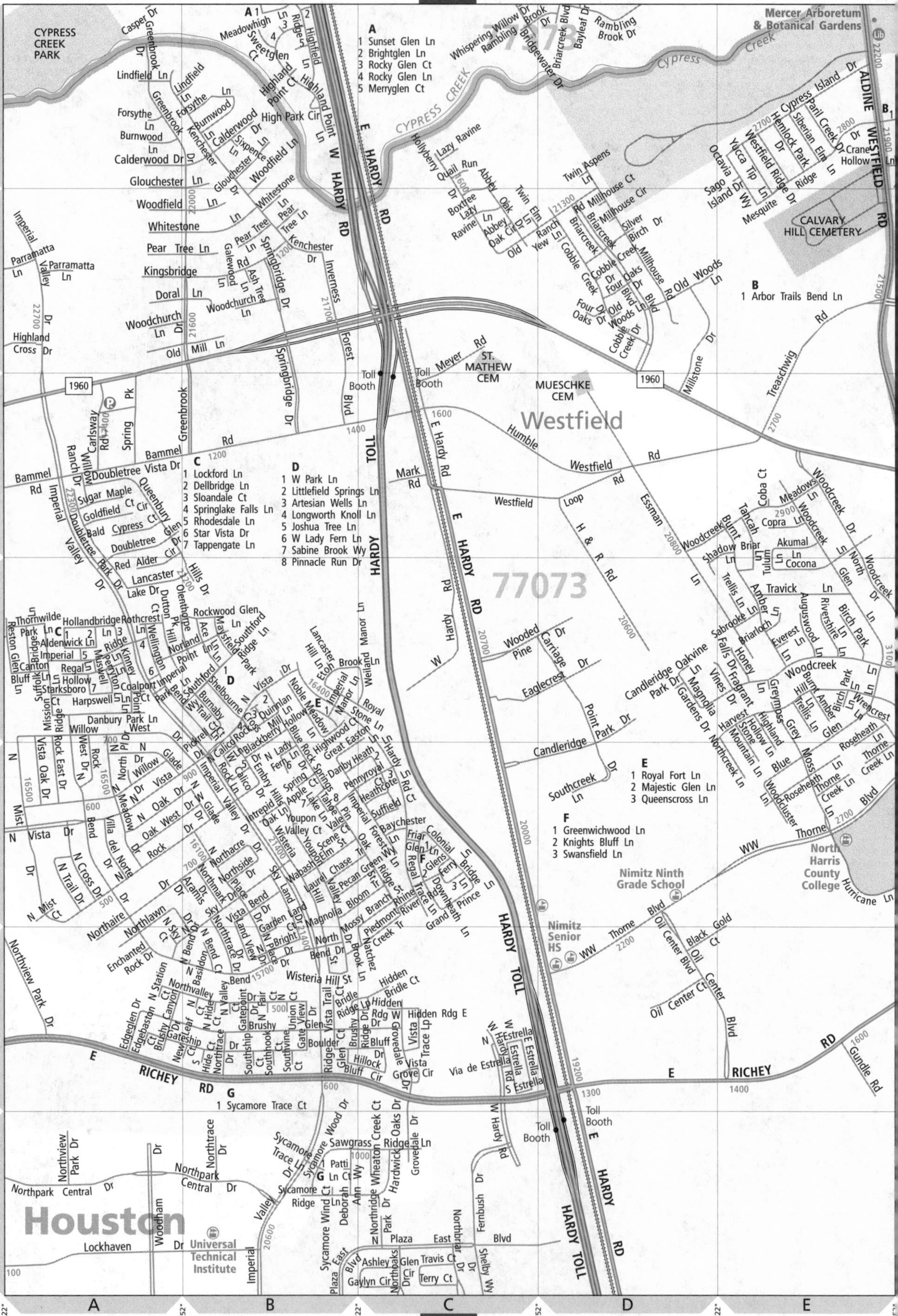
A
1 Sunset Glen Ln
2 Brightglen Ln
3 Rocky Glen Ct
4 Rocky Glen Ln
5 Merryglen Ct
B
1 Arbor Trails Bend Ln
C
1 Lockford Ln
2 Dellbridge Ln
3 Sloandale Ct
4 Springlake Falls Ln
5 Rhodesdale Ln
6 Star Vista Dr
7 Tappengate Ln
D
1 W Park Ln
2 Littlefield Springs Ln
3 Artesian Wells Ln
4 Longworth Knoll Ln
5 Joshua Tree Ln
6 W Lady Fern Ln
7 Sabine Brook Wy
8 Pinnacle Run Dr
E
1 Royal Fort Ln
2 Majestic Glen Ln
3 Queenscross Ln
F
1 Greenwichwood Ln
2 Knights Bluff Ln
3 Swansfield Ln
G
1 Sycamore Trace Ct
CYPRESS CREEK PARK
Mercer Arboretum & Botanical Gardens
Cypress Creek
CALVARY HILL CEMETERY
ST. MATHEW CEM
MUESCHKE CEM
Westfield
77073
77373
Nimitz Ninth Grade School
Nimitz Senior HS
North Harris County College
Universal Technical Institute
Houston
Toll Booth
HARDY TOLL RD
E HARDY RD
W HARDY RD
ALDINE WESTFIELD RD
E RICHEY RD
1960
Bammel Rd
Westfield Rd
Treaschwig Rd
Imperial Valley Dr
Northpark Central Dr
Lockhaven Dr
Thorne Blvd
WW Thorne Blvd
Humble Westfield Rd
Essman Rd
Candleridge Park Dr
Greenbrook Dr
Springbridge Dr
Inverness Forest Blvd

SEE 3258 MAP

30°02'20" 30°01'54" 30°01'28" 30°01'02" 30°00'36" 30°00'10" 29°59'43" 29°59'17"

95°25'22" 95°24'52" 95°24'22" 95°23'52" 95°23'22"

SEE 3403 MAP

1:24,000
1 in. = 2000 ft.
0 0.25 0.5
miles

SEE 3115 MAP

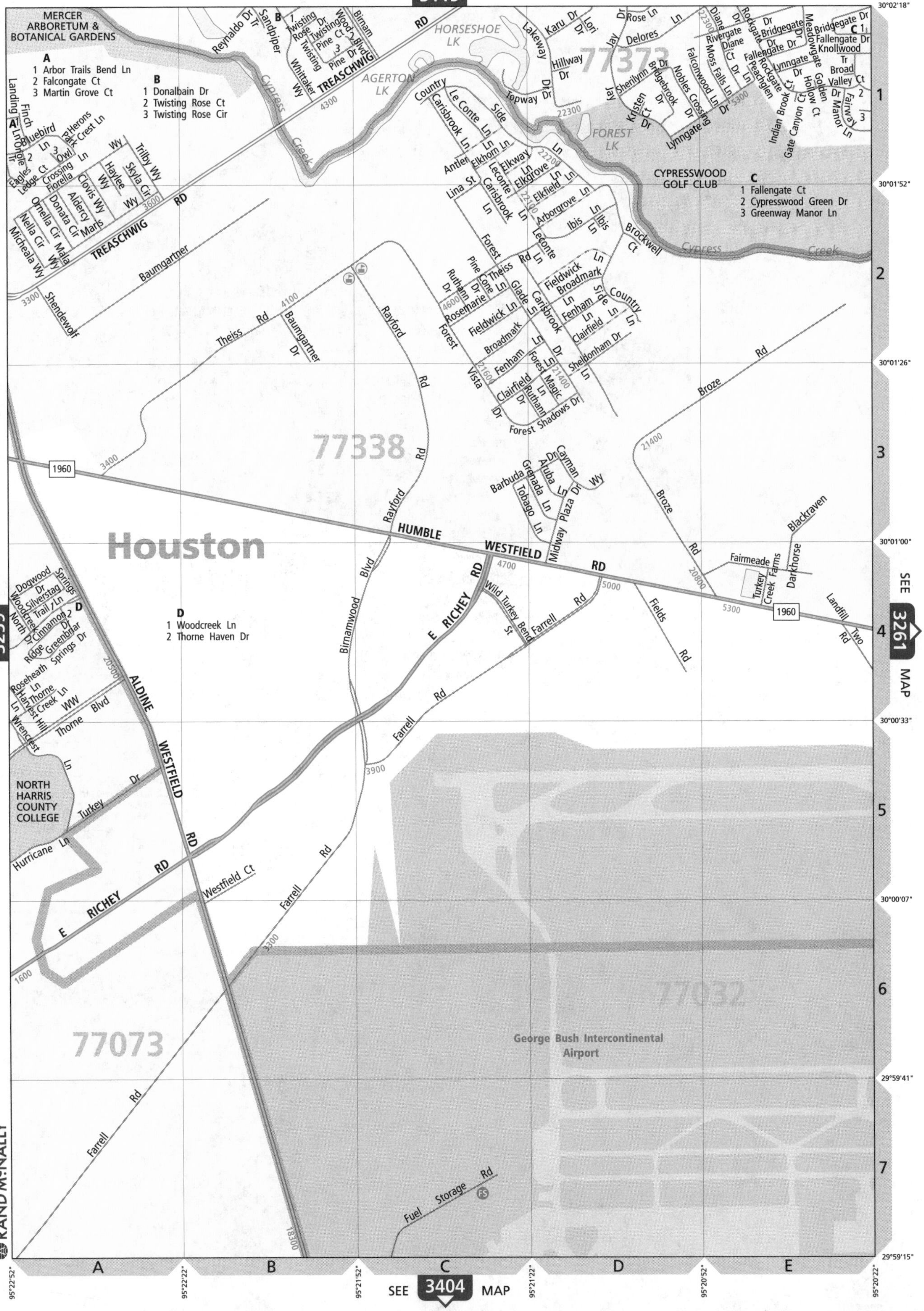
MERCER ARBORETUM & BOTANICAL GARDENS
A
1 Arbor Trails Bend Ln
2 Falcongate Ct
3 Martin Grove Ct
B
1 Donalbain Dr
2 Twisting Rose Ct
3 Twisting Rose Cir
C
1 Fallengate Ct
2 Cypresswood Green Dr
3 Greenway Manor Ln
D
1 Woodcreek Ln
2 Thorne Haven Dr
HORSESHOE LK
AGERTON LK
FOREST LK
CYPRESSWOOD GOLF CLUB
Cypress Creek
TREASCHWIG RD
77373
77338
77032
77073
Houston
HUMBLE WESTFIELD RD
1960
E RICHEY RD
ALDINE WESTFIELD RD
Rayford Rd
Birnamwood Blvd
Farrell Rd
Broze Rd
Theiss Rd
Baumgartner Dr
Shendewolf
Fields Rd
Landfill Two Rd
Turkey Creek Farms
Fairmeade
Blackraven
Darkhorse
Midway Plaza Dr
Wild Turkey Bend St
Westfield Ct
Hurricane Ln
Turkey Dr
NORTH HARRIS COUNTY COLLEGE
Thorne Blvd
Fuel Storage Rd
George Bush Intercontinental Airport
30°02'18"
30°01'52"
30°01'26"
30°01'00"
30°00'33"
30°00'07"
29°59'41"
29°59'15"
95°22'52"
95°22'22"
95°21'52"
95°21'22"
95°20'52"
95°20'22"
A B C D E
1 2 3 4 5 6 7

SEE 3261 MAP

SEE 3259 MAP

SEE 3404 MAP

1:24,000
1 in. = 2000 ft.
0 0.25 0.5
miles

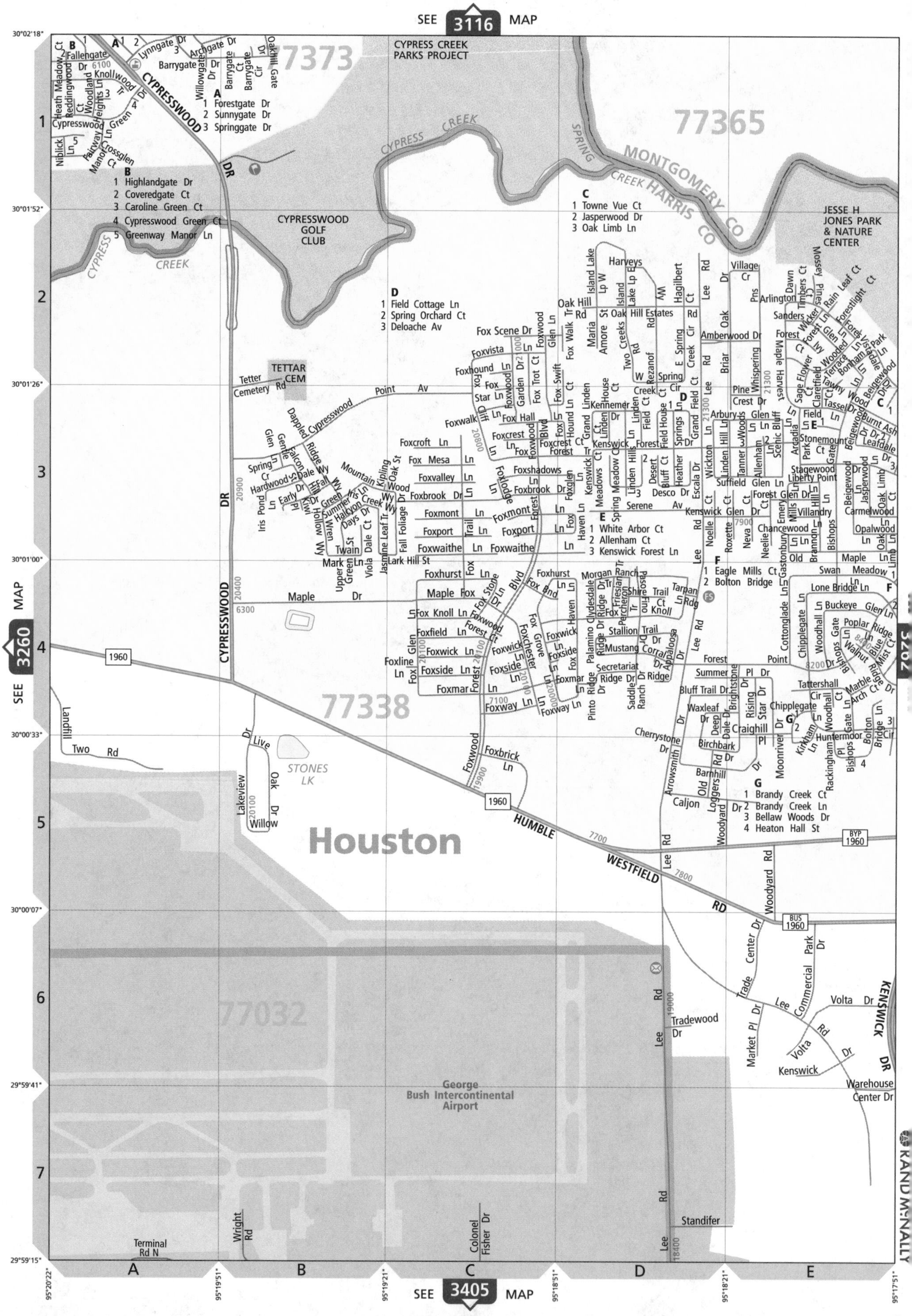
SEE 3116 MAP
SEE 3405 MAP
SEE 3260 MAP
CYPRESS CREEK PARKS PROJECT
77373
77365
77338
77032
CYPRESSWOOD GOLF CLUB
TETTAR CEM
JESSE H JONES PARK & NATURE CENTER
MONTGOMERY CO
HARRIS CO
CYPRESS CREEK
SPRING CREEK
STONES LK
Houston
George Bush Intercontinental Airport
CYPRESSWOOD DR
HUMBLE WESTFIELD RD
KENSWICK DR
Lee Rd
Woodyard Rd
Cypresswood Point Av
Maple Dr
Two Rd
Landfill
Terminal Rd N
Wright Rd
Colonel Fisher Dr
Standifer
Tradewood Dr
Trade Center Dr
Commercial Park Dr
Market Pl Dr
Volta Dr
Kenswick Dr
Warehouse Center Dr
A
1 Forestgate Dr
2 Sunnygate Dr
3 Springgate Dr
B
1 Highlandgate Dr
2 Coveredgate Ct
3 Caroline Green Ct
4 Cypresswood Green Ct
5 Greenway Manor Ln
C
1 Towne Vue Ct
2 Jasperwood Dr
3 Oak Limb Ln
D
1 Field Cottage Ln
2 Spring Orchard Ct
3 Deloache Av
E
1 White Arbor Ct
2 Allenham Ct
3 Kenswick Forest Ln
F
1 Eagle Mills Ct
2 Bolton Bridge
G
1 Brandy Creek Ct
2 Brandy Creek Ln
3 Bellaw Woods Dr
4 Heaton Hall St
30°02'18"
30°01'52"
30°01'26"
30°01'00"
30°00'33"
30°00'07"
29°59'41"
29°59'15"
95°20'22"
95°19'51"
95°19'21"
95°18'51"
95°18'21"
95°17'51"
1
2
3
4
5
6
7
A
B
C
D
E
RAND McNALLY

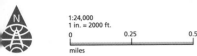

1:24,000
1 in. = 2000 ft.
0 0.25 0.5
miles

SEE 3117 MAP

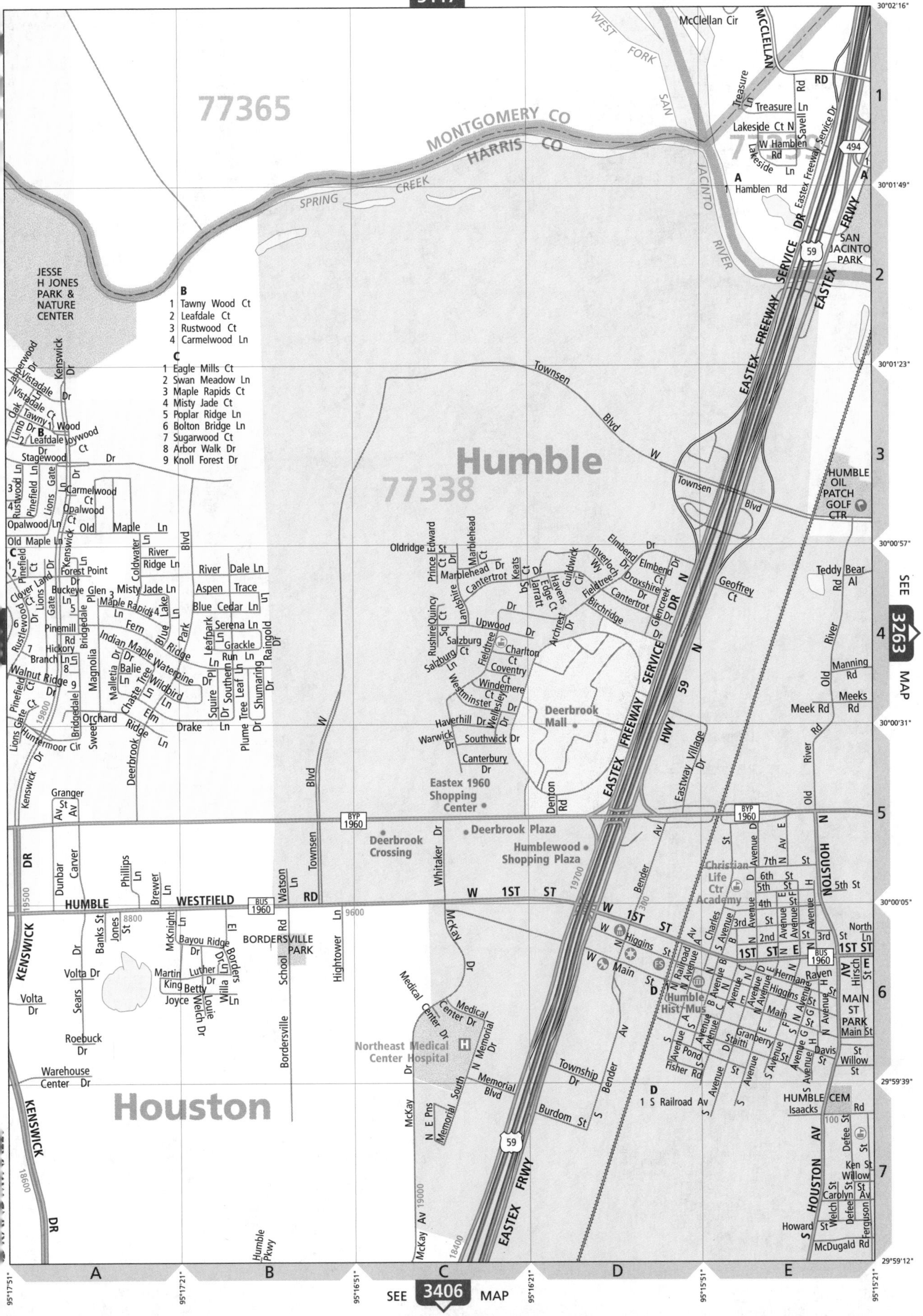
30°02'16"
30°01'49"
30°01'23"
30°00'57"
30°00'31"
30°00'05"
29°59'39"
29°59'12"
95°17'51"
95°17'21"
95°16'51"
95°16'21"
95°15'51"
95°15'21"
A
B
C
D
E
1
2
3
4
5
6
7
77365
77338
77339
Humble
Houston
MONTGOMERY CO
HARRIS CO
SPRING CREEK
WEST FORK SAN JACINTO RIVER
JESSE H JONES PARK & NATURE CENTER
SAN JACINTO PARK
HUMBLE OIL PATCH GOLF CTR
Deerbrook Mall
Eastex 1960 Shopping Center
Deerbrook Plaza
Deerbrook Crossing
Humblewood Shopping Plaza
Christian Life Ctr Academy
Humble Hist Mus
Northeast Medical Center Hospital
BORDERSVILLE PARK
MAIN ST PARK
HUMBLE CEM
B
1 Tawny Wood Ct
2 Leafdale Ct
3 Rustwood Ct
4 Carmelwood Ln
C
1 Eagle Mills Ct
2 Swan Meadow Ln
3 Maple Rapids Ct
4 Misty Jade Ct
5 Poplar Ridge Ln
6 Bolton Bridge Ln
7 Sugarwood Ct
8 Arbor Walk Dr
9 Knoll Forest Dr
A
1 Hamblen Rd
D
1 S Railroad Av
McClellan Cir
MCCLELLAN RD
Treasure Ln
Treasure Ln
Lakeside Ct N
W Hamblen Rd
Lakeside Ln
Savell Rd
Eastex Freeway Service Dr
EASTEX FRWY
EASTEX FREEWAY SERVICE DR
EASTEX FREEWAY SERVICE DR N
HWY 59 N
59
494
Townsen Blvd W
Townsen Blvd
Kenswick Dr
KENSWICK DR
Jasperwood Dr
Vistadale Dr
Oak Limb Dr
Stagewood Dr
Lions Gate Dr
Opalwood Ln
Old Maple Ln
Maple Ln
Coldwater Ln
River Ridge Ln
River Dale Ln
Aspen Trace Ln
Blue Cedar Ln
Serena Ln
Grackle Run Ln
Raingold Dr
Forest Point Dr
Buckeye Glen Dr
Misty Jade Ln
Maple Rapids Ln
Fern Lake Dr
Blue Ridge Park Dr
Indian Maple Dr
Waterpine Dr
Wildbird Ln
Pinemill Rd
Hickory Branch Ln
Walnut Ridge Dr
Bridgedale Dr
Magnolia
Malletia Dr
Balie Ln
Chaste Tree Ln
Elm Ridge Ln
Orchard Sweet
Deerbrook Dr
Drake Ln
Squire Dr
Southern Leaf Ln
Plume Tree Dr
Shumaring Dr
Huntermoor Cir
Granger St
Av
Dunbar
Carver
Phillips Ln
Brewer Ln
HUMBLE WESTFIELD RD
BYP 1960
BUS 1960
Watson Ln
Townsen
W Blvd
Whitaker Dr
W 1ST ST
McKay Dr
Banks St
Jones St
McKnight Ln
Bayou Ridge Dr
Martin Luther King Dr
Betty Ln
Joyce
Louie Welch Dr
Willa Ln
Borders
School Rd
Bordersville Rd
Hightower Ln
Volta Dr
Sears
Roebuck Dr
Warehouse Center Dr
Humble Pkwy
Oldridge Dr
Prince Edward Ct
Marblehead Ct
Marblehead Dr
Cantertrot Ct
Keats Ct
Guildwick Cir
Inverloch Wy
Elmbend Dr
Elmbend Ct
Droxshire Ct
Cantertrot Dr
Fieldtree Dr
Birchridge Dr
Glencreek Dr
Geoffrey Ct
Upwood Dr
Rushire
Quincy Sq
Landshire Ln
Salzburg Ct
Charlton Ct
Coventry Ct
Windemere Ct
Westminster Ct
Wellesley Dr
Haverhill Dr
Warwick Dr
Southwick Dr
Canterbury Dr
Denton Rd
Eastway Village Dr
Bender Av
Medical Center Dr
N Memorial Dr
Memorial Blvd
Township Dr
Burdom St
N E Pns
Memorial South
McKay Av
Teddy Bear Rd
River Al
Old River Rd
Manning Rd
Meeks Rd
Meek Rd
N HOUSTON AV
S HOUSTON AV
7th St
6th St
5th St
4th St
3rd St
2nd St
1ST ST E
North Ln
Higgins St
W Main St
Charles St
Railroad Av
Hirsch St
Raven St
Herman St
Davis St
Willow St
Staitti
Granberry St
Pond St
Fisher Rd
Isaacks Rd
Defee St
Ken St
Carolyn St
Welch St
Ferguson
Howard St
McDugald Rd
19500
19800
8800
9600
19700
300
19000
18400
18600
100

SEE 3263 MAP

SEE 3406 MAP

1:24,000
1 in. = 2000 ft.
0 0.25 0.5
miles

SEE 3118 MAP

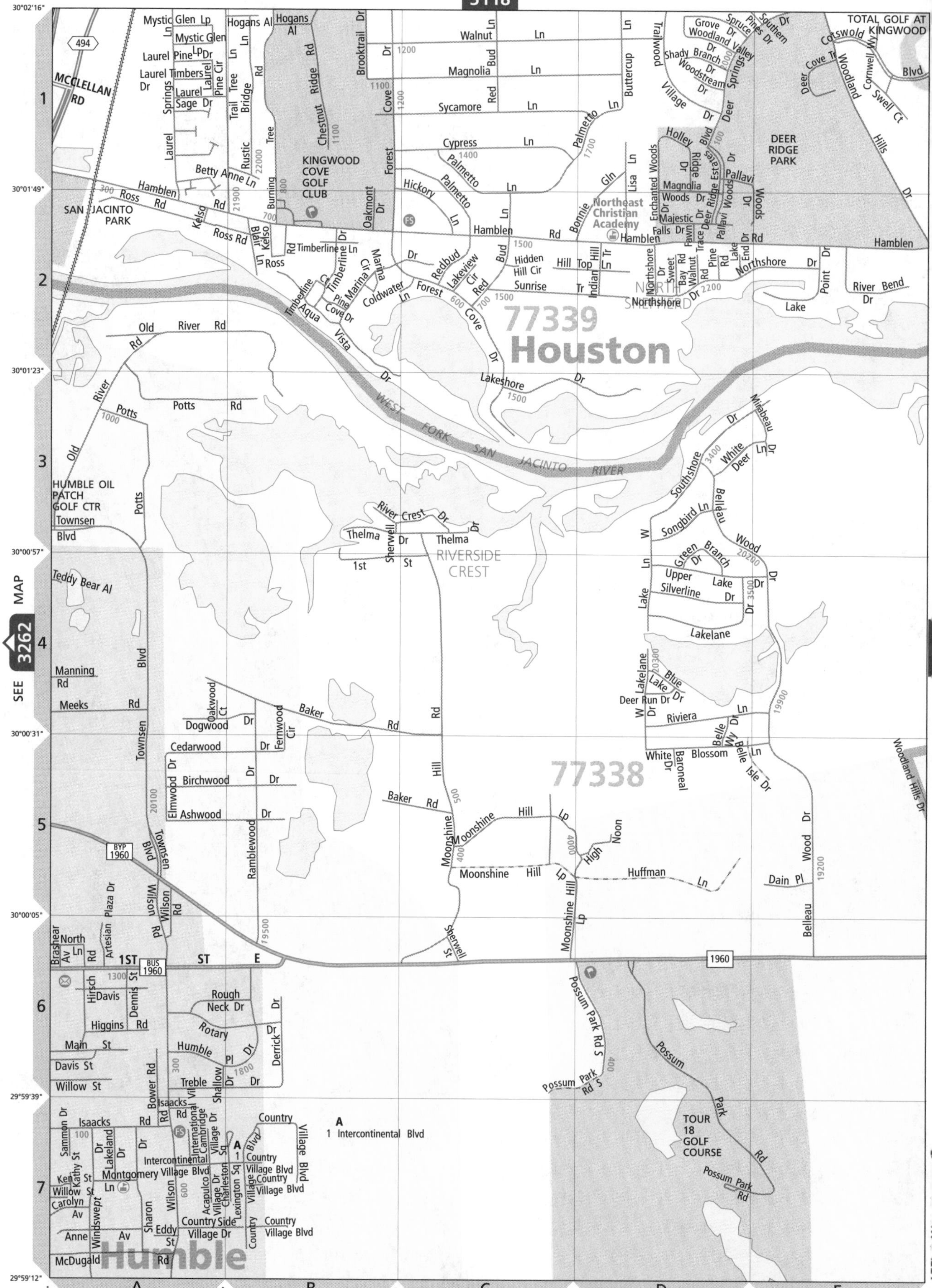
Houston
77339
77338
Humble
WEST FORK SAN JACINTO RIVER
KINGWOOD COVE GOLF CLUB
SAN JACINTO PARK
HUMBLE OIL PATCH GOLF CTR
DEER RIDGE PARK
TOTAL GOLF AT KINGWOOD
TOUR 18 GOLF COURSE
RIVERSIDE CREST
NORTH SHEPHERD
Northeast Christian Academy
McCLELLAN RD
494
Hamblen Rd
Ross Rd
Old River Rd
Potts Rd
Townsen Blvd
Baker Rd
Hill Rd
Moonshine Hill Lp
Huffman Ln
Belleau Wood Dr
Possum Park Rd
1960
BYP 1960
BUS 1960
1ST ST E
Wilson Rd
Northshore Dr
Lakeshore Dr
Forest Cove Dr
Aqua Vista Dr
Southshore Dr
Riviera Ln
Sherwell St
Intercontinental Vil
Country Village Blvd
Montgomery Village Blvd
A
1 Intercontinental Blvd
30°02'16"
30°01'49"
30°01'23"
30°00'57"
30°00'31"
30°00'05"
29°59'39"
29°59'12"
95°15'21"
95°14'51"
95°14'21"
95°13'51"
95°13'21"
95°12'51"
1
2
3
4
5
6
7
A
B
C
D
E

SEE 3262 MAP

SEE 3407 MAP

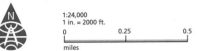

1:24,000
1 in. = 2000 ft.
0 0.25 0.5
miles

SEE 3119 MAP

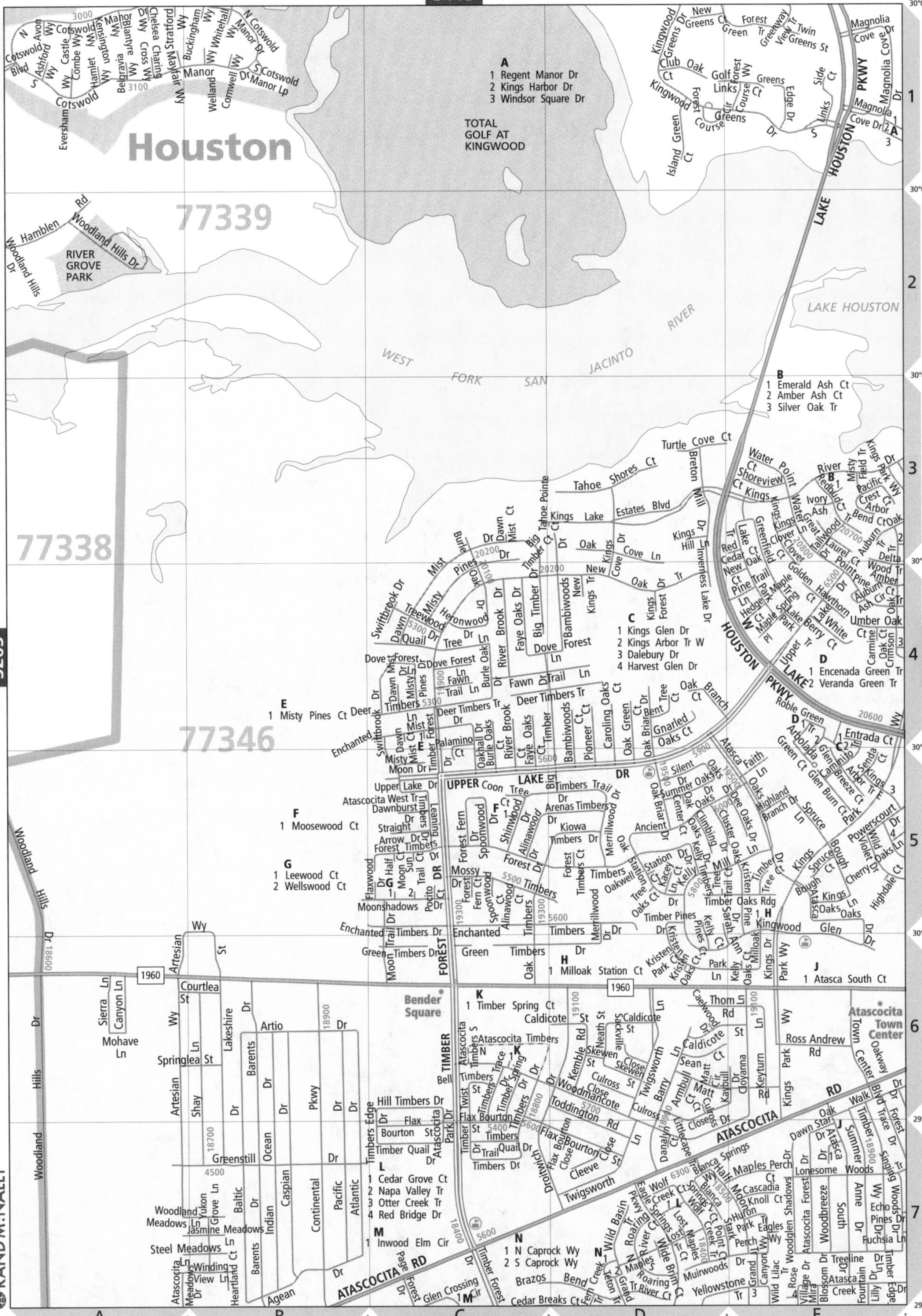
Houston
77339
77338
77346
RIVER GROVE PARK
TOTAL GOLF AT KINGWOOD
LAKE HOUSTON
WEST FORK SAN JACINTO RIVER
LAKE HOUSTON PKWY
UPPER LAKE DR
TIMBER FOREST DR
ATASCOCITA RD
Bender Square
Atascocita Town Center
Woodland Hills Dr
Kingwood Dr
Hamblen Rd
Woodland Hills Dr
Cotswold
Eversham
Manor
Tahoe Shores Ct
Turtle Cove Ct
Kings Lake Estates Blvd
Breton Mill Dr
Inverness Lake Dr
Atasca Oaks Dr
Kingwood Glen
Milloak Station Ct
Caldicote St
Toddington Rd
Twigsworth
Woodmancote
Greenstill
Continental Pkwy
Pacific Dr
Atlantic Dr
Caspian Dr
Ross Andrew Rd
Kings Park Wy
Summer Woods
Yellowstone
Brazos Bend
Cedar Breaks Ct
Glen Crossing Cir
1960
A
1 Regent Manor Dr
2 Kings Harbor Dr
3 Windsor Square Dr
B
1 Emerald Ash Ct
2 Amber Ash Ct
3 Silver Oak Tr
C
1 Kings Glen Dr
2 Kings Arbor Tr W
3 Dalebury Dr
4 Harvest Glen Dr
D
1 Encenada Green Tr
2 Veranda Green Tr
E
1 Misty Pines Ct
F
1 Moosewood Ct
G
1 Leewood Ct
2 Wellswood Ct
H
1 Milloak Station Ct
J
1 Atasca South Ct
K
1 Timber Spring Ct
L
1 Cedar Grove Ct
2 Napa Valley Tr
3 Otter Creek Tr
4 Red Bridge Dr
M
1 Inwood Elm Cir
N
1 N Caprock Wy
2 S Caprock Wy
1
2
3
4
5
6
7
A
B
C
D
E
30°02'13"
30°01'47"
30°01'20"
30°00'54"
30°00'28"
30°00'02"
29°59'36"
29°59'10"
95°12'51"
95°12'21"
95°11'51"
95°11'21"
95°10'51"
95°10'21"

SEE 3265 MAP

SEE 3408 MAP

1:24,000
1 in. = 2000 ft.
0 0.25 0.5
miles

SEE 3120 MAP

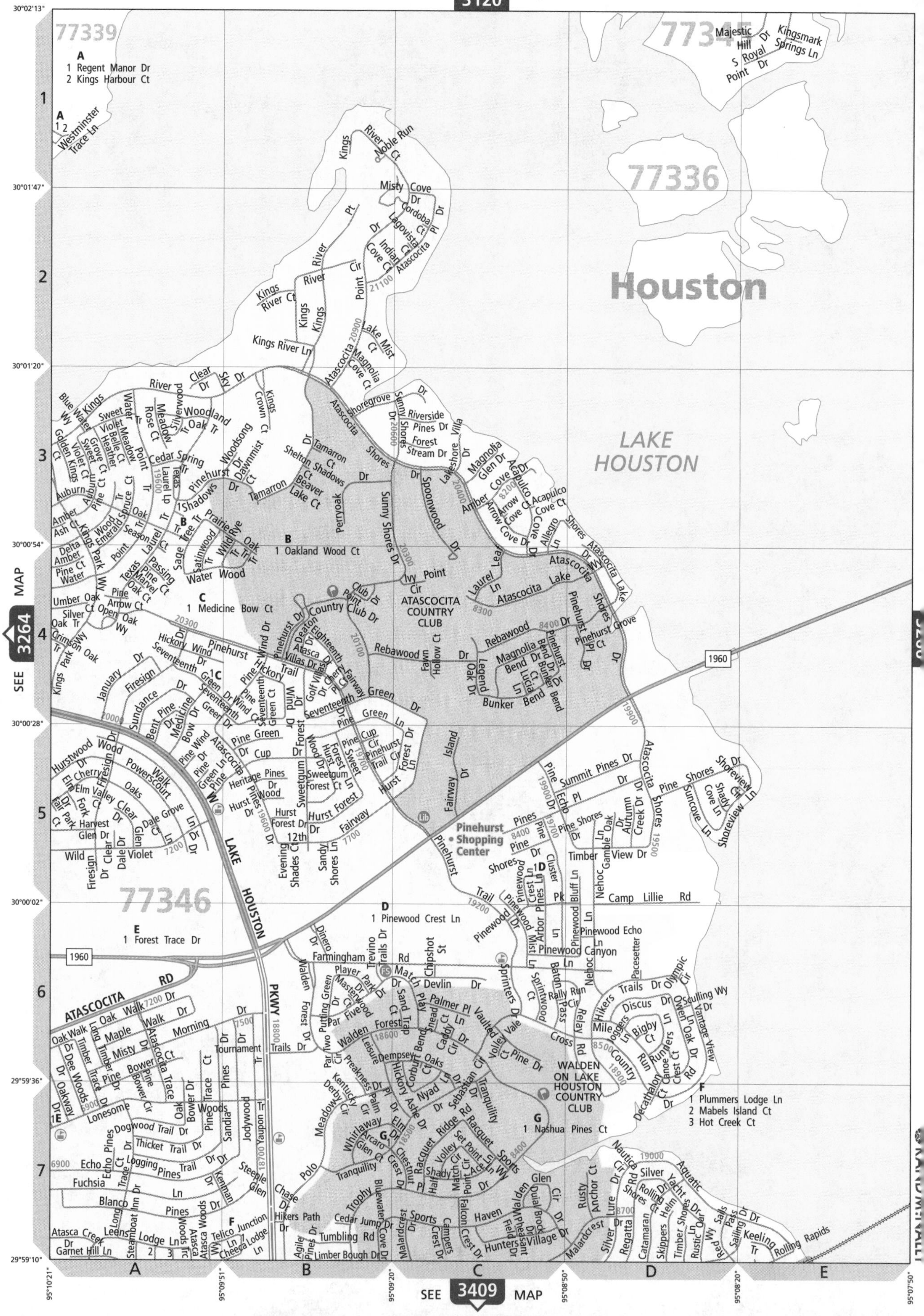
Houston
LAKE HOUSTON
77339
77345
77336
77346
A
1 Regent Manor Dr
2 Kings Harbour Ct
B
1 Oakland Wood Ct
C
1 Medicine Bow Ct
D
1 Pinewood Crest Ln
E
1 Forest Trace Dr
F
1 Plummers Lodge Ln
2 Mabels Island Ct
3 Hot Creek Ct
G
1 Nashua Pines Ct
ATASCOCITA COUNTRY CLUB
WALDEN ON LAKE HOUSTON COUNTRY CLUB
Pinehurst Shopping Center
LAKE HOUSTON PKWY
ATASCOCITA RD
1960
SEE 3264 MAP

SEE 3409 MAP

1:24,000
1 in. = 2000 ft.
0 0.25 0.5
miles
Houston
LAKE HOUSTON
77336
77532
ANDY ANDERSON PARK
INDIAN SHORES GC
LAKEWOOD HEIGHTS
Scotts Point
Atascocita Rd
Smith Rd
Walraven Dr
Guys
Twin Oaks Blvd
Saddle Creek Farms Dr
Big Deer Dr
Black Bear Dr
Elk Dr
Petromac
CROSBY HUFFMAN RD
1960
2100
1008
A
1 Woodland Lakes Dr
B
1 3rd St
2 2nd St
3 Pruett
30°02'10"
30°01'44"
30°01'18"
30°00'51"
30°00'25"
29°59'59"
29°59'33"
29°59'07"
95°07'50"
95°07'20"
95°06'50"
95°06'20"
95°05'50"
95°05'20"
A B C D E
1 2 3 4 5 6 7

SEE 3121 MAP

SEE 3267 MAP

SEE 3410 MAP

1:24,000
1 in. = 2000 ft.
0 0.25 0.5
miles

SEE 3122 MAP

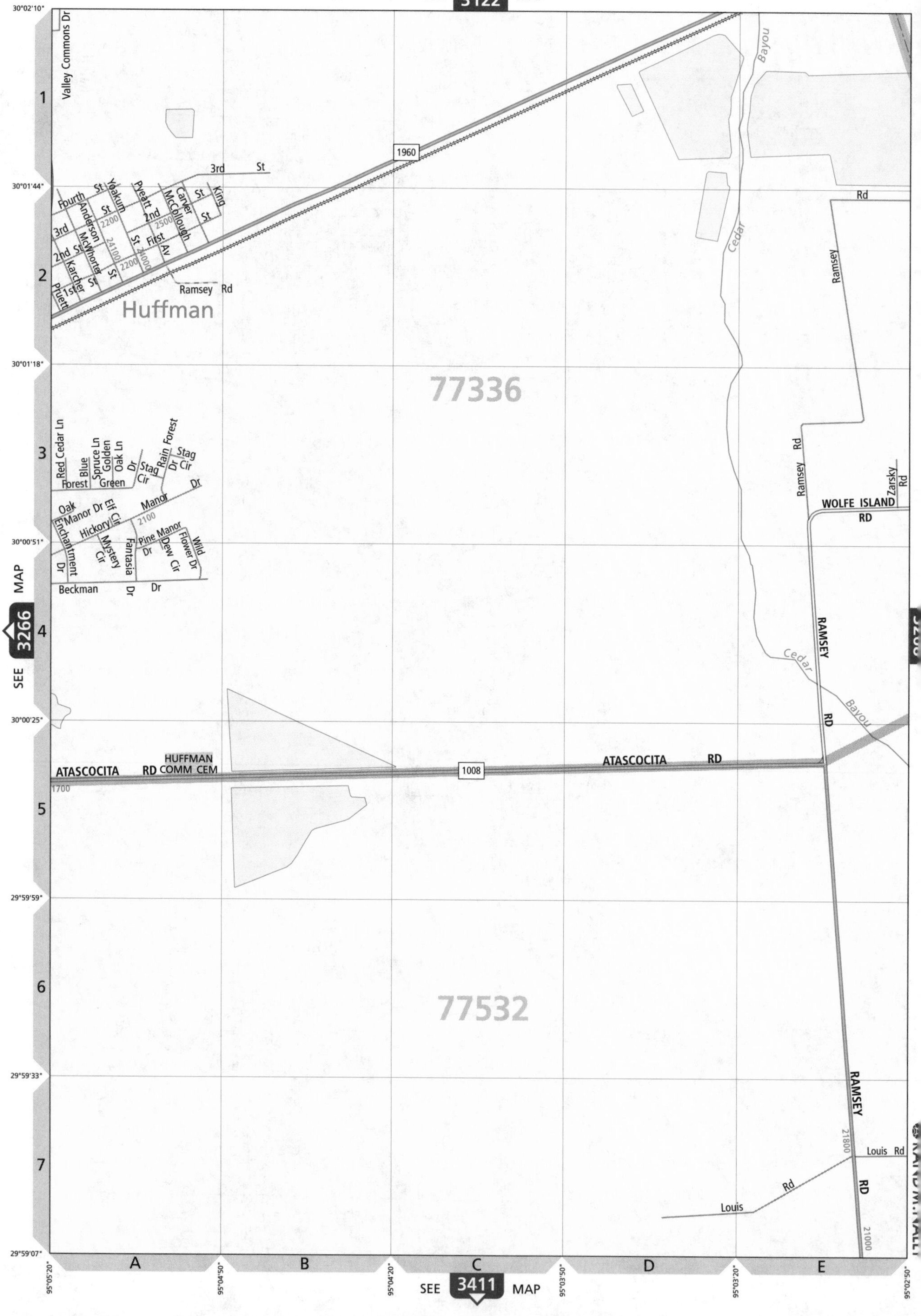
30°02'10"
30°01'44"
30°01'18"
30°00'51"
30°00'25"
29°59'59"
29°59'33"
29°59'07"
95°05'20"
95°04'50"
95°04'20"
95°03'50"
95°03'20"
95°02'50"
1
2
3
4
5
6
7
A
B
C
D
E
Valley Commons Dr
1960
3rd St
Fourth St
Yoakum
Pyeatt
Carver
McCollough
King
St
Anderson
2200
2nd
2500
St
3rd
McWhorter
24100
24000
First Av
2nd St
Karcher
St
2200
St
1st St
Pruett
Ramsey Rd
Huffman
Bayou
Cedar
Rd
Ramsey
77336
Red Cedar Ln
Blue
Spruce Ln
Golden
Oak Ln
Dr
Rain Forest
Stag Cir
Stag Dr
Cir
Forest
Green
Dr
Oak
Manor Dr
Elf Cir
Manor
2100
Enchantment
Hickory
Mystery Cir
Fantasia
Pine Manor Dr
Dew Cir
Wild Flower Dr
Dr
Beckman
Dr
Dr
Ramsey Rd
Zarsky Rd
WOLFE ISLAND RD
RAMSEY RD
Cedar Bayou
ATASCOCITA RD
HUFFMAN COMM CEM
1700
1008
ATASCOCITA RD
77532
RAMSEY
21800
Louis Rd
Rd
Louis
RD
21000

SEE 3266 MAP

SEE 3411 MAP

1:24,000
1 in. = 2000 ft.
0 0.25 0.5
miles

SEE B MAP

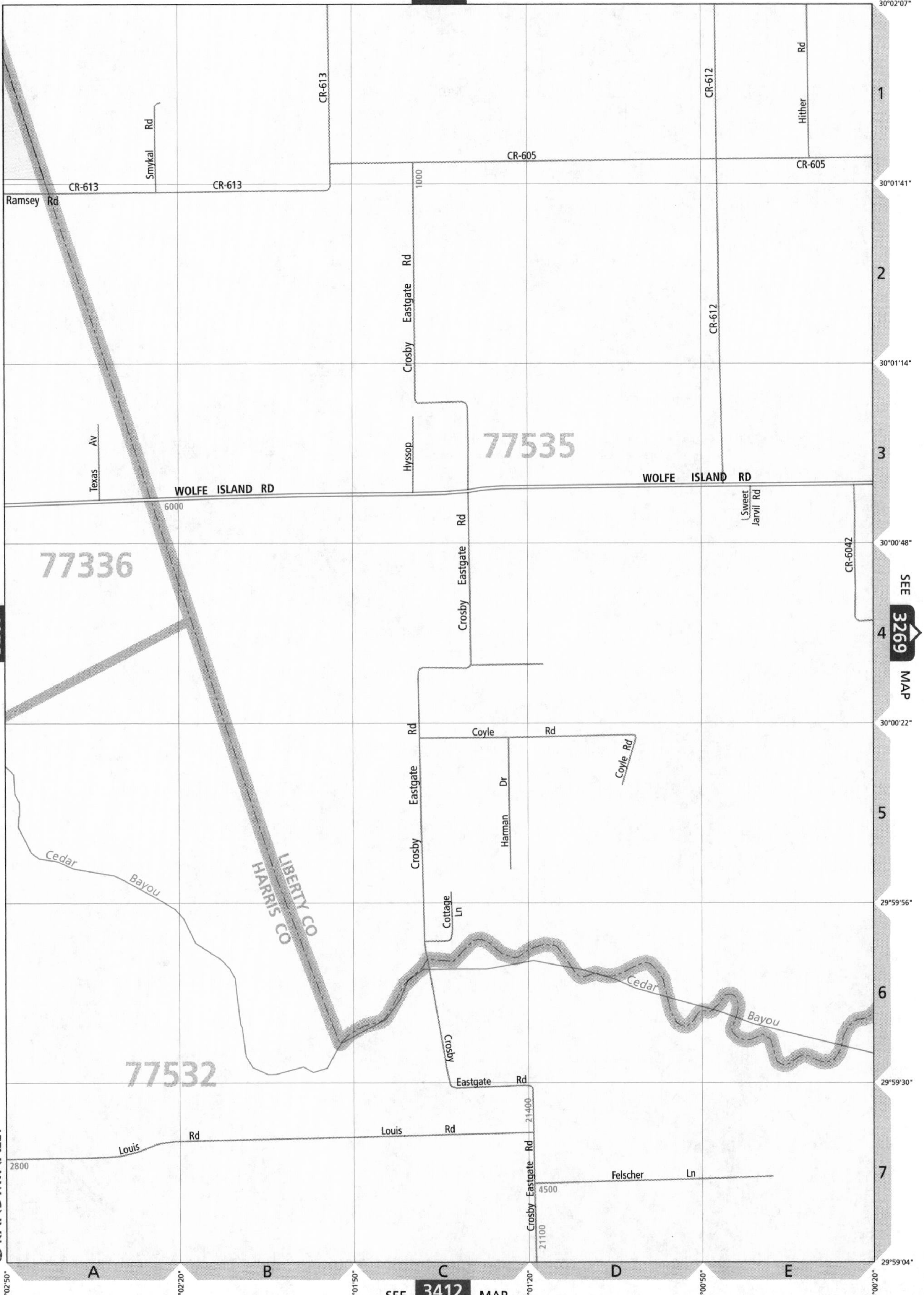

CR-613
Smykal Rd
CR-613
CR-613
Ramsey Rd
CR-605
CR-605
1000
CR-612
Hither Rd
Crosby Eastgate Rd
CR-612
77535
Texas Av
Hyssop
WOLFE ISLAND RD
WOLFE ISLAND RD
6000
Sweet
Jarvil Rd
77336
CR-6042
Crosby Eastgate Rd
Coyle Rd
Coyle Rd
Crosby Eastgate Rd
Harman Dr
Cedar Bayou
LIBERTY CO
HARRIS CO
Cottage Ln
Cedar Bayou
Crosby
77532
Eastgate Rd
21400
Louis Rd
Louis Rd
2800
Crosby Eastgate Rd
4500
Felscher Ln
21100
30°02'07"
30°01'41"
30°01'14"
30°00'48"
30°00'22"
29°59'56"
29°59'30"
29°59'04"
95°02'50"
95°02'20"
95°01'50"
95°01'20"
95°00'50"
95°00'20"
1
2
3
4
5
6
7
A
B
C
D
E

SEE 3269 MAP

SEE 3412 MAP

1:24,000
1 in. = 2000 ft.
0 0.25 0.5
miles

SEE B MAP

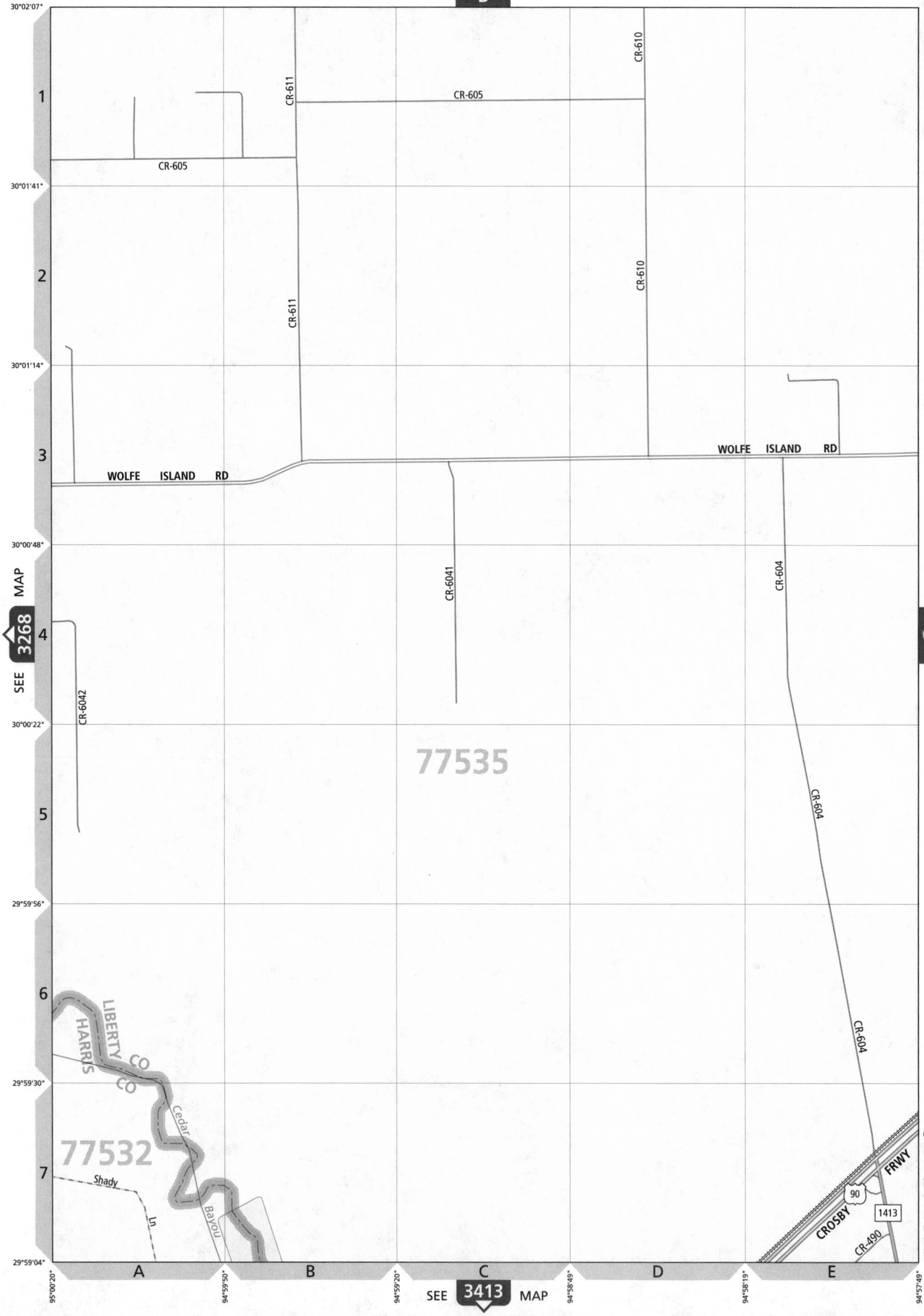
30°02'07"
30°01'41"
30°01'14"
30°00'48"
30°00'22"
29°59'56"
29°59'30"
29°59'04"
95°00'20"
94°59'50"
94°59'20"
94°58'49"
94°58'19"
94°57'49"
1
2
3
4
5
6
7
A
B
C
D
E
CR-605
CR-605
CR-611
CR-611
CR-610
CR-610
WOLFE ISLAND RD
WOLFE ISLAND RD
CR-6041
CR-604
CR-604
CR-604
CR-6042
77535
77532
LIBERTY CO
HARRIS CO
Cedar Bayou
Shady Ln
CROSBY FRWY
90
1413
CR-490

SEE 3268 MAP

SEE 3413 MAP

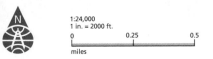

1:24,000
1 in. = 2000 ft.
0 0.25 0.5
miles

SEE 3251 MAP

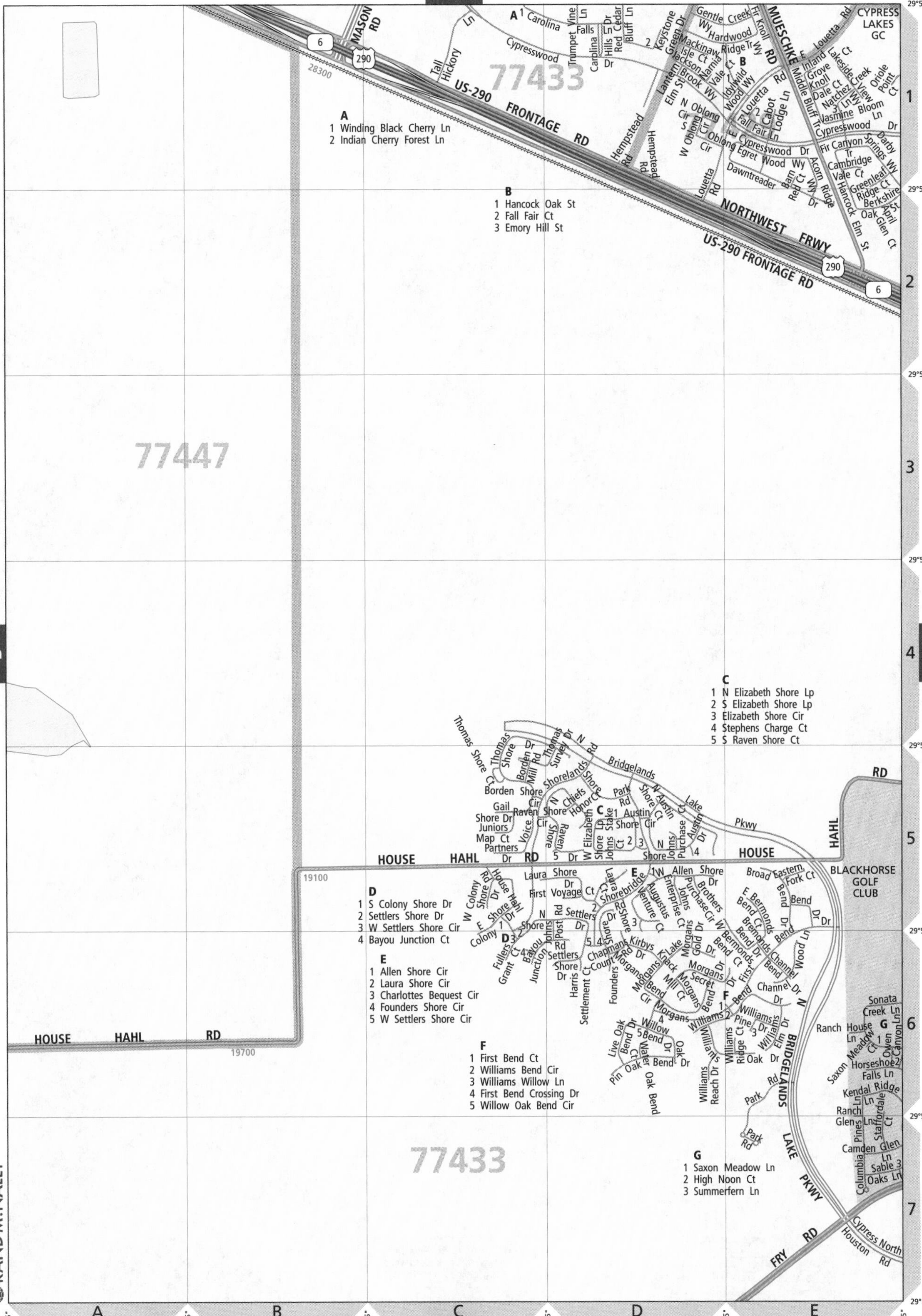
77433
77447
77433
US-290 FRONTAGE RD
NORTHWEST FRWY
US-290 FRONTAGE RD
MASON RD
MUESCHKE RD
HOUSE HAHL RD
HOUSE HAHL RD
HOUSE HAHL RD
HAHL RD
N BRIDGELANDS LAKE PKWY
FRY RD
Cypress North Houston Rd
CYPRESS LAKES GC
BLACKHORSE GOLF CLUB
28300
19100
19700
A
1 Winding Black Cherry Ln
2 Indian Cherry Forest Ln
B
1 Hancock Oak St
2 Fall Fair Ct
3 Emory Hill St
C
1 N Elizabeth Shore Lp
2 S Elizabeth Shore Lp
3 Elizabeth Shore Cir
4 Stephens Charge Ct
5 S Raven Shore Ct
D
1 S Colony Shore Dr
2 Settlers Shore Dr
3 W Settlers Shore Cir
4 Bayou Junction Ct
E
1 Allen Shore Cir
2 Laura Shore Cir
3 Charlottes Bequest Cir
4 Founders Shore Cir
5 W Settlers Shore Cir
F
1 First Bend Ct
2 Williams Bend Cir
3 Williams Willow Ln
4 First Bend Crossing Dr
5 Willow Oak Bend Cir
G
1 Saxon Meadow Ln
2 High Noon Ct
3 Summerfern Ln
29°59'24"
29°58'58"
29°58'32"
29°58'05"
29°57'39"
29°57'13"
29°56'47"
29°56'21"
95°45'25"
95°44'55"
95°44'25"
95°43'55"
95°43'25"
95°42'55"
A B C D E
1 2 3 4 5 6 7

SEE 3396 MAP

SEE B MAP

1:24,000
1 in. = 2000 ft.
0 0.25 0.5
miles

SEE 3252 MAP

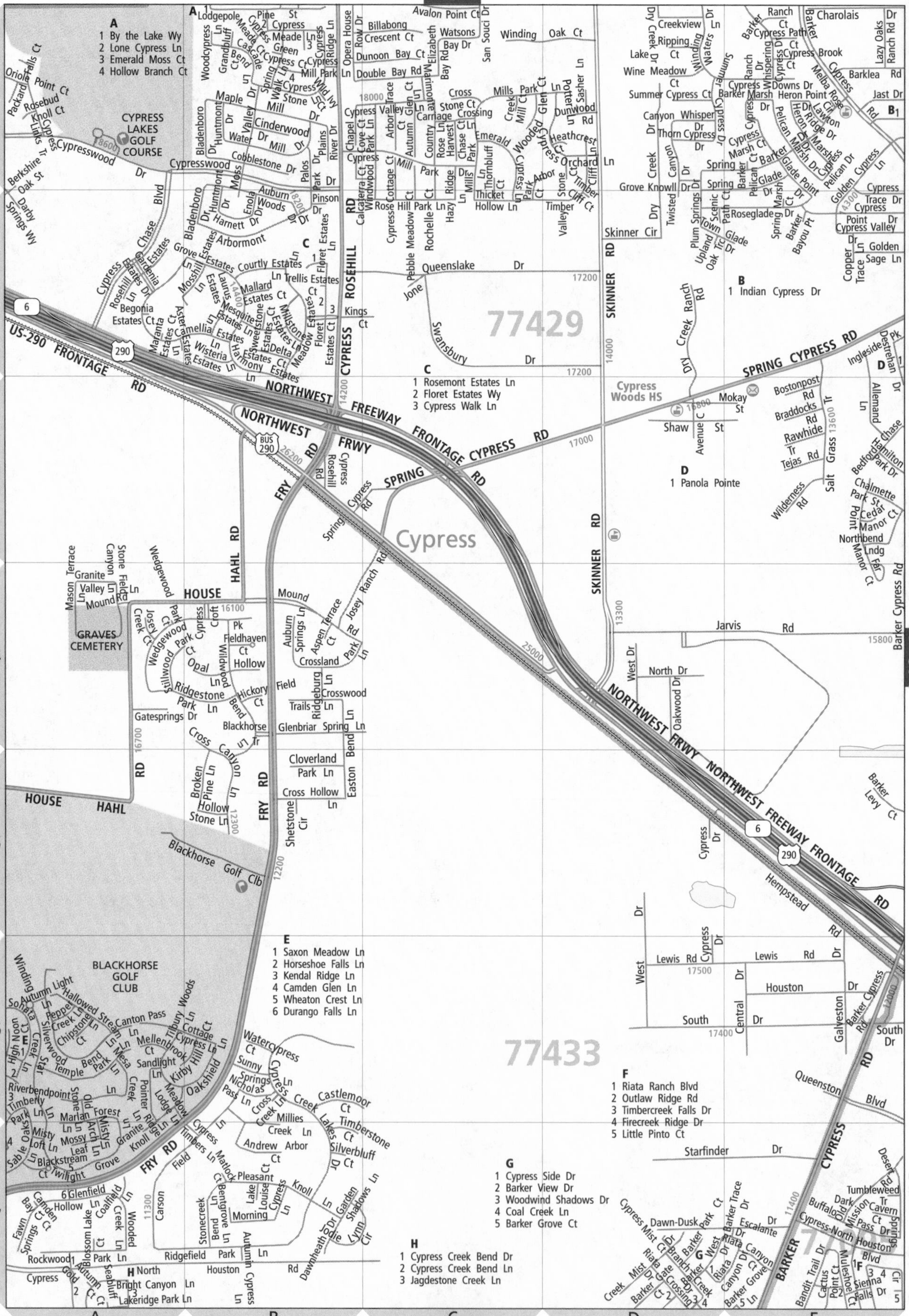
A
1 By the Lake Wy
2 Lone Cypress Ln
3 Emerald Moss Ct
4 Hollow Branch Ct
B
1 Indian Cypress Dr
C
1 Rosemont Estates Ln
2 Floret Estates Wy
3 Cypress Walk Ln
D
1 Panola Pointe
E
1 Saxon Meadow Ln
2 Horseshoe Falls Ln
3 Kendal Ridge Ln
4 Camden Glen Ln
5 Wheaton Crest Ln
6 Durango Falls Ln
F
1 Riata Ranch Blvd
2 Outlaw Ridge Rd
3 Timbercreek Falls Dr
4 Firecreek Ridge Dr
5 Little Pinto Ct
G
1 Cypress Side Dr
2 Barker View Dr
3 Woodwind Shadows Dr
4 Coal Creek Ln
5 Barker Grove Ct
H
1 Cypress Creek Bend Dr
2 Cypress Creek Bend Ln
3 Jagdestone Creek Ln
CYPRESS LAKES GOLF COURSE
BLACKHORSE GOLF CLUB
GRAVES CEMETERY
Cypress Woods HS
Cypress
77429
77433
NORTHWEST FREEWAY
US-290 FRONTAGE RD
SPRING CYPRESS RD
SKINNER RD
FRY RD
HOUSE HAHL RD
BARKER CYPRESS RD
29°59'24"
29°58'58"
29°58'32"
29°58'05"
29°57'39"
29°57'13"
29°56'47"
29°56'21"
95°42'55"
95°42'25"
95°41'55"
95°41'25"
95°40'55"
95°40'25"

SEE 3395 MAP

SEE 3537 MAP

1:24,000
1 in. = 2000 ft.
0 0.25 0.5
miles

SEE 3253 MAP

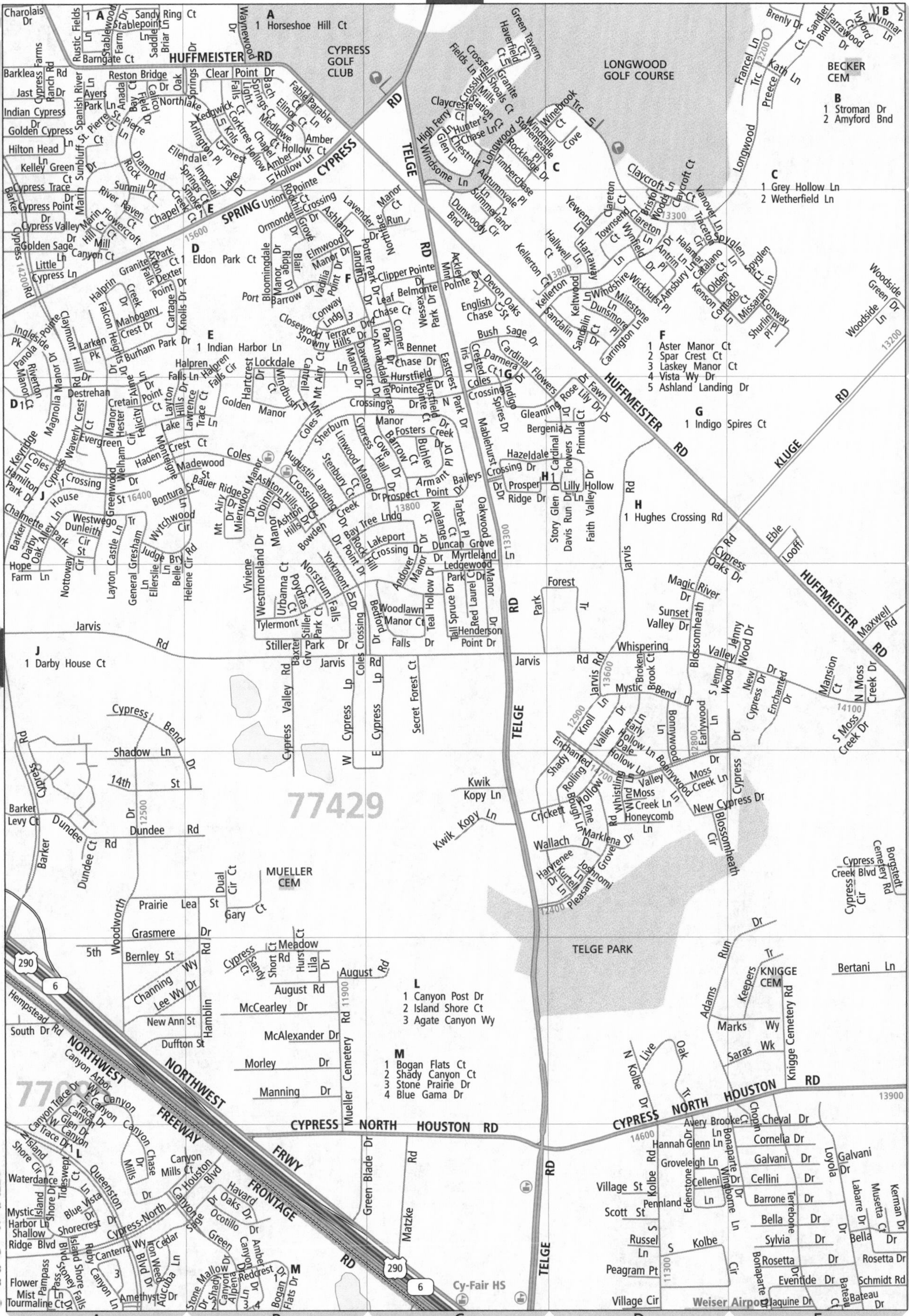
CYPRESS GOLF CLUB
LONGWOOD GOLF COURSE
BECKER CEM
MUELLER CEM
KNIGGE CEM
TELGE PARK
Cy-Fair HS
Weiser Airport
77429
HUFFMEISTER RD
SPRING CYPRESS
TELGE RD
KLUGE RD
Jarvis Rd
CYPRESS NORTH HOUSTON RD
NORTHWEST FREEWAY
NORTHWEST FRWY FRONTAGE RD
290
6
A
1 Horseshoe Hill Ct
B
1 Stroman Dr
2 Amyford Bnd
C
1 Grey Hollow Ln
2 Wetherfield Ln
D
1 Eldon Park Ct
E
1 Indian Harbor Ln
F
1 Aster Manor Ct
2 Spar Crest Ct
3 Laskey Manor Ct
4 Vista Wy Dr
5 Ashland Landing Dr
G
1 Indigo Spires Ct
H
1 Hughes Crossing Rd
J
1 Darby House Ct
L
1 Canyon Post Dr
2 Island Shore Ct
3 Agate Canyon Wy
M
1 Bogan Flats Ct
2 Shady Canyon Ct
3 Stone Prairie Dr
4 Blue Gama Dr
29°59'22"
29°58'56"
29°58'30"
29°58'04"
29°57'38"
29°57'12"
29°56'45"
29°56'19"
95°40'25"
95°39'55"
95°39'25"
95°38'55"
95°38'25"
95°37'55"
A B C D E
1 2 3 4 5 6 7

SEE 3398 MAP

SEE 3538 MAP

1:24,000
1 in. = 2000 ft.
0 0.25 0.5
miles

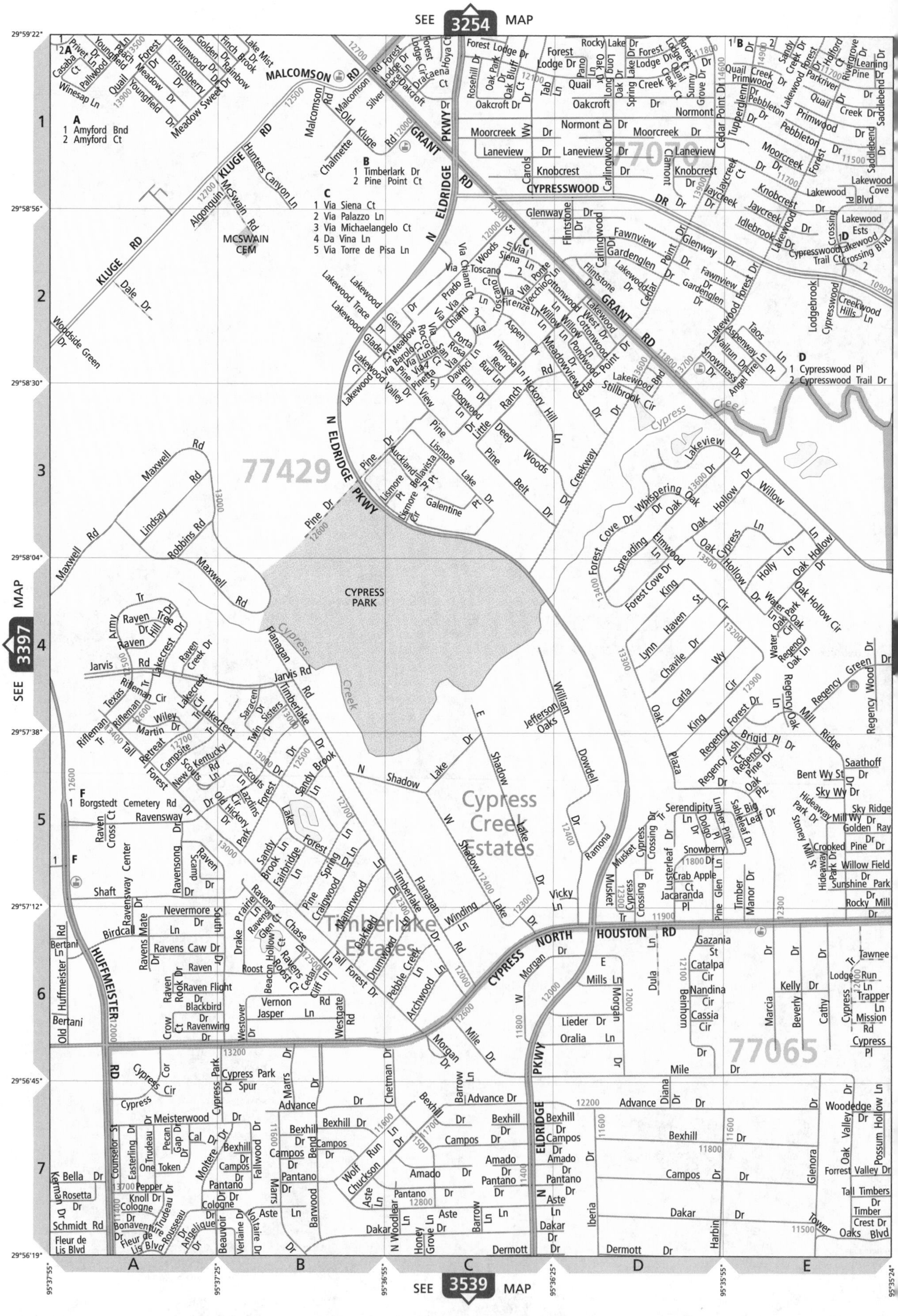
SEE 3254 MAP
SEE 3397 MAP
SEE 3539 MAP
A
1 Amyford Bnd
2 Amyford Ct
B
1 Timberlark Dr
2 Pine Point Ct
C
1 Via Siena Ct
2 Via Palazzo Ln
3 Via Michaelangelo Ct
4 Da Vina Ln
5 Via Torre de Pisa Ln
D
1 Cypresswood Pl
2 Cypresswood Trail Dr
F
1 Borgstedt Cemetery Rd
MALCOMSON RD
KLUGE RD
GRANT RD
N ELDRIDGE PKWY
CYPRESSWOOD DR
CYPRESS NORTH HOUSTON RD
HUFFMEISTER RD
MCSWAIN CEM
CYPRESS PARK
Cypress Creek
Cypress Creek Estates
Timberlake Estates
77429
77070
77065

1:24,000
1 in. = 2000 ft.
0 0.25 0.5
miles

SEE 3255 MAP

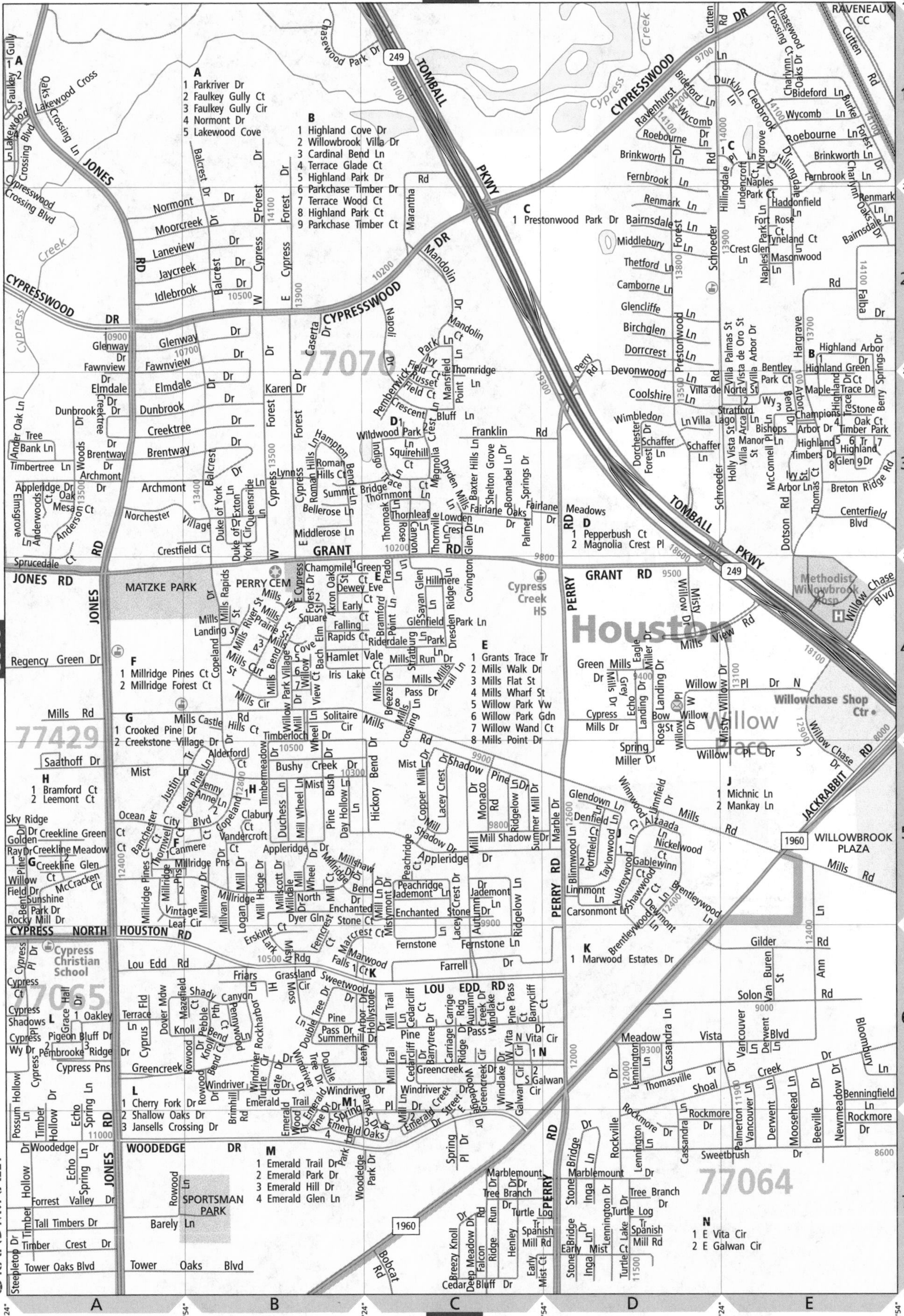
A
1 Parkriver Dr
2 Faulkey Gully Ct
3 Faulkey Gully Cir
4 Normont Dr
5 Lakewood Cove
B
1 Highland Cove Dr
2 Willowbrook Villa Dr
3 Cardinal Bend Ln
4 Terrace Glade Ct
5 Highland Park Dr
6 Parkchase Timber Dr
7 Terrace Wood Ct
8 Highland Park Ct
9 Parkchase Timber Ct
C
1 Prestonwood Park Dr
D
1 Pepperbush Ct
2 Magnolia Crest Pl
E
1 Grants Trace Tr
2 Mills Walk Dr
3 Mills Flat St
4 Mills Wharf St
5 Willow Park Vw
6 Willow Park Gdn
7 Willow Wand Ct
8 Mills Point Dr
F
1 Millridge Pines Ct
2 Millridge Forest Ct
G
1 Crooked Pine Dr
2 Creekstone Village Dr
H
1 Bramford Ct
2 Leemont Ct
J
1 Michnic Ln
2 Mankay Ln
K
1 Marwood Estates Dr
L
1 Cherry Fork Dr
2 Shallow Oaks Dr
3 Jansells Crossing Dr
M
1 Emerald Trail Dr
2 Emerald Park Dr
3 Emerald Hill Dr
4 Emerald Glen Ln
N
1 E Vita Cir
2 E Galwan Cir
TOMBALL PKWY
CYPRESSWOOD DR
JONES RD
GRANT RD
PERRY RD
CYPRESS NORTH HOUSTON RD
LOU EDD RD
WOODEDGE DR
JACKRABBIT RD
Houston
77070
77429
77065
77064
Willow Place
MATZKE PARK
PERRY CEM
Cypress Creek HS
Methodist Willowbrook Hosp
Willowchase Shop Ctr
WILLOWBROOK PLAZA
Cypress Christian School
SPORTSMAN PARK
RAVENEAUX CC
249
1960
1
2
3
4
5
6
7
A
B
C
D
E
29°59'20"
29°58'54"
29°58'28"
29°58'02"
29°57'36"
29°57'10"
29°56'44"
29°56'17"
95°35'24"
95°34'54"
95°34'24"
95°33'54"
95°33'24"
95°32'54"

SEE 3400 MAP

SEE 3398 MAP

SEE 3540 MAP

1:24,000
1 in. = 2000 ft.
0 0.25 0.5
miles

SEE 3256 MAP
SEE 3541 MAP
SEE 3399 MAP
3401
A
B
C
D
E
1
2
3
4
5
6
7
29°59'20"
29°58'54"
29°58'28"
29°58'02"
29°57'36"
29°57'10"
29°56'44"
29°56'17"
95°32'54"
95°32'24"
95°31'54"
95°31'24"
95°30'54"
95°30'24"
RAVENEAUX CC
CHAMPIONS GOLF CLUB
77069
77070
77066
77064
77086
77379
Champions Forest Plaza
Champions Village 3
Old Champions Vil
Banff School
Applause Theatre
SHILO CEM
CLASSIC 3 GOLF COURSE
The Commons at Willowbrook
Willowbrook Mall
Willowbrook Plaza
Deco
Houston
CHAMPION FOREST DR
1960
249
TOMBALL PKWY
JACKRABBIT RD
CUTTEN RD
BOURGEOIS RD
Greens Bayou
GREENS BAYOU
A
1 Hedgley Pl
B
1 S Cashel Oak Dr
C
1 Lawn Arbor Dr
D
1 Renmark Ln
2 Bairnsdale Ln
E
1 Champions Ct Wy
2 Barrington Fairway
3 Champions Colony W
4 Champions Colony Rd W
5 Champions Colony E
F
1 Champions Centre Ct
2 Grainger Sprs
3 Breton Glen Ln
4 Park Centre Ct
G
1 Tahoe Crossing Ln
2 N Wintersage Ln
3 S Wintersage Ln
4 Braxtons Bnd
Cutten Rd
Hargrave Rd
Falba Dr
Vermarion
Gessner Rd
Mills Rd
W Greens Rd
High Life Rd
Willowbrook Dr
Willow Centre Dr
Cockrum Blvd
Belgold St
Vinvale Rd
Haynes Rd
Nathan Rd
Theall Rd
Shiloh Church Rd
Duncan Rd
Scyrus Ln
Weeds Rd
Stamey Rd
Gant Rd
Alsay
Mitchell Ln
Mazen Rd
Rockland Rd
Champions Plaza Dr
Champion Centre Dr
Breton Ridge St
Willow Chase
Pebble Beach Dr
Boca Raton Dr
Coral Ridge Rd
Bermuda Dunes Dr
Paradise Valley Dr
Champions Dr
Tournament Dr
Cypress Creek
Mazen Rd
Cutten Rd

1:24,000
1 in. = 2000 ft.
0 0.25 0.5
miles

SEE 3257 MAP

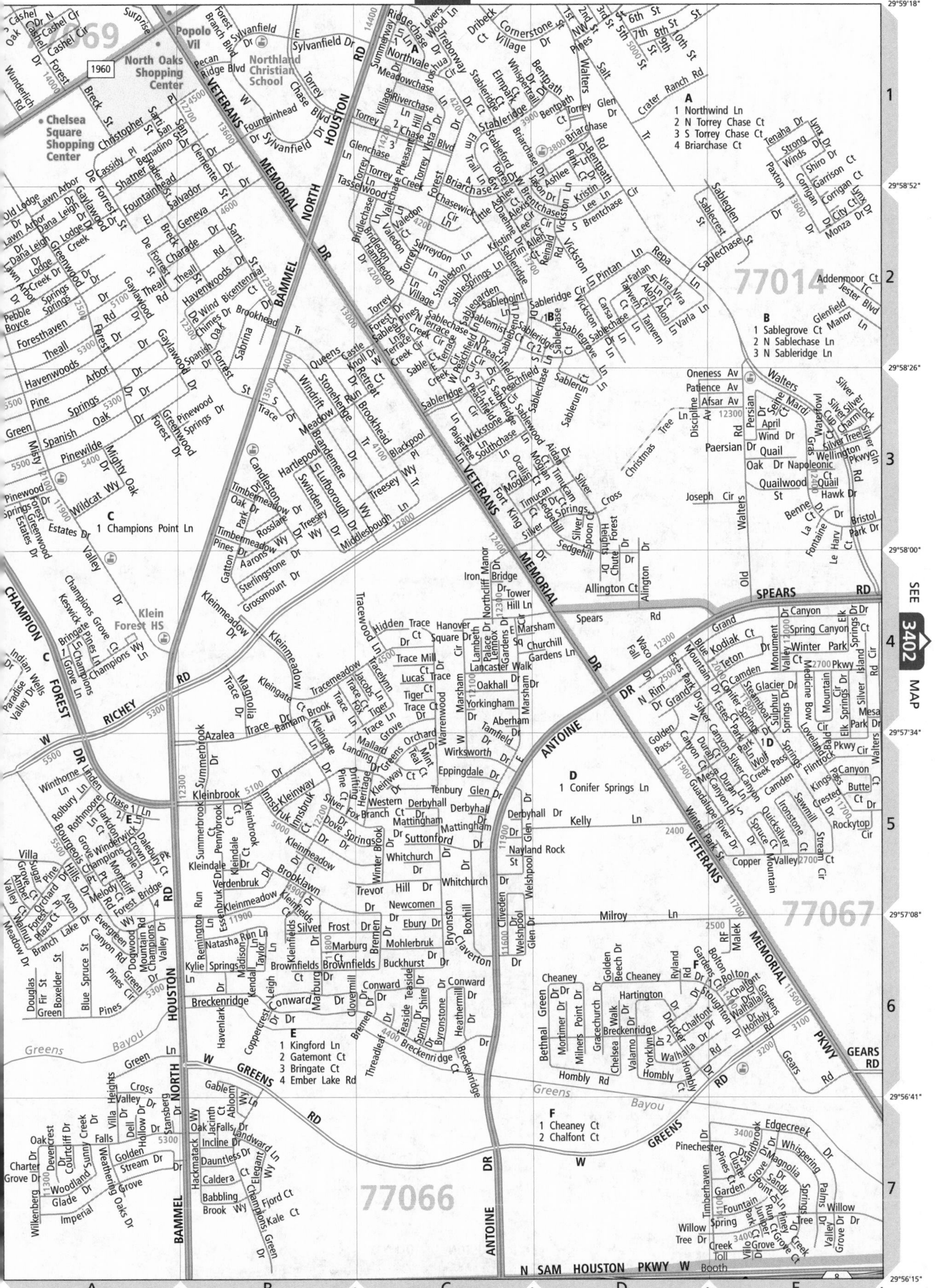
77069
77014
77067
77066
North Oaks Shopping Center
Northland Christian School
Chelsea Square Shopping Center
Popolo Vil
Klein Forest HS
1960
VETERANS MEMORIAL DR
NORTH HOUSTON RD
BAMMEL NORTH HOUSTON RD
CHAMPION FOREST DR
RICHEY RD
SPEARS RD
ANTOINE DR
W GREENS RD
GEARS RD
N SAM HOUSTON PKWY W
Greens Bayou
A
1 Northwind Ln
2 N Torrey Chase Ct
3 S Torrey Chase Ct
4 Briarchase Ct
B
1 Sablegrove Ct
2 N Sablechase Ln
3 N Sableridge Ln
C
1 Champions Point Ln
D
1 Conifer Springs Ln
E
1 Kingford Ln
2 Gatemont Ct
3 Bringate Ct
4 Ember Lake Rd
F
1 Cheaney Ct
2 Chalfont Ct
1
2
3
4
5
6
7
A
B
C
D
E
29°59'18"
29°58'52"
29°58'26"
29°58'00"
29°57'34"
29°57'08"
29°56'41"
29°56'15"
95°29'54"
95°29'24"
95°28'54"
95°28'24"
95°27'54"
SEE 3402 MAP

SEE 3542 MAP

1:24,000
1 in. = 2000 ft.
0 0.25 0.5
miles

SEE 3258 MAP

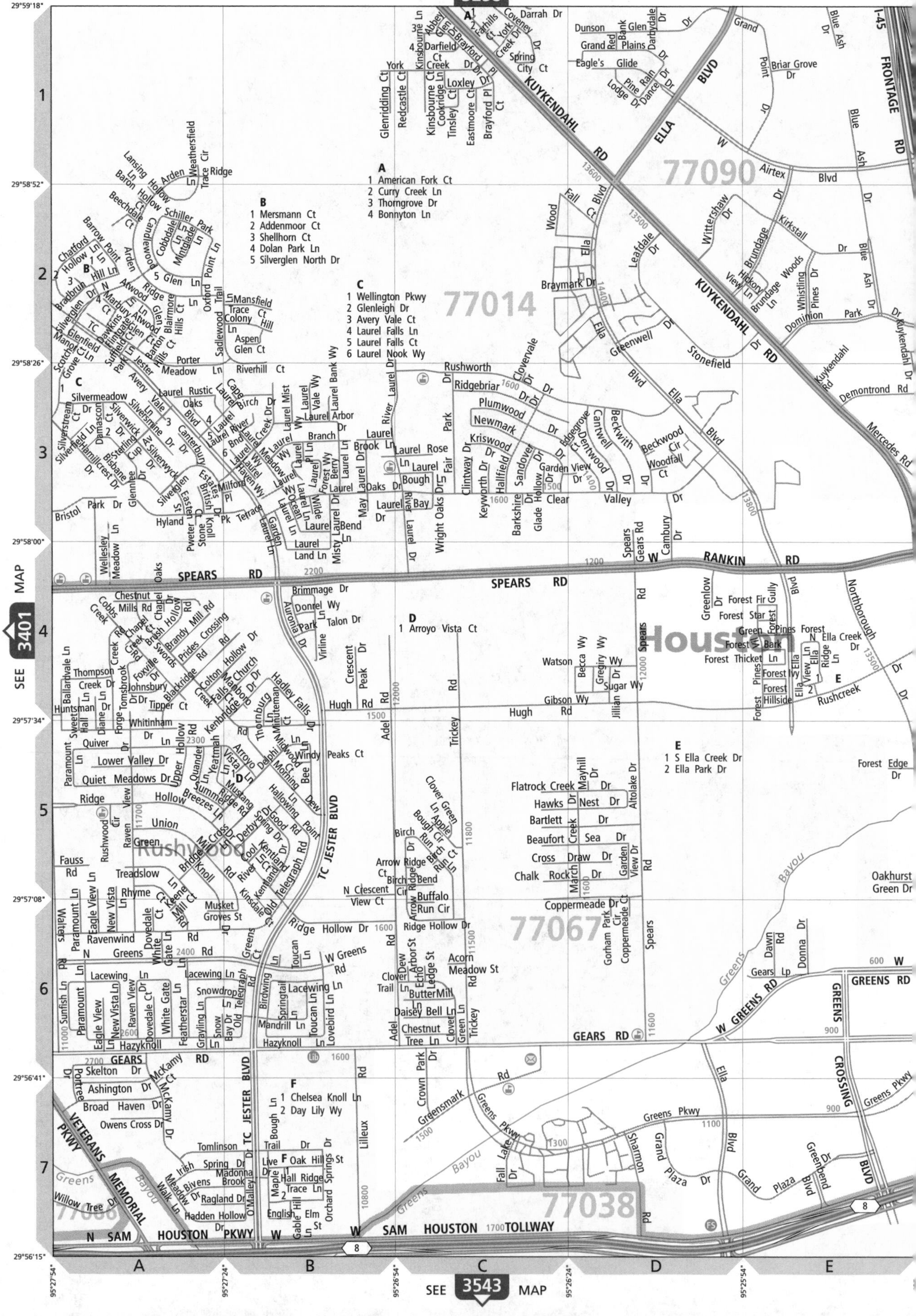
29°59'18"
29°58'52"
29°58'26"
29°58'00"
29°57'34"
29°57'08"
29°56'41"
29°56'15"
95°27'54"
95°27'24"
95°26'54"
95°26'24"
95°25'54"
A
B
C
D
E
1
2
3
4
5
6
7
77090
77014
77067
77038
Houston
Rushwood
KUYKENDAHL RD
ELLA BLVD
W Airtex Blvd
I-45
FRONTAGE RD
SPEARS RD
W RANKIN RD
TC JESTER BLVD
GEARS RD
W GREENS RD
GREENS RD
GREENS CROSSING BLVD
VETERANS MEMORIAL PKWY
N SAM HOUSTON PKWY W
W SAM HOUSTON TOLLWAY
Greens Bayou
Greens Pkwy
Hugh Rd
Rushworth
Clear Valley Dr
Ridge Hollow Dr
Ridgebriar Dr
Stonefield
Mercedes Rd
Demontrond Rd
Northborough
Rushcreek
Greensmark Rd
Lilleux Rd
Adel Rd
Trickey Rd
Spears Rd
Grand Plaza Dr
A
1 American Fork Ct
2 Curry Creek Ln
3 Thorngrove Dr
4 Bonnyton Ln
B
1 Mersmann Ct
2 Addenmoor Ct
3 Shellhorn Ct
4 Dolan Park Ln
5 Silverglen North Dr
C
1 Wellington Pkwy
2 Glenleigh Dr
3 Avery Vale Ct
4 Laurel Falls Ln
5 Laurel Falls Ct
6 Laurel Nook Wy
D
1 Arroyo Vista Ct
E
1 S Ella Creek Dr
2 Ella Park Dr
F
1 Chelsea Knoll Ln
2 Day Lily Wy
8

SEE 3401 MAP

SEE 3543 MAP

1:24,000
1 in. = 2000 ft.
0 0.25 0.5
miles

SEE 3259 MAP

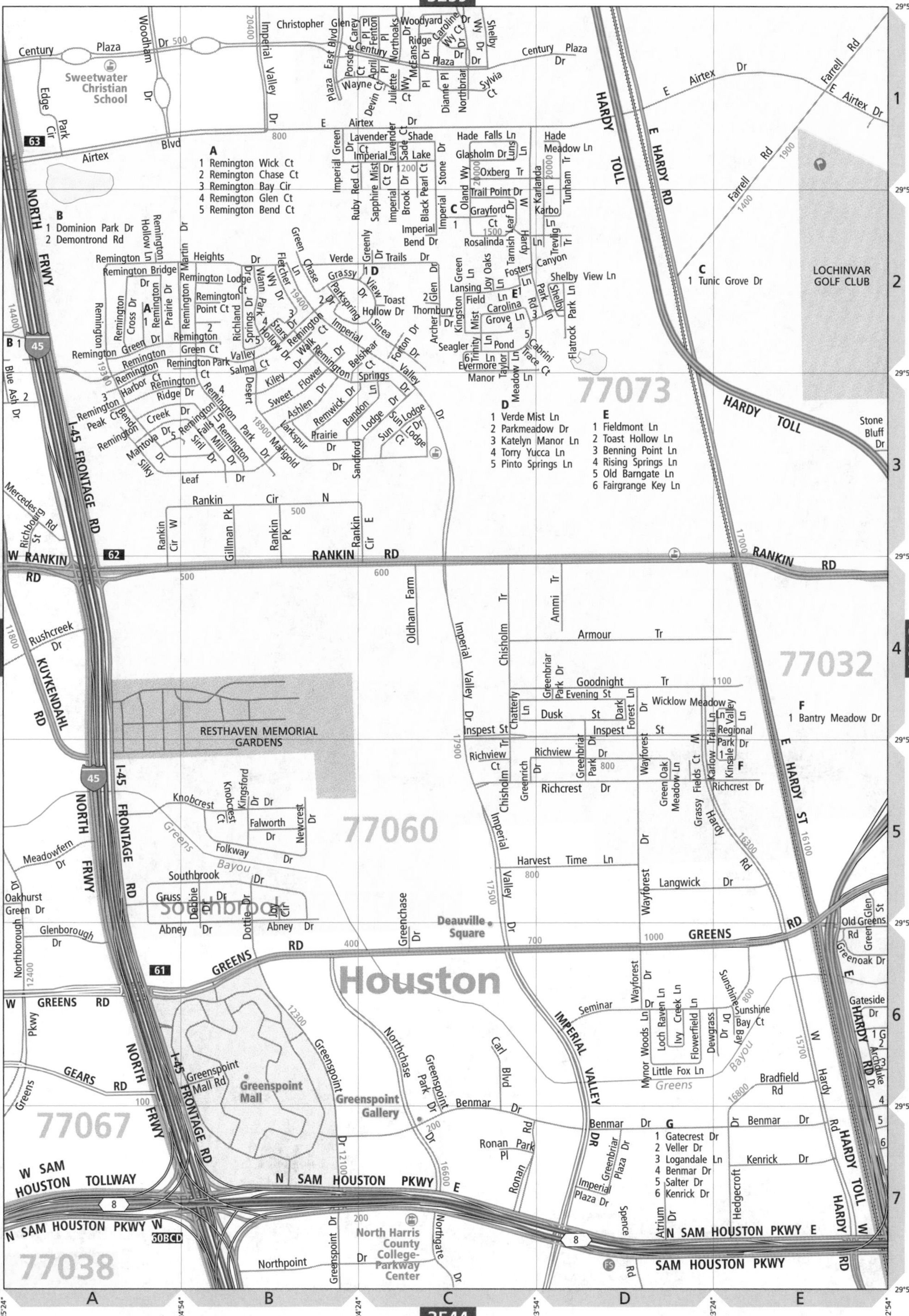
Houston
77073
77060
77032
77067
77038
Sweetwater Christian School
LOCHINVAR GOLF CLUB
RESTHAVEN MEMORIAL GARDENS
Greenspoint Mall
Greenspoint Gallery
Deauville Square
North Harris County College-Parkway Center
Southbrook
NORTH FRWY
I-45 FRONTAGE RD
HARDY TOLL
E HARDY RD
HARDY ST
W RANKIN RD
RANKIN RD
GREENS RD
W GREENS RD
N SAM HOUSTON PKWY E
N SAM HOUSTON PKWY W
W SAM HOUSTON TOLLWAY
SAM HOUSTON PKWY
IMPERIAL VALLEY DR
Century Plaza Dr
E Airtex Dr
Airtex Blvd
Farrell Rd
KUYKENDAHL RD
Greens Bayou
A
1 Remington Wick Ct
2 Remington Chase Ct
3 Remington Bay Cir
4 Remington Glen Ct
5 Remington Bend Ct
B
1 Dominion Park Dr
2 Demontrond Rd
C
1 Tunic Grove Dr
D
1 Verde Mist Ln
2 Parkmeadow Dr
3 Katelyn Manor Ln
4 Torry Yucca Ln
5 Pinto Springs Ln
E
1 Fieldmont Ln
2 Toast Hollow Ln
3 Benning Point Ln
4 Rising Springs Ln
5 Old Barngate Ln
6 Fairgrange Key Ln
F
1 Bantry Meadow Dr
G
1 Gatecrest Dr
2 Veller Dr
3 Logandale Ln
4 Benmar Dr
5 Salter Dr
6 Kenrick Dr
29°59'16"
29°58'50"
29°58'24"
29°57'58"
29°57'32"
29°57'05"
29°56'39"
29°56'13"
95°25'24"
95°24'54"
95°24'24"
95°23'54"
95°23'24"
95°22'54"

SEE 3404 MAP

SEE 3544 MAP

1:24,000
1 in. = 2000 ft.
0 0.25 0.5
miles

SEE 3260 MAP

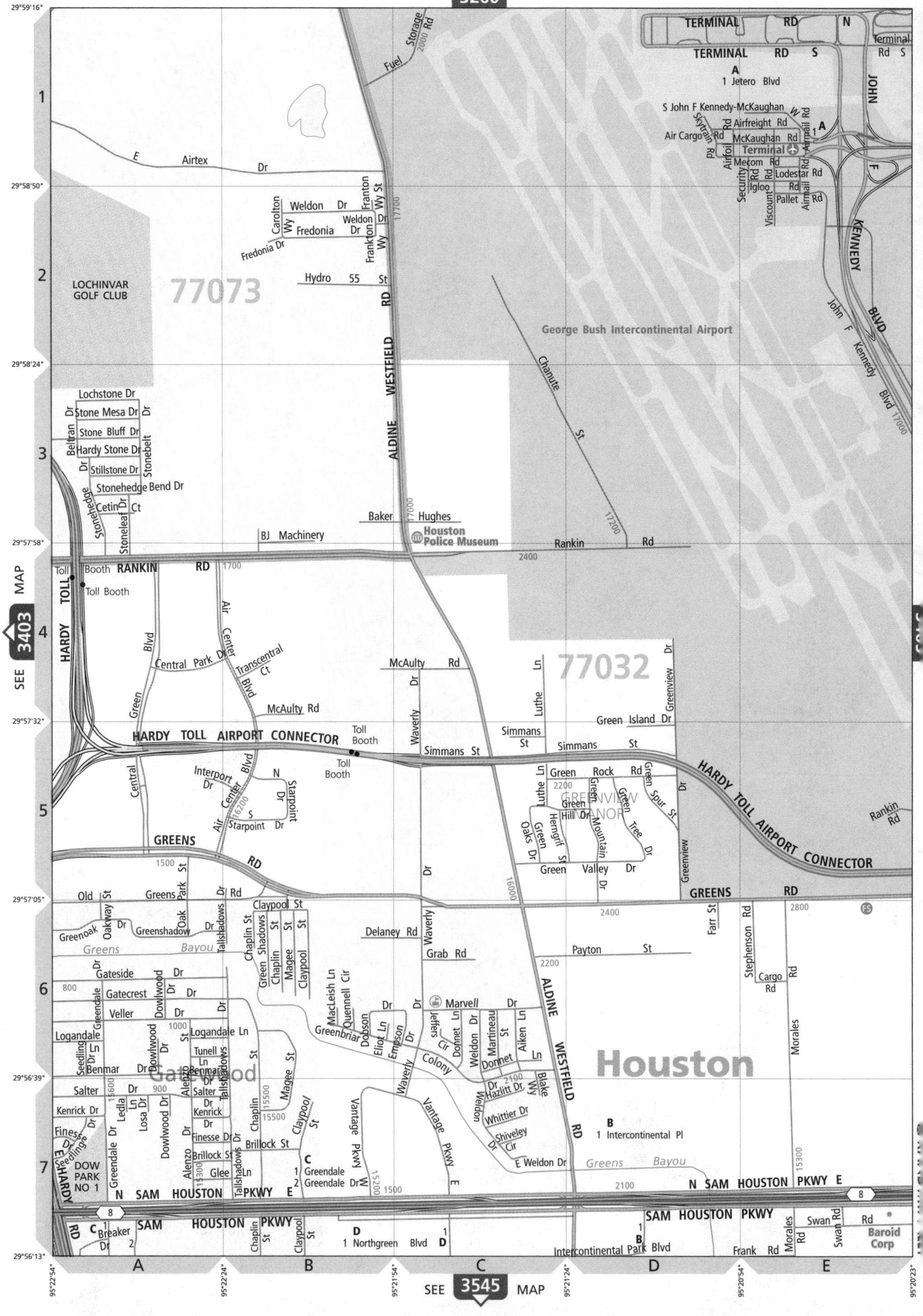
TERMINAL RD N
TERMINAL RD S
Terminal Rd S
1 Jetero Blvd
S John F Kennedy-McKaughan W
Airfreight Rd
Air Cargo Rd
Skytrain Rd
McKaughan Rd
Terminal
Airmail Rd
Airfoil Rd
Mecom Rd
Lodestar Rd
Security Rd
Igloo Rd
Pallet Rd
Viscount Rd
Airmail Rd
JOHN F KENNEDY BLVD
John F Kennedy Blvd
17000
Fuel Storage Rd
2000
E Airtex Dr
Weldon Dr
Carolton Wy
Fredonia Dr
Fredonia Dr
Weldon Dr
Franton Wy St
Frankton Wy
Hydro 55 St
LOCHINVAR GOLF CLUB
77073
ALDINE WESTFIELD RD
17700
George Bush Intercontinental Airport
Chanute St
17200
Lochstone Dr
Stone Mesa Dr
Stone Bluff Dr
Hardy Stone Dr
Stillstone Dr
Stonehedge Bend Dr
Cetin Dr Ct
Beltran Dr
Stonebelt Dr
Stonehedge
Stoneleaf Dr
Baker Hughes
Houston Police Museum
BJ Machinery
Rankin Rd
2400
Toll Booth
Toll Booth
RANKIN RD
1700
HARDY TOLL RD
Air Center Blvd
Transcentral Ct
Central Park Dr
Green Blvd
McAulty Rd
McAulty Rd
77032
Luthe Ln
Waverly Dr
Greenview Dr
Green Island Dr
Simmans St
Simmans St
Simmans St
HARDY TOLL AIRPORT CONNECTOR
Toll Booth
Toll Booth
Interport Dr
N Starpoint Dr
S Starpoint Dr
16200
Central
Green Rock Rd
Green Spur St
Luthe Ln
2200
GREENVIEW MANOR
Green Hill Dr
Green Mountain Dr
Green Tree Dr
Hemgrif St
Green Oaks Dr
Green Valley Dr
Greenview Dr
Rankin Rd
GREENS RD
1500
Greens Park St
Old Oak St
Greens Dr Rd
16000
GREENS RD
2400
2800
Oakway St
Greenoak Dr
Greenshadow Dr
Tallshadows Dr
Claypool St
Chaplin St
Green Shadows St
Chaplin St
Magee St
Claypool St
Delaney Rd
Waverly Dr
Grab Rd
Payton St
Farr St
Stephenson Rd
Cargo Rd
Greens Bayou
Gateside Dr
Gatecrest Dr
Dowlwood Dr
800
2200
Veller Dr
Greendale Dr
MacLeish Ln
Quennell Cir
Marvell Dr
ALDINE WESTFIELD RD
Morales Rd
Logandale
1000
Logandale Ln
Greenbriar Dr
Dobson Dr
Eliot Ln
Emerson Dr
Jeffers Cir
Donnet Ln
Weldon Dr
Martineau St
Aiken Ln
Seedling Ln
Benmar Dr
Tunell Ln
Benmar Dr
Gatewood
Colony
Donnet
Houston
Salter Dr
900
Alenzo Dr
Salter Dr
Tallshadows
Magee St
15500
Waverly
Hazlitt Dr
2100
Blake Wy
Kenrick Dr
Ledla Ln
Losa Dr
Dowlwood Dr
Kenrick Dr
Chaplin
15500
Claypool St
Vantage Pkwy W
Vantage Pkwy E
Weldon Dr
Whittier Dr
B
1 Intercontinental Pl
Finesse Dr
Seedlings Dr
Greendale Dr
Finesse Dr
Brillock St
Brillock St
Shiveley Cir
DOW PARK NO 1
Glee Ln
15300
C
1 Greendale
2 Greendale Dr
15200
E Weldon Dr
Greens Bayou
15300
E HARDY RD
N SAM HOUSTON PKWY E
1500
2100
N SAM HOUSTON PKWY E
8
8
SAM HOUSTON PKWY
SAM HOUSTON PKWY
C 1 Breaker Dr 2
Chaplin St
Claypool St
D
1 Northgreen Blvd
1 D
1 B
Intercontinental Park Blvd
Frank Rd
Morales Rd
Swan Rd
Swan Rd
Baroid Corp
1
2
3
4
5
6
7
A
B
C
D
E
29°59'16"
29°58'50"
29°58'24"
29°57'58"
29°57'32"
29°57'05"
29°56'39"
29°56'13"
95°22'54"
95°22'24"
95°21'54"
95°21'24"
95°20'54"
95°20'23"

SEE 3403 MAP

SEE 3545 MAP

1:24,000
1 in. = 2000 ft.
0 0.25 0.5
miles

SEE 3261 MAP

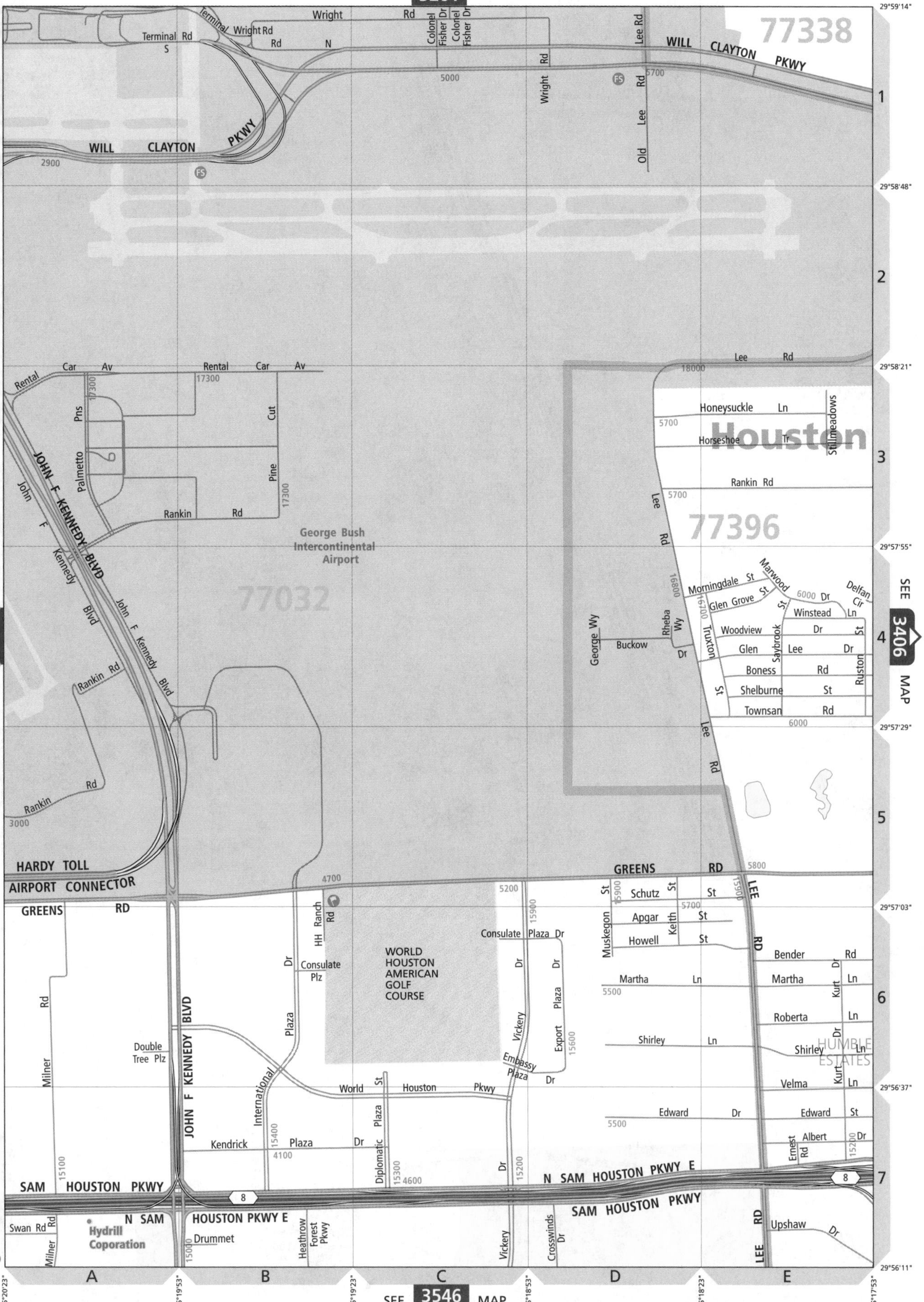
29°59'14"
29°58'48"
29°58'21"
29°57'55"
29°57'29"
29°57'03"
29°56'37"
29°56'11"
77338
77396
77032
Houston
George Bush Intercontinental Airport
WORLD HOUSTON AMERICAN GOLF COURSE
HUMBLE ESTATES
Hydrill Coporation
WILL CLAYTON PKWY
Wright Rd
Terminal Rd S
Terminal Wright Rd
Rd N
Colonel Fisher Dr
Lee Rd
Old Lee Rd
5000
5700
2900
Rental Car Av
17300
Pns
Palmetto
Cut
Pine
Rankin Rd
JOHN F KENNEDY BLVD
John F Kennedy Blvd
Lee Rd
18000
Honeysuckle Ln
Horseshoe Tr
Stillmeadows
Rankin Rd
Morningdale St
Marwood
Glen Grove St
Delfan Cir
6000 Dr
Winstead Ln
Woodview Dr
Glen Lee Dr
Saybrook St
Boness Rd
Shelburne St
Townsan Rd
Ruston St
Truxton St
Rheba Wy
Buckow Dr
George Wy
16800
16700
6000
3000
HARDY TOLL
AIRPORT CONNECTOR
GREENS RD
4700
5800
HH Ranch Rd
5200
15900
Consulate Plaza Dr
Consulate Plz
Plaza Dr
Muskegon St
Schutz St
Apgar St
Keith St
Howell St
LEE RD
Bender Rd
Martha Ln
5500
Kurt Dr
Roberta Ln
Shirley Ln
Velma Ln
Edward Dr
Edward St
Albert Dr
Ernest Rd
15200
Milner Rd
Double Tree Plz
JOHN F KENNEDY BLVD
International
Vickery Dr
Export Plaza Dr
15600
Embassy Plaza Dr
World Houston Pkwy
St
Kendrick Plaza Dr
15400
4100
Diplomatic Plaza
15300
4600
15100
SAM HOUSTON PKWY
N SAM HOUSTON PKWY E
8
SAM HOUSTON PKWY
N SAM HOUSTON PKWY E
Swan Rd
Drummet
Heathrow Forest Pkwy
Vickery
Crosswinds Dr
Upshaw Dr
1
2
3
4
5
6
7
A
B
C
D
E
95°20'23"
95°19'53"
95°19'23"
95°18'53"
95°18'23"
95°17'53"

SEE 3406 MAP

SEE 3546 MAP

1:24,000
1 in. = 2000 ft.
0 0.25 0.5
miles

SEE 3262 MAP

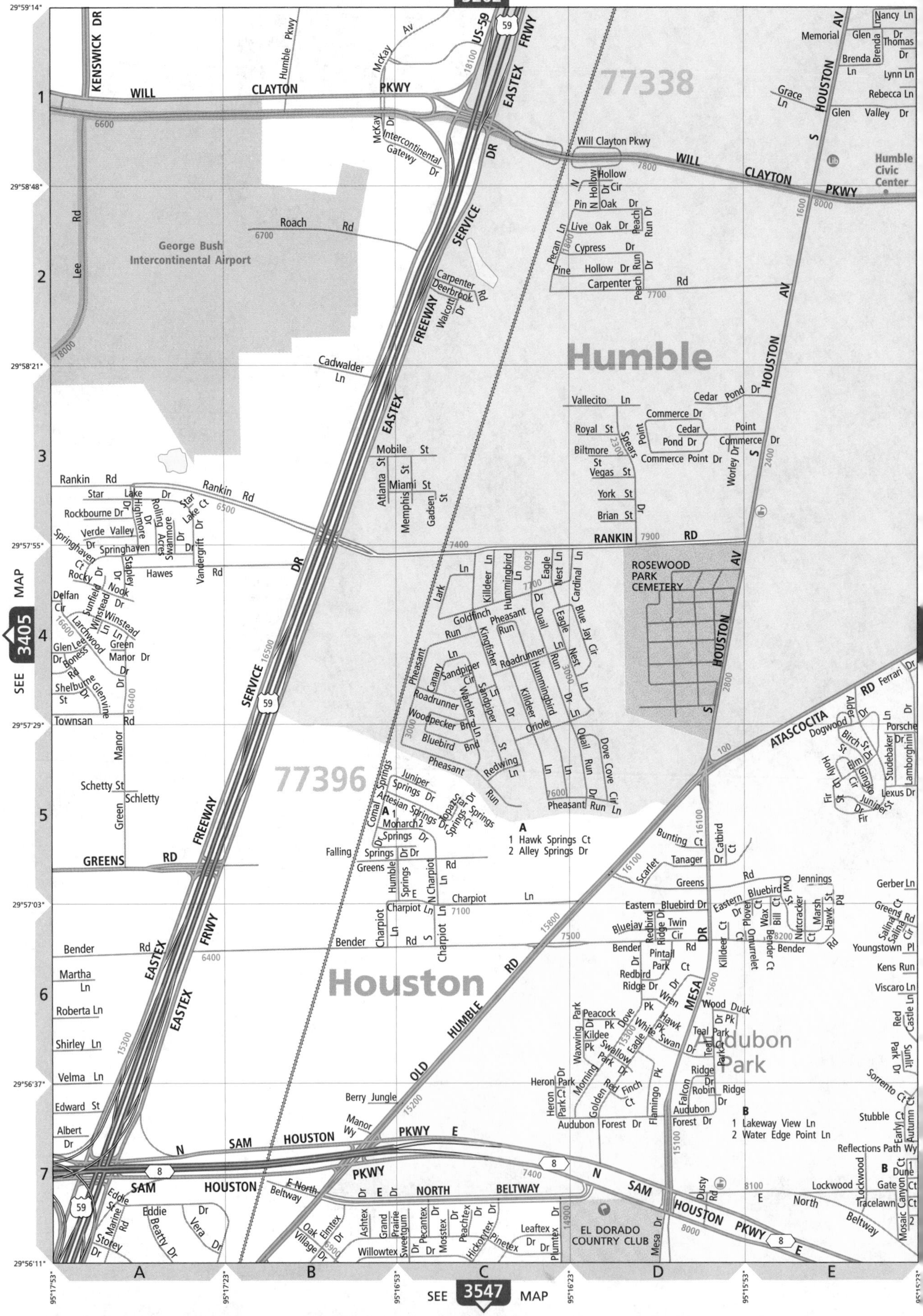

29°59'14"
29°58'48"
29°58'21"
29°57'55"
29°57'29"
29°57'03"
29°56'37"
29°56'11"
95°17'53"
95°17'23"
95°16'53"
95°16'23"
95°15'53"
95°15'23"
1
2
3
4
5
6
7
A
B
C
D
E
KENSWICK DR
WILL CLAYTON PKWY
Humble Pkwy
McKay Av
US-59
59
EASTEX FRWY
77338
Memorial
Glen
Nancy Ln
Dr Thomas Dr
Brenda Ln
Lynn Ln
Rebecca Ln
Grace Ln
Glen Valley Dr
S HOUSTON AV
6600
McKay Dr
Intercontinental Gateway Dr
Will Clayton Pkwy
7800
Humble Civic Center
8000
1600
Lee Rd
18000
Roach Rd
6700
George Bush Intercontinental Airport
SERVICE DR
N Hollow Dr Cir
Pin Oak Dr
Live Oak Dr
Peach Run Dr
Pecan Ln
1800
Cypress Dr
Pine Hollow Dr
Carpenter Rd
7700
Carpenter Rd
Deerbrook
Walcott Dr
FREEWAY
Humble
Cadwalder Ln
EASTEX
Vallecito Ln
Cedar Pond Dr
Commerce Dr
Royal St
Point
Cedar Pond Dr
Commerce Dr
Spears
2300
Biltmore St
Commerce Point Dr
Worley Dr
2400
Vegas St
Mobile St
Atlanta St
Miami St
Memphis St
Gadsen St
York St
Brian St
Rankin Rd
Star Lake Dr
Rockbourne Dr
Highmore Dr
Rolling Acres
Swanmore Dr
Star Lake Ct
Vandergrift Dr
6500
Verde Valley
Springhaven Dr
Springhaven
Stapley Dr
Hawes Rd
RANKIN RD
7400
7900
Lark Ln
Killdeer Ln
Hummingbird Ln
2600
Eagle Nest Ln
Cardinal Ln
ROSEWOOD PARK CEMETERY
Rocky Ct
Nook
Delfan Cir
Sunfield
Winstead Ln
Winstead
Larchwood
Green Manor Dr
Glen Lee Dr
Boness Rd
Shelburne St
Glenvine Dr
16600
16400
Townsan Rd
Goldfinch Run
Pheasant Run
Quail Dr
Blue Jay Cir
Kingfisher
Roadrunner Ln
Nest Ln
Canary Ln
Sandpiper Cir
Warbler Ln
Sandpiper St
Killdeer Dr
Hummingbird Dr
Oriole Ln
3000
Roadrunner
Woodpecker Bnd
Bluebird Bnd
Pheasant
Redwing Ln
Quail Run
Dove Cove Cir
Ln
Run Dr
7600
Pheasant Run Ln
SERVICE 16500
59
HOUSTON S AV
2800
ATASCOCITA RD
Ferrari Dr
Alder Dr
Porsche Dr
Lamborghini
Dogwood
Birch St
Elm Dr
Gingko Cir
Studebaker Ln
Holly Ln
Juniper St
Fir
Lexus Dr
100
77396
Manor Dr
Schetty St
Schletty
Green Dr
Juniper Springs Dr
Comal Springs
Artesian Springs Dr
Topaz Springs Ct
Star Springs
Monarch Springs Dr
A
1 Hawk Springs Ct
2 Alley Springs Dr
FREEWAY
GREENS RD
Falling Springs Dr
Greens Rd
Humble Springs
Charpiot Ln
16100
Bunting Ct
Catbird Ct
Tanager Dr
Scarlet
Greens Rd
Jennings
Gerber Ln
Charpiot Ln
7100
Eastern Bluebird Dr
Eastern Bluebird Dr
Owl St
Greens Ct
Bluejay Redbird Ridge Dr
Twin Cir
Plover Wax Ct
Bill Ct
Nutcracker Ct
Marsh Hawk St
Salina Cir
Salina Rd
Bender Rd
EASTEX FRWY
6400
Bender Rd
Charpiot Ln
Rd S
7500
15800
Bender Pintail Park Ct
Killdeer Ct
Omurrelet
Bender Ct
8200
Bender
Youngstown Pl
Martha Ln
Houston
Redbird Ridge Dr
Wren Dr
MESA DR
Kens Run
Roberta Ln
OLD HUMBLE RD
15600
Viscaro Ln
Waxwing Park Dr
Peacock Pk
Kildee Pk
Dove
Swallow Park
Eagle
White Pk
Hawk
Swan Dr
Wood Duck Dr Pk
Teal Park
Audubon Park
Castle Ln
Red Park
Shirley Ln
15300
Sunlit
Velma Ln
Heron Park Ct Dr
Morning Dr
Golden
Red Finch Ct
Flamingo Pk
Falcon
Ridge Robin Dr
Ridge
Sorrento Ct
Edward St
Berry Jungle
15200
Audubon Forest Dr
Audubon Forest Dr
B
1 Lakeway View Ln
2 Water Edge Point Ln
Stubble Ct
Early Autumn
Albert Dr
Manor Wy
N SAM HOUSTON PKWY E
15100
Reflections Path Wy
8
7400
8
Dusty Rd
8100
Lockwood
Lockwood
B Dune Ct
Gate Ct
SAM HOUSTON
E North Beltway
PKWY
Dr E Dr NORTH BELTWAY
N SAM HOUSTON PKWY E
E North Beltway
Tracelawn Ct
Mosaic Canyon
59
Eddie St
Eddie Dr
Marine Rd
Beatty Dr
Vera Dr
Storey Dr
Oak Village Dr
Elmtex Dr
6900
Ashtex
Grand Prairie
Sweetgum
Willowtex
Pecantex Dr
Mosstex Dr
Peachtex Dr
Hickorytex Dr
Pinetex
Leaftex Dr
Plumtex Dr
14900
EL DORADO COUNTRY CLUB
Mesa Dr
8000
8

SEE MAP 3405

SEE 3547 MAP

1:24,000
1 in. = 2000 ft.
0 0.25 0.5
miles

SEE 3263 MAP

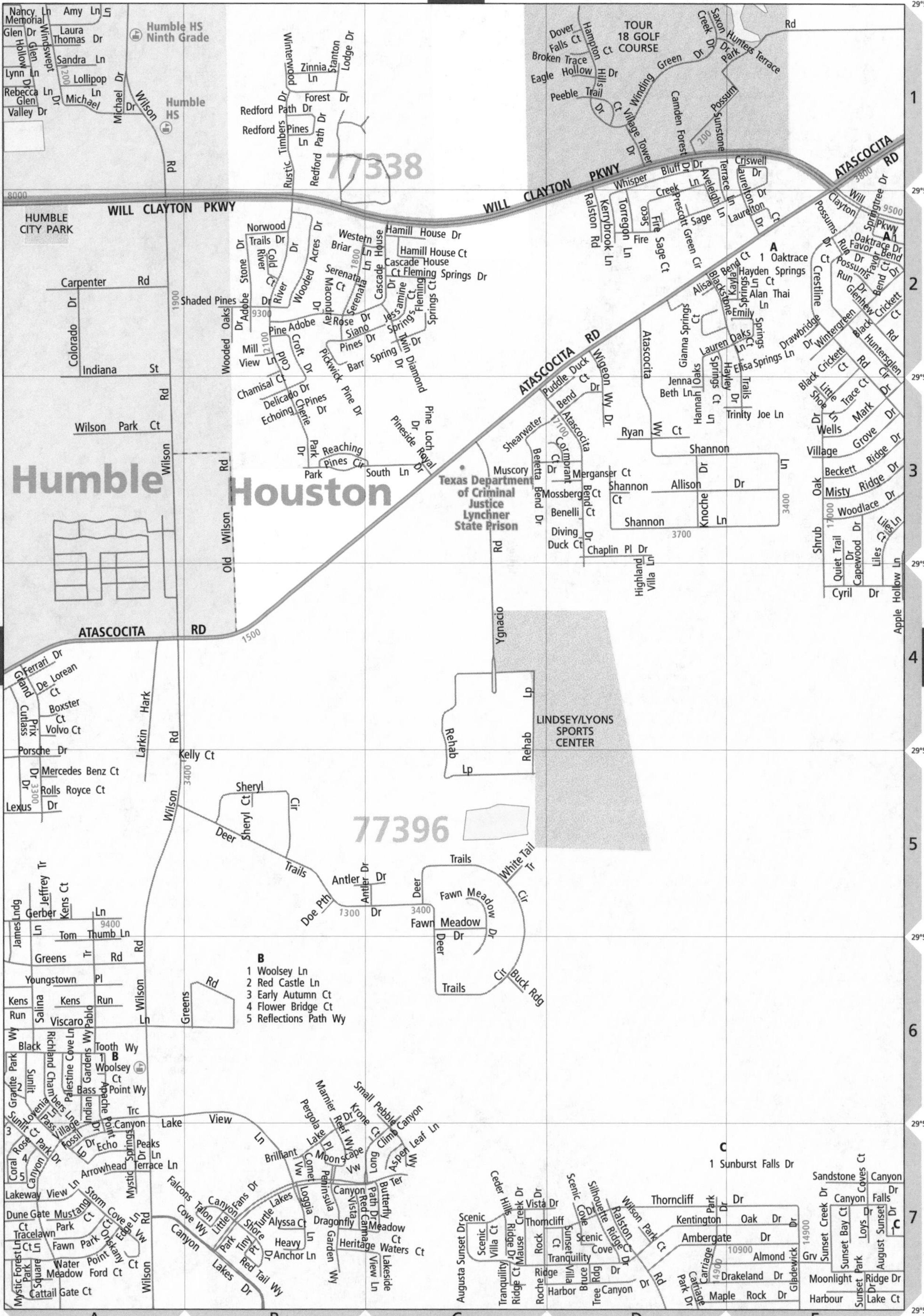
Humble
Houston
77338
77396
HUMBLE CITY PARK
Humble HS Ninth Grade
Humble HS
TOUR 18 GOLF COURSE
Texas Department of Criminal Justice Lynchner State Prison
LINDSEY/LYONS SPORTS CENTER
WILL CLAYTON PKWY
ATASCOCITA RD
Wilson Rd
Old Wilson Rd
Larkin
Hark
Kelly Ct
Ygnacio Rd
Rehab Lp
Carpenter Rd
Colorado Dr
Indiana St
Wilson Park Ct
Shannon Dr
Allison Dr
Knoche Ln
Ryan Ct
Trails Cir
Fawn Meadow Dr
Deer Trails
Antler Dr
Doe Pth
Sheryl Cir
Sheryl Ct
Lake View Dr
Thorncliff Dr
Kentington Dr
Ambergate Dr
Almond Dr
Drakeland Dr
Maple Rock Dr
Moonlight Ridge Dr
Harbour Lake Ct
Sunset Creek Dr
A
1 Oaktrace
B
1 Woolsey Ln
2 Red Castle Ln
3 Early Autumn Ct
4 Flower Bridge Ct
5 Reflections Path Wy
C
1 Sunburst Falls Dr
1
2
3
4
5
6
7
A
B
C
D
E
29°59'11"
29°58'45"
29°58'19"
29°57'53"
29°57'26"
29°57'00"
29°56'34"
29°56'08"
95°15'23"
95°14'53"
95°14'23"
95°13'53"
95°13'23"
95°12'53"

SEE 3408 MAP

SEE 3548 MAP

1:24,000
1 in. = 2000 ft.
0 0.25 0.5
miles

SEE 3264 MAP

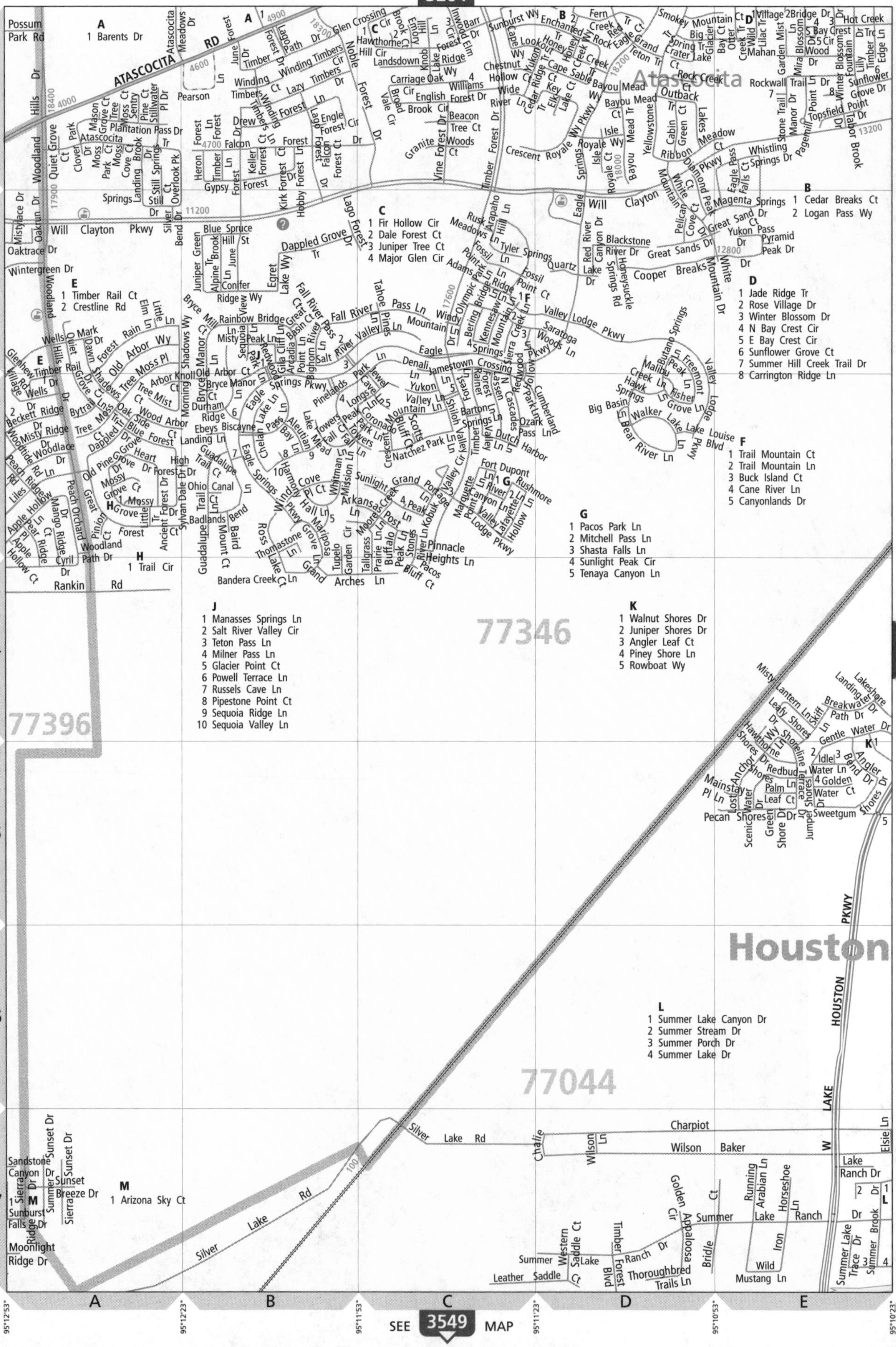
Atascocita
Houston
77346
77396
77044
Will Clayton Pkwy
Atascocita Rd
Woodland Hills Dr
Timber Forest Dr
Valley Lodge Pkwy
Eagle Springs Pkwy
Fall River Pass Ln
Old Arbor Wy
Rankin Rd
Silver Lake Rd
W Lake Houston Pkwy
Charpiot
Wilson Baker
Summer Lake Ranch Dr
Lake Ranch Dr
A
1 Barents Dr
B
1 Cedar Breaks Ct
2 Logan Pass Wy
C
1 Fir Hollow Cir
2 Dale Forest Ct
3 Juniper Tree Ct
4 Major Glen Cir
D
1 Jade Ridge Tr
2 Rose Village Dr
3 Winter Blossom Dr
4 N Bay Crest Cir
5 E Bay Crest Cir
6 Sunflower Grove Ct
7 Summer Hill Creek Trail Dr
8 Carrington Ridge Ln
E
1 Timber Rail Ct
2 Crestline Rd
F
1 Trail Mountain Ct
2 Trail Mountain Ln
3 Buck Island Ct
4 Cane River Ln
5 Canyonlands Dr
G
1 Pacos Park Ln
2 Mitchell Pass Ln
3 Shasta Falls Ln
4 Sunlight Peak Cir
5 Tenaya Canyon Ln
H
1 Trail Cir
J
1 Manasses Springs Ln
2 Salt River Valley Cir
3 Teton Pass Ln
4 Milner Pass Ln
5 Glacier Point Ct
6 Powell Terrace Ln
7 Russels Cave Ln
8 Pipestone Point Ct
9 Sequoia Ridge Ln
10 Sequoia Valley Ln
K
1 Walnut Shores Dr
2 Juniper Shores Dr
3 Angler Leaf Ct
4 Piney Shore Ln
5 Rowboat Wy
L
1 Summer Lake Canyon Dr
2 Summer Stream Dr
3 Summer Porch Dr
4 Summer Lake Dr
M
1 Arizona Sky Ct
29°59'11"
29°58'45"
29°58'19"
29°57'53"
29°57'26"
29°57'00"
29°56'34"
29°56'08"
95°12'53"
95°12'23"
95°11'53"
95°11'23"
95°10'53"
95°10'23"

SEE 3407 MAP

SEE 3549 MAP

1:24,000
1 in. = 2000 ft.
0 0.25 0.5
miles

SEE 3265 MAP

77346
77044
Houston
LAKE HOUSTON
77532
Lake Shadows
WALDEN ON LK HOUSTON COUNTRY CLUB
W LAKE HOUSTON PKWY
Clayton Pkwy
Will Clayton Pkwy
A
1 Garnet Hill Ln
2 Steamboat Inn Dr
3 Cheeca Lodge Ln
4 Castle Rain Dr
5 Sunset Crest Dr
B
1 Catamaran Dr
2 Catamaran Rd
3 Red Sails Pass
4 Kyack Ct
5 Lookout Ln
C
1 Sailfish Cove Dr
D
1 S Habour Bend Ln
2 Lakeshore Landing Dr
3 Gentle Water Dr
4 Winding Canyon Dr
5 Lake Excursion Ct
6 Rowboat Wy
Aerobic
Bronze Trail
Bluewater Cove Dr
Deerwood Lake Dr
Malardcrest
Silver
Crossing Dr
Lure
Nautic Cross
Mariner Pl
Regatta Rd
Sailing Dr
Rolling Rapids Rd
Rolling Rapids
Waters Edge Blvd
Superior Ln
Lake Michigan
Lake Sophie Ct
Rock Bend
Loramie Creek Ct
Baikal Ct
Chobee Dr
Tahoe
Livingston Dr
Boca Brook Ct
Coral Garden Ln
Sugar Dock
Pelican Beach
Gentle Winds
Copano
Breakwater Pass
Hillsboro Brook Ln
Delwood Dr
Stern Creek Ln
Springs
Explorer Dr
Redwood Shores Dr
Azalea Shores
Cedar Shores
Chart House
Elm
Finwood Ln
Lake Passage Ct
Summer Lake Canyon Dr
Summer Lake Home Dr
Summer Lake Ranch Dr
Bunde
Lakeside Terrace Dr
Indian Mound Ct
Foley Rd
Deep Anchor Wy
Windward Wy
Shadows
Crosswinds Wy
Metycove
Shoreside Dr
Steele
Skimmer Cote Wy
Little Skiff Dr
Metycove Dr
Metycove Ct
Shoreline Dr
3000
3600
18600
18500
18400
8700

SEE 3410 MAP

SEE 3550 MAP

1:24,000
1 in. = 2000 ft.
0 0.25 0.5
miles

SEE 3266 MAP

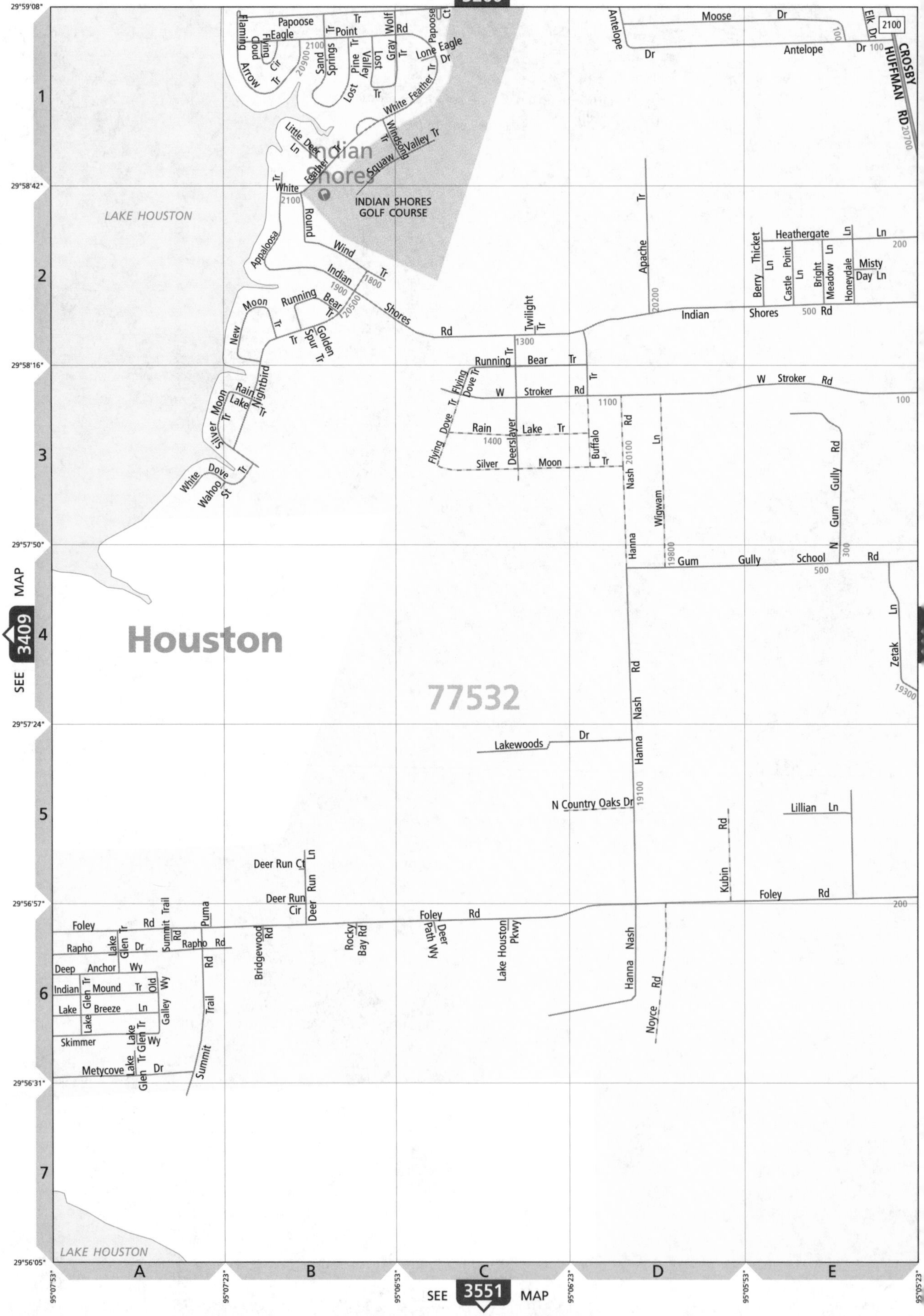
Houston
77532
LAKE HOUSTON
Indian Shores
INDIAN SHORES GOLF COURSE
CROSBY HUFFMAN RD
2100
Moose Dr
Antelope Dr
Elk Dr
Papoose Tr
Eagle Point
Papoose Ct
Flaming Arrow Tr
Flying Cloud Cir
Sand Springs
Pine Valley
Lost Valley
Gray Wolf Rd
Lone Eagle Dr
Lost Tr
White Feather Tr
Little Deer Ln
Windsong Tr
Squaw Valley Tr
White Feather Tr
Round Wind Tr
Appaloosa
Indian Shores Rd
Apache Tr
Heathergate Ln
Thicket Ln
Berry
Castle Point Ln
Bright Meadow Ln
Honeydale
Misty Day Ln
New Moon Tr
Running Bear Tr
Golden Spur Tr
Twilight Tr
Running Bear Tr
W Stroker Rd
Flying Dove Tr
Rain Lake Tr
Nightbird Tr
Silver Moon Tr
White Dove Tr
Wahoo St
Rain Lake Tr
Silver Moon
Deerslayer
Buffalo Tr
Hanna Nash Rd
Wigwam Ln
Gum Gully Rd
N Gum Gully Rd
Gum Gully School Rd
Zetak Ln
Lakewoods Dr
N Country Oaks Dr
Lillian Ln
Kubin Rd
Foley Rd
Deer Run Ct
Deer Run Ln
Deer Run Cir
Bridgewood Rd
Rocky Bay Rd
Deer Path Wy
Lake Houston Pkwy
Noyce Rd
Rapho Dr
Rapho Rd
Lake Glen Tr
Summit Trail Rd
Puma Rd
Deep Anchor Wy
Indian Mound Tr
Old Galley Wy
Lake Breeze Ln
Skimmer Wy
Lake Glen Tr
Metycove Dr
Summit Trail
29°59'08"
29°58'42"
29°58'16"
29°57'50"
29°57'24"
29°56'57"
29°56'31"
29°56'05"
95°07'53"
95°07'23"
95°06'53"
95°06'23"
95°05'53"
95°05'23"
A B C D E
1 2 3 4 5 6 7

SEE 3409 MAP

SEE 3551 MAP

1:24,000
1 in. = 2000 ft.
0 0.25 0.5
miles

SEE 3267 MAP

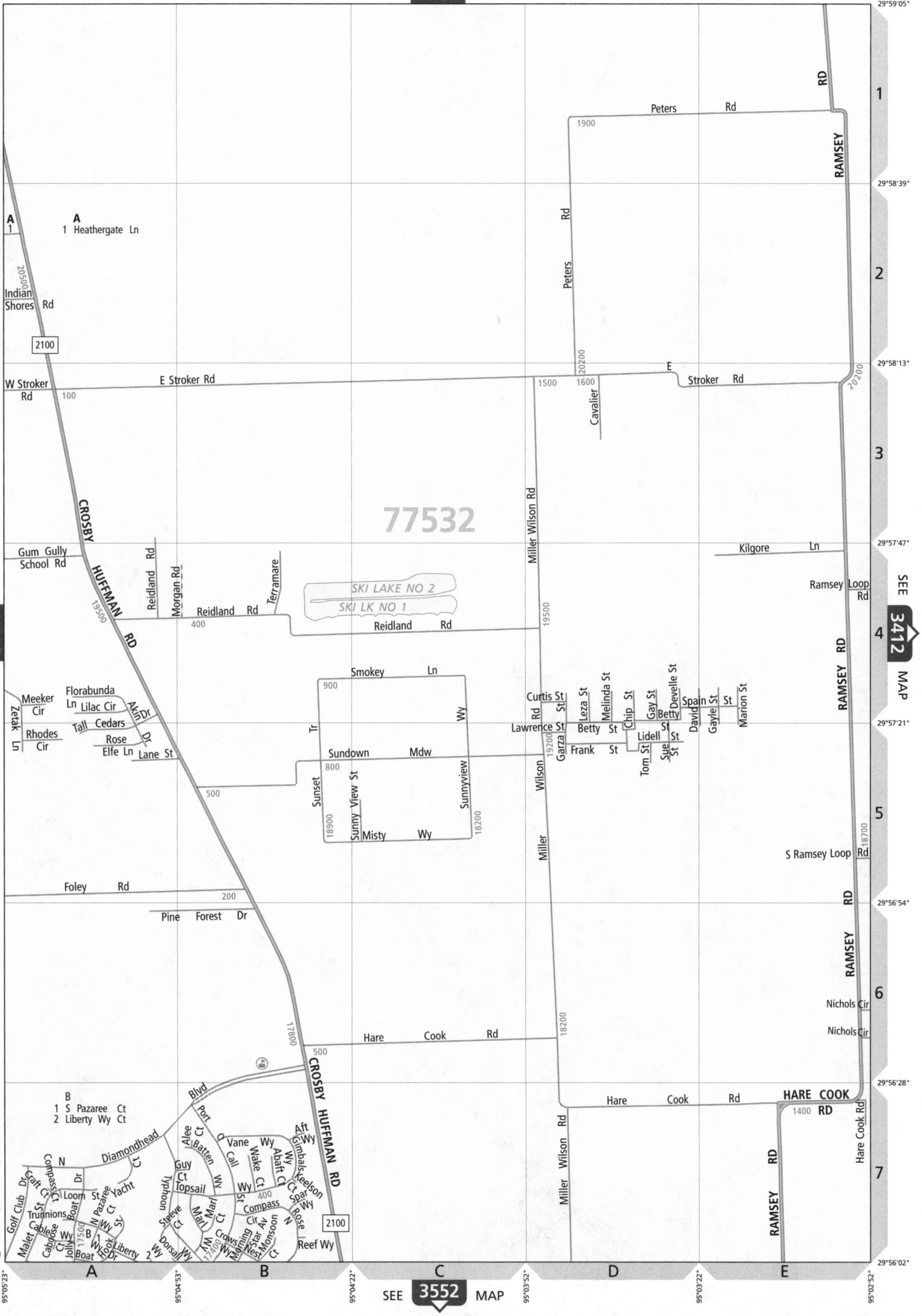
77532
A
1 Heathergate Ln
B
1 S Pazaree Ct
2 Liberty Wy Ct
Peters Rd
Ramsey Rd
Indian Shores Rd
2100
W Stroker Rd
E Stroker Rd
Cavalier
Crosby Huffman Rd
Miller Wilson Rd
Kilgore Ln
Ramsey Loop Rd
Gum Gully School Rd
Reidland Rd
Morgan Rd
Terramare
Ski Lake No 2
Ski Lk No 1
Smokey Ln
Sundown Mdw
Sunset Tr
Sunny View St
Sunnyview Wy
Misty Wy
Meeker Cir
Florabunda Ln
Lilac Cir
Akin Dr
Zetak Ln
Rhodes Cir
Tall Cedars Dr
Rose
Elfe Ln
Lane St
Curtis St
Lawrence St
Garza St
Leza St
Melinda St
Chip St
Gay St
Develle St
Spain St
Marion St
Betty St
Frank St
Lidell St
Tom St
Sue St
David St
Gayle St
S Ramsey Loop Rd
Foley Rd
Pine Forest Dr
Nichols Cir
Hare Cook Rd
Hare Cook Rd
Diamondhead Blvd
Port O Call
Vane Wy
Aft Wy
Alee Ct
Batten Wy
Wake Ct
Abaft Ct
Gimbal Ct
Keelson Wy
Guy Ct
Topsail Wy
Typhoon
Compass Cir
Spar Wy
Rose
Reef Wy
N Compass Dr
Craft Ct
Golf Club Dr
Loom St
N Pazaree St
Yacht
Trunnions
Boat
Cablose
Caboose Ct
Malet St
Jolly Boat Dr
Hook Wy
Liberty Wy
Steeve Ct
Dorsal Wy
Marl Ct
Crows Nest Ct
Morning Star Av
Monsoon Ct
20500 2100 100 19500 400 500 200 17800 500 900 800 18900 18200 19500 19200 18200 1900 20200 1500 1600 20200 18700 1400 17500 17400 400
1 2 3 4 5 6 7
A B C D E
29°59'05" 29°58'39" 29°58'13" 29°57'47" 29°57'21" 29°56'54" 29°56'28" 29°56'02"
95°05'23" 95°04'53" 95°04'22" 95°03'52" 95°03'22" 95°02'52"

SEE 3412 MAP

SEE 3552 MAP

1:24,000
1 in. = 2000 ft.
0 0.25 0.5
miles

SEE 3268 MAP

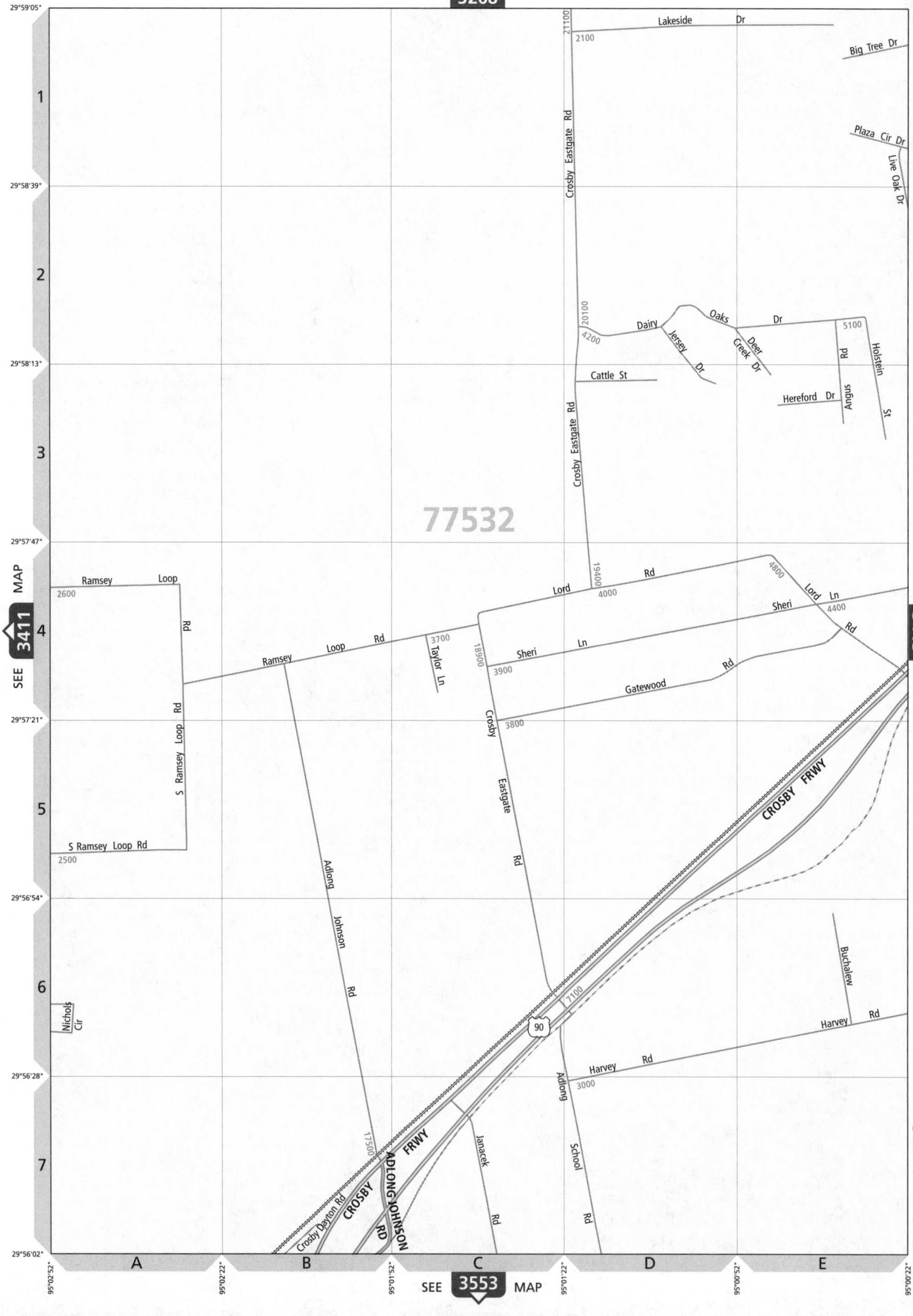
77532
Lakeside Dr
2100
21100
Big Tree Dr
Plaza Cir Dr
Live Oak Dr
Crosby Eastgate Rd
20100
4200
Dairy
Jersey Dr
Oaks Dr
Deer Creek Dr
5100
Angus Rd
Holstein St
Hereford Dr
Cattle St
Ramsey Loop Rd
2600
S Ramsey Loop Rd
2500
Lord Rd
19400
4000
4800
Lord Ln
Sheri Ln
4400
3700
Taylor Ln
18900
3900
Gatewood Rd
3800
Crosby Eastgate Rd
CROSBY FRWY
Adlong Johnson Rd
17500
ADLONG JOHNSON RD
Crosby Dayton Rd
7100
90
Nichols Cir
Buchalew Rd
Harvey Rd
3000
Adlong School Rd
Janacek Rd
1
2
3
4
5
6
7
A
B
C
D
E
29°59'05"
29°58'39"
29°58'13"
29°57'47"
29°57'21"
29°56'54"
29°56'28"
29°56'02"
95°02'52"
95°02'22"
95°01'52"
95°01'22"
95°00'52"
95°00'22"

SEE 3411 MAP

SEE 3553 MAP

1:24,000
1 in. = 2000 ft.
0 0.25 0.5
miles

SEE 3269 MAP

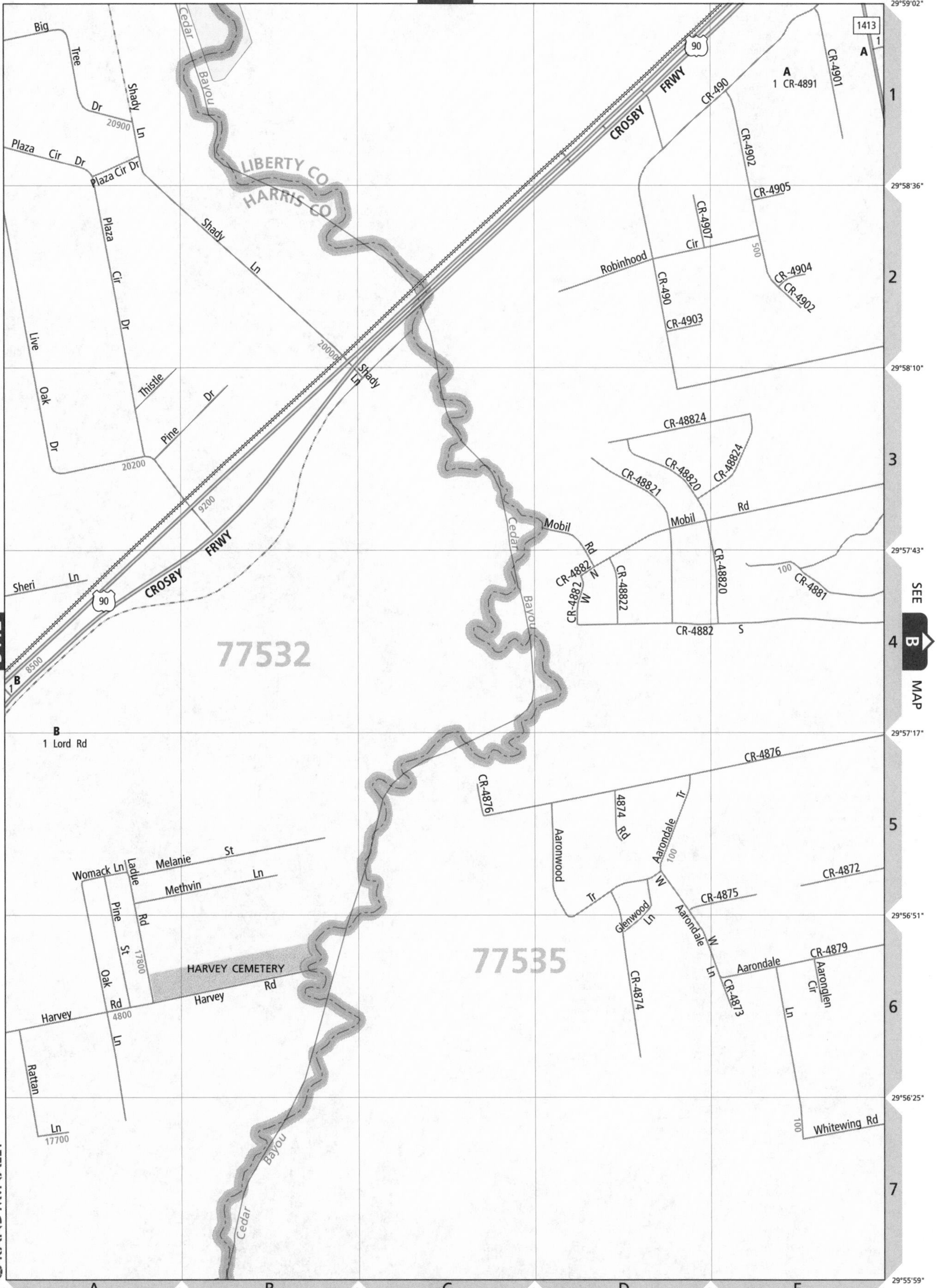
Big
Tree
Dr
Shady
Ln
20900
Plaza Cir Dr
Plaza Cir Dr
Plaza
Cir
Dr
Live
Oak
Dr
Thistle
Pine
Dr
20200
9200
Shady
Ln
20000
Shady
Ln
Cedar
Bayou
LIBERTY CO
HARRIS CO
90
CROSBY FRWY
Sheri Ln
8500
1 B
B
1 Lord Rd
77532
1413
1
A
A
1 CR-4891
CR-4901
CR-490
CR-4902
CR-4905
CR-4907
Robinhood Cir
500
CR-490
CR-4904
CR-4902
CR-4903
CR-48824
CR-48820
CR-48824
CR-48821
Mobil Rd
Mobil Rd
CR-4882 N
CR-4882 W
CR-48822
CR-48820
CR-4882 S
100
CR-4881
Cedar
Bayou
CR-4876
CR-4876
4874 Rd
Aaronwood Tr
Aarondale Tr
100
W
Glenwood Ln
Aarondale W Ln
CR-4875
CR-4872
CR-4874
CR-4873
Aarondale
CR-4879
Aaronglen Cir
Ln
100
Whitewing Rd
77535
Womack Ln
Ladue Rd
Melanie St
Methvin Ln
Pine St
17800
HARVEY CEMETERY
Harvey Rd
Harvey Rd
4800
Oak Ln
Rattan Ln
17700
Bayou
Cedar
29°59'02"
29°58'36"
29°58'10"
29°57'43"
29°57'17"
29°56'51"
29°56'25"
29°55'59"
1
2
3
4
5
6
7
A
B
C
D
E
95°00'22"
94°59'52"
94°59'22"
94°58'52"
94°58'22"
94°57'52"

SEE B MAP

SEE 3554 MAP

1:24,000
1 in. = 2000 ft.
0 0.25 0.5
miles

SEE 3396 MAP

SEE B MAP

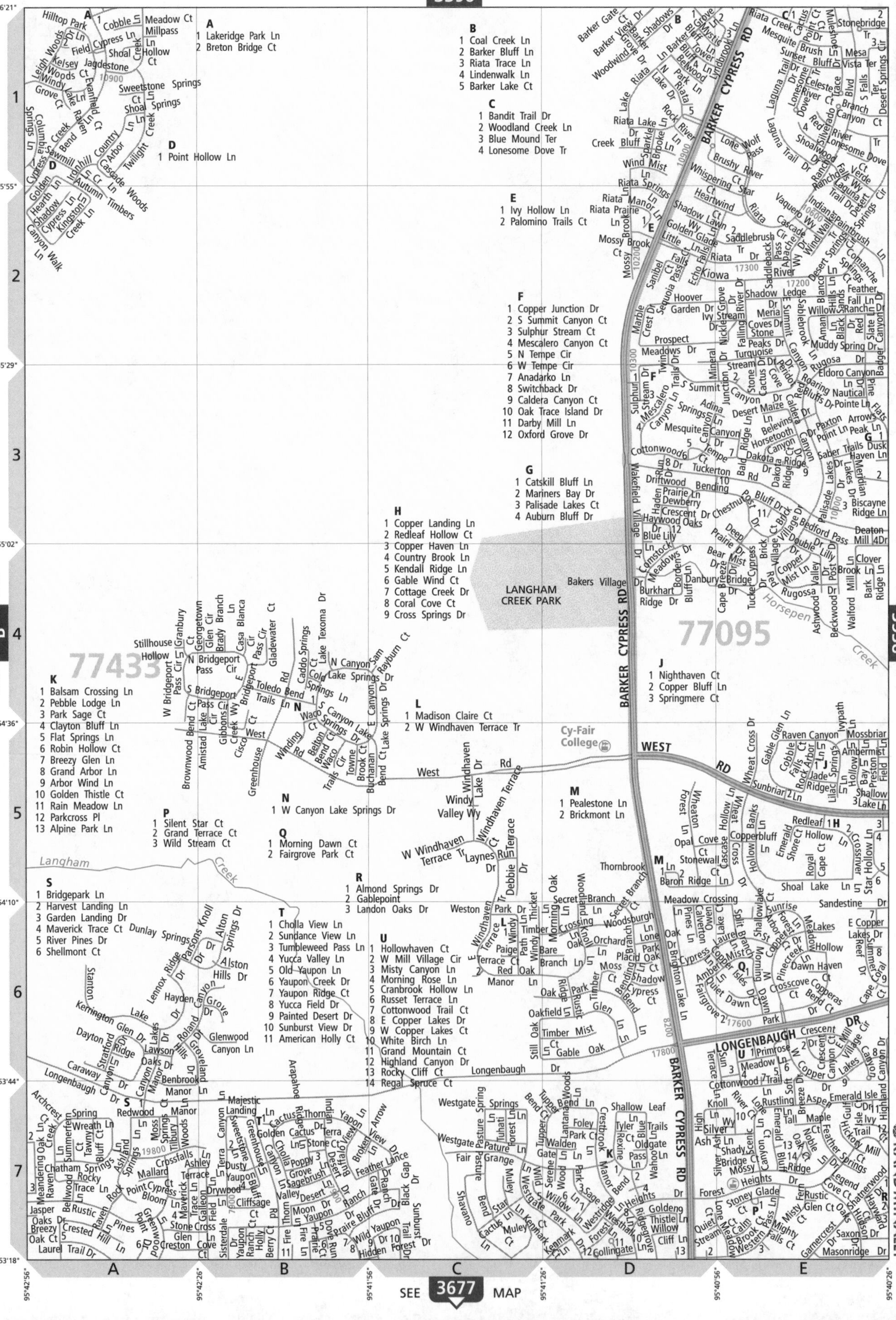
A
1 Lakeridge Park Ln
2 Breton Bridge Ct
B
1 Coal Creek Ln
2 Barker Bluff Ln
3 Riata Trace Ln
4 Lindenwalk Ln
5 Barker Lake Ct
C
1 Bandit Trail Dr
2 Woodland Creek Ln
3 Blue Mound Ter
4 Lonesome Dove Tr
D
1 Point Hollow Ln
E
1 Ivy Hollow Ln
2 Palomino Trails Ct
F
1 Copper Junction Dr
2 S Summit Canyon Ct
3 Sulphur Stream Ct
4 Mescalero Canyon Ct
5 N Tempe Cir
6 W Tempe Cir
7 Anadarko Ln
8 Switchback Dr
9 Caldera Canyon Ct
10 Oak Trace Island Dr
11 Darby Mill Ln
12 Oxford Grove Dr
G
1 Catskill Bluff Ln
2 Mariners Bay Dr
3 Palisade Lakes Ct
4 Auburn Bluff Dr
H
1 Copper Landing Ln
2 Redleaf Hollow Ct
3 Copper Haven Ln
4 Country Brook Ln
5 Kendall Ridge Ln
6 Gable Wind Ct
7 Cottage Creek Dr
8 Coral Cove Ct
9 Cross Springs Dr
J
1 Nighthaven Ct
2 Copper Bluff Ln
3 Springmere Ct
K
1 Balsam Crossing Ln
2 Pebble Lodge Ln
3 Park Sage Ct
4 Clayton Bluff Ln
5 Flat Springs Ln
6 Robin Hollow Ct
7 Breezy Glen Ln
8 Grand Arbor Ln
9 Arbor Wind Ln
10 Golden Thistle Ct
11 Rain Meadow Ln
12 Parkcross Pl
13 Alpine Park Ln
L
1 Madison Claire Ct
2 W Windhaven Terrace Tr
M
1 Pealestone Ln
2 Brickmont Ln
N
1 W Canyon Lake Springs Dr
P
1 Silent Star Ct
2 Grand Terrace Ct
3 Wild Stream Ct
Q
1 Morning Dawn Ct
2 Fairgrove Park Ct
R
1 Almond Springs Dr
2 Gablepoint
3 Landon Oaks Dr
S
1 Bridgepark Ln
2 Harvest Landing Ln
3 Garden Landing Dr
4 Maverick Trace Ct
5 River Pines Dr
6 Shellmont Ct
T
1 Cholla View Ln
2 Sundance View Ln
3 Tumbleweed Pass Ln
4 Yucca Valley Ln
5 Old Yaupon Ln
6 Yaupon Creek Dr
7 Yaupon Ridge Ct
8 Yucca Field Dr
9 Painted Desert Dr
10 Sunburst View Dr
11 American Holly Ct
U
1 Hollowhaven Ct
2 W Mill Village Cir
3 Misty Canyon Ln
4 Morning Rose Ln
5 Cranbrook Hollow Ln
6 Russet Terrace Ln
7 Cottonwood Trail Ct
8 E Copper Lakes Dr
9 W Copper Lakes Ct
10 White Birch Ln
11 Grand Mountain Ct
12 Highland Canyon Dr
13 Rocky Cliff Ct
14 Regal Spruce Ct
LANGHAM CREEK PARK
Cy-Fair College
77433
77095
BARKER CYPRESS RD
WEST RD
LONGENBAUGH DR
Langham Creek
Horsepen Creek
29°56'21"
29°55'55"
29°55'29"
29°55'02"
29°54'36"
29°54'10"
29°53'44"
29°53'18"
95°42'56"
95°42'26"
95°41'56"
95°41'26"
95°40'56"
95°40'26"

SEE 3677 MAP

1:24,000
1 in. = 2000 ft.
0 0.25 0.5
miles

SEE 3397 MAP

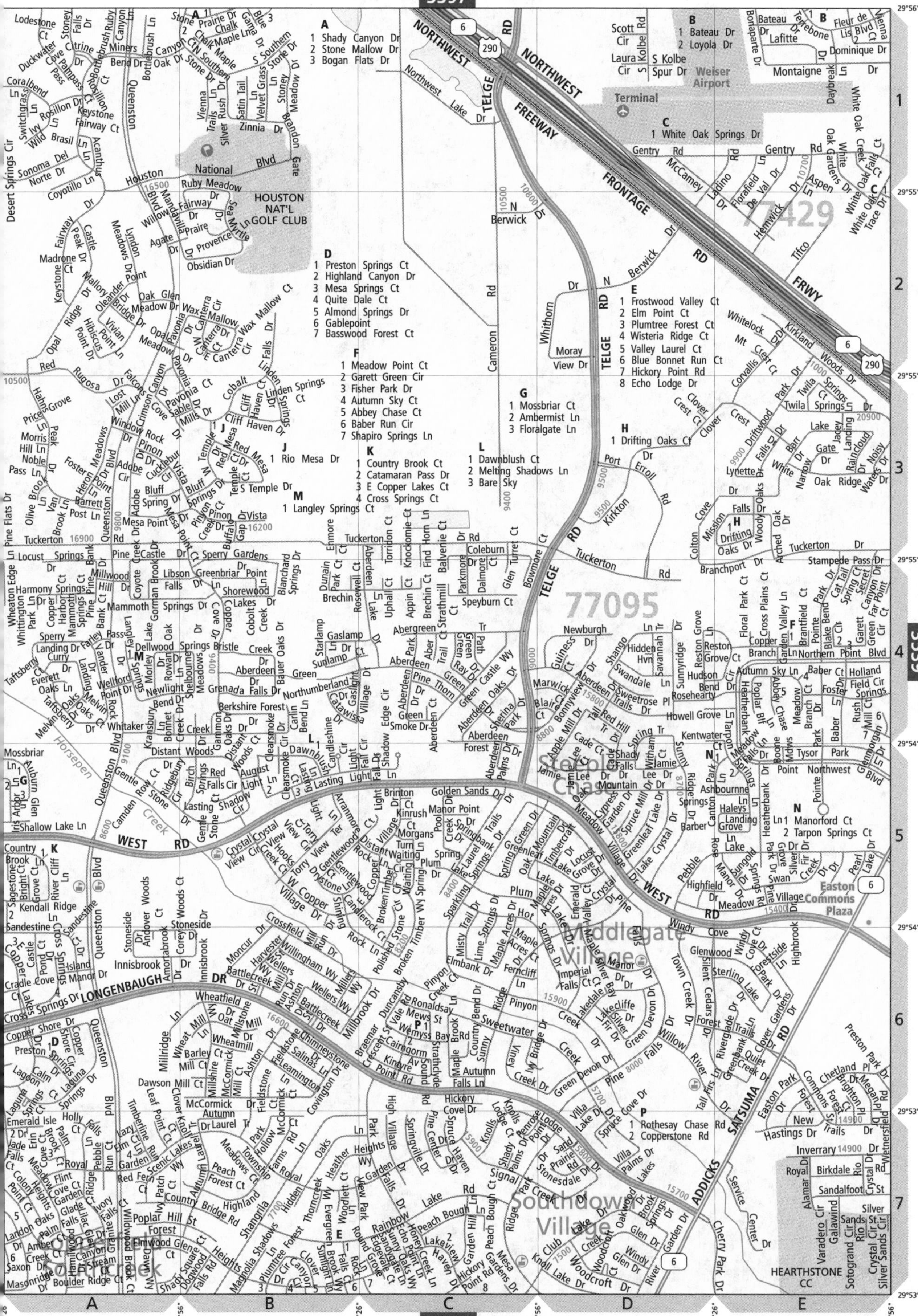
A
1 Shady Canyon Dr
2 Stone Mallow Dr
3 Bogan Flats Dr
B
1 Bateau Dr
2 Loyola Dr
C
1 White Oak Springs Dr
D
1 Preston Springs Ct
2 Highland Canyon Dr
3 Mesa Springs Ct
4 Quite Dale Ct
5 Almond Springs Dr
6 Gablepoint
7 Basswood Forest Ct
E
1 Frostwood Valley Ct
2 Elm Point Ct
3 Plumtree Forest Ct
4 Wisteria Ridge Ct
5 Valley Laurel Ct
6 Blue Bonnet Run Ct
7 Hickory Point Rd
8 Echo Lodge Dr
F
1 Meadow Point Ct
2 Garett Green Cir
3 Fisher Park Dr
4 Autumn Sky Ct
5 Abbey Chase Ct
6 Baber Run Cir
7 Shapiro Springs Ln
G
1 Mossbriar Ct
2 Ambermist Ln
3 Floralgate Ln
H
1 Drifting Oaks Ct
J
1 Rio Mesa Dr
K
1 Country Brook Ct
2 Catamaran Pass Dr
3 E Copper Lakes Ct
4 Cross Springs Ct
L
1 Dawnblush Ct
2 Melting Shadows Ln
3 Bare Sky
M
1 Langley Springs Ct
N
1 Manorford Ct
2 Tarpon Springs Ct
P
1 Rothesay Chase Rd
2 Copperstone Rd
HOUSTON NAT'L GOLF CLUB
Weiser Airport
Terminal
NORTHWEST FREEWAY
NORTHWEST FREEWAY FRONTAGE RD
FRWY
TELGE RD
WEST RD
LONGENBAUGH DR
SATSUMA RD
ADDICKS
77429
77095
Steeple Chase
Middlegate Village
Southdown Village
Easton Commons Plaza
HEARTHSTONE CC
Houston National Blvd
Gentry Rd
Tuckerton Rd
Queenston Blvd
Horsepen Creek
6
290
29°56'19"
29°55'53"
29°55'27"
29°55'01"
29°54'35"
29°54'08"
29°53'42"
29°53'16"
95°39'56"
95°39'26"
95°38'56"
95°38'26"
95°37'56"
1
2
3
4
5
6
7
A
B
C
D
E

SEE 3539 MAP

SEE 3678 MAP

1:24,000
1 in. = 2000 ft.
0 0.25 0.5
miles

N

SEE 3398 MAP

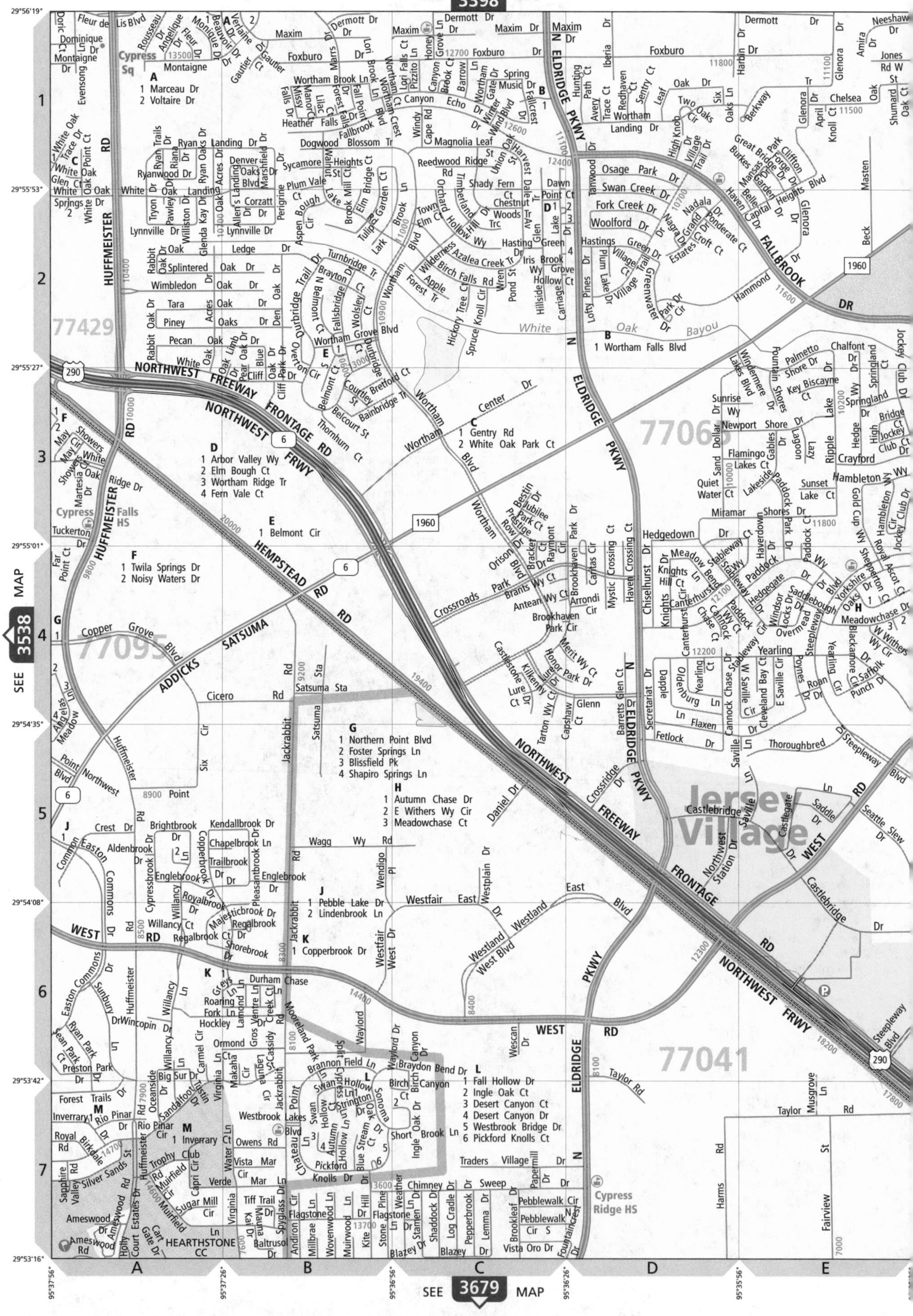
A
1 Marceau Dr
2 Voltaire Dr
B
1 Wortham Falls Blvd
C
1 Gentry Rd
2 White Oak Park Ct
D
1 Arbor Valley Wy
2 Elm Bough Ct
3 Wortham Ridge Tr
4 Fern Vale Ct
E
1 Belmont Cir
F
1 Twila Springs Dr
2 Noisy Waters Dr
G
1 Northern Point Blvd
2 Foster Springs Ln
3 Blissfield Pk
4 Shapiro Springs Ln
H
1 Autumn Chase Dr
2 E Withers Wy Cir
3 Meadowchase Ct
J
1 Pebble Lake Dr
2 Lindenbrook Ln
K
1 Copperbrook Dr
L
1 Fall Hollow Dr
2 Ingle Oak Ct
3 Desert Canyon Ct
4 Desert Canyon Dr
5 Westbrook Bridge Dr
6 Pickford Knolls Ct
M
1 Inverrary Ct
77429
77095
77065
77041
Jersey Village
NORTHWEST FREEWAY
NORTHWEST FRONTAGE RD
HEMPSTEAD RD
HUFFMEISTER RD
N ELDRIDGE PKWY
ELDRIDGE PKWY
FALLBROOK DR
WEST RD
ADDICKS SATSUMA
Cypress Sq
Cypress Falls HS
Cypress Ridge HS
HEARTHSTONE CC
White Oak Bayou
29°56'19"
29°55'53"
29°55'27"
29°55'01"
29°54'35"
29°54'08"
29°53'42"
29°53'16"
95°37'56"
95°37'26"
95°36'56"
95°36'26"
95°35'56"

SEE 3538 MAP

SEE 3679 MAP

1:24,000
1 in. = 2000 ft.
0 0.25 0.5
miles

SEE 3399 MAP

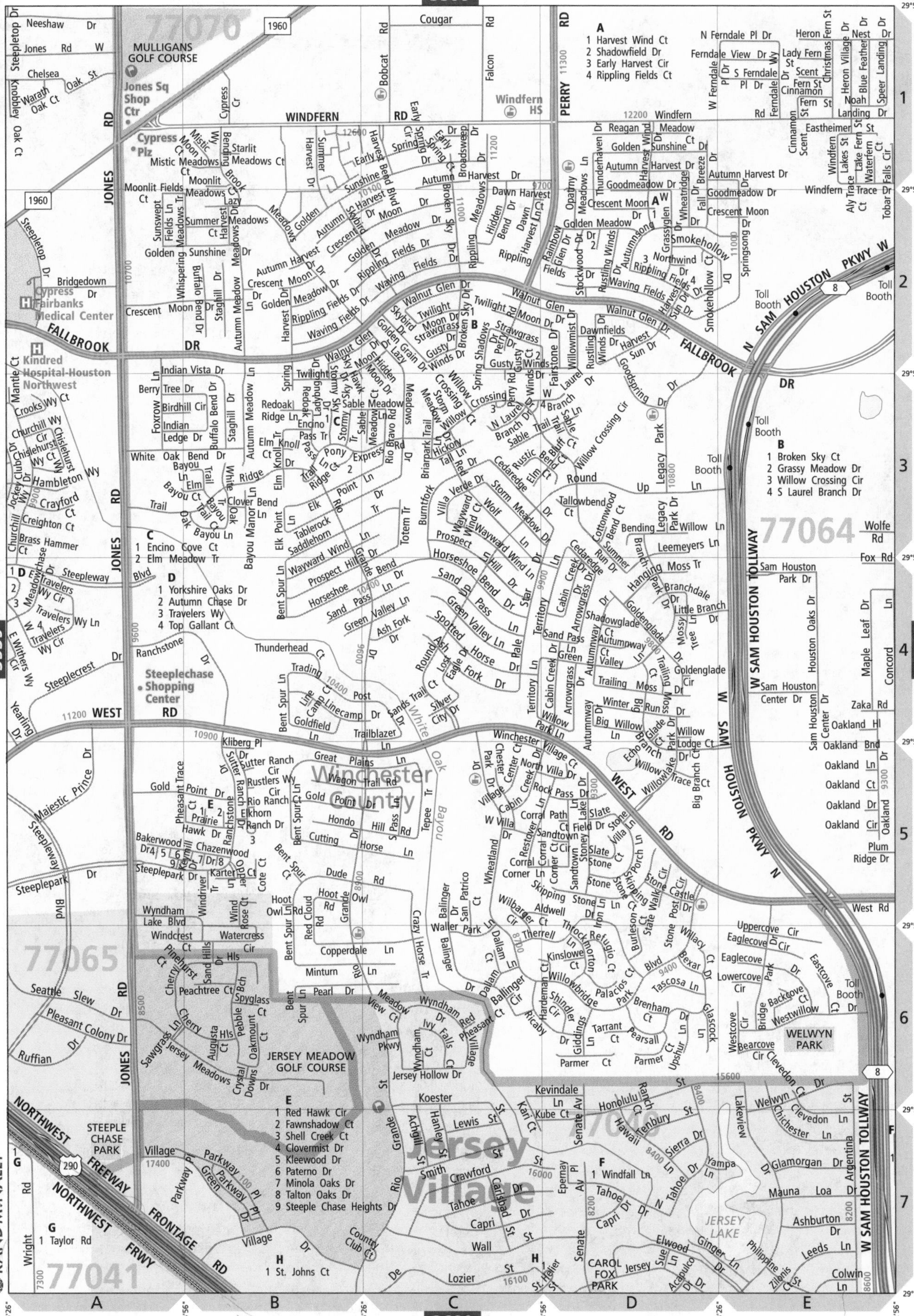
77070
MULLIGANS GOLF COURSE
Jones Sq Shop Ctr
Cypress Plz
WINDFERN RD
Windfern HS
PERRY RD
JONES RD
FALLBROOK DR
Cypress Fairbanks Medical Center
Kindred Hospital-Houston Northwest
N SAM HOUSTON PKWY W
Toll Booth
77064
W SAM HOUSTON TOLLWAY
WEST RD
Steeplechase Shopping Center
Winchester Country
77065
JERSEY MEADOW GOLF COURSE
WELWYN PARK
Jersey Village
JERSEY LAKE
CAROL FOX PARK
STEEPLE CHASE PARK
NORTHWEST FREEWAY
NORTHWEST FRWY FRONTAGE RD
77041
A
1 Harvest Wind Ct
2 Shadowfield Dr
3 Early Harvest Cir
4 Rippling Fields Ct
B
1 Broken Sky Ct
2 Grassy Meadow Dr
3 Willow Crossing Cir
4 S Laurel Branch Dr
C
1 Encino Cove Ct
2 Elm Meadow Tr
D
1 Yorkshire Oaks Dr
2 Autumn Chase Dr
3 Travelers Wy
4 Top Gallant Ct
E
1 Red Hawk Cir
2 Fawnshadow Ct
3 Shell Creek Ct
4 Clovermist Dr
5 Kleewood Dr
6 Paterno Dr
7 Minola Oaks Dr
8 Talton Oaks Dr
9 Steeple Chase Heights Dr
F
1 Windfall Ln
G
1 Taylor Rd
H
1 St. Johns Ct
A B C D E
1 2 3 4 5 6 7
29°56'17"
29°55'51"
29°55'25"
29°54'59"
29°54'33"
29°54'07"
29°53'40"
29°53'14"
95°35'26"
95°34'56"
95°34'26"
95°33'56"
95°33'26"
95°32'56"

SEE 3541 MAP

SEE 3680 MAP

1:24,000
1 in. = 2000 ft.
0 0.25 0.5
miles

SEE 3400 MAP

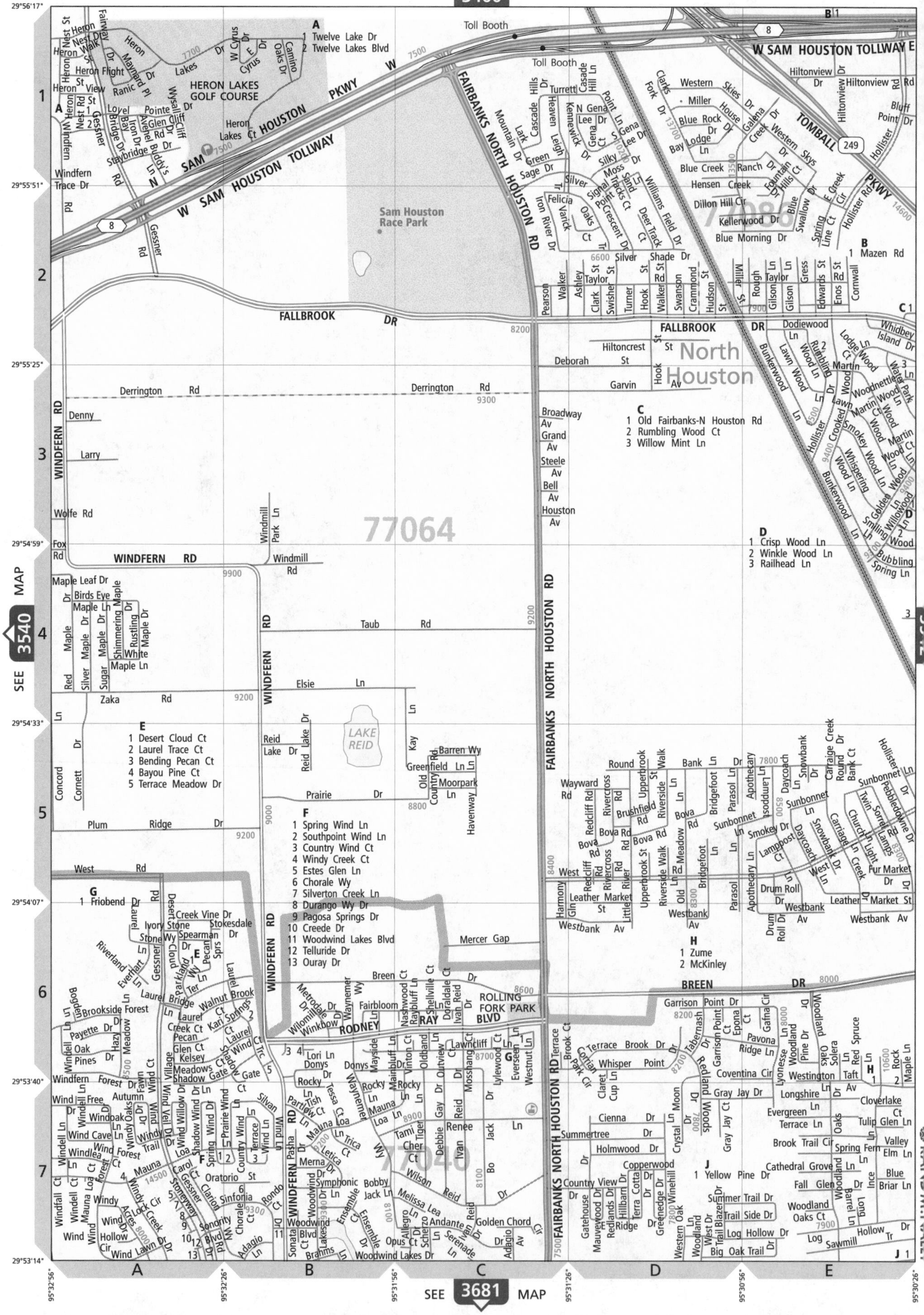
W SAM HOUSTON TOLLWAY
W SAM HOUSTON PKWY
HERON LAKES GOLF COURSE
Sam Houston Race Park
FAIRBANKS NORTH HOUSTON RD
TOMBALL PKWY
FALLBROOK DR
Derrington Rd
WINDFERN RD
Taub Rd
Elsie Ln
Zaka Rd
LAKE REID
Prairie Dr
Plum Ridge Dr
West Rd
BREEN DR
RODNEY RAY BLVD
ROLLING FORK PARK
North Houston
77064
77086
77040
Toll Booth
A
1 Twelve Lake Dr
2 Twelve Lakes Blvd
B
1 Mazen Rd
C
1 Old Fairbanks-N Houston Rd
2 Rumbling Wood Ct
3 Willow Mint Ln
D
1 Crisp Wood Ln
2 Winkle Wood Ln
3 Railhead Ln
E
1 Desert Cloud Ct
2 Laurel Trace Ct
3 Bending Pecan Ct
4 Bayou Pine Ct
5 Terrace Meadow Dr
F
1 Spring Wind Ln
2 Southpoint Wind Ln
3 Country Wind Ct
4 Windy Creek Ct
5 Estes Glen Ln
6 Chorale Wy
7 Silverton Creek Ln
8 Durango Wy Dr
9 Pagosa Springs Dr
10 Creede Dr
11 Woodwind Lakes Blvd
12 Telluride Dr
13 Ouray Dr
G
1 Friobend Dr
H
1 Zume
2 McKinley
J
1 Yellow Pine Dr

SEE 3540 MAP

SEE 3681 MAP

1:24,000
1 in. = 2000 ft.
0 0.25 0.5
miles

SEE 3401 MAP

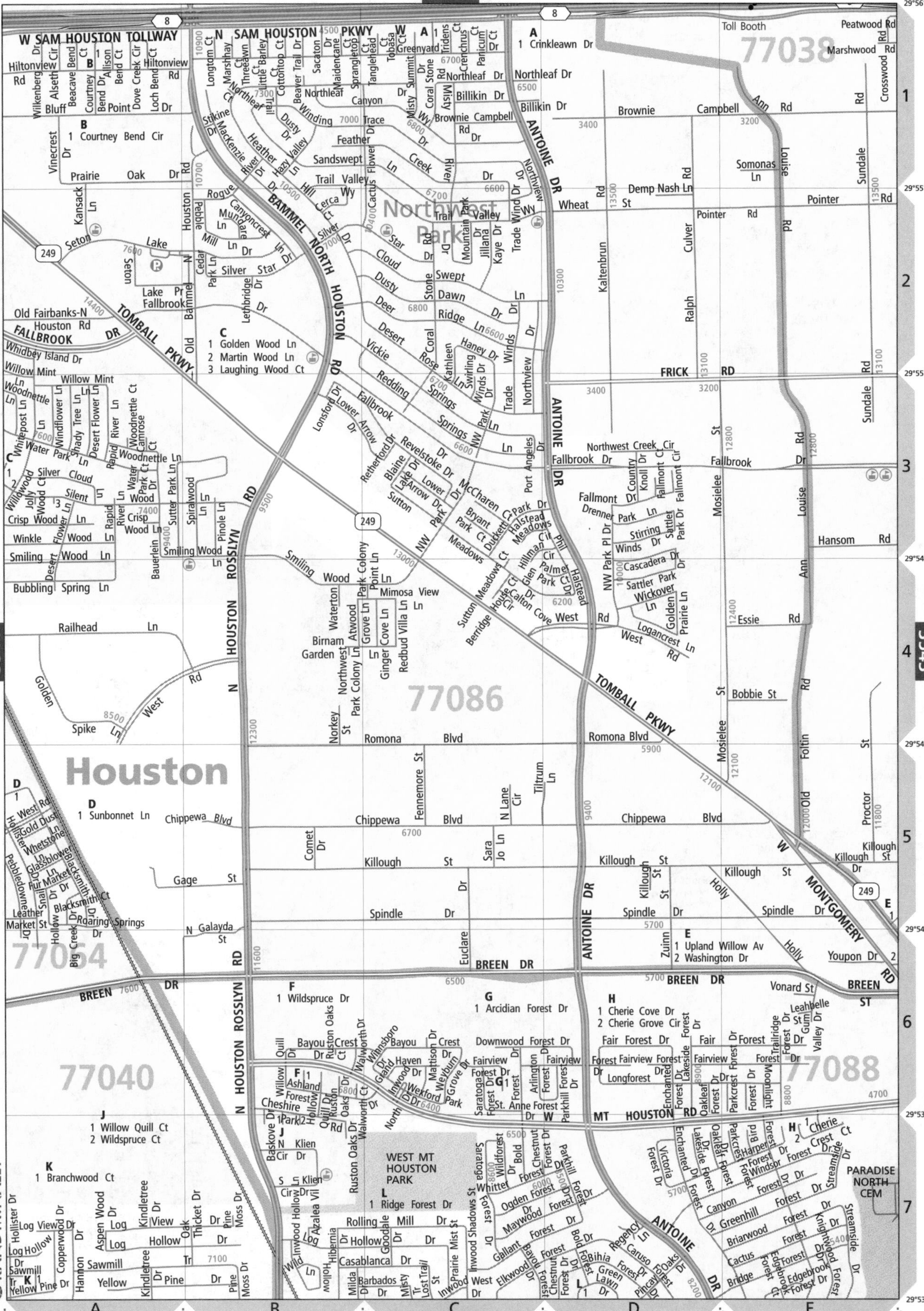
29°56'15"
29°55'49"
29°55'23"
29°54'57"
29°54'31"
29°54'05"
29°53'38"
29°53'12"
95°30'26"
95°29'56"
95°29'26"
95°28'56"
95°28'26"
95°27'56"
1
2
3
4
5
6
7
A
B
C
D
E
W SAM HOUSTON TOLLWAY
N SAM HOUSTON PKWY
8
Toll Booth
77038
Peatwood Rd
Marshwood Rd
Crosswood
Hiltonview Rd
Wilkenberg Dr
Alseth Cir
Beacave Bend Ct
Courtney Bend Dr
Allison Point Dr
Dove Creek Cir
Loch Bend Dr
Bluff
B
1 Courtney Bend Cir
Vinecrest Dr
Prairie Oak Dr
Kansack Ln
Longtom Ct
Marshhay
Threeawn Ct
Little Barley Ct
Cottontop Ct
Beaver Trail Dr
Sacaton Dr
Maidencane Ct
Sprangletop Ct
Tanglehead Ct
Tobasa Ct
Greenyard
Tridens Ct
Crenchrus Ct
Paricum Ct
A
1 Crinkleawn Dr
Northleaf Dr
Billikin Dr
Brownie Campbell Rd
Brownie
Campbell
Ann Rd
Northleaf
Canyon
Winding Trace
Feather Creek
Sandswept
Trail Valley Wy
Cactus Flower Dr
Misty Summit Dr
Coral Stone Rd
Stikine Dr
MacKenzie River Dr
Heather Hill
Hazy Valley Ln
Dusty Dr
Northwest Park
Trail Valley
Mountain Park Dr
Jillana Dr
Kaye Dr
Trade Wind Dr
Northview Dr
ANTOINE DR
Wheat St
Kaltenbrun
Demp Nash Ln
Culver Rd
Somonas Ln
Louise
Sundale
Pointer Rd
Pointer Rd
Rogue
Munguare Ln
Canyoncrest Ln
Mill Dr
BAMMEL NORTH HOUSTON RD
Silver Star Dr
Cerca Ct
Star Dr
Cloud
Swept
Dawn Dr
Dusty
Deer Ridge Ln
Desert
Vickie
Coral Rose
Kathleen Ln
Haney Dr
Swirling Winds Dr
Winds Dr
Redding Springs
Northview Dr
Trade
Ralph
FRICK RD
Seton
Lake
Seton
Houston
Pebble
Cedar Park Ln
Lethbridge Dr
Lake Pr
Fallbrook
Old Bammel
249
Old Fairbanks-N Houston Rd
FALLBROOK DR
TOMBALL PKWY
Whidbey Island Dr
Willow Mint Ln
Willow Mint
C
1 Golden Wood Ln
2 Martin Wood Ln
3 Laughing Wood Ct
Woodnettle Ln
Whitepost Ln
Windflower Ln
Shady Tree Ln
Desert Flower Ln
River Ln
Woodnettle Ct
Canrose Ct
Water Park Ln
Woodnettle Ln
Silver Cloud
Silent
Wildwood Dr
Jolly Wood Ct
Crisp Wood Ln
Winkle Wood Ln
Smiling Wood Ln
Desert Flower
Rapid River Ln
Water Park Ct
Crisp Wood Ln
Bauerlein
Sutter Park Ln
Spiralwood Ln
Pinole Ln
Smiling Wood
Bubbling Spring Ln
N HOUSTON ROSSLYN RD
Lonsford Dr
Lower Arrow Dr
Fallbrook
Retherford Dr
Revelstoke Dr
Blaine Lake Dr
Lower Arrow Dr
Sutton
McCharen Ct
Bryant Park Ct
Duckett Ct
NW Park Dr
Halstead Meadows Cir
Port Angeles Dr
Springs Ln
Park Ln
Northwest Creek Cir
Fallbrook Dr
Fallbrook Dr
Country Knoll Dr
Fallmont Ct
Fallmont Cir
Fallmont Dr
Drenner Park Ln
Stirring Winds Dr
Settler Park Dr
Mosielee St
Hansom Rd
Smiling Wood
Park Colony Dr
Point Ln
Mimosa View Ln
Meadows
Hillman Ct
Phil Halstead
Palmer Park Ct
Glen Park Ct
Calton Cove
West Rd
NW Park Pl Dr
Cascadera Dr
Sattler Park
Wickover Ln
Golden Prairie Ln
Logancrest Ln
West Rd
Essie Rd
Railhead Ln
Waterton
Birnam Garden
Atwood Grove Ln
Cove Ln
Redbud Villa Ln
Ginger Ln
Northwest Park Colony Ln
Sutton Meadows Ct
Berridge Cir
House Ct
Golden
West Rd
Spike Ln
Norkey St
77086
TOMBALL PKWY
Bobbie St
Romona Blvd
Romona Blvd
Houston
Fennemore St
Tiltrum Ln
Mosielee St
Foltin
Old Ann Rd
Proctor St
D
1 Sunbonnet Ln
Chippewa Blvd
Chippewa Blvd
N Lane Cir
Chippewa Blvd
West Rd
Hollister
Gold Dust Ln
Whetstone
Glassblower
Blacksmith Ln
Fur Market Dr
Pebbledowne Dr
Snail Hollow Dr
Blacksmith Ct
Roaring Springs
Leather Market St
Big Creek Dr
Gage St
Comet Dr
Killough St
Sara Jo Ln
Killough St
Killough St
Killough St
Killough Dr
Holly
W MONTGOMERY RD
249
Spindle Dr
Spindle Dr
Spindle Dr
Euclare Dr
N Galayda St
E
1 Upland Willow Av
2 Washington Dr
Zuinn Dr
Holly
Youpon Dr
77064
BREEN DR
BREEN DR
BREEN DR
BREEN ST
Vonard St
F
1 Wildspruce Dr
G
1 Arcidian Forest Dr
H
1 Cherie Cove Dr
2 Cherie Grove Cir
Leahbelle St
Gum Valley Dr
Trailridge Forest Dr
Quill Dr
Bayou Crest Dr
Ruston Oaks Ct
Walworth Dr
Wimbsboro
Bayou Crest
Mattison Dr
Grand Haven Dr
Inwood Dr
Wexford Park
Welburn
Grove Dr
Downwood Forest Dr
Fairview Forest Dr
Fairview
Fair Forest Dr
Fair Forest Dr
Fairview Forest
Longforest Dr
Lakeside Forest
Enchanted Forest Dr
77088
77040
Willow
Ashland Forest
Cheshire
Hollow
Ruston Oaks Dr
Walworth Ct
Saratoga Forest Dr
Arlington Forest Dr
Parkhill Forest Dr
St. Anne Forest Dr
Oakleaf Forest Dr
Parkcrest Forest Dr
Moonlight Forest
MT HOUSTON RD
J
1 Willow Quill Ct
2 Wildspruce Ct
Baskove Dr
N Klien Cir Dr
S Klien Cir Dr
Ruston Oaks Dr
WEST MT HOUSTON PARK
Wildforest Dr
Bold Forest Dr
Chestnut Forest Dr
Parkhill Forest Dr
Victoria Forest Dr
Enchanted Lakeside Forest
Oakleaf Forest Dr
Parkcrest Forest Dr
Bird Harper Forest
Windsor Forest Dr
Cherie Crest Ct
Streamside Dr
PARADISE NORTH CEM
K
1 Branchwood Ct
Hollister Dr
Log View Dr
Log Hollow Dr
Copperwood Dr
Aspen Wood Dr
Log View
Log Hollow
Kindletree Dr
Oak
Thicket Dr
Pine Dr
Moss Dr
Sawmill Dr
Yellow Pine Dr
Hannon Dr
Sawmill
Yellow Pine
Kindletree Dr
Pine Dr
Moss Dr
Azalea Vil
Inwood Hollow
Hibernia
Rolling Mill Dr
Goodale
Hollow Dr
Casablanca Dr
Barbados Dr
Milda Dr
Misty Tr
Lost Trail St
Prairie Mist St
Inwood West Dr
Inwood Shadows St
L
1 Ridge Forest Dr
Saratoga Forest
Whitter Forest
Ogden Forest Dr
Maywood Forest Dr
Gallant Forest
Elkwood Forest
Bayou Forest
Chestnut Forest
Bold Forest
Bihia Forest Dr
Green Lawn Dr
Regency Ln
Caruso Forest
Pincay Oaks Dr
ANTOINE DR
Canyon Forest Dr
Greenhill Forest Dr
Briarwood Forest Dr
Cactus Forest Dr
Bridge Forest Dr
Edgebrook Forest Ct
Knightwood Forest Dr
Streamside Dr
Edgebrook Forest Dr

SEE 3543 MAP

SEE 3682 MAP

1:24,000
1 in. = 2000 ft.
0 0.25 0.5
miles

SEE 3402 MAP

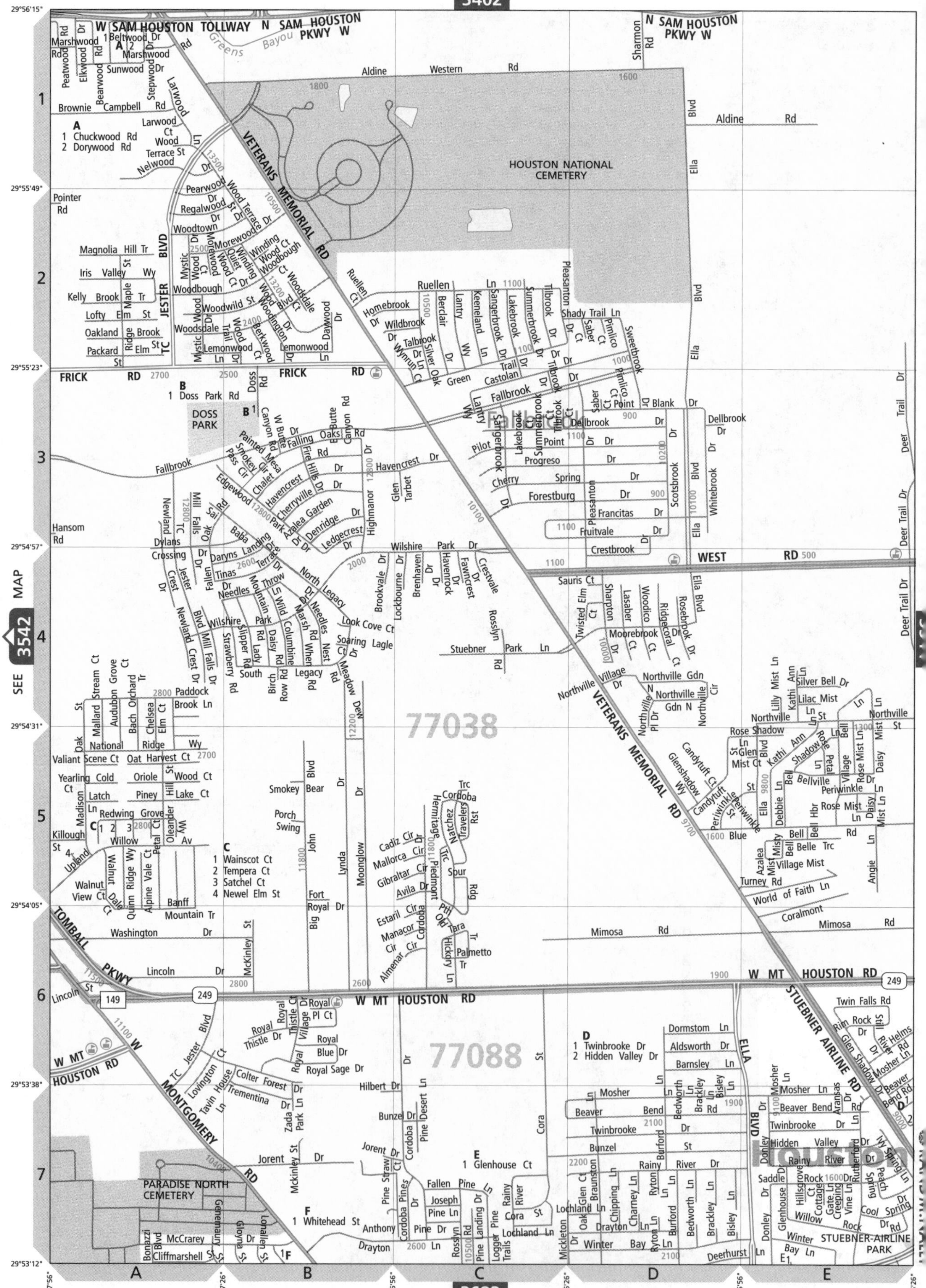
W SAM HOUSTON TOLLWAY N SAM HOUSTON PKWY W
N SAM HOUSTON PKWY W
Greens Bayou
HOUSTON NATIONAL CEMETERY
VETERANS MEMORIAL RD
Aldine Western Rd
Aldine Rd
Ella Blvd
TC JESTER BLVD
FRICK RD
DOSS PARK
Fallbrook
WEST RD
77038
77088
W MT HOUSTON RD
TOMBALL PKWY
MONTGOMERY RD
W MT HOUSTON RD
STUEBNER AIRLINE RD
PARADISE NORTH CEMETERY
STUEBNER-AIRLINE PARK
Houston
Mimosa Rd
Washington Dr
Lincoln Dr
249
149
1 2 3 4 5 6 7
A B C D E

SEE 3542 MAP

SEE 3683 MAP

1:24,000
1 in. = 2000 ft.
0 0.25 0.5
miles

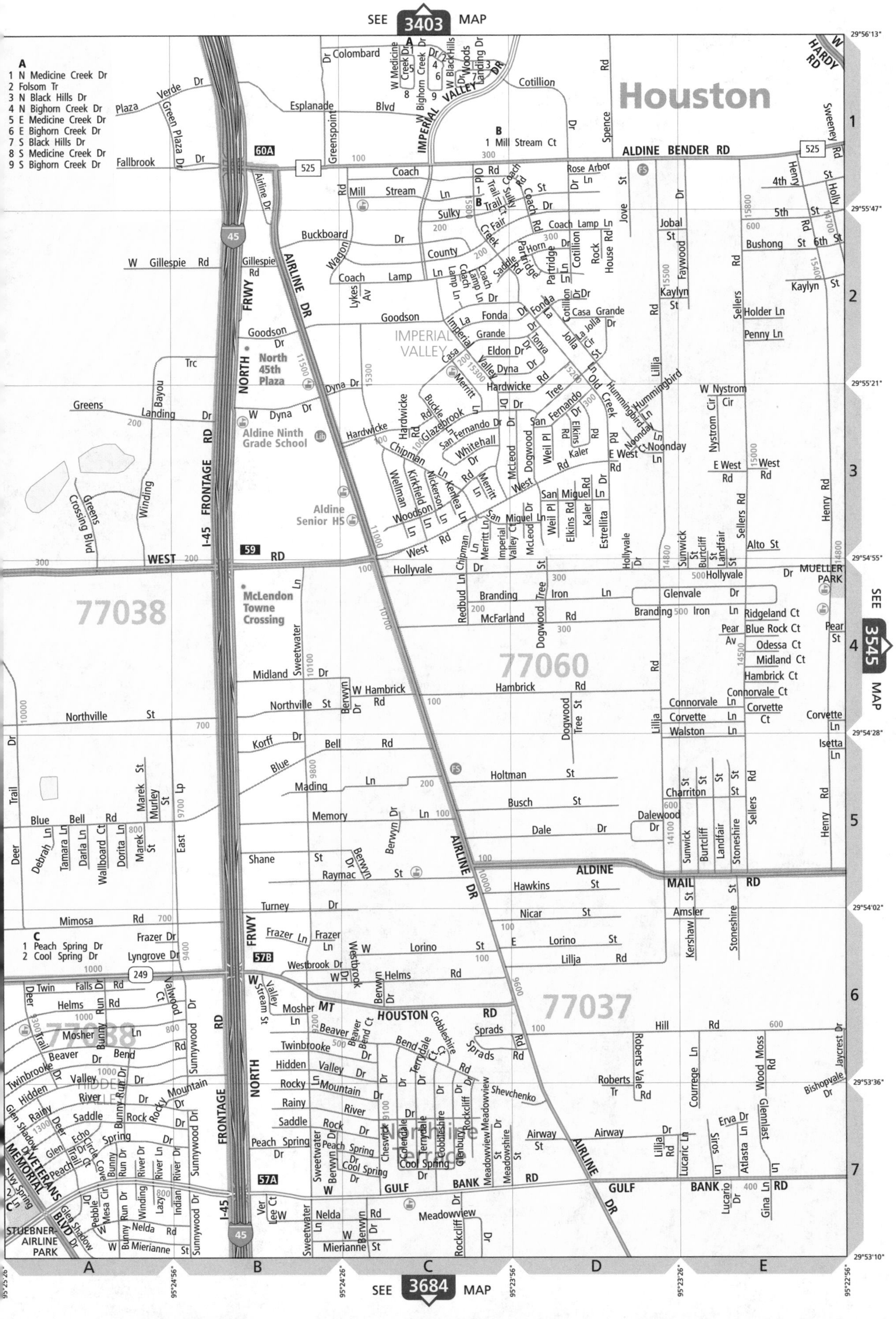
SEE 3403 MAP
SEE 3545 MAP
SEE 3684 MAP
Houston
A
1 N Medicine Creek Dr
2 Folsom Tr
3 N Black Hills Dr
4 N Bighorn Creek Dr
5 E Medicine Creek Dr
6 E Bighorn Creek Dr
7 S Black Hills Dr
8 S Medicine Creek Dr
9 S Bighorn Creek Dr
B
1 Mill Stream Ct
C
1 Peach Spring Dr
2 Cool Spring Dr
ALDINE BENDER RD
525
60A
IMPERIAL VALLEY DR
Esplanade Blvd
Colombard Dr
Cotillion
Plaza Verde Dr
Green Plaza Dr
Fallbrook Dr
W Gillespie Rd
Gillespie Rd
Airline Dr
AIRLINE DR
NORTH FRWY
I-45 FRONTAGE RD
45
Greenspoint
Coach Rd
Mill Stream Ln
Buckboard Dr
Wagon
Coach Lamp Ln
County
Goodson Dr
IMPERIAL VALLEY
North 45th Plaza
Aldine Ninth Grade School
Aldine Senior HS
McLendon Towne Crossing
Dyna Dr
W Dyna Dr
Hardwicke Rd
Greens Landing Dr
Bayou Trc
Winding
Greens Crossing Blvd
WEST RD
59
Hollyvale Dr
Branding Iron Ln
McFarland Rd
Glenvale Dr
Ridgeland Ct
Blue Rock Ct
Odessa Ct
Midland Ct
Hambrick Ct
Connorvale Ct
Corvette Ct
Connorvale Ln
Corvette Ln
Walston Ln
Isetta Ln
MUELLER PARK
77038
77060
77037
Midland Dr
W Hambrick Rd
Hambrick Rd
Northville St
Korff Dr
Bell Rd
Blue Bell Rd
Mading Ln
Memory Ln
Holtman St
Busch St
Dale Dr
Dalewood Dr
Charriton St
Shane St
Raymac St
Turney Dr
Mimosa Rd
Frazer Dr
Lyngrove Dr
ALDINE MAIL RD
Hawkins St
Nicar St
Amsler
Lorino St
Lillja Rd
Westbrook Dr
Helms Rd
249
57B
57A
MT HOUSTON RD
Sprads Rd
Hill Rd
Roberts Vale Rd
Courrege Ln
Wood Moss Rd
Bishopvale Dr
Jaycrest Dr
Airway Dr
Erva Dr
Glenmist
GULF BANK RD
AIRLINE DR
Meadowview
Northline Terrace
Twinbrooke Dr
Hidden Valley Dr
Rocky Mountain Dr
Rainy River Dr
Saddle Rock Dr
Peach Spring Dr
Cool Spring
Nelda Rd
Mierianne St
MEMORIAL
VETERANS BLVD
STUEBNER-AIRLINE PARK
Sellers Rd
Henry Rd
Sweeney Rd
W HARDY RD
Bushong St
Kaylyn St
Holder Ln
Penny Ln
W Nystrom Cir
E West Rd
West Rd
Alto St
Lillja Rd
Spence Rd
Jove St
Rose Arbor Ln
Jobal St
Faywood
Hummingbird Ln
Noonday Ln
Casa Grande Dr
Fonda Dr
Eldon Dr
Whitehall Dr
Glazebrook
San Fernando Dr
San Miguel Ln
Chipman
Woodson
Dogwood Tree St
Redbud Ln
Sweetwater
Berwyn Dr
A B C D E
1 2 3 4 5 6 7
29°56'13"
29°55'47"
29°55'21"
29°54'55"
29°54'28"
29°54'02"
29°53'36"
29°53'10"
95°24'56"
95°24'26"
95°23'56"
95°23'26"
95°22'56"

1:24,000
1 in. = 2000 ft.
0 0.25 0.5
miles

SEE 3404 MAP

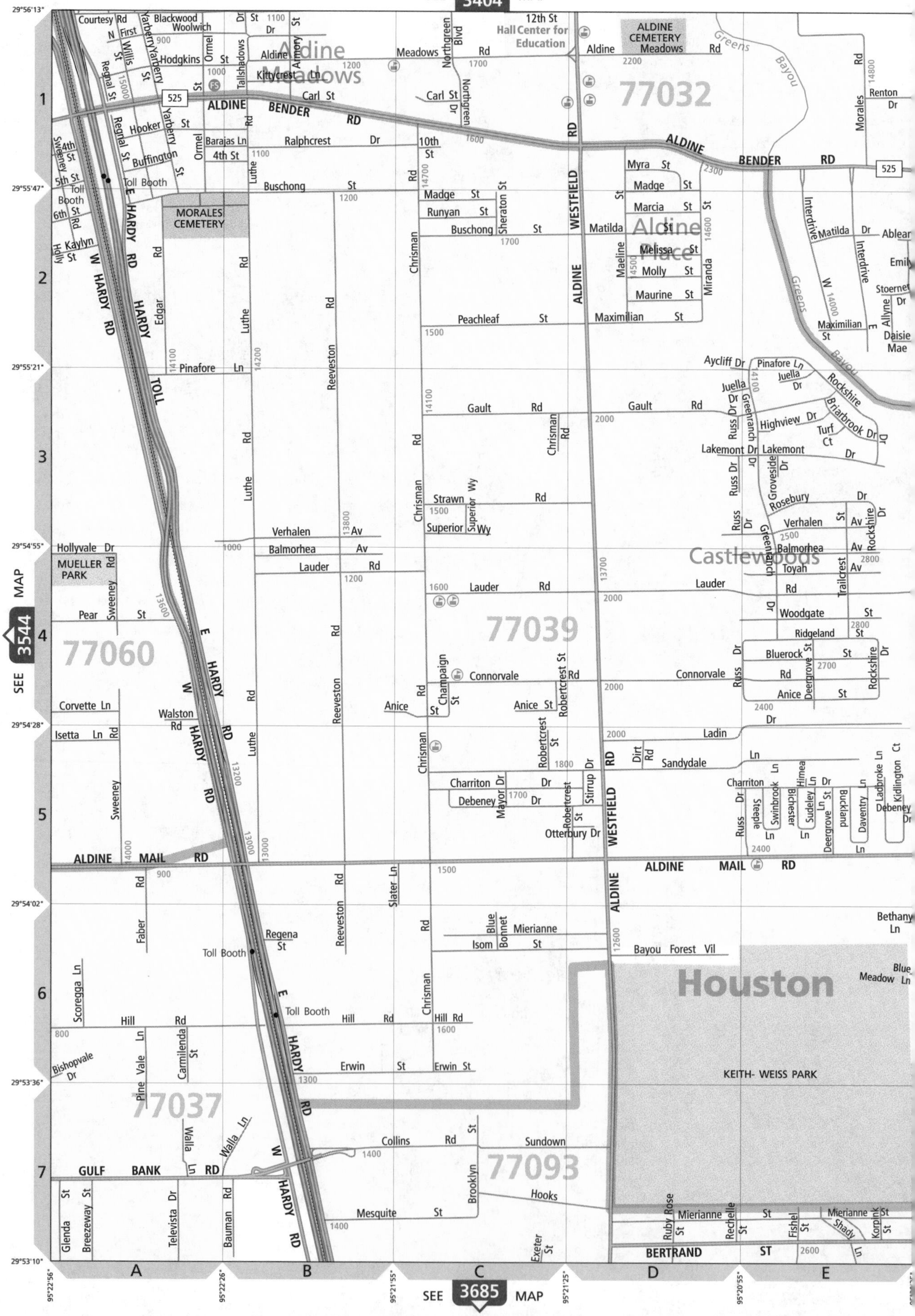
29°56'13"
Courtesy Rd
Blackwood
Woolwich
N First St
Willis St
Yarberry
Hodgkins St
Ormel
Tallshadows
Aldine Meadows
Aldine Dr
Armory
Kittycrest Ln
Carl St
Meadows
Northgreen Blvd
Hall Center for Education
12th St
ALDINE CEMETERY
Aldine
Meadows Rd
Greens Bayou
77032
Renton Dr
Morales Rd
525
ALDINE BENDER RD
Regnal St
Hooker St
Buffington
Barajas Ln
4th St
Ralphcrest Dr
10th St
Sweeney
5th St
Toll Booth
6th St
Buschong St
Myra St
Madge St
Marcia St
Matilda St
Aldine Place
Melissa St
Molly St
Maurine St
Maximilian St
Maeline St
Miranda St
Interdrive
Matilda Dr
Ablear
Emily
Stoerner
Allyne Dr
Daisie Mae
29°55'47"
MORALES CEMETERY
Runyan St
Sheraton St
Kaylyn St
Holly St
W HARDY RD
HARDY RD
HARDY TOLL
Edgar Rd
Luthe Rd
Reeveston Rd
Chrisman Rd
ALDINE WESTFIELD RD
Peachleaf St
29°55'21"
Pinafore Ln
Aycliff Dr
Pinafore Ln
Juella Dr
Rockshire
Briarbrook Dr
Gault Rd
Greenranch
Highview Dr
Turf Ct
Lakemont Dr
Russ Dr
Groveside Dr
Rosebury Dr
Strawn Rd
Superior Wy
Verhalen Av
Balmorhea Av
Lauder Rd
Castlewoods
Toyah Av
Trailcrest
29°54'55"
Hollyvale Dr
MUELLER PARK
Pear St
Woodgate St
Ridgeland St
77039
77060
Bluerock St
Deergrove St
Champaign St
Connorvale Rd
Robertcrest St
Anice St
Corvette Ln
Walston Rd
29°54'28"
Isetta Ln
Ladin Dr
Sandydale Ln
Dirt Rd
Charriton Dr
Debeney Dr
Mayor Dr
Stirrup Dr
Otterbury Dr
Steeple
Swinbrook Ln
Bichester
Himea
Sudeley Ln
Buckland
Daventry Ln
Ladbroke Ln
Kidlington Ct
ALDINE MAIL RD
Slater Ln
Faber Rd
29°54'02"
Bethany Ln
Blue Bonnet
Mierianne St
Isom St
Bayou Forest Vil
Regena St
Toll Booth
Houston
Blue Meadow Ln
Scoregga Ln
Hill Rd
Pine Vale Ln
Carmilenda St
Bishopvale Dr
Erwin St
KEITH- WEISS PARK
29°53'36"
77037
Walla Ln
Collins Rd
Sundown
GULF BANK RD
77093
Brooklyn St
Hooks
Glenda St
Breezeway St
Televista Dr
Bauman Rd
Mesquite St
Ruby Rose St
Mierianne St
Rechelle St
Fishel St
Shady Ln
Korpink St
Exeter St
BERTRAND ST
29°53'10"
A B C D E
1 2 3 4 5 6 7
95°22'56" 95°22'26" 95°21'55" 95°21'25" 95°20'55"

SEE 3544 MAP

SEE 3685 MAP

1:24,000
1 in. = 2000 ft.
0 0.25 0.5
miles

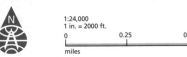

SEE 3405 MAP

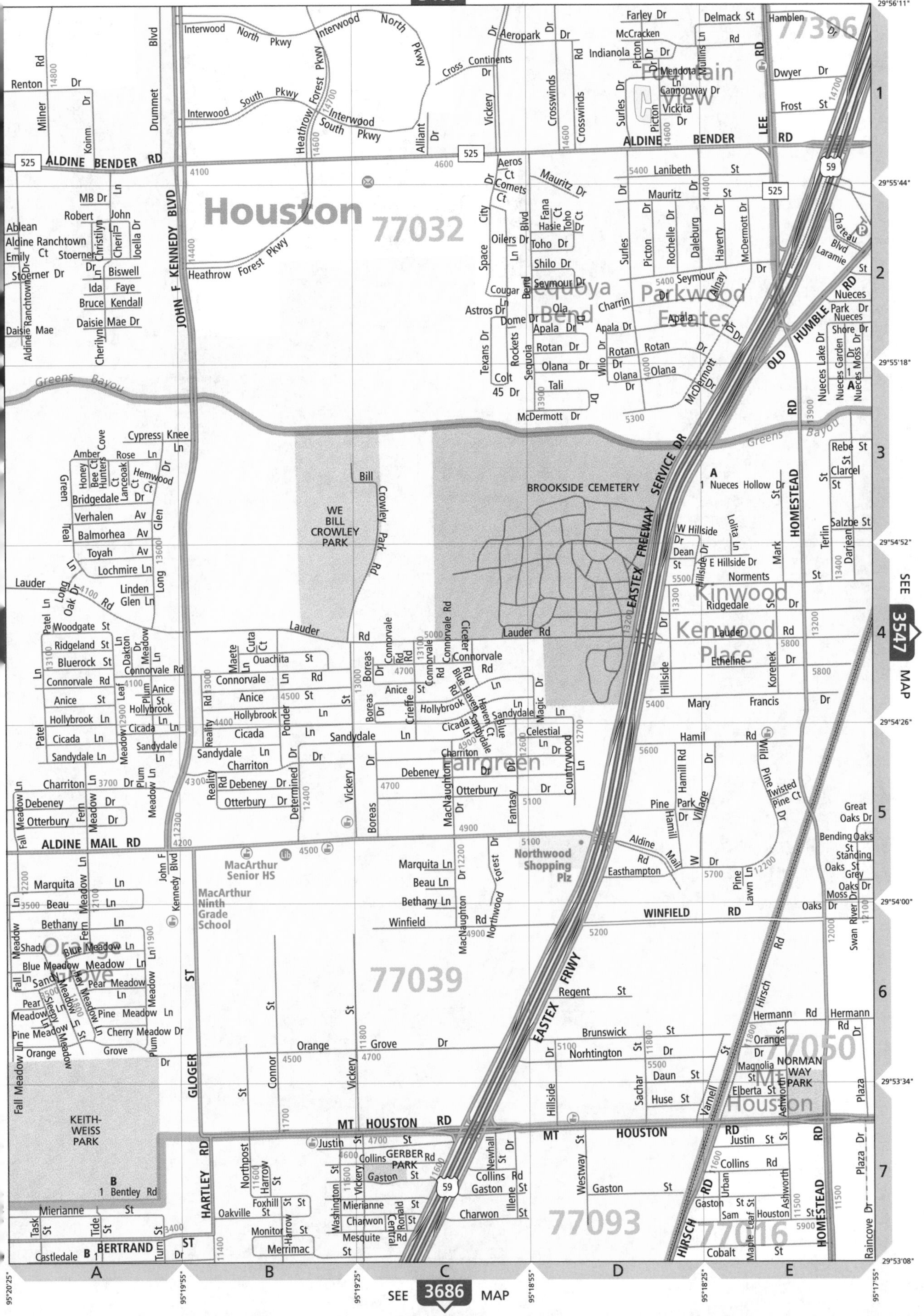
Houston
77032
77039
77093
77050
77016
77396
525
59
Fountain View
Sequoya Bend
Parkwood Estates
Kinwood
Kenwood Place
Fairgreen
Orange Grove
Mt Houston
ALDINE BENDER RD
JOHN F KENNEDY BLVD
EASTEX FREEWAY SERVICE DR
EASTEX FRWY
OLD HUMBLE RD
HOMESTEAD RD
LEE RD
ALDINE MAIL RD
WINFIELD RD
MT HOUSTON RD
HARTLEY RD
GLOGER ST
HIRSCH RD
BERTRAND ST
Greens Bayou
BROOKSIDE CEMETERY
WE BILL CROWLEY PARK
MacArthur Senior HS
MacArthur Ninth Grade School
Northwood Shopping Plz
KEITH-WEISS PARK
GERBER PARK
NORMAN WAY PARK
Interwood North Pkwy
Interwood South Pkwy
Heathrow Forest Pkwy
Cross Continents Dr
Aeropark Dr
Indianola
Mauritz Dr
Lanibeth St
Seymour Dr
Lauder Rd
Connorvale Rd
Sandydale Ln
Orange Grove Dr
Brunswick St
Regent St
Gaston St
Collins Rd
Justin St
Hermann Rd
Nueces Park Dr
Renton Dr
Milner Rd
Drummet Blvd
Vickery Dr
Crosswinds Rd
Alliant Dr
Surles Dr
Picton Dr
Space City Dr
McDermott Dr
Boreas Dr
Greens Teal
Long Oak Dr
Pine Park Dr
Great Oaks Dr
Swan River Dr
Plaza Dr
Raincove Dr
A
B
C
D
E
1
2
3
4
5
6
7
29°56'11"
29°55'44"
29°55'18"
29°54'52"
29°54'26"
29°54'00"
29°53'34"
29°53'08"
95°20'25"
95°19'55"
95°19'25"
95°18'55"
95°18'25"
95°17'55"

SEE 3547 MAP

SEE 3686 MAP

1:24,000
1 in. = 2000 ft.
0 0.25 0.5
miles

SEE 3406 MAP

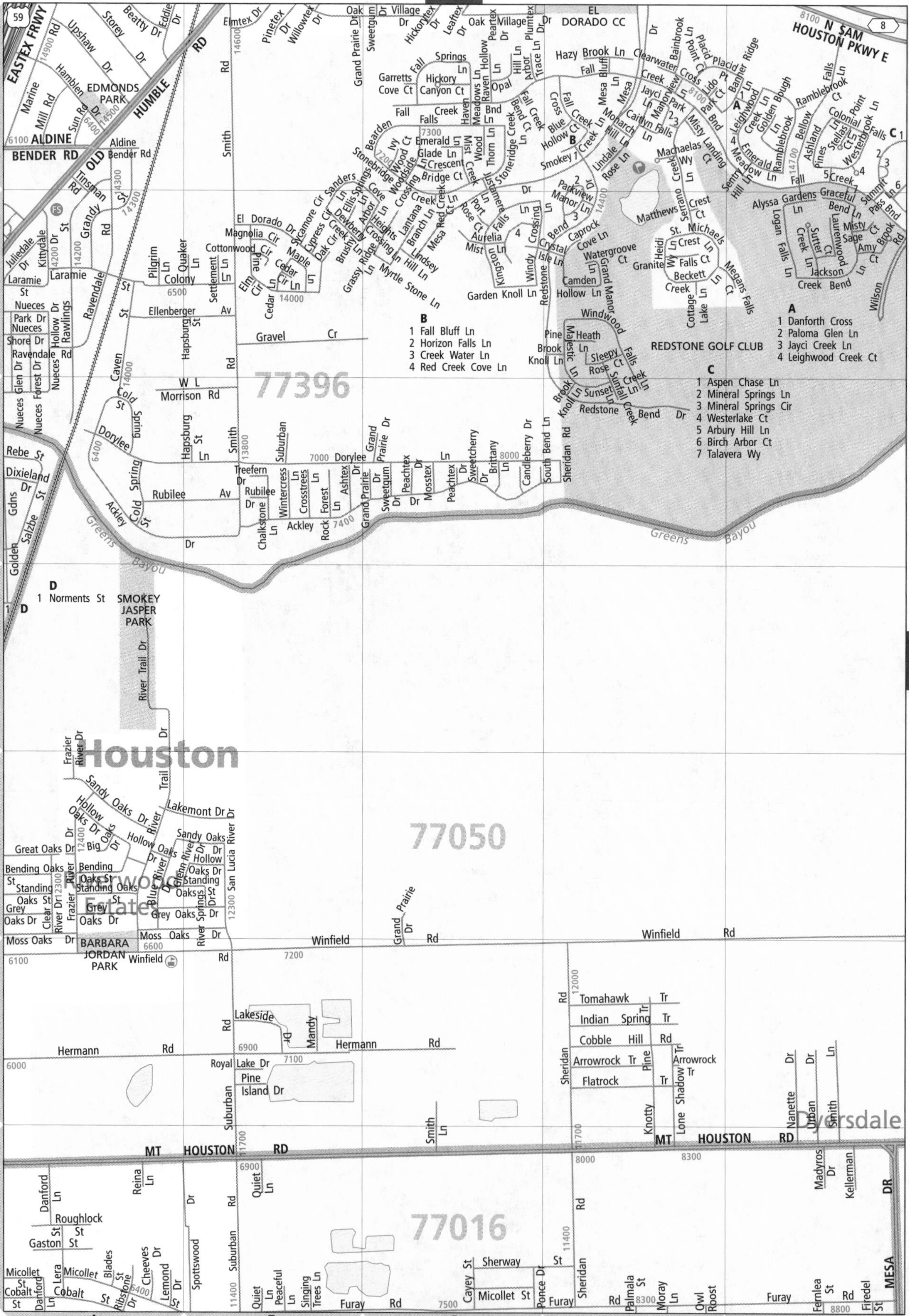
EASTEX FRWY
59
ALDINE
BENDER RD
Aldine Bender Rd
OLD HUMBLE RD
EDMONDS PARK
Upshaw Dr
Hamblen Dr
Storey Dr
Beatty Dr
Marine
Mill Rd
Sun Rd
Tinsman St
Grandy Rd
Kittydale Dr
Juliedale Dr
Laramie St
Nueces
Park Dr
Shore Dr
Ravendale Rd
Nueces Glen Dr
Nueces Forest Dr
Hollow Dr
Rawlings
Ravendale
Caven St
Cold Spring St
Dorylee
Rebe St
Dixieland Dr
Gdns
Salzbe St
Golden
Ackley Dr
Pilgrim Ln
Quaker Ln
Colony
Ellenberger Av
Hapsburg St
Settlement Ln
Smith Rd
W L Morrison Rd
Gravel Cr
El Dorado Dr
Magnolia Cir
Cottonwood Cir
Elm Cir
Cedar Dr
Sycamore Cir
Cypress Cir
Pine Cir
Maple
Oak Cir
Dewberry
Brushy Creek
Grassy Ridge
Ellis Springs
Sanders
Stonebridge Cove
Woodside Crossing
Myrtle Stone Ln
Lindsey
Lantana
Arbor
Heights
Crossing Ln
Hill Ln
Branch Ln
Mesa Red Creek Ct
Bearden
Ivy Wood Ct
Emerald Glade Ln
Crescent Bridge Ct
Mist Creek
Thorn Ln
Port Rose Ct
Aurelia Mist
Kingston
Falls
Garden Knoll Ln
Windy Crossing
Redstone
Crystal Isle Ln
Bend
Caprock Cove Ln
Camden Hollow Ln
Grand Manor Ct
Watergroove Ct
Windwood
Pine Brook Knoll Ln
Heath
Majestic Ln
Sleepy Rose Ct
Sunset
Sunfall Creek
Redstone Creek Bend Dr
Brook Knoll Ln
REDSTONE GOLF CLUB
Matthews Crest Ct
St. Michaels
Heidi Wy
Granite Falls Ct
Beckett Creek
Cottage Lake Ln
Megans Falls
Serrano Creek
Machaelas Wy
Alyssa Gardens Ln
Logan Falls Ln
Graceful Bend Ln
Sutter Creek Ln
Laurenwood Ln
Misty Sage Ct
Jackson Creek Bend
Amy Ct
Wilson
Elmtex Dr
Pinetex Dr
Willowtex Dr
Oak Village Dr
Sweetgum Dr
Grand Prairie Dr
Hickorytex Dr
Leaftex Dr
Oak Village Dr
Peartex Dr
Plumtex Dr
EL DORADO CC
Hazy Brook Ln
Fall Springs Ln
Hickory Canyon Ct
Garretts Cove Ct
Fall Falls Creek
Haven Meadows Ln
Hollow Raven Ln
Opal Bnd
Arbor Hill Ln
Trace Ln
Stoneridge Creek Ln
Fall Creek
Blue Cross
Hollow Ct
Smokey Creek
Parkview Manor Ln
Fall Creek Mesa Bluff Ln
Monarch Hill Ln
Lindale Rose Ln
Clearwater Creek
Bainbrook Ln
Jayci Ln
Manorview Park
Caitlyn Falls Ln
Misty Landing Ct
Placid Point Ct
Lido Pt
Park Ct
Bnd
Banner Ridge
Leighwood Creek Ln
Golden Bough Ln
Ramblebrook Ln
Emerald Meadow Ln
Sentry Hill Ln
Bellow Ln
Ashland Pines
Colonial Point Ln
Stellas Falls
Westerbrook Ln
Summit Pass
Birch Bnd
N SAM HOUSTON PKWY E
8
8100
B
1 Fall Bluff Ln
2 Horizon Falls Ln
3 Creek Water Ln
4 Red Creek Cove Ln
A
1 Danforth Cross
2 Paloma Glen Ln
3 Jayci Creek Ln
4 Leighwood Creek Ct
C
1 Aspen Chase Ln
2 Mineral Springs Ln
3 Mineral Springs Cir
4 Westerlake Ct
5 Arbury Hill Ln
6 Birch Arbor Ct
7 Talavera Wy
77396
Dorylee Dr
Grand Prairie Dr
Suburban
Treefern Dr
Rubilee Av
Rubilee Dr
Chalkstone Ln
Wintercress Ln
Crosstrees Ln
Forest Ln
Rock Forest Ln
Ashtex Dr
Grand Prairie Dr
Sweetgum Dr
Peachtex Dr
Mosstex Dr
Peachtex Dr
Sweetcherry Dr
Brittany Ln
Candleberry Dr
South Bend Ln
Sheridan Rd
Ackley
Greens Bayou
D
1 Norments St
SMOKEY JASPER PARK
River Trail Dr
Houston
Frazier River Dr
Sandy Oaks Dr
Hollow Oaks Dr
Trail Dr
Lakemont Dr
San Lucia River Dr
Great Oaks Dr
Big Oaks
Hollow Oaks Dr
Sandy Oaks Dr
Glenn River Dr
Hollow Oaks Dr
Standing Oaks St
Bending Oaks St
Bending Oaks St
Standing Oaks
Blue River Dr
Riverwood Estates
Grey Oaks Dr
Clear River Dr
Frazier River
Grey Oaks Dr
River Springs Dr
Moss Oaks Dr
77050
Winfield Rd
BARBARA JORDAN PARK
Winfield Rd
Grand Prairie Dr
Lakeside Dr
Mandy
Hermann Rd
Royal Lake Dr
Pine Island Dr
Suburban Rd
Smith Ln
Tomahawk Tr
Indian Spring Tr
Cobble Hill Rd
Arrowrock Tr
Flatrock Tr
Pine
Lone Shadow Tr
Knotty
Sheridan Rd
Nanette Dr
Urban Dr
Smith Ln
Dyersdale
MT HOUSTON RD
Danforth Ln
Reina Ln
Roughlock St
Gaston St
Micollet St
Cobalt St
Lera Ln
Blades St
Ribstone
Cheeves Dr
Lemond Dr
Spottswood Dr
Suburban Rd
Quiet Ln
Peaceful Ln
Singing Trees Ln
Furay Rd
77016
Cayey St
Sherway St
Micollet St
Ponce Dr
Furay
Sheridan Rd
Palmala St
Moray Ln
Owl Roost
Madyros Dr
Kellerman
Fernlea St
Firedel St
Furay Rd
MESA DR
29°56'11"
29°55'44"
29°55'18"
29°54'52"
29°54'26"
29°54'00"
29°53'34"
29°53'08"
95°17'55"
95°17'25"
95°16'55"
95°16'25"
95°15'55"
95°15'25"
A B C D E
1 2 3 4 5 6 7

SEE 3546 MAP

SEE 3687 MAP

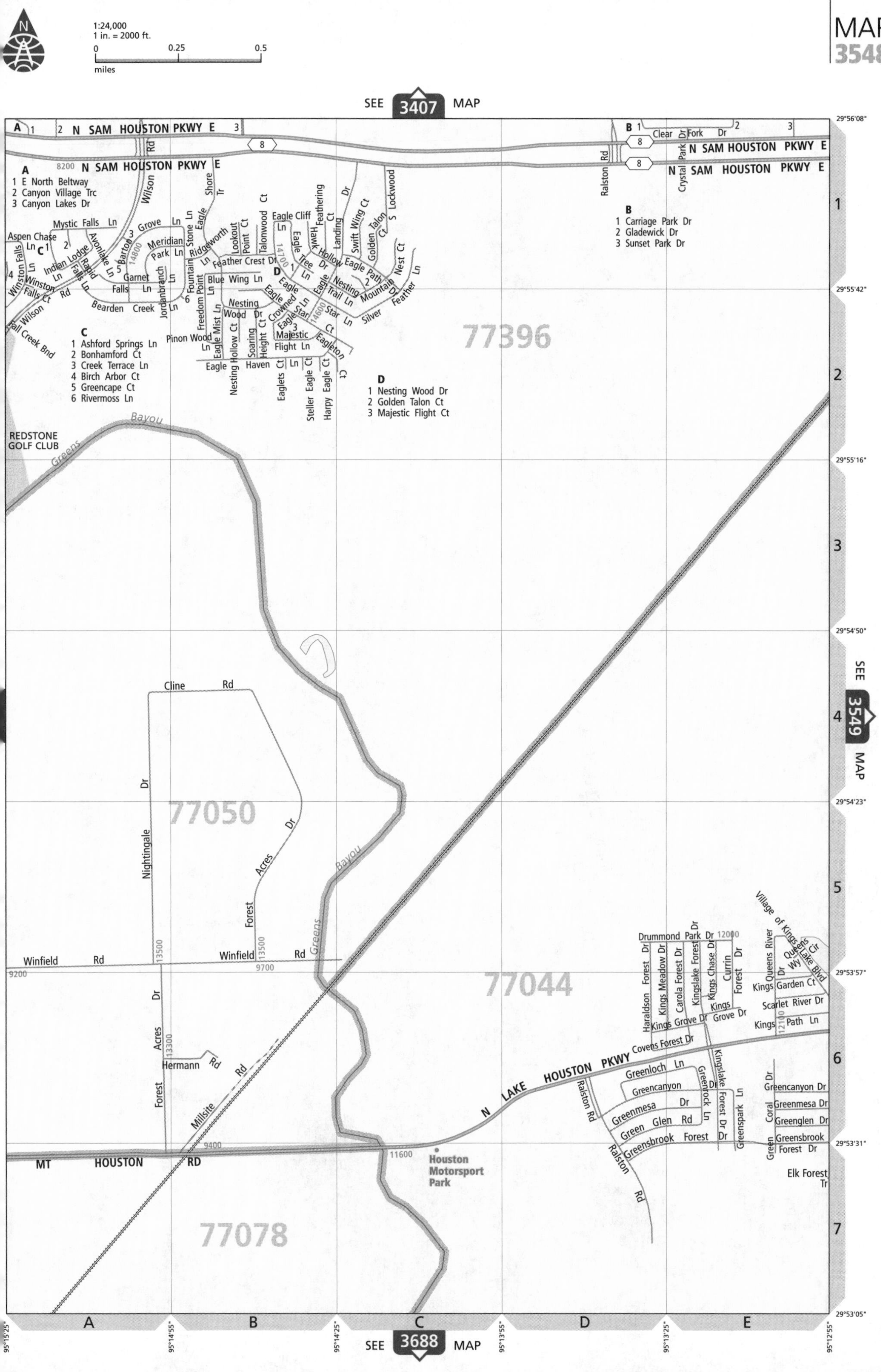

N
1:24,000
1 in. = 2000 ft.
0
0.25
0.5
miles
SEE 3407 MAP
SEE 3549 MAP
SEE 3688 MAP
N SAM HOUSTON PKWY E
8
8200
Wilson Rd
Ralston Rd
Crystal Park Dr
Clear Fork Dr
A
1 E North Beltway
2 Canyon Village Trc
3 Canyon Lakes Dr
B
1 Carriage Park Dr
2 Gladewick Dr
3 Sunset Park Dr
C
1 Ashford Springs Ln
2 Bonhamford Ct
3 Creek Terrace Ln
4 Birch Arbor Ct
5 Greencape Ct
6 Rivermoss Ln
D
1 Nesting Wood Dr
2 Golden Talon Ct
3 Majestic Flight Ct
Aspen Chase Ln
Mystic Falls Ln
Winston Falls Ln
Winston Falls Ct
Indian Lodge Ln
Rapid Falls Ln
Avonlake Ln
Barton Grove Ln
Meridian Park Ln
Garnet Falls Ln
Jordanbranch Ln
Bearden Creek
Fall Creek Bnd
Eagle Shore Tr
Stone Fountain
Ridgeworth
Lookout Point Ct
Talonwood Ct
Eagle Cliff Ln
Feathering Ct
Hawk Hollow Dr
Landing
Swift Wing Ct
Golden Talon Ct
S Lockwood Dr
Feather Crest Dr
Blue Wing Ln
Freedom Point
Eagle Mist Ln
Nesting Wood Dr
Nesting Hollow Ct
Soaring Height Ct
Pinon Wood
Eagle Haven
Majestic Flight Ln
Eaglets Ct
Steller Eagle Ct
Harpy Eagle Ct
Eagle Tree Ln
Eagle Path
Eagle Trail Ln
Nesting Mountain Dr
Nest Ct
Feather Ln
Silver Star Ln
Crowned Eagle
Eagle Star Ln
Eagleton Ct
14800
14700
14600
77396
REDSTONE GOLF CLUB
Greens Bayou
Cline Rd
Nightingale Dr
Forest Acres Dr
77050
Winfield Rd
9200
9700
13500
13300
Hermann Rd
Millsite Rd
MT HOUSTON RD
9400
11600
Houston Motorsport Park
77078
77044
N LAKE HOUSTON PKWY
Drummond Park Dr
12000
Haraldson Forest Dr
Kings Meadow Dr
Carola Forest Dr
Kingslake Forest Dr
Kings Chase Dr
Currin Forest Dr
Kings Grove Dr
Covens Forest Dr
Village of Kings Lake Blvd
Queens River Dr
Queens Wy
Lake Cir
Kings Garden Ct
Scarlet River Dr
Kings Path Ln
12100
Greenloch Ln
Greencanyon Dr
Greenmesa Dr
Green Glen Rd
Greensbrook Forest Dr
Greenlock Ln
Kingslake Forest Dr
Greenspark Ln
Ralston Rd
Coral Green Dr
Greencanyon Dr
Greenmesa Dr
Greenglen Dr
Greensbrook Forest Dr
Elk Forest Tr
A
B
C
D
E
1
2
3
4
5
6
7
29°56'08"
29°55'42"
29°55'16"
29°54'50"
29°54'23"
29°53'57"
29°53'31"
29°53'05"
95°15'25"
95°14'55"
95°14'25"
95°13'55"
95°13'25"
95°12'55"

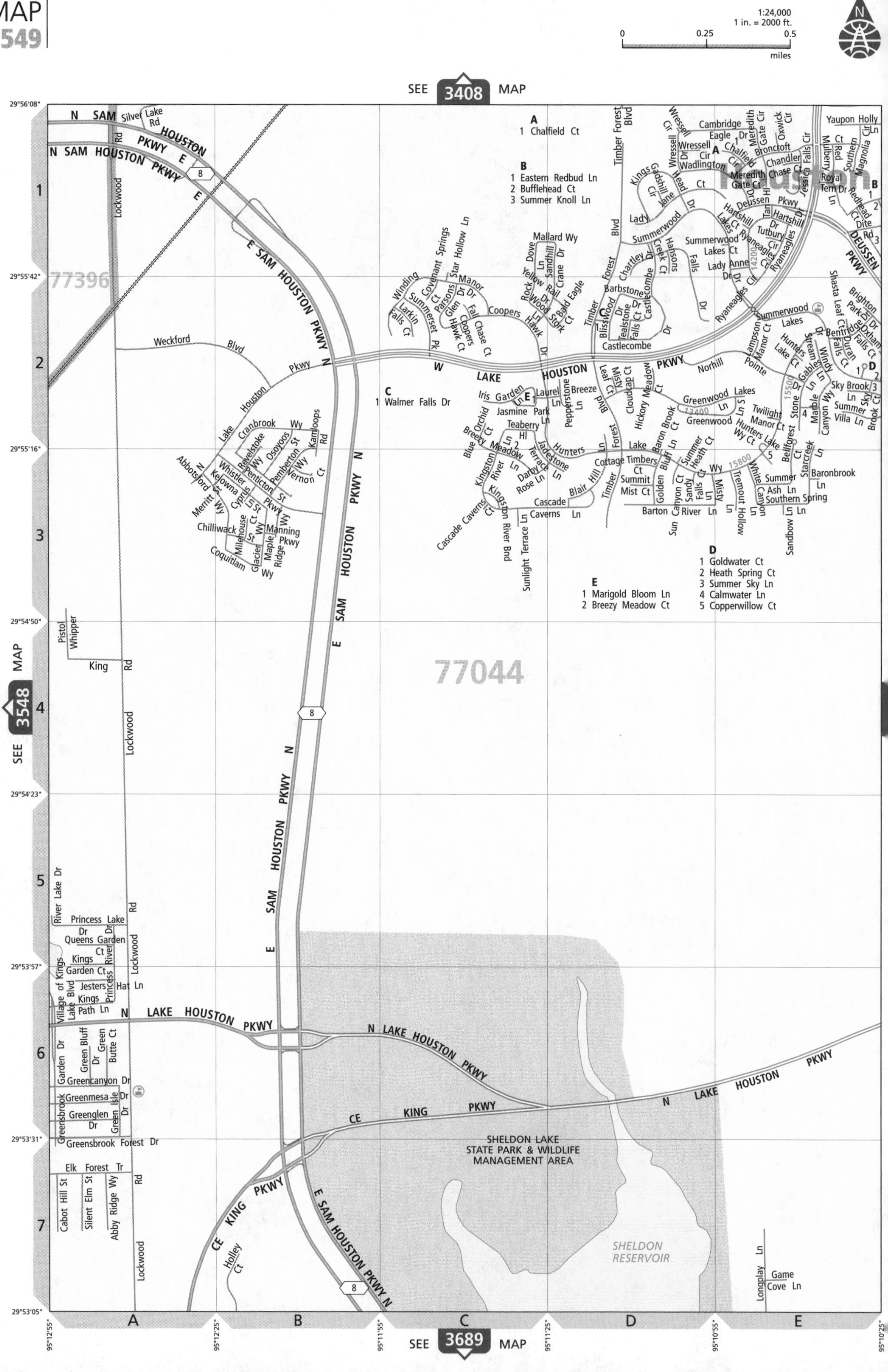
1:24,000
1 in. = 2000 ft.
0 0.25 0.5
miles
N
SEE 3408 MAP
SEE 3548 MAP
SEE 3689 MAP
A
1 Chalfield Ct
B
1 Eastern Redbud Ln
2 Bufflehead Ct
3 Summer Knoll Ln
C
1 Walmer Falls Dr
D
1 Goldwater Ct
2 Heath Spring Ct
3 Summer Sky Ln
4 Calmwater Ln
5 Copperwillow Ct
E
1 Marigold Bloom Ln
2 Breezy Meadow Ct
77396
77044
Houston
N SAM HOUSTON PKWY E
E SAM HOUSTON PKWY N
W LAKE HOUSTON PKWY
N LAKE HOUSTON PKWY
CE KING PKWY
DEUSSEN PKWY
Lockwood Rd
Weckford Blvd
Timber Forest Blvd
SHELDON LAKE
STATE PARK & WILDLIFE
MANAGEMENT AREA
SHELDON
RESERVOIR
29°56'08"
29°55'42"
29°55'16"
29°54'50"
29°54'23"
29°53'57"
29°53'31"
29°53'05"
95°12'55"
95°12'25"
95°11'55"
95°11'25"
95°10'55"
95°10'25"
A B C D E
1 2 3 4 5 6 7

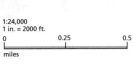

1:24,000
1 in. = 2000 ft.
0 0.25 0.5
miles

SEE 3409 MAP

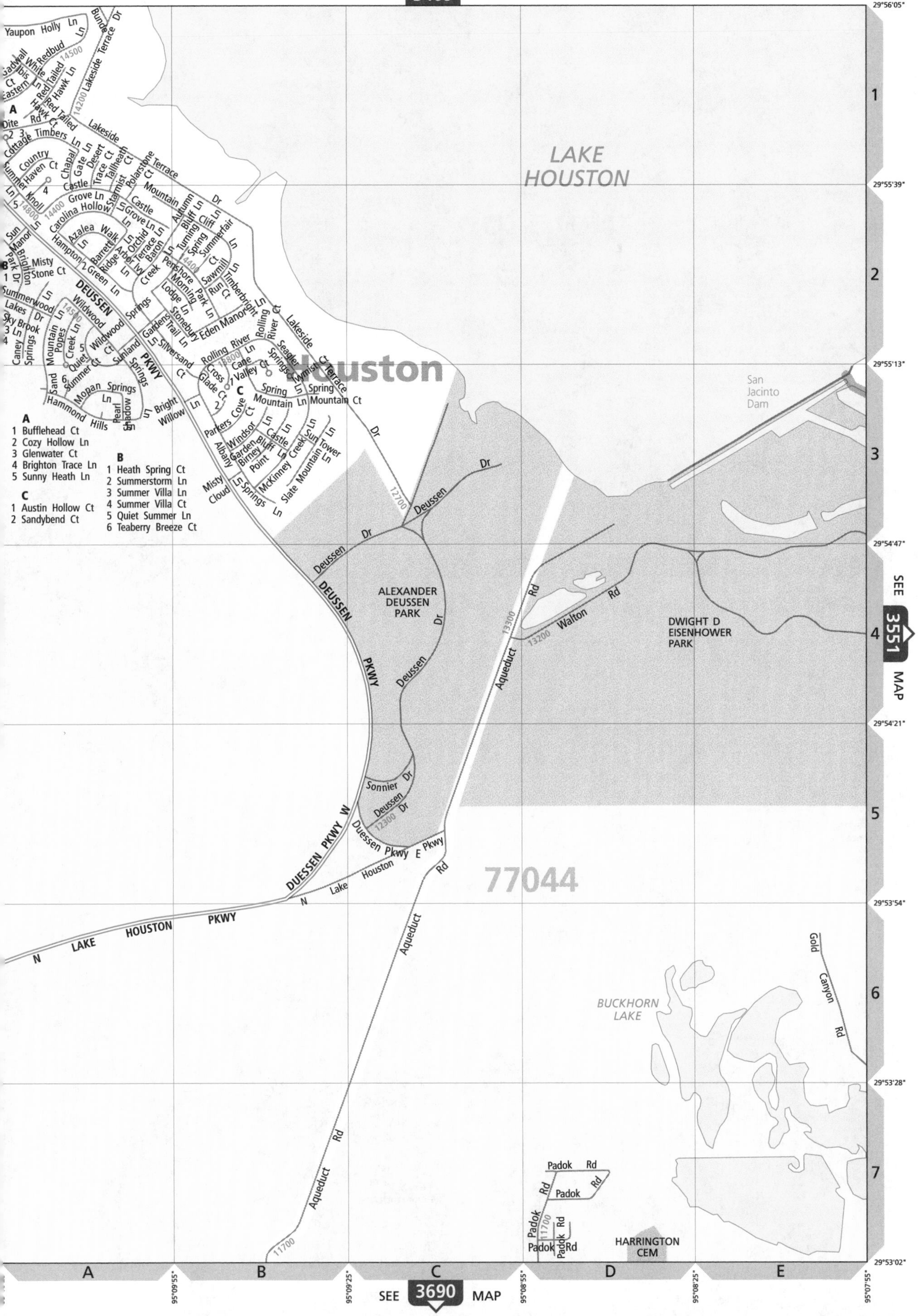
LAKE HOUSTON
Houston
San Jacinto Dam
ALEXANDER DEUSSEN PARK
DWIGHT D EISENHOWER PARK
DEUSSEN PKWY
DUESSEN PKWY W
N LAKE HOUSTON PKWY
N Lake Houston Pkwy E
Aqueduct Rd
Walton Rd
Deussen Dr
Sonnier Dr
77044
BUCKHORN LAKE
Gold Canyon Rd
Padok Rd
HARRINGTON CEM
Lakeside Terrace Dr
Yaupon Holly Ln
A
1 Bufflehead Ct
2 Cozy Hollow Ln
3 Glenwater Ct
4 Brighton Trace Ln
5 Sunny Heath Ln
B
1 Heath Spring Ct
2 Summerstorm Ln
3 Summer Villa Ln
4 Summer Villa Ct
5 Quiet Summer Ln
6 Teaberry Breeze Ct
C
1 Austin Hollow Ct
2 Sandybend Ct
1
2
3
4
5
6
7
A
B
C
D
E
29°56'05"
29°55'39"
29°55'13"
29°54'47"
29°54'21"
29°53'54"
29°53'28"
29°53'02"
95°09'55"
95°09'25"
95°08'55"
95°08'25"
95°07'55"

SEE 3551 MAP

SEE 3690 MAP

1:24,000
1 in. = 2000 ft.
0 0.25 0.5
miles

SEE 3410 MAP

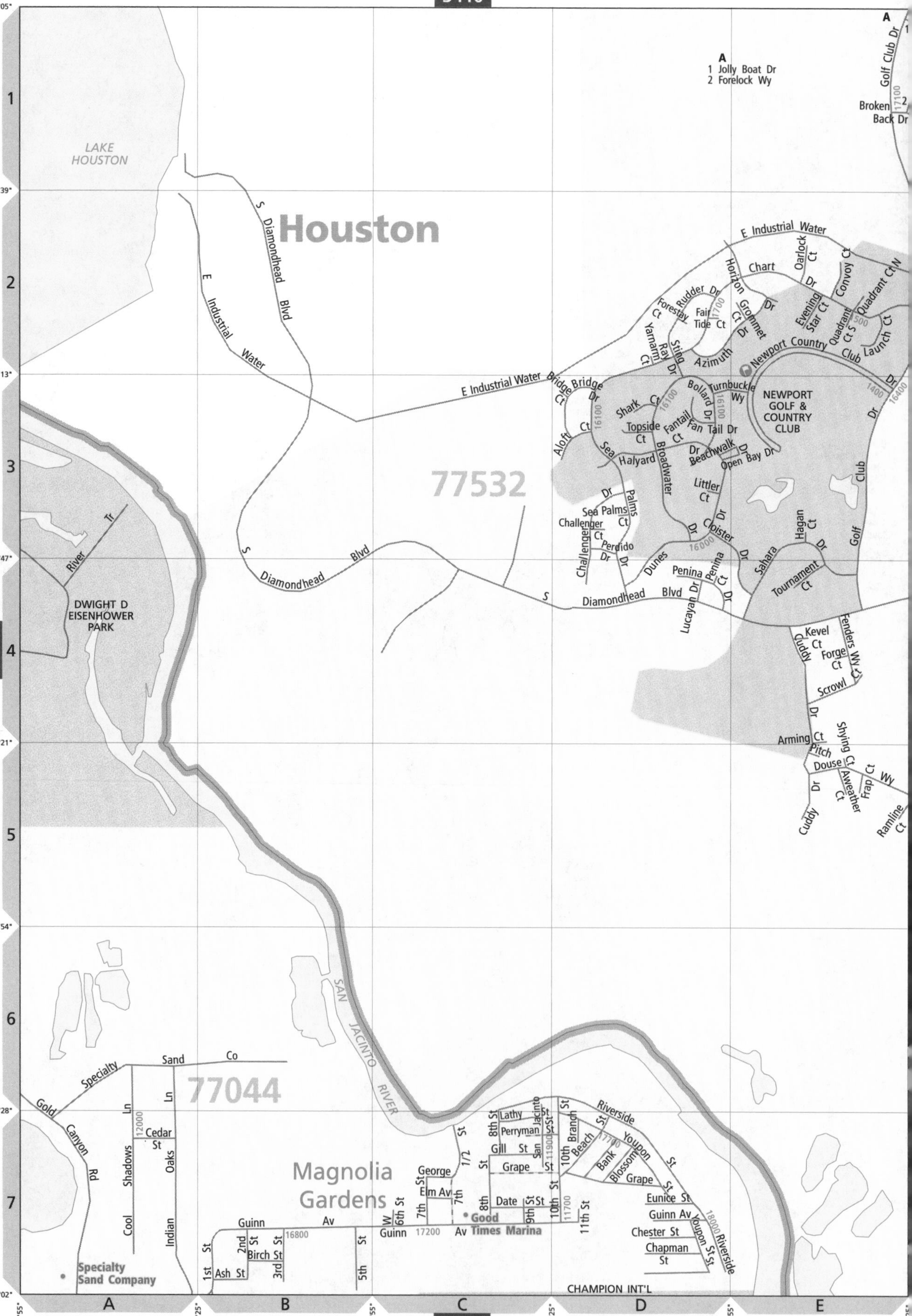
A
1 Jolly Boat Dr
2 Forelock Wy
LAKE HOUSTON
Houston
77532
77044
DWIGHT D EISENHOWER PARK
NEWPORT GOLF & COUNTRY CLUB
Magnolia Gardens
SAN JACINTO RIVER
S Diamondhead Blvd
E Industrial Water
River Tr
Newport Country Club Dr
Specialty Sand Company
Good Times Marina
CHAMPION INT'L
Gold Canyon Rd
Specialty Sand Co
Cool Shadows Ln
Indian Oaks Ln
Cedar St
Guinn Av
Riverside
Youpon St
Golf Club Dr
Broken Back Dr

SEE 3550 MAP

SEE 3691 MAP

1:24,000
1 in. = 2000 ft.
0 0.25 0.5
miles

SEE 3411 MAP

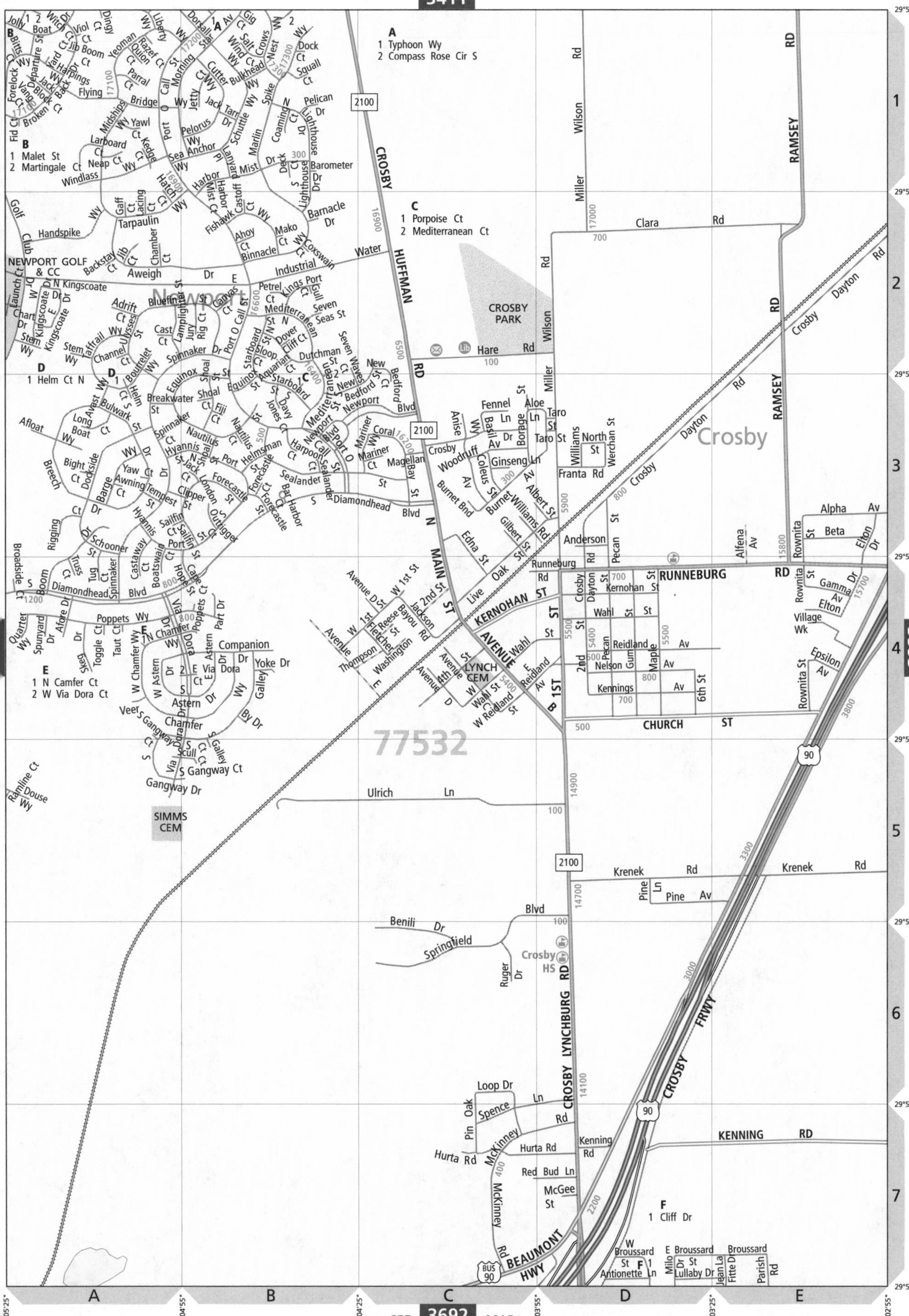
A
1 Typhoon Wy
2 Compass Rose Cir S
B
1 Malet St
2 Martingale Ct
C
1 Porpoise Ct
2 Mediterranean Ct
D
1 Helm Ct N
E
1 N Camfer Ct
2 W Via Dora Ct
F
1 Cliff Dr
CROSBY HUFFMAN RD
N MAIN ST
CROSBY LYNCHBURG RD
RAMSEY RD
Wilson Rd
Miller Rd
Clara Rd
Crosby Dayton Rd
RUNNEBURG RD
KERNOHAN ST
AVENUE B
1ST ST
CHURCH ST
Diamondhead Blvd
Industrial Dr
Water
Hare Rd
Ulrich Ln
Krenek Rd
Pine Av
Benili Dr
Springfield Blvd
Loop Dr
Spence Ln
Hurta Rd
McKinney Rd
KENNING RD
BEAUMONT HWY
CROSBY FRWY
CROSBY PARK
NEWPORT GOLF & CC
Newport
Crosby
77532
LYNCH CEM
SIMMS CEM
Crosby HS
Alpha Av
Beta
Gamma Av
Elton Av
Epsilon Av
Village Wk
Rownita St
Alfena Av
Anderson
Pecan St
W Broussard St
E Broussard St
Broussard Rd
Antionette Ln
Parish
2100
90
BUS 90
A B C D E
1 2 3 4 5 6 7
29°56'02"
29°55'36"
29°55'10"
29°54'44"
29°54'17"
29°53'51"
29°53'25"
29°52'59"
95°05'25"
95°04'55"
95°04'25"
95°03'55"
95°03'25"
95°02'55"

SEE 3553 MAP

SEE 3692 MAP

1:24,000
1 in. = 2000 ft.
0 0.25 0.5
miles

N

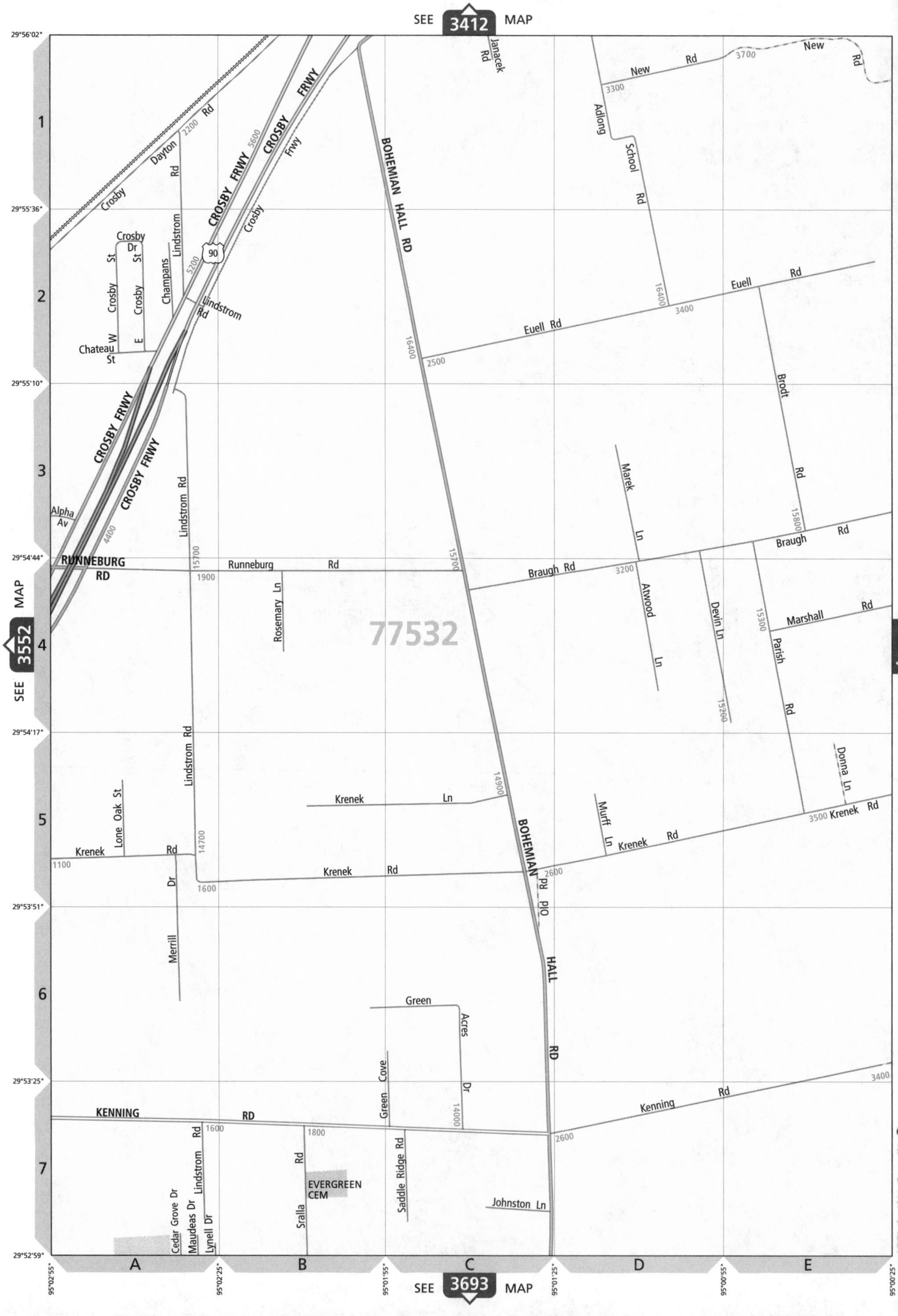
SEE 3412 MAP
SEE 3693 MAP
SEE 3552 MAP
29°56'02"
29°55'36"
29°55'10"
29°54'44"
29°54'17"
29°53'51"
29°53'25"
29°52'59"
95°02'55"
95°02'25"
95°01'55"
95°01'25"
95°00'55"
95°00'25"
1
2
3
4
5
6
7
A
B
C
D
E
77532
Janacek Rd
New Rd
3700
New Rd
3300
Adlong
School Rd
Crosby Dayton Rd
2200
CROSBY FRWY
5600
CROSBY FRWY
Crosby Frwy
Crosby Frwy
BOHEMIAN HALL RD
Crosby Dr
W Crosby St
E Crosby St
Lindstrom Rd
Champans
5200
90
Lindstrom Rd
Chateau St
16400
Euell Rd
3400
Euell Rd
16400
2500
Brodt Rd
CROSBY FRWY
CROSBY FRWY
Marek Ln
Alpha Av
4400
Lindstrom Rd
15800
Braugh Rd
RUNNEBURG RD
15700
Runneburg Rd
15700
Braugh Rd
3200
1900
Rosemary Ln
Atwood Ln
Devin Ln
15300
Marshall Rd
Parish Rd
15200
Lindstrom Rd
Lone Oak St
Krenek Ln
14900
Donna Ln
Murff Ln
BOHEMIAN
Krenek Rd
3500 Krenek Rd
Krenek Rd
1100
14700
Krenek Rd
2600
Old Rd
1600
Merrill Dr
HALL
Green Acres Dr
RD
Green Cove
KENNING RD
14000
3400
Kenning Rd
1600
1800
2600
Lindstrom Rd
Sralla Rd
Saddle Ridge Rd
EVERGREEN CEM
Johnston Ln
Cedar Grove Dr
Maudeas Dr
Lynell Dr

1:24,000
1 in. = 2000 ft.
0 0.25 0.5
miles

SEE 3413 MAP

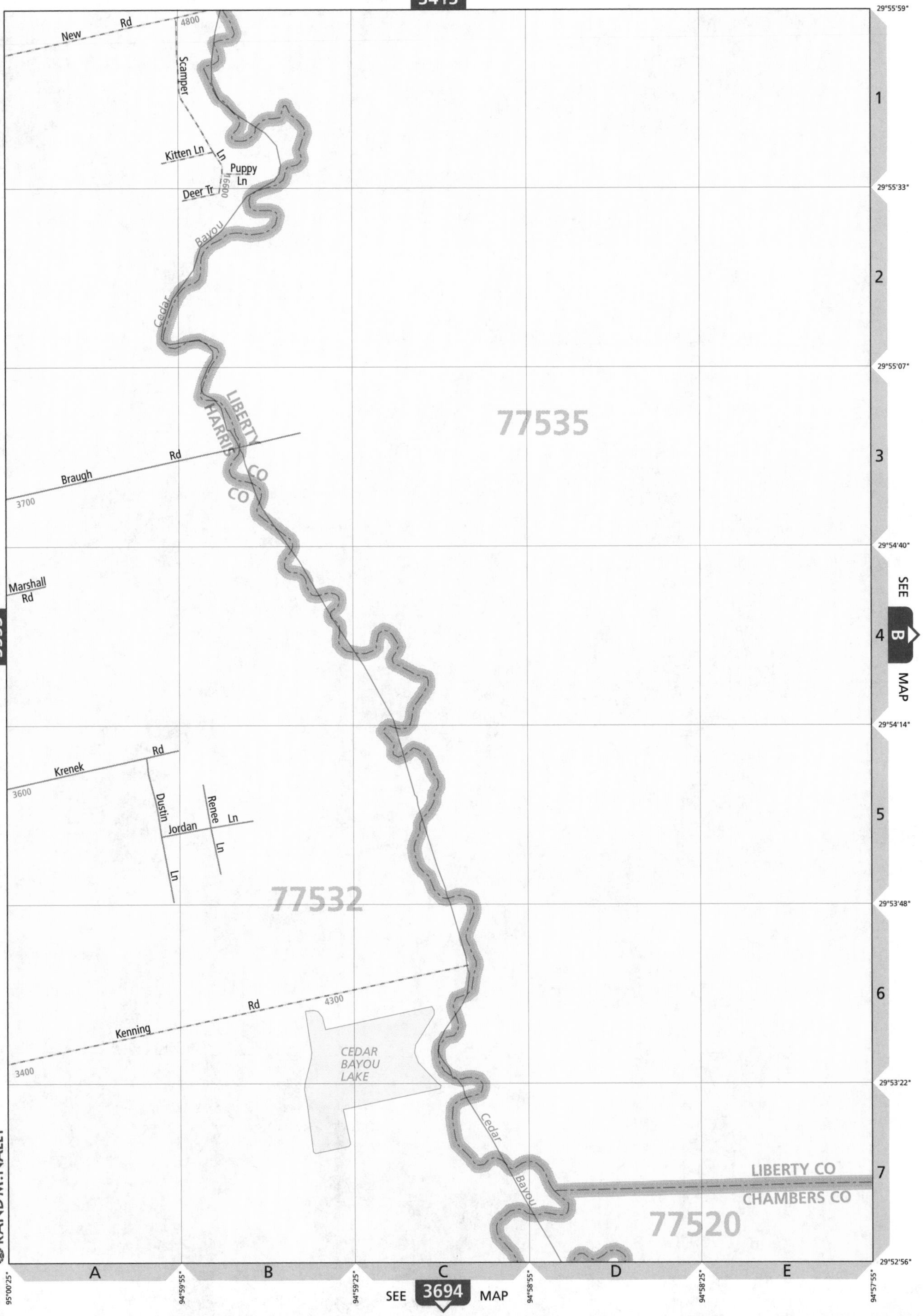
29°55'59"
New Rd
4800
Scamper
Kitten Ln
Ln
Puppy Ln
Deer Tr
6600
29°55'33"
Bayou
Cedar
29°55'07"
LIBERTY CO
HARRIS CO
77535
Braugh Rd
3700
29°54'40"
Marshall Rd
29°54'14"
Krenek Rd
3600
Dustin Ln
Jordan
Renee Ln
Ln
77532
29°53'48"
Kenning Rd
4300
3400
CEDAR BAYOU LAKE
29°53'22"
Cedar Bayou
LIBERTY CO
CHAMBERS CO
77520
29°52'56"
1
2
3
4
5
6
7
A
B
C
D
E
95°00'25"
94°59'55"
94°59'25"
94°58'55"
94°58'25"
94°57'55"

SEE B MAP

SEE 3694 MAP

3553

1:24,000
1 in. = 2000 ft.

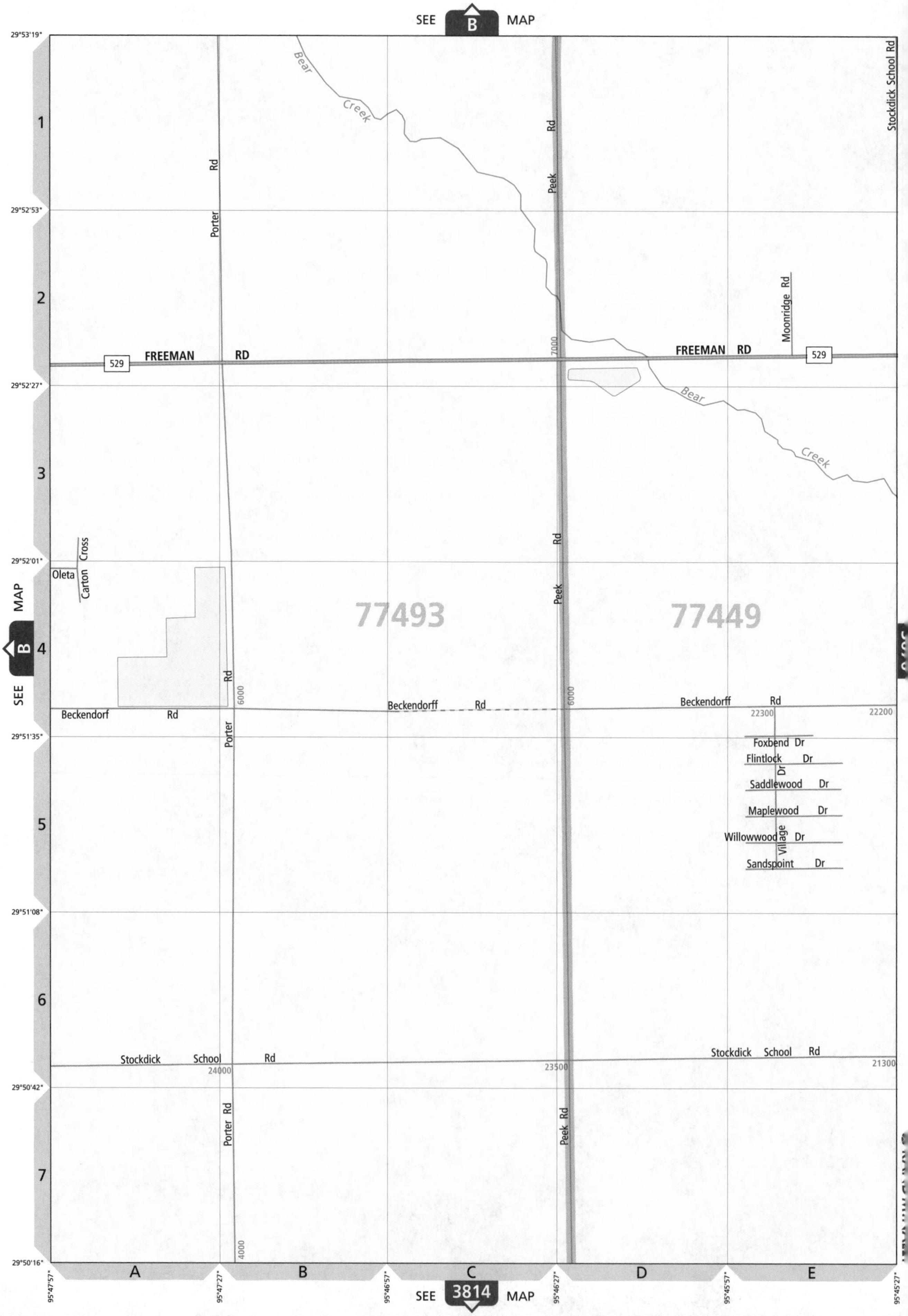
SEE B MAP
29°53'19"
29°52'53"
29°52'27"
29°52'01"
29°51'35"
29°51'08"
29°50'42"
29°50'16"
1
2
3
4
5
6
7
Bear Creek
Porter Rd
Peek Rd
Stockdick School Rd
Moonridge Rd
529
FREEMAN RD
7000
Oleta
Carton Cross
SEE B MAP
77493
77449
Beckendorf Rd
6000
Beckendorff Rd
22300
22200
Foxbend Dr
Flintlock Dr
Saddlewood Dr
Maplewood Dr
Willowwood Dr
Sandspoint Dr
Village Dr
Stockdick School Rd
24000
23500
21300
4000
A
B
C
D
E
95°47'57"
95°47'27"
95°46'57"
95°46'27"
95°45'57"
95°45'27"
SEE 3814 MAP

1:24,000
1 in. = 2000 ft.
0 0.25 0.5
miles

SEE B MAP

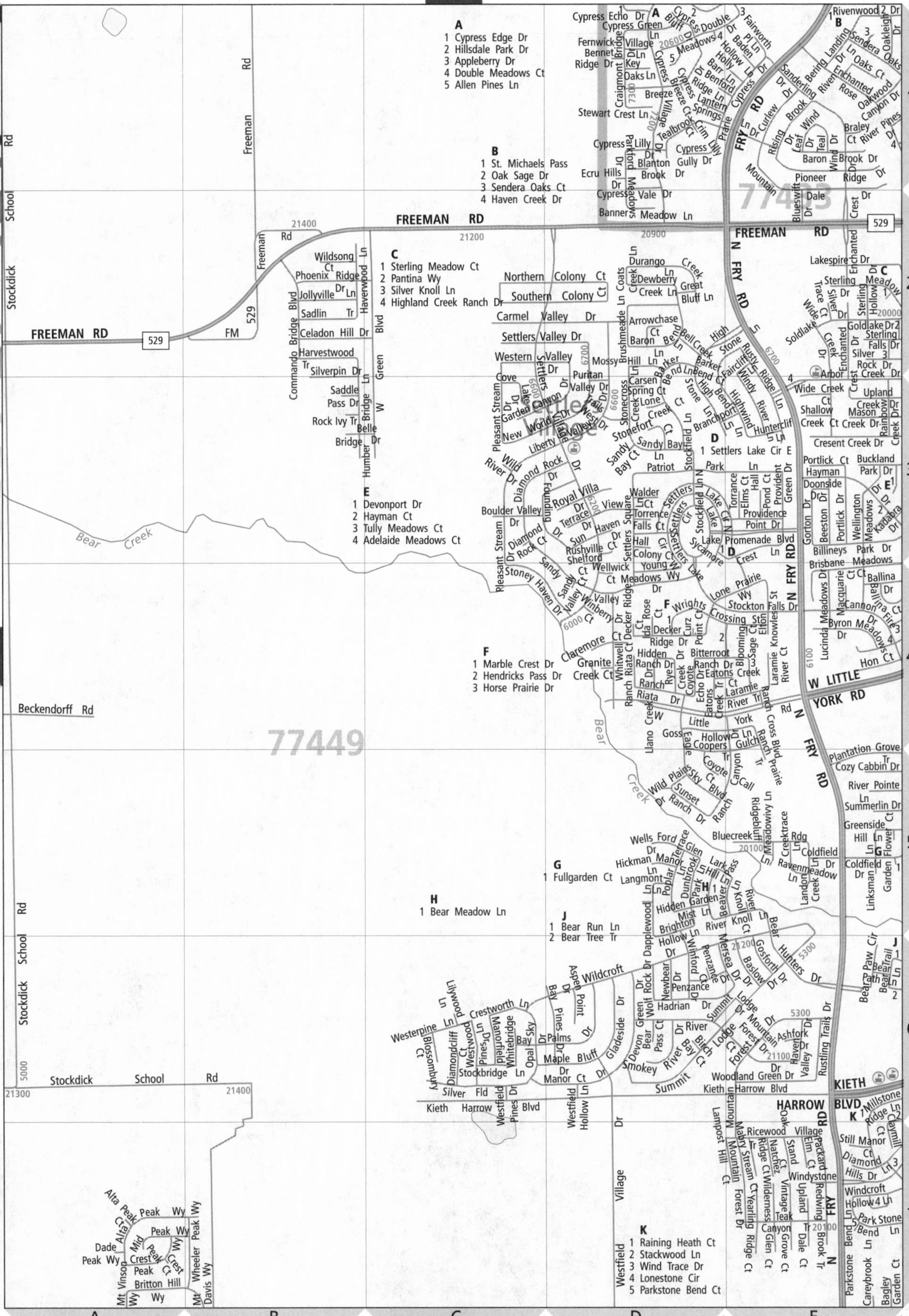
A
1 Cypress Edge Dr
2 Hillsdale Park Dr
3 Appleberry Dr
4 Double Meadows Ct
5 Allen Pines Ln
B
1 St. Michaels Pass
2 Oak Sage Dr
3 Sendera Oaks Ct
4 Haven Creek Dr
C
1 Sterling Meadow Ct
2 Pantina Wy
3 Silver Knoll Ln
4 Highland Creek Ranch Dr
D
1 Settlers Lake Cir E
E
1 Devonport Dr
2 Hayman Ct
3 Tully Meadows Ct
4 Adelaide Meadows Ct
F
1 Marble Crest Dr
2 Hendricks Pass Dr
3 Horse Prairie Dr
G
1 Fullgarden Ct
H
1 Bear Meadow Ln
J
1 Bear Run Ln
2 Bear Tree Tr
K
1 Raining Heath Ct
2 Stackwood Ln
3 Wind Trace Dr
4 Lonestone Cir
5 Parkstone Bend Ct
FREEMAN RD
FREEMAN RD
FM 529
529
N FRY RD
W LITTLE YORK RD
KIETH HARROW BLVD
Stockdick School Rd
Beckendorff Rd
Bear Creek
77449
77433
29°53'18"
29°52'52"
29°52'25"
29°51'59"
29°51'33"
29°51'07"
29°50'41"
29°50'15"
95°45'27"
95°44'57"
95°44'27"
95°43'57"
95°43'27"
95°42'57"
A B C D E
1 2 3 4 5 6 7

SEE 3677 MAP

SEE 3815 MAP

1:24,000
1 in. = 2000 ft.
0 0.25 0.5
miles

SEE 3537 MAP

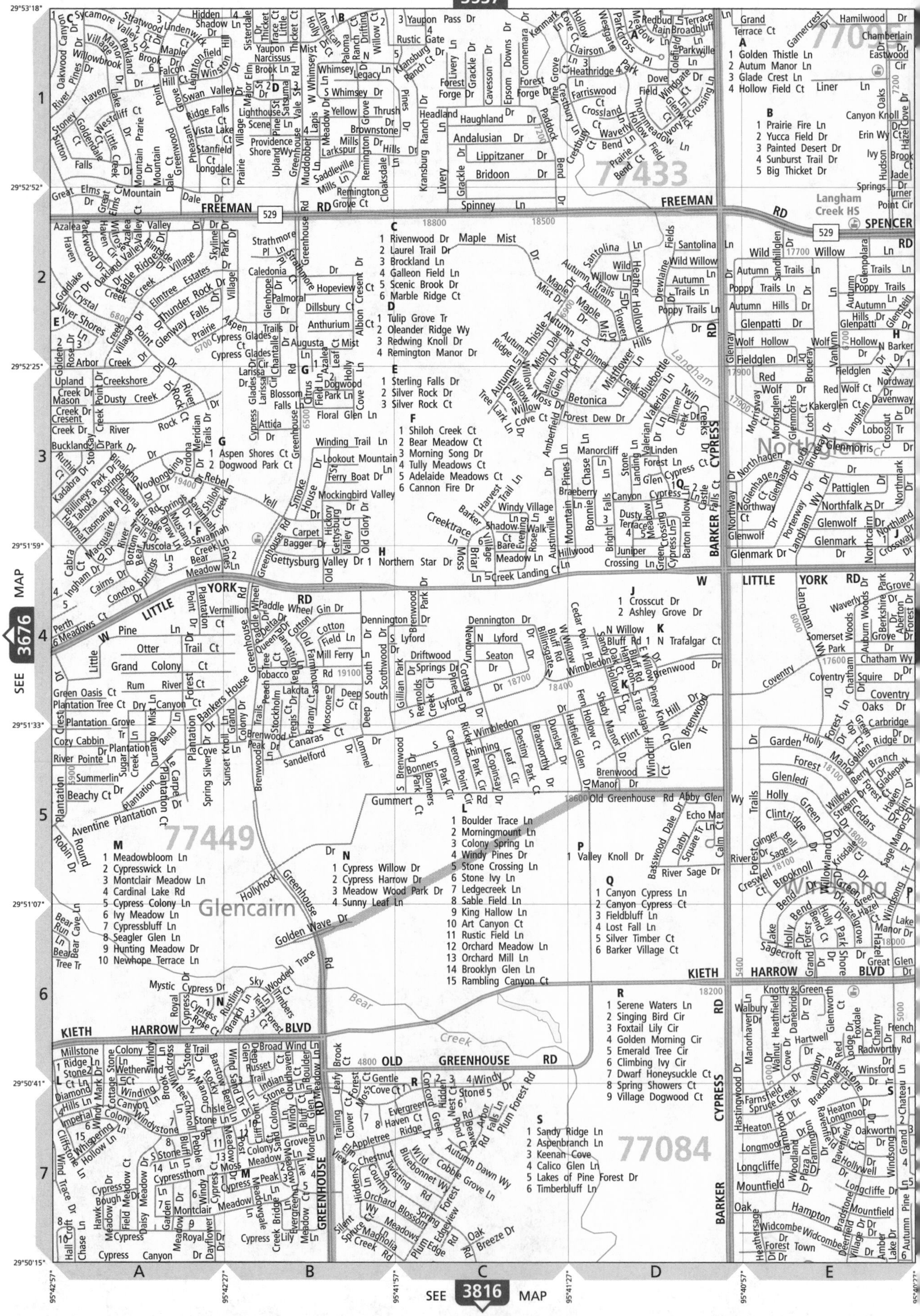
29°53'18"
29°52'52"
29°52'25"
29°51'59"
29°51'33"
29°51'07"
29°50'41"
29°50'15"
95°42'57"
95°42'27"
95°41'57"
95°41'27"
95°40'57"
95°40'27"
A
B
C
D
E
1
2
3
4
5
6
7
FREEMAN RD
529
SPENCER RD
W LITTLE YORK RD
KIETH HARROW BLVD
OLD GREENHOUSE RD
GREENHOUSE RD
BARKER CYPRESS RD
Langham Creek HS
Glencairn
Northglen
Windsong
77433
77449
77084
77095
Bear Creek
A
1 Golden Thistle Ln
2 Autum Manor Ln
3 Glade Crest Ln
4 Hollow Field Ct
B
1 Prairie Fire Ln
2 Yucca Field Dr
3 Painted Desert Dr
4 Sunburst Trail Dr
5 Big Thicket Dr
C
1 Rivenwood Dr
2 Laurel Trail Dr
3 Brockland Ln
4 Galleon Field Ln
5 Scenic Brook Dr
6 Marble Ridge Ct
D
1 Tulip Grove Tr
2 Oleander Ridge Wy
3 Redwing Knoll Dr
4 Remington Manor Dr
E
1 Sterling Falls Dr
2 Silver Rock Dr
3 Silver Rock Ct
F
1 Shiloh Creek Ct
2 Bear Meadow Ct
3 Morning Song Dr
4 Tully Meadows Ct
5 Adelaide Meadows Ct
6 Cannon Fire Dr
G
1 Aspen Shores Ct
2 Dogwood Park Ct
H
1 Northern Star Dr
J
1 Crosscut Dr
2 Ashley Grove Dr
K
1 N Trafalgar Ct
L
1 Boulder Trace Ln
2 Morningmount Ln
3 Colony Spring Ln
4 Windy Pines Dr
5 Stone Crossing Ln
6 Stone Ivy Ln
7 Ledgecreek Ln
8 Sable Field Ln
9 King Hallow Ln
10 Art Canyon Ct
11 Rustic Field Ln
12 Orchard Meadow Ln
13 Orchard Mill Ln
14 Brooklyn Glen Ln
15 Rambling Canyon Ct
M
1 Meadowbloom Ln
2 Cypresswick Ln
3 Montclair Meadow Ln
4 Cardinal Lake Rd
5 Cypress Colony Ln
6 Ivy Meadow Ln
7 Cypressbluff Ln
8 Seagler Glen Ln
9 Hunting Meadow Dr
10 Newhope Terrace Ln
N
1 Cypress Willow Dr
2 Cypress Harrow Dr
3 Meadow Wood Park Dr
4 Sunny Leaf Ln
P
1 Valley Knoll Dr
Q
1 Canyon Cypress Ln
2 Canyon Cypress Ct
3 Fieldbluff Ln
4 Lost Fall Ln
5 Silver Timber Ct
6 Barker Village Ct
R
1 Serene Waters Ln
2 Singing Bird Cir
3 Foxtail Lily Cir
4 Golden Morning Cir
5 Emerald Tree Cir
6 Climbing Ivy Cir
7 Dwarf Honeysuckle Ct
8 Spring Showers Ct
9 Village Dogwood Ct
S
1 Sandy Ridge Ln
2 Aspenbranch Ln
3 Keenan Cove
4 Calico Glen Ln
5 Lakes of Pine Forest Dr
6 Timberbluff Ln

SEE 3676 MAP

SEE 3816 MAP

1:24,000
1 in. = 2000 ft.
0 0.25 0.5
miles

SEE 3538 MAP

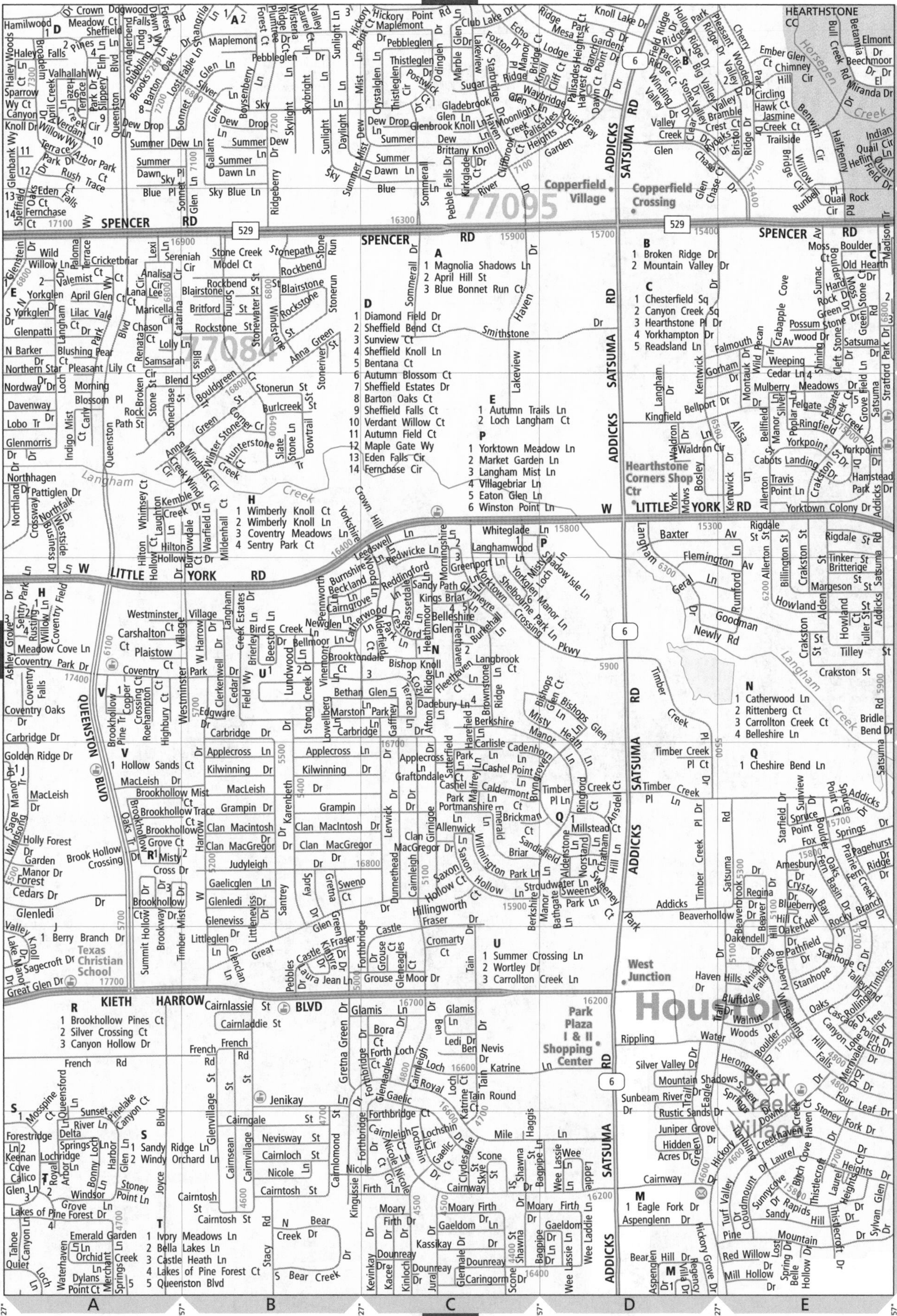

HEARTHSTONE CC
Copperfield Village
Copperfield Crossing
77095
77084
SPENCER RD
W LITTLE YORK RD
ADDICKS SATSUMA RD
QUEENSTON BLVD
KIETH HARROW BLVD
Langham Creek
Horsepen Creek
Hearthstone Corners Shop Ctr
Texas Christian School
West Junction
Houston
Park Plaza I & II Shopping Center
Bear Creek Village
A
1 Magnolia Shadows Ln
2 April Hill St
3 Blue Bonnet Run Ct
B
1 Broken Ridge Dr
2 Mountain Valley Dr
C
1 Chesterfield Sq
2 Canyon Creek Sq
3 Hearthstone Pl Dr
4 Yorkhampton Dr
5 Readsland Ln
D
1 Diamond Field Dr
2 Sheffield Bend Ct
3 Sunview Ct
4 Sheffield Knoll Ln
5 Bentana Ct
6 Autumn Blossom Ct
7 Sheffield Estates Dr
8 Barton Oaks Ct
9 Sheffield Falls Ct
10 Verdant Willow Ct
11 Autumn Field Ct
12 Maple Gate Wy
13 Eden Falls Cir
14 Fernchase Cir
E
1 Autumn Trails Ln
2 Loch Langham Ct
P
1 Yorktown Meadow Ln
2 Market Garden Ln
3 Langham Mist Ln
4 Villagebriar Ln
5 Eaton Glen Ln
6 Winston Point Ln
H
1 Wimberly Knoll Ct
2 Wimberly Knoll Ln
3 Coventry Meadows Ln
4 Sentry Park Ct
N
1 Catherwood Ln
2 Rittenberg Ct
3 Carrollton Creek Ct
4 Belleshire Ln
Q
1 Cheshire Bend Ln
V
1 Hollow Sands Ct
J
1 Berry Branch Dr
U
1 Summer Crossing Ln
2 Wortley Dr
3 Carrollton Creek Ln
R
1 Brookhollow Pines Ct
2 Silver Crossing Ct
3 Canyon Hollow Dr
S
1 Sandy Ridge Ln
2 Windy Orchard Ln
T
1 Ivory Meadows Ln
2 Bella Lakes Ln
3 Castle Heath Ln
4 Lakes of Pine Forest Ct
5 Queenston Blvd
M
1 Eagle Fork Dr
A B C D E
1 2 3 4 5 6 7
29°53'16"
29°52'50"
29°52'24"
29°51'58"
29°51'31"
29°51'05"
29°50'39"
29°50'13"
95°40'27"
95°39'57"
95°39'27"
95°38'57"
95°38'27"
95°37'57"

SEE 3679 MAP

SEE 3817 MAP

SEE 3539 MAP

1:24,000
1 in. = 2000 ft.
0
0.25
0.5
miles
N
77041
77084
Houston
Deerfield Village
HEARTHSTONE CC
Chimney Hill
Concord Bridge
SPENCER RD
W LITTLE YORK RD
N ELDRIDGE PKWY
HORSEPEN BAYOU
LANGHAM CREEK
Toshiba Int'l Corp
A
1 Fountaincrest Ct
2 Fountaincrest Dr
3 Burkridge Dr
4 Silver Meadow Ct
5 Meadow Mist Ct
6 Eldridge Chase Ct
B
1 Virginia Water Ln
2 W Suddley Castle St
C
1 Sunshine Creek Dr
2 Rainbow Star Dr
3 Boxwood Br
4 Daisy Meadow Ct
5 Boxwood Wy Ln
D
1 N Hearthstone Green Dr
2 Heflin Ln
E
1 Meadowbrook Sq
2 Jasmine Tr
3 Mariner Grv
4 Hertford Park Dr
F
1 Cotorra Cove Ct
2 Lago Royale Ln
3 Ensenada Canyon Ln
4 Grand Peak Ln
5 Arcadia Bend Ln
6 Paloma Park Ct
7 W Solano Bay Ln
8 E Solano Bay Ln
9 Diamond Bay Ct
G
1 Perdido Cove Ln
H
1 E Bristol Harbour Cir
2 Jamestown Colony Dr
3 S Bristol Harbour Cir
4 Bacons Castle Ln
5 W Rutledge Ct
6 Charlestown Colony Ct
7 E Stonegrove Lp
8 Cape Henry Ln
9 Old Lighthouse Ln
10 Cinnamon Creek Cir
11 White Hart Run
12 Golden Pond Dr
13 Towerglen Ct
14 Pipingwood Dr
J
1 Sonata Canyon Ln
2 Acacia Arbor Ln
K
1 Highlands View Ct
2 Rolling Timbers Ct
M
1 Laguna Pointe Ln
2 Eden Springs Ln
3 Ember Isles Ln
4 Sea Grove Ct
5 Green Cove Bend Ln
6 Harbor Rdg
7 Medina Bend Ln
8 Auburn Shores Ct
N
1 Chandlers Wy Dr
2 Coral Pointe Dr
3 Coral Crest Ct
4 Evening Shore Ct
5 Cherry Creek Bend Ct
6 Cardinal Bay
7 Lakeshore Ridge Ct
8 Silent Shore Ln
29°53'16"
29°52'50"
29°52'24"
29°51'58"
29°51'31"
29°51'05"
29°50'39"
29°50'13"
95°37'57"
95°37'27"
95°36'57"
95°36'27"
95°35'57"
95°35'27"
A
B
C
D
E
1
2
3
4
5
6
7

SEE 3678 MAP

SEE 3818 MAP

1:24,000
1 in. = 2000 ft.
0 0.25 0.5
miles

SEE 3540 MAP

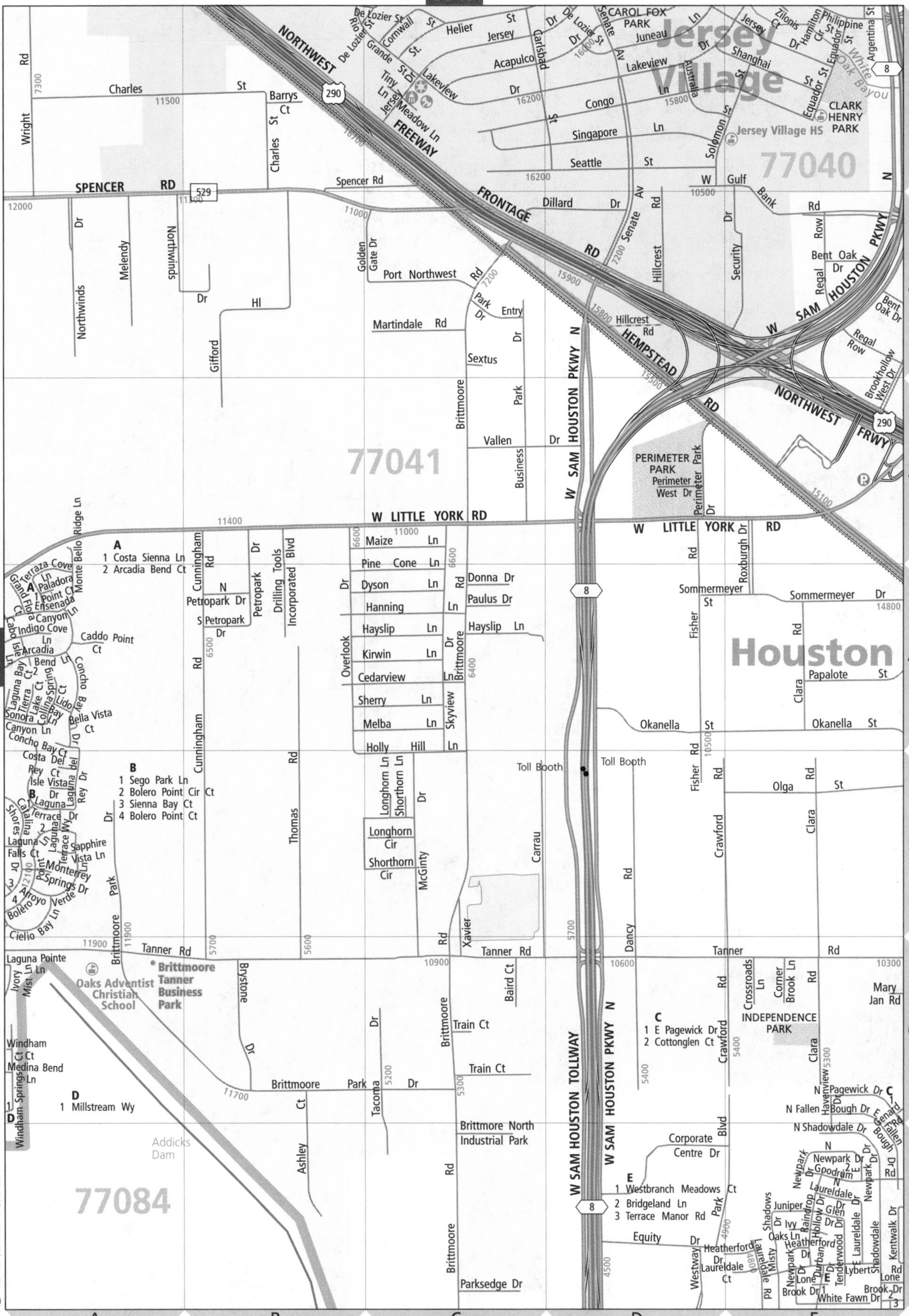
Jersey Village
77040
77041
77084
Houston
NORTHWEST FREEWAY
FRONTAGE RD
HEMPSTEAD RD
NORTHWEST FRWY
290
8
529
SPENCER RD
Spencer Rd
W SAM HOUSTON PKWY
W SAM HOUSTON PKWY N
W SAM HOUSTON TOLLWAY
W LITTLE YORK RD
W LITTLE YORK RD
Tanner Rd
Tanner Rd
Charles St
Barrys Ct
Wright Rd
Northwinds Dr
Melendy
Gifford
Golden Gate Dr
Port Northwest Rd
Martindale Rd
Park Entry Dr
Sextus
Brittmoore
Park
Vallen Dr
Business
Carol Fox Park
Clark Henry Park
Jersey Village HS
Perimeter Park
Perimeter West Dr
Gulf Bank Rd
Bent Oak Dr
Regal Row
Brookhollow West Dr
Dillard Dr
Senate Av
Hillcrest Rd
Security Dr
Seattle St
Singapore Ln
Congo
Lakeview
Acapulco
Jersey
Helier
Carlsbad
Juneau
Shanghai
Solomon St
Australia
Equador St
Philippine St
Zilonis
Argentina St
White Oak Bayou
Sommermeyer St
Sommermeyer Dr
Fisher Rd
Roxburgh Dr
Clara Rd
Papalote St
Okanella St
Olga St
Crawford
Dancy Rd
Toll Booth
Toll Booth
Maize Ln
Pine Cone Ln
Dyson Ln
Hanning Ln
Hayslip Ln
Kirwin Ln
Cedarview Ln
Sherry Ln
Melba Ln
Holly Hill Ln
Overlook Dr
Skyview
Donna Dr
Paulus Dr
Longhorn Cir
Shorthorn Cir
McGinty
Carrau
Xavier
Thomas Rd
Cunningham Rd
Petropark Dr
Drilling Tools
Incorporated Blvd
Caddo Point Ct
Bella Vista Ct
A
1 Costa Sienna Ln
2 Arcadia Bend Ct
B
1 Sego Park Ln
2 Bolero Point Cir Ct
3 Sienna Bay Ct
4 Bolero Point Ct
C
1 E Pagewick Dr
2 Cottonglen Ct
D
1 Millstream Wy
E
1 Westbranch Meadows Ct
2 Bridgeland Ln
3 Terrace Manor Rd
Brittmoore Tanner Business Park
Oaks Adventist Christian School
Brystone Dr
Brittmoore Park Dr
Tacoma
Ashley
Train Ct
Baird Ct
Brittmore North Industrial Park
Parksedge Dr
Addicks Dam
Windham Springs Ln
Medina Bend
Laguna Pointe
Independence Park
Crossroads Ln
Corner Brook Ln
Corporate Centre Dr
Equity Dr
Westway Park
Heatherford Dr
Laureldale Ct
N Pagewick Dr
N Fallen Bough Dr
N Shadowdale Dr
Newpark Dr
Goodrum
White Fawn Dr
1
2
3
4
5
6
7
A
B
C
D
E

SEE 3681 MAP

SEE 3819 MAP

1:24,000
1 in. = 2000 ft.
0 0.25 0.5
miles

SEE 3541 MAP

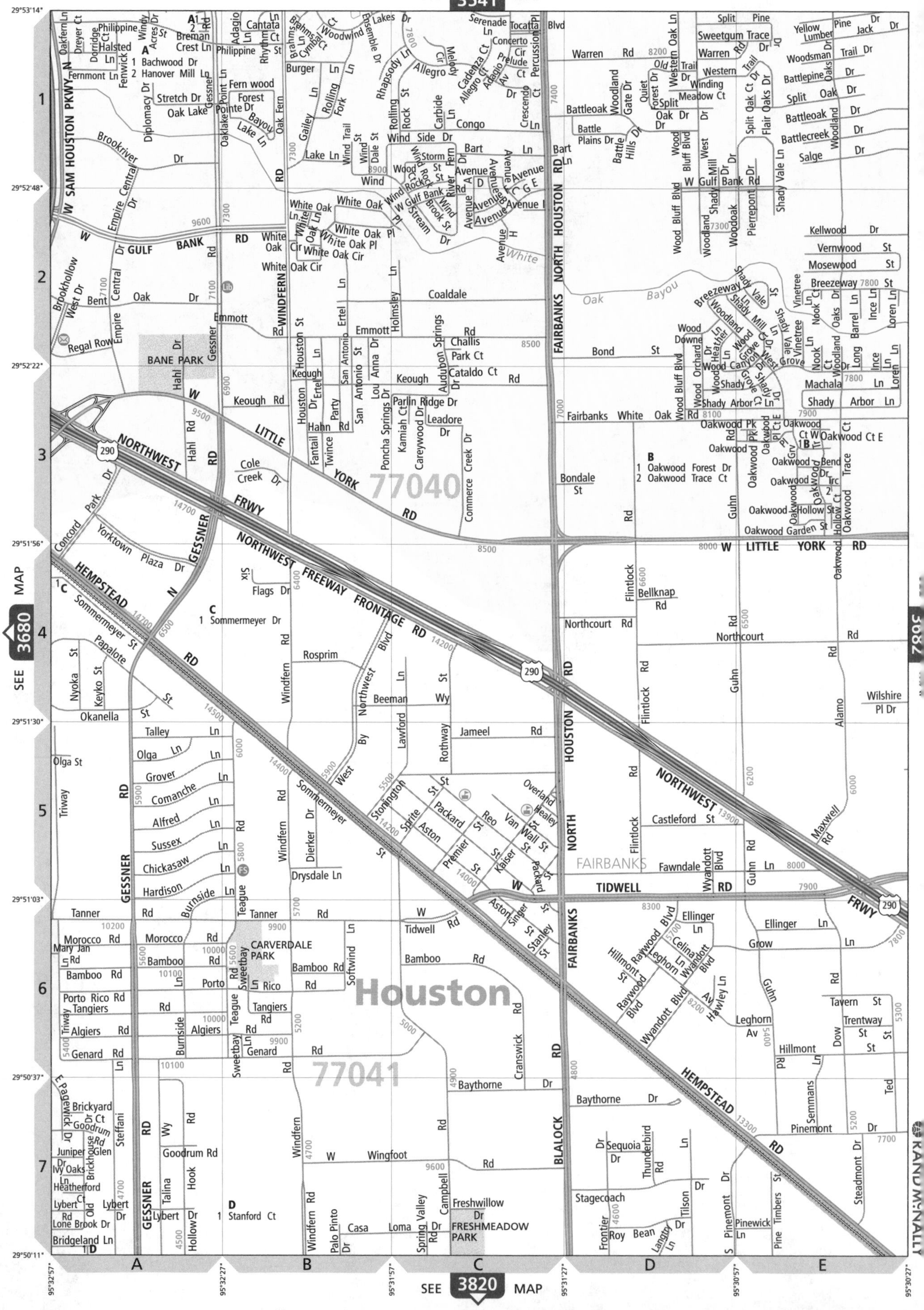
W SAM HOUSTON PKWY N
Brookriver Dr
Empire Central Dr
W GULF BANK RD
Bent Oak Dr
Regal Row
BANE PARK
Emmott Rd
WINDFERN RD
White Oak Cir
White Oak Pl
Coaldale
Keough Rd
Challis Park Ct
Cataldo Ct
Parlin Ridge Dr
Leadore Dr
W LITTLE YORK RD
77040
NORTHWEST FRWY
NORTHWEST FREEWAY FRONTAGE RD
HEMPSTEAD RD
GESSNER N
Yorktown Plaza Dr
Concord Park Dr
Cole Creek Dr
Commerce Creek Dr
NORTH HOUSTON RD
FAIRBANKS NORTH HOUSTON RD
White Oak Bayou
Bond St
Fairbanks White Oak Rd
Bondale St
Oakwood Forest Dr
Oakwood Trace Ct
Oakwood Garden St
Kellwood Dr
Vernwood St
Mosewood St
Breezeway
Machala Ln
Shady Arbor Ln
Northcourt Rd
Bellknap Rd
Flintlock Rd
Gessner Rd
Okanella St
Talley Ln
Olga Ln
Grover Ln
Comanche Ln
Alfred Ln
Sussex Ln
Chickasaw Ln
Hardison Ln
Tanner Rd
Rosprim
Beeman Wy
Jameel Rd
Drysdale Ln
Sommermeyer St
W TIDWELL RD
FAIRBANKS
Fawndale Ln
Castleford St
Wilshire Pl Dr
Maxwell Rd
CARVERDALE PARK
Morocco Rd
Bamboo Rd
Porto Rico Rd
Tangiers Rd
Algiers Rd
Genard Rd
Houston
77041
Baythorne Dr
Cranswick Rd
Ellinger Ln
Grow Ln
Tavern St
Trentway St
Hillmont St
Pinemont Dr
Steadmont Dr
Wingfoot Rd
Freshwillow Dr
FRESHMEADOW PARK
Goodrum Rd
Stanford Ct
BLALOCK RD
Sequoia Dr
Thunderbird Rd
Stagecoach
Roy Bean
Pinewick Ln
A B C D E
1 2 3 4 5 6 7

SEE 3680 MAP
3682
SEE 3820 MAP

1:24,000
1 in. = 2000 ft.
0 0.25 0.5
miles

SEE 3542 MAP

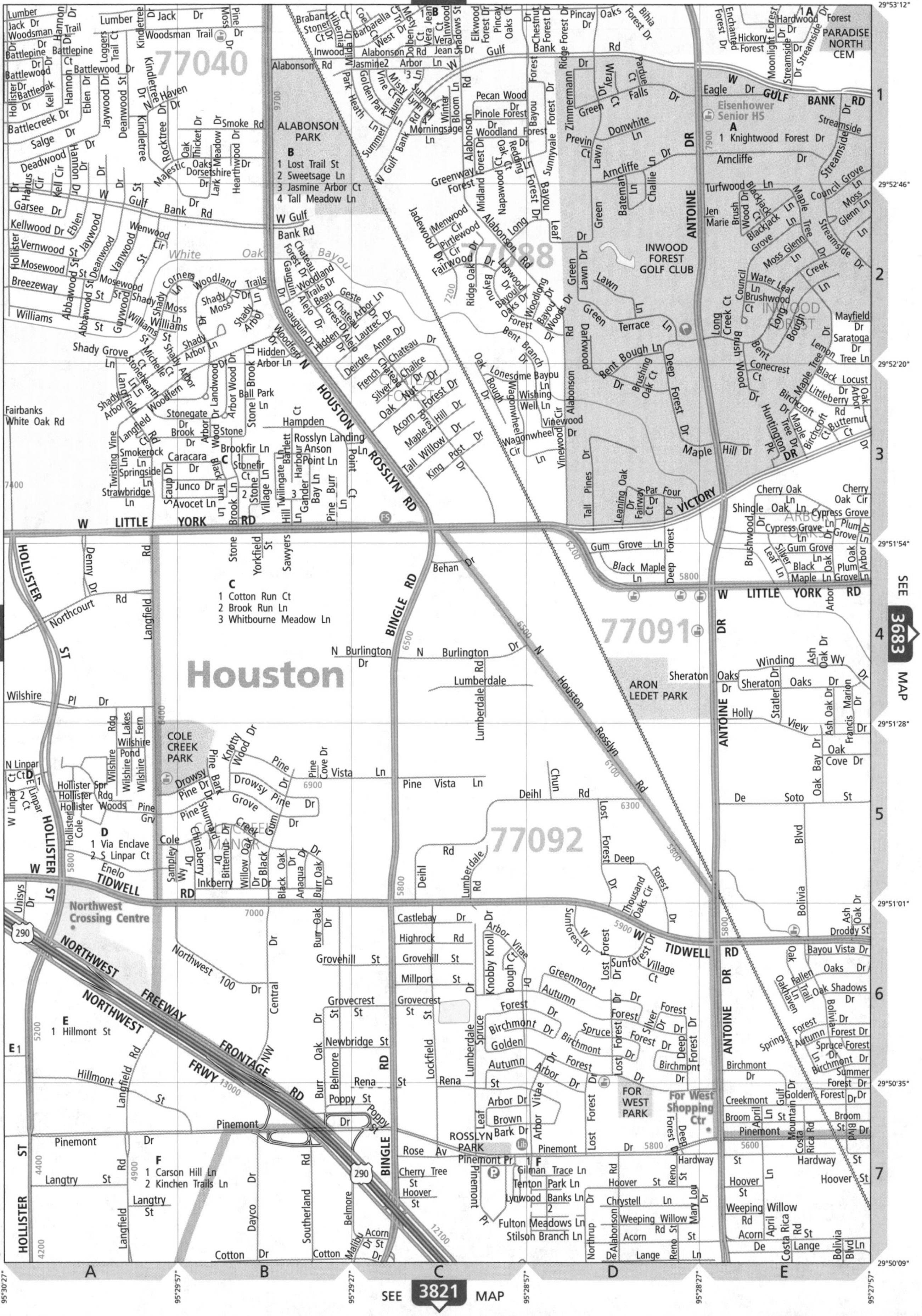
77040
77088
77091
77092
Houston
ALABONSON PARK
B
1 Lost Trail St
2 Sweetsage Ln
3 Jasmine Arbor Ct
4 Tall Meadow Ln
INWOOD FOREST GOLF CLUB
Eisenhower Senior HS
A
1 Knightwood Forest Dr
PARADISE NORTH CEM
C
1 Cotton Run Ct
2 Brook Run Ln
3 Whitbourne Meadow Ln
ARON LEDET PARK
COLE CREEK PARK
D
1 Via Enclave
2 S Linpar Ct
Northwest Crossing Centre
E
1 Hillmont St
F
1 Carson Hill Ln
2 Kinchen Trails Ln
ROSSLYN PARK
FOR WEST PARK
For West Shopping Ctr
W GULF BANK RD
W LITTLE YORK RD
W TIDWELL RD
HOLLISTER ST
BINGLE RD
ANTOINE DR
HOUSTON ROSSLYN RD
NORTHWEST FREEWAY
NORTHWEST FRWY FRONTAGE RD
VICTORY DR
Pinemont Dr
White Oak Bayou
SEE 3683 MAP
29°53'12"
29°52'46"
29°52'20"
29°51'54"
29°51'28"
29°51'01"
29°50'35"
29°50'09"
95°30'27"
95°29'57"
95°29'27"
95°28'57"
95°28'27"
95°27'57"
A
B
C
D
E
1
2
3
4
5
6
7

SEE 3821 MAP

1:24,000
1 in. = 2000 ft.
0 0.25 0.5
miles

SEE 3543 MAP

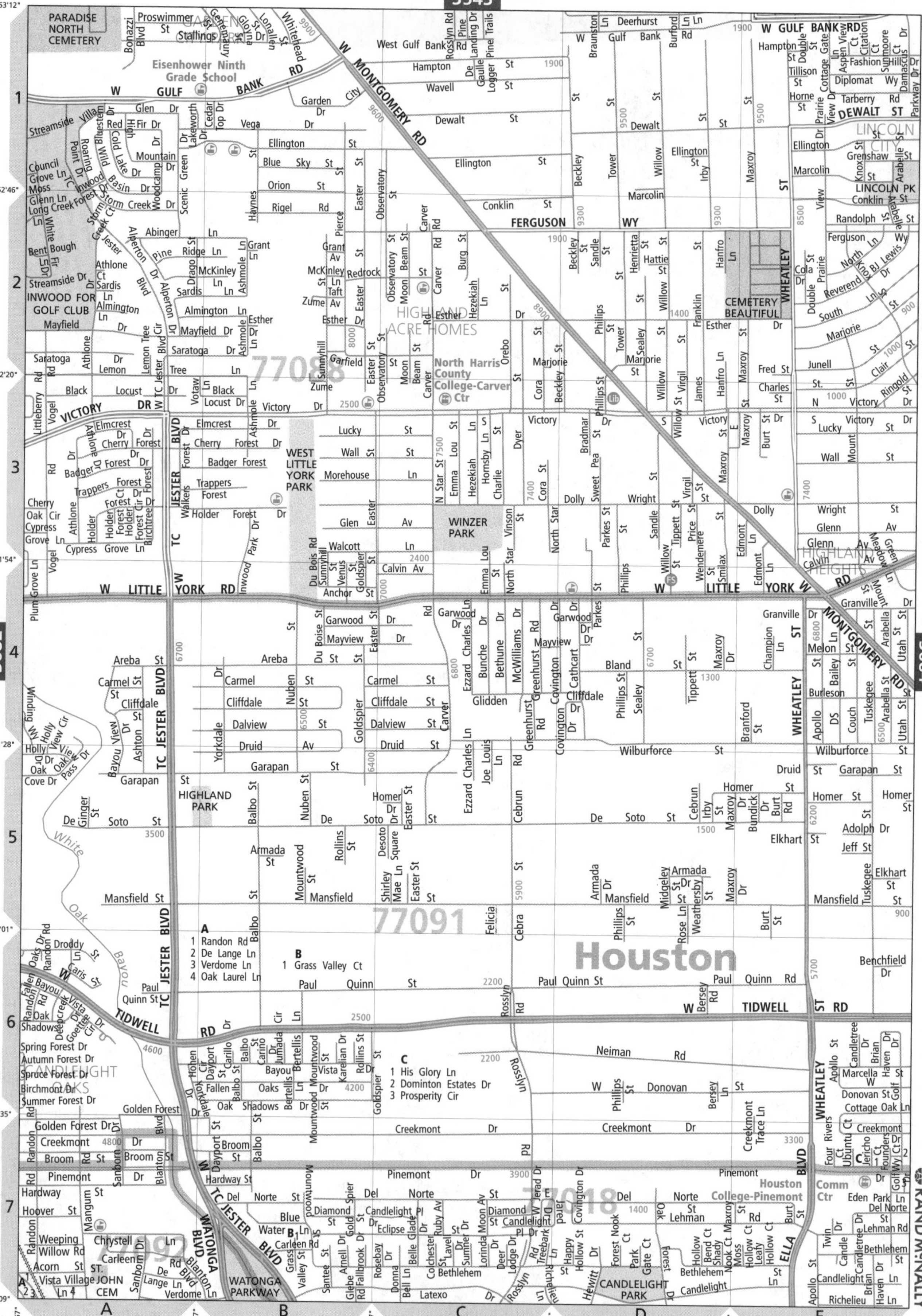
PARADISE NORTH CEMETERY
Eisenhower Ninth Grade School
W GULF BANK RD
W MONTGOMERY RD
West Gulf Bank Rd
Hampton St
Wavell St
Dewalt St
Ellington St
Conklin St
FERGUSON WY
Deerhurst Ln
W GULF BANK RD
DEWALT ST
LINCOLN CITY
LINCOLN PK
INWOOD FOREST GOLF CLUB
HIGHLAND ACRE HOMES
77088
North Harris County College-Carver Ctr
CEMETERY BEAUTIFUL
WHEATLEY
VICTORY DR
Victory Dr
WEST LITTLE YORK PARK
WINZER PARK
HIGHLAND HEIGHTS
W LITTLE YORK RD
TC JESTER BLVD
W TC JESTER BLVD
HIGHLAND PARK
77091
Houston
Paul Quinn St
W TIDWELL RD
Neiman Rd
Donovan St
Creekmont Dr
Pinemont Dr
Del Norte St
CANDLELIGHT OAKS
CANDLELIGHT PARK
Houston Community College-Pinemont
WATONGA BLVD
WATONGA PARKWAY
ST. JOHN CEM
Latexo Dr
77018
77092
White Oak Bayou
ELLA
A
1 Randon Rd
2 De Lange Ln
3 Verdome Ln
4 Oak Laurel Ln
B
1 Grass Valley Ct
C
1 His Glory Ln
2 Dominton Estates Dr
3 Prosperity Cir
29°53'12"
29°52'46"
29°52'20"
29°51'54"
29°51'28"
29°51'01"
29°50'35"
29°50'09"
95°27'57"
95°27'27"
95°26'57"
95°26'27"
95°25'57"
95°25'27"
A B C D E
1 2 3 4 5 6 7

SEE 3682 MAP
SEE 3684 MAP
SEE 3822 MAP

1:24,000
1 in. = 2000 ft.
0 0.25 0.5
miles

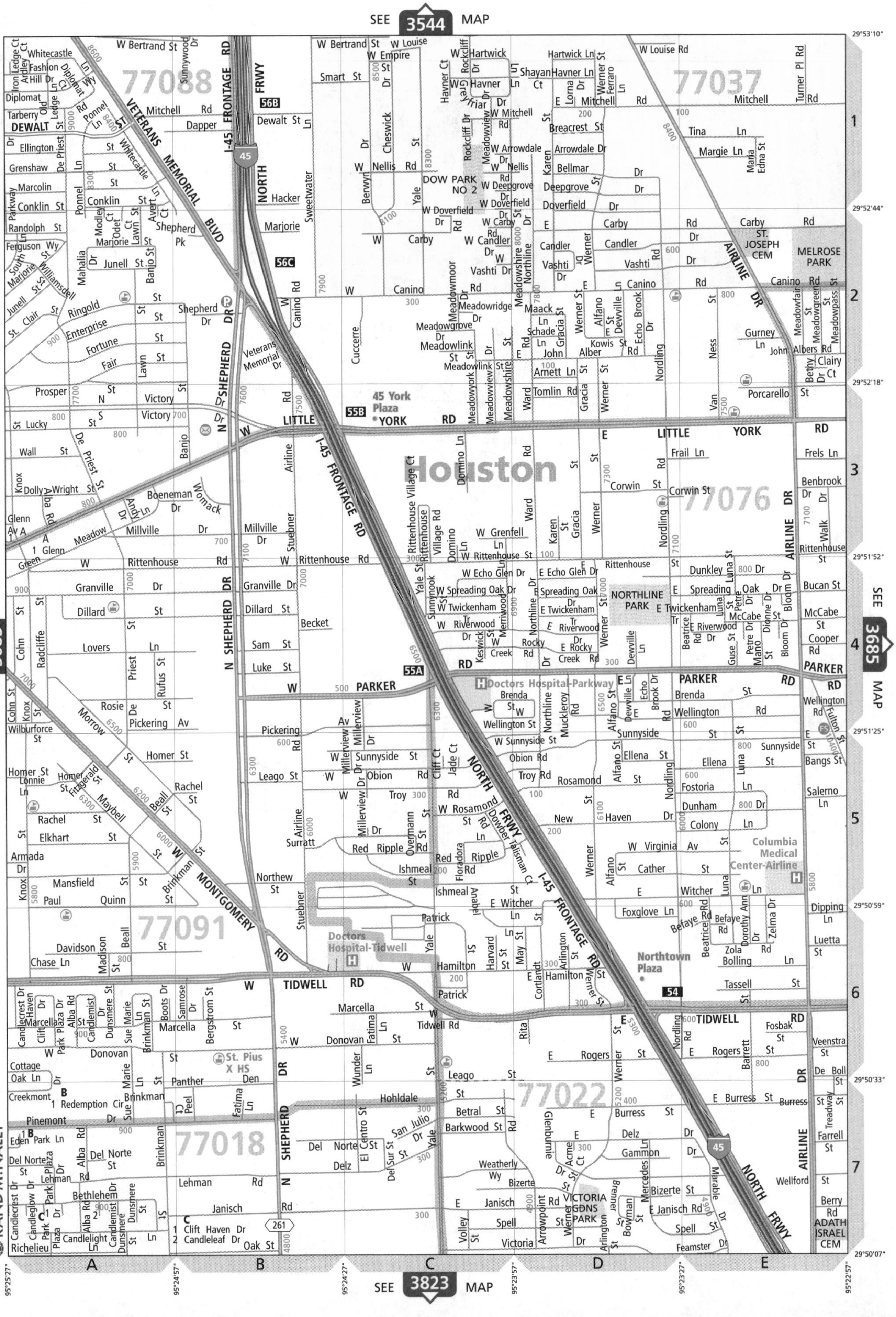
SEE 3544 MAP
SEE 3823 MAP
SEE 3685 MAP
Houston
77088
77037
77076
77091
77022
77018
I-45 FRONTAGE RD
NORTH FRWY
VETERANS MEMORIAL BLVD
N SHEPHERD DR
SHEPHERD DR
W LITTLE YORK RD
E LITTLE YORK RD
W PARKER RD
E PARKER RD
W MONTGOMERY RD
W TIDWELL RD
E TIDWELL RD
AIRLINE DR
DOW PARK NO 2
ST. JOSEPH CEM
MELROSE PARK
NORTHLINE PARK
45 York Plaza
Doctors Hospital-Parkway
Doctors Hospital-Tidwell
Columbia Medical Center-Airline
Northtown Plaza
St. Pius X HS
VICTORIA GDNS PARK
ADATH ISRAEL CEM
56B
56C
55B
55A
54
45
261
DEWALT
29°53'10"
29°52'44"
29°52'18"
29°51'52"
29°51'25"
29°50'59"
29°50'33"
29°50'07"
95°25'27"
95°24'57"
95°24'27"
95°23'57"
95°23'27"
95°22'57"
A
B
C
D
E
1
2
3
4
5
6
7

1:24,000
1 in. = 2000 ft.
0 0.25 0.5
miles

SEE 3545 MAP

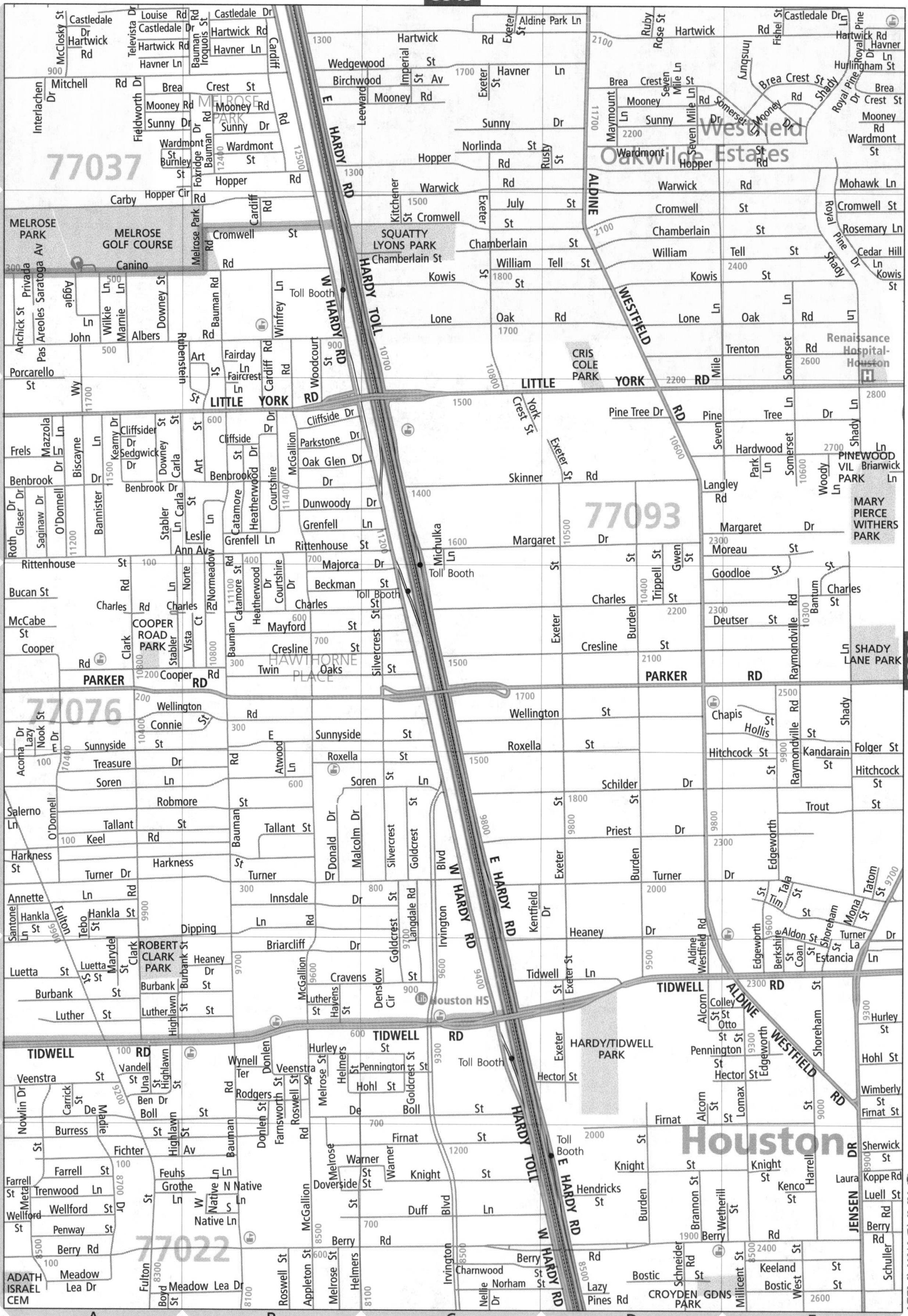
77037
77093
77076
77022
MELROSE PARK
MELROSE GOLF COURSE
SQUATTY LYONS PARK
CRIS COLE PARK
COOPER ROAD PARK
HAWTHORNE PLACE
ROBERT CLARK PARK
HARDY/TIDWELL PARK
PINEWOOD VIL PARK
MARY PIERCE WITHERS PARK
SHADY LANE PARK
ADATH ISRAEL CEM
Renaissance Hospital-Houston
Houston HS
Westfield Oakwilde Estates
Houston
CROYDEN GDNS PARK
HARDY TOLL RD
E HARDY RD
W HARDY RD
LITTLE YORK RD
PARKER RD
TIDWELL RD
ALDINE WESTFIELD RD
WESTFIELD RD
JENSEN DR
Toll Booth
Castledale Dr
Hartwick Rd
Havner Ln
Mitchell Rd
Brea Crest St
Mooney Rd
Sunny Dr
Wardmont St
Hopper Rd
Carby
Cromwell St
Canino Rd
Wedgewood
Birchwood
Norlinda St
Warwick Rd
July St
Chamberlain St
William Tell St
Kowis St
Lone Oak Rd
Trenton Rd
Porcarello St
Pine Tree Dr
Cliffside Dr
Parkstone Dr
Oak Glen Dr
Benbrook Dr
Dunwoody Dr
Grenfell Ln
Skinner Rd
Margaret Dr
Rittenhouse St
Majorca Dr
Beckman St
Charles Rd
Mayford St
Cresline St
Twin Oaks St
Bucan St
McCabe St
Cooper Rd
Wellington Rd
Connie St
Sunnyside St
Roxella St
Treasure Dr
Soren Ln
Robmore St
Schilder Dr
Tallant St
Keel Rd
Harkness St
Priest Dr
Turner Dr
Innsdale Dr
Dipping Ln
Briarcliff Dr
Heaney Dr
Cravens St
Burbank St
Luther St
Veenstra St
Rodgers St
Hohl St
Boll St
Burress St
Fichter Av
Firnat St
Knight St
Farrell St
Trenwood Ln
Wellford St
Penway St
Duff Ln
Berry Rd
Meadow Lea Dr
Native Ln
Hendricks St
Bostic St
Keeland St
Lazy Pines Rd
Norham St
Charnwood
Chapis St
Hitchcock St
Kandarain St
Folger St
Trout St
Estancia Ln
Hurley St
Wimberly St
Sherwick St
Luell St
Schuller Rd
95°22'57"
95°22'27"
95°21'57"
95°21'27"
95°20'57"
95°20'27"
29°53'10"
29°52'44"
29°52'18"
29°51'51"
29°51'25"
29°50'59"
29°50'33"
29°50'07"

SEE 3684 MAP

SEE 3824 MAP

1:24,000
1 in. = 2000 ft.
0 0.25 0.5
miles

SEE 3546 MAP

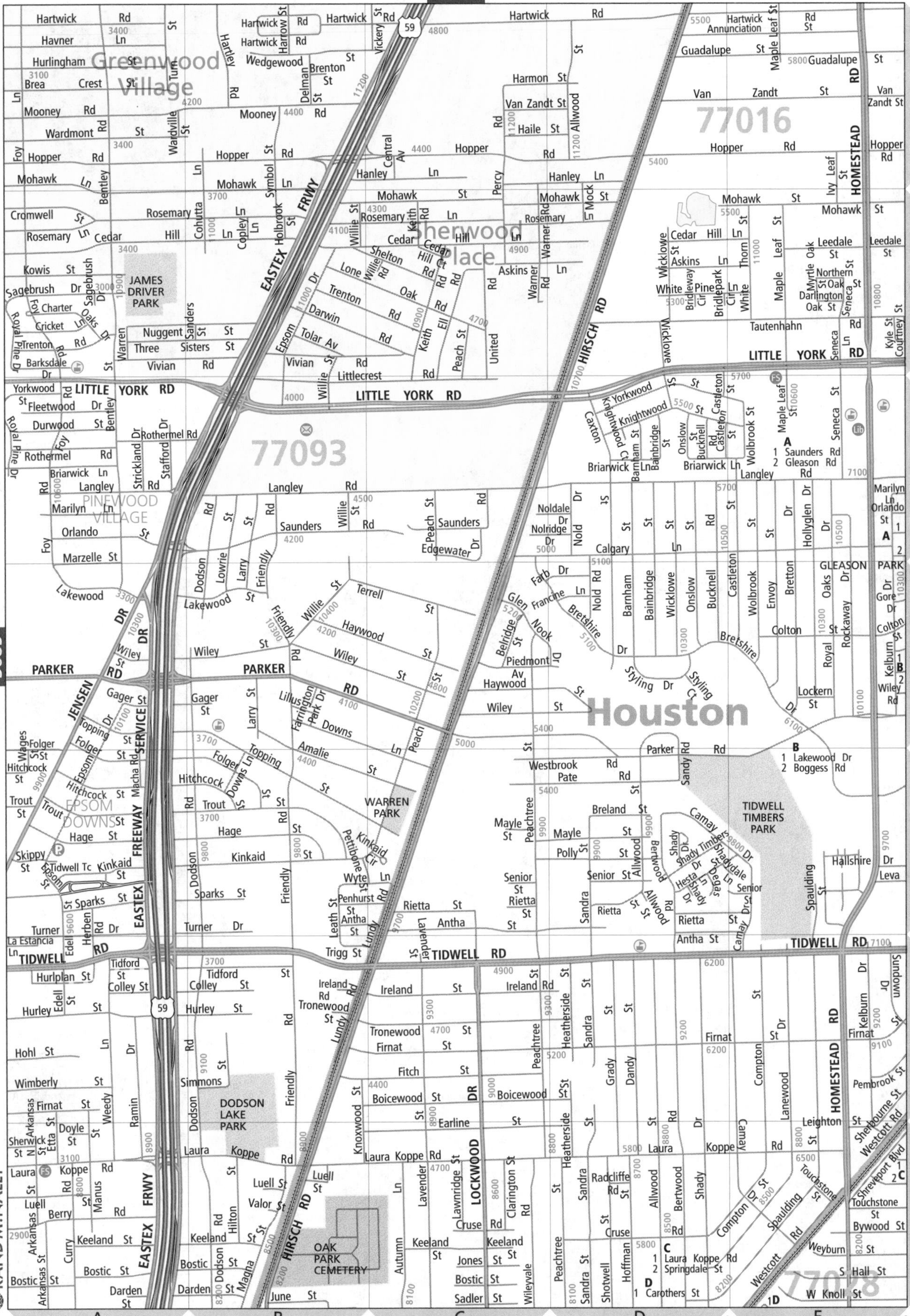
Greenwood Village
Sherwood Place
PINEWOOD VILLAGE
EPSOM DOWNS
Houston
77016
77093
77028
JAMES DRIVER PARK
WARREN PARK
TIDWELL TIMBERS PARK
DODSON LAKE PARK
OAK PARK CEMETERY
GLEASON PARK
EASTEX FRWY
EASTEX FREEWAY SERVICE
HIRSCH RD
HOMESTEAD RD
LITTLE YORK RD
PARKER RD
TIDWELL RD
JENSEN DR
LOCKWOOD DR
Hartwick Rd
Hopper Rd
Mohawk
Mooney Rd
Langley Rd
Saunders
Wiley St
Lakewood
Kinkaid
Laura Koppe Rd
Keeland St
Bostic St
Firnat
Ireland St
Guadalupe
Van Zandt St
Tautenhahn
Calgary Ln
Bretshire
Styling Dr
Westbrook
Pate
Breland St
Camay
Compton
Spaulding
Westcott
Shreveport Blvd
Touchstone
A 1 Saunders Rd 2 Gleason Rd
B 1 Lakewood Dr 2 Boggess Rd
C 1 Laura Koppe Rd 2 Springdale St
D 1 Carothers St
29°53'08"
29°52'41"
29°52'15"
29°51'49"
29°51'23"
29°50'57"
29°50'31"
29°50'04"
95°20'27"
95°19'57"
95°19'27"
95°18'57"
95°18'27"
95°17'57"
1
2
3
4
5
6
7
A
B
C
D
E

SEE 3687 MAP

SEE 3685 MAP

SEE 3825 MAP

1:24,000
1 in. = 2000 ft.
0 0.25 0.5 miles

SEE 3547 MAP

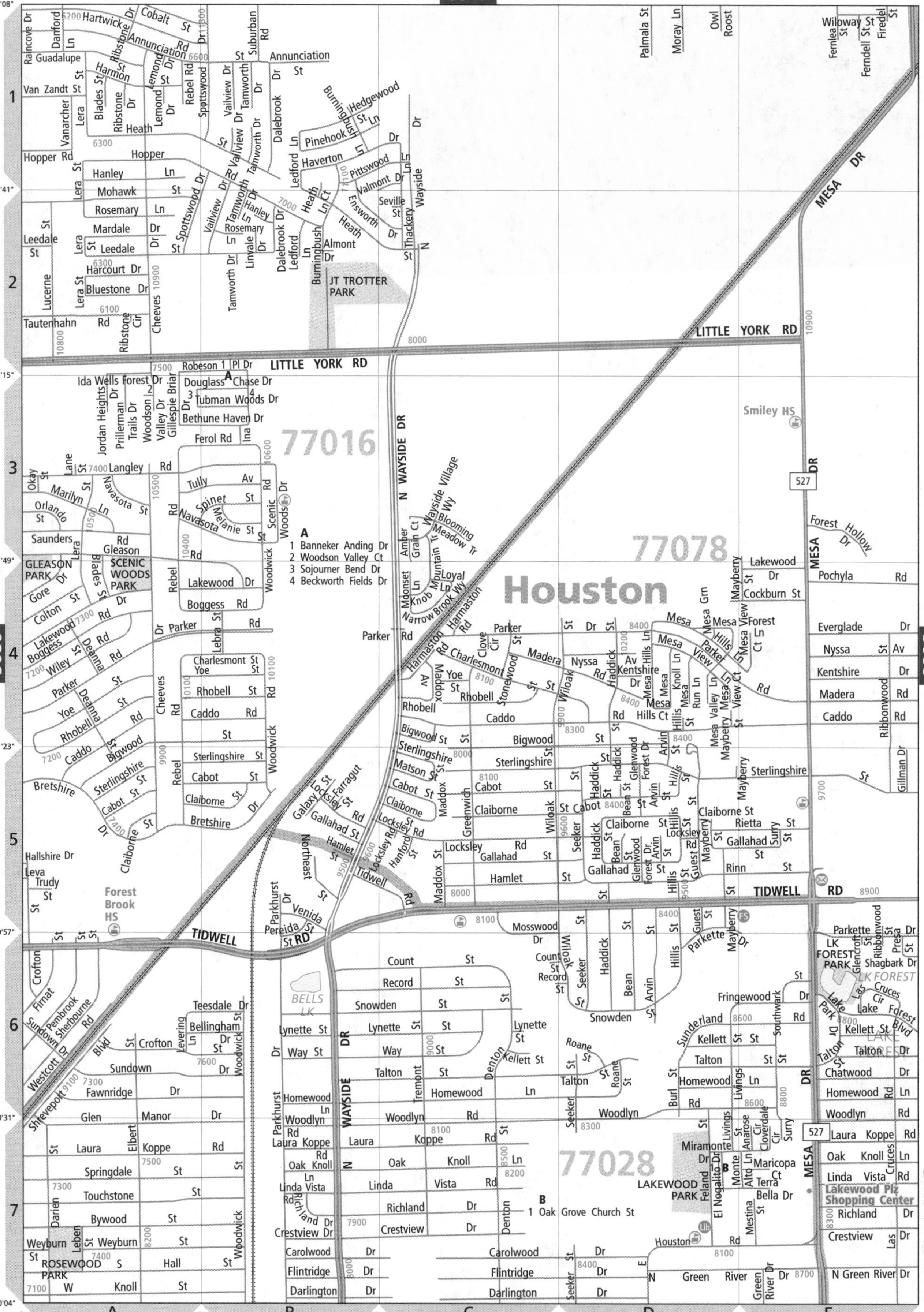
77016
77078
77028
Houston
LITTLE YORK RD
TIDWELL RD
N WAYSIDE DR
MESA DR
JT TROTTER PARK
GLEASON PARK
SCENIC WOODS PARK
Forest Brook HS
Smiley HS
BELLS LK
LAKEWOOD PARK
LK FOREST PARK
LK FOREST
Lakewood Plz Shopping Center
ROSEWOOD PARK
A
1 Banneker Anding Dr
2 Woodson Valley Ct
3 Sojourner Bend Dr
4 Beckworth Fields Dr
B
1 Oak Grove Church St
527
Hopper Rd
Parker Rd
Lakewood Dr
Caddo Rd
Bigwood St
Sterlingshire St
Cabot St
Claiborne St
Gallahad St
Hamlet St
Laura Koppe Rd
Oak Knoll Ln
Linda Vista Rd
Richland Dr
Crestview Dr
Carolwood Dr
Flintridge Dr
Darlington Dr
N Green River Dr
Woodlyn Rd
Homewood Ln
Talton St
Way St
Lynette St
Snowden St
Record St
Count St
Langley Rd
Saunders Rd
Gleason Rd
Mesa Hills Ln
Kentshire Dr
Madera Rd
Nyssa Av
Everglade Dr
Pochyla Rd
Cockburn St
Forest Hollow Dr
Tamworth Dr
Vailview Dr
Spottswood Dr
Leedale St
Harcourt Dr
Bluestone Dr
Tautenhahn Rd
Cheeves Dr
Rebel Rd
Woodwick St
Sundown Dr
Fawnridge Dr
Glen Manor Dr
Springdale St
Touchstone St
Bywood St
Weyburn St
Knoll St
Hall St
A B C D E
1 2 3 4 5 6 7

SEE 3686 MAP

SEE 3826 MAP

1:24,000
1 in. = 2000 ft.
0 0.25 0.5
miles

SEE 3548 MAP

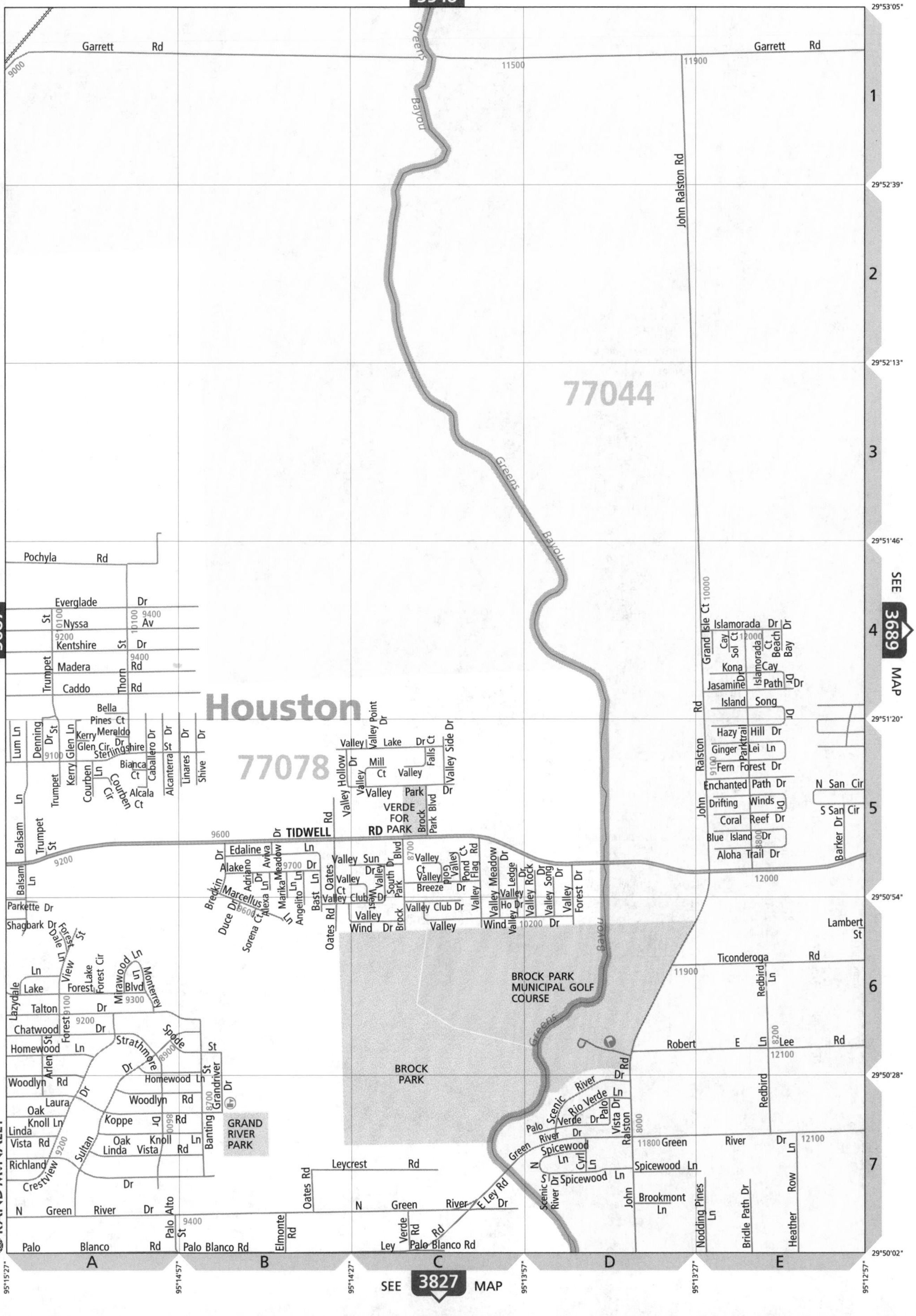
Garrett Rd
9000
11500
11900
Garrett Rd
Greens Bayou
John Ralston Rd
77044
Houston
77078
Pochyla Rd
Everglade Dr
Nyssa Av
Kentshire St Dr
Madera Rd
Caddo Rd
Trumpet St
Thorn
Bella Pines Ct
Kerry Meraldo Dr
Glen Cir
Sterlingshire
Bianca Ct
Caballero Dr
Alcantarra St
Linares Dr
Shive Dr
Lum Ln
Denning Dr St
Kerry Glen Ln
Courben Ln Cir
Courben Ct
Alcala Ct
Balsam Ln
Trumpet St
Valley Point Dr
Valley Lake Dr Ct
Valley Side Dr
Valley Hollow Dr
Mill Ct
Valley Falls Ct
Valley Park Dr
VERDE FOR PARK
Brock Park Blvd
TIDWELL RD
9600
9200
Edaline Ln
Alake
Adriano Dr
Aviva Ln
Meadow Ln
Marika Ln
Angelito Ln
Marcellus
Breckin
Duce Dr
Sorena Ct
Alexa Ln
Bast Ln
Oates Rd
Valley Sun Dr
Valley Club Dr
Valley Ct
West Valley
South Park Blvd
Valley Breeze Dr
Valley Gold
Pond Ct
Flag Rd
Valley Meadow Dr
Valley Ledge Dr
Valley Ho Dr
Valley Rock Dr
Valley Song Dr
Valley Forest Dr
Valley Wind Dr
10200
Parkette Dr
Shagbark Dr
Forest Dale Ln
Forest St
Lake Forest Cir
View Ln
Mirawood Ln
Monterrey
Lazydale
Lake Forest
Blvd
9300
Talton Dr
Chatwood Dr
Homewood Ln
Strathmore Dr
Spode
Arlen St
Woodlyn Rd
Homewood Ln
Grandriver Dr
Woodlyn Rd
Laura
Oak Knoll Ln
Linda Vista Rd
Koppe Dr Rd
Oak Knoll
Linda Vista Rd
Banting St
GRAND RIVER PARK
Richland
Crestview
Sultan
N Green River Dr
Palo Alto St
9400
Palo Blanco Rd
Elmonte Rd
Leycrest Rd
Oates Rd
N Green River E Ley Rd Dr
Verde Rd
Ley Rd
Palo Blanco Rd
BROCK PARK MUNICIPAL GOLF COURSE
BROCK PARK
Robert E Lee Rd
8200
12100
Ticonderoga Rd
11900
Redbird Ln
Redbird
Lambert St
Barker Dr
N San Cir
S San Cir
Grand Isle Ct
10000
Islamorada Dr
Cay
Sol Ct
Islamorada Ct
Beach Bay Dr
Kona Cay
Jasamine Dr
Path Dr
Island Song Dr
Hazy Hill Dr
Ginger Parktrail Lei Ln
Fern Forest Dr
Enchanted Path Dr
Drifting Winds Dr
Coral Reef Dr
Blue Island Dr
Aloha Trail Dr
12000
John Ralston Rd
9100
8800
Scenic River Dr
Rio Verde Ln
Palo Verde Dr
Vista Dr
Ralston
8000
11800 Green River Dr Ln
Spicewood Ln
Cyril Ln
N Spicewood
S Spicewood Ln
Scenic River Dr
Spicewood Ln
Brookmont Ln
John
Nodding Pines Ln
Bridle Path Dr
Heather Row
12100
1
2
3
4
5
6
7
A
B
C
D
E
29°53'05"
29°52'39"
29°52'13"
29°51'46"
29°51'20"
29°50'54"
29°50'28"
29°50'02"
95°15'27"
95°14'57"
95°14'27"
95°13'57"
95°13'27"
95°12'57"

SEE 3689 MAP

SEE 3827 MAP

1:24,000
1 in. = 2000 ft.
0 0.25 0.5
miles

SEE 3549 MAP

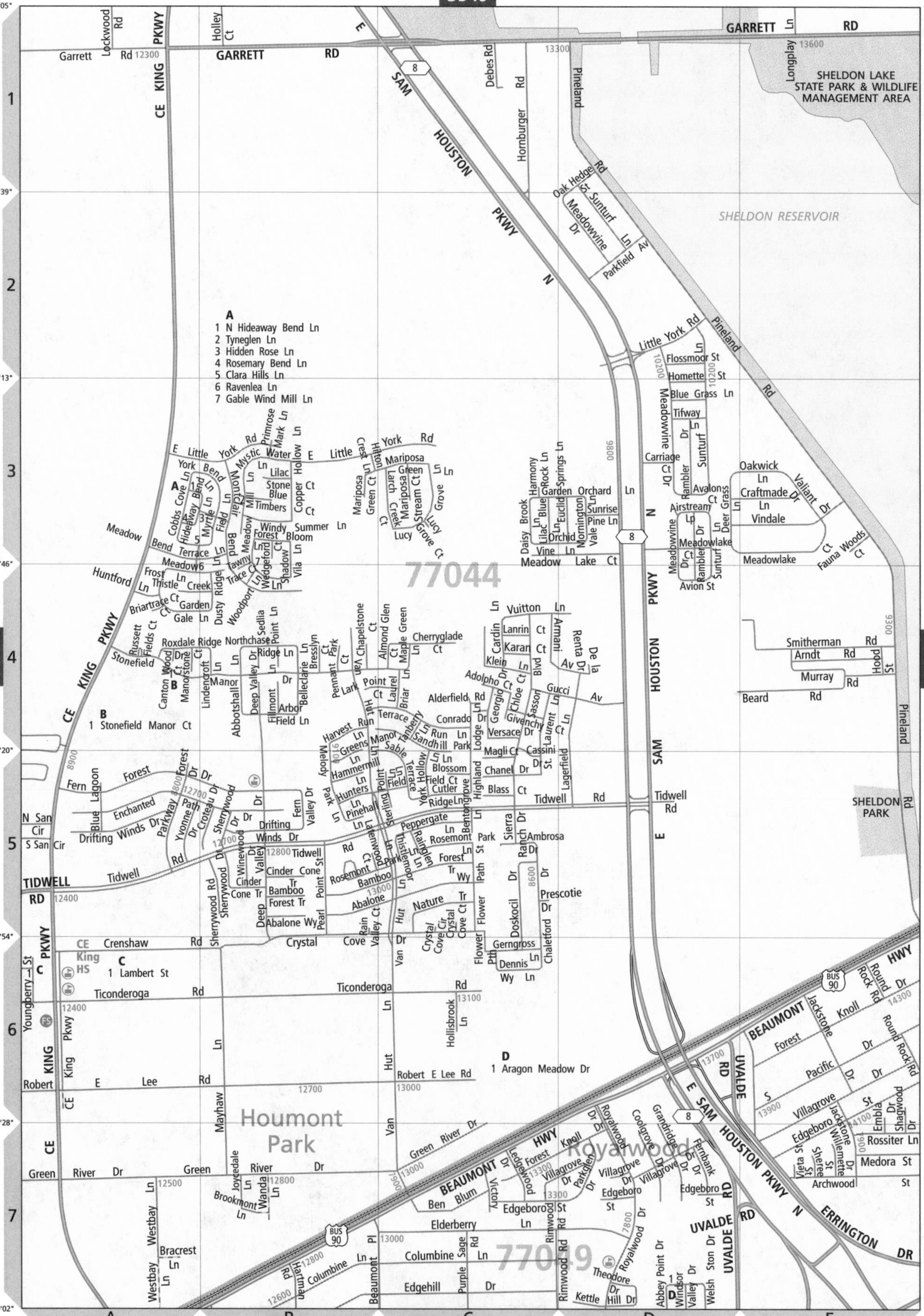
GARRETT RD
Garrett Rd 12300
Lockwood Rd
Holley Ct
CE KING PKWY
SAM HOUSTON PKWY N
E SAM HOUSTON PKWY
Debes Rd
Hornburger Rd
Pineland
SHELDON LAKE STATE PARK & WILDLIFE MANAGEMENT AREA
SHELDON RESERVOIR
Longplay
Oak Hedge Rd
Sunturf St
Meadowvine Dr
Parkfield Av
Little York Rd
Pineland Rd
Flossmoor St
Hometter St
Blue Grass Ln
Tifway
Carriage Ct
Oakwick Ln
Craftmade Dr
Valiant Dr
Vindale
Airstream Lp
Avalon Ct
Meadowlake
Fauna Woods Ct
Avion St
A
1 N Hideaway Bend Ln
2 Tyneglen Ln
3 Hidden Rose Ln
4 Rosemary Bend Ln
5 Clara Hills Ln
6 Ravenlea Ln
7 Gable Wind Mill Ln
E Little York Rd
Mariposa
Meadow Bend
Huntford Ln
Briartrace Ct
Gale Ln
Roxdale Ridge
Northchase
Stonefield
B
1 Stonefield Manor Ct
77044
Vuitton Ln
Alderfield Rd
Gucci Av
Smitherman Rd
Arndt Rd
Murray Rd
Beard Rd
Hood St
SHELDON PARK
Sheldon Rd
Tidwell Rd
TIDWELL RD
Fern Forest Dr
Enchanted Parkway
Drifting Winds Dr
N San Cir
S San Cir
Crystal Cove Dr
CE Crenshaw Rd
CE King HS
C
1 Lambert St
Ticonderoga Rd
Youngberry St
Robert E Lee Rd
Hut
Van
Hollisbrook Ln
D
1 Aragon Meadow Dr
Houmont Park
Mayhaw
Green River Dr
Joyedale Ln
Wanda Ln
Brookmont Ln
Westbay Ln
Bracrest Ln
BEAUMONT HWY
BUS 90
Royalwood
UVALDE RD
Elderberry Ln
Columbine Ln
Edgehill Dr
Beaumont Pl
Hartman Rd
77049
Theodore Dr
Kettle Dr
Hill Dr
Abbey Point Dr
Windsor Valley Dr
Welsh
Ston Dr
ERRINGTON DR
Round Rock Rd
Jackstone
Forest
Pacific Dr
Villagrove St
Edgeboro St
Rossiter Ln
Medora St
Archwood St
8
13300
13600
10200
9800
9300
8900
12700
12400
13100
13000
12800
12500
12600
14300
13900
13700

SEE 3688 MAP

SEE 3828 MAP

1:24,000
1 in. = 2000 ft.
0 0.25 0.5 miles

SEE 3550 MAP

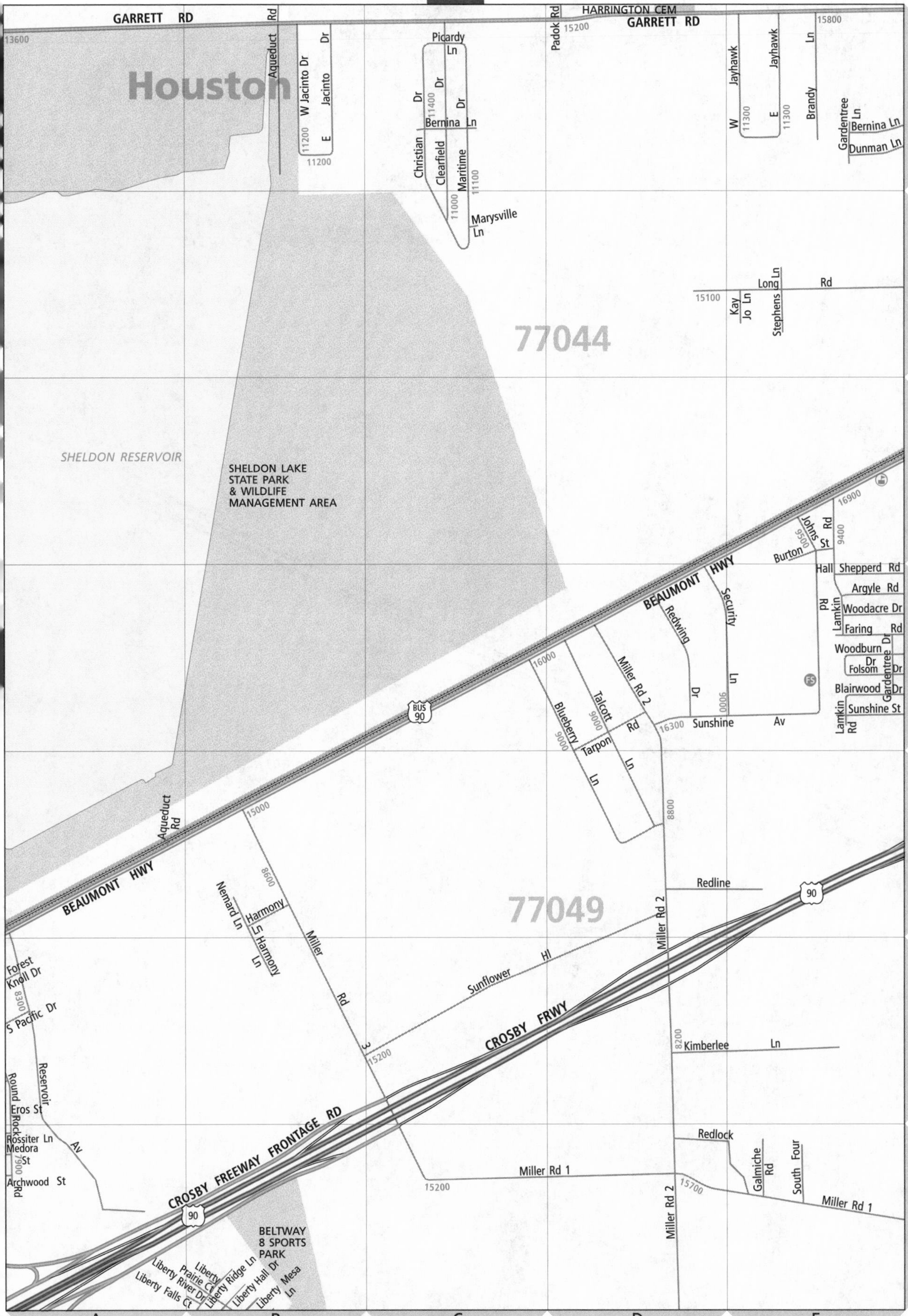

GARRETT RD
HARRINGTON CEM
Houston
Aqueduct Rd
W Jacinto Dr
E Jacinto Dr
Picardy Ln
Christian Dr
Clearfield Dr
Maritime Dr
Bernina Ln
Marysville Ln
Padok Rd
W Jayhawk
E Jayhawk
Brandy Ln
Gardentree Ln
Bernina Ln
Dunman Ln
Long Rd
Kay
Jo Ln
Stephens Ln
77044
SHELDON RESERVOIR
SHELDON LAKE STATE PARK & WILDLIFE MANAGEMENT AREA
BEAUMONT HWY
Johns Rd
Johns St
Burton
Hall
Shepperd Rd
Argyle Rd
Lamkin Rd
Woodacre Dr
Faring Rd
Woodburn Dr
Folsom Dr
Blairwood Dr
Sunshine St
Gardentree Dr
Redwing Dr
Security Ln
Miller Rd 2
Talcott Rd
Blueberry Ln
Tarpon Ln
Sunshine Av
77049
Nemard Ln
Harmony Ln
Miller Rd
Redline
Sunflower Hl
Forest Knoll Dr
S Pacific Dr
Reservoir Av
Round Rock Rd
Eros St
Rossiter Ln
Medora St
Archwood St
CROSBY FRWY
CROSBY FREEWAY FRONTAGE RD
Kimberlee Ln
Redlock
Galmiche Rd
South Four
Miller Rd 1
BELTWAY 8 SPORTS PARK
Liberty Falls Ct
Liberty River Dr
Prairie Ct
Liberty Ridge Ln
Liberty Hall Dr
Liberty Mesa Ln

SEE 3691 MAP

SEE 3829 MAP

SEE 3551 MAP

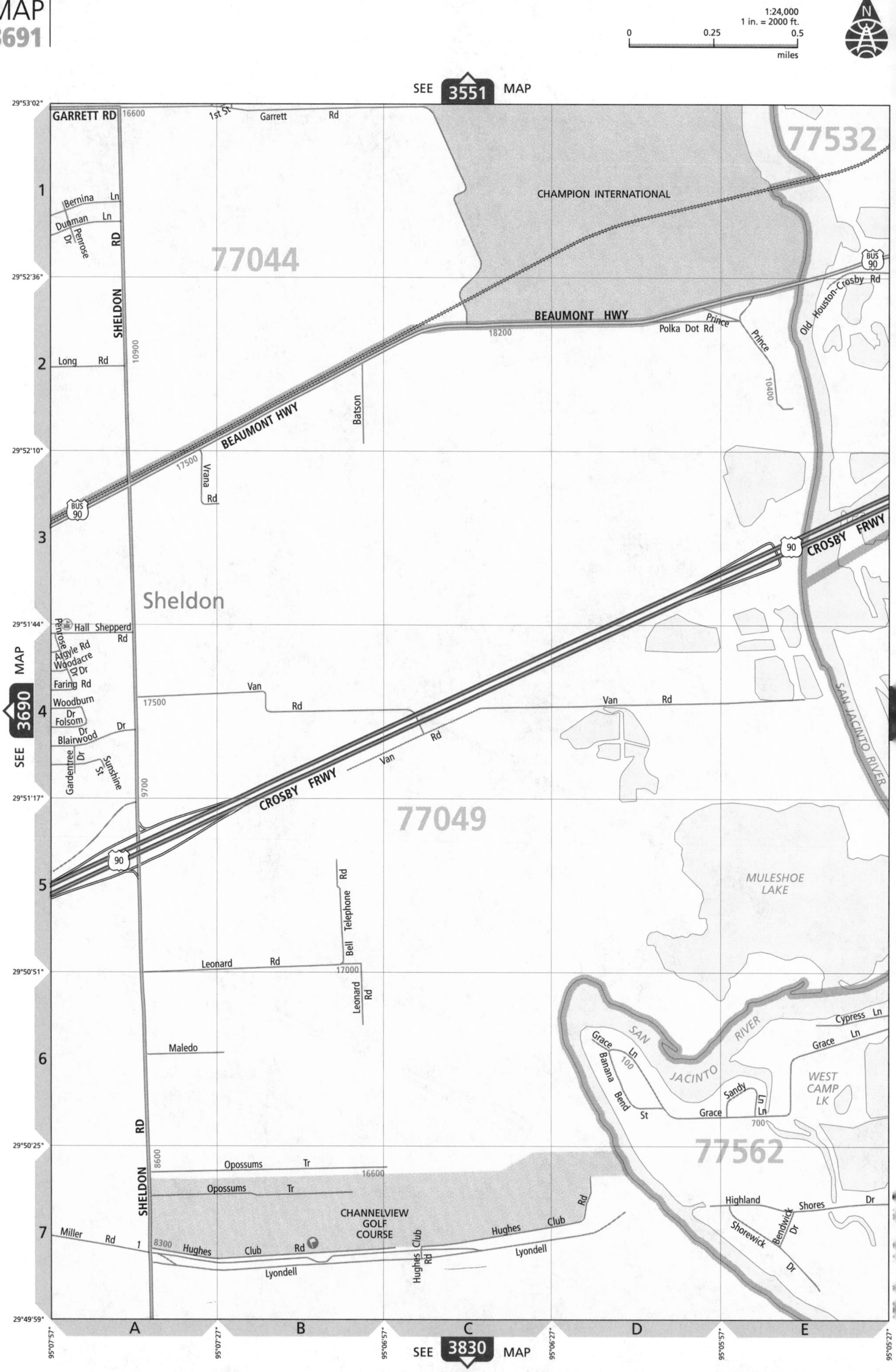
1:24,000
1 in. = 2000 ft.
0 0.25 0.5
miles
GARRETT RD
16600
1st St
Garrett Rd
77532
CHAMPION INTERNATIONAL
Bernina Ln
Dunman Ln
Penrose Dr
SHELDON RD
77044
BUS 90
Old Houston-Crosby Rd
BEAUMONT HWY
18200
Prince
Polka Dot Rd
Prince
10900
Long Rd
10400
Batson
BEAUMONT HWY
17500
Vrana Rd
CROSBY FRWY
90
Sheldon
Hall Shepperd Rd
Penrose
Argyle Rd
Woodacre Dr
Dr
Faring Rd
Van Rd
17500
Van Rd
Woodburn Dr
Folsom Dr
Blairwood Dr
Gardentree Dr
Sunshine St
Van Rd
SAN JACINTO RIVER
CROSBY FRWY
9700
77049
MULESHOE LAKE
Bell Telephone Rd
Leonard Rd
17000
Leonard Rd
Cypress Ln
Grace Ln
Grace Ln
SAN JACINTO RIVER
100
Banana Bend St
Maledo
Sandy Ln
Ln
Grace
700
WEST CAMP LK
77562
8600
Opossums Tr
16600
Opossums Tr
Highland Shores Dr
Shorewick Dr
Bendwick Dr
CHANNELVIEW GOLF COURSE
Miller Rd
8300
Hughes Club Rd
Hughes Club Rd
Hughes Club Rd
Lyondell
Lyondell
29°53'02"
29°52'36"
29°52'10"
29°51'44"
29°51'17"
29°50'51"
29°50'25"
29°49'59"
1
2
3
4
5
6
7
A
B
C
D
E
95°07'57"
95°07'27"
95°06'57"
95°06'27"
95°05'57"
95°05'27"

SEE 3690 MAP

SEE 3830 MAP

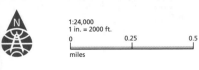

1:24,000
1 in. = 2000 ft.
0 0.25 0.5
miles

SEE 3552 MAP

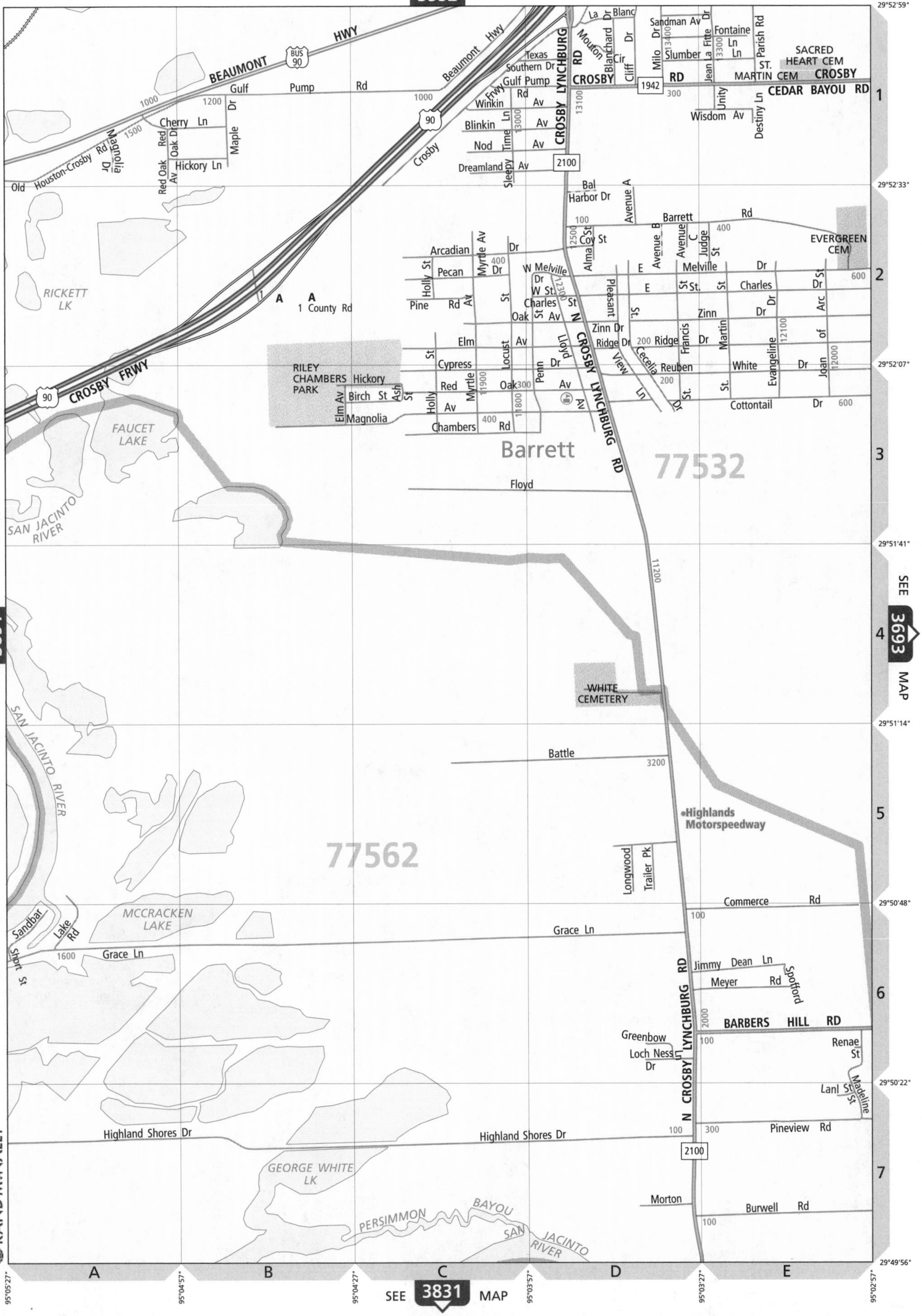
BEAUMONT HWY
BUS 90
Gulf Pump Rd
Beaumont Hwy
Texas Southern Dr
Gulf Pump Rd
Frwy
Winkin Av
Blinkin Av
Nod Av
Dreamland Av
Sleepy Ln
Time Ln
13000
Cherry Ln
Maple Dr
Red Oak Dr
Red Oak Av
Hickory Ln
Magnolia Dr
Old Houston-Crosby Rd
1000
1200
1500
90
Crosby
La Blanc
Mouton Cir
Blanchard Dr
Cliff Dr
Milo Dr
13400
Sandman Av
Slumber Ln
La Fitte Ln
Jean
Fontaine Ln
Parish Rd
3300
SACRED HEART CEM
ST. MARTIN CEM
CROSBY LYNCHBURG RD
13100
CROSBY 1942 RD
300
CROSBY CEDAR BAYOU RD
Unity
Wisdom Av
Destiny Ln
2100
Bal Harbor Dr
Avenue A
Barrett Rd
100
400
2500
Coy St
Alma St
Avenue B
Avenue C
Judge St
EVERGREEN CEM
Arcadian
Myrtle Av
Dr
400
Pecan Dr
W Melville Dr
Holly St
W St
12300
E Melville
E St.
St
Charles Dr
Dr
Arc St
600
Pine Rd
Av
St
Charles St
Oak St Av
Pleasant
St.
Zinn Dr
Dr
Francis
Martin
12100
of
Joan
12000
Elm Av
Locust
Lloyd
Zinn Dr
Ridge Dr
200 Ridge Dr
View
Cecelia
Reuben
200
White Dr
Evangeline
Cypress
St
RILEY CHAMBERS PARK
Hickory
Birch St
Ash St
Elm Av
Magnolia
Red
Myrtle
11900
Oak 300
Penn
Dr
Av
Ln
Dr
St.
St.
Cottontail Dr
600
Holly
Av
11800
Chambers 400 Rd
N CROSBY LYNCHBURG RD
A A
1 County Rd
CROSBY FRWY
90
RICKETT LK
FAUCET LAKE
Barrett
77532
Floyd
SAN JACINTO RIVER
11200
WHITE CEMETERY
Battle
3200
Highlands Motorspeedway
SAN JACINTO RIVER
77562
Longwood
Trailer Pk
Commerce Rd
100
Grace Ln
MCCRACKEN LAKE
Sandbar
Lake Rd
Short St
1600
Grace Ln
N CROSBY LYNCHBURG RD
Jimmy Dean Ln
Spofford
Meyer Rd
2000
BARBERS HILL RD
100
Greenbow Ln
Loch Ness Dr
Renae St
Lanl St
Madeline St
Highland Shores Dr
Highland Shores Dr
100
300
Pineview Rd
2100
GEORGE WHITE LK
Morton
Burwell Rd
100
PERSIMMON BAYOU
SAN JACINTO RIVER
1
2
3
4
5
6
7
A
B
C
D
E
29°52'59"
29°52'33"
29°52'07"
29°51'41"
29°51'14"
29°50'48"
29°50'22"
29°49'56"
95°05'27"
95°04'57"
95°04'27"
95°03'57"
95°03'27"
95°02'57"

SEE 3693 MAP

SEE 3831 MAP

1:24,000
1 in. = 2000 ft.
0 0.25 0.5
miles

SEE 3553 MAP

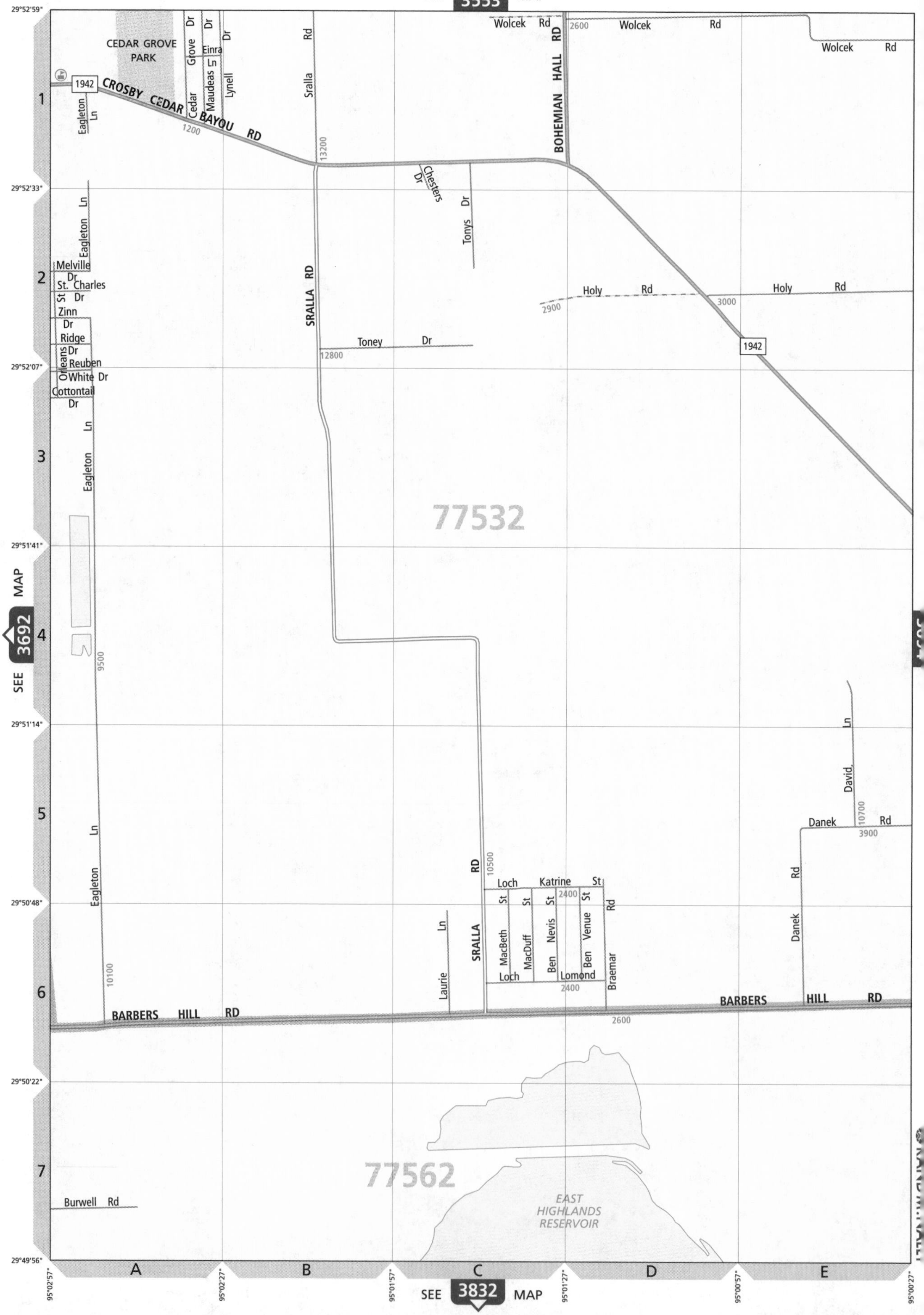
CEDAR GROVE PARK
1942
CROSBY CEDAR BAYOU RD
1200
Eagleton Ln
Cedar Grove Dr
Maudeas Ln
Einra Dr
Lynell Dr
Sralla Rd
13200
Wolcek Rd
2600
BOHEMIAN HALL RD
Chesters Dr
Tonys Dr
SRALLA RD
Melville Dr
St. Charles St
Dr
Zinn Dr
Ridge Dr
Orleans
Reuben
White Dr
Cottontail Dr
Toney Dr
12800
Holy Rd
2900
3000
77532
9500
David Ln
10700
Danek Rd
3900
10500
Loch St
Katrine St
2400
MacBeth St
MacDuff St
Ben Nevis St
Ben Venue St
Lomond
Braemar Rd
Laurie Ln
10100
BARBERS HILL RD
2600
77562
EAST HIGHLANDS RESERVOIR
Burwell Rd
29°52'59"
29°52'33"
29°52'07"
29°51'41"
29°51'14"
29°50'48"
29°50'22"
29°49'56"
95°02'57"
95°02'27"
95°01'57"
95°01'27"
95°00'57"
95°00'27"
1
2
3
4
5
6
7
A
B
C
D
E

SEE 3692 MAP

SEE 3832 MAP

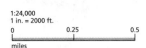

1:24,000
1 in. = 2000 ft.
0 0.25 0.5
miles

SEE 3554 MAP

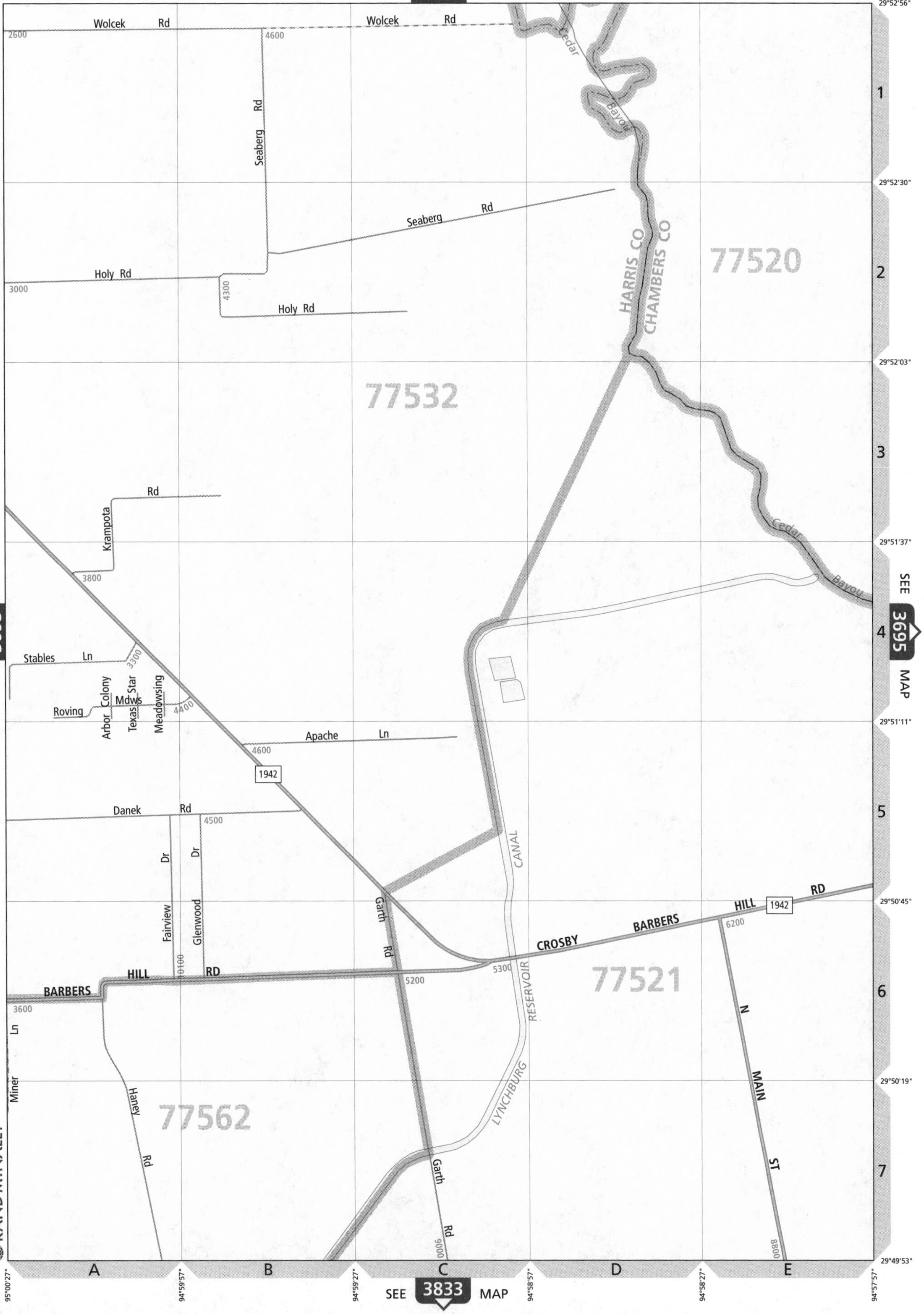
Wolcek Rd
2600
4600
Seaberg Rd
Seaberg Rd
Holy Rd
3000
4300
Holy Rd
Cedar Bayou
HARRIS CO
CHAMBERS CO
77520
77532
Krampota Rd
3800
Stables Ln
3300
Roving
Arbor
Colony
Mdws
Texas
Star
Meadowsing
4400
Apache Ln
4600
1942
Danek Rd
4500
Fairview Dr
Glenwood Dr
Garth Rd
CANAL
RESERVOIR
LYNCHBURG
CROSBY BARBERS HILL RD
1942
6200
5300
5200
10100
BARBERS HILL RD
3600
77521
N MAIN ST
Miner Ln
Haney Rd
77562
Garth Rd
9000
8800
1
2
3
4
5
6
7
A
B
C
D
E
29°52'56"
29°52'30"
29°52'03"
29°51'37"
29°51'11"
29°50'45"
29°50'19"
29°49'53"
95°00'27"
94°59'57"
94°59'27"
94°58'57"
94°58'27"
94°57'57"

SEE 3695 MAP

SEE 3833 MAP

SEE B MAP

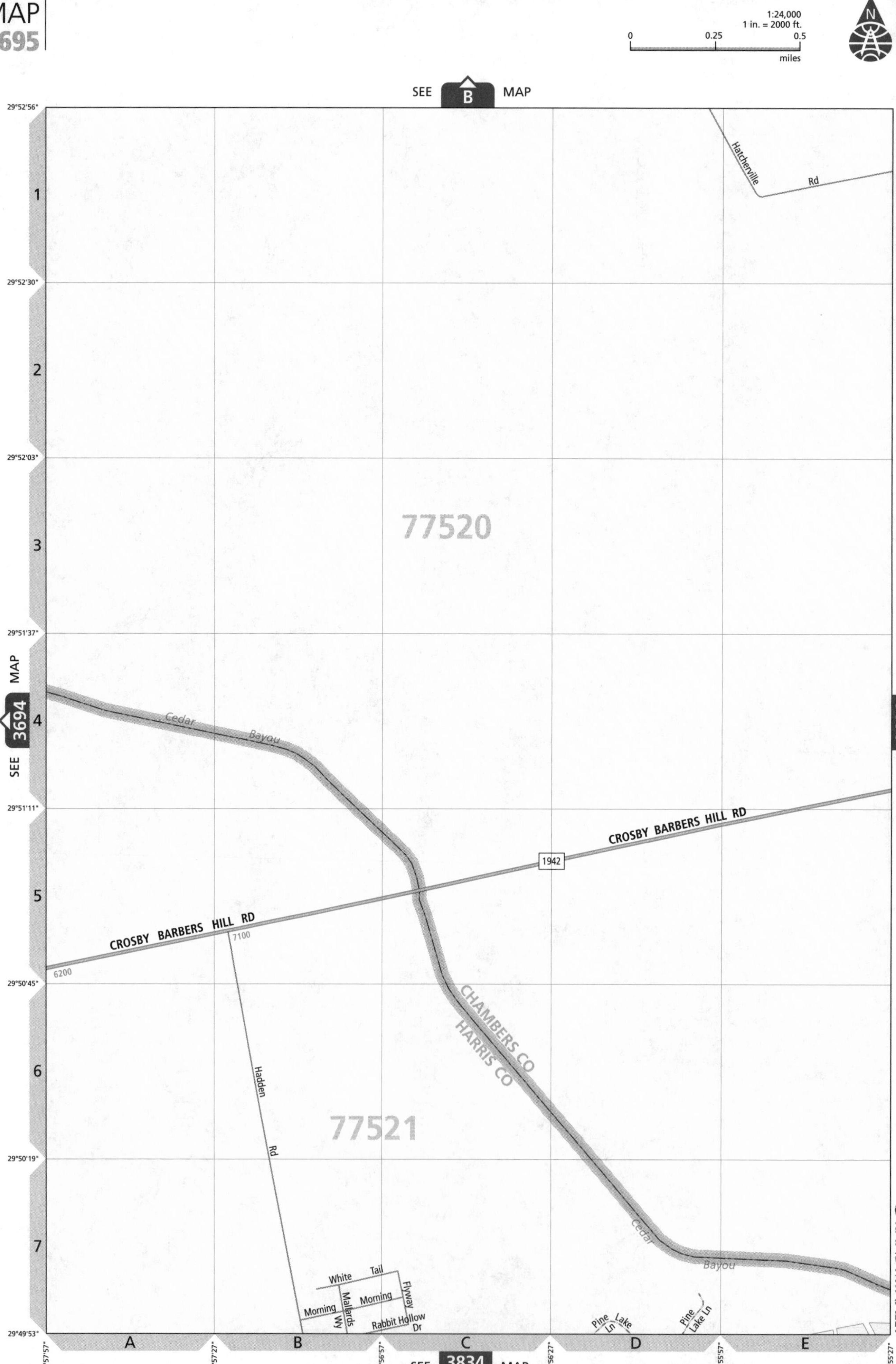
1:24,000
1 in. = 2000 ft.
0
0.25
0.5
miles
N
29°52'56"
29°52'30"
29°52'03"
29°51'37"
29°51'11"
29°50'45"
29°50'19"
29°49'53"
1
2
3
4
5
6
7
A
B
C
D
E
94°57'57"
94°57'27"
94°56'57"
94°56'27"
94°55'57"
94°55'27"
Hatcherville
Rd
77520
Cedar
Bayou
CROSBY BARBERS HILL RD
1942
CROSBY BARBERS HILL RD
7100
6200
CHAMBERS CO
HARRIS CO
Hadden
Rd
77521
Cedar
Bayou
White
Tail
Flyway
Morning
Mallards
Morning
Wy
Rabbit Hollow
Dr
Pine
Lake
Ln
Pine
Lake Ln

SEE 3694 MAP

SEE 3834 MAP

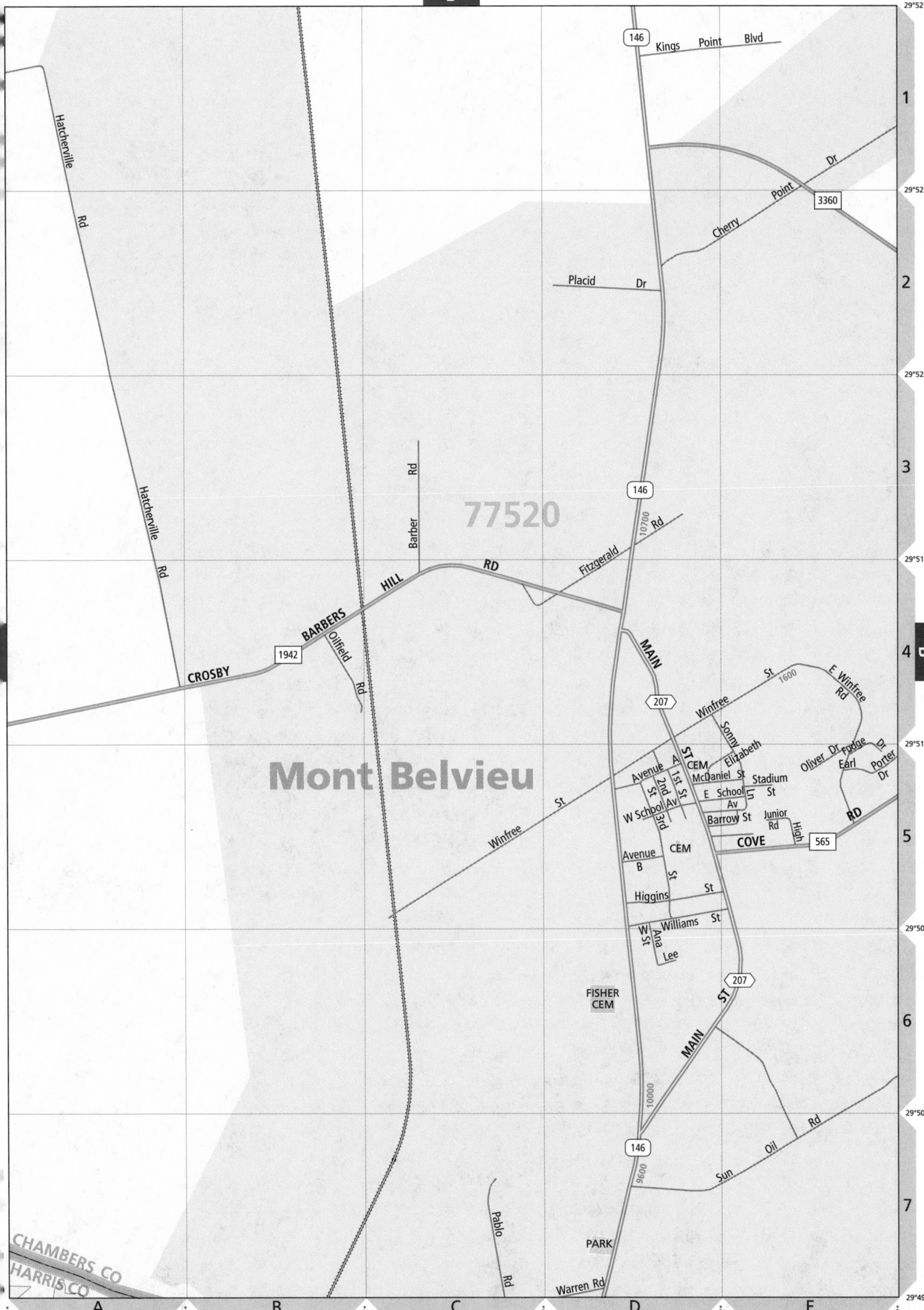
N
1:24,000
1 in. = 2000 ft.
0 0.25 0.5
miles
SEE B MAP
146
Kings Point Blvd
Hatcherville Rd
Dr
Point
3360
Cherry
Placid Dr
146
Barber Rd
77520
10700
Fitzgerald Rd
BARBERS HILL RD
Hatcherville Rd
1942
CROSBY
Oilfield Rd
MAIN
207
Winfree St
1600
E Winfree Rd
Sonny
Elizabeth
Mont Belvieu
Winfree St
Avenue A
ST
CEM
McDaniel St
2nd Av
1st St
3rd St
Stadium St
E School Av
Ln
W School
Barrow St
Junior High Rd
Oliver Dr
Fudge Dr
Earl
Porter Dr
RD
COVE
565
Avenue B
CEM
St
Higgins St
Williams St
W St
Ana Lee
207
FISHER CEM
ST
MAIN
10000
146
Rd
Oil
Sun
9600
Pablo Rd
PARK
Warren Rd
CHAMBERS CO
HARRIS CO
A B C D E
1 2 3 4 5 6 7
29°52'52"
29°52'26"
29°52'00"
29°51'34"
29°51'08"
29°50'42"
29°50'15"
29°49'49"
94°55'27"
94°54'57"
94°54'27"
94°53'57"
94°53'27"
94°52'57"

SEE B MAP

SEE 3835 MAP

1:24,000
1 in. = 2000 ft.

SEE B MAP

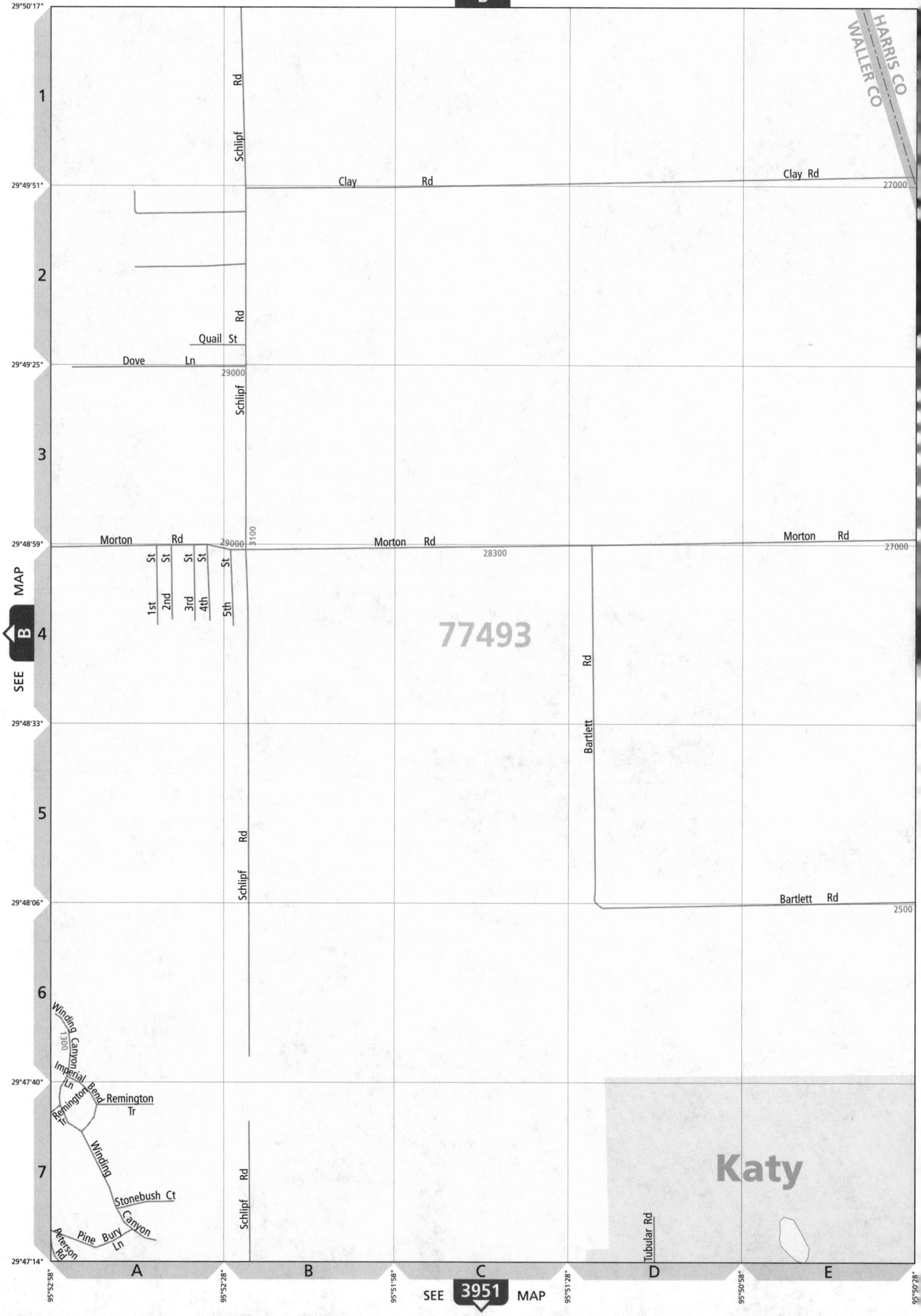
29°50'17"
29°49'51"
29°49'25"
29°48'59"
29°48'33"
29°48'06"
29°47'40"
29°47'14"
1
2
3
4
5
6
7
A
B
C
D
E
95°52'58"
95°52'28"
95°51'58"
95°51'28"
95°50'58"
95°50'28"
HARRIS CO
WALLER CO
Schlipf Rd
Clay Rd
Clay Rd
27000
Quail St
Dove Ln
29000
Morton Rd
29000
3100
Morton Rd
28300
Morton Rd
27000
1st St
2nd St
3rd St
4th St
5th St
77493
Bartlett Rd
Bartlett Rd
2500
Winding Canyon
1300
Imperial Ln
Bend
Remington Tr
Remington Tr
Winding
Stonebush Ct
Canyon
Pine Bury Ln
Peterson Rd
Tubular Rd
Katy

SEE B MAP

SEE 3951 MAP

N
1:24,000
1 in. = 2000 ft.
0 0.25 0.5
miles

SEE B MAP

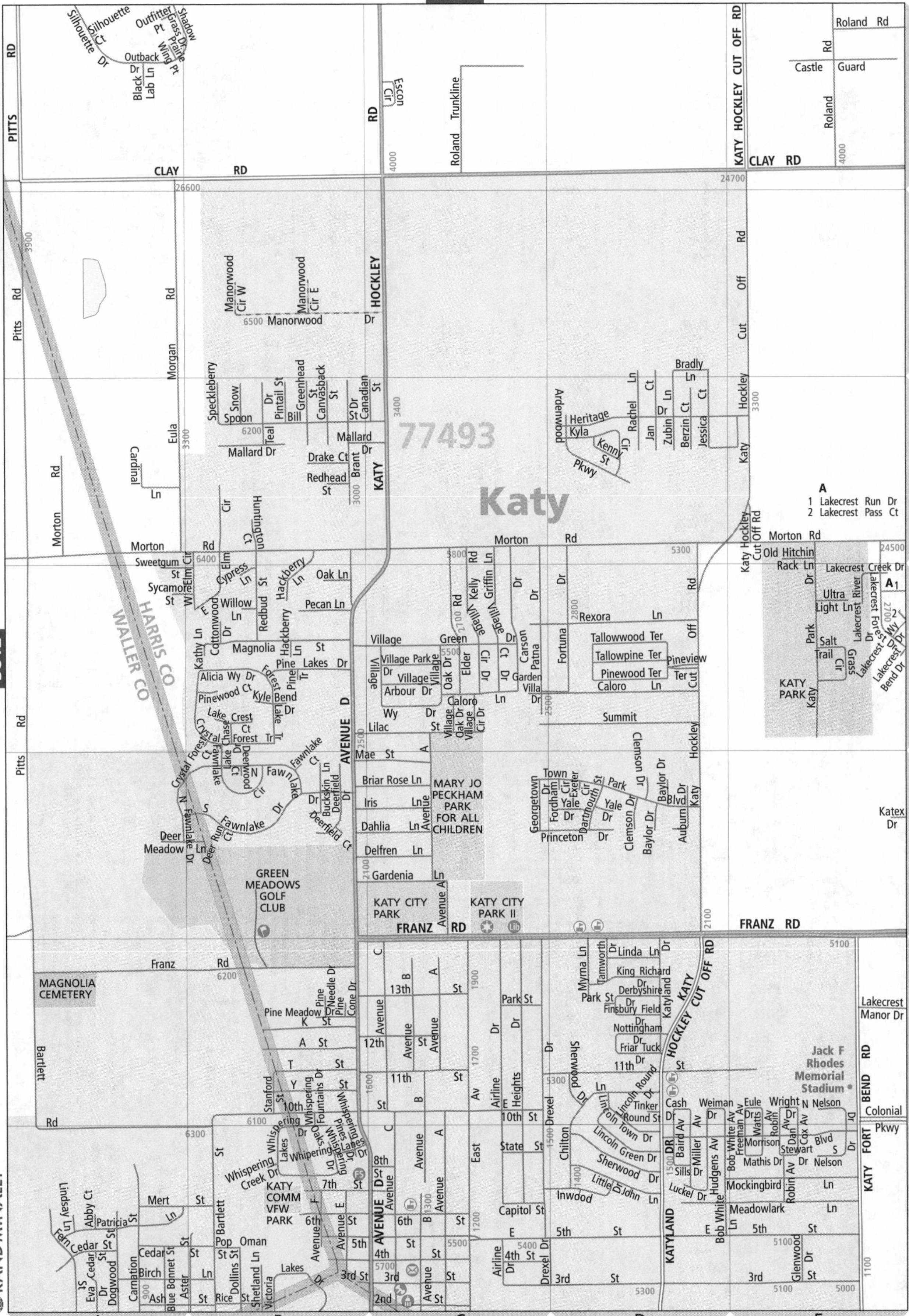
Katy
77493
CLAY RD
PITTS RD
KATY HOCKLEY RD
KATY HOCKLEY CUT OFF RD
Morton Rd
Roland Rd
Castle
Guard
Trunkline
Escon Cir
Manorwood
Manorwood Cir W
Manorwood Cir E
Morgan Rd
Eula
Cardinal Ln
Mallard Dr
Drake Ct
Redhead St
Brant Dr
Speckleberry
Snow
Spoon
Teal
Pintail St
Greenhead
Bill
Canvasback St
Canadian St
Huntington Ct
Heritage
Kyla
Kenny Cir
Ardenwood
Pkwy
Rachel Ct
Jan Dr
Zubin Ln
Berzin Ct
Jessica Ct
Bradly Ln
A
1 Lakecrest Run Dr
2 Lakecrest Pass Ct
Sweetgum St
Sycamore St
Elm
Cypress Ln
Willow Ln
Hackberry Ln
Oak Ln
Pecan Ln
Redbud St
Magnolia St
Kathy Ln
Cottonwood Dr
Pine Lakes Dr
Alicia Wy
Pinewood Ct
Kyle Bend Dr
Lake Crest Ct
Crystal Forest Ct
Forest Tr
Fawnlake Ct
Fawnlake Dr
Deerwood Ct
Deer Run Ct
Deer Meadow Ln
Buckskin Ln
Deerfield Dr
Deerfield Ct
HARRIS CO
WALLER CO
AVENUE D
Village
Village Park Dr
Arbour Dr
Green
Oak Dr
Elder
Kelly
Griffin Ln
Carson
Patna
Garden Villa Dr
Caloro Ln
Lilac St
Mae St
Briar Rose Ln
Iris Ln
Dahlia Ln
Delfren Ln
Gardenia Ln
Avenue A
MARY JO PECKHAM PARK FOR ALL CHILDREN
Fortuna Dr
Rexora Ln
Tallowood Ter
Tallowpine Ter
Pinewood Ter
Pineview Ter
Summit
Clemson Dr
Baylor Dr
Auburn Blvd
Town Park Dr
Georgetown
Fordham Cir
Exeter Cir
Yale Dr
Dartmouth St
Princeton Dr
Old Hitchin Rack Ln
Lakecrest Creek Dr
Ultra Light Ln
Salt Trail Cir
Grass
Lakecrest River Dr
Lakecrest Forest Dr
Lakecrest Bend Dr
KATY PARK
Katex Dr
GREEN MEADOWS GOLF CLUB
KATY CITY PARK
KATY CITY PARK II
FRANZ RD
Franz Rd
MAGNOLIA CEMETERY
Bartlett Rd
Pine Meadow Dr
Pine Needle Dr
Pine Cone Dr
K St
A St
T St
Y St
13th St
12th St
11th St
10th St
Stanford
Whispering Fountains Dr
Whispering Pines Dr
Whispering Oaks Dr
Whispering Lakes Dr
Whispering Creek Dr
KATY COMM VFW PARK
8th St
7th St
6th St
5th St
4th St
3rd St
2nd St
East Av
Airline Dr
Heights
Park St
State St
Capitol St
Drexel Dr
Chilton
Inwood
Sherwood Dr
Myrna Ln
Tamworth Dr
Linda Ln
King Richard Dr
Derbyshire Dr
Finsbury Field Dr
Nottingham Dr
Friar Tuck Dr
Lincoln Round Dr
Tinker Round St
Lincoln Town Dr
Lincoln Green Dr
Little John Ln
Luckel Dr
KATYLAND DR
Cash Dr
Baird Av
Miller Av
Sills Dr
Hudgens Av
Bob White Av
Freeman Av
Weiman Dr
Eule Dr
Watts Av
Morrison Dr
Mathis Dr
Wright Av
Robin Av
Cox Av
Stewart Blvd
Nelson
Mockingbird Ln
Meadowlark Ln
Glenwood Dr
Lakecrest Manor Dr
Colonial Pkwy
Jack F Rhodes Memorial Stadium
KATY FORT BEND RD
Mert St
Lindsay Ln
Abby Ct
Patricia St
Fern Ln
Cedar St
Eva Dr
Dogwood
Carnation
Cedar St
Birch
Blue Bonnet St
Aster
Ash
Pop Oman St
Dollins St
Rice St
Shetland Ln
Victoria
Lakes Dr
1 2 3 4 5 6 7
A B C D E
29°50'16"
29°49'50"
29°49'24"
29°48'58"
29°48'31"
29°48'05"
29°47'39"
29°47'13"
95°50'28"
95°49'59"
95°49'29"
95°48'59"
95°48'29"
95°47'59"

SEE 3814 MAP

SEE 3952 MAP

1:24,000
1 in. = 2000 ft.
0 0.25 0.5
miles

SEE 3675 MAP

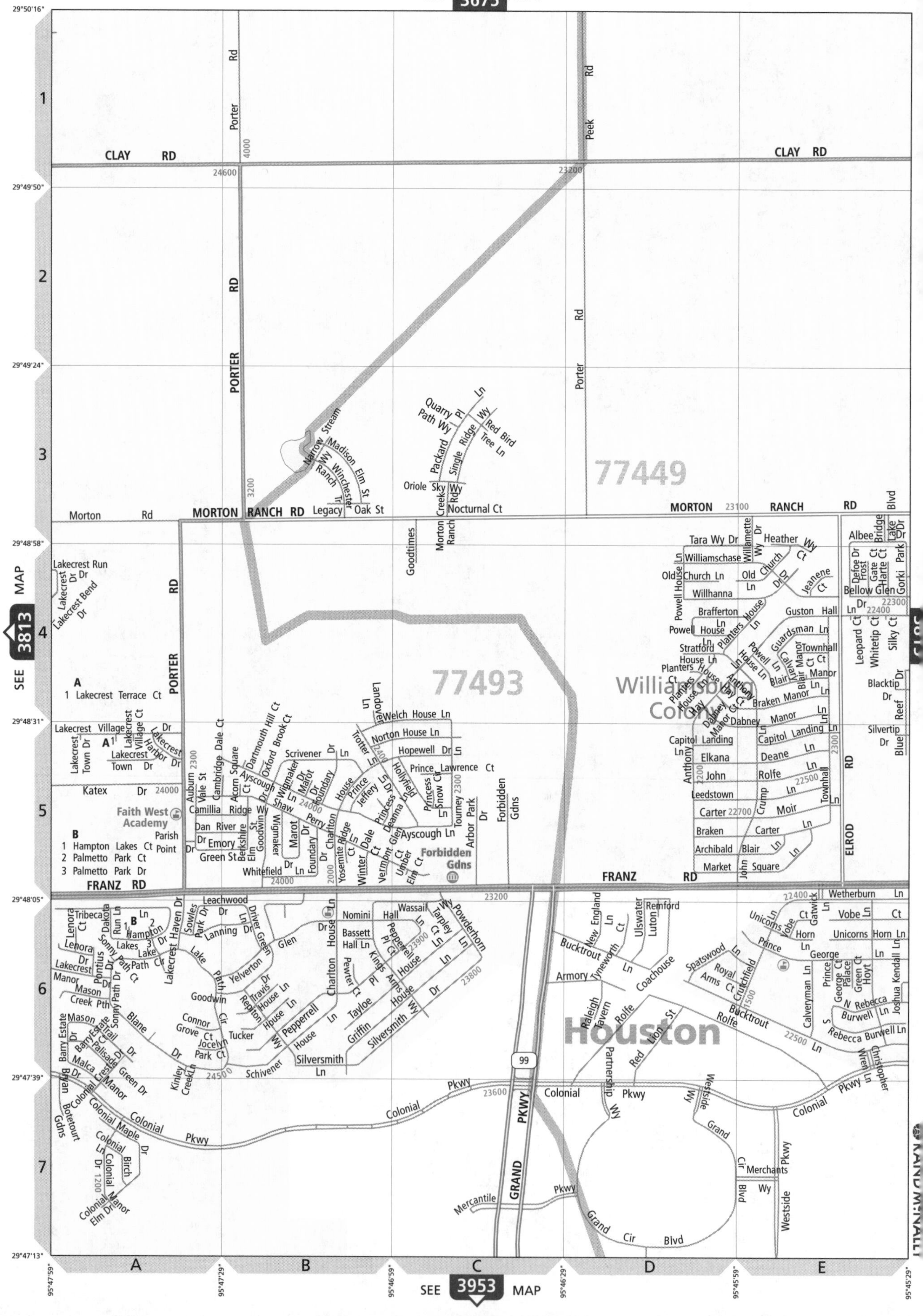
CLAY RD
Porter Rd
Peek Rd
PORTER RD
77449
77493
MORTON RANCH RD
Morton Rd
ELROD RD
FRANZ RD
Williamsburg Colony
Houston
Faith West Academy
Forbidden Gdns
GRAND PKWY
99
Colonial Pkwy
Grand Cir Blvd
Westside Pkwy
Merchants Wy
Mercantile Pkwy
Bucktrout Ln
Rolfe Ln
Powderhorn Ln
Goodtimes
Nocturnal Ct
Narrow Stream
Madison Elm St
Winchester Ranch Tr
Legacy Oak St
Quarry Path Wy
Packard Pl
Single Ridge Wy
Red Bird Tree Ln
Oriole Sky Wy
Morton Creek Ranch Rd
Lakecrest Run Dr
Lakecrest Bend Dr
Lakecrest Terrace Ct
Lakecrest Village Dr
Katex Dr
Hampton Lakes Ct
Palmetto Park Ct
Palmetto Park Dr
Parish Point
Colonial Maple Dr
Colonial Birch Ln
Colonial Manor Dr
Colonial Elm Dr
Botetourt Gdns
Bryan Dr
Lakecrest Haven Dr
Yelverton Glen Dr
Charlton House Ln
Wassail Ln
Silversmith Dr
Pepperrell Pl
Kings Arms Wy
Kinley Creek Ln
Christopher Wren Ln
Joshua Kendall Ln
Rebecca Burwell Ln
Wetherburn Ln
Westside Wy
Partnership Wy
Raleigh Tavern Ln
Red Lion St
Coachouse
New England Ct
Ulswater Luton
Remford
Armory
Tyneworth
Spatswood Ln
Royal Arms Ct
Crutchfield
Unicorns Horn Ln
Vobe Ct
Prince George Ct
Palace Green Ct
Calveryman Ln
Albee
Bellow Glen
Guston Hall Ln
Blacktip Dr
Silvertip Dr
Blue Reef
Leopard Ct
Whitetip Ct
Silky Ct
Welch House Ln
Norton House Ln
Hopewell Dr
Prince Lawrence Ct
Ayscough Ln
Scrivener Dr
Dartmouth Hill Ct
Oxford Brook Ct
Cambridge Dale Ct
Acorn Square
Camillia Ridge Wy
Dan River Dr
Emory Green St
Whitefield Dr
Foundary Dr
Capitol Landing Ln
Elkana
John
Leedstown
Carter
Braken
Archibald
Market Square
Deane Ln
Moir Ln
Townhall Ln
Tara Wy Dr
Williamschase
Willhanna
Bafferton
Powell House Ln
Heather Wy Ct
Jeanene Ct
Old Church Ln
A
B
C
D
E
1
2
3
4
5
6
7
RAND McNALLY

SEE 3813 MAP

SEE 3953 MAP

1:24,000
1 in. = 2000 ft.
0 0.25 0.5
miles

SEE 3676 MAP

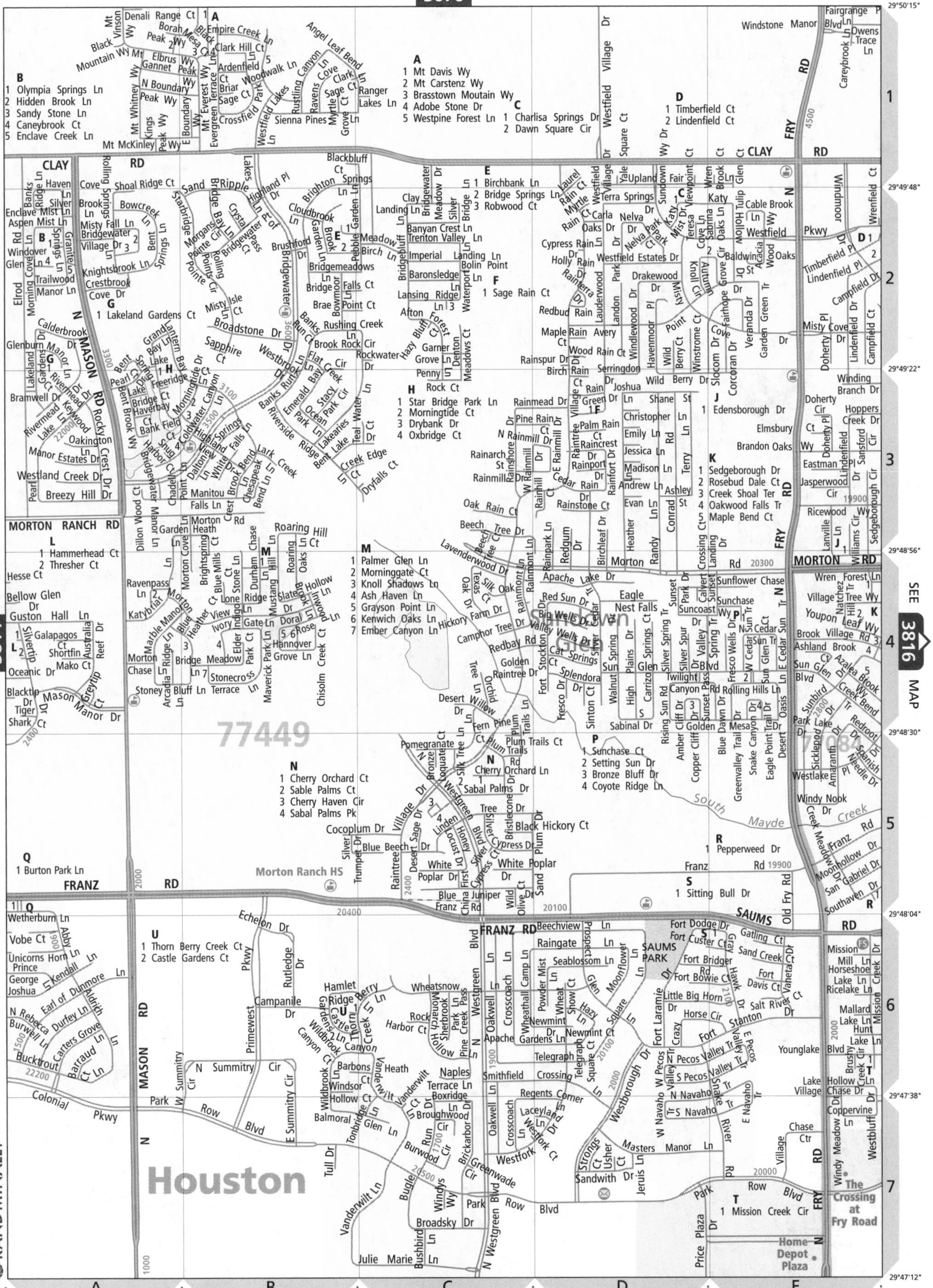
A
1 Mt Davis Wy
2 Mt Carstenz Wy
3 Brasstown Moutain Wy
4 Adobe Stone Dr
5 Westpine Forest Ln
B
1 Olympia Springs Ln
2 Hidden Brook Ln
3 Sandy Stone Ln
4 Caneybrook Ct
5 Enclave Creek Ln
C
1 Charlisa Springs Dr
2 Dawn Square Cir
D
1 Timberfield Ct
2 Lindenfield Ct
E
1 Birchbank Ln
2 Bridge Springs Ln
3 Robwood Ct
F
1 Sage Rain Ct
G
1 Lakeland Gardens Ct
H
1 Star Bridge Park Ln
2 Morningtide Ct
3 Drybank Dr
4 Oxbridge Ct
J
1 Edensborough Dr
K
1 Sedgeborough Dr
2 Rosebud Dale Ct
3 Creek Shoal Ter
4 Oakwood Falls Tr
5 Maple Bend Ct
L
1 Hammerhead Ct
2 Thresher Ct
M
1 Palmer Glen Ln
2 Morninggate Ct
3 Knoll Shadows Ln
4 Ash Haven Ln
5 Grayson Point Ln
6 Kenwich Oaks Ln
7 Ember Canyon Ln
N
1 Cherry Orchard Ct
2 Sable Palms Ct
3 Cherry Haven Cir
4 Sabal Palms Pk
P
1 Sunchase Ct
2 Setting Sun Dr
3 Bronze Bluff Dr
4 Coyote Ridge Ln
Q
1 Burton Park Ln
R
1 Pepperweed Dr
S
1 Sitting Bull Dr
T
1 Mission Creek Cir
U
1 Thorn Berry Creek Ct
2 Castle Gardens Ct
CLAY RD
MORTON RANCH RD
FRANZ RD
SAUMS RD
N MASON RD
N FRY RD
Colonial Pkwy
Park Row Blvd
Morton Ranch HS
SAUMS PARK
Houston
77449
Windstone Manor
The Crossing at Fry Road
Home Depot Plaza
South Mayde Creek
1 2 3 4 5 6 7
A B C D E
29°50'15"
29°49'48"
29°49'22"
29°48'56"
29°48'30"
29°48'04"
29°47'38"
29°47'12"
95°45'29"
95°44'59"
95°44'29"
95°43'59"
95°43'29"
95°42'59"

SEE 3816 MAP

SEE 3954 MAP

1:24,000
1 in. = 2000 ft.
0 0.25 0.5
miles

SEE 3677 MAP

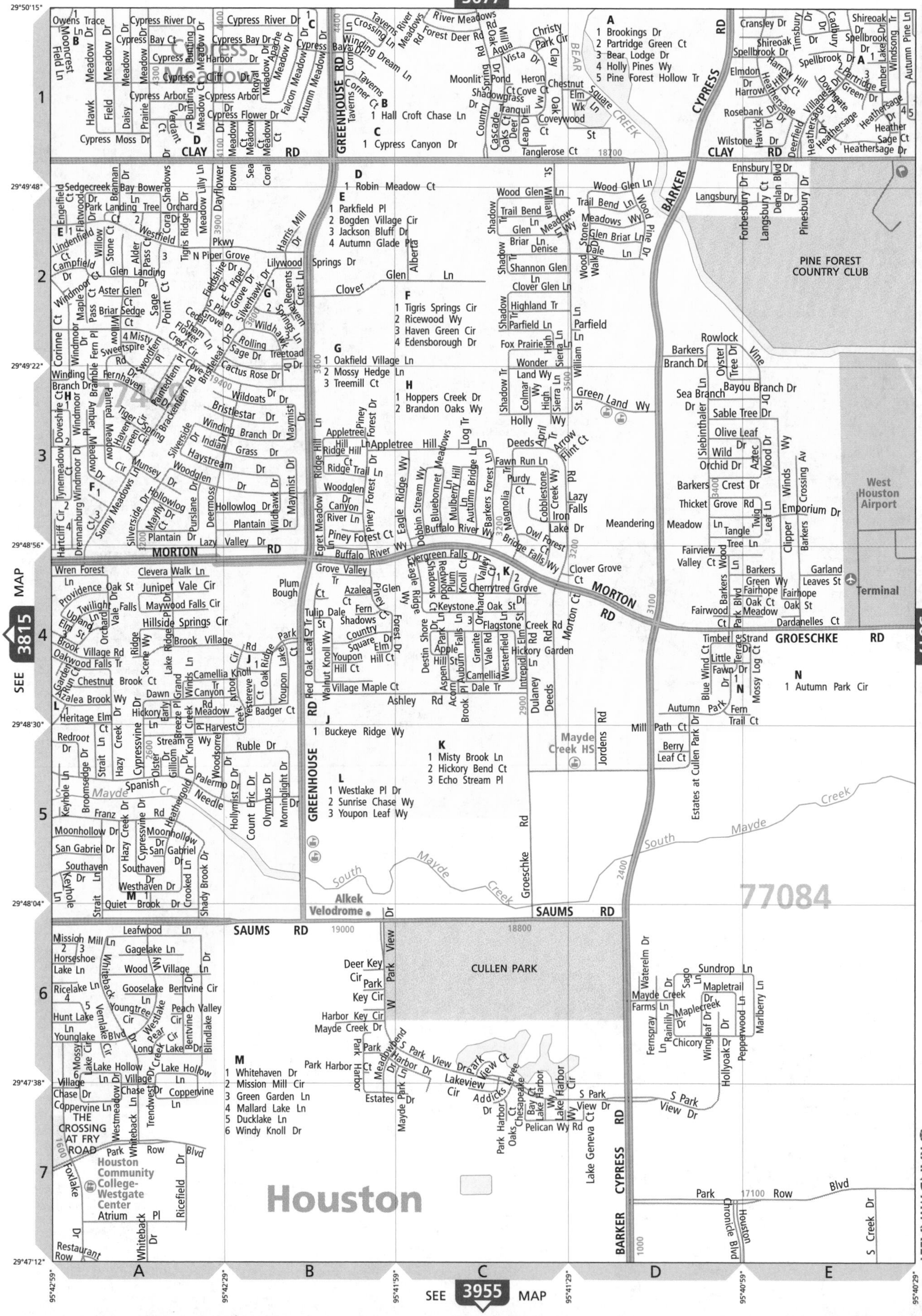
A
1 Brookings Dr
2 Partridge Green Ct
3 Bear Lodge Dr
4 Holly Pines Wy
5 Pine Forest Hollow Tr
B
1 Hall Croft Chase Ln
C
1 Cypress Canyon Dr
D
1 Robin Meadow Ct
E
1 Parkfield Pl
2 Bogden Village Cir
3 Jackson Bluff Dr
4 Autumn Glade Pl
F
1 Tigris Springs Cir
2 Ricewood Wy
3 Haven Green Cir
4 Edensborough Dr
G
1 Oakfield Village Ln
2 Mossy Hedge Ln
3 Treemill Ct
H
1 Hoppers Creek Dr
2 Brandon Oaks Wy
J
1 Buckeye Ridge Wy
K
1 Misty Brook Ln
2 Hickory Bend Ct
3 Echo Stream Pl
L
1 Westlake Pl Dr
2 Sunrise Chase Wy
3 Youpon Leaf Wy
M
1 Whitehaven Dr
2 Mission Mill Cir
3 Green Garden Ln
4 Mallard Lake Ln
5 Ducklake Ln
6 Windy Knoll Dr
N
1 Autumn Park Cir
CLAY RD
MORTON RD
GROESCHKE RD
SAUMS RD
GREENHOUSE RD
BARKER CYPRESS RD
PINE FOREST COUNTRY CLUB
West Houston Airport
Terminal
CULLEN PARK
Mayde Creek HS
Alkek Velodrome
THE CROSSING AT FRY ROAD
Houston Community College-Westgate Center
Houston
77084
Cypress Meadows
BEAR CREEK
South Mayde Creek

SEE 3815 MAP

SEE 3955 MAP

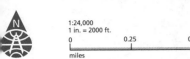

1:24,000
1 in. = 2000 ft.
0 0.25 0.5
miles

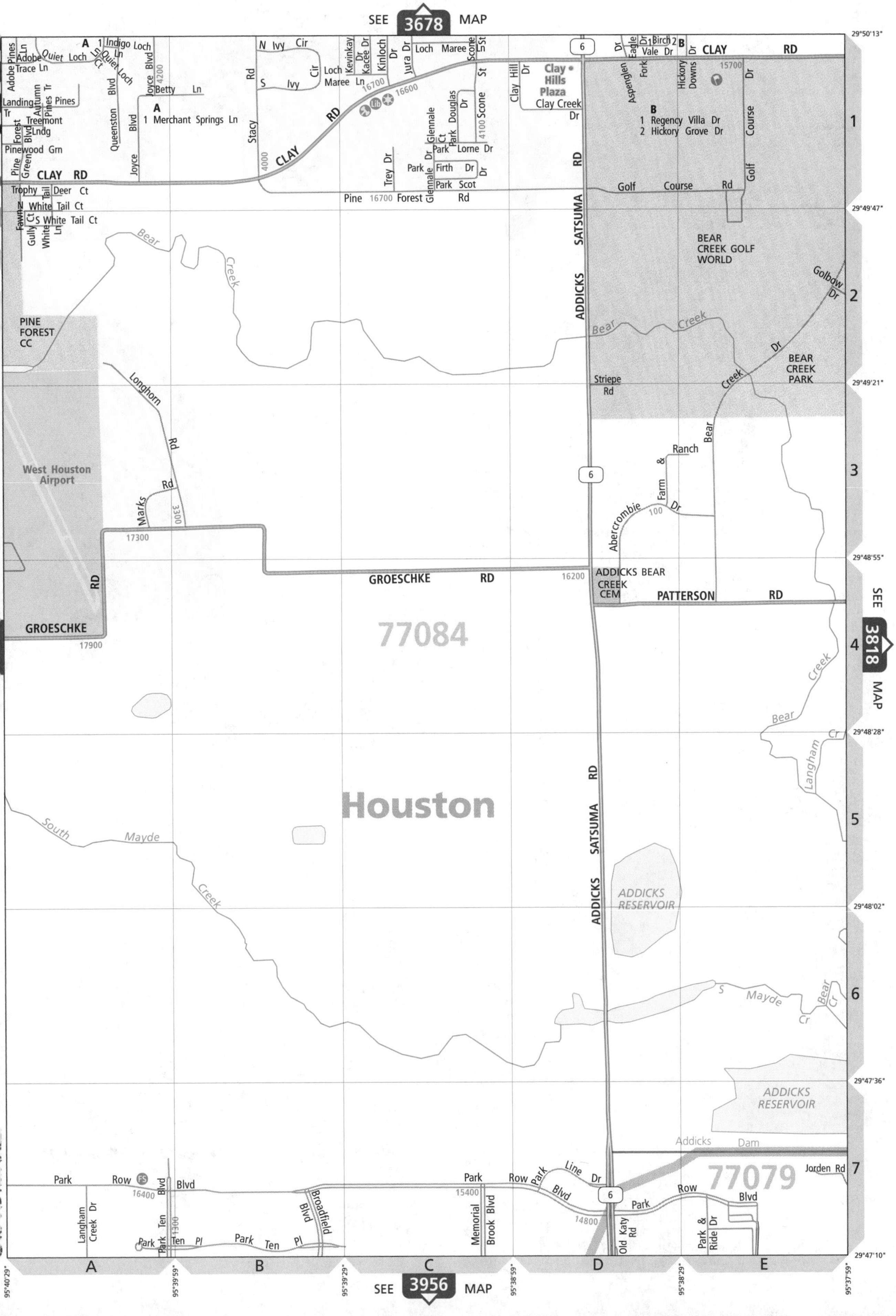
SEE 3678 MAP
SEE 3818 MAP
SEE 3956 MAP
CLAY RD
ADDICKS SATSUMA RD
GROESCHKE RD
PATTERSON RD
Park Row Blvd
Park Ten Blvd
Park Ten Pl
Broadfield Blvd
Memorial Brook Blvd
Langham Creek Dr
Old Katy Rd
Park & Ride Dr
Jorden Rd
Park Line Dr
Addicks Dam
Longhorn Rd
Marks Rd
Abercrombie Dr
Farm & Ranch Dr
Bear Creek Dr
Golbow Dr
Striepe Rd
Golf Course Rd
Golf Course Dr
Pine Forest Rd
Clay Hills Plaza
Clay Creek Dr
Clay Hill Dr
Stacy Rd
Joyce Blvd
Queenston Blvd
Betty Ln
1 Merchant Springs Ln
Indigo Loch
Quiet Loch Ln
Adobe Trace Ln
Adobe Pines Ln
Landing Pines Tr
Autumn Pines Tr
Treemont
Forest Lndg
Pinewood Grn
Pine Green
Trophy Deer Ct
N White Tail Ct
S White Tail Ct
Fawn Gully Ct
White Tail Ln
N Ivy Cir
S Ivy Cir
Loch Maree Ln
Kevinkay Dr
Kacee Dr
Kinloch Dr
Jura Dr
Scone St
Scone Dr
Glennale Ct
Glennale Dr
Douglas Dr
Park Lorne Dr
Park Firth Dr
Park Scot
Trey Dr
Aspenglen Dr
Eagle Fork Dr
1 Birch Vale Dr
Hickory Downs Dr
1 Regency Villa Dr
2 Hickory Grove Dr
PINE FOREST CC
West Houston Airport
BEAR CREEK GOLF WORLD
BEAR CREEK PARK
ADDICKS BEAR CREEK CEM
ADDICKS RESERVOIR
Bear Creek
South Mayde Creek
S Mayde Cr
Bear Cr
Langham Cr
77084
77079
Houston
17300
17900
16200
16700
16600
15700
15400
16400
14800
4200
4000
4100
3300
1300
100
A B C D E
1 2 3 4 5 6 7
29°50'13"
29°49'47"
29°49'21"
29°48'55"
29°48'28"
29°48'02"
29°47'36"
29°47'10"
95°40'29"
95°39'59"
95°39'29"
95°38'59"
95°38'29"
95°37'59"

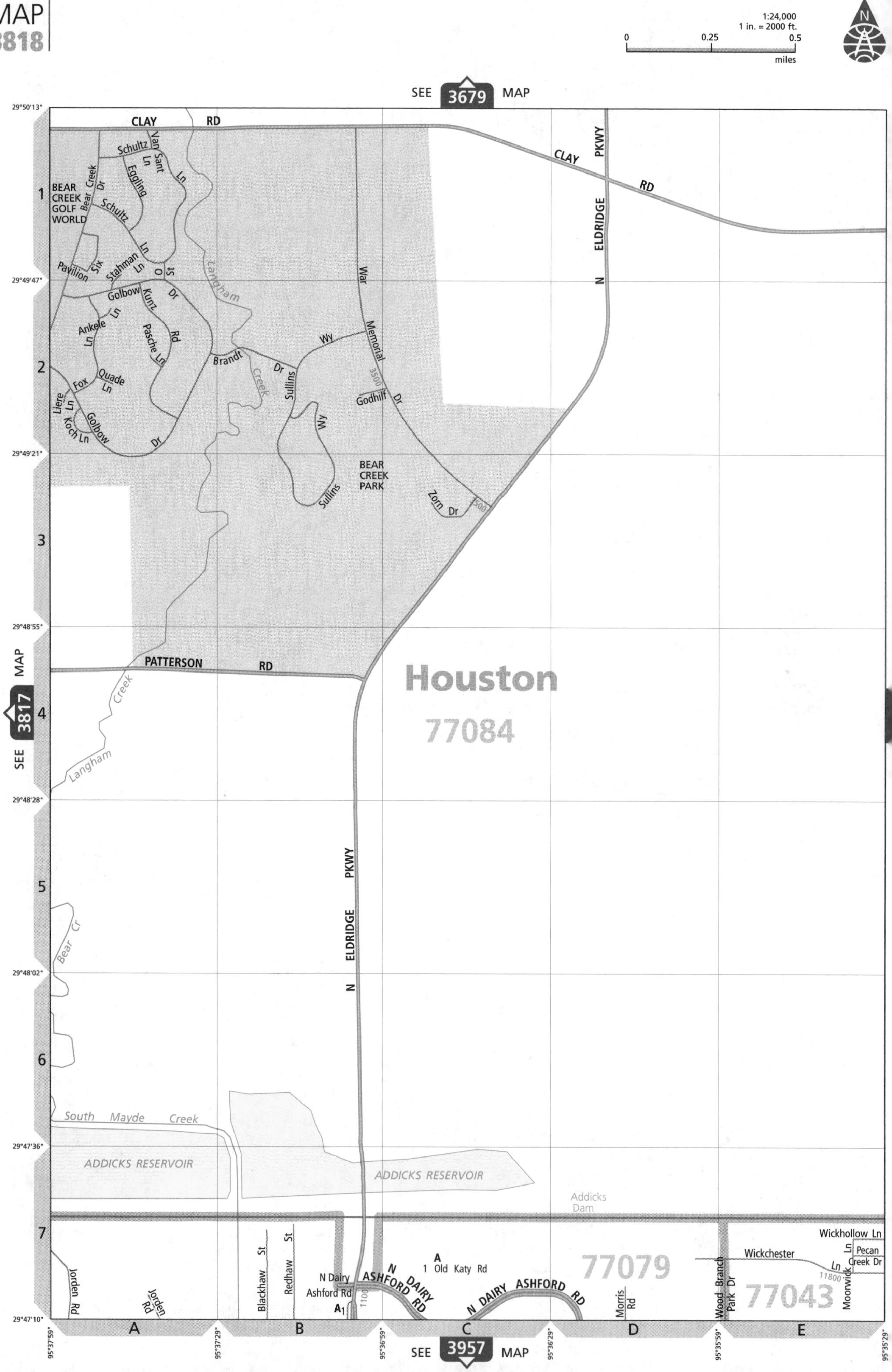
1:24,000
1 in. = 2000 ft.
0
0.25
0.5
miles
SEE 3679 MAP
SEE 3817 MAP
SEE 3957 MAP
CLAY RD
Schultz
Van Sant Ln
Eggling Ln
Bear Creek Dr
BEAR CREEK GOLF WORLD
Schultz
Ln
Pavilion
Six
Stahman Ln
O St
Golbow
Kunz
Dr
Langham
Ankele Ln
Pasche Ln
Rd
Brandt
Creek
Dr
Sullins
Wy
War
Memorial
Dr
3500
Godhilf
Fox
Quade Ln
Liere Ln
Koch Ln
Golbow
Dr
Wy
BEAR CREEK PARK
Sullins
Zorn Dr
3500
CLAY RD
N ELDRIDGE PKWY
PATTERSON RD
Creek
Langham
Houston
77084
N ELDRIDGE PKWY
Bear Cr
South Mayde Creek
ADDICKS RESERVOIR
ADDICKS RESERVOIR
Addicks Dam
Jorden Rd
Jorden Rd
Blackhaw St
Redhaw St
N Dairy Ashford Rd
A1
1100
N DAIRY ASHFORD RD
A
1 Old Katy Rd
N DAIRY ASHFORD RD
77079
Morris Rd
Wood Branch Park Dr
Wickchester
Wickhollow Ln
Ln
Pecan Creek Dr
Ln
11800
Moorwick
77043
1
2
3
4
5
6
7
A
B
C
D
E
29°50'13"
29°49'47"
29°49'21"
29°48'55"
29°48'28"
29°48'02"
29°47'36"
29°47'10"
95°37'59"
95°37'29"
95°36'59"
95°36'29"
95°35'59"
95°35'29"

1:24,000
1 in. = 2000 ft.
0 0.25 0.5
miles

SEE 3680 MAP

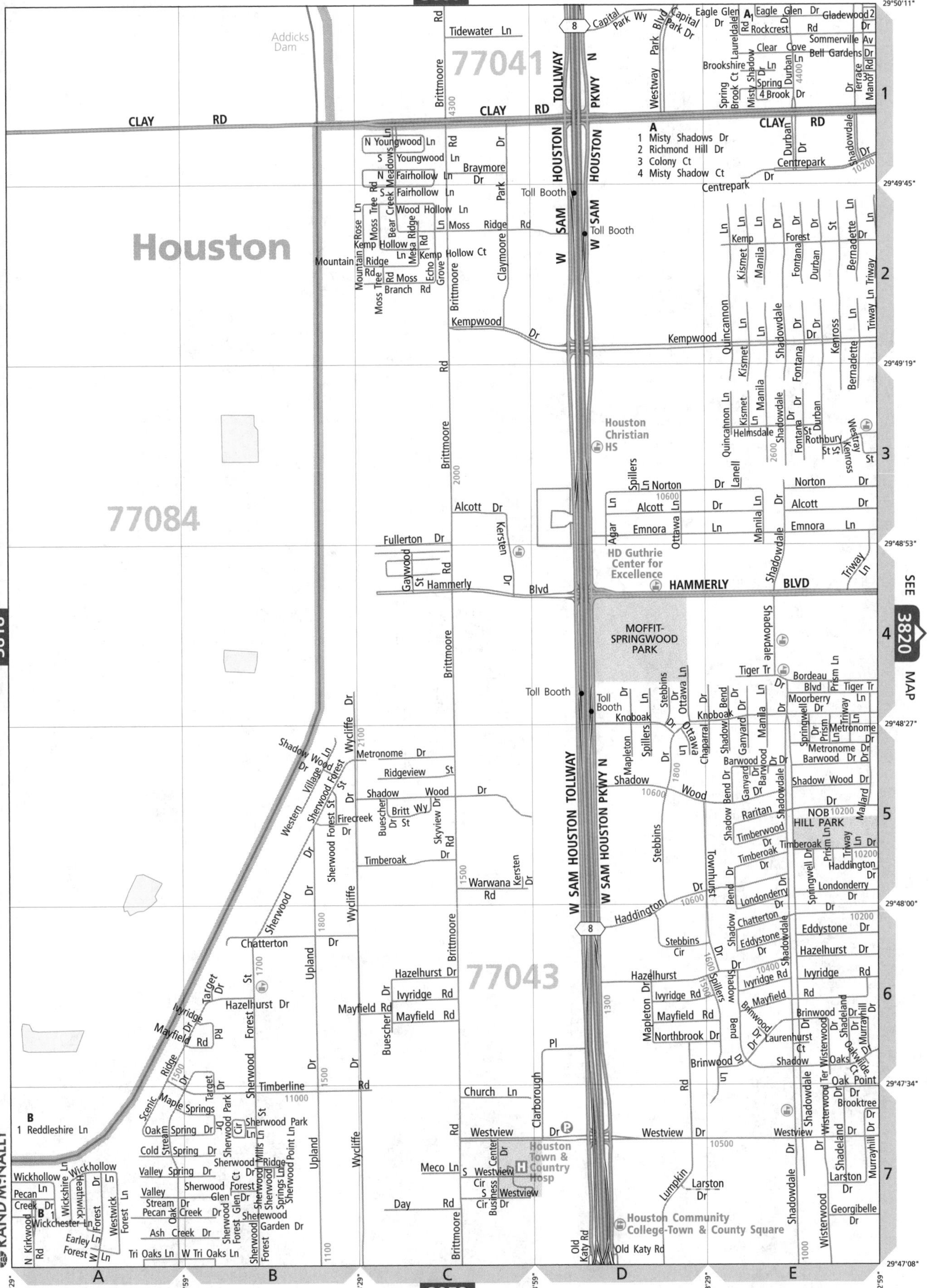
Houston
77041
77084
77043
Addicks Dam
CLAY RD
W SAM HOUSTON TOLLWAY
W SAM HOUSTON PKWY N
HAMMERLY BLVD
Brittmoore Rd
Kempwood Dr
Toll Booth
Houston Christian HS
HD Guthrie Center for Excellence
MOFFIT-SPRINGWOOD PARK
NOB HILL PARK
Houston Town & Country Hosp
Houston Community College-Town & County Square
Westview Dr
Centrepark Dr
Shadow Wood Dr
Haddington Dr
Hazelhurst Dr
Mayfield Rd
Ivyridge Rd
Timberline Rd
Church Ln
Day Rd
Old Katy Rd
Upland
Wycliffe Dr
Sherwood Forest
Shadowdale Dr
Tidewater Ln
Capital Park Wy
Eagle Glen Dr
A
1 Misty Shadows Dr
2 Richmond Hill Dr
3 Colony Ct
4 Misty Shadow Ct
B
1 Reddleshire Ln
1
2
3
4
5
6
7
A
B
C
D
E
29°50'11"
29°49'45"
29°49'19"
29°48'53"
29°48'27"
29°48'00"
29°47'34"
29°47'08"
95°35'29"
95°34'59"
95°34'29"
95°33'59"
95°33'29"
95°32'59"

SEE 3820 MAP

SEE 3958 MAP

1:24,000
1 in. = 2000 ft.
0 0.25 0.5
miles

SEE 3681 MAP

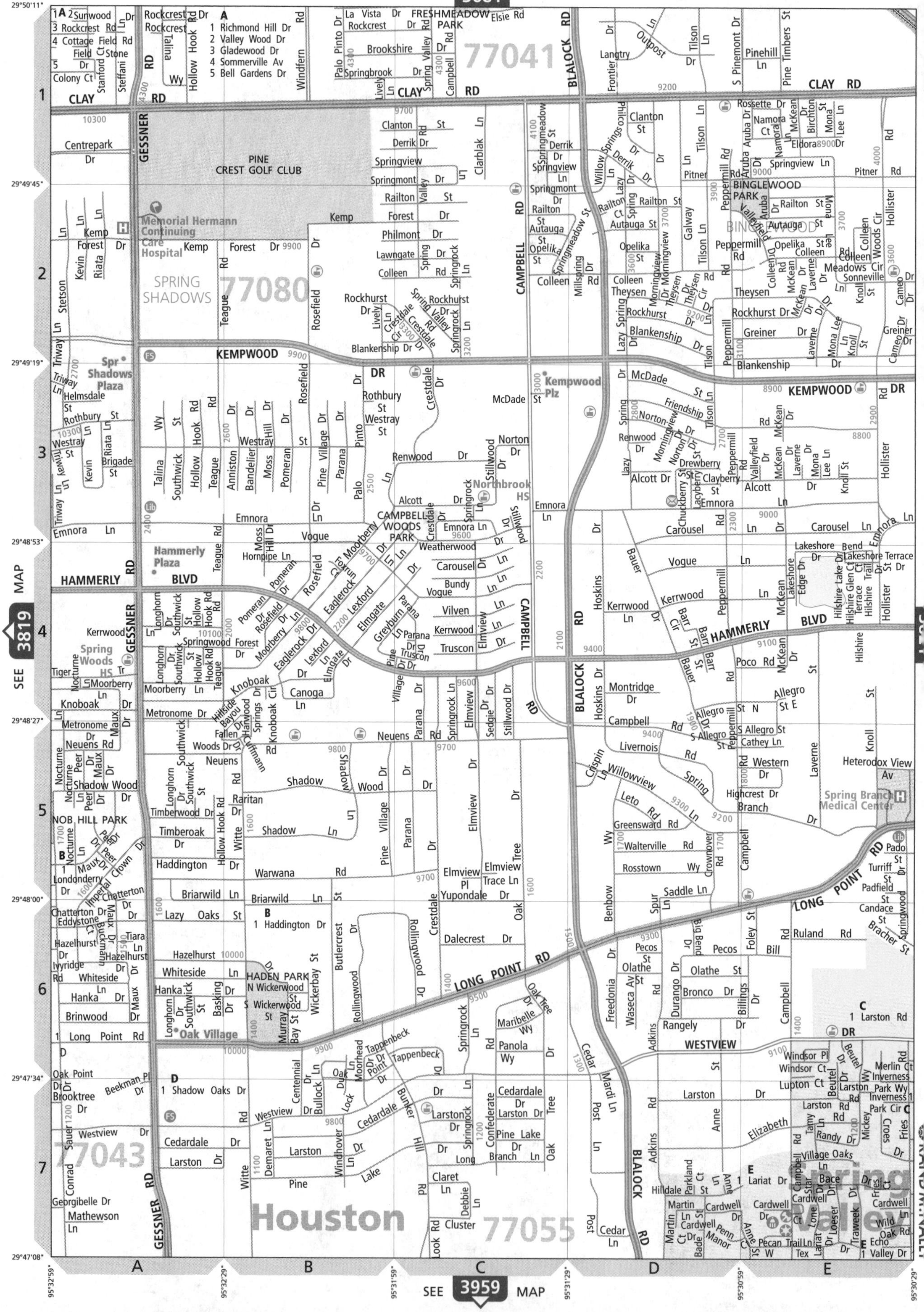
CLAY RD
GESSNER RD
BLALOCK RD
CAMPBELL RD
KEMPWOOD DR
HAMMERLY BLVD
LONG POINT RD
WESTVIEW DR
77041
77080
77043
77055
PINE CREST GOLF CLUB
Memorial Hermann Continuing Care Hospital
SPRING SHADOWS
BINGLEWOOD PARK
FRESHMEADOW PARK
CAMPBELL WOODS PARK
Spring Shadows Plaza
Kempwood Plz
Northbrook HS
Hammerly Plaza
Spring Woods HS
NOB HILL PARK
HADEN PARK
Oak Village
Spring Branch Medical Center
Houston
Spring Valley
1 Richmond Hill Dr
2 Valley Wood Dr
3 Gladewood Dr
4 Sommerville Av
5 Bell Gardens Dr
1 Haddington Dr
1 Shadow Oaks Dr
1 Larston Rd
1 Lariat Dr
1 Valley Dr
A
B
C
D
E
1
2
3
4
5
6
7
29°50'11"
29°49'45"
29°49'19"
29°48'53"
29°48'27"
29°48'00"
29°47'34"
29°47'08"
95°32'59"
95°32'29"
95°31'59"
95°31'29"
95°30'59"
95°30'29"

SEE 3819 MAP

SEE 3959 MAP

1:24,000
1 in. = 2000 ft.
0 0.25 0.5
miles

SEE 3682 MAP

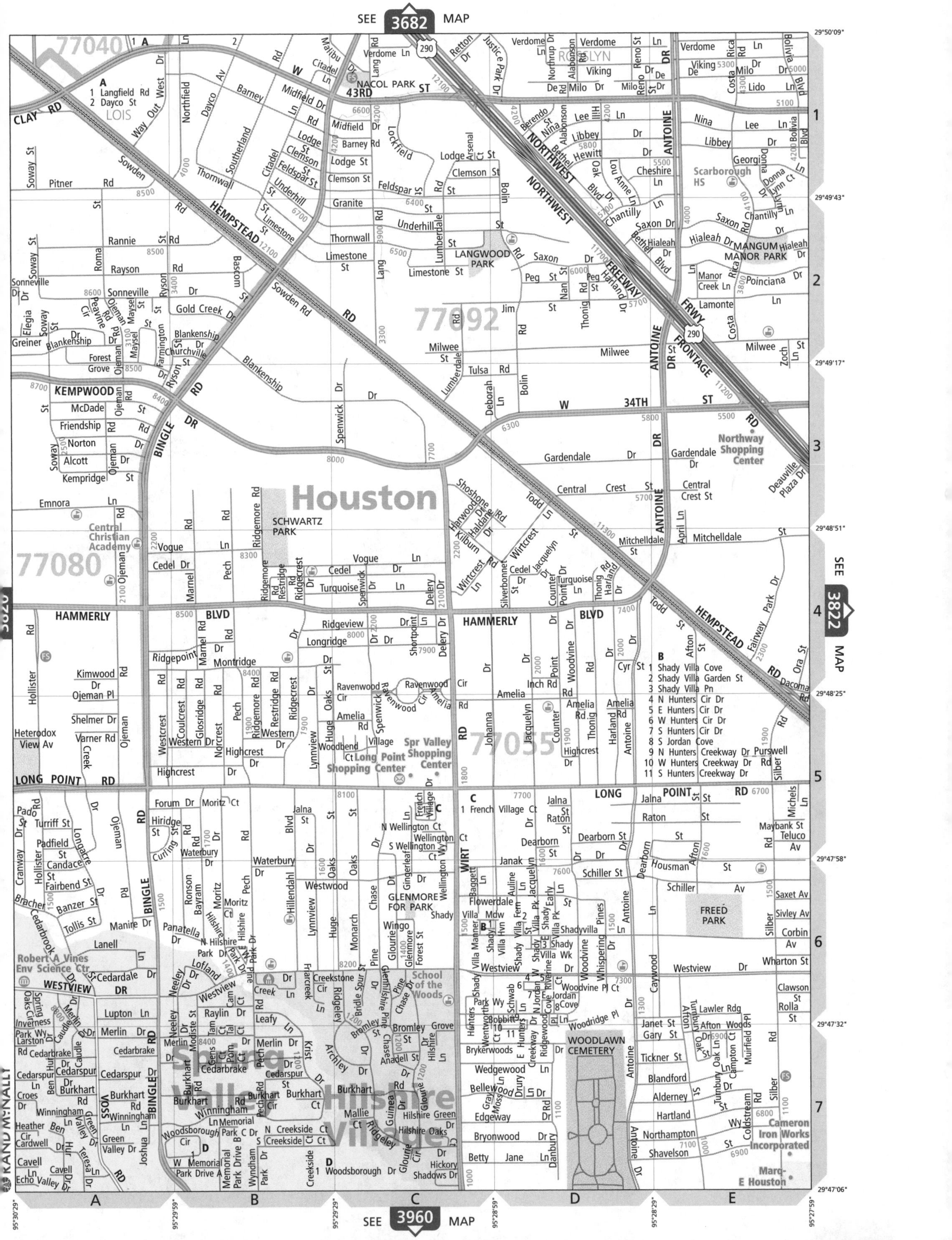
Houston
77040
77092
77080
77055
LOIS
ROSLYN
NACOL PARK
LANGWOOD PARK
MANGUM MANOR PARK
SCHWARTZ PARK
FREED PARK
WOODLAWN CEMETERY
GLENMORE FOR PARK
Spring Valley
Hilshire Village
Scarborough HS
Northway Shopping Center
Central Christian Academy
Spr Valley Shopping Center
Long Point Shopping Center
School of the Woods
Robert A Vines Env Science Ctr
Cameron Iron Works Incorporated
Marq-E Houston
CLAY RD
W 43RD ST
HEMPSTEAD RD
NORTHWEST FREEWAY
NORTHWEST FRWY FRONTAGE RD
ANTOINE DR
W 34TH ST
KEMPWOOD DR
BINGLE DR
HAMMERLY BLVD
LONG POINT RD
WIRT RD
WESTVIEW DR
VOSS RD
A
1 Langfield Rd
2 Dayco St
B
1 Shady Villa Cove
2 Shady Villa Garden St
3 Shady Villa Pn
4 N Hunters Cir Dr
5 E Hunters Cir Dr
6 W Hunters Cir Dr
7 S Hunters Cir Dr
8 S Jordan Cove
9 N Hunters Creekway Dr
10 W Hunters Creekway Dr
11 S Hunters Creekway Dr
C
1 French Village Ct
D
1 Woodsborough Dr
A B C D E
1 2 3 4 5 6 7
29°50'09"
29°49'43"
29°49'17"
29°48'51"
29°48'25"
29°47'58"
29°47'32"
29°47'06"
95°30'29"
95°29'59"
95°29'29"
95°28'59"
95°28'29"
95°27'59"
SEE 3822 MAP
3820
RAND McNALLY

SEE 3960 MAP

1:24,000
1 in. = 2000 ft.
0 0.25 0.5
miles

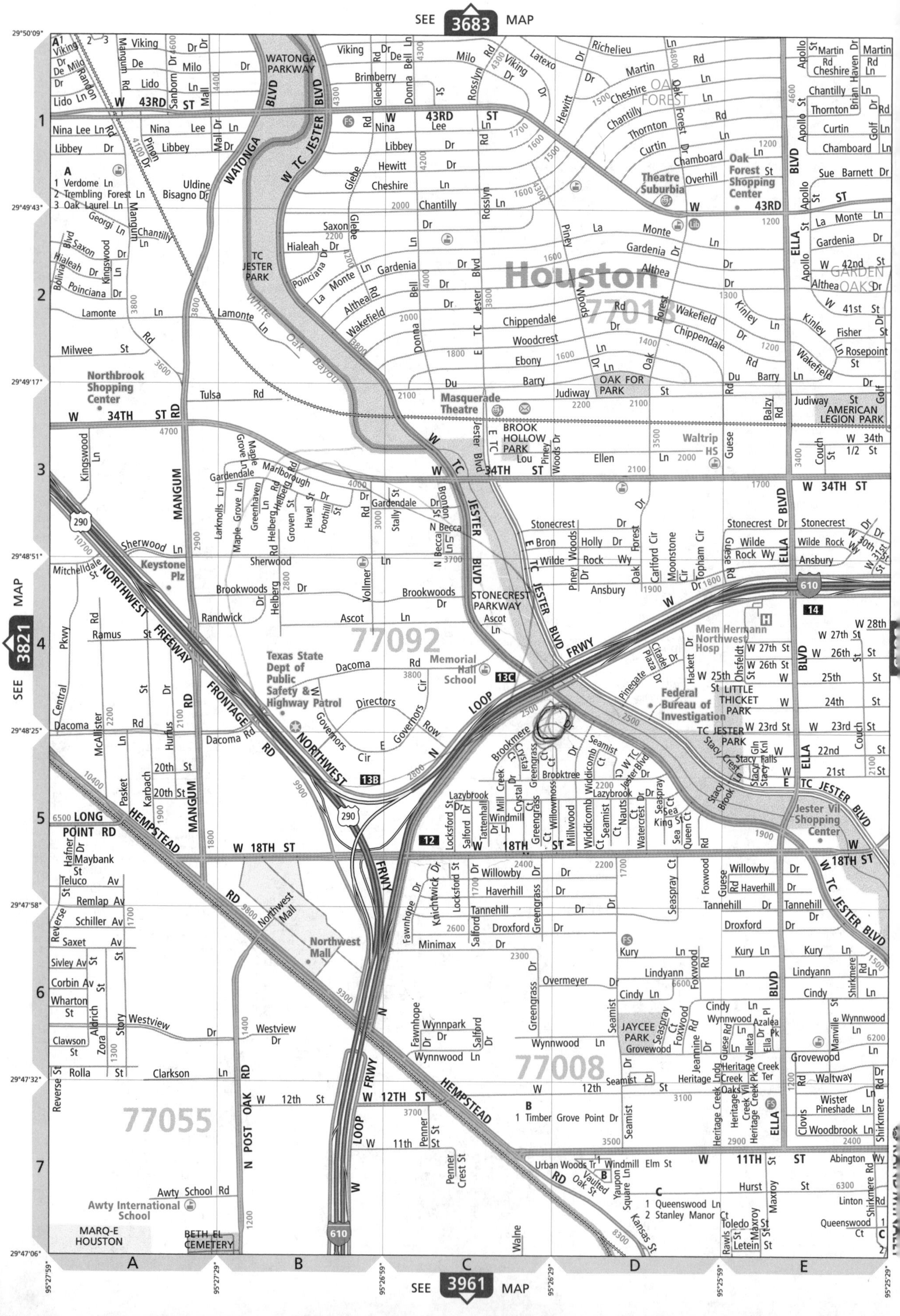
SEE 3683 MAP
SEE 3821 MAP
SEE 3961 MAP
Houston
77018
77092
77008
77055
WATONGA PARKWAY
TC JESTER PARK
White Oak Bayou
OAK FOREST
GARDEN OAKS
Theatre Suburbia
Oak Forest Shopping Center
Northbrook Shopping Center
Masquerade Theatre
OAK FOR PARK
BROOK HOLLOW PARK
Waltrip HS
AMERICAN LEGION PARK
Keystone Plz
STONECREST PARKWAY
Texas State Dept of Public Safety & Highway Patrol
Memorial Hall School
Mem Hermann Northwest Hosp
Federal Bureau of Investigation
LITTLE THICKET PARK
TC JESTER PARK
Jester Vil Shopping Center
Northwest Mall
JAYCEE PARK
Awty International School
MARQ-E HOUSTON
BETH EL CEMETERY
W 43RD ST
W 34TH ST
W 18TH ST
W 12TH ST
W 11TH ST
W TC JESTER BLVD
MANGUM RD
ELLA BLVD
NORTHWEST FREEWAY
LOOP N FRWY
W LOOP FRWY
HEMPSTEAD RD
LONG POINT RD
N POST OAK RD
290
610
A
1 Verdome Ln
2 Trembling Forest Ln
3 Oak Laurel Ln
B
1 Timber Grove Point Dr
C
1 Queenswood Ln
2 Stanley Manor Ct
13C
13B
12
14
29°50'09"
29°49'43"
29°49'17"
29°48'51"
29°48'25"
29°47'58"
29°47'32"
29°47'06"
95°27'59"
95°27'29"
95°26'59"
95°26'29"
95°25'59"
95°25'29"

1:24,000
1 in. = 2000 ft.
0 0.25 0.5
miles

SEE 3684 MAP

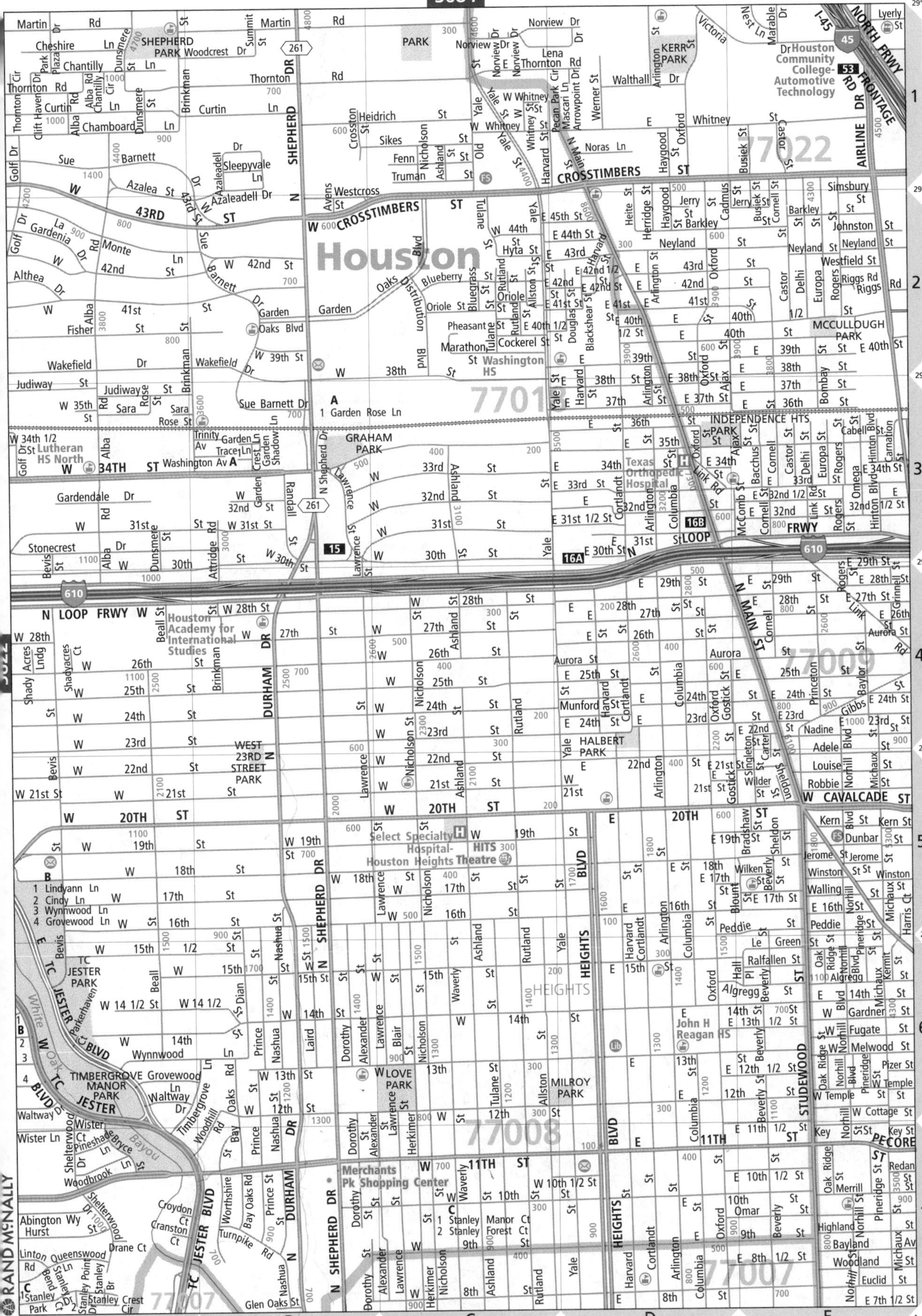
Houston
77022
77018
77009
77008
77007
Houston Community College-Automotive Technology
Lutheran HS North
Washington HS
Houston Academy for International Studies
Texas Orthopedic Hospital
Select Specialty Hospital-Houston Heights
HITS Theatre
John H Reagan HS
Merchants Pk Shopping Center
SHEPHERD PARK
KERR PARK
GRAHAM PARK
INDEPENDENCE HTS PARK
MCCULLOUGH PARK
HALBERT PARK
WEST 23RD STREET PARK
TC JESTER PARK
TIMBERGROVE MANOR PARK
LOVE PARK
MILROY PARK
HEIGHTS
White Oak Bayou
CROSSTIMBERS ST
W 43RD ST
W 34TH ST
N LOOP FRWY W
LOOP FRWY
NORTH FRWY
I-45
AIRLINE DR
N MAIN ST
SHEPHERD DR
N SHEPHERD DR
DURHAM DR
HEIGHTS BLVD
YALE
STUDEWOOD ST
W 20TH ST
E 20TH
W CAVALCADE ST
11TH ST
PECORE ST
TC JESTER BLVD
W TC JESTER BLVD
29°50'07"
29°49'41"
29°49'15"
29°48'48"
29°48'22"
29°47'56"
29°47'30"
29°47'04"
95°25'29"
95°24'59"
95°24'29"
95°23'59"
95°23'29"
95°22'59"
A
B
C
D
E
1
2
3
4
5
6
7

SEE 3824 MAP

SEE 3962 MAP

1:24,000
1 in. = 2000 ft.
0 0.25 0.5
miles

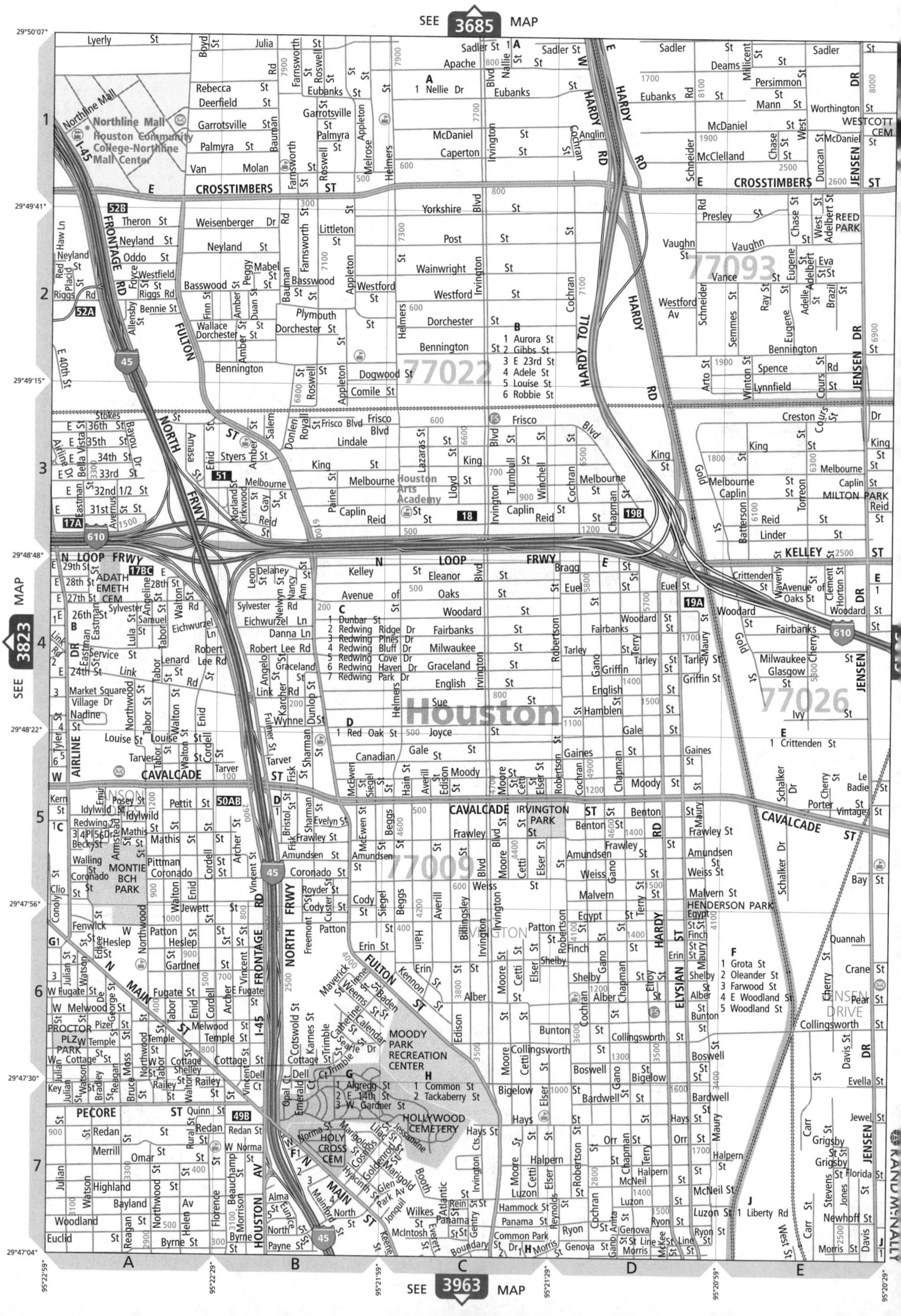
SEE 3685 MAP
SEE 3823 MAP
SEE 3963 MAP
Houston
77022
77093
77009
77026
Northline Mall
Houston Community College-Northline Mall Center
E CROSSTIMBERS ST
N LOOP FRWY
NORTH FRWY
HARDY TOLL RD
HARDY RD
FULTON ST
AIRLINE DR
CAVALCADE ST
JENSEN DR
N MAIN ST
PECORE ST
ELYSIAN ST
IRVINGTON PARK
MONTIE BCH PARK
MOODY PARK RECREATION CENTER
HOLLYWOOD CEMETERY
HOLY CROSS CEM
ADATH EMETH CEM
WESTCOTT CEM
REED PARK
MILTON PARK
HENDERSON PARK
PROCTOR PLZ PARK
Houston Arts Academy
JENSEN DRIVE
29°50'07"
29°49'41"
29°49'15"
29°48'48"
29°48'22"
29°47'56"
29°47'30"
29°47'04"
95°22'59"
95°22'29"
95°21'59"
95°21'29"
95°20'59"
95°20'29"
RAND McNALLY

1:24,000
1 in. = 2000 ft.
0 0.25 0.5
miles

SEE 3686 MAP

Houston
77093
77016
77028
77026
77020
EASTEX FRWY
CROSSTIMBERS ST
ERNIE RD
LANDOR ST
WEAVER RD
HIRSCH RD
LOCKWOOD DR
HOMESTEAD RD
KELLEY ST
LOOP FRWY E
N LOOP
610
59
CAVALCADE ST
LIBERTY RD
WALLISVILLE RD
Shreveport Blvd
Baton Rouge St
Lyndon B Johnson Gen Hosp
Kashmere HS
TRINITY GDNS PARK
BUSBY PARK
HOUSTON GDNS PARK
PELHAM PARK
CURRY STREET PARK
WESTCOTT CEM
HUTCHESON PARK
TUFFLY PARK
DELCE PARK
ENGLEWOOD
20AB
20C
21
22
A
1 Brackenridge St
C
1 Date St
2 Jewel St
3 Florida St
4 Kentucky St
5 Newhoff St
6 Liberty Rd
D
1 Hailey St
2 Bleker St
3 Pannell St
4 Hutton St
5 Leffingwell St
6 Abernathy St
A
B
C
D
E
1
2
3
4
5
6
7
29°50'04"
29°49'38"
29°49'12"
29°48'46"
29°48'20"
29°47'54"
29°47'28"
29°47'01"
95°20'29"
95°19'59"
95°19'29"
95°18'59"
95°18'29"
95°17'59"

SEE 3826 MAP

SEE 3964 MAP

1:24,000
1 in. = 2000 ft.
0 0.25 0.5
miles

SEE 3687 MAP

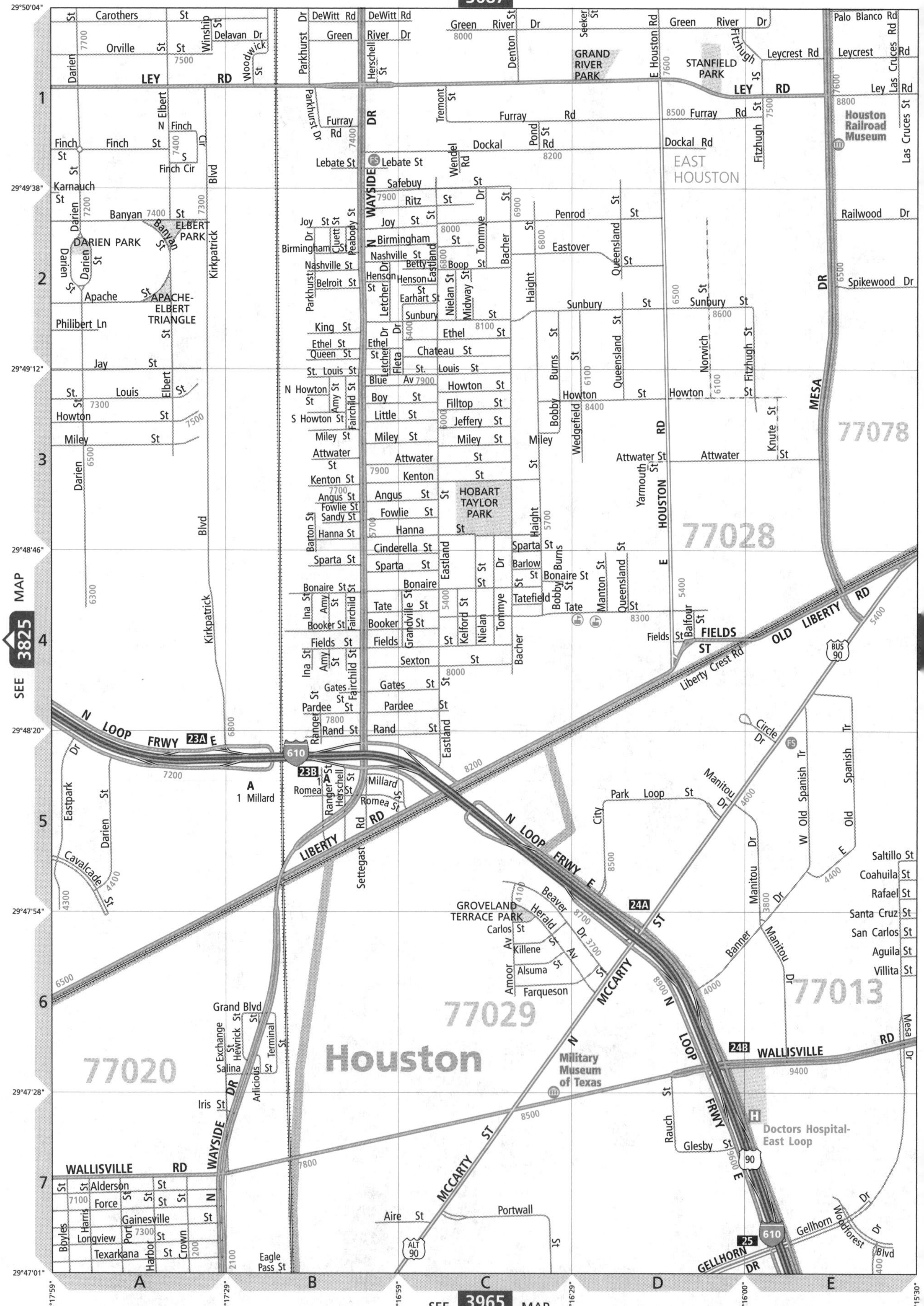
29°50'04"
29°49'38"
29°49'12"
29°48'46"
29°48'20"
29°47'54"
29°47'28"
29°47'01"
95°17'59"
95°17'29"
95°16'59"
95°16'29"
95°16'00"
95°15'30"
A
B
C
D
E
1
2
3
4
5
6
7
Carothers St
Orville St
Winship St
Delavan Dr
Woodwick St
LEY RD
Darien St
Parkhurst Dr
DeWitt Rd
Green River Dr
Herschell St
Denton St
Seeker St
GRAND RIVER PARK
E Houston Rd
STANFIELD PARK
Fitzhugh St
Leycrest Rd
Palo Blanco Rd
Las Cruces Rd
Ley Rd
Houston Railroad Museum
Tremont St
Furray Rd
Dockal Rd
Pond St
Finch St
N Elbert St
Finch Cir
Karnauch St
Lebate St
Wendel Rd
EAST HOUSTON
Safebury St
Ritz St
Banyan St
ELBERT PARK
DARIEN PARK
N WAYSIDE DR
Joy St
Birmingham St
Nashville St
Penrod St
Eastover St
Queensland St
Railwood Dr
Spikewood Dr
Apache St
APACHE-ELBERT TRIANGLE
Kirkpatrick Blvd
Belroit St
Sunbury St
Norwich St
Philibert Ln
King St
Ethel St
Chateau St
Queen St
St. Louis St
Jay St
Blue Av
Howton St
Filltop St
Jeffery St
Miley St
Little St
Boy St
Wedgefield St
Attwater St
Knute St
MESA DR
77078
Kenton St
Angus St
Fowlie St
Sandy St
Hanna St
HOBART TAYLOR PARK
Haight St
HOUSTON
Yarmouth St
77028
Cinderella St
Sparta St
Barlow St
Bonaire St
Tate St
Tatefield St
Manton St
Booker St
Fields St
Balfour St
FIELDS ST
OLD LIBERTY RD
Liberty Crest Rd
Sexton St
Gates St
Pardee St
Rand St
N LOOP FRWY E
23A
610
23B
1 Millard
Millard St
Romea St
LIBERTY RD
Eastpark Dr
Cavalcade St
Settegast
City Park Loop St
Circle Dr
Manitou Dr
W Old Spanish Tr
E Old Spanish Tr
Saltillo St
Coahuila St
Rafael St
Santa Cruz St
San Carlos St
Aguila St
Villita St
GROVELAND TERRACE PARK
Beaver Dr
Herald St
Carlos St
Killene Av
Alsuma St
Amoor Av
Farqueson St
24A
N MCCARTY ST
Banner Dr
77013
77029
77020
Houston
Grand Blvd
Exchange St
Hewrick St
Terminal St
Salina St
Ardicious St
Iris St
N WAYSIDE DR
Military Museum of Texas
24B
WALLISVILLE RD
Rauch St
Glesby St
Doctors Hospital-East Loop
90
WALLISVILLE RD
Alderson St
Force St
Gainesville St
Longview St
Texarkana St
Boyles St
Harris St
Harbor St
Crown St
Eagle Pass St
Aire St
Portwall St
ALT 90
GELLHORN DR
Gellhorn Dr
Woodforest Blvd
BUS 90
N LOOP FRWY E
25

SEE 3825 MAP

SEE 3965 MAP

1:24,000
1 in. = 2000 ft.
0 0.25 0.5
miles

SEE 3688 MAP

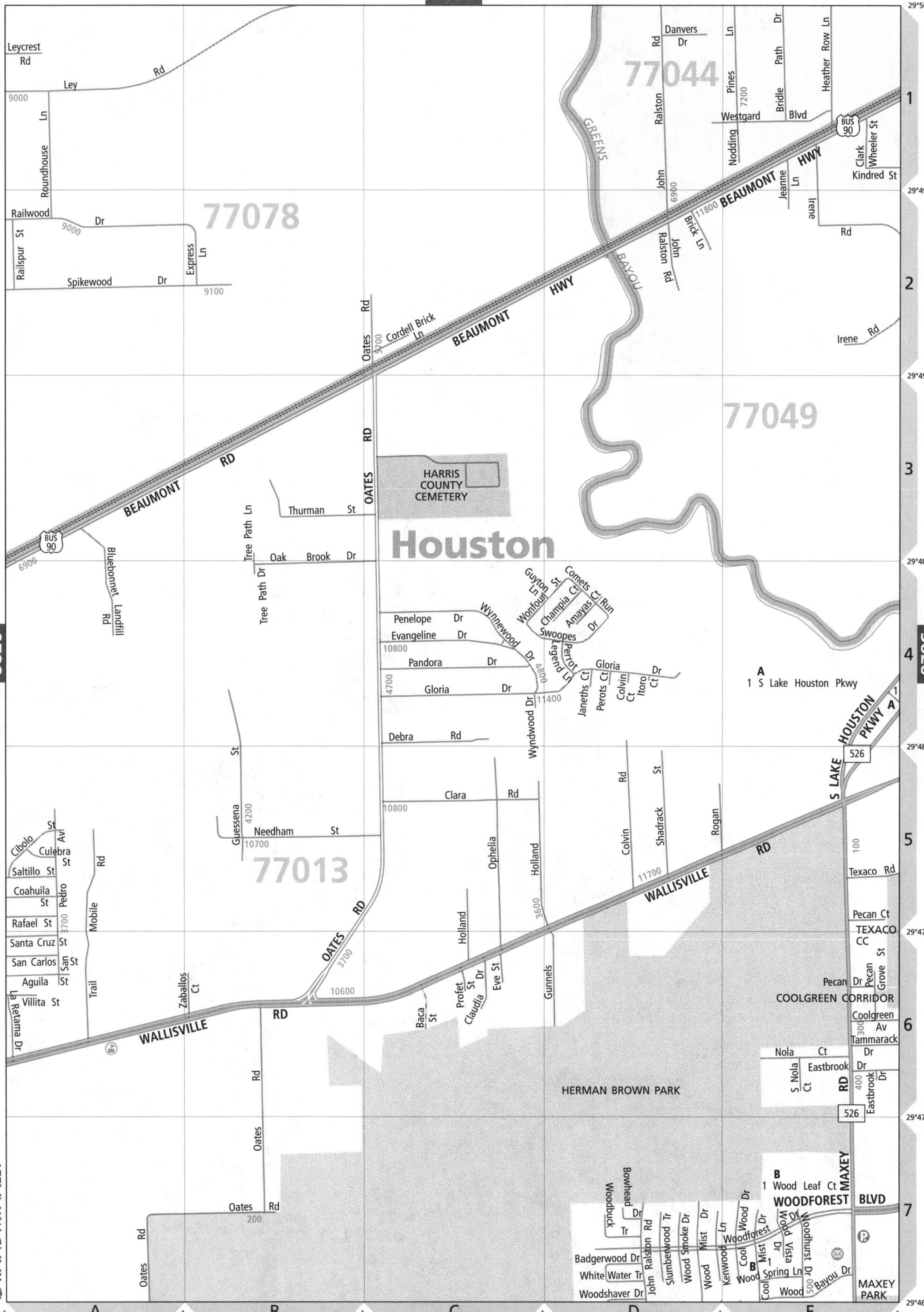
77044
77078
77049
77013
Houston
HARRIS COUNTY CEMETERY
HERMAN BROWN PARK
COOLGREEN CORRIDOR
MAXEY PARK
BEAUMONT HWY
BEAUMONT RD
WALLISVILLE RD
OATES RD
S LAKE HOUSTON PKWY
WOODFOREST BLVD
MAXEY RD
GREENS BAYOU
BUS 90
526
Leycrest Rd
Ley Rd
Roundhouse Ln
Railwood Dr
Railspur St
Spikewood Dr
Express Ln
Cordell Brick Ln
Thurman St
Tree Path Ln
Tree Path Dr
Oak Brook Dr
Bluebonnet Landfill Rd
Penelope Dr
Evangeline Dr
Pandora Dr
Gloria Dr
Debra Rd
Clara Rd
Needham St
Guessena St
Wynnewood Dr
Wyndwood Dr
Guyton Ln
Wonfour St
Comets Run
Champia Ct
Amayas Ct
Swoopes Dr
Legend Ln
Perrot Ct
Janeths Ct
Perots Ct
Colvin Ct
Itoro Ct
Gloria Dr
Colvin Rd
Shadrack St
Rogan
Holland Rd
Ophelia
Holland
Gunnels
Profet St
Claudia Dr
Eve St
Baca St
Zaballos Ct
Mobile Rd
Trail
Cibolo St
Culebra St
Saltillo St
Coahuila St
Pedro
Rafael St
Santa Cruz St
San Carlos St
San St
Aguila St
Villita St
La Retama Dr
Oates Rd
Danvers Dr
Ralston Rd
John Ralston Rd
Nodding Pines Ln
Bridle Path Dr
Heather Row Ln
Westgard Blvd
Clark St
Wheeler St
Kindred St
Jeanne Ln
Irene Rd
Brick Ln
A 1 S Lake Houston Pkwy
Texaco Rd
Pecan Ct
TEXACO CC
Pecan Dr
Pecan Grove St
Coolgreen Av
Tammarack Dr
Nola Ct
S Nola Ct
Eastbrook Dr
B 1 Wood Leaf Ct
Bowhead Dr
Woodbuck Tr
Badgerwood Dr
White Water Tr
Woodshaver Dr
Slumberwood Tr
Wood Smoke Dr
Wood Mist Dr
Kenwood Ln
Cool Wood Dr
Woodforest Dr
Wood Vista Dr
Woodhurst Dr
Wood Spring Ln
Bayou Dr
Cool Wood
9000
9100
6900
11800
7200
5700
10800
4700
4800
11400
4200
10700
11700
3600
3700
10600
200
100
300
400
500
1
2
3
4
5
6
7
A
B
C
D
E
29°50'02"
29°49'36"
29°49'10"
29°48'43"
29°48'17"
29°47'51"
29°47'25"
29°46'59"
95°15'30"
95°15'00"
95°14'30"
95°14'00"
95°13'30"
95°13'00"

SEE 3828 MAP

SEE 3966 MAP

1:24,000
1 in. = 2000 ft.
0 0.25 0.5
miles

SEE 3689 MAP

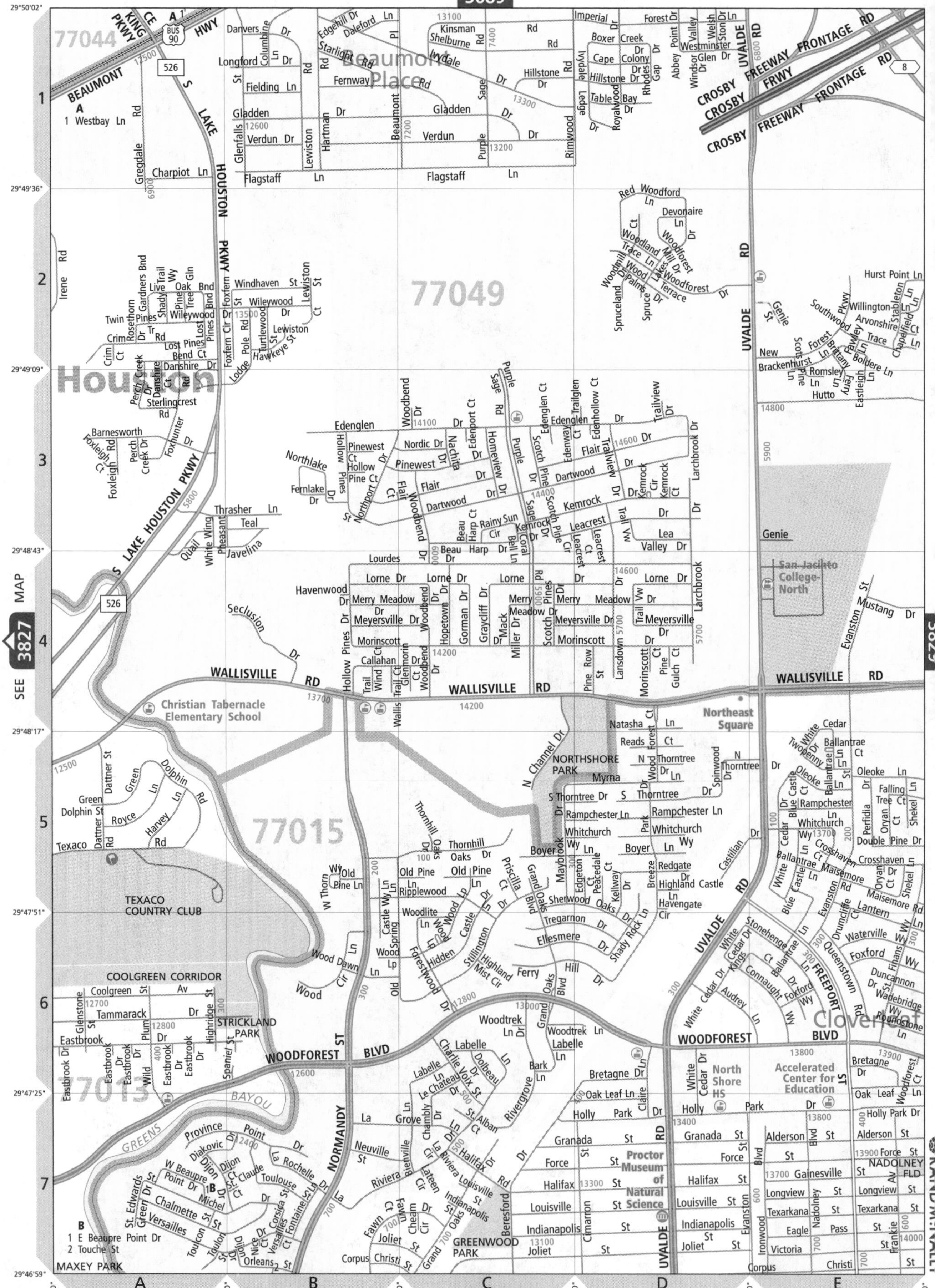
77044
77049
77015
77013
Houston
Beaumont Place
BEAUMONT HWY
KING PKWY
S LAKE HOUSTON PKWY
WALLISVILLE RD
WOODFOREST BLVD
UVALDE RD
NORMANDY ST
FREEPORT ST
CROSBY FREEWAY
CROSBY FRWY
FREEWAY FRONTAGE RD
Christian Tabernacle Elementary School
San Jacinto College-North
Northeast Square
NORTHSHORE PARK
TEXACO COUNTRY CLUB
COOLGREEN CORRIDOR
STRICKLAND PARK
GREENS BAYOU
North Shore HS
Accelerated Center for Education
Proctor Museum of Natural Science
GREENWOOD PARK
MAXEY PARK
Cloverleaf
NADOLNEY FLD
Flagstaff Ln
Gladden Dr
Verdun Dr
Edenglen Dr
Lorne Dr
Morinscott
Genie
Granada St
Halifax St
Louisville St
Indianapolis St
Joliet St
A
1 Westbay Ln
B
1 E Beaupre Point Dr
2 Touche St

SEE 3827 MAP

SEE 3967 MAP

1:24,000
1 in. = 2000 ft.
0 0.25 0.5
miles

SEE 3690 MAP

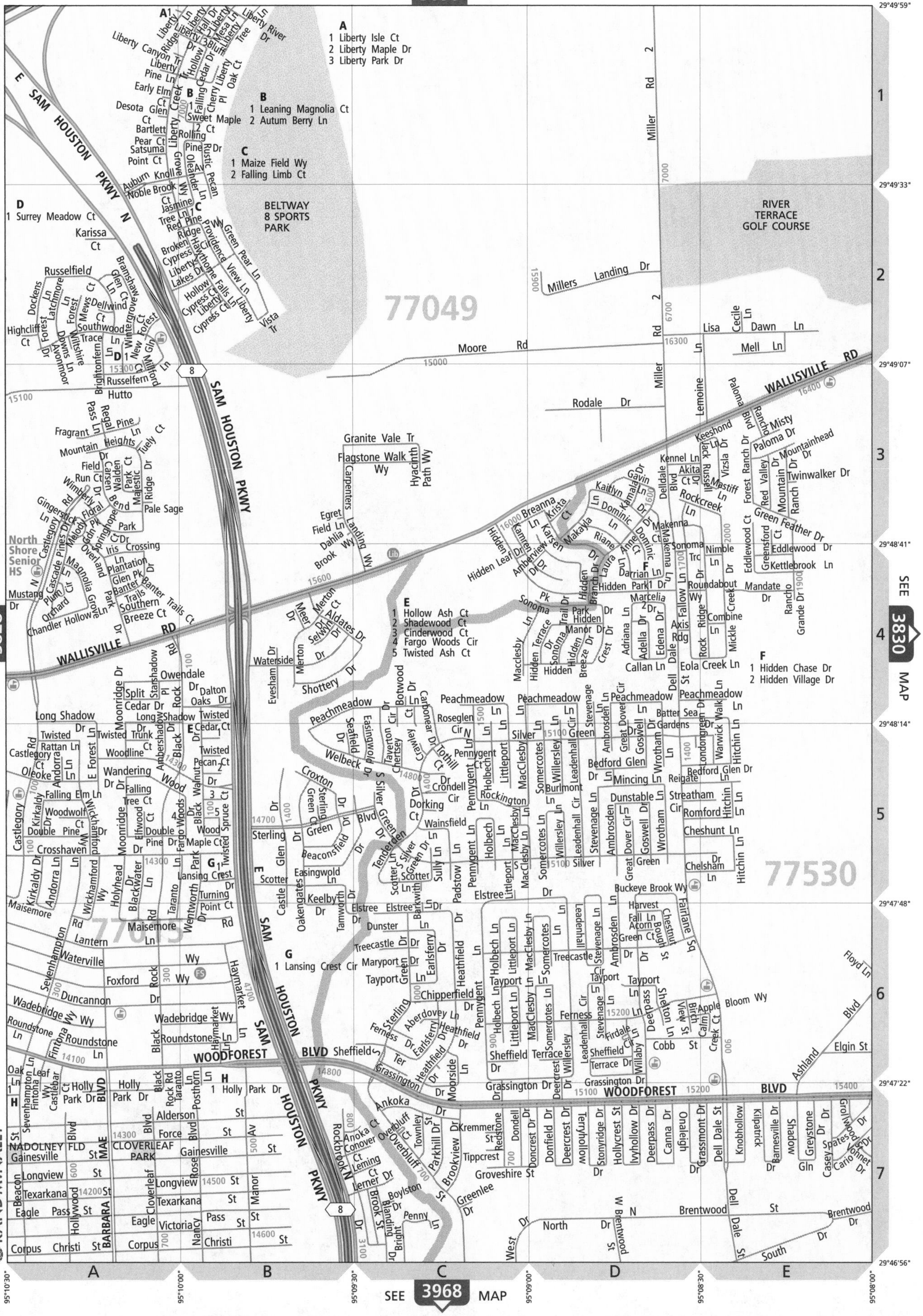
A
1 Liberty Isle Ct
2 Liberty Maple Dr
3 Liberty Park Dr
B
1 Leaning Magnolia Ct
2 Autum Berry Ln
C
1 Maize Field Wy
2 Falling Limb Ct
D
1 Surrey Meadow Ct
E
1 Hollow Ash Ct
2 Shadewood Ct
3 Cinderwood Ct
4 Fargo Woods Cir
5 Twisted Ash Ct
F
1 Hidden Chase Dr
2 Hidden Village Dr
G
1 Lansing Crest Cir
H
1 Holly Park Dr
BELTWAY 8 SPORTS PARK
RIVER TERRACE GOLF COURSE
77049
77530
North Shore Senior HS
E SAM HOUSTON PKWY N
SAM HOUSTON PKWY
WALLISVILLE RD
WOODFOREST BLVD
Miller Rd 2
Moore Rd
Rodale Dr
Millers Landing Dr
NADOLNEY FLD
CLOVERLEAF PARK
29°49'59"
29°49'33"
29°49'07"
29°48'41"
29°48'14"
29°47'48"
29°47'22"
29°46'56"
95°10'30"
95°10'00"
95°09'30"
95°09'00"
95°08'30"
95°08'00"
A
B
C
D
E
1
2
3
4
5
6
7

SEE 3830 MAP

SEE 3968 MAP

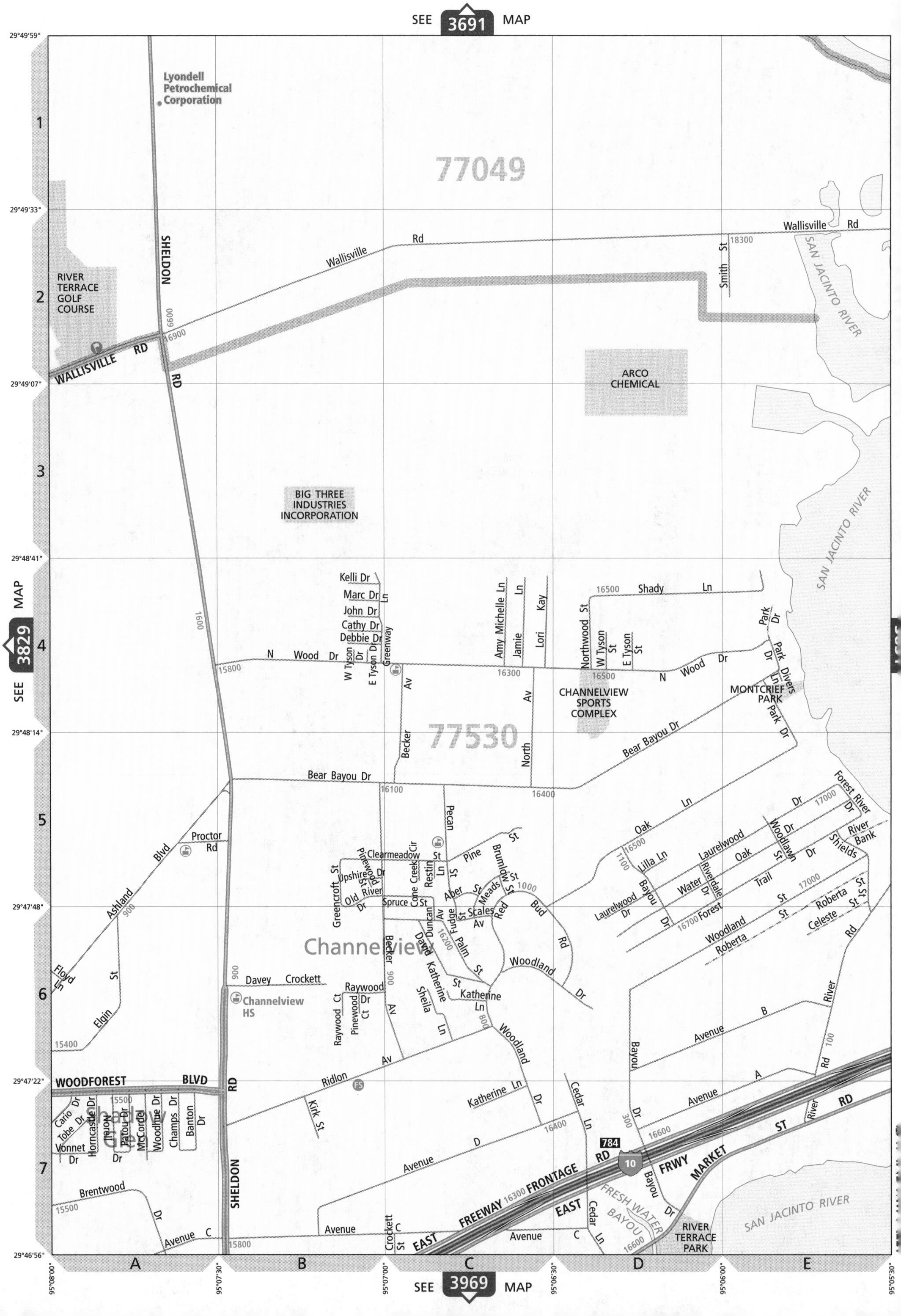
1:24,000
1 in. = 2000 ft.
0 0.25 0.5
miles
SEE 3691 MAP
SEE 3829 MAP
SEE 3969 MAP
Lyondell Petrochemical Corporation
77049
77530
RIVER TERRACE GOLF COURSE
SHELDON RD
WALLISVILLE RD
Wallisville Rd
ARCO CHEMICAL
SAN JACINTO RIVER
BIG THREE INDUSTRIES INCORPORATION
N Wood Dr
Shady Ln
CHANNELVIEW SPORTS COMPLEX
MONTCRIEF PARK
Bear Bayou Dr
Channelview
Channelview HS
WOODFOREST BLVD
Davey Crockett
Ridlon Av
Avenue D
Avenue C
Avenue B
Avenue A
EAST FREEWAY FRONTAGE RD
EAST FRWY
MARKET ST
FRESH WATER BAYOU
RIVER TERRACE PARK
River Rd
Ashland Blvd
Proctor Rd
Elgin St
Floyd Ln
Brentwood Dr
Shadow Glen
Kelli Dr
Marc Dr
John Dr
Cathy Dr
Debbie Dr
Greenway Ln
Becker Av
Amy Michelle Ln
Jamie Ln
Lori Kay
North Av
Northwood St
W Tyson St
E Tyson St
Park Dr
Divers Ln
Oak Ln
Lilla Ln
Laurelwood Dr
Woodland Dr
Woodlawn Dr
Forest River Dr
River Bank
Shields
Roberta St
Celeste St
Trail St
Katherine Ln
Woodland
Cedar Ln
Kirk St
Raywood Dr
Pinewood Ct
Bayou Dr
A B C D E
1 2 3 4 5 6 7

1:24,000
1 in. = 2000 ft.
0 0.25 0.5
miles

SEE 3692 MAP

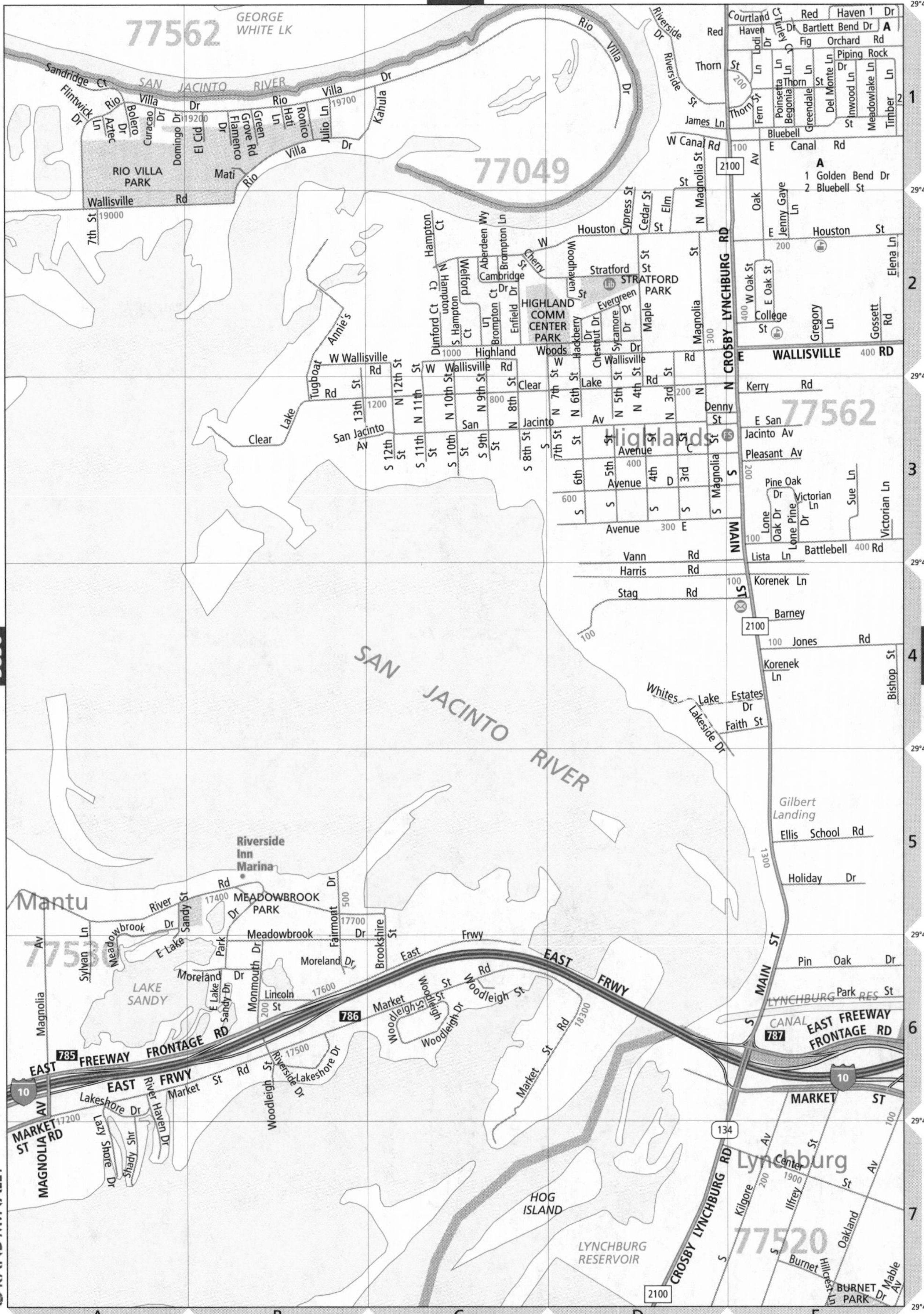
77562
GEORGE WHITE LK
SAN JACINTO RIVER
Sandridge Ct
Flintwick Dr
Rio Villa Dr
Bolero Dr
Aztec
Curacao Dr
Domingo Dr
El Cid
Flamenco
Grove Rd
Green
Hatt
Ronico
Julio Ln
Kahula
Mati
RIO VILLA PARK
Wallisville Rd
7th St
77049
Riverside Dr
Riverside St
Courtland Ct
Red Haven Dr
Bartlett Bend Dr
Fig
Orchard Rd
Piping Rock
Thorn St
Fern St
Poinsetta
Begonia
Greendale
Del Monte Ln
Inwood Ln
Meadowlake Ln
Timber
Bluebell
James Ln
W Canal Rd
E Canal Rd
A
1 Golden Bend Dr
2 Bluebell St
Oak
Jenny Gaye Ln
Houston St
Elena Ln
Hampton Ct
N Hampton Ct
Welford
Aberdeen Wy
Brompton Ln
Cambridge Dr
W Cherry St
Woodhaven St
Cypress St
Cedar St
Elm St
N Magnolia St
Stratford St
STRATFORD PARK
HIGHLAND COMM CENTER PARK
Evergreen Dr
Sycamore Dr
Maple
Chestnut Dr
Hackberry
Dunford Ct
S Hampton Ct
Brompton Ct
Enfield
Highland Woods Dr
W Wallisville Rd
Annie's
Tugboat Rd
Clear Lake
13th St
N 12th St
N 11th St
N 10th St
N 9th St
N 8th St
N 7th St
N 6th St
N 5th St
N 4th St
N 3rd St
San Jacinto Av
Highlands
S 12th St
S 11th St
S 10th St
S 9th St
S 8th St
S 7th St
S 6th St
S 5th St
S 4th St
S 3rd St
Avenue C
Avenue D
Avenue E
S Magnolia St
CROSBY LYNCHBURG RD
WALLISVILLE RD
Kerry Rd
Denny St
E San Jacinto Av
Pleasant Av
W Oak St
E Oak St
College St
Gregory Ln
Gossett Rd
77562
Pine Oak Dr
Victorian Ln
Sue Ln
Lone Oak Dr
Lone Pine Dr
Lista Ln
Battlebell Rd
MAIN ST
Vann Rd
Harris Rd
Stag Rd
Korenek Ln
Barney
Jones Rd
Bishop St
Whites Lake Estates Dr
Lakeside Dr
Faith St
SAN JACINTO RIVER
Gilbert Landing
Ellis School Rd
Holiday Dr
Riverside Inn Marina
Mantu
MEADOWBROOK PARK
River Rd
Sandy St
Meadowbrook Dr
E Lake Dr
Meadowbrook
Fairmont Dr
Brookshire St
Moreland Dr
Monmouth Dr
Park
77530
Sylvan Ln
Magnolia Av
LAKE SANDY
Lincoln St
East Frwy
EAST FRWY
Market St Rd
Woodleigh St
Woodleigh Dr
Pin Oak Dr
LYNCHBURG RES
CANAL
Park St
EAST FREEWAY FRONTAGE RD
EAST FRWY
Riverside Dr
Lakeshore Dr
River Haven Dr
Lazy Shore Dr
Shady Shr
MAGNOLIA AV
MARKET ST RD
MARKET ST
Lynchburg
Center St
Kilgore Av
Ilfrey St
Oakland Av
77520
HOG ISLAND
LYNCHBURG RESERVOIR
Burnet
Hillcrest Ln
Mable Av
BURNET PARK
A B C D E
1 2 3 4 5 6 7

SEE 3832 MAP

SEE 3970 MAP

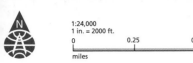

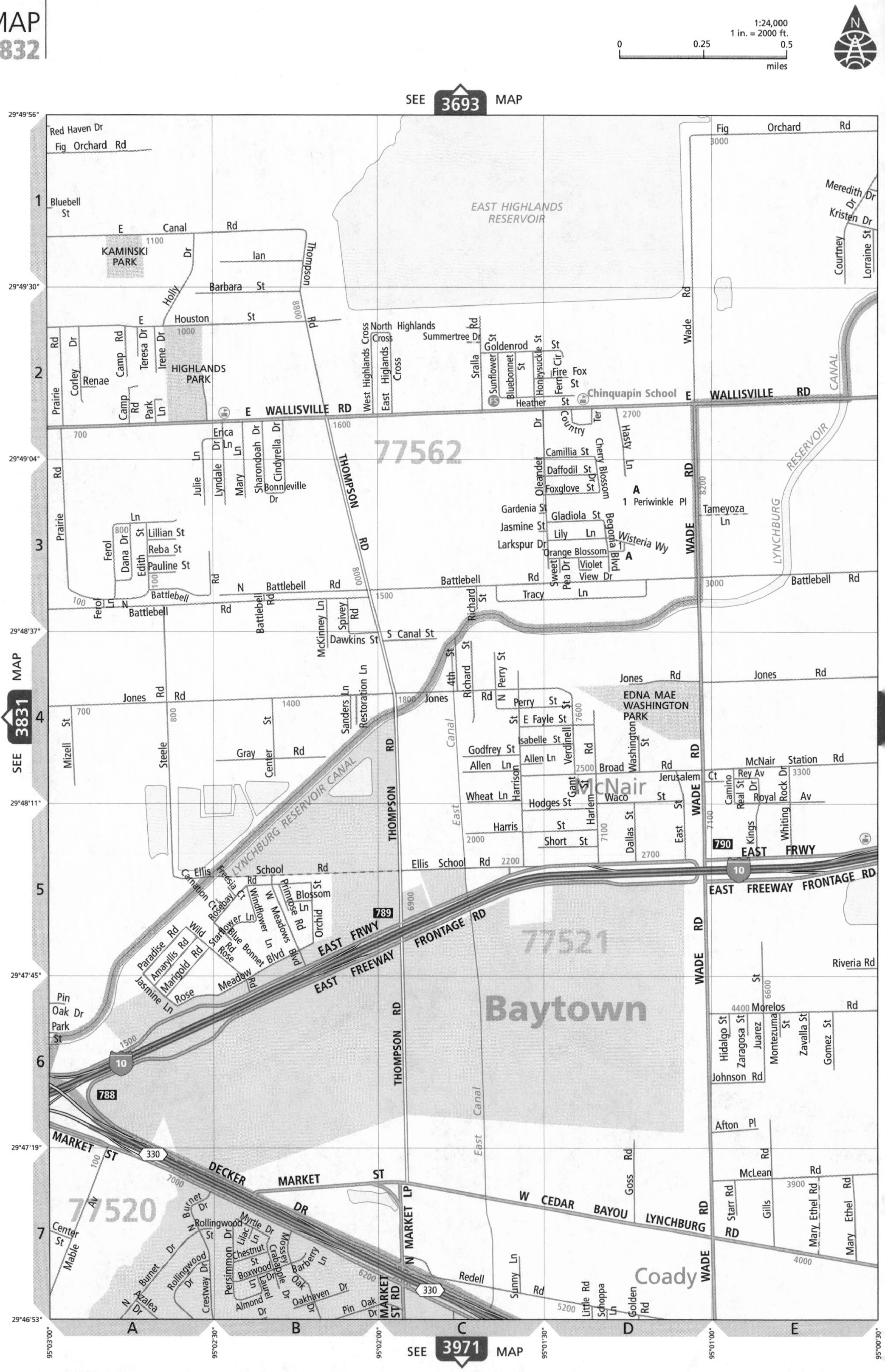
1:24,000
1 in. = 2000 ft.
0 0.25 0.5
miles
N
SEE 3693 MAP
SEE 3831 MAP
SEE 3971 MAP
29°49'56"
29°49'30"
29°49'04"
29°48'37"
29°48'11"
29°47'45"
29°47'19"
29°46'53"
95°03'00"
95°02'30"
95°02'00"
95°01'30"
95°01'00"
95°00'30"
A
B
C
D
E
1
2
3
4
5
6
7
Red Haven Dr
Fig Orchard Rd
Bluebell St
E Canal Rd
1100
KAMINSKI PARK
Holly Dr
Ian
Thompson Rd
Barbara St
E Houston St
1000
8800
HIGHLANDS PARK
Prairie Rd
Corley Dr
Renae
Camp Rd
Teresa Dr
Irene Dr
Park Ln
E WALLISVILLE RD
700
1600
Erica Ln
Lyndale Dr
Mary Ln
Julie Ln
Sharondoah Dr
Cindyrella Dr
Bonnieville Dr
THOMPSON RD
North Highlands Cross
West Highlands Cross
East Higlands Cross
Summertree Dr
Sralla Rd
Goldenrod St
Sunflower St
Bluebonnet St
Honeysuckle St
Fern Cir
Fire Fox St
Heather St
Chinquapin School
Country Ter
Oleander Dr
Cherry Blossom Dr
Hasty Ln
2700
77562
EAST HIGHLANDS RESERVOIR
Wade Rd
WADE RD
8200
E WALLISVILLE RD
CANAL
LYNCHBURG RESERVOIR
Fig Orchard Rd
3000
Meredith Dr
Kristen Dr
Courtney
Lorraine St
Camillia St
Daffodil St
Foxglove St
A
1 Periwinkle Pl
Gardenia St
Jasmine St
Larkspur Dr
Gladiola St
Lily Ln
Begonia Blvd
Wisteria Wy
Orange Blossom
Sweet Pea Dr
Violet View Dr
Tameyoza Ln
Ferol Ln
Dana Dr
Edith St
Lillian St
Reba St
Pauline St
800
100
N Battlebell Rd
Battlebell Rd
Battlebell Rd
Battlebell
Tracy Ln
Richard St
3000
Battlebell Rd
McKinney Ln
Spivey Rd
Dawkins St
S Canal St
1500
8000
Jones Rd
1800
Jones Rd
4th St
Richard St
N Perry St
Perry St
E Fayle St
Isabelle St
7600
Verdinell Rd
Godfrey St
Allen Ln
Allen Ln
Harrison
Wheat Ln
Gant St
Broad St
2500
Jerusalem Ct
Washington St
EDNA MAE WASHINGTON PARK
Jones Rd
McNair
Waco St
Hodges St
Harlem
Harris St
Short St
2000
Dallas St
East St
2700
7100
East Canal
Mizell St
700
1400
Steele
800
Gray Rd
Center St
Sanders Ln
Restoration Ln
THOMPSON RD
LYNCHBURG RESERVOIR CANAL
McNair Station Rd
Rey Av
Camino Real St
Kings Dr
Royal Rock Dr Av
3300
Whiting St
790
EAST FRWY
10
EAST FREEWAY FRONTAGE RD
Ellis School Rd
Ellis School Rd
2200
Carnation Ct
Freesia Ct
Rosebay Rd
Windflower Ln
W Meadows Blvd
Primrose Rd
Blossom St Ln
Orchid
Starflower Ln
Blue Bonnet Blvd
Rose Rd
Wild Rd
Paradise Rd
Amaryllis Rd
Marigold Rd
Jasmine Ln
Rose
Meadow Rd
789
6900
EAST FRWY
FRONTAGE RD
EAST FREEWAY
77521
Baytown
Riveria Rd
6600 St
4400 Morelos Rd
Hidalgo St
Zaragosa St
Juarez
Montezuma St
Zavalla St
Gomez St
Johnson Rd
Pin Oak Dr
Park St
1500
10
788
THOMPSON RD
East Canal
Afton Pl
MARKET ST
100
330
7000
DECKER DR
MARKET ST
N MARKET LP
W CEDAR BAYOU LYNCHBURG RD
Goss Rd
Rd
McLean Rd
3900
Starr Rd
Gills
Mary Ethel Rd
Mary Ethel Rd
4000
77520
Av
Center St
Mable
Burnet Dr
N Burnet Dr
Rollingwood St
Myrtle Dr
Lilac Ln
Chestnut St
Boxwood Dr
Crabapple Dr
Mossey Oak Dr
Barberry Ln
Laurel Ln
Almond Dr
Persimmon Dr
Crestway Dr
Rollingwood Dr
N Azalea Dr
Oakhaven Dr
Pin Oak Dr
6200
MARKET ST RD
330
Redell Rd
Sunny Ln
5200
Little Rd
Schoppa Ln
Golden Rd
Coady
WADE RD

1:24,000
1 in. = 2000 ft.
0 0.25 0.5
miles

SEE 3694 MAP

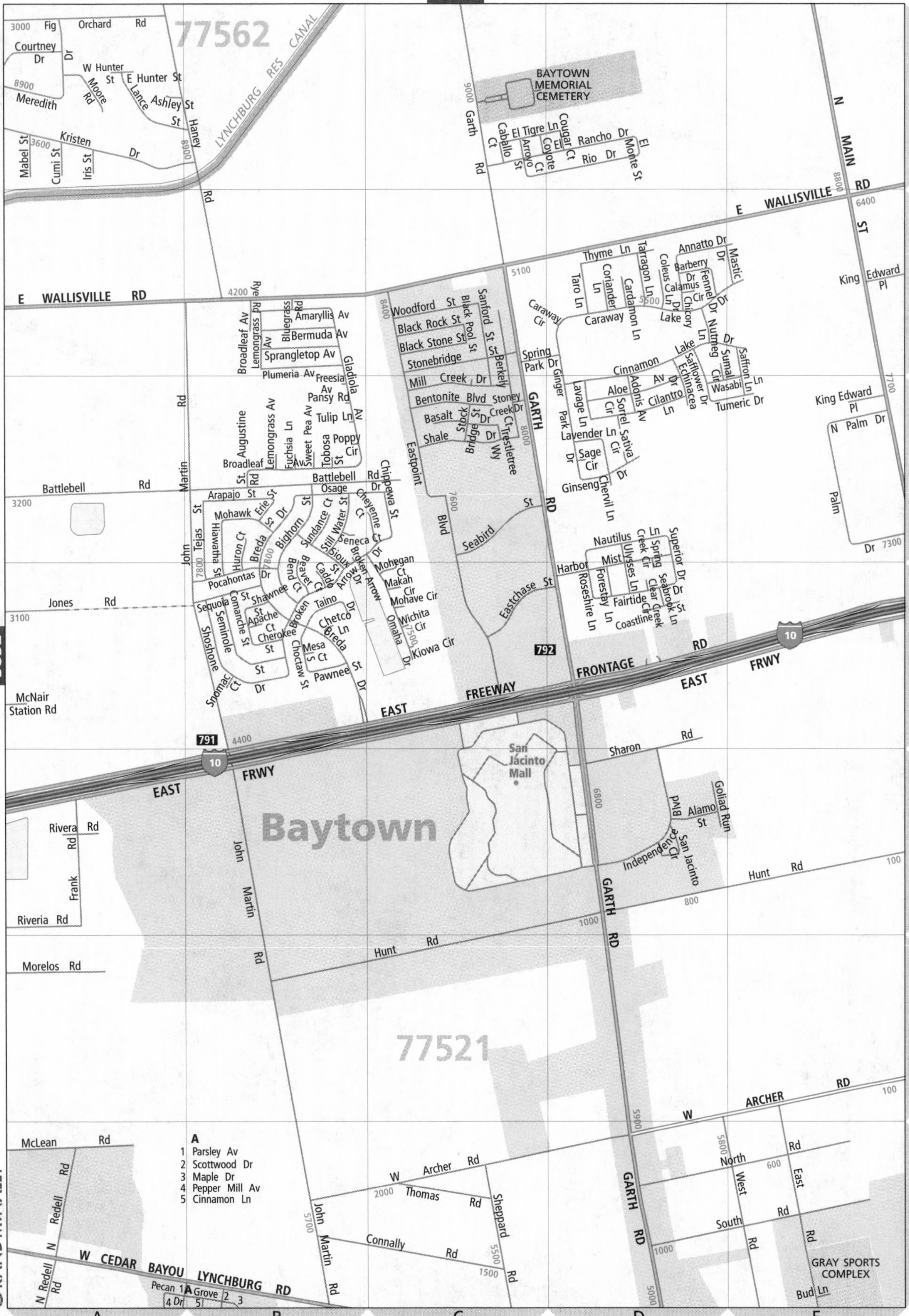
77562
LYNCHBURG RES CANAL
BAYTOWN MEMORIAL CEMETERY
E WALLISVILLE RD
N MAIN ST
Garth Rd
John Martin Rd
Battlebell Rd
Jones Rd
McNair Station Rd
EAST FREEWAY
FRONTAGE RD
EAST FRWY
San Jacinto Mall
Baytown
Hunt Rd
Rivera Rd
Riveria Rd
Frank Rd
Morelos Rd
77521
W ARCHER RD
W Archer Rd
Thomas Rd
Connally Rd
Sheppard Rd
McLean Rd
N Redell Rd
W CEDAR BAYOU LYNCHBURG RD
GRAY SPORTS COMPLEX
Bud Ln
North Rd
West Rd
East Rd
South Rd
Sharon Rd
Goliad Run
Alamo St
Independence Blvd
San Jacinto Cir
King Edward Pl
N Palm Dr
Palm Dr
Eastpoint Blvd
Seabird St
Eastchase St
Harbor Mist
Nautilus Ln
Superior Dr
Caraway Cir
Spring Park Dr
Cinnamon Ln
Thyme Ln
Annatto Dr
Woodford St
Black Rock St
Black Stone St
Stonebridge
Mill Creek Dr
Bentonite Blvd
Basalt
Shale
Sanford St
Amaryllis Av
Bermuda Av
Sprangleotop Av
Broadleaf Av
Gladiola Av
Arapajo St
Mohawk
Pocahontas Dr
Sequoia St
Shoshone
Comanche St
Seminole
Apache Ct
Cherokee Ct
Choctaw St
Pawnee St
Kiowa Cir
Wichita Cir
Omaha Dr
Mohave Cir
Makah Cir
Mohegan Ct
Seneca Ct
Cheyenne Ct
Chippewa St
Osage
A
1 Parsley Av
2 Scottwood Dr
3 Maple Dr
4 Pepper Mill Av
5 Cinnamon Ln
Pecan
Grove
10
791
792
29°49'53"
29°49'27"
29°49'00"
29°48'34"
29°48'08"
29°47'42"
29°47'16"
29°46'50"
95°00'30"
95°00'00"
94°59'30"
94°59'00"
94°58'30"
94°58'00"
1
2
3
4
5
6
7
A
B
C
D
E

SEE 3834 MAP

SEE 3972 MAP

SEE 3695 MAP

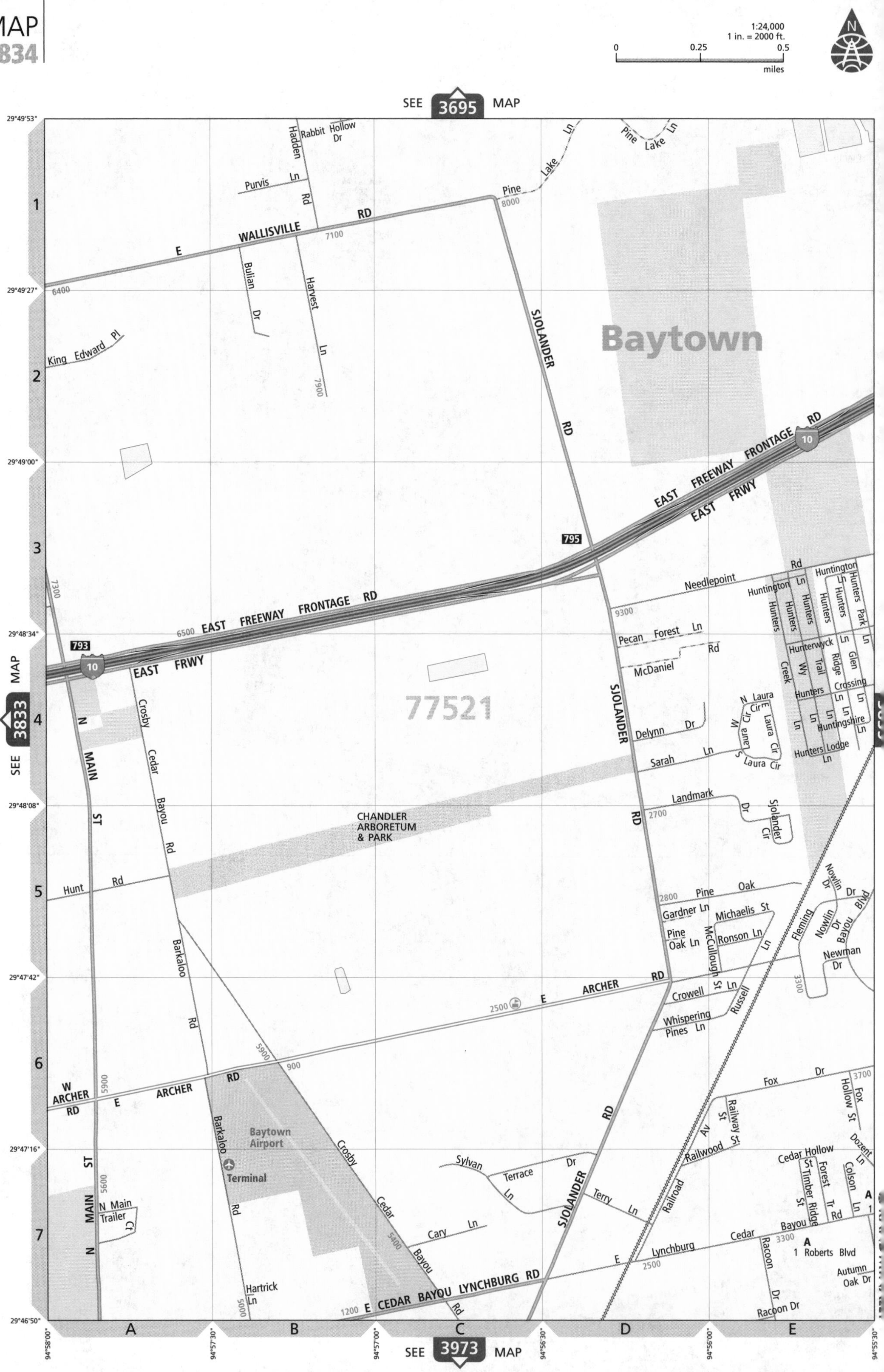
1:24,000
1 in. = 2000 ft.
0 0.25 0.5
miles
N
Baytown
77521
CHANDLER ARBORETUM & PARK
Baytown Airport
Terminal
E WALLISVILLE RD
7100
6400
Pine Lake Ln
8000
Pine Lake Ln
Rabbit Hollow Dr
Hadden Rd
Purvis Ln
Bulian Dr
Harvest Ln
7900
King Edward Pl
SJOLANDER RD
EAST FREEWAY FRONTAGE RD
EAST FRWY
10
795
793
7300
6500
9300
Needlepoint Rd
Huntington Ln
Hunters Creek
Hunters Wy
Hunters Trail
Hunters Ridge
Hunters Park Ln
Hunterwyck Ln
Glen Ln
Hunters Crossing
Hunters Ln
Huntingshire Ln
Hunters Lodge Ln
Pecan Forest Ln
McDaniel Rd
Delynn Dr
N Laura Cir
E Laura Cir
W Laura Cir
S Laura Cir
Sarah Ln
Landmark Dr
Sjolander Cir
2700
N MAIN ST
Crosby Cedar Bayou Rd
Hunt Rd
Pine Oak
2800
Gardner Ln
Michaelis St
Pine Oak Ln
McCullough St
Ronson Ln
Nowlin Dr
Bayou Blvd
Fleming
Newman Dr
3300
Barkaloo Rd
E ARCHER RD
2500
Crowell Ln
Russell
Whispering Pines Ln
W ARCHER RD
5900
900
5900
Fox Dr
3700
Fox Hollow St
Railway St
Av
Railwood St
Dozent Ln
Sylvan Terrace Dr
Ln
Terry Ln
Railroad
Cedar Hollow St
Forest Tr
Timber Ridge Rd
Colson Ln
5600
N Main Trailer Ct
Cary Ln
5400
Cedar Bayou
3300
Lynchburg
E
2500
Racoon Dr
Racoon Dr
A
1 Roberts Blvd
Autumn Oak Dr
Hartrick Ln
5000
1200
E CEDAR BAYOU LYNCHBURG RD
Rd
29°49'53"
29°49'27"
29°49'00"
29°48'34"
29°48'08"
29°47'42"
29°47'16"
29°46'50"
94°58'00"
94°57'30"
94°57'00"
94°56'30"
94°56'00"
94°55'30"
1
2
3
4
5
6
7
A
B
C
D
E

SEE 3833 MAP

SEE 3973 MAP

1:24,000
1 in. = 2000 ft.
0 0.25 0.5
miles

SEE 3696 MAP

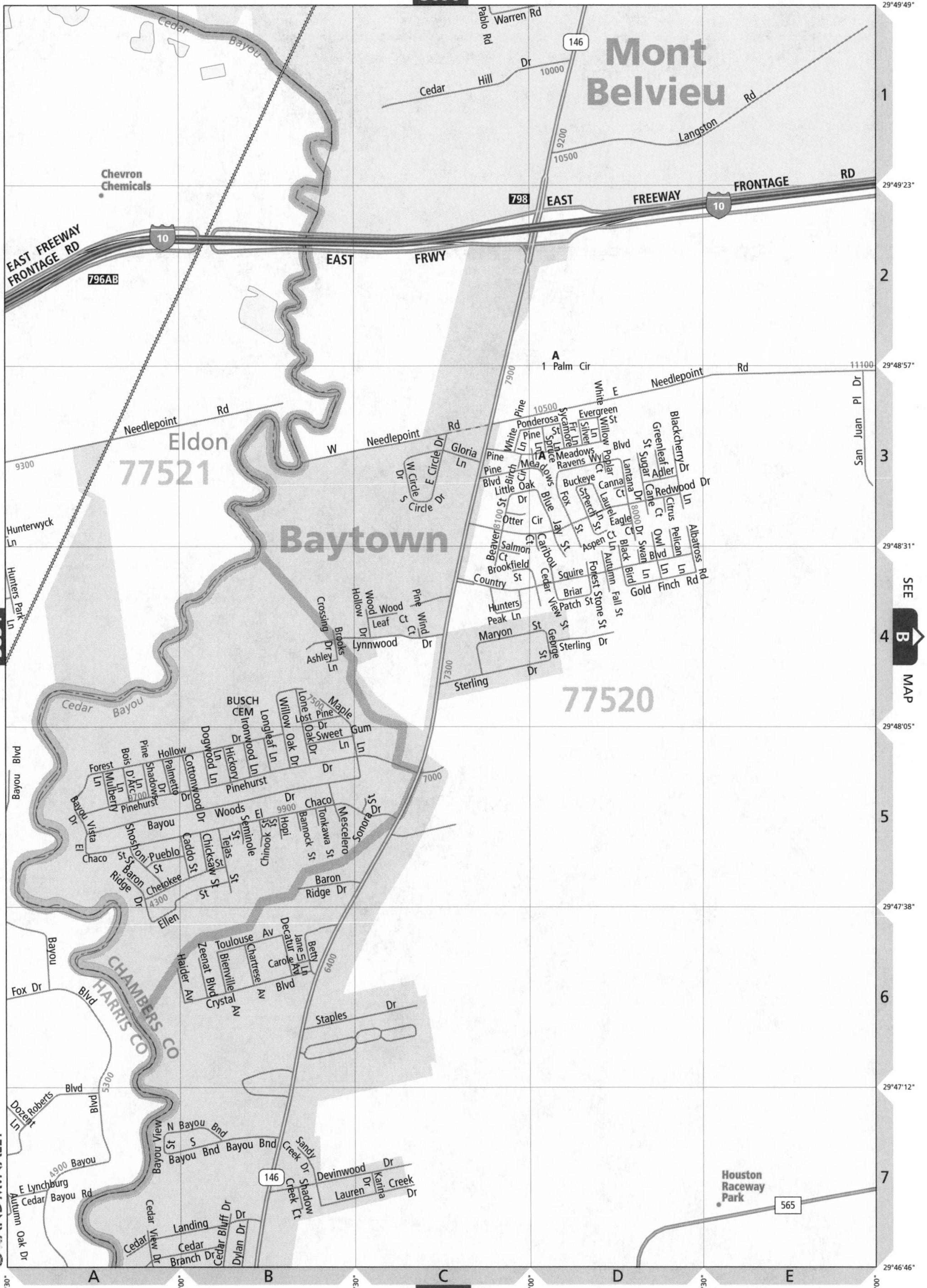
Mont
Belvieu
Eldon
77521
Baytown
77520
Chevron
Chemicals
Cedar Bayou
146
10
798
796AB
565
EAST FREEWAY FRONTAGE RD
EAST FRWY
Warren Rd
Pablo Rd
Cedar Hill Dr
Langston Rd
Needlepoint Rd
W Needlepoint Rd
E Needlepoint Rd
1 Palm Cir
San Juan Pl Dr
Gloria Ln
Pine Blvd
Hunterwyck Ln
Hunters Park Ln
BUSCH
CEM
Pinehurst
Bayou Woods Dr
Chaco
Baron Ridge Dr
Ellen
Toulouse Av
Decatur Av
Zeenat Blvd
Bienville
Chartrese Av
Carole
Crystal Av
Haider Av
Staples Dr
CHAMBERS CO
HARRIS CO
Bayou Blvd
Fox Dr
Roberts Blvd
Dozent Ln
Bayou View
N Bayou Bnd
S Bayou Bnd
Sandy Creek Dr
Shadow Creek Ct
Devinwood Dr
Lauren Dr
Karina
Creek Dr
E Lynchburg Cedar Bayou Rd
Autumn Oak Dr
Cedar View Dr
Landing
Cedar Branch Dr
Cedar Bluff Dr
Dylan Dr
Houston
Raceway
Park
Sterling Dr
Maryon St
George St
Lynnwood Dr
Albatross Rd
Gold Finch Rd
Fall St
Forest Stone St
Briar Patch St
Squire
Country
Brookfield St
Hunters Peak Ln
A B C D E
1 2 3 4 5 6 7
29°49'49"
29°49'23"
29°48'57"
29°48'31"
29°48'05"
29°47'38"
29°47'12"
29°46'46"
94°55'30"
94°55'00"
94°54'30"
94°54'00"
94°53'30"
94°53'00"

SEE B MAP

SEE 3974 MAP

1:24,000
1 in. = 2000 ft.
0 0.25 0.5
miles

SEE 3812 MAP

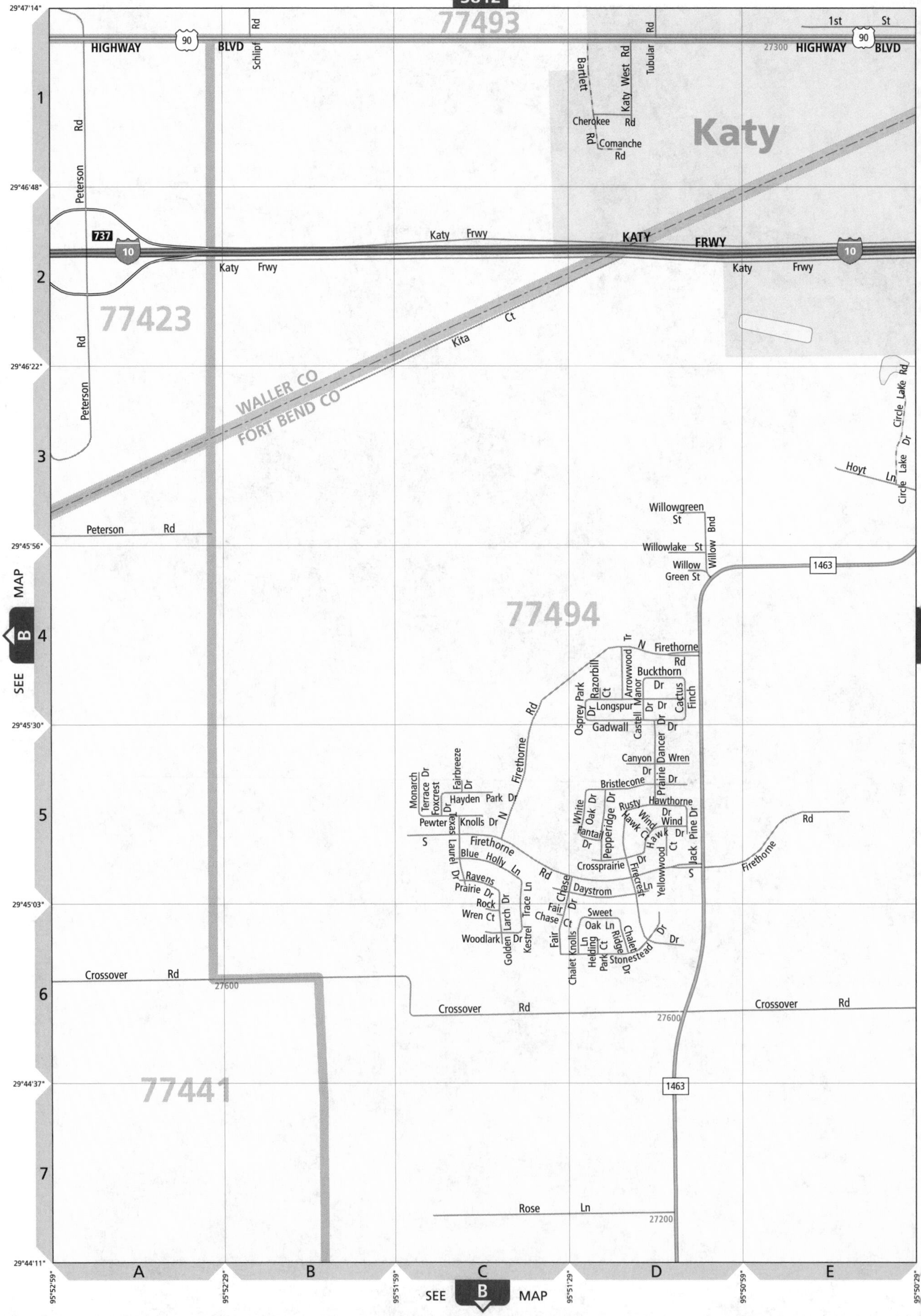
77493
HIGHWAY 90 BLVD
Schlipf Rd
Tubular Rd
1st St
27300 HIGHWAY 90 BLVD
Bartlett Rd
Katy West Rd
Cherokee Rd
Comanche Rd
Katy
Peterson Rd
737
10
Katy Frwy
KATY FRWY
77423
Kita Ct
WALLER CO
FORT BEND CO
Circle Lake Rd
Circle Lake Dr
Hoyt Ln
Willowgreen St
Willowlake St
Willow Green St
Willow Bnd
1463
77494
N Firethorne Rd
Buckthorn Dr
Arrowwood Tr
Razorbill Ct
Osprey Park Dr
Longspur Dr
Castell Manor Dr
Cactus Finch
Gadwall Dr
Prairie Dancer Dr
Canyon Wren Dr
Bristlecone Dr
Monarch Terrace Dr
Foxcrest Dr
Fairbreeze Dr
Hayden Park Dr
Pewter Knolls Dr
Texas Laurel Dr
S Firethorne Rd
Blue Holly Ln
White Oak Dr
Fantail Dr
Pepperidge Dr
Rusty Wind Dr
Hawk Ct
Hawthorne Dr
Wind Hawk Dr
Yellowwood Ct
Jack Pine Dr
Crossprairie Dr
Firecrest Ln
Ravens Prairie Dr
Rock Wren Ct
Woodlark Dr
Golden Larch Dr
Kestrel Trace Ln
Fair Chase Dr
Fair Chase Ct
Daystrom
Sweet Oak Ln
Chalet Knolls Ln
Helding Park Ct
Ridge
Chalet Stonestead Dr
Crossover Rd
27600
77441
Rose Ln
27200
A B C D E
1 2 3 4 5 6 7
29°47'14"
29°46'48"
29°46'22"
29°45'56"
29°45'30"
29°45'03"
29°44'37"
29°44'11"
95°52'59"
95°52'29"
95°51'59"
95°51'29"
95°50'59"
95°50'29"

SEE B MAP

SEE B MAP

1:24,000
1 in. = 2000 ft.
0 0.25 0.5
miles

SEE 3813 MAP

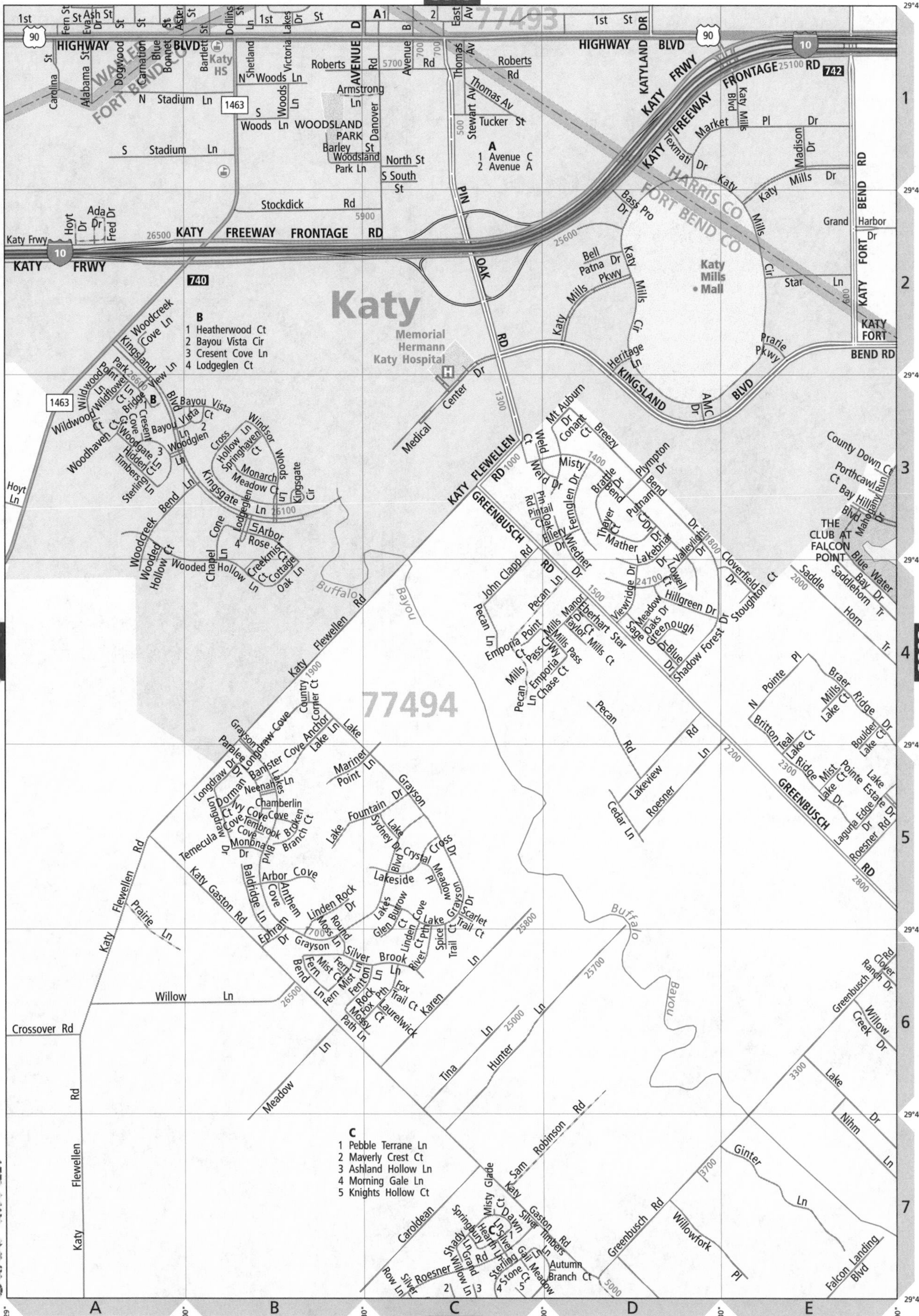
Katy
77493
77494
Katy HS
WOODSLAND PARK
Memorial Hermann Katy Hospital
Katy Mills Mall
THE CLUB AT FALCON POINT
HARRIS CO
FORT BEND CO
WALLER CO
FORT BEND CO
HIGHWAY BLVD
KATY FREEWAY FRONTAGE RD
KATY FRWY
PIN OAK RD
KINGSLAND BLVD
KATY FLEWELLEN RD
GREENBUSCH RD
KATYLAND DR
KATY FORT BEND RD
AVENUE D
Buffalo Bayou
A
1 Avenue C
2 Avenue A
B
1 Heatherwood Ct
2 Bayou Vista Cir
3 Cresent Cove Ln
4 Lodgeglen Ct
C
1 Pebble Terrane Ln
2 Maverly Crest Ct
3 Ashland Hollow Ln
4 Morning Gale Ln
5 Knights Hollow Ct
1
2
3
4
5
6
7
A
B
C
D
E
29°47'13"
29°46'47"
29°46'21"
29°45'55"
29°45'28"
29°45'02"
29°44'36"
29°44'10"
95°50'29"
95°50'00"
95°49'30"
95°49'00"
95°48'30"
95°48'00"

SEE 3953 MAP

SEE 4092 MAP

SEE 3814 MAP

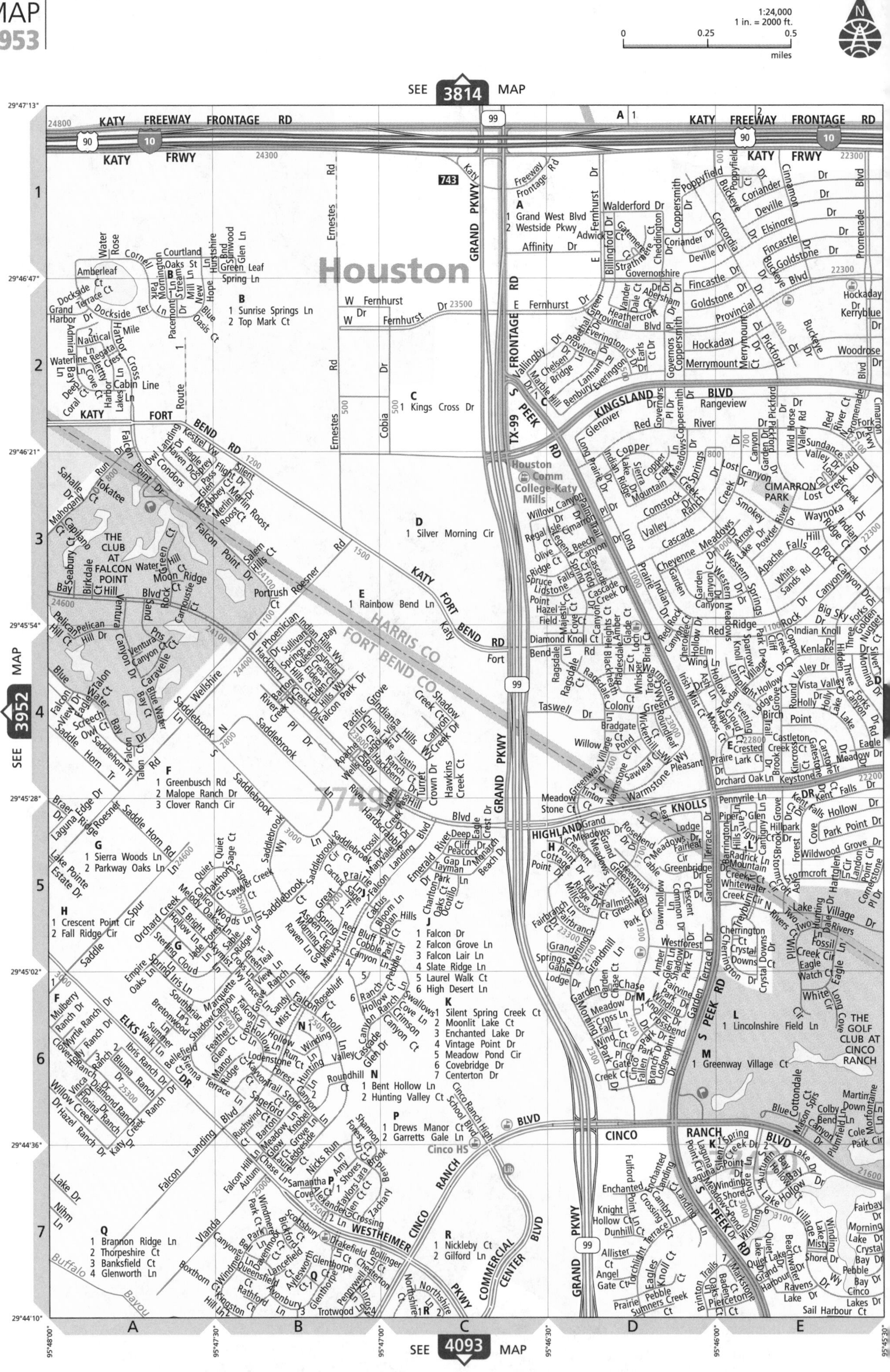
1:24,000
1 in. = 2000 ft.
0 0.25 0.5
miles
N
Houston
KATY FREEWAY FRONTAGE RD
KATY FRWY
GRAND PKWY
FRONTAGE RD
S PEEK RD
KINGSLAND BLVD
KATY FORT BEND RD
HARRIS CO
FORT BEND CO
HIGHLAND KNOLLS
CINCO RANCH BLVD
WESTHEIMER
COMMERCIAL CENTER BLVD
CINCO RANCH PKWY
TX-99
Houston Comm College-Katy Mills
THE CLUB AT FALCON POINT
THE GOLF CLUB AT CINCO RANCH
CIMARRON PARK
Cinco HS
Buffalo Bayou
A
1 Grand West Blvd
2 Westside Pkwy
B
1 Sunrise Springs Ln
2 Top Mark Ct
C
1 Kings Cross Dr
D
1 Silver Morning Cir
E
1 Rainbow Bend Ln
F
1 Greenbusch Rd
2 Malope Ranch Dr
3 Clover Ranch Cir
G
1 Sierra Woods Ln
2 Parkway Oaks Ln
H
1 Crescent Point Cir
2 Fall Ridge Cir
J
1 Falcon Dr
2 Falcon Grove Ln
3 Falcon Lair Ln
4 Slate Ridge Ln
5 Laurel Walk Ct
6 High Desert Ln
K
1 Silent Spring Creek Ct
2 Moonlit Lake Ct
3 Enchanted Lake Dr
4 Vintage Point Dr
5 Meadow Pond Cir
6 Covebridge Dr
7 Centerton Dr
L
1 Lincolnshire Field Ln
M
1 Greenway Village Ct
N
1 Bent Hollow Ln
2 Hunting Valley Ct
P
1 Drews Manor Ct
2 Garretts Gale Ln
Q
1 Brannon Ridge Ln
2 Thorpeshire Ct
3 Banksfield Ct
4 Glenworth Ln
R
1 Nickleby Ct
2 Gilford Ln
29°47'13"
29°46'47"
29°46'21"
29°45'54"
29°45'28"
29°45'02"
29°44'36"
29°44'10"
95°48'00"
95°47'30"
95°47'00"
95°46'30"
95°46'00"
95°45'30"
SEE 3952 MAP

SEE 4093 MAP

1:24,000
1 in. = 2000 ft.
0 0.25 0.5
miles

SEE 3815 MAP

KATY FRWY
KATY FREEWAY FRONTAGE RD
HOME DEPOT PLZ
10
90
745
746
747
Houston
Pointwest Shopping Center
Kingsland Vil Shopping Center
Mason Park Centre
One Mason Plaza Shopping Center
Green Tree Shopping Center
Christus St. Catherine Hosp
Taylor HS
KINGSLAND BLVD
MASON RD
WESTGREEN BLVD
FRY RD
HIGHLAND KNOLLS DR
CINCO RANCH BLVD
WESTHEIMER PKWY
77450
77094
THE GOLF CLUB AT CINCO RANCH
WILLOW FORK COUNTRY CLUB
GEORGE BUSH PARK
HARRIS CO
FORT BEND CO
FIRST LK
A 1 N Westgreen Blvd
B 1 Fish Creek Dr 2 Sterling Creek Cir 3 Sweet Pine Dr
C 1 Ivory Brook Dr 2 Partridge Run Dr
D 1 Western Hills Ct 2 Golden Nugget Ct 3 Silver Morning Ct 4 Cove Hollow Dr
E 1 Geronimo Ct
F 1 Barton Creek 2 Landmore Ct 3 Polly Creek Wy 4 Penrice Dr 5 Tretowner
G 1 Canyon Terrace Ct
H 1 Gulf Oil Big Creek Field Rd
J 1 Knolls Spring Dr 2 Highland Oak
K 1 Hidden Shore Cir 2 Golden Reed Dr 3 High Canyon Ct
L 1 Mission Hills Ct
M 1 Crossbrook Ct 2 Morning Lake Dr 3 Cloudbridge Dr
N 1 Cabot Point Dr 2 Sparrows Rdg 3 Meadow Arbor Ct
P 1 Crossing Nexus Ln 2 Avon Oaks Ln
Q 1 Prairie Stone Tr 2 Diamond Hollow Ct 3 Auburn Hollow Ln
R 1 Kelliwood Ct Dr 2 Kingsbriar Ct
29°47'12"
29°46'45"
29°46'19"
29°45'53"
29°45'27"
29°45'01"
29°44'35"
29°44'08"
95°45'30"
95°45'00"
95°44'30"
95°44'00"
95°43'30"
95°43'00"
A B C D E
1 2 3 4 5 6 7

SEE 3955 MAP

SEE 4094 MAP

1:24,000
1 in. = 2000 ft.
0 0.25 0.5
miles

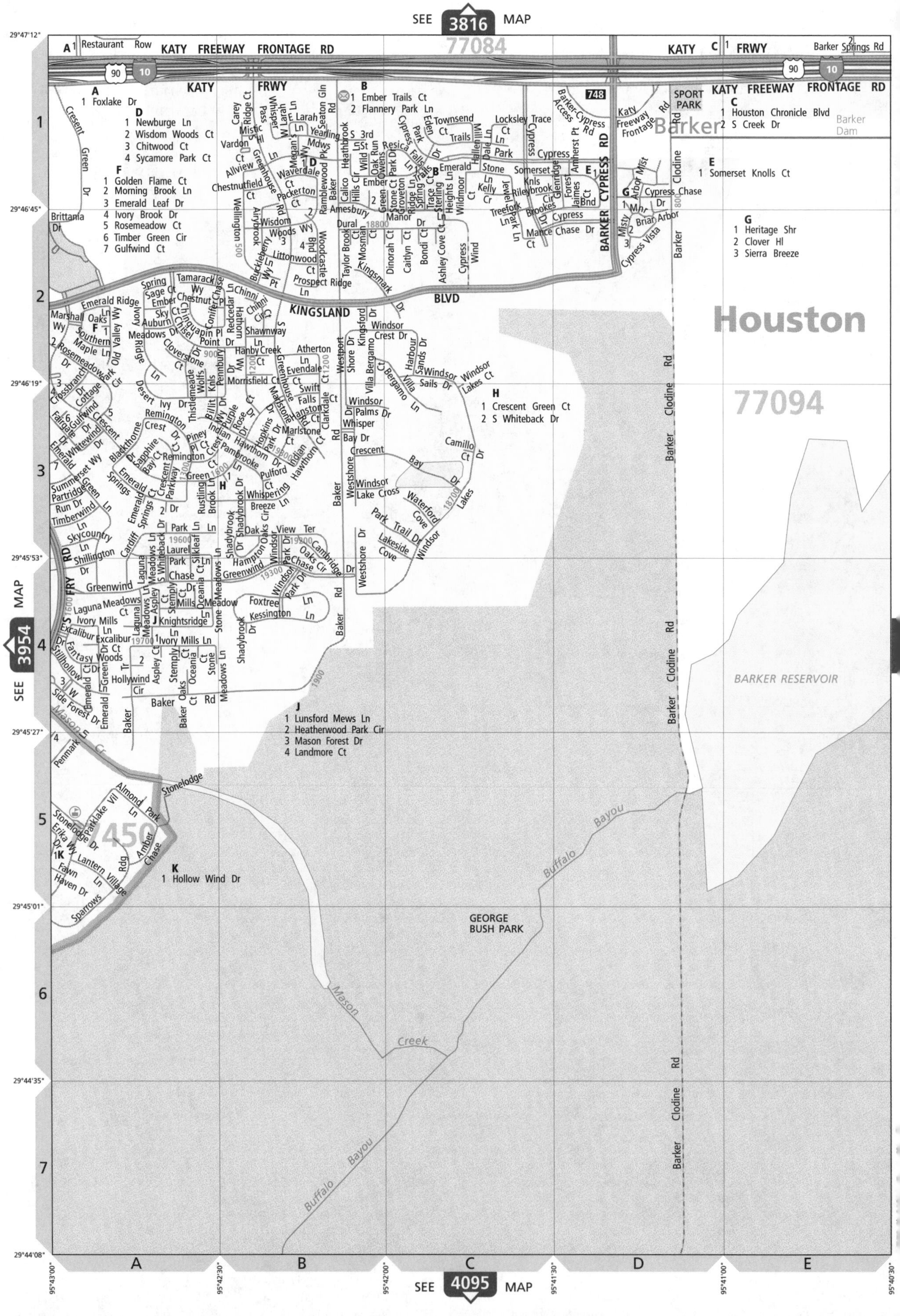
SEE 3816 MAP
77084
KATY FREEWAY FRONTAGE RD
KATY FRWY
KATY FREEWAY FRONTAGE RD
Barker Springs Rd
SPORT PARK
Barker
Barker Dam
KINGSLAND BLVD
BARKER CYPRESS RD
Houston
77094
Barker Clodine Rd
BARKER RESERVOIR
GEORGE BUSH PARK
Buffalo Bayou
Mason Creek
FRY RD
A
1 Foxlake Dr
B
1 Ember Trails Ct
2 Flannery Park Ln
C
1 Houston Chronicle Blvd
2 S Creek Dr
D
1 Newburge Ln
2 Wisdom Woods Ct
3 Chitwood Ct
4 Sycamore Park Ct
E
1 Somerset Knolls Ct
F
1 Golden Flame Ct
2 Morning Brook Ln
3 Emerald Leaf Dr
4 Ivory Brook Dr
5 Rosemeadow Ct
6 Timber Green Cir
7 Gulfwind Ct
G
1 Heritage Shr
2 Clover Hl
3 Sierra Breeze
H
1 Crescent Green Ct
2 S Whiteback Dr
J
1 Lunsford Mews Ln
2 Heatherwood Park Cir
3 Mason Forest Dr
4 Landmore Ct
K
1 Hollow Wind Dr
SEE 3954 MAP
SEE 4095 MAP
A B C D E
1 2 3 4 5 6 7
29°47'12" 29°46'45" 29°46'19" 29°45'53" 29°45'27" 29°45'01" 29°44'35" 29°44'08"
95°43'00" 95°42'30" 95°42'00" 95°41'30" 95°41'00" 95°40'30"

1:24,000
1 in. = 2000 ft.
0 0.25 0.5
miles

SEE 3817 MAP

KATY FREEWAY FRONTAGE RD
KATY FRWY
Barker Springs Rd
77084
77079
77094
77077
Houston
Barker Dam
BARKER RESERVOIR
GEORGE BUSH PARK
ADDICKS SATSUMA RD
MEMORIAL DR
TERRY HERSHY PARK
Buffalo Bayou
BRIAR FOREST DR
Westside HS
MAGEE CEM
National Guard Armory
Village at West Oaks
Westheimer Six Plaza
WESTHEIMER PKWY
WESTHEIMER RD
A
1 Langham Creek Dr
2 Park Ten Blvd
B
1 Broadfield Blvd
2 Memorial Brook Blvd
C
1 Park & Ride Dr
D
1 Atlantis Ct
2 E Fair Harbor Ln
3 Barkers Landing Ct
4 Lee Shore Ln
5 Marywood Chase
E
1 Bonniefield Ln
2 Shannon Marie Ln
F
1 Cottage Landing Ct
2 Bay Front Dr
3 Shore Meadows Ct
4 Arbor Canyon Ln
Grisby Rd
Hidden Cove
Barkers Landing
Fleetwood Oaks Dr
Walkwood Dr
Westway Ln
Kingston Cove Ln
Piping Rock Ln
Briarview Dr
Barker Oaks Dr
Chevy Chase Dr
Burgoyne Rd
Ella Lee Ln
Overbrook Ln
Locke Ln
Wickersham Ln
1 2 3 4 5 6 7
A B C D E

SEE 3957 MAP

SEE 4096 MAP

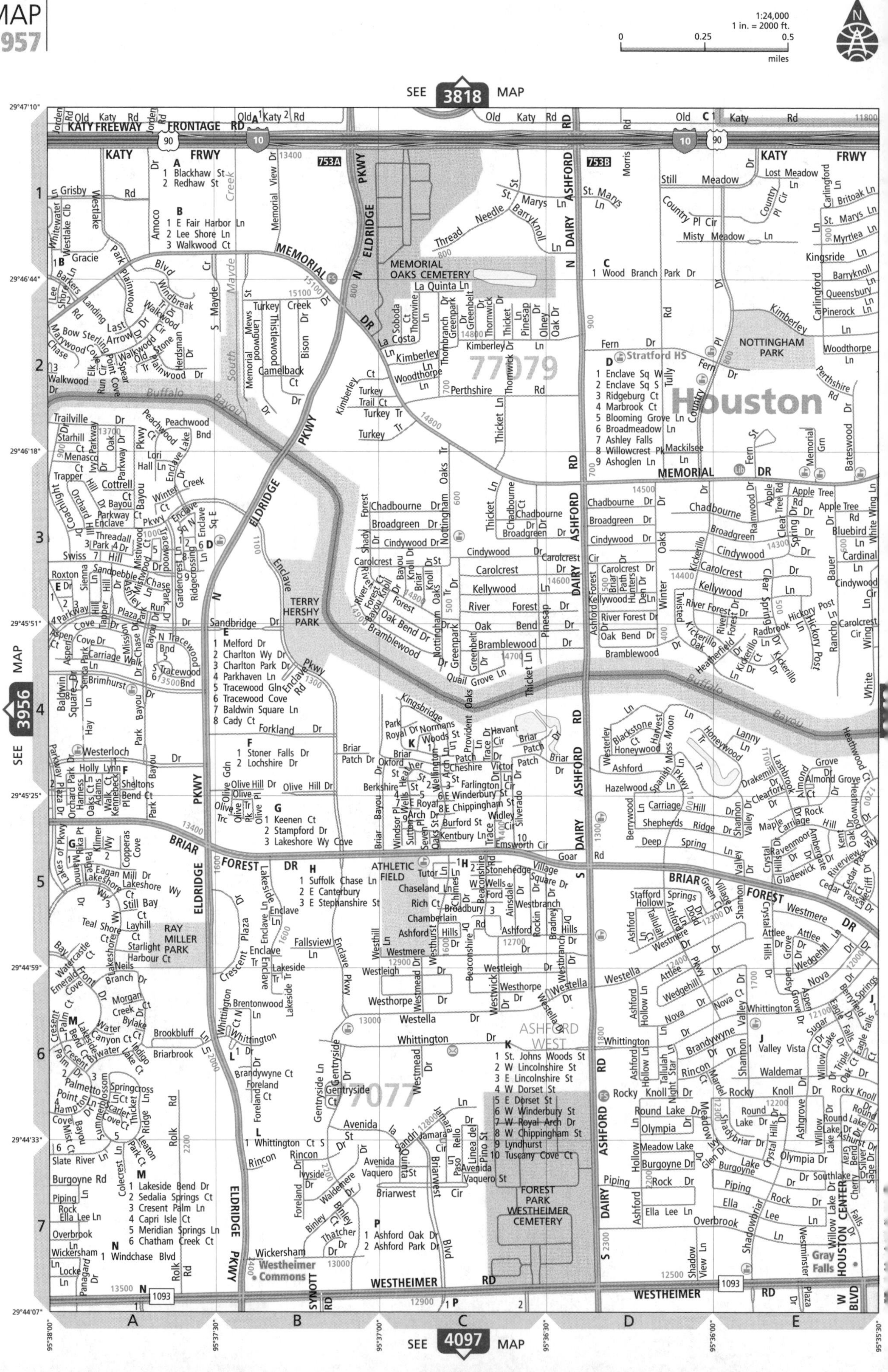
1:24,000
1 in. = 2000 ft.
0 0.25 0.5
miles
SEE 3818 MAP
SEE 4097 MAP
SEE 3956 MAP
KATY FREEWAY
FRONTAGE RD
Old Katy Rd
KATY FRWY
MEMORIAL DR
N ELDRIDGE PKWY
ELDRIDGE PKWY
N DAIRY ASHFORD RD
S DAIRY ASHFORD RD
BRIAR FOREST DR
WESTHEIMER RD
SYNOTT RD
MEMORIAL OAKS CEMETERY
77079
Houston
NOTTINGHAM PARK
Stratford HS
Buffalo Bayou
TERRY HERSHY PARK
ATHLETIC FIELD
RAY MILLER PARK
ASHFORD WEST
77077
FOREST PARK WESTHEIMER CEMETERY
Westheimer Commons
Gray Falls
HOUSTON CENTER BLVD
A 1 Blackhaw St 2 Redhaw St
B 1 E Fair Harbor Ln 2 Lee Shore Ln 3 Walkwood Ct
C 1 Wood Branch Park Dr
D 1 Enclave Sq W 2 Enclave Sq S 3 Ridgeburg Ct 4 Marbrook Ct 5 Blooming Grove Ln 6 Broadmeadow Ln 7 Ashley Falls 8 Willowcrest Pk 9 Ashoglen Ln
E 1 Melford Dr 2 Charlton Wy Dr 3 Charlton Park Dr 4 Parkhaven Ln 5 Tracewood Gln 6 Tracewood Cove 7 Baldwin Square Ln 8 Cady Ct
F 1 Stoner Falls Dr 2 Lochshire Dr
G 1 Keenen Ct 2 Stampford Dr 3 Lakeshore Wy Cove
H 1 Suffolk Chase Ln 2 E Canterbury 3 E Stephanshire St
J 1 Valley Vista
K 1 St. Johns Woods St 2 W Lincolnshire St 3 E Lincolnshire St 4 W Dorset St 5 E Dorset St 6 W Winderbury St 7 W Royal Arch Dr 8 W Chippingham St 9 Lyndhurst 10 Tuscany Cove Ct
L 1 Whittington Ct S
M 1 Lakeside Bend Dr 2 Sedalia Springs Ct 3 Cresent Palm Ln 4 Capri Isle Ct 5 Meridian Springs Ln 6 Chatham Creek Ct
N 1 Windchase Blvd
P 1 Ashford Oak Dr 2 Ashford Park Dr
29°47'10"
29°46'44"
29°46'18"
29°45'51"
29°45'25"
29°44'59"
29°44'33"
29°44'07"
95°38'00"
95°37'30"
95°37'00"
95°36'30"
95°36'00"
95°35'30"

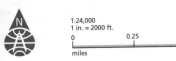

1:24,000
1 in. = 2000 ft.
0 0.25 0.5
miles

SEE 3819 MAP

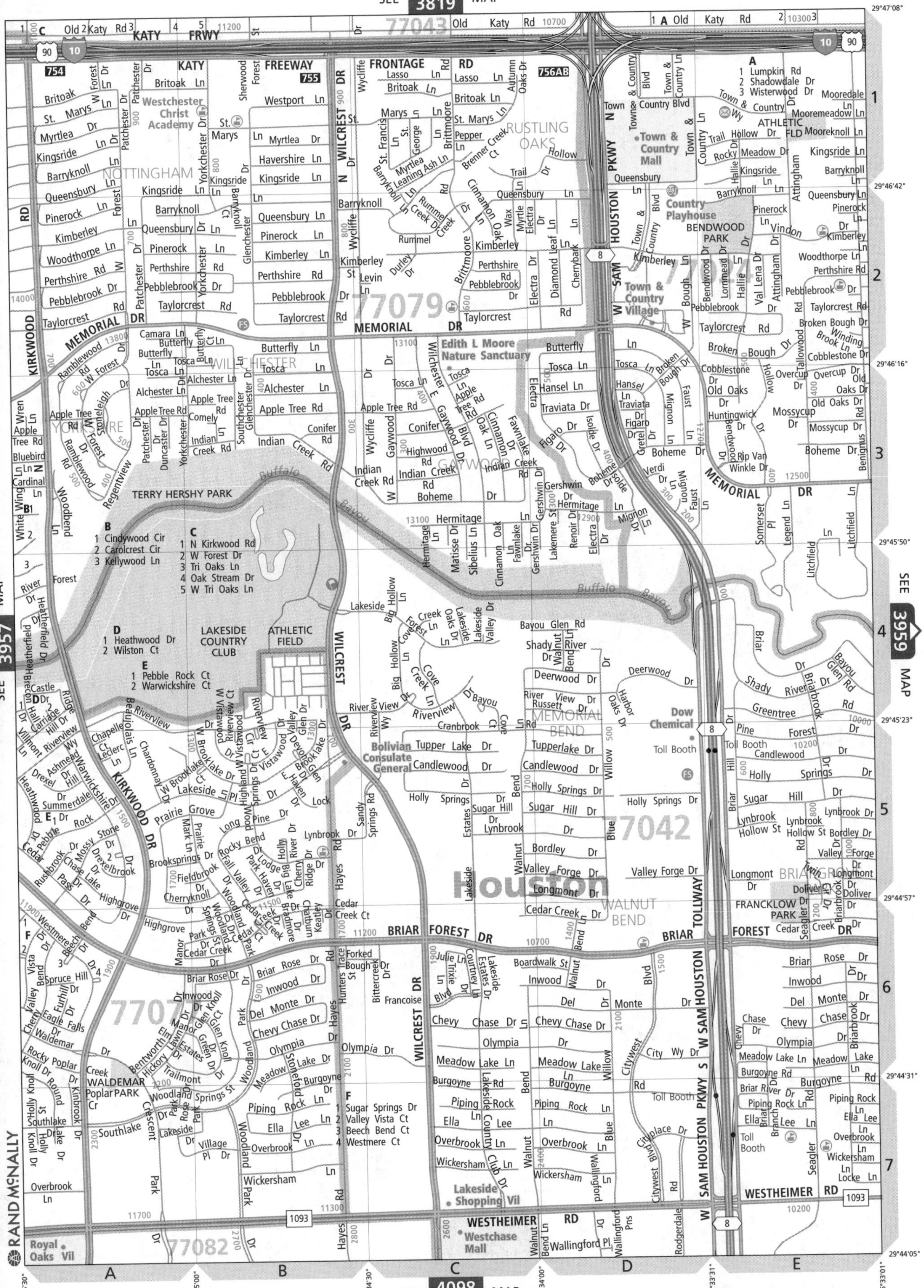
KATY FRWY
KATY FREEWAY
Old Katy Rd
MEMORIAL DR
KIRKWOOD RD
N WILCREST DR
WILCREST DR
BRIAR FOREST DR
WESTHEIMER RD
SAM HOUSTON PKWY
SAM HOUSTON TOLLWAY
W SAM HOUSTON PKWY S
NOTTINGHAM
RUSTLING OAKS
WILCHESTER
YORKSHIRE
GAYWOOD
BENDWOOD PARK
MEMORIAL BEND
BRIARGROVE
WALNUT BEND
TERRY HERSHY PARK
LAKESIDE COUNTRY CLUB
ATHLETIC FIELD
Buffalo Bayou
Edith L Moore Nature Sanctuary
Town & Country Mall
Town & Country Village
Country Playhouse
Westchester Christ Academy
Bolivian Consulate General
Dow Chemical
Toll Booth
Lakeside Shopping Vil
Westchase Mall
Royal Oaks Vil
FRANCKLOW PARK
WALDEMAR PARK
Houston
77043
77079
77024
77042
77077
77082

SEE 3959 MAP

SEE 3957 MAP

SEE 4098 MAP

1:24,000
1 in. = 2000 ft.
0 0.25 0.5
miles

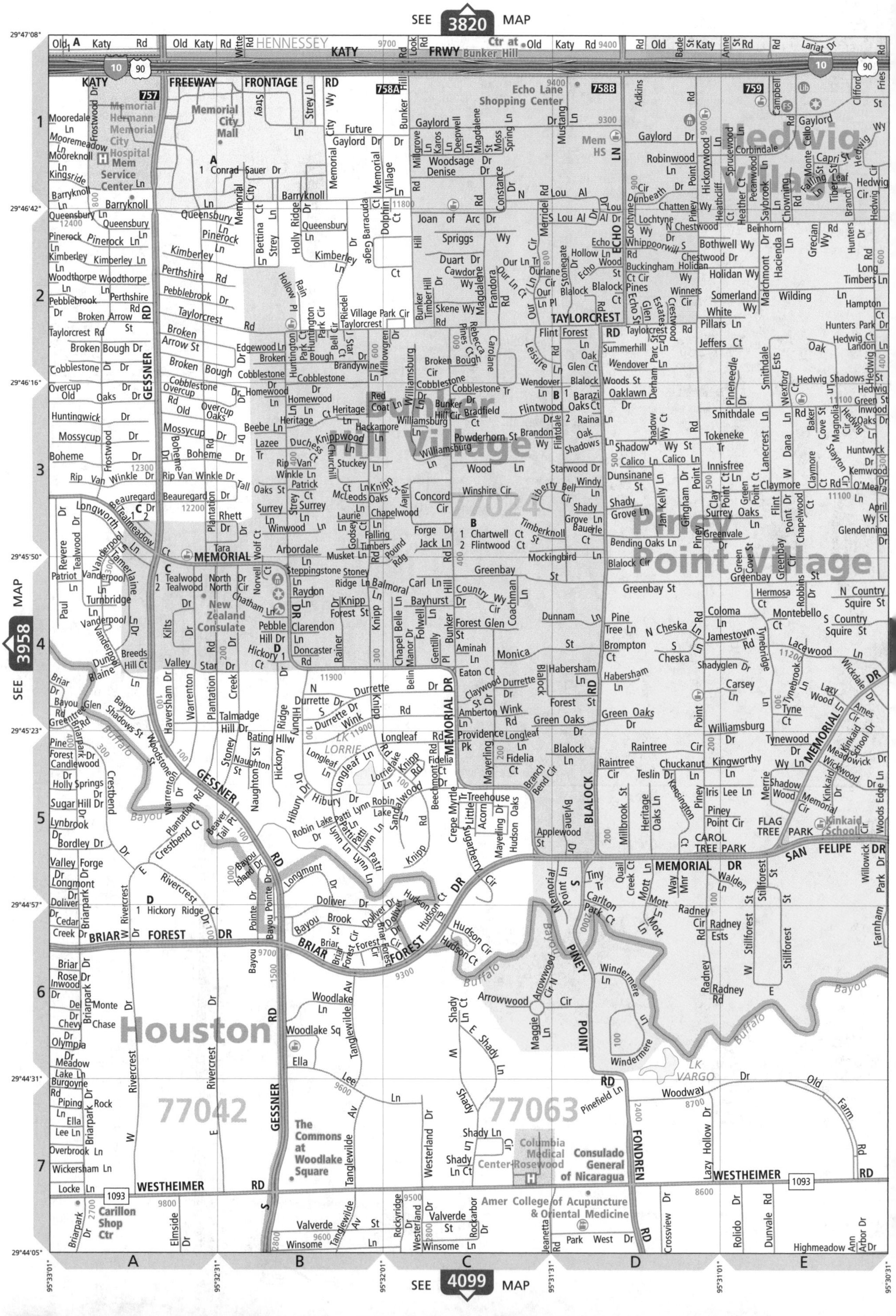
SEE 3820 MAP
SEE 3958 MAP
SEE 4099 MAP
KATY FRWY
KATY FREEWAY FRONTAGE RD
Old Katy Rd
Memorial City Mall
Memorial Hermann Memorial City Hospital
Mem Service Center
Echo Lane Shopping Center
Mem HS
Hedwig Village
Bunker Hill Village
Piney Point Village
Houston
77024
77042
77063
GESSNER RD
MEMORIAL DR
TAYLORCREST RD
BLALOCK RD
ECHO LN
SAN FELIPE DR
BRIAR FOREST DR
WESTHEIMER RD
FONDREN RD
PINEY POINT RD
New Zealand Consulate
Kinkaid School
LK LORRIE
LK VARGO
Buffalo Bayou
The Commons at Woodlake Square
Carillon Shop Ctr
Columbia Medical Center-Rosewood
Consulado General of Nicaragua
Amer College of Acupuncture & Oriental Medicine
CAROL TREE PARK
FLAG TREE PARK
Woodlake Sq
Woodway Dr
Old Farm Rd
A B C D E
1 2 3 4 5 6 7
29°47'08"
29°46'42"
29°46'16"
29°45'50"
29°45'23"
29°44'57"
29°44'31"
29°44'05"
95°33'01"
95°32'31"
95°32'01"
95°31'31"
95°31'01"
95°30'31"

1:24,000
1 in. = 2000 ft.
0 0.25 0.5
miles

SEE 3821 MAP

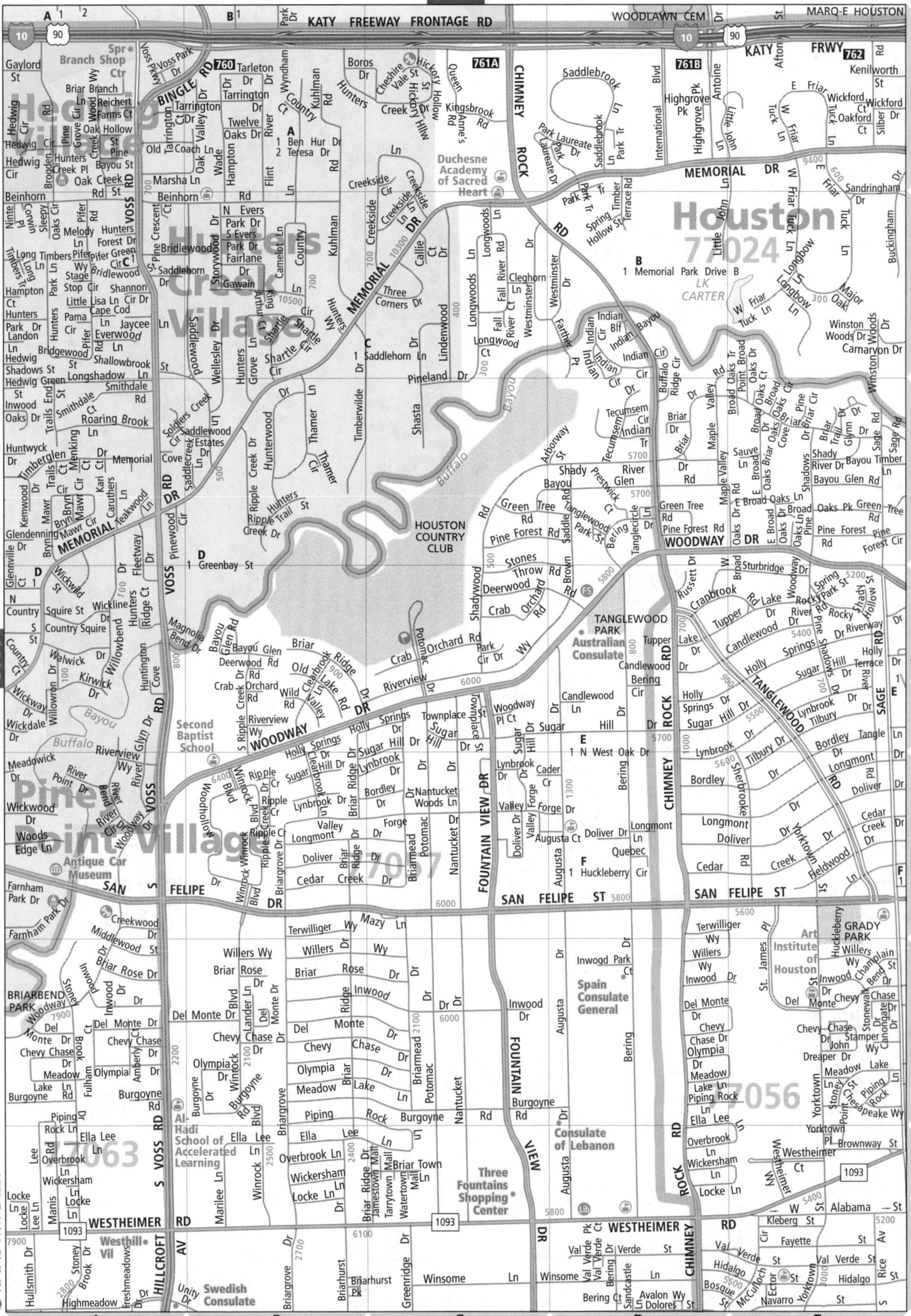
KATY FREEWAY FRONTAGE RD
KATY FRWY
WOODLAWN CEM
MARQ-E HOUSTON
Hedwig Village
Hunters Creek Village
Piney Point Village
Houston
77024
77057
77056
77063
MEMORIAL DR
WOODWAY DR
SAN FELIPE DR
SAN FELIPE ST
WESTHEIMER RD
VOSS RD
S VOSS RD
CHIMNEY ROCK RD
FOUNTAIN VIEW DR
TANGLEWOOD
SAGE RD
HILLCROFT AV
BINGLE RD
Buffalo Bayou
HOUSTON COUNTRY CLUB
TANGLEWOOD PARK
LK CARTER
Duchesne Academy of Sacred Heart
Branch Shop Ctr
Second Baptist School
Antique Car Museum
Australian Consulate
Spain Consulate General
Consulate of Lebanon
Art Institute of Houston
GRADY PARK
BRIARBEND PARK
Al-Hadi School of Accelerated Learning
Three Fountains Shopping Center
Westhill Vil
Swedish Consulate
A B C D E
1 2 3 4 5 6 7
29°47'06"
29°46'40"
29°46'14"
29°45'48"
29°45'21"
29°44'55"
29°44'29"
29°44'03"
95°30'31"
95°30'01"
95°29'31"
95°29'01"
95°28'31"
95°28'01"

SEE 3961 MAP

SEE 3959 MAP

SEE 4100 MAP

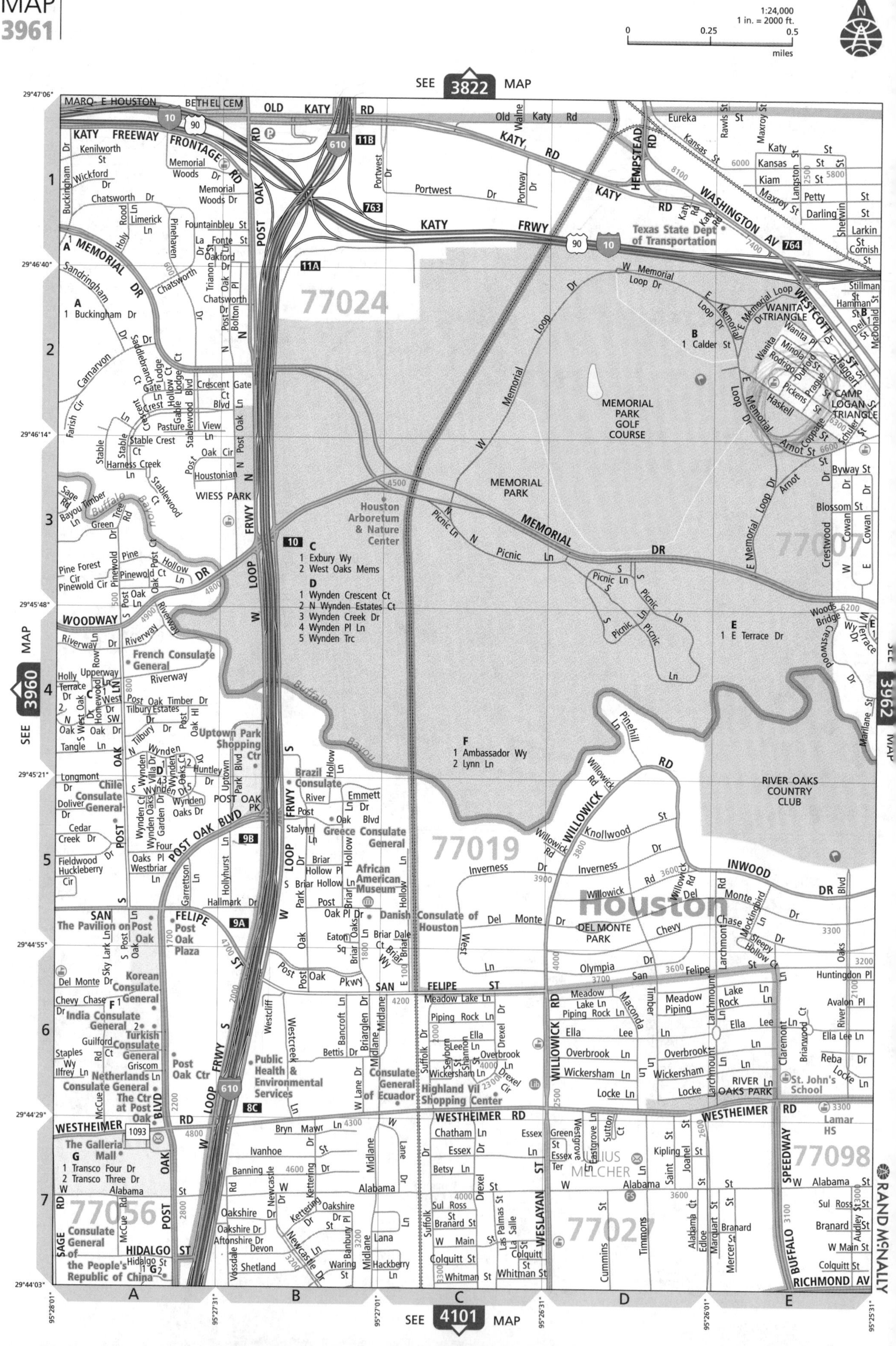
1:24,000
1 in. = 2000 ft.
0 0.25 0.5
miles
N
SEE 3822 MAP
SEE 3960 MAP
SEE 3962 MAP
SEE 4101 MAP
RAND McNALLY
29°47'06"
29°46'40"
29°46'14"
29°45'48"
29°45'21"
29°44'55"
29°44'29"
29°44'03"
95°28'01"
95°27'31"
95°27'01"
95°26'31"
95°26'01"
95°25'31"
77024
77007
77019
77098
77056
77027
Houston
KATY FREEWAY
FRONTAGE RD
OLD KATY RD
KATY FRWY
KATY RD
HEMPSTEAD RD
WASHINGTON AV
MEMORIAL DR
W LOOP N FRWY
W LOOP S FRWY
POST OAK BLVD
SAN FELIPE ST
WESTHEIMER RD
WILLOWICK RD
INWOOD DR
WESLAYAN ST
BUFFALO SPEEDWAY
RICHMOND AV
WOODWAY
SAGE RD
HIDALGO ST
Texas State Dept of Transportation
MEMORIAL PARK GOLF COURSE
MEMORIAL PARK
Houston Arboretum & Nature Center
WIESS PARK
WANITA TRIANGLE
CAMP LOGAN TRIANGLE
RIVER OAKS COUNTRY CLUB
DEL MONTE PARK
RIVER OAKS PARK
St. John's School
Lamar HS
JULIUS MELCHER
French Consulate General
Chile Consulate General
Brazil Consulate
Greece Consulate General
African American Museum
Danish Consulate of Houston
Uptown Park Shopping Ctr
The Pavilion on Post Oak
Post Oak Plaza
Korean Consulate General
India Consulate General
Turkish Consulate General
Netherlands Consulate General
The Ctr at Post Oak
Post Oak Ctr
Public Health & Environmental Services
Consulate General of Ecuador
Highland Vil Shopping Center
The Galleria Mall
Consulate General of the People's Republic of China
A
1 Buckingham Dr
B
1 Calder St
C
1 Exbury Wy
2 West Oaks Mems
D
1 Wynden Crescent Ct
2 N Wynden Estates Ct
3 Wynden Creek Dr
4 Wynden Pl Ln
5 Wynden Trc
E
1 E Terrace Dr
F
1 Ambassador Wy
2 Lynn Ln
G
1 Transco Four Dr
2 Transco Three Dr

1:24,000
1 in. = 2000 ft.
0 0.25 0.5
miles

SEE 3823 MAP

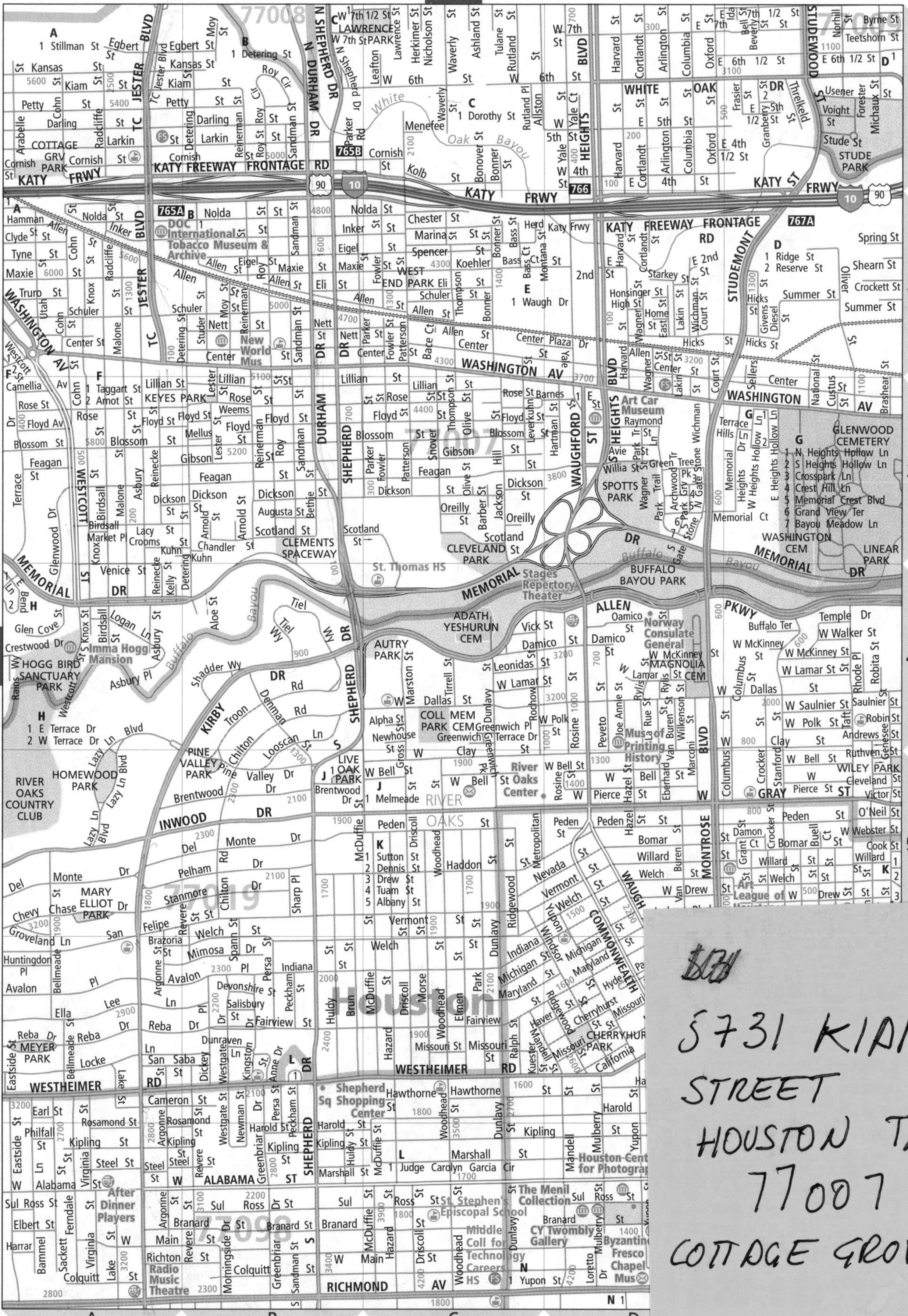

77008
77007
77019
77098
KATY FRWY
KATY FREEWAY FRONTAGE RD
WASHINGTON AV
MEMORIAL DR
ALLEN PKWY
INWOOD DR
WESTHEIMER RD
ALABAMA ST
RICHMOND AV
SHEPHERD DR
DURHAM DR
TC JESTER BLVD
HEIGHTS BLVD
STUDEMONT ST
WAUGHFORD ST
MONTROSE BLVD
KIRBY DR
WESTCOTT ST
COMMONWEALTH
White Oak Bayou
Buffalo Bayou
COTTAGE GRV PARK
STUDE PARK
DOC International Tobacco Museum & Archive
New World Mus
Art Car Museum
SPOTTS PARK
GLENWOOD CEMETERY
CLEMENTS SPACEWAY
St. Thomas HS
CLEVELAND PARK
Stages Repertory Theater
BUFFALO BAYOU PARK
LINEAR PARK
WASHINGTON CEM
ADATH YESHURUN CEM
Norway Consulate General
MAGNOLIA CEM
Imma Hogg Mansion
HOGG BIRD SANCTUARY PARK
AUTRY PARK
COLL MEM PARK CEM
Mus of Printing History
River Oaks Center
RIVER OAKS
PINE VALLEY PARK
HOMEWOOD PARK
RIVER OAKS COUNTRY CLUB
MARY ELLIOT PARK
MEYER PARK
Houston
CHERRYHURST PARK
Art League of Houston
WILEY PARK
Shepherd Sq Shopping Center
After Dinner Players
St. Stephen's Episcopal School
The Menil Collection
CY Twombly Gallery
Middle Coll for Technology Careers HS
Houston Center for Photography
Byzantine Fresco Chapel Mus
Radio Music Theatre
A
B
C
D
1
2
3
4
5
29°47'04"
29°46'38"
29°46'11"
29°45'45"
29°45'19"
95°25'31"
95°25'01"
95°24'31"
95°24'01"
95°23'
95°23'0"

SEE 3963 MAP

SEE 4102 MAP

5731 KIAM
STREET
HOUSTON TX
77007
COTTAGE GROVE

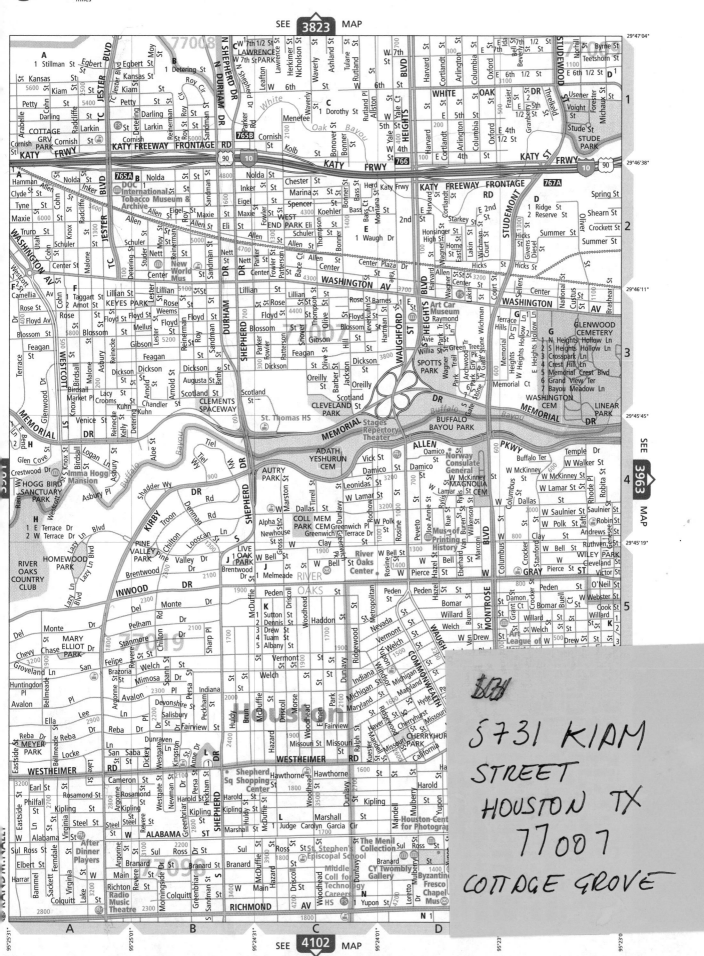

1:24,000
1 in. = 2000 ft.
0 0.25 0.5
miles

SEE 3824 MAP

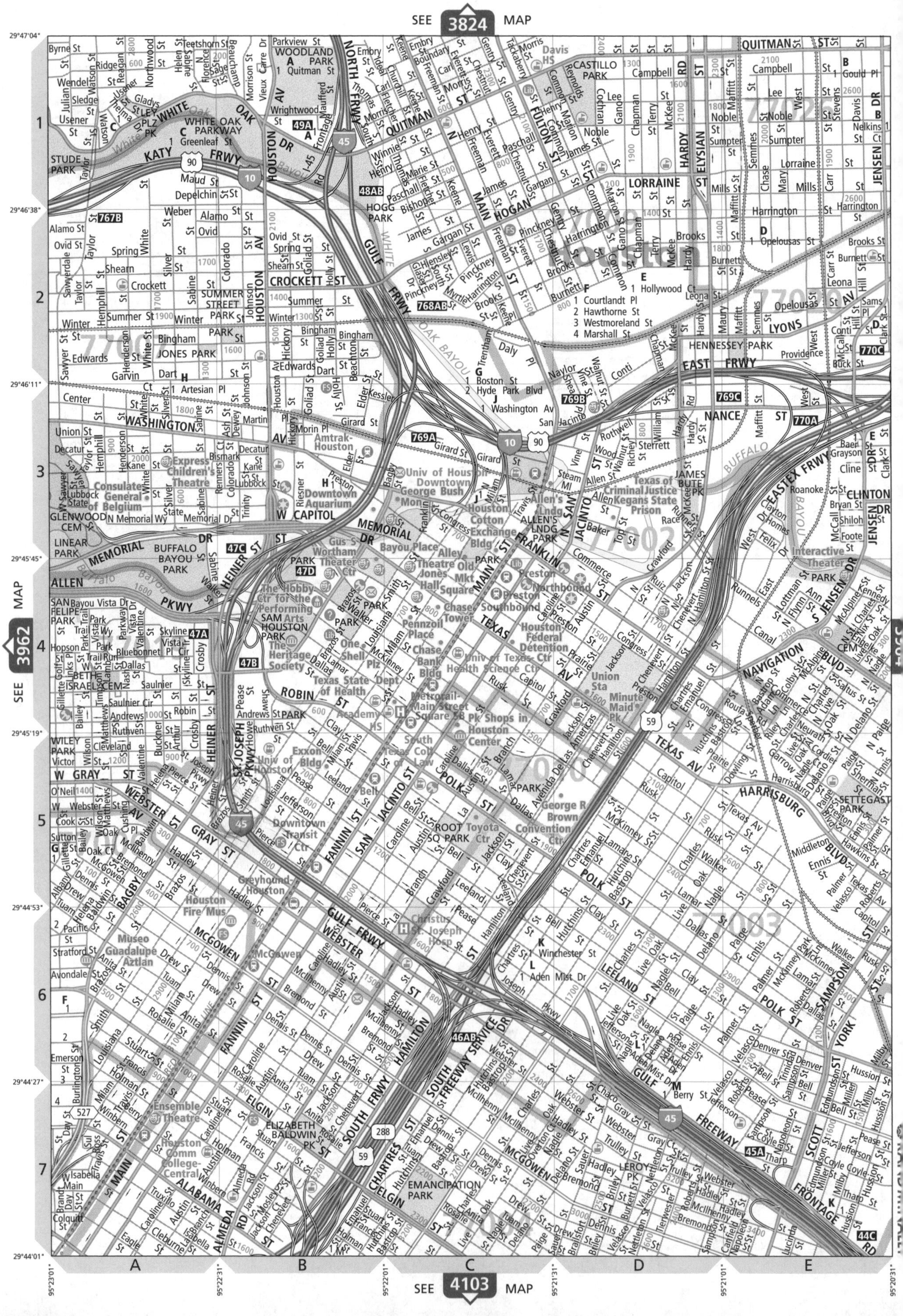
Houston
WOODLAND PARK
WHITE OAK PARKWAY
STUDE PARK
KATY FRWY
NORTH FRWY
HOGG PARK
GULF FRWY
HOUSTON AV
SUMMER STREET PARK
JONES PARK
WASHINGTON AV
MEMORIAL DR
BUFFALO BAYOU PARK
ALLEN PKWY
GLENWOOD CEM
LINEAR PARK
SAN FELIPE PARK
WILEY PARK
W GRAY ST
WEBSTER
GRAY ST
Amtrak-Houston
Downtown Aquarium
Univ of Houston-Downtown
George Bush Mon
Houston Cotton Exchange Bldg
ALLEN'S LNDG PARK
Texas Criminal Justice Kegans State Prison
JAMES BUTE PK
HENNESSEY PARK
EAST FRWY
EASTEX FRWY
CLINTON DR
Interactive Theater
Gus S. Wortham Theater Ctr
The Hobby Ctr for the Performing Arts
SAM HOUSTON PARK
The Heritage Society
Texas State Dept of Health
Alley Theatre
Jones Hall
Old Mkt Square
Chase Tower
Pennzoil Place
Chase Bank Bldg
One Shell Plz
Houston Federal Detention Ctr
Univ of Texas Health Science Ctr
Union Sta
Minute Maid Pk
Pk Shops in Houston Center
George R Brown Convention Ctr
Toyota Ctr
ROOT SQ PARK
South Texas Coll of Law
Exxon Bldg
Downtown Transit Ctr
Greyhound-Houston
Houston Fire Mus
Museo Guadalupe Aztlan
Christus St. Joseph Hosp
Ensemble Theatre
Houston Comm College-Central
ELIZABETH BALDWIN PK
EMANCIPATION PARK
SOUTH FRWY
GULF FREEWAY
NAVIGATION BLVD
HARRISBURG
SETTEGAST PARK
77002
77003
77004
77006
77007
77009
77020
77026

SEE 3962 MAP

SEE 4103 MAP

1:24,000
1 in. = 2000 ft.
0 0.25 0.5
miles

SEE 3825 MAP

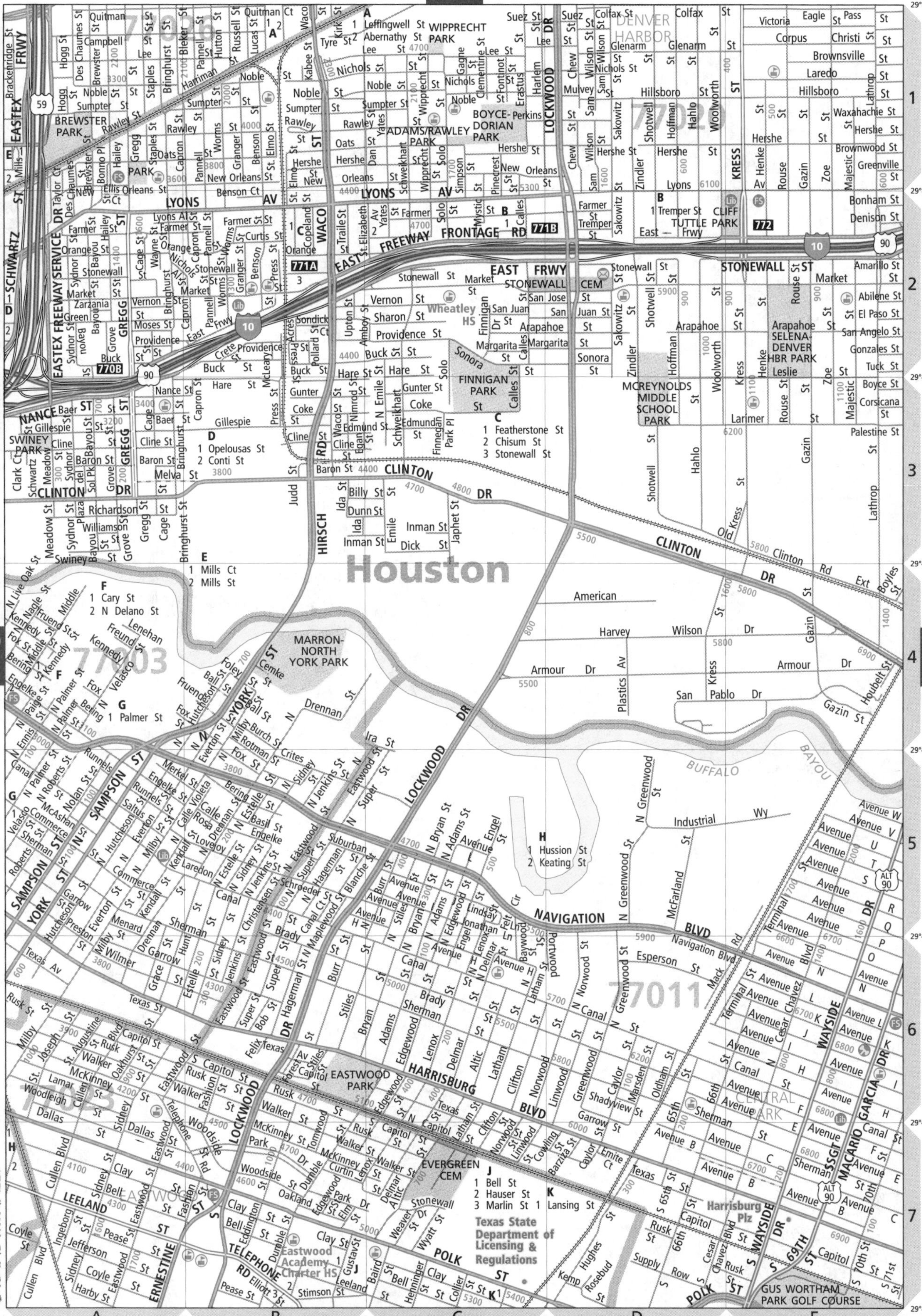
Houston
EASTEX FRWY
SCHWARTZ
EASTEX FREEWAY SERVICE DR
LYONS AV
EAST FREEWAY FRONTAGE RD
EAST FRWY
STONEWALL CEM
STONEWALL ST
CLINTON DR
NAVIGATION BLVD
HARRISBURG BLVD
POLK ST
LOCKWOOD DR
HIRSCH RD
WACO ST
YORK ST
SAMPSON ST
GREGG ST
KRESS ST
WAYSIDE DR
TELEPHONE RD
LEELAND ST
ERNESTINE
BREWSTER PARK
SWINEY PARK
WIPPRECHT PARK
ADAMS/RAWLEY PARK
BOYCE-DORIAN PARK
DENVER HARBOR
CLIFF TUTTLE PARK
Wheatley HS
FINNIGAN PARK
ARAPAHOE SELENA-DENVER HBR PARK
MCREYNOLDS MIDDLE SCHOOL PARK
MARRON-NORTH YORK PARK
BUFFALO BAYOU
EASTWOOD PARK
EVERGREEN CEM
CENTRAL PARK
Harrisburg Plz
GUS WORTHAM PARK GOLF COURSE
Eastwood Academy Charter HS
Texas State Department of Licensing & Regulations
77020
77029
77003
77011
77023
Industrial Wy
Armour Dr
San Pablo Dr
Harvey Wilson Dr
American
Clinton Rd Ext
29°47'01"
29°46'35"
29°46'09"
29°45'43"
29°45'17"
29°44'51"
29°44'24"
29°43'58"
95°20'31"
95°20'01"
95°19'31"
95°19'01"
95°18'31"
95°18'01"
A
B
C
D
E
1
2
3
4
5
6
7

SEE 3965 MAP

SEE 4104 MAP

1:24,000
1 in. = 2000 ft.
0 0.25 0.5
miles

SEE 3826 MAP

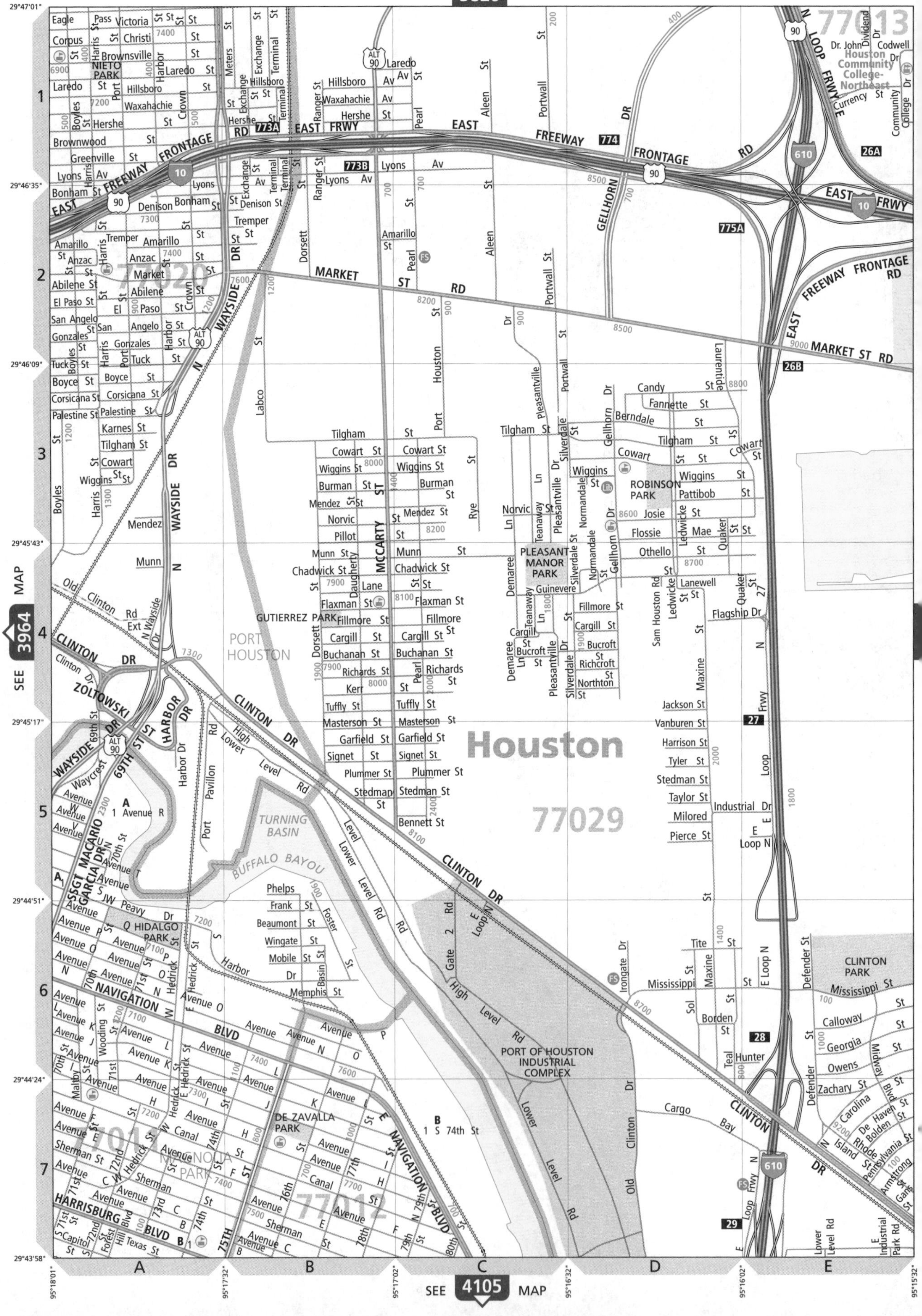
29°47'01"
29°46'35"
29°46'09"
29°45'43"
29°45'17"
29°44'51"
29°44'24"
29°43'58"
95°18'01"
95°17'32"
95°17'02"
95°16'32"
95°16'02"
95°15'32"
1
2
3
4
5
6
7
A
B
C
D
E
Houston
77013
77020
77029
77011
77012
NIETO PARK
ROBINSON PARK
PLEASANT MANOR PARK
GUTIERREZ PARK
PORT HOUSTON
TURNING BASIN
BUFFALO BAYOU
HIDALGO PARK
DE ZAVALLA PARK
MAGNOLIA PARK
CLINTON PARK
PORT OF HOUSTON INDUSTRIAL COMPLEX
Houston Community College-Northeast
EAST FRWY
EAST FREEWAY FRONTAGE RD
MARKET ST RD
N WAYSIDE DR
MCCARTY ST
GELLHORN DR
N LOOP FRWY E
CLINTON DR
ZOLTOWSKI ST
HARBOR DR
69TH ST
SSGT MACARIO GARCIA DR
NAVIGATION BLVD
N NAVIGATION BLVD
HARRISBURG BLVD
75TH ST
Old Clinton Rd
High Level Rd
Lower Level Rd
Gate 2 Rd
Industrial Dr
Cargo Bay
Sam Houston Rd
Maxine St
Laurentide
Tilgham St
Cowart St
Wiggins St
Fillmore St
Mississippi St
773A
773B
774
775A
26A
26B
27
28
29

SEE 3964 MAP

SEE 4105 MAP

1:24,000
1 in. = 2000 ft.
0 0.25 0.5
miles

SEE 3827 MAP

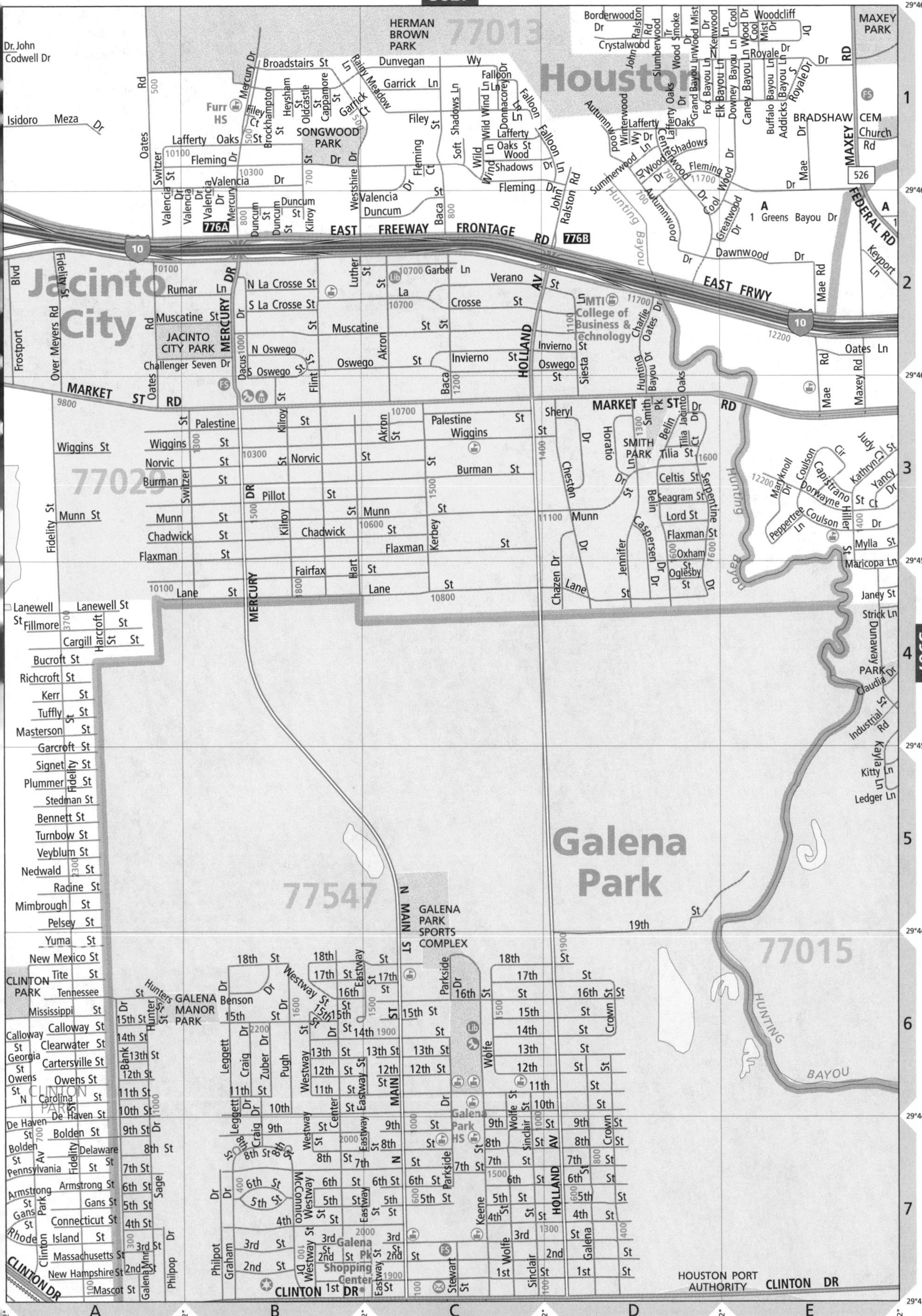
Houston
Jacinto City
Galena Park
77013
77029
77547
77015
HERMAN BROWN PARK
SONGWOOD PARK
JACINTO CITY PARK
SMITH PARK
GALENA MANOR PARK
CLINTON PARK
MAXEY PARK
GALENA PARK SPORTS COMPLEX
BRADSHAW CEM
Furr HS
Galena Park HS
MTI College of Business & Technology
Galena Pk Shopping Center
HOUSTON PORT AUTHORITY
EAST FREEWAY FRONTAGE RD
EAST FRWY
MARKET ST RD
MERCURY DR
HOLLAND AV
N MAIN ST
MAXEY RD
FEDERAL RD
CLINTON DR
HUNTING BAYOU
19th St
Oates Rd
Isidoro Meza Dr
Dr. John Codwell Dr
776A
776B
10
526
1
2
3
4
5
6
7
A
B
C
D
E
29°46'59"
29°46'33"
29°46'06"
29°45'40"
29°45'14"
29°44'48"
29°44'22"
29°43'56"
95°15'32"
95°15'02"
95°14'32"
95°14'02"
95°13'32"
95°13'02"

SEE 3967 MAP

SEE 4106 MAP

1:24,000
1 in. = 2000 ft.
0 0.25 0.5
miles

SEE 3828 MAP

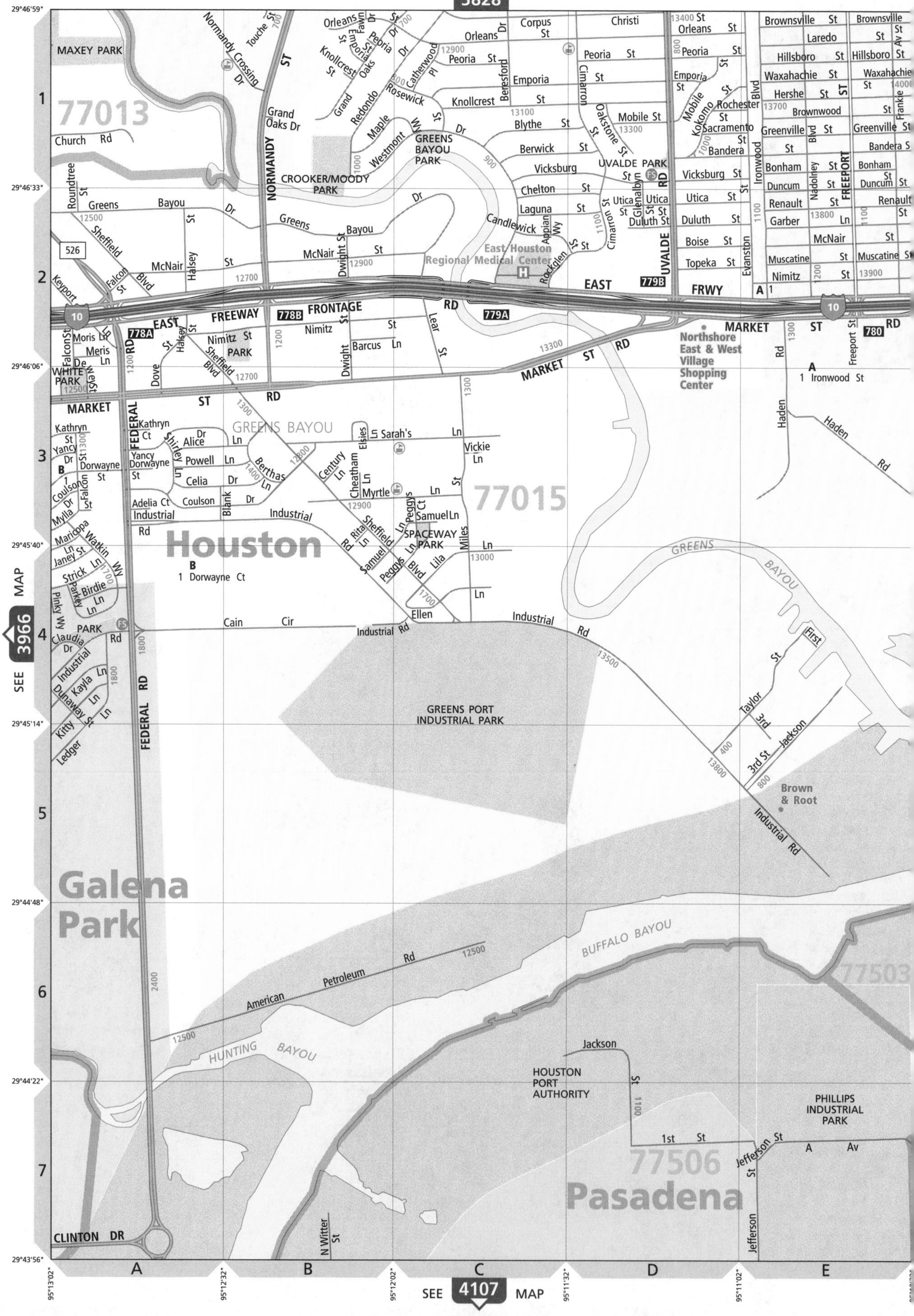
MAXEY PARK
77013
Church Rd
Roundtree St
Greens Bayou Dr
Sheffield
526
Keyport
Falcon St
McNair St
Halsey St
Normandy Crossing Dr
Touche St
NORMANDY ST
Grand Oaks Dr
CROOKER/MOODY PARK
Greens Bayou
Dwight St
Orleans
Peoria
Emporia
Knollcrest
Oaks
Redondo
Rosewick
Catherwood Pl
Maple
Westmont
Wy
GREENS BAYOU PARK
Orleans Dr
Peoria St
Corpus St
Christi
Beresford
Emporia
Knollcrest St
Blythe St
Berwick St
Vicksburg
Chelton St
Laguna St
Candlewick
Appian Wy
Rockglen St
Cimarron St
Oakstone St
Mobile St
UVALDE PARK
Glenalbyn Ln
Utica St
Duluth St
East Houston Regional Medical Center
UVALDE RD
Orleans St
Peoria St
Emporia St
Mobile
Kokomo St
Rochester St
Sacramento
Bandera
Vicksburg St
Utica St
Duluth St
Boise St
Topeka St
Evanston
Ironwood Blvd
Brownsville St
Laredo St
Hillsboro St
Waxahachie St
Hershe St
Brownwood
Greenville St
Bandera St
Bonham St
Duncum St
Renault St
Garber
McNair
Muscatine St
Nimitz St
Nadolney Blvd
FREEPORT ST
Frankie Av
EAST FRWY
779B
10
779A
778B
778A
FRONTAGE RD
EAST FREEWAY
Nimitz St
Nimitz PARK
Barcus Ln
Lear St
MARKET ST RD
Northshore East & West Village Shopping Center
780
Freeport St
A
1 Ironwood St
Haden Rd
Moris Ln
Meris Ln
De Wey St
WHITE PARK
Dove St
Sheffield Blvd
MARKET ST RD
FEDERAL RD
Kathryn Ct
Kathryn St
Yancy Dr
Dorwayne St
Coulson Dr
Mylla St
Falcon St
Shirley Ln
Alice Dr
Powell Ln
Celia Dr
Coulson Dr
Blank
Berthas Ln
Adelia Ct
Industrial Rd
GREENS BAYOU
Century Ln
Cheatham Ln
Elsies Ln
Sarah's Ln
Myrtle Ln
Vickie Ln
77015
Houston
B
1 Dorwayne Ct
Maricopa
Janey St
Watkin Wy
Strick Ln
Birdie Ln
Parkey Ln
Pinky Wy
PARK
Claudia Dr
Industrial
Kayla Ln
Dunaway St
Kitty
Ledger
Rita Ln
Sheffield
Samuel
Peggys Ct
Samuel Ln
SPACEWAY PARK
Peggys Blvd
Lila
Miles
Ellen
Cain Cir
Industrial Rd
GREENS BAYOU
First St
Taylor
3rd
3rd St
Jackson
Brown & Root
Industrial Rd
GREENS PORT INDUSTRIAL PARK
FEDERAL RD
Galena Park
BUFFALO BAYOU
American Petroleum Rd
HUNTING BAYOU
77503
Jackson St
HOUSTON PORT AUTHORITY
1st St
Jefferson St
PHILLIPS INDUSTRIAL PARK
A Av
77506
Pasadena
N Witter St
CLINTON DR
A
B
C
D
E
1
2
3
4
5
6
7
SEE 3966 MAP

SEE 4107 MAP

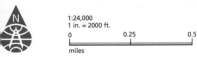

1:24,000
1 in. = 2000 ft.
0 0.25 0.5
miles

SEE 3829 MAP

Brownsville St
Laredo St
CLOVERLEAF PARK
Waxahachie St
Brownwood St
Greenville Blvd
Bandera
Bonham
Duncum
Renault
Garber
McNair St
Muscatine St
Nimitz St
MARKET ST RD
EAST FRWY
BARBARA BLVD
MAE
Cloverleaf
Hollywood
Beacon
Hillsboro St
Hershe Blvd
Rose
Nancy
Manor Av
SAN JACINTO MEMORIAL PARK
E SAM HOUSTON PKWY N
SAM HOUSTON PKWY
CHANNELWOOD PARK
Blanding Dr
Bright
Penny Ln
Woodford
Gloster Dr
Overbluff Dr
Lofton Dr
Lawther Dr
Belvoir Dr
Colville Dr
Arundel Dr
Brookview Dr
Deming
West Dr
South
W Brentwood Dr
Dell
Dale
Avenue C
Brentwood St
Colville St
Grand Av
77530
Sun Belt Regional Medical Center
782
781AB
EAST FREEWAY FRONTAGE RD
Carey Ln
Dell Dale St
MARKET ST
W Victorson Av
E Victorson Av
Antoinette Ln
Redmond St
Kenny St
Le May St
Patch
Waldine
Marwood St
Bomford Av
Talcott St
Penn City Rd
Jacintoport Blvd
Wadsworth
Appelt Dr
E Sam Houston Pkwy N
Haden Rd
Dean White Dr
77015
Jacintoport Blvd
GREENS BAYOU
Ship Channel Bridge Toll Plaza
Toll Booth
SAM HOUSTON TOLLWAY
HOUSTON PORT AUTHORITY
W SAM HOUSTON
N South St
BUFFALO BAYOU
Houston
Ethyl Rd
Corp Rd
HOUSTON SHIP CHANNEL BR
77503
ETHYL INDUSTRIAL PARK
Phillips Company Rd
PHILLIPS INDUSTRIAL PARK
Pasadena
Channel City Rd
GEORGIA PACIFIC INDUSTRIAL DISTRICT
TENNECO INDUSTRIAL PARK
W SAM HOUSTON TOLLWAY
SAM HOUSTON PKWY N
77536
A B C D E
1 2 3 4 5 6 7

SEE 3969 MAP

SEE 4108 MAP

1:24,000
1 in. = 2000 ft.
0 0.25 0.5
miles

SEE 3830 MAP

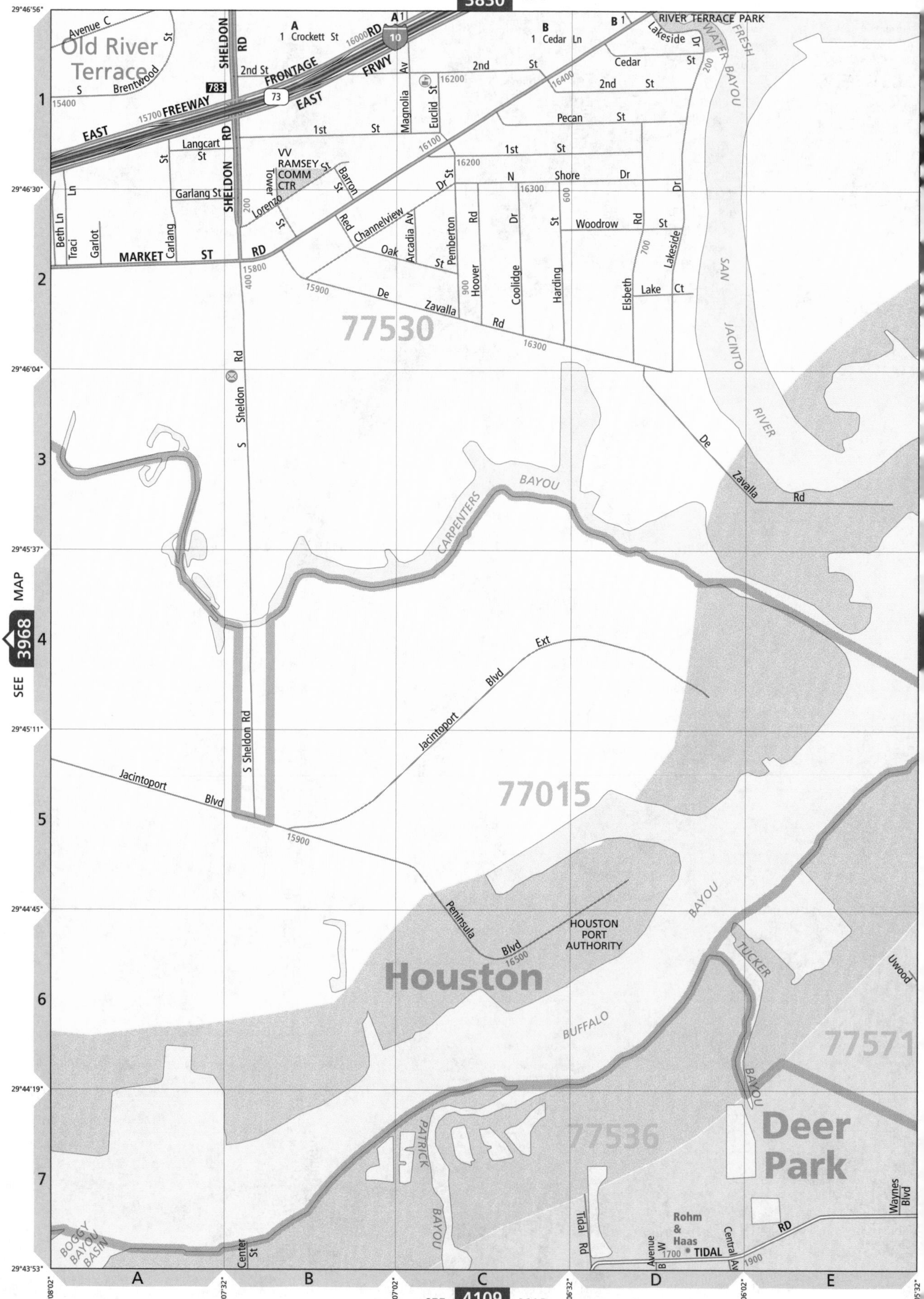
Old River Terrace
Avenue C
S Brentwood St
EAST FREEWAY
FRONTAGE RD
EAST FRWY
10
73
783
SHELDON RD
2nd St
1 Crockett St
1 Cedar Ln
RIVER TERRACE PARK
Lakeside Dr
Cedar St
2nd St
Magnolia Av
Euclid St
1st St
Pecan St
Langcart St
Garlang St
VV RAMSEY COMM CTR
Tower St
Lorenzo St
Barron St
Red Oak St
Channelview Dr
Arcadia Av
Pemberton St
Hoover Rd
Coolidge Dr
Harding St
N Shore Dr
Woodrow St
Elsbeth Rd
Lakeside Dr
Lake Ct
Beth Ln
Traci Ln
Garlot
Carlang
MARKET ST RD
De Zavalla Rd
77530
S Sheldon Rd
FRESH WATER BAYOU
SAN JACINTO RIVER
CARPENTERS BAYOU
Jacintoport Blvd Ext
Jacintoport Blvd
77015
Peninsula Blvd
HOUSTON PORT AUTHORITY
Houston
BUFFALO BAYOU
TUCKER BAYOU
Uwood
77571
Deer Park
77536
PATRICK BAYOU
BOGGY BAYOU BASIN
Center St
Tidal Rd
Avenue B
W
Rohm & Haas
TIDAL RD
Central Av
Waynes Blvd
A B C D E
1 2 3 4 5 6 7

SEE 3968 MAP

SEE 4109 MAP

1:24,000
1 in. = 2000 ft.
0 0.25 0.5
miles

SEE 3831 MAP

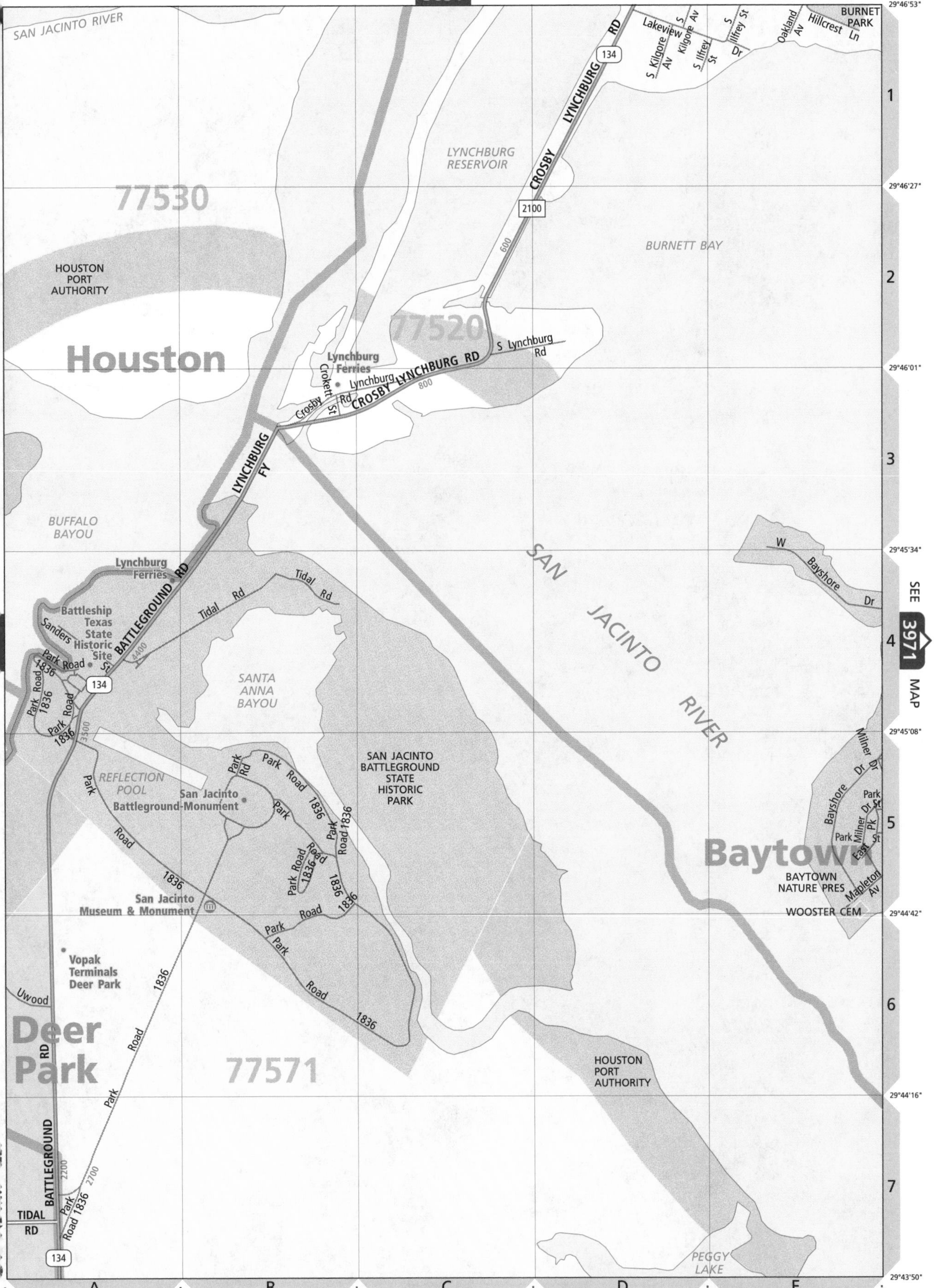
SAN JACINTO RIVER
LYNCHBURG RESERVOIR
CROSBY LYNCHBURG RD
134
2100
600
Lakeview
S Kilgore Av
Kilgore Av
S Ilfrey St
S Ilfrey St
Dr
Oakland Av
Hillcrest Ln
BURNET PARK
77530
HOUSTON PORT AUTHORITY
BURNETT BAY
77520
Houston
Lynchburg Ferries
S Lynchburg Rd
CROSBY LYNCHBURG RD
800
Crosby
Crokett St
Lynchburg Rd
LYNCHBURG FY
BUFFALO BAYOU
SAN JACINTO RIVER
W Bayshore Dr
Lynchburg Ferries
BATTLEGROUND RD
Tidal Rd
Tidal Rd
Battleship Texas State Historic Site
Sanders St
Park Road 1836
3400
134
SANTA ANNA BAYOU
3500
REFLECTION POOL
San Jacinto Battleground Monument
SAN JACINTO BATTLEGROUND STATE HISTORIC PARK
Park Rd
Park Road 1836
Park Road 1836
San Jacinto Museum & Monument
Vopak Terminals Deer Park
Uwood
Deer Park
77571
HOUSTON PORT AUTHORITY
Milner Dr
Bayshore Dr
Park St
Milner Dr
Park Pk
East
Mapleton Av
Baytown
BAYTOWN NATURE PRES
WOOSTER CEM
BATTLEGROUND RD
2200
2700
TIDAL RD
134
PEGGY LAKE
1
2
3
4
5
6
7
A
B
C
D
E
29°46'53"
29°46'27"
29°46'01"
29°45'34"
29°45'08"
29°44'42"
29°44'16"
29°43'50"
95°05'32"
95°05'02"
95°04'32"
95°04'02"
95°03'32"
95°03'02"

SEE 3971 MAP

SEE 4110 MAP

1:24,000
1 in. = 2000 ft.
0 0.25 0.5
miles

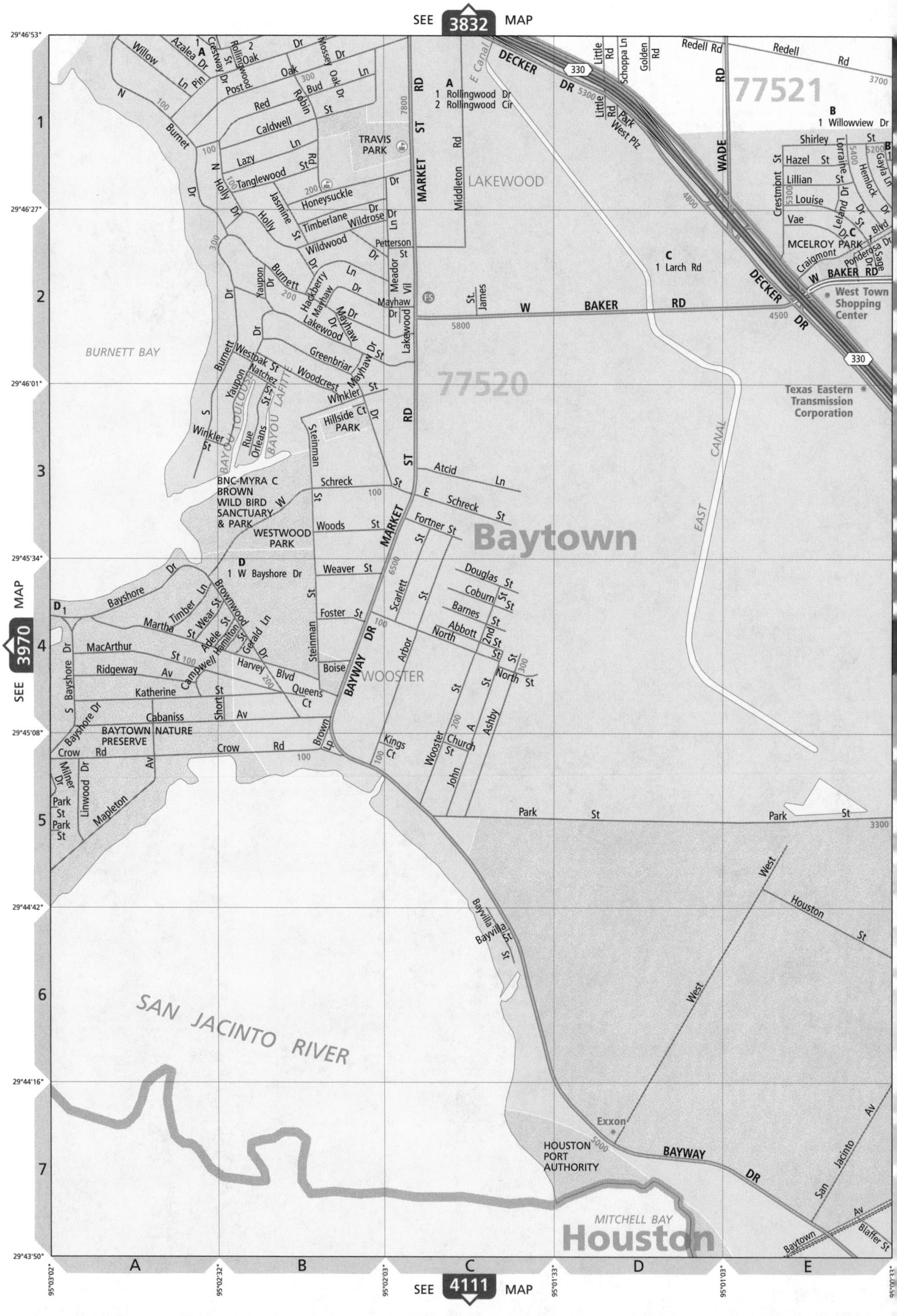
SEE 3832 MAP
SEE 3970 MAP
SEE 4111 MAP
Baytown
Houston
77520
77521
LAKEWOOD
WOOSTER
BURNETT BAY
SAN JACINTO RIVER
MITCHELL BAY
TRAVIS PARK
HILLSIDE CT PARK
BNC-MYRA C BROWN WILD BIRD SANCTUARY & PARK
WESTWOOD PARK
BAYTOWN NATURE PRESERVE
MCELROY PARK
West Town Shopping Center
Texas Eastern Transmission Corporation
HOUSTON PORT AUTHORITY
Exxon
BAYOU TOULOUSE
BAYOU LAFITTE
E Canal
EAST CANAL
A
1 Rollingwood Dr
2 Rollingwood Cir
B
1 Willowview Dr
C
1 Larch Rd
D
1 W Bayshore Dr
MARKET ST RD
BAYWAY DR
DECKER DR
W BAKER RD
WADE RD
Redell Rd
Park St
Schreck St
Atcid Ln
Woods St
Weaver St
Foster St
Boise
Steinman St
Fortner St
Douglas St
Coburn St
Barnes St
Abbott St
North St
2nd St
Scarlett St
Arbor St
Wooster St
Church St
John St
Ashby
Kings Ct
Bayshore Dr
S Bayshore Dr
MacArthur St
Ridgeway Av
Katherine St
Cabaniss Av
Crow Rd
Brown Lp
Harvey Blvd
Queens Ct
Gerald Ln
Brownwood
Martha St
Timber Ln
Milner Dr
Linwood Dr
Mapleton Av
Park St
N Burnet Dr
N Holly Dr
Willow Ln
Azalea Dr
Crestway Dr
Rollingwood
Oak Dr
Post Oak
Bud Oak Dr
Mossey Dr
Red Robin Rd
Caldwell St
Lazy Ln
Tanglewood St
Honeysuckle Dr
Timberlane Dr
Wildrose Dr
Wildwood Dr
Jasmine St
Holly
Petterson St
Meador Ln
Mayhaw Dr
Lakewood Vil
Hackberry
Burnett Dr
Yaupon Dr
Greenbriar
Woodcrest
Winkler St
Westbak St
Natchez
Rue Orleans
Middleton Rd
St. James
Little Rd
Schoppa Ln
Golden Rd
Little Park
West Plz
Shirley St
Hazel St
Lillian St
Louise
Vae
Crestmont St
Lorraine St
Hemlock
Leland Dr
Craigmont
Ponderosa Dr
West Houston St
San Jacinto Av
Baytown
Blaffer St
330
7800
5800
4500
4800
5300
3700
3300
5000
6500

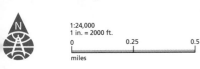

1:24,000
1 in. = 2000 ft.
0 0.25 0.5
miles

SEE 3833 MAP

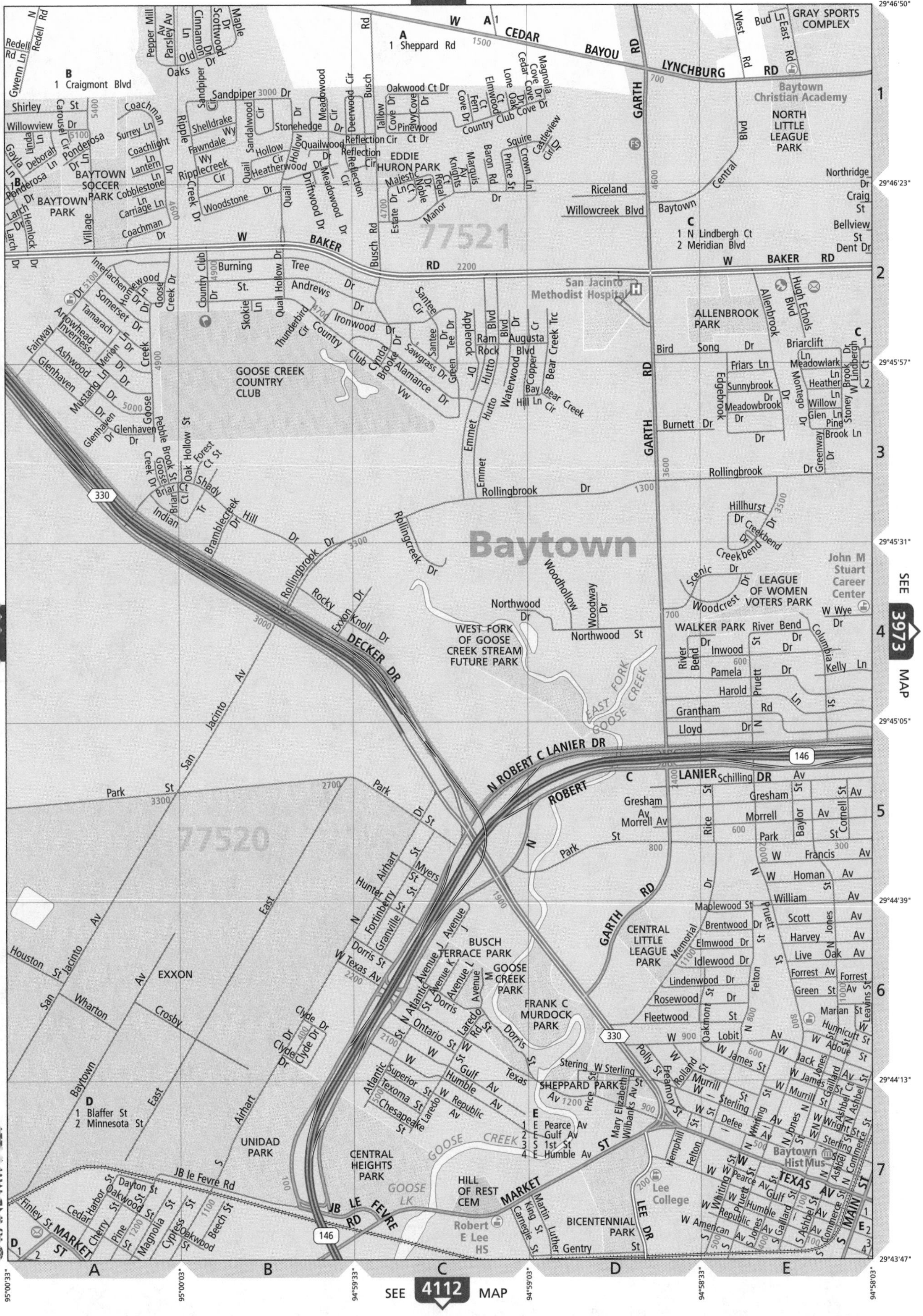

Baytown
77521
77520
W CEDAR BAYOU LYNCHBURG RD
GARTH RD
W BAKER RD
DECKER DR
N ROBERT C LANIER DR
MARKET ST
JB LE FEVRE RD
TEXAS AV
N MAIN ST
LEE DR
GRAY SPORTS COMPLEX
Baytown Christian Academy
NORTH LITTLE LEAGUE PARK
BAYTOWN SOCCER PARK
BAYTOWN PARK
EDDIE HURON PARK
San Jacinto Methodist Hospital
ALLENBROOK PARK
GOOSE CREEK COUNTRY CLUB
WEST FORK OF GOOSE CREEK STREAM FUTURE PARK
LEAGUE OF WOMEN VOTERS PARK
WALKER PARK
John M Stuart Career Center
EXXON
CENTRAL LITTLE LEAGUE PARK
BUSCH TERRACE PARK
GOOSE CREEK PARK
FRANK C MURDOCK PARK
SHEPPARD PARK
UNIDAD PARK
CENTRAL HEIGHTS PARK
HILL OF REST CEM
Robert E Lee HS
BICENTENNIAL PARK
Lee College
Baytown Hist Mus
EAST FORK GOOSE CREEK
GOOSE CREEK
GOOSE LK
A 1 Sheppard Rd
B 1 Craigmont Blvd
C 1 N Lindbergh Ct 2 Meridian Blvd
D 1 Blaffer St 2 Minnesota St
E 1 E Pearce Av 2 E Gulf Av 3 S 1st St 4 E Humble Av
330
146
29°46'50"
29°46'23"
29°45'57"
29°45'31"
29°45'05"
29°44'39"
29°44'13"
29°43'47"
95°00'33"
95°00'03"
94°59'33"
94°59'03"
94°58'33"
94°58'03"
A B C D E
1 2 3 4 5 6 7

SEE 3973 MAP

SEE 4112 MAP

1:24,000
1 in. = 2000 ft.
0 0.25 0.5
miles

SEE 3834 MAP

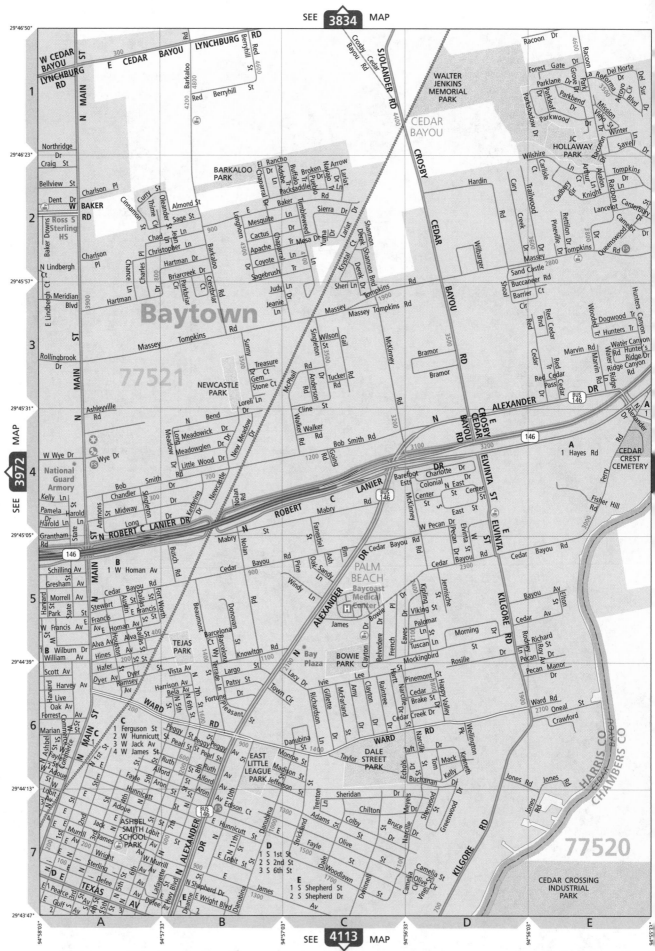

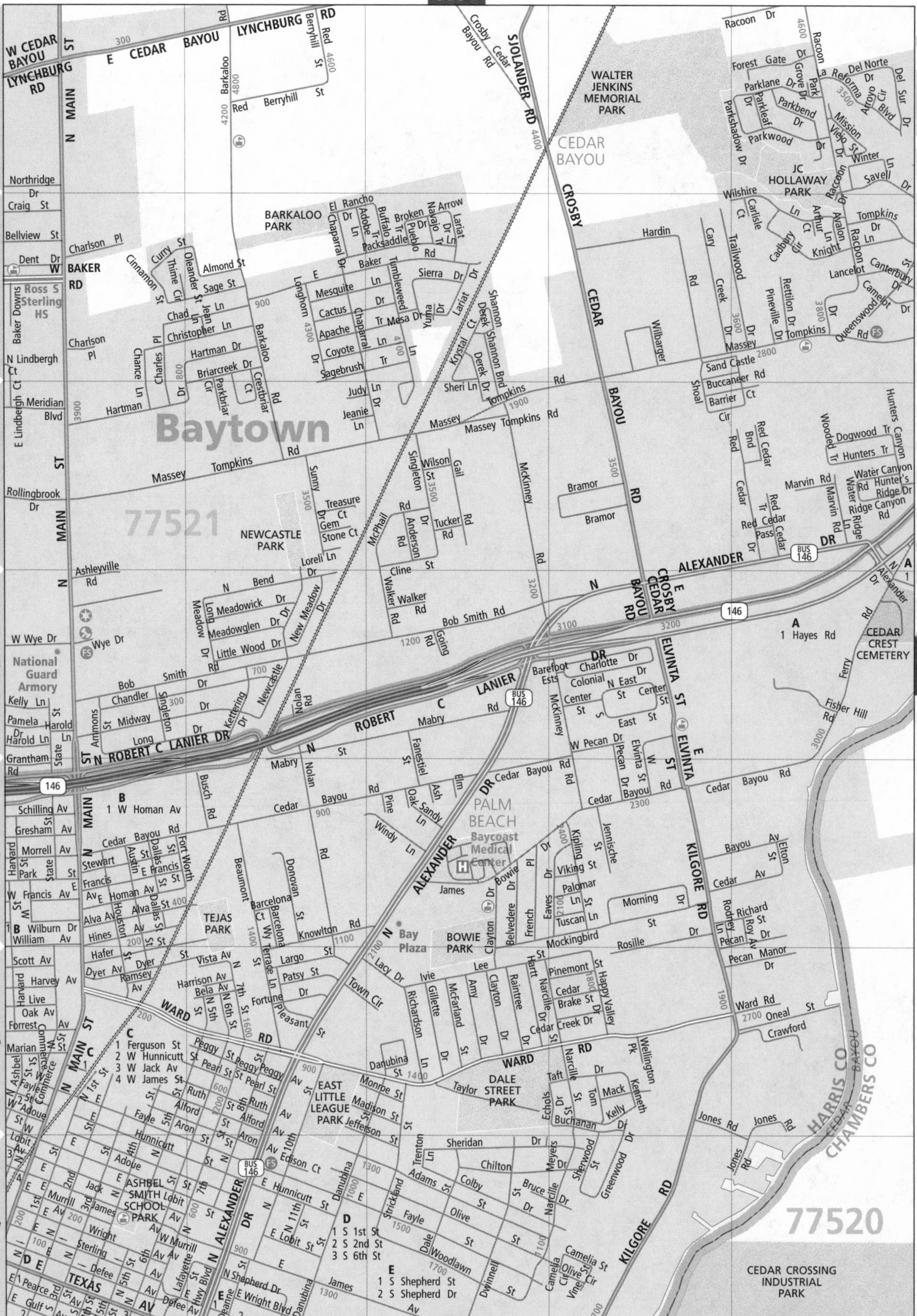
Baytown
77521
77520
WALTER JENKINS MEMORIAL PARK
CEDAR BAYOU
JC HOLLAWAY PARK
BARKALOO PARK
NEWCASTLE PARK
Ross S Sterling HS
National Guard Armory
CEDAR CREST CEMETERY
PALM BEACH
Baycoast Medical Center
Bay Plaza
BOWIE PARK
TEJAS PARK
EAST LITTLE LEAGUE PARK
DALE STREET PARK
ASHBEL SMITH SCHOOL PARK
CEDAR CROSSING INDUSTRIAL PARK
HARRIS CO
CHAMBERS CO
N MAIN ST
SJOLANDER RD
CROSBY CEDAR BAYOU RD
N ALEXANDER DR
ROBERT C LANIER DR
KILGORE RD
ELVINTA ST
E CEDAR BAYOU LYNCHBURG RD
W CEDAR BAYOU LYNCHBURG RD
W BAKER RD
WARD RD
TEXAS AV
Massey Tompkins Rd
Cedar Bayou Rd
A
1 Hayes Rd
B
1 W Homan Av
C
1 Ferguson St
2 W Hunnicutt St
3 W Jack Av
4 W James St
D
1 S 1st St
2 S 2nd St
3 S 6th St
E
1 S Shepherd St
2 S Shepherd Dr
29°46'50"
29°46'23"
29°45'57"
29°45'31"
29°45'05"
29°44'39"
29°44'13"
29°43'47"
94°58'03"
94°57'33"
94°57'03"
94°56'33"
94°56'03"
94°55'33"
1
2
3
4
5
6
7
A
B
C
D
E

SEE 3972 MAP

SEE 4113 MAP

1:24,000
1 in. = 2000 ft.
0 0.25 0.5
miles

SEE 3835 MAP

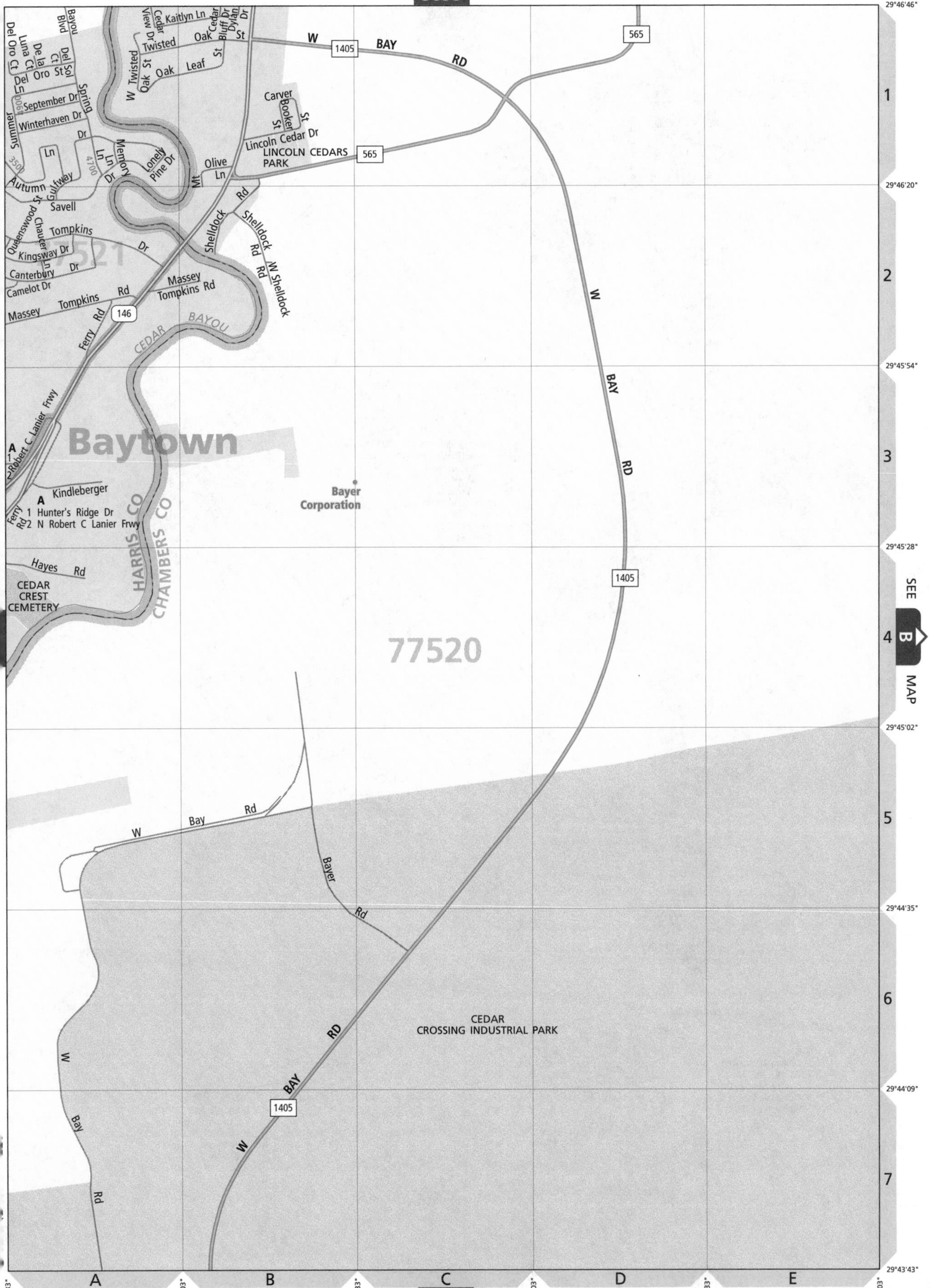
W BAY RD
1405
565
Bayou Blvd
Del Oro Ct
Luna Ct
De la Ct
Del Sol
Del Oro St
Ln
September Dr
Spring
Winterhaven Dr
Summer
Dr
Ln
Autumn
Gulfway
Savell
Queenswood St
Chaucer Ln
Tompkins
Kingsway Dr
Dr
Canterbury
Dr
Camelot Dr
Massey
Tompkins
Rd
Ferry Rd
146
Kaitlyn Ln
Cedar View Dr
Twisted
Oak
Cedar
Bluff Dr
Dylan Dr
St
W Twisted Oak St
Oak
Leaf
Memory Ln
Lonely Pine Dr
Mt
Olive Ln
Carver St
Booker St
Lincoln Cedar Dr
LINCOLN CEDARS PARK
Rd
Shelldock
Shelldock Rd
W Shelldock
Rd
Massey Tompkins Rd
CEDAR BAYOU
Dr
77521
N Robert C Lanier Frwy
Baytown
A
1
2
Kindleberger
A
1 Hunter's Ridge Dr
2 N Robert C Lanier Frwy
Ferry Rd
HARRIS CO
CHAMBERS CO
Hayes Rd
CEDAR CREST CEMETERY
Bayer Corporation
77520
W BAY RD
W Bay Rd
Bayer Rd
CEDAR CROSSING INDUSTRIAL PARK
W BAY RD
1405
W Bay Rd
1
2
3
4
5
6
7
A
B
C
D
E
29°46'46"
29°46'20"
29°45'54"
29°45'28"
29°45'02"
29°44'35"
29°44'09"
29°43'43"
94°55'33"
94°55'03"
94°54'33"
94°54'03"
94°53'33"
94°53'03"

SEE B MAP

SEE 4114 MAP

1:24,000
1 in. = 2000 ft.
0 0.25 0.5
miles

SEE 3952 MAP

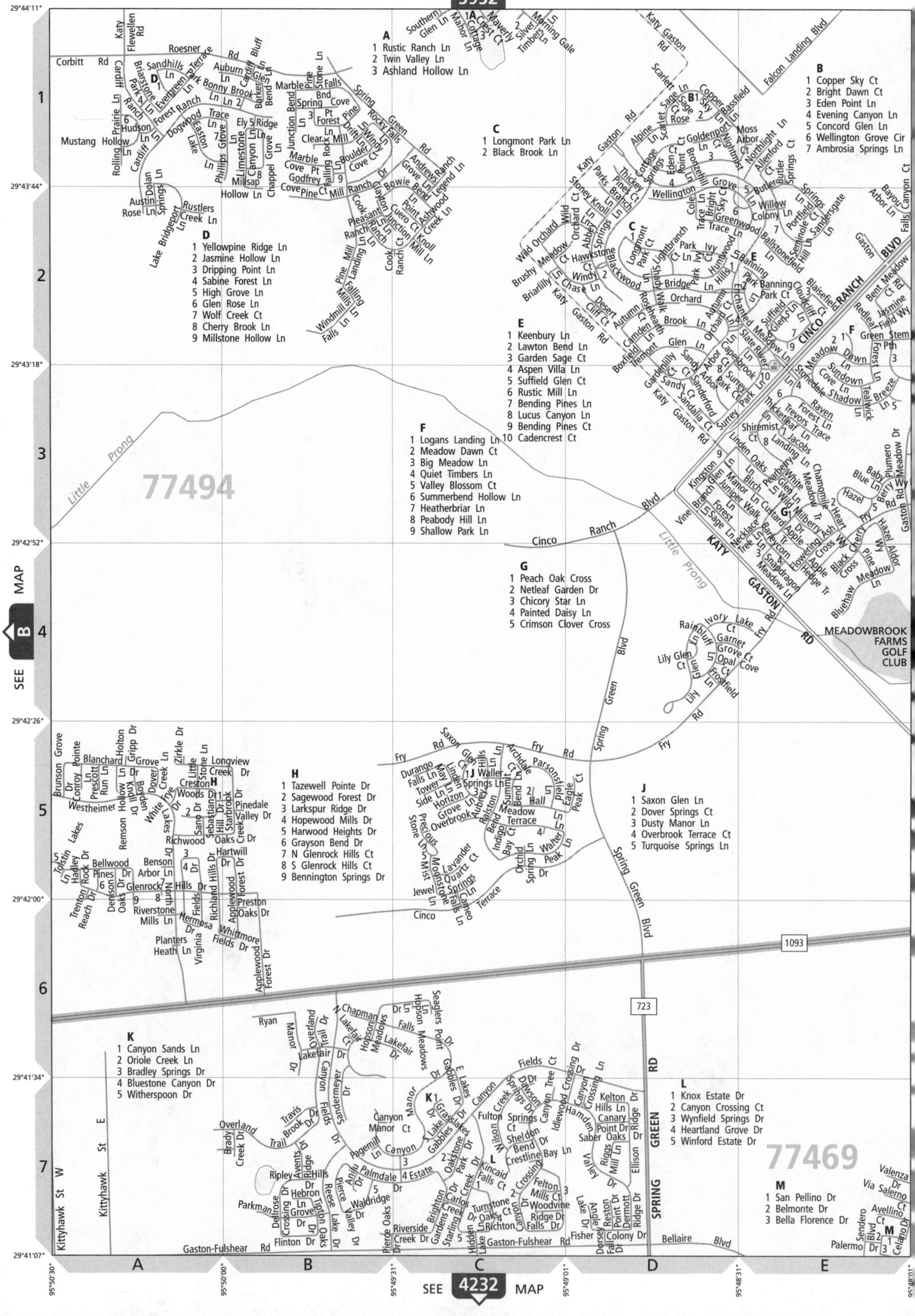
77494
77469
A
1 Rustic Ranch Ln
2 Twin Valley Ln
3 Ashland Hollow Ln
B
1 Copper Sky Ct
2 Bright Dawn Ct
3 Eden Point Ln
4 Evening Canyon Ln
5 Concord Glen Ln
6 Wellington Grove Cir
7 Ambrosia Springs Ln
C
1 Longmont Park Ln
2 Black Brook Ln
D
1 Yellowpine Ridge Ln
2 Jasmine Hollow Ln
3 Dripping Point Ln
4 Sabine Forest Ln
5 High Grove Ln
6 Glen Rose Ln
7 Wolf Creek Ct
8 Cherry Brook Ln
9 Millstone Hollow Ln
E
1 Keenbury Ln
2 Lawton Bend Ln
3 Garden Sage Ct
4 Aspen Villa Ln
5 Suffield Glen Ct
6 Rustic Mill Ln
7 Bending Pines Ln
8 Lucus Canyon Ln
9 Bending Pines Ct
10 Cadencrest Ct
F
1 Logans Landing Ln
2 Meadow Dawn Ct
3 Big Meadow Ln
4 Quiet Timbers Ln
5 Valley Blossom Ct
6 Summerbend Hollow Ln
7 Heatherbriar Ln
8 Peabody Hill Ln
9 Shallow Park Ln
G
1 Peach Oak Cross
2 Netleaf Garden Dr
3 Chicory Star Ln
4 Painted Daisy Ln
5 Crimson Clover Cross
H
1 Tazewell Pointe Dr
2 Sagewood Forest Dr
3 Larkspur Ridge Dr
4 Hopewood Mills Dr
5 Harwood Heights Dr
6 Grayson Bend Dr
7 N Glenrock Hills Ct
8 S Glenrock Hills Ct
9 Bennington Springs Dr
J
1 Saxon Glen Ln
2 Dover Springs Ct
3 Dusty Manor Ln
4 Overbrook Terrace Ct
5 Turquoise Springs Ln
K
1 Canyon Sands Ln
2 Oriole Creek Ln
3 Bradley Springs Dr
4 Bluestone Canyon Dr
5 Witherspoon Dr
L
1 Knox Estate Dr
2 Canyon Crossing Ct
3 Wynfield Springs Dr
4 Heartland Grove Dr
5 Winford Estate Dr
M
1 San Pellino Dr
2 Belmonte Dr
3 Bella Florence Dr
CINCO RANCH BLVD
KATY GASTON RD
SPRING GREEN RD
Spring Green Blvd
Cinco Ranch Blvd
Fry Rd
Gaston-Fulshear Rd
Bellaire Blvd
Little Prong
MEADOWBROOK FARMS GOLF CLUB
1093
723
29°44'11"
29°43'44"
29°43'18"
29°42'52"
29°42'26"
29°42'00"
29°41'34"
29°41'07"
95°50'30"
95°50'00"
95°49'31"
95°49'01"
95°48'31"
95°48'01"
A
B
C
D
E
1
2
3
4
5
6
7

SEE MAP B

SEE 4232 MAP

1:24,000
1 in. = 2000 ft.
0 0.25 0.5
miles

SEE 3953 MAP

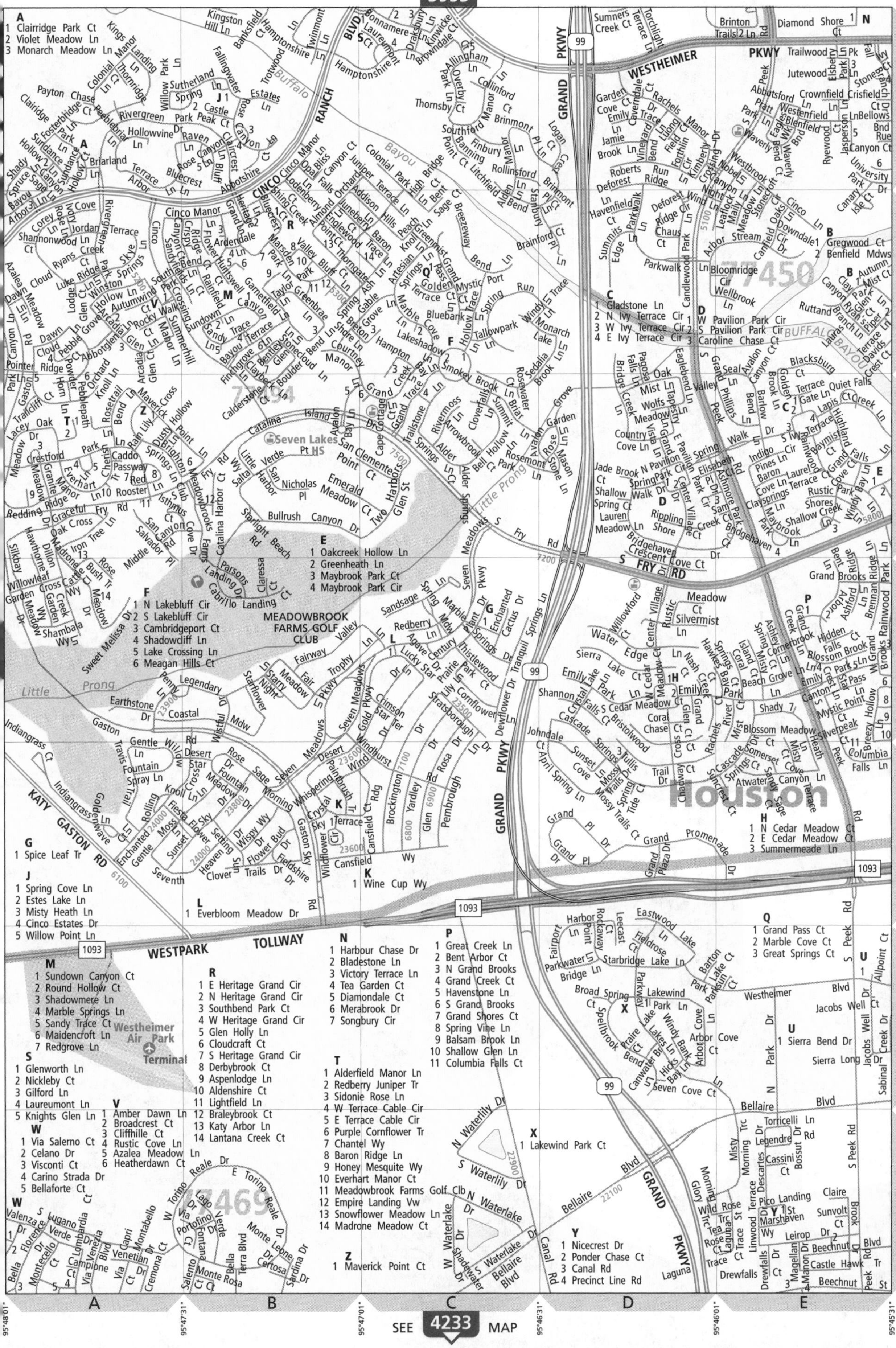

Houston
77450
77494
77469
WESTHEIMER PKWY
GRAND PKWY
S FRY RD
WESTPARK TOLLWAY
KATY GASTON RD
CINCO RANCH BLVD
MEADOWBROOK FARMS GOLF CLUB
Seven Lakes HS
Westheimer Air Park Terminal
A
1 Clairridge Park Ct
2 Violet Meadow Ln
3 Monarch Meadow Ln
B
1 Gregwood Ct
2 Benfield Mdws
C
1 Gladstone Ln
2 N Ivy Terrace Cir
3 W Ivy Terrace Cir
4 E Ivy Terrace Cir
D
1 W Pavilion Park Cir
2 S Pavilion Park Cir
3 Caroline Chase Ct
E
1 Oakcreek Hollow Ln
2 Greenheath Ln
3 Maybrook Park Ct
4 Maybrook Park Cir
F
1 N Lakebluff Cir
2 S Lakebluff Cir
3 Cambridgeport Ct
4 Shadowcliff Ln
5 Lake Crossing Ln
6 Meagan Hills Ct
G
1 Spice Leaf Tr
H
1 N Cedar Meadow Ct
2 E Cedar Meadow Ct
3 Summermeade Ln
J
1 Spring Cove Ln
2 Estes Lake Ln
3 Misty Heath Ln
4 Cinco Estates Dr
5 Willow Point Ln
K
1 Wine Cup Wy
L
1 Everbloom Meadow Dr
M
1 Sundown Canyon Ct
2 Round Hollow Ct
3 Shadowmere Ln
4 Marble Springs Ln
5 Sandy Trace Ct
6 Maidencroft Ln
7 Redgrove Ln
N
1 Harbour Chase Dr
2 Bladestone Ln
3 Victory Terrace Ln
4 Tea Garden Ct
5 Diamondale Ct
6 Merabrook Dr
7 Songbury Cir
P
1 Great Creek Ln
2 Bent Arbor Ct
3 N Grand Brooks
4 Grand Creek Ct
5 Havenstone Ln
6 S Grand Brooks
7 Grand Shores Ct
8 Spring Vine Ln
9 Balsam Brook Ln
10 Shallow Glen Ln
11 Columbia Falls Ct
Q
1 Grand Pass Ct
2 Marble Cove Ct
3 Great Springs Ct
R
1 E Heritage Grand Cir
2 N Heritage Grand Cir
3 Southbend Park Ct
4 W Heritage Grand Cir
5 Glen Holly Ln
6 Cloudcraft Ct
7 S Heritage Grand Cir
8 Derbybrook Ct
9 Aspenlodge Ln
10 Aldenshire Ct
11 Lightfield Ln
12 Braleybrook Ct
13 Katy Arbor Ln
14 Lantana Creek Ct
S
1 Glenworth Ln
2 Nickleby Ct
3 Gilford Ln
4 Laureumont Ln
5 Knights Glen Ln
T
1 Alderfield Manor Ln
2 Redberry Juniper Tr
3 Sidonie Rose Ln
4 W Terrace Cable Cir
5 E Terrace Cable Cir
6 Purple Cornflower Tr
7 Chantel Wy
8 Baron Ridge Ln
9 Honey Mesquite Wy
10 Everhart Manor Ct
11 Meadowbrook Farms Golf Clb
12 Empire Landing Vw
13 Snowflower Meadow Ln
14 Madrone Meadow Ct
U
1 Sierra Bend Dr
V
1 Amber Dawn Ln
2 Broadcrest Ct
3 Cliffhille Ct
4 Rustic Cove Ln
5 Azalea Meadow Ln
6 Heatherdawn Ct
W
1 Via Salerno Ct
2 Celano Dr
3 Visconti Ct
4 Carino Strada Dr
5 Bellaforte Ct
X
1 Lakewind Park Ct
Y
1 Nicecrest Dr
2 Ponder Chase Ct
3 Canal Rd
4 Precinct Line Rd
Z
1 Maverick Point Ct
29°44'09"
29°43'43"
29°43'17"
29°42'51"
29°42'25"
29°41'58"
29°41'32"
29°41'06"
95°48'01"
95°47'31"
95°47'01"
95°46'31"
95°46'01"
95°45'31"

SEE 4094 MAP

SEE 4233 MAP

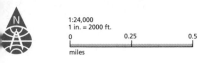

1:24,000
1 in. = 2000 ft.
0 0.25 0.5
miles

SEE 3954 MAP

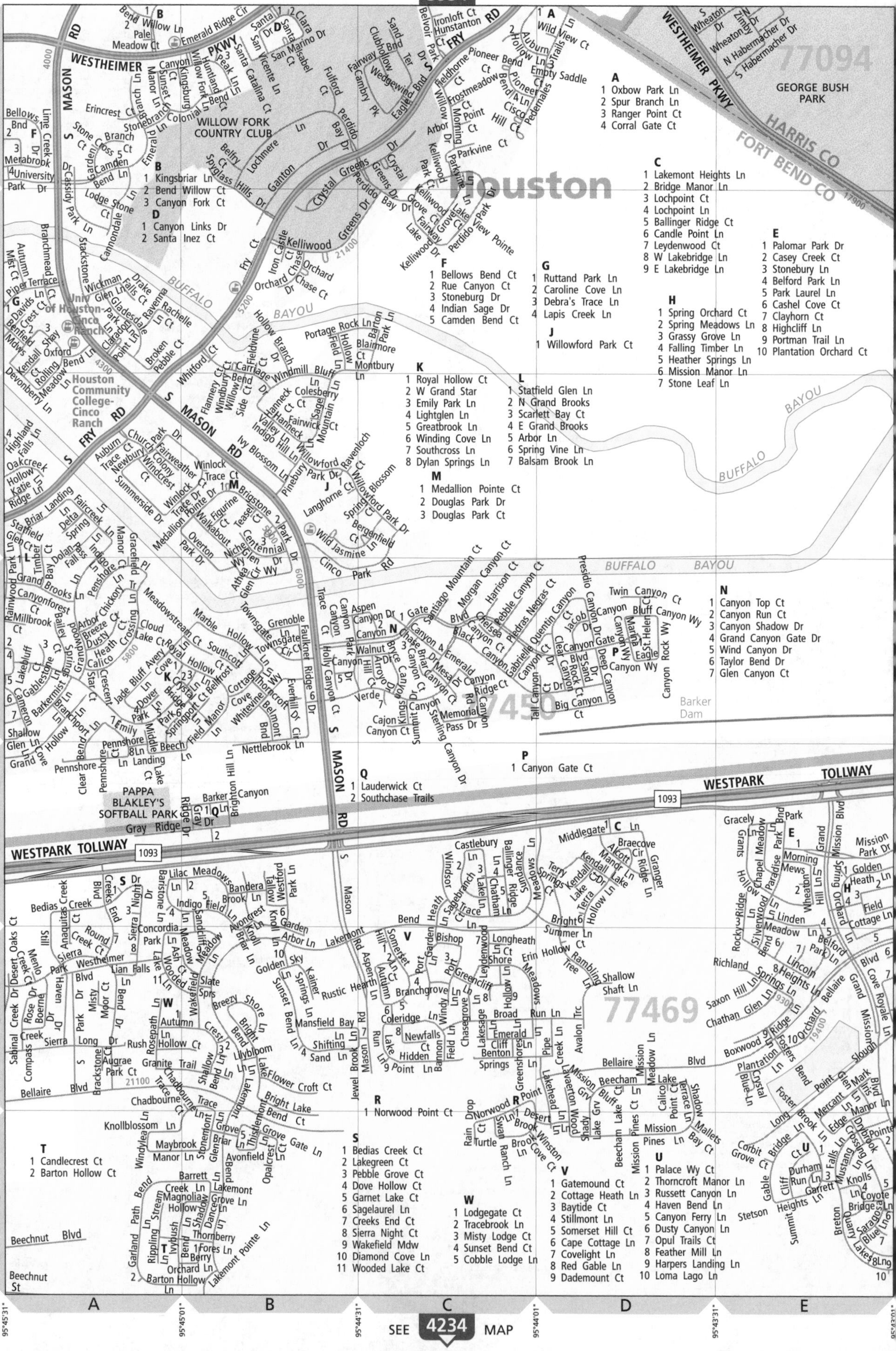
Houston
77094
77450
77469
GEORGE BUSH PARK
WILLOW FORK COUNTRY CLUB
Univ of Houston-Cinco Ranch
Houston Community College-Cinco Ranch
PAPPA BLAKLEY'S SOFTBALL PARK
HARRIS CO
FORT BEND CO
BUFFALO BAYOU
Barker Dam
WESTPARK TOLLWAY
1093
WESTHEIMER PKWY
S MASON RD
S FRY RD
A
1 Oxbow Park Ln
2 Spur Branch Ln
3 Ranger Point Ct
4 Corral Gate Ct
B
1 Kingsbriar Ln
2 Bend Willow Ct
3 Canyon Fork Ct
D
1 Canyon Links Dr
2 Santa Inez Ct
C
1 Lakemont Heights Ln
2 Bridge Manor Ln
3 Lochpoint Ct
4 Lochpoint Ln
5 Ballinger Ridge Ct
6 Candle Point Ln
7 Leydenwood Ct
8 W Lakebridge Ln
9 E Lakebridge Ln
E
1 Palomar Park Dr
2 Casey Creek Ct
3 Stonebury Ln
4 Belford Park Ln
5 Park Laurel Ln
6 Cashel Cove Ct
7 Clayhorn Ct
8 Highcliff Ln
9 Portman Trail Ln
10 Plantation Orchard Ct
F
1 Bellows Bend Ct
2 Rue Canyon Ct
3 Stoneburg Dr
4 Indian Sage Dr
5 Camden Bend Ct
G
1 Ruttand Park Ln
2 Caroline Cove Ln
3 Debra's Trace Ln
4 Lapis Creek Ln
H
1 Spring Orchard Ct
2 Spring Meadows Ln
3 Grassy Grove Ln
4 Falling Timber Ln
5 Heather Springs Ln
6 Mission Manor Ln
7 Stone Leaf Ln
J
1 Willowford Park Ct
K
1 Royal Hollow Ct
2 W Grand Star
3 Emily Park Ln
4 Lightglen Ln
5 Greatbrook Ln
6 Winding Cove Ln
7 Southcross Ln
8 Dylan Springs Ln
L
1 Statfield Glen Ln
2 N Grand Brooks
3 Scarlett Bay Ct
4 E Grand Brooks
5 Arbor Ln
6 Spring Vine Ln
7 Balsam Brook Ln
M
1 Medallion Pointe Ct
2 Douglas Park Dr
3 Douglas Park Ct
N
1 Canyon Top Ct
2 Canyon Run Ct
3 Canyon Shadow Dr
4 Grand Canyon Gate Dr
5 Wind Canyon Dr
6 Taylor Bend Dr
7 Glen Canyon Ct
P
1 Canyon Gate Ct
Q
1 Lauderwick Ct
2 Southchase Trails
R
1 Norwood Point Ct
S
1 Bedias Creek Ct
2 Lakegreen Ct
3 Pebble Grove Ct
4 Dove Hollow Ct
5 Garnet Lake Ct
6 Sagelaurel Ln
7 Creeks End Ct
8 Sierra Night Ct
9 Wakefield Mdw
10 Diamond Cove Ln
11 Wooded Lake Ct
T
1 Candlecrest Ct
2 Barton Hollow Ct
W
1 Lodgegate Ct
2 Tracebrook Ln
3 Misty Lodge Ct
4 Sunset Bend Ct
5 Cobble Lodge Ln
V
1 Gatemound Ct
2 Cottage Heath Ln
3 Baytide Ct
4 Stillmont Ln
5 Somerset Hill Ct
6 Cape Cottage Ln
7 Covelight Ln
8 Red Gable Ln
9 Dademount Ct
U
1 Palace Wy Ct
2 Thorncroft Manor Ln
3 Russett Canyon Ln
4 Haven Bend Ln
5 Canyon Ferry Ln
6 Dusty Canyon Ln
7 Opul Trails Ct
8 Feather Mill Ln
9 Harpers Landing Ln
10 Loma Lago Ln
A B C D E
1 2 3 4 5 6 7

SEE 4093 MAP

SEE 4234 MAP

1:24,000
1 in. = 2000 ft.
0 0.25 0.5
miles

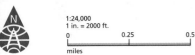

SEE 3955 MAP

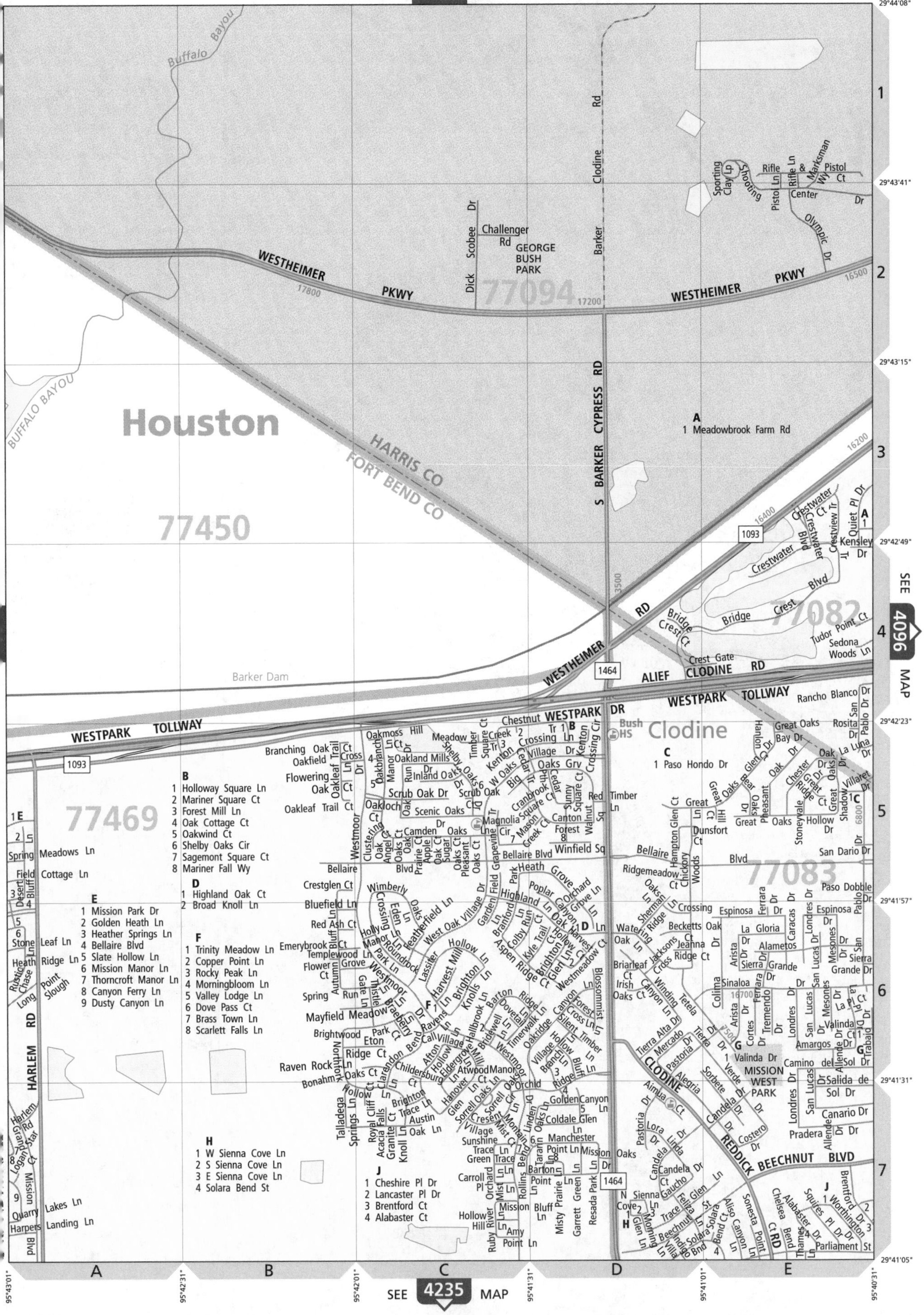
Houston
Clodine
77094
77450
77469
77082
77083
GEORGE
BUSH
PARK
HARRIS CO
FORT BEND CO
WESTHEIMER PKWY
WESTPARK TOLLWAY
S BARKER CYPRESS RD
Barker Clodine Rd
ALIEF CLODINE RD
WESTHEIMER RD
REDDICK RD
BEECHNUT BLVD
HARLEM RD
Barker Dam
Buffalo Bayou
BUFFALO BAYOU
1093
1464
MISSION
WEST
PARK
Bush HS
A
1 Meadowbrook Farm Rd
B
1 Holloway Square Ln
2 Mariner Square Ct
3 Forest Mill Ln
4 Oak Cottage Ct
5 Oakwind Ct
6 Shelby Oaks Cir
7 Sagemont Square Ct
8 Mariner Fall Wy
C
1 Paso Hondo Dr
D
1 Highland Oak Ct
2 Broad Knoll Ln
E
1 Mission Park Dr
2 Golden Heath Ln
3 Heather Springs Ln
4 Bellaire Blvd
5 Slate Hollow Ln
6 Mission Manor Ln
7 Thorncroft Manor Ln
8 Canyon Ferry Ln
9 Dusty Canyon Ln
F
1 Trinity Meadow Ln
2 Copper Point Ln
3 Rocky Peak Ln
4 Morningbloom Ln
5 Valley Lodge Ln
6 Dove Pass Ct
7 Brass Town Ln
8 Scarlett Falls Ln
G
1 Valinda Dr
H
1 W Sienna Cove Ln
2 S Sienna Cove Ln
3 E Sienna Cove Ln
4 Solara Bend St
J
1 Cheshire Pl Dr
2 Lancaster Pl Dr
3 Brentford Ct
4 Alabaster Ct
A B C D E
1 2 3 4 5 6 7
29°44'08"
29°43'41"
29°43'15"
29°42'49"
29°42'23"
29°41'57"
29°41'31"
29°41'05"
95°43'01"
95°42'31"
95°42'01"
95°41'31"
95°41'01"
95°40'31"

SEE 4096 MAP

SEE 4235 MAP

1:24,000
1 in. = 2000 ft.
0 0.25 0.5
miles

SEE 3956 MAP

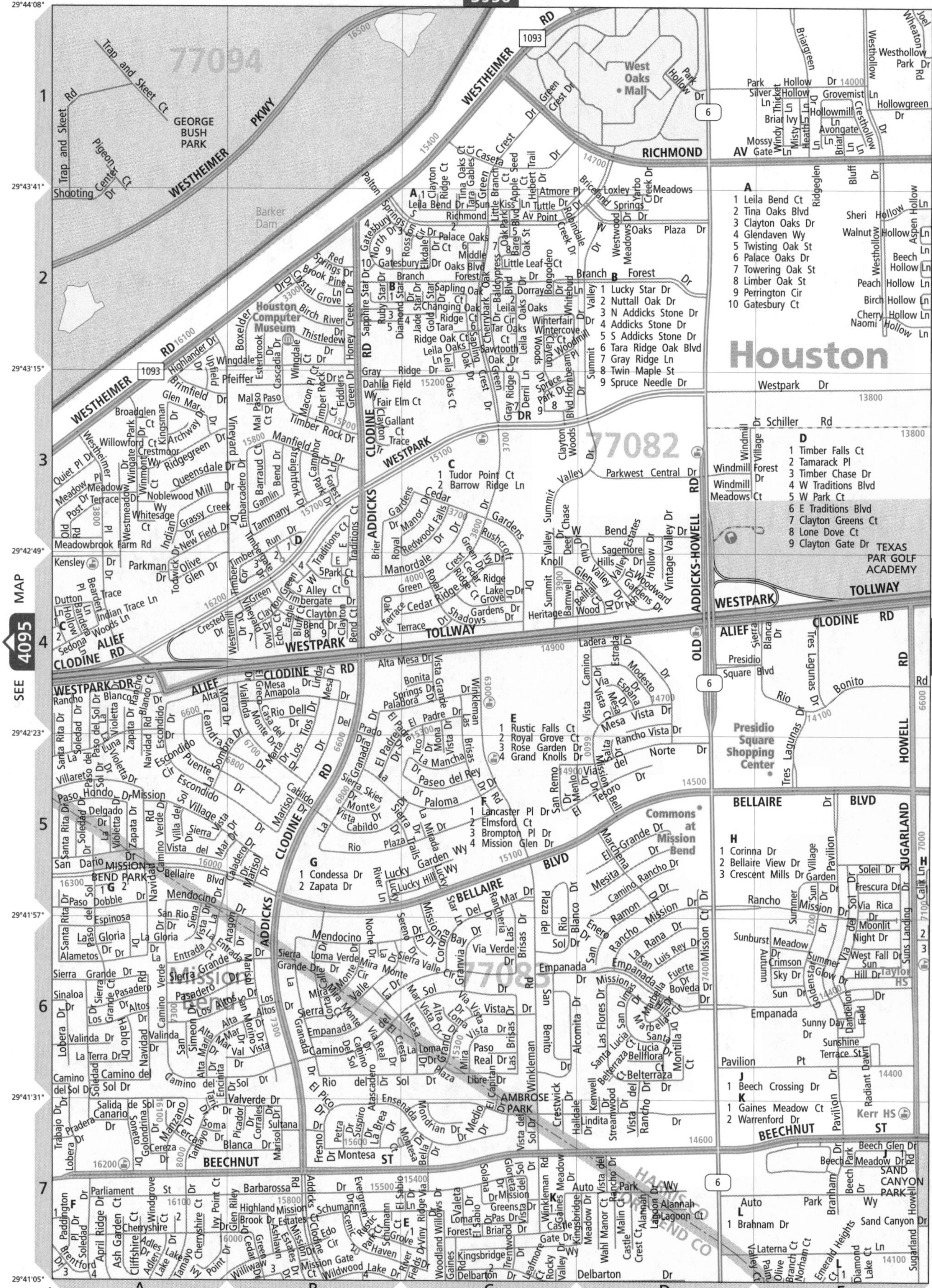
77094
GEORGE BUSH PARK
Trap and Skeet Ct
Trap and Skeet Rd
Pigeon Center Dr
Shooting Center Ct
WESTHEIMER PKWY
Barker Dam
WESTHEIMER RD
1093
West Oaks Mall
RICHMOND AV
6
Houston Computer Museum
Houston
77082
WESTPARK TOLLWAY
ADDICKS CLODINE RD
OLD ADDICKS-HOWELL RD
ALIEF CLODINE RD
TEXAS PAR GOLF ACADEMY
Presidio Square Shopping Center
Commons at Mission Bend
MISSION BEND PARK
Mission Bend
77083
BELLAIRE BLVD
BEECHNUT ST
SUGARLAND HOWELL RD
Kerr HS
Taylor HS
AMBROSE PARK
SAND CANYON PARK
HARRIS CO
FORT BEND CO
A
1 Leila Bend Ct
2 Tina Oaks Blvd
3 Clayton Oaks Dr
4 Glendaven Wy
5 Twisting Oak St
6 Palace Oaks Dr
7 Towering Oak St
8 Limber Oak St
9 Perrington Cir
10 Gatesbury Ct
B
1 Lucky Star Dr
2 Nuttall Oak Dr
3 N Addicks Stone Dr
4 Addicks Stone Dr
5 S Addicks Stone Dr
6 Tara Ridge Oak Blvd
7 Gray Ridge Ln
8 Twin Maple St
9 Spruce Needle Dr
C
1 Tudor Point Ct
2 Barrow Ridge Ln
D
1 Timber Falls Ct
2 Tamarack Pl
3 Timber Chase Dr
4 W Traditions Blvd
5 W Park Ct
6 E Traditions Blvd
7 Clayton Greens Ct
8 Lone Dove Ct
9 Clayton Gate Dr
E
1 Rustic Falls Ct
2 Royal Grove Ct
3 Rose Garden Dr
4 Grand Knolls Dr
F
1 Lancaster Pl Dr
2 Elmsford Ct
3 Brompton Pl Dr
4 Mission Glen Dr
G
1 Condessa Dr
2 Zapata Dr
H
1 Corinna Dr
2 Bellaire View Dr
3 Crescent Mills Dr
J
1 Beech Crossing Dr
K
1 Gaines Meadow Ct
2 Warrenford Dr
L
1 Brahnam Dr
29°44'08"
29°43'41"
29°43'15"
29°42'49"
29°42'23"
29°41'57"
29°41'31"
29°41'05"
95°40'31"
95°40'01"
95°39'31"
95°39'02"
95°38'32"
95°38'02"
1 2 3 4 5 6 7
A B C D E

SEE 4095 MAP

SEE 4236 MAP

1:24,000
1 in. = 2000 ft.
0 0.25 0.5
miles

SEE 3957 MAP

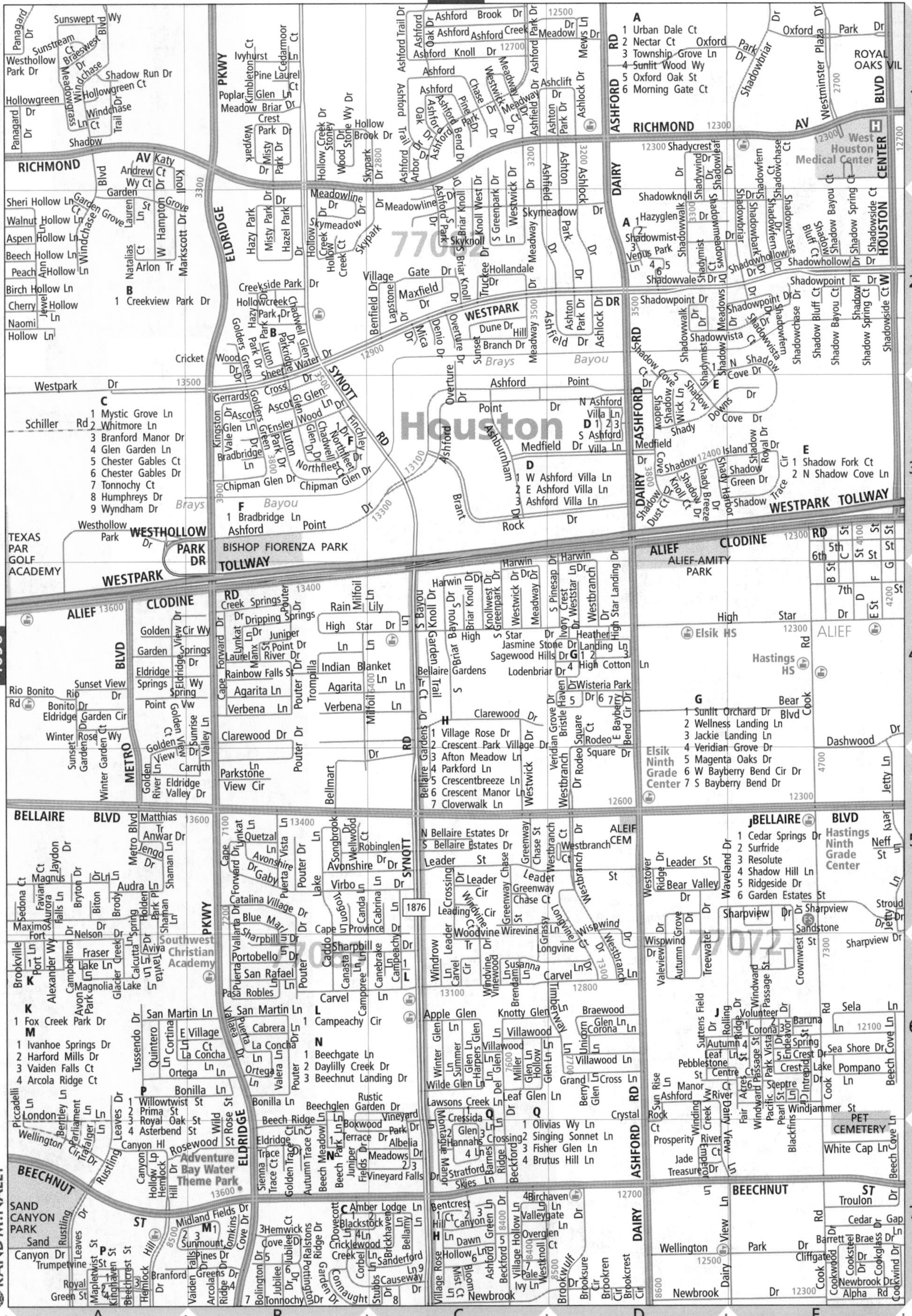
Houston
77082
77083
77072
RICHMOND AV
WESTPARK TOLLWAY
WESTPARK DR
ALIEF CLODINE RD
BELLAIRE BLVD
BEECHNUT ST
ELDRIDGE PKWY
DAIRY ASHFORD RD
SYNOTT RD
HOUSTON CENTER BLVD
METRO BLVD
WESTHOLLOW PARK DR
Brays Bayou
West Houston Medical Center
ROYAL OAKS VIL
TEXAS PAR GOLF ACADEMY
BISHOP FIORENZA PARK
ALIEF-AMITY PARK
ALIEF
Elsik HS
Hastings HS
Elsik Ninth Grade Center
Hastings Ninth Grade Center
ALIEF CEM
Southwest Christian Academy
Adventure Bay Water Theme Park
SAND CANYON PARK
PET CEMETERY
A
1 Urban Dale Ct
2 Nectar Ct
3 Township Grove Ln
4 Sunlit Wood Wy
5 Oxford Oak St
6 Morning Gate Ct
B
1 Creekview Park Dr
C
1 Mystic Grove Ln
2 Whitmore Ln
3 Branford Manor Dr
4 Glen Garden Ln
5 Chester Gables Ct
6 Chester Gables Dr
7 Tonnochy Ct
8 Humphreys Dr
9 Wyndham Dr
D
1 W Ashford Villa Ln
2 E Ashford Villa Ln
3 Ashford Villa Ln
E
1 Shadow Fork Ct
2 N Shadow Cove Ln
F
1 Bradbridge Ln
G
1 Sunlit Orchard Dr
2 Wellness Landing Ln
3 Jackie Landing Ln
4 Veridian Grove Dr
5 Magenta Oaks Dr
6 W Bayberry Bend Cir Dr
7 S Bayberry Bend Dr
H
1 Village Rose Dr
2 Crescent Park Village Dr
3 Afton Meadow Ln
4 Parkford Ln
5 Crescentbreeze Ln
6 Crescent Manor Ln
7 Cloverwalk Ln
J
1 Cedar Springs Dr
2 Surfride
3 Resolute
4 Shadow Hill Ln
5 Ridgeside Dr
6 Garden Estates St
K
1 Fox Creek Park Dr
L
1 Campeachy Cir
M
1 Ivanhoe Springs Dr
2 Harford Mills Dr
3 Vaiden Falls Ct
4 Arcola Ridge Ct
N
1 Beechgate Ln
2 Daylilly Creek Dr
3 Beechnut Landing Dr
P
1 Willowtwist St
2 Prima St
3 Royal Oak St
4 Asterbend St
Q
1 Olivias Wy Ln
2 Singing Sonnet Ln
3 Fisher Glen Ln
4 Brutus Hill Ln
29°44'06"
29°43'40"
29°43'14"
29°42'47"
29°42'21"
29°41'55"
29°41'29"
29°41'03"
95°38'02"
95°37'32"
95°37'02"
95°36'32"
95°36'02"
95°35'32"
A B C D E
1 2 3 4 5 6 7

SEE 4098 MAP

SEE 4237 MAP

1:24,000
1 in. = 2000 ft.
0 0.25 0.5
miles

SEE 3958 MAP

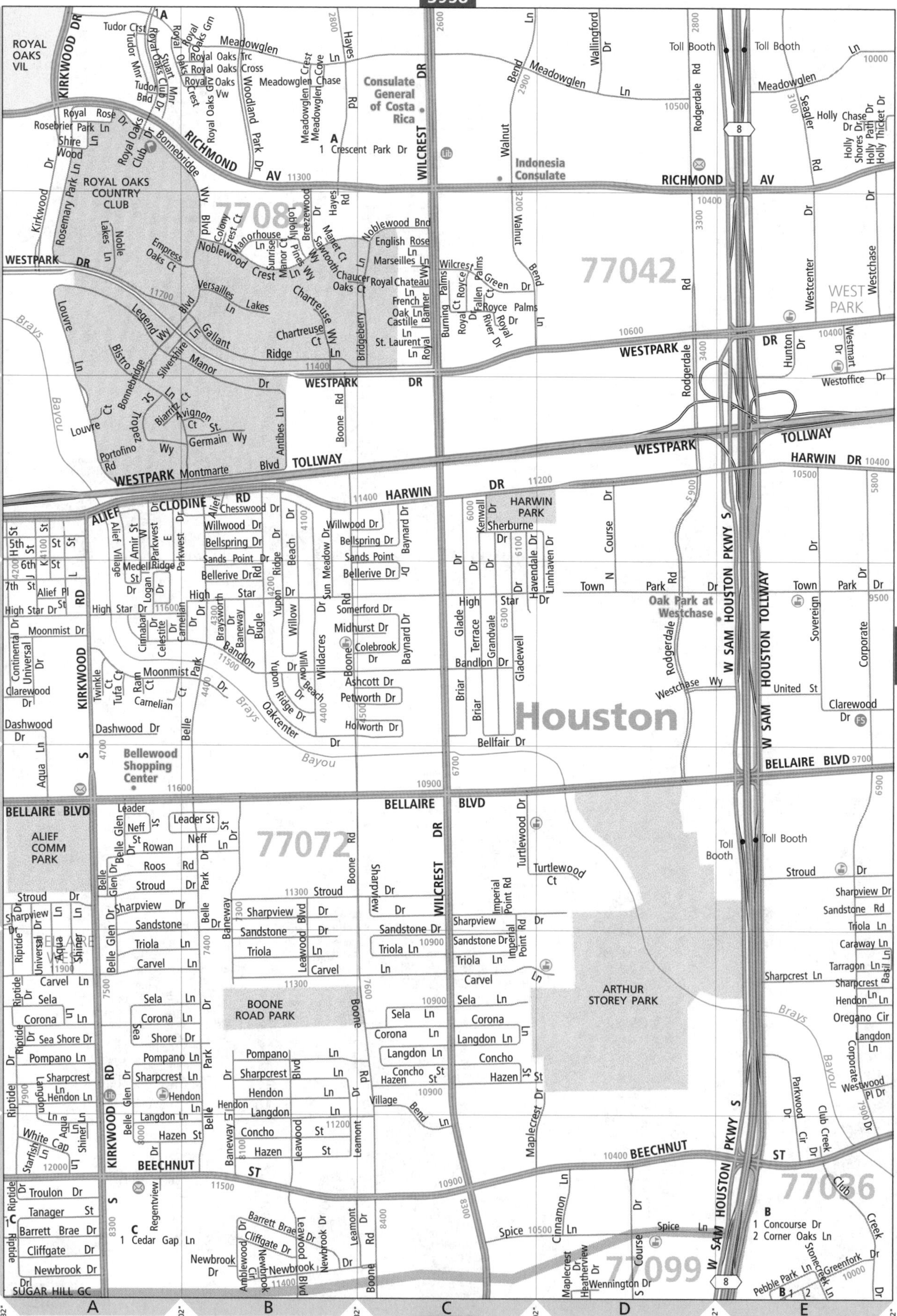
29°44'06"
29°43'40"
29°43'14"
29°42'47"
29°42'21"
29°41'55"
29°41'29"
29°41'03"
ROYAL OAKS VIL
KIRKWOOD DR
Tudor Crst
Royal Oaks Grn
Meadowglen
Royal Oaks Trc
Royal Oaks Cross
Royal Oaks Vw
Meadowglen Chase
Meadowglen Crest
Meadowglen Cove
Woodland Park Dr
Hayes Rd
Consulate General of Costa Rica
WILCREST DR
Walnut Bend
Meadowglen Ln
Wallingford Dr
Toll Booth
Rodgerdale Rd
Meadowglen
Holly Chase Dr
Seagler Rd
Holly Shores Dr
Holly Path Dr
Holly Thicket Dr
Royal Rose Dr
Rosebrier Park Ln
Shire Wood
Bonnebridge Wy
RICHMOND AV
1 Crescent Park Dr
Indonesia Consulate
RICHMOND AV
ROYAL OAKS COUNTRY CLUB
Kirkwood Dr
Rosemary Park Ln
Noble Lakes Ln
77082
Noblewood Bnd
English Rose Ln
Marseilles Ln
Wilcrest Palms
Green Dr
77042
Westcenter Dr
Westchase Dr
WEST PARK
WESTPARK DR
Empress Oaks Ct
Noblewood Crest
Versailles Ln
Lakes
Chartreuse Wy
Chaucer Oaks Ct
Royal Chateau Ln
French Oak Ln
Castille Ln
St. Laurent Ln
Burning Palms
Royce Palms Dr
Royal River Dr
Louvre Ln
Legend Wy
Gallant Ridge
Chartreuse Ct
Bridgeberry
Brays Bayou
WESTPARK DR
Hunton Dr
Westmart Dr
Westoffice Dr
Bistro
Bonnebridge
Silvershire
Manor Dr
St. Tropez
Biarritz Ct
Avignon Ct
St. Germain Wy
Louvre Ct
Portofino Rd
Antibes Ln
Boone Rd
WESTPARK TOLLWAY
Montmarte Blvd
TOLLWAY
HARWIN DR
ALIEF CLODINE RD
Chesswood Dr
Willwood Dr
Bellspring Dr
Sands Point Dr
Bellerive Dr
Baynard Dr
HARWIN PARK
Sherburne
Kenwall Dr
Havendale Dr
Linnhaven Dr
Course N Dr
Town Park Dr
Oak Park at Westchase
W SAM HOUSTON PKWY S
W SAM HOUSTON TOLLWAY
Sovereign
Corporate Dr
High Star Dr
Moonmist Dr
Continental Dr
Universal Dr
Clarewood Dr
Dashwood Dr
Amir St
Parkwest
Medell Ridge
Logan Dr
Cinnabar
Celestite
Carnelian
Braesworth
Baneway
Bugle
Yupon Ridge Dr
Willow Beach Dr
Sun Meadow Dr
Wildacres
Somerford Dr
Midhurst Dr
Colebrook Dr
Ashcott Dr
Petworth Dr
Holworth Dr
Glade Dr
Terrace Dr
Grandvale Dr
Gladewell
Bandlon Dr
Briar
Houston
Westchase Wy
United St
Clarewood Dr
Twinkle Ct
Tufa Ct
Ram Ct
Carnelian
Belle Park
Oakcenter
Bayou
Bellfair Dr
Aqua Ln
Bellewood Shopping Center
BELLAIRE BLVD
ALIEF COMM PARK
Leader St
Neff St
Rowan
Belle Glen Dr
Roos Rd
Stroud Dr
77072
Sharpview Dr
Turtlewood Dr
Turtlewood Ct
Toll Booth
Stroud Dr
Sharpview Dr
Sandstone Rd
Triola Ln
Caraway Ln
Tarragon Ln
Sharpcrest Ln
Hendon Ln
Oregano Cir
Langdon Ln
Sandstone
Triola
Carvel
Imperial Point Rd
Leawood Blvd
Riptide Dr
Shiner
Sela Ln
Corona Ln
Sea Shore Dr
Pompano Ln
Sharpcrest Ln
Hendon Ln
White Cap Ln
Starfish
BOONE ROAD PARK
ARTHUR STOREY PARK
Concho St
Hazen St
Village Bend Ln
Maplecrest Dr
Parkwood Dr
Club Creek Dr
Westwood Pl Dr
BEECHNUT ST
77036
Troulon Dr
Tanager St
Barrett Brae Dr
Cliffgate Dr
Newbrook Dr
SUGAR HILL GC
1 Cedar Gap Ln
Regentview
Leamont
Amblewood Cir
Cinnamon Ln
Spice Ln
Heatherview
Wennington Dr
77099
B
1 Concourse Dr
2 Corner Oaks Ln
Pebble Park Ln
Stonecreek Ln
Greenfork Dr
A B C D E
SEE 4097 MAP
95°35'32" 95°35'02" 95°34'32" 95°34'02" 95°33'32" 95°33'02"

SEE 4238 MAP

1:24,000
1 in. = 2000 ft.
0 0.25 0.5
miles

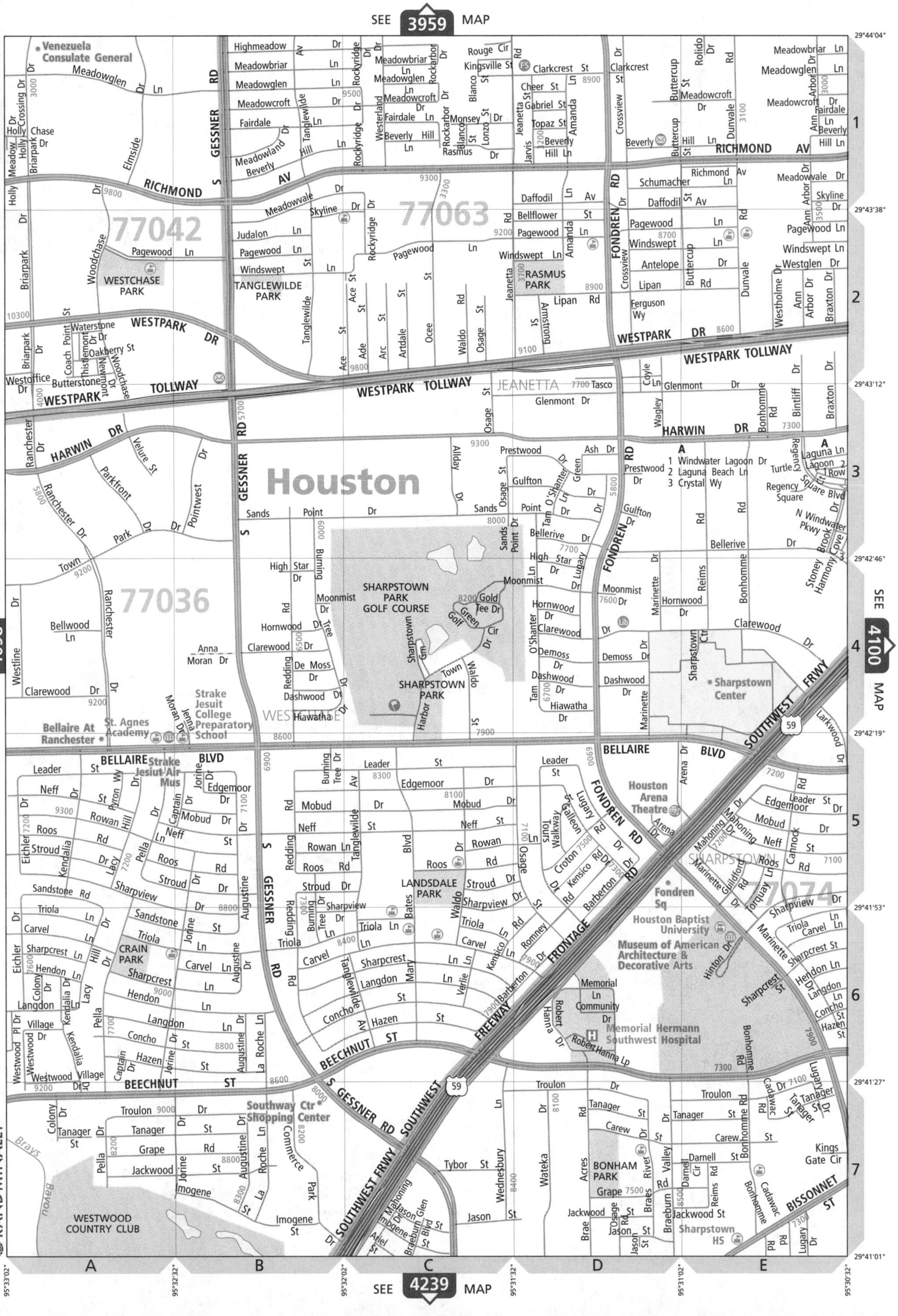
SEE 3959 MAP
SEE 4100 MAP
SEE 4239 MAP
Houston
77042
77063
77036
77074
RICHMOND AV
WESTPARK DR
WESTPARK TOLLWAY
HARWIN DR
BELLAIRE BLVD
BEECHNUT ST
BISSONNET ST
S GESSNER RD
FONDREN RD
SOUTHWEST FRWY
FRONTAGE
59
Venezuela Consulate General
WESTCHASE PARK
TANGLEWILDE PARK
RASMUS PARK
SHARPSTOWN PARK GOLF COURSE
SHARPSTOWN PARK
Sharpstown Center
Bellaire At Ranchester
St. Agnes Academy
Strake Jesuit College Preparatory School
Strake Jesuit Air Mus
WESTCHASE
JEANETTA
SHARPSTOWN
Houston Arena Theatre
LANDSDALE PARK
CRAIN PARK
Fondren Sq
Houston Baptist University
Museum of American Architecture & Decorative Arts
Memorial Hermann Southwest Hospital
Southway Ctr Shopping Center
WESTWOOD COUNTRY CLUB
BONHAM PARK
Sharpstown HS
Brays Bayou
A B C D E
1 2 3 4 5 6 7
29°44'04" 29°43'38" 29°43'12" 29°42'46" 29°42'19" 29°41'53" 29°41'27" 29°41'01"
95°33'02" 95°32'32" 95°32'02" 95°31'32" 95°31'02" 95°30'32"

1:24,000
1 in. = 2000 ft.

0 0.25 0.5
miles

SEE 3960 MAP

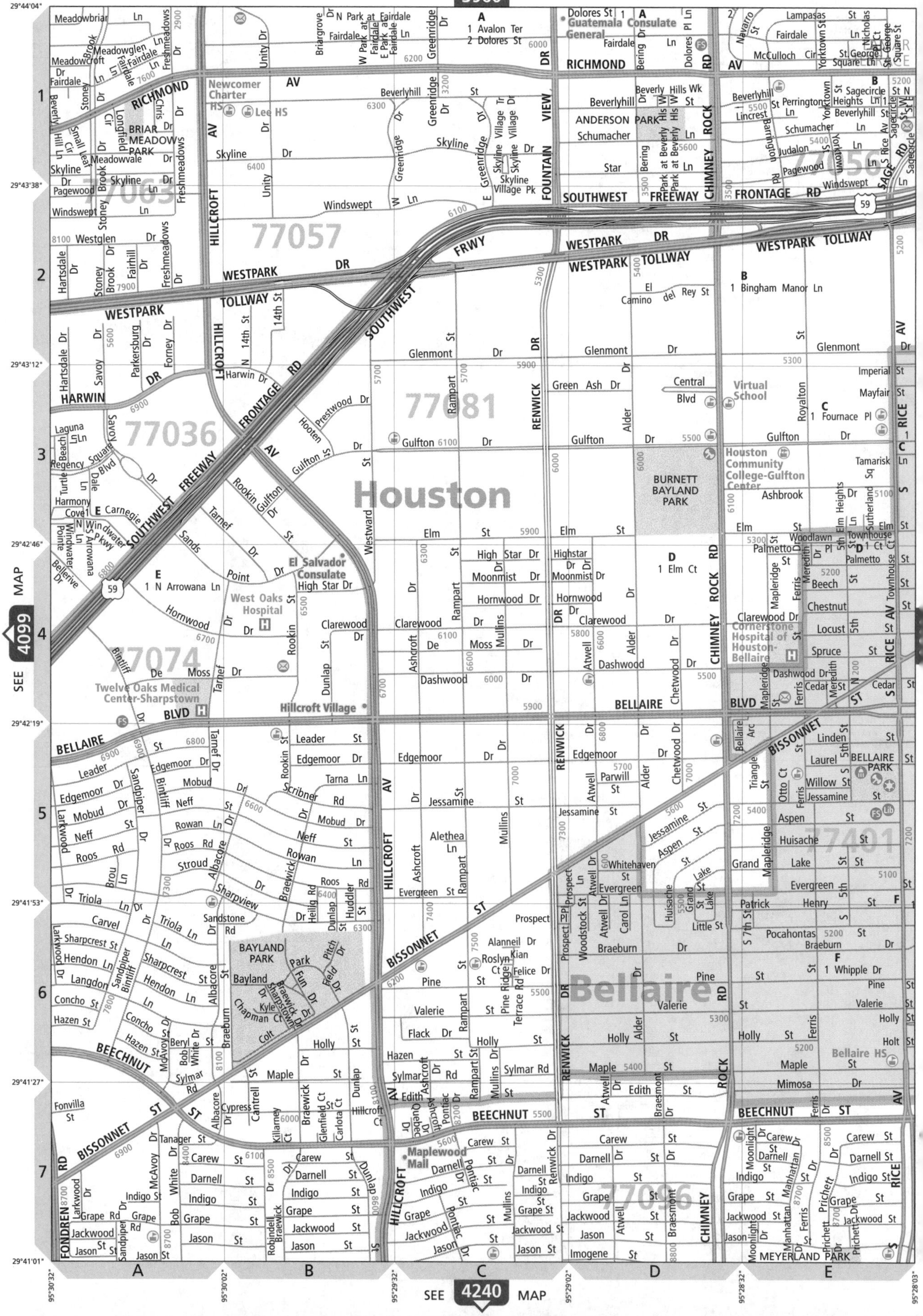

RICHMOND AV
SOUTHWEST FREEWAY
SOUTHWEST FRWY
FRONTAGE RD
WESTPARK TOLLWAY
WESTPARK DR
HARWIN DR
BELLAIRE BLVD
BISSONNET ST
BEECHNUT ST
HILLCROFT AV
FOUNTAIN VIEW DR
RENWICK DR
CHIMNEY ROCK RD
FONDREN RD
RICE AV
Houston
Bellaire
77057
77063
77036
77081
77074
77401
77096
77056
Newcomer Charter HS
Lee HS
BRIAR MEADOWS PARK
ANDERSON PARK
Guatemala Consulate General
Virtual School
Houston Community College-Gulfton Center
BURNETT BAYLAND PARK
El Salvador Consulate
West Oaks Hospital
Twelve Oaks Medical Center-Sharpstown
Hillcroft Village
Cornerstone Hospital of Houston-Bellaire
BELLAIRE PARK
BAYLAND PARK
Maplewood Mall
Bellaire HS
MEYERLAND PARK

SEE 4099 MAP

SEE 4240 MAP

1:24,000
1 in. = 2000 ft.
0 0.25 0.5
miles

SEE 3961 MAP

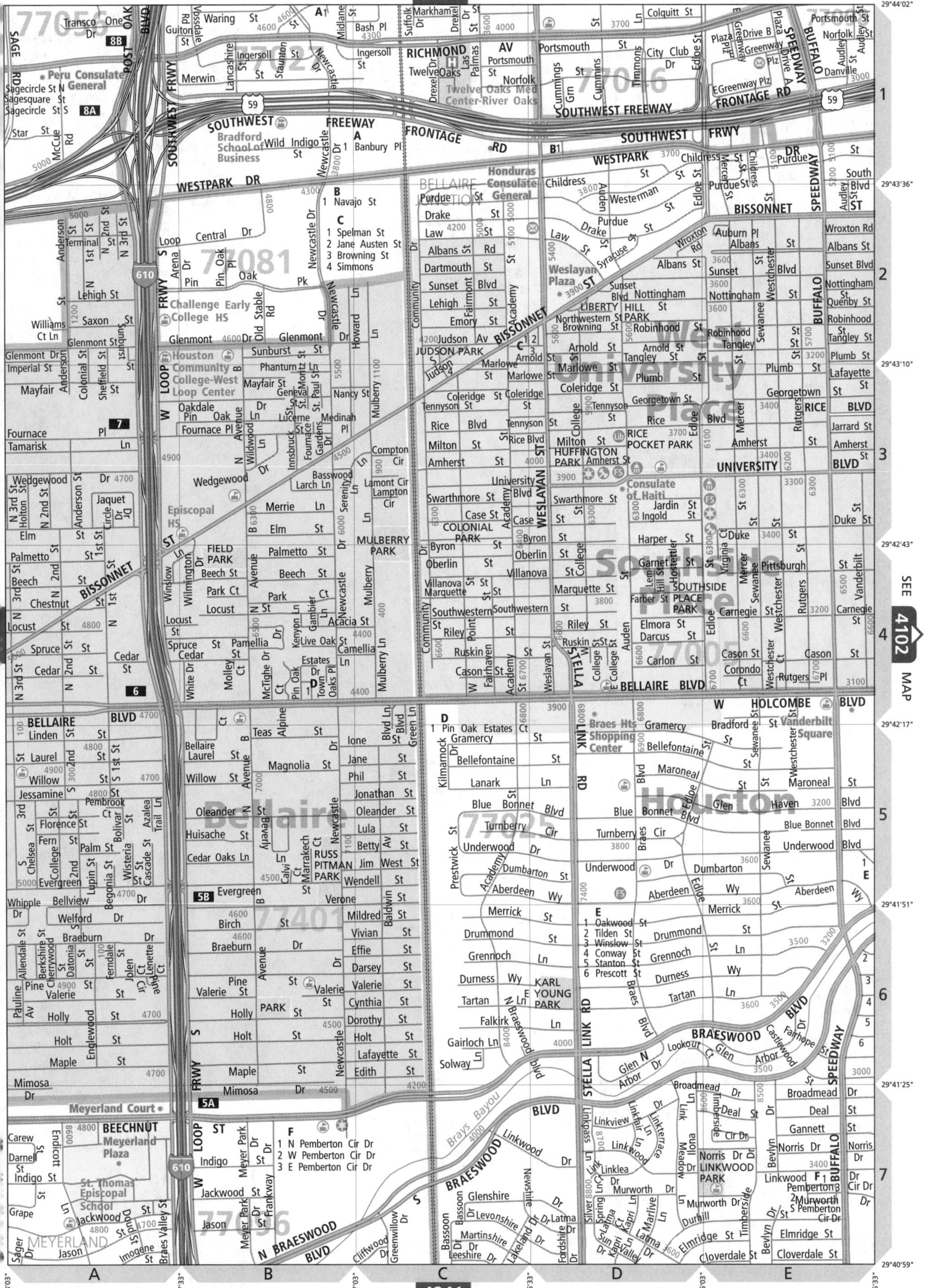
SOUTHWEST FREEWAY
WESTPARK DR
RICHMOND AV
BISSONNET ST
BELLAIRE BLVD
HOLCOMBE BLVD
BRAESWOOD BLVD
N BRAESWOOD BLVD
STELLA LINK RD
WESLAYAN ST
BUFFALO SPEEDWAY
S LOOP W FRWY
Bellaire
Houston
West University Place
Southside Place
Twelve Oaks Med Center-River Oaks
Bradford School of Business
Honduras Consulate General
Peru Consulate General
Consulate of Haiti
Houston Community College-West Loop Center
Challenge Early College HS
Episcopal HS
Weslayan Plaza
Braes Hts Shopping Center
Vanderbilt Square
Meyerland Plaza
Meyerland Court
St. Thomas' Episcopal School
BELLAIRE JUNCTION
JUDSON PARK
COLONIAL PARK
MULBERRY PARK
FIELD PARK
HUFFINGTON PARK
RICE POCKET PARK
LIBERTY HILL PARK
SOUTHSIDE PLACE PARK
RUSS PITMAN PARK
KARL YOUNG PARK
LINKWOOD PARK
MEYERLAND
Brays Bayou
77056
77027
77046
77081
77005
77025
77401
77096
A
B
C
D
E
1
2
3
4
5
6
7
29°44'02"
29°43'36"
29°43'10"
29°42'43"
29°42'17"
29°41'51"
29°41'25"
29°40'59"
95°28'03"
95°27'33"
95°27'03"
95°26'33"
95°26'03"
95°25'33"
B
1 Navajo St
C
1 Spelman St
2 Jane Austen St
3 Browning St
4 Simmons
D
1 Pin Oak Estates Ct
E
1 Oakwood St
2 Tilden St
3 Winslow St
4 Conway St
5 Stanton St
6 Prescott St
F
1 N Pemberton Cir Dr
2 W Pemberton Cir Dr
3 E Pemberton Cir Dr
SEE 4102 MAP

SEE 4241 MAP

1:24,000
1 in. = 2000 ft.
0 0.25 0.5
miles

SEE 3962 MAP

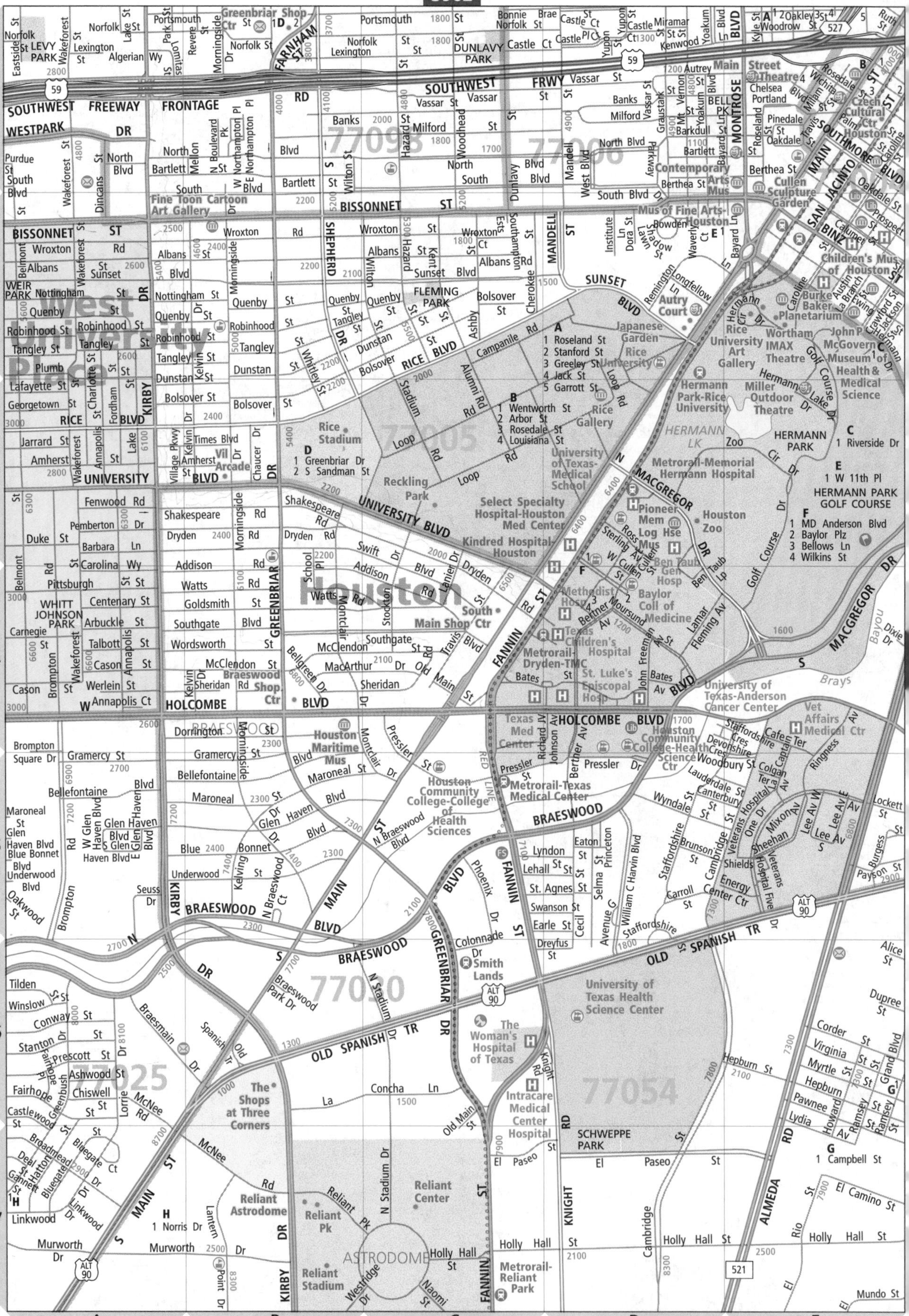
SOUTHWEST FREEWAY FRONTAGE RD
WESTPARK DR
BISSONNET ST
RICE BLVD
UNIVERSITY BLVD
HOLCOMBE BLVD
BRAESWOOD BLVD
OLD SPANISH TR
KIRBY DR
GREENBRIAR DR
SHEPHERD DR
MAIN ST
FANNIN ST
MONTROSE BLVD
SAN JACINTO
MACGREGOR DR
ALMEDA RD
KNIGHT RD
SUNSET BLVD
West University Place
Houston
LEVY PARK
DUNLAVY PARK
WEIR PARK
FLEMING PARK
WHITT JOHNSON PARK
Reckling Park
Rice Stadium
Rice University
Rice Gallery
Hermann Park-Rice University
HERMANN PARK
HERMANN PARK GOLF COURSE
Houston Zoo
Miller Outdoor Theatre
Burke Baker Planetarium
Wortham IMAX Theatre
John P McGovern Museum of Health & Medical Science
Children's Mus. of Houston
Mus of Fine Arts-Houston
Contemporary Arts Mus
Cullen Sculpture Garden
Japanese Garden
Autry Court
Pioneer Mem Log Hse
Metrorail-Memorial Hermann Hospital
Select Specialty Hospital-Houston Med Center
Kindred Hospital-Houston
Ben Taub Gen Hosp
Baylor Coll of Medicine
Methodist Hosp
Texas Children's Hospital
St. Luke's Episcopal Hosp
Metrorail-Dryden-TMC
University of Texas Medical School
University of Texas-Anderson Cancer Center
Texas Med Center
Houston Community College-Health Science Ctr
Metrorail-Texas Medical Center
Vet Affairs Medical Ctr
Houston Community College-College of Health Sciences
Houston Maritime Mus
Braeswood Shop. Ctr
Vil Arcade
Main Shop Ctr
Fine Toon Cartoon Art Gallery
Greenbriar Shop Ctr
Street Theatre
Czech Cultural Ctr Houston
University of Texas Health Science Center
The Woman's Hospital of Texas
Intracare Medical Center Hospital
SCHWEPPE PARK
The Shops at Three Corners
Reliant Astrodome
Reliant Pk
Reliant Center
Reliant Stadium
ASTRODOME
Metrorail-Reliant Park
Smith Lands
77098
77006
77005
77030
77025
77054
59
ALT 90
527
521

A B C D E

SEE 4101 MAP

SEE 4242 MAP

1:24,000
1 in. = 2000 ft.
0 0.25 0.5
miles

SEE 3963 MAP

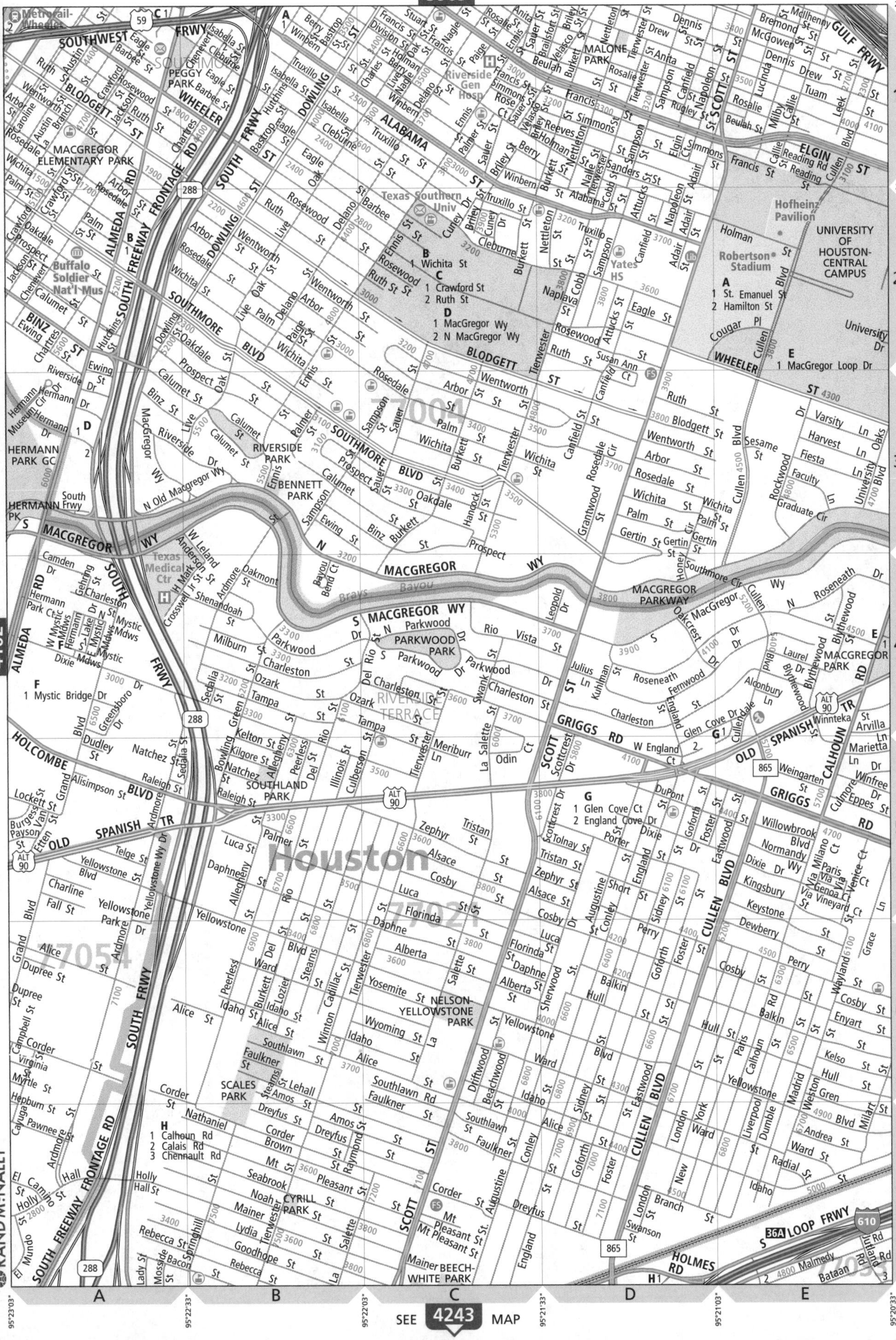
Houston
SOUTHWEST FRWY
SOUTH FRWY
GULF FRWY
LOOP FRWY
SOUTH FREEWAY FRONTAGE RD
MACGREGOR WY
N MACGREGOR WY
S MACGREGOR WY
OLD SPANISH TR
GRIGGS RD
HOLCOMBE BLVD
CULLEN BLVD
SCOTT ST
WHEELER ST
ALABAMA ST
ELGIN ST
BLODGETT ST
SOUTHMORE BLVD
ALMEDA RD
CALHOUN RD
HOLMES RD
DOWLING ST
Brays Bayou
MACGREGOR ELEMENTARY PARK
PEGGY PARK
MALONE PARK
Riverside Gen Hosp
Texas Southern Univ
Yates HS
Robertson Stadium
Hofheinz Pavilion
UNIVERSITY OF HOUSTON-CENTRAL CAMPUS
Buffalo Soldier Nat'l Mus
HERMANN PARK GC
HERMANN PK
Texas Medical Ctr
RIVERSIDE PARK
BENNETT PARK
PARKWOOD PARK
RIVERSIDE TERRACE
MACGREGOR PARKWAY
MACGREGOR PARK
SOUTHLAND PARK
NELSON-YELLOWSTONE PARK
SCALES PARK
CYRILL PARK
BEECH-WHITE PARK
77004
77021
77054
A 1 St. Emanuel St 2 Hamilton St
B 1 Wichita St
C 1 Crawford St 2 Ruth St
D 1 MacGregor Wy 2 N MacGregor Wy
E 1 MacGregor Loop Dr
F 1 Mystic Bridge Dr
G 1 Glen Cove Ct 2 England Cove Dr
H 1 Calhoun Rd 2 Calais Rd 3 Chennault Rd
29°44'00"
29°43'33"
29°43'07"
29°42'41"
29°42'15"
29°41'49"
29°41'23"
29°40'56"
95°23'03"
95°22'33"
95°22'03"
95°21'33"
95°21'03"
95°20'33"
A B C D E
1 2 3 4 5 6 7

SEE 4104 MAP

SEE 4243 MAP

1:24,000
1 in. = 2000 ft.
0 0.25 0.5
miles

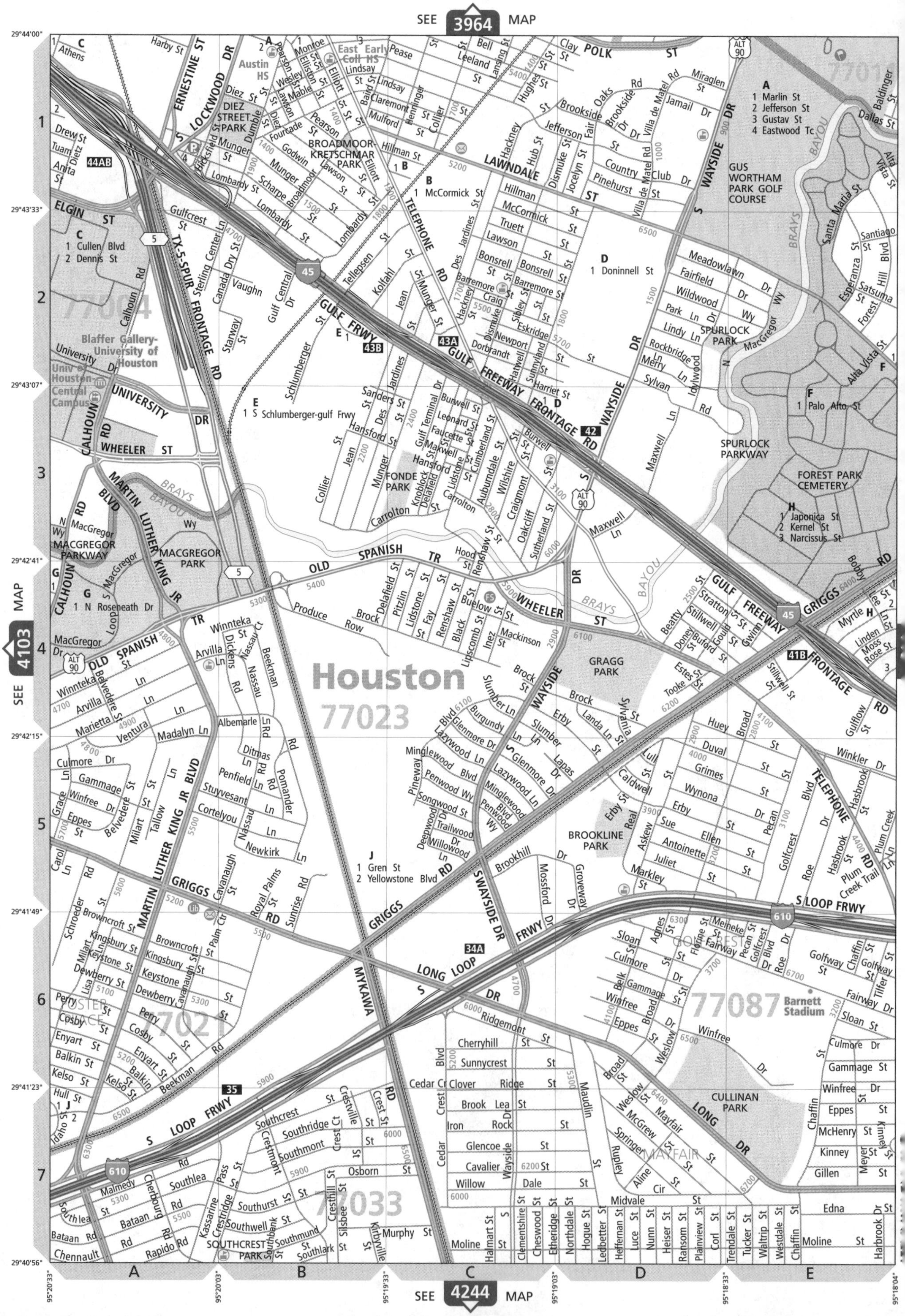
SEE 3964 MAP
SEE 4103 MAP
SEE 4244 MAP
Houston
77023
77004
77021
77087
77033
77011
GULF FRWY
GULF FREEWAY
S LOOP FRWY
OLD SPANISH TR
WHEELER ST
UNIVERSITY DR
ELGIN ST
LAWNDALE ST
POLK ST
TELEPHONE RD
WAYSIDE DR
S WAYSIDE DR
MARTIN LUTHER KING JR BLVD
GRIGGS RD
LONG DR
S LONG LOOP DR
MYKAWA RD
CALHOUN RD
ERNESTINE ST
LOCKWOOD DR
TX-5-SPUR FRONTAGE RD
BRAYS BAYOU
Austin HS
East Early Coll HS
DIEZ STREET PARK
BROADMOOR-KRETSCHMAR PARK
GUS WORTHAM PARK GOLF COURSE
SPURLOCK PARK
SPURLOCK PARKWAY
FOREST PARK CEMETERY
FONDE PARK
GRAGG PARK
BROOKLINE PARK
CULLINAN PARK
MACGREGOR PARK
MACGREGOR PARKWAY
Blaffer Gallery-University of Houston
Univ of Houston-Central Campus
Barnett Stadium
FOSTER PLACE
GOLFCREST
MAYFAIR
SOUTHCREST PARK
A
1 Marlin St
2 Jefferson St
3 Gustav St
4 Eastwood Tc
B
1 McCormick St
C
1 Cullen Blvd
2 Dennis St
D
1 Doninnell St
E
1 S Schlumberger-gulf Frwy
F
1 Palo Alto St
G
1 N Roseneath Dr
H
1 Japonica St
2 Kernel St
3 Narcissus St
J
1 Gren St
2 Yellowstone Blvd
29°44'00"
29°43'33"
29°43'07"
29°42'41"
29°42'15"
29°41'49"
29°41'23"
29°40'56"
95°20'33"
95°20'03"
95°19'33"
95°19'03"
95°18'33"
95°18'04"

1:24,000
1 in. = 2000 ft.
0 0.25 0.5
miles

SEE 3965 MAP

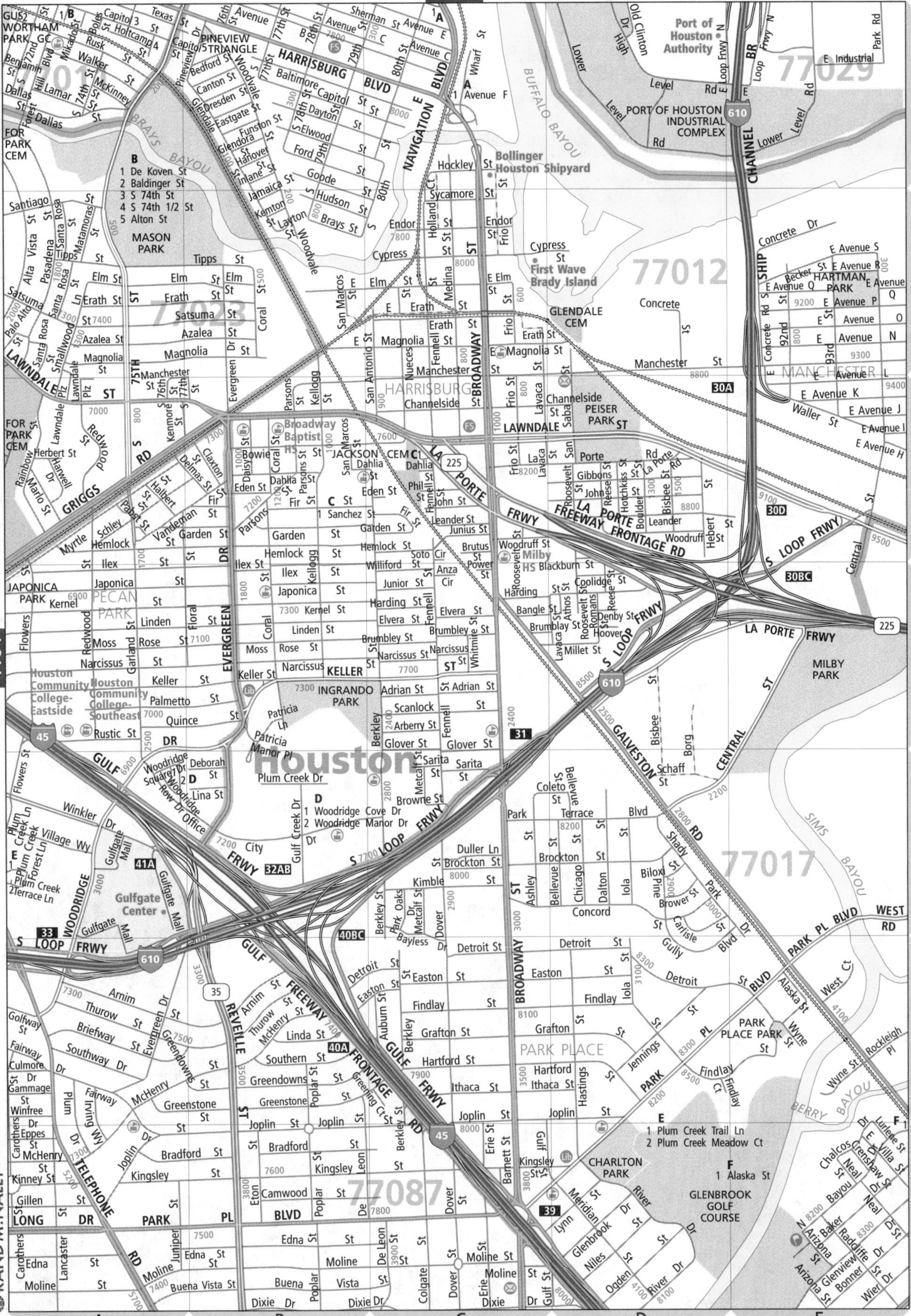
Port of Houston Authority
PORT OF HOUSTON INDUSTRIAL COMPLEX
77029
77012
77023
77017
77087
Houston
HARRISBURG
MANCHESTER
PARK PLACE
PECAN PARK
PINEVIEW TRIANGLE
MASON PARK
GLENDALE CEM
JACKSON CEM
PEISER PARK
MILBY PARK
INGRANDO PARK
HARTMAN PARK
PARK PLACE PARK
CHARLTON PARK
GLENBROOK GOLF COURSE
FOREST PARK CEM
JAPONICA PARK
GUS WORTHAM PARK GC
Bollinger Houston Shipyard
First Wave Brady Island
Broadway Baptist HS
Milby HS
Houston Community College-Eastside
Houston Community College-Southeast
Gulfgate Center
BUFFALO BAYOU
BRAYS BAYOU
SIMS BAYOU
BERRY BAYOU
HARRISBURG BLVD
NAVIGATION BLVD
BROADWAY ST
LAWNDALE ST
LA PORTE FRWY
S LOOP FRWY
GULF FRWY
GALVESTON RD
EVERGREEN DR
TELEPHONE RD
WOODRIDGE DR
REVEILLE ST
PARK PLACE BLVD
CENTRAL ST
SHIP CHANNEL BR
GRIGGS RD
75TH ST
B
1 De Koven St
2 Baldinger St
3 S 74th St
4 S 74th 1/2 St
5 Alton St
C
1 Sanchez St
D
1 Woodridge Cove Dr
2 Woodridge Manor Dr
E
1 Plum Creek Trail Ln
2 Plum Creek Meadow Ct
F
1 Alaska St
610
45
225
35
30A
30D
30BC
31
32AB
33
39
40A
40BC
41A
1
2
3
4
5
6
7
A
B
C
D
E
29°43'57"
29°43'31"
29°43'05"
29°42'39"
29°42'12"
29°41'46"
29°41'20"
29°40'54"
95°18'04"
95°17'34"
95°17'04"
95°16'34"
95°16'04"
95°15'34"

SEE 4106 MAP

SEE 4245 MAP

1:24,000
1 in. = 2000 ft.
0 0.25 0.5
miles

SEE 3966 MAP

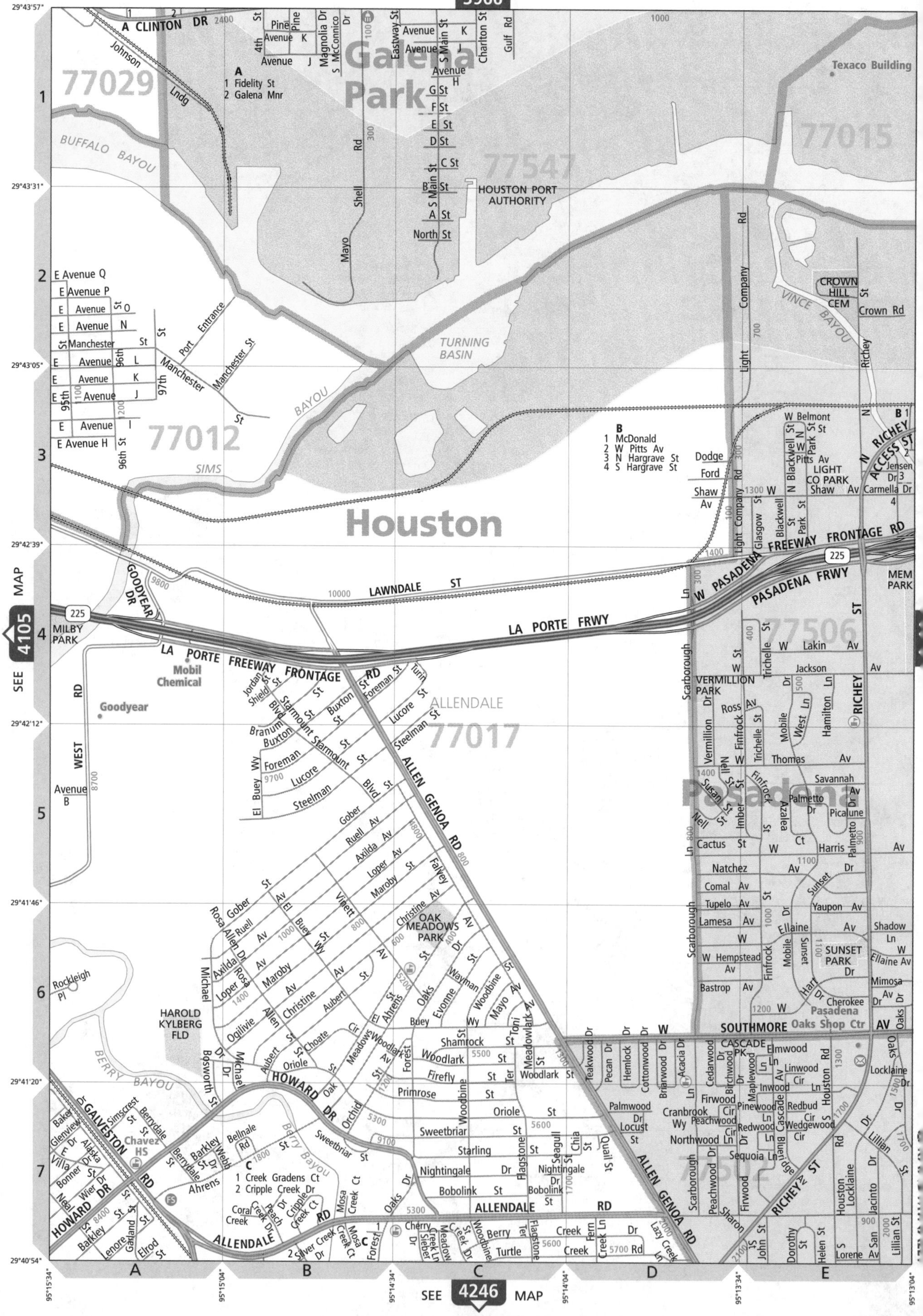
29°43'57"
29°43'31"
29°43'05"
29°42'39"
29°42'12"
29°41'46"
29°41'20"
29°40'54"
95°15'34"
95°15'04"
95°14'34"
95°14'04"
95°13'34"
95°13'04"
1
2
3
4
5
6
7
A
B
C
D
E
A CLINTON DR
2400
Johnson Lndg
77029
BUFFALO BAYOU
Galena Park
A
1 Fidelity St
2 Galena Mnr
Pine
Avenue K
Avenue J
4th St
Magnolia Dr
S McConnico Dr
Eastway St
S Main St
Charlton St
Gulf Rd
Avenue H
G St
F St
E St
D St
C St
B St
A St
North St
Mayo Shell Rd
300
77547
HOUSTON PORT AUTHORITY
1000
Texaco Building
77015
E Avenue Q
E Avenue P
E Avenue O
E Avenue N
Manchester St
E Avenue L
E Avenue K
E Avenue J
E Avenue I
E Avenue H
95th
96th St
97th St
Port Entrance
Manchester St
BAYOU
77012
SIMS
TURNING BASIN
Light Company Rd
700
CROWN HILL CEM
Crown Rd
VINCE BAYOU
Richey
B
1 McDonald
2 W Pitts Av
3 N Hargrave St
4 S Hargrave St
Dodge
Ford
Shaw Av
1300 W
W Belmont
N Blackwell St
N Park St
W Pitts Av
LIGHT CO PARK
Shaw Av
N RICHEY ACCESS ST
Jensen Dr
Carmella Dr
Glasgow St
Blackwell St
Park St
Houston
GOODYEAR DR
9800
10000
LAWNDALE ST
1400
W PASADENA FREEWAY FRONTAGE RD
225
W PASADENA FRWY
PASADENA FRWY
MEM PARK
LA PORTE FRWY
MILBY PARK
LA PORTE FREEWAY FRONTAGE RD
Mobil Chemical
Goodyear
WEST RD
8700
Avenue B
Scarborough Ln
77506
Trichelle St
W Lakin Av
W Jackson Av
VERMILLION PARK
RICHEY ST
ALLENDALE
77017
Jordan St
Shield St
Starmount Blvd
Buxton St
Foreman St
Turin
Lucore St
Steelman St
Branum
El Buey Wy
9700
ALLEN GENOA RD
800
Ross Av
Vermillion Dr
Finfrock St
Mobile Dr
West Ln
Hamilton Ln
Thomas Av
Savannah Av
Pasadena
Susan St
Nell St
Imber St
Azalea
Palmetto Dr
Picalune
Cactus St
W Ct
Harris Av
Natchez Av
Comal Av
Tupelo Av
Lamesa Av
W Hempstead Av
Bastrop Av
1100
Sunset
Yaupon Av
Shadow Ln
Ellaine Av
SUNSET PARK Dr
Ellaine Av
Mimosa Av
Hart Dr
Cherokee Dr
1200 W
Pasadena Oaks Shop Ctr
SOUTHMORE AV
Gober St
Ruell Av
Axilda Av
Loper Av
Maroby St
Falvey
Christine Av
OAK MEADOWS PARK
Vinett
Rosa Allen Dr
Michael
Ogilvie
Aubert
Ahrens
Evonne
Wayman
Woodbine
Mayo
Toni
Meadowlark Av
Rockleigh Pl
HAROLD KYLBERG FLD
BERRY BAYOU
Bosworth St
HOWARD DR
Shamrock St
Woodlark St
Firefly St
Primrose St
Oriole St
Sweetbriar St
Starling St
Nightingale Dr
Bobolink St
ALLENDALE RD
5500
5600
5300
9100
Teakwood Dr
Pecan Dr
Hemlock Dr
Cottonwood Dr
Briarwood Dr
Acacia Dr
Cedarwood Dr
Birchwood Dr
CASCADE PK
Elmwood
Linwood Cir
Inwood
Redbud
Houston Rd
Locklaine
Palmwood Dr
Locust St
Cranbrook Wy
Firwood
Pinewood
Peachwood
Redwood
Wedgewood Cir
Northwood Ln
Sequoia Ln
77502
Lillian
Jacinto
RICHEY ST
Baker
Glenview
GALVESTON RD
Simscrest
Berrydale
Chavez HS
Alaska
Villa
Bonner
Wier Dr
Neal
HOWARD DR
Barkley
Lenore
Garland
Elrod St
Bellnale Rd
Webb
C
1 Creek Gradens Ct
2 Cripple Creek Dr
Coral Creek
Peach Creek Dr
Mosa Creek Ct
Silver Creek
Forest
Cherry
Meadow Creek Ln
Berry Ln
Turtle
Flagstone
Creek Dr
Fern
Lazy Creek
5700 Rd
Sharon
John St
Dorothy St
Helen St
S Lorene Av
San
Lillian St
900
2000
2100

SEE 4105 MAP

SEE 4246 MAP

1:24,000
1 in. = 2000 ft.
0 0.25 0.5
miles

SEE 3967 MAP

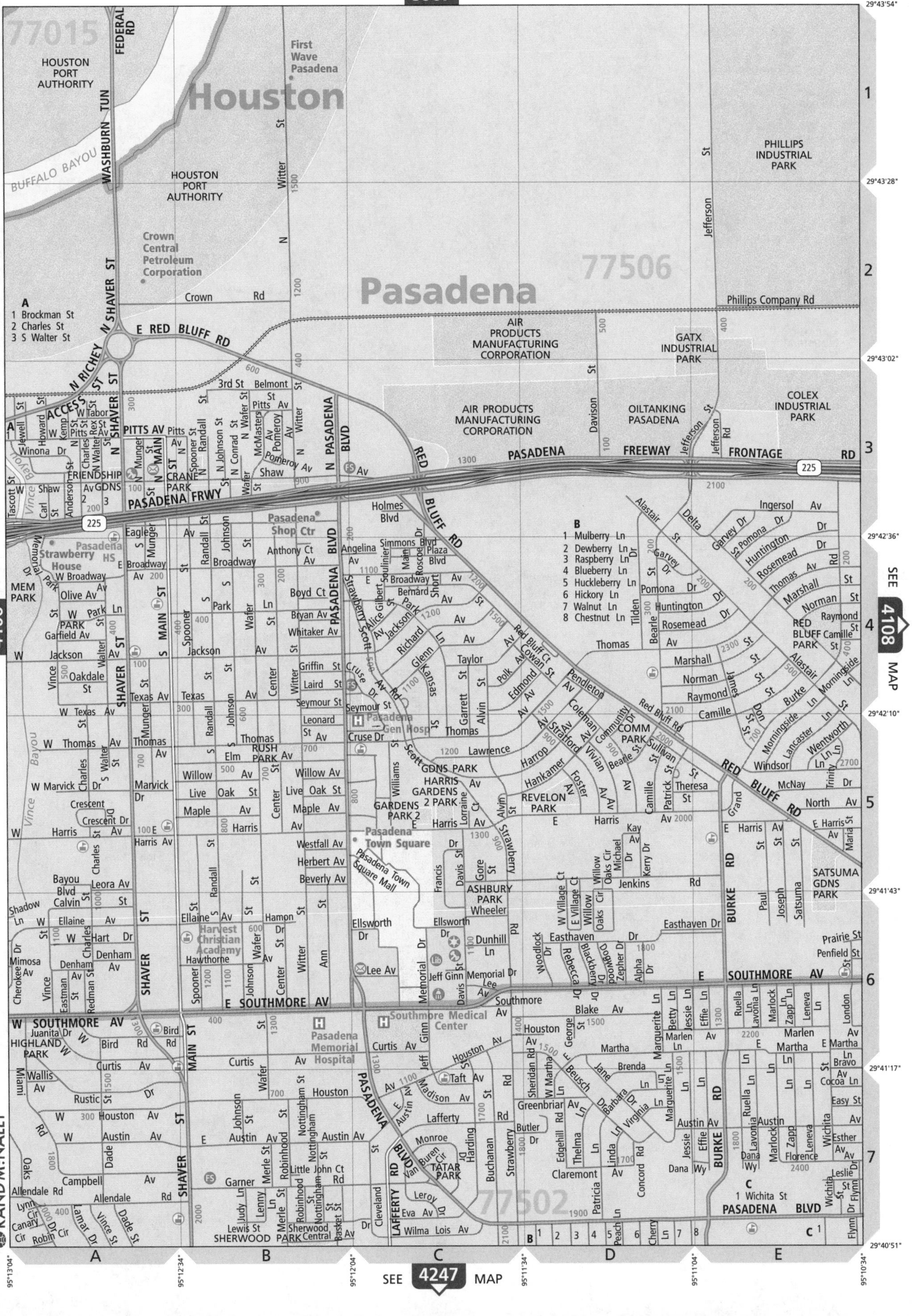
Houston
Pasadena
77015
77506
77502
HOUSTON PORT AUTHORITY
First Wave Pasadena
Crown Central Petroleum Corporation
PHILLIPS INDUSTRIAL PARK
AIR PRODUCTS MANUFACTURING CORPORATION
GATX INDUSTRIAL PARK
OILTANKING PASADENA
COLEX INDUSTRIAL PARK
BUFFALO BAYOU
WASHBURN TUN
FEDERAL RD
N SHAVER ST
N RICHEY ST
E RED BLUFF RD
PASADENA FRWY
PASADENA FREEWAY FRONTAGE RD
RED BLUFF RD
PASADENA BLVD
E SOUTHMORE AV
W SOUTHMORE AV
BURKE RD
SHAVER ST
MAIN ST
Phillips Company Rd
Crown Rd
Pasadena Shop Ctr
Pasadena Town Square
Pasadena Town Square Mall
Pasadena Gen Hosp
Pasadena Memorial Hospital
Southmore Medical Center
Strawberry House
Pasadena HS
Harvest Christian Academy
MEM PARK
FRIENDSHIP GDNS
CRANE PARK
RUSH PARK
GARDENS PARK 2
HARRIS GARDENS 2 PARK
REVELON PARK
ASHBURY PARK
COMM PARK
RED BLUFF PARK
SATSUMA GDNS PARK
HIGHLAND PARK
TATAR PARK
SHERWOOD PARK
A
1 Brockman St
2 Charles St
3 S Walter St
B
1 Mulberry Ln
2 Dewberry Ln
3 Raspberry Ln
4 Blueberry Ln
5 Huckleberry Ln
6 Hickory Ln
7 Walnut Ln
8 Chestnut Ln
C
1 Wichita St
225
1
2
3
4
5
6
7
A
B
C
D
E
29°43'54"
29°43'28"
29°43'02"
29°42'36"
29°42'10"
29°41'43"
29°41'17"
29°40'51"
95°13'04"
95°12'34"
95°12'04"
95°11'34"
95°11'04"
95°10'34"

SEE 4108 MAP

SEE 4247 MAP

1:24,000
1 in. = 2000 ft.
0 0.25 0.5
miles

SEE 3968 MAP

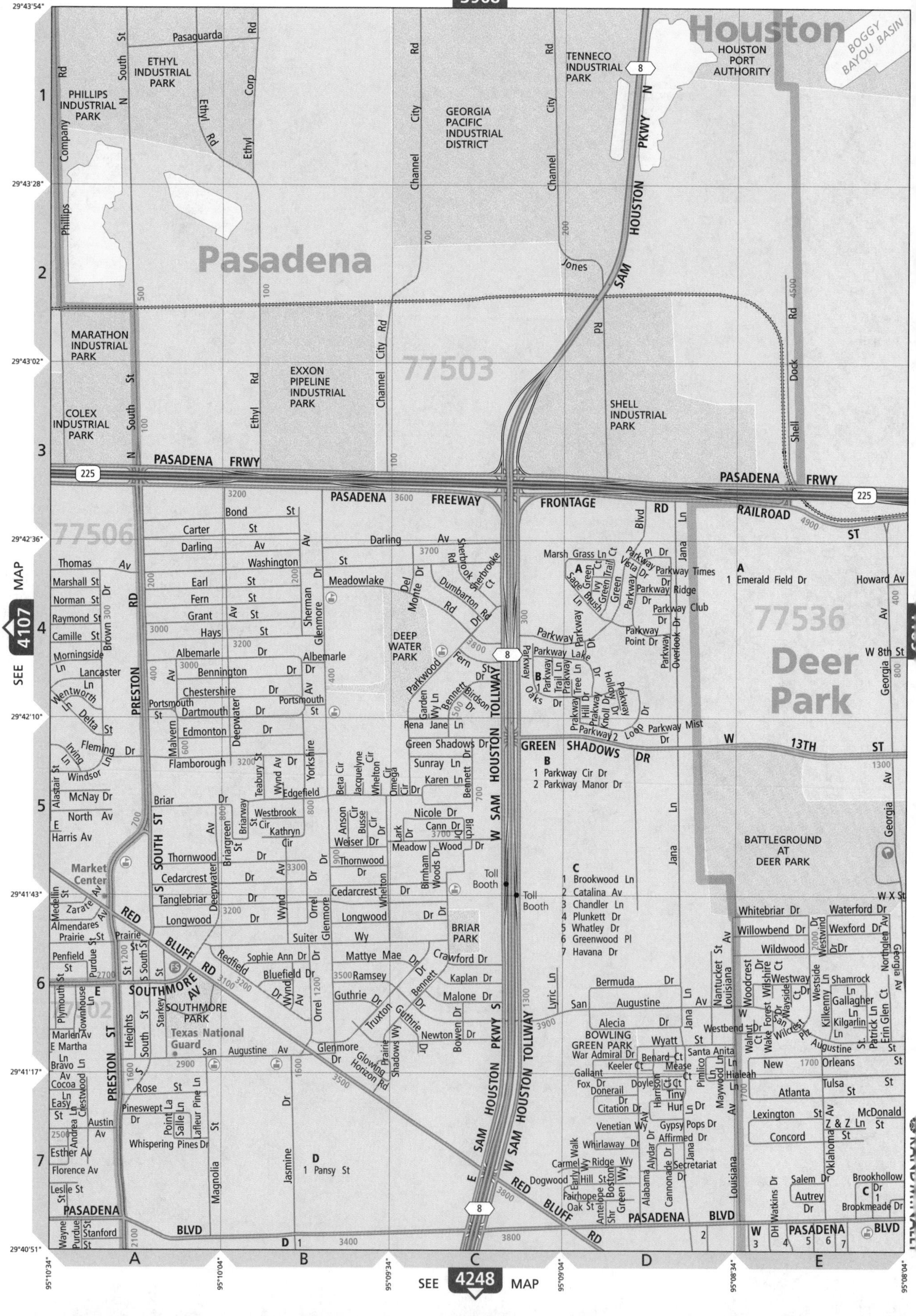
Houston
HOUSTON PORT AUTHORITY
BOGGY BAYOU BASIN
Pasadena
PHILLIPS INDUSTRIAL PARK
ETHYL INDUSTRIAL PARK
GEORGIA PACIFIC INDUSTRIAL DISTRICT
TENNECO INDUSTRIAL PARK
MARATHON INDUSTRIAL PARK
EXXON PIPELINE INDUSTRIAL PARK
COLEX INDUSTRIAL PARK
SHELL INDUSTRIAL PARK
77503
77506
77536
77502
Deer Park
DEEP WATER PARK
BRIAR PARK
SOUTHMORE PARK
BOWLING GREEN PARK
BATTLEGROUND AT DEER PARK
Market Center
Texas National Guard
Toll Booth
PASADENA FRWY
PASADENA FREEWAY
FRONTAGE RD
RAILROAD ST
SAM HOUSTON PKWY N
W SAM HOUSTON TOLLWAY
E SAM HOUSTON PKWY S
GREEN SHADOWS DR
W 13TH ST
RED BLUFF RD
SOUTHMORE AV
PASADENA BLVD
PRESTON RD
SOUTH ST
PRESTON ST
Pasaguarda Rd
Ethyl Rd
Corp Rd
Company Rd
Phillips Rd
Channel City Rd
Jones Rd
Dock Rd
Shell Rd
Howard Av
Georgia Av
W 8th St
225
8
A 1 Emerald Field Dr
B 1 Parkway Cir Dr 2 Parkway Manor Dr
C 1 Brookwood Ln 2 Catalina Av 3 Chandler Ln 4 Plunkett Dr 5 Whatley Dr 6 Greenwood Pl 7 Havana Dr
D 1 Pansy St
1 2 3 4 5 6 7
A B C D E

SEE 4107 MAP

SEE 4248 MAP

1:24,000
1 in. = 2000 ft.
0 0.25 0.5
miles

SEE 3969 MAP

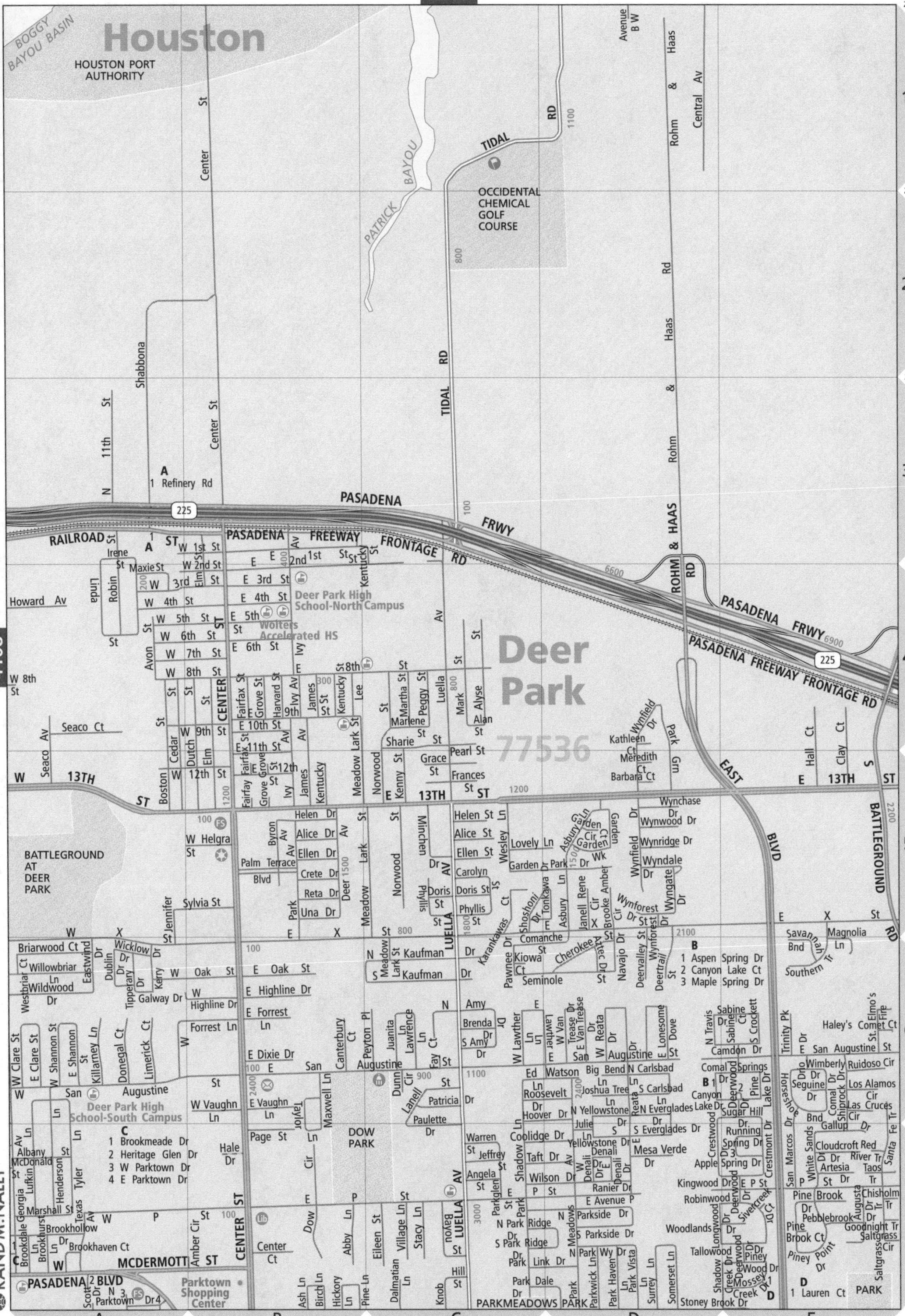
Houston
BOGGY BAYOU BASIN
HOUSTON PORT AUTHORITY
PATRICK BAYOU
OCCIDENTAL CHEMICAL GOLF COURSE
TIDAL RD
Center St
Rohm & Haas Rd
Central Av
PASADENA FRWY
225
PASADENA FREEWAY FRONTAGE RD
RAILROAD ST
Deer Park High School-North Campus
Wolters Accelerated HS
Deer Park
77536
W 13TH ST
E 13TH ST
CENTER ST
LUELLA AV
EAST BLVD
BATTLEGROUND RD
BATTLEGROUND AT DEER PARK
X ST
Deer Park High School-South Campus
DOW PARK
San Augustine St
Parktown Shopping Center
PASADENA BLVD
MCDERMOTT ST
PARKMEADOWS PARK
PARK
A 1 Refinery Rd
B 1 Aspen Spring Dr 2 Canyon Lake Ct 3 Maple Spring Dr
C 1 Brookmeade Dr 2 Heritage Glen Dr 3 W Parktown Dr 4 E Parktown Dr
D 1 Lauren Ct
1 2 3 4 5 6 7
A B C D E
29°43'51" 29°43'25" 29°42'59" 29°42'33" 29°42'07" 29°41'41" 29°41'14" 29°40'48"
95°08'04" 95°07'35" 95°07'05" 95°06'35" 95°06'05" 95°05'35"

SEE 4110 MAP

SEE 4249 MAP

1:24,000
1 in. = 2000 ft.
0 0.25 0.5
miles

SEE 3970 MAP

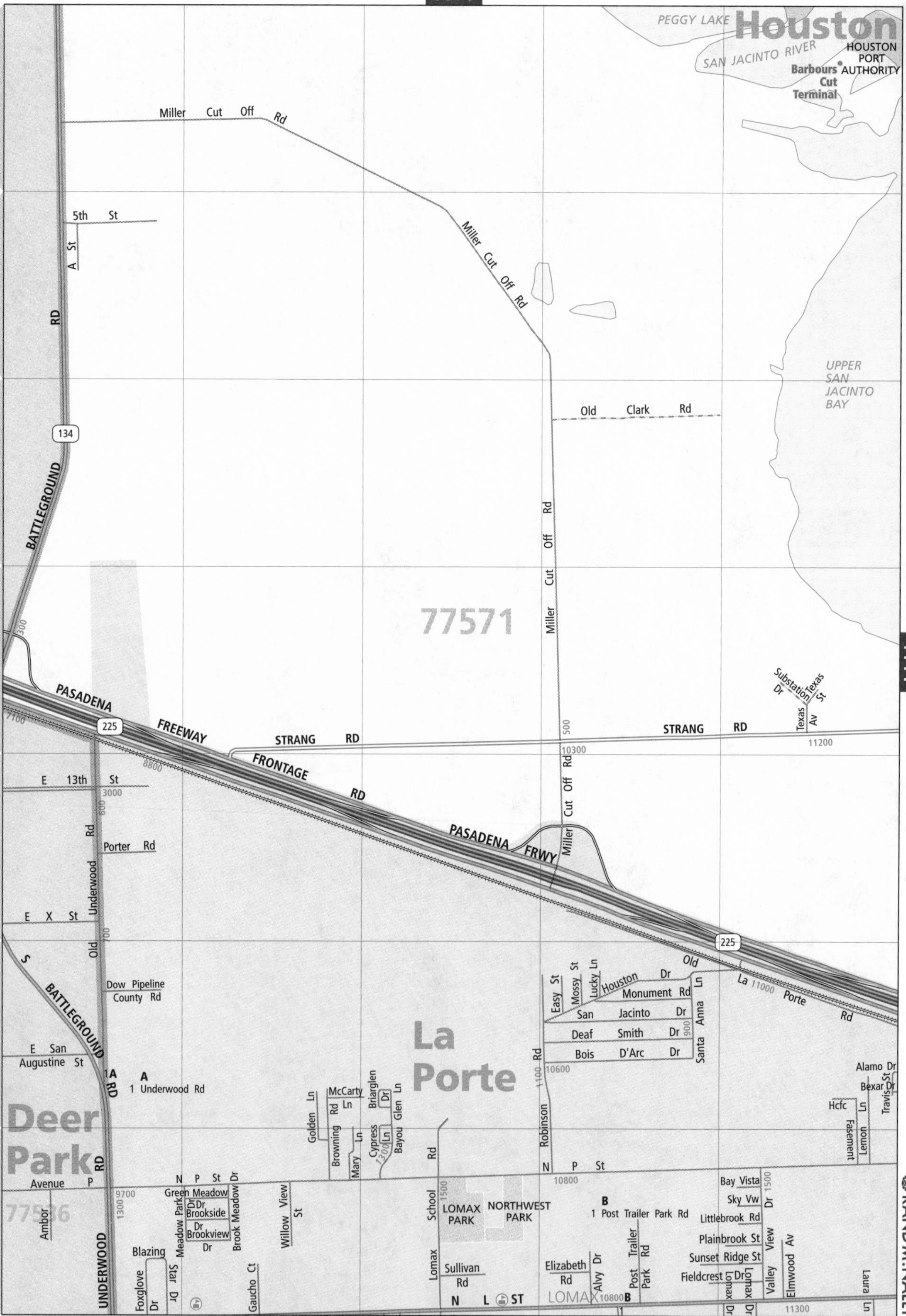
29°43'51"
29°43'25"
29°42'59"
29°42'33"
29°42'07"
29°41'41"
29°41'14"
29°40'48"
1
2
3
4
5
6
7
A
B
C
D
E
95°05'35"
95°05'05"
95°04'35"
95°04'05"
95°03'35"
95°03'05"
PEGGY LAKE
Houston
SAN JACINTO RIVER
HOUSTON PORT AUTHORITY
Barbours Cut Terminal
UPPER SAN JACINTO BAY
Miller Cut Off Rd
5th St
A St
BATTLEGROUND RD
134
Old Clark Rd
77571
PASADENA FREEWAY
225
STRANG RD
FRONTAGE RD
PASADENA FRWY
Substation Dr
Texas St
Texas Av
11200
10300
500
300
7100
8800
E 13th St
3000
600
Porter Rd
Old Underwood Rd
700
E X St
S BATTLEGROUND RD
Dow Pipeline County Rd
E San Augustine St
1A
A
1 Underwood Rd
Deer Park
77536
Avenue P
9700
1300
UNDERWOOD RD
Ambor
La Porte
Easy St
Mossy St
Lucky Ln
Houston Dr
Old La Porte Rd
11000
Monument Rd
San Jacinto Dr
Deaf Smith Dr
Bois D'Arc Dr
Santa Anna Ln
900
Robinson Rd
1100
10600
Golden Ln
McCarty Ln
Browning Rd
Mary Ln
Cypress Ln
1300
Briarglen Dr
Bayou Glen Ln
N P St
Green Meadow Dr
Meadow Park Dr
Brookside Dr
Brookview Dr
Brook Meadow Dr
Willow View St
Blazing Star Dr
Foxglove Dr
Gaucho Ct
School Rd
1500
Lomax School Rd
LOMAX PARK
NORTHWEST PARK
Sullivan Rd
N L ST
N P St
10800
B
1 Post Trailer Park Rd
Post Trailer Park Rd
Elizabeth Rd
Alvy Dr
LOMAX
10800
Bay Vista
Sky Vw
Littlebrook Rd
Plainbrook St
Sunset Ridge St
Fieldcrest Dr
Lomax Dr
Valley View
Elmwood Av
1500
Alamo Dr
Bexar Dr
Travis St
Hcfc
Fasement
Lemon Ln
Laura Ln
11300

SEE 4109 MAP

SEE 4250 MAP

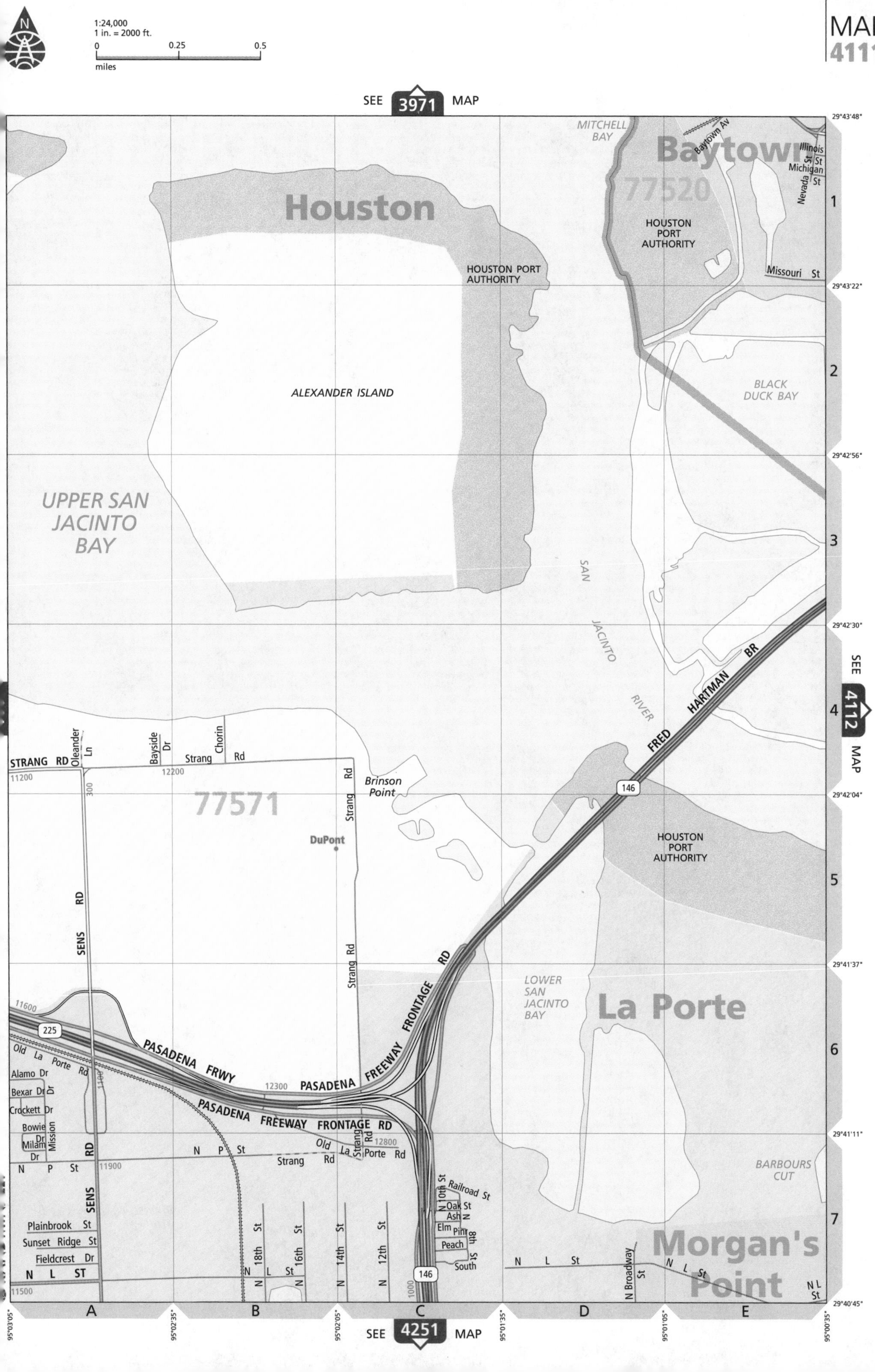
1:24,000
1 in. = 2000 ft.
0
0.25
0.5
miles
SEE 3971 MAP
Houston
Baytown
77520
MITCHELL BAY
Baytown Av
Illinois St
Michigan St
Nevada St
HOUSTON PORT AUTHORITY
Missouri St
HOUSTON PORT AUTHORITY
ALEXANDER ISLAND
BLACK DUCK BAY
UPPER SAN JACINTO BAY
SAN JACINTO RIVER
FRED HARTMAN BR
SEE 4112 MAP
STRANG RD
Oleander Ln
Bayside Dr
Strang Rd
Chorin
11200
12200
300
Brinson Point
Strang Rd
77571
DuPont
146
HOUSTON PORT AUTHORITY
SENS RD
Strang Rd
FREEWAY FRONTAGE RD
LOWER SAN JACINTO BAY
La Porte
11600
225
PASADENA FRWY
Old La Porte Rd
Alamo Dr
Bexar Dr
Crockett Dr
Bowie Dr
Milam Dr
Mission Dr
12300
PASADENA
PASADENA FREEWAY FRONTAGE RD
12800
N P St
Old La Porte Rd
Strang Rd
Strang Rd
N P St
11900
SENS RD
BARBOURS CUT
N 10th St
Railroad St
Oak St
Ash St
Elm St
Pine St
N 8th St
Peach St
South
Plainbrook St
Sunset Ridge St
Fieldcrest Dr
N L ST
N 18th St
N 16th St
N 14th St
N 12th St
N L St
146
1000
N L St
N Broadway St
N L St
Morgan's Point
N L St
11500
A
B
C
D
E
1
2
3
4
5
6
7
29°43'48"
29°43'22"
29°42'56"
29°42'30"
29°42'04"
29°41'37"
29°41'11"
29°40'45"
95°03'05"
95°02'35"
95°02'05"
95°01'35"
95°01'05"
95°00'35"
SEE 4251 MAP

1:24,000
1 in. = 2000 ft.
0 0.25 0.5
miles

SEE 3972 MAP

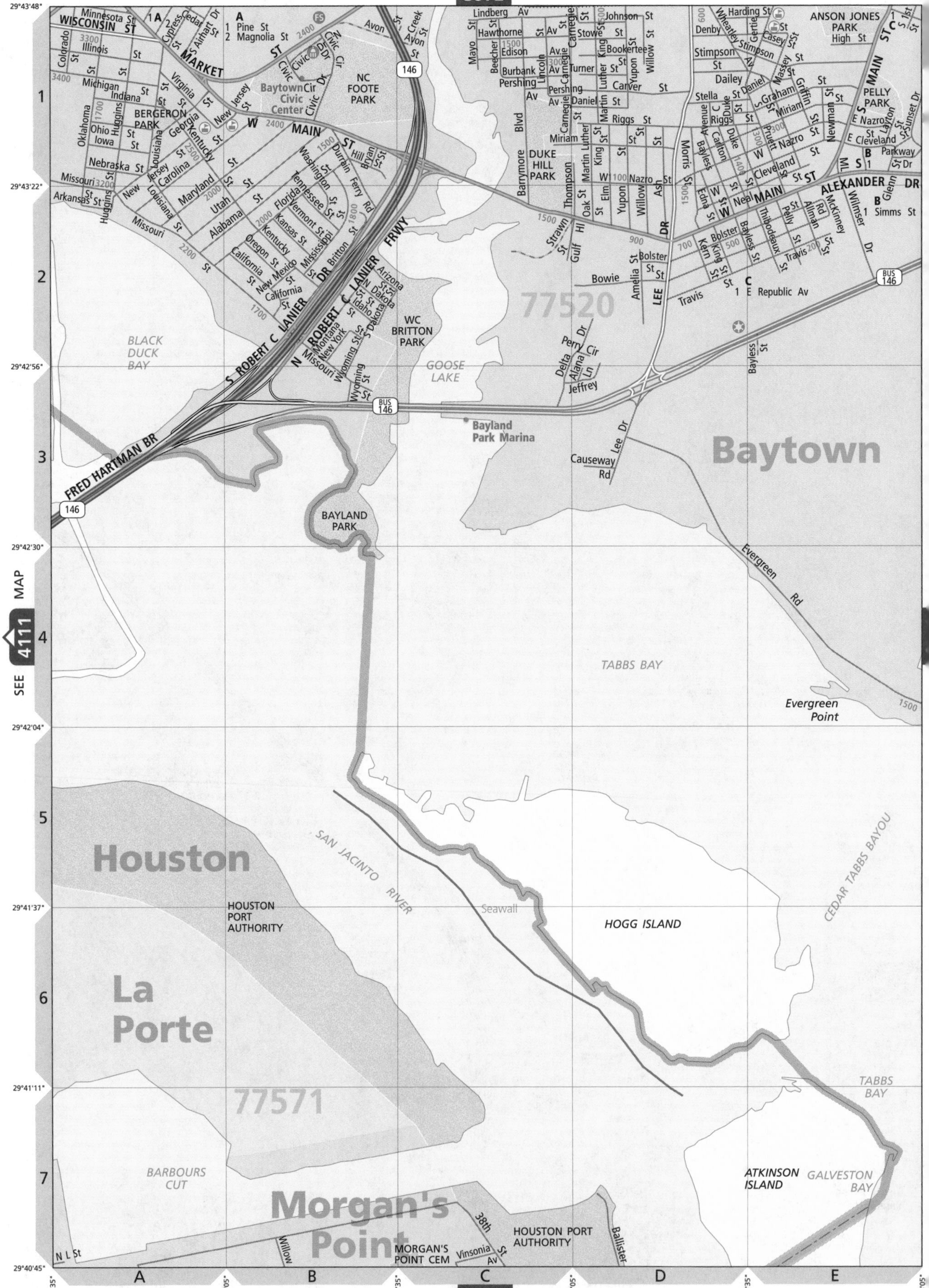
29°43'48"
29°43'22"
29°42'56"
29°42'30"
29°42'04"
29°41'37"
29°41'11"
29°40'45"
1
2
3
4
5
6
7
A
B
C
D
E
95°00'35"
95°00'05"
94°59'35"
94°59'05"
94°58'35"
94°58'05"
WISCONSIN ST
Minnesota St
Illinois St
Michigan St
Indiana St
Colorado St
Oklahoma St
Ohio St
Iowa St
Huggins St
Nebraska St
Missouri St
Arkansas St
BERGERON PARK
Georgia St
Kentucky St
Virginia St
Louisiana St
Jersey St
Carolina St
Maryland St
Utah St
Alabama St
MARKET ST
Cypress St
Cedar St
S Airhart Dr
Pine St
Magnolia St
New Jersey St
W MAIN ST
Civic Cir
Baytown Civic Center
NC FOOTE PARK
Avon St
Creek St
Washington St
Durain St
Ferry Rd
Hill St
Bryan St
Tennessee St
Vermont St
Florida St
Kansas St
Kentucky St
Oregon St
California St
New Mexico St
Mississippi St
Britton St
S ROBERT C LANIER DR
N ROBERT C LANIER FRWY
Arizona St
N Dakota St
S Dakota St
Idaho St
Montana St
New York St
Missouri St
Wyoming St
WC BRITTON PARK
BLACK DUCK BAY
GOOSE LAKE
FRED HARTMAN BR
146
BUS 146
Bayland Park Marina
BAYLAND PARK
Lindberg Av
Hawthorne Av
Edison Av
Burbank Av
Pershing Av
Mayo St
Beecher St
Lincoln St
Carnegie St
Johnson St
Stowe St
Bookertee St
Turner St
Carver St
Daniel St
Riggs St
Miriam St
Martin Luther King St
Yupon St
Willow St
Blvd
Barrymore Blvd
DUKE HILL PARK
Thompson St
Oak St
Elm St
W Nazro St
Ash St
Morris St
Strawn St
Gulf Hl
Bowie
Amelia St
Bolster St
LEE DR
Travis
77520
Delta Dr
Perry Cir
Alana Ln
Jeffrey
Lee Dr
Causeway Rd
Harding St
Denby
Wheatley St
Gertie St
Casey St
Stimpson St
Dailey
Stella St
Avenue C
Bayless St
Edna St
Carlton St
Duke St
W Main St
Graham St
Massey St
Griffin St
Pruett St
Nazro St
Cleveland St
Newman St
ANSON JONES PARK
High St
S MAIN ST
PELLY PARK
Lanier St
Sunset Dr
Parkway Dr
ALEXANDER DR
W Neal St
Kern St
King St
Thibodeaux St
Pelly St
Allman Rd
McKinney St
Wilmsee Dr
Glenn St
Simms St
Republic Av
Bayless St
Baytown
Evergreen Rd
TABBS BAY
Evergreen Point
SAN JACINTO RIVER
Seawall
HOGG ISLAND
CEDAR TABBS BAYOU
Houston
HOUSTON PORT AUTHORITY
La Porte
77571
TABBS BAY
ATKINSON ISLAND
GALVESTON BAY
BARBOURS CUT
Morgan's Point
38th St
Willow
MORGAN'S POINT CEM
Vinsonia Av
HOUSTON PORT AUTHORITY
Ballister
N L St

SEE 4111 MAP

SEE 4252 MAP

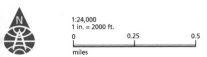

1:24,000
1 in. = 2000 ft.
0 0.25 0.5
miles

SEE 3973 MAP

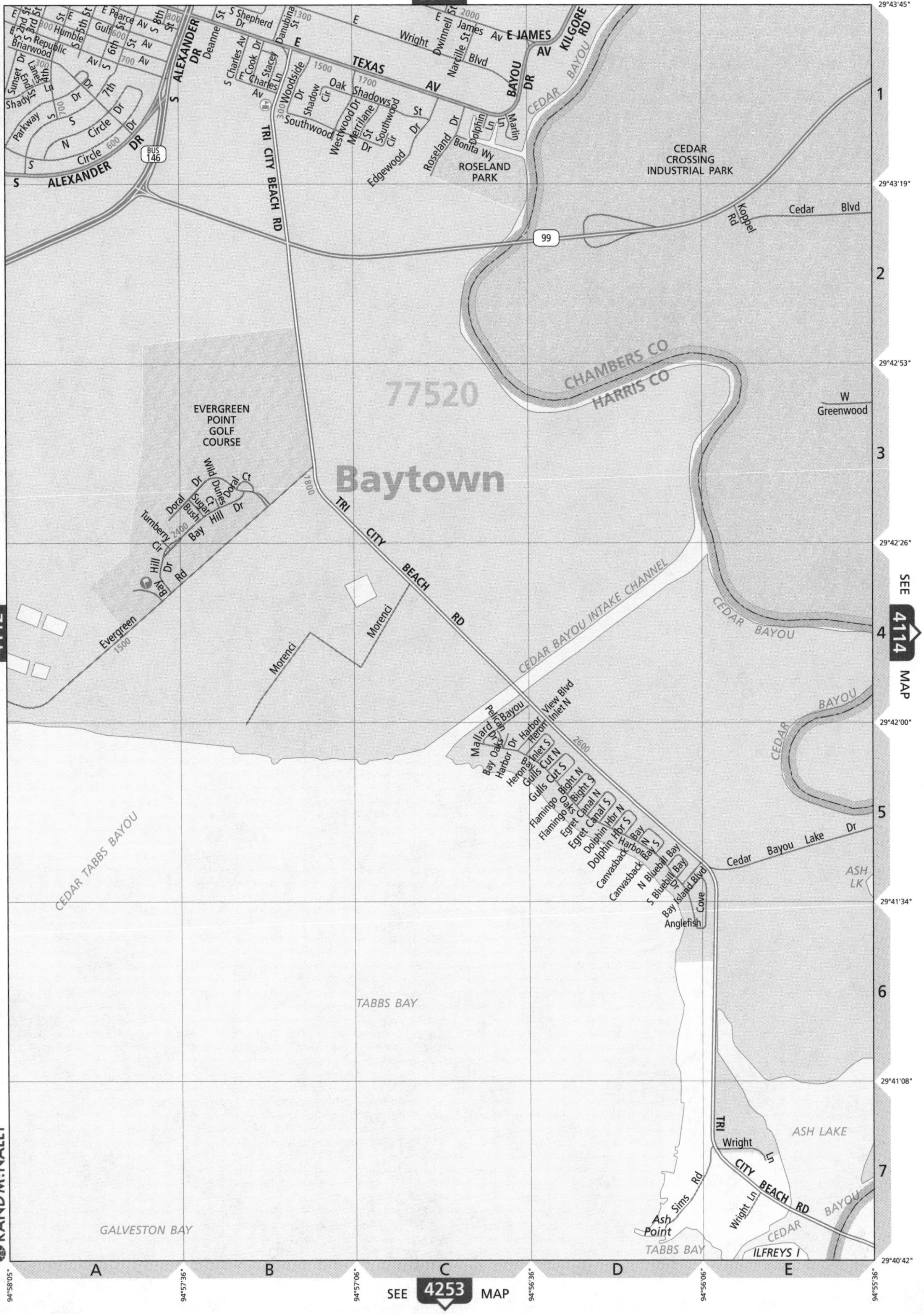
Baytown
77520
CEDAR CROSSING INDUSTRIAL PARK
ROSELAND PARK
EVERGREEN POINT GOLF COURSE
CHAMBERS CO
HARRIS CO
CEDAR BAYOU
CEDAR BAYOU INTAKE CHANNEL
CEDAR TABBS BAYOU
TABBS BAY
GALVESTON BAY
ASH LAKE
ASH LK
Ash Point
ILFREYS I
TRI CITY BEACH RD
S ALEXANDER DR
E TEXAS AV
E JAMES
BAYOU DR
KILGORE RD
Cedar Blvd
Koppel Rd
W Greenwood
Evergreen Rd
Morenci
Cedar Bayou Lake Dr
Wright Ln
Sims Rd
Bay Island Blvd
99
BUS 146
29°43'45"
29°43'19"
29°42'53"
29°42'26"
29°42'00"
29°41'34"
29°41'08"
29°40'42"
94°58'05"
94°57'36"
94°57'06"
94°56'36"
94°56'06"
94°55'36"
A
B
C
D
E
1
2
3
4
5
6
7

SEE 4114 MAP

SEE 4253 MAP

1:24,000
1 in. = 2000 ft.
0 0.25 0.5
miles

SEE 3974 MAP

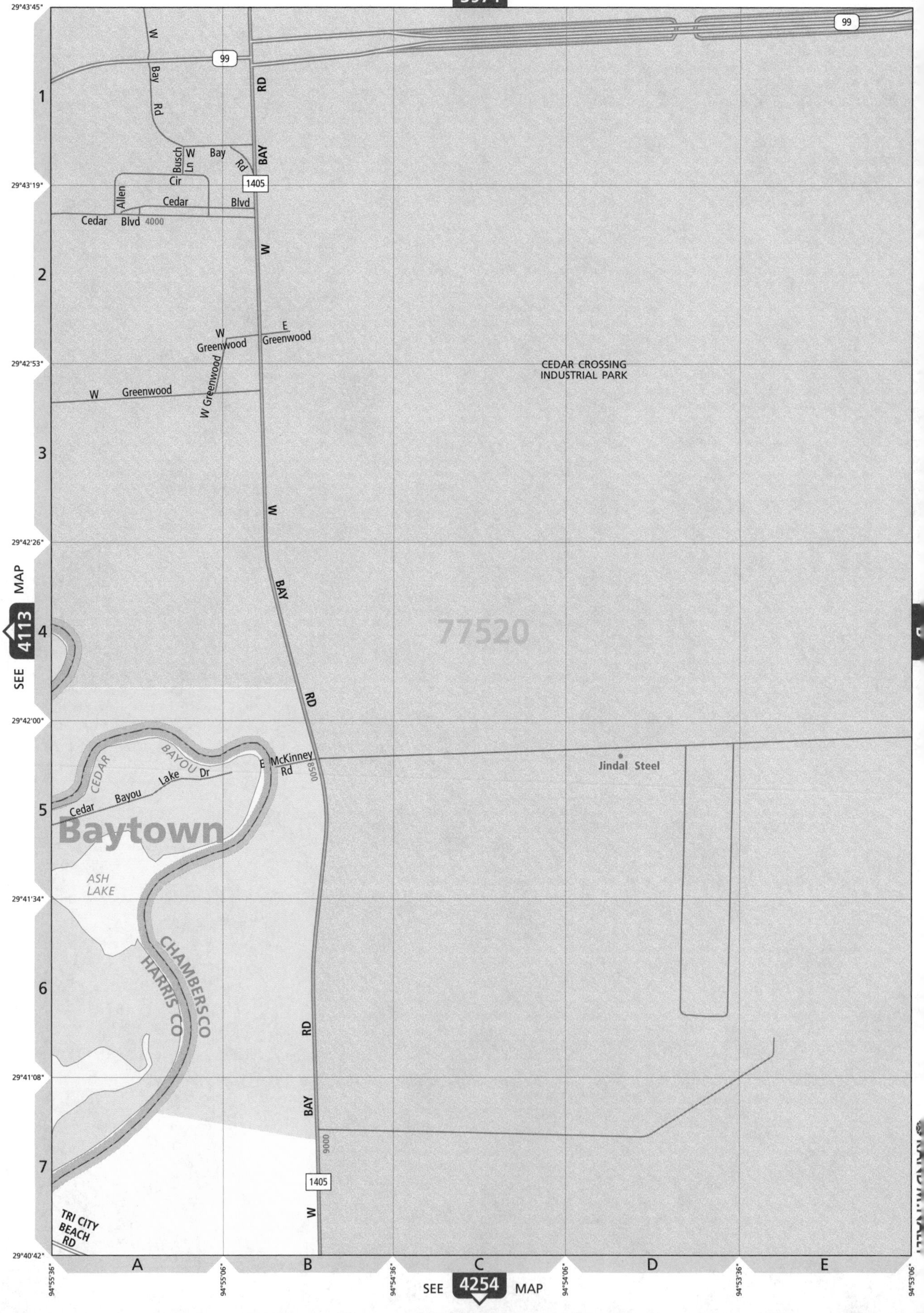
29°43'45"
29°43'19"
29°42'53"
29°42'26"
29°42'00"
29°41'34"
29°41'08"
29°40'42"
1
2
3
4
5
6
7
A
B
C
D
E
94°55'36"
94°55'06"
94°54'36"
94°54'06"
94°53'36"
94°53'06"
99
W Bay Rd
RD BAY
W Bay Rd
Busch Ln
Cir
1405
Allen
Cedar Blvd
Cedar Blvd 4000
W
W Greenwood
E Greenwood
W Greenwood
W Greenwood
CEDAR CROSSING
INDUSTRIAL PARK
W BAY RD
77520
E McKinney Rd
8500
Jindal Steel
CEDAR BAYOU
Bayou Lake Dr
Cedar Bayou
Baytown
ASH LAKE
CHAMBERSCO
HARRIS CO
RD
BAY
9000
1405
W
TRI CITY BEACH RD

SEE 4113 MAP

SEE 4254 MAP

1:24,000
1 in. = 2000 ft.
0 0.25 0.5
miles

SEE 4092 MAP

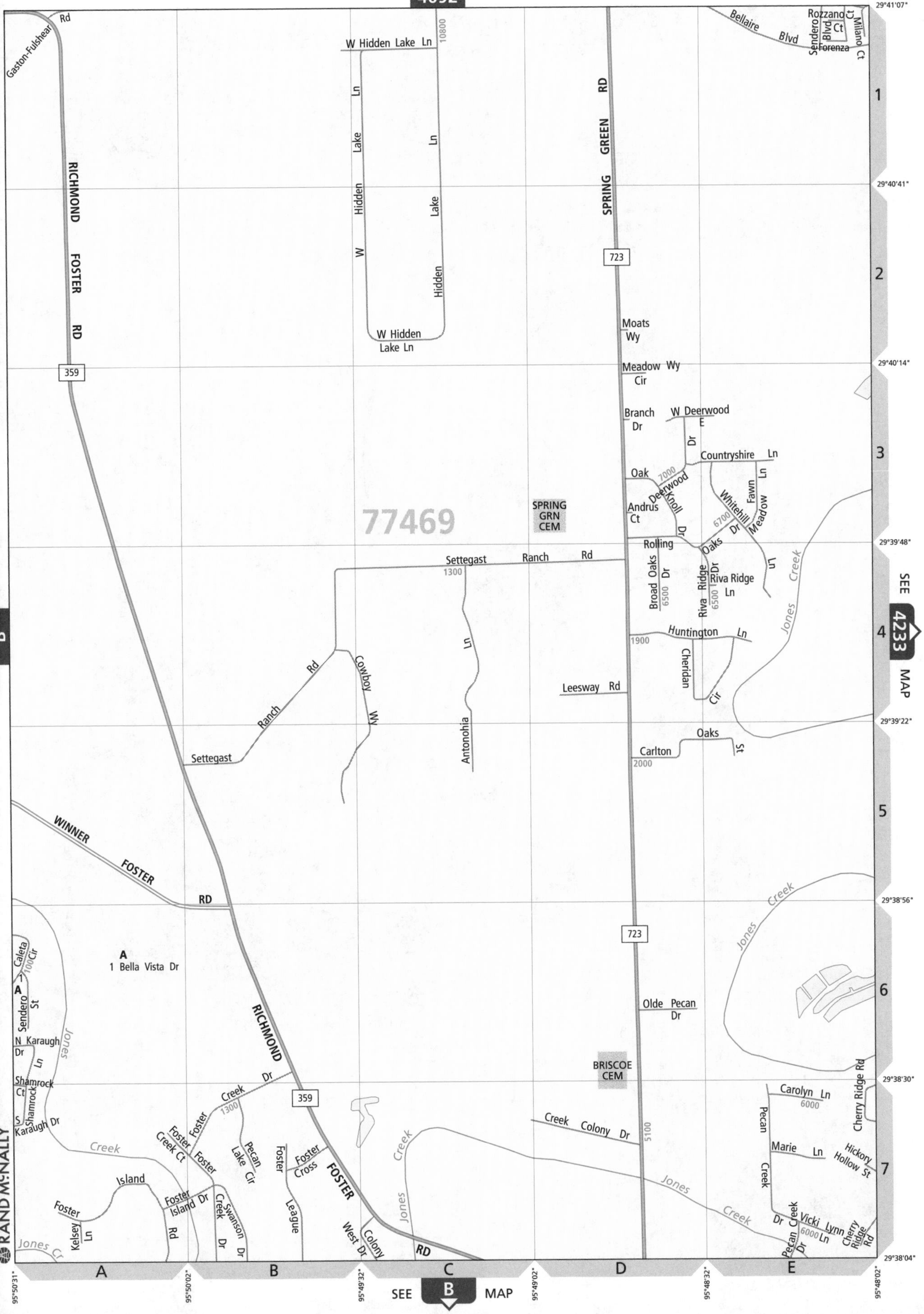
29°41'07"
Gaston-Fulshear Rd
W Hidden Lake Ln
10800
W Hidden Lake Ln
Hidden Lake Ln
W Hidden Lake Ln
SPRING GREEN RD
Bellaire Blvd
Rozzano Ct
Sendero Blvd
Milano Ct
Forenza
1
RICHMOND FOSTER RD
29°40'41"
723
2
Moats Wy
Meadow Wy Cir
359
29°40'14"
Branch Dr
W Deerwood
E
Dr
Countryshire Ln
Oak
7000
Deerwood
Knoll
Andrus Ct
Dr
Whitehill
Fawn
Meadow
Ln
6700
Dr
3
77469
SPRING GRN CEM
Rolling
Oaks
29°39'48"
Settegast Ranch Rd
1300
Broad Oaks Dr
6500
Riva Ridge Dr
6500
Riva Ridge Ln
Ln
Jones Creek
Huntington Ln
1900
Cheridan Cir
Ln
Cowboy Wy
Settegast Ranch Rd
Leesway Rd
4
Antonohia
29°39'22"
Oaks St
Carlton
2000
WINNER FOSTER RD
5
29°38'56"
Jones Creek
723
Caleta Cir
100
A
1 Bella Vista Dr
A
Sendero St
RICHMOND
Olde Pecan Dr
6
N Karaugh Dr
Ln
Jones
BRISCOE CEM
Shamrock Ct
S Shamrock Karaugh Dr
Creek Dr
1300
359
29°38'30"
Carolyn Ln
6000
Cherry Ridge Rd
Creek
Foster
Foster Creek Ct
Foster
Pecan Lake Cir
Foster
Foster Cross
FOSTER
Creek
Creek Colony Dr
5100
Pecan Creek
Marie Ln
Hickory Hollow St
7
Island
Foster Island Dr
Creek Dr
Swanson Dr
League
Jones
Jones Creek
Foster
Kelsey Ln
Rd
West Dr
Colony
RD
Dr
Pecan Creek Dr
Vicki Lynn Ln
6000
Cherry Ridge Rd
Jones Cr
29°38'04"
A B C D E
95°50'31" 95°50'02" 95°49'32" 95°49'02" 95°48'32" 95°48'02"

SEE 4233 MAP

SEE B MAP

1:24,000
1 in. = 2000 ft.
0 0.25 0.5
miles

SEE 4093 MAP

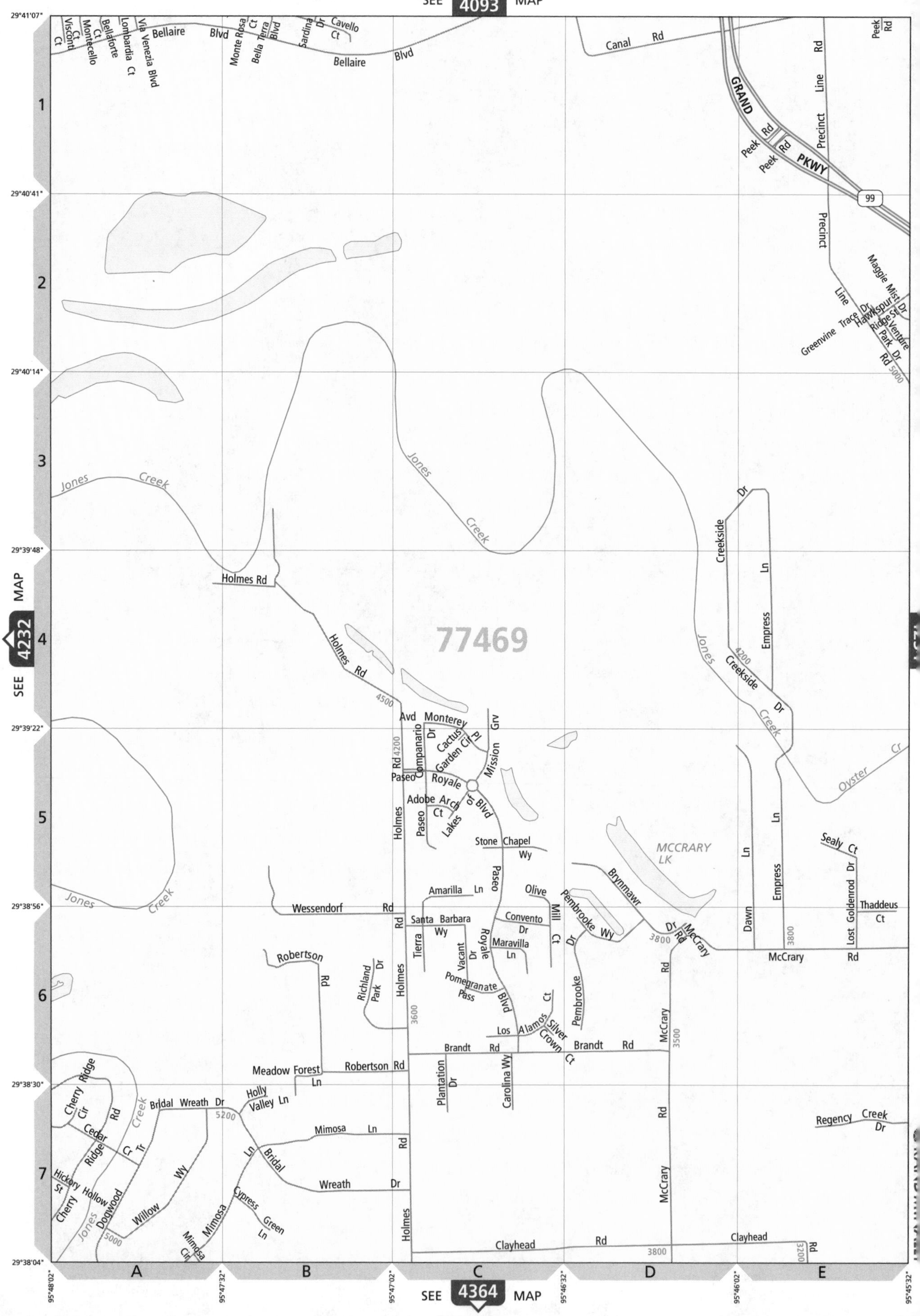

29°41'07"
29°40'41"
29°40'14"
29°39'48"
29°39'22"
29°38'56"
29°38'30"
29°38'04"
1
2
3
4
5
6
7
A
B
C
D
E
95°48'02"
95°47'32"
95°47'02"
95°46'32"
95°46'02"
95°45'32"
77469
Bellaire Blvd
Visconti Ct
Montecello Ct
Bellaforte Ct
Lombardia Ct
Via Venezia Blvd
Monte Rosa Ct
Bella Terra Blvd
Sardina Dr
Cavello Ct
Canal Rd
GRAND PKWY
99
Peek Rd
Precinct Line Rd
Maggie Mist Dr
Hawkspur Dr
Ridge St
Venture Dr
Park Rd
Greenvine Trace Dr
5000
Jones Creek
Holmes Rd
4500
4200
Creekside Dr
Empress Ln
Oyster Cr
Monterey Avd
Companario Dr
Cactus Pl
Garden Cir
Mission Grv
Paseo Royale
Adobe Arch Ct
Lakes of Mission Blvd
Stone Chapel Wy
MCCRARY LK
Sealy Ct
Lost Goldenrod Dr
Thaddeus Ct
Amarilla Ln
Olive Mill Ct
Pembrooke Wy
Brynmawr Dr
Dawn Ln
McCrary Rd
3800
Wessendorf Rd
Santa Barbara Wy
Tierra Rd
Convento Dr
Maravilla Ln
Vacant Dr
Royale Blvd
Pembrooke Dr
Robertson Rd
Richland Park Dr
Holmes Rd
Pomegranate Pass
3600
Los Alamos Ct
Silver Crown Ct
Brandt Rd
3500
Meadow Forest Ln
Robertson Rd
Plantation Dr
Carolina Wy
Cherry Ridge Cir
Cedar Ridge Rd
Cr Tr
Bridal Wreath Dr
5200
Holly Valley Ln
Mimosa Ln
Regency Creek Dr
Hickory St
Cherry Hollow
Dogwood
Willow Wy
Cypress Green Ln
Mimosa Cir
Clayhead Rd
3200

SEE 4232 MAP

SEE 4364 MAP

1:24,000
1 in. = 2000 ft.
0 0.25 0.5
miles

SEE 4094 MAP

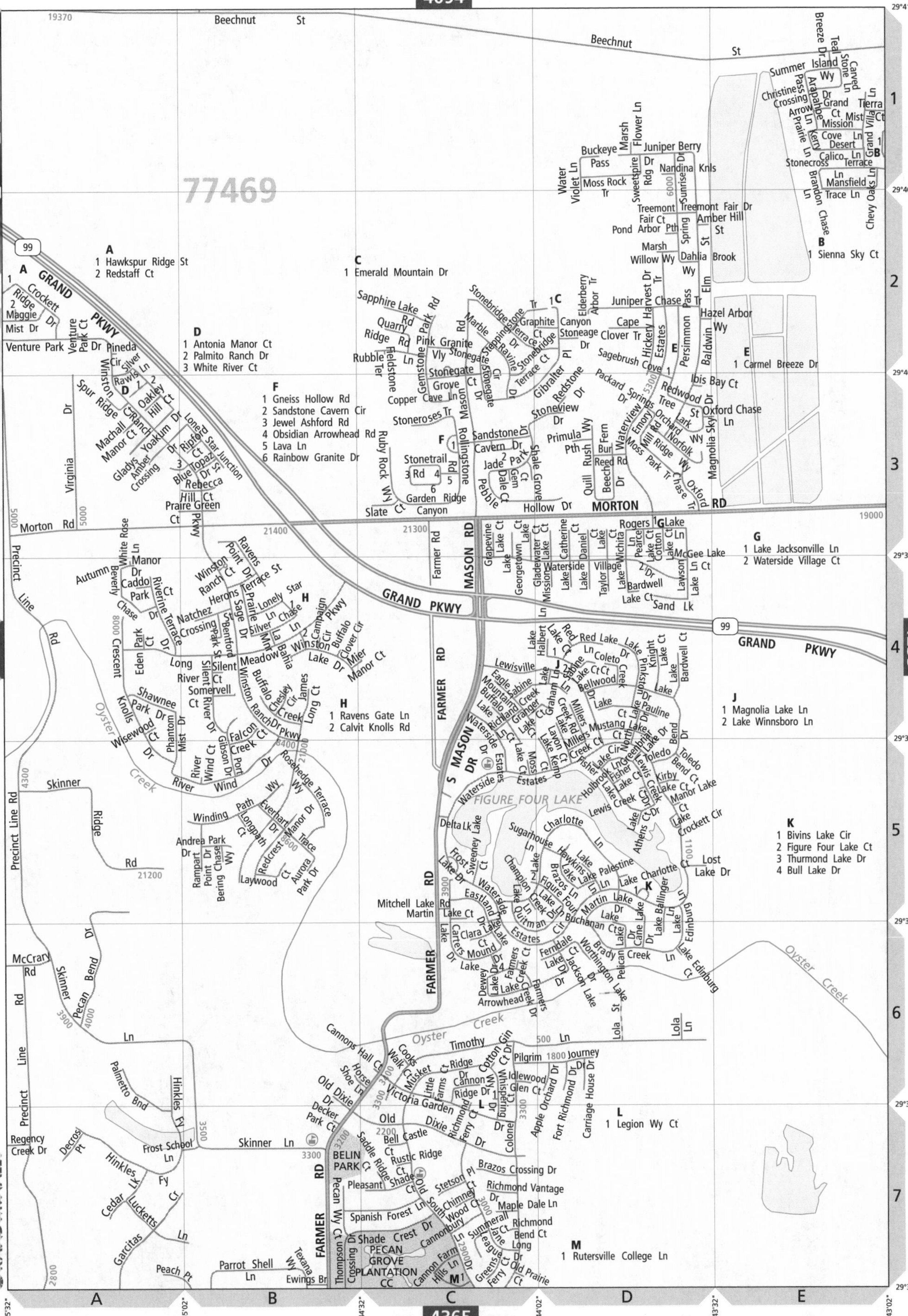
77469
Beechnut St
19370
1 2 3 4 5 6 7
A B C D E
29°41'05"
29°40'39"
29°40'13"
29°39'47"
29°39'21"
29°38'55"
29°38'28"
29°38'02"
95°45'32"
95°45'02"
95°44'32"
95°44'02"
95°43'32"
95°43'02"
A
1 Hawkspur Ridge St
2 Redstaff Ct
B
1 Sienna Sky Ct
C
1 Emerald Mountain Dr
D
1 Antonia Manor Ct
2 Palmito Ranch Dr
3 White River Ct
E
1 Carmel Breeze Dr
F
1 Gneiss Hollow Rd
2 Sandstone Cavern Cir
3 Jewel Ashford Rd
4 Obsidian Arrowhead Rd
5 Lava Ln
6 Rainbow Granite Dr
G
1 Lake Jacksonville Ln
2 Waterside Village Ct
H
1 Ravens Gate Ln
2 Calvit Knolls Rd
J
1 Magnolia Lake Ln
2 Lake Winnsboro Ln
K
1 Bivins Lake Cir
2 Figure Four Lake Ct
3 Thurmond Lake Dr
4 Bull Lake Dr
L
1 Legion Wy Ct
M
1 Rutersville College Ln
GRAND PKWY
99
MORTON RD
Morton Rd
MASON RD
S MASON DR
FARMER RD
Precinct Line Rd
Skinner Ln
Skinner Ridge Rd
FIGURE FOUR LAKE
Oyster Creek
BELIN PARK
PECAN GROVE PLANTATION CC
Venture Park Dr
Virginia Dr
Juniper Berry
Juniper Chase Dr
Hazel Arbor Wy
Oxford Chase Ln
Ibis Bay Ct
Magnolia Sky Dr
Packard Springs Dr
Stoneview Dr
Primula Wy
Sandstone Cavern Dr
Stonetrail Rd
Garden Ridge
Slate Canyon Ct
Hollow Dr
Waterside Village
Bardwell Lake Ct
Sand Lk
Red Lake Dr
Lewisville Lake
Lake Charlotte Ct
Lost Lake Dr
Sugarhouse Ln
Mitchell Lake Rd
Timothy Ln
Pilgrim Journey Dr
Victoria Garden Dr
Old Dixie Dr
Apple Orchard Dr
Fort Richmond Dr
Carriage House Dr
Brazos Crossing Dr
Richmond Vantage Dr
Maple Dale Ln
Richmond Bend Ct
Spanish Forest Ln
Shade Crest Dr
Thompson Crossing Dr
Pecan Wy
Parrot Shell Ln
Ewings Br
Texana Wy
Peach Pt
Garcitas
Lucketts Ln
Cedar Lk
Hinkles Fy
Frost School Ln
Decros Pt
Regency Creek Dr
Palmetto Bnd
McCrary Rd
Pecan Bend Dr
Winding Path Wy
Andrea Park Dr
Rosehedge Terrace
Falcon Creek Ct
River Wind Dr
Wisewood Dr
Shawnee Park Dr
Crescent Park Ct
Autumn Manor Dr
White Rose Ln
Prairie Green Ct
Lone Star Junction
Beechnut St
19000
21400
21300
5000
4300
21200
3900
4000
3500
3300
3200
2800
2200
500
1800
3300
1100
5300
6000
8000
8400
8600

SEE 4235 MAP

SEE 4365 MAP

SEE 4095 MAP

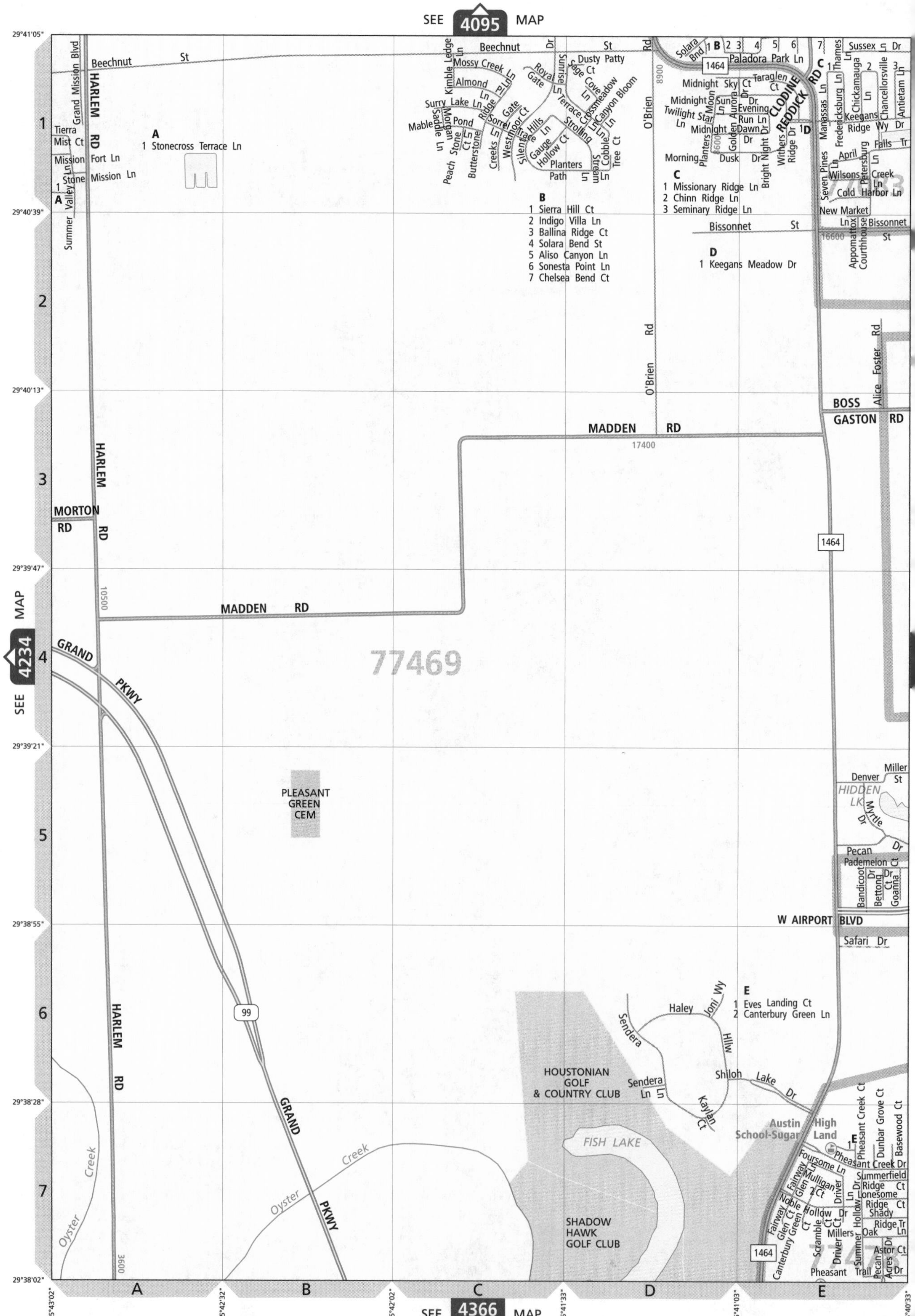
1:24,000
1 in. = 2000 ft.
0 0.25 0.5 miles
Beechnut St
HARLEM RD
Grand Mission Blvd
Tierra Mist Ct
Mission Fort Ln
Stone Mission Ln
Summer Valley Ln
A
1 Stonecross Terrace Ln
B
1 Sierra Hill Ct
2 Indigo Villa Ln
3 Ballina Ridge Ct
4 Solara Bend St
5 Aliso Canyon Ln
6 Sonesta Point Ln
7 Chelsea Bend Ct
C
1 Missionary Ridge Ln
2 Chinn Ridge Ln
3 Seminary Ridge Ln
D
1 Keegans Meadow Dr
E
1 Eves Landing Ct
2 Canterbury Green Ln
Paladora Park Ln
CLODINE REDDICK RD
O'Brien Rd
Bissonnet St
MADDEN RD
BOSS GASTON RD
Alice Foster Rd
MORTON RD
GRAND PKWY
77469
PLEASANT GREEN CEM
W AIRPORT BLVD
Safari Dr
HIDDEN LK
HOUSTONIAN GOLF & COUNTRY CLUB
FISH LAKE
SHADOW HAWK GOLF CLUB
Oyster Creek
Shiloh Lake Dr
Sendera Ln
Austin High School-Sugar Land
1464
99

SEE 4234 MAP

SEE 4366 MAP

1:24,000
1 in. = 2000 ft.
0 0.25 0.5
miles

SEE 4096 MAP

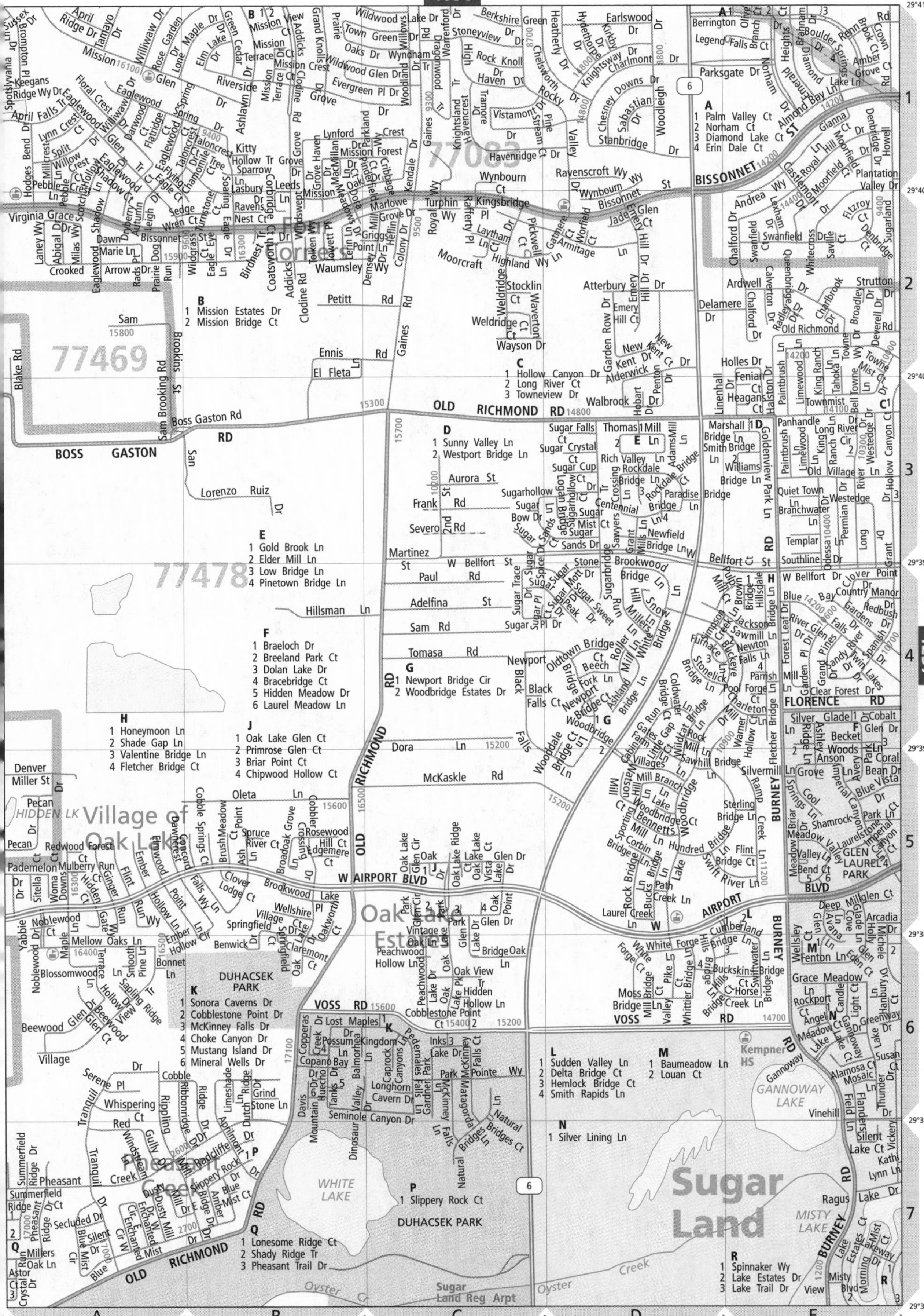
77083
77469
77478
Four Corners
Village of Oak Lake
Oak Lake Estates
Pheasant Creek
Sugar Land
DUHACSEK PARK
WHITE LAKE
GANNOWAY LAKE
MISTY LAKE
HIDDEN LK
Kempner HS
Sugar Land Reg Arpt
BISSONNET ST
OLD RICHMOND RD
BOSS GASTON RD
W AIRPORT BLVD
VOSS RD
BURNEY RD
FLORENCE RD
GLEN LAUREL PARK
A
1 Palm Valley Ct
2 Norham Ct
3 Diamond Lake Ct
4 Erin Dale Ct
B
1 Mission Estates Dr
2 Mission Bridge Ct
C
1 Hollow Canyon Dr
2 Long River Ct
3 Towneview Dr
D
1 Sunny Valley Ln
2 Westport Bridge Ln
E
1 Gold Brook Ln
2 Elder Mill Ln
3 Low Bridge Ln
4 Pinetown Bridge Ln
F
1 Braeloch Dr
2 Breeland Park Ct
3 Dolan Lake Dr
4 Bracebridge Ct
5 Hidden Meadow Dr
6 Laurel Meadow Ln
G
1 Newport Bridge Cir
2 Woodbridge Estates Dr
H
1 Honeymoon Ln
2 Shade Gap Ln
3 Valentine Bridge Ln
4 Fletcher Bridge Ct
J
1 Oak Lake Glen Ct
2 Primrose Glen Ct
3 Briar Point Ct
4 Chipwood Hollow Ct
K
1 Sonora Caverns Dr
2 Cobblestone Point Dr
3 McKinney Falls Dr
4 Choke Canyon Dr
5 Mustang Island Dr
6 Mineral Wells Dr
L
1 Sudden Valley Ln
2 Delta Bridge Ct
3 Hemlock Bridge Ct
4 Smith Rapids Ln
M
1 Baumeadow Ln
2 Louan Ct
N
1 Silver Lining Ln
P
1 Slippery Rock Ct
Q
1 Lonesome Ridge Ct
2 Shady Ridge Tr
3 Pheasant Trail Dr
R
1 Spinnaker Wy
2 Lake Estates Dr
3 Lake Trail Dr
29°41'04"
29°40'38"
29°40'11"
29°39'45"
29°39'19"
29°38'53"
29°38'27"
29°38'01"
95°40'33"
95°40'03"
95°39'33"
95°39'03"
95°38'33"
95°38'03"
A B C D E
1 2 3 4 5 6 7

SEE 4237 MAP

SEE 4367 MAP

1:24,000
1 in. = 2000 ft.
0 0.25 0.5
miles

SEE 4097 MAP

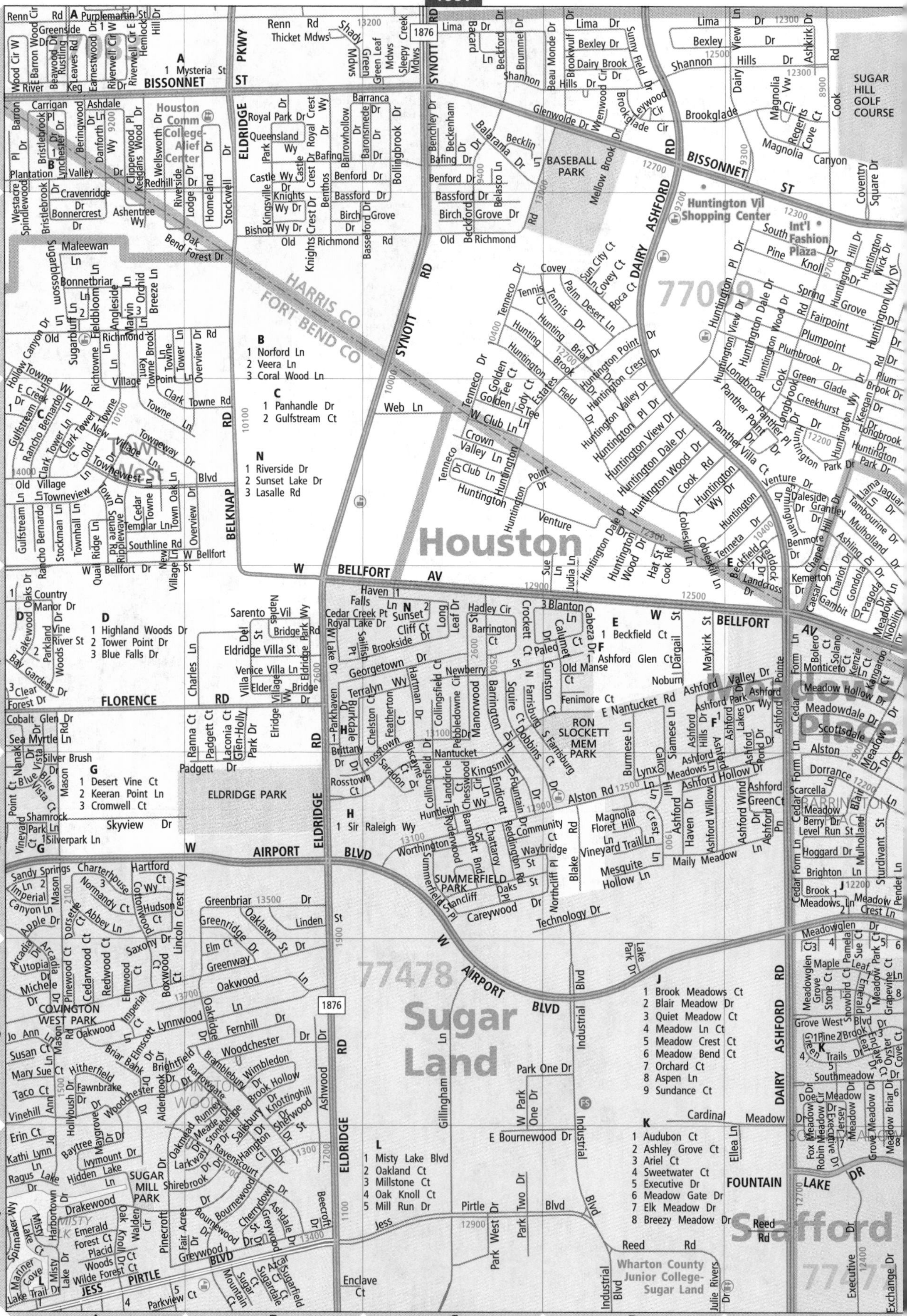
29°41'04"
29°40'38"
29°40'11"
29°39'45"
29°39'19"
29°38'53"
29°38'27"
29°38'01"
95°38'03"
95°37'33"
95°37'03"
95°36'33"
95°36'03"
A
B
C
D
E
1
2
3
4
5
6
7
BISSONNET ST
Houston Comm College-Alief Center
ELDRIDGE PKWY
SYNOTT RD
DAIRY ASHFORD RD
BASEBALL PARK
Huntington Vil Shopping Center
Int'l Fashion Plaza
SUGAR HILL GOLF COURSE
HARRIS CO
FORT BEND CO
77099
Houston
Town West
BELKNAP RD
W BELLFORT AV
FLORENCE RD
ELDRIDGE PARK
RON SLOCKETT MEM PARK
SUMMERFIELD PARK
Meadows Place
W AIRPORT BLVD
77478
Sugar Land
COVINGTON WEST PARK
SUGAR MILL PARK
JESS PIRTLE BLVD
Wharton County Junior College-Sugar Land
FOUNTAIN LAKE DR
Stafford
1876
A
1 Mysteria St
B
1 Norford Ln
2 Veera Ln
3 Coral Wood Ln
C
1 Panhandle Dr
2 Gulfstream Ct
N
1 Riverside Dr
2 Sunset Lake Dr
3 Lasalle Rd
D
1 Highland Woods Dr
2 Tower Point Dr
3 Blue Falls Dr
E
1 Beckfield Ct
F
1 Ashford Glen Ct
G
1 Desert Vine Ct
2 Keeran Point Ln
3 Cromwell Ct
H
1 Sir Raleigh Wy
J
1 Brook Meadows Ct
2 Blair Meadow Dr
3 Quiet Meadow Ct
4 Meadow Ln Ct
5 Meadow Crest Ct
6 Meadow Bend Ct
7 Orchard Ct
8 Aspen Ln
9 Sundance Ct
K
1 Audubon Ct
2 Ashley Grove Ct
3 Ariel Ct
4 Sweetwater Ct
5 Executive Dr
6 Meadow Gate Dr
7 Elk Meadow Dr
8 Breezy Meadow Dr
L
1 Misty Lake Blvd
2 Oakland Ct
3 Millstone Ct
4 Oak Knoll Ct
5 Mill Run Dr

SEE 4236 MAP

SEE 4368 MAP

1:24,000
1 in. = 2000 ft.
0 0.25 0.5
miles

SEE 4098 MAP

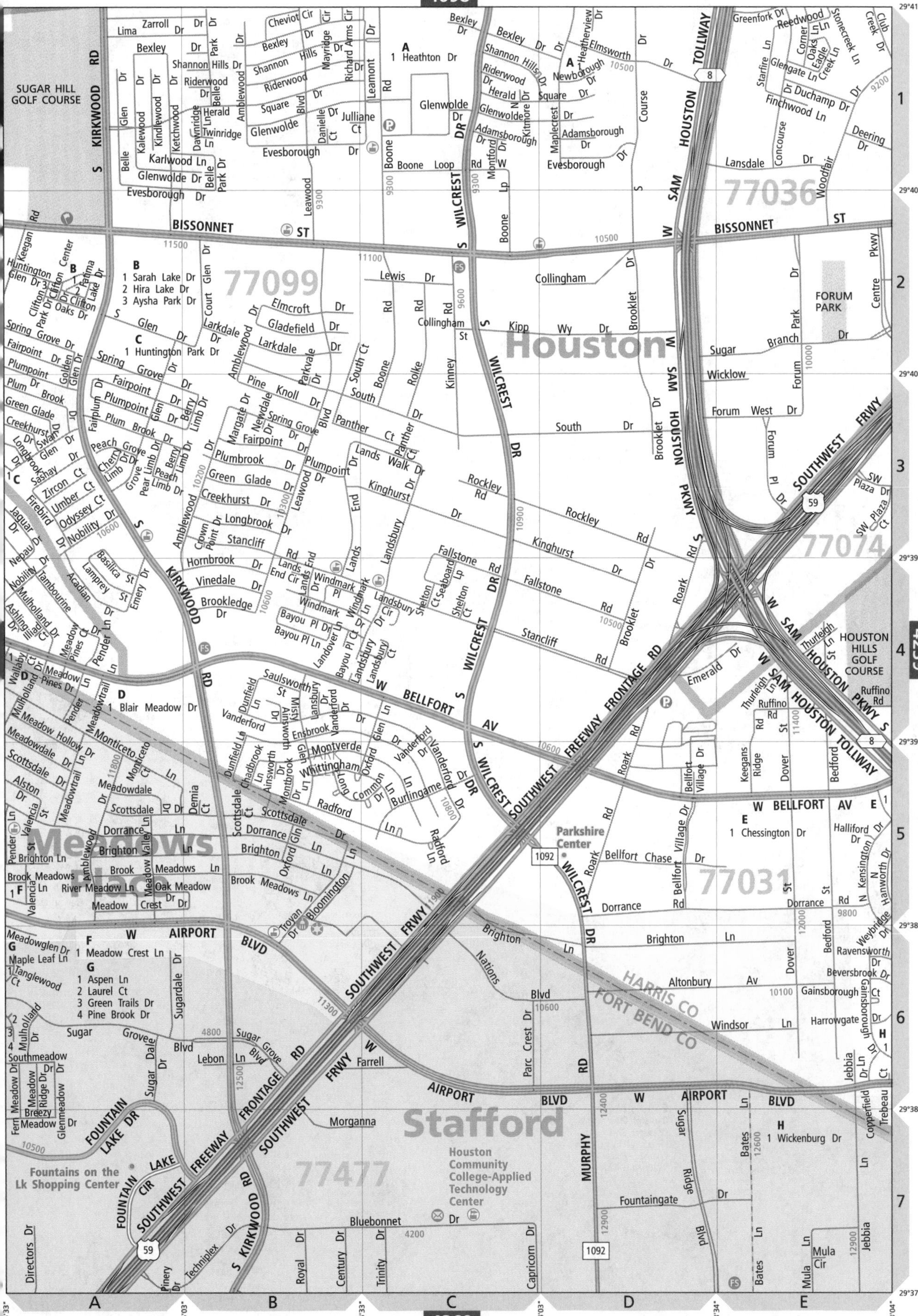
SUGAR HILL GOLF COURSE
S KIRKWOOD RD
BISSONNET ST
S WILCREST DR
W SAM HOUSTON TOLLWAY
W SAM HOUSTON PKWY
SOUTHWEST FRWY
SOUTHWEST FREEWAY FRONTAGE RD
W BELLFORT AV
W AIRPORT BLVD
MURPHY RD
FOUNTAIN LAKE DR
FOUNTAIN LAKE CIR
S KIRKWOOD RD
Houston
Meadows Place
Stafford
77099
77036
77074
77031
77477
FORUM PARK
HOUSTON HILLS GOLF COURSE
Parkshire Center
Fountains on the Lk Shopping Center
Houston Community College-Applied Technology Center
HARRIS CO
FORT BEND CO
A
1 Heathton Dr
B
1 Sarah Lake Dr
2 Hira Lake Dr
3 Aysha Park Dr
C
1 Huntington Park Dr
D
1 Blair Meadow Dr
E
1 Chessington Dr
F
1 Meadow Crest Ln
G
1 Aspen Ln
2 Laurel Ct
3 Green Trails Dr
4 Pine Brook Dr
H
1 Wickenburg Dr
Evesborough Dr
Glenwolde Dr
Collingham Dr
Kipp Wy
Sugar Branch Dr
Forum West Dr
South Dr
Rockley Rd
Kinghurst Dr
Fallstone Rd
Stancliff Rd
Brookledge Dr
Vinedale Dr
Hornbrook Dr
Landsbury Dr
Brighton Ln
Altonbury Av
Windsor Ln
Nations Blvd
Dorrance Rd
Bellfort Chase Dr
Farrell
Morganna
Bluebonnet Dr
Fountaingate Dr
Sugar Ridge Blvd
Sugar Grove Blvd
Lebon Ln
Directors Dr
Technipex Dr
Royal Dr
Century Dr
Trinity Dr
Capricorn Dr
Parc Crest Dr
Bates Ln
Mula Cir
Jebbia Ln
8
59
1092
29°41'02"
29°40'36"
29°40'10"
29°39'43"
29°39'17"
29°38'51"
29°38'25"
29°37'59"
95°35'33"
95°35'03"
95°34'33"
95°34'03"
95°33'34"
95°33'04"
A B C D E
1 2 3 4 5 6 7

SEE 4239 MAP

SEE 4369 MAP

1:24,000
1 in. = 2000 ft.
0 0.25 0.5
miles

SEE 4099 MAP

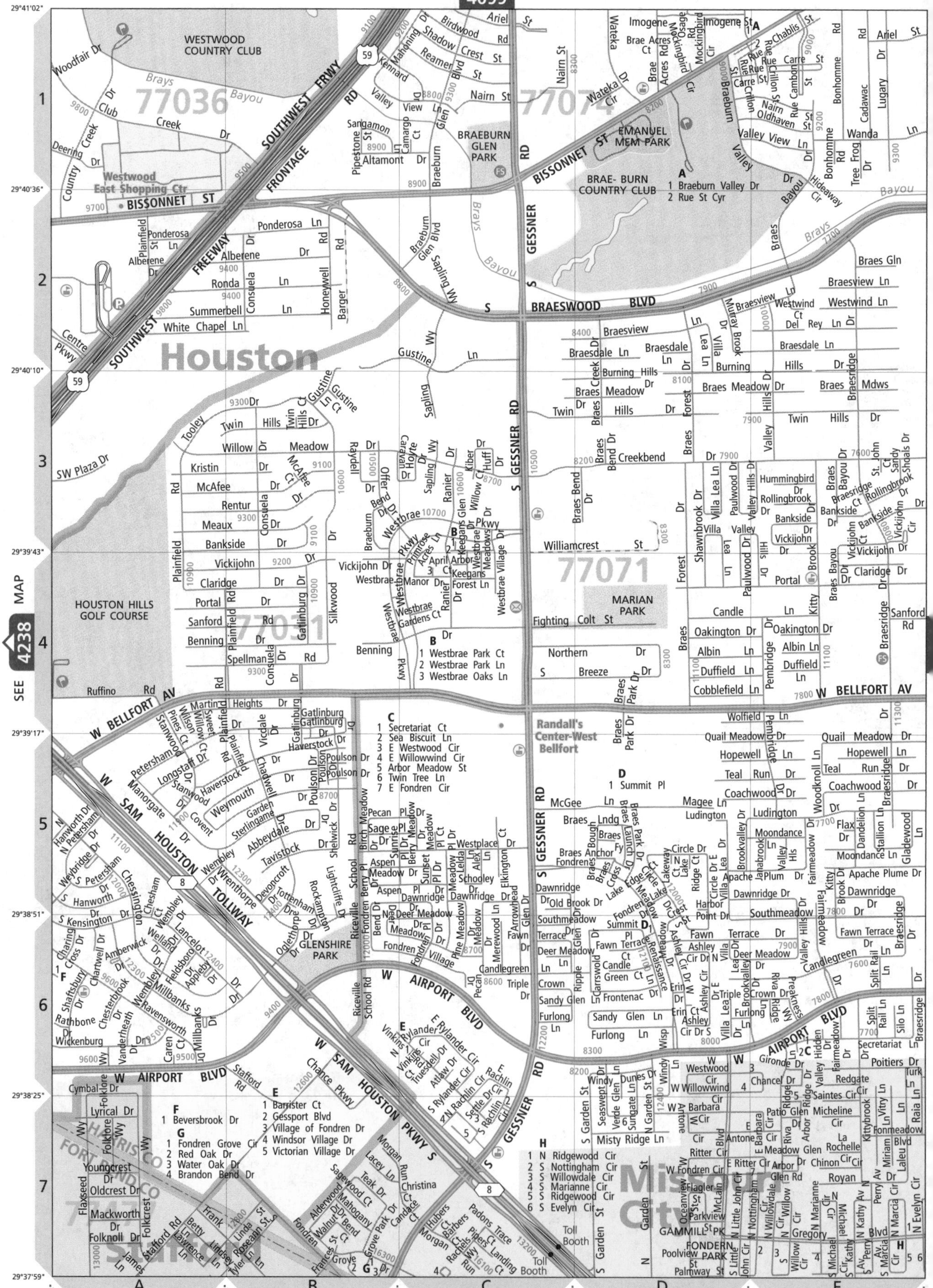
29°41'02"
29°40'36"
29°40'10"
29°39'43"
29°39'17"
29°38'51"
29°38'25"
29°37'59"
WESTWOOD COUNTRY CLUB
77036
77074
77071
77031
77477
Houston
Missouri City
Stafford
SOUTHWEST FRWY
SOUTHWEST FREEWAY
FRONTAGE RD
59
8
BISSONNET ST
S BRAESWOOD BLVD
GESSNER RD
S GESSNER RD
W BELLFORT AV
W SAM HOUSTON TOLLWAY
W SAM HOUSTON PKWY S
W AIRPORT BLVD
Brays Bayou
Westwood East Shopping Ctr
BRAEBURN GLEN PARK
EMANUEL MEM PARK
BRAE- BURN COUNTRY CLUB
MARIAN PARK
HOUSTON HILLS GOLF COURSE
Randall's Center-West Bellfort
GLENSHIRE PARK
HARRIS CO
FORT BEND CO
GAMMILL PK
FONDERN PARK
Toll Booth
A
1 Braeburn Valley Dr
2 Rue St Cyr
B
1 Westbrae Park Ct
2 Westbrae Park Ln
3 Westbrae Oaks Ln
C
1 Secretariat Ct
2 Sea Biscuit Ln
3 E Westwood Cir
4 E Willowwind Cir
5 Arbor Meadow St
6 Twin Tree Ln
7 E Fondren Cir
D
1 Summit Pl
E
1 Barrister Ct
2 Gessport Blvd
3 Village of Fondren Dr
4 Windsor Village Dr
5 Victorian Village Dr
F
1 Beversbrook Dr
G
1 Fondren Grove Cir
2 Red Oak Dr
3 Water Oak Dr
4 Brandon Bend Dr
H
1 N Ridgewood Cir
2 N Nottingham Cir
3 S Willowdale Cir
4 S Marianne Cir
5 S Ridgewood Cir
6 S Evelyn Cir
A
B
C
D
E
1
2
3
4
5
6
7
95°33'04"
95°32'34"
95°32'04"
95°31'34"
95°31'04"
95°30'34"

SEE 4238 MAP

SEE 4370 MAP

1:24,000
1 in. = 2000 ft.
0 0.25 0.5
miles

SEE 4100 MAP

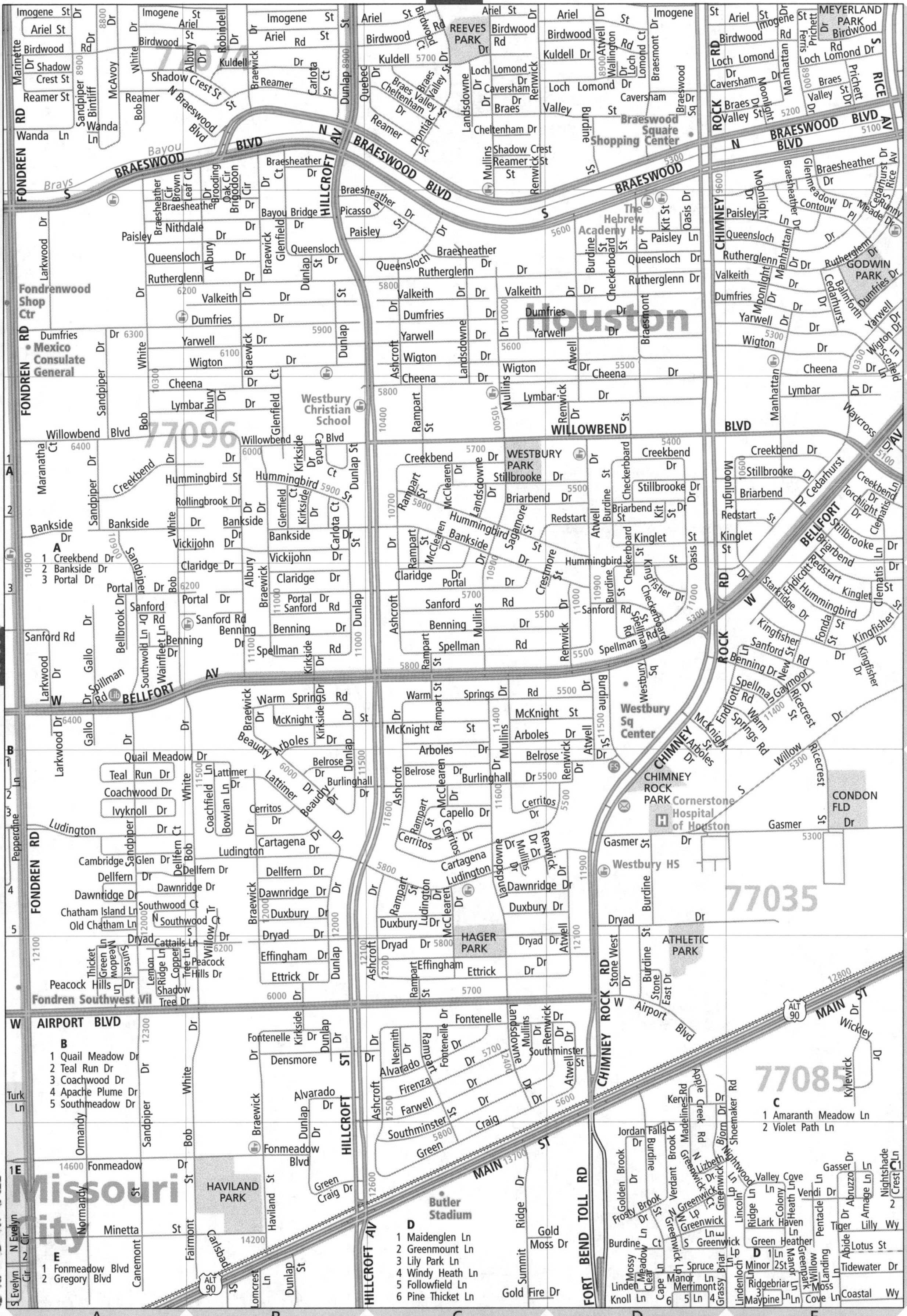
29°41'00"
29°40'34"
29°40'08"
29°39'41"
29°39'15"
29°38'49"
29°38'23"
29°37'57"
95°30'34"
95°30'04"
95°29'34"
95°29'04"
95°28'34"
95°28'04"
1
2
3
4
5
6
7
A
B
C
D
E
Houston
Missouri City
77074
77096
77035
77085
REEVES PARK
MEYERLAND PARK
GODWIN PARK
WESTBURY PARK
CHIMNEY ROCK PARK
CONDON FLD
HAGER PARK
ATHLETIC PARK
HAVILAND PARK
Braeswood Square Shopping Center
The Hebrew Academy HS
Fondrenwood Shop Ctr
Mexico Consulate General
Westbury Christian School
Westbury Sq Center
Cornerstone Hospital of Houston
Westbury HS
Fondren Southwest Vil
Butler Stadium
Brays Bayou
N BRAESWOOD BLVD
S BRAESWOOD BLVD
WILLOWBEND BLVD
W BELLFORT AV
W AIRPORT BLVD
MAIN ST
ALT 90
FONDREN RD
HILLCROFT AV
HILLCROFT ST
CHIMNEY ROCK RD
FORT BEND TOLL RD
RICE AV
S Willow Dr
Imogene St
Ariel St
Birdwood Rd
Kuldell Dr
Shadow Crest St
Reamer St
Loch Lomond Dr
Caversham Dr
Valley St
Cheltenham Dr
Wanda Ln
Braesheather Dr
Paisley St
Queensloch Dr
Rutherglenn Dr
Valkeith Dr
Dumfries Dr
Yarwell Dr
Wigton Dr
Cheena Dr
Lymbar Dr
Creekbend Dr
Hummingbird St
Stillbrooke Dr
Briarbend Dr
Bankside Dr
Vickijohn Dr
Claridge Dr
Portal Dr
Sanford Rd
Benning Dr
Spellman Rd
Warm Springs Rd
McKnight St
Arboles Dr
Belrose Dr
Burlinghall Dr
Cerritos Dr
Ludington Dr
Cartagena St
Dellfern Dr
Dawnridge Dr
Duxbury Dr
Dryad Dr
Effingham Dr
Ettrick Dr
Fontenelle Dr
Densmore Dr
Alvarado Dr
Firenza Dr
Farwell Dr
Southminster St
Craig Dr
Fonmeadow Blvd
Minetta St
Gasmer Dr
Airport Blvd
Wickley Dr
Kylewick Dr
Braewick Dr
Glenfield Ct
Dunlap St
Albury Dr
White Dr
Bob St
Sandpiper Dr
Gallo Dr
Larkwood Dr
Ashcroft Dr
Rampart St
McClearen Dr
Landsdowne Dr
Mullins Dr
Renwick Dr
Atwell Dr
Burdine St
Checkerboard Dr
Braesmont Dr
Moonlight Dr
Manhattan Dr
Cedarhurst Dr
Kingfisher Dr
Ridge Dr
Summit Dr
Gold Moss Dr
Gold Fire Dr
A
1 Creekbend Dr
2 Bankside Dr
3 Portal Dr
B
1 Quail Meadow Dr
2 Teal Run Dr
3 Coachwood Dr
4 Apache Plume Dr
5 Southmeadow Dr
C
1 Amaranth Meadow Ln
2 Violet Path Ln
D
1 Maidenglen Ln
2 Greenmount Ln
3 Lily Park Ln
4 Windy Heath Ln
5 Followfield Ln
6 Pine Thicket Ln
E
1 Fonmeadow Blvd
2 Gregory Blvd

SEE 4241 MAP

SEE 4371 MAP

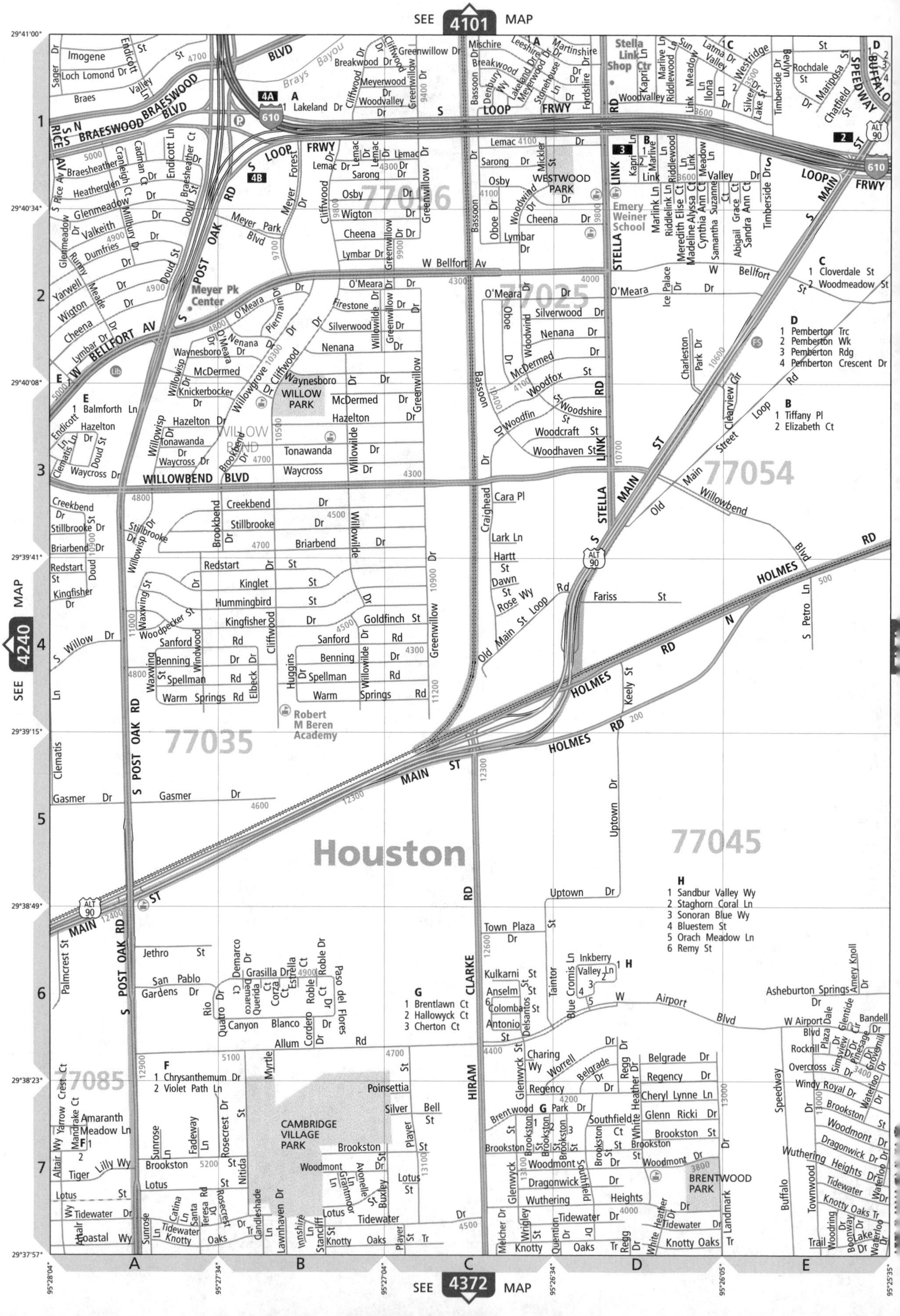
1:24,000
1 in. = 2000 ft.
0
0.25
0.5
miles
N
SEE 4101 MAP
SEE 4240 MAP
SEE 4372 MAP
Houston
77096
77025
77054
77035
77045
77085
S LOOP FRWY
S MAIN ST
S POST OAK RD
STELLA LINK RD
HIRAM CLARKE RD
W BELLFORT AV
WILLOWBEND BLVD
HOLMES RD
N BRAESWOOD BLVD
S BRAESWOOD BLVD
S RICE AV
BUFFALO SPEEDWAY
W Airport Blvd
Allum Rd
Uptown Dr
Gasmer Dr
Brays Bayou
Meyer Pk Center
Stella Link Shop Ctr
WESTWOOD PARK
WILLOW PARK
WILLOW BEND
Emery Weiner School
Robert M Beren Academy
CAMBRIDGE VILLAGE PARK
BRENTWOOD PARK
A
1 Lakeland Dr
B
1 Tiffany Pl
2 Elizabeth Ct
C
1 Cloverdale St
2 Woodmeadow St
D
1 Pemberton Trc
2 Pemberton Wk
3 Pemberton Rdg
4 Pemberton Crescent Dr
E
1 Balmforth Ln
F
1 Chrysanthemum Dr
2 Violet Path Ln
G
1 Brentlawn Ct
2 Hallowyck Ct
3 Cherton Ct
H
1 Sandbur Valley Wy
2 Staghorn Coral Ln
3 Sonoran Blue Wy
4 Bluestem St
5 Orach Meadow Ln
6 Remy St
29°41'00"
29°40'34"
29°40'08"
29°39'41"
29°39'15"
29°38'49"
29°38'23"
29°37'57"
95°28'04"
95°27'34"
95°27'04"
95°26'34"
95°26'05"
95°25'35"

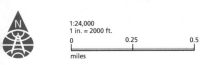

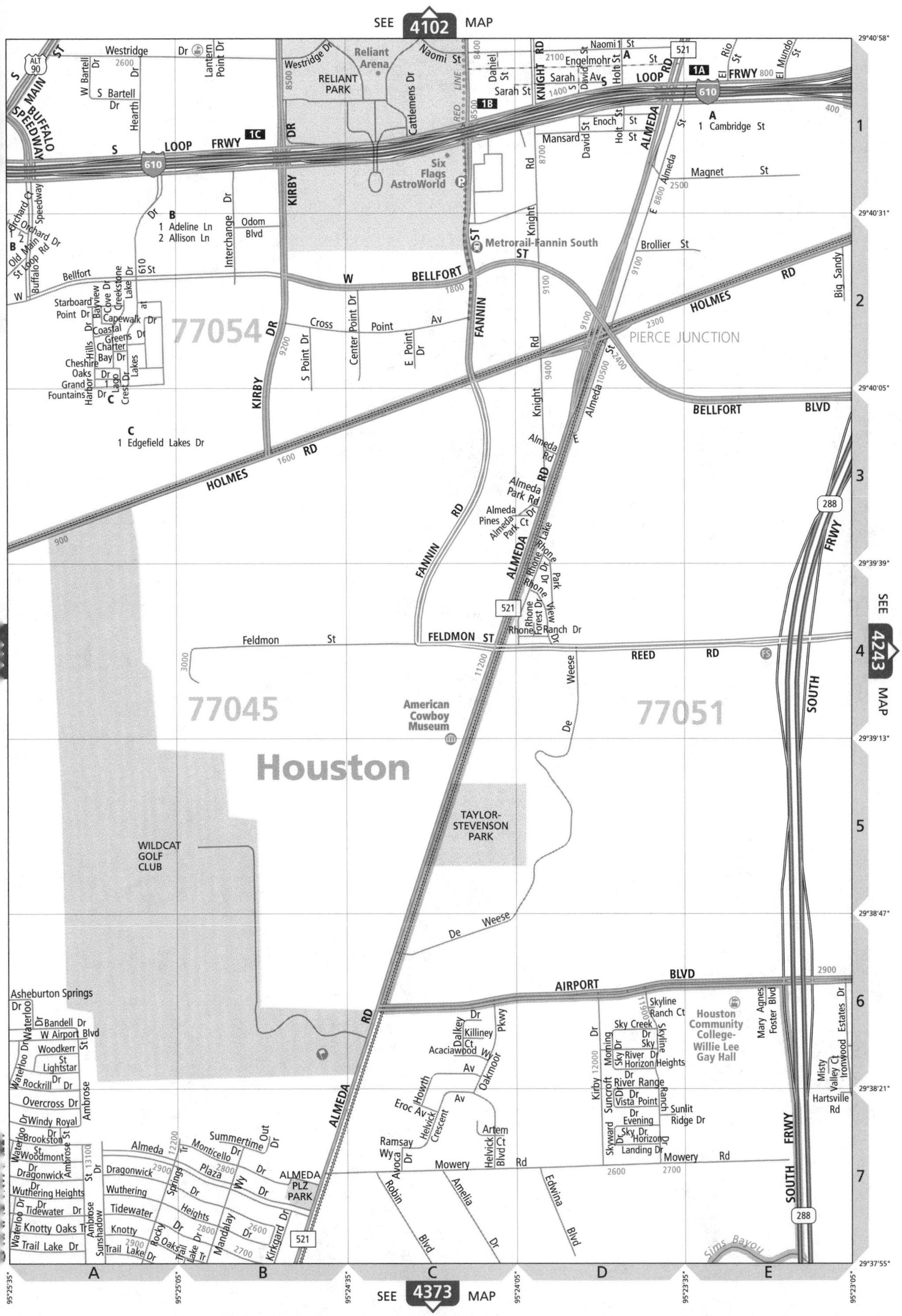
N
1:24,000
1 in. = 2000 ft.
0
0.25
0.5
miles
SEE 4102 MAP
SEE 4243 MAP
SEE 4373 MAP
29°40'58"
29°40'31"
29°40'05"
29°39'39"
29°39'13"
29°38'47"
29°38'21"
29°37'55"
95°25'35"
95°25'05"
95°24'35"
95°24'05"
95°23'35"
95°23'05"
A
B
C
D
E
1
2
3
4
5
6
7
Houston
77054
77045
77051
Reliant Arena
RELIANT PARK
Six Flags AstroWorld
Metrorail-Fannin South
PIERCE JUNCTION
American Cowboy Museum
TAYLOR-STEVENSON PARK
WILDCAT GOLF CLUB
Houston Community College-Willie Lee Gay Hall
ALMEDA PLZ PARK
S LOOP FRWY
610
1A
1B
1C
ALT 90
S MAIN ST
BUFFALO SPEEDWAY
KIRBY DR
FANNIN ST
KNIGHT RD
ALMEDA RD
W BELLFORT ST
BELLFORT BLVD
HOLMES RD
FELDMON ST
REED RD
AIRPORT BLVD
SOUTH FRWY
288
521
Westridge Dr
Westridge St
Naomi St
Cattlemens Dr
Lantern Point Dr
W Bartell Dr
S Bartell Dr
Hearth Dr
Odom Blvd
Interchange Dr
Cross Point Av
Center Point Dr
S Point Dr
E Point Dr
Engelmohr St
Sarah St
David St
Holt St
Enoch St
Mansard St
Daniel St
El Rio St
El Mundo St
Cambridge St
Magnet St
Brollier St
Big Sandy
1 Cambridge St
1 Adeline Ln
2 Allison Ln
1 Edgefield Lakes Dr
Orchard Ct
Orchard Dr
Old Main St
Buffalo Speedway
Starboard Point Dr
Bayview Cove Dr
Creekstone Dr
Capewalk Dr
Coastal Greens Dr
Charter Bay Dr
Cheshire Oaks Dr
Grand Fountains Dr
Almeda Park Rd
Almeda Pines
Almeda Park Ct
Rhone Lake
Rhone Park
Rhone Forest Dr
Rhone Ranch Dr
Rhone View Dr
De Weese
Feldmon St
Asheburton Springs Dr
Bandell Dr
W Airport Blvd
Woodkerr St
Lightstar St
Rockrill Dr
Overcross Dr
Windy Royal Dr
Brookston St
Woodmont St
Dragonwick Dr
Wuthering Heights Dr
Tidewater Dr
Knotty Oaks Trl
Trail Lake Dr
Waterloo Dr
Ambrose St
Sunshadow
Almeda Springs Tr
Monticello Dr
Summertime Dr
Out Dr
Plaza Wy
Mandalay Dr
Kirkgard Dr
Rocky Trail
Oaks Lake Dr
Dalkey Dr
Killiney Ct
Acaciawood Wy
Oakmoor Pkwy
Howth Av
Eroc Av
Helvick Crescent
Artem
Helvick Ct
Blvd Ct
Ramsay Wy
Avoca Dr
Mowery Rd
Robin Blvd
Amelia Dr
Edwina Blvd
Skyline Ranch Ct
Sky Creek Dr
Morning Sky Dr
River Horizon
Skyline Heights
River Range Dr
Vista Point Dr
Evening Dr
Sky Horizon Dr
Landing Dr
Skyward Dr
Suncroft Dr
Sunlit Ridge Dr
Kirby Dr
Mary Agnes Foster Blvd
Estates Dr
Ironwood
Misty Valley Ct
Hartsville Rd
Sims Bayou

1:24,000
1 in. = 2000 ft.
0 0.25 0.5
miles

SEE 4103 MAP

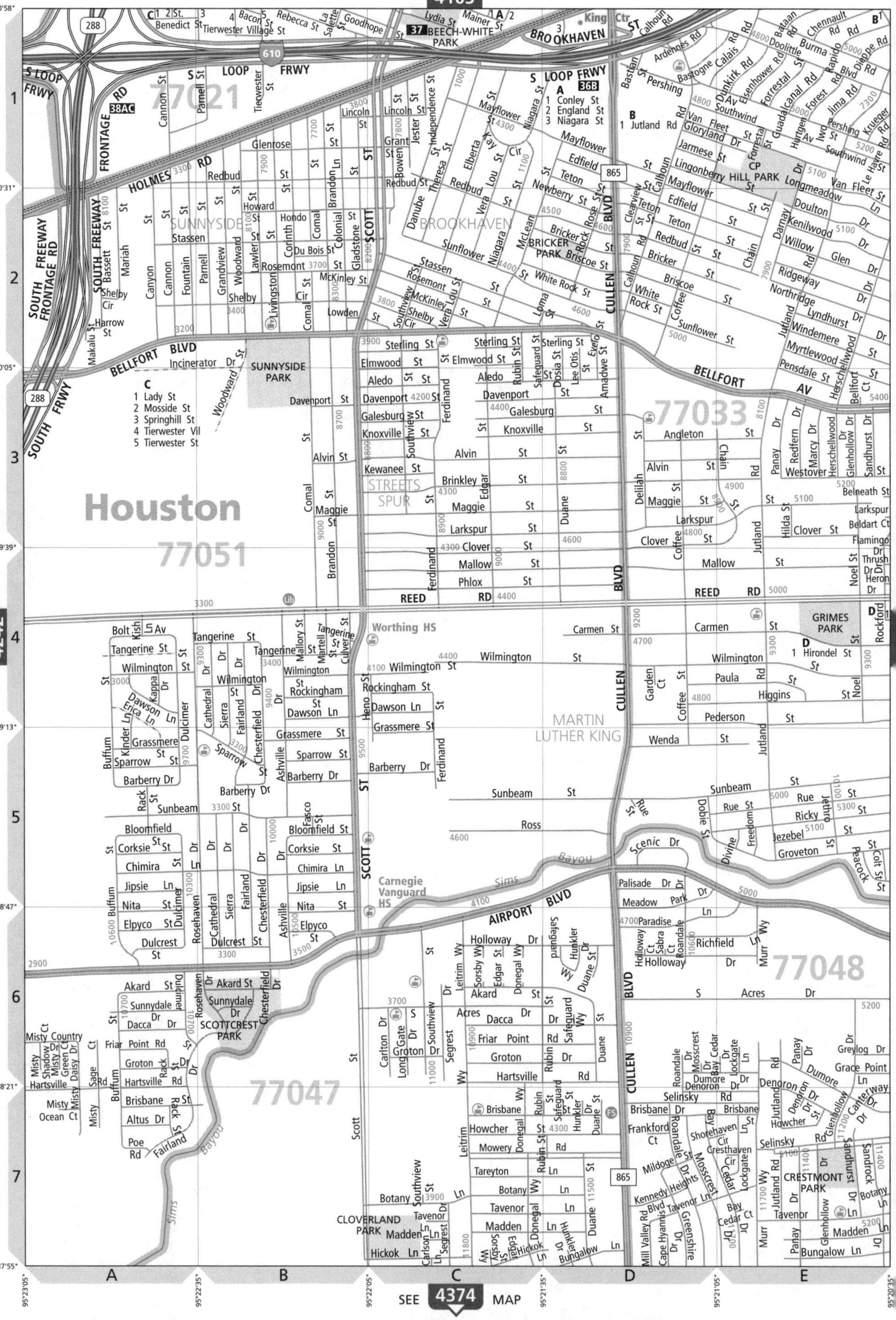
Houston
77051
77021
77033
77048
77047
SUNNYSIDE
SUNNYSIDE PARK
BROOKHAVEN
BRICKER PARK
BEECH-WHITE PARK
HILL PARK
STREETS SPUR
MARTIN LUTHER KING
GRIMES PARK
SCOTTCREST PARK
CLOVERLAND PARK
CRESTMONT PARK
Worthing HS
Carnegie Vanguard HS
S LOOP FRWY
SOUTH FREEWAY
SOUTH FRWY
BELLFORT BLVD
BELLFORT AV
REED RD
AIRPORT BLVD
SCOTT ST
CULLEN BLVD
HOLMES RD
BROOKHAVEN ST
Sims Bayou
610
288
865
1 Lady St
2 Mosside St
3 Springhill St
4 Tierwester Vil
5 Tierwester St
1 Conley St
2 England St
3 Niagara St
1 Jutland Rd
1 Hirondel St
29°40'58"
29°40'31"
29°40'05"
29°39'39"
29°39'13"
29°38'47"
29°38'21"
29°37'55"
95°23'05"
95°22'35"
95°22'05"
95°21'35"
95°21'05"
95°20'35"

SEE 4242 MAP

SEE 4374 MAP

1:24,000
1 in. = 2000 ft.
0 0.25 0.5
miles

SEE 4104 MAP

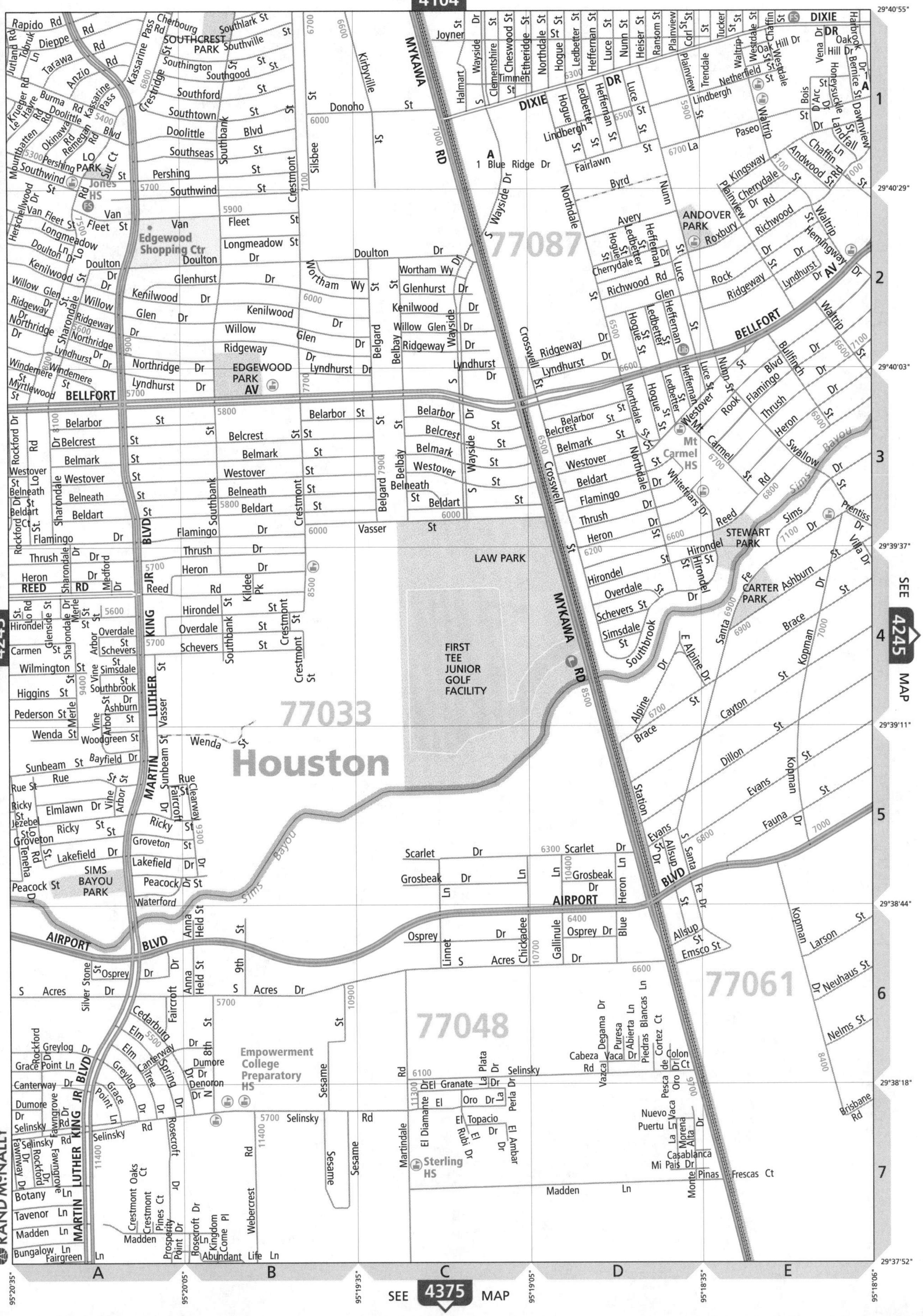

MYKAWA RD
BELLFORT AV
AIRPORT BLVD
MARTIN LUTHER KING JR BLVD
DIXIE DR
SOUTHCREST PARK
LO PARK
Jones HS
Edgewood Shopping Ctr
EDGEWOOD PARK
ANDOVER PARK
Mt Carmel HS
STEWART PARK
CARTER PARK
LAW PARK
FIRST TEE JUNIOR GOLF FACILITY
SIMS BAYOU PARK
Empowerment College Preparatory HS
Sterling HS
Sims Bayou
Houston
77087
77033
77061
77048
Wortham Wy
Glenhurst Dr
Kenilwood Dr
Willow Glen Dr
Ridgeway Dr
Lyndhurst Dr
Belarbor St
Belcrest St
Belmark St
Westover St
Belneath St
Beldart St
Flamingo Dr
Thrush Dr
Heron Dr
Reed Rd
Hirondel St
Overdale St
Schevers St
Crosswell St
Wayside Dr
Belgard St
Belbay St
Southbank St
Crestmont St
Vasser St
Scarlet Dr
Grosbeak Dr
Osprey Dr
S Acres Dr
Selinsky Rd
Madden Ln
Kopman Dr
Larson St
Neuhaus St
Nelms St
Brisbane Rd
Santa Fe Dr
Allsup St
Emsco St
Station
Brace St
Cayton St
Dillon St
Evans St
Fauna Dr
Alpine Dr
E Alpine Dr
Kingsway
Waltrip St
Paseo
Ashburn Dr
Sims Dr
Prentiss Dr
Villa Dr
Cedarburg
Canterway Dr
Greylog Dr
Grace Point Ln
Rosecroft Dr
Sesame St
Martindale Rd
Pinas
Frescas Ct
29°40'55"
29°40'29"
29°40'03"
29°39'37"
29°39'11"
29°38'44"
29°38'18"
29°37'52"
95°20'35"
95°20'05"
95°19'35"
95°19'05"
95°18'35"
95°18'06"
A B C D E
1 2 3 4 5 6 7

SEE 4245 MAP

SEE 4375 MAP

1:24,000
1 in. = 2000 ft.
0 0.25 0.5
miles

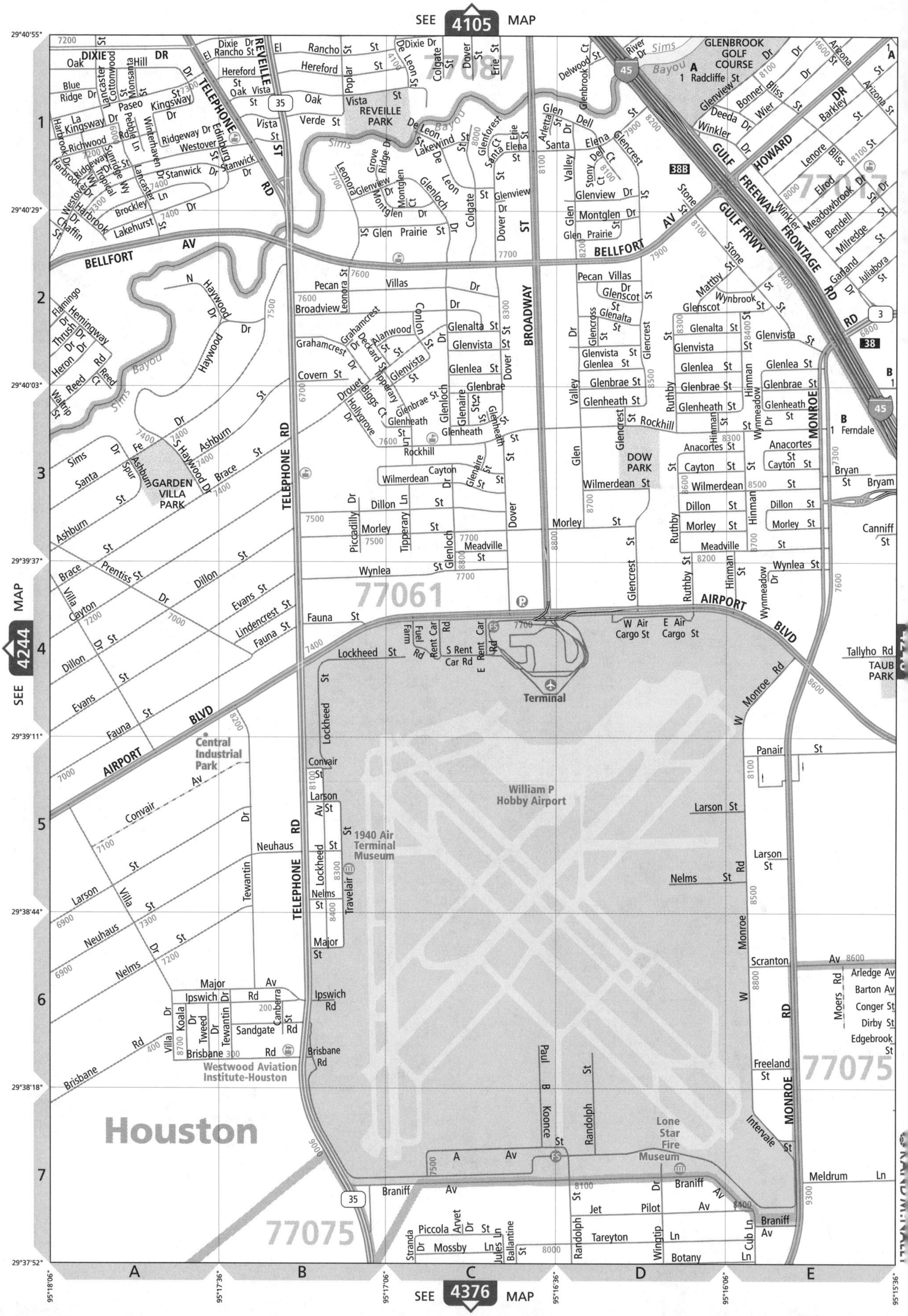
SEE 4105 MAP
SEE 4244 MAP
SEE 4376 MAP
77087
77061
77017
77075
Houston
William P Hobby Airport
Terminal
1940 Air Terminal Museum
Lone Star Fire Museum
Central Industrial Park
Westwood Aviation Institute-Houston
GLENBROOK GOLF COURSE
REVEILLE PARK
GARDEN VILLA PARK
DOW PARK
TAUB PARK
TELEPHONE RD
BROADWAY ST
BELLFORT AV
AIRPORT BLVD
GULF FREEWAY
GULF FRWY
MONROE RD
W Monroe Rd
HOWARD DR
DIXIE DR
REVEILLE ST
Sims Bayou
29°40'55"
29°40'29"
29°40'03"
29°39'37"
29°39'11"
29°38'44"
29°38'18"
29°37'52"
95°18'06"
95°17'36"
95°17'06"
95°16'36"
95°16'06"
95°15'36"
A
B
C
D
E
1
2
3
4
5
6
7

1:24,000
1 in. = 2000 ft.
0 0.25 0.5
miles

SEE 4106 MAP

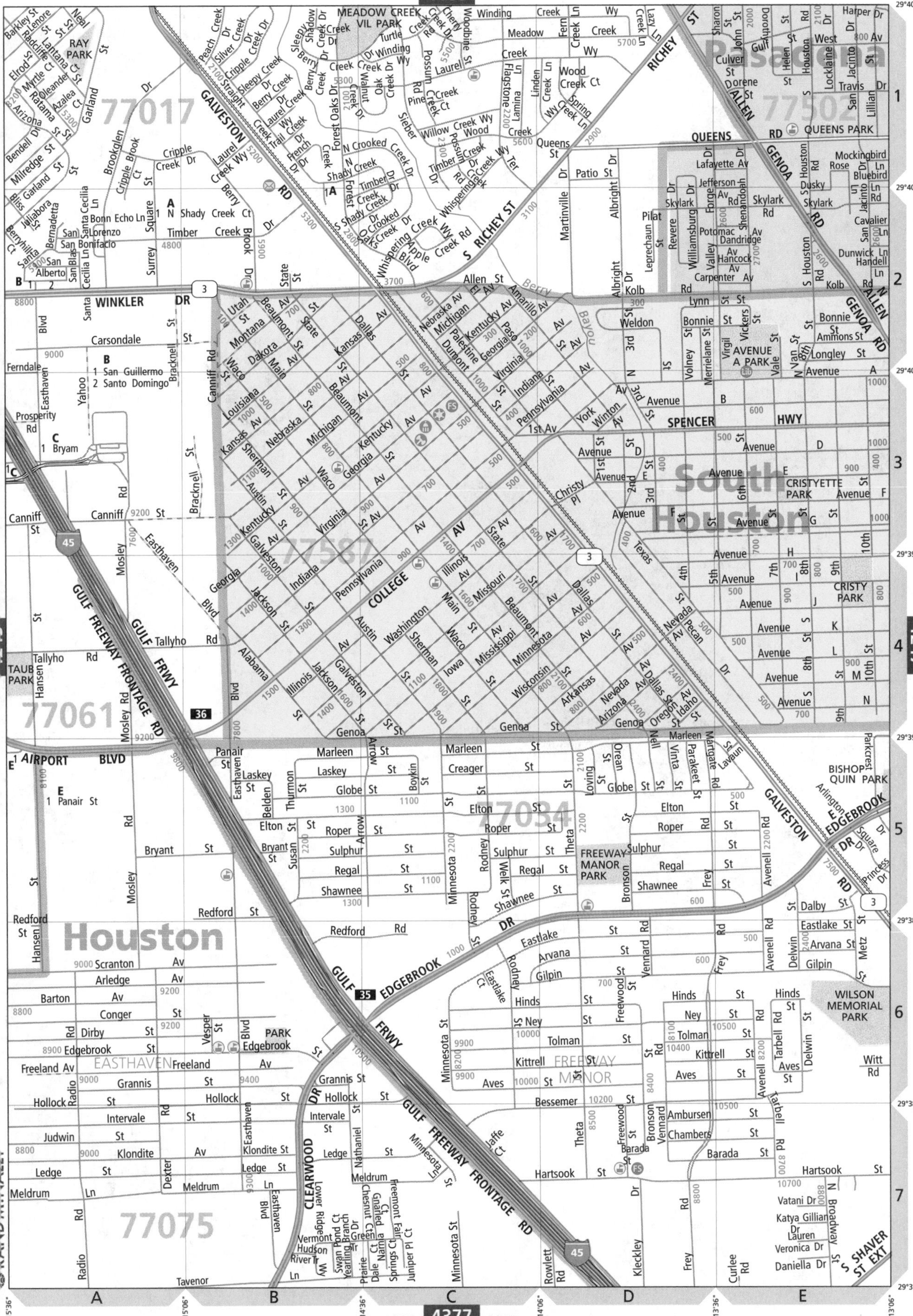
Houston
South Houston
Pasadena
77017
77502
77587
77061
77034
77075
RAY PARK
MEADOW CREEK VIL PARK
QUEENS PARK
AVENUE A PARK
CRISTYETTE PARK
CRISTY PARK
TAUB PARK
FREEWAY MANOR PARK
BISHOP QUIN PARK
WILSON MEMORIAL PARK
EASTHAVEN
FREEWAY MANOR
GALVESTON RD
S RICHEY ST
RICHEY ST
QUEENS RD
GENOA RD
ALLEN GENOA RD
WINKLER DR
SPENCER HWY
COLLEGE AV
GULF FREEWAY FRONTAGE RD
GULF FRWY
AIRPORT BLVD
EDGEBROOK DR
CLEARWOOD DR
S SHAVER ST EXT
Genoa
Canniff Rd
Mosley Rd
Easthaven Blvd
Tallyho Rd
Redford St
Scranton Av
Edgebrook St
Almeda Genoa
3
35
36
45
1
2
3
4
5
6
7
A
B
C
D
E
29°40'53"
29°40'26"
29°40'00"
29°39'34"
29°39'08"
29°38'42"
29°38'16"
29°37'49"
95°15'36"
95°15'06"
95°14'36"
95°14'06"
95°13'36"
95°13'06"

SEE 4247 MAP

SEE 4377 MAP

1:24,000
1 in. = 2000 ft.
0 0.25 0.5
miles

SEE 4107 MAP

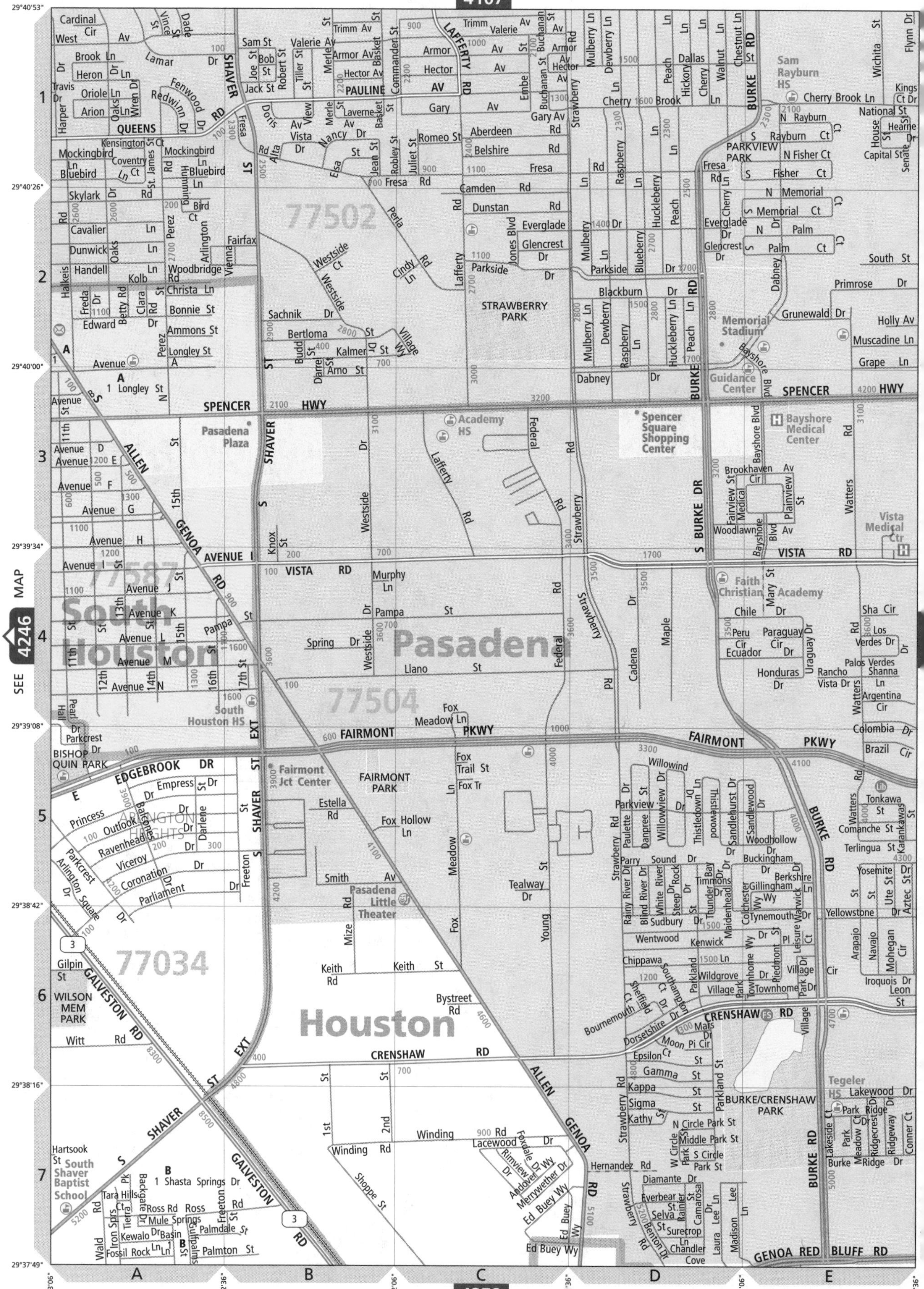
29°40'53"
29°40'26"
29°40'00"
29°39'34"
29°39'08"
29°38'42"
29°38'16"
29°37'49"
1
2
3
4
5
6
7
A
B
C
D
E
95°13'06"
95°12'36"
95°12'06"
95°11'36"
95°11'06"
95°10'36"
77502
77587
77504
77034
South Houston
Pasadena
Houston
SHAVER ST
SPENCER HWY
FAIRMONT PKWY
VISTA RD
AVENUE I
ALLEN GENOA RD
BURKE RD
S BURKE DR
CRENSHAW RD
GALVESTON RD
S SHAVER ST EXT
EDGEBROOK DR
QUEENS RD
PAULINE AV
LAFFERTY RD
GENOA RED BLUFF RD
Strawberry Rd
Pasadena Plaza
Academy HS
Spencer Square Shopping Center
Bayshore Medical Center
Memorial Stadium
Guidance Center
Sam Rayburn HS
PARKVIEW PARK
STRAWBERRY PARK
Faith Christian Academy
Vista Medical Ctr
South Houston HS
BISHOP QUIN PARK
Fairmont Jct Center
FAIRMONT PARK
ARLINGTON HEIGHTS
Pasadena Little Theater
WILSON MEM PARK
South Shaver Baptist School
Tegeler HS
BURKE/CRENSHAW PARK
3

SEE 4246 MAP

SEE 4378 MAP

N

1:24,000
1 in. = 2000 ft.
0 0.25 0.5
miles

SEE 4108 MAP

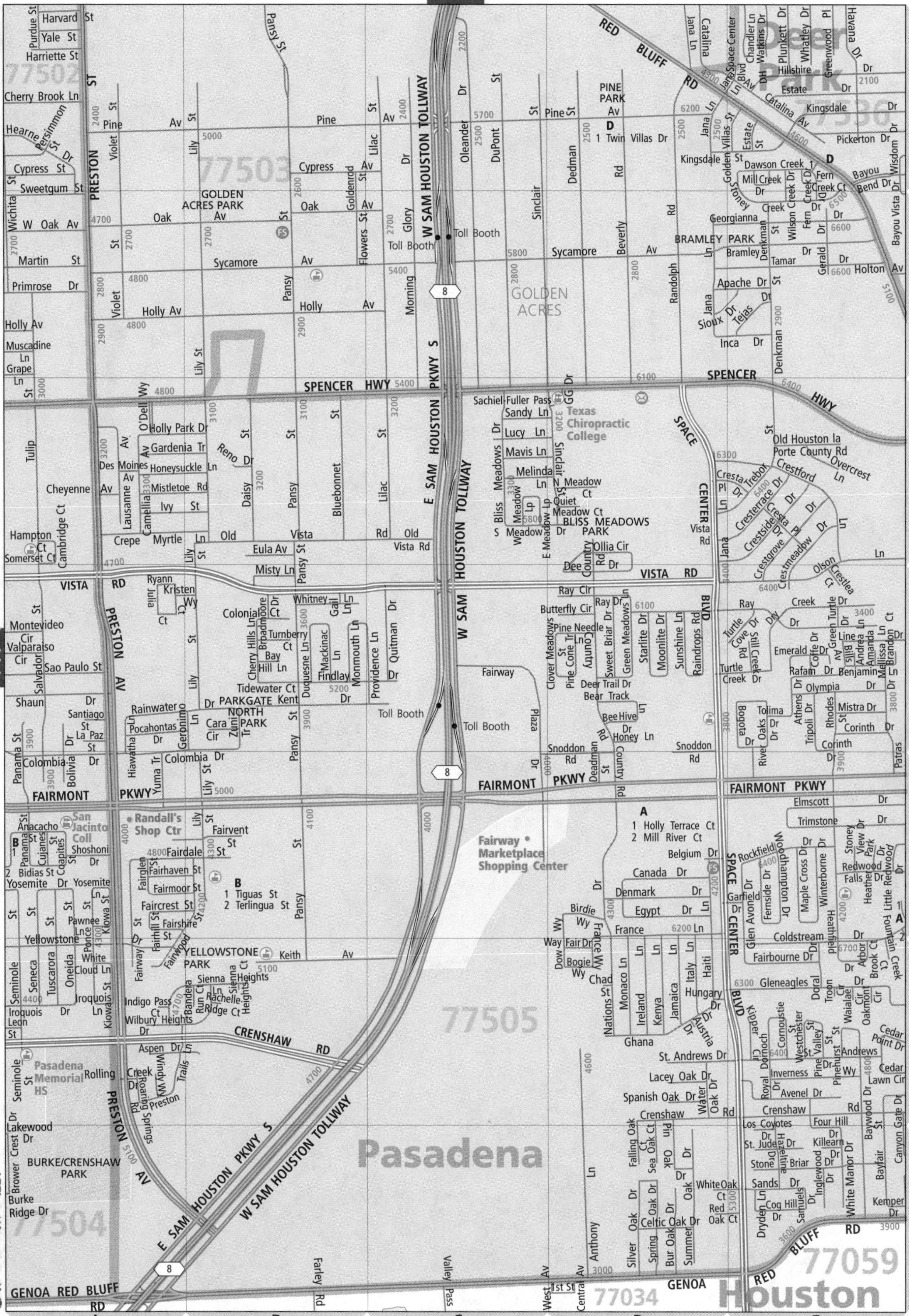
Purdue St
Harvard St
Yale St
Harriette St
77502
PRESTON ST
Cherry Brook Ln
Hearne St
Persimmon Dr
Cypress St
Sweetgum St
Wichita St
W Oak Av
Martin St
Primrose Dr
Holly Av
Muscadine Ln
Grape Ln
Violet St
Pine Av
Lily St
77503
Cypress Av
GOLDEN ACRES PARK
Oak Av
Sycamore Av
Holly Av
Pansy St
Lilac St
Goldenrod St
Flowers St
Glory Dr
Morning
Toll Booth
W SAM HOUSTON TOLLWAY
W SAM HOUSTON PKWY S
Oleander Dr
DuPont St
Sinclair St
Pine St
Dedman
PINE PARK Av
1 Twin Villas Dr
Beverly Rd
Randolph
GOLDEN ACRES
RED BLUFF RD
Jana Ln
Catalina
Space Center Blvd
Chandler Ln
Watkins Dr
Plunkett Dr
Whatley Dr
Greenwood Pl
Havana Dr
Deer Park
77536
Hillshire
Estate
Catalina Av
Kingsdale Dr
Pickerton Dr
Wisdom Dr
Kingsdale St
Dawson Creek
Mill Creek Dr
Fern Creek Ct
Bayou Bend Dr
Bayou Vista Dr
Georgianna
Stoney Creek
Wilson Creek Dr
BRAMLEY PARK
Bramley Dr
Denkman
Tamar
Gerald
Holton Av
Apache Dr
Sioux Dr
Tejas Dr
Inca Dr
SPENCER HWY
Sachiel-Fuller Pass
Sandy Ln
Lucy Ln
Mavis Ln
Melinda Ln
Bliss Meadows Dr
N Meadow Ct
Quiet Meadow Ct
BLISS MEADOWS PARK
S Meadow Dr
E Meadow Lp
Texas Chiropractic College
SPACE CENTER BLVD
Old Houston la Porte County Rd
Overcrest Ln
Crestford
Cresta Pl
Trebor Dr
Cresterrace Dr
Crestside Dr
Crestgrove
Crestmeadow Dr
Olson Ct
Crestlea
O'Dell Wy
Holly Park Dr
Gardenia Tr
Reno Dr
Des Moines Av
Honeysuckle Ln
Mistletoe Rd
Ivy St
Tulip
Cheyenne Av
Lausanne Av
Camellia
Daisy
Bluebonnet
Lilac Rd
Hampton Ct
Somerset Ct
Cambridge Ct
Crepe Myrtle Ln
Old Vista
Eula Av
Misty Ln
Old Vista Rd
VISTA RD
Ryann
Kristen Wy
Julia Ct
Whitney Ln
Gail Ln
Colonial Ct
Broadmoore Dr
Turnberry Ct
Bay Hill Ln
Cherry Hills Ln
Duquesne Ln
Mackinac Ln
Findlay Dr
Monmouth Ln
Providence Ln
Quitman Dr
Ollia Cir
Dee Country Dr
Ray Cir
Butterfly Cir
Ray Dr
Pine Needle Ln
Pine Cone Tr
Sweet Briar Dr
Green Meadows Ln
Starlite Dr
Moonlite Dr
Sunshine Ln
Raindrops Rd
Clover Meadows
Deer Trail Dr
Bear Track
Bee Hive Dr
Honey Ln
Fairway
Plaza Dr
Snoddon Rd
Deadman St
Country Rd
Ray Creek Dr
Turtle Cove Dr
Still Creek Rd
Green Turtle Dr
Emerald Dr
Coffee Dr
Line Av
Bills
Andrea
Amanda
Mellissa Ln
Brandon Dr
Turtle Creek Dr
Rafam Dr
Benjamin
Olympia Dr
Athens Dr
Tripoli Dr
Rhodes St
Mistra Dr
Corinth Dr
Tolima
Bogota Dr
River Oaks Dr
Patras
Montevideo Cir
Valparaiso Cir
Sao Paulo St
Salvador
Shaun Dr
Santiago St
La Paz St
Panama St
Colombia Dr
Bolivia
Rainwater Dr
Pocahontas Dr
Hiawatha Ln
Geronimo
Cara Cir
Zuni Tr
PARKGATE NORTH PARK
Tidewater Ct
Kent
Yuma Tr
Colombia Dr
Toll Booth
PRESTON AV
FAIRMONT PKWY
Elmscott Dr
Trimstone Dr
San Jacinto Coll
Randall's Shop Ctr
Anacacho St
Panama St
Cujanes St
Coapites St
Shoshoni Dr
Bidias St
Yosemite Dr
Fairvent St
Fairdale St
Fairglen
Fairhaven St
Fairmoor St
Faircrest St
Fairshire
1 Tiguas St
2 Terlingua St
Fairway Marketplace Shopping Center
A
1 Holly Terrace Ct
2 Mill River Ct
Belgium Dr
Canada Dr
Denmark Dr
Egypt Dr
France Ln
Birdie Wy
Fair Dr
Bogie Wy
Dow Wy
Chad St
Nations St
Monaco Ln
Ireland Ln
Kenya Ln
Jamaica Ln
Italy Ln
Haiti
Hungary Dr
Austria Dr
Ghana
Rockfield Dr
Woodhampton Dr
Maple Cross Dr
Winterborne Dr
Stoney View Dr
Park Dr
Redwood Falls Dr
Heather Dr
Little Redwood
Garfield Dr
Glen Avon Dr
Fernside Dr
Coldstream Dr
Heathfield
Fairbourne Dr
Arbor Brook Cir
Fountain Creek
Gleneagles Dr
Doral
Troon
Waialae Cir
Oakmont Cir
Yellowstone Dr
Pawnee
Kiowa St
Ponce Ln
White Cloud Ln
YELLOWSTONE PARK
Keith Av
Seminole
Seneca
Tuscarora
Oneida
Iroquois Dr
Leon St
Indigo Pass Ct
Bandera Run Ct
Sienna Heights
Rachelle Ridge Ct
Wilbury Heights Dr
Aspen Dr
Windy Wy
Trails
Rolling Creek Dr
Roaring Springs Rd
Preston
CRENSHAW RD
77505
Pasadena Memorial HS
Lakewood Dr
Brower Crest Dr
BURKE/CRENSHAW PARK
Burke Ridge Dr
77504
E SAM HOUSTON PKWY S
W SAM HOUSTON TOLLWAY
Pasadena
Kipper Cir
Royal Dornoch Dr
Cornoustie Dr
Westchester St
Pine Valley
Pinehurst St
Andrews Wy
Cedar Point Dr
Cedar Lawn Cir
Inverness Dr
Avenel Dr
St. Andrews Dr
Lacey Oak Dr
Spanish Oak Dr
Water Oak Dr
Crenshaw Rd
Los Coyotes Dr
St. Jude Dr
Hazeltine Dr
Four Hill Ct
Killearn Dr
Stone Briar Dr
Inglewood Dr
White Manor Dr
Baywood Dr
Bayfair
Canyon Gate Dr
Sands Dr
Dryden Ln
Cog Hill Dr
Samuels Dr
Kemper Dr
Falling Oak Ct
Sea Oak Ct
Pin Oak
White Oak Ct
Red Oak Ct
Silver Oak Dr
Spring Oak Dr
Celtic Oak Dr
Bur Oak
Summer
Anthony Ln
Farley Rd
Valley Pass
West Av
Central Av
1st St
77034
GENOA RED BLUFF RD
RED BLUFF RD
77059
Houston

A B C D E
1 2 3 4 5 6 7

29°40'50" 29°40'24" 29°39'57" 29°39'31" 29°39'05" 29°38'39" 29°38'13" 29°37'47"

95°10'36" 95°10'07" 95°09'37" 95°09'07" 95°08'37" 95°08'07"

SEE 4249 MAP

SEE 4379 MAP

1:24,000
1 in. = 2000 ft.
0 0.25 0.5
miles

SEE 4109 MAP

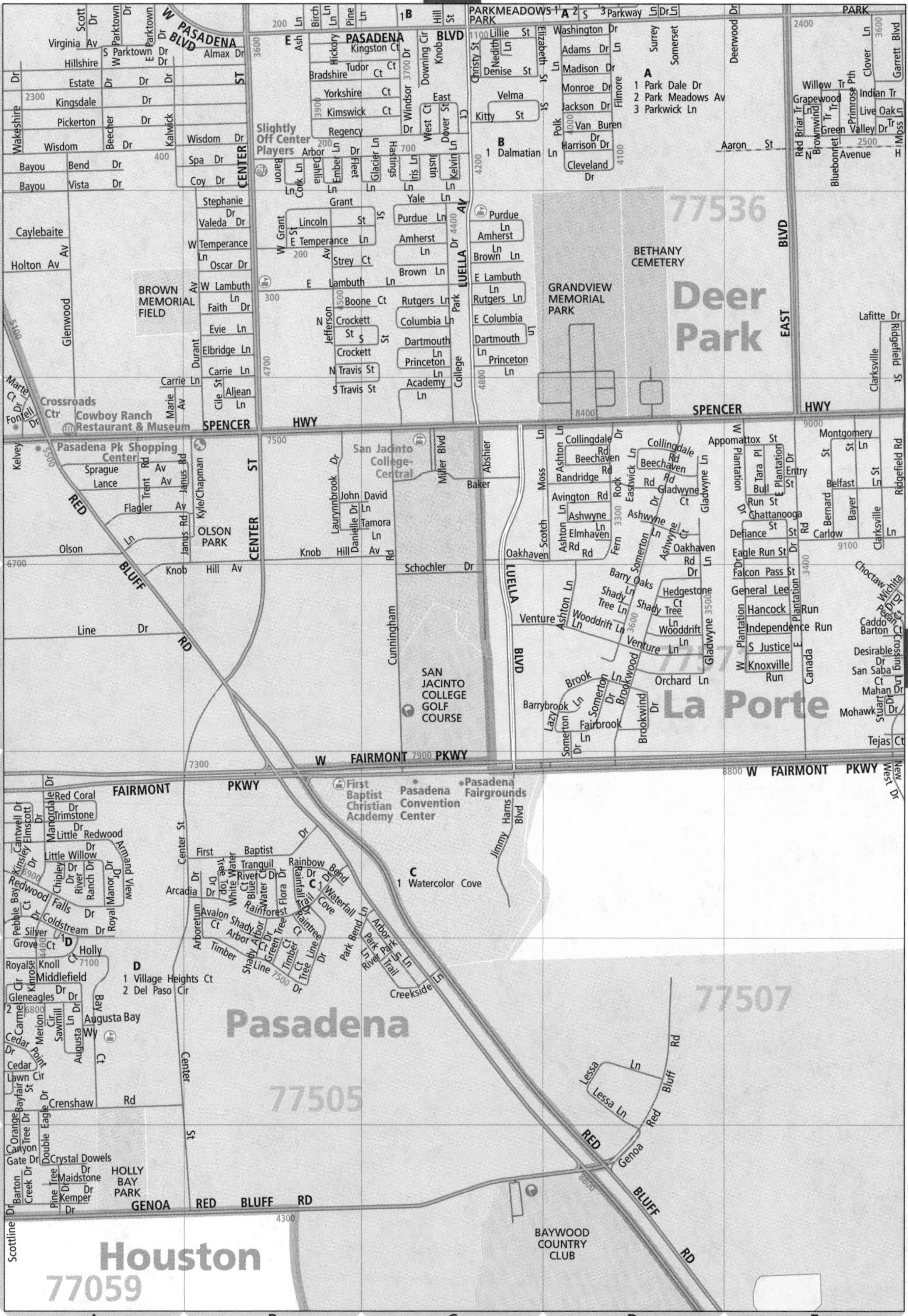
29°40'50"
29°40'24"
29°39'57"
29°39'31"
29°39'05"
29°38'39"
29°38'13"
29°37'47"
1
2
3
4
5
6
7
A
B
C
D
E
95°08'07"
95°07'37"
95°07'07"
95°06'37"
95°06'07"
95°05'37"
Deer Park
La Porte
Pasadena
Houston
77536
77507
77505
77059
W PASADENA BLVD
PASADENA BLVD
PARKMEADOWS PARK
Parkway
Virginia Av
Hillshire
Estate Dr
Kingsdale
Pickerton
Wisdom
Bayou Bend Dr
Bayou Vista Dr
Wakeshire
Beecher
Kalwick
Scott Dr
Parktown Dr
Almax Dr
CENTER ST
Wisdom Dr
Spa Dr
Coy Dr
Kingston Ct
Tudor Ct
Bradshire
Yorkshire Ct
Kimswick Ct
Regency
Slightly Off Center Players
Windsor Dr
Downing Cir
Hill St
East Knob
West Ct
Dover St
Christy St
Lillie St
Nedith Ln
Denise St
Velma
Kitty St
Elizabeth St
Washington Dr
Adams Dr
Madison Dr
Monroe Dr
Jackson Dr
Van Buren Dr
Harrison Dr
Cleveland Dr
Polk
Fillmore
Surrey
Somerset
Deerwood Dr
A
1 Park Dale Dr
2 Park Meadows Av
3 Parkwick Ln
B
1 Dalmatian Ln
Aaron St
Willow Tr
Grapewood Ln
Indian Tr
Live Oak Ln
Green Valley Dr
Avenue H
Clover
Garrett Blvd
Red Briar Tr
Bluebonnet
Brownwind
Moss
PARK
Stephanie Dr
Valeda Dr
Temperance
Oscar Dr
W Lambuth
Faith Dr
Evie Ln
Elbridge Ln
Carrie Ln
Aljean Ln
Carrie Ln
Caylebaite
Holton Av
Glenwood
Durant Av
Marie Av
Cile St
BROWN MEMORIAL FIELD
Grant
Lincoln St
E Temperance Ln
Strey Ct
E Lambuth Ln
Boone Ct
Crockett St
Travis St
Jefferson
Yale Ln
Purdue Ln
Amherst Ln
Brown Ln
Rutgers Ln
Columbia Ln
Dartmouth Ln
Princeton Ln
Academy Ln
LUELLA AV
Park
College
Purdue Ln
Amherst Ln
Brown Ln
E Lambuth Ln
Rutgers Ln
E Columbia
Dartmouth Ln
Princeton Ln
GRANDVIEW MEMORIAL PARK
BETHANY CEMETERY
EAST BLVD
Lafitte Dr
Ridgefield St
Clarksville
SPENCER HWY
Crossroads Ctr
Cowboy Ranch Restaurant & Museum
Marte Ct
Fontell Dr
Pasadena Pk Shopping Center
Kelvey
Sprague Av
Lance Av
Trent Rd
Janus Rd
Kyle/Chapman
Flagler Av
Olson Ln
OLSON PARK
Olson
Knob Hill Av
RED BLUFF RD
San Jacinto College-Central
Miller Blvd
Abshier
Baker
Laurynnbrook Dr
John David
Danielle Dr
Tamora Ln
Knob Hill Av
Schochler Dr
Cunningham
SAN JACINTO COLLEGE GOLF COURSE
LUELLA BLVD
Line Dr
Collingdale Rd
Beechaven Rd
Bandridge
Avington Rd
Ashwyne
Elmhaven Rd
Ashton
Scotch
Moss
Oakhaven
Rock
Eastwick
Fern
Gladwyne Ct
Ashwyne
Somerton
Barry Oaks
Shady Tree Ln
Hedgestone Ct
Woodrift Ln
Woodridft Ln
Venture Ln
Venture
Gladwyne
Orchard Ln
Brook Ln
Brookwood
Barrybrook
Lazy
Somerton Dr
Fairbrook
Brookwind Dr
Appomattox St
Plantation Dr
Tara Pl
Bull Run St
Entry St
Chattanooga
Defiance St
Eagle Run St
Falcon Pass St
General Lee
Hancock Run
Independence Run
S Justice
Knoxville Run
Canada
Montgomery St Ln
Belfast Ln
Bernard
Bayer
Carlow
Clarksville
Ridgefield Rd
Choctaw
Wichita
Pecan Dr
Caddo Dr
Barton Ct
Crossing
Desirable Dr
San Saba Ct
Mahan Dr
Mohawk Dr
Stuart
Tejas Ct
W FAIRMONT PKWY
FAIRMONT PKWY
New West Dr
First Baptist Christian Academy
Pasadena Convention Center
Pasadena Fairgrounds
Jimmy Harris Blvd
Red Coral Dr
Trimstone Dr
Little Redwood Dr
Little Willow Dr
Cantwell
Elmscott
Manordale
Kinsley
Chipley
River Ranch Dr
Manor Dr
Armand View
Redwood Falls Dr
Pebble Bay
Coldstream Dr
Royal
Silver Grove Ct
Holly Knoll
Royale
Kinrose
Middlefield
Gleneagles Dr
Carmel
Merion Cir
Sawmill Ln
Augusta Bay Wy
Augusta
Bay Ct
Cedar Point
Cedar Lawn Cir
Bayfair St
Crenshaw Rd
Eagle Dr
Orange Tree Dr
Canyon Gate Dr
Double
Crystal Dowels Dr
Maidstone Dr
Kemper Dr
Barton Creek Dr
Pine Tree
HOLLY BAY PARK
Scottline
D
1 Village Heights Ct
2 Del Paso Cir
First
Baptist
Tranquil
Center St
Arcadia Dr
Tree Top Dr
White Water
River Ct
Blue Water Ct
Flora Dr
Rainbow Bend
Rainfall Trail
Rainforest
Waterfall Cove
Arboretum
Avalon Ct
Shady Arbor
Green Tree
Timber Ct
Raintree
Timber Line
Shady Line
Park Bend Ln
Arbor Ln
Park Trail
River Park
Creekside Ln
C
1 Watercolor Cove
Lessa Ln
Red Bluff Rd
Genoa
GENOA RED BLUFF RD
BAYWOOD COUNTRY CLUB

SEE 4248 MAP

SEE 4380 MAP

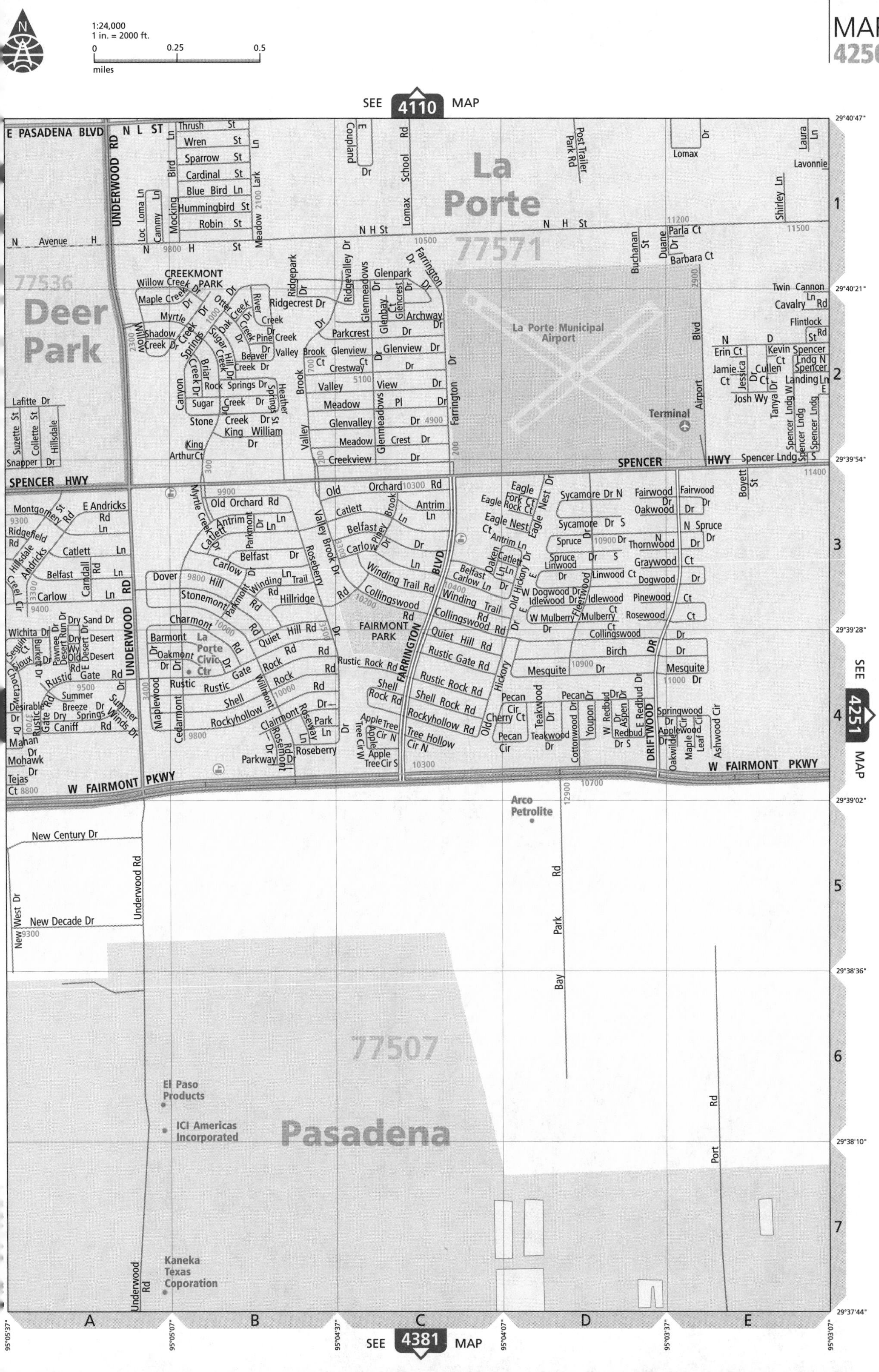
1:24,000
1 in. = 2000 ft.
0
0.25
0.5
miles
SEE 4110 MAP
SEE 4381 MAP
SEE 4251 MAP
La Porte
77571
Deer Park
77536
Pasadena
77507
La Porte Municipal Airport
Terminal
CREEKMONT PARK
FAIRMONT PARK
La Porte Civic Ctr
Arco Petrolite
El Paso Products
ICI Americas Incorporated
Kaneka Texas Coporation
E PASADENA BLVD
UNDERWOOD RD
N L ST
Thrush St
Wren St
Sparrow St
Cardinal St
Blue Bird Ln
Hummingbird St
Robin St
Lark Ln
Meadow
Bird Ln
Mocking
Cammy Ln
Loc Loma Ln
N H St
Avenue H
Coupland Dr
School Rd
Lomax
Post Trailer Park Rd
Lomax
Laura Ln
Lavonnie
Shirley Ln
Parla Ct
Barbara Ct
Buchanan St
Duane Dr
Twin Cannon Ln
Cavalry Rd
Flintlock St
Airport Blvd
Erin Ct
Kevin Spencer
Spencer Lndg N
Jamie Ct
Jessica Dr
Cullen Ct
Tanya Dr
Josh Wy
Spencer Lndg W
Spencer Lndg
Spencer Lndg E
Spencer Landing Ln
Spencer Lndg S
Willow Creek Dr
Maple Creek Dr
Myrtle
Shadow Creek Dr
Willow
Otter Creek
Oak Creek
River Creek
Ridgecrest Dr
Ridgepark Dr
Pine Creek
Sugar Hill Dr
Beaver Creek Dr
Briar Creek Dr
Valley Brook
Rock Springs Dr
Heather Springs St
Canyon
Sugar Creek Dr
Stone Creek Dr
King William Dr
King Arthur Ct
Lafitte Dr
Suzette St
Collette St
Hillsdale
Snapper Dr
Ridgevalley Dr
Glenpark Dr
Glenmeadows
Glenbay Ct
Glencrest Dr
Farrington
Archway Dr
Parkcrest Dr
Glenview Dr
Crestway Ct
Valley View Dr
Meadow Pl
Glenvalley Dr
Meadow Crest Dr
Creekview Dr
Farrington
SPENCER HWY
Boyett St
Montgomery St
E Andricks Rd
Ridgefield Rd
Hillsdale
Andricks
Catlett Ln
Belfast Ln
Camdall Rd
Creel Cir
Carlow Ln
Old Orchard Rd
Myrtle Creek Dr
Antrim Ln
Catlett Dr
Parkmont Dr
Belfast Dr
Carlow
Dover
Hill
Winding Trail
Hillridge Rd
Stonemont Rd
Parkmont
Charmont Rd
Quiet Hill Rd
Barmont
Oakmont Dr
Rustic Gate Rd
Rock Rd
Shell Rd
Rockyhollow
Maplewood
Cedarmont
Clairmont
Rosemont
Roseway Dr
Park Ln
Parkway Dr
Roseberry
Valley Brook Dr
Old Orchard Rd
Catlett Ln
Belfast
Pinecrest Dr
Antrim Ln
Carlow Dr
Winding Trail Rd
Collingswood Rd
Rustic Rock Rd
Shell Rock Rd
Apple Tree Cir N
Apple Tree Cir W
Apple Tree Cir S
Tree Hollow Cir N
Rockyhollow Rd
Wichita Dr
Seguin Ct
Sioux Dr
Choctaw Dr
Burkett Dr
Pawnee Dr
Desert Run Dr
Dry Sand Dr
Dry Desert Wy
Old Desert
E Desert Rd
Summer Breeze Dr
Dry Springs
Caniff Rd
Summer Winds Dr
Desirable Dr
Rustic Gate Rd
Mahan Dr
Mohawk Dr
Tejas Ct
FARRINGTON BLVD
Eagle Fork Ct
Eagle Rock Ct
Eagle Nest Dr
Eagle Nest Ct
Antrim Ln
Oaken Ln
Catlett
Belfast Carlow Ln
Winding Trail
Collingswood Rd
Quiet Hill Rd
Rustic Gate Rd
Rustic Rock Rd
Shell Rock Rd
Rockyhollow Rd
Tree Hollow
Old Hickory Dr
Hickory
Sycamore Dr N
Sycamore Dr S
Spruce Dr
Spruce Dr S
Linwood Dr
Linwood Ct
W Dogwood Dr
Idlewood Dr
Idlewood Ct
Fleetwood
W Mulberry Dr
Mulberry Ct
Collingswood
Mesquite Dr
Pecan Cir
Cherry Ct
Teakwood Dr
Pecan Dr
Cottonwood Dr
Youpon Dr
W Redbud Dr
Aspen Dr
E Redbud Dr
Redbud Dr S
Fairwood Dr
Oakwood Dr
N Spruce Dr
Thornwood Dr
Graywood Ct
Dogwood Dr
Pinewood Ct
Rosewood Ct
Birch Dr
Mesquite Dr
DRIFTWOOD DR
Springwood Dr
Applewood Dr
Oakwilde
Maple Cir
Leaf Cir
Ashwood Cir
W FAIRMONT PKWY
New Century Dr
New Decade Dr
New West Dr
Underwood Rd
Bay Park Rd
Port Rd
A
B
C
D
E
1
2
3
4
5
6
7
29°40'47"
29°40'21"
29°39'54"
29°39'28"
29°39'02"
29°38'36"
29°38'10"
29°37'44"
95°05'37"
95°05'07"
95°04'37"
95°04'07"
95°03'37"
95°03'07"

1:24,000
1 in. = 2000 ft.
0 0.25 0.5
miles

SEE 4111 MAP

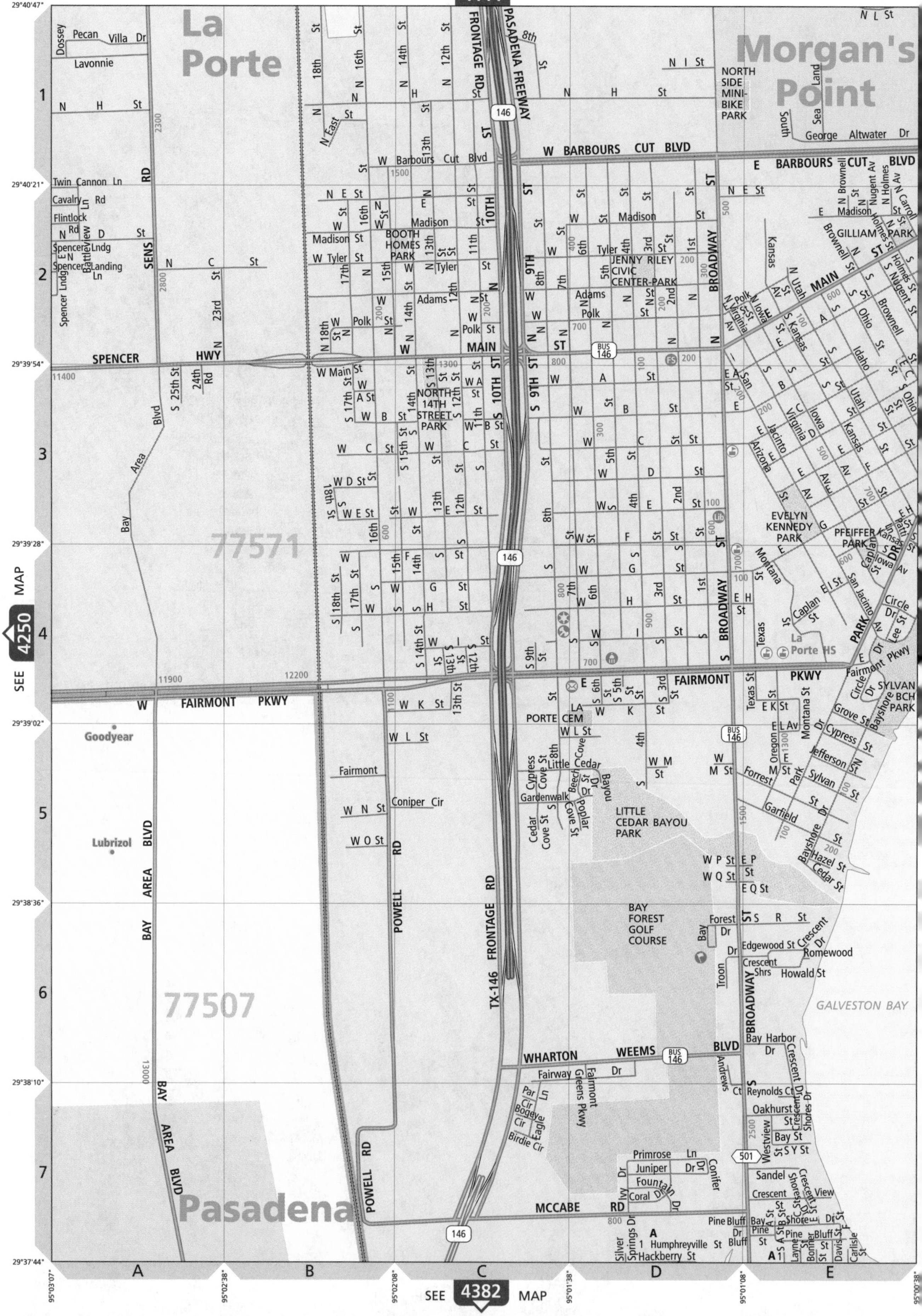
La Porte
Morgan's Point
Pasadena
77571
77507
GALVESTON BAY
SPENCER HWY
W FAIRMONT PKWY
E BARBOURS CUT BLVD
W BARBOURS CUT BLVD
PASADENA FREEWAY
FRONTAGE RD
TX-146 FRONTAGE RD
BAY AREA BLVD
SENS RD
POWELL RD
BROADWAY
MAIN ST
WHARTON WEEMS BLVD
MCCABE RD
NORTH SIDE MINI-BIKE PARK
BOOTH HOMES PARK
JENNY RILEY CIVIC CENTER-PARK
NORTH 14TH STREET PARK
EVELYN KENNEDY PARK
PFEIFFER PARK
SYLVAN BCH PARK
LITTLE CEDAR BAYOU PARK
BAY FOREST GOLF COURSE
PORTE CEM
La Porte HS
Goodyear
Lubrizol
146
BUS 146
501
A
B
C
D
E
1
2
3
4
5
6
7

SEE 4250 MAP

SEE 4382 MAP

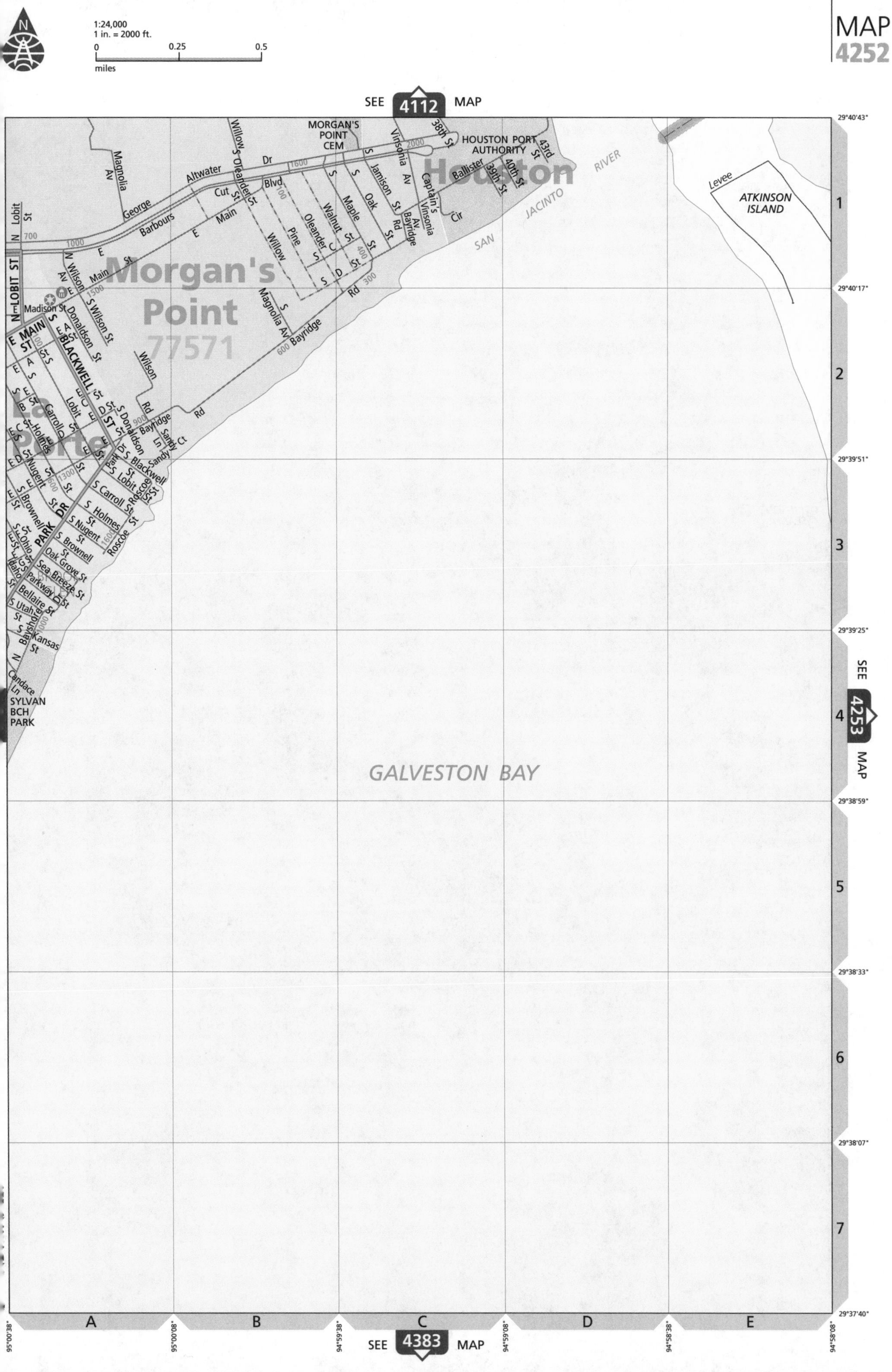
N
1:24,000
1 in. = 2000 ft.
0
0.25
0.5
miles
SEE 4112 MAP
MORGAN'S POINT CEM
HOUSTON PORT AUTHORITY
Houston
SAN JACINTO RIVER
Levee
ATKINSON ISLAND
Morgan's Point
77571
La Porte
Altwater Dr
George
Barbours Cut Blvd
E Main St
N Lobit St
N LOBIT ST
E MAIN ST
S BLACKWELL ST
Madison St
N Wilson Av
S Wilson St
Donaldson St
Magnolia Av
Willow
S Oleander St
Pine
Oleander
Walnut
Maple
Oak
S Jamison St
Vinsonia Av
Captain's Cir
Bayridge Rd
Ballister
38th St
39th St
40th St
43rd St
Sandy Ct
S Carroll St
S Holmes St
S Nugent St
S Brownell
S Lobit St
Roscoe St
PARK DR
Oak Grove St
Sea Breeze St
Parkway Dr
Bellaire St
S Utah St
S Kansas St
Candace Ln
SYLVAN BCH PARK
GALVESTON BAY
SEE 4253 MAP
SEE 4383 MAP
A
B
C
D
E
1
2
3
4
5
6
7
29°40'43"
29°40'17"
29°39'51"
29°39'25"
29°38'59"
29°38'33"
29°38'07"
29°37'40"
95°00'38"
95°00'08"
94°59'38"
94°59'08"
94°58'38"
94°58'08"

1:24,000
1 in. = 2000 ft.
0
0.25
0.5
miles
N
SEE 4113 MAP
77520
TABBS BAY
ILFREYS ISLAND
HARRIS CO
CHAMBERS CO
CEDAR CROSSING INDUSTRIAL PARK
Levee
ATKINSON ISLAND
GALVESTON BAY
Levee
SEE 4252 MAP
SEE B MAP
29°40'43"
29°40'17"
29°39'51"
29°39'25"
29°38'59"
29°38'33"
29°38'07"
29°37'40"
94°58'08"
94°57'38"
94°57'08"
94°56'38"
94°56'08"
1
2
3
4
5
6
7
A
B
C
D
E

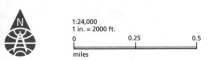

1:24,000
1 in. = 2000 ft.
0 0.25 0.5
miles

SEE 4114 MAP

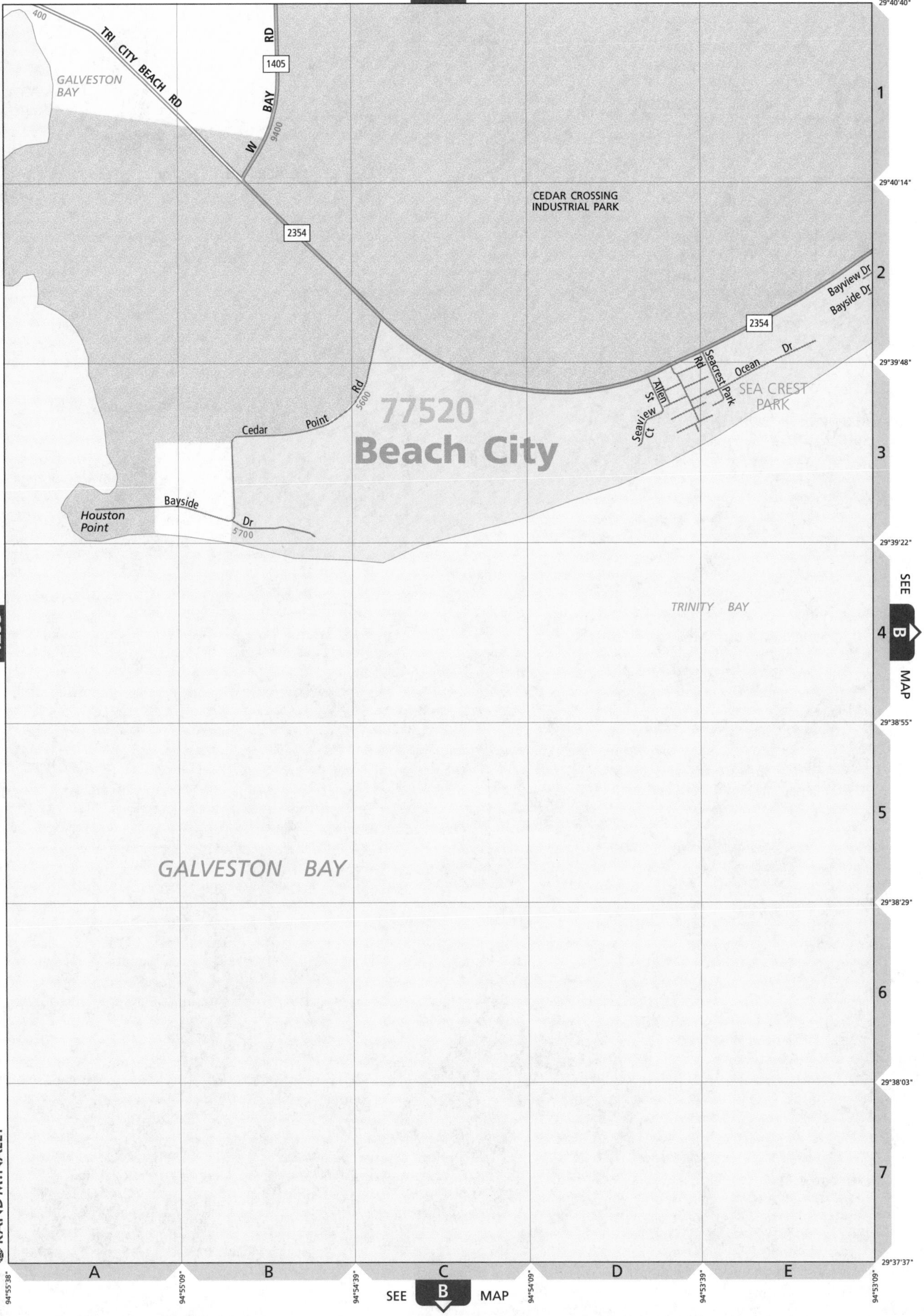
29°40'40"
29°40'14"
29°39'48"
29°39'22"
29°38'55"
29°38'29"
29°38'03"
29°37'37"
400
TRI CITY BEACH RD
RD
1405
GALVESTON BAY
W BAY
9400
CEDAR CROSSING
INDUSTRIAL PARK
2354
Bayview Dr
Bayside Dr
2354
Ocean Dr
Seacrest Park
Rd
Allen St
SEA CREST PARK
Seaview Ct
Rd
5600
77520
Beach City
Cedar Point
Bayside
Dr
5700
Houston Point
TRINITY BAY
GALVESTON BAY
1
2
3
4
5
6
7
A
B
C
D
E
94°55'38"
94°55'09"
94°54'39"
94°54'09"
94°53'39"
94°53'09"

SEE B MAP

SEE B MAP

1:24,000
1 in. = 2000 ft.
0 0.25 0.5
miles

SEE 4233 MAP

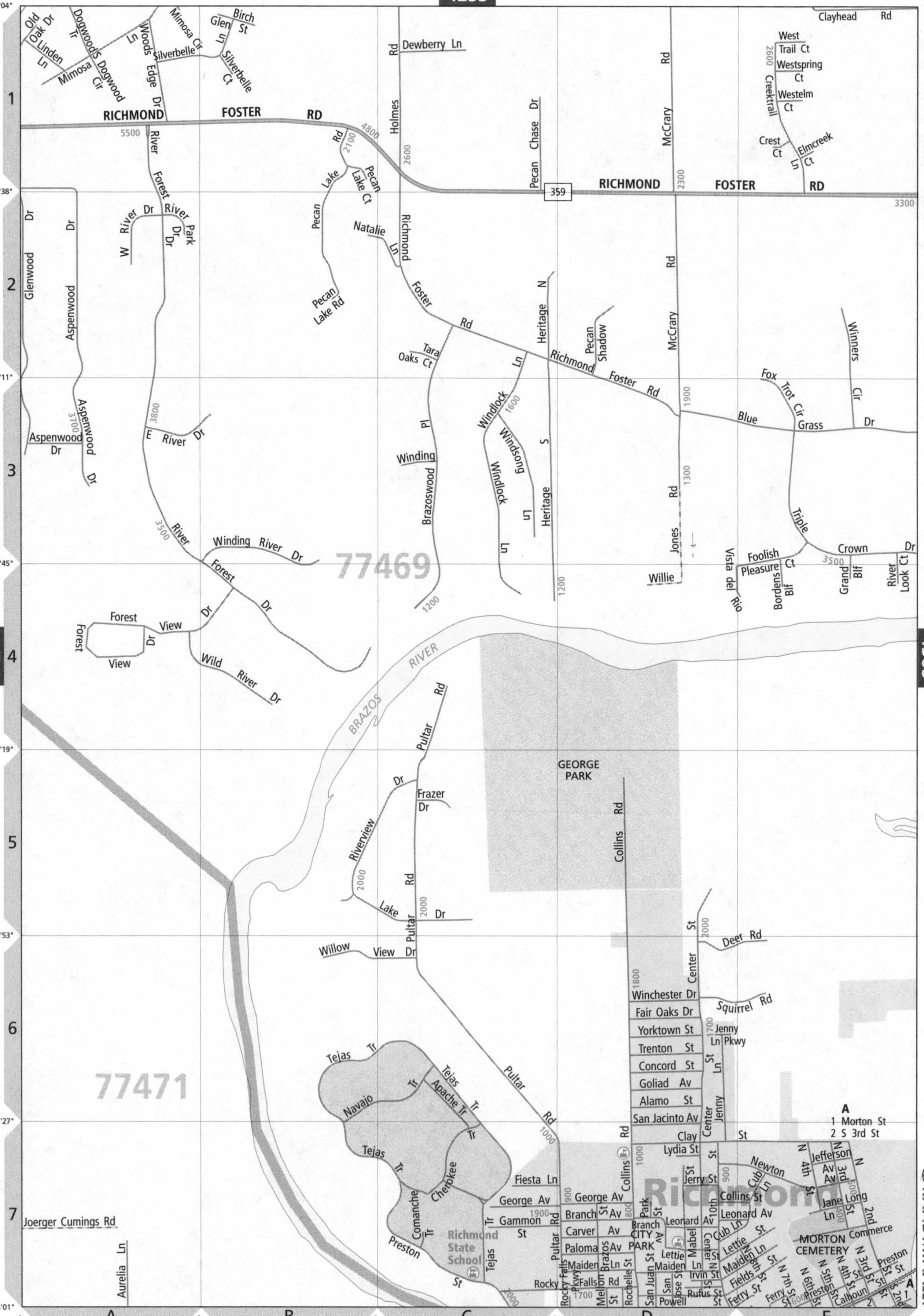
RICHMOND FOSTER RD
RICHMOND FOSTER RD
359
77469
77471
BRAZOS RIVER
GEORGE PARK
Richmond
Richmond State School
CITY PARK
MORTON CEMETERY
Old Oak Dr
Linden Ln
Dogwood Tr
Mimosa Ln
S Dogwood Cir
Woods Edge Dr
Silverbelle Ln
Mimosa Cir
Birch St
Glen Ln
Silverbelle Ct
Dewberry Ln
Holmes Rd
Pecan Chase Dr
McCrary Rd
Clayhead Rd
West Trail Ct
Westspring Ct
Westelm Ct
Creektrail
Crest Ct
Elmcreek Ct
Ln
River Forest Dr
Pecan Lake Rd
Pecan Lake Ct
Natalie Ln
Richmond Foster Rd
W River Dr
River Park Dr
Glenwood Dr
Aspenwood Dr
E River Dr
Tara Oaks Ct
Heritage N
Heritage S
Pecan Shadow
Windlock Ln
Windsong Ln
Winners Cir
Fox Trot Cir
Blue Grass Dr
Winding
Brazoswood Pl
Jones Rd
Triple Crown Dr
Foolish Pleasure Ct
Vista del Rio
Bordens Blf
Grand Blf
River Look Ct
Willie
Winding River Dr
Forest View Dr
Wild River Dr
Pultar Rd
Frazer Dr
Riverview Dr
Lake Dr
Willow View Dr
Collins Rd
Center St
Deer Rd
Squirrel Rd
Winchester Dr
Fair Oaks Dr
Yorktown St
Trenton St
Concord St
Goliad Av
Alamo St
San Jacinto Av
Jenny Ln
Jenny Pkwy
Clay St
Lydia St
Tejas Tr
Navajo Tr
Apache Tr
Cherokee Tr
Comanche Tr
Preston St
Fiesta Ln
George Av
Gammon St
Branch St
Carver Av
Paloma Av
Maiden Ln
Brazos St
Rocky Falls
Pkwy
Mellon St
Rd
Rochelle St
San Juan St
San Jose St
Powell
Park St
Leonard Av
Mabel Ln
Lettie
Irvin St
Rufus St
10th St
Jerry St
Collins St
Newton
Cub Ln
Fields
Ferry St
N 4th St
N 3rd St
N 2nd
Jefferson Av
Jane Ln
Long
Commerce
N 7th St
N 6th St
N 5th St
Calhoun
Preston St
Joerger Cumings Rd
Aurelia Ln
A
1 Morton St
2 S 3rd St
5500
4800
2100
2600
2300
3300
3800
3700
3500
1900
1600
1300
1200
2000
1800
1700
1000
900
800
600
400
500
29°38'04"
29°37'38"
29°37'11"
29°36'45"
29°36'19"
29°35'53"
29°35'27"
29°35'01"
95°48'03"
95°47'33"
95°47'03"
95°46'33"
95°46'03"
95°45'33"
1
2
3
4
5
6
7
A
B
C
D
E

SEE B MAP

SEE 4491 MAP

1:24,000
1 in. = 2000 ft.
0 0.25 0.5
miles

SEE 4234 MAP

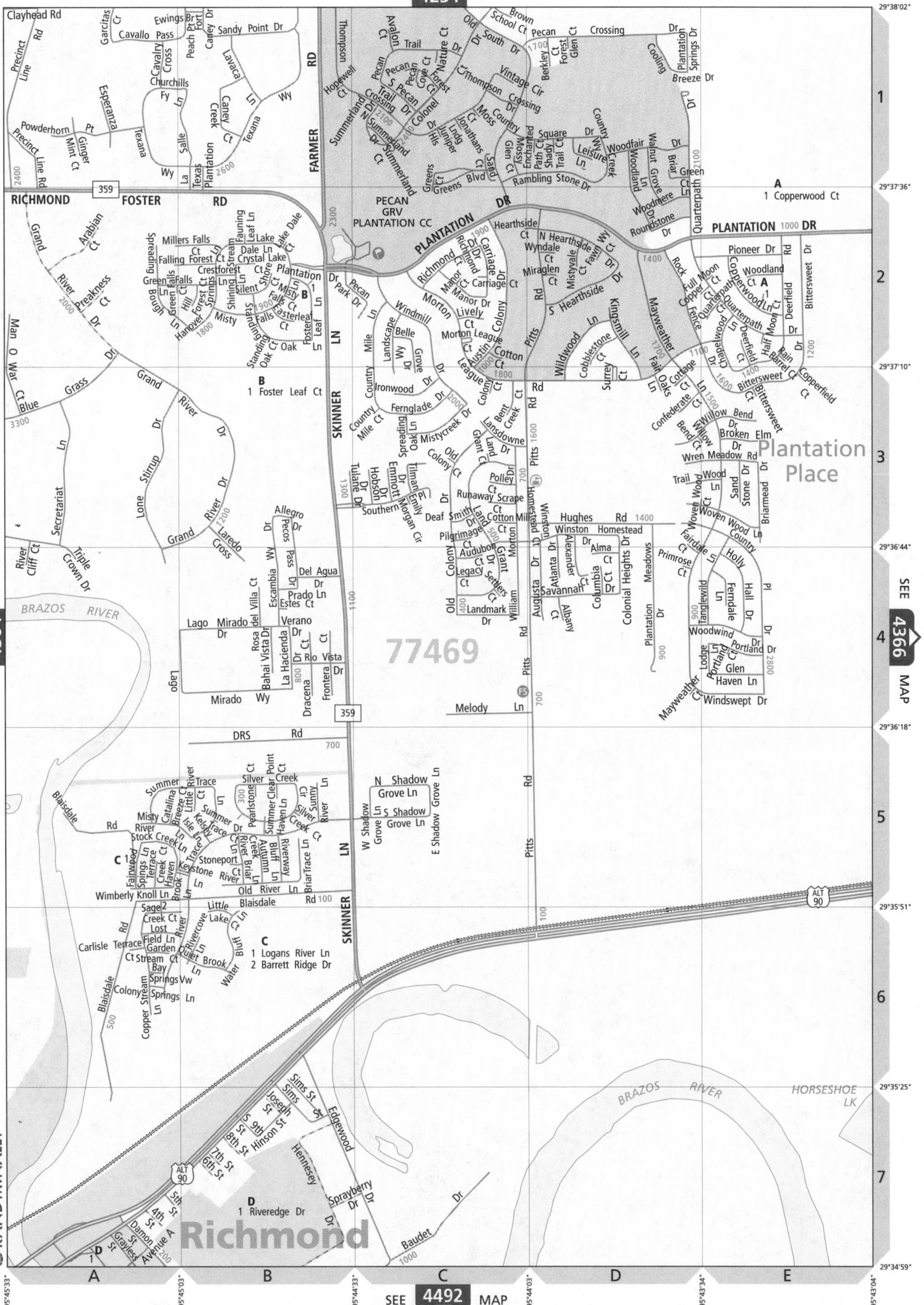
RICHMOND FOSTER RD
FARMER RD
SKINNER LN
PLANTATION DR
PECAN GRV PLANTATION CC
Plantation Place
77469
BRAZOS RIVER
HORSESHOE LK
Richmond
A
1 Copperwood Ct
B
1 Foster Leaf Ct
C
1 Logans River Ln
2 Barrett Ridge Dr
D
1 Riveredge Dr
Pitts Rd
Hughes Rd
DRS Rd
Blaisdale Rd
Melody Ln
Grand River Dr
Clayhead Rd
Sandy Point Dr
359
ALT 90
29°38'02"
29°37'36"
29°37'10"
29°36'44"
29°36'18"
29°35'51"
29°35'25"
29°34'59"
95°45'33"
95°45'03"
95°44'33"
95°44'03"
95°43'34"
95°43'04"
A
B
C
D
E
1
2
3
4
5
6
7

SEE 4366 MAP

SEE 4492 MAP

1:24,000
1 in. = 2000 ft.
0 0.25 0.5
miles

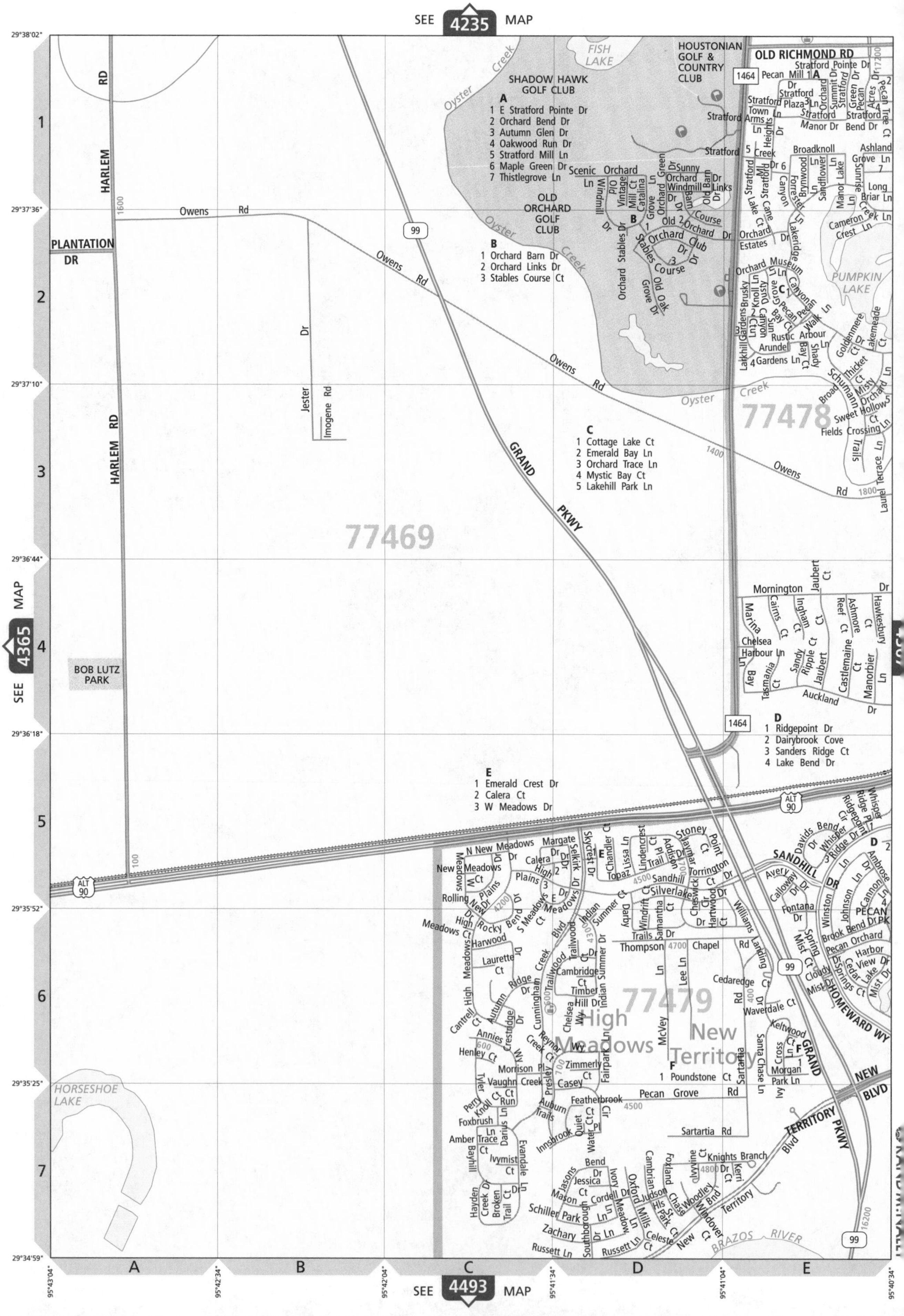
SEE 4235 MAP
SEE 4365 MAP
SEE 4493 MAP
29°38'02"
29°37'36"
29°37'10"
29°36'44"
29°36'18"
29°35'52"
29°35'25"
29°34'59"
95°43'04"
95°42'34"
95°42'04"
95°41'34"
95°41'04"
95°40'34"
A
B
C
D
E
1
2
3
4
5
6
7
HARLEM RD
PLANTATION DR
Owens Rd
Jester Dr
Imogene Rd
GRAND PKWY
99
1464
ALT 90
OLD RICHMOND RD
FISH LAKE
HOUSTONIAN GOLF & COUNTRY CLUB
SHADOW HAWK GOLF CLUB
OLD ORCHARD GOLF CLUB
Oyster Creek
PUMPKIN LAKE
BOB LUTZ PARK
HORSESHOE LAKE
BRAZOS RIVER
77469
77478
77479
High Meadows
New Territory
SANDHILL DR
HOMEWARD WY
NEW TERRITORY BLVD
PECAN PK
A
1 E Stratford Pointe Dr
2 Orchard Bend Dr
3 Autumn Glen Dr
4 Oakwood Run Dr
5 Stratford Mill Ln
6 Maple Green Dr
7 Thistlegrove Ln
B
1 Orchard Barn Dr
2 Orchard Links Dr
3 Stables Course Ct
C
1 Cottage Lake Ct
2 Emerald Bay Ln
3 Orchard Trace Ln
4 Mystic Bay Ct
5 Lakehill Park Ln
D
1 Ridgepoint Dr
2 Dairybrook Cove
3 Sanders Ridge Ct
4 Lake Bend Dr
E
1 Emerald Crest Dr
2 Calera Ct
3 W Meadows Dr
F
1 Poundstone Ct
Mornington
Auckland
Thompson
Chapel
Pecan Grove Rd
Sartartia Rd
Knights Branch
Zachary
Russett Ln

1:24,000
1 in. = 2000 ft.
0 0.25 0.5
miles

SEE 4236 MAP

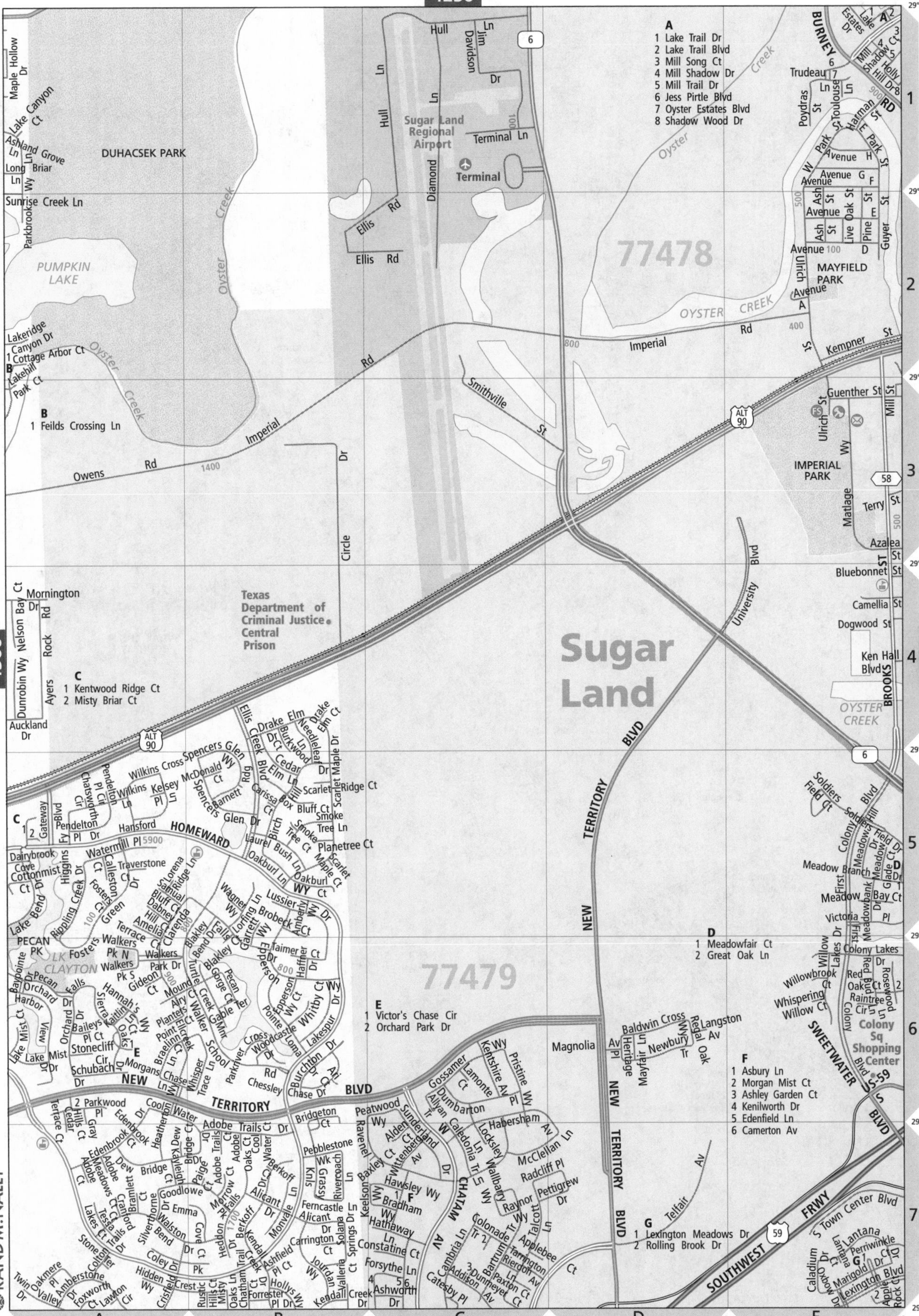
Sugar Land
77478
77479
Sugar Land Regional Airport
Terminal
DUHACSEK PARK
PUMPKIN LAKE
MAYFIELD PARK
IMPERIAL PARK
Texas Department of Criminal Justice Central Prison
Colony Sq Shopping Center
LK CLAYTON
PECAN PK
OYSTER CREEK
Imperial Rd
Owens Rd
Circle Dr
University Blvd
NEW TERRITORY BLVD
HOMEWARD WY
SWEETWATER BLVD
SOUTHWEST FRWY
BROOKS ST
BURNEY RD
Kempner St
Guenther St
Mill St
Terminal Ln
Ellis Rd
Smithville St
Magnolia Av
Baldwin Cross
Langston Av
Telfair Av
Town Center Blvd
Colony Lakes Dr
Soldiers Field Blvd
Ken Hall Blvd
A
1 Lake Trail Dr
2 Lake Trail Blvd
3 Mill Song Ct
4 Mill Shadow Dr
5 Mill Trail Dr
6 Jess Pirtle Blvd
7 Oyster Estates Blvd
8 Shadow Wood Dr
B
1 Feilds Crossing Ln
C
1 Kentwood Ridge Ct
2 Misty Briar Ct
D
1 Meadowfair Ct
2 Great Oak Ln
E
1 Victor's Chase Cir
2 Orchard Park Dr
F
1 Asbury Ln
2 Morgan Mist Ct
3 Ashley Garden Ct
4 Kenilworth Dr
5 Edenfield Ln
6 Camerton Av
G
1 Lexington Meadows Dr
2 Rolling Brook Dr
29°38'01"
29°37'34"
29°37'08"
29°36'42"
29°36'16"
29°35'50"
29°35'24"
29°34'58"
95°40'34"
95°40'04"
95°39'34"
95°39'04"
95°38'34"
95°38'04"
A B C D E
1 2 3 4 5 6 7

SEE 4368 MAP

SEE 4494 MAP

1:24,000
1 in. = 2000 ft.
0 0.25 0.5
miles

N

SEE 4237 MAP

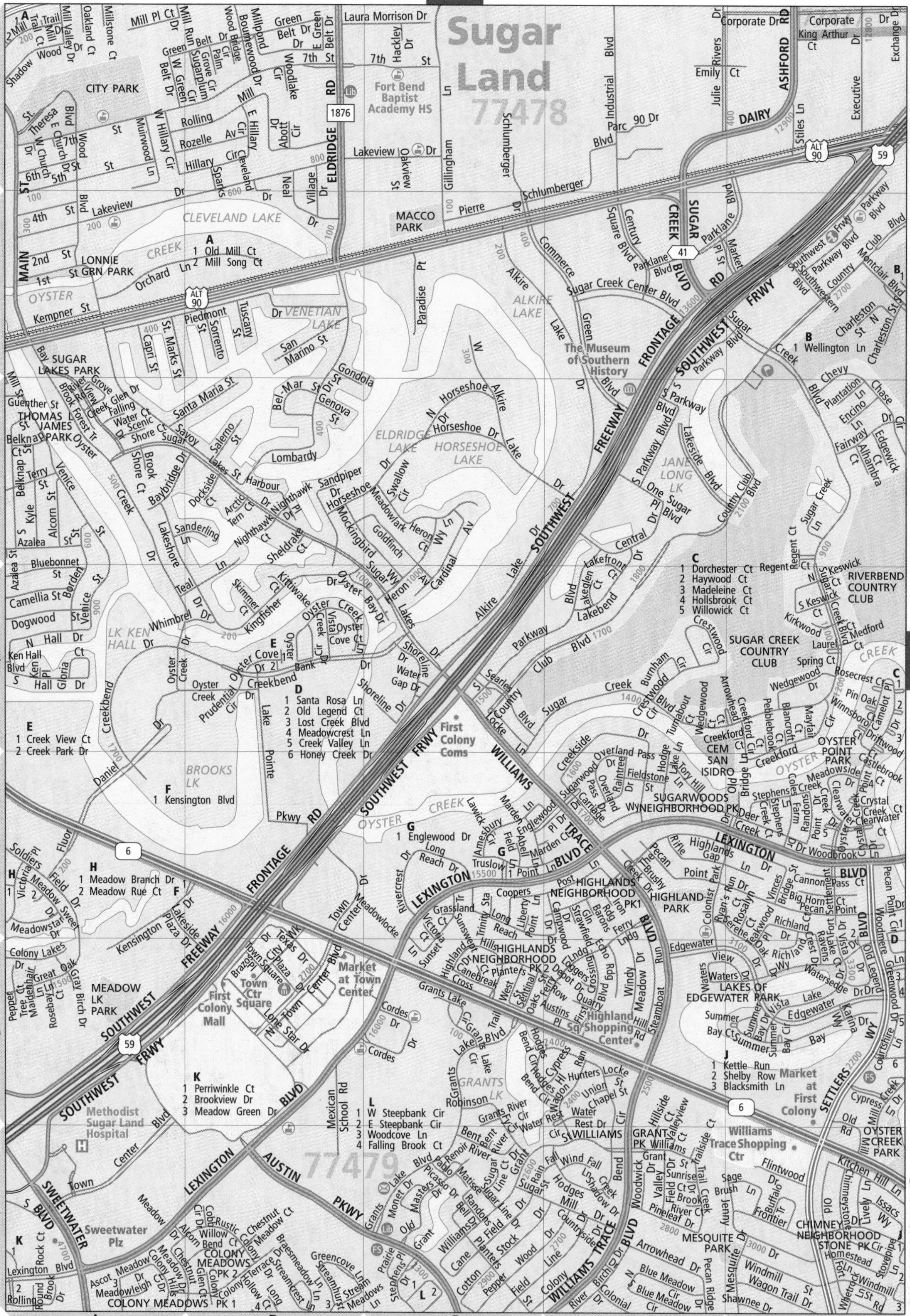
Sugar Land
77478
77479
CITY PARK
Fort Bend Baptist Academy HS
CLEVELAND LAKE
MACCO PARK
LONNIE GRN PARK
OYSTER CREEK
VENETIAN LAKE
SUGAR LAKES PARK
THOMAS L JAMES PARK
ELDRIDGE LAKE
HORSESHOE LAKE
ALKIRE LAKE
The Museum of Southern History
JANE LONG LK
RIVERBEND COUNTRY CLUB
SUGAR CREEK COUNTRY CLUB
LK KEN HALL
BROOKS LK
First Colony Coms
CEM SAN ISIDRO
OYSTER POINT PARK
SUGARWOODS NEIGHBORHOOD PK
HIGHLANDS NEIGHBORHOOD PK1
HIGHLAND PARK
HIGHLANDS NEIGHBORHOOD PK 2
LAKES OF EDGEWATER PARK
Highland Sq Shopping Center
Market at Town Center
First Colony Mall
Town Ctr Square
MEADOW LK PARK
Methodist Sugar Land Hospital
Sweetwater Plz
GRANTS LK
GRANT PK
Williams Trace Shopping Ctr
Market at First Colony
OYSTER CREEK PARK
CHIMNEY STONE NEIGHBORHOOD PK
MESQUITE PARK
COLONY MEADOWS PK 2
COLONY MEADOWS PK 1
SOUTHWEST FRWY
SOUTHWEST FREEWAY
FRONTAGE RD
ELDRIDGE RD
DAIRY ASHFORD RD
SUGAR CREEK BLVD
LEXINGTON BLVD
WILLIAMS TRACE BLVD
AUSTIN PKWY
SWEETWATER BLVD
SETTLERS WY
MAIN ST
1876
ALT 90
59
41
6
A
1 Old Mill Ct
2 Mill Song Ct
B
1 Wellington Ln
C
1 Dorchester Ct
2 Haywood Ct
3 Madeleine Ct
4 Hollsbrook Ct
5 Willowick Ct
D
1 Santa Rosa Ln
2 Old Legend Ct
3 Lost Creek Blvd
4 Meadowcrest Ln
5 Creek Valley Ln
6 Honey Creek Dr
E
1 Creek View Ct
2 Creek Park Dr
F
1 Kensington Blvd
G
1 Englewood Dr
H
1 Meadow Branch Dr
2 Meadow Rue Ct
J
1 Kettle Run
2 Shelby Row
3 Blacksmith Ln
K
1 Perriwinkle Ct
2 Brookview Dr
3 Meadow Green Dr
L
1 W Steepbank Cir
2 E Steepbank Cir
3 Woodcove Ln
4 Falling Brook Ct
29°38'01"
29°37'34"
29°37'08"
29°36'42"
29°36'16"
29°35'50"
29°35'24"
29°34'58"
95°38'04"
95°37'34"
95°37'05"
95°36'35"
95°36'05"
95°35'35"
A B C D E
1 2 3 4 5 6 7

SEE 4367 MAP

SEE 4495 MAP

1:24,000
1 in. = 2000 ft.
0 0.25 0.5
miles

SEE 4238 MAP

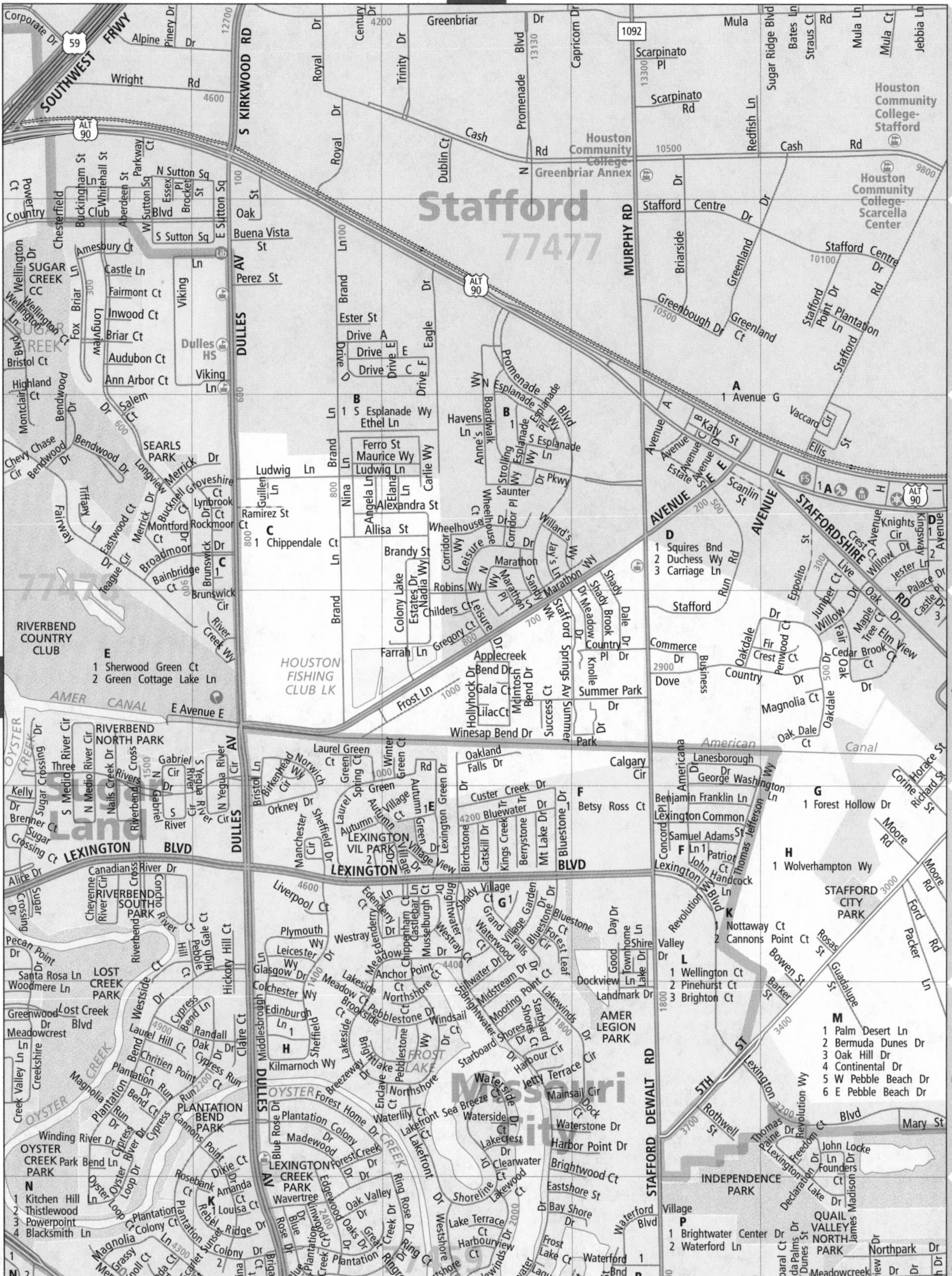
Stafford
77477
77478
Sugar Land
Missouri City
77459
SOUTHWEST FRWY
59
ALT 90
1092
6
3345
Corporate Dr
Alpine Dr
Pinery Dr
Wright Rd
4600
12700
S KIRKWOOD RD
Royal Dr
Century Dr
4200
Greenbriar Dr
Trinity Dr
Promenade Blvd
13130
Capricorn Dr
Scarpinato Pl
Scarpinato Rd
13300
Mula Rd
Sugar Ridge Blvd
Bates Ln
Straus Ct
Mula Ln
Mula Ct
Jebbia Ln
Redfish Ln
Houston Community College-Stafford
Cash Rd
10500
9800
Houston Community College-Greenbriar Annex
Houston Community College-Scarcella Center
Dublin Ct
Power Ct
Country Club Blvd
Chesterfield
Buckingham St
Whitehall St
Aberdeen St
Parkway Ct
N Sutton Sq
Essex Pl
Brocket St
W Sutton Sq
S Sutton Sq
E Sutton Sq
Oak St
Buena Vista St
MURPHY RD
Stafford Centre Dr
Briarside Dr
Greenland Dr
Greenland Ct
Greenbough Dr
Stafford Point Dr
Plantation Ln
Stafford Rd
10100
Wellington Dr
Amesbury Ct
Castle Ln
Fairmont Ct
Inwood Ct
Briar Ct
Audubon Ct
Ann Arbor Ct
SUGAR CREEK CC
Wellington Ct
Fox Briar Ln
Longview
Viking Ln
Dulles HS
Perez St
DULLES AV
Brand Ln
Ester St
Drive A
Drive E
Drive C
Drive D
Drive F
Eagle Dr
Bristol Ct
Highland Ct
Montclair Ct
Bendwood Dr
Salem Ct
Chevy Chase Cir
SEARLS PARK
Merrick Dr
Groveshire Ct
Lynbrook Ct
Rockmoor Ct
Montford Ct
Broadmoor
Bainbridge Ct
Brunswick Dr
Brunswick Cir
Tiffany Ln
Fairway
Eastwood Ct
Teague Cir
River Creek Wy
Ludwig Ln
Guillen Ln
Ramirez St
1 Chippendale Ct
Nina Ln
Angela Ln
Elena Ln
Ferro St
Maurice Wy
Ludwig Ln
Alexandra St
Carlie Wy
Allisa St
Brandy St
Colony Lake
Estates Dr
Nadia Wy
1 S Esplanade Wy
Ethel Ln
Havens Ln
Anne's Boardwalk
Promenade Blvd
Esplanade Wy
S Esplanade
Strolling Wy
Saunter
Willard's Wy
Wheelhouse Dr
Corridor Wy
Leisure Wy
Marathon Wy
Robins Wy
Childers Ct
Gregory Ct
Jay's Ln
Stafford Springs Av
Shady Brook Ln
Shady Dale Dr
Meadow Dr
Country Pl
Knolle Dr
Summer Park Dr
Farrah Ln
Frost Ln
Applecreek Bend Dr
Gala Ct
LilacCt
Mdntosh Bend Dr
Success Ct
Winesap Bend Dr
Hollyhock Dr
HOUSTON FISHING CLUB LK
AVENUE E
Avenue G
Avenue A
Avenue B
Avenue C
Estate Avenue
Katy St
Scanlin St
Vaccaro Cir
Ellis St
STAFFORDSHIRE RD
AVENUE F
1 Squires Bnd
2 Duchess Wy
3 Carriage Ln
Run Rd
Stafford
Eppolito St
Commerce Dr
2900
Dove
Business
Oakdale Dr
Country
Fir Crest Ct
Penwood Ct
Cedar Brook Ct
Fair Oak
Jumper Ct
Willow Dr
Maple Tree Ct
Elm View
Knights Cir
Kingsway
Jester Ln
Palace Dr
Castle Dr
Magnolia Ct
Oak Dale Ct
RIVERBEND COUNTRY CLUB
1 Sherwood Green Ct
2 Green Cottage Lake Ln
AMER CANAL
E Avenue E
RIVERBEND NORTH PARK
Oyster Creek Dr
Sugar Crossing
Three Rivers
S Medio River Cir
N Medio River Cir
Nails Creek Dr
Rivers Cross
Gabriel Cir
S Gabriel
N Gabriel
S Yegua River Cir
N Yegua River Cir
Kelly
Brenner Ct
Sugar Crossing Ct
LEXINGTON BLVD
Bristol Ln
Birkenhead Wy
Norwich Cir
Orkney Dr
Laurel Green Ct
Winter Green Ct
Laurel Spring Ct
Oakland Falls Dr
Custer Creek Dr
Bluewater Tr
Calgary Cir
Manchester Cir
Sheffield Dr
Autumn Village
LEXINGTON VIL PARK
Lexington Green Dr
Birchstone Dr
Catskill Dr
Kings Creek
Berrystone Dr
Mt Lake Dr
Bluestone Dr
1 Betsy Ross Ct
American Canal
Lanesborough
George Washington Ln
Benjamin Franklin Ln
Lexington Common
Samuel Adams St
Patriot Ct
Thomas Jefferson
John Handcock
Lexington Blvd
Concord Pl
1 Forest Hollow Dr
Horace St
Corine St
Richard St
Moore Rd
1 Wolverhampton Wy
STAFFORD CITY PARK
3000
Ford Rd
Packer Rd
Canadian River Dr
Concho River Dr
Alice Dr
Cheyenne River
RIVERBEND SOUTH PARK
Riverbend Cross
Hill Ct
Pebble Ct
High Gale Ct
Hickory Hill Ct
Liverpool Ct
4600
Plymouth
Leicester Wy
Glasgow Wy
Colchester Wy
Edinburgh Ln
Kilmarnoch Wy
Middlesbrough Ct
Westray
Anchor Point
Northshore
Pebblestone Dr
Windsail
Stillwater Dr
Midstream Dr
Mooring Point Ct
Lakewinds
Brightwater
Shady Village
Grand Falls
Village Garden
Bluestone Ct
Forest Leaf
Day Dr
Good
Townhome Ln
Shire Ct
Valley Dr
Dockview Ln
Landmark Dr
AMER LEGION PARK
Revolution Wy
1 Nottaway Ct
2 Cannons Point Ct
1 Wellington Ct
2 Pinehurst Ct
3 Brighton Ct
Bowen St
Barker St
Rosas St
Guadalupe St
Lexington
1 Palm Desert Ln
2 Bermuda Dunes Dr
3 Oak Hill Dr
4 Continental Dr
5 W Pebble Beach Dr
6 E Pebble Beach Dr
Pecan Point Dr
Santa Rosa Ln
Woodmere Ln
LOST CREEK PARK
Westside Ct
Greenwood Ct
Lost Creek Blvd
Meadowcrest Dr
Creekshire Ln
Creek Valley Ln
Cypress Bend Ln
Randall Ct
Laurel Hill Ct
Chritien Point Ct
Cypress Run
Oak Ct
Claire Ct
Sheffield
Magnolia Plantation
PLANTATION BEND PARK
Winding River Dr
OYSTER CREEK Park Bend Ln
OYSTER CREEK PARK
1 Kitchen Hill Ln
2 Thistlewood
3 Powerpoint
4 Blacksmith Ln
Cannons Point
Dixie Ct
Amanda
Louisa Ct
Rosebank Ct
Rebel Ridge Dr
Plantation Colony Ct
Scarlet Sunset Ct
Magnolia
Grassy Knoll Ct
Merriweather
Smada Ct
Tarlton
STAFFORD DEWALT RD
1800
2400
Waterford Blvd
Village
1 Brightwater Center Dr
2 Waterford Ln
INDEPENDENCE PARK
Thomas Paine
Freedom Ct
John Locke
Founders Ct
Declaration
Lake Dr
James Madison
QUAIL VALLEY NORTH PARK
Northpark Dr
Meadowcreek
Springhill
Greenridge
Ashmont
Valleyview Dr
N Pebble Beach Dr
3200
3300
Rothwell St
5TH ST
3700
Mary St
Blvd
Plantation Colony
Blue Rose Dr
Madewood
Forest Creek
LEXINGTON CREEK PARK
Wavertree
Edgewood
Oak Valley
Oaks Dr
Ring Rose Dr
Lakefront
Waterlily Ct
Sea Breeze
Waterside Dr
Lakecrest Dr
Clearwater
Shoreline Ct
Lakewood
Lake Terrace Ct
Harbouryiew
Westshore
Tradewinds Dr
Reflection Ct
Dockside Ct
Brightwood Ct
Eastshore St
Bay Shore Dr
Harbor Point Dr
Waterstone Dr
Mainsail Cir
Jetty Terrace Cir
Harbour Cir
Starboard Shores Dr
Frost Lake Ct
Laguna Cir
Waterview Ct
Waterford Bnd
Waterford Park St
Waterford Village Blvd
Warwick
Baron Ln
Pinehurst Ln
T Huxley Ln
Windsor Ct
Barcelona Ct
Chapparal Ct
Bermuda Palms Dr
Bermuda Dunes St
Bermuda Shores
QUAILVALLEY CC
Brigade
Justina
Cartwright Rd
Plantation Tr
Hidden Knoll Ct
Gray Moss Ct
Frost St
Connie's Ct
Kellyway
Gregway
Colonial Lakes Cory Ct
Cheryl Ct
Admiral
CARTWRIGHT RD
Ringrose
Frontier Dr
Kettle Run
Oil Field Rd
Shelby Row
Lakefield
Rainbow Run
Sky Sunshine Dr
Sea Breeze Ct
Lakeside Ct
Brookside
Brightlake
Enclave Ct
Breezeway
FROST LAKE
Edenderry
Meadow Ct
Chippenham Ct
Castlebar Dr
Musselburgh Ct
Brightwater Dr
A B C D E
1 2 3 4 5 6 7

SEE 4370 MAP

SEE 4496 MAP

1:24,000
1 in. = 2000 ft.
0 0.25 0.5
miles

SEE 4239 MAP

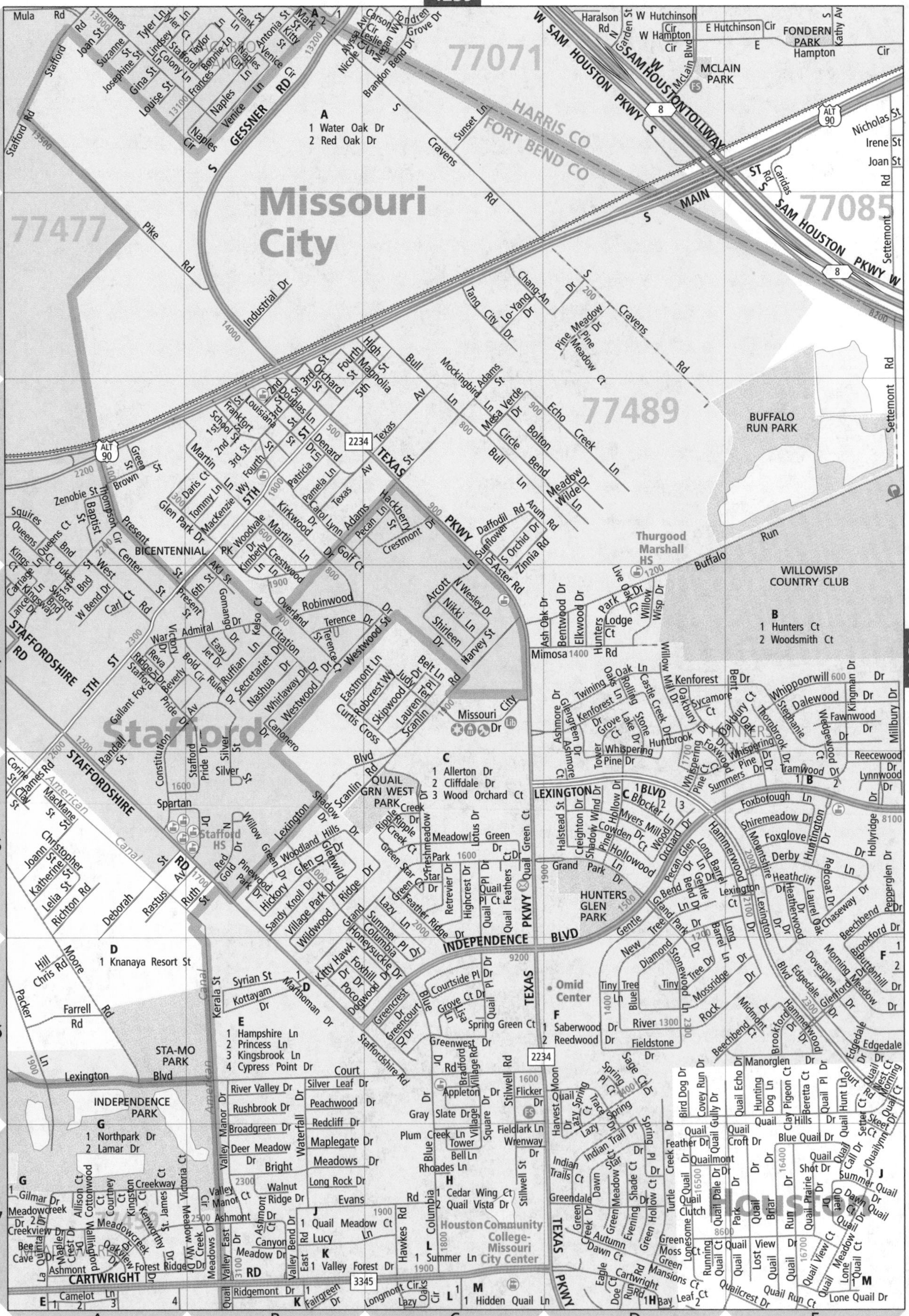
Missouri City
Stafford
Houston
77071
77477
77489
77085
HARRIS CO
FORT BEND CO
S GESSNER RD
S MAIN ST
W SAM HOUSTON PKWY S
SAM HOUSTON TOLLWAY
S SAM HOUSTON PKWY W
TEXAS PKWY
STAFFORDSHIRE RD
5TH ST
CARTWRIGHT RD
INDEPENDENCE BLVD
LEXINGTON BLVD
BICENTENNIAL PK
MCLAIN PARK
FONDERN PARK
BUFFALO RUN PARK
WILLOWISP COUNTRY CLUB
Thurgood Marshall HS
Stafford HS
QUAIL GRN WEST PARK
HUNTERS GLEN PARK
INDEPENDENCE PARK
STA-MO PARK
Omid Center
Houston Community College-Missouri City Center
American Canal
A
1 Water Oak Dr
2 Red Oak Dr
B
1 Hunters Ct
2 Woodsmith Ct
C
1 Allerton Dr
2 Cliffdale Dr
3 Wood Orchard Ct
D
1 Knanaya Resort St
E
1 Hampshire Ln
2 Princess Ln
3 Kingsbrook Ln
4 Cypress Point Dr
F
1 Saberwood Dr
2 Reedwood Dr
G
1 Northpark Dr
2 Lamar Dr
H
1 Cedar Wing Ct
2 Quail Vista Dr
K
1 Valley Forest Dr
L
1 Summer Ln
M
1 Hidden Quail Ln
29°37'59"
29°37'33"
29°37'07"
29°36'40"
29°36'14"
29°35'48"
29°35'22"
29°34'56"
95°33'05"
95°32'35"
95°32'05"
95°31'35"
95°31'05"
95°30'36"
1
2
3
4
5
6
7
A
B
C
D
E

SEE 4369 MAP

SEE 4497 MAP

1:24,000
1 in. = 2000 ft.
0 0.25 0.5
miles

SEE 4240 MAP

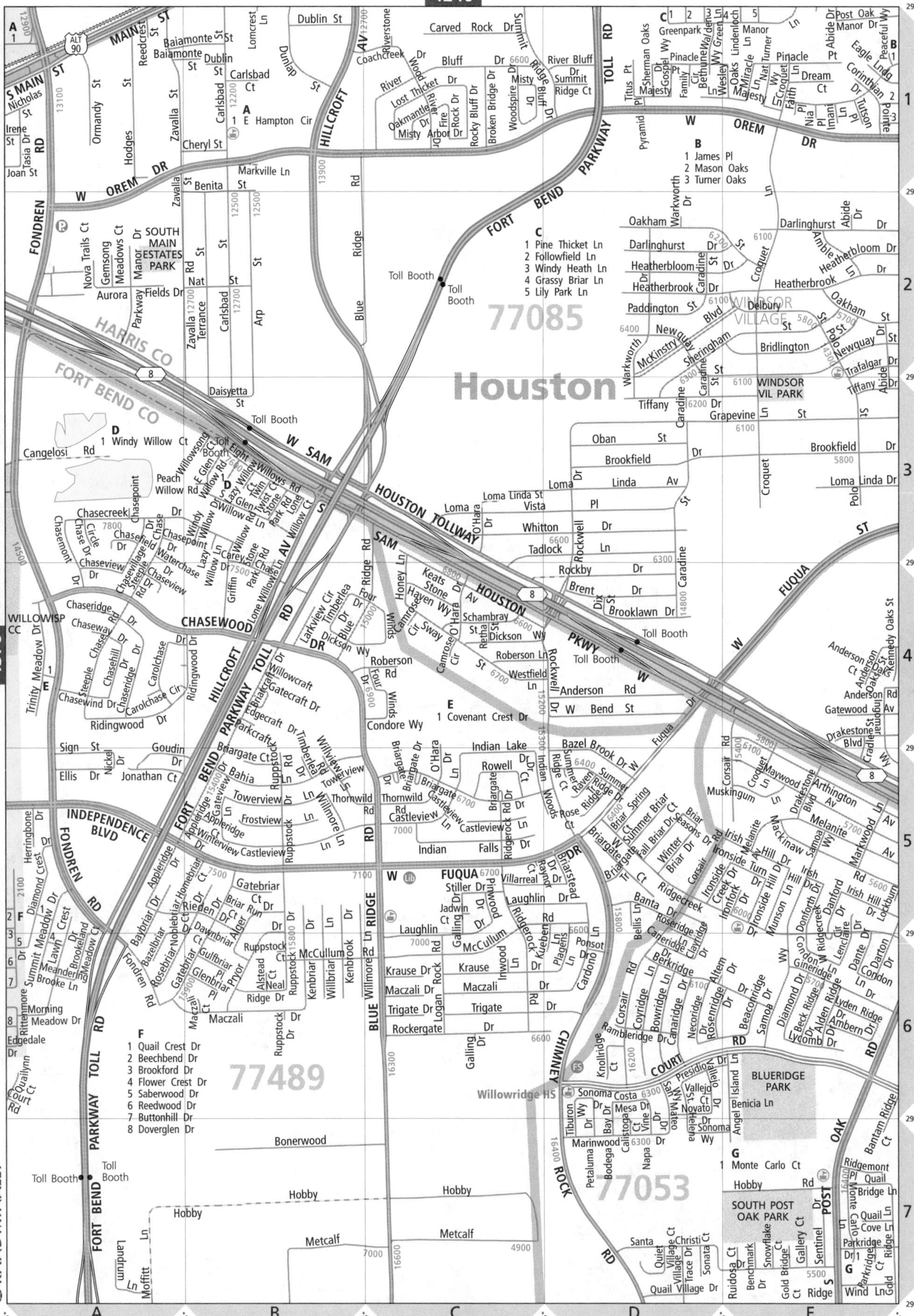
Houston
77085
77489
77053
HARRIS CO
FORT BEND CO
W SAM HOUSTON TOLLWAY
W SAM HOUSTON PKWY
FORT BEND PARKWAY TOLL RD
HILLCROFT AV
FONDREN RD
W OREM DR
S MAIN ST
MAIN ST
ALT 90
W FUQUA ST
INDEPENDENCE BLVD
CHASEWOOD DR
BLUE RIDGE RD
CHIMNEY ROCK RD
COURT RD
POST OAK RD
SOUTH MAIN ESTATES PARK
WINDSOR VILLAGE
WINDSOR VIL PARK
BLUERIDGE PARK
SOUTH POST OAK PARK
WILLOWISP CC
Willowridge HS
Toll Booth
A 1 E Hampton Cir
B 1 James Pl 2 Mason Oaks 3 Turner Oaks
C 1 Pine Thicket Ln 2 Followfield Ln 3 Windy Heath Ln 4 Grassy Briar Ln 5 Lily Park Ln
D 1 Windy Willow Ct
E 1 Covenant Crest Dr
F 1 Quail Crest Dr 2 Beechbend Dr 3 Brookford Dr 4 Flower Crest Dr 5 Saberwood Dr 6 Reedwood Dr 7 Buttonhill Dr 8 Doverglen Dr
G 1 Monte Carlo Ct
Dublin St
Carved Rock Dr
Bluff Dr
River Bluff Dr
Summit Ridge Ct
Carlsbad Ct
Cheryl St
Markville Ln
Benita St
Oakham Dr
Darlinghurst Dr
Heatherbloom Dr
Heatherbrook Dr
Paddington St
Newquay St
Bridlington
Tiffany Dr
Grapevine Ln
Oban St
Brookfield Dr
Loma Linda Av
Whitton Dr
Tadlock Ln
Rockby Dr
Brent Dr
Brooklawn Dr
Anderson Rd
Bend St
Indian Lake Dr
Rowell Dr
Castleview Ln
Indian Falls Dr
Laughlin Dr
McCullum Ln
Krause Dr
Maczali Dr
Trigate Dr
Rockergate Dr
Bonerwood
Hobby
Metcalf
Landrum Ln
Moffitt Ln
Cangelosi Rd
Chasecreek Dr
Chaseridge Dr
Chasewind Dr
Ridingwood Dr
Sign St
Ellis Dr
Jonathan Ct
Goudin Dr
Aurora Fields Dr
Roberson Rd
Condore Wy
Bazel Brook Dr
Muskingum Ln
Melanite Wy
Banta Dr
Ridgecreek Dr
Rambleridge Dr
Sonoma Costa
Marinwood Dr
Santa Christi Ct
Quail Village Dr
Benicia Ln
S Ridge
Wind Ln

SEE 4372 MAP

SEE 4498 MAP

1:24,000
1 in. = 2000 ft.
0 0.25 0.5
miles

SEE 4241 MAP

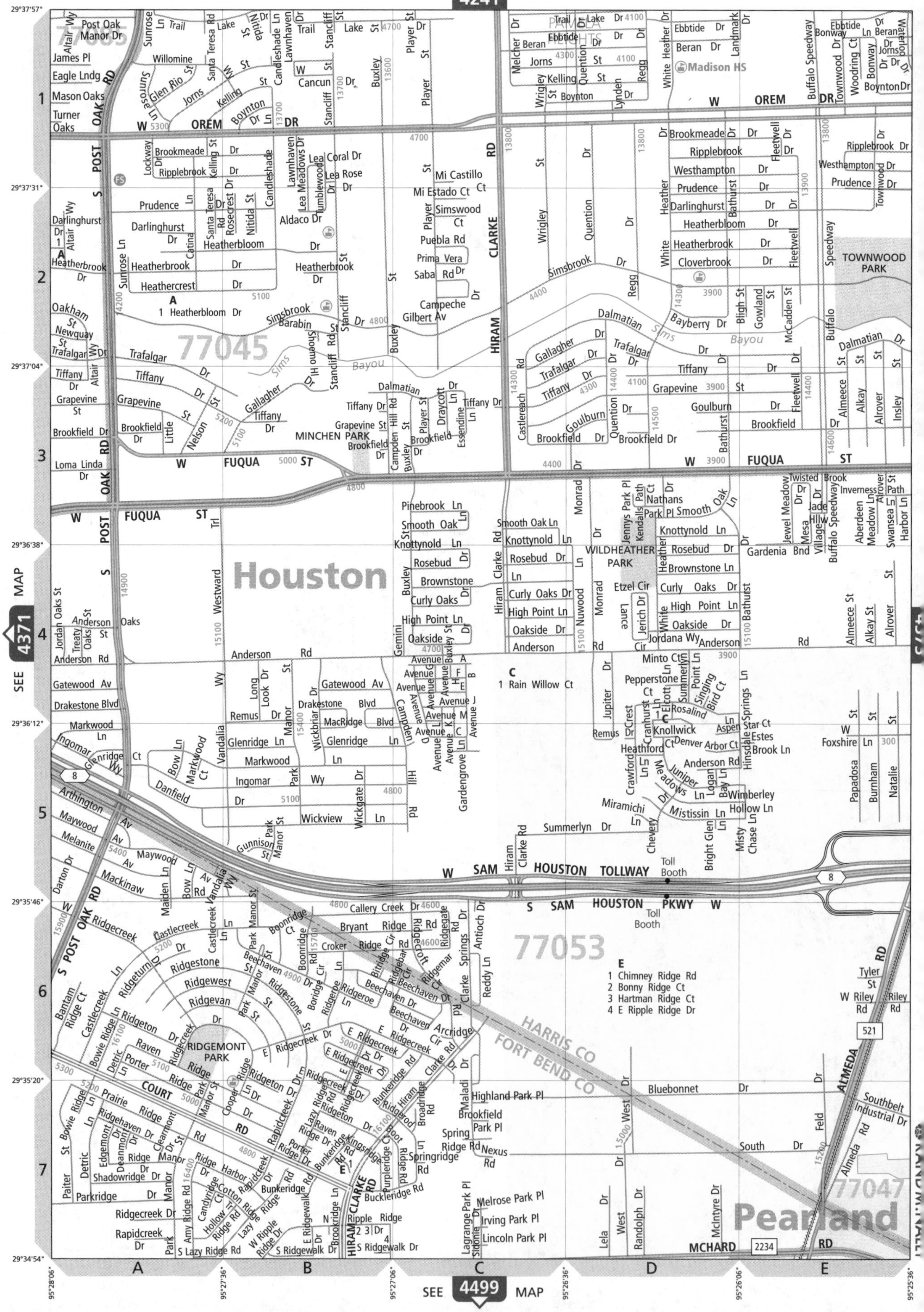
Houston
77045
77053
77047
77085
Pearland
W OREM DR
W FUQUA ST
S POST OAK RD
HIRAM CLARKE RD
W SAM HOUSTON TOLLWAY
S SAM HOUSTON PKWY W
Toll Booth
COURT RD
ALMEDA RD
MCHARD RD
Anderson Rd
Sims Bayou
Madison HS
TOWNWOOD PARK
MINCHEN PARK
WILDHEATHER PARK
RIDGEMONT PARK
HARRIS CO
FORT BEND CO
Buffalo Speedway
Westward
Bluebonnet Dr
Southbelt Industrial Dr
A
1 Heatherbloom Dr
C
1 Rain Willow Ct
E
1 Chimney Ridge Rd
2 Bonny Ridge Ct
3 Hartman Ridge Ct
4 E Ripple Ridge Dr
8
521
2234
1
2
3
4
5
6
7
A
B
C
D
E
29°37'57"
29°37'31"
29°37'04"
29°36'38"
29°36'12"
29°35'46"
29°35'20"
29°34'54"
95°28'06"
95°27'36"
95°27'06"
95°26'36"
95°26'06"
95°25'36"

SEE 4371 MAP

SEE 4499 MAP

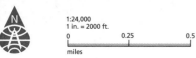

1:24,000
1 in. = 2000 ft.
0 0.25 0.5
miles

SEE 4242 MAP

77045
77051
77053
77047
77584
Houston
Pearland
W OREM DR
ALMEDA RD
ALMEDA GENOA RD
W FUQUA ST
ALMEDA SCHOOL RD
S SAM HOUSTON PKWY W
W SAM HOUSTON TOLLWAY
Sam Houston Southwest Toll Plaza
Toll Booth
WHITE RD
FELLOWS RD
Fellows Rd
Anderson Rd
Riley Rd
Fruge Rd
KIRBY DR
Hooper Rd
Del Papa St
Labrador Rd
Chris Rd
KINGSLEY DR
SOUTH FRWY
South Freeway Service Dr
Sims Bayou
Clear Creek
HARRIS CO
BRAZORIA CO
TOWNWOOD PARK
CANTERBURY VILLAGE PARK
ALMEDA PARK
BETH JACOB CEM
ALMEDA
A
1 Tidewater Dr
B
1 City Park Wy
2 Parc Monceau Ln
C
1 Bell Manor Ct
2 Highbury View Ct
3 Seagler Park Ln
4 Belvedere Park Ct
D
1 Fellows
Robin Blvd
Amelia Dr
Kilkenny Dr
Canterview Dr
Bayswater Dr
Elaine Rd
Anagnost Rd
Karalis Rd
Karalas Ln
Caribe Ln
Briggs Rd
Lew Briggs Rd
McGrath Dr
Van Cleve St
Janbar Rd
Schurmier Rd
Betty Sue Ln
Danfield Dr
Foxshire St
Broadhurst St
Grammar Rd
Southbelt Industrial Dr
Nautique Wy
Jersey Shore Dr
Commercial Rd
Bridgeport Rd
Cardiff Cliff Ln
Waterloo Dr
Gumas St
Ward St
Insley St
Industry St
Elmfield
Brookfield Dr
Goulburn Dr
Junction Dr
Ripplebrook Dr
Westhampton Dr
Prudence Dr
Ebbtide Dr
Jorns Dr
Kelling St
Boynton Dr
Steelhead
Umiak Dr
Meiko Dr
Knotty Oaks Dr
Tandy Park Wy
Cogburn Dr
Lingard Park Ct
Creegan Park Ct
Fergus Park Ct
Cressey Park Ct
Kessler Park Dr
Nichole Dr
Claremont Cir
Royal Chase Dr
Kew Garden Dr
Garnier Dr
Chanteloup Dr
City Park Central Ln
Brenford Dr
Staffordale Manor Ln
Westwood Glen Ln
Hampton Villa Ln
Canterlane Dr
Canterville Rd
Vernage Rd
Heatherton
Ridge Hill Ln
Riley Rd
12400
13400
13500
13600
13800
14100
14600
14700
1400
2000
1100
800
500
400
200
100
521
288
8
29°37'55"
29°37'28"
29°37'02"
29°36'36"
29°36'10"
29°35'44"
29°35'18"
29°34'51"
95°25'36"
95°25'06"
95°24'37"
95°24'07"
95°23'37"
95°23'07"
A
B
C
D
E
1
2
3
4
5
6
7

SEE 4374 MAP

SEE 4500 MAP

1:24,000
1 in. = 2000 ft.
0 0.25 0.5
miles

SEE 4243 MAP

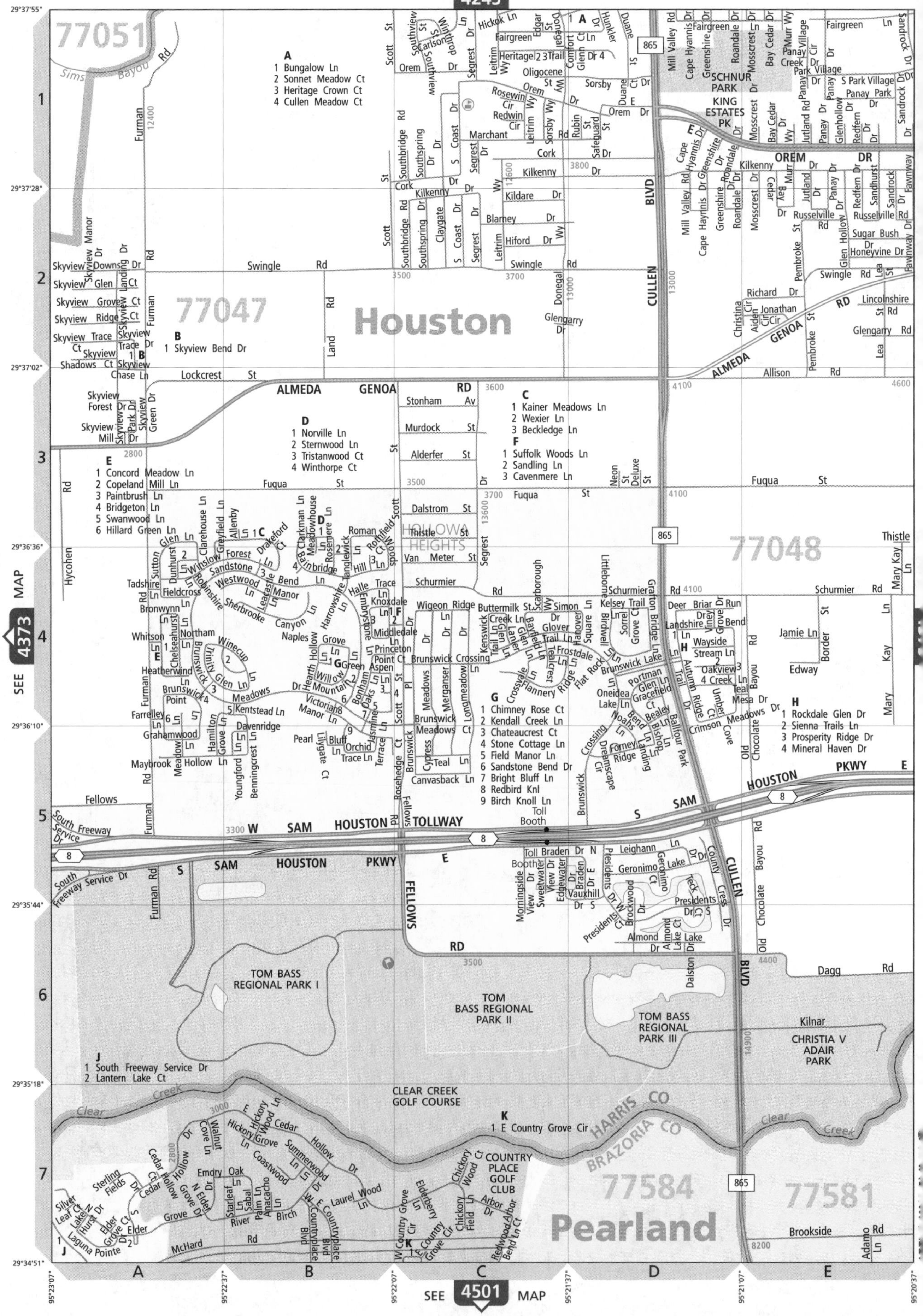
77051
77047
77048
77584
77581
Houston
Pearland
HOLLOWAY HEIGHTS
A
1 Bungalow Ln
2 Sonnet Meadow Ct
3 Heritage Crown Ct
4 Cullen Meadow Ct
B
1 Skyview Bend Dr
C
1 Kainer Meadows Ln
2 Wexier Ln
3 Beckledge Ln
D
1 Norville Ln
2 Sternwood Ln
3 Tristanwood Ct
4 Winthorpe Ct
E
1 Concord Meadow Ln
2 Copeland Mill Ln
3 Paintbrush Ln
4 Bridgeton Ln
5 Swanwood Ln
6 Hillard Green Ln
F
1 Suffolk Woods Ln
2 Sandling Ln
3 Cavenmere Ln
G
1 Chimney Rose Ct
2 Kendall Creek Ln
3 Chateaucrest Ct
4 Stone Cottage Ln
5 Field Manor Ln
6 Sandstone Bend Dr
7 Bright Bluff Ln
8 Redbird Knl
9 Birch Knoll Ln
H
1 Rockdale Glen Dr
2 Sienna Trails Ln
3 Prosperity Ridge Dr
4 Mineral Haven Dr
J
1 South Freeway Service Dr
2 Lantern Lake Ct
K
1 E Country Grove Cir
SCHNUR PARK
KING ESTATES PK
TOM BASS REGIONAL PARK I
TOM BASS REGIONAL PARK II
TOM BASS REGIONAL PARK III
CHRISTIA V ADAIR PARK
CLEAR CREEK GOLF COURSE
COUNTRY PLACE GOLF CLUB
HARRIS CO
BRAZORIA CO
Clear Creek
Sims Bayou
ALMEDA GENOA RD
CULLEN BLVD
W SAM HOUSTON TOLLWAY
S SAM HOUSTON PKWY E
FELLOWS RD
OREM DR
Swingle Rd
Fuqua St
Schurmier Rd
Lockcrest St
Furman Rd
Dagg Rd
Kilnar
Brookside Rd
McHard Rd
Toll Booth
865
8
1 2 3 4 5 6 7
A B C D E
29°37'55"
29°37'28"
29°37'02"
29°36'36"
29°36'10"
29°35'44"
29°35'18"
29°34'51"
95°23'07"
95°22'37"
95°22'07"
95°21'37"
95°21'07"
95°20'37"

SEE 4373 MAP

SEE 4501 MAP

1:24,000
1 in. = 2000 ft.
0 0.25 0.5
miles

SEE 4244 MAP

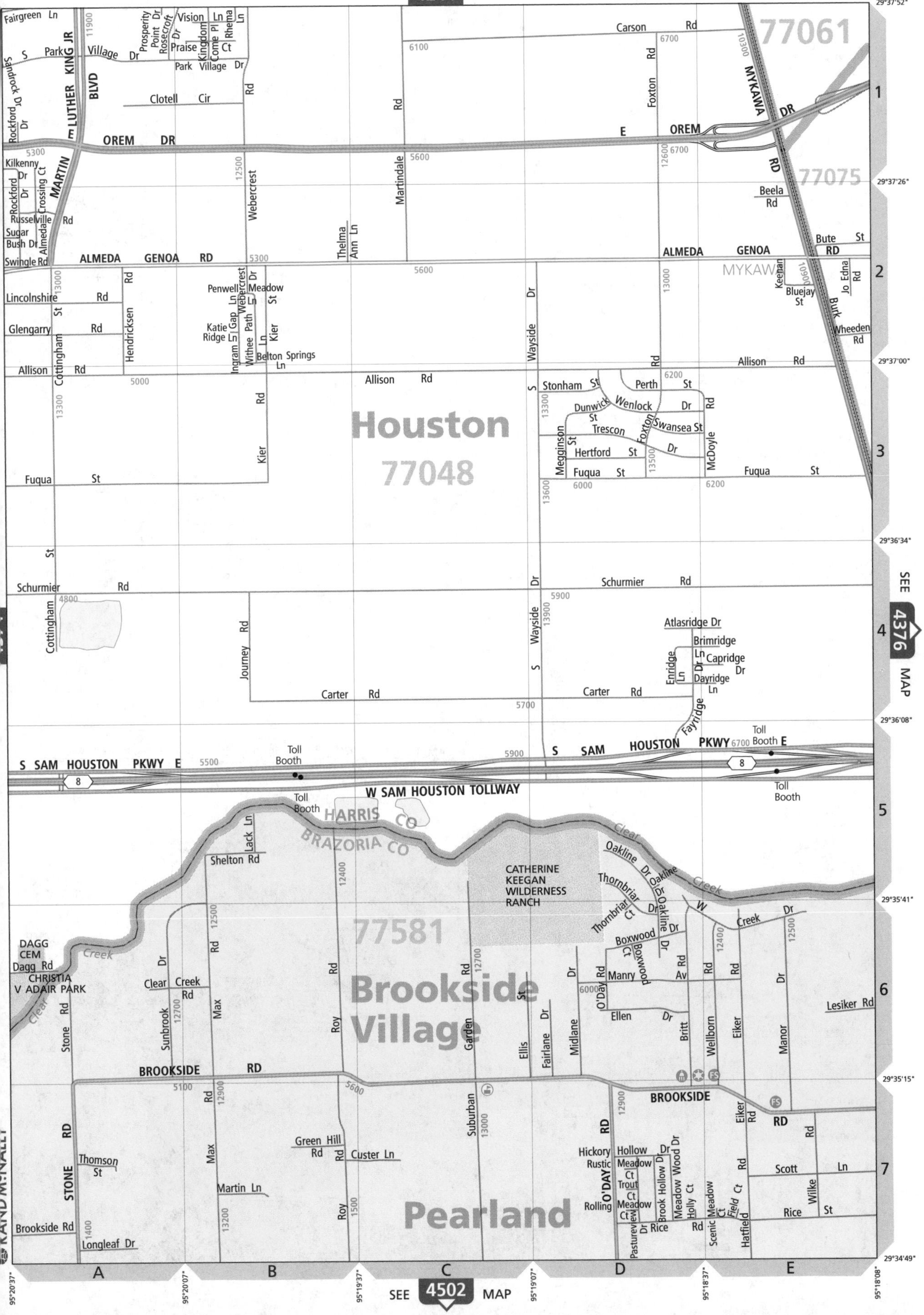
Houston
77048
77061
77075
77581
Brookside Village
Pearland
MYKAWA
HARRIS CO
BRAZORIA CO
CATHERINE KEEGAN WILDERNESS RANCH
DAGG CEM
CHRISTIA V ADAIR PARK
OREM DR
E OREM
MYKAWA DR
RD
MARTIN LUTHER KING JR BLVD
ALMEDA GENOA RD
S SAM HOUSTON PKWY E
W SAM HOUSTON TOLLWAY
Toll Booth
BROOKSIDE RD
STONE RD
O'DAY RD
Fairgreen Ln
Sandrock Dr
S Park Village Dr
Prosperity Point Dr
Rosecroft Dr
Vision Ln
Kingdom Come Pl
Rhema Ln
Praise Ct
Park Village Dr
Clotell Cir
Carson Rd
Foxton Rd
Martindale Rd
Webercrest Rd
Kilkenny Dr
Rockford Dr
Crossing Ct
Russelville Rd
Sugar Bush Dr
Almeda
Swingle Rd
Thelma Ann Ln
Beela Rd
Bute St
RD
Keenan
Bluejay St
Jo Edna Rd
Burk
Wheeden Rd
Lincolnshire Rd
Glengarry Rd
Cottingham St
Hendricksen Rd
Penwell Ln
Meadow St
Gap Ln
Katie Ridge Ln
Ingram
Withee Path
Kier Rd
Belton Springs Ln
Allison Rd
S Wayside Dr
Stonham St
Perth St
Dunwick St
Wenlock Dr
Trescon
Swansea St
Megginson St
Hertford St
McDoyle Rd
Fuqua St
Schurmier Rd
Journey Rd
Carter Rd
Atlasridge Dr
Brimridge Ln
Capridge Dr
Enridge Ln
Dayridge Ln
Fayridge
Lack Ln
Shelton Rd
Clear Creek
Oakline Dr
Thornbriar Dr
Thornbriar Ct
W Creek Dr
Boxwood Ct
Boxwood Dr
Manry Av
Dagg Rd
Clear Creek Rd
Sunbrook Dr
Max Rd
Roy Rd
Garden Rd
Ellis St
Fairlane Dr
Midlane Dr
Ellen Dr
Britt Rd
Wellborn Rd
Eiker Rd
Manor Dr
Lesiker Rd
Suburban
Green Hill Rd
Custer Ln
Thomson St
Martin Ln
Brookside Rd
Longleaf Dr
Hickory Hollow Dr
Rustic Meadow Ct
Trout Ct
Meadow Wood Dr
Rolling Meadow Ct
Brook Hollow Dr
Holly Ct
Scenic Meadow Ct
Field Ct
Hatfield Rd
Pastureview Dr
Rice Rd
Scott Ln
Wilke St
Rice St
A
B
C
D
E
1
2
3
4
5
6
7
8
29°37'52"
29°37'26"
29°37'00"
29°36'34"
29°36'08"
29°35'41"
29°35'15"
29°34'49"
95°20'37"
95°20'07"
95°19'37"
95°19'07"
95°18'37"
95°18'08"

SEE 4376 MAP

SEE 4502 MAP

1:24,000
1 in. = 2000 ft.
0 0.25 0.5
miles

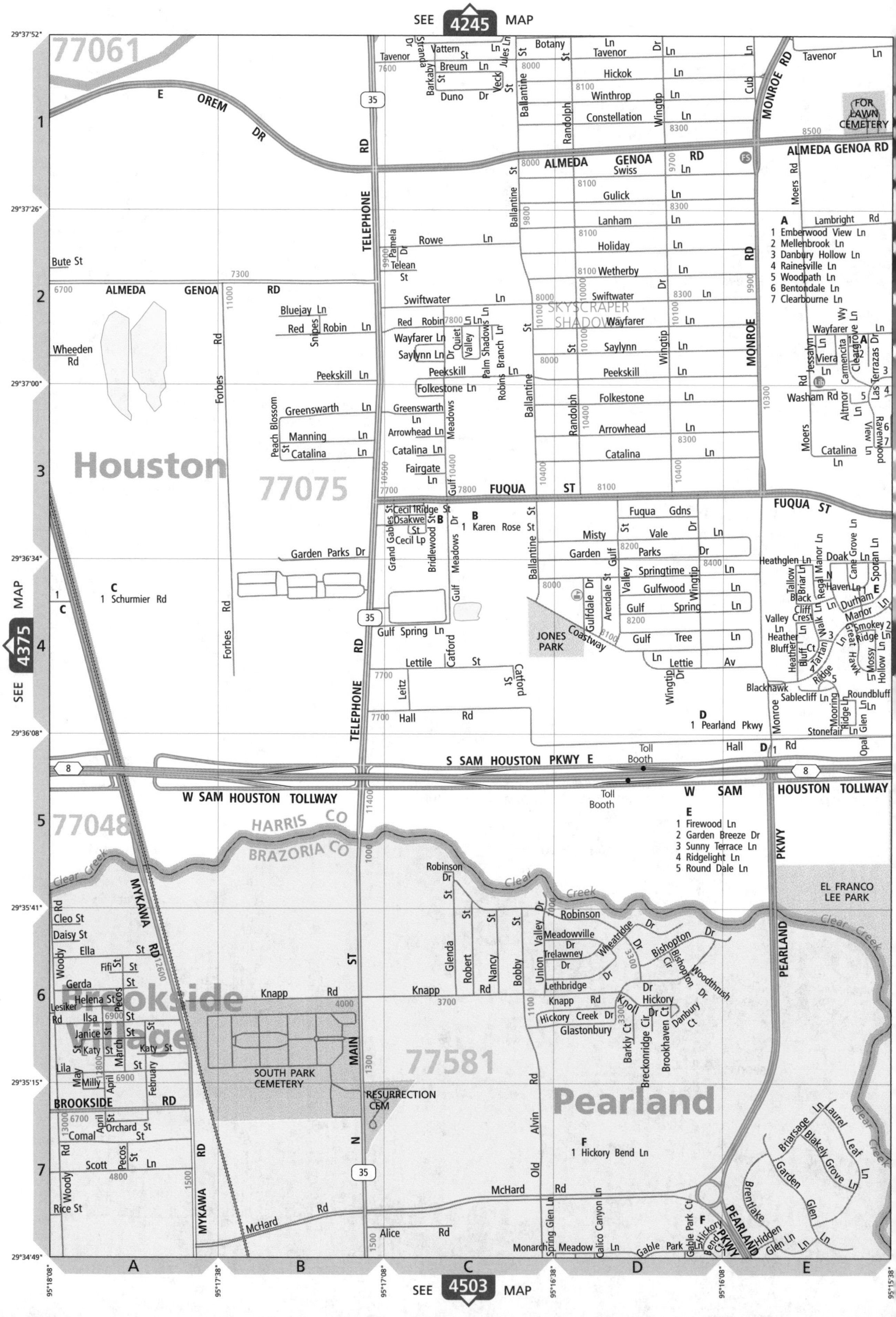
SEE 4245 MAP
SEE 4375 MAP
SEE 4503 MAP
Houston
77061
77075
77048
77581
Pearland
Brookside Village
SKYSCRAPER SHADOWS
HARRIS CO
BRAZORIA CO
Clear Creek
E OREM DR
ALMEDA GENOA RD
TELEPHONE RD
MONROE RD
FUQUA ST
S SAM HOUSTON PKWY E
W SAM HOUSTON TOLLWAY
Toll Booth
MYKAWA RD
N MAIN ST
PEARLAND PKWY
BROOKSIDE RD
Knapp Rd
McHard Rd
Alice Rd
Old Alvin Rd
Hall Rd
Gulf Spring Ln
Forbes Rd
Wheeden Rd
Bute St
Garden Parks Dr
FOR LAWN CEMETERY
JONES PARK
SOUTH PARK CEMETERY
RESURRECTION CEM
EL FRANCO LEE PARK
A
1 Emberwood View Ln
2 Mellenbrook Ln
3 Danbury Hollow Ln
4 Rainesville Ln
5 Woodpath Ln
6 Bentondale Ln
7 Clearbourne Ln
B
1 Karen Rose St
C
1 Schurmier Rd
D
1 Pearland Pkwy
E
1 Firewood Ln
2 Garden Breeze Dr
3 Sunny Terrace Ln
4 Ridgelight Ln
5 Round Dale Ln
F
1 Hickory Bend Ln
29°37'52"
29°37'26"
29°37'00"
29°36'34"
29°36'08"
29°35'41"
29°35'15"
29°34'49"
95°18'08"
95°17'38"
95°17'08"
95°16'38"
95°16'08"
95°15'38"

1:24,000
1 in. = 2000 ft.
0 0.25 0.5
miles

SEE 4246 MAP

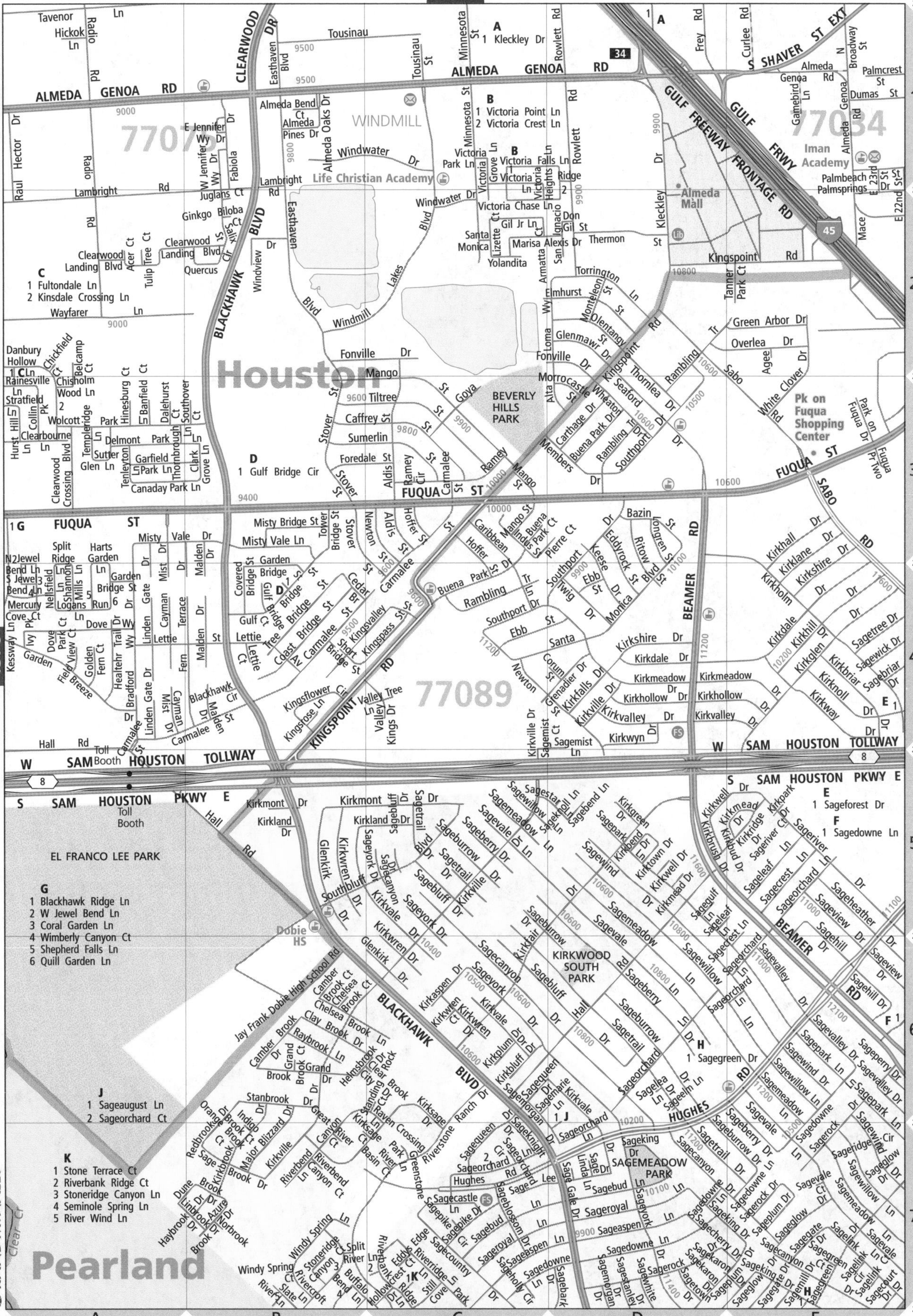

ALMEDA GENOA RD
CLEARWOOD DR
BLACKHAWK BLVD
GULF FREEWAY
GULF FRWY
FRONTAGE RD
S SHAVER ST EXT
KINGSPOINT RD
FUQUA ST
BEAMER RD
SABO RD
W SAM HOUSTON TOLLWAY
S SAM HOUSTON PKWY E
HUGHES RD
Houston
Pearland
77075
77034
77089
WINDMILL
Life Christian Academy
Iman Academy
Almeda Mall
BEVERLY HILLS PARK
Pk on Fuqua Shopping Center
EL FRANCO LEE PARK
Dobie HS
KIRKWOOD SOUTH PARK
SAGEMEADOW PARK
Toll Booth
A
1 Kleckley Dr
B
1 Victoria Point Ln
2 Victoria Crest Ln
C
1 Fultondale Ln
2 Kinsdale Crossing Ln
D
1 Gulf Bridge Cir
E
1 Sageforest Dr
F
1 Sagedowne Ln
G
1 Blackhawk Ridge Ln
2 W Jewel Bend Ln
3 Coral Garden Ln
4 Wimberly Canyon Ct
5 Shepherd Falls Ln
6 Quill Garden Ln
H
1 Sagegreen Dr
J
1 Sageaugust Ln
2 Sageorchard Ct
K
1 Stone Terrace Ct
2 Riverbank Ridge Ct
3 Stoneridge Canyon Ln
4 Seminole Spring Ln
5 River Wind Ln
29°37'49"
29°37'23"
29°36'57"
29°36'31"
29°36'05"
29°35'39"
29°35'13"
29°34'46"
95°15'38"
95°15'08"
95°14'38"
95°14'08"
95°13'38"
95°13'08"

SEE 4378 MAP

SEE 4504 MAP

1:24,000
1 in. = 2000 ft.
0 0.25 0.5
miles

SEE 4247 MAP

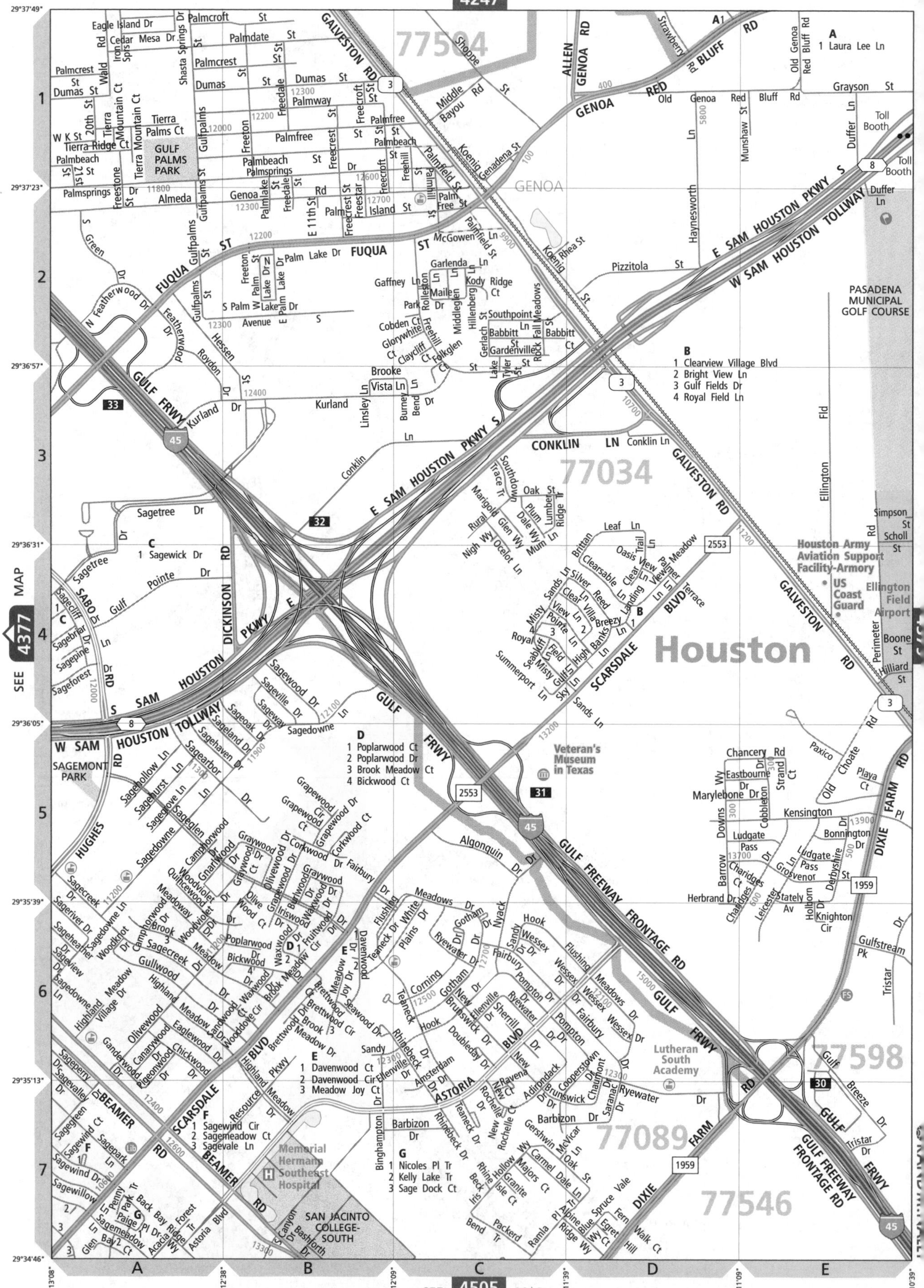
29°37'49"
29°37'23"
29°36'57"
29°36'31"
29°36'05"
29°35'39"
29°35'13"
29°34'46"
1
2
3
4
5
6
7
A
B
C
D
E
95°13'08"
95°12'38"
95°12'09"
95°11'39"
95°11'09"
95°10'39"
77504
77034
77598
77089
77546
Houston
GENOA
GULF PALMS PARK
PASADENA MUNICIPAL GOLF COURSE
Houston Army Aviation Support Facility-Armory
US Coast Guard
Ellington Field Airport
SAGEMONT PARK
Veteran's Museum in Texas
Lutheran South Academy
Memorial Hermann Southeast Hospital
SAN JACINTO COLLEGE-SOUTH
Toll Booth
Toll Booth
GALVESTON RD
GENOA RED BLUFF RD
ALLEN GENOA RD
FUQUA ST
E SAM HOUSTON PKWY S
W SAM HOUSTON TOLLWAY
GULF FRWY
GULF FREEWAY FRONTAGE RD
CONKLIN LN
DICKINSON RD
SABO RD
HUGHES RD
SCARSDALE BLVD
BEAMER RD
ASTORIA BLVD
DIXIE FARM RD
Kurland Dr
Sagetree Dr
Gulf Pointe Dr
Algonquin Dr
Kensington
Pizzitola St
Grayson St
Palmcroft St
Palmdate St
Dumas St
Almeda
Genoa
A
1 Laura Lee Ln
B
1 Clearview Village Blvd
2 Bright View Ln
3 Gulf Fields Dr
4 Royal Field Ln
C
1 Sagewick Dr
D
1 Poplarwood Ct
2 Poplarwood Dr
3 Brook Meadow Ct
4 Bickwood Ct
E
1 Davenwood Ct
2 Davenwood Cir
3 Meadow Joy Ct
F
1 Sagewind Cir
2 Sagemeadow Ct
3 Sagevale Ln
G
1 Nicoles Pl Tr
2 Kelly Lake Tr
3 Sage Dock Ct
3
8
45
33
32
31
30
2553
1959
SEE 4377 MAP

SEE 4505 MAP

1:24,000
1 in. = 2000 ft.
0 0.25 0.5
miles

SEE 4248 MAP

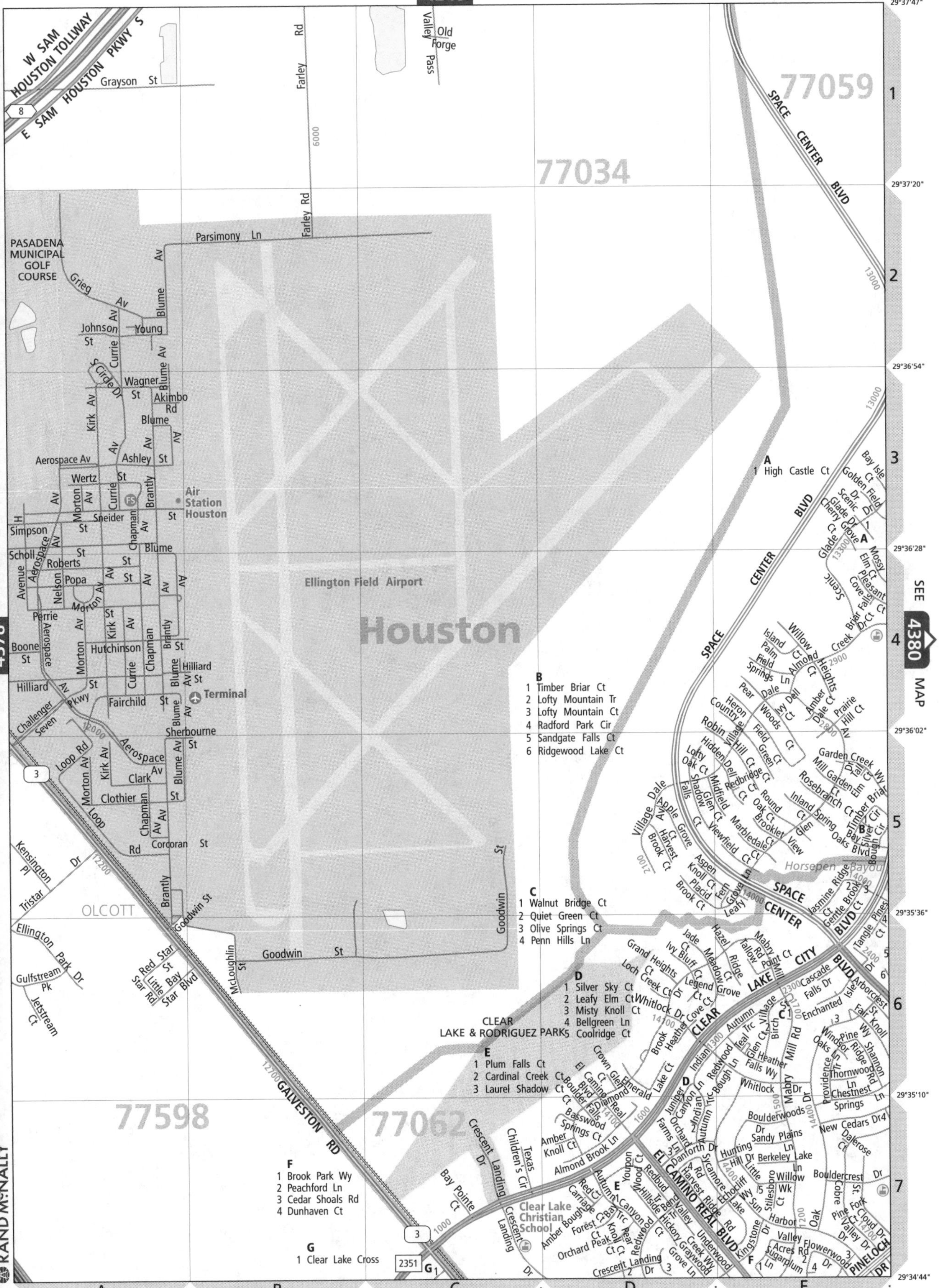
W SAM HOUSTON TOLLWAY
E SAM HOUSTON PKWY S
8
Grayson St
Farley Rd
6000
Valley Old Forge Pass
77059
77034
SPACE CENTER BLVD
13000
PASADENA MUNICIPAL GOLF COURSE
Parsimony Ln
Grieg Av
Johnson St
Young
Currie Av
Blume Av
Circle Dr
Wagner St
Akimbo Rd
Kirk Av
Blume
Aerospace Av
Ashley St
Wertz St
Morton Av
Brantly Av
Air Station Houston
Simpson St
Sneider St
Chapman Av
Scholl
Roberts St
Blume
Avenue H
Popa St
Nelson
Perrie
Boone St
Hutchinson
Hilliard Av
Fairchild St
Terminal
Challenger Seven Pkwy
12000
Sherbourne St
Aerospace Av
Loop Rd
Clark Av
Clothier
Corcoran St
3
Ellington Field Airport
Houston
A
1 High Castle Ct
Bay Isle Ct
Golden Field Dr
Scenic Glade Dr
Cherry Grove
Glade Ct
Mossy Elm Ct
Pleasant Cove Ct
Falls Dr
Scenic
Creek Brier Dr
Island Palm Ct
Willow Almond Ct
Field Springs Ln
Heights
B
1 Timber Briar Ct
2 Lofty Mountain Tr
3 Lofty Mountain Ct
4 Radford Park Cir
5 Sandgate Falls Ct
6 Ridgewood Lake Ct
Pear Dale Ct
Ivy Dell Ct
Amber Dale Ct
Prairie Hill Ct
Heron Country Ct
Robin Hill Ct
Village Woods
Field Green Ct
Garden Creek Wy
Mill Garden Ct
Rosebranch Ct
Inland Spring Ct
Timber Briar Cir
Oaks Blvd
Bay Silver Cir
Bough Cir
Village Dale
Apple Grove
Lofty Oak Ct
Hidden Dell Ct
Redbridge Ct
Midfield Ct
Marbledale Ct
Round Oak Ct
Brooklet View
Shadow Glen Ct
Falls Ct
Viewfield Ct
Harvest Brook Ct
Aspen Knoll Ct
Placid Brook Ct
Fern Grove Ln
Leafy Ct
Horsepen Bayou
Jasmine Ridge Ct
Gentle Brook Ct
Tangle Pines Ct
2100
14000
OLCOTT
Kensington Pl
Tristar Dr
12200
Ellington Park Dr
Gulfstream Pk
Jetstream Ct
Red Star St
Little Bay Star Rd
Star Blvd
Goodwin St
McLoughlin St
Goodwin St
C
1 Walnut Bridge Ct
2 Quiet Green Ct
3 Olive Springs Ct
4 Penn Hills Ln
Grand Heights Ct
Jade Ivy Bluff Ct
Loch Creek Ct
Hazel Meadow Ct
Legend Grove
Mabry Tallow Rd
Point Ct
Mill
LAKE CITY BLVD
Cascade Falls Dr
Arborcrest
Enchanted Isle
Fair Knoll
D
1 Silver Sky Ct
2 Leafy Elm Ct
3 Misty Knoll Ct
4 Bellgreen Ln
5 Coolridge Ct
Whitlock Dr
Heather Cove Ct
CLEAR
CLEAR LAKE & RODRIGUEZ PARK
E
1 Plum Falls Ct
2 Cardinal Creek Ct
3 Laurel Shadow Ct
Autumn Teal Trc
Village Glen Ct
Birch
Windsor Oaks Ln
Pine Ridge Tr
Shannon Wy
Heather Falls Wy
Mill Rd
Providence Ln
Thornwood Rd
Chestnest Springs Ln
Brook
Crown Glen
El Camino Blvd
Emerald Lake Ct
Indian Trc
Redwood Bough Ln
Whitlock
Diamond Real
Boulder Falls Ct
Basswood Springs Ct
Juniper Canyon
Farms Ln
Orchard
Autumn Trc
Boulderwoods Dr
Sandy Plains Ln
New Cedars Dr
Dalerose Ct
77598
77062
GALVESTON RD
12700
Crescent Dr
Children's Cir
Texas
Landing
Amber Knoll Ct
Almond Brook Ln
Danforth Dr
Hunting Hill Dr
Berkeley Lake Ln
Willow Wk
Bouldercrest Dr
EL CAMINO REAL BLVD
Sycamore
Echocliff Wy
Stilesboro Ct
Cobre St
Pine Fork Ct
Cloud Dr
Valley Dr
F
1 Brook Park Wy
2 Peachford Ln
3 Cedar Shoals Rd
4 Dunhaven Ct
Bay Pointe Ct
Clear Lake Christian School
Crescent Landing
Red Carriage
Amber Bough
Autumn Canyon
Youpon
Wood Ct
Redbud
Hillside Tr
Bend
Valley Creek
Hickory Grove
Harvest Ridge Rd
Underwood
Graywood
Kingstone Dr
Harbor
Oak
Valley Acres Rd
Flowerwood Dr
PINELOCH DR
Sugarplum
Forest Trc
Pear Knoll Ct
Orchard Peak Ct
Redwood Ct
Crescent Landing Dr
G
1 Clear Lake Cross
3
2351
1000
29°37'47"
29°37'20"
29°36'54"
29°36'28"
29°36'02"
29°35'36"
29°35'10"
29°34'44"
1
2
3
4
5
6
7
A
B
C
D
E
95°10'39"
95°10'09"
95°09'39"
95°09'09"
95°08'39"
95°08'09"

SEE 4380 MAP

SEE 4506 MAP

1:24,000
1 in. = 2000 ft.
0 0.25 0.5
miles

SEE 4249 MAP

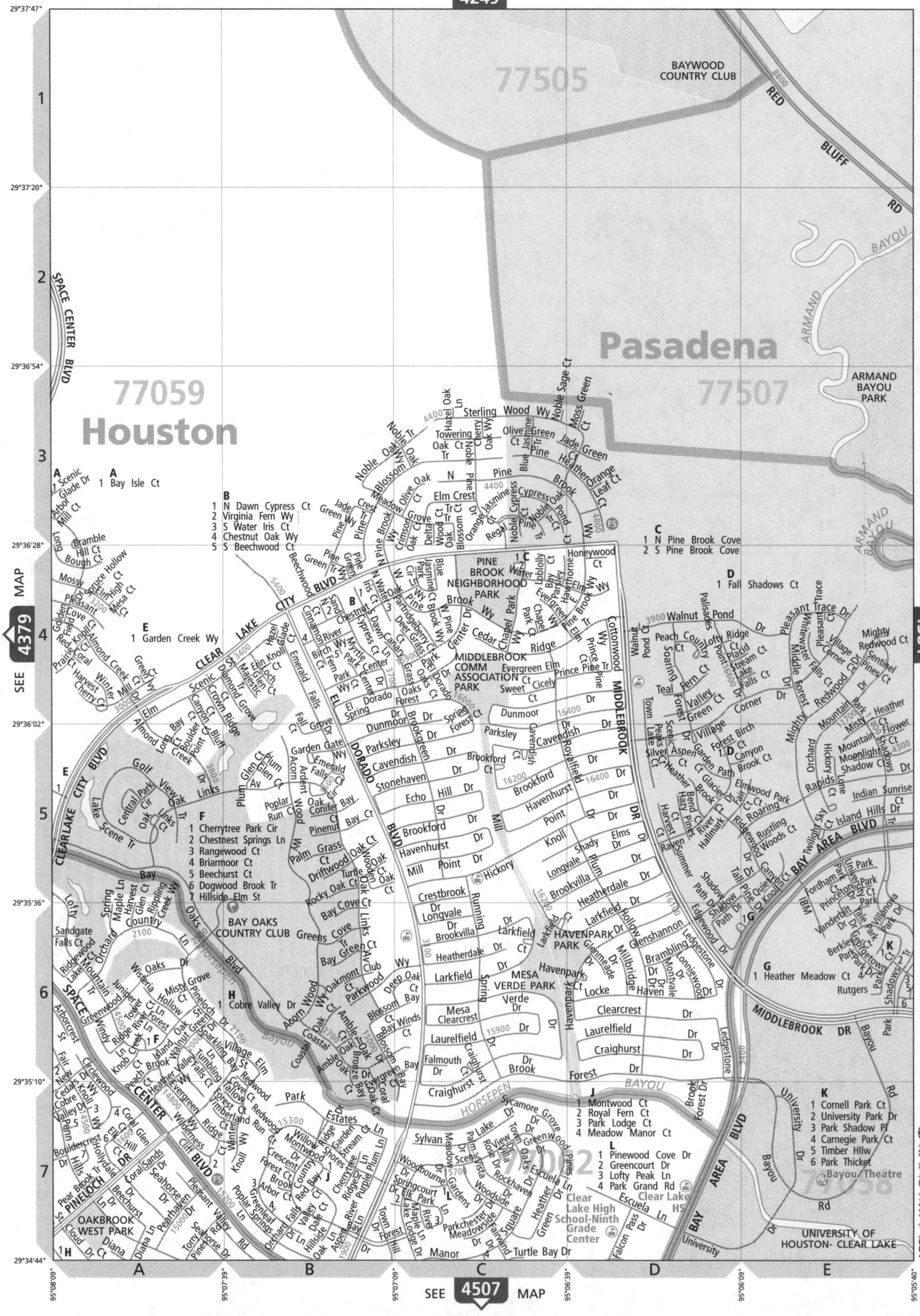
77505
BAYWOOD COUNTRY CLUB
RED BLUFF RD
Pasadena
77507
ARMAND BAYOU PARK
ARMAND BAYOU
77059
Houston
SPACE CENTER BLVD
CLEAR LAKE CITY BLVD
EL DORADO BLVD
MIDDLEBROOK DR
BAY AREA BLVD
PINE BROOK NEIGHBORHOOD PARK
MIDDLEBROOK COMM ASSOCIATION PARK
BAY OAKS COUNTRY CLUB
HAVENPARK PARK
MESA VERDE PARK
OAKBROOK WEST PARK
Clear Lake High School-Ninth Grade Center
Clear Lake HS
Bayou Theatre
UNIVERSITY OF HOUSTON- CLEAR LAKE
77062
77058
HORSEPEN BAYOU
A
1 Scenic Glade Dr
A
1 Bay Isle Ct
B
1 N Dawn Cypress Ct
2 Virginia Fern Wy
3 S Water Iris Ct
4 Chestnut Oak Wy
5 S Beechwood Ct
C
1 N Pine Brook Cove
2 S Pine Brook Cove
D
1 Fall Shadows Ct
E
1 Garden Creek Wy
F
1 Cherrytree Park Cir
2 Chestnest Springs Ln
3 Rangewood Ct
4 Briarmoor Ct
5 Beechurst Ct
6 Dogwood Brook Tr
7 Hillside Elm St
G
1 Heather Meadow Ct
H
1 Cobre Valley Dr
J
1 Montwood Ct
2 Royal Fern Ct
3 Park Lodge Ct
4 Meadow Manor Ct
K
1 Cornell Park Ct
2 University Park Dr
3 Park Shadow Pl
4 Carnegie Park Ct
5 Timber Hllw
6 Park Thicket
L
1 Pinewood Cove Dr
2 Greencourt Dr
3 Lofty Peak Ln
4 Park Grand Rd

SEE 4379 MAP

SEE 4507 MAP

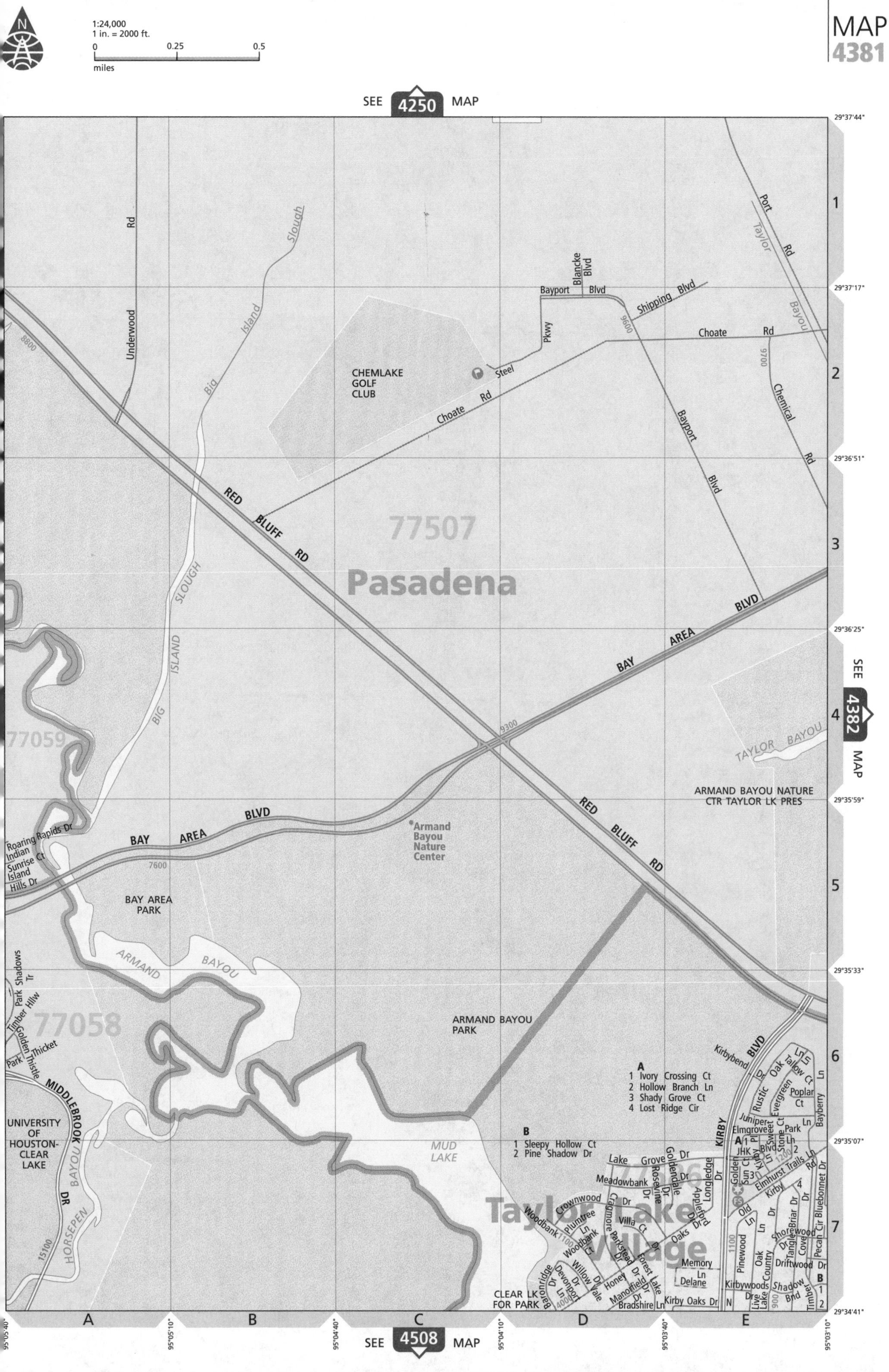
1:24,000
1 in. = 2000 ft.
0
0.25
0.5
miles
SEE 4250 MAP
SEE 4508 MAP
SEE 4382 MAP
Underwood Rd
Big Island Slough
CHEMLAKE GOLF CLUB
Steel
Choate Rd
Bayport Blvd
Blancke Blvd
Pkwy
Shipping Blvd
Port Taylor Rd
Taylor Bayou
Chemical Rd
RED BLUFF RD
77507
Pasadena
BAY AREA BLVD
Big Island Slough
77059
TAYLOR BAYOU
ARMAND BAYOU NATURE CTR TAYLOR LK PRES
Armand Bayou Nature Center
Roaring Rapids Dr
Indian
Sunrise Ct
Island
Hills Dr
BAY AREA PARK
ARMAND BAYOU
77058
ARMAND BAYOU PARK
Park Shadows Tr
Timber Hllw
Golden Thistle
Park Thicket
MIDDLEBROOK DR
UNIVERSITY OF HOUSTON-CLEAR LAKE
HORSEPEN BAYOU
MUD LAKE
A
1 Ivory Crossing Ct
2 Hollow Branch Ln
3 Shady Grove Ct
4 Lost Ridge Cir
B
1 Sleepy Hollow Ct
2 Pine Shadow Dr
Kirbybend
KIRBY BLVD
Lake Grove Dr
Meadowbank Dr
Crownwood Dr
Taylor Lake Village
Woodbank
Plumtree
Villa Ct
Oaks Dr
Memory Ln
Delane
Devonport Dr
Willow Vale
Honey Ln
Manorfield Dr
Forest Lake Dr
Bradshire Ln
Kirby Oaks Dr
CLEAR LK FOR PARK
Pinewood
Oak Country
Elmhurst Trails Ln
Driftwood Dr
Shadow Bnd
Kirbywoods Dr
Bluebonnet Dr
Pecan Cir
Bayberry Ln
Poplar Ct
Rustic Oak
Evergreen
Juniper
Elmgrove
Tallow Ct
Golden Sun Ct
Timber
A
B
C
D
E
1
2
3
4
5
6
7
29°37'44"
29°37'17"
29°36'51"
29°36'25"
29°35'59"
29°35'33"
29°35'07"
29°34'41"
95°05'40"
95°05'10"
95°04'40"
95°04'10"
95°03'40"
95°03'10"

1:24,000
1 in. = 2000 ft.
0 0.25 0.5
miles

SEE 4251 MAP

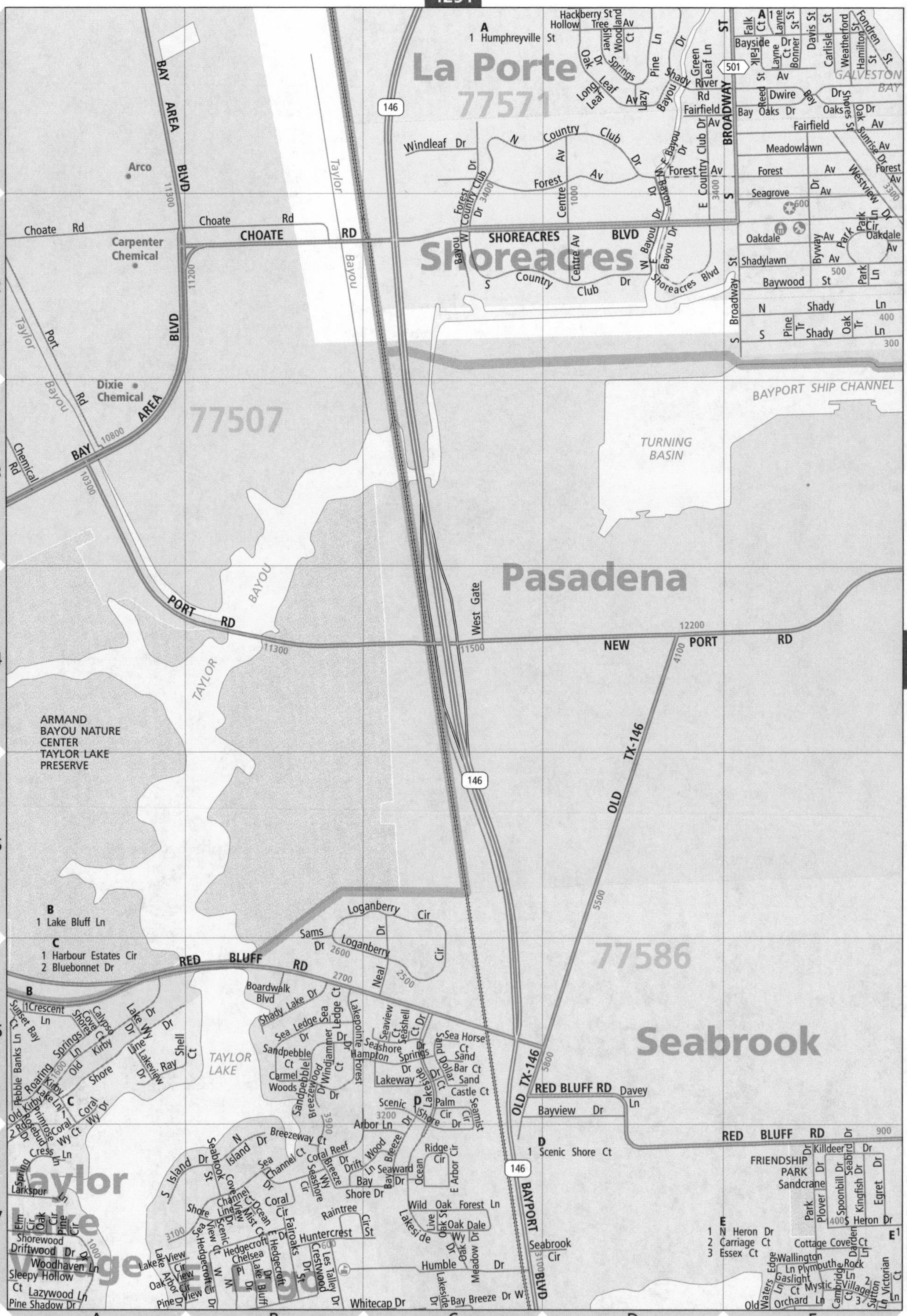
La Porte
77571
Shoreacres
77507
Pasadena
77586
Seabrook
Taylor Lake Village
El Lago
BAY AREA BLVD
CHOATE RD
Choate Rd
SHOREACRES BLVD
NEW PORT RD
PORT RD
RED BLUFF RD
OLD TX-146
BAYPORT BLVD
BROADWAY ST
146
501
Arco
Carpenter Chemical
Dixie Chemical
Chemical Rd
Port Rd
Taylor Bayou
BAYPORT SHIP CHANNEL
TURNING BASIN
GALVESTON BAY
ARMAND BAYOU NATURE CENTER TAYLOR LAKE PRESERVE
TAYLOR LAKE
FRIENDSHIP PARK
West Gate
N Country Club Dr
S Country Club Dr
Forest Av
Windleaf Dr
Fairfield Rd
Meadowlawn
Oakdale
Shadylawn
Baywood St
Loganberry Cir
Sams Dr
Neal
Boardwalk Blvd
Bayview Dr
Davey Ln
Humble Dr
Whitecap Dr
Seabrook Cir
A
1 Humphreyville St
B
1 Lake Bluff Ln
C
1 Harbour Estates Cir
2 Bluebonnet Dr
D
1 Scenic Shore Ct
E
1 N Heron Dr
2 Carriage Ct
3 Essex Ct
29°37'44"
29°37'17"
29°36'51"
29°36'25"
29°35'59"
29°35'33"
29°35'07"
29°34'41"
95°03'10"
95°02'40"
95°02'10"
95°01'40"
95°01'10"
95°00'40"
1
2
3
4
5
6
7
A
B
C
D
E

SEE 4381 MAP

SEE 4509 MAP

1:24,000
1 in. = 2000 ft.
0 0.25 0.5
miles

SEE 4252 MAP

A
1 Miramar Dr
2 Bay Shore Dr
3 Bay Oaks Dr
GALVESTON BAY
BAYPORT SHIP CHANNEL
Shoreacres
La Porte
Houston Yacht Club
Seawall
Pasadena
77586
Seabrook
NEW PORT RD
SUNRISE DR
TODVILLE RD
RED BLUFF RD
EL JARDIN DEL MAR
EL JARDIN PARK
SEABROOK CEM
PINE GULLEY PARK
Crimson Pt
Park Dr
Youpon Dr
Cruise Rd
Baywood Dr
Pine Gully Rd
Surf Oaks Dr
Casa Mara
N Flamingo Dr
Bay Club Dr
Hamblen Ct
Tharp St
Quintana Roo Pl
Elmen
Bradley
Loraine
Mystic Village Ln
A B C D E
1 2 3 4 5 6 7

SEE B MAP

SEE 4510 MAP

1:24,000
1 in. = 2000 ft.
0 0.25 0.5
miles

SEE B MAP

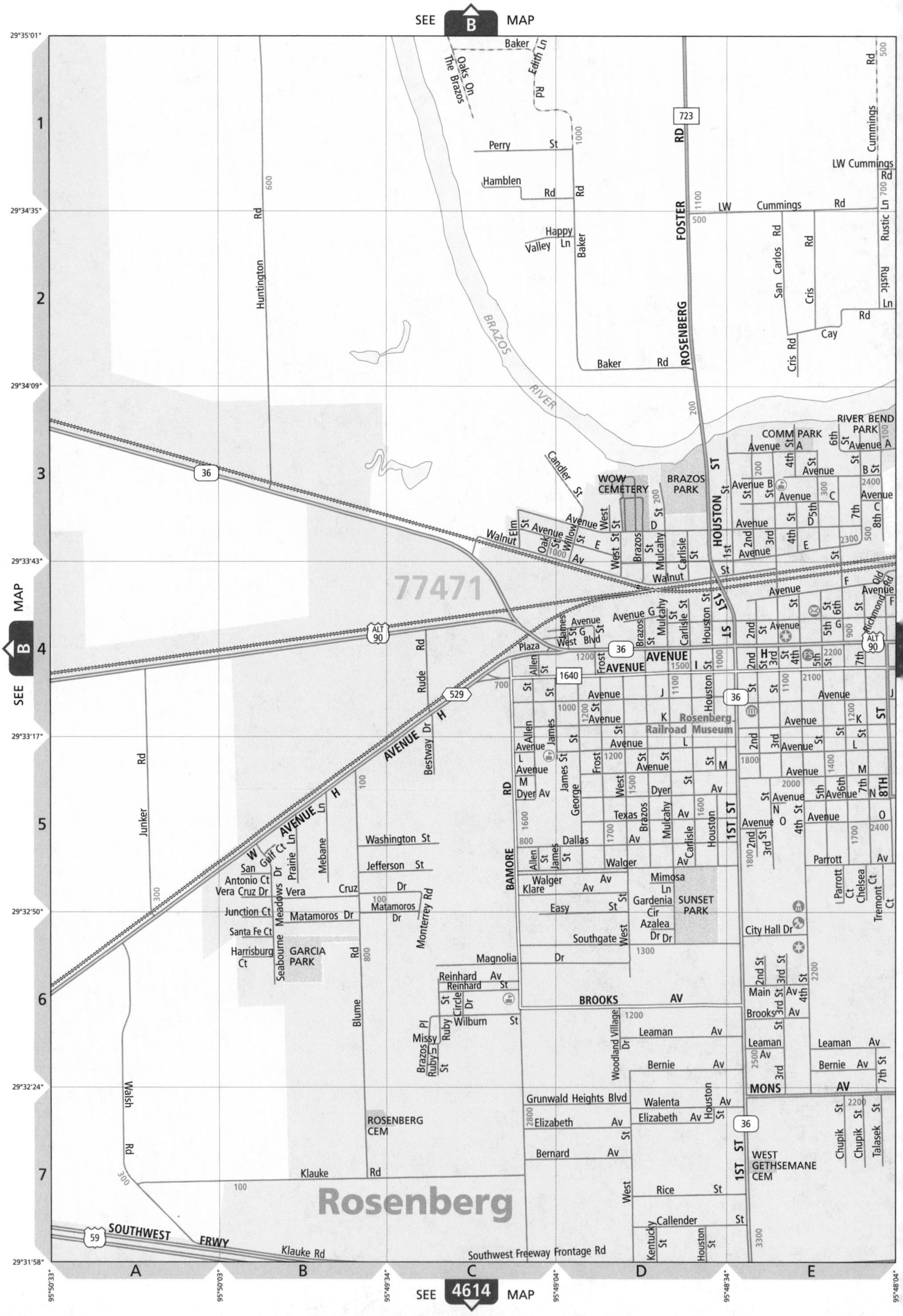
Rosenberg
77471
BRAZOS RIVER
FOSTER RD
ROSENBERG RD
723
36
ALT 90
529
1640
59
SOUTHWEST FRWY
Southwest Freeway Frontage Rd
Klauke Rd
AVENUE H
BAMORE RD
HOUSTON ST
1ST ST
8TH ST
BROOKS AV
MONS AV
WOW CEMETERY
BRAZOS PARK
RIVER BEND PARK
COMM PARK
Rosenberg Railroad Museum
SUNSET PARK
GARCIA PARK
ROSENBERG CEM
WEST GETHSEMANE CEM
Huntington Rd
Junker Rd
Walsh Rd
Blume Rd
Rude Rd
Bestway Dr
Mebane Ln
Prairie Ln
Seabourne Meadows Dr
Washington St
Jefferson St
Matamoros Dr
Monterrey Rd
Magnolia Dr
Reinhard Av
Wilburn St
Leaman Av
Bernie Av
Grunwald Heights Blvd
Elizabeth Av
Bernard Av
Rice St
Callender St
Walenta Av
Woodland Village Dr
Baker Rd
Perry St
Hamblen Rd
Happy Valley Ln
Oaks On The Brazos
Edith Ln
LW Cummings Rd
Cummings Rd
San Carlos Rd
Cris Rd
Cay Rd
Rustic Ln
Candler St
Walnut St
Plaza
Dallas Av
Walger Av
Dyer Av
Texas Av
Mimosa Ln
Gardenia Cir
Azalea Dr
Southgate Dr
City Hall Dr
Parrott Av
Chelsea Ct
Tremont Ct
Chupik St
Talasek St
Old Richmond Rd
SEE B MAP
1 2 3 4 5 6 7
A B C D E

SEE 4614 MAP

1:24,000
1 in. = 2000 ft.
0 0.25 0.5
miles

SEE 4364 MAP

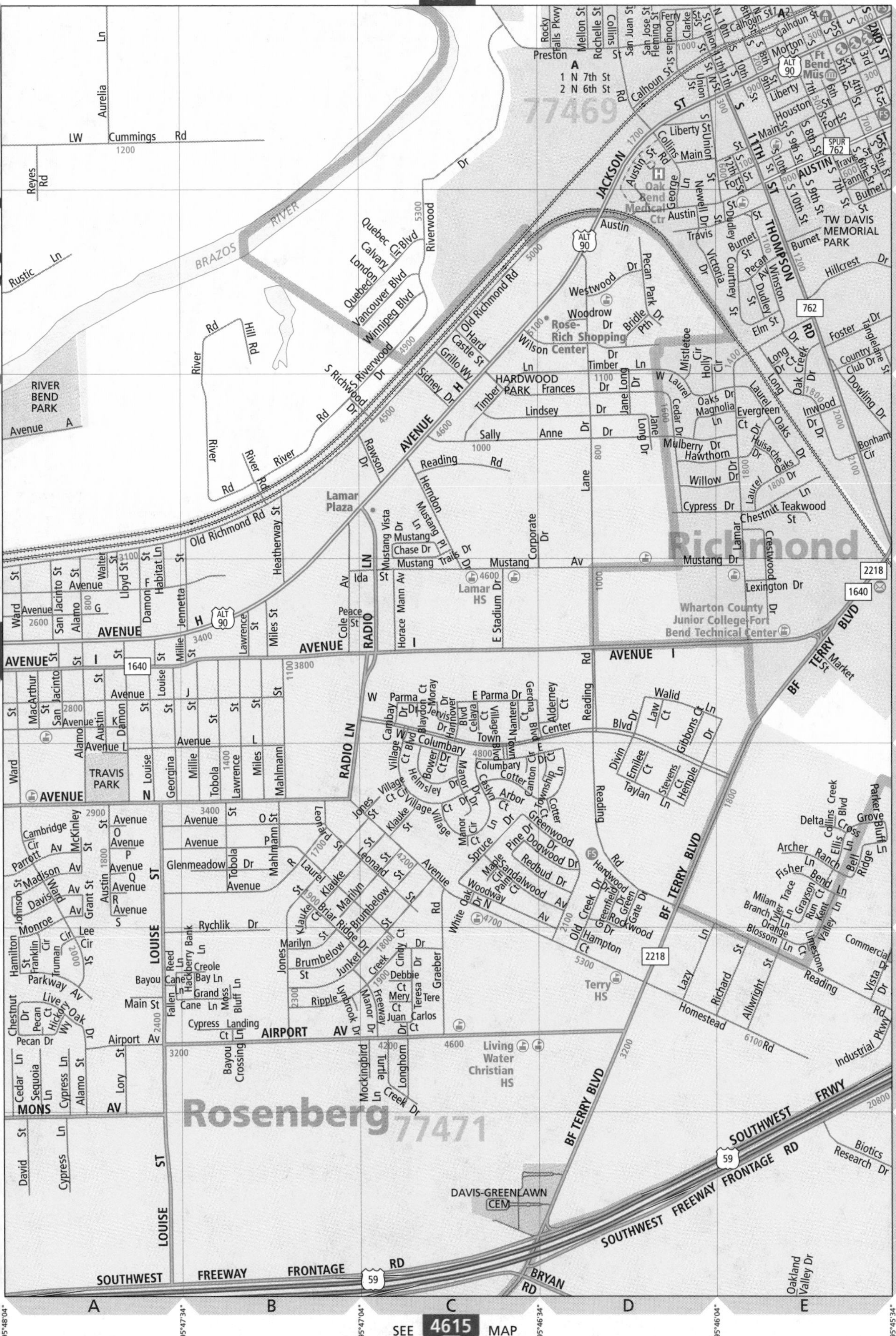
77469
Richmond
Rosenberg
77471
BRAZOS RIVER
RIVER BEND PARK
TRAVIS PARK
TW DAVIS MEMORIAL PARK
Oak Bend Medical Ctr
Ft Bend Mus
Rose-Rich Shopping Center
HARDWOOD PARK
Lamar Plaza
Lamar HS
Wharton County Junior College-Fort Bend Technical Center
Terry HS
Living Water Christian HS
DAVIS-GREENLAWN CEM
JACKSON ST
THOMPSON RD
AVENUE H
AVENUE I
RADIO LN
LOUISE ST
AIRPORT AV
MONS AV
BF TERRY BLVD
SOUTHWEST FREEWAY FRONTAGE RD
SOUTHWEST FRWY
BRYAN RD
Old Richmond Rd
Mustang Av
Reading Rd
Lane Dr
Cummings Rd
Riverwood Dr
Vancouver Blvd
Winnipeg Blvd
Quebec Blvd
Hillcrest Dr
Foster Dr
Homestead Rd
Industrial Pkwy
Biotics Research Dr
Commercial Dr
Airport Av
Avenue N
Avenue O
Avenue P
Avenue Q
Avenue R
Avenue S
Glenmeadow Dr
Rychlik Dr
Cypress Landing Ln
Columbary Dr
Town Center Blvd
Lexington Dr
Chestnut St
Teakwood St
Cypress Dr
Willow Dr
Hawthorn Dr
Mulberry Dr
Lindsey Dr
Sally Anne Dr
Timber Ln
Woodrow Dr
Westwood Dr
Pecan Park Dr
Austin St
Main St
Liberty St
Houston St
Morton St
Calhoun St
Preston
ALT 90
SPUR 762
762
1640
2218
59
4492

29°35'00"
29°34'34"
29°34'08"
29°33'41"
29°33'15"
29°32'49"
29°32'23"
29°31'57"
95°48'04"
95°47'34"
95°47'04"
95°46'34"
95°46'04"
95°45'34"

SEE 4492 MAP

SEE 4615 MAP

1:24,000
1 in. = 2000 ft.
0 0.25 0.5
miles

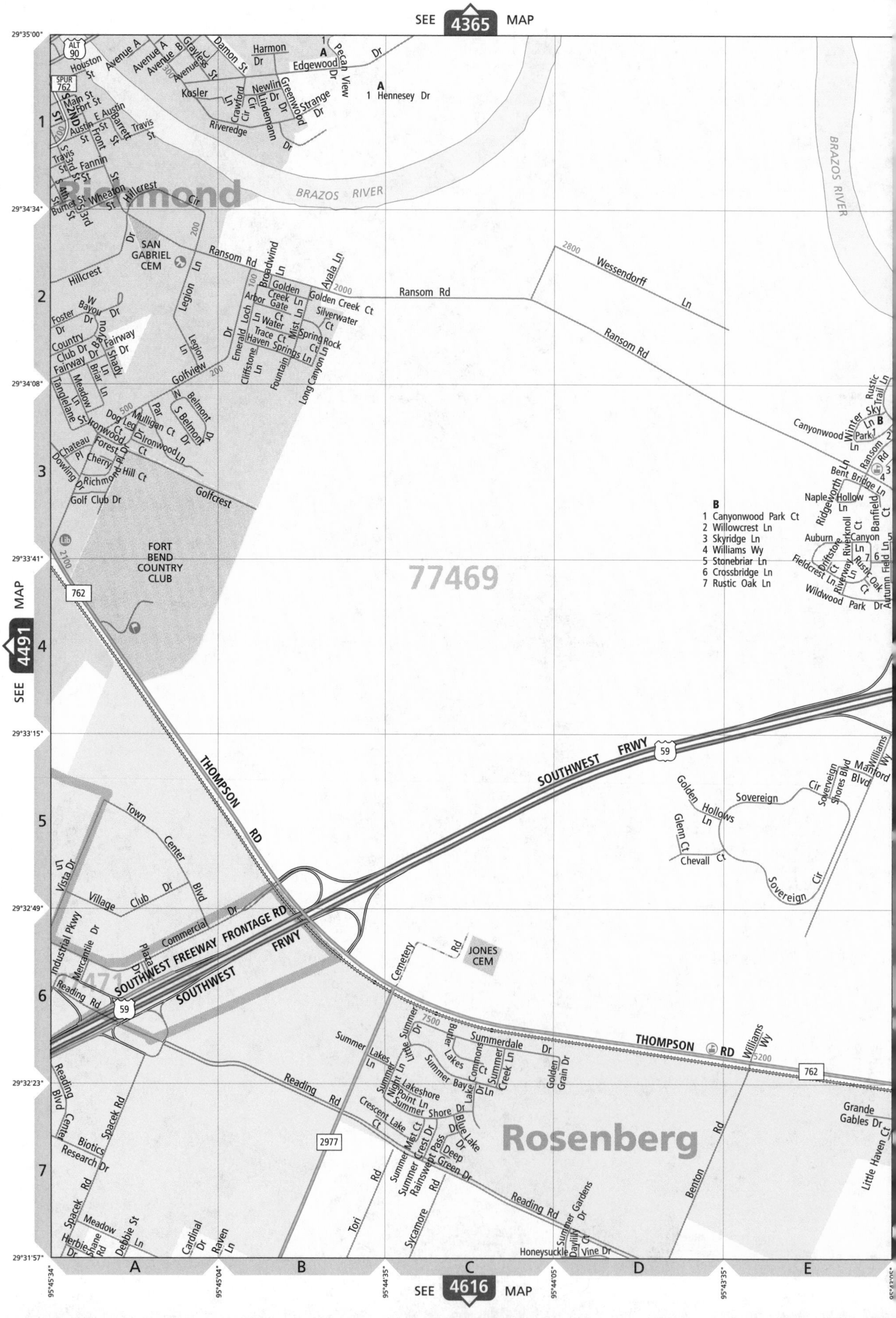
SEE 4365 MAP
SEE 4491 MAP
SEE 4616 MAP
Richmond
Rosenberg
77469
77471
BRAZOS RIVER
A
1 Hennesey Dr
B
1 Canyonwood Park Ct
2 Willowcrest Ln
3 Skyridge Ln
4 Williams Wy
5 Stonebriar Ln
6 Crossbridge Ln
7 Rustic Oak Ln
SAN GABRIEL CEM
FORT BEND COUNTRY CLUB
JONES CEM
SOUTHWEST FRWY
SOUTHWEST FREEWAY FRONTAGE RD
THOMPSON RD
Ransom Rd
Wessendorff Ln
Reading Rd
Golfcrest
Town Center Blvd
Village Club Dr
Commercial Dr
Industrial Pkwy
Mercantile Dr
Plaza Dr
Reading Blvd
Center Biotics Research Dr
Spacek Rd
Meadow Ln
Debbie St
Herbie Dr
Shane Rd
Cardinal Dr
Raven Ln
Tori Rd
Sycamore Rd
Cemetery Rd
Summerdale Dr
Golden Grain Dr
Summer Lakes Ln
Lakeshore Point Ln
Summer Shore Dr
Blue Lake Dr
Deep Green Dr
Rainswept Pass
Crescent Lake Ct
Summer Gardens Ct
Honeysuckle Vine Dr
Benton Rd
Williams Wy
Sovereign Cir
Golden Hollows Ln
Glenn Ct
Chevall Ct
Sovereign Shores Blvd
Manford Blvd
Williams Wy
Grande Gables Dr
Little Haven Ct
Canyonwood Park Ln
Bent Bridge Ln
Naple Hollow Ln
Ridgeworth Ln
Banfield Ct
Auburn Canyon Ln
Fieldcrest Ln
Driftstone Ct
Riverway Ln
Riverknoll Ct
Rustic Oak Ct
Autumn Field Ln
Wildwood Park Dr
Winter Sky Ln
Rustic Trail Ln
Golden Creek Ct
Silverwater Ct
Spring Rock Ct
Long Canyon Ln
Ayala Ln
Broadwind Ln
Arbor Gate Ct
Emerald Loch Dr
Cliffstone Ln
Fountain Mist Ln
Golfview Dr
Legion Ln
Hillcrest Dr
Hillcrest Cir
Foster Dr
W Bayou Dr
Country Club Dr
Fairway Dr
Bayou Shady Ln
Briar Ln
Meadow Ln
Tanglelane St
Belmont Dr
S Belmont Dr
Mulligan Ct
Par Dr
Dog Leg Ct
Ironwood Ln
Chateau Pl
Dowling Dr
Forest Cherry Hill Ct
Richmond Pl
Golf Club Dr
Houston St
Avenue A
Avenue B
Avenue C
Damon St
Harmon Dr
Edgewood Dr
Pecan View Dr
Kosler
Newlin Dr
Lindemann Dr
Greenwood Dr
Strange Dr
Crawford Ln
Riveredge Dr
Main St
Fort St
E Austin St
Front St
Barrett St
Travis St
Fannin St
Wheaton St
Burnet St
ALT 90
SPUR 762
762
59
2977
A B C D E
1 2 3 4 5 6 7

N

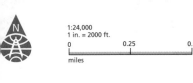

1:24,000
1 in. = 2000 ft.
0 0.25 0.5
miles

SEE 4366 MAP

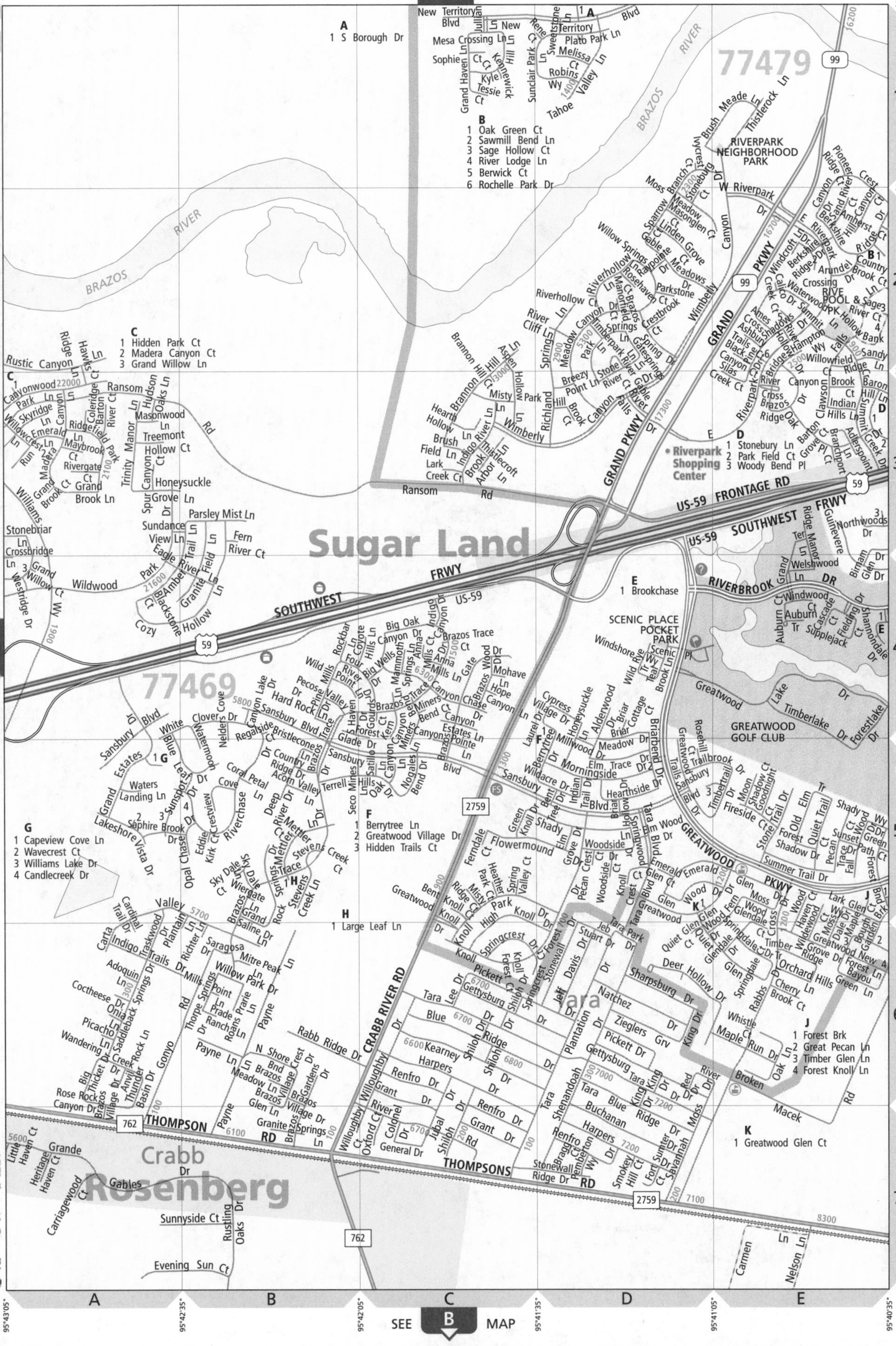
Sugar Land
Rosenberg
Crabb
Tara
77479
77469
BRAZOS RIVER
A
1 S Borough Dr
B
1 Oak Green Ct
2 Sawmill Bend Ln
3 Sage Hollow Ct
4 River Lodge Ln
5 Berwick Ct
6 Rochelle Park Dr
C
1 Hidden Park Ct
2 Madera Canyon Ct
3 Grand Willow Ln
D
1 Stonebury Ln
2 Park Field Ct
3 Woody Bend Pl
E
1 Brookchase
F
1 Berrytree Ln
2 Greatwood Village Dr
3 Hidden Trails Ct
G
1 Capeview Cove Ln
2 Wavecrest Ct
3 Williams Lake Dr
4 Candlecreek Dr
H
1 Large Leaf Ln
J
1 Forest Brk
2 Great Pecan Ln
3 Timber Glen Ln
4 Forest Knoll Ln
K
1 Greatwood Glen Ct
RIVERPARK NEIGHBORHOOD PARK
Riverpark Shopping Center
SCENIC PLACE POCKET PARK
GREATWOOD GOLF CLUB
US-59 FRONTAGE RD
US-59 SOUTHWEST FRWY
SOUTHWEST FRWY
GRAND PKWY
CRABB RIVER RD
GREATWOOD PKWY
RIVERBROOK DR
THOMPSON RD
THOMPSONS RD
99
59
762
2759
1
2
3
4
5
6
7
A
B
C
D
E
29°34'58"
29°34'32"
29°34'06"
29°33'40"
29°33'14"
29°32'48"
29°32'21"
29°31'55"
95°43'05"
95°42'35"
95°42'05"
95°41'35"
95°41'05"
95°40'35"

SEE 4494 MAP

SEE B MAP

1:24,000
1 in. = 2000 ft.
0 0.25 0.5
miles

SEE 4367 MAP

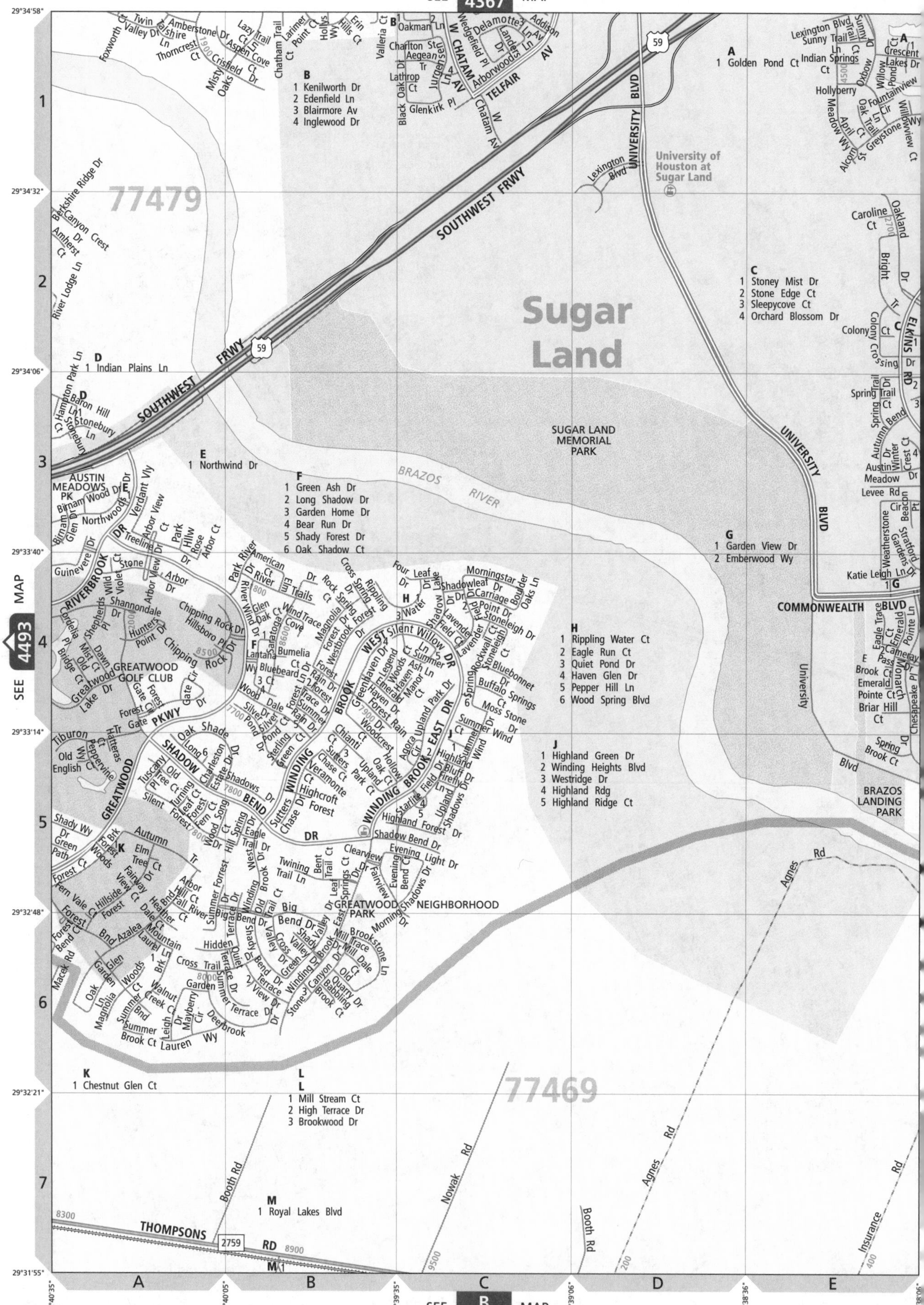

A
1 Golden Pond Ct
B
1 Kenilworth Dr
2 Edenfield Ln
3 Blairmore Av
4 Inglewood Dr
C
1 Stoney Mist Dr
2 Stone Edge Ct
3 Sleepycove Ct
4 Orchard Blossom Dr
D
1 Indian Plains Ln
E
1 Northwind Dr
F
1 Green Ash Dr
2 Long Shadow Dr
3 Garden Home Dr
4 Bear Run Dr
5 Shady Forest Dr
6 Oak Shadow Ct
G
1 Garden View Dr
2 Emberwood Wy
H
1 Rippling Water Ct
2 Eagle Run Ct
3 Quiet Pond Dr
4 Haven Glen Dr
5 Pepper Hill Ln
6 Wood Spring Blvd
J
1 Highland Green Dr
2 Winding Heights Blvd
3 Westridge Dr
4 Highland Rdg
5 Highland Ridge Ct
K
1 Chestnut Glen Ct
L
1 Mill Stream Ct
2 High Terrace Dr
3 Brookwood Dr
M
1 Royal Lakes Blvd
77479
77469
Sugar Land
SUGAR LAND MEMORIAL PARK
University of Houston at Sugar Land
SOUTHWEST FRWY
UNIVERSITY BLVD
COMMONWEALTH BLVD
BRAZOS RIVER
BRAZOS LANDING PARK
GREATWOOD GOLF CLUB
GREATWOOD PARK
NEIGHBORHOOD
AUSTIN MEADOWS PK
THOMPSONS RD
Booth Rd
Nowak Rd
Agnes Rd
Insurance Rd
29°34'58"
29°34'32"
29°34'06"
29°33'40"
29°33'14"
29°32'48"
29°32'21"
29°31'55"
95°40'35"
95°40'05"
95°39'35"
95°39'06"
95°38'36"
A B C D E
1 2 3 4 5 6 7

SEE 4493 MAP

SEE B MAP

1:24,000
1 in. = 2000 ft.
0 0.25 0.5
miles

SEE 4368 MAP

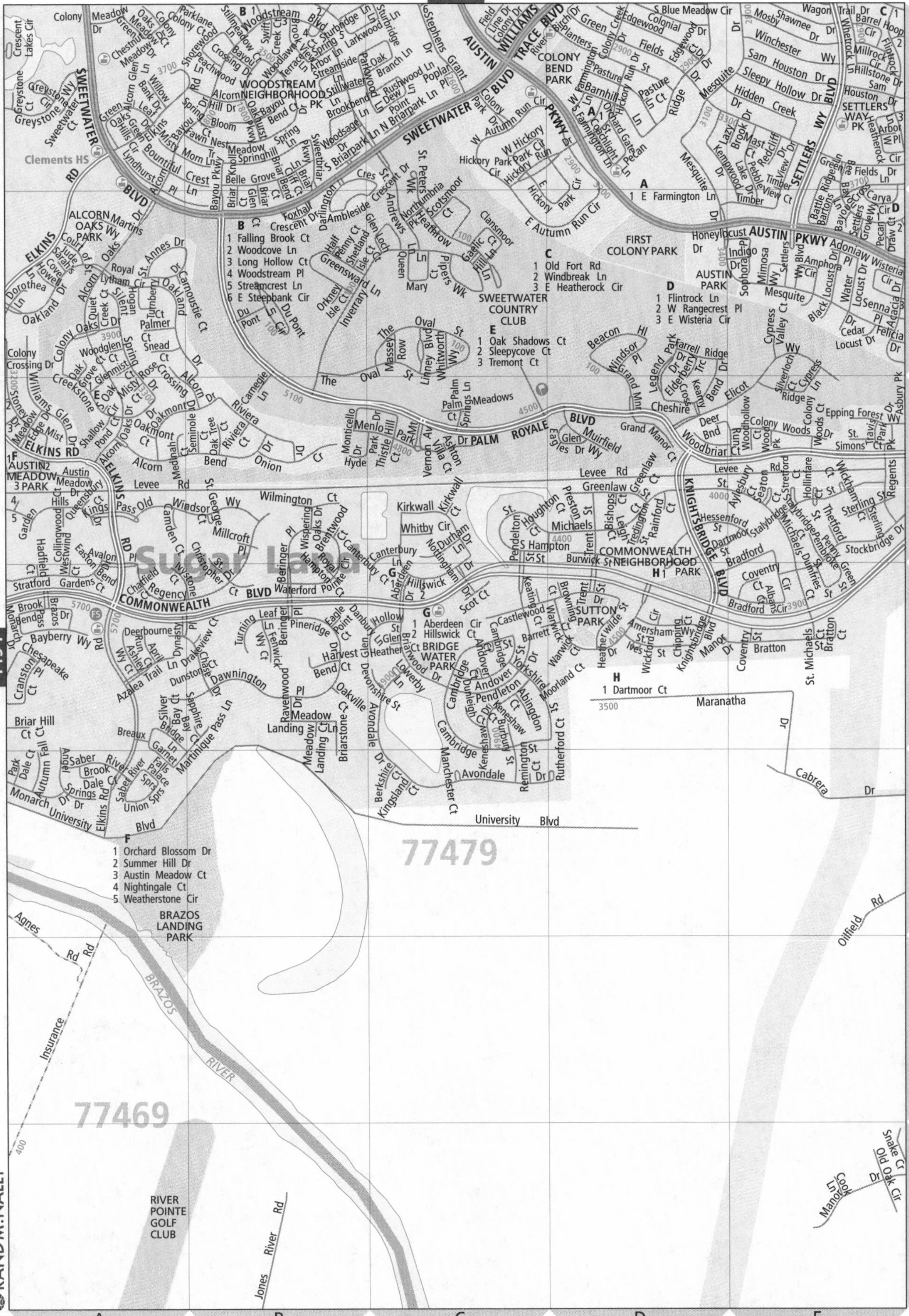
Sugar Land
77479
77469
SWEETWATER COUNTRY CLUB
WOODSTREAM NEIGHBORHOOD PK
COLONY BEND PARK
FIRST COLONY PARK
AUSTIN PARK
SETTLERS WAY PK
ALCORN OAKS PARK
AUSTIN MEADOW PARK
COMMONWEALTH NEIGHBORHOOD PARK
SUTTON PARK
BRIDGE WATER PARK
BRAZOS LANDING PARK
RIVER POINTE GOLF CLUB
Clements HS
BRAZOS RIVER
SWEETWATER BLVD
AUSTIN PKWY
WILLIAMS TRACE BLVD
ELKINS RD
PALM ROYALE BLVD
COMMONWEALTH BLVD
KNIGHTSBRIDGE BLVD
SETTLERS WY
University Blvd
Levee Rd
A
1 E Farmington Ln
B
1 Falling Brook Ct
2 Woodcove Ln
3 Long Hollow Ct
4 Woodstream Pl
5 Streamcrest Ln
6 E Steepbank Cir
C
1 Old Fort Rd
2 Windbreak Ln
3 E Heatherock Cir
D
1 Flintrock Ln
2 W Rangecrest Pl
3 E Wisteria Cir
E
1 Oak Shadows Ct
2 Sleepycove Ct
3 Tremont Ct
F
1 Orchard Blossom Dr
2 Summer Hill Dr
3 Austin Meadow Ct
4 Nightingale Ct
5 Weatherstone Cir
G
1 Aberdeen Cir
2 Hillswick Ct
H
1 Dartmoor Ct
29°34'57"
29°34'31"
29°34'04"
29°33'38"
29°33'12"
29°32'46"
29°32'20"
29°31'54"
95°38'06"
95°37'36"
95°37'06"
95°36'36"
95°36'06"
95°35'36"
A B C D E
1 2 3 4 5 6 7

SEE 4496 MAP

SEE B MAP

1:24,000
1 in. = 2000 ft.
0 0.25 0.5
miles

SEE 4369 MAP

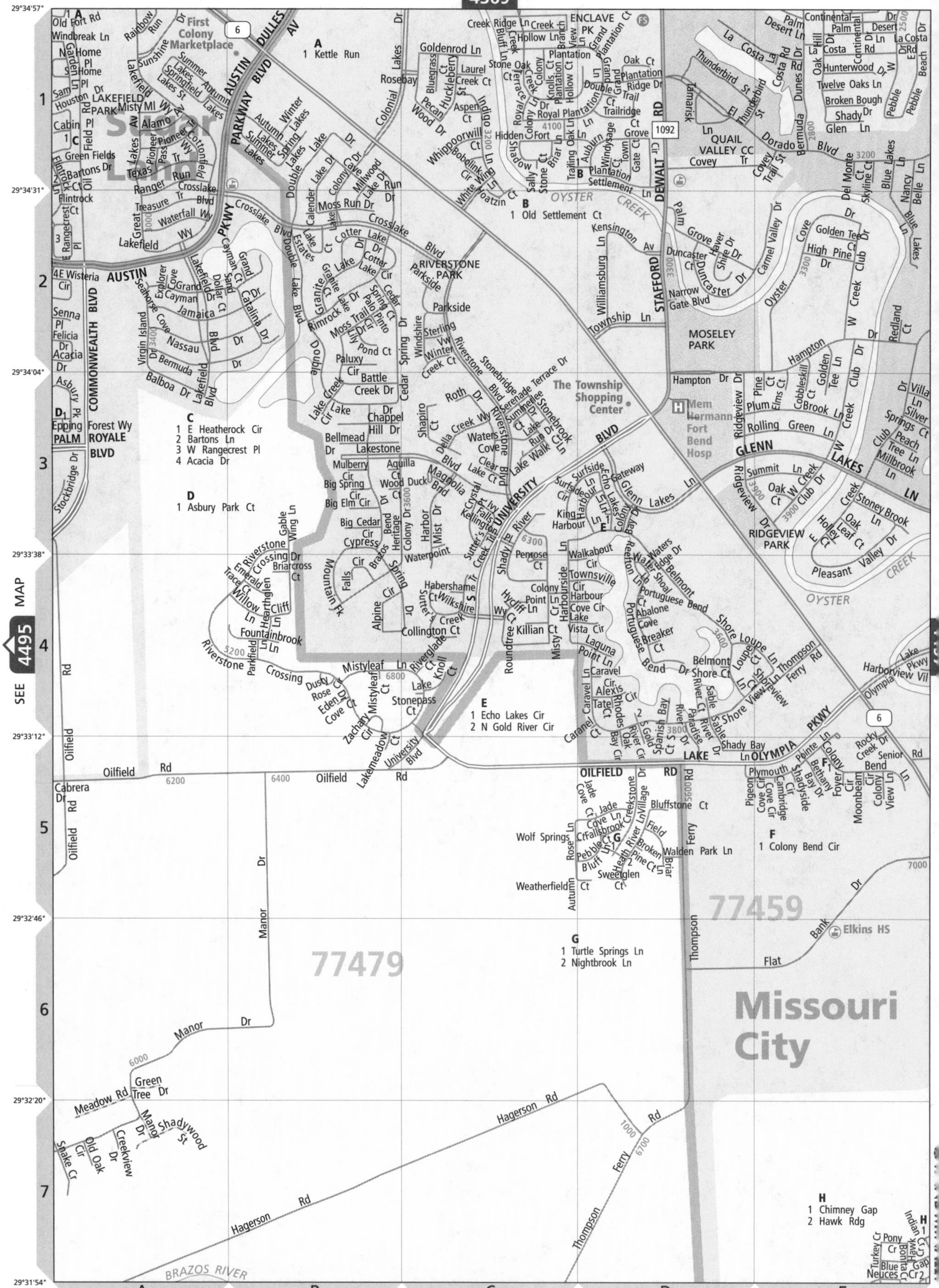
First Colony Marketplace
Sugar Land
LAKEFIELD PARK
AUSTIN PKWY
DULLES AV
AUSTIN PARKWAY BLVD
COMMONWEALTH BLVD
PALM ROYALE BLVD
RIVERSTONE PARK
ENCLAVE PK
QUAIL VALLEY CC
MOSELEY PARK
The Township Shopping Center
Mem Hermann Fort Bend Hosp
RIDGEVIEW PARK
UNIVERSITY BLVD
GLENN LAKES LN
STAFFORD RD
DEWALT RD
OLYMPIA PKWY
LAKE OLYMPIA PKWY
OILFIELD RD
Oilfield Rd
Manor Dr
Hagerson Rd
Ferry Rd
Thompson
Flat Bank Dr
Elkins HS
OYSTER CREEK
BRAZOS RIVER
77479
77459
Missouri City
A
1 Kettle Run
B
1 Old Settlement Ct
C
1 E Heatherock Cir
2 Bartons Ln
3 W Rangecrest Pl
4 Acacia Dr
D
1 Asbury Park Ct
E
1 Echo Lakes Cir
2 N Gold River Cir
F
1 Colony Bend Cir
G
1 Turtle Springs Ln
2 Nightbrook Ln
H
1 Chimney Gap
2 Hawk Rdg
29°34'57"
29°34'31"
29°34'04"
29°33'38"
29°33'12"
29°32'46"
29°32'20"
29°31'54"
95°35'36"
95°35'06"
95°34'36"
95°34'07"
95°33'37"
95°33'07"
A B C D E
1 2 3 4 5 6 7

SEE 4495 MAP

SEE B MAP

1:24,000
1 in. = 2000 ft.
0 0.25 0.5
miles

SEE 4370 MAP

A
1 Hampshire Ln
2 Cambridge Ln
3 Oak Pointe Blvd
4 Quail Creek Dr
5 Kissing Camel Ct
6 Quail Hollow Dr
B
1 Harborview Vil
2 Crow Valley Dr
C
1 Truesdale Ln
2 Antelope Hills Dr
3 Shiloh Ct
D
1 Hawk Rdg
77545
Missouri City
77459
77489
Houston
QUAIL VALLEY COUNTRY CLUB
MISSOURI CITY COMM PK
CRESCENT OAK VILLAGE PARK
FREEDOM TREE PK
LAKESHORE HARBOUR PARK
DEWALT CEM
KITTY HOLLOW PARK
KITTY HOLLOW LK
LAKE OLYMPIA
NORTH ROANE PK
SOUTH ROANE PK
TEXAS PKWY
MCHARD RD
GLENN LAKES LN
MISSION VALLEY DR
TURTLE CREEK DR
SIENNA PKWY
Olympia Pkwy
Senior Rd
Trammel-Fresno Rd
Kitty Hollow Park Dr
OYSTER CREEK
29°34'55"
29°34'29"
29°34'02"
29°33'36"
29°33'10"
29°32'44"
29°32'18"
29°31'52"
95°33'07"
95°32'37"
95°32'07"
95°31'37"
95°31'07"
95°30'37"
A B C D E
1 2 3 4 5 6 7

SEE 4498 MAP

SEE 4621 MAP

1:24,000
1 in. = 2000 ft.
0 0.25 0.5
miles

SEE 4371 MAP

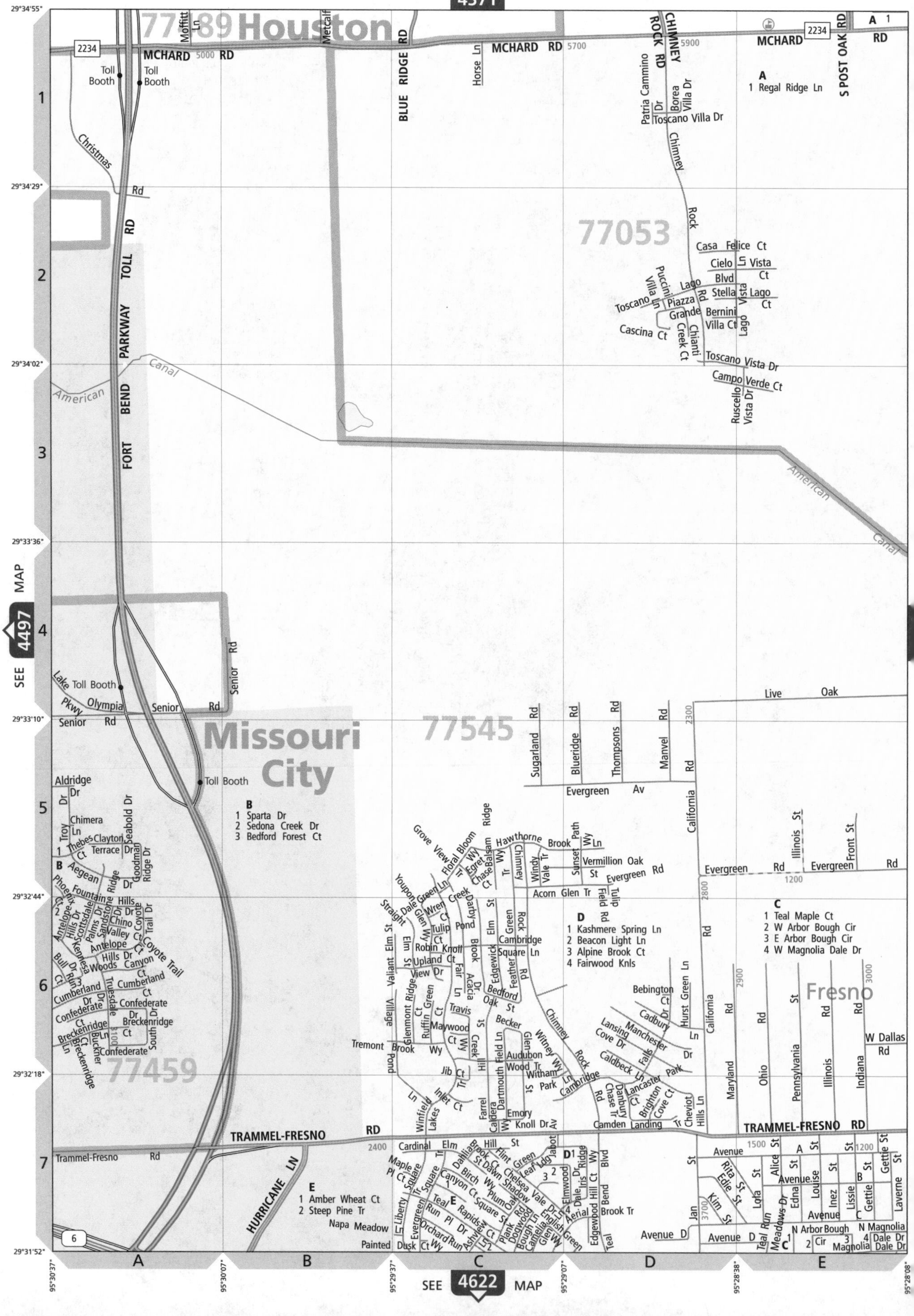
Houston
77489
77053
77545
77459
Missouri City
Fresno
MCHARD RD
FORT BEND PARKWAY TOLL RD
BLUE RIDGE RD
CHIMNEY ROCK RD
S POST OAK RD
TRAMMEL-FRESNO RD
HURRICANE LN
American Canal
Toll Booth
A
1 Regal Ridge Ln
B
1 Sparta Dr
2 Sedona Creek Dr
3 Bedford Forest Ct
C
1 Teal Maple Ct
2 W Arbor Bough Cir
3 E Arbor Bough Cir
4 W Magnolia Dale Dr
D
1 Kashmere Spring Ln
2 Beacon Light Ln
3 Alpine Brook Ct
4 Fairwood Knls
E
1 Amber Wheat Ct
2 Steep Pine Tr
Evergreen Av
Evergreen Rd
Live Oak
Senior Rd
Olympia
Lake Olympia Pkwy
Sugarland Rd
Blueridge Rd
Thompsons Rd
Manvel Rd
California Rd
Maryland Rd
Ohio Rd
Pennsylvania St
Illinois Rd
Indiana Rd
W Dallas Rd
Trammel-Fresno Rd
Toscano Vista Dr
Campo Verde Ct
Casa Felice Ct
Toscano Villa Dr
Cambridge Square Ln
Tremont Brook Wy
Confederate Ct
Breckenridge Ct
Aldridge Dr
Chimera Ln
Avenue D
Painted Dusk Ct
Napa Meadow
Cardinal Elm
Hill St
29°34'55"
29°34'29"
29°34'02"
29°33'36"
29°33'10"
29°32'44"
29°32'18"
29°31'52"
95°30'37"
95°30'07"
95°29'37"
95°29'07"
95°28'38"
95°28'08"

SEE 4497 MAP

SEE 4622 MAP

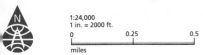

1:24,000
1 in. = 2000 ft.
0 0.25 0.5
miles

SEE 4372 MAP

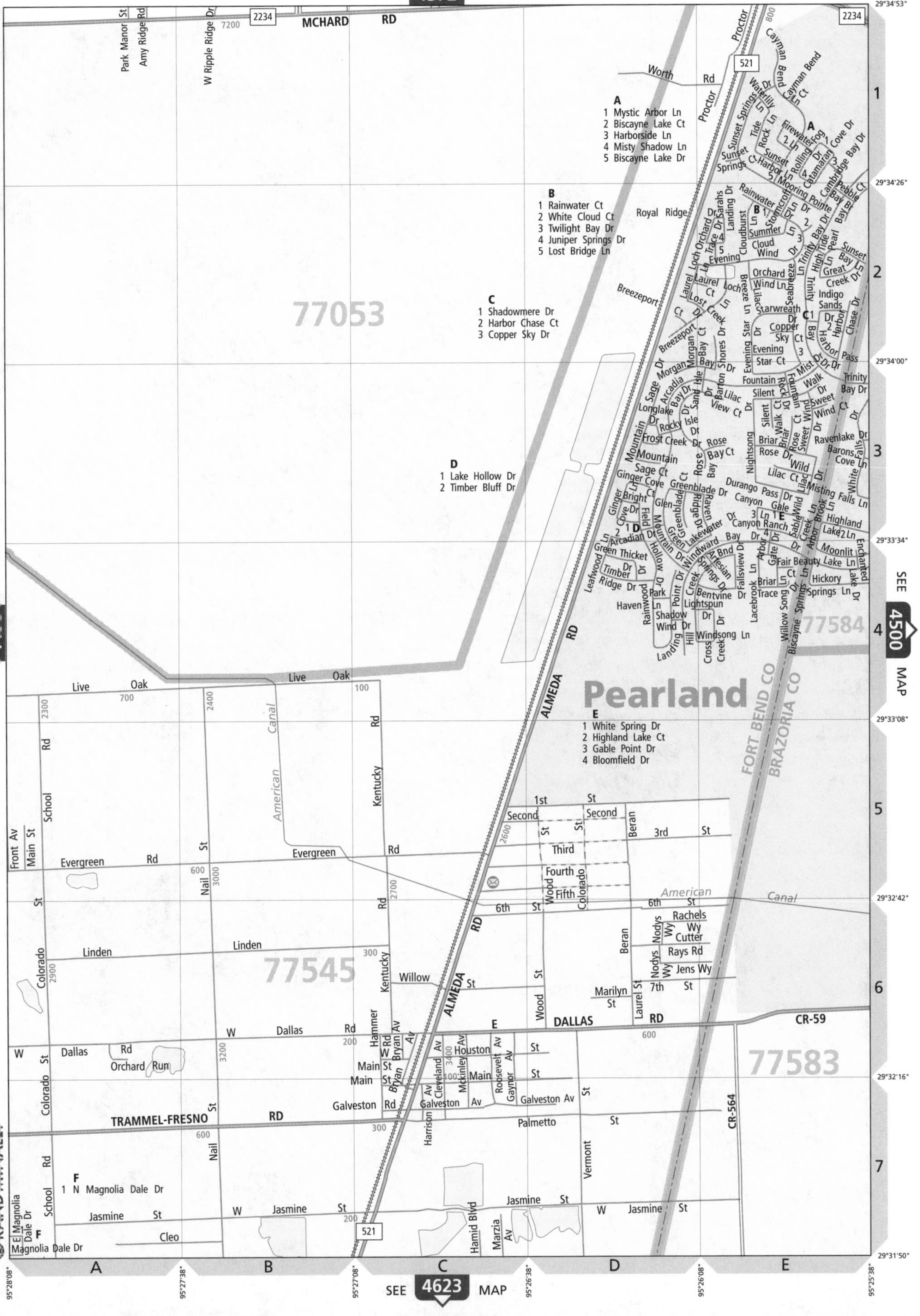
MCHARD RD
2234
7200
Park Manor St
Amy Ridge Rd
W Ripple Ridge Dr
Worth Rd
Proctor
521
800
77053
A
1 Mystic Arbor Ln
2 Biscayne Lake Ct
3 Harborside Ln
4 Misty Shadow Ln
5 Biscayne Lake Dr
B
1 Rainwater Ct
2 White Cloud Ct
3 Twilight Bay Dr
4 Juniper Springs Dr
5 Lost Bridge Ln
C
1 Shadowmere Dr
2 Harbor Chase Ct
3 Copper Sky Dr
D
1 Lake Hollow Dr
2 Timber Bluff Dr
E
1 White Spring Dr
2 Highland Lake Ct
3 Gable Point Dr
4 Bloomfield Dr
F
1 N Magnolia Dale Dr
Royal Ridge
Breezeport
Pearland
77584
FORT BEND CO
BRAZORIA CO
ALMEDA RD
Live Oak
700
100
2300
2400
School Rd
Kentucky Rd
American Canal
Front Av
Main St
Evergreen Rd
Nail St
Colorado St
Linden
77545
Willow St
W Dallas Rd
DALLAS RD
CR-59
77583
Orchard Run
TRAMMEL-FRESNO RD
Galveston Rd
Palmetto St
CR-564
Vermont St
Jasmine St
W Jasmine St
Cleo
Magnolia Dale Dr
Hamid Blvd
Marzia Av
1st St
Second St
3rd St
Third
Fourth
Fifth
6th St
Beran
Rachels Wy
Cutter
Rays Rd
Jens Wy
7th St
Marilyn St
Laurel St
Wood St
Houston St
Main St
Galveston Av
Harrison
Cleveland Av
Mckinley Av
Roosevelt Av
Gaynor Av
Bryan Av
Hammer
600
3000
3200
2900
2700
2600
300
200
29°34'53"
29°34'26"
29°34'00"
29°33'34"
29°33'08"
29°32'42"
29°32'16"
29°31'50"
95°28'08"
95°27'38"
95°27'08"
95°26'38"
95°26'08"
95°25'38"
1
2
3
4
5
6
7
A
B
C
D
E

SEE 4500 MAP

SEE 4623 MAP

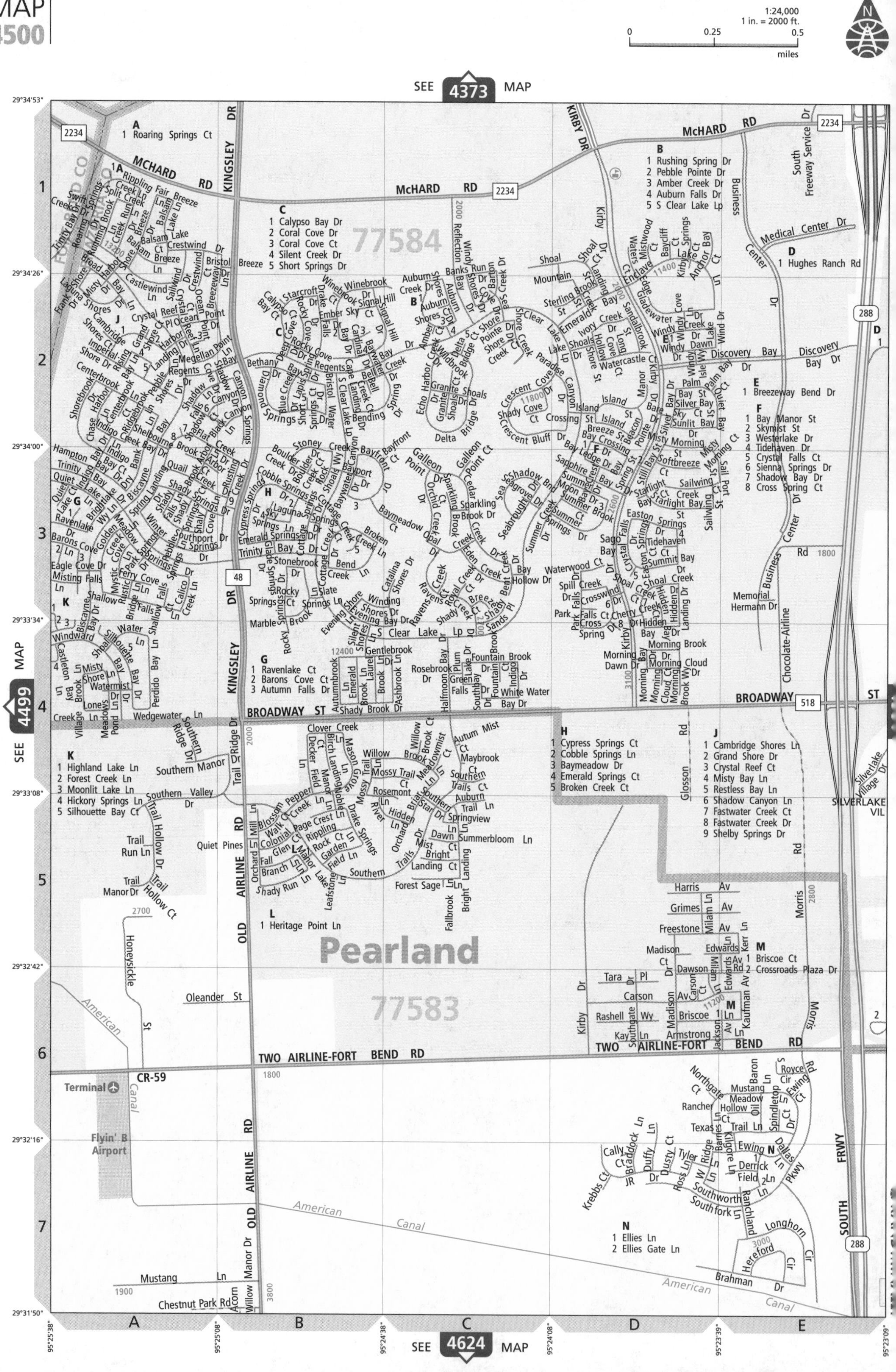
1:24,000
1 in. = 2000 ft.
0
0.25
0.5
miles
N
SEE 4373 MAP
SEE 4624 MAP
SEE 4499 MAP
77584
77583
Pearland
MCHARD RD
McHARD RD
2234
KINGSLEY DR
KIRBY DR
BROADWAY ST
BROADWAY
518
48
288
OLD AIRLINE RD
TWO AIRLINE-FORT BEND RD
CR-59
SOUTH FRWY
South Freeway Service Dr
Business Center Dr
Chocolate-Airline
Morris Rd
Glosson Rd
Medical Center Dr
Discovery Bay Dr
Memorial Hermann Dr
SILVERLAKE VIL
Silverlake Village Dr
Terminal
Flyin' B Airport
American Canal
Oleander St
Honeysickle St
Mustang Ln
Chestnut Park Rd
Willow Manor Dr
A
1 Roaring Springs Ct
B
1 Rushing Spring Dr
2 Pebble Pointe Dr
3 Amber Creek Dr
4 Auburn Falls Dr
5 S Clear Lake Lp
C
1 Calypso Bay Dr
2 Coral Cove Dr
3 Coral Cove Ct
4 Silent Creek Dr
5 Short Springs Dr
D
1 Hughes Ranch Rd
E
1 Breezeway Bend Dr
F
1 Bay Manor St
2 Skymist St
3 Westerlake Dr
4 Tidehaven Dr
5 Crystal Falls Ct
6 Sienna Springs Dr
7 Shadow Bay Dr
8 Cross Spring Ct
G
1 Ravenlake Ct
2 Barons Cove Ct
3 Autumn Falls Dr
H
1 Cypress Springs Ct
2 Cobble Springs Ln
3 Baymeadow Dr
4 Emerald Springs Ct
5 Broken Creek Ct
J
1 Cambridge Shores Ln
2 Grand Shore Dr
3 Crystal Reef Ct
4 Misty Bay Ln
5 Restless Bay Ln
6 Shadow Canyon Ln
7 Fastwater Creek Ct
8 Fastwater Creek Dr
9 Shelby Springs Dr
K
1 Highland Lake Ln
2 Forest Creek Ln
3 Moonlit Lake Ln
4 Hickory Springs Ln
5 Silhouette Bay Ct
L
1 Heritage Point Ln
M
1 Briscoe Ct
2 Crossroads Plaza Dr
N
1 Ellies Ln
2 Ellies Gate Ln
1
2
3
4
5
6
7
A
B
C
D
E
29°34'53"
29°34'26"
29°34'00"
29°33'34"
29°33'08"
29°32'42"
29°32'16"
29°31'50"
95°25'38"
95°25'08"
95°24'38"
95°24'08"
95°23'39"
95°23'09"

1:24,000
1 in. = 2000 ft.
0 0.25 0.5
miles

SEE 4374 MAP

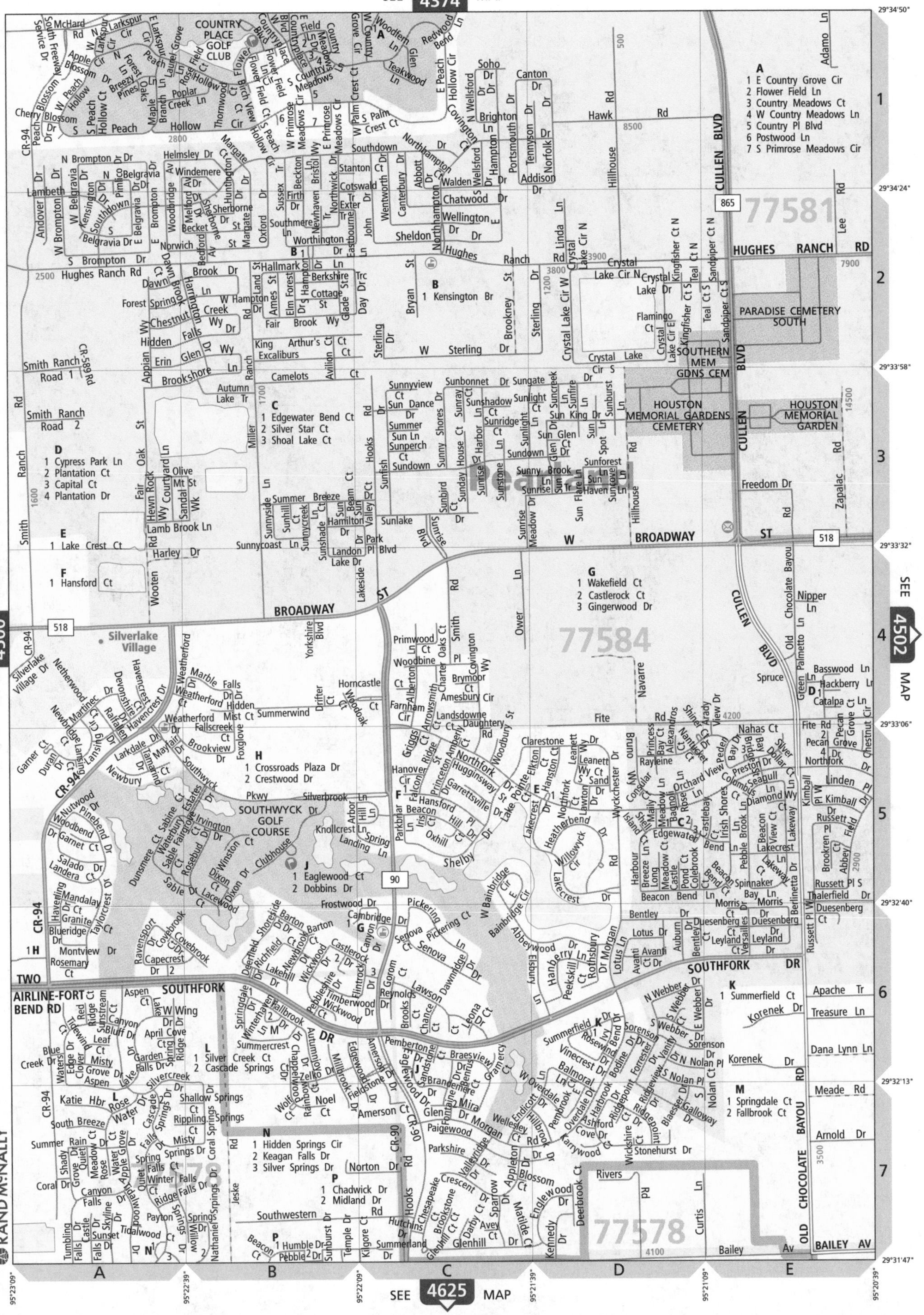
A
1 E Country Grove Cir
2 Flower Field Ln
3 Country Meadows Ct
4 W Country Meadows Ln
5 Country Pl Blvd
6 Postwood Ln
7 S Primrose Meadows Cir
B
1 Kensington Br
C
1 Edgewater Bend Ct
2 Silver Star Ct
3 Shoal Lake Ct
D
1 Cypress Park Ln
2 Plantation Ct
3 Capital Ct
4 Plantation Dr
E
1 Lake Crest Ct
F
1 Hansford Ct
G
1 Wakefield Ct
2 Castlerock Ct
3 Gingerwood Dr
H
1 Crossroads Plaza Dr
2 Crestwood Dr
J
1 Eaglewood Ct
2 Dobbins Dr
K
1 Summerfield Ct
L
1 Silver Creek Ct
2 Cascade Springs Ct
M
1 Springdale Ct
2 Fallbrook Ct
N
1 Hidden Springs Cir
2 Keagan Falls Dr
3 Silver Springs Dr
P
1 Chadwick Dr
2 Midland Dr
COUNTRY PLACE GOLF CLUB
SOUTHWYCK GOLF COURSE
PARADISE CEMETERY SOUTH
SOUTHERN MEM GDNS CEM
HOUSTON MEMORIAL GARDENS CEMETERY
HOUSTON MEMORIAL GARDEN
Pearland
Silverlake Village
77581
77584
77578
CULLEN BLVD
HUGHES RANCH RD
BROADWAY ST
W BROADWAY ST
SOUTHFORK DR
TWO AIRLINE-FORT BEND RD
CHOCOLATE BAYOU RD
OLD CHOCOLATE BAYOU
BAILEY AV
Hughes Ranch Rd
Smith Ranch Road
CR-94
CR-90
865
518
90
SEE 4502 MAP
SEE 4500 MAP
A B C D E
1 2 3 4 5 6 7
29°34'50"
29°34'24"
29°33'58"
29°33'32"
29°33'06"
29°32'40"
29°32'13"
29°31'47"
95°23'09"
95°22'39"
95°22'09"
95°21'39"
95°21'09"
95°20'39"
RAND McNALLY

SEE 4625 MAP

1:24,000
1 in. = 2000 ft.
0 0.25 0.5
miles

SEE 4375 MAP

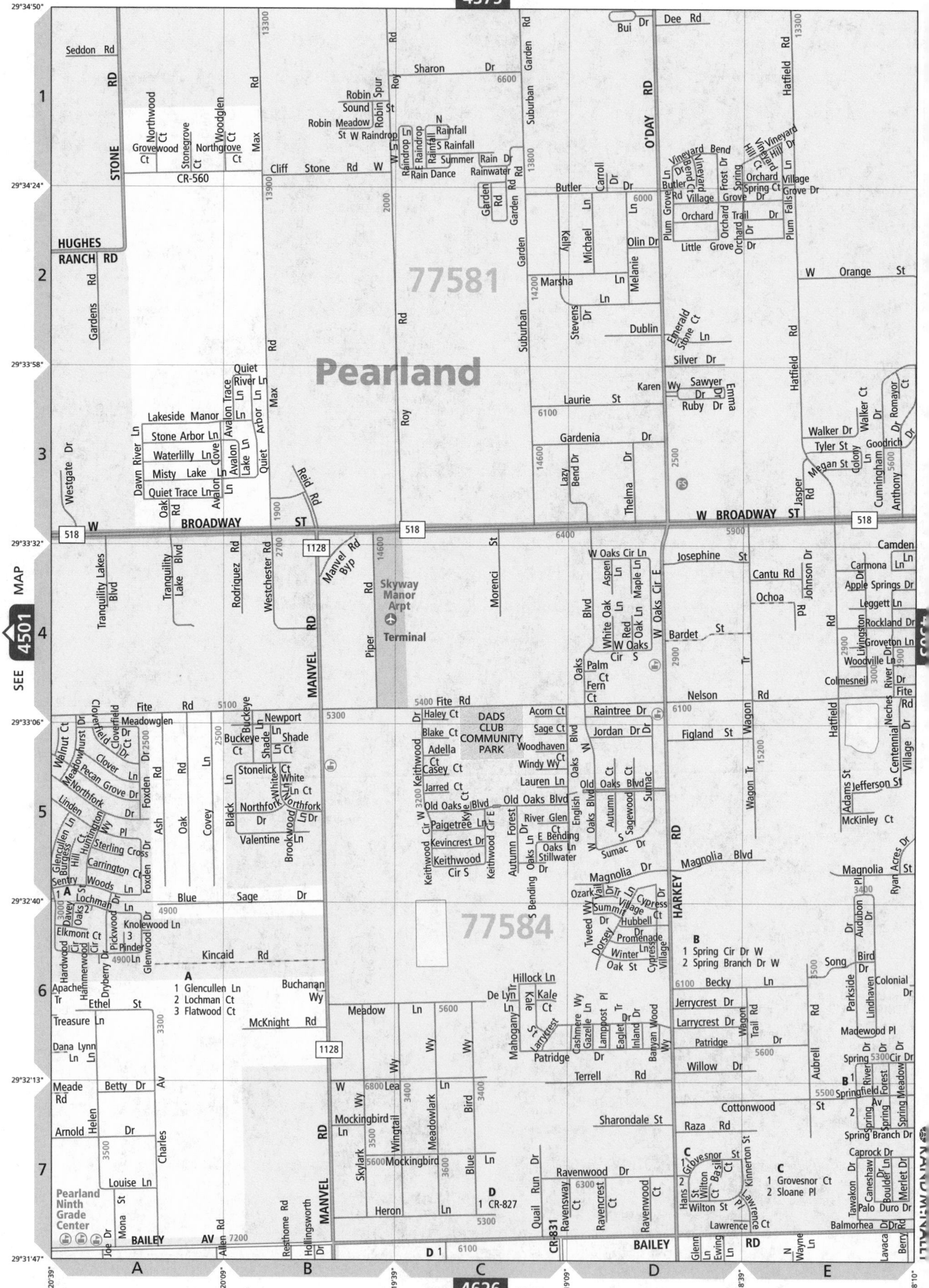
Pearland
77581
77584
Skyway Manor Arpt
Terminal
DADS CLUB COMMUNITY PARK
Pearland Ninth Grade Center
W BROADWAY ST
518
1128
MANVEL RD
O'DAY RD
HARKEY RD
STONE RD
HUGHES RANCH RD
BAILEY AV
BAILEY RD
CR-560
CR-831
Seddon Rd
Sharon Dr
Dee Rd
Bui Dr
Robin Spur
Robin Sound
Robin St
Robin Meadow St
W Raindrop Ln
Rainfall
S Rainfall
Summer Rain Dr
Rain Dance
Rainwater Rd
Cliff Stone Rd W
Grovewood Ct
Northwood Ct
Stonegrove Ct
Woodglen Ct
Northgrove Ct
Max Rd
Garden Rd
Suburban Garden Rd
Butler Dr
Carroll Dr
Kelly Ln
Michael Ln
Olin Dr
Melanie
Marsha Ln
Stevens Dr
Dublin
Emerald Stone Ct
Silver Dr
Karen Wy
Sawyer Dr
Ruby Dr
Emma Dr
Laurie St
Gardenia Dr
Lazy Bend Dr
Thelma Dr
Vineyard Bend
Vineyard Hill Dr
Orchard Village
Spring Grove Dr
Plum Grove Ln
Plum Falls
Little Grove
Orchard Trail Dr
Hatfield Rd
W Orange St
Walker Dr
Walker Ct
Tyler St
Megan St
Goodrich
Romayor Ct
Colony Ln
Cunningham Dr
Anthony
Jasper Rd
Westgate Dr
Lakeside Manor
Stone Arbor Ln
Waterlilly Ln
Misty Lake Ln
Quiet Trace Ln
Dawn River Ln
Oak Rd
Avalon Trace
Avalon Cove
Avalon Lake Ln
Quiet River Ln
Arbor Ln
Quiet
Reid Rd
Roy Rd
Tranquility Lakes Blvd
Tranquility Lake Blvd
Rodriguez Rd
Westchester Rd
Manvel Rd Byp
Piper Rd
Morenci St
W Oaks Cir Ln
Aspen Ln
Maple Ln
White Oak Ln
Red Oak Ln
W Oaks Cir S
W Oaks Cir E
Oaks Blvd
Palm Ct
Fern Ct
Josephine St
Cantu Rd
Ochoa
Johnson Dr
Bardet St
Nelson Rd
Wagon Tr
Camden
Carmona Ln
Apple Springs Dr
Leggett Ln
Rockland Dr
Livingston
Groveton Ln
Woodville Ln
Colmesneil
Fite Rd
Neches River Dr
Centennial Dr
Village
Fite
Meadowglen
Cloverfield
Walnut Ct
Meadowhurst Dr
Clover Ln
Pecan Grove Dr
Northfork
Linden Dr
Huntington Wy
Sterling Cross
Carrington Ct
Woods Ln
Foxden Dr
Ash
Oak
Covey Ln
Black Ln
Buckeye Ct
Shade Ln
Newport
Shade Ct
Stonelick Ct
White Ln Ct
Northfork Dr
Valentine Ln
Brookwood
Haley Ct
Blake Ct
Adella Ct
Casey Ct
Jarred Ct
Keithwood Dr
Old Oaks Blvd
Paigetree Ln
Kevincrest Dr
Keithwood Cir S
Keithwood Cir E
Acorn Ct
Sage Ct
Woodhaven
Windy Wy
Lauren Ln
River Glen Ct
E Bending Oaks Ln
Stillwater Dr
Autumn Forest Dr
Raintree Dr
Jordan Dr
English Oaks Blvd
Autumn Ct
Sagewood
Sumac Dr
Figland St
Adams St
Jefferson St
McKinley Ct
Magnolia Dr
Magnolia Blvd
Magnolia St
Ryan Acres Dr
Ozark
Tweed Wy
Summit
Cypress Ct
Hubbell
Dorsey
Promenade
Winter Ln
Oak St
Cypress Village
Blue Sage Dr
Lochman
Knolewood Ln
Elkmont Ct
Pickwood Dr
Pinder
Glenwood Dr
Kincaid Rd
Hardwood Cir
Apache Tr
Ethel St
Treasure Ln
Dana Lynn Ln
Meade Rd
Betty Dr
Arnold
Helen Dr
Charles Av
Louise Ln
Mona St
Joe Dr
Allen Rd
Resthome Rd
Hollingsworth Dr
Buchanan Wy
McKnight Rd
Meadow Ln
Lea Wy
Mockingbird Ln
Skylark Wy
Wingtail
Meadowlark Wy
Bird Wy
Blue Ln
Heron Ln
CR-827
Hillock Ln
De Lyn Tr
Kale Ct
Larrycrest
Mahogany Ln
Patridge Dr
Cashmere Wy
Gazelle Ln
Lamppost Pl
Eagle Tr
Inland Dr
Banyan Wood Wy
Terrell Rd
Sharondale St
Quail Run Dr
Ravenwood Dr
Ravensway Ct
Ravencrest Ct
Ravenwood Ct
Becky Ln
Jerrycrest Dr
Larrycrest Dr
Patridge Dr
Willow Dr
Cottonwood St
Raza Rd
Grovesnor St
Wilton Ct
Basil Ct
Kinnerton St
Lawrence Ct
Hans St
Glenn Ln
Ewing Ln
Wayne Ln
Song
Bird Dr
Colonial Dr
Parkside Dr
Lindhaven Dr
Audubon Dr
Madewood Pl
Aubrell Rd
Spring Cir Dr
Spring River
Springfield Av
Spring Forest
Spring Meadow
Spring Branch Dr
Caprock Dr
Tawakon Dr
Caneshaw
Boulder Ln
Merlet Dr
Palo Duro Dr
Balmorhea
Lavaca
Berry Rd
A
1 Glencullen Ln
2 Lochman Ct
3 Flatwood Ct
B
1 Spring Cir Dr W
2 Spring Branch Dr W
C
1 Grovesnor Ct
2 Sloane Pl
D
1 CR-827
A B C D E
1 2 3 4 5 6 7

SEE 4501 MAP

SEE 4626 MAP

1:24,000
1 in. = 2000 ft.
0 0.25 0.5
miles

SEE 4376 MAP

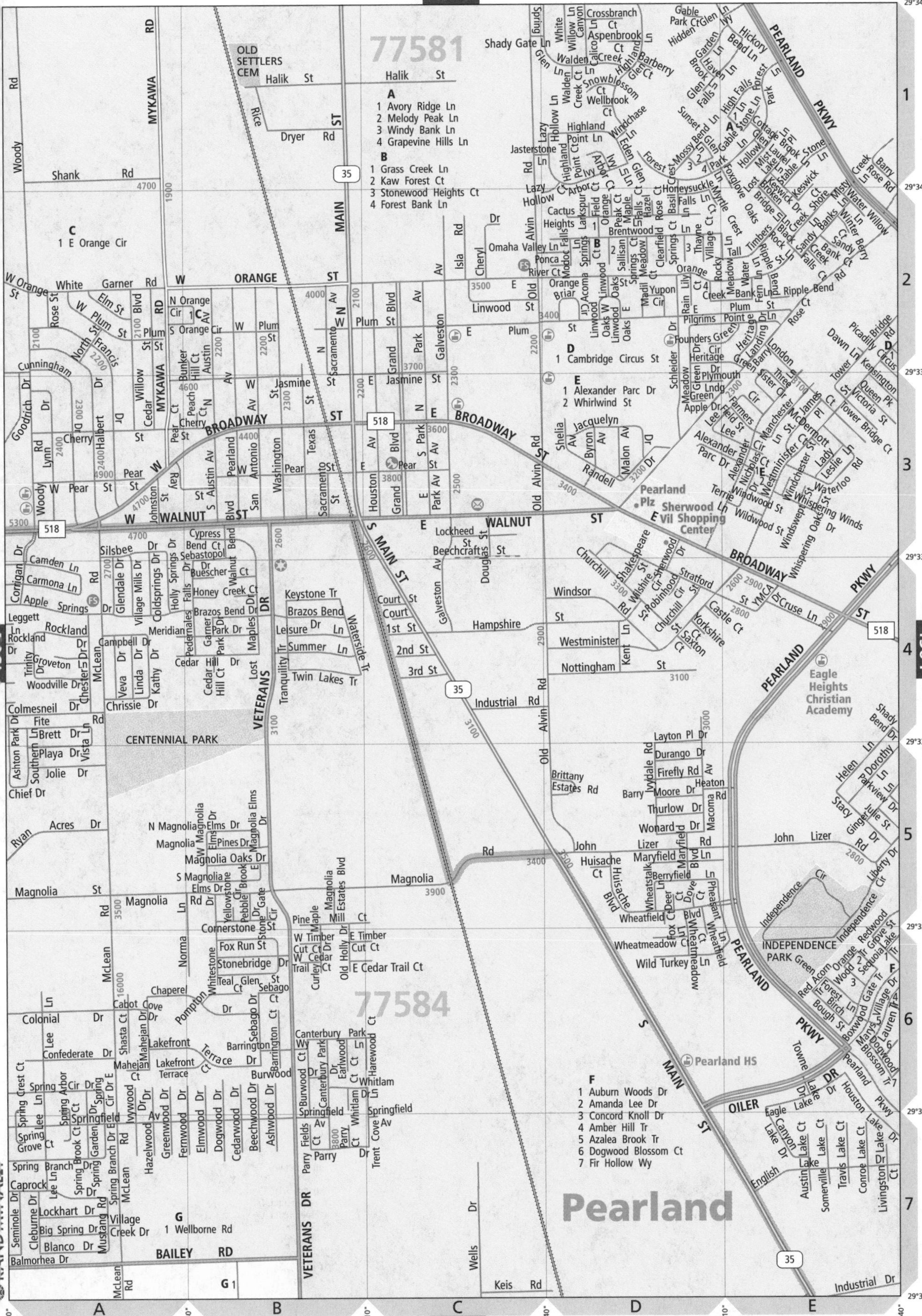
77581
77584
Pearland
OLD SETTLERS CEM
CENTENNIAL PARK
INDEPENDENCE PARK
Pearland HS
Eagle Heights Christian Academy
Pearland Plz
Sherwood Vil Shopping Center
YMCA
MAIN ST
S MAIN ST
W BROADWAY ST
E BROADWAY ST
W WALNUT ST
E WALNUT ST
W ORANGE ST
MYKAWA RD
VETERANS DR
PEARLAND PKWY
OILER DR
BAILEY RD
John Lizer Rd
Old Alvin Rd
Magnolia St
Halik St
Dryer Rd
Shank Rd
Industrial Rd
Keis Rd
35
518
A
1 Avory Ridge Ln
2 Melody Peak Ln
3 Windy Bank Ln
4 Grapevine Hills Ln
B
1 Grass Creek Ln
2 Kaw Forest Ct
3 Stonewood Heights Ct
4 Forest Bank Ln
C
1 E Orange Cir
D
1 Cambridge Circus St
E
1 Alexander Parc Dr
2 Whirlwind St
F
1 Auburn Woods Dr
2 Amanda Lee Dr
3 Concord Knoll Dr
4 Amber Hill Tr
5 Azalea Brook Tr
6 Dogwood Blossom Ct
7 Fir Hollow Wy
G
1 Wellborne Rd
A B C D E
1 2 3 4 5 6 7
29°34'48"
29°34'22"
29°33'55"
29°33'29"
29°33'03"
29°32'37"
29°32'11"
29°31'45"
95°18'10"
95°17'40"
95°17'10"
95°16'40"
95°16'10"
95°15'40"

SEE 4504 MAP

SEE 4627 MAP

1:24,000
1 in. = 2000 ft.
0 0.25 0.5
miles

SEE 4377 MAP

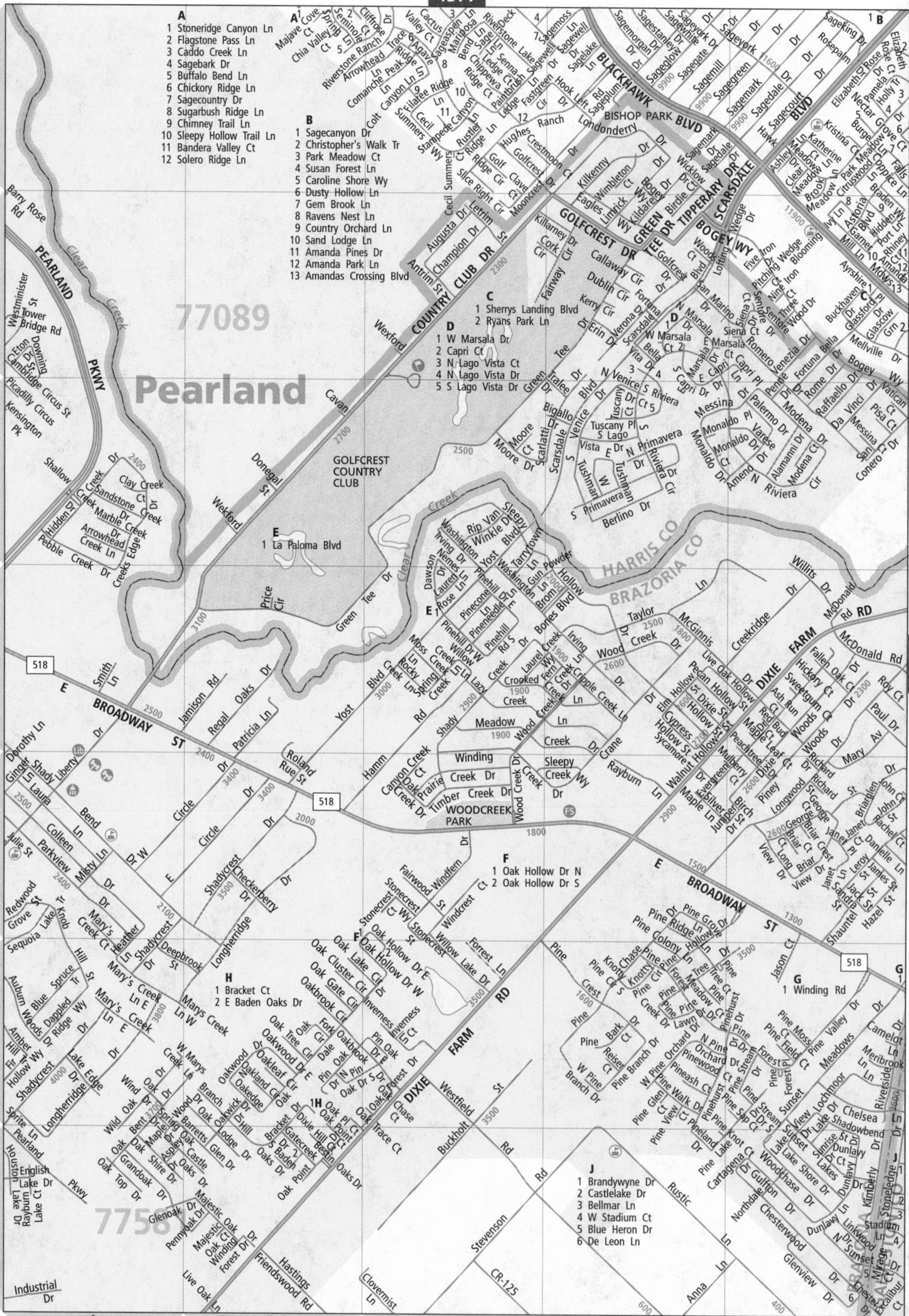
A
1 Stoneridge Canyon Ln
2 Flagstone Pass Ln
3 Caddo Creek Ln
4 Sagebark Dr
5 Buffalo Bend Ln
6 Chickory Ridge Ln
7 Sagecountry Dr
8 Sugarbush Ridge Ln
9 Chimney Trail Ln
10 Sleepy Hollow Trail Ln
11 Bandera Valley Ct
12 Solero Ridge Ln
B
1 Sagecanyon Dr
2 Christopher's Walk Tr
3 Park Meadow Ct
4 Susan Forest Ln
5 Caroline Shore Wy
6 Dusty Hollow Ln
7 Gem Brook Ln
8 Ravens Nest Ln
9 Country Orchard Ln
10 Sand Lodge Ln
11 Amanda Pines Dr
12 Amanda Park Ln
13 Amandas Crossing Blvd
C
1 Sherrys Landing Blvd
2 Ryans Park Ln
D
1 W Marsala Dr
2 Capri Ct
3 N Lago Vista Ct
4 N Lago Vista Dr
5 S Lago Vista Dr
E
1 La Paloma Blvd
F
1 Oak Hollow Dr N
2 Oak Hollow Dr S
G
1 Winding Rd
H
1 Bracket Ct
2 E Baden Oaks Dr
J
1 Brandywyne Dr
2 Castlelake Dr
3 Bellmar Ln
4 W Stadium Ct
5 Blue Heron Dr
6 De Leon Ln
77089
Pearland
GOLFCREST COUNTRY CLUB
WOODCREEK PARK
HARRIS CO
BRAZORIA CO
BLACKHAWK BLVD
BISHOP PARK BLVD
COUNTRY CLUB DR
GOLFCREST DR
SCARSDALE BLVD
PEARLAND PKWY
E BROADWAY ST
DIXIE FARM RD
518
77581

SEE 4503 MAP

SEE 4628 MAP

1:24,000
1 in. = 2000 ft.
0 0.25 0.5
miles

SEE 4378 MAP

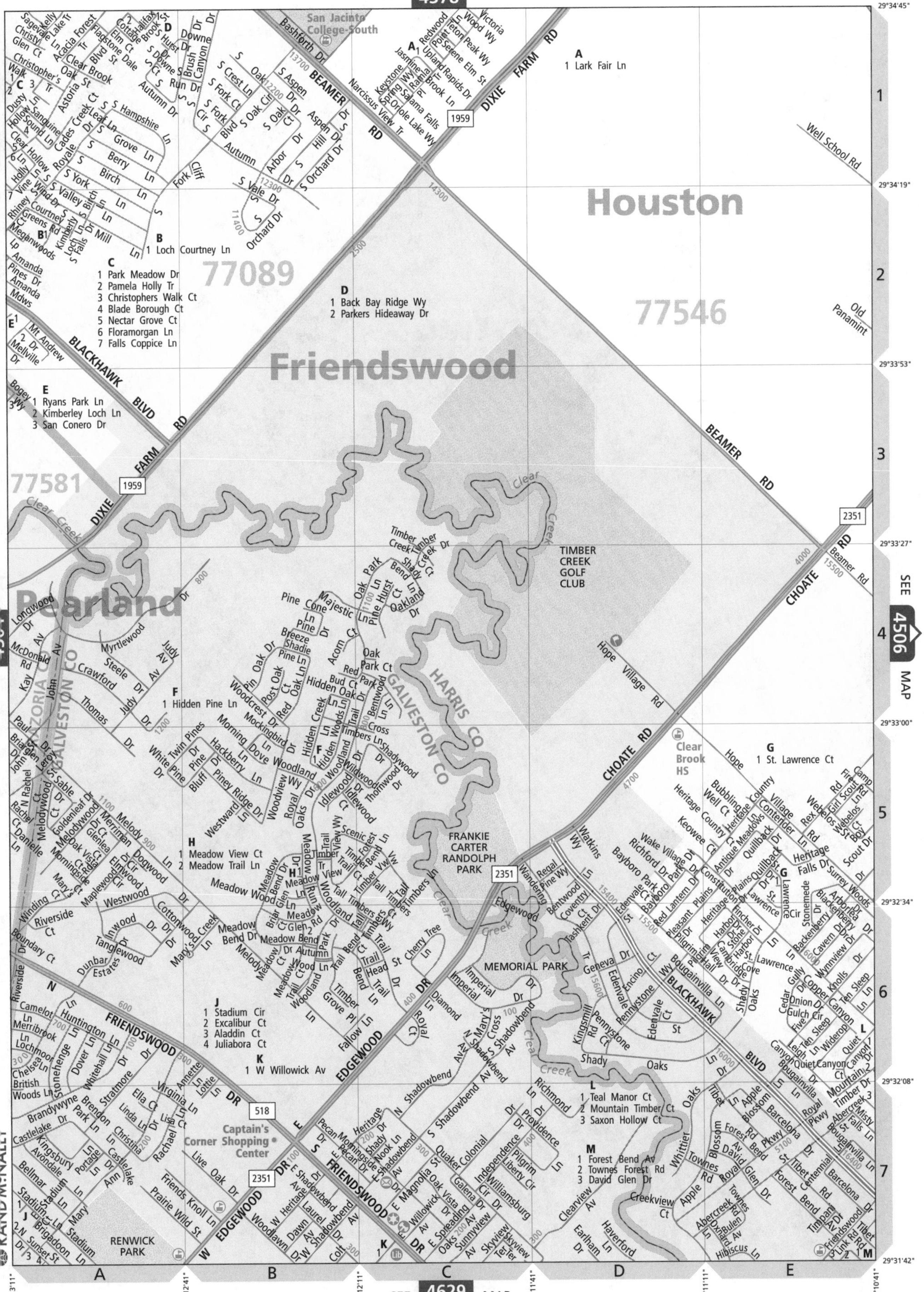
Houston
Friendswood
Pearland
77089
77546
77581
San Jacinto College-South
TIMBER CREEK GOLF CLUB
FRANKIE CARTER RANDOLPH PARK
MEMORIAL PARK
RENWICK PARK
Clear Brook HS
Captain's Corner Shopping Center
BEAMER RD
DIXIE FARM RD
BLACKHAWK BLVD
CHOATE RD
FRIENDSWOOD DR
EDGEWOOD DR
HARRIS CO
GALVESTON CO
BRAZORIA CO
Clear Creek
1959
2351
518
A
1 Lark Fair Ln
B
1 Loch Courtney Ln
C
1 Park Meadow Dr
2 Pamela Holly Tr
3 Christophers Walk Ct
4 Blade Borough Ct
5 Nectar Grove Ct
6 Floramorgan Ln
7 Falls Coppice Ln
D
1 Back Bay Ridge Wy
2 Parkers Hideaway Dr
E
1 Ryans Park Ln
2 Kimberley Loch Ln
3 San Conero Dr
F
1 Hidden Pine Ln
G
1 St. Lawrence Ct
H
1 Meadow View Ct
2 Meadow Trail Ln
J
1 Stadium Cir
2 Excalibur Ct
3 Aladdin Ct
4 Juliabora Ct
K
1 W Willowick Av
L
1 Teal Manor Ct
2 Mountain Timber Ct
3 Saxon Hollow Ct
M
1 Forest Bend Av
2 Townes Forest Rd
3 David Glen Dr
29°34'45"
29°34'19"
29°33'53"
29°33'27"
29°33'00"
29°32'34"
29°32'08"
29°31'42"
95°13'11"
95°12'41"
95°12'11"
95°11'41"
95°11'11"
95°10'41"
A B C D E
1 2 3 4 5 6 7

SEE 4506 MAP

SEE 4629 MAP

1:24,000
1 in. = 2000 ft.
0 0.25 0.5
miles

SEE 4379 MAP

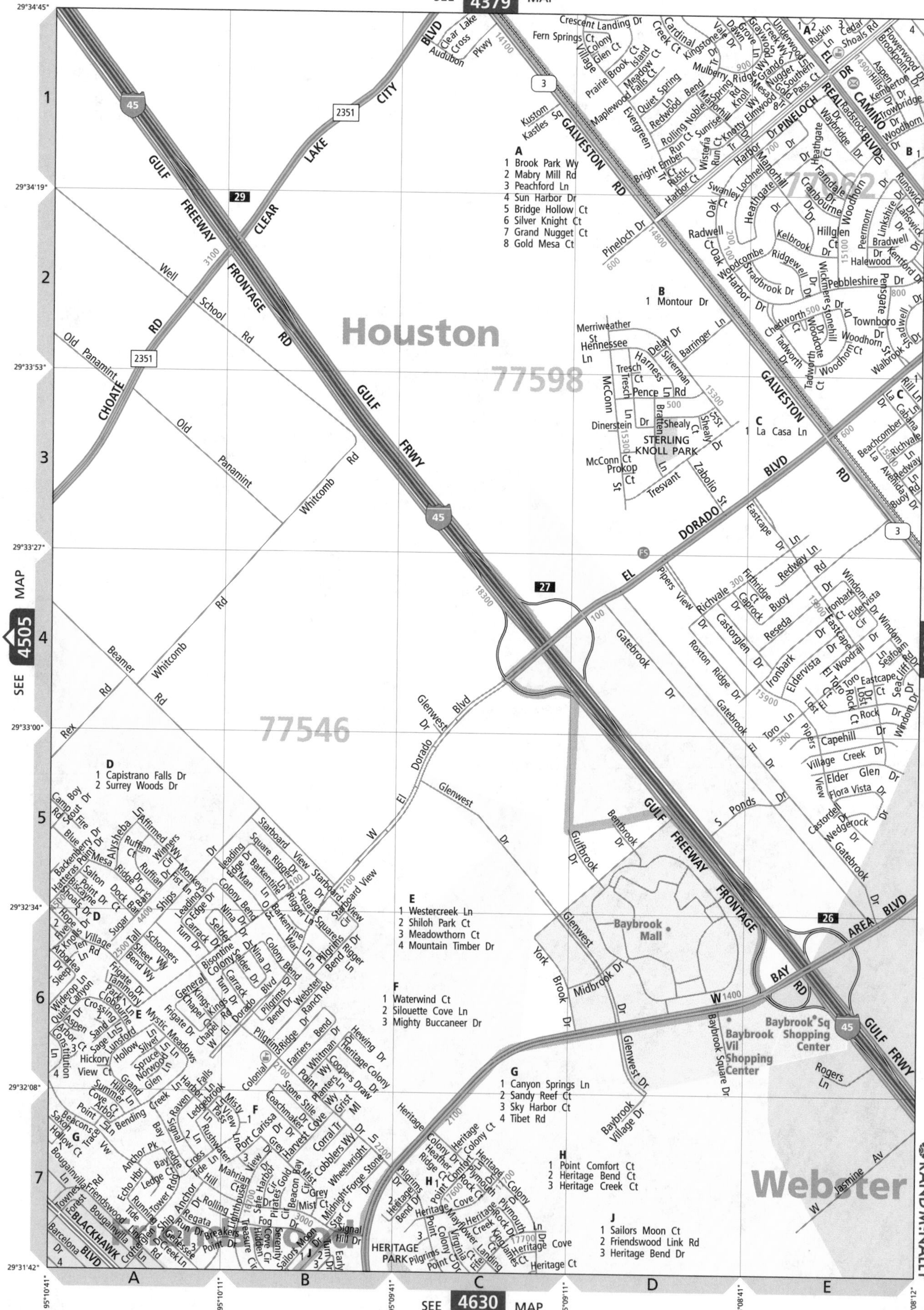
Houston
77598
77546
77062
Webster
Friendswood
GULF FREEWAY FRONTAGE RD
GULF FRWY
CLEAR LAKE CITY BLVD
CHOATE RD
GALVESTON RD
EL DORADO BLVD
BAY AREA BLVD
W BAY AREA BLVD
EL CAMINO REAL
PINELOCH DR
BLACKHAWK BLVD
Old Panamint Rd
Well School Rd
Whitcomb Rd
Beamer Rd
Rex Rd
W El Dorado Blvd
Glenwest Dr
Gatebrook Dr
Baybrook Mall
Baybrook Sq Shopping Center
Baybrook Vil Shopping Center
STERLING KNOLL PARK
HERITAGE PARK
A
1 Brook Park Wy
2 Mabry Mill Rd
3 Peachford Ln
4 Sun Harbor Dr
5 Bridge Hollow Ct
6 Silver Knight Ct
7 Grand Nugget Ct
8 Gold Mesa Ct
B
1 Montour Dr
C
1 La Casa Ln
D
1 Capistrano Falls Dr
2 Surrey Woods Dr
E
1 Westercreek Ln
2 Shiloh Park Ct
3 Meadowthorn Ct
4 Mountain Timber Dr
F
1 Waterwind Ct
2 Silouette Cove Ln
3 Mighty Buccaneer Dr
G
1 Canyon Springs Ln
2 Sandy Reef Ct
3 Sky Harbor Ct
4 Tibet Rd
H
1 Point Comfort Ct
2 Heritage Bend Ct
3 Heritage Creek Ct
J
1 Sailors Moon Ct
2 Friendswood Link Rd
3 Heritage Bend Dr
29°34'45"
29°34'19"
29°33'53"
29°33'27"
29°33'00"
29°32'34"
29°32'08"
29°31'42"
95°10'41"
95°10'11"
95°09'41"
95°09'11"
95°08'41"
95°08'12"

SEE 4505 MAP

SEE 4630 MAP

1:24,000
1 in. = 2000 ft.
0 0.25 0.5
miles

SEE 4380 MAP

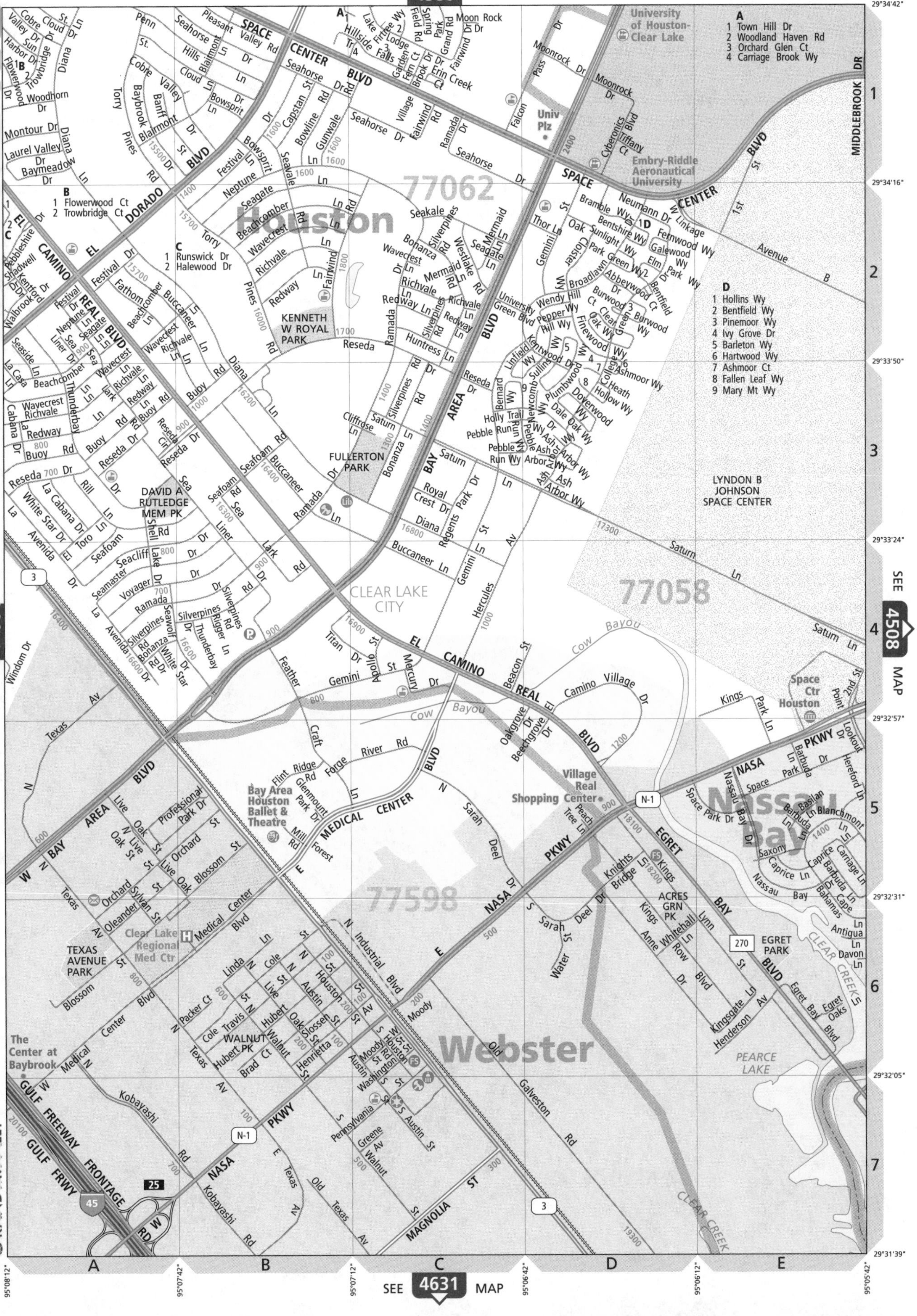

A
1 Town Hill Dr
2 Woodland Haven Rd
3 Orchard Glen Ct
4 Carriage Brook Wy
B
1 Flowerwood Ct
2 Trowbridge Ct
C
1 Runswick Dr
2 Halewood Dr
D
1 Hollins Wy
2 Bentfield Wy
3 Pinemoor Wy
4 Ivy Grove Dr
5 Barleton Wy
6 Hartwood Wy
7 Ashmoor Ct
8 Fallen Leaf Wy
9 Mary Mt Wy
Houston
77062
77058
77598
University of Houston-Clear Lake
Embry-Riddle Aeronautical University
Univ Plz
KENNETH W ROYAL PARK
FULLERTON PARK
DAVID A RUTLEDGE MEM PK
CLEAR LAKE CITY
LYNDON B JOHNSON SPACE CENTER
Space Ctr Houston
Nassau Bay
Village Real Shopping Center
Bay Area Houston Ballet & Theatre
Clear Lake Regional Med Ctr
TEXAS AVENUE PARK
ACRES GRN PK
EGRET PARK
WALNUT PK
The Center at Baybrook
Webster
PEARCE LAKE
CLEAR CREEK
Cow Bayou
SPACE CENTER BLVD
EL CAMINO REAL
EL DORADO BLVD
BAY AREA BLVD
NASA PKWY
MEDICAL CENTER BLVD
GULF FREEWAY
GULF FRWY FRONTAGE RD W
EGRET BAY BLVD
MAGNOLIA ST
MIDDLEBROOK DR
Saturn Ln
Old Galveston Rd
N-1
3
45
270
25

SEE 4508 MAP

SEE 4631 MAP

1:24,000
1 in. = 2000 ft.
0 0.25 0.5
miles

SEE 4381 MAP

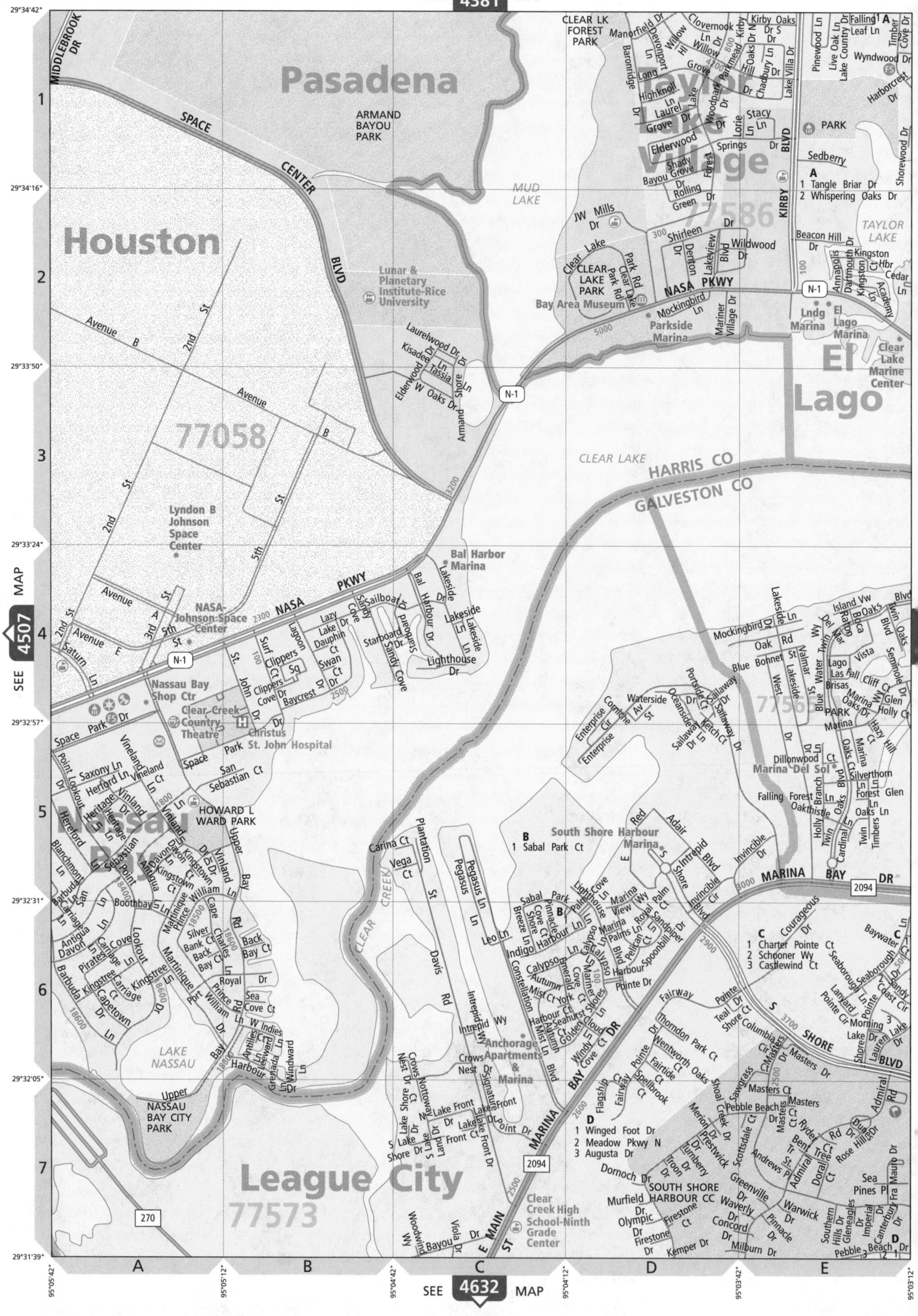
Pasadena
Houston
Taylor Lake Village
El Lago
Nassau Bay
League City
77058
77586
77565
77573
ARMAND BAYOU PARK
MUD LAKE
CLEAR LAKE
TAYLOR LAKE
LAKE NASSAU
CLEAR CREEK
HARRIS CO
GALVESTON CO
SPACE CENTER BLVD
NASA PKWY
MARINA BAY DR
S SHORE BLVD
KIRBY BLVD
E MAIN ST
MIDDLEBROOK DR
Lunar & Planetary Institute-Rice University
Lyndon B Johnson Space Center
NASA-Johnson Space Center
Bay Area Museum
CLEAR LAKE PARK
CLEAR LK FOREST PARK
Parkside Marina
Lndg Marina
El Lago Marina
Clear Lake Marine Center
Bal Harbor Marina
Nassau Bay Shop Ctr
Clear Creek Country Theatre
Christus St. John Hospital
HOWARD L WARD PARK
NASSAU BAY CITY PARK
South Shore Harbour Marina
Marina Del Sol
Anchorage Apartments & Marina
SOUTH SHORE HARBOUR CC
Clear Creek High School-Ninth Grade Center
A
1 Tangle Briar Dr
2 Whispering Oaks Dr
B
1 Sabal Park Ct
C
1 Charter Pointe Ct
2 Schooner Wy
3 Castlewind Ct
D
1 Winged Foot Dr
2 Meadow Pkwy N
3 Augusta Dr
N-1
2094
270
29°34'42"
29°34'16"
29°33'50"
29°33'24"
29°32'57"
29°32'31"
29°32'05"
29°31'39"
95°05'42"
95°05'12"
95°04'42"
95°04'12"
95°03'42"
95°03'12"
A B C D E
1 2 3 4 5 6 7

SEE 4507 MAP

SEE 4632 MAP

1:24,000
1 in. = 2000 ft.
0 0.25 0.5
miles

SEE 4382 MAP

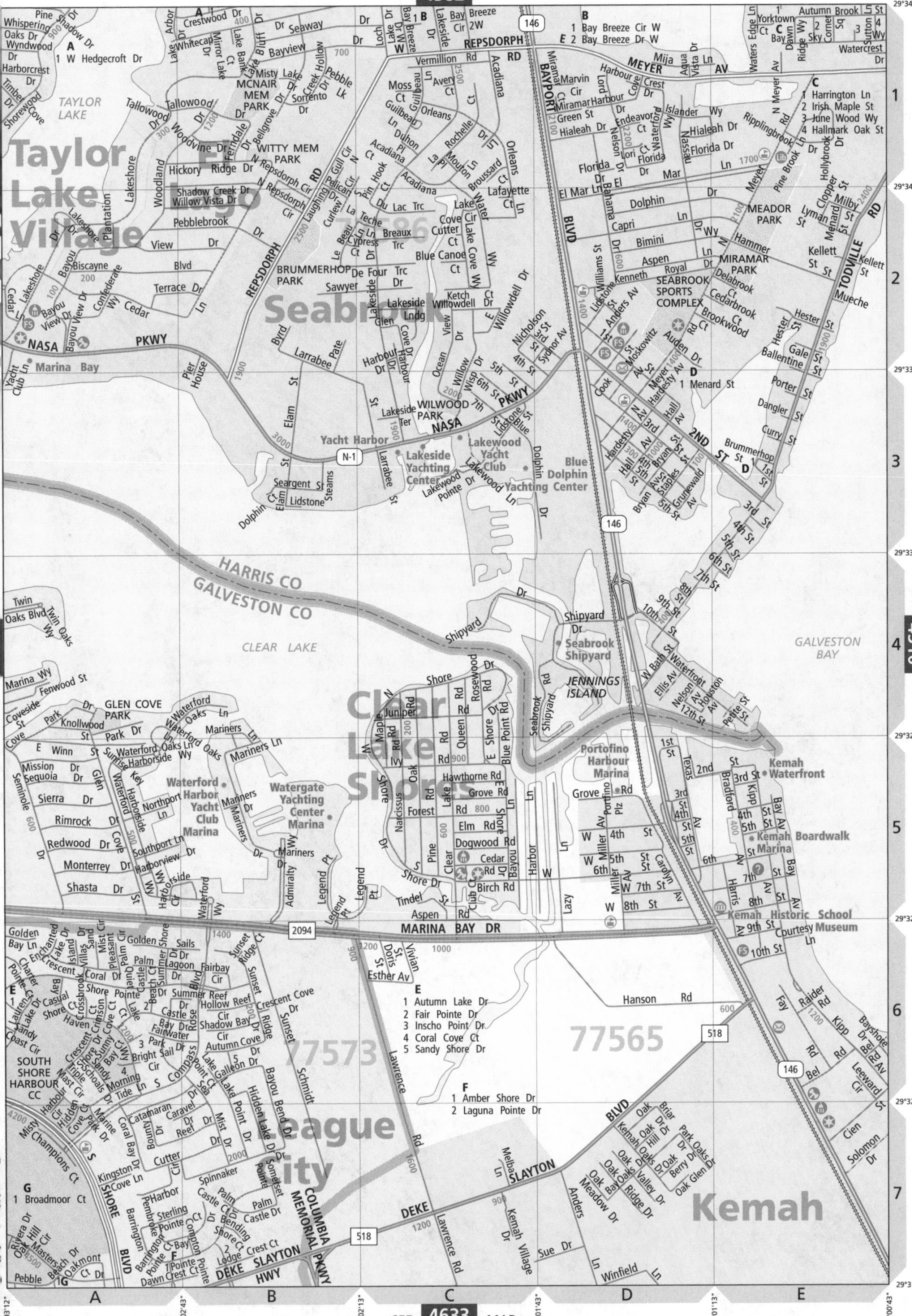
Taylor Lake Village
TAYLOR LAKE
El Lago
Seabrook
77586
NASA PKWY
REPSDORPH RD
BAYPORT BLVD
MEYER AV
TODVILLE RD
2ND ST
MCNAIR MEM PARK
WITTY MEM PARK
BRUMMERHOP PARK
MEADOR PARK
MIRAMAR PARK
SEABROOK SPORTS COMPLEX
WILWOOD PARK
Lakeside Yachting Center
Lakewood Yacht Club
Blue Dolphin Yachting Center
Marina Bay
Yacht Harbor
HARRIS CO
GALVESTON CO
CLEAR LAKE
GALVESTON BAY
Seabrook Shipyard
JENNINGS ISLAND
Clear Lake Shores
GLEN COVE PARK
Waterford Harbor Yacht Club Marina
Watergate Yachting Center Marina
Portofino Harbour Marina
Kemah Waterfront
Kemah Boardwalk Marina
Kemah Historic School Museum
MARINA BAY DR
77573
77565
League City
SOUTH SHORE HARBOUR CC
COLUMBIA MEMORIAL PKWY
DEKE SLAYTON HWY
SLAYTON BLVD
Kemah
146
N-1
2094
518
A
1 W Hedgecroft Dr
B
1 Bay Breeze Cir W
2 Bay Breeze Dr W
C
1 Harrington Ln
2 Irish Maple St
3 June Wood Wy
4 Hallmark Oak St
D
1 Menard St
E
1 Autumn Lake Dr
2 Fair Pointe Dr
3 Inscho Point Dr
4 Coral Cove Ct
5 Sandy Shore Dr
F
1 Amber Shore Dr
2 Laguna Pointe Dr
G
1 Broadmoor Ct
29°34'39"
29°34'13"
29°33'47"
29°33'21"
29°32'54"
29°32'28"
29°32'02"
29°31'36"
95°03'12"
95°02'43"
95°02'13"
95°01'43"
95°01'13"
95°00'43"
1
2
3
4
5
6
7
A
B
C
D
E

SEE 4510 MAP

SEE 4633 MAP

1:24,000
1 in. = 2000 ft.
0 0.25 0.5
miles

SEE 4383 MAP

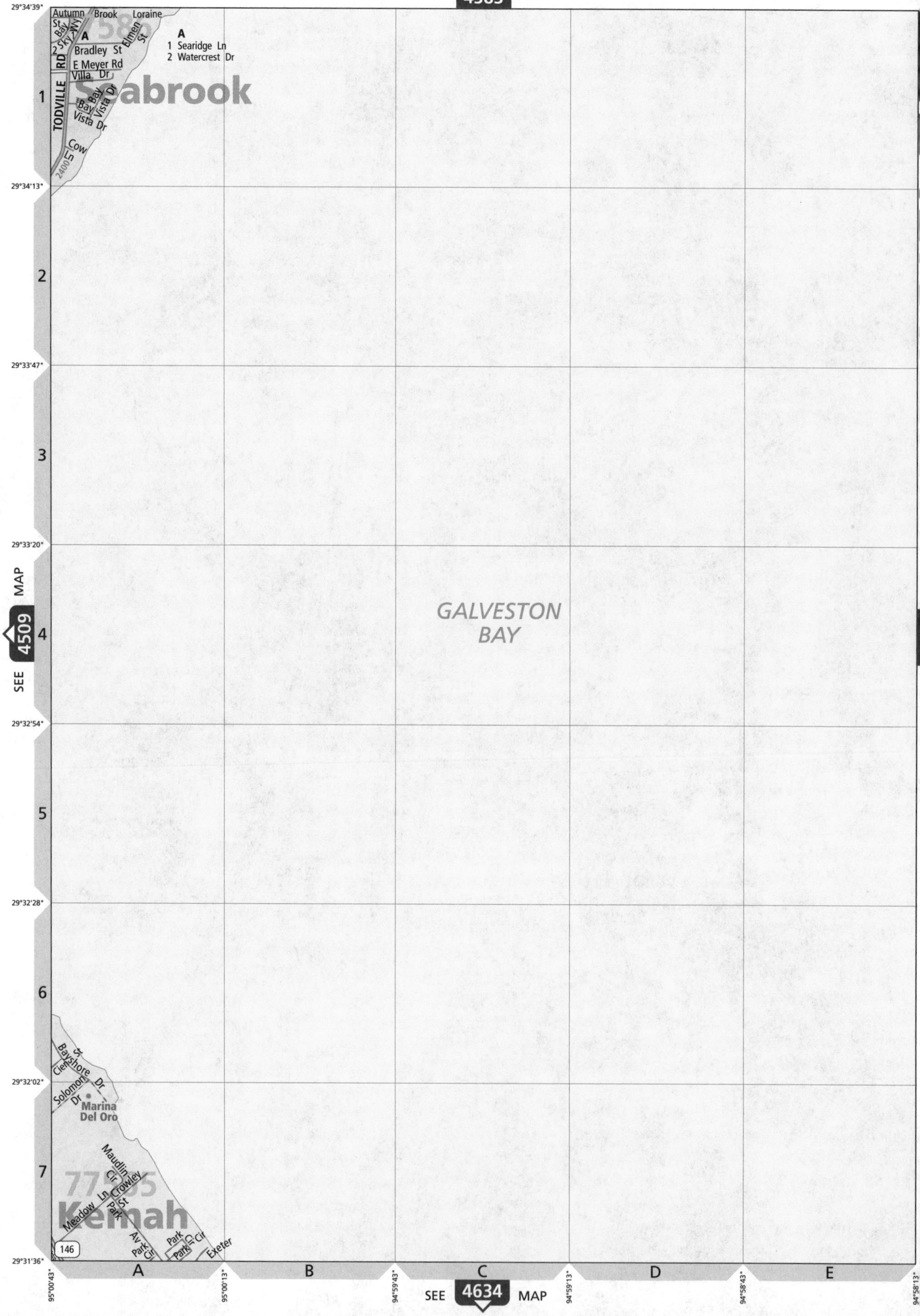
29°34'39"
29°34'13"
29°33'47"
29°33'20"
29°32'54"
29°32'28"
29°32'02"
29°31'36"
1
2
3
4
5
6
7
A
B
C
D
E
95°00'43"
95°00'13"
94°59'43"
94°59'13"
94°58'43"
94°58'13"
Autumn
Brook
Loraine
St
Bay
Sky Wy
Elmen St
A
1 Searidge Ln
2 Watercrest Dr
Bradley St
E Meyer Rd
Villa Dr
TODVILLE RD
Seabrook
Bay Vista Dr
Bay Vista Dr
Cow Ln
2400
GALVESTON
BAY
Bayshore Dr
Cienega St
Solomon Dr
Marina Del Oro
Maudlin Cir
Crowley St
Meadow Ln
Park
77565
Kemah
Av
Park Cir
Park Cir
Exeter
146

SEE 4509 MAP

SEE 4634 MAP

1:24,000
1 in. = 2000 ft.
0 0.25 0.5
miles

SEE 4490 MAP

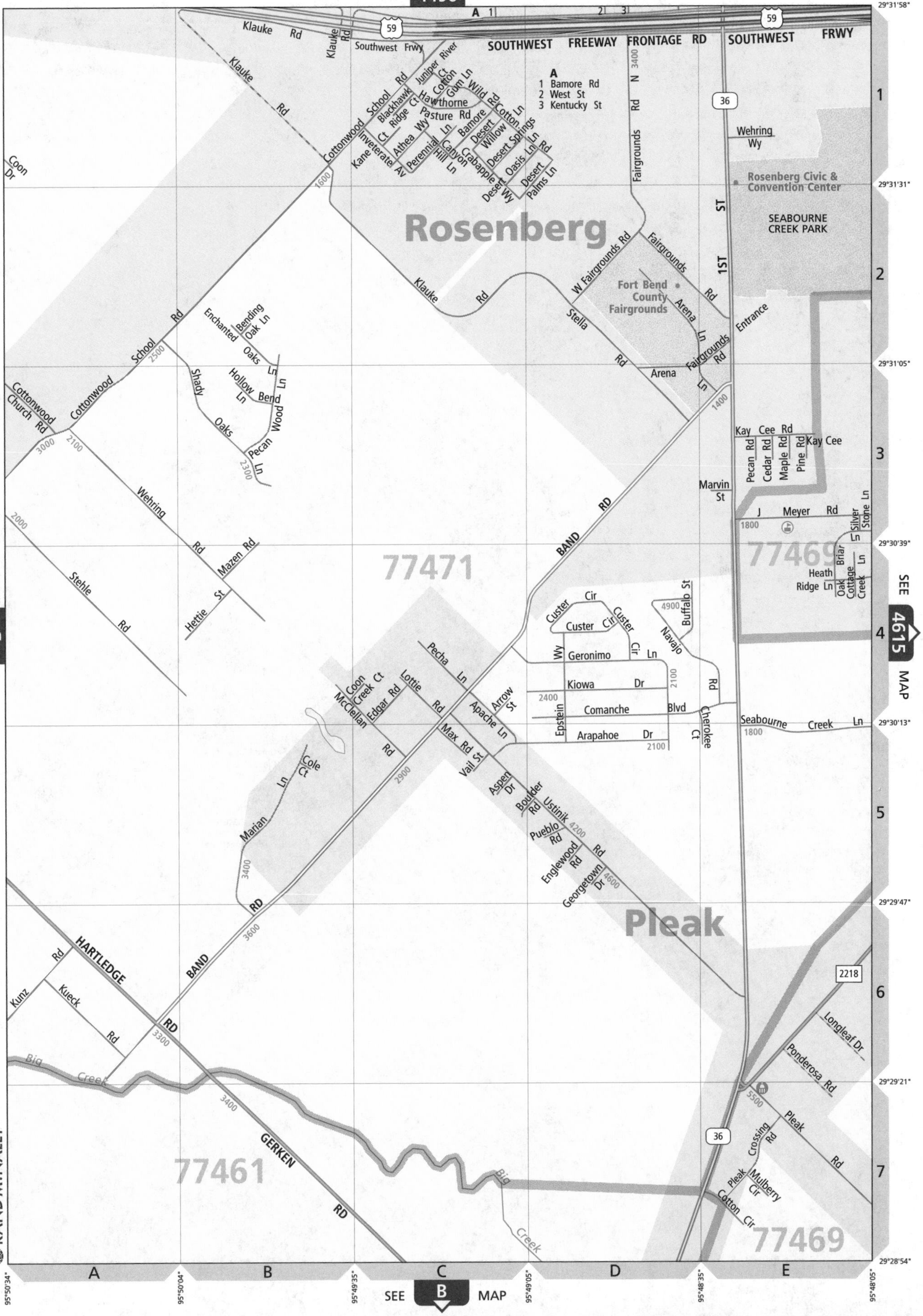
Klauke Rd
Klauke Rd
Southwest Frwy
59
SOUTHWEST FREEWAY FRONTAGE RD
SOUTHWEST FRWY
A
1 Bamore Rd
2 West St
3 Kentucky St
Juniper River Ct
Cotton Gum Ln
Wild Cotton Rd
Hawthorne
Pasture Rd
Bamore
Blackhawk Ridge Ct
School Rd
Cottonwood
Kane Ct
Inveterate Av
Athea Wy
Perennial Ln
Hill Canyon Ln
Grabapple
Desert Willow Ln
Desert Springs
Oasis Ln
Desert Palms Ln
Desert Wy
Fairgrounds Rd N
3400
36
Wehring Wy
Rosenberg Civic & Convention Center
SEABOURNE CREEK PARK
1ST ST
Coon Dr
1600
Rosenberg
Klauke Rd
W Fairgrounds Rd
Fairgrounds Rd
Fort Bend County Fairgrounds
Arena Ln
Entrance
Stella Rd
Arena
Fairgrounds Rd
Cottonwood School Rd
2500
Enchanted Oaks Ln
Bending Oak Ln
Shady Oaks
Hollow Bend Ln
Pecan Wood Ln
Pecan Ln
2300
Cottonwood Church Rd
3000
2100
1400
Kay Cee Rd
Kay Cee
Pecan Rd
Cedar Rd
Maple Rd
Pine Rd
Marvin St
BAND RD
Wehring Rd
Mazen Rd
2000
J Meyer Rd
1800
Silver Stone Ln
77469
Briar Ln
Heath Ridge Ln
Oak Cottage Creek Ln
77471
Stehle Rd
Hettie St
Custer Cir
Custer Cir
Custer Cir
Buffalo St
4900
Navajo
Wy
Geronimo Ln
Pecha Ln
Coon Creek Ct
Lottie Rd
Edgar Rd
McClellan Rd
Arrow St
Apache Ln
Kiowa Dr
2100
2400
Epstein
Comanche Blvd
Rd
Cherokee Ct
Seabourne Creek Ln
1800
Max Rd
Vail St
Arapahoe Dr
2100
2900
Cole Ct
Marian Ln
Aspen Dr
Boulder Rd
Ustinik Rd
4200
Pueblo Rd
Englewood Rd
Georgetown Dr
4600
3400
RD
3600
Pleak
HARTLEDGE RD
Rd
BAND
Kunz
Kueck Rd
3300
2218
Longleaf Dr
Ponderosa Rd
Big Creek
3400
GERKEN RD
5500
Pleak Rd
36
Crossing Rd
77461
Big Creek
Pleak Mulberry Cir
Cotton Cir
77469
29°31'58"
29°31'31"
29°31'05"
29°30'39"
29°30'13"
29°29'47"
29°29'21"
29°28'54"
1
2
3
4
5
6
7
A
B
C
D
E
95°50'34"
95°50'04"
95°49'35"
95°49'05"
95°48'35"
95°48'05"

SEE 4615 MAP

SEE B MAP

1:24,000
1 in. = 2000 ft.
0 0.25 0.5
miles

SEE 4491 MAP

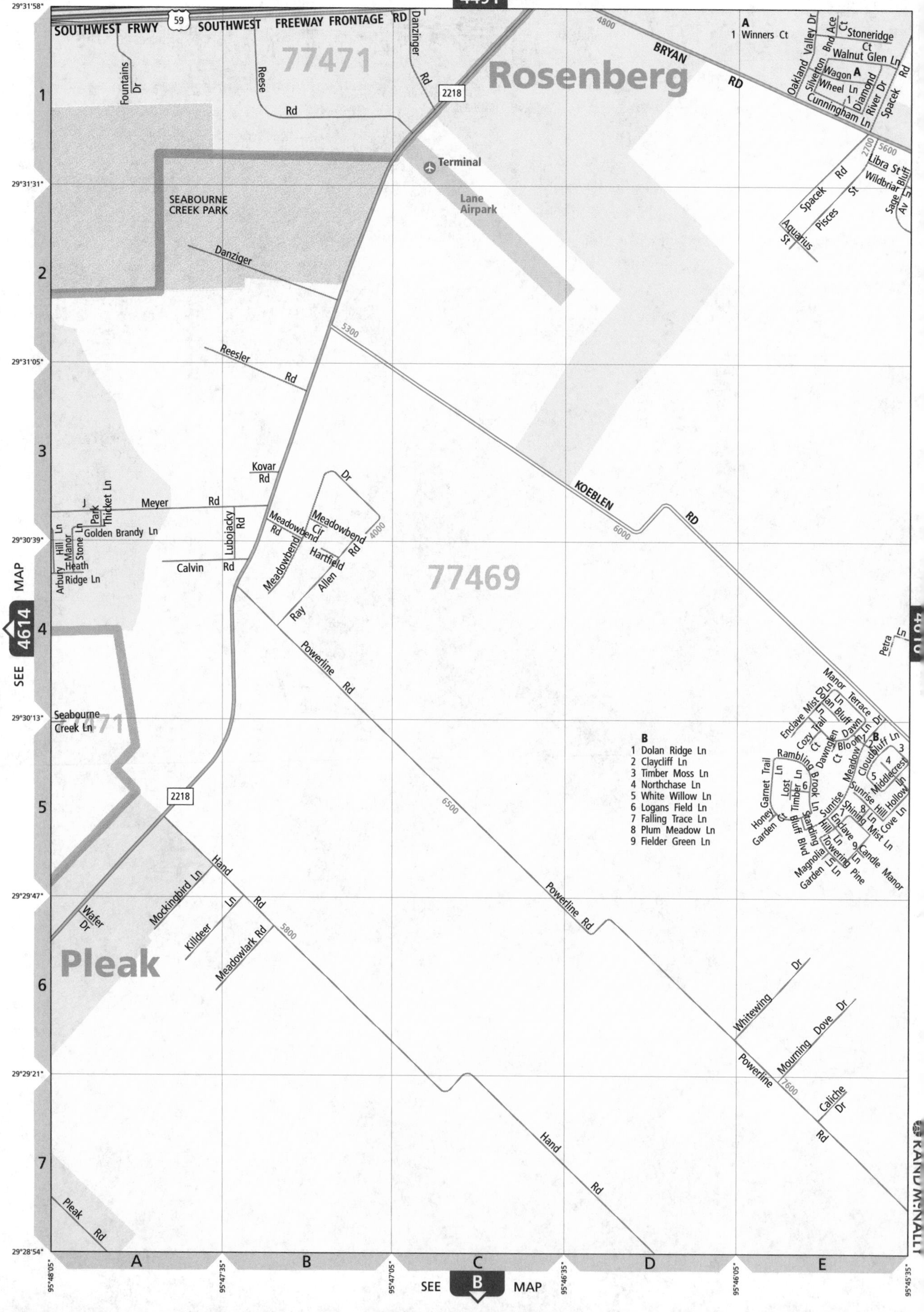

SOUTHWEST FRWY
59
SOUTHWEST FREEWAY FRONTAGE RD
Danzinger Rd
Fountains Dr
Reese Rd
77471
Rosenberg
2218
4800
BRYAN RD
A
1 Winners Ct
Oakland Valley Dr
Silverton Bnd
Ace Ct
Stoneridge Ct
Walnut Glen Ln
Wagon
Wheel Ln
Diamond
River Dr
Cunningham Ln
Spacek Rd
Terminal
Lane Airpark
SEABOURNE CREEK PARK
2700
5600
Libra St
Wildbriar
Bluff
Sage Av
Spacek Rd
Pisces St
Aquarius St
Danziger
5300
Reesler Rd
KOEBLEN RD
6000
Kovar Rd
Meyer Rd
Thicket Ln
Park
J
Golden Brandy Ln
Arbury Hill Ln
Manor
Stone Ln
Heath
Ridge Ln
Lubojacky Rd
Calvin Rd
Meadowbend Rd
Meadowbend Cir
Meadowbend Rd
Dr
4000
Hartfield
Allen
Ray
77469
Powerline Rd
Petra Ln
Manor Terrace
Seabourne Creek Ln
471
B
1 Dolan Ridge Ln
2 Claycliff Ln
3 Timber Moss Ln
4 Northchase Ln
5 White Willow Ln
6 Logans Field Ln
7 Falling Trace Ln
8 Plum Meadow Ln
9 Fielder Green Ln
Enclave Mist Dr
Dolan Bluff
Cozy Trail
Dawngten Ct
Dawn Bloom Ln
Meadow
Cloudbluff Ln
Middlecrest Ln
Rambling Brook Ln
Garnet Trail
Lost Timber Ln
Honey Garden Ct
Bluff Blvd
Standing Hill Ln
Sunrise
Shining Mist Ln
Sunrise Hill
Hollow Cove Ln
Enclave
Towering Pine
Candle Manor
Magnolia Garden Ln
2218
6500
Hand Rd
Mockingbird Ln
Killdeer Ln
Wafer Dr
Meadowlark Rd
5800
Pleak
Powerline Rd
Whitewing Dr
Mourning Dove Dr
Powerline Rd
7600
Caliche Dr
Hand Rd
Pleak Rd
29°31'58"
29°31'31"
29°31'05"
29°30'39"
29°30'13"
29°29'47"
29°29'21"
29°28'54"
95°48'05"
95°47'35"
95°47'05"
95°46'35"
95°46'05"
95°45'35"
A
B
C
D
E
1
2
3
4
5
6
7

SEE 4614 MAP

SEE B MAP

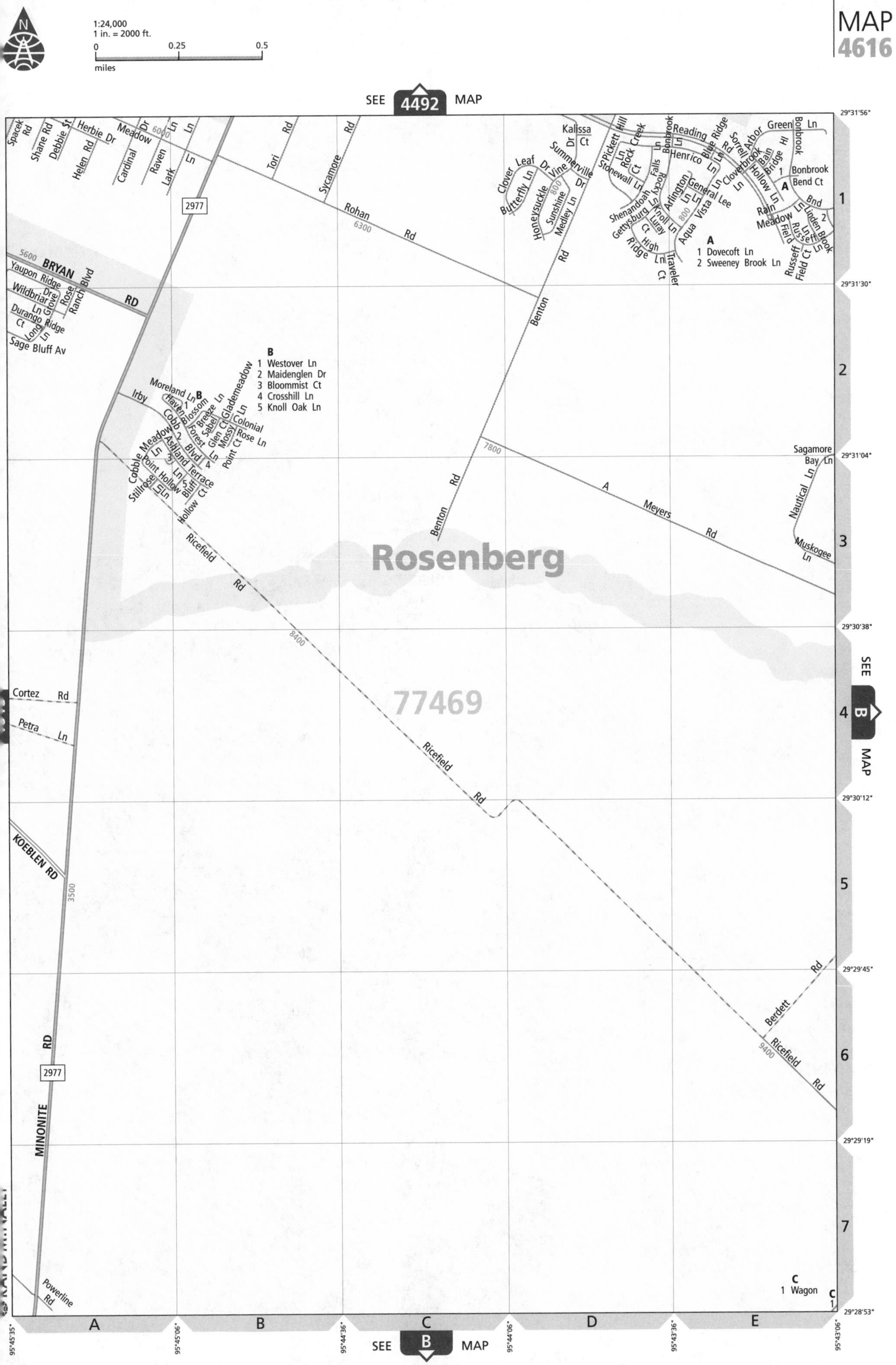
1:24,000
1 in. = 2000 ft.
0
0.25
0.5
miles
SEE 4492 MAP
Rosenberg
77469
2977
BRYAN RD
MINONITE RD
KOEBLEN RD
Rohan Rd
Benton Rd
A Meyers Rd
Ricefield Rd
Cortez Rd
Petra Ln
Powerline Rd
Berdett Rd
Tori Rd
Sycamore Rd
Irby
Sagamore Bay Ln
Nautical Ln
Muskogee Ln
Kalissa Ct
Summerville Dr
Clover Leaf Dr
Butterfly Ln
Honeysuckle
Sunshine
Medley Ln
Vine
Pickett Hill
Rock Creek Ct
Stonewall Ln
Shenandoah Ln
Gettysburg Ct
Ridge Ln
High Ct
Traveler Ct
Luray
Rocky Knoll Ln
Falls
Arlington Ln
Aqua Vista Ln
General Lee
Bonbrook Ln
Reading
Henrico
Blue Ridge Rd
Sorrell Ln
Cloverbrook Ln
Arbor Hollow Ln
Bain Bridge
Green Ln
Bonbrook Hl
Bonbrook Bend Ct
Bnd
Rain Meadow Ln
Linden Brook Ln
Russeff Field Ct
Russeff Field Ln
A
1 Dovecoft Ln
2 Sweeney Brook Ln
B
1 Westover Ln
2 Maidenglen Dr
3 Bloommist Ct
4 Crosshill Ln
5 Knoll Oak Ln
Moreland Ln
Haven
Blossom
Breeze Ln
Sabel
Glademeadow
Glen Ct
Colonial
Mossy Rose Ln
Point Ct
Forest
Cobb Blvd
Cobble Meadow Ln
Ashland Terrace
Point Hollow Ln
Stillrose Ln
Bluff
Hollow Ct
Spacek Rd
Shane Rd
Debbie St
Herbie Dr
Helen Rd
Meadow
Cardinal Dr
Raven Ln
Lark Ln
Yaupon Ridge Dr
Wildbriar Ln
Rose Grove
Ranch Blvd
Durango Ridge Ct
Long Ln
Sage Bluff Av
C
1 Wagon
5600
6000
6300
800
7800
8400
9400
3500
A B C D E
1 2 3 4 5 6 7
29°31'56"
29°31'30"
29°31'04"
29°30'38"
29°30'12"
29°29'45"
29°29'19"
29°28'53"
95°45'35"
95°45'06"
95°44'36"
95°44'06"
95°43'36"
95°43'06"
SEE B MAP

1:24,000
1 in. = 2000 ft.
0 0.25 0.5
miles

SEE 4497 MAP

29°31'53"

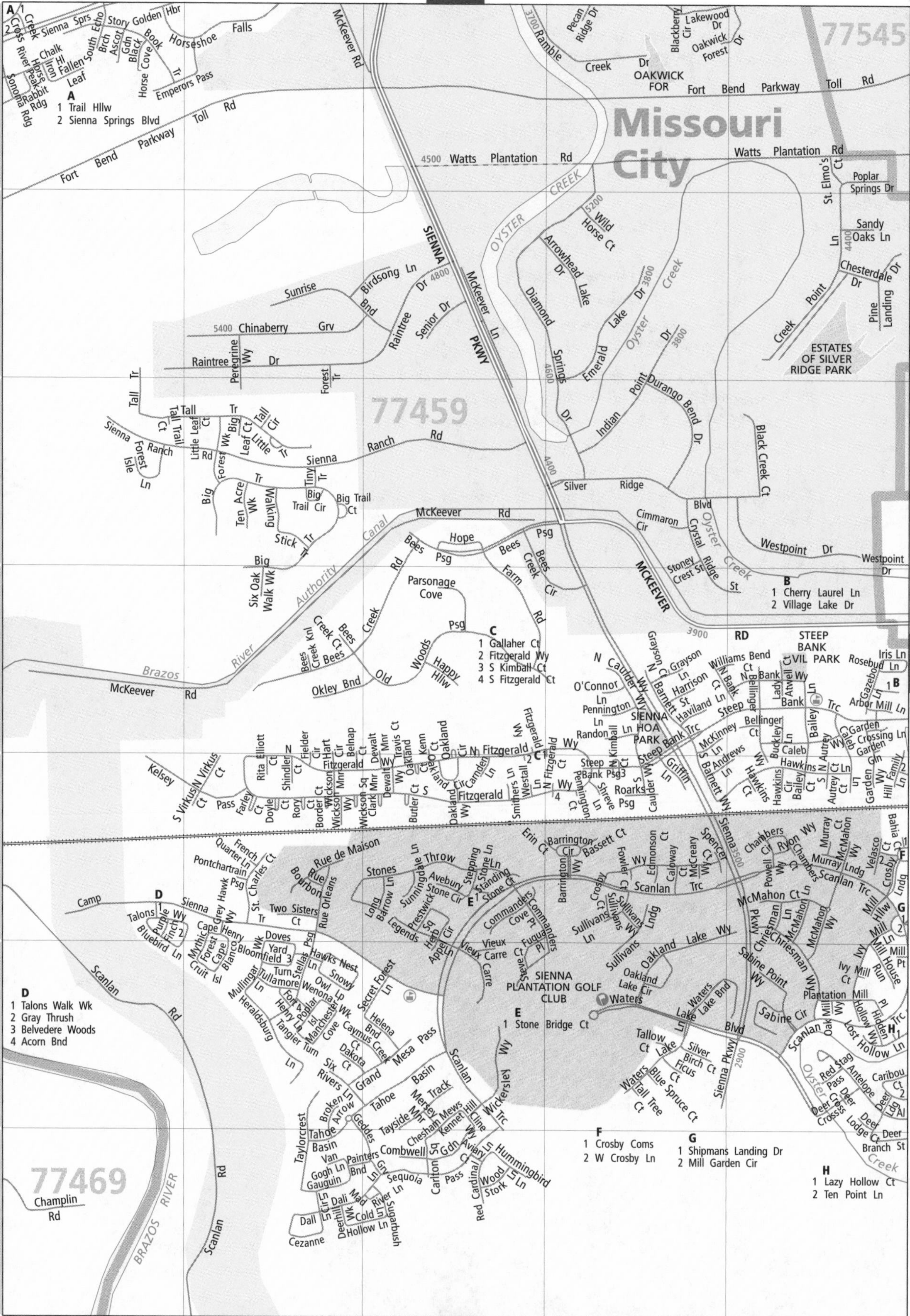
Missouri City
77545
77459
77469
SIENNA PKWY
MCKEEVER RD
McKeever Rd
Fort Bend Parkway Toll Rd
Watts Plantation Rd
4500
OAKWICK FOR
Oakwick Forest Dr
Lakewood Dr
Blackberry Cir
Pecan Ridge Dr
Ramble Creek Dr
OYSTER CREEK
Oyster Creek
Wild Horse Ct
Arrowhead Lake Dr
Diamond Springs Dr
Emerald Lake Dr
Indian Point Dr
Durango Bend Dr
Black Creek Ct
Silver Ridge Blvd
Cimmaron Cir
Crystal Ridge
Stoney Crest St
Westpoint Dr
Poplar Springs Dr
Sandy Oaks Ln
St. Elmo's Ct
Chesterdale Dr
Creek Point Dr
Pine Landing
ESTATES OF SILVER RIDGE PARK
Sunrise
Birdsong Ln
Chinaberry Grv
5400
Raintree Dr
Peregrine Wy
Senior Dr
Forest Tr
Sienna Ranch Rd
Sienna Forest Isle Ln
Tall Tr
Tall Trail Ct
Little Leaf Ct
Big Leaf Ct
Tall Cir
Little Tr
Big Forest Wk
Big Trail Cir
Big Trail Ct
Ten Acre Wk
Walking Stick Tr
Six Oak Walk Wk
Brazos River Authority Canal
Hope
Bees Psg
Bees Creek Cir
Farm Rd
Parsonage Cove
Old Woods Psg
Happy Hllw
Oakley Bnd
Bees Creek Knl
STEEP BANK CIVIL PARK
SIENNA HOA PARK
Fitzgerald
Rita Elliott Ct
Kelsey
Virkus Ct
Scanlan Trc
SIENNA PLANTATION GOLF CLUB
Waters Lake Blvd
Sienna Pkwy
Rue de Maison
Camp Sienna
Bluebird Ln
Scanlan Rd
BRAZOS RIVER
Champlin Rd
A
1 Trail Hllw
2 Sienna Springs Blvd
B
1 Cherry Laurel Ln
2 Village Lake Dr
C
1 Gallaher Ct
2 Fitzgerald Wy
3 S Kimball Ct
4 S Fitzgerald Ct
D
1 Talons Walk Wk
2 Gray Thrush
3 Belvedere Woods
4 Acorn Bnd
E
1 Stone Bridge Ct
F
1 Crosby Coms
2 W Crosby Ln
G
1 Shipmans Landing Dr
2 Mill Garden Cir
H
1 Lazy Hollow Ct
2 Ten Point Ln

29°31'27"
29°31'00"
29°30'34"
29°30'08"
29°29'42"
29°29'16"
29°28'50"

1 2 3 4 5 6 7

SEE B MAP

A B C D E

95°33'08" 95°32'38" 95°32'08" 95°31'39" 95°31'09" 95°30'39"

SEE B MAP

1:24,000
1 in. = 2000 ft.
0 0.25 0.5
miles

SEE 4498 MAP

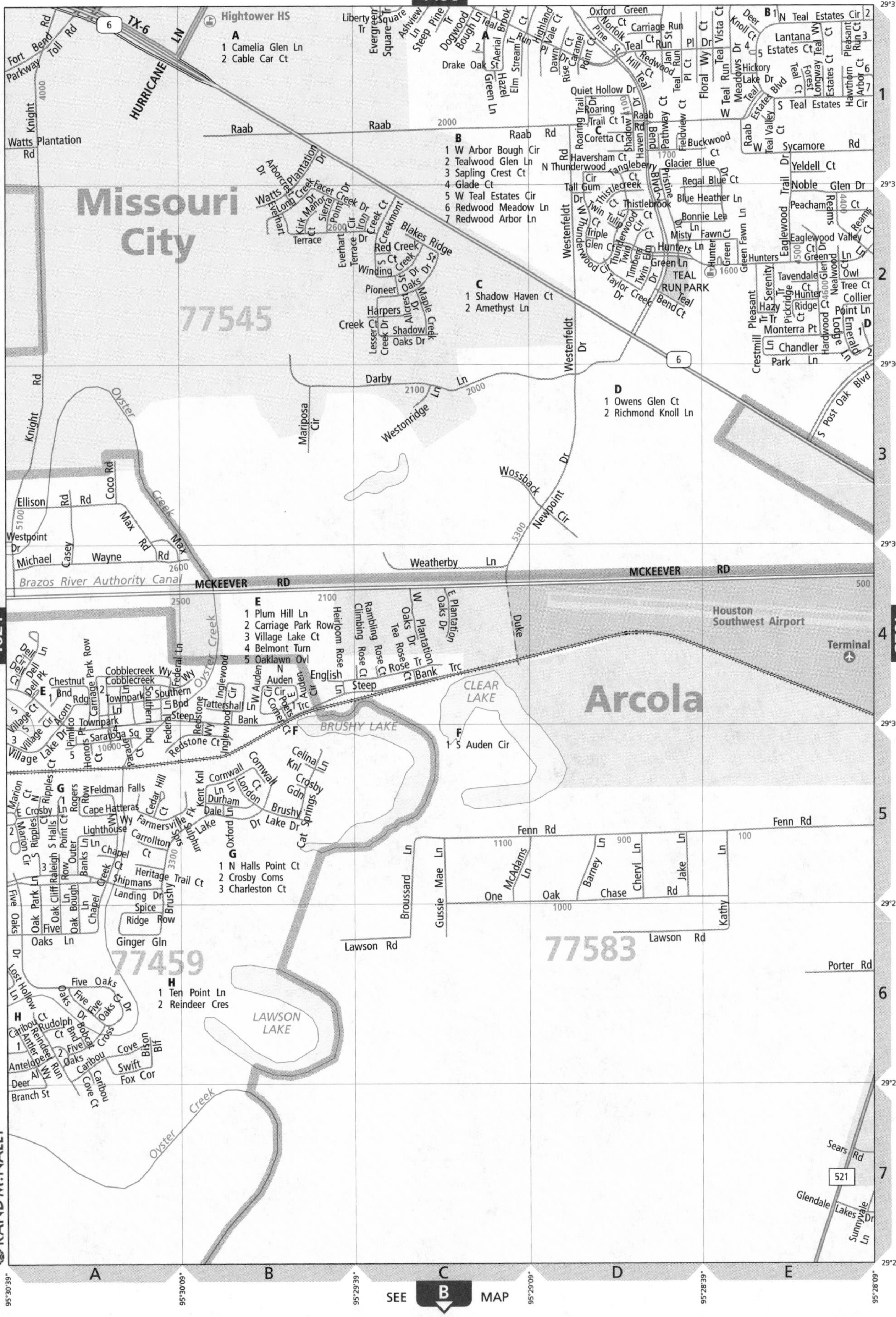

Missouri City
Arcola
77545
77583
77459
Hightower HS
TEAL RUN PARK
Houston Southwest Airport
Terminal
CLEAR LAKE
BRUSHY LAKE
LAWSON LAKE
Brazos River Authority Canal
Oyster Creek
MCKEEVER RD
HURRICANE LN
TX-6
Fort Bend Parkway Toll Rd
Raab Rd
Knight Rd
Watts Plantation Rd
Westenfeldt Dr
Darby Ln
Weatherby Ln
Fenn Rd
Lawson Rd
Porter Rd
Sears Rd
Glendale Lakes Dr
S Post Oak Blvd
A
1 Camelia Glen Ln
2 Cable Car Ct
B
1 W Arbor Bough Cir
2 Tealwood Glen Ln
3 Sapling Crest Ct
4 Glade Ct
5 W Teal Estates Cir
6 Redwood Meadow Ln
7 Redwood Arbor Ln
C
1 Shadow Haven Ct
2 Amethyst Ln
D
1 Owens Glen Ct
2 Richmond Knoll Ln
E
1 Plum Hill Ln
2 Carriage Park Row
3 Village Lake Ct
4 Belmont Turn
5 Oaklawn Ovl
F
1 S Auden Cir
G
1 N Halls Point Ct
2 Crosby Coms
3 Charleston Ct
H
1 Ten Point Ln
2 Reindeer Cres
29°31'51"
29°31'24"
29°30'58"
29°30'32"
29°30'06"
29°29'40"
29°29'14"
29°28'48"
95°30'39"
95°30'09"
95°29'39"
95°29'09"
95°28'39"
95°28'09"
A B C D E
1 2 3 4 5 6 7

SEE 4623 MAP

SEE B MAP

1:24,000
1 in. = 2000 ft.
0 0.25 0.5
miles

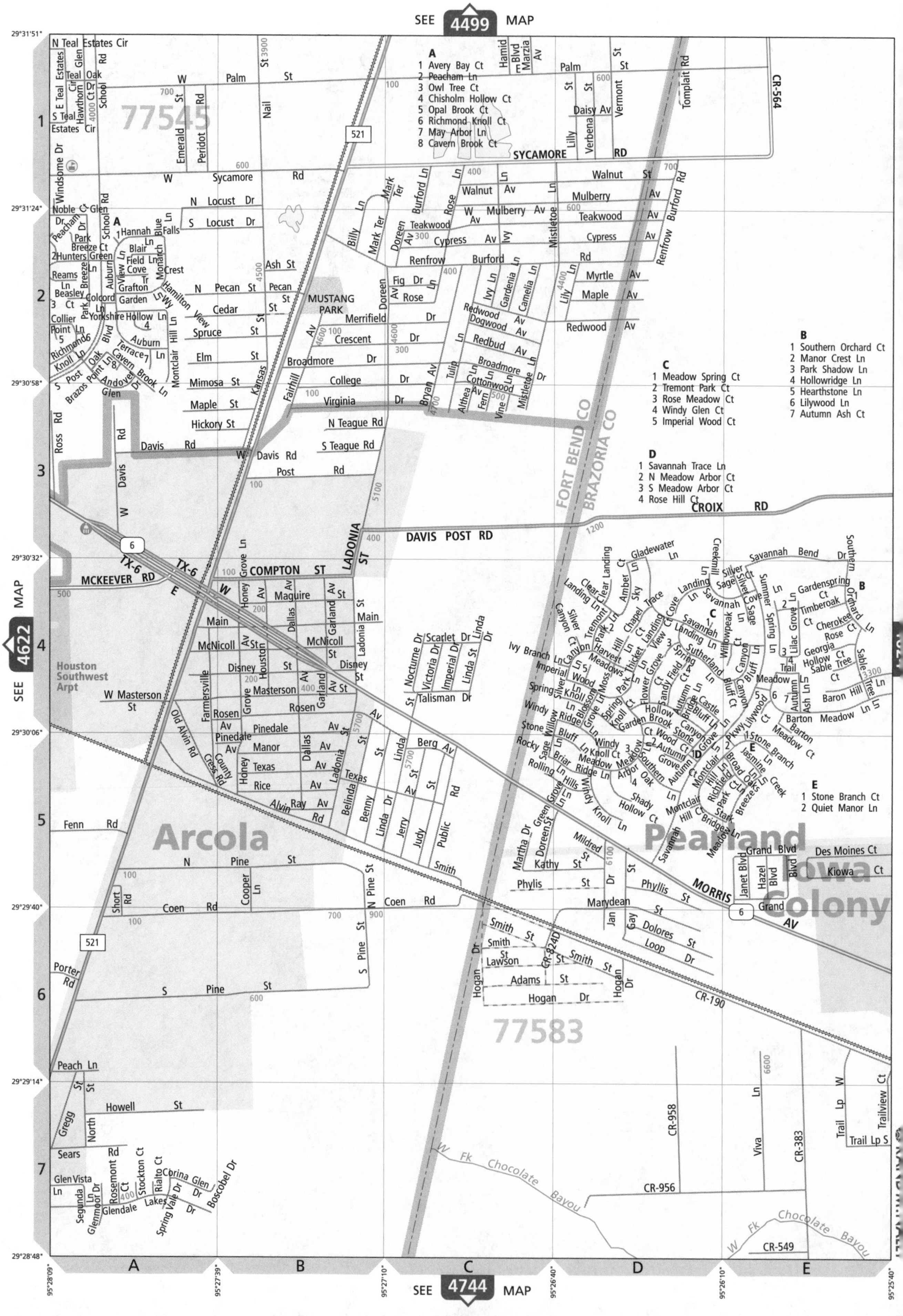
SEE 4499 MAP
SEE 4622 MAP
SEE 4744 MAP
77545
77583
Arcola
Pearland
Iowa Colony
MUSTANG PARK
Houston Southwest Arpt
FORT BEND CO
BRAZORIA CO
SYCAMORE RD
DAVIS POST RD
CROIX RD
COMPTON ST
LADONIA ST
MCKEEVER RD
TX-6 E
TX-6 W
MORRIS AV
CR-564
CR-190
CR-958
CR-956
CR-383
CR-549
CR-824D
W Fk Chocolate Bayou
A
1 Avery Bay Ct
2 Peacham Ln
3 Owl Tree Ct
4 Chisholm Hollow Ct
5 Opal Brook Ct
6 Richmond Knoll Ct
7 May Arbor Ln
8 Cavern Brook Ct
B
1 Southern Orchard Ct
2 Manor Crest Ln
3 Park Shadow Ln
4 Hollowridge Ln
5 Hearthstone Ln
6 Lilywood Ln
7 Autumn Ash Ct
C
1 Meadow Spring Ct
2 Tremont Park Ct
3 Rose Meadow Ct
4 Windy Glen Ct
5 Imperial Wood Ct
D
1 Savannah Trace Ln
2 N Meadow Arbor Ct
3 S Meadow Arbor Ct
4 Rose Hill Ct
E
1 Stone Branch Ct
2 Quiet Manor Ln
29°31'51"
29°31'24"
29°30'58"
29°30'32"
29°30'06"
29°29'40"
29°29'14"
29°28'48"
95°28'09"
95°27'39"
95°27'10"
95°26'40"
95°26'10"
95°25'40"

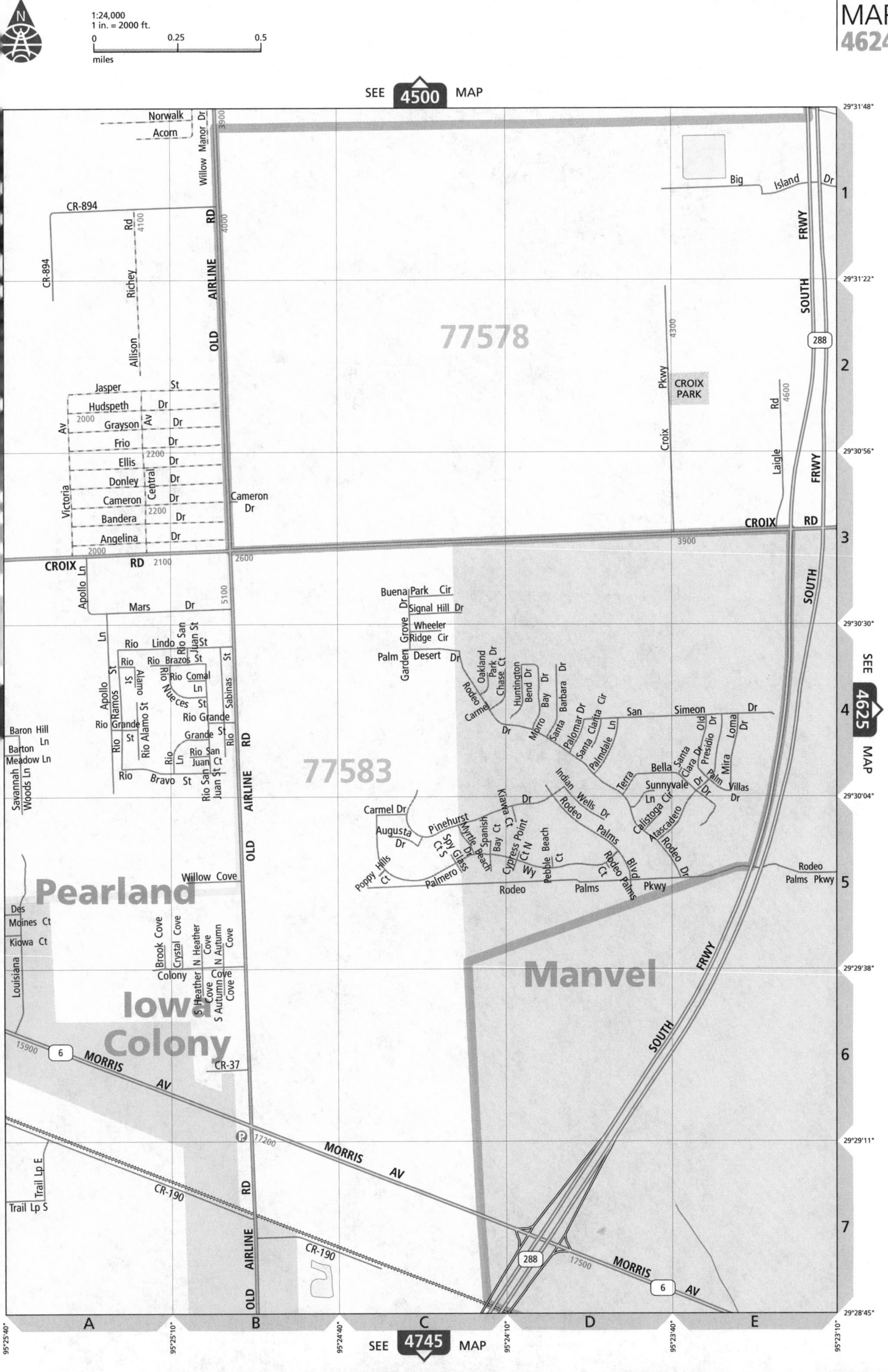
1:24,000
1 in. = 2000 ft.
0
0.25
0.5
miles
SEE 4500 MAP
SEE 4625 MAP
SEE 4745 MAP
77578
77583
Pearland
Iowa Colony
Manvel
CROIX PARK
OLD AIRLINE RD
SOUTH FRWY
288
6
MORRIS AV
CROIX RD
CR-894
CR-37
CR-190
Norwalk
Acorn
Willow Manor Dr
Richey Rd
Allison
Jasper St
Hudspeth Dr
Grayson Dr
Frio Dr
Ellis Dr
Donley Dr
Cameron Dr
Bandera Dr
Angelina Dr
Victoria Av
Central Av
Big Island Dr
Croix Pkwy
Laigle Rd
Apollo Ln
Mars Dr
Rio Lindo St
Rio San Juan St
Rio Brazos St
Rio Comal Ln
Rio Nueces St
Rio Grande St
Rio Ramos St
Rio Alamo St
Rio Bravo St
Sabinas St
Baron Hill Ln
Barton Meadow Ln
Savannah Woods Ln
Buena Park Cir
Signal Hill Dr
Wheeler Ridge Cir
Garden Grove Dr
Palm Desert Dr
Oakland Park Dr
Chase Ct
Huntington Bend Dr
Morro Bay Dr
Santa Barbara Dr
Palomar Dr
Santa Clarita Cir
Palmdale Ln
San Simeon Dr
Old Presidio Dr
Loma Dr
Carmel Dr
Rodeo Dr
Terra Bella Dr
Santa Clara Dr
Palm Villas Dr
Mira Dr
Sunnyvale Ln
Calistoga Cir
Atascadero Dr
Indian Wells Dr
Rodeo Palms Blvd
Rodeo Palms Pkwy
Rodeo Ct
Kiawa Ct
Pinehurst Dr
Augusta Dr
Poppy Hills Ct
Spy Glass Ct S
Myrtle Beach Dr
Spanish Bay Ct
Cypress Point Ct N
Pebble Beach Ct
Palmero Wy
Willow Cove
Brook Cove
Crystal Cove
Colony Cove
N Heather Cove
N Autumn Cove
S Heather Cove
S Autumn Cove
Des Moines Ct
Kiowa Ct
Louisiana
Trail Lp E
Trail Lp S
A
B
C
D
E
1
2
3
4
5
6
7
29°31'48"
29°31'22"
29°30'56"
29°30'30"
29°30'04"
29°29'38"
29°29'11"
29°28'45"
95°25'40"
95°25'10"
95°24'40"
95°24'10"
95°23'40"
95°23'10"

1:24,000
1 in. = 2000 ft.
0 0.25 0.5 miles

SEE 4501 MAP

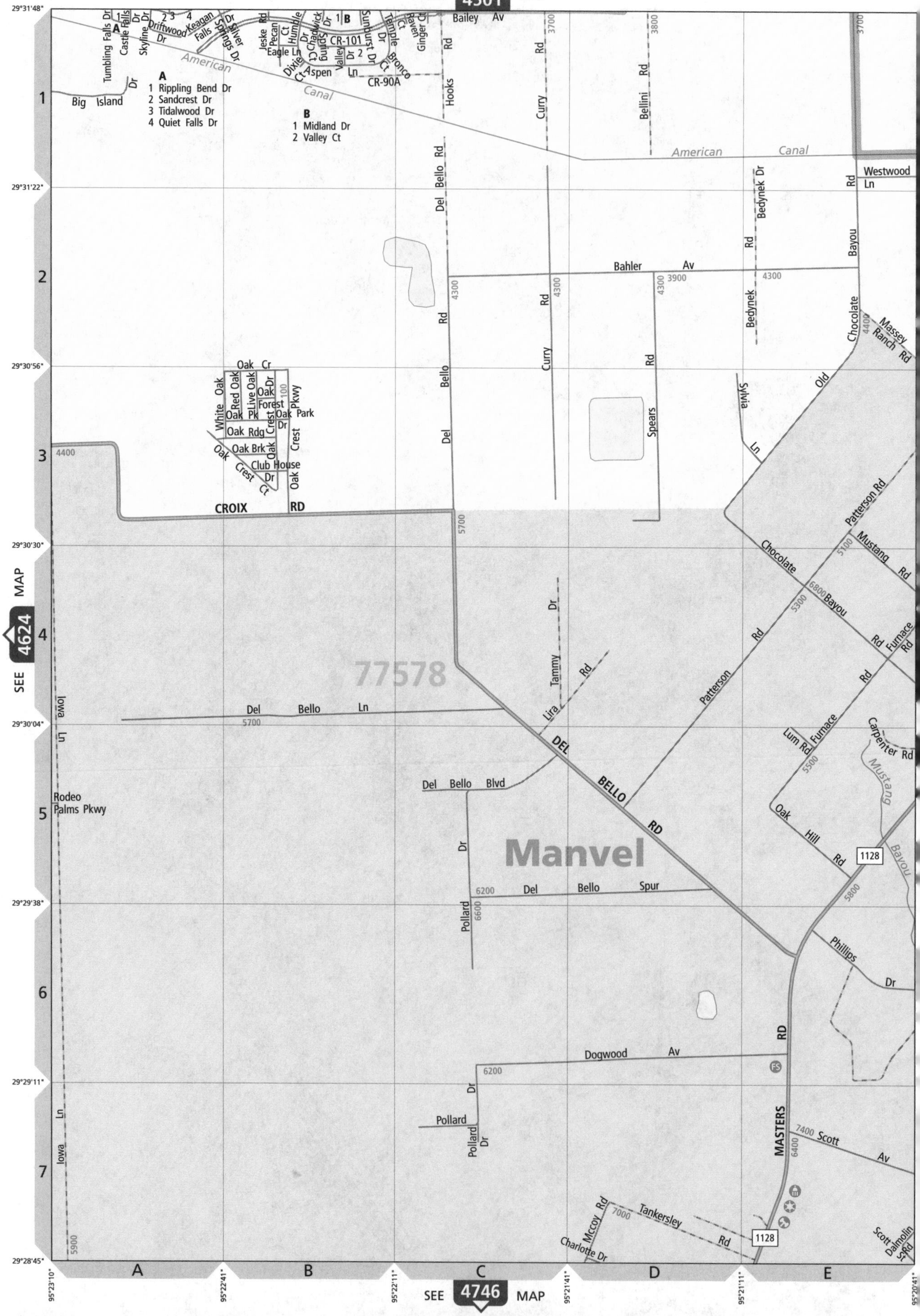
A
1 Rippling Bend Dr
2 Sandcrest Dr
3 Tidalwood Dr
4 Quiet Falls Dr
B
1 Midland Dr
2 Valley Ct
American Canal
Big Island Dr
Del Bello Rd
Hooks Rd
Curry Rd
Bellini Rd
Westwood Ln
Bedynek Dr
Bahler Av
Bedynek Rd
Chocolate Bayou Rd
Massey Ranch Rd
Spears Rd
Sylvia Ln
Old Chocolate Bayou Rd
Oak Cr
White Oak
Red Oak
Live Oak
Oak Forest Dr
Oak Pk
Oak Park Pkwy
Oak Rdg
Oak Brk
Oak Crest Ct
Club House Dr
Oak Crest Dr
CROIX RD
77578
Patterson Rd
Mustang Rd
Furnace Rd
Tammy Dr
Lira Rd
Del Bello Ln
DEL BELLO RD
Del Bello Blvd
Lum Rd
Carpenter Rd
Mustang Bayou
Iowa Ln
Rodeo Palms Pkwy
Oak Hill Rd
1128
Manvel
Pollard Dr
Del Bello Spur
Phillips Dr
Dogwood Av
MASTERS RD
Pollard
Scott Av
Tankersley Rd
Mccoy Rd
Charlotte Dr
Scott Rd
Dalmolin

SEE 4624 MAP

SEE 4746 MAP

1:24,000
1 in. = 2000 ft.
0 0.25 0.5
miles

SEE 4502 MAP

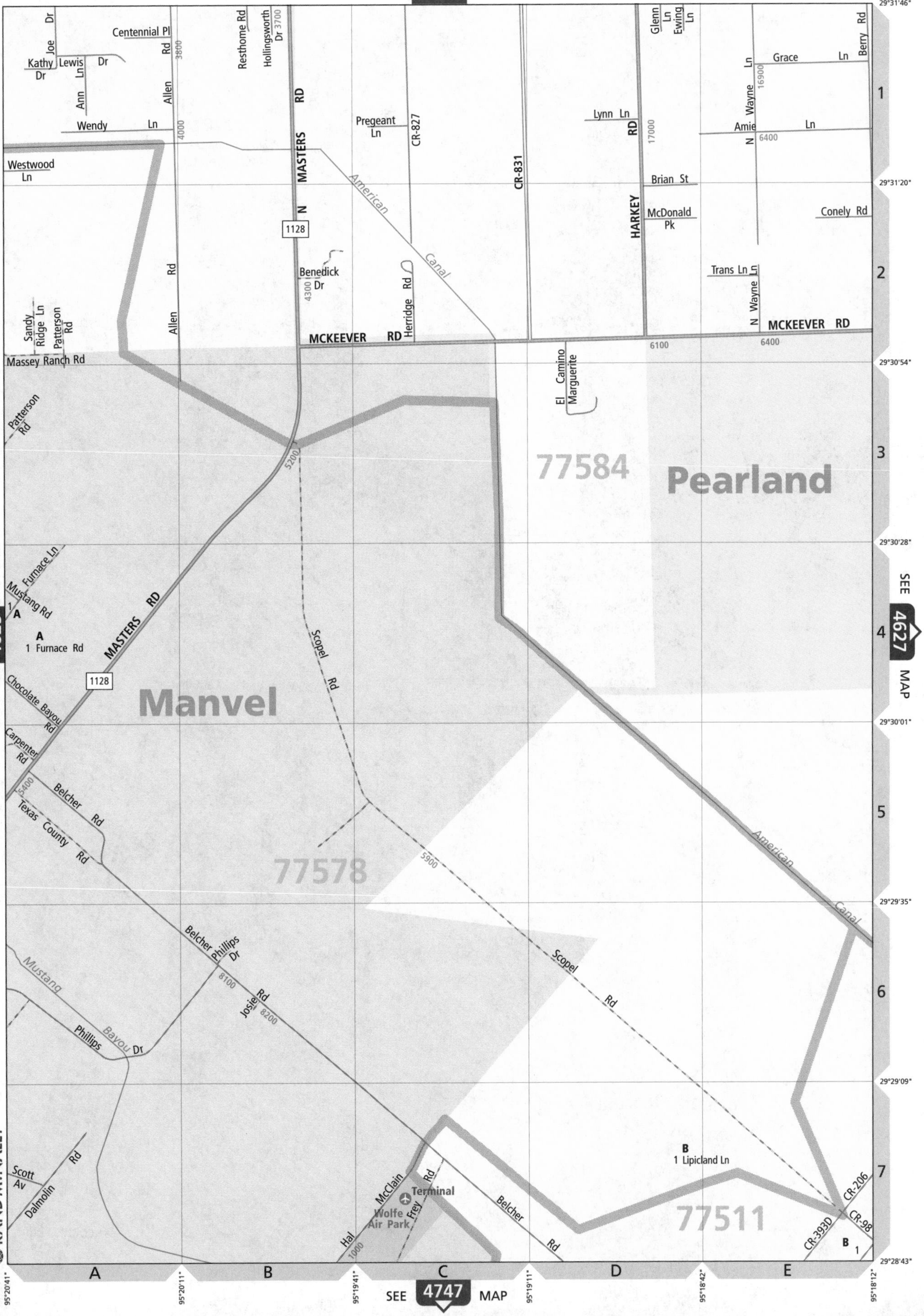
Joe Dr
Centennial Pl
Kathy Dr
Lewis Dr
Ann Ln
Allen Rd
Resthome Rd
Hollingsworth Dr
3700
3800
Wendy Ln
4000
Westwood Ln
N MASTERS RD
1128
Pregeant Ln
CR-827
American Canal
Benedick Dr
4300
Herridge Rd
CR-831
Glenn Ln
Ewing Ln
Lynn Ln
HARKEY RD
17000
Brian St
McDonald Pk
Grace Ln
Berry Rd
N Wayne Ln
16900
Amie Ln
6400
Conely Rd
Trans Ln
MCKEEVER RD
6100
Sandy Ridge Ln
Patterson Rd
Massey Ranch Rd
El Camino Marguerite
77584
Pearland
5200
Furnace Ln
Mustang Rd
A
1 Furnace Rd
MASTERS RD
Scopel Rd
Manvel
Chocolate Bayou Rd
Carpenter Rd
5400
Belcher Rd
Texas County Rd
77578
5900
Belcher Phillips Dr
Mustang Bayou Dr
Phillips
8100
Josie Rd
8200
B
1 Lipicland Ln
Scott Av
Dalmolin Rd
McClain Rd
Terminal
Wolfe Air Park
Frey
Hal
1000
77511
CR-206
CR-98
CR-393D
B
1
1
2
3
4
5
6
7
A
B
C
D
E
29°31'46"
29°31'20"
29°30'54"
29°30'28"
29°30'01"
29°29'35"
29°29'09"
29°28'43"
95°20'41"
95°20'11"
95°19'41"
95°19'11"
95°18'42"
95°18'12"

SEE 4627 MAP

SEE 4747 MAP

4625

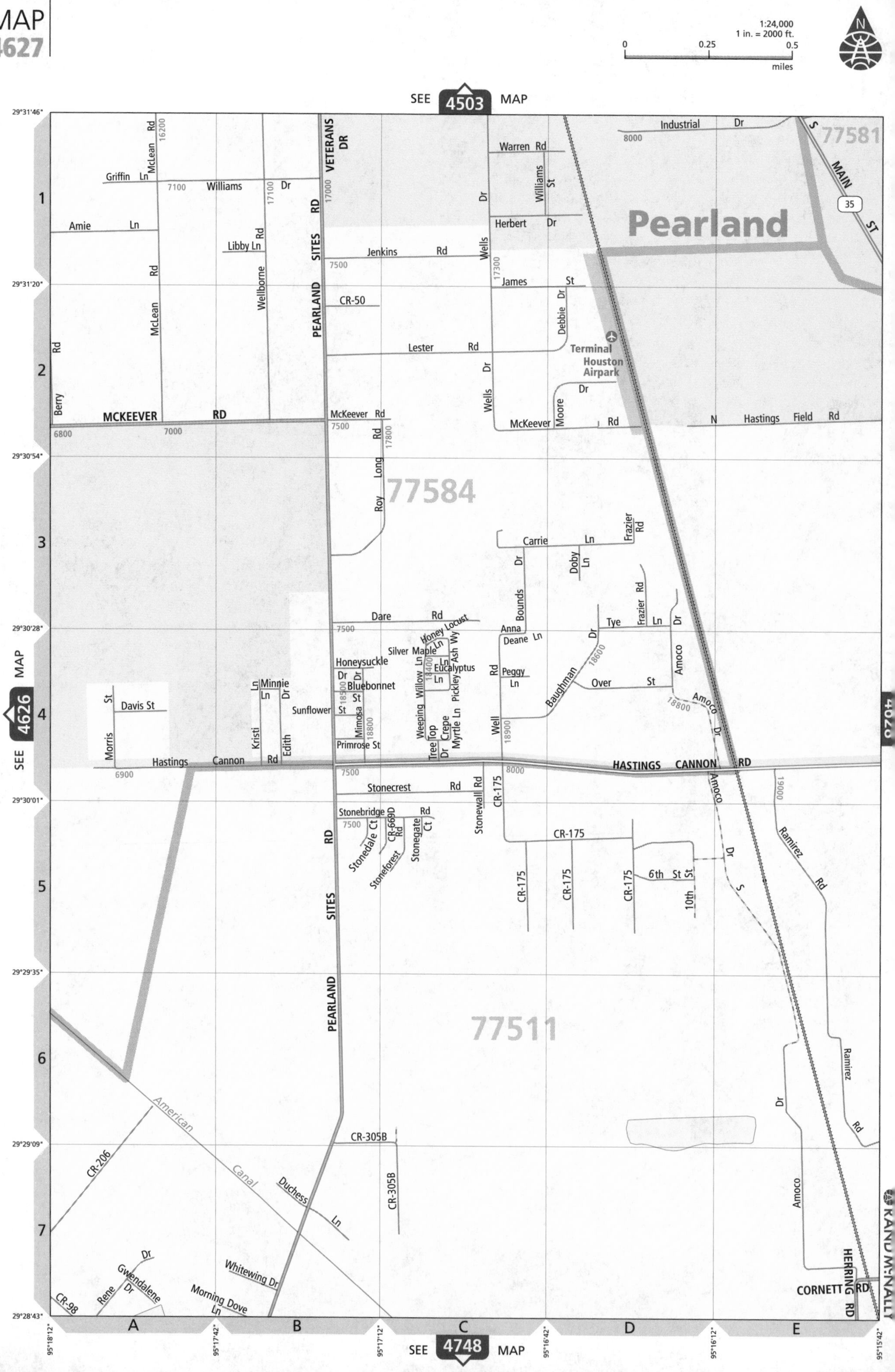
1:24,000
1 in. = 2000 ft.
0 0.25 0.5
miles
N
SEE 4503 MAP
SEE 4748 MAP
SEE 4626 MAP
Pearland
77581
77584
77511
S MAIN ST
35
Industrial Dr
8000
Warren Rd
Williams St
Herbert Dr
Wells Dr
17300
James St
Debbie Dr
Terminal
Houston
Airpark
Moore Dr
McKeever Rd
N Hastings Field Rd
Griffin Ln
McLean Rd
16200
7100
Williams Dr
17100
Amie Ln
Libby Ln
Wellborne Rd
McLean Rd
PEARLAND SITES RD
VETERANS DR
17000
Jenkins Rd
7500
CR-50
Lester Rd
Berry Rd
MCKEEVER RD
6800
7000
McKeever Rd
7500
Roy Long Rd
17800
Carrie Ln
Frazier Rd
Doby Ln
Bounds Dr
Frazier Rd
Tye Ln
Dr
Dare Rd
7500
Honey Locust
Silver Maple
Ash Wy
Honeysuckle
Dr
Bluebonnet
St
Eucalyptus
Ln
18400
Weeping Willow Ln
Pickley
Anna
Deane Ln
Peggy Ln
Baughman
18600
Over St
Amoco Dr
Amoco
18800
Davis St
Morris St
Minnie Ln
Dr
Kristi Ln
Edith
Sunflower St
18500
Mimosa
18800
Primrose St
Tree Top Dr
Crepe Myrtle Ln
Well
18900
Hastings Cannon Rd
6900
7500
HASTINGS CANNON RD
8000
Stonecrest Rd
Stonewall Rd
CR-175
Stonebridge
7500
Stonedale Ct
CR-669D Rd
Stoneforest
Stonegate Ct
Rd
CR-175
CR-175
CR-175
CR-175
6th St
St
10th
Amoco Dr
S
19000
Ramirez Rd
PEARLAND SITES RD
Ramirez Rd
Dr
Amoco
American Canal
CR-305B
CR-305B
CR-206
Duchess Ln
Whitewing Dr
Gwendalene Dr
Dr
Rene
CR-98
Morning Dove Ln
HERRING RD
CORNETT RD
RAND McNALLY
1
2
3
4
5
6
7
A
B
C
D
E
29°31'46"
29°31'20"
29°30'54"
29°30'28"
29°30'01"
29°29'35"
29°29'09"
29°28'43"
95°18'12"
95°17'42"
95°17'12"
95°16'42"
95°16'12"
95°15'42"

1:24,000
1 in. = 2000 ft.
0 0.25 0.5
miles

SEE 4504 MAP

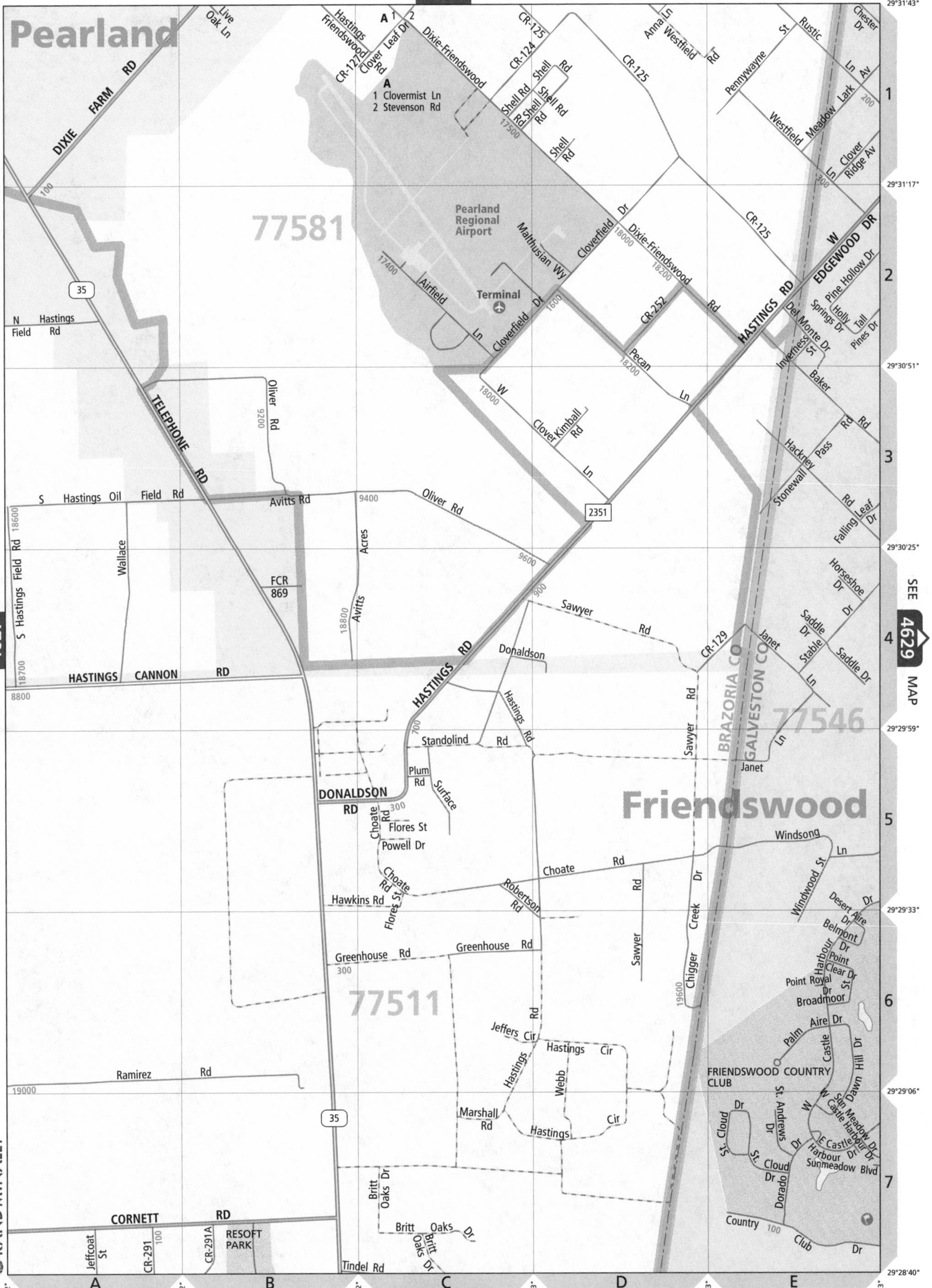
Pearland
Friendswood
77581
77511
77546
Pearland Regional Airport
Terminal
A
1 Clovermist Ln
2 Stevenson Rd
DIXIE FARM RD
TELEPHONE RD
HASTINGS RD
HASTINGS CANNON RD
DONALDSON RD
CORNETT RD
W EDGEWOOD DR
Dixie-Friendswood Rd
Cloverfield Dr
Malthusian Wy
Airfield Ln
CR-125
CR-124
CR-127
CR-252
CR-129
Shell Rd
Pecan Ln
W Clover Ln
Kimball Rd
Oliver Rd
Avitts Rd
S Hastings Oil Field Rd
N Hastings Field Rd
S Hastings Field Rd
Wallace
Acres
Avitts
FCR 869
Sawyer Rd
Donaldson
Standolind Rd
Plum Rd
Surface
Choate Rd
Flores St
Powell Dr
Hawkins Rd
Robertson Rd
Greenhouse Rd
Jeffers Cir
Hastings Cir
Webb
Marshall Rd
Ramirez Rd
Britt Oaks Dr
Tindel Rd
Jeffcoat St
CR-291
CR-291A
RESOFT PARK
Chigger Creek Dr
Windsong Ln
Windwood St
Janet Ln
Saddle Dr
Stable Ln
Horseshoe Dr
Falling Leaf Dr
Stonewall
Hackney Pass
Baker Rd
Inverness St
Del Monte Dr
Pine Hollow Dr
Holly Springs Dr
Tall Pines Dr
Clover Ridge Av
Meadow Lark Ln
Westfield Ln
Pennywayne St
Rustic Ln
Chester Dr
Anna Ln
Westfield Rd
Live Oak Ln
BRAZORIA CO
GALVESTON CO
FRIENDSWOOD COUNTRY CLUB
Country Club Dr
St. Cloud Dr
St. Andrews Dr
Dorado Dr
Sunmeadow Blvd
Castle Harbour Dr
Dawn Hill Dr
Palm Aire Dr
Broadmoor Dr
Point Royal St
Clear Dr
Point Harbour Dr
Belmont Dr
Desert Aire Dr
35
2351
29°31'43"
29°31'17"
29°30'51"
29°30'25"
29°29'59"
29°29'33"
29°29'06"
29°28'40"
95°15'42"
95°15'12"
95°14'42"
95°14'13"
95°13'43"
95°13'13"
A B C D E
1 2 3 4 5 6 7

SEE 4629 MAP

SEE 4749 MAP

1:24,000
1 in. = 2000 ft.
0 0.25 0.5
miles

SEE 4505 MAP

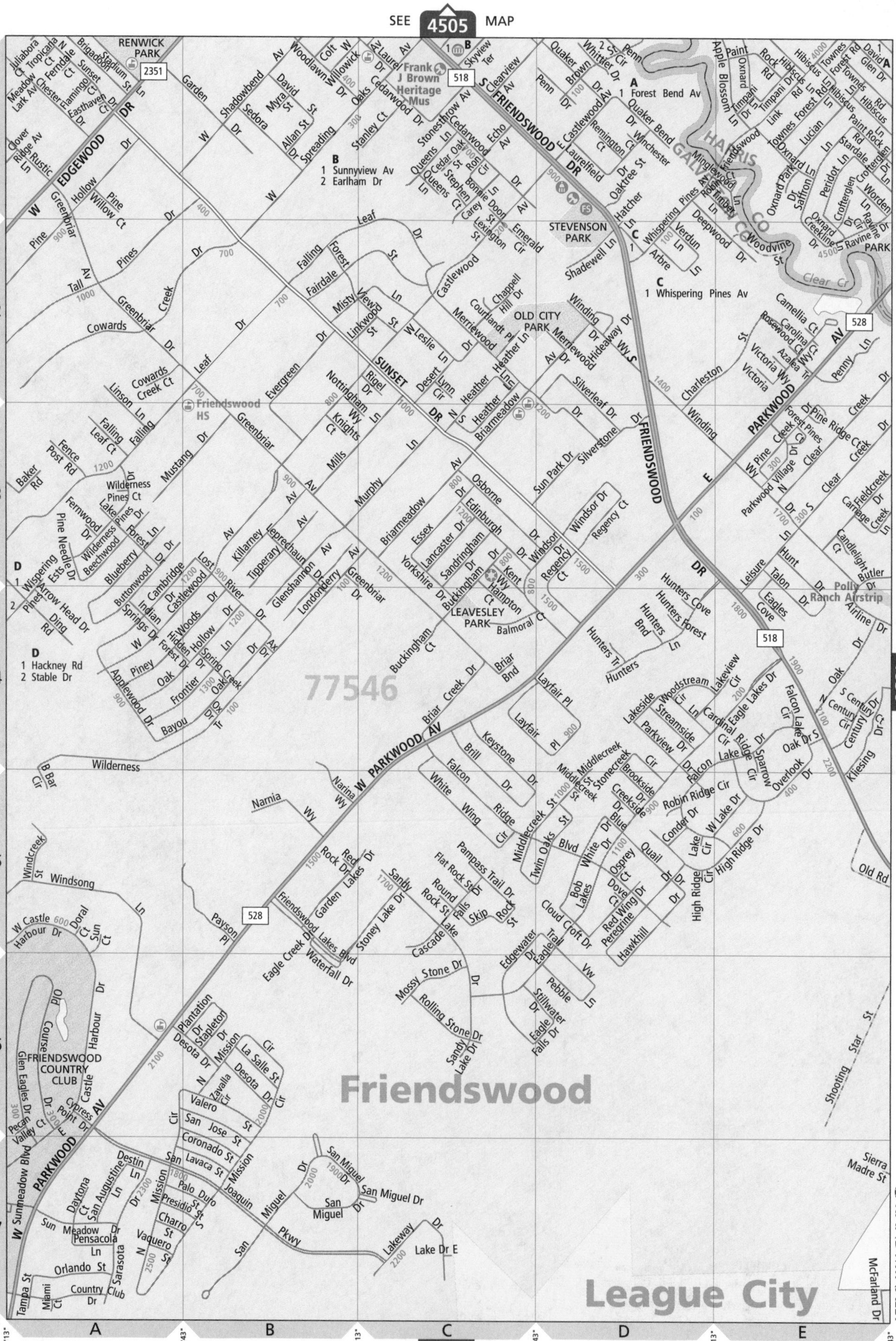
29°31'43"
29°31'17"
29°30'51"
29°30'25"
29°29'59"
29°29'33"
29°29'06"
29°28'40"
95°13'13"
95°12'43"
95°12'13"
95°11'43"
95°11'13"
95°10'43"
A
B
C
D
E
1
2
3
4
5
6
7
RENWICK PARK
2351
518
528
Frank J Brown Heritage Mus
STEVENSON PARK
OLD CITY PARK
LEAVESLEY PARK
Friendswood HS
77546
Friendswood
League City
FRIENDSWOOD COUNTRY CLUB
Polly Ranch Airstrip
HARRIS CO
GALVESTON CO
Clear Cr
PARK
W EDGEWOOD DR
S FRIENDSWOOD DR
SUNSET DR
W PARKWOOD AV
E PARKWOOD AV
PARKWOOD AV
A
1 Forest Bend Av
B
1 Sunnyview Av
2 Earlham Dr
C
1 Whispering Pines Av
D
1 Hackney Rd
2 Stable Dr
Juliabora Ct
Tropicana
Meadow Lark Av
Ferndale
Chester
Brigadoon
Flamingo
Sunset
Easthaven
Stadium
Clover Ridge Av
Rustic Ln
Greenbriar
Hollow
Willow Ct
Pine
Pines
Tall Av
Cowards Creek
Cowards Creek Ct
Linson Ln
Falling Leaf Ct
Fence Post Rd
Baker Rd
Wilderness Pines Ct
Mustang Dr
Fernwood Dr
Pine Needle Dr
Wilderness
Beechwood
Blueberry
Buttonwood
Cambridge
Castlewood
Lost River
Wispering Pines
Arrow Head Dr
Ding Rd
Indian Springs Dr
Woods
Hidden Hollow
Spring Creek
Piney
Oak
Frontier
Applewood Dr
Bayou
Wilderness
B Bar Cir
Garden
Shadowbend
Sedora
David
Myra St
Allan St
Spreading Oaks
Woodlawn
Colt
Willowick
Laurel
Cedarwood Dr
Stanley Ct
Leaf
Falling
Forest
Fairdale
Misty
View
Linkwood
Leslie
Evergreen
Nottingham
Rigel
Knights Ct
Mills
Murphy
Killarney
Tipperary
Leprechaun
Glenshannon
Londonderry
Briarmeadow
Essex
Lancaster Dr
Sandringham
Edinburgh
Osborne
Yorkshire Dr
Buckingham
Hampton
Kent
Windsor
Regency Ct
Balmoral Ct
Briar Creek Dr
Briar Bnd
Layfair Pl
Keystone
Brill
Falcon
White Wing
Ridge
Narnia Wy
Stonesthrow Av
Cedarwood
Queens Ln
Queens Ct
Cedar Oak
Stephen
Bonnie Doon
Carey
Lexington
Emerald Cir
Echo
Castlewood
Chappell Hill Dr
Courtlandt Pl
Merriewood
Heather Ln
Briarmeadow
Desert Lynn Cir
Winding Wy
Hideaway Dr
Silverleaf Dr
Silverstone
Sun Park Dr
Windsor Dr
Regency Ct
Skyview Ter
Clearview Av
Quaker
Brown
Whittier
Penn
Castlewood Av
Laurelfield
Remington Ct
Winchester
Quaker Bend
Oaktree St
Hatcher
Shadewell Ln
Whispering Pines Av
Verdun
Arbre
Deepwood
Woodvine
Apple Blossom Ln
Oxnard
Timpani
Paint Rock Rd
Hibiscus
Townes Forest Rd
Lucian
Saffron
Peridot Ln
Stardale
Crofton
Worden
Ravine
Camellia Ct
Carolina
Rosewood
Azalea
Victoria Wy
Charleston
Winding
Penny Ln
Creek Dr
Pine Ridge Ct
Forest Pines
Clear Creek
Parkwood Village Dr
Fieldcreek
Carriage Ln
Candlelight
Butler
Leisure
Hunt
Talon
Eagles Cove
Airline Dr
Hunters Cove
Hunters Forest
Hunters Bnd
Hunters Tr
Hunters
Lakeside
Woodstream
Lakeview
Eagle Lakes Dr
Streamside
Parkview
Cardinal Ridge Cir
Falcon Lake
Oak Dr S
S Century Dr
Century
Kliesing
Middlecreek St
Stonecreek
Brookside
Creekside
Robin Ridge Cir
Sparrow
Overlook
Conder Dr
W Lake Dr
Lake Cir
High Ridge Dr
High Ridge Cir
Quail
Osprey Ct
Dove Ct
Red Wing Dr
Peregrine
Hawkhill
Blue
White
Bob Lakes
Twin Oaks
Cloud Croft Dr
Pebble Ln
Old Rd
Pampass Trail Dr
Flat Rock St
Round Rock St
Falls
Skip Rock St
Sandy Lake
Cascade
Mossy Stone Dr
Rolling Stone Dr
Sandy Lake Dr
Edgewater
Eagle Trail
Stillwater Dr
Eagle Falls Dr
Red Rock Dr
Garden Lakes Dr
Stoney Lake Dr
Friendswood Lakes Blvd
Eagle Creek Dr
Waterfall Dr
Payson Pl
Windcreek St
Windsong
W Castle Harbour Dr
Doral Ct
Sun Ct
Harbour Dr
Old Course
Glen Eagles Dr
Castle
Cypress Point Dr
Pecan Valley Ct
Plantation Dr
Stapleton
Desota Dr
Mission
La Salle St
Desota
Zavalla
Valero
San Jose St
Coronado St
San Lavaca St
Palo Duro
Presidio St
Charro St
Joaquin
Miguel
San Miguel Dr
San Miguel
Pkwy
Lakeway
Lake Dr E
Destin Ln
Daytona
San Augustine
Sunmeadow Blvd
Sun Meadow Dr
Pensacola Ln
Vaquero St
Sarasota
Orlando St
Country Club Dr
Tampa St
Miami Ct
Shooting Star St
Sierra Madre St
McFarland Dr

SEE 4628 MAP

SEE 4750 MAP

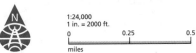

1:24,000
1 in. = 2000 ft.
0 0.25 0.5
miles

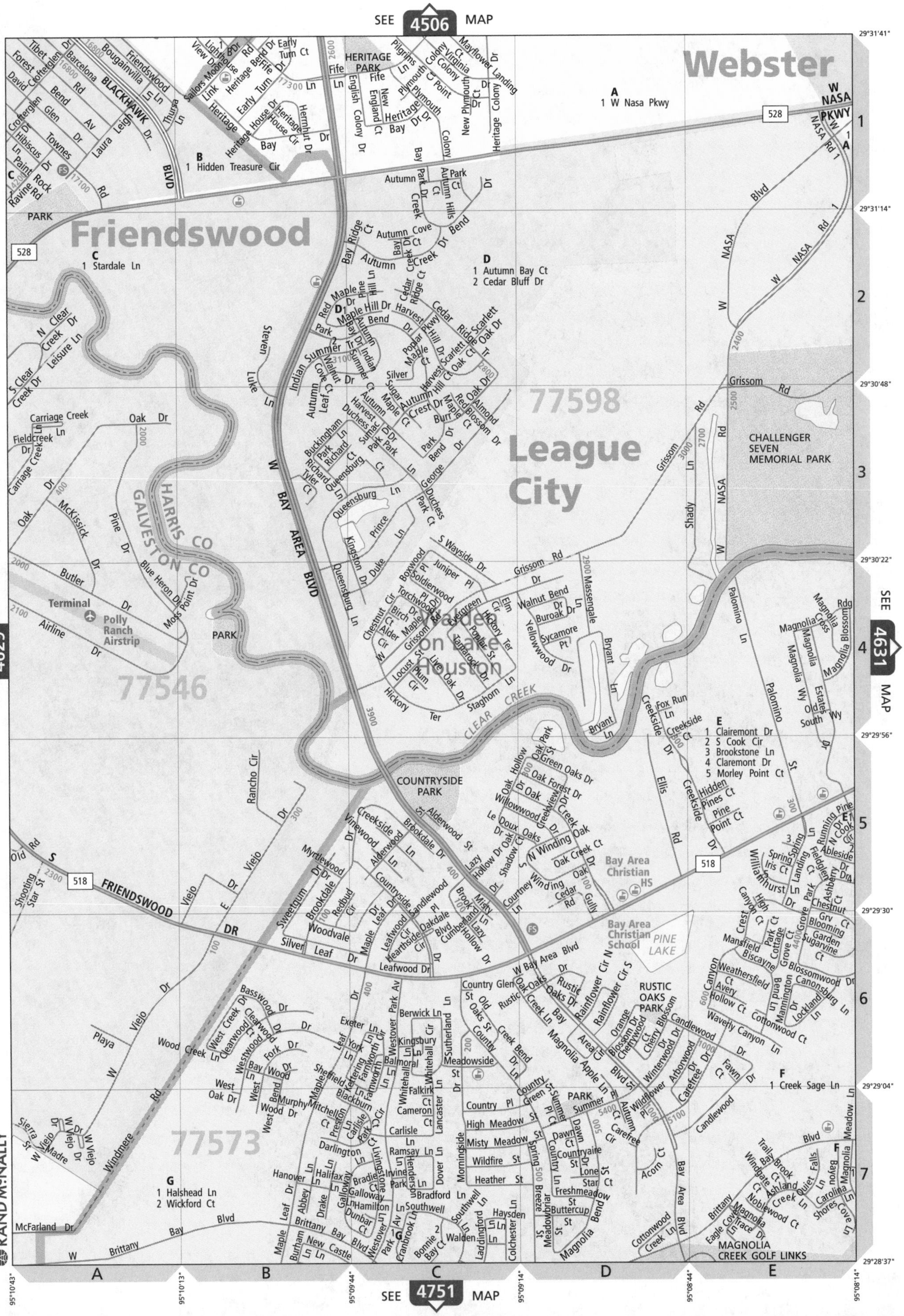
SEE 4506 MAP
Webster
Friendswood
League City
77598
77546
77573
HARRIS CO
GALVESTON CO
HERITAGE PARK
CHALLENGER SEVEN MEMORIAL PARK
COUNTRYSIDE PARK
RUSTIC OAKS PARK
MAGNOLIA CREEK GOLF LINKS
Polly Ranch Airstrip
Bay Area Christian HS
Bay Area Christian School
PINE LAKE
CLEAR CREEK
Wedgewood on Lake Houston
A
1 W Nasa Pkwy
B
1 Hidden Treasure Cir
C
1 Stardale Ln
D
1 Autumn Bay Ct
2 Cedar Bluff Dr
E
1 Clairemont Dr
2 S Cook Cir
3 Brookstone Ln
4 Claremont Dr
5 Morley Point Ct
F
1 Creek Sage Ln
G
1 Halshead Ln
2 Wickford Ct
W BAY AREA BLVD
FRIENDSWOOD DR
W NASA PKWY
Grissom Rd
SEE 4631 MAP
SEE 4629 MAP
SEE 4751 MAP
29°31'41"
29°31'14"
29°30'48"
29°30'22"
29°29'56"
29°29'30"
29°29'04"
29°28'37"
95°10'43"
95°10'13"
95°09'44"
95°09'14"
95°08'44"
95°08'14"
A B C D E
1 2 3 4 5 6 7
RAND McNALLY

1:24,000
1 in. = 2000 ft.
0 0.25 0.5
miles

SEE 4507 MAP

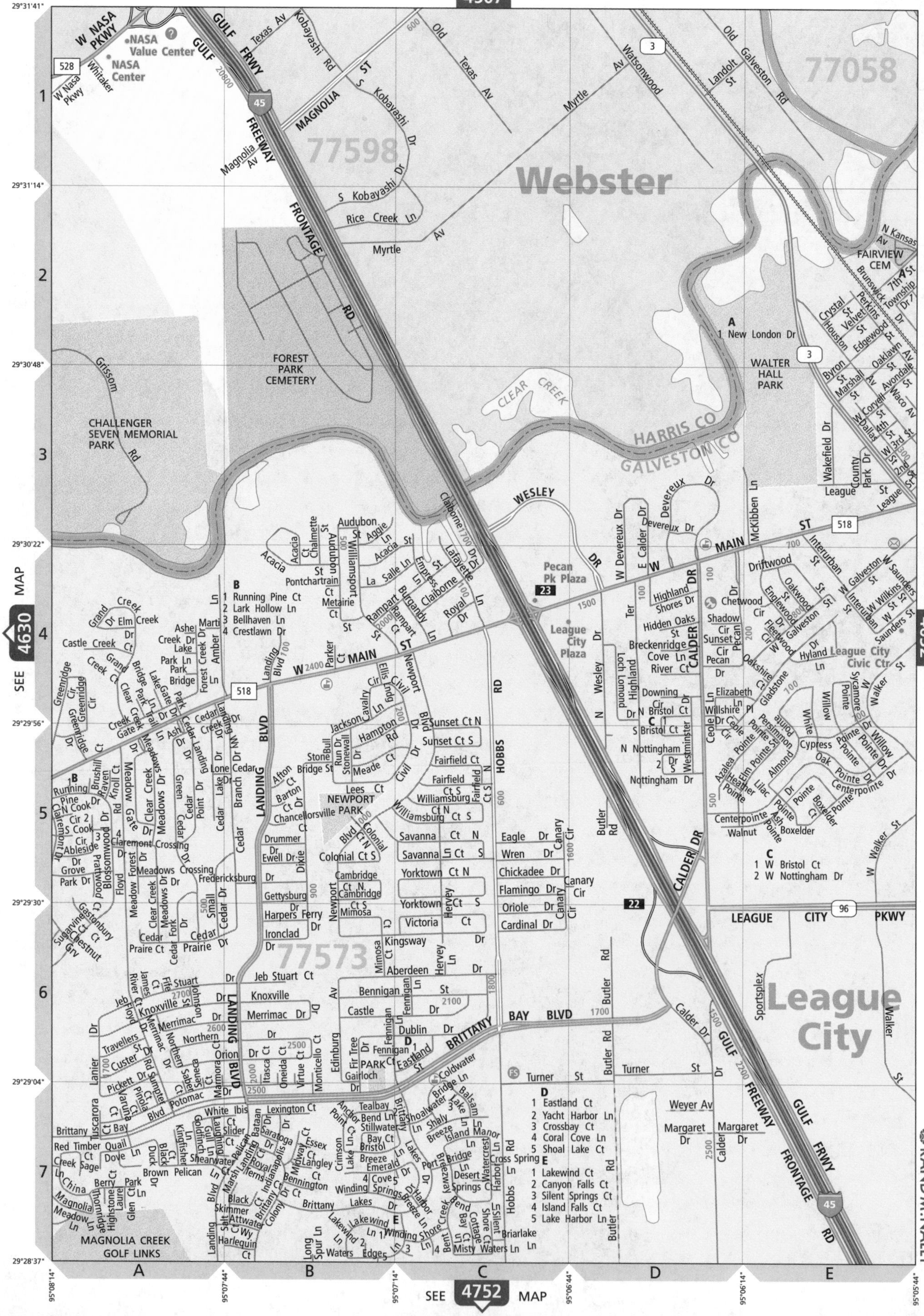
Webster
League City
77058
77598
77573
W NASA PKWY
NASA Value Center
NASA Center
GULF FRWY
GULF FREEWAY
FRONTAGE RD
MAGNOLIA ST
Kobayashi Rd
S Kobayashi Dr
Rice Creek Ln
Myrtle Av
Old Texas Av
Watsonwood
Old Galveston Rd
Landolt St
FOREST PARK CEMETERY
CHALLENGER SEVEN MEMORIAL PARK
Grissom Rd
CLEAR CREEK
HARRIS CO
GALVESTON CO
WALTER HALL PARK
FAIRVIEW CEM
A
1 New London Dr
B
1 Running Pine Ct
2 Lark Hollow Ln
3 Bellhaven Ln
4 Crestlawn Dr
C
1 W Bristol Ct
2 W Nottingham Dr
D
1 Eastland Ct
2 Yacht Harbor Ln
3 Crossbay Ct
4 Coral Cove Ln
5 Shoal Lake Ct
E
1 Lakewind Ct
2 Canyon Falls Ct
3 Silent Springs Ct
4 Island Falls Ct
5 Lake Harbor Ln
W MAIN ST
WESLEY DR
CALDER DR
HOBBS RD
LANDING BLVD
BRITTANY BAY BLVD
LEAGUE CITY PKWY
Pecan Pk Plaza
League City Plaza
League City Civic Ctr
NEWPORT PARK
Sportsplex
MAGNOLIA CREEK GOLF LINKS
Butler Rd
Walker St
Turner St
518
528
3
96
45
23
22
A B C D E
1 2 3 4 5 6 7

SEE 4630 MAP

SEE 4752 MAP

1:24,000
1 in. = 2000 ft.
0 0.25 0.5
miles

SEE 4508 MAP

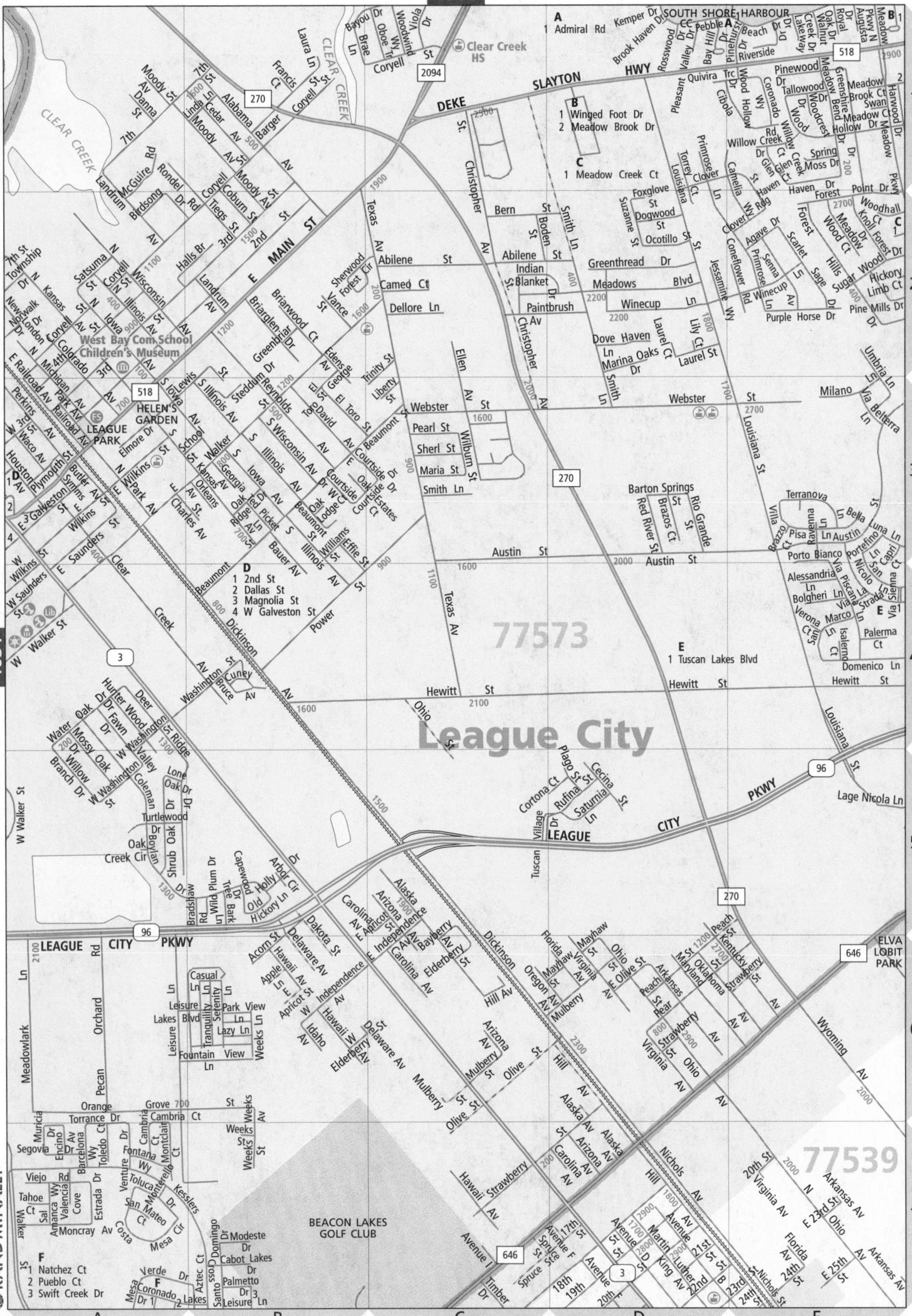
League City
77573
77539
DEKE SLAYTON HWY
E MAIN ST
LEAGUE CITY PKWY
SOUTH SHORE HARBOUR
Clear Creek HS
CLEAR CREEK
West Bay Com School
Children's Museum
HELEN'S GARDEN
LEAGUE PARK
BEACON LAKES GOLF CLUB
ELVA LOBIT PARK
Dickinson Av
Louisiana St
Texas Av
Webster St
Austin St
Hewitt St
Christopher Av
Wyoming Av
A
1 Admiral Rd
B
1 Winged Foot Dr
2 Meadow Brook Dr
C
1 Meadow Creek Ct
D
1 2nd St
2 Dallas St
3 Magnolia St
4 W Galveston St
E
1 Tuscan Lakes Blvd
F
1 Natchez Ct
2 Pueblo Ct
3 Swift Creek Dr

SEE 4631 MAP
SEE 4633 MAP
SEE 4753 MAP

1:24,000
1 in. = 2000 ft.
0 0.25 0.5
miles

SEE 4509 MAP

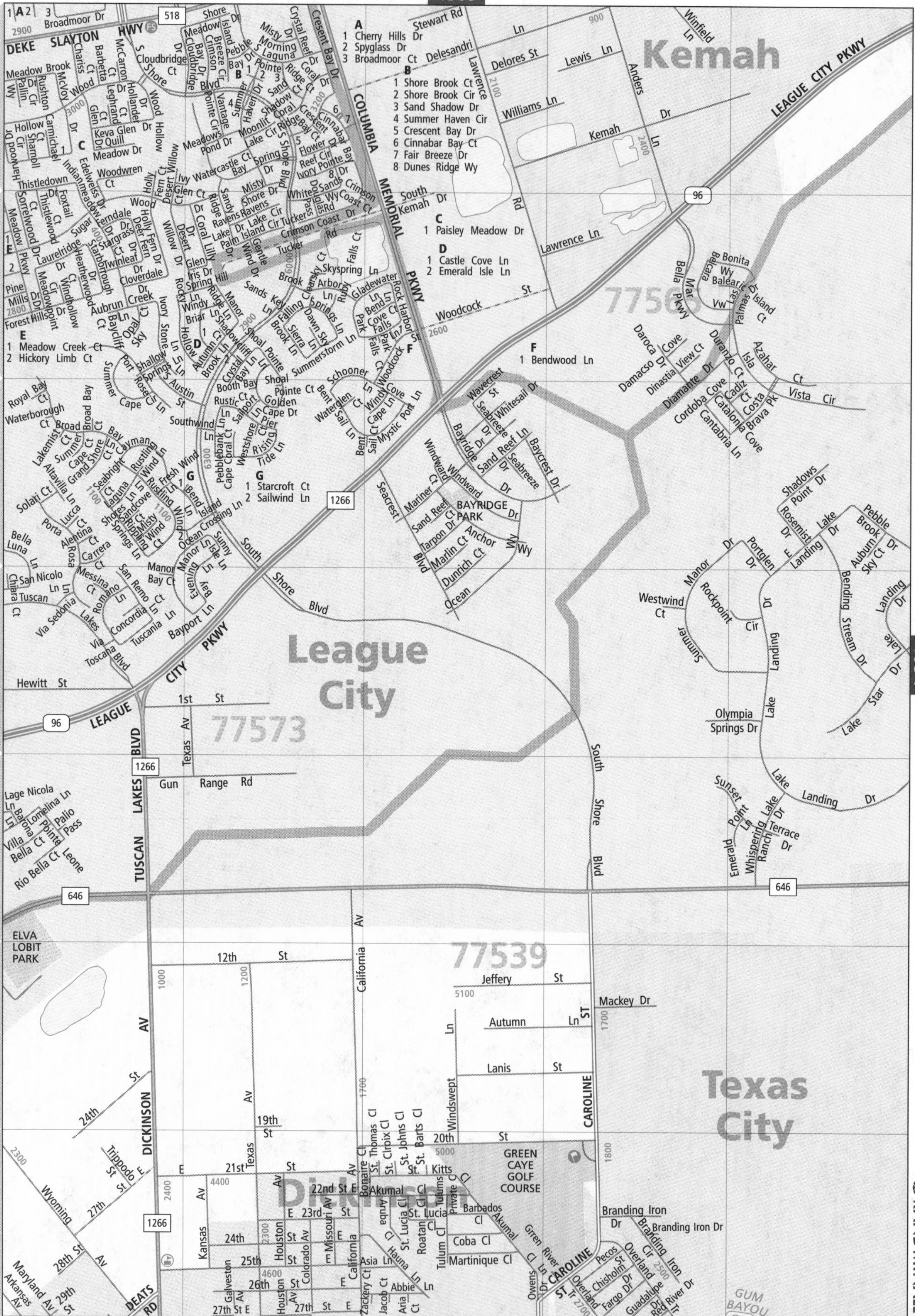
Kemah
League City
Texas City
Dickinson
77565
77573
77539
LEAGUE CITY PKWY
DEKE SLAYTON HWY
COLUMBIA MEMORIAL PKWY
South Shore Blvd
TUSCAN LAKES BLVD
DICKINSON AV
DEATS RD
CAROLINE ST
BAYRIDGE PARK
ELVA LOBIT PARK
GREEN CAYE GOLF COURSE
GUM BAYOU
Gun Range Rd
Hewitt St
1st St
12th St
Jeffery St
Mackey Dr
Autumn Ln
Lanis St
20th St
21st St
22nd St E
23rd St
24th St
25th St
26th St
27th St
28th St
29th St
Olympia Springs Dr
Lake Landing Dr
Kemah Dr
Lawrence Rd
Lawrence Ln
Delores St
Lewis Ln
Williams Ln
Anders Ln
Woodcock St
Stewart Rd
A
1 Cherry Hills Dr
2 Spyglass Dr
3 Broadmoor Ct
B
1 Shore Brook Ct
2 Shore Brook Cir
3 Sand Shadow Dr
4 Summer Haven Cir
5 Crescent Bay Dr
6 Cinnabar Bay Ct
7 Fair Breeze Dr
8 Dunes Ridge Wy
C
1 Paisley Meadow Dr
D
1 Castle Cove Ln
2 Emerald Isle Ln
E
1 Meadow Creek Ct
2 Hickory Limb Ct
F
1 Bendwood Ln
G
1 Starcroft Ct
2 Sailwind Ln
96
518
1266
646
29°31'37"
29°31'11"
29°30'45"
29°30'19"
29°29'53"
29°29'27"
29°29'01"
29°28'34"
95°03'15"
95°02'45"
95°02'15"
95°01'45"
95°01'15"
95°00'56"
A B C D E
1 2 3 4 5 6 7

SEE 4632 MAP

4634

SEE 4754 MAP

1:24,000
1 in. = 2000 ft.
0 0.25 0.5
miles

SEE 4510 MAP

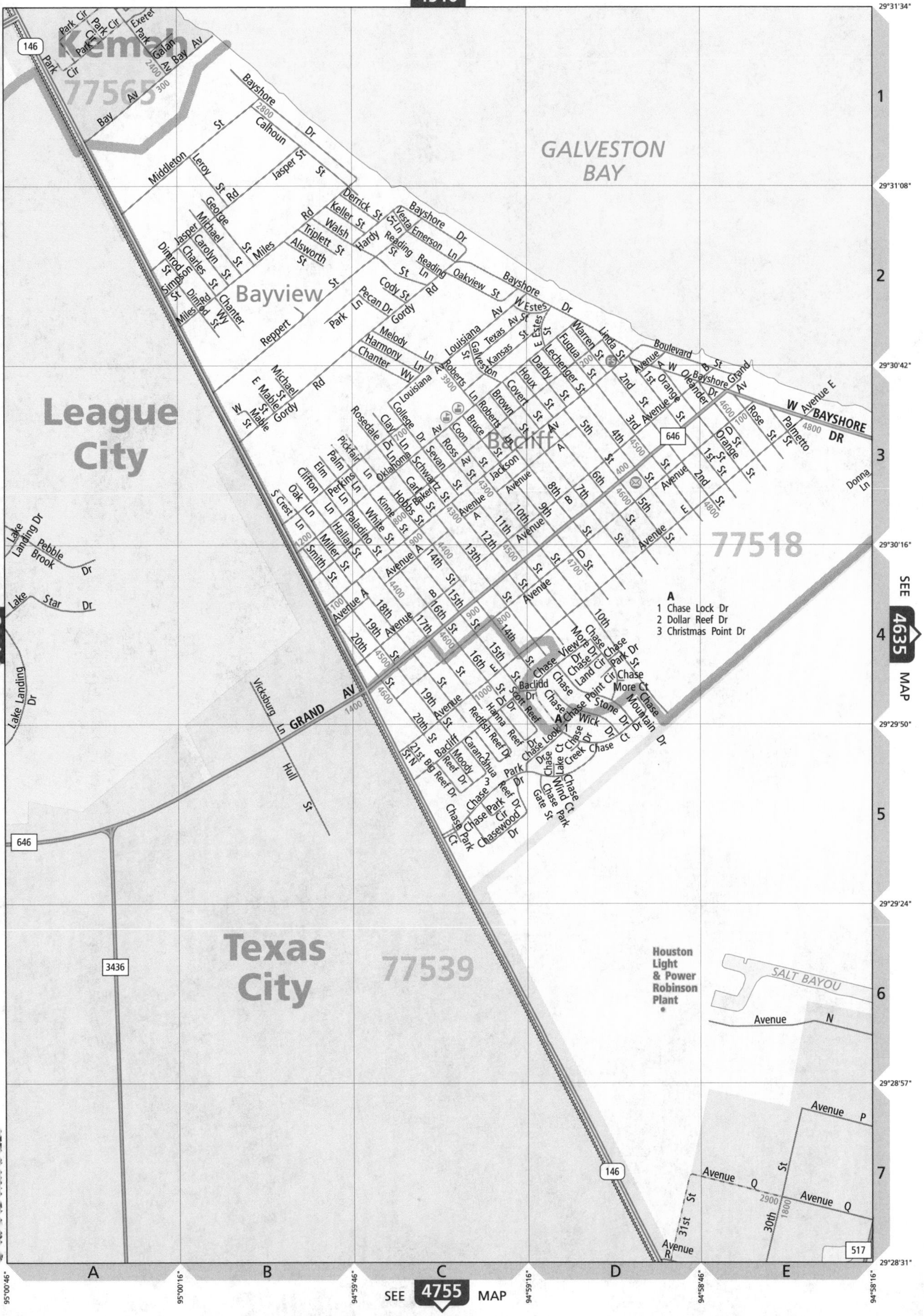
Kemah
77565
GALVESTON BAY
Bayview
League City
Bacliff
77518
Texas City
77539
Houston Light & Power Robinson Plant
SALT BAYOU
GRAND AV
W BAYSHORE DR
Bayshore Dr
A
1 Chase Lock Dr
2 Dollar Reef Dr
3 Christmas Point Dr
Avenue N
Avenue P
Avenue Q
Avenue R
146
646
3436
517
1
2
3
4
5
6
7
A
B
C
D
E
29°31'34"
29°31'08"
29°30'42"
29°30'16"
29°29'50"
29°29'24"
29°28'57"
29°28'31"
95°00'46"
95°00'16"
94°59'46"
94°59'16"
94°58'46"
94°58'16"

SEE 4635 MAP

SEE 4755 MAP

1:24,000
1 in. = 2000 ft.
0 0.25 0.5
miles

SEE B MAP

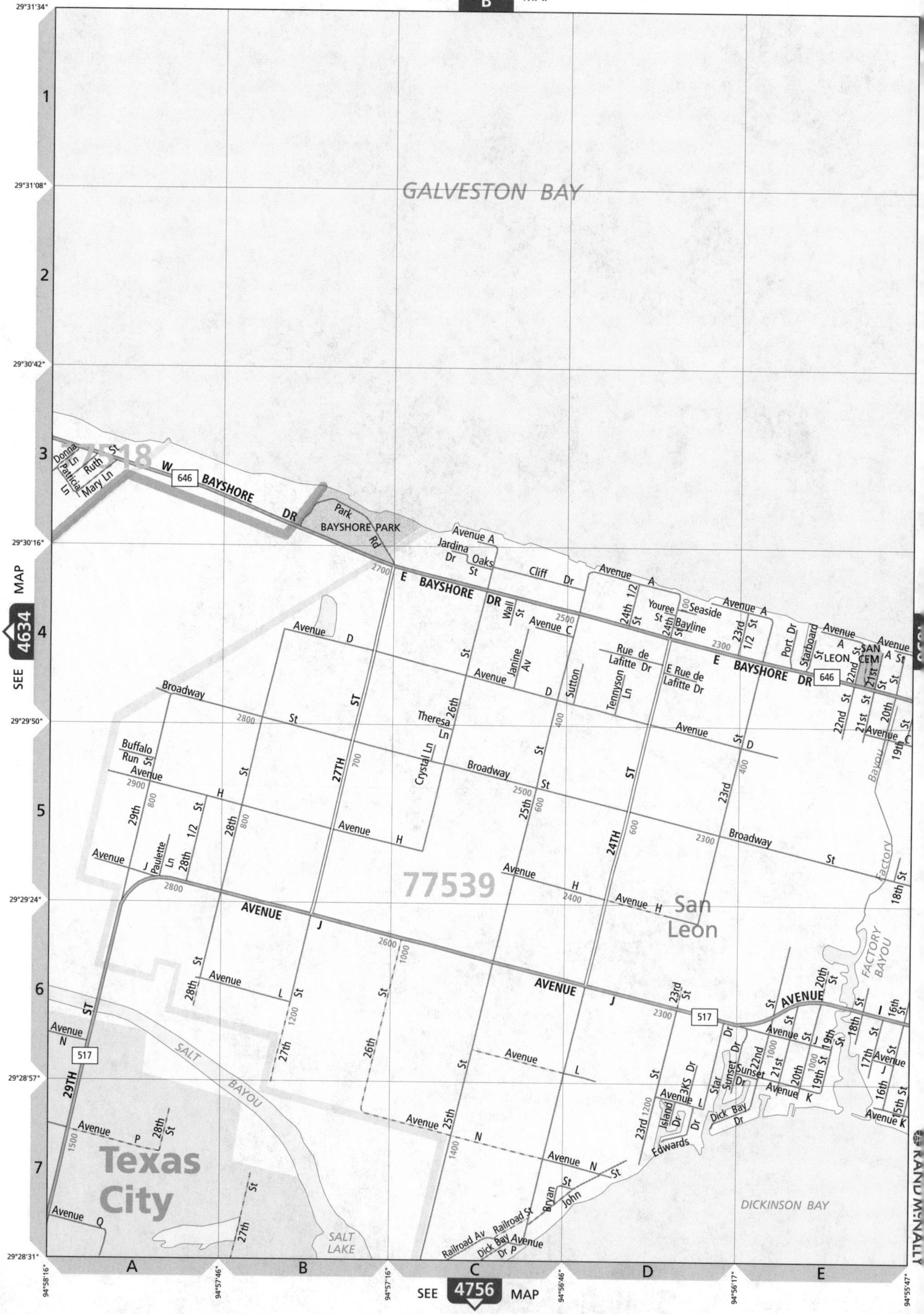
GALVESTON BAY
Donna Ln
Ruth St
Patricia Ln
Mary Ln
77518
W BAYSHORE DR
646
BAYSHORE PARK
Park Rd
Avenue A
Jardina Dr
Oaks St
Cliff Dr
E BAYSHORE DR
Wall St
Avenue C
24th 1/2 St
Youree St
24th St
Seaside
Bayline
23rd 1/2 St
Port Dr
Starboard St
SAN LEON CEM
Avenue D
Janine Av
Sutton
Rue de Lafitte Dr
E Rue de Lafitte Dr
Tennyson Ln
Broadway St
Theresa Ln
26th St
27TH ST
Crystal Ln
Buffalo Run St
Avenue H
29th
28th St
28th 1/2 St
Paulette Ln
Avenue J
25th St
24TH ST
23rd
22nd St
21st St
20th
19th
Bayou
Factory
18th St
77539
San Leon
AVENUE J
AVENUE
Avenue L
27th St
26th St
23rd St
20th St
FACTORY BAYOU
517
Avenue N
29TH ST
SALT BAYOU
3KS Dr
Island Dr
Star Dr
Sunset Dr
Dick Bay Dr
Edwards
Avenue K
Avenue P
Texas City
Bryan St
John St
Railroad Av
Railroad St
Dick Bay Dr
Avenue P
Avenue Q
SALT LAKE
DICKINSON BAY
A B C D E
1 2 3 4 5 6 7
29°31'34"
29°31'08"
29°30'42"
29°30'16"
29°29'50"
29°29'24"
29°28'57"
29°28'31"
94°58'16"
94°57'46"
94°57'16"
94°56'46"
94°56'17"
94°55'47"

SEE 4634 MAP

SEE 4756 MAP

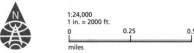

1:24,000
1 in. = 2000 ft.
0 0.25 0.5
miles

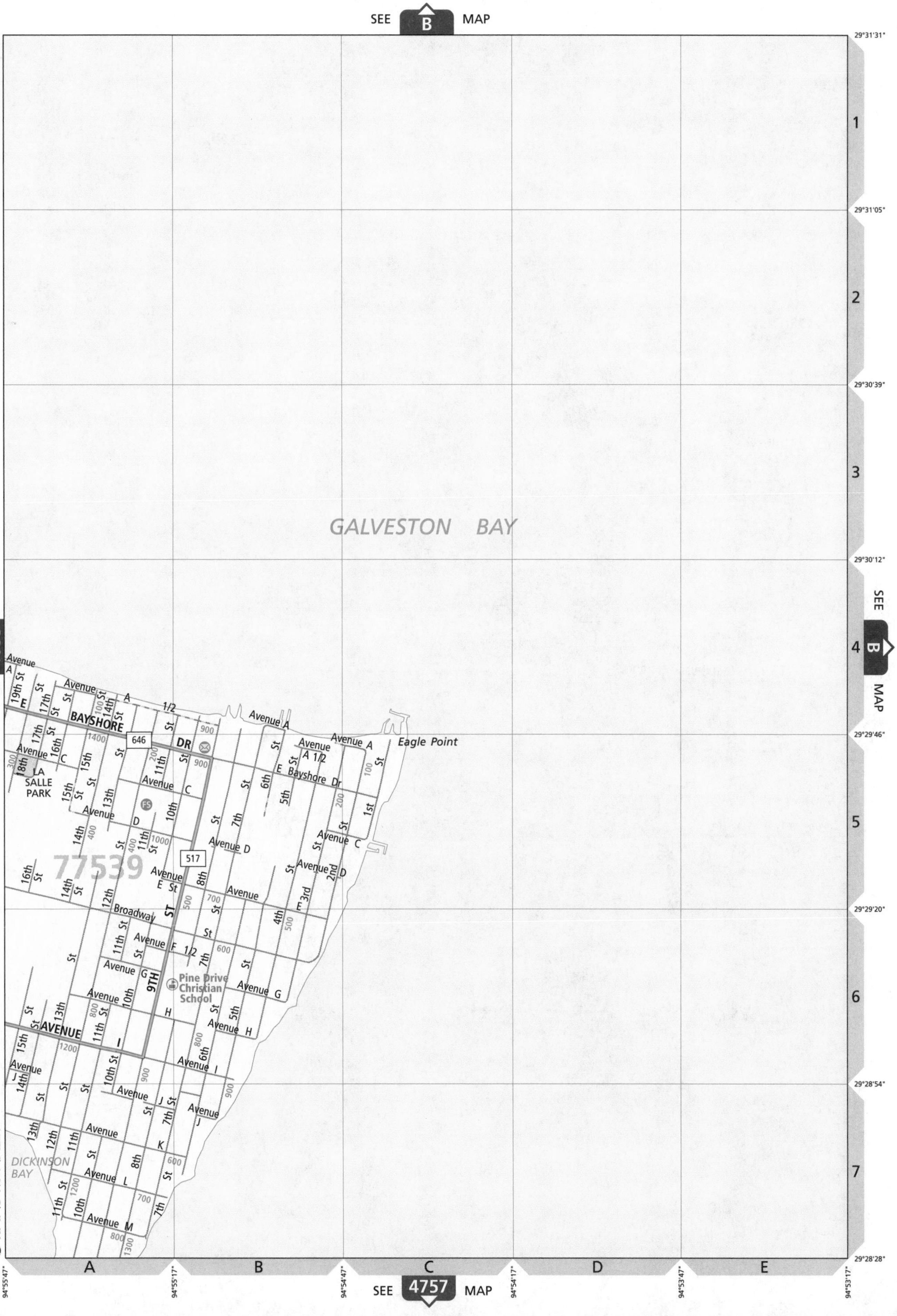
SEE B MAP
SEE B MAP
SEE 4757 MAP
GALVESTON BAY
Eagle Point
DICKINSON BAY
LA SALLE PARK
77539
Pine Drive Christian School
BAYSHORE DR
AVENUE I
9TH ST
646
517
Avenue A
Avenue A 1/2
E Bayshore Dr
Avenue C
Avenue D
Avenue E
Broadway
Avenue F 1/2
Avenue G
Avenue H
Avenue J
Avenue K
Avenue L
Avenue M
1st
2nd
E 3rd
4th
5th
6th
7th
8th
10th
11th
12th
13th
14th
15th
16th
17th
18th
19th St
29°31'31"
29°31'05"
29°30'39"
29°30'12"
29°29'46"
29°29'20"
29°28'54"
29°28'28"
94°55'47"
94°55'17"
94°54'47"
94°54'17"
94°53'47"
94°53'17"
1
2
3
4
5
6
7
A
B
C
D
E

SEE 4623 MAP

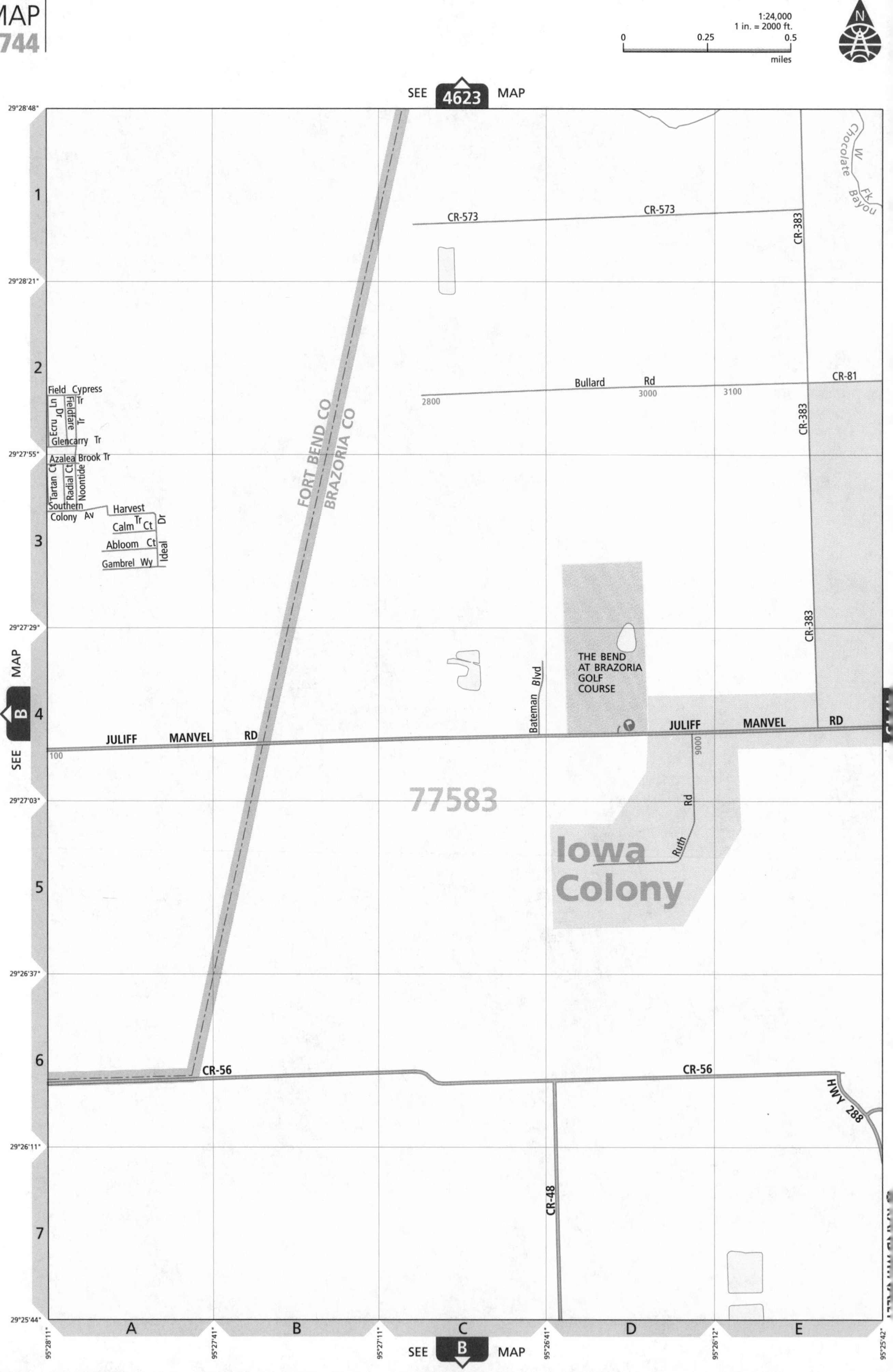
1:24,000
1 in. = 2000 ft.
0 0.25 0.5
miles
N
29°28'48"
29°28'21"
29°27'55"
29°27'29"
29°27'03"
29°26'37"
29°26'11"
29°25'44"
95°28'11"
95°27'41"
95°27'11"
95°26'41"
95°26'12"
95°25'42"
1
2
3
4
5
6
7
A
B
C
D
E
W Chocolate Fk Bayou
CR-573
CR-573
CR-383
Bullard Rd
CR-81
2800
3000
3100
CR-383
Field Cypress Tr
Ecru Ln
Dr
Fieldfare Tr
Glencarry Tr
Azalea Brook Tr
Tartan Ct
Radial Ct
Noontide
Southern Colony Av
Harvest Tr
Calm Ct
Dr
Abloom Ct
Ideal
Gambrel Wy
FORT BEND CO
BRAZORIA CO
CR-383
THE BEND AT BRAZORIA GOLF COURSE
Bateman Blvd
JULIFF MANVEL RD
100
JULIFF MANVEL RD
9000
77583
Rd
Ruth
Iowa Colony
CR-56
CR-56
HWY 288
CR-48

SEE B MAP

SEE B MAP

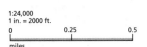

1:24,000
1 in. = 2000 ft.
0 0.25 0.5
miles

SEE 4624 MAP

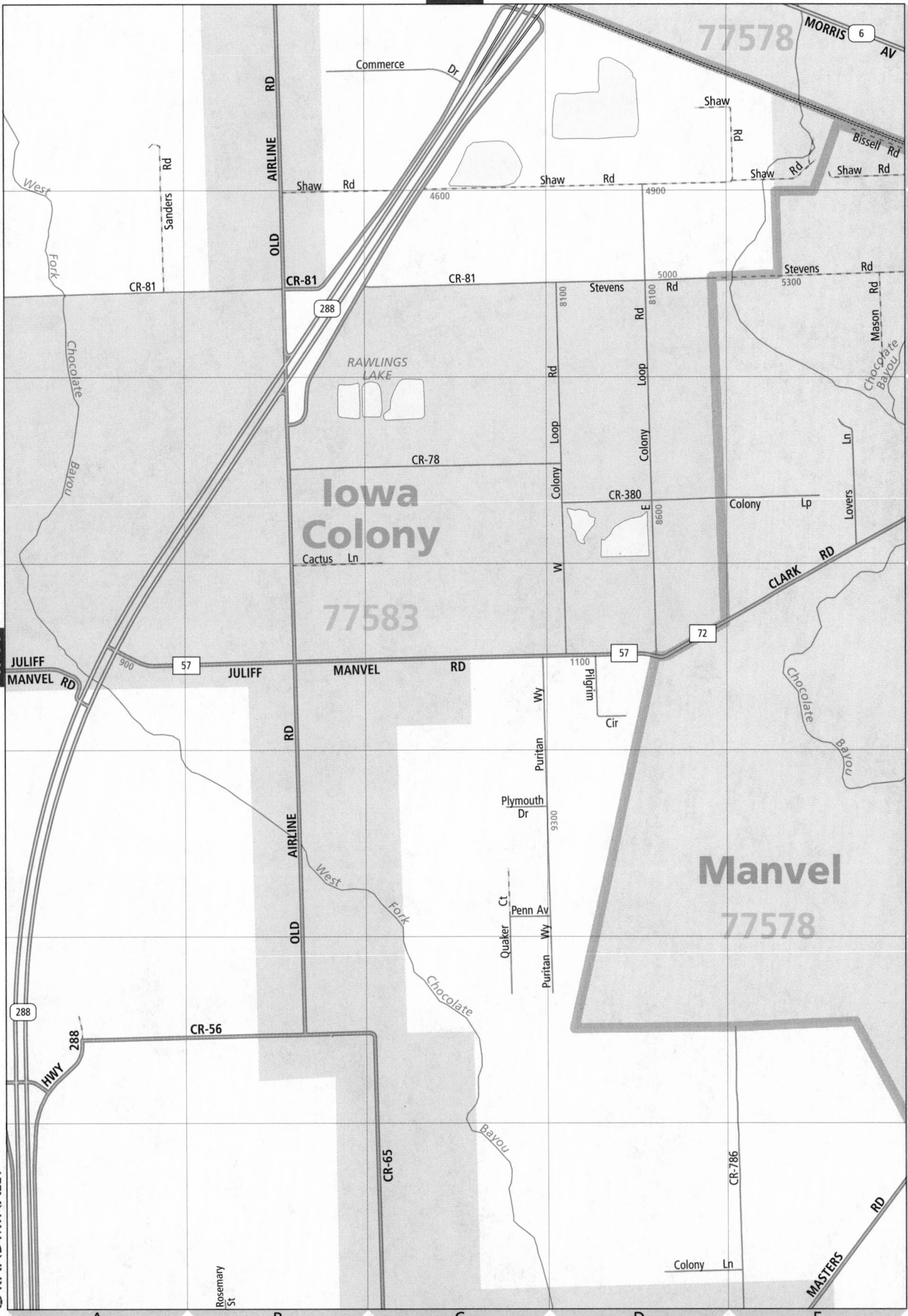
MORRIS AV
6
77578
Commerce Dr
Shaw Rd
Bissell Rd
OLD AIRLINE RD
Sanders Rd
West Fork Chocolate Bayou
Shaw Rd
4600
4900
CR-81
288
5000
5300
Stevens Rd
8100
Mason Rd
RAWLINGS LAKE
Chocolate Bayou
W Colony Loop Rd
E Colony Loop Rd
CR-78
CR-380
Colony Lp
8600
Lovers Ln
Iowa Colony
Cactus Ln
77583
CLARK RD
72
JULIFF MANVEL RD
900
57
1100
Pilgrim Cir
Puritan Wy
Plymouth Dr
9300
Manvel
77578
Quaker Ct
Penn Av
HWY 288
CR-56
CR-65
CR-786
Colony Ln
MASTERS RD
Rosemary St
29°28'45"
29°28'19"
29°27'53"
29°27'27"
29°27'01"
29°26'35"
29°26'08"
29°25'42"
95°25'42"
95°25'12"
95°24'42"
95°24'12"
95°23'42"
95°23'12"
1
2
3
4
5
6
7
A
B
C
D
E

SEE 4746 MAP

SEE B MAP

1:24,000
1 in. = 2000 ft.
0 0.25 0.5
miles

SEE 4625 MAP

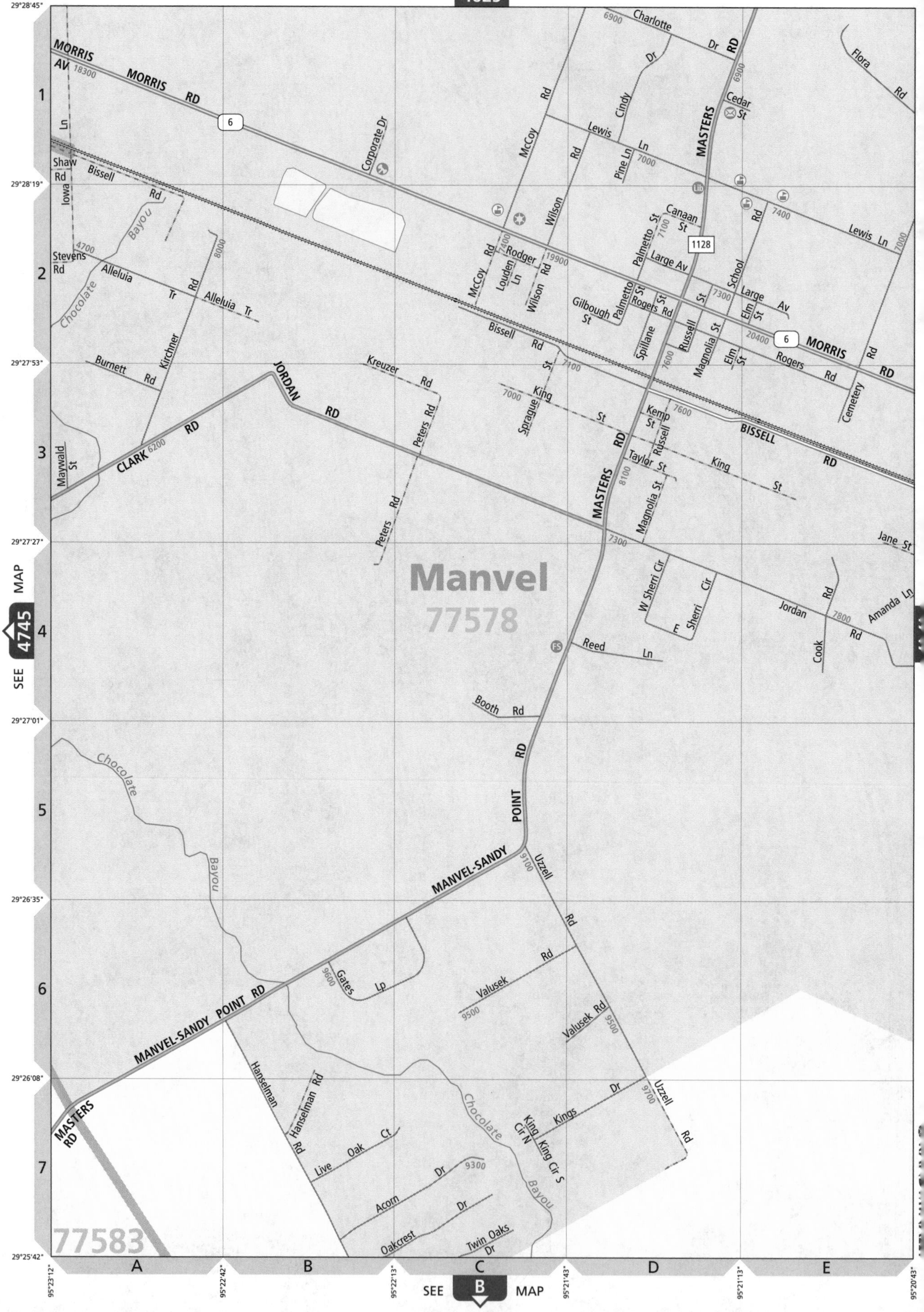
Manvel
77578
77583
MORRIS AV
MORRIS RD
6
1128
Corporate Dr
Charlotte Dr
Cindy Dr
McCoy Rd
Lewis Ln
Pine Ln
MASTERS RD
Cedar St
Flora Rd
Wilson Rd
Shaw Rd
Iowa Ln
Bissell Rd
Stevens Rd
Bayou
Chocolate
Alleluia Tr
Kirchner Rd
Canaan St
Palmetto St
Large Av
School Rd
Lewis Ln
Rodger Rd
Louden Ln
Gilbough St
Rogers Rd
Spillane
Russell St
Magnolia St
Elm St
Cemetery Rd
Burnett Rd
JORDAN RD
Kreuzer Rd
Peters Rd
Sprague St
King St
Kemp St
BISSELL RD
Taylor St
CLARK RD
Maywald St
Jane St
W Sherri Cir
E Sherri Cir
Jordan Rd
Amanda Ln
Cook Rd
Reed Ln
Booth Rd
POINT RD
MANVEL-SANDY POINT RD
Uzzell Rd
Gates Lp
Valusek Rd
Hanselman Rd
Kings Dr
King Cir N
King Cir S
Live Oak Ct
Acorn Dr
Oakcrest Dr
Twin Oaks Dr
A
B
C
D
E
1
2
3
4
5
6
7
29°28'45"
29°28'19"
29°27'53"
29°27'27"
29°27'01"
29°26'35"
29°26'08"
29°25'42"
95°23'12"
95°22'42"
95°22'13"
95°21'43"
95°21'13"
95°20'43"

SEE 4745 MAP

SEE B MAP

1:24,000
1 in. = 2000 ft.
0 0.25 0.5
miles

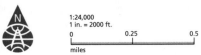

SEE 4626 MAP

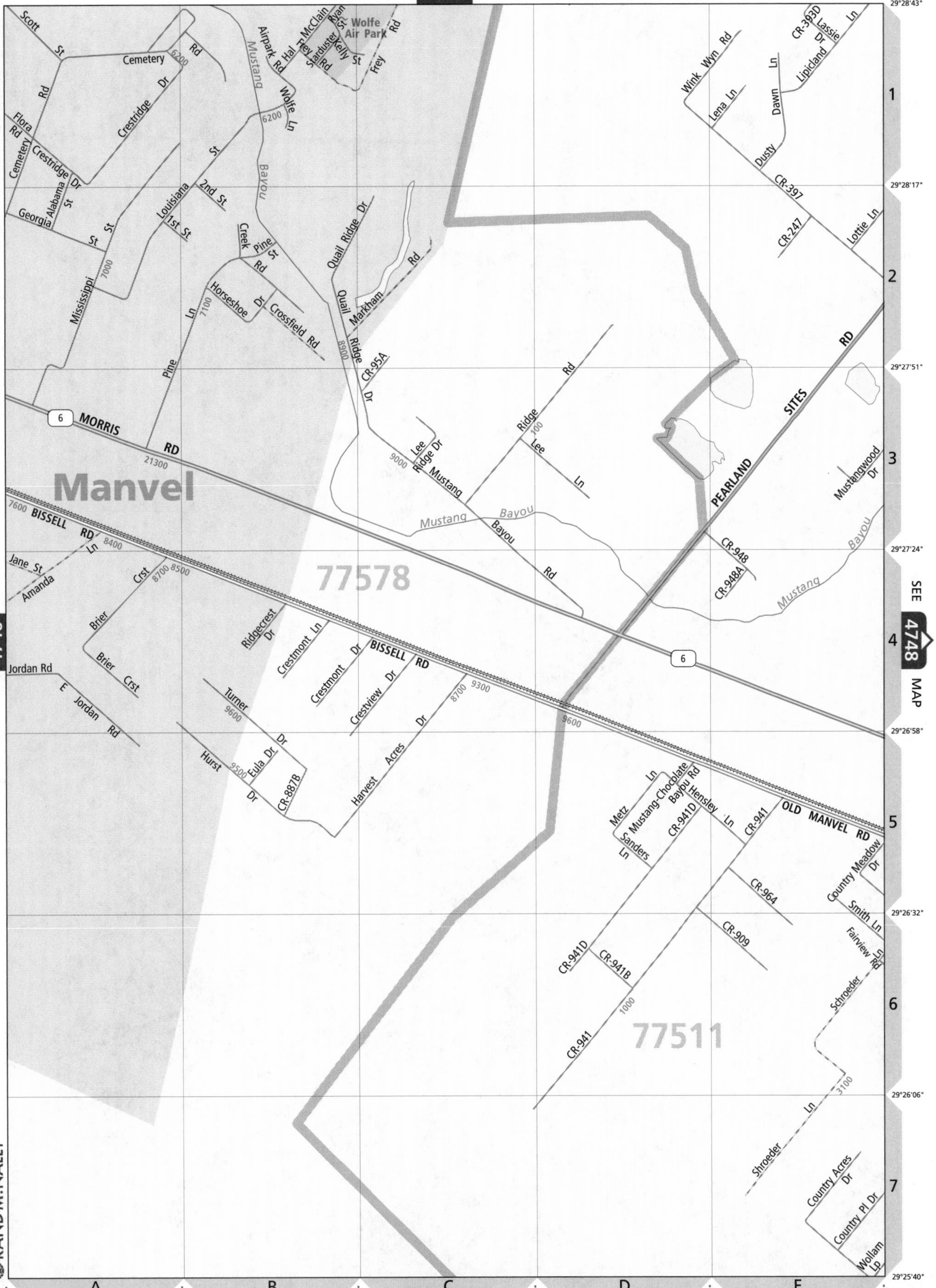
Manvel
77578
77511
MORRIS RD
21300
6
BISSELL RD
7600
8400
8500
8700
9300
9600
PEARLAND SITES RD
OLD MANVEL RD
Wolfe Air Park
Scott St
Cemetery Rd
6200
Crestridge Dr
Flora Rd
Cemetery
Crestridge Dr
Alabama St
Georgia St
Mississippi St
7000
Louisiana St
2nd St
1st St
Airpark Rd
Hal
McClain
Frey
Starduster Rd
Ryan St
Kelly St
Frey
Rd
Wolfe Ln
Mustang Bayou
Creek Rd
Pine St
Horseshoe Dr
Crossfield Rd
Pine Ln
7100
Quail Ridge Dr
Markham Rd
8900
CR-95A Dr
Lee Ridge Dr
9000
Mustang Bayou Rd
Ridge Rd
100
Lee Ln
Wink Wyn Rd
Lena Ln
Dawn Ln
Dusty
CR-397
CR-393D
Lassie Dr
Ln
Lipicland
CR-247
Lottie Ln
Mustangwood Dr
CR-948
CR-948A
Mustang Bayou
Jane St
Amanda
Brier Crst
Brier Crst
Jordan Rd
E Jordan Rd
Ridgecrest Dr
Crestmont Ln
Crestmont Dr
Crestview Dr
Harvest Acres Dr
Turner Dr
9600
Hurst Dr
9500
Eula Dr
CR-887B
Metz Ln
Mustang-Chocolate Bayou Rd
CR-941D
Hensley Ln
Sanders Ln
CR-941
Country Meadow Dr
Smith Ln
Fairview Rd
CR-964
CR-909
CR-941D
CR-941B
1000
CR-941
Schroeder
3100
Shroeder Ln
Country Acres Dr
Country Pl Dr
Wollam Lp
1
2
3
4
5
6
7
A
B
C
D
E
29°28'43"
29°28'17"
29°27'51"
29°27'24"
29°26'58"
29°26'32"
29°26'06"
29°25'40"
95°20'43"
95°20'13"
95°19'43"
95°19'13"
95°18'44"
95°18'14"

SEE 4748 MAP

SEE B MAP

1:24,000
1 in. = 2000 ft.
0 0.25 0.5
miles

SEE 4627 MAP

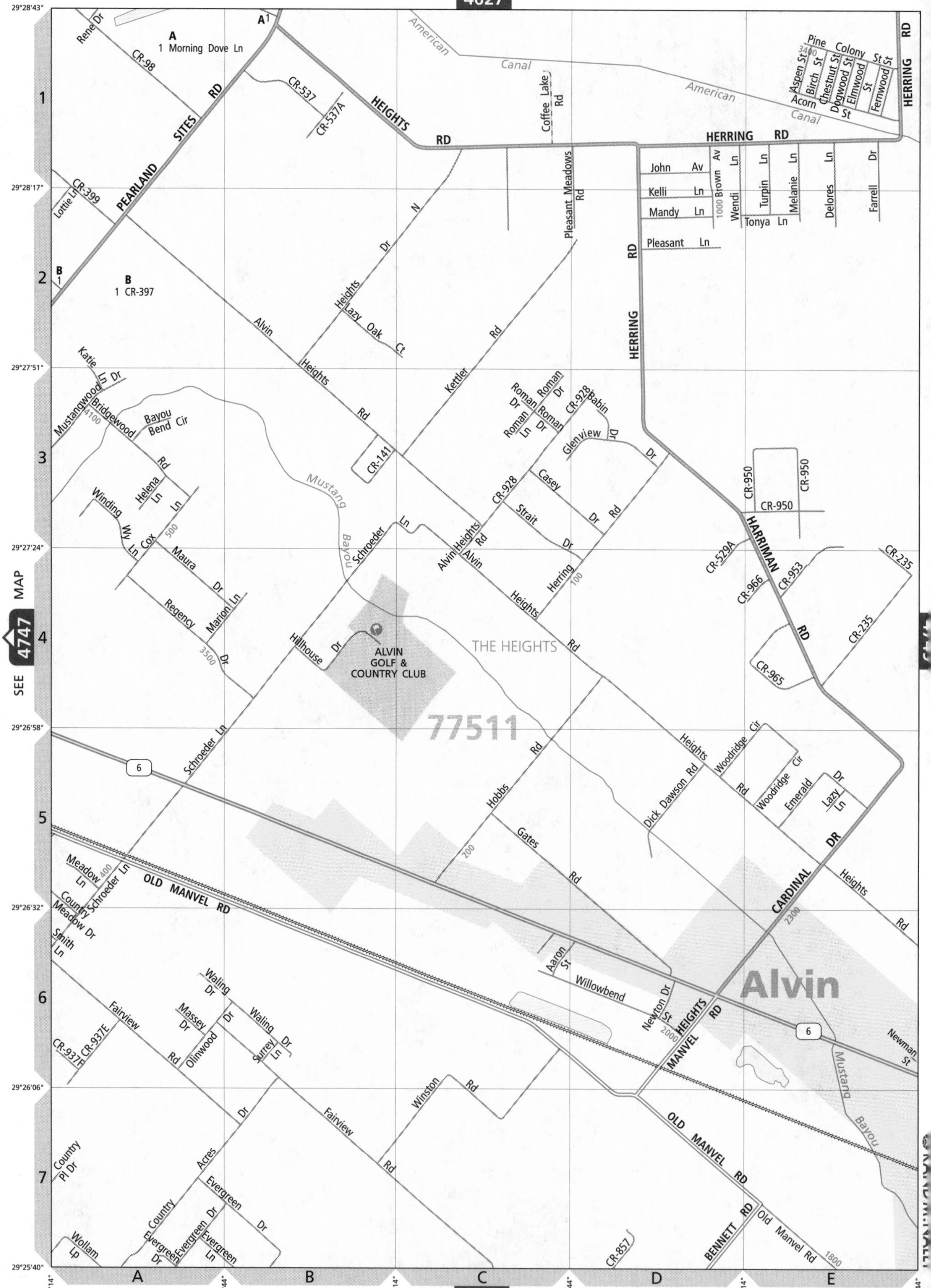
29°28'43"
29°28'17"
29°27'51"
29°27'24"
29°26'58"
29°26'32"
29°26'06"
29°25'40"
1
2
3
4
5
6
7
A
B
C
D
E
95°18'14"
95°17'44"
95°17'14"
95°16'44"
95°16'14"
95°15'44"
A
1 Morning Dove Ln
B
1 CR-397
Rene Dr
CR-98
PEARLAND SITES RD
CR-399
Lottie Ln
CR-537
CR-537A
HEIGHTS RD
American Canal
Coffee Lake Rd
Pleasant Meadows Rd
HERRING RD
John Av
Kelli Ln
Mandy Ln
Pleasant Ln
Brown Av
Wendi Ln
Turpin Ln
Tonya Ln
Melanie Ln
Delores Ln
Farrell Dr
Pine
Colony St
Aspen St
Birch St
Chestnut St
Dogwood St
Elmwood St
Fernwood St
Acorn St
3400
1000
Heights Dr N
Lazy Oak Ct
Alvin Heights Rd
Kettler Rd
CR-141
Katie Ln
Dr
Mustangwood
Bridgewood Rd
4100
Bayou Bend Cir
Helena Ln
Winding Wy Ln
Cox Ln
500
Maura Dr
Regency Dr
Marion Ln
3500
Roman Dr
Roman Ln
CR-928
Babin Dr
Glenview Dr
Casey Dr
Strait Dr
Rd
Herring
100
Mustang Bayou
Schroeder Ln
Alvin Heights Rd
CR-950
HARRIMAN RD
CR-529A
CR-966
CR-953
CR-235
CR-965
Hillhouse Dr
ALVIN GOLF & COUNTRY CLUB
THE HEIGHTS
77511
6
Schroeder Ln
Hobbs Rd
Dick Dawson Rd
Woodridge Cir
Heights Rd
Emerald Dr
Lazy Ln
CARDINAL DR
2300
Gates Rd
200
Meadow Ln
400
Country Meadow Dr
Smith Ln
OLD MANVEL RD
Aaron St
Willowbend
Newton Dr
St
2000
MANVEL HEIGHTS RD
Alvin
Newman St
Mustang Bayou
Fairview Rd
CR-937E
CR-937F
Waling Dr
Massey Dr
Olinwood Dr
Surrey Ln
Winston Rd
Acres Dr
Country Evergreen Dr
Evergreen Dr
Evergreen Ln
Evergreen Dr
Country Pl Dr
Wollam Lp
CR-857
BENNETT RD
Old Manvel Rd
1800

SEE 4747 MAP

SEE 4866 MAP

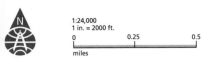

1:24,000
1 in. = 2000 ft.
0 0.25 0.5
miles

SEE 4628 MAP

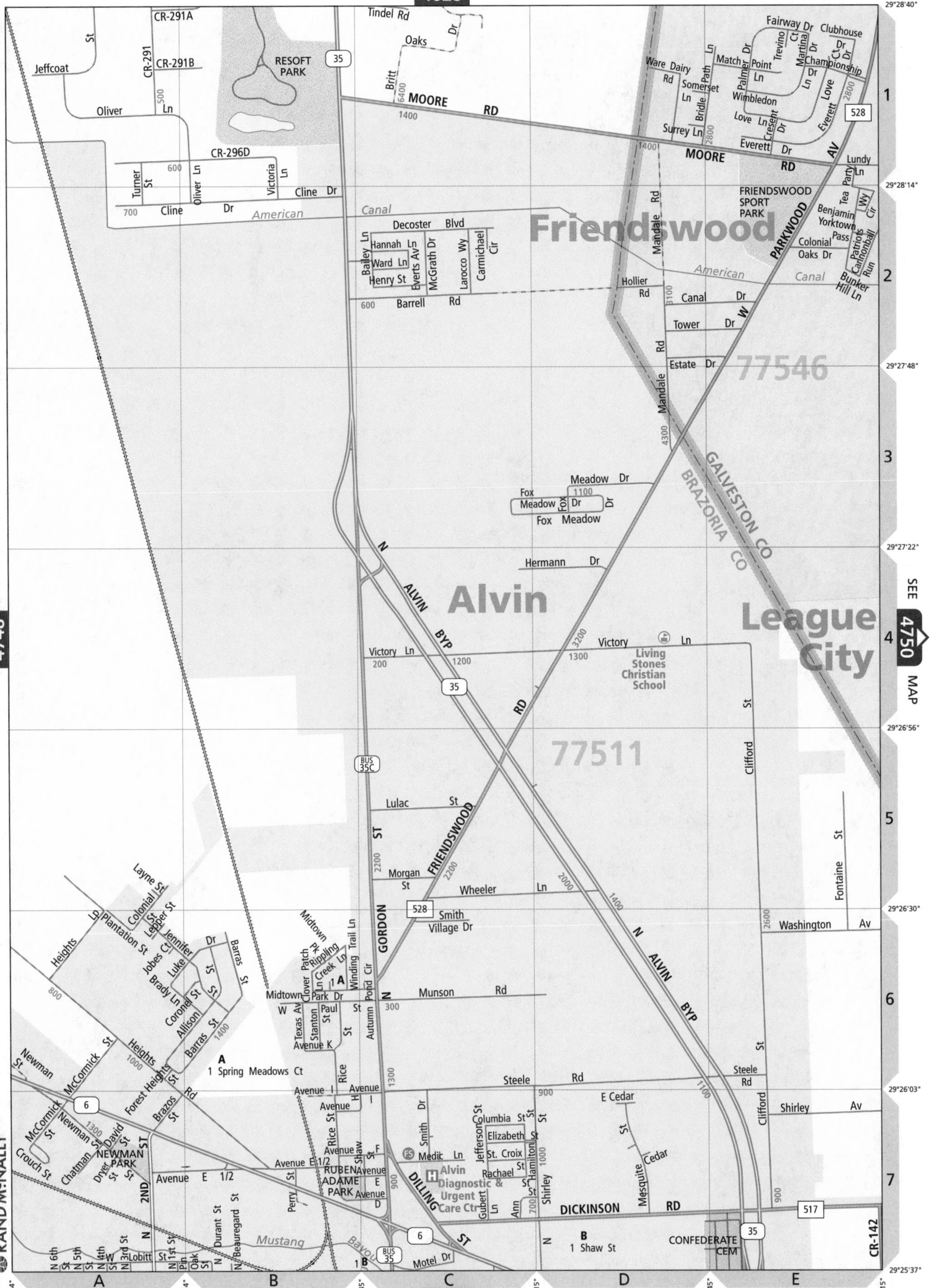
Friendswood
Alvin
League City
77546
77511
GALVESTON CO
BRAZORIA CO
RESOFT PARK
FRIENDSWOOD SPORT PARK
MOORE RD
N ALVIN BYP
FRIENDSWOOD RD
PARKWOOD AV
GORDON ST
DICKINSON RD
DILLING ST
American Canal
Mustang Bayou
Living Stones Christian School
Alvin Diagnostic & Urgent Care Ctr
RUBEN ADAME PARK
NEWMAN PARK
CONFEDERATE CEM
CR-291A
CR-291B
CR-291
CR-296D
CR-142
Victory Ln
Steele Rd
Munson Rd
Wheeler Ln
Washington Av
Shirley Av
Clifford St
Mandale Rd
Hermann Dr
Meadow Dr
Fox Meadow
Lulac St
Morgan St
Smith Village Dr
Barrell Rd
Decoster Blvd
Cline Dr
Oliver Ln
Jeffcoat
Tindel Rd
Oaks Dr
Britt
Hollier Rd
Canal Dr
Tower Dr
Estate Dr
Heights
McCormick St
Newman St
Avenue E 1/2
A 1 Spring Meadows Ct
B 1 Shaw St
1 2 3 4 5 6 7
A B C D E
29°28'40"
29°28'14"
29°27'48"
29°27'22"
29°26'56"
29°26'30"
29°26'03"
29°25'37"
95°15'44"
95°15'14"
95°14'45"
95°14'15"
95°13'45"
95°13'15"

SEE 4750 MAP

SEE 4867 MAP

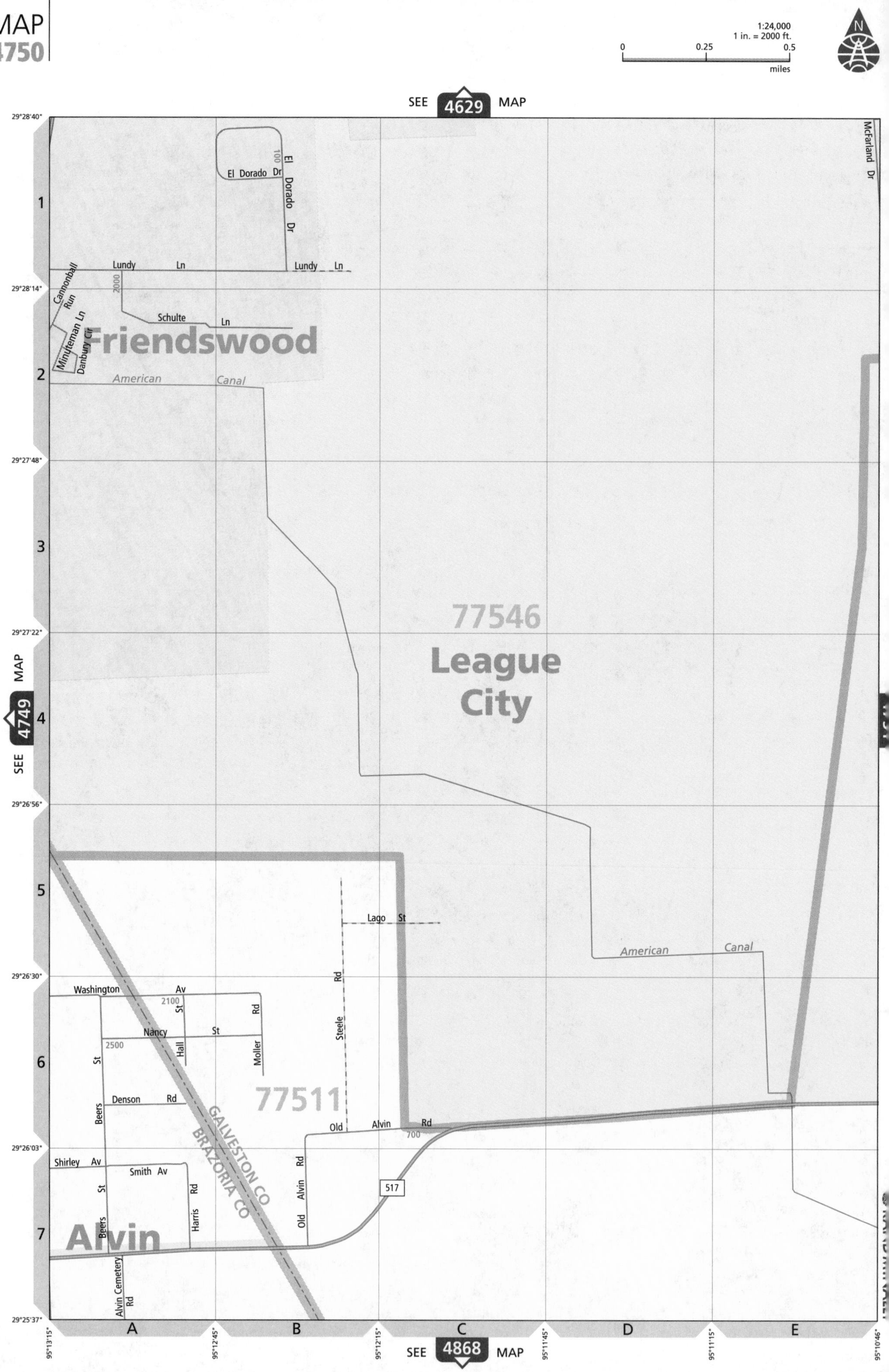
1:24,000
1 in. = 2000 ft.
0
0.25
0.5
miles
N
SEE 4629 MAP
SEE 4749 MAP
SEE 4868 MAP
29°28'40"
29°28'14"
29°27'48"
29°27'22"
29°26'56"
29°26'30"
29°26'03"
29°25'37"
95°13'15"
95°12'45"
95°12'15"
95°11'45"
95°11'15"
95°10'46"
1
2
3
4
5
6
7
A
B
C
D
E
El Dorado Dr
100
El Dorado Dr
Lundy Ln
Lundy Ln
2000
Cannonball Run
Schulte Ln
Minuteman Ln
Danbury Cir
Friendswood
American Canal
McFarland Dr
77546
League City
Lago St
American Canal
Washington Av
2100
St
Hall
Nancy St
2500
Rd
Moller
Steele Rd
St
Beers
Denson Rd
77511
Old Alvin Rd
700
GALVESTON CO
BRAZORIA CO
Shirley Av
Smith Av
Beers St
Harris Rd
Old Alvin Rd
517
Alvin
Alvin Cemetery Rd

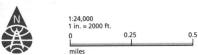

1:24,000
1 in. = 2000 ft.
0 0.25 0.5
miles

SEE 4630 MAP

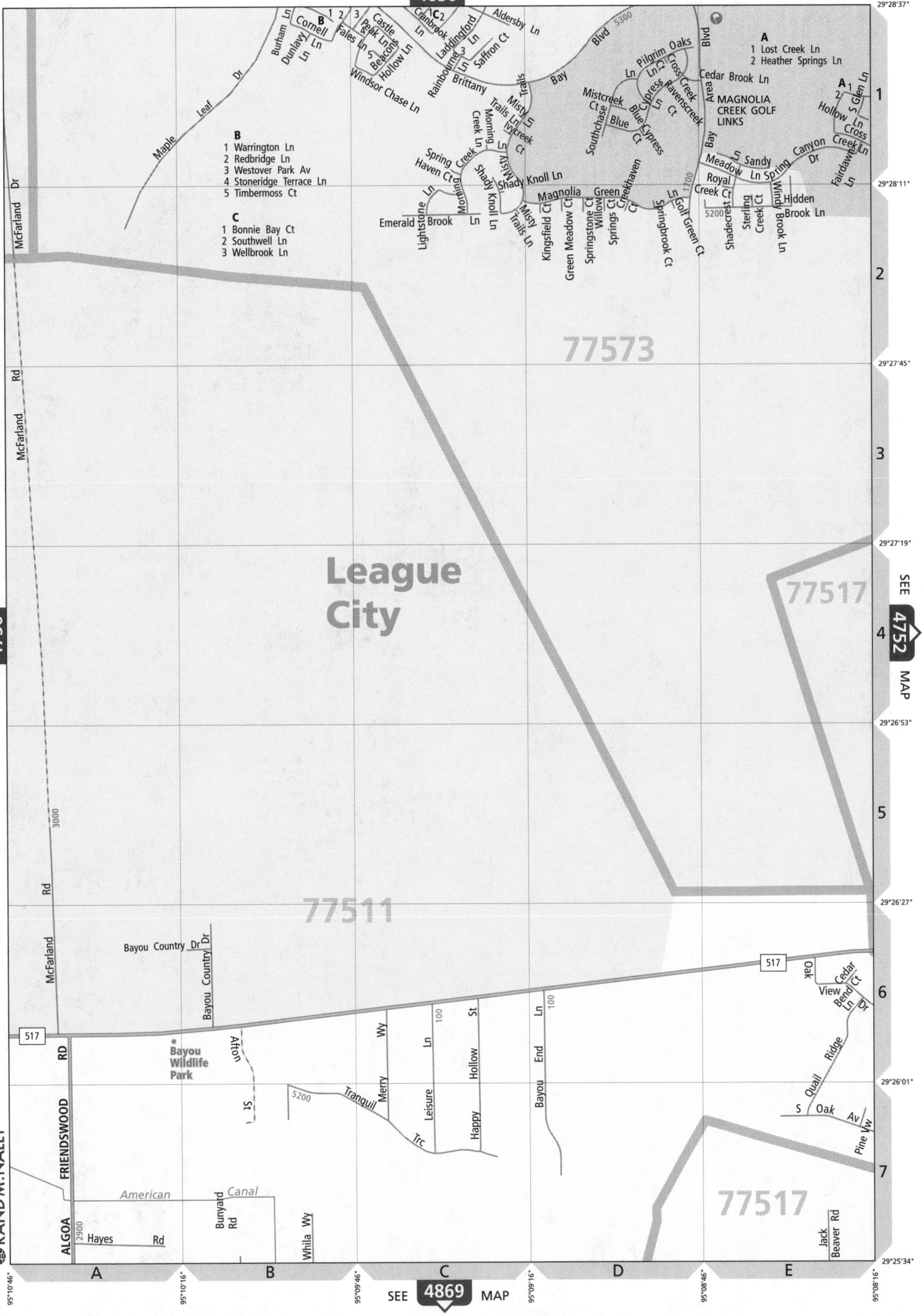
League City
77573
77511
77517
77517
MAGNOLIA CREEK GOLF LINKS
A
1 Lost Creek Ln
2 Heather Springs Ln
B
1 Warrington Ln
2 Redbridge Ln
3 Westover Park Av
4 Stoneridge Terrace Ln
5 Timbermoss Ct
C
1 Bonnie Bay Ct
2 Southwell Ln
3 Wellbrook Ln
Maple Leaf Dr
McFarland Dr
McFarland Rd
Burham Ln
Dunlavy Ln
Cornell Ln
Fales Ln
Castle Peak Ln
Beacons Hollow Ln
Windsor Chase Ln
Cranbrook Ln
Laddingford Ln
Rainbourne Ln
Saffron Ct
Aldersby Ln
Brittany Bay Blvd
Misty Trails Ln
Ivycreek Ct
Morning Creek Ln
Spring Creek
Haven Ct
Shady Knoll Ln
Emerald Brook Ln
Lightstone Ln
Kingsfield Ct
Magnolia
Green Meadow Ct
Green Willow
Springstone Ct
Springs Ct
Creekhaven Ct
Springbrook Ct
Golf Green Ct
Mistcreek Ct
Southchase
Blue Cypress Ct
Pilgrim Oaks Ln
Cross Creek Ct
Ravenscreek
Bay Area Blvd
Cedar Brook Ln
Sandy Meadow Ln
Royal Creek Ct
Spring Canyon Dr
Shadecrest
Sterling Creek Ct
Windy Brook Ln
Hidden Brook Ln
Hollow Cross Creek Ln
S Glen Ln
Fairdawn Ln
Bayou Country Dr
517
Bayou Wildlife Park
Afton St
Tranquil Trc
Merry Wy
Leisure Ln
Happy Hollow St
Bayou End Ln
Oak View Dr
Cedar Bend Ct
Quail Ridge
S Oak Av
Pine Vw
FRIENDSWOOD RD
ALGOA
Hayes Rd
American Canal
Bunyard Rd
Whila Wy
Jack Beaver Rd
A B C D E
1 2 3 4 5 6 7
29°28'37" 29°28'11" 29°27'45" 29°27'19" 29°26'53" 29°26'27" 29°26'01" 29°25'34"
95°10'46" 95°10'16" 95°09'46" 95°09'16" 95°08'46" 95°08'16"
SEE 4752 MAP

SEE 4869 MAP

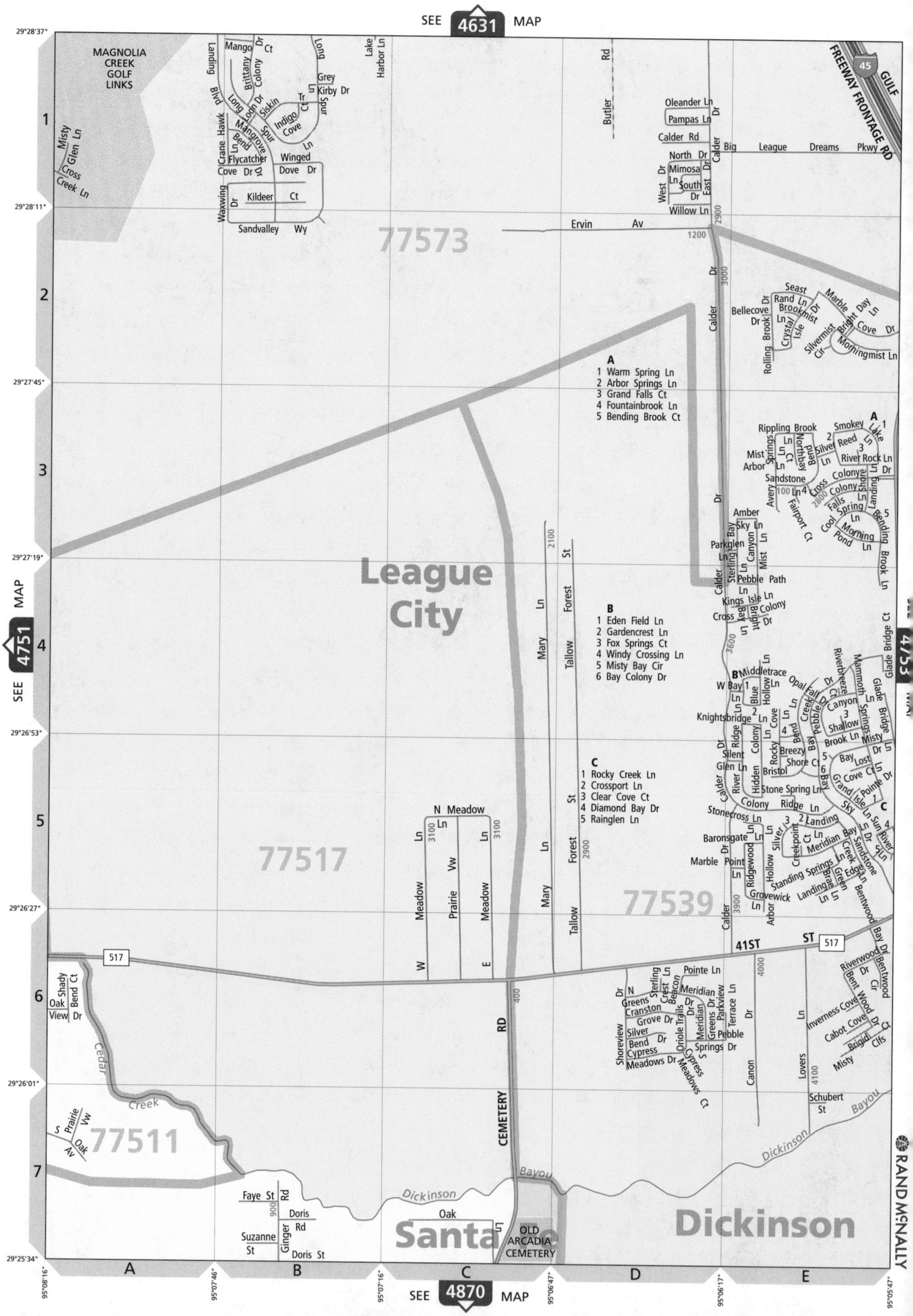
1:24,000
1 in. = 2000 ft.
0 0.25 0.5
miles
N
SEE 4631 MAP
SEE 4751 MAP
SEE 4870 MAP
MAGNOLIA CREEK GOLF LINKS
League City
Dickinson
Santa Fe
77573
77517
77539
77511
FREEWAY FRONTAGE RD
GULF
45
Big League Dreams Pkwy
Ervin Av
Calder Dr
Calder Rd
Butler Rd
CEMETERY RD
41ST ST
517
Dickinson Bayou
Cedar Creek
OLD ARCADIA CEMETERY
A
1 Warm Spring Ln
2 Arbor Springs Ln
3 Grand Falls Ct
4 Fountainbrook Ln
5 Bending Brook Ct
B
1 Eden Field Ln
2 Gardencrest Ln
3 Fox Springs Ct
4 Windy Crossing Ln
5 Misty Bay Cir
6 Bay Colony Dr
C
1 Rocky Creek Ln
2 Crossport Ln
3 Clear Cove Ct
4 Diamond Bay Dr
5 Rainglen Ln
N Meadow Ln
W Meadow Ln
E Meadow Ln
Prairie Vw
Mary Ln
Tallow Forest St
Shady Oak Bend Ct
View Dr
Faye St
Doris Rd
Doris St
Suzanne St
Ginger Rd
Oak Ln
Schubert St
Lovers Ln
Canon Dr
Misty Glen Ln
Cross Creek Ln
Sandvalley Wy
Kildeer Ct
Waxwing Dr
Flycatcher Dr
Dove Dr
Winged Dove Dr
Oleander Ln
Pampas Ln
North Dr
Mimosa Ln
South Dr
West Dr
East Dr
Willow Ln
29°28'37"
29°28'11"
29°27'45"
29°27'19"
29°26'53"
29°26'27"
29°26'01"
29°25'34"
95°08'16"
95°07'46"
95°07'16"
95°06'47"
95°06'17"
95°05'47"
A B C D E
1 2 3 4 5 6 7
RAND McNALLY

SEE 4632 MAP

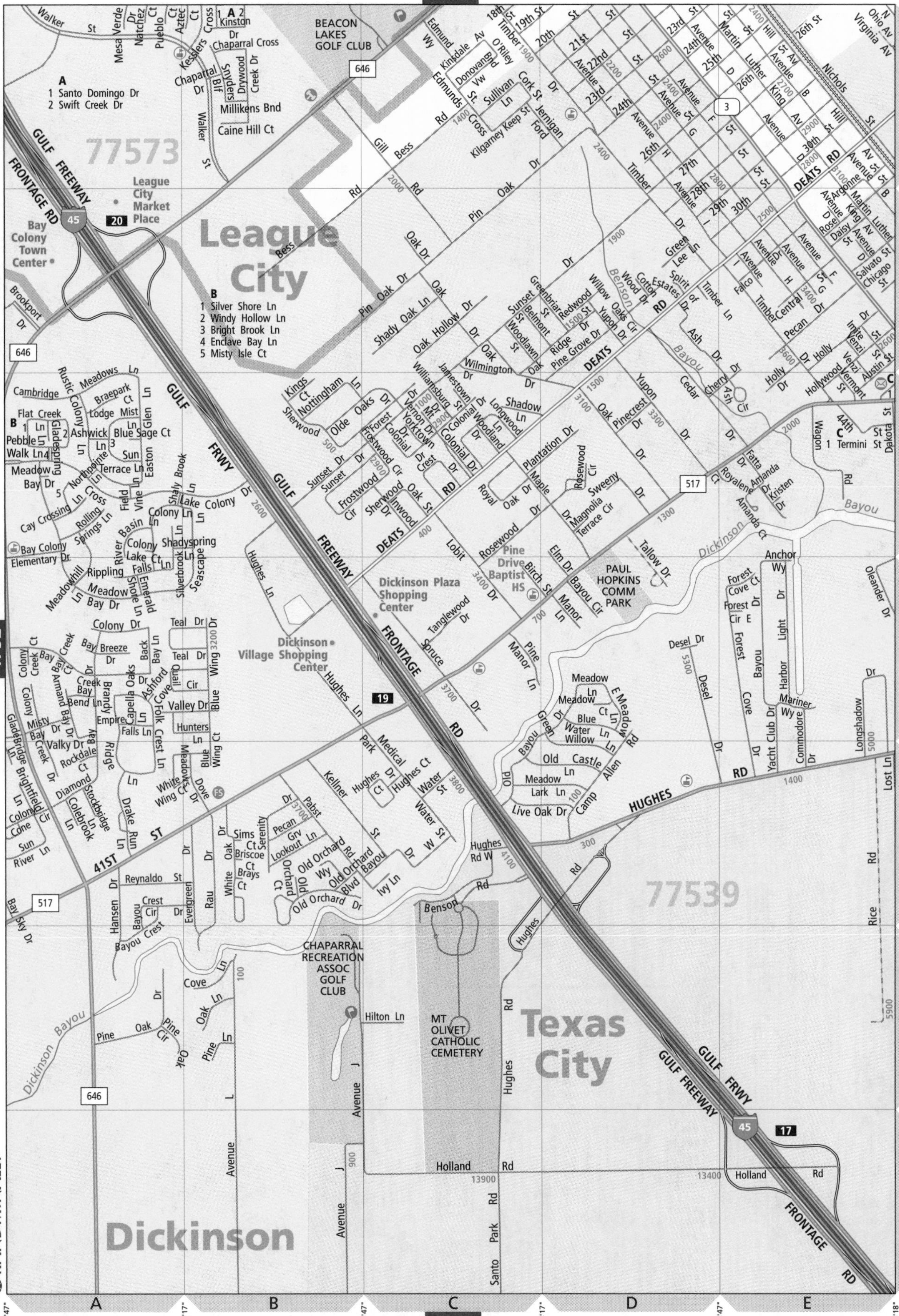
1:24,000
1 in. = 2000 ft.
0 0.25 0.5
miles
League City
Texas City
Dickinson
77573
77539
BEACON LAKES GOLF CLUB
League City Market Place
Bay Colony Town Center
Dickinson Plaza Shopping Center
Dickinson Village Shopping Center
PAUL HOPKINS COMM PARK
Pine Drive Baptist HS
CHAPARRAL RECREATION ASSOC GOLF CLUB
MT OLIVET CATHOLIC CEMETERY
Bay Colony Elementary
GULF FREEWAY
FRONTAGE RD
GULF FRWY
DEATS RD
HUGHES RD
41ST ST
Holland Rd
A
1 Santo Domingo Dr
2 Swift Creek Dr
B
1 Silver Shore Ln
2 Windy Hollow Ln
3 Bright Brook Ln
4 Enclave Bay Ln
5 Misty Isle Ct
C
1 Termini St
29°28'34"
29°28'08"
29°27'42"
29°27'16"
29°26'50"
29°26'24"
29°25'58"
29°25'31"
95°05'47"
95°05'17"
95°04'47"
95°04'17"
95°03'47"
95°03'18"
A B C D E
1 2 3 4 5 6 7

SEE 4754 MAP

SEE 4871 MAP

1:24,000
1 in. = 2000 ft.
0 0.25 0.5
miles

SEE 4633 MAP

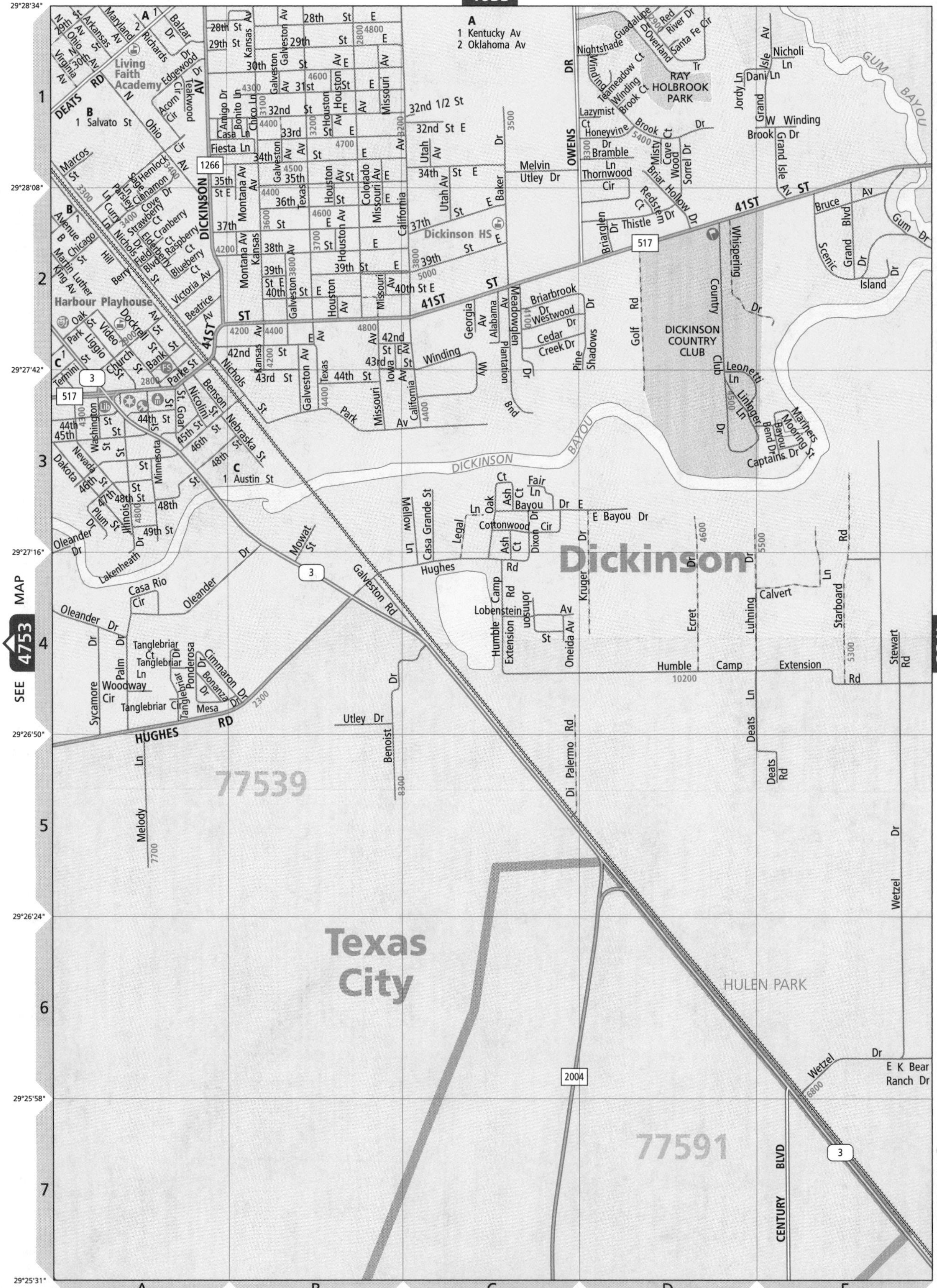
Dickinson
Texas City
77539
77591
HULEN PARK
DICKINSON COUNTRY CLUB
RAY HOLBROOK PARK
Living Faith Academy
Harbour Playhouse
Dickinson HS
DICKINSON BAYOU
GUM BAYOU
DEATS RD
DICKINSON AV
41ST ST
OWENS DR
HUGHES RD
CENTURY BLVD
Galveston Rd
Humble Camp Extension
Country Club Dr
Whispering Dr
Golf Rd
Wetzel Dr
Stewart Rd
Deats Ln
Deats Rd
Di Palermo Rd
Benoist Dr
Utley Dr
Melody Ln
Oleander Dr
Casa Rio Cir
Lakenheath Dr
Tanglebriar Ct
Woodway Cir
Sycamore Dr
Palm Dr
Ponderosa Dr
Bonanza Dr
Cimmaron Dr
Mesa Dr
Mowat St
Nichols St
Nebraska St
Benson St
Minnesota St
Illinois St
Dakota St
Nevada St
Washington St
Parke St
Bank St
Church St
Liggio St
Video St
Dockrell St
Chicago St
Martin Luther King Av
Hill St
Berry St
Kansas Av
Galveston Av
Houston Av
Missouri Av
California Av
Colorado Av
Montana Av
Texas Av
Utah Av
Baker Dr
Iowa Av
Winding Wy
Georgia Av
Alabama Av
Meadowglen Dr
Plantation Bnd
Briarbrook Dr
Westwood Dr
Cedar Creek Dr
Pine Shadows Dr
Melvin Utley Dr
Thornwood Cir
Bramble Ln
Briarglen Dr
Thistle Ct
Redstem Ct
Briar Hollow Dr
Misty Cove Ct
Wood Sorrel Dr
Honeyvine Ct
Lazymist Ct
Brook Dr
Nightshade
Guadalupe Dr
Overland Dr
Red River Dr
Santa Fe Cir
Teameadow Ct
Winding Brook Ct
Jordy Ln
Dani Ln
Nicholi Ln
Grand Isle Av
W Winding Brook Dr
Bruce Av
Gum Dr
Scenic Grand Blvd
Island Dr
Leonetti Ln
Linlinger Dr
Mariners Mooring St
Bayou Bend Dr
Captains Dr
Fair Ln
Ash Ct
Oak Ln
Legal Ln
Cottonwood Cir
Dixon Dr
E Bayou Dr
Mellow Ln
Casa Grande St
Hughes Rd
Lobenstein Av
Johnson St
Oneida Av
Kruger Dr
Ecret Dr
Luhning Dr
Calvert Ln
Starboard Rd
E K Bear Ranch Dr
Wetzel Dr
A 1 Kentucky Av 2 Oklahoma Av
B 1 Salvato St
C 1 Austin St
3
517
1266
2004
1
2
3
4
5
6
7
A
B
C
D
E
29°28'34"
29°28'08"
29°27'42"
29°27'16"
29°26'50"
29°26'24"
29°25'58"
29°25'31"
95°03'17"
95°02'48"
95°02'18"
95°01'48"
95°01'18"
95°00'48"

SEE 4753 MAP

SEE 4872 MAP

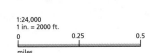

1:24,000
1 in. = 2000 ft.
0 0.25 0.5
miles

SEE 4634 MAP

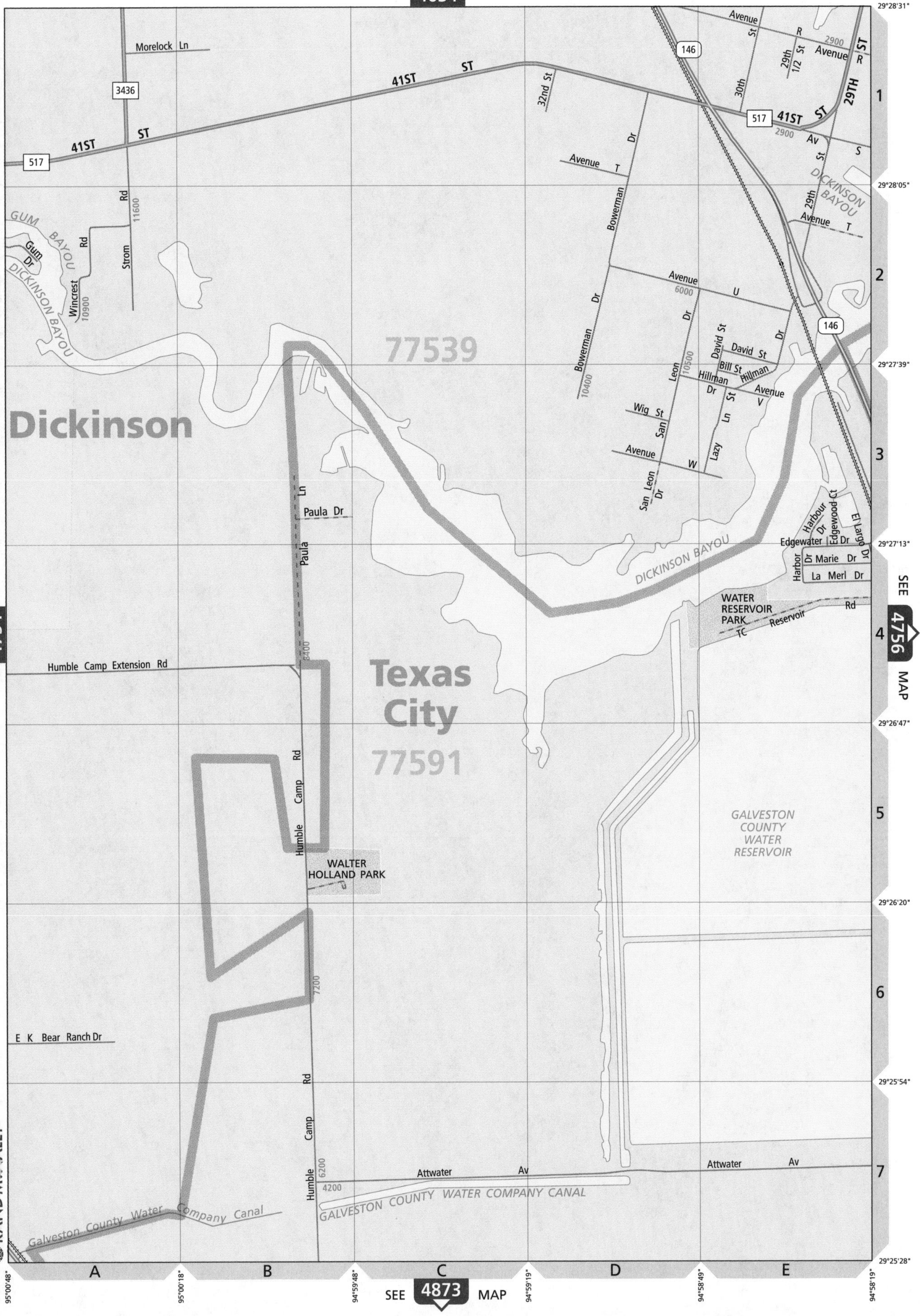
Dickinson
Texas City
77539
77591
41ST ST
517
3436
146
Morelock Ln
Strom Rd
11600
Wincrest Rd
10900
Gum Dr
GUM BAYOU
DICKINSON BAYOU
32nd St
Avenue T
Bowerman Dr
10400
Avenue U
6000
Leon Dr
10500
David St
David St
Bill St
Hillman Dr
Hillman
Avenue V
Wig St
San Leon Dr
Lazy Ln
Avenue W
Avenue R
2900
Avenue
30th St
29th 1/2 St
29TH ST
2900
Av S
29th St
Paula Ln
Paula Dr
Harbour Dr
Edgewood Ct
El Largo Dr
Edgewater Dr
Harbor Dr
Marie Dr
La Merl Dr
WATER RESERVOIR PARK
TC
Reservoir Rd
Humble Camp Extension Rd
8400
Humble Camp Rd
WALTER HOLLAND PARK
7200
E K Bear Ranch Dr
6200
4200
GALVESTON COUNTY WATER RESERVOIR
Attwater Av
GALVESTON COUNTY WATER COMPANY CANAL
Galveston County Water Company Canal
A
B
C
D
E
1
2
3
4
5
6
7
29°28'31"
29°28'05"
29°27'39"
29°27'13"
29°26'47"
29°26'20"
29°25'54"
29°25'28"
95°00'48"
95°00'18"
94°59'48"
94°59'19"
94°58'49"
94°58'19"

SEE 4756 MAP

SEE 4873 MAP

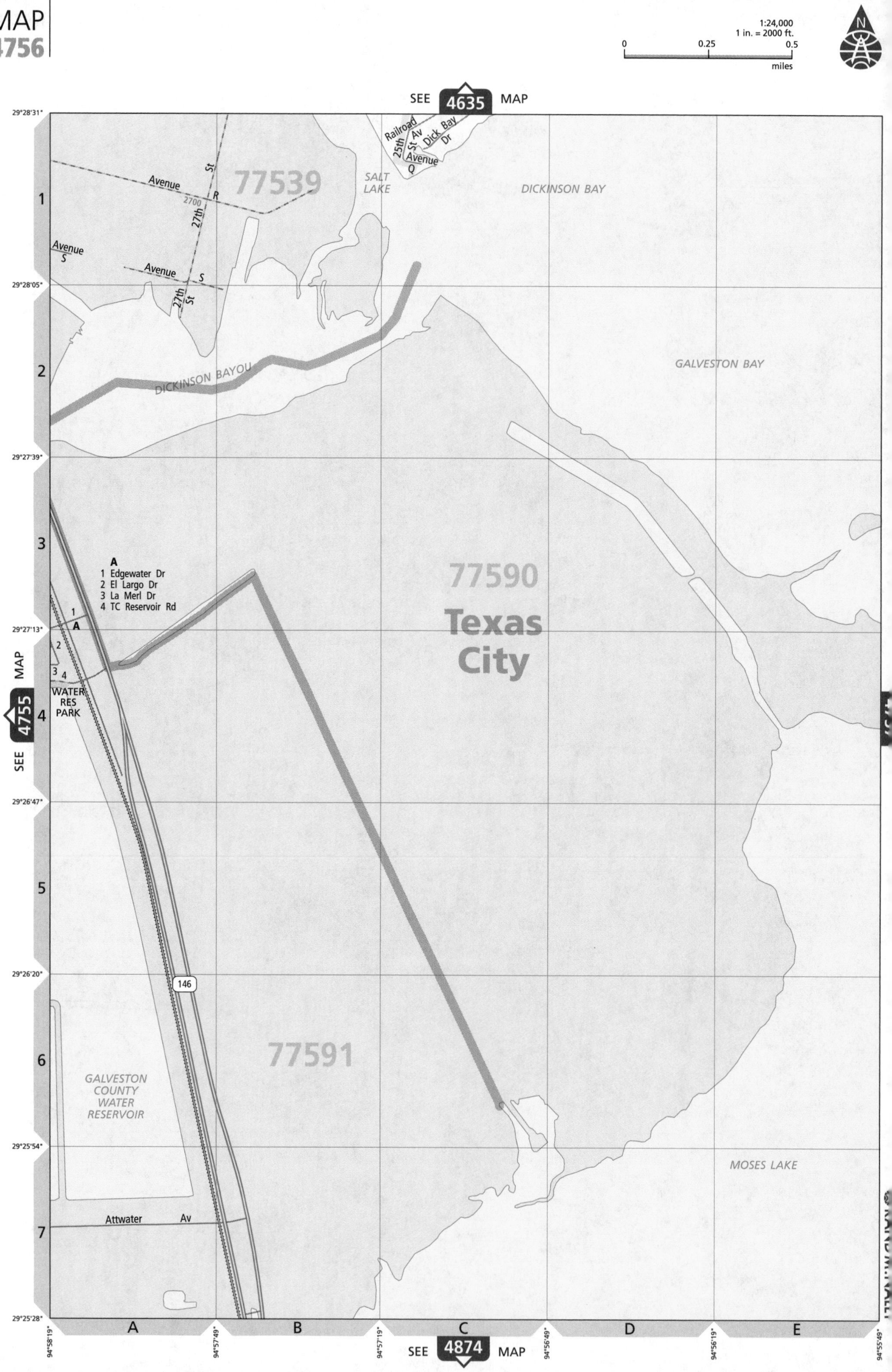
1:24,000
1 in. = 2000 ft.
0
0.25
0.5
miles
N
SEE 4635 MAP
SEE 4874 MAP
SEE 4755 MAP
29°28'31"
29°28'05"
29°27'39"
29°27'13"
29°26'47"
29°26'20"
29°25'54"
29°25'28"
94°58'19"
94°57'49"
94°57'19"
94°56'49"
94°56'19"
94°55'49"
1
2
3
4
5
6
7
A
B
C
D
E
77539
77590
77591
Texas City
SALT LAKE
DICKINSON BAY
GALVESTON BAY
DICKINSON BAYOU
MOSES LAKE
GALVESTON COUNTY WATER RESERVOIR
WATER RES PARK
Railroad
25th St
Av
Dick Bay Dr
Avenue Q
Avenue R
2700
27th St
Avenue S
Avenue S
27th St
146
Attwater Av
A
1 Edgewater Dr
2 El Largo Dr
3 La Merl Dr
4 TC Reservoir Rd

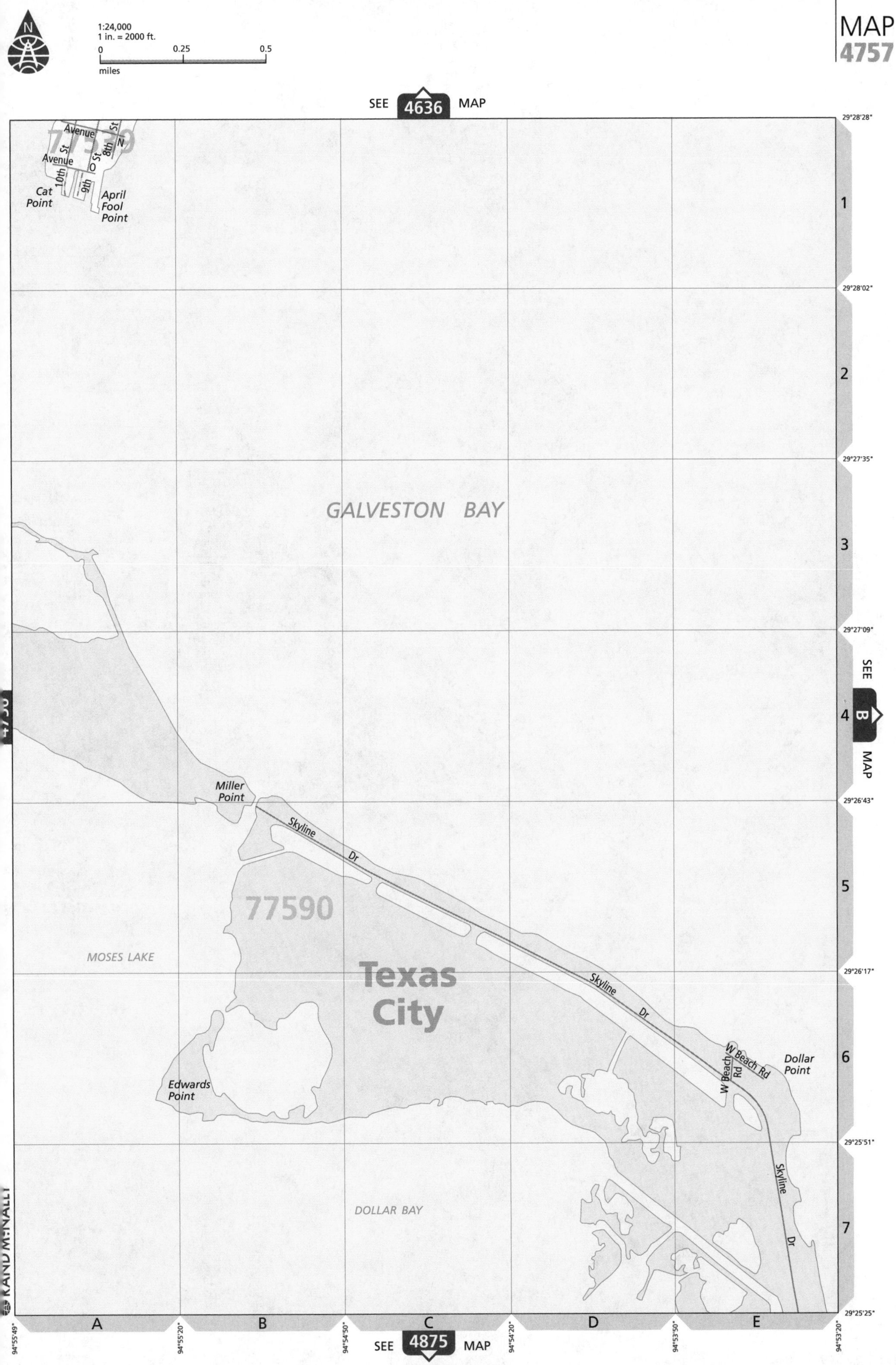
1:24,000
1 in. = 2000 ft.
0
0.25
0.5
miles
SEE 4636 MAP
29°28'28"
29°28'02"
29°27'35"
29°27'09"
29°26'43"
29°26'17"
29°25'51"
29°25'25"
1
2
3
4
5
6
7
A
B
C
D
E
94°55'49"
94°55'20"
94°54'50"
94°54'20"
94°53'50"
94°53'20"
SEE B MAP
SEE 4875 MAP
Avenue
Avenue
10th St
9th
O St
8th St
N
Cat Point
April Fool Point
GALVESTON BAY
Miller Point
Skyline Dr
77590
MOSES LAKE
Texas City
Skyline Dr
W Beach Rd
W Beach Rd
Dollar Point
Edwards Point
Skyline Dr
DOLLAR BAY
RAND McNALLY

1:24,000
1 in. = 2000 ft.
0 0.25 0.5
miles

SEE 4748 MAP

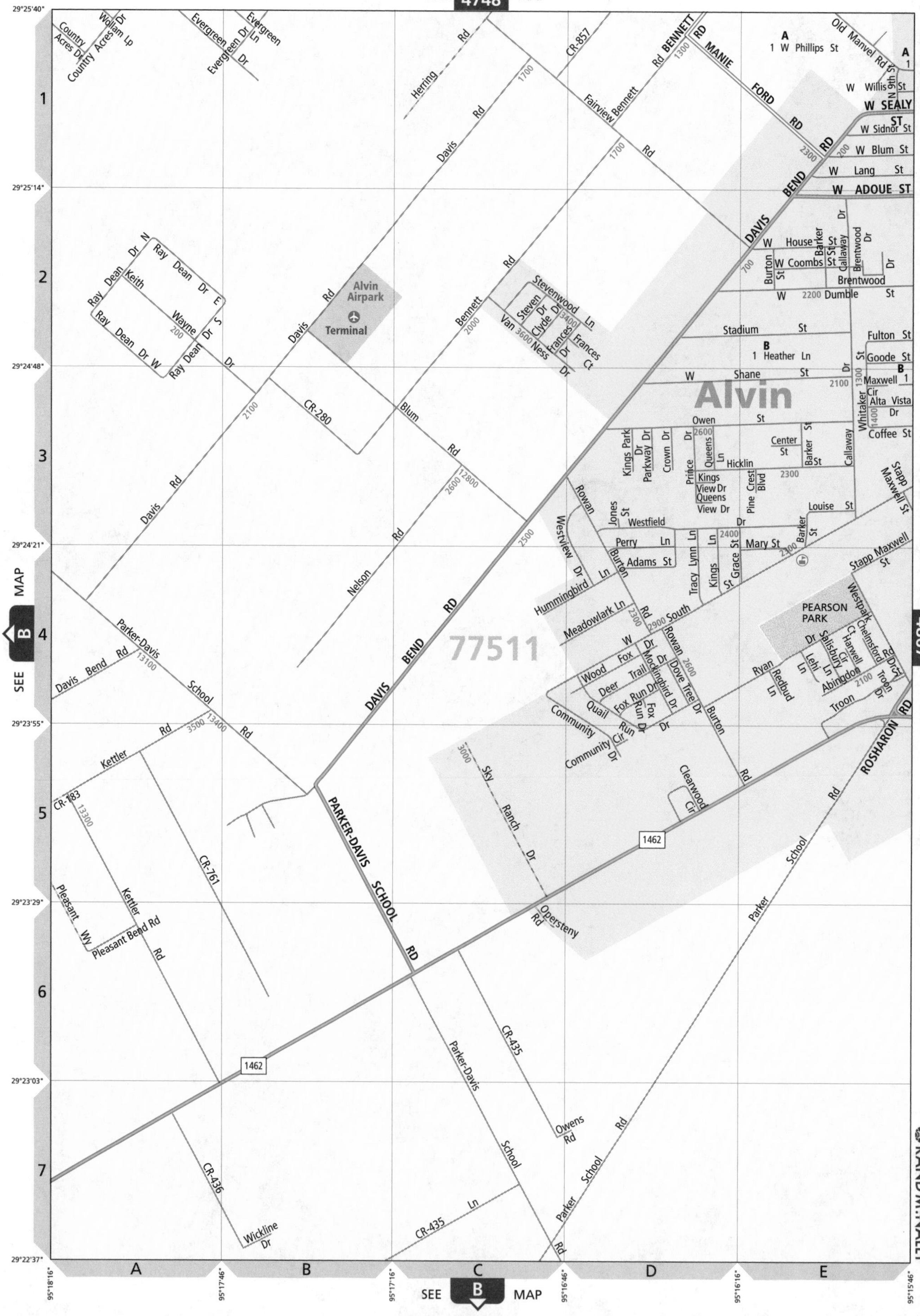
Alvin
77511
Alvin Airpark
Terminal
PEARSON PARK
Davis Bend Rd
Parker-Davis School Rd
Rosharon Rd
Bennett Rd
Manie Ford Rd
W Sealy St
W Adoue St
W Sidnor St
W Blum St
W Lang St
W Willis St
Old Manvel Rd
W Phillips St
W House St
W Coombs St
W Dumble St
Brentwood Dr
Callaway Dr
Barker St
Burton St
Stadium St
Heather Ln
W Shane St
Owen St
Fulton St
Goode St
Maxwell Cir
Alta Vista Dr
Whitaker Dr
Coffee St
Kings Park Dr
Parkway Dr
Crown Dr
Prince Dr
Queens Ln
Hicklin
Center St
Kings View Dr
Queens View Dr
Pine Crest Blvd
Louise St
Stapp Maxwell St
Westfield Dr
Jones St
Perry Ln
Adams St
Mary St
Tracy Lynn Ln
Kings Ln
Grace St
Westview Dr
Rowan Rd
Burton Ln
Hummingbird Ln
Meadowlark Ln
W South St
Fox Dr
Wood Trail
Deer Trail
Mockingbird Dr
Dove Tree Dr
Fox Run Dr
Quail Run Dr
Community Cir
Community Dr
Ryan Ln
Redbud Ln
Westpark
Chelmsford Rd
Salisbury Ct
Harwell Cir
Lehi Ln
Abingdon Dr
Troon Dr
Troon
Clearwood Cir
Sky Ranch Dr
Opersteny Rd
Stevenwood Ln
Steven Dr
Clyde Dr
Frances Dr
Frances Ct
Van Ness Dr
Blum Rd
CR-280
Davis Rd
Nelson Rd
Herring Rd
Fairview
CR-857
Ray Dean Dr N
Ray Dean Dr E
Ray Dean Dr S
Ray Dean Dr W
Ray Dean Dr
Keith
Wayne
Country Acres Dr
Country Acres Lp
Wollam Dr
Evergreen Dr
Evergreen Ln
Parker-Davis School Rd
Davis Bend Rd
Kettler Rd
CR-183
CR-761
Pleasant Wy
Pleasant Bend Rd
CR-435
CR-435 Ln
Owens Rd
CR-436
Wickline Dr
Parker School Rd
1462
A B C D E
1 2 3 4 5 6 7
29°25'40"
29°25'14"
29°24'48"
29°24'21"
29°23'55"
29°23'29"
29°23'03"
29°22'37"
95°18'16"
95°17'46"
95°17'16"
95°16'46"
95°16'16"
95°15'46"

SEE B MAP

SEE B MAP

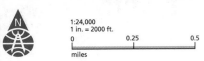

1:24,000
1 in. = 2000 ft.
0 0.25 0.5
miles

SEE 4749 MAP

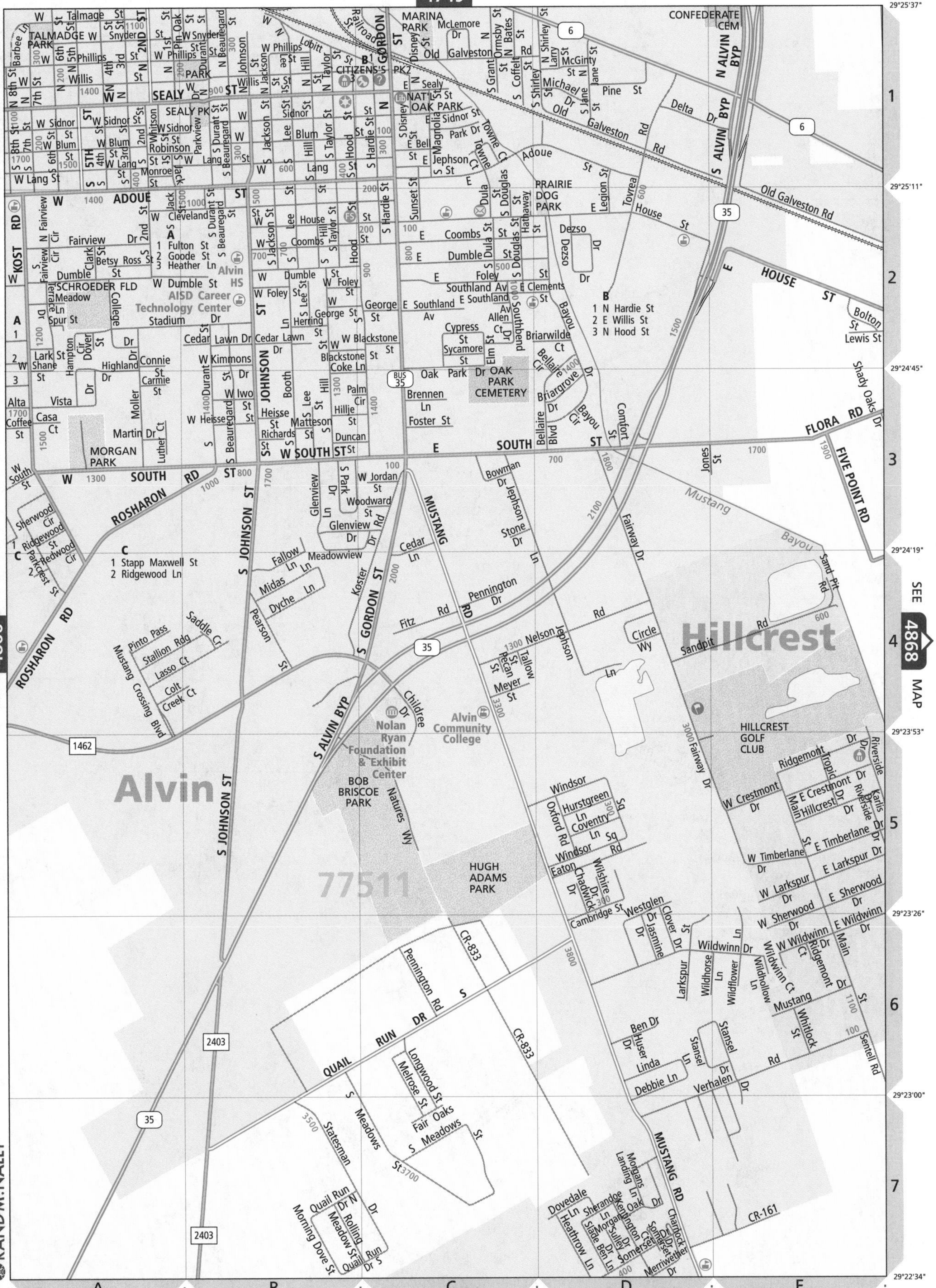
Alvin
Hillcrest
77511
TALMADGE PARK
MARINA PARK
CONFEDERATE CEM
CITIZENS'S PK
NAT'L OAK PARK
SEALY PK
PRAIRIE DOG PARK
SCHROEDER FLD
Meadow
Alvin HS
AISD Career Technology Center
Stadium
OAK PARK CEMETERY
MORGAN PARK
Nolan Ryan Foundation & Exhibit Center
Alvin Community College
BOB BRISCOE PARK
HUGH ADAMS PARK
HILLCREST GOLF CLUB
ADOUE
SEALY ST
W SOUTH ST
E SOUTH ST
ROSHARON RD
S JOHNSON ST
S GORDON ST
S ALVIN BYP
N ALVIN BYP
MUSTANG RD
FLORA RD
FIVE POINT RD
E HOUSE ST
QUAIL RUN DR
KOST RD
CR-833
CR-161
Old Galveston Rd
Mustang Bayou
6
35
BUS 35
1462
2403
A
1 Fulton St
2 Goode St
3 Heather Ln
B
1 N Hardie St
2 E Willis St
3 N Hood St
C
1 Stapp Maxwell St
2 Ridgewood Ln
29°25'37"
29°25'11"
29°24'45"
29°24'19"
29°23'53"
29°23'26"
29°23'00"
29°22'34"
95°15'46"
95°15'17"
95°14'47"
95°14'17"
95°13'47"
95°13'17"
A
B
C
D
E
1
2
3
4
5
6
7

SEE 4868 MAP

SEE B MAP

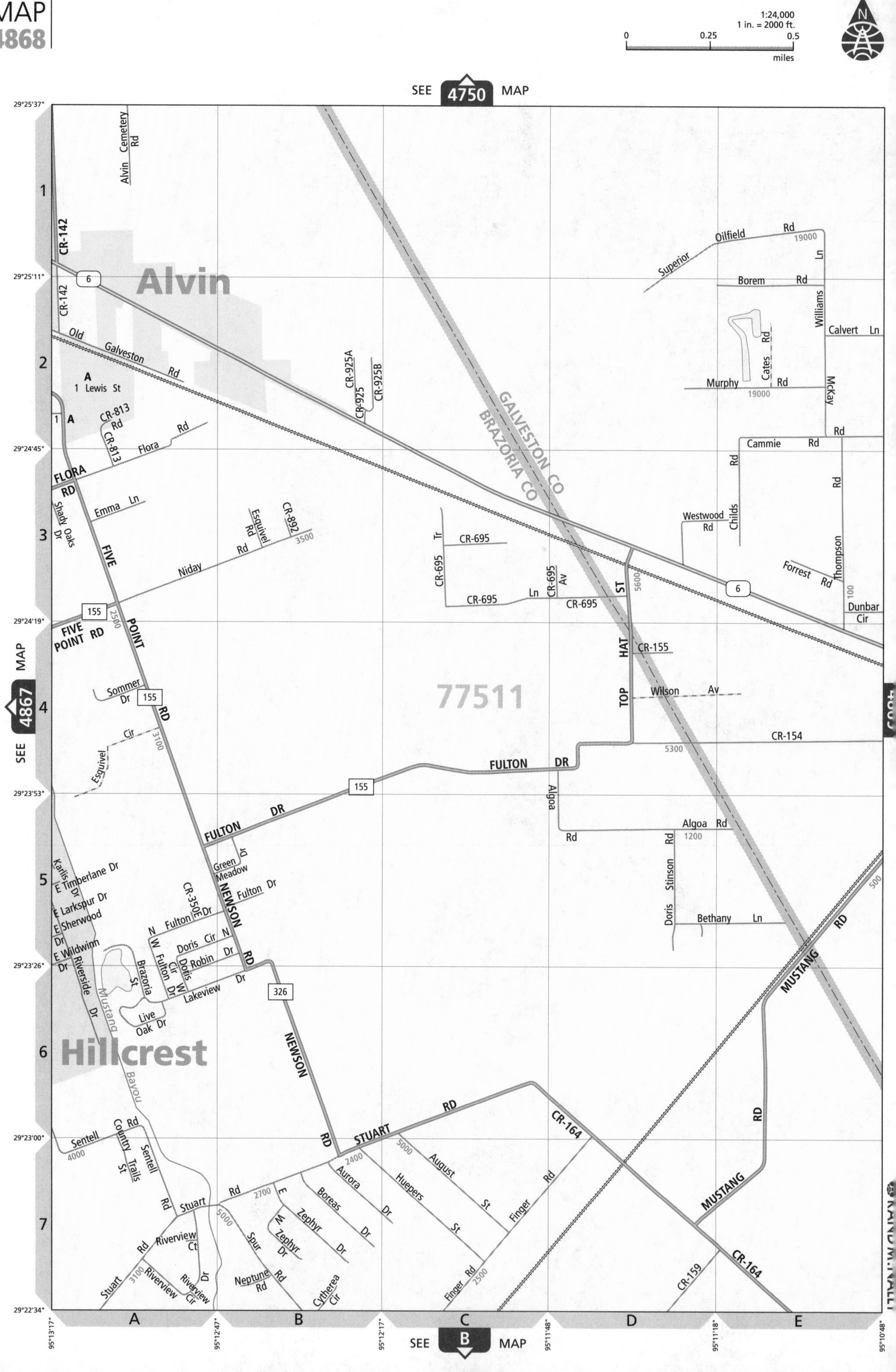
1:24,000
1 in. = 2000 ft.
0
0.25
0.5
miles
N
SEE 4750 MAP
SEE 4867 MAP
SEE B MAP
29°25'37"
29°25'11"
29°24'45"
29°24'19"
29°23'53"
29°23'26"
29°23'00"
29°22'34"
95°13'17"
95°12'47"
95°12'17"
95°11'48"
95°11'18"
95°10'48"
1
2
3
4
5
6
7
A
B
C
D
E
Alvin
Hillcrest
77511
GALVESTON CO
BRAZORIA CO
Alvin Cemetery Rd
CR-142
6
Old Galveston Rd
A
1 Lewis St
1
CR-813 Rd
CR-813
Flora Rd
FLORA RD
Shady Oaks Dr
Emma Ln
FIVE POINT RD
Niday Rd
Esquivel Rd
CR-892
3500
CR-925A
CR-925
CR-925B
155
2500
Sommer Dr
Esquivel Cir
3100
FULTON DR
Green Meadow Dr
Fulton Dr
NEWSON RD
CR-350E
Karlis Dr
E Timberlane Dr
E Larkspur Dr
E Sherwood Dr
E Wildwind Dr
Riverside Dr
N Fulton Dr
W Fulton Dr
Doris Cir N
Doris Cir W
Robin Dr
Brazoria St
Lakeview Dr
Live Oak Dr
326
Mustang Bayou
CR-695 Tr
CR-695
CR-695 Ln
CR-695 Av
TOP HAT ST
5600
CR-155
Wilson Av
CR-154
5300
Algoa Rd
1200
Stinson Rd
Doris
Bethany Ln
Superior
Oilfield Rd
19000
Borem Rd
Williams Ln
Calvert Ln
Cates Rd
Murphy Rd
McKay Rd
Cammie Rd
Childs Rd
Thompson Rd
Westwood Rd
Forrest Rd
100
Dunbar Cir
500
MUSTANG RD
Sentell Rd
4000
Country Trails St
Sentell Rd
Stuart Rd
Riverview Ct
Riverview Dr
Riverview Cir
3100
5000
Spur Rd
Neptune Rd
2700
E Zephyr Dr
W Zephyr Dr
Boreas Dr
Cytherea Cir
2400
Aurora Dr
Huepers St
August St
Finger Rd
2500
STUART RD
CR-164
CR-159
RAND McNALLY

1:24,000
1 in. = 2000 ft.
0 0.25 0.5
miles

SEE 4751 MAP

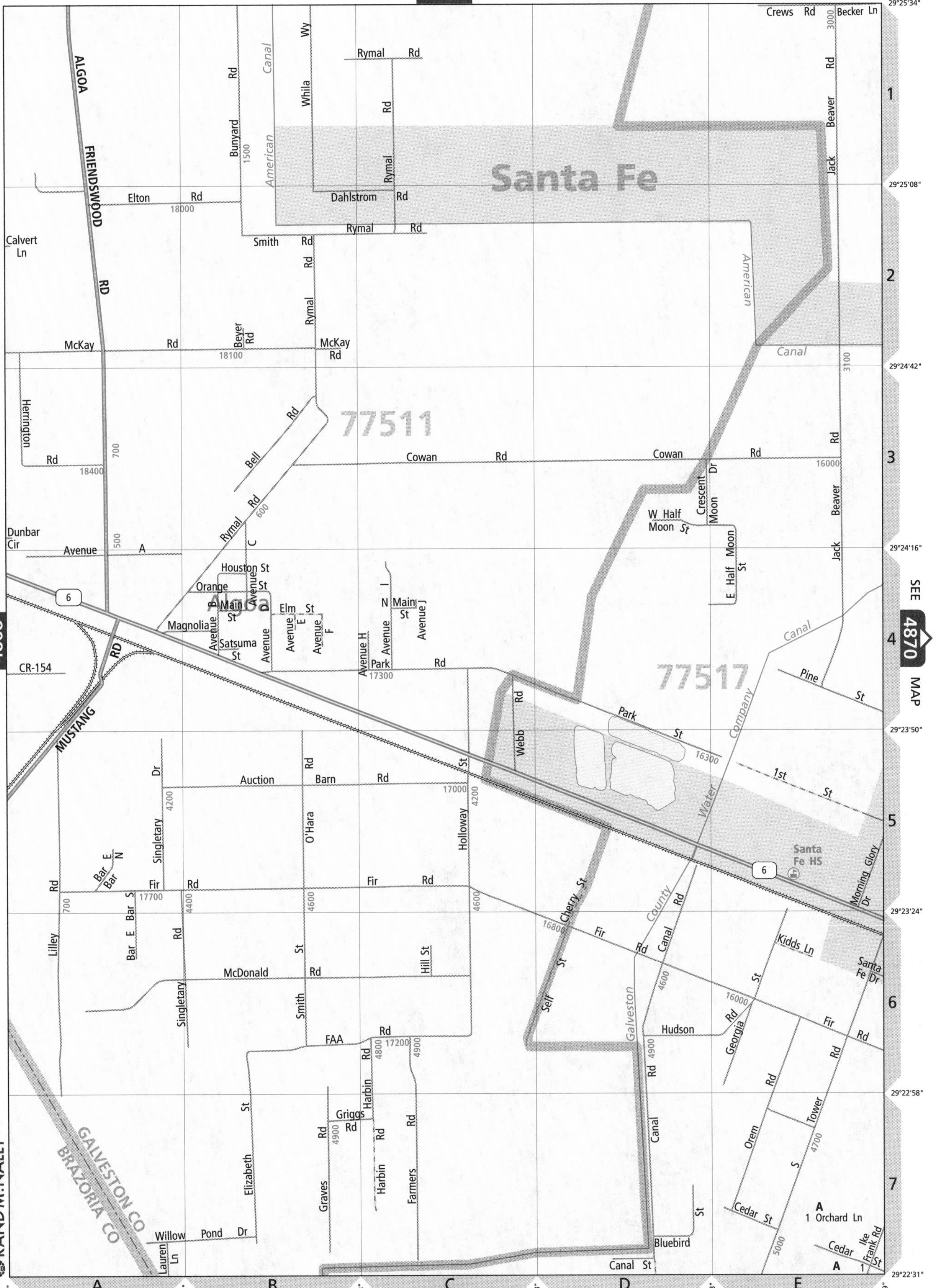
Santa Fe
77511
77517
Algoa
ALGOA FRIENDSWOOD RD
MUSTANG RD
Crews Rd
Becker Ln
Jack Beaver Rd
Rymal Rd
Whila Wy
Bunyard Rd
American Canal
Dahlstrom Rd
Elton Rd
Calvert Ln
Smith Rd
McKay Rd
Beyer Rd
Herrington Rd
Bell Rd
Cowan Rd
Crescent Moon Dr
W Half Moon St
E Half Moon St
Dunbar Cir
Avenue A
Avenue C
Houston St
Orange St
Main St
Magnolia
Satsuma St
Elm St
Avenue B
Avenue D
Avenue E
Avenue F
Avenue H
Avenue I
Avenue J
Avenue N
CR-154
Park Rd
Park St
Webb Rd
1st St
Company Canal
Water
Pine St
Santa Fe HS
Morning Glory Dr
Auction Barn Rd
O'Hara Rd
Singletary Dr
Holloway St
Bar E N
Bar E Bar S
Fir Rd
Lilley Rd
Cherry St
Self St
County Canal Rd
Galveston Canal Rd
Kidds Ln
Santa Fe Dr
McDonald Rd
Smith St
Hill St
FAA Rd
Harbin Rd
Griggs Rd
Graves Rd
Farmers Rd
Hudson
Georgia Rd
Orem Rd
Tower S
Elizabeth St
Willow Pond Dr
Lauren Ln
Bluebird St
Canal St
Cedar St
Orchard Ln
Ike Frank Rd
GALVESTON CO
BRAZORIA CO
6
A B C D E
1 2 3 4 5 6 7
29°25'34" 29°25'08" 29°24'42" 29°24'16" 29°23'50" 29°23'24" 29°22'58" 29°22'31"
95°10'48" 95°10'18" 95°09'48" 95°09'18" 95°08'48" 95°08'19"
RAND McNALLY

SEE 4870 MAP

SEE B MAP

4868

1:24,000
1 in. = 2000 ft.
0 0.25 0.5
miles

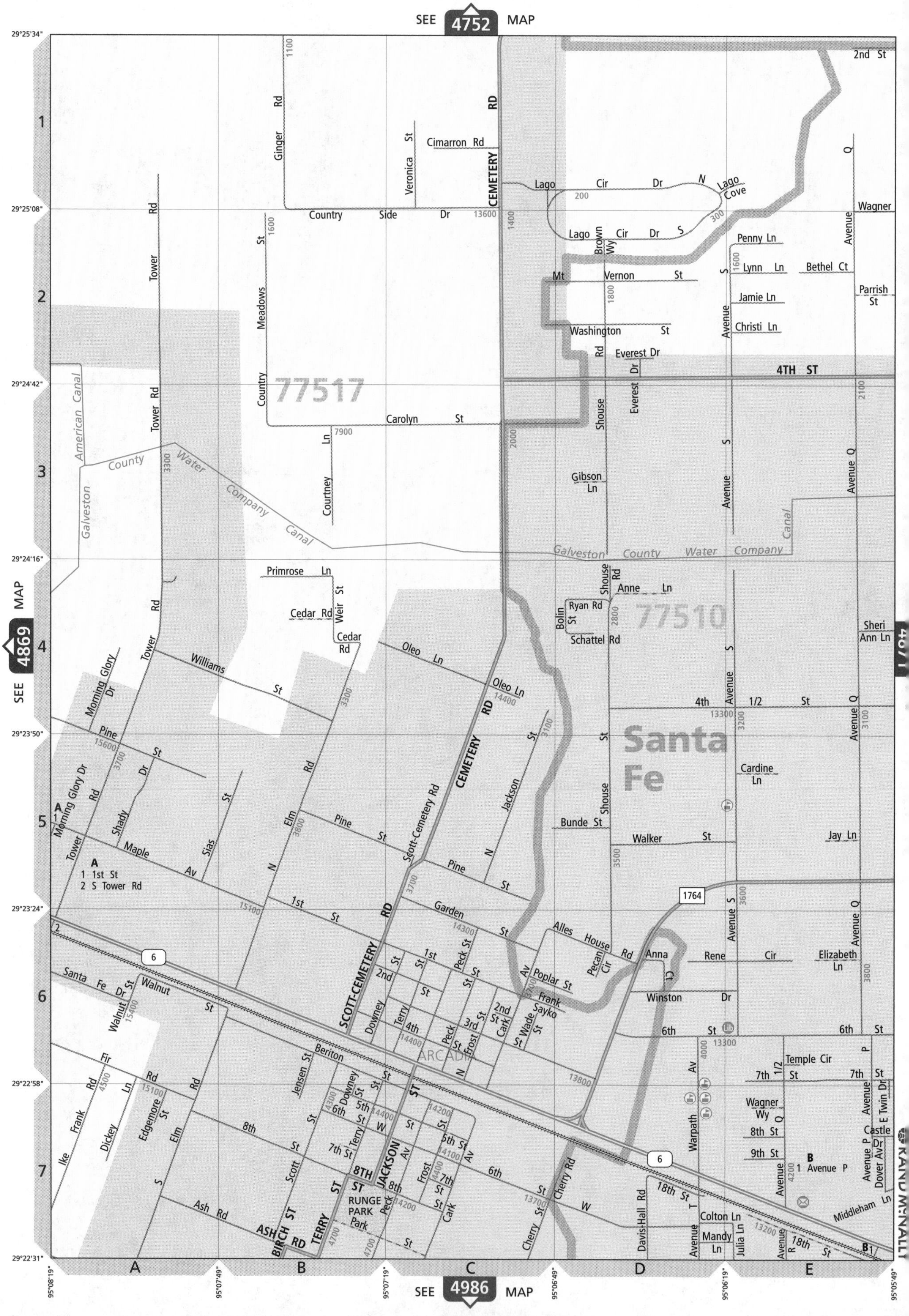
SEE 4752 MAP
SEE 4869 MAP
SEE 4986 MAP
4871
77517
77510
Santa Fe
ARCADIA
Cemetery Rd
Scott-Cemetery Rd
Tower Rd
Ginger Rd
Veronica St
Cimarron Rd
Country Side Dr
Country Meadows St
Carolyn St
Courtney Ln
Lago Cir Dr N
Lago Cir Dr S
Lago Cove
Brown Wy
Mt Vernon St
Washington St
Everest Dr
Shouse Rd
Penny Ln
Lynn Ln
Bethel Ct
Jamie Ln
Christi Ln
Parrish St
Wagner
2nd St
Avenue S
Avenue Q
4TH ST
Gibson Ln
American Canal
Galveston County Water Company Canal
Primrose Ln
Cedar Rd
Weir St
Anne Ln
Ryan Rd
Bolin St
Schattel Rd
Sheri Ann Ln
Williams St
Oleo Ln
Morning Glory Dr
Pine St
Shady Dr
Maple Av
Sias St
N Elm Rd
N Jackson St
4th 1/2 St
Cardine Ln
Bunde St
Walker St
Jay Ln
1st St
Garden St
Alles House Rd
Pecan Cir
Anna Ct
Rene Cir
Elizabeth Ln
Poplar St
Frank Sayko St
Winston Dr
6th St
Temple Cir
7th 1/2 St
7th St
Wagner Wy
8th St
9th St
Twin Dr
Castle Dr
Dover Av
Avenue P
Middleham Ln
Santa Fe Dr
Walnut St
Beriton St
Jensen St
Downey St
Terry St
Peck St
Frost St
Cark St
Wade St
Fir Rd
Frank Rd
Dickey Ln
Edgemore St
Elm St
Ike
8th St
Scott St
Ash Rd
Birch St
Terry Rd
8th St
Jackson Av
Runge Park
Cherry Rd
Cherry St
Davis-Hall Rd
18th St
Warpath Av
Colton Ln
Mandy Ln
Julia Ln
Avenue R
Avenue T
1764
6
A 1 1st St 2 S Tower Rd
B 1 Avenue P
A B C D E
1 2 3 4 5 6 7
29°25'34" 29°25'08" 29°24'42" 29°24'16" 29°23'50" 29°23'24" 29°22'58" 29°22'31"
95°08'19" 95°07'49" 95°07'19" 95°06'49" 95°06'19" 95°05'49"

1:24,000
1 in. = 2000 ft.
0 0.25 0.5
miles

SEE 4753 MAP

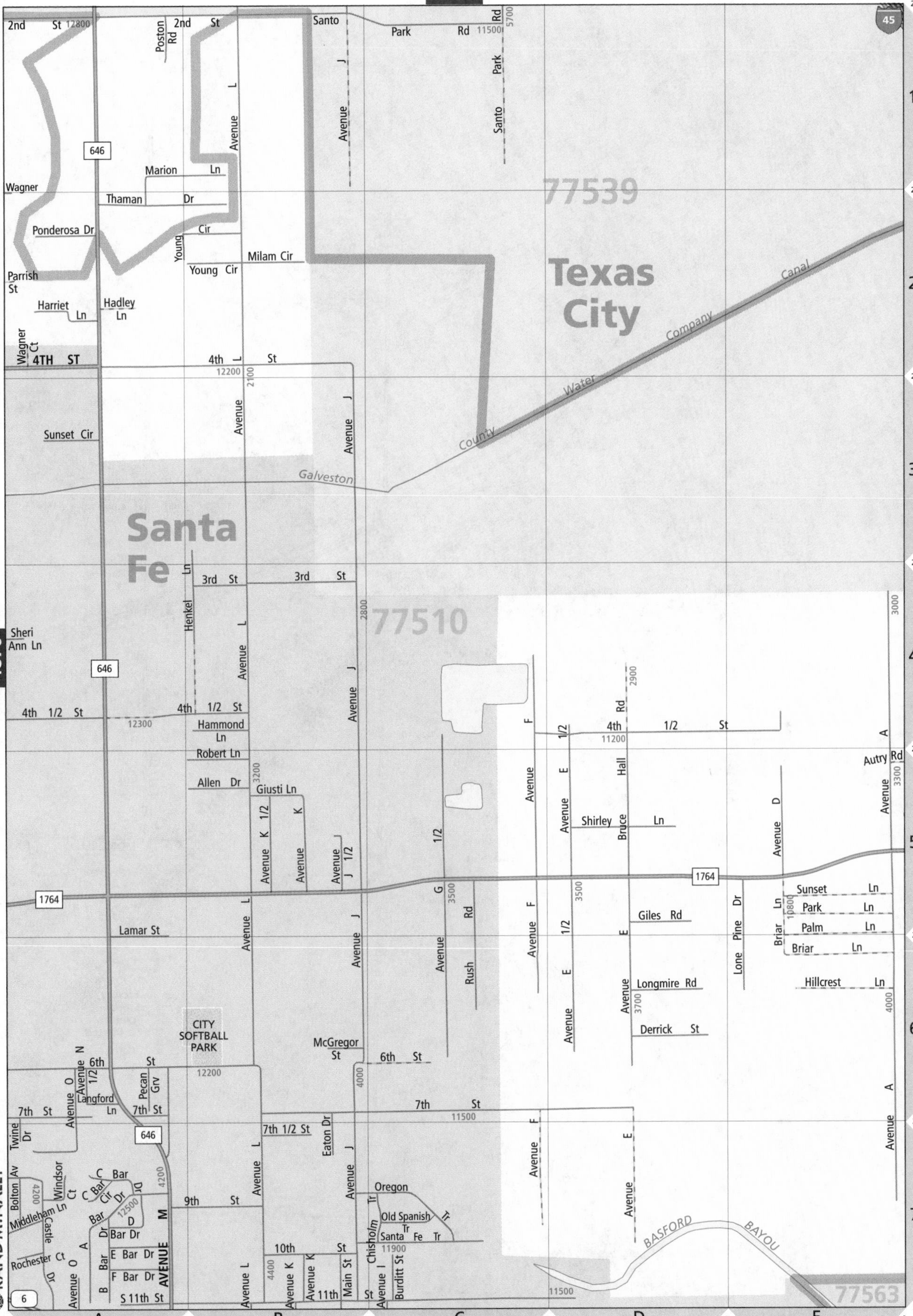
Texas City
Santa Fe
77539
77510
77563
2nd St 12800
Poston Rd
2nd St
Santo Park Rd 11500
Santo Park Rd
5700
Avenue L
Avenue J
646
Marion Ln
Wagner
Thaman Dr
Ponderosa Dr
Young Cir
Milam Cir
Young Cir
Parrish St
Harriet Ln
Hadley Ln
Wagner Ct
4TH ST
4th L St
12200
2100
Sunset Cir
Galveston
County Water Company Canal
3rd St
3rd St
Henkel Ln
2800
Sheri Ann Ln
4th 1/2 St
12300
4th 1/2 St
Hammond Ln
Robert Ln
Allen Dr
3200
Giusti Ln
Avenue K 1/2
Avenue K
Avenue J 1/2
1/2
Avenue G
3500
Rush Rd
Avenue F
Avenue E 1/2
Avenue E
4th 1/2 St
11200
Hall Rd
2900
Shirley Ln
Bruce
Avenue D
Avenue A
Autry Rd
3300
3000
1764
Lamar St
Giles Rd
Lone Pine Dr
Briar Ln
10800
Sunset Ln
Park Ln
Palm Ln
Briar Ln
Hillcrest Ln
Longmire Rd
3700
4000
Derrick St
CITY SOFTBALL PARK
McGregor St
6th St
6th St
12200
Avenue N
Avenue O
Avenue N 1/2
Langford Ln
Pecan Grv
7th St
7th St
7th St
11500
7th 1/2 St
Eaton Dr
Twine Dr
Bolton Av
4200
Windsor Ct
C Bar Cir
C Bar Dr
D Bar Dr
12500
Middleham Ln
Castle
Rochester Ct
Dr
Avenue O
B Bar
A
E Bar Dr
F Bar Dr
S 11th St
AVENUE M
9th St
Oregon
Old Spanish Tr
Santa Fe Tr
Chisholm Tr
11900
10th St
Avenue L
4400
Avenue K
11th St
Main St
St
Avenue I
Burditt St
BASFORD BAYOU
11500
45
6
1 2 3 4 5 6 7
A B C D E
29°25'31"
29°25'05"
29°24'39"
29°24'13"
29°23'47"
29°23'21"
29°22'54"
29°22'28"
95°05'49"
95°05'19"
95°04'50"
95°04'20"
95°03'50"
95°03'20"

SEE 4872 MAP

SEE 4987 MAP

4870

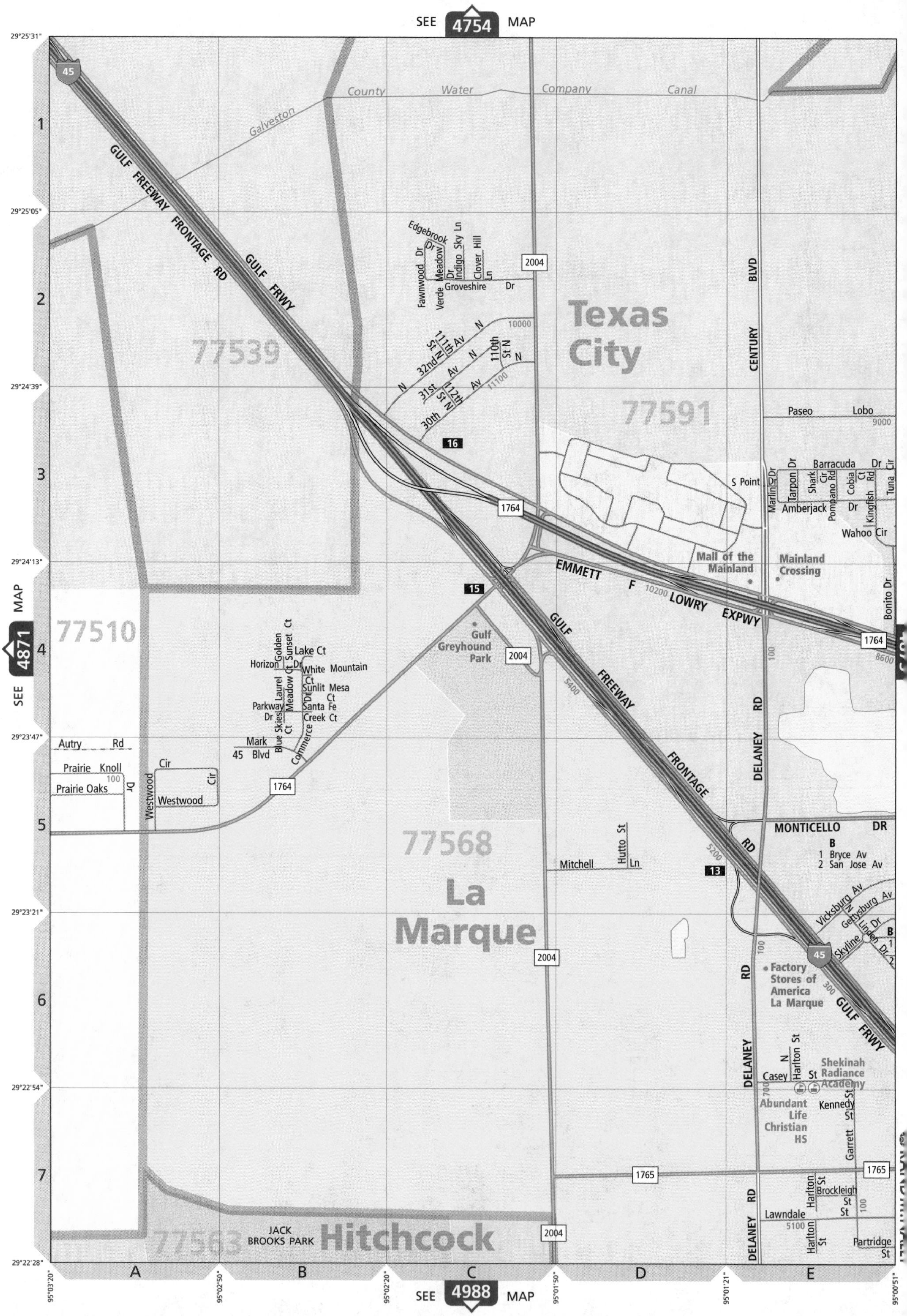
1:24,000
1 in. = 2000 ft.
0 0.25 0.5 miles
SEE 4754 MAP
SEE 4871 MAP
SEE 4988 MAP
Galveston County Water Company Canal
GULF FREEWAY FRONTAGE RD
GULF FRWY
Texas City
La Marque
Hitchcock
77539
77591
77510
77568
77563
CENTURY BLVD
DELANEY RD
EMMETT F LOWRY EXPWY
MONTICELLO DR
Mall of the Mainland
Mainland Crossing
Gulf Greyhound Park
Factory Stores of America La Marque
Shekinah Radiance Academy
Abundant Life Christian HS
JACK BROOKS PARK
Edgebrook Dr
Fawnwood Dr
Verde Meadow Dr
Indigo Sky Ln
Clover Hill Ln
Groveshire Dr
32nd St N
31st St N
30th St N
111th Av N
112th Av N
110th St N
Paseo
Lobo
Barracuda Dr
S Point
Marlin Dr
Tarpon Dr
Shark Cir
Pompano Rd
Cobia Ct
Kingfish Rd
Tuna Cir
Amberjack Dr
Wahoo Cir
Bonito Dr
Golden Sunset Ct
Lake Ct
Horizon Dr
White Mountain Ct
Laurel Meadow Ct
Sunlit Mesa Ct
Parkway Dr
Santa Fe Creek Ct
Blue Skies Ct
Mark Blvd
Commerce
Autry Rd
Prairie Knoll Dr
Prairie Oaks
Westwood Cir
Mitchell
Hutto St
Ln
1 Bryce Av
2 San Jose Av
Vicksburg Av
Gettysburg Av
Linden Dr
Skyline Dr
Casey St
Harlton St
Kennedy St
Garrett St
Brockleigh St
Lawndale
Partridge St
2004
1764
1765
45
16
15
13
10000
11100
10200
9000
8600
5400
5200
5100
700
300
100
29°25'31"
29°25'05"
29°24'39"
29°24'13"
29°23'47"
29°23'21"
29°22'54"
29°22'28"
95°03'20"
95°02'50"
95°02'20"
95°01'50"
95°01'21"
95°00'51"
A B C D E
1 2 3 4 5 6 7

1:24,000
1 in. = 2000 ft.
0 0.25 0.5
miles

SEE 4755 MAP

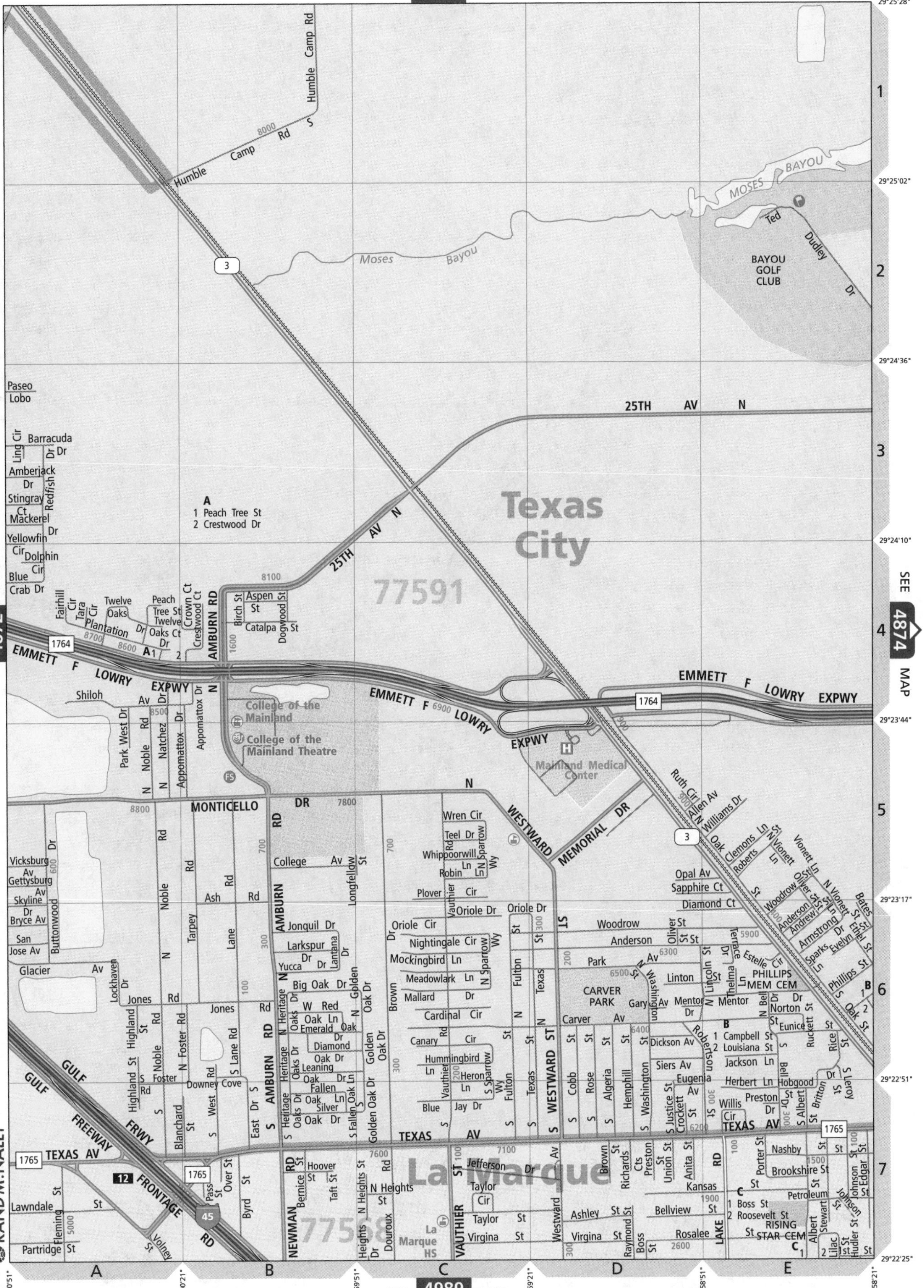
29°25'28"
29°25'02"
29°24'36"
29°24'10"
29°23'44"
29°23'17"
29°22'51"
29°22'25"
95°00'51"
95°00'21"
94°59'51"
94°59'21"
94°58'51"
94°58'21"
1
2
3
4
5
6
7
A
B
C
D
E
Texas City
77591
La Marque
77568
Humble Camp Rd
8000
S Humble Camp Rd
Moses Bayou
MOSES BAYOU
Ted Dudley Dr
BAYOU GOLF CLUB
3
25TH AV N
8100
Paseo Lobo
Ling Cir
Barracuda Dr
Amberjack Dr
Redfish Dr
Stingray Ct
Mackerel
Yellowfin Dr
Cir Dolphin
Blue Cir
Crab Dr
A
1 Peach Tree St
2 Crestwood Dr
Fairhill Cir
Tara Cir
Twelve Oaks
Plantation Dr
Peach Tree St
Twelve Oaks Ct
Crown Ct
Crestwood Ct
Birch St
Aspen St
Catalpa St
Dogwood St
AMBURN RD
1600
1764
8700
8600
EMMETT F LOWRY EXPWY
6900
Shiloh Av
Park West Dr
N Noble Rd
8500
N Natchez Dr
N Appomattox Dr
Appomattox Dr
College of the Mainland
College of the Mainland Theatre
FS
Mainland Medical Center
MONTICELLO DR
8800
7800
N WESTWARD
MEMORIAL DR
Ruth Cir
Allen Av
Williams Dr
Oak
Clemons Ln
Roberts St
N Vionett Ln
Vionett Ln
Wren Cir
Teel Dr
Whippoorwill Rd
Robin Ln
N Sparrow Wy
Vicksburg Dr
Gettysburg Av
Skyline Av
Bryce Av
San Jose Av
Buttonwood Dr
Glacier Av
Lockhaven Dr
Jones Rd
Noble Rd
Tarpey Rd
Ash Rd
Lane Rd
AMBURN RD
College Av
Longfellow St
Jonquil Dr
Larkspur Dr
Yucca Dr
Lantana Dr
Big Oak Dr
W Red Oak Ln
Emerald Oak Dr
Diamond Oak Dr
N Heritage Oaks Dr
N Golden Oak Dr
Plover Cir
Vauthier
Oriole Dr
Oriole Cir
Nightingale Cir
Mockingbird Ln
Meadowlark Ln
Mallard Dr
Cardinal Cir
Canary Rd
Hummingbird Ln
Heron Ln
S Sparrow Wy
Jay Dr
Blue
N Sparrow Wy
Oriole Dr
Fulton St
Texas St
Brown Dr
Opal Av
Sapphire Ct
Diamond Ct
Woodrow
Oliver St
Anderson St
Park Av
Linton St
Lincoln St
Washington
CARVER PARK
Gary Av
Mentor Dr
Mentor
Carver Av
Dixson Av
Siers Av
Eugenia Av
Robertson
Thelma Ln
Terrace Dr
Estelle Cir
PHILLIPS MEM CEM
Norton St
Eunice St
B
1 Campbell St
2 Louisiana St
Jackson Ln
Herbert Ln
Hobgood Dr
Preston Dr
Willis Cir
Britton
S Leroy
Rice St
Ruckett St
Woodrow St
Oliver St
Anderson St
Andrew St
Armstrong Dr
Sparks Ln
Evelyn
Ethel St
Bates St
N Vionett St
Phillips St
S Oak St
5900
6300
6500
6400
6200
Highland St
Blanchard St
S Foster Rd
N Foster Rd
Downey Cove
S West St
S Lane Rd
East Dr S
S AMBURN
Heritage Oaks Dr
Fallen Oak Ln
Leaning
Silver Oak Dr
S Fallen Oak Ln
Golden Oak Dr
Vauthier
Fulton
Texas
S WESTWARD ST
Cobb St
Rose St
Algeria St
Hemphill St
Washington St
S Justice St
Crockett St
TEXAS AV
1765
GULF FREEWAY
GULF FRWY
FRONTAGE RD
12
45
1765
Pass St
Over St
Byrd St
TEXAS AV
Lawndale St
Fleming St
5000
Partridge St
Volney St
NEWMAN RD
Bernice St
Hoover St
Taft St
N Heights St
Heights Dr
Douroux
7600
7100
VAUTHIER ST
Jefferson Dr
Taylor Cir
Taylor St
Virgina St
La Marque HS
Westward Av
Brown St
Ashley St
Virgina St
Richards St
Raymond St
Preston Cts
Union St
Anita St
Kansas
Bellview St
Boss St
Rosalee St
2600
1900
LAKE RD
C
1 Boss St
2 Roosevelt St
RISING STAR CEM
Porter St
Nashby St
Brookshire St
Petroleum St
Albert St
Stewart St
Lilac St
Johnson St
Edgar St
Hudler St
1500
100
C1

SEE 4874 MAP

SEE 4989 MAP

1:24,000
1 in. = 2000 ft.
0 0.25 0.5
miles

SEE 4756 MAP

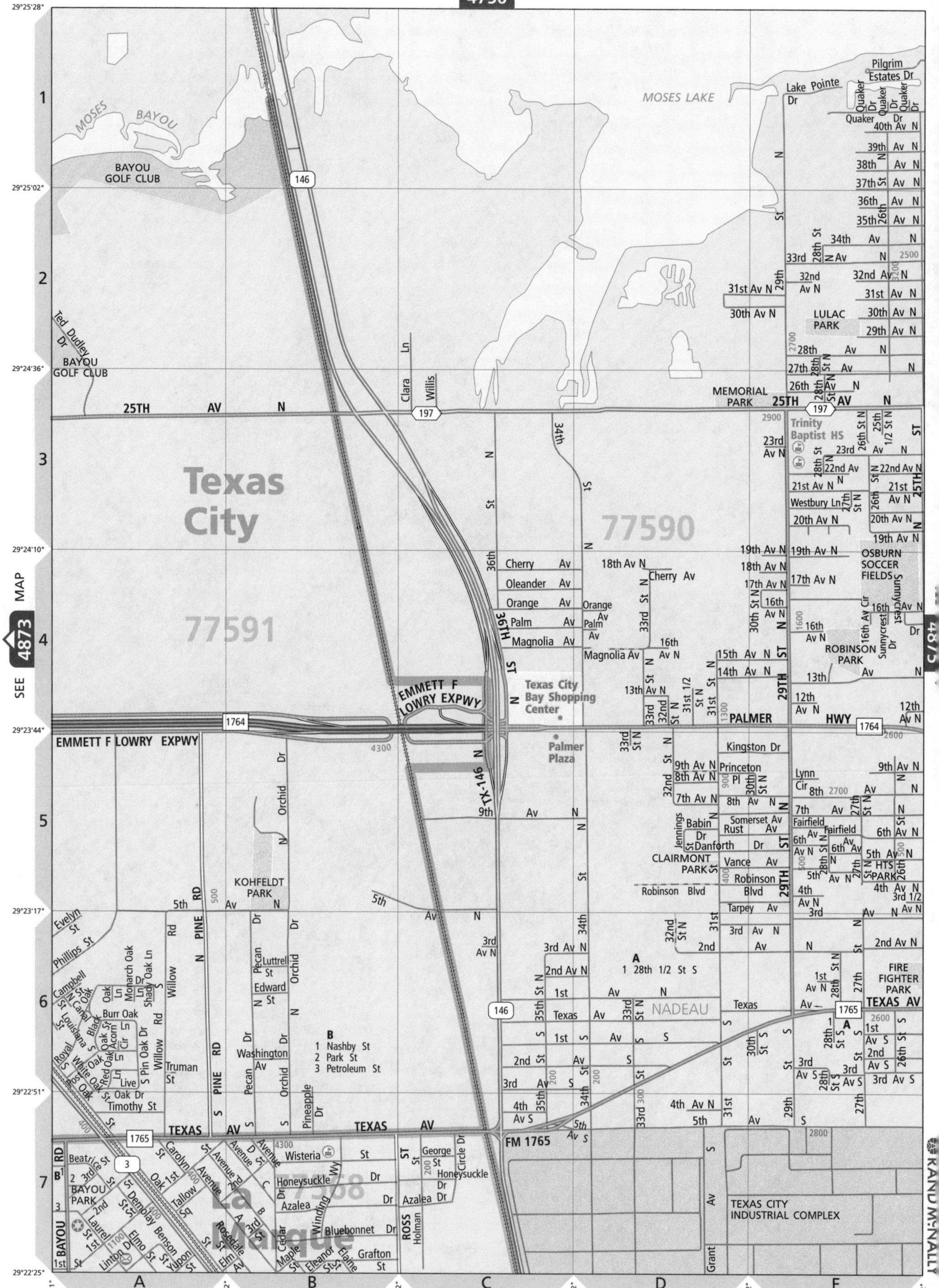
29°25'28"
29°25'02"
29°24'36"
29°24'10"
29°23'44"
29°23'17"
29°22'51"
29°22'25"
1
2
3
4
5
6
7
A
B
C
D
E
94°58'21"
94°57'52"
94°57'22"
94°56'52"
94°56'22"
94°55'52"
MOSES BAYOU
BAYOU GOLF CLUB
MOSES LAKE
Lake Pointe Dr
Pilgrim Estates Dr
Quaker Dr
40th Av N
39th Av N
38th Av N
37th Av N
36th Av N
35th Av N
34th Av N
33rd Av N
32nd Av N
31st Av N
30th Av N
29th Av N
28th Av N
27th Av N
26th Av N
LULAC PARK
Ted Dudley Dr
Clara Ln
Willis
25TH AV N
197
146
MEMORIAL PARK
Trinity Baptist HS
23rd Av N
22nd Av N
21st Av N
Westbury Ln
20th Av N
19th Av N
18th Av N
17th Av N
16th Av N
15th Av N
14th Av N
13th Av N
12th Av N
OSBURN SOCCER FIELDS
Sunnycrest Dr
ROBINSON PARK
Texas City
77590
77591
36th St N
34th St N
33rd St N
29TH ST
25TH ST
Cherry Av
Oleander Av
Orange Av
Palm Av
Magnolia Av
36TH ST N
Texas City Bay Shopping Center
EMMETT F LOWRY EXPWY
1764
PALMER HWY
Palmer Plaza
TX-146 N
Kingston Dr
Princeton Pl
9th Av N
8th Av N
7th Av N
Lynn Cir
Somerset Av
Babin Dr
Rust Av
Fairfield Av
Danforth Dr
Vance Av
CLAIRMONT PARK
Robinson Blvd
Tarpey Av
HTS PARK
4th Av N
3rd Av N
2nd Av N
1st Av N
FIRE FIGHTER PARK
TEXAS AV
1765
NADEAU
Texas Av
1 28th 1/2 St S
Orchid Dr
Pecan Dr
KOHFELDT PARK
5th Av N
PINE RD
Evelyn St
Phillips St
Campbell St
Monarch Oak
Shady Oak Ln
Willow Rd
Burr Oak
Luttrell St
Edward St
Washington Av
Truman St
Timothy St
Live Oak Dr
1 Nashby St
2 Park St
3 Petroleum St
Pineapple Dr
TEXAS AV
FM 1765
3
Beatrice St
Carolyn St
BAYOU PARK
Wisteria
Honeysuckle Dr
Azalea Dr
Bluebonnet Dr
Grafton St
George St
Circle Dr
ROSS Holman
Cedar
Maple St
Eleanor St
Elaine St
Winding Wy
La Marque
77568
Laurel St
Linton Dr
Elmo St
Benson St
Yupon St
Rosedale
Elm Av
BAYOU
Grant Av
TEXAS CITY INDUSTRIAL COMPLEX
RAND McNALLY

SEE 4873 MAP

SEE 4990 MAP

1:24,000
1 in. = 2000 ft.
0 0.25 0.5
miles

SEE 4757 MAP

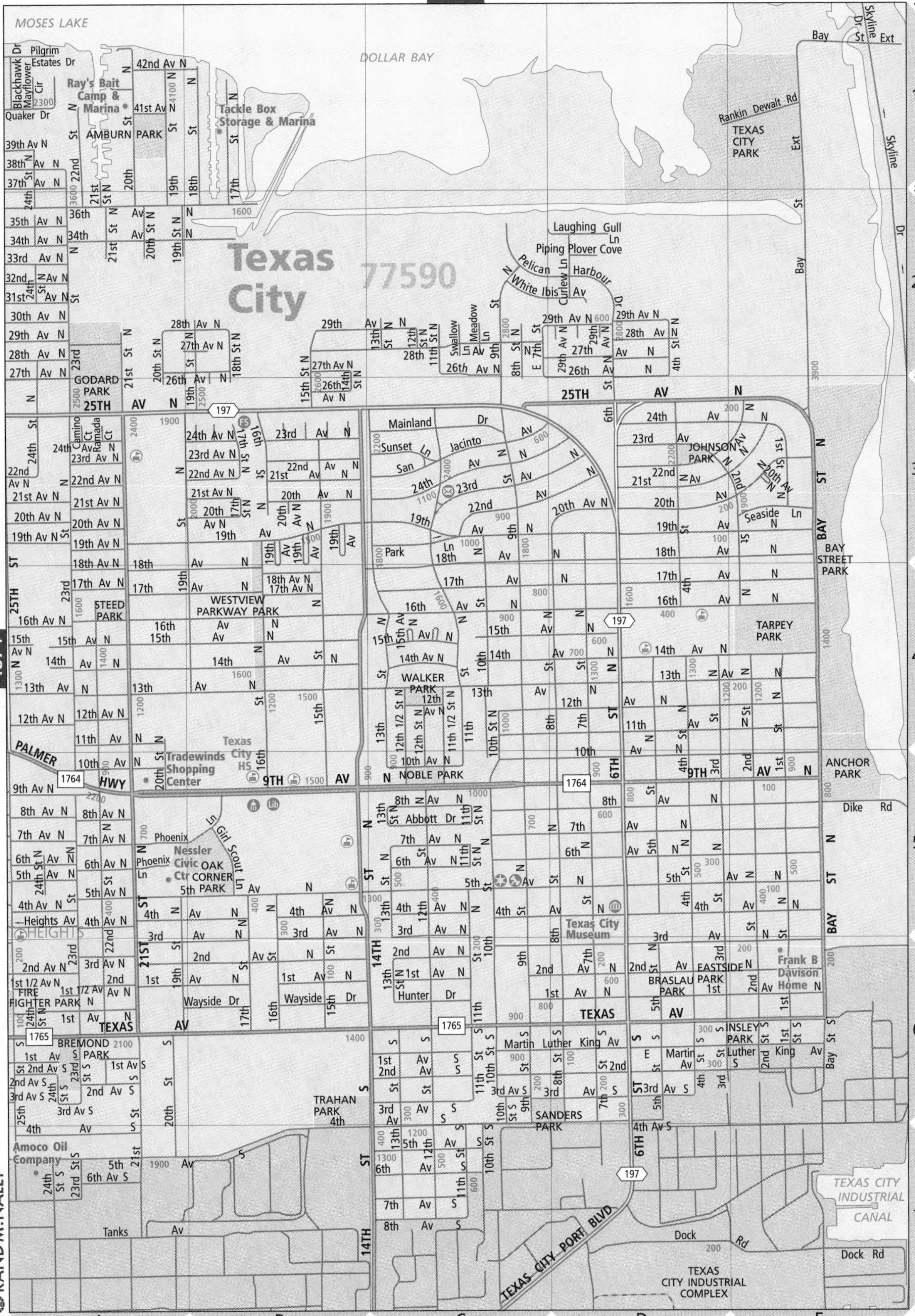
MOSES LAKE
DOLLAR BAY
Texas City
77590
Ray's Bait Camp & Marina
Tackle Box Storage & Marina
AMBURN PARK
TEXAS CITY PARK
Rankin Dewalt Rd
Skyline Dr
GODARD PARK
25TH AV N
Mainland Dr
JOHNSON PARK
STEED PARK
WESTVIEW PARKWAY PARK
BAY STREET PARK
TARPEY PARK
WALKER PARK
NOBLE PARK
Tradewinds Shopping Center
Texas City HS
PALMER HWY
9TH AV N
ANCHOR PARK
Dike Rd
Nessler Civic Ctr
OAK CORNER PARK
Texas City Museum
HEIGHTS
FIRE FIGHTER PARK
EASTSIDE PARK
BRASLAU PARK
Frank B Davison Home
TEXAS AV
BREMOND PARK
INSLEY PARK
Martin Luther King Av
TRAHAN PARK
SANDERS PARK
Amoco Oil Company
Tanks Av
TEXAS CITY PORT BLVD
TEXAS CITY INDUSTRIAL CANAL
Dock Rd
TEXAS CITY INDUSTRIAL COMPLEX
14TH ST
6TH ST
21ST ST
BAY ST
A
B
C
D
E
1
2
3
4
5
6
7
29°25'25"
29°24'59"
29°24'32"
29°24'06"
29°23'40"
29°23'14"
29°22'48"
29°22'22"
94°55'52"
94°55'22"
94°54'52"
94°54'23"
94°53'53"
94°53'23"

SEE 4876 MAP

4874

SEE 4991 MAP

1:24,000
1 in. = 2000 ft.
0 0.25 0.5
miles

SEE B MAP

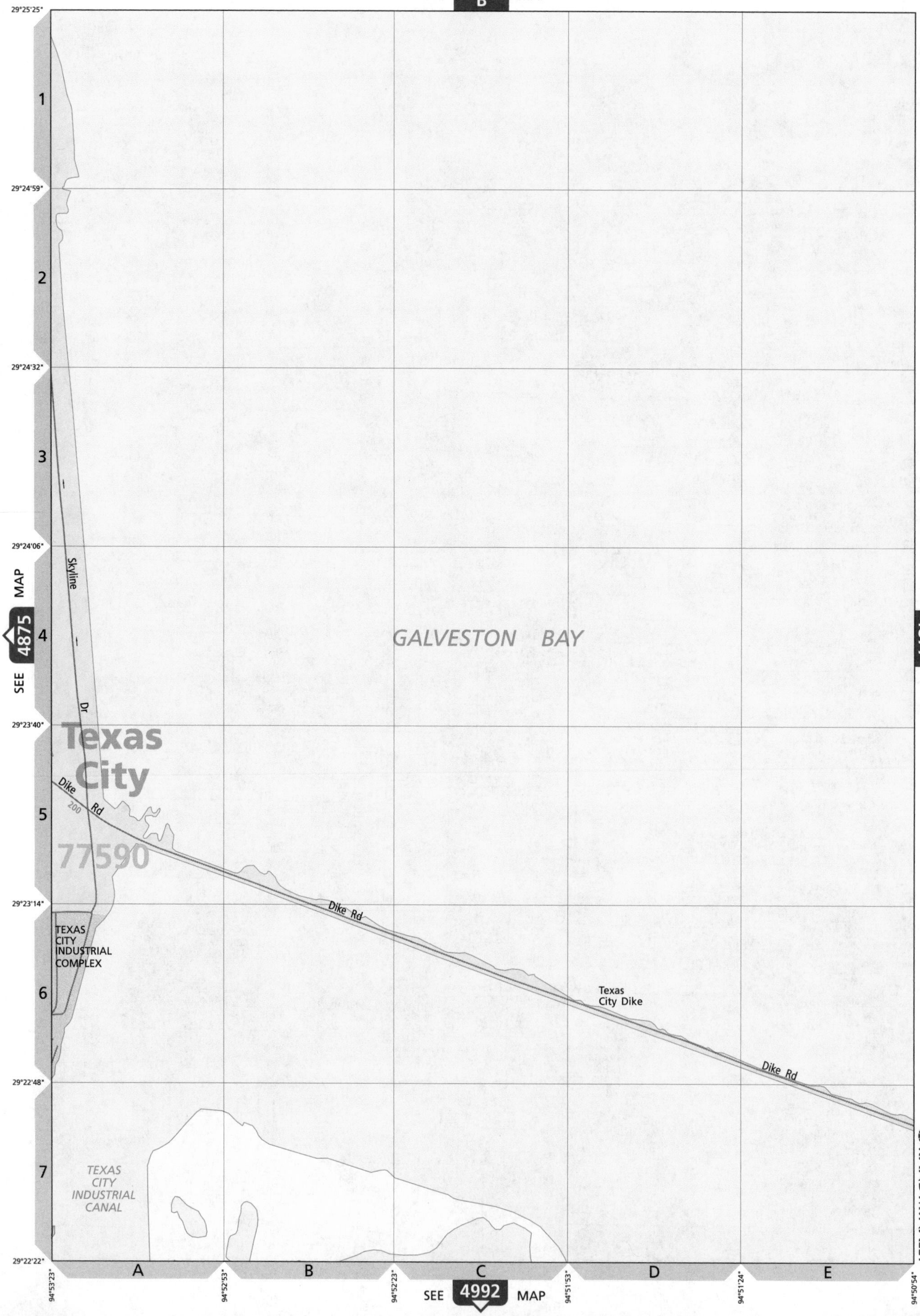
29°25'25"
29°24'59"
29°24'32"
29°24'06"
29°23'40"
29°23'14"
29°22'48"
29°22'22"
1
2
3
4
5
6
7
A
B
C
D
E
94°53'23"
94°52'53"
94°52'23"
94°51'53"
94°51'24"
94°50'54"
Skyline
Dr
GALVESTON BAY
Texas
City
77590
Dike
200
Rd
Dike Rd
TEXAS
CITY
INDUSTRIAL
COMPLEX
Texas
City Dike
Dike Rd
TEXAS
CITY
INDUSTRIAL
CANAL

SEE 4875 MAP

4877

SEE 4992 MAP

1:24,000
1 in. = 2000 ft.
0 0.25 0.5
miles

SEE B MAP

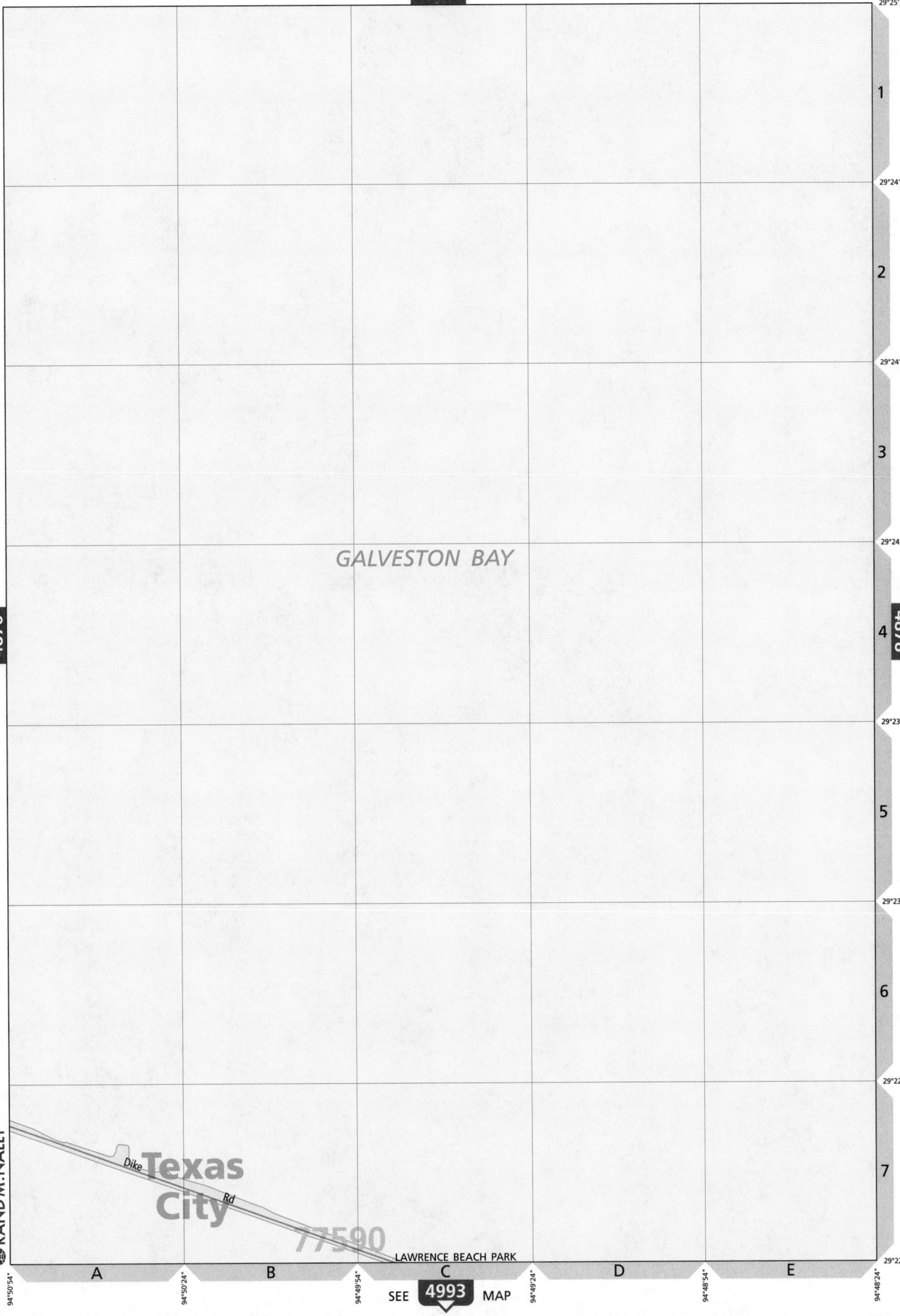
GALVESTON BAY
Texas City
Dike Rd
77590
LAWRENCE BEACH PARK
29°25'21"
29°24'55"
29°24'29"
29°24'03"
29°23'36"
29°23'10"
29°22'44"
29°22'18"
1
2
3
4
5
6
7
A
B
C
D
E
94°50'54"
94°50'24"
94°49'54"
94°49'24"
94°48'54"
94°48'24"

SEE 4876 MAP

SEE 4878 MAP

SEE 4993 MAP

1:24,000
1 in. = 2000 ft.
0 0.25 0.5
miles

SEE B MAP

GALVESTON BAY
Baffle Point
GOAT ISLAND
INTRACOASTAL WATERWAY
77650
HORSESHOE LAKE
BROADWAY
7TH ST
108
Rankin Av
S 16th St
Charles Av
Al
Pickney Al
Av
14th St
15th St
Quarles St
Pickney
1400
Al 13th St
Av
1300
Nelson Av
14th St
12th
Overton
St
10th Av
Pickney Av
Quarles
9th St
1400
900
Av
Pickney
8th Av
St
6th Pickney
5th Av
Overton
500
7th St
Nelson St
8th St
800 Madison
5th
St
3rd St
4th St
700
8th St
1200
29°25'21"
29°24'55"
29°24'29"
29°24'03"
29°23'37"
29°23'10"
29°22'44"
29°22'18"
94°48'24"
94°47'55"
94°47'25"
94°46'55"
94°46'25"
94°45'55"
1
2
3
4
5
6
7
A
B
C
D
E

SEE 4877 MAP

SEE 4879 MAP

SEE 4994 MAP

1:24,000
1 in. = 2000 ft.
0 0.25 0.5
miles

SEE B MAP

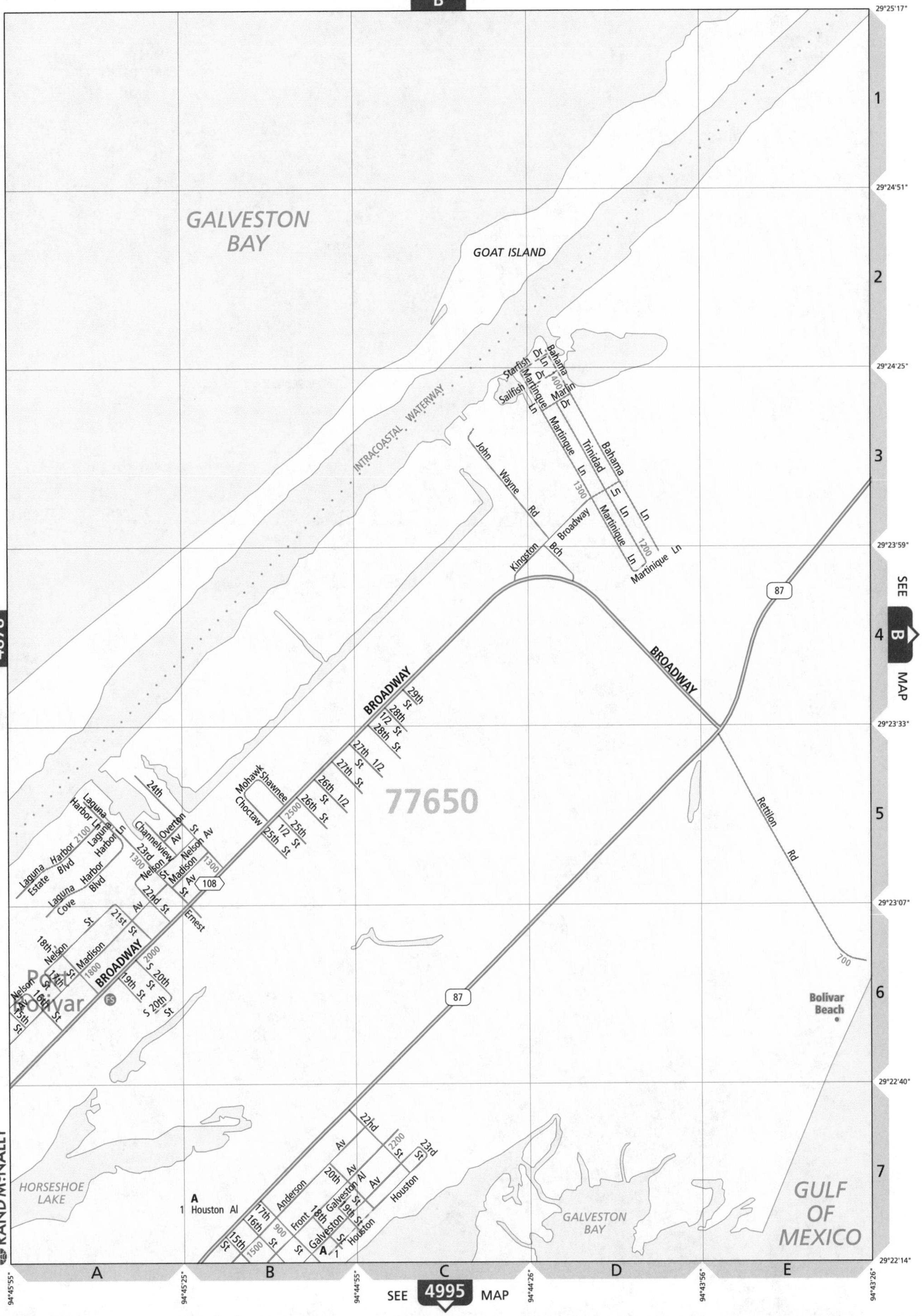
GALVESTON
BAY
GOAT ISLAND
INTRACOASTAL WATERWAY
77650
BROADWAY
Port Bolivar
Bolivar Beach
HORSESHOE LAKE
GALVESTON BAY
GULF OF MEXICO
87
108
Rettilon Rd
John Wayne Rd
Kingston Bch
Broadway
Martinique Ln
Trinidad Ln
Bahama Ln
Marlin Dr
Sailfish Dr
Starfish Dr
Laguna Harbor Estate Blvd
Laguna Harbor Ln
Laguna Harbor Cove Blvd
Channelview
Overton Av
Nelson Av
Madison Av
24th
23rd St
22nd St
21st St
S 20th St
19th St
18th
Ernest
Mohawk
Shawnee
Choctaw
25th St
25th 1/2 St
26th St
26th 1/2
27th St
27th 1/2
28th St
28th 1/2 St
29th St
A 1 Houston Al
Anderson
Front
Galveston Al
Galveston
Houston
Av
15th
16th St
17th St
18th St
19th St
20th
22nd
23rd St
1
2
3
4
5
6
7
A
B
C
D
E
29°25'17"
29°24'51"
29°24'25"
29°23'59"
29°23'33"
29°23'07"
29°22'40"
29°22'14"
94°45'55"
94°45'25"
94°44'55"
94°44'26"
94°43'56"
94°43'26"

SEE 4878 MAP

SEE B MAP

SEE 4995 MAP

1:24,000
1 in. = 2000 ft.
0 0.25 0.5
miles

SEE 4870 MAP

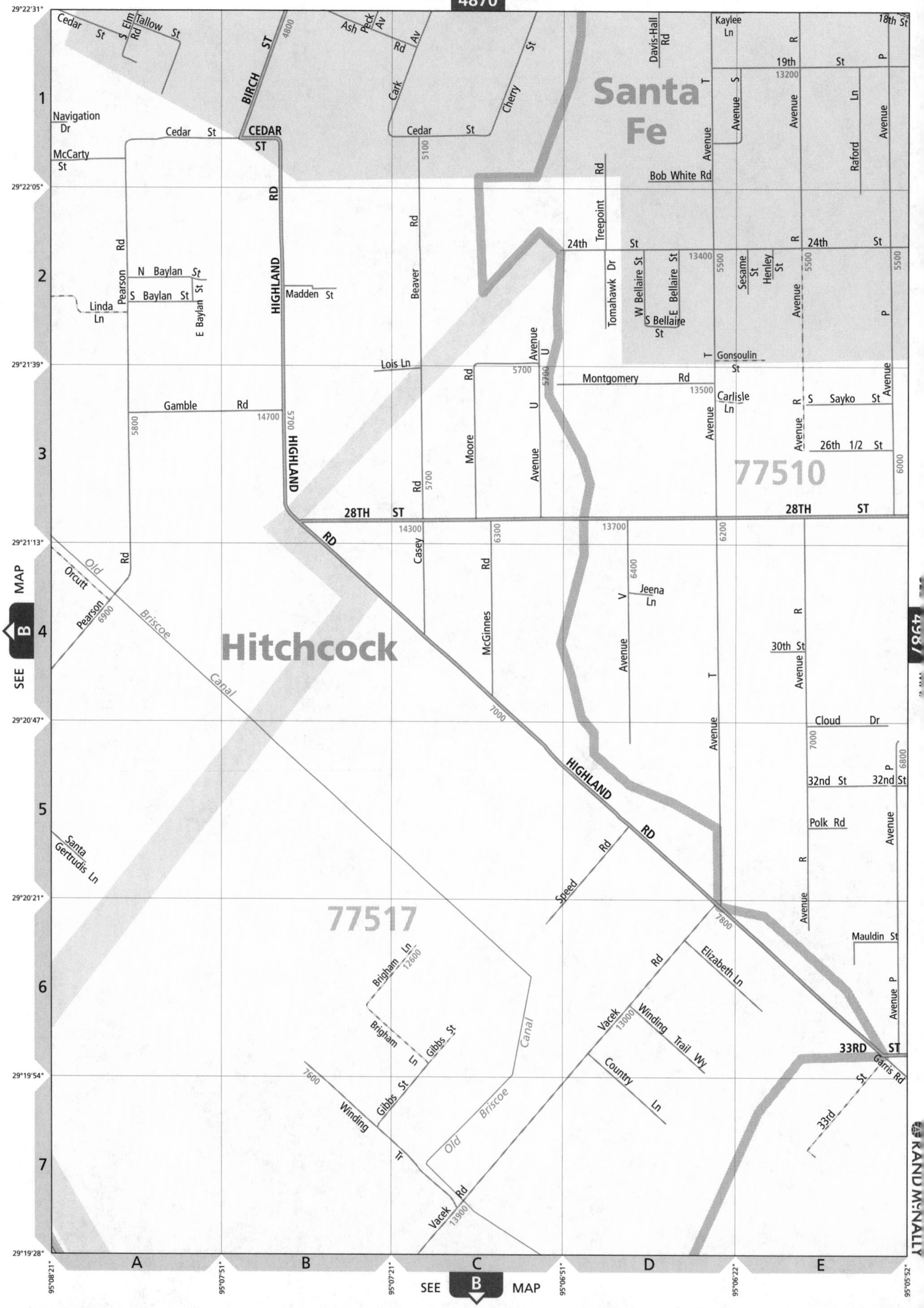
Santa Fe
Hitchcock
77510
77517
Cedar St
Elm Rd
Tallow St
Ash
Peck Av
Rd
Av
BIRCH ST
4800
Cark
Cherry St
Navigation Dr
McCarty St
Cedar St
CEDAR ST
Cedar St
5100
Davis-Hall Rd
Kaylee Ln
18th St
19th St
13200
Avenue T
Avenue S
Avenue R
Raford Ln
Avenue P
Bob White Rd
Treepoint Rd
HIGHLAND RD
Beaver Rd
24th St
24th St
13400
5500
5500
5500
Tomahawk Dr
W Bellaire St
E Bellaire St
S Bellaire St
Sesame St
Henley St
Pearson Rd
N Baylan St
S Baylan St
E Baylan St
Linda Ln
Madden St
Lois Ln
Avenue U
5700
5700
Gonsoulin St
Montgomery Rd
13500
Carlisle Ln
Sayko St
Gamble Rd
14700
5800
5700 HIGHLAND
Moore Rd
26th 1/2 St
6000
5700
28TH ST
28TH ST
14300
13700
6300
6200
6400
RD
Casey Rd
McGinnes Rd
Old Orcutt
Pearson Rd
6900
Briscoe Canal
Jeena Ln
Avenue V
30th St
7000
Cloud Dr
7000
6800
32nd St
32nd St
HIGHLAND RD
Polk Rd
Santa Gertrudis Ln
Speed Rd
7800
Mauldin St
Elizabeth Ln
Brigham Ln
12600
Brigham Ln
Gibbs St
Vacek Rd
13000
Winding Trail Wy
33RD ST
Garris Rd
Country Ln
Canal
7600
Winding Tr
Gibbs St
Old Briscoe
33rd St
Vacek Rd
13900
29°22'31"
29°22'05"
29°21'39"
29°21'13"
29°20'47"
29°20'21"
29°19'54"
29°19'28"
95°08'21"
95°07'51"
95°07'21"
95°06'51"
95°06'22"
95°05'52"
1
2
3
4
5
6
7
A
B
C
D
E

SEE B MAP

SEE 4987 MAP

SEE B MAP

1:24,000
1 in. = 2000 ft.
0 0.25 0.5
miles

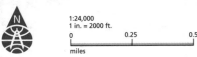

SEE 4871 MAP

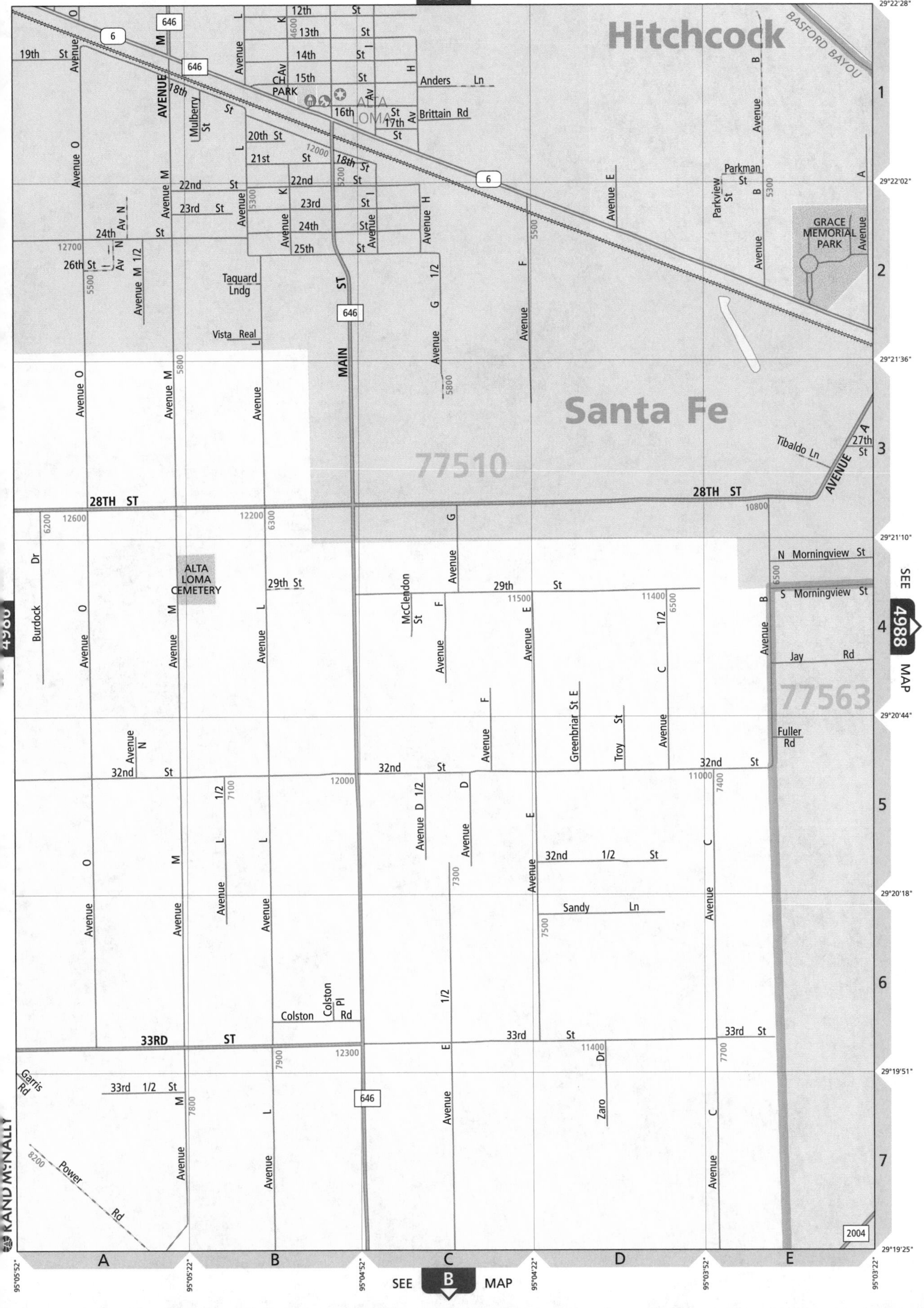
Hitchcock
Santa Fe
77510
77563
BASFORD BAYOU
GRACE MEMORIAL PARK
ALTA LOMA CEMETERY
ALTA LOMA
CH PARK
28TH ST
33RD ST
MAIN ST
AVENUE M
AVENUE A
Avenue O
Avenue M
Avenue L
Avenue K
Avenue H
Avenue G 1/2
Avenue G
Avenue F
Avenue E
Avenue D 1/2
Avenue D
Avenue C 1/2
Avenue C
Avenue B
Avenue A
Avenue N
Avenue M 1/2
Avenue L 1/2
Avenue E 1/2
12th St
13th St
14th St
15th St
16th St
17th St
18th St
19th St
20th St
21st St
22nd St
23rd St
24th St
25th St
26th St
27th St
29th St
32nd St
32nd 1/2 St
33rd St
33rd 1/2 St
Anders Ln
Brittain Rd
Parkman St
Parkview St
Mulberry St
Taquard Lndg
Vista Real
Tibaldo Ln
N Morningview St
S Morningview St
Jay Rd
Fuller Rd
McClendon St
Greenbriar St E
Troy St
Sandy Ln
Colston
Colston Pl Rd
Zaro Dr
Burdock Dr
Garris Rd
Power Rd
6
646
2004
12700
12600
12200
12000
11500
11400
11000
10800
12300
5300
5200
5500
5800
6200
6300
6500
7100
7300
7400
7500
7700
7800
7900
8200
4600
1
2
3
4
5
6
7
A
B
C
D
E
29°22'28"
29°22'02"
29°21'36"
29°21'10"
29°20'44"
29°20'18"
29°19'51"
29°19'25"
95°05'52"
95°05'22"
95°04'52"
95°04'22"
95°03'52"
95°03'22"
SEE 4988 MAP
SEE B MAP
4986
RAND McNALLY

1:24,000
1 in. = 2000 ft.
0 0.25 0.5
miles

SEE 4872 MAP

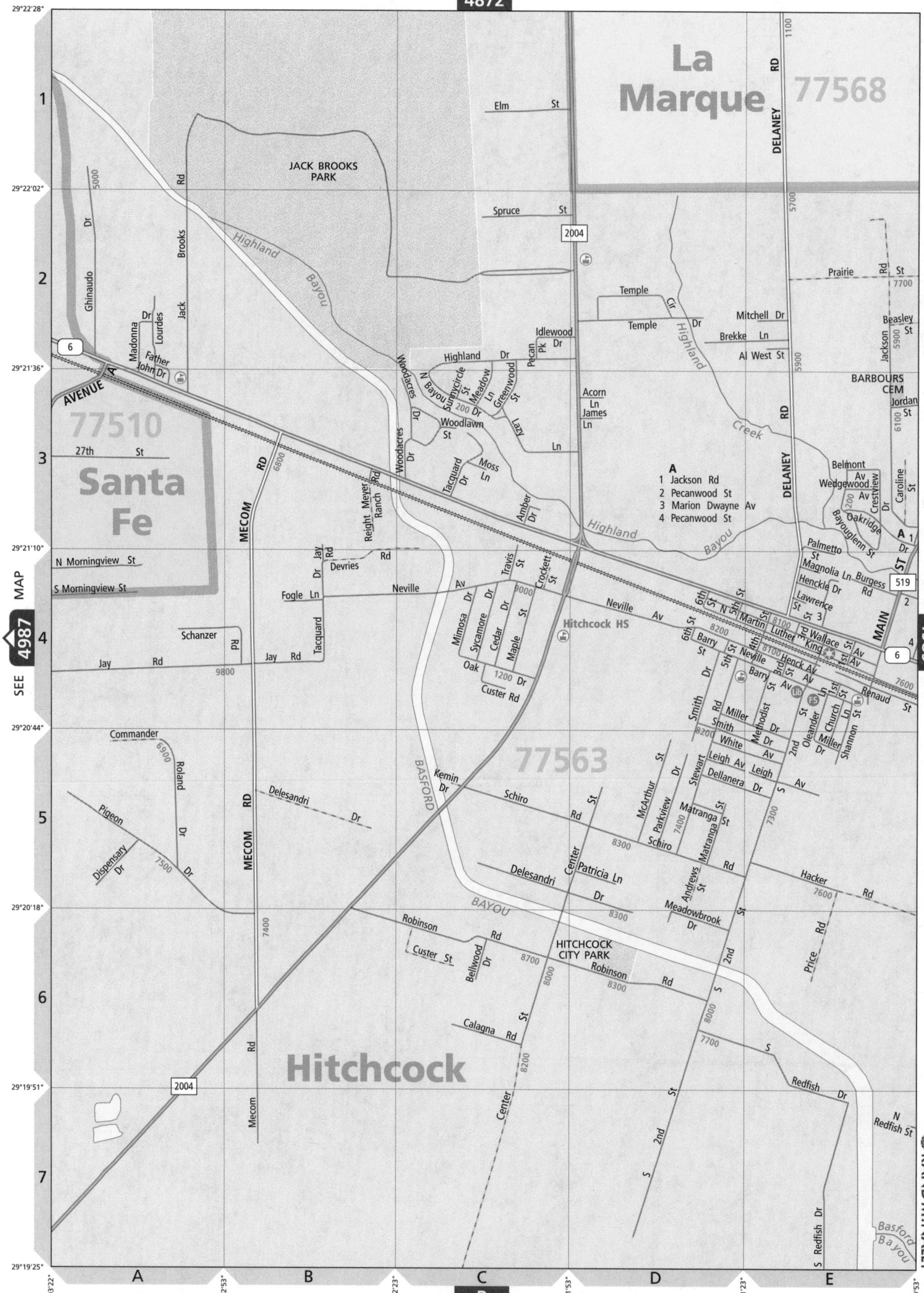
29°22'28"
29°22'02"
29°21'36"
29°21'10"
29°20'44"
29°20'18"
29°19'51"
29°19'25"
95°03'22"
95°02'53"
95°02'23"
95°01'53"
95°01'23"
95°00'53"
A
B
C
D
E
1
2
3
4
5
6
7
La Marque
77568
Santa Fe
77510
77563
Hitchcock
JACK BROOKS PARK
HITCHCOCK CITY PARK
BARBOURS CEM
Hitchcock HS
Elm St
Spruce St
Highland Bayou
Highland Creek
Highland Dr
Basford Bayou
BASFORD BAYOU
Ghinaudo Dr
Madonna Dr
Lourdes
Father John Dr
Jack Brooks Rd
AVENUE A
27th St
N Morningview St
S Morningview St
Schanzer Rd
Jay Rd
Fogle Ln
Neville Av
Devries Rd
Jay Rd
Tacquard Dr
Tacquard Dr
Reight Meyer Ranch Rd
MECOM RD
Mecom Rd
Woodacres Dr
N Bayou
Sunnycircle St
Meadow Ln
Greenwood St
Woodlawn St
Lazy Ln
Moss Ln
Pecan Pk
Idlewood Dr
Acorn Ln
James Ln
Amber Dr
Travis St
Crockett St
Mimosa Dr
Sycamore Dr
Cedar Dr
Maple St
Oak Dr
Custer Rd
Temple Cir
Temple Dr
Mitchell Dr
Brekke Ln
Al West St
Prairie Rd St
Beasley St
Jackson St
Jordan St
DELANEY RD
Belmont Av
Wedgewood Av
Crestview Dr
Caroline St
Oakridge
Bayouglenn St
Palmetto St
Magnolia Ln
Henckle Dr
Burgess Rd
Lawrence St
MAIN ST
6th St
5th St
4th St
3rd St
2nd St
1st St
Martin Luther King
Wallace St
N Neville
Henck Av
Barry St
Barry Av
Renaud St
Smith Dr
Miller Dr
Methodist Dr
White Av
Oleander Dr
Church Ln
Miller Dr
Shannon St
Leigh Av
Dellanera Dr
McArthur St
Parkview Dr
Stewart St
Matranga St
Schiro Rd
Kemin Dr
Commander
Roland Dr
Pigeon Dr
Dispensary Dr
Delesandri Dr
Center St
Patricia Ln
Andrews St
Meadowbrook Dr
Hacker Rd
Price Rd
Robinson Rd
Custer St
Bellwood Dr
Calagna Rd
S 2nd St
Redfish Dr
N Redfish St
S Redfish Dr
A
1 Jackson Rd
2 Pecanwood St
3 Marion Dwayne Av
4 Pecanwood St
2004
6
519
5000
6800
6900
7500
7400
9800
9000
1200
8200
8100
8300
7300
7600
8000
8700
7700
1100
5700
5900
6100
7700
200

SEE 4987 MAP

SEE B MAP

1:24,000
1 in. = 2000 ft.
0 0.25 0.5
miles

SEE 4873 MAP

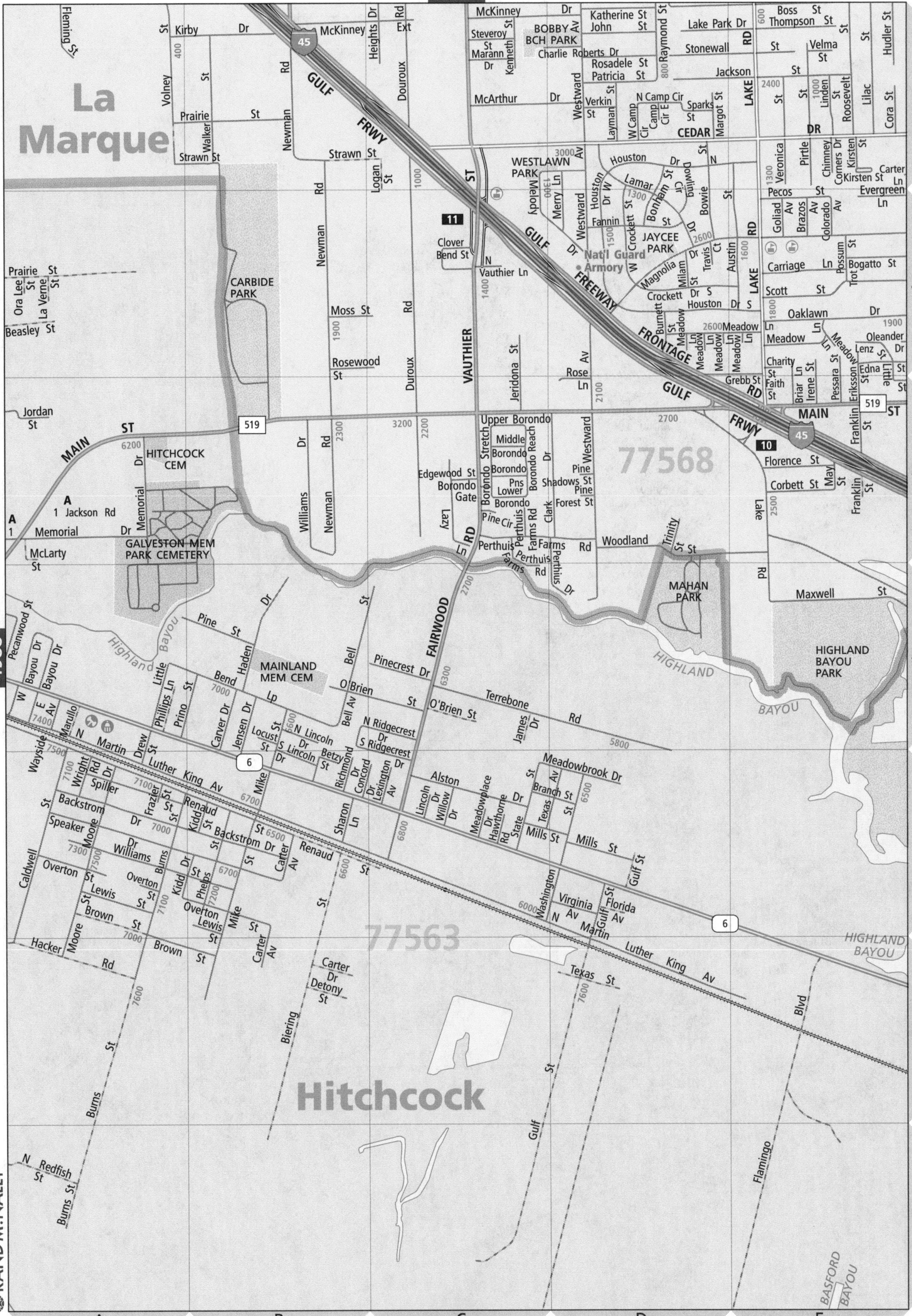
La Marque
Hitchcock
77568
77563
GULF FRWY
GULF FREEWAY FRONTAGE RD
VAUTHIER ST
FAIRWOOD RD
MAIN ST
LAKE RD
CEDAR DR
WESTLAWN PARK
BOBBY BCH PARK
JAYCEE PARK
Nat'l Guard Armory
CARBIDE PARK
HITCHCOCK CEM
GALVESTON MEM PARK CEMETERY
MAINLAND MEM CEM
MAHAN PARK
HIGHLAND BAYOU PARK
HIGHLAND BAYOU
BASFORD BAYOU
Highland Bayou
McKinney Dr
Katherine St
Lake Park Dr
Boss Thompson St
Stonewall
Jackson
McArthur Dr
Kirby Dr
Prairie St
Strawn St
Newman Rd
Duroux Rd
Moss St
Rosewood St
Jordan St
Jackson Rd
Memorial Dr
McLarty St
Upper Borondo
Woodland Rd
Perthuis Farms Rd
Maxwell St
Pinecrest Dr
O'Brien St
Terrebone Rd
Martin Luther King Av
Mills St
Texas St
Biering St
Burns St
Gulf St
Flamingo Blvd
Redfish St
Hacker Rd
Caldwell
Overton St
Backstrom Dr
Renaud St
Florence St
Corbett St
Oaklawn Dr
Carriage Ln
Scott St
Pecos St
Meadowbrook Dr
Carter Dr
Detony St
Williams Dr
Wayside
1 2 3 4 5 6 7
A B C D E
29°22'25"
29°21'59"
29°21'33"
29°21'07"
29°20'41"
29°20'14"
29°19'48"
29°19'22"
95°00'53"
95°00'23"
94°59'54"
94°59'24"
94°58'54"
94°58'24"

SEE 4990 MAP

SEE 4988 MAP

SEE 5104 MAP

SEE 4874 MAP

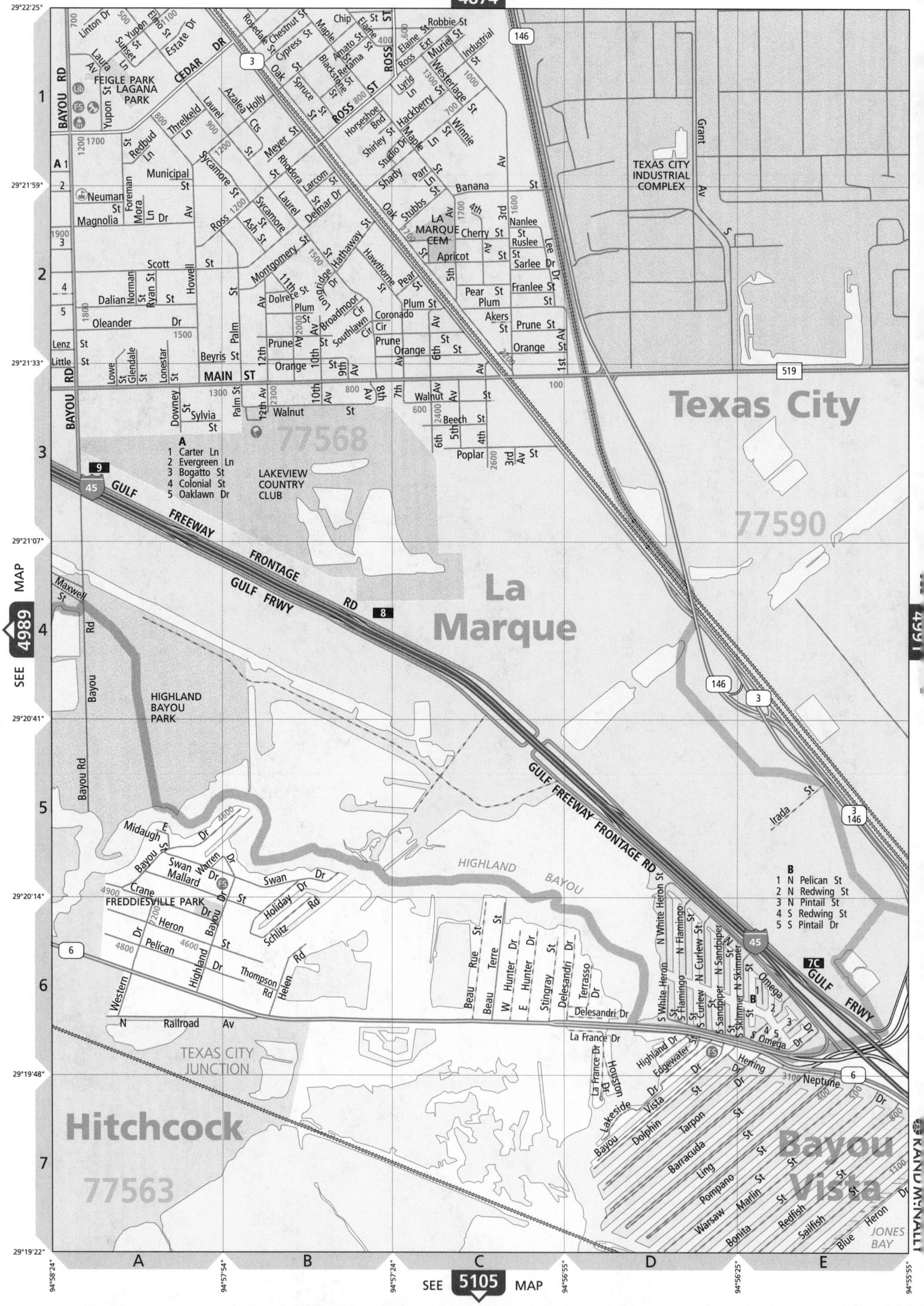
1:24,000
1 in. = 2000 ft.
0 0.25 0.5
miles
Texas City
77590
La Marque
77568
Hitchcock
77563
Bayou Vista
TEXAS CITY INDUSTRIAL COMPLEX
LAKEVIEW COUNTRY CLUB
HIGHLAND BAYOU PARK
FEIGLE PARK
LAGANA PARK
LA MARQUE CEM
FREDDIESVILLE PARK
TEXAS CITY JUNCTION
GULF FREEWAY
FRONTAGE RD
GULF FRWY
GULF FREEWAY FRONTAGE RD
HIGHLAND BAYOU
JONES BAY
MAIN ST
CEDAR DR
ROSS ST
BAYOU RD
A
1 Carter Ln
2 Evergreen Ln
3 Bogatto St
4 Colonial St
5 Oaklawn Dr
B
1 N Pelican St
2 N Redwing St
3 N Pintail St
4 S Redwing St
5 S Pintail Dr
RAND McNALLY

SEE 4989 MAP

SEE 4991 MAP

SEE 5105 MAP

1:24,000
1 in. = 2000 ft.
0 0.25 0.5
miles

SEE 4875 MAP

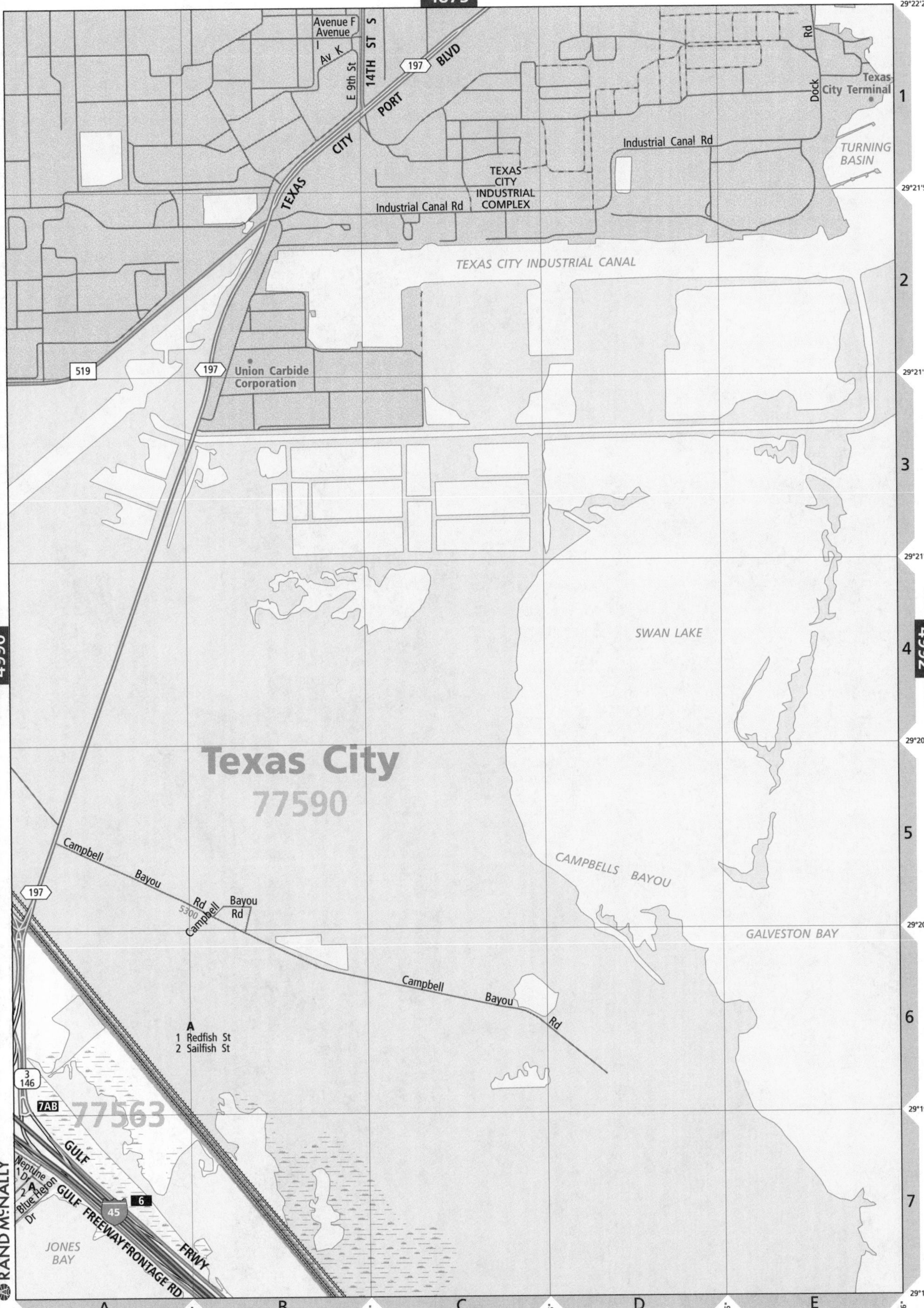
Avenue F
Avenue
Av K
E 9th St
14TH ST S
197
BLVD
PORT
CITY
TEXAS
Dock Rd
Texas City Terminal
Industrial Canal Rd
TURNING BASIN
TEXAS CITY INDUSTRIAL COMPLEX
Industrial Canal Rd
TEXAS CITY INDUSTRIAL CANAL
519
197
Union Carbide Corporation
SWAN LAKE
Texas City
77590
Campbell Bayou Rd
CAMPBELLS BAYOU
197
5300
Campbell Bayou Rd
GALVESTON BAY
Campbell Bayou Rd
A
1 Redfish St
2 Sailfish St
3
146
7AB
77563
GULF
Neptune Dr
Blue Heron Dr
GULF FREEWAY FRONTAGE RD
45
6
FRWY
JONES BAY
29°22'22"
29°21'56"
29°21'29"
29°21'03"
29°20'37"
29°20'11"
29°19'45"
29°19'19"
1
2
3
4
5
6
7
A
B
C
D
E
94°55'55"
94°55'25"
94°54'55"
94°54'25"
94°53'56"
94°53'26"

SEE 4992 MAP

SEE 4990 MAP

SEE 5106 MAP

1:24,000
1 in. = 2000 ft.
0 0.25 0.5
miles

SEE 4876 MAP

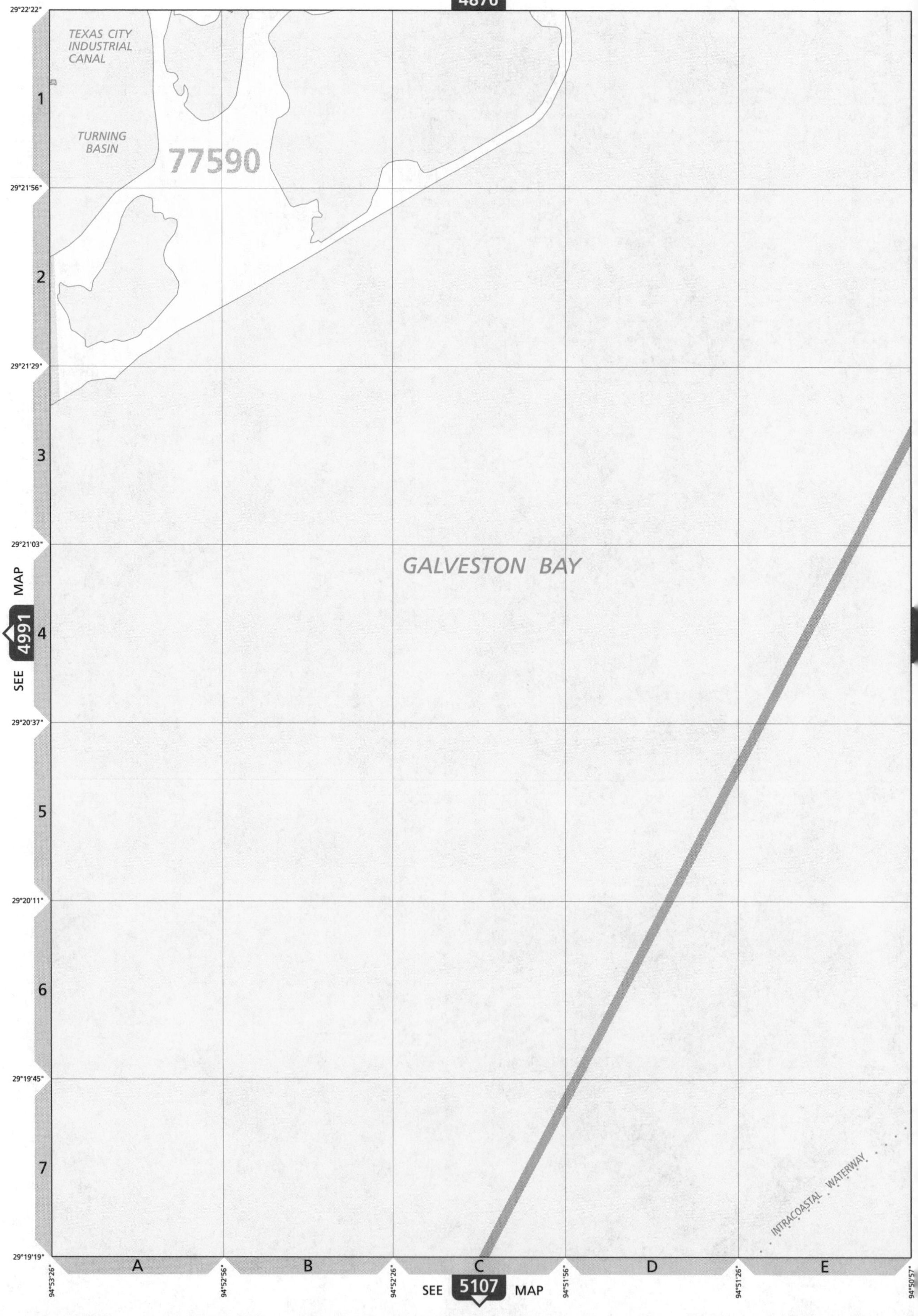
TEXAS CITY INDUSTRIAL CANAL
TURNING BASIN
77590
GALVESTON BAY
INTRACOASTAL WATERWAY
1
2
3
4
5
6
7
A
B
C
D
E
29°22'22"
29°21'56"
29°21'29"
29°21'03"
29°20'37"
29°20'11"
29°19'45"
29°19'19"
94°53'26"
94°52'56"
94°52'26"
94°51'56"
94°51'26"
94°50'57"

SEE 4991 MAP

SEE 5107 MAP

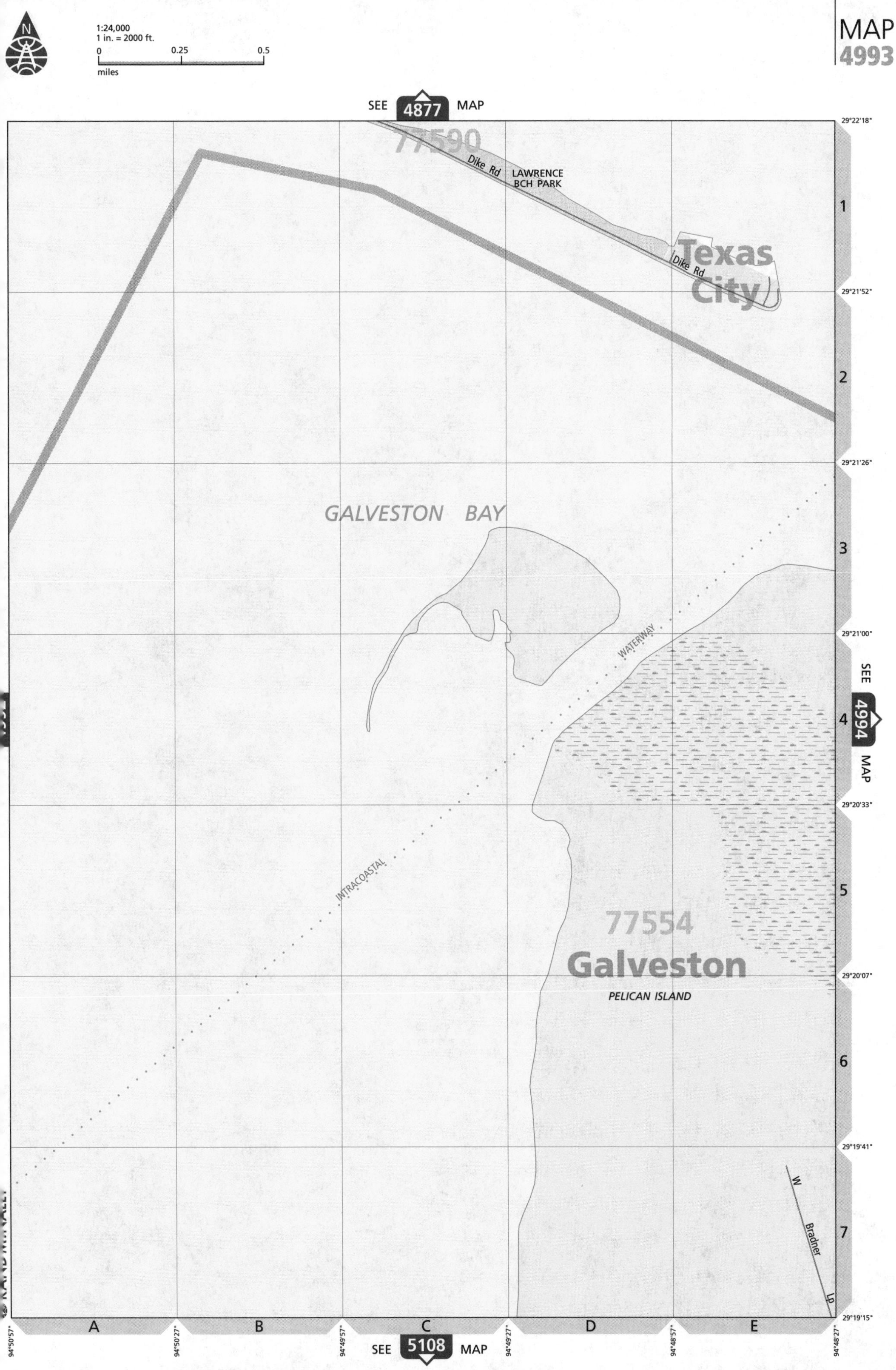
1:24,000
1 in. = 2000 ft.
0
0.25
0.5
miles
SEE 4877 MAP
77590
Dike Rd
LAWRENCE
BCH PARK
Texas
City
Dike Rd
GALVESTON BAY
WATERWAY
INTRACOASTAL
77554
Galveston
PELICAN ISLAND
W
Bradner
Lp
SEE 4994 MAP
SEE 5108 MAP
A
B
C
D
E
1
2
3
4
5
6
7
29°22'18"
29°21'52"
29°21'26"
29°21'00"
29°20'33"
29°20'07"
29°19'41"
29°19'15"
94°50'57"
94°50'27"
94°49'57"
94°49'27"
94°48'57"
94°48'27"

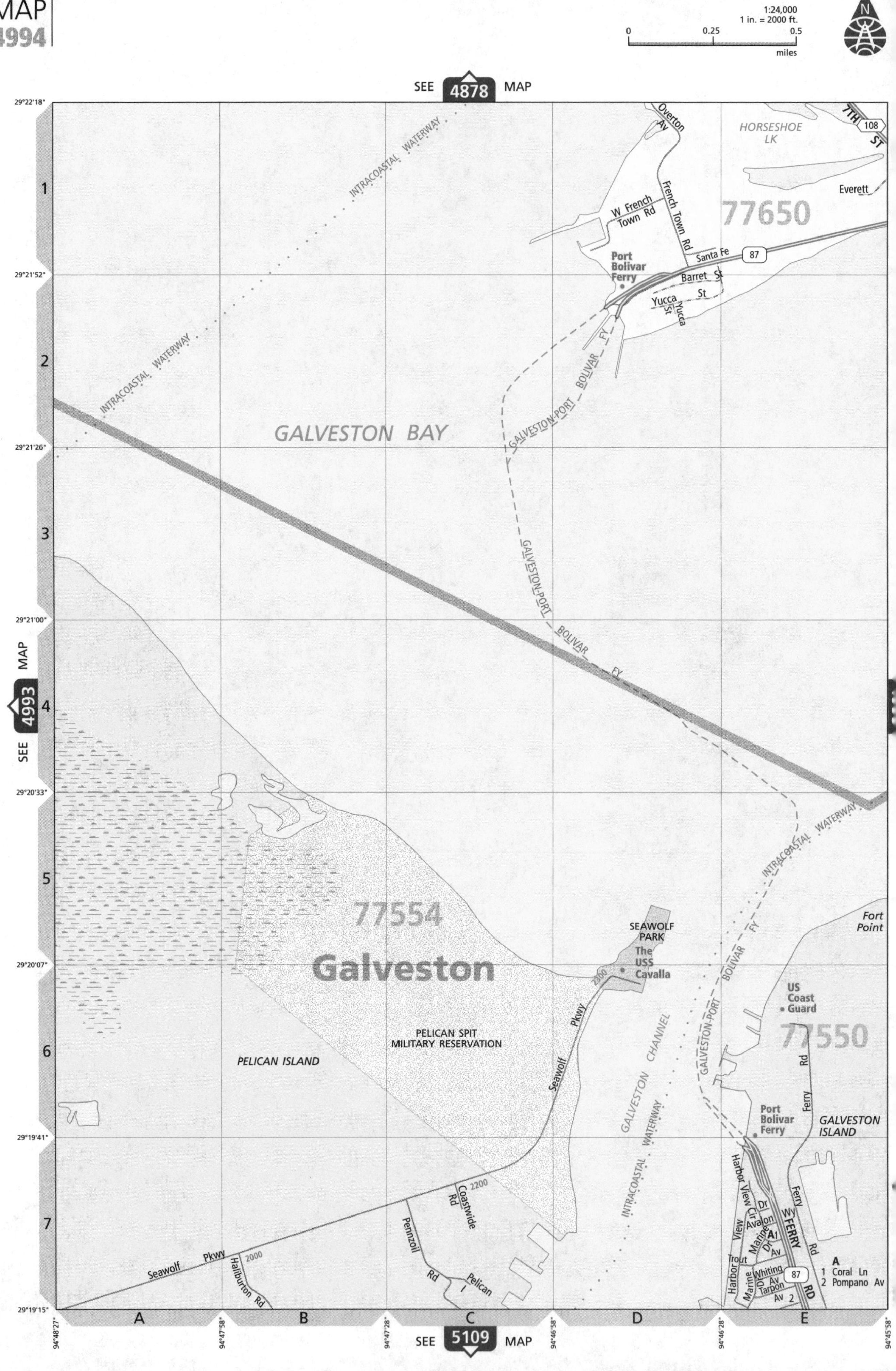
1:24,000
1 in. = 2000 ft.
0
0.25
0.5
miles
N
SEE 4878 MAP
SEE 4993 MAP
SEE 5109 MAP
29°22'18"
29°21'52"
29°21'26"
29°21'00"
29°20'33"
29°20'07"
29°19'41"
29°19'15"
94°48'27"
94°47'58"
94°47'28"
94°46'58"
94°46'28"
94°45'58"
1
2
3
4
5
6
7
A
B
C
D
E
INTRACOASTAL WATERWAY
GALVESTON BAY
HORSESHOE LK
Overton Av
7TH ST
108
Everett
W French Town Rd
French Town Rd
77650
Santa Fe
87
Port Bolivar Ferry
Barret St
Yucca St
Yucca St
GALVESTON-PORT BOLIVAR FY
77554
Galveston
SEAWOLF PARK
The USS Cavalla
Fort Point
US Coast Guard
77550
PELICAN SPIT MILITARY RESERVATION
PELICAN ISLAND
Seawolf Pkwy
2300
GALVESTON CHANNEL
Ferry Rd
GALVESTON ISLAND
Harbor View Cir
Dr
Avalon
Marine Dr
A1
Av
Wy
FERRY RD
Trout
Harbor
Marine
Whiting Av
Tarpon
Av 2
87
A
1 Coral Ln
2 Pompano Av
Coastwide Rd
2200
Pennzoil Rd
Pelican
Halliburton Rd
2000

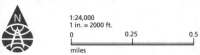

1:24,000
1 in. = 2000 ft.
0 0.25 0.5
miles

SEE 4879 MAP

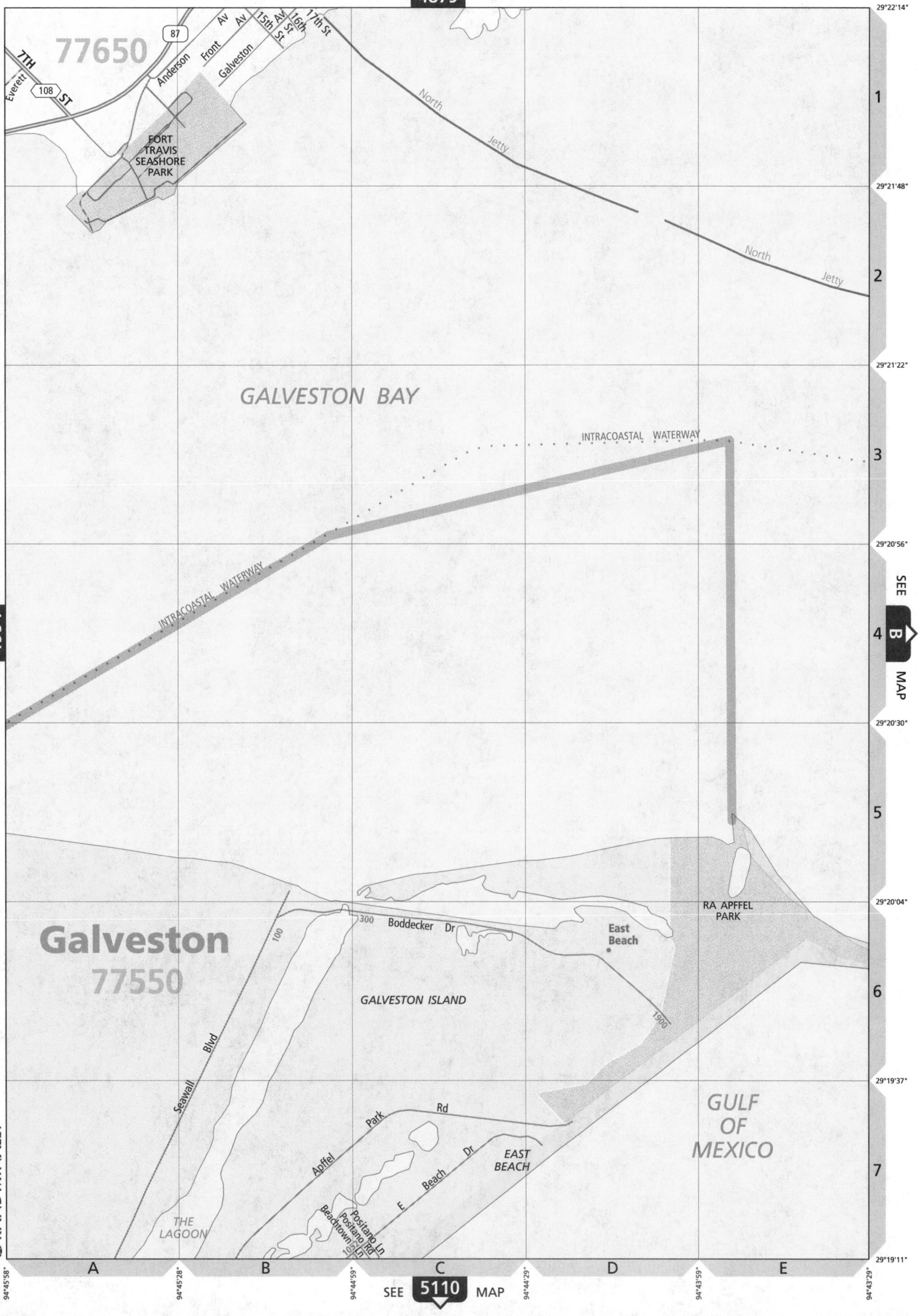
77650
7TH ST
Everett
108
87
Anderson
Front Av
Av
15th Av
16th St
St
17th St
Galveston
FORT TRAVIS SEASHORE PARK
North Jetty
North Jetty
GALVESTON BAY
INTRACOASTAL WATERWAY
INTRACOASTAL WATERWAY
RA APFFEL PARK
300
Boddecker Dr
East Beach
Galveston
77550
100
GALVESTON ISLAND
1900
Seawall Blvd
Park Rd
Apffel
GULF OF MEXICO
E Beach Dr
EAST BEACH
THE LAGOON
Beachtown Ln
Positano Ln
Positano Rd
1052
29°22'14"
29°21'48"
29°21'22"
29°20'56"
29°20'30"
29°20'04"
29°19'37"
29°19'11"
1
2
3
4
5
6
7
A
B
C
D
E
94°45'58"
94°45'28"
94°44'59"
94°44'29"
94°43'59"
94°43'29"

SEE B MAP

SEE 5110 MAP

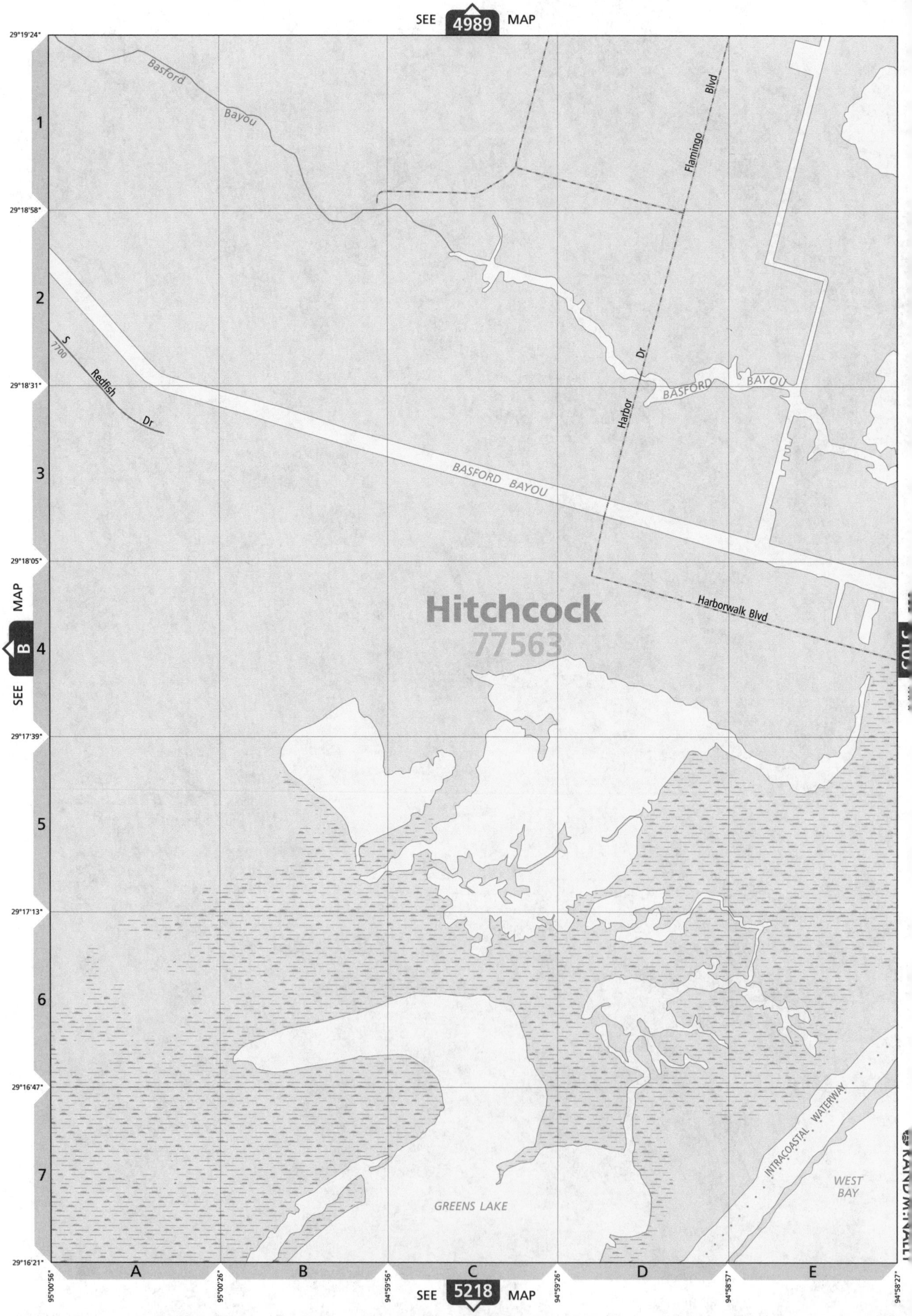
1:24,000
1 in. = 2000 ft.
0
0.25
0.5
miles
N
SEE 4989 MAP
SEE 5218 MAP
SEE B MAP
29°19'24"
29°18'58"
29°18'31"
29°18'05"
29°17'39"
29°17'13"
29°16'47"
29°16'21"
95°00'56"
95°00'26"
94°59'56"
94°59'26"
94°58'57"
94°58'27"
1
2
3
4
5
6
7
A
B
C
D
E
Basford
Bayou
S
7700
Redfish
Dr
BASFORD BAYOU
Flamingo
Blvd
Harbor
Dr
BASFORD
BAYOU
Harborwalk Blvd
Hitchcock
77563
GREENS LAKE
INTRACOASTAL WATERWAY
WEST
BAY

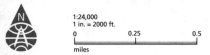

1:24,000
1 in. = 2000 ft.
0 0.25 0.5
miles

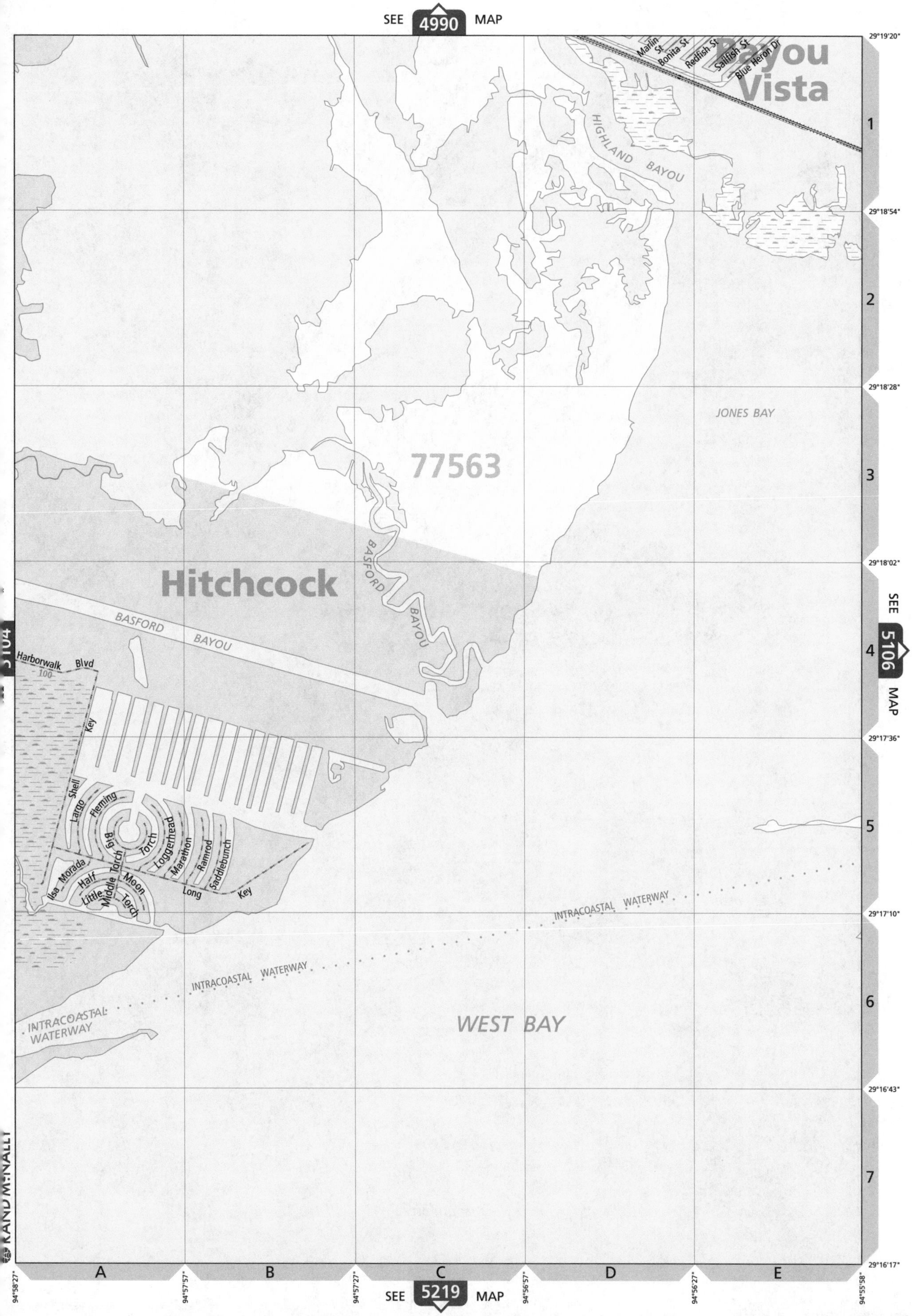
SEE 4990 MAP
Bayou Vista
Marlin St
Bonita St
Redfish St
Sailfish St
Blue Heron Dr
HIGHLAND BAYOU
JONES BAY
77563
Hitchcock
BASFORD BAYOU
Harborwalk Blvd
100
Key
Shell
Largo
Fleming
Big
Torch
Loggerhead
Marathon
Ramrod
Saddlebunch
Ilsa Morada
Half
Little
Middle Torch
Moon
Torch
Long
Key
INTRACOASTAL WATERWAY
WEST BAY
29°19'20"
29°18'54"
29°18'28"
29°18'02"
29°17'36"
29°17'10"
29°16'43"
29°16'17"
94°58'27"
94°57'57"
94°57'27"
94°56'57"
94°56'27"
94°55'58"
A
B
C
D
E
1
2
3
4
5
6
7
SEE 5106 MAP
5104
SEE 5219 MAP
RAND McNALLY

1:24,000
1 in. = 2000 ft.
0 0.25 0.5
miles

SEE 4991 MAP

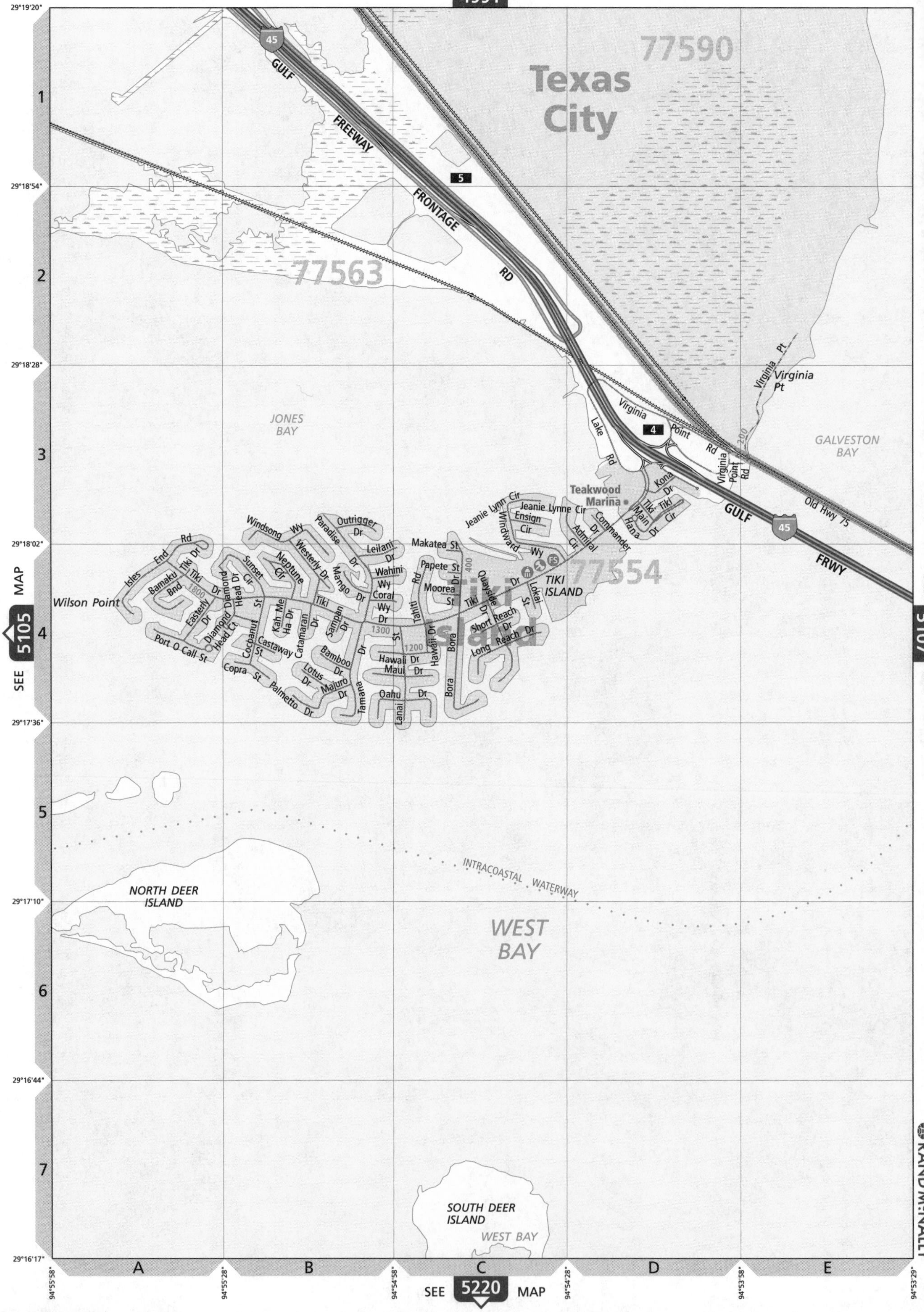
Texas City
77590
77563
77554
GULF FREEWAY
FRONTAGE RD
JONES BAY
GALVESTON BAY
Virginia Pt
Virginia Point Rd
Lake Rd
Teakwood Marina
Tiki Island
TIKI ISLAND
Wilson Point
GULF FRWY
Old Hwy 75
Commander
Admiral Cir
Windward Wy
Jeanie Lynn Cir
Jeanie Lynne Cir
Ensign Cir
Kona Dr
Tiki Cir
Main Dr
Hana
Makatea St
Papete St
Moorea St
Tiki Dr
Quayside Dr
Lokai St
Short Reach Dr
Long Reach Dr
Bora
Hawaii Dr
Maui Dr
Oahu Dr
Lanai St
Tahiti Rd
Tamana Dr
Maluro Dr
Lotus Dr
Bamboo Dr
Sampan Dr
Catamaran Dr
Mango Dr
Leilani Dr
Wahini Wy
Coral Wy
Outrigger Dr
Paradise Dr
Westerly Dr
Neptune Cir
Windsong Wy
Sunset Cir
Kah Me Ha Dr
Castaway St
Cocoanut St
Copra St
Palmetto Dr
Port O Call St
Diamond Head Cir
Diamond Head Ct
Easterly Dr
Tiki Dr
Bamaku Bnd
Isles End Rd
NORTH DEER ISLAND
INTRACOASTAL WATERWAY
WEST BAY
SOUTH DEER ISLAND
1, 2, 3, 4, 5, 6, 7
A, B, C, D, E

SEE 5105 MAP

SEE 5220 MAP

1:24,000
1 in. = 2000 ft.
0
0.25
0.5
miles
SEE 4992 MAP
SEE 5108 MAP
SEE 5221 MAP
GALVESTON BAY
INTRACOASTAL
WATERWAY
GULF
FRWY
Old
Hwy
75
Galveston
HARBORSIDE
DR
275
Channelview
Dr
67th
St
Channel View Dr
Pruitt
Dr
81st
St
79th
St
77th
St
Bayside
Av
77551
77554
71st
St
GALVESTON
ISLAND
BROADWAY
ST
1B
1C
Palm Cove Ct
Walsh
Ln
Harborside
Dr
Lillian
Commodore
Ln
Payco
Marina
Blume
Dr
Lewis
Ln
W Bay
Rd
93rd
St
91st
Teichman
Rd
89th
1/2 St
89th
St
91st
St
Skinner
Ln
Bamar
Ln
Cozy Cove Ln
Schattel
Ln
Cozy
Ln
Teichman Rd
Teichman
Point
TEICHMAN
COVE
WEST BAY
COZY
COVE
OFFATTS BAYOU
Scholes
International
Airport
at Galveston
Moody Gdns
IMAX 3D
Theater
Moody Gardens
Moody Gardens Convention
Center
Lockheed
Dr
Hope Blvd
GALVESTON ISLAND
MELAGER
COVE
SYDNOR BAYOU
Airway
Ln
Airways Ln
Travel Air
Pilot
Ln
Darcy Dr
103rd
St
A
B
C
D
E
1
2
3
4
5
6
7
29°19'17"
29°18'51"
29°18'25"
29°17'58"
29°17'32"
29°17'06"
29°16'40"
29°16'14"
94°53'29"
94°52'59"
94°52'29"
94°51'59"
94°51'29"
94°50'59"

1:24,000
1 in. = 2000 ft.
0 0.25 0.5
miles

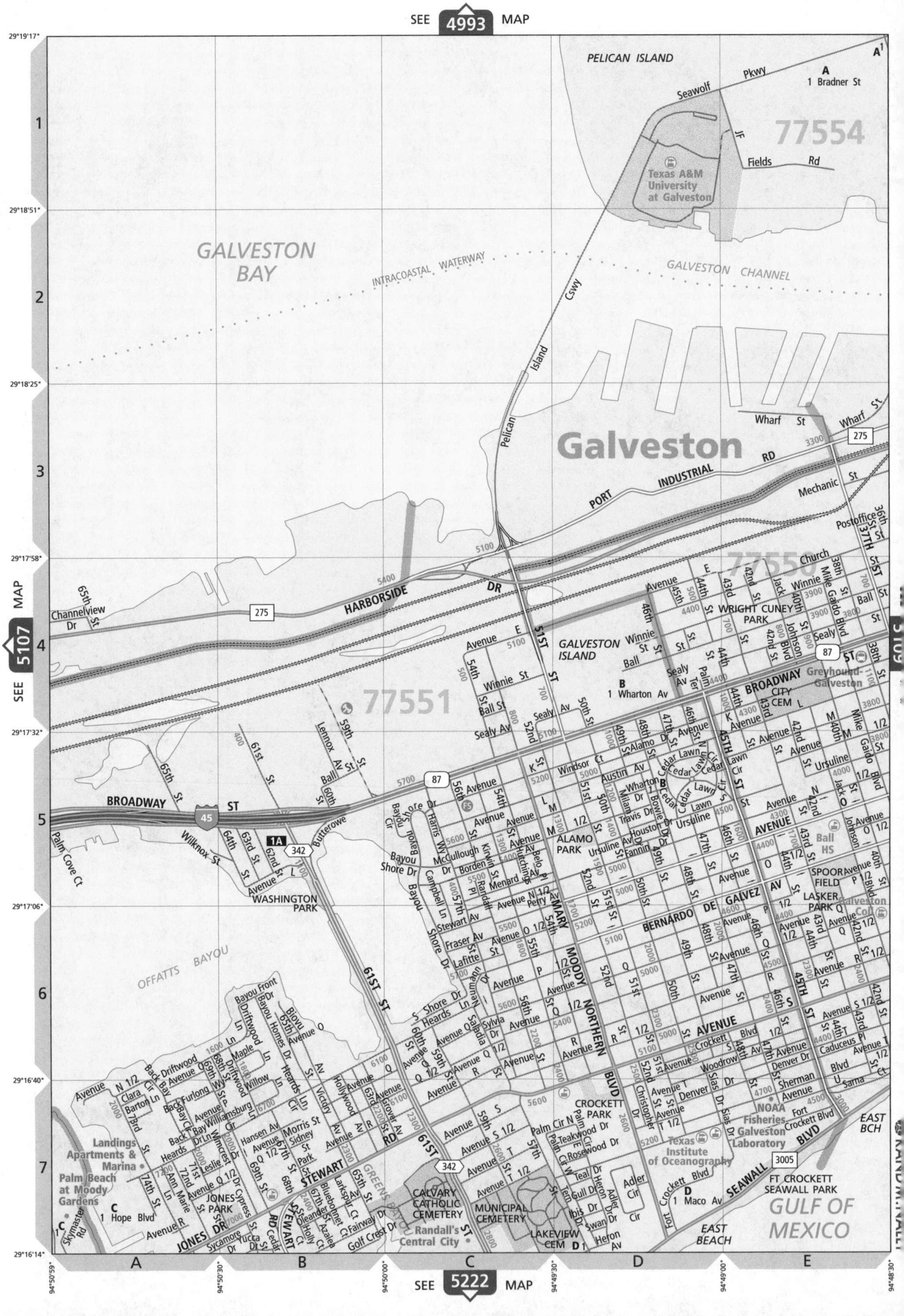
SEE 4993 MAP
SEE 5107 MAP
SEE 5222 MAP
PELICAN ISLAND
Seawolf Pkwy
1 Bradner St
77554
Fields Rd
Texas A&M University at Galveston
GALVESTON BAY
INTRACOASTAL WATERWAY
GALVESTON CHANNEL
Pelican Island Cswy
Galveston
Wharf St
PORT INDUSTRIAL RD
Mechanic St
HARBORSIDE DR
Channelview Dr
65th St
77550
77551
GALVESTON ISLAND
1 Wharton Av
BROADWAY
BROADWAY ST
CITY CEM
Greyhound-Galveston
WRIGHT CUNEY PARK
51ST ST
45TH ST
Palm Cove Ct
Wilknox St
Butterowe
WASHINGTON PARK
OFFATTS BAYOU
ALAMO PARK
Cedar Lawn Cir
BERNARDO DE GALVEZ AV
MOODY
MARY
NORTHERN BLVD
Ball HS
SPOOR FIELD
LASKER PARK
Galveston Coll
61ST ST
STEWART RD
JONES DR
JONES PARK
Landings Apartments & Marina
Palm Beach at Moody Gardens
1 Hope Blvd
CALVARY CATHOLIC CEMETERY
Randall's Central City
MUNICIPAL CEMETERY
LAKEVIEW CEM
CROCKETT PARK
Texas Institute of Oceanography
NOAA Fisheries Galveston Laboratory
1 Maco Av
SEAWALL BLVD
FT CROCKETT SEAWALL PARK
EAST BEACH
EAST BCH
GULF OF MEXICO
29°19'17"
29°18'51"
29°18'25"
29°17'58"
29°17'32"
29°17'06"
29°16'40"
29°16'14"
94°50'59"
94°50'30"
94°50'00"
94°49'30"
94°49'00"
94°48'30"

1:24,000
1 in. = 2000 ft.
0 0.25 0.5
miles

SEE 4994 MAP

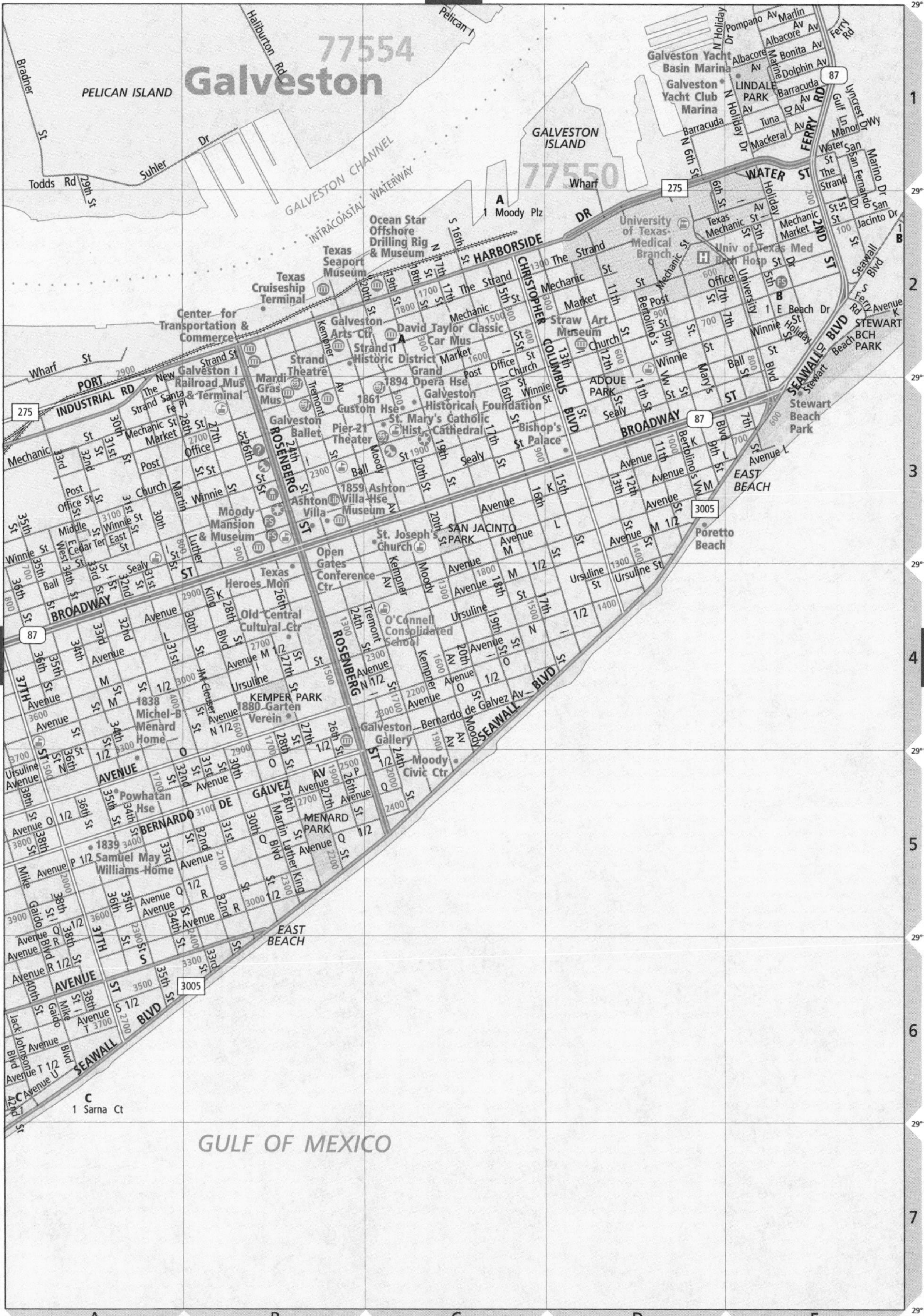
Galveston
77554
77550
PELICAN ISLAND
GALVESTON ISLAND
GALVESTON CHANNEL
INTRACOASTAL WATERWAY
GULF OF MEXICO
Galveston Yacht Basin Marina
Galveston Yacht Club Marina
LINDALE PARK
University of Texas-Medical Branch
Univ of Texas Med Brch Hosp
Ocean Star Offshore Drilling Rig & Museum
Texas Seaport Museum
Texas Cruiseship Terminal
Center for Transportation & Commerce
Galveston Arts Ctr
David Taylor Classic Car Mus
Strand Historic District
Strand Theatre
Grand 1894 Opera Hse
Galveston Historical Foundation
1861 Custom Hse
Galveston Railroad Mus & Terminal
Mardi Gras Mus
Galveston Ballet
Pier 21 Theater
St. Mary's Catholic Cathedral
Bishop's Palace
Straw Art Museum
ADOUE PARK
1859 Ashton Villa Hse Museum
Moody Mansion & Museum
St. Joseph's Church
SAN JACINTO PARK
Open Gates Conference Ctr
Texas Heroes Mon
Old Central Cultural Ctr
O'Connell Consolidated School
KEMPER PARK
1880 Garten Verein
1838 Michel-B Menard Home
Galveston Gallery
Moody Civic Ctr
Powhatan Hse
MENARD PARK
1839 Samuel May Williams Home
EAST BEACH
Stewart Beach Park
STEWART BCH PARK
Poretto Beach
HARBORSIDE DR
BROADWAY
ROSENBERG ST
CHRISTOPHER COLUMBUS BLVD
SEAWALL BLVD
FERRY RD
WATER ST
PORT INDUSTRIAL RD
AVENUE O
BERNARDO DE GALVEZ AV
37TH ST
2ND ST
87
275
3005
A 1 Moody Plz
B 1 E Beach Dr
C 1 Sarna Ct
1 2 3 4 5 6 7
A B C D E
29°19'13"
29°18'47"
29°18'21"
29°17'55"
29°17'29"
29°17'02"
29°16'36"
29°16'10"
94°48'30"
94°48'01"
94°47'31"
94°47'01"
94°46'31"
94°46'01"

SEE 5110 MAP

SEE B MAP

SEE 4995 MAP

1:24,000
1 in. = 2000 ft.
0 0.25 0.5
miles
N
29°19'13"
29°18'47"
29°18'21"
29°17'55"
29°17'29"
29°17'02"
29°16'36"
29°16'10"
94°46'01"
94°45'31"
94°45'02"
94°44'32"
94°44'02"
94°43'32"
1
2
3
4
5
6
7
A
B
C
D
E
77550
THE LAGOON
Galveston
GALVESTON ISLAND
Seawall Blvd
Park Rd
E Beach Dr
Apffel Dr
Lakeside
400
EAST BEACH
E Beach Dr
400
STEWART BEACH PARK
Seabreeze Ln
Ramsar Rd
Seaside
Positano Rd
Beachtown Ln
GULF OF MEXICO

SEE 5109 MAP

SEE B MAP

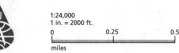

1:24,000
1 in. = 2000 ft.
0 0.25 0.5
miles

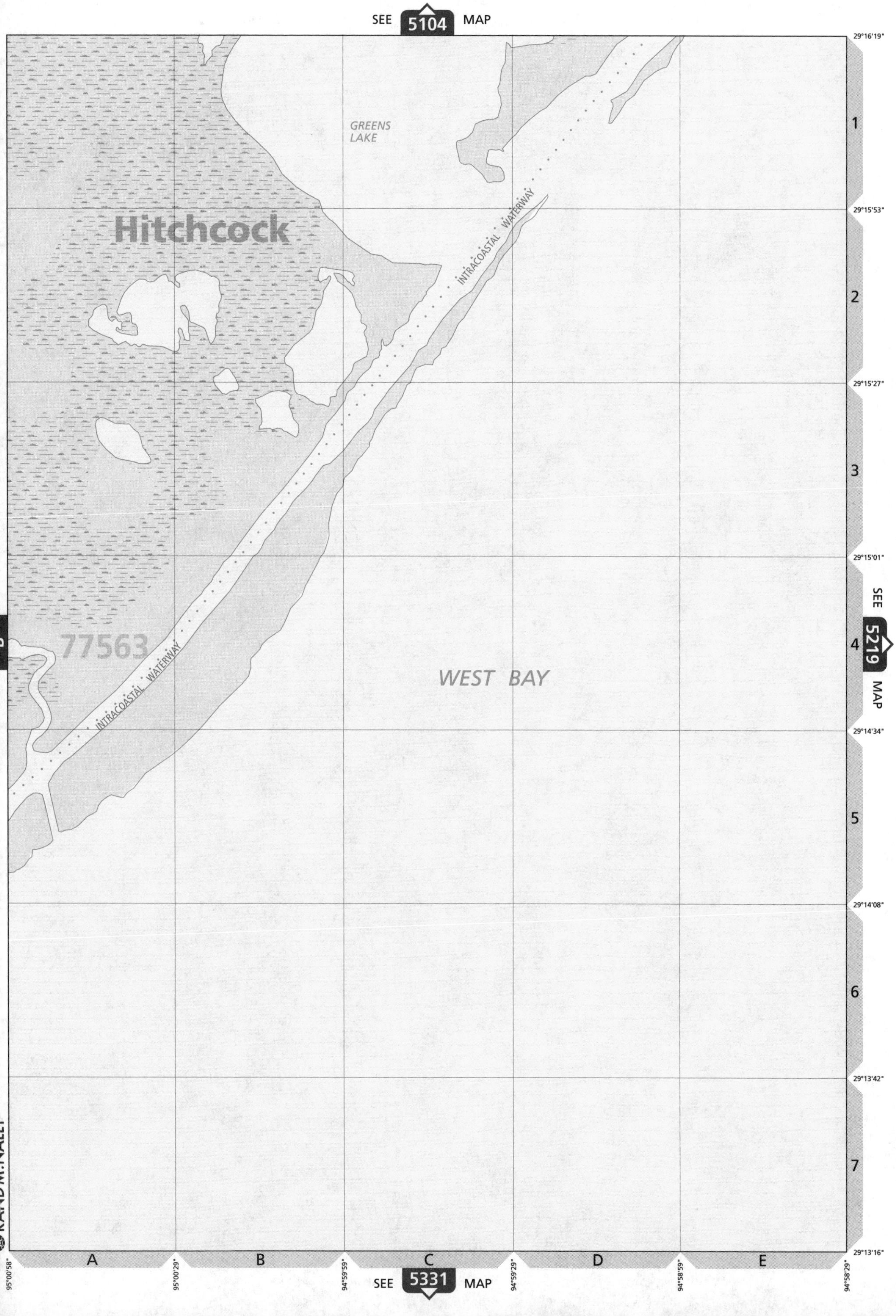
SEE 5104 MAP
GREENS
LAKE
Hitchcock
INTRACOASTAL WATERWAY
77563
INTRACOASTAL WATERWAY
WEST BAY
SEE 5219 MAP
29°16'19"
29°15'53"
29°15'27"
29°15'01"
29°14'34"
29°14'08"
29°13'42"
29°13'16"
1
2
3
4
5
6
7
A
B
C
D
E
95°00'58"
95°00'29"
94°59'59"
94°59'29"
94°58'59"
94°58'29"
SEE 5331 MAP

SEE 5105 MAP

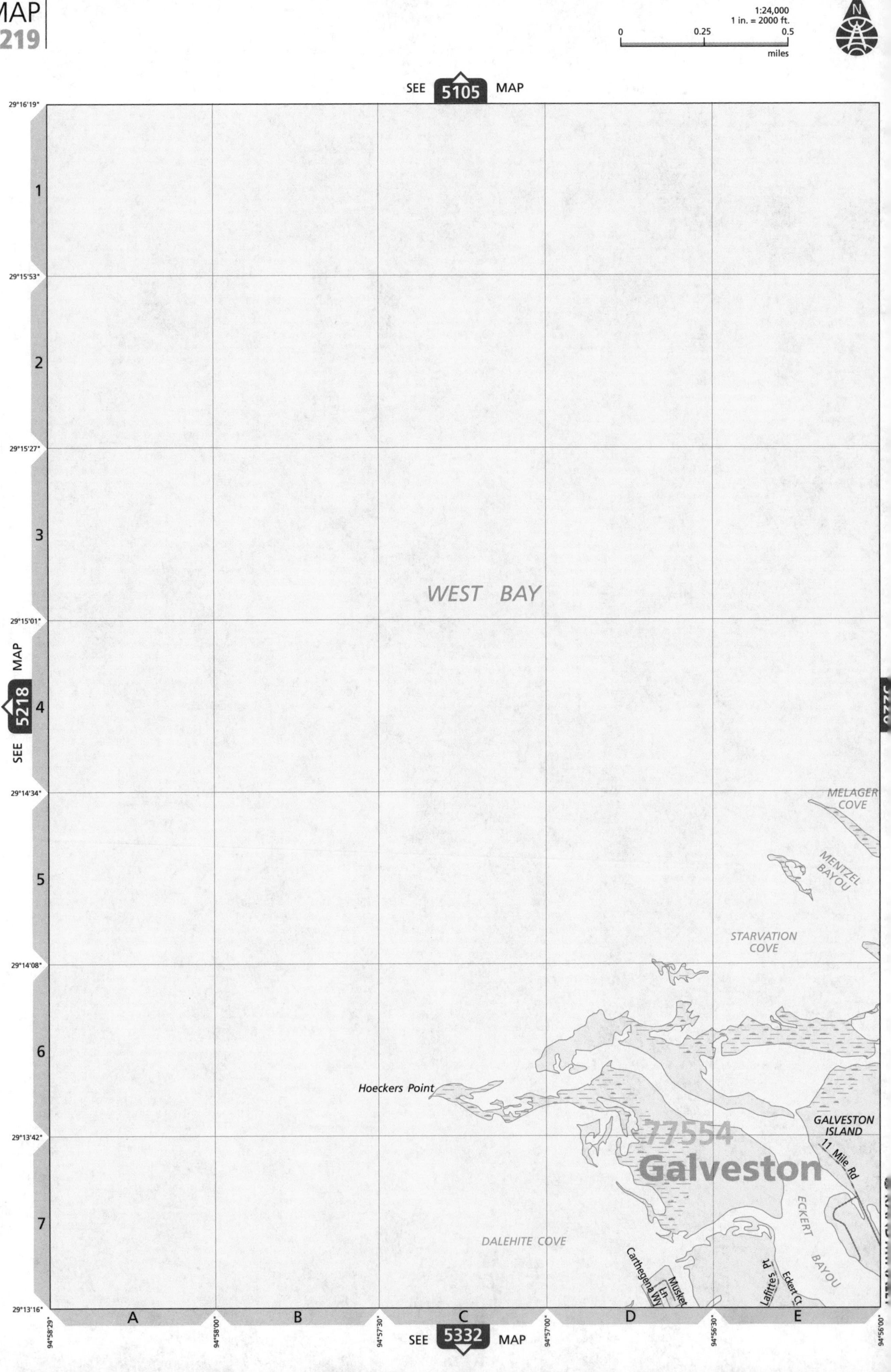
1:24,000
1 in. = 2000 ft.
0
0.25
0.5
miles
N
29°16'19"
29°15'53"
29°15'27"
29°15'01"
29°14'34"
29°14'08"
29°13'42"
29°13'16"
94°58'29"
94°58'00"
94°57'30"
94°57'00"
94°56'30"
94°56'00"
1
2
3
4
5
6
7
A
B
C
D
E
WEST BAY
MELAGER COVE
MENTZEL BAYOU
STARVATION COVE
Hoeckers Point
GALVESTON ISLAND
77554
Galveston
11 Mile Rd
ECKERT BAYOU
DALEHITE COVE
Carthegena Wy
Musket Ln
Lafittes Pt
Eckert Ct

SEE 5218 MAP

SEE 5332 MAP

SEE 5106 MAP

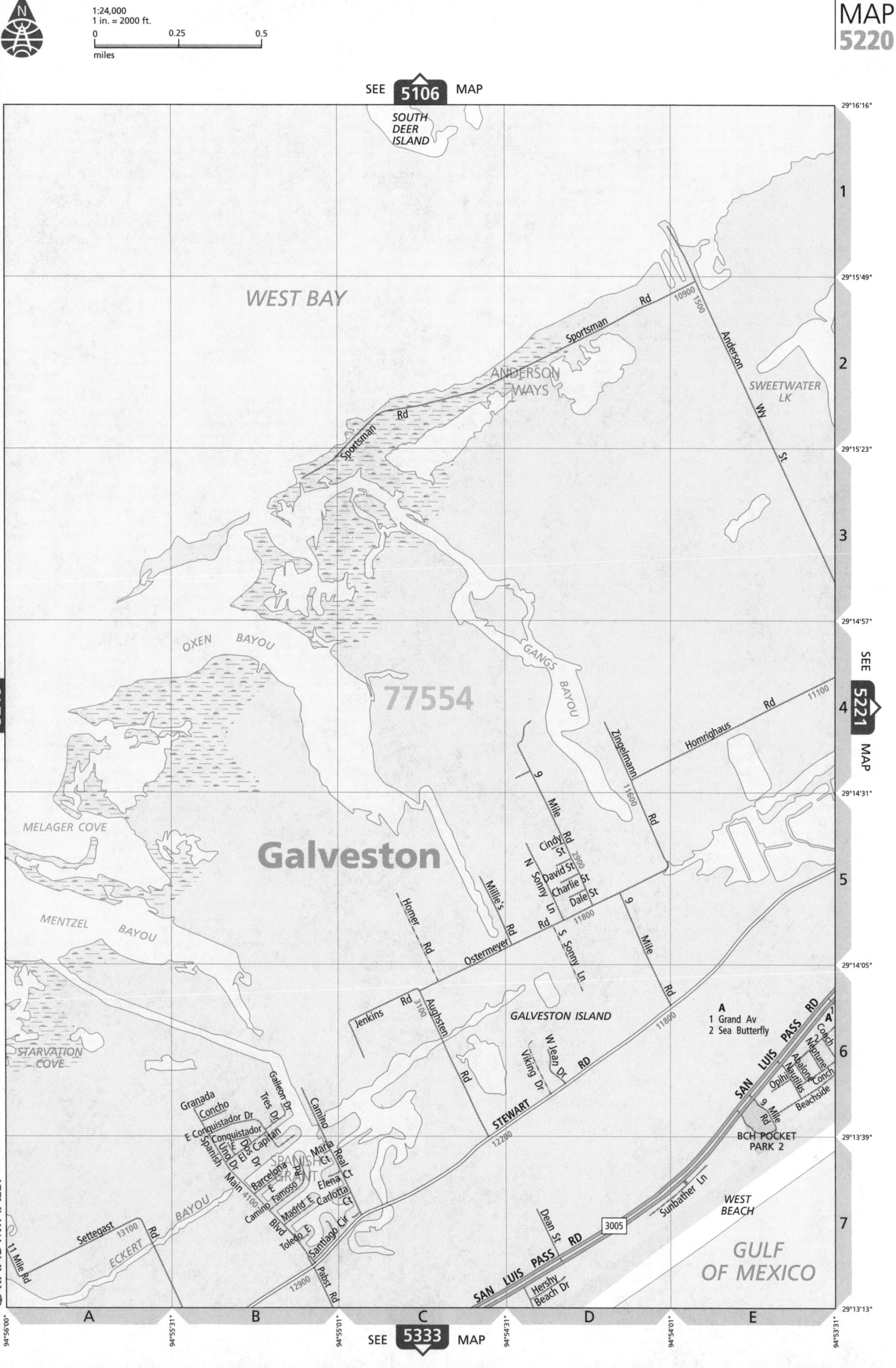
1:24,000
1 in. = 2000 ft.
0 0.25 0.5
miles
WEST BAY
SOUTH DEER ISLAND
Sportsman Rd
Anderson Wy St
ANDERSON WAYS
SWEETWATER LK
OXEN BAYOU
GANGS BAYOU
77554
MELAGER COVE
Galveston
MENTZEL BAYOU
STARVATION COVE
Homrighaus Rd
Zingelmann Rd
9 Mile Rd
Cindy St
David St
Charlie St
Dale St
N Sonny Ln
S Sonny Ln
Millie's Rd
Homer Rd
Ostermeyer Rd
Jenkins Rd
Aughsten Rd
GALVESTON ISLAND
Viking Dr
W Jean Dr
STEWART RD
A
1 Grand Av
2 Sea Butterfly
SAN LUIS PASS RD
Conch
Neptune
Abalone
Nautilus
Ophir
Beachside
BCH POCKET PARK 2
Sunbather Ln
WEST BEACH
GULF OF MEXICO
Dean St
3005
Hershy Beach Dr
Granada
Concho
Galleon Dr
Tres Dr
E Conquistador Dr
Conquistador
Camino Real
Spanish Main
Uno Dr
Dos Dr
El Capitan
SPANISH GRANT
Maria Ct
Elena Ct
Carlotta Ct
Barcelona Rd
Camino Famoso E
Blvd
Madrid E
Toledo E
Santiago Cir
Pabst Rd
Settegast Rd
11 Mile Rd
ECKERT BAYOU
29°16'16"
29°15'49"
29°15'23"
29°14'57"
29°14'31"
29°14'05"
29°13'39"
29°13'13"
94°56'00"
94°55'31"
94°55'01"
94°54'31"
94°54'01"
94°53'31"
A B C D E
1 2 3 4 5 6 7

SEE 5221 MAP

SEE 5333 MAP

1:24,000
1 in. = 2000 ft.
0 0.25 0.5
miles

SEE 5107 MAP

WEST BAY
Galveston
GALVESTON ISLAND
77554
SWEETWATER LAKE
GALVESTON I MUNICIPAL GOLF COURSE
SYDNOR BAYOU
Lone Star Flight Mus
Schlitterbahn Water Park
Terminal
DOT WATSON ATHLETIC FLD
SCHREIBER PARK
Scholes International Airport at Galveston
A
1 Cherokee Dr
B
1 Terminal Dr
C
1 Meridan Wy
D
1 Yucatan Dr
2 Mayapan Ct
3 Cadena Ct
E
1 E Gafftoppers
F
1 Sand Dollar
2 Grand Av
STEWART RD
SEAWALL BLVD
SAN LUIS PASS RD
3005
EAST BEACH
WEST BEACH
BCH POCKET PARK 1
GULF OF MEXICO
Avenue V 1/2
Quintana Dr
Maceo Wy
Cove View Blvd
7 Mile Rd
Beall Ln
Anderson Wy
Homrighaus Rd
Sydnor Ln
99th St
103rd St
Broome Rd
Baymeadows Dr
Cloud Ln
Seawall Blvd
A B C D E
1 2 3 4 5 6 7

SEE 5220 MAP

SEE B MAP

1:24,000
1 in. = 2000 ft.
0 0.25 0.5
miles

SEE 5108 MAP

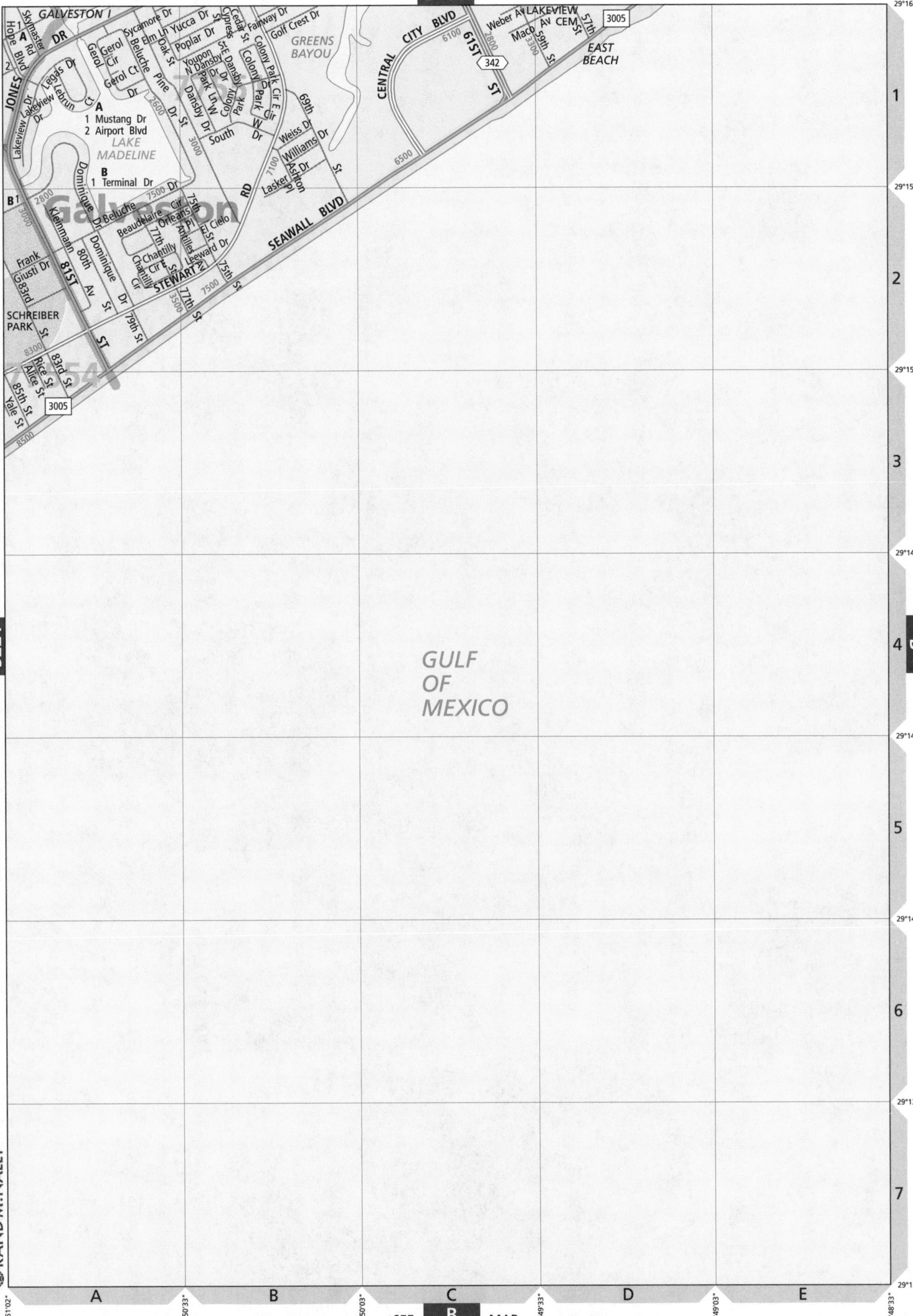
GALVESTON I
Skymaster
Hope Blvd
A
DR
JONES
Lakeview Dr
Lakeview
Legas Dr
Lebrun Ct
Gerol Cir
Gerol
Gerol Ct
Sycamore Dr
Elm Ln
Beluche
Pine Dr
Oak St
Yucca Dr
Poplar Dr
Youpon
N Dansby
Dansby Dr
Park Ln W
Cedar St
Cypress
E Dansby
Colony Park
Colony Park Cir E
Fairway Dr
Golf Crest Dr
GREENS BAYOU
South
W Dr
69th
Weiss Dr
Williams Dr
Ashton Dr
Lasker Pl
St
RD
A
1 Mustang Dr
2 Airport Blvd
LAKE MADELINE
B
1 Terminal Dr
Dominique Dr
Galveston
Beluche
Beaudelaire Cir
Orleans
75th
El Cielo
Antilles
Leeward Dr
77th
Chantilly Cir
Chantilly Cir
STEWART RD
Kleinmann
80th Av
Dominique Dr
79th St
81ST ST
Frank Giusti Dr
83rd St
SCHREIBER PARK
83rd St
Rice St
Alice St
85th St
Yale St
3005
SEAWALL BLVD
CENTRAL CITY BLVD
61ST ST
342
Weber Av
LAKEVIEW CEM
Maco Av
59th St
57th St
3005
EAST BEACH
GULF OF MEXICO
1
2
3
4
5
6
7
A
B
C
D
E
29°16'12"
29°15'46"
29°15'20"
29°14'54"
29°14'27"
29°14'01"
29°13'35"
29°13'09"
94°51'02"
94°50'33"
94°50'03"
94°49'33"
94°49'03"
94°48'33"

SEE B MAP

SEE B MAP

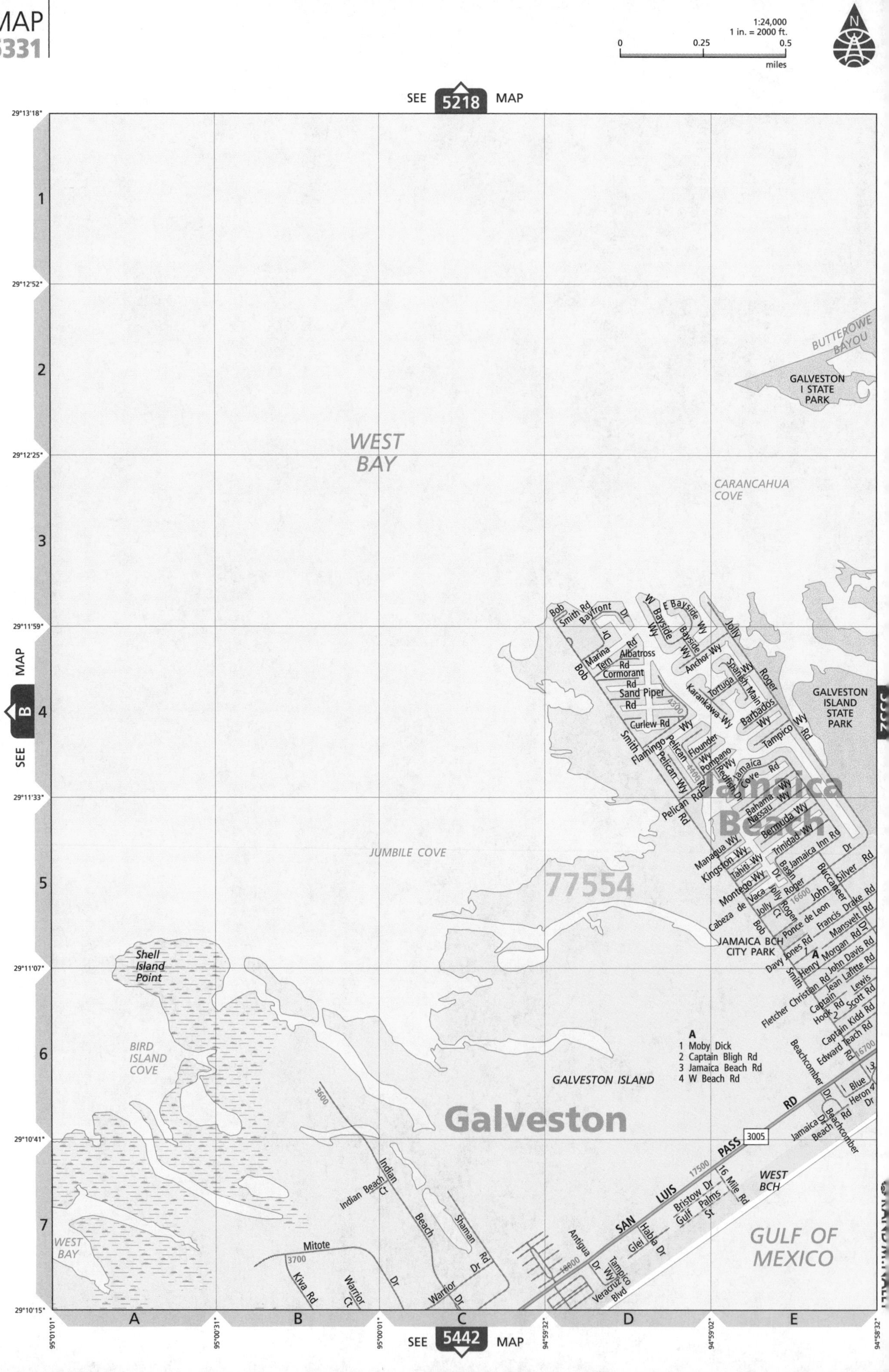
1:24,000
1 in. = 2000 ft.
0 0.25 0.5
miles
N
SEE 5218 MAP
SEE 5442 MAP
SEE B MAP
WEST BAY
BUTTEROWE BAYOU
GALVESTON I STATE PARK
CARANCAHUA COVE
GALVESTON ISLAND STATE PARK
Jamaica Beach
JUMBILE COVE
77554
Shell Island Point
BIRD ISLAND COVE
GALVESTON ISLAND
Galveston
JAMAICA BCH CITY PARK
WEST BCH
GULF OF MEXICO
WEST BAY
SAN LUIS PASS RD
3005
Bob Smith Rd
Bayfront Dr
E Bayside Wy
W Bayside Wy
Bayside Wy
Jolly Roger
Marina Tern
Albatross Rd
Cormorant Rd
Sand Piper Rd
Curlew Rd
Anchor Wy
Spanish Main Wy
Tortuga Wy
Karankawa Wy
Barbados Wy
Tampico Wy
Flamingo Wy
Pelican Wy
Pelican Rd
Flounder Wy
Pompano Wy
Redfish Dr
Jamaica Cove Rd
Bahama Wy
Nassau Wy
Bermuda Wy
Trinidad Wy
Jamaica Inn Rd
Managua Wy
Kingston Wy
Tahiti Wy
Montego Wy
Cabeza de Vaca Dr
Bayan Dr
Jolly Roger Ct
Buccaneer Dr
John Silver Rd
Ponce de Leon
Francis Drake Rd
Mansvelt Rd
Davy Jones Rd
Henry Morgan Rd
John Davis Rd
Jean Lafitte Rd
Lewis
Scott Rd
Captain Hook Rd
Captain Kidd Rd
Edward Teach Rd
Fletcher Christian Rd
Beachcomber Dr
Blue Heron Dr
Jamaica Beach Rd
Indian Beach Ct
Indian Beach Dr
Shaman Rd
Mitote Dr
Kiva Rd
Warrior Ct
Warrior Dr
Bristow Dr
Gulf Palms St
16 Mile Rd
Habla Dr
Glei
Antigua Dr
Tampico Wy
Veracruz Blvd
3600
3700
4300
4400
16600
16700
17500
18800
A
1 Moby Dick
2 Captain Bligh Rd
3 Jamaica Beach Rd
4 W Beach Rd
1
2
3
4
5
6
7
A
B
C
D
E
29°13'18"
29°12'52"
29°12'25"
29°11'59"
29°11'33"
29°11'07"
29°10'41"
29°10'15"
95°01'01"
95°00'31"
95°00'01"
94°59'32"
94°59'02"
94°58'32"

1:24,000
1 in. = 2000 ft.
0 0.25 0.5
miles

SEE 5219 MAP

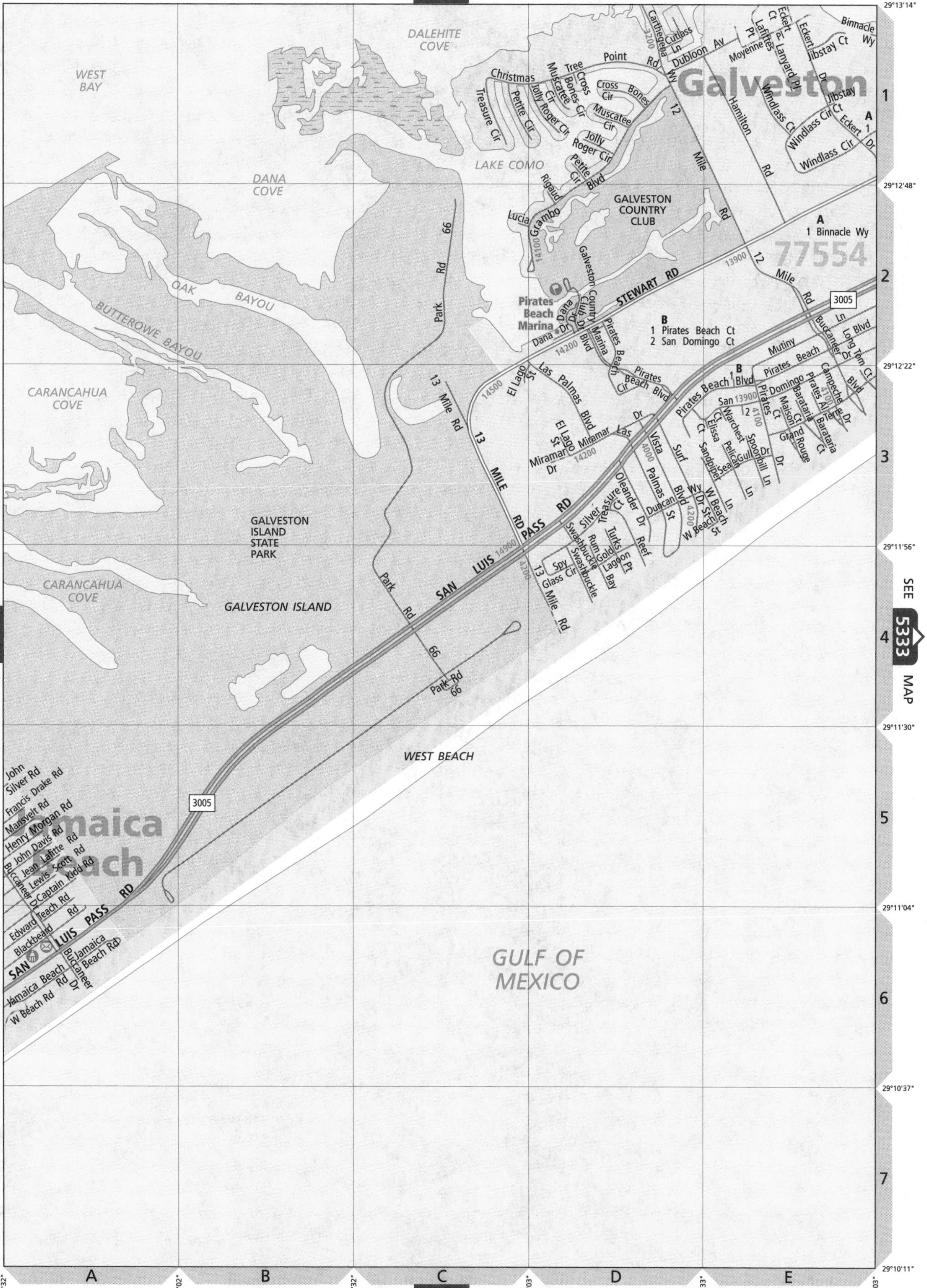
DALEHITE COVE
WEST BAY
DANA COVE
LAKE COMO
Galveston
77554
GALVESTON COUNTRY CLUB
Pirates Beach Marina
STEWART RD
OAK BAYOU
BUTTEROWE BAYOU
CARANCAHUA COVE
GALVESTON ISLAND STATE PARK
CARANCAHUA COVE
GALVESTON ISLAND
SAN LUIS PASS RD
13 MILE RD
12 Mile Rd
Park Rd 66
3005
WEST BEACH
Jamaica Beach
GULF OF MEXICO
A
1 Binnacle Wy
B
1 Pirates Beach Ct
2 San Domingo Ct
Christmas
Treasure Cir
Petite Cir
Jolly Roger Cir
Muscatee Cir
Tree Cross Bones Cir
Cross Bones Cir
Muscatee Cir
Jolly Roger Cir
Petite Cir
Rigaud Blvd
Lucia
Grambo
Point Rd
Carthegena Wy
Cutlass Ln
Dubloon Av
Moyenne Pt
Lafittes Ct
Eckert Pl
Lanyard Pl
Eckert Dr
Jibstay Ct
Binnacle Wy
Hamilton Rd
Windlass Ct
Windlass Cir
Jibstay Ct
Eckert Dr
Galveston Country Club Dr
Dana Dr
Marina Blvd
Pirates Beach Cir
Pirates Beach Blvd
El Lago St
Las Palmas Blvd
El Lago St
Miramar Dr
Buccaneer Dr
Long Tom Ct
Mutiny Ln
Campeche Blvd
San Domingo
Pirates Al
Barataria Dr
Maison Rouge
Grand Terre
Warchest
Elissa Ct
Sandpiper
Pelican
Sea Gull
Spoonbill Ln
Vista Dr
Surf Dr
Oleander Dr
Palmas St
Duncan
W Beach St
Treasure Ct
Silver
Swashbuckle
Rum
Gold
Turks Pt
Lagoon
Reef
Bay
Spy Glass Cir
13 Mile Rd
John Silver Rd
Francis Drake Rd
Mansvelt Rd
Henry Morgan Rd
John Davis Rd
Jean Lafitte Rd
Lewis Scott Rd
Captain Kidd Rd
Buccaneer
Edward Teach Rd
Blackbeard Rd
Jamaica Beach Rd
Buccaneer Dr
Jamaica Beach Rd
W Beach Rd
13900
14100
14200
14500
14900
4000
4100
4200
3200
1
2
3
4
5
6
7
A
B
C
D
E
29°13'14"
29°12'48"
29°12'22"
29°11'56"
29°11'30"
29°11'04"
29°10'37"
29°10'11"
94°58'32"
94°58'02"
94°57'32"
94°57'03"
94°56'33"
94°56'03"

SEE 5333 MAP

SEE B MAP

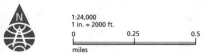

1:24,000
1 in. = 2000 ft.
0 0.25 0.5
miles

SEE 5220 MAP

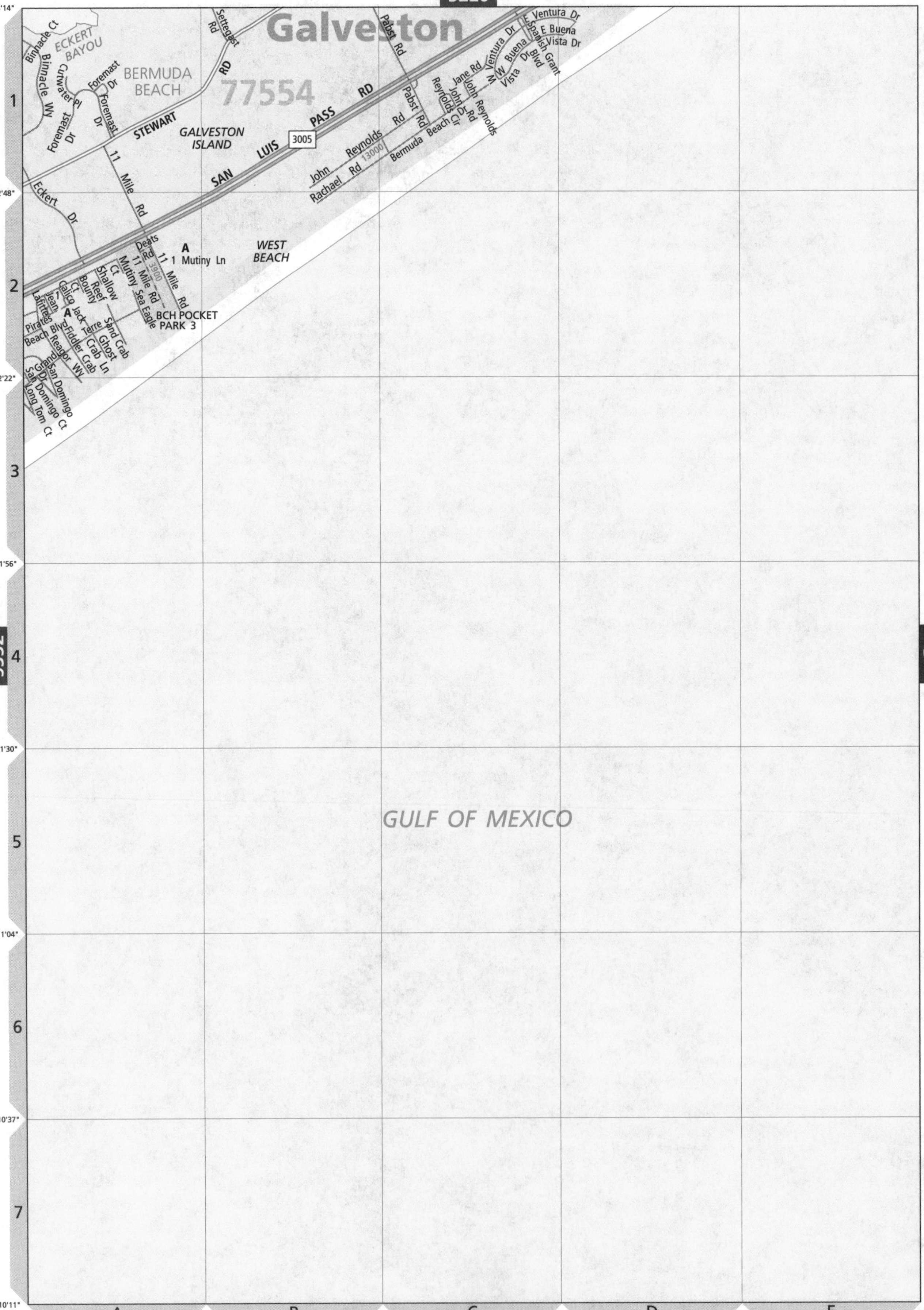
Galveston
77554
ECKERT BAYOU
BERMUDA BEACH
GALVESTON ISLAND
WEST BEACH
GULF OF MEXICO
SAN LUIS PASS RD
3005
STEWART RD
11 Mile Rd
Eckert Dr
Settegast Rd
Pabst Rd
Binnacle Ct
Binnacle Wy
Cutwater Pl
Foremast Dr
E Ventura Dr
E Buena Vista Dr
Sand Grant
Spanish Blvd
W Buena Vista Dr
Ventura Dr
Jane Rd
John Dr
Reynolds Cir
John Reynolds Rd
Bermuda Beach
John Reynolds Rd
Rachael Rd
13000
Deats Rd
3900
1 Mutiny Ln
11 Mile Rd
Mutiny
Sea Eagle
Shallow Ct
Reef
Bounty
Calico Jack Ct
Jean
Lafitte
Pirates Beach Blvd
Reador Wy
Fiddler Crab
Terre
Ghost Crab Ln
Sand Crab
BCH POCKET PARK 3
Grand Dr
San Domingo
San Domingo Ct
Long Tom Ct
A
1
2
3
4
5
6
7
A
B
C
D
E
29°13'14"
29°12'48"
29°12'22"
29°11'56"
29°11'30"
29°11'04"
29°10'37"
29°10'11"
94°56'03"
94°55'33"
94°55'04"
94°54'34"
94°54'04"
94°53'34"

SEE 5332 MAP

SEE B MAP

1:24,000
1 in. = 2000 ft.
0 0.25 0.5
miles

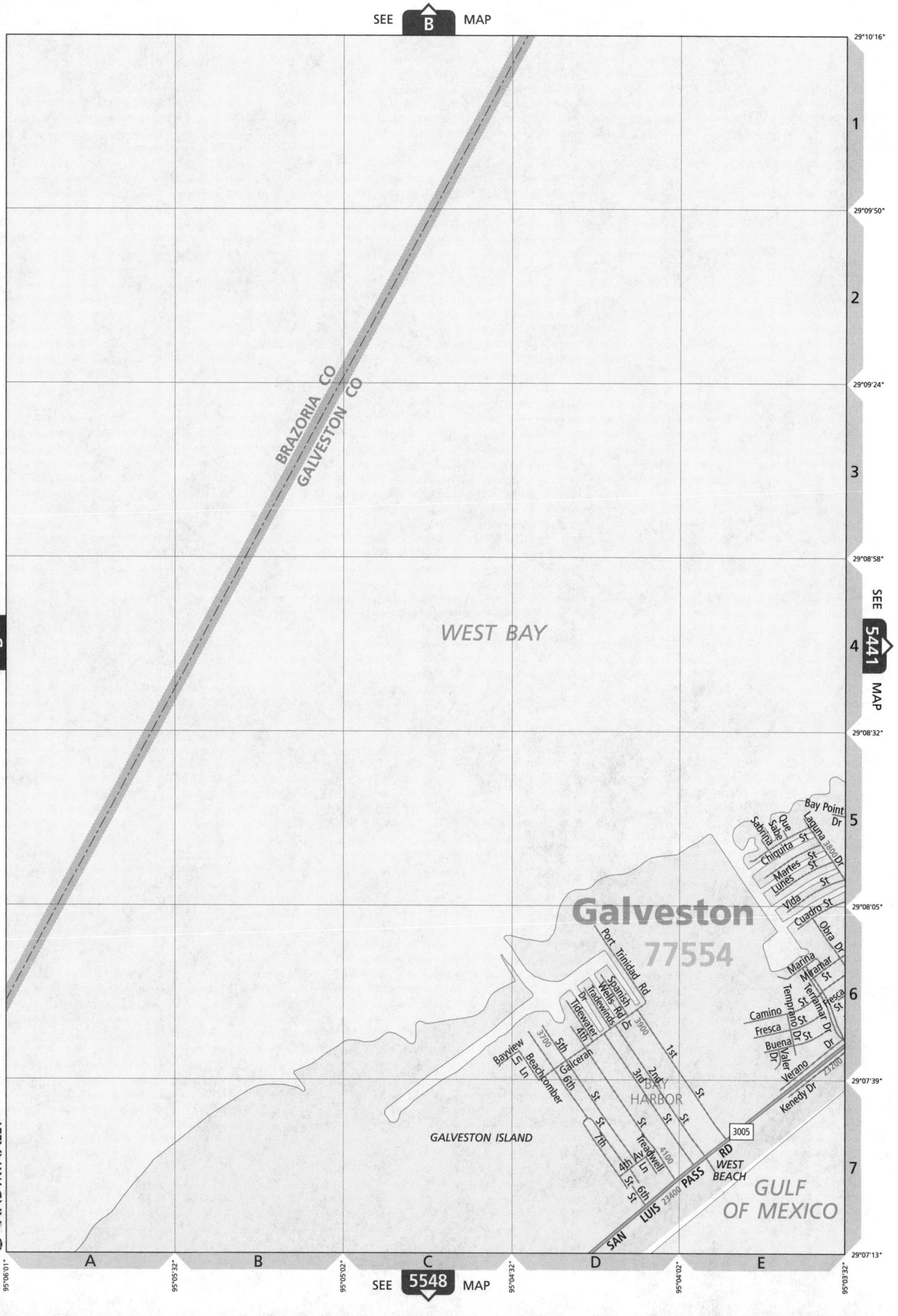
SEE B MAP
SEE 5548 MAP
SEE 5441 MAP
WEST BAY
BRAZORIA CO
GALVESTON CO
Galveston
77554
GALVESTON ISLAND
GULF OF MEXICO
BAY HARBOR
WEST BEACH
SAN LUIS PASS RD
23400
23200
3005
Kenedy Dr
Bay Point Dr
Laguna 3800 Dr
Que Sabe
Sabrina
Chiquita St
Martes St
Lunes St
Vida St
Cuadro St
Obra Dr
Marina
Miramar St
Terramar Dr
Fresca St
Camino
Temprano Dr
Fresca St
Buena
Valer
Dr
Verano
Dr
Port Trinidad Rd
Spanish
Wells Rd
Tradewinds Dr
3900
Tidewater Dr
4th
5th
3700
Bayview Ln
Beachcomber Ln
Galceran
6th St
7th St
1st St
2nd St
3rd St
St
Treadwell Ln
4100
4th Av
St
6th St
N
A B C D E
1 2 3 4 5 6 7
29°10'16"
29°09'50"
29°09'24"
29°08'58"
29°08'32"
29°08'05"
29°07'39"
29°07'13"
95°06'01"
95°05'32"
95°05'02"
95°04'32"
95°04'02"
95°03'32"

1:24,000
1 in. = 2000 ft.
0 0.25 0.5
miles

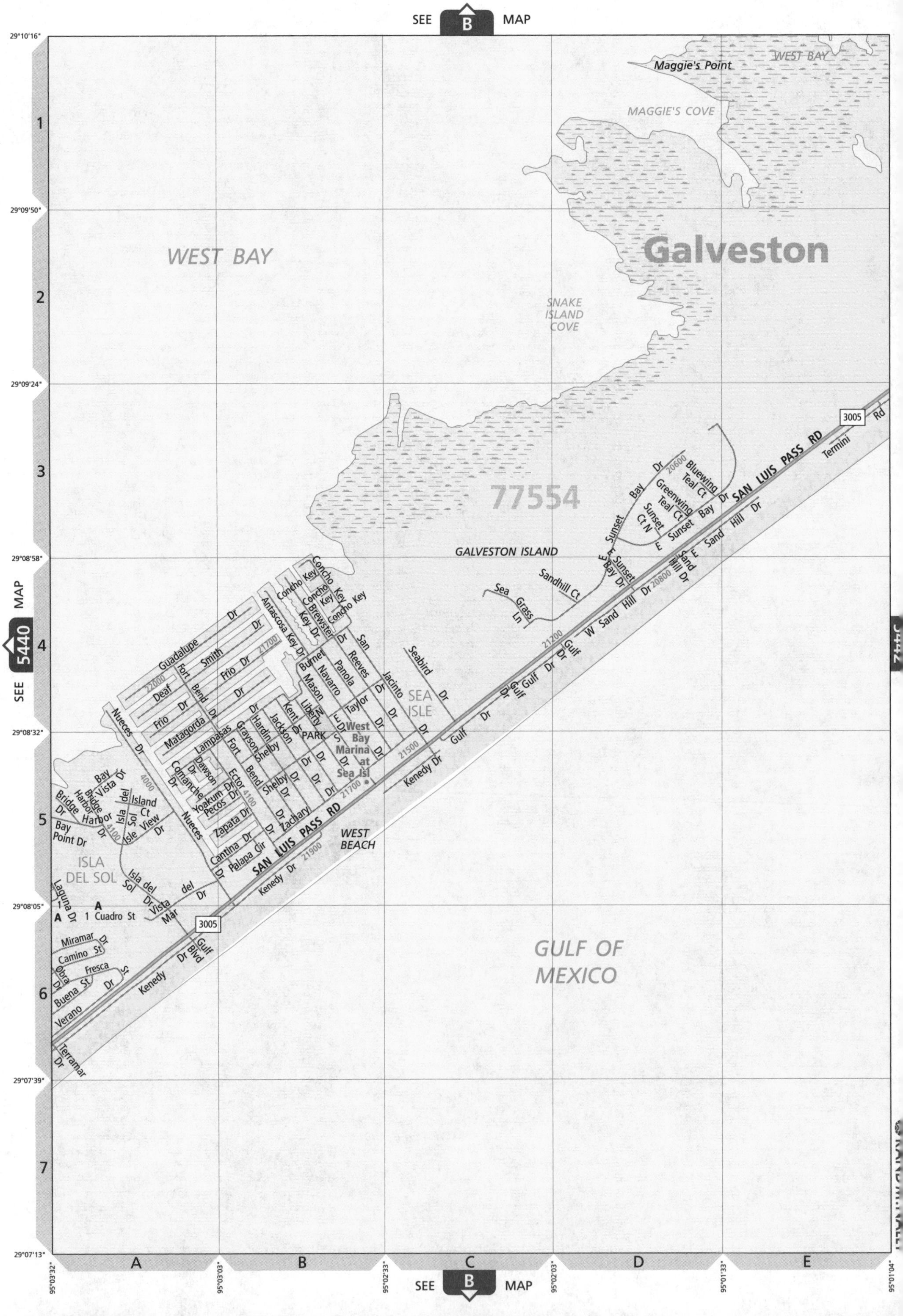
SEE B MAP
SEE 5440 MAP
SEE B MAP
5442
WEST BAY
Maggie's Point
MAGGIE'S COVE
Galveston
SNAKE ISLAND COVE
77554
GALVESTON ISLAND
GULF OF MEXICO
SEA ISLE
ISLA DEL SOL
WEST BEACH
West Bay Marina at Sea Isl
PARK
SAN LUIS PASS RD
3005
Termini Rd
Bluewing Teal Ct
Greenwing Teal Ct
Bay Dr
Sunset Ct N
E Sunset Bay Dr
Sunset Bay Dr
E Sand Hill Dr
W Sand Hill Dr
Sandhill Ct
Sea Grass Ln
Seabird Dr
Gulf Dr
Kenedy Dr
Jacinto Dr
San Reeves Dr
Taylor Dr
Panola Dr
Navarro Dr
Mason Dr
Burnet Dr
Liberty Dr
Kent Ct
Jackson Dr
Shelby Dr
Hardin Dr
Grayson Dr
Fort Bend Dr
Zachary Dr
Ector Dr
Zapata Dr
Cantina Dr
Palapa Cir
Pecos Dr
Yoakum Dr
Dawson Dr
Comanche Dr
Lampasas Dr
Matagorda Dr
Frio Dr
Deaf Smith Dr
Guadalupe Dr
Nueces Dr
Antascosa Key Dr
Concho Key Dr
Brewster Key Dr
Bay Vista Dr
Harbor Bridge Dr
Bridge Harbor Dr
Bay Point Dr
Isla del Sol Dr
Island Ct
Isle View Dr
Vista del Mar Dr
Laguna Dr
Cuadro St
Gulf Blvd
Miramar Dr
Camino St
Fresca St
Obra Dr
Buena St
Verano Dr
Terramar Dr
20600
20800
21200
21500
21700
21900
22000
4000
4100
29°10'16"
29°09'50"
29°09'24"
29°08'58"
29°08'32"
29°08'05"
29°07'39"
29°07'13"
95°03'32"
95°03'03"
95°02'33"
95°02'03"
95°01'33"
95°01'04"
1
2
3
4
5
6
7
A
B
C
D
E

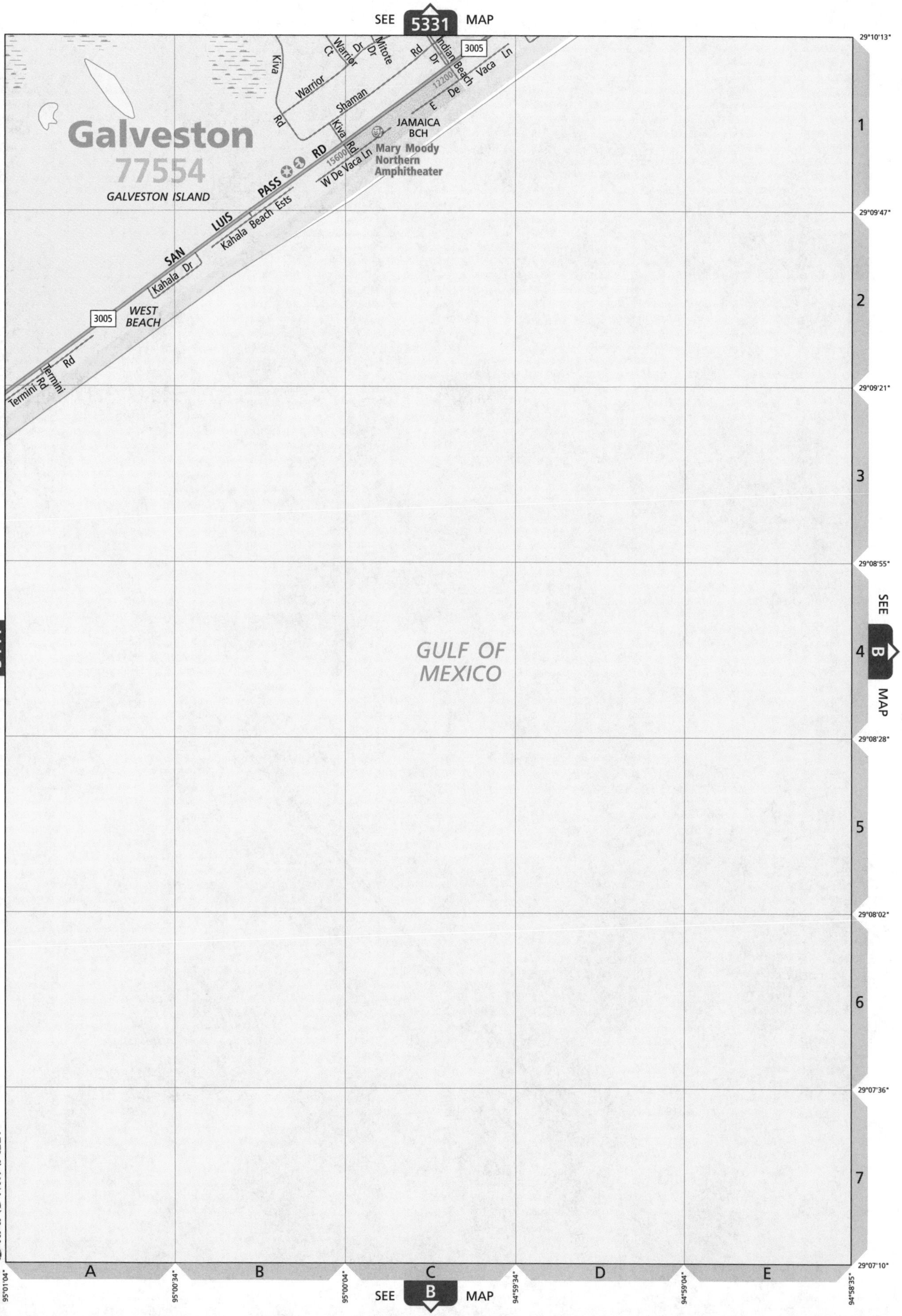
1:24,000
1 in. = 2000 ft.
0
0.25
0.5
miles
SEE 5331 MAP
Galveston
77554
GALVESTON ISLAND
SAN LUIS PASS RD
3005
WEST BEACH
Kahala Dr
Kahala Beach Ests
Termini Rd
Kiva Rd
Warrior Ct
Warrior Dr
Mitote Dr
Shaman
Indian Beach Dr
E De Vaca Ln
W De Vaca Ln
12200
15600
JAMAICA BCH
Mary Moody Northern Amphitheater
GULF OF MEXICO
SEE B MAP
SEE B MAP
29°10'13"
29°09'47"
29°09'21"
29°08'55"
29°08'28"
29°08'02"
29°07'36"
29°07'10"
95°01'04"
95°00'34"
95°00'04"
94°59'34"
94°59'04"
94°58'35"
A
B
C
D
E
1
2
3
4
5
6
7

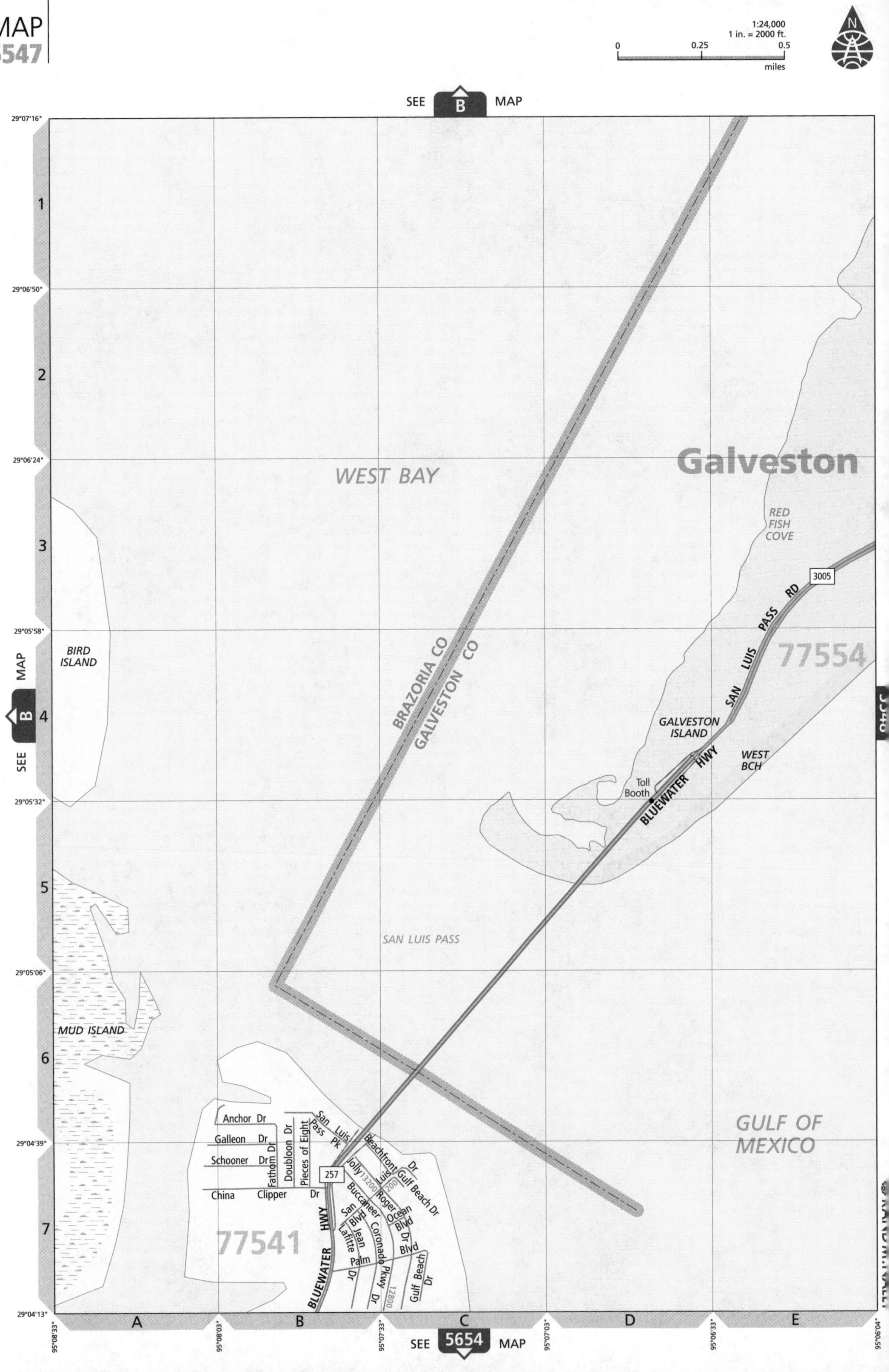
1:24,000
1 in. = 2000 ft.
0
0.25
0.5
miles
N
SEE B MAP
SEE 5654 MAP
SEE B MAP
29°07'16"
29°06'50"
29°06'24"
29°05'58"
29°05'32"
29°05'06"
29°04'39"
29°04'13"
95°08'33"
95°08'03"
95°07'33"
95°07'03"
95°06'33"
95°06'04"
A
B
C
D
E
1
2
3
4
5
6
7
WEST BAY
Galveston
RED FISH COVE
3005
SAN LUIS PASS RD
77554
BRAZORIA CO
GALVESTON CO
BIRD ISLAND
GALVESTON ISLAND
WEST BCH
Toll Booth
BLUEWATER HWY
SAN LUIS PASS
MUD ISLAND
GULF OF MEXICO
Anchor Dr
Galleon Dr
Schooner Dr
Fathom Dr
Doubloon Dr
Pieces of Eight
San Luis Pass Pk
Beachfront Dr
Gulf Beach Dr
257
Jolly Roger
Luis
13200
China
Clipper
Dr
Buccaneer
Ocean Dr
Blvd
San
Blvd
Jean
Coronado
Lafitte
Palm
Dr
Pkwy
Dr
12800
Gulf Beach Dr
77541
BLUEWATER HWY

1:24,000
1 in. = 2000 ft.
0 0.25 0.5
miles

SEE 5440 MAP

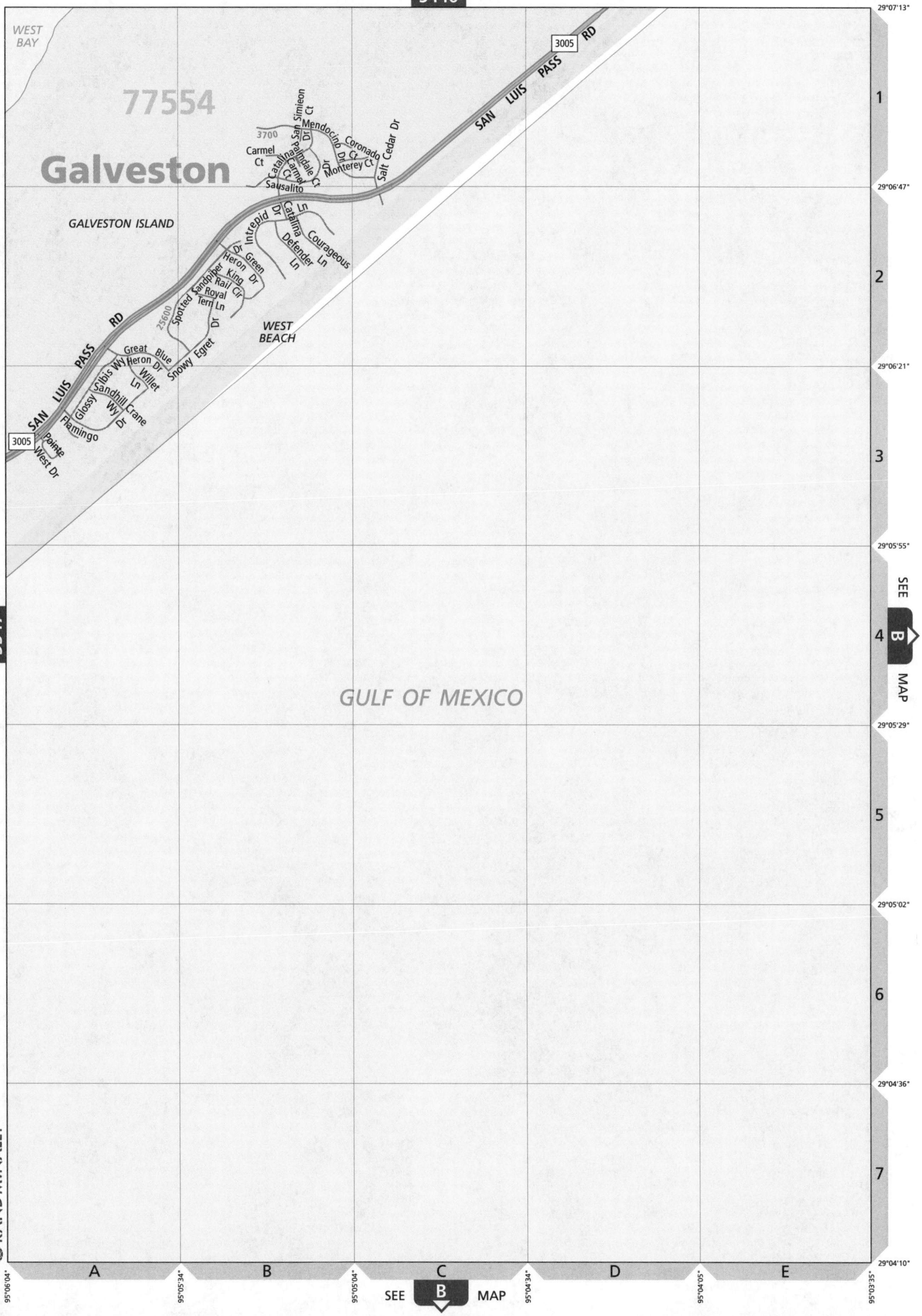
WEST BAY
77554
Galveston
GALVESTON ISLAND
SAN LUIS PASS RD
3005
3700
Carmel Ct
Catalina
San Simieon Dr
Ct
Mendocino Dr
Palmdale Ct
Carmel Ct
Ct
Coronado Ct
Monterey Ct
Dr
Salt Cedar Dr
Sausalito
Intrepid Dr
Catalina Ln
Defender Ln
Courageous Ln
Green Dr
Heron Dr
King Dr
Rail Cir
Royal Tern Ln
Spotted Sandpiper Dr
25600
WEST BEACH
Great Blue Heron Dr
Ibis Wy
Willet Ln
Snowy Egret Dr
Glossy
Sandhill Crane Wy Dr
Flamingo
Pointe West Dr
GULF OF MEXICO
1
2
3
4
5
6
7
A
B
C
D
E
29°07'13"
29°06'47"
29°06'21"
29°05'55"
29°05'29"
29°05'02"
29°04'36"
29°04'10"
95°06'04"
95°05'34"
95°05'04"
95°04'34"
95°04'05"
95°03'35"

SEE B MAP

SEE B MAP

1:24,000
1 in. = 2000 ft.
0 0.25 0.5
miles

SEE 5547 MAP

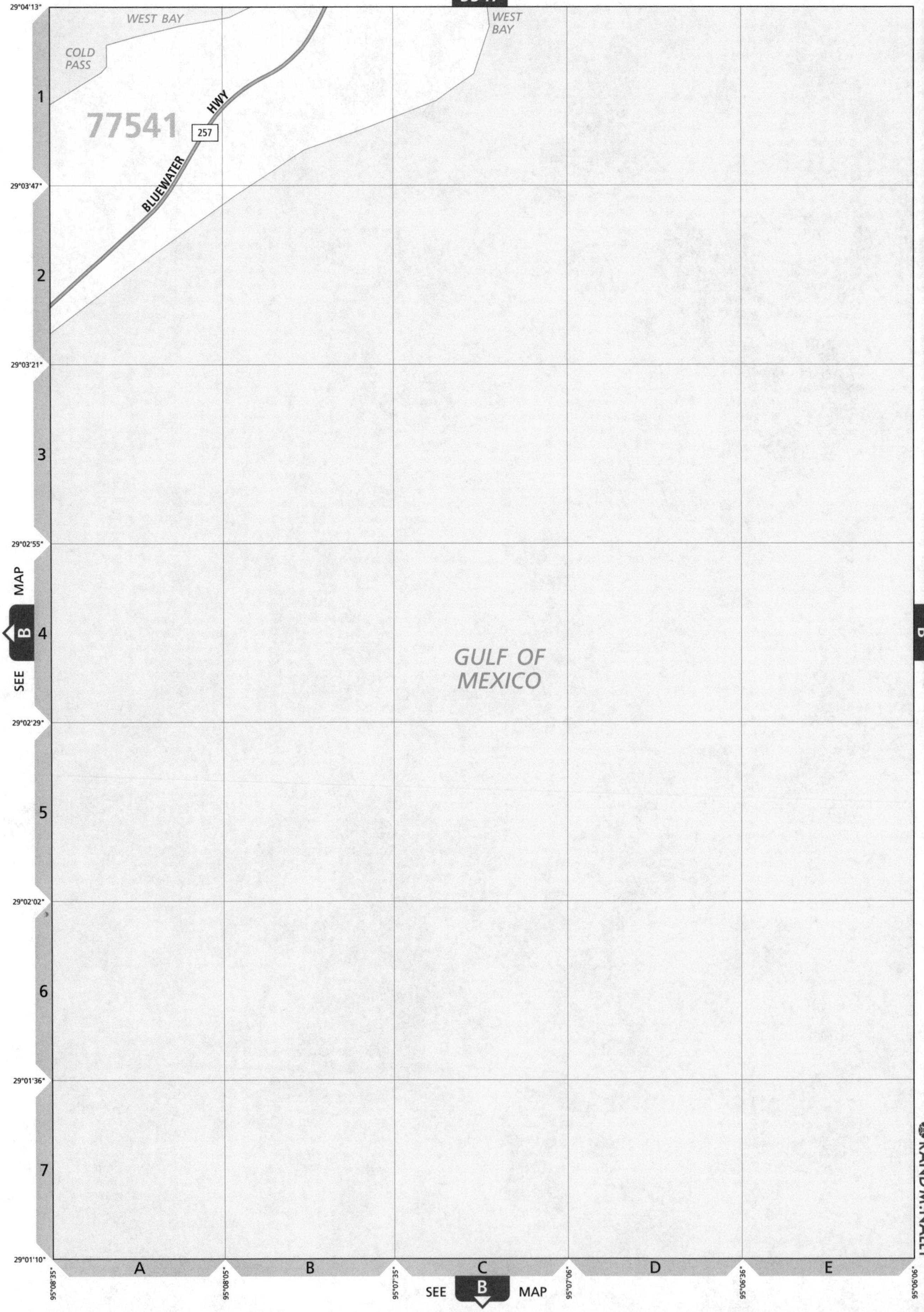
29°04'13"
WEST BAY
COLD PASS
WEST BAY
77541
BLUEWATER HWY
257
29°03'47"
29°03'21"
29°02'55"
GULF OF MEXICO
29°02'29"
29°02'02"
29°01'36"
29°01'10"
1
2
3
4
5
6
7
A
B
C
D
E
95°08'35"
95°08'05"
95°07'35"
95°07'06"
95°06'36"
95°06'06"

SEE B MAP

SEE B MAP

Cities and Communities

Community Name	Abbr.	County	ZIP Code	Map Page
Adams Oaks		Montgomery	77365	2974
Aldine Meadows		Harris	77032	3545
Aldine Place		Harris	77039	3545
Algoa		Galveston	77511	4869
Alvin	ALVN	Brazoria	77511	4867
Arcola	ARLA	Fort Bend	77583	4623
Artesian Forest		Montgomery	77304	2383
Atascocita		Harris	77346	3408
Audubon Park		Harris	77396	3406
Austin County	AusC			
Autumn Woods		Montgomery	77362	2963
Bacliff		Galveston	77518	4634
Bammel		Harris	77090	3258
Barker		Harris	77094	3955
Barrett		Harris	77532	3692
Bayou Vista	BYUV	Galveston	77563	4990
Baytown	BYTN	Chambers	77520	3835
Baytown	BYTN	Harris	77520	4112
Bayview		Galveston	77518	4634
Beach City	BHCY	Chambers	77520	4254
Bear Creek Village		Harris	77084	3678
Beaumont Place		Harris	77049	3828
Bellaire	BLAR	Harris	77401	4100
Bennett Estates		Montgomery	77302	2824
Birnam Wood		Harris	77373	3115
Brazoria County	BzaC			
Brook Forest		Montgomery	77357	2827
Brookside Village	BKVL	Brazoria	77581	4375
Bunker Hill Village	BKHV	Harris	77024	3959
Caney Creek Estates		Montgomery	77357	2827
Castlewoods		Harris	77039	3545
Chambers County	CmbC			
Channelview		Harris	77530	3830
Chateau Woods	CHTW	Montgomery	77385	2823
Chimney Hill		Harris	77041	3679
C H Rouse Estates		Montgomery	77365	2972
Clear Lake Shores	CRLS	Galveston	77565	4509
Clodine		Fort Bend	77083	4095
Cloverleaf		Harris	77015	3828
Coady		Harris	77521	3832
Concord Bridge		Harris	77041	3679
Conroe	CNRO	Montgomery	77301	2384
Copperfield Southcreek		Harris	77095	3538
Country Colony		Montgomery	77372	2537
Country Place Acres		Montgomery	77355	2815
Crabb		Fort Bend	77469	4493
Creekwood Addition		Montgomery	77372	2682
Cripple Creek Farms		Montgomery	77362	2963
Cripple Creek North		Montgomery	77354	2816
Crosby		Harris	77532	3552
Crystal Creek Forest		Montgomery	77303	2385
Cut & Shoot	CTSH	Montgomery	77303	2385
Cypress		Harris	77429	3396
Cypress Creek Estates		Harris	77429	3398
Cypress Meadow		Harris	77449	3816
Decker Prairie		Montgomery	77362	2963
Deco		Harris	77069	3400
Deerfield Village		Harris	77084	3679
Deer Park	DRPK	Harris	77536	4109
Dickinson	DKSN	Galveston	77539	4754
Dyersdale		Harris	77016	3547
Egypt		Montgomery	77354	2673
Eldon		Harris	77521	3835
El Lago	ELGO	Harris	77586	4509
Fairgreen		Harris	77039	3546
Fallbrook		Harris	77038	3543
Forest Hills		Montgomery	77385	2676
Fort Bend County	FBnC			
Fountain View		Harris	77032	3546
Four Corners		Fort Bend	77478	4236
Fox Run		Montgomery	77386	2969
Foxwood		Montgomery	77362	2963
Freeway Oaks Estates		Montgomery	77365	2972
Fresno		Fort Bend	77545	4498
Friendswood	FRDW	Galveston	77546	4629
Friendswood	FRDW	Harris	77546	4505
Galena Park	GNPK	Harris	77547	4106
Galveston	GLSN	Galveston	77550	5109
Galveston County	GlsC			
Gatewood		Harris	77032	3404
Glencairn		Harris	77449	3677
Grangerland		Montgomery	77306	2533
Greenwood Village		Harris	77093	3686
Harris County	HarC			
Harvest Acres		Montgomery	77372	2537
Hazy Hollow		Montgomery	77354	2670
Hedwig Village	HDWV	Harris	77024	3959
Hempstead	HMPD	Waller	77445	2953
Highlands		Harris	77562	3831
High Meadows		Fort Bend	77479	4366
Hill & Dale Acres		Montgomery	77372	2683
Hillcrest	HLCS	Brazoria	77511	4867
Hilshire Village	HLSV	Harris	77055	3821
Hitchcock	HTCK	Galveston	77563	4989

Community Name	Abbr.	County	ZIP Code	Map Page
Hockley		Harris	77447	3248
Holiday Oaks		Montgomery	77372	2683
Holly Terrace		Montgomery	77365	2974
Houmont Park		Harris	77044	3689
* Houston	HOUS	Montgomery	77339	3117
* Houston	HOUS	Fort Bend	77489	4371
* Houston	HOUS	Harris	77002	3963
Huffman		Harris	77336	3267
Hufsmith		Harris	77375	2964
* Humble	HMBL	Harris	77338	3262
* Hunters Creek Village	HNCV	Harris	77024	3960
Hunters Retreat		Montgomery	77355	2816
Indian Shores		Harris	77532	3410
Indian Woods		Montgomery	77355	2962
* Iowa Colony	IWCY	Brazoria	77583	4745
* Jacinto City	JTCY	Harris	77029	3966
* Jamaica Beach	JMAB	Galveston	77554	5332
* Jersey Village	JRSV	Harris	77040	3680
* Katy	KATY	Harris	77493	3813
* Katy	KATY	Waller	77493	3813
* Katy	KATY	Fort Bend	77494	3952
* Kemah	KMAH	Galveston	77565	4509
Kenwood Place		Harris	77039	3546
Kingwood		Harris	77339	3119
Kinwood		Harris	77039	3546
Klein		Harris	77379	3111
Kohrville		Harris	77070	3255
Lake Creek Estates		Montgomery	77384	2529
Lakeland		Montgomery	77384	2676
Lake Shadows		Harris	77532	3409
Lake Splendora		Montgomery	77372	2682
Lakewood Estates		Montgomery	77384	2674
* La Marque	LMQU	Galveston	77568	4990
* La Porte	LPRT	Harris	77571	4251
Lazy Forest		Montgomery	77303	2239
* League City	LGCY	Galveston	77573	4632
* League City	LGCY	Harris	77598	4630
Lexington Woods		Harris	77373	3114
-- Liberty County	LbyC			
Long Lake		Montgomery	77354	2818
Louetta		Harris	77379	3255
Lynchburg		Harris	77520	3831
* Magnolia	MAGA	Montgomery	77354	2669
Magnolia Bend		Montgomery	77302	2677
Magnolia Gardens		Harris	77044	3551
Mantu		Harris	77530	3831
* Manvel	MNVL	Brazoria	77578	4625
McNair		Harris	77521	3832
* Meadows Place	MDWP	Fort Bend	77477	4238
Middlegate Village		Harris	77095	3538
Mill Creek Forest		Montgomery	77354	2816
Mission Bend		Fort Bend	77083	4096
* Missouri City	MSCY	Fort Bend	77489	4370
* Missouri City	MSCY	Harris	77071	4239
* Mont Belvieu	MTBL	Chambers	77520	3696
Monte Oaks		Montgomery	77357	2974
-- Montgomery County	MtgC			
* Morgans Point	MRGP	Harris	77571	4252
Mostyn		Montgomery	77354	2670
Mt Houston		Harris	77050	3546
* Nassau Bay	NSUB	Harris	77058	4508
New Caney		Montgomery	77357	2828
New Caney Heights		Montgomery	77357	2827
Newport		Harris	77532	3552
New Territory		Fort Bend	77479	4366
Northampton		Harris	77389	2966
Northglen		Harris	77084	3677
North Houston		Harris	77086	3541
North Line Oaks		Montgomery	77382	2675
Northline Terrace		Harris	77037	3544
North Spring		Harris	77373	3114
Northwest Park		Harris	77086	3542
Oak Hills Acres		Montgomery	77362	2816
Oak Lake Estates		Fort Bend	77478	4236
* Oak Ridge North	ORDN	Montgomery	77385	2822
Oak Terrace		Montgomery	77365	2973
Oakwilde		Harris	77093	3685
Oakwood Glen		Harris	77379	3256
Oklahoma		Montgomery	77354	2818
Old River Terrace		Harris	77530	3969
Orange Grove		Harris	77039	3546
* Panorama Village	PNVL	Montgomery	77304	2237
Parkwood Estates		Harris	77032	3546
* Pasadena	PASD	Harris	77506	4107
* Patton Village	PTVL	Montgomery	77372	2682
Peach Creek Estates		Montgomery	77372	2537
* Pearland	PRLD	Brazoria	77581	4504
* Pearland	PRLD	Fort Bend	77545	4499
* Pearland	PRLD	Harris	77047	4373
Pheasant Creek		Fort Bend	77478	4236
Pine Acres		Montgomery	77357	2828
Pinehurst		Montgomery	77354	2816
* Pine Island	PNIS	Waller	77445	3099
Pinewood Estates		Montgomery	77372	2682

Community Name	Abbr.	County	ZIP Code	Map Page
Piney Point		Montgomery	77301	2385
* Piney Point Village	PNPV	Harris	77024	3960
Pioneer Trails		Montgomery	77302	2679
Plantation Place		Fort Bend	77469	4365
* Pleak	PLEK	Fort Bend	77469	4614
Pleasant Valley Acres		Montgomery	77354	2817
* Plum Grove	PLMG	Liberty	77327	2684
Port Bolivar		Galveston	77650	4879
Porter		Montgomery	77365	2973
Porter Heights		Montgomery	77365	2825
Porterville Timbers		Montgomery	77365	2973
* Prairie View	PRVW	Waller	77445	3100
Rayford		Montgomery	77386	2968
* Richmond	RHMD	Fort Bend	77469	4491
Rimwick Forest		Montgomery	77354	2817
River Brook		Montgomery	77385	2676
River Plantation		Montgomery	77302	2530
River Terrace		Harris	77336	2975
Riverwood Estates		Harris	77050	3547
* Roman Forest	RMFT	Montgomery	77357	2829
Rose Hill		Harris	77377	3107
* Rosenberg	RSBG	Fort Bend	77471	4490
Royal Oaks		Montgomery	77354	2671
Royalwood		Harris	77049	3689
Rushwood		Harris	77067	3402
San Leon		Galveston	77539	4635
* Santa Fe	STFE	Galveston	77510	4987
* Seabrook	SEBK	Harris	77586	4509
Sequoya Bend		Harris	77032	3546
Settlers Village		Harris	77449	3676
Shadow Glen		Harris	77530	3830
Shadow Lake Estates		Montgomery	77365	2974
Shady Brook Acres		Montgomery	77355	2814
Sheldon		Harris	77049	3691
* Shenandoah	SHEH	Montgomery	77381	2822
Sherwood Place		Harris	77093	3686
* Shoreacres	SRAC	Harris	77571	4382
Southbrook		Harris	77060	3403
Southdown Village		Harris	77095	3538
* South Houston	SHUS	Harris	77587	4246
* Southside Place	SSPL	Harris	77005	4101
* Splendora	SPLD	Montgomery	77372	2683
Splendora Farms		Montgomery	77372	2536
Spring		Harris	77373	3115
Spring Creek Estates		Montgomery	77354	2818
Spring Forest		Montgomery	77386	2969
Spring Hills		Montgomery	77386	2969
* Spring Valley	SPVL	Harris	77055	3820
* Stafford	STAF	Fort Bend	77477	4369
* Stafford	STAF	Harris	77477	4239
* Stagecoach	SGCH	Montgomery	77355	2961
Steeple Chase		Harris	77095	3538
* Sugar Land	SGLD	Fort Bend	77479	4368
Sundown Glen		Harris	77449	3815
Tamina		Montgomery	77385	2822
Tanglewood Manor		Montgomery	77357	2827
Tara		Fort Bend	77469	4493
* Taylor Lake Village	TYLV	Harris	77586	4508
Terranova		Harris	77379	3257
* Texas City	TXCY	Galveston	77590	4875
* The Woodlands	WDLD	Montgomery	77381	2821
* Tiki Island	TKIS	Galveston	77554	5106
Timberlake Estates		Harris	77429	3398
Timber Lakes		Montgomery	77380	2967
Timberlane Acres		Montgomery	77365	3118
Timber Ridge		Montgomery	77380	2967
* Tomball	TMBL	Harris	77375	2964
Town West		Fort Bend	77478	4237
Ventura		Montgomery	77354	2817
Village of Oak Lake		Fort Bend	77478	4236
Walden on Lake Houston		Harris	77598	4630
* Waller	WALR	Waller	77484	3101
* Waller	WALR	Harris	77484	3102
-- Waller County	WlrC			
Walnut Creek		Montgomery	77355	2961
Walnut Springs		Montgomery	77355	2961
* Webster	WEBS	Harris	77598	4507
Westfield		Harris	77073	3259
Westfield Estates		Harris	77093	3685
* West University Place	WUNP	Harris	77005	4101
Westwood Three		Montgomery	77354	2673
Whispering Pines		Montgomery	77302	2680
White Oak Valley Estates		Montgomery	77306	2533
Williamsburg Colony		Harris	77449	3814
Willow Place		Harris	77070	3399
Wimbledon Estates		Harris	77379	3256
Winchester Country		Harris	77064	3540
Windsong		Harris	77084	3677
* Woodbranch	WDBR	Montgomery	77357	2828
Wood Hollow		Montgomery	77365	2972
Woodland Lakes		Montgomery	77355	2814
* Woodloch	WDLC	Montgomery	77385	2677
Woody Acres		Montgomery	77365	3119

* Indicates incorporated city

List of Abbreviations

Admin	Administration	Cto	Cut Off	Lp	Loop	Ste.	Sainte
Agri	Agricultural	Dept	Department	Mnr	Manor	Sci	Science
Ag	Agriculture	Dev	Development	Mkt	Market	Sci	Sciences
AFB	Air Force Base	Diag	Diagonal	Mdw	Meadow	Sci	Scientific
Arpt	Airport	Div	Division	Mdws	Meadows	Shop Ctr	Shopping Center
Al	Alley	Dr	Drive	Med	Medical	Shr	Shore
Amer	American	Drwy	Driveway	Mem	Memorial	Shrs	Shores
Anx	Annex	E	East	Metro	Metropolitan	Skwy	Skyway
Arc	Arcade	El	Elevation	Mw	Mews	S	South
Arch	Archaeological	Env	Environmental	Mil	Military	Spr	Spring
Aud	Auditorium	Est	Estate	Ml	Mill	Sprs	Springs
Avd	Avenida	Ests	Estates	Mls	Mills	Sq	Square
Av	Avenue	Exh	Exhibition	Mon	Monument	Stad	Stadium
Bfld	Battlefield	Expm	Experimental	Mtwy	Motorway	St For	State Forest
Bch	Beach	Expo	Exposition	Mnd	Mound	St Hist Site	State Historic Site
Bnd	Bend	Expwy	Expressway	Mnds	Mounds	St Nat Area	State Natural Area
Bio	Biological	Ext	Extension	Mt	Mount	St Pk	State Park
Blf	Bluff	Frgds	Fairgrounds	Mtn	Mountain	St Rec Area	State Recreation Area
Blvd	Boulevard	ft	Feet	Mtns	Mountains	Sta	Station
Brch	Branch	Fy	Ferry	Mun	Municipal	St	Street
Br	Bridge	Fld	Field	Mus	Museum	Smt	Summit
Brk	Brook	Flds	Fields	Nat'l	National	Sys	Systems
Bldg	Building	Flt	Flat	Nat'l For	National Forest	Tech	Technical
Bur	Bureau	Flts	Flats	Nat'l Hist Pk	National Historic Park	Tech	Technological
Byp	Bypass	For	Forest	Nat'l Hist Site	National Historic Site	Tech	Technology
Bywy	Byway	Fk	Fork	Nat'l Mon	National Monument	Ter	Terrace
Cl	Calle	Ft	Fort	Nat'l Park	National Park	Terr	Territory
Cljn	Callejon	Found	Foundation	Nat'l Rec Area	National Recreation Area	Theol	Theological
Cmto	Caminito	Frwy	Freeway	Nat'l Wld Ref	National Wildlife Refuge	Thwy	Throughway
Cm	Camino	Gdn	Garden	Nat	Natural	Toll Fy	Toll Ferry
Cap	Capitol	Gdns	Gardens	NAS	Naval Air Station	TIC	Tourist Information Center
Cath	Cathedral	Gen Hosp	General Hospital	Nk	Nook	Trc	Trace
Cswy	Causeway	Gln	Glen	N	North	Trfwy	Trafficway
Cem	Cemetery	GC	Golf Course	Orch	Orchard	Tr	Trail
Ctr	Center	Grn	Green	Ohwy	Outer Highway	Tun	Tunnel
Ctr	Centre	Grds	Grounds	Ovl	Oval	Tpk	Turnpike
Cir	Circle	Grv	Grove	Ovlk	Overlook	Unps	Underpass
Crlo	Circulo	Hbr	Harbor/Harbour	Ovps	Overpass	Univ	University
CH	City Hall	Hvn	Haven	Pk	Park	Vly	Valley
Clf	Cliff	HQs	Headquarters	Pkwy	Parkway	Vet	Veterans
Clfs	Cliffs	Ht	Height	Pas	Paseo	Vw	View
Clb	Club	Hts	Heights	Psg	Passage	Vil	Village
Cltr	Cluster	HS	High School	Pass	Passenger	Wk	Walk
Col	Coliseum	Hwy	Highway	Pth	Path	Wall	Wall
Coll	College	Hl	Hill	Pn	Pine	Wy	Way
Com	Common	Hls	Hills	Pns	Pines	W	West
Coms	Commons	Hist	Historical	Pl	Place	WMA	Wildlife Management Area
Comm	Community	Hllw	Hollow	Pln	Plain		
Co.	Company	Hosp	Hospital	Plns	Plains		
Cons	Conservation	Hse	House	Plgnd	Playground		
Conv & Vis Bur	Convention and Visitors Bureau	Ind Res	Indian Reservation	Plz	Plaza		
Cor	Corner	Info	Information	Pt	Point		
Cors	Corners	Inst	Institute	Pnd	Pond		
Corp	Corporation	Int'l	International	PO	Post Office		
Corr	Corridor	I	Island	Pres	Preserve		
Cte	Corte	Is	Islands	Prov	Provincial		
CC	Country Club	Isl	Isle	Rwy	Railway		
Co	County	Jct	Junction	Rec	Recreation		
Ct	Court	Knl	Knoll	Reg	Regional		
Ct Hse	Court House	Knls	Knolls	Res	Reservoir		
Cts	Courts	Lk	Lake	Rst	Rest		
Cr	Creek	Lndg	Landing	Rdg	Ridge		
Cres	Crescent	Ln	Lane	Rd	Road		
Cross	Crossing	Lib	Library	Rds	Roads		
Curv	Curve	Ldg	Lodge	St.	Saint		

Houston Street Index

STREET
Block City ZIP Map# Grid

HIGHWAYS

ALT - Alternate Route
BIA - Bureau of Indian Affairs
BUS - Business Route
CO - County Highway/Road
FM - Farm To Market Road
HIST - Historic Highway
I - Interstate Highway
LP - State Loop
PK - Park & Recreation Road
PROV - Provincial Highway
RTE - Other Route
SPR - State Spur
SR - State Route/Highway
TCH - Trans-Canada Highway
US - United States Highway

CO-48
- PRLD 77047 4373 B7
- PRLD 77583 4500 B4
- PRLD 77584 4373 B7
- PRLD 77584 4500 B3
CO-48 Kingsley Dr
- PRLD 77047 4373 B7
- PRLD 77583 4500 B4
- PRLD 77584 4373 B7
- PRLD 77584 4500 B3
CO-56
- BzaC 77583 4744 E6
CO-56 CR-56
- BzaC 77583 4744 E6
CO-57
900 IWCY 77583 4744 E4
900 IWCY 77583 4745 B4
1100 BzaC 77583 4745 D4
1100 MNVL 77578 4745 D4
1100 MNVL 77583 4745 D4
CO-57 Juliff Manvel Rd
900 IWCY 77583 4744 E4
900 IWCY 77583 4745 A4
1100 BzaC 77583 4745 D4
1100 MNVL 77578 4745 D4
1100 MNVL 77583 4745 D4
CO-72
5700 BzaC 77583 4745 D4
5700 IWCY 77583 4745 D4
5700 MNVL 77578 4745 D4
5700 MNVL 77583 4745 D4
CO-72 Clark Rd
5700 BzaC 77583 4745 D4
5700 IWCY 77583 4745 D4
5700 MNVL 77578 4745 D4
5700 MNVL 77583 4745 D4
CO-79
8500 IWCY 77583 4745 D3
8600 BzaC 77583 4745 D4
CO-79 W Colony Loop Rd
8500 IWCY 77583 4745 D3
8600 BzaC 77583 4745 D4
CO-89
- PRLD 77584 4501 E4
CO-89 Old Chocolate Bayou Rd
- PRLD 77584 4501 E4
CO-90
- BzaC 77584 4501 C5
- PRLD 77584 4501 C6
CO-90 CR-90
- BzaC 77584 4501 C6
- PRLD 77584 4501 C6
CO-127
1500 BzaC 77581 4504 B7
1500 PRLD 77581 4504 B7
16700 BzaC 77581 4628 B1
18000 BzaC 77511 4628 D2
18200 BzaC 77546 4628 E2
CO-127 Dixie-Friendswood Rd
18000 BzaC 77511 4628 D2
18000 BzaC 77581 4628 D2
18200 BzaC 77546 4628 E2
CO-127 Hastings Friendswood Rd
1500 BzaC 77581 4504 B7
1500 PRLD 77581 4504 B7
16700 BzaC 77581 4628 B1
CO-128
7500 BzaC 77511 4627 B4
7500 BzaC 77584 4627 B4
7500 PRLD 77584 4627 B4
CO-128 Hastings Cannon Rd
7500 BzaC 77511 4627 B4
7500 BzaC 77584 4627 B4
7500 PRLD 77584 4627 B4
CO-155
1200 ALVN 77511 4867 D3
1700 BzaC 77511 4867 E3
1900 BzaC 77511 4868 B4
CO-155 Five Point Rd
1900 BzaC 77511 4867 E3
1900 BzaC 77511 4868 A4
CO-155 Fulton Dr
- BzaC 77511 4868 B4
CO-155 E South St
1200 ALVN 77511 4867 D3
1700 BzaC 77511 4867 E3
CO-158
3800 ALVN 77511 4867 D6
4900 BzaC 77511 4867 D7
CO-158 Mustang Rd
3800 ALVN 77511 4867 D6
4900 BzaC 77511 4867 D7
CO-257
- GlsC 77554 5547 C6
10200 BzaC 77541 5547 B7
10200 BzaC 77541 5654 A1
CO-257 Bluewater Hwy
- GlsC 77554 5547 C6
10200 BzaC 77541 5547 B7
10200 BzaC 77541 5654 A1
CO-326
3200 BzaC 77511 4868 B6
CO-326 Newson Rd
3200 BzaC 77511 4868 B6
CO-397
10 BzaC 77511 4747 E1
CO-397 Wink Rd
10 BzaC 77511 4747 E1
CO-397 Wink Wyn Rd
1400 BzaC 77511 4747 E1
CO-413
2200 BzaC 77511 4628 A2
2200 PRLD 77511 4628 A2
9100 BzaC 77511 4627 E2
9100 PRLD 77511 4627 E2
CO-413 N Hastings Field Rd
2200 BzaC 77511 4628 A2
2200 PRLD 77511 4628 A2
9100 BzaC 77511 4627 E2
9100 PRLD 77511 4627 E2
CO-560
5200 BzaC 77581 4502 B1
5200 PRLD 77581 4502 B1
CO-560 CR-560
5200 BzaC 77581 4502 B1
5200 PRLD 77581 4502 B1
CO-562
10400 PRLD 77584 4501 A2
CO-562 Smith Ranch Road 1
10400 PRLD 77584 4501 A2
CO-648K
2600 BzaC 77584 4501 D5
CO-648K Lakecrest Dr
2600 BzaC 77584 4501 D5
CO-824A
5900 BzaC 77583 4623 C5
5900 PRLD 77583 4623 C5
CO-824A Martha Dr
5900 BzaC 77583 4623 C5
5900 PRLD 77583 4623 C5
CO-824D
- BzaC 77583 4623 C6
CO-870H
100 BzaC 77511 4748 E1
CO-879B
16700 BzaC 77584 4626 E1
17300 PRLD 77584 4626 E2
CO-879B N Wayne Ln
16700 BzaC 77584 4626 E1
17300 PRLD 77584 4626 E2
CO-922
- BzaC 77578 4501 B6
- BzaC 77584 4501 B6
- PRLD 77584 4501 B6
CO-922 Jeske Rd
- BzaC 77584 4501 B6
- PRLD 77584 4501 B6
3900 BzaC 77578 4501 B7
FM-149
2900 HarC 77038 3543 A6
2900 HarC 77086 3543 A6
2900 HarC 77088 3543 A6
4100 MtgC 77354 2670 D5
35700 MtgC 77362 2816 D3
37100 MtgC 77362 2670 E7
FM-149 SPUR
37500 MtgC 77354 2670 D5
FM-149 W Mt Houston Rd
2900 HarC 77038 3543 A6
2900 HarC 77086 3543 A6
2900 HarC 77088 3543 A6
FM-149 SPUR Spur Rd
37500 MtgC 77354 2670 D5
FM-188
8200 GLSN 77554 5107 D6
FM-188 Harborside Dr
- GLSN 77554 5107 D6
FM-188 Teichman Rd
8200 GLSN 77554 5107 D6
FM-270
- LGCY 77539 4632 E6
- LGCY 77573 4507 E6
- LGCY 77573 4508 A7
- LGCY 77573 4632 B1
18100 WEBS 77058 4507 E6
FM-270 Egret Bay Blvd
- LGCY 77573 4507 E6
18100 WEBS 77058 4507 E6
FM-275
200 GLSN 77550 5109 D2
3100 GLSN 77550 5108 E3
3100 GLSN 77551 5108 E3
5200 GLSN 77554 5108 C4
5400 GLSN 77554 5107 E4
FM-275 Harborside Dr
400 GLSN 77550 5109 E1
5400 GLSN 77551 5108 C4
5400 GLSN 77554 5107 E4
5400 GLSN 77554 5108 B4
FM-275 Port Industrial Rd
2900 GLSN 77550 5109 A3
3100 GLSN 77550 5108 E3
3100 GLSN 77551 5108 E3
5200 GLSN 77554 5108 C4
FM-275 Water St
200 GLSN 77550 5109 D2
FM-359
- PNIS 77445 3099 B7
- WlrC 77445 2954 A7
- WlrC 77445 3099 A1
- WlrC 77445 3244 B6
100 FBnC 77469 4365 B4
400 RHMD 77469 4365 B5
3300 FBnC 77469 4364 C2
6700 FBnC 77469 4232 A3
FM-359 Richmond Foster Rd
2600 FBnC 77469 4365 A2
3300 FBnC 77469 4364 C2
6700 FBnC 77469 4232 A3
FM-359 Skinner Ln
100 FBnC 77469 4365 B4
400 RHMD 77469 4365 B5
FM-362
- WALR 77484 3101 D5
- WlrC 77484 2956 D6
- WlrC 77484 3101 D3
- WlrC 77484 3246 C6
FM-517
- DKSN 77539 4752 E6
- GlsC 77511 4751 A6
- GlsC 77511 4752 A6
- LGCY 77511 4750 C7
- LGCY 77511 4751 A6
- LGCY 77517 4751 E6
- LGCY 77517 4752 A6
- LGCY 77539 4752 E6
- LGCY 77539 4753 B5
- LGCY 77546 4750 C7
- TXCY 77539 4754 E1
100 DKSN 77539 4753 D3
200 GlsC 77539 4636 B5
600 ALVN 77511 4749 E7
600 BzaC 77511 4749 E7
800 ALVN 77511 4750 A7
1000 GlsC 77539 4635 A6
1000 TXCY 77539 4635 D6
1100 GlsC 77511 4750 C7
1700 TXCY 77539 4634 E7
1700 TXCY 77539 4755 E1
2500 DKSN 77539 4754 A3
FM-517 9th St
200 GlsC 77539 4636 B5
FM-517 29th St
1000 GlsC 77539 4635 A6
1000 TXCY 77539 4635 D6
1700 TXCY 77539 4634 E7
1700 TXCY 77539 4755 E1
FM-517 41st St
- DKSN 77539 4752 E6
- DKSN 77539 4753 B5
- DKSN 77539 4754 D2
- LGCY 77539 4752 E6
- LGCY 77539 4753 B5
- TXCY 77539 4754 E1
- TXCY 77539 4755 D1
FM-517 Avenue I
900 GlsC 77539 4636 A6
1600 GlsC 77539 4635 E6
FM-517 Avenue J
2200 GlsC 77539 4635 D6
FM-517 Dickinson Rd
- ALVN 77511 4749 E7
FM-518
- LGCY 77573 4509 B7
- PRLD 77581 4505 B7
100 FRDW 77546 4505 B7
100 LGCY 77573 4631 B4
100 LGCY 77573 4632 A3
500 FRDW 77546 4629 E4
900 GlsC 77565 4509 D6
900 KMAH 77565 4509 D6
900 LGCY 77565 4509 C7
1100 PRLD 77581 4504 E6
2300 FRDW 77546 4630 A5
2500 PRLD 77581 4503 A3
2600 LGCY 77573 4630 E5
2900 LGCY 77573 4633 A1
4800 PRLD 77584 4503 A3
5300 PRLD 77581 4502 C3
5300 PRLD 77584 4502 C3
7900 PRLD 77581 4501 A4
7900 PRLD 77584 4501 A4
9000 BzaC 77584 4501 C4
10500 PRLD 77584 4500 E4
10800 PRLD 77583 4500 C4
FM-518 Broadway St
9300 BzaC 77584 4501 C4
9300 PRLD 77584 4501 C4
10500 PRLD 77584 4500 E4
10800 PRLD 77583 4500 C4
FM-518 E Broadway St
1100 PRLD 77581 4504 E6
2500 PRLD 77581 4503 A3
FM-518 W Broadway St
4000 PRLD 77581 4503 B3
4800 PRLD 77584 4503 A3
5300 PRLD 77581 4502 C3
5300 PRLD 77584 4502 C3
7900 PRLD 77581 4501 A4
7900 PRLD 77584 4501 A4
9000 BzaC 77584 4501 C4
FM-518 Deke Slayton Blvd
- LGCY 77573 4509 B7
900 GlsC 77565 4509 D6
900 KMAH 77565 4509 D6
900 LGCY 77565 4509 C7
FM-518 Deke Slayton Hwy
- LGCY 77565 4509 B7
- LGCY 77573 4509 B7
2200 LGCY 77573 4632 E1
2900 LGCY 77573 4633 A1
FM-518 N Friendswood Dr
- PRLD 77581 4505 B7
100 FRDW 77546 4505 B7
FM-518 S Friendswood Dr
100 FRDW 77546 4505 B7
500 FRDW 77546 4629 E4
2300 FRDW 77546 4630 A5
2600 LGCY 77573 4630 B6
FM-518 E Main St
100 LGCY 77573 4632 A3
FM-518 W Main St
100 LGCY 77573 4631 B4
FM-519
- TXCY 77590 4991 A2
10 LMQU 77568 4990 D3
10 TXCY 77590 4990 E3
2500 LMQU 77568 4989 B3
4000 HTCK 77563 4989 B3
6400 HTCK 77563 4988 E4
FM-519 Main St
10 LMQU 77568 4990 D3
10 TXCY 77590 4990 D3
2500 LMQU 77568 4989 B3
4000 HTCK 77563 4989 B3
6400 HTCK 77563 4988 E4
FM-521
- HOUS 77021 4102 E7
300 FBnC 77545 4372 E7
300 PRLD 77053 4372 E7
800 FBnC 77545 4499 E1
800 PRLD 77545 4499 E1
3700 FBnC 77545 4623 B1
4700 ARLA 77545 4623 B3
4700 ARLA 77583 4623 B1
4700 FBnC 77583 4623 B3
6600 ARLA 77583 4622 E7
6900 FBnC 77583 4622 E7
7000 HOUS 77030 4102 E7
7000 HOUS 77054 4102 E7
8500 HOUS 77054 4242 B7
10600 HOUS 77045 4242 D3
12300 HOUS 77045 4373 B1
13400 HOUS 77053 4373 B1
13700 HarC 77053 4373 A4
14300 HarC 77053 4372 E6
15200 HarC 77047 4372 E7
15200 PRLD 77047 4372 E7
FM-521 Almeda Rd
- HOUS 77021 4102 E7
300 FBnC 77545 4372 E7
300 PRLD 77053 4372 E7
800 FBnC 77545 4499 E1
800 PRLD 77545 4499 E1
7000 HOUS 77030 4102 E7
7000 HOUS 77054 4102 E7
8500 HOUS 77054 4242 B7
10600 HOUS 77045 4242 D3
12300 HOUS 77045 4373 B1
13400 HOUS 77053 4373 B1
13700 HarC 77053 4373 A4
14300 HarC 77053 4372 E6
15200 HarC 77047 4372 E7
15200 PRLD 77047 4372 E7
FM-525
- HOUS 77038 3544 B1
10 HOUS 77037 3544 B1
10 HOUS 77060 3544 E1
400 HarC 77060 3544 E1
700 HarC 77060 3545 A1
700 HOUS 77060 3545 A1
800 HarC 77032 3545 E1
800 HarC 77039 3545 E1
800 HOUS 77032 3545 A1
2900 HarC 77032 3546 E2
3400 HOUS 77032 3546 A1
14200 HarC 77396 3546 E2
14500 HOUS 77396 3546 E2
FM-525 Aldine Bender Rd
- HarC 77396 3546 E2
- HOUS 77396 3546 E2
10 HOUS 77037 3544 B1
10 HOUS 77060 3544 E1
400 HarC 77060 3544 E1
700 HarC 77060 3545 A1
700 HOUS 77060 3545 A1
800 HarC 77032 3545 E1
800 HarC 77039 3545 E1
800 HOUS 77032 3545 A1
2900 HarC 77032 3546 E2
3400 HOUS 77032 3546 A1
FM-525 Fallbrook Dr
- HOUS 77037 3544 B1
- HOUS 77038 3544 B1
- HOUS 77060 3544 B1
FM-525 Lee Rd
14200 HarC 77032 3546 E2
14200 HarC 77396 3546 E2
14500 HOUS 77396 3546 E1
FM-526
- HarC 77044 3828 A1
10 HOUS 77013 3827 E6
600 HOUS 77013 3966 E1
700 HOUS 77015 3966 E2
900 HOUS 77015 3967 A2
5000 HOUS 77013 3828 A4
5000 HOUS 77049 3828 A4
6700 HarC 77049 3828 A1
FM-526 CE King Pkwy
- HarC 77044 3828 A1
- HarC 77049 3828 A1
FM-526 Federal Rd
700 HOUS 77015 3966 E2
900 HOUS 77015 3967 A2
FM-526 S Lake Houston Pkwy
5000 HOUS 77013 3827 E5
5000 HOUS 77013 3828 A4
5000 HOUS 77049 3828 A4
6700 HarC 77049 3828 A2
FM-526 Maxey Rd
10 HOUS 77013 3827 E6
600 HOUS 77013 3966 E1
700 HOUS 77015 3966 E1
FM-527
9400 HOUS 77028 3687 E7
9400 HOUS 77078 3687 E7
10900 HarC 77078 3687 E2
FM-527 Mesa Dr
9400 HOUS 77028 3687 E7
9400 HOUS 77078 3687 E7
10900 HarC 77078 3687 E2
FM-528
- WEBS 77598 4507 A7
100 FRDW 77546 4629 E2
1400 HarC 77598 4630 A2
1400 HarC 77598 4631 A1
1400 LGCY 77598 4630 A2
1400 WEBS 77598 4630 A2
1400 WEBS 77598 4631 A1
1600 FRDW 77598 4630 D1
1800 ALVN 77511 4749 C6
1900 HOUS 77058 4508 A4
1900 NSUB 77058 4508 A4
2200 SEBK 77586 4509 C3
2500 FRDW 77546 4749 C6
3200 FRDW 77546 4630 B1
3200 HarC 77546 4630 B1
3700 ELGO 77586 4509 A2
FM-528 Friendswood Rd
- FRDW 77546 4749 D3
1800 ALVN 77511 4749 C6
FM-528 NASA Pkwy
1900 HOUS 77058 4508 A4
1900 NSUB 77058 4508 A4
3700 ELGO 77586 4509 A2
3700 SEBK 77586 4509 A2
FM-528 W NASA Pkwy
- FRDW 77598 4630 E1
- WEBS 77598 4507 A7
1400 HarC 77598 4630 A2
1400 HarC 77598 4631 A1
1400 LGCY 77598 4630 A2
1400 WEBS 77598 4630 A2
1400 WEBS 77598 4631 A1
FM-528 W NASA Rd 1
- WEBS 77598 4507 C6
FM-528 NASA Road 1
2200 SEBK 77586 4509 C3
FM-528 E Parkwood Av
100 FRDW 77546 4629 D3
FM-528 W Parkwood Av
100 FRDW 77546 4629 B5
2500 FRDW 77546 4749 C6
3200 ALVN 77511 4749 D3
FM-529
- HarC 77449 3675 E2
- HarC 77493 3675 A2
10900 HarC 77040 3680 C2
10900 HarC 77041 3680 B2
10900 JRSV 77040 3680 C2
11300 JRSV 77041 3680 A2
12100 HarC 77041 3679 D2
13200 HarC 77095 3679 B2
14100 HarC 77084 3679 A2
15000 HarC 77084 3678 D2
15000 HarC 77095 3678 B2
17400 HarC 77084 3677 E2
17400 HarC 77095 3677 E2
17700 HarC 77433 3677 B2
17700 HarC 77449 3677 B2
20500 HarC 77433 3676 A2
20500 HarC 77449 3676 A2
FM-529 Freeman Rd
- HarC 77084 3677 E2
- HarC 77449 3675 E2
- HarC 77493 3675 A2
18000 HarC 77095 3677 E2
18000 HarC 77433 3677 B2
18000 HarC 77449 3677 B2
20500 HarC 77433 3676 A2
20500 HarC 77449 3676 A2
FM-529 Spencer Rd
10900 HarC 77040 3680 C2
10900 HarC 77041 3680 B2
10900 JRSV 77040 3680 C2
11300 JRSV 77041 3680 A2
12100 HarC 77041 3679 D2
13200 HarC 77095 3679 B2
14100 HarC 77084 3679 A2
15000 HarC 77084 3678 D2
15000 HarC 77095 3678 B2
17400 HarC 77084 3677 E2
17400 HarC 77095 3677 E2
FM-565
100 MTBL 77520 3696 E5
300 BYTN 77520 3974 B1
300 CmbC 77520 3974 C1
2300 CmbC 77520 3835 E7
FM-565 Cove Rd
100 MTBL 77520 3696 E5
FM-646
- DKSN 77510 4871 A4
- DKSN 77539 4871 A4
- GlsC 77510 4987 B2
- LGCY 77539 4632 C7
- LGCY 77539 4633 E5
- LGCY 77539 4634 A5
- LGCY 77573 4632 C7
- LGCY 77573 4633 A5
- TXCY 77539 4633 E5
100 GlsC 77518 4634 D3
900 GlsC 77539 4636 A5
1000 GlsC 77539 4634 C4
1200 TXCY 77539 4634 A5
1600 GlsC 77510 4871 A4
1600 GlsC 77539 4871 A4
1800 LGCY 77539 4753 B1
1800 LGCY 77573 4753 B1
1900 LGCY 77539 4752 E3
2000 GlsC 77539 4635 E4
2000 STFE 77510 4871 A2
2700 TXCY 77539 4635 B4
4500 STFE 77510 4987 B1
4800 GlsC 77518 4635 A3
5200 TXCY 77518 4635 A3
5600 DKSN 77539 4753 A6
FM-646 Avenue M
4200 STFE 77510 4871 A7
4500 STFE 77510 4987 A1
FM-646 E Bayshore Dr
900 GlsC 77539 4636 A5
2000 GlsC 77539 4635 E4
2700 TXCY 77539 4635 B4
FM-646 W Bayshore Dr
4600 GlsC 77518 4634 E3
4800 GlsC 77518 4635 A3
5200 TXCY 77518 4635 A3
5600 GlsC 77539 4635 B3
FM-646 Grand Av
100 GlsC 77518 4634 D3
1000 GlsC 77539 4634 C4
1200 TXCY 77539 4634 C4
FM-646 Main St
5000 STFE 77510 4987 B1
FM-723
- FBnC 77494 4092 D6
200 FBnC 77471 4490 D1
300 RSBG 77471 4490 D3
4700 FBnC 77469 4232 D6
9200 FBnC 77469 4092 D6
FM-723 Houston St
300 RSBG 77471 4490 D3
FM-723 Rosenberg Foster Rd
- RSBG 77471 4490 D3
200 FBnC 77471 4490 D1
FM-723 Spring Green Rd
- FBnC 77494 4092 D6
6700 FBnC 77469 4232 D6
9200 FBnC 77469 4092 D6
FM-762
- RHMD 77469 4492 A4
300 RHMD 77469 4491 E2
2100 FBnC 77469 4491 E3
3700 FBnC 77469 4492 E6
5200 FBnC 77469 4493 B7
7000 RSBG 77469 4493 B7
FM-762 SPUR
200 RHMD 77469 4492 A1
400 RHMD 77469 4491 E1
FM-762 SPUR S 2nd St
300 RHMD 77469 4491 E1
500 RHMD 77469 4492 A1
FM-762 S 11th St
300 RHMD 77469 4491 E2
FM-762 SPUR Austin St
200 RHMD 77469 4492 A1
400 RHMD 77469 4491 E1
FM-762 Thompson Rd
- RHMD 77469 4492 A4
900 RHMD 77469 4491 E2
2100 FBnC 77469 4491 E3
3700 FBnC 77469 4492 E6
5200 FBnC 77469 4493 A7
FM-762 Thompsons Rd
6100 FBnC 77469 4493 B7
FM-830
1000 CNRO 77303 2237 D1
1000 CNRO 77304 2237 A1
1000 CNRO 77378 2237 A1
1000 MtgC 77378 2237 A1
1000 PNVL 77304 2237 B1
1000 PNVL 77318 2237 B1
9700 MtgC 77304 2237 A1
9700 MtgC 77318 2237 A1
9800 MtgC 77304 2236 E1
9800 MtgC 77318 2236 E1
FM-830 Seven Coves Rd
1000 CNRO 77304 2237 B1
1000 MtgC 77378 2237 B1
1000 PNVL 77304 2237 B1
1000 PNVL 77318 2237 B1
9700 MtgC 77304 2237 A1
9700 MtgC 77318 2237 A1
FM-865
100 HarC 77047 4374 D3
100 HarC 77584 4374 D7
100 HOUS 77047 4374 D3
100 PRLD 77581 4374 D7
100 PRLD 77584 4374 D7
500 PRLD 77581 4501 E2
500 PRLD 77584 4501 E2
5700 HOUS 77021 4103 D7
7200 HOUS 77033 4103 D7
7200 HOUS 77051 4103 D7
7300 HOUS 77033 4243 D1
7300 HOUS 77051 4243 D1
10100 HOUS 77047 4243 D7
10100 HOUS 77048 4243 D7
11800 HOUS 77048 4374 D7
13900 HarC 77048 4374 D4
FM-865 Cullen Blvd
100 HarC 77047 4374 D3
100 HarC 77584 4374 D7
100 HOUS 77047 4374 D3
100 PRLD 77581 4374 D7
100 PRLD 77584 4374 D7
500 PRLD 77581 4501 E2
500 PRLD 77584 4501 E2
5700 HOUS 77021 4103 D7
7200 HOUS 77033 4103 D7
7200 HOUS 77051 4103 D7
7300 HOUS 77033 4243 D1
7300 HOUS 77051 4243 D1
10100 HOUS 77047 4243 D7
10100 HOUS 77048 4243 D7
11800 HOUS 77048 4374 D7
13900 HarC 77048 4374 D4
FM-1008
1700 HarC 77336 3266 E5
1700 HarC 77336 3267 C5
1700 HarC 77532 3266 E5
1700 HarC 77532 3267 C5
FM-1008 Atascocita Rd
1700 HarC 77336 3266 E5
1700 HarC 77336 3267 C5
1700 HarC 77532 3266 E5
1700 HarC 77532 3267 C5
FM-1010
- LbyC 77327 2538 E1
- LbyC 77327 2684 D1
- PLMG 77327 2684 D2
FM-1092
1000 FBnC 77477 4369 D4
1000 MSCY 77459 4369 D5
1000 MSCY 77477 4369 D4
3000 MSCY 77459 4496 D1
11800 HOUS 77031 4238 D7
11900 HarC 77031 4238 D5
12100 STAF 77477 4238 D6
13200 STAF 77477 4369 D1
FM-1092 Murphy Rd
12100 HarC 77031 4238 D6
12100 STAF 77477 4238 D6
13200 STAF 77477 4369 D1
FM-1092 Stafford Dewalt Rd
1000 FBnC 77477 4369 D4
1000 MSCY 77459 4369 D5
1000 MSCY 77477 4369 D4
3000 MSCY 77459 4496 D1
FM-1092 Wilcrest Dr
11800 HOUS 77031 4238 D7
11900 HarC 77031 4238 D5
FM-1093
4800 HOUS 77027 3961 A7
4800 HOUS 77056 3961 A7
5100 HOUS 77056 3960 E7
5700 HOUS 77057 3960 D7
6500 HOUS 77063 3960 A7
7900 HOUS 77063 3959 E7
9700 HOUS 77042 3959 A7
10000 HOUS 77042 3958 B7
11100 HOUS 77077 3958 B7
11100 HOUS 77082 3958 C7
11900 HOUS 77077 3957 A7
11900 HOUS 77082 3957 E7
13100 HarC 77077 3957 B7
13100 HarC 77082 3957 B7
13700 HOUS 77077 3956 E7
13700 HOUS 77082 3956 E7
14800 HOUS 77082 4096 C1
15500 HarC 77082 4096 A3
16200 HarC 77082 4095 E3
16200 HOUS 77082 4095 E3
16800 HOUS 77450 4095 D4
16800 HOUS 77469 4095 D4
19100 FBnC 77469 4094 A5
19100 FBnC 77469 4095 A5
21000 HOUS 77469 4094 A5
21600 FBnC 77469 4093 E5
21600 HOUS 77469 4093 E5
24000 FBnC 77494 4093 A6
24300 FBnC 77469 4092 E6
24300 FBnC 77494 4092 E6
FM-1093 Westheimer Rd
- FBnC 77469 4095 D4
4800 HOUS 77027 3961 A7
4800 HOUS 77056 3961 A7
5100 HOUS 77056 3960 E7
5700 HOUS 77057 3960 D7
6500 HOUS 77063 3960 A7
7900 HOUS 77063 3959 E7
9700 HOUS 77042 3959 A7
10000 HOUS 77042 3958 B7
11100 HOUS 77077 3958 B7
11100 HOUS 77082 3958 C7
11900 HOUS 77077 3957 E7
11900 HOUS 77082 3957 E7
13100 HarC 77082 3957 B7
13200 HarC 77077 3957 B7
13700 HOUS 77077 3956 E7
13700 HOUS 77082 3956 E7
14700 HOUS 77082 4096 A3
15400 HarC 77082 4096 C1
16200 HarC 77082 4095 E3
16200 HOUS 77082 4095 E3
16800 HOUS 77450 4095 D4
16800 HOUS 77469 4095 D4
FM-1093 Westpark Tollway
24000 FBnC 77469 4093 A6
24000 FBnC 77494 4093 A6
FM-1098
- PRVW 77445 2955 B6
- WlrC 77445 2955 B5
100 PRVW 77445 3100 A1
FM-1098 Owens Rd
- PRVW 77445 3100 B1
FM-1098 University Dr
100 PRVW 77445 3100 C1
FM-1098 Williams St
- PRVW 77445 3100 A1
FM-1128
2100 PRLD 77581 4502 B4
2100 PRLD 77584 4502 B6
3200 BzaC 77584 4502 B6
4300 BzaC 77584 4626 B2
4300 MNVL 77584 4626 B2
4300 PRLD 77584 4626 B2
4600 MNVL 77578 4626 A4
5400 MNVL 77578 4625 E7
6700 MNVL 77578 4746 D2
FM-1128 Manvel Rd
2100 PRLD 77581 4502 B4
2100 PRLD 77584 4502 B6
3200 BzaC 77584 4502 B6
FM-1128 Masters Rd
- BzaC 77584 4626 B2
- PRLD 77584 4626 B2
4600 MNVL 77578 4626 A4
4600 MNVL 77584 4626 B3
5400 MNVL 77578 4625 E7
6700 MNVL 77578 4746 D2
FM-1128 N Masters Rd
4300 BzaC 77584 4626 B2
4300 MNVL 77584 4626 B2
4300 PRLD 77584 4626 B2
FM-1266
- LGCY 77565 4633 A7
- LGCY 77573 4633 B3
900 GlsC 77539 4633 A6
900 LGCY 77539 4633 A5
2400 DKSN 77539 4633 A7
2700 DKSN 77539 4754 A1
FM-1266 Dickinson Av
- LGCY 77573 4633 A5
900 GlsC 77539 4633 A6
900 LGCY 77539 4633 A5
2400 DKSN 77539 4633 A7
2700 DKSN 77539 4754 A1
FM-1266 League City Pkwy
- LGCY 77565 4633 A7
- LGCY 77573 4633 B3
FM-1266 Tuscan Lakes Blvd
- LGCY 77539 4633 A5
- LGCY 77573 4633 A5
FM-1314
100 CNRO 77301 2384 D7
1800 CNRO 77301 2530 E2
11600 CNRO 77302 2530 E2
11600 MtgC 77302 2530 E2
11700 CNRO 77301 2531 A3
11700 CNRO 77302 2531 A3
11700 MtgC 77302 2531 C5
14500 MtgC 77302 2677 E1
14900 MtgC 77302 2678 B2
17900 MtgC 77302 2825 A1
19200 MtgC 77365 2825 E6
19800 MtgC 77357 2825 D5
20800 MtgC 77365 2826 A7
21200 MtgC 77365 2972 A1
23400 MtgC 77365 2973 A5
FM-1314 Conroe Porter Rd
11600 CNRO 77301 2530 E2
11600 CNRO 77302 2530 E2
11600 MtgC 77302 2530 E2
11700 CNRO 77301 2531 A3
11700 CNRO 77302 2531 A3
11700 MtgC 77302 2531 C5
14500 MtgC 77302 2677 E1
14900 MtgC 77302 2678 B2
17900 MtgC 77302 2825 A1
19200 MtgC 77365 2825 C3
FM-1314 Porter Rd
100 CNRO 77301 2384 D7
1800 CNRO 77301 2530 E2
FM-1405
- BYTN 77520 3974 B7
- CmbC 77520 3974 D4
- CmbC 77520 4114 B2
8500 BYTN 77520 4114 B6
9000 CmbC 77520 4254 B1
FM-1405 W Bay Rd
- BYTN 77520 3974 B7
- CmbC 77520 3974 D4
- CmbC 77520 4114 B2
8500 BYTN 77520 4114 B6
9000 CmbC 77520 4254 B1
FM-1413
- LbyC 77535 3269 E7
- LbyC 77535 3413 E1
FM-1462
900 ALVN 77511 4867 A5
2000 ALVN 77511 4866 D5
10300 BzaC 77511 4866 A7
FM-1462 Parker-Davis School Rd
- BzaC 77511 4866 C6
FM-1463
100 KATY 77493 3952 B1
100 KATY 77494 3952 A3
1000 FBnC 77494 3952 A3
1400 FBnC 77494 3951 D7
FM-1464
- HOUS 77082 4095 D4
- HOUS 77469 4095 D4
6500 FBnC 77082 4095 D4
6500 FBnC 77083 4095 D7
6500 FBnC 77469 4095 D7
8600 FBnC 77083 4235 E3
8600 FBnC 77469 4235 E3
9500 FBnC 77478 4235 E2
13000 FBnC 77469 4366 E1
13000 FBnC 77478 4366 E1
FM-1464 S Barker Cypress Rd
- FBnC 77082 4095 D4
- FBnC 77083 4095 D4
- FBnC 77469 4095 D4
- HOUS 77082 4095 D4
- HOUS 77469 4095 D4
FM-1484
200 CNRO 77301 2384 D1
2200 CNRO 77303 2384 D1
2300 MtgC 77303 2384 D1
2600 CNRO 77303 2238 E6
2600 MtgC 77303 2238 E6
10100 CNRO 77303 2239 A5
10200 MtgC 77303 2239 A4
FM-1484 N 10th St
200 CNRO 77301 2384 B4
FM-1484 Airport Rd
1100 CNRO 77301 2384 D1
2200 CNRO 77303 2384 D1
2300 MtgC 77303 2384 D1
2600 CNRO 77303 2238 E6
2600 MtgC 77303 2238 E6
10100 CNRO 77303 2239 A5
10200 MtgC 77303 2239 A5
FM-1485
- CNRO 77301 2385 B3
- CNRO 77303 2385 B3
- CTSH 77303 2385 E4
- HarC 77336 2830 C7
1000 CTSH 77301 2385 E4
1000 CTSH 77306 2385 E4
1000 MtgC 77301 2385 C3
1000 MtgC 77306 2385 C3
11000 MtgC 77306 2532 E1
11200 MtgC 77306 2533 D6
14300 MtgC 77306 2679 E1
14500 MtgC 77302 2679 E1
14800 MtgC 77302 2680 E6
14800 MtgC 77306 2680 E6
16600 MtgC 77357 2680 C5
17300 MtgC 77357 2681 A7
17600 MtgC 77357 2827 A2

Block	City	ZIP	Map#	Grid
FM-1485				
23200	MtgC	77357	2828	A6
25300	MtgC	77357	2829	E6
28100	MtgC	77357	2830	B7
FM-1485 Old TX-105 E				
-	CNRO	77301	2385	B3
-	CNRO	77303	2385	B3
-	CTSH	77301	2385	C3
-	CTSH	77303	2385	B3
FM-1486				
100	MtgC	77354	2668	D2
1400	MtgC	77316	2668	D2
FM-1488				
-	CNRO	77384	2676	A1
-	CNRO	77385	2676	A1
-	HMPD	77445	2953	C7
-	HMPD	77445	2954	A5
-	MtgC	77384	2676	A1
-	MtgC	77385	2676	A1
-	WlrC	77363	2813	B1
-	WlrC	77445	2953	E6
-	WlrC	77445	2954	C4
-	WlrC	77445	2955	E2
-	WlrC	77445	2956	A1
100	CNRO	77384	2675	A2
100	MtgC	77384	2675	A2
800	MAGA	77355	2669	A5
2200	MAGA	77354	2669	E3
2400	MtgC	77354	2669	C4
2500	MtgC	77384	2674	A3
2500	WDLD	77384	2674	A3
3300	MtgC	77382	2674	D2
3300	WDLD	77382	2674	D2
4000	WDLD	77354	2674	C3
4600	MtgC	77354	2674	A3
5100	MtgC	77354	2673	A4
8400	MtgC	77354	2672	A4
10000	MtgC	77354	2671	D3
13700	MtgC	77354	2670	E3
18800	MAGA	77355	2668	E6
19000	MtgC	77355	2668	C7
20900	MtgC	77355	2814	B1
21500	MtgC	77355	2813	A2
21800	WlrC	77447	2813	E1
FM-1488 Magnolia Blvd				
800	MAGA	77355	2669	A5
FM-1488 Magnolia Pkwy				
2200	MAGA	77354	2669	E3
2400	MtgC	77354	2669	C4
18700	MAGA	77355	2669	A5
18800	MAGA	77355	2668	E6
19000	MtgC	77355	2668	C7
20900	MtgC	77355	2814	B1
21500	MtgC	77355	2813	A2
21800	WlrC	77447	2813	A2
FM-1640				
800	RSBG	77471	4490	D4
1700	RHMD	77469	4491	E4
1700	RSBG	77469	4491	E4
1700	RSBG	77471	4491	A4
5300	FBnC	77469	4491	E4
FM-1640 Avenue I				
800	RSBG	77471	4490	D4
2600	RSBG	77471	4491	A4
4900	RSBG	77469	4491	D4
5000	RHMD	77469	4491	D4
FM-1640 BF Terry Blvd				
5300	FBnC	77469	4491	E4
5300	RHMD	77469	4491	E4
FM-1736				
-	WlrC	77445	2952	B2
FM-1764				
-	GlsC	77510	4871	D5
-	GlsC	77510	4872	A5
-	LMQU	77510	4872	A5
-	LMQU	77568	4872	B5
-	STFE	77510	4870	D6
-	STFE	77510	4871	D5
-	STFE	77517	4870	D5
-	TXCY	-	4872	C3
-	TXCY	-	4873	A4
-	TXCY	-	4874	B4
600	TXCY	77590	4875	D5
3200	TXCY	77590	4874	E4
FM-1764 9th Av N				
600	TXCY	77590	4875	D5
FM-1764 Emmett F Lowry Expwy				
-	TXCY	-	4872	C3
-	TXCY	-	4873	A4
-	TXCY	-	4874	A4
FM-1764 Palmer Hwy				
2100	TXCY	77590	4875	A5
3200	TXCY	77590	4874	E4
FM-1765				
-	LMQU	77568	4872	D7
10	TXCY	77590	4875	A6
100	LMQU	77568	4874	C7
100	TXCY	77591	4874	C7
1900	LMQU	77568	4873	B7
1900	TXCY	77591	4873	B7
2500	TXCY	77590	4874	E6
FM-1765 5th Av S				
3500	TXCY	77590	4874	C7
FM-1765 Texas Av				
10	TXCY	77590	4875	A6
100	LMQU	77568	4874	C7
100	TXCY	77591	4874	C7
1900	LMQU	77568	4873	B7
1900	TXCY	77591	4873	B7
2500	TXCY	77590	4874	E6
FM-1774				
10	MAGA	77355	2669	A5
100	MtgC	77355	2669	D7
27200	MtgC	77362	2816	D3
35800	MtgC	77355	2816	A1
38100	MtgC	77355	2815	E1
40900	MAGA	77354	2668	E5
40900	MAGA	77354	2669	A5
40900	MtgC	77354	2668	E5
FM-1774 Magnolia Blvd				
200	MAGA	77355	2669	A5
FM-1774 S Magnolia Blvd				
10	MAGA	77355	2669	B6
100	MtgC	77355	2669	B6
FM-1876				
100	SGLD	77478	4368	B1
900	SGLD	77478	4237	B6
2400	FBnC	77478	4237	B6
6800	HOUS	77072	4097	C5
6800	HOUS	77083	4097	C5
7800	HarC	77072	4097	C6
7800	HarC	77083	4097	C6
8700	HarC	77072	4237	C1
8700	HarC	77083	4237	C1
9300	HarC	77099	4237	C1
9700	HOUS	77099	4237	C2
9900	HOUS	77478	4237	B6
FM-1876 Eldridge Rd				
-	HOUS	77478	4237	B6
100	SGLD	77478	4368	B1
900	SGLD	77478	4237	B6
2400	FBnC	77478	4237	B6
FM-1876 Synott Rd				
6800	HOUS	77072	4097	C5
6800	HOUS	77083	4097	C5
7800	HarC	77072	4097	C6
7800	HarC	77083	4097	C6
8700	HarC	77072	4237	C1
8700	HarC	77083	4237	C1
9300	HarC	77099	4237	C1
9600	HOUS	77099	4237	C2
9900	HOUS	77478	4237	C2
10400	SGLD	77478	4237	B4
FM-1887				
-	HMPD	77445	2953	B7
-	HMPD	77445	3098	B1
-	WlrC	77445	3098	B3
-	WlrC	77445	3243	A7
FM-1887 11th St				
-	HMPD	77445	2953	B7
-	HMPD	77445	3098	B1
FM-1942				
100	HarC	77532	3692	D1
600	HarC	77532	3693	E2
2700	HarC	77532	3694	B5
4800	HarC	77521	3694	C5
6200	HarC	77521	3695	C5
7100	CmbC	77520	3695	C5
7500	CmbC	77520	3696	A4
9500	MTBL	77520	3696	B4
FM-1942 Crosby Rd				
100	HarC	77532	3692	D1
FM-1942 Crosby Barbers Hill Rd				
5300	HarC	77521	3694	D6
6200	HarC	77521	3695	C5
7100	CmbC	77520	3695	C5
7500	CmbC	77520	3696	A4
9500	MTBL	77520	3696	B4
FM-1942 Crosby Cedar Bayou Rd				
500	HarC	77532	3692	D1
600	HarC	77532	3693	A1
FM-1959				
-	FRDW	77546	4505	C1
-	HarC	77089	4505	A3
-	HarC	77546	4505	C1
-	HOUS	77089	4505	A3
-	HOUS	77546	4505	C1
100	HOUS	77034	4378	E5
100	HOUS	77598	4378	E5
1100	HOUS	77089	4378	D7
1100	HOUS	77546	4378	D7
2500	FRDW	77089	4505	C2
2500	PRLD	77089	4505	A3
2800	PRLD	77581	4505	A3
FM-1959 Dixie Farm Rd				
-	FRDW	77089	4505	C1
-	HarC	77089	4505	A3
-	HOUS	77089	4505	A3
-	HOUS	77546	4505	C1
300	HOUS	77034	4378	E5
1000	HOUS	77598	4378	E6
1100	HOUS	77089	4378	D7
1100	HOUS	77546	4378	D7
2500	FRDW	77546	4505	C2
2500	HarC	77546	4505	C2
2500	PRLD	77089	4505	A3
2800	PRLD	77581	4505	A3
FM-1960				
-	HarC	77066	3400	E1
-	HarC	77069	3400	E1
-	HOUS	77014	3258	A5
-	HOUS	77068	3258	A5
-	HOUS	77084	3817	D7
10	HarC	77073	3258	A5
10	HarC	77090	3258	E3
10	HOUS	77090	3258	A5
100	HMBL	77338	3262	E6
400	HarC	77073	3259	A3
1100	HMBL	77338	3263	A6
1700	HarC	77338	3263	D6
2300	HOUS	77014	3257	E5
2300	HOUS	77068	3257	E5
2300	HOUS	77338	3263	C6
2400	HarC	77014	3257	E5
2400	HarC	77068	3257	E5
2400	HOUS	77073	3259	E3
3100	HarC	77338	3260	E4
3100	HOUS	77073	3260	A3
3100	HOUS	77338	3260	E4
3700	HarC	77338	3264	D6
3700	HarC	77346	3264	D6
4400	HarC	77014	3401	A1
4400	HarC	77066	3401	A1
4400	HarC	77068	3401	A1
4400	HarC	77069	3401	A1
5600	HarC	77338	3261	C5
5600	HOUS	77338	3261	C5
6800	HarC	77346	3265	A6
7300	HOUS	77064	3400	B4
7300	HOUS	77066	3400	B4
7300	HOUS	77069	3400	B4
7300	HOUS	77070	3400	B4
8200	HOUS	77064	3399	C7
8200	HOUS	77070	3399	C7
8600	HarC	77064	3399	D6
8600	HarC	77070	3399	E5
8800	HOUS	77336	3265	D4
9600	HOUS	77338	3262	C5
9900	HarC	77064	3540	B1
9900	HarC	77070	3540	B1
10600	HOUS	77336	3266	B3
10900	HarC	77065	3540	A1
11300	HarC	77065	3539	E2
11600	HarC	77336	3266	D3
12500	HarC	77336	3267	C1
13000	HarC	77336	3122	E7
14400	LbyC	77535	3122	E7
FM-1960 BUS				
8000	HarC	77338	3261	E6
8000	HOUS	77338	3261	E6
8600	HarC	77338	3262	A6
8900	HOUS	77338	3262	B6
9100	HMBL	77338	3262	B6
FM-1960 BYP				
1000	HMBL	77338	3262	B5
1000	HMBL	77338	3263	A5
1500	HarC	77338	3263	A5
7600	HarC	77338	3261	E5
7600	HOUS	77338	3261	D5
8500	HarC	77338	3262	A5
8500	HOUS	77338	3262	A5
FM-1960 1st St E				
200	HMBL	77338	3262	E6
1100	HMBL	77338	3263	A6
1700	HarC	77338	3263	A6
FM-1960 W 1st St				
100	HMBL	77338	3262	D6
FM-1960 Bammel Rd				
-	HarC	77090	3258	A5
-	HOUS	77014	3258	A5
-	HOUS	77068	3258	A5
-	HOUS	77090	3258	A5
2300	HOUS	77014	3257	E5
2300	HOUS	77068	3257	E5
2400	HarC	77014	3257	E5
2400	HarC	77068	3257	E5
FM-1960 Humble Westfield Rd				
4500	HarC	77338	3260	E4
4500	HOUS	77338	3260	E4
7300	HarC	77338	3261	C5
7300	HOUS	77338	3261	C5
9600	HMBL	77338	3262	C5
9600	HOUS	77338	3262	C5
FM-1960 BUS Humble Westfld Rd				
8000	HarC	77338	3261	E6
8000	HOUS	77338	3261	E6
8600	HarC	77338	3262	A6
8900	HOUS	77338	3262	B6
9100	HMBL	77338	3262	B6
FM-1960A BUS				
-	HMBL	77338	3262	B6
-	HOUS	77338	3262	B6
8000	HarC	77338	3261	E6
8000	HOUS	77338	3261	E6
FM-1960A BUS Humble Westfld Rd				
-	HMBL	77338	3262	B6
-	HOUS	77338	3262	B6
8000	HarC	77338	3261	E6
8000	HOUS	77338	3261	E6
FM-2004				
-	HTCK	77563	4872	C6
-	HTCK	77563	4987	E7
-	HTCK	77563	4988	C2
-	LMQU	77568	4872	C4
-	LMQU	77568	4988	C2
-	TXCY	77539	4754	C6
-	TXCY	77591	4754	C6
-	TXCY	77591	4872	C2
FM-2090				
-	PLMG	77327	2684	D4
15800	MtgC	77302	2533	A6
15800	MtgC	77306	2533	B6
17600	MtgC	77306	2534	A5
20200	MtgC	77372	2534	E5
23400	MtgC	77372	2535	C5
23400	MtgC	77372	2536	B7
24700	MtgC	77372	2682	E1
24700	SPLD	77372	2682	E1
25400	SPLD	77372	2683	A2
26600	MtgC	77372	2683	C2
27400	MtgC	77372	2684	B4
28700	LbyC	77327	2684	B4
FM-2094				
200	GlsC	77565	4509	D6
200	KMAH	77565	4509	D6
600	CRLS	77565	4509	C6
1200	LGCY	77565	4509	B6
1200	LGCY	77573	4509	B6
2200	LGCY	77573	4632	C1
2400	LGCY	77573	4508	C7
3000	LGCY	77565	4508	E5
FM-2094 E Main St				
2200	LGCY	77573	4632	C1
2400	LGCY	77573	4508	C7
FM-2094 Marina Bay Dr				
200	GlsC	77565	4509	D6
200	KMAH	77565	4509	D6
600	CRLS	77565	4509	C6
1200	LGCY	77565	4509	B6
1200	LGCY	77573	4509	B6
2500	LGCY	77573	4508	C7
3000	LGCY	77565	4508	E5
FM-2100				
100	HarC	77520	3831	E6
100	HarC	77562	3831	D7
200	HarC	77520	3970	C2
600	HOUS	77520	3970	C2
1000	HOUS	77571	3970	B3
1200	HarC	77562	3692	D7
5200	HarC	77532	3552	C3
10500	HarC	77532	3692	D7
16900	HarC	77532	3411	B7
20700	HarC	77532	3410	E1
21300	HarC	77532	3266	E7
24300	HarC	77336	3267	A1
24700	HarC	77336	3266	E1
26000	HarC	77336	3122	A5
26600	HarC	77336	3121	D3
26900	HOUS	77336	3121	D3
29800	HarC	77336	2976	C1
FM-2100 Avenue B				
5200	HarC	77532	3552	D4
FM-2100 Crosby Huffman Rd				
6100	HarC	77532	3552	C3
16900	HarC	77532	3411	B7
20700	HarC	77532	3410	E1
21300	HarC	77532	3266	E7
24300	HarC	77336	3267	A1
24700	HarC	77336	3266	E1
26000	HarC	77336	3122	A5
26600	HarC	77336	3121	D3
26900	HOUS	77336	3121	D3
FM-2100 Crosby Lynchburg Rd				
100	HarC	77520	3831	E6
100	HarC	77562	3831	E6
200	HarC	77520	3970	C2
600	HOUS	77520	3970	C2
1000	HOUS	77571	3970	B3
13100	HarC	77532	3692	D1
13600	HarC	77532	3552	D7
FM-2100 N Crosby Lynchburg Rd				
100	HarC	77562	3831	D1
1200	HarC	77562	3692	D7
10500	HarC	77532	3692	D7
FM-2100 Huffman New Caney Rd				
29800	HarC	77336	2976	C1
FM-2100 N Main St				
5700	HarC	77532	3552	C4
FM-2100 S Main St				
100	HarC	77562	3831	D7
FM-2218				
-	PLEK	77469	4614	E6
-	PLEK	77471	4614	E7
1500	FBnC	77469	4491	E4
1500	FBnC	77471	4491	E4
1500	RHMD	77469	4491	E4
1500	RHMD	77471	4491	E4
1500	RSBG	77469	4491	E5
1500	RSBG	77471	4491	D6
2700	RSBG	77469	4615	C1
2700	RSBG	77471	4615	C1
3200	FBnC	77469	4615	A5
5500	PLEK	77469	4615	A5
FM-2218 BF Terry Blvd				
1500	FBnC	77471	4491	E4
1500	RHMD	77471	4491	E4
1500	RSBG	77469	4491	E5
1500	RSBG	77471	4491	D6
5300	FBnC	77469	4491	E4
5300	RHMD	77469	4491	E4
FM-2234				
-	PRLD	77053	4372	E7
-	PRLD	77053	4499	E1
-	PRLD	77053	4500	A1
-	PRLD	77545	4372	E7
-	PRLD	77545	4499	E1
-	PRLD	77545	4500	A1
200	MSCY	77489	4370	C6
700	STAF	77477	4370	C3
700	STAF	77489	4370	C3
1400	MSCY	77477	4370	C4
3000	MSCY	77489	4497	D1
3400	HOUS	77489	4497	E1
4100	FBnC	77489	4497	E1
4100	FBnC	77545	4497	E1
4100	FBnC	77545	4498	A1
4100	HOUS	77489	4498	A1
4100	HOUS	77545	4498	A1
5000	FBnC	77053	4498	A1
5000	HOUS	77053	4498	A1
6500	FBnC	77053	4499	B1
6500	HOUS	77053	4499	B1
8200	FBnC	77053	4372	E7
8600	FBnC	77545	4372	E7
10800	BzaC	77584	4500	E1
10800	PRLD	77584	4500	C1
FM-2234 McHard Rd				
-	MSCY	77489	4497	D1
-	PRLD	77053	4372	E7
-	PRLD	77053	4499	E1
-	PRLD	77053	4500	A1
-	PRLD	77545	4372	E7
-	PRLD	77545	4499	E1
-	PRLD	77545	4500	A1
3700	HOUS	77489	4497	E1
4100	FBnC	77489	4497	E1
4100	FBnC	77545	4497	E1
4100	FBnC	77545	4498	A1
4100	HOUS	77489	4498	A1
4100	HOUS	77545	4498	A1
5000	FBnC	77053	4498	A1
5000	HOUS	77053	4498	A1
6500	FBnC	77053	4499	B1
6500	HOUS	77053	4499	B1
8200	FBnC	77053	4372	E7
8600	FBnC	77545	4372	E7
10800	BzaC	77584	4500	E1
11700	PRLD	77584	4500	C1
FM-2234 Shadow Creek Pkwy				
-	PRLD	77053	4500	A1
-	PRLD	77545	4500	A1
-	PRLD	77584	4500	E1
FM-2234 Texas Pkwy				
200	MSCY	77489	4370	C6
700	STAF	77477	4370	C3
700	STAF	77489	4370	C3
1400	MSCY	77477	4370	C4
3000	MSCY	77489	4497	D1
3400	HOUS	77489	4497	D1
FM-2351				
100	HOUS	77062	4379	C7
100	HOUS	77598	4379	C7
100	HOUS	77598	4506	B1
200	BzaC	77511	4628	D3
400	FRDW	77546	4629	A1
700	BzaC	77581	4628	C4
700	PRLD	77511	4628	C4
700	PRLD	77581	4628	C4
900	FRDW	77546	4628	E2
1200	BzaC	77546	4628	D3
3000	HOUS	77546	4505	E3
3000	HOUS	77546	4506	A2
3900	FRDW	77546	4505	C5
3900	HarC	77546	4505	E3
FM-2351 Choate Rd				
3000	HOUS	77546	4505	E3
3000	HOUS	77546	4506	B1
3900	FRDW	77546	4505	C5
3900	HarC	77546	4505	E4
FM-2351 Clear Lake City Blvd				
-	HOUS	77546	4506	B2
100	HOUS	77062	4379	C7
100	HOUS	77598	4379	C7
100	HOUS	77598	4506	B1
FM-2351 Donaldson Rd				
200	BzaC	77511	4628	D3
FM-2351 E Edgewood Dr				
100	FRDW	77546	4505	B7
FM-2351 W Edgewood Dr				
100	FRDW	77546	4505	B7
400	FRDW	77546	4629	A1
900	FRDW	77546	4628	E2
1100	PRLD	77581	4628	E2
FM-2351 Hastings Rd				
700	BzaC	77511	4628	C4
700	BzaC	77581	4628	C4
700	PRLD	77511	4628	C4
700	PRLD	77581	4628	C4
1200	BzaC	77546	4628	D3
2100	FRDW	77546	4628	E2
FM-2354				
-	BHCY	77520	4254	B2
-	CmbC	77520	4254	B2
FM-2403				
3100	ALVN	77511	4867	B6
3100	BzaC	77511	4867	B7
FM-2432				
10200	MtgC	77303	2239	A1
FM-2432 Willis Waukegan Rd				
10900	MtgC	77303	2239	D3
FM-2553				
13100	HOUS	77034	4378	C5
FM-2553 Scarsdale Blvd				
13100	HOUS	77034	4378	C5
FM-2759				
-	FBnC	77469	4493	D3
-	SGLD	77469	4493	C5
-	SGLD	77479	4493	C5
700	FBnC	77479	4493	C6
8300	FBnC	77469	4494	B7
FM-2759 Crabb River Rd				
-	FBnC	77469	4493	D3
-	SGLD	77469	4493	C5
-	SGLD	77479	4493	C5
700	FBnC	77479	4493	C6
FM-2759 Thompsons Rd				
7100	FBnC	77469	4493	E7
8300	FBnC	77469	4494	A7
FM-2854				
600	CNRO	77301	2383	E5
1100	CNRO	77304	2383	A5
2000	CNRO	77304	2382	E5
6200	MtgC	77304	2382	E5
FM-2854 Old Montgomery Rd				
600	CNRO	77301	2383	E5
1100	CNRO	77304	2383	A5
2000	CNRO	77304	2382	E5
FM-2920				
-	HarC	77388	3112	E3
-	HarC	77447	3103	A4
-	WALR	77484	3102	B5
100	TMBL	77375	2964	E6
1000	HarC	77375	2964	E6
1200	TMBL	77375	3109	A1
1300	TMBL	77375	3108	E1
1500	HarC	77388	3113	A3
6000	HarC	77379	3111	A3
6000	HarC	77388	3111	E3
7300	HarC	77379	3110	E3
8600	HarC	77375	3110	B1
9800	HarC	77375	2965	A7
14000	HarC	77377	3108	E1
14000	TMBL	77377	3108	E1
16300	HarC	77377	3107	D2
18600	HarC	77377	3106	E2
20300	HarC	77447	3106	A2
21200	HarC	77447	3105	A4
24900	HarC	77447	3104	E4
27900	HarC	77484	3103	C4
29000	HarC	77484	3102	B6
FM-2920 E Main St				
100	TMBL	77375	2964	E6
1000	HarC	77375	2964	E6
FM-2920 W Main St				
-	TMBL	77377	3108	E1
100	TMBL	77375	2964	B7
1200	TMBL	77375	3109	A1
1300	TMBL	77375	3108	E1
FM-2920 Spring Cypress Rd				
1500	HarC	77388	3113	C3
FM-2920 Stuebner Airline Rd				
8400	HarC	77379	3110	E3
8600	HarC	77375	3110	B1
9800	HarC	77375	2965	B7
FM-2920 Waller Tomball Rd				
-	HarC	77447	3103	A4
14000	HarC	77377	3108	E1
14000	TMBL	77375	3108	E1
14000	TMBL	77377	3108	E1
16300	HarC	77377	3107	D2
18600	HarC	77377	3106	E2
19100	WALR	77484	3102	B6
20300	HarC	77447	3106	A2
21200	HarC	77447	3105	A4
24900	HarC	77447	3104	E4
27900	HarC	77484	3103	C4
29000	HarC	77484	3102	B6
FM-2977				
-	FBnC	77469	4492	B7
-	RSBG	77469	4492	B7
-	RSBG	77469	4616	A6
3500	FBnC	77469	4616	A6
FM-2977 Minonite Rd				
3500	FBnC	77469	4616	A6
FM-2978				
23200	HarC	77375	2964	E6
23200	TMBL	77375	2964	E6
26000	MtgC	77354	2818	D4
26000	MtgC	77354	2964	D1
30200	WDLD	77354	2818	E1
30400	MtgC	77354	2672	E7
30400	WDLD	77354	2672	E7
30400	WDLD	77382	2672	E7
30600	MtgC	77354	2673	B5
30600	WDLD	77382	2673	B5
31200	MtgC	77382	2673	B5
31300	WDLD	77354	2673	B6
FM-2978 Hufsmith Kohrville Rd				
23200	HarC	77375	2964	E6
23200	TMBL	77375	2964	E6
FM-3005				
-	GLSN	77554	5220	D7
-	GLSN	77554	5333	B1
-	GLSN	77554	5547	E3
-	GLSN	77554	5548	D1
300	GLSN	77550	5109	D3
4100	GLSN	77550	5108	E7
4100	GLSN	77551	5108	E7
5300	GLSN	77551	5222	D1
7900	GLSN	77554	5222	D1
8500	GLSN	77554	5221	E3
12200	GLSN	77554	5442	A2
14900	GLSN	77554	5332	E2
16700	GLSN	77554	5331	E7
16700	JMAB	77554	5331	E7
16700	JMAB	77554	5332	A6
21200	GLSN	77554	5441	A6
23200	GLSN	77554	5440	E7
FM-3005 San Luis Pass Rd				
-	GLSN	77554	5220	D7
-	GLSN	77554	5333	B1
-	GLSN	77554	5547	E3
-	GLSN	77554	5548	D1
10300	GLSN	77554	5221	B5
12200	GLSN	77554	5442	A2
14900	GLSN	77554	5332	E2
16700	GLSN	77554	5331	E7
16700	JMAB	77554	5331	E7
16700	JMAB	77554	5332	A6
21200	GLSN	77554	5441	D4
23200	GLSN	77554	5440	E7
FM-3005 Seawall Blvd				
300	GLSN	77550	5109	D3
4100	GLSN	77550	5108	E7
4100	GLSN	77551	5108	E7
5300	GLSN	77551	5222	D1
7900	GLSN	77554	5222	D1
8500	GLSN	77554	5221	E3
FM-3005 Termini Rd				
-	GLSN	77554	5441	A6
-	GLSN	77554	5442	A2
FM-3083				
-	CNRO	77304	2382	E2
-	CNRO	77304	2383	A1
100	CNRO	77301	2384	D1
100	CNRO	77301	2385	A4
100	CNRO	77303	2238	C7
300	MtgC	77303	2238	D7
700	CNRO	77303	2237	E7
1000	CNRO	77303	2384	D1
1000	MtgC	77303	2384	D1
1100	CNRO	77304	2237	E7
11600	MtgC	77301	2385	C6
11700	MtgC	77302	2385	D6
11900	MtgC	77306	2385	E7
12500	MtgC	77302	2531	E1
12500	MtgC	77306	2531	E1
12700	MtgC	77302	2532	D5
14800	MtgC	77306	2532	E5
15500	MtgC	77302	2533	B7
15500	MtgC	77306	2533	B7
16600	MtgC	77302	2679	C1
16600	MtgC	77306	2679	C1
FM-3083 Beach Airport Rd				
100	CNRO	77301	2384	D1
1500	CNRO	77303	2384	D1
2500	MtgC	77303	2384	D1
FM-3083 Teas Rd				
100	CNRO	77303	2238	C7
300	MtgC	77303	2238	D7
700	CNRO	77303	2237	E7
1000	CNRO	77301	2384	D1
1000	CNRO	77303	2384	D1
1000	MtgC	77303	2384	D1
1500	CNRO	77304	2237	E7
FM-3083 Tink Calfee Rd				
-	CNRO	77304	2382	E2
FM-3155				
1700	RHMD	77469	4491	D1
FM-3155 Preston St				
1700	RHMD	77469	4491	D1
FM-3345				
1600	MSCY	77489	4370	B7
2400	MSCY	77459	4370	B7
3200	MSCY	77459	4369	E7
FM-3345 Cartwright Rd				
1600	MSCY	77489	4370	B7
2400	MSCY	77459	4370	B7
3200	MSCY	77459	4369	E7
FM-3346				
-	PNIS	77445	3098	D6
-	PNIS	77445	3099	A6
-	WlrC	77445	3097	E6
-	WlrC	77445	3098	D6
FM-3360				
-	CmbC	77520	3696	E2
-	MTBL	77520	3696	E2
FM-3436				
-	TXCY	77539	4634	A6
-	TXCY	77539	4755	A1
I-10				
-	BYTN	-	3832	B6
-	BYTN	-	3833	B5
-	BYTN	-	3834	E3
-	CmbC	-	3835	E2
-	HarC	-	3830	D7
-	HarC	-	3831	A6
-	HarC	-	3832	A6
-	HarC	-	3833	B5
-	HarC	-	3834	E2
-	HarC	-	3835	A2
-	HarC	-	3952	E1
-	HarC	-	3953	A1
-	HarC	-	3955	A1
-	HarC	-	3956	E1
-	HarC	-	3959	D1
-	HarC	-	3967	E2
-	HarC	-	3968	E2
-	HarC	-	3969	B1
-	HDWV	-	3959	E1
-	HDWV	-	3960	A1
-	HOUS	-	3953	B1
-	HOUS	-	3954	A1
-	HOUS	-	3955	A1
-	HOUS	-	3956	A1
-	HOUS	-	3957	B1
-	HOUS	-	3958	E1
-	HOUS	-	3959	E1
-	HOUS	-	3960	A1
-	HOUS	-	3961	A1
-	HOUS	-	3962	E2
-	HOUS	-	3963	D2
-	HOUS	-	3964	E2
-	HOUS	-	3965	B1
-	HOUS	-	3966	E2
-	HOUS	-	3967	A2
-	KATY	-	3951	E2
-	KATY	-	3952	E1
-	MTBL	-	3835	E2
-	SPVL	-	3959	D1
-	SPVL	-	3960	A1
-	WlrC	-	3951	A2
I-10 East Frwy				
-	BYTN	-	3832	B6
-	BYTN	-	3833	B5
-	BYTN	-	3834	E3
-	CmbC	-	3835	E2
-	HarC	-	3830	D7
-	HarC	-	3831	A6
-	HarC	-	3832	A6
-	HarC	-	3833	B5
-	HarC	-	3834	E2
-	HarC	-	3835	A2
-	HarC	-	3967	E2
-	HarC	-	3968	E2
-	HarC	-	3969	B1
-	HOUS	-	3963	E2
-	HOUS	-	3964	E2
-	HOUS	-	3965	B1
-	HOUS	-	3966	A2
-	HOUS	-	3967	A2
-	MTBL	-	3835	E2
I-10 Katy Frwy				
-	HarC	-	3952	E1
-	HarC	-	3953	E1
-	HarC	-	3955	A1
-	HarC	-	3956	E1
-	HarC	-	3959	D1
-	HDWV	-	3959	E1
-	HDWV	-	3960	A1
-	HOUS	-	3953	C1
-	HOUS	-	3954	A1
-	HOUS	-	3955	E1
-	HOUS	-	3956	E1
-	HOUS	-	3957	B1
-	HOUS	-	3958	B1
-	HOUS	-	3959	A1
-	HOUS	-	3960	A1
-	HOUS	-	3961	D1
-	HOUS	-	3962	E2
-	HOUS	-	3963	B1
-	KATY	-	3951	A2
-	KATY	-	3952	E1
-	SPVL	-	3959	D1
-	SPVL	-	3960	A1
-	WlrC	-	3951	A2
I-45				
-	CNRO	-	2237	B1
-	CNRO	-	2383	E7
-	CNRO	-	2529	E1
-	CNRO	-	2530	A7
-	CNRO	-	2676	A4
-	DKSN	-	4753	B4
-	GlsC	-	4990	E6
-	GlsC	-	4991	A7
-	GlsC	-	5106	E3
-	GlsC	-	5107	A4
-	GLSN	-	5107	E5
-	GLSN	-	5108	A5
-	HarC	-	2968	D5
-	HarC	-	3113	D1
-	HarC	-	3258	E7
-	HarC	-	3402	E1
-	HarC	-	3403	A4
-	HarC	-	4506	E6
-	HOUS	-	3113	E7
-	HOUS	-	3258	E7
-	HOUS	-	3403	A4
-	HOUS	-	3544	B7
-	HOUS	-	3684	C3
-	HOUS	-	3823	E1
-	HOUS	-	3824	B5
-	HOUS	-	3963	B1
-	HOUS	-	4103	E1
-	HOUS	-	4104	E4
-	HOUS	-	4105	B5
-	HOUS	-	4245	D1
-	HOUS	-	4246	A3
-	HOUS	-	4377	E2
-	HOUS	-	4378	C5
-	HOUS	-	4506	E6
-	LGCY	-	4631	B1
-	LGCY	-	4752	E1
-	LGCY	-	4753	E7
-	LMQU	-	4872	E6
-	LMQU	-	4873	B7
-	LMQU	-	4989	B1
-	LMQU	-	4990	E6
-	MtgC	-	2237	B1
-	MtgC	-	2530	A5
-	MtgC	-	2676	A7
-	MtgC	-	2822	B7
-	MtgC	-	2968	D6
-	ORDN	-	2822	B5
-	SHEH	-	2676	B7
-	SHEH	-	2822	B7
-	TXCY	-	4753	C5
-	TXCY	-	4871	E1
-	TXCY	-	4872	B3
-	TXCY	-	4873	B7
-	WEBS	-	4506	E6
-	WEBS	-	4507	A7
-	WEBS	-	4631	C3
I-45 Gulf Frwy				
-	DKSN	-	4753	B3
-	GlsC	-	4990	E6
-	GlsC	-	4991	A7
-	GlsC	-	5106	D3
-	GlsC	-	5107	A4
-	GLSN	-	5107	A4
-	HarC	-	4506	E6
-	HOUS	-	3963	C6
-	HOUS	-	4103	E1
-	HOUS	-	4104	B2
-	HOUS	-	4105	C7
-	HOUS	-	4245	D1
-	HOUS	-	4246	A3
-	HOUS	-	4377	E2
-	HOUS	-	4378	C5
-	HOUS	-	4506	E6
-	LGCY	-	4631	C3
-	LGCY	-	4752	E1
-	LGCY	-	4753	E7
-	LMQU	-	4872	E6
-	LMQU	-	4873	B7
-	LMQU	-	4989	B1
-	LMQU	-	4990	E6
-	TXCY	-	4753	C5
-	TXCY	-	4871	E1
-	TXCY	-	4872	E6
-	TXCY	-	4873	B7
-	WEBS	-	4506	E6
-	WEBS	-	4507	A7
-	WEBS	-	4631	C3
I-45 Gulf Freeway Frontage Rd				
-	HOUS	-	4506	B3
I-45 North Frwy				
-	CNRO	-	2383	E6
-	CNRO	-	2529	E1
-	CNRO	-	2530	A5
-	CNRO	-	2676	A4
-	HarC	-	2968	D5
-	HarC	-	3113	D3
-	HarC	-	3258	E1
-	HarC	-	3402	E1
-	HarC	-	3403	A4
-	HOUS	-	3113	E7
-	HOUS	-	3258	E7
-	HOUS	-	3403	A4
-	HOUS	-	3544	B1
-	HOUS	-	3684	B1
-	HOUS	-	3823	E1
-	HOUS	-	3824	B5
-	HOUS	-	3963	B1
-	MtgC	-	2530	A5
-	MtgC	-	2676	A1
-	MtgC	-	2822	B4
-	MtgC	-	2968	C2
-	ORDN	-	2822	B4
-	SHEH	-	2676	B7
-	SHEH	-	2822	B7
I-610				
-	BLAR	-	4101	A7
-	HOUS	-	3822	B7
-	HOUS	-	3823	D3
-	HOUS	-	3824	A3
-	HOUS	-	3825	E4
-	HOUS	-	3826	C5
-	HOUS	-	3961	B1
-	HOUS	-	3965	E7
-	HOUS	-	4101	A1
-	HOUS	-	4103	E7
-	HOUS	-	4104	A7
-	HOUS	-	4105	E2
-	HOUS	-	4241	E1
-	HOUS	-	4242	E1
-	HOUS	-	4243	B1

STREET
Block City ZIP Map# Grid

I-610 Ship Channel Br
- HOUS - 4105 E1
LP-8
- HarC - 3401 E7
- HarC - 3402 C7
- HarC - 3405 B7
- HarC - 3540 E2
- HarC - 3541 A2
- HarC - 3542 A1
- HarC - 3543 A1
- HarC - 3680 D4
- HarC - 3681 A1
- HarC - 3829 B7
- HarC - 3968 D6
- HarC - 4239 B6
- HarC - 4372 D5
- HarC - 4373 A5
- HarC - 4374 A5
- HarC - 4377 D5
- HarC 77044 3549 A1
- HarC 77049 3828 E1
- HOUS - 3402 B7
- HOUS - 3403 E7
- HOUS - 3404 E7
- HOUS - 3405 B7
- HOUS - 3406 A7
- HOUS - 3680 D7
- HOUS - 3819 D1
- HOUS - 3958 D2
- HOUS - 3968 D7
- HOUS - 4098 E7
- HOUS - 4108 D1
- HOUS - 4238 E4
- HOUS - 4239 A5
- HOUS - 4248 A7
- HOUS - 4370 E2
- HOUS - 4371 C4
- HOUS - 4372 E5
- HOUS - 4374 C5
- HOUS - 4375 E5
- HOUS - 4376 E5
- HOUS - 4377 E5
- HOUS - 4378 A5
- HOUS - 4379 A1
- JRSV - 3680 E2
- MSCY - 4239 C7
- MSCY - 4370 E2
- PASD - 4108 C4
- PASD - 4248 A7
7000 HarC 77396 3406 C7
8000 HarC 77049 3689 D6
8100 HarC 77396 3547 E1
8100 HarC 77396 3548 B1
8700 HarC 77044 3689 C1
11000 HarC 77396 3549 A1
LP-8 Houston Ship Channel Br
- HOUS - 3968 D7
LP-8 Sam Houston Pkwy
- HarC - 3405 E7
- HarC - 3406 B7
- HarC - 3829 B7
- HarC - 3968 B1
- HOUS - 3403 B7
- HOUS - 3404 E7
- HOUS - 3405 E7
- HOUS - 3406 A7
LP-8 E Sam Houston Pkwy N
- HarC 77044 3549 B7
- HarC 77049 3828 E1
7700 HarC 77049 3829 B3
8000 HarC 77049 3689 D6
8700 HarC 77044 3689 C1
LP-8 N Sam Houston Pkwy E
- HarC 77044 3549 A1
7000 HarC 77396 3406 C7
8100 HarC 77396 3547 E1
8100 HarC 77396 3548 B1
11000 HarC 77396 3549 A1
LP-8 W Sam Houston Tollway
- HarC - 3401 E7
- HarC - 3402 C7
- HarC - 3540 E7
- HarC - 3541 A2
- HarC - 3542 B1
- HarC - 3543 A1
- HarC - 3680 D4
- HarC - 3681 A1
- HarC - 3968 D6
- HarC - 4239 B6
- HarC - 4372 D5
- HarC - 4373 E5
- HarC - 4374 A5
- HarC - 4377 B5
- HOUS - 3402 E7
- HOUS - 3403 B7
- HOUS - 3680 D3
- HOUS - 3819 D1
- HOUS - 3958 D2
- HOUS - 3968 D7
- HOUS - 4098 E7
- HOUS - 4108 D1
- HOUS - 4238 E4
- HOUS - 4239 C7
- HOUS - 4248 A7
- HOUS - 4370 E2
- HOUS - 4371 C4
- HOUS - 4372 A5
- HOUS - 4374 C5
- HOUS - 4375 E5
- HOUS - 4376 E5
- HOUS - 4377 A5
- HOUS - 4378 E1
- HOUS - 4379 A1
- JRSV - 3680 E2
- MSCY - 4239 C7
- MSCY - 4370 E2
- PASD - 4108 C4
- PASD - 4248 C5
LP-8 W Sam Houston Tollway E
- HarC - 3541 E1
LP-8 W Sam Houston Tollway W
- HarC - 3541 E1
LP-108
- GlsC 77650 4994 E1
- GlsC 77650 4995 A1
700 GlsC 77650 4878 E7
700 GlsC 77650 4879 B5
LP-108 7th St
- GlsC 77650 4878 E7
- GlsC 77650 4994 E1
- GlsC 77650 4995 A1
LP-108 Broadway
700 GlsC 77650 4878 E7
700 GlsC 77650 4879 B5

LP-197
- GlsC 77563 4991 A5
- LMQU 77563 4991 A6
- LMQU 77590 4991 A5
- TXCY 77563 4991 A5
- TXCY 77590 4991 B2
10 TXCY 77590 4875 B3
2500 TXCY 77590 4874 C3
LP-197 6th St N
10 TXCY 77590 4875 D6
LP-197 6th St S
10 TXCY 77590 4875 D6
LP-197 25th Av N
800 TXCY 77590 4875 C3
2500 TXCY 77590 4874 C3
LP-197 Texas City Port Blvd
- TXCY 77590 4875 D7
- TXCY 77590 4991 B2
LP-201
- BYTN - 4112 A3
LP-201 N Robert C Lanier Frwy
- BYTN - 4112 A3
LP-207
- MTBL 77520 3696 E6
LP-207 Main St
- MTBL 77520 3696 E6
LP-336
- CNRO 77301 2530 A3
- CNRO 77301 2531 A1
- MtgC 77301 2385 B2
100 CNRO 77301 2384 E1
200 CNRO 77304 2530 A2
300 CNRO 77301 2383 E1
300 CNRO 77303 2383 E1
900 CNRO 77304 2529 B1
1300 CNRO 77304 2383 C2
1700 CNRO 77303 2384 E1
1700 MtgC 77303 2384 E1
1900 CNRO 77301 2385 B2
1900 CNRO 77303 2385 B2
1900 MtgC 77303 2385 B2
2700 CNRO 77304 2382 E5
LP-336 Cartwright Rd
- MtgC 77301 2385 B2
1700 CNRO 77301 2384 E1
1700 CNRO 77303 2384 E1
1700 MtgC 77303 2384 E1
1900 CNRO 77301 2385 B2
1900 CNRO 77303 2385 B2
1900 MtgC 77303 2385 B2
LP-494
- HOUS 77339 3262 E1
20000 MtgC 77357 2828 A5
20400 MtgC 77357 2827 E7
21100 MtgC 77357 2973 E1
22000 HOUS 77339 3118 C1
22000 HOUS 77339 3263 A1
22400 MtgC 77365 2973 C7
24700 MtgC 77365 3118 C1
25300 MtgC 77339 3118 C1
25500 HOUS 77365 3118 B3
LP-512
10 SPLD 77372 2683 A2
13500 MtgC 77372 2537 B7
13500 SPLD 77372 2537 B7
SPR-5
- HOUS - 4104 A2
100 HOUS 77021 4104 B3
SPR-41
13100 SGLD 77478 4368 D2
SPR-41 Dairy Ashford Rd
13100 SGLD 77478 4368 D2
SPR-58
100 SGLD 77478 4367 E3
SPR-58 Brooks St
100 SGLD 77478 4367 E3
SPR-261
2900 HOUS 77018 3823 B1
4800 HOUS 77018 3684 B7
SPR-261 N Durham Dr
2900 HOUS 77018 3823 B4
SPR-261 N Shepherd Dr
2900 HOUS 77018 3823 B1
4800 HOUS 77018 3684 B7
SPR-330
- BYTN - 3832 C7
- BYTN - 3971 E2
- BYTN - 3972 A3
- HarC - 3832 A7
2200 BYTN 77521 3972 D6
SPR-330 Decker Dr
900 BYTN 77520 3972 D6
2200 BYTN 77521 3972 D6
SPR-342
1000 GLSN 77551 5108 C7
2800 GLSN 77551 5222 C1
SPR-342 61st St
1000 GLSN 77551 5108 C7
2800 GLSN 77551 5222 C1
SPR-501
2300 LPRT 77571 4251 E7
3200 LPRT 77571 4382 E1
3200 SRAC 77571 4382 E1
3800 HarC 77571 4382 E2
3900 PASD 77571 4382 E2
SPR-501 S Broadway St
2300 LPRT 77571 4251 D7
3200 LPRT 77571 4382 E1
3200 SRAC 77571 4382 E1
3800 HarC 77571 4382 E2
3900 PASD 77571 4382 E2
SPR-527
- HOUS 77002 3962 E7
- HOUS 77002 3963 A7
- HOUS 77002 4102 E1
- HOUS 77006 3962 E7
- HOUS 77006 3963 A7
- HOUS 77006 4102 E1
SPR-529
10 RSBG 77471 4490 C4
1100 FBnC 77471 4490 A5
SPR-529 Avenue H
10 RSBG 77471 4490 C4
SPR-529 W Avenue H
700 RSBG 77471 4490 B5
SR-3
- GlsC 77563 4991 A6
- LGCY 77573 4632 D7
- LMQU 77563 4991 A6
- LMQU 77568 4990 E4
- LMQU 77590 4990 D4
- LMQU 77590 4991 A5
- TXCY 77539 4873 B2
- TXCY 77591 4754 E7
- TXCY 77591 4873 B2
100 LMQU 77568 4874 A7

SR-3
100 SHUS 77017 4246 B2
100 TXCY 77591 4874 A7
1700 GlsC 77539 4632 D7
1700 LGCY 77539 4632 D7
1900 DKSN 77539 4632 D7
2200 DKSN 77539 4753 E1
2200 GlsC 77539 4753 E1
2500 HOUS 77034 4246 E5
3800 DKSN 77539 4754 A3
5200 TXCY 77539 4754 E7
6800 HOUS 77017 4245 E2
7600 HOUS 77034 4247 A6
8800 HOUS 77017 4246 B2
8800 HOUS 77034 4378 E4
9300 SHUS 77587 4246 D4
11700 HOUS 77034 4379 C7
11700 HOUS 77598 4379 C7
12700 HOUS 77062 4379 C7
14100 HOUS 77598 4506 E3
15200 HOUS 77062 4506 E3
15800 HOUS 77062 4507 A4
15800 HOUS 77598 4507 A4
16200 WEBS 77598 4507 D7
16600 HarC 77598 4507 A5
18400 WEBS 77598 4631 D1
19600 LGCY 77573 4631 E2
19600 WEBS 77573 4631 E1
SR-3 Galveston Rd
400 HOUS 77017 4246 C2
400 SHUS 77017 4246 C2
400 SHUS 77587 4246 C2
2500 HOUS 77034 4246 E5
7600 HOUS 77034 4247 A6
9900 HOUS 77034 4378 E4
11700 HOUS 77034 4379 C7
11700 HOUS 77598 4379 C7
12700 HOUS 77062 4379 C7
14100 HOUS 77598 4506 E3
15200 HOUS 77062 4506 E5
SR-3 Monroe Rd
6800 HOUS 77017 4245 E2
SR-3 Old Galveston Rd
- HOUS 77034 4378 C2
SR-3 Winkler Dr
- HOUS 77017 4245 E2
100 SHUS 77017 4246 B2
8800 HOUS 77017 4246 B2
9300 SHUS 77587 4246 D4
SR-6
- FBnC 77083 4096 D7
- FBnC 77083 4236 D1
- FBnC 77459 4497 D7
- FBnC 77478 4236 C7
- GlsC 77563 4991 A7
- HarC - 3102 E6
- HarC - 3103 A6
- HarC - 3248 E2
- HarC - 3249 E5
- HarC - 3250 D6
- HarC - 3251 B7
- HarC - 3395 B1
- HarC - 3396 B3
- HarC - 3397 C7
- HarC - 3538 C1
- HarC - 3539 B3
- HMPD - 2953 D5
- HMPD - 2954 A6
- HOUS 77079 3956 D1
- HOUS 77082 4096 D7
- HOUS 77083 4096 D4
- HTCK 77510 4987 D2
- HTCK 77510 4988 A2
- HTCK 77563 4988 A2
- HTCK 77563 4989 B5
- HTCK 77563 4990 A6
- MSCY 77545 4497 E7
- MSCY 77545 4498 A7
- PRVW - 3099 D1
- PRVW - 3100 A2
- SGLD 77478 4236 C6
- SGLD 77479 4367 E5
- STFE 77510 4871 A7
- STFE 77510 4987 A1
- WALR - 3102 A4
- WlrC - 2954 B7
- WlrC - 3099 D1
- WlrC - 3100 E3
- WlrC - 3101 E4
- WlrC 77445 2953 C2
100 ALVN 77511 4749 C7
600 ALVN 77511 4867 E1
1000 HOUS 77077 3956 D6
1200 HOUS 77079 3817 D7
1200 HOUS 77084 3817 D3
1800 BzaC 77511 4867 E1
2200 HOUS 77082 3956 D7
2300 SGLD 77478 4368 E6
2300 SGLD 77479 4368 A5
2600 ALVN 77511 4868 A2
2600 BzaC 77511 4868 E3
2900 GlsC 77563 4990 E7
2900 GlsC 77568 4990 E6
2900 LMQU 77568 4990 E6
3300 LMQU 77563 4990 D6
3800 SGLD 77478 4369 A7
3800 SGLD 77479 4369 A7
4000 HarC 77084 3817 D1
4300 HOUS 77084 3678 D7
4400 SGLD 77478 4496 B1
4400 SGLD 77479 4496 B1
4500 HarC 77084 3678 D7
4700 MSCY 77459 4496 B1
6600 HarC 77095 3678 D4
7300 MSCY 77459 4497 A6
7400 HarC 77095 3538 E5
8600 HarC 77095 3539 A5
10100 MSCY 77545 4622 D2
11500 FBnC 77545 4622 D2
12200 ARLA 77583 4622 E3
13100 ARLA 77583 4623 A3
13600 STFE 77510 4870 D7
13600 STFE 77517 4870 D7
13800 SGLD 77478 4367 C1
14000 FBnC 77583 4623 A3
14900 PRLD 77583 4623 D5
14900 IWCY 77583 4623 B6
15700 STFE 77517 4869 E6
15800 BzaC 77583 4624 A6
15800 IWCY 77583 4624 A6
16800 GlsC 77511 4869 E5
17200 MNVL 77583 4624 D7
17200 MNVL 77583 4624 C7
17500 MNVL 77578 4745 E1
18300 MNVL 77578 4746 E2
19900 HarC 77065 3539 B4
20700 MNVL 77578 4747 A3
21300 BzaC 77578 4747 D4

SR-6
22300 BzaC 77511 4747 D4
22400 BzaC 77511 4748 A5
24000 ALVN 77511 4748 E6
SR-6 Addicks Satsuma Rd
- HOUS 77079 3956 D1
1200 HOUS 77079 3817 D7
1200 HOUS 77084 3817 D7
4000 HarC 77084 3817 D1
4300 HOUS 77084 3678 D7
4500 HarC 77084 3678 D7
6600 HarC 77095 3678 D4
7400 HarC 77095 3538 E5
8800 HarC 77095 3539 A5
13200 HarC 77065 3539 B4
SR-6 Morris Av
14600 BzaC 77583 4623 C5
14900 PRLD 77583 4623 D5
15400 IWCY 77583 4623 E6
15800 BzaC 77583 4624 A6
15800 IWCY 77583 4624 A6
17200 MNVL 77578 4624 D7
17200 MNVL 77583 4624 C7
17500 MNVL 77578 4745 E1
SR-6 Morris Rd
18300 MNVL 77578 4746 E2
20700 MNVL 77578 4747 A3
21300 BzaC 77578 4747 B3
SR-6 Northwest Frwy
- HarC - 3249 E5
- HarC - 3250 D6
- HarC - 3251 B7
- HarC - 3395 B1
- HarC - 3396 B3
- HarC - 3397 C7
- HarC - 3538 E2
- HarC - 3539 B3
SR-6 Old Addicks-Howell Rd
- FBnC 77083 4236 D1
- HOUS 77082 4096 D2
SR-35
- PRLD 77581 4628 A2
600 ALVN 77511 4749 E7
1400 ALVN 77511 4867 A7
1600 PRLD 77581 4503 B1
3000 BzaC 77511 4867 A7
3100 PRLD 77584 4503 D5
3300 HOUS 77087 4105 B6
4200 PRLD 77581 4627 E1
4200 PRLD 77584 4627 E1
4600 HOUS 77087 4245 B7
5600 BzaC 77511 4749 B1
6400 HOUS 77061 4245 B2
9000 HOUS 77075 4245 B7
9200 HOUS 77061 4376 B1
9200 HOUS 77075 4376 B7
11400 PRLD 77581 4376 B5
19300 BzaC 77511 4628 B4
19300 PRLD 77511 4628 A2
SR-35 BUS
100 ALVN 77511 4867 C3
400 ALVN 77511 4749 C7
SR-35 N Alvin Byp
- ALVN 77511 4867 A7
600 ALVN 77511 4749 E7
SR-35 S Alvin Byp
- ALVN 77511 4749 E7
1400 ALVN 77511 4867 C4
SR-35 BUS S Alvin Byp
- ALVN 77511 4867 B4
SR-35 BUS N Gordon St
100 ALVN 77511 4867 C1
400 ALVN 77511 4749 C7
SR-35 BUS S Gordon St
100 ALVN 77511 4867 C3
SR-35 N Main St
1000 HOUS 77075 4376 B5
1000 PRLD 77581 4376 B6
1600 PRLD 77581 4503 B1
SR-35 S Main St
2400 PRLD 77581 4503 B3
3100 PRLD 77584 4503 D5
4200 PRLD 77581 4627 E1
4200 PRLD 77584 4627 E1
SR-35 Reveille St
3300 HOUS 77087 4105 B6
4600 HOUS 77087 4245 B7
SR-35 Telephone Rd
- BzaC 77511 4628 B4
- HOUS 77087 4245 B2
- PRLD 77511 4628 A2
- PRLD 77581 4628 A2
6400 HOUS 77061 4245 B2
9000 HOUS 77075 4245 B7
9200 HOUS 77061 4376 B1
9200 HOUS 77075 4376 B7
11400 PRLD 77581 4376 B5
SR-35C BUS
1800 ALVN 77511 4749 C5
SR-35C BUS N Gordon St
1800 ALVN 77511 4749 C5
SR-36
- FBnC 77471 4490 A3
500 RSBG 77471 4490 E7
3400 RSBG 77471 4614 E1
4700 RSBG 77469 4614 E3
4900 FBnC 77471 4614 E4
6000 PLEK 77471 4614 E7
6500 PLEK 77469 4614 E7
6700 PLEK 77461 4614 E7
SR-36 1st St
- RSBG 77471 4614 E1
1000 RSBG 77471 4490 E7
SR-36 Avenue H
1100 RSBG 77471 4490 D4
SR-73
- BYTN - 3832 B6
- BYTN - 3833 D4
- HarC - 3831 E6
- HarC - 3833 D4
- HarC - 3967 E2
- HarC - 3968 D2
- HarC - 3969 B1
- HOUS - 3967 D2
SR-73 East Frwy
- BYTN - 3832 B6
- BYTN - 3833 D4
- HarC - 3831 D6
- HarC - 3967 E2
- HarC - 3968 D2
- HarC - 3969 B1
- HOUS - 3967 D2
SR-75
100 CNRO 77301 2384 A7
300 CNRO 77301 2383 E5
1000 CNRO 77301 2530 A1

SR-75
2100 CNRO 77303 2383 E1
2400 CNRO 77303 2237 D7
4400 MtgC 77303 2237 D7
4800 CNRO 77304 2237 C2
4800 MtgC 77304 2237 C2
7800 CNRO 77378 2237 D1
7800 MtgC 77378 2237 D1
SR-75 N Frazier St
100 CNRO 77301 2384 A7
300 CNRO 77301 2383 E5
2100 CNRO 77303 2383 D1
2400 CNRO 77303 2237 D7
4400 MtgC 77303 2237 D7
4800 CNRO 77304 2237 C2
4800 MtgC 77304 2237 C2
7800 CNRO 77378 2237 D1
7800 MtgC 77378 2237 D1
SR-75 S Frazier St
100 CNRO 77301 2384 A6
1000 CNRO 77301 2530 A1
SR-87
- GlsC 77650 4879 E4
- GlsC 77650 4994 E1
- GlsC 77650 4995 A1
- GLSN 77550 4994 E7
- GLSN 77554 4994 E7
10 GLSN 77550 5109 E1
3700 GLSN 77550 5108 E4
4400 GLSN 77551 5108 C5
SR-87 2nd St
100 GLSN 77550 5109 E1
SR-87 Broadway
- GlsC 77650 4879 E5
SR-87 Broadway St
600 GLSN 77550 5109 E3
3700 GLSN 77550 5108 E4
4400 GLSN 77551 5108 C5
SR-87 Ferry Rd
- GLSN 77550 4994 E7
- GLSN 77554 4994 E7
10 GLSN 77550 5109 E1
SR-87 Seawall Blvd
300 GLSN 77550 5109 E1
SR-96
- GlsC 77565 4633 D2
- KMAH 77565 4633 E1
- KMAH 77565 4634 A1
- LGCY 77565 4633 A4
100 LGCY 77573 4632 A5
900 LGCY 77573 4631 E6
1700 LGCY 77573 4633 A4
SR-96 League City Pkwy
- GlsC 77565 4633 D2
- KMAH 77565 4633 E1
- KMAH 77565 4634 A1
- LGCY 77565 4633 A4
100 LGCY 77573 4632 A5
900 LGCY 77573 4631 E6
1700 LGCY 77573 4633 A4
SR-99
- BYTN 77520 4113 D2
- CmbC 77520 4113 E1
- CmbC 77520 4114 B1
- FBnC 77469 4093 D6
- FBnC 77469 4233 E2
- FBnC 77469 4234 A2
- FBnC 77469 4235 B6
- FBnC 77469 4366 C2
- FBnC 77478 4366 E6
- FBnC 77479 4366 C2
- FBnC 77494 4093 C5
- HarC 77449 3814 C5
- HarC 77493 3814 C5
- HarC 77494 3953 C4
- HOUS 77449 3814 C5
- HOUS 77450 3953 C1
- HOUS 77450 4093 D1
- HOUS 77469 4093 D6
- HOUS 77493 3814 C6
- HOUS 77493 3953 C1
- HOUS 77494 3953 C1
- HOUS 77494 4093 D1
16200 FBnC 77479 4493 E1
17400 FBnC 77469 4493 D3
SR-99 Grand Pkwy
- FBnC 77469 4093 D6
- FBnC 77469 4233 E2
- FBnC 77469 4234 A2
- FBnC 77469 4235 B6
- FBnC 77469 4366 C2
- FBnC 77478 4366 E6
- FBnC 77479 4366 C2
- FBnC 77494 4093 C5
- HarC 77449 3814 C5
- HarC 77493 3814 C5
- HarC 77494 3953 C4
- HOUS 77449 3814 C5
- HOUS 77450 3953 C1
- HOUS 77450 4093 D1
- HOUS 77469 4093 D7
- HOUS 77493 3814 C6
- HOUS 77493 3953 C1
- HOUS 77494 3953 C1
- HOUS 77494 4093 C4
16200 FBnC 77479 4493 E1
17400 FBnC 77469 4493 D3
SR-105
400 CNRO 77301 2383 E5
700 CNRO 77301 2384 D4
1300 CNRO 77304 2383 C4
2500 CNRO 77301 2385 E3
4200 CNRO 77304 2382 A1
11000 CNRO 77303 2385 E3
11000 CTSH 77301 2385 E3
11000 CTSH 77303 2385 E3
11500 CTSH 77306 2385 C3
SR-105 E Davis St
700 CNRO 77301 2384 D4
2500 CNRO 77301 2385 E3
11000 CNRO 77303 2385 E3
11000 CTSH 77301 2385 E3
11000 CTSH 77303 2385 E3
SR-105 W Davis St
100 CNRO 77301 2384 A5
600 CNRO 77301 2383 E5
1300 CNRO 77304 2383 C4
4200 CNRO 77304 2382 E3
SR-105 E Phillips St
100 CNRO 77301 2384 A5
SR-105 W Phillips St
100 CNRO 77301 2384 A5
400 CNRO 77301 2383 E5
SR-134
- DRPK 77536 4109 E4
- HarC 77536 4109 E4
- HarC 77571 4109 E4
100 HarC 77520 3831 D7

SR-134
100 HarC 77562 3831 E6
200 DRPK 77536 4110 A3
200 DRPK 77571 4110 A3
200 HarC 77520 3970 D1
200 HarC 77536 4110 A3
200 HarC 77571 4110 A3
600 HOUS 77520 3970 C2
1700 DRPK 77536 3970 A7
1700 HarC 77536 3970 A7
1700 HarC 77571 3970 A7
2200 DRPK 77571 3970 A6
2200 HOUS 77571 3970 A4
SR-134 Battleground Rd
- DRPK 77536 4109 E4
- HarC 77536 4109 E4
- HarC 77571 4109 E4
200 DRPK 77536 4110 A3
200 DRPK 77571 4110 A3
200 HarC 77536 4110 A3
200 HarC 77571 4110 A3
1700 DRPK 77536 3970 A7
1700 HarC 77536 3970 A7
1700 HarC 77571 3970 A7
2200 DRPK 77571 3970 A6
2200 HOUS 77571 3970 A4
SR-134 Crosby Lynchburg Rd
100 HarC 77520 3831 D7
100 HarC 77562 3831 E6
200 HarC 77520 3970 D1
600 HOUS 77520 3970 C2
1000 HOUS 77571 3970 B3
SR-146
- BYTN - 3972 B7
- BYTN - 4112 C1
- BYTN 77521 3974 A2
- GlsC 77563 4991 A6
- GlsC 77565 4509 D4
- GlsC 77565 4634 A1
- HarC - 4111 E4
- HarC - 4112 A3
- HarC 77571 4382 C2
- HOUS - 4111 D4
- KMAH 77539 4634 A1
- KMAH 77565 4509 D4
- KMAH 77565 4510 A7
- KMAH 77565 4634 A1
- LMQU 77563 4991 A6
- LMQU 77568 4990 E5
- LMQU 77590 4990 D4
- LMQU 77590 4991 A6
- LPRT - 4111 D4
- LPRT - 4251 C4
- LPRT 77571 4382 C1
- PASD 77571 4382 C2
- SEBK 77565 4509 D4
- SRAC 77571 4382 C1
- TXCY 77568 4990 D4
- TXCY 77590 4755 E2
- TXCY 77590 4756 A6
- TXCY 77590 4874 C6
- TXCY 77590 4990 C1
- TXCY 77591 4755 E2
- TXCY 77591 4756 A6
- TXCY 77591 4874 B1
900 SEBK 77586 4509 D3
1400 TXCY 77539 4755 D1
2900 SEBK 77586 4382 C7
3000 GlsC 77518 4634 A2
3000 LGCY 77539 4634 A2
3100 BYTN 77520 3974 A2
3200 BYTN 77520 3973 E4
3200 BYTN 77521 3973 D4
3200 GlsC 77539 4634 D7
3400 TXCY 77539 4634 D7
5300 PASD 77586 4382 C1
7000 BYTN 77521 3835 C5
8600 BYTN 77520 3835 D2
8600 CmbC 77520 3835 B7
8900 MTBL 77520 3835 D1
9500 MTBL 77520 3696 D3
11000 CmbC 77520 3696 D1
SR-146 BUS
100 BYTN 77520 3973 E3
100 BYTN 77520 4113 A1
100 LPRT 77571 4251 D6
1000 BYTN 77520 4112 B3
3000 BYTN 77521 3973 C4
SR-146 BUS N Alexander Dr
100 BYTN 77520 3973 E3
100 BYTN 77520 4113 A1
3000 BYTN 77521 3973 C4
SR-146 BUS S Alexander Dr
100 BYTN 77520 4113 B1
SR-146 Bayport Blvd
900 SEBK 77586 4509 C1
2900 SEBK 77586 4382 C7
SR-146 BUS S Broadway St
100 LPRT 77571 4251 D5
SR-146 Fred Hartman Br
- HarC - 4111 E4
- HarC - 4112 A3
- HOUS - 4111 D4
- LPRT - 4111 D4
SR-146 BUS W Main St
100 LPRT 77571 4251 D2
SR-146 N Robert C Lanier Frwy
- BYTN - 4112 A3
- HarC - 4112 A3
SR-146 TX-146 Frontage Rd
- LPRT 77571 4251 C7
SR-146 BUS Wharton Weems Blvd
- LPRT 77571 4251 D6
SR-159
- HMPD 77445 3098 A1
- WlrC 77445 3098 A3
200 HMPD 77445 2953 A7
11000 WlrC 77445 3097 D6
SR-159 13th St
- HMPD 77445 2953 A7
- HMPD 77445 3098 A1
- WlrC 77445 3098 A3
SR-159 Austin St
200 HMPD 77445 2953 A7
SR-225
- DRPK - 4108 D3
- DRPK - 4109 E4
- HarC - 4109 E4
- HarC - 4110 A4
- HOUS - 4105 E4
- HOUS - 4106 A4
- LPRT - 4110 E6
- LPRT - 4111 A6
- PASD - 4106 E4
- PASD - 4107 A3

SR-225
- PASD - 4108 A3
7900 HOUS 77012 4105 C3
SR-225 La Porte Frwy
- HOUS - 4105 E4
- HOUS - 4106 A4
- PASD - 4106 D4
7900 HOUS 77012 4105 E4
SR-225 La Porte Hwy
- HOUS - 4105 E4
SR-225 Pasadena Frwy
- DRPK - 4108 E3
- DRPK - 4109 E4
- HarC - 4109 E4
- HarC - 4110 A4
- HOUS - 4106 D4
- LPRT - 4110 E6
- LPRT - 4111 A6
- PASD - 4106 E4
- PASD - 4107 A3
- PASD - 4108 A3
SR-242
- MtgC 77302 2677 E4
- MtgC 77306 2681 A4
- PTVL 77357 2682 B7
- WDLD 77385 2676 B5
3000 MtgC 77384 2676 A5
3000 WDLD 77384 2676 A5
3100 WDLD 77384 2675 E5
3800 WDLD 77382 2675 E5
6300 MtgC 77384 2675 A5
8300 MtgC 77382 2674 E4
8300 WDLD 77382 2674 E4
9000 MtgC 77385 2676 A5
9400 MtgC 77384 2674 E2
10600 MtgC 77385 2677 A5
15900 MtgC 77302 2678 E4
15900 MtgC 77302 2679 E4
18600 MtgC 77302 2680 B4
18600 MtgC 77306 2680 E4
21800 MtgC 77357 2681 E7
21900 MtgC 77357 2682 B7
SR-242 College Park Dr
3000 MtgC 77384 2676 A5
3000 WDLD 77384 2676 A5
4200 WDLD 77384 2675 E5
4200 WDLD 77384 2675 E5
6300 MtgC 77384 2675 A5
8300 MtgC 77382 2674 E4
8300 WDLD 77382 2674 E4
9400 MtgC 77384 2674 E2
SR-242 Lazy River Rd
- MtgC 77302 2677 E4
- MtgC 77302 2678 B5
10700 MtgC 77385 2677 E4
SR-242 Needham Rd
- MtgC 77384 2676 A5
- WDLD 77385 2676 B5
9000 MtgC 77385 2676 A5
10600 MtgC 77385 2677 A5
SR-249
- HarC - 3399 C1
- HarC - 3400 C7
- HarC 77377 2963 E7
- HarC 77377 3108 E2
- HOUS - 3399 C1
- HOUS - 3400 A4
700 HOUS 77037 3544 A6
700 HOUS 77038 3544 B6
700 HOUS 77088 3544 B6
800 HarC 77038 3544 A6
1300 HarC 77038 3543 A6
1300 HOUS 77038 3543 E6
1300 HOUS 77088 3543 E6
1800 HarC 77088 3543 A6
2800 HarC 77086 3543 A6
11700 HarC 77038 3542 E5
12300 HOUS 77086 3542 B3
14600 HarC 77086 3541 E1
14600 HarC 77086 3542 E5
22000 HarC 77070 3255 A5
22100 HOUS 77070 3255 B7
22400 HarC 77070 3254 E4
22400 HOUS 77070 3254 E4
22400 HOUS 77377 3255 B7
22500 HOUS 77377 3254 E4
22600 HarC 77375 3254 E4
22600 HarC 77377 3254 D2
24300 HarC 77375 3109 C7
24300 HarC 77377 3109 C7
26900 TMBL 77375 3109 A2
26900 TMBL 77377 3109 A2
28100 TMBL 77375 3108 E1
28100 TMBL 77375 3108 E1
28800 TMBL 77375 2963 E7
28800 TMBL 77377 2963 E7
29400 HarC 77375 2963 E6
30500 MtgC 77362 2963 B4
31900 MtgC 77355 2963 C2
32400 MtgC 77362 2817 A5
33800 MtgC 77362 2816 E4
33800 SGCH 77362 2816 E4
SR-249 W Mt Houston Rd
700 HOUS 77037 3544 A6
700 HOUS 77038 3544 B6
700 HOUS 77088 3544 B6
800 HarC 77038 3544 A6
1300 HarC 77038 3543 A6
1300 HOUS 77038 3543 E6
1300 HOUS 77088 3543 E6
1800 HarC 77088 3543 A6
2800 HarC 77086 3543 A6
SR-249 Tomball Pkwy
- HarC - 3399 C1
- HarC - 3400 C7
- HOUS - 3399 E4
- HOUS - 3400 C7
11500 HarC 77038 3543 A6
11500 HarC 77086 3543 A6
11500 HarC 77088 3543 A6
11700 HarC 77038 3542 E5
12300 HOUS 77086 3542 B3
14600 HarC 77086 3541 E1
14600 HarC 77086 3542 E5
22000 HarC 77070 3255 A5
22000 HOUS 77070 3255 A5
22400 HarC 77070 3254 E4
22400 HOUS 77070 3254 E4
22400 HOUS 77377 3255 B7
22500 HOUS 77377 3254 E4
22600 HarC 77375 3254 E4
22600 HarC 77377 3254 D2
24300 HarC 77375 3109 C7
24300 HarC 77377 3109 C7
26900 TMBL 77375 3109 A2
26900 TMBL 77377 3109 A2
28100 HarC 77377 3108 E2
28100 TMBL 77375 3108 E1

Houston Street Index

STREET Block	City	ZIP	Map#	Grid
SR-249 Tomball Pkwy				
28100	TMBL	77377	3108	E1
28800	HarC	77377	2963	E7
28800	TMBL	77375	2963	E7
28800	TMBL	77377	2963	E7
29400	HarC	77375	2963	E6
30500	MtgC	77362	2963	E7
SR-288				
-	BzaC	-	4373	E7
-	BzaC	-	4500	E2
-	BzaC	77583	4745	A6
-	HarC	-	4373	E5
-	HOUS	-	3963	C6
-	HOUS	-	4103	A7
-	HOUS	-	4242	E7
-	HOUS	-	4243	A1
-	HOUS	-	4373	E1
-	IWCY	77583	4745	B3
-	MNVL	77578	4624	D7
-	MNVL	77583	4624	E3
-	PRLD	-	4373	E6
17600	BzaC	77583	4500	E7
17600	PRLD	77583	4500	E5
17600	PRLD	77584	4500	E2
17700	BzaC	77578	4500	E7
17700	BzaC	77578	4624	D7
17700	BzaC	77583	4624	D7
SR-288 South Frwy				
-	HarC	-	4373	E5
-	HOUS	-	3963	B7
-	HOUS	-	4103	A3
-	HOUS	-	4242	E3
-	HOUS	-	4243	A1
-	HOUS	-	4373	E6
-	MNVL	77578	4624	E3
-	MNVL	77583	4624	E3
-	PRLD	-	4373	E7
17700	BzaC	77578	4500	E7
17700	BzaC	77578	4624	D7
17700	BzaC	77583	4500	E7
17700	BzaC	77583	4624	D7
17700	BzaC	77584	4500	E6
SR-N-1				
100	WEBS	77598	4507	B7
700	WEBS	77058	4507	D5
1000	NSUB	77058	4507	D5
1200	HOUS	77058	4507	D5
1700	HOUS	77058	4508	A4
2200	SEBK	77586	4509	B3
2800	NSUB	77058	4508	A4
3000	PASD	77058	4508	C3
3200	PASD	77586	4508	C3
3800	ELGO	77586	4509	A2
4100	ELGO	77586	4508	E2
4100	TYLV	77586	4508	E2
SR-N-1 NASA Pkwy				
1300	HOUS	77058	4507	D5
1300	NSUB	77058	4507	E5
1300	WEBS	77058	4507	E5
1700	HOUS	77058	4508	A4
2200	SEBK	77586	4509	B3
2800	NSUB	77058	4508	A4
3000	PASD	77058	4508	C3
3200	PASD	77586	4508	C3
3800	ELGO	77586	4509	A2
4100	ELGO	77586	4508	E2
4100	TYLV	77586	4508	E2
SR-N-1 E NASA Pkwy				
100	WEBS	77598	4507	C6
700	WEBS	77058	4507	D5
1000	NSUB	77058	4507	D5
1200	HOUS	77058	4507	E5
SR-N-1 W NASA Pkwy				
100	WEBS	77598	4507	B7
US-59				
-	FBnC	-	4492	B6
-	FBnC	-	4493	B4
-	HarC	-	3546	E1
-	HarC	-	3686	C1
-	HarC	-	4238	C5
-	HMBL	-	3262	E2
-	HMBL	-	3406	B4
-	HOUS	-	3117	E7
-	HOUS	-	3118	A6
-	HOUS	-	3262	C7
-	HOUS	-	3406	A7
-	HOUS	-	3546	E1
-	HOUS	-	3547	A1
-	HOUS	-	3686	A5
-	HOUS	-	3825	A7
-	HOUS	-	3963	C6
-	HOUS	-	3964	A1
-	HOUS	-	4099	C7
-	HOUS	-	4100	D2
-	HOUS	-	4101	E1
-	HOUS	-	4102	C1
-	HOUS	-	4103	A1
-	HOUS	-	4238	D4
-	HOUS	-	4239	B1
-	LbyC	77327	2537	E2
-	LbyC	77327	2538	A1
-	LbyC	77328	2537	E2
-	LbyC	77328	2538	A1
-	MtgC	-	2537	D3
-	MtgC	-	2682	E4
-	MtgC	-	2827	E5
-	MtgC	-	2828	B2
-	MtgC	-	2973	B7
-	MtgC	-	3118	B1
-	PTVL	-	2682	D5
-	RSBG	-	4491	E7
-	RSBG	-	4492	A6
-	RSBG	-	4614	C1
-	RSBG	-	4615	A1
-	RSBG	77471	4490	A7
-	SGLD	-	4367	E7
-	SGLD	-	4368	A6
-	SGLD	-	4369	A1
-	SGLD	-	4493	D3
-	SGLD	-	4494	B2
-	SPLD	-	2537	B7
-	SPLD	-	2682	E3
-	SPLD	-	2683	A1
-	STAF	-	4238	C5
-	STAF	-	4369	A1
-	WDBR	-	2682	C7
-	WDBR	-	2828	A4
US-59 BUS				
10	SPLD	77372	2683	A2
13500	MtgC	77372	2537	B7
13500	SPLD	77372	2537	B7
US-59 Eastex Frwy				
-	HarC	-	3546	E2
-	HarC	-	3686	A6
-	HMBL	-	3262	D4
-	HMBL	-	3406	B4
-	HOUS	-	3117	E7
-	HOUS	-	3118	A6
US-59 Eastex Frwy				
-	HOUS	-	3262	C7
-	HOUS	-	3406	A7
-	HOUS	-	3546	E1
-	HOUS	-	3547	A1
-	HOUS	-	3686	A4
-	HOUS	-	3825	A7
-	HOUS	-	3963	B7
-	HOUS	-	3964	A1
-	MtgC	-	2973	C5
-	MtgC	-	3118	B1
US-59 Southwest Frwy				
-	FBnC	-	4492	B6
-	FBnC	-	4493	B4
-	HarC	-	4238	C5
-	HOUS	-	3963	B7
-	HOUS	-	4099	E4
-	HOUS	-	4100	E2
-	HOUS	-	4101	E1
-	HOUS	-	4102	A1
-	HOUS	-	4103	A1
-	HOUS	-	4238	D4
-	HOUS	-	4239	B1
-	RSBG	-	4491	E7
-	RSBG	-	4492	B6
-	RSBG	-	4614	C1
-	RSBG	-	4615	A1
-	RSBG	77471	4490	A7
-	SGLD	-	4367	E7
-	SGLD	-	4368	A6
-	SGLD	-	4369	A1
-	SGLD	-	4493	D3
-	SGLD	-	4494	B2
-	STAF	-	4238	C5
-	STAF	-	4369	A1
US-90				
-	HarC	-	3552	D7
-	HarC	-	3690	B7
-	HarC	-	3691	E3
-	HarC	-	3692	C1
-	HarC	-	3952	E1
-	HarC	-	3953	A1
-	HarC	-	3955	E1
-	HarC	-	3956	E1
-	HarC	-	3959	D1
-	HDWV	-	3959	E1
-	HDWV	-	3960	A1
-	HOUS	-	3826	E7
-	HOUS	-	3953	D1
-	HOUS	-	3954	A1
-	HOUS	-	3955	E1
-	HOUS	-	3956	E1
-	HOUS	-	3957	E1
-	HOUS	-	3958	B1
-	HOUS	-	3959	E1
-	HOUS	-	3960	E1
-	HOUS	-	3961	A1
-	HOUS	-	3962	E2
-	HOUS	-	3963	A1
-	HOUS	-	3964	E2
-	HOUS	-	3965	B1
-	LbyC	77535	3269	E7
-	LbyC	77535	3413	D1
-	SPVL	-	3959	D1
-	SPVL	-	3960	A1
5100	HarC	77532	3553	A2
5600	HarC	77532	3412	C6
6300	KATY	77493	3952	D1
6300	KATY	77494	3952	D1
6800	HOUS	77013	3826	E4
6900	HOUS	77013	3827	B3
8500	HarC	77532	3413	A4
10900	HarC	77049	3827	E1
10900	HOUS	77049	3827	D2
12100	HarC	77049	3828	A1
12600	HarC	77049	3689	B7
26900	KATY	77493	3951	E1
26900	KATY	77494	3951	E1
27700	WlrC	77493	3951	A1
27700	WlrC	77494	3951	D1
30600	WlrC	77423	3951	A1
US-90 ALT				
-	HOUS	77013	3826	D5
-	HOUS	77020	3965	A5
-	HOUS	77071	4370	E1
-	HOUS	77085	4370	E1
-	MSCY	77071	4370	D1
-	MSCY	77085	4370	D1
-	MSCY	77489	4370	A3
-	SGLD	77478	4369	A1
-	STAF	77477	4369	C2
-	STAF	77477	4370	A3
10	RHMD	77469	4365	A7
10	RHMD	77469	4492	A1
100	HOUS	77011	3964	E7
100	HOUS	77029	3826	C7
100	RHMD	77469	4491	E1
100	RSBG	77471	4490	B4
200	FBnC	77469	4365	B7
200	HOUS	77029	3965	B1
300	HOUS	77023	3964	E7
700	HOUS	77023	4104	D3
800	FBnC	77471	4490	A4
1000	HOUS	77054	4102	A7
1100	HOUS	77030	4102	B6
1700	RSBG	77471	4491	B4
1900	FBnC	77469	4366	E5
2300	HOUS	77011	3965	A5
2300	HOUS	77021	4102	A7
2900	HOUS	77054	4103	A5
3300	HOUS	77021	4103	C5
4400	FBnC	77479	4366	A5
5000	FBnC	77478	4366	E5
5000	HOUS	77021	4104	A4
5400	FBnC	77478	4367	A5
5400	FBnC	77479	4367	A5
5700	SGLD	77478	4367	E3
6300	SGLD	77479	4367	B4
8100	SGLD	77478	4368	E1
8500	HOUS	77025	4102	A6
9200	HOUS	77025	4242	A1
9200	HOUS	77054	4242	A1
9600	HOUS	77025	4241	D4
9600	HOUS	77054	4241	A6
11800	HOUS	77045	4241	C5
12200	HOUS	77035	4241	C4
12400	HOUS	77085	4241	A6
12600	HOUS	77035	4240	B7
12600	HOUS	77085	4240	E6
14300	HOUS	77035	4371	A1
14300	HOUS	77085	4371	A1
14700	HOUS	77071	4371	A1
US-90 BUS				
10	HarC	77532	3691	E1
10	HarC	77532	3692	B1
1000	HarC	77532	3552	C7
3900	HOUS	77029	3826	D6
4500	HOUS	77013	3826	E4
US-90 BUS				
6900	HOUS	77013	3827	B3
10900	HarC	77049	3827	E1
10900	HOUS	77049	3827	D2
12100	HarC	77049	3828	A1
12600	HarC	77049	3689	E6
14500	HarC	77049	3690	C4
17000	HarC	77049	3691	E1
17800	HarC	77044	3691	E1
US-90 ALT 69th St				
-	HOUS	77020	3965	A5
2200	HOUS	77011	3965	A5
US-90 ALT S 69th St				
-	HOUS	77023	4104	E1
100	HOUS	77011	3964	E7
300	HOUS	77023	3964	E7
US-90 ALT Avenue H				
1100	RSBG	77471	4490	B4
2600	RSBG	77471	4491	B4
5200	RHMD	77469	4491	D2
US-90 Beaumont Hwy				
10900	HarC	77049	3827	E1
10900	HOUS	77013	3827	C2
10900	HOUS	77049	3827	D2
12100	HarC	77049	3828	A1
12600	HarC	77049	3689	B7
US-90 BUS Beaumont Hwy				
10	HarC	77532	3691	E1
10	HarC	77532	3692	B1
1000	HarC	77532	3552	C7
10900	HarC	77049	3827	E1
10900	HOUS	77013	3827	C2
10900	HOUS	77049	3827	D2
12100	HarC	77049	3828	A1
12600	HarC	77049	3689	E6
14500	HarC	77049	3690	C4
17000	HarC	77049	3691	E1
17800	HarC	77044	3691	E1
US-90 Beaumont Rd				
6800	HOUS	77013	3826	E4
6900	HOUS	77013	3827	B3
US-90 BUS Beaumont Rd				
6800	HOUS	77013	3826	E4
6900	HOUS	77013	3827	B3
US-90 Crosby Frwy				
-	HarC	-	3552	D7
-	HarC	-	3690	B7
-	HarC	-	3691	A5
-	HarC	-	3692	C1
-	LbyC	77535	3269	E7
-	LbyC	77535	3413	D1
5100	HarC	77532	3553	A2
5600	HarC	77532	3412	C6
8500	HarC	77532	3413	A4
US-90 East Frwy				
-	HOUS	-	3963	C2
-	HOUS	-	3964	E2
-	HOUS	-	3965	A2
US-90 ALT East Frwy				
-	HOUS	-	3965	B1
-	HOUS	77029	3965	B1
US-90 Highway Blvd				
6300	KATY	77493	3952	D1
6300	KATY	77494	3952	D1
26900	KATY	77493	3951	E1
26900	KATY	77494	3951	E1
27700	WlrC	77494	3951	D1
30600	WlrC	77423	3951	A1
30600	WlrC	77493	3951	A1
US-90 ALT Jackson St				
100	RHMD	77469	4491	E1
1700	RSBG	77471	4491	D2
US-90 Katy Frwy				
-	HarC	-	3952	E1
-	HarC	-	3953	A1
-	HarC	-	3955	E1
-	HarC	-	3956	E1
-	HarC	-	3959	D1
-	HDWV	-	3959	E1
-	HDWV	-	3960	A1
-	HOUS	-	3953	C1
-	HOUS	-	3954	E1
-	HOUS	-	3955	E1
-	HOUS	-	3956	B1
-	HOUS	-	3957	D1
-	HOUS	-	3958	A1
-	HOUS	-	3959	E1
-	HOUS	-	3960	A1
-	HOUS	-	3961	A1
-	HOUS	-	3962	E2
-	HOUS	-	3963	C3
-	KATY	-	3952	E1
-	SPVL	-	3959	D1
-	SPVL	-	3960	A1
US-90 ALT Main St				
-	HOUS	77071	4371	A1
12100	HOUS	77045	4241	B5
12200	HOUS	77035	4241	C4
12400	HOUS	77085	4241	A6
12600	HOUS	77035	4240	B7
12600	HOUS	77085	4240	E6
14300	HOUS	77035	4371	A1
14300	HOUS	77085	4371	A1
US-90 ALT S Main St				
8400	HOUS	77054	4102	B6
8500	HOUS	77025	4102	A6
9200	HOUS	77025	4242	A1
9200	HOUS	77054	4242	A1
9600	HOUS	77025	4241	E1
9600	HOUS	77054	4241	A6
14700	HOUS	77035	4371	A1
14700	HOUS	77071	4371	A1
14700	HOUS	77085	4371	A1
US-90 ALT McCarty St				
100	HOUS	77029	3826	C7
200	HOUS	77029	3965	B1
US-90 N McCarty St				
-	HOUS	77013	3826	D5
US-90 ALT N McCarty St				
-	HOUS	77013	3826	D5
3300	HOUS	77029	3826	C6
US-90 BUS N McCarty St				
3900	HOUS	77029	3826	D6
4500	HOUS	77013	3826	D5
US-90 ALT Old Spanish Tr				
1000	HOUS	77025	4102	B6
1000	HOUS	77054	4102	E5
1100	HOUS	77030	4102	B6
2300	HOUS	77021	4102	A7
2900	HOUS	77054	4103	A5
3300	HOUS	77021	4103	C5
5000	HOUS	77021	4104	A4
5300	HOUS	77023	4104	B4
US-90 ALT SSgt M Garcia Dr				
100	HOUS	77011	3964	E7
1600	HOUS	77011	3965	A6
US-90 ALT Wayside Dr				
-	HOUS	77020	3965	A5
100	HOUS	77011	3964	E5
2300	HOUS	77011	3965	A5
US-90 ALT N Wayside Dr				
100	HOUS	77020	3965	A2
US-90 ALT S Wayside Dr				
100	HOUS	77011	3964	E7
300	HOUS	77023	3964	E7
700	HOUS	77023	4104	D3
US-290				
-	HarC	-	3102	E6
-	HarC	-	3103	A7
-	HarC	-	3248	C1
-	HarC	-	3249	A3
-	HarC	-	3250	D7
-	HarC	-	3251	B7
-	HarC	-	3395	B1
-	HarC	-	3396	A2
-	HarC	-	3397	A6
-	HarC	-	3538	C1
-	HarC	-	3539	E6
-	HarC	-	3680	E3
-	HarC	-	3681	E6
-	HMPD	-	2954	A6
-	HMPD	77445	2952	D4
-	HMPD	77445	2953	A4
-	HOUS	-	3681	C4
-	HOUS	-	3682	A6
-	HOUS	-	3821	C1
-	HOUS	-	3822	A3
-	JRSV	-	3539	D5
-	JRSV	-	3540	A7
-	JRSV	-	3680	E3
-	PRVW	-	3099	C1
-	PRVW	-	3100	D2
-	WALR	-	3102	A4
-	WlrC	-	2954	B7
-	WlrC	-	3099	C1
-	WlrC	-	3100	E3
-	WlrC	-	3101	E4
-	WlrC	77445	2952	A3
-	WlrC	77445	2953	A4
US-290 BUS				
-	HarC	77447	3248	E3
-	HarC	77447	3249	A3
-	HarC	77484	3247	E1
-	HarC	77484	3248	A1
-	HMPD	77445	3098	D1
-	PRVW	77445	3099	E3
-	PRVW	77445	3100	D4
-	PRVW	77484	3100	D4
-	WlrC	77445	2953	B5
-	WlrC	77445	3098	E1
-	WlrC	77445	3099	C2
-	WlrC	77484	3100	E4
10	HMPD	77445	2953	B5
1900	WALR	77484	3102	D7
2200	WALR	77484	3101	E6
3200	WlrC	77484	3101	C5
25000	HarC	77429	3396	C4
26100	HarC	77433	3396	B3
37900	HarC	77484	3102	C7
US-290 BUS 10th St				
-	WlrC	77445	2953	B5
200	HMPD	77445	2953	B5
US-290 BUS Austin St				
10	HMPD	77445	2953	C7
US-290 BUS Hempstead Rd				
-	HarC	77447	3248	A1
-	HarC	77484	3247	E1
-	HarC	77484	3248	A1
37900	HarC	77484	3102	C7
39500	WALR	77484	3102	B6
US-290 Northwest Frwy				
-	HarC	-	3249	A3
-	HarC	-	3250	D7
-	HarC	-	3251	B7
-	HarC	-	3395	B1
-	HarC	-	3396	E5
-	HarC	-	3397	A6
-	HarC	-	3538	C1
-	HarC	-	3539	E6
-	HarC	-	3680	E3
-	HarC	-	3681	C4
-	HOUS	-	3681	C4
-	HOUS	-	3682	C7
-	HOUS	-	3821	C1
-	HOUS	-	3822	A3
-	JRSV	-	3539	D5
-	JRSV	-	3540	A7
-	JRSV	-	3680	E3

A

STREET Block	City	ZIP	Map#	Grid
A Av				
-	PASD	77503	3967	E7
-	PASD	77506	3967	E7
7500	HOUS	77061	4245	C7
A Dr				
-	HarC	77388	3111	D1
A St				
-	HarC	77571	4110	A2
-	HOUS	77547	4106	C2
-	WlrC	77484	3101	E4
100	WALR	77484	3101	E6
2800	LPRT	77571	4251	E7
5900	KATY	77493	3813	B6
E A St				
100	LPRT	77571	4251	E2
1100	LPRT	77571	4252	A2
S A St				
2900	LPRT	77571	4251	E7
W A St				
-	LPRT	77571	4251	B3
Aaron St				
100	ALVN	77511	4748	C6
100	BzaC	77511	4748	C6
2300	DRPK	77536	4249	E1
W Aarondale Ln				
10	LbyC	77535	3413	D5
Aarondale Tr				
10	LbyC	77535	3413	D5
Aaronglen Cir				
10	LbyC	77535	3413	E6
Aarons Wy				
12400	HarC	77066	3401	B4
Aaronwood Tr				
10	LbyC	77535	3413	D5
Abaft Ct				
17700	HarC	77532	3411	B7
Abalone				
3800	GLSN	77554	5220	E6
Abalone Wy				
12900	HarC	77044	3689	B5
Abalone Cove				
3800	MSCY	77459	4496	D4
Abana Ln				
1000	HarC	77090	3258	B3
A Bar Dr				
4300	STFE	77510	4871	A7
Abbawood St				
-	HOUS	77040	3682	A2
Abberton Hill Dr				
15900	HarC	77379	3256	B5
Abbey Ln				
-	WDLD	77382	2674	C5
400	LGCY	77573	4630	B7
13800	SGLD	77478	4237	A5
Abbey Brook Pl				
10	WDLD	77381	2820	D3
Abbey Chase Ct				
15400	HarC	77095	3538	B3
Abbey Chase Ln				
9200	HarC	77095	3538	E4
Abbeydale Dr				
8800	HOUS	77031	4239	B5
Abbey Field Dr				
2700	PRLD	77584	4501	E5
Abbey Field Ln				
3200	MtgC	77365	2974	C7
Abbey Oak Cir				
21200	HarC	77073	3259	C2
Abbey Oak Dr				
1600	HarC	77073	3259	C1
Abbey Point Dr				
-	HarC	77049	3689	D7
-	HarC	77049	3828	D1
Abbey Springs Ln				
26400	FBnC	77494	4092	D2
Abbeywood Dr				
3600	BzaC	77584	4501	C6
3900	PRLD	77584	4501	D6
16600	HOUS	77058	4507	D2
Abbie Ln				
5000	DKSN	77539	4633	C7
Abbotglen Ln				
25700	FBnC	77494	4093	A2
Abbotsford Wy				
-	HarC	77044	3549	A3
Abbotshall Ln				
-	HarC	77090	3258	C5
9300	HarC	77044	3689	B4
Abbotshire Ct				
25000	FBnC	77494	4093	B1
Abbotswood Ct				
600	HarC	77450	3954	C1
Abbott Dr				
1000	PRLD	77584	4501	C1
1000	TXCY	77590	4875	C5
Abbott St				
300	BYTN	77520	3971	C4
Abbott Lakes Dr				
3200	MtgC	77386	2969	D2
Abbutsford Ln				
22700	FBnC	77450	4093	E1
Abby Ct				
1100	KATY	77493	3813	A7
Abby Ln				
3000	DRPK	77536	4109	B7
17800	HarC	77379	3256	A2
Abby Aldrich Ln				
1500	HarC	77449	3815	A6
Abby Glen Wy				
18200	HarC	77084	3677	D5
Abby Ln Cir				
8100	HarC	77379	3256	A3
Abby Ridge Wy				
11600	HarC	77044	3549	A7
Abby Ruins Ct				
24900	HarC	77389	2966	A3
Abel Rd				
20600	MtgC	77355	2961	B5
Abelia Creek Dr				
-	HarC	77379	3257	A2
Abell Field Ln				
1700	SGLD	77478	4368	C5
Aber St				
16200	HarC	77530	3830	C5
Abercreek St				
4900	FRDW	77546	4505	D7
4900	HarC	77546	4505	E7
Abercrombie Dr				
10	HOUS	77084	3817	D3
Aberdeen Cir				
4900	SGLD	77479	4495	C4
Aberdeen Ct				
8800	HarC	77095	3538	C5
Aberdeen Dr				
-	SGLD	77479	4495	C4
2000	LGCY	77573	4631	B6
28800	MtgC	77354	2818	A1
Aberdeen Rd				
1100	PASD	77502	4247	C1
Aberdeen St				
200	STAF	77477	4369	A2
Aberdeen Wy				
500	HarC	77562	3831	C2
3100	HOUS	77025	4101	E5
Aberdeen Crossing Pl				
10	WDLD	77381	2820	C2
Aberdeen Forest Dr				
16000	HarC	77095	3538	C4
Aberdeen Green Dr				
16000	HarC	77095	3538	C4
Aberdeen Hollow Ln				
18700	HarC	77377	3254	B2
Aberdeen Lake Dr				
9200	HarC	77095	3538	C3
Aberdeen Meadow Ln				
14800	HOUS	77053	4372	E3
Aberdeen Oaks Dr				
8800	HarC	77095	3538	C4
Aberdeen Palms Dr				
8700	HarC	77095	3538	C5
Aberdeen Park Dr				
8800	HarC	77095	3538	C4
Aberdeen Trails Dr				
15700	HarC	77095	3538	D4
Aberdovey Ln				
15000	HarC	77530	3829	C6
Abergreen Tr				
16100	HarC	77095	3538	C4
Aberham Dr				
3600	HarC	77066	3401	C4
Abernathy St				
2200	HOUS	77026	3964	C1
2700	HOUS	77026	3825	B7
Abersham Ct				
400	HarC	77450	3953	D2
Aberton Ct				
19700	HarC	77379	3112	A4
Aberton Ln				
5100	HarC	77379	3112	A5
Aberton Forest Dr				
6100	HarC	77084	3677	E4
Aber Trail Ct				
8900	HarC	77095	3538	C4
Abide Dr				
12900	HOUS	77085	4240	E7
13800	HOUS	77085	4371	E2
Abigail Grace Ct				
9800	HOUS	77025	4241	E2
Abigal Dr				
9500	FBnC	77478	4236	A2
Abilene Dr				
-	MAGA	77354	2669	A4
-	MtgC	77354	2669	A4
Abilene St				
1900	LGCY	77573	4632	C2
6900	HOUS	77020	3964	E2
6900	HOUS	77020	3965	A2
29500	MtgC	77354	2818	A2
29800	MtgC	77354	2817	E2
Abingdon Ct				
4700	SGLD	77479	4495	C4
Abingdon Rd				
2100	ALVN	77511	4866	E4
Abinger Ln				
3400	HOUS	77088	3683	A2
Abington Wy				
6100	HOUS	77008	3822	E7
6100	HOUS	77008	3823	A7
Abington Cove Dr				
20700	MtgC	77365	3118	A1
Ablean				
2800	HarC	77032	3545	E2
2900	HarC	77032	3546	A2
Ableside Dr				
4300	LGCY	77573	4631	A5
4400	LGCY	77573	4630	E5
Abloom Ct				
600	FBnC	77583	4744	A3
Abloom Wy				
-	HarC	77066	3401	B7
Abney Dr				
100	HarC	77060	3403	B5
Abney Ln				
100	MtgC	77355	2668	C7
100	MtgC	77355	2814	D1
Abott Cir				
400	SGLD	77478	4368	B1
N Abram Cir				
10	WDLD	77382	2819	B2
S Abram Cir				
10	WDLD	77382	2819	B2
Abril Vista St				
5100	MtgC	77354	2673	E4
5100	MtgC	77354	2674	A4
Abruzzo Dr				
12800	HOUS	77085	4240	E7
Abshier				
-	DRPK	77536	4249	C3
-	LPRT	77536	4249	C3
-	LPRT	77571	4249	C3
-	PASD	77505	4249	C3
-	PASD	77571	4249	C3
Abundant Life Ln				
5500	HOUS	77048	4244	B7
Acacia Ct				
500	LGCY	77573	4631	B4
Acacia Dr				
-	MtgC	77355	2960	B2
-	SGLD	77479	4496	A3
1300	HOUS	77017	4106	D6
1300	PASD	77017	4106	D6
1300	PASD	77502	4106	D6
3500	SGLD	77479	4495	E2
22600	SGCH	77355	2960	B2
Acacia Pl				
700	MSCY	77459	4497	A6
Acacia St				
2200	LGCY	77573	4631	B4
4400	BLAR	77401	4101	B4
Acacia Arbor Ln				
12400	HarC	77041	3679	D5
Acacia Fair Ln				
2700	FBnC	77545	4498	C6
Acacia Falls Ct				
7900	FBnC	77469	4095	C7
Acacia Forest Tr				
10300	HarC	77089	4505	A1
10600	HarC	77089	4378	A7
N Acacia Park Cir				
10	WDLD	77382	2674	B4
S Acacia Park Cir				
100	WDLD	77382	2674	B4
Acacia Park Dr				
100	WDLD	77382	2674	C4
Acacia Park Pl				
10	WDLD	77382	2674	C4
Acaci Arbor Ln				
12200	HarC	77041	3679	E5
Acacia Wood Wy				
3700	HarC	77449	3815	E2
Acaciawood Wy				
1800	HOUS	77045	4242	C6
Academy Dr				
100	CNRO	77301	2384	A2
Academy Ln				
700	DRPK	77536	4249	C3
4300	TYLV	77586	4508	E2
4900	DRPK	77505	4249	C3
4900	PASD	77505	4249	C3
Academy St				
5000	HOUS	77005	4101	C2
5100	WUNP	77005	4101	C4
6700	SSPL	77025	4101	C5
6800	HOUS	77025	4101	C5
Acadia Branch Pl				
10	WDLD	77382	2674	E4
Acadian Dr				
11700	HOUS	77099	4238	A4
Acadiana Ct				
2200	SEBK	77586	4509	C1
Acadiana Ln				
2400	SEBK	77586	4509	C1
Acanthus Ln				
11000	HarC	77095	3538	A1
Acapulco Dr				
15700	JRSV	77040	3540	D7
15700	JRSV	77040	3680	C1
Acapulco Cove Ct				
8300	HarC	77346	3265	C3
Acapulco Cove Dr				
20300	HarC	77346	3265	C3
Acapulco Village Dr				
600	HMBL	77338	3263	A7
Ace Ct				
2400	RSBG	77469	4615	E1
Ace Ln				
21900	HarC	77073	3259	B4
Ace St				
3700	HOUS	77063	4099	C2
Acer Ct				
10000	HOUS	77075	4377	A2
Achgill St				
8300	JRSV	77040	3540	C7
Achievement Dr				
10	WDLD	77384	2675	E6
Achievement Ln				
10	WDLD	77384	2675	D6
Acker St				
100	MAGA	77354	2669	A5
Ackley Dr				
6400	HarC	77396	3547	A3
Ackley Mnr				
13900	HarC	77429	3397	C2
Acme Ct				
300	HOUS	77022	3684	D7
Acoma Dr				
10500	HOUS	77076	3685	A5
Acoma Springs Ct				
2100	PRLD	77581	4503	D2
Acorn				
200	BzaC	77583	4500	B7
200	BzaC	77583	4624	A1
Acorn Bnd				
-	FBnC	77459	4621	A6
Acorn Cir				
3200	DKSN	77539	4754	A1
5000	TXCY	77591	4874	A6
Acorn Ct				
1000	FRDW	77546	4505	B4
1400	MSCY	77489	4497	D1
5300	LGCY	77573	4630	D7
6400	PRLD	77584	4502	C4
33300	MtgC	77354	2671	B4
Acorn Dr				
9300	BzaC	77578	4746	B7
9300	MNVL	77578	4746	B7
Acorn Ln				
3700	HOUS	77365	3119	E3
8700	HTCK	77563	4988	D3
Acorn Rdg				
3900	FBnC	77459	4622	A4
Acorn St				
200	LGCY	77573	4632	B6
3300	BzaC	77511	4748	E1
4900	HOUS	77092	3683	A7
6700	HOUS	77092	3682	C7
Acorn Brook Pl				
2800	HarC	77084	3816	C4
Acornchase Dr				
22200	HarC	77389	3112	D1
Acorn Cluster Ct				
10	WDLD	77381	2821	C3
Acorn Forest Dr				
6300	HOUS	77088	3682	C3
Acorn Glen Tr				
-	FBnC	77545	4498	C5
Acorn Green Ct				
15300	HarC	77530	3829	D6
Acorn Grove Dr				
22300	HarC	77389	3112	D1
Acorn Hill Rd				
18100	MtgC	77302	2680	C6
18100	MtgC	77357	2680	C6
Acorn Meadow St				
1500	HarC	77067	3402	C6
Acorn Oak St				
12000	WDLD	77380	2967	E1
Acorn Ridge Wy				
14300	HarC	77429	3395	E1
Acornrun Ln				
3500	HarC	77389	3112	E1
Acorn Springs Ln				
3400	HarC	77389	3112	D
Acorn Square Ct				
2200	HarC	77493	3814	B5
Acorn Tree Ct				
200	HarC	77388	3113	D
Acorn Valley Dr				
22200	HarC	77389	3112	D
22700	HarC	77389	2967	D
Acorn Valley Ln				
6000	FBnC	77469	4493	B5
Acorn Wood Wy				
2800	HOUS	77059	4380	B6
Acorn Wy Ln				
3400	HarC	77389	3112	D
Acreman Rd				
10800	MtgC	77306	2532	A
Acres				
1000	HOUS	77020	3964	B
S Acres Dr				
4700	HOUS	77047	4243	E6
4700	HOUS	77048	4243	E6
5200	HOUS	77048	4244	B6
Acrewoods Pl				
10	WDLD	77382	2673	B6
Acuna Ln				
14400	HOUS	77045	4373	A
Ada Dr				
100	KATY	77494	3952	A
Ada Ln				
20000	MtgC	77357	2829	A
Adagio Av				
7700	HarC	77040	3681	C
7800	HarC	77040	3541	C
Adagio Ln				
9300	HarC	77040	3541	B
9300	HarC	77040	3681	B
Adair St				
3100	HOUS	77004	4103	D
Adam Ct				
200	TMBL	77375	3109	C
Adam Ln				
100	HOUS	77002	3963	E
Adambury Ct				
23300	HarC	77373	2968	E
Adamo Ln				
1700	PRLD	77581	4374	E
1700	PRLD	77581	4501	E
Adams Dr				
1500	DRPK	77536	4249	D
22200	MtgC	77355	2960	E
22200	MtgC	77355	2961	A
Adams Ln				
13700	MtgC	77362	2816	C
Adams St				
10	HOUS	77011	3964	C
900	MSCY	77489	4370	B
1200	BYTN	77520	3973	C
1200	BzaC	77583	4623	C
1200	CNRO	77301	2383	E
1300	STAF	77477	4370	B
1300	STAF	77489	4370	B
1900	ALVN	77511	4866	D
3200	PRLD	77584	4502	E

TREET
ock City ZIP Map# Grid
dams St
21900 MtgC 77365 3118 C2
Adams St
100 HOUS 77011 3964 C5
Adams St
700 LPRT 77571 4251 D2
damsborough Dr
10600 HOUS 77099 4238 C1
dams Mill Ln
10100 FBnC 77478 4236 D3
dams Ridge Ln
12400 HarC 77346 3408 C2
dams Run Dr
12000 HarC 77429 3397 D6
dams Walk Ct
1500 HOUS 77077 3957 A5
damwood Ct
3600 HarC 77388 3112 D6
ddenmoor Ct
1300 HarC 77014 3401 E2
1300 HarC 77014 3402 B2
ddicks Bayou Ln
10 HOUS 77013 3966 E1
ddicks Clodine Rd
- FBnC 77083 4236 B1
- HOUS 77082 4096 B2
- HOUS 77094 3956 B1
3300 HarC 77082 4096 B3
7100 FBnC 77083 4096 B7
9400 FBnC 77478 4236 B2
ddicks Howell Rd
200 HOUS 77079 3956 D2
ddicks Levee Dr
- HOUS 77084 3816 C7
ddicks Satsuma Rd
- HarC 77065 3539 A4
- HOUS 77079 3956 D1
1200 HOUS 77079 3817 D7
1200 HOUS 77084 3817 D6
4000 HarC 77084 3817 D1
4300 HOUS 77084 3678 D7
5000 HarC 77084 3678 E3
6600 HarC 77095 3678 D5
7400 HarC 77095 3538 D7
8800 HarC 77095 3539 A4
ddicks Satsuma Rd SR-6
- HarC 77065 3539 A4
- HOUS 77079 3956 D1
1200 HOUS 77079 3817 D7
1200 HOUS 77084 3817 D6
4000 HarC 77084 3817 D1
4300 HOUS 77084 3678 D7
4500 HarC 77084 3678 D7
6600 HarC 77095 3678 D5
7400 HarC 77095 3538 D7
8800 HarC 77095 3539 A4
ddicks Stone Dr
15100 HarC 77082 4096 D2
Addicks Stone Dr
15300 HarC 77082 4096 D2
Addicks Stone Dr
15300 HarC 77082 4096 D2
ddie Gee Rd
38900 WlrC 77445 3243 D7
38900 WlrC 77445 3244 A6
ddington Ct
3600 HarC 77336 3121 D3
dd Inn Ln
- HarC 77069 3400 A1
ddison Av
6800 SGLD 77479 4367 C7
7000 SGLD 77479 4494 C1
ddison Dr
3800 PRLD 77584 4501 C1
ddison Pl
100 FBnC 77479 4366 D5
ddison Rd
2300 HOUS 77030 4102 A4
2400 WUNP 77005 4102 A4
ddison Hills Ln
5200 FBnC 77494 4093 B2
ddison Park Ln
1000 HarC 77373 2968 D4
de St
3700 HOUS 77063 4099 C2
del Rd
- HOUS 77067 3402 C6
11400 HarC 77067 3402 C6
delaide Meadows Ct
19600 HarC 77449 3676 C3
19600 HarC 77449 3677 C3
delbert St
7300 HOUS 77093 3824 E2
dele St
- BYTN 77520 3971 A4
800 HOUS 77009 3824 C2
900 HOUS 77009 3823 E5
1200 HOUS 77008 3823 E5
delfina St
15000 FBnC 77478 4236 C4
delia Ct
12600 HOUS 77015 3967 A3
delia St
3000 HOUS 77026 3825 A7
deline Ln
9900 HOUS 77054 4242 A2
della Ct
6800 PRLD 77584 4502 C5
della Dr
1700 HarC 77530 3829 D4
delle St
7200 HOUS 77093 3824 E2
den
29600 MtgC 77354 2818 B2
den Dr
1700 HOUS 77003 3963 D6
den Mist Dr
1700 HOUS 77003 3963 C6
dina Springs Ln
17400 HarC 77095 3537 D3
dirondack Dr
12500 HOUS 77089 4378 C7
dkins Rd
1000 HOUS 77055 3820 D6
1000 HOUS 77055 3959 D1
1000 SPVL 77055 3820 D7
1000 SPVL 77055 3959 D1
1500 HOUS 77080 3820 D6
dkins St
600 CNRO 77301 2384 B3
dkins Forest Dr
19400 HarC 77379 3110 D6
dler Cir
10 GLSN 77551 5108 D7
dler Dr
10700 CmbC 77520 3835 D3
13200 HOUS 77047 4373 C3
Adler Lake Dr
8200 FBnC 77083 4096 A7
Adlerspoint Ln
2600 FBnC 77479 4493 E3
Adles Lake Dr
8300 FBnC 77083 4096 A7
Adlong Johnson Rd
17500 HarC 77532 3412 B7
Adlong School Rd
16400 HarC 77532 3553 D1
17100 HarC 77532 3412 C7
Admiral Cir
300 TKIS 77554 5106 D3
Admiral Ct
4100 MSCY 77459 4369 C7
Admiral Rd
- LGCY 77573 4632 D1
2600 LGCY 77573 4508 E7
Admiral Bay Ln
600 HarC 77494 3953 A2
Admiralty Dr
3600 HarC 77336 3121 D3
Admiralty Wy
- LGCY 77573 4509 B6
300 CRLS 77565 4509 B5
300 LGCY 77565 4509 B5
Adobe Cir
16500 HarC 77095 3538 A3
Adobe Ct
7100 FBnC 77479 4367 A7
Adobe Dr
9900 HarC 77095 3538 A3
Adobe Ln
4500 BYTN 77521 3973 B2
Adobe Arch Ct
4000 FBnC 77469 4233 C5
Adobe Canyon Ln
19200 HarC 77377 3109 A7
Adobe Falls Dr
1800 HarC 77388 3113 B2
29900 MtgC 77386 2969 D2
Adobe Meadows Ct
7100 FBnC 77479 4367 A7
Adobe Oaks Ct
7000 FBnC 77479 4367 B7
Adobe Pines Ln
4600 HarC 77084 3678 A7
4600 HarC 77084 3817 A1
Adobe Rose Dr
9400 HarC 77396 3407 B2
Adobe Stone Dr
- HarC 77449 3815 C1
1700 HarC 77396 3407 B2
Adobe Trace Ln
17900 HarC 77084 3817 A1
Adobe Trails Ct
7000 FBnC 77479 4367 B7
Adobe Trails Dr
6400 FBnC 77479 4367 B7
Adolph Dr
1000 HOUS 77091 3683 E5
Adolpho Ct
- HarC 77044 3689 C4
Adonia Pl
3700 SGLD 77479 4495 E2
Adonis Av
8000 HarC 77521 3833 D3
Adonis Dr
4800 HarC 77373 3115 C6
Adoquin Ln
5700 FBnC 77469 4493 A6
E Adoue St
100 ALVN 77511 4867 C1
100 BYTN 77520 3973 A7
W Adoue St
10 BYTN 77520 3973 A6
100 ALVN 77511 4867 A2
200 BYTN 77520 3972 E6
1800 ALVN 77511 4866 E2
Adowa Spring Lp
700 HarC 77373 3114 A3
Adrian St
7900 HOUS 77012 4105 C4
Adriana Ln
1700 HarC 77530 3829 D4
Adriano Dr
8600 HOUS 77078 3688 B5
Adrift Ct
1000 HarC 77532 3552 A2
Advance Dr
11500 HarC 77065 3398 D7
Adventure Green Dr
16900 HarC 77433 3250 E4
Adwick Ct
23000 HarC 77450 3953 D1
Aegean Dr
3200 MSCY 77459 4498 A5
Aegean Tr
6600 SGLD 77479 4494 C1
Aerial Brook Tr
3800 FBnC 77545 4498 D7
3900 FBnC 77545 4622 C1
Aerie Dr
11800 HarC 77377 3109 B7
Aerobic Av
7500 HarC 77346 3409 B1
Aerobic Dr
- HarC 77346 3409 B1
Aeropark Dr
5200 HarC 77032 3546 C1
Aeros Ct
- HOUS 77032 3546 C1
Aerospace Av
11100 HOUS 77034 4379 A4
Aestival St
23400 MtgC 77365 2972 B6
Affinity Dr
- HOUS 77450 3953 C1
- HOUS 77494 3953 C1
Affirmed Dr
4200 PASD 77503 4108 D7
Affirmed Wy
16100 HarC 77546 4506 A5
Afloat Wy
1200 HarC 77532 3552 A3
Afore Dr
15800 HarC 77532 3552 A4
Aft Wy
300 HarC 77532 3411 B7
Afton Ct
1000 TMBL 77375 2964 D5
2500 LGCY 77573 4631 B5
Afton Pl
- HarC 77521 3832 E6
Afton St
200 GlsC 77511 4751 B6
200 LGCY 77511 4751 B6
1000 HOUS 77024 3960 E1
Afton St
1000 HOUS 77055 3960 E1
1800 HOUS 77055 3821 E4
Afton Wy
27100 HarC 77336 3121 E3
Afton Estates Dr
- MtgC 77386 2969 B1
Afton Forest Ln
- HarC 77449 3815 C2
Afton Hollow Ln
18100 FBnC 77469 4095 C6
Afton Meadow Ln
13000 HarC 77072 4097 C5
Afton Oak Ln
2700 MtgC 77386 2823 C7
Afton Ridge Ln
5600 HarC 77084 3678 C4
Aftonshire Dr
4700 HOUS 77027 3961 B7
Afton Woods Dr
6900 HOUS 77055 3821 E7
African Violets Pl
10 WDLD 77382 2673 C6
Afsar Av
3000 HarC 77014 3401 D3
Agar Ln
2400 HOUS 77043 3819 D3
Agarita Ln
13200 HOUS 77072 4097 B4
13200 HOUS 77083 4097 B4
13400 HarC 77083 4097 B4
Agarita Rd
- WlrC 77447 2813 A7
- WlrC 77447 2959 A1
Agassi Ct
31500 MtgC 77354 2672 E5
Agassi Ace Ct
6200 HarC 77379 3257 A3
Agate St
23400 HarC 77389 2967 A5
Agate Canyon Wy
11500 HarC 77095 3397 C6
Agate Praire Dr
16500 HarC 77095 3538 A2
Agate Stream Pl
10 WDLD 77381 2820 C4
Agave Dr
2500 LGCY 77573 4632 E2
7200 FBnC 77494 4093 C4
Agave Ridge Ln
11200 HarC 77089 4504 C1
Ag Cleaver St
1700 PRVW 77445 2955 B7
Agean Dr
- HarC 77346 3264 B7
Agee
- HOUS 77089 4377 E2
Agg Rd
100 TMBL 77375 3109 C2
Aggie Ln
1900 LGCY 77573 4631 B3
11900 HOUS 77037 3685 A2
11900 HOUS 77076 3685 A2
Agile Pines Dr
18600 HarC 77346 3265 B7
18600 HarC 77346 3409 B1
Agnes Rd
200 FBnC 77469 4494 D7
200 FBnC 77469 4495 A5
200 SGLD 77469 4494 D7
Agnes St
3600 HOUS 77087 4104 D6
Agora Cir
8000 FBnC 77479 4494 C5
Agua Vista Dr
18600 HarC 77084 3816 C1
Aguila St
9600 HOUS 77013 3826 E6
9600 HOUS 77013 3827 A6
Agusta Ct
16400 HarC 77379 3255 E6
Ahoy Ct
400 HarC 77532 3552 B2
Ahrens St
300 HOUS 77017 4106 B6
Aidan Ct
- HarC 77014 3401 D3
Aiden Cir
- HOUS 77048 4374 E2
Aiken Ln
15500 HarC 77032 3404 C6
Aikins & Owen Rd
- HarC 77377 3107 B2
22500 HarC 77377 2962 A7
Aimua Ct
7600 FBnC 77083 4095 D7
Ainsdale Dr
1500 HOUS 77077 3957 C5
Ainslie
3000 MtgC 77380 2967 C1
3000 WDLD 77380 2821 C7
3000 WDLD 77380 2967 C1
Ainsworth Dr
11500 HOUS 77099 4238 B4
11800 MDWP 77477 4238 B5
Air Cargo Rd
2800 HOUS 77032 3404 D1
E Air Cargo St
7900 HOUS 77061 4245 D4
W Air Cargo St
8100 HOUS 77061 4245 D4
Air Center Blvd
16100 HOUS 77032 3404 A4
16600 HarC 77073 3404 A4
16600 HOUS 77073 3404 A4
Aire St
- HOUS 77029 3826 B7
Airfield Ln
17300 BzaC 77581 4628 C2
17800 BzaC 77511 4628 C2
20200 MtgC 77365 2825 C5
Airfoil Rd
- HOUS 77032 3404 D1
Airfreight Rd
3000 HOUS 77032 3404 D1
N Airhart Dr
100 BYTN 77520 3972 C5
S Airhart Dr
100 BYTN 77520 3972 B7
1200 BYTN 77520 4112 A1
Airline Dr
- HOUS 77022 3824 A3
600 CNRO 77301 2384 E2
1300 KATY 77493 3813 C6
1400 HOUS 77009 3824 A5
2000 FRDW 77546 4629 E4
2100 FRDW 77546 4630 A4
3900 HOUS 77022 3823 E1
Airline Dr
4700 HOUS 77022 3684 E7
5400 HOUS 77076 3684 E6
7400 HOUS 77037 3684 E4
7700 HarC 77037 3684 E3
8700 HarC 77037 3544 D7
10000 HarC 77060 3544 C5
10900 HOUS 77037 3544 C5
11000 HOUS 77060 3544 B2
Airmail Rd
18600 HOUS 77032 3404 E1
Airpark Rd
6000 MNVL 77578 4747 B1
Airport Av
2900 RSBG 77471 4491 A6
Airport Blvd
- GLSN 77554 5222 A1
- HOUS 77045 4242 C6
100 LPRT 77571 4250 E2
1900 HOUS 77051 4242 D6
2900 HOUS 77051 4243 A6
4100 HOUS 77047 4243 C6
4100 HOUS 77048 4243 C6
5000 HOUS 77048 4244 A6
6700 HOUS 77061 4244 A6
7000 HOUS 77061 4245 A5
8300 GLSN 77554 5221 E1
8600 HOUS 77061 4246 A5
9200 HOUS 77017 4246 A5
9200 HOUS 77034 4246 A5
9200 HOUS 77075 4246 A5
W Airport Blvd
- FBnC 77469 4235 E5
- FBnC 77478 4235 E5
- FBnC 77478 4237 B5
- HarC 77477 4238 E6
- HOUS 77045 4242 A6
- SGLD 77478 4236 D5
3400 HOUS 77045 4241 D6
5200 HOUS 77035 4240 D6
6600 HOUS 77071 4240 A6
7600 HOUS 77071 4239 A6
9400 HOUS 77031 4239 A6
9700 HarC 77031 4238 E6
9700 HOUS 77031 4238 E6
10200 STAF 77031 4238 E6
10200 STAF 77477 4238 C6
11300 MDWP 77477 4238 A6
12000 MDWP 77477 4237 E5
12300 MDWP 77478 4237 E5
12300 SGLD 77478 4237 B5
15500 FBnC 77478 4236 B5
Airport Pkwy
19500 CNRO 77303 2238 E7
19500 MtgC 77303 2238 E7
Airport Rd
600 CNRO 77301 2384 C4
2200 CNRO 77303 2384 D1
2300 MtgC 77303 2384 D1
2600 CNRO 77303 2238 D7
2600 MtgC 77303 2238 D7
10100 CNRO 77303 2239 A5
10200 MtgC 77303 2239 A5
Airport Rd FM-1484
1100 CNRO 77301 2384 C4
2200 CNRO 77303 2384 D1
2300 MtgC 77303 2384 D1
2600 CNRO 77303 2238 D7
2600 MtgC 77303 2238 D7
10100 CNRO 77303 2239 A5
10200 MtgC 77303 2239 A5
Airstream Lp
13700 HarC 77044 3689 D3
Airtex Blvd
100 HarC 77073 3403 A1
100 HarC 77090 3403 A1
100 HOUS 77073 3403 A1
W Airtex Blvd
100 HarC 77090 3402 E1
E Airtex Dr
800 HarC 77073 3403 E1
2000 HarC 77073 3404 A1
2000 HOUS 77032 3404 A1
Airway Dr
10 HarC 77037 3544 D7
Airway Ln
10000 GLSN 77554 5107 B7
Airway St
9100 HarC 77037 3544 D7
Airways Ln
9600 GLSN 77554 5107 B7
Airybrook Ln
400 HarC 77094 3955 B2
Ajax St
3600 HOUS 77022 3823 D3
AJ Foyt Rd
23800 HarC 77447 3104 E4
23800 HarC 77447 3105 A3
AJ Lloyd Ln
- MtgC 77447 2960 A4
Ajuga Ct
17100 HarC 77377 3254 B4
Akard St
3000 HOUS 77051 4243 A6
4100 HOUS 77047 4243 C6
Akers St
300 LMQU 77568 4990 C2
Akimbo Rd
- HOUS 77034 4379 A3
Akin Dr
19100 HarC 77532 3411 A4
Akita Ct
- HarC 77530 3829 D3
AKJ St
500 MSCY 77489 4370 B4
500 STAF 77477 4370 B3
Akron St
900 HOUS 77029 3966 C2
900 JTCY 77029 3966 C2
Akron Oak St
13200 HarC 77070 3399 B4
Akumal Cl
5000 DKSN 77539 4633 C7
Akumal Ln
2800 HarC 77073 3259 E3
Alabama Av
100 LGCY 77573 4632 B1
1600 PASD 77503 4108 D7
4100 DKSN 77539 4754 C2
Alabama Ct
3000 HOUS 77027 3961 D7
Alabama Pk
500 MtgC 77302 2530 A5
Alabama St
700 KATY 77493 3952 A1
700 KATY 77494 3952 A1
900 HOUS 77002 3963 A7
1000 HOUS 77004 3963 A7
Alabama St
1100 HOUS 77017 4246 B4
1100 HOUS 77587 4246 B4
1100 SHUS 77017 4246 B4
1100 SHUS 77587 4246 B4
1500 BYTN 77520 4112 A2
1800 HOUS 77004 4103 C1
6900 MNVL 77578 4747 A2
W Alabama St
100 HOUS 77002 3963 A7
200 HOUS 77006 3963 A7
300 HOUS 77006 3962 B7
1600 HOUS 77098 3962 A7
3200 HOUS 77098 3961 D7
3400 HOUS 77027 3961 B7
4900 HOUS 77056 3961 A7
5200 HOUS 77056 3960 E7
Alabaster Ct
16800 FBnC 77083 4095 C7
Alabaster Dr
8200 FBnC 77083 4095 E7
Alabonson Rd
- HOUS 77040 3682 B1
- HOUS 77091 3682 D3
- HOUS 77092 3682 D7
- HOUS 77092 3821 D1
6800 HOUS 77088 3682 B1
7200 HarC 77088 3682 D3
Aladdin Ct
700 FRDW 77546 4505 B6
Alake Dr
9600 HOUS 77078 3688 B5
Alamance Dr
4300 BYTN 77521 3972 C3
14200 HarC 77090 3258 C7
Alamanni Dr
2400 PRLD 77581 4504 E3
Alamar Dr
7800 HarC 77095 3538 E7
Alameda Point Ln
6200 HarC 77041 3679 E4
Alametos Dr
16100 FBnC 77083 4096 A6
16600 FBnC 77083 4095 E6
Alamo Av
4400 SGLD 77479 4496 A1
Alamo Dr
4700 GLSN 77551 5108 D5
11700 LPRT 77571 4110 E6
11700 LPRT 77571 4111 A6
Alamo Rd
6000 HOUS 77040 3681 E4
6500 HarC 77040 3681 E3
Alamo St
700 BYTN 77521 3833 D5
700 RSBG 77471 4491 A5
1100 FBnC 77469 4364 D6
1100 RHMD 77469 4364 D6
2300 HOUS 77007 3963 A2
Alamo Wy
25100 WlrC 77447 2813 D1
Alamosa Ct
14200 SGLD 77478 4236 E6
Alamosa Ln
5200 HarC 77379 3257 B1
Alan St
1100 DRPK 77536 4109 C4
Alana Ln
- BYTN 77520 4112 D3
300 ORDN 77386 2822 C6
400 MtgC 77385 2822 D6
400 ORDN 77385 2822 D6
Alana Springs Dr
1900 HarC 77450 3954 E5
Alannah Lagoon Ct
14600 HarC 77083 4096 D7
Alannah Lagoon Dr
8200 FBnC 77083 4096 D7
Alanneil Dr
5500 HOUS 77081 4100 C6
Alan Thai Ln
3200 HarC 77396 3407 E2
Alanwood St
7700 HOUS 77061 4245 B2
Alaska Av
1600 LGCY 77573 4632 C5
3000 LGCY 77539 4632 D7
Alaska St
4000 HOUS 77017 4105 E6
4300 HOUS 77017 4106 A7
Alassio Isle Ct
2200 MSCY 77459 4497 D5
Alastair St
100 PASD 77506 4107 D3
600 PASD 77506 4108 A5
Alba Rd
4600 HOUS 77018 3823 A1
4900 HOUS 77018 3684 A7
5100 HOUS 77091 3684 A7
7300 HOUS 77088 3684 A3
Albacore Av
100 GLSN 77550 5109 E1
Albacore Dr
7400 HOUS 77074 4100 A7
Albans Ct
10 SGLD 77479 4495 E4
Albans Rd
1700 HOUS 77005 4102 C2
4100 WUNP 77005 4101 C2
Albans St
2400 HOUS 77005 4102 A2
2600 WUNP 77005 4102 A2
3700 WUNP 77005 4101 D2
Albany Ct
1000 FBnC 77469 4365 D4
Albany St
- DRPK 77536 4109 A7
2600 HOUS 77006 3963 A5
2900 HOUS 77006 3962 C5
Albany Park Ln
21000 HarC 77379 3111 C3
Albany Springs Ln
13900 HOUS 77044 3550 B3
Albatross Dr
4300 SEBK 77586 4383 A7
Albatross Rd
7700 CmbC 77520 3835 D3
16700 JMAB 77554 5331 D4
Albee Dr
22300 HarC 77449 3814 E3
Albelia Meadows Dr
13200 HarC 77083 4097 C7
Albemarle Dr
3000 PASD 77503 4108 A4
3000 PASD 77506 4108 A4
Albemarle Ln
5100 HOUS 77021 4104 B4
Alber St
1000 HOUS 77009 3824 D6
Alberene Dr
- HOUS 77036 4239 A2
9200 HOUS 77074 4239 B2
Albert Dr
5800 HarC 77032 3405 E7
5800 HOUS 77032 3405 E7
5800 HOUS 77396 3405 E7
6000 HOUS 77396 3406 A7
23100 MtgC 77365 2973 E7
23100 MtgC 77365 3118 E1
Albert St
- HarC 77532 3552 C3
100 LMQU 77568 4873 E7
100 TXCY 77591 4873 E7
S Albert St
300 LMQU 77568 4873 E7
300 TXCY 77591 4873 E7
Alberta
3700 HarC 77084 3816 C2
Alberta St
3600 HOUS 77021 4103 C6
Albert Miller Ln
31700 MtgC 77354 2672 E5
Alberton Ln
2200 BzaC 77584 4501 C4
Albin Ln
7800 HOUS 77071 4239 E4
Albion Cresent Dr
6600 HarC 77449 3677 B2
Albright Dr
2400 HOUS 77017 4246 D2
2600 SHUS 77017 4246 D2
2600 SHUS 77587 4246 D2
Albury Dr
8900 HOUS 77074 4240 B1
9400 HOUS 77096 4240 B2
11100 HOUS 77035 4240 B4
Albury Park Ln
10000 HarC 77375 3110 A4
Alcala Ct
9400 HOUS 77078 3688 A5
Alcanterra Dr
9700 HOUS 77078 3688 A5
Alcea Ct
20100 HarC 77379 3110 D5
Alchester Ln
13300 HOUS 77079 3958 B3
Alcomita Dr
7400 HarC 77083 4096 D6
Alconbury Ln
4300 HOUS 77021 4103 E4
Alcorn St
500 SGLD 77478 4368 A3
7400 SGLD 77479 4494 E1
9400 HOUS 77093 3685 D6
Alcorn Bayou Dr
1600 SGLD 77479 4495 A1
Alcorn Bend Dr
3500 SGLD 77479 4495 A3
Alcorn Crossing Dr
3300 SGLD 77479 4495 B3
Alcorn Glen Ln
4200 SGLD 77479 4495 A1
Alcorn Hill Dr
3800 SGLD 77479 4495 B1
Alcorn Meadow Dr
- SGLD 77479 4368 A7
Alcorn Oaks Dr
2800 SGLD 77479 4495 A3
Alcott Dr
8500 HOUS 77055 3821 A3
8500 HOUS 77080 3821 A3
8800 HOUS 77080 3820 E3
10800 HOUS 77043 3819 C3
Alcott Glen Ln
- HarC 77377 3253 E3
- HarC 77377 3254 A3
Alcott Manor Ln
7000 FBnC 77469 4094 D5
Alcove
17000 HarC 77090 3258 A4
17000 HOUS 77090 3258 A4
Alcove Ln
17000 HarC 77090 3258 B4
Alcove Glen Ln
10100 HarC 77375 3255 A1
Aldaco Dr
- HOUS 77045 4372 B2
Aldates Dr
1800 HarC 77015 3829 B4
1900 HarC 77049 3829 B4
Aldeburgh Ct
8600 HarC 77379 3256 B5
Alden Ct
6800 SGLD 77479 4367 C7
Alden St
6100 HarC 77084 3678 E4
Alden Bend Dr
7800 WDLD 77381 2674 C5
7800 WDLD 77382 2674 C5
Alden Bridge Dr
- WDLD 77381 2674 D6
- WDLD 77382 2673 D5
- WDLD 77382 2674 B5
Aldenbrook Dr
- HarC 77095 3539 A5
Alden Glen Ct
10 WDLD 77382 2674 D4
Alden Glen Dr
10 WDLD 77382 2674 D4
Aldenham Pl
16600 HarC 77379 3256 E3
Alden Manor Ln
3300 FBnC 77494 4093 C2
Alden Ridge Dr
16000 HOUS 77053 4371 E6
Aldenshire Ct
25100 FBnC 77494 4093 B6
Aldenstone Ln
5200 HarC 77084 3678 D5
Aldenwale Ln
13300 HOUS 77047 4373 B3
Aldenwick Ln
600 HarC 77073 3259 A4
Alden Woods Dr
- WDLD 77382 2675 C6
5700 MtgC 77384 2675 B6
5700 WDLD 77384 2675 B6
Alder
10900 MtgC 77372 2536 E1
Alder Cir
1200 LGCY 77598 4630 C4
Alder Dr
- BLAR 77401 4100 D6
- HOUS 77096 4100 D6
- HOUS 77401 4100 D6
Alder Dr
5400 HOUS 77057 4100 D3
5400 HOUS 77081 4100 D6
Alder Pl
10 WDLD 77380 2968 A1
Alder St
- HarC 77396 3406 E4
- HMBL 77396 3406 E4
Alderbrook Dr
1500 SGLD 77478 4237 A6
Aldercy
21500 HarC 77338 3260 A2
Alderete Dr
15500 HarC 77068 3257 A6
Alderfer St
3500 HOUS 77047 4374 C3
Alderfield Ct
5800 HarC 77084 3678 C4
Alderfield Rd
13200 HarC 77044 3689 C4
Alderfield Manor Ln
5300 FBnC 77494 4093 B6
Alderford Ct
10600 HarC 77070 3399 B5
Aldergrove Dr
3400 HarC 77388 3112 E7
Alderleaf Pl
2700 HarC 77388 3113 B6
Alderly Dr
7400 HarC 77389 2966 B2
Aldermoor Dr
18300 HarC 77388 3258 A1
Alderney Ct
5100 RSBG 77471 4491 D4
Alderney Dr
6900 HOUS 77055 3821 E7
Alderon Woods Pl
10 WDLD 77382 2674 E3
Alder Pass Ct
3800 HarC 77449 3816 A2
Aldersby Ln
6000 LGCY 77573 4751 C1
6100 LGCY 77573 4630 C7
Aldersgate Ct
600 HarC 77450 3954 E1
Alderson St
6200 HOUS 77020 3825 E7
7100 HOUS 77020 3826 A7
13700 HarC 77015 3828 E7
14100 HarC 77015 3829 A7
Alder Springs Ct
7200 FBnC 77494 4093 C3
Alder Springs Ln
7300 FBnC 77494 4093 C3
Alderwick Dr
14700 FBnC 77478 4236 D3
Alderwood Dr
1400 FBnC 77479 4493 D4
3600 HarC 77388 3257 E1
12600 MSCY 77071 4239 B7
Alderwood St
100 LGCY 77573 4630 C5
Aldine Rd
- HarC 77038 3543 D1
Aldine Bender Rd
10 HOUS 77037 3544 B1
10 HOUS 77060 3544 D1
400 HarC 77060 3544 D1
700 HarC 77060 3545 A1
700 HOUS 77060 3545 A1
800 HarC 77032 3545 D1
800 HarC 77039 3545 D1
800 HOUS 77032 3545 A1
2900 HarC 77032 3546 D1
3400 HOUS 77032 3546 A1
5800 HarC 77396 3546 D1
5800 HOUS 77396 3546 D1
6100 HarC 77396 3547 A1
6100 HOUS 77396 3547 A1
Aldine Bender Rd FM-525
- HarC 77396 3546 D1
- HOUS 77396 3546 D1
10 HOUS 77037 3544 B1
10 HOUS 77060 3544 D1
400 HarC 77060 3544 D1
700 HarC 77060 3545 A1
700 HOUS 77060 3545 A1
800 HarC 77032 3545 D1
800 HarC 77039 3545 D1
800 HOUS 77032 3545 A1
2900 HarC 77032 3546 D1
3400 HOUS 77032 3546 A1
Aldine Mail Rd
100 HarC 77037 3544 D5
100 HarC 77060 3544 D5
800 HarC 77037 3545 A5
800 HarC 77060 3545 A5
1100 HarC 77039 3545 D5
3400 HarC 77039 3546 D5
Aldine Meadows Rd
1100 HarC 77032 3545 B1
1100 HOUS 77032 3545 B1
Aldine Park Ln
1700 HarC 77093 3685 C1
Aldine Ranchtown Ct
2900 HarC 77032 3546 A2
Aldine Ranchtown Dr
13900 HarC 77032 3546 A2
Aldine Western Rd
1600 HarC 77038 3543 B1
Aldine Westfield Rd
9000 HOUS 77093 3685 D6
10700 HarC 77093 3685 D1
11900 HarC 77093 3545 D7
12000 HarC 77039 3545 D2
12000 HOUS 77039 3545 D7
12000 HOUS 77093 3545 D7
14700 HarC 77032 3545 D1
15000 HOUS 77032 3545 D1
15100 HarC 77032 3404 C3
15100 HOUS 77032 3404 C3
16800 HarC 77073 3404 C4
18100 HarC 77073 3260 A4
18100 HOUS 77032 3260 B7
18100 HOUS 77338 3260 A4
19400 HarC 77338 3260 B5
20700 HOUS 77073 3260 A3
21100 HarC 77073 3259 E1
21100 HarC 77338 3259 E1
21100 HOUS 77073 3259 E1
22200 HarC 77073 3114 E7
22200 HarC 77338 3114 E7
24000 HarC 77373 3114 A1
27600 HarC 77373 2969 A7
29900 MtgC 77386 2969 C3
30900 MtgC 77386 2823 C7
31300 MtgC 77385 2823 C6

STREET
Block City ZIP Map# Grid

Aldis St
10400 HOUS 77075 4377 C3
Aldon St
2400 HOUS 77093 3685 E5
Aldrich St
1300 HOUS 77055 3822 A6
16500 MtgC 77302 2678 D5
Aldridge Dr
- MSCY 77459 4498 A5
3500 MSCY 77459 4497 E5
Aldridge Creek Ct
15800 HarC 77429 3253 B5
Aldsworth Dr
1900 HarC 77088 3543 D6
Aldwell Ct
9900 HarC 77064 3540 C5
Aleah Ct
2500 HarC 77388 3113 A3
Alecia Dr
4100 PASD 77503 4108 D6
Aledo St
4300 HOUS 77051 4243 C3
4600 HOUS 77033 4243 C3
Alee Ct
17900 HarC 77532 3411 B7
Aleen St
600 HOUS 77029 3965 C2
Alegria Dr
7400 FBnC 77083 4095 D6
Alejo Dr
8900 HOUS 77088 3682 B2
Alemarble Oak St
18200 HarC 77429 3252 B7
Alentina Ct
2800 LGCY 77573 4633 A3
Alenzo Dr
15300 HarC 77032 3404 A7
15300 HOUS 77032 3404 A7
Alenzo St
15400 HarC 77032 3404 A7
Alessandria Ln
2700 LGCY 77573 4632 E4
Aleta Dr
7800 HarC 77379 3256 A2
Alethea Ln
6100 HOUS 77081 4100 C5
Aleutian Bay Ln
17300 HarC 77346 3408 B3
Alex Ln
11800 HOUS 77071 4239 C5
Alexa Ln
8600 HOUS 77078 3688 B6
Alexa Forest Dr
21500 MtgC 77365 2973 A4
Alexander Ct
1100 FBnC 77469 4365 D3
N Alexander Dr
100 BYTN 77520 3973 E4
3000 BYTN 77521 3973 C5
N Alexander Dr SR-146 BUS
100 BYTN 77520 3973 D4
3000 BYTN 77521 3973 C5
S Alexander Dr
100 BYTN 77520 4113 B1
600 BYTN 77520 4112 E2
S Alexander Dr SR-146 BUS
100 BYTN 77520 4113 B1
Alexander Ln
2100 PRLD 77581 4503 E3
20100 MtgC 77365 2825 C7
Alexander St
800 HOUS 77007 3823 C7
800 HOUS 77008 3823 C7
Alexander Crossing Ln
24400 FBnC 77494 3953 B7
Alexander Parc Dr
3100 PRLD 77581 4503 D3
Alexandra St
900 FBnC 77477 4369 C3
Alexandra Park Dr
1300 HarC 77379 3255 D1
Alexandria Ct
7900 HarC 77379 3110 E7
Alexandria Dr
17700 MtgC 77302 2678 D7
17700 MtgC 77302 2824 D1
Alexandros Ct
3100 PRLD 77584 4501 D5
Alexis Cir
4000 HarC 77014 3401 C2
Alexis Tate Cir
4000 MSCY 77459 4496 D4
Alfano St
6500 HOUS 77076 3684 D4
7700 HOUS 77037 3684 D2
Alfena Av
15800 HarC 77532 3552 E3
Alfonso Ct
20600 HarC 77388 3113 C4
Alford Av
800 BYTN 77520 3973 B6
Alford Rd
18100 MtgC 77355 2814 B4
Alford St
300 BYTN 77520 3973 A6
Alfred Ln
10000 HOUS 77041 3681 A5
Alger Dr
15800 HOUS 77489 4371 B6
S Algeria St
10 LMQU 77568 4873 D7
10 TXCY 77591 4873 D7
Algerian Wy
2500 HOUS 77098 4102 A1
Algernon Dr
4800 HarC 77373 3115 C6
Algiers Rd
9900 HOUS 77041 3681 A6
10200 HarC 77041 3681 A6
Algoa Rd
700 BzaC 77511 4868 D4
Algoa Friendswood Rd
300 GlsC 77511 4869 A1
1800 GlsC 77511 4751 A7
2900 LGCY 77511 4751 A7
Algonquin
- HarC 77429 3398 A2
Algonquin Dr
11700 HOUS 77089 4378 C5
Algrave Ln
16000 HarC 77379 3256 A6
Algregg St
600 HOUS 77008 3823 D6
800 HOUS 77009 3823 D6
900 HOUS 77009 3824 B7
Alhambra Ct
800 SGLD 77478 4368 E3
Alhaven Dr
17300 HarC 77388 3257 E2
Alicant Dr
6600 FBnC 77479 4367 B7
Alice Av
1100 PASD 77506 4107 C4
Alice Dr
300 DRPK 77536 4109 B5
4000 SGLD 77478 4369 A5
Alice Ln
12600 HOUS 77015 3967 A3
20100 MtgC 77357 2827 D5
31000 TMBL 77375 2963 D4
Alice Rd
3600 PRLD 77581 4376 C7
13700 HarC 77377 3108 D2
13700 HarC 77377 3109 A2
13700 TMBL 77375 3109 A2
Alice St
- HOUS 77054 4102 E6
- HOUS 77054 4103 A6
1100 DRPK 77536 4109 C5
3200 HOUS 77021 4103 A6
3500 GLSN 77554 5222 A2
3600 FBnC 77545 4498 E7
Alice Foster Rd
16600 FBnC 77469 4235 E3
16600 FBnC 77478 4235 E3
Alicia Wy Dr
6300 KATY 77493 3813 B4
Alief
11500 HOUS 77072 4098 B3
11500 HOUS 77082 4098 B3
Alief Clodine Rd
11200 HOUS 77072 4098 A3
11200 HOUS 77082 4098 A3
12000 HOUS 77072 4097 A4
12000 HOUS 77082 4097 A4
13000 HOUS 77083 4097 C4
13200 HarC 77082 4097 B4
13200 HarC 77083 4097 B4
13600 HarC 77083 4096 D4
14600 HarC 77082 4096 A4
14600 HOUS 77082 4096 A4
14600 HOUS 77083 4096 A4
16700 FBnC 77082 4095 D4
16900 FBnC 77469 4095 D4
Alief Pl Dr
11900 HOUS 77072 4098 A4
Alief Pl St
11900 HOUS 77072 4098 A4
Alief Village Dr
4100 HOUS 77072 4098 A3
4100 HOUS 77082 4098 A3
Alinawood Ct
19300 HarC 77346 3264 C5
Alinawood Dr
19500 HarC 77346 3264 C5
Aline St
4500 HOUS 77087 4104 D7
Alington Dr
12200 HarC 77014 3401 D4
12200 HarC 77067 3401 D4
Alisa Ln
6400 HarC 77084 3678 E3
Alisa Bend Ct
3100 HarC 77396 3407 D2
Alisimpson St
3000 HOUS 77021 4103 A5
Aliso Bend Ln
12400 HarC 77041 3679 D5
Aliso Canyon Ln
8200 FBnC 77083 4095 E7
8300 FBnC 77083 4235 C2
Alison Ln
500 CNRO 77303 2383 E1
500 CNRO 77303 2384 A1
Alivia Ct
24100 HarC 77373 3114 D5
Aljean Ln
7400 DRPK 77536 4249 B3
7400 PASD 77536 4249 B3
Alkay St
14400 HOUS 77045 4372 E3
15100 HarC 77053 4372 E4
15100 HOUS 77053 4372 E4
Alkire Lake Dr
200 SGLD 77478 4368 C4
W Alkire Lake Dr
300 SGLD 77478 4368 C3
Alladdin Ln
10 WDLD 77380 2967 C1
Allan St
400 FRDW 77546 4629 B1
Allcrest St
4600 MSCY 77545 4622 C2
Allday Dr
5800 HOUS 77036 4099 C3
Alleda Rd
100 PRVW 77445 3100 D3
Allegheny St
6200 HOUS 77021 4103 B5
Allegro Ct
7600 HarC 77040 3681 C1
Allegro Dr
2400 FBnC 77469 4365 B3
4500 SEBK 77586 4383 A7
7500 HarC 77040 3681 C1
7900 HarC 77040 3541 C7
Allegro St E
1900 HOUS 77080 3820 E4
Allegro St N
9100 HOUS 77080 3820 D4
S Allegro St
9100 HOUS 77080 3820 E5
Allegro Shores Ln
20300 HarC 77346 3265 C3
Alleluia Tr
4700 MNVL 77578 4746 A2
Allemand Ln
16700 HarC 77429 3396 E3
Allen
- HMPD 77445 3097 E1
Allen Av
6100 TXCY 77591 4873 D5
Allen Cir
- CmbC 77520 4114 A2
Allen Ct
500 ALVN 77511 4867 C2
Allen Dr
4700 MtgC 77304 2382 C4
12300 STFE 77510 4871 B5
Allen Ln
2300 HarC 77521 3832 C4
Allen Pkwy
300 HOUS 77002 3963 B4
1500 HOUS 77019 3963 A4
1700 HOUS 77019 3962 D4
Allen Rd
3700 BzaC 77584 4502 B7
3700 BzaC 77584 4626 A1
3700 PRLD 77584 4502 B7
4000 MNVL 77578 4626 B3
4000 MNVL 77584 4626 B2
Allen St
- BHCY 77520 4254 D3
- CmbC 77520 4254 D3
- HOUS 77002 3963 D3
100 HMPD 77445 3098 C1
200 HOUS 77017 4246 C2
200 SHUS 77017 4246 C2
200 SHUS 77587 4246 C2
400 CNRO 77301 2384 A5
1000 RSBG 77471 4490 C4
4700 HOUS 77007 3962 A2
Allenbrook Dr
3700 BYTN 77521 3972 E2
Allenby Ln
- HarC 77047 4374 B3
Allen Dale Rd
14800 MtgC 77302 2678 D5
Allendale Rd
700 PASD 77502 4107 A7
800 PASD 77502 4106 E7
4800 HOUS 77017 4106 A7
5700 HOUS 77502 4106 D7
Allendale St
100 BLAR 77401 4101 A6
Allende Dr
- FBnC 77083 4095 E7
Allene Dr
30600 MtgC 77355 2961 E5
30600 SGCH 77355 2961 E5
Allenford Ct
26100 FBnC 77494 4092 E1
Allen Genoa Rd
- SHUS 77504 4247 B4
- SHUS 77587 4247 B4
100 HOUS 77017 4106 C5
1200 PASD 77017 4106 C6
1900 HOUS 77502 4106 D7
1900 PASD 77502 4106 D7
2100 HOUS 77017 4246 D1
2100 HOUS 77502 4246 D1
2100 PASD 77502 4246 E1
2300 PASD 77017 4246 E1
2600 SHUS 77502 4246 E2
2600 SHUS 77587 4246 E2
3600 PASD 77504 4247 C6
4300 HOUS 77504 4247 C6
5100 HOUS 77034 4247 D7
5300 HOUS 77034 4378 D1
N Allen Genoa Rd
100 SHUS 77587 4247 A2
300 SHUS 77587 4246 E2
400 PASD 77502 4246 E2
400 SHUS 77502 4246 E2
S Allen Genoa Rd
100 SHUS 77587 4247 A3
1100 PASD 77504 4247 B4
1100 SHUS 77504 4247 B4
Allenham Ct
21200 HarC 77338 3261 D3
Allenham Ln
21100 HarC 77338 3261 E3
Allen Pines Ln
7400 HarC 77433 3676 C1
Allensby St
7000 HOUS 77022 3824 A2
Allen Shore Cir
- HarC 77433 3395 C6
W Allen Shore Dr
12100 HarC 77433 3395 D5
Allen's Landing Dr
10700 HarC 77065 3539 B2
Allentown Dr
6000 HarC 77389 2966 D6
Allenwick Ln
16000 HarC 77084 3678 C5
Allerton Dr
1800 MSCY 77489 4370 C5
Allerton St
6200 HarC 77084 3678 E4
Alles House Rd
13800 STFE 77510 4870 D6
13800 STFE 77517 4870 D6
Alley Ct
500 HarC 77388 3113 C6
S Alley Ct
15700 HarC 77082 4096 B4
Alley Ln
16100 MtgC 77302 2679 B7
Alley Springs Dr
- HOUS 77396 3406 C5
Alliance St
- WlrC 77484 3101 E4
100 WALR 77484 3101 E5
Alliant Dr
100 HarC 77032 3546 C1
100 HOUS 77032 3546 C1
Allingham Ln
23700 FBnC 77494 4093 C1
Allington Ct
3300 HarC 77014 3401 D4
Allis St
200 HarC 77373 3113 E7
Allisa St
900 FBnC 77477 4369 B3
Allison Ct
2200 MSCY 77459 4370 A7
Allison Dr
3000 HarC 77396 3407 D3
Allison Ln
9900 HOUS 77054 4242 A2
Allison Rd
4100 HOUS 77048 4374 E3
4600 HOUS 77048 4375 A3
Allison St
1400 ALVN 77511 4749 A6
Allison Bend Ct
10900 HarC 77086 3542 A1
Allison Richey Rd
- HarC 77583 4624 A2
Allister Ct
23300 FBnC 77494 3953 D7
Allman St
1700 BYTN 77520 4112 E2
Allpoint Ct
7200 FBnC 77469 4093 E6
Allston St
500 HOUS 77007 3962 C1
800 HOUS 77007 3823 C7
800 HOUS 77008 3823 C6
4100 HOUS 77018 3823 C2
Allsup St
7400 HOUS 77048 4244 D6
7400 HOUS 77061 4244 D6
Allum Rd
4600 HOUS 77045 4241 B6
5100 HOUS 77085 4241 A6
Allview Ln
19000 HarC 77094 3955 B1
Allwood St
7900 HOUS 77016 3825 D1
9500 HOUS 77016 3686 D5
11200 HarC 77093 3686 D1
Allwright St
2400 RSBG 77469 4491 E6
2400 RSBG 77471 4491 E6
Allyan Tr
1300 SGLD 77479 4367 C6
Allyne
14000 HarC 77032 3545 E2
Allyson Ct
2600 HarC 77373 3114 E4
Allyson Ln
2800 HarC 77373 3114 E4
Allysum Ct
13200 HarC 77429 3254 A7
Allysum Ln
13100 HarC 77429 3254 A7
Alma
4200 HarC 77389 2967 C7
Alma Ct
1500 FBnC 77469 4365 D4
Alma St
100 HOUS 77009 3824 B7
800 TMBL 77375 3109 A1
1100 CNRO 77301 2530 A1
12400 HarC 77532 3692 D2
Almahurst Cir
13800 HarC 77429 3253 E6
Almahurst Ln
13800 HarC 77429 3253 E6
13800 HarC 77429 3254 B5
Almarie Dr
25400 MtgC 77357 2828 E6
25400 MtgC 77357 2829 A6
Almax Dr
2700 DRPK 77536 4249 B1
Almeda Rd
10 HarC 77047 4372 E7
10 HarC 77053 4372 E7
10 PRLD 77047 4372 E7
10 PRLD 77053 4372 E7
300 FBnC 77545 4372 E7
800 FBnC 77545 4499 D4
800 PRLD 77545 4499 D4
3500 HOUS 77004 3963 B7
4000 HOUS 77004 4103 A2
5700 HOUS 77030 4103 A5
6100 HOUS 77021 4103 A4
6400 HOUS 77021 4102 E7
6400 HOUS 77030 4102 E4
6900 HOUS 77054 4102 E7
8500 HOUS 77054 4242 D1
9100 HOUS 77045 4242 D3
12300 HOUS 77045 4373 B1
13400 HOUS 77053 4373 A3
13700 HarC 77053 4373 A4
Almeda Rd FM-521
300 FBnC 77545 4372 E7
300 PRLD 77053 4372 E7
800 FBnC 77545 4499 D4
800 PRLD 77545 4499 D4
7000 HOUS 77021 4102 E7
7000 HOUS 77030 4102 E5
7000 HOUS 77054 4102 E7
8500 HOUS 77054 4242 D1
10600 HOUS 77045 4242 B7
12300 HOUS 77045 4373 B2
13400 HOUS 77053 4373 A4
13700 HarC 77053 4373 A4
14300 HarC 77053 4372 E7
15200 HarC 77047 4372 E7
15200 PRLD 77047 4372 E7
E Almeda St
8800 HOUS 77054 4242 D1
9100 HOUS 77045 4242 D3
9100 HOUS 77051 4242 D3
Almeda Bend Ct
9500 HOUS 77075 4377 B1
Almeda Crossing Ct
12700 HOUS 77048 4375 A2
Almeda Genoa Rd
100 HOUS 77045 4373 D3
100 HOUS 77047 4373 D3
100 HOUS 77053 4373 D3
2600 HOUS 77047 4374 B3
4100 HOUS 77048 4374 D3
4600 HOUS 77048 4375 A2
6700 HOUS 77075 4375 A2
7700 HOUS 77075 4376 E1
8800 HOUS 77075 4377 C1
10500 HOUS 77034 4377 E1
11100 HOUS 77034 4378 A2
Almeda Oaks Dr
9800 HOUS 77075 4377 B1
Almeda Park Dr
10800 HOUS 77045 4242 C3
Almeda Park Rd
- HOUS 77045 4242 C3
Almeda Pines Ct
2600 HOUS 77045 4242 C3
Almeda Pines Dr
9500 HOUS 77075 4377 B1
Almeda Plaza Dr
2600 HOUS 77045 4242 A7
Almeda School Rd
13400 HOUS 77047 4373 B4
14500 HarC 77047 4373 B7
14500 PRLD 77047 4373 B7
14700 PRLD 77584 4373 B7
Almeece St
14400 HOUS 77045 4372 E3
15100 HarC 77053 4372 E4
15100 HOUS 77053 4372 E4
Almenar Cir
2500 HarC 77038 3543 B6
Almendares Av
2600 PASD 77506 4108 A6
Almington Ln
3800 HOUS 77088 3683 A2
Almond Ct
3900 MtgC 77386 2970 C7
Almond Dr
200 BYTN 77520 3832 B7
Almond Grv
10900 HarC 77396 3407 E7
Almond St
900 BYTN 77521 3973 B2
900 HarC 77521 3973 B2
Almond Bay Ln
14100 FBnC 77083 4236 E1
Almond Blossom Dr
2800 FRDW 77598 4630 C3
Almond Branch Pl
10 WDLD 77382 2673 E4
Almond Brook Ln
1400 HOUS 77062 4379 D7
Almond Creek Dr
2900 HOUS 77059 4379 E4
3300 HOUS 77059 4380 A5
Almond Dale Ct
10 WDLD 77382 2673 C4
Almond Glen Ct
9500 HarC 77044 3689 C4
Almond Grove Ct
12100 HOUS 77077 3957 E4
Almond Grove Dr
1200 HOUS 77077 3957 E4
Almond Lake Ct
14700 HarC 77047 4374 D6
Almond Lake Dr
4000 HarC 77047 4374 D6
Almond Orchard Ln
24800 FBnC 77494 4093 B2
Almond Park Ln
19800 HarC 77450 3955 A5
Almond Pl Ln
- FBnC 77469 4235 C1
Almond Pointe
700 LGCY 77573 4631 E5
Almond Springs Dr
7500 HarC 77095 3538 B2
7600 HarC 77095 3537 B5
Almondwood Ln
3400 HarC 77389 3112 D1
Almont Dr
7100 HOUS 77016 3687 B2
Almonte Dr
18100 HarC 77377 3254 C2
Alnay
- HarC 77032 3546 E2
Aloe Av
5300 HarC 77521 3833 D3
Aloe Ln
500 HarC 77532 3552 C3
Aloe St
10 HOUS 77007 3962 B4
Aloft Ct
2000 HarC 77532 3551 D3
Aloha Trail Dr
11900 HarC 77044 3688 E5
Alon Ct
13700 HarC 77014 3401 D2
Alon Ln
13600 HarC 77014 3401 D2
Alonzo St
- PRVW 77445 3100 B3
Alpena Ln
11500 HarC 77095 3397 B7
Alperton Dr
7700 HOUS 77088 3683 A2
Alpestrine Dr
24500 MtgC 77357 2828 C7
Alpha Av
1300 HarC 77532 3552 E3
1400 HarC 77532 3553 A3
Alpha Dr
1100 PASD 77502 4107 D6
1100 PASD 77506 4107 D6
Alpha Rd
12100 HOUS 77072 4097 E7
Alpha St
3600 HOUS 77019 3962 C4
Alpine Cir
3800 MSCY 77459 4496 B4
Alpine Ct
10 BLAR 77401 4101 B5
Alpine Dr
4600 STAF 77477 4369 A1
6700 HOUS 77061 4244 D4
E Alpine Dr
7000 HOUS 77061 4244 D4
Alpine Hts
5600 MtgC 77365 2974 C6
Alpine Brook Ct
2100 FBnC 77545 4498 D6
Alpine Brook Ln
17800 HarC 77346 3408 B2
Alpine Park Ln
7500 HarC 77433 3537 A5
Alpine Ridge Wy
- HOUS 77546 4378 D7
12500 HOUS 77089 4378 C7
Alpine Rose Ln
26300 FBnC 77494 4092 D1
Alpine Vale Ct
11600 HarC 77038 3543 A6
Alp Springs Ct
1000 HarC 77373 3114 B4
Alp Springs Ln
25600 HarC 77373 3114 A3
Alrover St
14400 HOUS 77045 4372 E3
15000 HarC 77053 4372 E4
15000 HOUS 77053 4372 E4
Alsace St
3600 HOUS 77021 4103 C5
Alsay
12100 HarC 77066 3400 D5
Alseth Cir
10900 HarC 77086 3542 A1
Alshire Dr
4000 HarC 77373 3115 B7
Alstead Ct
15900 HOUS 77489 4371 B6
Alstead Dr
6100 HarC 77041 3679 C4
Alston Dr
6200 HTCK 77563 4989 C5
12000 MDWP 77477 4237 E4
12000 MDWP 77477 4238 A5
Alston Rd
- MDWP 77477 4237 E5
12400 MDWP 77477 4237 D5
12400 SGLD 77478 4237 D5
12600 FBnC 77478 4237 D5
Alston Hills Dr
8400 HarC 77433 3537 B6
Alsuma St
8500 HOUS 77029 3826 C6
Alsworth St
3200 GlsC 77518 4634 B2
Alta Rd
13100 MtgC 77372 2536 D6
Altair Dr
14200 TMBL 77375 2963 E4
Altair Wy
- HOUS 77085 4372 A2
13000 HOUS 77085 4241 A7
Alta Loma Wy
10200 HOUS 77075 4377 D3
10400 HOUS 77089 4377 D3
Altalr Wy
13100 HOUS 77085 4241 A7
13400 HOUS 77085 4372 A1
Alta Mar Dr
15800 FBnC 77083 4096 A6
Alta Mesa Dr
15300 HarC 77083 4096 B4
Altamont Dr
8900 HOUS 77074 4239 B1
Alta Peak Ct
4600 HarC 77449 3676 A7
Alta Peak Wy
21600 HarC 77449 3676 A7
Altavilla Ln
- LGCY 77573 4633 A3
Alta Vista Dr
300 PASD 77502 4247 B1
1500 ALVN 77511 4867 A3
1700 ALVN 77511 4866 E3
Alta Vista St
1700 HOUS 77023 4104 E1
1700 HOUS 77023 4105 A1
Altem Dr
- HOUS 77053 4371 D6
Althea Dr
900 HOUS 77018 3823 A2
1000 HOUS 77018 3822 E2
Althea Ln
4700 FBnC 77545 4623 C3
4700 FBnC 77583 4623 C3
Altic Ln
11500 HarC 77066 3400 E5
Altic St
10 HOUS 77011 3964 C6
500 HOUS 77023 3964 C7
Altmor Ln
10200 HOUS 77075 4376 E3
Alto Dr
400 CNRO 77301 2384 E4
400 CNRO 77301 2385 A5
Alto St
700 HarC 77060 3544 E3
Altolake Dr
11700 HarC 77067 3402 D5
Alton St
100 HOUS 77012 4105 A2
Altonbury Av
10100 HarC 77031 4238 D6
10100 STAF 77477 4238 D6
Alton Springs Dr
19500 HarC 77433 3537 B6
Alton Wright Dr
33100 MtgC 77355 2962 A1
33400 SGCH 77355 2962 A1
Altoona St
3000 HOUS 77026 3825 B7
Altus Dr
3000 HOUS 77051 4243 A7
N Altwood Cir
10 WDLD 77382 2819 E2
S Altwood Cir
10 WDLD 77382 2819 D2
Alumni Rd
- HOUS 77005 4102 C2
Alva Av
10 BYTN 77520 3973 A5
Alva Ct
- MtgC 77357 2829 D3
Alva St
200 BYTN 77520 3973 A5
Alvarado Dr
5700 HOUS 77035 4240 C6
N Alvin Byp
400 ALVN 77511 4867 E1
600 ALVN 77511 4749 D6
N Alvin Byp SR-35
- ALVN 77511 4867 E1
600 ALVN 77511 4749 D6
S Alvin Byp
- ALVN 77511 4749 E7
1400 ALVN 77511 4867 B5
S Alvin Byp SR-35
- ALVN 77511 4749 E7
1400 ALVN 77511 4867 B5
S Alvin Byp SR-35 BUS
- ALVN 77511 4867 B4
Alvin Rd
- FBnC 77583 4623 B5
100 ARLA 77583 4623 B5
Alvin St
500 PASD 77506 4107 C5
3700 HOUS 77051 4243 B3
4600 HOUS 77033 4243 C3
Alvin A Klien Blvd
- HarC 77379 3111 E4
- HarC 77388 3111 E3
Alvin A Klien Dr
- HarC 77379 3111 B3
Alvin Cemetery Rd
- ALVN 77511 4750 A7
- BzaC 77511 4750 A7
- BzaC 77511 4868 A1
Alvin Heights Rd
1500 BzaC 77511 4748 C4
Alvy Dr
1700 LPRT 77571 4110 D7
Al West St
8100 HTCK 77563 4988 D2
Alydar Dr
2000 PASD 77503 4108 D7
Alyse St
600 DRPK 77536 4109 C4
Alysheba Ln
4200 HarC 77546 4506 A5
Alyssa Av
12700 MSCY 77071 4370 B1
12700 MSCY 77489 4370 B1
Alyssa Ct
9700 HarC 77396 3407 B7
Alyssa Ln
- MtgC 77365 2826 D7
19200 MtgC 77365 2972 D1
Alyssa Gardens Ln
8400 HarC 77396 3547 E2
Aly Trace Ct
10800 HarC 77064 3540 E2
Alzaada Ln
9300 HarC 77070 3399 D5
Amado Dr
12300 HarC 77065 3398 C7
Amadwe St
8500 HOUS 77051 4243 D3
Amalie St
4000 HOUS 77093 3686 B
Amanda Ct
3900 DKSN 77539 4753 E
4800 SGLD 77478 4369 B
Amanda Dr
3800 DKSN 77539 4753 E
Amanda Ln
3400 HOUS 77063 4099 D
8700 MNVL 77578 4747 A
8800 MNVL 77578 4746 E
Amanda Mdws
12200 HarC 77089 4504 E
12300 HarC 77089 4505 A
Amanda St
100 CNRO 77304 2383 D
Amanda Grace Ln
13800 HarC 77429 3253 D
Amanda Lee Dr
2900 PRLD 77581 4503 D
Amanda Mellissa Ln
3600 PASD 77505 4248 E
Amanda Park Ln
9900 HarC 77089 4504 B
Amanda Pines Dr
12200 HarC 77089 4504 B
12200 HarC 77089 4505 A
Amandas Wy
28500 MtgC 77386 2970 B
Amandas Crossing Blvd
9900 HarC 77089 4504 B
Amani Ln
10300 HarC 77095 3537 E
Amapola Dr
15600 HarC 77083 4096 B
Amara Ct
10 WDLD 77381 2821 B
Amaranth Dr
2600 HarC 77084 3815 E
Amaranth Meadow Ln
5500 HOUS 77085 4241 A
5600 HOUS 77085 4240 E
Amargos Dr
16400 FBnC 77083 4095 E
Amarillo Dr
100 MAGA 77354 2668 E
Amarillo St
- HOUS 77017 4246 C
- HOUS 77020 3964 E
- HOUS 77587 4246 C
- SHUS 77017 4246 C
1400 SHUS 77587 4246 C
7300 HOUS 77020 3965 A
8100 HOUS 77029 3965 B
29500 MtgC 77354 2818 A
29800 MtgC 77354 2817 E
Amarose Dr
17000 HarC 77090 3258 A
Amaryllis Av
4200 HarC 77521 3833 B
Amaryllis Rd
800 BYTN 77521 3832 A
800 HarC 77521 3832 A
E Amaryllis St
43600 PRVW 77484 3100 D
W Amaryllis St
- PRVW 77445 3100 C
Amasa St
6500 HOUS 77022 3824 A
Amato St
700 LMQU 77568 4990 B
Amayas Ct
11600 HOUS 77013 3827 D
Amazon Dr
22800 MtgC 77365 2971 C
E Ambassador Bnd
10 WDLD 77382 2673 B
W Ambassador Bnd
10 WDLD 77382 2673 B
Ambassador Ct
1800 MSCY 77459 4497 C
Ambassador Wy
5000 HOUS 77056 3961 C
Amber Cir
300 DRPK 77536 4109 B
Amber Ct
6900 HarC 77069 3400 A
Amber Dr
6300 HTCK 77563 4988 C
Amber Ln
200 LGCY 77573 4631 A
Amber St
7000 HOUS 77022 3824 B
Amber Alcove Ct
4600 HOUS 77345 3119 D
Amber Ash Ct
6800 HarC 77346 3264 E
6800 HarC 77346 3265 A
Amber Bay Dr
- HarC 77377 3254 A
Amber Bough Ct
800 HOUS 77062 4379 D
Amber Canyon Dr
11500 HarC 77095 3397 B
Amber Chase
1700 HarC 77450 3955 A
Amber Cliff Dr
2900 HarC 77449 3815 D
Amber Cove Dr
8200 HarC 77346 3265 C
Amber Creek Ct
2200 PRLD 77584 4500 C
17300 HarC 77095 3538 A
Amber Creek Dr
12100 PRLD 77584 4500 D
Ambercrest Ct
6500 HarC 77389 2966 C
Ambercrest Dr
6600 HarC 77389 2966 C
Ambercrombie Pl
- CNRO 77384 2675 B
Amber Crossing Dr
21000 FBnC 77469 4234 A
Amber Daisy Ln
16200 HarC 77433 3251 A
Amber Dale Ct
2800 HOUS 77059 4379 E
Amber Dawn Ln
- FBnC 77494 4093 A
Amber Elm Tr
21900 HarC 77433 3251 C
Amberfield Ln
6500 HarC 77449 3677 C
Amber Fire Pl
10 WDLD 77381 2675 A
Amber Forest Dr
3200 HarC 77068 3257 E

Houston Street Index

STREET
Block City ZIP Map# Grid

nbergate Dr
1300 HOUS 77077 3957 E5
10700 HarC 77396 3407 D7
nber Glade Ct
1100 HarC 77494 3953 D4
nber Glen Ln
2000 FBnC 77494 3953 D5
Amberglow Cir
10 WDLD 77381 2674 E6
Amberglow Cir
100 WDLD 77381 2674 E6
nberglow Ct
10 WDLD 77381 2674 E6
nber Grain Ct
- HOUS 77016 3687 C3
nber Grain Ln
21500 HarC 77433 3250 E4
nber Grove Ct
14100 HarC 77083 4236 E1
nber Hill St
9700 FBnC 77469 4234 D2
nber Hill Tr
2900 PRLD 77581 4503 D7
2900 PRLD 77581 4504 A6
nber Hollow Ct
14100 HarC 77429 3397 B1
nber Hollow Ln
15400 HarC 77429 3397 B1
nber Holly Ct
3200 HOUS 77345 3119 E1
nberjack Dr
9000 TXCY 77591 4872 E3
9000 TXCY 77591 4873 A3
nber Knoll Ct
1400 HOUS 77062 4379 D7
nber Lake Dr
4200 HarC 77084 3816 E1
4400 HarC 77084 3677 E7
nber Leaf Ct
10 WDLD 77381 2821 B2
nberleaf Ct
24600 HarC 77494 3953 A1
nberlee Ct
4000 MtgC 77386 2970 C6
nber Leigh Pl
10 WDLD 77382 2673 E4
nberlight Ln
20100 HarC 77450 3954 D4
nber Lodge Ln
13300 HarC 77083 4097 B7
nberly Ct
2000 HOUS 77063 3960 A6
2400 BzaC 77584 4501 C5
nberly Wy
- FBnC 77479 4367 B5
nber Meadow Dr
3100 HarC 77449 3816 A3
nber Mist Ln
17600 HarC 77095 3537 D6
nbermist Ln
17200 HarC 77095 3537 E5
17200 HarC 77095 3538 C3
nbern Dr
5500 HOUS 77053 4371 E6
nber Park Dr
1100 MtgC 77303 2239 D3
nber Pine Ct
5700 HarC 77346 3264 E4
6800 HarC 77346 3265 A4
nber Queen Ct
5700 HarC 77041 3679 C5
nber Queen Ln
13400 HarC 77041 3679 C5
nber Ridge Dr
7000 FBnC 77478 4236 B7
nber Rose Ln
3600 HarC 77039 3546 A3
nbershadow Dr
100 HarC 77015 3829 A5
nber Shore Dr
- LGCY 77573 4509 C6
nber Sky Ln
3000 LGCY 77539 4752 E3
3300 BzaC 77583 4623 D4
nber Sky Pl
10 WDLD 77381 2820 C2
nberson Cir
25100 MtgC 77365 3117 E1
nber Springs Dr
2200 HarC 77450 3954 D6
nberstone Dr
10 FBnC 77479 4367 A7
10 FBnC 77479 4494 A1
nberton Ln
- BKHV 77024 3959 C4
- HOUS 77024 3959 C4
nber Trace Ct
4100 FBnC 77479 4366 C7
nber Trail Ln
1700 FBnC 77469 4493 A4
nber Valley Ct
1400 HarC 77066 3401 A5
nberview Dr
- HarC 77049 3829 C4
nbervine Cir
20000 HarC 77450 3954 E3
nber Wheat Ct
2300 FBnC 77545 4498 B7
nberwick Dr
9600 HOUS 77031 4239 A6
Amber Willow Tr
6300 HarC 77433 3251 C3
Amber Willow Tr
20800 HarC 77433 3251 A5
nberwood Dr
- HarC 77338 3261 D2
23200 MtgC 77372 2682 A5
nble Ln
3900 HOUS 77085 4371 E2
nble Oak Ct
4500 HOUS 77059 4380 B6
nble Oak Tr
- HOUS 77059 4380 B6
nbler Dr
6600 HarC 77379 3256 D2
nbleside Crescent Dr
10 SGLD 77479 4495 B2
nblewood Dr
8300 HOUS 77072 4098 B7
8600 HOUS 77099 4238 B1
1800 MDWP 77477 4238 A5
nbor
- DRPK 77536 4110 A7
nboy St
1100 HOUS 77020 3964 C2
2900 HOUS 77026 3825 B7
nbrosa Dr
3200 HarC 77044 3689 C5

Ambrosden Ln
1400 HarC 77530 3829 D5
Ambrose Dr
5400 FBnC 77479 4366 E5
Ambrose St
- HOUS 77053 4373 A3
12800 HOUS 77045 4242 A7
13500 HOUS 77045 4373 A1
Ambrosia Pl
10 WDLD 77381 2820 B3
Ambrosia Falls Dr
19400 HarC 77375 3109 E7
Ambrosia Springs Ln
4500 FBnC 77494 4092 E1
N Amburn Rd
1000 TXCY 77591 4873 B4
S Amburn Rd
10 TXCY 77591 4873 B7
300 LMQU 77568 4873 B7
Ambursen St
10400 HOUS 77034 4246 D7
AMC Dr
- KATY 77494 3952 D3
Amcreek Rd
16200 HarC 77068 3257 D4
Amelia Dr
12200 HOUS 77045 4242 C7
12200 HOUS 77045 4373 C1
Amelia Rd
7900 HOUS 77055 3821 C4
Amelia St
- HOUS 77055 3821 C5
1700 BYTN 77520 4112 D2
Amelia Springs Dr
6300 HarC 77379 3256 D2
Amelia Terrace Ct
6000 FBnC 77479 4367 A5
Ameno Dr
2400 PRLD 77581 4504 E3
American
5500 HOUS 77020 3964 D4
W American Av
300 BYTN 77520 3972 D7
Americana Dr
1000 MSCY 77459 4369 D4
American Beauty Ct
5400 HarC 77041 3679 C6
American Elm Ct
1800 FBnC 77479 4494 B4
American Fork Ct
1300 HarC 77090 3402 B1
American Holly Ct
7500 HarC 77433 3677 B1
7700 HarC 77433 3537 B6
American Petroleum Rd
12500 GNPK 77015 3967 A6
12500 HOUS 77015 3967 B6
Amersham Ct
25800 HarC 77389 2966 B1
Amersham Wy
4100 SGLD 77479 4495 D4
Amerson Ct
3900 BzaC 77584 4501 C7
3900 PRLD 77584 4501 B7
Amerson Dr
3100 BzaC 77584 4501 C6
Amery Knoll Dr
12600 HOUS 77045 4241 E6
Ames Cir
10 PNPV 77024 3959 E4
Ames Cross
5700 FBnC 77479 4493 E2
Ames St
500 HarC 77373 3114 A7
2200 PRLD 77584 4501 B2
Amesbury Cir
3500 BzaC 77584 4501 C4
Amesbury Ct
3100 SGLD 77478 4369 A2
3100 STAF 77478 4369 A2
Amesbury Dr
15800 HarC 77084 3678 E5
Amesbury Ln
15300 SGLD 77478 4368 C5
Amesbury Manor Ln
18500 HarC 77094 3955 B2
Amesbury Meadow Ln
21300 HarC 77379 3111 D2
Ameswood Dr
- HarC 77095 3539 A7
Ameswood Rd
7600 HarC 77095 3539 A7
7600 HarC 77095 3679 A1
Amethyst Dr
- HarC 77095 3397 A7
Amethyst Ln
- FBnC 77545 4622 C2
A Meyers Rd
7800 FBnC 77469 4616 D3
Amherst Ct
10 PNVL 77304 2237 B2
5900 FBnC 77479 4493 E2
5900 FBnC 77479 4494 A2
Amherst Ln
1100 DRPK 77536 4249 C2
Amherst Pt
- HarC 77094 3955 D1
- HOUS 77094 3955 D1
Amherst St
2600 HOUS 77005 4102 A3
2600 WUNP 77005 4102 A3
3200 WUNP 77005 4101 E3
4200 HOUS 77005 4101 C3
Amici St
15200 MtgC 77355 2962 B6
Amidon Dr
16800 HarC 77379 3256 D2
Amie Ln
6300 BzaC 77584 4626 E1
6800 BzaC 77584 4627 A1
Amigo Dr
100 DKSN 77539 4754 B1
Aminah Ln
- BKHV 77024 3959 C4
Amir St
4100 HOUS 77072 4098 A3
Amira Dr
11200 HarC 77065 3539 E1
Amistad Ct
12000 HarC 77375 3109 D6
Amistad Dr
19100 HarC 77375 3109 D7
Amistad Lake Cir
9100 HarC 77433 3537 B5
Ammi Tr
18100 HarC 77060 3403 D4
18100 HarC 77073 3403 D4

Ammick Ct
22900 HarC 77389 2966 D6
Ammons St
700 SHUS 77587 4246 E2
1500 SHUS 77587 4247 A2
2700 BYTN 77521 3973 A4
Amoco Dr
- HOUS 77079 3957 A1
18100 BzaC 77584 4627 D4
18800 BzaC 77511 4627 D4
18800 PRLD 77511 4627 D4
18800 PRLD 77584 4627 D4
Amoco Dr S
19000 BzaC 77511 4627 D4
19000 PRLD 77511 4627 D4
19000 PRLD 77584 4627 D4
Amoor Av
3600 HOUS 77029 3826 C6
Amorgas Isle Dr
4900 HarC 77388 3112 B2
Amortabrook Dr
- HarC 77095 3538 A6
Amos St
3500 HOUS 77021 4103 B6
Amphora Cir
3400 SGLD 77479 4495 E2
Ampton Dr
- HarC 77379 3256 E4
Amsbury Ln
13600 HarC 77429 3397 D2
Amsler
600 HarC 77037 3544 D6
Amsterdam Dr
12300 HOUS 77089 4378 C7
Amudarya Dr
23000 MtgC 77365 2972 B5
Amulet Oaks Ct
10 WDLD 77382 2819 C2
Amulet Oaks Pl
10 WDLD 77382 2819 D2
Amundsen St
3700 MtgC 77339 3118 B4
Amur Dr
22900 MtgC 77365 2971 D5
Amurwood Ln
8100 HarC 77375 2965 E7
8100 HarC 77375 2966 A7
Amwell Rd
6000 HarC 77389 2966 E3
Amy Dr
1600 BYTN 77520 3973 C6
N Amy Dr
900 DRPK 77536 4109 C6
S Amy Dr
1100 DRPK 77536 4109 C6
Amy Ln
1400 HMBL 77338 3407 A1
17800 HarC 77429 3252 C1
17800 HarC 77433 3252 C1
19200 MtgC 77365 2972 D1
Amy St
6200 HOUS 77028 3826 B3
Amy Ann Ln
3700 HarC 77336 3121 D1
Amy Brook Ct
8600 HarC 77396 3547 E2
Amyford Bnd
11700 HarC 77429 3254 A7
11800 HarC 77429 3253 B7
11800 HarC 77429 3397 E1
11800 HarC 77429 3398 A1
Amyford Ct
14300 HarC 77429 3398 A1
Amy Lee Dr
2500 CNRO 77304 2382 E2
2500 CNRO 77304 2383 A2
Amy Michelle Ln
1700 HarC 77530 3830 C4
Amy Point Ln
17900 FBnC 77469 4095 C7
Amy Ridge Rd
16400 HOUS 77053 4372 A7
16800 FBnC 77053 4499 A1
16800 HOUS 77053 4499 A1
Amy Shores Ct
2900 FBnC 77494 3953 B7
Anabel Ln
100 HOUS 77076 3684 C5
Anacacho Dr
500 MtgC 77386 2968 D2
Anacacho Ln
400 BzaC 77584 4374 B7
Anacacho St
4400 PASD 77504 4248 A5
Anacortes St
8100 HOUS 77061 4245 D3
Anada Bay Ct
14400 HarC 77429 3397 A1
Anadarko Ln
17400 HarC 77095 3537 C3
Anadell St
8000 HLSV 77055 3821 C7
Anagnost Rd
13700 HOUS 77047 4373 D4
Ana Lee St
- MTBL 77520 3696 D6
Analisa Cir
17000 HarC 77084 3678 A2
Anaqua Dr
5800 HOUS 77092 3682 B5
Anaquitas Creek Ct
7100 FBnC 77469 4094 A6
Anark Ct
7100 HarC 77379 3111 B2
Anarose Cir
- HOUS 77028 3687 E7
Anchick St
11900 HOUS 77037 3685 A2
11900 HOUS 77076 3685 A2
Anchor Dr
- BzaC 77541 5547 B6
Anchor Pk
16800 HarC 77546 4506 A7
Anchor St
2500 HOUS 77088 3683 B4
Anchor Wy
300 LGCY 77573 4633 C3
1900 DKSN 77539 4753 E4
10700 MtgC 77354 2671 D5
16500 GLSN 77554 5331 D4
16500 JMAB 77554 5331 D4
Anchorage Ln
500 HOUS 77079 3956 E2
Anchor Bay Ct
2000 PRLD 77584 4500 D1
Anchor Lake Ln
1900 FBnC 77494 3952 B4

Anchor Point Ct
2100 LGCY 77573 4631 B7
4500 MSCY 77459 4369 B5
Anchor Point Pl
10 WDLD 77381 2821 C4
Anchor Ranch Dr
24000 HarC 77447 3249 E4
Ancient Forest Dr
16300 HarC 77346 3408 A3
Ancient Oaks Dr
5700 HarC 77346 3264 D5
Ancient Willow Dr
8700 HarC 77375 3110 E1
8700 HarC 77375 3111 A1
Ancla Ln
22000 HarC 77532 3266 D6
Andalusian Dr
18500 HarC 77433 3677 C1
Andante Dr
8700 HarC 77040 3541 C7
Andante Trail Pl
10 SHEH 77381 2821 E2
Ander Oak Ln
13600 HarC 77070 3399 A3
Anders Av
1100 SEBK 77586 4509 D2
Anders Ln
- GlsC 77565 4509 D7
- LGCY 77565 4633 D2
2000 KMAH 77565 4509 D7
2100 KMAH 77565 4633 D1
11600 STFE 77510 4987 C1
Andershire Dr
4800 CNRO 77304 2237 B6
Anderson
500 HarC 77532 3552 D3
Anderson Av
1100 GlsC 77650 4995 A1
1500 GlsC 77650 4879 B7
Anderson Cir
3700 MtgC 77339 3118 B4
Anderson Rd
600 MtgC 77339 3118 B4
1500 CNRO 77304 2383 C6
3100 HarC 77053 4373 A4
3100 HOUS 77053 4373 A4
3300 HOUS 77053 4372 A4
3400 BYTN 77521 3973 C3
3800 HarC 77053 4372 D5
5500 HOUS 77053 4371 E4
6200 HOUS 77085 4371 D4
26300 MtgC 77354 2817 E6
E Anderson Rd
100 HarC 77047 4373 A4
100 HarC 77053 4373 A4
100 HOUS 77047 4373 C4
100 HOUS 77053 4373 A4
Anderson St
100 PASD 77506 4107 A3
800 BLAR 77401 4101 A3
1100 HOUS 77081 4101 A3
1100 HOUS 77401 4101 A3
5700 TXCY 77591 4873 E6
24000 HarC 77336 3267 A2
Anderson Oaks Ct
5600 HOUS 77053 4371 E4
Anderson Oaks St
5500 HOUS 77053 4372 A4
5600 HOUS 77053 4371 E4
Anderson Woods Dr
- HarC 77429 3399 A4
13300 HarC 77070 3399 A3
Anderson Wy St
- GLSN 77554 5221 A5
1500 GLSN 77554 5220 E2
Anderwoods Ct
13400 HarC 77070 3399 A3
Andiron Cir
7500 HarC 77041 3539 B7
7500 HarC 77041 3679 B1
Andorra Ln
100 HarC 77015 3829 A5
Andover Ct
4600 SGLD 77479 4495 C4
Andover Dr
1000 PRLD 77584 4501 A2
Andover St
600 HarC 77373 3113 E6
600 HarC 77373 3114 A6
4700 SGLD 77479 4495 C4
Andover Wy
- HOUS 77504 4247 C7
Andover Glen Dr
900 FBnC 77545 4623 A3
Andover Manor Dr
13000 HarC 77429 3397 C4
Andover Woods Ct
8300 HarC 77095 3538 A6
Andrea Ln
1800 PASD 77502 4108 A7
3600 PASD 77505 4248 E4
Andrea St
4900 HOUS 77021 4103 E7
Andrea Park Dr
21200 FBnC 77469 4234 A5
Andrea Wy Ln
14200 FBnC 77083 4236 E2
Andrew Ln
20500 HarC 77449 3815 D3
22900 MtgC 77365 2973 A4
23000 MtgC 77365 2972 E5
Andrew Rd
44400 WlrC 77445 2952 C2
Andrew St
5600 TXCY 77591 4873 E6
Andrew Arbor Ct
26300 HarC 77433 3396 B7
Andrew Chase Ln
1500 MtgC 77386 2969 D7
Andrew Ridge Ln
100 MtgC 77384 2675 A1
Andrews Ct
- LPRT 77571 4251 D6
Andrews Ln
9700 FBnC 77459 4621 D5
Andrews St
400 HOUS 77002 3963 B4
700 HOUS 77019 3963 A4
1600 HOUS 77019 3962 E4
7600 HTCK 77563 4988 D5
Andrews Grove Ln
3800 FBnC 77494 4092 C1
Andrew Springs Ln
2600 MtgC 77386 2969 E7
Andrew Wy Ct
13500 HarC 77082 4097 A1
Andricks Rd
3100 LPRT 77571 4250 A3

E Andricks Rd
9600 LPRT 77571 4250 A3
Andrus Ct
10 FBnC 77469 4232 D3
Andwood St
6100 HOUS 77087 4244 E1
Andy Dr
7300 HOUS 77088 3684 A3
7300 HOUS 77091 3684 A3
Andy Ln
26000 MtgC 77354 2817 D6
Angara Ct
19200 MtgC 77365 2971 D5
Angela Ct
9800 HarC 77379 3110 C4
Angela Dr
25700 MtgC 77355 2814 B5
Angela Ln
200 FBnC 77477 4369 B3
200 STAF 77477 4369 B3
Angela St
1100 DRPK 77536 4109 C7
Angela Brook Tr
10 MtgC 77385 2676 C6
Angela Faye Wy
2500 CNRO 77304 2382 E2
2500 CNRO 77304 2383 A2
Angelas Meadow Ln
9100 HarC 77095 3539 A5
Angel Dove Pl
10 WDLD 77382 2819 C1
Angel Falls Ln
5900 HarC 77041 3679 B5
Angel Fire Ln
13800 HarC 77070 3398 E3
Angel Gate Ct
23300 FBnC 77494 3953 D7
Angeli Dr
19800 HarC 77377 3251 C1
Angeli Rd E
17800 HarC 77377 3251 D1
Angeli Rd W
20400 HarC 77377 3251 C1
Angelina Av
1000 PASD 77506 4107 B4
Angelina Ct
10 MtgC 77302 2530 D7
Angelina Dr
10 MtgC 77302 2530 D7
2000 BzaC 77583 4624 A3
2200 BzaC 77578 4624 B3
2200 PRLD 77578 4624 B3
2200 PRLD 77583 4624 B3
Angelina Ln
10 MtgC 77302 2530 D7
Angeline St
1800 HOUS 77009 3824 A4
Angelique Dr
11200 HarC 77065 3539 A1
11300 HarC 77065 3398 A7
Angelique Wy
10 WDLD 77382 2820 A1
Angel Island Ln
16300 HOUS 77053 4371 E7
Angelito Ln
8600 HOUS 77078 3688 B6
Angel Leaf Rd
100 WDLD 77380 2967 E4
100 WDLD 77380 2968 A4
Angel Leaf Bend Ln
4100 HarC 77449 3815 B1
Angel Meadow Ct
14300 SGLD 77478 4236 E6
Angelo St
5300 HOUS 77009 3824 B4
Angel Oaks Cir
30700 MtgC 77355 2815 C1
Angel Oaks Ct
7000 FBnC 77469 4095 C5
Angel Oaks Dr
38600 MtgC 77355 2815 C1
38700 MAGA 77355 2815 C1
Angel Shores Ln
12300 HarC 77041 3679 E6
Angel Springs Dr
4000 SGLD 77479 4495 A5
Angels Rest Ct
3300 HarC 77373 3115 B3
Angeni Tr
23800 MtgC 77365 2974 B7
Angie Ln
9600 HarC 77038 3543 E5
Anglefish Cove
3100 BYTN 77520 4113 D6
Angle Lake Dr
10900 FBnC 77469 4092 D7
Angler Dr
7600 HarC 77346 3409 B1
Angler Pk
23400 MtgC 77385 2823 B6
Angler Bend Dr
- HOUS 77044 3408 E5
Anglerbend Lndg
7300 HarC 77095 3678 A1
Angler Leaf Ct
16000 HOUS 77044 3408 D4
Anglers Wy
36900 MtgC 77362 2816 D1
37100 MtgC 77362 2670 D7
Angleside Ln
9700 FBnC 77478 4237 A2
Angleton St
4700 HOUS 77033 4243 D3
Anglin
1200 HOUS 77022 3824 D1
Angling Ln
4100 MtgC 77386 3115 C1
Angus Rd
19800 HarC 77532 3412 E3
Angus St
7800 HOUS 77028 3826 B3
Anice St
2400 HarC 77039 3545 E4
4700 HarC 77039 3546 C4
Anilu Dr
1300 FBnC 77469 4092 B7
Animal Cracker Dr
- MtgC 77339 3118 D3
Anise Av
6000 HarC 77532 3552 C3
Anise Tree Pl
10 WDLD 77382 2675 A4
Anita St
- HOUS 77004 3963 B7
- HOUS 77009 3824 D7
100 LMQU 77568 4873 D7
100 TXCY 77591 4873 D7
300 HOUS 77006 3963 A6

Anita St
1000 HOUS 77002 3963 A6
2800 HOUS 77004 4103 C1
4100 HOUS 77004 4104 A1
Ankele Ln
- HOUS 77084 3818 A2
Ankoka Dr
14800 HarC 77530 3829 C7
Anmar Dr
10700 MtgC 77303 2239 B3
12100 MtgC 77372 2537 B5
Ann Cir
21800 MtgC 77355 2960 E7
Ann Ct
27200 ORDN 77385 2822 B4
Ann Ln
3900 BzaC 77584 4626 A1
12100 HarC 77064 3399 E6
12400 HOUS 77064 3399 E6
Ann St
700 ALVN 77511 4749 C7
1000 PASD 77502 4107 B6
1000 PASD 77506 4107 B6
2100 HOUS 77003 3963 E4
20200 MtgC 77357 2827 B6
Anna Ct
3800 STFE 77510 4870 D6
3800 STFE 77517 4870 D6
Anna Ln
- BzaC 77581 4504 D7
- BzaC 77581 4628 D1
Anna St
100 TMBL 77375 3109 C1
Anna Deane Ln
- BzaC 77584 4627 C4
Anna Green St
16800 HarC 77084 3678 A3
Anna Held St
10500 HOUS 77048 4244 B6
Anna Mills Ct
1600 FBnC 77469 4493 C4
Anna Mills Ln
6300 FBnC 77469 4493 C4
Anna Moran Dr
- HOUS 77036 4099 B4
Annandale Terrace Dr
13900 HarC 77429 3397 C2
Annapolis
- ELGO 77586 4508 E2
- TYLV 77586 4508 E2
Annapolis Ct
10 WUNP 77005 4102 A4
Annapolis St
5800 WUNP 77005 4102 A3
6700 HOUS 77025 4102 A4
6700 WUNP 77025 4102 A4
Ann Arbor Ct
3100 SGLD 77478 4369 A2
Ann Arbor Dr
2800 HOUS 77063 3959 E7
2900 HOUS 77063 4099 E1
Annatto Dr
5600 HarC 77521 3833 D2
Annawood Cir
- HarC 77388 3257 D2
Anne Av
1200 HMBL 77338 3263 A7
Anne Dr
18100 WEBS 77058 4507 D6
18100 WEBS 77598 4507 D6
Anne Ln
1200 SPVL 77055 3820 D7
13400 STFE 77510 4870 D4
32000 MtgC 77362 2963 C1
Anne St
- HOUS 77055 3820 D7
- SPVL 77055 3959 E1
1100 SPVL 77055 3820 E7
Annendale Cir
20900 MtgC 77365 3118 A1
Anne's Ct
10 WDLD 77380 2822 B6
Anne's Wy
100 STAF 77477 4369 C3
Annette Ln
10 HOUS 77076 3685 A5
100 FRDW 77546 4505 A7
Annfran Cir
11900 HarC 77429 3253 E7
Annice Ln
32000 MtgC 77362 2963 C1
Annies Wy
600 FBnC 77479 4366 C6
Anniston Dr
2500 HOUS 77080 3820 B3
Ann Louise Rd
12500 HarC 77038 3542 E4
12500 HarC 77086 3542 E4
Ann Marie Ln
- GLSN 77551 5108 A7
Annola Ln
7900 HarC 77379 3256 C4
Annunciation St
5500 HarC 77093 3686 D1
5500 HOUS 77016 3686 D1
5500 HOUS 77093 3686 D1
6200 HOUS 77016 3687 B1
Anoka Ct
14700 HarC 77015 3829 B7
Ansbury Dr
1200 HOUS 77018 3822 D4
Ansdell Ct
5400 HarC 77084 3678 D5
Anselm St
4400 HOUS 77045 4241 C6
Ansley Rd
33500 MtgC 77355 2962 D1
33500 SGCH 77355 2816 D7
33500 SGCH 77355 2962 D1
Anson Cir
800 PASD 77503 4108 B5
Anson Falls Ct
20100 HarC 77450 3954 E3
Anson Grove Ln
14100 SGLD 77478 4236 E5
Anson Point Ln
6800 HOUS 77040 3682 B3
Antascosa Key Dr
3600 GLSN 77554 5441 B4
Antean Wy Ct
12500 HarC 77065 3539 C4
Antelope Al
10100 FBnC 77459 4621 E6
10300 FBnC 77459 4622 A6
Antelope Dr
100 HarC 77532 3410 E1
800 HarC 77532 3266 D7
8600 HOUS 77063 4099 D2

Antelope Ln
15300 SGCH 77355 2961 C3
Antelope Shr
- PASD 77503 4108 D7
Antelope St
15300 SGCH 77355 2961 C3
Antelope Hills Dr
- MSCY 77459 4497 D5
2800 MSCY 77459 4498 A6
Antha St
4400 HOUS 77016 3686 B5
4400 HOUS 77093 3686 B5
Anthem Cove
1500 FBnC 77494 3952 B5
Anthony Ct
900 PASD 77506 4107 B4
Anthony Dr
2300 PRLD 77581 4502 E3
2500 PRLD 77584 4502 E3
Anthony Ln
4600 HOUS 77034 4248 D7
4600 PASD 77034 4248 D7
4600 PASD 77505 4248 D7
Anthony Hay Ct
22700 HarC 77449 3814 D4
Anthony Hay Ln
2000 HarC 77449 3814 D5
Anthony Pine Dr
2500 HarC 77088 3543 B7
Anthurium Ct
19200 HarC 77449 3677 B2
Antibes Ln
3800 HOUS 77082 4098 B3
Antico Ct
10 WDLD 77382 2819 A2
Antietam Ln
8400 FBnC 77083 4235 E1
Antigua Dr
4400 GLSN 77554 5331 D7
Antigua Ln
1300 NSUB 77058 4507 E6
1600 NSUB 77058 4508 A5
Antilles Av
- GLSN 77551 5222 A2
Antilles Ln
10 NSUB 77058 4508 B6
Antioch Dr
15700 HOUS 77053 4372 C6
Antionette Ln
100 HarC 77532 3552 D7
Antiqua Estates Ln
22900 MtgC 77385 2823 A6
Antique Ln
22700 MtgC 77357 2827 E7
Antique Meadows Dr
4600 HarC 77546 4505 E5
Antique Rose Ct
- WDLD 77382 2673 C6
Antler Dr
1400 HarC 77396 3407 B5
Antler Ln
4800 HarC 77338 3260 C1
Antler Wy
3000 FBnC 77459 4622 A6
Antlers Cir
24400 MtgC 77365 2974 A7
Antoine Dr
- HarC 77086 3401 C7
- HOUS 77055 3960 D1
700 HOUS 77024 3960 D1
1000 HOUS 77055 3821 D6
2800 HOUS 77092 3821 E3
4900 HOUS 77092 3682 E7
5300 HOUS 77091 3682 E7
6800 HOUS 77088 3682 E5
8000 HarC 77088 3682 D1
8200 HarC 77088 3542 D7
9200 HarC 77086 3542 D3
9500 HOUS 77086 3542 D3
11600 HarC 77066 3401 C7
12000 HarC 77067 3401 D5
12400 HarC 77014 3401 E4
Antoinette Ln
100 HarC 77015 3968 A3
Antoinette St
4000 HOUS 77087 4104 D5
Anton Dr
15500 HarC 77429 3253 C4
E Antone Cir
15300 MSCY 77071 4239 D7
W Antone Cir
15400 MSCY 77071 4239 D7
Antonia Ln
31100 TMBL 77375 2963 D5
Antonia St
- MSCY 77071 4239 B7
- STAF 77477 4239 B7
12700 MSCY 77071 4370 B1
12700 STAF 77477 4370 B1
Antonia Manor Ct
21000 FBnC 77469 4234 B2
Antonio St
4400 HOUS 77045 4241 C6
Antonohia Ln
6100 FBnC 77469 4232 C5
Antrim Ln
10300 LPRT 77571 4250 C3
Antrim Pl
14400 HarC 77429 3397 D2
Antrim St
2600 PRLD 77581 4504 C2
Antwerp Cove
9300 HarC 77070 3255 C6
Anvil Cir
17400 HarC 77090 3258 A3
Anvil Ct
17400 HarC 77090 3258 A3
Anvil Dr
1400 HarC 77090 3258 A3
1900 HarC 77090 3257 E4
Anvil Ln
21600 MtgC 77365 2972 B1
Anvil Rock Ln
100 FBnC 77469 4493 A6
Anwar Dr
11700 HarC 77083 4097 A5
Any Wy
- HOUS 77339 3119 C1
Anza Cir
7900 HOUS 77012 4105 C4
Anzac St
7300 HOUS 77020 3965 A2
Anzalone Dr
2500 HarC 77373 3114 D7
Anzio Rd
5200 HOUS 77033 4244 A1
Aodoban Park Dr
9600 HarC 77379 3255 B1

STREET
Block City ZIP Map# Grid

Apache Cir
100 PNVL 77304 2237 A3
Apache Ct
4200 HarC 77521 3833 B4
Apache Dr
6300 PASD 77503 4248 D2
Apache Ln
3400 FBnC 77471 4614 C4
3400 PLEK 77471 4614 C4
4600 HarC 77532 3694 B5
Apache Pth
20700 MtgC 77357 2681 A6
Apache St
500 HOUS 77022 3824 C1
6900 HOUS 77028 3825 D2
7100 HOUS 77028 3826 A2
27300 MtgC 77372 2683 D2
Apache Tr
- FBnC 77469 4364 C6
1100 BYTN 77521 3973 B2
4500 BzaC 77584 4501 E6
4500 BzaC 77584 4502 A6
18200 MtgC 77365 2972 C5
20200 HarC 77532 3410 D2
26600 MtgC 77354 2818 C7
Apache Bluff Ln
- HarC 77429 3253 A6
Apache Falls Dr
1000 HarC 77450 3953 E3
Apache Gardens Ln
20100 HarC 77449 3815 C6
Apache Hills Dr
17300 HarC 77377 3254 D4
Apache Lake Dr
20300 HarC 77449 3815 D4
Apache Meadow Dr
4300 HarC 77449 3816 B1
Apache Plum Dr
7800 HOUS 77071 4239 D5
Apache Plume Dr
7500 HOUS 77071 4239 E5
7500 HOUS 77071 4240 A6
Apache Point Dr
4500 HarC 77396 3407 A6
Apache Wells Dr
- FBnC 77494 3953 B4
Apache Wy Dr
10400 HarC 77095 3537 E2
Apala Dr
5300 HarC 77032 3546 D2
Apffel Park Rd
- GLSN 77550 4995 B7
- GLSN 77550 5110 A1
Apgar St
5500 HOUS 77032 3405 D6
Apollo Ln
5000 BzaC 77583 4624 A3
Apollo St
800 HarC 77058 4507 C4
800 HOUS 77058 4507 C4
900 RMFT 77357 2829 A1
4700 HOUS 77018 3822 E1
4800 HOUS 77018 3683 E7
6500 HOUS 77091 3683 E4
Apothecary Ln
8500 HarC 77064 3541 E5
Appalachian Tr
3200 HOUS 77339 3119 C2
3200 HOUS 77345 3119 D2
Appaloosa Av
14800 HarC 77084 3679 A4
Appaloosa Tr
20500 HarC 77532 3410 B2
Appaloosa Ridge Dr
20000 HarC 77338 3261 D4
Appelt Dr
2200 HarC 77015 3968 D4
2200 HarC 77530 3968 D4
Appian Rdg
24400 MtgC 77365 2974 A7
Appian Wy
- MtgC 77357 2829 C2
1100 HOUS 77015 3967 C2
1600 RMFT 77357 2829 B2
2200 PRLD 77584 4501 A3
Appian Oak St
14800 HarC 77433 3251 E7
Appin Ct
9200 HarC 77095 3538 C4
Appin Falls Dr
9100 HarC 77379 3256 A5
9200 HarC 77379 3255 E6
Apple Ct
27500 MtgC 77386 3115 D1
Apple Dr
3100 MSCY 77459 4497 C2
14000 SGLD 77478 4237 A5
Apple Hbr
23000 HarC 77373 3114 C7
Apple Ln
- LGCY 77573 4632 B6
700 LGCY 77573 4630 D6
Applebee Ct
7000 SGLD 77479 4367 C7
Appleberry Dr
7500 HarC 77433 3676 C1
Apple Bloom Wy
15300 HarC 77530 3829 E6
Apple Blossom
- MtgC 77357 2828 C7
Apple Blossom Dr
700 BzaC 77584 4501 A1
Apple Blossom Ln
5000 FRDW 77546 4505 E7
5000 HarC 77546 4505 E7
5400 FRDW 77546 4629 D1
Apple Bough Cir
11700 HarC 77067 3402 C5
Appleby Dr
12200 HOUS 77031 4239 A6
Apple Creek Rd
- HOUS 77035 4240 D6
- HOUS 77085 4240 D6
5400 HOUS 77017 4246 C2
Applecreek Bend Dr
4100 FBnC 77477 4369 C4
Applecrest Wy
19100 HarC 77388 3112 C5
Applecross Ln
17000 HarC 77084 3678 B5
Appleford Dr
1100 TYLV 77586 4381 E7
Apple Forest Ct
2800 HOUS 77345 3120 A2
3000 HOUS 77345 3119 E1
Apple Forest Tr
12800 HarC 77065 3539 C2
Applegate Dr
22600 HarC 77373 3116 A7
Apple Glen Ln
13000 HOUS 77072 4097 C6
13100 HOUS 77083 4097 C6
Apple Grove Ct
13600 HOUS 77059 4379 D5
Apple Grove Dr
3500 BzaC 77578 4501 A7
Apple Hedge Tr
- FBnC 77494 4092 E4
Apple Hill St
18700 HarC 77084 3816 C4
Apple Hollow Ct
16400 HarC 77396 3408 A3
Apple Hollow Ln
3600 HarC 77396 3407 E4
3700 HarC 77396 3408 A3
Apple Mill Dr
8700 HarC 77095 3538 D5
Applemint Cir
20600 HarC 77433 3251 B3
Apple Oak Ct
7000 FBnC 77469 4095 C5
Apple Orchard Dr
3400 FBnC 77469 4234 D7
Apple Orchard Tr
1400 CNRO 77301 2384 E6
Apple Park Dr
- HarC 77450 3954 B4
Appleridge Ct
7500 HOUS 77489 4371 B5
Appleridge Dr
11100 HarC 77070 3399 A3
15300 HOUS 77489 4371 B5
Apple Rock Ct
4700 SGLD 77479 4367 E4
Applerock Dr
4000 BYTN 77521 3972 C2
Applerock Tr
15800 HarC 77433 3251 B6
Apple Seed Ct
2900 HarC 77082 4096 C2
Apple Spring Dr
2100 DRPK 77536 4109 D7
N Apple Springs Cir
10 WDLD 77382 2673 D4
S Apple Springs Cir
10 WDLD 77382 2673 D5
Apple Springs Dr
4800 PRLD 77584 4503 A4
5600 PRLD 77584 4502 E4
Appleton Dr
1900 MSCY 77489 4370 C6
3300 BzaC 77584 4501 C7
Appleton St
7100 HOUS 77022 3824 B2
8100 HOUS 77022 3685 B7
Apple Tree Cir N
10300 LPRT 77571 4250 C4
Apple Tree Cir S
10300 LPRT 77571 4250 C4
Apple Tree Cir W
3700 LPRT 77571 4250 C4
Apple Tree Rd
13600 HOUS 77079 3958 B3
14200 HOUS 77079 3957 E3
Appletree Hill Ln
19000 HarC 77084 3816 B3
Appletree Ridge Rd
18600 HarC 77084 3677 B7
Applevale Ct
5200 HOUS 77345 3119 D2
Apple Valley Dr
200 PNVL 77304 2237 A4
Apple Valley Ln
3000 MSCY 77459 4497 A2
6100 HarC 77069 3400 C2
Apple Valley Rd
- PNVL 77304 2237 A4
Applewhite Dr
100 HarC 77450 3954 A2
100 HOUS 77450 3954 A1
Applewood Dr
300 FRDW 77546 4629 A4
11000 LPRT 77571 4250 D4
Applewood St
11600 BKHV 77024 3959 C5
11600 HOUS 77024 3959 C5
Applewood Forest Dr
6300 FBnC 77494 4092 B6
26200 FBnC 77469 4092 B6
Appleyard Ln
16100 HarC 77447 3248 D7
Appomattox Dr
800 MtgC 77380 2968 A2
1500 TXCY 77591 4873 B5
Appomattox Pk
400 MtgC 77302 2530 C5
Appomattox St
8900 HarC 77521 4249 D3
Appomattox Courthouse
- FBnC 77083 4235 E2
- FBnC 77478 4235 E2
Apricot St
300 LMQU 77568 4990 C2
E Apricot St
1700 LGCY 77573 4632 B6
April Ln
3000 HOUS 77092 3821 E4
5000 HOUS 77092 3682 E7
5300 HOUS 77091 3682 E7
April Pl
20200 HarC 77073 3403 C1
April St
12600 BKVL 77581 4376 A7
13000 PRLD 77581 4376 A7
April Tr
- HarC 77084 3816 C3
April Arbor Ct
8700 HOUS 77031 4239 C4
April Cove Ct
2700 BzaC 77578 4501 A6
April Creek Ln
7200 HarC 77095 3678 A1
April Falls Tr
16300 FBnC 77083 4236 A1
16600 FBnC 77083 4235 E1
April Glen Ct
14100 HarC 77429 3395 E2
17200 HarC 77084 3678 A2
April Hill St
16600 HarC 77095 3678 C2
April Knoll Ct
10900 HarC 77065 3539 E1
April Meadow Wy
4300 SGLD 77479 4494 E1
N April Mist Cir
10 WDLD 77385 2676 C3
S April Mist Cir
10 WDLD 77385 2676 B4
April Mist Ct
13200 HarC 77429 3254 A7
Aprilmont Dr
2300 FBnC 77478 4236 B7
April Rain Ct
10 WDLD 77382 2673 C4
E April Rain Ct
1300 MSCY 77489 4497 D1
W April Rain Ct
1400 MSCY 77489 4370 D7
1400 MSCY 77489 4497 D1
April Ridge Dr
16100 FBnC 77083 4236 A1
16200 FBnC 77083 4096 A7
April Run Ct
2600 HOUS 77345 3120 C5
5300 SGLD 77479 4495 A4
April Spring Ln
22600 FBnC 77494 4093 D5
April Wind Dr
3000 HarC 77014 3401 E3
April Wy St
11000 HNCV 77024 3959 E3
11000 PNPV 77024 3959 E3
Aqua Ln
- HOUS 77072 4098 A5
Aquagate Dr
5000 HarC 77373 3115 C5
Aquarian Ct
16400 HarC 77532 3552 B3
Aquarius St
5600 FBnC 77469 4615 E2
Aquatic Dr
18800 HarC 77346 3265 D7
18800 HOUS 77346 3265 D7
Aqua Vista Dr
- SEBK 77586 4509 D1
900 HOUS 77339 3263 B2
Aqua Vista Ln
700 FBnC 77469 4616 E1
Aqueduct Rd
8900 HarC 77049 3690 A5
11500 HarC 77044 3690 B1
11500 HOUS 77044 3690 B1
11700 HarC 77044 3550 B7
11700 HOUS 77044 3550 B7
Aquiline Oaks Pl
10 WDLD 77382 2819 A1
Aquilla Ct
5000 MSCY 77459 4496 B3
Arabella St
6500 HOUS 77091 3683 E4
8600 HOUS 77088 3683 E1
Arabelle St
2000 HOUS 77007 3962 A1
8700 HOUS 77088 3683 E1
Arabian Cir
14800 HarC 77084 3679 A4
Arabian Ct
3000 FBnC 77469 4365 A2
Arabian Tr
21200 TMBL 77375 3109 E3
Arady View Dr
- PRLD 77584 4501 E4
Aragon Dr
7100 FBnC 77083 4096 B6
Aragon Green Dr
15100 HarC 77433 3250 E5
Aragon Meadow Dr
- HarC 77049 3689 C6
Aramis Dr
16000 HarC 77073 3259 B5
Aransas Dr
9100 HOUS 77088 3543 E7
Arapaho Tr
24100 MtgC 77365 2974 B7
Arapahoe Dr
2100 FBnC 77471 4614 D5
2400 PLEK 77471 4614 C5
Arapahoe St
5200 HOUS 77020 3964 C2
Arapahoe Pass Ln
8700 FBnC 77469 4234 E1
Arapahoe Ridge Ln
8000 HarC 77433 3537 B6
Arapaho Hiill Ln
- HarC 77346 3408 C2
Arapaho Shadow Ct
13800 HarC 77429 3253 E5
Arapajo St
4100 HarC 77521 3833 B3
4200 PASD 77504 4247 E6
Arberry St
7700 HOUS 77012 4105 C4
Arbolada Green Ct
20200 HarC 77346 3264 E4
Arboles Dr
5700 HOUS 77035 4240 C5
Arbor Cir
300 LGCY 77573 4632 B5
E Arbor Cir
2200 SEBK 77586 4382 C7
Arbor Cross
900 CNRO 77303 2384 C1
Arbor Ct
500 BzaC 77584 4374 C7
4800 RSBG 77471 4491 C5
Arbor Dr
100 DRPK 77536 4249 B1
3800 BzaC 77584 4374 C7
S Arbor Dr
11400 HarC 77089 4505 B1
Arbor Gln
1800 CNRO 77303 2238 C7
1800 CNRO 77303 2384 C1
Arbor Ln
3300 SEBK 77586 4382 B7
4400 PASD 77505 4249 C5
6000 FBnC 77450 4094 C3
Arbor Pl
3500 SGLD 77479 4495 E1
Arbor Pn
800 TMBL 77375 2964 A6
Arbor St
100 BYTN 77520 3971 C4
1000 HOUS 77002 4102 E1
1000 HOUS 77004 4102 C3
3800 HOUS 77004 4103 D3
Arbor Wy
900 CNRO 77303 2238 C7
Arbor Bend Ct
20700 HarC 77346 3264 E3
Arbor Bend Dr
10 HarC 77070 3399 E3
E Arbor Bough Cir
3800 FBnC 77545 4498 E6
N Arbor Bough Cir
1200 FBnC 77545 4498 E7
W Arbor Bough Cir
3800 FBnC 77545 4498 E6
3800 FBnC 77545 4622 C1
Arbor Breeze Ct
5700 FBnC 77450 4094 A4
19300 HarC 77379 3112 A6
Arbor Bridge Ct
5300 HOUS 77345 3119 C1
Arbor Brook Ct
4400 PASD 77505 4248 E6
Arbor Brook Ln
2800 PRLD 77584 4499 E4
Arbor Canyon Ln
- HOUS 77077 3956 D5
Arbor Colony
- HarC 77532 3694 A5
Arbor Cove
2000 FBnC 77494 3952 B5
Arbor Cove Ct
23400 FBnC 77469 4093 D6
Arbor Cove Ln
22800 FBnC 77469 4093 D6
Arbor Creek Dr
19700 HarC 77449 3677 A2
20000 HarC 77449 3676 E3
Arborcrest Dr
- MSCY 77545 4622 B1
Arborcrest St
14200 HOUS 77062 4379 E6
14300 HOUS 77062 4380 A6
Arbordale Ln
11900 BKHV 77024 3959 B3
Arboretum Dr
4200 PASD 77505 4249 B6
Arbor Falls Ln
4900 HarC 77084 3677 C7
Arbor Field Ln
12700 HarC 77044 3689 B4
Arbor Forest Tr
1700 HOUS 77345 3120 D6
Arborg Dr
30400 MtgC 77386 2969 B2
Arbor Gate Ct
- RHMD 77469 4492 B2
Arbor Gate Dr
- PRLD 77545 4499 E4
Arborgate Dr
22500 HarC 77373 3116 A7
Arbor Glen Rd
7900 MSCY 77071 4239 E7
Arbor Green Ln
300 FBnC 77469 4616 E1
Arbor Grove Ln
- HarC 77379 3111 D4
Arborgrove Ln
5000 HarC 77338 3260 D2
Arbor Hill Ct
100 MtgC 77384 2675 A1
7900 FBnC 77479 4494 A5
Arbor Hill Ln
2600 BzaC 77584 4501 B5
Arbor Hollow Ln
- HarC 77377 3254 A1
6800 LGCY 77539 4752 E6
Arbor Ivy Ln
14500 HOUS 77044 3550 A2
Arbor Knoll Ct
4200 HarC 77346 3408 A3
Arbor Lake Dr
15800 HarC 77377 3254 E5
Arborlea Dr
16000 HarC 77546 4505 E5
16000 HarC 77546 4506 A6
Arbor Meadow St
7900 MSCY 77071 4239 B5
Arbor Mill Ct
3200 HOUS 77059 4380 A3
Arbor Mill Ln
10200 FBnC 77459 4621 E4
Arbor Mist
- HarC 77094 3955 D1
Arbormont Dr
18100 HarC 77429 3396 B2
Arbor Oak Dr
7000 HOUS 77088 3682 E4
7000 HOUS 77091 3682 E4
Arbor Oaks Cir
17700 MtgC 77357 2827 A1
17800 MtgC 77357 2826 E1
Arbor Park Ct
7200 HarC 77095 3678 A1
Arbor Park Dr
2100 HarC 77493 3814 C5
Arbor Pines Ln
19300 HarC 77346 3265 C6
Arbor Point Ct
3600 FBnC 77450 4094 C1
Arbor Point Ln
3700 HarC 77546 4506 A7
Arbor Ridge Ct
100 MtgC 77384 2675 A1
Arbor Ridge Dr
12700 MSCY 77071 4239 E7
Arbor Ridge Ln
300 MtgC 77384 2529 B7
300 MtgC 77384 2675 A1
Arbor Rose Ct
26000 KATY 77494 3952 B3
Arbor Rose Ln
6300 HarC 77379 3111 C4
E Arbor Rose Ln
7000 HarC 77379 3111 B3
W Arbor Rose Ln
7100 HarC 77379 3111 B3
Arbor Spring Ct
17400 HarC 77379 3111 E7
Arbor Springs Ln
100 LGCY 77539 4752 D2
Arbor Stream Dr
22500 FBnC 77450 4093 D2
Arbor Stream Ln
10 MtgC 77384 2675 B1
Arbor Terrace Ct
3500 HarC 77388 3257 E1
Arbor Terrace Dr
18300 HarC 77388 3257 E1
18300 HarC 77388 3258 A1
Arbor Trace Ct
14700 HarC 77429 3396 C1
Arbor Trace Ln
14700 HarC 77396 3547 C1
Arbor Trail Ln
300 MtgC 77384 2529 B7
300 MtgC 77384 2675 B1
Arbor Trails Bend Ln
3300 HarC 77073 3259 E2
3300 HarC 77338 3259 E2
3300 HarC 77338 3260 A1
Arbor Valley Tr
100 MtgC 77384 2675 B1
Arbor Valley Wy
12000 HarC 77065 3539 A3
Arbor View Ct
1900 FBnC 77479 4494 A3
Arbor View Dr
1800 FBnC 77479 4494 A4
Arbor Vitae Dr
5200 HOUS 77092 3682 D7
Arbor Walk Dr
8600 HarC 77338 3262 A3
Arborway St
200 HOUS 77057 3960 D3
Arbor Wind Ln
7600 HarC 77433 3537 A5
Arbor Wood Dr
8800 HOUS 77040 3682 B3
Arborwood Dr
1000 LGCY 77573 4630 D6
Arborwood Ln
6800 SGLD 77479 4494 C1
Arbre Ln
1200 FRDW 77546 4629 D2
Arbroath Ct
24900 HarC 77389 2966 A3
Arbuckle St
2600 HOUS 77030 4102 A4
2600 WUNP 77005 4102 A4
Arbury Glen Ln
7800 HarC 77338 3261 D3
Arbury Hill Ln
- RSBG 77469 4615 A4
14700 HarC 77396 3547 D3
Arc St
3700 HOUS 77063 4099 C2
Arcade Dr
9500 HarC 77379 3255 E6
9500 HarC 77379 3256 A6
Arcadia Av
700 HarC 77530 3969 C2
Arcadia Dr
1900 SGLD 77478 4237 A6
2100 SGLD 77478 4236 E5
7300 PASD 77505 4249 A5
Arcadia St
2400 HOUS 77026 3825 A7
Arcadia Wy
10 CNRO 77384 2675 E3
10 CNRO 77384 2676 A3
Arcadia Bay Dr
- PRLD 77545 4499 D3
Arcadia Bend Ct
6400 HarC 77041 3680 A4
Arcadia Bend Ln
11900 HarC 77041 3680 A4
12000 HarC 77041 3679 D3
Arcadia Glen Ct
25600 FBnC 77494 4093 A3
Arcadia Glen Ln
5200 FBnC 77494 4093 A2
Arcadian Dr
- PRLD 77545 4499 D4
200 HarC 77532 3692 C2
Arcadian Shores Dr
6100 HarC 77084 3679 A4
Arcadian Springs Ln
- HarC 77375 3255 B1
Arcadia Park Ln
21100 HarC 77338 3261 E3
Arcadia Point Ln
17600 HarC 77346 3408 B2
Arcadia Ridge Ln
2500 HarC 77449 3815 A4
Arcane Ct
25100 HarC 77389 2966 D3
Arcaro Glen Ct
18700 HarC 77346 3265 B7
Archbriar Pl
10 WDLD 77382 2675 C7
Archcrest Ct
8000 HarC 77433 3537 A7
Archdale Ct
25400 FBnC 77494 4092 C5
Archduke Dr
15800 HarC 77032 3403 E6
Arched Oak Dr
- HarC 77095 3538 E3
Archer Pk
32100 MtgC 77385 2823 B6
E Archer Rd
10 HarC 77521 3834 D6
W Archer Rd
100 HarC 77521 3833 C7
100 HarC 77521 3834 A6
800 BYTN 77521 3833 C7
Archer St
1000 HOUS 77009 3824 B5
Archer Glen Dr
19300 HarC 77073 3403 C2
Archer Oak Pl
10 WDLD 77382 2819 C3
Archer Ranch Ln
- RSBG 77469 4491 E5
- RSBG 77471 4491 E5
Archgate Dr
6400 HarC 77373 3116 B7
6400 HarC 77373 3261 A1
Archibald Blair Ln
22500 HarC 77449 3814 D5
Archie Ln
25200 WlrC 77445 2952 D1
Archley Dr
1200 HLSV 77055 3821 B7
Archmont Dr
10500 HarC 77070 3399 A3
Archrest Dr
- HMBL 77338 3262 D4
Archway Dr
4900 LPRT 77571 4250 C2
16100 HarC 77082 4096 A3
Archwood Ln
12600 HarC 77429 3398 C6
Archwood St
13900 HarC 77049 3689 E7
14100 HarC 77049 3690 A7
Archwood Tr
500 HOUS 77007 3962 D3
N Archwyck Cir
10 WDLD 77382 2819 A3
S Archwyck Cir
10 WDLD 77382 2819 B3
W Archwyck Cir
10 WDLD 77382 2819 A2
Arcidian Forest Dr
8900 HarC 77088 3542 C6
Arcola Ridge Ct
13800 HarC 77083 4097 A6
Arcola Ridge Dr
8600 HarC 77083 4097 B7
Arcott Ln
1600 MSCY 77489 4370 C3
1600 STAF 77477 4370 C4
1600 STAF 77489 4370 C3
Arcridge Cir
4700 HOUS 77053 4372 C6
Arctic Cir
11100 MtgC 77306 2532 D1
Arctic Tern Ct
400 SGLD 77478 4368 B3
Ardendale Ln
- FBnC 77494 4093 B2
Ardenfield Ct
21400 HarC 77449 3815 B1
Arden Forest Dr
1100 HarC 77379 3255 B1
Ardennes Rd
7300 HOUS 77033 4243 D1
Arden Ridge Ln
12700 HarC 77014 3402 A1
Ardent Oak Cir
3400 HOUS 77059 4380 B5
Ardenwood Pkwy
- KATY 77493 3813 D3
Ardfield Dr
13600 HarC 77070 3400 A3
13600 HOUS 77070 3400 A3
Ardley Ct
8600 HOUS 77088 3684 A1
Ardmore St
5400 HOUS 77004 4103 B3
5400 HOUS 77021 4103 B4
6600 HOUS 77054 4103 A7
16600 MtgC 77302 2678 C5
Ardsley Square Pl
10 WDLD 77382 2674 B5
E Ardsley Square Pl
10 WDLD 77382 2674 B5
W Ardsley Square Pl
10 WDLD 77382 2674 B4
Ardwell Dr
14300 FBnC 77478 4236 E2
Ardwick Ct
24100 HarC 77375 2965 D5
Areba St
2400 HOUS 77091 3683 A4
Arena Dr
- HOUS 77081 4101 B2
7200 HOUS 77036 4099 E5
7200 HOUS 77074 4099 E5
Arena Ln
- RSBG 77471 4614 D3
Arenas Timbers Dr
5600 HarC 77346 3264 D5
Arendale Ln
2100 MtgC 77386 2969 B4
Arendale St
10900 HOUS 77075 4376 D4
Argentina Cir
4200 PASD 77504 4247 E4
Argentina St
7900 JRSV 77040 3540 E7
7900 JRSV 77040 3680 E1
8600 HarC 77040 3540 E7
8600 HarC 77064 3540 E7
Argo St
1800 CNRO 77301 2384 D7
Argone Pl
10 WDLD 77382 2674 B6
Argonne St
2000 HOUS 77019 3962 A6
2900 HOUS 77098 3962 A7
3000 DKSN 77539 4753 E2
3000 GlsC 77539 4753 E2
Argonne Stone Ln
8900 MtgC 77302 2530 C4
Argos Ct
3400 MSCY 77459 4497 E5
Argos Dr
2500 MSCY 77459 4497 E5
Argyle Rd
16900 HarC 77049 3690 E4
16900 HarC 77049 3691 A4
Ari Ct
1100 FBnC 77479 4367 B6
Aria Ct
2600 DKSN 77539 4633 C7
Aria Ln
10 WDLD 77382 2674 C5
Arica Ln
2600 HarC 77373 3114 D5
Ariel Ct
12100 STAF 77477 4237 D7
Ariel St
5500 HOUS 77096 4240 C1
6100 HOUS 77074 4240 B1
8300 HOUS 77074 4239 C1
8800 HOUS 77074 4099 C7
Arion Ln
600 PASD 77502 4247 A1
Arista Dr
7200 FBnC 77083 4095 E6
Aristis Pth
10 WDLD 77382 2673 C6
Arizona Av
500 SHUS 77587 4246 D4
1600 LGCY 77573 4632 C5
2900 LGCY 77539 4632 D7
Arizona St
- HOUS 77017 4105 E7
400 LPRT 77571 4251 E3
1300 BYTN 77520 4112 B2
4600 HOUS 77017 4245 E1
5100 HOUS 77017 4246 A1
Arizona Sky Ct
14900 HarC 77396 3408 A7
Ark Dr
- CNRO 77301 2383 D7
- CNRO 77304 2383 D7
Arkansas Av
500 SHUS 77587 4246 D4
2200 GlsC 77539 4632 E7
2600 LGCY 77573 4632 D6
2700 DKSN 77539 4633 A7
2700 DKSN 77539 4754 A1
2700 GlsC 77539 4633 A7
Arkansas Pk
500 MtgC 77302 2530 B5
Arkansas St
2400 HOUS 77026 3825 A7
3200 BYTN 77520 4112 A2
8000 HOUS 77093 3825 A1
Arkansas St
8600 HOUS 77093 3686 A
N Arkansas St
8900 HOUS 77093 3686 A
Arkansas Post Ln
17200 HarC 77346 3408 B
Arkdale Ct
15900 HarC 77379 3256 B
Arlan Lake Dr
18700 HarC 77388 3113 C
18700 HarC 77388 3258 C
Arledge Av
8800 HOUS 77075 4245 E
8800 HOUS 77075 4246 A
Arlen St
8700 HOUS 77078 3688 A
Arlene Dr
21600 MtgC 77355 2960 E
Arlene St
37000 MtgC 77355 2816 A
Arletta St
8000 HOUS 77061 4245 C
Arlicious St
3300 HOUS 77020 3826 B
Arlington
- PASD 77502 4247 A
Arlington Ln
700 FBnC 77469 4616 B
Arlington Pl
14300 HarC 77429 3397 B
Arlington St
10 CNRO 77301 2384 A
300 HOUS 77007 3962 D
800 HOUS 77007 3823 D
800 HOUS 77008 3823 D
3000 HOUS 77018 3823 D
4600 HOUS 77022 3823 D
4700 HOUS 77022 3684 D
5500 HOUS 77076 3684 D
Arlington Fores Ln
- HarC 77338 3261 E
Arlington Forest Dr
8900 HarC 77088 3542 C
Arlington Meadows Ln
12600 HarC 77377 3254 A
Arlington Square Dr
3900 HOUS 77034 4246 E
4000 HOUS 77034 4247 A
Arlon Tr
13300 HarC 77082 4097 A
Armada Dr
900 HOUS 77091 3684 A
1500 HOUS 77091 3683 D
Armada St
3100 HOUS 77091 3683 E
Armadillo Dr
14900 HarC 77429 3252 E
Armand Bay Dr
200 LGCY 77539 4753 A
Armand Shore Dr
- PASD 77058 4508 C
Armand View Dr
4200 PASD 77505 4249 A
Armani Av
- HarC 77044 3689 C
Armant Pl Dr
14000 HarC 77429 3397 C
Armatta Ct
10000 HOUS 77075 4377 D
Armbull Ct
18900 HarC 77346 3264 D
Arming Ct
- HarC 77532 3551 E
Armitage Ln
14700 FBnC 77478 4236 E
Armor Av
1300 PASD 77502 4247 C
Armor Oaks Dr
26800 HarC 77339 3118 D
Armor Smith Dr
26900 MtgC 77339 3118 E
Armory
- HOUS 77449 3814 C
- HOUS 77493 3814 C
Armory St
- HarC 77032 3545 B
- HarC 77039 3545 B
Armour Dr
5500 HOUS 77020 3964 C
Armour Tr
800 HarC 77060 3403 E
Armstead St
1200 HOUS 77009 3824 A
Armstrong Dr
5500 TXCY 77591 4873 E
Armstrong Ln
200 KATY 77494 3952 E
11100 PRLD 77583 4500 D
Armstrong St
100 HOUS 77029 3965 E
300 HOUS 77029 3966 A
3800 HOUS 77063 4099 C
Arnage Ln
12900 HOUS 77085 4240 E
Arncliffe Dr
5400 HOUS 77088 3682 D
Arndt Rd
14300 HarC 77044 3689 E
Arndt Wy
21300 MtgC 77355 2960 E
21300 MtgC 77447 2960 E
Arnell Dr
4400 HOUS 77018 3683 E
Arnett Ln
100 HOUS 77037 3684 D
Arneway Dr
9000 HarC 77375 2965 D
Arnica Ct
10 WDLD 77381 2820 E
Arnim St
7300 HOUS 77087 4105 A
7600 HOUS 77017 4105 E
Arno St
400 PASD 77502 4247 E
Arnold Dr
4500 BzaC 77584 4501 E
4500 BzaC 77584 4502 A
Arnold Rd
- MAGA 77355 2669 A
- MtgC 77355 2669 A
300 HOUS 77376 3120 E
Arnold St
100 HOUS 77007 3962 E
700 CNRO 77301 2383 E
800 TMBL 77375 2964 E
3700 WUNP 77005 4101 E
Arnot St
6200 HOUS 77007 3962 E

STREET Block City ZIP Map# Grid

Arnot St
6400 HOUS 77007 3961 E3
Arnsworth Rd
1800 CNRO 77304 2383 C6
Aron Av
800 BYTN 77520 3973 B7
Aron St
300 BYTN 77520 3973 A6
Arp St
12500 HOUS 77085 4371 B2
Arranmore Ln
8600 HarC 77095 3538 B5
Arriola Lk
- HarC 77377 3106 D5
Arromanches Ln
3300 HarC 77388 3112 E4
Arrondi Cir
12400 HarC 77065 3539 D4
Arrow
2100 HOUS 77034 4246 C5
2100 SHUS 77034 4246 C5
2100 SHUS 77587 4246 C4
Arrow St
2500 FBnC 77471 4614 C4
2500 PLEK 77471 4614 C4
N Arrowana Ln
6000 HOUS 77036 4100 A4
S Arrowana Ln
6100 HOUS 77036 4100 A3
Arrowbrook Ct
7300 FBnC 77494 4093 C3
Arrowby Ln
- CNRO 77304 2529 D1
Arrowchase Ct
6800 HarC 77449 3676 D2
Arrow Cove Ct
8200 HarC 77346 3265 C3
Arrow Cove Dr
20300 HarC 77346 3265 C3
Arrow Creek Ln
7000 HarC 77379 3111 B4
Arrowdale Dr
200 HarC 77037 3684 D1
W Arrowdale Dr
100 HarC 77037 3684 C1
Arrow Field Ln
20500 HarC 77450 3954 C7
Arrow Flint Ct
18400 HarC 77084 3816 C3
Arrow Grand Ct
19300 FBnC 77469 4234 E1
Arrowgrass Dr
9800 HarC 77064 3540 D4
Arrowhead Ct
10 SGLD 77478 4368 D4
1800 MSCY 77459 4497 C2
Arrow Head Dr
700 FRDW 77546 4629 A4
Arrowhead Dr
2700 SGLD 77479 4368 D7
5000 BYTN 77521 3972 A2
Arrowhead Ln
8000 HOUS 77075 4376 D3
Arrowhead Pl
10 PNVL 77304 2237 B4
Arrowhead Pt
23800 MtgC 77357 2681 C7
Arrowhead Tr
28000 MtgC 77355 2815 B3
Arrowhead Creek Ln
2600 PRLD 77581 4504 A3
Arrowhead Glen Dr
12000 HOUS 77071 4239 C6
Arrowhead Lake Dr
4700 MSCY 77459 4621 D2
Arrowhead Terrace Ln
9400 HarC 77396 3407 A7
Arrowhead Trace Ln
9200 HarC 77089 4504 B1
Arrow Hill Rd
1000 HOUS 77077 3956 E3
Arrow Lake Dr
900 HarC 77450 3953 E3
Arrowmill Ln
18900 HarC 77377 3253 E2
Arrowood Dr
- RMFT 77357 2828 E3
400 WDBR 77357 2828 E3
Arrowpoint Dr
4600 HOUS 77022 3823 D1
Arrowpoint Rd
4800 HOUS 77022 3684 D7
Arrow Ridge Cir
- HarC 77429 3253 A7
Arrow Ridge Ct
1500 HarC 77067 3402 B5
Arrow Ridge Dr
11600 HarC 77067 3402 C6
Arrowrock Tr
- HarC 77050 3547 D6
Arrowsmith Ct
2400 BzaC 77584 4501 C4
Arrowsmith Dr
19800 HarC 77338 3261 D5
Arrows Peak Ln
17000 HarC 77095 3537 E3
Arrow Wood
12200 MtgC 77362 2817 C7
Arrowwood Cir
11600 PNPV 77063 3959 C6
Arrowwood Cir N
2000 PNPV 77063 3959 C6
Arrowwood Tr
2200 FBnC 77494 3951 D4
Arroyo Cir
10 BYTN 77521 3973 E1
Arroyo Dr
22200 HOUS 77532 3266 C6
Arroyo St
8700 HarC 77521 3833 C1
Arroyo Creek Ln
11500 HarC 77377 3109 C7
Arroyo Hill Ct
6400 FBnC 77450 4094 C4
Arroyo Verde Ln
11900 HarC 77041 3680 A5
Arroyo Vista Ct
2000 HarC 77067 3402 C4
Arroyo Vista Ln
11900 HarC 77067 3402 B5
Arsenal Ct
4200 HOUS 77092 3821 C1
Art St
11500 HOUS 77076 3685 B3
Art Canyon Ct
4800 HarC 77449 3677 C6
Artdale St
3700 HOUS 77063 4099 C2

Artem Ct
1800 HOUS 77045 4242 C7
Artesia
10 CNRO 77304 2383 A6
Artesia Dr
2500 DRPK 77536 4109 E7
Artesia St
- HarC 77373 3114 A7
400 HarC 77373 3113 E7
Artesian Pl
10 HOUS 77002 3963 A3
Artesian Wy
10 RMFT 77357 2829 A3
18600 HarC 77346 3264 A6
Artesian Forest Dr
10 CNRO 77304 2383 B6
Artesian Oaks Dr
10 CNRO 77304 2383 A6
Artesian Plaza Dr
400 HMBL 77338 3263 A6
Artesian Springs Dr
- HOUS 77396 3406 B5
- PRLD 77545 4499 E4
Artesian Springs Ln
3500 FBnC 77494 4093 C2
Artesian Wells Ln
- HarC 77073 3259 B3
Arthington Av
5500 HOUS 77053 4372 A5
5700 HOUS 77053 4371 E5
Arthur Ct
4100 BYTN 77521 3973 E2
Arthur Rd
26600 HarC 77373 3114 A1
Arthur St
900 HOUS 77019 3963 A5
Arthurian Dream Ct
11000 HarC 77375 3110 A4
Artio Dr
- HarC 77346 3264 B6
E Artists Grove Cir
10 WDLD 77382 2819 B2
W Artists Grove Cir
10 WDLD 77382 2819 B2
E Artists Grove Ct
10 WDLD 77382 2819 B2
Arto St
6800 HOUS 77093 3824 D2
Artoys Dr
15500 HarC 77377 3255 A6
Artwood Ln
17000 HOUS 77489 4497 D1
Aruba Cl
2100 DKSN 77539 4633 C7
Aruba Dr
4100 HOUS 77080 3820 E1
4200 HOUS 77041 3820 E1
Aruba Ln
- HarC 77338 3260 D3
Arum Rd
1000 MSCY 77489 4370 C3
Arundel Dr
14900 HarC 77530 3968 C1
Arundel Crossing Dr
2100 FBnC 77479 4493 E2
Arundel Gardens Ln
3700 FBnC 77478 4366 E2
Arvana St
300 HOUS 77034 4246 E6
Arvet Dr
9100 HOUS 77075 4245 C7
Arvilla Ln
4700 HOUS 77021 4103 E4
4700 HOUS 77021 4104 A4
Arvin St
9100 HOUS 77028 3687 D6
9800 HOUS 77078 3687 D5
Arvonshire Ct
14900 HarC 77049 3828 E2
Asbury Ln
- SGLD 77479 4367 E6
1300 DRPK 77536 4109 D5
Asbury Pk
10 SGLD 77479 4495 E3
10 SGLD 77479 4496 A3
Asbury Pl
10 HOUS 77007 3962 A4
Asbury St
100 HOUS 77007 3962 A3
Asbury Park Ct
10 SGLD 77479 4496 A3
Ascalon Cir
5600 HarC 77069 3400 D1
Ascot Gdn
7900 FBnC 77459 4621 A1
Ascot Ln
3700 HOUS 77018 3822 B4
3700 HOUS 77092 3822 B4
Ascot Farms Rd
28100 MtgC 77354 2818 B2
Ascot Glen Ln
13200 HOUS 77082 4097 B3
Ascot Meadow Dr
16900 SGLD 77479 4368 A7
Ascot Way Ct
100 WDLD 77382 2674 B5
Ascot Wy Ct
100 WDLD 77382 2674 B4
Ash
800 LPRT 77571 4111 C7
2700 BYTN 77520 3973 C5
Ash Cir
3500 DKSN 77539 4753 E3
Ash Ct
5100 DKSN 77539 4754 C3
Ash Dr
100 LGCY 77573 4631 A5
3100 DKSN 77539 4753 D2
Ash Ln
3400 DRPK 77536 4109 B7
3400 DRPK 77536 4249 B1
Ash Pl
- MtgC 77302 2677 C2
10 HarC 77357 2830 E7
Ash Rd
2500 BzaC 77584 4502 A5
2500 PRLD 77584 4502 A5
8000 TXCY 77591 4873 B5
14200 STFE 77517 4986 B1
14500 STFE 77517 4870 B7
Ash St
- KATY 77493 3813 A7
400 TMBL 77375 2964 C7
500 FBnC 77545 4623 B2
500 SGLD 77478 4367 E2
700 HMPD 77445 2953 B6
700 WALR 77484 3101 E6
1000 HOUS 77007 3963 B3

Ash St
1100 BYTN 77520 4112 D2
1300 LMQU 77568 4990 B2
6800 KATY 77493 3952 A1
11900 HarC 77532 3692 C3
16600 HarC 77044 3551 B7
33000 MtgC 77362 2817 B7
33000 MtgC 77362 2963 B1
Ash Arbor Wy
16800 HOUS 77058 4507 D3
Ashbel Ct
300 BYTN 77520 3972 E7
N Ashbel St
300 BYTN 77520 3972 E7
900 BYTN 77520 3973 A6
S Ashbel St
10 BYTN 77520 3972 E7
Ashberry Ct
400 LGCY 77573 4630 E5
Ashbournne Springs Ln
15600 HarC 77095 3538 D5
Ash Branch Ct
10 WDLD 77381 2821 A1
Ashbridge Ct
16800 HarC 77379 3255 E5
Ashbrook Dr
5100 BLAR 77401 4100 E3
5100 HOUS 77081 4100 E3
5100 HOUS 77401 4100 E3
Ashbrook Ln
2900 PRLD 77584 4500 C4
28700 MtgC 77355 2814 E4
Ashburn Spur
6700 HOUS 77061 4245 A3
Ashburn St
5600 HOUS 77033 4244 A4
6900 HOUS 77061 4244 E4
7400 HOUS 77061 4245 A3
Ashburnham Dr
3900 HOUS 77082 4097 C3
Ashburton Ct
- HarC 77377 3253 E1
Ashburton Dr
15300 JRSV 77040 3540 E7
Ashbury Park Ct
13900 HOUS 77077 3956 E5
Ashbury Park Dr
1500 HOUS 77077 3956 E5
Ashbury Trails Ct
5700 FBnC 77479 4493 E2
Ash Butte Dr
17200 HarC 77090 3258 A4
Ashby St
100 BYTN 77520 3971 C4
5300 HOUS 77005 4102 C2
5300 HOUS 77098 4102 C2
Ashclift Dr
12600 HOUS 77082 4097 C1
Ashcott Dr
11000 HOUS 77072 4098 B4
Ash Creek Dr
3400 MSCY 77459 4497 E6
11200 HOUS 77043 3819 A7
Ashcroft Dr
- HOUS 77096 4240 C2
6300 HOUS 77081 4100 C4
8300 HOUS 77096 4100 C7
11400 HOUS 77035 4240 C5
Ashdale Dr
1100 SGLD 77478 4237 B7
Ashdale Ln
13900 HarC 77083 4237 A1
Ashdown Forest Dr
9500 HarC 77379 3255 B1
Asheboro Dr
100 HarC 77450 3954 A1
600 HOUS 77450 3954 A2
Asheburton Springs Dr
3300 HOUS 77045 4241 E6
3300 HOUS 77045 4242 A6
Ashe Creek Dr
- LGCY 77573 4631 A4
Ashentree Wy
13800 FBnC 77083 4237 A2
Ashfield Dr
3100 HOUS 77082 4097 C2
Ashfield Pl Ct
6500 FBnC 77479 4367 B7
Ashford Ln
- SGLD 77478 4237 D4
Ashford Pkwy
900 HOUS 77077 3957 D5
Ashford Pn
11400 SGLD 77478 4237 E5
Ashford St
2000 WALR 77484 3101 E4
Ashford Wy
- MDWP 77477 4237 E4
- MDWP 77478 4237 E4
- SGLD 77478 4237 E4
1200 HOUS 77339 3264 A1
Ashford Arbor Dr
3100 HOUS 77082 4097 C1
Ashford Bend Dr
3000 HOUS 77082 4097 C1
Ashford Brook Dr
12700 HOUS 77082 4097 C1
Ashford Chase Dr
12600 HOUS 77082 4097 C1
Ashford Cove
400 LGCY 77539 4753 A4
Ashford Cove Dr
- BzaC 77584 4501 D7
Ashford Creek Dr
12500 HOUS 77082 4097 C1
Ashford Forest Dr
400 HOUS 77079 3957 D4
Ashford Glen Ct
12300 SGLD 77478 4237 D4
Ashford Green Ct
12300 SGLD 77478 4237 E5
Ashford Green Ln
8400 HarC 77072 4097 C7
Ashford Grove Ln
21600 HarC 77450 3954 B5
Ashford Haven Dr
11400 SGLD 77478 4237 D5
Ashford Hills Dr
11200 SGLD 77478 4237 D4
12600 HOUS 77077 3957 C5
Ashford Hollow Dr
12300 SGLD 77478 4237 D5
Ashford Hollow Ln
1500 HOUS 77077 3957 D5
Ashford Knoll Dr
12700 HOUS 77082 4097 C1
Ashford Lakes Dr
11200 SGLD 77478 4237 E4

Ashford Meadow Dr
12500 HOUS 77082 4097 C1
Ashford Meadows Dr
12200 SGLD 77478 4237 D5
Ashford Oak Dr
- HOUS 77077 3957 C7
- HOUS 77082 3957 B7
2700 HOUS 77082 4097 C1
Ashford Park Dr
- HOUS 77077 3957 B7
- HOUS 77082 3957 B7
2900 HOUS 77082 4097 C1
12200 SGLD 77478 4237 D4
Ashford Pine Dr
12600 HOUS 77082 4097 C1
Ashford Point Dr
12600 HOUS 77082 4097 C3
Ashford Pointe
11200 SGLD 77478 4237 E4
Ashford Pond Dr
11300 SGLD 77478 4237 E5
Ashford Ridge Ln
5600 FBnC 77450 4093 E4
Ashford River
12500 HOUS 77072 4097 D6
Ashford Springs Ln
14800 HarC 77396 3548 A2
Ashford Trail Dr
2700 HOUS 77082 4097 C1
Ashford Valley Dr
12200 SGLD 77478 4237 D4
Ashford Villa Ln
3700 HOUS 77082 4097 C3
E Ashford Villa Ln
3700 HOUS 77082 4097 C3
N Ashford Villa Ln
12500 HOUS 77082 4097 D3
S Ashford Villa Ln
12500 HOUS 77082 4097 D3
W Ashford Villa Ln
3700 HOUS 77082 4097 C3
Ashford Willow
11400 SGLD 77478 4237 D5
Ashford Wind Dr
11400 SGLD 77478 4237 E5
Ash Forest Dr
1800 HarC 77450 3953 E5
Ash Fork Dr
10200 HarC 77064 3540 C4
Ashfork Dr
21100 HarC 77449 3676 E6
Ash Garden Ct
8200 FBnC 77083 4096 A7
Ashgate Dr
5500 HarC 77373 3115 E7
Ash Glade Ct
3800 HOUS 77345 3119 E2
Ash Glen Ct
20200 HarC 77388 3112 D6
Ash Glen Dr
3500 HarC 77388 3112 D5
Ashgrove Dr
2000 HOUS 77077 3957 E6
Ash Haven Ln
2600 HarC 77449 3815 C4
Ash Hollow Dr
3900 HarC 77082 4096 D4
Ashington Dr
2600 HarC 77067 3402 A7
Ashkirk Dr
8700 HOUS 77099 4237 E1
Ashland Blvd
800 HarC 77530 3829 E6
900 HarC 77530 3830 A6
Ashland Dr
1200 MtgC 77385 2677 A7
Ashland St
700 HOUS 77007 3962 C1
800 HOUS 77007 3823 C7
2600 HOUS 77008 3823 C4
2900 HOUS 77018 3823 C3
Ashland Bridge Ln
10800 FBnC 77478 4236 D4
Ashland Brook Ct
19800 HarC 77084 3815 E4
Ashland Creek Ln
- LGCY 77573 4630 E7
Ashland Forest Dr
6600 HarC 77088 3542 B6
Ashland Grove Ln
3300 FBnC 77478 4366 E1
3300 FBnC 77478 4367 A1
Ashland Hollow Ln
- FBnC 77494 3952 B7
- FBnC 77494 4092 B1
Ashland Landing Dr
13900 HarC 77429 3397 D3
Ashland Park Ln
- MtgC 77386 2823 C7
Ashland Pines Ln
14700 HarC 77396 3547 E1
Ashland Springs Ln
7800 HarC 77433 3537 A7
Ashland Terrace Ln
6400 FBnC 77469 4616 A2
Ashlane Wy
- WDLD 77382 2819 C2
Ashlar Pt
10 WDLD 77381 2820 C1
Ashlawn Dr
8200 FBnC 77083 4096 B7
8300 FBnC 77083 4236 B1
Ashlee Ln
3700 HarC 77014 3401 D1
Ashlen Dr
600 HarC 77073 3403 B3
Ashley
10000 HarC 77064 3541 D2
23600 HarC 77389 2966 C5
Ashley Ct
1400 TMBL 77375 3109 C2
3600 MSCY 77459 4497 E6
5000 HarC 77041 3680 B7
Ashley Dr
- WlrC 77447 2813 C4
Ashley Grn
- WDLD 77382 2674 B4
S Ashley Grn
10 WDLD 77382 2674 B5
Ashley Ln
9900 BYTN 77521 3835 B4
9900 HarC 77089 4504 E1
14800 MtgC 77372 2682 D2
Ashley Rd
18600 HarC 77084 3816 B4
Ashley Run
13600 HOUS 77077 3957 A3

Ashley St
2700 HOUS 77017 4105 C5
2700 LMQU 77568 4873 D7
4000 HarC 77562 3833 A1
14500 HOUS 77034 4379 A3
20200 HarC 77449 3815 D3
Ashley Trc
- HarC 77375 2964 C2
Ashley Bay Ln
13500 HOUS 77070 3400 A3
Ashley Cir Dr E
12100 HOUS 77071 4239 D6
Ashley Cir Dr N
8000 HOUS 77071 4239 D6
Ashley Cir Dr S
8000 HOUS 77071 4239 D6
Ashley Cir Dr W
12100 HOUS 77071 4239 D6
Ashley Cove Ct
600 HarC 77094 3955 C2
Ashley Falls
1000 HOUS 77077 3957 D2
Ashley Garden Ct
1900 SGLD 77479 4367 E6
Ashley Glen Cir
1000 HarC 77073 3259 C7
Ashley Grove Ct
12100 STAF 77477 4237 D7
Ashley Grove Dr
- HarC 77084 3677 D4
6000 HarC 77084 3678 A4
Ashley Hall Ct
6300 HarC 77084 3679 A4
Ashley Manor Dr
6300 HarC 77389 2966 D2
Ashley Oak Dr
31800 HarC 77447 3250 A7
Ashley Pines Dr
22700 HarC 77373 2968 E7
Ashley Ridge Ln
2300 SGLD 77478 4236 E4
Ashley Row Dr
23800 HarC 77389 2966 C5
Ashley Spring Ct
5700 FBnC 77494 4093 E4
Ashley Terrace Ln
19700 HarC 77433 3537 A7
Ashleyville Rd
10 BYTN 77521 3973 A4
Ashley Wy Ct
5300 SGLD 77479 4495 A4
Ashling Dr
12200 HOUS 77477 4237 E4
12200 HOUS 77477 4238 A4
12500 HOUS 77099 4237 E3
Ashlock Dr
3100 HOUS 77082 4097 D2
Ashlyn Grv
10 WDLD 77382 2820 A2
Ashlyn Ridge Ln
28400 MtgC 77386 2969 C6
Ashlyn Timbers Ct
31400 SGCH 77355 2961 E4
Ashlyn Timbers Ln
16300 SGCH 77355 2961 D4
Ashmead Dr
11900 HOUS 77077 3958 A5
Ash Meadow Dr
1400 HarC 77090 3258 B4
Ashmere Ln
5200 HarC 77379 3257 B2
Ashmole Ln
7700 HOUS 77088 3683 B2
Ashmond Ln
9500 HarC 77375 3110 C3
Ashmont Ct
2200 MSCY 77489 4370 B7
Ashmont Dr
2300 MSCY 77489 4370 B7
2400 MSCY 77459 4370 A7
3200 MSCY 77459 4369 E7
Ashmoor Ct
16700 HOUS 77058 4507 E3
Ashmoor Wy
16800 HOUS 77058 4507 D3
Ashmore Ct
1700 MSCY 77489 4370 D4
Ashmore Dr
1500 MSCY 77489 4370 D4
6700 HarC 77069 3400 B2
Ashmore Estates Ct
22900 MtgC 77385 2823 A6
Ashmore Park Dr
5200 FBnC 77494 4093 E3
Ashmore Reef Ct
14200 FBnC 77478 4366 E4
Ash Oak Dr
1400 MSCY 77489 4370 D4
6400 HOUS 77091 3682 E4
Ashoglen Ln
13500 HOUS 77077 3957 D3
Ash Park Dr
3600 HOUS 77339 3119 B7
Ash Point Ln
16300 FBnC 77478 4236 B5
Ash Pointe
900 LGCY 77573 4631 E5
Ashridge Park Dr
8600 HarC 77379 3256 A6
Ash Run Ct
1500 PRLD 77581 4504 E4
Ashtex Dr
13700 HarC 77396 3547 B3
14900 HOUS 77396 3406 B7
Ashton Ct
32000 MtgC 77362 2963 C2
Ashton Dr
7800 HarC 77095 3538 B6
Ashton Ln
3100 LPRT 77571 4249 D3
32000 MtgC 77362 2963 C2
Ashton Pl
3300 GLSN 77551 5222 B1
Ashton St
6400 HOUS 77091 3683 A5
Ashton Hills Ct
13500 HarC 77429 3397 B3
Ashton Hills Dr
15800 HarC 77429 3397 B3
Ashton Lake Ln
12800 HarC 77041 3679 D3
Ashton Park Dr
3000 PRLD 77584 4503 A5
3100 PRLD 77584 4097 D2
Ashton Pines Ln
6800 HarC 77379 3111 B4
Ashton Villa Ct
4000 SGLD 77479 4495 C3

Ashton Village Ct
31300 MtgC 77386 2823 A7
Ashton Village Dr
1500 MtgC 77385 2823 A7
1500 MtgC 77386 2823 A7
Ash Tree Ln
21800 HarC 77073 3259 B2
Ashurst Dr
12000 HOUS 77077 3957 E6
Ash Vale Dr
16000 HarC 77377 3254 E5
Ashvale Dr
29600 MtgC 77354 2818 C2
Ash Valley Dr
8000 HarC 77379 3256 A2
8200 HarC 77379 3255 E2
Ashview Ln
4000 FBnC 77545 4498 C7
4900 FBnC 77545 4622 C1
Ashville Dr
9200 HOUS 77051 4243 B5
Ashway Dr
14600 MtgC 77372 2682 D2
Ashway St
1300 CHTW 77385 2823 A5
Ashwell Ct
7800 HarC 77389 2966 A3
Ashwick Ln
100 LGCY 77539 4753 A3
Ashwood Cir
3800 LPRT 77571 4250 E4
Ashwood Dr
1200 SGLD 77478 4237 B6
3900 PRLD 77584 4503 B7
5000 BYTN 77521 3972 A2
11200 HarC 77338 3263 A5
11200 HMBL 77338 3263 A5
Ashwood St
2800 HOUS 77025 4102 A6
Ashwood Creek Ln
26500 FBnC 77494 4092 C2
Ashwood Valley Dr
9600 HarC 77095 3537 E4
Ashworth Ct
10 WDLD 77385 2676 C3
Ashworth Dr
6700 SGLD 77479 4367 C7
Ashworth St
11500 HOUS 77016 3546 E7
11600 HarC 77050 3546 E7
11600 HOUS 77050 3546 E7
Ashwyne Ct
3300 LPRT 77571 4249 D3
Ashwyne Ln
8400 LPRT 77571 4249 D3
Asia Ln
5000 DKSN 77539 4633 C7
Askew St
2900 HOUS 77087 4104 D5
Askins Ln
4800 HarC 77093 3686 C2
5200 HOUS 77016 3686 D2
Aspen Cir
6800 HarC 77389 2966 C5
Aspen Ct
4300 MSCY 77459 4496 C1
8000 CmbC 77520 3835 D4
Aspen Dr
2700 PLEK 77471 4614 C5
3800 LPRT 77571 4250 D4
4800 PASD 77505 4248 A6
12000 HarC 77429 3398 C2
12700 MtgC 77362 2963 B1
S Aspen Dr
12200 HarC 77089 4505 B1
Aspen Ln
1700 SEBK 77586 4509 D2
2700 PRLD 77584 4502 D4
2800 BzaC 77578 4625 B1
12000 STAF 77477 4238 A6
12100 STAF 77477 4237 D6
21400 HarC 77429 3538 E1
Aspen Rd
900 CRLS 77565 4509 C5
Aspen St
100 BzaC 77511 4748 E1
5100 BLAR 77401 4100 D5
5300 HOUS 77081 4100 D5
8000 TXCY 77591 4873 B4
11100 MtgC 77372 2536 E1
Aspen Arbor Ct
16200 HarC 77546 4506 A6
Aspen Bend Dr
3200 HarC 77068 3257 B5
Aspen Bough Cir
13200 HarC 77065 3539 B2
Aspenbranch Ln
17900 HarC 77084 3677 C7
Aspenbrook Ct
3300 PRLD 77581 4503 D1
Aspen Brook Ln
4300 HarC 77388 3112 C3
Aspen Canyon Dr
20500 FBnC 77450 4094 B4
Aspen Chase Ln
14800 HarC 77396 3547 D3
14800 HarC 77396 3548 A1
Aspen Cove Ct
6300 FBnC 77479 4494 B1
13900 HOUS 77077 3957 A4
Aspen Cove Dr
13700 HOUS 77077 3957 A4
Aspen Creek Ct
2900 HOUS 77345 3119 D1
Aspen Fair Tr
3000 HarC 77389 3113 A1
3100 HarC 77389 3112 E1
Aspenfield Ln
2300 HarC 77450 3954 B6
Aspen Glade Dr
2000 HOUS 77339 3118 E3
Aspen Glen Ct
- HarC 77014 3402 B2
Aspenglen Dr
- HOUS 77084 3817 D1
4300 HarC 77084 3678 D7
4300 HarC 77084 3817 D1
Aspen Glen Ln
3600 HarC 77388 3112 D5
Aspenglenn Dr
16000 HarC 77084 3678 D7
16000 HOUS 77084 3678 D7
Aspen Grove Dr
1600 HOUS 77077 3957 E6
Aspen Hills Dr
14900 HOUS 77062 4506 E1
Aspen Hollow Ln
3000 FBnC 77479 4493 C2

Aspen Hollow Ln
13800 HOUS 77082 4096 E2
13800 HOUS 77082 4097 A2
Aspen Knoll Ct
13800 HOUS 77059 4379 D5
Aspen Lake Ct
3100 BzaC 77578 4501 A6
5300 HOUS 77345 3119 D2
Aspen Lake Dr
3100 BzaC 77578 4501 A6
Aspen Leaf Ln
4500 HarC 77396 3407 C7
Aspenlodge Ln
5200 FBnC 77494 4093 B6
Aspen Meadow Dr
8800 HOUS 77071 4239 B5
Aspen Mist Ln
21800 HarC 77449 3815 A2
Aspen Mountain Tr
3900 HOUS 77345 3119 E5
Aspen Oak Ct
17400 HarC 77379 3111 E7
Aspen Park Ln
2900 HarC 77084 3816 C4
Aspen Pine Tr
- HarC 77433 3251 A6
Aspen Pine Wy
- HarC 77433 3251 A6
Aspen Pl Dr
8800 HOUS 77071 4239 B5
Aspen Point Dr
5200 HarC 77449 3676 D6
Aspen Ridge Ct
17400 FBnC 77469 4095 C6
Aspen River Ln
1900 HOUS 77062 4380 B7
Aspen Shores Ct
6500 HarC 77449 3677 B3
Aspen Spring Dr
2400 DRPK 77536 4109 D6
Aspen Star Ct
- HarC 77053 4372 D5
Aspen Terrace Ct
12800 HarC 77433 3396 B4
Aspen Trace Ln
- HarC 77338 3262 B4
Aspen Trails Dr
19300 HarC 77449 3677 B2
Aspen View Ct
8600 HOUS 77088 3683 E1
Aspen Villa Ln
- FBnC 77494 4092 C3
Aspenway Dr
11500 HarC 77070 3398 E2
Aspenwilde Dr
20300 HarC 77433 3251 C6
Aspen Wood Dr
10200 HOUS 77040 3542 A7
Aspenwood Dr
3700 FBnC 77469 4364 A3
Asphodel Ct
5700 HarC 77379 3257 A2
Asphodel Ln
17800 HarC 77379 3257 B2
Aspley Ct
1900 HarC 77094 3955 A4
Aspley Dr
- PRLD 77581 4504 A7
Asprey Ct
8600 HarC 77379 3256 B5
Aste Ln
12300 HarC 77065 3398 C7
Aster Rd
1000 MSCY 77489 4370 C4
Aster St
800 KATY 77493 3952 B1
900 KATY 77493 3813 A7
Asterbend St
13800 HarC 77083 4097 A7
Aster Crest Ct
10500 HarC 77379 3110 A7
Aster Estates Ln
14100 HarC 77429 3396 A2
Aster Glen Ct
19400 HarC 77449 3816 A2
Aster Manor Ct
15900 HarC 77429 3397 D2
E Astern Dr
15700 HarC 77532 3552 B4
S Astern Dr
800 HarC 77532 3552 A4
W Astern Dr
15700 HarC 77532 3552 A4
Aster Petal Ct
15000 HarC 77433 3250 C5
Astilbe Ct
19900 HarC 77379 3110 C6
Astipalia Dr
21500 HarC 77388 3112 B2
Astley Ln
7900 HarC 77379 3256 B3
Aston St
13800 HOUS 77040 3681 C6
Astor Ct
3100 FBnC 77478 4235 E7
3100 FBnC 77478 4236 A7
Astoria Blvd
- HOUS 77034 4378 D6
10000 HarC 77089 4504 E2
10200 HarC 77089 4505 A1
11500 HarC 77089 4378 A7
11500 HOUS 77089 4378 C7
Astros Dr
- HarC 77032 3546 C2
Astwood Ct
4200 HarC 77068 3257 A6
8300 HarC 77379 3256 B5
Atasca Creek Dr
6600 HarC 77346 3264 E7
6800 HarC 77346 3265 A7
Atascadero Dr
10 MNVL 77583 4624 D5
7700 FBnC 77083 4096 B7
Atasca Oaks Dr
19400 HarC 77346 3264 D4
Atasca South Ct
6700 HarC 77346 3264 E6
Atasca South Dr
18600 HarC 77346 3264 E7
Atasca Villas Dr
20000 HarC 77346 3265 B4
Atasca Woods Trc
18300 HarC 77346 3409 A1
18400 HarC 77346 3265 A7
Atasca Woods Wy
18400 HarC 77346 3409 A1
18500 HarC 77346 3265 A7

STREET
Block City ZIP Map# Grid

Atascocita Rd
100 HarC 77396 3406 E5
100 HMBL 77396 3406 E5
100 HOUS 77336 3266 C5
500 HarC 77336 3266 C5
500 HarC 77396 3407 A4
500 HarC 77532 3266 C5
500 HMBL 77396 3407 A4
1300 HOUS 77396 3407 B4
1700 HarC 77336 3267 D5
1700 HarC 77532 3267 D5
3400 HarC 77338 3407 E1
3800 HarC 77338 3408 A1
3800 HarC 77346 3408 A1
3800 HarC 77396 3408 A1
5100 HarC 77346 3264 B7
6400 HarC 77346 3265 A6
Atascocita Rd FM-1008
1700 HarC 77336 3266 E5
1700 HarC 77336 3267 D5
1700 HarC 77532 3266 E5
1700 HarC 77532 3267 D5
Atascocita Tr
- HarC 77396 3408 A1
4400 HarC 77346 3408 A1
Atascocita Wy
3900 HarC 77396 3407 D2
Atascocita Bend Dr
16700 HarC 77396 3407 D3
Atascocita Forest Dr
18600 HarC 77346 3264 E7
Atascocita Lake Dr
20100 HarC 77346 3265 D4
Atascocita Lake Wy
8300 HarC 77346 3265 C4
Atascocita Meadows Dr
18300 HarC 77346 3264 A7
18300 HarC 77346 3408 A1
Atascocita Park Dr
18600 HarC 77346 3264 C7
Atascocita Pines Dr
19600 HarC 77346 3265 A5
Atascocita Pl Dr
21100 HarC 77346 3265 C2
Atascocita Point Dr
20900 HarC 77346 3265 B3
Atascocita Shores Dr
19900 HarC 77346 3265 B3
20000 HOUS 77346 3265 D4
20100 HOUS 77336 3265 D4
Atascocita Timbers N
5400 HarC 77346 3264 C6
Atascocita Timbers S
18900 HarC 77346 3264 C6
Atascocita Trace Dr
18900 HarC 77346 3265 A6
Atascocita West Tr
5300 HarC 77346 3264 B5
At Chison St
5600 HarC 77389 2966 E5
Atcid Ln
100 BYTN 77520 3971 C3
Athea Wy
1200 RSBG 77471 4614 C1
Athea Glen Cir
20800 FBnC 77450 4094 B4
Athens
4000 HOUS 77023 4104 A1
Athens Dr
1600 RMFT 77357 2828 E3
1900 RMFT 77357 2829 A3
3700 PASD 77505 4248 E4
Atherington Pl
17200 HarC 77379 3256 B2
Atherstone St
29400 MtgC 77386 2969 C4
Atherton Ln
19200 HarC 77094 3955 B2
Atherton Canyon Ln
3100 HarC 77014 3257 D7
Athlone Ct
3900 HOUS 77088 3683 A2
Athlone Dr
7400 HOUS 77088 3683 A3
Athos St
1900 HOUS 77012 4105 D4
Atkinson Rd
18100 MtgC 77384 2676 A7
18100 MtgC 77384 2821 E1
18100 MtgC 77384 2822 A1
18100 SHEH 77384 2821 E1
18100 SHEH 77384 2822 A1
18100 WDLD 77384 2676 A7
Atlanta Dr
1100 FBnC 77469 4365 D4
Atlanta Pk
600 MtgC 77302 2530 C5
Atlanta St
1300 DRPK 77536 4108 E7
17000 HMBL 77396 3406 B3
Atlantic Av
29700 MtgC 77354 2818 A1
Atlantic Dr
- HarC 77346 3264 B7
Atlantic St
10 BYTN 77520 3972 C7
2600 HOUS 77009 3824 C7
N Atlantic St
10 BYTN 77520 3972 C6
Atlantis Ct
15600 HOUS 77079 3956 C1
Atlas Dr
2500 MSCY 77459 4497 E5
Atlas Cedar Dr
32600 WlrC 77484 3246 C2
Atlasridge Dr
- HOUS 77048 4375 D4
Atlasta Ln
13200 HarC 77037 3544 E7
Atlaw Dr
12400 HOUS 77071 4239 C6
Atmore Forest Dr
- HarC 77379 3255 D6
- HarC 77379 3256 C6
Atmore Pl Dr
14900 HOUS 77082 4096 C2
Atrium Dr
500 HOUS 77060 3403 D7
Atrium Pl
10 WDBR 77357 2828 C2
19400 HOUS 77084 3816 A7
Atrium Woods Ct
10 WDLD 77381 2821 C3
Atterbury Dr
14700 FBnC 77478 4236 D2
Attica Dr
- HarC 77449 3677 B3
Attingham Dr
800 HOUS 77024 3958 E2
Attlee Dr
- HOUS 77077 3957 E5
Attridge Rd
2900 HOUS 77018 3823 B4
Attucks St
3500 HOUS 77004 4103 D2
Attwater Av
- TXCY 77591 4756 A7
4200 TXCY 77591 4755 E7
Attwater St
- HOUS 77078 3826 E3
7700 HOUS 77028 3826 B3
Attwater Wy
2500 LGCY 77573 4631 B7
Atwater Canyon Ln
22000 FBnC 77494 4093 E5
Atwell Dr
- HOUS 77096 4100 D7
600 BLAR 77401 4100 D5
6300 HOUS 77081 4100 D5
7200 HOUS 77401 4100 D5
9700 HOUS 77096 4240 D2
12300 HOUS 77035 4240 D6
Atwood Ln
10300 HOUS 77076 3685 B5
15200 HarC 77532 3553 D4
Atwood Glen Ct
12900 HarC 77014 3402 A2
Atwood Glen Ln
2400 HarC 77014 3402 A2
Atwood Grove Ln
12600 HarC 77086 3542 B4
Atwood Manor Ct
7700 FBnC 77469 4095 C6
Aubert St
900 HOUS 77017 4106 B6
Aubrell Rd
3500 PRLD 77584 4502 E6
Aubrey Falls Ct
2400 HarC 77450 3954 D6
Aubrey Hills Ln
9700 FBnC 77494 4092 C5
Aubreywood Ln
12300 HarC 77070 3399 D5
Aubrun Creek Ln
2900 LGCY 77573 4633 A2
Auburn Ct
1900 FBnC 77479 4493 E4
Auburn Dr
2000 KATY 77493 3813 D5
2900 PRLD 77584 4501 D6
18100 HarC 77375 2965 E7
18100 HarC 77375 2966 A7
18100 HarC 77375 3111 A1
Auburn Pl
10 WUNP 77005 4101 E2
Auburn St
3200 HOUS 77017 4105 C6
Auburn Tr
1800 FBnC 77479 4493 E4
Auburn Ash Cir
6500 HarC 77346 3264 E4
Auburn Bluff Dr
9800 HarC 77095 3537 C3
Auburn Canyon Ln
22200 FBnC 77469 4492 E3
Auburn Creek Dr
12100 PRLD 77584 4500 C2
Auburndale St
2300 HOUS 77023 4104 C3
Auburn Falls Dr
- PRLD 77584 4500 D1
Auburn Falls Ln
2900 HarC 77084 3816 C4
Auburn Forest Dr
7500 HarC 77379 3256 B1
Auburn Glen Ln
- FBnC 77494 4092 A1
8700 HarC 77095 3538 A5
Auburn Grove Cir
3700 MSCY 77459 4496 D1
Auburn Grove Ln
12800 HarC 77041 3679 D3
Auburn Hills Dr
12000 HarC 77377 3254 D6
Auburn Hollow Ln
3200 FBnC 77450 3954 D7
3300 FBnC 77450 4094 C1
Auburn Knoll Av
- HarC 77049 3829 A2
Auburn Lakes Dr
6600 HarC 77389 2966 D3
Auburn Mane Dr
8700 HarC 77375 2965 D2
Auburn Meadows Dr
19600 HarC 77094 3955 A2
Auburn Oak Tr
6700 HarC 77346 3264 E3
6700 HarC 77346 3265 A3
Auburn Park Ln
19700 HarC 77379 3112 A5
Auburn Path Dr
10 WDLD 77382 2674 B5
N Auburn Path Dr
10 WDLD 77382 2674 B5
Auburn Pine Ct
20600 HarC 77346 3265 A3
Auburn Point Ct
- HarC 77389 2966 D2
Auburn Ridge Ln
20900 HarC 77379 3111 D4
Auburn Run Ln
- HarC 77379 3111 E4
Auburn Shores Ct
12100 HarC 77041 3679 B7
12100 PRLD 77584 4500 C2
Auburn Shores Dr
2100 PRLD 77584 4500 C2
Auburn Shores Ln
- HarC 77041 3679 E6
Auburn Sky Ct
2000 LGCY 77539 4633 E3
Auburn Springs Ln
12700 HarC 77433 3396 B4
Auburn Terrace Ct
6300 HarC 77389 2966 D2
Auburn Terrace Dr
24800 HarC 77389 2966 D3
Auburn Terrace Ln
900 FBnC 77545 4623 A2
Auburn Trace Ct
20900 FBnC 77450 4094 A3
Auburn Trail Ln
11900 PRLD 77583 4500 C5
Auburn Trails
- FBnC 77479 4366 C7
Auburn Vale St
2100 HarC 77493 3814 A5
Auburn View Ln
1200 FBnC 77545 4623 A2
Auburn Woods Dr
2900 PRLD 77581 4503 D6
2900 PRLD 77581 4504 A6
6100 HarC 77084 3677 E4
18200 HarC 77429 3396 B2
Auckland Dr
5200 FBnC 77478 4366 E4
5300 FBnC 77478 4367 A4
Auckland Pt
12000 HarC 77429 3398 C3
Auction Barn Rd
10500 LbyC 77328 2537 C1
10500 MtgC 77372 2537 C1
17000 GlsC 77511 4869 B5
Aucuba Ln
11500 HarC 77095 3397 A7
E Auden Cir
3900 FBnC 77459 4622 B4
N Auden Cir
11000 FBnC 77459 4622 B4
S Auden Cir
11000 FBnC 77459 4622 C5
W Auden Cir
3900 FBnC 77459 4622 B4
Auden Dr
1400 SEBK 77586 4509 D2
Auden St
5000 HOUS 77005 4101 D4
5400 WUNP 77005 4101 D4
6300 SSPL 77005 4101 D3
6700 SSPL 77025 4101 D4
Audley St
3000 HOUS 77098 3961 E7
3700 HOUS 77098 4101 E1
5200 HOUS 77005 4101 E2
5200 WUNP 77005 4101 E2
Audra Ln
13700 HarC 77083 4097 A5
Audrain Ln
- MtgC 77354 2672 D1
Audrey Ct
12000 MtgC 77362 2963 C1
Audrey Ln
300 HarC 77015 3828 D6
300 HOUS 77015 3828 D6
Audubon Ct
1900 FBnC 77469 4365 C4
3100 SGLD 77478 4369 A2
12100 STAF 77477 4237 D7
Audubon Pkwy
13800 HOUS 77598 4506 C1
Audubon Pl
3300 PRLD 77584 4502 E6
3400 HOUS 77006 3962 E7
Audubon St
500 LGCY 77573 4631 B3
Audubon Forest Dr
7600 HarC 77396 3406 C7
Audubon Grove Ct
- HarC 77038 3543 A4
Audubon Grove Ln
- HarC 77429 3253 C4
Audubon Park Dr
9600 HarC 77379 3255 C1
Audubon Springs Dr
7900 HarC 77040 3681 C3
Audubon Wood Tr
2200 FBnC 77545 4498 C6
Audust Mdws
17700 HarC 77379 3255 E3
Auger Pl
10900 WDLD 77380 2821 C7
Aughsten Rd
3100 GLSN 77554 5220 C6
Aughton Ct
24800 HarC 77389 2965 E3
Aughton Dr
25000 HarC 77389 2965 E3
25000 HarC 77389 2966 A3
Augrae Park Ct
21400 FBnC 77469 4094 A6
August Rd
15600 HarC 77429 3397 B6
August St
5000 BzaC 77511 4868 C7
Augusta Blvd
1700 BYTN 77521 3972 C2
Augusta Ct
10 JRSV 77065 3540 B6
5800 HOUS 77057 3960 C5
Augusta Dr
- BzaC 77583 4624 C5
600 HOUS 77057 3960 D6
1000 FBnC 77469 4365 D4
2100 LGCY 77573 4508 D7
2100 LGCY 77573 4632 E1
2300 PRLD 77581 4504 C2
2500 DRPK 77536 4109 E7
4200 PASD 77505 4249 A6
Augusta Pk
600 MtgC 77302 2530 C5
Augusta St
4900 HOUS 77007 3962 B3
Augusta Bay Wy
- PASD 77505 4249 A6
Augusta Meadows Ln
23900 HarC 77389 2965 E4
Augusta Mist Ln
19200 HarC 77449 3677 B2
Augusta Pines Dr
- HarC 77375 2965 E1
- HarC 77389 2965 E1
10 HarC 77389 2966 A1
Augusta Pines Pkwy E
6500 HarC 77389 2966 B2
Augusta Pines Pkwy W
7100 HarC 77389 2966 A2
Augusta Pines Cove
6900 HarC 77389 2966 B2
Augusta Sunset Dr
15000 HarC 77396 3407 C7
August Hill Dr
- HOUS 77345 3120 E6
Augustine Dr
7000 HOUS 77036 4099 B6
Augustin Landing Dr
15900 HarC 77429 3397 B3
August Leaf Dr
22500 HarC 77375 2965 E7
August Light Ln
- HarC 77095 3538 B5
August Sunset Dr
14900 HarC 77396 3407 E7
Augustus St
- RMFT 77357 2829 B1
Augustus Venture Ct
12200 HarC 77433 3395 D5
Auguswood Ln
20800 HarC 77073 3259 E4
Auline Ln
1500 HOUS 77055 3821 D6
Aura Dr
- HarC 77433 3250 E5
Aurelia Ln
900 FBnC 77471 4364 A7
900 FBnC 77471 4491 A1
Aurelia Mist Ln
7400 HarC 77396 3547 C2
Auronia Dr
12200 HarC 77067 3402 B4
Aurora Dr
10 BzaC 77511 4868 B7
Aurora St
100 HOUS 77008 3823 D4
1200 HOUS 77009 3823 E4
1200 HOUS 77009 3824 C2
15100 FBnC 77478 4236 C3
Aurora Falls Ln
7100 HarC 77083 4097 A5
Aurora Fields Dr
- HOUS 77085 4371 A2
Aurora Park Dr
21300 FBnC 77469 4234 B5
Austin Av
1900 PASD 77502 4107 D7
2500 PASD 77502 4108 A7
2700 PASD 77503 4108 A7
4800 GLSN 77551 5108 D5
E Austin Av
1000 PASD 77502 4107 B7
N Austin Av
2100 PRLD 77581 4503 B2
S Austin Av
2400 PRLD 77581 4503 B3
2500 PRLD 77584 4503 B3
W Austin Av
100 PASD 77502 4107 A7
Austin Dr
6200 MSCY 77459 4497 A7
Austin Pkwy
1800 SGLD 77479 4368 B7
2400 SGLD 77479 4495 E2
4300 SGLD 77479 4496 A2
4400 MSCY 77459 4496 A2
Austin Rd
100 CNRO 77301 2529 E1
Austin St
10 HMPD 77445 2953 D7
100 HOUS 77002 3963 B6
100 RHMD 77469 4492 A1
600 HOUS 77017 4246 B3
600 SHUS 77587 4246 B3
700 HOUS 77010 3963 C5
1100 RSBG 77471 4491 A4
1300 BYTN 77520 3973 A5
1300 LMQU 77568 4989 E2
1500 LGCY 77573 4632 C3
1700 RHMD 77469 4491 D2
1900 RHMD 77471 4491 D2
2000 HMPD 77445 2952 E7
2200 HOUS 77004 3963 A7
2400 DKSN 77539 4753 E3
2600 DKSN 77539 4754 B3
4200 HOUS 77004 4103 A1
5200 HOUS 77004 4102 E2
5700 HOUS 77030 4102 E2
27000 HarC 77447 3248 E3
Austin St FM-762 SPUR
200 RHMD 77469 4492 A1
300 RHMD 77469 4491 E1
Austin St SR-159
200 HMPD 77445 2953 B7
Austin St US-290 BUS
10 HMPD 77445 2953 D7
E Austin St
100 RHMD 77469 4492 A1
N Austin St
100 WEBS 77598 4507 B6
S Austin St
100 WEBS 77598 4507 B6
2900 LGCY 77573 4633 A3
W Austin St
100 CNRO 77301 2384 A4
600 CNRO 77301 2383 E4
Austin Bluff Ln
19100 HarC 77377 3254 A1
Austin Branch Rd
43300 HMPD 77445 2953 A6
44100 HMPD 77445 2952 E6
45300 WlrC 77445 2952 A5
Austin Colony Dr
1000 FBnC 77469 4365 C2
Austin Hollow Ct
14100 HOUS 77044 3550 A3
Austin Lake Ct
3800 PRLD 77581 4503 E7
Austin Manor Ct
1100 HarC 77379 3110 A7
Austin Meadow Ct
3600 SGLD 77479 4495 A5
Austin Meadow Dr
4000 SGLD 77479 4495 A3
4200 SGLD 77479 4494 E3
Austin Oak Ln
18300 FBnC 77469 4095 C7
Austin Parkway Blvd
4600 MSCY 77459 4496 B1
4600 SGLD 77478 4496 B1
4600 SGLD 77479 4496 B1
Austin Rose Ln
26800 FBnC 77494 4092 A2
Austins Pl
2600 SGLD 77478 4368 D6
Austin Shore Cir
18200 HarC 77433 3395 D5
N Austin Shore Ct
12500 HarC 77433 3395 D5
N Austin Shore Dr
12400 HarC 77433 3395 D5
Austinville Dr
6300 HarC 77449 3677 C4
Australia St
15600 JRSV 77040 3680 D1
Australia Reef Dr
2500 HarC 77449 3815 A4
Austria Dr
4600 PASD 77505 4248 D6
Austrian Pine Pl
8500 HarC 77375 3110 D2
Autauga St
8900 HOUS 77080 3820 E2
Auto Park Wy
14300 HarC 77083 4096 D7
N Autrey Ct
3700 FBnC 77459 4621 E5
S Autrey Ct
3600 FBnC 77459 4621 E5
Autrey Dr
1700 DRPK 77536 4108 E7
Autrey St
1000 HOUS 77006 4102 D1
Autry Rd
10400 GlsC 77510 4871 E5
10400 GlsC 77510 4872 A5
Autum Berry Ln
7000 HarC 77049 3829 B1
Autum Glow Ct
2900 FBnC 77494 3953 B7
Autumin Cypress Ln
- HarC 77433 3396 B7
Autum Manor Ln
- HarC 77433 3677 E1
Autum Mist Ct
- PRLD 77583 4500 C4
Autumn Cres
10 WDLD 77381 2820 D1
Autumn Ct
1000 LGCY 77573 4630 D7
3200 PRLD 77584 4502 D5
S Autumn Dr
12000 HarC 77089 4505 A1
Autumn Ln
- MtgC 77362 2963 C2
3500 BYTN 77521 3974 A1
5200 GlsC 77539 4633 C6
5200 TXCY 77539 4633 C6
8100 HOUS 77016 3686 C7
8100 HOUS 77016 3825 C1
10800 MtgC 77372 2537 C2
Autumn St
19200 MtgC 77357 2827 C3
Autumn Tr
7700 FBnC 77479 4494 A5
Autumn Alcove Ct
4700 HOUS 77345 3119 E1
Autumn Arbor Dr
6000 HOUS 77092 3682 C6
Autumn Ash Ct
13500 BzaC 77583 4623 E3
Autumn Ash Dr
- CNRO 77302 2530 E4
Autumn Ash Ln
5500 BzaC 77583 4623 E4
Autumn Aspen Ln
7300 FBnC 77469 4094 C6
Autumn Bay Ct
3200 FRDW 77598 4630 C2
Autumn Bay Dr
- FRDW 77598 4630 C2
Autumn Bend Dr
3400 SGLD 77479 4494 E3
11000 MtgC 77303 2239 B4
Autumn Blossom Ct
17200 HarC 77095 3678 C3
Autumn Bluff Ln
7100 FBnC 77469 4095 B6
13900 HOUS 77044 3550 B2
Autumn Brair Ln
19200 HarC 77377 3254 A1
Autumn Branch Ct
3700 FBnC 77494 3952 D7
Autumn Branch Dr
- WDLD 77382 2674 C4
E Autumn Branch Dr
10 WDLD 77382 2674 C4
Autumn Breeze Ct
5300 HarC 77379 3257 A1
Autumn Breeze Dr
18600 HarC 77379 3112 A7
18600 HarC 77379 3257 A1
Autumn Bridge Ln
- BzaC 77583 4623 D4
3200 HarC 77084 3816 C3
Autumnbrook Dr
15500 HarC 77068 3257 B5
Autumn Brook Ln
2900 LGCY 77573 4633 B2
Autumnbrook Ln
2900 PRLD 77584 4500 B4
Autumn Brook St
900 SEBK 77586 4509 E1
900 SEBK 77586 4510 A1
Autumn Canyon Ln
30900 MtgC 77386 2969 D1
31000 MtgC 77386 2823 C7
Autumn Canyon Trc
14300 HOUS 77062 4379 D7
Autumn Chase Dr
11400 HarC 77065 3540 A4
11500 HarC 77065 3539 C5
N Autumn Cove
6200 BzaC 77583 4624 B5
S Autumn Cove
6300 BzaC 77583 4624 B6
Autumn Cove Ct
2900 FRDW 77598 4630 C2
Autumn Cove Dr
2100 LGCY 77573 4509 B6
Autumn Creek Dr
- FRDW 77546 4630 B2
2900 FRDW 77598 4630 C2
12000 HarC 77070 3399 C6
19500 HarC 77346 3265 D5
Autumn Creek Ln
200 FBnC 77469 4365 B5
Autumncrest Ct
24400 SGCH 77355 2961 A2
Autumn Crest Dr
2900 FRDW 77598 4630 C3
Autumn Crest Ln
21100 FBnC 77469 4094 A6
Autumn Dawn Ct
1400 MSCY 77489 4370 D7
Autumn Dawn Wy
4700 HarC 77084 3677 C7
Autumn Day Ct
7200 MtgC 77354 2673 A3
Autumn Dogwood Wy
5800 HOUS 77345 3120 C6
Autumn Fall Ct
5800 SGLD 77479 4495 A5
Autumn Fall St
7800 CmbC 77520 3835 D4
Autumn Falls Dr
2700 PRLD 77584 4500 B4
Autumn Falls Ln
16000 HarC 77095 3538 C6
Autumn Fern Dr
2000 HarC 77450 3954 D5
Autumn Field Ct
17300 HarC 77095 3678 C3
Autumn Field Ln
1900 FBnC 77469 4492 E4
Autumn Flowers Dr
6600 HarC 77449 3677 D2
Autumn Forest Ct
32400 MtgC 77354 2672 B5
Autumn Forest Dr
3200 PRLD 77584 4502 C5
5000 HOUS 77091 3682 E6
5000 HOUS 77091 3683 A6
5800 HOUS 77092 3682 D6
Autumn Forest Ln
100 MtgC 77384 2675 B1
Autumn Garden Ct
2500 HOUS 77345 3120 C5
Autumn Glade Pl
19600 HarC 77449 3816 B2
Autumn Glen Ct
14700 HarC 77429 3396 C1
Autumn Glen Dr
12700 FBnC 77478 4366 C1
Autumn Gold Ct
26900 HarC 77433 3396 A7
Autumn Green Dr
1100 MSCY 77459 4369 C5
Autumn Grove Ct
13900 BzaC 77583 4623 D5
Autumn Grove Dr
7100 HOUS 77072 4097 D6
Autumn Grove Ln
5600 BzaC 77583 4623 D5
Autumn Harvest Dr
2900 FRDW 77598 4630 C3
9100 HarC 77064 3540 D1
Autumn Haze Ln
13100 HarC 77429 3254 A4
Autumn Hills Ct
3000 FRDW 77598 4630 C1
Autumn Hills Dr
17700 HarC 77084 3677 D2
18000 HarC 77449 3677 C2
Autumn Hollow Ln
7800 HarC 77095 3539 B7
Autumn Joy Dr
9400 HarC 77379 3110 C6
Autumnjoy Dr
3100 BzaC 77584 4501 B6
Autumn Knoll Cir
3700 HarC 77449 3815 D2
Autumn Lake Dr
2000 LGCY 77573 4509 C6
2600 FBnC 77450 3953 E7
Autumn Lake Tr
9900 PRLD 77584 4501 B3
Autumn Lakes
4700 MSCY 77459 4496 B1
4700 SGLD 77479 4496 A1
Autumn Laurel Tr
7800 HarC 77095 3538 B7
Autumn Leaf Dr
3100 FRDW 77598 4630 B3
Autumn Leaf Ln
12500 HOUS 77072 4097 D6
Autumn Leigh Dr
16200 FBnC 77083 4236 A2
Autumn Light Ln
- HarC 77433 3396 A6
Autumn Manor Dr
21300 FBnC 77469 4234 A4
Autumn Meadow Dr
4200 HarC 77449 3816 B1
Autumn Meadow Ln
10200 HarC 77064 3540 B3
Autumn Mill Dr
12500 HarC 77070 3399 C6
Autumn Mist
14100 HarC 77429 3253 E6
Autumn Mist Ct
2300 LGCY 77573 4508 C6
4300 FBnC 77450 4093 E2
4300 FBnC 77450 4094 A2
Autumn Mist Ln
2300 LGCY 77573 4508 C6
13200 MtgC 77302 2530 D4
Autumn Mist Cove
10900 MtgC 77354 2671 D4
Autumn Oak Ct
17300 HarC 77379 3111 D7
Autumn Oak Dr
10 HarC 77521 3834 E7
10 HarC 77521 3835 A7
Autumn Oak St
300 RMFT 77357 2829 A3
Autumn Oak Wy
17300 HarC 77379 3111 E7
Autumn Oaks Dr
900 HOUS 77079 3958 C1
Autumn Orchard Ct
26500 FBnC 77494 4092 D2
Autumn Orchard Ln
4700 FBnC 77494 4092 D2
Autumn Park Cir
- HarC 77084 3816 E4
Autumn Park Ct
2800 FRDW 77598 4630 C1
Autumn Park Dr
18300 HarC 77084 3816 D4
Autumn Pine Ln
4600 HarC 77084 3677 E7
4600 HarC 77084 3816 E1
Autumn Pines Tr
3900 HarC 77084 3817 A1
Autumn Point Ln
800 HarC 77373 2968 E6
Autumn Pond Cir
- ALVN 77511 4749 C6
Autumn Rain Ln
6800 HarC 77379 3111 C4
Autumn Redwood Ln
20800 HarC 77433 3251 B6
Autumn Ridge Dr
1900 CNRO 77304 2237 A5
4100 FBnC 77479 4366 C6
Autumn Ridge Ln
- HarC 77449 3677 C2
Autumn Ridge Trail Dr
13900 HOUS 77048 4374 D4
Autumn Rose Ln
- FBnC 77479 4496 C5
E Autumn Run Cir
2900 SGLD 77479 4495 C2
W Autumn Run Cir
2900 SGLD 77479 4495 C1
Autumn Run Ln
10300 CNRO 77304 2236 E4
Autumn Sage Ln
2300 HOUS 77345 3120 A3
Autumn Shore Cir
2500 HarC 77450 3954 D6
Autumn Shore Dr
20400 HarC 77450 3954 D6
Autumn Sky Ct
15400 HarC 77095 3538 B3
Autumn Sky Ln
15400 HarC 77095 3538 E4
Autumnsong Dr
9000 HarC 77064 3540 D2
Autumn Springs Dr
1600 MSCY 77459 4497 D3
Autumn Springs Ln
2200 HarC 77373 3114 D4
Autumn Stream
22400 HarC 77375 3109 E1
Autumn Sun Dr
7200 HarC 77083 4096 E6
Autumn Sunset Ln
6500 HarC 77379 3111 C3
Autumn Terrace Ln
20400 HarC 77450 3954 D5
Autumn Thistle Dr
6400 HarC 77449 3677 C3
Autumn Timbers Ln
26800 HarC 77433 3537 A1
Autumn Trace Ct
8100 HarC 77083 4097 B7
Autumn Trails Ln
17400 HarC 77084 3677 E2
17400 HarC 77084 3678 C3
18000 HarC 77449 3677 D2
Autumnvale Ln
14900 HarC 77429 3397 C1
Autumn Valley Dr
13200 HarC 77429 3254 A6
Autumn Village Ct
4600 MSCY 77459 4369 B5
Autumn Village Dr
1100 MSCY 77459 4369 B5
Autumnway Ct
10100 HarC 77064 3540 D4
Autumnway Dr
9700 HarC 77064 3540 D4
Autumn Willow Dr
8100 HarC 77375 2965 E7
8100 HarC 77375 2966 A7
Autumn Wind Dr
8300 HarC 77040 3541 A7
16200 HarC 77090 3258 D5
Autumnwood Dr
600 HOUS 77013 3966 D1
Autumn Wood Ln
- FRDW 77546 4505 B6
Autumnwood Wy
- WDLD 77380 2821 D7
N Autumnwood Wy
10 WDLD 77380 2821 D6
Autumn Woods Dr
22200 MtgC 77357 2973 D3
22200 MtgC 77365 2973 D3
Autumwind Ct
25500 FBnC 77494 4093 A2
Avalange Ct
13100 HarC 77429 3397 C3
Avalon Ct
2700 FBnC 77469 4365 C1
7300 PASD 77505 4249 B5
13700 HarC 77044 3689 D3
Avalon Ln
4100 BYTN 77521 3973 E2
Avalon Pl
10 SGLD 77479 4495 A3
2100 HOUS 77019 3962 A6
3200 HOUS 77019 3961 E6
Avalon Ter
3000 HOUS 77057 4100 C1
Avalon Trc
- FBnC 77469 4094 D6
Avalon Wy
100 GLSN 77550 4994 E7
5600 HOUS 77057 3960 D7
Avalon Bay Ln
23000 FBnC 77494 4093 B3
Avalon Bend Cir
7100 HarC 77379 3111 B3
Avalon Canyon Ct
22200 FBnC 77450 4093 E2
Avalon Castle Dr
3500 MtgC 77386 2969 E3
Avalon Cove Ln
2500 BzaC 77581 4502 A3
Avalon Crest Dr
22000 HarC 77379 3111 B1
Avalon Forest Ct
2600 MtgC 77386 2823 C7
Avalon Garden Ln
3900 FBnC 77494 4093 D3
Avalon Lake Ln
- BzaC 77581 4502 B3
Avalon Lords Cir
7100 HarC 77379 3111 B1
Avalon Oaks Ct
10 SHEH 77381 2821 E2
Avalon Oaks Pl
- WDLD 77381 2821 E2
10 SHEH 77381 2821 E2
Avalon Point Ct
17900 HarC 77429 3252 C7
17900 HarC 77429 3396 C1
Avalon Queen Dr
21400 HarC 77379 3111 B1
Avalon Springs Dr
19000 HarC 77375 3109 D6
19000 HarC 77375 3254 E1
Avalon Trace Ln
- BzaC 77581 4502 B3
Avana Glen Ln
2000 SGLD 77478 4236 E5
Avanak Rd
5500 HarC 77389 3111 E1
5500 HarC 77389 3112 A1
Avanti Ct
3000 PRLD 77584 4501 D6
Avanti Dr
2900 PRLD 77584 4501 D6
Avast Wy
16200 HarC 77532 3552 A3
Avebury Ct
10 WDLD 77384 2675 D5
2100 HarC 77450 3954 E6
Avebury Stone Cir
9000 FBnC 77459 4621 C1
Aveleigh Ln
17800 HarC 77396 3407 D1

Houston Street Index

STREET
Block City ZIP Map# Grid

Avellino Ct
24500 FBnC 77469 4092 E7
Avenel Dr
6300 PASD 77505 4248 E6
Avenel Iron Dr
10800 HarC 77064 3541 A1
Avenell Rd
2200 HOUS 77034 4246 E6
Avenfield Rd
16400 HarC 77377 3254 C5
Avenida De Las Americas
- HOUS 77002 3963 D4
800 HOUS 77003 3963 D5
800 HOUS 77010 3963 C5
Avenida la Quinta St
2100 HOUS 77077 3957 B6
Avenida Monterey Pl
4500 FBnC 77469 4233 C5
Avenida Vaquero St
12700 HOUS 77077 3957 C7
Avenplace Rd
16200 HarC 77377 3254 C5
Avens
4300 HOUS 77018 3823 B2
Avenstone St
- HarC 77377 3254 C4
Avenswood Pl
10 WDLD 77382 2673 A7
Aventine Plantation Dr
19400 HarC 77449 3677 A5
Avents Ridge Dr
11100 FBnC 77469 4092 B7
Avenue E
- SGLD 77478 4367 E2
2300 RSBG 77471 4490 E3
Avenue W
6700 HOUS 77011 3964 E5
6800 HOUS 77011 3965 A5
N Avenue E
300 HMBL 77338 3262 E6
S Avenue E
100 HMBL 77338 3262 E6
Avenue A
- GlsC 77539 4634 B4
- HarC 77040 3681 C2
- HOUS 77053 4372 C4
- HOUS 77058 4508 A4
- KATY 77494 3952 C1
- MTBL 77520 3696 D5
- PRVW 77445 2955 B7
- TXCY 77539 4634 B4
10 SGLD 77478 4367 E2
100 CNRO 77301 2384 A5
100 GlsC 77518 4634 D3
100 RHMD 77469 4492 A1
100 STAF 77477 4369 D3
200 FBnC 77469 4365 A7
200 RHMD 77469 4365 A7
300 SHUS 77587 4246 E3
400 LMQU 77568 4874 A7
800 KATY 77493 3952 C1
1100 FBnC 77545 4498 D7
1100 SHUS 77587 4247 A3
1800 GlsC 77539 4636 A4
2100 KATY 77493 3813 C5
2300 RSBG 77471 4490 E3
2400 GlsC 77539 4635 D4
2600 FBnC 77471 4491 A3
2600 RSBG 77471 4491 A3
3000 GlsC 77510 4871 E7
3000 TXCY 77510 4871 E5
4900 HTCK 77510 4987 E2
5900 HTCK 77510 4988 A3
5900 HTCK 77563 4988 A3
5900 STFE 77510 4987 E3
5900 STFE 77510 4988 A3
12600 HarC 77532 3692 D2
16700 HarC 77530 3830 D7
18200 GlsC 77511 4869 A4
Avenue A
- HarC 77373 3113 E1
- HarC 77373 3114 A1
100 HMBL 77338 3262 D6
Avenue A
100 HMBL 77338 3262 D6
Avenue A St
10 CNRO 77301 2384 C5
2000 GlsC 77539 4635 E4
Avenue A 1/2
400 GlsC 77539 4636 B5
Avenue B
- HarC 77040 3681 C1
- HOUS 77017 4106 A5
- HOUS 77053 4372 C5
- HOUS 77058 4507 E2
- HOUS 77058 4508 A2
- MTBL 77520 3696 D5
- PASD 77058 4508 B3
- PRVW 77445 2955 B7
- PRVW 77445 3100 B1
- RHMD 77469 4492 A1
100 STAF 77477 4369 D3
200 GlsC 77511 4869 B4
200 LMQU 77568 4874 A7
300 SHUS 77587 4246 D3
700 KATY 77493 3952 C1
700 KATY 77494 3952 C1
900 GlsC 77518 4634 C4
1100 SHUS 77587 4247 A3
1200 GlsC 77539 4634 C4
1200 TXCY 77539 4634 C4
1400 FBnC 77545 4498 E7
1700 KATY 77493 3813 C6
1800 GlsC 77539 4632 D7
2000 RSBG 77471 4490 E3
2300 GlsC 77539 4753 E1
2400 FBnC 77471 4490 E3
3200 DKSN 77539 4753 E1
3300 DKSN 77539 4754 A2
5200 HarC 77532 3552 C4
5200 HTCK 77510 4987 E2
6300 STFE 77510 4987 E4
6500 GlsC 77510 4987 E4
6500 HOUS 77011 3964 D7
6500 HTCK 77563 4987 E4
7100 HOUS 77011 3965 A7
7300 BLAR 77401 4101 B6
7500 HOUS 77012 3965 B7
7600 HOUS 77012 4105 B1
12400 HarC 77532 3692 D2
16700 HarC 77530 3830 D6
Avenue B FM-2100
5200 HarC 77532 3552 C4
Avenue B W
- DRPK 77536 3969 D7
- DRPK 77536 4109 D1
Avenue B
- HOUS 77081 4101 B3

N Avenue B
- HOUS 77401 4101 B3
100 HMBL 77338 3262 E6
6300 BLAR 77401 4101 B5
S Avenue B
- HarC 77373 3113 E1
- HarC 77373 3114 A1
300 HMBL 77338 3262 E6
Avenue C
- BYTN 77520 4112 D1
- GlsC 77539 4635 E5
- HarC 77040 3681 C1
- HOUS 77053 4372 C5
- STAF 77477 4369 D3
100 HarC 77562 3831 D3
300 FBnC 77469 4492 A1
300 RHMD 77469 4492 A1
400 GlsC 77511 4869 B4
400 LMQU 77568 4874 B7
400 TXCY 77591 4874 B7
800 KATY 77493 3952 C1
800 KATY 77494 3952 C1
1100 FBnC 77545 4498 E7
1500 GlsC 77539 4636 A5
1600 KATY 77493 3813 C6
2400 FBnC 77471 4490 E3
2400 RSBG 77471 4490 E3
5400 HarC 77532 3552 C4
6400 HOUS 77011 3964 E7
7000 HOUS 77011 3965 A7
7400 GlsC 77510 4987 E6
7500 HOUS 77012 3965 B7
7600 HOUS 77012 4105 B1
12500 HarC 77532 3692 D2
13600 HarC 77429 3396 D3
15400 HarC 77530 3968 E1
15400 HarC 77530 3969 A1
16200 HarC 77530 3830 C7
N Avenue C
100 HMBL 77338 3262 E6
S Avenue C
- HarC 77373 3113 E1
100 HMBL 77338 3262 E6
Avenue C 1/2
6500 GlsC 77510 4987 D5
Avenue D
- HarC 77040 3681 C1
- HarC 77373 3113 E1
- HOUS 77053 4372 C4
- KATY 77494 3952 C1
- STAF 77477 4369 D3
100 ALVN 77511 4749 B7
100 GlsC 77518 4634 D4
100 HarC 77562 3831 D3
100 SGLD 77478 4367 E2
100 SHUS 77587 4246 D3
400 GlsC 77511 4869 B4
400 LMQU 77568 4874 B7
400 TXCY 77591 4874 B7
800 FBnC 77471 4490 D3
800 GlsC 77539 4634 C4
800 KATY 77493 3952 B1
800 RSBG 77471 4490 E3
900 GlsC 77539 4636 A5
900 KATY 77493 3813 B5
1000 HMBL 77338 3262 E5
1100 SHUS 77587 4247 A3
1800 FBnC 77545 4498 D7
1800 GlsC 77539 4632 D7
1800 LGCY 77539 4632 D7
2000 GlsC 77539 4753 D1
2700 GlsC 77539 4635 B4
3200 DKSN 77539 4753 E2
3200 GlsC 77510 4871 E5
5900 HarC 77532 3552 B4
7100 GlsC 77510 4987 C5
15900 HarC 77530 3830 C7
N Avenue D
100 HMBL 77338 3262 E6
S Avenue D
100 HMBL 77338 3262 E7
Avenue D 1/2
7100 GlsC 77510 4987 C5
Avenue E
- HarC 77040 3681 C1
- HarC 77373 3113 E1
- HOUS 77053 4372 C4
- HOUS 77058 4508 A4
10 GlsC 77518 4634 E3
100 ALVN 77511 4749 C7
100 HarC 77562 3831 D3
100 SHUS 77587 4246 D3
200 GlsC 77511 4869 B4
200 GlsC 77539 4636 B5
800 GlsC 77539 4634 D4
1000 KATY 77493 3813 B7
1100 SHUS 77587 4247 A3
1200 TXCY 77539 4634 C5
3500 GlsC 77510 4871 D6
4100 GLSN 77550 5108 C4
4500 GLSN 77551 5108 C4
5200 HTCK 77510 4987 D2
5700 HarC 77532 3552 B4
6500 HOUS 77011 3964 E7
6700 GlsC 77510 4987 D5
7000 HOUS 77011 3965 A7
7400 HOUS 77012 3965 B7
7800 HOUS 77012 4105 C1
Avenue E E
- FBnC 77459 4369 B4
- SGLD 77478 4369 B4
100 SGLD 77478 4367 E2
100 STAF 77477 4369 D3
200 FBnC 77477 4369 D3
200 MSCY 77477 4369 D3
1100 RSBG 77471 4490 D3
E Avenue E
- FBnC 77477 4369 A4
1600 SGLD 77478 4369 A4
Avenue E St
300 CNRO 77301 2384 B5
900 GlsC 77539 4636 A5
Avenue E 1/2
200 ALVN 77511 4749 B7
3100 GlsC 77510 4871 D6
7300 GlsC 77510 4987 C7
Avenue F
- HarC 77040 3681 C2
- HOUS 77053 4372 C4
- TXCY 77590 4991 B1
100 ALVN 77511 4749 B7
100 SGLD 77478 4367 E1
100 SHUS 77587 4246 D3
100 STAF 77477 4369 E3
200 GlsC 77511 4869 B4
1100 SHUS 77587 4247 A3
1200 KATY 77493 3813 B7
1300 CNRO 77301 2384 C5

Avenue F
1600 LGCY 77539 4632 C7
1600 LGCY 77573 4632 C7
1800 GlsC 77539 4632 D7
1800 RSBG 77471 4490 E4
2000 DKSN 77539 4753 D1
2600 RSBG 77471 4491 A4
3000 GlsC 77510 4871 C5
5500 STFE 77510 4987 C2
6500 HOUS 77011 3964 E7
6800 GlsC 77510 4987 C5
7000 HOUS 77011 3965 A7
7400 HOUS 77012 3965 B7
8000 HOUS 77012 4105 C1
N Avenue F
100 HMBL 77338 3262 E6
S Avenue F
100 HMBL 77338 3262 E6
Avenue F St
200 CNRO 77301 2384 B5
Avenue F 1/2
800 GlsC 77539 4636 A6
Avenue G
- HarC 77040 3681 C2
- HOUS 77030 4102 D6
- HOUS 77053 4372 C4
- PRVW 77445 3100 C1
100 SGLD 77478 4367 E1
100 STAF 77477 4369 D3
200 SHUS 77587 4246 E3
900 GlsC 77539 4636 A6
1100 SHUS 77587 4247 A3
1500 RSBG 77471 4490 E4
2000 DKSN 77539 4753 E2
2000 GlsC 77539 4753 D1
2600 RSBG 77471 4491 A4
6300 GlsC 77510 4987 C4
6300 STFE 77510 4987 C4
N Avenue G
100 HMBL 77338 3262 E6
S Avenue G
100 HMBL 77338 3262 E6
W Avenue G
100 CNRO 77301 2384 A6
500 CNRO 77301 2383 E6
Avenue G St
500 CNRO 77301 2384 B5
Avenue G 1/2
3100 STFE 77510 4871 C6
5600 STFE 77510 4987 C2
Avenue H
- HarC 77040 3681 C2
- HOUS 77034 4379 A4
- HOUS 77053 4372 C4
- STAF 77477 4369 E3
- RSBG 77471 4491 B5
100 ALVN 77511 4749 B7
100 GlsC 77511 4869 C4
100 SGLD 77478 4367 E1
300 SHUS 77587 4246 E4
400 GlsC 77539 4636 B6
1100 RSBG 77471 4490 D4
1100 SHUS 77587 4247 A3
1800 GNPK 77547 4106 C1
2000 DKSN 77539 4753 D1
2000 GlsC 77539 4753 D1
2600 GlsC 77539 4635 B5
2600 RSBG 77471 4491 A4
2900 TXCY 77539 4635 A5
4700 HOUS 77011 3964 B5
5200 RHMD 77469 4491 C3
5300 STFE 77510 4987 C2
7000 HOUS 77011 3965 A7
7400 HOUS 77012 3965 B7
Avenue H SPR-529
10 RSBG 77471 4490 C5
Avenue H SR-36
1100 RSBG 77471 4490 D4
Avenue H US-90 ALT
1100 RSBG 77471 4490 D4
2600 RSBG 77471 4491 A4
5200 RHMD 77469 4491 C3
E Avenue H
9400 HOUS 77012 4105 E3
9400 HOUS 77012 4106 A3
N Avenue H
100 HMBL 77338 3262 E6
2400 DRPK 77536 4249 E1
2400 DRPK 77536 4250 A1
2400 LPRT 77536 4250 A1
2400 LPRT 77571 4250 A1
S Avenue H
200 HMBL 77338 3262 E6
W Avenue H
700 RSBG 77471 4490 B5
W Avenue H SPR-529
700 RSBG 77471 4490 B5
Avenue H St
500 CNRO 77301 2384 B6
Avenue I
- HarC 77040 3681 C2
- STAF 77477 4369 E3
- TXCY 77590 4991 B1
100 ALVN 77511 4749 B7
100 GlsC 77511 4869 C4
300 SHUS 77587 4246 E4
400 GlsC 77539 4636 B6
600 RSBG 77471 4490 D4
1100 SHUS 77587 4247 A4
1500 LGCY 77539 4632 C7
1500 LGCY 77573 4632 C7
1600 GlsC 77539 4635 E6
1600 PASD 77504 4247 A4
1600 SHUS 77504 4247 A4
2000 DKSN 77539 4753 D1
2600 RSBG 77471 4491 A4
4700 HOUS 77011 3964 C5
4900 RSBG 77469 4491 B4
5000 RHMD 77469 4491 D4
5200 STFE 77510 4987 C2
6900 HOUS 77011 3965 A6
7600 HOUS 77012 3965 B7
Avenue I FM-517
900 GlsC 77539 4636 A6
1600 GlsC 77539 4635 E6
Avenue I FM-1640
800 RSBG 77471 4490 D4
2600 RSBG 77471 4491 A4
4900 RSBG 77469 4491 B4
5000 RHMD 77469 4491 D4
E Avenue I
9400 HOUS 77012 4105 E3
9400 HOUS 77012 4106 A3
Avenue I St
500 CNRO 77301 2384 B6
Avenue J
- GlsC 77539 4636 A6
- HOUS 77053 4372 C4

Avenue J
100 TXCY 77539 4753 B7
300 BYTN 77520 3972 C6
400 GlsC 77511 4869 C4
400 SHUS 77587 4246 E4
800 RSBG 77471 4490 D4
1100 SHUS 77587 4247 A4
1100 TXCY 77539 4871 B1
1700 GNPK 77547 4106 C1
1900 GlsC 77539 4635 E6
2100 TXCY 77510 4871 B6
2400 HOUS 77547 4106 B1
2600 RSBG 77471 4491 A4
2800 STFE 77510 4871 B4
4900 HOUS 77011 3964 C5
7000 HOUS 77011 3965 A7
7400 HOUS 77012 3965 B7
Avenue J FM-517
2200 GlsC 77539 4635 C6
E Avenue J
9300 HOUS 77012 4105 E3
9400 HOUS 77012 4106 A3
Avenue J Pl
500 CNRO 77301 2384 B6
Avenue J St
500 CNRO 77301 2384 B6
Avenue J 1/2
3400 STFE 77510 4871 B5
Avenue K
- HOUS 77053 4372 C5
- TXCY 77590 4991 B1
100 BYTN 77520 3972 C6
200 GLSN 77550 5109 E2
300 ALVN 77511 4749 B6
500 SHUS 77587 4246 E4
600 GlsC 77539 4636 A7
800 RSBG 77471 4490 D4
1100 SHUS 77587 4247 A4
1700 GNPK 77547 4106 C1
1800 GlsC 77539 4635 E7
2600 RSBG 77471 4491 A4
3300 STFE 77510 4871 B5
3800 GLSN 77550 5108 D5
4400 GLSN 77551 5108 C5
5100 STFE 77510 4987 B2
6500 HOUS 77011 3964 E6
7000 HOUS 77011 3965 A6
7400 HOUS 77012 3965 B7
E Avenue K
9200 HOUS 77012 4105 E3
9400 HOUS 77012 4106 A3
Avenue K 1/2
3300 STFE 77510 4871 B5
Avenue L
- HOUS 77053 4372 C5
- RSBG 77471 4491 B5
100 BYTN 77520 3972 C6
100 DKSN 77539 4753 B7
500 SHUS 77587 4246 E4
600 GlsC 77539 4636 A7
700 GLSN 77550 5109 A4
800 CNRO 77301 2384 B6
1000 RSBG 77471 4490 D5
1100 DKSN 77510 4871 B1
1100 DKSN 77539 4871 B1
1100 GlsC 77510 4871 B1
1100 GlsC 77539 4871 B1
1100 SHUS 77587 4247 A4
2100 STFE 77510 4871 B3
2700 GlsC 77539 4635 A6
3800 GLSN 77550 5108 E4
4400 GLSN 77551 5108 C5
4500 STFE 77510 4987 B1
5200 HOUS 77011 3964 C5
5700 GlsC 77510 4987 B7
7000 HOUS 77011 3965 A6
7400 HOUS 77012 3965 B7
E Avenue L
9100 HOUS 77012 4105 E3
9500 HOUS 77012 4106 A3
Avenue L 1/2
7100 GlsC 77510 4987 B6
Avenue M
- HOUS 77053 4372 C4
100 BYTN 77520 3972 C6
600 SHUS 77587 4246 E4
700 GlsC 77539 4636 A7
900 GLSN 77550 5109 A4
1100 RSBG 77471 4490 D5
1100 SHUS 77587 4247 A4
1200 CNRO 77301 2384 C6
1600 PASD 77504 4247 A4
1600 SHUS 77504 4247 A4
3800 GLSN 77550 5108 E5
4000 STFE 77510 4871 A7
4500 STFE 77510 4987 A2
5000 GLSN 77551 5108 C5
5500 GlsC 77510 4987 A7
Avenue M FM-646
4200 STFE 77510 4871 A7
4500 STFE 77510 4987 A1
E Avenue M
100 CNRO 77301 2384 D6
Avenue M Ext
2800 CNRO 77301 2384 E6
2800 CNRO 77301 2385 A5
Avenue M 1/2
1000 GLSN 77550 5109 C4
3800 GLSN 77550 5108 E5
5000 GLSN 77551 5108 C5
5500 STFE 77510 4987 A2
Avenue N
- GlsC 77539 4634 E6
- TXCY 77539 4634 E6
- TXCY 77539 4635 A6
600 SHUS 77587 4246 E4
700 GlsC 77539 4757 A1
1100 SHUS 77587 4247 A4
1600 PASD 77504 4247 A4
1600 SHUS 77504 4247 A4
2100 RSBG 77471 4490 E5
2300 GlsC 77539 4635 C7
2600 RSBG 77471 4491 C5
5300 STFE 77510 4987 A2
6500 HOUS 77011 3964 E6
7000 GlsC 77510 4987 A5
7200 HOUS 77011 3965 B6
7400 HOUS 77012 3965 B6
E Avenue N
9100 HOUS 77012 4105 E2
9500 HOUS 77012 4106 A2
Avenue N 1/2
1300 GLSN 77550 5109 C4
3800 GLSN 77550 5108 E5
4000 STFE 77510 4871 A6
4300 GLSN 77551 5108 C6
Avenue O
- STFE 77510 4987 A1

Avenue O
1000 GlsC 77539 4757 A1
1500 GLSN 77550 5109 A5
2100 RSBG 77471 4490 E5
3200 RSBG 77471 4491 B5
3900 GLSN 77550 5108 E5
4000 STFE 77510 4871 A6
4400 GLSN 77551 5108 E5
5500 GlsC 77510 4987 A6
6600 HOUS 77011 3964 E5
7400 HOUS 77011 3965 B6
7400 HOUS 77012 3965 B6
E Avenue O
9100 HOUS 77012 4105 E2
9500 HOUS 77012 4106 A2
Avenue O 1/2
1600 GLSN 77550 5109 B5
3900 GLSN 77550 5108 E5
4400 GLSN 77551 5108 C6
Avenue of Oaks St
100 HOUS 77009 3824 B4
2400 HOUS 77026 3824 E4
Avenue P
2400 GlsC 77539 4635 C7
2500 DRPK 77536 4110 A7
2500 LPRT 77571 4110 A7
2800 TXCY 77539 4635 A7
2900 TXCY 77539 4634 E7
3000 RSBG 77471 4491 A5
4000 STFE 77510 4870 E7
4600 STFE 77510 4986 E3
6600 HOUS 77011 3964 E5
6800 GlsC 77510 4986 E6
6900 GLSN 77551 5108 A7
7400 HOUS 77011 3965 B6
7400 HOUS 77012 3965 B6
E Avenue P
1600 DRPK 77536 4109 D7
9100 HOUS 77012 4105 E2
9500 HOUS 77012 4106 A2
Avenue P 1/2
2300 GLSN 77550 5109 A5
4100 GLSN 77550 5108 E5
4400 GLSN 77551 5108 C6
Avenue Q
1500 GlsC 77510 4870 E2
1900 STFE 77510 4870 E4
2400 GlsC 77539 4756 C1
2400 GLSN 77550 5109 B5
2400 TXCY 77539 4756 C1
2800 TXCY 77539 4635 A7
2900 GlsC 77539 4634 E7
2900 TXCY 77539 4634 E7
3000 RSBG 77471 4491 A5
3900 GLSN 77550 5108 C6
4400 GLSN 77551 5108 C6
6600 HOUS 77011 3964 E5
6900 HOUS 77011 3965 A6
E Avenue Q
9400 HOUS 77012 4105 E2
9400 HOUS 77012 4106 A2
Avenue Q 1/2
2800 GLSN 77550 5109 B5
4000 STFE 77510 4870 E7
4100 GLSN 77550 5108 E6
4400 GLSN 77551 5108 C6
Avenue R
- GlsC 77539 4634 D7
- TXCY 77539 4634 D7
1700 RSBG 77471 4491 B5
2600 TXCY 77539 4756 A1
2700 TXCY 77539 4755 E1
2800 GLSN 77550 5109 A6
4100 GLSN 77550 5108 D6
4400 GLSN 77551 5108 C6
4400 STFE 77510 4870 E7
4400 STFE 77510 4986 E3
5700 GlsC 77510 4986 E3
6600 HOUS 77011 3964 E5
6800 HOUS 77011 3965 A5
E Avenue R
9200 HOUS 77012 4105 E2
Avenue R 1/2
2800 GLSN 77550 5109 B5
4000 GLSN 77550 5108 D6
4400 GLSN 77551 5108 D6
Avenue S
- RSBG 77471 4491 A5
1600 GlsC 77510 4870 E2
2600 STFE 77510 4870 E4
2800 TXCY 77539 4755 E1
2800 TXCY 77539 4756 A1
3000 GLSN 77550 5109 A6
4100 GLSN 77550 5108 D6
4700 STFE 77510 4986 E1
5700 GLSN 77551 5108 C7
6600 HOUS 77011 3964 E5
6800 HOUS 77011 3965 A5
12300 HOUS 77034 4378 B2
E Avenue S
9300 HOUS 77012 4105 E2
Avenue S 1/2
3500 GLSN 77550 5109 A6
4100 GLSN 77550 5108 D6
4300 GLSN 77551 5108 D6
Avenue T
2800 TXCY 77539 4755 E2
3700 GLSN 77550 5109 A6
4200 GLSN 77550 5108 E6
4200 STFE 77510 4870 D7
4400 GLSN 77551 5108 E6
4500 STFE 77510 4986 D3
5500 GlsC 77510 4986 D5
6200 GlsC 77517 4986 D5
6600 HOUS 77011 3964 E5
6800 HOUS 77011 3965 A5
Avenue T 1/2
4100 GLSN 77550 5108 E6
4100 GLSN 77550 5108 D6
5100 GLSN 77551 5108 D7
Avenue U
3900 GLSN 77550 5109 A6
4200 GLSN 77550 5108 E7
4300 GLSN 77551 5108 E7
5500 TXCY 77539 4755 D2
5700 GlsC 77517 4986 C3
6600 HOUS 77011 3964 E5
6800 HOUS 77011 3965 A5
Avenue V
5500 TXCY 77539 4755 E3
6400 GlsC 77510 4986 D4
6600 HOUS 77011 3964 E5
6800 HOUS 77011 3965 A5
Avenue V 1/2
9500 GLSN 77554 5221 D3
Avenue W
6000 TXCY 77539 4755 D3

Averill St
3700 HOUS 77009 3824 C6
Avernus St
3000 HOUS 77022 3824 A3
Avert Ct
8200 HOUS 77088 3684 A2
Avery
6600 HOUS 77087 4244 D2
Avery Ct
2600 SEBK 77586 4509 C1
Avery Dr
500 FBnC 77479 4366 E5
Avery St
16500 MtgC 77302 2678 D5
Avery Bay Ct
4500 FBnC 77545 4623 C1
Avery Brooke Ln
14400 HarC 77429 3397 D7
Avery Cove Ln
20800 FBnC 77450 4094 A4
Avery Hill Ln
25300 HarC 77373 3114 E2
Avery Hollow Ct
4500 LGCY 77573 4630 E6
Avery Park Dr
2300 SGLD 77478 4236 E5
Avery Point Dr
20200 HarC 77449 3815 D2
Avery Ridge Ln
13000 HarC 77377 3254 A3
Avery Springs Ln
100 LGCY 77539 4752 E3
Avery Trace Ct
11000 HarC 77065 3539 D1
Avery Vale Ct
12400 HarC 77014 3402 B2
Avery Vale Ln
12500 HarC 77014 3402 A3
Aves St
10700 HOUS 77034 4246 E6
Avetex
- HarC 77377 3106 D4
Avey Ct
3600 BzaC 77584 4501 C7
Aviary Ct
- FBnC 77459 4621 C7
Avie St
3300 HOUS 77007 3962 D3
Avignon Ct
11500 HOUS 77082 4098 B3
Avila Dr
2500 HarC 77038 3543 C5
Avila Bend Dr
14800 HarC 77095 3679 A2
Avilion Ct
2400 PRLD 77584 4501 B3
Avington Rd
8400 LPRT 77571 4249 D3
Avion St
13700 HarC 77044 3689 D4
Avitts Rd
9900 BzaC 77581 4628 B3
9900 PRLD 77511 4628 B3
Avitts Acres
18600 BzaC 77581 4628 C4
Aviva Ln
13700 HarC 77083 4097 A6
Aviva Meadow Dr
8700 HOUS 77078 3688 B5
Avoca Dr
- HOUS 77045 4242 C7
Avocet Ln
7200 HOUS 77040 3682 B3
Avocet Wy
1600 MSCY 77489 4497 C1
Avon Pl
11300 HarC 77066 3401 A5
Avon St
400 DRPK 77536 4109 A4
1500 BYTN 77520 4112 B1
Avon Wy
1300 HOUS 77339 3264 A1
Avonbury Ln
24500 FBnC 77494 3953 B7
Avoncrest Ln
7100 FBnC 77469 4094 B6
Avondale Dr
4900 SGLD 77479 4495 C4
Avondale Ln
300 FRDW 77546 4505 A7
Avondale St
100 HOUS 77006 3963 A6
200 HOUS 77006 3962 E6
400 LGCY 77573 4631 E3
Avonelle Ln
13200 HOUS 77045 4241 B7
Avonfield Ln
- FBnC 77469 4094 B7
Avongate Ln
14100 HOUS 77082 4096 E1
Avonglen Ln
22000 HarC 77389 3112 D1
Avonlake Ln
14800 HarC 77396 3548 A1
N Avonlea Cir
10 WDLD 77382 2675 D6
S Avonlea Cir
10 WDLD 77382 2675 C6
Avonlea Ct
100 WDLD 77382 2675 D6
Avonlea Dr
100 WDLD 77382 2675 C6
Avonmoor Dr
6600 HarC 77049 3829 A2
Avon Oaks Ln
21100 HarC 77450 3954 E7
Avon Park Ln
- HarC 77083 4097 A6
Avonshire Dr
13200 HOUS 77083 4097 B5
13500 HarC 77083 4097 B5
Avory Ridge Ln
3100 PRLD 77581 4503 C1
AV Sallas Ln
- MtgC 77357 2827 B7
Aweather Ct
- HarC 77532 3551 E5
Aweigh Dr
500 HarC 77532 3552 A2
Awning Ct
1000 HarC 77532 3552 A3
Awty School Rd
7400 HOUS 77055 3822 A7
Ax Dr
- FRDW 77546 4629 B4
Axilda Av
200 HOUS 77017 4106 A6

Axis Rdg
16300 HarC 77530 3829 D4
Axleridge Dr
1400 MtgC 77384 2529 A6
Axton Falls
- HarC 77429 3397 A2
Ayala Ln
1900 FBnC 77469 4492 B2
Aycliff Dr
2400 HarC 77039 3545 D2
Ayers Ln
25600 MtgC 77365 3118 A3
Ayers Park Ln
- HarC 77429 3397 A1
Ayers Rock Ln
- HarC 77373 2968 E6
Ayers Rock Rd
14200 FBnC 77478 4367 A4
Aylesbury Ct
10 SGLD 77479 4495 E3
Aylesbury Ln
7900 HarC 77379 3256 A2
26900 HarC 77447 3248 E6
Aylesworth Ct
3000 FBnC 77494 3953 B7
Ayrshire Pl
12200 HarC 77089 4504 E2
Ayscough Ln
23700 HarC 77493 3814 B5
Aysha Park Dr
12000 HOUS 77099 4238 A2
Ayston Dr
18900 HarC 77375 3255 A1
Azahar Ct
- LGCY 77539 4633 E2
Azale St
- PRVW 77484 3100 D5
- WlrC 77484 3100 D5
Azalea Bnd
1100 FBnC 77479 4494 A6
Azalea Ct
1200 PASD 77506 4106 E5
2500 GLSN 77551 5108 B7
8200 HOUS 77017 4246 A1
27000 MtgC 77354 2817 D4
Azalea Cts
800 LMQU 77568 4990 B1
Azalea Dr
- HarC 77389 2966 A2
100 LMQU 77568 4874 C7
400 BYTN 77520 3832 A7
400 BYTN 77520 3971 A1
1400 RSBG 77471 4490 D6
Azalea Ln
20900 MtgC 77357 2827 A1
Azalea Pk
6500 HOUS 77008 3822 E6
Azalea St
100 SGLD 77478 4367 E3
100 SGLD 77478 4368 A4
800 HOUS 77018 3823 A1
7400 HOUS 77023 4105 A2
Azalea Tr
1500 FRDW 77546 4629 E2
37100 MtgC 77354 2816 B1
Azalea Vil
10200 HOUS 77088 3542 B7
Azalea Wy
18900 HarC 77379 3110 E6
Azalea Brook Tr
- PRLD 77581 4503 D7
400 FBnC 77583 4744 A3
Azalea Brook Wy
19600 HarC 77084 3816 A4
19700 HarC 77084 3815 E4
Azalea Creek Tr
12700 HarC 77065 3539 C2
Azaleadell Dr
400 HOUS 77018 3823 B1
Azalea Garden Dr
2300 HarC 77038 3543 B3
Azalea Glen Ct
19000 HarC 77084 3816 B4
Azalea Leaf Ct
6500 HarC 77449 3677 B3
Azalea Meadow Ln
- FBnC 77494 4093 A2
Azalea Mist
- HarC 77038 3543 E5
Azalea Pointe
900 LGCY 77573 4631 D5
Azalea Sands Dr
3400 MtgC 77386 2969 D2
Azalea Shores Ct
15800 HOUS 77044 3409 A5
Azalea Shores Dr
15600 HarC 77070 3255 C6
Azalea Trace Dr
5100 HarC 77066 3401 B5
Azalea Trail Ln
10 BLAR 77401 4101 A5
5500 SGLD 77479 4495 A4
Azalea Valley Ct
6900 HarC 77449 3677 A2
Azalea Valley Dr
19400 HarC 77449 3677 A2
Azalea Walk Ln
- HOUS 77044 3550 A2
Azcar Ct
800 SGLD 77478 4237 B7
Azimuth Dr
16300 HarC 77532 3551 D2
Azrock Rd
- HarC 77375 2965 E1
- HarC 77389 2965 E1
Aztec Ct
- LGCY 77573 4632 B7
- LGCY 77573 4753 B1
Aztec Dr
1900 DRPK 77536 4109 D6
Aztec Ln
7000 HarC 77049 3831 A1
18300 MtgC 77365 2972 B5
Aztec St
4200 PASD 77504 4247 E6
29000 HarC 77484 3248 A2
Aztec Canyon Dr
30200 MtgC 77386 2969 C2
Aztec Wood Dr
3400 HarC 77084 3816 E3
Azure Ln
18800 MtgC 77365 2972 B6
Azure Brook Dr
8100 HarC 77089 4377 B7
8100 PRLD 77089 4377 B7
Azure Crystal Ct
2000 HarC 77373 3114 D5

STREET Block City ZIP Map# Grid

Azure Lake Dr
9500 MtgC 77354 2672 B5
Azure Sky Dr
24100 HarC 77373 3114 D5

B

B Dr
- HarC 77388 3111 D1
B St
- HOUS 77547 4106 C2
- PRVW 77445 3100 C2
- WlrC 77484 3101 D6
700 WALR 77484 3101 E6
2800 LPRT 77571 4251 E7
4100 HOUS 77072 4097 E4
4100 HOUS 77082 4097 E4
E B St
- LPRT 77571 4252 A2
100 LPRT 77571 4251 E3
W B St
100 LPRT 77571 4251 D3
Babbitt Ct
13400 HOUS 77034 4378 C2
Babbitt St
13200 HOUS 77034 4378 C2
Babbling Brook Ct
8500 FBnC 77479 4494 B6
Babbling Brook Wy
5000 HarC 77066 3401 B7
Babbling Creek Dr
- HOUS 77339 3119 C3
3500 HOUS 77345 3119 C3
Babbling Spring Ct
9600 HarC 77375 3255 B2
Baber Ct
15300 HarC 77095 3538 E4
Baber Dr
9100 HarC 77095 3538 E4
Baber Run Cir
9200 HarC 77095 3538 B3
Babin Dr
- BzaC 77511 4748 D3
3100 TXCY 77590 4874 D5
Babling Brooks Ct
- WDLD 77382 2819 C1
Baby Blue Ln
- FBnC 77494 4092 E3
Baca St
10 HOUS 77013 3827 C6
500 HOUS 77013 3966 C2
800 HOUS 77029 3966 C2
1000 JTCY 77029 3966 C3
Bacard Ln
13000 HarC 77099 4237 C1
Baccara Pl
10 WDLD 77384 2674 E3
Bacchus St
3300 HOUS 77022 3823 E3
Bace Ct
10 HOUS 77007 3962 C2
Bace Dr
8900 SPVL 77055 3820 E7
Bach Elm St
13000 HarC 77070 3399 B4
Bacher St
5200 HOUS 77028 3826 C2
Bach Orchard Tr
12000 HarC 77038 3543 A5
Bach Springs Ct
14400 HarC 77429 3397 B1
Bachwood Dr
7900 HarC 77040 3681 A1
Back Bay Cir
10 GLSN 77551 5108 A6
Back Bay Ct
2000 NSUB 77058 4508 B6
Back Bay Dr
1900 GLSN 77551 5108 A7
Back Bay Ln
500 LGCY 77539 4753 A4
Back Bay Ridge Wy
12000 HarC 77089 4378 A7
12000 HarC 77089 4505 B2
Backcove Ct
- HarC 77064 3540 E6
Backenberry Dr
4500 HarC 77546 4505 E6
4500 HarC 77546 4506 A5
Backgate Dr
8900 HOUS 77034 4247 A7
Backland Ct
1000 HarC 77373 2968 D5
Backstay Ct
800 HarC 77532 3552 A2
Backstrom Dr
6600 HTCK 77563 4989 B5
Baclidd Dr
900 GlsC 77518 4634 C4
900 GlsC 77539 4634 C4
Bacliff Dr
900 GlsC 77518 4634 C5
900 GlsC 77539 4634 C5
1200 TXCY 77539 4634 C5
Bacon St
3400 HOUS 77021 4103 A7
3500 HOUS 77021 4243 B1
Bacons Castle Ln
14900 HarC 77084 3679 A5
Bade St
1000 SPVL 77055 3820 D7
1000 SPVL 77055 3959 D1
Baden St
3800 HOUS 77009 3824 B6
Baden Hollow Ln
20500 HarC 77433 3676 E1
Baden Oaks Ct
3300 FBnC 77494 3953 E7
E Baden Oaks Dr
4100 PRLD 77581 4504 B6
S Baden Oaks Dr
1700 PRLD 77581 4504 B7
Badger Ct
19100 HarC 77084 3816 B4
Badger Canyon Dr
10500 HarC 77095 3537 E3
Badger Forest
3300 HOUS 77088 3683 B3
Badger Forest Dr
3700 HOUS 77088 3683 A3
Badger Hollow Dr
21700 MtgC 77355 2960 E1
Badgerwood Dr
11600 HOUS 77013 3827 D7
Badlands Bend Ln
11900 HarC 77346 3408 B3
Badtke Rd
17000 HarC 77447 3249 A3
Baer St
2600 HOUS 77020 3963 E3
2700 HOUS 77020 3964 A3
Baethe Rd
32500 WlrC 77484 3246 A5
33000 WlrC 77484 3245 E5
Baffin Ln
1000 HarC 77090 3258 A2
Baffin Bay Ct
- HarC 77379 3111 E6
Bafing Dr
13100 HarC 77083 4237 B1
13100 HarC 77099 4237 C1
Bagby St
100 HOUS 77002 3963 C3
2200 HOUS 77006 3963 A5
Baggett Ln
1500 HOUS 77055 3821 C6
Bagley Garden Ct
- HarC 77449 3676 E7
Bagnoli Rose Ln
- PRLD 77584 4501 D5
Bagpipe Ln
4400 HarC 77084 3678 D7
Bagpipe Wy
10 CNRO 77384 2675 E3
Bahai Vista Dr
900 FBnC 77469 4365 B4
Bahama Dr
1500 SEBK 77586 4509 D2
Bahama Ln
1200 GlsC 77650 4879 D3
Bahama Wy
16600 JMAB 77554 5331 E5
Bahia Ct
3500 FBnC 77459 4621 E5
Bahia Ln
7100 HOUS 77489 4371 B5
Bahler Av
3500 BzaC 77578 4625 D2
Baiamonte St
- HOUS 77085 4371 A1
Baikal Ct
16800 HOUS 77044 3409 B3
Bailey Av
3500 BzaC 77578 4501 C7
3500 BzaC 77578 4625 C1
3500 BzaC 77584 4501 C7
3500 PRLD 77578 4501 E7
3500 PRLD 77578 4625 C1
3500 PRLD 77584 4501 E7
3500 PRLD 77584 4625 C1
7500 BzaC 77584 4502 A7
7500 PRLD 77584 4502 A7
Bailey Ct
3600 FBnC 77459 4621 E5
Bailey Ln
3700 FBnC 77459 4621 E4
5200 ALVN 77511 4749 C2
Bailey Rd
4300 BzaC 77584 4503 A7
4300 PRLD 77584 4503 A7
5300 BzaC 77584 4502 D7
5300 PRLD 77584 4502 D7
23300 HarC 77375 2965 D6
Bailey St
1000 HOUS 77019 3963 A5
1800 HOUS 77006 3963 A5
Baileys Crossing Dr
- HarC 77429 3397 C3
Baileys Pl Ct
10 FBnC 77479 4367 A6
Bailey Springs Ct
5800 FBnC 77450 4094 A4
Bain St
3000 HOUS 77026 3825 A6
E Bainbridge Cir
2700 BzaC 77584 4501 C6
W Bainbridge Cir
2600 BzaC 77584 4501 C5
Bainbridge Ct
3000 SGLD 77478 4369 A3
Bain Bridge Hl
600 FBnC 77469 4616 E1
Bainbridge Ln
19700 HarC 77379 3112 A5
Bainbridge St
10600 HOUS 77016 3686 D3
Bainbridge Tr
13000 HarC 77065 3539 B3
Bainbridge Estates Dr
3500 HarC 77388 3112 D6
Bainbridge Hill Ln
- HarC 77047 4374 B4
Bainbrook Ln
14700 HarC 77396 3547 D1
Baird Av
1400 KATY 77493 3813 D7
Baird Ct
5600 HarC 77041 3680 C6
Baird St
- HOUS 77023 3964 C7
1600 HOUS 77023 4104 B1
Baird Mount Ct
12100 HarC 77346 3408 B3
Bairnsdale Ln
7400 HarC 77070 3399 E2
7400 HarC 77070 3400 A2
Baker
- HMPD 77445 3097 E1
- LPRT 77571 4249 C3
- PASD 77505 4249 C3
- PASD 77571 4249 C3
Baker Av
100 GlsC 77518 4634 C3
1200 GlsC 77539 4634 B4
1200 TXCY 77539 4634 B4
Baker Dr
- TMBL 77377 2963 D5
100 TMBL 77375 2964 A7
1400 TMBL 77375 2963 E5
3500 DKSN 77539 4754 C2
8200 HOUS 77017 4105 E7
8500 HOUS 77017 4106 A7
Baker Rd
- HarC 77338 3263 B4
100 HarC 77094 3955 A4
200 FBnC 77471 4490 C1
1600 HOUS 77094 3955 B4
2400 HOUS 77338 3263 B4
18600 BzaC 77546 4628 E3
18600 BzaC 77581 4628 E3
18600 FRDW 77546 4628 E3
18600 PRLD 77546 4628 E3
18900 FRDW 77546 4629 A3
E Baker Rd
900 BYTN 77521 3973 B2
W Baker Rd
100 BYTN 77521 3973 A2
300 BYTN 77521 3972 E2
4200 BYTN 77521 3971 E2
4300 BYTN 77520 3971 E2
Baker St
100 HMPD 77445 3098 C1
1100 HOUS 77002 3963 D3
Baker Tr
1900 HarC 77094 3955 A4
Baker Cemetery Rd
25200 MtgC 77355 2962 E4
Baker Cove St
10 PNPV 77024 3959 E3
Baker Downs
- BYTN 77521 3973 A2
Baker Hughes
- HarC 77073 3404 B3
- HOUS 77032 3404 B3
Bakerlake Dr
31100 MtgC 77386 2823 A7
31100 MtgC 77386 2969 A1
Baker Oaks Ct
1900 HarC 77094 3955 A4
Bakers Village Dr
17600 HarC 77095 3537 D4
17600 HarC 77433 3537 D4
Bakerswood Dr
3400 MtgC 77386 2969 D2
Bakerwood Dr
- HarC 77064 3540 A5
Bala Lake Ct
1200 HarC 77379 3255 C2
Balarama Dr
12900 HarC 77099 4237 C1
12900 HOUS 77099 4237 C1
Balbo St
4900 HOUS 77018 3683 B7
5600 HOUS 77091 3683 B5
Balboa Dr
4400 SGLD 77479 4496 A3
Balch Sprs
700 HarC 77373 3114 A4
Balcones Dr
3900 HOUS 77034 4247 A5
Balcones Pine St
19000 HarC 77433 3251 E7
Balcrest Dr
14200 HarC 77070 3399 B1
Baldcypress Blvd
- HarC 77082 4096 C2
Bald Cypress Ct
900 HarC 77073 3259 A3
Bald Eagle Ct
14100 HarC 77044 3549 D2
Baldinger St
200 HOUS 77011 4105 A1
400 HOUS 77011 4104 E1
Bald Mountain Cir
11900 HarC 77067 3401 E5
Bald Ridge Ln
10000 HarC 77095 3537 E3
Baldridge Ln
1400 FBnC 77494 3952 B5
Baldsprings Tr
1700 HOUS 77345 3120 D6
Baldswelle Dr
15500 HarC 77377 3254 E6
Baldwin Av
- BLAR 77401 4101 C6
Baldwin Cross
7400 SGLD 77479 4367 D6
Baldwin Ln
20400 MtgC 77365 2972 E4
20400 MtgC 77365 2973 A4
Baldwin St
1900 HOUS 77002 3963 A5
2400 HOUS 77006 3963 A6
Baldwin Elm St
5200 FBnC 77469 4234 D2
Baldwin Oaks St
20100 HarC 77449 3815 E2
Baldwin Square Dr
1400 HOUS 77077 3957 A4
Baldwin Square Ln
1400 HOUS 77077 3957 B4
Balearic Island Ct
- LGCY 77565 4633 D2
Balfour St
5300 HOUS 77028 3826 D4
Bal Harbor Dr
100 HarC 77532 3692 D2
Bal Harbour Dr
18000 HOUS 77058 4508 C4
18000 NSUB 77058 4508 C4
Balie Ln
8700 HarC 77338 3262 A4
Balinger Dr
8600 HarC 77064 3540 C5
Balkin St
4100 HOUS 77021 4103 D6
4900 HOUS 77021 4104 A6
Ball St
400 GLSN 77550 5109 A4
3500 HOUS 77003 3964 B4
3600 GLSN 77550 5108 E4
4500 GLSN 77551 5108 D4
Ballantine St
- HOUS 77075 4245 C7
9500 HOUS 77075 4376 C4
Ballantrae Ct
13600 HarC 77015 3828 E5
Ballantrae Ln
100 HarC 77015 3828 E5
Ballard Cir
100 CNRO 77304 2382 B1
Ballard Ct
2400 HarC 77388 3113 A3
Ballardvale Ln
12000 HarC 77067 3402 A4
Ballardwood Ct
900 HarC 77373 2968 E5
Ballast Rd
13500 HOUS 77044 3409 A5
Ballentine St
600 CmbC 77586 4509 E2
600 SEBK 77586 4509 E2
Balley Castle
16900 HarC 77070 3255 C4
Ballfour Park Ln
14000 HarC 77047 4374 D4
Ballina Ct
6300 HarC 77449 3676 E4
6300 HarC 77449 3677 A4
Ballina Dr
19600 HarC 77449 3676 E4
Ballina Canyon Ct
12300 HarC 77041 3679 E4
Ballina Canyon Ln
5600 HarC 77041 3679 D4
Ballina Ridge Ct
8300 FBnC 77083 4235 C2
Ballin David Dr
9500 HarC 77379 3255 C4
Ballinger Cir
10100 HarC 77064 3540 C6
Ballinger Ridge Ct
20000 FBnC 77469 4094 D2
Ballinger Ridge Ln
7000 FBnC 77469 4094 C5
Ballister
3300 HarC 77571 4112 D7
3300 HOUS 77571 4112 D7
3300 HOUS 77571 4252 C1
3300 MRGP 77571 4252 C1
Ball Park Ln
- HOUS 77040 3682 B3
Ballstonefield Ln
4600 FBnC 77494 4092 E2
Balmforth Ln
- HOUS 77035 4241 A3
9900 HOUS 77096 4240 E2
10300 HOUS 77096 4241 A3
Balmoral Ct
700 FRDW 77546 4629 C4
Balmoral Ln
3800 BzaC 77584 4501 D6
6100 LGCY 77573 4630 C6
11800 BKHV 77024 3959 B4
Balmoral Pl
10 WDLD 77382 2819 E1
Balmoral Glen Ln
20800 HarC 77449 3815 B7
Balmore Cir
13300 HarC 77069 3400 D1
13600 HarC 77069 3256 D7
Balmorhea Av
1200 HarC 77039 3545 B4
3600 HarC 77039 3546 A3
Balmorhea Dr
5200 PRLD 77584 4502 E7
5200 PRLD 77584 4503 A7
Balmorhea Ln
11800 FBnC 77478 4236 B6
Balsam Ln
9300 HOUS 77078 3688 A5
Balsam Breeze Ln
13000 PRLD 77584 4500 A1
Balsam Brook Ln
21600 FBnC 77450 4093 C6
21600 FBnC 77450 4094 C3
Balsam Crossing Ln
7700 HarC 77433 3537 A4
W Balsam Fir Cir
27200 MtgC 77386 3116 A2
Balsam Fir Ct
5400 MtgC 77386 3115 E2
5400 MtgC 77386 3116 A2
Balsam Fir Ln
4000 MtgC 77386 3115 C1
Balsam Lake Ct
13000 PRLD 77584 4500 A1
Balsam Lake Ln
2000 PRLD 77584 4500 A1
2100 LGCY 77573 4631 C7
Balsam Ridge Wy
2500 FBnC 77545 4498 C5
Balsam Spruce Cir
1700 CNRO 77301 2384 E6
Balthamwood Ln
11600 HarC 77377 3254 D4
Balthasar St
23300 HarC 77373 3115 C6
Baltic Av
29800 MtgC 77354 2818 A1
Baltic Dr
- HarC 77346 3264 B7
Baltic Ln
700 HarC 77090 3258 B2
Baltimore St
7600 HOUS 77012 4105 B1
Baltimore Ohio
25400 MtgC 77355 2963 A4
Baltrusol Dr
14000 HarC 77095 3539 B7
Baltzell Dr
7800 HarC 77389 2966 A4
8000 HarC 77389 2965 E3
Baltzell Rd
- MtgC 77362 2816 E5
300 SGCH 77362 2816 E5
Balvenie Ct
9300 HarC 77095 3538 C4
Balzar Dr
3100 DKSN 77539 4754 A1
Balzy Rd
3500 HOUS 77018 3822 E3
Bamaku Bnd
100 TKIS 77554 5106 A4
Bamar Ln
1000 GLSN 77554 5107 B6
Bambi Cir
10 HOUS 77336 3266 A1
Bambiwoods Ct
19700 HarC 77346 3264 D5
Bambiwoods Dr
19900 HarC 77346 3264 D4
Bamboo Dr
1400 TKIS 77554 5106 B4
Bamboo Rd
10000 HOUS 77041 3681 A6
10200 HarC 77041 3681 A6
Bamboo Forest Tr
12900 HarC 77044 3689 B5
Bambriar Dr
18100 HarC 77090 3258 A2
Bambridge Dr
18000 HarC 77090 3258 A2
18100 HarC 77090 3257 E1
Bambrook Ln
18000 HarC 77090 3257 E2
Bamcrest Dr
2000 HarC 77090 3258 A2
Bammel Ln
2700 HOUS 77019 3962 A7
2700 HOUS 77098 3962 A7
Bammel Rd
- HOUS 77014 3258 A5
- HOUS 77068 3258 A5
100 HarC 77090 3258 D3
100 HOUS 77090 3258 D3
300 HarC 77073 3258 E3
300 HarC 77073 3259 A3
2300 HOUS 77014 3257 C6
2300 HOUS 77068 3257 C7
2400 HarC 77014 3257 E5
Bammel Rd
2400 HarC 77068 3257 E5
Bammel Rd FM-1960
- HarC 77090 3258 A5
- HOUS 77014 3258 A5
- HOUS 77068 3258 A5
- HOUS 77090 3258 A5
2300 HOUS 77014 3257 C7
2300 HOUS 77068 3257 C7
2400 HarC 77014 3257 E5
2400 HarC 77068 3257 E5
Bammel Fields Ct
15400 HarC 77014 3257 E6
15400 HarC 77014 3258 A6
Bammel North Houston Rd
- HarC 77066 3542 B1
- HOUS 77086 3542 B3
10800 HarC 77086 3542 B2
11000 HarC 77066 3401 B7
13900 HarC 77014 3401 B7
15100 HarC 77014 3257 C7
Bammel Oaks Ct
15400 HarC 77014 3257 E6
Bammel Timbers Ln
2400 HarC 77068 3257 E5
Bammel Village Dr
15700 HarC 77014 3257 E5
15700 HarC 77014 3258 A5
15700 HOUS 77014 3257 E5
15700 HOUS 77068 3257 E5
Bammel Westfield Rd
100 HarC 77090 3258 D3
100 HOUS 77090 3258 D3
Bammelwood Dr
2300 HarC 77014 3258 A6
2300 HarC 77090 3258 A6
2800 HarC 77014 3257 E6
Bamore Rd
1100 RSBG 77471 4490 C5
3100 RSBG 77471 4614 D1
Bampton Dr
9300 HarC 77379 3255 D4
Bamwick Dr
2000 HarC 77090 3258 A2
Bamwood Rd
17000 HarC 77090 3258 A2
17000 HOUS 77090 3258 A2
Banana St
100 LMQU 77568 4990 C2
100 TXCY 77590 4990 C2
Banana Bend St
100 HarC 77562 3691 D6
Banbury Pl
3100 HOUS 77027 3961 B7
3400 HOUS 77027 4101 C1
Banchester Ct
12600 HarC 77070 3399 A5
Banchory Av
17000 HarC 77379 3255 D4
Bancock Ct
21000 MtgC 77355 2960 D1
Bancroft Ln
2000 HOUS 77027 3961 B6
Band Rd
1400 RSBG 77471 4614 D4
1500 FBnC 77471 4614 B6
2400 PLEK 77471 4614 C4
Bandelier Dr
2500 HOUS 77080 3820 B3
Bandell Dr
3000 HOUS 77045 4241 E6
3000 HOUS 77045 4242 A6
Bandera Dr
2000 BzaC 77583 4624 A3
2200 BzaC 77578 4624 B3
2200 PRLD 77578 4624 B3
2200 PRLD 77583 4624 B3
Bandera St
13400 HOUS 77015 3967 D1
13700 HarC 77015 3967 D1
14000 HarC 77015 3968 A1
Bandera Brook Ln
20900 FBnC 77469 4094 B5
Bandera Creek Ln
- HarC 77346 3408 B4
Bandera Falls Bnd
15200 HarC 77429 3253 D5
Bandera Hollow Ln
4200 HarC 77082 4096 A4
Bandera Run Ct
4500 PASD 77505 4248 B6
Bandera Valley Ct
11400 HarC 77089 4504 A1
Bandicoot Dr
16300 FBnC 77478 4235 E5
Bandit Trail Dr
11100 HarC 77095 3396 E7
11100 HarC 77095 3537 C1
Bandlon Dr
11000 HOUS 77072 4098 C4
Bandon Ln
700 HarC 77073 3403 B3
Bandridge Rd
8400 LPRT 77571 4249 D3
Bane Berry Dr
23000 HarC 77373 3114 D7
Baneberry Rd
22200 MtgC 77355 2960 A2
22200 MtgC 77447 2960 D3
22700 SGCH 77355 2960 C3
23600 MtgC 77355 2959 E2
23600 MtgC 77447 2959 E2
Baneway Dr
4300 HOUS 77072 4098 B4
Banff St
15400 HOUS 77062 4507 A1
Banff Mountain Tr
- HarC 77038 3543 A6
Banfield Ct
2100 FBnC 77469 4492 E3
10300 HOUS 77075 4377 A3
Bangle St
8100 HOUS 77012 4105 C4
Bangs St
10 HOUS 77076 3684 E5
Banister Cove
2100 FBnC 77494 3952 B5
Banjo St
7500 HOUS 77091 3684 B3
8400 HOUS 77088 3684 A2
Bank
11900 HarC 77044 3551 D7
N Bank Ct
3900 FBnC 77459 4621 D4
Bank Dr
200 GNPK 77547 3966 A6
Bank St
2900 DKSN 77539 4754 A2
N Bank Wy
9800 FBnC 77459 4621 E4
Bank Birch Pl
10 WDLD 77381 2674 D7
Bankers House Dr
19300 HarC 77449 3677 A4
Bank Field Ct
21700 HarC 77449 3815 A3
Bankford Dr
- HarC 77447 3249 D6
Banks St
1000 HOUS 77006 4102 D1
1600 HOUS 77098 4102 B1
19400 HOUS 77338 3262 A6
Banksfield Ct
3200 FBnC 77494 3953 A7
3200 FBnC 77494 4093 B1
Bank Shade Ct
22900 HarC 77375 2966 A7
Bankside Dr
7400 HOUS 77096 4240 A3
7600 HOUS 77071 4240 A4
7700 HOUS 77071 4239 E3
9100 HOUS 77031 4239 A3
Banks Ridge Ln
3800 HarC 77449 3815 A2
Banks Run Ct
- HarC 77449 3815 B2
Banks Run Dr
12000 PRLD 77584 4500 C1
Banks Run Ln
3500 HarC 77449 3815 B3
Banna Dr
1900 HarC 77090 3258 B6
Banneker Anding Dr
10700 HOUS 77016 3687 B3
Banner Dr
4000 HOUS 77013 3826 D6
4000 HOUS 77029 3826 D6
Banner Meadow Ln
20700 HarC 77433 3676 D2
Banner Ridge Ln
14700 HarC 77396 3547 E1
Banning Dr
4500 HOUS 77027 3961 B7
Banning Park Ct
4700 FBnC 77494 4092 E2
Banning Park Ln
26300 FBnC 77494 4092 E2
Banning Point Ct
23600 FBnC 77494 4093 C1
Bannister Ln
11200 HOUS 77076 3685 A3
Bannock St
7100 BYTN 77521 3835 B5
Bannon Field Ln
7400 FBnC 77469 4094 C6
Banquo Dr
22800 HarC 77373 3115 C6
Banta Dr
- HOUS 77053 4371 D5
6400 HOUS 77489 4371 D5
Bantam Brook Ln
4900 HarC 77066 3401 B4
Bantam Ridge Ct
16100 HOUS 77053 4372 A6
16300 HOUS 77053 4371 E7
N Bantam Woods Cir
10 WDLD 77382 2819 D1
S Bantam Woods Cir
10 WDLD 77382 2819 D1
Bantam Woods Dr
100 WDLD 77382 2819 D1
Banter Trails Ct
15400 HarC 77049 3829 A4
Banter Trails Dr
300 HarC 77049 3829 A4
Banting St
8400 HOUS 77078 3688 B7
Banton Dr
700 HarC 77530 3830 A7
Bantry Meadow Dr
1200 HarC 77060 3403 E4
Bantum St
10400 HOUS 77093 3685 E4
Banty Falls Ct
15500 HarC 77068 3257 C4
Banyan St
6900 HOUS 77028 3825 E2
7200 HOUS 77028 3826 A2
Banyan Crest Ln
20800 HarC 77449 3815 C2
Banyan Wood Wy
3700 PRLD 77584 4502 D6
Banzer St
8700 HOUS 77055 3821 A6
Baptist St
200 STAF 77477 4370 A3
Baptist Encampment Rd
20500 MtgC 77357 2828 D7
20800 MtgC 77357 2974 D2
E Bar Dr
12500 STFE 77510 4871 A7
Barabin St
- HOUS 77045 4372 B2
Barada St
10300 HOUS 77034 4246 D7
Barajas Ln
1000 HarC 77039 3545 A1
Barany Ct
6000 HarC 77449 3677 B5
Barataria Ct
4100 GLSN 77554 5332 E3
Barazi Oaks Ct
10 BKHV 77024 3959 D3
10 PNPV 77024 3959 D3
Barbados Cl
500 DKSN 77539 4633 C7
Barbados Dr
6600 HOUS 77088 3542 B7
Barbados Wy
16500 GLSN 77554 5331 E4
16500 JMAB 77554 5331 E4
E Barbara Cir
15300 MSCY 77071 4239 E7
W Barbara Cir
15400 HOUS 77071 4239 D7
15400 MSCY 77071 4239 D7
Barbara Ct
- LPRT 77571 4250 E1
1800 DRPK 77536 4109 D5
Barbara Ln
500 CNRO 77301 2384 D5
1700 PASD 77502 4107 D7
2600 HOUS 77030 4102 A3
2600 WUNP 77005 4102 A3
15900 MtgC 77355 2961 E3
15900 SGCH 77355 2961 E3
Barbara St
700 TMBL 77375 3109 B1
800 TMBL 77375 2964 A7
1300 HarC 77562 3832 B2
37100 MtgC 77355 2816 A2
Barbara Mae Blvd
500 HarC 77015 3829 A7
700 HarC 77015 3968 A2
Barbarella Ct
6600 HOUS 77088 3682 C1
Barbarossa Dr
15100 FBnC 77083 4096 B7
Barbee Ln
400 ALVN 77511 4867 A1
Barbee St
1500 HOUS 77004 4103 A1
Barber Rd
- MTBL 77520 3696 C3
Barber St
400 HOUS 77007 3962 C3
Barber Grove Ln
15600 HarC 77095 3538 D5
Barberry Ct
3300 PRLD 77581 4503 D1
Barberry Dr
3800 HOUS 77051 4243 C5
5600 HarC 77521 3833 D2
Barberry Ln
400 BYTN 77520 3832 B7
Barbers Ct
12800 MSCY 77071 4239 C7
Barbers Hill Rd
100 HarC 77562 3692 E6
600 HarC 77532 3693 A6
600 HarC 77562 3693 A6
3600 HarC 77532 3694 A6
3600 HarC 77562 3694 A6
5200 HarC 77521 3694 A6
Barberton Dr
7400 HOUS 77036 4099 D6
Barbetta Ct
100 LGCY 77573 4633 A1
Barbil Ln
100 HOUS 77336 3121 D4
Barbizon Dr
12600 HOUS 77089 4378 C7
Barbons Heath Ct
20900 HarC 77449 3815 B6
E Barbours Cut Blvd
- LPRT 77571 4252 A1
10 LPRT 77571 4251 E1
10 MRGP 77571 4251 E1
1000 MRGP 77571 4252 A1
2000 HOUS 77571 4252 A1
W Barbours Cut Blvd
100 LPRT 77571 4251 C1
100 MRGP 77571 4251 D1
Barbstone Dr
13300 HarC 77044 3549 D2
Barbuda Dr
- HarC 77338 3260 C3
Barbuda Ln
18000 HOUS 77058 4507 E5
18100 NSUB 77058 4507 E5
18300 NSUB 77058 4508 A6
Barcan Cir
21700 HarC 77450 3954 B5
Barcarole Dr
21300 HarC 77388 3112 D3
Barcelona E
12800 GLSN 77554 5220 B7
Barcelona Ct
10 MSCY 77459 4369 E7
700 BYTN 77520 3973 B5
Barcelona Dr
16100 FRDW 77546 4505 E7
16600 FRDW 77546 4506 A7
16600 FRDW 77546 4630 A1
Barcelona Wy
- LGCY 77573 4632 A7
1500 BYTN 77520 3973 B5
Barco Ct
4000 MtgC 77386 2970 C7
4000 MtgC 77386 3115 C1
Barcus Ln
12900 HOUS 77015 3967 B2
Bardet St
5900 PRLD 77584 4502 D4
N Bardsbrook Cir
10 WDLD 77382 2819 A2
S Bardsbrook Cir
10 WDLD 77382 2819 A2
Bardwell St
1100 HOUS 77009 3824 D7
Bardwell Lake Ct
1500 FBnC 77469 4234 D4
Bar E Bar N
700 GlsC 77511 4869 A5
Bar E Bar S
900 GlsC 77511 4869 A6
Bare Branch Ln
18100 HarC 77433 3537 D6
Barefoot Ests
- BYTN 77520 3973 C4
Barely Ln
10700 HarC 77070 3399 A7
10800 HarC 77065 3399 A7
Barely Rose Ct
21700 HarC 77433 3250 E3
Bare Meadow Ln
18500 HarC 77449 3677 C4
Barents Dr
- HarC 77346 3264 B7
- HarC 77346 3408 A1
Bare Oak St
3000 HarC 77082 4096 C2
Bare Sky
- HarC 77095 3538 C3
Bare Sky Dr
- PRLD 77584 4500 D2
Barge Wy
16100 HarC 77532 3552 A3
Barger Rd
9600 HOUS 77074 4239 B2
Barger St
1900 LGCY 77573 4632 B1
Bar Harbor Ct
- HarC 77532 3552 B3
Baristone Ln
7000 FBnC 77469 4094 A5
Bark Ln
13000 HarC 77015 3828 C6
Barkaby St
9300 HOUS 77075 4376 C1
Barkaloo Rd
3700 BYTN 77521 3973 B1
4200 HarC 77521 3973 B2
5000 BYTN 77521 3834 B7

STREET
Block City ZIP Map# Grid
Barkaloo Rd
5900 HarC 77521 3834 A5
Bar Kay Ln
24000 HarC 77447 3249 E4
Bark Bend Pl
- WDLD 77385 2676 B4
Barkdull St
900 HOUS 77006 4102 D1
Barkentine Ln
16700 HarC 77546 4506 B5
Barker Dr
8700 HarC 77044 3688 E5
N Barker Dr
17300 HarC 77084 3677 E2
17300 HarC 77084 3678 A2
Barker St
1000 FBnC 77477 4369 E6
1000 MSCY 77477 4369 E6
1600 ALVN 77511 4866 E3
Barker 1 St
700 PTVL 77372 2682 E7
Barker 2 St
17200 PTVL 77372 2682 E7
Barker Bayou Pt
14200 HarC 77429 3396 E2
Barker Bend Ct
20500 HarC 77449 3676 D2
Barker Bend Ln
- FBnC 77494 4092 B1
6600 HarC 77449 3676 D2
Barker Bluff Ln
17700 HarC 77433 3537 C1
Barker Canyon Ln
21000 FBnC 77450 4094 B5
Barker Clodine Rd
- HOUS 77094 4095 D2
200 HarC 77094 3955 D4
200 HOUS 77094 3955 D4
Barker Cypress
- HarC 77429 3252 E7
Barker Cypress Rd
- HarC 77095 3396 E6
- HarC 77433 3396 E6
- HOUS 77094 3955 D1
300 HarC 77094 3955 D2
1000 HOUS 77084 3816 D7
1000 HOUS 77084 3955 D1
2400 HarC 77084 3816 D2
4300 HarC 77084 3677 D7
5500 HarC 77449 3677 D4
6900 HarC 77095 3677 D4
6900 HarC 77433 3677 D4
7600 HarC 77433 3537 D6
10200 HarC 77095 3537 D1
13000 HarC 77429 3396 E4
14100 HarC 77429 3397 A2
14900 HarC 77429 3252 E7
S Barker Cypress Rd
- FBnC 77082 4095 D4
- FBnC 77083 4095 D4
- FBnC 77469 4095 D4
- HOUS 77469 4095 D4
3500 HOUS 77082 4095 D3
3500 HOUS 77094 4095 D3
3500 HOUS 77450 4095 D3
S Barker Cypress Rd FM-1464
- FBnC 77082 4095 D4
- FBnC 77083 4095 D4
- FBnC 77469 4095 D4
- HOUS 77082 4095 D4
- HOUS 77469 4095 D4
Barker-Cypress Access Rd
- HarC 77094 3955 D1
- HOUS 77094 3955 D1
Barker Gate Ct
10700 HarC 77433 3396 D7
10700 HarC 77433 3537 D1
Barker Grove Ct
17700 HarC 77433 3396 C7
Barker Grove Dr
- HarC 77433 3537 D1
Barker Grove Ln
10900 HarC 77433 3537 D1
11000 HarC 77433 3396 E7
Barker Lake Ct
10700 HarC 77433 3537 C1
Barker Levy Ct
- HarC 77429 3396 E5
- HarC 77429 3397 A5
Barker Marsh Dr
16500 HarC 77429 3396 D1
Barkermist Ln
6100 FBnC 77450 4094 A4
Barker Oaks Dr
- HOUS 77077 3956 D7
- HOUS 77082 3956 D7
Barker Park Ct
11100 HarC 77433 3396 D7
Barker Pelican Ct
14400 HarC 77429 3396 E1
Barker Ranch Ct
16500 HarC 77429 3396 E1
Barker Ridge Ct
10 WDLD 77382 2819 A3
Barkers Branch Dr
18400 HarC 77084 3816 D2
Barkers Cove
500 HOUS 77079 3956 E2
Barkers Crest Dr
18200 HarC 77084 3816 D3
Barkers Crossing Av
3000 HarC 77084 3816 E4
3000 HOUS 77084 3816 E4
Barkers Forest Ln
3200 HarC 77084 3816 C3
Barkers Green Wy
18200 HarC 77084 3816 E4
Barkers Landing Ct
400 HOUS 77079 3956 C1
Barkers Landing Rd
- HOUS 77079 3957 A1
15600 HOUS 77079 3956 E1
N Barkers Landing Rd
15800 HOUS 77079 3956 E1
S Barkers Landing Rd
15800 HOUS 77079 3956 D1
Barkers Point Ln
16000 HOUS 77079 3956 D2
Barker Springs Rd
16600 HOUS 77084 3955 E1
16600 HOUS 77084 3956 A1
Barkers Wood Ln
3000 HarC 77084 3816 D4
Barker Trace Dr
- HarC 77433 3396 E7
Barkerview Ct
14100 HarC 77084 3679 B5
Barker View Dr
10700 HarC 77433 3537 D1
10800 HarC 77433 3396 C7
Barker Village Ct
18600 HarC 77449 3677 D6
Barker Village Ln
6400 HarC 77449 3677 C3
Barker West Dr
11100 HarC 77433 3396 D7
Barklea Rd
16100 HarC 77429 3396 E1
16100 HarC 77429 3397 A1
Barkley St
900 HOUS 77022 3823 E2
4900 HOUS 77017 4106 A7
8000 HOUS 77017 4245 E1
8300 HOUS 77017 4246 A1
Barkley Park Ct
10 WDLD 77384 2675 C5
Barkly Ct
1100 PRLD 77581 4376 D6
Bark Ridge Ln
9700 HarC 77095 3537 E4
Barksdale Dr
2900 HOUS 77093 3686 A2
40000 MtgC 77354 2671 B3
Barksdale Rd
10300 MtgC 77354 2672 A3
Barkshire Dr
- HarC 77014 3402 C3
Barkston Ct
20600 HarC 77450 3954 D3
Barkston Dr
1000 HarC 77450 3954 D3
Barkwith Ln
- HarC 77530 3829 C6
Barkwood St
10 CNRO 77304 2383 C3
200 HOUS 77018 3684 C7
200 HOUS 77022 3684 C7
Barleton Wy
1700 HOUS 77058 4507 E2
Barley Ln
- HarC 77065 3399 A7
- HarC 77070 3399 A7
Barley St
5800 KATY 77494 3952 B1
Barleycorn Ln
- FBnC 77494 4092 D4
Barley Hall St
10 WDLD 77382 2820 B2
Barley Mill Ct
16600 HarC 77095 3538 B6
Barlow Ct
10 WDLD 77382 2819 A2
Barlow St
8200 HOUS 77028 3826 C4
Barlow Bend Ln
5100 FBnC 77450 4093 E3
Barmby Ct
8400 HarC 77389 2965 E3
Barmby Dr
24900 HarC 77389 2965 E3
25000 HarC 77375 2965 E3
Barmont Dr
9700 LPRT 77571 4250 A4
Barnacle Dr
16800 HarC 77532 3552 B2
Barn Course Dr
13000 FBnC 77469 4366 D1
Barnes Ln
3300 BzaC 77583 4500 E7
Barnes St
300 BYTN 77520 3971 C4
3800 HOUS 77007 3962 C3
Barnes Ridge Ln
7900 HarC 77072 4097 C7
Barnesville Dr
700 HarC 77530 3829 E7
Barnesworth Dr
13200 HOUS 77049 3828 A3
Barnett Rdg
6200 FBnC 77479 4367 B5
Barnett St
3800 HOUS 77017 4105 C7
27900 MtgC 77357 2829 E4
N Barnett St
26600 SGCH 77355 2961 B2
S Barnett St
22500 SGCH 77355 2961 B2
N Barnett Wy
3900 FBnC 77459 4621 D4
S Barnett Wy
3700 FBnC 77459 4621 D5
Barney
- HarC 77562 3831 E4
Barney Ln
6000 FBnC 77583 4622 D5
Barney Rd
6600 HOUS 77092 3821 C1
Barngate Ct
16100 HarC 77429 3397 A1
Barnham St
10600 HOUS 77016 3686 D3
Barnhart Blvd
13900 HOUS 77077 3957 A5
14100 HOUS 77077 3956 E6
Barnhill Dr
7800 HarC 77338 3261 D5
Barnhill Ln
2900 SGLD 77479 4495 D1
Barn Lantern Pl
10 WDLD 77382 2674 C5
Barn Red Ct
14300 HarC 77429 3395 E1
Barnsford Ln
9200 HarC 77375 3110 D3
Barnsley Ln
1900 HarC 77088 3543 D6
Barnstable Ct
10500 HarC 77379 3110 A7
Barnstable Pl
10 WDLD 77381 2820 D3
Barnston St
6000 HOUS 77026 3825 A3
Barnwell Dr
4100 HarC 77082 4096 C4
Barometer Dr
- HarC 77532 3552 B1
Barometer Close
10 GLSN 77554 5221 C2
Barometr Bend Dr
13400 HOUS 77044 3409 A5
Baron Ln
10 MSCY 77459 4369 D7
4200 DRPK 77536 4249 B1
W Baron Ln
10 MSCY 77459 4369 D7
Baron Rd
4500 BYTN 77521 3972 C1
Baron St
3200 HOUS 77020 3964 B3
Barona Ln
- LGCY 77573 4633 A5
Baron Bend Ln
20400 HarC 77449 3676 D2
Baron Brook Ct
- HarC 77044 3549 D2
Baron Brook Dr
20100 HarC 77433 3676 E1
Baronbrook Ln
13800 HarC 77044 3549 E3
Baron Brook Wy
- HarC 77429 3252 B7
Baron Cove Ln
22200 FBnC 77450 4093 E3
Baron Creek Ln
14300 HOUS 77044 3550 A2
Baroneal Dr
600 HOUS 77338 3263 D5
Baronet Woods Ct
10 WDLD 77382 2819 D2
Baron Gate Ct
6800 HarC 77379 3111 C2
Barongate Ct
10 WDLD 77382 2674 D4
Baron Grove Dr
- HOUS 77345 3120 E6
Baron Hill Ln
6000 FBnC 77479 4493 E3
6000 FBnC 77479 4494 A3
13200 BzaC 77583 4623 E4
13200 BzaC 77583 4624 A4
Baron Hollow Ct
13100 HarC 77014 3402 A1
Baronial Cir
10 WDLD 77382 2673 D7
Baron Oaks Ct
5500 HarC 77069 3256 C7
Baron Oaks Dr
14200 HarC 77069 3256 C7
Baron Ridge Dr
- BYTN 77520 3835 B5
- BYTN 77521 3835 B5
Baronridge Dr
600 TYLV 77586 4508 D1
1000 TYLV 77586 4381 D7
Baron Ridge Ln
- HarC 77095 3537 D5
5500 FBnC 77494 4093 B7
Barons Gln
1900 SGLD 77478 4368 D5
Barons Pl
10 CNRO 77304 2529 D1
Barons Bridge Dr
13700 HarC 77069 3256 C7
Barons Cove
5200 HarC 77041 3679 D7
Barons Cove Ct
2700 PRLD 77584 4500 B4
Barons Cove Ln
13200 PRLD 77584 4500 A3
13300 PRLD 77584 4499 E3
Baronsgate Ln
3000 LGCY 77539 4752 D5
Baronshire Dr
17200 HarC 77070 3255 C4
Baronshire Round
9900 HarC 77070 3255 B4
Barons Lake Ln
13500 HarC 77429 3254 A5
Baronsledge Ln
20800 HarC 77449 3815 C2
Baronsmede Dr
9200 HarC 77083 4237 C1
Baron Trace Ln
5300 FBnC 77494 4093 C2
Barque Ln
10 GLSN 77554 5221 C2
Bar R Blvd
34000 MtgC 77355 2668 A7
Barr Cir
9200 HOUS 77080 3820 D4
Barr St
2000 HOUS 77080 3820 D4
Barracuda Av
100 GLSN 77550 5109 E1
Barracuda Ct
10 HOUS 77024 3959 B2
Barracuda Dr
8900 TXCY 77591 4873 A3
9100 TXCY 77591 4872 E3
Barracuda Ln
3800 LPRT 77571 4383 A2
3800 PASD 77571 4383 A2
Barracuda St
- GlsC 77563 4990 E6
200 BYUV 77563 4990 D7
Barranca Dr
13200 HarC 77083 4237 B1
Barras St
1400 ALVN 77511 4749 B6
1400 BzaC 77511 4749 B6
Barraud Ct
1500 HarC 77449 3815 A6
3700 HarC 77082 4096 B3
Barrel Hoop Cir
3900 SGLD 77479 4495 E1
Barrell Rd
600 ALVN 77511 4749 C2
Barrell Springs Ln
22400 HarC 77375 3109 E1
Barremore St
5500 HOUS 77023 4104 C2
Barren Wy
8700 HarC 77064 3541 C5
Barren Springs Dr
200 HarC 77090 3258 D7
Barret St
100 GlsC 77650 4994 D2
Barrett Ct
4600 SGLD 77479 4495 C4
Barrett Rd
100 HarC 77532 3692 D2
Barrett St
700 RHMD 77469 4492 A1
5200 HOUS 77022 3684 E6
5400 HOUS 77076 3684 E6
Barretta Dr
100 CNRO 77301 2384 B7
100 CNRO 77301 2530 B1
Barrett Brae Dr
11900 HOUS 77072 4098 A7
12100 HOUS 77072 4097 E7
Barrett Creek Ln
- FBnC 77469 4094 A7
Barrett Post Ln
16600 HarC 77095 3538 A3
Barrett Ridge Dr
- FBnC 77469 4365 B6
Barrett Ridge Ln
- HOUS 77044 3550 A2
Barretts Crossing Dr
16900 HarC 77379 3256 C3
Barretts Glen Ct
9500 HarC 77065 3539 D5
Barretts Glen Dr
1800 PRLD 77581 4504 B6
Barr Forest Dr
12400 HarC 77346 3408 C1
Barrier Ct
- BYTN 77521 3973 D3
Barringer Ln
500 HOUS 77598 4506 D2
Barrington Cir
9200 FBnC 77459 4621 D5
Barrington Ct
2600 SGLD 77478 4237 C4
3500 PRLD 77584 4503 B6
Barrington Gdn
6600 HarC 77069 3400 B2
Barrington Grn
6600 HarC 77069 3400 B2
Barrington Rd
3300 HOUS 77056 4100 E1
Barrington Wy
- FBnC 77459 4621 D5
- PRLD 77584 4503 B6
Barrington Fairway
13800 HarC 77069 3400 D3
Barrington Hills Ln
1600 HarC 77450 3953 E5
Barrington Pl Dr
2100 SGLD 77478 4237 C4
2600 HOUS 77099 4237 C4
2600 HOUS 77478 4237 C4
Barrington Pointe Ct
100 LGCY 77573 4509 A7
Barrington Pointe Dr
2000 LGCY 77573 4509 A7
Barrister Ct
12500 HOUS 77071 4239 B7
Barrister Creek Dr
22900 HarC 77377 2962 E7
Barr Lake Dr
9900 HarC 77095 3538 E3
Barron St
10 HarC 77530 3969 B1
Barrone Dr
14100 HarC 77429 3397 E7
Barronett Bnd
1900 SGLD 77478 4237 C5
Barronton Dr
6600 HarC 77389 2966 C6
Barron Wood Cir W
8700 HarC 77083 4237 A1
E Barron Wood Cir
8500 HarC 77083 4237 A1
Barrow Ln
11100 HarC 77065 3539 C1
11700 HarC 77065 3398 C7
Barrow St
- MTBL 77520 3696 D5
Barrow Cove Dr
15800 HarC 77429 3397 C3
Barrow Downs Wy
300 HOUS 77034 4378 D5
Barrowgate Dr
1100 SGLD 77478 4237 B6
Barrowhollow Dr
9200 HarC 77083 4237 B1
Barrow Point Ln
13200 HarC 77014 3402 A2
Barrow Ridge Ln
4200 HarC 77082 4096 C3
Barr Spring Dr
9600 HarC 77396 3407 B2
Barry Av
7800 HTCK 77563 4988 E4
Barry Ln
18700 HarC 77346 3264 D6
31800 HarC 77484 3103 B3
Barry St
7000 HTCK 77563 4988 D4
Barrybrook Ln
8500 LPRT 77571 4249 C4
Barrycliff Ct
12000 HarC 77070 3399 C6
Barry Estate Ct
1500 HarC 77493 3814 A6
Barry Estate Dr
1500 HarC 77493 3814 A6
Barrygate Cir
22200 HarC 77373 3261 B1
Barrygate Ct
22200 HarC 77373 3261 B1
Barrygate Dr
6400 HarC 77373 3261 A1
Barryknoll Ct
800 HOUS 77079 3958 B1
Barryknoll Ln
11800 HDWV 77024 3959 C1
11800 HOUS 77024 3959 B1
12600 HOUS 77024 3958 E2
13300 HOUS 77079 3958 A2
14700 HOUS 77079 3957 C1
Barry Moore Dr
3200 PRLD 77581 4503 D5
Barrymore Blvd
700 BYTN 77520 4112 C2
Barry Oaks Ln
8600 LPRT 77571 4249 D4
Barry Rose Rd
1900 PRLD 77581 4503 E2
1900 PRLD 77581 4504 A2
Barrys Ct
11100 HarC 77041 3680 B1
Barrys Wy
24500 HOUS 77336 3266 C2
Barrytree Dr
12000 HarC 77070 3399 C6
Barstow St
23600 HarC 77389 2966 E5
23800 HarC 77389 2967 A5
Barstow Bend Ln
4900 HarC 77449 3677 A6
Bart Ln
8500 HarC 77040 3681 C1
S Bartell Dr
2800 HOUS 77054 4242 A1
W Bartell Dr
8400 HOUS 77054 4242 A1
Bartle St
100 CNRO 77301 2384 D3
Bartlett Dr
1200 HarC 77067 3402 C5
Bartlett Rd
1500 KATY 77493 3813 A6
1500 WlrC 77493 3813 A6
2500 WlrC 77493 3812 E5
27900 KATY 77493 3951 D1
27900 KATY 77494 3951 D1
27900 WlrC 77493 3951 D1
27900 WlrC 77494 3951 D1
Bartlett St
- KATY 77494 3952 B1
800 KATY 77493 3952 B1
900 HOUS 77006 4102 D1
900 KATY 77493 3813 B7
2100 HOUS 77098 4102 B1
Bartlett Bend Dr
300 HarC 77562 3831 E1
Bartlett Harbour Ct
8500 HOUS 77040 3682 B3
Bartlett Landing Dr
15200 HarC 77433 3251 E6
Bartlett Pear Ct
15500 HarC 77049 3829 A1
Barton Av
8800 HOUS 77075 4245 E6
8800 HOUS 77075 4246 A6
Barton Ct
2500 LGCY 77573 4631 B5
2900 BzaC 77584 4501 B6
2900 LPRT 77571 4249 E4
Barton Dr
3000 BzaC 77584 4501 B6
Barton St
5600 HOUS 77028 3826 B3
Barton Creek Ct
20000 HarC 77450 3954 C4
Barton Creek Dr
- FBnC 77494 3953 B4
2100 PRLD 77584 4500 C2
5100 PASD 77505 4249 A7
Barton Creek Tr
1600 HarC 77450 3954 E5
Barton Falls
5600 HarC 77041 3679 E6
Barton Grove Ct
2600 FBnC 77479 4493 E3
Barton Grove Ln
14700 HarC 77396 3548 A1
Barton Hills Ct
2600 HarC 77014 3402 A2
Barton Hollow Ct
- FBnC 77469 4094 A7
Barton Hollow Ln
- FBnC 77469 4094 A7
6300 HarC 77449 3677 D4
Barton Lake Ct
7400 FBnC 77469 4093 D6
Barton Meadow Ct
13600 BzaC 77583 4623 E4
Barton Meadow Ln
2800 FBnC 77494 3953 B6
13200 BzaC 77583 4623 E4
13200 BzaC 77583 4624 A4
Barton Oaks Ct
17000 HarC 77095 3678 C3
Barton Oaks Dr
7200 HarC 77095 3678 A1
Barton Park Ln
21800 FBnC 77450 4094 C2
Barton Point Ln
17600 FBnC 77469 4095 D7
Barton Ridge Ln
17900 FBnC 77469 4095 C6
Barton River Ct
2300 FBnC 77469 4493 A3
Barton River Ln
- HarC 77044 3549 D3
Bartons Ct
3900 SGLD 77479 4496 A1
Bartons Ln
3600 SGLD 77479 4495 E2
3800 SGLD 77479 4496 A3
Barton Shores Dr
2400 PRLD 77545 4499 E3
Barton Springs Ln
- HarC 77346 3408 C3
Barton Springs St
2500 LGCY 77573 4632 D3
Bartrum Tr
1600 SGLD 77479 4367 C7
Baruna
- HOUS 77072 4097 E6
Barwick Dr
19500 HarC 77373 3113 E6
Barwood Dr
10200 HOUS 77043 3819 E5
Barwood St
3200 MtgC 77380 2967 B4
Barwood Bend Dr
11300 HarC 77065 3398 B7
11800 HarC 77429 3398 B6
Barziza St
400 HOUS 77011 3964 D7
Basal Briar Ct
10 WDLD 77381 2821 A6
Basalt Dr
4700 BYTN 77521 3833 C3
Basalt Ln
14400 HOUS 77077 3956 E3
Bascom St
8400 HOUS 77055 3821 B2
8400 HOUS 77080 3821 B2
Base
- MtgC 77302 2678 D5
Basewood Ct
16800 FBnC 77478 4235 E7
Bash Pl
10 HOUS 77027 3961 C7
10 HOUS 77027 4101 C1
Bashaw Dr
30000 MtgC 77386 2969 A2
Bashforth Dr
- HOUS 77089 4378 B7
- HOUS 77089 4505 B1
Basil Ct
3900 PRLD 77584 4502 D7
Basil Ln
7500 HOUS 77036 4098 E6
Basil St
4100 HOUS 77003 3964 B5
Basil Wy
6200 HarC 77532 3552 C3
Basilan Ln
1300 NSUB 77058 4507 E5
Basil Crest Ln
- PRLD 77581 4503 D2
N Basildon Ct
21100 HarC 77073 3259 B6
Basilica St
11700 HOUS 77099 4238 A3
Basin Dr
- JMAB 77554 5331 E5
Basin St
100 HOUS 77365 2974 E6
100 HOUS 77365 2975 A7
1600 HOUS 77011 3965 B6
Basket St
2000 PASD 77502 4107 B7
2100 PASD 77502 4247 B1
Basket Flower Dr
20000 HarC 77375 3110 C5
20000 HarC 77379 3110 C5
Basket Oak Dr
24100 HOUS 77336 3266 D2
Baskin Dr
- MtgC 77355 2962 C3
Basking Dr
- HOUS 77080 3820 A6
Baskove Dr
8800 HarC 77088 3542 B7
Baslow Dr
5400 HarC 77449 3676 E6
Bass Ct
1500 HOUS 77007 3962 C2
Bass St
1600 HOUS 77007 3962 C2
Bassbrook Dr
21300 HarC 77388 3112 E3
Bassdale Dr
11300 HarC 77070 3254 E7
11300 HarC 77070 3255 A7
Basselford Dr
9600 HarC 77083 4237 C2
Bassetdale Ln
6000 HarC 77084 3678 C4
Bassett Ct
3500 FBnC 77459 4621 D5
Bassett St
8100 HOUS 77051 4243 A2
Bassett Hall Ln
24100 HarC 77493 3814 B6
Bassfield Ln
26100 FBnC 77494 4092 D1
Bassford Dr
13000 HarC 77099 4237 C2
13200 HarC 77083 4237 B2
Bassingham Dr
2900 HOUS 77339 3119 B3
Bassoon Dr
9100 HOUS 77025 4101 C7
9200 HOUS 77025 4241 C1
Bass Point Wy
9400 HarC 77396 3407 A6
Bass Pro Dr
- KATY 77494 3952 D2
Basswood Dr
- LGCY 77573 4630 B6
200 MtgC 77386 2822 C7
Basswood Ln
- PRLD 77584 4501 E4
4400 BLAR 77401 4101 B3
Basswood St
300 HOUS 77022 3824 B2
Basswood Dale Dr
5500 HarC 77084 3677 D5
5700 HarC 77449 3677 D5
Basswood Forest Ct
7500 HarC 77095 3538 B2
Basswood Springs Ct
1400 HOUS 77062 4379 D7
Bast Ln
8500 HOUS 77078 3688 B6
Bastian St
7300 HOUS 77033 4243 D1
Bastogne Rd
7300 HOUS 77033 4243 D1
Bastrop Av
1300 HOUS 77017 4106 D6
1300 PASD 77506 4106 D6
Bastrop Ln
30600 MtgC 77355 2815 C1
Bastrop St
2300 HOUS 77003 3963 C7
2300 HOUS 77004 3963 C7
3500 HOUS 77004 4103 B1
N Bastrop St
10 HOUS 77002 3963 E4
10 HOUS 77003 3963 E4
Bataan Dr
2500 LGCY 77573 4631 B7
Bataan Rd
4900 HOUS 77033 4103 E7
4900 HOUS 77033 4243 E1
5100 HOUS 77033 4104 A7
Bateau Ct
11300 HarC 77429 3397 E7
Bateau Dr
14100 HarC 77429 3397 E7
14100 HarC 77429 3538 D1
Bateman Blvd
8800 BzaC 77583 4744 C4
Bateman Ln
7700 HOUS 77088 3682 D2
Bates Av
1300 HOUS 77030 4102 D4
Bates Ln
12600 STAF 77477 4238 E7
12700 STAF 77477 4369 E1
Bates Rd
25200 MtgC 77372 2536 E4
25200 MtgC 77372 2537 A4
Bates St
400 TXCY 77591 4873 E6
1100 HOUS 77030 4102 C4
N Bates St
200 ALVN 77511 4867 C1
Batesbrooke Ct
10 WDLD 77381 2820 C3
Bateswood Dr
700 HOUS 77079 3957 E3
W Bath St
- CmbC 77586 4509 D4
100 SEBK 77586 4509 D4
Bathgate Ln
5200 HarC 77084 3678 D6
Bathurst Dr
14200 HOUS 77045 4372 D2
14800 HOUS 77053 4372 E4
15100 HarC 77053 4372 E4
Bathurst Ln
3000 HarC 77014 3257 E6
Bating Hllw
12000 HOUS 77024 3959 B5
Baton Pass
19100 HarC 77346 3265 C6
Baton Rouge St
4600 HOUS 77028 3825 C3
Batson
- HarC 77049 3691 B2
Batten Wy
500 HarC 77532 3411 B7
Batter Sea Gardens Dr
15300 HarC 77530 3829 D4
Batterson St
6000 HOUS 77026 3824 E3
Battle
3200 HarC 77562 3692 D5
Battlebell Rd
100 HarC 77562 3831 E3
1500 HarC 77562 3832 C3
2700 HarC 77521 3832 E3
3200 HarC 77521 3833 B3
N Battlebell Rd
1100 HarC 77562 3832 B3
Battle Creek Dr
3300 MSCY 77459 4496 B3
Battlecreek Dr
7600 HarC 77040 3682 A1
7600 HOUS 77040 3682 A1
7800 HarC 77040 3681 E1
16500 HarC 77095 3538 B6
Battleground Rd
- DRPK 77536 4109 E4
- HarC 77536 4109 E4
- HarC 77571 4109 E4
200 DRPK 77536 4110 A3
200 DRPK 77571 4110 A3
200 HarC 77536 4110 A3
200 HarC 77571 4110 A3
1700 DRPK 77536 3970 A7
1700 HarC 77536 3970 A7
1700 HarC 77571 3970 A7
2200 DRPK 77571 3970 A7
2200 HOUS 77571 3970 A7
Battleground Rd SR-134
- DRPK 77536 4109 E4
- HarC 77536 4109 E4
- HarC 77571 4109 E4
200 DRPK 77536 4110 A3
200 DRPK 77571 4110 A3
200 HarC 77536 4110 A3
200 HarC 77571 4110 A3
1700 DRPK 77536 3970 A7
1700 HarC 77536 3970 A7
1700 HarC 77571 3970 A7
2200 DRPK 77571 3970 A7
2200 HOUS 77571 3970 A7
S Battleground Rd
- DRPK 77571 4109 E5
- DRPK 77571 4110 A6
- HarC 77571 4109 E5
- LPRT 77571 4110 A6
2200 DRPK 77536 4109 E5
2300 DRPK 77536 4110 A6
Battle Hills Dr
7200 HarC 77040 3681 D1
Battleoak Dr
7600 HarC 77040 3682 A1
7600 HOUS 77040 3682 A1
8200 HarC 77040 3681 D1
Battlepine Ct
7500 HOUS 77040 3682 A1
Battlepine Dr
7600 HarC 77040 3682 A1
7600 HOUS 77040 3682 A1
7800 HarC 77040 3681 E1
Battle Plains Dr
8400 HarC 77040 3681 D1
Battle Ridge Ln
3100 SGLD 77479 4495 E2
Battleview Ln
300 LPRT 77571 4251 A2
Battlewood Dr
7300 HOUS 77040 3682 A1
7700 HarC 77040 3682 A1
Baudet Dr
1000 FBnC 77469 4365 C7
Bauer Av
800 LGCY 77573 4632 B3
Bauer Dr
1900 HOUS 77080 3820 D4
Bauer Rd
16700 HarC 77447 3250 B4
17600 HarC 77433 3250 C1
18100 HarC 77447 3105 B5
Bauer Hockley Rd
- HarC 77447 3248 D2
19900 HarC 77377 3251 D1
19900 HarC 77433 3251 D1
22800 HarC 77433 3250 A1
22800 HarC 77447 3250 A1
24000 HarC 77447 3249 B1
Bauerle Ct
10 BKHV 77024 3959 D3
10 PNPV 77024 3959 D3
Bauerlein Dr
9400 HarC 77086 3542 A4
Bauer Oaks Dr
9300 HarC 77095 3538 B4
Bauer Ridge Dr
16000 HarC 77429 3397 B3
Baughman Dr
18600 BzaC 77584 4627 D4
Bauman Rd
6900 HOUS 77022 3824 B2
8100 HOUS 77022 3685 B7
9400 HOUS 77076 3685 B5
12700 HOUS 77037 3685 B1
12900 HarC 77037 3545 B7
12900 HOUS 77037 3545 B7
Baumeadow Ln
1900 SGLD 77478 4236 D6
Baumgartner
- HarC 77338 3260 A2
Baumgartner Dr
21800 HarC 77338 3260 B2
Bauxhall Ct
300 HarC 77450 3954 E1
300 HOUS 77450 3954 E1
Bavaria Dr
9600 HarC 77070 3255 C6
Baxley Ct
6700 SGLD 77479 4367 B7
Baxter Av
15300 HarC 77084 3678 D3
Baxter Grv
- HarC 77429 3397 B4
Baxter Rd
14200 MtgC 77306 2532 D2
Baxter Hills Ln
13600 HarC 77070 3399 C3

STREET Block City ZIP Map# Grid
Bay Av
100 CmbC 77565 4634 B1
100 KMAH 77565 4634 A1
200 KMAH 77565 4509 E5
300 GlsC 77518 4634 A1
300 KMAH 77539 4634 A1
Bay Ct
100 PNVL 77304 2237 B3
Bay Ln
11100 MtgC 77372 2537 A2
20700 MtgC 77365 2825 A6
W Bay Ln
- LGCY 77539 4752 E4
W Bay Rd
- BYTN 77520 3974 C1
- CmbC 77520 3974 B5
- CmbC 77520 4114 B1
5000 CmbC 77520 4114 B1
8500 BYTN 77520 4114 B7
9000 CmbC 77520 4254 B1
9200 GLSN 77554 5107 C6
W Bay Rd FM-1405
- BYTN 77520 3974 C1
- CmbC 77520 3974 B7
8500 BYTN 77520 4114 B7
8500 CmbC 77520 4114 B7
9000 CmbC 77520 4254 B1
Bay St
200 LPRT 77571 4251 E7
2000 CNRO 77301 2384 D3
2800 HOUS 77026 3824 E5
2900 HOUS 77026 3825 A5
Bay St N
10 TXCY 77590 4875 E3
Bay St S
10 TXCY 77590 4875 E6
Bayard Ln
4900 HOUS 77006 4102 E2
5200 HOUS 77005 4102 E2
Bay Area Blvd
- HarC 77598 4507 A5
- WEBS 77598 4507 A5
200 LGCY 77573 4630 D6
400 HarC 77058 4507 B4
400 HarC 77062 4507 B4
400 HOUS 77058 4507 C3
400 HOUS 77062 4507 B4
1500 LGCY 77573 4751 E1
2500 HOUS 77058 4380 D7
2500 HOUS 77062 4380 D7
2800 HOUS 77059 4380 D7
3400 PASD 77058 4380 E5
3400 PASD 77059 4380 E5
4300 PASD 77058 4381 A5
4300 PASD 77059 4381 A5
4300 PASD 77507 4381 D4
10200 PASD 77507 4382 A3
11300 HarC 77507 4251 A6
11300 PASD 77507 4251 A7
13000 LPRT 77571 4251 A6
W Bay Area Blvd
100 HarC 77598 4507 A5
100 HOUS 77062 4507 A5
100 LGCY 77573 4630 D6
100 WEBS 77598 4507 A5
700 WEBS 77598 4506 E6
1200 HarC 77546 4506 D6
1200 HarC 77598 4506 E6
1200 HOUS 77546 4506 E6
2600 HarC 77598 4630 B1
2900 FRDW 77546 4630 B3
2900 FRDW 77598 4630 B3
2900 HarC 77546 4630 B1
3700 LGCY 77598 4630 C5
Bay Bend Ln
3000 LGCY 77539 4753 A4
Bayberry
- LGCY 77573 4632 C6
Bayberry Ct
11700 HarC 77377 3254 D4
Bayberry Dr
3900 HOUS 77045 4372 D2
Bayberry Ln
1400 PASD 77586 4381 E6
1400 TYLV 77586 4381 E7
Bayberry Wy
5700 SGLD 77479 4495 A4
S Bayberry Bend Dr
12700 HOUS 77072 4097 D5
E Bayberry Bend Cir Dr
6500 HOUS 77072 4097 D4
W Bayberry Bend Cir Dr
6500 HOUS 77072 4097 D5
Bayberry Creek Dr
19900 MtgC 77355 2814 C2
Bayberry Park Ln
9800 HarC 77375 3110 B4
Bay Blue Wy
- HarC 77433 3251 A4
Bayboro Park Ct
15500 HarC 77546 4505 D5
Bayboro Park Dr
4800 HarC 77546 4505 D6
Bay Bower Ln
19400 HarC 77449 3816 A2
Bay Branch Dr
- WDLD 77381 2674 C6
- WDLD 77382 2674 C6
Bay Breeze Cir W
- SEBK 77586 4509 C1
Bay Breeze Dr
3000 LGCY 77539 4753 A4
3400 SEBK 77586 4382 C7
Bay Breeze Dr W
- SEBK 77586 4382 C7
- SEBK 77586 4509 C1
Baybriar Dr
15700 HOUS 77489 4371 A6
Bay Bridge Dr
10800 HarC 77064 3541 A1
Baybridge Dr
200 SGLD 77478 4368 A3
Bay Bridge St
- PRLD 77584 4501 E5
Baybrook Dr
15300 HOUS 77062 4507 A1
Baybrook Square Dr
- HarC 77546 4506 D6
- HarC 77598 4506 D6
- HOUS 77546 4506 D6
Baybrook Village Dr
- HarC 77598 4506 D7
Bay Cedar Ct
5000 HOUS 77048 4243 E7
Bay Cedar Dr
11300 HOUS 77048 4243 D7
11700 HOUS 77048 4374 E1
Bay Chapel Ct
10 WDLD 77385 2676 C4

STREET Block City ZIP Map# Grid
Baychester Ln
1400 HarC 77073 3259 C5
Bay Cliff Ct
14200 HOUS 77077 3956 E6
Baycliff Ct
500 LGCY 77573 4633 A2
2000 PRLD 77584 4500 D1
Bay Club Dr
600 SEBK 77586 4383 B6
Bay Colony Cir
200 LPRT 77571 4383 B2
Bay Colony Dr
100 LPRT 77571 4383 A2
100 PASD 77571 4383 B2
2800 LGCY 77539 4752 D4
Bay Colony Elementary Dr
- LGCY 77539 4753 A3
Bay Cove Ct
15400 HOUS 77059 4380 B6
Bay Creek Ct
100 LGCY 77539 4753 A4
Bay Creek Dr
- FRDW 77598 4630 C2
100 LGCY 77539 4752 E5
3000 LGCY 77539 4753 A4
E Bay Crest Cir
7000 HarC 77346 3408 E2
N Bay Crest Cir
6700 HarC 77346 3408 E2
S Bay Crest Cir
6700 HarC 77346 3408 E1
Bay Crest Dr
- PRLD 77584 4500 D3
Baycrest Dr
300 LGCY 77573 4633 C3
2300 NSUB 77058 4508 B4
Bay Crossing Dr
11500 PRLD 77584 4500 D2
Bayer
17900 HarC 77377 2962 B7
17900 HarC 77377 3107 B1
Bayer Rd
- CmbC 77520 3974 B5
- MtgC 77355 2961 C4
- SGCH 77355 2961 C4
200 HarC 77373 3114 A2
Bayer St
- DRPK 77536 4249 E3
- LPRT 77536 4249 E3
3200 LPRT 77571 4249 E3
Bayers
23900 HarC 77447 3105 A3
Bayeux Ln
20900 HarC 77388 3112 D4
Bayfair St
4700 PASD 77505 4248 E7
4700 PASD 77505 4249 A6
Bayfield Dr
5600 HOUS 77033 4244 A5
Bayfield Glen Ln
- HarC 77047 4374 C4
Bay Forest Dr
200 LPRT 77571 4251 D6
15700 HOUS 77062 4380 B7
Bayfront Ct
12300 PRLD 77584 4500 C3
Bay Front Dr
- HOUS 77077 3956 D5
13500 HOUS 77077 3957 A5
Bayfront Dr
2400 PRLD 77584 4500 B3
16600 JMAB 77554 5331 D3
Bay Gardens Dr
13800 FBnC 77478 4237 A4
14000 FBnC 77478 4236 E4
Bayginger Pl
10 WDLD 77381 2674 D6
Bayglen Ct
4200 HarC 77068 3257 A6
Bay Green Ct
15400 HOUS 77059 4380 B6
Bay Harbor Dr
10 LPRT 77571 4251 E6
Bay Haven Wy
1900 LGCY 77573 4509 A6
Bay Hill Blvd
24100 FBnC 77494 3953 A3
24600 FBnC 77494 3952 E3
Bay Hill Dr
2100 LGCY 77573 4632 D1
2300 BYTN 77520 4113 B3
Bayhill Dr
900 FBnC 77479 4366 C7
Bay Hill Ln
300 PNVL 77304 2237 A2
1700 BYTN 77521 3972 D3
5100 PASD 77505 4248 B4
Bay Hollow Ct
2900 FBnC 77450 3953 E7
Bay Hollow Dr
- PRLD 77584 4500 C3
22500 FBnC 77450 3953 E7
Bayhurst Dr
11800 BKHV 77024 3959 C4
Bayland Av
200 HOUS 77009 3824 A7
900 HOUS 77009 3823 E7
1100 HOUS 77007 3823 E7
Bayland Park Dr
- HOUS 77074 4100 B6
Baylark Pl
10 WDLD 77382 2674 E5
Bay Leaf Ct
1300 MSCY 77489 4370 D7
Bayleaf Dr
22700 HarC 77373 3259 D1
23000 HarC 77373 3114 D6
W Bayleaf Dr
9900 MtgC 77385 2676 D7
Bayleaf Ln
10 WDLD 77380 2821 E6
Bay Ledge
3500 HarC 77546 4506 A7
Bay Ledge Ct
16800 HarC 77546 4506 A7
Bay Ledge Dr
11500 PRLD 77584 4500 D2

STREET Block City ZIP Map# Grid
Bayless Dr
7800 HOUS 77017 4105 C6
Bayless St
1200 BYTN 77520 4112 D2
Bayline
2300 GlsC 77539 4635 D4
Bay Lodge Ln
15400 HarC 77086 3541 D1
Baylor Dr
2200 KATY 77493 3813 D5
Baylor Plz
10 HOUS 77030 4102 E3
Baylor St
2100 BYTN 77520 3972 E5
2200 HOUS 77009 3823 E4
Bay Manor St
2400 PRLD 77584 4500 E2
Baymeadow Ct
12300 PRLD 77584 4500 B3
Baymeadow Dr
1000 HOUS 77062 4507 A1
12400 PRLD 77584 4500 D4
Baymeadows Dr
1200 GLSN 77554 5221 B1
Baymist Ct
22100 FBnC 77450 4093 E3
Baynard Dr
4100 HOUS 77072 4098 C3
Bay Oaks Blvd
14000 HOUS 77059 4379 E5
14500 HOUS 77059 4380 A5
Bay Oaks Dr
10 LPRT 77571 4383 A1
10 SRAC 77571 4383 A1
100 LPRT 77571 4382 E1
300 SRAC 77571 4382 E1
600 KMAH 77565 4509 D7
Bay Oaks Rd
800 HOUS 77008 3823 B7
Bay Oaks Harbor Dr
2300 BYTN 77520 4113 C5
Bayonne Cir
13300 HarC 77377 3109 A5
Bayonne Dr
5800 HarC 77389 2966 D6
Bayou Av
2500 BYTN 77520 3973 D5
Bayou Blvd
- PASD 77506 4107 A5
3800 BYTN 77521 3974 A1
3800 HarC 77521 3974 A1
5600 HarC 77521 3834 E5
6300 HarC 77521 3835 A5
Bayou Bnd
400 BYTN 77520 3835 B7
N Bayou Bnd
200 BYTN 77520 3835 B7
S Bayou Bnd
200 BYTN 77520 3835 A7
Bayou Cir
800 ALVN 77511 4867 D3
1000 GLSN 77551 5108 C5
3700 DKSN 77539 4753 D4
Bayou Cross
3200 SGLD 77479 4495 E2
Bayou Dr
- BYTN 77520 4113 C1
10 CNRO 77304 2382 E3
500 RHMD 77469 4492 A2
700 ALVN 77511 4867 D2
900 HarC 77530 3830 D5
2200 LGCY 77573 4508 C7
2200 LGCY 77573 4632 B1
3000 LPRT 77571 4382 D1
3300 HOUS 77022 3824 A3
4600 GlsC 77563 4990 A5
4900 DKSN 77539 4753 E4
Bayou Dr E
3300 DKSN 77539 4754 C3
Bayou Dr W
2600 DKSN 77539 4753 C5
E Bayou Dr
3300 SRAC 77571 4382 D1
3400 DKSN 77539 4754 D3
6700 HTCK 77563 4989 A4
N Bayou Dr
100 HTCK 77563 4988 C3
8200 HOUS 77017 4105 E7
W Bayou Dr
500 RHMD 77469 4492 A2
3300 SRAC 77571 4382 D1
6700 HTCK 77563 4989 A4
Bayou Ln
10 CRLS 77565 4509 C5
10 GlsC 77565 4509 C5
Bayou Pkwy
- SGLD 77479 4495 B2
900 HOUS 77077 3957 A3
Bayou Rd
- HOUS 77058 4380 E7
- PASD 77058 4380 E7
100 LMQU 77568 4874 A7
100 TXCY 77591 4874 A7
700 LMQU 77568 4990 A3
2700 HTCK 77563 4990 A5
2700 LMQU 77563 4990 A5
Bayou St
1200 HOUS 77020 3964 A2
3000 DRPK 77536 4109 C7
Bayou Arbor Ln
25700 FBnC 77494 4093 A2
25800 FBnC 77494 4092 E2
Bayou Bend Cir
- BzaC 77511 4748 A3
Bayou Bend Ct
3700 SGLD 77479 4495 B1
5800 HOUS 77004 4103 B4
Bayou Bend Dr
- DRPK 77503 4248 E1
- DRPK 77536 4248 E1
- PASD 77503 4248 E1
100 LGCY 77573 4509 B6
600 DRPK 77536 4249 A1
4500 DKSN 77539 4754 E3
Bayou Bluff Ct
17100 HarC 77379 3255 E5
Bayou Bluff Dr
9000 HarC 77379 3255 E5
Bayou Branch Dr
18200 HarC 77084 3816 D3
Bayou Bridge Dr
- HOUS 77096 4240 B2
Bayou Brook St
9500 HOUS 77063 3959 B6
Bayou Cane Ln
3100 RSBG 77471 4491 A6
N Bayou Club Ct
- HarC 77389 2820 B6

STREET Block City ZIP Map# Grid
S Bayou Club Ct
10 HarC 77389 2820 B6
Bayou Country Dr
400 GlsC 77511 4751 B6
400 LGCY 77511 4751 B6
Bayou Cove Ct
400 HOUS 77042 3958 C4
Bayou Cove Ln
- LGCY 77573 4630 E7
Bayou Crest Cir
600 DKSN 77539 4753 A5
Bayou Crest Dr
600 DKSN 77539 4753 A6
6600 HarC 77088 3542 B6
Bayou Crossing Dr
3200 SGLD 77479 4495 B1
Bayou Crossing Ln
2400 RSBG 77471 4491 B6
Bayou Elm Dr
22700 HarC 77373 3114 D7
Bayou End Ln
100 GlsC 77511 4751 D7
100 LGCY 77511 4751 D7
Bayou Forest Dr
3400 SRAC 77571 4382 C2
7100 HOUS 77088 3682 C2
7800 HarC 77088 3682 D2
8200 HarC 77088 3542 C7
Bayou Forest Vil
- HarC 77039 3545 D6
- HOUS 77039 3545 D6
Bayou Front Dr
6500 GLSN 77551 5108 B6
Bayou Glen Dr
200 LPRT 77571 4110 C7
Bayou Glen Rd
5600 HOUS 77056 3960 D3
6400 HOUS 77057 3960 B4
10000 HOUS 77042 3958 E4
10000 HOUS 77042 3959 A4
Bayouglenn St
100 HTCK 77563 4988 E3
Bayou Green Ln
7700 FBnC 77469 4493 E6
7700 FBnC 77479 4493 E6
Bayou Grove Dr
4000 TYLV 77586 4508 D1
Bayou Homes Dr
1500 GLSN 77551 5108 B6
Bayou Island Dr
1000 HOUS 77024 3959 B5
1000 HOUS 77042 3959 B5
Bayou Junction Ct
18500 HarC 77433 3395 C6
Bayou Junction Rd
12000 HarC 77433 3395 C6
Bayou Knoll Dr
500 HOUS 77079 3957 C3
S Bayou Knoll Dr
6200 HOUS 77072 4097 C4
Bayou Lake Ln
9400 HarC 77040 3681 B1
Bayou Manor Ln
10100 HarC 77064 3540 B4
Bayou Mead Ct
12600 HarC 77346 3408 D1
Bayou Mead Tr
18000 HarC 77346 3408 D1
Bayou Mead Wy
12600 HarC 77346 3408 D1
Bayou Meadow Ln
3400 HOUS 77007 3962 E3
Bayou Mist Ct
2300 HOUS 77077 3957 A6
Bayou Oak Dr
1200 FRDW 77546 4629 A4
Bayou Oaks Dr
7200 HOUS 77088 3682 C2
Bayou Parkway Ct
13700 HOUS 77077 3957 A3
Bayou Pine Ct
8400 HarC 77040 3541 A5
Bayou Pl Ct
10700 HOUS 77099 4238 B4
Bayou Pl Dr
11100 HOUS 77099 4238 B4
Bayou Pl Ln
11200 HOUS 77099 4238 B4
Bayou Pointe Dr
10 HOUS 77024 3959 B6
10 HOUS 77042 3959 B6
10 HOUS 77063 3959 B6
Bayou Ridge Dr
8900 HOUS 77338 3262 B6
Bayou River Ct
15900 HOUS 77079 3956 D2
Bayou River Dr
800 HOUS 77079 3956 E2
Bayou St. John
4800 CNRO 77304 2382 D3
Bayou Shadows
- HOUS 77024 3959 A4
Bayou Shadows St
- HOUS 77024 3959 A4
Bayou Shore Dr
1000 GLSN 77551 5108 C5
Bayou Springs Ct
10 WDLD 77382 2675 C7
Bayou Teche Ct
600 MtgC 77302 2530 A5
Bayou Terrace Ln
25200 FBnC 77494 4093 B2
Bayou Tesch Dr
26400 MtgC 77354 2817 D5
Bayou Timber Ln
5000 HOUS 77056 3960 E3
5000 HOUS 77056 3961 A3
Bayou Trail Ct
10100 HarC 77064 3540 B3
Bayou Trail Ln
10200 HarC 77064 3540 A3
Bayou View Dr
100 ELGO 77586 4509 A2
100 SEBK 77586 4509 A2
6400 HOUS 77091 3683 A5
Bayou View St
- BYTN 77520 3835 A7
Bayou Vista Cir
16400 KATY 77494 3952 B2
Bayou Vista Ct
1000 KATY 77494 3952 B3
Bayou Vista Dr
- GlsC 77568 4990 D7
- LMQU 77568 4990 D7
10 GlsC 77563 4990 D7
600 DRPK 77536 4249 A1
900 DRPK 77536 4248 E2
1200 HOUS 77019 3963 A4

STREET Block City ZIP Map# Grid
Bayou Vista Dr
4700 HOUS 77091 3683 A6
5000 HOUS 77091 3682 E6
7200 BYTN 77521 3835 A5
Bayou Vista Ln
1000 KATY 77494 3952 A3
Bayou Woods Dr
7200 HOUS 77088 3682 D2
9000 BYTN 77521 3835 A5
Bay Palms Dr
21600 HarC 77449 3676 C6
Bay Park Dr
- FRDW 77598 4630 C1
- HarC 77598 4630 C1
Bay Park Rd
12900 HarC 77507 4250 D6
12900 LPRT 77571 4250 D6
Bay Pines Dr
5200 HarC 77449 3676 D6
Bay Point Dr
22500 GLSN 77554 5440 E5
22500 GLSN 77554 5441 A5
Bay Pointe Ct
14100 HOUS 77062 4379 C7
Baypointe Dr
- FBnC 77479 4367 A6
Bayport Blvd
900 SEBK 77586 4509 D1
2900 SEBK 77586 4382 C7
9500 PASD 77507 4381 D2
Bayport Blvd SR-146
900 SEBK 77586 4509 D1
2900 SEBK 77586 4382 C7
Bayport Ct
3800 MtgC 77386 2970 B6
Bayport Dr
12300 PRLD 77584 4500 B3
Bayport Ln
1300 LGCY 77573 4633 A4
Bayram Rd
1500 HOUS 77055 3821 B6
Bay Ridge Ct
3100 FRDW 77598 4630 C2
Bayridge Dr
200 LGCY 77565 4633 C3
300 LGCY 77573 4633 C3
Bayridge Rd
10 MRGP 77571 4252 C1
1000 LPRT 77571 4252 A2
Bayshore Blvd
3000 PASD 77502 4247 E3
3000 PASD 77504 4247 E3
Bay Shore Dr
10 LPRT 77571 4251 E7
2600 SEBK 77586 4382 B7
3200 LPRT 77571 4383 A1
4000 MSCY 77459 4369 C7
Bayshore Dr
- BYTN 77520 3970 E5
- BYTN 77520 3971 A5
100 LPRT 77571 4251 E5
1400 KMAH 77565 4509 E6
1400 KMAH 77565 4510 A6
2600 GlsC 77518 4634 B1
E Bayshore Dr
100 GlsC 77539 4636 B5
2000 GlsC 77539 4635 C4
2700 TXCY 77539 4635 C4
E Bayshore Dr FM-646
900 GlsC 77539 4636 A4
2000 GlsC 77539 4635 C4
2700 TXCY 77539 4635 C4
N Bayshore Dr
100 LPRT 77571 4251 E5
800 LPRT 77571 4252 A4
S Bayshore Dr
- BYTN 77520 3971 A4
W Bayshore Dr
- BYTN 77520 3970 E4
- BYTN 77520 3971 B4
4300 GlsC 77518 4634 E3
4800 GlsC 77518 4635 A3
5200 TXCY 77518 4635 A3
5600 GlsC 77539 4635 B3
W Bayshore Dr FM-646
4600 GlsC 77518 4634 E3
4800 GlsC 77518 4635 A3
5200 TXCY 77518 4635 A3
5600 GlsC 77539 4635 B3
Bayside Av
7700 GLSN 77554 5107 D5
Bayside Dr
100 HarC 77571 4111 A4
100 LPRT 77571 4382 E1
5100 CmbC 77520 4254 A3
6000 BHCY 77520 4254 E2
Bayside Wy
4200 JMAB 77554 5331 D4
E Bayside Wy
4100 JMAB 77554 5331 D3
W Bayside Wy
4100 JMAB 77554 5331 D3
Bay Sky Dr
200 LGCY 77539 4752 E5
400 DKSN 77539 4753 A5
400 LGCY 77539 4753 A5
Bay Sky Wy
900 SEBK 77586 4509 E1
900 SEBK 77586 4510 A1
Bay Spring Dr
300 LGCY 77573 4633 B1
22100 FBnC 77450 3954 A7
Bay Spring St
2400 PRLD 77584 4500 D3
Bay Springs Vw
- FBnC 77469 4365 A6
Bay St Ext
3900 TXCY 77590 4875 E1
Bay Star Blvd
800 HOUS 77034 4379 A6
800 HOUS 77598 4379 A6
Bayswater Dr
1200 HOUS 77047 4373 C3
Baythorne Dr
9400 HOUS 77041 3681 C7
Baytide Ct
20300 FBnC 77469 4094 D7
Baytown Av
- BYTN 77520 3972 A7
1800 BYTN 77520 3971 E7
1800 BYTN 77520 4111 E1
Baytown Central Blvd
- BYTN 77521 3972 D2
- HarC 77521 3972 D2
Baytree Dr
13800 SGLD 77478 4237 A7
15900 HarC 77070 3255 B6

STREET Block City ZIP Map# Grid
Bay Tree Lndg
15400 HarC 77429 3397 B3
Bayview Ct
4600 MSCY 77459 4497 C4
Bay View Dr
100 SGLD 77478 4368 A2
Bayview Dr
500 ELGO 77586 4509 B1
1900 SEBK 77586 4382 D6
7900 BHCY 77520 4254 E2
Bayview Ln
23500 GLSN 77554 5440 C6
Bayview Cove Dr
9000 HOUS 77054 4242 A2
Bayvilla St
10 BYTN 77520 3971 C6
Bay Vista
11200 LPRT 77571 4110 E7
Bay Vista Dr
600 SEBK 77586 4510 A1
22300 GLSN 77554 5441 A5
Baywater Ct
2000 LGCY 77573 4508 E6
Baywater Dr
- PRLD 77584 4500 B2
Baywater Canyon Dr
2500 PRLD 77584 4500 B3
Bayway Dr
- BYTN 77520 4111 E1
3500 BYTN 77520 3971 D7
5700 HarC 77520 3971 C5
Baywick Dr
24800 HarC 77389 2965 E3
Bay Winds Ct
2500 HOUS 77059 4380 B6
Baywood Ct
200 MtgC 77386 2822 C7
Baywood Dr
400 CmbC 77586 4383 C5
400 SEBK 77586 4383 C5
4700 PASD 77505 4248 E7
5100 HOUS 77059 4248 E7
5100 PASD 77059 4248 E7
Bay Wood Ln
- LGCY 77573 4630 B6
Baywood St
100 SRAC 77571 4383 A2
200 HOUS 77011 3964 C6
400 SRAC 77571 4382 E2
Baywood Park Dr
3000 HarC 77068 3257 C4
Bazelbriar Dr
15800 HOUS 77489 4371 A6
Bazel Brook Dr
6400 HOUS 77489 4371 D5
Bazin St
10800 HOUS 77089 4377 D3
B Bar Cir
- FRDW 77546 4629 A5
B Bar Dr
4300 STFE 77510 4871 A7
B Boggs Rd
25000 HarC 77375 2964 E3
Beacave Bend Ct
10900 HarC 77086 3542 A1
E Beach Dr
- GLSN 77550 5109 E2
400 GLSN 77550 5110 A2
1000 GLSN 77550 4995 C7
W Beach Rd
4300 TXCY 77590 4757 E6
16700 JMAB 77554 5331 D6
16700 JMAB 77554 5332 A6
Beach St
11900 HarC 77044 3551 D7
W Beach St
4200 GLSN 77554 5332 E3
Beach Airport Rd
100 CNRO 77301 2384 E1
1500 CNRO 77303 2384 D1
2500 MtgC 77303 2384 D1
Beach Airport Rd FM-3083
100 CNRO 77301 2384 E1
1500 CNRO 77303 2384 D1
2500 MtgC 77303 2384 D1
Beacham Dr
15100 HarC 77070 3255 A7
Beach Bay Dr
9400 HarC 77044 3688 E4
Beachcomber Dr
- GLSN 77554 5331 E6
16800 JMAB 77554 5331 E6
Beachcomber Ln
700 HOUS 77062 4506 E3
1400 HOUS 77062 4507 B2
3800 GLSN 77554 5440 D6
Beachfront Dr
12800 BzaC 77541 5547 B6
Beach Grove Ln
22000 FBnC 77494 4093 E4
Beachside
11400 GLSN 77554 5221 A6
11500 GLSN 77554 5220 E6
Beachton St
1300 HOUS 77007 3963 B2
Beachtown Ln
700 GLSN 77550 4995 B7
700 GLSN 77550 5110 C1
Beachtown Psg
700 GLSN 77550 5110 C1
Beachwalk Dr
1700 HarC 77532 3551 D3
Beachwater Dr
3200 FBnC 77450 3953 E7
Beachwood St
6800 HOUS 77021 4103 C6
Beachy Ct
19600 HarC 77449 3677 A5
Beacon Ct
3600 BzaC 77578 4501 B7
Beacon Dr
- GLSN 77554 5221 E1
Beacon Hl
10 SGLD 77479 4495 D2
Beacon Pt
5100 SGLD 77479 4494 E3
Beacon St
600 HarC 77015 3829 A7
800 HarC 77015 3968 A2
1000 HarC 77058 4507 C4
Beacon Bay Cir
2700 HarC 77546 4506 B7
Beacon Bend Ct
3400 PRLD 77584 4501 E5
Beacon Bend Ln
3500 PRLD 77584 4501 D5
Beacon Chase Ct
2000 HarC 77373 3114 C6

STREET Block City ZIP Map# Grid
Beacon Cove Ct
1700 HarC 77450 3954 D4
Beacon Falls Dr
5800 HOUS 77345 3120 B5
Beacon Grove St
2900 HarC 77389 3113 A1
3100 HarC 77389 3112 E1
Beacon Hill Dr
- PASD 77586 4508 E2
3400 BzaC 77584 4501 C5
4400 TYLV 77586 4508 E2
Beacon Hollow Ct
12300 HarC 77429 3398 B6
Beacon Light Ln
2100 FBnC 77545 4498 D6
Beacon Manor Ln
6700 HarC 77041 3679 D3
Beacon Pointe
2300 PRLD 77584 4500 D2
Beacon Pointe Ln
- DKSN 77539 4752 D6
Beaconridge Dr
5900 HOUS 77053 4371 E6
Beacons Vw
3500 HarC 77546 4506 A7
Beaconsfield Ct
10 MtgC 77355 2814 E3
Beaconsfield Dr
14800 HarC 77015 3829 B5
Beaconshire Rd
1600 HOUS 77077 3957 C5
Beacons Hollow Ln
- LGCY 77573 4751 C1
Beacons Trace Ct
14300 HarC 77069 3256 C6
Beacons Trace Dr
- HarC 77069 3256 C6
Beacon Tree Ct
12200 HarC 77346 3408 C1
Beacon View Ct
3300 PRLD 77584 4501 E5
Bealey Ln
4000 HarC 77047 4374 D4
Beall Ln
3300 GLSN 77554 5221 B4
Beall St
1300 HOUS 77008 3823 A6
5500 HOUS 77091 3684 A6
Beamer Rd
- FRDW 77089 4505 C1
10900 HOUS 77089 4377 D4
11500 HarC 77089 4377 D5
12300 HarC 77089 4378 A7
12300 HOUS 77089 4378 A7
13500 HarC 77089 4505 B1
13500 HOUS 77089 4505 B1
14000 FRDW 77546 4505 E3
14000 HarC 77546 4505 E4
14000 HOUS 77546 4505 E4
15500 HarC 77546 4506 A4
15500 HOUS 77546 4506 A4
Bean St
300 PRVW 77445 2955 A6
9200 HOUS 77028 3687 D6
9700 HOUS 77078 3687 D5
Bear Blvd
12300 HOUS 77072 4097 E4
Bear Bayou Dr
15800 HarC 77530 3830 B5
Bearborough Dr
25700 MtgC 77386 2968 D1
Bear Branch Ln
32800 MtgC 77354 2673 E4
Bear Brook Dr
2300 HOUS 77345 3120 A6
Bear Cave Ln
5500 HarC 77449 3677 A6
Bearclaw Ct
27100 MtgC 77355 2961 D1
Bearcove Cir
9100 HarC 77064 3540 E6
Bear Creek Cir
1700 BYTN 77521 3972 D3
Bear Creek Dr
10 HOUS 77084 3817 E3
10 HOUS 77084 3818 A1
N Bear Creek Dr
17000 HarC 77084 3678 B7
S Bear Creek Dr
17000 HarC 77084 3678 B7
Bear Creek Trc
4000 BYTN 77521 3972 D3
Bear Creek Meadows Ln
- HOUS 77041 3819 C1
3800 HOUS 77043 3819 C2
Bear Cub Ln
21400 HOUS 77532 3266 B7
Beard Dr
11200 GLSN 77554 5221 B5
Beard Rd
14000 HarC 77044 3689 E4
Bearden Ln
10 HarC 77336 2977 A1
10 LbyC 77327 2977 A1
100 HarC 77336 2976 E1
Bearden Creek Ln
9300 HarC 77396 3548 A2
Bearden Falls Ln
7100 HarC 77396 3547 C1
Bearden Lake Dr
- HarC 77377 3254 C5
Bearden Pl Ln
4200 HarC 77082 4096 A4
Bear Hill Dr
16000 HarC 77084 3678 D7
Bear Hunters Dr
5400 HarC 77449 3676 E5
Bearing Star Ln
31300 TMBL 77375 2963 E4
Bear Lake Dr
3600 HOUS 77345 3119 D3
Bearle St
100 PASD 77506 4107 D5
Bear Lodge Dr
4200 HarC 77084 3816 D1
Bear Meadow Ct
19300 HarC 77449 3677 C3
Bear Meadow Ln
5600 HarC 77449 3676 C5
19400 HarC 77449 3677 A4
Bear Mist Dr
17300 HarC 77095 3537 D4
Bear Oaks Dr
6900 FBnC 77083 4095 E5
Bear Pass Ct
5200 HarC 77449 3676 D6
Bear Path Ln
- HarC 77449 3676 E6

Houston Street Index

STREET
Block City ZIP Map# Grid

ear Paw Cir
5500 HarC 77449 3676 E6
ear River Ln
17400 HarC 77346 3408 D3
ear Run Dr
- FBnC 77479 4494 B3
ear Run Ln
21100 HarC 77449 3676 D5
21100 HarC 77449 3677 A6
ear Springs Dr
19300 HarC 77449 3677 A4
ear Springs Pl
10 WDLD 77381 2675 B7
ear Track Ln
6000 PASD 77505 4248 D4
ear Trail Ln
5500 HarC 77449 3676 E6
ear Tree Tr
21100 HarC 77449 3676 D6
21100 HarC 77449 3677 A6
ear Valley Dr
12400 HOUS 77072 4097 D5
earwood Rd
13800 HarC 77038 3543 A1
easley Ct
1100 FBnC 77545 4623 A2
easley St
2600 CNRO 77301 2384 E3
2600 CNRO 77301 2385 A3
7500 HTCK 77563 4988 E2
7500 HTCK 77563 4989 A2
eatrice Av
3900 DKSN 77539 4754 A2
eatrice Rd
- HOUS 77076 3684 E4
eatrice St
200 LMQU 77568 4874 A7
eatty Dr
14800 HOUS 77396 3406 A7
14800 HOUS 77396 3547 A1
eatty St
2400 HOUS 77023 4104 D4
eau Ln
4800 HarC 77039 3546 C5
eaubridge Ln
- HarC 77379 3112 B5
eauchamp St
2600 HOUS 77009 3963 B1
2800 HOUS 77009 3824 B7
eaudelaire Cir
7500 GLSN 77551 5222 A2
eaudry Dr
5900 HOUS 77035 4240 B5
eau Forest Ln
23200 HarC 77447 3105 B5
eaufort Dr
7800 HarC 77379 3256 A2
eaufort Sea Dr
1200 HarC 77067 3402 C5
eau Geste Dr
6300 HOUS 77088 3682 B2
eau Harp Ct
6000 HarC 77049 3828 C3
eau Harp Dr
14200 HarC 77049 3828 C4
eaujolais Ln
1300 HOUS 77077 3958 A4
eauline Abbey St
12500 HarC 77377 3254 B5
eau Monde Dr
8700 HarC 77099 4237 D1
eaumont Hwy
10 HarC 77532 3691 C2
1000 HarC 77532 3552 C7
10900 HarC 77049 3827 C2
10900 HOUS 77013 3827 C2
10900 HOUS 77049 3827 D2
12100 HarC 77049 3828 A1
12600 HarC 77049 3689 E6
13300 HarC 77049 3692 C1
14500 HarC 77049 3690 D4
17000 HarC 77049 3691 B2
17800 HarC 77044 3691 B2
eaumont Hwy US-90
10900 HarC 77049 3827 C2
10900 HOUS 77013 3827 C2
10900 HOUS 77049 3827 D2
12100 HarC 77049 3828 A1
12600 HarC 77049 3689 E6
eaumont Hwy US-90 BUS
10 HarC 77532 3691 C2
10 HarC 77532 3692 B1
1000 HarC 77532 3552 C7
10900 HarC 77049 3827 C2
10900 HOUS 77013 3827 C2
10900 HOUS 77049 3827 D2
12100 HarC 77049 3828 A1
12600 HarC 77049 3689 E6
14500 HarC 77049 3690 D4
17000 HarC 77049 3691 B2
17800 HarC 77044 3691 B2
eaumont Pl
7200 HarC 77049 3828 C1
7600 HarC 77049 3689 B7
eaumont Rd
- HOUS 77013 3826 E4
6900 HOUS 77013 3827 A3
eaumont Rd US-90
6900 HOUS 77013 3827 A3
eaumont Rd US-90 BUS
6900 HOUS 77013 3827 A3
aumont St
200 HOUS 77017 4246 B2
200 MAGA 77354 2669 A4
200 SHUS 77017 4246 B2
200 SHUS 77587 4246 C4
600 LGCY 77573 4632 C3
1300 BYTN 77520 3973 B5
7400 HOUS 77011 3965 B6
Beaupre Point Dr
600 HarC 77015 3828 A7
Beaupre Point Dr
12400 HarC 77015 3828 A7
auregard Ct
3400 MSCY 77459 4497 E6
auregard Dr
500 MtgC 77302 2530 B5
12100 HOUS 77024 3959 A3
Beauregard St
100 ALVN 77511 4867 B1
400 ALVN 77511 4749 B7
Beauregard St
100 ALVN 77511 4867 B1
au Rivage Dr
1600 CNRO 77304 2382 D3
au Rue St
7100 GlsC 77563 4990 C6

Beau Terre St
7000 GlsC 77563 4990 C6
Beauty Bower Pl
10 WDLD 77382 2819 B2
Beauvoir Dr
11200 HarC 77065 3539 A1
11300 HarC 77065 3398 B7
Beaver Dr
3600 HOUS 77029 3826 C5
Beaver Ln
15900 SGCH 77355 2961 C3
Beaver Rd
5100 GlsC 77517 4986 C2
5100 HTCK 77517 4986 C2
5100 STFE 77517 4986 C2
Beaver St
7900 CmbC 77520 3835 C4
31900 SGCH 77355 2961 B3
Beaver Bend Ct
7600 HarC 77521 3833 B3
9200 HarC 77037 3544 C6
Beaver Bend Rd
200 HarC 77037 3544 B6
500 HOUS 77037 3544 B6
800 HOUS 77088 3544 A6
1200 HOUS 77088 3543 E7
1900 HarC 77088 3543 D7
Beaverbrook Dr
5200 HarC 77084 3678 E6
Beaver Creek Dr
5400 LPRT 77571 4250 B2
17900 HarC 77090 3257 E2
17900 HarC 77090 3258 A3
Beaver Dam Dr
- HOUS 77532 3266 B7
Beaver Dam St
23000 HarC 77389 2967 B6
Beaverdell Dr
18000 HarC 77377 3254 C2
Beaver Falls Dr
5800 HOUS 77345 3120 C6
Beaver Glen Dr
3100 HOUS 77339 3119 B2
Beaverhead Cir
3200 MtgC 77380 2967 B2
Beaverhead Ct
3300 MtgC 77380 2967 B2
Beaver Hill Dr
5100 HarC 77084 3678 E5
Beaverhollow Dr
5100 HarC 77084 3678 D5
Beaver Lake Ct
7800 HarC 77346 3265 B3
Beaver Lodge Dr
5300 HOUS 77345 3120 B6
Beaver Pass Ln
5600 HarC 77449 3676 E5
Beaver Pond Cir
4800 HarC 77084 3677 C7
Beaver Run Dr
25600 HarC 77336 3121 C7
Beaver Springs Cir
1600 HarC 77090 3258 A4
Beaver Springs Ct
1700 HarC 77090 3258 A4
Beaver Springs Dr
17000 HarC 77090 3258 A4
17000 HOUS 77090 3258 B4
Beaver Tail Pt
10 HOUS 77024 3959 A5
Beaver Trail Dr
11000 HarC 77086 3542 B1
Beaverwood Dr
1700 MtgC 77354 2673 B1
23800 HarC 77373 3115 A4
25300 HarC 77373 3114 D2
Beawood Dr
8800 HarC 77083 4237 A1
Bebington Ct
- FBnC 77545 4498 D6
N Becca Ln
2900 HOUS 77092 3822 C3
Becca Wy
12000 HarC 77067 3402 D4
Beck St
1300 HOUS 77009 3824 A5
Beckendorf Rd
- HarC 77493 3675 A4
Beckendorff Rd
21900 HarC 77449 3676 A4
22100 HarC 77449 3675 C4
22300 HarC 77493 3675 C4
Beckenham Dr
9200 HarC 77099 4237 C1
Becker Av
- HarC 77530 3830 C5
Becker Ln
15900 GlsC 77517 4869 E1
Becker Rd
17900 HarC 77447 3249 E3
17900 HarC 77447 3250 A1
18000 HarC 77447 3104 E5
24200 WlrC 77445 2955 A2
Becker St
9100 HOUS 77012 4105 E2
Becker Cemetery Rd
13400 HarC 77429 3254 A7
Becker Glen St
3100 FBnC 77545 4498 C6
Becker Line Dr
6200 HarC 77379 3256 E3
6200 HarC 77379 3257 A3
Becket
- HOUS 77091 3684 B4
Becket St
2900 PRLD 77584 4501 B2
Becket Hill Pl
10 WDLD 77382 2674 B4
Beckets Crossing Ln
700 HarC 77373 2968 C6
Beckett Creek Ln
8100 HarC 77396 3547 D2
Beckett Ridge Dr
3600 HarC 77396 3407 E3
3700 HarC 77396 3408 A3
3800 HarC 77346 3408 A3
Becketts Oak Ct
16900 FBnC 77083 4095 D6
Becket Woods Ln
14000 SGLD 77478 4236 E4
Beckfield Ct
12200 HOUS 77099 4237 D4
Beckfield Dr
10600 HOUS 77099 4237 E4
Beckford Dr
- HarC 77072 4097 C7
- HarC 77072 4237 C1
- HOUS 77072 4097 C6

Beckford Dr
- HOUS 77099 4237 C2
8700 HarC 77099 4237 C2
Beckham Springs Ct
25700 HarC 77373 3114 A4
Beckins Cliff Dr
10 HarC 77379 3255 C1
Beckland Ln
16500 HarC 77084 3678 B4
Beckledge Ln
- HarC 77047 4374 C3
Beckley St
9300 HOUS 77088 3683 D1
Becklin Ln
12900 HarC 77099 4237 C1
Beckman Dr
1600 HarC 77336 3266 E4
1600 HarC 77336 3267 A4
Beckman St
700 HOUS 77076 3685 B4
Beck Masten
10700 HarC 77065 3539 E2
E Beckonvale Cir
10 WDLD 77382 2819 D1
W Beckonvale Cir
10 WDLD 77382 2819 D1
Beckonvale Ct
10 WDLD 77382 2819 D1
Beck Pl Ln
- HarC 77090 3258 D2
- HOUS 77090 3258 D2
Beck Ridge Dr
16000 HOUS 77053 4371 E6
Beckton Ln
1000 PRLD 77584 4501 B1
Beckwith Dr
13800 HarC 77014 3402 D3
Beckwood Cir
1200 HarC 77014 3402 D3
Beckwood Post Dr
9600 HarC 77095 3537 E4
Beckworth Fields Dr
10700 HOUS 77016 3687 B4
Becky Ln
5600 PRLD 77584 4502 D6
30400 MtgC 77354 2672 D7
Becky St
100 CNRO 77301 2384 A2
Becurtesy Ct
14600 HarC 77429 3253 D4
Bedford
19100 MtgC 77357 2829 A4
Bedford Av
- PRLD 77584 4501 B2
Bedford Dr
- HOUS 77031 4238 E4
Bedford Ln
200 CNRO 77303 2238 C7
200 CNRO 77303 2384 D1
15400 MtgC 77384 2674 A2
Bedford St
100 HOUS 77012 4105 B1
11300 HOUS 77031 4238 E6
11600 HarC 77031 4238 E6
Bedford Chase
13400 HarC 77429 3396 E3
Bedford Falls Dr
12800 HarC 77429 3397 C4
Bedford Forest Ct
3300 MSCY 77459 4497 E6
3300 MSCY 77459 4498 B5
Bedford Glen Dr
15300 HarC 77530 3829 D5
Bedford Oak St
2300 FBnC 77545 4498 C6
Bedford Pass Dr
17200 HarC 77095 3537 E3
Bedias Creek Ct
7000 FBnC 77469 4094 B7
Bedias Creek Dr
21400 FBnC 77469 4094 A5
Bedworth Ln
9200 HarC 77088 3543 D7
Bedynek Dr
- BzaC 77578 4625 E2
Bedynek Rd
3900 BzaC 77578 4625 E2
Bee Ln
11800 HarC 77067 3402 B5
Bee Bayou Ln
3600 SGLD 77479 4495 E1
Beebe Ln
10 BKHV 77024 3959 B3
Bee Cave Dr
3000 MSCY 77459 4370 A7
Beech Dr
1300 CHTW 77385 2823 A4
Beech St
400 LMQU 77568 4990 C3
1100 BYTN 77520 3972 B7
2100 GLSN 77554 5221 E1
4600 BLAR 77401 4101 B4
5100 BLAR 77401 4100 E4
5200 HOUS 77081 4100 E4
Beecham Cir
3000 HarC 77068 3257 C5
Beecham Dr
15100 HarC 77068 3257 C4
Beecham Lake Ct
7400 FBnC 77469 4094 D7
Beecham Lake Ln
19700 FBnC 77469 4094 D6
Beechaven Dr
4900 HOUS 77053 4372 B6
Beechaven Rd
8400 LPRT 77571 4249 D3
Beech Bark Pl
10 WDLD 77382 2673 D5
Beech Bend Ct
1700 HOUS 77077 3958 B7
Beech Bend Dr
1900 HOUS 77077 3958 A6
Beechbend Dr
500 MSCY 77489 4370 E5
500 MSCY 77489 4371 A6
1200 HOUS 77489 4370 D6
Beech Canyon Dr
23100 HarC 77450 3953 D3
23100 HarC 77494 3953 D3
Beech Cove Ln
7600 HOUS 77072 4097 E6
Beech Cove St
1400 LPRT 77571 4251 D5
Beechcraft St
3400 PRLD 77581 4503 C3
4500 SEBK 77586 4383 A7
Beechcrest St
8600 HarC 77083 4097 A7

Beech Crossing Dr
8300 HarC 77083 4096 D6
Beechdale Ct
13100 HarC 77014 3402 A2
Beecher Dr
4000 DRPK 77536 4249 A1
Beecher St
700 BYTN 77520 4112 C1
Beech Fern Dr
4900 FBnC 77469 4234 D3
Beech Fork Ln
15100 FBnC 77478 4236 D4
Beechgate Ln
13400 HarC 77083 4097 B6
Beech Glen Dr
14100 HarC 77083 4096 E7
Beechglen Ln
13400 HarC 77083 4097 B6
Beechgrove Dr
900 HarC 77058 4507 C5
Beech Hill Dr
3400 HarC 77388 3258 A1
3500 HarC 77388 3257 E1
Beech Hollow Ln
13800 HOUS 77082 4096 E2
13800 HOUS 77082 4097 A2
Beechknoll Ln
4900 HarC 77449 3677 A7
Beech Landing Ln
21000 FBnC 77469 4094 A5
Beech Meadow Dr
14100 HarC 77083 4096 E7
Beech Meadow Ln
7900 HarC 77083 4097 B7
Beechmont Rd
100 HOUS 77024 3959 C5
Beechmoor Dr
14800 HarC 77095 3679 A1
14900 HarC 77095 3678 E1
Beechnut Blvd
- FBnC 77469 4093 E7
- FBnC 77469 4094 A7
16300 FBnC 77083 4095 E7
Beechnut St
- FBnC 77083 4095 D7
- FBnC 77083 4235 D1
4200 BLAR 77096 4101 C7
4200 BLAR 77401 4101 A7
4200 HOUS 77025 4101 A7
4200 HOUS 77096 4101 A7
4200 HOUS 77401 4101 C7
5100 HOUS 77096 4100 E7
5700 HOUS 77074 4100 C7
6900 HOUS 77074 4099 E6
8000 HOUS 77036 4099 B6
9200 HOUS 77036 4098 A7
9800 HOUS 77036 4098 E7
12200 HOUS 77072 4097 E7
12800 HarC 77072 4097 D7
13100 HarC 77083 4097 C7
14500 HarC 77083 4096 E7
14500 HOUS 77083 4096 A7
19300 FBnC 77469 4093 E7
19300 FBnC 77469 4094 A7
19300 FBnC 77469 4234 B1
19300 FBnC 77469 4235 A1
Beechnut Landing Dr
13200 HarC 77083 4097 B6
Beech Park Dr
8300 HarC 77083 4096 E7
Beech Park Ln
7900 HarC 77083 4097 B7
Beech Point Dr
3300 HOUS 77345 3119 D5
Beech Ridge Ln
13500 HarC 77083 4097 B7
Beech Tree Ct
3100 HarC 77449 3815 C3
Beech Tree Dr
20700 HarC 77449 3815 C3
Beechurst Ct
1500 HOUS 77062 4380 A5
Beechurst Dr
14900 HOUS 77062 4380 A7
Beechview Ln
20000 HarC 77449 3815 D6
N Beechwood Ct
4000 HOUS 77059 4380 B4
S Beechwood Ct
3900 HOUS 77059 4380 B4
Beechwood Dr
1200 FRDW 77546 4629 A3
3900 PRLD 77584 4503 B7
Beechwood Chase Ln
- CNRO 77302 2530 C4
- MtgC 77302 2530 C4
Beechwood Park Dr
- HarC 77447 3249 D5
Beecroft Dr
1100 SGLD 77478 4237 B7
Beef Canyon Dr
24000 HarC 77447 3249 E3
Bee Hive Dr
6000 PASD 77505 4248 D4
Beekman Rd
4900 HOUS 77021 4104 B4
Beekman Pl Dr
10100 HOUS 77043 3820 A7
10100 HOUS 77055 3820 A7
Beela Rd
6800 HOUS 77048 4375 E2
Beeman Wy
9200 HOUS 77040 3681 B4
Beemeadow Ln
8300 FBnC 77489 4497 E1
8300 FBnC 77545 4497 E1
8300 HOUS 77489 4497 E1
Beers St
- ALVN 77511 4750 A7
- BzaC 77511 4750 A6
Bees Psg
- FBnC 77459 4621 C3
- MSCY 77459 4621 C3
Bees Creek Cir
- MSCY 77459 4621 C3
Bees Creek Ct
10 FBnC 77459 4621 B4
Bees Creek Knl
10 FBnC 77459 4621 B4
Bees Creek Rd
10 FBnC 77459 4621 B4
Beeson Rd
18200 MtgC 77302 2680 A2
18200 MtgC 77306 2680 A2
Beeston Dr
6500 HarC 77449 3676 E3
Beeston Ln
5800 HarC 77084 3678 B4

Beeston Hall Ct
- HarC 77388 3111 E2
Beetle Rd
28500 HarC 77336 3121 C3
28500 HOUS 77336 3121 C4
Beeville Dr
11700 HarC 77064 3399 E7
Beewood Glen Ct
16500 FBnC 77478 4236 A6
Beewood Glen Dr
16300 FBnC 77478 4236 A6
Befaye Rd
600 HOUS 77076 3684 E6
Beggs St
3800 HOUS 77009 3824 C6
Begonia Blvd
8000 HarC 77562 3832 D3
Begonia Ln
100 HarC 77562 3831 E1
Begonia St
- PRVW 77445 3100 C2
500 BLAR 77401 4101 A5
Begonia Creek Ct
2100 HarC 77433 3251 A5
Begonia Estates Ct
14200 HarC 77429 3396 A2
Begonia Meadows Dr
25100 HarC 77375 2965 C3
Behan Dr
- HOUS 77091 3682 C4
- HOUS 77092 3682 C4
Beigewood Dr
20700 HarC 77338 3261 E3
Beigewood Ln
20300 HarC 77338 3261 E3
Beinhorn Dr
11800 HarC 77065 3398 D6
12100 HarC 77429 3398 D6
Beinhorn Rd
- HNCV 77024 3959 E2
10500 HNCV 77024 3960 A2
10800 HDWV 77024 3960 A2
11100 HDWV 77024 3959 E2
11100 PNPV 77024 3959 E2
Bekonscot Dr
1100 HarC 77379 3255 C2
Bel Rd
1300 KMAH 77565 4509 E6
Bela Av
500 BYTN 77520 3973 B6
Belarbor St
5900 HOUS 77033 4244 B3
6200 HOUS 77087 4244 D3
Belasco Ln
9400 HarC 77099 4237 C2
Belaya Ln
1000 HarC 77090 3258 A2
Belbay St
7600 HOUS 77033 4244 C3
Belcamp Ct
10200 HOUS 77075 4377 A2
Bel Canto Grn
10 WDLD 77382 2674 B3
Belcara Vw
- LGCY 77539 4633 D2
- LGCY 77565 4633 D2
Belcarra Pl
10 WDLD 77382 2673 E5
Belcher Rd
8100 MNVL 77578 4626 B6
8200 BzaC 77511 4626 C7
Belcourt St
10400 HarC 77065 3539 B3
Belcrest St
5600 HOUS 77033 4244 A3
6200 HOUS 77087 4244 D3
Beldart Ct
5400 HOUS 77033 4243 E3
5400 HOUS 77033 4244 A3
Beldart St
6000 HOUS 77033 4244 C3
6200 HOUS 77087 4244 D3
Belden
2100 HOUS 77034 4246 B5
Belevins Dr
- HarC 77095 3537 E3
N Belfar Pl
10 WDLD 77382 2674 B5
S Belfar Pl
10 WDLD 77382 2674 B5
Belfast Dr
10200 LPRT 77571 4250 C3
Belfast Ln
9100 LPRT 77571 4249 E3
9200 LPRT 77571 4250 A3
Belford Park Ln
7100 FBnC 77469 4094 E2
Belfry Ct
4100 FBnC 77450 4094 B1
Belgard St
7600 HOUS 77033 4244 C3
Belgium Dr
6200 PASD 77505 4248 D5
Belgold St
7000 HarC 77066 3400 B4
Belgrade Dr
3800 HOUS 77045 4241 D6
Belgrave Dr
12900 HarC 77429 3254 C7
E Belgravia Dr
1000 PRLD 77584 4501 A2
N Belgravia Dr
2700 PRLD 77584 4501 A1
S Belgravia Dr
2600 PRLD 77584 4501 A2
W Belgravia Dr
1000 PRLD 77584 4501 A2
Belgravia Wy
1200 HOUS 77339 3264 A1
Belham Ridge Ct
1300 HarC 77379 3255 C1
Belhaven Dr
13400 HarC 77069 3400 E1
Belin Dr
1300 JTCY 77029 3966 D3
Belinda Ct
13600 HarC 77069 3400 B2
Belinda St
5700 ARLA 77583 4623 B5
5700 FBnC 77583 4623 B5
Belin Manor Dr
300 BKHV 77024 3959 C4
300 HOUS 77024 3959 C4
Belk St
3700 HOUS 77087 4104 D6
Belknap Ct
100 SGLD 77478 4368 A3

Belknap Rd
9900 FBnC 77478 4237 B2
9900 HarC 77083 4237 B3
9900 HOUS 77478 4237 B2
S Belknap St
300 SGLD 77478 4368 A3
Bell
- HarC 77388 3113 D3
Bell Av
6300 HTCK 77563 4989 B4
8400 HarC 77064 3541 C3
24100 MtgC 77365 2974 B7
Bell Cir
- BKHV 77024 3959 B2
- HOUS 77024 3959 B2
Bell Ct
14500 MtgC 77302 2678 D5
N Bell Dr
10 TXCY 77591 4873 E6
S Bell Dr
10 TXCY 77591 4873 E6
300 LMQU 77568 4873 E7
Bell Hbr
- HarC 77038 3543 E5
Bell Rd
500 GlsC 77511 4869 B3
Bell St
- PRVW 77445 3100 B3
600 HOUS 77002 3963 C5
1500 HOUS 77003 3963 C5
4100 HOUS 77023 3964 A7
5300 HOUS 77023 4104 C1
6100 HTCK 77563 4989 B4
17000 HarC 77447 3248 D3
21400 HarC 77388 3113 D3
E Bell St
100 ALVN 77511 4867 C1
W Bell St
300 HOUS 77019 3962 E5
Bella Dr
- HarC 77065 3398 A7
13800 HarC 77429 3398 A7
14100 HarC 77429 3397 E7
Bella Cascata
18700 SHEH 77384 2822 A1
Bella Donna
100 SHEH 77384 2822 A1
Bella Dulce Ct
21300 HarC 77379 3111 C3
Bella Flora Ct
21300 HarC 77379 3111 C3
Bella Florence Dr
24200 FBnC 77469 4093 A7
24500 FBnC 77469 4092 E7
Bellaforte Ct
10900 FBnC 77469 4093 A7
10900 FBnC 77469 4233 A1
Bellaire Blvd
- FBnC 77083 4095 B5
- FBnC 77469 4092 D7
- FBnC 77469 4094 E6
- FBnC 77469 4095 A6
- FBnC 77469 4232 E1
1400 ALVN 77511 4867 D3
3700 SSPL 77005 4101 A5
3700 SSPL 77025 4101 A5
3800 WUNP 77005 4101 D4
4200 HOUS 77005 4101 C4
4200 HOUS 77025 4101 C4
4300 BLAR 77401 4101 C4
4300 HOUS 77401 4101 C4
5000 BLAR 77401 4100 D4
5400 BLAR 77081 4100 D4
5400 HOUS 77081 4100 D4
6300 HOUS 77074 4100 A5
7100 HOUS 77074 4099 E5
7300 HOUS 77036 4099 D5
9300 HOUS 77036 4098 E5
9700 HOUS 77072 4098 A5
12100 HOUS 77072 4097 E5
12900 HOUS 77083 4097 C5
13300 HarC 77083 4097 E5
16000 FBnC 77083 4096 A5
16000 HOUS 77083 4096 A5
21600 FBnC 77469 4093 E7
22100 FBnC 77469 4093 D7
23000 FBnC 77469 4233 A1
Bellaire Cir
600 ALVN 77511 4867 D2
Bellaire Ct
100 BLAR 77401 4101 B5
Bellaire St
- LPRT 77571 4252 A3
E Bellaire St
5500 STFE 77510 4986 D2
S Bellaire St
13400 STFE 77510 4986 D2
W Bellaire St
5500 STFE 77510 4986 D2
N Bellaire Estates Dr
13100 HOUS 77072 4097 C5
13100 HOUS 77083 4097 C5
S Bellaire Estates Dr
13100 HOUS 77072 4097 C5
13100 HOUS 77083 4097 C5
Bellaire Gardens Dr
6600 HOUS 77072 4097 C5
6600 HOUS 77083 4097 C5
Bellaire Gardens Tr
13100 HOUS 77072 4097 C4
13100 HOUS 77083 4097 C4
Bellaire Triangle Arc
10 BLAR 77401 4100 E5
10 HOUS 77081 4100 E5
Bellaire View Dr
- HarC 77083 4096 D5
Bella Jess Dr
21300 HarC 77379 3111 C3
Bella Lakes Ln
- HarC 77084 3678 A7
Bella Luce
100 MtgC 77384 2822 A1
100 SHEH 77384 2822 A1
Bella Luna
100 SHEH 77381 2822 A2
100 SHEH 77384 2822 A2
Bella Luna Ct
21300 HarC 77379 3111 D3
Bella Luna Ln
1200 LGCY 77573 4632 E3
1200 LGCY 77573 4633 A3
Bella Mountain Dr
21300 HarC 77379 3111 D3
Bellamy Ln
8400 HarC 77083 4097 C7
Bella Noche Dr
6400 HarC 77379 3111 C2

Bella Pines Ct
9300 HOUS 77078 3688 A4
Bellario Ln
12100 HarC 77041 3679 E5
Bella Sera Dr
6400 HarC 77379 3111 C3
Bella Sole
100 SHEH 77384 2822 A2
Bella Terra Blvd
11100 FBnC 77469 4093 B7
11100 FBnC 77469 4233 B1
Bella Vista
100 MtgC 77384 2822 A1
100 SHEH 77384 2822 A1
Bella Vista Ct
12000 HarC 77041 3680 A4
Bella Vista Dr
200 FBnC 77469 4232 A6
Bellavista Pt
13300 HarC 77429 3398 C3
Bella Vista St
3300 HOUS 77022 3824 A3
Bella Vita Dr
- PRLD 77581 4504 D2
Bellaw Woods Dr
19700 HarC 77338 3261 E5
Bellbird Ct
10 WDLD 77380 2968 B1
Bellbrook Dr
11000 HOUS 77096 4240 A4
Bell Canyon Ln
1000 FBnC 77494 3953 B7
Bell Castle Ct
2200 FBnC 77469 4234 C7
Bellchase Cir
25400 HarC 77373 3114 B3
Bellchase Dr
2900 HarC 77373 3114 D2
Bell Creek Ct
2300 PRLD 77584 4500 B2
Bell Creek Dr
12200 PRLD 77584 4500 B2
Bell Creek Ln
- HarC 77449 3676 D2
Belle Ct
11800 MtgC 77362 2963 C1
25100 HarC 77375 2964 D2
Belle Trc
- HarC 77038 3543 E5
Belleau Wood Dr
19100 HarC 77338 3263 E6
19200 HOUS 77338 3263 D3
Belle Bridge Dr
- HarC 77449 3676 B3
Belleclarie Ln
9300 HarC 77044 3689 B4
Belle Cote Dr
18400 HarC 77532 3409 E6
Bellecove Dr
2800 LGCY 77539 4752 E2
Bellefield Ct
2800 FBnC 77494 3953 A6
W Bellefointaine Wy
15900 HarC 77377 3254 C6
15900 HarC 77429 3254 C6
Bellefontaine Blvd
2600 HOUS 77025 4102 A5
2600 HOUS 77030 4102 A5
Bellefontaine St
3200 HOUS 77025 4101 D5
Belle Glade Dr
4400 HOUS 77018 3683 C7
Belle Glen Dr
6800 HOUS 77072 4098 A5
8700 HOUS 77099 4238 A1
Belle Grove Dr
2100 FBnC 77469 4365 C2
Belle Grove Ln
3600 SGLD 77479 4495 B1
Belle Haven Dr
10800 HarC 77065 3539 E2
Belle Helene Cir
13400 HarC 77429 3397 A4
Belle Hollow Dr
4400 HarC 77084 3678 E7
Belle Isle Dr
19500 HarC 77338 3263 E5
19500 HOUS 77338 3263 D5
E Bellemeade Pl
10 WDLD 77382 2674 B4
W Bellemeade Pl
10 WDLD 77382 2674 B4
Belle Park Dr
- HOUS 77082 4098 B4
3900 HOUS 77072 4098 B7
8600 HOUS 77099 4238 B1
Bellerine Ct
- HarC 77377 3253 E3
Bellerine Ln
- HarC 77377 3253 D3
Bellerive Dr
7100 HOUS 77036 4099 E3
7100 HOUS 77036 4100 A4
7100 HOUS 77074 4100 A4
11000 HOUS 77072 4098 B4
Belle River Ln
14300 HOUS 77077 3956 E5
Bellerose Ln
10400 HarC 77070 3399 B3
Belleshire Ln
16000 HarC 77084 3678 E4
Belleshire Glen Ln
16000 HarC 77084 3678 C4
Belle Terre
- HarC 77336 3121 E6
Belle Vernon Dr
23500 HarC 77389 2966 C5
Bellevue St
2800 HOUS 77017 4105 D5
Bellewood Dr
7600 HOUS 77055 3821 C7
7800 HLSV 77055 3821 C7
Belle Wy Dr
19800 HOUS 77338 3263 D5
Bellfair Dr
10700 HOUS 77072 4098 C5
Bellfall Ct
14900 HarC 77082 4096 D4
Bellfield Manor Ln
6500 HarC 77084 3678 E3
Bellflora Ct
14800 HarC 77083 4096 D6
Bellflower St
8900 HOUS 77063 4099 D2
Bellforest Ct
15700 HarC 77044 3549 E3
Bellfort Av
- HOUS 77017 4245 D2

STREET
Block City ZIP Map# Grid

Bellfort Av
4800 HOUS 77033 4243 D3
4800 HOUS 77051 4243 D3
5400 HOUS 77033 4244 A3
6200 HOUS 77087 4244 A3
7200 HOUS 77087 4245 A2
7300 HOUS 77061 4245 A2
W Bellfort Av
- HOUS 77071 4240 A4
4000 HOUS 77025 4241 C2
4300 HOUS 77035 4241 C2
4300 HOUS 77096 4241 C2
5000 HOUS 77035 4240 E3
5300 HOUS 77096 4240 D4
7500 HOUS 77071 4239 E4
8600 HOUS 77031 4239 E4
10000 HOUS 77031 4238 E5
10600 HOUS 77099 4238 C5
11700 HOUS 77477 4238 C4
12300 HOUS 77099 4237 E4
12300 HOUS 77477 4237 E4
12300 MDWP 77477 4237 E4
12300 SGLD 77478 4237 B4
12400 FBnC 77099 4237 D4
12400 FBnC 77478 4237 D4
12400 SGLD 77099 4237 E4
12600 HOUS 77478 4237 B4
Bellfort Blvd
2400 HOUS 77045 4242 E3
2400 HOUS 77051 4242 E3
2400 HOUS 77054 4242 D2
3000 HOUS 77051 4243 A3
4600 HOUS 77033 4243 D2
Bellfort Ct
5300 HOUS 77033 4243 E3
W Bellfort Dr
- FBnC 77478 4236 E4
13800 FBnC 77478 4237 A4
W Bellfort St
- HOUS 77045 4242 D2
- HOUS 77051 4242 D2
1600 HOUS 77054 4242 C2
3000 HOUS 77054 4241 E2
3100 HOUS 77025 4241 E2
13700 FBnC 77478 4237 B3
13700 HOUS 77478 4237 B3
15000 FBnC 77478 4236 C4
Bellfort Chase Dr
10300 HOUS 77031 4238 D5
Bellfort Village Dr
- HarC 77031 4238 D5
- HOUS 77031 4238 D5
Bellfrost Ln
20800 FBnC 77450 4094 B4
Bell Gardens Dr
10300 HOUS 77041 3819 E1
10300 HOUS 77041 3820 B1
Bellgate Ct
22400 HarC 77373 3115 C7
Bellgreen Dr
6800 HOUS 77030 4102 B4
Bellgreen Ln
1000 HOUS 77062 4379 D6
Bellgrove Dr
1300 ELGO 77586 4509 B1
1300 SEBK 77586 4509 B1
Bellhaven Ln
- LGCY 77573 4631 B4
Bell Hollow Ln
3800 FBnC 77494 4093 C3
Bellinger Ct
9900 FBnC 77459 4621 E4
Bellinger Wy
3700 FBnC 77459 4621 E4
Bellingham Dr
7600 HOUS 77028 3687 A6
Bellingrath Pk
600 MtgC 77302 2530 C5
Bellington Ct
4400 HOUS 77345 3119 E7
Bellini Rd
3800 BzaC 77578 4625 D1
Bellis Ln
15800 HOUS 77489 4371 D6
Bellisima Ct
10 WDLD 77384 2674 E2
Bellknap Rd
8200 HOUS 77040 3681 D4
Bell Manor Ct
13000 HOUS 77047 4373 B3
Bellmar Dr
200 HarC 77037 3684 D1
Bellmar Ln
300 FRDW 77546 4504 D7
300 FRDW 77546 4505 A7
Bellmart Dr
- HOUS 77072 4097 C5
- HOUS 77083 4097 B5
Bellmead Dr
4900 MSCY 77459 4496 B3
Bellmeade St
2500 HOUS 77019 3962 A6
2500 HOUS 77098 3962 A6
Bellmoor Ln
16800 HarC 77084 3678 B4
Bellnale Rd
4800 HOUS 77017 4106 B7
Bellow Falls Ln
14600 HarC 77396 3547 E1
Bellow Glen Dr
22200 HarC 77449 3814 E4
22200 HarC 77449 3815 A4
Bellows Bnd
22300 FBnC 77450 4094 A1
22400 FBnC 77450 4093 E1
Bellows Ln
6300 HOUS 77030 4102 E3
Bellows Bend Ct
3900 FBnC 77450 4094 C2
Bell Patna Dr
- KATY 77494 3952 D2
Bellport Dr
15300 HarC 77084 3678 D3
Bell Ridge Ln
- RSBG 77471 4491 E5
Bell Shadow Ln
1400 HarC 77038 3543 E5
Bellshire Dr
- CNRO 77301 2384 A7
800 CNRO 77301 2383 E7
Bellspring Dr
11000 HOUS 77072 4098 B3
Bell Telephone Rd
- HarC 77049 3691 B5
Bell Timbers St
5400 HarC 77346 3264 C6
Bell Towne Ln
10000 FBnC 77478 4236 E3

Bellview Dr
4700 BLAR 77401 4101 A5
Bellview St
10 BYTN 77521 3972 E2
10 BYTN 77521 3973 A2
1900 LMQU 77568 4873 D7
Bellville Dr
1300 HarC 77038 3543 E5
Bellweather Ct
10 WDLD 77381 2821 C5
Bellwood Dr
8000 HTCK 77563 4988 C6
Bellwood Ln
7800 HarC 77433 3537 A7
9200 HOUS 77036 4099 A4
Bellwood Lake Dr
1400 FBnC 77469 4234 D4
Bellwood Pines Dr
- FBnC 77494 4092 A5
Bel-Mar St
800 SGLD 77478 4368 B3
Belmark St
5700 HOUS 77033 4244 B3
6200 HOUS 77087 4244 D3
Belmont Av
100 HTCK 77563 4988 E3
Belmont Bnd
6500 FBnC 77450 4094 B4
Belmont Cir
13000 HarC 77065 3539 B3
N Belmont Ct
10700 HarC 77065 3539 B2
S Belmont Ct
10500 HarC 77065 3539 B3
Belmont Dr
500 FRDW 77546 4628 E6
N Belmont Dr
2200 RHMD 77469 4492 A3
S Belmont Dr
2200 RHMD 77469 4492 A3
Belmont St
200 TMBL 77375 2964 C7
300 TMBL 77375 3109 B1
700 PASD 77506 4107 B3
2700 DKSN 77539 4753 C2
5100 HOUS 77005 4102 A2
5100 WUNP 77005 4102 A2
6700 HOUS 77025 4102 A4
W Belmont St
1100 PASD 77506 4106 E3
Belmonte Dr
11000 FBnC 77469 4092 E7
Belmonte Pointe Dr
15700 HarC 77429 3397 C2
Belmont Farms Dr
21200 HarC 77375 3110 B2
Belmont Legend Ct
12900 HOUS 77047 4373 C2
Belmont Pointe Dr
- HarC 77429 3397 C2
Belmont Shore Ct
3600 MSCY 77459 4496 D4
Belmont Shore Ln
3500 MSCY 77459 4496 D4
Belmont Turn
- FBnC 77459 4622 B4
Belmore
4800 HOUS 77092 3682 C7
Belmore St
- HOUS 77092 3682 B7
Belnap Ct
3900 FBnC 77459 4621 B4
Belneath St
5400 HOUS 77033 4243 E3
5400 HOUS 77033 4244 A3
Belo Pl
1400 GLSN 77551 5108 C5
Belridge St
10400 HOUS 77016 3686 C4
Belroit St
7800 HOUS 77028 3826 B2
Belrose Dr
5500 HOUS 77035 4240 C5
Belshear Ct
- HarC 77073 3403 B2
Belshire Rd
1100 PASD 77502 4247 C1
Belt Ln
1200 MSCY 77489 4370 C4
Belterraza Ct
7900 HarC 77083 4096 D6
Belterraza Dr
14700 HarC 77083 4096 D6
Belton Bend Ct
9100 HarC 77433 3537 B5
Belton Springs Ln
- HOUS 77048 4375 B2
Beltran Dr
17400 HarC 77073 3404 A3
Beltwood Dr
2700 HarC 77038 3543 A1
Beluche Dr
2400 GLSN 77551 5222 A2
8000 GLSN 77554 5222 A2
Belvan Ct
14500 HarC 77429 3253 B7
14500 HarC 77429 3254 A6
Belvedere Dr
100 CNRO 77301 2384 B7
2100 BYTN 77520 3973 C5
Belvedere St
5300 HOUS 77021 4104 A4
Belvedere Park Ct
13300 HOUS 77047 4373 B3
Belvedere Woods
- FBnC 77459 4621 A6
Belvoir Dr
14900 HarC 77530 3968 C1
Belvoir Park Dr
4000 FBnC 77450 3954 C7
4000 FBnC 77450 4094 C1
Belvon Valley Dr
20700 MtgC 77365 3118 A1
Belvon Valley Ln
24600 MtgC 77365 3118 A1
Belwin Dr
- HOUS 77450 3954 A2
500 HarC 77450 3954 A2
Belwood Park Ln
17600 HarC 77433 3537 D1
Bembridge Dr
1600 MtgC 77386 2969 A1
Ben Dr
100 HOUS 77022 3685 A6
1000 ALVN 77511 4867 D6
Benard Ct
4100 PASD 77503 4108 D6

Ben Blum
13000 HarC 77049 3689 C7
Benbow Wy
1700 HOUS 77055 3820 D6
1700 HOUS 77080 3820 D6
Benbrook Dr
100 HOUS 77076 3684 E3
400 HOUS 77076 3685 A3
Benbrook Manor Ln
19700 HarC 77433 3537 A7
Benbury Dr
22900 HarC 77450 3953 D2
Benchfield Dr
900 HOUS 77091 3683 E6
Benchley Dr
9200 HarC 77099 4237 C1
Benchmark Dr
16700 HOUS 77053 4371 E7
Bend Ct
4900 SGLD 77478 4369 A6
N Bend Ct
15800 HarC 77073 3259 B6
Bend Dr
- HarC 77433 3395 E5
N Bend Dr
600 BYTN 77521 3973 B4
15800 HarC 77073 3259 B6
W Bend Dr
2300 STAF 77477 4370 A4
14600 HarC 77082 4096 D3
14600 HOUS 77082 4096 D3
E Bend Ln
10 HOUS 77007 3962 A4
W Bend St
6200 HOUS 77085 4371 D4
6200 HOUS 77489 4371 D4
Bendbough Ln
- HarC 77377 3253 E1
Bend Cove Ct
3200 LGCY 77573 4633 C2
Bend Creek Ln
3500 PRLD 77584 4500 B3
Bendell Dr
8000 HOUS 77017 4245 E2
8100 HOUS 77017 4246 A1
N Bender Av
100 HMBL 77338 3262 D5
S Bender Av
400 HMBL 77338 3262 D7
Bender Ct
15800 HarC 77396 3406 E6
Bender Rd
5800 HOUS 77032 3405 E6
5800 HOUS 77396 3405 E6
6400 HOUS 77396 3406 B6
7500 HarC 77396 3406 E6
Benders Ln
3800 MtgC 77386 2970 B5
Benders Crossing Ct
3700 MtgC 77386 2970 A4
Benders Crossing Dr
28600 MtgC 77386 2970 A4
Benders Dock Ct
28500 MtgC 77386 2970 A4
Benders Landing Blvd
- MtgC 77386 2970 A4
E Benders Landing Blvd
27300 MtgC 77386 2970 C7
27300 MtgC 77386 3115 C1
W Benders Landing Blvd
3100 MtgC 77386 2970 B5
Benderwood Ct
28600 MtgC 77386 2970 A4
Bending Birch Ct
20300 HarC 77433 3251 E6
Bending Birch Dr
15600 HarC 77433 3251 C6
Bending Bough Dr
500 HarC 77388 3113 B6
Bending Bough Ln
1900 HarC 77388 3113 C6
Bending Branch Ln
8300 HarC 77433 3537 D6
Bending Branch Pl
10 WDLD 77381 2820 C2
Bending Brook Ct
100 LGCY 77539 4752 D3
Bending Brook Ln
100 LGCY 77539 4752 E3
Bending Brook Wy
- HarC 77064 3540 B1
Bending Creek Ln
16700 HarC 77546 4506 A7
Bending Cypress Rd
17300 HarC 77429 3252 C4
Bending Green Wy
21200 HarC 77450 3954 C5
Bending Oak Ct
17200 HarC 77429 3252 C7
Bending Oak Ln
- FBnC 77471 4614 B2
Bending Oaks Dr
16700 MtgC 77385 2676 C5
Bending Oaks Ln
10 BKHV 77024 3959 D3
10 PNPV 77024 3959 D3
E Bending Oaks Ln
6400 PRLD 77584 4502 C5
S Bending Oaks Ln
3300 PRLD 77584 4502 C6
Bending Oaks St
6100 HOUS 77050 3546 E5
6400 HOUS 77050 3547 A5
Bending Pecan Ct
8400 HarC 77040 3541 A5
Bending Pines Ct
4900 FBnC 77494 4092 C3
Bending Pines Ln
20700 HarC 77379 3111 B4
26300 FBnC 77494 4092 C3
Bending Post Dr
17300 HarC 77095 3537 D3
Bending Shore Ct
100 LGCY 77573 4509 B7
Bending Spring Dr
2300 PRLD 77584 4500 B2
Bending Stream Dr
1800 LGCY 77573 4633 E4
Bending Willow Ln
9500 HarC 77064 3540 D3
Bend Rock Wy
13700 HOUS 77044 3409 B3
N Bendrook Lp
10 CNRO 77384 2675 E3
10 CNRO 77384 2676 A3
S Bendrook Lp
10 CNRO 77384 2676 A3

Bendstone Cir
2000 HarC 77450 3954 E6
Bendwick Dr
1500 HarC 77562 3691 E7
Bend Willow Ct
21900 FBnC 77450 4094 A2
Bend Willow Ln
3200 FBnC 77450 3954 A7
3300 FBnC 77450 4094 A1
Bendwood Dr
10 SGLD 77478 4369 A3
600 HOUS 77024 3958 E2
Bendwood Ln
800 LGCY 77573 4633 C2
Benedick Dr
4200 BzaC 77584 4626 B2
4200 PRLD 77584 4626 B2
Benedict Canyon Lp
10 WDLD 77382 2819 A4
Benelli Ct
2600 HarC 77396 3407 D3
Benevolent Wy
11100 HarC 77375 3110 A3
Benfer Rd
14400 HarC 77069 3256 E7
14400 HarC 77069 3400 E1
Benfield Dr
3400 HOUS 77082 4097 C2
Benfield Mdws
- FBnC 77450 4093 E2
- FBnC 77450 4094 A2
Benford Dr
13000 HarC 77099 4237 C1
13200 HarC 77083 4237 B1
Benford Ridge Ln
20500 HarC 77433 3676 D1
Ben Hur Dr
1000 SPVL 77055 3960 B1
1200 SPVL 77055 3821 A7
Benicia Ln
- HOUS 77053 4371 E6
Benignus Rd
400 HOUS 77024 3958 E3
Benili Dr
14600 HarC 77532 3552 C6
Benita St
14200 HOUS 77085 4371 B1
Benjamin Cir
1600 FRDW 77546 4749 E2
Benjamin Ln
6700 PASD 77505 4248 E4
Benjamin St
- HOUS 77011 4105 A1
Benjamin Franklin Ln
3500 MSCY 77459 4369 D5
Ben Ledi Dr
16600 HarC 77084 3678 C6
Benmar Dr
200 HOUS 77060 3403 D7
800 HarC 77032 3403 D7
800 HarC 77032 3404 A6
Benmore Dr
12100 HOUS 77099 4237 E3
Benne Ct
2900 HarC 77014 3401 E3
Bennet Chase Dr
15800 HarC 77429 3397 C2
Bennet Ridge Dr
20800 HarC 77433 3676 D1
Bennett Dr
400 PASD 77503 4108 C4
Bennett Rd
1000 BzaC 77511 4748 D7
1000 BzaC 77511 4866 D1
1700 ALVN 77511 4866 C2
Bennett St
8100 HOUS 77029 3965 C5
9700 HOUS 77029 3966 A5
Bennette Woods Rd
15000 MtgC 77302 2678 E7
15300 MtgC 77302 2824 E1
Bennetts Mill Ln
14900 FBnC 77478 4236 D5
Ben Nevis Dr
16600 HarC 77084 3678 C6
Ben Nevis St
10200 HarC 77532 3693 C6
Bennie St
100 HOUS 77022 3824 A2
11600 HarC 77375 2964 E3
Bennigan St
2000 LGCY 77573 4631 B6
Benning Dr
4300 HOUS 77035 4241 B4
5200 HOUS 77035 4240 E4
5500 HOUS 77096 4240 C4
8600 HOUS 77071 4239 C4
9100 HOUS 77031 4239 A4
Benningcrest Ln
14400 HarC 77047 4374 B5
Benningfield Ln
8500 HarC 77064 3400 A6
8500 HOUS 77064 3400 A6
8600 HarC 77064 3399 E6
Benning Point Ln
1600 HarC 77073 3403 D3
Bennington Ct
2500 LGCY 77573 4631 B7
Bennington Dr
3100 PASD 77503 4108 A4
Bennington St
600 HOUS 77022 3824 C2
1700 HOUS 77093 3824 E2
3000 HOUS 77093 3825 A2
3600 HOUS 77016 3825 A2
4900 HOUS 77028 3825 D3
Bennington Springs Dr
- FBnC 77494 4092 B5
Benny St
5700 FBnC 77583 4623 B5
Benoist Dr
8300 TXCY 77539 4754 B5
8400 DKSN 77539 4754 B5
Benrus Ct
3200 BzaC 77584 4501 C6
Bens Ln
800 HOUS 77336 3266 D2
Bens Branch Dr
2700 HOUS 77339 3119 D6
Benson Ct
10 HOUS 77020 3964 B2
Benson Dr
2200 GNPK 77547 3966 B6
Benson Rd
100 TXCY 77539 4753 C5
Benson St
600 LMQU 77568 4874 A7
1200 HOUS 77020 3964 B2

Benson St
4300 DKSN 77539 4754 A3
Benson Arbor Ln
- FBnC 77494 4092 A5
Benson Landing Dr
15100 HarC 77433 3251 E6
Benson Springs Ln
29600 MtgC 77386 2969 C3
Bens Town Dr
- HOUS 77339 3119 D6
- HOUS 77345 3119 D6
Bens View Ln
- HOUS 77339 3119 D7
- HOUS 77345 3119 E7
Bens View Tr
2200 HOUS 77339 3119 E7
Bentana Ct
17000 HarC 77095 3678 C2
Bent Arbor Ct
21800 FBnC 77450 4093 C6
Bent Arbor Ln
5600 FBnC 77450 4093 E3
Bent Aspen Ct
20300 HarC 77433 3251 C6
Ben Taub Lp
1500 HOUS 77030 4102 D4
Bent Bough Ln
5200 HOUS 77088 3683 A2
5400 HOUS 77088 3682 E2
Bent Branch Dr
6900 HOUS 77088 3682 C2
Bent Bridge Ln
22200 FBnC 77469 4492 E3
Bentbrook Dr
- HarC 77598 4506 D5
- HOUS 77546 4506 D5
Bent Brook Wy
3200 HarC 77449 3815 A3
Bent Creek Ln
900 FBnC 77469 4365 C3
Bent Creek Dr
2700 PRLD 77584 4500 C3
Bent Creek Ln
1800 LGCY 77573 4631 C7
Bentcrest Ct
13100 HarC 77072 4097 C7
Bent Cypress Dr
17600 HarC 77388 3257 D1
Bent Elm Dr
18400 HarC 77388 3112 C7
Bentfield Ct
16800 HOUS 77058 4507 D2
Bentfield Wy
16700 HOUS 77058 4507 E2
Bentford Dr
- HOUS 77339 3117 E6
- HOUS 77339 3118 A6
Bentford Park St
- FBnC 77469 4234 B4
Bentgate Dr
24200 HarC 77373 3115 B5
Bentgrass Ct
21400 FBnC 77450 3954 B7
Bentgrass Dr
3000 FBnC 77450 3954 B7
Bentgrass Pl
10 WDLD 77381 2675 A7
Bent Green Ln
7800 HarC 77389 2966 A3
Bentgrove Ln
11300 HarC 77433 3396 B7
Bent Hollow Ln
24700 FBnC 77494 3953 B6
Bent Horn Ln
27700 MtgC 77355 2815 A6
Benthos Dr
9100 HarC 77083 4237 B2
Bent Knoll Ct
800 FBnC 77479 4493 C5
Bent Lake Dr
21000 HarC 77449 3815 B3
Bentley Ct
2900 PRLD 77584 4501 D6
Bentley Dr
- MtgC 77447 2960 B3
4000 BzaC 77584 4501 D6
4000 PRLD 77584 4501 D6
Bentley Ln
8200 HarC 77083 4097 A7
Bentley Rd
- HarC 77093 3546 A7
11000 HarC 77093 3686 A2
Bentley St
10300 HOUS 77093 3686 A3
10900 HarC 77093 3686 A3
Bentley Glen Ln
25200 FBnC 77494 4093 B2
Bentley Park Ct
10 HarC 77070 3399 E2
Bent Meadow Ct
26100 FBnC 77494 4092 E2
Bent Oak Dr
1600 MSCY 77489 4370 E4
9700 HarC 77040 3681 A2
10100 HarC 77040 3680 E2
27500 MtgC 77354 2819 C5
Bent Oak Ln
- HarC 77379 3256 B4
Benton Dr
5100 PASD 77504 4247 D7
Benton Rd
- FBnC 77469 4492 D7
- RSBG 77469 4492 D7
1600 FBnC 77469 4616 D2
1900 RSBG 77469 4616 D2
Benton St
1100 HOUS 77009 3824 D5
Bentondale Ln
10300 HOUS 77075 4376 E2
Bentongrove Ln
8700 HarC 77044 3689 C5
Bentonite Blvd
4700 BYTN 77521 3833 C3
Benton Park Ln
12700 HarC 77377 3254 A1
Benton Springs Ln
20000 FBnC 77469 4094 C6
N Benton Woods Cir
10 WDLD 77382 2674 A6
S Benton Woods Cir
10 WDLD 77382 2674 A6
Benton Woods Ct
10 WDLD 77382 2674 A6
Benton Woods Dr
10 WDLD 77382 2674 A6
Bentpath Ct
- HarC 77014 3401 D1

Bentpath Dr
- HarC 77014 3401 D1
Bent Pine Dr
12300 HarC 77429 3399 A5
17200 MtgC 77302 2680 B7
19800 HarC 77346 3265 A5
Bentridge Dr
15100 HarC 77044 3549 E2
Bent River Cir
2800 SGLD 77479 4368 C7
Bent River Dr
2200 SGLD 77479 4368 C7
Bent Sage Ct
24700 FBnC 77494 4093 C2
Bent Sail Ct
3100 LGCY 77573 4633 B3
Bent Sail Ln
800 LGCY 77573 4633 B3
Bentshire Wy
16600 HOUS 77058 4507 D2
Bent Spring Ct
3300 HarC 77449 3815 A2
Bent Springs Ln
3600 HarC 77449 3815 A2
Bent Spur Ct
10600 HarC 77064 3540 B5
Bent Spur Ln
8700 JRSV 77065 3540 B6
9800 HarC 77064 3540 B4
Bent Trail Ct
1500 FBnC 77479 4494 B5
11500 HarC 77066 3400 D6
Bent Tree Ct
5900 HarC 77346 3264 D4
Bent Tree Dr
- FBnC 77479 4493 D5
Bent Tree Tr
2700 LGCY 77573 4508 E7
Bent Twig Wy
15300 HarC 77433 3251 A5
Bentvine Cir
19300 HarC 77084 3816 A6
Bentvine Dr
- PRLD 77545 4499 E4
1900 HarC 77084 3816 A6
Bentwood Cir
- DKSN 77539 4752 E6
Bent Wood Dr
- DKSN 77539 4752 E6
Bentwood Dr
- WlrC 77447 2813 B4
1400 MSCY 77489 4370 D4
Bentwood Ln
900 FRDW 77546 4505 C4
Bentwood Pkwy
- HOUS 77339 3117 E3
- HOUS 77339 3118 A3
- HOUS 77365 3117 E3
- HOUS 77365 3118 A3
- MtgC 77365 3117 E2
- MtgC 77365 3118 A1
Bentwood Bay Dr
- DKSN 77539 4752 E5
- LGCY 77539 4752 E5
Bentwood Elm St
5500 HarC 77379 3112 A6
Bentwood Oaks Cir
20400 MtgC 77365 3117 E2
Bentwood Oaks Dr
19900 MtgC 77365 3117 E1
21000 MtgC 77365 3118 A2
Bentworth Dr
2000 HOUS 77077 3958 A6
Bent Wy St
11400 HarC 77429 3398 E5
Ben Venue St
10200 HarC 77532 3693 D6
Benwest Ct
20500 HarC 77388 3112 D5
Benwich Cir
7100 HarC 77095 3678 E1
Benwick Dr
16800 FBnC 77478 4236 B6
Benwick St
9100 HarC 77379 3255 D3
Beran
2400 FBnC 77545 4499 D5
2400 PRLD 77545 4499 D5
Beran Dr
3100 HOUS 77045 4373 A1
4100 HOUS 77045 4372 C1
Berclair Dr
10500 HarC 77038 3543 C2
Berdett Rd
1700 FBnC 77469 4616 E6
Berendo St
6000 HOUS 77092 3821 D1
Beresford Dr
- HOUS 77015 3967 C1
400 HarC 77015 3828 C7
400 HOUS 77015 3828 C7
Beretta Ct
16300 HOUS 77489 4370 E6
Beretta Bend Dr
17100 HarC 77396 3407 C3
Berg Av
800 FBnC 77583 4623 C5
Bergenfield Ct
5600 FBnC 77450 4094 B3
Bergenia Dr
14400 HarC 77429 3397 C3
Bergin St
3000 HOUS 77026 3825 A6
Bergman Ct
1200 MtgC 77384 2529 B7
Bergman Dr
22400 MtgC 77355 2961 A6
Bergstrom St
5400 HOUS 77091 3684 B6
Bering
3100 HOUS 77003 3964 A4
Bering Cir
5700 HOUS 77056 3960 D4
5700 HOUS 77057 3960 D4
Bering Ct
5700 HOUS 77057 3960 D7
Bering Dr
500 HOUS 77056 3960 D3
500 HOUS 77057 3960 D6
3000 HOUS 77057 4100 D1
Bering St
3800 HOUS 77003 3964 B5
Bering Bridge Ln
17500 HarC 77346 3408 C2
Bering Chase Wy
8600 FBnC 77469 4234 B5
Beringer Pl
10 SGLD 77479 4495 B4

Bering Landing Dr
7400 HarC 77433 3676 E
Beringwood Dr
9200 FBnC 77083 4237 A
Beriton St
14100 STFE 77517 4870 E
Berkeley Lake Ln
1200 HOUS 77062 4379 E
Berkely Ct
8000 BYTN 77521 3833 C
Berkley Ct
10 HarC 77389 2819 E
10 HarC 77389 2820 A
2500 FBnC 77469 4365 D
Berkley St
1200 HOUS 77012 4105 C
2900 HOUS 77017 4105 C
3600 HOUS 77087 4105 C
Berkley Park Ct
3800 PASD 77058 4380 E
Berkoff Ct
6500 FBnC 77479 4367 B
Berkoff Dr
1600 FBnC 77479 4367 B
Berkridge Dr
5800 HOUS 77053 4371 D
Berkshire Ct
5000 SGLD 77479 4495 C
Berkshire Ln
- PASD 77504 4247 E
Berkshire St
100 BLAR 77401 4101 A
9500 HOUS 77093 3685 E
12800 HOUS 77077 3957 B
Berkshire Trc
9700 PRLD 77584 4501 B
Berkshire Elm St
2100 HarC 77493 3814 B
Berkshire Forest Dr
16500 HarC 77095 3538 B
Berkshire Green Dr
15000 FBnC 77083 4236 C
Berkshire Hills Dr
5800 HOUS 77345 3120 B
Berkshire Manor Ln
15400 HarC 77084 3678 C
Berkshire Oak St
- HarC 77429 3396 A
19100 HarC 77429 3395 E
Berkshire Park Dr
6100 HarC 77084 3677 E
Berkshire Ridge Dr
2200 FBnC 77479 4493 E
5900 FBnC 77479 4494 A
Berkway Tr
11500 HarC 77065 3539 E
Berkwood Ct
13100 HarC 77038 3543 B
Berlin Ct
9600 HarC 77070 3255 C
Berlinetta Dr
2900 PRLD 77584 4501 E
Berlino Dr
- PRLD 77581 4504 D
Bermar St
31200 SGCH 77355 2961 D
E Bermonds Bend Ct
17500 HarC 77433 3395 E
W Bermonds Bend Ct
17500 HarC 77433 3395 D
Bermondsey Ct
17500 HarC 77377 3254 D
Bermondsey Dr
11500 HarC 77377 3254 D
Bermuda Av
4300 HarC 77521 3833 B2
Bermuda Dr
4100 PASD 77503 4108 D6
4400 SGLD 77479 4496 A2
Bermuda Wy
16600 JMAB 77554 5331 E5
Bermuda Beach Dr
12600 GLSN 77554 5333 C1
Bermuda Dunes Ct
13600 HarC 77069 3400 C1
Bermuda Dunes Dr
2500 MSCY 77459 4369 E6
2500 MSCY 77459 4496 E1
5700 HarC 77069 3400 C1
Bermuda Dunes St
2200 MSCY 77459 4369 E7
Bermuda Palms Dr
2200 MSCY 77459 4369 E7
Bermuda Shores Dr
2200 MSCY 77459 4369 E7
Bern St
2300 LGCY 77573 4632 C2
Bernadette Ln
2900 HOUS 77043 3819 E2
Bernard Av
800 RSBG 77471 4490 C7
Bernard Ct
18900 MtgC 77365 2972 B3
Bernard St
1200 PASD 77506 4107 C4
3100 LPRT 77571 4249 E3
Bernard Wy
1600 HOUS 77058 4507 C3
Bernardo de Galvez Av
1800 GLSN 77550 5109 A5
3900 GLSN 77550 5108 E5
4400 GLSN 77551 5108 D6
Berndale St
8500 HOUS 77029 3965 D3
Berners-lee Av
2700 MtgC 77381 2821 D2
Bernice Dr
11200 GLSN 77554 5221 B5
34500 MtgC 77362 2816 D5
34500 SGCH 77362 2816 D5
Bernice St
100 LMQU 77568 4873 B7
100 TXCY 77591 4873 B7
5900 HOUS 77087 4244 E1
Bernie Av
1300 RSBG 77471 4490 D6
Bernina Ln
- HarC 77044 3690 C1
16100 HarC 77044 3691 A1
Bernini Villa Ct
- FBnC 77053 4498 D2
Bernley St
16200 HarC 77429 3397 A6
Berridge House Ct
9600 HarC 77086 3542 C4
Berrington Dr
14100 FBnC 77083 4236 D1

REET
ock City ZIP Map# Grid
erry Ct
16600 MtgC 77302 2678 D5
erry Ln
11100 MtgC 77302 2677 B2
23700 HarC 77389 2966 A5
Berry Ln
12000 HarC 77089 4505 A1
erry Rd
- HOUS 77022 3685 C7
10 HOUS 77022 3684 E7
1500 HOUS 77093 3685 D7
2900 HOUS 77093 3686 A7
16600 BzaC 77584 4502 E7
16600 BzaC 77584 4626 E1
16600 PRLD 77584 4502 E7
17200 BzaC 77584 4627 A2
17200 PRLD 77584 4627 A2
erry St
700 HOUS 77002 3963 A7
700 HOUS 77006 3963 A7
2000 HOUS 77004 3963 D7
2000 HOUS 77004 4103 B1
erry Blossom Ct
10 MtgC 77380 2822 D7
erry Blossom Dr
10 MtgC 77380 2822 A7
erry Branch Dr
18000 HarC 77084 3677 E5
18000 HarC 77084 3678 A6
errybriar Ln
10000 HarC 77375 3110 B5
erry Brook Dr
5500 HOUS 77017 4246 B2
5900 SHUS 77017 4246 B2
5900 SHUS 77587 4246 B2
erry Creek Dr
5200 HOUS 77017 4246 B1
5500 HOUS 77017 4106 C7
erry Cresent Dr
22300 HarC 77389 3112 E1
errydale St
4500 HOUS 77017 4106 A7
erry Field Blvd
- DKSN 77539 4754 A2
erryfield Dr
1800 HOUS 77077 3957 E6
erryfield Ln
3100 PRLD 77581 4503 D5
errryfrost Ln
10 WDLD 77380 2968 A1
erry Glen Ln
7700 HOUS 77072 4097 D6
erry Grove Dr
3400 HarC 77388 3112 E2
erryhill Ct
5400 HOUS 77017 4246 A2
erry Hill Dr
8600 HarC 77377 3109 B7
18600 HarC 77377 3254 B1
erry Hill Ln
10200 HarC 77375 3110 B4
erryhill Ln
3100 HarC 77388 3112 E2
erry Jungle
- HarC 77396 3406 B7
- HOUS 77396 3406 B7
erry Knoll Ct
4900 HOUS 77345 3120 A1
erry Laurel Ln
12500 HarC 77014 3402 B3
erry Leaf Ct
18500 HarC 77084 3816 D5
erry Limb Dr
9900 HOUS 77099 4238 B3
Berryline Cir
10 WDLD 77381 2821 C3
Berryline Cir
10 WDLD 77381 2821 C4
erry Meadow Dr
11800 HOUS 77071 4239 C5
erry Oaks Ln
17800 HarC 77379 3255 D2
erry Orchard Ln
- FBnC 77469 4094 B7
9800 HarC 77375 3110 A4
errypatch Ct
20900 HarC 77375 3110 C4
errypatch Ln
9800 HarC 77375 3110 B3
errypick Ln
10 WDLD 77380 2821 C7
10 WDLD 77380 2967 C1
erry Pine Dr
23000 HarC 77373 3114 C7
erry Pl Dr
1900 HOUS 77071 4239 B5
erry Ridge Ln
21300 HarC 77375 3110 A4
erry Shoals Ln
17600 HarC 77377 3254 C3
erry Springs Dr
3600 HarC 77070 3399 E3
errystone Ln
9800 HarC 77375 3110 C3
errystone Tr
1200 MSCY 77459 4369 C5
erry Thicket Ln
20500 HarC 77532 3410 E2
erry Tree Dr
10800 HarC 77064 3540 A3
errytree Dr
1300 FBnC 77479 4493 D5
errytree Ln
6600 FBnC 77479 4493 C5
erryview Ct
10 MtgC 77380 2822 D7
10 MtgC 77380 2968 B3
10 WDLD 77380 2968 B3
erry Vine St
21200 HarC 77375 3110 B4
errywick
- HarC 77375 2965 D5
errywood Ln
1200 HOUS 77077 3957 D5
errywood Bend Dr
20900 HarC 77375 3110 C4
ersey Ln
5300 HOUS 77091 3683 D6
ersey Rd
5600 HOUS 77091 3683 D6
rtani
- HarC 77429 3398 A6
rtani Ln
14100 HarC 77429 3397 E6
14100 HarC 77429 3398 A6
rt Brown Rd
3000 MtgC 77302 2531 D6

STREET
Block City ZIP Map# Grid
Bertell Ln
11600 HarC 77429 3253 E7
Bertellis Ln
5500 HOUS 77091 3683 B6
Bertha St
4000 HOUS 77026 3825 B6
Berthas Ln
1400 HOUS 77015 3967 B3
Berthea St
900 HOUS 77006 4102 E1
Bertloma St
200 PASD 77502 4247 B2
200 SHUS 77587 4247 B2
Bertner Av
6500 HOUS 77030 4102 D5
Bertolino's Vw
400 GLSN 77550 5109 D3
Bertrand St
1000 CNRO 77301 2384 A7
2000 HarC 77093 3545 D7
2800 HarC 77093 3546 A7
W Bertrand St
400 HarC 77037 3684 B1
500 HOUS 77037 3684 B1
900 HOUS 77088 3684 A1
Bertwood Rd
7900 HOUS 77016 3825 D1
8200 HOUS 77016 3686 D7
Berwick Ct
5700 FBnC 77479 4493 C1
N Berwick Dr
- HarC 77429 3538 D2
22200 HarC 77095 3538 C2
Berwick Ln
6100 LGCY 77573 4630 C6
Berwick St
13100 HOUS 77015 3967 C1
Berwick Manor Ct
1200 HarC 77379 3110 A6
Berwyn Dr
7900 HarC 77037 3684 C1
7900 HOUS 77037 3684 C2
10300 HarC 77037 3544 C4
Beryl St
6600 HOUS 77074 4100 A6
Berzin Ct
3200 KATY 77493 3813 D3
Bess Rd
1100 DKSN 77539 4753 B2
1100 GlsC 77539 4753 B2
1100 LGCY 77573 4753 B2
Bessdale Ct
- WDLD 77382 2673 B7
Bessemer Ct
2700 MtgC 77381 2821 D2
Bessemer St
9900 HOUS 77034 4246 D7
Bestin Dr
9700 HarC 77065 3539 C3
Bestin Oaks Dr
- PRLD 77581 4504 B7
Bestway Dr
500 RSBG 77471 4490 C5
Beta
1300 HarC 77532 3552 E3
Beta Cir
700 PASD 77503 4108 B5
Betannia Dr
7400 HarC 77095 3678 E1
Beth
- HarC 77375 2964 E3
Beth Ln
100 HarC 77530 3969 A2
12000 MtgC 77354 2817 C5
Bethal Green Dr
400 HarC 77450 3953 D2
Bethan Glen Ln
16700 HarC 77084 3678 B4
Bethany Ln
1000 BzaC 77511 4868 D5
3400 HarC 77039 3545 E6
4800 HarC 77039 3546 C6
Bethany Bay Dr
7200 MSCY 77459 4496 E5
12500 PRLD 77584 4500 B2
N Bethany Bend Cir
10 WDLD 77382 2674 A5
S Bethany Bend Cir
10 WDLD 77382 2674 A5
Bethany Bend Ct
10 WDLD 77382 2674 A5
Bethany Bend Dr
10 WDLD 77382 2674 A5
Bethany Park Ln
- MtgC 77386 2823 B7
- MtgC 77386 2969 D1
Bethel Blvd
4100 HOUS 77092 3821 D1
Bethel Ct
13000 GlsC 77510 4870 E2
Bethel Baptist Rd
19900 MtgC 77357 2828 A5
Bethje St
100 HOUS 77007 3962 B3
Bethlehem St
900 HOUS 77018 3684 A7
1000 HOUS 77018 3683 E7
Beth Marie
28200 MtgC 77355 2815 E6
Bethnal Green Dr
11300 HarC 77066 3401 D6
Bethune Dr
6500 HOUS 77088 3683 C4
6500 HOUS 77091 3683 C4
Bethune Wy
13300 HOUS 77085 4371 D1
Bethune Haven Dr
7600 HOUS 77016 3687 A3
Bethy Dr
11800 HOUS 77076 3684 E2
Betka Rd
- PNIS 77445 3099 D7
- PNIS 77445 3244 E1
- WlrC 77445 3099 D7
- WlrC 77445 3244 E1
12700 WlrC 77484 3246 A3
24000 WlrC 77484 3245 E3
26100 HarC 77447 3248 A3
26100 HarC 77447 3249 A3
28800 HarC 77447 3247 C3
28800 HarC 77484 3247 C3
28800 HarC 77484 3248 A3
29000 PNIS 77445 3245 C3
29000 WlrC 77445 3245 D3
Betonica Ln
6500 HarC 77449 3677 D3
Betony Pl
10 WDLD 77382 2674 B6

STREET
Block City ZIP Map# Grid
Betral St
100 HOUS 77022 3684 C7
200 HOUS 77018 3684 C7
Betsy Ln
4000 HOUS 77027 3961 C7
Betsy Ross Ct
1200 MSCY 77459 4369 D5
Betsy Ross St
1200 ALVN 77511 4867 A2
Bettes St
1600 CNRO 77301 2383 D3
Bettina Ct
800 BKHV 77024 3959 B2
800 HOUS 77024 3959 B2
Bettis Dr
4200 HOUS 77027 3961 B6
Bettong Ct
16300 FBnC 77478 4235 E5
Betty Dr
4800 BzaC 77584 4502 A7
Betty Ln
1300 PASD 77502 4107 D6
1300 PASD 77506 4107 D6
13000 STAF 77477 4239 A7
17400 HarC 77084 3817 A1
22100 MtgC 77357 2827 D5
Betty Rd
400 PASD 77502 4247 A2
400 SHUS 77502 4247 A2
400 SHUS 77587 4247 A2
Betty St
100 CNRO 77301 2384 A2
1800 HarC 77532 3411 D4
4300 BLAR 77401 4101 C5
4300 HOUS 77401 4101 C5
Betty Anne Ln
700 HOUS 77339 3263 A1
Betty Boop St
7900 HOUS 77028 3826 C2
Betty Jane Ln
6600 BYTN 77520 3835 B6
7600 HLSV 77055 3821 C7
7600 HOUS 77055 3821 C7
Betty Joyce Ln
8800 HOUS 77338 3262 B6
Betty Sue Ln
500 HOUS 77047 4373 B5
Bettywood Ct
8000 HarC 77375 2966 B6
Bettywood Ln
23300 HarC 77375 2966 A6
Betzy St
6500 HTCK 77563 4989 B5
Beufort Wy
6000 HarC 77389 2966 E3
Beulah St
3000 HOUS 77004 4103 D1
Beusch Dr
1400 PASD 77502 4107 D7
Beutel Dr
1300 SPVL 77055 3820 E7
Beverly Av
900 PASD 77506 4107 B5
Beverly Cir
600 STAF 77477 4370 A4
Beverly Dr
11800 HarC 77065 3398 E6
12000 HarC 77429 3398 E6
Beverly Ln
100 BLAR 77401 4101 B5
Beverly Rd
2400 PASD 77503 4248 D2
2800 PASD 77505 4248 D2
Beverly St
700 HOUS 77007 3962 E1
800 HOUS 77007 3823 E7
1700 HOUS 77008 3823 E5
Beverly Chase Dr
21300 FBnC 77469 4234 A4
Beverly Hill Ln
- HOUS 77042 4099 B1
7900 HOUS 77063 4100 A1
9300 HOUS 77063 4099 C1
Beverlyhill St
5300 HOUS 77056 4100 E1
5600 HOUS 77057 4100 D1
6400 HOUS 77063 4100 A1
Beverly Hills Wk
5700 HOUS 77057 4100 D1
Beversbrook Dr
9700 HOUS 77031 4238 E6
9700 HOUS 77031 4239 A7
Bevington Oaks Cir
1900 HarC 77450 3954 B6
Bevington Oaks Ct
21700 HarC 77450 3954 B5
Bevis St
1300 HOUS 77018 3823 A4
1500 HOUS 77008 3823 A6
Bevken Ct
- HarC 77429 3253 E7
Bevlyn Dr
9200 HOUS 77025 4101 E7
9500 HOUS 77025 4241 E1
Bexar Dr
8700 HarC 77064 3540 D6
11700 LPRT 77571 4110 E6
11700 LPRT 77571 4111 A6
Bexhill Dr
12900 HarC 77065 3398 B7
Bexley Dr
11200 HOUS 77099 4238 B1
12300 HOUS 77099 4237 D1
Beyer Rd
1100 GlsC 77511 4869 B2
Beyette Rd
30100 MtgC 77355 2815 D2
Beyris St
1400 LMQU 77568 4990 A2
BF Terry Blvd
1500 FBnC 77471 4491 E4
1500 RHMD 77469 4491 E4
1500 RHMD 77471 4491 E4
1500 RSBG 77469 4491 E5
1500 RSBG 77471 4491 D7
5300 FBnC 77469 4491 D5
BF Terry Blvd FM-1640
5300 FBnC 77469 4491 E4
5300 RHMD 77469 4491 E4
BF Terry Blvd FM-2218
1500 FBnC 77471 4491 E4
1500 RHMD 77471 4491 E4
1500 RSBG 77469 4491 E5
1500 RSBG 77471 4491 D7
5300 FBnC 77469 4491 D5
5300 RHMD 77469 4491 D5
Bianca Ct
9400 HOUS 77078 3688 A5

STREET
Block City ZIP Map# Grid
Biarritz Ct
3500 HOUS 77082 4098 A3
Bibb Dr
13300 HarC 77069 3400 E1
Bicentennial Ct
4700 HarC 77066 3401 B2
Bichester Ln
12300 HarC 77039 3545 E5
Bickett Ln
200 HarC 77373 3113 E7
400 HarC 77373 3114 A7
Bickford Ct
24500 FBnC 77494 3953 B7
Bickford Pl
- HarC 77069 3256 E7
Bickwood Ct
11300 HarC 77089 4378 B5
Bickwood Dr
11500 HarC 77089 4378 B6
Bideford Ln
7600 HarC 77070 3399 E1
Bidias St
4500 PASD 77504 4248 A5
Bienville Av
6700 BYTN 77520 3835 B6
Bienville Ln
500 HarC 77015 3828 C7
Biering St
6600 HTCK 77563 4989 B6
Big Pns
1300 TMBL 77375 2963 E5
1300 TMBL 77375 2964 A5
Big Tr
10 FBnC 77459 4621 B4
Bigallo Dr
1700 PRLD 77581 4504 D3
Big Basin Ln
17500 HarC 77346 3408 D3
Big Bend Dr
1500 HOUS 77055 3820 D6
1500 HOUS 77080 3820 D6
8300 FBnC 77479 4494 A6
Big Bend Ln
1600 DRPK 77536 4109 D6
Big Branch Ct
9400 HarC 77064 3540 D5
Big Branch Dr
- HarC 77064 3540 D4
Bigby Ct
8500 HarC 77346 3265 D6
Big Canyon Ct
19800 FBnC 77450 4094 D4
Big Cedar Cir
4900 MSCY 77459 4496 B3
Big Cedar Dr
2500 HOUS 77345 3120 A5
Big Creek Dr
8300 HarC 77064 3542 A6
Big Creek Falls Ct
16600 HarC 77379 3256 B4
Big Cypress Dr
18300 HarC 77388 3258 A1
18800 HarC 77388 3112 E6
Big Deer Dr
100 HarC 77532 3266 B7
1200 HOUS 77532 3266 C7
Big Elm Cir
4900 MSCY 77459 4496 B3
Bigelow St
600 HOUS 77009 3824 C7
E Bigelow Oak Ct
10 WDLD 77381 2821 A5
W Bigelow Oak Ct
10 WDLD 77381 2821 A5
Big Falls Dr
4800 HOUS 77345 3119 E6
Big Fir Dr
3200 HOUS 77345 3120 B4
Biggs Ct
6700 HOUS 77061 4245 B3
16700 MtgC 77302 2678 D5
Big Hickory Dr
3400 HOUS 77345 3120 A4
Big Hollow Ln
100 HOUS 77042 3958 C4
Big Holly Ln
11400 MtgC 77385 2823 B2
Big Horn Ct
3300 SGLD 77478 4368 E5
Big Horn Dr
1400 HarC 77090 3258 A3
1800 HarC 77090 3257 E3
Big Horn Ln
25200 WlrC 77447 2813 D1
Bighorn St
7600 HarC 77521 3833 B3
E Bighorn Creek Dr
- HOUS 77060 3544 A1
N Bighorn Creek Dr
- HOUS 77060 3544 A1
S Bighorn Creek Dr
- HOUS 77060 3544 A1
W Bighorn Creek Dr
- HOUS 77060 3544 C1
Bighorn River Ln
11900 HarC 77346 3408 B3
Bight Ct
1100 HarC 77532 3552 A3
Big Island Dr
- BzaC 77578 4624 E1
- BzaC 77578 4625 A1
Big John Blvd
11600 HarC 77038 3543 B6
11600 HarC 77088 3543 B6
Big Lake Dr
1600 HOUS 77077 3958 B5
Big Leaf Ct
10 FBnC 77459 4621 B3
Big Leaf Dr
- HarC 77429 3398 E5
Big League Dreams Pkwy
- LGCY 77573 4752 D1
Big Meadow Ln
5000 FBnC 77494 4092 C3
Big Meadows Dr
2900 HOUS 77339 3118 E5
Big Oak Cir
16200 MtgC 77355 2961 D6
Big Oak Dr
1800 CNRO 77301 2384 E7
1800 CNRO 77301 2530 E1
7800 TXCY 77591 4873 B6
19000 MtgC 77302 2680 B7
19000 MtgC 77357 2680 B7
Big Oak Ln
26300 MtgC 77354 2817 D6
Big Oak Canyon Dr
6300 FBnC 77469 4493 C4

STREET
Block City ZIP Map# Grid
Big Oaks Dr
1900 MtgC 77385 2676 C5
12400 HOUS 77050 3547 A5
Big Oaks Grv
17400 FBnC 77469 4095 C5
Big Oak Trail Dr
8000 HarC 77040 3541 D7
Big Piney Dr
3600 HOUS 77345 3120 A4
Big Reef Dr
4800 GlsC 77539 4634 C5
Big River Dr
2300 HOUS 77345 3120 A6
21800 MtgC 77355 2960 E1
Big Rock Ct
19300 HarC 77377 3254 E2
Big Sandy
8100 HOUS 77051 4242 E2
Big Sky Dr
22600 HarC 77450 3953 E3
Big Spring Cir
4900 MSCY 77459 4496 B3
Big Spring Dr
5000 PRLD 77584 4503 A7
Big Spring Tr
12700 HarC 77346 3408 D1
Big Springs Dr
2900 HOUS 77339 3118 E5
Big Spruce Dr
3200 HOUS 77339 3119 C3
Big Stone Dr
12600 HarC 77066 3400 E2
Big Sur Dr
14400 HarC 77095 3539 A6
Big Thicket Dr
100 FBnC 77469 4493 A6
7400 HarC 77433 3677 E1
Big Timber Ct
20200 HarC 77346 3264 C3
Big Timber Dr
19900 HarC 77346 3264 C4
Big Torch
10 HTCK 77563 5105 A5
Big Trail Cir
100 FBnC 77459 4621 B3
Big Trail Ct
100 FBnC 77459 4621 B3
Big Tree Dr
20900 HarC 77532 3412 E1
20900 HarC 77532 3413 A1
Big Valley Dr
7300 HarC 77095 3678 D1
Big Wells Dr
- FBnC 77469 4493 C4
20500 HarC 77449 3815 D4
Big Willow Ln
9700 HarC 77064 3540 D4
Bigwood St
7300 HOUS 77016 3687 A5
8000 HOUS 77078 3687 C4
Big Wood Springs Dr
21500 HarC 77450 3954 B5
Bihia Forest Dr
5800 HarC 77088 3682 D1
5900 HarC 77088 3542 D7
Bill St
5600 TXCY 77539 4755 E3
Billabong Crescent Ct
18000 HarC 77429 3396 C1
Billandrea Ln
100 PNVL 77304 2237 B1
100 PNVL 77318 2237 B1
Bill Crowley Park Rd
- HarC 77039 3546 C3
Billie Bess Ln
100 CNRO 77301 2383 E3
100 CNRO 77301 2384 B2
Billie Lee Dr
25000 MtgC 77357 2974 D1
Billie Lou Ln
200 HOUS 77336 3121 D5
Billikin Dr
6500 HarC 77086 3542 C1
Billineys Park Dr
19400 HarC 77449 3677 A3
19600 HarC 77449 3676 E3
Billingford Dr
200 HarC 77450 3953 D1
Billingham Ct
6800 HarC 77379 3256 D4
Billings Dr
1400 HOUS 77055 3820 E6
Billingsley St
3500 HOUS 77009 3824 C6
Billington St
6200 HarC 77084 3678 E4
Billingsgate Dr
6200 HarC 77449 3677 C4
Billit Wy Dr
1300 HarC 77094 3955 A3
Bills Av
3600 PASD 77505 4248 E4
Bill Smith Rd
2100 MtgC 77384 2675 D7
2100 MtgC 77384 2821 D1
2100 WDLD 77384 2675 D7
2100 WDLD 77384 2821 D1
Billy Ln
4200 FBnC 77545 4623 B2
Billy St
4400 HOUS 77020 3964 B3
Biloxi Ct
700 MtgC 77302 2530 D7
Biloxi St
8500 HOUS 77017 4105 D5
Biltmore St
7800 HMBL 77396 3406 D3
Bimbo Ln
14000 MtgC 77302 2531 C7
14600 MtgC 77302 2677 C1
Bimini Wy
1700 SEBK 77586 4509 D2
Bimms Dr
9400 MtgC 77385 2822 D2
Binalong Dr
6400 HarC 77449 3677 A3
Binefield St
29400 MtgC 77386 2969 C4
Binford Cir
21300 HarC 77484 3102 C1
Binford Pl
30000 HarC 77484 3102 D2
Binford Rd
800 WALR 77484 3102 A6
20000 HarC 77484 3102 D5
21300 HarC 77484 2957 D7
Bingham St
1000 HOUS 77002 3963 B2

STREET
Block City ZIP Map# Grid
Bingham St
1200 HOUS 77007 3963 B2
Bingham Manor Ln
3300 HOUS 77056 4100 E2
Binghampton Dr
11900 HOUS 77089 4378 B7
Bingle Rd
- HNCV 77024 3960 B1
1000 SPVL 77024 3960 A1
1000 SPVL 77055 3821 A7
1000 SPVL 77055 3960 A1
1400 HOUS 77055 3821 A6
1700 HOUS 77080 3821 A6
4000 HOUS 77092 3821 A3
4600 HOUS 77092 3682 C7
6800 HOUS 77040 3682 C7
6800 HOUS 77088 3682 C7
Bink Ct
13800 HarC 77014 3401 D1
Binley Ct
13000 HOUS 77077 3957 B7
Binley Dr
2300 HOUS 77077 3957 B7
Binnacle Ct
3400 GLSN 77554 5333 A1
Binnacle Wy
300 HarC 77532 3552 B2
13200 GLSN 77554 5332 E1
13200 GLSN 77554 5333 A1
Bintliff Dr
5600 HOUS 77036 4099 E3
6600 HOUS 77074 4100 A4
8800 HOUS 77074 4240 A1
Binz St
1000 HOUS 77004 4102 E2
1000 HOUS 77005 4102 E2
1000 HOUS 77006 4102 E2
1600 HOUS 77004 4103 A2
Biotics Research Dr
6500 RSBG 77469 4491 E7
6500 RSBG 77469 4492 A7
Biovu Av
1500 GLSN 77551 5108 B6
Birch Cir
- CmbC 77520 3835 C3
Birch Ct
1200 LGCY 77598 4630 C4
Birch Dr
800 PASD 77503 4108 C5
10800 LPRT 77571 4250 D4
Birch Ln
- KATY 77493 3813 A7
3400 DRPK 77536 4109 B7
3400 DRPK 77536 4249 B1
25100 MtgC 77372 2536 E1
S Birch Ln
12000 HarC 77089 4505 A1
Birch Pl
10 HarC 77357 2830 E7
Birch Rd
800 CRLS 77565 4509 C5
Birch St
- HarC 77396 3406 E5
100 BzaC 77511 4748 E1
600 TMBL 77375 2964 B6
700 HarC 77532 3692 C3
1300 PRLD 77581 4504 E5
1700 TXCY 77591 4873 B4
3400 DKSN 77539 4753 C4
4500 BLAR 77401 4101 B6
4800 GlsC 77517 4986 B1
4800 STFE 77517 4870 B7
4800 STFE 77517 4986 B1
16600 HarC 77044 3551 B7
22800 MtgC 77365 3118 E1
Birch Arbor Ct
14700 HarC 77396 3547 D3
14700 HarC 77396 3548 A2
Birchaven Ln
12900 HarC 77072 4097 C7
Birchbank Ln
21100 HarC 77449 3815 C1
Birchbark Dr
7800 HarC 77338 3261 D5
Birch Bay Ct
21400 HarC 77449 3676 D6
Birch Bend Cir
1500 HarC 77067 3402 B5
Birch Bough Ct
4900 HOUS 77345 3120 B2
Birch Bough St
2900 PRLD 77581 4503 E6
Birchbrook Ct
10 WDLD 77380 2967 C2
N Birchcane Ct
10 WDLD 77381 2821 A5
Birchcane Dr
10 WDLD 77381 2821 A5
Birch Canyon Ct
2300 FBnC 77545 4498 C7
13600 HarC 77095 3539 C7
Birch Canyon Dr
8000 HarC 77095 3539 C7
Birch Cluster Ct
500 CNRO 77301 2384 E3
Birch Cove
4600 HarC 77084 3678 E7
Birch Creek Dr
2900 HOUS 77339 3119 C3
Birchcroft Ct
4300 HOUS 77088 3682 E3
Birchcroft Dr
4300 HOUS 77088 3682 E3
E Birchdale Dr
2700 MSCY 77489 4497 B1
W Birchdale Dr
2700 MSCY 77489 4497 B1
Birch Falls Rd
12700 HarC 77065 3539 C2
Birch Forest Ln
17800 HarC 77379 3256 A2
Birchgate Dr
5500 HarC 77373 3115 D7
Birch Glen Dr
12900 HarC 77429 3254 A6
Birchglen Ln
8100 HarC 77070 3399 D2
Birch Glen St
5200 FBnC 77469 4364 B1
Birch Grove Dr
13000 HarC 77099 4237 C2
13200 HarC 77083 4237 B2
Birch Haven Dr
4000 HOUS 77339 3119 B3
Birch Hill Dr
100 FBnC 77479 4367 B5
100 SGLD 77479 4367 B5

STREET
Block City ZIP Map# Grid
Birch Hollow Ln
13800 HOUS 77082 4096 E2
13800 HOUS 77082 4097 A2
Birch Knoll Ln
14300 HarC 77047 4374 C5
Birchland Ct
3300 HOUS 77345 3120 A4
Birch Landing Ct
- PRLD 77583 4500 B4
Birchleaf Dr
3100 HarC 77449 3815 D4
Birchline Dr
10200 HarC 77379 3110 B7
Birch Manor Ln
5000 FBnC 77494 4092 E3
Birch Meadow Dr
11700 HOUS 77071 4239 B5
Birchmere Ct
2600 HarC 77450 3954 D6
Birchmont Dr
5000 HOUS 77091 3682 E6
5000 HOUS 77091 3683 A6
5800 HOUS 77092 3682 D6
Birchmoor Ct
2100 HOUS 77345 3120 B2
Birch Park Ln
3100 HarC 77073 3259 E4
Birch Point Dr
22500 HarC 77450 3953 E4
Birch Rain Ct
20600 HarC 77449 3815 D3
Birchridge Dr
- HarC 77336 3121 E3
10200 HMBL 77338 3262 D4
Birch River Dr
15700 HarC 77082 4096 B2
Birch Row Rd
12400 HarC 77038 3543 B4
Birch Run Ct
1500 HarC 77067 3402 C5
Birch Run Ln
11600 HarC 77067 3402 C5
Birchsa Manor Dr
- HarC 77379 3110 B7
Birch Springs Dr
8700 HarC 77095 3538 B5
Birchstone Dr
1000 FBnC 77459 4369 C5
1000 MSCY 77459 4369 C5
Birchton St
4100 HOUS 77080 3820 E1
Birchtree Forest Dr
7200 HOUS 77088 3683 A3
Birch Vale Dr
16000 HarC 77084 3817 D1
Birch Valley Ct
1200 HarC 77450 3954 A4
Birch Valley Dr
22000 HarC 77450 3954 A4
Birch View Ct
800 BzaC 77584 4501 B1
Birchview Dr
15600 HarC 77377 3254 D5
Birch View St
900 HarC 77530 3829 D6
Birch Villa Dr
3600 HOUS 77345 3119 D4
Birchwood Av
1400 HarC 77093 3685 B1
1400 HOUS 77093 3685 B1
Birchwood Dr
10 HarC 77336 2976 A4
100 HarC 77336 2975 D5
200 MtgC 77386 2822 C7
1300 PASD 77502 4106 D7
1300 PASD 77506 4106 D7
11200 HarC 77338 3263 A5
11200 HMBL 77338 3263 A5
Birchwood Park Pl
10 WDLD 77382 2819 A1
Bird Rd
100 PASD 77502 4107 A6
W Bird Rd
100 PASD 77502 4107 A6
200 PASD 77506 4107 A6
Bird St
32000 WlrC 77484 3246 D6
Birdcall Ln
13300 HarC 77429 3398 A6
Bird Creek Dr
16900 HarC 77084 3678 B4
Bird Dog Dr
16300 HOUS 77489 4370 D6
Bird Forest Dr
8800 HarC 77088 3542 E7
Birdhaven Ln
16900 HOUS 77489 4497 E1
Birdhill Cir
10900 HarC 77064 3540 A3
Birdie Cir
900 LPRT 77571 4251 C7
Birdie Ct
2100 PRLD 77581 4504 D2
Birdie Dr
100 HMPD 77445 2952 D4
Birdie Ln
12400 GNPK 77015 3967 A4
Birdie Wy
5900 PASD 77505 4248 D5
Bird Meadow Ln
8300 HOUS 77489 4497 E1
Birdnest Tr
9600 FBnC 77083 4236 B2
9600 FBnC 77478 4236 B2
Bird Run Dr
8500 HOUS 77489 4497 D1
Birdsall St
10 HOUS 77007 3962 A4
Birdsall Market Pl
5800 HOUS 77007 3962 A3
Birds Eye Maple Ln
9600 HarC 77064 3541 A4
Birdson Dr
- PASD 77503 4108 C4
Bird Song Dr
8900 BYTN 77521 3972 D2
Birdsong Dr
500 LGCY 77573 4632 A2
Birdsong Ln
4900 MSCY 77459 4621 C2
Birdwing Ln
11300 HarC 77067 3402 B6
Birdwood Ct
8900 HOUS 77096 4240 C1
Birdwood Rd
5500 HOUS 77096 4240 C1
5800 HOUS 77074 4240 A1
8600 HOUS 77074 4239 C1

STREET
Block City ZIP Map# Grid

Birkdale Ct
1200 FBnC 77494 3953 A3
Birkenhead Cir
4700 MSCY 77459 4369 B5
Birksbridge Dr
9700 HarC 77379 3110 B6
Birmingham St
7900 HOUS 77028 3826 B2
Birnam Garden Ln
6800 HarC 77086 3542 B4
Birnam Glen Dr
1800 FBnC 77479 4493 E4
1800 FBnC 77479 4494 A3
Birnam Wood Blvd
22800 HarC 77373 3115 B6
22800 HarC 77373 3260 C1
Birnamwood Blvd
- HarC 77338 3260 C3
- HOUS 77338 3260 B4
Birnam Wood Dr
2000 FBnC 77479 4494 A3
Birnamwood Dr
23700 HarC 77373 3115 A4
25000 HarC 77373 3114 E3
Birney Point Ln
13700 HOUS 77044 3550 B3
Birnham Bend Cir
3700 MtgC 77386 2970 A5
Birnham Woods Dr
- MtgC 77386 2969 E4
900 PASD 77503 4108 C5
28300 MtgC 77386 2970 A4
Birsay St
9600 HarC 77379 3255 D4
Bisbane Dr
2500 HarC 77014 3402 A3
Bisbee St
1200 HOUS 77012 4105 D3
2500 HOUS 77017 4105 D4
Biscay Ct
10 WDLD 77381 2675 A6
Biscay Pl
10 WDLD 77381 2675 A7
Biscayne Blvd
200 ELGO 77586 4509 A2
Biscayne Ct
2200 SGLD 77478 4237 C4
Biscayne Wy
11200 HOUS 77076 3685 A3
Biscayne Bay Dr
- PRLD 77545 4500 A1
2600 PRLD 77584 4500 A4
Biscayne Bend Ln
600 LGCY 77573 4630 E6
Biscayne Hill Ct
20100 HarC 77379 3112 A5
Biscayne Lake Ct
- PRLD 77545 4499 D1
Biscayne Lake Dr
- PRLD 77545 4499 D1
Biscayne Pass Ln
11800 HarC 77346 3408 B3
Biscayne Ridge Ln
17000 HarC 77095 3537 E3
Biscayne Shoals Dr
16000 HarC 77546 4506 A5
Biscayne Springs Ln
2900 PRLD 77584 4499 E4
Bishop St
100 HarC 77562 3831 E4
300 HOUS 77009 3963 C2
Bishop Bend Ln
14100 HarC 77047 4374 D5
Bishop Knoll Ln
16600 HarC 77084 3678 C4
Bishops Ct
10 SGLD 77479 4495 D3
Bishops Gate Ln
20300 HarC 77338 3261 E3
Bishops Glen Ct
5700 HarC 77084 3678 D4
Bishops Glen Ln
15800 HarC 77084 3678 D4
Bishops Manor Ln
10 HarC 77070 3399 E3
Bishops Pl Dr
1300 HarC 77379 3255 C2
Bishops Terrace Dr
3400 HarC 77336 3121 D3
Bishopton Cir
3300 PRLD 77581 4376 D6
Bishopton Dr
3100 PRLD 77581 4376 D6
Bishopvale Dr
800 HarC 77037 3544 E7
800 HarC 77037 3545 A6
Bishop Wy Dr
13400 HarC 77083 4237 B2
Bisley Ln
9200 HarC 77088 3543 D7
Bismark
- HOUS 77007 3963 A3
Bison
25600 SPLD 77372 2683 A4
Bison Blf
2900 FBnC 77459 4622 A6
Bison Dr
700 HOUS 77079 3957 B2
Bison Back Dr
18400 HarC 77346 3409 A1
Bisontine St
2100 HarC 77546 4506 A6
Bissell Rd
5800 MNVL 77578 4745 E1
5800 MNVL 77583 4745 E1
5800 MNVL 77583 4746 A1
7000 MNVL 77578 4746 E3
7600 MNVL 77578 4747 C4
8500 BzaC 77578 4747 A3
9300 BzaC 77511 4747 A3
Bissonnet St
- HOUS 77004 4102 E2
1000 HOUS 77005 4102 B2
1000 HOUS 77006 4102 B2
2600 HOUS 77098 4102 A2
2600 WUNP 77005 4102 A2
3000 HOUS 77005 4101 A4
3000 WUNP 77005 4101 C2
4300 BLAR 77401 4101 C3
4300 HOUS 77401 4101 C3
5400 BLAR 77081 4100 E5
5400 BLAR 77401 4100 E5
5400 HOUS 77081 4100 E5
5600 HOUS 77401 4100 D5
6300 HOUS 77074 4100 A7
7200 HOUS 77074 4099 E7
8200 HOUS 77074 4239 A2
9500 HOUS 77036 4239 A2
Bissonnet St
9800 HOUS 77036 4238 E2
10100 HOUS 77099 4238 A2
12100 HOUS 77099 4237 A1
12800 HarC 77099 4237 A1
13000 HarC 77083 4237 C1
14200 FBnC 77083 4236 D2
14200 FBnC 77478 4236 A2
16500 FBnC 77083 4235 E2
16700 FBnC 77469 4235 D2
16700 FBnC 77478 4235 D2
Bistro Ln
11400 HOUS 77082 4098 A2
Biswell
3300 HarC 77032 3546 A2
Biton Dr
7000 HarC 77083 4097 A5
Bitridge Cir
15800 HOUS 77053 4372 B6
Bittercreek Dr
1900 HOUS 77042 3958 C6
Bitternut Dr
5800 HOUS 77092 3682 B5
Bitter Root Dr
20100 MtgC 77365 2972 D7
Bitterroot Ranch Dr
20100 HarC 77449 3676 D4
Bittersweet Ct
1400 FBnC 77469 4365 E3
Bittersweet Dr
1000 FBnC 77469 4365 E2
Bitterwood Cir
10 WDLD 77381 2821 A6
Bitterwood Ct
10 WDLD 77381 2821 A6
Bitts Ct
17300 HarC 77532 3552 A1
Bivens Bnd
18400 HarC 77379 3256 A1
Bivens Brook Dr
2100 HarC 77067 3402 A7
Bivins Lake Cir
3900 FBnC 77469 4234 E5
Bizerte St
100 HOUS 77022 3684 C7
BJ Machinery
- HarC 77073 3404 B3
Bjorn Dr
- HOUS 77085 4240 D7
Black Ln
- PRLD 77584 4502 B5
Black St
2800 HOUS 77023 4104 C4
25300 PTVL 77372 2682 E7
25300 PTVL 77372 2683 A7
Blackamore Cir
9600 HarC 77065 3539 E4
Black Bass Dr
- MtgC 77384 2675 E6
Black Bear Dr
1400 HOUS 77532 3266 B7
Black Bear St
2100 MtgC 77385 2823 B3
Blackbeard Rd
16500 JMAB 77554 5332 A6
Blackberry Cir
3600 MSCY 77459 4497 D7
3600 MSCY 77459 4621 D1
Blackberry Dr
1100 PASD 77502 4107 D6
1100 PASD 77506 4107 D6
Blackberry Ln
18100 MtgC 77306 2534 A6
26300 MtgC 77357 2829 B6
Blackberry Hollow Dr
1200 HarC 77073 3259 B5
Blackbird Dr
13300 HarC 77429 3398 A6
Black Bird Ln
7900 CmbC 77520 3835 D3
Blackbird Ln
- WDLD 77382 2674 C4
Blackbluff Ct
21100 HarC 77449 3815 B1
Blackbristle Ln
20900 HarC 77379 3111 C4
Black Brook Ln
- FBnC 77494 4092 C1
Blackbrook Ln
12800 HarC 77041 3679 D3
Black Buck Ln
9100 MtgC 77303 2239 E4
Blackburn Ct
6100 LGCY 77573 4630 B7
Blackburn Dr
1400 PASD 77502 4247 D2
24900 MtgC 77372 2536 D4
25400 MtgC 77372 2537 A4
Blackburn St
8400 HOUS 77012 4105 C4
Blackburn Cove Ct
15100 HarC 77429 3253 B7
Black Canyon Ct
5700 FBnC 77479 4493 E2
Black Canyon Dr
19800 FBnC 77450 4094 C4
Black Canyon Ln
2400 PRLD 77584 4500 A2
Blackcastle Dr
3100 HarC 77068 3257 C5
Black Cherry Cross
- FBnC 77494 4092 E4
Black Cherry Ct
10 WDLD 77381 2821 A6
Blackcherry Ln
8000 CmbC 77520 3835 D3
Black Cherry St
30000 MtgC 77354 2671 E7
30000 MtgC 77354 2817 E1
Black Cherry Bend Ct
19800 HarC 77433 3251 D7
Black Cliff Ln
8600 HOUS 77075 4376 E4
Black Creek Ct
3900 MSCY 77459 4621 E3
Black Crickett Ct
3800 HarC 77396 3407 E2
Black Duck Dr
2100 LGCY 77573 4631 A7
Blackenberry Dr
15900 HarC 77546 4505 E5
Black Falcon Ct
33100 WlrC 77484 3246 B5
Black Falcon Rd
16000 WlrC 77484 3246 B5
Black Falls Ct
11000 FBnC 77478 4236 C4
Black Falls Ln
15100 FBnC 77478 4236 C4
Blackfins Ln
7800 HOUS 77072 4097 E7
Blackfoot Trail Run
13800 HarC 77429 3253 E5
Black Forest Ct
10200 MtgC 77385 2822 E4
Black Forest Dr
200 HarC 77388 3113 D7
7000 MtgC 77354 2673 A5
8300 HarC 77389 2965 E1
8300 HarC 77389 2966 A1
Black Gap Dr
7800 HarC 77433 3537 C7
Black Gold Ct
2400 HarC 77073 3259 D6
Black Gum Dr
5800 HOUS 77092 3682 B5
Blackgum Dr
22600 MtgC 77355 2960 C1
22600 SGCH 77355 2960 C1
Blackhaw St
1000 HOUS 77079 3818 B7
1000 HOUS 77079 3957 A1
Blackhawk Blvd
- FRDW 77089 4505 A3
- HarC 77089 4505 A2
- PRLD 77089 4505 A3
9600 HOUS 77075 4377 B2
10000 HarC 77089 4377 C6
10600 HOUS 77089 4377 C6
11400 HarC 77089 4504 D1
15300 FRDW 77546 4505 D6
16600 FRDW 77546 4506 A7
16800 FRDW 77546 4630 A1
17200 HarC 77546 4630 B1
Blackhawk Cir
9300 HOUS 77075 4377 B4
Blackhawk Dr
4100 TXCY 77590 4875 A1
Blackhawk Ridge Ct
1200 RSBG 77471 4614 C1
Blackhawk Ridge Ln
- HOUS 77075 4376 E4
- HOUS 77075 4377 A5
Blackhawk Trail Ct
3100 HarC 77373 3115 A3
Black Hearth Tr
21800 HarC 77433 3251 C4
Blackheath Ct
1300 HarC 77494 3953 D4
Black Hickory Ct
20200 HarC 77449 3815 C5
N Black Hills Dr
- HOUS 77060 3544 A1
S Black Hills Dr
- HOUS 77060 3544 A1
W Black Hills Dr
- HOUS 77060 3544 C1
Blackhorse Tr
- HarC 77433 3396 B4
Black Horse Cove
7900 FBnC 77459 4621 A1
Blackhorse Golf Clb
- HarC 77433 3396 A5
Blackjack Ct
7800 HOUS 77088 3682 E2
Black Jack Ln
28000 MtgC 77354 2819 C4
Blackjack Ln
5500 HOUS 77088 3682 E2
N Blackjack Oak Cir
11900 WDLD 77380 2967 E1
S Blackjack Oak Cir
12000 WDLD 77380 2967 E2
Blackjack Oak Pl
2500 WDLD 77380 2967 E2
Black Knight Dr
- WDLD 77382 2673 B6
E Black Knight Dr
10 WDLD 77382 2673 C7
W Black Knight Dr
- WDLD 77382 2673 C6
Black Lab Ln
4500 HarC 77493 3813 A1
Black Locust Dr
3300 SGLD 77479 4495 E2
3800 HOUS 77088 3683 A3
4200 HOUS 77088 3682 E3
Black Maple Ln
5900 HOUS 77088 3682 D4
Black Mesa Ct
4200 HarC 77449 3815 B1
Black Mountain Wy
21800 HarC 77449 3815 A1
Black Oak Dr
2100 SGLD 77479 4494 C1
5800 HOUS 77092 3682 B5
7700 MtgC 77354 2819 B4
S Black Oak St
10 TXCY 77591 4874 A6
Black Opal Ln
21500 MtgC 77339 3118 C4
Black Pearl Ct
19900 HarC 77073 3403 C2
Blackpool Pl
12900 HarC 77014 3401 C3
12900 HarC 77066 3401 C3
Black Pool St
8200 BYTN 77521 3833 C2
Blackraven
- HarC 77338 3260 E3
Blackridge Rd
2400 HarC 77067 3402 A4
Black Rock Ln
3000 PRLD 77581 4503 E2
Black Rock Rd
10 HarC 77015 3829 B5
10 HarC 77049 3829 B5
Black Rock St
4700 BYTN 77521 3833 C2
Black Rose Tr
17600 HarC 77429 3252 C6
Black Sands Dr
10400 HarC 77095 3537 E2
Blacksburg Ct
22100 FBnC 77450 4093 E2
Blackshear St
200 TMBL 77375 2964 D7
4100 HOUS 77018 3823 D2
Black Skimmer Ct
2500 LGCY 77573 4631 B7
Blacksmith Ct
7500 HarC 77064 3542 A5
Blacksmith Dr
8300 HarC 77064 3542 A5
Blacksmith Ln
4000 SGLD 77479 4368 E6
4000 SGLD 77479 4369 A7
Blackstar Pl
10 WDLD 77382 2673 E4
Blackstock Ln
13400 HarC 77083 4097 B7
Blackstone Ct
12500 HOUS 77077 3957 D4
21700 FBnC 77469 4493 A4
Black Stone St
4700 BYTN 77521 3833 C2
Blackstone St
1200 LMQU 77568 4990 B1
W Blackstone St
100 ALVN 77511 4867 C2
Blackstone Creek Ln
5800 HOUS 77345 3120 D7
Blackstone River Dr
12600 HarC 77346 3408 D2
Blackstone Trails Dr
17200 HarC 77396 3407 D2
Blackstream Ct
13800 HarC 77433 3396 A7
Blacktail Ct
26800 HarC 77447 3248 E7
Black Tern Ln
8500 HOUS 77040 3682 B3
Blackthorne Dr
1300 HarC 77094 3955 A3
Blacktip Dr
22200 HarC 77449 3814 E4
22200 HarC 77449 3815 A4
Black Tooth Wy
9200 HarC 77396 3407 A6
Black Walnut Dr
100 HarC 77015 3829 B5
Blackwater Ln
200 HarC 77015 3829 A6
Blackwell St
100 PASD 77506 4106 E3
N Blackwell St
100 PASD 77506 4106 E3
S Blackwell St
100 LPRT 77571 4252 A2
Black Willow Dr
22600 HarC 77375 2966 A7
22700 HarC 77375 2965 E7
Blackwood St
900 HarC 77032 3545 A1
Blackwood Bridge Ln
- FBnC 77494 4092 D2
Blade Borough Ct
12000 HarC 77089 4505 A2
Bladenboro Dr
14600 HarC 77429 3396 B1
Blades St
11200 HOUS 77016 3687 A1
11400 HOUS 77016 3547 A7
Bladesdale Ct
1200 HarC 77494 3953 D4
Bladestone Ln
- FBnC 77450 4093 B6
- FBnC 77494 4093 B6
Blaesser Dr
3200 PRLD 77584 4501 D7
Blaffer St
- BYTN 77520 3971 E7
- BYTN 77520 3972 A7
4500 HOUS 77026 3825 E5
Blaine Lake Dr
9800 HarC 77086 3542 C3
Blair Cross
10000 MtgC 77385 2822 D6
Blair Ln
100 HOUS 77339 3263 B2
Blair Rd
21000 MtgC 77385 2822 D6
Blair St
1300 HOUS 77008 3823 C6
N Blair Bridge Dr
- WDLD 77385 2676 B4
S Blair Bridge Dr
- WDLD 77385 2676 C4
Blaire Ct
15900 HarC 77095 3538 D4
Blair Field Ln
900 FBnC 77545 4623 A2
Blair Hill Ln
- HarC 77044 3549 D3
Blair Manor Ct
2500 HarC 77449 3814 E4
Blair Manor Ln
22500 HarC 77449 3814 E4
Blair Meadow Dr
11600 HOUS 77477 4237 E5
11600 HOUS 77477 4238 A4
11600 MDWP 77477 4237 E5
11600 MDWP 77477 4238 A4
Blairmont Ln
- HOUS 77062 4507 B1
Blairmore Av
6900 SGLD 77479 4494 B1
Blairmore Ct
5400 FBnC 77450 4094 C2
Blairmore Hills Ct
2500 HarC 77014 3402 A2
Blair Ridge Dr
14100 HarC 77429 3397 B2
Blairstone
- HarC 77084 3678 B2
Blairstone St
16800 HarC 77084 3678 B2
Blairwood Dr
16900 HarC 77049 3690 E4
17100 HarC 77049 3691 A4
Blaisdale Rd
100 FBnC 77469 4365 A6
Blaisefield Ct
4900 FBnC 77494 4092 E2
Blake Av
1400 PASD 77502 4107 D6
Blake Ct
6800 PRLD 77584 4502 C5
Blake Rd
1900 FBnC 77478 4237 D5
1900 SGLD 77478 4237 D5
16500 FBnC 77478 4236 A3
Blake Wy
15400 HarC 77032 3404 C7
Blake Bend Cir
9100 HarC 77095 3538 E4
Blakely Grove Ln
1400 PRLD 77581 4376 E7
Blakes Ridge St
4500 MSCY 77545 4622 C2
Blake Valley Ln
18100 HarC 77429 3252 B6
Blakewood Ct
3400 HarC 77068 3257 B4
Blakley Ct
800 FBnC 77479 4367 B6
Blakley Bend Dr
800 FBnC 77479 4367 B6
Blalock Cir
10 BKHV 77024 3959 D4
10 PNPV 77024 3959 D4
Blalock Ln
11600 BKHV 77024 3959 D5
11600 PNPV 77024 3959 D5
Blalock Rd
- HDWV 77024 3959 D5
- HOUS 77024 3959 D1
- HOUS 77055 3959 D1
200 PNPV 77024 3959 D5
700 BKHV 77024 3959 D2
1000 HOUS 77055 3820 D7
1400 HOUS 77080 3820 D4
4100 HOUS 77041 3820 D4
4300 HOUS 77041 3681 C7
4800 HOUS 77040 3681 C7
Blalock Forest St
11600 BKHV 77024 3959 C4
11600 PNPV 77024 3959 C4
Blalock Pines Ct
10 HDWV 77024 3959 D2
Blalock Woods St
10 BKHV 77024 3959 D3
10 PNPV 77024 3959 D3
Blanca Springs Ct
18500 HarC 77346 3264 D7
Blanca Springs Wy
12800 HarC 77346 3264 D7
Blanchard Dr
13200 HarC 77532 3692 D1
Blanchard St
200 LMQU 77568 4873 B7
200 TXCY 77591 4873 B7
Blanchard Grove Dr
- FBnC 77494 4092 A5
Blanchard Hill Ln
800 HOUS 77047 4373 B3
Blanchard Springs Dr
9600 HarC 77095 3538 B4
Blanche St
200 HOUS 77011 3964 B5
Blanchmont Ln
18200 NSUB 77058 4507 E5
18200 NSUB 77058 4508 A5
Blancke Blvd
- PASD 77507 4381 D1
Blanco Dr
5000 PRLD 77584 4503 A7
Blanco St
- HOUS 77063 4099 C1
Blanco Falls Ln
13900 HarC 77429 3253 D6
Blanco Hills Ln
- HarC 77095 3537 E2
Blanco Lake Ct
19200 HarC 77388 3112 D7
Blanco Pines Dr
6900 HarC 77346 3265 A7
Blanco River Ct
28700 MtgC 77386 2970 B2
Blanco Terrace Ln
12600 HarC 77041 3679 E4
Blanco Trails Ln
15700 HarC 77429 3253 D7
Blancroft Ct
100 SGLD 77478 4368 E4
Bland St
1100 HOUS 77091 3683 D4
4700 PASD 77586 4383 C5
Blandford Ln
6900 HOUS 77055 3821 D7
Blanding Dr
600 HarC 77015 3829 C7
600 HarC 77015 3968 C1
Blane Dr
24500 HarC 77493 3814 A6
Blanefield Ct
22600 HarC 77375 3110 D2
Blanefield Ln
9000 HarC 77375 3110 D3
Blank
1400 HOUS 77015 3967 B3
Blankenship Dr
7700 HOUS 77055 3821 B2
8600 HOUS 77080 3821 A2
9700 HOUS 77080 3820 B2
Blanketflower Ct
10 WDLD 77381 2821 C3
Blanks Rd
16200 MtgC 77306 2680 D4
Blanton Blvd
- HOUS 77091 3683 A7
4700 HOUS 77092 3683 A7
Blanton Ln
12700 SGLD 77478 4237 D4
Blanton Brook Dr
20700 HarC 77433 3676 D1
Blantyre Wy
1300 HOUS 77339 3264 A1
Blarney Dr
3600 HOUS 77047 4374 C2
Blasingane Rd
200 HMPD 77445 2953 A6
300 WlrC 77445 2953 A6
Blass Ct
13200 HarC 77044 3689 C5
Blaydon Ct
1200 RSBG 77471 4491 C4
Blazey Cir
7600 HarC 77095 3679 B1
Blazey Dr
13300 HarC 77041 3539 C7
13600 HarC 77041 3679 B1
13900 HarC 77095 3679 B1
Blazing Tr
21900 MtgC 77357 2827 E1
21900 MtgC 77357 2828 A2
Blazing Gap
7800 FBnC 77459 4497 A7
Blazing Star Ct
10 WDLD 77380 2821 D6
Blazing Star Dr
- LPRT 77571 4110 A7
Bledsoe St
100 PRVW 77445 3100 B1
Bleker St
2000 HOUS 77026 3964 B1
2900 HOUS 77026 3825 A7
6900 HOUS 77016 3825 A2
6900 HOUS 77093 3825 A2
Blend Stone
16800 HarC 77084 3678 A3
Blenfield
22700 FBnC 77450 4093 E1
Blenheim Dr
6900 HarC 77379 3256 D3
Blenheim Palace Ct
14300 HarC 77095 3679 A1
Blenheim Palace Ln
- HarC 77041 3679 B1
7100 HarC 77095 3679 B1
Bligh St
14200 HOUS 77045 4372 E2
Blindlake Dr
1700 HarC 77084 3816 A6
Blind River Dr
4200 PASD 77504 4247 D6
Blinka Cir
34000 WlrC 77484 3245 E1
Blinka Rd
14000 WlrC 77484 3245 E1
19800 WlrC 77484 3100 E5
Blinkin Av
100 HarC 77532 3692 C1
Blinnwood Ln
12400 HarC 77070 3399 D5
Bliss St
- HOUS 77017 4245 E1
5400 HOUS 77017 4246 A2
Bliss Tr
6600 HarC 77084 3678 B2
Bliss Canyon Ct
24900 FBnC 77494 4093 B1
Blissfield Ln
21300 HarC 77450 3954 C5
Blissfield Pk
- HarC 77095 3539 B5
Blissfull Valley Ln
- HarC 77375 3255 B1
Bliss Meadows Dr
3200 PASD 77503 4248 C3
3200 PASD 77505 4248 C3
Blisswood Dr
14000 HarC 77044 3549 D2
Blocker Ln
1100 MSCY 77489 4370 D5
Blodgett St
- HOUS 77002 4102 E1
1000 HOUS 77004 4102 E1
1100 HOUS 77004 4103 C2
Bloom Dr
6900 HOUS 77076 3684 E4
Bloombury Ct
10 CNRO 77384 2675 E3
Bloombury Ln
8600 HarC 77064 3399 E6
8600 HarC 77064 3400 A6
Bloomfield Dr
1300 PRLD 77545 4499 D5
Bloomfield St
3000 HOUS 77051 4243 A5
Bloomfield Turn
8600 FBnC 77459 4621 B6
Bloomingdale Manor Dr
14100 HarC 77429 3397 B2
Blooming Garden Ct
4400 LGCY 77573 4630 E6
Blooming Grove Ln
10 HOUS 77077 3957 D2
Blooming Ivy Ln
9900 HarC 77089 4504 E2
Blooming Meadow Tr
- HOUS 77016 3687 C3
Blooming Orchard Ln
- FBnC 77450 3954 A7
Blooming Park Ln
1900 HarC 77450 3954 C5
Blooming Pear Ct
20900 HarC 77433 3251 D5
E Blooming Rose Ct
17300 HarC 77429 3252 D5
W Blooming Rose Ct
17400 HarC 77429 3252 D5
Blooming Sage Ct
6000 HarC 77449 3676 E4
Bloomington Ln
11800 HarC 77099 4238 B5
11800 MDWP 77477 4238 B5
Bloom Meadow Tr
16200 HarC 77433 3251 B5
Bloom Mist Ct
8500 HarC 77072 4097 C7
Bloommist Ct
6500 FBnC 77469 4616 B2
Bloomridge Cir
22700 FBnC 77450 4093 D2
Blossom
11900 HarC 77044 3551 D7
Blossom Ct
3800 BzaC 77584 4501 C7
Blossom Ln
1500 HarC 77521 3832 B5
Blossom Rd
- PRVW 77484 3100 D5
Blossom St
- HOUS 77007 3961 E3
100 HarC 77598 4507 B5
100 WEBS 77598 4507 B5
3800 HOUS 77007 3962 C3
Blossom Bay Ct
2500 HOUS 77059 4380 B6
Blossom Bay Dr
15000 HOUS 77059 4380 B6
Blossom Bell Ln
8500 HOUS 77489 4497 D1
Blossom Breeze Ln
1900 FBnC 77469 4616 B2
Blossom Brook Ln
21800 FBnC 77450 4093 E4
Blossombury Ct
5100 HarC 77449 3676 C6
Blossom Creek Ct
1600 HOUS 77339 3118 D3
Blossom Creek Dr
2000 HOUS 77339 3118 C7
Blossom Creek Tr
2100 HOUS 77339 3118 C6
Blossom Crest Ln
23900 HarC 77373 3115 C5
Blossom Falls Ln
6500 HarC 77449 3677 B3
Blossom Field Ct
13100 HarC 77044 3689 C5
16200 HarC 77433 3251 B5
Blossom Grove Ln
- BzaC 77583 4623 D4
21900 HarC 77379 3111 C1
Blossomheath Cir
12500 HarC 77429 3397
Blossomheath Rd
12800 HarC 77429 3397
Blossom Lake Ct
11300 HarC 77433 3396
Blossom Meadow Ct
22100 FBnC 77494 4093
Blossommist Ln
7400 FBnC 77469 4095
Blossom Walk Ct
- PRLD 77583 4500
Blossom Walk Ln
12600 HarC 77041 3679
Blossomwood Dr
200 LGCY 77573 4631
4400 LGCY 77573 4630
Blossomwood Ln
16300 FBnC 77478 4236
Blosson Green Ln
- HarC 77433 3251
Blount St
1600 HOUS 77008 3823
Blue Av
7900 HOUS 77028 3826
Blue & Gold
- HarC 77379 3256
Blue Aaron Ct
18900 HarC 77433 3250
Blue Agave Wy
19700 HarC 77379 3110
Blue Ash Dr
- HarC 77090 3403
14100 HOUS 77090 3402
14100 HOUS 77090 3403
15200 HarC 77090 3258
15200 HarC 77090 3402
Bluebank Ln
- FBnC 77494 4093
Bluebeard Ct
1700 FBnC 77479 4494
Blue Beech Dr
20400 HarC 77449 3815
Blue Bell Dr
10500 MtgC 77318 2236
Blue Bell Rd
100 HarC 77037 3544
100 HarC 77060 3544
100 HOUS 77037 3544
700 HarC 77038 3544
700 HOUS 77038 3544
1200 HarC 77038 3543
Bluebell St
600 HarC 77562 3831
600 HarC 77562 3832
Blueberry Ct
- DKSN 77539 4754
Blueberry Ln
1200 FRDW 77546 4629
2100 PASD 77502 4107
2100 PASD 77502 4247
3000 PASD 77504 4247
8800 HarC 77049 3690
Blueberry St
100 HOUS 77018 3823
Blueberry Hill Ct
15800 HarC 77084 3678
Blueberry Hill Dr
4700 HarC 77084 3678
4700 HarC 77084 3679
Blue Berry Hill Dr
27000 MtgC 77385 2822
27000 ORDN 77385 2822
N Bluebill Bay
100 BYTN 77520 4113
S Bluebill Bay
100 BYTN 77520 4113
Bluebird Bnd
7300 HMBL 77396 3406
Blue Bird Ln
9800 LPRT 77571 4250
20800 HarC 77447 3106
Bluebird Ln
100 PASD 77502 4247
700 PASD 77502 4246
8200 FBnC 77459 4621
14100 HOUS 77079 3957
14100 HOUS 77079 3958
18800 HarC 77377 3106
W Bluebird Ln
18000 HarC 77377 3107
18800 HarC 77377 3106
Bluebird Pl
10900 CHTW 77385 2823
Bluebird St
16100 GlsC 77517 4869
Blue Bird Wy
3200 PRLD 77584 4502
Bluebird Park Ln
3300 HarC 77338 3260
Blue Bonnet
- HarC 77039 3545
Blue Bonnet Blvd
2300 HOUS 77030 4102
3000 HOUS 77025 4102
4000 HOUS 77025 4101
Bluebonnet Bnd
14100 HarC 77429 3253
Bluebonnet Ct
2500 GLSN 77551 5108
Bluebonnet Dr
400 LMQU 77568 4874
1200 TYLV 77586 4381
1200 TYLV 77586 4382
3600 HarC 77053 4372
3900 STAF 77477 4238
4200 HOUS 77053 4372
Bluebonnet Ln
30900 MtgC 77354 2816
31200 MtgC 77354 2670
Blue Bonnet Rd
7000 HarC 77521 3832
Blue Bonnet St
800 KATY 77493 3952
900 KATY 77493 3813
2700 LGCY 77565 4508
Bluebonnet St
100 SGLD 77478 4367
100 SGLD 77478 4368
3100 PASD 77503 4248
3100 PASD 77505 4248
7500 BzaC 77584 4627
8500 HarC 77562 3832
Blue Bonnet Tr
18200 HarC 77389 2819
18200 HarC 77389 2820
Bluebonnet Tr
3900 DRPK 77536 4249

Houston Street Index

STREET
Block City ZIP Map# Grid

uebonnet Dale Dr
15500 HarC 77433 3251 B6
uebonnet Landfill Rd
- HOUS 77013 3827 A3
uebonnet Meadow Ln
21500 HarC 77388 3112 C3
uebonnet Meadows Ln
3200 HarC 77084 3816 C3
uebonnet Pl Cir
1000 HOUS 77019 3963 A4
uebonnet Pond Ln
6100 HOUS 77345 3120 D6
ue Bonnet Run Ct
7500 HarC 77095 3538 D2
7500 HarC 77095 3678 C2
uebottle Ln
6600 HarC 77449 3677 D3
ue Briar Ln
7700 HarC 77040 3541 E7
ue Candle Dr
3400 HarC 77388 3112 E6
3400 HarC 77388 3113 A4
ue Canoe Ct
2400 SEBK 77586 4509 C2
ue Canyon Dr
22500 FBnC 77450 3953 E6
ue Castle Ct
100 HarC 77015 3828 E5
ue Castle Ln
200 HarC 77015 3828 E5
ue Cedar
27400 MtgC 77386 3115 E1
ue Cedar Ct
4400 MtgC 77386 3115 D2
ue Cedar Ln
- HarC 77338 3262 B4
27200 MtgC 77386 3115 D2
ue Crab Dr
9000 TXCY 77591 4873 A4
ue Creek Ct
10 WDLD 77382 2819 C2
ue Creek Dr
- BzaC 77578 4501 A6
2300 PRLD 77584 4500 B2
5100 HOUS 77345 3120 A5
ue Creek Pl
10 WDLD 77382 2819 C1
uecreek Rdg
20000 HarC 77449 3676 D5
ue Creek Ranch Dr
15100 HarC 77086 3541 D1
uecrest Ln
- FBnC 77494 4093 A1
ue Cromis Ln
12700 HOUS 77045 4241 D6
ue Cruls Wy
9700 HarC 77379 3110 C6
ue Cypress Ct
5300 LGCY 77573 4751 D1
ue Cypress Dr
3400 HarC 77388 3257 E1
3400 HarC 77388 3258 A1
ue Cypress Ln
5200 LGCY 77573 4751 D1
ue Dawn Dr
2900 HarC 77449 3815 E5
ue Diamond Dr
1100 MSCY 77489 4370 D6
ue Dolphin Dr
300 SEBK 77586 4509 C3
ue Dusk Dr
16400 HarC 77433 3251 A4
ue Egret Dr
14700 HarC 77433 3250 D4
ue Falls Dr
13800 FBnC 77478 4237 A4
13800 SGLD 77478 4237 A4
13900 FBnC 77478 4236 E4
ue Feather Dr
11000 HarC 77064 3540 E1
uefield Dr
3300 PASD 77503 4108 B6
uefield Ln
18100 FBnC 77469 4095 B6
uefin St
16500 HarC 77532 3552 A2
ue Forest Dr
4100 HarC 77346 3408 A3
ue Fovant Ct
2900 HarC 77388 3113 A5
3000 HarC 77388 3112 E5
ue Fox Ct
10 WDLD 77380 2968 A2
ue Fox Rd
10 WDLD 77380 2968 A1
ue Gama Dr
11400 HarC 77095 3397 C6
11400 HarC 77095 3538 B1
ue Gap
7400 FBnC 77459 4496 E7
7500 FBnC 77459 4497 A7
uegate Ct
8400 HOUS 77025 4102 A7
uegate St
8400 HOUS 77025 4102 A7
ue Gill Rd
- WDLD 77384 2675 E6
3100 MtgC 77384 2675 E6
ue Ginger
- WDLD 77381 2674 B7
ue Glen Ln
2700 HarC 77073 3259 E5
uegrass Ct
2900 MSCY 77459 4496 C1
ue Grass Dr
2900 FBnC 77469 4365 A3
3300 FBnC 77469 4364 E3
ue Grass Ln
13700 HarC 77044 3689 D3
uegrass Rd
8400 HarC 77521 3833 B2
uegrass St
4100 HOUS 77018 3823 C2
ue Haven Ct
12700 HarC 77039 3546 C5
ue Haven Rd
12800 HarC 77039 3546 C4
uehaw Meadow Ln
- FBnC 77494 4092 E4
ue Heather Ct
21600 HarC 77449 3815 B4
ue Heather Ln
1600 FBnC 77545 4622 D2
ue Heron Dr
10 GLSN 77554 5331 E6
10 JMAB 77554 5331 E6
100 FRDW 77546 4630 A4
1200 BYUV 77563 4990 E7

Blue Heron Dr
1200 BYUV 77563 4991 A7
1200 BYUV 77563 5105 E1
1200 GlsC 77563 4990 E7
1200 GlsC 77563 4991 A7
1200 GlsC 77563 5105 E1
3900 PRLD 77581 4504 D7
Blue Heron Ln
10400 HOUS 77048 4244 D6
Blue Hills Dr
3100 MSCY 77459 4497 C2
Blue Hills Rd
6500 HarC 77069 3400 B2
Blue Hollow Ct
7600 HarC 77396 3547 D1
Blue Hollow Ln
6600 LGCY 77539 4752 E4
Blue Holly Ln
28400 FBnC 77494 3951 C5
N Blue Hyacinth Dr
- HarC 77433 3251 B4
S Blue Hyacinth Dr
- HarC 77433 3251 B4
W Blue Hyacinth Dr
- HarC 77433 3251 B4
Blue Island Dr
11900 HarC 77044 3688 E5
Blue Jack Ln
28500 MtgC 77354 2819 B3
Blue Jasmine Ct
4000 HOUS 77059 4380 C4
Blue Jasmine Tr
- PASD 77059 4380 C3
Blue Jay Cir
2700 HMBL 77396 3406 D4
Blue Jay Dr
7200 TXCY 77591 4873 C7
N Blue Jay Dr
16700 MtgC 77385 2676 D4
Blue Jay Ln
25100 MtgC 77365 3117 D1
Bluejay Ln
7400 HOUS 77075 4376 B2
31600 MtgC 77362 2963 D3
Blue Jay St
10 MtgC 77385 2676 D4
8000 CmbC 77520 3835 D3
Bluejay St
6600 HOUS 77048 4375 E2
Bluejay Trails Ct
17000 HarC 77447 3249 E4
Bluejay Twin Cir
7700 HarC 77396 3406 D6
Blue Juniper Dr
20200 HarC 77449 3815 C5
Blue Lagoon
- HarC 77044 3689 A5
Blue Lagoon Ct
3000 MSCY 77459 4497 D6
Blue Lake Dr
10 HarC 77336 2976 A5
100 HarC 77336 2975 D5
3100 HOUS 77338 3263 D4
3500 HarC 77388 3113 A7
3700 HarC 77388 3112 E7
7700 RSBG 77469 4492 C7
Blue Lake Ln
- HarC 77338 3262 A4
Blue Lakes Ln
2900 MSCY 77459 4496 E2
Blue Lapis Wy
- WDLD 77382 2819 E1
Blue Leaf Dr
1100 FBnC 77469 4493 A5
Blue Lily Ln
17600 HarC 77095 3537 D3
Blue Marlin Ln
13500 HarC 77083 4097 B5
N Blue Meadow Cir
2800 SGLD 77479 4368 D7
S Blue Meadow Cir
2800 SGLD 77479 4368 D7
2800 SGLD 77479 4495 D1
Blue Meadow Ln
3400 HarC 77039 3545 E6
3400 HOUS 77039 3545 E6
3600 HarC 77039 3546 A6
Blue Mesa Ridge Dr
15900 HarC 77546 4506 A5
Blue Mills Ct
2700 HarC 77449 3815 B4
Blue Mist Cir
16900 FBnC 77478 4236 A7
Blue Mist Ct
2400 FBnC 77478 4236 B7
19900 HarC 77338 3261 E4
Blue Mist Dr
2500 FBnC 77478 4236 A7
Blue Morning Dr
15200 HarC 77086 3541 D2
Blue Mound Ter
17200 HarC 77095 3537 C1
Blue Mountain Dr
12000 HarC 77067 3401 D4
Blue Oak Cir
18400 MAGA 77355 2815 B1
N Blue Oak Cir
18400 MAGA 77355 2815 B1
S Blue Oak Cir
18400 MAGA 77355 2815 B1
Blue Oak Dr
10300 HarC 77065 3539 B2
Blue Oasis Ct
600 HarC 77494 3953 A2
Blue Orchid Ct
- HarC 77044 3549 C3
Blue Point Rd
200 CRLS 77565 4509 C5
Blue Quail Dr
1800 FRDW 77546 4629 D5
8300 HOUS 77489 4370 E7
Blue Reef Dr
2300 HarC 77449 3814 E5
Blueridge Av
1500 PASD 77502 4106 E7
Blue Ridge Dr
500 SHEH 77381 2822 A2
700 SHEH 77381 2821 E2
700 WDLD 77381 2821 E2
6600 FBnC 77469 4493 C6
7200 HOUS 77087 4244 C1
7200 HOUS 77087 4245 A1
Blueridge Dr
- BzaC 77584 4501 A6
Blue Ridge Ln
- FBnC 77469 4616 E1
Blue Ridge Rd
13800 HOUS 77085 4371 B2

Blue Ridge Rd
15100 HOUS 77489 4371 C6
16000 FBnC 77053 4498 C1
16000 HOUS 77053 4498 C1
16000 HOUS 77489 4498 C1
Blueridge Rd
2300 FBnC 77545 4498 D5
Blue Ridge Park Ln
30900 MtgC 77386 2969 C1
31000 MtgC 77386 2823 D7
Blue River Dr
12200 HOUS 77050 3547 A5
Blue River Pass Dr
- HarC 77373 3115 B3
Blue Rock Ct
700 HarC 77060 3544 E4
Blue Rock Dr
15600 HarC 77086 3541 D1
Bluerock St
2400 HarC 77039 3545 E4
3500 HarC 77039 3546 A4
Blue Rock Springs Dr
16200 HarC 77073 3259 B4
Blue Rose Cir
4600 MSCY 77459 4369 B7
Blue Rose Dr
2200 MSCY 77459 4369 B6
Blue Sage Ct
100 LGCY 77539 4753 A3
Blue Sage Dr
1800 FBnC 77494 3952 D4
4900 BzaC 77584 4502 A6
4900 PRLD 77584 4502 A6
Blue Sage Ter
4200 HarC 77388 3112 C7
Blue Shadow Ln
2400 HarC 77388 3113 A3
Blue Shimmering Tr
21800 HarC 77433 3250 E4
Blue Shine Tr
16500 HarC 77433 3250 E4
Blue Skies Ct
- LMQU 77568 4872 B5
Blue Sky St
2800 HOUS 77088 3683 B1
Blue Spring Dr
3800 HarC 77068 3257 B6
Blue Spring Wy
- HarC 77379 3256 E1
Blue Spruce Ct
9600 FBnC 77459 4621 D6
Blue Spruce Ln
23500 HarC 77336 3267 A3
Blue Spruce St
11900 HarC 77066 3401 A6
Blue Spruce Tr
3400 PRLD 77581 4504 A6
Blue Spruce Hill St
- HarC 77346 3408 B2
Blue Spruce Vale Wy
12400 HOUS 77089 4378 D7
Bluestem Dr
- HOUS 77088 3683 A1
Bluestem St
4200 HOUS 77045 4241 D6
Bluestone Ct
4100 MSCY 77459 4369 C5
Bluestone Dr
1100 MSCY 77459 4369 C5
6300 HOUS 77016 3687 A2
Bluestone Canyon Dr
11100 FBnC 77469 4092 A7
Bluestone Hollow Ln
18900 HarC 77377 3253 E2
Bluestone Springs Ln
6500 HarC 77379 3111 C3
Blue Stream Ct
7800 HarC 77095 3539 B7
Blue Swallow Dr
13400 HarC 77086 3541 E2
Blueswift Dr
7000 HarC 77433 3676 E2
7000 HarC 77449 3676 E2
Blue Tail Dr
24300 HOUS 77336 3266 B2
Blue Thistle Dr
15100 HarC 77433 3250 E5
15200 HarC 77433 3251 C4
Blue Timbers Ct
12700 HarC 77044 3689 B3
Blue Topaz Dr
21000 FBnC 77469 4234 B3
Blue Vista Ct
2200 SGLD 77478 4237 A5
Blue Vista Dr
13700 SGLD 77478 4237 A5
14000 SGLD 77478 4236 E5
16600 HarC 77095 3397 A7
Blue Wahoo Ln
7800 HarC 77433 3537 D7
Blue Water Ct
4200 PASD 77505 4249 B5
Bluewater Dr
4100 MSCY 77459 4369 C5
Bluewater Hwy
- GlsC 77554 5547 C6
- GLSN 77554 5547 D5
10200 BzaC 77541 5547 B7
10200 BzaC 77541 5654 A2
Bluewater Hwy CO-257
- GlsC 77554 5547 C6
10200 BzaC 77541 5547 B7
10200 BzaC 77541 5654 A2
Blue Water Ln
2300 HOUS 77018 3683 B7
4900 DKSN 77539 4753 D4
Blue Water Wy
- HarC 77346 3265 A3
100 LGCY 77565 4508 E4
Blue Water Bay Ct
2600 FBnC 77494 3953 A4
Blue Water Bay Dr
1800 FBnC 77494 3952 E4
1900 FBnC 77494 3953 A4
Bluewater Cove Dr
18200 HarC 77346 3409 B1
18400 HarC 77346 3265 B7
Blue Willow Dr
100 HOUS 77042 3958 D5
Blue Wind Ct
2700 HarC 77084 3816 D4
Blue Wing Ct
3600 LGCY 77539 4753 B5
Blue Wing Dr
3200 LGCY 77539 4753 B4
Blue Wing Ln
9600 HarC 77396 3548 B1

Bluewing Teal Ct
4100 GLSN 77554 5441 D3
Bluff Ct
26800 MtgC 77365 3117 C5
Bluff Canyon Wy
19700 FBnC 77450 4094 D4
Bluff Creek Cir
- WDLD 77382 2673 C5
N Bluff Creek Cir
10 WDLD 77382 2673 C5
S Bluff Creek Cir
10 WDLD 77382 2673 C5
Bluff Creek Ct
10 WDLD 77382 2673 C5
Bluff Creek Dr
2100 HOUS 77345 3120 A7
Bluff Creek Pl
10 WDLD 77382 2673 C5
Bluffdale Dr
15900 HarC 77084 3678 E6
Bluff Hollow Ct
2000 FBnC 77469 4616 B3
Bluffton Ln
2000 HarC 77450 3954 B5
Bluff Point Dr
- HarC 77086 3541 E1
7600 HarC 77086 3542 A1
Bluffridge Cir
14800 HarC 77095 3679 A1
Bluff Spring Dr
16400 HarC 77095 3538 A3
Bluff Springs Dr
16400 HarC 77095 3538 B3
Bluffstone Ct
- FBnC 77479 4496 D5
Bluff Trail Dr
7800 HarC 77338 3261 D4
Bluff View Ct
25300 WlrC 77447 2813 D1
Bluff View Dr
18400 HarC 77532 3409 D6
Blum Rd
12200 BzaC 77511 4866 C3
W Blum St
100 ALVN 77511 4867 B1
1800 ALVN 77511 4866 E1
Bluma Ranch Dr
25100 FBnC 77494 3953 A6
Blumberg Rd
41700 WlrC 77445 2953 C4
Blume Av
11800 HOUS 77034 4379 A4
Blume Dr
500 GLSN 77554 5107 C5
Blume Rd
100 RSBG 77471 4490 B6
Blundell Dr
18000 HarC 77388 3257 C1
Blush Hill Dr
10 PNVL 77304 2237 A2
Blushing Pear Ct
17200 HarC 77084 3678 A2
Blushwood Pl
200 WDLD 77382 2675 A5
Blythe St
13000 HOUS 77015 3967 C1
Blythewood St
5400 HOUS 77021 4103 E4
Board Cross
7700 CNRO 77304 2236 E3
Boardwalk Blvd
- SEBK 77586 4382 B6
E Boardwalk Dr
30000 MtgC 77354 2818 B1
W Boardwalk Dr
30000 MtgC 77354 2818 B1
Boardwalk Pkwy
100 STAF 77477 4369 C3
Boardwalk St
10700 HOUS 77042 3958 C6
Boat Hook St
17600 HarC 77532 3411 A7
Boatswain Ct
15900 HarC 77532 3552 A4
Bob Ln
20100 MtgC 77357 2827 C5
Bob St
300 HOUS 77011 3964 B6
400 PASD 77502 4247 B1
Bobbie St
3200 HarC 77086 3542 E4
Bobbitt Ln
7600 HOUS 77055 3821 C6
7800 HLSV 77055 3821 C6
Bobby Ln
17000 MtgC 77365 2825 C5
Bobby St
1100 PRLD 77581 4376 C6
11300 HarC 77375 2964 E3
Bobby Burns St
6000 HOUS 77028 3826 C3
Bobby Jack Ln
- HarC 77040 3541 B7
Bobby Lee Ln
- HOUS 77023 4104 E4
- HOUS 77087 4104 E3
Bobcat Bnd
3000 FBnC 77459 4622 A6
Bobcat Ln
31900 SGCH 77355 2961 B3
Bobcat Rd
11400 HarC 77064 3399 C7
11400 HarC 77064 3540 C1
11400 HarC 77070 3399 C7
Bobcat Tr
16500 HarC 77429 3107 D7
16500 HarC 77429 3252 D2
Bob Link St
500 MtgC 77355 2960 A2
Bobolink Cir
4300 MSCY 77459 4496 C1
22600 HarC 77377 3107 A1
Bobolink Dr
9800 MtgC 77385 2676 D4
Bobolink St
5600 HOUS 77017 4106 C7
Bob Smith Rd
100 BYTN 77521 3973 A4
4100 GLSN 77554 5331 D4
4100 JMAB 77554 5331 D4
Bob White
16800 MtgC 77385 2676 D4
Bob White Av
1300 KATY 77493 3813 E7
Bob White Dr
1100 FRDW 77546 4629 D5
8100 HOUS 77074 4100 A6
8700 HOUS 77074 4240 A1

Bob White Dr
9400 HOUS 77096 4240 A3
11500 HOUS 77035 4240 B7
N Bob White Dr
16700 MtgC 77385 2676 D4
Bob White Ln
1300 KATY 77493 3813 D7
Bob White Rd
13400 STFE 77510 4986 D1
Bob White St
2200 MtgC 77385 2823 C4
Boca Ct
3600 MSCY 77459 4497 B3
10300 HOUS 77099 4237 D2
Boca Grande Ln
13800 HOUS 77044 3409 B4
Boca Raton
- LGCY 77565 4508 E4
Boca Raton Dr
200 PNVL 77304 2237 A3
3300 MSCY 77459 4497 B2
13500 HarC 77069 3400 C2
Bodart Cir
1600 HarC 77090 3258 A4
Bodart Ct
1700 HarC 77090 3258 A4
Bodart Dr
1400 HarC 77090 3258 B4
Boddecker Dr
10 GLSN 77550 4995 C6
Bodega Bay Dr
16300 HOUS 77053 4371 D7
Boden Ln
3900 MtgC 77386 2970 C6
Boden St
2100 LGCY 77573 4632 C2
Bodie Perry Rd
16000 MtgC 77306 2533 B6
Bodine Dr
3200 BzaC 77584 4501 D6
3200 PRLD 77584 4501 D6
Boeneman Dr
700 HOUS 77091 3684 A3
Boerne Canyon Ln
13600 HarC 77429 3253 D7
Boerne Country Dr
- HarC 77429 3253 C5
Boerne Creek Dr
7300 FBnC 77469 4094 A6
Bogan Flats Ct
16400 HarC 77095 3397 C6
Bogan Flats Dr
11400 HarC 77095 3397 B7
11400 HarC 77095 3538 B1
Bogatto St
1900 LMQU 77568 4989 E2
1900 LMQU 77568 4990 A3
Bogden Ln
- HarC 77040 3541 A6
Bogden Village Cir
3900 HarC 77449 3816 B2
Bogey Cir
1000 LPRT 77571 4251 C7
Bogey Wy
- HarC 77581 4504 E2
11700 HarC 77089 4504 E2
11900 PRLD 77089 4504 E2
12000 PRLD 77581 4504 D1
12100 PRLD 77089 4505 A3
12100 PRLD 77581 4505 A3
Boggess Rd
7200 HOUS 77016 3686 E5
7600 HOUS 77016 3687 A4
Bogie
- WlrC 77484 3246 D6
Bogie Wy
5900 PASD 77505 4248 D6
Bogota Dr
3800 PASD 77505 4248 E4
Bogs Ct
11700 HarC 77375 2964 D2
Bogs Rd
11300 HarC 77375 2964 E2
Boheme Dr
12100 HOUS 77024 3959 A3
12700 HOUS 77024 3958 D3
13000 HOUS 77079 3958 C3
Bohemian Hall Rd
13000 HarC 77532 3693 C1
13600 HarC 77532 3553 C5
Bohlssen Rd
31500 HarC 77357 2830 B7
31500 HarC 77357 2976 B1
Bohlssen Wy
1100 HarC 77336 2976 B1
1100 HarC 77357 2976 B1
Bohnhof Strasse St
16300 HarC 77070 3255 B5
Boicewood St
4500 HOUS 77016 3686 C6
Bois D'Arc
- WALR 77484 3101 E5
- WALR 77484 3102 A5
- WlrC 77484 3101 D5
300 CNRO 77301 2384 B7
Bois D'Arc Dr
300 CNRO 77301 2384 B7
10600 LPRT 77571 4110 D6
Bois D'Arc Ln
7300 BYTN 77521 3835 A5
Bois D'Arc St
5900 HOUS 77087 4244 E1
Boise
100 BYTN 77520 3971 B4
Boise St
13400 HOUS 77015 3967 D2
Bo Jack Dr
8100 HarC 77040 3541 C7
Bolden St
100 HOUS 77029 3965 E7
300 HOUS 77029 3966 A7
400 GNPK 77029 3966 A7
400 GNPK 77547 3966 A7
Boldere Ln
14700 HarC 77049 3828 E2
Bold Forest Dr
8600 HarC 77088 3542 C7
Bold River Rd
19300 HarC 77375 3110 A7
Bold Ruler Dr
600 STAF 77477 4370 B4
Bolero Ct
11700 MDWP 77477 4237 E4
Bolero Dr
7000 HarC 77049 3831 A1
Bolero Point Ct
5700 HarC 77041 3680 A5

Bolero Point Ln
12000 HarC 77041 3680 A5
Bolero Point Cir Ct
5800 HarC 77041 3680 A5
Boles Rd
- LbyC 77327 2538 A1
- LbyC 77328 2538 A1
Boles St
300 HOUS 77011 4105 A1
Bolgheri Ln
2700 LGCY 77573 4632 E4
Bolin Rd
3500 HOUS 77092 3821 D3
Bolin St
2800 STFE 77510 4870 D4
Bolinas Ct
28300 MtgC 77386 2970 B4
Bolington Dr
8500 HarC 77083 4097 B7
Bolin Point Ln
20700 HarC 77449 3815 C2
Bolivar St
400 BLAR 77401 4101 A5
Bolivia Blvd
3800 HOUS 77092 3822 A2
4200 HOUS 77092 3821 E1
4900 HOUS 77092 3682 E7
5600 HOUS 77091 3682 E6
Bolivia Dr
3900 PASD 77504 4248 A5
Bolla Rdg
- MtgC 77355 2962 A5
Bollard Dr
16000 HarC 77532 3551 D3
Bolling Ln
700 HOUS 77076 3684 E6
Bollingbrook Dr
9200 HarC 77083 4237 C1
Bollinger Ct
24200 FBnC 77494 3953 B7
Bollinger Park Ct
11700 HOUS 77047 4373 C1
Bolsa Chica Ln
6300 HarC 77041 3679 B4
Bolsover St
1700 HOUS 77005 4102 C2
2500 WUNP 77005 4102 A3
Bolster St
100 BYTN 77520 4112 D2
Bolt Av
3000 HOUS 77051 4243 A4
Bolton Av
4200 STFE 77510 4871 A7
Bolton Ct
900 TMBL 77375 2964 D5
Bolton Dr
900 MSCY 77489 4370 C3
Bolton Pl
500 HOUS 77024 3961 B2
Bolton St
2000 BzaC 77511 4867 E2
Bolton Bridge Ln
19900 HarC 77338 3261 D4
19900 HarC 77338 3262 A3
Bolton Gardens Ct
11500 HarC 77066 3401 E6
Bolton Gardens Dr
3200 HarC 77066 3401 E6
Bomar St
300 HOUS 77006 3962 E5
Bombay St
- HOUS 77022 3823 E3
Bomford Av
14800 HarC 77015 3968 C2
Bonaham Oaks Ct
18200 FBnC 77469 4095 B7
Bonaire Cl
2000 DKSN 77539 4633 C7
2000 GlsC 77539 4633 C7
Bonaire St
8300 HOUS 77028 3826 C4
Bonann Dr
10100 HarC 77070 3255 B5
Bonanza Dr
- GLSN 77554 5221 E1
5300 DKSN 77539 4754 A4
Bonanza Rd
1600 HOUS 77062 4507 C2
Bonaparte Dr
11200 HarC 77429 3538 E1
11600 HarC 77429 3397 D7
Bonaventure Dr
13700 HarC 77065 3398 A7
Bonazzi Blvd
9800 HOUS 77088 3683 A1
10000 HOUS 77088 3543 A7
Bonbrook Bnd
8900 FBnC 77469 4616 E1
Bonbrook Ln
- FBnC 77469 4616 E1
Bonbrook Bend Ct
500 FBnC 77469 4616 E1
Bond St
3000 PASD 77503 4108 B3
3000 PASD 77506 4108 A3
4300 HOUS 77026 3825 B7
8200 HarC 77040 3681 D2
Bondale St
8400 HarC 77040 3681 D3
Bondi Ct
600 HarC 77094 3955 C2
Bonds Creek Ln
20500 HarC 77388 3112 D5
Bonerwood
- HOUS 77489 4371 B7
Boness Rd
5800 HOUS 77396 3405 E4
6100 HOUS 77396 3406 A4
Boney Rd
300 MtgC 77385 2676 B5
Bongodero Dr
- HarC 77082 4096 C2
Bonham Cir
1000 RHMD 77469 4491 E3
Bonham St
1300 LMQU 77568 4989 D2
6900 HOUS 77020 3964 E2
7200 HOUS 77020 3965 A2
13700 HarC 77015 3967 E1
14100 HarC 77015 3968 A1
Bonhamford Ct
14800 HarC 77396 3548 A2
Bonham Oaks Ln
14100 HarC 77047 4374 B4
Bonham Park Ln
20800 HarC 77338 3261 E2
Bonhill Ct
8300 HarC 77379 3256 B5

Bonhomme Rd
5600 HOUS 77036 4099 E3
7900 HOUS 77074 4099 E6
8700 HOUS 77074 4239 E1
Bonilla Ln
13500 HarC 77083 4097 B6
Bonita Av
100 GLSN 77550 5109 E1
Bonita Cr
5900 FBnC 77459 4496 E7
Bonita Ln
3800 LPRT 77571 4383 B2
3800 PASD 77571 4383 B2
Bonita St
800 BYUV 77563 4990 D7
800 BYUV 77563 5105 D1
800 GlsC 77563 4990 D7
7500 HOUS 77016 3825 C1
Bonita Wy
- LGCY 77539 4633 D2
- LGCY 77565 4633 D2
2200 STFE 77520 4113 C1
Bonita Springs Dr
15300 HarC 77083 4096 C4
Bonito Dr
1900 TXCY 77591 4872 E4
Bonito Ln
100 DKSN 77539 4754 B1
Bonnabel Ln
13600 HarC 77070 3399 C3
Bonnaire Dr
10 WDLD 77382 2674 B4
Bonnamere Ln
23900 FBnC 77494 4093 C1
Bonnard Cir
17200 HarC 77379 3256 B2
Bonnebridge Wy Blvd
3000 HOUS 77082 4098 A1
Bonn Echo Ln
6000 HOUS 77017 4246 A2
Bonner Dr
8000 HOUS 77017 4245 E1
8200 HOUS 77017 4105 E7
8400 HOUS 77017 4106 A7
Bonner St
1800 HOUS 77007 3962 C1
3000 LPRT 77571 4251 E7
3000 LPRT 77571 4382 E1
Bonnercrest Dr
13900 FBnC 77083 4237 A2
Bonners Park Cir
18800 HarC 77449 3677 C5
Bonners Park Ct
5900 HarC 77449 3677 C5
Bonnet Ln
16300 FBnC 77478 4236 A6
Bonnetbriar Ln
13800 FBnC 77478 4237 A2
Bonnet Creek Dr
9200 HarC 77095 3538 A4
Bonney
600 MtgC 77385 2823 C1
11400 MtgC 77385 2677 B7
Bonney Briar Dr
3000 MSCY 77459 4497 A1
14100 HarC 77069 3400 B1
14200 HarC 77069 3256 B7
E Bonneymead Cir
10 WDLD 77381 2820 C3
S Bonneymead Cir
10 WDLD 77381 2820 C3
W Bonneymead Cir
10 WDLD 77381 2820 C2
Bonnie Gln
900 HOUS 77339 3263 D2
Bonnie Ln
12800 STAF 77477 4370 B1
27800 MtgC 77357 2829 E5
Bonnie St
800 SHUS 77587 4246 E2
1500 SHUS 77587 4247 A2
Bonnie Bay Ct
400 LGCY 77573 4630 C7
400 LGCY 77573 4751 B2
Bonnie Brae St
1400 HOUS 77006 4102 C1
1600 HOUS 77098 4102 C1
Bonnie Chase Ln
6300 HarC 77449 3677 D3
Bonnie Doon St
800 FRDW 77546 4629 C1
Bonniefield Ln
1100 HOUS 77077 3956 D4
Bonnie Lea Ln
1600 FBnC 77545 4622 D2
Bonnie Park Ct
15500 HarC 77068 3257 B5
Bonnie Sean Dr
16700 HarC 77379 3255 C3
Bonnieville Dr
1300 HarC 77562 3832 B3
Bonnington Dr
13900 HOUS 77034 4378 E5
Bonno Pl
1700 HOUS 77020 3964 A1
E Bonny Branch St
10 WDLD 77382 2820 B1
W Bonny Branch St
10 WDLD 77382 2820 B1
Bonnybrook Ct
23900 HarC 77373 2968 E5
Bonny Brook Ln
- FBnC 77494 4092 A1
Bonny Heights Dr
3500 HarC 77068 3257 C6
Bonny Loch Ln
4800 HarC 77084 3678 A7
Bonny Ridge Ct
16600 HOUS 77053 4372 D6
Bonnyton Ln
- HarC 77014 3402 B2
Bonnyview Dr
8800 HarC 77095 3538 D4
Bonnywood Ln
12800 HarC 77429 3397 D4
Bonover St
1800 HOUS 77007 3962 C1
Bonsrell St
5500 HOUS 77023 4104 C2
Bontura St
16200 HarC 77429 3397 A3
Bonway Dr
13500 HOUS 77045 4372 E1
Bonway Ln
3400 HOUS 77045 4372 E1
Bonwick Ct
10 WDLD 77382 2673 A6

STREET
Block City ZIP Map# Grid

Booker Dr
100 HarC 77373 3114 A1
400 HarC 77373 3113 D1
Booker Rd
900 HarC 77373 3113 E1
Booker St
100 BYTN 77520 3974 B1
7600 HOUS 77028 3826 B4
Bookertee St
1100 BYTN 77520 4112 D1
Boom Dr
15900 HarC 77532 3552 A4
Boone Ct
400 DRPK 77536 4249 B2
Boone Lp
- HOUS 77099 4238 C2
Boone Mdws
- HarC 77095 3538 E5
Boone Rd
- HOUS 77082 4098 B3
3900 HOUS 77072 4098 C7
8500 HOUS 77099 4098 C7
8500 HOUS 77099 4238 C3
Boone St
11400 HOUS 77034 4378 E4
11400 HOUS 77034 4379 A4
Boone Loop Rd W
10900 HOUS 77099 4238 C1
Boonridge Ct
4900 HOUS 77053 4372 B6
Boonridge Rd
- HOUS 77053 4372 B6
Boonway Dr
13400 HOUS 77045 4241 E7
S Booth Ln
900 ALVN 77511 4867 B3
Booth Rd
100 FBnC 77469 4494 D7
7100 MNVL 77578 4746 C4
Booth St
700 HOUS 77009 3824 C7
Booth Bay Ct
800 LGCY 77573 4633 B3
Boothbay Ln
1700 NSUB 77058 4508 A6
Boot Hill Rd
15900 SGCH 77355 2815 E7
Boothill Rd
15900 SGCH 77355 2815 E6
Boot Ridge Rd
16100 HOUS 77053 4372 B7
Boots Dr
5400 HOUS 77091 3684 A6
Boquilla Canyon Dr
19200 HarC 77377 3254 B1
Bora Ct
16800 HarC 77084 3678 C6
Bora Bora Dr
100 TKIS 77554 5106 C4
Borage St
6100 HarC 77532 3552 C3
Borah Peak Wy
21500 HarC 77449 3815 A1
Bordace Ct
7200 HarC 77379 3111 B2
Bordeau Blvd
- HOUS 77043 3819 E4
Borden Av
5300 GLSN 77551 5108 C5
Borden St
600 SGLD 77478 4368 A4
9000 HOUS 77029 3965 D6
Borden Bluff Ln
9400 HarC 77095 3537 D4
Borden Manor Dr
17200 HarC 77090 3258 A4
Borden Mill Rd
12500 HarC 77433 3395 C5
Bordens Blf
1400 FBnC 77469 4364 E4
Borden Shore Cir
12400 HarC 77433 3395 C5
Border Ct
3700 FBnC 77459 4621 B5
Border St
13900 HOUS 77048 4374 E4
26400 HarC 77373 3114 A2
26800 HarC 77373 3113 E1
E Border Oak Ct
33200 MtgC 77354 2671 B4
E Border Oak Dr
11900 MtgC 77354 2671 B5
W Border Oak Dr
11700 MtgC 77354 2670 E4
11700 MtgC 77354 2671 A4
E Border Oak Pk
33200 MtgC 77354 2671 B5
W Border Oaks Dr
- MtgC 77354 2670 E5
- MtgC 77354 2671 A5
Bordersville School Rd
19100 HOUS 77338 3262 B6
19200 HMBL 77338 3262 B6
Borderwood Dr
11600 HOUS 77013 3966 D1
Bordley Dr
5300 HOUS 77056 3960 D5
6100 HOUS 77057 3960 C5
9900 HOUS 77042 3959 A5
10000 HOUS 77042 3958 E5
Boreas Dr
5000 BzaC 77511 4868 B7
13000 HarC 77039 3546 C4
Borea Villa Dr
- FBnC 77053 4498 D1
Borem Rd
19000 GlsC 77511 4868 E2
Borg
2600 HOUS 77017 4105 D5
Borg Breakpoint Dr
6200 HarC 77379 3257 A4
Borgstedt Cemetery Rd
- HarC 77429 3398 A5
14100 HarC 77429 3397 E5
Boridge Cir
15800 HOUS 77053 4372 B6
Borondo Pns
10 LMQU 77568 4989 C3
Borondo Gate
10 LMQU 77568 4989 C3
Borondo Reach
10 LMQU 77568 4989 C3
Borondo Stretch
10 LMQU 77568 4989 C3
Boros Dr
900 HNCV 77024 3960 B1
S Borough Dr
- FBnC 77479 4493 C1

Borough Ln
- HarC 77379 3256 B3
Borough Park Dr
25200 MtgC 77380 2968 C2
Borthwick Ln
- CNRO 77301 2530 B3
Boscobel Dr
6900 FBnC 77583 4623 A7
Bosley Ln
6400 HarC 77084 3678 D3
Bosque Rd
39500 WlrC 77445 3243 B2
Bosque St
- HOUS 77057 3960 D7
5500 HOUS 77056 3960 D7
Boss St
2200 LMQU 77568 4989 E1
2500 LMQU 77568 4873 D7
Boss Gaston Rd
15300 FBnC 77478 4236 A3
15900 FBnC 77469 4236 A3
16500 FBnC 77469 4235 E3
16500 FBnC 77478 4235 E3
Bossut Dr
6100 FBnC 77469 4093 E7
Bostic St
1700 HOUS 77093 3685 D7
3600 HOUS 77093 3686 A7
4700 HOUS 77016 3686 C7
Boston St
800 DRPK 77536 4109 A5
2600 HOUS 77006 3963 C2
2700 HOUS 77006 3962 E5
Boston Green Wy
- PASD 77503 4108 D7
Bostonpost Rd
16500 HarC 77429 3396 E3
Boswell St
1100 HOUS 77009 3824 D6
Bosworth St
5100 HOUS 77017 4106 A6
Botany Ln
3700 HOUS 77047 4243 C7
5300 HOUS 77048 4243 E7
5300 HOUS 77048 4244 A7
8000 HOUS 77075 4376 C1
8100 HOUS 77075 4245 D7
Botany Bay Ln
- HarC 77450 3954 E6
Botetourt
1600 HarC 77493 3814 A7
Bothwell Wy
11300 HDWV 77024 3959 D2
11300 PNPV 77024 3959 D2
Botkins Rd
23300 HarC 77447 3105 A6
24200 HarC 77447 3104 D6
Bottlebrush Ct
12100 HarC 77095 3538 A1
Bottlebrush Ln
11400 HarC 77095 3538 A1
Botwood Dr
- HarC 77530 3829 C4
Boudreaux Cir
25800 HarC 77377 3109 A6
Boudreaux Rd
7000 HarC 77379 3111 B1
7000 HarC 77388 3111 C1
7100 HarC 77389 3111 B1
7300 HarC 77375 3111 B1
7600 HarC 77375 3110 A5
7600 HarC 77379 3110 E3
11300 HarC 77375 3109 B6
13000 HarC 77377 3109 A7
14500 HarC 77377 3108 D7
14500 HarC 77429 3108 E7
Boudreaux Estates Dr
13200 HarC 77377 3109 A6
13600 HarC 77377 3108 E6
Bougainvilla Ln
15700 FRDW 77546 4505 D6
16400 FRDW 77546 4506 A7
16800 FRDW 77546 4630 A1
Bouganvillia Blossom Ln
20500 HarC 77433 3251 B5
Bough Ct
5600 HOUS 77092 3682 C6
W Bough Ln
600 HOUS 77024 3958 D2
Bough Knoll Ct
- HarC 77429 3253 C4
Bough Leaf Pl
10 WDLD 77381 2674 D7
Boulder Ln
4100 PRLD 77584 4502 E7
Boulder Rd
2700 PLEK 77471 4614 C5
Boulder St
1200 HOUS 77012 4105 D3
Boulder Bend Ln
25200 FBnC 77494 4093 B3
Boulder Bluff Dr
700 HarC 77073 3259 B6
Boulder Cove Ct
26500 FBnC 77494 4092 B1
Boulder Creek Ct
2500 PRLD 77584 4500 B3
Boulder Creek Dr
2900 HOUS 77339 3118 E5
12500 PRLD 77584 4500 B3
Bouldercrest Dr
1400 HOUS 77062 4379 E7
1400 HOUS 77062 4380 A7
Boulder Falls Ct
14000 HOUS 77062 4379 D6
Boulder Lake Ct
6000 HOUS 77345 3120 B4
24800 FBnC 77494 3952 E5
Boulder Meadow Ln
4900 HarC 77449 3677 B6
Boulder Oaks Dr
15500 HarC 77084 3678 E5
Boulder Oaks Ln
1900 FBnC 77479 4494 C4
Boulder Park Ct
32500 MtgC 77385 2823 C6
Boulder Point Ct
3100 HOUS 77059 4380 A5
Boulder Ridge Ct
17200 HarC 77095 3538 A7
Boulder Ridge Dr
1900 CNRO 77304 2237 A4
Boulder Springs Dr
8800 HarC 77083 4236 E1
Boulder Springs Ln
2000 HOUS 77077 3956 E6
22200 HarC 77375 3109 D2

Boulder Trace Ln
4800 HarC 77449 3677 C5
Boulder Valley Dr
20500 HarC 77449 3676 C3
Boulderwoods Dr
1200 HOUS 77062 4379 E7
Bouldgreen St
16600 HarC 77084 3678 B3
Boulevard Ln
10 BLAR 77401 4101 C4
N Boulevard Pk
4100 HOUS 77098 4102 B1
Boulevard St
4300 GlsC 77518 4634 D2
Boulevard Green Ln
- BLAR 77401 4101 C4
Boundary Ct
900 FRDW 77546 4505 A6
900 PRLD 77581 4505 A6
Boundary St
400 HOUS 77009 3963 C1
1000 HOUS 77009 3824 C7
E Boundary Wy
4000 HarC 77449 3815 B1
N Boundary Peak Wy
21500 HarC 77449 3815 A1
Bounds Dr
18200 BzaC 77584 4627 C3
Bounds Ln
10 HarC 77336 2976 A2
Bounds Rd
17300 MtgC 77302 2679 D2
Bountiful Crest Ln
3900 SGLD 77479 4495 A1
Bounty Ct
4000 GLSN 77554 5333 A2
Bounty Dr
100 LGCY 77573 4509 A7
Bounty Ln
12600 HarC 77377 3254 B5
Bourelle Cir
21800 MtgC 77355 2960 E4
Bourgain Dr
25900 HarC 77377 3109 A5
Bourgeois Rd
5300 HarC 77066 3401 A5
6000 HarC 77066 3400 D6
Bourgeois Forest Rd
11600 HarC 77066 3400 E4
Bourland Blvd
- HarC 77429 3253 D4
Bournemouth Dr
1200 PASD 77504 4247 D6
Bournewood Dr
900 SGLD 77478 4368 B1
1100 SGLD 77478 4237 B7
E Bournewood Dr
12800 SGLD 77478 4237 C7
Bourrelet Wy
16200 HarC 77532 3552 A3
Bova Rd
7900 HarC 77064 3541 D5
Boveda Dr
14700 HarC 77083 4096 D6
Bovington Dr
24900 HarC 77389 2966 A3
Bow Ln
15700 HOUS 77053 4372 A5
Bowcreek Ln
21500 HarC 77449 3815 A2
Bowden
- HOUS 77005 4102 D2
Bowden Ct
2800 MSCY 77459 4497 E6
Bowden Dr
22000 MtgC 77357 2827 C5
Bowden Chase Ct
1300 HarC 77379 3110 A6
Bowden Chase Dr
1300 HarC 77379 3110 A6
Bowden Creek Dr
13700 HarC 77429 3397 B3
Bowdin Crest Dr
17000 HarC 77433 3251 A3
Bowdoin Rd
14400 MtgC 77372 2681 C1
Bowen Dr
- PASD 77503 4108 C6
Bowen St
1100 FBnC 77477 4369 E5
1100 MSCY 77477 4369 E5
1700 HOUS 77051 4243 C1
Bower Ct
1400 RSBG 77471 4491 C5
Bower Rd
300 HMBL 77338 3263 A7
Bowerman Dr
10400 TXCY 77539 4755 D3
Bowfin Rd
10100 HarC 77070 3255 B6
Bowhead Dr
11600 HOUS 77013 3827 D7
Bowie Dr
1200 GLSN 77551 5108 D5
11700 LPRT 77571 4111 A6
Bowie Ln
24000 MtgC 77365 2973 C7
Bowie St
100 BYTN 77520 4112 D2
1200 LMQU 77568 4989 D2
7200 HOUS 77012 4105 B3
7200 HOUS 77087 4105 B3
Bowie Bend Ct
10 WDLD 77385 2676 C4
Bowie Bend Ln
3800 FBnC 77494 4092 C2
Bowie Ridge Ln
16100 HOUS 77053 4372 A7
Bowing Oaks Dr
12800 HarC 77429 3254 C7
Bowlan Ln
11500 HOUS 77035 4240 B5
Bowles Ct
5500 HarC 77388 3112 A1
Bowline Rd
1600 HOUS 77062 4507 B1
Bowling Green Dr
1600 MtgC 77385 2677 B7
Bowling Green St
5600 HOUS 77021 4103 B5
Bowman Ct
5000 HarC 77388 3112 B3
Bowman Dr
300 ALVN 77511 4867 C3
Bowman St
100 CNRO 77301 2530 A1
4900 HOUS 77022 3684 D7

Bowmoor Ln
- HarC 77449 3815 B2
Bowmore Ct
9300 HarC 77095 3538 C4
Bo Wood Rd
13100 MtgC 77302 2532 E5
13100 MtgC 77306 2532 E5
Bowridge Ln
16100 HOUS 77053 4371 D6
Bowsman Dr
12100 HarC 77377 3254 B2
Bowsprit Ln
15500 HOUS 77062 4507 B1
Bow Sterling Cove
700 HOUS 77079 3957 A2
Bowtrail St
6400 HarC 77084 3678 B3
Bow Willow St
14000 HOUS 77070 3399 D4
Bow Wood Ct
25000 HarC 77389 2966 D3
Boxberry Ct
10 WDLD 77380 2822 B6
Box Bluff Ct
6300 FBnC 77479 4367 B5
Box Canyon Dr
17200 HarC 77447 3249 E4
Box Canyon Ln
17700 HarC 77447 3249 E3
Boxelder Ct
600 LGCY 77573 4631 E5
Box Elder Dr
800 MtgC 77354 2673 D2
Boxelder Dr
3200 HarC 77082 4096 B2
Boxelder St
11900 HarC 77066 3401 A6
Boxelder Pointe
800 LGCY 77573 4631 E5
Boxer Creek Dr
- HarC 77049 3828 D1
Boxfield Ln
- FBnC 77494 4092 D3
Boxford Ct
1100 HarC 77373 2968 D5
Boxhill Dr
11600 HarC 77066 3401 C6
Box M
- MtgC 77372 2683 D1
Box Oak Pl
2400 WDLD 77380 2967 E1
Boxridge Ln
20400 HarC 77449 3815 C7
Boxster Ct
800 HarC 77396 3407 A4
Boxthorn Ct
24600 FBnC 77494 3953 A7
Boxtree
21200 HarC 77073 3259 C2
Box Turtle Ln
10 WDLD 77380 2822 A6
Boxwood Br
6600 HarC 77041 3679 E2
Boxwood Ct
1800 SGLD 77478 4237 A6
12500 BKVL 77581 4375 D6
Boxwood Dr
200 BYTN 77520 3832 B7
1100 BKVL 77581 4375 D6
Boxwood Pl
- LGCY 77598 4630 C4
Boxwood Gate Tr
3500 PRLD 77581 4503 E6
Boxwood Ridge Ln
7400 FBnC 77469 4094 E6
Boxwood Terrace Dr
13200 HarC 77083 4097 B7
Boxwood Wy Ln
12500 HarC 77041 3679 E2
Boy St
7800 HOUS 77028 3826 B3
Boyce St
6900 HOUS 77020 3964 E3
6900 HOUS 77020 3965 A3
Boyce Springs Dr
5100 HarC 77066 3401 A2
5500 HarC 77066 3400 E3
Boyd Ct
900 PASD 77506 4107 B4
Boyd St
8200 HOUS 77022 3685 A7
8200 HOUS 77022 3824 A1
Boyden Knoll Dr
- FBnC 77494 4092 A5
Boyer Ln
13300 HarC 77015 3828 D5
Boyett St
3200 LPRT 77571 4250 E3
Boykin St
2100 HOUS 77034 4246 C5
Boyles St
100 HOUS 77020 3826 A7
300 HOUS 77020 3965 A1
1400 HOUS 77020 3964 E4
Boylston Dr
14700 HarC 77015 3829 C7
Boynton Dr
3100 HOUS 77045 4373 A1
4100 HOUS 77045 4372 C1
Boys Country Dr
- HarC 77447 3104 D7
Boy Scout Dr
4400 HarC 77546 4505 E5
4400 HarC 77546 4506 A5
Boysenberry Ln
7300 HarC 77095 3678 B1
Boyton Ln
17000 HarC 77379 3255 D3
Brabant Ct
6900 HOUS 77088 3682 B1
Brabner Wy
- CNRO 77301 2530 B3
Brace Rd
23100 HarC 77447 3105 B7
Brace St
6700 HOUS 77061 4244 D5
7200 HOUS 77061 4245 A4
E Bracebridge Cir
10 WDLD 77382 2819 E3
100 WDLD 77382 2820 A3
W Bracebridge Cir
10 WDLD 77382 2819 E3
Bracebridge Ct
14100 SGLD 77478 4236 B4
Bracebridge Dr
- WDLD 77382 2820 A3
10 WDLD 77382 2819 E3

Bracher St
1400 HOUS 77055 3821 A6
1400 SPVL 77055 3821 A6
1500 HOUS 77055 3820 E6
Bracken Fern Ct
10 WDLD 77380 2822 A7
Brackenfern Rd
3300 HarC 77449 3816 A3
Brackenfield Dr
18400 HarC 77388 3112 E7
18400 HarC 77388 3257 E1
Brackenhurst Ln
14400 HarC 77049 3828 E3
Brackenridge St
1700 HOUS 77026 3964 A1
5600 HOUS 77026 3825 A3
Brackenton Crest Ct
20000 HarC 77379 3110 B5
Brackenton Crest Dr
9200 HarC 77379 3110 C5
Bracket Ct
1700 PRLD 77581 4504 B6
9700 HarC 77065 3539 C4
Bracket Dr
3900 PRLD 77581 4504 B7
Brackley Ln
9200 HarC 77088 3543 D7
Bracknell St
6100 HOUS 77017 4246 A3
Brackstone Ct
7500 FBnC 77469 4094 A6
Bracrest Ln
12600 HarC 77044 3689 A7
Brad Ct
500 WEBS 77598 4507 B6
Brad Pk
1000 CNRO 77304 2529 D1
Bradbridge Ln
13100 HOUS 77082 4097 B3
Bradbrun Hill Ln
2500 HarC 77014 3402 A2
Bradbury Ln
20000 MtgC 77355 2813 E3
Bradbury Rd
25200 WlrC 77447 2813 A4
Bradbury Forest Dr
2500 HarC 77373 3114 D4
Bradbury Path Ct
2100 HarC 77373 3114 D4
Braddock Ln
3500 BzaC 77583 4500 D7
Braddocks Rd
16500 HarC 77429 3396 E3
Braden Dr E
14500 HarC 77047 4374 D5
Braden Dr N
3800 HarC 77047 4374 C5
Braden Wy
12100 HarC 77089 4504 E1
Bradenhall Ln
- HarC 77379 3111 B3
Bradfield Ct
10 BKHV 77024 3959 C3
Bradfield Rd
700 HOUS 77060 3403 E6
Bradford Av
200 KMAH 77565 4509 E5
Bradford Cir
10 SGLD 77479 4495 E4
Bradford Dr
2300 MSCY 77489 4497 B1
Bradford Ln
6100 LGCY 77573 4630 C7
Bradford St
3400 HOUS 77025 4101 E5
7600 HOUS 77087 4105 B7
Bradford Colony Dr
14500 HarC 77084 3679 A3
Bradford Creek Ct
20700 HarC 77433 3251 A5
Bradford Shores Dr
16100 HarC 77433 3251 A5
Bradford Village Dr
31300 MtgC 77386 2823 A7
Bradford Village Rd
2500 MSCY 77489 4370 C6
Bradford Wy Dr
10800 HOUS 77075 4377 A4
Bradgate Ct
23200 HarC 77494 3953 D4
Bradham Wy
6700 SGLD 77479 4367 C7
Bradie Ct
6100 LGCY 77573 4630 C7
Bradley
- SEBK 77586 4383 A7
Bradley St
600 SEBK 77586 4510 A1
3700 HOUS 77009 3824 A7
Bradley Springs Dr
- FBnC 77469 4092 A6
Bradly Ln
5200 KATY 77493 3813 D2
Bradmar St
7500 HOUS 77088 3683 D3
Bradmore Dr
1800 HOUS 77077 3958 B6
W Bradner Lp
- GLSN 77554 4993 E7
Bradner St
- GLSN 77554 5108 E1
- GLSN 77554 5109 A1
Bradney Dr
1500 HOUS 77077 3957 D5
Bradshaw Rd
1400 LGCY 77573 4632 B5
Bradshaw St
1900 HOUS 77008 3823 E5
Bradshire Ct
200 DRPK 77536 4249 B1
Bradshire Ln
4200 TYLV 77586 4381 D7
Bradstone Ct
4900 HarC 77084 3677 E7
Bradstone Dr
4700 HarC 77084 3677 E7
Bradwell Dr
800 HOUS 77062 4506 E2
Bradworthy Dr
5900 HarC 77449 3677 C5
Brady Ct
17700 MtgC 77302 2679 E1
Brady Ln
900 ALVN 77511 4749 A6
10100 HarC 77375 2965 A7
Brady St
4400 HOUS 77003 3964 B5
4400 HOUS 77011 3964 C6

Brady St
31400 MAGA 77355 2669 A6
Brady Branch Ln
9300 HarC 77433 3537 B4
Brady Creek Dr
- FBnC 77469 4092 B7
Brady Creek Ln
1400 FBnC 77469 4234 D6
Brae Ln
2200 LGCY 77573 4632 B1
Brae Acres Ct
7600 HOUS 77074 4239 D1
Brae Acres Rd
8100 HOUS 77074 4099 D7
8600 HOUS 77074 4239 D1
Braeberry Ct
7500 FBnC 77469 4095 C6
Braeberry Ln
18300 HarC 77449 3677 C3
Braeburn Dr
4700 BLAR 77401 4101 A6
5100 BLAR 77401 4100 D6
5400 HOUS 77081 4100 C6
5400 HOUS 77401 4100 C6
Braeburn St
- HOUS 77074 4100 B6
Braeburn Bend Dr
10800 HOUS 77031 4239 B3
Braeburn Glen Blvd
- HOUS 77074 4099 C7
9200 HOUS 77074 4239 C2
Braeburn Valley Dr
- HOUS 77074 4239 D1
8000 HOUS 77074 4099 D7
Braecove Cir
19800 FBnC 77469 4094 D5
Braelinn Ln
1100 FBnC 77479 4367 A6
Braeloch Dr
2500 FBnC 77478 4236 B4
2500 SGLD 77478 4236 B4
Braemar Rd
10100 HarC 77532 3693 D6
10100 HarC 77562 3693 D6
Braemar Crescent St
7800 HarC 77095 3538 C6
Braemar Forest St
10 WDLD 77381 2821 A3
Braepark Ct
- LGCY 77539 4753 A3
Brae Point Ct
21100 HarC 77449 3815 B2
Braer Ridge Dr
2200 FBnC 77494 3952 E4
2500 FBnC 77494 3953 A5
Braes Blvd
6800 HOUS 77025 4101 D6
6800 SSPL 77025 4101 D6
Braes Cross
11900 HOUS 77071 4239 D5
Braes Fy
11900 HOUS 77071 4239 D5
Braes Gln
7600 HOUS 77071 4239 E2
Braes Lndg
- HOUS 77071 4239 C5
Braes Mdws
7600 HOUS 77071 4239 E3
Braes Anchor
- HOUS 77071 4239 C5
Braes Bayou Dr
9100 HOUS 77074 4239 E2
10700 HOUS 77071 4239 E3
Braes Bend Dr
- HOUS 77071 4239 D3
Braes Bough
- HOUS 77071 4239 D5
Braes Creek Dr
- HOUS 77071 4239 D3
- HOUS 77074 4239 D2
Braesdale Ln
7800 HOUS 77071 4239 E2
Braes Forest Dr
- HOUS 77074 4239 D2
10000 HOUS 77071 4239 D3
Braesheather Cir
6200 HOUS 77096 4240 A2
Braesheather Ct
9400 HOUS 77096 4241 A1
Braesheather Dr
- HOUS 77096 4240 B1
4900 HOUS 77096 4241 A1
Braes Launch Dr
11900 HOUS 77071 4239 D5
Braesmain Dr
- HOUS 77054 4102 B6
8000 HOUS 77025 4102 A6
Braes Meadow Dr
7800 HOUS 77071 4239 D3
Braesmeadow Ln
2000 SGLD 77479 4368 B7
Braesmont Dr
- BLAR 77401 4100 D7
- HOUS 77401 4100 D7
8800 HOUS 77096 4100 D7
8800 HOUS 77096 4240 D1
Braes Park Dr
11900 HOUS 77071 4239 D5
Braesridge Ct
7700 HOUS 77071 4239 E3
Braesridge Dr
- HOUS 77074 4239 E2
10700 HOUS 77071 4239 E5
Braes River Dr
8100 HOUS 77074 4099 D7
Braes Valley St
4700 HOUS 77096 4101 A7
4700 HOUS 77096 4241 A1
5700 HOUS 77096 4240 C1
Braesview Dr
3200 BzaC 77584 4501 C6
Braesview Ln
7600 HOUS 77071 4239 E2
Braeswest Dr
13500 HarC 77082 4097 A1
Braeswood Blvd
1300 HOUS 77030 4102 C5
N Braeswood Blvd
2300 HOUS 77030 4102 B5
2700 HOUS 77025 4102 A6
3100 HOUS 77025 4101 C6
4400 HOUS 77401 4101 C7
4400 HOUS 77096 4101 B7
4500 HOUS 77096 4241 A1
5100 HOUS 77096 4240 E1
5900 HOUS 77074 4240 A1
S Braeswood Blvd
- HOUS 77071 4240 A2

S Braeswood Blvd
1000 HOUS 77030 4102 E
2500 HOUS 77025 4102 A
3000 HOUS 77025 4101 C
4100 HOUS 77096 4101 C
5000 HOUS 77096 4241 A
5100 HOUS 77096 4240 A
5900 HOUS 77074 4240 A
7500 HOUS 77071 4239 E
7500 HOUS 77074 4239 C
8600 HOUS 77031 4239 C
N Braeswood Ct
2300 HOUS 77030 4102 B
Braeswood Sq
10 HOUS 77096 4240 D
Braeswood Park Dr
2200 HOUS 77030 4102 B
Braewick Dr
- HOUS 77074 4100 B
8700 HOUS 77074 4240 E
9400 HOUS 77096 4240 E
11400 HOUS 77035 4240 B
Braewin Ct
3600 HarC 77068 3257 B
Braewood Glen Ln
12700 HOUS 77072 4097 D
Brafferton Ln
22700 HarC 77449 3814 D
Braford Lake Tr
- HarC 77433 3251 A
Bragg Ct
200 FBnC 77469 4493 D
Bragg St
1100 HOUS 77009 3824 D
Brahman Dr
2900 BzaC 77583 4500 E
Brahms Ct
7800 HarC 77040 3681 B
Brahms Ln
9100 HarC 77040 3541 B
9200 HarC 77040 3681 B
Brahnam Dr
8700 HarC 77083 4096 D
8700 HarC 77083 4236 E
Braidwood Dr
20200 HarC 77450 3954 E
20200 HOUS 77450 3954 E
Brailsfort St
2300 HOUS 77004 3963 D
2900 HOUS 77004 4103 D
Brainford Ct
23500 FBnC 77494 4093 C
Braken Carter Ln
22500 HarC 77449 3814 D
Braken Manor Ln
22500 HarC 77449 3814 E
Braley Ct
20100 HarC 77433 3676 E
Braleybrook Ct
25100 FBnC 77494 4093 B
Braley Park Ln
2500 MtgC 77385 2823 C
Bramble Ln
5300 DKSN 77539 4754 D
Bramble Wy
16500 HOUS 77058 4507 D
Bramblebury Dr
1100 SGLD 77478 4237 B
Bramblecreek Dr
- BYTN 77520 3972 E
- BYTN 77521 3972 E
Bramble Crest Ct
15400 HarC 77095 3678 D
Bramble Fern Pl
3500 HarC 77449 3816 A
Bramble Hill Ct
3100 HOUS 77059 4380 A
Bramble Rose Ln
30900 MtgC 77354 2670 B
Bramblevine Dr
22600 SGCH 77355 2960 B
22700 MtgC 77355 2960 C
Bramblewood Dr
14800 HOUS 77079 3957 B
Brambling Dr
16400 HOUS 77059 4380 D
Bramford Ct
10600 HarC 77070 3399 A
Bramford Point Ln
12900 HarC 77070 3399 C
Bramlett Ct
7100 FBnC 77479 4367 A
Bramley Dr
6200 PASD 77503 4248 C
6600 DRPK 77503 4248 E
6600 DRPK 77536 4248 D
Bramor
- BYTN 77521 3973 D
Brampton Ct
10 CNRO 77304 2236 C
15900 HarC 77379 3256 A
Bramshaw Glen Ct
15200 HarC 77049 3829 A
Bramwell Dr
- HarC 77449 3815 A
Branard St
300 HOUS 77006 3962 E
2200 HOUS 77098 3962 A
3200 HOUS 77098 3961 E
4000 HOUS 77027 3961 C
Branch
1300 HarC 77373 3114 A
12000 HarC 77044 3551 D
Branch Av
1500 RHMD 77469 4364 D
Branch Cross W
- WDLD 77382 2819 A
Branch Dr
10 FBnC 77469 4232 D
Branch St
4500 HOUS 77021 4103 D
5900 HTCK 77563 4989 C
27200 HarC 77373 3113 E
Branch Bend Cir
10 BKHV 77024 3959 C
10 HOUS 77024 3959 C
Branchberry Ln
4700 HarC 77388 3112 B
Branch Canyon Ct
17200 HarC 77095 3537 B
Branch Creek Dr
17900 HarC 77433 3396 D
Branch Crossing Dr
- WDLD 77354 2819 E
- WDLD 77382 2674 A
8700 WDLD 77382 2673 D
11100 WDLD 77382 2819 E

STREET
Block City ZIP Map# Grid

Branchdale Dr
9500 HarC 77064 3540 D4
Branchdale Ln
18400 HarC 77379 3256 B1
Branch Forest Dr
14600 HarC 77082 4096 B2
14600 HOUS 77082 4096 D2
Branchgrove Ln
20300 FBnC 77469 4094 C6
Branch Hill Dr
1800 PRLD 77581 4504 B6
Branching Oak Ct
18100 FBnC 77469 4095 B5
Branch Lake Dr
5900 HarC 77066 3401 A6
Branchmead Ct
4400 FBnC 77450 4094 A2
Branch Park Dr
- HarC 77064 3540 D3
Branch Point Dr
7400 HarC 77095 3678 D1
Branchport Ct
2700 FBnC 77479 4493 E3
2700 SGLD 77479 4493 E3
Branchport Dr
- HarC 77095 3538 D4
Branchport Ln
- HarC 77449 3676 D3
6400 FBnC 77450 4094 A4
Branch View Ln
2500 MSCY 77459 4496 C1
Branchwater Ln
14300 FBnC 77478 4236 E3
Branch Wood
34800 SGCH 77362 2816 D4
Branchwood Ct
10100 HOUS 77040 3542 A7
Brand Ln
100 STAF 77477 4369 B3
700 FBnC 77477 4369 B3
Brandemere Dr
3500 BzaC 77584 4501 C7
Brandemere Wy
4000 HarC 77066 3401 B3
Brandenberry Pl
10 WDLD 77381 2820 E1
Branding Iron Cir
2400 TXCY 77539 4633 D7
Branding Iron Dr
5500 DKSN 77539 4633 D7
5500 TXCY 77539 4633 D7
Branding Iron Ln
200 HarC 77060 3544 C4
27700 MtgC 77355 2815 B7
Brandon Ct
3600 PASD 77505 4248 E4
Brandon Dr
20600 MtgC 77357 2828 A7
Brandon Rd
10 MtgC 77302 2530 C7
Brandon St
7700 HOUS 77051 4243 B4
Brandon Wy
11700 BKHV 77024 3959 C3
Brandon Bend Dr
12600 MSCY 77071 4239 A7
12600 MSCY 77071 4370 C1
12700 MSCY 77489 4370 C1
Brandon Bluff Ln
- HarC 77377 3253 E1
Brandon Chase Ln
9200 FBnC 77469 4234 E1
Brandon Gate
11100 HarC 77095 3538 B1
Brandon Oaks Wy
19700 HarC 77449 3816 C3
19800 HarC 77449 3815 E3
Brandonwood Ct
15400 HarC 77069 3256 D6
Brandonwood Pl
15300 HarC 77069 3256 D6
Brandt Dr
- HOUS 77084 3818 B2
Brandt Rd
500 HarC 77373 3113 E2
3900 FBnC 77469 4233 C6
Brandt St
3800 HOUS 77006 3963 A7
4100 HOUS 77002 3963 A7
Brandy Dr
11900 HarC 77377 3254 D6
Brandy Ln
11300 HarC 77044 3690 E1
Brandy St
900 FBnC 77477 4369 C3
Brandy Bend Dr
900 HarC 77373 2968 D7
Brandy Creek Ct
8100 HarC 77338 3261 E5
Brandy Creek Ln
19800 HarC 77338 3261 E5
Brandygate Ct
23100 HarC 77373 2968 E7
Brandy Mill Rd
2400 HarC 77067 3402 A4
Brandy Ridge Ln
200 LGCY 77539 4753 A4
Brandywine Ln
11800 BKHV 77024 3959 B2
Brandywood Cir
9900 HarC 77070 3255 B3
Brandywyne Ct
13300 HOUS 77077 3957 B6
Brandywyne Dr
100 FRDW 77546 4505 A7
400 FRDW 77546 4504 D7
12300 HOUS 77077 3957 D6
Branford St
6500 HOUS 77091 3683 E4
Branford Greens Dr
13700 HarC 77083 4097 A7
Branford Hills Ln
21200 HarC 77450 3954 C5
Branford Manor Dr
13700 HarC 77083 4097 A3
Branford Park Ln
7200 FBnC 77469 4095 C6
Branham Dr
- HOUS 77083 4096 E7
8400 HarC 77083 4096 E7
Braniff Av
7700 HOUS 77061 4245 D7
7700 HOUS 77075 4245 D7
Brannan Dr
3900 HarC 77449 3816 A2
Brannon St
8600 HOUS 77093 3685 D7
Brannon Field Ln
13700 HarC 77095 3539 B6
Brannon Hill Ct
5000 FBnC 77479 4493 C2
Brannon Hill Ln
2900 FBnC 77479 4493 C3
20900 HarC 77338 3261 E3
Brannon Park Ln
1000 HarC 77373 2968 D7
Brannon Ridge Ln
- FBnC 77494 3953 A7
Branns Fern
10 CNRO 77304 2236 E6
Branson Ln
13600 HarC 77429 3253 E6
Brant Dr
3000 KATY 77493 3813 B3
Brantdale Rd
- WDLD 77381 2821 A4
Brantfield Ct
9400 HarC 77095 3538 E4
Brantfield Park Ln
13100 HarC 77377 3253 D1
13100 HarC 77377 3254 A2
Brantley Ln
100 MAGA 77354 2669 A5
5300 HarC 77389 2967 A7
Brantley Haven Dr
11800 HarC 77375 3254 D1
Brantly Av
- HOUS 77598 4379 A6
10500 HOUS 77034 4379 A3
Brant Rock Dr
12700 HOUS 77082 4097 C3
Brants Wy Ct
12500 HarC 77065 3539 C4
Brantwood Dr
- HarC 77388 3111 E3
Branum St
9700 HOUS 77017 4106 B5
Brashear Av
400 HMBL 77338 3263 A6
Brashear St
1000 HOUS 77007 3962 E3
Brasil Ln
16600 HarC 77095 3538 A1
Brass Hammer Ct
11300 HarC 77065 3540 A3
Brassie Dr
200 HMPD 77445 2952 C4
Brass Nail
15100 CNRO 77384 2676 A2
Brass Town Ln
- FBnC 77469 4095 B6
Brasstown Moutain Wy
21400 HarC 77449 3815 C1
Brasswood Ct
22200 MtgC 77355 2960 D1
Brat Pass Dr
23300 HarC 77373 3115 A5
Bratten Ln
15200 HOUS 77598 4506 D3
Brattle Dr
24700 FBnC 77494 3952 D3
Bratton Ct
3700 SGLD 77479 4495 E4
Bratton St
3800 SGLD 77479 4495 E4
Braugh Rd
2700 HarC 77532 3553 C4
3700 HarC 77532 3554 A3
3700 LbyC 77535 3554 A3
Braunston Ln
8700 HarC 77088 3543 D7
8700 HarC 77088 3683 D1
Brautigam Rd
24400 MtgC 77355 2962 D4
Bravery Dr
21800 HarC 77447 3105 E2
Bravo Av
2500 PASD 77502 4107 E6
2500 PASD 77502 4108 A6
Braxton Dr
3900 HOUS 77063 4099 E2
5600 HOUS 77036 4099 E3
Braxton Bragg Ln
10 MtgC 77302 2530 B5
Braxton Grove Ln
- HarC 77379 3257 A2
Braxtons Bnd
11600 HarC 77066 3400 D4
Braxtonshire Ct
5400 HarC 77069 3256 D7
Braybend Ln
2200 HarC 77450 3954 C5
Braydon Ct
27700 MtgC 77386 2970 C6
Braydon Bend Dr
13600 HarC 77095 3539 C6
Brayford Pl Ct
13900 HarC 77014 3402 C1
Brayford Pl Dr
14000 HarC 77014 3402 C1
Bray Hofffart Rd
- HarC 77375 3109 E6
Braymark Dr
- HarC 77014 3402 C2
Braymore Dr
10800 HOUS 77043 3819 C1
Braypark Ln
2300 HarC 77450 3954 C6
Brays Ct
- DKSN 77539 4753 B5
Brays St
7900 HOUS 77012 4105 B2
Braysworth Dr
4300 HOUS 77072 4098 B4
Brayton Ct
13000 HarC 77065 3539 B2
Brazeal St
2000 HarC 77484 3102 A4
2000 WALR 77484 3101 E4
2000 WALR 77484 3102 A4
2700 WlrC 77484 3101 D4
Brazil Cir
4200 PASD 77504 4247 E5
Brazil St
7000 HOUS 77093 3824 E2
Brazoria St
100 BzaC 77511 4868 A6
2400 HOUS 77019 3962 A6
Brazos Av
1400 LMQU 77568 4989 E2
Brazos Ct
1000 LGCY 77573 4632 D3
Brazos Dr
15900 SGLD 77479 4368 B6
20000 MtgC 77357 2826 E7
Brazos Dr
20000 MtgC 77357 2827 A7
22800 MtgC 77365 2972 C4
Brazos Pl
10 RSBG 77471 4490 C6
Brazos St
- ALVN 77511 4749 A7
- BzaC 77511 4749 A7
500 RHMD 77469 4364 D7
500 RSBG 77471 4490 D3
900 HOUS 77002 3963 B4
1400 HMPD 77445 2953 A6
2200 HOUS 77006 3963 A6
Brazos Bend Dr
4200 PRLD 77584 4503 B4
4500 MSCY 77459 4496 B4
Brazos Bend Tr
12400 HarC 77346 3264 C7
Brazos Crossing Dr
1900 FBnC 77469 4234 C7
Brazos Estates Dr
23200 WlrC 77445 3097 E6
Brazos Gardens Dr
100 FBnC 77469 4493 B7
Brazos Gate Dr
1500 FBnC 77469 4493 C5
Brazos Glen Ln
6400 FBnC 77469 4493 B6
Brazos Meadow Ln
6400 FBnC 77469 4493 B6
Brazos Pass
- SGLD 77479 4495 A4
Brazos Point Ln
4700 FBnC 77545 4623 A3
Brazos Ridge Dr
2600 FBnC 77479 4493 E3
Brazos River Blvd
- MtgC 77386 2970 B2
Brazos Spring Dr
5500 FBnC 77479 4493 D2
Brazos Trace Ct
6300 FBnC 77469 4493 C4
Brazos Trace Dr
- FBnC 77469 4493 B5
Brazos Village Dr
10 FBnC 77469 4493 A7
Brazos Wood Dr
1500 FBnC 77469 4493 C4
Brazoswood Pl
1200 FBnC 77469 4364 C3
Brazzel St
3100 HarC 77336 3122 C7
Brazzo Ct
- LGCY 77573 4632 E3
Brea Ct
3800 MtgC 77386 2970 B5
Brea Crest St
1100 HOUS 77037 3685 A1
2100 HarC 77093 3685 D1
3100 HarC 77093 3686 A1
Breacrest St
200 HarC 77037 3684 D1
Breaker Ct
3800 MSCY 77459 4496 D4
Breaker Dr
700 HarC 77032 3404 A7
Breakers Point Dr
3000 HarC 77546 4506 A7
Breakwater St
800 HarC 77532 3552 A3
Breakwater Pass Dr
13200 HOUS 77044 3409 A4
Breakwater Path Dr
- HOUS 77044 3408 E4
Breakwood Dr
4000 HOUS 77025 4241 C1
4300 HOUS 77096 4241 B1
Breanna Ln
15900 HarC 77049 3829 D3
Breaux Trc
2500 SEBK 77586 4509 C2
Breaux Bridge Ln
3900 SGLD 77479 4495 A4
Breccia Dr
7300 HarC 77041 3679 C1
Brechin Ct
9200 HarC 77095 3538 C4
Brechin Ln
16200 HarC 77095 3538 B4
Breck St
13800 HarC 77066 3401 A1
13800 HarC 77069 3401 A1
Breckan Ct
11600 HarC 77429 3254 A7
Breckenridge Ct
3200 MSCY 77459 4498 A6
4100 HarC 77066 3401 C6
Breckenridge Dr
4100 HarC 77066 3401 C6
9000 MtgC 77354 2672 D7
9000 MtgC 77354 2673 A6
Breckenridge Ln
3300 MSCY 77459 4498 A6
Breckenridge Cove Ln
1100 LGCY 77573 4631 D4
Breckenridge Forest Ct
3000 HarC 77373 3115 C3
Breckenridge Forest Dr
23500 HarC 77373 3115 A3
Breckin Dr
8600 HOUS 77078 3688 B6
Breckonridge Cir
1100 PRLD 77581 4376 D6
Brecon Hall Dr
1100 HOUS 77077 3958 A4
Breda Dr
- BYTN 77521 3833 C4
7300 HarC 77521 3833 B3
Bredon Springs Ct
- HarC 77388 3111 E2
Breech Dr
900 HarC 77532 3552 A3
Breeds Hill Ct
200 BKHV 77024 3959 A4
Breeland Park Ct
14200 SGLD 77478 4236 B4
Breen Dr
5100 HarC 77086 3542 D6
5100 HarC 77088 3542 D6
6500 HOUS 77086 3542 B6
6500 HOUS 77088 3542 B6
7500 HarC 77040 3542 A6
7500 HarC 77064 3542 A6
7600 HarC 77040 3541 B6
7600 HarC 77064 3541 B6
Breen St
4800 HarC 77086 3542 E6
4800 HarC 77088 3542 E6
S Breeze Dr
- HOUS 77031 4239 C4
8300 HOUS 77071 4239 D4
Breeze Wy
3800 SEBK 77586 4382 B7
Breeze Park Dr
300 HarC 77015 3828 D5
Breezeport Ct
- PRLD 77545 4499 D2
Breezeport Ln
- PRLD 77545 4499 D2
Breezeway Ct
3800 SEBK 77586 4382 B7
Breezeway Dr
- MSCY 77459 4369 B6
Breezeway Ln
2100 PRLD 77584 4500 A2
Breezeway St
7400 HOUS 77040 3682 A2
7500 HarC 77040 3682 A2
7800 HarC 77040 3681 E2
12900 HarC 77037 3545 A7
Breezeway Bend Dr
2200 PRLD 77584 4500 E2
Breezeway Bend Ln
7600 FBnC 77494 4093 C2
Breezewood Dr
3200 HOUS 77082 4098 B2
3900 SEBK 77586 4382 B6
Breezin Ct
1800 WDLD 77380 2968 A1
Breezway Bend Ln
300 LGCY 77573 4631 C7
Breezy Ct
18600 MtgC 77365 2972 A5
28300 MtgC 77355 2815 D6
Breezy Wy
200 WDLD 77380 2821 C5
E Breezy Wy
10 WDLD 77380 2821 D5
W Breezy Wy
100 WDLD 77380 2821 C6
Breezy Bend Dr
1200 FBnC 77494 3952 D3
Breezy Cove Ct
19800 HarC 77375 3109 E6
Breezy Glen Ln
18200 HarC 77433 3537 A5
Breezy Hill Dr
21900 HarC 77449 3815 A3
Breezy Hollow Ln
6100 FBnC 77450 4093 E5
Breezy Knoll Dr
11500 HarC 77064 3399 C7
Breezy Landing Ln
13500 HOUS 77034 4378 D4
Breezy Meadow Ct
- HarC 77044 3549 D3
Breezy Meadow Dr
12000 STAF 77477 4237 D7
12000 STAF 77477 4238 A7
Breezy Meadow Ln
13000 HarC 77044 3549 C2
Breezy Oak Ct
20100 HarC 77433 3537 A7
Breezy Pines Ct
3100 HOUS 77339 3119 B7
Breezy Pines Ln
2700 BzaC 77584 4501 A1
Breezy Point Dr
4600 HOUS 77345 3119 E7
Breezy Point Ln
5200 FBnC 77479 4493 D3
Breezy Point Pl
10 WDLD 77381 2820 D4
Breezy Shore Ct
100 LGCY 77539 4752 E5
Breezy Shore Ln
21100 FBnC 77469 4094 B6
Brekke Ln
8100 HTCK 77563 4988 D2
Breland St
5700 HOUS 77016 3686 D5
Breman Crest Ln
7800 HarC 77040 3681 A1
Bremen Dr
11800 HarC 77066 3401 C6
Bremerton Ln
19300 HarC 77388 3112 D6
Bremerton Falls Dr
3300 MSCY 77459 4497 E5
Bremond St
200 HOUS 77006 3963 A5
1000 HOUS 77002 3963 B6
1600 HMPD 77445 2953 A7
2000 HMPD 77445 2952 E7
3000 HOUS 77004 3963 D7
3500 HOUS 77004 4103 E1
Bremonds Bend Dr
7200 HarC 77433 3395 E5
Brenda Dr
1100 DRPK 77536 4109 C6
Brenda Ln
300 ORDN 77385 2822 C4
900 HMBL 77338 3406 E1
1600 PASD 77502 4107 D7
E Brenda Ln
800 MtgC 77354 2668 D3
N Brenda Ln
41400 MtgC 77354 2668 D3
S Brenda Ln
41300 MtgC 77354 2668 E3
W Brenda Ln
800 MtgC 77354 2668 D3
Brenda St
500 HOUS 77076 3684 E4
W Brenda St
100 HOUS 77076 3684 C4
Brendam Ln
7300 HOUS 77072 4097 C6
Brendan Woods Ln
10 MtgC 77384 2675 A1
Brendon Ct
16600 HarC 77379 3256 D3
Brendon Park Ln
500 FRDW 77546 4505 A7
Brendon Trace Ln
10 MtgC 77386 2969 D7
Brendon Trail Ct
28000 MtgC 77386 2969 D7
Brendon Trail Ln
- MtgC 77386 2969 D7
Brendon Trails Ct
10800 HarC 77379 3110 B6
Brendon Trails Dr
1300 HarC 77379 3110 A6
Brenford Dr
1100 HOUS 77047 4373 C2
Brenham Ct
9400 HarC 77064 3540 D6
Brenhaven Dr
12600 HarC 77038 3543 C4
Brenly Dr
14700 HarC 77429 3397 E1
14800 HarC 77429 3253 E7
Brennan Ridge Ln
5600 FBnC 77450 4093 E4
Brennen Ln
100 ALVN 77511 4867 C3
Brenner Ct
4000 SGLD 77478 4369 A5
Brenner St
4900 HOUS 77022 3684 D7
Brenner Creek Ct
10800 HOUS 77079 3958 C1
Brent Dr
6300 HOUS 77085 4371 D4
S Brentchase Cir
- HarC 77014 3401 D2
W Brentchase Cir
- HarC 77014 3401 C2
Brentcross Dr
11600 HarC 77377 3254 D4
Brentford Ct
16500 FBnC 77083 4095 C7
Brentford Dr
8100 FBnC 77083 4095 E7
8200 FBnC 77083 4096 A7
Brenthaven Springs Ln
9600 HarC 77375 3255 B2
Brentlake Ln
1400 PRLD 77581 4376 E7
Brentlawn Ct
13000 HOUS 77045 4241 C6
Brentleywood Ln
12300 HarC 77070 3399 D6
Brenton St
4500 HarC 77093 3686 B1
N Brenton Knoll Ct
11900 HarC 77375 3109 D6
N Brenton Knoll Dr
12000 HarC 77375 3109 D7
S Brenton Knoll Dr
11800 HarC 77375 3109 D7
Brenton Oaks Dr
16600 HarC 77379 3256 E3
Brentonridge Ln
19600 HarC 77379 3112 A5
Brentonwood Ln
13300 HOUS 77077 3957 B6
Brentshire Ln
14200 HarC 77069 3256 C6
Brentway Dr
10500 HarC 77070 3399 A3
Brentwood Ct
10 SGLD 77479 4495 B3
Brentwood Dr
700 BYTN 77520 3972 E6
2000 ALVN 77511 4866 E2
2000 HOUS 77019 3962 B5
11400 MtgC 77303 2239 C3
15500 HarC 77530 3829 E7
15500 HarC 77530 3830 A7
Brentwood Ln
3200 PRLD 77581 4503 D2
16100 SPLD 77372 2683 A5
Brentwood Rd
26200 MtgC 77372 2683 C4
N Brentwood St
15200 HarC 77530 3829 D7
S Brentwood St
15200 HarC 77530 3968 E1
15400 HarC 77530 3969 A1
W Brentwood St
400 HarC 77530 3968 D1
600 HarC 77530 3829 D7
Brentwood Lakes Cir
9300 HarC 77375 3255 C3
Brentwood Lakes Dr
- HarC 77379 3255 C2
Brentwood Oaks Ct
10 WDLD 77381 2821 A3
Brentwood Park Dr
4200 HOUS 77045 4241 C7
Brenwick Ct
600 HarC 77450 3954 E2
Brenwood Dr
- HarC 77449 3677 D4
18100 HarC 77084 3677 D4
S Brenwood Dr
5900 HarC 77449 3677 C5
Brenwood Glen Tr
5600 HarC 77449 3677 D5
Brenwood Manor Dr
8300 HarC 77449 3677 D5
Brenwood Park Dr
6400 HarC 77449 3677 C4
Brenwood Peak Dr
19200 HarC 77449 3677 B5
Brenwood Trails Ln
5800 HarC 77449 3677 B5
Bressingham Dr
18900 HarC 77375 3255 A1
Bresslyn Ct
9500 HarC 77044 3689 B4
Bresslyn Ln
16200 HarC 77429 3252 B6
Bretagne Dr
13300 HarC 77015 3828 D6
Bretford Ct
13000 HarC 77065 3539 B3
Breton Bridge Ct
27000 HarC 77433 3537 B1
Breton Falls Ln
19100 FBnC 77469 4094 E7
Breton Glen Ln
13600 HOUS 77070 3400 C3
Breton Hill Ln
- HarC 77377 3253 E3
Breton Mill Dr
20900 HarC 77346 3264 D3
Breton Point Dr
22900 HarC 77373 2968 E7
Breton Ridge Rd
- HarC 77070 3399 E3
- HarC 77070 3400 A3
Breton Ridge St
13100 HOUS 77064 3400 B4
13100 HOUS 77070 3400 A3
13600 HarC 77070 3400 A3
Breton Shore Ln
3800 FBnC 77494 4093 B2
Bretonwood Ln
25100 FBnC 77494 3953 A6
Bretshire Dr
5000 HOUS 77016 3686 D4
Bretshire Dr
7100 HOUS 77016 3687 A5
Brett Dr
5100 PRLD 77584 4503 A4
Brett Creek Ct
15800 HarC 77429 3253 B5
Bretton Dr
10100 HOUS 77016 3686 E4
Brettwood Cir
11700 HarC 77089 4378 B6
Brettwood Ct
11700 HarC 77089 4378 B6
Brettwood Dr
11200 HarC 77089 4378 B6
11200 HOUS 77089 4378 B6
Breum Ln
7800 HOUS 77075 4376 C1
Brewer Ln
19500 HOUS 77338 3262 A5
Brewster St
10 CNRO 77301 2384 A2
1600 HOUS 77020 3964 A1
1900 HOUS 77026 3964 A1
3200 HOUS 77026 3825 A6
6800 HOUS 77093 3825 A2
Brewster Key Dr
3600 GLSN 77554 5441 B4
Briac Ln
1000 CNRO 77301 2530 B2
Brian Blvd
13300 MtgC 77372 2537 D7
Brian St
6100 BzaC 77584 4626 D2
7800 HMBL 77396 3406 D3
Brian Haven Dr
4700 HOUS 77018 3822 E1
4800 HOUS 77018 3683 E7
5400 HOUS 77091 3683 E6
Brianwood Ct
18400 HarC 77388 3112 C7
Briar Bnd
1500 FRDW 77546 4629 C4
Briar Cir
2100 PRLD 77581 4503 D2
23900 MtgC 77365 2973 A6
Briar Ct
10 PNVL 77304 2237 B3
1400 PRLD 77581 4504 E5
3100 SGLD 77478 4369 A2
3200 BYTN 77521 3972 A3
Briar Dr
3000 PASD 77503 4108 A5
3000 PASD 77506 4108 A5
5200 HOUS 77056 3960 D3
10000 HOUS 77042 3958 E4
10000 HOUS 77042 3959 A4
Briar Ln
2000 RHMD 77469 4492 A2
2100 LMQU 77568 4989 E3
4000 MtgC 77354 2674 C3
10800 GlsC 77510 4871 E6
26100 MtgC 77357 2829 A5
Briar Sq
6800 HarC 77084 3679 A2
Briar Wy
10 HOUS 77027 3961 C6
Briar Arbor
17700 HarC 77094 3955 D2
Briar Bank Dr
1500 SGLD 77478 4237 A6
Briar Bark Ln
23800 MtgC 77365 2973 A6
Briar Bayou Dr
1100 HOUS 77077 3957 C5
S Briar Bayou Dr
6100 HOUS 77072 4097 C4
Briar Bend Ct
2700 SGLD 77479 4495 B1
Briarbend Dr
1400 FBnC 77479 4493 D4
4300 HOUS 77035 4241 B3
5100 HOUS 77035 4240 E3
5400 HOUS 77096 4240 D3
Briar Berry Ln
23800 MtgC 77365 2973 A7
Briar Bluff Ln
2800 HOUS 77082 4096 E1
Briar Branch Dr
2200 HOUS 77042 3958 E7
Briar Branch Ln
10800 HNCV 77024 3960 A1
Briarbrook Dr
- HOUS 77042 3958 E4
5000 DKSN 77539 4754 C2
14000 HarC 77039 3545 E3
Briarbrook Ln
13500 HOUS 77077 3957 A6
Briar Canyon Ct
6300 FBnC 77450 4094 C4
11600 HarC 77377 3254 D5
Briarchase Ct
14200 HarC 77014 3401 D1
Briar Chase Dr
20800 MtgC 77365 2972 E6
20800 MtgC 77365 2973 A6
Briarchase Dr
- HarC 77014 3401 D1
Briarchester Dr
1700 HarC 77450 3954 A5
Briar Cliff Ct
2700 SGLD 77479 4495 B1
Briarcliff Dr
300 HOUS 77076 3685 B6
Briar Cliff St
1300 CHTW 77385 2823 A5
Briarclift Ln
600 BYTN 77521 3972 E2
Briar Cottage Ct
1500 FBnC 77479 4493 D4
Briar Cove Cir
- MtgC 77365 2972 E6
- MtgC 77365 2973 A6
Briarcraft Dr
15100 HOUS 77489 4371 B4
Briarcreek Blvd
- HarC 77373 3114 C6
1800 HarC 77073 3259 D2
2200 HOUS 77073 3259 D2
22600 HarC 77373 3259 D1
Briar Creek Cir
23600 MtgC 77365 2973 A6
Briar Creek Dr
600 LPRT 77571 4250 B2
1000 FRDW 77546 4629 C4
Briarcreek Dr
800 BYTN 77521 3973 B2
Briar Crest Dr
1400 PRLD 77581 4504 E5
Briarcrest Dr
- MtgC 77386 2968 C1
2000 HOUS 77077 3956 E7
Briar Cross Ct
6300 HarC 77084 3679 A4
Briarcross Ct
5100 FBnC 77479 4496 B4
Briar Dale Ct
10 HOUS 77027 3961 B5
Briar Falls Ct
13500 HOUS 77059 4379 E4
Briarfield Dr
6700 HarC 77379 3256 D2
Briar Forest Cir
9300 HOUS 77063 3959 B6
Briar Forest Dr
- BKHV 77024 3959 B6
- PNPV 77024 3959 C5
8900 HOUS 77024 3959 B6
9100 HOUS 77063 3959 C6
9500 HOUS 77042 3959 A6
10000 HOUS 77042 3958 D6
11200 HOUS 77077 3958 C6
12000 HOUS 77077 3957 D5
13900 HOUS 77077 3956 D5
Briargate Ct
15600 HOUS 77489 4371 D5
Briargate Dr
6600 HOUS 77489 4371 C5
Briargate Tr
6500 HOUS 77489 4371 D5
Briar Glade Dr
6000 HOUS 77072 4098 C4
Briar Glen Ct
400 FRDW 77546 4505 B6
2700 SGLD 77479 4495 B2
Briarglen Dr
100 LGCY 77573 4632 B2
2000 HOUS 77027 3961 B6
2500 PRLD 77581 4504 E5
2500 PRLD 77581 4505 A5
4000 DKSN 77539 4754 D2
Briarglen Ln
200 LPRT 77571 4110 C6
Briar Green Ct
1300 FBnC 77469 4365 D1
Briargreen Dr
- HOUS 77082 3956 E7
- HOUS 77082 4096 E1
2000 HOUS 77077 3956 E7
Briargreen St
800 PASD 77503 4108 B5
Briar Grove Ct
10 CNRO 77301 2384 C2
Briar Grove Dr
- CNRO 77303 2384 C1
- HarC 77090 3402 E1
2000 CNRO 77301 2384 C2
Briargrove Dr
- MtgC 77354 2673 B1
700 ALVN 77511 4867 D3
2600 HOUS 77057 3960 B7
2700 HOUS 77057 4100 B1
Briar Harbor Dr
12700 HarC 77377 3254 A4
Briar Heath Dr
14000 HOUS 77077 3956 E5
Briar Hill Ct
5900 SGLD 77479 4495 A4
6000 SGLD 77479 4494 E4
Briar Hill Dr
10 HOUS 77042 3958 E5
Briarhills Pkwy
13900 HOUS 77077 3956 E3
Briar Hollow Dr
- FBnC 77479 4493 D5
3800 DKSN 77539 4754 D1
Briar Hollow Ln
10 HOUS 77027 3961 B5
E Briar Hollow Ln
10 HOUS 77027 3961 C6
S Briar Hollow Ln
10 HOUS 77027 3961 B5
Briar Hollow Pl
4500 HOUS 77027 3961 B5
Briar Home Dr
1700 HOUS 77077 3956 E5
Briarhorn Dr
22900 HarC 77389 2966 C6
Briarhurst Dr
2300 HOUS 77057 3960 B7
Briarhurst Pk
2700 HOUS 77057 3960 B7
Briar Ivy Ln
14200 HOUS 77082 4096 E1
Briar Knoll Ct
2700 SGLD 77479 4495 B2
Briar Knoll Dr
500 HOUS 77079 3957 C3
S Briar Knoll Dr
3200 HOUS 77082 4097 C2
6200 HOUS 77072 4097 C4
Briarlake Ln
2000 LGCY 77573 4631 C7
Briarland Ln
- FBnC 77494 4093 A1
Briar Landing Ln
21600 FBnC 77450 4094 A3
Briarleaf Ct
17000 FBnC 77083 4095 D6
Briarlee Dr
1900 HOUS 77077 3956 E7
Briarlilly Ln
- FBnC 77494 4092 C2
Briarloch Ln
2700 HarC 77073 3259 E4
Briar Lodge Dr
- MtgC 77365 2973 A7
Briarmead Dr
1000 HOUS 77057 3960 C5
1100 FBnC 77469 4365 E3
Briarmeadow Av
300 FRDW 77546 4629 C3
Briar Meadow Dr
6900 FBnC 77479 4493 D4
Briar Meadow Ln
20000 WlrC 77484 3101 A2
Briar Meadow Rd
27800 HarC 77377 3108 E2
Briarmoor Ct
1700 HOUS 77062 4380 A5
Briar Moss Ln
6500 HarC 77449 3677 C4
Briar Oak Dr
21300 HarC 77338 3261 E2
Briar Oaks Ln
1800 HOUS 77027 3961 B6

STREET
Block City ZIP Map# Grid

Briar Oaks Cove
200 HOUS 77056 3960 E3
Briarpark Dr
200 HOUS 77042 3959 A4
2700 HOUS 77042 4099 A2
N Briarpark Ln
3300 SGLD 77479 4495 C1
S Briarpark Ln
3400 SGLD 77479 4495 B1
Briarpark Trail Ln
10000 HarC 77064 3540 C3
Briar Patch Dr
- HOUS 77077 3957 B4
Briar Patch St
7800 CmbC 77520 3835 D4
Briar Path Dr
500 HOUS 77079 3957 D3
Briarpine Ct
12900 HarC 77041 3679 D3
Briar Pl Dr
13900 HOUS 77077 3956 E6
Briar Point Ct
11500 FBnC 77478 4236 B5
Briarport Dr
2200 HOUS 77077 3956 D7
Briar Ridge Dr
800 HOUS 77057 3960 B4
1900 RSBG 77471 4491 B5
Briar River Dr
10300 HOUS 77042 3958 E7
Briar Rock Rd
300 MtgC 77380 2968 B2
Briar Rose Ct
2600 PRLD 77545 4499 E3
Briar Rose Dr
1300 PRLD 77545 4499 E3
6300 HOUS 77057 3960 B6
7500 HOUS 77063 3960 A6
10000 HOUS 77042 3958 E6
10000 HOUS 77042 3959 A6
11600 HOUS 77077 3958 A6
Briar Rose Ln
5600 KATY 77493 3813 B5
Briar Rose Tr
- HarC 77429 3252 C6
Briar Run Ct
7500 HOUS 77489 4371 B5
Briar Sage Ct
- HarC 77449 3815 B1
Briarsage Ct
14000 HOUS 77077 3956 E6
Briarsage Dr
2100 HOUS 77077 3956 E6
Briarsage Ln
3000 PRLD 77581 4376 E7
Briar Seasons Dr
6200 HOUS 77489 4371 D5
Briar Sedge Ct
19400 HarC 77449 3816 A2
Briarside Dr
- STAF 77477 4369 D2
Briar Spring Ct
15500 HOUS 77489 4371 D5
Briarstead Dr
15700 HOUS 77489 4371 D5
Briarstem Dr
2000 HOUS 77077 3956 E7
Briarstone
5000 SGLD 77479 4495 B5
Briarstone Ct
20000 HarC 77379 3111 D5
Briarstone Ln
6400 HarC 77379 3111 D5
Briarstone Park Ln
4100 FBnC 77494 4092 A1
Briar Summit Ln
6900 FBnC 77494 4093 C3
Briar Terrace Dr
6100 HOUS 77072 4098 C4
Briar Thicket Dr
24000 MtgC 77365 2973 A6
Briar Thistle Ln
23700 MtgC 77365 2973 A6
Briar Timber Dr
20900 MtgC 77365 2973 A6
Briar Town Ln
6100 HOUS 77057 3960 C7
Briartrace Ct
9600 HarC 77044 3689 A4
Briar Trace Dr
1300 PRLD 77545 4499 E4
Briar Trace Ln
200 FBnC 77469 4365 B5
Briar Trail Dr
10 HOUS 77056 3960 E3
Briar Tree Dr
23800 MtgC 77365 2973 A6
Briarturn Dr
1900 HOUS 77077 3956 E6
Briar View Dr
2600 PRLD 77581 4504 E5
Briarview Dr
2000 HOUS 77077 3956 D6
Briarvine Ct
22000 HarC 77389 3112 D1
Briar Walk Dr
20900 MtgC 77365 2973 A6
Briarway St
800 PASD 77503 4108 B5
Briarwest Blvd
2200 HOUS 77077 3957 C7
Briarwest Cir
12800 HOUS 77077 3957 C7
Briarwick Dr
19400 MtgC 77365 2972 C2
Briarwick Ln
2900 HOUS 77093 3685 E3
2900 HOUS 77093 3686 A3
5600 HOUS 77016 3686 D3
19700 MtgC 77357 2829 A5
Briarwild Ln
10000 HOUS 77080 3820 A5
Briarwilde Ct
600 ALVN 77511 4867 C2
Briar Willow Dr
20100 MtgC 77365 2973 A6
Briar Wood
- MtgC 77362 2816 C5
Briarwood Ct
10 HOUS 77019 3961 E6
100 LGCY 77573 4632 B2
900 DRPK 77536 4109 A6
Briarwood Dr
200 BYTN 77520 4113 A1
1300 HOUS 77017 4106 D7
1300 PASD 77017 4106 D7
1300 PASD 77502 4106 D7
4500 SGLD 77479 4495 C4
Briarwood Dr E
10 CNRO 77301 2384 A3
W Briarwood Dr
10 CNRO 77301 2384 A3
Briarwood Forest Dr
5400 HarC 77088 3542 E7
Briarworth Dr
13900 HOUS 77077 3956 D6
Brice Ln
26200 SPLD 77372 2537 C5
Briceland Springs Dr
14700 HOUS 77082 4096 D1
Bricelyn Ln
13100 HOUS 77047 4373 C2
Brick Ln
10 HarC 77049 3827 D2
Brickarbor Dr
1400 HarC 77449 3815 C7
Bricker St
4500 HOUS 77051 4243 D2
4600 HOUS 77033 4243 D2
Brickhaven Ln
8400 HarC 77083 4097 C7
Brickhill Dr
25800 HarC 77389 2966 A1
Brickman Ct
15800 HarC 77084 3678 C5
Brickmont Ln
- HarC 77095 3537 D5
Brickstone Ct
800 MtgC 77386 2968 D1
Brick Village Ct
- HarC 77095 3537 E4
Brick Village Dr
9800 HarC 77095 3537 E3
Brickyard Ct
10300 HOUS 77041 3681 A7
Bridal Wreath Dr
4800 FBnC 77469 4233 A7
Briden Oak Ct
18100 HarC 77379 3256 A1
Bridenwood Ct
7600 HarC 77379 3256 A1
Bridewell Ln
- FBnC 77469 4095 C6
Bridge Ct
2000 HarC 77532 3551 C3
Bridge Dr
16100 HarC 77532 3551 D3
Bridge Ln
15300 MtgC 77354 2669 E2
Bridge Wy
24000 HarC 77389 2966 D5
Bridge Bay Ln
3800 HarC 77449 3815 B1
Bridgeberry Ct
10 WDLD 77381 2820 C2
Bridgeberry Ln
3200 HOUS 77082 4098 C2
Bridgeberry Pl
10 WDLD 77381 2820 C2
Bridgebluff Ln
3600 HarC 77449 3815 C2
Bridgebrook Dr
22100 HarC 77373 3260 D1
Bridge Creek Ln
4900 FBnC 77494 4093 D2
Bridge Creek Falls Ct
16600 HarC 77379 3256 B4
Bridge Crest Blvd
100 HarC 77082 4095 E4
Bridge Crest Ct
10 HarC 77082 4095 D4
Bridge Cross Ln
2000 HarC 77067 3402 A5
Bridgecrossing Ct
5000 HarC 77379 3112 C5
Bridgedale Dr
3600 HarC 77039 3546 A3
Bridgedale Ln
20000 HarC 77338 3262 A4
Bridgedown Dr
- HarC 77064 3540 A2
11000 HarC 77065 3540 A2
Bridge End Ln
21800 HarC 77388 3112 C4
Bridge Falls Ct
21100 HarC 77449 3815 B2
Bridge Falls Wy
18500 HarC 77084 3816 C3
Bridgefield Ln
- HarC 77379 3111 B5
Bridgefoot Ln
8500 HarC 77064 3541 D5
Bridge Forest Dr
- HarC 77088 3682 D1
5400 HarC 77088 3542 E7
Bridgegate Dr
5800 HarC 77373 3260 E1
6300 HarC 77373 3116 A7
Bridge Hampton Wy
2500 FBnC 77479 4493 E3
Bridgeharbor Ct
5000 HarC 77379 3112 A5
Bridge Harbor Dr
3900 GLSN 77554 5441 A5
Bridgehaven Ct
5500 FBnC 77494 4093 E3
Bridgehaven Dr
22300 FBnC 77494 4093 D3
Bridge Hollow Ct
900 HOUS 77062 4506 C2
Bridge Lake Blvd
2900 HarC 77449 3814 E3
Bridgeland Ln
4100 HarC 77388 3112 C4
10200 HOUS 77041 3680 D7
10200 HOUS 77041 3681 A7
N Bridgelands Lake Pkwy
16900 HarC 77433 3395 E6
Bridge Manor Ln
20200 FBnC 77469 4094 D2
Bridge Meadow Ln
21500 HarC 77449 3815 A4
Bridgemeadows Ln
21100 HarC 77449 3815 B2
Bridgemont Ln
4700 HarC 77388 3112 B4
Bridge Oak Ln
15200 FBnC 77478 4236 C6
Bridge Park Dr
8600 HarC 77064 3540 E6
Bridgepark Ln
- HarC 77433 3537 A5
Bridgepath Ct
13300 HarC 77041 3679 C5
Bridgepath Ln
13400 HarC 77041 3679 C5
Bridgepath Cove
13500 HarC 77041 3679 C5
Bridgepoint Ln
21300 HarC 77388 3112 B4
Bridgeport Rd
13500 HOUS 77047 4373 A5
14200 HarC 77047 4373 A5
E Bridgeport Pass Cir
9200 HarC 77433 3537 B4
N Bridgeport Pass Cir
19600 HarC 77433 3537 B4
S Bridgeport Pass Cir
19600 HarC 77433 3537 B4
W Bridgeport Pass Cir
9200 HarC 77433 3537 A4
Bridges Fairway Ln
15900 HarC 77068 3257 D5
Bridge Springs Ln
21100 HarC 77449 3815 C2
Bridgestone Lk
- CNRO 77304 2236 D4
Bridgestone Ln
10400 CNRO 77304 2236 D4
10400 MtgC 77304 2236 D4
21500 HarC 77388 3112 C4
Bridgestone Bend Dr
4600 HarC 77388 3112 B3
Bridgestone Canyon Dr
22300 HarC 77388 3112 C2
Bridgestone Cedar Dr
4300 HarC 77388 3112 C3
Bridgestone Cliff Ct
4500 HarC 77388 3112 B3
Bridgestone Crossing Dr
22000 HarC 77388 3112 C3
Bridgestone Eagle Ct
22000 HarC 77388 3112 C3
Bridgestone Hawk Ct
22000 HarC 77388 3112 C3
Bridgestone Hill Dr
- HarC 77388 3112 C2
Bridgestone Lakes Dr
4200 HarC 77388 3112 C3
Bridgestone Maple Dr
4300 HarC 77388 3112 C3
Bridgestone Oak Dr
22000 HarC 77388 3112 C3
Bridgestone Palm Ct
22300 HarC 77388 3112 C2
Bridgestone Park Ln
2400 MtgC 77386 2823 C7
Bridgestone Path Dr
- HarC 77388 3112 B2
Bridgestone Pine Ct
22000 HarC 77388 3112 C3
Bridgestone Point Dr
4500 HarC 77388 3112 B3
Bridgestone Ranch Dr
- HarC 77388 3112 B3
Bridgestone Ridge Dr
22300 HarC 77388 3112 B3
Bridgestone Shadow Ct
4200 HarC 77388 3112 C3
Bridgestone Trails Dr
22200 HarC 77388 3112 C3
Bridgestone Valley Dr
4500 HarC 77388 3112 C2
Bridgestone Wy Ct
22000 HarC 77388 3112 C2
Bridgeton Ct
10 FBnC 77479 4367 B6
Bridgeton Ln
- HarC 77047 4374 A3
Bridgevalley Ct
5000 HarC 77379 3112 C5
Bridgeview Cir
21000 HarC 77388 3112 B5
Bridge View Ln
1100 KATY 77494 3952 A3
Bridgeview Ln
- HarC 77379 3112 A5
4600 HarC 77388 3112 B5
Bridgevillage Dr
4400 HarC 77373 3115 B5
Bridgeville Ln
4800 HarC 77388 3112 B3
Bridgewalk Ln
13300 HarC 77041 3679 C5
Bridgewalk Cove
13500 HarC 77041 3679 C5
Bridgewater Cir
22800 HarC 77373 3114 C7
Bridgewater Dr
22000 SGCH 77355 2960 E2
22400 HarC 77373 3259 C1
22800 HarC 77373 3114 C7
24700 MtgC 77355 2960 E2
25100 MtgC 77355 2961 A1
Bridgewater Pt
21400 HarC 77449 3815 B2
Bridgewater Manor Ln
3000 HarC 77449 3815 A3
Bridgewater Meadow Dr
- HarC 77449 3815 C2
Bridgewater Village Dr
- HarC 77449 3815 A2
Bridgewood Rd
3900 BzaC 77511 4748 A3
18600 HarC 77532 3410 B6
Bridgewood St
10900 HNCV 77024 3960 A2
Bridgewood Cove Ct
10 WDLD 77384 2821 E1
Bridle Ct
14500 HarC 77044 3408 D7
Bridle Pth
200 RSBG 77471 4491 D2
Bridle Bend Dr
- HarC 77084 3678 E4
14800 HarC 77084 3679 A4
Bridle Canyon
23700 MtgC 77355 2962 C5
Bridlechase Ln
14000 HarC 77014 3401 C2
Bridle Creek Dr N
25600 MtgC 77355 2962 C5
S Bridle Creek Dr
25600 MtgC 77355 2962 C5
Bridledon Ln
4100 HarC 77014 3401 C2
Bridle Falls
25700 MtgC 77355 2962 C6
Bridle Oak Ct
10 WDLD 77380 2967 D4
Bridle Oak Dr
16400 HarC 77433 3251 C4
Bridlepark Cir
10900 HOUS 77016 3686 D2
Bridle Path Dr
7200 HarC 77044 3688 E7
7200 HarC 77044 3827 E1
Bridle Path Ln
2800 FRDW 77546 4749 D1
Bridle Ridge Lp
700 HarC 77073 3259 B6
Bridle Run Ln
- HarC 77429 3253 B7
Bridle Spur St
1300 HLSV 77055 3821 C6
1300 HOUS 77055 3821 C6
Bridleway Cir
10900 HOUS 77016 3686 D2
26900 MtgC 77355 2961 D1
Bridlewood
10700 HNCV 77024 3960 A2
Bridlewood St
- HOUS 77075 4376 C4
10700 HNCV 77024 3960 A2
15000 MtgC 77384 2674 B3
15000 WDLD 77354 2674 B3
15000 WDLD 77384 2674 B3
Bridlington St
5700 HOUS 77085 4371 E2
Bridoon Dr
18500 HarC 77433 3677 C1
Briefway St
7300 HOUS 77087 4105 A6
Brier Crst
8700 MNVL 77578 4747 A4
Brier Gardens Dr
3600 HarC 77082 4096 B4
Brierley Ln
5800 HarC 77084 3678 B4
Briervine Ct
10 WDLD 77381 2821 A5
Brigade Ct
2500 SGLD 77478 4369 B7
Brigade St
- HOUS 77043 3820 A3
- HOUS 77080 3820 A3
Brigade Trails Dr
6400 HarC 77449 3677 A3
Brigadoon St
100 FRDW 77546 4505 A7
100 FRDW 77546 4629 A1
Brigham Ln
12600 GlsC 77517 4986 B6
N Bright Dr
800 HarC 77073 3259 B6
Bright Tr
2700 SGLD 77479 4494 E2
Bright Bay Ln
- LGCY 77539 4752 E4
Bright Bloom Ln
6300 HarC 77379 3111 D3
Bright Bluff Ln
14300 HarC 77047 4374 C5
Brightbrook Dr
14900 HarC 77095 3539 A5
Bright Brook Ln
- LGCY 77539 4753 B2
Bright Canyon Ln
11200 HarC 77433 3396 A7
Bright Dawn Ct
26200 FBnC 77494 4092 E1
Bright Day Ln
200 LGCY 77539 4752 E2
Bright Ember Ct
800 HOUS 77062 4506 D1
Bright Falls Ln
6300 HarC 77449 3677 D4
Brightfield Dr
13700 SGLD 77478 4237 A6
Brightfield Ln
300 LGCY 77539 4753 A5
Bright Glen Dr
1400 PRLD 77545 4499 D3
Bright Glen Ln
- HarC 77053 4372 D5
Brightglen Ln
1500 HarC 77373 3259 C1
Bright Grove Ct
8500 HarC 77095 3538 A5
Bright Hollow Ln
25200 FBnC 77494 3953 A5
Brightlake Wy
1700 MSCY 77459 4369 B6
Bright Lake Bend Ct
- FBnC 77469 4094 B6
Bright Lake Bend Ln
7400 FBnC 77469 4094 B6
Brightlake Wy Ln
2600 PRLD 77584 4500 A3
Bright Landing Ct
12000 PRLD 77583 4500 C5
Bright Landing Ln
3000 PRLD 77583 4500 C5
Brightling Ln
16500 HarC 77090 3258 D5
Bright Meadow Ln
20500 HarC 77532 3410 E2
Bright Meadows Dr
2000 MSCY 77489 4370 B7
Bright Night Dr
8500 FBnC 77469 4235 E1
Bright Oak Ct
5100 HarC 77373 3115 C5
Brighton Ct
10 MSCY 77459 4369 D6
Brighton Ln
- MDWP 77478 4237 E5
- SGLD 77478 4237 E5
3700 PRLD 77584 4501 C1
10600 HarC 77031 4238 C6
10600 STAF 77477 4238 C6
11300 MDWP 77477 4238 A5
12100 MDWP 77477 4237 E5
Brighton Cove Ct
3400 FBnC 77545 4498 D7
Brightonfern Ln
6500 HarC 77049 3829 A3
Brighton Gardens Dr
10900 FBnC 77469 4092 C7
Brighton Glen Ln
7300 FBnC 77469 4095 D6
Brighton Hill Ln
6800 FBnC 77450 4094 B5
6800 FBnC 77469 4094 B5
Brighton Hollow Ln
21400 HarC 77449 3676 D5
Brighton Knolls Ln
7500 FBnC 77469 4095 C6
Brighton Lake Ln
8300 HarC 77095 3537 D6
Brighton Park Dr
13600 HarC 77044 3550 A2
13900 HarC 77044 3549 E2
Brighton Pl Ct
8100 HarC 77095 3538 E6
Brighton Springs Ln
- FBnC 77494 4093 A3
3700 HarC 77449 3815 B2
Brighton Trace Ln
- FBnC 77469 4095 C7
14400 HOUS 77044 3550 A3
Brighton Trail Ct
12700 HarC 77377 3254 A2
Brighton Trail Ln
18800 HarC 77377 3254 A1
Brightonwood Ct
6600 HarC 77379 3111 C5
Brightonwood Ln
20300 HarC 77379 3111 D4
Bright Penny Ln
600 HarC 77015 3829 C7
600 HarC 77015 3968 C1
Bright Point Ct
20300 HarC 77375 3109 D4
Brightridge Ln
6900 HarC 77379 3111 C3
Brights Bnd
4300 MSCY 77459 4497 A4
Bright Sail Cir
2000 LGCY 77573 4509 A6
Bright Sky Ct
2900 MtgC 77386 2823 D7
26400 FBnC 77494 4092 D2
Brightspring Ct
2900 HarC 77449 3815 B4
Bright Spring Ln
6700 HarC 77379 3111 C2
Bright Star Rd
23100 HarC 77373 3115 E6
Brightstone Dr
19800 HarC 77338 3261 E4
Bright Summer Ln
7100 FBnC 77469 4094 D5
Bright View Ln
13500 HOUS 77034 4378 D3
Brightwater Dr
1900 MSCY 77459 4369 C6
Brightwater Center Dr
- MSCY 77459 4369 D7
Bright Willow Ln
- HarC 77044 3550 A3
- HOUS 77044 3550 A3
Brightwood Ct
4000 MSCY 77459 4369 C6
Brightwood Dr
3900 HarC 77068 3257 A6
4300 HarC 77068 3256 E6
4300 HarC 77069 3256 E6
Brightwood Ln
25100 HarC 77336 3121 E7
25100 HarC 77336 3266 E1
Brightwood Park Ln
18100 FBnC 77469 4095 B6
Brigid Ct
1000 DKSN 77539 4752 E6
Brigid Pl Dr
12900 HarC 77429 3398 E5
Brigodoon Cir
9400 HOUS 77096 4240 B2
Brigstone Park Dr
5600 FBnC 77450 4094 B3
Briley St
2000 HOUS 77003 3963 D7
2000 HOUS 77004 3963 D7
2800 HOUS 77004 4103 D1
Brill Dr
1600 FRDW 77546 4629 C4
Brill Ln
10900 HarC 77375 2965 A3
Brill St
3300 HOUS 77026 3825 A6
Brilliant Lake Dr
9600 HarC 77396 3407 B7
Brillock St
1100 HarC 77032 3404 B7
Brim St
6900 HOUS 77028 3825 E2
Brimberry St
1900 HOUS 77018 3822 B1
Brimfield Dr
16000 HarC 77082 4096 A3
Brimhill Rd
- HarC 77070 3399 B7
Brimhurst Dr
- HOUS 77077 3956 E4
- HOUS 77077 3957 A4
Brimmage Dr
2200 HarC 77067 3402 B4
Brimridge Ln
- HOUS 77048 4375 D4
Brim Stone Ct
10 WDLD 77380 2967 C2
Brimwood Dr
3400 HarC 77068 3257 B6
Brindisi Ct
4000 MSCY 77459 4497 C5
Bringate Ct
12200 HarC 77066 3401 B6
Bringate Ln
5300 HarC 77066 3401 A4
Bringewood Chase Dr
1000 HarC 77379 3255 D2
Bringhurst St
1000 HOUS 77020 3964 A2
1900 HOUS 77026 3964 A1
2400 HOUS 77026 3825 A7
Brinkley St
4100 HOUS 77051 4243 C3
4600 HOUS 77033 4243 C3
Brinkman Ct
5200 HOUS 77018 3684 A7
5200 HOUS 77091 3684 A7
Brinkman St
2500 HOUS 77008 3823 B4
4500 HOUS 77018 3823 B1
4800 HOUS 77018 3684 A7
6000 HOUS 77091 3684 A5
Brinkwood Dr
16200 HarC 77090 3258 D5
Brinkworth Ln
8100 HarC 77070 3399 D1
Brinmont Pl Ct
23500 FBnC 77494 4093 D1
Brinmont Pl Ln
3200 FBnC 77494 4093 C1
Brinson Ct
1200 HarC 77379 3110 B7
Brinton Ct
16200 HarC 77095 3538 C5
Brinton Oaks Ct
2100 HarC 77450 3954 B6
Brinton Trails Ln
3200 FBnC 77494 3953 D7
3400 FBnC 77494 4093 E1
Brinwood Dr
10100 HOUS 77043 3820 A6
10100 HOUS 77080 3820 A6
10300 HOUS 77043 3819 E6
Brisbane Dr
4800 HOUS 77048 4243 D7
Brisbane Rd
200 HOUS 77061 4245 A6
400 HOUS 77061 4244 E7
Brisbane St
3000 HOUS 77051 4243 A7
4100 HOUS 77047 4243 C7
4900 HOUS 77048 4243 E7
Brisbane Meadows Ct
19600 HarC 77449 3676 E4
Briscoe Ct
- DKSN 77539 4753 B5
3600 PRLD 77583 4500 E5
Briscoe Ln
11100 PRLD 77583 4500 D6
Briscoe St
4500 HOUS 77051 4243 D2
4600 HOUS 77033 4243 D2
Brisk Spring Ct
25500 HarC 77373 3114 B5
Bristlebrook Dr
9200 FBnC 77083 4237 A1
Bristlecone Dr
2700 HarC 77449 3815 C5
28000 FBnC 77494 3951 D5
Bristlecone Ln
6000 FBnC 77469 4493 B4
Bristlecone Pl
2000 WDLD 77380 2967 C1
Bristle Cone Tr
3300 MtgC 77380 2967 B2
Bristle Creek Dr
16500 HarC 77095 3538 B4
Bristle Haven Dr
6400 HOUS 77072 4097 D4
Bristleleaf Dr
3600 HarC 77449 3816 A3
N Bristle Pine Dr
8400 HarC 77379 3256 C4
S Bristle Pine Dr
17200 HarC 77379 3256 C4
Bristlestar Dr
19200 HarC 77449 3816 A3
Bristol Ct
2700 SGLD 77478 4369 A2
19100 MtgC 77357 2829 E3
N Bristol Ct
1100 LGCY 77573 4631 D4
S Bristol Ct
1100 LGCY 77573 4631 D5
W Bristol Ct
400 LGCY 77573 4631 E5
Bristol Ln
- SGLD 77478 4369 A3
1000 MSCY 77459 4369 B5
Bristol Pk
12500 HarC 77041 3679 E3
Bristol St
4600 HOUS 77009 3824 B5
Bristol Wy
1000 PRLD 77584 4501 B1
Bristol Bank Ct
5200 HarC 77041 3679 E6
Bristol Bay Ct
18400 HarC 77346 3409 B1
Bristol Bend Cir
100 WDLD 77382 2674 D5
Bristol Bend Ln
100 LGCY 77539 4752 E5
2200 HarC 77450 3954 C6
Bristolberry Dr
12900 HarC 77429 3398 A1
13100 HarC 77429 3254 A7
Bristol Breeze Dr
- PRLD 77584 4500 A1
Bristol Breeze Ln
2100 LGCY 77573 4631 B7
N Bristol Gate Pl
10 WDLD 77380 2822 A7
10 WDLD 77380 2968 B3
S Bristol Gate Pl
10 MtgC 77380 2968 A1
10 WDLD 77380 2968 A1
E Bristol Harbour Cir
6200 HarC 77084 3679 A5
S Bristol Harbour Cir
14700 HarC 77084 3679 A5
Bristol Lake Dr
15600 HarC 77070 3255 B6
Bristol Ln Ct
11500 HarC 77066 3400 D6
S Bristol Oak Cir
10 WDLD 77382 2674 D5
W Bristol Oak Cir
100 WDLD 77382 2674 D4
S Bristol Oak Ct
10 WDLD 77382 2674 D4
Bristol Park Dr
2500 HarC 77014 3401 E3
2500 HarC 77014 3402 A3
Bristol Point Ln
- HarC 77377 3254 A3
18500 HarC 77377 3253 E2
Bristol Ridge Dr
7100 HarC 77095 3678 E1
Bristol Water Dr
2300 PRLD 77584 4500 B2
Bristol Waters
- HarC 77041 3679 E6
Bristolwood Ct
22400 FBnC 77494 4093 D4
Bristol Woods Ln
- HarC 77429 3397 D2
Bristow Dr
17400 GLSN 77554 5331 D7
Britannia Dr
20000 HarC 77450 3954 E2
20000 HOUS 77094 3954 E2
20000 HOUS 77450 3954 E2
Brite Ct
7100 HarC 77379 3111 B2
Britford St
16700 HarC 77084 3678 B2
British Knoll Ct
12600 HarC 77014 3402 A3
British Woods Ln
700 FRDW 77546 4505 A7
Britoak Ln
13700 HOUS 77079 3958 A1
14000 HOUS 77079 3957 E1
Briton Centre Ct
7000 HarC 77069 3400 A3
Briton Cove Dr
14500 HarC 77084 3679 A3
Britt Rd
12400 BKVL 77581 4375 D6
Brittain Rd
11700 STFE 77510 4987 C1
Brittania Dr
19600 HOUS 77094 3955 A2
19700 HOUS 77094 3954 E2
19900 HarC 77450 3954 E2
19900 HOUS 77450 3954 E2
Brittan Leaf Ln
11000 HOUS 77034 4378 D4
Brittany Dr
13400 SGLD 77478 4237 B5
Brittany Ln
13700 HarC 77396 3547 C3
Brittany Bay Blvd
1700 LGCY 77573 4631 A7
3000 LGCY 77573 4630 E7
5300 LGCY 77573 4751 C1
W Brittany Bay Blvd
6200 LGCY 77546 4630 A7
6200 LGCY 77546 4750 E1
6200 LGCY 77573 4630 A7
Brittany Colony Dr
2100 LGCY 77573 4631 B7
2100 LGCY 77573 4752 B1
Brittany Creek Dr
19300 HarC 77388 3113 B6
Brittany Estates Rd
3200 PRLD 77581 4503 D5
Brittany Ferry Ln
6600 HarC 77049 3828 E2
Brittany Knoll Dr
16000 HarC 77095 3678 C1
Brittany Lakes Dr
2100 LGCY 77573 4631 B7
Brittany Park Ln
6300 HarC 77066 3400 E6
Britterige St
15000 HarC 77084 3678 E4
Brittmoore Rd
- HOUS 77043 3958 C1
- JRSV 77040 3680 C2
- JRSV 77041 3680 C2
600 HOUS 77079 3958 C1
1000 HOUS 77043 3819 C7
4000 HOUS 77041 3819 C1
4500 HarC 77041 3680 C6
4500 HOUS 77041 3680 C4
7200 HarC 77040 3680 C2
Brittmoore Park Dr
10900 HarC 77041 3680 A6
Brittmore North Ind Park
- HarC 77041 3680 C7
Britt Oaks Dr
- BzaC 77511 4628 C7
6400 ALVN 77511 4749 C1
6400 BzaC 77511 4749 C1
Britton Dr
100 TXCY 77591 4873 E7
Britton St
1800 BYTN 77520 4112 B2
Britton Hill Wy
21600 HarC 77449 3676 A7
Britton Ridge Dr
2200 FBnC 77494 3952 E4
Britt Wy St
10900 HOUS 77043 3819 C5
Broad Rd
2300 HarC 77521 3832 D4
Broad St
2400 HOUS 77087 4104 D6
Broad Bay Ct
2900 LGCY 77573 4633 A3
Broad Bay Ln
1000 LGCY 77573 4633 A3
13100 PRLD 77584 4500 A1
Broad Bend Dr
17500 HarC 77433 3395 E5
Broadbluff Ln
18000 HarC 77433 3677 D1
Broad Branch Ct
24600 HarC 77373 3114 D3
Broadbury
- HOUS 77077 3957 C5
Broadcrest Ct
25600 FBnC 77494 4093 A7
Broadelm Dr
7200 HarC 77095 3678 A1
Broadfield Blvd
1200 HOUS 77084 3956 B1
1300 HOUS 77084 3817 B7
Broadford
27000 MtgC 77355 2963 B4
Broadglen Ct
16200 HarC 77082 4096 A3
Broadgreen Dr
2300 MSCY 77489 4370 B7
14500 HOUS 77079 3957 D3
Broad Haven Dr
2500 HarC 77067 3402 A7
2900 HarC 77066 3402 A7
Broadhead Manor Ct
9300 HarC 77379 3110 B5
Broadhead Manor Dr
19700 HarC 77379 3110 C6
Broad Hollow Ct
20900 HarC 77379 3111 A4
Broadhurst St
- HarC 77047 4373 A4
- HarC 77053 4373 A4
10 HOUS 77047 4373 A4
Broad Knoll Ln
17300 FBnC 77469 4095 B6
Broadknoll Ln
3400 FBnC 77478 4366 E1
Broadlawn Dr
2100 HOUS 77058 4507 D2
Broadleaf Av
4200 HarC 77521 3833 B3
Broadleaf St
4200 HOUS 77345 3119 E3
Broadley Dr
9700 FBnC 77478 4236 B2
Broadmark Ln
4500 HarC 77338 3260 C2
Broadmead Dr
- HOUS 77054 4102 A7
2800 HOUS 77025 4102 A7
3000 HOUS 77025 4101 E7

STREET
Block City ZIP Map# Grid

Broadmeadow Ln
13500 HOUS 77077 3957 D2
Broadmoor Cir
10 LMQU 77568 4990 B2
2700 MSCY 77459 4497 A1
Broadmoor Ct
10 CNRO 77304 2382 D3
2100 LGCY 77573 4509 A7
2100 LGCY 77573 4633 B1
Broadmoor Dr
3000 SGLD 77478 4369 A3
3100 FBnC 77477 4369 B3
3100 SGLD 77477 4369 B3
4700 LGCY 77573 4633 A1
Broadmoor St
400 FRDW 77546 4628 E6
1600 HOUS 77023 4104 B1
Broadmoore Dr
3600 PASD 77505 4248 B4
Broadmore Dr
100 FBnC 77545 4623 C2
Broad Oak Ct
15900 HarC 77377 3254 E5
Broadoak Grove Ln
16600 FBnC 77478 4236 B5
Broad Oaks Cir
100 HOUS 77056 3960 E3
Broad Oaks Ct
100 HOUS 77056 3960 E3
Broad Oaks Dr
6500 FBnC 77469 4232 D4
E Broad Oaks Dr
10 HOUS 77056 3960 E3
W Broad Oaks Dr
10 HOUS 77056 3960 E4
Broad Oaks Ln
1300 CNRO 77301 2384 D2
13700 BzaC 77583 4623 E5
E Broad Oaks Ln
10 HOUS 77056 3960 E3
Broad Oaks Pk
5400 HOUS 77056 3960 E3
Broad Oaks Tr
100 HOUS 77056 3960 E3
Broad Pine Dr
800 HOUS 77336 3266 D2
Broadridge Rd
16000 HOUS 77053 4372 C7
Broad Ripple Dr
900 HOUS 77336 3266 D2
Broad Run Ln
19900 FBnC 77469 4094 C6
Broadside Ct
15900 HarC 77532 3552 A3
Broadsky Dr
- HOUS 77449 3815 C7
20300 HarC 77449 3815 C7
Broad Spring Ct
23100 FBnC 77469 4093 D6
Broadstairs St
10300 HOUS 77013 3966 B1
Broadstone Dr
21500 HarC 77449 3815 B2
Broadsweep Dr
11200 HarC 77064 3540 C1
Broad Thicket Ct
3900 FBnC 77478 4366 E3
Broad Timbers Dr
2400 HarC 77373 3114 D4
Broad Vale Cir
18200 HarC 77346 3408 C1
Broad Valley Ct
5800 HarC 77373 3260 E1
Broadview Dr
7600 HOUS 77061 4245 B2
Broadwater Dr
16000 HarC 77532 3551 D3
Broadway
700 GlsC 77650 4878 E7
700 GlsC 77650 4879 D4
Broadway LP-108
700 GlsC 77650 4878 E7
700 GlsC 77650 4879 D4
Broadway SR-87
- GlsC 77650 4879 E5
Broadway Av
300 PASD 77506 4107 B4
8400 HarC 77064 3541 C3
9300 MtgC 77385 2822 D2
E Broadway Av
100 PASD 77506 4107 A4
W Broadway Av
100 PASD 77506 4107 A4
Broadway Ln
2300 GlsC 77650 4879 D3
Broadway St
100 HOUS 77012 4105 C3
200 GlsC 77539 4636 A6
600 GLSN 77550 5109 D3
1700 GlsC 77539 4635 A4
2600 HOUS 77017 4105 C6
2900 TXCY 77539 4635 A4
3700 GLSN 77550 5108 E4
3900 HOUS 77087 4105 C7
4100 HOUS 77061 4245 C2
4100 HOUS 77087 4245 C1
4400 GLSN 77551 5108 E4
7000 GLSN 77551 5107 E5
7000 GLSN 77554 5107 D5
9300 BzaC 77584 4501 B4
9300 PRLD 77584 4501 B4
10500 PRLD 77584 4500 E4
10800 PRLD 77583 4500 E4
Broadway St FM-518
9300 BzaC 77584 4501 B4
9300 PRLD 77584 4501 B4
10500 PRLD 77584 4500 E4
10800 PRLD 77583 4500 E4
Broadway St SR-87
600 GLSN 77550 5109 D3
3700 GLSN 77550 5108 E4
4400 GLSN 77551 5108 E4
E Broadway St
1100 PRLD 77581 4504 D5
2500 PRLD 77581 4503 E4
E Broadway St FM-518
1100 PRLD 77581 4504 D5
2500 PRLD 77581 4503 E3
N Broadway St
100 LPRT 77571 4251 D2
600 MRGP 77571 4251 D1
700 LPRT 77571 4111 D7
700 MRGP 77571 4111 D7
8800 HOUS 77034 4246 E7
9100 HOUS 77034 4377 E1
S Broadway St
100 LPRT 77571 4251 E6
2900 LPRT 77571 4382 E1
3200 SRAC 77571 4382 E2
3800 HarC 77571 4382 E2
3900 PASD 77571 4382 E2
S Broadway St SPR-501
2300 LPRT 77571 4251 E7
3200 LPRT 77571 4382 E1
3200 SRAC 77571 4382 E2
3800 HarC 77571 4382 E2
3900 PASD 77571 4382 E2
S Broadway St SR-146 BUS
100 LPRT 77571 4251 E6
W Broadway St
4000 PRLD 77581 4503 B3
4800 PRLD 77584 4503 A3
5300 PRLD 77581 4502 D3
5300 PRLD 77584 4502 D3
7900 PRLD 77581 4501 D3
7900 PRLD 77584 4501 D3
9000 BzaC 77584 4501 C4
W Broadway St FM-518
4000 PRLD 77581 4503 B3
4800 PRLD 77584 4503 A3
5300 PRLD 77581 4502 D3
5300 PRLD 77584 4502 D3
7900 PRLD 77581 4501 D3
7900 PRLD 77584 4501 D3
9000 BzaC 77584 4501 C4
Broad Weather Pl
10 WDLD 77382 2673 E5
Broad Wind Ln
19100 HarC 77449 3677 B6
Broadwind Ln
- FBnC 77469 4492 B2
- RHMD 77469 4492 B2
Brobeck Ct
6400 FBnC 77479 4367 B5
Brock St
5500 HOUS 77023 4104 B4
Brock Creek Wy
15300 HarC 77429 3253 B5
Brocket St
200 STAF 77477 4369 A2
Brockhampton St
500 HOUS 77013 3966 B1
Brockington Dr
6800 FBnC 77494 4093 C5
Brockland Ln
19900 HarC 77433 3677 C2
Brockleigh St
5000 LMQU 77568 4872 E7
Brockley Ln
7300 HOUS 77087 4245 A2
Brockman St
200 PASD 77506 4107 A2
Brock Park Blvd
8800 HOUS 77078 3688 C5
Brockton St
8000 HOUS 77017 4105 C5
Brockwell Ct
- HarC 77338 3260 D2
Brockwood Dr
14600 HarC 77047 4374 D6
Brodie Ln
2000 CNRO 77301 2530 C3
Brodt Rd
15800 HarC 77532 3553 E2
Brody Ln
7000 HarC 77083 4097 A5
Brogan Ct
8600 HarC 77375 2965 D4
Brogden Rd
- SPVL 77024 3960 A1
700 HDWV 77024 3960 A1
700 HNCV 77024 3960 A1
Broken Arrow
2800 FBnC 77459 4621 B6
Broken Arrow Dr
1500 BYTN 77521 3973 C2
7700 HarC 77521 3833 B3
Broken Arrow Ln
19000 HarC 77433 3537 B7
Broken Arrow St
12300 HOUS 77024 3959 A2
Broken Back Dr
17000 HarC 77532 3551 E1
17100 HarC 77532 3552 A1
Broken Bough Cir
11700 BKHV 77024 3959 C2
Broken Bough Dr
3200 MSCY 77459 4496 E1
11900 BKHV 77024 3959 B2
12300 HOUS 77024 3959 A2
12500 HOUS 77024 3958 E2
N Broken Bough Dr
3600 MtgC 77380 2967 B2
S Broken Bough Dr
25000 MtgC 77380 2967 B2
Broken Bough Ln
100 CNRO 77304 2383 B4
19600 MtgC 77357 2829 D5
Broken Bow Dr
24200 HarC 77447 3249 E3
Broken Bow Ln
12100 MtgC 77362 2963 B1
24000 HarC 77447 3249 E3
Broken Branch Ct
2000 FBnC 77494 3952 B5
Broken Bridge Dr
13600 HOUS 77085 4371 C1
Broken Bridge Ln
- PRLD 77581 4503 E2
Broken Brook Ct
13000 HarC 77429 3397 D4
Broken Creek Ct
2600 PRLD 77584 4500 D4
Broken Creek Ln
12300 PRLD 77584 4500 B3
Broken Cypress Cir
15500 HarC 77049 3829 A2
Broken Elm Dr
2400 FBnC 77469 4365 E3
3800 HarC 77388 3112 C7
4700 HarC 77388 3257 C1
N Brokenfern Dr
10 WDLD 77380 2822 A6
S Brokenfern Dr
10 WDLD 77380 2822 A7
Broken Limb Tr
21800 HarC 77433 3251 A5
E Broken Oak Ct
10 WDLD 77381 2821 A5
W Broken Oak Ct
10 WDLD 77381 2821 A5
Broken Oak Ln
7400 FBnC 77479 4493 E6
Broken Pebble Ct
22100 FBnC 77450 4094 A2
Broken Pine Ct
- FBnC 77479 4496 D5
300 CNRO 77304 2383 A6
Broken Pine Ln
12300 HarC 77433 3396 B5
Broken Ridge Dr
7400 HarC 77095 3678 D2
Broken Sky Ct
9800 HarC 77064 3540 E3
Broken Sky Dr
10800 HarC 77064 3540 C2
Broken Spear Ln
21400 MtgC 77365 2973 A3
Broken Stone St
6500 HarC 77084 3678 A3
Broken Timber Cir
16200 HarC 77095 3538 C5
Broken Timber Wy
8200 HarC 77095 3538 C6
Broken Trace Ct
10200 HarC 77338 3407 C1
Broken Trail Ct
1000 FBnC 77479 4366 C7
Brollier St
2400 HOUS 77054 4242 D2
Brom Bones Blvd
2600 PRLD 77581 4504 C4
Bromel Station St
4500 HOUS 77053 4372 C7
Bromley St
8100 HLSV 77055 3821 C7
Brompton Ct
10 BKHV 77024 3959 D4
10 PNPV 77024 3959 D4
300 HarC 77562 3831 C2
E Brompton Dr
1000 PRLD 77584 4501 A2
N Brompton Dr
2600 PRLD 77584 4501 A1
S Brompton Dr
2600 PRLD 77584 4501 A2
W Brompton Dr
1000 PRLD 77584 4501 A2
Brompton Ln
500 HarC 77562 3831 C2
Brompton Rd
6300 WUNP 77005 4102 A5
6700 HOUS 77025 4102 A5
Brompton Pl Dr
8300 FBnC 77083 4096 C5
8300 FBnC 77083 4236 A1
Brompton Square Dr
2900 HOUS 77025 4102 A4
Bronco Ct
3200 BzaC 77578 4625 B1
Bronco Dr
9100 HOUS 77055 3820 D6
Bronco Bluff Ct
3100 HarC 77450 3954 D7
Broncroft Ct
12900 HarC 77044 3549 E1
13100 HOUS 77044 3549 E1
Brondesbury Dr
20100 HarC 77450 3954 E4
Bron Holly Dr
2000 HOUS 77018 3822 C3
Bronson St
2100 HOUS 77034 4246 D5
Bronton St
3000 HOUS 77092 3822 C3
Bronwynn Ln
- HarC 77047 4374 A4
Bronze Bay Ct
15100 HOUS 77059 4380 B6
Bronze Bluff Dr
20200 HarC 77449 3815 D5
Bronze Finch Dr
14700 HarC 77433 3250 D4
Bronzehill Ln
26200 FBnC 77494 4092 D1
Bronze Leaf Ct
15300 HarC 77433 3251 A5
Bronze Leaf Dr
21900 HarC 77433 3251 C3
Bronze Loquate Ct
2700 HarC 77449 3815 C5
Bronze Sunset Ct
1700 HOUS 77345 3120 D6
Bronze Trail Dr
7600 HarC 77346 3409 B1
Brooding Oak Cir
9400 HOUS 77096 4240 B2
E Brook Ct
6000 SGLD 77479 4494 E4
Brook Ln
600 PASD 77502 4247 A1
Brook St
- HarC 77015 3829 C7
Brook Arbor Ct
12800 PRLD 77584 4500 A3
15300 HOUS 77062 4380 B7
Brook Arbor Ln
- PRLD 77584 4500 A3
800 LGCY 77573 4633 B2
3200 FBnC 77479 4493 C3
Brook Bank Dr
12100 HarC 77068 3257 B5
Brook Bend Dr
5400 FBnC 77479 4366 E6
5700 SGLD 77479 4495 A4
Brookbend Dr
10600 HOUS 77035 4241 B3
Brookbend Ln
3400 SGLD 77479 4495 B1
E Brookberry Ct
10 WDLD 77381 2821 A4
S Brookberry Ct
10 WDLD 77381 2821 A4
Brookbluff Ln
13500 HOUS 77077 3957 A6
Brookchase
- FBnC 77479 4493 D4
Brookchase Dr
29100 MtgC 77386 2969 C4
Brookchase Lp
21500 HarC 77433 3251 D5
Brookchase Wy
15600 HarC 77433 3251 A6
Brookchester St
7100 HarC 77450 3954 A5
Brook Cove
6100 BzaC 77583 4624 A5
Brookcrest Cir
8600 HOUS 77072 4097 D7
Brook Dale Ct
4000 SGLD 77479 4495 A5
Brookdale Dr
100 LGCY 77573 4630 C5
2900 HOUS 77339 3119 C3
Brookdale Ln
3100 DRPK 77536 4109 A7
Brooke Amber Cir
1700 DRPK 77536 4109 D5
Brookefield Cir
10 MtgC 77355 2814 E3
10 MtgC 77355 2815 A3
Brookeland Meadow Ct
- HOUS 77489 4371 A6
Brookes Bnd
18000 HarC 77094 3955 C2
Brooke Vista Ln
12600 HOUS 77034 4378 B3
Brookfield Dr
3200 HOUS 77045 4373 A3
4100 HOUS 77045 4372 D3
5500 HOUS 77085 4371 D3
5500 HOUS 77085 4372 A3
Brookfield Ln
13200 MtgC 77302 2530 C4
Brookfield Pk
12600 HarC 77041 3679 E3
Brookfield St
7800 CmbC 77520 3835 C4
Brookfield Park Pl
4500 HOUS 77053 4372 C7
Brookfir Ln
7000 HOUS 77040 3682 B3
Brookflower Rd
10 WDLD 77380 2822 B6
Brookford Ct
16200 HOUS 77059 4380 C5
Brookford Dr
500 MSCY 77489 4370 E6
500 MSCY 77489 4371 A6
16200 HOUS 77059 4380 C5
16400 PASD 77059 4380 C5
Brook Forest Ct
900 MtgC 77385 2676 C2
Brook Forest Dr
- HOUS 77058 4380 D6
900 MtgC 77385 2676 C2
15700 HOUS 77059 4380 C6
Brook Forest Rd
22000 MtgC 77357 2827 C3
22700 MtgC 77357 2828 A2
Brook Forest Tr
200 SGLD 77478 4368 A3
Brook Garden Ln
3800 HarC 77449 3815 B2
Brookgate Dr
6100 HarC 77373 3116 A7
Brookglade Cir
12300 HOUS 77099 4237 D1
Brookglen Dr
5100 HOUS 77017 4246 A1
Brookgreen Dr
- HOUS 77059 4380 C4
3200 HOUS 77339 3119 C4
Brookgreen Falls Dr
21500 HarC 77450 3954 B5
Brook Grove Dr
1200 HarC 77450 3953 E4
3100 HOUS 77345 3120 A4
Brookhaven Av
3900 PASD 77504 4247 D3
Brookhaven Ct
1100 PRLD 77581 4376 D6
3100 DRPK 77536 4109 A7
Brook Haven Dr
100 MtgC 77385 2676 B3
2100 LGCY 77573 4632 D1
Brook Haven St
25500 MtgC 77386 2968 C2
Brookhaven St
4300 HOUS 77033 4243 C1
4300 HOUS 77051 4243 C1
Brookhaven Park Cir
12500 HarC 77065 3539 C4
Brookhaven Park Dr
9500 HarC 77065 3539 D4
Brookhead Tr
4000 HarC 77066 3401 C3
Brookhill Dr
6100 HOUS 77087 4104 C5
Brook Hollow Dr
200 MtgC 77385 2676 C2
1500 PRLD 77581 4375 D7
13500 SGLD 77478 4237 B6
Brookhollow Dr
- WlrC 77447 2813 B5
1000 DRPK 77536 4109 A7
1300 DRPK 77536 4108 E7
Brook Hollow Crossing Dr
17200 HarC 77084 3678 A5
Brookhollow Ct Dr
17200 HarC 77084 3678 A5
Brookhollow Grove Ct
17200 HarC 77084 3678 A5
Brookhollow Mist Ct
17100 HarC 77084 3678 A5
Brookhollow Oaks Tr
5500 HarC 77084 3678 A5
Brookhollow Pine Tr
5700 HarC 77084 3678 A5
Brookhollow Pines Ct
5500 HarC 77084 3678 A6
Brookhollow Trace Ct
17200 HarC 77084 3678 A5
Brookhollow West Dr
6900 HarC 77040 3680 E3
7000 HarC 77040 3681 A2
Brookhurst Ln
3100 DRPK 77536 4109 A7
Brookings Dr
18000 HarC 77084 3816 D1
Brook Knoll Ln
- HarC 77396 3547 D3
W Brooklake Ct
1400 HOUS 77077 3958 A5
E Brooklake Dr
1300 HOUS 77077 3958 B5
W Brooklake Dr
1300 HOUS 77077 3958 B5
Brooklawn Dr
4700 HarC 77066 3401 B5
6200 HOUS 77085 4371 D4
Brook Lea St
6000 HOUS 77087 4104 C7
Brookleaf Dr
7400 HarC 77041 3679 C1
7500 HarC 77041 3539 C7
Brookledge Dr
11400 HOUS 77099 4238 B4
Brooklet Dr
9900 HOUS 77099 4238 D2
Brooklet View Ct
13800 HOUS 77059 4379 E5
Brookline Cir
2800 MSCY 77459 4497 A1
Brookline Ct
10 WDLD 77381 2821 B2
Brooklyn St
11400 HarC 77093 3545 C7
Brooklyn Glen Ln
4800 HarC 77449 3677 C6
Brookmeade Dr
1300 DRPK 77536 4108 E7
1300 DRPK 77536 4109 A7
3700 HOUS 77045 4372 D1
Brook Meadow Cir
11300 HarC 77089 4378 B6
Brook Meadow Ct
11200 HarC 77089 4378 B5
Brook Meadow Dr
1500 LPRT 77571 4110 B7
11400 HarC 77089 4378 A6
Brook Meadow Ln
9900 HarC 77089 4504 E2
Brook Meadows Ct
12100 MDWP 77477 4237 D6
Brook Meadows Ln
11300 MDWP 77477 4238 B5
12400 MDWP 77477 4237 E5
Brookmere Dr
2300 HOUS 77008 3822 C5
Brook Mill Ct
11100 HarC 77065 3539 B2
Brookmist Ln
2800 LGCY 77539 4752 E2
Brookmont Ln
11800 HarC 77044 3688 D7
12700 HarC 77044 3689 B7
Brookney St
1300 PRLD 77584 4501 C2
Brooknoll Dr
18000 HarC 77084 3677 E5
Brook Park Wy
14700 HOUS 77062 4379 B7
14700 HOUS 77062 4506 C1
N Brook Pebble Ct
10 WDLD 77380 2968 B4
S Brook Pebble Ct
10 WDLD 77380 2968 A3
Brook Pine Ln
15700 HarC 77082 4096 B2
Brookpoint Dr
14900 HOUS 77062 4506 E1
Brookport Dr
200 LGCY 77539 4753 A2
Brookren Cir
8600 HOUS 77072 4097 D7
Brookren Ct
4500 PRLD 77584 4501 E5
Brookridge Ln
16600 HOUS 77053 4372 B7
Brook Rise Ln
20700 HarC 77433 3251 B7
Brook River Ct
2800 SGLD 77479 4368 D7
Brookriver Dr
9800 HarC 77040 3681 A1
Brook Rock Cir
21100 HarC 77449 3815 B2
Brook Run Ln
7000 HOUS 77040 3682 B4
Brooks Av
1800 RSBG 77471 4490 E6
Brooks Ct
3000 BzaC 77584 4501 C6
S Brooks Rd
12100 MtgC 77302 2677 D1
Brooks St
100 SGLD 77478 4367 E4
500 HOUS 77009 3963 C2
1600 HOUS 77026 3963 D2
2700 HOUS 77020 3963 E2
Brooks St SPR-58
100 SGLD 77478 4367 E4
Brooksburg Ln
13700 HarC 77429 3254 A5
Brooks Crossing Dr
7700 BYTN 77520 3835 B4
7700 BYTN 77521 3835 B4
N Brooksedge Cir
10 WDLD 77382 2673 E5
S Brooksedge Cir
100 WDLD 77382 2673 E5
Brooksedge Ct
10 WDLD 77382 2673 E5
Brooksedge Dr
- WDLD 77382 2673 E4
Brooksfalls Dr
11600 HarC 77070 3254 E7
Brook Shadow Dr
3400 HOUS 77339 3119 D4
3400 HOUS 77345 3119 D4
4500 HOUS 77345 3120 A3
Brookshire Dr
9700 HOUS 77041 3820 B1
Brookshire Ln
10600 HOUS 77041 3819 E1
Brookshire St
300 HarC 77530 3831 C6
500 HarC 77562 3831 C5
1700 LMQU 77568 4873 E7
Brook Shore Ct
400 SGLD 77478 4368 A3
3000 HOUS 77345 3120 A1
Brookshore Ln
10000 PRLD 77584 4501 A3
Brookside Ct
4700 MSCY 77459 4369 B6
Brookside Dr
100 SRAC 77571 4383 A2
1800 FRDW 77546 4629 D4
6300 HOUS 77023 4104 D1
9800 LPRT 77571 4110 B7
13100 SGLD 77478 4237 C4
Brookside Ln
20500 MtgC 77357 2830 A7
Brookside Rd
5000 BKVL 77581 4375 D7
5000 PRLD 77581 4375 A6
6700 BKVL 77581 4376 A7
7000 PRLD 77581 4376 A7
7900 PRLD 77581 4374 E7
8200 PRLD 77584 4374 E7
Brookside Forest Dr
14700 HarC 77040 3541 A6
Brookside Pine Ln
3100 HOUS 77345 3120 B6
Brook Springs Dr
7700 HarC 77095 3538 D7
Brooksprings Dr
11600 HOUS 77077 3958 A5
Brookston St
3000 HOUS 77045 4242 A7
3300 HOUS 77045 4241 E7
5300 HOUS 77085 4241 A7
Brookstone Ct
3500 BzaC 77584 4501 C7
Brook Stone Dr
7100 HOUS 77040 3682 A3
Brookstone Ln
1500 FBnC 77479 4494 B6
4500 LGCY 77573 4630 E5
Brooksure Cir
8600 HOUS 77072 4097 D7
Brooktondale Ct
16800 HarC 77084 3678 B4
Brook Trail Cir
7800 HarC 77040 3541 E7
Brooktrail Dr
1300 HOUS 77339 3263 B1
1500 HOUS 77339 3118 B7
Brooktree Dr
2000 HOUS 77008 3822 C5
10200 HOUS 77043 3819 E7
10200 HOUS 77043 3820 A7
Brooktree Ln
3200 MtgC 77380 2967 B1
Brookvale Ct
3700 HOUS 77345 3119 E3
Brookvale Dr
12600 HarC 77038 3543 B4
Brookvalley Dr
11800 HOUS 77071 4239 D5
Brookview Dr
200 HarC 77015 3968 C2
400 HarC 77530 3968 C1
500 HarC 77530 3829 C7
2900 BzaC 77584 4501 B5
4700 SGLD 77479 4368 B6
9800 LPRT 77571 4110 B7
Brook View Ln
2200 SGLD 77479 4495 B1
Brookvilla Dr
16200 HOUS 77059 4380 C5
16400 PASD 77059 4380 C5
Brook Village Rd
19200 HarC 77084 3816 A4
19800 HarC 77084 3815 E4
19800 HarC 77449 3815 E4
Brookville Ln
- HarC 77083 4097 A6
Brookwater Dr
400 HarC 77336 3121 C6
Brookway Dr
5300 HarC 77084 3678 A6
Brookway Berch Ct
19800 HarC 77379 3112 A5
Brookway Cedar Ct
19800 HarC 77379 3112 A5
Brookway Cypress Ct
19800 HarC 77379 3112 A4
Brookway Knoll Ct
- HarC 77379 3112 A4
Brookway Maple Ct
19800 HarC 77379 3112 A3
Brookway Oaks Ct
- HarC 77379 3111 D6
Brookway Park Ct
- HarC 77379 3111 D6
Brookway Pine Ct
19900 HarC 77379 3112 A5
Brookway Willow Dr
5200 HarC 77379 3112 A5
5800 HarC 77379 3111 E6
Brookway Wind Ct
- HarC 77379 3111 E6
Brookwind Dr
3800 LPRT 77571 4249 D4
Brookwood Ct
1400 SEBK 77586 4509 D2
Brookwood Dr
- FBnC 77479 4494 B7
- HarC 77507 4249 D5
3400 LPRT 77571 4249 D4
Brookwood Ln
- PRLD 77584 4502 B5
3100 DRPK 77536 4108 D5
Brookwood St
10 CNRO 77304 2383 C3
Brookwood Bridge Ln
15000 FBnC 77478 4236 D4
Brookwood Lake Pl
15600 FBnC 77478 4236 B5
Brookwoods Dr
3700 HOUS 77018 3822 C4
3700 HOUS 77092 3822 B4
Brookwulf Dr
8400 HOUS 77072 4097 D7
8600 HOUS 77072 4237 D1
8600 HOUS 77099 4237 D1
Brook Wy St
17700 HarC 77447 3250 B1
Broom St
- HOUS 77092 3682 E7
4700 HOUS 77092 3683 A7
4800 HOUS 77091 3683 A7
5000 HOUS 77091 3682 E7
Broome Rd
2500 GLSN 77554 5221 C2
Broomsedge Dr
2600 HarC 77084 3816 A5
Brothers Purchase Cir
12200 HarC 77433 3395 D5
Brou Ln
7300 HOUS 77074 4100 A5
Broughton St
25100 HarC 77373 3114 D2
Broughwood Cir
20500 HarC 77449 3815 C7
Broussard
400 HarC 77532 3552 E7
Broussard Ct
2600 SEBK 77586 4509 C2
Broussard Ln
6000 FBnC 77583 4622 C6
E Broussard St
300 HarC 77532 3552 D7
W Broussard St
100 HarC 77532 3552 D7
Broway Ln
16300 HarC 77429 3252 B5
Browder St
500 CNRO 77301 2384 B4
Brower St
8500 HOUS 77017 4105 D5
Brower Crest Dr
4900 PASD 77504 4248 A7
Brown Av
1000 BzaC 77511 4748 D1
Brown Dr
200 PASD 77506 4108 A4
300 LMQU 77568 4873 C6
300 TXCY 77591 4873 C6
Brown Ln
1100 DRPK 77536 4249 C2
23400 HarC 77375 2965 E7
34600 MtgC 77362 2816 C7
34600 SGCH 77362 2816 C7
Brown Lp
- BYTN 77520 3971 B5
Brown Rd
14100 HarC 77377 2963 D6
14100 TMBL 77375 2963 D6
14100 TMBL 77377 2963 D6
16100 WlrC 77484 3245 E5
17500 MtgC 77306 2533 E7
17500 MtgC 77306 2534 A7
Brown St
100 FRDW 77546 4629 D1
100 LMQU 77568 4873 D7
100 TXCY 77591 4873 D7
2000 MSCY 77489 4370 A3
2100 STAF 77477 4370 A3
2100 STAF 77489 4370 A3
4100 GlsC 77518 4634 C3
6700 HTCK 77563 4989 A6
Brown Tr
11400 HarC 77377 3254 D5
Brown Wy
- GlsC 77510 4870 D2
- GlsC 77517 4870 D2
Brown Bark Dr
6100 HOUS 77092 3682 C7
6600 MtgC 77354 2673 A1
Brown Bridge Ct
10600 FBnC 77478 4236 E4
Brown Cone Ln
36800 MtgC 77354 2816 B1
Browncroft St
5100 HOUS 77021 4104 A6
Browndale Ct
23800 FBnC 77494 4093 C1
Browne St
- HOUS 77012 4105 C5
- HOUS 77017 4105 C5
N Brownell St
100 LPRT 77571 4251 E2
S Brownell St
100 LPRT 77571 4251 E2
400 LPRT 77571 4252 A3
Brown Eyed Susan Ct
15100 HarC 77433 3250 E5
15200 HarC 77433 3251 C4
Brownfields Ct
4900 HarC 77066 3401 B6
Brownfields Dr
4700 HarC 77066 3401 B6
Brown Hill Dr
2600 HarC 77373 3114 E4
Brownie Campbell Rd
2700 HarC 77038 3542 D1
2700 HarC 77038 3543 A1
6600 HarC 77086 3542 C1
Browning Ct
4300 SGLD 77479 4495 D4
Browning Rd
1200 LPRT 77571 4110 B7
Browning St
3800 WUNP 77005 4101 D2
Brown Leaf Cir
9400 HOUS 77096 4240 A2
Brownlee Ln
5200 HarC 77379 3257 B2
Brown Meadow Ct
4100 HarC 77449 3816 B1
Brown Pelican Ln
2600 LGCY 77573 4631 A7
Brown Plantation
100 CNRO 77304 2383 B5
Brown Saddle Rd
300 HOUS 77057 3960 D4
Brown School Ct
1900 FBnC 77469 4234 C7
1900 FBnC 77469 4365 C1
Brownstone Ln
3900 HOUS 77053 4372 D4
Brownstone Mills Dr
18900 HarC 77433 3677 B1
Brownstone Ridge Ln
5700 HarC 77084 3678 C4
Brownsville St
6500 HOUS 77020 3964 E1
6900 HOUS 77020 3965 A1
13700 HarC 77015 3967 E1
14100 HarC 77015 3968 A1
29500 MtgC 77354 2818 A2
29800 MtgC 77354 2817 E2
Brownway St
5200 HOUS 77056 3960 E7
Brownwind Tr
3800 DRPK 77536 4249 E1
Brownwood Ct
40200 MtgC 77354 2671 C3
Brownwood Dr
10 BYTN 77520 3971 A4
11800 MtgC 77354 2671 C3
Brownwood Ln
23200 HarC 77377 2962 C7
Brownwood St
6900 HOUS 77020 3964 E1
6900 HOUS 77020 3965 A1
13700 HarC 77015 3967 E1
14000 HarC 77015 3968 A1
Brownwood Bend Ct
9100 HarC 77433 3537 A5
Broyles St
3400 HOUS 77026 3825 B6
Broze Rd
20800 HarC 77338 3260 D3
20800 HOUS 77338 3260 D3
Bruce Av
900 LGCY 77573 4632 B4
5000 DKSN 77539 4754 E2
Bruce Dr
2000 BYTN 77520 3973 C7
Bruce St
3700 HOUS 77009 3824 A7
4100 GlsC 77518 4634 C3
Bruce Hall Rd
2900 GlsC 77510 4871 D5
Bruce Kendall
3300 HarC 77032 3546 A2
Bruce Tree Rdg
14900 HarC 77396 3407 D7

STREET
Block City ZIP Map# Grid

Brumbelow St
1600 RSBG 77471 4491 B5
Brumblay St
8200 HOUS 77012 4105 C4
Brumbley St
7900 HOUS 77012 4105 C4
Brumlow Rd
- PNIS 77484 3100 B5
- WlrC 77484 3100 B5
35000 PNIS 77445 3100 D6
36100 PNIS 77445 3099 C5
Brumlow St
1000 HarC 77530 3830 C5
Brummel Dr
8700 HarC 77099 4237 C1
Brummerhop St
700 SEBK 77586 4509 E3
Brun St
1700 HOUS 77019 3962 B6
2400 HOUS 77098 3962 B6
Brundage Dr
2100 HarC 77014 3402 D2
2100 HarC 77090 3402 E2
Brundage Woods Ln
2200 HarC 77090 3402 E2
Bruno Wy
3100 PRLD 77584 4501 D5
Brunson St
1900 HOUS 77030 4102 D5
Brunson Grove Dr
- FBnC 77494 4092 A5
Brunswick Cir
900 SGLD 77478 4369 B4
Brunswick Dr
600 LGCY 77573 4631 E2
800 SGLD 77478 4369 B3
Brunswick St
5100 HarC 77039 3546 D6
Brunswick Crossing Ln
3500 HarC 77047 4374 C4
Brunswick Lake Ln
- HarC 77047 4374 D4
- HarC 77048 4374 D4
- HOUS 77047 4374 D4
- HOUS 77048 4374 D4
Brunswick Meadows Ct
3500 HarC 77047 4374 C4
Brunswick Meadows Dr
2700 HarC 77047 4374 A4
Brunswick Pl Dr
13900 HarC 77047 4374 C5
Brunswick Point Ln
14200 HarC 77047 4374 A4
S Brush Dr
11500 HarC 77089 4505 B1
Brush Hl
6000 HarC 77379 3111 D4
Brush Canyon Dr
11800 HarC 77377 3254 D5
Brush Field Ln
5000 FBnC 77479 4493 C3
Brushfield Rd
8100 HarC 77064 3541 D5
Brushford Dr
- HarC 77449 3815 B2
Brush Hollow Rd
2400 HarC 77067 3402 A4
Brushill Ct
100 LGCY 77573 4631 A5
Brushing Oak Ct
7500 HOUS 77088 3682 D3
Brush Meade Ln
2100 FBnC 77479 4493 D1
Brushmeade Ln
- HarC 77449 3676 A3
Brush Meadow Ct
16300 FBnC 77478 4236 B5
Brushton Dr
- HarC 77379 3112 A4
Brushwood Ct
10 WDLD 77380 2822 B7
5600 HOUS 77088 3682 E2
Brush Wood Dr
7000 HOUS 77088 3682 E2
Brushwood Dr
7200 HOUS 77088 3682 E4
Brushy Arbor Ln
14300 HarC 77396 3547 B2
Brushy Canyon Dr
20900 HarC 77073 3259 A6
Brushy Creek Cir
1900 HarC 77084 3815 E6
Brushy Creek Dr
1800 SGLD 77478 4368 D5
25000 WlrC 77447 2813 A5
Brushy Forest Dr
- MtgC 77447 2960 A6
Brushy Glen Dr
300 HarC 77073 3259 B6
300 HOUS 77073 3259 B6
Brushy Lake Dr
3200 FBnC 77459 4622 A6
Brushy Meadow Ct
26700 FBnC 77494 4092 C2
Brushy Oaks St
23600 MtgC 77447 2960 A6
Brushy Pines St
23300 MtgC 77447 2960 A6
Brushy Ridge Dr
- HarC 77073 3259 B6
Brushy River Ct
10600 HarC 77095 3537 E1
Brushy Trail St
23600 MtgC 77447 2960 B6
Brushy Woods St
23600 MtgC 77447 2960 A6
Brusky Knoll Ln
13200 FBnC 77478 4366 E2
Brutus Dr
2400 RMFT 77357 2829 A1
Brutus St
7900 HOUS 77012 4105 C3
Brutus Hill Ln
13000 HarC 77072 4097 C7
Bryam
8800 HOUS 77061 4245 E3
8800 HOUS 77061 4246 A3
Bryan Av
800 SEBK 77586 4509 D3
900 PASD 77506 4107 B4
3200 FBnC 77545 4499 C7
4500 FBnC 77545 4623 C3
4700 FBnC 77583 4623 C3
Bryan Gdns
1500 HarC 77493 3814 A6
Bryan Rd
4700 RSBG 77469 4491 C7
4700 RSBG 77471 4491 C7
4800 FBnC 77469 4615 D1
4800 RSBG 77469 4615 D1
5600 FBnC 77469 4616 A1
5600 RSBG 77469 4616 A1
10200 GLSN 77554 5221 B1
Bryan St
- BYTN 77520 4112 B1
- HOUS 77061 4245 E3
10 HOUS 77011 3964 C6
900 SEBK 77586 4509 D3
2200 PRLD 77584 4501 C2
2300 GlsC 77539 4635 C7
2600 HOUS 77020 3963 E3
31400 MAGA 77355 2669 A6
N Bryan St
100 HOUS 77011 3964 C5
Bryanhurst Ln
5200 HarC 77379 3257 B1
Bryant Cir
16600 MtgC 77306 2680 D5
16600 MtgC 77357 2680 D5
Bryant Ln
2700 LGCY 77598 4630 D4
Bryant Rd
300 CNRO 77303 2383 E1
300 CNRO 77303 2384 A1
Bryant St
9200 HOUS 77034 4246 A5
9200 HOUS 77075 4246 A5
Bryant Crossing Ln
10 MtgC 77386 2969 E7
Bryant Park Ct
6500 HarC 77086 3542 C3
Bryant Pond Dr
5800 HarC 77041 3679 B4
Bryant Ridge Rd
4600 HOUS 77053 4372 B6
Bryberry Ct
10 WDLD 77381 2821 A3
Bryce Av
9000 TXCY 77591 4872 E5
9000 TXCY 77591 4873 A6
Bryce St
- HOUS 77008 3823 A7
Bryce Branch Cir
100 WDLD 77382 2819 A1
Bryce Canyon Dr
6300 FBnC 77450 4094 C4
Bryce Manor Ct
- HarC 77346 3408 B3
Bryce Manor Ln
- HarC 77346 3408 B3
Bryce Mill Ct
- HarC 77346 3408 B2
Bryce Pecan Wy
- HarC 77447 3250 A6
Brydan Dr
11700 HarC 77429 3253 E7
11700 HarC 77429 3254 A7
Brykerwoods Dr
7500 HOUS 77055 3821 C7
7500 HLSV 77055 3821 C7
Brymoor Ct
3500 BzaC 77584 4501 C4
Bryngrove Ln
2400 HarC 77084 3678 D5
Bryn Mawr Cir
200 HNCV 77024 3960 A3
Brynmawr Dr
3800 FBnC 77469 4233 D5
Bryn Mawr Ln
4500 HOUS 77027 3961 B7
Brynwood Ln
13000 FBnC 77478 4366 E1
Bryonston Dr
11600 HarC 77066 3401 C6
Bryonwood Dr
7600 HLSV 77055 3821 C7
7600 HOUS 77055 3821 C7
Brystone Dr
5300 HarC 77041 3680 B6
Bryton Dr
7000 HarC 77083 4097 A5
Brywood Pl
10 WDLD 77382 2820 A2
Bubbling Brooks Ln
7200 HarC 77095 3678 A1
Bubbling Spring Ln
7500 HarC 77086 3542 A4
7600 HarC 77086 3541 E4
Bubbling Well Ct
15500 HarC 77546 4505 E5
Bucan St
10 HOUS 77076 3684 E4
10 HOUS 77076 3685 A4
Buccaneer Blvd
- GLSN 77554 5332 E2
Buccaneer Dr
- JMAB 77554 5331 E5
- JMAB 77554 5332 A5
Buccaneer Ln
15700 HOUS 77062 4507 A2
16600 HOUS 77058 4507 C4
Buccaneer Pkwy
12800 BzaC 77541 5547 B7
Buccaneer Rd
- BYTN 77521 3973 D3
Buchalew
- HarC 77532 3412 E6
Buchanan Dr
2100 BYTN 77520 3973 D6
7000 FBnC 77469 4493 D7
Buchanan St
1500 PASD 77502 4107 C7
2100 PASD 77502 4247 C1
2300 LPRT 77571 4250 D1
7900 HOUS 77029 3965 B4
Buchanan Wy
5100 BzaC 77584 4502 B6
5100 PRLD 77584 4502 B6
Buchanan Bend Ct
9100 HarC 77433 3537 C5
Buchans Dr
1300 MtgC 77386 2968 E1
1300 MtgC 77386 2969 A1
Buck Rd
25000 SPLD 77372 2682 D4
33200 MtgC 77355 2962 C2
Buck Rdg
- HarC 77396 3407 C6
N Buck Rdg
10 WDLD 77381 2821 B3
S Buck Rdg
10 WDLD 77381 2821 B3
Buck St
2600 HOUS 77020 3963 E2
4200 HOUS 77020 3964 B2
15900 SGCH 77355 2961 C3
Buckboard Dr
10 HOUS 77037 3544 B2
10 HOUS 77060 3544 B2
Buckeye Ct
7400 PRLD 77584 4502 B5
Buckeye Dr
100 HarC 77450 3953 E1
100 HOUS 77450 3953 E1
Buckeye Ln
3100 PRLD 77584 4502 B5
Buckeye Pl
800 MSCY 77459 4497 B5
Buckeye St
10500 CmbC 77520 3835 D3
Buckeye Brook Wy
15300 HarC 77530 3829 D5
Buckeye Creek Rd
4000 HOUS 77339 3119 C4
Buckeye Furnace Ln
10700 FBnC 77478 4236 E4
Buckeye Glen Ln
8200 HarC 77338 3261 E4
8600 HarC 77338 3262 A4
Buckeye Pass
20100 FBnC 77469 4234 D1
Buckeye Ridge Wy
19200 HarC 77084 3816 B5
Buckhaven Dr
9800 HarC 77089 4504 E2
Buckhead Ct
16100 HarC 77377 3254 E5
Buck Hollow Dr
1000 HarC 77532 3266 C7
Buckholt St
2200 BzaC 77581 4504 C7
2200 PRLD 77581 4504 C7
Buckhorn Ln
800 MtgC 77354 2668 E3
S Buckhorn Ln
41500 MtgC 77354 2668 E3
Buckhurst Dr
3800 HarC 77066 3401 C6
Buckingham Ct
10 CNRO 77304 2529 C1
1000 FRDW 77546 4629 C4
Buckingham Dr
300 HOUS 77024 3960 E2
600 HOUS 77024 3961 A2
800 FRDW 77546 4629 C4
1600 PASD 77504 4247 E5
13900 TMBL 77375 2964 A5
Buckingham Ln
14000 TMBL 77375 2963 E5
Buckingham Pl
12900 MtgC 77306 2533 D5
Buckingham St
200 STAF 77477 4369 A2
Buckingham Wy
1300 HOUS 77339 3264 B1
Buckingham Ct Cir
10 HDWV 77024 3959 D2
Buckingham Park Ln
3300 FRDW 77598 4630 B3
Buck Island Ct
17500 HarC 77346 3408 E3
Buck Knoll Rd
20700 MtgC 77372 2681 A1
Buckland Ln
12300 HarC 77039 3545 E5
Buckland Park Dr
19400 HarC 77449 3677 A3
19600 HarC 77449 3676 E3
Buckle Ln
15200 HOUS 77060 3544 C3
Buckleberry Wy
- HarC 77094 3955 B2
Buckleridge Rd
4500 HOUS 77053 4372 B7
Buckley Ln
3800 FBnC 77459 4621 E4
Buckmann Ct
1500 HOUS 77043 3820 A6
Buckminster Dr
2500 MtgC 77386 2969 C5
Bucknell Ct
3000 SGLD 77478 4369 A3
Bucknell Rd
10000 HOUS 77016 3686 D3
Buckner Ct
3100 MSCY 77459 4498 A6
Buckner St
1000 HOUS 77019 3963 A5
Buckow Dr
5600 HOUS 77396 3405 D4
Bucks Run
15500 HarC 77377 2963 B6
Bucks Bridge Ln
11300 FBnC 77478 4236 D5
Buck Shot Ln
33200 MtgC 77354 2674 C4
33200 WDLD 77382 2674 C4
33500 MtgC 77384 2674 C3
33500 WDLD 77382 2674 C3
33500 WDLD 77384 2674 C3
Buckskin Dr
12000 HarC 77377 3109 B7
Buckskin Ln
2300 KATY 77493 3813 B5
Buckskin Bridge Ct
14800 FBnC 77478 4236 D6
Buckskin Trail Ct
20500 HarC 77450 3954 D7
Buck Springs Tr
11600 HarC 77377 3254 E5
Buckthorn Dr
28000 FBnC 77494 3951 D4
Buckthorne Pl
2100 WDLD 77380 2821 E7
2100 WDLD 77380 2967 D1
Bucktrout Ln
22000 HarC 77449 3815 A6
22300 HarC 77449 3814 D6
22900 HOUS 77449 3814 D6
22900 HOUS 77493 3814 C6
Buckwood Ct
1600 FBnC 77545 4622 D1
Bucroft St
8400 HOUS 77029 3965 D4
9700 HOUS 77029 3966 A4
9800 GNPK 77547 3966 A4
Bud Ln
300 BYTN 77521 3833 E7
300 BYTN 77521 3972 E1
Budd St
2900 PASD 77502 4247 B2
Budde Rd
500 MtgC 77380 2968 B4
500 WDLD 77380 2968 B4
Budde Cemetery Rd
20300 HarC 77388 3113 B4
Buddy Riley Blvd
- MAGA 77355 2669 A5
17600 MAGA 77354 2669 A5
Buddy's Ln
- HarC 77064 3541 A1
Buell Ct
10 HOUS 77006 3962 E5
Buelow St
5900 HOUS 77023 4104 C4
Buena St
22800 GLSN 77554 5441 A6
23100 GLSN 77554 5440 E6
Buena Wy
27400 MtgC 77386 2970 C7
27400 MtgC 77386 3115 B1
Buena Park Cir
10 BzaC 77583 4624 C3
10 MNVL 77583 4624 C3
Buena Park Ct
9900 HOUS 77089 4377 C3
Buena Park Dr
- HOUS 77075 4377 C4
10200 HOUS 77089 4377 D3
E Buena Vista Dr
12400 GLSN 77554 5333 C1
W Buena Vista Dr
12500 GLSN 77554 5333 C1
Buena Vista St
4300 STAF 77477 4369 B2
7600 HOUS 77087 4105 B7
Buescher Ct
4700 PRLD 77584 4503 B4
Buescher Dr
1600 HOUS 77043 3819 C5
Buescher Rd
22000 HarC 77377 3107 E2
Buffalo Run
1200 MSCY 77489 4370 D4
1200 STAF 77477 4370 C4
1200 STAF 77489 4370 C4
2900 GlsC 77539 4635 A5
13100 HOUS 77489 4370 D4
Buffalo St
5000 FBnC 77471 4614 D4
Buffalo Ter
2000 HOUS 77019 3962 E4
Buffalo Tr
2500 SGLD 77479 4368 E7
4500 BYTN 77521 3973 C2
20100 HarC 77532 3410 D3
Buffalo Bayou Ln
10 HOUS 77013 3966 E1
Buffalo Bend Dr
10600 HarC 77064 3540 B2
Buffalo Bend Ln
9200 HarC 77089 4504 A1
9400 HarC 77089 4377 B7
Buffalo Canyon Dr
29700 MtgC 77386 2969 E2
Buffalo Clover Cir
8200 FBnC 77469 4234 B4
Buffalo Creek Dr
8300 FBnC 77469 4234 B4
Buffalo Gap
5700 FBnC 77459 4497 A7
Buffalo Gap Dr
9800 HarC 77095 3538 B3
Buffalo Lake Ct
4400 FBnC 77469 4234 C4
Buffalo Pass Dr
17200 HarC 77095 3396 E7
Buffalo Peak Ln
- HarC 77346 3408 C4
Buffalo Ridge Cir
10 HOUS 77056 3960 D3
10 HOUS 77057 3960 D3
Buffalo River Wy
19000 HarC 77084 3816 B4
Buffalo Run Cir
1500 HarC 77067 3402 C6
Buffalo Speedway
- HOUS 77053 4372 E4
- HOUS 77054 4241 E1
2700 HOUS 77019 3961 E7
2700 HOUS 77027 3961 E7
2700 HOUS 77098 3961 E7
3100 HOUS 77046 3961 E7
3700 HOUS 77046 4101 E1
3700 HOUS 77098 4101 E1
3800 HOUS 77027 4101 E1
5100 HOUS 77005 4101 E2
5200 WUNP 77005 4101 E2
7900 HOUS 77025 4101 E7
9500 HOUS 77025 4241 E1
9800 HOUS 77025 4242 A1
9800 HOUS 77054 4242 A2
12900 HOUS 77045 4241 E7
12900 HOUS 77045 4372 E1
Buffalo Springs Ct
8100 FBnC 77479 4494 C4
25500 HarC 77373 3114 B5
Buffalo Springs Wy
900 HarC 77373 3114 A4
Buffalo View Ln
7900 HarC 77433 3537 B7
Buffington
800 HarC 77039 3545 A1
Buffkin Ln
6900 HarC 77069 3400 A1
Bufflehead Ct
13200 HOUS 77044 3549 C1
13200 HOUS 77044 3550 A3
Buffum St
10700 HOUS 77051 4243 A7
Buford St
6300 HOUS 77023 4104 D4
Buggy Ln
15700 MtgC 77302 2679 D3
Bugle Rd
4100 HOUS 77072 4098 B4
4100 HOUS 77082 4098 B4
Bugle Run Dr
1400 HarC 77449 3815 C7
Buhler Ct
15800 HarC 77429 3397 C3
Bui Dr
6100 PRLD 77581 4502 D1
Bulen Av
5300 FRDW 77546 4505 E7
Bulian Dr
8200 HarC 77521 3834 B1
Bulkhead Wy
17300 HarC 77532 3552 B1
Bull Ln
400 MSCY 77489 4370 C2
Bullard Rd
2800 BzaC 77583 4744 D2
3100 IWCY 77583 4744 D2
Bull Creek Rd
7400 HarC 77095 3678 E1
Bulldog Ln
11200 MtgC 77306 2533 E1
Bullfinch St
6400 HOUS 77087 4244 E2
Bullfrog Ln
600 MtgC 77384 2675 E7
600 MtgC 77384 2676 A7
Bullinger Dr
6800 HarC 77379 3256 D2
Bullis Gap Dr
17200 HarC 77447 3249 E3
Bull Lake Dr
- FBnC 77469 4234 E5
Bullock Ln
1300 HOUS 77055 3820 B7
Bull Pine Dr
18400 HarC 77379 3257 A1
Bull Ridge Cir
20800 MtgC 77365 3118 A2
Bull Ridge Dr
25100 MtgC 77365 3118 A1
Bull Run Ct
500 MtgC 77302 2530 B6
2900 MSCY 77459 4498 A6
Bull Run Dr
300 LGCY 77573 4631 B5
Bull Run St
8900 LPRT 77571 4249 E3
Bullrush Canyon Dr
7500 FBnC 77494 4093 B3
Bullwood Pl
10 WDLD 77382 2674 A5
Bulwark Dr
900 HarC 77532 3552 A3
Bumble Bee Ct
24400 MtgC 77355 2960 E3
24400 SGCH 77355 2960 E3
Bumelia Ct
1700 FBnC 77479 4494 B4
Bunche Dr
6500 HOUS 77088 3683 C4
6500 HOUS 77091 3683 C4
Bundage Rd
14500 MtgC 77354 2670 C3
Bunde
- HOUS 77044 3409 A7
- HOUS 77044 3550 A1
Bunde St
13600 STFE 77510 4870 D5
Bundick Dr
6200 HOUS 77091 3683 E5
Bundy Ln
9500 HOUS 77080 3820 C4
Bungalow Ln
4300 HOUS 77047 4374 B1
4500 HOUS 77047 4243 D7
4500 HOUS 77048 4243 D7
5300 HOUS 77048 4244 A7
Bunker Ln
32000 WlrC 77484 3246 D6
Bunker Bend Ct
20000 HarC 77346 3265 C4
Bunker Bend Dr
8300 HarC 77346 3265 C4
Bunker Hill Cir
11800 BKHV 77024 3959 C3
Bunker Hill Ct
2200 PRLD 77581 4503 B3
Bunker Hill Ln
1600 FRDW 77546 4749 E2
Bunker Hill Rd
- HOUS 77055 3959 C1
200 BKHV 77024 3959 C4
600 HDWV 77024 3959 C4
700 HOUS 77024 3959 C2
1000 HOUS 77055 3820 C7
1300 HOUS 77080 3820 C7
Bunkeridge Rd
15900 HOUS 77053 4372 B7
Bunker Oak Ln
- HarC 77336 3122 B2
Bunkerwood Ln
7900 HarC 77086 3541 E2
Bunnelle Wy
10 WDLD 77382 2819 D2
Bunny Ln
12000 MtgC 77362 2963 C1
Bunny Hill Ct
16500 MtgC 77302 2679 B4
Bunny Run Dr
- HarC 77038 3544 A6
- HOUS 77038 3544 A6
- HOUS 77088 3544 A6
Bunte St
5400 HOUS 77026 3825 D5
Bunting Ct
8000 HarC 77396 3406 D5
Bunting Meadow Ct
4200 HarC 77449 3816 A1
Bunting Meadow Dr
4300 HarC 77449 3816 A1
Bunton St
900 HOUS 77009 3824 C6
Bunyard Rd
1400 GlsC 77511 4869 B1
1500 GlsC 77511 4751 B7
Bunyard St
1400 GlsC 77511 4869 B2
Bunzel Dr
2400 HarC 77088 3543 B7
Bunzel St
1900 HarC 77088 3543 D7
Buoy Rd
300 HOUS 77598 4506 E4
700 HOUS 77062 4506 E3
1000 HOUS 77062 4507 B3
Burbank Av
1300 BYTN 77520 4112 C1
Burbank St
100 HOUS 77076 3685 B6
E Burberry Cir
10 WDLD 77384 2674 E2
W Burberry Cir
100 WDLD 77384 2674 D2
N Burberry Park Cir
100 WDLD 77382 2819 A3
S Burberry Park Cir
10 WDLD 77382 2819 A1
W Burberry Park Cir
10 WDLD 77382 2819 A4
Burbury St
4800 SGLD 77479 4495 C4
Burcan Ct
23000 HarC 77373 2968 E7
Burch St
3800 HOUS 77003 3964 B4
Burchton Dr
900 FBnC 77479 4367 B6
Burden St
9500 HOUS 77093 3685 D5
Burdine Ct
6400 HOUS 77085 4240 D7
Burdine St
- HOUS 77085 4240 D7
9100 HOUS 77096 4240 D1
11500 HOUS 77035 4240 D4
Burditt St
4400 STFE 77510 4871 C7
Burdock Dr
6200 GlsC 77510 4987 A4
Burdom St
- HMBL 77338 3262 D7
Burford Ln
4200 FBnC 77545 4623 C2
8600 HarC 77088 3683 D1
9200 HarC 77088 3543 D7
Burford St
12700 HOUS 77077 3957 C5
Burg St
8300 HOUS 77088 3683 C2
Burgandy Ln
100 LGCY 77573 4631 C4
Burgandy Vine Ct
10 WDLD 77384 2674 E3
Burge Ln
- HarC 77089 4504 E1
Burger Ln
9100 HarC 77040 3681 B1
Burgess Rd
7800 HTCK 77563 4988 E4
Burgess St
6900 HOUS 77021 4102 E5
6900 HOUS 77021 4103 A5
6900 HOUS 77054 4102 E5
Burgess Hill Ct
2800 PRLD 77584 4502 A5
Burgh Castle Dr
25000 HarC 77389 2965 E3
25000 HarC 77389 2966 A3
Burgoyne Dr
6400 HOUS 77057 3960 B6
11300 HOUS 77077 3958 B6
12400 HOUS 77077 3957 D7
Burgoyne Rd
5800 HOUS 77057 3960 C6
7500 HOUS 77063 3960 A6
10000 HOUS 77042 3959 A7
10300 HOUS 77042 3958 E6
13700 HOUS 77077 3957 A7
14200 HOUS 77077 3956 D7
Burgundy Ln
3500 HOUS 77023 4104 C4
Burgundy Sky Wy
18400 HarC 77429 3252 B7
Burham Ln
- LGCY 77573 4630 B7
- LGCY 77573 4751 B1
Burham Park Dr
16300 HarC 77429 3397 A2
Burk
10900 HOUS 77048 4375 E2
10900 HOUS 77075 4375 E2
Burk Wy
10 HarC 77357 2830 C7
Burkdale Dr
2300 SGLD 77478 4237 B4
S Burke Dr
3100 PASD 77502 4247 D3
3100 PASD 77504 4247 D3
Burke Rd
100 PASD 77506 4107 E4
1100 PASD 77502 4107 E7
2100 PASD 77502 4247 D3
4000 PASD 77504 4247 E7
5000 HOUS 77034 4247 E7
5000 PASD 77034 4247 E7
Burke Forest Dr
14000 HarC 77070 3399 E1
Burkegate Dr
4300 HarC 77373 3115 B6
Burkehall Ln
15900 HarC 77084 3678 C4
Burke Ridge Dr
4200 PASD 77504 4247 E7
4300 PASD 77504 4248 A7
Burkes Garden Dr
10800 HarC 77065 3539 D1
Burkett Dr
3400 LPRT 77571 4250 A4
Burkett St
2300 HOUS 77004 3963 D7
2800 HOUS 77004 4103 C2
6600 HOUS 77021 4103 B6
Burkette Rd
23200 MtgC 77357 2973 E4
Burkhardt Rd
18000 HarC 77377 3107 A3
Burkhart Cir
8300 SPVL 77055 3821 B7
Burkhart Ct
8300 SPVL 77055 3821 B7
Burkhart Rd
8000 HLSV 77055 3821 C7
8800 SPVL 77055 3821 A7
Burkhart Ridge Dr
17500 HarC 77095 3537 D4
Burklin Ln
16500 SGCH 77355 2961 D3
Burkridge Dr
7300 HarC 77041 3679 D1
Burkwood Ct
200 FBnC 77479 4367 B4
Burl St
8800 HOUS 77028 3687 D6
Burlcreek St
16500 HarC 77084 3678 B3
Burle Oak Dr
20000 HarC 77346 3264 C3
Burle Oaks Ct
19700 HarC 77346 3264 C5
Burleson Ct
8800 HarC 77064 3540 D6
Burleson St
900 HOUS 77091 3683 E4
Burlingame Dr
11800 HOUS 77099 4238 C5
Burlinghall Dr
5500 HOUS 77035 4240 B5
Burlington
25500 MtgC 77355 2963 A
N Burlington Dr
6400 HOUS 77091 3682 D
6400 HOUS 77092 3682 C
Burlington St
3400 HOUS 77006 3963 A
Burlmont Ln
15100 HarC 77530 3829 D
Burlwood Dr
11500 HarC 77089 4378 B
Burma Rd
4800 HOUS 77033 4243 E1
5100 HOUS 77033 4244 A1
Burman St
7900 HOUS 77029 3965 B3
10100 JTCY 77029 3966 A3
Burmese Ln
11200 SGLD 77478 4237 D5
E Burnaby Cir
24700 HarC 77373 3114 D3
N Burnaby Cir
2500 HarC 77373 3114 E3
W Burnaby Cir
24700 HarC 77373 3114 D3
Burnaby St
25100 HarC 77373 3114 D2
Burnaby Trail Ct
21800 HarC 77073 3259 B4
Burnell Oaks Ln
16500 HarC 77090 3258 C5
Burnet
- RHMD 77469 4491 E2
Burnet Av
100 HarC 77532 3552 C3
Burnet Bnd
6000 HarC 77532 3552 C3
Burnet Dr
1700 HarC 77520 3831 E7
21500 GLSN 77554 5441 B4
N Burnet Dr
100 BYTN 77520 3971 A1
300 BYTN 77520 3832 A7
Burnet St
300 RHMD 77469 4492 A2
1200 RHMD 77469 4491 E2
Burnett Dr
100 BYTN 77520 3971 B2
600 BYTN 77521 3972 D3
S Burnett Dr
300 BYTN 77520 3971 B2
Burnett Rd
5700 MNVL 77578 4746 A3
Burnett St
600 HOUS 77009 3963 D2
1700 HOUS 77026 3963 D2
2700 HOUS 77020 3963 E2
2900 LMQU 77568 4989 D2
Burney Rd
700 SGLD 77478 4368 A1
900 SGLD 77478 4367 E1
1100 SGLD 77478 4236 B5
10800 FBnC 77478 4236 E5
Burney Bend Ln
10500 HOUS 77034 4378 C3
Burnham Cir
10 SGLD 77478 4368 D4
Burnham St
14100 HarC 77053 4372 E5
Burningbush Ln
- HOUS 77016 3687 B1
Burning Cypress Dr
19700 HarC 77433 3251 D7
Burning Hills Dr
7800 HOUS 77071 4239 D7
Burning Palms Ct
3600 HOUS 77042 4098 C2
Burning Tree Dr
4600 BYTN 77521 3972 B2
5900 HOUS 77036 4099 B3
Burning Tree Ln
2800 MSCY 77459 4497 A2
27100 MtgC 77357 2829 D5
Burning Tree Rd
800 HOUS 77339 3263 B2
1400 HOUS 77339 3118 B7
Burnley St
1100 HOUS 77037 3685 A1
Burns St
6900 HTCK 77563 4989 A6
Burnshire Ln
- HarC 77084 3678 B4
Burnside Ln
10000 HOUS 77041 3681 A6
Burns Lake Dr
32100 HarC 77447 3250 A6
Burnt Amber Ln
- HOUS 77073 3259 E3
20800 HarC 77073 3259 E3
Burnt Ash Dr
8200 HarC 77338 3261 E3
Burnt Candle Dr
- HarC 77388 3113 A7
18600 HarC 77388 3258 B1
Burntfork Dr
9900 HarC 77064 3540 C3
Burnt Leaf Ln
17800 HarC 77379 3257 A3
Burnwood Ln
1200 HarC 77073 3259 B1
Bur Oak Ct
17100 HarC 77379 3111 E7
Bur Oak Dr
5000 PASD 77505 4248 D7
5300 HOUS 77034 4248 D7
5300 PASD 77034 4248 D7
6000 HarC 77379 3111 E7
6000 HarC 77379 3256 E1
Buroak Dr
- LGCY 77598 4630 D4
Burr St
10 HOUS 77011 3964 B6
N Burr St
100 HOUS 77011 3964 C5
Burrard St
25100 HarC 77373 3114 D2
Bur Reed Rd
- FBnC 77469 4234 D3
Burress St
10 HOUS 77022 3684 E7
10 HOUS 77022 3685 A7
E Burress St
700 HOUS 77022 3684 E7
Burris Park Dr
200 HarC 77373 3113 E7
Burr Oak Dr
2800 FRDW 77598 4630 C3
5700 HOUS 77092 3682 B6

STREET
Block City ZIP Map# Grid
urr Oak Ln
5000 TXCY 77591 4874 A6
urr Oak Trc
7000 MtgC 77354 2819 C3
Burrowdale Ct
17000 HarC 77084 3678 B4
urt Rd
6200 HOUS 77091 3683 E5
urt St
5100 HOUS 77018 3683 E7
5800 HOUS 77091 3683 E5
7500 HOUS 77088 3683 E3
urtcliff St
14000 HarC 77037 3544 E5
14800 HarC 77060 3544 E4
Burton St
700 ALVN 77511 4866 E2
16700 HarC 77049 3690 E3
Burton Cemetery Rd
29000 HarC 77447 3248 A1
29000 HarC 77484 3247 C1
29000 HarC 77484 3248 A1
Burton Forest Ct
100 MtgC 77384 2675 B1
Burton Park Ln
- HarC 77449 3815 A5
Burton Ridge Dr
- MtgC 77386 2969 D1
Burwell Rd
100 HarC 77562 3692 E7
100 HarC 77562 3693 A7
Burwell St
5600 HOUS 77023 4104 C3
Burwick St
10 SGLD 77479 4495 D3
Burwood Cir
20500 HarC 77449 3815 C7
Burwood Ct
3600 PRLD 77584 4503 B6
16700 HOUS 77058 4507 D2
Burwood Dr
- PRLD 77584 4503 B6
Burwood Wy
16800 HOUS 77058 4507 D2
Burwood Park Dr
8300 HarC 77379 3256 A5
Bus Barn Rd
- CNRO 77301 2383 E7
- CNRO 77301 2384 A7
Busch Ln
2100 CmbC 77520 4114 A1
Busch Rd
2100 BYTN 77520 3973 B5
4500 BYTN 77521 3972 C2
4900 HarC 77521 3972 C2
Busch St
100 HarC 77037 3544 D5
100 HarC 77060 3544 C5
Buschong St
800 HarC 77039 3545 B2
Bushbird Ln
1300 HarC 77449 3815 C7
Bushell Mill Pl
10 WDLD 77382 2819 A1
Bush Oak Ln
10 WDLD 77380 2822 B6
Bush Oaks Tr
16100 SGCH 77355 2961 E5
Bushong St
500 HarC 77060 3544 E2
Bush Sage Dr
14300 HarC 77429 3397 C2
Bushwood Dr
19100 HarC 77388 3112 C5
Bushy Creek Dr
10300 HarC 77070 3399 B5
Busiek St
4300 HOUS 77022 3823 E2
Business Center Dr
1100 HOUS 77043 3819 C7
2000 PRLD 77584 4500 E3
Business Park Dr
6700 HarC 77041 3680 C3
6700 HOUS 77041 3680 C3
Busse Cir
800 PASD 77503 4108 B5
Buster Cir
900 TMBL 77375 2964 D6
Butano Springs Ln
17600 HarC 77346 3408 D2
Bute St
3800 HOUS 77006 3962 E7
4200 HOUS 77002 3962 E7
6700 HOUS 77075 4375 E2
6700 HOUS 77075 4376 A2
Butera Rd
15900 SGCH 77355 2961 E2
16000 MtgC 77355 2961 E2
Butler Av
- LGCY 77573 4632 A3
Butler Ct
3700 FBnC 77459 4621 C5
Butler Dr
- FRDW 77546 4629 E3
10 CNRO 77303 2237 D6
1400 PASD 77502 4107 C7
2000 FRDW 77546 4630 A4
5800 PRLD 77581 4502 C2
Butler Rd
- PRLD 77581 4502 D2
100 CNRO 77303 2237 D6
2500 LGCY 77573 4631 D6
2500 LGCY 77573 4752 D1
3300 CNRO 77301 2385 B5
3800 MtgC 77301 2385 C5
Butlercrest St
1400 HOUS 77055 3820 B6
1400 HOUS 77080 3820 B6
Butler Hill Ct
25000 HarC 77375 2964 D3
Butler Lakes Ct
7600 RSBG 77469 4492 C6
Butler Oaks Ct
6600 HarC 77389 2966 C3
Butler Rd Ext
9600 CNRO 77301 2385 C5
9600 MtgC 77301 2385 C5
Butlers Ct
100 MtgC 77385 2676 C3
Butlersburg
- CNRO 77301 2384 C3
Butlers Island St
100 MtgC 77302 2530 C7
Butler Springs Ct
26100 FBnC 77494 4092 E1
Butler Springs Ln
4500 FBnC 77494 4092 E2

STREET
Block City ZIP Map# Grid
E Butte Canyon Rd
12800 HarC 77038 3543 B3
W Butte Canyon Rd
12800 HarC 77038 3543 B3
Butte Creek Rd
17000 HOUS 77090 3258 A4
17400 HarC 77090 3258 A3
17900 HarC 77090 3257 E3
Buttercup Ln
1200 HOUS 77339 3263 D1
1700 HOUS 77339 3118 D7
27000 MtgC 77354 2817 D4
Buttercup St
- HOUS 77063 4099 D1
5600 LGCY 77573 4630 D7
Butterfield Rd
- HarC 77090 3258 D4
- HOUS 77090 3258 D4
Butterfly Cir
5900 PASD 77505 4248 C4
18400 MtgC 77365 2972 A7
Butterfly Ct
400 HOUS 77079 3958 B2
Butterfly Ln
800 FBnC 77469 4616 D1
12900 HOUS 77024 3958 D2
13600 HOUS 77079 3958 A2
24100 MtgC 77365 2972 A6
Butterfly Branch Pl
10 WDLD 77382 2674 C3
Butterfly Path Dr
4700 HarC 77396 3407 C7
Buttergrove Dr
5700 HarC 77041 3679 C5
Buttermilk Creek Ln
- HarC 77047 4374 C4
Butter Mill Ln
1500 HarC 77067 3402 C6
Butternut Ct
4200 HOUS 77088 3682 E3
Butternut Ln
- MtgC 77354 2819 B4
Butteroak Dr
16800 HarC 77379 3256 E1
Butterowe
- GLSN 77551 5108 B5
Butterstone
- HOUS 77042 4099 A3
Butterstone Ridge Ln
- FBnC 77469 4235 C1
Butterwick Dr
24800 HarC 77389 2965 E3
Buttonbush Ct
10 WDLD 77380 2821 E6
Buttonhill Dr
2300 MSCY 77489 4370 E6
2400 MSCY 77489 4371 A7
Buttonwood Dr
300 TXCY 77591 4873 A6
1200 FRDW 77546 4629 A4
Buvinghausen St
100 HarC 77377 3254 D4
100 TMBL 77375 2964 A7
100 TMBL 77375 3109 A1
Buxley St
13000 HOUS 77045 4241 C7
14400 HOUS 77045 4372 C4
14700 HOUS 77053 4372 C4
Buxton St
9700 HOUS 77017 4106 B5
By Dr
9700 HarC 77532 3552 B4
Bybee Dr
100 CNRO 77301 2384 C3
Bycreek Dr
2500 HarC 77068 3257 D3
Bylake Ct
13600 HOUS 77077 3957 A6
Bylane Dr
- PNPV 77024 3959 D5
200 BKHV 77024 3959 D5
Byrd
2100 SEBK 77586 4509 B2
6600 HOUS 77087 4244 D1
Byrd St
200 LMQU 77568 4873 B7
200 TXCY 77591 4873 B7
Byrdsong Ct
1100 CNRO 77301 2384 D2
Byrne St
100 HOUS 77009 3824 B7
900 HOUS 77009 3962 E1
900 HOUS 77009 3963 A1
Byron Av
1300 DRPK 77536 4109 B5
2400 PRLD 77581 4503 D3
Byron Ln
7800 HarC 77379 3111 A7
Byron St
100 LGCY 77573 4631 E3
3800 SSPL 77005 4101 D3
4100 WUNP 77005 4101 C4
4200 HOUS 77005 4101 C3
Byron Meadows Dr
19700 HarC 77449 3676 E4
Byronstone Dr
11500 HarC 77066 3401 C6
Bystreet Rd
800 HOUS 77504 4247 C6
800 PASD 77504 4247 C6
By the Lake Ct
8400 HarC 77429 3252 B7
By the Lake Wy
8400 HarC 77429 3252 B7
8400 HarC 77429 3396 A1
Bytrail Ct
400 HarC 77346 3408 A3
Bywater Dr
1900 HOUS 77077 3957 A6
Byway Dr
3400 SRAC 77571 4382 E2
Byway St
6400 HOUS 77007 3961 E3
Bywood St
7000 HOUS 77028 3686 E7
7100 HOUS 77028 3687 A7

C

C Dr
- HarC 77388 3111 D1
C St
- HOUS 77547 4106 C1
- WALR 77484 3101 E5
2800 LPRT 77571 4251 E7
4100 HOUS 77072 4097 E3
4100 HOUS 77082 4097 E3

STREET
Block City ZIP Map# Grid
E C St
- LPRT 77571 4252 A2
200 LPRT 77571 4251 E3
N C St
12000 LPRT 77571 4251 A2
S C St
2000 MRGP 77571 4252 C1
W C St
100 LPRT 77571 4251 D3
Caballero Dr
9700 HOUS 77078 3688 A5
Caballo Ct
8800 HarC 77521 3833 C1
Cabango Dr
19200 MtgC 77365 2971 E5
Cabaniss Av
10 BYTN 77520 3971 A4
Cabaniss Cir
18500 HarC 77379 3257 A1
Cabanna Rd
22700 HarC 77389 2967 A7
Cabbage St
5000 HarC 77379 3112 A7
Cabbott Cove Ct
11300 HarC 77375 3110 A6
Cabell St
1200 HOUS 77022 3823 E3
Cabeza Dr
2500 SGLD 77478 4237 D4
Cabeza de Vaca
16700 GLSN 77554 5331 E5
16700 JMAB 77554 5331 E5
Cabeza Vaca Dr
6400 HOUS 77048 4244 D6
Cabildo Dr
15400 HarC 77083 4096 B5
Cabin Pl
3500 SGLD 77479 4496 A1
Cabin Creek Ct
100 WDLD 77385 2676 D4
Cabin Creek Dr
9900 HarC 77064 3540 D4
Cabin Green Ct
18000 HarC 77346 3408 D1
Cabin Line Ln
- HarC 77494 3953 A2
Cabin Run Ln
14900 FBnC 77478 4236 D5
Cable St
600 CNRO 77301 2383 E5
Cable Wy
1100 HarC 77532 3411 A7
Cable Brook Ln
20100 HarC 77449 3815 E2
Cable Car Ct
2200 FBnC 77545 4622 B1
Cable Terrace Dr
- FBnC 77494 3953 D5
Cabo Blanco Ct
12200 HarC 77041 3679 E5
Cabo Isle Ln
6500 HarC 77041 3680 A4
Caboose Ct
17500 HarC 77532 3411 A7
Cabot St
7600 HOUS 77016 3687 A5
7900 HOUS 77078 3687 C5
Cabot Cove
- DKSN 77539 4752 E6
Cabot Cove Dr
- PRLD 77584 4503 A6
Cabot Creek Cir
15600 HarC 77070 3255 B6
Cabot Hill St
11600 HarC 77044 3549 A7
Cabot Lakes Dr
- LGCY 77573 4632 B7
Cabot Lodge Ln
14300 HarC 77429 3395 E1
Cabot Point Dr
2000 HarC 77450 3954 D7
Cabots Landing Dr
15000 HarC 77084 3678 E3
Cabotway
29500 HarC 77375 2964 D4
29500 TMBL 77375 2964 D4
Cabra Ct
19500 HarC 77449 3677 A4
Cabrera Dr
3800 FBnC 77479 4495 E5
3800 SGLD 77479 4495 E5
4000 FBnC 77479 4496 A5
4000 SGLD 77479 4496 A5
Cabrera Ln
13500 HarC 77083 4097 B6
Cabrillo Landing Ct
8100 FBnC 77494 4093 B4
Cabrina Ln
7200 HOUS 77083 4097 C5
Cabrini Trace Ct
1600 HarC 77073 3403 C2
Cactus Dr
300 CHTW 77385 2822 D4
1100 BYTN 77521 3973 B2
Cactus Ln
4000 IWCY 77583 4745 B3
Cactus Rd
22900 MtgC 77357 2973 E3
Cactus St
1300 HOUS 77017 4106 D5
1300 PASD 77506 4106 D5
3100 HOUS 77026 3825 A6
Cactus Bloom Ln
2100 FBnC 77494 3953 B5
Cactus Creek Dr
3400 MtgC 77386 2969 D2
Cactus Finch
2200 FBnC 77494 3951 D4
Cactus Flower Dr
10400 HarC 77086 3542 C2
Cactus Forest Dr
5400 HarC 77088 3542 E7
Cactus Garden Cir
4500 FBnC 77469 4233 C5
Cactus Heights Ln
- PRLD 77581 4503 D2
Cactus Point Ct
11100 HarC 77095 3396 E7
11100 HarC 77095 3537 E1
Cactus Rose Dr
19200 HarC 77449 3816 B3
Cactus Sage Tr
24900 FBnC 77494 3953 B5
Cactus Thorn Dr
19200 HarC 77433 3537 B7
Cactus Valley Ct
11200 HarC 77089 4504 C1

STREET
Block City ZIP Map# Grid
Cactus Wren Ln
14700 HarC 77377 2963 C6
Cadawac Rd
8100 HOUS 77074 4099 E7
8700 HOUS 77074 4239 E1
Cadbury Cir
4100 BYTN 77521 3973 E2
Cadbury Dr
18100 HarC 77084 3816 E1
Cadbury Ln
- FBnC 77545 4498 D6
Caddo Ct
7600 HarC 77521 3833 B4
9200 LPRT 77571 4249 E4
Caddo Dr
9900 MtgC 77354 2818 B6
Caddo Rd
7600 HOUS 77016 3687 A4
7900 HOUS 77078 3687 E4
9000 HOUS 77078 3688 A4
Caddo St
7100 BYTN 77521 3835 B5
Caddo Tr
10200 MtgC 77354 2818 A6
Caddo Creek Ln
11200 HarC 77089 4504 A1
Caddo Lake Ln
6800 HOUS 77083 4097 B6
Caddo Park Ct
21300 FBnC 77469 4234 A4
Caddo Passway
25700 FBnC 77494 4093 A3
Caddo Point Ct
11900 HarC 77041 3680 A4
Caddo Springs Ct
9200 HarC 77433 3537 B4
Caddo Terrace Ln
5900 HarC 77041 3679 E5
Caddy Cir
19000 HarC 77346 3265 C6
Cade Ct
15800 HarC 77095 3538 D4
Cade Dr
8700 HarC 77095 3538 D5
Cade Hills Ln
28100 MtgC 77386 2969 D6
Cadena Ct
10 GLSN 77554 5221 D3
10300 HarC 77379 3110 B7
Cadena Dr
10 GLSN 77554 5221 C3
3500 PASD 77504 4247 D4
Cadena Pl
10 GLSN 77554 5221 C3
Caden Creek Ln
22100 MtgC 77365 2973 B3
Cadencrest Ct
4900 FBnC 77494 4092 C3
Cadenhead Rd
23800 MtgC 77357 2828 A6
Cadenhorn Ln
15800 HarC 77084 3678 C5
Cadenza Ct
7700 HarC 77040 3681 C1
Cader Cr
5800 HOUS 77057 3960 C5
Cades Cove Dr
2300 HarC 77373 3114 C6
Cades Creek Ct
10200 HarC 77089 4505 A1
Cadillac St
6600 HOUS 77021 4103 B6
Cadiz Cir
2500 HarC 77038 3543 B5
Cadiz Ct
- LGCY 77539 4633 E3
Cadiz Landing Cir
1300 HOUS 77336 3121 C5
Cadman Ct
9400 HOUS 77096 4241 A1
Cadmus St
100 HOUS 77022 3823 E2
Cadogan Ct
20200 HarC 77450 3954 E4
Cadogan Ln
1600 HarC 77450 3954 E4
Caduceus Pl
4300 GLSN 77550 5108 E6
4300 GLSN 77551 5108 E6
Cadwalder Ln
6900 HOUS 77396 3406 B2
Cady Ct
13800 HOUS 77077 3957 B4
Caelin Ct
10 WDLD 77382 2673 A6
Caelwood Dr
5900 HarC 77346 3264 D6
Caesar Dr
11400 HOUS 77477 4237 E4
Caesars Cir
400 RMFT 77357 2829 A3
Cafe Ter
- HOUS 77030 4102 E4
Cafe Dumonde
1600 CNRO 77304 2382 D2
Caffrey St
9600 HOUS 77075 4377 B3
Cage St
1400 HOUS 77020 3964 A2
Cahill Ct
13700 HarC 77429 3254 A6
Cahill Ln
13500 HarC 77429 3254 A6
Cain Cir
12600 GNPK 77015 3967 A4
12600 HarC 77015 3967 B4
12600 HOUS 77015 3967 A4
Caine Hill Ct
- LGCY 77573 4753 B1
Cairngale St
16900 HarC 77084 3678 B7
Cairngorm Av
16100 HarC 77095 3538 C6
Cairngrove Ln
16500 HarC 77084 3678 B4
Cairnladdie St
17000 HarC 77084 3678 B6
Cairnlassie St
17000 HarC 77084 3678 B6
Cairnleigh Ct
16700 HarC 77084 3678 C7
Cairnleigh Dr
4600 HarC 77084 3678 C6
Cairnloch St
16900 HarC 77084 3678 B7
Cairnlomond St
4600 HarC 77084 3678 B7

STREET
Block City ZIP Map# Grid
Cairn Meadows Dr
10000 HarC 77379 3110 B7
Cairn Oaks Pl
10 WDLD 77381 2821 E3
Cairns Ct
14200 FBnC 77478 4366 E4
Cairns Dr
19500 HarC 77449 3677 A4
Cairnsean St
4600 HarC 77084 3678 B7
Cairntosh St
16900 HarC 77084 3678 B7
Cairnvillage St
4600 HarC 77084 3678 B7
Cairnway Dr
16000 HarC 77084 3678 C7
16000 HOUS 77084 3678 D7
Caitlyn Ct
600 HarC 77094 3955 C2
Caitlyn Falls Ln
8000 HarC 77396 3547 D1
Cajon Cir
22100 HarC 77532 3266 D6
Cajon Canyon Ct
20400 FBnC 77450 4094 C4
Cal Dr
13400 HarC 77065 3398 A7
Calabria Bay Ct
4000 MSCY 77459 4497 D5
Caladero Dr
7000 HarC 77083 4096 B5
Caladium Dr
4800 SGLD 77479 4367 E7
Calagna Rd
8800 HTCK 77563 4988 C6
Calais Rd
7200 HOUS 77033 4103 A7
7200 HOUS 77033 4243 E1
Calamus Cir
5600 HarC 77521 3833 D2
Calaway Cove Ct
12200 HarC 77041 3679 E6
Calcaterra Ct
18100 HarC 77429 3396 C2
Calcutta Spring Dr
7200 HarC 77083 4097 A6
Caldbeck Ln
1700 FBnC 77545 4498 D6
Calder Dr
100 LGCY 77573 4631 D6
2500 LGCY 77573 4752 D4
2900 LGCY 77539 4752 E5
3900 DKSN 77539 4752 E6
E Calder Dr
- LGCY 77573 4631 D4
Calder Rd
1200 LGCY 77573 4752 D1
Calder St
6300 HOUS 77007 3961 D2
Caldera Ct
- HarC 77066 3401 B7
Caldera Wy
3400 FBnC 77545 4498 C7
Caldera Canyon Ct
17100 HarC 77095 3537 C3
Caldera Canyon Dr
10000 HarC 77095 3537 E3
Calderbrook Dr
21900 HarC 77449 3815 A2
Caldermont Ct
15800 HarC 77084 3678 C5
Calderstone Ct
25300 FBnC 77494 4093 B3
Calderwood Dr
900 HarC 77073 3259 A1
Caldicote St
5800 HarC 77346 3264 D6
Caldwell
- HOUS 77087 4104 D5
Caldwell St
100 BYTN 77520 3971 B1
6900 HTCK 77563 4989 A5
Caleb Ln
3600 FBnC 77459 4621 E4
Caleb Wy
9900 FBnC 77459 4621 E4
Caledonia Dr
19100 HarC 77449 3677 B2
Caledonia Tr
1500 SGLD 77479 4367 C7
Calendar St
3800 HOUS 77009 3824 B6
Calender Lake Dr
2800 MSCY 77459 4496 B2
Calera Ct
100 FBnC 77479 4366 C5
Calera Dr
4300 FBnC 77479 4366 C5
Caleta Cir
100 FBnC 77469 4232 A6
Calfee Rd
11500 MtgC 77304 2236 B2
Calgary Cir
3700 MSCY 77459 4369 D4
Calgary Ln
5000 HOUS 77016 3686 D3
Calgary Pointe Dr
26800 MtgC 77339 3118 C3
Calhoun Rd
- HOUS 77033 4103 D7
- HOUS 77033 4243 D1
4500 HOUS 77004 4104 A2
5000 HOUS 77021 4104 A3
5200 HOUS 77021 4103 E6
8200 HOUS 77051 4243 D2
12500 MtgC 77302 2823 E1
12500 MtgC 77302 2824 A1
15400 MtgC 77302 2678 E7
Calhoun St
200 RHMD 77469 4364 E7
600 RHMD 77469 4491 E1
3000 GlsC 77518 4634 B1
Cali Dr
17000 HarC 77090 3258 B2
17000 HOUS 77090 3258 C3
Caliche Dr
5200 FBnC 77469 4615 E7
Calico Ln
11400 PNPV 77024 3959 D3
Calico Canyon Dr
8200 HarC 77375 3110 E2
Calico Canyon Ln
1600 PRLD 77581 4376 D7
1600 PRLD 77581 4503 D1
Calico Corners Ln
23100 HarC 77373 3115 D6
Calico Creek Ct
5700 FBnC 77479 4493 E2

STREET
Block City ZIP Map# Grid
Calico Creek Ln
2700 PRLD 77584 4500 A3
Calico Crossing Ln
5600 FBnC 77450 4094 A4
Calico Falls Ln
12400 HarC 77041 3679 E5
Calico Field Dr
14400 HarC 77429 3397 A1
Calico Glen Ln
17900 HarC 77084 3677 C7
17900 HarC 77084 3678 A7
Calico Hill Ln
2000 SGLD 77478 4237 D5
Calico Hills Cir
400 HarC 77094 3955 B1
Calico Jack
4000 GLSN 77554 5333 A2
Calico Peak Wy
17100 HarC 77433 3251 A3
Calico Point Ct
7400 FBnC 77469 4094 D6
Calico Ridge Ln
22900 HarC 77373 2968 E7
N Calico Rock Ln
1100 HarC 77073 3259 B5
W Calico Rock Ln
16400 HarC 77073 3259 B5
Calico Woods Ln
- FBnC 77494 3953 A5
6600 HarC 77041 3679 D3
California Av
900 LGCY 77539 4633 B5
2000 DKSN 77539 4633 B7
2000 GlsC 77539 4633 B7
2800 DKSN 77539 4754 C3
California Rd
2300 FBnC 77545 4498 D6
California St
1000 HOUS 77006 3962 E6
1600 BYTN 77520 4112 B2
Calistoga Cir
10 MNVL 77583 4624 D5
Calistoga Ct
16300 HOUS 77053 4371 D7
Calix Ln
7100 HarC 77083 4096 E5
Caljon Dr
- HarC 77338 3261 D5
Callahan Av
800 CNRO 77301 2383 E4
Callahan Dr
14000 HarC 77049 3828 B4
Callan Ln
16100 HarC 77530 3829 D4
Callaway Cir
2300 PRLD 77581 4504 D2
Callaway Dr
700 ALVN 77511 4866 E2
Calle Lozano Dr
6400 HarC 77041 3679 C3
Callender St
1300 RSBG 77471 4490 D7
Callepine Ln
18900 HarC 77377 3254 C3
Calle Rosa
3900 HOUS 77003 3964 B5
Callery Creek Dr
4600 HOUS 77053 4372 B6
Calles St
1100 HOUS 77020 3964 C2
Calleston Ct
10 FBnC 77479 4367 A5
Calle Violeta
200 HOUS 77003 3964 A5
Callie Ct
10 HNCV 77024 3960 C2
Callie St
2300 HOUS 77004 4103 E1
Calloway Dr
500 FBnC 77479 4366 E5
Calloway St
100 HOUS 77029 3965 E6
300 HOUS 77029 3966 A6
400 GNPK 77547 3966 A6
Cally Ct
2700 BzaC 77583 4500 D7
Calm Ct
600 FBnC 77583 4744 A3
5500 HarC 77084 3677 D5
Calmar Dr
1600 MtgC 77386 2969 A3
Calm Brook Ct
17900 HarC 77095 3537 E7
Calm Creek Ct
900 HarC 77530 3829 E6
Calm Lagoon Ct
17000 HarC 77095 3538 A6
Calmwater Ln
- HarC 77044 3549 D3
Caloro Ln
- HarC 77493 3813 D4
5400 KATY 77493 3813 C4
Caloway Ct
3400 FBnC 77459 4621 D5
Calthorte Ct
700 HarC 77450 3954 E2
Calton Cove Cir
6300 HarC 77086 3542 C4
Calumet Dr
2300 SGLD 77478 4237 D4
Calumet St
1000 HOUS 77006 4102 E1
1200 HOUS 77004 4102 E2
1600 HOUS 77004 4103 A2
6800 HarC 77389 2966 C5
Calvary
- FBnC 77469 4491 C2
Calvary Ln
2500 HarC 77449 3814 E4
Calvert Ln
5200 DKSN 77539 4754 E4
19000 GlsC 77511 4868 E2
19000 GlsC 77511 4869 A2
Calvert Rd
27300 HarC 77377 3108 D3
Calvert Cove Ct
4100 MtgC 77386 2970 D6
Calvert Crossing Ct
3000 HarC 77449 3815 D4
Calverton Dr
9700 FBnC 77478 4236 E2
Calverton Pines Ln
8500 HarC 77095 3537 D6
Calveryman Ln
1500 HarC 77449 3814 E6
Calveston
- HMPD 77445 3097 E1

STREET
Block City ZIP Map# Grid
Calvi Ct
100 BLAR 77401 4101 B5
Calvin Av
900 HOUS 77088 3683 E3
900 HOUS 77091 3683 E4
Calvin Rd
2500 FBnC 77469 4615 A4
15700 HarC 77090 3258 D6
21800 HOUS 77336 3120 E5
Calvin St
100 PASD 77506 4107 A6
Calvit St
- HMPD 77445 2952 E6
- WlrC 77445 2953 C6
100 HMPD 77445 2953 A6
Calvit Knolls Rd
- FBnC 77469 4234 B4
Calwood Cir
9400 HarC 77379 3255 E5
Calypso Ln
200 LGCY 77573 4508 C6
Calypso Bay Ct
2100 PRLD 77584 4500 B2
Calypso Bay Dr
2200 PRLD 77584 4500 B1
Calypso Cove Ct
1800 PASD 77586 4382 A6
Cam Ct
10 SPVL 77055 3821 B6
Camara Ln
13700 HOUS 77079 3958 A2
Camargo Ct
9400 HOUS 77074 4239 C1
Camarosa Dr
5100 PASD 77504 4247 D7
Camay Dr
9500 HOUS 77016 3686 D5
Cambay Dr
1200 RSBG 77471 4491 C4
Camber Brook Ct
8800 HarC 77089 4377 B6
Camber Brook Dr
8600 HarC 77089 4377 B6
Camberleigh Ln
5000 HarC 77388 3112 A4
Camber Pines Pl
10 WDLD 77382 2674 B4
Camberwell Ct
10 WDLD 77380 2967 E4
Camberwell Green Ct
10000 HarC 77070 3255 C4
Camberwell Green Ln
16900 HarC 77070 3255 C4
Camborn Pl
10 WDLD 77384 2675 A4
Camborne Ln
8200 HarC 77070 3399 D2
Cambria Ct
- LGCY 77573 4632 A6
Cambria Ln
1800 SGLD 77479 4367 C7
Cambrian Park Ct
1100 FBnC 77479 4366 D7
Cambria Pine Ct
10 WDLD 77382 2819 B1
Cambridge Blvd
- MtgC 77357 2828 E4
27900 MtgC 77357 2829 E4
28200 MtgC 77357 2830 A4
Cambridge Cir
2700 RSBG 77471 4491 A5
Cambridge Ct
1200 SEBK 77586 4382 E7
3500 PASD 77504 4248 A3
4400 FBnC 77479 4366 D6
4500 SGLD 77479 4495 C4
15700 MtgC 77384 2674 A2
Cambridge Ct N
2200 LGCY 77573 4631 B5
Cambridge Ct S
2200 LGCY 77573 4631 B5
Cambridge Dr
- BzaC 77584 4501 B6
800 HarC 77562 3831 C2
1200 FRDW 77546 4629 A4
Cambridge Ln
2800 MSCY 77459 4497 D2
Cambridge Rd
10 CNRO 77304 2529 D1
Cambridge St
300 ALVN 77511 4867 D6
4700 SGLD 77479 4495 C4
7200 HOUS 77030 4102 D7
7200 HOUS 77054 4102 D7
8300 HOUS 77054 4242 E1
Cambridge Bay Dr
- PRLD 77545 4499 E2
Cambridge Circus St
2900 PRLD 77581 4503 D2
2900 PRLD 77581 4504 A2
Cambridge Cove Cir
7200 MSCY 77459 4496 E5
Cambridge Dale Ct
2200 HarC 77493 3814 B5
Cambridge Eagle Dr
12800 HarC 77044 3549 D1
Cambridge Falls Dr
3000 FBnC 77545 4498 D7
Cambridge Glen Dr
6300 HOUS 77035 4240 A5
Cambridge Meadows Ln
- LGCY 77539 4753 A3
Cambridge Oaks Cir
1600 HarC 77094 3955 B3
Cambridgeport Ct
3800 FBnC 77494 4093 A4
Cambridge Shores Ct
13100 PRLD 77584 4500 A2
Cambridge Shores Ln
2200 PRLD 77584 4500 D4
Cambridge Square Ln
2300 FBnC 77545 4498 C6
Cambridge Vale Ct
19000 HarC 77429 3395 E1
Cambridge View Dr
15800 HarC 77546 4505 E6
Cambridge Village Dr
500 HMBL 77338 3263 A7
Cambry Pk
4100 FBnC 77450 4094 B1
Cambry Crossing Ct
2900 FBnC 77494 3953 D7
Cambury Dr
13700 HarC 77014 3402 D4
13700 HOUS 77014 3402 D4
13700 HOUS 77067 3402 D4
Camby St
17200 HarC 77447 3248 D3

STREET Block City ZIP Map# Grid

Camby Park Dr
11800 HOUS 77047 4373 C2
Camden Cir
10200 MtgC 77354 2672 B6
Camden Ct
10 SGLD 77479 4495 A3
Camden Dr
- HOUS 77030 4103 A4
2300 HOUS 77021 4103 A4
Camden Hl
14700 MtgC 77372 2682 D2
Camden Ln
5000 PRLD 77584 4503 A4
5300 PRLD 77584 4502 E4
N Camden Pkwy
- HarC 77066 3401 D5
2400 HarC 77067 3401 E4
S Camden Pkwy
- HarC 77066 3401 D5
2500 HarC 77067 3401 E5
Camden Rd
1000 PASD 77502 4247 C2
Camden Bay Ct
11400 HarC 77433 3396 A7
Camden Bend Ct
4100 FBnC 77450 4094 C2
Camden Bend Ln
22000 FBnC 77450 4094 A1
Camden Brook Ln
4500 FBnC 77494 4092 D2
Camden Cross Ln
10500 HarC 77379 3110 B6
Camden Forest Dr
17800 HarC 77338 3407 D1
17800 HarC 77396 3407 D1
Camden Glen Ln
27100 HarC 77433 3395 E7
27100 HarC 77433 3396 B6
Camden Hollow Ln
7800 HarC 77396 3547 D2
Camden Landing Tr
1700 FBnC 77545 4498 D7
Camden Meadow Dr
12200 HarC 77375 3109 D7
Camden Oaks Ln
17700 FBnC 77469 4095 C5
Camden Park Dr
- MtgC 77386 2823 B7
2500 MtgC 77385 2823 B7
Camden Row Ct
8700 HarC 77095 3538 A5
Camden Village Dr
31400 MtgC 77386 2823 A7
Camden Woods Ct
19100 HarC 77377 3254 A1
Camdon Dr
2100 DRPK 77536 4109 D6
Camelback Ct
10 PNVL 77304 2237 A3
15100 HOUS 77079 3957 B2
Camelia Cir
2200 BYTN 77520 3973 D7
Camelia Ct
26300 MtgC 77354 2817 D4
Camelia Ln
4400 FBnC 77545 4623 C2
Camelia St
2300 BYTN 77520 3973 D7
Camelia Wy
300 LGCY 77573 4632 E1
Camelia Glen Ln
3900 FBnC 77545 4498 C7
3900 FBnC 77545 4622 B1
Camellia Av
3200 PASD 77505 4248 A3
6000 HOUS 77007 3962 A3
Camellia Ct
1500 FRDW 77546 4629 E2
Camellia Ln
4400 BLAR 77401 4101 B4
18200 HarC 77429 3108 A7
18200 HarC 77429 3253 A1
Camellia St
- SGLD 77478 4367 E4
100 SGLD 77478 4368 A4
Camellia Bend Cir
19100 HarC 77379 3111 E6
19100 HarC 77379 3112 A6
Camellia Dale Tr
18600 HarC 77084 3816 C4
Camellia Estates Ln
18300 HarC 77429 3396 A2
N Camellia Grove Cir
10 WDLD 77382 2674 E3
S Camellia Grove Cir
10 WDLD 77382 2674 D3
Camellia Grove Pl
- WDLD 77382 2674 D3
Camellia Knoll Tr
19300 HarC 77084 3816 A4
Camelot Ct
- HarC 77379 3111 A1
Camelot Dr
3500 BYTN 77521 3973 E2
3500 BYTN 77521 3974 A2
Camelot Ln
700 HNCV 77024 3960 B2
800 FRDW 77546 4505 A6
1100 PRLD 77581 4504 E6
2800 MSCY 77459 4370 A7
25200 WlrC 77447 2813 C7
Camelot Pl
1300 SGLD 77478 4368 E4
Camelot St
100 CNRO 77304 2383 C4
Camelot Centre Ct
13700 HarC 77069 3400 A2
Camelot Grove Dr
22100 HarC 77339 3118 C3
Camelot Oaks Ct
10 WDLD 77382 2673 D7
Camelots Ct
9600 PRLD 77584 4501 B3
Cameo Ct
- LGCY 77573 4632 C2
Cameo Dr
3300 HOUS 77080 3820 E2
Cameo Wy
9300 MtgC 77384 2529 A7
Cameo Falls Ln
- FBnC 77494 4092 C5
Cameray Pass
- SGLD 77479 4494 E4
Cameray Pass Dr
- SGLD 77479 4494 E4
Cameron Ct
6100 LGCY 77573 4630 C7

Cameron Dr
2000 BzaC 77583 4624 A3
2200 BzaC 77578 4624 A3
2200 PRLD 77578 4624 A3
2200 PRLD 77583 4624 A3
Cameron Rd
- PRVW 77445 2955 D6
- WlrC 77445 2955 E6
9400 HarC 77095 3538 C2
33000 WlrC 77445 2956 C6
33000 WlrC 77484 2956 C6
Cameron St
2600 HOUS 77098 3962 A6
Cameron Cove Ln
6100 FBnC 77450 4094 A4
Cameron Crest Ln
13100 FBnC 77478 4366 E2
Cameron Point Cir
5900 HarC 77449 3677 C5
E Cameron Ridge Dr
20800 HarC 77433 3251 A3
W Cameron Ridge Dr
21000 HarC 77433 3251 A3
Camerton Av
6800 SGLD 77479 4367 E7
N Camfer Ct
15800 HarC 77532 3552 A4
Camille
2100 PASD 77506 4107 D5
Camille Dr
28100 TMBL 77375 2963 D4
Camille St
1700 MtgC 77362 2816 C7
1700 SGCH 77362 2816 C7
2700 PASD 77506 4107 E4
2700 PASD 77506 4108 A4
Camillia St
2300 HarC 77562 3832 D2
Camillia Tr
15900 HarC 77377 3254 D5
Camillia Ridge Wy
24200 HarC 77493 3814 A5
Camillo Ct
18900 HarC 77094 3955 C3
Caminito Tr
6400 HarC 77346 3264 E5
Camino Ct
10 WDLD 77382 2819 E2
2400 TXCY 77590 4875 A3
Camino St
22800 GLSN 77554 5441 A6
23000 GLSN 77554 5440 E6
Camino Del Sol
15600 FBnC 77083 4096 B6
Camino del Sol Dr
15500 FBnC 77083 4096 A6
16300 FBnC 77083 4095 E6
Camino Famoso Rd
12700 GLSN 77554 5220 B7
Camino Oaks Dr
11100 HarC 77064 3541 B1
Camino Rancho Dr
14700 HarC 77083 4096 D5
Camino Real
3900 GLSN 77554 5220 B6
Camino Real St
7300 HarC 77521 3832 E4
Camino Verde Dr
7000 HarC 77083 4096 A5
Cammie Rd
18900 GlsC 77511 4868 E2
Cammy Ln
2100 LPRT 77571 4250 A1
Camp Cir E
1000 LMQU 77568 4989 D1
N Camp Cir
2600 LMQU 77568 4989 D1
W Camp Cir
1000 LMQU 77568 4989 D1
Camp Rd
400 HarC 77562 3832 A2
Campaign Cir
8200 FBnC 77469 4234 B4
Camp Allen Rd
100 DKSN 77539 4753 D5
100 TXCY 77539 4753 D5
Campanile Dr
- HarC 77449 3815 B6
- HOUS 77449 3815 B6
Campanile Rd
- HOUS 77005 4102 C2
Campbell Av
100 PASD 77502 4107 A7
Campbell Dr
4800 PRLD 77584 4503 A4
Campbell Ln
1500 GLSN 77551 5108 C5
Campbell Rd
- SPVL 77055 3959 E1
900 HDWV 77024 3959 E1
900 SPVL 77024 3959 E1
1000 SPVL 77055 3820 E7
1200 HOUS 77055 3820 E6
1700 HOUS 77080 3820 E5
4300 HOUS 77041 3820 C1
4500 HOUS 77041 3681 C7
5700 HOUS 77040 3681 C7
20000 MtgC 77357 2828 B5
Campbell St
1200 HOUS 77009 3963 D1
2000 HOUS 77026 3963 E1
3000 HOUS 77026 3964 A1
5200 TXCY 77591 4874 A6
5300 TXCY 77591 4873 E6
7300 HOUS 77054 4102 E7
7300 HOUS 77054 4103 A6
Campbell Bayou Rd
1600 TXCY 77590 4991 A5
Campbellford Dr
18100 HarC 77377 3254 C2
Campbell Pit Rd
- MtgC 77357 2974 D2
Campbellton Dr
- HarC 77083 4097 A6
Camp Cove Dr
17800 HarC 77429 3252 C7
Campden Ct
16000 HarC 77379 3256 E4
Campden Dr
6600 HarC 77379 3256 E4
Campden Hill Rd
14400 HOUS 77045 4372 C3
15200 HOUS 77053 4372 C4
Campeachy Cir
13200 HOUS 77083 4097 B6
Campeachy Ln
7100 HOUS 77083 4097 C6

Campeche Cir
10 GLSN 77554 5221 C3
Campeche Dr
- HOUS 77045 4372 C2
10 GLSN 77554 5221 C3
4100 GLSN 77554 5332 E3
Campeche Ests
10 GLSN 77554 5221 C3
Campers Crest Dr
18500 HarC 77346 3265 C7
Campfield Ct
3500 HarC 77449 3815 E2
Campfield Dr
19700 HarC 77449 3815 E2
19700 HarC 77449 3816 A2
Camp Fire Rd
15800 HarC 77546 4505 E5
15800 HarC 77546 4506 A5
Camphor Dr
3700 HarC 77082 4096 B3
Camphor Tree Dr
20700 HarC 77449 3815 C4
Camphorwood Dr
11300 HarC 77089 4378 A5
Campione Ct
24200 FBnC 77469 4093 A7
Camp Lillie Rd
100 HarC 77346 3265 D5
100 HOUS 77346 3265 D5
Camporee Ln
7400 HOUS 77083 4097 B6
Campos Dr
12300 HarC 77065 3398 C7
Campo Verde Ct
- FBnC 77053 4498 D3
Camp Sienna Tr
7700 FBnC 77459 4621 A5
7700 MSCY 77459 4621 A5
Campsite Tr
12500 HarC 77429 3398 A5
Camp Strake Rd
13300 CNRO 77302 2530 A5
13300 CNRO 77304 2530 A5
13500 MtgC 77304 2529 E5
13500 MtgC 77304 2530 A5
Campton Ct
1200 HOUS 77055 3821 E7
Camptown Cir
6600 HarC 77069 3400 B1
W Campus Dr
- CNRO 77384 2675 D5
- WDLD 77384 2675 D5
Campwell
- BYTN 77520 3971 A4
Camp Wood Cir
11600 MtgC 77354 2817 C1
Campwood Dr
1900 SGLD 77478 4368 D5
30000 MtgC 77354 2817 C1
Campwood Ln
13800 HarC 77429 3253 D5
Camrose Cir
10500 HOUS 77085 4371 C4
Camrose Ct
1100 HarC 77373 2968 E5
9600 HarC 77086 3542 A3
Camway St
7100 HOUS 77028 3825 D2
Camwood St
100 MtgC 77355 2960 A2
7600 HOUS 77087 4105 B7
Canaan St
7200 MNVL 77578 4746 D2
Canaan Bridge Dr
13300 HarC 77041 3679 B4
Canabury Dr
28500 HarC 77336 3121 E3
Canada Dr
6000 PASD 77505 4248 D5
Canada Rd
- HarC 77507 4249 E5
3200 DRPK 77536 4249 E4
3200 LPRT 77536 4249 E4
3200 LPRT 77571 4249 E4
Canada Dry St
2100 HOUS 77023 4104 B2
Canaday Park Ln
9200 HOUS 77075 4377 A3
Canadian St
200 HOUS 77009 3824 B5
3200 KATY 77493 3813 C3
Canadian River Ct
4600 MtgC 77386 2970 B2
Canadian River Dr
4300 SGLD 77478 4369 A5
Canal Ct
10 HOUS 77011 3964 B5
Canal Dr
100 FRDW 77546 4749 D2
Canal Rd
4400 GlsC 77517 4869 D6
4400 STFE 77517 4869 D6
22000 FBnC 77469 4093 D1
22000 FBnC 77469 4233 D1
22000 HOUS 77469 4093 C7
E Canal Rd
100 HarC 77562 3831 E1
600 HarC 77562 3832 A1
W Canal Rd
100 HarC 77562 3831 D1
Canal St
2000 HOUS 77003 3963 E4
2900 HOUS 77003 3964 B5
4400 HOUS 77011 3964 E7
5500 GlsC 77517 4869 D7
7000 HOUS 77011 3965 B7
7400 HOUS 77012 3965 B7
N Canal St
10 TXCY 77591 4874 A6
S Canal St
1800 HarC 77562 3832 C4
Canaras Ct
19100 HarC 77449 3677 B5
Canaridge Dr
16100 HOUS 77053 4371 D6
Canario Dr
16200 FBnC 77083 4096 A7
16400 FBnC 77083 4095 E7
Canary Cir
700 PASD 77502 4107 A7
1600 LGCY 77573 4631 C5
7200 TXCY 77591 4873 C6
20400 MtgC 77365 3117 E1
Canary Ct
100 MtgC 77385 2676 D4
Canary Ln
2800 HMBL 77396 3406 C4
25100 MtgC 77365 3117 E2

Canary St
10 MtgC 77385 2676 D4
300 RMFT 77357 2829 A3
Canary Grass Ln
3700 HOUS 77059 4380 B4
Canary Isle Ct
4200 FBnC 77450 4093 E2
Canary Point Dr
25200 FBnC 77469 4092 D7
Canarywood Dr
10900 HarC 77089 4378 A6
E Canary Yellow Cir
22000 HarC 77433 3250 E4
S Canary Yellow Cir
14800 HarC 77433 3250 E5
W Canary Yellow Cir
22000 HarC 77433 3250 E4
Canasta Ln
7400 HOUS 77083 4097 B6
Canbay Dr
- RSBG 77471 4491 C4
Canberra St
8800 HOUS 77061 4245 B6
Canby Point Ln
15300 HarC 77433 3251 D7
W Cancun Dr
- HOUS 77045 4372 B1
Canda Ln
7200 HOUS 77083 4097 B5
Candace Ct
12800 MSCY 77071 4239 B7
Candace Ln
- LPRT 77571 4251 E3
- LPRT 77571 4252 A4
Candace St
8700 HOUS 77055 3821 A6
8900 HOUS 77055 3820 E6
Candela Ct
7700 FBnC 77083 4095 D7
Candela Dr
17300 FBnC 77083 4095 D7
Candice Ct
11700 MtgC 77304 2382 A4
Candle Ln
7800 HOUS 77071 4239 D4
Candle Bend Dr
3000 HarC 77388 3113 B7
Candleberry Dr
13700 HarC 77396 3547 C3
Candlebrook Cir
19200 HarC 77388 3113 A6
Candlebrook Dr
3400 HarC 77388 3113 A4
Candle Cabin Ln
3100 HarC 77388 3113 A7
Candlechase Dr
18600 HarC 77388 3113 B7
18600 HarC 77388 3258 B1
Candlecreek Dr
5700 FBnC 77469 4493 A5
18900 HarC 77388 3113 A6
19900 HarC 77388 3112 E5
Candlecrest Ct
- FBnC 77469 4094 A7
Candlecrest Dr
4900 HOUS 77018 3684 A7
5400 HOUS 77091 3684 A6
Candleglow Dr
4900 HOUS 77018 3684 A7
Candle Green Ct
8200 HOUS 77071 4239 D6
Candlegreen Ln
7600 HOUS 77071 4239 E6
Candle Grove Dr
3000 HarC 77388 3113 C2
Candle Hill Dr
3000 HarC 77388 3113 C2
Candle Hollow Dr
3000 HarC 77388 3113 C2
Candleknoll Dr
3300 HarC 77388 3113 A7
Candleleaf Dr
4900 HOUS 77018 3684 B7
Candle Light Ct
1800 SGLD 77478 4236 E6
Candlelight Ct
1900 FRDW 77546 4629 E3
Candlelight Ln
900 HOUS 77018 3684 A7
1000 HOUS 77018 3683 E7
19700 MtgC 77357 2829 A5
Candlelight Crescent Rd
18900 HarC 77388 3113 A4
Candlelight Pl Dr
1900 HOUS 77018 3683 B7
Candlelon Dr
3300 HarC 77388 3113 A6
Candle Manor Ln
7300 FBnC 77469 4615 E5
Candlemist Dr
4900 HOUS 77018 3684 A7
5400 HOUS 77091 3684 A6
Candlenut Dr
- WDLD 77382 2674 C5
Candlenut Pl
10 WDLD 77381 2674 D7
Candleoak Dr
3300 HarC 77388 3113 A7
Candle Park Dr
- HarC 77388 3113 B7
Candlepine Dr
3200 HarC 77388 3113 A7
Candle Pine Pl
10 WDLD 77381 2674 C6
Candle Pl Dr
3000 HarC 77388 3113 C2
Candle Point Ln
- FBnC 77469 4094 D2
Candle Pond Ln
3100 HarC 77388 3113 A7
Candler Dr
400 HarC 77037 3684 D2
600 HOUS 77037 3684 D2
W Candler Dr
100 HarC 77037 3684 C2
Candler St
1000 FBnC 77471 4490 C3
1000 RSBG 77471 4490 C3
Candleridge Ct
25400 WlrC 77447 2813 C1
Candleridge Dr
3300 HarC 77388 3113 A7
Candleridge Park Dr
- HarC 77073 3259 D4
Candle River Ln
19000 HarC 77388 3113 A4
Candlerock Ct
16300 HarC 77095 3538 B5

Candleshade Ln
- HOUS 77045 4372 B1
13300 HOUS 77045 4241 B7
Candleshine Cir
8700 HarC 77095 3538 B5
Candlespice Pl
10 WDLD 77382 2673 D4
Candleston Dr
4100 HarC 77066 3401 B3
Candleston Ln
1600 HarC 77450 3954 E5
Candletrail Dr
19100 HarC 77388 3113 A7
Candletree Dr
5000 HOUS 77018 3683 E7
5400 HOUS 77091 3683 E6
Candleview Dr
19000 HarC 77388 3113 A6
Candleway Dr
3200 HarC 77388 3113 A7
Candlewick St
13100 HOUS 77015 3967 C2
Candlewisp Cir
3300 HarC 77388 3113 A7
Candlewisp Dr
3400 HarC 77388 3113 A7
Candlewood Dr
700 LGCY 77573 4630 E7
5400 HOUS 77056 3960 D4
10000 HOUS 77042 3958 E5
10000 HOUS 77042 3959 A5
Candlewood Ln
5800 HOUS 77057 3960 D4
Candlewood Glen Ln
12800 HarC 77014 3402 A2
Candlewood Oaks Ln
19600 HarC 77379 3110 C6
Candlewood Park Ln
4300 FBnC 77450 4093 D2
Candover Ct
400 HarC 77450 3954 D1
Candy Ct
9800 HarC 77379 3110 D4
Candy Ln
25500 MtgC 77355 2963 A4
Candy St
2000 SGCH 77362 2816 C7
8600 HOUS 77029 3965 D3
Candyridge Ct
16500 HOUS 77053 4372 A7
Candytuft Ct
1600 HarC 77038 3543 D5
Candytuft St
1500 HarC 77038 3543 D5
Canebrake Ln
7400 HOUS 77083 4097 C6
Canebreak Cross
2200 SGLD 77478 4368 C6
Cane Creek Ct
16100 HarC 77070 3255 C6
Cane Creek Dr
9500 HarC 77070 3255 C6
Cane Field Dr
2700 SGLD 77479 4368 C7
Cane Grove Ln
10800 HOUS 77075 4376 E4
Cane Lake Ct
13100 FBnC 77478 4366 E1
Cane Lake Dr
3700 FBnC 77469 4234 D6
Cane Mill Pl
10 WDLD 77382 2674 E4
Canemont St
11400 HOUS 77035 4240 A7
Caneridge Dr
6200 HOUS 77053 4371 D6
Cane River Ln
500 MtgC 77302 2530 D5
12400 HarC 77346 3408 E3
Caneshaw Dr
4100 PRLD 77584 4502 E7
Cane Valley Ct
13800 HOUS 77044 3550 B3
Caney Dr
21000 MtgC 77357 2828 C7
21900 MtgC 77357 2827 C4
Caney Bayou Ln
10 HOUS 77013 3966 E1
Caneybrook Ct
21800 HarC 77449 3815 A1
Caney Creek Ct
2400 FBnC 77469 4365 B1
Caney Springs Ln
13400 HarC 77044 3550 A2
Canfield St
2100 HOUS 77003 3963 E7
2100 HOUS 77004 3963 E7
2600 HOUS 77004 4103 D1
Canfield Oaks Ln
4200 FBnC 77450 4093 E2
Canford Ct
4600 HOUS 77345 3119 E6
Cangelosi Rd
- HOUS 77489 4371 A3
Caniff Rd
- LPRT 77571 4250 A4
Canino Rd
100 HarC 77037 3684 E2
100 HOUS 77037 3684 E2
100 HOUS 77076 3684 E2
300 HOUS 77037 3685 A2
300 HOUS 77076 3685 A2
E Canino Rd
100 HarC 77037 3684 D2
100 HOUS 77037 3684 D2
800 HOUS 77076 3684 D2
W Canino Rd
10 HarC 77037 3684 C2
10 HOUS 77037 3684 C2
Canmere Ct
10700 HarC 77070 3399 A5
Canmore Springs Dr
- MtgC 77386 2969 C1
Cann Dr
3700 PASD 77503 4108 C5
Canna Ct
10600 CmbC 77520 3835 D3
Canna Dr
700 HarC 77530 3829 D7
Cannaberry Wy
20500 HarC 77388 3113 A5
Cannady Ct
13600 HarC 77069 3400 B2
Canna Lily Ct
3200 HOUS 77345 3119 E1
Cannata Dr
14400 HOUS 77045 4373 A3

Canneberry Wy
- HarC 77388 3113 B6
Canniff Rd
200 HOUS 77017 4246 B3
200 SHUS 77587 4246 B3
Canniff St
8700 HOUS 77061 4245 E3
8700 HOUS 77061 4246 A3
9100 HOUS 77017 4246 A3
9300 SHUS 77587 4246 A3
Cannion Falls Dr
15600 HarC 77377 3254 D6
Cannock Ct
19200 MtgC 77357 2829 D4
Cannock Rd
7300 HOUS 77074 4099 E5
Cannock Chase Ct
9700 HarC 77065 3539 D4
Cannock Chase Dr
9400 HarC 77065 3539 D5
Cannon Ct
19900 MSCY 77459 4497 D7
Cannon Knls
6300 HarC 77084 3679 A4
Cannon Ln
600 FBnC 77479 4366 E5
Cannon St
7700 HOUS 77021 4243 A1
7700 HOUS 77051 4243 A2
Cannonade Dr
2000 PASD 77503 4108 D7
Cannon Ball Dr
700 MtgC 77380 2968 A1
Cannonball Run
2900 FRDW 77546 4749 E2
2900 FRDW 77546 4750 A2
Cannon Bridge Dr
- HarC 77041 3679 B4
Cannonbury Ln
2000 FBnC 77469 4234 C7
Cannon Creek Tr
23300 HarC 77377 2963 B6
Cannondale Ln
4200 FBnC 77450 4094 A2
Cannon Farm Hills Ln
2100 FBnC 77469 4234 C7
Cannon Fire Dr
- HarC 77449 3677 C3
19800 HarC 77449 3676 E4
Cannongate Dr
4400 HarC 77373 3115 B5
Cannon Pass Ct
3300 SGLD 77478 4368 E5
Cannon Ridge Dr
3100 FBnC 77469 4234 C6
Cannons Hall Ct
2400 FBnC 77469 4234 B6
Cannons Point Ct
2300 SGLD 77478 4369 D5
Cannons Point Dr
2300 SGLD 77478 4369 A6
Cannonway Dr
5500 HarC 77032 3546 D1
Canoe Birch Pl
10 WDLD 77382 2674 A5
Canoe Crest Ct
18900 HarC 77346 3265 D6
Canoga Ln
9800 HOUS 77080 3820 B4
Canon Dr
4000 DKSN 77539 4752 E6
4000 LGCY 77539 4752 E6
Canonero Dr
900 MSCY 77489 4370 B4
900 STAF 77477 4370 B4
900 STAF 77489 4370 B4
Canongate Dr
2000 HOUS 77056 3960 E6
Canonsburg Ln
4400 LGCY 77573 4630 E6
Canopy Ln
18400 MtgC 77365 2972 A6
Canopy Oaks Dr
- WDLD 77384 2674 E3
Cansfield Ct
6800 FBnC 77494 4093 C5
Cansfield Wy
23400 FBnC 77494 4093 B5
Canston Ct
24900 HarC 77389 2966 C3
Cantabria Ln
- LGCY 77539 4633 D3
Cantata Ct
9300 HarC 77040 3681 B1
Canter Ct
2400 MtgC 77384 2528 E7
Canter Ln
2400 MtgC 77384 2529 A5
E Canterbury
- HOUS 77077 3957 B5
Canterbury Cir
24600 WlrC 77447 2813 E7
Canterbury Ct
10 CNRO 77304 2529 C1
2100 DRPK 77536 4109 B6
4200 SGLD 77479 4495 B3
Canterbury Dr
100 CNRO 77301 2384 C1
100 CNRO 77303 2384 C1
200 CNRO 77303 2238 C7
1000 PRLD 77584 4501 C2
2200 LGCY 77573 4508 E7
3500 BYTN 77521 3973 E2
3500 BYTN 77521 3974 A2
9800 HMBL 77338 3262 C5
12700 HarC 77014 3402 A3
Canterbury Ln
4900 SGLD 77479 4495 C3
Canterbury Rd
20100 MtgC 77365 2972 D5
20400 MtgC 77365 2973 A5
Canterbury St
1900 HOUS 77030 4102 D5
Canterbury Wy
4800 HarC 77069 3256 E6
Canterbury Forest Dr
15300 HarC 77070 3255 A6
15300 HarC 77377 3255 A6
Canterbury Green Ct
17100 FBnC 77478 4235 E7
Canterbury Green Ln
17000 FBnC 77478 4235 E6
Canterbury Park Dr
3600 PRLD 77584 4503 B6
Canterbury Park Ln
4000 PRLD 77584 4503 B6
Canterbury Ranch Rd
31000 MtgC 77354 2817 C1

Canterdale St
1100 HOUS 77047 4373 C
Canterhurst Cir
9800 HarC 77065 3539 D
Canterhurst Wy
12000 HarC 77065 3539 D
Canterlane Dr
1200 HOUS 77047 4373 C
E Canterra Cir
16500 HarC 77095 3538 B
W Canterra Cir
10500 HarC 77095 3538 B
Canterra Ct
10400 HarC 77095 3538 B
Canterra Wy
16600 HarC 77095 3397 A
Cantertrot Dr
9700 HMBL 77338 3262 D
Canterview Dr
1200 HOUS 77047 4373 C
Canterville Rd
1200 HOUS 77047 4373 C
Canterway Dr
5200 HOUS 77048 4243 E
5200 HOUS 77048 4244 A
Canterwell Rd
13400 HOUS 77047 4373 C
Canterwood Dr
4200 HarC 77068 3257 A
Cantigny Ct
22800 HarC 77450 3953 E
Cantigny Ln
1600 HarC 77450 3953 E
Cantina Dr
- GLSN 77554 5441 A
Canton Cir
1400 RSBG 77471 4491 C
Canton Dr
3800 PRLD 77584 4501 C
Canton St
100 HOUS 77012 4105 B
Canton Bluff Ln
400 HarC 77073 3259 A
Canton Forest
17300 FBnC 77469 4095 D
Canton Oaks Ct
3500 HarC 77068 3257 B
Canton Park Ln
9000 HarC 77095 3538 E
Canton Pass Ln
21800 FBnC 77450 4093 E
26700 HarC 77433 3396 A
Canton Wood Ct
9500 HarC 77044 3689 A
Cantor Cir
14800 HarC 77084 3679 A
Cantrell Blvd
1600 CNRO 77301 2384 D
Cantrell Ct
4200 FBnC 77479 4366 C
Cantrell Mnr
13900 HarC 77429 3397 B
Cantrell St
8200 HOUS 77074 4100 B
Cantu Rd
5700 PRLD 77584 4502 E
Cantwell Bnd
14700 HarC 77429 3253 E
Cantwell Dr
4200 PASD 77505 4249 A
13800 HarC 77014 3402 D
Cantwell Wy
10 WDLD 77382 2819 D
Cantwell Forest Dr
- SHEH 77381 2821 D
- WDLD 77381 2821 D
Canty Rd
38000 PNIS 77445 3099 A
Canvas Ct
600 HarC 77532 3552 B
Canvasback Ln
3500 HarC 77047 4374 C
16100 HarC 77447 3248 D
Canvasback St
3200 KATY 77493 3813 B
Canvasback Bay N
100 BYTN 77520 4113 D
Canvasback Bay S
100 BYTN 77520 4113 D
Canwater Br
23000 FBnC 77469 4093 D
Canyon Cir
11600 MtgC 77385 2823 A
Canyon Cr
- MtgC 77362 2963 C
Canyon Cross
11400 MtgC 77385 2823 B
Canyon Ct
3000 MSCY 77459 4497 A
Canyon Dr
2800 BzaC 77584 4501 C
N Canyon Dr
19000 HarC 77377 3254 C
19100 HarC 77377 3109 C
S Canyon Dr
- HOUS 77089 4378 B
11500 HarC 77089 4505 B
11600 HarC 77089 4378 B
Canyon Hl
13800 HarC 77083 4097 A
Canyon Ln
18900 HarC 77346 3264 A
Canyon St
7900 HOUS 77051 4243 A
Canyon Vw
28200 MtgC 77355 2815 B
Canyon Arbor Wy
12100 HarC 77095 3397 A
Canyonback Ln
22700 HarC 77373 2968 E
Canyon Bay Ct
19300 HarC 77377 3254 E
Canyon Bay Dr
19200 HarC 77377 3254 E
Canyon Bend Dr
11500 HarC 77377 3109 C
11600 HarC 77377 3254 C
Canyon Blanco Dr
4700 HOUS 77045 4241 B
Canyon Bloom Ln
17700 FBnC 77469 4235 D
Canyon Bluff Ct
3800 HOUS 77059 4380 A
5500 BzaC 77583 4623 E
Canyon Bluff Dr
2600 BzaC 77578 4501 A
Canyon Bluff Ln
5500 BzaC 77583 4623 E

Houston Street Index

STREET
Block City ZIP Map# Grid

Canyon Branch Ct
30100 MtgC 77386 2969 C3
Canyon Breeze Dr
11600 HarC 77377 3254 C1
Canyon Brook Ct
4000 PASD 77059 4380 E5
5900 FBnC 77479 4493 E3
11100 HarC 77065 3539 C1
Canyon Chase Dr
6200 FBnC 77469 4493 C4
6300 FBnC 77450 4094 C4
16400 HarC 77095 3397 A7
Canyon Cliff Ct
6500 HarC 77041 3679 E4
Canyon Cove Dr
18400 HarC 77532 3409 D6
Canyon Creek Ct
1900 PRLD 77581 4504 C5
Canyon Creek Dr
- FBnC 77494 3953 C4
Canyon Creek Ln
6100 CNRO 77304 2236 E6
Canyon Creek Rd
17900 HarC 77090 3257 E2
17900 HarC 77090 3258 A2
Canyon Creek Sq
6900 HarC 77084 3678 D2
Canyon Crest Dr
600 LGCY 77573 4630 E6
1900 FBnC 77479 4494 A2
2000 FBnC 77479 4493 E2
Canyon Crest Ln
13200 MtgC 77302 2530 C4
Canyoncrest Ln
10400 HarC 77086 3542 B2
Canyon Crossing Ct
25500 FBnC 77469 4092 D7
Canyon Crossing Dr
25500 FBnC 77469 4092 C7
Canyon Crossing Ln
11100 FBnC 77469 4092 D7
Canyon Cypress Ct
6400 HarC 77449 3677 D6
Canyon Cypress Ln
18000 HarC 77084 3677 D3
18000 HarC 77449 3677 D3
Canyon Drop Dr
11700 HarC 77377 3254 C1
Canyon Echo Dr
12500 HarC 77065 3539 C1
Canyon Estates Ln
6400 FBnC 77469 4493 C4
Canyon Falls Ct
2200 LGCY 77573 4631 C7
Canyon Falls Dr
2600 BzaC 77578 4501 A7
11300 HarC 77396 3407 E7
11800 HarC 77375 3109 D5
Canyon Ferry Ln
19100 FBnC 77469 4094 D7
19100 FBnC 77469 4095 A6
Canyon Fields Dr
- FBnC 77469 4092 C7
- FBnC 77494 4092 C7
Canyonforest Ct
21600 FBnC 77450 4094 A4
Canyon Forest Dr
5400 HarC 77088 3542 D7
Canyon Fork Ct
3600 FBnC 77450 4094 A2
Canyon Gale Ln
1300 PRLD 77545 4499 E3
Canyon Garden Dr
700 HarC 77450 3953 E3
Canyon Gate Blvd
20300 FBnC 77450 4094 C4
Canyon Gate Ct
19700 FBnC 77450 4094 C5
Canyon Gate Dr
- HarC 77375 3109 C7
- HarC 77377 3109 B7
- HarC 77377 3254 B1
4900 PASD 77505 4248 E7
4900 PASD 77505 4249 A7
Canyon Glen Dr
12100 HarC 77095 3397 A6
Canyon Green Dr
- HarC 77095 3397 A7
Canyon Heights Ct
1100 HarC 77494 3953 D4
Canyon Hill Ln
700 RSBG 77471 4614 C1
Canyon Hollow Dr
5300 HarC 77084 3678 A6
Canyon Hollow Lp
13700 HarC 77083 4097 A7
Canyon Knoll Dr
17300 HarC 77095 3678 A1
17400 HarC 77095 3677 E1
Canyon Lake Ct
2100 DRPK 77536 4109 D6
Canyon Lake Dr
1200 FBnC 77469 4493 B4
2100 DRPK 77536 4109 D6
3800 PRLD 77581 4503 E7
20400 HarC 77377 3106 D5
22800 HarC 77373 3114 D7
Canyon Lake Creek Dr
1700 CNRO 77304 2383 A2
Canyon Lakes Dr
- HarC 77396 3407 A7
- HarC 77396 3548 A1
Canyon Lakes Manor Dr
- HarC 77433 3537 A7
E Canyon Lake Springs Dr
9200 HarC 77433 3537 C4
N Canyon Lake Springs Dr
19100 HarC 77433 3537 B4
S Canyon Lake Springs Dr
19100 HarC 77433 3537 B4
W Canyon Lake Springs Dr
9200 HarC 77433 3537 B5
Canyonlands Dr
- HarC 77346 3408 E3
Canyon Laurel Ct
16900 HarC 77379 3256 D5
Canyon Links Ct
21600 FBnC 77450 3954 B7
Canyon Links Dr
- FBnC 77450 4094 A2
3100 FBnC 77450 3954 B7
Canyon Manor Ct
- FBnC 77469 4092 B7
Canyon Manor Dr
- FBnC 77469 4092 B7
Canyon Maples Ln
13900 HarC 77429 3253 D6
Canyon Meadow Dr
2300 MSCY 77489 4370 B7
Canyon Mill Ln
11900 HarC 77377 3254 B1
Canyon Mills Ct
16300 HarC 77095 3397 A7
Canyon Mills Dr
11600 HarC 77095 3397 A6
Canyon Mist Ln
6500 LGCY 77539 4752 E3
11700 HarC 77377 3254 C1
Canyon Oak Ct
3100 HarC 77068 3257 D6
Canyon Oak Dr
- HarC 77095 3538 A1
Canyon Oak Pl
10 WDLD 77380 2967 E2
Canyon Park Dr
6200 FBnC 77450 4094 B4
Canyon Peak Ln
21700 FBnC 77450 4094 A1
Canyon Pine Dr
8400 HarC 77379 3256 A4
Canyon Pointe Ln
6400 FBnC 77469 4493 C4
Canyon Post Dr
- HarC 77095 3397 C6
Canyon Ranch Dr
- MtgC 77386 2969 C3
1300 PRLD 77545 4499 E3
Canyon Ranch Ln
- FBnC 77494 3953 B6
Canyon Ridge Ct
16900 HarC 77379 3256 A4
20200 FBnC 77450 4094 C4
Canyon Ridge Dr
8500 HarC 77379 3256 D5
17100 HarC 77379 3255 E4
Canyon Ridge Ln
6100 CNRO 77304 2236 E6
Canyon River Ln
19000 HarC 77084 3816 B3
Canyon Rock Ln
11900 HarC 77377 3254 E2
Canyon Rock Wy
6200 FBnC 77450 4094 D4
Canyon Rose Dr
18900 HarC 77377 3254 C1
Canyon Rose Ln
10200 HarC 77070 3399 C3
Canyon Royal Dr
18900 HarC 77377 3254 B1
Canyon Run Ct
6200 FBnC 77450 4094 E4
Canyon Sage Ln
- HarC 77429 3253 A7
4800 FBnC 77494 4093 A1
Canyon Sands Ln
- FBnC 77469 4092 A6
Canyon Shadow Dr
20400 FBnC 77450 4094 E4
Canyon Shore Dr
4700 HarC 77396 3407 B7
Canyon Side Ct
30000 MtgC 77386 2969 B3
Canyon Side Ln
30100 MtgC 77386 2969 C3
Canyon Springs Dr
500 LPRT 77571 4250 B2
2300 PRLD 77584 4500 B2
17200 HarC 77090 3258 A3
Canyon Springs Ln
16900 HarC 77546 4506 C6
Canyon Square Dr
2900 MtgC 77386 2969 C3
Canyon Star Ct
19000 HarC 77377 3254 E3
Canyon Star Ln
11900 HarC 77377 3254 C1
Canyon Stream Ct
17100 HarC 77095 3538 A7
Canyon Summer Ln
30100 MtgC 77386 2969 C2
Canyon Sun Ln
11700 HarC 77377 3109 A7
Canyon Terrace Ct
1600 HarC 77450 3954 B6
Canyon Terrace Ln
21500 HarC 77450 3954 B5
Canyon Timbers Dr
11900 HarC 77377 3254 B1
Canyon Top Ct
6200 FBnC 77450 4094 E4
Canyon Trace Ct
6200 FBnC 77450 4094 B4
E Canyon Trace Dr
12100 HarC 77095 3397 A6
N Canyon Trace Dr
16500 HarC 77095 3397 A7
W Canyon Trace Dr
12000 HarC 77095 3397 A7
Canyon Trail Dr
- HarC 77066 3400 D5
Canyon Tree Ct
11100 FBnC 77469 4092 C7
Canyon Valley Ct
19000 HarC 77377 3254 E2
Canyon Valley Dr
11900 HarC 77377 3254 B1
Canyon View Ct
37800 MtgC 77355 2815 B5
Canyonview Ct
2900 HarC 77450 3954 C7
Canyon Village Trc
- HarC 77396 3407 A7
- HarC 77396 3548 A1
Canyon Vista Ct
19100 HarC 77377 3254 B1
Canyon Vista Ln
11700 HarC 77377 3254 C1
Canyon Walk Ln
26800 HarC 77433 3537 A2
Canyon Whisper Dr
16700 HarC 77429 3396 D1
Canyonwood Park Ct
2400 FBnC 77469 4492 D3
Canyonwood Park Ln
21900 FBnC 77469 4493 A3
22100 FBnC 77469 4492 E3
Canyon Woods Dr
11500 HarC 77377 3109 C7
Canyon Wren Dr
28000 FBnC 77494 3951 D5
Canyon Wy Dr
6600 HarC 77086 3542 B1
Cape Bahamas Ln
18200 NSUB 77058 4507 E6
Cape Blanco
3000 FBnC 77459 4621 B6
Cape Breeze Dr
9700 HarC 77095 3537 E4
9800 HarC 77070 3255 B6
Cape Charles Ln
18600 NSUB 77058 4508 A6
Cape Chestnut Dr
10 WDLD 77381 2821 B6
Cape Clover Tr
- FBnC 77469 4234 D2
Cape Cod Ln
10 HNCV 77024 3960 A2
Cape Colony Dr
- HarC 77049 3828 D1
Cape Coral Ct
800 LGCY 77573 4633 B3
17200 HarC 77095 3537 E6
Cape Cottage Ct
3900 FBnC 77494 4093 C3
23300 HarC 77373 2968 D5
Cape Cottage Ln
700 HarC 77373 2968 E6
7300 FBnC 77469 4094 D7
Capecrest Dr
2800 BzaC 77584 4501 A6
Cape Forest Dr
3300 HOUS 77345 3119 D5
Cape Forward Dr
6300 HarC 77083 4097 B4
Cape Hatteras Dr
5900 HarC 77041 3679 B5
Cape Hatteras Wy
10300 FBnC 77459 4622 A5
Cape Haynnis Dr
12700 HOUS 77048 4374 D2
Cape Henry
8400 FBnC 77459 4621 B5
Cape Henry Ln
6100 HarC 77084 3679 A6
Capehill Dr
300 HOUS 77598 4506 E5
Cape Hope St
15900 HarC 77532 3552 B4
Cape Hyannis Dr
11700 HOUS 77048 4243 D7
11700 HOUS 77048 4374 D1
Cape Jasmine Ct
200 WDLD 77381 2674 A6
Cape Jasmine Pl
10 WDLD 77381 2674 C6
Cape Landing Dr
2300 PRLD 77584 4500 B2
Cape Laurel
12700 HarC 77014 3402 B3
Capella Cir
31200 TMBL 77375 2963 E4
Capella Oaks Ln
300 LGCY 77539 4753 A4
Capella Park Dr
5600 HarC 77379 3112 A5
Capello Dr
5700 HOUS 77035 4240 C5
Cape Lookout Wy
18300 HarC 77346 3408 C1
Cape Province Dr
13200 HOUS 77083 4097 B5
Caperidge Ct
27200 HarC 77336 3121 E3
Caperidge Dr
27200 HarC 77336 3121 E3
Caperton St
600 HOUS 77022 3824 C1
Cape Sable Ct
12500 HarC 77346 3408 D1
Capesbrook Ct
4900 FBnC 77494 4092 D2
Capetown Dr
18500 NSUB 77058 4508 A6
Capeview Cove Ln
- FBnC 77469 4493 A5
Capewalk Dr
2600 HOUS 77054 4242 A2
Capewood Ct
10 WDLD 77381 2821 A5
Capewood Dr
300 LGCY 77573 4632 B5
16600 HarC 77396 3407 E4
Capilano Ct
24600 FBnC 77494 3953 A3
Capistrano St
12300 HOUS 77015 3966 E3
Capistrano Falls Dr
16000 HarC 77546 4506 A5
Capital Ct
3100 PRLD 77584 4501 A3
Capital St
2300 PASD 77502 4247 E1
Capital Heights Blvd
11700 HarC 77065 3539 E2
Capital Park Dr
- HOUS 77041 3819 D1
Capital Park Wy
11000 HOUS 77041 3819 D1
Capitol St
- KATY 77493 3813 C7
600 HOUS 77002 3963 C4
3300 HOUS 77003 3963 E6
3900 HOUS 77003 3964 A6
3900 HOUS 77023 3964 A6
4700 HOUS 77011 3964 B6
7100 HOUS 77011 3965 A7
7200 HOUS 77011 4105 A1
7500 HOUS 77012 4105 A1
N Capitol St
5100 HOUS 77011 3964 C7
5100 HOUS 77023 3964 C7
S Capitol St
4400 HOUS 77003 3964 B6
4400 HOUS 77023 3964 B6
5200 HOUS 77011 3964 C7
W Capitol St
- HOUS 77002 3963 B3
- HOUS 77007 3963 B3
Capitol Landing Ln
22500 HarC 77449 3814 E5
Caplan St
800 LPRT 77571 4251 E4
Caplin St
100 HOUS 77022 3824 C3
1800 HOUS 77026 3824 D3
2800 HOUS 77026 3825 A3
Cappamore St
500 HOUS 77013 3966 B1
Capri Cir
7800 HarC 77095 3539 A7
Capri Ct
1200 LGCY 77573 4632 E3
2200 PRLD 77581 4504 C2
Capri Dr
15900 JRSV 77040 3540 D7
E Capri Dr
2200 PRLD 77581 4504 D2
S Capri Dr
2300 PRLD 77581 4504 D3
Capri Ln
1700 SEBK 77586 4509 D2
Capri St
100 SGLD 77478 4368 A2
11000 HDWV 77024 3959 E1
Caprice Ln
- NSUB 77058 4507 E5
Capricorn Dr
12700 STAF 77477 4238 C7
12700 STAF 77477 4369 D1
Capridge Dr
- HOUS 77048 4375 E4
Capri Isle Ct
2200 HOUS 77077 3957 A7
Capri Pl Ln
1400 PRLD 77581 4504 E2
Caprock Ct
- HarC 77429 3253 A7
Caprock Dr
5000 PRLD 77584 4503 A7
5300 PRLD 77584 4502 E7
15700 HOUS 77598 4506 D4
N Caprock Wy
12400 HarC 77346 3264 C7
S Caprock Wy
12400 HarC 77346 3264 C7
Caprock Canyons Ln
11800 FBnC 77478 4236 C6
Caprock Cove Ln
14200 HarC 77396 3547 D2
Capron St
1100 HOUS 77020 3964 B2
Capshaw Ct
10 WDLD 77385 2676 C4
9400 HarC 77065 3539 D5
Capstan St
1600 HOUS 77062 4507 B1
Capstone Cir
100 WDLD 77381 2674 D7
E Capstone Cir
100 WDLD 77381 2674 E7
N Capstone Cir
- WDLD 77381 2674 D7
W Capstone Cir
- WDLD 77381 2674 D7
Captain Dr
7000 HOUS 77036 4099 B5
Captain Bligh Rd
16700 GLSN 77554 5331 D6
16700 JMAB 77554 5331 D6
Captain Hook Rd
16700 GLSN 77554 5331 E6
16700 JMAB 77554 5331 E6
Captain Kidd Rd
16500 JMAB 77554 5332 A5
16600 JMAB 77554 5331 E6
Captain's Cir
- HOUS 77571 4252 C1
- MRGP 77571 4252 C1
Captains Ct
4400 MSCY 77459 4497 A4
Captains Dr
5000 DKSN 77539 4754 D3
Captains Wk
300 HOUS 77079 3956 E1
Capulet Ct
10 WDLD 77382 2819 A2
Cara Cir
5000 PASD 77505 4248 B4
Cara Pl
4100 HOUS 77025 4241 C3
Caracara Dr
7200 HOUS 77040 3682 A3
Caracas Dr
7200 FBnC 77083 4095 E6
Caradine St
- HOUS 77085 4371 D2
Caradoc Springs Ct
27500 MtgC 77386 2969 E7
Caramel Point Ct
3900 FBnC 77545 4622 D1
Carancahua Reef Dr
4800 GlsC 77539 4634 C5
Caranel Ct
4100 MSCY 77459 4496 C5
Caraquet Ct
30900 MtgC 77386 2969 A1
Caraquet Dr
- MtgC 77385 2823 A7
- MtgC 77386 2823 A7
1200 MtgC 77386 2969 A1
Caravan Dr
10500 HOUS 77031 4239 C3
Caravel Cir
4000 MSCY 77459 4496 D4
Caravel Dr
2000 LGCY 77573 4509 A7
Caravel Ln
6700 MSCY 77459 4496 D4
Caravelle Ct
1300 FBnC 77494 3953 A4
Caravelle St
10 GLSN 77554 5221 C2
Caraway Ct
8300 HarC 77521 3833 C2
Caraway Dr
19900 HarC 77433 3537 A6
Caraway Ln
9500 HOUS 77036 4098 E6
Caraway Lake Dr
5200 HarC 77521 3833 D2
Carbide Ln
7400 HarC 77040 3681 C1
Carbon Canyon Ln
11700 HarC 77377 3109 B7
Carbonear Dr
1500 HarC 77530 3829 C4
Carbridge Dr
16600 HarC 77084 3678 B4
18000 HarC 77084 3677 E5
Carbrook Ct
4700 HarC 77388 3112 C7
Carby Rd
100 HarC 77037 3684 E2
100 HOUS 77037 3684 E2
200 HarC 77037 3685 A2
200 HOUS 77037 3685 A2
E Carby Rd
200 HarC 77037 3684 D2
600 HOUS 77037 3684 E2
W Carby Rd
100 HarC 77037 3684 C2
Cardamon Ln
8300 HarC 77521 3833 D2
Cardiff Rd
12200 HOUS 77076 3685 B2
12400 HOUS 77037 3685 B1
Cardiff Bluff Ln
- FBnC 77494 4092 B1
Cardiff Cliff Ln
14800 HOUS 77053 4373 A4
Cardiff Park Ln
19500 HarC 77094 3955 A3
Cardiff Ranch Ln
4000 FBnC 77494 4092 A1
Cardigan Bay Cir
1200 HarC 77379 3255 C2
Cardin Ln
- HarC 77044 3689 C4
Cardinal Av
1000 SGLD 77478 4368 C4
Cardinal Cir
700 PASD 77502 4247 A1
7200 TXCY 77591 4873 C6
Cardinal Dr
1100 FBnC 77469 4492 A7
1100 FBnC 77469 4616 A1
1300 ALVN 77511 4748 E5
1300 BzaC 77511 4748 E6
1800 LGCY 77573 4631 C6
21900 HarC 77447 3106 A2
22500 HarC 77447 2961 A7
22500 MtgC 77355 2961 A7
Cardinal Ln
2600 HMBL 77396 3406 D4
14100 HOUS 77079 3957 E3
14100 HOUS 77079 3958 A3
22600 HarC 77377 3107 A1
26600 HarC 77493 3813 A3
26600 KATY 77493 3813 A3
Cardinal St
9800 LPRT 77571 4250 B1
Cardinal Tr
15000 MtgC 77302 2680 A3
15400 MtgC 77302 2679 E3
Cardinal Bay
5500 HarC 77041 3679 E7
Cardinal Bay Dr
- PRLD 77584 4500 B2
Cardinal Bend Ln
10 HarC 77070 3399 B1
Cardinal Brook Wy
4500 HOUS 77345 3120 A2
Cardinal Cove Ct
- HarC 77429 3253 E7
Cardinal Creek Ct
14500 HOUS 77062 4379 D7
14600 HOUS 77062 4506 D1
Cardinal Creek Wy
5900 HOUS 77345 3120 C5
Cardinal Elm St
2300 FBnC 77545 4498 C7
Cardinal Flowers Dr
13500 HarC 77429 3397 C2
Cardinal Grove Ct
19100 HarC 77433 3251 E7
Cardinal Lake Rd
- HarC 77084 3677 A5
- HarC 77449 3677 A5
Cardinal Meadow Dr
- STAF 77477 4237 E6
12500 SGLD 77478 4237 D6
12500 STAF 77478 4237 D6
Cardinal Oaks Ln
400 LGCY 77565 4508 E5
Cardinal Point Dr
- HOUS 77339 3117 E7
Cardinal Ridge Cir
2000 FRDW 77546 4629 D4
Cardinal Trail Dr
500 FBnC 77469 4493 A5
Cardine Ln
13200 STFE 77510 4870 E5
Cardono Ln
15800 HOUS 77489 4371 D6
Cardston Ct
12200 HarC 77377 3254 C2
Cardwell Ct
10 SPVL 77055 3820 E7
Cardwell Dr
8800 SPVL 77055 3821 A7
9100 SPVL 77055 3820 E7
Cardwell Ln
8900 SPVL 77055 3820 E7
Carefree Cir
5400 LGCY 77573 4630 D7
Carefree Dr
1200 LGCY 77573 4630 D7
Carelia Ln
17700 HarC 77379 3256 B2
Caren Ct
12400 HOUS 77031 4239 A6
Carew St
5000 HOUS 77096 4101 A7
5100 HOUS 77096 4100 E7
5700 HOUS 77074 4100 B7
7200 HOUS 77074 4099 E7
Carey Ln
100 HarC 77530 3968 E2
200 FRDW 77546 4629 C1
Carey Pl
20300 HarC 77073 3403 C1
Carey St
5300 HOUS 77028 3825 D2
Careybrook Ln
- HarC 77449 3676 E7
- HarC 77449 3815 E1
Carey Chase Dr
7500 HOUS 77489 4371 B3
Carey Ridge Ct
200 HarC 77094 3955 B1
Careywood Dr
6900 HarC 77040 3681 C3
12800 SGLD 77478 4237 C5
Cargill St
8500 HOUS 77029 3965 D4
9700 HOUS 77029 3966 A4
Cargo Rd
- HOUS 77032 3404 E6
Cargo Bay
8700 HOUS 77029 3965 D7
Caribbean Ln
11000 HOUS 77075 4377 C3
11000 HOUS 77089 4377 C3
Caribe Ln
1400 HOUS 77047 4373 D5
Caribou Ct
8000 CmbC 77520 3835 D3
10400 FBnC 77459 4621 E6
10400 FBnC 77459 4622 A6
Caribou St
5100 HarC 77389 2967 A5
Caribou Cove
10300 FBnC 77459 4622 A6
Caribou Cove Ct
2900 FBnC 77459 4622 A6
Caribou Ridge Dr
19100 HarC 77375 3254 D1
19200 HarC 77375 3109 D7
Caridas Rd
12300 HOUS 77071 4370 E1
12300 HOUS 77085 4370 E1
Carillion Pns
- WDLD 77381 2674 E7
Carillo Dr
5500 HOUS 77091 3683 B6
Carina Ct
2300 LGCY 77573 4508 B5
Caringorm Dr
16500 HarC 77084 3678 C7
Carino Dr
5500 HOUS 77091 3683 B6
Carino Strada Dr
24200 FBnC 77469 4093 A7
Cario Dr
700 HarC 77530 3829 E7
700 HarC 77530 3830 A7
Caris St
4800 HOUS 77091 3683 A6
Carisbrook Ln
22000 HarC 77338 3260 C2
Carissa Ct
6300 FBnC 77479 4367 B5
Caritas Cir
9600 HarC 77065 3539 D4
Cark Av
3600 STFE 77510 4870 C6
3700 STFE 77517 4870 C6
4700 STFE 77517 4986 C1
Carl Blvd
16800 HOUS 77060 3403 C6
Carl Ct
2300 STAF 77477 4370 A4
Carl Ln
300 BKHV 77024 3959 C4
Carl St
100 PASD 77506 4107 A3
800 HOUS 77009 3963 C1
1100 HarC 77039 3545 B1
1600 HarC 77032 3545 C1
4100 GlsC 77518 4634 C3
Carla Ct
14600 MtgC 77302 2678 D7
14600 MtgC 77302 2824 D1
Carla Ln
23500 MtgC 77357 2974 A2
Carla St
11500 HOUS 77076 3685 A3
Carla Wy
12900 HarC 77429 3398 D4
Carlang St
100 HarC 77530 3969 A2
Carla Oaks Dr
- HarC 77449 3815 D2
Carlaris Ct
12900 HarC 77041 3679 D3
Carleen Rd
2300 HOUS 77018 3683 B7
4600 HOUS 77092 3683 A7
Carlene Rd
25900 MtgC 77355 2962 D3
Carley Cove Ct
1800 MtgC 77386 2969 C7
Carley Cove Ln
28500 MtgC 77386 2969 C6
Carlford Cir
3000 HOUS 77018 3822 D4
Carlie Wy
100 FBnC 77477 4369 C3
100 STAF 77477 4369 C3
Carlin Bend Ln
9200 HarC 77095 3538 B4
Carlingford Ln
- HOUS 77079 3957 E1
Carlingwood Dr
- HarC 77070 3398 D1
Carlisle Ct
4200 BYTN 77521 3973 E2
Carlisle Ln
5800 GlsC 77510 4986 D3
6100 LGCY 77573 4630 C7
Carlisle St
- MtgC 77385 2677 A7
500 RSBG 77471 4490 D4
3000 LPRT 77571 4251 E7
3000 LPRT 77571 4382 E1
8500 HOUS 77017 4105 D5
Carlisle Park Cir
300 LGCY 77573 4630 C7
Carlisle Park Ln
16000 HarC 77084 3678 C5
Carlisle Terrace Ct
- FBnC 77469 4365 A6
Carlon St
3700 SSPL 77005 4101 D4
Carlos St
8500 HOUS 77029 3826 C6
Carlos Creek Dr
25700 FBnC 77469 4092 C7
Carlota Ct
10 HOUS 77074 4100 B7
9000 HOUS 77074 4240 B1
10600 HOUS 77096 4240 B3
Carlotta Ct
12700 GLSN 77554 5220 B7
Carlow Ln
9000 LPRT 77571 4249 E3
9800 LPRT 77571 4250 B3
Carl Pickering Memorial Dr
9800 CNRO 77303 2238 C7
9800 MtgC 77303 2238 C7
10200 CNRO 77303 2239 A6
Carl Rd Ext
6800 HarC 77373 3116 B6
Carlsbad Ct
10 HOUS 77085 4371 B1
N Carlsbad Ln
1800 DRPK 77536 4109 D6
S Carlsbad Ln
1800 DRPK 77536 4109 D6
Carlsbad St
- JRSV 77040 3540 C7
- JRSV 77040 3680 C1
12000 HOUS 77035 4240 B7
12000 HOUS 77085 4240 B7
12000 HOUS 77085 4371 B2
Carlson Ln
3700 HOUS 77047 4374 C1
3800 HOUS 77047 4243 C7
Carlsway Rd
17400 HarC 77073 3259 A3
Carlton Dr
10800 HOUS 77047 4243 C6
Carlton Rd
24100 MtgC 77365 2974 A7
Carlton Sq
10 FBnC 77459 4621 C7
Carlton St
500 CNRO 77301 2383 E3
1300 BYTN 77520 4112 D1
Carlton Oaks St
2000 FBnC 77469 4232 D5
12400 HarC 77377 3254 C5
Carlton Park Ct
10 PNPV 77024 3959 D5
Carlton Vale Ct
16400 HarC 77377 3254 B5
Carlton Woods Dr
- WDLD 77382 2819 E1
10 WDLD 77382 2673 E7
Carlyle Pl
10 WDLD 77382 2820 A2
Carly Park Wy
6500 HarC 77084 3678 A3
Carmalee St
9600 HOUS 77075 4377 C4
Carmel Cir
4600 PASD 77505 4249 A6
8000 HarC 77095 3539 A6
Carmel Ct
- GLSN 77554 5548 B1
Carmel Dr
10 BzaC 77583 4624 C5
Carmel St
2400 HOUS 77091 3683 B4
Carmel Breeze Dr
19800 FBnC 77469 4234 E2
Carmel Chase Ct
10 MNVL 77583 4624 C4
Carmel Cove Ct
6000 HarC 77041 3679 E5
Carmel Dale Ln
12300 HOUS 77089 4378 C7
Carmeline Dr
10 WDLD 77382 2819 B2
Carmelite Ct
20100 HarC 77450 3954 E2
Carmella Dr
600 PASD 77506 4106 E3
Carmel Ridge Wy
4000 PASD 77503 4108 C7
Carmel Valley Dr
3100 MSCY 77459 4496 E2
20900 HarC 77449 3676 C2
Carmelwood Ct
8500 HarC 77338 3262 A3
Carmelwood Ln
8300 HarC 77338 3261 E3
8300 HarC 77338 3262 B2
Carmel Woods Dr
2700 SEBK 77586 4382 B6
Carmen Ln
100 FBnC 77469 4493 E7
23600 MtgC 77365 2973 D6
Carmen St
4600 HOUS 77033 4243 D4
4600 HOUS 77051 4243 D4
5200 HOUS 77033 4244 A4
Carmencita Wy
10200 HOUS 77075 4376 E2
Carmichael Cir
- ALVN 77511 4749 C2
Carmichael Ct
200 LGCY 77573 4633 A1
Carmie St
1100 ALVN 77511 4867 A3
Carmilenda St
13500 HarC 77037 3545 A6
Carmine Oak Ct
20600 HarC 77346 3264 E4
Carmita St
1400 MtgC 77385 2822 D3
Carmona Ln
5000 PRLD 77584 4503 A4
5500 PRLD 77584 4502 E4
Carnarvon Dr
100 HOUS 77024 3960 E2
100 HOUS 77024 3961 A2
Carnation Ct
7100 HarC 77521 3832 A5
Carnation St
800 KATY 77493 3952 A1
900 KATY 77493 3813 A7
3400 HOUS 77022 3823 E3
Carndall Rd
- LPRT 77571 4250 A3
Carnden Ln
9300 FBnC 77459 4621 C5
Carnegie Ln
- SGLD 77479 4495 B3
Carnegie St
- BYTN 77520 3972 C7
600 BYTN 77520 4112 C1
2800 WUNP 77005 4102 A4
3000 WUNP 77005 4101 E4
3600 SSPL 77005 4101 E4
Carnegie Park Ct
3800 PASD 77058 4380 E7
Carnelian Ct
4400 HOUS 77072 4098 A4
Carnelian Dr
4300 HOUS 77072 4098 B4
Carnes St
300 CNRO 77301 2384 A4
Carnes Woods Ln
14000 TMBL 77375 2963 E5
Carneys Point Ln
6200 HarC 77379 3111 D3
Carnoustie Ct
1200 FBnC 77494 3953 A3
2900 SGLD 77479 4495 A2
Carnoustie Dr
2800 MSCY 77459 4497 A2
Carol Ct
- HarC 77040 3541 A7
Carol Dr
26900 HarC 77336 3121 D4
Carol Ln
800 BLAR 77401 4100 D6
4900 HOUS 77021 4104 A5
12000 MtgC 77362 2963 B1

Houston Street Index

STREET
Block City ZIP Map# Grid

Carol Ln
26200 MtgC 77372 2683 B3
Carol Rd
21600 MtgC 77357 2974 D2
Carola Forest Dr
12100 HarC 77044 3548 E6
Carolane Tr
10 BKHV 77024 3959 C2
10 HDWV 77024 3959 C2
Carolchase Cir
15200 HOUS 77489 4371 A4
Carolchase Dr
15000 HOUS 77489 4371 A4
Carolcrest Cir
14100 HOUS 77079 3958 A4
14500 HOUS 77079 3957 C3
Carolcrest Dr
14200 HOUS 77079 3957 D3
Carolcrest St
14800 HOUS 77079 3957 B3
Caroldean
- FBnC 77494 3952 C7
Carole Ln
10000 BYTN 77520 3835 B6
Carolina Av
1700 LGCY 77573 4632 C6
N Carolina Av
30000 MtgC 77354 2818 B1
Carolina Ct
1500 FRDW 77546 4629 E2
N Carolina Pk
600 MtgC 77302 2530 A5
S Carolina Pk
500 MtgC 77302 2530 A5
Carolina St
700 KATY 77494 3952 A1
1700 BYTN 77520 4112 A1
6800 KATY 77493 3952 A1
16400 MtgC 77372 2682 A5
N Carolina St
10 HOUS 77029 3965 E7
200 HOUS 77029 3966 A6
400 GNPK 77547 3966 A6
Carolina Wy
2600 HOUS 77030 4102 A4
2600 WUNP 77005 4102 A4
3300 FBnC 77469 4233 C7
Carolina Cherry Ct
26000 HarC 77389 2966 C1
Carolina Cherry Ln
6900 HarC 77389 2966 C1
Carolina Falls Ln
14600 HarC 77433 3395 C1
Carolina Green Dr
21500 HarC 77433 3250 E5
Carolina Grove Ln
1400 HarC 77073 3403 C2
Carolina Hills Dr
- HarC 77433 3251 D7
14900 HarC 77433 3395 D1
Carolina Hollow Ln
- HOUS 77044 3550 A2
Carolina Oaks Dr
15100 HarC 77433 3251 C7
Carolina Shores Ln
- LGCY 77573 4630 E7
Caroline Ct
4200 SGLD 77479 4494 E2
Caroline St
100 HarC 77373 3114 A1
200 HOUS 77002 3963 B6
400 HarC 77373 3113 E1
700 HOUS 77010 3963 C5
1600 GlsC 77539 4633 D6
1600 LGCY 77539 4633 D5
1600 TXCY 77539 4633 D6
2200 DKSN 77539 4633 D7
2200 HOUS 77004 3963 B6
4300 HOUS 77004 4103 A1
4700 PASD 77586 4383 B4
4900 HOUS 77004 4102 E1
5800 HOUS 77030 4102 E2
6200 HTCK 77563 4988 E3
Caroline Chase Ct
22400 FBnC 77494 4093 D2
Caroline Cove Ln
22300 FBnC 77450 4094 D2
Caroline Green Ct
6100 HarC 77373 3261 A2
Caroline Oaks Ct
20200 HarC 77433 3251 D6
Caroline Park Ln
2200 MtgC 77386 2969 D6
Caroline Shore Wy
11900 HarC 77089 4504 B1
Caroline Wy Ct
20300 HarC 77073 3403 C1
Caroling Oaks Ct
19700 HarC 77346 3264 D4
Carol Lee Ln
1700 CNRO 77301 2384 D5
Carol Lynn Dr
600 MSCY 77489 4370 B3
600 STAF 77477 4370 B3
600 STAF 77489 4370 B3
Carols St
13000 MtgC 77306 2534 B6
Carols Wy Cir
12200 HarC 77070 3254 C7
Carols Wy Dr
14600 HarC 77070 3398 C1
14700 HarC 77070 3254 C7
Carolton Ct
10 MtgC 77355 2814 E3
Carolton Wy
17800 HarC 77073 3404 B2
Carolwood Dr
7800 HOUS 77028 3687 B7
Carolyn Av
- GlsC 77565 4509 D6
500 KMAH 77565 4509 D5
1000 HMBL 77338 3262 E7
1300 HMBL 77338 3263 A7
Carolyn Ct
9800 HarC 77379 3110 D4
Carolyn Ln
6000 FBnC 77469 4232 E7
Carolyn St
100 LMQU 77568 4874 A7
800 TXCY 77591 4874 A7
1100 DRPK 77536 4109 C5
3000 GlsC 77518 4634 B2
7800 GlsC 77517 4870 C3
7900 STFE 77510 4870 C3
7900 STFE 77517 4870 C3
Carothers St
3300 HOUS 77087 4105 A7
6800 HOUS 77028 3686 D7

Carothers St
6800 HOUS 77028 3825 E1
7000 HOUS 77028 3826 A1
Carousel Cir
5400 BYTN 77521 3972 A1
Carousel Ct
13300 HarC 77041 3679 C6
Carousel Ln
8800 HOUS 77080 3820 D3
Carousel Creek Ct
18500 HarC 77429 3252 B7
Carpenter Av
1300 PASD 77502 4246 D2
Carpenter Rd
- HMBL 77396 3406 C2
- HOUS 77396 3406 C2
1000 HMBL 77396 3407 A2
7100 MNVL 77578 4625 E4
7100 MNVL 77578 4626 A5
14100 MtgC 77302 2532 C7
Carpenters Landing Wy
- HarC 77015 3829 C4
- HarC 77049 3829 B3
Carpet Bagger Dr
19200 HarC 77449 3677 B3
Carr St
1300 HOUS 77020 3963 E2
1500 HOUS 77026 3963 E2
3200 HOUS 77026 3824 E7
Carrack Turn Dr
16700 HarC 77546 4506 A6
Carraige Creek Dr
- HarC 77064 3541 E5
Carrau
5500 HarC 77041 3680 C5
Carraway Ct
15000 HarC 77429 3253 D4
Carraway Ln
8700 MtgC 77354 2818 C6
Carrell St
200 TMBL 77375 2964 C6
Carrera Ct
2800 LGCY 77573 4633 A3
Carriage Ct
1100 SEBK 77586 4382 E7
2000 FBnC 77469 4365 C2
13600 HarC 77044 3689 D3
18600 NSUB 77058 4508 A6
Carriage Dr
1200 FBnC 77469 4365 C2
Carriage Ln
- NSUB 77058 4508 A6
100 MtgC 77385 2676 B3
2200 LMQU 77568 4989 E2
2500 STAF 77477 4369 E4
2500 STAF 77477 4370 A4
3400 BYTN 77521 3972 A2
18200 NSUB 77058 4507 E5
Carriage Run E
1300 MtgC 77384 2529 A6
Carriage Run W
1300 MtgC 77384 2529 A5
Carriage Wy
1700 SGLD 77478 4368 D5
Carriage Bend Dr
5100 FBnC 77450 4094 B2
Carriage Brook Wy
1900 HOUS 77062 4507 E1
Carriage Creek Dr
8300 HarC 77064 3541 E5
Carriage Creek Ln
300 FRDW 77546 4629 E3
1900 FRDW 77546 4630 A3
Carriage Crossing Ln
17800 HarC 77429 3396 C1
Carriage Dale Ct
17100 HarC 77379 3256 A3
Carriage Glen Dr
12600 HarC 77377 3254 A3
Carriage Hill Dr
- HOUS 77042 3958 A4
11800 HOUS 77077 3958 A4
12400 HOUS 77077 3957 D5
Carriage Hills Blvd
100 MtgC 77384 2675 A2
900 MtgC 77384 2529 A7
Carriage House Dr
3400 FBnC 77469 4234 D7
Carriage House Wy
10 CNRO 77384 2675 E3
Carriage Lake Dr
11100 HarC 77065 3539 D2
Carriage Lamp Ln
2400 MtgC 77384 2529 A5
Carriage Manor Ln
26900 HarC 77339 3118 D5
Carriage Oak Cir
12100 HarC 77346 3408 C1
Carriage Park Dr
14700 HarC 77396 3548 D1
14900 HarC 77396 3407 D7
Carriage Park Row
3900 FBnC 77459 4622 B4
Carriage Pines Ct
10 WDLD 77381 2821 C3
Carriage Point Dr
9000 FBnC 77479 4494 C4
20500 HarC 77073 3259 D4
Carriage Ridge Dr
11900 HarC 77070 3399 C6
Carriage Ridge Ln
2400 MtgC 77384 2529 A5
Carriage Run Ct
1700 FBnC 77545 4622 D1
Carriage Walk Ln
13700 HOUS 77077 3957 A4
Carriagewood Ct
6700 RSBG 77469 4493 A7
Carrick St
9200 HOUS 77022 3685 A6
Carrick Bend Dr
25000 HarC 77389 2966 C2
Carrie
1600 WALR 77484 3102 A6
Carrie Ln
7400 DRPK 77536 4249 B2
7800 BzaC 77584 4627 C3
22300 MtgC 77355 2960 C3
22300 MtgC 77447 2960 C3
Carrie St
100 HOUS 77047 4373 A3
Carrie Cove Ct
3000 MtgC 77386 2970 C6
Carrigan Pl
14000 HarC 77083 4237 A1
Carrige Rdg
- HarC 77070 3399 C6

Carrington Ct
4900 PRLD 77584 4502 A5
6600 FBnC 77479 4367 B7
Carrington Dr
30700 MtgC 77354 2672 B6
Carrington Ln
13800 HarC 77429 3397 D2
Carrington Ridge Ln
6700 HarC 77346 3408 E3
Carrizo Fall Ct
6500 HarC 77041 3679 E4
Carrizo Springs Ct
2900 HarC 77449 3815 D4
N Carrol Ln
26600 SGCH 77355 2961 B2
S Carrol Ln
26500 SGCH 77355 2961 B2
Carroll Dr
2000 PRLD 77581 4502 D1
Carroll St
1900 HOUS 77030 4102 D5
N Carroll St
100 LPRT 77571 4251 E2
S Carroll St
100 LPRT 77571 4252 A3
Carroll Lake Dr
17100 HarC 77379 3255 E4
Carroll Pl Ln
17900 FBnC 77469 4095 C7
Carrollton Ct
10500 FBnC 77459 4622 A5
Carrollton Creek Ct
5700 HarC 77084 3678 E4
Carrollton Creek Ln
16700 HarC 77084 3678 C6
Carrolton St
2700 HOUS 77023 4104 C3
Carrot St
18400 HarC 77379 3112 B7
18400 HarC 77379 3257 B1
Carrswold Dr
12100 HOUS 77071 4239 D6
Carruth Ln
13400 HarC 77083 4097 A5
Carsa Ln
13600 HarC 77014 3401 D2
Carsen Bnd
14700 HarC 77429 3253 E7
Carsen Bend Dr
15000 HarC 77049 3829 A3
Carsen Spring Ct
20800 HarC 77449 3676 D3
Carsey Ln
10 PNPV 77024 3959 E4
Carshalton Ct
17100 HarC 77084 3678 A4
Carson Av
11100 PRLD 77583 4500 D6
Carson Cir
16200 MSCY 77071 4370 C1
Carson Ct
3500 PRLD 77583 4500 D6
Carson Dr
800 MtgC 77354 2673 A2
2600 KATY 77493 3813 C4
Carson Rd
6100 HOUS 77048 4375 D1
Carsondale St
- SHUS 77587 4246 B2
9000 HOUS 77017 4246 A2
Carson Field Ln
11300 HarC 77433 3396 A7
Carson Hill Ln
5100 HOUS 77092 3682 A7
Carsonmont Ln
9400 HarC 77070 3399 D5
Carson Ridge Dr
400 MtgC 77386 2968 D1
Carstairs Dr
11200 HarC 77070 3255 A7
Carstone Ct
1500 HarC 77450 3953 E4
Cartage Knolls Dr
13000 HarC 77429 3397 A2
Cartagena Dr
4000 PRLD 77581 4504 D7
5500 HOUS 77035 4240 C5
Carta Valley Ln
5300 FBnC 77469 4493 A6
Carter Av
7000 HTCK 77563 4989 B5
Carter Dr
6300 HTCK 77563 4989 B6
Carter Ln
1900 LMQU 77568 4989 E1
1900 LMQU 77568 4990 A3
Carter Rd
5300 HOUS 77048 4375 B4
10100 HarC 77070 3255 A5
10200 HOUS 77070 3255 B5
20700 MtgC 77372 2535 A4
26400 MtgC 77354 2817 E5
Carter St
2100 HOUS 77008 3823 E5
3000 PASD 77503 4108 A3
3000 PASD 77506 4108 A3
Carter Gate Dr
22700 HarC 77373 3115 E7
Carter Moir Ln
22500 HarC 77449 3814 D5
Carters Grv
100 MtgC 77302 2530 C7
Carters Grove Ln
- HOUS 77449 3815 A6
1500 HarC 77449 3815 A6
Carters Lake Dr
3800 FBnC 77469 4234 C6
Cartersville St
300 HOUS 77029 3966 A6
400 GNPK 77029 3966 A6
400 GNPK 77547 3966 A6
Cart Gate Ct
14500 HarC 77095 3679 A1
Cart Gate Dr
7200 HarC 77095 3679 A1
7500 HarC 77095 3539 A7
Cartgate Ln
10 WDLD 77381 2820 C2
Carthage Dr
10200 HOUS 77089 4377 D3
Carthegena Wy
3200 GLSN 77554 5219 D7
3200 GLSN 77554 5332 D1
Carton Cross
- HarC 77493 3675 A4
E Cartouche Cir
10 WDLD 77382 2820 B1

W Cartouche Cir
10 WDLD 77382 2820 B1
Cartouche Dr
- WDLD 77382 2820 A1
Cartwright Rd
- MtgC 77301 2385 B3
1600 MSCY 77489 4370 A7
1700 CNRO 77301 2384 E1
1700 CNRO 77303 2384 E1
1700 MtgC 77303 2384 E1
1900 CNRO 77301 2385 B3
1900 CNRO 77303 2385 B3
1900 MtgC 77303 2385 B3
2400 MSCY 77459 4370 B7
3200 MSCY 77459 4369 C7
4700 SGLD 77478 4369 C7
Cartwright Rd FM-3345
1600 MSCY 77489 4370 A7
2400 MSCY 77459 4370 B7
3100 MSCY 77459 4369 E7
Cartwright Rd LP-336
- MtgC 77301 2385 B3
1700 CNRO 77301 2384 E1
1700 CNRO 77303 2384 E1
1700 MtgC 77303 2384 E1
1900 CNRO 77301 2385 B3
1900 CNRO 77303 2385 B3
1900 MtgC 77303 2385 B3
W Cartwright Rd
300 CNRO 77301 2384 A2
Cartwright Rdg
25900 MtgC 77380 2821 A7
Caruso Forest Dr
5800 HarC 77088 3542 D7
Caruthers Ln
200 HNCV 77024 3960 A3
Carved Rock Dr
6600 HOUS 77085 4371 C1
Carved Stone Ln
8700 FBnC 77469 4234 E1
Carvel Cir
7300 HOUS 77072 4097 C6
Carvel Ln
6700 HOUS 77074 4100 A6
7100 HOUS 77074 4099 E6
9200 HOUS 77036 4099 A6
11600 HOUS 77072 4098 A6
12700 HOUS 77072 4097 D6
13100 HOUS 77083 4097 B6
13400 HarC 77083 4097 B6
Carver
24000 HarC 77336 3267 A2
Carver Av
1500 RHMD 77469 4364 D7
5900 TXCY 77591 4873 D6
19500 HOUS 77338 3262 A5
19700 HarC 77338 3262 A5
Carver Dr
6600 HTCK 77563 4989 B4
Carver Rd
6200 HOUS 77091 3683 C4
6800 HOUS 77088 3683 C4
Carver St
100 BYTN 77520 3974 B1
800 BYTN 77520 4112 D1
Cary Ln
1500 HarC 77521 3834 C7
Cary St
2800 HOUS 77003 3964 A4
Carya Cir
3700 SGLD 77479 4495 E2
Cary Creek Dr
3800 BYTN 77521 3973 D2
Cary Douglas Dr
31700 HarC 77447 3250 A6
Casa Ct
1600 ALVN 77511 4867 A3
Casa Ln
100 DKSN 77539 4754 A1
Casaba Ct
13700 HarC 77429 3398 A1
Casablanca
6800 HOUS 77048 4244 D7
Casa Blanca Cir
9300 HarC 77433 3537 B4
Casablanca Dr
6600 HOUS 77088 3542 B7
Casade Hill Ln
10400 HarC 77064 3541 D1
Casa del Lago Dr
4100 MSCY 77459 4497 C4
Casa del Monte Dr
6600 HarC 77083 4096 B4
Casa del Sol
7800 HarC 77375 2965 E5
7800 HarC 77389 2965 E5
7800 HarC 77389 2966 A5
Casa Felice Ct
- FBnC 77053 4498 D2
Casa Grande Dr
300 HOUS 77060 3544 D2
Casa Grande St
5000 DKSN 77539 4754 C4
Casa Loma Dr
9700 HOUS 77041 3681 B7
Casa Mara
- SEBK 77586 4383 B6
Casa Rio Cir
2100 DKSN 77539 4754 A4
Casa Tejas Ln
300 HarC 77532 3266 D6
Cascada Dr
- HOUS 77532 3266 B6
Cascade Av
- PASD 77506 4106 E7
1200 PASD 77502 4106 E7
Cascade Cir
17300 HarC 77095 3537 E2
Cascade Ct
1800 FBnC 77479 4493 E4
37000 MtgC 77354 2670 D5
Cascade Rdg
900 HarC 77494 3953 D3
Cascade St
500 BLAR 77401 4101 A5
Cascade Basin Falls
9100 HarC 77375 2965 C4
Cascade Bay Dr
14600 HarC 77377 2963 D7
Cascade Bend Ln
14800 HarC 77429 3396 B1
Cascade Canyon Dr
- WDLD 77382 2819 E3
Cascade Caverns Ct
- HarC 77044 3549 C3
- HarC 77429 3253 C5
Cascade Caverns Ln
- HarC 77044 3549 C3

Cascade Creek Dr
- HarC 77494 3953 D3
- HOUS 77345 3119 C3
700 HarC 77450 3953 D3
3100 HOUS 77339 3119 C3
Cascade Falls
700 HOUS 77373 3113 E3
Cascade Falls Dr
1300 FRDW 77546 4629 C6
14100 HOUS 77062 4379 E6
Cascade Glen Dr
- FBnC 77494 3953 B6
Cascade Hills Dr
10200 HarC 77064 3541 C1
Cascade Hollow Ln
21900 HarC 77379 3111 C1
Cascade House Ct
9600 HarC 77396 3407 C2
Cascade House Dr
- HarC 77338 3407 C2
- HarC 77396 3407 C2
Cascade Oaks Ct
4100 HarC 77084 3816 C1
Cascade Pines Dr
100 HarC 77049 3829 A4
Cascade Point Dr
15600 HarC 77084 3678 E6
15600 HarC 77084 3679 A6
Cascadera Dr
5900 HarC 77086 3542 D4
N Cascades Ln
17300 HarC 77346 3408 C3
Cascade Springs Ct
2800 BzaC 77578 4501 B6
Cascade Springs Dr
3400 BzaC 77578 4501 A7
22100 FBnC 77494 4093 D4
Cascade Springs Pl
10 WDLD 77381 2821 A2
Cascade Timbers Ln
18400 HarC 77377 3254 A2
Cascade Woods Ln
26800 HarC 77433 3537 A1
Cascadia Dr
3400 HarC 77082 4096 B3
Cascadia Knoll Ct
12900 HarC 77346 3264 E7
Cascading Brook Ct
20600 HarC 77433 3251 B6
Cascading Brook Wy
15500 HarC 77433 3251 B6
Cascase Hollow Ln
8600 HarC 77095 3537 E5
Cascet Ct
700 HarC 77450 3954 D1
Cascina Ct
- FBnC 77053 4498 D2
Case St
3800 SSPL 77005 4101 D3
4100 WUNP 77005 4101 C3
Casemont Dr
4700 HarC 77388 3257 C1
Caserta Dr
- HarC 77070 3399 B2
Caseta Dr
15000 HOUS 77082 4096 C1
Casey Cir
4000 FBnC 77479 4366 D7
Casey Ct
6800 PRLD 77584 4502 C5
Casey Dr
- BzaC 77511 4748 C3
700 HarC 77530 3829 E7
Casey Rd
5000 FBnC 77583 4622 A4
5600 GlsC 77517 4986 C4
5600 HTCK 77517 4986 C3
27700 MtgC 77357 2829 E5
31700 HarC 77357 2830 A7
Casey St
400 BYTN 77520 4112 E1
5100 LMQU 77568 4872 E6
Casey Creek Ct
19300 FBnC 77469 4094 E2
Cash Dr
5200 KATY 77493 3813 D6
Cash Rd
9800 STAF 77477 4369 E1
Cashel Cir
4600 HarC 77069 3401 A1
N Cashel Cir
4600 HarC 77069 3401 A1
Cashel Castle Dr
4600 HarC 77069 3257 A7
Cashel Cove Ct
7200 FBnC 77469 4094 E2
Cashel Forest Dr
14000 HarC 77066 3401 A1
14000 HarC 77069 3401 A1
14300 HarC 77069 3256 E7
14300 HarC 77069 3257 A7
Cashel Glen Dr
4600 HarC 77068 3257 A7
4600 HarC 77069 3257 A7
4700 HarC 77069 3256 E7
N Cashel Oak Dr
14200 HarC 77069 3257 A7
S Cashel Oak Dr
- HarC 77069 3400 D2
4700 HarC 77069 3257 A7
4700 HarC 77069 3401 A1
Cashel Park Ln
16000 HarC 77084 3678 C5
Cashel Point Ln
15800 HarC 77084 3678 C5
Cashel Spring Dr
4600 HarC 77069 3257 A7
Cashel Wood Dr
14200 HarC 77069 3257 A7
14200 HarC 77069 3401 A1
Cashmere Wy
3700 PRLD 77584 4502 D6
Cash Oaks Dr
6200 HarC 77379 3257 A4
Casita Dr
7000 MtgC 77354 2673 A2
Caslyn Dr
1400 RSBG 77471 4491 C5
Cason St
2600 HOUS 77030 4102 A4
2600 WUNP 77005 4102 A4
3100 WUNP 77005 4101 E4
Casper Ct
600 HarC 77373 3114 A7
700 MtgC 77302 2530 C6
Casper Dr
18700 HarC 77373 3114 A7
18700 HarC 77373 3259 A1

Caspersen Dr
1600 JTCY 77029 3966 D3
Caspian Dr
- HarC 77346 3264 B7
Caspian Ln
1000 HarC 77090 3258 B3
Cass Ct
27200 MtgC 77386 3115 C1
Cassandra Ln
12000 HarC 77064 3399 D6
Cassandra Park St
16000 HarC 77379 3256 D5
Casselberry Dr
24600 MtgC 77365 2973 A7
24600 MtgC 77365 3118 A1
Cassia Cir
11800 HarC 77065 3398 D6
Cassidy Pl
4800 HarC 77066 3401 A1
Cassidy Creek Ct
8300 HarC 77095 3539 B6
Cassidy Park Ln
4100 FBnC 77450 4094 A1
Cassina Dr
17400 HarC 77388 3257 D1
Cassina Ln
17700 HarC 77388 3257 D1
18300 HarC 77388 3112 D7
Cassini Ct
2700 MtgC 77381 2821 D2
22100 FBnC 77469 4093 E7
Cassini Dr
13300 HarC 77044 3689 C5
Cassius Ct
2500 RMFT 77357 2829 B2
Cassowary Ct
3100 HarC 77373 3114 E6
Cassowary Dr
200 MtgC 77385 2676 D4
Cassowary Ln
10 WDLD 77380 2822 B7
Cast Ct
800 HarC 77532 3552 A2
Castaway Ct
15900 HarC 77532 3552 A4
Castaway Ln
15700 HOUS 77044 3409 A5
Castaway St
1600 TKIS 77554 5106 B4
Castell Manor Dr
2200 FBnC 77494 3951 D5
Castilian Dr
13400 HarC 77015 3828 D5
13400 HOUS 77015 3828 D5
Castille Ln
11200 HOUS 77082 4098 C2
Casting Springs Wy
1000 HarC 77373 3114 A3
Castle
2500 WALR 77484 3101 E6
Castle Ct
1300 HOUS 77006 4102 D1
1600 HOUS 77098 4102 C1
2900 PRLD 77581 4503 D4
Castle Dr
2000 LGCY 77573 4631 B6
4000 STFE 77510 4870 E7
4000 STFE 77510 4871 A7
Castle Ln
3100 SGLD 77478 4369 A2
3100 STAF 77478 4369 A2
24900 WlrC 77447 2959 D1
Castle Pl
2500 STAF 77477 4369 E4
Castle Rd
29200 HarC 77484 2957 D5
29200 HarC 77484 2958 A5
Castle Arc Ct
27100 HarC 77339 3118 C3
Castlebar Ct
400 HarC 77015 3829 A7
Castlebar Ln
- MSCY 77459 4369 C5
Castlebay Ct
3300 PRLD 77584 4501 E5
Castle Bay Dr
2200 LGCY 77573 4509 A6
Castlebay Dr
6500 HOUS 77092 3682 C6
Castle Beach Ct
2100 LGCY 77573 4509 A6
Castle Bend Dr
20600 HarC 77450 3954 D4
Castle Bluff Ln
- HOUS 77044 3550 B3
13800 BzaC 77583 4623 D4
Castlebridge Dr
12100 HarC 77065 3539 E6
12200 JRSV 77065 3539 E5
Castlebrook Ct
3400 SGLD 77478 4368 E5
Castlebrook St
5000 HarC 77389 2967 A7
Castlebury Ln
20200 FBnC 77469 4094 C5
Castlecliff Ln
26800 MtgC 77339 3118 B5
Castlecombe Dr
13200 HarC 77044 3549 D2
Castle Combe Wy
1300 HOUS 77339 3264 A1
Castle Cove Ln
600 LGCY 77573 4633 C2
Castle Creek Ct
- LGCY 77573 4631 A4
Castle Creek Dr
1600 MSCY 77489 4370 D4
Castlecreek Ln
5000 HOUS 77053 4372 A6
Castle Crest Ct
8200 FBnC 77083 4096 D7
Castle Crest Dr
9800 HarC 77083 4237 B1
Castle Ct Pl
4400 HOUS 77006 4102 D1
Castledale Dr
1000 HarC 77037 3685 A1
1000 HOUS 77037 3685 A1
2600 HarC 77093 3685 E1
3100 HarC 77093 3546 A7
Castle Falls Ct
6400 HarC 77449 3677 D3
Castle Falls Dr
3600 BzaC 77578 4501 A7
3700 BzaC 77578 4625 A1
Castleford St
8100 HOUS 77040 3681 D5

Castle Forest Dr
30200 MtgC 77386 2969 E2
Castle Fraser Dr
16500 HarC 77084 3678 C6
Castlegap Ct
19700 HarC 77379 3110 B5
Castlegap Dr
9300 HarC 77379 3110 D6
Castle Gardens Ct
21000 HarC 77449 3815 A6
Castle Gardens Ln
2100 HarC 77449 3815 B6
Castle Gate Dr
15100 FBnC 77083 4096 C7
Castlegate Ln
100 HarC 77065 3539 E5
100 JRSV 77065 3539 E5
Castle Glen Dr
1200 HarC 77015 3829 B6
Castlegory Ct
14000 HarC 77015 3829 A5
Castlegory Rd
- HarC 77049 3829 A4
100 HarC 77015 3829 A5
N Castlegory Rd
- HarC 77015 3829 A4
- HarC 77049 3829 A4
S Castlegreen Cir
10 WDLD 77381 2820 C2
Castlegreen Dr
19900 HarC 77388 3113 A4
20000 HarC 77388 3112 E5
Castlegrove Ct
16100 HarC 77377 3254 D5
Castle Grove Ln
14400 HOUS 77044 3550 A2
Castle Guard
- HarC 77493 3813 E1
E Castle Harbour Dr
10 FRDW 77546 4628 E7
200 FRDW 77546 4629 A6
W Castle Harbour Dr
200 FRDW 77546 4628 E6
600 FRDW 77546 4629 A5
Castle Hawk Tr
21900 FBnC 77469 4093 E7
Castlehead Dr
9300 HarC 77375 3110 C3
Castleheath Ct
2100 HarC 77450 3954 E6
Castle Heath Ln
17900 HarC 77084 3678 A7
Castle Hill Blvd
22000 HarC 77377 2961 D7
22000 HarC 77377 3106 D2
Castle Hill Tr
600 HOUS 77339 3118 A6
Castle Hills Ct
10700 HarC 77070 3399 B4
Castle Hollow Ln
6900 HarC 77389 2966 C2
Castle Knoll Dr
12900 HarC 77014 3401 B2
12900 HarC 77066 3401 B2
Castlelake Dr
200 FRDW 77546 4505 A7
600 FRDW 77546 4504 D7
Castle Ln Dr
6300 HarC 77066 3400 E6
Castlemaine Ct
14300 FBnC 77478 4366 E4
Castle Manor Dr
3300 MtgC 77386 2969 D2
Castle Meadow Ln
26000 MtgC 77339 3118 C4
Castlemills Ct
20600 HarC 77450 3954 D5
Castlemist Dr
1300 MtgC 77386 2822 E7
1400 MtgC 77386 2823 A7
Castlemont Dr
- FBnC 77083 4236 E1
Castlemont Ln
21100 HarC 77388 3112 B4
Castlemoor Ct
26000 HarC 77433 3396 B6
Castle Oaks Dr
1800 PRLD 77581 4504 B7
Castle Peak Ct
25000 FBnC 77494 4093 B1
Castle Peak Dr
10900 HarC 77095 3538 A2
Castle Peak Ln
- LGCY 77573 4751 C1
Castle Point Ln
20500 HarC 77532 3410 E2
Castle Pond Ct
3300 PRLD 77584 4501 D5
8300 HarC 77095 3538 A6
Castle Rain Dr
18100 HarC 77346 3409 A1
Castlereach Rd
14300 HOUS 77045 4372 C3
Castle Ridge Dr
11800 HOUS 77077 3958 A4
Castlerock Ct
2900 BzaC 77584 4501 D4
2900 PRLD 77584 4501 D4
Castlerock Dr
3100 BzaC 77584 4501 B6
Castlerock Rd
1400 HarC 77090 3258 A3
1800 HarC 77090 3257 E3
Castlerock Springs Ln
9600 HarC 77375 3255 C2
Castle Springs Dr
22000 HarC 77450 3954 A4
Castlestone Dr
12500 HarC 77065 3539 C4
Castle Terrace Ct
6600 HarC 77379 3111 D2
Castleton St
10800 HOUS 77016 3686 D3
Castleton Bay Ln
2900 PRLD 77584 4500 A4
Castleton Creek Ct
22500 HarC 77450 3953 E4
Castleton Farms Rd
16900 HarC 77379 3256 B3
Castletown Park Ct
16000 HarC 77379 3256 E4
Castleview Cir
4500 BYTN 77521 3972 D1
Castleview Ln
6700 HOUS 77489 4371 B5
Castlewind Cir
22000 FBnC 77450 3954 A7

STREET
Block City ZIP Map# Grid

Castlewind Ct
2000 LGCY 77573 4508 E6
22000 FBnC 77450 3954 A7
Castlewind Dr
3100 FBnC 77450 3954 A7
Castlewind Ln
12900 PRLD 77584 4500 A2
E Castlewood Av
200 FRDW 77546 4629 D1
W Castlewood Av
100 FRDW 77546 4629 C2
Castlewood Dr
200 ORDN 77386 2822 C6
4400 SGLD 77479 4495 C4
17200 MtgC 77306 2533 D4
Castlewood St
3000 HOUS 77025 4101 E6
3000 HOUS 77025 4102 A6
Castle Wy Dr
13400 HarC 77083 4237 B1
Castle Wy Ln
200 HarC 77015 3828 B6
Castoff Ct
16800 HarC 77532 3552 B2
Castolan Dr
1000 HarC 77038 3543 C3
Castor St
4000 HOUS 77022 3823 E2
14100 TMBL 77375 2963 E4
Castordell Dr
200 HOUS 77598 4506 E5
Castorglen Dr
15700 HOUS 77598 4506 D4
Casual Ln
- LGCY 77573 4632 B6
Casual Shore Ct
100 LGCY 77573 4509 A6
Caswell Ct
900 HarC 77450 3954 C3
Catacombs Dr
2300 RMFT 77357 2829 A1
Catalano Ct
13500 HarC 77429 3397 D2
Cataldo Ct
8700 HarC 77040 3681 C3
Catalina Av
2100 DRPK 77503 4248 D1
2100 DRPK 77536 4248 E1
2100 PASD 77503 4108 D5
2100 PASD 77503 4248 D1
Catalina Dr
- GLSN 77554 5548 B2
- SGLD 77479 4496 B2
Catalina Ln
7700 HOUS 77075 4376 C3
Catalina Breeze Ct
400 FBnC 77469 4365 A5
Catalina Grove Ln
13000 FBnC 77469 4366 D1
Catalina Harbor Ct
23000 FBnC 77494 4093 B3
Catalina Island Dr
7500 FBnC 77494 4093 B3
Catalina Leaf Ln
9600 HarC 77379 3110 C7
Catalina Shores Dr
- HarC 77041 3679 E5
- HarC 77041 3680 A5
2700 PRLD 77584 4500 C3
Catalina Village Dr
13500 HarC 77083 4097 B5
Catalonia Cove
- LGCY 77539 4633 D3
Catalpa Cir
11800 HarC 77065 3398 D6
Catalpa Ln
- PRLD 77584 4501 E4
Catalpa Pl
800 MSCY 77459 4497 B5
Catalpa St
7900 TXCY 77591 4873 B4
Catamaran Dr
200 TKIS 77554 5106 B4
2000 LGCY 77573 4509 A7
18500 HarC 77346 3265 D7
18500 HarC 77346 3409 C1
18700 HOUS 77346 3265 D7
Catamaran Rd
18300 HarC 77346 3409 C1
Catamaran Cove Dr
- PRLD 77545 4499 E2
Catamaran Pass Dr
8400 HarC 77095 3538 C3
Catamore St
11300 HOUS 77076 3685 B3
Catarina Cir
6700 HarC 77084 3678 B2
Catawissa Dr
8800 HarC 77095 3538 B4
Catbird Ct
16100 HarC 77396 3406 D5
Caterpillar Ct
18800 MtgC 77365 2972 A6
Cates Rd
19000 GlsC 77511 4868 E2
Cates St
31800 MtgC 77362 2963 D2
Catesby Pl
6800 SGLD 77479 4367 C7
Catfeet Ct
10 WDLD 77381 2820 E3
Cat Fish Ln
3000 MtgC 77384 2675 E7
3000 MtgC 77384 2676 A7
Catfish Ln
22900 WlrC 77445 2953 C4
Catford
11000 HOUS 77075 4376 C4
Catford St
11000 HOUS 77075 4376 C4
Cathcart Dr
6500 HOUS 77091 3683 D4
6800 HOUS 77088 3683 D4
Cathedral Dr
9300 HOUS 77051 4243 B4
Cathedral Grove Ln
7800 HarC 77040 3541 E7
Cather St
400 HOUS 77076 3684 D5
Catherine St
200 HOUS 77009 3824 B6
Catherwood Ln
5600 HarC 77084 3678 B4
Catherwood Pl
800 HOUS 77015 3967 C1
Cathey Ln
9100 HOUS 77080 3820 E5
Cathy Dr
11800 HarC 77065 3398 E6
12000 HarC 77429 3398 E6
16000 HarC 77530 3830 B4
25500 WlrC 77447 2813 C6
Cathys Wy
20000 MtgC 77365 2825 B5
Catina Ln
13200 HOUS 77045 4241 A7
13900 HOUS 77045 4372 A2
Catlett Ln
9800 LPRT 77571 4250 B3
Catoosa Dr
21800 HarC 77388 3111 E2
Catrose Ln
11700 HarC 77429 3253 E7
Cat's Cradle Dr
- WDLD 77381 2675 A7
Catskill Dr
1200 MSCY 77459 4369 C5
Catskill Bluff Ln
17000 HarC 77095 3537 C3
Catskill Crest Dr
12100 HarC 77375 3109 C6
Cat Springs Ct
20500 HarC 77449 3815 D4
Cat Springs Ln
3500 FBnC 77459 4622 B5
Cattail Pl
10 WDLD 77381 2820 D5
Cattail Gate Ct
9200 HarC 77396 3407 A7
Cattail Park Ct
31700 MtgC 77385 2823 C6
Cattails Ln
6300 HOUS 77035 4240 A6
Cat Tail Spring Ct
9500 HarC 77095 3538 E4
Cattle Dr
1400 MtgC 77354 2673 D1
Cattle St
4200 HarC 77532 3412 D3
Cattle Creek Rd
35000 PNIS 77445 3100 B7
35000 WlrC 77484 3100 B7
Cattlemens Dr
- HOUS 77054 4242 C1
Cattle Wy Cl
- FBnC 77494 4093 A4
Caudle Dr
1300 SPVL 77055 3821 A7
N Caulder Wy
3900 FBnC 77459 4621 D4
S Caulder Wy
3800 FBnC 77459 4621 D5
Causeway Dr
- HarC 77072 4097 C7
8500 HarC 77083 4097 C7
Causeway Rd
2400 BYTN 77520 4112 D3
Cavalcade St
200 HOUS 77009 3824 C5
1900 HOUS 77026 3824 E5
2800 HOUS 77026 3825 A5
6800 HOUS 77028 3825 E5
7000 HOUS 77028 3826 A5
W Cavalcade St
100 HOUS 77009 3824 A5
800 HOUS 77009 3823 E5
1100 HOUS 77008 3823 E5
Cavalier
- HarC 77532 3411 D3
Cavalier Ln
300 PASD 77502 4247 A2
700 PASD 77502 4246 E2
Cavalier St
6000 HOUS 77087 4104 C7
Cavallo Pass
2700 FBnC 77469 4365 A1
Cavalry Cir
100 LGCY 77573 4631 B4
Cavalry Cross
2600 FBnC 77469 4365 A1
Cavalry Rd
11500 LPRT 77571 4250 E2
11500 LPRT 77571 4251 A2
Cavalry Charge Ln
25100 WlrC 77447 2813 E1
Cavan
- PRLD 77089 4504 B3
- PRLD 77581 4504 B3
Cavanaugh St
5600 HOUS 77021 4104 B5
Cavehill Ct
800 HOUS 77047 4373 C3
Cavell Ln
8800 SPVL 77055 3821 A7
Cavello Ct
23600 FBnC 77469 4233 B1
Caven St
13800 HarC 77396 3547 A2
Cavendish Ct
16200 HOUS 77059 4380 C5
Cavendish Dr
16200 HOUS 77059 4380 C5
16400 PASD 77059 4380 C5
Cavenmere Ln
- HarC 77047 4374 C3
Cavern Dr
4700 HarC 77546 4505 E6
Cavern Brook Ct
4700 FBnC 77545 4623 C1
Cavern Brook Ln
900 FBnC 77545 4623 A2
Caverndale Ct
4000 FBnC 77494 4093 D1
Cavern Springs Dr
19400 HarC 77375 3109 E7
Caversham Dr
5200 HOUS 77096 4240 D1
Cave Run Dr
4900 MSCY 77459 4496 B1
Cave Springs Dr
3300 HOUS 77339 3118 D4
Cavesson Dr
7400 HarC 77433 3677 C1
Cawdor Wy
11700 HDWV 77024 3959 C2
Cawood Pl
- HarC 77379 3256 B3
Caxton St
10200 HOUS 77016 3686 D3
Cay Rd
400 FBnC 77471 4490 E2
Cay Crossing Ln
200 LGCY 77539 4753 A3
Cayey St
11200 HarC 77016 3547 C7
Caylebaite
- DRPK 77536 4249 A2
Caylor St
10 HOUS 77011 3964 D7
Cayman Ests
22900 MtgC 77385 2823 A6
Cayman Wy
- HarC 77338 3260 D3
Cayman Bend Ct
- PRLD 77545 4499 E1
Cayman Bend Ln
- PRLD 77545 4499 E1
1000 LGCY 77573 4633 A3
Cayman Mist Dr
10900 HOUS 77075 4377 A4
Cayman Point Dr
21700 FBnC 77450 3954 A7
Caymus Creek Ct
- FBnC 77459 4621 B6
Cay Sol Ct
9400 HarC 77044 3688 E4
Cayton St
6700 HOUS 77061 4244 E4
7500 HOUS 77061 4245 C3
Cayuga St
7300 HOUS 77054 4103 A7
Caywood Ln
1300 HOUS 77055 3821 E6
C Bar Cir
12600 STFE 77510 4871 A7
C Bar Dr
12500 STFE 77510 4871 A7
Ceal Rd
19600 MtgC 77365 2972 C7
Cebra St
5700 HOUS 77091 3683 C6
Cebrun
6200 HOUS 77091 3683 D5
Cebrun Rd
6200 HOUS 77091 3683 C5
Cece Glen Ct
28500 MtgC 77386 2969 D6
Cecil Lp
7700 HOUS 77075 4376 C3
Cecil St
7000 HOUS 77030 4102 D5
Cecile Ln
6500 HarC 77049 3829 E2
Cecilia Ct
16200 MtgC 77355 2961 D5
16200 SGCH 77355 2961 D5
Cecil Ridge St
7700 HOUS 77075 4376 C3
Cecil Summers Ct
11600 HarC 77089 4504 C2
Cecil Summers Wy
11400 HarC 77089 4504 C1
Cecina St
- LGCY 77573 4632 D5
Cedar
- ALVN 77511 4749 D7
E Cedar
1200 ALVN 77511 4749 D7
Cedar Av
500 LGCY 77573 4632 B1
2500 BYTN 77520 3973 D5
Cedar Blvd
- CmbC 77520 4113 E2
4000 CmbC 77520 4114 A2
Cedar Br
10900 HOUS 77075 4377 B4
Cedar Cir
200 WDBR 77357 2828 C2
4600 MtgC 77302 2677 C1
7000 HarC 77396 3547 B2
16600 MtgC 77372 2683 A6
Cedar Cr
4000 HOUS 77087 4104 C6
5600 FBnC 77469 4233 A7
Cedar Ct
- WlrC 77447 2813 A3
Cedar Dr
100 LMQU 77568 4874 B7
100 TXCY 77591 4874 B7
200 HTCK 77563 4988 C4
900 LMQU 77568 4990 A1
1600 RHMD 77469 4491 D3
1600 RHMD 77471 4491 D3
1600 RSBG 77471 4491 D3
1900 LMQU 77568 4989 D1
3000 DKSN 77539 4753 D3
Cedar Lk
2700 FBnC 77469 4234 A7
Cedar Ln
100 ALVN 77511 4867 C3
100 ELGO 77586 4509 A2
100 HarC 77530 3830 D7
100 HarC 77530 3969 C1
100 TYLV 77586 4508 E2
100 TYLV 77586 4509 A2
2000 CNRO 77301 2383 D2
2000 FBnC 77494 3952 D5
2500 RSBG 77471 4491 A6
14100 HarC 77396 3547 B2
17400 SGCH 77355 2961 B3
19100 HarC 77377 3107 E6
25300 MtgC 77372 2683 A6
Cedar Pth
6700 FBnC 77469 4095 D5
Cedar Rd
800 CRLS 77565 4509 C5
4600 RSBG 77471 4614 E3
15100 GlsC 77517 4870 B4
Cedar Run
- HarC 77041 3679 D6
Cedar St
- BYTN 77520 4112 A1
100 HarC 77562 3831 D2
100 LPRT 77571 4251 E5
500 FBnC 77545 4623 B2
800 DRPK 77536 4109 A5
2100 PRLD 77581 4503 A3
2500 GLSN 77551 5108 B7
2500 GLSN 77551 5222 B1
2900 HOUS 77339 3119 D6
3100 BYTN 77520 3972 A7
3100 HarC 77053 4373 A4
4600 BLAR 77401 4101 B4
4700 PASD 77586 4383 B4
5100 BLAR 77401 4100 E4
6500 KATY 77493 3813 A7
7300 MNVL 77578 4746 D1
10900 MtgC 77372 2536 E1
14600 STFE 77517 4986 A1
15100 GlsC 77517 4986 A1
15600 GlsC 77517 4869 E7
16200 HarC 77044 3551 A7
16500 HarC 77530 3969 D1
Cedar Ter
10 GLSN 77550 5109 A3
Cedar Tr
- FBnC 77469 4095 C5
Cedar Vw
25000 MtgC 77362 2963 C1
Cedar Bay Dr
5500 HOUS 77345 3120 B6
Cedar Bayou Rd
100 BYTN 77520 3973 A5
Cedar Bayou Lake Dr
- BYTN 77520 4113 E5
- BYTN 77520 4114 A5
E Cedar Bayou Lynchburg Rd
10 BYTN 77521 3973 A1
10 HarC 77521 3973 A1
1200 HarC 77521 3834 C7
W Cedar Bayou Lynchburg Rd
10 BYTN 77521 3972 E1
10 BYTN 77521 3973 A1
300 HarC 77521 3972 C1
2400 BYTN 77521 3833 B7
2400 HarC 77521 3833 A7
3700 HarC 77521 3832 D7
Cedar Bend Cr
5200 HarC 77041 3679 D6
Cedar Bend Ct
100 GlsC 77511 4751 E6
Cedar Bend Dr
4100 MSCY 77459 4497 C3
Cedarberry Ln
9900 HarC 77375 3110 C4
Cedar Bluff Dr
- FRDW 77598 4630 C2
5700 BYTN 77520 3835 B7
5700 BYTN 77520 3974 B1
9600 HarC 77064 3399 C7
Cedarbrake Dr
8600 SPVL 77055 3821 A7
Cedar Brake Rd
10 WDLD 77381 2820 D6
Cedar Brake St
2100 BYTN 77520 3973 D6
Cedar Branch Dr
100 LGCY 77573 4631 B5
9800 BYTN 77520 3835 B7
Cedar Breaks Ct
12400 HarC 77346 3264 C7
12400 HarC 77346 3408 C1
Cedar Brook Ct
2600 FBnC 77477 4369 E4
2600 STAF 77477 4369 E4
Cedarbrook Ct
1400 SEBK 77586 4509 E2
Cedarbrook Dr
1400 SPVL 77055 3821 A6
Cedar Brook Ln
5200 LGCY 77573 4751 E1
Cedar Brush Cir
8000 HarC 77379 3256 A3
Cedarburg Dr
5500 HOUS 77048 4244 A6
Cedar Canyon Dr
21000 HarC 77433 3251 B6
Cedar Chase Pl
10 WDLD 77381 2820 D3
Cedarcliff Ct
12000 HarC 77070 3399 C6
Cedarcliff Dr
11700 HarC 77070 3399 C6
Cedar Cliff Ln
12800 HarC 77429 3398 B6
Cedar Cove Ct
1700 HarC 77450 3954 B4
Cedar Cove Dr
4900 BYTN 77521 3972 C1
21500 HarC 77450 3954 B5
Cedar Cove St
1500 LPRT 77571 4251 C5
Cedar Creek Ct
200 MtgC 77362 2816 E5
11200 HOUS 77042 3958 B6
11200 HOUS 77077 3958 B6
Cedar Creek Dr
- LGCY 77573 4631 A4
2100 BYTN 77520 3973 C6
5000 DKSN 77539 4754 C2
5000 HOUS 77056 3961 A5
5200 HOUS 77056 3960 D5
6100 HOUS 77057 3960 B5
10000 HOUS 77042 3959 A6
11300 HOUS 77042 3958 B6
11600 HOUS 77077 3958 A6
11900 PRLD 77584 4500 C3
Cedar Creek Pt
13300 SGLD 77478 4237 B4
Cedar Crest Blvd
4000 HOUS 77087 4104 C7
Cedarcrest Dr
3000 PASD 77503 4108 A5
Cedardale Dr
8600 SPVL 77055 3821 A6
9600 HOUS 77055 3820 C7
10000 HOUS 77043 3820 A7
Cedardale St
31500 MtgC 77355 2668 C6
Cedaredge Ct
5500 FBnC 77479 4366 D6
Cedar Edge Dr
18500 HarC 77379 3111 A7
Cedaredge Dr
10000 HarC 77064 3540 C3
Cedar Elm Ln
200 FBnC 77479 4367 B5
Cedar Falls Dr
2200 HOUS 77339 3118 E7
Cedar Fern Ct
2100 MtgC 77386 2969 D6
Cedar Field Wy
5700 HarC 77084 3678 B4
Cedar Flats Ln
3600 MtgC 77386 2969 E2
Cedar Forest Dr
3900 HOUS 77339 3119 C3
Cedar Fork Dr
500 LGCY 77573 4631 A6
Cedar Form Ln
11900 MDWP 77477 4237 E4
Cedar Gap Ln
12100 HOUS 77072 4097 E7
12100 HOUS 77072 4098 A7
Cedar Gardens Dr
3600 HarC 77082 4096 C3
Cedar Glen Ln
3600 HarC 77388 3112 D5
Cedar Greens Dr
- HarC 77068 3257 D5
Cedar Grove Ct
12700 HarC 77346 3264 C7
Cedar Grove Dr
13300 HarC 77532 3693 A1
13500 HarC 77532 3553 A7
Cedar Gully Dr
16000 HarC 77546 4505 E6
Cedar Gully Rd
10 LGCY 77573 4630 D5
Cedar Hill Ct
2900 PRLD 77584 4503 B4
3500 FBnC 77459 4622 A5
4100 HarC 77093 3686 C2
Cedar Hill Dr
4500 PRLD 77584 4503 A4
9000 MTBL 77520 3835 C1
Cedar Hill Ln
10 CNRO 77303 2237 C2
10 CNRO 77304 2237 C2
10 MtgC 77303 2237 C2
2800 HarC 77093 3685 E2
2800 HarC 77093 3686 A2
5400 HOUS 77016 3686 D2
Cedar Hollow Ct
300 BzaC 77584 4374 A7
E Cedar Hollow Dr
2900 BzaC 77584 4374 B7
S Cedar Hollow Dr
2700 BzaC 77584 4374 A7
Cedar Hollow St
3300 HarC 77521 3834 E7
Cedarhurst Dr
9600 HOUS 77096 4240 E2
Cedar Isle Dr
14700 HarC 77084 3679 A4
Cedar Jump Dr
7600 HarC 77346 3265 B7
Cedar Key Tr
12500 HarC 77346 3408 C1
Cedar Knolls Dr
3000 HOUS 77339 3119 A5
Cedar Lake Dr
100 LGCY 77573 4631 A5
Cedar Lake Rd
100 HOUS 77336 3266 C5
Cedar Landing Dr
- LGCY 77573 4631 A4
9800 BYTN 77520 3835 A7
Cedar Lawn N
10 GLSN 77551 5108 D5
Cedar Lawn S
10 GLSN 77551 5108 D5
Cedar Lawn Cir
- GLSN 77550 5108 D5
10 GLSN 77551 5108 D5
6800 PASD 77505 4248 E6
6800 PASD 77505 4249 A6
Cedar Lawn Dr
700 ALVN 77511 4867 B2
Cedarloch Dr
8400 HarC 77379 3255 E1
Cedar Locust Dr
3500 SGLD 77479 4495 E2
Cedar Lodge Ct
5300 HOUS 77345 3119 D2
Cedar Manor Ct
16600 HarC 77429 3396 E3
E Cedar Meadow Ct
- FBnC 77494 4093 E5
N Cedar Meadow Ct
- FBnC 77494 4093 E5
S Cedar Meadow Ct
- FBnC 77494 4093 D4
W Cedar Meadow Ct
- FBnC 77494 4093 D4
Cedar Mesa Dr
11700 HOUS 77034 4378 A1
Cedar Mill Ct
3400 HOUS 77345 3120 A4
Cedar Mills Dr
3500 HOUS 77345 3120 A4
Cedarmont Dr
3200 LPRT 77571 4250 B4
Cedarmoor Ct
2600 HOUS 77082 4097 B1
Cedar Oak St
200 FRDW 77546 4629 C1
Cedar Oaks Dr
18600 HarC 77379 3111 A7
Cedar Oaks Ln
4600 BLAR 77401 4101 B5
Cedar Park Ln
10400 HarC 77086 3542 B2
Cedar Park Forest
- HarC 77070 3255 B5
Cedar Pass Ct
1400 HOUS 77077 3957 E5
Cedar Pass Dr
11800 HOUS 77077 3958 A5
12100 HOUS 77077 3957 E5
Cedar Placid Cir
2900 HarC 77068 3257 C4
Cedar Placid Ln
17200 HarC 77068 3257 C4
Cedar Point Cir
9300 HarC 77070 3255 C5
Cedar Point Dr
200 LGCY 77573 4631 A5
6800 PASD 77505 4248 E6
6800 PASD 77505 4249 A6
11700 HarC 77070 3398 D3
13500 HarC 77429 3398 D3
14800 HarC 77070 3254 D7
Cedar Point Pl
6200 HarC 77449 3677 D4
Cedar Point Rd
5400 BHCY 77520 4254 B3
5400 CmbC 77520 4254 B3
Cedar Pond Dr
100 HMBL 77396 3406 D3
Cedar Post Ct
1000 TMBL 77375 2964 D5
Cedar Post Ln
1200 HOUS 77055 3820 D6
1300 HOUS 77080 3820 D6
Cedar Praire Ct
500 LGCY 77573 4631 A6
Cedar Prairie Dr
3400 LGCY 77573 4631 A6
Cedar Rain Dr
20500 HarC 77449 3815 D3
Cedar Ridge Ct
3200 FRDW 77598 4630 C2
4000 HarC 77082 4096 C4
Cedar Ridge Dr
15000 HarC 77082 4096 C4
Cedar Ridge St
100 MtgC 77354 2671 E3
Cedar Ridge Tr
2800 FRDW 77598 4630 C2
4200 HOUS 77059 4380 C4
4500 PASD 77059 4380 C4
Cedar Rock Dr
17500 HarC 77447 3249 D3
Cedar Run Falls
8600 HarC 77375 2965 D4
Cedar Sage Dr
16400 HarC 77095 3397 A7
Cedarshade Ln
10 WDLD 77380 2821 E6
Cedar Sham Ln
19200 HarC 77449 3816 A2
Cedar Shoals Rd
1100 HOUS 77062 4379 E7
1100 HOUS 77062 4506 E1
Cedar Shores Ln
15900 HOUS 77044 3409 B5
Cedar Spring Ct
- MSCY 77459 4496 B2
Cedar Spring Dr
4900 MSCY 77459 4496 C3
Cedar Spring Tr
- HarC 77346 3265 A3
Cedar Springs Ct
10 FBnC 77479 4366 E6
Cedar Springs Dr
- HOUS 77072 4097 E5
Cedar Springs Pl
25500 HarC 77373 3113 E4
Cedarspur Dr
8800 SPVL 77055 3821 A7
Cedarspur Ln
8800 SPVL 77055 3821 A7
Cedarspur St
8300 SPVL 77055 3821 B7
E Cedar Sun Tr
3000 HarC 77449 3815 E4
N Cedar Sun Tr
20000 HarC 77449 3815 E4
W Cedar Sun Tr
3000 HarC 77449 3815 E4
Cedar Terrace Ct
1300 FBnC 77479 4367 A6
Cedar Top Dr
8900 HOUS 77088 3683 B1
Cedar Towne Ln
10400 FBnC 77478 4237 A3
Cedar Trace Dr
8400 HarC 77379 3256 A4
8700 HarC 77379 3255 B4
E Cedar Trail Ct
4000 PRLD 77584 4503 C6
W Cedar Trail Ct
4200 PRLD 77584 4503 B6
Cedarvale Ln
11600 HarC 77377 3254 E5
Cedar Valley Dr
3700 MSCY 77459 4497 A3
4200 HOUS 77345 3119 E5
4200 HOUS 77345 3120 A5
Cedar View Dr
5700 BYTN 77520 3974 A1
5800 BYTN 77520 3835 A7
Cedarview Ln
11000 HarC 77041 3680 B4
Cedar View St
7800 CmbC 77520 3835 D4
Cedar Village Ct
22700 HarC 77450 3953 E4
Cedar Village Dr
3000 HOUS 77345 3119 E4
Cedarville Dr
2700 HOUS 77345 3120 A5
Cedar Vine Ln
- HarC 77377 3254 D4
Cedar Walk Dr
8600 HarC 77375 2965 D3
Cedar Wing Ct
3000 MSCY 77489 4370 C7
Cedarwing Ln
10 WDLD 77380 2822 A6
Cedarwood Ct
1800 SGLD 77478 4237 A6
Cedarwood Dr
500 FRDW 77546 4629 C1
1300 PASD 77502 4106 D6
1300 PASD 77506 4106 D7
3900 PRLD 77584 4503 B7
11200 HarC 77338 3263 A5
11200 HMBL 77338 3263 A5
29100 SHEH 77381 2821 E1
29200 SHEH 77384 2821 E1
Cedar Woods Pl
2800 HarC 77068 3257 C4
Cedel Dr
- HOUS 77080 3821 A4
8500 HOUS 77055 3821 A4
Ceder Hills Ridge Dr
15000 HarC 77396 3407 C7
CE King Pkwy
- HarC 77044 3549 B7
7400 HarC 77044 3689 A7
7400 HarC 77044 3828 A1
7400 HarC 77049 3828 A1
CE King Pkwy FM-526
- HarC 77044 3828 A1
- HarC 77049 3828 A1
Celadon Hill Dr
- HarC 77449 3676 B2
Celano Dr
11100 FBnC 77469 4092 E7
11100 FBnC 77469 4093 A7
Celaya Ct
1200 RSBG 77471 4491 C4
Celeste Ct
1200 FBnC 77479 4366 D7
Celeste St
17000 HarC 77530 3830 E6
Celeste River Ct
17300 HarC 77095 3537 E1
Celestial Ln
5100 HarC 77039 3546 D5
Celestite Dr
4300 HOUS 77072 4098 A4
Celia Dr
12600 HOUS 77015 3967 A3
Celina Knl
3300 FBnC 77459 4622 B5
Celina Ln
8200 HOUS 77040 3681 D6
Celleni Dr
14400 HarC 77429 3397 D7
Cellini Dr
14100 HarC 77429 3397 E7
Celtic Oak Dr
6000 PASD 77505 4248 D7
Celtis St
11500 JTCY 77029 3966 D3
Cembra Wk
20300 HarC 77379 3112 A4
Cemetery Rd
- FBnC 77469 4492 C6
400 GlsC 77517 4752 C7
400 LGCY 77517 4752 C7
400 LGCY 77539 4752 C7
400 STFE 77517 4752 C7
400 STFE 77539 4752 C7
600 GlsC 77517 4870 C1
600 STFE 77517 4870 C1
1900 STFE 77510 4870 C3
6200 MNVL 77578 4747 A1
7000 MNVL 77578 4746 E3
Cemetery St
18500 MAGA 77354 2669 A5
Cemke St
3700 HOUS 77003 3964 B4
Centenary St
2600 HOUS 77030 4102 A4
2600 WUNP 77005 4102 A4
Centennial Dr
1300 HOUS 77055 3820 B7
1300 HOUS 77080 3820 B7
Centennial Ln
5000 FRDW 77546 4505 E7
Centennial Pl
4900 BzaC 77584 4626 A1
Centennial Bridge Ln
15100 FBnC 77478 4236 D3
Centennial Glen Dr
5800 FBnC 77450 4094 B3
Centennial Village Dr
3000 PRLD 77584 4502 E5
Center Ct
100 DRPK 77536 4109 B7
Center Dr
100 GNPK 77547 3966 B7
Center St
- BYTN 77520 3973 D4
- HOUS 77015 3969 B7
- HOUS 77059 4249 A6
- HOUS 77505 4249 A6
- HOUS 77536 3969 B7
- HOUS 77536 4109 B1
10 DRPK 77536 4109 B3
100 ALVN 77511 4866 E3
200 PASD 77506 4107 B4
300 STAF 77477 4370 A3
400 HarC 77562 3832 B4
500 RHMD 77469 4364 D7
1100 PASD 77502 4107 B6
1500 HOUS 77007 3963 A3
1700 FBnC 77469 4364 D6
1700 HarC 77520 3831 E7
1700 HarC 77520 3832 A7
2600 WALR 77484 3101 E5
3400 DRPK 77536 4249 B1
5100 PASD 77505 4249 A6
5100 PASD 77536 4249 B3
5500 HOUS 77007 3962 A2
7500 HTCK 77563 4988 C7
26500 MtgC 77372 2683 C7
26500 PTVL 77372 2683 C7
Centerbrook Ct
2400 PRLD 77584 4500 A2
Centerbrook Ln
2200 HarC 77450 3954 D5
13000 PRLD 77584 4500 A2
Center Ct Cir
17300 HarC 77379 3111 E7
Center Ct Dr
5800 HarC 77379 3111 E7
6100 HarC 77379 3256 D1
Centerfield Blvd
- HarC 77070 3399 E3
- HOUS 77070 3399 E3
- HOUS 77070 3400 A4
Center Hill Dr
700 HOUS 77079 3956 E2
Centerlake Dr
- HarC 77070 3400 A3
- HOUS 77070 3399 E3
- HOUS 77070 3400 A3
Centerlake Ln
- HarC 77379 3112 A5
Centerline Rd
2400 MtgC 77384 2675 D7
Center Park Dr
19100 HarC 77373 3113 E7
Center Plaza Dr
3800 HOUS 77007 3962 C2
Center Point Dr
9100 HOUS 77054 4242 C2
Centerpointe Dr
800 LGCY 77573 4631 E5
Center Site Dr
- CNRO 77304 2383 D5
Center Spring Ct
25800 HarC 77373 3113 C1
Centerton Dr
- FBnC 77450 3953 C6
- FBnC 77494 3953 C6
Center Village Dr
- HOUS 77494 4093 D4
5300 FBnC 77494 4093 D3
Centerwood Dr
600 HOUS 77013 3966 D1
900 HOUS 77015 3966 D1
Central
11400 HarC 77093 3546 C7
Central Av
- BzaC 77583 4624 A3
- DRPK 77536 3969 D7
- HarC 77093 3686 C1
- HOUS 77034 4248 D7
- PASD 77034 4248 D7
- PASD 77505 4248 D7
600 PASD 77502 4107 B7
1000 DRPK 77536 4109 D1
Central Blvd
- HOUS 77081 4100 D3
Central Dr
- SGLD 77478 4368 D3
11900 HarC 77433 3396 E6
NW Central Dr
5400 HOUS 77040 3682 B6
5400 HOUS 77092 3682 B6
Central Pkwy
2200 HOUS 77092 3822 A4
4700 CNRO 77303 2238 E7
Central St
300 HOUS 77012 4105 E4
1600 HOUS 77017 4105 E4

STREET
Block City ZIP Map# Grid

Central St
2300 DKSN 77539 4753 E2
Central City Blvd
6100 GLSN 77551 5222 C1
Central Crest St
5600 HOUS 77092 3821 D3
Central Falls Dr
5900 HarC 77041 3679 B5
Central Green Blvd
- HarC 77073 3404 A4
- HOUS 77073 3404 A4
16500 HOUS 77032 3404 A5
Central Park Cir
2300 HOUS 77059 4380 A5
Central Park Dr
- HOUS 77032 3404 A4
Centre Av
1000 SRAC 77571 4382 D2
Centre Ct
12400 HOUS 77072 4097 D6
Centre Pkwy
- HOUS 77036 4239 A2
- HOUS 77074 4239 A2
9800 HOUS 77036 4238 E2
Centre Ct Pl
- HarC 77379 3256 E3
Centre Grove Ct
7100 HarC 77069 3400 A3
Centre Grove Dr
7000 HarC 77069 3400 B3
Centre Oaks Dr
7000 HarC 77069 3400 A3
Centrepark Dr
10200 HOUS 77043 3819 E1
10200 HOUS 77043 3820 A1
10200 HOUS 77080 3820 A1
Centre Pl Cir
6500 HarC 77379 3256 E3
Centurian Cir
2200 RMFT 77357 2829 A1
Century Blvd
- TXCY 77539 4754 E7
- TXCY 77591 4754 E7
- TXCY 77591 4872 E2
N Century Cir
2100 FRDW 77546 4629 E4
S Century Ct
2200 FRDW 77546 4629 E4
Century Dr
100 FRDW 77546 4629 E4
12700 STAF 77477 4238 B7
12700 STAF 77477 4369 B1
Century Ln
12900 HOUS 77015 3967 B3
Century Oaks Ct
34100 MtgC 77355 2668 A5
Century Plant Dr
23100 FBnC 77494 4093 C4
Century Plaza Dr
- HarC 77090 3403 A1
300 HOUS 77073 3403 A1
900 HarC 77073 3403 C1
Century Square Blvd
- SGLD 77478 4368 D2
Ceole Cir
1000 LGCY 77573 4631 D4
Ceole Ln
400 LGCY 77573 4631 D5
Cerca Ct
7000 HarC 77086 3542 B2
Cerca Blanca Dr
15800 FBnC 77083 4096 A7
Cercina Dr
2100 MtgC 77386 2969 B2
Cereza Dr
16100 FBnC 77083 4096 A7
Cerritos Dr
6000 HOUS 77035 4240 B5
Certosa Dr
23600 FBnC 77469 4093 B7
N Cesar Chavez Blvd
100 HOUS 77011 3964 E6
S Cesar Chavez Blvd
100 HOUS 77011 3964 D7
Cessna Dr
- GLSN 77554 5221 E2
Cetin Ct
1400 HarC 77073 3404 A3
Cetti St
4400 HOUS 77009 3824 C5
Cezanne Cir
2300 FBnC 77459 4621 B7
Cezanne Woods Dr
10 WDLD 77382 2819 B2
Chaco St
2600 HOUS 77003 3963 D7
2600 HOUS 77004 3963 D7
Chad Ct
16200 SGCH 77355 2961 E4
Chad Ln
900 BYTN 77521 3973 A2
20100 MtgC 77357 2827 D5
Chad St
- PASD 77505 4248 D6
Chad Arbor Tr
20100 HarC 77433 3251 C4
Chadbourne Ct
600 HOUS 77079 3957 C3
Chadbourne Dr
14500 HOUS 77079 3957 D3
Chadbourne Trace Ct
7700 FBnC 77469 4094 A6
Chadbourne Trace Ln
21100 FBnC 77469 4094 A6
Chadbrook Ln
11700 HOUS 77099 4238 B5
Chadbury Ln
800 TYLV 77586 4508 E1
Chadbury Park Dr
20400 HarC 77450 3954 D5
Chadell Point Ln
3000 HarC 77449 3815 A3
Chadington Ln
3300 HarC 77388 3112 E6
3300 HarC 77388 3113 A6
Chadway Cross
- FBnC 77494 4093 D5
Chadwell Dr
11900 HOUS 77031 4239 B5
Chadwell Glen Dr
3700 HOUS 77082 4097 B3
Chadwick Dr
3600 BzaC 77578 4501 B7
3600 BzaC 77578 4625 B1
3700 ALVN 77511 4867 D5
Chadwick St
7900 HOUS 77029 3965 B4
10100 JTCY 77029 3966 A3

Chaffin St
3100 HOUS 77087 4104 E6
5700 HOUS 77087 4244 E1
6200 HOUS 77087 4245 A2
Chagall Ln
17000 HarC 77379 3256 B3
Chain St
5700 HOUS 77033 4243 E2
Chalcos Dr
8500 HOUS 77017 4105 E7
Chalet Rd
2100 HarC 77038 3543 B3
Chalet St
16500 MtgC 77355 2961 D5
16500 SGCH 77355 2961 D5
Chaletford Dr
8500 HarC 77044 3689 C6
Chalet Knolls Ln
2800 FBnC 77494 3951 D6
Chalet Ridge Dr
2800 FBnC 77494 3951 D6
Chalfield Cir
12900 HarC 77044 3549 E1
Chalfield Ct
14600 HarC 77044 3549 C1
Chalfont Ct
3400 HarC 77066 3401 D7
Chalfont Dr
3200 HarC 77066 3401 E6
11500 HarC 77065 3539 E2
Chalford Dr
9500 FBnC 77083 4236 E2
9600 FBnC 77478 4236 E2
Chalie
- HarC 77044 3408 D7
Chalk Hl
7500 FBnC 77459 4621 A1
Chalk Maple Ct
11400 HarC 77095 3538 B1
Chalk Maple Ln
16500 HarC 77095 3538 B1
Chalk Rock Dr
1200 HarC 77067 3402 C5
Chalkstone Ln
13700 HarC 77396 3547 B3
Challe Cir E
19000 HarC 77373 3113 E7
Challe Cir W
19000 HarC 77373 3113 E7
Challenger Ct
2000 HarC 77532 3551 D3
Challenger Dr
15100 HarC 77532 3551 D4
Challenger Rd
- HOUS 77094 4095 C2
Challenger Seven Dr
10100 JTCY 77029 3966 A2
Challenger Seven Pkwy
- HOUS 77034 4379 A4
- HOUS 77598 4379 A5
Challie Ln
7700 HOUS 77088 3682 D2
Challis Park Ct
8700 HarC 77040 3681 C2
Chalmette
- HarC 77429 3398 B1
Chalmette St
500 LGCY 77573 4631 B4
12400 HarC 77015 3828 A7
Chalmette Park St
16500 HarC 77429 3397 A3
16600 HarC 77429 3396 E3
Chalton Ct
8300 HarC 77379 3256 B5
Chamber Ct
16700 HarC 77532 3552 A2
Chamberlain Dr
12800 HOUS 77077 3957 C5
17400 HarC 77095 3677 E1
Chamberlain St
1300 HOUS 77093 3685 C2
1700 HarC 77093 3685 C2
Chamberlin Cove
2100 FBnC 77494 3952 B5
Chambers Cir
3400 FBnC 77459 4621 E5
Chambers Ct
3400 FBnC 77459 4621 E5
Chambers Rd
300 HarC 77532 3692 C3
Chambers St
100 CNRO 77301 2384 A3
10400 HOUS 77034 4246 D7
Chambler Ct
5200 HarC 77069 3256 C6
Chambly Dr
500 HarC 77015 3828 C7
Chamboard Ln
900 HOUS 77018 3823 A1
1100 HOUS 77018 3822 E1
Chamfer Wy
700 HarC 77532 3552 A4
N Chamfer Wy
800 HarC 77532 3552 A4
W Chamfer Wy
15700 HarC 77532 3552 A4
Chamisal Ct
9300 HarC 77396 3407 B3
Chamomile Ct
10 WDLD 77382 2819 D1
16100 FBnC 77083 4236 B1
Chamomile Green Ct
10400 HarC 77070 3399 B4
Chamomile Meadow Tr
- FBnC 77494 4092 E3
E Champagne Cir
21600 HarC 77377 3108 B2
S Champagne Cir
21500 HarC 77377 3108 B2
W Champagne Cir
21600 HarC 77377 3108 B2
W Champagne Ct
15500 HarC 77377 3108 C2
Champagne Dr
15600 HarC 77377 3108 B2
Champagne Falls Ct
16600 HarC 77379 3256 B4
Champagne Falls Dr
- HarC 77379 3256 C5
Champaign St
13400 HarC 77039 3545 C4
Champans
- HarC 77532 3553 A2
Champia Ct
11500 HOUS 77013 3827 D4
Champion Dr
2300 PRLD 77581 4504 C2
15800 HarC 77379 3256 A6

Champion Dr
16700 HarC 77379 3255 E5
Champion Ln
6700 HOUS 77091 3683 E4
Champion Centre Dr
13100 HOUS 77066 3400 B3
13100 HOUS 77069 3400 B3
13400 HarC 77069 3400 A2
Champion Creek Ln
3900 FBnC 77469 4234 C5
Champion Forest Cir
8300 HarC 77379 3256 D4
Champion Forest Dr
11100 HarC 77375 3110 A3
11600 HarC 77066 3401 A4
12000 HarC 77066 3400 E3
12800 HarC 77069 3400 D1
13600 HarC 77069 3256 D7
15800 HarC 77379 3256 B5
17700 HarC 77379 3255 D1
19000 HarC 77379 3110 C6
Champion Forest Lp
10000 MtgC 77303 2239 D2
Champion Lake Ct
25600 MtgC 77380 2968 B1
Champion Lake Dr
- HarC 77068 3257 C6
400 MtgC 77380 2968 B1
Champion Oaks Rd
28400 MtgC 77354 2818 C3
Champion Pines Dr
7700 HarC 77379 3256 B3
Champion Rod & Gun Club Rd
- MtgC 77357 2829 B7
- MtgC 77357 2975 A1
Champions Ct
4400 LGCY 77573 4509 A7
Champions Dr
2200 MSCY 77459 4497 B2
13000 HarC 77066 3400 C3
13000 HarC 77069 3400 B1
14300 HarC 77069 3256 B7
28000 MtgC 77355 2815 D3
Champions Ln
100 PNVL 77304 2237 B3
Champions Pt
- HarC 77066 3401 A5
Champions Arbor Dr
- HarC 77070 3399 E3
Champions Bend Cir
10 HarC 77069 3256 C7
10 HarC 77069 3400 C1
Champions Bend Dr
- HarC 77069 3256 B7
Champions Centre Ct
7000 HarC 77069 3400 C3
Champions Centre Ests
1000 HarC 77069 3400 B3
Champions Colony
300 HarC 77069 3256 C7
Champions Colony E
10 HarC 77069 3400 D3
Champions Colony W
10 HarC 77069 3400 D3
Champions Colony Rd W
10 HarC 77069 3400 D3
E Champions Colony Rd
10 HarC 77069 3400 D1
Champions Cove Cir
16500 HarC 77379 3255 E5
Champions Cove Ct
16500 HarC 77379 3255 E5
Champions Cove Dr
9600 HarC 77379 3255 E6
Champions Ct Pl
10 HarC 77069 3400 B1
Champions Ct Tr
10 HarC 77069 3400 B1
Champions Ct Wy
- HarC 77069 3400 D3
Champions Glen Dr
5600 HarC 77069 3256 C7
Champions Green Dr
- HarC 77066 3401 B7
Champions Grove Ct
11700 HarC 77066 3401 A4
Champions Grove Ln
11700 HarC 77066 3401 A4
Championship Dr
- FRDW 77546 4749 E1
Championship Ln
14200 HarC 77069 3400 A1
Champions Lakes Ests
- HarC 77070 3255 A4
Champions Lakes Tr
10600 HarC 77070 3255 A3
10600 HarC 77375 3255 A3
Champions Lakeway
17000 HarC 77070 3255 A3
17000 HarC 77375 3255 A3
Champions Park Dr
13000 HarC 77066 3400 C3
13000 HarC 77069 3400 B2
13000 HOUS 77069 3400 C3
Champions Pl Dr
- HarC 77069 3400 B1
Champions Plaza Dr
6800 HarC 77069 3400 B3
6800 HOUS 77069 3400 B3
Champions Point Ln
5200 HarC 77066 3401 A3
Champion Springs Cir
8800 HarC 77379 3256 A5
Champion Springs Ct
8800 HarC 77379 3256 A5
Champion Springs Dr
- HarC 77379 3256 C5
Champions Ridge Rd
28300 MtgC 77354 2818 B2
Champions Trace Ln
6200 HarC 77066 3400 E5
Champions Trailview Dr
16600 HarC 77379 3255 D5
Champions Valley Dr
12000 HarC 77066 3401 A6
Champions Walk Ln
11600 HarC 77066 3400 E4
Champions Wy Ln
5300 HarC 77066 3401 A4
Champion Villa Dr
10 HarC 77069 3256 C7
Champion Village Ct
6800 HarC 77069 3400 B1
Champion Village Dr
10100 MtgC 77303 2239 C1
14100 HarC 77069 3400 A1

Champion Village Rd
10000 MtgC 77303 2239 C2
Champion Woods Dr
11200 HarC 77375 3255 A3
Champlain Dr
16700 HOUS 77044 3409 B3
Champlain Bend St
5200 HOUS 77056 3960 E6
Champlin Rd
1500 FBnC 77469 4621 A7
Champs Dr
700 HarC 77530 3830 A7
Chanas Ct
21700 HarC 77388 3112 A2
Chanay Ln
2100 HOUS 77339 3118 E3
2100 MtgC 77339 3118 E3
2200 HOUS 77339 3119 A3
Chance Ct
3000 BzaC 77584 4501 C6
29200 MtgC 77354 2818 B1
Chance Ln
700 BYTN 77521 3973 A2
Chance Pkwy
10600 HarC 77031 4239 B6
10600 HOUS 77031 4239 B6
Chancel Dr
7900 MSCY 77071 4239 E6
Chancel Arch Cts S
- MtgC 77357 2829 C3
Chancellor Dr
6600 HarC 77379 3256 D4
Chancellor Crest Ln
- HarC 77433 3396 A4
Chancellorsville Ct
2500 LGCY 77573 4631 B5
Chancellorsville Ln
8400 FBnC 77083 4235 E1
Chancellorsville Pk
400 MtgC 77302 2530 C5
Chancery Pl
10 WDLD 77381 2674 C7
Chancery Rd
13700 HOUS 77034 4378 D5
Chancewood Ln
8100 HarC 77338 3261 E3
Chandler Ct
100 FBnC 77479 4366 D5
Chandler Dr
100 BYTN 77521 3973 A4
Chandler Ln
3300 DRPK 77536 4108 D6
3300 DRPK 77536 4248 E1
12400 MtgC 77302 2531 D6
Chandler St
5200 HOUS 77007 3962 B3
Chandler Chase Ct
13000 HarC 77044 3549 E1
Chandler Cove
1300 PASD 77504 4247 D7
Chandler Creek Cir
- WDLD 77381 2820 B3
N Chandler Creek Cir
10 WDLD 77381 2820 B3
S Chandler Creek Cir
10 WDLD 77381 2820 B3
Chandler Creek Ct
10 WDLD 77381 2820 B3
Chandler Hollow Ln
15100 HarC 77049 3829 A4
Chandler Park Ln
1400 FBnC 77545 4622 E2
Chandler Point Dr
16300 HarC 77447 3250 A6
Chandler Ridge Ln
16300 HarC 77429 3252 B6
Chandlers Wy
10 MtgC 77355 2961 E3
10 MtgC 77355 2962 A3
10 SGCH 77355 2961 E3
Chandlers Wy Dr
12600 HarC 77041 3679 E7
Chanel Dr
13200 HarC 77044 3689 C5
Chang-An Dr
100 MSCY 77489 4370 C2
Changing Oak Ridge Ct
15000 HarC 77082 4096 C2
Channel Ct
1100 HarC 77532 3552 A2
N Channel Dr
- HarC 77049 3828 C5
Channel Bend Dr
17200 HarC 77433 3395 E6
Channelbrook Ln
6200 HarC 77379 3111 D3
Channel City Rd
200 HOUS 77015 3968 C7
200 HOUS 77503 4108 C2
200 PASD 77503 4108 C2
900 PASD 77503 3968 C7
1000 HOUS 77503 3968 C7
Channelside St
7700 HOUS 77012 4105 C3
Channelview
1300 GlsC 77650 4879 A5
Channel View Dr
7700 GLSN 77554 5107 D4
Channelview Dr
6500 GLSN 77554 5108 A4
6600 GLSN 77554 5107 E4
15900 HarC 77530 3969 B2
Channel Wood Ln
17900 HarC 77433 3395 E6
Channelwood Ln
2300 HarC 77450 3954 B6
Channing Wy
16200 HarC 77429 3397 A6
Chantalle Dr
6600 HarC 77449 3677 B3
Chantel Wy
- FBnC 77494 4093 B7
Chanteloup Dr
11700 HOUS 77047 4373 E2
11700 HOUS 77051 4373 E2
Chanter Wy
3200 GlsC 77518 4634 B2
Chantilly Cir
4600 HOUS 77018 3823 A1
7700 GLSN 77551 5222 A2
Chantilly Cir E
7600 GLSN 77551 5222 A2
Chantilly Ln
900 HOUS 77018 3823 A1
1100 HOUS 77018 3822 E1
2300 MtgC 77384 2528 E7
2300 MtgC 77384 2529 A7
4800 HOUS 77092 3822 A2

Chantilly Ln
5500 HOUS 77092 3821 D2
Chantilly St
10 CNRO 77303 2237 E5
Chantry Dr
5000 HarC 77084 3677 E6
N Chantsong Cir
10 WDLD 77382 2819 E2
10 WDLD 77382 2820 A2
S Chantsong Cir
10 WDLD 77382 2820 A2
Chanty Wy
1800 CNRO 77301 2530 B2
Chanute St
17200 HOUS 77032 3404 C2
Chapal Gate Ln
14800 HOUS 77044 3550 A1
Chaparral Cir
22800 MtgC 77365 2973 E5
Chaparral Cross
- LGCY 77573 4753 B1
Chaparral Ct
22800 MtgC 77365 2973 E5
Chaparral Dr
- LGCY 77573 4753 A1
1900 HOUS 77043 3819 E5
4500 BYTN 77521 3973 B2
22800 MtgC 77365 2973 E4
Chaparral Ln
23100 MtgC 77365 2973 E4
Chaparral Wy
3200 MtgC 77380 2967 B3
Chapel Ct
10300 FBnC 77459 4622 A5
Chapel Ln
- PRVW 77445 2954 E7
Chapel Belle Ln
300 BKHV 77024 3959 C4
300 HOUS 77024 3959 C4
Chapel Bend Dr
3200 HarC 77068 3257 C5
Chapel Brook Dr
5400 HarC 77069 3256 B7
Chapelbrook Ln
14700 HarC 77095 3539 A5
Chapel Cone Ln
- KATY 77494 3952 B4
Chapel Cove Ct
14700 HarC 77429 3396 B1
Chapel Creek Ct
2500 HarC 77067 3402 A4
Chapel Creek Wy
3200 FBnC 77459 4622 A6
Chapel Crest Dr
- MtgC 77339 3118 C3
Chapelfield Ln
6800 HarC 77049 3828 E2
Chapel Glen Ct
20400 HarC 77450 3954 D5
Chapel Hill Dr
600 MtgC 77302 2530 C6
10500 HOUS 77099 4237 E4
Chapel Hollow Ln
14200 HarC 77429 3397 B1
Chapel Lake Dr
15000 HarC 77429 3397 A2
Chapelle Ct
11700 HOUS 77077 3958 A5
Chapel Meadow Ln
6900 FBnC 77469 4094 E5
Chapel Oaks Dr
12100 HarC 77067 3402 A4
Chapel Park Ct
17000 HOUS 77059 4380 C4
Chapel Park Wy
17000 HOUS 77059 4380 C4
17100 PASD 77059 4380 C4
Chapel Pine Ct
9400 HarC 77379 3255 D3
Chapel Pine St
17200 HarC 77379 3255 D3
Chapel Pines Dr
16800 HarC 77379 3256 B3
Chapel Ridge Ln
26100 HarC 77373 3114 C1
Chapel Square Dr
3400 HarC 77388 3112 E7
4000 HarC 77388 3257 D1
Chapelstone Ct
9500 HarC 77044 3689 B4
Chapel Trace Ct
5400 BzaC 77583 4623 D4
Chapelwood Ct
400 PNPV 77024 3959 E3
Chapelwood Ln
1600 FBnC 77469 4365 E2
11800 BKHV 77024 3959 B3
Chaperel Dr
4600 PRLD 77584 4503 A6
Chapis St
2300 HOUS 77093 3685 D4
Chaplin St
15100 HOUS 77032 3404 B7
16100 HarC 77032 3404 B6
Chaplin Pl Dr
2600 HarC 77396 3407 D3
Chapman Av
- HOUS 77034 4379 A4
Chapman Rd
22000 WlrC 77445 2952 B7
Chapman St
1000 HOUS 77002 3963 D2
1500 HOUS 77009 3963 D2
2500 HOUS 77009 3824 D6
6100 HOUS 77022 3824 D3
17800 HarC 77044 3551 D7
Chapman Falls Dr
25700 FBnC 77469 4092 B6
Chapmans Count Rd
18300 HarC 77433 3395 D6
Chapparal Ct
10 MSCY 77459 4369 E7
Chappel Grove Ln
4200 FBnC 77494 4092 B2
Chappel Hill Dr
4900 MSCY 77459 4496 B3
Chappell Ln
2100 MSCY 77459 4497 B5
Chappell Hill Dr
300 FRDW 77546 4629 C2
Chappell Knoll Dr
- HarC 77433 3251 C6
Chappelwood Dr
3100 BzaC 77584 4501 B6
Chappel Wood Ln
13200 MtgC 77302 2530 C4
Chapwood Ct
900 HarC 77373 2968 D5

Charade Dr
4700 HarC 77066 3401 A2
Chardonnay Dr
1300 HOUS 77077 3958 A5
Charidges Ct
13700 HOUS 77034 4378 D5
Charidges Dr
400 HOUS 77034 4378 D6
Charing Wy
- HOUS 77045 4241 C6
Charing Cross Dr
12200 HOUS 77031 4239 A6
Charing Cross Wy
1200 HOUS 77339 3264 A1
Chariot Dr
11400 HOUS 77477 4237 E4
Chariot Ln
200 RMFT 77357 2828 E3
300 WDBR 77357 2828 E3
Charis Pl
10 HarC 77388 3113 B7
Chariss Glen Dr
100 LGCY 77573 4633 A1
Charity St
2400 LMQU 77568 4989 E2
Charlbrook Dr
9800 FBnC 77478 4236 E2
Charlemagne Rd
- PRVW 77445 3100 B3
Charles
- HOUS 77088 3683 E3
Charles Al
1400 GlsC 77650 4878 E6
Charles Av
3300 BzaC 77584 4502 A7
3600 PRLD 77584 4502 A7
E Charles Av
10 BYTN 77520 4113 B1
S Charles Av
10 BYTN 77520 4113 B1
Charles Cir
21800 MtgC 77447 3105 E1
Charles Ln
2600 FBnC 77478 4237 B4
2600 HOUS 77478 4237 B4
Charles Pl
700 BYTN 77521 3973 A2
Charles Rd
200 HOUS 77076 3685 A4
Charles St
200 HMBL 77338 3262 E6
300 HOUS 77076 3685 B4
900 PASD 77506 4107 A6
1100 HOUS 77088 3683 E3
2600 HOUS 77093 3685 E4
3000 GlsC 77518 4634 B2
4700 PASD 77586 4383 C5
7000 HarC 77041 3680 B1
11400 JRSV 77041 3680 A1
N Charles St
100 PASD 77506 4107 A3
Charlesmont St
7600 HOUS 77016 3687 A4
8000 HOUS 77078 3687 C4
Charles Ray Ln
15300 MtgC 77302 2679 B2
Charleston Ct
3300 FBnC 77459 4622 B5
Charleston Dr
16300 MtgC 77372 2682 A6
Charleston Pk
400 MtgC 77302 2530 B5
Charleston Sq
500 HMBL 77338 3263 B7
Charleston St
- PRVW 77445 3100 C2
100 FRDW 77546 4629 D2
2400 HOUS 77021 4103 A4
Charleston St N
10 SGLD 77478 4368 E2
Charleston St S
10 SGLD 77478 4368 E2
Charleston Estate Dr
- FBnC 77479 4494 A5
Charleston Park Dr
10 HOUS 77025 4241 D2
Charlestown Colony Ct
6000 HarC 77084 3679 A5
Charlestown Colony Dr
5500 HarC 77084 3679 A4
Charleton Mill Ln
14800 FBnC 77478 4236 E4
Charlie Ln
30000 MtgC 77355 2815 B2
Charlie St
100 MAGA 77354 2669 C4
100 MtgC 77354 2669 C4
7400 HOUS 77088 3683 C3
11800 GLSN 77554 5220 D5
Charlie Oates Dr
- HOUS 77029 3966 D2
- JTCY 77029 3966 D2
Charlie Roberts Dr
3000 LMQU 77568 4989 C1
Charlie Voix St
500 HarC 77015 3828 C6
Charline
- HOUS 77054 4103 A5
Charlisa Springs Dr
20400 HarC 77449 3815 C1
Charlmont Dr
14700 FBnC 77083 4236 D1
Charlotte Dr
2000 BYTN 77520 3973 D4
6900 MNVL 77578 4625 D7
6900 MNVL 77578 4746 D1
21800 SGCH 77355 2960 E2
Charlotte St
5800 WUNP 77005 4102 A3
Charlottes Bequest Cir
12000 HarC 77433 3395 C6
Charlson Pl
100 BYTN 77521 3973 A2
Charlton Ct
9800 HMBL 77338 3262 C4
Charlton St
100 GNPK 77547 4106 C1
6700 SGLD 77479 4494 B1
Charlton House Ln
1700 HarC 77493 3814 B6
Charlton Oaks Ct
1700 FBnC 77494 3953 C5
Charlton Park Dr
1200 HOUS 77077 3957 B4
Charlton Wy Dr
13900 HOUS 77077 3957 B4
Charlyn Oaks Dr
14600 HarC 77070 3399 E1

Charmine Wy
10 WDLD 77382 2820 A1
Charming Creek Ct
6000 HOUS 77345 3120 D7
Charming River Dr
2600 HarC 77373 3114 D6
Charmont Rd
9700 LPRT 77571 4250 B3
Charney Ln
8700 HarC 77088 3543 D7
Charnock Dr
4900 ALVN 77511 4867 D7
Charnwick Ct
5200 HarC 77069 3256 D6
Charnwood St
1100 HOUS 77022 3685 C7
Charolais Dr
15600 HarC 77429 3253 B7
16100 HarC 77429 3396 E1
16100 HarC 77429 3397 A1
Charpiot
- HarC 77044 3408 E7
- HOUS 77044 3408 D7
Charpiot Ln
7100 HarC 77396 3406 C5
7100 HOUS 77396 3406 C5
12500 HarC 77049 3828 A1
E Charpiot Ln
- HOUS 77396 3406 B6
N Charpiot Ln
16000 HOUS 77396 3406 C5
S Charpiot Ln
15800 HOUS 77396 3406 C6
Charred Pine Dr
7000 MtgC 77354 2673 A4
Charrin Dr
5300 HarC 77032 3546 D2
Charrington Dr
6000 HarC 77389 2966 E3
Charriton Dr
1500 HarC 77039 3545 C5
4700 HarC 77039 3546 C5
Charriton St
600 HarC 77060 3544 D5
Charro St
1800 FRDW 77546 4629 A7
Chart Dr
1400 HarC 77532 3551 E2
1400 HarC 77532 3552 A2
Charter Ln
31500 WlrC 77484 3246 E1
31500 WlrC 77484 3247 A1
Charter Bay Dr
2600 HOUS 77054 4242 A2
Charter Club Dr
10 WDLD 77384 2675 C5
Charter Grove Dr
- HarC 77066 3401 A7
Charterhouse Wy
13700 SGLD 77478 4237 A5
Charterlawn Cir
9300 HarC 77070 3255 C5
Chartermoss Cir
9400 HarC 77070 3255 C4
Charter Oaks Ct
100 MtgC 77302 2530 D5
2400 BzaC 77584 4501 C4
Charter Oaks Dr
700 MtgC 77302 2530 D5
2900 HOUS 77093 3686 A2
Charter Pine St
9300 HarC 77070 3255 C6
Charter Pointe Ct
2000 LGCY 77573 4508 E6
2000 LGCY 77573 4509 A6
Charter Ridge Dr
9400 HarC 77070 3255 C5
Charter Rock Dr
16100 HarC 77070 3255 C6
Charterstone Dr
16000 HarC 77070 3255 C5
Charterwood Dr
10200 HOUS 77070 3255 B6
16300 HarC 77070 3255 C5
23200 MtgC 77372 2682 A6
Chart House Ct
15900 HOUS 77044 3409 A5
Chartley Falls Dr
14100 HarC 77044 3549 D1
Chartres St
10 HOUS 77002 3963 D4
10 HOUS 77003 3963 C6
2900 HOUS 77004 3963 B7
4000 HOUS 77004 4103 A1
Chartrese Av
6700 BYTN 77520 3835 B6
Chartreuse Ct
11400 HOUS 77082 4098 B2
Chartreuse Wy
3300 HOUS 77082 4098 B2
Chartwell Ct
11600 BKHV 77024 3959 C3
Chartwell Dr
12200 HOUS 77031 4239 A6
Charwell Cross
13500 HarC 77069 3400 D1
13600 HarC 77069 3256 D7
Charwon St
4400 HarC 77093 3546 B7
Charwood Ct
3600 HarC 77068 3257 B6
Chase Ct
900 CNRO 77301 2383 E3
Chase Hbr
5500 HarC 77041 3679 E6
Chase Ln
800 HOUS 77091 3684 A6
Chase St
1500 HOUS 77026 3963 E1
7700 HOUS 77093 3824 E1
Chasebrook Tr
2300 HOUS 77345 3120 B2
Chase Creek Dr
900 GlsC 77539 4634 D5
Chasecreek Dr
7600 HOUS 77489 4371 A3
Chase Ct Dr
4900 GlsC 77518 4634 D4
4900 GlsC 77539 4634 D5
Chasefield Dr
7800 HOUS 77489 4371 A3
Chasegrove Ln
7200 FBnC 77469 4094 C6
Chase Harbor Ln
2400 PRLD 77584 4500 A2
Chasehill Dr
15100 HOUS 77489 4371 A4

STREET
Block City ZIP Map# Grid

Chase Lake Ct
5000 GlsC 77539 4634 D5
Chase Lake Dr
11800 HOUS 77077 3958 A5
Chase Land Cir
700 GlsC 77518 4634 D4
Chaseland Ln
12800 HOUS 77077 3957 C5
Chaseloch St
17200 HarC 77379 3255 D3
Chase Lock Dr
800 GlsC 77518 4634 D4
800 GlsC 77539 4634 D4
Chase Look Dr
- GlsC 77539 4634 D5
Chasemont Dr
14500 HOUS 77489 4371 A3
Chase More Ct
600 GlsC 77518 4634 D4
Chase More Dr
4800 GlsC 77518 4634 D4
Chasemore Dr
16100 HarC 77379 3255 E6
Chase Mountain Dr
5000 GlsC 77539 4634 D4
Chase Park Cir
5100 GlsC 77539 4634 C5
Chase Park Ct
5000 GlsC 77539 4634 C5
Chase Park Dr
- TXCY 77539 4634 C5
600 GlsC 77518 4634 D4
900 GlsC 77539 4634 C5
Chase Park Gate St
5000 GlsC 77539 4634 D5
Chasepoint
- HOUS 77489 4371 A3
Chase Point Cir
700 GlsC 77518 4634 D4
Chasepoint Dr
7700 HOUS 77489 4371 A3
Chaseridge Dr
14900 HOUS 77489 4371 A4
Chasestone Ct
20000 HarC 77450 3954 E3
Chase Stone Dr
5000 GlsC 77518 4634 D4
5000 GlsC 77539 4634 D4
Chase View Dr
700 GlsC 77518 4634 D4
Chaseview Dr
7800 HOUS 77489 4371 A4
Chasevillage Dr
14500 HOUS 77489 4371 A4
Chaseway Dr
500 MSCY 77489 4370 E5
7700 HOUS 77489 4371 A4
Chasewick Cir
4100 HarC 77014 3401 C2
Chase Wick Dr
4900 GlsC 77518 4634 D4
4900 GlsC 77539 4634 D4
Chase Wind Ct
5000 GlsC 77539 4634 D5
Chasewind Dr
7700 HOUS 77489 4371 A4
Chasewood Blvd
9400 MtgC 77304 2382 A4
Chase Wood Ct
5000 GlsC 77539 4634 C5
Chasewood Dr
5100 GlsC 77539 4634 C5
7500 HOUS 77489 4371 B4
Chasewood Crossing Ct
- HarC 77070 3399 E1
Chasewood Park Dr
20300 HarC 77070 3255 B7
20300 HarC 77070 3399 B1
Chason Ct
17000 HarC 77084 3678 A2
Chaste Tree Ln
19900 HarC 77338 3262 A4
Chaston Dr
13200 HarC 77041 3679 C1
Chasworth Dr
13200 HarC 77041 3679 C1
W Chatam Av
- SGLD 77479 4367 C7
2300 SGLD 77479 4494 C1
Chatanooga
26800 MtgC 77355 2963 A4
Chatburn Dr
1800 HOUS 77077 3958 B5
Chatdale Ln
16500 HarC 77429 3252 B5
Chateau Blvd
- HarC 77396 3546 E2
Chateau Dr
13500 HarC 77377 3109 A5
13600 HarC 77377 3108 E5
Chateau Ln
700 CHTW 77385 2822 D4
Chateau Pl
800 RHMD 77469 4492 A3
Chateau St
1300 HarC 77532 3553 A2
7900 HOUS 77028 3826 C2
Chateau Tr
11800 HarC 77377 3254 D5
Chateau Bend Ct
1700 HarC 77450 3954 E4
Chateau Bend Dr
20100 HarC 77450 3954 E4
Chateau Cove
3700 MtgC 77386 2970 B5
Chateau Creek Wy
4400 MtgC 77386 3115 D2
Chateaucrest Ct
3400 HarC 77047 4374 C5
Chateau Forest Dr
- HOUS 77091 3682 C3
9000 HOUS 77088 3682 B2
Chateau Park Ln
- MtgC 77386 2823 C6
Chateau Point Ln
7700 HarC 77095 3539 B7
Chateau Ridge Ct
19300 HarC 77377 3106 D1
Chateau Springs Ct
28500 MtgC 77386 2969 C6
Chateau Woods Parkway Dr
- CHTW 77385 2823 A4
200 CHTW 77385 2822 D4
200 MtgC 77385 2822 C4
Chatea Woods Ln
23200 HarC 77447 3105 B6
Chatfield Ct
3900 SGLD 77479 4495 A4
Chatfield St
9500 HOUS 77025 4241 E1
Chatfield Manor Ln
13000 HarC 77377 3254 A2
13100 HarC 77377 3253 E2
Chatford Hollow Ln
2500 HarC 77014 3402 A2
Chatham Ln
4000 HOUS 77027 3961 C7
12000 BKHV 77024 3959 B4
Chatham Creek Ct
2400 HOUS 77077 3957 A7
Chatham Hill Ln
5200 HarC 77084 3678 D5
Chatham Island Ln
6400 HOUS 77035 4240 A5
Chatham Lake Ln
7000 FBnC 77469 4094 C5
Chatham Springs Ln
7700 HarC 77433 3537 A7
Chatham Trail Ct
1800 FBnC 77479 4367 B7
1800 FBnC 77479 4494 B1
Chatham Woods Dr
6000 HarC 77084 3677 E4
Chatham Wy Dr
17500 HarC 77084 3677 E4
Chathan Glen Ln
7400 FBnC 77469 4094 D6
Chatman St
800 ALVN 77511 4749 A7
Chatsworth Cir
100 FBnC 77479 4367 A5
Chatsworth Dr
8600 HOUS 77024 3961 A2
Chattanooga Pk
300 MtgC 77302 2530 D5
Chattanooga St
8900 LPRT 77571 4249 E3
Chattaroy Pl
1900 SGLD 77478 4237 C5
Chatten Wy
11400 HDWV 77024 3959 D2
Chatterbird Ln
10 WDLD 77380 2822 A7
Chatterly Ln
18000 HarC 77060 3403 C4
Chatterton Dr
10100 HOUS 77043 3820 A6
10200 HOUS 77043 3819 E6
Chatwood Dr
3500 PRLD 77584 4501 C2
8800 HOUS 77028 3687 E6
8800 HOUS 77078 3687 E6
9000 HOUS 77078 3688 A6
Chaucer Dr
5400 HOUS 77005 4102 B3
5400 HOUS 77030 4102 B3
Chaucer Ln
- BYTN 77521 3974 A2
Chaucer Oaks Ct
11400 HOUS 77082 4098 B2
Chaumont Dr
12700 HOUS 77089 4378 D7
Chauncey Ct
10 CNRO 77384 2675 E3
Chaus Ct
22800 FBnC 77450 4093 D2
Chavile Dr
12900 HarC 77429 3398 D4
Chazen Dr
1600 JTCY 77029 3966 D4
Chazenwood Dr
- HarC 77064 3540 B5
Cheam Cir
700 HOUS 77015 3828 C7
Cheaney Ct
11500 HarC 77066 3401 D7
Cheaney Dr
3300 HarC 77066 3401 D6
Cheatham Ln
1400 HOUS 77015 3967 B3
Cheatham Rd
400 HOUS 77336 3120 E4
400 HOUS 77336 3121 A4
Cheatum Rd
25500 PTVL 77372 2683 A7
Checkerberry Dr
- PRLD 77581 4504 B5
Checkerberry Park Ln
10000 HarC 77375 3110 B5
Checkerboard St
- HOUS 77035 4240 D4
- HOUS 77096 4240 D4
Cheddar Ct
24100 HarC 77375 2965 D4
Cheddar Ridge Dr
1000 HarC 77379 3255 D1
Cheddington Dr
200 HarC 77450 3953 D1
Chedworth Dr
400 HOUS 77062 4506 E2
Cheeca Lodge Ln
7400 HarC 77346 3265 B7
7400 HarC 77346 3409 A1
Cheena Dr
4000 HOUS 77025 4241 C2
4300 HOUS 77096 4241 B2
5100 HOUS 77096 4240 E2
Cheer St
9000 HOUS 77063 4099 D1
Cheeves Dr
10800 HOUS 77016 3687 A2
11400 HOUS 77016 3547 A7
Chelmsford Ct
2300 ALVN 77511 4866 E4
Chelmsford Ln
8700 HarC 77379 3256 B6
Chelsea Blvd
10 HOUS 77006 4102 E1
700 HOUS 77002 4102 E1
Chelsea Ct
1900 RSBG 77471 4490 E5
Chelsea Ln
200 FRDW 77546 4505 A6
400 FRDW 77546 4504 E6
400 PRLD 77581 4504 E6
W Chelsea Pl
400 ELGO 77586 4382 B7
Chelsea Rd
100 CNRO 77304 2383 C4
Chelsea St
500 BLAR 77401 4101 A5
Chelsea Wy
- FBnC 77479 4366 D6
1300 HOUS 77339 3119 A7
1300 HOUS 77339 3264 A1
Chelsea Bend Ct
8200 FBnC 77083 4095 E7
8300 FBnC 77083 4235 C2
Chelsea Bridge Ct
10 WDLD 77382 2674 A5
Chelsea Brook Ct
8800 HarC 77089 4377 B6
Chelsea Brook Ln
10300 HarC 77089 4377 B6
Chelsea Canyon Ct
20200 FBnC 77450 4094 C4
Chelsea Creek Ln
2000 MtgC 77386 2969 D6
Chelsea Elm Ct
- HarC 77038 3543 A5
Chelsea Fair Ln
5400 HarC 77379 3112 B6
Chelsea Harbour Ln
- FBnC 77469 4366 E4
- FBnC 77478 4366 E4
Chelseahurst Ln
- HarC 77047 4374 A4
Chelsea Knoll Ln
10900 HarC 77067 3402 B7
Chelsea Oak St
11000 HarC 77065 3540 A1
11000 HarC 77070 3540 A1
11200 HarC 77065 3539 E1
Chelsea Park Ct
20400 HarC 77450 3954 D4
Chelsea Park Dr
- HarC 77450 3954 D5
Chelsea Ridge Ct
2200 HarC 77450 3954 C5
Chelsea Vale Dr
2100 FBnC 77545 4498 C7
Chelsea Walk Dr
11300 HarC 77066 3401 D6
Chelsen Bridge Ln
23000 HarC 77450 3953 D2
Chelsham Ln
15300 HarC 77530 3829 D5
Chelshurst Wy
1100 HarC 77379 3110 A7
Chelshurst Wy Ct
10300 HarC 77379 3110 B7
Chelston Ct
2300 SGLD 77478 4237 C4
Chelsworth Dr
- FBnC 77083 4236 C1
Cheltenham Dr
700 HarC 77450 3954 D2
5600 HOUS 77096 4240 C1
Chelton St
13100 HOUS 77015 3967 C2
Chelwood Pl
13700 HarC 77069 3256 D7
Chemawa Tr
10 HarC 77375 3110 A3
Chemical Rd
9600 PASD 77507 4381 E2
9700 PASD 77507 4382 A3
Chenevert St
10 HOUS 77002 3963 D4
600 HOUS 77003 3963 D5
700 HOUS 77010 3963 D5
3400 HOUS 77004 3963 B7
3900 HOUS 77004 4103 B1
N Chenevert St
10 HOUS 77002 3963 D4
Chennault Rd
4900 HOUS 77033 4103 E7
4900 HOUS 77033 4243 E1
5100 HOUS 77033 4104 A7
Cher Ct
8900 HarC 77040 3541 C7
Cheranna Dr
1100 HarC 77090 3258 D7
Cherbourg Rd
- HOUS 77033 4244 A1
4900 HOUS 77033 4104 A7
Cheridan Cir
6400 FBnC 77469 4232 D4
Cherie Cove Dr
8700 HarC 77088 3542 D6
Cherie Crest Dr
5300 HarC 77088 3542 E7
Cherie Grove Cir
8700 HarC 77088 3542 D6
Cherie Park Dr
- HarC 77396 3407 B3
- HOUS 77396 3407 B3
Cheril Ln
14400 HarC 77032 3546 A2
Cherilyn Ln
14100 HarC 77032 3546 A2
Cherish Tr
5800 FBnC 77494 4093 A3
Cherokee Ct
5500 FBnC 77471 4614 E4
Cherokee Dr
- GLSN 77554 5221 D1
10 PNVL 77304 2237 A4
700 PASD 77506 4106 E6
1000 PASD 77506 4107 A6
17000 MtgC 77357 2681 A6
23600 MtgC 77365 2972 C5
29000 HarC 77484 3248 A2
Cherokee Ln
10 PNVL 77304 2237 A4
26600 MtgC 77354 2818 C7
Cherokee Rd
7600 KATY 77494 3951 D1
Cherokee St
1300 DRPK 77536 4109 D6
4200 HarC 77521 3833 B4
4300 BYTN 77521 3835 A5
5300 HOUS 77005 4102 C2
5300 HOUS 77006 4102 C2
Cherokee Tr
- FBnC 77469 4364 C7
Cherokee Trc
24000 MtgC 77365 2974 B7
Cherokee Bluff Dr
19400 HarC 77375 3109 D7
Cherokee Hollow Dr
1200 HarC 77450 3953 D4
Cherokee Rose Ct
13400 BzaC 77583 4623 E4
Cherokee Rose Ln
30900 MtgC 77354 2670 B7
Cherrington Ct
23000 FBnC 77450 3953 E5
Cherrington Dr
2000 FBnC 77450 3953 E5
Cherry Av
3400 TXCY 77590 4874 C4
Cherry Ct
300 LPRT 77571 4250 C4
Cherry Dr
1900 DKSN 77539 4753 D3
Cherry Hl
- WlrC 77447 2813 C4
Cherry Hls
10 JRSV 77065 3540 A6
Cherry Ln
1200 HarC 77532 3692 A1
2100 PASD 77502 4107 D7
2100 PASD 77502 4247 D1
Cherry Rd
4300 STFE 77510 4870 D7
4300 STFE 77517 4870 D7
Cherry Run
6300 HarC 77084 3679 A3
Cherry St
- BYTN 77520 4112 A1
- CNRO 77301 2384 D6
- HarC 77562 3831 C2
10 HarC 77336 2975 C6
300 LMQU 77568 4990 C2
1100 BYTN 77520 3972 A7
2000 WALR 77484 3102 A5
2200 WALR 77484 3101 E5
4300 STFE 77510 4870 C7
4300 STFE 77517 4870 C7
4300 STFE 77517 4986 C1
4400 GlsC 77511 4869 D6
4400 GlsC 77517 4869 D6
4500 PRLD 77581 4503 A3
5000 HOUS 77026 3824 E4
21100 MtgC 77357 2827 B6
N Cherry St
100 TMBL 77375 2964 B6
S Cherry St
100 TMBL 77375 2964 B7
800 TMBL 77375 3109 C1
2400 HarC 77375 3109 C4
Cherrybark Ln
600 HOUS 77079 3958 D2
Cherrybark Oak Dr
3200 HarC 77082 4096 C2
Cherry Bend Dr
1700 HOUS 77077 3958 A6
2100 HOUS 77077 3957 E7
Cherry Blossom Dr
- BzaC 77584 4501 A1
700 LGCY 77573 4630 D6
8200 HarC 77562 3832 D2
Cherry Blossom Pl
10 WDLD 77381 2674 D6
Cherry Brook Ct
7400 FBnC 77479 4493 E6
Cherry Brook Ln
1400 PASD 77502 4247 E1
2600 PASD 77502 4248 A1
2600 PASD 77503 4248 A1
26600 FBnC 77494 4092 A2
Cherry Canyon Ln
21200 HarC 77375 3110 B4
Cherry Creek Ct
1400 MSCY 77459 4497 D2
Cherry Creek Dr
- PRLD 77584 4500 D3
3100 MSCY 77459 4497 D1
3300 MSCY 77545 4497 D2
5400 HOUS 77017 4106 C7
5400 HOUS 77017 4246 C1
Cherry Creek Bend Ct
5500 HarC 77041 3679 E7
Cherry Creek Bend Ln
12500 HarC 77041 3679 E6
Cherrydale Dr
6800 HOUS 77087 4244 E2
Cherrydown St
13600 SGLD 77478 4237 B7
Cherry Forest Dr
3200 HOUS 77088 3683 A3
Cherry Fork Dr
11100 HarC 77065 3399 A6
Cherryglade Ct
13000 HarC 77044 3689 C4
Cherry Glen Ct
2500 HOUS 77345 3120 C5
Cherry Grove Ct
3000 HOUS 77059 4379 E3
Cherry Haven Cir
20400 HarC 77449 3815 B5
Cherry Hill Ct
- RHMD 77469 4492 A3
Cherryhill St
6000 HOUS 77087 4104 C6
Cherry Hills Dr
10 PNVL 77304 2237 B2
2100 LGCY 77573 4633 B1
3100 MSCY 77459 4497 D1
Cherry Hills Ln
3700 PASD 77505 4248 B4
6300 HarC 77069 3400 B1
Cherry Hills Rd
6800 HarC 77069 3400 A2
Cherry Hollow Ln
13700 HarC 77082 4097 A2
13700 HOUS 77082 4097 A2
13800 HOUS 77082 4096 E2
Cherryhurst St
1600 HOUS 77006 3962 D6
Cherryknoll Dr
11600 HOUS 77077 3958 A5
Cherry Laurel Cir
24100 MtgC 77365 2974 B6
Cherry Laurel Dr
1800 HOUS 77339 3118 D4
1800 MtgC 77386 2969 A3
Cherry Laurel Ln
10200 FBnC 77459 4621 E4
18000 MtgC 77357 2827 B1
Cherry Laurel Rd
300 TMBL 77375 3109 B1
Cherry Limb Dr
10200 HOUS 77099 4238 A3
Cherry Meadow Dr
3700 HarC 77039 3546 A6
Cherry Mill Ct
2900 HOUS 77059 4380 A4
Cherry Mound Rd
14000 HOUS 77077 3956 E3
Cherry Oak Cir
4100 HOUS 77088 3682 E3
4100 HOUS 77088 3683 A3
Cherry Oak Ln
4400 HOUS 77088 3682 E3
Cherry Oak Wy
- HOUS 77059 4380 C3
Cherry Oaks Ln
19700 HarC 77346 3265 A5
20200 HarC 77346 3264 E5
Cherry Orchard Ct
2800 HarC 77449 3815 B5
Cherry Orchard Ln
20300 HarC 77449 3815 C5
Cherry Park Dr
7100 HarC 77095 3678 E1
7500 HarC 77095 3538 E7
Cherry Pl Ct
7800 HarC 77346 3265 B4
Cherry Point Dr
10 MTBL 77520 3696 D2
Cherry Ridge Cir
- FBnC 77469 4233 A7
Cherry Ridge Dr
1600 HOUS 77077 3958 B5
Cherry Ridge Rd
5100 FBnC 77469 4232 E7
5100 FBnC 77469 4233 A7
Cherryshire Ct
8200 FBnC 77083 4096 A7
Cherryshire Dr
16000 FBnC 77083 4096 A7
Cherry Spring Dr
900 HarC 77038 3543 C3
Cherry Springs Ct
1400 MSCY 77459 4497 D2
Cherry Springs Dr
2900 MSCY 77459 4497 D1
2900 MSCY 77489 4497 D1
Cherry Springs Ln
400 HarC 77373 3113 E4
Cherrystone Dr
- HarC 77338 3261 D4
Cherry Tree Ln
100 FRDW 77546 4505 C6
Cherry Tree St
6600 HOUS 77092 3682 C7
Cherrytree Grove Dr
18500 HarC 77084 3816 C4
Cherrytree Park Cir
1900 HOUS 77062 4380 A5
Cherrytree Ridge Ln
2100 HOUS 77062 4380 B7
Cherryvale Ct
10 WDLD 77382 2673 C5
Cherry Valley Dr
600 HOUS 77336 3266 C2
Cherryville Dr
2100 HarC 77038 3543 B3
Cherrywood Ct
5100 LGCY 77573 4630 D6
Cherrywood Ln
29000 SHEH 77381 2821 E2
Cherrywood St
100 BLAR 77401 4101 A6
Cherton Ct
13000 HOUS 77045 4241 C6
Chertsey Cir
1400 HarC 77530 3829 C5
Chervil Ln
7700 HarC 77521 3833 D3
Cheryl Ct
2700 MSCY 77459 4369 C7
Cheryl Dr
2000 PRLD 77581 4503 C2
Cheryl Ln
6000 FBnC 77583 4622 D5
Cheryl St
14300 HOUS 77085 4371 B1
31000 MtgC 77362 2963 C4
Cheryl Lynne Ln
3800 HOUS 77045 4241 D7
Chesapeak Bend Ln
3000 HarC 77449 3815 B3
Chesapeake Ct
3500 BzaC 77584 4501 C7
Chesapeake Pl
5400 SGLD 77479 4494 E4
5400 SGLD 77479 4495 A4
Chesapeake St
1800 BYTN 77520 3972 C7
Chesapeake Wy
5200 HOUS 77056 3960 E6
Chesapeake Bay Ct
1700 HOUS 77084 3816 C7
Chesham Ct
12100 HOUS 77031 4239 A5
Chesham Mews
10 FBnC 77459 4621 C7
Cheshire Gln
- WDLD 77382 2674 A4
Cheshire Ln
1000 HOUS 77018 3822 E1
1000 HOUS 77018 3823 A1
5500 HOUS 77092 3821 D1
Cheshire St
12700 HOUS 77077 3957 C4
Cheshire Bend Dr
10 SGLD 77479 4495 D3
Cheshire Bend Ln
15700 HarC 77084 3678 E5
Cheshire Gln Ct
10 WDLD 77382 2674 B5
Cheshire Grove Ln
16500 HarC 77090 3258 C4
Cheshire Oaks Dr
2600 HOUS 77054 4242 A2
Cheshire Park Rd
6800 HOUS 77088 3542 B6
7100 HOUS 77088 3542 B6
Cheshire Pl Dr
16700 FBnC 77083 4095 C7
Cheshire Vale St
8300 HNCV 77024 3960 C1
Cheshunt Ln
15300 HarC 77530 3829 D5
N Cheska Ln
10 PNPV 77024 3959 D4
S Cheska Ln
10 PNPV 77024 3959 D4
Chesley Cir
21000 FBnC 77469 4234 B4
Cheslyn Ct
9400 HarC 77375 3110 C3
Chesney Downs Dr
9000 FBnC 77083 4236 D1
Chessgate Ct
1800 HarC 77450 3954 B5
Chessington Dr
11600 HOUS 77031 4238 E5
11600 HOUS 77031 4239 A5
Chessley Chase Dr
6800 FBnC 77479 4367 B6
Chessnut Glen Dr
3500 HarC 77388 3112 D5
Chesswood Cir
2100 SGLD 77478 4237 C5
Chesswood Dr
11500 HOUS 77072 4098 B3
11600 HOUS 77082 4098 B3
Chesswood Ln
100 CNRO 77301 2384 C7
Chester Dr
100 FRDW 77546 4504 E7
100 FRDW 77546 4628 E1
100 FRDW 77546 4629 A1
2800 PRLD 77584 4503 A4
Chester St
4200 HOUS 77007 3962 C2
17800 HarC 77044 3551 D7
Chesterbrook Dr
12300 HOUS 77031 4239 A6
Chesterdale Dr
3700 MSCY 77459 4621 E2
Chesterfield Dr
9300 HOUS 77051 4243 B5
Chesterfield Ln
3100 STAF 77477 4369 A2
3100 STAF 77478 4369 A2
Chesterfield Sq
- HarC 77084 3678 D2
Chester Fort Dr
2100 HarC 77373 3114 C4
Chester Gables Ct
13700 HarC 77083 4097 A3
Chester Gables Dr
13600 HarC 77083 4097 A3
Chestergate Dr
4200 HarC 77373 3115 B6
Chester Oak Dr
6800 FBnC 77083 4095 E5
Chester Park Dr
9100 HarC 77064 3540 C5
Chesterpoint Dr
1300 MtgC 77386 2822 E7
1400 MtgC 77386 2823 A7
Chesters Dr
13000 HarC 77532 3693 C1
Chestershire Dr
3100 PASD 77503 4108 A4
Chesterton Ct
24200 FBnC 77494 3953 B7
Chesterwick Dr
21900 HarC 77450 3954 A5
Chesterwood Dr
900 PRLD 77581 4504 E7
Chestnest Springs Ln
1300 HOUS 77062 4379 E7
1500 HOUS 77062 4380 A5
Chestnut Bnd
3900 FBnC 77459 4622 A4
Chestnut Cir
2500 PRLD 77584 4501 E5
4400 LGCY 77598 4630 C4
Chestnut Dr
200 HarC 77562 3831 D2
2400 RSBG 77471 4491 A6
Chestnut Grv
4300 LGCY 77573 4630 E5
4300 LGCY 77573 4631 A6
Chestnut Ln
1500 RHMD 77469 4491 E3
2100 PASD 77502 4107 D4
2100 PASD 77502 4247 D1
25600 MtgC 77372 2683 A6
Chestnut Pl
19500 HarC 77094 3955 A2
Chestnut St
100 BzaC 77511 4748 E1
200 BYTN 77520 3832 D7
800 LMQU 77568 4874 B7
800 LMQU 77568 4990 B1
1500 HOUS 77009 3963 C2
4800 BLAR 77401 4101 A4
5100 BLAR 77401 4100 E4
5200 HOUS 77081 4100 E4
N Chestnut St
100 TMBL 77375 2964 C6
S Chestnut St
100 TMBL 77375 2964 C6
Chestnut Tr
16200 HarC 77377 3254 D5
17400 FBnC 77469 4095 C5
Chestnut Bluff Dr
17300 HarC 77095 3537 E3
Chestnut Bough St
1100 HarC 77530 3829 D6
Chestnut Brook Ct
19600 HarC 77084 3816 A4
Chestnut Creek Ct
17100 HarC 77379 3256 D4
Chestnut Creek Wy
10000 PRLD 77584 4501 A2
Chestnut Crest Dr
18700 HarC 77346 3265 C7
Chestnut Falls Dr
14900 HarC 77433 3251 C6
Chestnutfield Ct
19400 HarC 77094 3955 B1
Chestnut Forest Dr
8200 HarC 77088 3682 D1
8600 HarC 77088 3542 C7
Chestnut Glen Ct
1700 CNRO 77301 2384 E6
7700 FBnC 77479 4494 A6
Chestnut Glen Ln
15000 HarC 77429 3397 C1
Chestnut Grove Ln
1400 HOUS 77345 3120 C6
Chestnut Hill Ct
10 WDLD 77380 2967 C3
Chestnut Hills Ct
700 HarC 77450 3954 D1
Chestnut Hills Dr
20600 HarC 77450 3954 C1
Chestnut Hollow Ct
12400 HarC 77346 3408 C1
Chestnut Isle Ct
5400 HOUS 77345 3119 D2
Chestnut Meadow Ct
16600 SGLD 77479 4368 B7
Chestnut Meadow Dr
4400 SGLD 77479 4495 A1
4500 SGLD 77479 4368 A7
Chestnut Mills Rd
2400 HarC 77067 3402 A4
Chestnut Oak Ln
- HOUS 77059 4380 B4
Chestnut Oak Pl
2300 WDLD 77380 2967 E2
Chestnut Oak Wy
- HOUS 77059 4380 B3
Chestnut Park Rd
- PRLD 77583 4500 A7
100 BzaC 77583 4500 A7
Chestnut Peace Ct
6200 HOUS 77345 3120 C4
Chestnut Ridge Ct
4400 MSCY 77459 4497 D4
Chestnut Ridge Dr
2700 HOUS 77339 3118 B6
Chestnut Ridge Rd
10 WDBR 77357 2828 C2
1100 HOUS 77339 3263 B1
1800 HOUS 77339 3118 B7
Chestnut Square Ln
18500 HarC 77084 3816 C1
Chestnut Tree Ln
1500 HarC 77067 3402 C6
Chestnut Woods Tr
11200 HarC 77065 3539 C2
Cheston Dr
1300 JTCY 77029 3966 D3
N Chestwood Dr
11400 HDWV 77024 3959 D2
11400 PNPV 77024 3959 D2
S Chestwood Dr
11400 HDWV 77024 3959 D2
11400 PNPV 77024 3959 D2
Cheswick Cir
200 FBnC 77479 4366 D6
Cheswick Dr
8100 HarC 77037 3684 C1
9000 HarC 77037 3544 C7
Cheswood St
5600 HOUS 77087 4104 C7
5700 HOUS 77087 4244 C1
Chetco Ln
4500 HarC 77521 3833 B4
Chetland Pl Dr
14800 HarC 77095 3538 E6
14800 HarC 77095 3539 A6
Chetman Dr
11500 HarC 77065 3398 C7
Chetwood Cir
900 LGCY 77573 4631 D4
Chetwood Dr
6600 HOUS 77081 4100 D4
Cheval Dr
14100 HarC 77429 3397 E6
Chevall Ct
10 FBnC 77469 4492 D5
Chevery Dr
- HarC 77053 4372 D5
Cheviot Cir
11400 HOUS 77099 4238 B1
Cheviot Hills Ln
3400 FBnC 77545 4498 D7
Chevy Chase Cir
600 SGLD 77478 4368 E2
800 SGLD 77478 4369 A3
Chevy Chase Dr
- HOUS 77056 3960 E6
2900 HOUS 77019 3962 A5
3200 HOUS 77019 3961 D5
5100 HOUS 77056 3961 A6
6100 HOUS 77057 3960 B6
7500 HOUS 77063 3960 A6
10000 HOUS 77042 3959 A6
10800 HOUS 77042 3958 C6
11300 HOUS 77077 3958 B6
13900 HOUS 77077 3956 E7
Chevy Chase St
22000 MtgC 77365 2972 C2
Chevy Oaks Ln
9200 FBnC 77469 4234 E2
Chew St
2000 HOUS 77020 3964 D1
2000 HOUS 77020 3825 D7
Chewton Ct
- HarC 77377 3254 B4
Chewton Glen St
16600 HarC 77377 3254 B5
Cheyene Bend Dr
- HarC 77429 3253 E5
Cheyenne Av
4700 PASD 77504 4248 A3
4700 PASD 77505 4248 A3
Cheyenne Ct
10 PNVL 77304 2237 A4
7900 HarC 77521 3833 B3
Cheyenne Meadows Dr
900 HarC 77450 3953 D3
Cheyenne River Cir
1800 SGLD 77478 4369 A5
Cheyne Cir
7600 HarC 77379 3256 C4
Chia St
1500 HOUS 77017 4106 D7
Chianti Ct
7900 FBnC 77479 4494 B4
Chianti Creek Ct
- FBnC 77053 4498 D2
Chiara Ct
1200 LGCY 77573 4633 A4
Chia Valley Ct
9200 HarC 77089 4504 B1
Chicadee Ln
14400 MtgC 77302 2679 D1
14400 MtgC 77306 2679 D1
Chicago St
2100 DKSN 77539 4753 E2
2800 HOUS 77017 4105 D5
2900 DKSN 77539 4754 A2
Chichester Ln
15300 JRSV 77040 3540 E6
15500 HarC 77064 3540 E7
Chickadee Dr
1800 LGCY 77573 4631 C5
Chickadee Ln
10400 HOUS 77048 4244 C6
18800 HarC 77377 3106 E1
18800 HarC 77377 3107 A1
Chickamauga Ln
8400 FBnC 77083 4235 E1
Chickasaw Ln
10000 HOUS 77041 3681 A5
Chickasaw Tr
24100 MtgC 77365 2974 B7
Chickering St
3100 HOUS 77026 3825 A5
Chickfield Ct
10200 HOUS 77075 4377 A2
Chickory Tr
21300 FBnC 77450 4094 A4
Chickory Field Ln
500 BzaC 77584 4374 C7
Chickory Ridge Ln
- HarC 77089 4504 A1

STREET
Block City ZIP Map# Grid

Chickory Wood Ct
400 BzaC 77584 4374 C7
Chickory Woods Ln
6900 FBnC 77083 4095 D5
Chicksaw St
7100 BYTN 77521 3835 B5
Chickwood Dr
11500 HarC 77089 4378 A6
11600 HOUS 77089 4378 A6
Chico Ln
100 DKSN 77539 4754 B1
Chicora Wood Ct
700 MtgC 77302 2530 C7
Chicory Dr
8300 HarC 77521 3833 D2
17400 HOUS 77084 3816 D6
Chicory Star Ln
- FBnC 77494 4092 C4
Chief Dr
5200 PRLD 77584 4503 A5
Chiefs Honor Ct
18400 HarC 77433 3395 D5
Chigger Creek Dr
19600 BzaC 77511 4628 D6
19600 FRDW 77546 4628 D6
Childers Ct
800 STAF 77477 4369 C4
Childers Ln
1300 HarC 77373 3114 B6
Childersburg Ct
7600 FBnC 77469 4095 C6
Childree Dr
- ALVN 77511 4867 C4
Childress St
3500 HOUS 77027 4101 E1
3700 HOUS 77005 4101 D2
4300 WUNP 77005 4101 C2
Childs Rd
600 GlsC 77511 4868 E3
Chile Dr
3900 PASD 77504 4247 D4
Chilliwack St
- HarC 77044 3549 A3
Chilton Dr
1700 BYTN 77520 3973 C7
Chilton Ln
1400 KATY 77493 3813 D7
Chilton Rd
2000 HOUS 77019 3962 B5
Chiltren Cir
15900 HarC 77379 3256 A6
Chimera Ln
- MSCY 77459 4498 A5
Chimes Dr
12800 HOUS 77077 3957 C5
Chimira Ln
3000 HOUS 77051 4243 B5
Chimney Brook Ln
3200 HarC 77068 3257 B4
Chimney Corners Dr
10 LMQU 77568 4989 E1
Chimney Gap
7600 FBnC 77459 4496 E7
7600 FBnC 77459 4497 A7
Chimney Hill Cir
15200 HarC 77095 3678 E1
Chimney Ridge Rd
4600 HOUS 77053 4372 D6
Chimney Rock Rd
- BLAR 77096 4100 D7
- BLAR 77401 4100 D6
- HOUS 77085 4240 D6
- HOUS 77401 4100 D6
200 HOUS 77056 3960 D5
200 HOUS 77057 3960 D5
800 HOUS 77024 3960 C1
2400 FBnC 77545 4498 C6
3000 HOUS 77056 4100 D7
3000 HOUS 77057 4100 D2
5300 HOUS 77081 4100 D7
6600 BLAR 77081 4100 D4
8600 HOUS 77096 4100 D7
8800 HOUS 77096 4240 D6
11300 HOUS 77035 4240 D5
15300 HOUS 77085 4371 D4
16000 HOUS 77053 4371 D6
16000 HOUS 77489 4371 D6
16700 FBnC 77053 4498 D1
16700 HOUS 77053 4498 D1
Chimney Rose Ct
3200 HarC 77047 4374 C4
Chimneystone Cir
2400 SGLD 77479 4368 E7
Chimneystone Dr
16300 HarC 77095 3538 B6
Chimney Sweep Dr
13100 HarC 77041 3539 C7
Chimney Trail Ln
11300 HarC 77089 4504 A1
Chimney Vine Ln
1700 HOUS 77339 3118 C7
Chimney Wood Ct
2000 FBnC 77469 4234 C7
China Sprs
25400 HarC 77373 3114 A4
Chinaberry Dr
5800 HOUS 77092 3682 B5
Chinaberry Grv
5100 MSCY 77459 4621 B2
China Berry Park Ln
2600 LGCY 77573 4631 A7
Chinaberry Park Ln
9900 HarC 77375 3110 A5
China Blue Ln
16700 HarC 77433 3250 E4
China Clipper Dr
100 BzaC 77541 5547 A7
China Doll Ct
5400 HarC 77041 3679 C6
China First
- HarC 77449 3815 C5
China Green Ln
16900 HarC 77433 3250 E3
China Lake Ct
23800 FBnC 77494 3953 B4
China Rose Ct
10 WDLD 77381 2821 C3
China Yellow Tr
17000 HarC 77433 3250 E3
Chinkapin Oak Dr
500 MtgC 77386 2968 D2
Chinni Cir
19400 HarC 77094 3955 B2
Chinni Ct
900 HarC 77094 3955 B2
Chinn Ridge Ln
16600 FBnC 77083 4235 D1

Chinon Cir
7800 MSCY 77071 4239 E7
Chinook St
7100 BYTN 77521 3835 B5
Chino Valley Ct
3200 MSCY 77459 4498 A6
Chinquapin Ln
20500 HarC 77357 2830 A7
20600 HarC 77357 2976 A1
Chinquapin Pl
900 HarC 77094 3955 A2
Chip St
400 LMQU 77568 4990 B1
19200 HarC 77532 3411 D5
Chipley Dr
4200 PASD 77505 4249 A5
Chipman Ln
14900 HOUS 77060 3544 C3
Chipman Glen Dr
13400 HOUS 77082 4097 B3
Chippawa Ln
1200 PASD 77504 4247 D6
17900 MtgC 77365 2972 B6
Chippendale Ct
3100 SGLD 77478 4369 B3
Chippendale Rd
1200 HOUS 77018 3822 C2
Chippenham Ct
1300 MSCY 77459 4369 C5
Chippenham Dr
900 HarC 77450 3954 D3
Chipperfield Dr
15000 HarC 77530 3829 C6
Chippewa Blvd
5400 HarC 77086 3542 D5
7100 HOUS 77086 3542 B5
Chippewa St
7900 HarC 77521 3833 C3
Chippewa Ridge Ct
11400 HarC 77089 4504 C1
Chipping Ct
4400 SGLD 77479 4495 D4
Chipping Ln
8800 HarC 77088 3543 D7
E Chippingham St
12700 HOUS 77077 3957 C5
W Chippingham St
12800 HOUS 77077 3957 C6
Chipping Rock Dr
8500 FBnC 77479 4494 A4
Chipplegate Ln
19800 HarC 77338 3261 E4
Chipshot St
- HarC 77346 3265 C6
Chipstead Cir
9700 HarC 77379 3255 D6
Chipstead Ct
9700 HarC 77379 3255 E6
Chipstead Dr
16200 HarC 77379 3255 E6
Chipstone Ct
26800 HarC 77433 3396 A6
Chipwood Dr
24400 MtgC 77355 2960 E2
24400 SGCH 77355 2960 E2
Chipwood Hollow Ct
11500 FBnC 77478 4236 B5
Chipwyck Wy
10 WDLD 77382 2673 A7
Chiquita St
22800 GLSN 77554 5440 E5
Chirping Sparrow Ct
500 MtgC 77362 2816 E5
Chirping Squirrel Ct
200 MtgC 77362 2817 A6
Chiselhurst Dr
9700 HarC 77065 3539 D4
Chisel Point Dr
800 HarC 77094 3955 A2
Chisholm Dr
5500 DKSN 77539 4633 D7
Chisholm Tr
2600 DRPK 77536 4109 E7
4200 STFE 77510 4871 C7
17900 HarC 77060 3403 C5
18200 HarC 77073 3403 C4
Chisholm Hollow Ct
4700 FBnC 77545 4623 C1
Chisholm Wood Ln
8900 HOUS 77075 4377 A3
Chislehurst Wy
10000 HarC 77065 3540 A3
Chislehurst Wy Ct
11300 HarC 77065 3540 A3
Chisle Stone Ln
19300 HarC 77449 3677 A7
Chisolm Creek Ct
2600 HarC 77449 3815 B4
Chisos Tr
600 HarC 77388 3113 D7
600 HarC 77388 3258 C1
Chisum St
4500 HOUS 77020 3964 C3
Chiswell St
2800 HOUS 77025 4102 A6
Chiswick Rd
12600 HOUS 77047 4373 C3
Chitwood Ct
500 HarC 77094 3955 A1
Chivary Oaks Ct
10 WDLD 77382 2673 C7
Chloe Ct
- HarC 77044 3689 C4
Choate Cir
1100 HOUS 77017 4106 B6
Choate Rd
- FRDW 77546 4628 D5
- SRAC 77571 4382 B2
400 BzaC 77511 4628 C5
3000 HOUS 77546 4505 E3
3000 HOUS 77546 4506 A3
3900 HarC 77546 4505 E4
4000 FRDW 77546 4505 E4
8600 PASD 77507 4382 A2
9000 PASD 77507 4381 E2
11300 HarC 77507 4382 B2
Choate Rd FM-2351
3000 HOUS 77546 4505 E3
3000 HOUS 77546 4506 A3
3900 HarC 77546 4505 E4
4000 FRDW 77546 4505 E4
Chocolate-Airline Rd
1800 PRLD 77584 4500 E4
Chocolate Bayou Rd
6400 MNVL 77578 4625 E4
7100 MNVL 77578 4626 A4
Choctaw
1300 GlsC 77650 4879 B5

Choctaw Dr
3500 LPRT 77571 4249 E4
3500 LPRT 77571 4250 A4
Choctaw St
18400 MtgC 77365 2972 C5
S Choctaw St
7300 HarC 77521 3833 B4
Choctaw Tr
23800 MtgC 77365 2974 B7
Choke Canyon Dr
11800 FBnC 77478 4236 B6
Cholla Canyon Ln
8000 HarC 77433 3537 B7
Cholla View Ln
19400 HarC 77433 3537 B6
Chopin Ct
11900 HarC 77429 3397 E6
Chorale Ct
8000 HarC 77040 3541 B7
Chorale Wy
8000 HarC 77040 3541 B5
Chorale Grove Ct
100 WDLD 77384 2675 A3
Chorin
200 HarC 77571 4111 B4
200 LPRT 77571 4111 B4
Chowning Rd
800 HDWV 77024 3959 E2
800 PNPV 77024 3959 E2
Chriesman Ln
3300 FBnC 77459 4621 E6
Chriesman Wy
9700 FBnC 77459 4621 E5
Chris Ct
37000 MtgC 77355 2815 E6
Chris Dr
3200 HOUS 77063 4100 A1
Chris Ln
22300 MtgC 77357 2973 E3
28100 TMBL 77375 2963 D4
Chris Rd
15200 PRLD 77047 4373 D7
15200 PRLD 77584 4373 D7
Chris Carrie Ln
10 CNRO 77303 2237 C6
Chrisman Rd
12300 HarC 77039 3545 C6
14700 HarC 77032 3545 C1
Chris Ridge Ct
27500 MtgC 77386 2969 E7
Chrissie Dr
4800 PRLD 77584 4503 A4
Christa Ln
1500 SHUS 77587 4247 A2
Christensen St
100 HOUS 77003 3964 B5
Christi Ln
13200 GlsC 77510 4870 E2
Christian Dr
11000 HarC 77044 3690 C1
Christiana Cir
27500 MtgC 77355 2963 B2
Christie St
2900 HOUS 77026 3825 A6
Christilyn
14300 HarC 77032 3546 A2
Christina Cir
- HOUS 77048 4374 D2
Christina Ct
12800 MSCY 77071 4239 C7
Christina Ln
300 FRDW 77546 4505 A7
Christine Av
300 HOUS 77017 4106 C6
E Christine Dr
25600 MtgC 77372 2537 A5
26400 SPLD 77372 2537 C5
W Christine Dr
24700 MtgC 77372 2536 E5
25200 MtgC 77372 2537 A5
Christine Crossing Dr
19200 FBnC 77469 4234 E1
Christmas Rd
- FBnC 77489 4497 E1
- FBnC 77545 4497 E1
- FBnC 77545 4498 A1
- HOUS 77489 4497 E1
- HOUS 77489 4498 A1
- HOUS 77545 4498 A1
Christmas Fern St
11000 HarC 77064 3540 E1
Christmas Point Dr
1100 GlsC 77539 4634 D4
Christmas Tree Ln
10300 CNRO 77304 2382 D2
12300 HarC 77014 3401 D3
Christmas Tree Point Rd
3400 GLSN 77554 5332 C1
Christopher Dr
2600 GLSN 77551 5108 D7
Christopher Ln
800 BYTN 77521 3973 A2
20500 HarC 77449 3815 D3
Christopher Pl
4500 HarC 77066 3401 A1
Christopher St
1400 FBnC 77477 4370 A5
Christopher Columbus Blvd
100 GLSN 77550 5109 C2
Christopher Glen Pl
1000 HarC 77073 3403 B1
Christopher Lake Ct
21600 HarC 77433 3250 E4
Christopher Park St
16300 HarC 77447 3250 A6
Christophers Walk Ct
12000 HarC 77089 4505 A2
Christopher's Walk Tr
11900 HarC 77089 4504 B1
11900 HarC 77089 4505 A1
Christopher Wren Ln
- HarC 77449 3814 E6
- HOUS 77449 3814 E6
Christy Pl
300 SHUS 77587 4246 D3
Christy St
3600 DRPK 77536 4249 C1
Christy Glen Ct
11800 HarC 77089 4505 A1
Christy Lynn Ln
900 CNRO 77304 2529 D1
Christy Mill Ct
12200 HarC 77070 3254 C7
12300 HarC 77429 3254 C7
Christy Park Cir
18600 HarC 77084 3816 C1
Chriswood Dr
12600 HarC 77377 3254 C6

Chriswood Dr
12600 HarC 77429 3254 C6
Chritien Point Ct
4900 SGLD 77478 4369 A6
Chrysanthemum Dr
12900 HOUS 77085 4241 A7
Chrystell Ln
4600 HOUS 77092 3683 A7
5700 HOUS 77092 3682 D7
Chuckanut Ln
10 PNPV 77024 3959 D5
Chuckberry St
2400 HOUS 77080 3820 D3
Chuckson Dr
11500 HarC 77065 3398 B7
Chuckwagon Tr
28000 MtgC 77355 2815 B6
Chuckwagon Ride Ln
11400 TMBL 77375 3109 E3
Chuckwood Rd
13800 HarC 77038 3543 A1
Chun
6200 HOUS 77092 3682 D5
Chupik St
2700 RSBG 77471 4490 E7
E Church Dr
600 SGLD 77478 4368 A1
W Church Dr
600 SGLD 77478 4368 A1
Church Ln
7000 HTCK 77563 4988 E4
10800 HOUS 77043 3819 C7
Church Rd
12400 HOUS 77013 3966 E1
12400 HOUS 77013 3967 A1
Church St
- BYTN 77520 3971 C5
200 GLSN 77550 5109 A3
500 HarC 77532 3552 D4
2700 DKSN 77539 4754 A3
3600 GLSN 77550 5108 E4
4500 GLSN 77551 5108 D4
23600 MtgC 77365 2973 B6
Church Colony
- FBnC 77450 4094 A3
Churchdale Pl
10 WDLD 77382 2674 D5
Churchhill Falls Ct
16600 HarC 77379 3256 B4
Churchill St
2300 HOUS 77009 3963 C1
2700 PRLD 77581 4503 D4
Churchill Ct Ln
11900 BKHV 77024 3959 B3
Churchill Gardens Ln
3500 HarC 77066 3401 C4
Churchills Fy
2400 FBnC 77469 4365 A1
Churchill Wy Cir
11300 HarC 77065 3540 A3
Churchill Wy Dr
9800 HarC 77065 3540 A3
Church Light Ln
8300 HarC 77064 3541 E5
Churchville St
8400 HOUS 77055 3821 A2
8400 HOUS 77080 3821 A2
Chute Forest Dr
12300 HarC 77014 3401 D4
Cias Trail Ln
- MtgC 77386 2969 D6
Cibola Rd
- LGCY 77573 4632 D1
Cibola Park Ln
6200 HarC 77041 3679 E4
Cibolo St
9600 HOUS 77013 3827 A5
Cicada Cir E
23800 MtgC 77357 2974 A4
Cicada Cir W
23800 MtgC 77357 2974 A4
Cicada Dr
7600 MSCY 77459 4497 B5
Cicada Ln
4700 HarC 77039 3546 C5
Cicero Rd
14000 HarC 77041 3539 A4
14000 HarC 77095 3539 A4
Ciceter Rd
12900 HarC 77039 3546 C4
Cider Creek Ln
21100 HarC 77375 3110 B4
Cider Mill Ct
10 WDLD 77382 2673 D4
Ciderwood Dr
2500 HarC 77373 3114 D7
3200 HarC 77373 3115 A6
Cielio Bay Ct
5700 HarC 77041 3679 E5
Cielio Bay Ln
12100 HarC 77041 3680 A6
Cielo Vista Ct
- FBnC 77053 4498 D2
Cien St
- KMAH 77565 4510 A6
400 KMAH 77565 4509 E7
Cienna Dr
8200 HarC 77040 3541 D7
Cilantro Ln
5300 HarC 77521 3833 D3
Cile St
3000 DRPK 77536 4249 B3
3000 PASD 77536 4249 B3
Cimarron Pkwy
21000 HarC 77450 3954 B3
21700 HOUS 77450 3954 B3
22300 HarC 77450 3953 E2
Cimarron Rd
14000 GlsC 77517 4870 C1
14000 STFE 77517 4870 C1
Cimarron St
- HarC 77015 3828 D7
- HOUS 77015 3828 D7
800 HOUS 77015 3967 D1
Cimarron Wy
39300 MtgC 77354 2672 E3
Cimarron Falls
9100 HarC 77375 2965 D5
Cimarron Pass Dr
3000 HarC 77373 3115 B4
Cimarron Pl Dr
- HarC 77450 3953 D3
- HarC 77494 3953 D3
Cimber Ln
23100 HarC 77373 3115 C7
Cimmaron Cir
3700 MSCY 77459 4621 D3

Cimmaron Dr
5300 DKSN 77539 4754 A4
5400 TXCY 77539 4754 B4
16200 SGCH 77355 2815 E6
16200 SGCH 77355 2816 A6
Cimmaron Creek Ct
5800 HarC 77379 3256 E1
Cinco Blvd
21600 FBnC 77450 3954 B7
Cinco Crossing Ln
- FBnC 77494 4093 A2
Cinco Estates Dr
- FBnC 77494 4093 A6
Cinco Lakes Ct
22200 FBnC 77450 3954 A7
Cinco Lakes Dr
3200 FBnC 77450 3954 A7
3400 FBnC 77450 3953 E7
Cinco Manor Ln
24900 FBnC 77494 4093 B1
Cinco Park Pl
- HOUS 77494 3953 D6
2300 FBnC 77494 3953 D6
Cinco Park Rd
15000 FBnC 77450 4094 B4
15000 HOUS 77450 4094 B4
Cinco Park Pl Ct
23200 FBnC 77494 3953 D6
Cinco Ranch Blvd
- FBnC 77494 4092 E2
- FBnC 77494 4093 B2
20300 FBnC 77450 3954 A7
21600 FBnC 77450 3953 D6
23100 FBnC 77494 3953 C7
23100 HOUS 77450 3953 D6
23100 HOUS 77494 3953 D6
Cinco Ranch High School Blvd
- FBnC 77494 3953 C6
Cinco Terrace Dr
25300 FBnC 77494 4092 C6
Cinder Cone Tr
12800 HarC 77044 3689 B5
Cinder Creek Ct
22900 HarC 77375 2966 A7
Cinderella St
7900 HOUS 77028 3826 B4
Cinderwood Ct
14600 HarC 77015 3829 C4
Cinderwood Dr
18200 HarC 77429 3396 B1
Cindy Ct
4400 RSBG 77471 4491 C6
Cindy Dr
6800 MNVL 77578 4746 D1
Cindy Ln
- PASD 77502 4247 C2
300 PRVW 77445 2955 A7
1700 CNRO 77304 2382 E2
1700 CNRO 77304 2383 A2
6200 HOUS 77008 3822 D6
6200 HOUS 77008 3823 A5
18000 MtgC 77302 2679 B7
18000 MtgC 77302 2825 B1
Cindy St
11800 GLSN 77554 5220 D5
Cindy Ann Wy
8000 HarC 77375 2819 E6
8000 HarC 77389 2819 E6
8000 HarC 77389 2820 A6
Cindy Lynn Ln
22200 MtgC 77447 2960 C3
22300 MtgC 77355 2960 C3
Cindyrella Dr
400 HarC 77562 3832 B3
Cindywood Cir
14100 HOUS 77079 3957 E3
14100 HOUS 77079 3958 A3
Cindywood Dr
14500 HOUS 77079 3957 D3
Cinnabar Dr
4300 HOUS 77072 4098 A4
Cinnabar Bay Ct
200 LGCY 77573 4633 C1
Cinnabar Bay Dr
200 LGCY 77573 4633 B1
Cinnaberry Ln
10200 HarC 77375 3110 B4
Cinnamon Dr
100 HarC 77450 3953 E1
100 HOUS 77450 3953 E1
Cinnamon Ln
5100 BYTN 77521 3833 B7
5100 BYTN 77521 3972 B1
8300 HOUS 77072 4098 D7
Cinnamon Run
8200 HarC 77375 2819 E6
8200 HarC 77389 2819 E6
8200 HarC 77389 2820 A6
Cinnamon St
4200 BYTN 77521 3973 A2
4200 HarC 77521 3973 A2
Cinnamon Cove Dr
3300 DKSN 77539 4754 A2
Cinnamon Creek Cir
5800 HarC 77084 3679 A6
Cinnamon Fern Ct
3900 HOUS 77059 4380 B4
Cinnamon Fern St
8900 HarC 77064 3540 E1
Cinnamon Lake Dr
5200 HarC 77521 3833 D2
Cinnamon Oak Ln
700 HOUS 77079 3958 C1
Cinnamon Ridge Dr
3000 HarC 77073 3260 A4
Cinnamon Scent St
11000 HarC 77064 3540 E1
Cinnamon Teal Pl
10 WDLD 77382 2675 B6
Circle Dr
- RSBG 77471 4490 C6
- SGLD 77478 4367 B3
- SGLD 77479 4367 B3
- TXCY 77591 4874 C7
10 CNRO 77301 2383 D2
10 HOUS 77013 3826 E4
300 LMQU 77568 4874 C7
700 LPRT 77571 4251 E4
800 BLAR 77401 4101 A3
Circle Dr E
12000 HOUS 77071 4239 D5
Circle Dr N
8000 HOUS 77071 4239 D5
Circle Dr S
12000 HOUS 77071 4239 D5
E Circle Dr
200 BYTN 77520 3835 C3

E Circle Dr
3400 PRLD 77581 4504 B5
N Circle Dr
400 BYTN 77520 4113 A1
S Circle Dr
100 BYTN 77520 3835 C3
400 BYTN 77520 4113 A1
10600 HOUS 77034 4379 A3
W Circle Dr
100 BYTN 77520 3835 C3
3400 PRLD 77581 4504 A5
Circle Wy
600 ALVN 77511 4867 D4
600 HLCS 77511 4867 D4
Circle Bend Ln
900 MSCY 77489 4370 C3
Circle C Dr
25100 PTVL 77372 2682 E6
Circle Chase Dr
14500 HOUS 77489 4371 A3
Circle Cove Ct
9000 HOUS 77088 3544 A7
Circlegate Dr
5500 HarC 77373 3115 E7
Circle H St
26700 MtgC 77372 2683 C2
Circle Lake Dr
1100 FBnC 77494 3951 E3
Circle Lake Rd
1100 FBnC 77494 3951 E3
Circle Lake Retreat
- MtgC 77362 2816 E4
- MtgC 77362 2817 A3
- SGCH 77362 2816 E4
N Circle Park St
1400 PASD 77504 4247 D7
S Circle Park St
1400 PASD 77504 4247 D7
W Circle Park St
5000 PASD 77504 4247 D7
Circle Six Dr
10 CTSH 77303 2385 D3
10 CTSH 77306 2385 D3
10 MtgC 77303 2385 D3
N Circlewood Gln
10 WDLD 77381 2821 A5
S Circlewood Gln
10 WDLD 77381 2821 A5
Circlewood Wy
14400 HOUS 77062 4380 A6
Circling Hawk Ct
15200 HarC 77095 3678 E1
Circular Quay Ln
17800 HarC 77429 3252 C7
Cirrus Ct
10 WDLD 77380 2967 E3
Cirus Ln
- WlrC 77484 3101 D4
Cisco Ct
19500 HarC 77433 3537 B5
Cisco Hill Ct
20400 FBnC 77450 4094 C1
Citadel Ln
3600 HOUS 77092 3821 B1
Citadel Plaza Dr
2600 HOUS 77008 3822 D4
Citation Ct
8600 HOUS 77088 3683 E1
Citation Dr
700 STAF 77477 4370 B4
4100 PASD 77503 4108 D7
Citrine Dr
- HarC 77095 3538 A1
Citrus Ct
8000 CmbC 77520 3835 D3
Citrus Field Ln
6500 HarC 77449 3677 B3
W Citrus Rose Ct
21700 HarC 77433 3250 E4
Citruswood Ln
10000 HarC 77089 4504 E1
City Ct
3300 HarC 77014 3401 E2
City Wk
- SGLD 77478 4368 B6
15900 SGLD 77479 4368 B6
City Club Dr
10 HOUS 77046 4101 D1
City Hall Dr
1800 RSBG 77471 4490 E6
City Park Dr
- HOUS 77051 4373 D1
11700 HOUS 77047 4373 D1
City Park Lp
- HOUS 77047 4373 D1
City Park Wy
11900 HOUS 77047 4373 D2
City Park Central Ln
11700 HOUS 77047 4373 E2
11700 HOUS 77051 4373 E1
City Park Loop St
- HOUS 77029 3826 D5
8500 HOUS 77013 3826 D5
Cityplace Dr
- HOUS 77042 3958 D7
Citywest Blvd
1500 HOUS 77042 3958 D7
City Wy Dr
- HOUS 77042 3958 D6
Civic Cir
- BYTN 77520 4112 B1
Civic Dr
- BYTN 77520 4112 B1
Civic Dr N
- BYTN 77520 4112 B1
Civic Cir Dr
- BYTN 77520 4112 B1
Civil Dr
100 LGCY 77573 4631 B4
Clabury Ct
12600 HarC 77070 3399 B5
E Clady Ct
800 MtgC 77386 2968 D1
W Clady Dr
700 MtgC 77386 2968 D1
Claiborne Dr
1700 LGCY 77573 4631 C4
Claiborne St
7400 HOUS 77016 3687 A5
8500 HOUS 77078 3687 D5
Claircrest Ln
- FBnC 77494 4093 B1
Claire Ct
2000 SGLD 77478 4369 B6
Claire Ln
400 HarC 77015 3828 D7
Claire Brook Dr
6500 FBnC 77469 4093 E7

Clairemont Dr
- LGCY 77573 4630 E4
- LGCY 77573 4631 A5
Clairfield Ln
4900 HarC 77338 3260 D2
Clairidge Park Ln
4800 FBnC 77494 4093 A1
Clairmont Dr
9700 LPRT 77571 4250 B4
Clairridge Park Ct
25500 FBnC 77494 4093 A1
Clairson Ln
7300 HarC 77433 3677 D1
Clairy Ct
100 HOUS 77076 3684 E2
Clamont Dr
13900 HarC 77070 3398 D1
Clan MacGregor Dr
16100 HarC 77084 3678 C5
Clan Macintosh Dr
17000 HarC 77084 3678 B5
Clansmoor Ct
10 SGLD 77479 4495 C2
Clanton Rd
2600 CNRO 77301 2385 A4
Clanton St
9200 HOUS 77080 3820 D1
Clara Ln
2500 TXCY 77590 4874 C3
12100 MtgC 77362 2963 C2
Clara Rd
400 PASD 77502 4247 A2
400 SHUS 77502 4247 A2
400 SHUS 77587 4247 A2
600 HarC 77532 3552 D2
5300 HarC 77041 3680 E6
6300 HOUS 77041 3680 E4
10800 HOUS 77013 3827 C5
Clara Barton Ln
10 GLSN 77551 5108 A7
Claradon Point Ln
22100 FBnC 77450 4094 A2
Clara Hills Ln
12400 HarC 77044 3689 B3
Clara Lake Ct
2000 FBnC 77469 4234 C6
Clarblak Ln
4000 HOUS 77041 3820 C1
4000 HOUS 77080 3820 C1
Clarborough Dr
- HOUS 77043 3819 D7
Clarborough Pl
10700 HOUS 77043 3819 D7
Clarcel St
- HarC 77039 3546 E3
E Clare St
2200 DRPK 77536 4109 A6
W Clare St
2200 DRPK 77536 4109 A6
Clarehouse Ln
- HarC 77047 4374 A4
Claremont Av
1500 PASD 77502 4107 D7
Claremont Ct
15600 FBnC 77478 4236 B6
Claremont Dr
- LGCY 77573 4630 E5
Claremont Ln
2000 HOUS 77019 3961 E6
2000 HOUS 77027 3961 E6
2500 HOUS 77098 3961 E6
Claremont St
5100 HOUS 77023 4104 B1
Claremont Crossing Dr
- LGCY 77573 4631 A5
Claremont Garden Cir
1500 HOUS 77047 4373 D2
Claremore Ct
21000 HarC 77449 3676 D4
Clarence St
500 TMBL 77375 2964 B7
3300 HOUS 77093 3825 A2
Clarenda Falls Dr
600 FBnC 77479 4367 A6
Clarendon Ln
11900 BKHV 77024 3959 B4
Clarendon Bend Ln
7500 FBnC 77469 4095 C7
Claresholm Dr
12200 HarC 77377 3254 B2
Claressa Ct
23200 FBnC 77494 4093 B4
Clarestone Dr
3700 BzaC 77584 4501 C5
Claret Ln
9600 HOUS 77055 3820 C7
Claret Cup Ln
7800 HarC 77040 3541 D7
Claretfield Ct
21300 HarC 77338 3261 E3
Clareton Ct
14700 HarC 77429 3397 D2
Clareton Ln
13500 HarC 77429 3397 D2
Clarewood Ct
10 WDLD 77385 2676 B4
Clarewood Dr
- HOUS 77074 4100 B4
5300 BLAR 77401 4100 E4
5300 HOUS 77081 4100 B4
7100 HOUS 77036 4099 D4
7100 HOUS 77074 4099 E4
9600 HOUS 77036 4098 E4
12000 HOUS 77072 4098 A4
12800 HOUS 77072 4097 C4
13100 HOUS 77083 4097 C4
13400 HarC 77083 4097 B4
Claridge Ct
10 CNRO 77304 2236 C7
Claridge Dr
5700 HOUS 77096 4240 C4
7600 HOUS 77071 4239 E4
9200 HOUS 77031 4239 A4
Claridge Oak Ct
100 WDLD 77384 2675 D4
Claridge Park Ln
4800 FBnC 77494 4093 A1
Clarington St
8600 HOUS 77016 3686 C7
Clarion Rdg
10 WDLD 77382 2674 D4
Clarion Wy
7900 HarC 77040 3541 A7
Clark
- HOUS 77034 4379 A5
Clark Ct
400 HOUS 77020 3964 A3

Houston Street Index

STREET
Block City ZIP Map# Grid

Clark Dr
- SEBK 77586 4383 A7
2200 LMQU 77568 4989 D3
Clark Ln
200 MtgC 77385 2677 D7
Clark Mnr
3700 FBnC 77459 4621 C5
Clark Rd
5700 BzaC 77583 4745 D4
5700 IWCY 77583 4745 D4
5700 MNVL 77578 4745 E4
5700 MNVL 77583 4745 D4
5900 MNVL 77578 4746 A3
9400 HOUS 77022 3685 A6
9400 HOUS 77076 3685 A6
10900 MtgC 77302 2531 A6
Clark Rd CO-72
5700 BzaC 77583 4745 D4
5700 IWCY 77583 4745 D4
5700 MNVL 77578 4745 D4
5700 MNVL 77583 4745 D4
Clark St
- HOUS 77020 3963 E2
100 PRVW 77445 3100 C2
700 ALVN 77511 4867 A2
10000 HarC 77064 3541 D2
18700 MtgC 77302 2825 B3
Clarkcrest St
8900 HOUS 77063 4099 D1
Clarkdale Ct
1200 HarC 77094 3955 B3
Clarkdon Ct
- HarC 77066 3401 A5
Clarke Dr
10 CNRO 77301 2384 A2
Clarke St
200 RHMD 77469 4491 D1
Clarke Springs Dr
15700 HOUS 77053 4372 C6
Clarkgate Dr
4200 HarC 77373 3115 B7
Clark Grove Ln
10400 HOUS 77075 4377 B3
Clark Hill Ct
21400 HarC 77449 3815 B1
Clarkman Ln
- HarC 77047 4374 B3
Clark Sage Ct
21000 HarC 77449 3815 B1
Clarks Fork Dr
13600 HarC 77086 3541 D1
Clarkson Ln
6100 HOUS 77055 3822 A6
Clarkston Ln
5200 HarC 77379 3112 A5
Clarksville
- DRPK 77536 4249 E3
- LPRT 77536 4249 E3
- LPRT 77571 4249 E3
Clarksville St
3100 DRPK 77536 4249 E3
3100 LPRT 77536 4249 E3
3100 LPRT 77571 4249 E3
Clark Tower Ct
10300 FBnC 77478 4237 A3
Clark Tower Ln
10300 FBnC 77478 4237 A3
Clark Towne Rd
- HOUS 77478 4237 A3
13800 FBnC 77478 4237 A3
Clark Wheeler St
7100 HarC 77049 3827 E1
Clary Sage Ct
10 WDLD 77382 2819 E3
Classic Oaks Pl
10 WDLD 77382 2674 D6
Clatt Wy
- CNRO 77301 2530 B3
Claudia Dr
10 HOUS 77013 3827 C6
12400 GNPK 77015 3966 E4
12400 GNPK 77015 3967 A4
Clave Ct
2500 HarC 77089 4504 C1
Claverton Dr
3500 HarC 77066 3401 C6
Clawson St
6500 HOUS 77055 3821 E6
6500 HOUS 77055 3822 A6
Clawson Falls Ln
2200 FBnC 77479 4493 E3
Claxton St
1000 HOUS 77023 4105 B3
1000 HOUS 77087 4105 B3
Clay Ct
1000 DRPK 77536 4109 E5
Clay Ln
3900 GlsC 77518 4634 C3
Clay Rd
- HOUS 77080 3821 A1
- HOUS 77092 3821 A1
8700 HOUS 77041 3820 C1
8700 HOUS 77041 3821 A1
8700 HOUS 77080 3820 C1
10100 HOUS 77043 3820 A1
10300 HOUS 77041 3819 A1
10300 HOUS 77043 3819 E1
13000 HOUS 77084 3818 A1
13000 HOUS 77084 3819 A1
15400 HOUS 77084 3817 B1
15700 HarC 77084 3817 A1
18000 HarC 77084 3816 D1
19000 HarC 77449 3816 D1
19900 HarC 77449 3815 A1
23200 HarC 77449 3814 A1
23200 HarC 77493 3814 A1
24600 HarC 77493 3813 A1
24600 KATY 77493 3813 A1
27000 HarC 77493 3812 E1
Clay St
200 FBnC 77469 4364 D7
200 RHMD 77469 4364 D7
300 HOUS 77002 3963 B4
1200 FBnC 77477 4370 A5
1700 HOUS 77003 3963 C5
3900 HOUS 77023 3964 A7
5400 HOUS 77023 4104 D1
W Clay St
300 HOUS 77019 3962 C5
Claybeck Ln
5600 FBnC 77494 4093 B2
Clayberry St
9200 HOUS 77080 3820 D3
Clay Brook Dr
10300 HarC 77089 4377 B6
Clay Canyon
4300 FBnC 77450 4093 E2
Claycliff Ct
12800 HOUS 77034 4378 C2
Claycliff Ln
7000 FBnC 77469 4615 D5
Clay Creek Ct
2600 PRLD 77581 4504 A3
Clay Creek Dr
16200 HarC 77084 3817 D1
16200 HOUS 77084 3817 D1
Claycreste Ct
15100 HarC 77429 3397 C1
Claycroft Ct
14600 HarC 77429 3397 D2
Claygate Dr
12400 HOUS 77047 4374 C2
Clayhead Rd
3200 FBnC 77469 4233 D7
3200 FBnC 77469 4364 E1
3200 FBnC 77469 4365 A1
Clay Hill Dr
4200 HarC 77084 3817 D1
4200 HOUS 77084 3817 D1
Clayhorn Ct
7200 FBnC 77469 4094 E2
Clay Landing Ln
20800 HarC 77449 3815 C2
Claymill Ct
4800 HarC 77449 3676 E6
Claymont Hill Dr
13800 HarC 77429 3397 A2
Claymoore Park Dr
3000 HOUS 77043 3819 C2
3900 HOUS 77041 3819 C2
Claymore Ct
10 PNPV 77024 3959 E3
Claymore Rd
11100 HNCV 77024 3959 E3
11100 PNPV 77024 3959 E3
Clay Oak St
400 HarC 77084 3816 C1
Clay Pigeon Ct
16300 HOUS 77489 4370 E7
Clay Point Ct
400 PNPV 77024 3959 D3
Claypool St
- HarC 77032 3404 B6
15100 HOUS 77032 3404 B7
Clayridge Dr
6200 HOUS 77053 4371 D6
6200 HOUS 77489 4371 D6
Claysprings Ln
22200 FBnC 77450 4093 E3
Clayton Dr
2100 BYTN 77520 3973 C6
Clayton St
500 TMBL 77375 2964 B7
Clayton Bend Ct
4000 HarC 77082 4096 B4
Clayton Bend Dr
15700 HarC 77082 4096 B4
Clayton Bluff Ln
- HarC 77433 3537 A5
Clayton Gate Dr
3900 HarC 77082 4096 E3
Clayton Green Dr
16000 HarC 77082 4096 B4
Clayton Greens Ct
4000 HarC 77082 4096 E3
Clayton Hill Rd
13500 HarC 77041 3679 C5
Clayton Homes
- HOUS 77003 3963 E3
Clayton Junction Ln
3800 FBnC 77494 4092 B2
Clayton Oaks Dr
- HarC 77082 4096 D2
Clayton Ridge Ct
2900 HarC 77082 4096 C2
Claytons Bend Ct
1600 MtgC 77386 2969 D7
Claytons Cove Ct
1700 MtgC 77386 2969 C6
Clayton Terrace Dr
3200 MSCY 77459 4498 A5
Clayton Trace Tr
3500 HarC 77082 4096 B3
Clayton Woods Blvd
3400 HarC 77082 4096 C3
3400 HOUS 77082 4096 C3
Clayton Woods Dr
3200 HarC 77082 4096 C2
Claywood St
11700 BKHV 77024 3959 C4
11700 HOUS 77024 3959 C4
Clear Bend Ln
6400 FBnC 77450 4094 A5
Clearbend Pl
10 WDLD 77384 2675 A5
Clearbourne Ln
8700 HOUS 77075 4376 E2
8800 HOUS 77075 4377 A3
Clearbrook Dr
2200 MSCY 77489 4497 B1
Clearbrook Ln
900 HOUS 77057 3960 B5
19000 MtgC 77355 2814 E4
Clear Brook City Dr
- HarC 77089 4377 C6
Clear Brook Oak St
11900 HarC 77089 4505 A1
Clear Canyon Dr
6200 FBnC 77450 4094 D4
Clear Cape Ln
13000 HOUS 77085 4240 D7
Clear Cove Ct
400 LGCY 77539 4752 D5
Clear Cove Ln
10400 HOUS 77041 3819 E1
Clear Creek Av
200 LGCY 77573 4632 A3
Clear Creek Cir
7400 HarC 77521 3833 D4
24100 WlrC 77447 2959 D3
N Clear Creek Dr
300 FRDW 77546 4629 E3
300 FRDW 77546 4630 A2
S Clear Creek Dr
300 FRDW 77546 4629 E3
300 FRDW 77546 4630 A2
Clear Creek Rd
- BKVL 77581 4375 A6
- PRLD 77581 4375 A6
24000 WlrC 77447 2959 D4
N Clear Creek Rd
24500 WlrC 77447 2959 C2
S Clear Creek Rd
24800 WlrC 77447 2959 C3
Clear Creek Wy
- HOUS 77345 3119 E1
Clear Creek Meadows Dr
- LGCY 77573 4631 A4
Clearcrest Dr
15700 HOUS 77059 4380 C6
Clear Dale Dr
19700 HarC 77346 3265 A5
Clear Falls Dr
3700 HOUS 77339 3119 B4
Clearfield Dr
11000 HarC 77044 3690 C1
Clearfield Springs Ct
2100 PRLD 77581 4503 D2
Clear Forest Dr
13900 FBnC 77478 4237 A4
14000 FBnC 77478 4236 E4
Clear Fork Dr
10800 HarC 77396 3548 D1
Clearfork Dr
12200 HOUS 77077 3957 E5
Clear Glen Dr
19700 HarC 77346 3265 A5
Cleargrove Ln
10100 HOUS 77075 4376 E2
Clearhaven Ct
15300 HarC 77429 3253 C6
Clear Hollow Ln
12100 HarC 77089 4505 A1
Clear Lake Cross
900 HOUS 77598 4379 B7
900 HOUS 77598 4506 C1
Clear Lake Ct
4300 MSCY 77459 4496 C3
Clear Lake Lp
- PRLD 77584 4500 C2
S Clear Lake Lp
- PRLD 77584 4500 D1
Clear Lake Rd
10 HarC 77562 3831 B3
100 CRLS 77565 4509 C5
800 GlsC 77565 4509 C6
Clear Lake City Blvd
- HOUS 77059 4379 E5
- HOUS 77062 4380 A5
- HOUS 77546 4506 B2
100 HOUS 77062 4379 D6
100 HOUS 77598 4506 B2
200 HOUS 77598 4379 C7
4400 HOUS 77059 4380 A4
4400 PASD 77059 4380 C4
Clear Lake City Blvd FM-2351
- HOUS 77546 4506 B2
100 HOUS 77062 4379 C7
100 HOUS 77598 4379 C7
100 HOUS 77598 4506 B2
Clear Lake Park Rd
- PASD 77586 4508 D2
Clear Landing Ct
5300 BzaC 77583 4623 D4
Clear Landing Ln
14000 BzaC 77583 4623 D4
Clearlight Ln
17800 HarC 77379 3256 B1
Clear Meadow Ln
9900 HarC 77089 4504 E1
Clearmeadow St
16000 HarC 77530 3830 B5
Clear Mill Ln
26400 FBnC 77494 4092 B1
Clearmont Dr
16300 HOUS 77053 4372 A7
Clear Oak Wy
16700 HOUS 77058 4507 D2
Clear Point Ct
500 FBnC 77469 4365 B5
Clear Point Dr
15600 HarC 77429 3397 B1
Clear Ridge Dr
2400 HOUS 77339 3119 A2
Clear River Dr
12200 HOUS 77050 3547 A5
Clearsable Ln
11000 HOUS 77034 4378 D4
Clearsky Ct
3100 LGCY 77573 4633 B2
Clear Sky Dr
19200 HarC 77346 3265 A3
Clearsmoke Cir
8700 HarC 77095 3538 B5
Clearsmoke Dr
9100 HarC 77095 3538 B5
Clear Spring Dr
- HOUS 77079 3957 E3
Clear Springs Wy
25700 HarC 77373 3113 E4
Clear Trail Ln
13700 HOUS 77034 4378 D4
Clear Valley Dr
1200 HarC 77014 3402 C3
15400 HarC 77095 3678 D1
Clearview Av
100 FRDW 77546 4629 C1
300 FRDW 77546 4505 D7
Clearview Cir
3000 HOUS 77025 4241 E3
3000 HOUS 77054 4241 E3
Clearview Dr
- FBnC 77479 4494 B5
Clearview St
7800 HOUS 77033 4243 D2
Clearview Village Blvd
10900 HOUS 77034 4378 D2
Clear Villa Ln
10900 HOUS 77034 4378 C4
Clearwater Cross
8000 HarC 77396 3547 D1
Clear Water Ct
32800 MtgC 77354 2672 A4
Clearwater Ct
3400 SGLD 77478 4368 E5
4200 MSCY 77459 4369 C6
Clearwater St
300 HOUS 77029 3966 A6
Clearwater Creek Dr
1600 SGLD 77478 4368 E5
Clear Water Park Dr
3000 FBnC 77450 3954 A7
Clearway Dr
9200 HOUS 77033 4244 B5
Clear Wing St
3100 HarC 77373 3114 E6
Clearwood Ct
3000 ALVN 77511 4866 D5
Clearwood Ct
- LGCY 77573 4630 B6
Clearwood Dr
- LGCY 77573 4630 B6
8900 HOUS 77034 4246 B7
8900 HOUS 77075 4246 B6
9600 HOUS 77075 4377 B1
Clearwood Crossing Blvd
10400 HOUS 77075 4377 A3
Clearwood Landing Blvd
9000 HOUS 77075 4377 A2
Cleburne Dr
4100 PRLD 77584 4503 A7
Cleburne St
1000 HOUS 77002 3963 A7
1000 HOUS 77004 3963 A7
1500 HOUS 77004 4103 C2
Clee Ln
6800 HarC 77379 3256 D2
Cleerebrook Pl
10 WDLD 77382 2673 E6
10 WDLD 77382 2674 A6
Cleeve Close
18700 HarC 77346 3264 D7
Cleft Stone Dr
6700 HarC 77084 3678 E2
Cleghorn Ln
10100 HOUS 77024 3960 C2
Clematis Ln
- HOUS 77035 4240 E4
- HOUS 77035 4241 A3
Clement St
5600 HOUS 77026 3824 E4
Clementine St
2100 HOUS 77020 3964 C1
2800 HOUS 77026 3825 C7
E Clements St
600 ALVN 77511 4867 C2
Clementshire St
5600 HOUS 77087 4104 C7
5800 HOUS 77087 4244 C1
Clemons Ln
5800 TXCY 77591 4873 E5
Clemson Dr
2200 KATY 77493 3813 D4
Clemson St
6600 HOUS 77092 3821 C1
Clennie Needham Rd
23900 MtgC 77365 2973 C7
Cleo
600 FBnC 77545 4499 A7
Cleo St
6700 BKVL 77581 4376 A6
Cleobrook Dr
14000 HarC 77070 3399 E1
Clepper Dr
13200 HarC 77375 2964 B2
13200 TMBL 77375 2964 B2
Clepper St
100 MAGA 77355 2669 A5
Clepper Wood
300 SGCH 77362 2816 E5
Clerkenwell Dr
5700 HarC 77084 3678 B4
Clermont Ct
10 SGCH 77355 2961 C2
Clevedon Ct
15400 JRSV 77040 3540 E6
Clevedon Ln
15300 JRSV 77040 3540 E7
Cleveland Av
3200 FBnC 77545 4499 C7
Cleveland Dr
10 SGLD 77478 4368 B1
1500 DRPK 77536 4249 D1
Cleveland St
700 HOUS 77002 3963 A5
700 HOUS 77019 3963 A5
1700 HOUS 77019 3962 E5
1800 PASD 77502 4107 C7
E Cleveland St
10 BYTN 77520 4112 E1
W Cleveland St
10 BYTN 77520 4112 E1
100 ALVN 77511 4867 A2
Cleveland Bay Ct
9600 HarC 77065 3539 E4
Clevera Walk Ln
19400 HarC 77084 3816 A4
Cliff
12200 HarC 77089 4505 B1
Cliff Ct
10 HOUS 77076 3684 C5
Cliff Dr
2500 GlsC 77539 4635 C4
13200 HarC 77532 3692 D1
13400 HarC 77532 3552 D7
Cliffbrook Ct
15700 HarC 77095 3678 C1
Cliffdale Dr
1800 MSCY 77489 4370 C5
1900 HOUS 77091 3683 D4
Cliffdale St
2400 HOUS 77091 3683 B4
Cliffgate Dr
- HOUS 77072 4097 E7
11900 HOUS 77072 4098 A7
Cliff Haven Ct
10300 HarC 77095 3538 B3
Cliff Haven Dr
16200 HarC 77095 3538 B3
Cliffhille Ct
25600 FBnC 77494 4093 A7
Cliffmarshell St
3200 HOUS 77088 3543 A7
Clifford
- HDWV 77024 3959 E1
- SPVL 77024 3959 E1
Clifford St
900 ALVN 77511 4749 E7
Clifton Forge Dr
10800 HarC 77065 3539 E1
Cliff Park Dr
1200 HarC 77450 3953 E4
10200 HarC 77065 3539 B3
Cliff Point Ct
4800 HarC 77449 3677 B7
Cliffrose Ct
11100 HarC 77089 4504 B1
Cliffrose Ln
16500 HOUS 77062 4507 B3
Cliffsage Ct
19500 HarC 77433 3537 B7
Cliffshire Ct
8200 FBnC 77083 4096 A7
Cliffside Dr
700 HOUS 77076 3685 B3
Cliffsider Dr
400 HOUS 77076 3685 A3
Cliffstone Ln
- RHMD 77469 4492 B2
4700 HarC 77449 3677 A7
Cliff Stone Rd W
7000 BzaC 77581 4502 B1
7000 PRLD 77581 4502 B1
Cliff Swallow Ct
3100 HarC 77373 3114 E6
Cliffwood Dr
9000 HOUS 77096 4101 C7
9000 HOUS 77096 4241 C1
9600 HOUS 77035 4241 B4
Cliffwood St
23200 MtgC 77357 2827 E7
23200 MtgC 77357 2828 A7
Clift Haven Dr
4700 HOUS 77018 3823 A1
4900 HOUS 77018 3684 B7
5400 HOUS 77091 3684 A6
Clifton Ln
3900 GlsC 77518 4634 B3
Clifton St
10 HOUS 77011 3964 C6
Clifton Center Dr
9700 HOUS 77099 4238 A2
Clifton Oaks Dr
11900 HOUS 77099 4238 A2
Clifton Park Dr
9700 HOUS 77099 4238 A2
Climber Ct
5300 HarC 77041 3679 B6
Climbing Branch Ct
3100 HarC 77068 3257 C4
Climbing Branch Dr
15100 HarC 77068 3257 C5
Climbing Ivy Cir
4900 HarC 77084 3677 D6
Climbing Oaks Dr
19400 HarC 77346 3264 D5
Climbing Rose Ct
10 WDLD 77385 2676 B4
3900 FBnC 77583 4622 C4
Cline Dr
100 ALVN 77511 4749 B2
100 BzaC 77511 4749 B2
Cline Ln
27900 MtgC 77357 2829 E5
Cline Rd
9600 HarC 77050 3548 A4
Cline St
2500 HOUS 77020 3963 E3
3300 BYTN 77521 3973 C4
4100 HOUS 77020 3964 B3
Cline Wy
10 FBnC 77459 4621 C6
Clingstone Pl
10 WDLD 77382 2673 E5
Clint Neidigk Rd
10200 MtgC 77354 2818 B6
Clinton Dr
300 GNPK 77547 3966 B7
300 GNPK 77547 3967 A7
300 HOUS 77015 3967 A7
300 HOUS 77547 3966 B7
2300 GNPK 77547 4106 A1
2300 HOUS 77547 4106 A1
2700 HOUS 77020 3964 B3
5500 HOUS 77020 3964 D3
6900 HOUS 77020 3965 C5
7300 HOUS 77029 3965 B4
9600 HOUS 77029 3966 A7
9700 HOUS 77029 4106 A1
9800 GNPK 77029 4106 A1
Clinton St
100 CNRO 77301 2383 E6
200 CNRO 77301 2384 A6
Clinton Park Av
200 HOUS 77029 3966 A7
Clintridge Dr
5500 HarC 77084 3677 E5
Clintway Dr
13800 HarC 77014 3402 C3
Clio St
700 HOUS 77009 3824 A5
Clipper St
- HarC 77532 3552 A3
Clipper Hill Ct
5200 HarC 77373 3115 C4
Clipper Hill Ln
23900 HarC 77373 3115 C4
Clipper Pointe Dr
15900 HarC 77429 3397 C2
Clippers Sq
2400 NSUB 77058 4508 B4
Clippers Cove Dr
2400 NSUB 77058 4508 B4
Clipper Winds Wy
3100 HarC 77084 3816 E4
Clipperwood Pl
9200 HarC 77083 4237 A1
Cliveden Dr
11600 HarC 77066 3401 C6
Cloaksdale Ln
7100 HarC 77433 3677 B2
Clobourne Crossing Ln
3800 HarC 77546 4506 A6
Clodine Reddick Rd
- FBnC 77083 4235 E1
- FBnC 77469 4095 D6
- FBnC 77469 4235 E1
7300 FBnC 77083 4095 D6
Cloister Dr
1600 HarC 77532 3551 D3
Clopper St
1900 SEBK 77586 4509 E2
Closewood Terrace Dr
16000 HarC 77429 3397 B2
Clotell Cir
10 HOUS 77048 4375 A1
Clothier St
14700 HOUS 77034 4379 A5
Cloud Dr
12900 GlsC 77510 4986 E5
Cloud Ln
10300 GLSN 77554 5221 B1
Cloud Bank Pl
10 WDLD 77382 2673 C5
Cloudberry Ln
9900 HarC 77375 3110 A4
Cloudbluff Ln
3800 FBnC 77469 4615 E5
Cloudbridge Ct
100 LGCY 77573 4633 A1
Cloudbridge Dr
- FBnC 77450 3954 C7
100 LGCY 77573 4633 B1
Cloudbrook Ln
- HarC 77449 3815 B2
Cloudburst Ln
2200 PRLD 77545 4499 E2
Cloudcap Ct
13900 HarC 77044 3549 D2
Cloud Cliff Ln
14200 HOUS 77077 3956 E6
Cloudcliff Ln
4900 FBnC 77494 4092 E2
Cloudcraft Ct
5200 FBnC 77494 4093 B6
Cloud Croft Dr
1800 FRDW 77546 4629 D5
Cloudcroft Dr
2500 DRPK 77536 4109 E7
Cloudhaven Ct
4900 HarC 77449 3677 B7
Cloud Lake Ct
21200 FBnC 77450 4094 A4
Cloudleap Pl
10 WDLD 77381 2821 A1
Cloudmount Dr
4500 HarC 77084 3678 E7
Cloud Peak Dr
19300 HarC 77377 3109 B7
Clouds Rst
23900 MtgC 77355 2962 C5
Clouds Hill Ct
1300 HarC 77379 3255 B2
Cloud Swept Ln
6600 HarC 77086 3542 C2
Cloudy Mist Dr
- FBnC 77479 4366 E6
Clove Cir
10100 HOUS 77078 3687 C4
Clover Dr
3800 ALVN 77511 4867 D5
Clover Hl
17900 HarC 77094 3955 E2
Clover Ln
3600 DRPK 77536 4249 E1
4800 PRLD 77584 4502 A5
W Clover Ln
18000 BzaC 77511 4628 D3
18000 BzaC 77581 4628 D3
Clover Pth
18600 MtgC 77365 2972 A5
Clover Rdg
2500 LGCY 77573 4632 E2
Clover St
- LGCY 77573 4632 D1
4100 HOUS 77051 4243 C4
5000 HOUS 77033 4243 E3
Clover Bend Ln
- HarC 77064 3540 B3
Clover Bend St
10 LMQU 77568 4989 C2
Cloverbrook Dr
3700 HOUS 77045 4372 D2
Clover Brook Ln
17100 HarC 77095 3537 E4
Cloverbrook Ln
- FBnC 77469 4616 E1
Clover Canyon Cir
7600 HarC 77095 3538 B7
Clovercreek Blvd
19000 MtgC 77355 2815 A4
Clover Creek Dr
3500 HOUS 77345 3120 A4
Clover Creek Ln
- PRLD 77583 4500 B4
Clover Crest Ct
- HarC 77095 3538 D3
Clover Crest Dr
21200 HarC 77095 3538 D3
Cloverdale Cir
- HOUS 77028 3687 E7
Cloverdale Dr
3000 LGCY 77573 4633 A2
Cloverdale St
3200 HOUS 77025 4101 E7
3500 HOUS 77025 4241 E2
Cloverfalls Ln
- FBnC 77494 4093 C3
Cloverfield Ct
2600 PRLD 77584 4502 A5
Cloverfield Dr
1600 BzaC 77511 4628 D2
1600 BzaC 77581 4628 D2
1900 FBnC 77494 3952 E3
4800 PRLD 77584 4502 A4
Clover Gardens Dr
8100 HarC 77095 3538 E6
S Clovergate Cir
10 WDLD 77382 2674 A5
Clover Glade Pl
10 WDLD 77381 2820 C1
Clover Glen Ln
18700 HarC 77084 3816 C2
19000 HarC 77449 3816 B2
Clover Green Ln
11300 HOUS 77067 3402 C6
11700 HarC 77067 3402 C5
Clover Grove Ct
18400 HarC 77084 3816 D4
Clover Hill Ln
3300 TXCY 77591 4872 C2
Clover Hills Cir
25500 MtgC 77380 2968 A2
Clover Knoll Ct
7800 HarC 77095 3538 A6
Cloverlake Ct
7700 HarC 77040 3541 E7
Clover Land Ct
8500 HarC 77338 3262 A4
Cloverland Park Ln
- HarC 77433 3396 B5
Cloverleaf Blvd
500 HarC 77015 3829 A7
800 HarC 77015 3968 A2
Clover Leaf Ct
3200 BzaC 77578 4501 A6
Clover Leaf Dr
8200 FBnC 77469 4616 D1
2600 BzaC 77581 4628 C1
Cloverleaf Dr
19100 MtgC 77355 2814 E4
19300 MtgC 77355 2815 A3
Clover Ln Ct
11500 HarC 77066 3400 D5
Clover Lodge Ct
16400 FBnC 77478 4236 B5
Clovermeadow Ln
20900 HarC 77379 3111 D4
Clover Meadows St
3700 PASD 77505 4248 D4
Clovermill Dr
11500 HarC 77066 3401 B6
Clovermist Dr
- HarC 77064 3540 B7
Clovermist Ln
17000 BzaC 77581 4504 C7
17000 BzaC 77581 4628 C1
Clovernook Ln
4100 TYLV 77586 4381 D7
4100 TYLV 77586 4508 D1
Clover Park Dr
18000 HarC 77346 3408 A1
Clover Patch Ln
- ALVN 77511 4749 B6
Clover Point Dr
14100 FBnC 77478 4236 E4
Clover Ranch Cir
3100 FBnC 77494 3953 A5
Clover Ranch Dr
25300 FBnC 77494 3953 A6
25400 FBnC 77494 3952 E6
Clover Ridge Av
900 FRDW 77546 4628 E1
900 FRDW 77546 4629 A1
Clover Ridge St
6000 HOUS 77087 4104 C6
Clover Spring Dr
1800 HOUS 77339 3118 D5
Cloverstone Ct
19500 HarC 77094 3955 A2
Clover Trail Ln
1500 HarC 77067 3402 B6
Clover Trails Dr
23800 FBnC 77494 4093 B5
Clovervale Dr
- HarC 77014 3402 C3
Clover Valley Dr
3300 HOUS 77345 3120 A4
Cloverview Dr
17600 HarC 77377 3254 B3
Clover Walk Ln
12500 HarC 77041 3679 E3
Cloverwalk Ln
12900 HarC 77072 4097 C5
Cloverwick Ln
16300 HarC 77379 3256 E4
Cloverwood Dr
12600 HarC 77429 3254 B6
12700 HarC 77377 3254 B6
19100 MtgC 77355 2814 E4
19100 MtgC 77355 2815 A3
Clovis Rd
1100 HOUS 77008 3822 E7
Clovis Wy
21500 HarC 77338 3260 A1
Clow Rd
4200 HarC 77068 3256 E6
4200 HarC 77068 3257 A5
4200 HarC 77069 3256 E6
Cloyanna Ln
18900 HarC 77346 3264 E6
Cloyd Dr
700 MAGA 77355 2668 E6
Club Ct
700 CRLS 77565 4509 C5
Club Ln
12700 HOUS 77099 4237 C3
W Club Ln
12700 HOUS 77099 4237 C3
Club Creek Dr
- HOUS 77074 4239 B1
9700 HOUS 77036 4239 A1
9800 HOUS 77036 4098 E7
9800 HOUS 77036 4238 E1
Clubhollow
4100 FBnC 77450 4094 C1
Clubhouse Cir
- MtgC 77354 2672 C4
Club House Dr
10 BzaC 77578 4625 B3
Clubhouse Dr
1500 FRDW 77546 4749 E1
2900 BzaC 77584 4501 B5
Clubhouse Ln
37300 MtgC 77355 2815 D5
Club Lake Dr
- HarC 77095 3678 C1
7500 HarC 77095 3538 D7
Club Oak Ct
10 HOUS 77339 3264 D1
Club Point Dr
8000 HarC 77346 3265 B4
Club Ridge Ct
10 WDLD 77382 2673 E6
Club Valley Dr
3900 HarC 77082 4096 D3
Clubview Ct
10 WDLD 77382 2673 C7
Cluett St
6900 HOUS 77028 3826 B2
Cluny Ct
10 WDLD 77382 2820 A1
Cluster
9600 HOUS 77055 3820 C7
Cluster Ct
17800 HarC 77379 3257 C2
Clustering Oak Ct
7000 FBnC 77469 4095 C5
Cluster Oaks Dr
18700 MtgC 77355 2815 A2
19400 HarC 77346 3264 D5
Cluster Pine Dr
12900 HarC 77429 3254 B6
Cluster Pines Ct
14200 HarC 77066 3401 E7
Clyburn Ct
3100 MSCY 77459 4497 E6
Clyde Dr
300 BYTN 77520 3972 B6
1000 ALVN 77511 4866 C2
20200 MtgC 77357 2827 D6
Clyde St
6000 HOUS 77007 3962 A2
Clydesdale St
4600 HarC 77084 3678 C7
Clydesdale Ridge Dr
- HarC 77338 3261 D4
CO-48 Kingsley Dr
- PRLD 77047 4373 B7
- PRLD 77583 4500 B4
- PRLD 77584 4373 B7
- PRLD 77584 4500 B3
CO-56 CR-56
- BzaC 77583 4744 E6
CO-57 Juliff Manvel Rd
900 IWCY 77583 4744 E4
900 IWCY 77583 4745 A4
1100 BzaC 77583 4745 D4
1100 MNVL 77578 4745 D4
1100 MNVL 77583 4745 D4

STREET
Block City ZIP Map# Grid

CO-72 Clark Rd
5700 BzaC 77583 4745 D4
5700 IWCY 77583 4745 D4
5700 MNVL 77578 4745 D4
5700 MNVL 77583 4745 D4
CO-79 W Colony Loop Rd
8500 IWCY 77583 4745 D3
8600 BzaC 77583 4745 D4
CO-89 Old Chocolate Bayou Rd
- PRLD 77584 4501 E4
CO-90 CR-90
- BzaC 77584 4501 C6
- PRLD 77584 4501 C6
CO-127 Dixie-Friendswood Rd
18000 BzaC 77511 4628 D2
18000 BzaC 77581 4628 D2
18200 BzaC 77546 4628 E2
CO-127 Hastings Friendswood Rd
1500 BzaC 77581 4504 B7
1500 PRLD 77581 4504 B7
16700 BzaC 77581 4628 B1
CO-128 Hastings Cannon Rd
7500 BzaC 77511 4627 B4
7500 BzaC 77584 4627 B4
7500 PRLD 77584 4627 B4
CO-155 Five Point Rd
1900 BzaC 77511 4867 E3
1900 BzaC 77511 4868 A4
CO-155 Fulton Dr
- BzaC 77511 4868 B4
CO-155 E South St
1200 ALVN 77511 4867 D3
1700 BzaC 77511 4867 E3
CO-158 Mustang Rd
3800 ALVN 77511 4867 D6
4900 BzaC 77511 4867 D7
CO-257 Bluewater Hwy
- GlsC 77554 5547 C6
10200 BzaC 77541 5547 B7
10200 BzaC 77541 5654 A1
CO-326 Newson Rd
3200 BzaC 77511 4868 B6
CO-397 Wink Rd
10 BzaC 77511 4747 E1
CO-397 Wink Wyn Rd
1400 BzaC 77511 4747 E1
CO-413 N Hastings Field Rd
2200 BzaC 77511 4628 A2
2200 PRLD 77511 4628 A2
9100 BzaC 77511 4627 E2
9100 PRLD 77511 4627 E2
CO-560 CR-560
5200 BzaC 77581 4502 B1
5200 PRLD 77581 4502 B1
CO-562 Smith Ranch Road 1
10400 PRLD 77584 4501 A2
CO-648K Lakecrest Dr
2600 BzaC 77584 4501 D5
CO-824A Martha Dr
5900 BzaC 77583 4623 C5
5900 PRLD 77583 4623 C5
CO-824D
- BzaC 77583 4623 C6
CO-870H
100 BzaC 77511 4748 E1
CO-879B N Wayne Ln
16700 BzaC 77584 4626 E1
17300 PRLD 77584 4626 E2
CO-922 Jeske Rd
- BzaC 77584 4501 B6
- PRLD 77584 4501 B6
3900 BzaC 77578 4501 B7
Coach Rd
100 HOUS 77060 3544 D1
Coachcreek Dr
7000 HOUS 77085 4371 B1
Coachfield Ln
11500 HOUS 77035 4240 B5
Coachgate Dr
6000 HarC 77373 3116 A7
Coach Lamp Ln
100 HOUS 77060 3544 C2
Coachlight Dr
900 HOUS 77077 3957 A3
Coach Light Ln
600 MtgC 77357 2829 C5
Coachlight Ln
2400 MtgC 77384 2529 A5
3000 SGLD 77479 4495 D1
3400 BYTN 77521 3972 A1
Coachmaker Dr
17000 HarC 77546 4506 B7
Coachman Dr
2400 MtgC 77384 2529 A6
3400 BYTN 77521 3972 A1
Coachman Ln
400 BKHV 77024 3959 C4
Coachman Rdg
10 WDLD 77382 2674 B5
Coachmans Ln
12200 MtgC 77362 2963 B1
Coachouse
- HOUS 77449 3814 D6
Coach Point St
- HOUS 77042 4099 A2
Coachwood Dr
6300 HOUS 77035 4240 A5
7500 HOUS 77071 4239 E5
7500 HOUS 77071 4240 A6
Coahuila St
9600 HOUS 77013 3826 E5
9600 HOUS 77013 3827 A5
Coal St
3000 HOUS 77026 3825 A5
Coal Creek Ln
17800 HarC 77433 3396 C7
17800 HarC 77433 3537 C1
Coaldale
8500 HarC 77040 3681 C2
Coalfield Ln
11400 HarC 77433 3396 A7
Coalport Ct
800 HarC 77073 3259 A4
Coaming Ct
17000 HarC 77532 3552 B1
Coan St
9500 HOUS 77093 3685 E6
Coapites St
4000 PASD 77504 4248 A5
S Coast Dr
12400 HOUS 77047 4374 C1
Coastal Mdw
23700 FBnC 77494 4093 A4

STREET
Block City ZIP Map# Grid

Coastal Wy
5400 HOUS 77045 4241 A7
5400 HOUS 77085 4241 A7
5600 HOUS 77085 4240 E7
Coastal Greens Dr
2600 HOUS 77054 4242 A2
Coastal Oak Ct
15300 HOUS 77059 4380 B6
Coastal Oak Dr
2500 HOUS 77059 4380 B6
Coast Bridge St
9400 HOUS 77075 4377 B4
Coaster Ln
10800 MtgC 77306 2385 E7
10800 MtgC 77306 2531 E1
10800 MtgC 77306 2532 A1
10900 MtgC 77302 2531 E1
Coastline St
5300 HarC 77521 3833 D4
Coastway Ln
8100 HOUS 77075 4376 D4
Coastwide Rd
- GLSN 77554 4994 C7
Coastwood Ln
3300 BzaC 77584 4374 B7
Coats Creek Ln
- HarC 77449 3676 D2
Coatsworth Dr
9400 FBnC 77478 4236 B2
Coba Cl
5100 DKSN 77539 4633 C7
Coba Ct
21300 HarC 77073 3259 E3
Cobalt St
5600 HarC 77093 3546 D7
5600 HOUS 77016 3546 E7
6100 HOUS 77016 3547 A7
6400 HOUS 77016 3687 A1
Cobalt Falls Dr
10200 HarC 77095 3538 B3
Cobalt Glen Dr
14000 SGLD 77478 4236 E4
14000 SGLD 77478 4237 A4
Cobalt Green Dr
15000 HarC 77433 3250 E5
Cobb St
- HarC 77530 3829 D6
3500 HOUS 77004 4103 D2
S Cobb St
10 LMQU 77568 4873 D7
10 TXCY 77591 4873 D7
Cobb Cir Dr
4600 SGLD 77479 4368 B7
Cobbdale Ln
2300 HarC 77014 3402 A2
Cobble Ln
5200 HarC 77379 3257 B1
Cobble Canyon Ln
24800 FBnC 77494 3953 B5
Cobble Creek Ct
1200 MtgC 77384 2529 B7
Cobble Creek Dr
1700 HarC 77073 3259 D2
2300 MtgC 77384 2529 A7
Cobblecreek Wy
10600 FBnC 77459 4622 A4
Cobble Falls Ct
9000 HarC 77095 3537 E5
Cobblefield Ln
7900 HOUS 77071 4239 D4
Cobble Gate Pl
10 WDLD 77381 2821 E2
Cobble Grove Ln
4600 HarC 77084 3677 C7
E Cobble Hill Cir
10 WDLD 77381 2820 C5
S Cobble Hill Cir
10 WDLD 77381 2820 D3
W Cobble Hill Cir
10 WDLD 77381 2820 D3
S Cobble Hill Pl
10 WDLD 77381 2820 C5
Cobble Hill Rd
8000 HarC 77050 3547 D6
Cobble Lodge Ln
- FBnC 77469 4094 C7
Cobble Manor Ln
6300 HarC 77379 3111 C4
Cobble Meadow Ct
26800 HarC 77433 3537 A1
Cobble Meadow Ln
2000 FBnC 77469 4616 A3
Cobbler Ln
10100 HarC 77375 3110 B4
Cobbler Crossing Dr
16600 FBnC 77478 4236 B5
Cobble Ridge Dr
2500 FBnC 77478 4236 A6
Cobblers Wy
2500 HarC 77546 4506 B7
Cobbleshire Ct
9300 HarC 77037 3544 C6
23400 MtgC 77357 2828 A2
Cobbleshire Dr
9100 HarC 77037 3544 C7
Cobble Shores Dr
17100 HarC 77377 3254 B4
Cobbleskill Ct
3500 MSCY 77459 4496 E3
Cobble Springs Ct
16300 FBnC 77478 4236 B5
Cobble Springs Dr
- HarC 77450 3954 D5
12500 PRLD 77584 4500 B3
Cobble Springs Ln
2600 PRLD 77584 4500 D4
Cobblestone Ct
1700 FBnC 77469 4365 D3
Cobblestone Dr
12000 BKHV 77024 3959 B2
12100 HOUS 77024 3959 A3
12400 HOUS 77024 3958 E2
18200 HarC 77429 3396 B1
Cobblestone Ln
3400 BYTN 77521 3972 A2
Cobblestone Pth
6900 HarC 77084 3679 A2
Cobblestone Creek Wy
3200 HarC 77084 3816 C3
Cobblestone Hill St
6500 HOUS 77345 3120 B4
Cobblestone Point Ct
15300 FBnC 77478 4236 C6
Cobblestone Point Dr
11700 FBnC 77478 4236 B6
Cobble Terrace Ln
- HarC 77377 3253 E3

STREET
Block City ZIP Map# Grid

Cobbleton Dr
300 HOUS 77034 4378 E5
Cobble Tree Ct
- FBnC 77469 4235 D1
Cobbs Cove Ln
9900 HarC 77044 3689 A3
Cobbs Creek Rd
12000 HarC 77067 3402 A4
Cobden Ct
12800 HOUS 77034 4378 B2
Cobia Ct
2400 TXCY 77591 4872 E3
Cobia Dr
200 HarC 77494 3953 C2
200 HOUS 77494 3953 C2
Cobles Cor
5100 HarC 77069 3256 D7
Cobleskill Ln
10500 HOUS 77099 4237 D3
Cobolt Creek Ln
9600 HarC 77095 3538 B4
Cobre Valley Dr
14500 HOUS 77062 4379 E7
14500 HOUS 77062 4380 A7
14900 HOUS 77062 4507 A1
Coburn St
300 BYTN 77520 3971 C4
300 LGCY 77573 4632 B2
Cochet Spring Dr
16100 HarC 77379 3256 E3
Cochise Ct
100 PNVL 77304 2237 A3
Cochiti Tr
16700 HOUS 77044 3409 B3
Cochran Dr
23000 MtgC 77365 2973 E7
Cochran Rd
16700 PNIS 77445 3245 B7
17400 WlrC 77484 3245 C3
17500 PNIS 77445 3100 B5
17500 WlrC 77445 3245 B1
17500 WlrC 77484 3100 B5
17800 PNIS 77484 3100 B5
17800 WlrC 77445 3100 B5
19700 PRVW 77445 3100 B4
Cochran St
100 CNRO 77301 2384 A5
1900 HOUS 77009 3963 D1
3200 HOUS 77009 3824 D6
7600 HOUS 77022 3824 D1
Cochrans Crossing Dr
- WDLD 77381 2675 A6
- WDLD 77381 2820 C3
7300 WDLD 77381 2674 C7
N Cochrans Green Cir
10 WDLD 77381 2674 D6
S Cochrans Green Cir
100 WDLD 77381 2674 D7
Cockburn St
8500 HOUS 77078 3687 E4
Cockerel St
200 HOUS 77018 3823 C2
Cockrum Blvd
7000 HarC 77066 3400 B4
7200 HOUS 77066 3400 B4
Coco Ln
31000 MtgC 77362 2963 C4
Coco Rd
5000 FBnC 77583 4622 A3
5000 MSCY 77583 4622 A3
30500 HarC 77433 3250 C5
30500 HarC 77447 3250 C5
Cocoa Ln
2500 PASD 77502 4107 E7
2500 PASD 77502 4108 A7
Cocoanut St
100 TKIS 77554 5106 B4
Cocona Ln
2800 HarC 77073 3259 E4
Coconino Ln
11700 HarC 77377 3109 B7
Cocoplum Dr
20500 HarC 77449 3815 B5
Coctheese Dr
5700 FBnC 77469 4493 A6
Cody Dr
100 TMBL 77375 2964 A7
Cody St
10 GlsC 77518 4634 C2
300 HOUS 77009 3824 B5
Codys Run
14900 HarC 77429 3253 D7
Coe Ct
10000 HOUS 77088 3682 C1
Coe Ln
33000 MtgC 77354 2673 D4
Coe Lp
15100 MtgC 77355 2962 A5
15100 SGCH 77355 2962 A5
15600 MtgC 77355 2961 E5
15600 SGCH 77355 2961 E5
Coe Rd
10 MtgC 77362 2816 E5
10 SGCH 77362 2816 C7
Coen Rd
100 ARLA 77583 4623 A6
900 BzaC 77583 4623 A6
Coffe Dr
3600 PASD 77505 4248 E4
Coffee St
1700 ALVN 77511 4866 E3
1700 ALVN 77511 4867 A3
7400 HOUS 77033 4243 D2
Coffee Lake Rd
700 BzaC 77511 4748 C1
S Coffelt St
100 ALVN 77511 4867 C1
Cogburn Park Dr
1700 HOUS 77047 4373 C1
Cog Hill Dr
6300 PASD 77505 4248 E7
Cohn St
1300 HOUS 77007 3962 A2
6600 HOUS 77091 3684 A4
Coho Ln
12600 HOUS 77045 4373 A1
Cohutta Ln
11000 HarC 77093 3686 B2
Coke Ln
300 ALVN 77511 4867 B3
Coke St
4600 HOUS 77020 3964 C3
Cokeberry Ct
10 WDLD 77380 2968 A1
Cokeberry St
10 MtgC 77380 2822 A7
10 MtgC 77380 2968 A1
10 WDLD 77380 2822 A7

STREET
Block City ZIP Map# Grid

Cokeberry St
10 WDLD 77380 2968 A1
Cola Dr
1000 HOUS 77088 3683 E2
Colbert Ct
8500 HarC 77375 2965 D3
Colbury Ct
2000 HarC 77450 3954 E6
Colby Dr
1500 BYTN 77520 3973 C7
Colby Ln
10000 HarC 77375 2965 A7
Colby St
10 HOUS 77002 3963 E4
10 HOUS 77003 3963 E4
Colby Bend Ln
2400 FBnC 77450 3953 E6
Colby Lodge Dr
- HarC 77450 3954 D6
Colby Run Ct
7300 FBnC 77469 4095 C6
Colchester Ln
400 LGCY 77573 4630 C7
Colchester St
4400 HOUS 77018 3683 C7
Colchester Wy
4300 PASD 77504 4247 E6
4600 MSCY 77459 4369 B6
Colcord Ln
- FBnC 77545 4623 A2
Coldale Glen Ln
17900 FBnC 77469 4095 D7
E Coldbrook Cir
10 WDLD 77381 2674 E6
W Coldbrook Cir
10 WDLD 77381 2674 E6
Coldbrook Ct
10 WDLD 77381 2674 E6
Coldde Meadow Ln
21100 HarC 77379 3111 C3
Coldfield Dr
19700 HarC 77449 3676 E5
Cold Harbor Ln
16600 FBnC 77083 4235 E1
Cold Hollow Ln
9200 FBnC 77459 4621 B7
Cold Lake Dr
8500 HOUS 77088 3683 A1
Cold River Ct
9300 HarC 77396 3407 B2
Cold River Dr
- HarC 77338 3407 B2
1600 HarC 77396 3407 B2
Cold Spring Dr
11200 HOUS 77043 3819 A7
Cold Spring Ln
2900 HarC 77373 3115 A4
Cold Spring St
13800 HarC 77396 3547 A3
Coldsprings Ct
10 WDLD 77380 2967 C4
Coldsprings Dr
2700 PRLD 77584 4503 A4
Cold Springs Ln
9200 HarC 77433 3537 B4
Coldstream Dr
6300 PASD 77505 4248 E6
6900 PASD 77505 4249 A5
Coldstream Rd
1100 HOUS 77055 3821 E7
Coldwater Ln
- HarC 77338 3262 A4
1200 HOUS 77339 3263 B2
Coldwater Bridge Ct
10900 FBnC 77478 4236 D4
Coldwater Bridge Ln
2100 LGCY 77573 4631 C6
Coldwater Canyon Ln
3200 HarC 77449 3815 B3
Cole Av
800 RSBG 77471 4491 B4
Cole Ct
3200 PLEK 77471 4614 B5
Cole Dr
11800 MtgC 77372 2537 C4
11800 SPLD 77372 2537 C4
Cole St
100 WEBS 77598 4507 B6
Cole Bridge Ct
- HarC 77429 3252 B5
Cole Bridge Ln
16100 HarC 77429 3252 B5
Colebrook Ct
3400 PRLD 77584 4501 D5
Colebrook Dr
11000 HOUS 77072 4098 C4
Colebrook Ln
10 PNVL 77304 2237 B2
300 LGCY 77539 4753 A5
Coleburn Dr
16000 HarC 77095 3538 C3
Colechester Ct
900 HarC 77373 2968 D4
Cole Creek Dr
6900 HOUS 77092 3682 A5
7100 HOUS 77040 3682 A5
9200 HarC 77040 3681 B3
Colecrest Ct
15200 HarC 77429 3253 D7
Colecrest Ln
2400 HOUS 77077 3957 A7
Colefield Ln
- HarC 77433 3677 D1
Coleman Av
900 PASD 77506 4107 D4
Coleman Dr
25300 MtgC 77372 2536 E6
25300 MtgC 77372 2537 A6
25700 SPLD 77372 2537 B6
Coleman Rd
- MtgC 77355 2816 B2
26000 SPLD 77372 2683 A2
36500 MtgC 77362 2816 C2
Coleman St
500 CNRO 77301 2384 A4
Coleman Boylan Dr
1200 LGCY 77573 4632 A5
Colendale Dr
9100 HarC 77037 3544 C7
Cole Park Cir
22200 FBnC 77450 3954 A6
22300 FBnC 77450 3953 E6
Coleridge Ct
2300 FBnC 77469 4493 A3
Coleridge Ln
20400 FBnC 77469 4094 C6
Coleridge St
3800 WUNP 77005 4101 D3

STREET
Block City ZIP Map# Grid

Colesberry Ct
5300 FBnC 77450 4094 B3
Coles Crossing Dr
14300 HarC 77429 3397 C3
Coles Crossing Dr N
13700 HarC 77429 3397 B3
Coles Farm Dr
1700 SGLD 77478 4368 E5
Coleto St
8100 HOUS 77017 4105 C5
Coleto Creek Ct
4500 FBnC 77469 4234 D4
Cole Trace Ln
26400 FBnC 77494 4092 D2
Colette Ln
24900 MtgC 77365 3118 E2
Colette St
33000 MtgC 77355 2962 A2
Coleus Ln
8300 HarC 77521 3833 D2
Coleus St
6000 HarC 77532 3552 C3
Cole Valley Dr
31500 MtgC 77354 2670 A7
Colewick Ct
900 HarC 77373 2968 E5
Colewood Ct
10 WDLD 77382 2673 A6
Coley Pk
6300 FBnC 77479 4367 A7
Colfax Rd
40000 MtgC 77354 2672 D2
Colfax St
5700 HOUS 77020 3964 D1
Colgan Ter
- HOUS 77030 4102 E5
Colgate St
3700 HOUS 77017 4105 C7
3700 HOUS 77087 4105 C7
4000 HOUS 77087 4245 C1
8000 HOUS 77061 4245 C2
Colima Dr
7200 FBnC 77083 4095 E6
Colin Springs Ln
27500 MtgC 77386 2969 E7
Colleen Dr
2300 PRLD 77581 4504 A5
Colleen Rd
8900 HOUS 77080 3820 E2
Colleen Meadows Cir
3500 HOUS 77080 3820 E2
Colleen Woods Cir
3500 HOUS 77080 3820 E2
College Av
500 SHUS 77587 4246 C4
1500 HOUS 77017 4246 B4
1500 HOUS 77587 4246 B4
7700 TXCY 77591 4873 B5
18500 WlrC 77484 3246 C1
College Dr
100 FBnC 77545 4623 B3
1100 ALVN 77511 4867 A2
3900 GlsC 77518 4634 C3
College St
- HarC 77562 3831 E2
500 BLAR 77401 4101 A5
600 CNRO 77301 2384 B4
5600 HOUS 77005 4101 D3
5600 WUNP 77005 4101 D4
E College St
6700 WUNP 77005 4101 D4
W College St
6700 WUNP 77005 4101 D4
College Green Dr
1800 HOUS 77058 4507 D3
College Park Dr
3000 MtgC 77384 2676 A5
3000 WDLD 77384 2676 A6
3100 WDLD 77384 2675 D6
4200 WDLD 77382 2675 A5
4300 DRPK 77536 4249 C3
4900 PASD 77505 4249 C3
6300 MtgC 77384 2675 A5
8300 WDLD 77382 2674 E2
8300 WDLD 77384 2674 E2
9400 MtgC 77384 2674 E2
College Park Dr SR-242
3000 MtgC 77384 2676 A5
3000 WDLD 77384 2676 A6
3100 WDLD 77384 2675 D6
4200 WDLD 77382 2675 A5
6300 MtgC 77384 2675 A5
8300 WDLD 77382 2674 E2
8300 WDLD 77384 2674 E2
9400 MtgC 77384 2674 E2
Collette St
- DRPK 77536 4250 A2
Colleville Sur Mer Ln
3200 HarC 77388 3112 D3
Colley St
2300 HOUS 77093 3685 D6
3600 HOUS 77093 3686 B6
Collier St
1200 HOUS 77023 3964 C7
1500 HOUS 77023 4104 C1
Collier Point Ln
1200 FBnC 77545 4622 E2
1200 FBnC 77545 4623 A2
Collier Smith Rd
30000 MtgC 77354 2817 D2
Collin Pk
10300 HOUS 77075 4377 A3
Collina Spring Ct
6300 HarC 77041 3680 A4
Collinford Ct
23700 FBnC 77494 4093 C1
Collingate Ln
- HarC 77433 3537 D7
Collingdale Rd
8400 LPRT 77571 4249 D3
Collingham
10500 HOUS 77099 4238 D2
Collingham St
- HOUS 77099 4238 C2
Colling Park Dr
11700 HOUS 77047 4373 C2
Collingsfield Ct
2300 SGLD 77478 4237 C4
Collingsfield Dr
2100 SGLD 77478 4237 C5
Collingswood Dr
10800 LPRT 77571 4250 D4
Collingswood Rd
10200 LPRT 77571 4250 C3
Collingsworth St
600 HOUS 77009 3824 C6
1800 HOUS 77026 3824 E6
2800 HOUS 77026 3825 D6

STREET
Block City ZIP Map# Grid

Collington Ct
4500 MSCY 77459 4496 C4
Collingtree Dr
25100 HarC 77389 2965 E3
Collingwood Ct
5000 SGLD 77479 4495 A3
Collins Dr
100 HOUS 77336 3120 E5
Collins Ln
21600 MtgC 77372 2535 C3
Collins Rd
- HarC 77037 3545 B7
- HOUS 77037 3545 B7
- HOUS 77093 3545 B7
100 RHMD 77469 4491 D1
300 RHMD 77469 4364 D5
1000 FBnC 77469 4364 D7
1400 HarC 77093 3545 B7
4400 HarC 77093 3546 C7
5500 HOUS 77016 3546 E7
Collins St
100 CNRO 77301 2384 A5
800 RHMD 77469 4364 D7
Collins Creek Blvd
- RSBG 77469 4491 E5
Collinsville Dr
15800 HarC 77377 3254 C6
Colmar Wy
3500 HarC 77084 3816 C3
Colmesneil Dr
5000 PRLD 77584 4503 A4
5600 PRLD 77584 4502 E4
Cologne Dr
13300 HarC 77065 3398 A7
Coloma Ln
11300 PNPV 77024 3959 D4
Colomba St
4400 HOUS 77045 4241 C6
Colombard Dr
- HOUS 77060 3544 C1
Colombia Dr
- PASD 77504 4248 A5
4200 PASD 77504 4247 E5
4800 PASD 77505 4248 A5
Colon Ct
6700 HOUS 77048 4244 D6
Colonade Tr
6800 SGLD 77479 4367 C7
Colonel Dr
100 FBnC 77469 4493 C7
Colonel Ct Dr
2400 FBnC 77469 4365 C1
2800 FBnC 77469 4234 C7
Colonel Fisher Dr
18800 HOUS 77032 3261 C7
18800 HOUS 77032 3405 C1
Colonial
100 PRVW 77445 3100 C3
Colonial Ct
200 PNVL 77304 2237 A3
2300 MSCY 77459 4497 B3
5100 PASD 77505 4248 B4
Colonial Ct N
2200 LGCY 77573 4631 B5
Colonial Ct S
2200 LGCY 77573 4631 B5
Colonial Dr
300 FRDW 77546 4505 C7
2000 BYTN 77520 3973 D4
2800 DKSN 77539 4753 C3
2800 SGLD 77479 4368 D7
2900 SGLD 77479 4495 D1
6600 PRLD 77584 4502 E6
6600 PRLD 77584 4503 A6
Colonial Ln
7700 HOUS 77051 4243 B2
Colonial Pkwy
- HarC 77449 3814 C7
- HarC 77449 3815 A6
- HarC 77493 3813 E6
- HOUS 77449 3814 E7
- HOUS 77449 3815 A7
- KATY 77493 3813 E6
23000 HOUS 77493 3814 A7
23300 HarC 77493 3814 A7
Colonial St
1100 BLAR 77401 4101 A3
1900 LMQU 77568 4990 A3
2100 ALVN 77511 4749 A6
2100 BzaC 77511 4749 A6
Colonial Bend Ln
21700 FBnC 77450 4094 A1
Colonial Birch Ln
24500 HarC 77493 3814 A7
Colonial Bridge Ln
15700 HarC 77073 3259 C5
Colonial Crest Dr
1500 HarC 77493 3814 A7
Colonial Elm Dr
24600 HarC 77493 3814 A7
Colonial Falls Ln
8500 HarC 77396 3547 E1
Colonial Forest Cir
18100 HarC 77379 3255 E2
Colonial Forest Ln
8200 HarC 77379 3255 E3
Colonialgate Dr
22500 HarC 77373 3116 A7
Colonial Glen Ct
- PRLD 77583 4500 B5
Colonial Heights Dr
1200 FBnC 77469 4365 D4
Colonial Lakes Dr
- MSCY 77459 4496 B1
2600 MSCY 77459 4369 B7
Colonial Manor Dr
1100 HarC 77493 3814 A7
Colonial Manor Ln
- FBnC 77494 4093 A1
Colonial Maple Dr
24500 HarC 77493 3814 A7
Colonial Oaks Dr
1500 FRDW 77546 4749 E2
Colonial Oaks Ln
8200 HarC 77379 3255 E2
Colonial Park Dr
- WDLD 77380 2821 D5
Colonial Park Ln
5200 FBnC 77494 4093 C1
Colonial Pines Ct
25600 HarC 77389 2966 C2
Colonial Ridge Dr
2300 HarC 77546 4506 B6
Colonial Rose Ln
6500 FBnC 77469 4616 B2
Colonial Springs Ln
2300 MtgC 77386 2969 E6

STREET
Block City ZIP Map# Grid

Colonial Trail Dr
11300 HarC 77066 3400 E6
Colonist Park Dr
2000 SGLD 77478 4368 D5
Colonnade Dr
1700 HOUS 77030 4102 C6
Colony Ct
900 FBnC 77469 4365 C3
4200 SGLD 77479 4494 E2
10200 HOUS 77041 3819 D1
10200 HOUS 77041 3820 A1
Colony Dr
2700 SGLD 77479 4368 D7
2900 SGLD 77479 4495 C1
3000 LGCY 77539 4753 A4
7700 HOUS 77036 4099 A6
Colony Ln
- MtgC 77357 2827 C4
600 HOUS 77076 3684 E5
2400 PRLD 77581 4502 E3
4900 BzaC 77583 4745 D7
6500 HarC 77396 3547 A2
Colony Lp
- IWCY 77583 4745 E3
- MNVL 77578 4745 E3
Colony Bay Dr
- MSCY 77459 4496 D3
Colony Bend Cir
7200 MSCY 77459 4496 E5
Colony Bend Dr
16800 HarC 77546 4506 B6
Colony Bend Ln
7200 MSCY 77459 4496 E5
Colony Cone Cir
2800 LGCY 77539 4753 A5
Colony Cove
2300 BzaC 77583 4624 A6
Colony Cove Dr
9100 HarC 77379 3255 D4
Colony Creek Ct
100 LGCY 77539 4753 A4
Colony Creek Dr
- SGLD 77479 4495 D1
200 LGCY 77539 4753 A4
16800 HarC 77379 3255 E4
Colony Crest Ct
3200 HOUS 77082 4098 B2
Colony Crossing Dr
- SGLD 77479 4495 A2
3000 SGLD 77479 4494 E2
Colony Falls Ln
2800 LGCY 77539 4752 E3
Colony Forest Dr
4900 HarC 77373 3115 B4
Colony Glen Ct
800 HOUS 77062 4506 D1
4400 SGLD 77479 4368 B7
Colony Green Dr
- HarC 77450 3953 D4
23100 HarC 77494 3953 D4
Colony Grove Ln
19100 HarC 77449 3677 B7
Colony Heath Ln
12800 HOUS 77085 4240 E7
Colony Hill Ln
12600 HarC 77014 3402 B2
Colony Hills Dr
4500 SGLD 77479 4368 A7
Colony Knolls Ct
2600 MSCY 77459 4496 C1
Colony Lake Ct
200 LGCY 77539 4753 A3
Colony Lake Ln
100 LGCY 77539 4753 A3
Colony Lake Estates Dr
400 FBnC 77477 4369 C4
Colony Lakes Dr
1200 SGLD 77479 4367 E6
1300 SGLD 77479 4368 A6
E Colony Loop Rd
8100 BzaC 77583 4745 D3
8100 IWCY 77583 4745 D3
8600 MNVL 77578 4745 D4
8600 MNVL 77583 4745 D4
W Colony Loop Rd
8100 BzaC 77583 4745 D3
8100 IWCY 77583 4745 D3
W Colony Loop Rd CO-79
8500 IWCY 77583 4745 D3
8600 BzaC 77583 4745 D4
Colony Meadow Dr
- SGLD 77479 4495 A1
Colony Oaks Ct
4500 SGLD 77479 4495 A1
8400 HarC 77379 3256 C4
Colony Oaks Dr
4000 SGLD 77479 4495 A2
Colony Park Cir E
10 GLSN 77551 5222 B1
Colony Park Cir W
10 GLSN 77551 5222 B1
Colony Park Dr
10 GLSN 77551 5222 B1
2700 SGLD 77479 4495 C1
Colony Point Ct
7700 HarC 77095 3538 A7
Colony Point Ln
- MSCY 77459 4496 C4
Colonypond Dr
9200 HarC 77379 3255 D4
Colony Ridge Ln
2900 LGCY 77539 4752 E5
E Colony Shore Dr
12100 HarC 77433 3395 C5
S Colony Shore Dr
18600 HarC 77433 3395 C5
W Colony Shore Dr
12200 HarC 77433 3395 C5
Colony Spring Ln
- HarC 77449 3677 C5
Colony Springs Ln
2700 FBnC 77469 4365 A6
Colony Stream Dr
17400 HarC 77379 3255 D4
Colony Terrace Dr
16600 SGLD 77479 4368 B7
Colony Trail Ln
19300 HarC 77449 3677 A6
Colony View Ln
7300 MSCY 77459 4496 E5
Colonyway Ct
9200 HarC 77379 3255 D4
Colony West Dr
4300 FBnC 77469 4232 C7
Colony Wood Pl
10800 WDLD 77380 2821 D7
Colony Woods Ct
- SGLD 77479 4495 E3

STREET Block City ZIP Map# Grid

Colony Woods Dr
3700 SGLD 77479 4495 E3
Colorado Av
100 LGCY 77573 4632 A2
1400 LMQU 77568 4989 E2
2300 DKSN 77539 4633 B7
2800 DKSN 77539 4754 B2
Colorado Dr
2100 HMBL 77396 3407 A2
22800 MtgC 77365 2972 C4
Colorado Ln
- LbyC 77327 2537 E4
- LbyC 77372 2537 E4
Colorado St
1300 BYTN 77520 4112 A1
1300 HOUS 77007 3963 B2
1500 HMPD 77445 3098 A2
2200 HMPD 77445 3097 E2
2400 PRLD 77545 4499 D6
2700 FBnC 77545 4499 A7
Colorado River Dr
- MtgC 77386 2970 B2
Colorado Springs Ct
900 HarC 77373 3114 A3
Colosseum Ct
2600 MtgC 77357 2829 B2
2600 RMFT 77357 2829 B2
Colquitt St
100 HOUS 77002 3963 A7
300 HOUS 77002 3962 E7
400 HOUS 77006 3962 D7
2600 HOUS 77098 3962 A7
3100 HOUS 77098 3961 E7
3700 HOUS 77027 4101 D1
3900 HOUS 77027 3961 C7
Colson Ln
5000 HarC 77521 3834 E7
Colson Springs Dr
15400 HarC 77433 3251 D6
Colston Pl
7700 GlsC 77510 4987 B6
Colston Rd
12100 GlsC 77510 4987 B6
Colt
- FRDW 77546 4505 B7
- FRDW 77546 4629 B1
Colt Ct
12400 MtgC 77354 2671 B3
Colt Dr
- HOUS 77074 4100 B6
Colt St
10300 HOUS 77033 4243 E5
Colt 45 Dr
- HarC 77032 3546 C3
Colt Canyon Ln
9200 HarC 77089 4504 C1
Colt Creek Ct
- ALVN 77511 4867 A4
Colter Forest Dr
- HarC 77088 3543 B6
Colter Stone Dr
21700 HarC 77388 3111 D2
Coltfield Ct
- HarC 77429 3253 A6
Colton Ln
13300 STFE 77510 4870 D7
Colton St
7200 HOUS 77016 3686 E4
7200 HOUS 77016 3687 A4
Colton Cove Dr
- HarC 77095 3538 D3
Colton Hollow Dr
2400 HarC 77067 3402 A4
Colton Trails Dr
10 FBnC 77479 4367 A7
Colt Springs Ct
16100 HarC 77429 3253 A7
Colt Springs Ln
16100 HarC 77429 3253 A6
Coltwood Dr
- HarC 77388 3113 A6
3500 HarC 77388 3112 E7
4000 HarC 77388 3257 D1
Columba Ct
31200 TMBL 77375 2963 E4
E Columbary Dr
4800 RSBG 77471 4491 C5
W Columbary Dr
4400 RSBG 77471 4491 C5
Columbia Cir
2400 LGCY 77573 4508 E6
Columbia Ct
1100 FBnC 77469 4365 D4
Columbia Ln
700 DRPK 77536 4249 C2
E Columbia Ln
1100 DRPK 77536 4249 C2
Columbia St
- BYTN 77520 3972 E5
10 CNRO 77301 2384 A2
300 HOUS 77007 3962 D1
600 ALVN 77511 4749 C7
1000 HOUS 77007 3823 D7
1300 HOUS 77008 3823 D6
3000 BYTN 77521 3972 E4
3000 HOUS 77018 3823 D3
Columbia Blue Dr
- STAF 77477 4370 C5
1000 MSCY 77489 4370 C7
Columbia Crest Pl
10 WDLD 77382 2820 A2
Columbia Falls Ct
21800 FBnC 77450 4093 C6
Columbia Falls Ln
6100 FBnC 77450 4093 E5
Columbia Glen Ct
7000 HarC 77389 2966 C1
Columbia Memorial Pkwy
- LGCY 77565 4509 B7
- LGCY 77565 4633 B1
- LGCY 77573 4509 B7
- LGCY 77573 4633 C3
Columbia Pines Ln
11400 HarC 77433 3395 E7
Columbia Springs Ln
- HarC 77433 3537 A1
Columbine Ln
7400 HarC 77049 3828 B1
12600 HarC 77049 3689 B7
Columbus
900 HOUS 77019 3962 E4
Columbus Ct
8400 PRLD 77584 4501 E5
Columbus St
1000 HOUS 77019 3962 E5
1300 HOUS 77006 3962 E5
Columnberry Ct
10 WDLD 77384 2675 A4

Colville Dr
14900 HarC 77530 3968 C1
Colville St
- HarC 77530 3968 E1
Colvin Ct
4700 HOUS 77013 3827 D4
Colvin Rd
3700 HOUS 77013 3827 D5
Colwell Rd
- HOUS 77090 3257 E4
2300 HarC 77068 3257 D5
2300 HarC 77090 3257 D5
Colwin Ln
15300 JRSV 77040 3540 E7
Comal
4700 MtgC 77386 2970 B2
Comal Av
1300 HOUS 77017 4106 D5
1300 PASD 77506 4106 D5
Comal Dr
2400 DRPK 77536 4109 E6
Comal St
4700 PRLD 77581 4376 A7
4800 BKVL 77581 4376 A7
7700 HOUS 77051 4243 B2
Comal Bend Ln
16000 HarC 77429 3253 C7
Comal River Ct
28800 MtgC 77386 2970 B2
Comal River Lp
4600 MtgC 77386 2970 B2
Comal Springs Dr
- HOUS 77396 3406 B5
2100 DRPK 77536 4109 D6
Comanche
20700 MtgC 77357 2681 A6
Comanche Blvd
1900 FBnC 77471 4614 D4
Comanche Dr
3900 GLSN 77554 5441 A5
18300 MtgC 77365 2972 C5
Comanche Ln
10000 HOUS 77041 3681 A5
Comanche Rd
- KATY 77494 3951 D1
Comanche St
- GLSN 77554 5221 E2
1200 DRPK 77536 4109 C6
4200 PASD 77504 4247 E5
7400 HarC 77521 3833 B4
Comanche Tr
- FBnC 77469 4364 C7
33500 MtgC 77355 2962 E1
33500 SGCH 77355 2816 E7
33500 SGCH 77355 2962 E1
Comanche Peak Ln
9200 HarC 77089 4504 B1
Comanche Springs Ct
10400 HarC 77095 3537 E2
Combine Ln
16300 HarC 77530 3829 E4
Combwell Gdn
10 FBnC 77459 4621 C7
Comely Ln
13600 HOUS 77079 3958 B3
Comer Reinhart Rd
- MtgC 77357 2828 A5
Comet Dr
11900 HarC 77086 3542 B5
Comet Vw
4600 HarC 77396 3407 B7
Comets Ct
- HOUS 77032 3546 C2
Comets Run
4900 HOUS 77013 3827 D4
Comfort Ct
15500 HarC 77429 3253 D5
Comfort St
- ALVN 77511 4867 D3
Comfort Glenn Ct
12000 HOUS 77047 4374 D1
Comic Wy
8800 HarC 77375 2965 D3
Comile St
500 HOUS 77022 3824 B3
Commander Dr
200 TKIS 77554 5106 D3
Commander St
2100 PASD 77502 4247 C1
Commander Roland Dr
6900 HTCK 77563 4988 A5
Commanders Pt
10 FBnC 77459 4621 C5
Commanders Cove
10 FBnC 77459 4621 C5
Commando Bridge Blvd
- HarC 77449 3676 B3
Commerce
200 RHMD 77469 4364 E7
Commerce Av
23500 MtgC 77365 2973 C5
Commerce Dr
- BzaC 77583 4745 B1
- LMQU 77568 4872 B5
Commerce Rd
100 HarC 77562 3692 E6
Commerce St
- MAGA 77355 2668 E5
100 MAGA 77355 2669 A6
100 TMBL 77375 2964 B7
800 HOUS 77002 3963 E4
1900 HOUS 77003 3963 E4
3000 HOUS 77003 3964 A5
17800 WEBS 77598 4507 B6
N Commerce St
10 BYTN 77520 3972 E7
300 BYTN 77520 3973 A6
S Commerce St
100 BYTN 77520 3972 E7
W Commerce St
1000 BYTN 77520 3973 A6
Commerce Business Dr
- FBnC 77477 4369 D4
- MSCY 77477 4369 D4
Commerce Creek Dr
6800 HarC 77040 3681 C3
Commerce Green Blvd
400 SGLD 77478 4368 C2
Commerce Park Dr
8100 HOUS 77036 4099 B7
8700 HOUS 77074 4099 B7
Commercial Cir
100 CNRO 77304 2383 C5
Commercial Ct
- CNRO 77301 2384 B2
Commercial Dr
23700 FBnC 77469 4492 B5
23700 RSBG 77469 4492 B5

Commercial Dr
24000 RSBG 77471 4492 A6
24400 RSBG 77471 4491 E6
Commercial Ln
22700 HarC 77375 3110 B1
Commercial Rd
13700 HOUS 77047 4373 A4
Commercial Center Blvd
- FBnC 77494 3953 C7
- FBnC 77494 4093 C1
- HOUS 77494 3953 C7
- HOUS 77494 4093 C1
Commercial Park Dr
19100 HarC 77338 3261 E6
19100 HOUS 77338 3261 E6
27700 TMBL 77375 3109 B2
Commodore Dr
1000 GLSN 77554 5107 D6
5500 DKSN 77539 4753 E5
5500 TXCY 77539 4753 E5
Commodore Wy
300 HOUS 77079 3956 E2
Commoms Water Dr
1000 HarC 77336 3121 B3
Common St
1600 HOUS 77009 3963 D1
2400 HOUS 77009 3824 C7
Common Crest Dr
14800 HarC 77095 3539 A5
Common Park Dr
1200 HOUS 77009 3824 C7
Commons Ct
800 HarC 77336 3121 B1
Commons Breeze Dr
700 HarC 77336 2976 B6
Commons Enclave
400 HarC 77336 2975 E7
Commons Forest Ct
30000 HarC 77336 2976 B7
Commons Forest Dr
29100 HarC 77336 3121 A1
29600 HarC 77336 2976 A7
Commons Lake Dr
100 HarC 77336 3120 C1
Commons Lake Edge Dr
700 HarC 77336 2976 B6
Commons Lakeview Dr
500 HarC 77336 2976 A6
Commons Oak Ln
30500 HarC 77336 2976 B6
Commons Oaks Dr
- HarC 77336 3121 A3
Commons Park Dr
30100 HarC 77336 2976 A7
Commons Pine Ln
900 HarC 77336 2976 B6
Commons Royal View Dr
30100 HarC 77336 2976 B7
Commons Scenic View Dr
30000 HarC 77336 2976 C7
Commons Spring Creek Dr
800 HarC 77336 2976 B6
Commons Superior Dr
29400 HarC 77336 2976 B7
29400 HarC 77336 3121 B1
Commons Trail Ln
400 HarC 77336 2976 A7
N Commons View Dr
1000 HarC 77336 3121 B4
1000 HOUS 77336 3121 B4
S Commons View Dr
900 HarC 77336 3121 A3
900 HOUS 77336 3121 B4
Commons Vista Dr
300 HarC 77336 2975 E7
300 HarC 77336 2976 A7
300 HarC 77336 3121 B1
Commons Woods Ct
30000 HarC 77336 2976 A7
Commons Wy Ct
800 HarC 77336 2976 B7
Commonwealth Blvd
- SGLD 77479 4494 E4
- SGLD 77479 4496 A3
3900 SGLD 77479 4495 A4
Commonwealth St
1600 HOUS 77006 3962 D5
Community Cir
3100 ALVN 77511 4866 D5
41100 MtgC 77354 2671 A1
Community Ct
- SGLD 77478 4237 C5
Community Dr
- HOUS 77074 4099 D6
1600 PASD 77506 4107 D5
2800 ALVN 77511 4866 C4
2800 BzaC 77511 4866 C4
5300 HOUS 77005 4101 C2
5300 WUNP 77005 4101 C4
22400 MtgC 77357 2973 D2
27600 MtgC 77355 2963 B2
27600 MtgC 77362 2963 B2
E Community Dr
22800 MtgC 77357 2973 E2
23100 MtgC 77357 2974 A2
Community Rd
40000 MtgC 77354 2670 E3
40000 MtgC 77354 2671 A3
Community College Dr
500 HOUS 77013 3965 E1
Comoro Ln
17700 HarC 77379 3256 A2
Companion Dr
600 HarC 77532 3552 B4
Compaq Center Dr
- HarC 77070 3255 C7
W Compaq Center Dr
- HarC 77070 3255 A7
- HarC 77377 3255 A6
- HOUS 77070 3255 A6
- HOUS 77377 3255 A6
Compass Cir
10 GLSN 77554 5221 C2
Compass Ct
17600 HarC 77532 3411 A7
Compass Cove Cir
1000 HarC 77379 3255 D2
S Compass Rose Blvd
- LGCY 77565 4509 B6
1900 LGCY 77573 4509 A6
Compass Rose Cir N
400 HarC 77532 3411 B7
Compass Rose Cir S
17500 HarC 77532 3411 B7
17500 HarC 77532 3552 C1
Compass Rose Dr
7300 FBnC 77469 4094 A6

Compton Cir
4300 BLAR 77401 4101 C3
Compton St
100 ARLA 77583 4623 B4
500 FBnC 77583 4623 B4
8300 HOUS 77016 3686 E6
Compton Manor Dr
10 HarC 77379 3110 D6
Compton Pointe
- LGCY 77573 4509 B7
Comstock Cir
17400 HarC 77090 3257 E4
Comstock Meadows Dr
9400 HarC 77095 3537 D4
Comstock Springs Dr
800 HarC 77450 3953 D3
Conant Ct
24600 FBnC 77494 3952 D3
Conastoga Ct
2400 MtgC 77384 2529 A4
Concerto Cir
8600 HarC 77040 3681 C1
Conch
3800 GLSN 77554 5220 E6
3800 GLSN 77554 5221 A6
Concho
12900 GLSN 77554 5220 B6
Concho Mtn
7100 HarC 77069 3400 A2
Concho St
7000 HOUS 77074 4099 E6
7000 HOUS 77074 4100 A6
8000 HOUS 77036 4099 B6
10700 HOUS 77072 4098 C6
Concho Bay Ct
12000 HarC 77041 3680 A4
Concho Bay Dr
6300 HarC 77041 3680 A4
Concho Key
3700 GLSN 77554 5441 B4
Concho River Ct
1800 SGLD 77478 4369 A5
Concho Springs Dr
19400 HarC 77449 3677 A4
Concord Cir
10 BKHV 77024 3959 C3
Concord Dr
10 MtgC 77385 2676 E6
2600 LGCY 77573 4508 D7
6700 HTCK 77563 4989 B5
Concord Grv
14400 HarC 77084 3679 A4
Concord Ln
9200 HarC 77064 3541 A5
9500 HarC 77064 3540 E4
Concord Pl
1100 MSCY 77459 4369 D5
Concord Rd
1900 PASD 77502 4107 D7
Concord St
1100 FBnC 77469 4364 D6
1100 RHMD 77469 4364 D6
1500 DRPK 77536 4108 E7
8100 HOUS 77017 4105 D5
Concord Bridge Dr
5700 HarC 77041 3679 C4
Concord Falls Ln
16300 FBnC 77478 4236 A5
N Concord Forest Cir
10 WDLD 77381 2674 D7
S Concord Forest Cir
10 WDLD 77381 2674 D7
Concord Glen Ln
26300 FBnC 77494 4092 E1
Concord Green Dr
4800 HarC 77084 3677 C6
Concord Hill Dr
20200 HarC 77433 3251 C7
Concordia Ct
2800 LGCY 77573 4633 A4
Concordia Dr
100 HarC 77450 3953 D1
Concordia Park Ln
21100 FBnC 77469 4094 A6
Concord Knoll Dr
2900 PRLD 77581 4503 D7
Concord Meadow Ln
- HarC 77047 4374 A3
Concord Park Dr
- HarC 77040 3681 A4
6500 HOUS 77040 3681 A4
6500 HOUS 77041 3681 A4
E Concord Valley Cir
100 WDLD 77382 2819 A4
N Concord Valley Cir
10 WDLD 77382 2819 B2
S Concord Valley Pl
10 WDLD 77382 2819 C2
Concourse Dr
9300 HOUS 77036 4098 E7
9300 HOUS 77036 4238 E1
Concrete Dr
100 HOUS 77012 4105 E2
E Concrete Rd S
- HOUS 77012 4105 E2
Concrete St
100 HOUS 77012 4105 D2
Conder Dr
800 FRDW 77546 4629 D5
Condessa Dr
16200 FBnC 77083 4096 B5
16200 HOUS 77083 4096 B5
Condon Ln
5600 HOUS 77053 4371 E6
Condor Ct
10 CNRO 77304 2236 C6
Condor Dr
200 MtgC 77385 2676 D5
Condore Wy
7000 HOUS 77489 4371 C4
Condors Nest
24300 HarC 77494 3953 A3
Condrey Ct
18700 HarC 77377 3254 A2
Cone Creek Cir
- HarC 77530 3830 C5
Cone Creek Dr
2000 HarC 77090 3257 E3
Conecrest Ct
5600 HOUS 77088 3682 E3
Conefall Ct
23900 HarC 77373 3114 E5
Coneflower Rd
400 LGCY 77573 4632 E2
Conely Rd
6600 BzaC 77584 4626 E2
Conestoga Cir
700 HarC 77450 3954 A3

Conestog Ln Ct
11500 HarC 77066 3400 D6
Confederate Ct
2300 FBnC 77469 4365 D3
3300 MSCY 77459 4498 A6
Confederate Dr
3200 MSCY 77459 4498 A6
5000 PRLD 77584 4503 A6
Confederate Rd
1100 HOUS 77055 3820 C7
Confederate Wy
200 ELGO 77586 4509 A2
Confederate South Dr
3100 MSCY 77459 4498 A6
Conference Center Rd
12500 MtgC 77304 2529 D3
Conger St
8800 HOUS 77075 4245 E6
8800 HOUS 77075 4246 A6
Congo Ln
8600 HarC 77040 3681 C1
15400 JRSV 77040 3680 D1
Congress St
600 HOUS 77002 3963 D4
2100 HOUS 77003 3963 D4
Congressional Cir
10 HarC 77389 2820 A5
Conica Ct
5600 HarC 77379 3112 A4
Conifer Dr
2900 LPRT 77571 4251 D7
Conifer Rd
13000 HOUS 77079 3958 C3
Conifer Bay Ct
15400 HOUS 77059 4380 B5
Conifer Chase
- HarC 77094 3955 A2
Conifer Creek Tr
1900 HOUS 77345 3120 D6
Conifer Ridge Wy
4700 HarC 77346 3408 B2
Conifer Springs Ct
11900 HarC 77067 3401 E4
Conifer Springs Ln
11900 HarC 77067 3401 D5
Coniper Cir
1400 LPRT 77571 4251 C5
Conklin Ln
13200 HOUS 77034 4378 C3
Conklin St
800 HOUS 77088 3684 A1
900 HOUS 77088 3683 E2
Conlan Bay Dr
6100 HarC 77041 3679 B4
Conley St
5800 HOUS 77021 4103 D6
7200 HOUS 77021 4243 D1
Conlon St
6600 HOUS 77061 4245 C2
Connally Rd
1500 HarC 77521 3833 C7
Connaught Wy
300 HarC 77015 3828 D6
Connaught Garden Dr
8600 HarC 77083 4097 B7
Connecticut Av
29000 MtgC 77354 2818 B1
Connecticut St
300 HOUS 77029 3966 A7
Connemara Dr
7400 HarC 77433 3677 C1
Conner Ct
4900 PASD 77504 4247 E7
Conner Park Dr
13900 HarC 77429 3397 C2
Conners Rd
10 HarC 77336 2976 E1
Conners Ace Dr
15900 HarC 77379 3257 A3
Connie St
200 HOUS 77076 3685 A4
1100 ALVN 77511 4867 A2
18400 MtgC 77355 2815 A1
18400 MtgC 77355 2815 A1
Connie's Ct Ln
4500 MSCY 77459 4369 B7
Connor St
11700 HarC 77039 3546 B6
11700 HarC 77093 3546 B7
Connordale Ln
28500 MtgC 77386 2969 C7
Connor Grove Ct
22500 HarC 77493 3814 A6
Connor Reinhardt Rd
23300 MtgC 77357 2828 B5
Connorvale Ct
700 HarC 77060 3544 E4
Connorvale Ln
500 HarC 77060 3544 D4
Connorvale Rd
1500 HarC 77039 3545 C4
4900 HarC 77039 3546 C4
Conoly St
100 HOUS 77009 3824 A6
Conover Ct
14700 HarC 77015 3829 B7
Conquistador E
12900 GLSN 77554 5220 B7
Conquistador Dr
22000 HarC 77532 3266 E6
E Conquistador Dr
12700 GLSN 77554 5220 B7
Conrad Rd
3100 HarC 77449 3815 D3
N Conrad St
100 PASD 77506 4107 B3
Conrado Dr
13200 HarC 77044 3689 C4
Conrad Sauer Dr
- HOUS 77024 3959 A1
1000 HOUS 77043 3820 A7
1000 HOUS 77043 3959 A1
Conroe Dr
200 CNRO 77301 2384 A4
15200 MtgC 77384 2674 A2
Conroe Hufsmith Rd
26000 MtgC 77354 2818 E7
26000 MtgC 77354 2964 E1
33900 MtgC 77354 2673 C3
Conroe Lake Ct
3800 PRLD 77581 4503 E7
Conroe Marketplace Dr
- CNRO 77303 2237 C7
- CNRO 77304 2237 C7
Conroe Park North Dr
8900 CNRO 77303 2238 B6
Conroe Park West Dr
- CNRO 77303 2238 A6

Conroe Pipleline Rd
12100 MtgC 77302 2531 D7
12100 MtgC 77302 2677 D1
Conroe Porter Rd
11600 CNRO 77301 2530 E1
11600 CNRO 77302 2530 E1
11600 MtgC 77302 2530 E2
11700 CNRO 77301 2531 A3
11700 CNRO 77302 2531 A3
11700 MtgC 77302 2531 D7
14500 MtgC 77302 2677 E1
14900 MtgC 77302 2678 D6
17900 MtgC 77302 2825 B2
19200 MtgC 77365 2825 C3
Conroe Porter Rd FM-1314
11600 CNRO 77301 2530 E1
11600 CNRO 77302 2530 E1
11600 MtgC 77302 2530 E1
11700 CNRO 77301 2531 A3
11700 CNRO 77302 2531 A3
11700 MtgC 77302 2531 D7
14500 MtgC 77302 2677 E1
14900 MtgC 77302 2678 D6
17900 MtgC 77302 2825 B2
19200 MtgC 77365 2825 C3
Conroy St
4100 HOUS 77026 3825 B6
Conroy Pointe Ln
- FBnC 77494 4092 A5
Constance Dr
900 HDWV 77024 3959 C1
Constance Knolls Dr
24600 HOUS 77336 3266 C2
Constantine Dr
2500 RMFT 77357 2829 B1
2700 MtgC 77357 2829 B1
Constantine St
2500 MtgC 77357 2829 C1
2500 RMFT 77357 2829 C1
Constatine Ct
6700 SGLD 77479 4367 B7
Constellation Blvd
400 LGCY 77573 4508 C6
Constellation Ln
8000 HOUS 77075 4376 D1
Constitution Av
1300 STAF 77477 4370 A5
Constitution Ln
15500 HarC 77546 4505 D5
16200 HarC 77546 4506 A6
Consuela Dr
- HOUS 77031 4239 B3
9900 HOUS 77074 4239 B2
Consul Ct
- MtgC 77357 2829 D3
Consular Ct
3200 PRLD 77584 4501 D5
Consulate Plz
- HOUS 77032 3405 B6
Consulate Plaza Dr
5300 HOUS 77032 3405 C6
Contado Ct
13500 HarC 77429 3397 D2
Contender Ln
15500 HarC 77546 4505 E5
Conti St
1300 HOUS 77002 3963 D2
2600 HOUS 77020 3963 E2
2800 HOUS 77020 3964 B3
Continental Dr
10 MSCY 77459 4496 E1
3200 MSCY 77459 4369 E6
4300 HOUS 77072 4098 A4
Continental Pkwy
18400 HarC 77346 3264 B7
Contour Pl
5100 HOUS 77096 4240 E2
Contoy Ct
2900 GLSN 77554 5221 D3
Convair Av
7100 HOUS 77061 4245 A5
Convair St
100 HOUS 77061 4245 B5
Convento Dr
4400 FBnC 77469 4233 C6
Converse St
1900 HOUS 77006 3962 E6
Convoy Ct
16600 HarC 77532 3551 E2
Conward Dr
4200 HarC 77066 3401 C6
Conway Lndg
14000 HarC 77429 3397 B2
Conway Pl
13900 HarC 77429 3397 E2
Conway St
2800 HOUS 77025 4102 A6
3000 HOUS 77025 4101 D6
N Cook Cir
4300 LGCY 77573 4631 A5
4400 LGCY 77573 4630 E5
S Cook Cir
4300 LGCY 77573 4631 A5
4400 LGCY 77573 4630 E5
Cook Dr
10 BYTN 77520 4113 B1
Cook Ln
5200 FBnC 77479 4495 E7
Cook Rd
4100 HOUS 77072 4097 E7
4100 HOUS 77082 4097 E4
7800 MNVL 77578 4746 E4
8600 HOUS 77072 4237 E1
8600 HOUS 77099 4237 D3
20000 HarC 77377 3106 B5
Cook St
1100 SEBK 77586 4509 D3
1400 HOUS 77006 3963 A5
1600 HOUS 77006 3962 E5
Cooke Rd
40300 WlrC 77445 3098 B5
Cookglass Dr
8500 HOUS 77072 4097 E7
Cook Ranch Ct
4000 FBnC 77494 4092 B2
Cook Ranch Ln
3900 FBnC 77494 4092 B2
Cookridge Ln
- HarC 77014 3402 C1
Cooksteel Dr
8400 HOUS 77072 4097 E7
Cooks Walk Ct
2300 FBnC 77469 4234 C6
Cookwind Dr
8400 HOUS 77072 4097 E7
Cookwood Dr
8400 HOUS 77072 4097 E7

Cool Creek Ct
6000 HOUS 77345 3120 D7
Coolgreen Av
12400 HOUS 77013 3827 E6
12500 HOUS 77013 3828 A6
Coolgrove Dr
7900 HarC 77049 3689 D6
Coolidge Dr
600 HarC 77530 3969 C2
1400 DRPK 77536 4109 C7
Coolidge St
8400 HOUS 77012 4105 D4
Cooling Breeze Dr
2400 FBnC 77469 4365 D1
Cool Mist Dr
500 HOUS 77013 3827 E7
600 HOUS 77013 3966 E1
Coolridge Ct
14600 HOUS 77062 4379 D6
Cool River Ln
1900 HarC 77067 3402 B5
Cool Shadows Ln
11700 HarC 77044 3551 A7
Coolshire Ln
8200 HarC 77070 3399 D3
Cool Spring Ct
7100 MtgC 77354 2673 B3
Cool Spring Dr
300 HarC 77037 3544 C7
1400 HOUS 77088 3543 E7
1400 HOUS 77088 3544 A6
Cool Spring Ln
2800 LGCY 77539 4752 E3
Cool Springs Ln
2300 SGLD 77478 4236 E5
Cool Water Ct
7000 FBnC 77479 4367 B7
Cool Water Dr
6300 FBnC 77479 4367 A6
Cool Wood Dr
500 HOUS 77013 3827 E7
600 HOUS 77013 3966 E1
E Coombs St
100 ALVN 77511 4867 C2
W Coombs St
100 ALVN 77511 4867 B2
2100 ALVN 77511 4866 E2
Coon Dr
1200 FBnC 77471 4614 A1
Coon St
4100 GlsC 77518 4634 C3
Coon Creek Ct
2700 PLEK 77471 4614 C4
Coon Hollow Rd
- MtgC 77302 2532 D3
11000 MtgC 77306 2532 D3
Coon Massey Rd
12600 MtgC 77302 2532 E5
12600 MtgC 77306 2532 E5
12600 MtgC 77306 2533 A4
Coons Ln
- MtgC 77306 2532 E1
Coons Rd
23500 HarC 77070 3254 E2
23500 HarC 77375 3254 E2
Coon Tree Ct
5500 HarC 77346 3264 C5
Cooper Ln
- ARLA 77583 4623 B5
Cooper Rd
10 HOUS 77076 3684 E4
10 HOUS 77076 3685 A4
17800 MtgC 77302 2680 B7
17800 MtgC 77302 2826 A1
Cooper Breaks Dr
12600 HarC 77346 3408 D2
Cooper Ridge Ln
4800 HOUS 77053 4372 B7
Coopers Draw Ln
17100 HarC 77546 4506 B6
Coopers Gulch Tr
20100 HarC 77449 3676 D5
Coopers Hawk Ct
14000 HarC 77044 3549 C2
Coopers Hawk Dr
12700 HarC 77044 3549 C2
Coopers Post Ln
2500 SGLD 77478 4368 C5
Cooper Springs Dr
900 HarC 77373 3113 D1
Cooperstown Dr
12500 HOUS 77089 4378 C7
N Cooter Ct
15900 SGCH 77355 2961 C3
N Cooter St
32000 SGCH 77355 2961 C3
S Cooter St
31900 SGCH 77355 2961 C3
Copano Bay Dr
15600 FBnC 77478 4236 B6
Copano Sands Ln
16200 HOUS 77044 3409 B4
Copeland Dr
12700 HarC 77070 3399 B4
Copeland Ln
17300 MtgC 77365 2825 D6
Copeland St
1400 HOUS 77020 3964 B2
Copeland Mill Ln
2700 HarC 77047 4374 A3
Copeland Oaks Blvd
13400 HarC 77429 3254 A5
13800 HarC 77429 3253 E6
Copilot Ln
10000 GLSN 77554 5221 B1
Copinsay Dr
5900 HarC 77449 3677 C5
Copley Ln
11000 HarC 77093 3686 B2
Coppage St
6200 HOUS 77007 3961 E3
Copper
23300 HarC 77447 3105 B7
Copper Cr
3900 BYTN 77521 3972 D3
Copper Ct
1300 FBnC 77469 4365 D2
Copperas Bend Ct
8200 HarC 77095 3537 E6
Copperas Cove
1600 HOUS 77077 3957 A5
Copperas Creek Dr
11800 FBnC 77478 4236 B6
Copper Bean Dr
19100 HarC 77375 3109 C7
Copper Bluff Ln
8900 HarC 77095 3537 D4

STREET Block City ZIP Map# Grid

Copperbluff Ln
17600 HarC 77095 3537 E5
Copper Branch Ln
15400 HarC 77095 3538 E4
Copperbrook Dr
8500 HarC 77095 3539 A5
Copper Canyon Dr
12000 HarC 77377 3254 B1
16000 HarC 77546 4505 E6
Copper Cave Ln
20500 FBnC 77469 4234 C3
Copper Cliff Dr
2900 HarC 77449 3815 D5
Copper Cove
10 CNRO 77304 2383 B7
10 CNRO 77304 2529 B1
Copper Cove Dr
9300 HarC 77095 3538 B4
Copper Creek Cir
1100 HarC 77450 3953 E4
Copper Creek Dr
600 HarC 77450 3953 D3
Copper Creek Ln
22900 HarC 77450 3953 D3
Coppercrest Dr
- HarC 77066 3401 B6
1300 MtgC 77386 2822 E7
1400 MtgC 77386 2823 A7
Copper Crossing Ct
17100 HarC 77084 3678 A4
Copperdale Ln
10200 HarC 77064 3540 B6
Copperfield Ct
1400 FBnC 77469 4365 E3
Copperfield Dr
12400 HOUS 77031 4238 E7
Copper Gables Ln
16100 HarC 77429 3253 A7
Copper Grove Blvd
- HarC 77095 3539 A4
Copper Harbor Ct
9600 HarC 77095 3538 A4
Copper Haven Ln
8500 HarC 77095 3537 C4
Copperhead Rd
10300 MtgC 77303 2239 E2
Copper Hollow Ln
10000 HarC 77044 3689 B3
Copper Isles Ln
- HarC 77095 3537 D6
Copper Junction Dr
- HarC 77095 3537 C2
- HarC 77433 3537 C2
N Copperknoll Cir
10 WDLD 77381 2820 D2
S Copperknoll Cir
100 WDLD 77381 2820 D2
E Copper Lakes Ct
17000 HarC 77095 3538 C3
W Copper Lakes Ct
8000 HarC 77095 3537 C6
E Copper Lakes Dr
8000 HarC 77095 3537 C5
8200 HarC 77095 3538 A6
W Copper Lakes Dr
14500 HarC 77095 3537 E6
Copper Landing Ln
8800 HarC 77095 3537 C3
Copperleaf Dr
10 WDLD 77381 2820 D2
31100 MtgC 77386 2822 E7
31100 MtgC 77386 2968 E1
Coppermeade Ct
11500 HarC 77067 3402 D6
Coppermeade Dr
1200 HarC 77067 3402 C6
Copper Mill Dr
12600 HarC 77070 3399 C5
Copper Mist Ln
9700 HarC 77095 3537 E4
Copper Point Ln
7700 FBnC 77469 4095 B6
E Copper Sage Cir
10 WDLD 77381 2820 C2
S Copper Sage Cir
10 WDLD 77381 2820 B2
W Copper Sage Cir
10 WDLD 77381 2820 B2
Copper Shore Cir
8100 HarC 77095 3538 A6
Copper Shore Dr
16900 HarC 77095 3538 A6
Copper Sky Ct
1300 PRLD 77545 4499 E2
26200 FBnC 77494 4092 E1
Copper Sky Dr
2400 PRLD 77545 4499 C2
Copper Sky Ln
4200 FBnC 77494 4092 D1
Coppersmith Dr
100 HarC 77450 3953 D1
Copperstone Rd
- HarC 77095 3538 D7
Copper Stream Ln
- FBnC 77469 4365 A6
Copper Trace Ln
14200 HarC 77429 3396 E2
Copper Tree Ln
12100 HOUS 77035 4240 A6
Copper Valley Ct
2500 HarC 77067 3401 E5
E Copper Village Dr
8300 HarC 77095 3538 C5
W Copper Village Dr
8200 HarC 77095 3538 B5
Coppervine Ln
19300 HarC 77084 3816 A7
19700 HarC 77084 3815 E7
Copperwillow Ct
14000 HarC 77044 3549 D3
Copperwood Ct
1100 FBnC 77469 4365 E2
Copperwood Dr
8200 HarC 77040 3541 D7
10100 HOUS 77040 3542 A7
Copperwood Ln
1600 FBnC 77469 4365 E2
Copperwood Park Ln
2000 MtgC 77386 2823 B7
Copra Ln
2800 HarC 77073 3259 E3
Copra St
1600 TKIS 77554 5106 B4
Coquitlam Wy
- HarC 77044 3549 B3
Cora St
1100 LMQU 77568 4989 E1
7700 HOUS 77088 3683 C3
10600 HarC 77088 3543 C7
10700 HarC 77038 3543 C7
Coral Cir
3800 SEBK 77586 4382 B7
Coral Ct
100 PNVL 77304 2237 A2
Coral Dr
- BzaC 77578 4501 A7
500 LPRT 77571 4251 D7
Coral Ln
100 GLSN 77550 4994 E7
Coral Pt
- HarC 77041 3679 D6
Coral St
500 HOUS 77023 4105 B2
1000 HOUS 77012 4105 B3
27400 MtgC 77372 2683 D2
Coral Wy
1300 TKIS 77554 5106 B4
Coral Bay Dr
100 LGCY 77573 4509 A7
Coral Bay St
16100 HarC 77532 3552 C3
Coral Bean Dr
14000 SGLD 77478 4236 E5
14000 SGLD 77478 4237 A5
Coral Bell Ln
6000 HarC 77049 3828 C3
Coralbend Ln
16800 HarC 77095 3538 A1
Coralberry Ct
10 WDLD 77381 2821 A6
Coralberry Rd
10 WDLD 77381 2821 A6
Coral Bridge Ln
20900 HarC 77388 3112 E4
Coral Canyon
15400 HarC 77377 2963 B6
Coral Chase Ct
22400 FBnC 77494 4093 D4
Coral Cove Ct
2000 LGCY 77573 4509 C6
12300 PRLD 77584 4500 B1
17100 HarC 77095 3537 C4
Coral Cove Dr
2100 PRLD 77584 4500 B1
Coral Cove Ln
- LGCY 77573 4631 C7
Coral Creek Dr
5100 HOUS 77017 4106 B7
Coral Crest Ct
12900 HarC 77041 3679 E7
Coral Gables Dr
5000 HarC 77069 3400 E1
Coral Garden Ln
10800 HOUS 77075 4377 A5
13900 HOUS 77044 3409 B4
Coral Glen Ct
14800 HOUS 77062 4380 A7
Coral Leaf Tr
15300 HarC 77433 3251 A6
Coral Lilly Dr
400 LGCY 77573 4633 B2
Coral Meadow Ct
4100 HarC 77449 3816 B1
Coralmont
1500 HarC 77038 3543 E6
Coral Oak Ct
15100 HOUS 77059 4380 B7
Coral Oak Wy
- HOUS 77345 3119 E1
- HOUS 77365 3119 E1
Coral Park Dr
30800 MtgC 77386 2969 A1
Coral Petal Ln
5900 FBnC 77469 4493 B5
Coral Pointe Dr
5600 HarC 77041 3679 E7
Coral Reef Dr
3700 SEBK 77586 4382 B7
11900 HarC 77044 3688 E5
Coral Ridge Ct
3200 LGCY 77573 4633 B1
13100 HarC 77069 3400 D1
Coral Ridge Dr
3200 LGCY 77573 4633 B1
Coral Ridge Rd
5400 HarC 77069 3400 D2
Coral Rocks Ct
2900 MSCY 77459 4497 D6
Coral Rose Ct
4500 HarC 77396 3407 A7
Coral Sands Dr
15000 HOUS 77062 4380 A7
Coral Shadows Dr
3900 HarC 77449 3816 A2
Coral Springs Ct
5800 FBnC 77494 4093 E4
Coral Springs Dr
3400 BzaC 77578 4501 B7
Coral Stone Rd
10700 HarC 77086 3542 C1
Coral Tree Pl
800 MSCY 77459 4497 B6
Coralville Ct
12800 HarC 77041 3679 D6
Coralvine Ct
10 WDLD 77380 2822 A7
Coral Wood Ln
13800 FBnC 77478 4237 B3
Coral Wy Ct
1500 TYLV 77586 4382 A7
Coral Wy Dr
- PASD 77586 4382 A6
1300 TYLV 77586 4382 A6
Corbel Ln
8500 HarC 77083 4097 B7
Corbett Dr
3500 MSCY 77459 4497 E6
Corbett St
2400 LMQU 77568 4989 E3
Corbin Av
6500 HOUS 77055 3821 E6
6500 HOUS 77055 3822 A6
Corbin Dr
200 MAGA 77354 2669 A4
Corbin Bridge Ln
14900 FBnC 77478 4236 D5
Corbindale Rd
900 HDWV 77024 3959 E1
900 SPVL 77024 3959 E1
Corbingate Dr
24800 HarC 77389 2966 D3
Corbit Grove Ct
- FBnC 77469 4094 E7
Corbitt Rd
- FBnC 77494 4092 A1
Corbridge Ct
9200 FBnC 77083 4236 B1
Corburt Bend Ct
8300 HarC 77346 3265 C7
Corcoran Dr
3600 HarC 77449 3815 E3
Corcoran St
- HOUS 77034 4379 A5
Cordelia Pl
2000 FBnC 77479 4494 A4
Cordell Dr
4800 FBnC 77479 4366 D7
Cordell St
200 HOUS 77009 3824 A6
Cordella Pl
10 WDLD 77382 2819 A3
Cordell Brick Ln
10900 HOUS 77078 3827 C2
Corder St
2800 HOUS 77054 4102 E6
3000 HOUS 77054 4103 A6
3400 HOUS 77021 4103 C7
Cordero Dr
12800 HOUS 77045 4241 B6
Cordes Dr
100 HOUS 77336 3121 B5
2500 SGLD 77479 4368 C6
Cordier Ct
2500 HOUS 77003 3963 E5
Cordoba
12000 HarC 77038 3543 C5
Cordoba Ct
7700 HarC 77346 3265 C2
Cordoba Dr
- HarC 77088 3543 C7
11500 HarC 77038 3543 C6
Cordoba Cove
- LGCY 77539 4633 D3
Cordoba Pines Dr
10600 HarC 77088 3543 C7
Cordon St
2900 HOUS 77026 3825 A5
Cordona Dr
6400 HarC 77449 3677 A3
Coreland Ln
18200 HarC 77429 3252 B5
Coretta Ct
1800 FBnC 77545 4622 D1
Corey Cove Ln
25600 FBnC 77494 4093 A2
Corey Woods Ct
8300 HarC 77095 3538 B6
Coriander Ct
30000 SGCH 77355 2960 B1
Coriander Dr
22000 HarC 77450 3954 A1
22300 HarC 77450 3953 E1
22600 MtgC 77355 2960 C2
22600 SGCH 77355 2960 C2
Coriander Ln
8300 HarC 77521 3833 D2
Corina Glen Dr
600 FBnC 77583 4623 A7
Corine St
900 FBnC 77477 4369 E4
900 STAF 77477 4369 E4
1100 FBnC 77477 4370 A5
Corinna Dr
- HarC 77083 4096 D5
Corinne Ct
3500 HarC 77449 3816 A2
Corinth Dr
6700 PASD 77505 4248 E4
Corinth St
7800 HOUS 77051 4243 B2
Corinthian Park Dr
5900 HarC 77379 3111 E5
5900 HarC 77379 3112 A5
Corinthian Pointe Dr
13400 HOUS 77085 4371 E1
Cork Cir
2400 PRLD 77581 4504 C2
Cork Dr
- HOUS 77048 4374 D1
3500 HOUS 77047 4374 C2
Cork Ln
4200 DRPK 77536 4249 B2
Cork St
2000 DKSN 77539 4753 C1
Corksie St
3000 HOUS 77051 4243 A5
Corktree Knls
14300 HarC 77429 3397 B1
Corkwood Ct
11800 HarC 77089 4378 B5
Corkwood Dr
11500 HarC 77089 4378 B5
Corl St
5600 HOUS 77087 4104 D7
5700 HOUS 77087 4244 D1
Corley Dr
300 HarC 77562 3832 A2
Cormorant Cres
1700 MSCY 77489 4497 C1
Cormorant Ct
17300 HarC 77396 3407 D3
Cormorant Rd
16700 GLSN 77554 5331 D4
16700 JMAB 77554 5331 D4
Cornelia Dr
14100 HarC 77429 3397 E7
Cornell Ln
- LGCY 77573 4751 B1
Cornell St
- BYTN 77520 3972 E5
2500 HOUS 77009 3823 E4
4300 HOUS 77022 3823 E2
Cornell Park Ct
3900 PASD 77058 4380 E7
Cornell Park Ln
24200 HarC 77494 3953 A1
Corner Cr
16700 HarC 77084 3678 B3
Corner Sq
800 SEBK 77586 4509 E1
Corner Brook Ln
- HarC 77041 3680 E6
- HOUS 77041 3680 E6
Cornerbrook Ln
- FBnC 77494 4093 E4
Cornerbrook Pl
10 WDLD 77381 2821 A2
Corner Oaks Ln
9300 HOUS 77036 4098 E7
9300 HOUS 77036 4238 E1
Cornerstone St
4500 PRLD 77584 4503 B6
Cornerstone Park Dr
- HarC 77014 3257 D7
Cornerstone Pl Dr
1700 HarC 77450 3954 A4
1900 HarC 77450 3953 E5
Cornerstone Village Dr
14100 HarC 77014 3401 C1
14400 HarC 77014 3257 C7
Cornett Dr
9200 HarC 77064 3541 A5
Cornett Rd
- BzaC 77511 4627 E7
- BzaC 77511 4628 A7
Cornflower Dr
10 WDLD 77384 2675 A5
Cornflower Ln
7000 FBnC 77494 4093 C4
Corniche St
1600 LGCY 77573 4508 D4
Corning Dr
12400 HOUS 77089 4378 C6
Cornish St
4500 HOUS 77007 3962 A1
5700 HOUS 77007 3961 E1
Cornoustie St
4700 PASD 77505 4248 E6
Cornwall
- MtgC 77357 2829 D3
10000 HarC 77086 3541 E2
26000 MtgC 77357 2830 A3
Cornwall Ct
3500 FBnC 77459 4622 B5
Cornwall Ln
10800 FBnC 77459 4622 B5
Cornwall St
16400 JRSV 77040 3680 C1
Cornwall Bridge Ln
7300 HarC 77041 3679 C1
Cornwell Wy
- HOUS 77339 3263 E1
1200 HOUS 77339 3264 B1
Corola Trail Dr
11300 HarC 77066 3400 E5
Corona Ln
11600 HOUS 77072 4098 A6
12700 HOUS 77072 4097 D6
Corona Del Mar Dr
1700 MSCY 77459 4497 C3
15100 HarC 77083 4096 C6
Coronado Cir
10 LMQU 77568 4990 B2
Coronado Ct
25000 GLSN 77554 5548 B1
Coronado Dr
12800 BzaC 77541 5547 B7
Coronado St
100 HOUS 77009 3824 B5
1800 FRDW 77546 4629 B7
4500 SEBK 77586 4383 A7
Coronado Wy
- LGCY 77573 4632 E1
Coronado Lakes Dr
1500 LGCY 77573 4632 A7
Coronado Park Ln
17300 HarC 77346 3408 C3
Coronado Springs Dr
16800 HarC 77379 3256 D2
Coronation Dr
10 HOUS 77034 4247 A5
Corondo Ct
3500 WUNP 77005 4101 E4
Coronel St
1800 ALVN 77511 4749 A6
Corporate Dr
1200 RSBG 77471 4491 C3
5800 HOUS 77036 4098 E6
7200 MNVL 77578 4746 B1
10400 SGLD 77478 4368 D1
10500 STAF 77477 4368 E1
10700 STAF 77477 4369 A1
Corporate Centre Dr
10900 HOUS 77041 3680 D7
Corporate Woods Dr
- MtgC 77354 2671 E1
10 MtgC 77354 2672 B3
Corpus Dr
200 MAGA 77354 2669 A5
Corpus Christi St
6300 HOUS 77020 3964 E1
7100 HOUS 77020 3965 A1
12800 HOUS 77015 3828 B7
12900 HOUS 77015 3967 C1
13700 HarC 77015 3828 E7
14100 HarC 77015 3829 A7
Corral Ct
21000 TMBL 77375 3109 E3
Corral Dr
1400 HarC 77090 3258 A3
1800 HarC 77090 3257 E4
17100 HarC 77433 3252 B4
Corral Tr
2500 HarC 77546 4506 B7
Corral Corner Ct
9100 HarC 77064 3540 D5
Corral Corner Ln
9800 HarC 77064 3540 C5
Corrales Dr
7900 FBnC 77083 4096 B7
Corral Gate Ct
3500 FBnC 77450 4094 D1
Corral Path Ct
9800 HarC 77064 3540 C5
Corrian Park Cir
7900 HarC 77040 3541 D6
Corridor Pl
300 STAF 77477 4369 C3
Corridor Wy
400 STAF 77477 4369 C3
Corrigan Ct
3300 HarC 77014 3401 E2
Corrigan Dr
- PRLD 77581 4503 A3
- PRLD 77584 4503 A4
13600 HarC 77014 3401 E1
Corsair Rd
15300 HOUS 77053 4371 E5
15700 HOUS 77489 4371 D6
Corsica St
700 HarC 77015 3828 B7
Corsicana Lk
5900 HarC 77041 3679 E5
Corsicana St
6900 HOUS 77020 3964 E3
6900 HOUS 77020 3965 A3
Corta Calle Dr
7000 HarC 77083 4096 B6
Cortelyou Ln
5100 HOUS 77021 4104 A5
Cortes Dr
7400 FBnC 77083 4095 E6
Cortez Ct
11300 HOUS 77048 4244 D6
Cortez Rd
7300 FBnC 77469 4616 A4
Cortina Ln
7600 HarC 77083 4097 A6
Cortlandt St
300 HOUS 77007 3962 D1
800 HOUS 77007 3823 D7
2300 HOUS 77008 3823 D4
2900 HOUS 77018 3823 D3
4000 HOUS 77022 3823 D3
5500 HOUS 77022 3684 D6
5500 HOUS 77076 3684 D6
Corto St
3800 HOUS 77093 3825 A2
4200 HOUS 77016 3825 B2
Cortona Ct
- LGCY 77573 4632 C5
Corum St
11300 HOUS 77089 4377 C4
Coruthers St
- PRVW 77445 3100 B2
Corvallis Dr
10000 HarC 77095 3538 E3
Corvette Ct
700 HarC 77060 3544 E4
Corvette Ln
800 HarC 77060 3544 E4
800 HarC 77060 3545 A4
Corwin Pl
10 HDWV 77024 3960 A2
10 HNCV 77024 3960 A2
Corwin St
300 HOUS 77076 3684 D3
Cory Ln
4400 MSCY 77459 4369 C7
Cory St
100 CNRO 77301 2384 C6
Cory Crossing Ln
2000 MtgC 77386 2969 D5
Corydon Dr
900 HOUS 77336 3266 D2
Coryell St
2200 LGCY 77573 4632 C1
W Coryell St
- LGCY 77573 4631 E3
Cory Terrace Ct
28500 MtgC 77386 2969 D6
Corza Ct
12600 HOUS 77045 4241 B6
Corzatt Dr
13300 HarC 77065 3539 B2
Cosby St
4500 HOUS 77021 4103 E6
4900 HOUS 77021 4104 A6
Cosmos St
100 HOUS 77009 3824 B7
Cossey Rd
9400 HarC 77070 3255 A5
Costa Brava Pk
- LGCY 77539 4633 E3
Costa Del Rey Ct
12000 HarC 77041 3680 A5
Costa Mesa Cir
- LGCY 77573 4632 A7
Costa Mesa Dr
6300 HOUS 77053 4371 D6
Costa Rica Rd
3700 HOUS 77092 3821 E2
5200 HOUS 77091 3682 E7
5200 HOUS 77092 3682 E7
Costa Sienna Ln
6500 HarC 77041 3680 A3
Costero Dr
17000 FBnC 77083 4095 E7
Cote Ct
8900 HarC 77064 3540 B5
Cotillion Ct
10 WDLD 77382 2820 A1
Cotillion Dr
16000 HOUS 77060 3544 D2
Cotorra Cove Ct
6500 HarC 77041 3679 D3
6500 HarC 77041 3680 A4
Cotswald Tr
3000 PRLD 77584 4501 B1
Cotswold Blvd
- HOUS 77339 3263 E1
- HOUS 77339 3264 A1
Cotswold St
3900 HOUS 77009 3824 B6
N Cotswold Manor Dr
2700 HOUS 77339 3264 A1
3400 HOUS 77339 3119 A7
S Cotswold Manor Dr
3000 HOUS 77339 3264 A1
N Cotswold Manor Lp
1400 HOUS 77339 3119 B7
1400 HOUS 77339 3264 B1
S Cotswold Manor Lp
1100 HOUS 77339 3264 B1
Cottage Ct
2300 FBnC 77469 4365 D3
W Cottage Grn
10 WDLD 77382 2674 C5
Cottage Ln
10 LbyC 77535 3268 C6
Cottage St
100 HOUS 77009 3824 B6
9700 PRLD 77584 4501 B2
W Cottage St
600 HOUS 77009 3824 A6
1000 HOUS 77009 3823 E6
1100 HOUS 77008 3823 E6
Cottage Arbor Ct
13600 FBnC 77478 4367 A2
Cottage Bay Ct
1800 LGCY 77573 4631 C7
Cottage Brook Ln
- PRLD 77581 4503 E1
Cottage Cove Ct
1400 SEBK 77586 4382 E7
Cottage Cove Ln
20800 FBnC 77450 4094 B4
Cottage Creek Ct
2600 PRLD 77584 4500 B3
Cottage Creek Dr
- HarC 77095 3537 C4
2600 PRLD 77584 4500 B3
Cottage Creek Ln
- RSBG 77469 4614 E4
Cottage Cypress Ln
26400 HarC 77433 3396 B6
Cottage Elm Ct
12000 HarC 77089 4505 A1
Cottage Field Rd
10200 HOUS 77041 3820 A1
Cottage Gate
23500 MtgC 77447 2960 B5
Cottage Gate Ln
8500 HOUS 77088 3683 E1
8800 HOUS 77088 3543 E7
Cottage Glen Ct
5000 HOUS 77345 3120 A2
E Cottage Green St
10 WDLD 77382 2674 C5
Cottage Grove Ct
500 LGCY 77573 4630 E6
Cottage Grove Pl
10 WDLD 77381 2820 D2
Cottage Heath Ln
20500 FBnC 77469 4094 D7
Cottage Hill Ln
25200 HarC 77373 3114 C2
Cottage Ivy Cir
15800 HarC 77377 3254 C6
15800 HarC 77429 3254 C6
Cottage Lake Ct
3600 FBnC 77478 4366 D3
Cottage Lake Ln
14200 HarC 77396 3547 D2
Cottage Landing Ct
13700 HOUS 77077 3956 D5
Cottage Landing Ln
1600 HOUS 77077 3956 E5
Cottage Manor Ln
- FBnC 77494 4092 C1
Cottage Mill Pl
10 WDLD 77382 2674 E5
Cottage Oak Ln
1000 HOUS 77091 3683 E6
1000 HOUS 77091 3684 A6
1200 KATY 77494 3952 B4
Cottage Park Cir
19600 HarC 77094 3955 A3
Cottage Pines Dr
6200 HarC 77449 3677 C4
Cottage Point Dr
1600 FBnC 77494 3953 C5
Cottage Rose Tr
16600 HarC 77429 3252 C5
Cottage Springs Ct
26300 FBnC 77494 4092 D1
Cottage Springs Dr
2600 PRLD 77584 4500 B3
Cottage Stone Ln
4800 HarC 77449 3677 A7
Cottage Stream Ct
21000 HarC 77379 3111 D3
Cottage Stream Ln
6200 HarC 77379 3111 D3
Cottage Timbers Ct
- HarC 77044 3549 D3
Cottage Timbers Ln
14400 HOUS 77044 3550 A1
Cotter Ct
1600 RSBG 77471 4491 D5
Cotter Dr
600 HarC 77373 3113 E6
Cotter Ln
4800 RSBG 77471 4491 C5
Cotter Lake Cir
3000 MSCY 77459 4496 B2
Cotter Lake Dr
4900 MSCY 77459 4496 B2
Cottingham St
13000 HOUS 77048 4375 A3
Cotton Cir
2600 MSCY 77489 4497 B1
5700 PLEK 77461 4614 E7
5700 PLEK 77469 4614 E7
5700 PLEK 77471 4614 E7
5800 FBnC 77469 4614 E7
Cotton Ct
1800 FBnC 77469 4365 C2
Cotton Dr
- HOUS 77092 3821 C1
6700 HOUS 77092 3682 B7
Cotton Brook Ct
11700 HarC 77375 3109 E6
Cotton Creek Dr
19500 HarC 77375 3109 D6
Cottondale Ct
2500 FBnC 77450 3953 E6
20700 HarC 77450 3954 C6
Cotton Field Ln
6100 HarC 77449 3677 B4
Cottonfield Wy
2900 SGLD 77479 4496 A1
Cotton Gin Ct
3500 FBnC 77469 4234 C6
Cotton Gin Dr
19100 HarC 77449 3677 B4
Cottonglade Ln
20000 HarC 77338 3261 E4
Cottonglen Ct
5000 HOUS 77041 3680 D6
Cotton Gum Ln
1100 RSBG 77471 4614 C1
Cotton Lake Ct
4900 FBnC 77469 4234 D4
Cotton Mill Ct
1800 FBnC 77469 4365 C3
Cottonmist Ct
5600 FBnC 77479 4367 A5
Cotton Ridge Tr
4800 HOUS 77053 4372 A7
Cotton Run Ct
8700 HOUS 77040 3682 B4
Cottonshire Dr
3000 HarC 77373 3114 E6
Cotton Stock Dr
2700 SGLD 77479 4368 C7
Cottontail Dr
200 HarC 77532 3692 E3
700 HarC 77532 3693 A3
Cottontop Ct
11000 HarC 77086 3542 B1
Cotton Valley Ln
21500 MtgC 77365 2973 B3
Cottonwood Av
400 FBnC 77545 4623 C2
Cotton Wood Bnd
33200 MtgC 77354 2673 B3
Cottonwood Cir
5100 DKSN 77539 4754 C3
6900 HarC 77396 3547 B2
16600 MtgC 77372 2683 A6
Cottonwood Ct
- FBnC 77478 4237 A5
1800 SGLD 77478 4237 A5
2200 MSCY 77459 4370 A7
4400 LGCY 77573 4630 E6
Cotton Wood Dr
2900 DKSN 77539 4753 D2
10400 MtgC 77302 2676 E2
10400 MtgC 77302 2677 A2
Cottonwood Dr
400 FRDW 77546 4505 A6
1300 HOUS 77017 4106 D7
1300 PASD 77017 4106 D7
1300 PASD 77502 4106 D7
2800 KATY 77493 3813 B4
3800 LPRT 77571 4250 D4
7300 BYTN 77521 3835 B5
Cottonwood Ln
12000 HarC 77429 3398 C2
14000 MtgC 77306 2533 D7
16000 MtgC 77372 2682 E6
16000 PTVL 77372 2682 E6
31700 MtgC 77355 2669 B7
Cottonwood Pk
- HarC 77041 3679 E4
Cottonwood Pl
16700 MtgC 77372 2682 E6
16700 MtgC 77372 2683 A6
Cottonwood St
5500 PRLD 77584 4502 D7
5900 HOUS 77087 4245 A1
Cottonwood Wy
16900 HOUS 77059 4380 D6
Cottonwood Bend Ct
10300 HarC 77064 3540 D3
Cottonwood Canyon Dr
10100 HarC 77095 3537 D3
Cottonwood Church Rd
1200 FBnC 77471 4614 A3
1200 RSBG 77471 4614 A3
Cottonwood Cove Ln
24400 MtgC 77380 2967 B3
Cottonwood Creek Ln
5200 LGCY 77573 4630 D7
Cottonwood Heights Ln
14300 HarC 77090 3258 C7
Cottonwood Park Ln
6400 HarC 77041 3679 E3
Cottonwood School Rd
700 RSBG 77471 4614 A3
1600 FBnC 77471 4614 B2
Cottonwood Trail Ct
8100 HarC 77095 3537 C6
Cottonwood Trail Ln
17600 HarC 77095 3537 D7
Cottonwood Walk Ct
2700 HarC 77388 3113 B6
Cottrell Ct
13700 HOUS 77077 3957 A3
Couch St
2100 HOUS 77008 3822 E5
3400 HOUS 77018 3822 E3
6500 HOUS 77091 3683 E4
Cougar
12700 HarC 77064 3540 C1
Cougar Ct
8800 HarC 77521 3833 D1
Cougar Ln
- HOUS 77032 3546 C2
Cougar Pl
10 HOUS 77004 4103 E2
Cougar St
24000 MtgC 77355 2962 C5
Cougar Creek St
10 MtgC 77385 2823 C4
Cougar Falls Ct
16600 HarC 77379 3256 B4
Cougar Peak Dr
19200 HarC 77377 3109 C7
19200 HarC 77377 3254 E2
Coulcrest Rd
1900 HOUS 77055 3821 B5
Coulson Cir
12000 HOUS 77015 3966 E3
Coulson Dr
12200 HOUS 77015 3966 E3
12600 HOUS 77015 3967 A3
Council Grove Ln
5200 HOUS 77088 3682 E2
5200 HOUS 77088 3683 A1
Counselor St
11500 HarC 77065 3398 A7
Count St
8200 HOUS 77028 3687 C6
Count Eric Dr
2600 HarC 77084 3816 B5
Counter Point Dr
1900 HOUS 77055 3821 D5
N Country
- HarC 77389 2966 E4
Country Bnd
17700 SGCH 77355 2961 B2
Country Cir
13500 TMBL 77375 2964 A4
Country Ct
10 HNCV 77024 3960 B1
10 PNPV 77024 3960 A4
5200 MtgC 77354 2673 E1
5200 MtgC 77354 2674 A1
Country Dr
100 MtgC 77354 2818 B5
N Country Dr
15600 MtgC 77365 2824 E5
15600 MtgC 77365 2825 A5
Country Flds
17800 SGCH 77355 2961 A2
Country Grv
17600 SGCH 77355 2961 A2
Country Hllw
26500 SGCH 77355 2961 A2
Country Ln
- WlrC 77447 2813 D4
100 LGCY 77573 4630 D7
700 HNCV 77024 3960 B2
3800 MtgC 77384 2675 E7
3800 MtgC 77384 2676 A7
3800 SHEH 77384 2676 A7
3800 WDLD 77384 2676 A7
7800 GlsC 77517 4986 D6
13500 TMBL 77375 2964 A4
Country Mdw
17400 SGCH 77355 2961 A2
Country Pl
5800 LGCY 77573 4630 C7
Country Rd
3300 PASD 77505 4248 D4
Country Ter
- HarC 77562 3832 D2
Country Tr
15800 HarC 77377 3254 E6
Country Vil
- MtgC 77302 2679 D7

STREET
Block City ZIP Map# Grid

Country Acres Dr
- BzaC 77511 4748 A7
- BzaC 77511 4866 A1
5400 BzaC 77511 4747 E7
Countryaire St
5600 LGCY 77573 4630 D7
Country Arbor Ln
10600 HarC 77433 3537 A1
12500 HarC 77041 3679 E3
Country Bend Dr
16000 HarC 77095 3538 C6
Country Birch
17500 SGCH 77355 2961 B3
Country Boy Ct
3000 HarC 77373 3115 A4
Countrybreeze Ct
19500 HarC 77388 3112 C6
Country Bridge Rd
16800 HarC 77095 3538 A7
Country Brook Ct
5900 FBnC 77479 4493 E2
8600 HarC 77095 3538 C3
Country Brook Ln
17100 HarC 77095 3538 A5
17200 HarC 77095 3537 C4
Countrycanyon Dr
19500 HarC 77388 3112 B6
Country Cedar
17500 SGCH 77355 2961 B2
Country Club Blvd
2500 SGLD 77478 4368 E2
2900 SGLD 77478 4369 A2
3100 STAF 77477 4369 A2
3100 STAF 77478 4369 A2
Country Club Ct
16000 JRSV 77040 3540 B7
Country Club Dr
- HarC 77346 3265 B4
10 FRDW 77546 4628 E7
500 MtgC 77302 2530 C6
500 MtgC 77357 2829 D2
500 RMFT 77357 2829 D2
600 RHMD 77469 4491 E2
600 RHMD 77469 4492 A2
1600 FRDW 77546 4629 A7
2000 PRLD 77581 4504 C2
4100 DKSN 77539 4754 D2
4300 BYTN 77521 3972 B2
6400 HOUS 77023 4104 D1
E Country Club Dr
3300 SRAC 77571 4382 D1
N Country Club Dr
900 SRAC 77571 4382 D1
S Country Club Dr
800 SRAC 77571 4382 C2
W Country Club Dr
3200 SRAC 77571 4382 C2
Country Club Vw
4300 BYTN 77521 3972 B2
Country Club Cove Dr
1500 BYTN 77521 3972 C1
Country Club Green Blvd
- HarC 77375 3109 D2
- TMBL 77375 3109 D2
Country Club Green Cir
21500 HarC 77375 3109 D2
N Country Club Green Dr
11300 HarC 77375 3109 E2
11300 HarC 77375 3110 A2
S Country Club Green Dr
11100 HarC 77375 3110 A2
11200 HarC 77375 3109 E2
Country Club Green Wy
21600 HarC 77375 3109 E2
Country Colony Dr
27300 MtgC 77372 2537 D7
Country Corner Ct
1900 FBnC 77494 3952 B4
Country Cove Ln
22500 FBnC 77494 4093 D3
Country Creek Ct
1700 MtgC 77354 2673 D1
Country Creek Dr
8800 HOUS 77036 4239 A2
Country Creek Wy
2200 FBnC 77469 4365 D1
Country Crest St
17700 SGCH 77355 2961 A3
Countrycrossing Dr
4300 HarC 77388 3112 C7
Country Dell Ln
4000 HarC 77388 3112 D6
Country Elm
17500 SGCH 77355 2961 B2
Country Estates Dr
24600 MtgC 77357 2828 D5
Country Fair Ln
15600 HarC 77433 3251 B6
N Country Fair Ln
- HarC 77433 3251 C5
Country Falls Ln
5900 HOUS 77345 3120 C6
Country Forest Ct
10 WDLD 77380 2968 A3
Country Forest Dr
40300 MtgC 77354 2671 C2
N Country Gate Cir
10 WDLD 77384 2675 E5
W Country Gate Cir
10 WDLD 77384 2675 D5
Countrygate Dr
25100 HarC 77375 2965 C3
Country Glen St
5600 LGCY 77573 4630 C6
Country Green Ct
13500 HOUS 77059 4379 E4
Country Green Dr
4000 HarC 77388 3112 D6
Country Green St
5600 LGCY 77573 4630 D7
E Country Grove Cir
600 BzaC 77584 4374 C7
600 BzaC 77584 4501 E1
W Country Grove Cir
600 BzaC 77584 4374 C7
600 BzaC 77584 4501 C1
Country Haven Ct
14400 HOUS 77044 3550 A1
Countryheights Ct
4200 HarC 77388 3112 C6
Country Heights St
26200 SGCH 77355 2961 A3
Country Hill Ct
13600 TMBL 77375 2964 A4
Country Hill Ln
10 CNRO 77304 2383 B2
Countryhills Ct
19200 HarC 77388 3112 D6

Country Hills Dr
17800 HarC 77377 2962 C7
Country Hollow St
26100 SGCH 77355 2961 A2
Country Knoll Dr
- HarC 77086 3542 D3
Country Lake Dr
19000 MtgC 77355 2815 A5
19200 MtgC 77355 2814 E5
Country Lake Estates Dr
19200 HarC 77388 3112 C6
Countryland Ct
19500 HarC 77388 3112 C6
Country Ln Rd
- WlrC 77447 2813 D3
Country Manor Dr
13900 FBnC 77478 4237 A4
14100 FBnC 77478 4236 E4
Country Meadow Dr
10500 BzaC 77511 4747 E5
10500 BzaC 77511 4748 A5
30500 TMBL 77375 2964 A4
Country Meadow Ln
10700 HarC 77375 3254 E1
10700 HarC 77375 3255 A1
Countrymeadow Ln
19300 HarC 77388 3112 C6
Country Meadows Ct
3300 BzaC 77584 4501 E1
Country Meadows Dr
700 BzaC 77584 4501 B1
Countrymeadows Dr
4500 HarC 77388 3112 B7
S Country Meadows Ln
3300 BzaC 77584 4501 B1
W Country Meadows Ln
800 BzaC 77584 4501 E1
Country Meadows St
1600 GlsC 77517 4870 B3
Country Mile Ct
2000 FBnC 77469 4365 C3
Country Mile Ln
2100 FBnC 77469 4365 C3
Country Mill Wy
4100 HarC 77388 3112 D6
Countrymountain Ct
19500 HarC 77388 3112 B6
Country Oak
17500 SGCH 77355 2961 B2
Countryoaks Ct
4300 HarC 77388 3112 C6
N Country Oaks Dr
1500 HarC 77532 3410 C5
Country Orchard Ln
12000 HarC 77089 4504 B2
Country Park Ct
21700 HarC 77450 3954 B4
Country Park Dr
1400 HarC 77450 3954 B4
Country Park Rd
4100 HarC 77388 3112 C7
Country Park Wy
15700 HarC 77433 3251 B6
Country Pine Ct
13600 TMBL 77375 2964 A4
Country Pines Ct
25800 MtgC 77355 2814 B4
Countrypines Dr
4300 HarC 77388 3112 C6
4700 HarC 77379 3112 B7
Country Pines Rd
20500 MtgC 77355 2814 B5
Country Pl Blvd
800 BzaC 77584 4501 E1
Country Pl Cir
- HOUS 77079 3957 D1
Country Pl Dr
10 BzaC 77511 4747 E7
10 BzaC 77511 4748 A7
700 HOUS 77079 3957 D2
2300 FBnC 77469 4365 E3
3700 FBnC 77477 4369 D4
3700 MSCY 77477 4369 D4
17800 MtgC 77302 2825 E2
17800 MtgC 77302 2826 A2
Country Pl Rd
- MtgC 77355 2815 A3
29400 MtgC 77355 2814 E2
E Countryplace Blvd
- BzaC 77584 4374 B7
- BzaC 77584 4501 B1
W Countryplace Blvd
- BzaC 77584 4374 B7
- BzaC 77584 4501 B1
Countryranch Ct
19500 HarC 77388 3112 B6
Country Redbird
17500 SGCH 77355 2961 B2
Country Ridge Dr
2000 HOUS 77062 4380 B7
6000 FBnC 77469 4493 B5
Countryridge Dr
19600 HarC 77388 3112 C6
Country Ridge Ln
26200 SGCH 77355 2961 A2
Countryroad Dr
19400 HarC 77388 3112 C7
Country Rose Ln
14700 HarC 77429 3396 C1
Country Run Ct
19900 MSCY 77459 4497 E7
Countryshire Ln
2000 FBnC 77469 4232 E3
Country Side Dr
13600 GlsC 77517 4870 B2
13600 STFE 77517 4870 B2
Countryside Dr
- SGLD 77479 4368 D7
6100 LGCY 77573 4630 C5
Country Side Ln
21500 HarC 77338 3260 D2
Country Side Village Dr
- HMBL 77338 3263 A7
Country Spring Rd
4100 HarC 77084 3816 C1
4500 HarC 77084 3677 B7
Country Square Dr
1500 FBnC 77469 4365 C1
19000 HarC 77084 3816 B4
Country Squire Blvd
- BYTN 77520 3835 C4
10200 CmbC 77520 3835 C4
N Country Squire St
11000 HNCV 77024 3960 A4
11000 PNPV 77024 3959 E4
11000 PNPV 77024 3960 A4
S Country Squire St
11000 HNCV 77024 3960 A4

S Country Squire St
11000 PNPV 77024 3959 E4
11000 PNPV 77024 3960 A4
Country Timbers
26000 SGCH 77355 2961 B3
Country Time Cir
13600 TMBL 77375 2964 A4
Countrytrails Dr
4300 HarC 77388 3112 C6
Country Trails St
4000 BzaC 77511 4868 A6
Country View Dr
8300 HarC 77040 3541 C7
Country View Ln
22000 WlrC 77445 2952 D6
Country Village Blvd
1800 HarC 77338 3263 B7
1800 HMBL 77338 3263 B7
Country Village Dr
19200 HarC 77388 3112 D6
Country Walk Dr
17900 HarC 77379 3256 A1
Country West Dr
14600 MtgC 77302 2679 E2
14600 MtgC 77306 2679 E2
Country Wind Ct
8100 HarC 77040 3541 B5
Country Wind Ln
8300 HarC 77040 3541 B7
Countrywood Ln
12300 HarC 77039 3546 D5
Country Woods Tr
17500 SGCH 77355 2961 B3
Country Wy Cir
11700 BKHV 77024 3959 C4
County Rd
- HarC 77532 3692 B2
County Cress Dr
14500 HarC 77047 4374 D5
County Cress Rd
5500 ARLA 77583 4623 A5
County Down Ct
24700 FBnC 77494 3952 E3
County Fair Dr
100 HOUS 77060 3544 C2
23700 MtgC 77447 2960 B5
County Park Dr
300 LGCY 77573 4631 E3
E Coupland Dr
1900 LPRT 77571 4250 C1
Couples Ct
32800 MtgC 77354 2672 B4
Courageous Dr
100 LGCY 77573 4508 E6
20300 HarC 77447 3105 E1
Courageous Ln
4100 GLSN 77554 5548 B2
Courben Cir
9300 HOUS 77078 3688 A5
Courben Ln
9700 HOUS 77078 3688 A5
Courrege Ln
13400 HarC 77037 3544 E7
Cours St
- HOUS 77026 3824 E3
6800 HOUS 77093 3824 E3
N Course Dr
5800 HOUS 77072 4098 D3
S Course Dr
8300 HOUS 77072 4098 D7
8300 HOUS 77099 4098 D7
8400 HOUS 77099 4238 D1
Courseview Ct
24700 HarC 77389 2966 D4
Course View Ln
6500 HarC 77389 2966 C4
Court
3900 PRLD 77581 4503 C4
N Court Dr
19700 MtgC 77365 2825 A4
Court Rd
- HOUS 77489 4370 E6
- MSCY 77489 4370 E6
2500 MSCY 77459 4370 A6
2500 MSCY 77477 4370 A6
4600 HOUS 77053 4372 A7
5400 HOUS 77053 4371 D6
7300 HOUS 77489 4371 A6
Court St
- PRLD 77581 4503 C4
1200 HOUS 77007 3962 D2
Court Amber Tr
15300 HarC 77433 3251 A5
Courtcliff Dr
11400 HarC 77066 3401 A7
Court Dale Dr
10 WDLD 77381 2821 E1
10 WDLD 77384 2821 E1
Courtesy Ln
700 KMAH 77565 4509 E6
Courtesy Rd
800 HarC 77032 3545 A1
Court Glen Dr
9700 HOUS 77099 4238 B2
Court Green Tr
15300 HarC 77433 3251 A5
Courtland Cir
16500 HarC 77379 3256 C4
Courtland Ct
100 HarC 77562 3831 E1
Courtland Grn
10 WDLD 77382 2674 C4
Courtland Oaks St
24100 HarC 77494 3953 A1
Courtlandt Pl
10 HOUS 77006 3962 E6
10 HOUS 77006 3963 D2
300 FRDW 77546 4629 C2
Courtlea St
- HarC 77346 3264 A6
Courtley St
10400 HarC 77065 3539 B3
Courtly Estates Ln
18100 HarC 77429 3396 B2
Courtney Ct
2200 MSCY 77459 4370 A7
Courtney Dr
8900 HarC 77562 3832 E1
9100 HarC 77562 3833 A1
Courtney Ln
2100 GlsC 77517 4870 B3
5200 LGCY 77573 4630 C5
Courtney Rd
14500 SGCH 77362 2816 C7
Courtney St
- HOUS 77016 3686 E2
1100 RHMD 77469 4491 E2
3600 HOUS 77026 3825 B7

Courtney Bend Cir
10900 HarC 77086 3542 A1
Courtney Bend Dr
- HarC 77086 3542 A1
Courtney Greens Rd
12200 HarC 77089 4505 A2
Courtney Ln Dr
1900 HOUS 77042 3958 C6
Courtney Manor Ln
7700 FBnC 77494 4093 B2
Courtney Pine Cir
17400 HarC 77379 3255 D3
Court of Lions St
5600 HarC 77069 3400 D1
Court of Lords St
13800 HarC 77069 3256 D7
Court of Regents St
14000 HarC 77069 3256 D7
Court of St. Jude
10 SGLD 77479 4495 A2
Court of York St
5200 HarC 77069 3256 C7
Courtshire Dr
11300 HOUS 77076 3685 B3
Courtshire Ln
2100 SGLD 77478 4368 E6
Courtside Dr
- LGCY 77573 4632 B3
Courtside Dr E
- LGCY 77573 4632 B3
Courtside Dr W
- LGCY 77573 4632 B3
Courtside Pl Dr
1800 MSCY 77489 4370 C6
Courtyard Cir
10 MtgC 77304 2236 B4
Courtyard Ln
2600 PRLD 77584 4501 A3
Coushatta Ct
13800 HarC 77429 3253 E5
Cove Ln
12200 DKSN 77539 4753 B6
Cove Rd
100 MTBL 77520 3696 E5
Cove Rd FM-565
100 MTBL 77520 3696 E5
Covebridge Dr
- FBnC 77450 3953 C6
Covebrook Ct
2800 BzaC 77584 4501 A6
Covebrook Dr
2900 BzaC 77584 4501 A6
Cove Creek Ln
100 HOUS 77042 3958 C4
Covecrest Dr
100 HOUS 77336 3266 B4
Cove Crest Tr
900 FBnC 77545 4623 A2
Cove Hollow Dr
22300 HarC 77450 3953 E5
22300 HarC 77450 3954 B2
Cove Lake Dr
6600 HarC 77449 3676 C3
Cove Landing Ln
13800 BzaC 77583 4623 D4
Covelight Ln
20700 FBnC 77469 4094 D7
Covenant Crest Dr
7900 HOUS 77489 4371 C4
Covenant Springs Ct
14100 HarC 77044 3549 C2
Coveney Dr
14000 HarC 77090 3402 C1
14200 HarC 77090 3258 C7
Covens Forest Dr
11900 HarC 77044 3548 D6
Covent Garden Dr
8700 HOUS 77031 4239 A5
8700 HOUS 77071 4239 A5
Coventina Cir
8000 HarC 77040 3541 D6
Coventry Blvd
7600 HarC 77389 2966 A1
Coventry Ct
- MtgC 77357 2829 C4
10 SGLD 77479 4495 E4
300 PASD 77502 4247 A1
5100 FRDW 77546 4505 D6
9800 HMBL 77338 3262 C4
Coventry Ln
300 ALVN 77511 4867 D5
Coventry St
- SGLD 77479 4495 E4
Coventry Falls
6000 HarC 77084 3678 A4
Coventry Field Ln
6200 HarC 77084 3678 A4
Coventry Meadows Ln
- HarC 77084 3678 B3
Coventry Oaks Dr
17400 HarC 77084 3678 A4
17500 HarC 77084 3677 E4
Coventry Park Dr
17000 HarC 77084 3678 A4
17500 HarC 77084 3677 E4
17700 HarC 77449 3677 D4
Coventry Square Dr
9400 HOUS 77099 4237 E2
Coventry Squire Dr
17500 HarC 77084 3677 E4
Cove Park Dr
1800 LGCY 77565 4509 A5
Coverdale Park Pl
10 WDLD 77382 2819 C1
Covered Bridge St
10900 HOUS 77075 4377 B4
Coveredgate Ct
22200 HarC 77373 3261 A1
Coverlea Ct
1900 HarC 77388 3113 C5
Covern St
100 HOUS 77061 4245 B2
Cove Royale Ln
7400 FBnC 77469 4094 E6
Covert St
4100 GlsC 77518 4634 C3
Coveside St
2100 LGCY 77565 4509 A4
Covesville Ln
14800 HarC 77084 3679 A3
Cove Timbers Ct
22900 HarC 77375 2966 A7
Cove Timbers Ln
8100 HarC 77375 2966 A7
Cove View Blvd
3100 GLSN 77554 5221 C4
Cove View Cir
3400 GLSN 77554 5221 C4

Cove View Dr
2900 SEBK 77586 4382 B7
Coveview Dr
100 HOUS 77336 3266 C4
Cove Wood Dr
2100 HOUS 77339 3118 E4
Covey Cir
2900 MSCY 77459 4497 B1
Covey Ct
10300 HOUS 77099 4237 D2
Covey Ln
2500 BzaC 77584 4502 A5
2500 PRLD 77584 4502 A5
12700 HOUS 77099 4237 D2
Covey Tr
3400 MSCY 77459 4496 D1
Covey Run Dr
16300 HOUS 77489 4370 D6
Covey Trail St
- MSCY 77459 4496 E1
Coveywood Ct
18600 HarC 77084 3816 C1
Covington Ct
1000 PRLD 77584 4501 C1
Covington Dr
5100 HOUS 77018 3683 D7
6600 HOUS 77091 3683 D4
6800 HOUS 77088 3683 D4
7700 HarC 77095 3538 B7
Covington Wy
2400 BzaC 77584 4501 C4
Covington Bridge Ln
21100 HarC 77388 3112 E3
Covington Glen Dr
13500 HarC 77070 3399 C4
Cow Ln
- SEBK 77586 4510 A1
Cowan Av
800 CNRO 77301 2383 E4
E Cowan Dr
100 HOUS 77007 3961 E3
W Cowan Dr
100 HOUS 77007 3961 E3
Cowan Rd
16000 GlsC 77511 4869 D3
16000 GlsC 77517 4869 D3
Cowan St
500 PASD 77506 4107 D4
Cowards Creek Ct
1000 FRDW 77546 4629 A2
Cowards Creek Dr
700 FRDW 77546 4629 A2
Cowart St
7200 HOUS 77020 3965 A3
7900 HOUS 77029 3965 B3
Cowart Creek Ln
18800 FRDW 77546 4628 E2
18800 PRLD 77546 4628 E2
Cowboy Ct
11600 TMBL 77375 3109 D3
Cowboy Wy
10 FBnC 77469 4232 B4
11600 TMBL 77375 3109 D3
Cowden Ct
1100 MSCY 77489 4370 D5
Cowling St
400 HOUS 77011 3964 C7
Cow Oak Dr
23800 HarC 77389 2966 A5
Cox Ln
300 BzaC 77511 4748 A3
Cox Rd
- MtgC 77386 2822 D6
- ORDN 77386 2822 D6
200 MtgC 77385 2822 D6
Cox St
14000 SPLD 77372 2537 B7
14000 SPLD 77372 2683 B1
22500 MtgC 77357 2973 E3
Coxswain Ct
16700 HarC 77532 3552 B2
Coxwold Ln
19100 HarC 77375 3255 A1
Coy Dr
2700 DRPK 77536 4249 B1
Coy St
100 HarC 77532 3692 D2
Coyle
5600 HOUS 77036 4099 D2
Coyle Rd
10 LbyC 77535 3268 D5
Coyle St
3400 HOUS 77003 3963 E7
3900 HOUS 77003 3964 A7
3900 HOUS 77023 3964 A7
Coyote Ct
8800 HarC 77521 3833 C1
Coyote Ln
1100 BYTN 77521 3973 B2
Coyote Bridge Ln
- FBnC 77469 4094 E7
Coyote Call Ct
5700 HarC 77449 3676 D5
Coyote Creek Dr
9600 HarC 77095 3538 A4
Coyote Echo Dr
5800 HarC 77449 3676 D4
Coyote Hills Ln
1500 FBnC 77469 4493 C4
Coyote Ridge Ln
20000 HarC 77449 3815 D5
Coyote Springs Ct
25800 HarC 77373 3113 E3
Coyote Trail Ct
2900 MSCY 77459 4498 A6
Coyote Trail Dr
2700 MSCY 77459 4498 A6
Coyotillo Ln
16700 HarC 77095 3538 A2
Coyridge Ln
16100 HOUS 77053 4371 D6
Cozumel Cir
10 GLSN 77554 5221 C3
Cozy Ln
- GLSN 77554 5107 B6
Cozy Cabbin Dr
19600 HarC 77449 3677 A5
19700 HarC 77449 3676 E5
Cozy Cove Ln
1000 GLSN 77554 5107 B6
Cozy Hollow Ln
15000 HOUS 77044 3550 A3
21400 FBnC 77469 4493 A4
Cozy Terrace Ln
5600 HarC 77084 3678 C4
Cozy Trail Ct
4000 FBnC 77469 4615 E5

CR-37
- BzaC 77583 4624 B6
- IWCY 77583 4624 B6
CR-48
10500 BzaC 77583 4744 D7
CR-50
- BzaC 77584 4627 B2
CR-56
100 BzaC 77583 4744 D6
3500 BzaC 77583 4745 B6
3500 IWCY 77583 4745 B6
CR-56 CO-56
- BzaC 77583 4744 E6
CR-59
900 BzaC 77583 4499 E6
900 PRLD 77545 4499 E6
1000 BzaC 77583 4500 A6
1000 PRLD 77583 4499 E6
1000 PRLD 77583 4500 A6
CR-65
10000 IWCY 77583 4745 C7
CR-78
3900 IWCY 77583 4745 C3
CR-81
- BzaC 77583 4744 E2
- BzaC 77583 4745 A2
- IWCY 77583 4744 E2
- IWCY 77583 4745 C2
CR-90
3600 BzaC 77578 4501 C7
3600 BzaC 77584 4501 C7
3600 PRLD 77578 4501 C7
3600 PRLD 77584 4501 C7
CR-90 CO-90
- BzaC 77584 4501 C7
- PRLD 77584 4501 C7
CR-90A
- BzaC 77578 4625 B1
CR-94
2400 BzaC 77584 4501 A4
2600 BzaC 77578 4501 A6
2600 PRLD 77584 4501 A6
CR-95A
- BzaC 77578 4747 C3
CR-98
- BzaC 77511 4626 E7
- BzaC 77511 4627 A7
- BzaC 77511 4748 A1
- BzaC 77578 4626 E7
CR-101
- BzaC 77578 4625 B1
- PRLD 77578 4625 C1
- PRLD 77584 4625 C1
CR-124
2100 BzaC 77581 4628 C1
CR-125
17100 BzaC 77581 4504 C7
17100 BzaC 77581 4628 C1
18000 FRDW 77546 4628 E2
18000 PRLD 77581 4628 E2
CR-127
17000 BzaC 77581 4628 B1
CR-129
1000 BzaC 77511 4628 D4
1000 PRLD 77511 4628 E4
1000 PRLD 77546 4628 E4
1100 FRDW 77546 4628 E4
CR-141
1500 BzaC 77511 4748 B3
CR-142
200 ALVN 77511 4868 A2
200 BzaC 77511 4868 A2
700 ALVN 77511 4749 E7
700 BzaC 77511 4749 E7
CR-154
- GlsC 77511 4869 A4
5300 BzaC 77511 4868 E4
CR-155
5500 BzaC 77511 4868 D4
CR-159
2100 BzaC 77511 4868 D7
CR-161
3500 ALVN 77511 4867 E7
3500 BzaC 77511 4867 E7
CR-164
2000 BzaC 77511 4868 E7
CR-175
7800 BzaC 77511 4627 D5
18900 BzaC 77584 4627 C4
18900 PRLD 77584 4627 C5
CR-183
- BzaC 77511 4866 A5
CR-190
1200 BzaC 77583 4623 D6
3200 IWCY 77583 4624 A7
4000 BzaC 77583 4624 B7
CR-206
- BzaC 77511 4626 E7
- BzaC 77511 4627 A7
- BzaC 77578 4626 E7
CR-235
2300 BzaC 77511 4748 E4
CR-247
1300 BzaC 77511 4747 E2
CR-252
1900 BzaC 77511 4628 D2
1900 BzaC 77581 4628 D2
CR-280
12200 BzaC 77511 4866 B3
CR-291
100 BzaC 77511 4628 A7
100 BzaC 77511 4749 A1
CR-291A
100 BzaC 77511 4628 B7
100 BzaC 77511 4749 A1
CR-291B
300 BzaC 77511 4749 A1
CR-296D
300 BzaC 77511 4749 B1
CR-305B
- BzaC 77511 4627 C7
CR-343
10 PLMG 77327 2684 E3
CR-347
10 PLMG 77327 2684 E6
CR-347 S
10 PLMG 77327 2684 E6
CR-347 N
1600 PLMG 77327 2684 E5
CR-349
- PLMG 77327 2684 D6
CR-350E
- BzaC 77511 4868 A5
CR-351
10 PLMG 77327 2684 D7
CR-352
10 PLMG 77327 2830 D1

CR-353
- MtgC 77357 2830 D3
- PLMG 77327 2830 D3
CR-354
- MtgC 77357 2830 D3
2100 PLMG 77327 2830 D3
10 LbyC 77327 2830 D3
CR-360
10 LbyC 77327 2684 C4
CR-361
200 LbyC 77327 2684 C5
CR-366
200 LbyC 77327 2684 B3
CR-379
10 LbyC 77327 2538 A1
10 LbyC 77328 2537 E1
10 LbyC 77328 2538 A1
700 MtgC 77372 2537 D1
CR-380
4700 IWCY 77583 4745 D3
CR-383
10 LbyC 77327 2538 A1
6500 BzaC 77583 4623 E7
7200 BzaC 77583 4744 E2
7700 IWCY 77583 4744 E2
CR-393D
- BzaC 77511 4626 E7
- BzaC 77511 4747 E1
- BzaC 77578 4626 E7
CR-397
4600 BzaC 77511 4747 E1
4600 BzaC 77511 4748 A2
CR-399
4600 BzaC 77511 4748 A1
CR-435
14400 BzaC 77511 4866 C6
CR-435 Ln
4600 BzaC 77511 4866 C7
CR-436
14000 BzaC 77511 4866 A7
CR-490
10 LbyC 77535 3269 E7
10 LbyC 77535 3413 D2
CR-529A
- BzaC 77511 4748 D4
CR-537
4400 BzaC 77511 4748 B1
CR-537A
2200 BzaC 77511 4748 B1
CR-549
2700 BzaC 77583 4623 E7
CR-560
5200 BzaC 77581 4502 A1
5200 PRLD 77581 4502 B1
CR-560 CO-560
5200 BzaC 77581 4502 A1
5200 PRLD 77581 4502 B1
CR-564
3200 BzaC 77583 4499 E7
3800 BzaC 77583 4623 E1
CR-573
1700 BzaC 77583 4744 C1
CR-589 Rd
2700 PRLD 77584 4501 A2
CR-604
10 LbyC 77535 3269 E6
CR-605
4200 LbyC 77535 3269 C1
5600 LbyC 77535 3268 C1
CR-610
700 LbyC 77535 3269 D1
CR-611
10 LbyC 77535 3269 B1
CR-612
200 LbyC 77535 3268 E2
CR-613
500 LbyC 77535 3268 B2
1900 HarC 77336 3268 A2
CR-624
600 HarC 77336 3122 E3
CR-669D
- BzaC 77511 4627 C5
CR-695
1000 BzaC 77511 4868 D3
CR-695 Av
2000 BzaC 77511 4868 D3
CR-695 Ln
- BzaC 77511 4868 C3
CR-695 Tr
100 BzaC 77511 4868 C3
CR-761
13300 BzaC 77511 4866 A5
CR-786
10000 BzaC 77583 4745 E7
10000 MNVL 77578 4745 E7
10600 IWCY 77583 4745 E7
CR-813
2300 ALVN 77511 4868 A2
2300 BzaC 77511 4868 A2
CR-813 Rd
- ALVN 77511 4868 A2
CR-824D
- BzaC 77583 4623 C6
CR-827
16500 BzaC 77584 4502 C7
16500 BzaC 77584 4626 C1
16500 PRLD 77584 4502 C7
CR-831
16800 BzaC 77584 4502 C7
16800 BzaC 77584 4626 C1
16800 PRLD 77584 4502 C7
CR-833
3700 BzaC 77511 4867 C6
4000 ALVN 77511 4867 C6
CR-857
1200 BzaC 77511 4748 D7
1200 BzaC 77511 4866 D1
CR-887B
- BzaC 77578 4747 B5
CR-892
- BzaC 77511 4868 B3
CR-894
1600 BzaC 77583 4624 A1
1600 PRLD 77578 4624 A1
1600 PRLD 77583 4624 A1
CR-909
- BzaC 77511 4747 E6
CR-925
- BzaC 77511 4868 B2
CR-925A
- BzaC 77511 4868 B2
CR-925B
- BzaC 77511 4868 B2
CR-928
1600 BzaC 77511 4748 C3
CR-937E
- BzaC 77511 4748 A6

STREET
Block City ZIP Map# Grid
CR-937F
- BzaC 77511 4748 A6
CR-941
1000 BzaC 77511 4747 E5
CR-941B
- BzaC 77511 4747 D6
CR-941D
- BzaC 77511 4747 D6
CR-948
- BzaC 77511 4747 E3
- BzaC 77578 4747 E3
CR-948A
- BzaC 77511 4747 E4
CR-950
1800 BzaC 77511 4748 E3
CR-953
- BzaC 77511 4748 E4
CR-956
- BzaC 77583 4623 D7
CR-958
- BzaC 77583 4623 D7
CR-964
- BzaC 77511 4747 E5
CR-965
1600 BzaC 77511 4748 E4
CR-966
- BzaC 77511 4748 E4
CR-3470 N
10 PLMG 77327 2684 E5
CR-3470 Rd
- PLMG 77327 2684 E5
CR-3472
10 PLMG 77327 2684 E7
CR-3600
10 LbyC 77327 2684 C4
CR-3610
10 LbyC 77327 2684 C5
CR-3611
10 LbyC 77327 2684 C5
CR-3612
10 LbyC 77327 2684 C5
CR-3640
- LbyC 77327 2684 B5
CR-3661
10 LbyC 77327 2684 C3
CR-3662 A
10 LbyC 77372 2684 B2
CR-3663
10 LbyC 77372 2684 B3
CR-3664
10 LbyC 77372 2684 B2
CR-3665 E
10 LbyC 77372 2684 B2
CR-3665 W
10 LbyC 77372 2684 A2
CR-3666
10 LbyC 77372 2684 B2
CR-3667
10 LbyC 77372 2684 B2
CR-3668
10 LbyC 77372 2684 B2
CR-3669
10 LbyC 77372 2684 B2
CR-3669 N
10 LbyC 77372 2684 B2
CR-3669 A
10 LbyC 77372 2684 A2
CR-3701
10 LbyC 77372 2538 A6
CR-3702
10 LbyC 77372 2538 A6
CR-3703
10 LbyC 77372 2538 A6
CR-3704
10 LbyC 77372 2538 B7
CR-3704 A
10 LbyC 77372 2538 A7
CR-3704B
10 LbyC 77372 2538 A7
CR-3705
10 LbyC 77372 2538 C6
CR-3706
10 LbyC 77372 2538 C6
CR-3706A
10 LbyC 77372 2538 B7
CR-3709A
10 LbyC 77372 2537 E6
CR-3709B
10 LbyC 77372 2538 A6
CR-3731
10 LbyC 77372 2538 C5
CR-3742
12600 LbyC 77372 2537 E5
CR-3743
12600 LbyC 77372 2537 E5
CR-3744
12600 LbyC 77372 2537 E4
12600 LbyC 77372 2538 A4
CR-3745
12600 LbyC 77372 2537 E4
12600 LbyC 77372 2538 A4
CR-3746
21600 LbyC 77372 2537 E4
CR-3747
21600 LbyC 77372 2537 E4
21600 LbyC 77372 2538 A4
CR-3748
21600 LbyC 77372 2537 E4
21600 LbyC 77372 2538 A4
CR-3749
21500 LbyC 77327 2537 E4
21500 LbyC 77327 2538 A4
CR-3750
10 LbyC 77328 2537 D3
10 MtgC 77372 2537 D3
CR-3755
10 LbyC 77328 2537 D3
CR-3770
10 LbyC 77327 2538 A2
CR-3791
10 LbyC 77328 2537 D1
CR-3792
200 LbyC 77328 2537 D1
CR-3793
10 LbyC 77328 2537 D1
CR-3794
10 LbyC 77328 2537 D1
200 MtgC 77372 2537 C1
CR-3794A
10 LbyC 77328 2537 D1
CR-3794B
10 LbyC 77328 2537 D1
CR-3795
10 LbyC 77328 2537 C1
10 MtgC 77372 2537 C1
CR-3799
10 LbyC 77328 2537 E1
CR-4872
10 LbyC 77535 3413 E5
CR-4873
600 LbyC 77535 3413 E6
CR-4874
10 LbyC 77535 3413 D6
CR-4875
10 LbyC 77535 3413 D5
CR-4876
100 LbyC 77535 3413 C5
CR-4879
100 LbyC 77535 3413 E6
CR-4881
10 LbyC 77535 3413 E4
CR-4882 N
500 LbyC 77535 3413 D4
CR-4882 S
10 LbyC 77535 3413 D4
CR-4882 W
10 LbyC 77535 3413 D4
CR-4891
10 LbyC 77535 3413 E1
CR-4901
10 LbyC 77535 3413 E1
CR-4902
10 LbyC 77535 3413 E2
CR-4903
10 LbyC 77535 3413 D2
CR-4904
10 LbyC 77535 3413 E2
CR-4905
10 LbyC 77535 3413 E2
CR-4907
10 LbyC 77535 3413 D2
CR-6041
10 LbyC 77535 3269 C4
CR-6042
10 LbyC 77535 3268 E4
10 LbyC 77535 3269 A4
CR-6243
700 HarC 77336 3122 D1
700 LbyC 77535 3122 D1
CR-6245
10 LbyC 77535 3122 E1
CR-37491
21500 LbyC 77327 2537 E3
21500 LbyC 77327 2538 A3
CR-37492
21500 LbyC 77327 2537 E3
21500 LbyC 77327 2538 A3
CR-37493
12600 LbyC 77327 2538 A3
CR-48820
10 LbyC 77535 3413 E4
CR-48821
10 LbyC 77535 3413 D3
CR-48822
10 LbyC 77535 3413 D4
CR-48824
10 LbyC 77535 3413 D3
Crab Apple Ct
11900 HarC 77429 3398 D5
Crabapple Dr
100 BYTN 77520 3832 B7
Crabapple Wy
800 RSBG 77471 4614 C1
Crabapple Cove
6700 HarC 77084 3678 E2
Crabb River Rd
- SGLD 77469 4493 D3
- SGLD 77479 4493 D3
100 FBnC 77469 4493 C6
700 FBnC 77479 4493 C6
Crabb River Rd FM-2759
- SGLD 77469 4493 D3
- SGLD 77479 4493 D3
100 FBnC 77469 4493 C6
700 FBnC 77479 4493 C6
Crab Orchard Rd
5900 HOUS 77057 3960 C4
Crabtree Ct
10 WDLD 77382 2819 A3
Craddock Dr
10700 HOUS 77099 4237 E3
Cradle St
15300 HOUS 77053 4371 E5
Cradle Cove Ct
17100 HarC 77095 3538 A6
Craft Ct
17700 HarC 77532 3411 A7
Craftmade Ln
14000 HarC 77044 3689 E3
Craftwood Dr
- WDLD 77382 2819 B2
Crag Ct
10 CNRO 77301 2530 C3
Craggy Bark Dr
1900 HarC 77388 3113 C6
1900 HOUS 77388 3113 C6
Craggy Rock St
10 WDLD 77381 2820 E1
Cragmore Dr
1000 TYLV 77586 4381 D7
Craig Dr
1200 GNPK 77547 3966 B6
Craig St
10 BYTN 77521 3972 E2
10 BYTN 77521 3973 A2
5500 HOUS 77023 4104 C2
Craigchester Ln
19400 HarC 77388 3113 C6
Craighead Dr
10600 HOUS 77025 4241 C3
Craighill Pl
8000 HarC 77338 3261 E4
Craighurst Ct
3500 HOUS 77059 4380 C6
Craighurst Dr
15700 HOUS 77059 4380 C7
Craigmont Blvd
3800 BYTN 77521 3972 A1
3900 BYTN 77521 3971 E2
4200 BYTN 77520 3971 E2
Craigmont St
2400 HOUS 77023 4104 C3
Craigmont Bridge Dr
7300 HarC 77433 3676 D1
Craigshire Ct
16100 HarC 77379 3256 C5
Craigway Rd
6000 HarC 77389 2966 D6
Craigwood Ln
12600 HarC 77429 3398 B6
Crail Dr
9600 HarC 77379 3255 D4
Crakston St
6200 HarC 77084 3678 E4
Cramer Ct
700 HarC 77450 3954 E2
Crammond St
10000 WlrC 77064 3541 D2
Crampton Ln
- HarC 77379 3111 D7
17000 HarC 77379 3256 D1
Cranberry Bnd
10 WDLD 77381 2820 B3
Cranberry Cir
2300 HarC 77373 3114 C6
Cranberry Ct
- DKSN 77539 4754 A2
Cranberry Tr
23400 HarC 77373 3114 C6
Cranberry Crossing Ln
10100 HarC 77375 3110 B4
Cranberry Hill Ct
900 HOUS 77079 3956 E2
Cranberry Hill Dr
1000 HOUS 77079 3956 E2
Cranbourne Dr
15100 HOUS 77062 4506 E1
Cranbrook Ln
400 LGCY 77573 4630 C7
400 LGCY 77573 4751 C1
Cranbrook Rd
5500 HOUS 77056 3960 D4
10600 HOUS 77042 3958 C5
Cranbrook Wy
- HarC 77044 3549 B2
1400 PASD 77502 4106 D7
Cranbrook Hollow Ln
8100 HarC 77095 3537 C6
Cranbrook Square Ct
6800 FBnC 77469 4095 C5
Crandon St
3100 HOUS 77026 3825 A5
Crane Ct
10 MtgC 77385 2676 D6
Crane Dr
2500 PRLD 77581 4504 D5
4500 GlsC 77563 4990 A5
4900 HTCK 77563 4990 A5
Crane St
2800 HOUS 77026 3824 E6
2900 HOUS 77026 3825 A6
Cranebrook Dr
- WDLD 77382 2819 B2
Crane Hawk Ln
2100 LGCY 77573 4752 B1
Crane Hollow Ln
3200 HarC 77073 3259 E1
3200 HarC 77338 3259 E1
Cranes Park St
12500 HarC 77377 3254 B5
Cranfield Ct
600 HarC 77450 3954 D1
Cranfield Dr
- HOUS 77450 3954 C2
20600 HarC 77450 3954 C2
Cranford Ct
7100 FBnC 77479 4367 A7
Cranhurst Ln
15400 HarC 77053 4372 D5
Cranleigh Ct
9400 HOUS 77096 4241 A1
Crannog Wy
900 CNRO 77301 2530 B2
Cransley Dr
18200 HarC 77084 3816 E1
Cranston Ct
2000 HOUS 77008 3823 A7
5400 SGLD 77479 4495 A4
Cranston Grove Dr
- DKSN 77539 4752 D6
- LGCY 77539 4752 D6
Cranswick Rd
4800 HOUS 77041 3681 C6
Cranway Dr
1600 HOUS 77055 3821 A6
Cranwood Dr
16100 HarC 77379 3256 E3
Cranwood Rd
16300 HarC 77379 3256 E3
Crappie Tr
500 MtgC 77384 2675 E6
500 WDLD 77384 2675 E6
700 MtgC 77384 2676 A6
Crater Hill Rd
- MtgC 77302 2532 C2
- MtgC 77306 2532 C2
Crater Lake Ct
12700 HarC 77346 3408 D1
Crater Ranch Rd
- HarC 77014 3401 D1
Cravenridge Dr
13900 FBnC 77083 4237 A2
S Cravens Rd
- HarC 77031 4239 B7
- HarC 77477 4239 B7
- MSCY 77071 4239 B7
- MSCY 77071 4370 B1
- STAF 77031 4370 B1
- STAF 77477 4239 B7
- STAF 77477 4370 B1
200 MSCY 77489 4370 D2
Cravens St
600 HOUS 77076 3685 B6
Crawford
2600 BYTN 77520 3973 E6
Crawford Cir
600 FBnC 77469 4492 B1
600 RHMD 77469 4492 B1
Crawford Dr
1200 FRDW 77546 4505 A4
3700 PASD 77503 4108 C6
Crawford Rd
5400 HarC 77041 3680 E6
5400 HOUS 77041 3680 E6
Crawford St
700 HOUS 77010 3963 C4
1600 HOUS 77002 3963 C5
1600 HOUS 77003 3963 C5
2200 HOUS 77004 3963 B6
4800 HOUS 77004 4103 A1
5500 HOUS 77004 4102 E2
5700 HOUS 77030 4102 E3
16000 JRSV 77040 3540 C7
N Crawford St
10 HOUS 77002 3963 D4
Crawford Crest Ln
- HarC 77053 4372 D5
Crawley Ct
1500 HarC 77530 3829 C5
Crayford Ct
11200 HarC 77065 3540 A3
Crayford Dr
11400 HarC 77065 3539 E3
Crayton Rd
30700 WlrC 77484 3247 A7
Crazy Horse Cir
20000 HarC 77449 3815 D6
Crazy Horse Tr
8700 HarC 77040 3540 C6
8700 HarC 77064 3540 C5
8700 JRSV 77040 3540 C6
Creager St
800 HOUS 77034 4246 C5
Creede Dr
8000 HarC 77040 3541 B6
Creegan Park Ct
1800 HOUS 77047 4373 D2
Creek Bnd
15900 MtgC 77355 2962 A2
15900 SGCH 77355 2962 A2
E Creek Cir
13500 HarC 77086 3541 E2
Creek Cross
- FBnC 77459 4621 A1
600 MtgC 77355 2669 B7
Creek Ct
- MtgC 77380 2967 B1
Creek Dr
1700 HOUS 77055 3821 A5
1700 HOUS 77080 3821 A5
11100 MtgC 77372 2537 A2
19300 MtgC 77357 2827 D4
E Creek Dr
13900 FBnC 77478 4237 A3
N Creek Dr
100 CNRO 77301 2384 C7
27300 MtgC 77354 2818 B6
S Creek Dr
1200 HOUS 77084 3816 E7
1200 HOUS 77084 3955 E1
26100 MtgC 77354 2964 B1
26600 MtgC 77354 2818 B7
W Creek Dr
6200 BKVL 77581 4375 E6
Creek Rd
21100 MNVL 77578 4747 B2
Creek St
2200 BYTN 77520 4112 C1
Creek Tr
16600 HarC 77084 3678 B3
Creek Arbor Cir
2700 HarC 77084 3816 B5
Creek Bank Ln
3100 PRLD 77581 4503 D2
Creek Bend Dr
300 LGCY 77573 4630 C6
2800 FRDW 77598 4630 C1
19300 HarC 77388 3113 A6
Creekbend Dr
- SGLD 77478 4368 B4
3400 BYTN 77521 3972 E3
4300 HOUS 77035 4241 B3
5100 HOUS 77035 4240 E3
7500 HOUS 77071 4239 D3
7500 HOUS 77071 4240 A3
7500 HOUS 77096 4240 A3
Creek Bend Rd
24400 WlrC 77447 2959 C3
Creek Bend Tr
19700 HarC 77084 3815 E4
Creek Bluff Ln
2500 MSCY 77459 4496 C1
17600 HarC 77433 3537 D1
Creek Branch Ln
- HarC 77375 2965 E7
Creekbriar Ct
15600 HarC 77068 3257 B5
Creekbriar Dr
3400 HarC 77068 3257 B5
Creekbridge Ct
5000 HarC 77379 3112 C5
Creek Bridge Ln
4500 HarC 77449 3677 B7
E Creek Club Dr
3500 MSCY 77459 4496 E3
W Creek Club Dr
3100 MSCY 77459 4496 E2
Creek Colony Dr
6700 FBnC 77469 4232 D7
Creek Crest Dr
7200 HarC 77095 3679 A1
Creek Crossing Ln
18000 MtgC 77365 2972 B5
Creekdale Dr
2300 HarC 77068 3257 D4
Creek Edge Ct
21000 HarC 77449 3815 B3
Creek Falls Ct
2900 PRLD 77581 4503 E2
Creekfield Ct
18500 HarC 77379 3256 B1
Creekfield Dr
7400 HarC 77379 3256 A1
Creekford Cir
1200 SGLD 77478 4368 E5
Creekford Ct
1300 SGLD 77478 4368 D4
Creek Forest Cir
700 MtgC 77380 2968 A2
Creek Forest Ln
10 MtgC 77384 2528 B6
600 MtgC 77380 2968 A2
Creek Gate Dr
- LGCY 77573 4631 A5
Creek Gate St
2100 MtgC 77385 2823 B2
Creek Glen Dr
7500 HarC 77095 3538 D7
8200 SGLD 77478 4368 A3
Creek Gradens Ct
5200 HOUS 77017 4106 B7
Creek Grove Ct
14000 HarC 77066 3401 E7
Creek Grove Dr
3300 HarC 77066 3401 E7
Creek Haven Ct
4800 HarC 77084 3678 E7
Creekhaven Ct
5400 LGCY 77573 4751 D2
Creekhaven Dr
15500 HarC 77084 3678 E7
Creek Hickory Rd
2300 HarC 77068 3257 D4
2300 HarC 77090 3257 D4
Creek Hill Ct
15900 HarC 77429 3252 C6
Creek Hill Ln
15800 HarC 77429 3252 C6
Creek Hollow Dr
1300 ELGO 77586 4509 B1
Creek Hollow Ln
4000 MSCY 77459 4496 C1
Creekhurst Dr
11900 HOUS 77099 4238 A3
12100 HOUS 77099 4237 E3
Creek Knoll Blvd
- HarC 77373 2968 E5
Creek Landing Ct
18500 HarC 77449 3677 C4
Creekleaf Rd
2300 HarC 77068 3257 D3
2300 HarC 77090 3257 D3
Creekline Dr
16900 FRDW 77546 4629 E2
Creekline Glen Ct
11000 HarC 77429 3399 A5
Creekline Green Ct
11000 HarC 77429 3399 A5
Creekline Meadow Ct
11000 HarC 77429 3399 A5
Creek Manor Ct
5500 HOUS 77339 3119 A2
Creek Manor Dr
2800 HOUS 77339 3119 B2
Creek Meadow Dr
2400 HarC 77084 3815 E5
Creek Meadows Dr
2300 MSCY 77459 4370 B7
Creek Mill Ct
14800 HarC 77429 3396 C1
Creekmill Ln
5300 BzaC 77583 4623 D3
Creekmist Ct
- KATY 77494 3952 B4
Creek Mist Dr
10800 HarC 77433 3396 D7
N Creekmist Pl
10 WDLD 77385 2676 B4
S Creekmist Pl
10 WDLD 77385 2676 B4
S Creekmont
4400 MSCY 77545 4622 C2
Creekmont Dr
- HOUS 77092 3682 E7
1000 HOUS 77091 3683 E7
1000 HOUS 77091 3684 A7
4600 HOUS 77092 3683 A7
5000 HOUS 77091 3682 E7
Creekmont Trace Ln
5300 HOUS 77091 3683 E7
Creek Park Dr
1000 SGLD 77478 4368 A5
Creekpine Ln
- HarC 77377 3253 E4
- HarC 77377 3254 A4
11800 HarC 77375 3109 D5
Creekpoint Ct
400 LGCY 77539 4752 E5
Creek Point Dr
- HarC 77449 3677 A3
Creek Point Ln
4300 MSCY 77459 4621 E2
Creek Ridge Dr
23800 HarC 77373 3114 E4
Creekridge Dr
2400 PRLD 77581 4504 E4
Creek Ridge Ln
4000 MSCY 77459 4496 C1
Creek Run Dr
1900 PRLD 77584 4500 A1
19300 HarC 77388 3113 A6
Creek Sage Ln
- LGCY 77573 4630 E7
- LGCY 77573 4631 A7
Creeks Edge Dr
2400 PRLD 77581 4504 A4
Creeks End Blvd
7000 FBnC 77469 4094 A5
7000 HOUS 77469 4094 A5
Creeks End Ct
21400 FBnC 77469 4094 B7
Creeks Gate Ct
8900 FBnC 77469 4235 C1
Creek Shade Dr
3300 HarC 77388 3112 E6
Creek Shadow Dr
2600 SGLD 77479 4368 D7
3200 HOUS 77339 3119 B2
Creekshire Dr
1800 SGLD 77478 4369 A6
Creek Shoal Ter
3000 HarC 77084 3815 E3
Creekshore Dr
19700 HarC 77449 3677 A3
Creek Shore Ln
2000 PRLD 77581 4503 E2
Creekside
- RMFT 77357 2828 E3
Creekside Cir
10 HNCV 77024 3960 B1
Creekside Ct
10 SPVL 77055 3821 B7
10 LGCY 77573 4630 D4
N Creekside Ct
10 SPVL 77055 3821 B7
S Creekside Ct
10 SPVL 77055 3821 B7
Creekside Dr
100 CNRO 77304 2383 A2
100 MtgC 77354 2671 D3
300 LGCY 77573 4630 D4
1600 SGLD 77478 4368 D5
1800 FRDW 77546 4629 D5
4100 FBnC 77469 4233 D4
12100 MtgC 77362 2817 C7
Creekside Ln
- PASD 77507 4249 C6
700 HNCV 77024 3960 C2
6100 LGCY 77573 4630 C5
7500 PASD 77505 4249 C6
Creekside Gate Ct
22900 HarC 77375 2966 A7
Creekside Park Dr
- HarC 77082 4097 B2
13100 HOUS 77082 4097 B2
Creekside Timbers Dr
- HarC 77389 2966 A7
8200 HarC 77375 2966 A7
Creekside Willow Ct
8200 HarC 77375 2966 A7
Creekside Willow Dr
22900 HarC 77375 2966 A7
Creeksouth Rd
16200 HarC 77068 3257 D4
Creek Springs Dr
13400 HarC 77083 4097 B4
Creekstone Cir
8300 HLSV 77055 3821 B6
Creekstone Dr
3200 SGLD 77479 4495 A3
Creekstone Lake Dr
9000 HOUS 77054 4242 A2
Creekstone Village Dr
- FBnC 77459 4496 D5
- FBnC 77479 4496 D5
- HarC 77429 3399 A5
- MSCY 77459 4496 D5
Creek Terrace Dr
2600 MSCY 77459 4496 C1
Creek Terrace Ln
9400 HarC 77396 3548 A2
Creektrace Ln
5800 HarC 77449 3676 E5
18700 HarC 77449 3677 C3
Creektrail Ln
2300 FBnC 77469 4364 E1
Creektree Dr
10500 HarC 77070 3399 A3
Creek Valley Ln
1900 SGLD 77478 4368 B4
1900 SGLD 77478 4369 A6
Creek View Ct
1000 SGLD 77478 4368 A4
Creekview Ct
16200 FRDW 77546 4505 D7
Creekview Dr
200 LGCY 77573 4630 D5
3000 MSCY 77459 4370 A7
4900 LPRT 77571 4250 B3
6100 FBnC 77479 4496 A7
23500 HarC 77389 2966 E5
Creek View Ln
11600 CHTW 77385 2823 B5
11600 MtgC 77385 2823 B5
Creekview Ln
16700 HarC 77429 3396 D1
Creekview Park Dr
13100 HOUS 77082 4097 A2
Creek Village Dr
- HarC 77433 3677 A2
6700 HarC 77449 3677 A2
Creek Vine Dr
9400 HarC 77040 3541 A6
Creek Water Dr
8800 HarC 77379 3255 E3
Creek Water Ln
7700 HarC 77396 3547 C2
Creekway Cir
2500 MSCY 77459 4370 A7
Creekway Dr
13300 HarC 77429 3398 D3
13600 HarC 77070 3398 D3
Creek Willow Dr
8300 HarC 77375 2965 E7
8800 HarC 77375 3110 E1
Creek Wind Cir
6400 HarC 77084 3678 A3
Creek Wood Dr
23500 HarC 77375 2966 A6
23500 HarC 77389 2966 A6
Creekwood Dr
7500 HOUS 77057 3960 A5
7500 HOUS 77063 3960 A5
23800 MtgC 77372 2682 B5
24200 PTVL 77372 2682 B5
Creekwood Ln
- CNRO 77304 2236 D4
- MtgC 77304 2236 D4
Creek Wood Wy
800 HNCV 77024 3960 A1
Creekwood Hills Ln
11400 HarC 77070 3398 E2
Creekwood Village Ln
- WDLD 77381 2821 A6
Creel Cir
3200 LPRT 77571 4250 A3
Creeping Vine Ln
8800 HOUS 77088 3543 E7
Creighton Ct
11300 HarC 77065 3540 A3
Creighton Dr
1800 MSCY 77489 4370 D5
Creighton Rd
- MtgC 77302 2530 C4
10100 CNRO 77301 2530 E3
10100 CNRO 77301 2531 B2
10100 CNRO 77302 2530 C4
10100 CNRO 77302 2531 A3
12900 MtgC 77302 2531 B2
14200 MtgC 77301 2531 B2
Cremona Ct
11000 FBnC 77469 4093 A7
Crenchrus Ct
11000 HarC 77086 3542 C1
Crenshaw Rd
- PASD 77505 4249 A6
400 HOUS 77034 4247 B6
400 HOUS 77504 4247 B6
1200 PASD 77504 4247 D6
4400 PASD 77504 4248 A6
4400 PASD 77505 4248 B6
12500 HarC 77044 3689 A6
Crenshaw St
4200 HOUS 77017 4105 E7
Creole Bay Ln
3200 RSBG 77471 4491 B6
Crepe Myrtle Ln
4700 PASD 77504 4248 A3
4700 PASD 77505 4248 A3
7800 BzaC 77584 4627 C4
Crepe Myrtle Tr
200 HOUS 77024 3959 C5
Crescendo Ct
7600 HarC 77040 3681 C1
N Crescendo Path Pl
10 SHEH 77381 2821 D2
S Crescendo Path Pl
10 SHEH 77381 2821 E2
Crescent Dr
100 FBnC 77545 4623 B2
100 PASD 77506 4107 A5
1900 LPRT 77571 4251 E6
3500 BzaC 77584 4501 C7
Crescent Shrs
- LPRT 77571 4251 E6
Crescent Sq
7000 HarC 77084 3679 A2
Crescent Arbor Ln
20500 HarC 77379 3111 B4
Crescent Bay Ct
3200 LGCY 77573 4633 B1
Crescent Bay Dr
3200 LGCY 77573 4633 C1
18900 HarC 77094 3955 B3
Crescent Bluff Dr
11700 PRLD 77584 4500 C2
Crescent Bluff Ln
10100 HarC 77070 3399 C3
Crescentbreeze Ln
- HarC 77072 4097 C5
Crescent Bridge Ct
7300 HarC 77396 3547 C1
Crescent Canyon Ct
8000 HarC 77095 3537 E6
Crescent Canyon Dr
17000 HarC 77095 3537 E6
Crescent Clover Dr
- HarC 77379 3110 C6
Crescent Common Dr
1900 FBnC 77494 3953 D5
Crescent Coral Dr
2100 LGCY 77573 4509 A6
Crescent Cove Ct
22400 FBnC 77494 4093 B2
Crescent Cove Dr
2100 LGCY 77573 4509 B6
11700 PRLD 77584 4500 C2
Crescent Falls Ct
10 WDLD 77381 2821 B4
Crescent Forest Ct
15300 HOUS 77062 4380 B7
Crescent Fountain Rd
18900 HarC 77388 3113 A4
Crescent Gate Ct
8600 HOUS 77024 3961 A2
Crescent Gate Ln
8700 HOUS 77024 3961 A2
Crescent Green Ct
1400 HarC 77094 3955 C3
Crescent Green Dr
- HOUS 77094 3955 A2
1400 HarC 77094 3955 A3
Crescent Heights St
21600 HarC 77388 3112 B4
Crescent Hollow Ct
2500 HarC 77388 3113 B2
Crescent Knolls Dr
8000 FBnC 77469 4234 A4
Crescent Lake Ct
7500 RSBG 77469 4492 B7
Crescent Lakes Cir
4500 SGLD 77479 4495 A1
Crescent Lakes Dr
- SGLD 77479 4494 E1
Crescent Landing Dr
14200 HOUS 77062 4379 C7
14200 HOUS 77062 4506 C1
Crescent Lilly Dr
15100 HarC 77433 3250 E6
Crescent Manor Ln
13000 HarC 77072 4097 C5
Crescent Mills Dr
- HarC 77083 4096 D5
Crescent Moon Dr
3200 GlsC 77511 4869 D3
3200 GlsC 77517 4869 D3
9200 HarC 77064 3540 D2
10800 HarC 77065 3540 A2
Crescent Moon Rd
2900 HarC 77388 3113 A7
Crescent Mountain Ln
12200 HarC 77346 3408 C3
Crescent Oak Dr
1400 MSCY 77459 4497 C4
Crescent Oaks Park Ln
2900 MtgC 77386 2823 D7
3000 MtgC 77386 2969 D1
Crescent Park Dr
- HOUS 77082 3958 A7
- HOUS 77082 4098 B1
2300 HOUS 77077 3958 A7
Crescent Park Village Dr
8200 HarC 77072 4097 C5
Crescent Parkway Ct
1300 HarC 77094 3955 A3
Crescent Pass Dr
19100 HarC 77375 3109 D7
Crescent Peak Dr
12000 HarC 77067 3402 B4
Crescent Plaza Dr
- HOUS 77077 3957 B6
Crescent Point Cir
23400 FBnC 77494 3953 A5
Crescent Point Dr
1600 FBnC 77494 3953 D5
N Crescent Ridge Dr
2600 WDLD 77381 2821 C3
Crescent Royale Wy
18000 HarC 77346 3408 C1
Crescent Shore Dr
1900 LGCY 77573 4509 A6
Crescent Shores Dr
2500 LPRT 77571 4251 E7
Crescent Shores Ln
1500 PASD 77586 4382 A6
Crescent Springs Dr
19000 HOUS 77339 3118 A6
Crescent Star Ct
21200 FBnC 77450 4094 A4
Crescent Star Rd
2800 HarC 77388 3113 A7
Crescent View Ct
10 WDLD 77381 2821 B3
N Crescent View Ct
1600 HarC 77067 3402 B5
Crescent View St
100 LPRT 77571 4251 E7
Crescent Wood Ln
8400 HarC 77379 3255 E3
Cresent Dr
- FRDW 77546 4749 E1
14000 TMBL 77375 2963 E4
14000 TMBL 77375 2964 A4
Cresent Bay Dr
100 LGCY 77573 4633 B1
Cresent Cove Ct
1200 KATY 77494 3952 A3
Cresent Cove Ln
26300 KATY 77494 3952 B3
Cresent Creek Dr
19900 HarC 77449 3677 A3
20000 HarC 77449 3676 E3
Cresent Green Dr
- HOUS 77094 3955 A1
Cresent Hollow Ct
2300 HarC 77388 3113 A3
Cresent Hollow Dr
- HarC 77388 3113 B3
Cresent Mill Ln
2100 CNRO 77304 2383 A1
Cresent Oaks Ct
15400 HarC 77068 3257 C4

STREET
Block City ZIP Map# Grid

Cresent Palm Ct
2000 HOUS 77077 3957 A6
Cresent Palm Dr
2100 HOUS 77077 3957 A6
Cresent Palm Ln
2200 HOUS 77077 3957 A7
Cresent Point Dr
21600 HarC 77450 3954 B5
Cresent Village Ln
7800 FBnC 77469 4095 C7
Cresline St
300 HOUS 77076 3685 B4
1500 HOUS 77093 3685 D4
Cressey Park Ct
1800 HOUS 77047 4373 C2
Cressida Glen Ln
13000 HarC 77072 4097 C7
Cresswell Ct
3500 MSCY 77459 4497 E6
Crest Ct
100 STAF 77477 4369 E3
3600 FBnC 77469 4364 E1
5900 HOUS 77033 4104 B7
Crest Dr
3000 DKSN 77539 4753 C3
S Crest Ln
3900 GlsC 77518 4634 B3
12100 HarC 77089 4505 B1
Crest St
6300 HOUS 77033 4104 B7
Cresta Pl Dr
6300 PASD 77505 4248 D3
Crestbend Ct
300 HOUS 77042 3959 A5
Crestbend Dr
100 HOUS 77042 3959 A5
Crestbriar Ct
10 BYTN 77521 3973 B2
Crestbridge Ln
3200 HarC 77388 3112 E4
Crestbrook Ct
2700 FBnC 77479 4493 D2
Crestbrook Dr
900 HarC 77038 3543 D4
15700 HOUS 77059 4380 C5
Crest Brook Bend Ln
2800 HarC 77449 3815 B3
Crestbrook Cove Dr
- HarC 77449 3815 A2
Crestbrook Manor Ln
7600 HarC 77433 3537 D7
Crestbrook Park Ln
11100 HarC 77375 3110 A1
11200 HarC 77375 3109 E1
Crestbury Ct
7200 HarC 77433 3677 D1
Crestbury Ln
7200 HarC 77433 3677 C1
Crestdale Cir
9700 HOUS 77080 3820 B2
Crestdale Dr
1400 HOUS 77055 3820 C6
1400 HOUS 77080 3820 C6
Crested Butte Ct
2700 HarC 77067 3401 E5
Crested Cloud Ct
10 WDLD 77380 2967 E3
Crested Green Dr
16000 HarC 77082 4096 A4
Crested Hill Ln
19800 HarC 77433 3537 A7
Crested Iris Dr
13700 HarC 77429 3397 C2
Crested Jay Ln
10 WDLD 77380 2822 B7
Crested Lark Ct
22800 HarC 77450 3953 E4
Crested Pines Ct
10 WDLD 77381 2821 C3
Crested Tern Ct
10 WDLD 77380 2968 A1
Cresterrace Dr
6300 PASD 77505 4248 E3
Crestfield Ct
10700 HarC 77070 3399 A3
Crestford Ln
6300 PASD 77505 4248 E3
Crestford Park Ln
5800 HarC 77084 3678 C4
25800 FBnC 77494 4093 A3
Crestforest Ln
- FBnC 77469 4365 B2
Crest Gate
10 FBnC 77082 4095 D4
Crestglen Ct
18100 FBnC 77469 4095 B5
Crest Glen Ln
- HarC 77070 3399 E2
Crestgrove Dr
3300 PASD 77505 4248 E4
Cresthaven Cir
5000 HOUS 77048 4243 D7
Crest Hill Dr
200 CNRO 77301 2384 D5
Crest Hill Ln
3400 HOUS 77007 3962 E3
Cresthill St
6600 HOUS 77033 4104 B7
Cresthollow Ln
2700 HOUS 77082 4096 E1
Crestlake Blvd
32800 MtgC 77354 2672 A4
Crest Lake Dr
12300 HOUS 77072 4097 E6
Crestlawn Dr
4200 LGCY 77573 4631 B4
Crestlea Ct
3400 PASD 77505 4248 E4
Crestline Rd
17200 HarC 77396 3407 E2
17200 HarC 77396 3408 A2
Crestline Bay Ln
11100 FBnC 77469 4092 C7
Crestmeadow Dr
3300 PASD 77505 4248 E4
Crestmill Ln
4800 FBnC 77545 4622 E3
Crestmont Cir
2000 MSCY 77459 4497 C2
Crestmont Dr
1600 MSCY 77489 4370 C3
1600 STAF 77477 4370 C3
1600 STAF 77489 4370 C3
2600 DRPK 77536 4109 E7
8700 BzaC 77578 4747 B4
E Crestmont Dr
100 HLCS 77511 4867 E5

W Crestmont Dr
100 ALVN 77511 4867 E5
100 HLCS 77511 4867 E5
Crestmont Ln
8700 BzaC 77578 4747 B4
Crestmont St
5300 BYTN 77520 3971 E2
5300 BYTN 77521 3971 E2
6400 HOUS 77033 4104 B7
6700 HOUS 77033 4244 B3
Crestmont Oaks Ct
- HOUS 77048 4244 A7
Crestmont Pines Ct
- HOUS 77048 4244 A7
Crestmoon Ct
2100 HarC 77089 4504 C1
Crestmoor Wy
16200 HarC 77082 4096 A3
Crestmore St
11000 HOUS 77096 4240 C4
Creston Dr
1700 HOUS 77026 3824 E3
1900 MtgC 77386 2969 B2
2900 HOUS 77026 3825 A3
Creston Cove Ct
19800 HarC 77433 3537 A7
Crestone Pl
10 WDLD 77381 2820 E2
Creston Springs Ct
- HarC 77379 3257 A2
Creston Woods Dr
26300 FBnC 77494 4092 A5
Crest Park Dr
2800 HOUS 77082 4097 B1
Crest Peak Ct
4400 HarC 77449 3676 A7
Crest Peak Wy
21600 HarC 77449 3676 A7
Crestridge Dr
4100 FBnC 77479 4366 C6
6200 MNVL 77578 4747 A1
Crestridge St
6300 HOUS 77033 4104 B7
6600 HOUS 77033 4244 A1
Crestside Dr
6300 PASD 77505 4248 E3
Crestvale Dr
12600 HarC 77038 3543 C4
Crestview Ct
1800 MSCY 77459 4497 C2
Crestview Dr
100 HTCK 77563 4988 E3
7800 HOUS 77028 3687 B7
8700 BzaC 77578 4747 C4
8800 HOUS 77078 3687 E7
9000 HOUS 77078 3688 A7
Crestview Ln
10000 CNRO 77304 2236 D5
Crestview Tr
10 HarC 77082 4095 E4
Crestview Cove
5800 FBnC 77469 4493 B5
Crestville St
6300 HOUS 77033 4104 B7
Crestwater Blvd
- HarC 77082 4095 E3
- HOUS 77082 4095 E3
Crestwater Cir
9600 MtgC 77354 2672 A4
10500 MtgC 77354 2671 E5
Crestwater Ct
500 HarC 77082 4095 E3
Crestwater Tr
100 HarC 77082 4095 E4
Crestway Dr
100 BYTN 77520 3832 A7
100 BYTN 77520 3971 A1
4900 LPRT 77571 4250 B2
Crestwick Dr
8000 HarC 77083 4096 C7
Crestwind Ct
2100 PRLD 77584 4500 A2
Crestwind Dr
12800 PRLD 77584 4500 A1
Crestwood Cir
10 SGLD 77478 4368 D4
Crestwood Ct
1600 TXCY 77591 4873 B4
Crestwood Dr
- BzaC 77578 4501 A6
- BzaC 77584 4501 B5
- HOUS 77007 3962 A4
- PRLD 77584 4501 B5
10 HOUS 77007 3961 E4
300 ELGO 77586 4509 B1
400 ELGO 77586 4382 B7
600 SHEH 77381 2822 A2
1600 TXCY 77591 4873 B3
2000 RHMD 77469 4491 E3
2600 DRPK 77536 4109 D7
Crestwood Ln
700 MSCY 77489 4370 B3
1600 PASD 77502 4108 A7
Crestwood Pk
31500 MtgC 77385 2823 B6
Crestwood Estates Dr
10 HDWV 77024 3959 D2
10 PNPV 77024 3959 D2
Crestworth Ln
21900 HarC 77449 3676 C6
Creswell Ct
18200 HarC 77084 3677 E5
Cretain Point Ct
16300 HarC 77429 3397 A3
Crete Dr
300 DRPK 77536 4109 B5
Crete St
900 HOUS 77020 3964 B2
Crews Rd
16000 GlsC 77517 4869 E1
Cribbage Ct
- FBnC 77083 4236 C1
E Cricket Cir
21800 HarC 77388 3112 C2
N Cricket Cir
4300 HarC 77388 3112 C2
S Cricket Cir
4300 HarC 77388 3112 C2
Cricket Dr
21800 HarC 77388 3112 C2
21900 HarC 77389 3112 C2
Cricket Hllw
13700 HarC 77069 3256 D7
Cricket Ln
2900 HOUS 77093 3686 A2
12200 MtgC 77303 2239 E6
Cricketbriar Ct
17200 HarC 77084 3678 A2

Cricket Hollow Pl
10 WDLD 77381 2820 E3
10 WDLD 77381 2821 B2
Crickett Hollow Ln
12800 HarC 77429 3397 C5
Cricket Wood Dr
13400 HOUS 77082 4097 A2
Cricklewood Ln
1100 HarC 77379 3255 B1
Cricklewood Creek Ln
13400 HarC 77083 4097 B7
Crieffe Rd
13000 HarC 77039 3546 C4
Crighton Crossing Dr
8900 MtgC 77302 2530 D4
9000 CNRO 77302 2530 D4
Crighton Ridge Cir
8800 MtgC 77302 2530 B4
Crighton Ridge Dr
13100 CNRO 77302 2530 B4
13100 MtgC 77302 2530 B4
Crim Ct
6400 HOUS 77049 3828 A2
Crim Rd
13200 HOUS 77049 3828 A2
Criminal Justice Dr
10 CNRO 77301 2384 A2
Crim Lilly Ct
7100 HarC 77433 3676 D1
Crimson Pt
- PASD 77586 4383 C4
Crimson Tr
14800 HarC 77084 3679 A2
Crimson Bay Dr
100 LGCY 77573 4633 B1
Crimson Berry Tr
1900 HOUS 77345 3120 D6
Crimson Canyon Ct
- FBnC 77494 3953 C6
Crimson Canyon Dr
10300 HarC 77095 3538 A3
N Crimson Clover Cir
100 WDLD 77381 2821 B2
S Crimson Clover Cir
200 WDLD 77381 2821 B2
Crimson Clover Cross
- FBnC 77494 4092 C4
S Crimson Clover Ct
200 WDLD 77381 2821 B2
Crimson Coast Ct
400 LGCY 77573 4633 B1
Crimson Coast Dr
400 LGCY 77573 4633 B2
Crimson Cove Ct
2200 LGCY 77573 4509 A6
Crimson Elm Dr
- HarC 77433 3251 A5
Crimson Flower Ln
16400 HarC 77433 3251 B5
Crimson Lake Ln
2100 LGCY 77573 4631 B7
Crimson Leaf Ct
20700 HarC 77433 3251 B5
Crimson Leaf Ln
- HarC 77433 3251 A5
Crimson Maple Ct
3300 HOUS 77345 3119 E1
Crimson Meadows Dr
4100 HOUS 77048 4374 D5
Crimson Oak Ct
4100 HOUS 77059 4380 C4
Crimson Oak Tr
20400 HarC 77346 3264 E4
20400 HarC 77346 3265 A4
Crimson Ridge Ct
10 WDLD 77381 2820 B4
Crimson Sky Dr
7200 HarC 77083 4096 E6
Crimson Star Ter
23400 FBnC 77494 4093 C4
Crimson Valley Ct
2300 HOUS 77345 3120 A3
Crinkleawn Dr
11000 HarC 77086 3542 C1
Crinkleroot Ct
10 WDLD 77380 2822 A7
Crinum Lily Dr
- HarC 77377 3254 C4
Criolla Ct
10 GLSN 77554 5221 C2
Cripple Cr N
30500 MtgC 77354 2815 E1
30500 MtgC 77355 2815 E1
31000 MtgC 77354 2669 E7
31000 MtgC 77354 2670 A7
Cripple Brook Ct
5500 HOUS 77017 4246 A2
Cripple Creek Ct
5200 HOUS 77017 4106 B7
Cripple Creek Dr
5100 HOUS 77017 4106 B7
5100 HOUS 77017 4246 B1
12200 MtgC 77362 2817 B7
32600 MtgC 77362 2963 B1
Cripple Creek Ln
1800 PRLD 77581 4504 D4
Cris Rd
500 FBnC 77471 4490 E2
Crisfield Ct
22400 FBnC 77450 4093 E1
Crisfield Dr
- FBnC 77479 4367 A7
1900 FBnC 77479 4494 A1
Crispin Ln
9400 HOUS 77080 3820 D5
N Crisp Morning Cir
10 WDLD 77382 2673 B6
S Crisp Morning Cir
10 WDLD 77382 2673 C5
Crisp Morning Ct
100 WDLD 77382 2673 C5
Crisp Springs Ln
25600 HarC 77373 3114 A4
Crisp Wood Ln
7400 HarC 77086 3542 A3
7600 HarC 77086 3541 E4
Crispy Canyon Ct
5100 FBnC 77494 4093 B2
Cristal Ln
- MtgC 77357 2829 D3
Cristiwood Ct
19700 HarC 77379 3110 C6
Criswell Dr
10600 HarC 77396 3407 E1
Crites St
4100 HOUS 77003 3964 B5
4400 HOUS 77011 3964 B5

Crittenden St
2400 HOUS 77026 3824 E4
2900 HOUS 77026 3825 A4
Crocale Patch Dr
- HOUS 77336 3266 C1
Crocker St
1000 HOUS 77019 3962 E5
1800 HOUS 77006 3962 E5
Crockett
21200 MtgC 77357 2827 B7
S Crockett
- DRPK 77536 4109 E6
Crockett Blvd
4700 GLSN 77551 5108 D6
Crockett Ct
2500 SGLD 77478 4237 C4
Crockett Dr
11700 LPRT 77571 4111 A6
Crockett Dr S
2600 LMQU 77568 4989 D2
Crockett St
- HarC 77530 3830 C7
- HarC 77530 3969 B1
300 LMQU 77568 4873 D7
300 TXCY 77591 4873 D7
1000 HOUS 77007 3963 A2
2400 HOUS 77007 3962 E2
6500 HTCK 77563 4988 C4
N Crockett St
400 DRPK 77536 4249 B2
S Crockett St
400 DRPK 77536 4249 B2
W Crockett St
1400 LMQU 77568 4989 D2
Crockett Martin Rd
9200 MtgC 77306 2533 D4
Crockett Ridge Dr
7000 FBnC 77469 4234 A2
Crocus Petal St
10 WDLD 77382 2674 C5
Croes Dr
8800 SPVL 77055 3821 A7
8900 SPVL 77055 3820 E7
Croft Ct
11700 HarC 77065 3539 D2
Crofterglen Dr
- FRDW 77546 4506 A7
- FRDW 77546 4629 E1
- FRDW 77546 4630 A1
- HarC 77546 4506 A7
Crofton St
7400 HOUS 77028 3687 A6
9400 HOUS 77016 3687 A6
Croftwood Dr
14900 HarC 77068 3257 B6
Croger Dr
9900 MtgC 77354 2672 B7
Croix Pkwy
4300 BzaC 77578 4624 D2
4300 MNVL 77583 4624 D2
Croix Rd
1200 BzaC 77583 4623 D3
1200 PRLD 77583 4623 D3
1700 BzaC 77583 4624 A3
2100 BzaC 77578 4624 A3
2100 PRLD 77578 4624 A3
2100 PRLD 77583 4624 A3
2600 MNVL 77578 4624 E3
2600 MNVL 77583 4624 E3
4400 BzaC 77578 4625 A3
4400 MNVL 77578 4625 A3
Croker Ridge Rd
4600 HOUS 77053 4372 B6
Crokett St
- HOUS 77520 3970 B2
Cromarty Ct
16600 HarC 77084 3678 C6
Cromdale Manor Ct
10400 HarC 77379 3110 C7
Cromwell Ct
2000 SGLD 77478 4237 A5
Cromwell St
1000 HOUS 77037 3685 B2
1000 HOUS 77076 3685 B2
1400 HOUS 77093 3685 C2
2800 HarC 77093 3685 E2
2800 HarC 77093 3686 A2
Crondell Cir
14900 HarC 77530 3829 C5
Crooke St
400 CNRO 77301 2384 A6
Crooked Ln
2300 HarC 77084 3816 A5
Crooked Arrow Dr
15700 FBnC 77478 4236 A2
Crooked Creek Ct
23500 MtgC 77447 2960 C5
N Crooked Creek Dr
5400 HOUS 77017 4246 C1
S Crooked Creek Dr
5400 HOUS 77017 4246 C2
Crooked Creek Ln
1800 PRLD 77581 4504 C4
Crooked Creek Rd
24100 MtgC 77355 2960 C4
24100 MtgC 77447 2960 C4
Crooked Lake Wy N
16100 HarC 77433 3251 A5
Crooked Lake Wy S
15800 HarC 77433 3251 A6
Crooked Oak Dr
17000 HarC 77429 3252 D6
Crooked Oak Wy
18400 HarC 77379 3257 B1
Crooked Pine Ct
300 CNRO 77304 2383 A6
Crooked Pine Dr
11200 HarC 77429 3398 E5
11200 HarC 77429 3399 A4
Crooked Post Rd
5800 HarC 77373 3115 E6
Crooked Wood Ln
9400 HarC 77086 3541 E3
Crooks Wy Ct
10200 HarC 77065 3540 A3
Crooms St
5400 HOUS 77007 3962 A3
Croquet Ln
- HOUS 77053 4371 E5
13300 HOUS 77085 4371 E2
Crosby
- BYTN 77520 3972 A6
700 HOUS 77019 3963 A4
24000 HarC 77336 3266 E2
Crosby Coms
10100 FBnC 77459 4621 D7
10100 FBnC 77459 4622 B5

Crosby Dr
- HarC 77532 3553 A2
100 HarC 77532 3552 C3
Crosby Frwy
- HarC - 3552 D6
- HarC - 3690 C6
- HarC - 3691 E3
- HarC - 3692 A3
- HarC - 3828 D1
- HarC 77532 3413 A4
- LbyC 77535 3269 E7
- LbyC 77535 3413 D1
4300 HarC 77532 3553 A3
5600 HarC 77532 3412 B7
Crosby Frwy US-90
- HarC - 3552 D6
- HarC - 3690 C6
- HarC - 3691 E3
- HarC - 3692 A3
- HarC 77532 3413 A4
- HarC 77532 3553 B1
- LbyC 77535 3269 E7
- LbyC 77535 3413 D1
5600 HarC 77532 3412 B7
Crosby Gdn
3400 FBnC 77459 4622 B5
Crosby Ln
12100 HarC 77336 3266 E2
E Crosby Ln
10100 FBnC 77459 4622 A5
W Crosby Ln
- FBnC 77459 4621 D7
Crosby Lndg
3400 FBnC 77459 4621 E5
Crosby Rd
100 HarC 77532 3692 D1
24000 HarC 77336 3266 E2
Crosby Rd FM-1942
100 HarC 77532 3692 D1
Crosby St
800 HOUS 77019 3963 A5
1500 HOUS 77002 3963 A5
E Crosby St
16400 HarC 77532 3553 A2
W Crosby St
16400 HarC 77532 3553 A2
Crosby Wy
9300 FBnC 77459 4621 D5
Crosby Barbers Hill Rd
5300 HarC 77521 3694 D6
6200 HarC 77521 3695 A5
7100 CmbC 77520 3695 A5
7500 CmbC 77520 3696 A4
9500 MTBL 77520 3696 B4
Crosby Barbers Hill Rd FM-1942
5300 HarC 77521 3694 D6
6200 HarC 77521 3695 A5
7100 CmbC 77520 3695 A5
7500 CmbC 77520 3696 A4
9500 MTBL 77520 3696 B4
Crosby Cedar Bayou Rd
500 HarC 77532 3692 E1
600 HarC 77532 3693 A1
3200 BYTN 77521 3973 D2
3800 HarC 77521 3973 C1
4600 HarC 77521 3834 B6
6400 BYTN 77521 3834 A4
Crosby Cedar Bayou Rd FM-1942
500 HarC 77532 3692 E1
600 HarC 77532 3693 A1
E Crosby Cedar Bayou Rd
3100 BYTN 77520 3973 D4
3100 BYTN 77521 3973 D3
Crosby Dayton Rd
800 HarC 77532 3552 D4
1200 HarC 77532 3553 A1
2200 HarC 77532 3412 B7
Crosby Eastgate Rd
10 LbyC 77535 3268 C5
2400 HarC 77532 3268 D7
19400 HarC 77532 3412 D2
Crosby Freeway Frontage Rd
- HarC 77049 3689 E7
- HarC 77049 3690 A7
- HarC 77049 3828 D1
- HarC 77049 3829 A1
Crosby Huffman Rd
6100 HarC 77532 3552 C1
16900 HarC 77532 3411 B6
20700 HarC 77532 3410 E1
21300 HarC 77532 3266 E6
24300 HarC 77336 3267 A1
24700 HarC 77336 3266 E1
26000 HarC 77336 3122 A4
26600 HarC 77336 3121 C2
26900 HOUS 77336 3121 D3
Crosby Huffman Rd FM-2100
6100 HarC 77532 3552 C1
16900 HarC 77532 3411 B6
20700 HarC 77532 3410 E1
21300 HarC 77532 3266 E6
24300 HarC 77336 3267 A1
24700 HarC 77336 3266 E1
26000 HarC 77336 3122 A4
26600 HarC 77336 3121 C2
26900 HOUS 77336 3121 D3
Crosby Lynchburg Rd
100 HarC 77520 3831 D7
100 HarC 77562 3831 E6
200 HarC 77520 3970 C3
600 HOUS 77520 3970 D1
1000 HOUS 77571 3970 D2
13100 HarC 77532 3692 D1
13600 HarC 77532 3552 D6
Crosby Lynchburg Rd FM-2100
100 HarC 77520 3831 D7
100 HarC 77562 3831 E6
200 HarC 77520 3970 B3
600 HOUS 77520 3970 D2
1000 HOUS 77571 3970 D2
13100 HarC 77532 3692 D1
13600 HarC 77532 3552 D7
Crosby Lynchburg Rd SR-134
100 HarC 77520 3831 D7
100 HarC 77562 3831 E6
200 HarC 77520 3970 B3
600 HOUS 77520 3970 D2
1000 HOUS 77520 3970 D2
N Crosby Lynchburg Rd
100 HarC 77562 3831 E2
1200 HarC 77562 3692 D7
10500 HarC 77532 3692 D2

N Crosby Lynchburg Rd FM-2100
100 HarC 77562 3831 E2
1200 HarC 77562 3692 D7
10500 HarC 77532 3692 D2
N Cross Dr
16200 HarC 77073 3259 A5
S Cross Ln
7000 HarC 77379 3111 B4
Cross St
21300 MtgC 77357 2974 A1
Crossbay Ct
2100 LGCY 77573 4631 C7
Crossbend Dr
23100 FBnC 77494 3953 D6
Cross Bones Cir
3400 GLSN 77554 5332 D1
Crossbow Dr
300 MtgC 77386 2968 C1
Crossbranch Ct
3400 PRLD 77581 4503 D1
Crossbranch Dr
19600 HarC 77094 3955 A3
Crossbridge Dr
800 HarC 77373 2968 D6
1100 HarC 77389 2968 D6
Crossbridge Ln
22100 FBnC 77469 4492 D4
22100 FBnC 77469 4493 A3
Crossbrook Ct
2200 LGCY 77573 4509 A6
3000 FBnC 77450 3954 C7
Crossbrook Dr
22000 FBnC 77450 3954 A7
Cross Canyon Ln
12300 HarC 77433 3396 B4
Crosscoach Ln
1900 HarC 77449 3815 C6
Cross Colony Dr
3000 LGCY 77539 4753 A3
3300 LGCY 77539 4752 D4
Cross Continents Dr
4600 HarC 77032 3546 C1
4600 HOUS 77032 3546 C1
Cross Country Dr
8100 HarC 77346 3265 C6
8700 HOUS 77346 3265 D7
Crosscove Ct
17400 HarC 77095 3537 E6
Cross Creek Ct
5200 LGCY 77573 4751 D1
Crosscreek Ct
3500 MSCY 77459 4497 B2
Cross Creek Dr
- PRLD 77545 4499 E4
Cross Creek Ln
- HarC 77433 3396 B6
4900 LGCY 77573 4751 E1
4900 LGCY 77573 4752 A1
Cross Creek Rd
5600 CNRO 77304 2237 A5
Crosscut Dr
- HarC 77084 3677 E3
Crosscut Pass Dr
23300 HarC 77373 3115 A4
Cross Draw Dr
1200 HarC 77067 3402 C5
N Crossed Birch Pl
10 WDLD 77381 2674 E7
S Crossed Birch Pl
10 WDLD 77381 2674 E7
Crossfair Dr
- HarC 77450 3954 D6
Crossfalls Ln
19700 HarC 77433 3537 A7
Crossfell Dr
3400 HarC 77388 3112 E2
Crossfell Rd
2500 HarC 77388 3113 A2
3200 HarC 77388 3112 E2
Crossfell Fields Ln
- HarC 77429 3397 C1
Crossfence Dr
8800 HarC 77375 2965 D2
Crossfield Dr
900 HarC 77450 3954 D3
16300 HarC 77095 3538 B5
Crossfield Rd
21300 MNVL 77578 4747 B2
Crossfield Park Ln
4200 HarC 77449 3815 B1
Cross Fox Ln
10 WDLD 77380 2821 C7
Crossgate Blvd
- HarC 77373 2968 D6
Cross Glade Ct
14100 HOUS 77044 3550 B3
Crossglen Ct
21800 HarC 77373 3261 A1
Cross Green Ln
3600 HarC 77373 3114 E1
Cross Grove Ln
2700 FBnC 77494 3953 B6
Crosshaven Ct
13700 HarC 77015 3828 E5
Crosshaven Dr
13800 HarC 77015 3828 E5
13900 HarC 77015 3829 A5
Crosshill Ln
1900 FBnC 77469 4616 B2
Cross Hollow Ln
- KATY 77494 3952 B3
26100 HarC 77433 3396 B5
Crossing Dr
13000 HarC 77041 3679 C1
Crossing Pl
- CNRO 77304 2529 D2
- MtgC 77304 2529 D3
Crossing Nexus Ln
2000 HarC 77450 3954 E7
Cross Junction St
14500 HarC 77084 3679 A4
Crosslake Blvd
- MSCY 77459 4496 B2
- SGLD 77479 4496 B2
Cross Lake Dr
10 WDLD 77382 2674 B5
Crossland Ct
18200 HarC 77433 3677 D1
Crossland Park Ln
26100 HarC 77433 3396 B4
Crosslyn Ln
13400 HarC 77429 3397 C1
Crossman St
3200 MtgC 77365 2974 C6
Crossmeadow Ln
- FBnC 77469 4235 D1

Crossmill Ln
2100 HarC 77450 3954 C6
Crossno Dr
10900 MtgC 77372 2537 B2
Cross Oak Rd
- WDLD 77381 2820 E6
Crosson Ln
- HarC 77389 2966 A1
Crossout Ct
3100 HarC 77373 3115 A4
Crossover Rd
- FBnC 77494 3952 A6
27600 FBnC 77441 3951 C6
27600 FBnC 77494 3951 C6
Crosspark Ln
3300 HOUS 77007 3962 E3
Cross Pasture Rd
20100 WlrC 77484 3100 D5
20200 PRVW 77484 3100 D6
Cross Plains Ct
9400 HarC 77095 3538 E4
Cross Point Av
1600 HOUS 77054 4242 B2
Crossport Ln
400 LGCY 77539 4752 D5
Crossprairie Dr
28100 FBnC 77494 3951 D5
Crossridge Dr
- HarC 77065 3539 D5
- JRSV 77065 3539 D5
Crossriver Ln
8600 HarC 77095 3537 E5
Crossroads
17000 PTVL 77372 2683 B7
17400 RMFT 77357 2683 B7
Crossroads Dr
700 HOUS 77079 3956 D2
Crossroads Ln
- HarC 77041 3680 E6
- HOUS 77041 3680 E6
Crossroads Park Dr
12600 HarC 77065 3539 C4
Crossroads Plaza Dr
- BzaC 77584 4500 E6
- PRLD 77584 4500 E6
10600 BzaC 77584 4501 B5
Cross Saddle Ct
1000 HarC 77373 2968 D7
Cross Spring Ct
11500 PRLD 77584 4500 E3
Cross Spring Dr
1800 FBnC 77479 4494 B4
11600 PRLD 77584 4500 D4
17100 HarC 77095 3538 A6
Cross Spring Ln
- LGCY 77573 4631 C7
Cross Spring Park Ln
32300 MtgC 77385 2823 C6
Cross Springs Ct
8200 HarC 77095 3538 C3
Cross Springs Dr
16900 HarC 77095 3538 A6
17100 HarC 77095 3537 C4
Cross Stone Ct
14800 HarC 77429 3396 C1
Cross Tide Ln
2600 HarC 77546 4506 A7
Cross Timbers Ln
700 FRDW 77546 4505 C5
Crosstimbers St
100 HOUS 77018 3823 C1
200 HOUS 77022 3823 D1
1300 HOUS 77022 3824 A1
E Crosstimbers St
10 HOUS 77022 3824 A1
1700 HOUS 77093 3824 E1
3000 HOUS 77093 3825 A1
3700 HOUS 77016 3825 B1
W Crosstimbers St
100 HOUS 77018 3823 B2
Crosston St
4400 HOUS 77018 3823 B1
Cross Trail Dr
8000 FBnC 77479 4494 A6
Crosstrees Ln
13700 HarC 77396 3547 B3
Crossvale Ln
14000 HarC 77047 4374 C4
Cross Valley Dr
1300 FBnC 77479 4494 B6
5400 HarC 77066 3401 A6
Crossview Dr
2700 HOUS 77063 3959 D7
2700 HOUS 77063 4099 D2
Crossvine Cir
2600 WDLD 77380 2821 C7
2900 MtgC 77380 2821 C7
Crossvine Trail Ct
21200 HarC 77433 3251 A6
Crossvine Trail Ln
20000 HarC 77433 3251 C7
Crossway Dr
- HarC 77084 3678 A3
6300 HarC 77084 3677 E4
Crossway Oaks
28000 MtgC 77355 2815 B3
Crosswell St
6400 HOUS 77087 4244 D3
Crosswick Ln
- HarC 77373 2968 D6
Crosswind Dr
- PRLD 77584 4500 D3
Crosswinds Dr
14600 HarC 77032 3546 D1
14900 HarC 77032 3405 D7
Crosswinds Rd
- HarC 77032 3546 D1
Crosswinds Wy
18400 HarC 77532 3409 D6
Crosswood Rd
13900 HarC 77038 3542 E1
Crosswood Trails Ln
26100 HarC 77433 3396 B4
Croteau Dr
8700 HarC 77044 3689 B5
Croton Rd
7500 HOUS 77036 4099 D5
Crouch St
100 ALVN 77511 4749 A7
Crow Ct
12000 HarC 77429 3398 A6
Crow Rd
10 BYTN 77520 3971 A5
100 HarC 77520 3971 B5
Crowell Ln
2600 HarC 77521 3834 D6
Crowley St
100 KMAH 77565 4510 A7

STREET
Block City ZIP Map# Grid

Crown Ct
1700 TXCY 77591 4873 B4
Crown Dr
1500 ALVN 77511 4866 D3
Crown Ln
4500 BYTN 77521 3972 C1
Crown Rd
- HOUS 77506 4106 E2
300 HOUS 77506 4107 B2
300 PASD 77506 4107 B2
Crown St
100 HOUS 77020 3826 A7
100 HOUS 77020 3965 A1
1300 GNPK 77547 3966 D6
Crownberry Ct
10 WDLD 77381 2821 B6
Crown Brook Ct
8800 HarC 77083 4236 E1
Crown Chase Dr
27000 MtgC 77339 3118 B5
Crown Colony St
5400 HarC 77069 3400 E1
Crown Dale
- HarC 77066 3401 A5
Crowned Eagle Ln
- HarC 77396 3548 B2
Crowned Oak Ct
10 WDLD 77381 2674 D7
Crownfield Ln
22500 FBnC 77450 4093 E1
Crown Forest Dr
3000 HOUS 77345 3120 B4
Crown Glen Ct
14000 HOUS 77062 4379 D6
Crown Haven Ct
26900 MtgC 77339 3118 C3
Crown Haven Dr
26900 MtgC 77339 3118 B5
Crown Hill Ln
16100 HarC 77084 3678 B3
Crown Meadow Ct
17100 HarC 77095 3678 A1
Crownover Rd
1700 HOUS 77055 3820 D6
1700 HOUS 77080 3820 D5
Crown Park Dr
11200 HarC 77067 3402 C7
11200 HOUS 77067 3402 C7
Crown Point Dr
10500 HOUS 77099 4238 B3
Crown Ridge Ct
3900 HOUS 77059 4380 A4
Crownridge Dr
8100 WDLD 77382 2674 B4
Crown Rock Dr
27000 MtgC 77339 3118 B5
Crowns Cove Ln
26900 HarC 77339 3118 C3
Crownsedge Dr
10600 HarC 77379 3110 A6
Crown Valley Ln
12700 HOUS 77099 4237 C3
Crownwest Dr
7100 HOUS 77072 4097 E6
Crownwood Dr
4100 TYLV 77586 4381 D7
Crow Ridge Ct
13900 HarC 77429 3253 E4
Crows Nest Dr
2100 LGCY 77573 4508 C6
Crows Nest Wy
17300 HarC 77532 3552 B1
17400 HarC 77532 3411 B7
Crowson Dr
30200 TMBL 77375 2963 E5
Crow Valley Dr
3400 MSCY 77459 4497 A4
Croxton Dr
14800 HarC 77015 3829 B5
Croydon Ct
2000 HOUS 77008 3823 A7
Cruise Rd
12800 PASD 77586 4383 B3
Cruit Isl
8400 FBnC 77459 4621 B6
Cruse Dr
500 PASD 77506 4107 C5
Cruse Ln
- PRLD 77581 4503 E4
Cruse Rd
4700 HOUS 77016 3686 C7
Crutchfield Ln
- HOUS 77449 3814 E6
1500 HarC 77449 3814 E6
Cry Baby Ln
10 HarC 77336 3121 E6
10 HOUS 77336 3121 D5
Crystal Blvd
9800 BYTN 77520 3835 B6
Crystal Ct
- HarC 77429 3253 D2
2000 HOUS 77008 3822 C5
Crystal Ln
600 GlsC 77539 4635 C5
11600 MtgC 77303 2385 C2
Crystal Pt
6400 MSCY 77459 4496 C3
Crystal St
300 LGCY 77573 4631 E2
Crystal Tr
12700 MtgC 77306 2385 E3
Crystal Wy
7100 HOUS 77036 4099 E3
Crystal Bay Dr
5100 HarC 77084 3678 E5
22300 FBnC 77450 3953 E7
22300 FBnC 77450 3954 A7
Crystal Bay Ln
800 LGCY 77573 4633 B3
Crystal Blue Ln
7400 FBnC 77469 4094 E6
Crystal Bridge Ln
- FBnC 77450 4094 A4
Crystal Brook Dr
15800 HarC 77068 3257 A4
Crystal Cascade Ln
18700 HarC 77379 3111 B6
Crystal Cove
3400 HarC 77388 3112 D2
6200 BzaC 77583 4624 B5
Crystal Cove Cir
8600 HarC 77044 3689 C6
9300 HarC 77070 3255 C5
Crystal Cove Ct
8600 HarC 77044 3689 C5
Crystal Cove Dr
10500 MtgC 77354 2671 E4
10500 MtgC 77354 2672 A4
12700 HarC 77044 3689 B6
Crystal Creek Ct
3300 SGLD 77478 4368 E5
16200 HarC 77379 3256 B5
Crystal Creek Dr
3400 SGLD 77478 4368 E5
11600 MtgC 77303 2385 D1
Crystal Dowels Dr
6900 PASD 77505 4249 A7
Crystal Downs
- JRSV 77065 3540 B6
Crystal Downs Ct
23000 FBnC 77450 3953 E5
Crystal Downs Dr
2000 FBnC 77450 3953 E6
Crystal Falls Ct
2700 PRLD 77584 4500 E3
Crystal Falls Dr
2600 PRLD 77584 4500 D3
2700 HOUS 77345 3119 E5
3700 MSCY 77459 4497 A3
Crystal Forest Cir
2500 MtgC 77306 2385 E3
Crystal Forest Ct
2500 KATY 77493 3813 A5
Crystal Forest Dr
- CTSH 77303 2385 E3
- CTSH 77306 2385 E3
900 MtgC 77306 2385 E3
Crystal Forest Tr
6200 KATY 77493 3813 B4
Crystalglen Ln
7300 HarC 77095 3678 C1
Crystal Greens Dr
21000 FBnC 77450 4094 C1
Crystal Grove Dr
- HOUS 77082 4096 B2
15700 HarC 77082 4096 B2
Crystal Hills Dr
1300 HOUS 77077 3957 E5
Crystal Isle Dr
200 LGCY 77539 4752 E5
Crystal Isle Ln
7600 HarC 77396 3547 C2
Crystal Lake Cir E
1200 PRLD 77584 4501 D2
Crystal Lake Cir N
3900 PRLD 77584 4501 D2
Crystal Lake Cir S
3900 PRLD 77584 4501 D2
Crystal Lake Cir W
1200 PRLD 77584 4501 D2
Crystal Lake Ct
2500 FBnC 77469 4365 B2
Crystal Lake Dr
- PRLD 77581 4501 D2
- PRLD 77584 4501 D2
Crystal Lake Ln
- FBnC 77494 4093 D4
800 MtgC 77380 2968 A1
800 WDLD 77380 2968 A1
Crystal Meadow Pl
- FBnC 77494 3952 C5
Crystal Moon Dr
7800 HarC 77040 3541 D7
Crystal Park Dr
14600 HarC 77396 3548 E1
Crystal Pass Ct
3900 HarC 77449 3815 B2
Crystal Point Dr
6600 HarC 77449 3677 A2
Crystal Reef Ct
12900 PRLD 77584 4500 D4
Crystal Reef Dr
100 LGCY 77573 4633 B1
Crystal Reef Ln
2200 PRLD 77584 4500 A2
Crystal Reef Pl
13000 PRLD 77584 4500 A2
Crystal Ridge St
4200 MSCY 77459 4621 D3
Crystal River Dr
2000 HOUS 77345 3120 A6
Crystal Rock Ct
12600 HOUS 77072 4097 D6
Crystal Run Dr
17100 FBnC 77478 4236 A7
Crystal Sky
23700 FBnC 77494 4093 B5
N Crystal Springs Cir
9800 MtgC 77303 2238 A2
S Crystal Springs Cir
3000 MtgC 77303 2238 A3
Crystal Springs Ct
- HarC 77373 3113 C1
- HarC 77373 3114 A3
Crystal Springs Dr
1900 HOUS 77339 3118 D7
9000 MtgC 77303 2238 A2
9100 MtgC 77303 2237 E3
Crystal Stream Tr
- HOUS 77345 3120 D6
Crystal View Cir
16600 HarC 77095 3538 B5
Crystal View Ct
16500 HarC 77095 3538 B5
Crystalwood Cir
17800 MtgC 77357 2826 C1
Crystalwood Ct
17800 MtgC 77357 2826 D1
Crystalwood Dr
11600 HOUS 77013 3966 D1
Crystalwood Estates Dr
17800 MtgC 77357 2826 C1
19700 MtgC 77357 2680 D7
Crysti Ct
11700 MtgC 77304 2382 A3
Crystola Pk
19100 HarC 77373 3113 E7
Cuadro St
22800 GLSN 77554 5440 E6
22800 GLSN 77554 5441 A6
Cub Ln
700 RHMD 77469 4364 D7
9300 HOUS 77061 4245 E7
9300 HOUS 77075 4245 E7
9400 HOUS 77075 4376 E1
Cuba Libra Ln
22000 HarC 77532 3266 D6
Cuccerre
7700 HarC 77037 3684 C2
7700 HOUS 77037 3684 C2
Cucklebur Cir
10000 HarC 77095 3538 A3
Cuddy Dr
- HarC 77532 3551 E5
Cuffley
21900 MtgC 77357 2827 C5
Cuffmann Dr
1900 HOUS 77080 3820 B5
Cujanes St
4000 PASD 77504 4248 A5
Culberson St
6200 HOUS 77021 4103 B5
Culebra St
9700 HOUS 77013 3827 A5
Cullen
29000 MtgC 77354 2818 B2
Cullen Blvd
- HOUS 77023 4103 E1
- PRLD 77584 4501 E4
100 HarC 77047 4374 D5
100 HarC 77584 4374 D7
100 HOUS 77048 4374 D5
100 PRLD 77581 4374 D7
100 PRLD 77584 4374 D7
500 PRLD 77581 4501 E1
700 HOUS 77003 3964 A7
700 HOUS 77023 3964 A7
1800 HOUS 77023 4104 A2
2100 HOUS 77004 4103 E2
5800 HOUS 77021 4103 D6
7200 HOUS 77033 4103 D7
7200 HOUS 77051 4103 D7
7400 HOUS 77033 4243 D2
7400 HOUS 77051 4243 D2
10300 HOUS 77047 4243 D6
10300 HOUS 77048 4243 D7
11800 HOUS 77047 4374 D2
13900 HarC 77048 4374 D4
Cullen Blvd FM-865
- PRLD 77584 4501 E4
100 HarC 77047 4374 D5
100 HarC 77584 4374 D7
100 HOUS 77047 4374 D5
100 HOUS 77048 4374 D5
100 PRLD 77581 4374 D7
100 PRLD 77584 4374 D7
500 PRLD 77581 4501 E2
5800 HOUS 77021 4103 D6
7200 HOUS 77033 4103 D7
7200 HOUS 77051 4103 D7
7400 HOUS 77033 4243 D2
7400 HOUS 77051 4243 D2
10300 HOUS 77047 4243 D7
10300 HOUS 77048 4243 D7
13900 HarC 77048 4374 D4
W Cullen Cir
- HOUS 77030 4102 D4
Cullen Ct
200 LPRT 77571 4250 E2
E Cullen St
6400 HOUS 77030 4102 D4
W Cullen St
6400 HOUS 77030 4102 D4
Cullen Ter
28200 MtgC 77386 2969 C7
Cullendale
5700 HOUS 77021 4103 E5
Cullen Meadow Ct
12000 HOUS 77047 4374 B1
Culmore Dr
4800 HOUS 77021 4103 E5
4800 HOUS 77021 4104 A5
6300 HOUS 77087 4104 D6
7200 HOUS 77087 4105 A6
Culross Ct
18900 HarC 77346 3264 D6
Culross Close
5800 HarC 77346 3264 D6
Culver St
1300 PASD 77502 4246 E1
9200 HOUS 77051 4243 B4
Culverdale Pl
10 WDLD 77382 2819 D2
Cumberland Blvd
18000 MtgC 77365 2971 E1
18100 MtgC 77365 2972 A1
Cumberland Ct
500 MtgC 77302 2530 D5
3200 MSCY 77459 4498 A6
Cumberland Dr
2800 MSCY 77459 4497 E6
3300 MSCY 77459 4498 A6
5200 LGCY 77573 4630 C6
Cumberland Pkwy
- MtgC 77384 2673 E2
11400 MtgC 77384 2674 A2
Cumberland St
2000 HOUS 77023 4104 C3
Cumberland Tr
300 MtgC 77302 2530 D6
16100 HarC 77433 3251 B5
Cumberland Wy
21300 HarC 77433 3251 A6
Cumberland Bridge Ln
14800 FBnC 77478 4236 D5
Cumberland Oak Ct
2300 HOUS 77345 3120 A2
15700 HarC 77433 3251 B6
Cumberland Oak Wy
15300 HarC 77433 3251 A6
Cumberland Park Ln
12500 HarC 77346 3408 C3
Cumberland Ridge Dr
21300 HarC 77433 3250 E4
21300 HarC 77433 3251 C3
Cumbre Dr
22800 MtgC 77365 2972 B4
Cumbria Dr
15900 HarC 77379 3256 A6
Cumi St
8900 HarC 77562 3833 A1
Cummings Grn
- HOUS 77027 4101 D1
- HOUS 77046 4101 D1
Cummings Ln
20200 MtgC 77357 2827 C6
Cummings Rd
500 FBnC 77471 4490 E1
Cummins St
3100 HOUS 77027 3961 D7
3100 HOUS 77027 4101 D1
3100 HOUS 77046 4101 D1
Cuney
- LGCY 77573 4632 B4
Cuney Dr
3900 HOUS 77004 4103 C2
Cunningham Dr
2300 PRLD 77581 4503 A2
2500 PRLD 77584 4503 A3
5300 PRLD 77581 4502 E3
24300 MtgC 77365 2973 D7
24700 MtgC 77365 3118 D1
Cunningham Ln
5400 RSBG 77469 4615 E1
Cunningham Rd
- PASD 77507 4249 C5
3200 DRPK 77505 4249 C4
3200 DRPK 77536 4249 C4
3200 PASD 77505 4249 C4
3200 PASD 77536 4249 C4
5700 HarC 77041 3680 B5
Cunningham Creek Blvd
- FBnC 77469 4366 D5
600 FBnC 77479 4366 C6
Cupids Bower Ct
5000 HarC 77388 3112 B3
Curacao Dr
- HarC 77049 3831 A1
Curlee Rd
- HOUS 77034 4377 E1
9000 HOUS 77034 4246 E7
Curlew Cir S
2200 SEBK 77586 4509 B2
Curlew Ct
2100 MSCY 77489 4497 C1
Curlew Dr
7100 HarC 77433 3676 E1
Curlew Ln
3000 TXCY 77590 4875 D2
Curlew Rd
16600 JMAB 77554 5331 D4
16700 GLSN 77554 5331 D4
N Curlew St
10 LMQU 77568 4990 D6
S Curlew St
10 LMQU 77568 4990 D6
Curley Maple Dr
3400 PRLD 77584 4503 B6
Curling St
8500 HOUS 77055 3821 A5
Curly Oaks Dr
3900 HOUS 77053 4372 D4
Currency St
- HOUS 77029 3965 E1
9300 HOUS 77013 3965 E1
Currie Av
- HOUS 77034 4379 A4
Currin Forest Dr
12200 HarC 77044 3548 E6
Curry Ln
3600 DKSN 77539 4754 A2
Curry Rd
- ORDN 77385 2822 D5
3700 BzaC 77578 4625 C1
6900 HOUS 77093 3825 A2
8300 HOUS 77093 3686 A7
20600 MtgC 77385 2822 D5
Curry St
600 CmbC 77586 4509 E3
600 SEBK 77586 4509 E3
900 BYTN 77521 3973 A2
Curry Creek Ln
14100 HarC 77090 3402 B2
Curry Landing Dr
9300 HarC 77095 3538 A4
Currymead Pl
10 WDLD 77382 2674 E4
Curry Ridge Ln
11600 HarC 77377 3109 B7
Curt Ln
12900 HarC 77041 3679 D1
Curtin Ln
700 HOUS 77018 3823 B1
1000 HOUS 77018 3822 E1
Curtin St
4900 HOUS 77023 3964 B7
Curtis Av
100 PASD 77502 4107 B6
W Curtis Av
100 PASD 77502 4107 A6
200 PASD 77506 4107 A6
Curtis Cross
1100 MSCY 77489 4370 B4
Curtis Ln
3500 BzaC 77578 4501 D7
3500 PRLD 77578 4501 D7
Curtis St
- HarC 77532 3411 D4
3900 HOUS 77020 3964 B2
Curtis Creek Ct
10 CNRO 77304 2236 D6
Curwood
- WDLD 77380 2967 D3
Curz Point Ct
6000 HarC 77449 3676 D4
Cushing St
1100 HOUS 77019 3963 A5
1800 HOUS 77006 3963 A5
2900 HOUS 77026 3825 C7
Custard Apple Tr
- FBnC 77494 4092 E3
Custer Cir
4800 FBnC 77471 4614 D4
Custer Dr
2800 LGCY 77573 4631 A6
Custer Ln
- BKVL 77581 4375 B7
- PRLD 77581 4375 B7
Custer Rd
6800 HTCK 77563 4988 C4
Custer St
4300 HOUS 77009 3824 B6
8000 HTCK 77563 4988 C6
Custer Creek Dr
4100 MSCY 77459 4369 C5
Custers Ct
10 PNVL 77304 2237 B3
Custus St
- HOUS 77007 3962 E3
Cuta Ct
13100 HarC 77039 3546 B4
Cutlass Dr
3100 HarC 77396 3407 A4
Cutlass Ln
3200 GLSN 77554 5332 D1
Cutler Ridge Ln
13100 HarC 77044 3689 C5
Cutten Pkwy
6700 HarC 77069 3400 A2
Cutten Rd
- HarC 77069 3255 E7
- HarC 77069 3399 E1
- HarC 77086 3400 D7
- HarC 77379 3255 E7
10700 HarC 77066 3400 C4
12700 HOUS 77066 3400 B4
13000 HOUS 77069 3400 B3
13100 HarC 77069 3400 A1
14500 HarC 77070 3255 D6
14500 HarC 77070 3399 D1
Cutter Ct
2400 SEBK 77586 4509 C2
Cutter Dr
2000 LGCY 77573 4509 A7
12900 MtgC 77372 2536 E6
Cutter Wy
17100 HarC 77532 3552 B1
Cutter Rays Rd
600 FBnC 77545 4499 D6
Cutting Horse Ln
10200 HarC 77064 3540 B5
Cuttler Rd
22200 MtgC 77357 2827 D7
22200 MtgC 77357 2973 D1
Cutwater Pl
3500 GLSN 77554 5333 A1
Cyan Sky Dr
- HarC 77433 3250 E4
Cyberonics Blvd
100 HOUS 77058 4507 D1
Cymbal Ct
9200 HarC 77040 3681 B1
Cymbal Dr
9700 STAF 77477 4239 A6
Cynda Brooke Dr
4300 BYTN 77521 3972 C3
Cynthia St
4300 BLAR 77401 4101 B6
4300 HOUS 77401 4101 B6
Cynthia Ann Ct
9800 HOUS 77025 4241 D2
Cypress Av
500 FBnC 77545 4623 D2
600 BzaC 77583 4623 D2
600 PRLD 77545 4623 D2
5200 PASD 77503 4248 B1
Cypress Cir
- HarC 77065 3398 A6
12500 HarC 77429 3397 E5
14200 HarC 77396 3547 B2
17000 MtgC 77302 2825 C2
31600 WALR 77484 3102 A5
Cypress Cor
- HarC 77065 3398 A7
- HarC 77429 3398 A7
Cypress Cr
11300 HarC 77064 3540 B1
11300 HarC 77070 3540 B1
Cypress Ct
2600 SEBK 77586 4509 B2
11200 HarC 77065 3399 A6
Cypress Dr
- HarC 77429 3396 D5
100 HarC 77532 3692 C3
200 PNVL 77304 2237 A4
300 HarC 77094 3955 C1
1700 RHMD 77469 4491 D3
1900 RHMD 77471 4491 D3
1900 RSBG 77471 4491 D3
7500 HMBL 77396 3406 D2
12200 HarC 77433 3396 D6
14700 MtgC 77302 2677 B1
Cypress Gdns
15300 HarC 77069 3256 D5
Cypress Hl
2400 SGLD 77479 4368 D6
Cypress Ln
- MtgC 77372 2682 E6
- MtgC 77372 2683 A6
- PTVL 77372 2682 E6
- SGLD 77478 4368 E6
100 CNRO 77301 2384 B7
100 CNRO 77301 2530 B1
300 LPRT 77571 4110 C7
1200 HarC 77562 3691 E6
1200 HOUS 77339 3263 C1
2500 RSBG 77471 4491 A6
6300 KATY 77493 3813 B4
12800 HarC 77377 3254 A1
13500 HarC 77429 3398 E3
E Cypress Lp
12700 HarC 77429 3397 C4
W Cypress Lp
12700 HarC 77429 3397 B4
Cypress Mdws
15500 HarC 77377 3108 B4
Cypress Pl
11700 HarC 77065 3398 E6
11700 HarC 77065 3399 A6
Cypress Pns
10 HarC 77065 3399 A6
10 HarC 77070 3399 A6
Cypress Rd
26700 MtgC 77365 3117 D4
Cypress St
10 HarC 77336 2975 C6
100 HarC 77562 3831 D2
100 LPRT 77571 4251 E5
300 ALVN 77511 4867 C2
800 LMQU 77568 4990 B1
1100 BYTN 77520 3972 A7
1200 BYTN 77520 4112 A1
2400 GLSN 77551 5108 B7
2500 GLSN 77551 5222 B1
2600 PASD 77502 4248 A1
5800 HOUS 77074 4100 B7
7800 HOUS 77012 4105 C2
Cypress Tr
11800 HarC 77065 3398 E6
12100 HarC 77429 3398 E6
Cypress Arbor Dr
19300 HarC 77449 3816 A1
Cypress Bank Dr
18900 HarC 77388 3112 E6
Cypress Bay Ct
19400 HarC 77449 3816 A1
Cypress Bay Dr
- HarC 77084 3816 B1
19200 HarC 77449 3816 A1
Cypress Bayou Ct
10 WDLD 77382 2675 C6
Cypress Bend Ct
4600 PRLD 77584 4503 B3
Cypress Bend Dr
16200 HarC 77429 3397 A4
Cypress Bend Ln
2000 SGLD 77478 4369 A6
Cypress Bloom Ln
- HarC 77433 3537 A7
Cypress Bluff Dr
7400 HarC 77433 3676 D1
Cypressbluff Ln
4700 HarC 77449 3677 A6
Cypress Bough Dr
19600 HarC 77449 3677 A7
Cypress Branch Dr
14400 HarC 77429 3253 D7
Cypress Breeze Ct
7300 HarC 77433 3676 D1
14000 HarC 77429 3254 A5
Cypressbreeze Ct
7200 HarC 77379 3111 B3
Cypress Breeze Dr
20600 HarC 77433 3676 D1
Cypress Bridge Dr
16500 HarC 77429 3252 D7
Cypress Brook Ct
16500 HarC 77429 3396 E1
Cypressbrook Dr
8700 HarC 77095 3539 A6
Cypress Canyon Dr
19100 HarC 77449 3816 B1
19200 HarC 77449 3677 A7
Cypress Chase Blvd
18000 HarC 77429 3396 A2
18000 HarC 77433 3396 A2
Cypress Chase Dr
- HarC 77094 3955 D1
Cypress Chateau Dr
18800 HarC 77388 3112 E6
Cypress Church Rd
18200 HarC 77429 3252 A6
19500 HarC 77433 3251 D5
19500 HarC 77433 3252 A5
Cypress Cliff Dr
19200 HarC 77449 3816 A1
Cypress Colony Ln
4500 HarC 77449 3677 A6
Cypress Cottage Ct
14600 HarC 77429 3396 C2
Cypress Cove St
- HarC 77090 3258 A2
1400 LPRT 77571 4251 C5
1500 HarC 77090 3257 E2
Cypress Creek Blvd
14100 HarC 77429 3397 E5
Cypress Creek Bend Dr
11200 HarC 77433 3396 C7
Cypress Creek Bend Ln
- HarC 77433 3396 C7
- HarC 77433 3537 A1
Cypress Creek Lakes Dr
11300 HarC 77433 3396 B6
Cypress Crest Dr
- HarC 77429 3253 D7
Cypress Croft
- HarC 77433 3396 B4
Cypress Crossing Dr
12300 HarC 77065 3398 D6
12400 HarC 77429 3398 D5
Cypressdale Dr
3400 HarC 77388 3112 E6
4700 HarC 77388 3257 C1
4800 HarC 77379 3257 C1
Cypress Downs Dr
16500 HarC 77429 3396 E1
Cypress Echo Dr
20700 HarC 77433 3676 D1
Cypressedge Ct
15300 HarC 77429 3253 D7
Cypress Edge Dr
7500 HarC 77433 3676 C1
N Cypress Estates Cir
300 HarC 77388 3113 D7
S Cypress Estates Cir
300 HarC 77388 3113 E7
Cypress Estates Ct
19100 HarC 77388 3113 D7
Cypress Estates Dr
18900 HarC 77388 3113 D7
Cypress Falls Dr
14000 HarC 77429 3253 E7
Cypress Farms Ranch Rd
16000 HarC 77429 3397 A1
Cypress Fields Av
17000 HarC 77429 3252 E7
Cypress Flower Dr
19100 HarC 77449 3816 A1
E Cypress Forest Dr
13300 HarC 77070 3399 B3
W Cypress Forest Dr
13300 HarC 77070 3399 B3
Cypress Garden Dr
- HarC 77429 3253 E6
8600 HarC 77095 3538 D5
15500 HarC 77377 3108 B5
Cypressgate Dr
22500 HarC 77373 3115 E7
Cypress Glade Dr
17000 HarC 77429 3252 D5
Cypress Glades Cir
19300 HarC 77449 3677 A2
Cypress Glades Ct
19300 HarC 77449 3677 A2
Cypress Glades Dr
- HarC 77449 3677 B3
Cypress Glen St
17500 HarC 77429 3252 D4
Cypress Glenn Rd
- HarC 77429 3252 C3
Cypress Green Dr
14200 HarC 77429 3253 D7
Cypress Green Ln
5100 FBnC 77469 4233 B7
20600 HarC 77433 3676 D1
Cypress Grove Ln
4100 HOUS 77088 3682 E3
4100 HOUS 77088 3683 A3
Cypress Gully Dr
20500 HarC 77433 3676 D1
Cypress Hall Dr
15700 HarC 77429 3397 B3
Cypress Harbor Dr
19200 HarC 77449 3816 A1
Cypress Harrow Dr
19400 HarC 77449 3677 B5
Cypress Heath Ct
13500 HarC 77429 3254 A5
E Cypress Hill Cir
17900 HarC 77433 3252 A2
W Cypress Hill Cir
17700 HarC 77433 3252 A2
Cypress Hill Ct
17300 HarC 77388 3257 E1
Cypress Hill Dr
3700 HarC 77388 3257 D2
4300 HarC 77379 3257 D2
Cypress Hollow St
1600 PRLD 77581 4504 D4
17500 HarC 77429 3252 D3
Cypress Huffmeister Rd
19100 HarC 77433 3251 E6
19100 HarC 77433 3252 A5
Cypress Island Dr
2500 HarC 77073 3259 E1
2800 HarC 77338 3259 E1
Cypress Key Dr
3700 HarC 77388 3112 D5
Cypress Knee Dr
17000 HarC 77429 3252 D6
Cypress Knee Ln
3900 HarC 77039 3546 A3
Cypress Knoll Dr
- HarC 77429 3253 D6
Cypress Lake Dr
3900 HarC 77388 3257 D2
Cypress Lake Village Dr
18400 HarC 77429 3252 B7
18600 HarC 77433 3252 B7
Cypress Landing Ct
3300 RSBG 77471 4491 B6
Cypress Landing Dr
- HarC 77014 3258 A6
2100 HarC 77090 3258 A5
2100 HOUS 77090 3258 A6
Cypress Laurel St
- HarC 77433 3537 D6
17500 HarC 77095 3537 D6
Cypress Leaf Dr
14400 HarC 77429 3253 D7
Cypress Lilly Dr
20600 HarC 77433 3676 D1
Cypress Lily Ln
19100 HarC 77449 3677 B7
Cypress Links Tr
- HarC 77433 3252 A6
14400 HarC 77429 3396 A1
Cypress Ln Pl
10 WDLD 77382 2674 D4
Cypress Loch Dr
18700 HarC 77379 3255 E1
Cypress Manor Dr
1700 HarC 77336 3266 E3
Cypress Marsh Ct
16000 HarC 77429 3396 E1
Cypress Meade Ct
14900 HarC 77429 3396 B1
Cypress Meade Ln
18200 HarC 77429 3396 B1
Cypress Meadow Dr
14200 HarC 77429 3253 E6
Cypress Meadow Rd
15600 HarC 77429 3397 B6
Cypress Meadows Ct
- DKSN 77539 4752 D6
Cypress Meadows Dr
- DKSN 77539 4752 D6
- LGCY 77539 4752 D6
13900 HarC 77047 4374 C5
Cypress Mill Park Dr
17800 HarC 77429 3396 B1
Cypress Mill Park Ln
- HarC 77429 3396 B1
Cypress Mills Dr
9400 HarC 77070 3399 D4
9400 HOUS 77070 3399 D4
Cypress Mist Ct
18100 HarC 77433 3396 D7
Cypress Moss Dr
19500 HarC 77449 3816 A1
Cypress Mound Ct
5800 HarC 77379 3257 A2
Cypress Mountain Dr
18800 HarC 77388 3112 E6
Cypress North Houston Blvd
- HarC 77095 3397 A7
Cypress-North Houston Blvd
16400 HarC 77095 3397 A7
16400 HarC 77429 3397 A7
16700 HarC 77095 3396 E7
17300 HarC 77433 3396 E7
Cypress North Houston Rd
11000 HarC 77065 3399 A6
11000 HarC 77070 3399 A6
11000 HarC 77429 3399 A6
11200 HarC 77065 3398 C6
11200 HarC 77429 3398 C6
13900 HarC 77429 3397 D7
19000 HarC 77433 3396 A7
19200 HarC 77433 3395 E7
Cypress Oaks Dr
500 HarC 77388 3113 D7
500 HarC 77388 3258 C1
14400 HarC 77429 3397 D3
Cypress Orchard Ln
14700 HarC 77429 3396 D1
Cypress Park Dr
11800 HarC 77065 3398 B7
11900 HarC 77065 3398 B7
Cypress Park Ln
- PRLD 77584 4501 A3
Cypress Park Spur
13300 HarC 77065 3398 B6
Cypresspark Glen Ln
24500 HarC 77447 3249 D4
Cypress Path Ct
16500 HarC 77429 3396 E1
Cypress Peak Ln
19200 HarC 77449 3677 B7
Cypress Pelican Dr
16500 HarC 77429 3396 E1
N Cypress Pine Dr
10 WDLD 77381 2820 D6
S Cypress Pine Dr
10 WDLD 77381 2820 E5
Cypress Pl Dr
12200 HarC 77065 3399 A6
12200 HarC 77429 3399 A6
Cypress Plantation Dr
- HarC 77429 3252 D1
Cypress Point Ct N
10 MNVL 77578 4624 D5
Cypress Point Dr
- FRDW 77546 4629 A6
2700 MSCY 77459 4370 B6
2700 MSCY 77459 4497 A1
6500 HarC 77069 3400 B2
16100 HarC 77429 3397 A2
16200 HarC 77429 3396 E2
Cypress Pointe Dr
700 LGCY 77573 4631 E5
Cypress Pond Cir
13700 HarC 77429 3254 A6
Cypress Pond Ct
4400 PASD 77059 4380 C3
Cypress Pond Dr
13300 HarC 77429 3254 A6
Cypress Post Ln
15100 HarC 77429 3253 C7

STREET
Block City ZIP Map# Grid

Cypress Prarie Dr
7100 HarC 77433 3676 E1
Cypress Rain Dr
- HarC 77449 3815 D2
Cypress Ranch Dr
- HarC 77429 3396 E1
Cypress Ridge Dr
14200 HarC 77429 3253 D7
Cypress Ridge Ln
10 SGLD 77479 4495 E3
14800 HarC 77429 3396 B1
Cypress River Dr
- SGLD 77478 4369 A6
19200 HarC 77449 3816 B1
Cypress Rose Ct
19400 HarC 77449 3677 A6
Cypress Rosehill Rd
14100 HarC 77433 3396 B3
14200 HarC 77429 3396 B2
16100 HarC 77429 3252 B7
16400 HarC 77433 3252 C2
18500 HarC 77429 3107 C7
18500 HarC 77433 3107 C7
22000 HarC 77377 3107 B2
22500 HarC 77377 2962 B7
22700 MtgC 77355 2962 B6
Cypress Royal Dr
19300 HarC 77449 3677 A7
Cypress Run Ct
4800 SGLD 77478 4369 B6
Cypress Run Dr
1900 SGLD 77478 4369 A6
Cypress Shadows
11200 HarC 77065 3399 A6
Cypress Shores Dr
12200 HarC 77375 3109 C6
Cypress Side Dr
17900 HarC 77433 3396 C7
Cypress Spring Dr
4900 MSCY 77459 4496 B3
17300 HarC 77388 3257 D1
Cypress Springs Ct
2500 PRLD 77584 4500 D4
Cypress Springs Dr
2600 PRLD 77584 4500 B3
Cypress Square Ct
8700 HarC 77379 3255 B4
8700 HarC 77379 3256 A4
Cypress Square Dr
8900 HarC 77379 3255 E4
Cypress Station Dr
100 HarC 77073 3258 D1
1000 HOUS 77090 3258 D3
1400 HarC 77090 3258 D3
Cypress Stone Ln
18300 HarC 77429 3396 B1
Cypress Terrace Dr
- HarC 77429 3252 D1
Cypress Thicket Dr
16500 HarC 77429 3252 E7
Cypressthorn Ln
19400 HarC 77449 3677 A7
Cypress Timber Dr
- HarC 77429 3252 E7
Cypress Timbers Ln
11400 HarC 77433 3396 B7
Cypress Trace Dr
16100 HarC 77429 3397 A2
16200 HarC 77429 3396 E1
Cypress Trace Rd
18000 HarC 77090 3258 C1
18000 HOUS 77090 3258 C1
Cypresstree Dr
2000 HarC 77373 3114 C7
Cypress Tree Ln
20600 HarC 77388 3112 D5
Cypress Vale Dr
20700 HarC 77433 3676 D2
Cypress Valley Ct
10 SGLD 77479 4495 E2
Cypress Valley Dr
14200 HarC 77429 3253 D7
16100 HarC 77429 3397 A2
16200 HarC 77429 3396 E2
Cypress Valley Ln
17900 HarC 77429 3396 B1
Cypress Valley Rd
12700 HarC 77429 3397 B5
Cypress View Dr
14400 HarC 77429 3253 D7
Cypress Village Ct
6100 PRLD 77584 4502 D5
Cypress Village Dr
3400 PRLD 77584 4502 D6
6600 FBnC 77479 4493 D4
7000 HarC 77433 3676 D1
7000 HarC 77449 3676 D2
S Cypress Villas Dr
17700 HarC 77379 3257 C2
W Cypress Villas Dr
4400 HarC 77379 3257 C2
4400 HarC 77388 3257 C2
Cypressvine Dr
2600 HarC 77084 3816 A5
Cypress Vista
300 HarC 77094 3955 D2
Cypress Walk Ln
- HarC 77429 3396 C3
Cypress Waters Ct
16500 HarC 77429 3252 D7
Cypress Waters Dr
14900 HarC 77429 3252 D7
Cypresswell Ct
5800 HarC 77379 3257 A2
Cypresswick Cir
5800 HarC 77379 3257 A2
Cypresswick Ln
4700 HarC 77449 3677 A5
16600 HarC 77379 3257 A4
Cypress Willow Dr
5000 HarC 77449 3677 B5
Cypress Wind
300 HarC 77094 3955 C2
Cypresswood Bnd
800 HarC 77373 3113 E4
Cypresswood Brk
500 HarC 77373 3113 D4
Cypresswood Cr
19900 HarC 77373 3113 E4
Cypresswood Ct
19600 HarC 77388 3113 D5
19600 HOUS 77388 3113 D5
Cypresswood Dr
- HarC 77429 3395 E1
- HarC 77433 3251 A7
- HarC 77433 3395 C1
- HarC 77447 3249 D5
100 HarC 77388 3113 C7
100 HOUS 77388 3113 C7
500 HarC 77373 3113 E6
500 HOUS 77373 3113 E6
700 HarC 77373 3114 A5
4200 HarC 77388 3257 C1
4300 HarC 77379 3257 A3
6600 HarC 77379 3256 D5
7800 HarC 77069 3256 B6
9600 HarC 77069 3255 E7
9600 HarC 77070 3255 E7
9600 HarC 77379 3255 E7
9700 HarC 77070 3399 A2
9800 HOUS 77070 3399 D1
10900 HarC 77070 3398 C1
12300 HarC 77429 3398 C1
18100 HarC 77429 3396 A1
20200 HarC 77338 3261 A1
20200 HOUS 77338 3261 B4
21700 HarC 77433 3250 E6
21900 HarC 77373 3261 A1
22100 HarC 77373 3116 A7
22200 HarC 77373 3115 E7
Cypresswood Gln
19900 HarC 77373 3113 D4
Cypresswood Hl
500 HarC 77373 3113 D4
Cypresswood Hvn
400 HarC 77373 3113 D5
Cypresswood Knl
500 HarC 77373 3113 D4
Cypresswood Ml
700 HarC 77373 3113 E5
Cypresswood Pl
11500 HarC 77070 3398 E2
Cypresswood Rdg
600 HarC 77373 3113 E4
Cypresswood Shr
19800 HarC 77373 3113 D4
Cypresswood Sprs
19800 HarC 77373 3113 E4
Cypresswood Sq
19900 HarC 77373 3113 E4
Cypresswood Trc
500 HarC 77373 3113 E5
Cypresswood Bough
800 HarC 77373 3113 D4
Cypresswood Chase
20300 HarC 77373 3113 E4
Cypresswood Cove
700 HarC 77373 3113 E5
Cypresswood Crossing Blvd
13900 HarC 77070 3398 E2
14000 HarC 77070 3399 A1
Cypresswood Crossong Blvd
13700 HarC 77070 3398 E2
Cypresswood Dale
19800 HarC 77373 3113 E5
Cypresswood Estates Ln
600 HarC 77373 3113 E5
Cypresswood Estates Run
19800 HarC 77373 3113 E4
Cypresswood Falls
19800 HarC 77373 3113 D5
Cypresswood Forest Ct
18900 HarC 77388 3113 A7
Cypresswood Glen Dr
20000 HarC 77388 3112 E5
Cypresswood Glen Tr
17000 HarC 77447 3249 D4
Cypresswood Green Ct
21900 HarC 77373 3261 A2
Cypresswood Green Dr
5800 HarC 77373 3260 E2
5800 HarC 77373 3261 A1
Cypresswood Grove Rd
- HOUS 77345 3119 D1
- HOUS 77365 3119 D1
Cypresswood Harbor Cir
500 HarC 77373 3113 E5
Cypresswood Lake Ct
700 HarC 77373 3113 E5
Cypresswood Lake Dr
- HarC 77373 3114 A5
19700 HarC 77373 3113 E4
Cypresswood Manor St
6800 HarC 77379 3256 D5
Cypresswood Meadows Ct
3700 HarC 77388 3112 C5
Cypresswood Meadows Dr
20500 HarC 77388 3112 D5
Cypresswood Point Av
6300 HarC 77338 3261 B3
Cypress Woods Dr
- HarC 77014 3257 E6
- HarC 77068 3257 E6
Cypresswood Shadows
700 HarC 77373 3113 E5
Cypress Woods Medical Dr
15000 HarC 77014 3257 E6
15000 HarC 77068 3257 E6
Cypresswood Trail Ct
11500 HarC 77070 3398 E2
Cypresswood Trail Dr
11400 HarC 77070 3398 E2
Cypress Wy Dr
6000 MtgC 77354 2673 C2
11200 HarC 77065 3399 A6
Cyprus Fld
12000 HarC 77070 3399 A6
Cyprus Ln
- HarC 77044 3549 B3
Cyprus Cedar Ct
17900 WlrC 77484 3246 D1
Cyprus Cedar Ln
17800 WlrC 77484 3246 D2
Cyr St
- HOUS 77055 3821 D4
Cyress Hllw
- HarC 77357 2830 B6
Cyril Dr
3600 HarC 77396 3407 E4
3800 HarC 77396 3408 A4
Cyrl Ln
7900 HarC 77044 3688 D7
E Cyrus Dr
11100 HarC 77064 3541 B1
W Cyrus Dr
11100 HarC 77064 3541 B1
Cytherea Cir
2800 BzaC 77511 4868 B7

D

D Dr
- HarC 77388 3111 D2
D St
- HOUS 77547 4106 C1
- WALR 77484 3101 D5
4100 HOUS 77072 4097 E4
4100 HOUS 77082 4097 E4
E D St
200 LPRT 77571 4251 E3
900 LPRT 77571 4252 A3
N D St
11100 LPRT 77571 4250 E2
11600 LPRT 77571 4251 A2
S D St
2400 MRGP 77571 4252 C1
W D St
100 LPRT 77571 4251 D3
Dabney Dr
1400 PASD 77502 4247 E2
Dabney St
3400 HOUS 77026 3825 D6
Dabney Hill Ct
6000 FBnC 77479 4367 A5
Dabney Manor Ct
2400 HarC 77449 3814 D5
Dabney Manor Ln
22500 HarC 77449 3814 D5
Dacca Dr
- HOUS 77048 4243 D6
3000 HOUS 77051 4243 A6
4100 HOUS 77047 4243 C6
Dacoma Rd
- HOUS 77092 3821 E4
3700 HOUS 77018 3822 B4
3700 HOUS 77092 3822 A4
Dacus Dr
900 JTCY 77029 3966 B2
Dade St
1400 PASD 77502 4107 A7
2000 PASD 77502 4247 A1
Dadebrook Ct
12800 HarC 77041 3679 D3
Dadebury Ln
- HarC 77084 3678 C4
Dademount Ct
20600 FBnC 77469 4094 D7
Dade Peak Wy
21800 HarC 77449 3676 A7
Daehne Dr
13700 HarC 77014 3401 C2
Daffodil Av
8600 HOUS 77063 4099 D1
Daffodil Ct
18600 MtgC 77365 2972 A5
Daffodil Ln
23500 MtgC 77365 2972 A5
Daffodil Rd
1400 MSCY 77489 4370 C3
Daffodil St
2300 HarC 77562 3832 D3
Daffodill Ln
23700 MtgC 77365 2972 B6
Dagg Rd
4300 HarC 77047 4374 E6
4300 HOUS 77047 4374 E6
4300 HOUS 77048 4374 E6
4400 HOUS 77048 4375 A6
Dahila St
500 PRVW 77445 3100 C2
Dahlia Ln
4200 DRPK 77536 4249 B1
5600 KATY 77493 3813 B5
Dahlia St
7200 HOUS 77087 4105 B3
7500 HOUS 77012 4105 B3
Dahlia Brook Ln
16900 MtgC 77385 2676 E5
Dahlia Brook Wy
- HarC 77049 3829 B4
19800 FBnC 77469 4234 D2
Dahlia Field Wy
3500 HarC 77082 4096 B3
Dahlia Glen Ln
- HarC 77433 3252 A7
Dahlia Hill St
3500 FBnC 77545 4498 C7
Dahlia Trail Pl
10 WDLD 77382 2819 C3
Dahlstrom Rd
1600 STFE 77511 4869 B2
Dailey St
500 BYTN 77520 4112 D1
Dain Pl
3500 HarC 77338 3263 E5
Dairy Ashford Rd
- HOUS 77077 3957 D4
- SGLD 77477 4237 E6
300 HOUS 77079 3957 D3
2600 HOUS 77082 3957 D7
2600 HOUS 77082 4097 D1
4000 HOUS 77072 4097 D3
8600 HOUS 77072 4237 D1
8600 HOUS 77099 4237 D2
11000 HOUS 77477 4237 E4
11000 MDWP 77477 4237 E4
11000 MDWP 77478 4237 E4
11000 SGLD 77099 4237 E4
11000 SGLD 77478 4237 E6
12700 SGLD 77478 4368 E1
12700 STAF 77477 4237 E7
12700 STAF 77477 4368 E1
12700 STAF 77478 4237 E6
Dairy Ashford Rd SPR-41
13100 SGLD 77478 4368 D2
N Dairy Ashford Rd
200 HOUS 77079 3957 D1
400 HOUS 77079 3818 C7
400 HOUS 77084 3818 C7
S Dairy Ashford Rd
- HOUS 77079 3957 D5
1000 HOUS 77077 3957 D5
Dairy Brook Dr
12700 HOUS 77099 4237 D1
Dairybrook Cove
5600 FBnC 77479 4366 E5
5600 FBnC 77479 4367 A5
Dairy Gate Dr
22700 HarC 77373 3115 E7
Dairy Oaks Dr
4200 HarC 77532 3412 D2
Dairy View Ln
7800 HOUS 77072 4097 E7
9300 HOUS 77099 4237 E1
Daisey Ln
18400 MtgC 77365 2972 A6
Daisey Bell Ln
1500 HarC 77067 3402 C6
Daisie Mae
2800 HarC 77032 3545 E2
2900 HarC 77032 3546 A2
Daisie Mae Dr
3300 HarC 77032 3546 A2
Daisy Av
600 FBnC 77545 4623 D1
Daisy St
1000 HOUS 77012 4105 B3
2700 DKSN 77539 4753 E2
3100 PASD 77503 4248 B3
3100 PASD 77505 4248 B3
6700 BKVL 77581 4376 A6
Daisy Bloom Ct
20500 HarC 77433 3251 A4
Daisy Brook Ln
9500 HarC 77044 3689 C3
Daisy Chain
- HarC 77377 3107 E5
- HarC 77377 3108 A5
Daisy Creek Tr
16300 HarC 77433 3251 A5
Daisyetta St
14200 HOUS 77085 4371 B3
Daisy Meadow Ct
12500 HarC 77041 3679 E2
Daisy Meadow Dr
4200 HarC 77449 3816 A1
4700 HarC 77449 3677 A7
Daisy Mist Ln
9800 HarC 77038 3543 E5
Daisy View Ct
16200 MtgC 77302 2679 B4
Dakar Dr
11500 HarC 77065 3398 D7
Dakota Ct
8900 FBnC 77459 4621 B6
Dakota St
600 SHUS 77587 4246 B2
1000 HOUS 77017 4246 B2
1600 LGCY 77573 4632 B5
4200 DKSN 77539 4753 E3
4500 DKSN 77539 4754 A3
N Dakota St
1300 BYTN 77520 4112 B2
S Dakota St
1900 BYTN 77520 4112 B2
Dakota Bend Dr
14400 HarC 77429 3253 E4
Dakota Ridge Ct
10000 HarC 77095 3537 E3
Dakota Ridge Dr
17200 HarC 77095 3537 E3
Dakota Ridge Pl
10 WDLD 77381 2820 B3
Dakota Run Ln
1900 HarC 77493 3814 A6
Dakota Springs Dr
19500 HarC 77377 3109 B7
Dakton Dr
13100 HarC 77039 3546 A4
Dalby St
300 HOUS 77034 4246 E5
Dale Dr
100 HarC 77037 3544 D5
100 HarC 77060 3544 D5
12500 HarC 77429 3398 A2
Dale St
1200 BYTN 77520 3973 C7
11800 GLSN 77554 5220 D5
Dalea Pl
10 WDLD 77382 2674 A4
Dalebrook Dr
11100 HOUS 77016 3687 B1
Daleburg Dr
14300 HarC 77032 3546 D2
Dalebury Ct
12200 HarC 77066 3401 A5
Dalebury Dr
- HarC 77346 3264 D4
Dale Carnegie Ln
6000 HOUS 77036 4100 A3
6000 HOUS 77074 4100 A3
Dalecrest Dr
9500 HOUS 77080 3820 C6
Daleford Ln
12900 HarC 77049 3828 B1
Dale Forest Ct
18400 HarC 77346 3408 C2
Dale Green Ln
2500 FBnC 77545 4498 C6
Dale Grove Ct
7200 HarC 77346 3265 A5
Dale Hollow Ln
14600 HarC 77429 3397 D4
Dalehurst Ct
10300 HOUS 77075 4377 A3
Dale Oak Wy
16700 HOUS 77058 4507 D3
Dalerose Ct
1300 HOUS 77062 4379 E7
Daleside Dr
12100 HOUS 77099 4237 E3
Dalewood Dr
500 HarC 77060 3544 D5
500 MSCY 77489 4370 E4
Dali Ln
2200 FBnC 77459 4621 B7
Dalian St
1500 LMQU 77568 4990 A2
Dalkey Dr
11900 HOUS 77045 4242 C6
Dall Ln
2700 FBnC 77459 4621 B7
Dallam Ct
8700 HarC 77064 3540 C6
Dallam Ln
10100 HarC 77064 3540 C6
Dallas Av
800 RSBG 77471 4490 D5
5300 ARLA 77583 4623 B5
Dallas Ln
3100 BzaC 77583 4500 E7
E Dallas Rd
100 FBnC 77545 4499 D6
500 BzaC 77583 4499 D6
500 PRLD 77545 4499 D6
W Dallas Rd
100 FBnC 77545 4499 A6
1000 FBnC 77545 4498 E6
Dallas St
- BYTN 77520 3973 A5
200 LGCY 77573 4632 B4
300 LGCY 77573 4631 E3
400 HOUS 77002 3963 B4
400 HOUS 77017 4246 B2
400 SHUS 77017 4246 B2
400 SHUS 77587 4246 D4
1200 HOUS 77010 3963 C5
1400 PASD 77502 4247 D1
1500 HOUS 77003 3963 D6
3900 HOUS 77023 3964 A6
7000 HOUS 77011 4104 E1
7100 HarC 77521 3832 D5
7100 HOUS 77011 4105 A1
7400 HOUS 77023 4105 A1
21200 MtgC 77357 2827 B6
29500 MtgC 77354 2818 A2
29800 MtgC 77354 2817 E2
E Dallas St
100 CNRO 77301 2384 C3
W Dallas St
100 CNRO 77301 2384 A4
100 HOUS 77002 3963 B4
500 CNRO 77301 2383 E4
700 HOUS 77019 3963 A4
1600 HOUS 77019 3962 C4
Dallie-Sue St
26400 MtgC 77372 2683 C2
26400 SPLD 77372 2683 B2
Dalmally St
9500 HarC 77379 3255 C3
Dalmatian Dr
3200 HOUS 77045 4373 A2
4600 HOUS 77045 4372 B3
Dalmatian Ln
3400 DRPK 77536 4109 C7
3400 DRPK 77536 4249 C1
Dalmolin Rd
7600 MNVL 77578 4626 A7
7700 MNVL 77578 4625 E7
Dalmore Ct
9300 HarC 77095 3538 C4
Dalston Dr
- HarC 77047 4374 D6
Dalstrom St
3500 HarC 77047 4374 C3
Dalton St
2700 HOUS 77017 4105 D5
Dalton Oaks Dr
- HarC 77015 3829 B4
Daltonridge Dr
4100 MtgC 77386 3115 B1
Dalton Springs Ln
21500 HarC 77449 3815 B3
Dalton Trace Ct
2000 HarC 77373 3114 C6
Dalview St
2400 HOUS 77091 3683 B4
Daly Dr
14400 HOUS 77077 3956 E3
Daly Pl
10 HOUS 77009 3963 C2
Damacso Cove
- LGCY 77565 4633 D3
Damascon Ct
12500 HarC 77014 3402 A3
Damascus Dr
- HOUS 77088 3543 E7
8600 HOUS 77088 3683 E1
Damask Rose Wy
10 WDLD 77382 2673 E7
10 WDLD 77382 2819 E1
Damico Ln
11100 MtgC 77306 2532 E1
Damico St
3000 HOUS 77019 3962 C4
Damon Ct
800 HOUS 77006 3962 E5
32100 MtgC 77354 2673 B5
Damon St
100 FBnC 77469 4365 A7
100 RHMD 77469 4365 A7
300 FBnC 77469 4492 A1
300 RHMD 77469 4492 A1
700 RSBG 77471 4491 A4
Dan Ln
21700 MtgC 77355 2960 E6
Dan Rd
29500 MtgC 77354 2672 A7
Dan St
1600 HOUS 77020 3964 C1
Dana Dr
10 GLSN 77554 5332 D2
100 HarC 77562 3832 A3
22600 HarC 77377 3108 E2
W Dana Ln
500 PNPV 77024 3959 E3
Dana Wy
2000 PASD 77502 4107 D7
Dana Leigh Dr
5100 HarC 77066 3401 A2
Danalyn Ct
18800 HarC 77346 3264 D7
Dana Lynn Ln
4500 BzaC 77584 4501 E6
4500 BzaC 77584 4502 A6
Danbridge Ct
18900 HarC 77377 3254 A1
Danbury Cir
1700 FRDW 77546 4750 A2
Danbury Ct
1100 PRLD 77581 4376 D6
Danbury Ln
4400 SGLD 77479 4495 B4
Danbury Rd
900 HOUS 77055 3821 D7
Danbury Bridge Dr
17300 HarC 77095 3537 D4
Danbury Chase Tr
3400 FBnC 77545 4498 D7
Danbury Hollow Ln
8700 HOUS 77075 4376 E2
8700 HOUS 77075 4377 A2
Danbury Park Ln
500 HarC 77073 3259 A4
Danbury Run Dr
13600 HarC 77041 3679 B4
Danby Heath Ln
1400 HarC 77073 3259 B5
Dancing Breeze Pl
10 WDLD 77382 2673 C6
Dan Cox Av
1400 KATY 77493 3813 E7
Dancy Rd
5400 HarC 77041 3680 D6
5400 HOUS 77041 3680 D6
Dandelion Ln
11800 HOUS 77071 4239 E5
Dandelion Field
7600 HarC 77083 4096 E6
Dandridge Av
1300 PASD 77502 4246 E2
Dandy St
7800 HOUS 77016 3825 D1
8800 HOUS 77016 3686 D6
Dandyline Wy
10200 HarC 77375 3110 B4
Dandy Park Ct
11700 HOUS 77047 4373 D1
Dane St
7200 HOUS 77093 3825 A2
Danebridge Dr
5100 HarC 77084 3677 E6
Dane Hill Dr
7400 HarC 77389 2966 A2
Danek Rd
3300 HarC 77532 3693 E6
3300 HarC 77562 3693 E6
3900 HarC 77532 3694 A5
Daneswood Ct
2300 HarC 77388 3113 A3
Danette Ct
8000 HarC 77379 3255 E2
8000 HarC 77379 3256 A2
Danfield Dr
100 HOUS 77047 4373 B5
4800 HOUS 77053 4372 A5
Danford Dr
15700 HOUS 77053 4371 E5
Danford Ln
- HOUS 77016 3687 A1
11600 HarC 77050 3547 A7
11600 HOUS 77016 3547 A7
Danforth Cross
- HarC 77396 3547 E2
Danforth Dr
1000 HOUS 77062 4379 D7
2900 TXCY 77590 4874 D5
Danforth Wy
9200 FBnC 77083 4237 A1
Dangler St
600 SEBK 77586 4509 E3
Dani Ln
200 DKSN 77539 4754 D1
Daniel Dr
- HarC 77041 3539 C5
- HarC 77065 3539 C5
Daniel Rd
22100 MtgC 77357 2973 E3
Daniel St
200 BYTN 77520 4112 D1
8500 HOUS 77054 4242 C1
15100 MtgC 77354 2669 C1
Daniella Dr
10600 HOUS 77034 4246 E7
Danielle Ct
9100 HOUS 77099 4238 B1
Danielle Dr
5200 PASD 77505 4249 B3
Danielle Ln
1300 PRLD 77581 4504 E5
1300 PRLD 77581 4505 A5
E Daniel Oak Cir
22300 HarC 77389 3112 E1
N Daniel Oak Cir
3400 HarC 77389 3112 C1
S Daniel Oak Cir
3400 HarC 77389 3112 C1
Danna Ln
200 HOUS 77009 3824 B4
Danna St
800 LGCY 77573 4632 A1
Danover Rd
400 KATY 77494 3952 C1
700 KATY 77493 3952 C1
Danphe Landing Ct
19200 HarC 77375 3110 A7
Danpree St
3900 PASD 77504 4247 D5
Dan River Dr
24200 HarC 77493 3814 A5
Dans Ln
17900 MtgC 77302 2678 E7
17900 MtgC 77302 2824 E1
E Dansby Dr
10 GLSN 77551 5222 B1
N Dansby Dr
10 GLSN 77551 5222 B1
W Dansby Dr
10 GLSN 77551 5222 B1
Danshire Ct
6300 HOUS 77049 3828 A3
Danshire Dr
13300 HOUS 77049 3828 A3
Dante Dr
15900 HOUS 77053 4371 E6
Danton Falls Dr
13900 HarC 77041 3679 B4
Danube St
1000 HOUS 77051 4243 C2
Danubina St
10 BYTN 77520 4113 B1
600 BYTN 77520 3973 B7
Danvers Dr
11800 HarC 77044 3827 D1
12600 HarC 77049 3828 B1
Danville
- HOUS 77046 4101 E1
- HOUS 77098 4101 E1
Danville Crossing Ct
10 WDLD 77385 2676 C3
Danziger
- FBnC 77469 4615 A2
- RSBG 77469 4615 A2
Danzinger Rd
3200 RSBG 77469 4615 C1
3200 RSBG 77471 4615 C1
Daphne St
3200 HOUS 77021 4103 B5
Dapper
600 HOUS 77037 3684 B1
600 HOUS 77088 3684 B1
Dapple Ln
9600 HarC 77065 3539 D4
Dappled Tr
4000 HarC 77346 3408 A3
Dappled Filly Dr
25200 HarC 77375 2965 D2
Dappled Glen Ct
8100 MtgC 77385 2676 B6
Dappled Grove Tr
4800 HarC 77346 3408 B2
Dappled Ridge Wy
3500 PRLD 77581 4504 A6
20700 HarC 77338 3261 B3
Dappled Sun
10 WDLD 77381 2821 D4
Dapple Gray St
10 WDLD 77382 2820 B1
Dapplewood Ln
5500 HarC 77449 3676 D6
Darbey Trace Dr
9600 HarC 77379 3255 D5
Darby Cir
100 MtgC 77385 2822 E6
100 MtgC 77385 2823 A6
Darby Ct
3500 BzaC 77584 4501 C7
Darby Ln
1600 FBnC 77545 4622 C3
2000 MSCY 77545 4622 C3
Darby Lp
11000 MtgC 77385 2823 A6
Darby St
4100 GlsC 77518 4634 D2
Darby Brook Dr
2700 FBnC 77545 4498 C6
Darby Cove
13900 HOUS 77077 3956 E5
Darbydale Dr
14800 HarC 77090 3258 D7
14800 HarC 77090 3402 D1
Darbydale Crossing Ln
800 HarC 77090 3258 D7
Darby House Ct
13500 HarC 77429 3397 A4
Darby House St
16400 HarC 77429 3397 A3
Darby Mill Ln
9800 HarC 77095 3537 C3
Darby Ridge Ct
19200 HarC 77379 3112 A6
Darby Rose Ln
- HarC 77044 3549 C3
Darby Springs Wy
14100 HarC 77429 3396 A2
14200 HarC 77429 3395 E1
Darby Square Tr
5500 HarC 77084 3677 D5
Darby Trails Dr
200 FBnC 77479 4366 D5
Darby Wy Dr
6000 HarC 77389 2966 D6
Darcus St
3700 SSPL 77005 4101 D4
Darcy Dr
1000 GLSN 77554 5107 B7
Dardanelles Ct
18100 HarC 77084 3816 E4
Darden Dr
1200 HarC 77336 3266 E1
Darden Ln
1300 SEBK 77586 4382 E7
Darden St
3600 HOUS 77093 3686 A7
Dardenelle Ct
10 CNRO 77384 2676 A3
Dare Rd
7500 BzaC 77584 4627 B3
Darfield Ct
1400 HarC 77014 3402 C1
Dargail St
11000 FBnC 77099 4237 D4
11000 FBnC 77478 4237 D4
11000 HOUS 77099 4237 D4
11100 SGLD 77478 4237 D4
Daria Ct
700 HOUS 77079 3956 E2
Daria Dr
800 HOUS 77079 3956 E3
Darien St
7400 HOUS 77028 3826 A1
8000 HOUS 77028 3687 A7
Daris Ct
1900 MSCY 77489 4370 B3
Darius Ln
- FBnC 77479 4366 C7
Darjean St
13400 HarC 77039 3546 E4
13900 HarC 77396 3546 E3
Dark Cavern Ct
17200 HarC 77095 3396 E7
Dark Forest Ln
18000 HarC 77060 3403 D4
Darkhorse
- HarC 77338 3260 E4
Darkwood Dr
5900 HOUS 77088 3682 D2
Darla Ln
9600 HarC 77038 3544 A5
Darla Knolls Dr
11100 HarC 77375 3110 A3
Darlene Ln
19800 MtgC 77365 2972 D3
Darlene St
- HOUS 77034 4247 A5
Darling Av
3000 PASD 77506 4108 A4
3500 PASD 77503 4108 B4
Darling St
4900 HOUS 77007 3962 A1
5700 HOUS 77007 3961 E1
Darlinghurst Dr
- CNRO 77384 2675 E3
- CNRO 77384 2676 A4
3500 HOUS 77045 4372 D2
5700 HOUS 77085 4371 E2
5700 HOUS 77085 4372 A2
Darling Point Ct
18000 HarC 77429 3252 B7
Darlington Cres
10 SGLD 77479 4495 B2
Darlington Ct
6100 LGCY 77573 4630 B7
Darlington Dr
7800 HOUS 77028 3687 B7
Darlington Oak St
5800 HOUS 77016 3686 E2
Darmera Ct
14300 HarC 77429 3397 C2
Darnay Dr
7600 HOUS 77033 4243 E2
Darnell Cir
7400 HOUS 77074 4099 E7
Darnell Ct
3600 MSCY 77459 4497 E6
Darnell St
10 CNRO 77301 2384 A2
5000 HOUS 77096 4101 A7
5600 HOUS 77096 4100 C7
5800 HOUS 77074 4100 B7
7300 HOUS 77074 4099 E7
Darnley Ln
1500 HOUS 77077 3956 E4
Daroca Dr
- LGCY 77539 4633 D3
- LGCY 77565 4633 D2
Darone Ct
700 MtgC 77386 2968 D1
Darrah Dr
14100 HarC 77090 3258 C7
14100 HarC 77090 3402 C1

STREET Block City ZIP Map# Grid
Darrel St
2900 PASD 77502 4247 B3
Darrell Springs Ln
10000 HarC 77375 3255 A2
Darrian Ln
16100 HarC 77530 3829 D4
Darrington Ln
13700 HarC 77069 3400 B2
Darschelle Ct
14400 HarC 77069 3256 C6
Darschelle Dr
5400 HarC 77069 3256 C6
Darsey St
4300 BLAR 77401 4101 C6
4300 HOUS 77401 4101 B6
Dart St
900 HOUS 77002 3963 C3
900 HOUS 77007 3963 B2
Dartford Ct
6900 HarC 77379 3256 D3
Dartmaker Ct
25600 MtgC 77365 3117 E3
Dartmoor Ct
10 SGLD 77479 4495 D4
Dartmoor St
10 SGLD 77479 4495 D3
Dartmouth Dr
100 TYLV 77586 4508 E2
3100 PASD 77503 4108 A4
Dartmouth Ln
1100 DRPK 77536 4249 C2
Dartmouth St
2200 KATY 77493 3813 D5
4100 WUNP 77005 4101 C2
Dartmouth Field Ln
3200 FBnC 77545 4498 C7
Dartmouth Hill Ct
2300 HarC 77493 3814 B5
Darton Dr
15800 HOUS 77053 4371 E5
15800 HOUS 77053 4372 A5
Dartwood Dr
14100 HarC 77049 3828 C3
Darwin Rd
3900 HarC 77093 3686 B2
Darwood Ct
16100 FBnC 77083 4236 A1
Daryns Landing Dr
2600 HarC 77038 3543 A4
Dashwood Dr
- HOUS 77072 4097 E4
- HOUS 77074 4100 B4
5300 BLAR 77401 4100 D4
5300 HOUS 77081 4100 C4
5400 BLAR 77081 4100 D4
7600 HOUS 77036 4099 D4
11800 HOUS 77072 4098 A4
Dashwood Forest St
10 WDLD 77381 2821 A3
Date St
3500 HOUS 77026 3825 E6
17400 HarC 77044 3551 C7
Date Meadow Ln
10000 HarC 77375 3110 A4
Datewood Ln
9900 HarC 77375 3110 C4
Datonia St
100 BLAR 77401 4101 A6
Dattner Rd
10 HOUS 77013 3828 A5
Dattner St
10 HOUS 77013 3828 A5
Daubern Ct
14700 HarC 77429 3253 E7
Daugherty St
1300 HOUS 77029 3965 B4
2000 WALR 77484 3102 A4
2100 WALR 77484 3101 E4
Daughtery Rd
- BzaC 77584 4501 C5
- PRLD 77584 4501 C5
Daughtie Ln
- MtgC 77354 2818 E6
Daun St
5500 HarC 77039 3546 D6
Dauntless Dr
- HarC 77066 3401 B7
Dauphin Ct
2500 NSUB 77058 4508 B4
Davenmoor Ct
3100 FBnC 77494 3953 B7
Davenport St
4300 HOUS 77051 4243 C3
4600 HOUS 77033 4243 C3
Davenport Manor Dr
- HarC 77429 3397 B2
Davenridge Ln
- HarC 77047 4374 B5
Daventry Ln
12300 HarC 77039 3545 E5
Davenway Dr
17300 HarC 77084 3677 E3
17300 HarC 77084 3678 A3
Davenwood Cir
11700 HarC 77089 4378 B7
Davenwood Ct
11700 HarC 77089 4378 B6
Davenwood Dr
11400 HarC 77089 4378 B6
Davey Ln
1900 SEBK 77586 4382 D6
Davey Crockett
15900 HarC 77530 3830 B6
Davey Oaks St
3000 PRLD 77584 4502 A6
David
19200 HarC 77532 3411 D5
David Av
500 LGCY 77573 4632 B3
David Ln
3800 MAGA 77355 2669 C7
3800 MtgC 77355 2669 C7
10700 HarC 77532 3693 E5
20100 MtgC 77357 2827 C6
22700 MtgC 77357 2973 D3
David St
- ALVN 77511 4749 A7
- HOUS 77054 4242 D1
300 FRDW 77546 4629 B1
2700 RSBG 77471 4491 A7
5500 TXCY 77539 4755 E2
11800 GLSN 77554 5220 D5
16200 HarC 77530 3830 C6
S David St
- HOUS 77054 4242 D1
David Forest Ln
100 MtgC 77384 2675 A1

STREET Block City ZIP Map# Grid
David Glen Dr
16100 FRDW 77546 4505 E7
16600 FRDW 77546 4629 E1
16600 FRDW 77546 4630 A1
David Hill Ln
16100 HarC 77447 3250 A7
David Memorial Dr
- MtgC 77385 2822 B2
- SHEH 77385 2822 B2
Davids Bend Dr
5400 FBnC 77479 4366 E5
Davids Crest Ct
22300 FBnC 77450 4094 A2
22400 FBnC 77450 4093 E2
Davidson Ln
10 HarC 77336 2976 A2
Davidson St
700 HOUS 77091 3684 A6
David Vetter Blvd
- SHEH 77385 2822 B3
Da Vina Ln
12000 HarC 77429 3398 B2
Da Vince St
2800 MtgC 77357 2829 B1
2800 RMFT 77357 2829 B1
Da Vinci Dr
2300 PRLD 77089 4504 E3
2300 PRLD 77581 4504 E3
Da Vinci Wy
- RMFT 77357 2829 C1
2800 MtgC 77357 2829 C1
Davis
100 HMBL 77338 3263 A6
Davis Av
2500 RSBG 77471 4491 A5
Davis Rd
100 LGCY 77573 4508 C6
600 ARLA 77545 4623 A3
600 ARLA 77583 4623 A3
600 FBnC 77545 4623 A3
600 FBnC 77583 4623 A3
1700 BzaC 77511 4866 A3
21400 MtgC 77372 2535 C4
W Davis Rd
- ARLA 77545 4623 B3
- FBnC 77545 4623 B3
4800 ARLA 77583 4623 A3
4800 FBnC 77583 4623 A3
Davis St
100 HMBL 77338 3262 E6
100 HMBL 77338 3263 A6
900 PASD 77506 4107 C5
1200 PASD 77502 4107 C6
1600 HOUS 77026 3963 E1
2400 HOUS 77026 3824 E7
3000 LPRT 77571 4251 E7
3000 LPRT 77571 4382 E1
6900 BzaC 77584 4627 A4
29900 MtgC 77355 2816 A3
E Davis St
100 CNRO 77301 2384 C5
2500 CNRO 77301 2385 B3
11000 CNRO 77303 2385 B3
11000 CTSH 77301 2385 B3
11000 CTSH 77303 2385 B3
E Davis St SR-105
700 CNRO 77301 2384 E4
2500 CNRO 77301 2385 B3
11000 CNRO 77303 2385 B3
11000 CTSH 77301 2385 B3
11000 CTSH 77303 2385 B3
W Davis St
100 CNRO 77301 2384 A5
600 CNRO 77301 2383 E5
1300 CNRO 77304 2383 E5
5100 CNRO 77304 2382 A1
W Davis St SR-105
100 CNRO 77301 2384 A5
600 CNRO 77301 2383 E5
1300 CNRO 77304 2383 E5
4200 CNRO 77304 2382 A1
Davis Bend Rd
100 ALVN 77511 4866 E2
2000 BzaC 77511 4866 B4
Davis Cottage Ct
10 WDLD 77385 2676 C4
Davis-Hall Rd
4200 STFE 77510 4870 D7
4500 STFE 77510 4986 D1
Davis Mountain Dr
11900 FBnC 77478 4236 B6
Davison St
100 PASD 77506 4107 D3
Davis Post Rd
400 ARLA 77583 4623 C3
400 FBnC 77583 4623 C3
600 PRLD 77583 4623 C3
Davis Run Dr
- HarC 77429 3397 D3
Davon Ln
1300 NSUB 77058 4507 E6
1800 NSUB 77058 4508 A5
Davy Jones Ct
16300 HarC 77532 3552 B3
Davy Jones Rd
16700 GLSN 77554 5331 E6
16700 JMAB 77554 5331 E6
Daw Collins Rd
10300 MtgC 77372 2535 B5
Dawkins Ln
2500 HarC 77014 3402 A2
Dawkins St
1700 HarC 77562 3832 B4
Dawn Av
200 FRDW 77546 4505 B7
Dawn Ct
5600 LGCY 77573 4630 D7
Dawn Dr
500 LGCY 77573 4630 D7
Dawn Ln
- PRLD 77581 4503 E2
3800 FBnC 77469 4233 E6
Dawn Rd
12400 HarC 77067 3402 E6
12400 HOUS 77067 3402 E6
Dawn St
4100 HOUS 77025 4241 C4
Dawn Bloom Ln
6800 FBnC 77469 4615 E5
Dawnblush Ct
16400 HarC 77095 3538 C3
Dawnblush Ln
8700 HarC 77095 3538 B5
Dawnbriar Ct
7500 HOUS 77489 4371 B5
Dawn Brook Ct
2200 PRLD 77584 4501 A2

STREET Block City ZIP Map# Grid
Dawn Brook Dr
1900 PRLD 77584 4501 A2
Dawnbrook Dr
15500 HarC 77068 3257 B4
Dawn Brook Ln
300 MtgC 77384 2675 A1
Dawnburst Dr
5200 HarC 77346 3264 C5
Dawn Canyon Rd
19300 HarC 77084 3816 A4
Dawnchase Ct
5500 HarC 77069 3256 C7
Dawnchase Dr
- HarC 77069 3256 C7
Dawn Cloud Ln
25800 FBnC 77494 4093 A2
Dawn Creek Ln
4200 HarC 77388 3112 C4
Dawn Crest Ct
2000 LGCY 77573 4509 A7
Dawncrest Wy
16300 FBnC 77478 4236 A5
N Dawn Cypress Ct
4000 HOUS 77059 4380 B3
S Dawn Cypress Ct
3900 HOUS 77059 4380 B4
Dawn-Dusk Dr
- HarC 77095 3396 D7
- HarC 77433 3396 D7
Dawnfields Dr
9200 HarC 77064 3540 D2
Dawngate Dr
5000 HarC 77373 3115 C5
Dawnglen Ct
4000 FBnC 77469 4615 E5
6600 HarC 77379 3111 C4
Dawn Harvest Ct
9600 HarC 77064 3540 C2
Dawn Harvest Ln
11100 HarC 77064 3540 C2
Dawn Haven Ct
17300 HarC 77095 3537 E6
Dawnheath Dr
11300 HarC 77433 3396 B7
Dawn Heath Ln
6800 HarC 77379 3111 B3
Dawn Hill Dr
300 FRDW 77546 4628 E7
Dawn Hollow Ln
13000 HarC 77072 4097 C7
Dawnhollow Ln
1900 FBnC 77494 3953 D5
Dawnington Pl
5200 SGLD 77479 4495 B4
Dawn Lily Dr
5000 HarC 77388 3112 B3
Dawn Marie Ln
16100 FBnC 77478 4236 A2
Dawn Meadows Dr
15100 HarC 77068 3257 B5
Dawn Mist Ct
7500 FBnC 77479 4494 A4
12000 PRLD 77583 4500 C5
14600 MtgC 77354 2670 B1
20200 HarC 77346 3264 C3
Dawnmist Ct
20400 HarC 77346 3265 B3
Dawn Mist Dr
20000 HarC 77346 3264 C4
Dawn Point Ct
12500 HarC 77065 3539 C1
Dawn Quail Ct
8200 HOUS 77489 4370 E7
Dawnridge Dr
2800 BzaC 77584 4501 C6
6300 HOUS 77035 4240 A5
8500 HOUS 77071 4239 C5
Dawnridge Ln
9000 HOUS 77099 4238 B1
Dawn Ridge Wy
800 SEBK 77586 4509 E1
Dawn Rise Ct
3900 FBnC 77545 4622 D1
Dawn River Ln
2500 BzaC 77581 4502 A3
Dawn Rose Ct
20600 HarC 77379 3111 B4
Dawn Shadow Wy
2200 FBnC 77545 4498 C7
Dawn Shadows Dr
17000 HarC 77346 3408 A2
Dawn Sky Ln
800 LGCY 77573 4633 B2
Dawn Square Cir
20300 HarC 77449 3815 C1
Dawn Star Dr
2600 MSCY 77489 4370 D7
6700 HarC 77346 3264 E7
Dawn Timbers Ct
21600 HarC 77338 3261 E2
Dawntreader Dr
19100 HarC 77429 3395 E1
Dawn Vale Dr
14600 HOUS 77062 4506 D1
Dawnview St
6000 HOUS 77087 4244 E1
Dawn Wind Ln
2200 MtgC 77386 2969 D6
Dawnwood Dr
3200 MtgC 77380 2821 A7
3700 MtgC 77381 2821 A7
3700 WDLD 77381 2821 A7
11800 HOUS 77013 3966 E2
Dawson Dr
2600 PRLD 77581 4504 C4
3900 GLSN 77554 5441 A5
Dawson Ln
3000 HOUS 77051 4243 A4
Dawson Rd
11100 PRLD 77583 4500 D6
Dawson Creek Dr
6300 PASD 77503 4248 E1
Dawson Mill Ct
16500 HarC 77095 3538 A6
Dawson Springs Dr
11100 FBnC 77469 4092 C7
Day Dr
2200 PRLD 77584 4501 C2
12000 MtgC 77303 2239 D6
Day Ln
40500 WlrC 77445 2954 A3
Day Rd
10900 HOUS 77043 3819 C7
Day St
- HOUS 77006 3963 A7
4000 HOUS 77002 3963 A7
Daybreak Ln
11100 HarC 77429 3538 E1

STREET Block City ZIP Map# Grid
Dayco Av
4000 HOUS 77092 3821 B1
Dayco Dr
4700 HOUS 77040 3682 B7
4700 HOUS 77092 3682 B7
Dayco St
4300 HOUS 77092 3821 A1
Daycoach Ln
8600 HarC 77064 3541 E5
Dayflower Dr
- HarC 77449 3677 A7
3900 HarC 77449 3816 A2
Dayhill Dr
7300 HarC 77379 3256 B3
Day Hollow Ln
12600 HarC 77070 3399 B5
Daylight Ln
7200 HarC 77095 3678 B1
Daylight Ridge Ct
- WDLD 77382 2819 B1
Daylilly Ct
600 FBnC 77469 4492 D7
Daylilly Creek Dr
7900 HarC 77083 4097 B6
Day Lily Pl
10 WDLD 77381 2674 E7
Day Lily Wy
1800 HarC 77067 3402 B7
Daylily Hills Dr
21400 HarC 77388 3113 B2
Dayport St
5000 HOUS 77018 3683 B7
5500 HOUS 77091 3683 B6
Dayridge Ln
- HOUS 77048 4375 D4
Days Dawn Dr
12500 HarC 77377 3254 B3
Daystrom Ln
28100 FBnC 77494 3951 D5
Dayton St
- BYTN 77520 3972 A7
7700 HOUS 77012 4105 B1
Daytona Ct
2400 FRDW 77546 4629 A7
Dayton Ridge Ln
19900 HarC 77433 3537 A6
Dayton Springs Dr
19700 HarC 77433 3251 E7
Day Trail Ln
10500 HarC 77379 3110 B5
Day Trip Tr
15300 HarC 77429 3252 B7
Daywood Dr
13100 HarC 77038 3543 B2
D Bar Dr
12500 STFE 77510 4871 A7
Deadman St
4000 PASD 77505 4248 D5
Deadwood Dr
7400 HOUS 77040 3682 A1
7600 HarC 77040 3682 A1
Deadwood Ln
29000 SHEH 77381 2822 A2
Deaf Smith Dr
1900 FBnC 77469 4365 C3
10600 LPRT 77571 4110 D6
21700 GLSN 77554 5441 A4
De Akins
23900 HarC 77447 3105 A4
Deal St
3000 HOUS 77025 4101 E7
3000 HOUS 77025 4102 A7
Deams St
1700 HOUS 77093 3824 D1
Dean Ct
17600 MtgC 77302 2679 E2
Dean St
4700 GLSN 77554 5220 D7
5500 HarC 77039 3546 D4
22500 HarC 77373 3113 E2
Deanmont Dr
16300 HOUS 77053 4372 A7
Deanna St
- HOUS 77016 3687 A4
Deanne St
10 BYTN 77520 4113 B1
200 BYTN 77520 3973 B7
Dean White Dr
- HarC 77015 3968 C4
Deanwood Dr
9300 HOUS 77040 3682 A2
Deanwood St
9700 HOUS 77040 3682 A1
Dearborn St
7400 HOUS 77055 3821 D5
Deasa Dr
2300 HarC 77373 3114 D7
Deaton Dr
7900 HarC 77346 3265 B4
Deaton Mill Dr
17100 HarC 77095 3537 E3
Deats Ln
- TXCY 77539 4754 D5
Deats Rd
- GLSN 77554 5333 A2
100 DKSN 77539 4753 E1
2600 GlsC 77539 4753 E2
3100 DKSN 77539 4754 A1
4000 DKSN 77539 4633 A7
4000 GlsC 77539 4633 A7
7700 TXCY 77539 4754 E5
Deauville Dr
20700 HarC 77388 3112 E4
Deauville Plaza Dr
5500 HOUS 77092 3821 E3
Debbi Ln
31000 SGCH 77355 2961 E3
Debbie Ct
4300 RSBG 77471 4491 C6
Debbie Dr
- HarC 77060 3403 B5
16000 HarC 77530 3830 B4
17500 BzaC 77584 4627 D2
Debbie Ln
400 ALVN 77511 4867 D6
1100 HOUS 77055 3820 C7
9700 HarC 77038 3543 E5
32500 MtgC 77362 2963 C1
Debbie St
2100 FBnC 77469 4492 A7
2100 FBnC 77469 4616 A1
2100 RSBG 77469 4492 A7
Debbie Gay Dr
8100 HarC 77040 3541 C7
Debbies Cir
20100 MtgC 77357 2828 B6
Debbie's Pl
- WlrC 77447 2813 D4

STREET Block City ZIP Map# Grid
Debbie Terrace Dr
8600 HarC 77433 3537 C5
Debeney Dr
1500 HarC 77039 3545 C5
4700 HarC 77039 3546 C5
Debes Rd
11400 HarC 77044 3689 C1
De Boll St
10 HOUS 77022 3684 E6
10 HOUS 77022 3685 A6
Deborah Ln
3500 HOUS 77092 3821 D3
5100 BYTN 77521 3972 A1
Deborah St
2600 FBnC 77477 4370 A5
2600 STAF 77477 4370 A5
7100 HOUS 77012 4105 B5
7100 HOUS 77087 4105 B5
8200 HarC 77064 3541 C2
Deborah Ann Wy
20700 HOUS 77073 3259 B7
Debra Ln
23600 MtgC 77365 2973 D6
Debra Rd
10800 HOUS 77013 3827 C4
Debrah Ln
9600 HarC 77038 3544 A5
Debra's Trace Ln
4600 FBnC 77450 4094 D2
Debra Terrace Ct
1000 HOUS 77077 3956 E3
Debray Dr
21700 HarC 77388 3112 A2
Decathalon Ct
18800 HarC 77346 3265 D7
18800 HOUS 77346 3265 D7
Decatur Av
6700 BYTN 77520 3835 B6
Decatur Ct
2400 MtgC 77384 2529 A4
Decatur St
1500 HOUS 77002 3963 B3
1800 HOUS 77007 3963 A3
December Pine Ln
17600 HarC 77379 3256 A3
De Chirico Cir
17200 HarC 77379 3256 B3
Decision Dr
21800 HarC 77447 3105 E2
Deck Ct
16800 HarC 77532 3552 B1
Deckard St
6600 HOUS 77061 4245 B2
Decker Dr
900 BYTN 77520 3972 B4
2200 BYTN 77521 3972 B4
3700 BYTN 77520 3971 E2
3900 BYTN 77521 3971 E2
5000 HarC 77521 3971 D1
5100 HarC 77520 3971 D1
5500 HarC 77521 3832 A7
5600 BYTN 77520 3832 C7
6900 BYTN 77521 3832 A7
7100 HarC 77520 3832 B7
13400 MtgC 77355 2962 D1
Decker Dr SPR-330
900 BYTN 77520 3972 D7
2200 BYTN 77521 3972 C5
N Decker Dr
13100 MtgC 77355 2817 A7
13100 MtgC 77362 2817 A7
S Decker Dr
13100 MtgC 77355 2817 A7
W Decker Dr
33600 MtgC 77355 2817 A7
33600 MtgC 77362 2817 A7
Decker St
1600 CNRO 77301 2384 B2
Decker Field Ln
- PRLD 77583 4500 B4
Decker Forrest Blvd
800 MtgC 77354 2817 E5
Decker Hills Dr
- MtgC 77354 2818 A2
29500 MtgC 77354 2817 E3
Decker Industrial Cir
31700 MtgC 77362 2963 C2
Decker Oaks Dr
32000 MtgC 77362 2963 C1
Decker Park Ct
2400 FBnC 77469 4234 B7
Decker Pines St
32100 MtgC 77355 2963 B2
Decker Prairie Rd
32200 MtgC 77355 2963 A2
32200 MtgC 77362 2963 B2
32900 MtgC 77355 2962 E2
Decker Prairie Cemetery Rd
- MtgC 77355 2963 A2
Decker Prairie Rosehill Rd
22900 HarC 77377 2962 B6
22900 MtgC 77355 2962 B5
27600 MtgC 77355 2963 B2
27800 MtgC 77362 2963 B2
Decker Ridge Ct
6000 HarC 77449 3676 D4
Decker Ridge Dr
20200 HarC 77449 3676 D4
Decker Woods Dr
26800 MtgC 77354 2817 D4
Declaration Dr
2000 MSCY 77459 4369 E7
Decoster Blvd
- ALVN 77511 4749 C2
Decros Pt
2800 FBnC 77469 4234 A7
Dedman St
2400 PASD 77503 4248 D1
2800 PASD 77505 4248 D1
Dee Dr
5900 PASD 77505 4248 D4
Dee Rd
6100 PRLD 77581 4502 D1
Dee St
1500 CNRO 77301 2384 D7
Deeda Dr
4500 HOUS 77017 4245 D1
Deeds Rd
2800 HarC 77084 3816 C4
2800 HOUS 77084 3816 C4
Deen Dr
200 HarC 77336 3121 B6
Dee Oaks Dr
19400 HarC 77346 3264 E5
Deep Anchor Wy
2700 HarC 77532 3410 A6

STREET Block City ZIP Map# Grid
Deep Anchor Wy
3000 HarC 77532 3409 E6
Deep Brook Dr
17600 HarC 77379 3257 B2
Deepbrook St
2000 PRLD 77581 4504 A6
Deep Canyon Dr
6300 FBnC 77450 4094 D4
Deep Cliff Dr
23500 FBnC 77494 3953 C5
Deep Coral Ct
- HarC 77494 3953 A2
Deep Cove Dr
- PRLD 77584 4500 B2
Deep Cove Ln
14200 SGLD 77478 4236 E5
Deepcreek Ln
5600 HOUS 77091 3683 A6
Deep Dale Dr
19800 HarC 77338 3261 D4
Deepdale Dr
- WDLD 77384 2675 A3
Deep Dale Ln
200 PNVL 77304 2237 A4
Deep Forest Dr
- HOUS 77092 3682 D5
2500 HarC 77373 3114 D3
7000 HOUS 77091 3682 D4
7400 HOUS 77088 3682 D2
Deep Glen Ln
4800 HarC 77449 3677 B6
Deep Green Dr
7700 RSBG 77469 4492 C7
Deepgrove Dr
200 HarC 77037 3684 D1
W Deepgrove Dr
100 HarC 77037 3684 C1
Deep Lake Dr
2400 HOUS 77345 3120 B5
Deep Meadow Dr
11500 HarC 77064 3399 C7
23300 HarC 77375 2965 A5
Deep Oak Ct
2500 HOUS 77059 4380 B6
Deep Pines Ct
21700 MtgC 77365 2972 A1
Deep Pines Dr
16800 HarC 77379 3256 B3
21700 MtgC 77365 2972 A1
Deep Prairie Dr
17300 HarC 77095 3537 E3
Deep River Ct
3200 HOUS 77339 3119 B7
Deep River Dr
1100 FBnC 77469 4493 B5
Deep South Ct
19100 HarC 77449 3677 B4
Deep South Dr
5900 HarC 77449 3677 B4
Deep Spring Ln
12400 HOUS 77077 3957 D5
Deep Valley Dr
9500 HarC 77044 3689 B4
Deepwater Av
100 PASD 77503 4108 B5
Deepwell Ln
900 HDWV 77024 3959 C1
Deepwood Dr
1200 FRDW 77546 4629 D1
6000 HOUS 77023 4104 C5
Deep Woods Dr
11800 HarC 77429 3398 C3
Deepwoods Dr
25300 MtgC 77355 2814 C2
Deep Woods Tr
16800 MtgC 77302 2679 C3
Deer Av
1300 DRPK 77536 4109 B5
Deer Cr
29000 MtgC 77355 2815 E4
29100 MtgC 77355 2816 A4
Deer Cross
3000 FBnC 77459 4621 E6
Deer Ct
3400 PRLD 77581 4503 D5
30500 MtgC 77354 2817 D1
Deer Gln
2900 HarC 77068 3257 B4
Deer Ldg
3000 FBnC 77459 4621 E6
Deer Ln
31600 MtgC 77362 2963 D3
Deer Rd
900 FBnC 77469 4364 D6
Deer Tr
400 WlrC 77447 2813 A5
4800 HarC 77532 3554 B2
10400 MtgC 77302 2530 E6
13600 MtgC 77302 2531 A6
Deer Trc
2400 MtgC 77384 2674 E2
Deer Vly
36000 MtgC 77355 2816 A4
Deerbend Ct
3700 MtgC 77386 2970 A5
Deerberry Ct
10 WDLD 77380 2821 E6
Deerbourne Chase Dr
5300 SGLD 77479 4495 A4
Deer Branch St
10300 FBnC 77459 4621 E7
10300 FBnC 77459 4622 A7
Deer Briar Run Dr
4100 HOUS 77048 4374 D4
Deerbrook
10 HMBL 77396 3406 C2
10 HOUS 77396 3406 C2
Deerbrook Ct
3500 BzaC 77584 4501 D7
Deerbrook Dr
- WlrC 77447 2813 B4
1200 FBnC 77479 4494 A6
3500 HOUS 77339 3119 C5
25000 MtgC 77372 2682 E5
25000 PTVL 77372 2682 E5
25000 SPLD 77372 2682 E5
25600 SPLD 77372 2683 A5
Deerbrook Park Blvd
- HOUS 77338 3262 A5
20100 HarC 77338 3262 A5
Deer Chase Dr
3900 HarC 77082 4096 C3
Deer Cove Ln
12800 HarC 77041 3679 D4
Deer Cove Tr
2200 HOUS 77339 3263 E1
Deer Creek Ct
7100 HarC 77379 3256 D3

STREET Block City ZIP Map# Grid
Deer Creek Dr
2900 SGLD 77478 4368 E5
16900 HarC 77379 3256 C2
19900 HarC 77532 3412 E2
Deer Creek Wy
33500 SGCH 77355 2962 B1
33700 SGCH 77355 2816 B7
Deercrest Dr
800 HarC 77530 3829 D7
Deer Crossing Dr
18400 HarC 77346 3409 C1
Deer Falls Dr
3800 HOUS 77345 3119 D4
Deer Fern Dr
400 LGCY 77573 4633 A2
Deerfern Pl
10 WDLD 77381 2674 D6
Deerfield Ct
1600 FBnC 77469 4365 E2
5900 KATY 77493 3813 B5
Deerfield Dr
- BzaC 77584 4501 B6
- PRLD 77584 4501 B6
2200 KATY 77493 3813 B5
Deerfield Rd
1000 FBnC 77469 4365 E2
Deerfield St
100 HOUS 77022 3824 A1
Deerfield Village Dr
- HarC 77084 3677 E7
4000 HarC 77084 3816 E1
N Deerfoot Cir
- MtgC 77380 2822 B6
10 WDLD 77380 2822 B6
S Deerfoot Cir
100 WDLD 77380 2822 B6
Deerfoot Ct
10 WDLD 77380 2822 A6
Deer Glen Dr
18700 MtgC 77302 2680 B7
18700 MtgC 77357 2680 B7
Deer Glen Ln
15600 MtgC 77302 2679 E3
Deer Glen West Dr
17300 MtgC 77302 2679 D4
17300 MtgC 77302 2680 A4
Deer Grass Ct
3800 HOUS 77059 4380 C4
Deer Grass Ln
9500 HarC 77044 3689 D3
Deergrove St
- HarC 77039 3545 E4
Deerhaven Dr
21300 HarC 77388 3112 E3
Deerhill Wk
- FBnC 77459 4621 B7
Deer Hollow Dr
500 FBnC 77479 4493 D6
800 FBnC 77469 4493 D6
2800 HOUS 77345 3119 E5
Deerhurst Ln
1900 HarC 77088 3543 D7
1900 HarC 77088 3683 D1
Deering Dr
9300 HOUS 77036 4238 E1
9300 HOUS 77036 4239 A1
Deer Key Cir
18800 HOUS 77084 3816 B6
Deer Knoll Ct
1400 FBnC 77545 4622 E1
Deer Lake Ct
10 WDLD 77381 2821 B3
25000 HarC 77373 3115 A2
Deer Lake Rd
100 HOUS 77336 3266 A1
N Deer Lake Rd
100 HOUS 77336 3266 A1
Deer Lake Tr
3700 HarC 77373 3114 E2
3800 HarC 77373 3115 A2
Deerland Ct
3400 HOUS 77345 3119 E4
Deer Leap Dr
4100 HarC 77084 3816 C1
Deerlick Dr
16100 HarC 77090 3258 D5
Deer Lodge Ct
10300 FBnC 77459 4621 E6
Deer Lodge Dr
4400 HOUS 77018 3683 C7
Deer Lodge Rd
8200 MtgC 77354 2672 D2
8200 MtgC 77354 2673 A2
Deer Meadow Dr
2300 MSCY 77489 4370 B7
8700 HOUS 77071 4239 B5
N Deer Meadow Dr
8900 HOUS 77071 4239 C6
Deer Meadow Ln
6300 KATY 77493 3813 A5
8500 HOUS 77071 4239 C6
Deermoss Dr
- HarC 77084 3816 A4
3200 HarC 77449 3816 A3
Deer Mountain Ct
2500 HOUS 77345 3120 C5
Deerpass Dr
900 HarC 77530 3829 D6
Deerpath Ct
15800 HarC 77377 3254 D5
Deer Path Dr
5000 CNRO 77303 2237 C4
Deer Path Ln
9400 MtgC 77354 2672 B4
Deer Path Wy
18600 HarC 77532 3410 C6
Deer Point Dr
4900 HarC 77389 2967 A6
Deer Ridge Dr
1200 LGCY 77573 4632 A4
15500 MtgC 77306 2680 D3
Deer Ridge Ln
6600 HarC 77086 3542 C2
Deer Ridge Estates Blvd
10 HOUS 77339 3263 D2
Deer Run Bnd
3800 SGLD 77479 4495 D3
Deer Run Cir
2300 HarC 77532 3410 B5
Deer Run Ct
2200 KATY 77493 3813 B5
2300 HarC 77532 3410 B5
Deer Run Dr
3100 HOUS 77338 3263 D4
Deer Run Ln
18700 HarC 77532 3410 B6
19600 MtgC 77357 2829 C5

STREET
Block City ZIP Map# Grid

Deer Run St
14000 MtgC 77355 2962 D2
Deer Sage Ct
12900 HarC 77041 3679 D5
Deer Shadow Ct
5700 HarC 77041 3679 D5
Deerslayer Tr
20100 HarC 77532 3410 C3
Deer Springs Dr
2000 HOUS 77339 3263 D1
2100 HOUS 77339 3118 E7
Deer Timbers Ln
5300 HarC 77346 3264 B4
Deer Timbers Tr
5500 HarC 77346 3264 C4
Deer Track Ct
10000 HarC 77064 3541 D2
Deer Trail Dr
- HOUS 77038 3544 A6
2900 ALVN 77511 4866 D4
6000 PASD 77505 4248 D4
8100 HarC 77389 2966 A2
8200 HarC 77389 2965 E2
9300 HOUS 77088 3544 A6
9500 HarC 77038 3544 A5
10000 HarC 77038 3543 E4
Deertrail St
1800 DRPK 77536 4109 D6
Deer Trails Cir
3400 HarC 77396 3407 C5
Deer Trails Dr
1000 HarC 77396 3407 B5
Deer Valley Dr
3000 HarC 77373 3114 D2
Deervalley St
1800 DRPK 77536 4109 D6
Deerwick Ct
9000 HarC 77375 2965 D5
W Deerwood E
1900 FBnC 77469 4232 D3
Deerwood Cir
4900 BYTN 77521 3972 C1
Deerwood Ct
2400 KATY 77493 3813 B5
Deerwood Dr
- DRPK 77536 4109 E7
- DRPK 77536 4249 E1
7000 FBnC 77469 4232 D3
10600 HOUS 77042 3958 D4
Deerwood Ln
3300 MSCY 77459 4497 B2
Deerwood Rd
5900 HOUS 77057 3960 C4
Deer Wood Tr
12200 MtgC 77362 2963 B1
Deerwood Lake Dr
7800 HarC 77346 3409 B1
Deerwood Park Ln
31000 MtgC 77386 2969 D1
31100 MtgC 77386 2823 B7
Dee Woods Dr
18900 HarC 77346 3265 A6
E Defee Av
10 BYTN 77520 3973 A7
W Defee Av
10 BYTN 77520 3972 E7
Defee St
500 HMBL 77338 3262 E7
Defender Ln
4100 GLSN 77554 5548 B2
Defender St
700 HOUS 77029 3965 E6
Defiance St
8900 LPRT 77571 4249 E3
Defoe Dr
2700 HarC 77449 3814 E4
Defoor Rd
2400 CNRO 77301 2385 A5
Deforest Ridge Cir
4200 FBnC 77450 4093 D2
Deforest Ridge Ln
22800 FBnC 77450 4093 D2
De Forrest St
12600 HarC 77066 3401 A1
De Four Trc
2500 SEBK 77586 4509 C2
Degas Ln
9800 HOUS 77016 3686 D5
Degas Park Dr
- WDLD 77382 2819 B2
De Gaulle
9700 HOUS 77088 3683 C1
De George St
4100 HOUS 77009 3824 A6
De Haven St
100 HOUS 77029 3965 E7
300 HOUS 77029 3966 A7
Deihl Rd
6300 HOUS 77091 3682 C5
6300 HOUS 77092 3682 C5
Deirdre Anne Dr
6300 HOUS 77088 3682 C3
Dekadine Ct
7100 HarC 77379 3111 B2
Deke Slayton Blvd
- LGCY 77573 4509 B7
900 GlsC 77565 4509 D7
900 KMAH 77565 4509 C7
900 LGCY 77565 4509 C7
Deke Slayton Blvd FM-518
- LGCY 77573 4509 B7
900 GlsC 77565 4509 D7
900 KMAH 77565 4509 C7
900 LGCY 77565 4509 C7
Deke Slayton Hwy
- LGCY 77565 4509 B7
- LGCY 77573 4509 B7
- LGCY 77573 4632 C1
2200 LGCY 77573 4632 C1
2900 LGCY 77573 4633 A1
Deke Slayton Hwy FM-518
- LGCY 77565 4509 B7
- LGCY 77573 4509 B7
2200 LGCY 77573 4632 C1
2900 LGCY 77573 4633 A1
De Koven St
200 HOUS 77011 4105 A1
Delabrook Ct
1400 SEBK 77586 4509 E2
Delacey Ln
13600 HarC 77429 3253 E6
Delachase Cir
8500 HarC 77379 3256 A5
Delafield St
2300 HOUS 77023 4104 C3
Del Agua Dr
- FBnC 77469 4365 B4
De la Luna Ct
10 BYTN 77521 3974 A1

Delamere Dr
- FBnC 77478 4236 D2
Delamotte Ln
6800 SGLD 77479 4494 C1
Delane
10 TYLV 77586 4381 E7
Delaney Rd
- HarC 77032 3404 B6
10 TXCY 77591 4872 E5
100 LMQU 77568 4872 E7
1100 HTCK 77563 4988 E3
1100 LMQU 77568 4988 E1
Delaney St
100 HOUS 77009 3824 B4
De Lange Ln
4500 HOUS 77092 3683 A7
5000 HOUS 77092 3682 E7
Delano St
100 HOUS 77003 3963 E5
2400 HOUS 77004 3963 C7
3100 HOUS 77004 4103 B2
N Delano St
10 HOUS 77003 3963 E4
200 HOUS 77003 3964 A4
De la Paz
- HarC 77041 3679 C3
De la Renta Dr
- HarC 77044 3689 D4
Delavan Dr
7500 HOUS 77028 3826 A1
Delaware Av
1600 LGCY 77573 4632 B5
Delaware St
300 HOUS 77029 3966 A7
Delay Dr
- HOUS 77598 4506 D2
Delbarton Dr
15000 FBnC 77083 4096 C7
Del Bello Blvd
- MNVL 77578 4625 C5
Del Bello Ln
5400 MNVL 77578 4625 B4
Del Bello Rd
3700 BzaC 77578 4625 C5
4300 MNVL 77578 4625 C5
Del Bello Spur
6200 MNVL 77578 4625 C5
Delbury St
5800 HOUS 77085 4371 E2
Del Clair Cir
2800 MSCY 77489 4497 B1
De Leon Ln
4100 PRLD 77581 4504 D7
De Leon St
3600 HOUS 77087 4105 B7
4000 HOUS 77087 4245 C1
8000 HOUS 77061 4245 C1
Deleon Field Dr
30200 MtgC 77386 2969 D2
Deleon Trails Dr
- HarC 77379 3257 A2
Delery Dr
2000 HOUS 77055 3821 C4
Delesandri Dr
7000 GlsC 77563 4990 D6
7100 HTCK 77563 4988 B5
Delesandri Ln
900 KMAH 77565 4633 C1
900 LGCY 77565 4633 C1
Delfan Cir
6100 HOUS 77396 3405 E4
6100 HOUS 77396 3406 A4
Delfren Ln
5600 KATY 77493 3813 C5
Delgado Dr
16200 FBnC 77083 4096 A5
Del Glen Ln
7500 HOUS 77072 4097 C6
7800 HarC 77072 4097 C6
Delhi St
1900 HarC 77067 3402 B5
Delia Ln
4000 HOUS 77022 3823 E2
Delia St
3000 HOUS 77026 3825 A7
Delicado Dr
9300 HarC 77396 3407 B3
Delilah St
8700 HOUS 77033 4243 D3
Dell Cir
10300 FBnC 77459 4622 A4
Dell Ct
200 HOUS 77009 3824 B6
10300 FBnC 77459 4622 A4
Dell Ln
3900 FBnC 77459 4622 A4
Dell Pk
3900 FBnC 77459 4622 A4
Dell St
6200 HOUS 77007 3961 E2
Della St
6700 HOUS 77093 3825 A2
Della Creek Wy
4300 MSCY 77459 4496 C3
Dellanera Dr
8000 HTCK 77563 4988 D5
Dellbridge Ln
16900 HarC 77073 3259 B3
Dellbrook Dr
700 HarC 77038 3543 D3
Delldale Blvd
1600 HarC 77530 3829 D3
1800 HarC 77049 3829 D3
Dell Dale St
100 HarC 77530 3968 E2
600 HarC 77530 3829 D4
Dellfern Ct
11800 HOUS 77035 4240 A5
Dellfern Dr
6300 HOUS 77035 4240 B5
Dellforest Ct
10 WDLD 77381 2821 A5
Dellhaven Ln
8700 HarC 77379 3255 E1
Dell Hollow Dr
11700 HarC 77066 3401 A7
Dellore Ln
1900 LGCY 77573 4632 C2
Dellrose Crossing Dr
2100 FBnC 77469 4092 B7
Dellwind Ct
15200 HarC 77049 3829 A2
Dellwood Ln
6000 HarC 77379 3111 E5
Dellwood Springs Dr
16700 HarC 77095 3538 A4
Delmack St
5600 HarC 77032 3546 E1
5600 HOUS 77396 3546 E1

Delman St
11000 HarC 77093 3686 B1
Del Mar
100 LGCY 77565 4508 E4
Delmar Dr
1000 LMQU 77568 4990 B2
Delmar St
10 HOUS 77011 3964 C6
500 HOUS 77023 3964 C7
N Delmar St
200 HOUS 77011 3964 C6
Delmar Green Pl
10 SHEH 77381 2821 E1
Delmas St
1000 HOUS 77087 4105 A3
N Delmont Dr E
100 CNRO 77301 2384 A2
N Delmont Dr W
100 CNRO 77301 2384 B2
S Delmont Dr E
100 CNRO 77301 2384 A2
S Delmont Dr W
100 CNRO 77301 2384 B2
Del Monte Ct
2900 MSCY 77459 4496 E2
Del Monte Dr
100 BzaC 77581 4628 E2
100 FRDW 77546 4628 E2
100 PRLD 77546 4628 E2
100 PRLD 77581 4628 E2
200 PASD 77503 4108 C4
2100 HOUS 77019 3962 A5
3200 HOUS 77019 3961 C5
5100 HOUS 77056 3961 A6
5200 HOUS 77056 3960 E6
6400 HOUS 77057 3960 A6
7500 HOUS 77063 3960 A6
10000 HOUS 77042 3959 A6
10600 HOUS 77042 3958 D6
11300 HOUS 77077 3958 B6
Del Monte Ln
100 HarC 77562 3831 E1
Delmont Park Ln
9100 HOUS 77075 4377 A3
Del Norte Dr
3300 BYTN 77521 3973 E1
Del Norte St
400 HOUS 77018 3684 B7
2300 HOUS 77018 3683 B7
Del Norte Canyon Dr
- HarC 77377 3109 B7
- HarC 77377 3254 B1
Deloache Av
7400 HarC 77338 3261 C2
De Lorean Ct
800 HarC 77396 3407 A4
Delores Dr
2500 MtgC 77384 2674 D2
Delores Ln
1000 BzaC 77511 4748 E2
5200 HarC 77373 3260 D1
Delores St
100 CNRO 77301 2384 A2
1100 KMAH 77565 4633 C1
1100 LGCY 77565 4633 C1
Del Oro Ct
10 BYTN 77521 3974 A1
Del Oro St
3700 BYTN 77521 3974 A1
De Lozier St
16100 JRSV 77040 3540 C7
16500 JRSV 77040 3680 B1
Del Papa St
13400 HOUS 77047 4373 C7
13800 HarC 77047 4373 C5
14600 PRLD 77047 4373 C6
Del Paso Cir
4600 PASD 77505 4249 A6
Delphi Ln
1900 HarC 77067 3402 B5
Delphinium Pl
10 WDLD 77382 2819 C3
Del Prado Dr
15300 HarC 77083 4096 B4
Del Rey Ln
7600 HOUS 77071 4239 E2
Delridge Ln
21400 HarC 77388 3113 A3
Del Rio St
5600 HOUS 77021 4103 B6
Delsantos St
12700 HOUS 77045 4241 C6
Del Sol Ct
10 BYTN 77521 3974 A1
Del Sur Dr
3500 BYTN 77521 3973 E1
Del Sur St
5100 HOUS 77018 3684 C7
Delta Cross
- RSBG 77469 4491 E5
Delta Dr
- ALVN 77511 4867 D1
- BYTN 77520 4112 C3
22800 MtgC 77365 2971 E4
Delta Lk
- FBnC 77469 4234 C5
Delta St
100 PASD 77506 4107 D3
200 CNRO 77301 2383 E6
400 CNRO 77301 2384 A6
500 PASD 77506 4108 A5
Delta Bridge Ct
2200 PRLD 77584 4500 C2
11500 FBnC 77478 4236 D6
Delta Bridge Dr
2200 PRLD 77584 4500 C2
Delta Estates Ct
18100 HarC 77429 3396 B2
N Delta Mill Cir
100 WDLD 77385 2676 C4
S Delta Mill Cir
100 WDLD 77385 2676 C4
Delta Mill Ct
10 WDLD 77385 2676 C4
Delta Queen Dr
19200 HarC 77449 3677 B4
Delta Spring Ln
21500 FBnC 77450 4094 A3
Delta Springs Ln
17700 HarC 77084 3678 A7
Delta Wood Ct
4100 HOUS 77059 4380 C3
Delta Wood Tr
20400 HarC 77346 3264 E3
20500 HarC 77346 3265 A4
Delucia Ln
14700 HarC 77377 3108 E7

Deluxe St
13500 HarC 77047 4374 D3
13500 HOUS 77047 4374 D3
Delwin St
2400 HOUS 77034 4246 E6
Delwood St
8000 HOUS 77087 4245 D1
Delwood Springs Ln
- HOUS 77044 3409 A4
De Lyn Ln
- PRLD 77584 4502 C6
Delynn Dr
7800 HarC 77521 3834 D4
E Delz Dr
300 HOUS 77022 3684 D7
Delz St
300 HOUS 77018 3684 B7
300 HOUS 77022 3684 B7
Demarco Ct
12600 HOUS 77045 4241 B6
Demarco Dr
12500 HOUS 77045 4241 B6
Demaree Ln
1400 HOUS 77029 3965 C4
Demaret Ln
1200 HOUS 77055 3820 B7
Dement Rd
10800 HarC 77375 2964 E5
10800 HarC 77375 2965 A5
10800 TMBL 77375 2964 E5
Demia Ct
11800 MDWP 77477 4238 B5
De Milo Dr
1700 HOUS 77018 3822 C1
4300 HOUS 77092 3822 A1
5000 HOUS 77092 3821 E1
Deming Dr
14900 HarC 77530 3968 C1
Deming St
- HarC 77373 3114 B7
Democracy Ct
8000 HarC 77379 3256 B1
Demolay St
1100 LMQU 77568 4874 A7
Demontrond Rd
- HarC 77090 3403 A2
- HOUS 77090 3403 A2
200 HarC 77014 3402 E3
200 HOUS 77090 3402 E3
De Moss Dr
5900 HOUS 77081 4100 C4
6500 HOUS 77074 4100 A4
8500 HOUS 77036 4099 B4
Demoss Dr
7600 HOUS 77036 4099 D4
Dempley Dr
13600 HarC 77041 3679 B4
Demp Nash Ln
3300 HarC 77086 3542 D2
Dempsey Oaks Dr
18700 HarC 77346 3265 B6
Demsey Mill Dr
9400 FBnC 77478 4236 C2
Denali Dr
2700 DRPK 77536 4109 D7
E Denali Dr
2700 DRPK 77536 4109 D7
W Denali Dr
2700 DRPK 77536 4109 D7
Denali Ln
12300 HarC 77346 3408 C2
Denali Range Ct
21700 HarC 77449 3815 A1
Denard Dr
500 MSCY 77489 4370 B3
Denbridge Ct
14100 FBnC 77083 4236 E2
Denbridge Dr
9200 FBnC 77083 4236 E1
Denbrook Dr
- HarC 77068 3257 A6
Denbury Wy
9400 HOUS 77025 4241 C1
Denby St
400 BYTN 77520 4112 D1
8400 HOUS 77012 4105 D4
Denfield Ct
9500 HarC 77070 3399 D5
Denford Ct
20600 HarC 77450 3954 D4
Denham Av
100 PASD 77506 4107 A6
Denio Dr
3500 HOUS 77082 4097 C2
Denise Dr
11600 HDWV 77024 3959 C1
11700 HOUS 77024 3959 C1
Denise Ln
9200 HarC 77375 2965 C3
Denise Rd
17100 MtgC 77306 2533 D6
Denise St
1100 DRPK 77536 4249 C1
31000 MtgC 77362 2963 C4
Denise Dale Ln
18400 HarC 77084 3816 C2
Denise Terrace Dr
- HarC 77447 3250 A6
Denison St
6900 HOUS 77020 3964 E2
7200 HOUS 77020 3965 A2
Denison Oaks Dr
- FBnC 77494 4092 A6
Denkman St
2700 PASD 77503 4248 E2
3000 PASD 77505 4248 E3
Denlan Blvd
- HarC 77084 3816 E2
Denman St
1300 HOUS 77019 3962 B4
Denmark Dr
6000 PASD 77505 4248 D5
Denmark Rd
3200 HOUS 77093 3825 A2
4000 HOUS 77016 3825 B2
Denmark St
5400 HOUS 77028 3825 D2
Denmere Ct
4400 HOUS 77345 3119 E6
Denning Dr
9800 HOUS 77078 3688 A5
Dennington Dr
18800 HarC 77449 3677 B4
Dennis St
10 HOUS 77006 3962 C5
10 HOUS 77006 3963 A6
200 HMBL 77338 3263 A6
1000 HOUS 77002 3963 B6

Dennis St
1200 HOUS 77004 3963 B6
1400 HOUS 77004 4103 E1
4100 HOUS 77004 4104 A2
Dennis Wy Ln
13100 HarC 77044 3689 C6
Denny
9700 HarC 77064 3541 A3
Denny Dr
- HOUS 77040 3682 A4
7300 HarC 77040 3682 A3
Denny Rd
5400 HarC 77389 2967 A7
Denny St
100 HarC 77562 3831 D3
Den Oak Dr
10300 HarC 77065 3539 B2
Denoron Dr
5100 HOUS 77048 4243 E7
5600 HOUS 77048 4244 B7
Denridge Dr
2100 HarC 77038 3543 B3
Denslow Cir
9600 HOUS 77076 3685 C6
Densmore Dr
5900 HOUS 77035 4240 B6
Denson Rd
1900 BzaC 77511 4750 A6
Dent Dr
10 BYTN 77521 3972 E2
10 BYTN 77521 3973 A2
Denton Dr
100 PASD 77586 4508 D2
Denton Rd
- HMBL 77338 3262 D5
Denton St
7600 HOUS 77028 3826 C1
7900 HOUS 77028 3687 C7
29600 MtgC 77354 2818 A2
29700 MtgC 77354 2817 E2
Denton Meadows Ct
- HarC 77449 3815 C2
Dentwood Dr
13800 HarC 77014 3402 D3
Denver Dr
4500 GLSN 77550 5108 E6
4500 GLSN 77551 5108 D7
Denver St
3500 HOUS 77003 3963 E6
Denver Arbor Ct
- HarC 77053 4372 D5
Denver Miller St
16000 FBnC 77469 4235 E5
16000 FBnC 77469 4236 A5
16000 FBnC 77478 4236 A5
Denver Oaks Dr
13300 HarC 77065 3539 B1
Departure St
17300 HarC 77532 3552 A1
Depelchin St
1600 HOUS 77007 3963 A1
De Priest St
6200 HOUS 77091 3684 A4
7200 HOUS 77088 3684 A4
Derby Dr
1900 HarC 77067 3402 B5
2000 CNRO 77301 2384 C1
2000 CNRO 77303 2384 C1
Derby Ln
500 MSCY 77489 4370 E5
Derbybrook Ct
25100 FBnC 77494 4093 B6
Derbyhall Dr
3800 HarC 77066 3401 C5
Derbyshire Dr
400 HOUS 77034 4378 E5
5300 KATY 77493 3813 D6
Derek Dr
3700 BYTN 77521 3973 C2
Derham Parc St
10 HDWV 77024 3959 D3
10 PNPV 77024 3959 D3
Dering Ct
20100 HarC 77450 3954 E1
Dermott Dr
12300 HarC 77065 3398 C7
12600 HarC 77065 3539 C1
Dermott Ridge Dr
- FBnC 77469 4092 D7
Derquen Dr
- WlrC 77447 2813 D4
Derrick Dr
100 HarC 77338 3263 B6
Derrick St
3200 GlsC 77518 4634 B2
10700 GlsC 77510 4871 D6
Derrick Field Ln
3000 BzaC 77583 4500 E7
Derrik Dr
9600 HOUS 77080 3820 C1
Derril Ln
3500 HarC 77082 4096 C3
Derrington Rd
9300 HarC 77064 3541 A3
Derwent Ln
12000 HarC 77064 3399 E6
Descartes Dr
6800 FBnC 77469 4093 E7
Des Chaumes St
1700 HOUS 77020 3964 A2
1800 HOUS 77026 3964 A1
3500 HOUS 77026 3825 A6
Desco Dr
7600 HarC 77338 3261 D3
Desel Dr
5100 DKSN 77539 4753 D4
5300 TXCY 77539 4753 D4
Desert Dr
500 FRDW 77546 4629 C2
E Desert Dr
3600 LPRT 77571 4250 A4
Desert Aire Dr
500 FRDW 77546 4628 E5
Desert Bluff Ct
21100 HarC 77338 3261 D3
Desert Bluff Ln
7000 FBnC 77469 4095 A5
Desert Brook Ln
20000 FBnC 77469 4094 C7
Desert Calico Ln
19200 FBnC 77469 4234 E1
Desert Canyon Ct
7800 HarC 77095 3539 C7
Desert Canyon Dr
13800 HarC 77095 3539 C7
Desert Cliff Ct
4400 FBnC 77494 4092 D2

Desert Cloud Ct
9400 HarC 77040 3541 A5
Desert Cloud Ln
8700 HarC 77040 3541 A5
Desert Flower Ln
9600 HarC 77086 3542 A3
Desert Gold Dr
23400 FBnC 77494 4093 B5
Desert Ivy Dr
19400 HarC 77094 3955 A3
Desert Maize Ln
17200 HarC 77095 3537 E3
Desert Marigold Dr
18500 HarC 77073 3403 B3
Desert Moon Dr
19100 HarC 77433 3537 B7
Desert Oak Ct
17300 HarC 77379 3111 D7
Desert Oak Wy
5700 HarC 77379 3111 E7
Desert Oaks Ct
7200 FBnC 77469 4094 A6
Desert Oasis Ln
1100 RSBG 77471 4614 C2
2900 HarC 77449 3815 E5
Desert Palms Dr
8700 HarC 77379 3255 B4
8700 HarC 77379 3256 C4
Desert Palms Ln
1100 RSBG 77471 4614 D1
Desert Park Ln
- MtgC 77385 2823 B6
Desert Rose
10 WDLD 77382 2819 C2
Desert Rose Ln
6400 HarC 77086 3542 C2
Desert Rose Pl
800 MSCY 77459 4497 B6
Desert Run Dr
3600 LPRT 77571 4250 A4
Desert Sage Dr
2500 HarC 77449 3815 C5
Desert Springs Cir
10600 HarC 77095 3538 A2
10900 HarC 77095 3537 E1
11300 HarC 77095 3396 E7
Desert Springs Ct
2000 LGCY 77573 4631 C7
Desert Springs Ln
1100 RSBG 77471 4614 C1
Desert Star
7200 FBnC 77494 4093 B5
Desert Star Ct
15200 HarC 77429 3253 C6
16400 MtgC 77302 2679 B4
Desert Star Dr
16500 MtgC 77302 2679 B4
Desert Trace Ct
- HOUS 77044 3550 A1
Desert Vine Ct
9200 SGLD 77478 4237 A5
Desert Willow Ct
300 LGCY 77573 4633 A2
30000 SGCH 77355 2960 C1
Desert Willow Dr
400 LGCY 77573 4633 A2
20300 HarC 77449 3815 C4
22200 MtgC 77355 2960 C2
22600 SGCH 77355 2960 C2
Desert Willow Ln
1100 RSBG 77471 4614 C1
Desirable Dr
- LPRT 77571 4250 A4
9200 LPRT 77571 4249 E4
Desirable Ln
900 HarC 77336 3121 E7
Des Jardines St
1200 HOUS 77023 4104 C2
Des Moines Av
- PASD 77505 4248 A3
Des Moines Ct
100 IWCY 77583 4623 E5
100 IWCY 77583 4624 A5
Desna Ct
19300 MtgC 77365 2971 E5
19300 MtgC 77365 2972 A5
Desna Dr
19300 MtgC 77365 2971 E5
19300 MtgC 77365 2972 B5
Desota Dr
- FRDW 77546 4629 A6
De Sota Rd
40000 MtgC 77354 2672 E2
40000 MtgC 77354 2673 A2
Desota Glen Ct
15500 HarC 77049 3829 A1
Desoto Dr
25700 WlrC 77447 2813 A7
De Soto St
1100 HOUS 77091 3683 A5
5200 HOUS 77091 3682 E5
Desoto Square Dr
- HOUS 77091 3683 C5
Destin Ln
1700 FRDW 77546 4629 A7
Destin Shore Dr
2900 HarC 77084 3816 C4
Destiny Ln
12900 HarC 77532 3692 E1
Destiny Cove
10 WDLD 77381 2821 D4
Destiny Park Ct
5900 HarC 77449 3677 C5
Destrehan Dr
16300 HarC 77429 3397 A3
16800 HarC 77429 3396 E2
Detering St
2000 HOUS 77007 3962 B1
Determined Dr
12300 HarC 77039 3546 B5
Detony St
6300 HTCK 77563 4989 B6
Detric Ln
16200 HOUS 77053 4372 A6
Detroit St
8000 HOUS 77017 4105 C6
Deussen Dr
- HarC 77044 3550 B4
12300 HOUS 77044 3550 C5
Deussen Pkwy
- HarC 77044 3549 E1
- HOUS 77044 3549 E1
14200 HarC 77044 3550 A2
Deuster Ln
20100 MtgC 77365 2825 C6
Deutser St
2300 HOUS 77093 3685 D4

E De Vaca Ln
18200 GLSN 77554 5442 C1
W De Vaca Ln
18000 GLSN 77554 5442 B1
De Val Dr
10500 HarC 77429 3538 E2
Develle St
19200 HarC 77532 3411 D4
Devencrest Dr
11400 HarC 77066 3401 A7
Devereaux Ct
20100 HarC 77450 3954 E1
Deverell Dr
9700 FBnC 77083 4236 E2
9700 FBnC 77478 4236 E2
Devereux Dr
1100 LGCY 77573 4631 D3
W Devereux Dr
- LGCY 77573 4631 D4
Deveron
29600 MtgC 77354 2818 B2
Deveron Ln
700 HarC 77090 3258 D5
Deville Dr
22100 HarC 77450 3953 E1
22100 HarC 77450 3954 A1
Devin Ct
- HarC 77073 3403 C1
Devin Ln
15200 HarC 77532 3553 D4
Devinwood Dr
10200 BYTN 77520 3835 B7
10400 CmbC 77520 3835 C7
Devlin Dr
7800 HarC 77346 3265 C6
Devon Ln
19100 MtgC 77357 2829 E4
Devon St
4500 HOUS 77027 3961 B7
Devonaire Ln
- HarC 77049 3828 D2
Devonberry Ln
4600 FBnC 77450 4094 A3
Devoncroft Dr
9100 HOUS 77031 4239 B5
Devon Glen Dr
1400 HOUS 77077 3958 B5
Devon Green Dr
5100 HarC 77449 3676 D6
Devon Mill Pl
- WDLD 77382 2674 B5
Devon Oaks St
13900 HarC 77429 3397 C2
Devonport Dr
6700 HarC 77449 3676 C3
Devonport Ln
800 TYLV 77586 4508 D1
1000 TYLV 77586 4381 D7
Devonshire Cres
1800 HOUS 77030 4102 D4
Devonshire Dr
10 CNRO 77304 2529 C2
2400 BzaC 77584 4501 A4
Devonshire St
2200 HOUS 77019 3962 B6
4500 SGLD 77479 4495 B4
Devonwood Ln
8100 HarC 77070 3399 D3
Devries Rd
6500 HTCK 77563 4988 B4
Dew Cir
23300 HarC 77336 3267 A4
Dewalt Mnr
3900 FBnC 77459 4621 C5
Dewalt St
600 HarC 77037 3684 B1
600 HOUS 77037 3684 B1
800 HOUS 77088 3684 A1
1900 HOUS 77088 3683 C1
Dewalt Wy
3800 FBnC 77459 4621 C5
Dew Arbor St
11400 HarC 77067 3402 C6
Dewberry Ln
2100 PASD 77502 4107 D4
2100 PASD 77502 4247 D1
3000 PASD 77504 4247 D3
4500 FBnC 77469 4364 C1
12000 MtgC 77302 2532 E7
15400 MtgC 77302 2533 A7
Dewberry St
4500 HOUS 77021 4103 E6
5100 HOUS 77021 4104 A6
Dewberry Brook Ct
1700 HOUS 77345 3120 C6
Dewberry Creek Ln
7000 HarC 77396 3547 B2
20700 HarC 77449 3676 D2
Dewberry Crescent Dr
17500 HarC 77095 3537 D3
Dew Bridge Ct
7000 FBnC 77479 4367 A7
Dew Bridge Dr
6200 FBnC 77479 4367 A7
Dew Crest Dr
6700 HarC 77449 3677 D2
Dewdrift Pl
10 WDLD 77382 2674 A5
Dewdrop Ct
25200 MtgC 77355 2960 C1
Dew Drop Ln
16200 HarC 77095 3678 C1
De Weese
- HOUS 77045 4242 C6
- HOUS 77051 4242 D4
Dewey Ln
- WALR 77484 3101 E5
2000 WALR 77484 3102 A5
Dewey St
- HOUS 77007 3963 B3
1200 HOUS 77015 3967 A3
Dewey Eve Ct
10400 HarC 77070 3399 B4
Dewey Lake Dr
3600 FBnC 77469 4234 C6
Dew Fall Ct
10 WDLD 77380 2968 A4
Dewflower Dr
23200 FBnC 77494 4093 C4
Dewgrass Dr
17000 HOUS 77060 3403 E6
DeWitt Rd
7800 HOUS 77028 3826 B1
Dew Mist Ln
7200 HarC 77095 3678 C1
Dewmont Ln
9300 HarC 77070 3399 D5

STREET
Block City ZIP Map# Grid
Dew Point Ln
3300 SGLD 77479 4495 C1
Dewthread Ct
10 WDLD 77380 2821 D6
Dewville Ln
6600 HOUS 77076 3684 D4
7600 HOUS 77037 3684 D2
7700 HarC 77037 3684 D2
Dew Wood Ln
23100 HarC 77373 3115 D6
Dexter Rd
8700 HOUS 77075 4246 A7
Dexter Point Dr
16300 HarC 77429 3397 A2
De Zavalla Rd
- HOUS 77530 3969 D3
15900 HarC 77530 3969 B2
Dezso Dr
700 ALVN 77511 4867 D2
DH Watkins Dr
3300 DRPK 77536 4108 E7
3300 DRPK 77536 4248 E1
Diablo Dr
1200 HOUS 77532 3266 B7
Diablo Canyon Ln
19200 HarC 77377 3109 C7
Diakovic Dr
12400 HarC 77015 3828 A7
Diamante Dr
- LGCY 77539 4633 D3
- LGCY 77565 4633 D2
1300 PASD 77504 4247 D7
8800 MtgC 77354 2672 C3
Diamond Ct
6000 TXCY 77591 4873 D6
20000 MtgC 77355 2814 D3
Diamond Dr
16000 HOUS 77053 4371 E6
Diamond Ln
100 FRDW 77546 4505 C6
12600 SGLD 77478 4367 C2
Diamond Sq
26700 MtgC 77372 2683 C2
26700 SPLD 77372 2683 C2
Diamond St
2100 HOUS 77018 3683 B7
Diamond Wy
100 HOUS 77336 3120 E4
Diamondale Ct
3900 FBnC 77450 4093 B6
Diamond Bay Ct
6000 HarC 77041 3679 D4
Diamond Bay Dr
200 LGCY 77539 4753 A5
2800 LGCY 77539 4752 D5
Diamond Brook Dr
1400 HOUS 77062 4379 D7
Diamond C
26900 MtgC 77372 2683 C1
Diamondcliff Ct
5000 HarC 77449 3676 C6
Diamond Cove Ln
7200 FBnC 77469 4094 B7
Diamond Creek Dr
28400 MtgC 77355 2814 D4
Diamond Crest Dr
2000 HOUS 77489 4371 A5
2200 MSCY 77489 4371 A6
Diamond Falls Ln
7100 HarC 77389 2966 B1
Diamond Field Dr
7400 HarC 77095 3678 C2
Diamond Grove Ct
3900 HOUS 77059 4380 A4
N Diamondhead Blvd
500 HarC 77532 3411 A7
S Diamondhead Blvd
- HOUS 77532 3551 B2
100 HarC 77532 3552 A4
1300 HarC 77532 3551 B4
Diamond Head Ct
1700 TKIS 77554 5106 A4
Diamond Head Dr
1700 TKIS 77554 5106 B4
Diamond Hills Ln
19700 HarC 77449 3677 A7
19800 HarC 77449 3676 E7
Diamond Hollow Ct
3100 HarC 77450 3954 D7
Diamond Knoll Ct
23200 HarC 77494 3953 C4
Diamond Lake Ct
8700 HarC 77083 4096 E7
8700 HarC 77083 4236 D1
Diamond Lake Ln
8800 FBnC 77083 4236 E1
Diamond Leaf Ln
600 HOUS 77079 3958 D2
Diamond Oak Ct
10 WDLD 77381 2820 E6
10 WDLD 77381 2821 A6
Diamond Oak Dr
7800 TXCY 77591 4873 B6
Diamond Oaks Dr
37200 MtgC 77355 2815 C6
Diamond Park Cir
19300 HarC 77373 3113 E7
Diamond Park Dr
19300 HarC 77373 3113 E6
Diamond Peak Ct
17900 HarC 77346 3408 D1
Diamond Ranch Dr
25100 FBnC 77494 3953 A6
Diamond River Dr
2400 RSBG 77469 4615 E1
Diamond Rock Ct
21100 HarC 77449 3676 C3
Diamond Rock Dr
6200 HarC 77449 3676 C3
16000 HarC 77429 3397 A1
Diamond Shore Ct
22500 FBnC 77450 4093 E1
Diamond Springs Dr
2000 HOUS 77077 3956 E6
2300 PRLD 77584 4500 B2
4400 MSCY 77459 4621 C2
Diamond Star Dr
3200 HarC 77082 4096 C2
Diamond T
26700 MtgC 77372 2683 D1
Diamond Wy Ct
8300 PRLD 77584 4501 E5
Dian St
1300 HOUS 77008 3823 B6
Diana Ct
1400 HOUS 77062 4380 A7
1400 HOUS 77062 4507 A1

STREET
Block City ZIP Map# Grid
Diana Dr
- HarC 77065 3398 D7
Diana Ln
15000 HOUS 77062 4380 A7
15100 HOUS 77062 4507 B3
16600 HOUS 77058 4507 C3
Diane Ct
5400 HarC 77373 3260 E1
Diane Dr
22100 HarC 77373 3260 E1
22400 HarC 77373 3115 D7
Diane Ln
12000 HarC 77067 3402 A5
Diane St
100 CNRO 77301 2384 A2
1800 MtgC 77355 2816 C7
1800 MtgC 77362 2816 C7
1800 SGCH 77355 2816 C7
1800 SGCH 77362 2816 C7
Diane Oaks Dr
5700 HarC 77373 3115 D6
Dianeshire Ct
400 HarC 77388 3113 C7
Dianeshire Dr
19100 HarC 77388 3113 C6
Dianne Pl
- HarC 77073 3403 C1
Dibello Forest Ln
5400 HarC 77373 3115 C6
Dick St
400 HOUS 77020 3964 C3
Dick Bay Dr
1200 GlsC 77539 4635 D7
1200 GlsC 77539 4756 C1
Dick Dawson Rd
1200 BzaC 77511 4748 D5
Dickens Rd
4900 HOUS 77021 4104 B4
Dickey Ln
4600 GlsC 77517 4870 A7
Dickey Pl
2100 HOUS 77019 3962 B6
2500 HOUS 77098 3962 B6
Dickinson Av
- LGCY 77573 4633 A7
300 LGCY 77573 4632 C6
900 GlsC 77539 4633 A7
900 LGCY 77539 4633 A7
2300 LGCY 77539 4632 D7
2400 DKSN 77539 4633 A7
2700 DKSN 77539 4754 A2
Dickinson Av FM-1266
- LGCY 77573 4633 A7
900 GlsC 77539 4633 A7
900 LGCY 77539 4633 A7
2400 DKSN 77539 4633 A7
2700 DKSN 77539 4754 A2
Dickinson Rd
- HOUS 77034 4378 B4
300 ALVN 77511 4749 D7
11800 HOUS 77089 4378 B4
Dickinson Rd FM-517
- ALVN 77511 4749 E7
Dick Scobee Dr
- HOUS 77094 4095 C2
Dickson Av
6200 TXCY 77591 4873 D6
Dickson St
3900 HOUS 77007 3962 C3
Dickson Wy
6600 HOUS 77085 4371 C4
7000 HOUS 77489 4371 B4
Dickson Park Dr
19200 HarC 77373 3113 E6
Diego Springs Dr
9900 HarC 77375 3255 B2
Diehlwood Pl
4800 HarC 77388 3112 B4
Dieppe Rd
5000 HOUS 77033 4243 E1
5100 HOUS 77033 4244 A1
Dierker Dr
5800 HOUS 77041 3681 B5
Diesel St
1200 HOUS 77007 3962 E2
Dietz
2700 HOUS 77004 4104 A1
Diez St
1200 HOUS 77023 4104 B1
Dijon Ct
12500 HarC 77015 3828 A7
Dijon Dr
600 HarC 77015 3828 A7
Dike Rd
- TXCY 77590 4877 A7
- TXCY 77590 4993 C1
200 TXCY 77590 4875 E5
200 TXCY 77590 4876 A5
Dillard Dr
- JRSV 77040 3680 D2
Dillard St
600 HOUS 77091 3684 A4
Dilling St
700 ALVN 77511 4749 C7
Dillion Creek Ln
- FBnC 77494 4093 A3
Dillon Dr
6600 MtgC 77354 2673 B1
Dillon St
6700 HOUS 77061 4244 E5
7500 HOUS 77061 4245 B3
10500 MtgC 77303 2239 B1
Dillon Creek Ln
- FBnC 77494 4093 A3
Dillon Hill Cir
15400 HarC 77086 3541 D2
Dillon Wood Ct
3000 HarC 77449 3815 A3
Dillonwood Ct
2000 LGCY 77565 4508 E5
Dillsbury Ct
19200 HarC 77449 3677 B2
Di Mambro Ln
21200 HarC 77377 3106 A5
Dimmett Wy
21700 HarC 77388 3112 A2
Dimrod St
3000 GlsC 77518 4634 B2
Dinastia View Ct
- LGCY 77565 4633 D3
Dincans St
5000 HOUS 77005 4102 A2
5000 HOUS 77098 4102 A2
5100 WUNP 77005 4102 A2
Dinero Dr
19200 HarC 77346 3265 B6
Dinerstein Dr
- HOUS 77598 4506 D3

STREET
Block City ZIP Map# Grid
Ding Rd
- FRDW 77546 4629 A4
Dingy Ct
17500 HarC 77532 3552 A1
Dinner Creek Ct
6600 HarC 77449 3677 D3
Dinner Creek Dr
18100 HarC 77084 3677 D3
18100 HarC 77449 3677 D2
Dinorah Ct
600 HarC 77094 3955 C2
Dinosaur Valley Dr
11900 FBnC 77478 4236 B7
Dionne Dr
6900 HOUS 77076 3684 E4
Diorio Rd
- WlrC 77445 3243 B4
Di Palermo Rd
7800 TXCY 77539 4754 C5
Diplomacy Dr
7600 HarC 77040 3681 A1
Diplomat Ct
8600 HOUS 77088 3684 A1
Diplomat Wy
1300 HOUS 77088 3684 A1
1400 HOUS 77088 3683 E1
Diplomatic Plaza St
15300 HOUS 77032 3405 C7
Dipping Ln
10 HOUS 77076 3684 E6
10 HOUS 77076 3685 B5
20500 HarC 77357 2830 A7
20800 HarC 77357 2976 A1
Dirby St
8800 HOUS 77075 4245 E6
8800 HOUS 77075 4246 A6
Directors Dr
- STAF 77477 4369 A1
12700 STAF 77477 4238 A7
Directors Row
4000 HOUS 77092 3822 B4
Dirt Rd
- HarC 77039 3545 D5
Discipline Av
12800 HarC 77014 3401 D3
Discover Ln
14900 HarC 77084 3679 A4
Discovery Bay Dr
- PRLD 77584 4500 D2
11200 BzaC 77584 4500 E2
Discus Cir
500 MtgC 77357 2829 C2
Discus Dr
8500 HarC 77346 3265 D6
Disher Cir
10 HarC 77336 2976 A2
Dismuke St
1100 HOUS 77023 4104 C2
Disney St
- FBnC 77583 4623 B4
10 ARLA 77583 4623 B4
N Disney St
100 ALVN 77511 4867 C1
S Disney St
100 ALVN 77511 4867 C1
Dispensary Dr
7500 HTCK 77563 4988 A5
Distant Rock Ln
16300 HarC 77095 3538 C5
Distant Woods Ct
8800 HarC 77095 3538 B5
Distant Woods Dr
8700 HarC 77095 3538 A5
Distribution Blvd
3800 HOUS 77018 3823 C2
Dite Rd
13900 HarC 77044 3549 E1
13900 HOUS 77044 3549 E1
13900 HOUS 77044 3550 A1
Ditmas Ln
5100 HOUS 77021 4104 B5
Dittmans Ct
3100 HOUS 77020 3964 A2
Divellec Ln
20800 HarC 77388 3112 D4
Diven Cir
14600 HarC 77429 3253 E7
Divers Ln
1500 HarC 77530 3830 E4
Diversion Dr
19300 HarC 77375 3109 C7
Dividend Dr
- HOUS 77013 3826 E7
400 HOUS 77013 3965 E1
Divin Dr
1200 RSBG 77471 4491 D5
Divine
10200 HOUS 77033 4243 E5
Diving Duck Ct
2600 HarC 77396 3407 D3
Division St
2400 HOUS 77004 4103 C1
Divot St
32100 WlrC 77484 3246 D6
Dix St
- HOUS 77085 4371 D4
Dixie Ct
3800 BzaC 77578 4625 B1
4800 SGLD 77478 4369 B6
Dixie Dr
300 LGCY 77573 4631 B5
2200 HOUS 77030 4102 E4
2200 HOUS 77030 4103 A4
4000 HOUS 77021 4103 D5
6100 HOUS 77033 4244 C1
6100 HOUS 77087 4244 E1
7800 HOUS 77087 4245 C1
7900 HOUS 77087 4105 C7
E Dixie Dr
100 DRPK 77536 4109 B6
Dixie Farm Rd
- HOUS 77089 4505 C1
- HOUS 77546 4505 C1
100 PRLD 77511 4628 A2
100 PRLD 77581 4628 A1
300 HOUS 77034 4378 E5
300 HOUS 77598 4378 E5
800 PRLD 77581 4504 C6
1000 HOUS 77546 4378 D7
1100 HOUS 77089 4378 D7
2300 FRDW 77546 4505 A3
2300 PRLD 77581 4505 A4
2500 FRDW 77089 4505 A3
2500 HarC 77089 4505 A3
2500 HarC 77546 4505 A3
2500 PRLD 77089 4505 A3
Dixie Farm Rd FM-1959
- HOUS 77089 4505 C1

STREET
Block City ZIP Map# Grid
Dixie Farm Rd FM-1959
- HOUS 77546 4505 C1
300 HOUS 77034 4378 E5
300 HOUS 77598 4378 E5
1000 HOUS 77546 4378 D7
1100 HOUS 77089 4378 D7
2500 FRDW 77089 4505 A3
2500 FRDW 77546 4505 A3
2500 HarC 77089 4505 A3
2500 HarC 77546 4505 A3
2500 PRLD 77089 4505 A3
2800 PRLD 77581 4505 A3
Dixie-Friendswood Rd
17100 BzaC 77581 4628 D2
18000 BzaC 77511 4628 D2
18200 BzaC 77546 4628 D2
Dixie-Friendswood Rd CO-127
18000 BzaC 77511 4628 D2
18000 BzaC 77581 4628 D2
18200 BzaC 77546 4628 D2
Dixie Hill Ct
1600 PRLD 77581 4504 B6
Dixie Hollow St
1600 PRLD 77581 4504 D4
Dixieland Dr
6000 HarC 77039 3547 A3
Dixie Woods Dr
2300 PRLD 77581 4504 E5
Dixon Ct
2900 BzaC 77584 4501 B5
Dixon Dr
2800 BzaC 77584 4501 B5
5000 DKSN 77539 4754 C3
D-Jon Dr
25900 HarC 77377 3108 E5
Doak Ln
8800 HOUS 77075 4376 E3
Dobbin Dr
15400 MtgC 77384 2674 A2
Dobbin Huffsmith Rd
29800 MtgC 77354 2817 D1
29800 MtgC 77354 2818 A2
32000 MtgC 77354 2671 A5
33600 MtgC 77354 2670 E5
Dobbin Hufsmith Rd
26000 MtgC 77354 2964 D1
26200 MtgC 77354 2818 D6
Dobbins Dr
- BzaC 77584 4501 B5
Dobbin Springs Ln
4900 HOUS 77345 3119 E2
Dobbin Stream Wy
3200 HarC 77084 3816 C3
Dobie St
- HOUS 77033 4243 D5
Dobson Dr
15500 HarC 77032 3404 B6
Doby Ln
18000 BzaC 77584 4627 D3
Dobyns Dr
19300 MtgC 77306 2680 C1
Dock Ct
300 HarC 77532 3552 B1
4000 MSCY 77459 4369 D6
Dock Rd
100 TXCY 77590 4875 D7
1800 TXCY 77590 4991 E1
Dockal Rd
7900 HOUS 77028 3826 D1
Dock Bar Ct
16100 HarC 77546 4506 A5
Dockens Forest Ln
6700 HarC 77049 3829 A2
Dockrell St
4100 DKSN 77539 4754 A2
Dockside Cir
21400 HOUS 77450 3954 B2
Dockside Ct
400 SGLD 77478 4368 B3
4300 MSCY 77459 4369 C7
Dockside St
15900 HarC 77532 3552 A3
Dockside Ter
400 HarC 77494 3953 A2
Dockside Terrace Ct
24700 HarC 77494 3953 A2
Dockview Ln
3800 MSCY 77459 4369 D6
Dodar Cedar Ln
32800 WlrC 77484 3246 C1
Dodd Ln
1500 HOUS 77077 3957 D5
Dodd Rd
12700 MtgC 77372 2535 A5
26200 SPLD 77372 2683 B1
Doddridge Ln
600 HarC 77090 3258 D4
Dodge
- HOUS 77017 4106 D3
- HOUS 77506 4106 D3
- PASD 77506 4106 D3
Dodiewood Ln
8000 HarC 77086 3541 E2
Dodson Rd
8200 HOUS 77093 3825 B1
10300 HOUS 77093 3686 B4
10500 HarC 77093 3686 B4
Doe Cir
10 HOUS 77336 3266 B1
24400 MtgC 77365 2974 A7
Doe Ct
14500 MtgC 77355 2962 B2
Doe Dr
32300 MtgC 77355 2962 B2
Doe Pth
- HarC 77396 3407 B5
Doe Tr
24500 MtgC 77355 2961 B5
24500 SGCH 77355 2961 B5
Doe Meadow Dr
12200 STAF 77477 4237 E6
Doerner Ln
9600 MtgC 77354 2672 D7
Doerre Rd
18900 HarC 77379 3111 B5
Doe Run Dr
10 WDLD 77380 2821 E6
S Doe Run Dr
10 WDLD 77380 2821 E6
Doe Run Rd
3000 MSCY 77489 4370 D7
Doeskin Pl
10 WDLD 77382 2673 E4
Dog Run
22500 MtgC 77357 2973 E3
Dog Leg Ct
700 RHMD 77469 4492 A3

STREET
Block City ZIP Map# Grid
Dogwood
- MtgC 77357 2829 B1
- RMFT 77357 2829 B1
Dogwood Av
500 FBnC 77545 4623 C2
6200 MNVL 77578 4625 D6
Dogwood Cir
400 FRDW 77546 4505 A5
S Dogwood Cir
4700 FBnC 77469 4364 A1
Dogwood Dr
- HarC 77396 3406 E5
- WlrC 77447 2813 B2
1200 PASD 77502 4107 D6
1200 PASD 77506 4107 D6
3900 PRLD 77584 4503 B7
4700 RSBG 77471 4491 C5
8700 HarC 77375 2965 D6
9400 MSCY 77459 4370 B6
10900 LPRT 77571 4250 D3
11200 HarC 77338 3263 A4
21200 MtgC 77357 2827 B6
W Dogwood Dr
10800 LPRT 77571 4250 D3
Dogwood Ln
- MtgC 77372 2537 A2
10 HOUS 77345 2974 E7
10 HOUS 77365 2974 E7
200 MtgC 77357 2829 B3
200 RMFT 77357 2829 B3
7300 BYTN 77521 3835 B5
12000 HarC 77429 3398 C3
14600 MtgC 77372 2682 D2
20600 HOUS 77345 3119 E1
20600 HOUS 77365 3119 E1
20600 MtgC 77365 2825 A6
20700 HOUS 77365 2975 A7
25200 PTVL 77372 2682 E6
25500 MtgC 77372 2683 A6
N Dogwood Ln
26600 MtgC 77355 2961 B1
26600 SGCH 77355 2961 B2
S Dogwood Ln
26500 MtgC 77355 2961 B2
26500 SGCH 77355 2961 B2
Dogwood Rd
800 CRLS 77565 4509 C5
Dogwood St
100 BzaC 77511 4748 E1
100 SGLD 77478 4367 E4
100 SGLD 77478 4368 A4
500 HOUS 77022 3824 B2
800 KATY 77493 3952 A1
900 KATY 77493 3813 A7
1400 LbyC 77372 2538 D5
1700 TXCY 77591 4873 B4
2200 LGCY 77573 4632 D2
33100 MtgC 77362 2817 B7
Dogwood Tr
10 PNVL 77304 2237 A3
100 WDBR 77357 2828 C2
3700 BYTN 77521 3973 E3
4700 FBnC 77469 4233 A7
4700 FBnC 77469 4364 A1
18400 HarC 77377 3107 A4
32500 MtgC 77355 2962 A2
Dogwood Bloom Ct
19200 HarC 77379 3112 A6
Dogwood Blossom Ct
3600 PRLD 77581 4503 D7
Dogwood Blossom Tr
2900 PRLD 77581 4503 E6
13000 HarC 77065 3539 B1
Dogwood Bough Ln
3900 FBnC 77545 4498 C7
4000 FBnC 77545 4622 C1
Dogwood Branch Ln
2300 MtgC 77386 2823 B7
Dogwood Brook Tr
1600 HOUS 77062 4380 A5
Dogwood Cluster Ct
500 CNRO 77301 2384 E3
Dogwood Falls Rd
7300 HarC 77095 3678 A1
7400 HarC 77095 3538 B7
Dogwood Forest
10 MtgC 77385 2677 A6
Dogwood Glen Ct
13000 HarC 77429 3254 A6
Dogwood Hill St
4900 PASD 77503 4108 C7
Dogwood Mountain Rd
12000 HarC 77066 3401 A6
Dogwood Park Ct
6500 HarC 77449 3677 B3
Dogwood Park Ln
6500 HarC 77449 3677 B3
Dogwood Ridge Ln
4500 HOUS 77345 3119 D3
Dogwood Springs Dr
3100 HarC 77073 3260 A4
Dogwood Trace Ln
26700 FBnC 77494 4092 A1
Dogwood Trail Dr
7200 HarC 77346 3265 A7
23500 MtgC 77447 2959 E3
Dogwood Trails
200 MAGA 77354 2669 A3
Dogwood Tree St
14300 HarC 77060 3544 D5
14700 HOUS 77060 3544 D4
Dogwood Walk Ct
19600 HarC 77388 3113 B7
Doherty Cir
20000 HarC 77449 3815 E3
Doherty Pl
3500 HarC 77449 3815 E2
Doire Dr
900 CNRO 77301 2530 B2
Dolan Bluff Ln
6800 FBnC 77469 4615 E4
Dolan Fall Ln
21400 FBnC 77450 4094 A4
Dolan Hills Ct
2200 FBnC 77494 3953 C5
Dolan Lake Dr
2300 SGLD 77478 4236 B4
Dolan Park Ln
- HarC 77014 3402 B2
Dolan Ridge Ln
6900 FBnC 77469 4615 D5
Dolan Springs Dr
19300 HarC 77377 3109 B7
Dolan Springs Ln
4400 FBnC 77494 4092 A2
Dolbeau Dr
500 HarC 77015 3828 C6

STREET
Block City ZIP Map# Grid
Dolben Ct
9900 HOUS 77088 3682 C1
Dolben Meadows Ln
20200 HarC 77433 3251 D7
Dolgo Dr
12500 HarC 77429 3398 D5
Doliver Dr
- HOUS 77042 3958 E5
5000 HOUS 77056 3961 A5
5200 HOUS 77056 3960 D5
5800 HOUS 77057 3960 C5
9400 HOUS 77024 3959 C6
9400 HOUS 77063 3959 B5
10000 HOUS 77042 3959 A6
Dollar Reef Dr
4800 GlsC 77539 4634 D4
Dollins St
800 KATY 77493 3952 B1
900 KATY 77493 3813 B7
Dolly Wright St
800 HOUS 77088 3684 A3
900 HOUS 77088 3683 D3
Dolores St
1600 BzaC 77583 4623 D6
5500 HOUS 77056 3960 D7
5500 HOUS 77056 4100 C1
5600 HOUS 77057 3960 D7
5800 HOUS 77057 4100 D1
Dolores Pl Ln
3000 HOUS 77057 4100 D1
Dolphin Av
100 GLSN 77550 5109 E1
Dolphin Cir
9000 TXCY 77591 4873 A4
Dolphin Ct
10 HOUS 77024 3959 C2
3000 SEBK 77586 4509 B3
Dolphin Dr
1700 SEBK 77586 4509 D2
Dolphin Hbr N
100 BYTN 77520 4113 D5
Dolphin Hbr S
100 BYTN 77520 4113 D5
Dolphin Ln
10 BYTN 77520 4113 C1
3800 LPRT 77571 4383 A2
3800 PASD 77571 4383 A2
Dolphin St
- LMQU 77568 4990 D7
10 BYUV 77563 4990 D7
10 GlsC 77563 4990 D7
Dolphin Arc Dr
7600 HarC 77346 3409 B1
Dolrece St
1100 LMQU 77568 4990 B2
Dome Dr
- HarC 77032 3546 C2
Domenico Ln
2700 LGCY 77573 4632 E4
Domer Dr
8300 HarC 77379 3256 B5
Domineco Ln
2500 HarC 77450 3954 D6
Domingo Dr
- HarC 77049 3831 A1
Dominic Ct
1700 HarC 77530 3829 D3
Dominic Ln
1800 HarC 77530 3829 D3
Dominion Dr
10 HarC 77450 3954 D1
10 HOUS 77450 3954 D1
Dominion Park Dr
100 HarC 77090 3402 E2
100 HarC 77090 3403 A2
300 HarC 77014 3402 E2
Dominion Ridge Dr
- CNRO 77304 2237 A4
- PNVL 77304 2237 A4
Dominique Dr
2800 GLSN 77551 5222 A1
2800 GLSN 77554 5222 A1
13900 HarC 77429 3538 E1
13900 HarC 77429 3539 A1
Domino Ln
7300 HOUS 77037 3684 C3
7300 HOUS 77076 3684 C3
Domino Rd
- HarC 77373 3115 A3
10 WlrC 77484 3245 E1
10 WlrC 77484 3246 A2
Dominton Estates Dr
1100 HOUS 77091 3683 C6
Don St
600 PASD 77506 4107 E4
Donalbain Dr
4000 HarC 77373 3260 B1
4400 HarC 77373 3115 C7
Donald Dr
10100 HOUS 77076 3685 B5
Donald Rd
26600 HarC 77373 3114 A1
Donald St
4700 PASD 77586 4383 C4
S Donaldson
500 LPRT 77571 4252 A2
Donaldson Rd
200 BzaC 77511 4628 B5
Donaldson Rd FM-2351
200 BzaC 77511 4628 B5
Donaldson St
100 LPRT 77571 4252 A2
100 MRGP 77571 4252 A2
700 BzaC 77511 4628 C4
700 PRLD 77511 4628 C4
Donata Cir
21500 HarC 77338 3260 A2
Doncaster Dr
200 CNRO 77301 2384 C1
200 CNRO 77303 2238 C7
200 CNRO 77303 2384 C1
Doncaster Rd
11900 BKHV 77024 3959 B4
Doncrest Dr
700 HarC 77530 3829 D7
Dondell Dr
700 HarC 77530 3829 C7
Donegal Ct
2200 DRPK 77536 4109 A6
Donegal St
2300 PRLD 77089 4504 B3
2300 PRLD 77581 4504 B3
Donegal Wy
11100 HOUS 77047 4243 C7
11900 HOUS 77047 4374 C2
Donelson Ln
- HarC 77429 3253 E7
- HarC 77429 3254 A7

STREET
Block City ZIP Map# Grid
Donerail Dr
4100 PASD 77503 4108 D7
Doney St
2700 HOUS 77023 4104 D4
Donfield Dr
700 HarC 77530 3829 D7
Donforth Dr
15700 HOUS 77053 4371 E5
Don Gil St
10000 HOUS 77075 4377 D2
Doninnell St
5700 HOUS 77023 4104 D2
Donlen
- HOUS 77022 3685 B6
Donlen St
- HOUS 77022 3685 B7
6700 HOUS 77022 3824 B1
Donley Dr
2000 BzaC 77583 4624 A3
2200 PRLD 77578 4624 B3
2200 PRLD 77583 4624 B3
8900 HOUS 77088 3543 E7
Donna Dr
10800 HarC 77041 3680 C4
12400 HarC 77067 3402 E6
12400 HOUS 77067 3402 E6
Donna Ln
100 GlsC 77518 4634 E3
100 GlsC 77518 4635 A3
14700 HarC 77532 3553 E5
Donna Rd
11000 MtgC 77306 2532 B1
Donna Ana Rd
40300 MtgC 77354 2672 C2
Donna Bell Ln
3600 HOUS 77018 3822 C2
4300 HOUS 77018 3683 C7
Donnacorey Dr
500 HOUS 77013 3966 C1
Donna Farms
- HarC 77375 2965 D2
Donna Lynn Ct
5100 HOUS 77092 3821 E1
Donna Lynn Dr
4100 HOUS 77092 3821 E1
Donnet Ln
15500 HarC 77032 3404 C6
Donoho St
- HMPD 77445 3097 E2
100 HMPD 77445 3098 C2
6000 HOUS 77033 4244 B1
Donovan St
1500 BYTN 77520 3973 B5
W Donovan St
300 HOUS 77022 3684 C6
300 HOUS 77091 3684 A6
1000 HOUS 77091 3683 E6
Donovan Vw
2400 GlsC 77539 4753 C1
Donrel Wy
2200 HarC 77067 3402 B4
Donwell Ln
- HarC 77429 3253 E6
Donwhite Ln
5900 HOUS 77088 3682 D1
Donwick Dr
16500 MtgC 77385 2676 C5
16500 WDLD 77385 2676 C5
Donys Dr
8700 HarC 77040 3541 B6
Doolan Dr
2000 CNRO 77301 2530 B4
Dooley St
- PRVW 77445 3100 B1
Doolittle Blvd
4700 HOUS 77033 4243 E1
5200 HOUS 77033 4244 A1
Doonside Dr
19800 HarC 77449 3676 E3
Dora Ln
15200 FBnC 77478 4236 C5
Dora St
5300 HOUS 77005 4102 D2
5300 HOUS 77006 4102 D2
Dorado Cir
31200 TMBL 77375 2963 E4
Dorado Dr
10 FRDW 77546 4628 E7
Doral Ct
700 FRDW 77546 4629 A5
1400 BYTN 77520 4113 B3
2900 LGCY 77573 4508 E7
Doral Dr
2400 BYTN 77520 4113 A3
4300 PASD 77505 4248 E6
N Doral Dr
2700 MSCY 77459 4497 A1
S Doral Dr
2800 MSCY 77459 4497 A1
Doral Ln
900 HarC 77073 3259 A2
Doraldale Ct
8500 HarC 77040 3541 C6
Doral Rose Ln
21300 HarC 77449 3815 B4
Dora Meadows Dr
- FBnC 77083 4236 B2
9400 FBnC 77478 4236 B2
Dorantes Ln
- HOUS 77336 3266 C1
Dorbrandt Rd
10100 CNRO 77303 2238 C6
Dorbrandt St
5500 HOUS 77023 4104 C2
Dorchester Ct
3400 SGLD 77478 4368 D4
Dorchester St
600 HOUS 77022 3824 C2
3700 HOUS 77016 3825 A2
3700 HOUS 77093 3825 A2
Dorchester Wy
- CNRO 77304 2529 D1
Dorchester Forest Dr
13200 HarC 77070 3399 D3
13200 HOUS 77070 3399 D3
Doreen Av
4400 FBnC 77545 4623 C2
4700 FBnC 77583 4623 C3
4800 ARLA 77583 4623 C3
Doreen St
6000 BzaC 77583 4623 C5
6000 PRLD 77583 4623 C5
Dorene St
- HOUS 77017 4246 E1
1100 HOUS 77502 4246 E1
1300 PASD 77502 4246 E1
Doric Ct
11200 HarC 77429 3539 A1

STREET Block City ZIP Map# Grid
ris Av
400 PASD 77502 4247 B1
ris Cir N
10 BzaC 77511 4868 A5
ris Cir W
10 BzaC 77511 4868 A5
ris Rd
3800 GlsC 77517 4752 B7
ris St
- CNRO 77304 2383 B4
- CRLS 77565 4509 C6
900 GlsC 77565 4509 C6
1000 DRPK 77536 4109 C5
3900 GlsC 77517 4752 B7
ris Stinson Rd
3400 BzaC 77511 4868 D5
rita Ln
9600 HarC 77038 3544 A5
rking Ct
4900 HarC 77530 3829 C5
rman Ct
2200 FBnC 77494 3952 B5
rmstom Ln
1900 HarC 77088 3543 D6
rnoch Dr
2100 LGCY 77573 4508 D7
9400 HarC 77379 3255 D4
9800 HarC 77070 3255 C4
rothea Ln
10 SGLD 77479 4495 A2
rothy Ln
3600 PRLD 77581 4503 E5
3600 PRLD 77581 4504 A5
20200 MtgC 77357 2829 A6
rothy St
700 HOUS 77007 3962 C1
800 HOUS 77007 3823 B7
1300 HOUS 77008 3823 B6
2000 PASD 77502 4106 E7
2000 PASD 77502 4246 E1
4300 BLAR 77401 4101 B6
4300 HOUS 77401 4101 B6
rothy Ann Dr
5600 HOUS 77076 3684 E6
orrance Ln
- MDWP 77478 4237 E5
- SGLD 77478 4237 E5
11000 MDWP 77477 4238 A5
11000 STAF 77477 4238 C5
12100 MDWP 77477 4237 E5
orrance Rd
10100 HarC 77031 4238 E5
10100 HOUS 77031 4238 E5
orray Ln
14800 HarC 77082 4096 C2
orrcrest Ln
8100 HarC 77070 3399 D2
orridge Ct
- HarC 77040 3681 A1
orrington St
- HOUS 77025 4102 A4
2200 HOUS 77030 4102 A4
orrington Estates Ln
23800 MtgC 77385 2823 A7
orris St
2300 BYTN 77520 3972 C6
orriss Rd
19200 MtgC 77355 2813 E2
orsall Wy
400 HarC 77532 3552 B1
600 HarC 77532 3411 A7
orset
19100 MtgC 77357 2829 B4
Dorset Ct
- MtgC 77357 2829 D3
Dorset Sq
10 WDLD 77381 2821 B5
E Dorset St
12800 HOUS 77077 3957 C6
W Dorset St
12800 HOUS 77077 3957 C6
Dorsetshire Dr
1200 PASD 77504 4247 D6
7100 HOUS 77040 3682 B1
Dorsett St
700 HOUS 77029 3965 B2
2300 HOUS 77020 3965 B5
Dorsette Ct
- SGLD 77478 4237 A5
Dorsey Dr
5900 MtgC 77354 2673 D2
Dorsey Ln
3400 PRLD 77584 4502 D6
Dorsey Fall Dr
- FBnC 77469 4092 D7
Dorston Dr
20200 MtgC 77357 2829 A6
Dorwayne Ct
12200 HOUS 77015 3966 E3
12300 HOUS 77015 3967 A4
Dorwayne St
12500 HOUS 77015 3967 A3
Dorylee Ln
6300 HarC 77396 3547 B3
Dorywood Dr
13900 HarC 77038 3543 A1
Dorywood Rd
13800 HarC 77038 3543 A1
Dos Dr
3900 GLSN 77554 5220 B7
Dosia St
8500 HOUS 77051 4243 D3
Doskocil Dr
8500 HarC 77044 3689 C5
Doss Rd
- HarC 77038 3543 B3
Dossey
- LPRT 77571 4251 A1
Doss Park Rd
13000 HarC 77038 3543 A3
Dotson Rd
13200 HarC 77070 3399 E3
13200 HOUS 77070 3399 E3
Dottie Dr
- HOUS 77060 3403 B6
12600 HarC 77060 3403 B6
Double St
9200 HOUS 77088 3683 E1
Double B
14100 MtgC 77372 2683 E1
Double Bay Rd
17000 HarC 77429 3396 B1
Doubleday Dr
12000 HOUS 77089 4378 C6
Double Eagle Dr
4900 PASD 77505 4249 A7
E Double Green Cir
10 WDLD 77382 2673 D6
W Double Green Cir
10 WDLD 77382 2673 D6
Double Jack Ct
3100 HarC 77373 3115 A4
Double Lake Blvd
3000 MSCY 77459 4496 B2
Double Lake Dr
2600 MSCY 77459 4496 B2
Double Lilly Dr
17200 HarC 77095 3537 E3
Double Meadows Ct
7400 HarC 77433 3676 C1
Double Meadows Dr
20500 HarC 77433 3676 D1
Double Pine Dr
13800 HarC 77015 3828 E5
14000 HarC 77015 3829 A5
Double Shoals Cir
14300 HarC 77090 3258 C7
Double Six St
14500 MtgC 77372 2683 C2
Double T St
27100 MtgC 77372 2683 D1
Double Trail Ct
3900 MSCY 77459 4496 D1
Double Tree Dr
12000 HarC 77070 3399 B6
Double Tree Plz
- HOUS 77032 3405 A6
Doubletree Glen Dr
800 HarC 77073 3259 A3
Doubletree Park Dr
22200 HarC 77073 3259 A3
Doubletree Vista Dr
900 HarC 77073 3259 A3
Double X St
27200 MtgC 77372 2683 D2
Doubloon Dr
100 BzaC 77541 5547 B7
Doud St
- HOUS 77096 4101 A7
- HOUS 77096 4241 A2
10600 HOUS 77035 4241 A3
Douget Rd
11800 CTSH 77303 2385 C3
11800 CTSH 77306 2385 C3
11800 MtgC 77303 2385 C3
Douglas Ln
300 MSCY 77489 4370 B3
Douglas Rd
- PNIS 77445 3245 A1
- WlrC 77445 3245 A1
34100 PNIS 77445 3100 A7
Douglas St
100 RHMD 77469 4491 D1
300 BYTN 77520 3971 C4
2400 PRLD 77581 4503 C4
4000 HOUS 77018 3823 D2
S Douglas St
600 ALVN 77511 4867 C2
Douglas Creek Ln
3000 MtgC 77386 2969 D2
Douglas Fir Dr
400 MtgC 77354 2673 E2
Douglas Fir St
11900 HarC 77066 3401 A6
Douglas Park Ct
20700 FBnC 77450 4094 C3
Douglas Park Dr
- FBnC 77450 4094 C3
Douglas Pass
- LGCY 77573 4633 B1
Douglass Chase Dr
7600 HOUS 77016 3687 A3
Doulton Dr
5000 HOUS 77033 4243 E2
5600 HOUS 77033 4244 A2
Dounreay Dr
16300 HarC 77084 3678 C7
Douroux Rd
100 LMQU 77568 4873 C7
100 TXCY 77591 4873 C7
300 LMQU 77568 4989 C1
Douse Wy
- HarC 77532 3551 E5
- HarC 77532 3552 A5
Douvaine Ct
10 WDLD 77382 2820 A1
Dove Ct
10 MtgC 77385 2676 D6
1900 FRDW 77546 4629 D5
3400 PRLD 77581 4503 D5
Dove Ln
29000 WlrC 77493 3812 A2
Dove St
1200 HOUS 77015 3967 A3
Dove Tr
- TMBL 77375 2964 A6
- WDLD 77381 2674 E6
1300 TMBL 77375 2963 E6
Dove Wy
9100 HOUS 77075 4377 A4
Dove Brook Ct
12800 HarC 77041 3679 D4
Dove Call Ct
10 WDLD 77382 2819 B3
Dove Canyon Ln
22000 MtgC 77357 2973 B2
Dovecoft Ln
600 FBnC 77469 4616 E1
Dovecote Ct
- WDLD 77382 2819 B1
Dovecott Ln
8400 HarC 77083 4097 B7
Dove Country Dr
2700 FBnC 77477 4369 D4
2900 MSCY 77477 4369 D4
Dove Cove Cir
3200 HMBL 77396 3406 D5
Dove Creek Cir
10900 HarC 77086 3542 A1
Dovedale Ct
11500 HarC 77067 3402 A6
Dovedale Ln
400 ALVN 77511 4867 D7
Dove Fern Ct
6100 HarC 77041 3679 D4
Dove Field Ln
18000 HarC 77433 3677 D1
Dove Forest Ln
5500 HarC 77346 3264 C4
Dove Haven Ct
21400 MtgC 77357 2973 B2
21400 MtgC 77365 2973 B2
Dove Haven Ln
2200 LGCY 77573 4632 D2
Dove Hollow Ct
7100 FBnC 77469 4094 B7
Dove Lake Dr
37400 MtgC 77354 2816 A1
37600 MtgC 77354 2669 E7
37600 MtgC 77354 2670 A7
37600 MtgC 77354 2815 E1
Dove Manor Ct
10 HarC 77379 3110 D7
Dove Meadows Dr
3600 DKSN 77539 4753 B5
3600 LGCY 77539 4753 B5
Dove Oaks Ct
12900 HarC 77041 3679 D5
Dove Park Ct
10900 HOUS 77075 4377 A4
Dove Pass Ct
17800 FBnC 77469 4095 B6
Doveplum Pl
10 WDLD 77382 2674 D5
Dove Point Ln
12800 HarC 77041 3679 D4
Dove Prairie Ct
6200 HarC 77041 3679 D4
Dover Av
4200 STFE 77510 4870 E7
Dover Dr
10 CNRO 77304 2529 C1
Dover Ln
200 FRDW 77546 4505 A6
300 LGCY 77573 4630 C7
400 HarC 77373 3113 E7
400 HarC 77373 3114 A7
Dover Mdw
12000 HarC 77070 3399 A6
Dover St
1100 ALVN 77511 4867 A2
2800 HOUS 77017 4105 C5
3700 HOUS 77087 4105 C7
3900 DRPK 77536 4249 C1
4100 HOUS 77087 4245 C1
8100 HOUS 77061 4245 C2
11300 HOUS 77031 4238 E6
11600 HarC 77031 4238 E6
Dover Wy
6600 HarC 77389 2966 C5
Doverbrook Dr
27200 HarC 77336 3122 A3
27500 HarC 77336 3121 E2
Dover Cliff Ct
16500 HarC 77532 3552 B2
Dover Creek Ln
- FBnC 77494 4092 A5
Dover Falls Ct
10200 HarC 77338 3407 D1
Doverfield Dr
200 HarC 77037 3684 D2
W Doverfield Dr
100 HarC 77037 3684 C1
Doverglen Dr
2300 MSCY 77489 4370 E6
2400 MSCY 77489 4371 A7
Dover Hill Rd
9700 LPRT 77571 4250 A3
Dover House Wy
6000 HarC 77389 2966 D3
Dove Ridge Ln
5700 HarC 77041 3679 D5
Dover Mills Dr
16500 HarC 77379 3256 E2
Dover Park Ln
21100 FBnC 77450 4094 A4
Doversgreen Ln
19900 HarC 77388 3112 E5
19900 HarC 77388 3113 A4
Dovershire
24200 HarC 77389 2966 E4
Doverside St
600 HOUS 77022 3685 B7
Dover Springs Ct
9700 FBnC 77494 4092 D5
Doverton Ln
16300 HarC 77377 3254 B6
Dove Run Ct
7700 HarC 77433 3537 B7
Doverwick Dr
24000 HarC 77375 2965 D5
Doverwood Wy
16700 HOUS 77058 4507 D3
Doves Lndg
19200 HarC 77375 3110 A7
Doveshire Ct
3300 HarC 77449 3816 A3
Dove Springs Dr
4600 HarC 77066 3401 B5
Doves Yard
8600 FBnC 77459 4621 B5
Dovetail Ln
7700 FBnC 77469 4095 C6
Dovetail Pl
10 WDLD 77381 2820 C2
Doveton Ln
19100 HarC 77388 3112 C5
Dove Trace Cir
- WDLD 77382 2820 A2
S Dove Trace Cir
10 WDLD 77382 2820 A2
Dove Trail Ct
16000 HarC 77429 3252 C6
Dove Tree Dr
2700 ALVN 77511 4866 D4
Dove Tree Ln
17700 HarC 77379 3256 A3
Dovewing Pl
10 WDLD 77382 2674 C6
Dovewood Ln
2700 HarC 77373 3114 D6
Dovewood Pl
10 WDLD 77381 2820 E2
Dovewood Springs Ln
- HarC 77375 3255 B1
Dovie Dr
3300 MtgC 77380 2967 B2
Dovington Ct
21700 HarC 77388 3112 B4
Dow Cir
2600 DRPK 77536 4109 B7
Dow Rd
5200 HOUS 77040 3681 E6
Dow Wy
4300 PASD 77505 4248 D6
Dowber Rd
6000 HOUS 77076 3684 C5
Dowcrest Dr
6600 HarC 77389 2966 C6
Dowdell Rd
7600 HarC 77375 2966 A7
7600 HarC 77389 2966 A7
8400 HarC 77375 2965 E7
8700 HarC 77375 3110 D1
Dowling Cir
10 LMQU 77568 4989 D1
Dowling Dr
1900 RHMD 77469 4491 E3
1900 RHMD 77469 4492 A3
Dowling St
200 HOUS 77003 3963 E5
2200 HOUS 77004 3963 C7
3300 HOUS 77004 4103 A2
Dowlwood Dr
- HarC 77032 3404 A6
Downdale Cir
22500 FBnC 77450 4093 E2
S Downe Ct
12000 HarC 77089 4505 A1
S Downe Dr
11500 HarC 77089 4505 B1
Downey St
2300 LMQU 77568 4990 A3
3800 STFE 77517 4870 B6
11900 HOUS 77037 3685 A2
11900 HOUS 77076 3685 A2
Downey Bayou Ln
10 HOUS 77013 3966 E1
Downey Cove
100 TXCY 77591 4873 B7
Downford Dr
15500 HarC 77377 3254 E6
Downgate Dr
4100 HarC 77084 3816 E1
Downheath Ln
15700 HarC 77073 3259 C5
Downing Cir
1100 LGCY 77573 4631 D4
3600 DRPK 77536 4249 C1
Downing St
2900 PRLD 77581 4504 A2
5700 HOUS 77020 3825 D7
Downington Ct
8000 HarC 77379 3255 E2
8000 HarC 77379 3256 B1
Downs Ln
4300 HOUS 77093 3686 B4
4800 HOUS 77016 3686 C5
Downwood Forest Dr
6000 HarC 77088 3542 C6
N Downy Willow Cir
- WDLD 77382 2673 D5
S Downy Willow Cir
10 WDLD 77382 2673 D5
Dow Pipeline County Rd
- DRPK 77536 4110 A6
- DRPK 77571 4110 A6
- LPRT 77571 4110 A6
Doyle Ct
3700 FBnC 77459 4621 B5
4100 PASD 77503 4108 D7
Doyle St
3200 HOUS 77093 3686 A7
Dozent Ln
100 HarC 77521 3834 E6
100 HarC 77521 3835 A7
Dr. John Codwell Dr
- HOUS 77013 3965 E1
- HOUS 77013 3966 A1
Dracaena Ct
14400 HarC 77070 3398 C1
Dracena Ct
800 FBnC 77469 4365 B4
Drago St
- HOUS 77088 3683 A2
Dragonfly Dr
800 CNRO 77301 2384 C7
Dragon Fly Ln
30000 HarC 77377 2963 C5
Dragonfly Meadow Ct
9900 HarC 77396 3407 B7
Dragon Hill Pl
10 WDLD 77381 2821 D1
Dragon Spruce Pl
10 WDLD 77382 2673 D5
Dragonwick Dr
3100 HOUS 77045 4242 A7
3300 HOUS 77045 4241 E7
N Dragonwood Pl
10 WDLD 77381 2674 E6
S Dragonwood Pl
10 WDLD 77381 2674 C7
Dragonwood Tr
9000 FBnC 77083 4236 C1
Drake Ct
6000 KATY 77493 3813 B3
Drake Ln
400 LGCY 77573 4630 B7
Drake St
3700 HOUS 77005 4101 D2
Drake Book Ln
19200 HarC 77433 3251 E7
Drake Elm Ct
100 FBnC 77479 4367 B4
Drake Elm Dr
6300 FBnC 77479 4367 B4
Drake Falls Ct
4600 FBnC 77450 4094 A2
Drake Falls Dr
2100 PRLD 77584 4500 B2
Drakefield Ct
24400 FBnC 77494 3953 B7
Drakeford Ct
- HarC 77047 4374 B4
Drakeland Dr
10800 HarC 77396 3407 D7
Drakemill Dr
12200 HOUS 77077 3957 E4
Drake Oak St
2100 FBnC 77545 4622 C1
Drake Prairie Ln
12300 HarC 77429 3398 B6
Drake Run Ln
200 DKSN 77539 4753 A5
200 LGCY 77539 4753 A5
Drake Springs Ln
- PRLD 77583 4500 B5
Drakestone Blvd
5500 HOUS 77053 4371 E4
5500 HOUS 77053 4372 A4
Drakeview Ct
5400 SGLD 77479 4495 B4
Drakewood Dr
13700 SGLD 77478 4237 A7
20400 HarC 77449 3815 D2
Draksbury Ln
- FBnC 77494 4093 C1
Drane Ct
900 HOUS 77008 3823 A7
Draper Rd
15000 HarC 77014 3257 D6
15000 HarC 77068 3257 D6
20200 HarC 77377 3106 B3
Drava Ln
1000 HarC 77090 3258 B2
Drawbridge Dr
3600 HarC 77396 3407 E2
Draycott Ln
14400 HOUS 77045 4372 C3
Drayton Ln
2100 HarC 77088 3543 D7
2600 HOUS 77088 3543 B7
Dream Ct
5900 HOUS 77085 4371 E1
Dreamland Av
100 HarC 77532 3692 C1
Dreamscape Cir
14200 HarC 77047 4374 D5
N Dreamweaver Cir
100 WDLD 77380 2968 A3
200 WDLD 77380 2967 E3
S Dreamweaver Cir
- WDLD 77380 2967 E3
10 WDLD 77380 2968 A3
Drennan Dr
25300 MtgC 77372 2536 E4
25300 MtgC 77372 2537 A4
Drennan Rd
- CNRO 77303 2383 D1
Drennan St
10 HOUS 77003 3964 A6
N Drennan St
100 HOUS 77003 3964 B4
Drennanburg Ct
3100 HarC 77449 3816 A4
Drennen Rd
- CNRO 77303 2383 D1
Drenner Park Ln
5900 HarC 77086 3542 D3
Dresden Pl
10 WDLD 77382 2820 A2
Dresden St
100 HOUS 77012 4105 B1
Dresden Ridge Ln
12900 HarC 77070 3399 C4
Dresher Dr
600 HarC 77373 3113 E6
600 HarC 77373 3114 A6
Drew Ln
6500 MtgC 77304 2382 D4
Drew St
10 HOUS 77006 3962 C5
1000 HOUS 77002 3963 A6
1000 HOUS 77006 3963 A6
1400 HOUS 77004 3963 B6
3200 HOUS 77004 4103 D1
4100 HOUS 77004 4104 A1
6800 HTCK 77563 4989 A5
W Drew St
1000 HOUS 77006 3962 D5
Drewberry St
9200 HOUS 77080 3820 D3
Drewdale Ct
- WDLD 77382 2819 A1
Drewfalls Ct
22100 FBnC 77469 4093 E7
Drewfalls Dr
6500 FBnC 77469 4093 E7
Drew Forest Ln
4800 HarC 77346 3408 B1
Drew Haven Ln
8300 HarC 77379 3256 A1
Drewlaine Fields Dr
6700 HarC 77449 3677 D2
Drews Manor Ct
2900 FBnC 77494 3953 C6
Drexel Cir
2300 HOUS 77027 3961 C6
Drexel Dr
1200 KATY 77493 3813 D6
2000 HOUS 77019 3961 C6
2000 HOUS 77027 3961 C7
3500 HOUS 77027 4101 C1
Drexelbrook Dr
11800 HOUS 77077 3958 A5
Drexel Hill Dr
11900 HOUS 77077 3958 A5
Dreyer Ct
- HarC 77040 3681 A1
Dreyfus St
1000 HOUS 77030 4102 C6
3600 HOUS 77021 4103 B7
Dribeck Ct
- HarC 77014 3257 C7
- HarC 77014 3401 C1
Drifter Ct
2400 BzaC 77584 4501 B4
N Drifting Leaf Ct
10 WDLD 77380 2968 B4
S Drifting Leaf Ct
10 WDLD 77380 2968 A4
Drifting Oaks Ct
- HarC 77095 3538 D3
Drifting Oaks Dr
- HarC 77095 3538 E3
Drifting Pine Ct
12200 HarC 77066 3401 B5
Drifting Rose Cir
16000 HarC 77429 3252 D6
Drifting Rose Dr
15800 HarC 77429 3252 D6
Drifting Shadows Cir
10 WDLD 77385 2676 B3
W Drifting Shadows Cir
10 WDLD 77385 2676 B3
Drifting Shadows Ct
10 WDLD 77385 2676 C3
Drifting Willow Ct
7500 HarC 77433 3677 B1
Drifting Winds Dr
11900 HarC 77044 3688 E5
12400 HarC 77044 3689 A5
Driftoak Cir
10 WDLD 77381 2674 D7
Driftstone Dr
8800 HarC 77379 3255 E4
Driftstore Ct
1900 FBnC 77469 4492 E4
Driftwood Ct
3400 SGLD 77478 4368 E4
Driftwood Dr
- HarC 77507 4250 D4
- LPRT 77571 4250 D4
- TYLV 77586 4381 E7
100 TYLV 77586 4382 A7
2700 BzaC 77578 4625 A1
4600 BYTN 77521 3972 B1
Drift Wood Ln
2600 SEBK 77586 4382 B7
Driftwood Ln
1500 GLSN 77551 5108 B6
28900 SHEH 77381 2821 E2
28900 SHEH 77381 2822 A2
Driftwood St
200 LGCY 77573 4631 E4
6700 HOUS 77021 4103 C6
Driftwood Oak Ct
15400 HOUS 77059 4380 B5
Driftwood Park Dr
9900 HarC 77095 3538 E3
Driftwood Prairie Ln
17500 HarC 77095 3537 D3
Driftwood Springs Dr
18700 HarC 77449 3677 C4
Drilling Tools Inc Blvd
6600 HarC 77041 3680 B4
Drio Dr
- DRPK 77536 4109 E6
Dripping Point Ln
3500 FBnC 77494 4092 A2
Dripping Springs Dr
13400 HarC 77083 4097 B4
Driscoll St
1300 HOUS 77019 3962 C5
3800 HOUS 77098 3962 C7
Dristone Dr
2200 HOUS 77339 3119 A4
Drive A
- STAF 77477 4369 B2
Drive C
- STAF 77477 4369 B2
Drive D
- STAF 77477 4369 B2
Drive E
- STAF 77477 4369 C2
Drive F
- STAF 77477 4369 C2
Driver Ct
17100 FBnC 77478 4235 E7
Driver Ln
16900 FBnC 77478 4235 E7
Driver Green Ln
1800 HarC 77493 3814 B6
Drivers Rd
24300 MtgC 77372 2536 D7
24300 MtgC 77372 2682 C1
Dr Martin Luther King Jr Pl N
800 CNRO 77301 2384 C6
Dr Martin Luther King Jr Pl S
200 CNRO 77301 2384 B6
Droddy St
4800 HOUS 77091 3683 A6
5000 HOUS 77091 3682 E6
Droitwich Dr
18600 HarC 77346 3264 D7
Drouet St
7500 HOUS 77061 4245 B3
Drowsy Pine Dr
- MtgC 77357 2829 A5
7100 HOUS 77040 3682 B5
7100 HOUS 77092 3682 B5
Droxford Dr
1500 HOUS 77008 3822 E6
Droxshire Dr
10100 HMBL 77338 3262 D4
DRS Rd
700 FBnC 77469 4365 B5
Drucker Dr
- HarC 77066 3401 D6
Druid Av
2500 HOUS 77091 3683 B5
Druid St
2400 HOUS 77091 3683 C5
14000 MtgC 77302 2678 D7
15000 MtgC 77302 2824 D1
Druids Glen Pl
10 WDLD 77382 2819 C2
Drumcliffe Ct
300 HarC 77015 3828 E6
Drum Heller Ln
17900 HarC 77377 3254 B2
Drummer Dr
2500 LGCY 77573 4631 B5
Drummet
15100 HarC 77032 3405 B7
15100 HOUS 77032 3405 B7
Drummet Blvd
- HarC 77032 3546 A1
Drummond St
3200 HOUS 77025 4101 C6
Drummond Park Dr
11900 HarC 77044 3548 D5
Drumoak
28800 MtgC 77354 2818 C2
Drum Roll Dr
8300 HarC 77064 3541 E5
Drumwood Ln
12600 HarC 77429 3398 B6
Drury Ln
1200 HOUS 77055 3821 D7
Dryad Dr
4700 HOUS 77035 4240 D5
Drybank Dr
3100 HarC 77449 3815 C3
Dry Bank Ln
2400 PRLD 77584 4500 A3
Dryberry Ct
16200 FBnC 77083 4236 A2
Dryberry Dr
- PRLD 77584 4502 A6
Drybrook Rd
25900 HarC 77389 2966 A2
Drybrook Crossing Ln
7800 FBnC 77469 4094 E7
Dryburgh Ct
3400 HarC 77336 3121 D2
Dry Canyon Ct
19400 HarC 77449 3677 A4
Dry Creek Dr
3400 PASD 77505 4248 E4
14200 HarC 77429 3396 D2
14500 HarC 77429 3252 D7
20400 MtgC 77357 2680 E7
20400 MtgC 77357 2827 A1
27100 MtgC 77354 2819 A4
Dry Creek Ranch Rd
13800 HarC 77429 3396 D2
Dryden Ln
5200 PASD 77505 4248 E7
Dryden Rd
2100 HOUS 77030 4102 B3
2400 HOUS 77005 4102 A3
2400 WUNP 77005 4102 A3
Dryden Mills Ln
13600 HarC 77070 3399 C3
Dry Desert Wy
9500 LPRT 77571 4250 A4
Dryer St
800 ALVN 77511 4749 A7
Dryer Park Dr
- HarC 77373 3115 B3
Dryfalls Ct
21000 HarC 77449 3815 C3
Dry Sand Dr
9500 LPRT 77571 4250 A3
Drysdale Ln
9800 HOUS 77041 3681 B5
Dry Spring Ln
- HarC 77373 3114 E3
Dry Springs Dr
9500 LPRT 77571 4250 A4
Drystone Ln
16300 HarC 77095 3538 B5
Drywood Ln
- HarC 77433 3537 B7
Drywood Creek Dr
- LGCY 77573 4753 B1
Drywood Crossing Ct
23200 HarC 77373 2968 C6
DS Bailey Ln
6500 HOUS 77091 3683 E4
Dual Cir Ct
12200 HarC 77429 3397 B5
Duan St
7000 HOUS 77022 3824 B2
Duane Ct
12200 HOUS 77047 4374 D1
Duane Dr
2200 LPRT 77571 4250 E1
Duane St
8600 HOUS 77051 4243 D3
11100 HOUS 77047 4243 D7
11900 HOUS 77047 4374 D1
Duart Dr
11700 HDWV 77024 3959 C2
Du Barry Ln
1100 HOUS 77018 3822 E2
Dublin Cir
2300 PRLD 77581 4504 D2
Dublin Ct
13600 STAF 77477 4369 C1
Dublin Dr
1800 LGCY 77573 4631 C6
1900 DRPK 77536 4109 A6
Dublin Ln
5900 PRLD 77581 4502 D2
Dublin St
14000 HOUS 77085 4371 B1
Dubloon Av
13800 GLSN 77554 5332 D1
Du Bois Rd
7100 HOUS 77088 3683 B4
Du Bois St
3600 HOUS 77051 4243 B2
Du Boise St
6800 HOUS 77091 3683 B4
6900 HOUS 77088 3683 B4
Duce Dr
8500 HOUS 77078 3688 B6
Duchamp Dr
10100 HOUS 77036 4238 E1
Duchess Ct
10 BKHV 77024 3959 B3
Duchess Ln
4000 BzaC 77511 4627 B7
12600 HarC 77070 3399 B5
Duchess Wy
2400 STAF 77477 4369 D3
Duchess Park Ct
3400 FRDW 77598 4630 C3
Duchess Park Ln
3100 FRDW 77598 4630 B3
Duckett Park Dr
6400 HarC 77086 3542 C3
6400 HOUS 77086 3542 C3
Ducklake Ln
2100 HarC 77084 3816 B7
Duck Tail Ln
16100 HarC 77447 3248 E7
Duckwater Cove
16800 HarC 77095 3538 A1
Duclair Ln
16200 HarC 77447 3248 E6
Dude Rd
10200 HarC 77064 3540 B5
Dudley St
800 RHMD 77469 4491 E2
3000 HOUS 77021 4103 A5
Duer Ln
- CNRO 77301 2530 C3
Duesenberg Ct
4500 PRLD 77584 4501 E6
Duesenberg Dr
4400 PRLD 77584 4501 E6
Duessen Pkwy
18100 HarC 77346 3409 B1
Duessen Pkwy E
- HarC 77044 3550 C5
Duessen Pkwy W
- HarC 77044 3550 B5
Duff Ln
600 HOUS 77022 3685 C7
Duffer Ln
1000 HOUS 77034 4378 E2
Duffield Ln
7800 HOUS 77071 4239 E4
Duffton St
16200 HarC 77429 3397 A6
Duffy Ln
3300 BzaC 77583 4500 D7
11300 MtgC 77302 2531 C6
Duh Oak Cir
8000 HarC 77379 3256 A3
Duhon Pl
2400 SEBK 77586 4509 C1
Duial Brock Dr
18500 HarC 77346 3265 C7
Duke
- ARLA 77583 4622 C4
- FBnC 77583 4622 C4
Duke Ln
3300 FRDW 77598 4630 C4
Duke Rd
14600 MtgC 77372 2682 D3
14600 SPLD 77372 2682 E2
Duke St
1100 BYTN 77520 4112 D1
2800 WUNP 77005 4102 A3
3000 WUNP 77005 4101 E3
Duke Alexander Dr
21500 MtgC 77339 3118 C4
Dukedale Dr
10 WDLD 77382 2674 A5

STREET
Block City ZIP Map# Grid

Duke Lake Dr
18700 HarC 77388 3113 B7
18700 HarC 77388 3258 B1
Duke of York Cir
- HarC 77070 3399 B3
Duke of York Ln
10600 HarC 77070 3399 B3
Dukes Bnd
300 STAF 77477 4370 A4
Dukes Run Dr
22300 HarC 77373 3115 A5
Dula Ln
11800 HarC 77065 3398 D6
11800 HarC 77429 3398 D6
Dula St
500 ALVN 77511 4867 C2
S Dula St
700 ALVN 77511 4867 C2
Du Lac Trc
2500 SEBK 77586 4509 C2
Dulaney Rd
2900 HarC 77084 3816 C4
2900 HOUS 77084 3816 C5
Dulaney St
25700 SPLD 77372 2683 A2
N Dulcet Hollow Cir
10 WDLD 77382 2819 D1
S Dulcet Hollow Cir
10 WDLD 77382 2819 C1
Dulcet Hollow Ct
10 WDLD 77382 2819 C2
Dulcimer St
9200 HOUS 77051 4243 A5
Dulcimer Woods Dr
- SHEH 77381 2821 E2
- WDLD 77381 2821 E2
Dulcrest St
3300 HOUS 77051 4243 B6
Duller Ln
8000 HOUS 77017 4105 C5
Dulles Av
- FBnC 77459 4369 B6
100 STAF 77477 4369 B2
300 SGLD 77477 4369 B2
300 SGLD 77478 4369 B6
600 FBnC 77477 4369 B6
1500 MSCY 77459 4369 B6
1500 SGLD 77459 4369 B5
1700 MSCY 77478 4369 B6
2800 MSCY 77459 4496 B1
2800 SGLD 77478 4496 B1
2800 SGLD 77479 4496 B1
Du Lock Ln
1300 HOUS 77055 3820 B7
Duluth St
13300 HOUS 77015 3967 D2
Dumaine Ct
10 CNRO 77304 2382 E3
Dumas St
11200 HOUS 77034 4377 E1
12000 HOUS 77034 4378 B1
Dumbarton Pl
6900 SGLD 77479 4367 C6
Dumbarton Rd
3700 PASD 77503 4108 C4
Dumbarton St
4000 HOUS 77025 4101 C5
Dumble St
400 HOUS 77011 3964 B7
500 HOUS 77023 3964 B7
1600 HOUS 77023 4104 B1
6300 HOUS 77021 4103 E7
E Dumble St
100 ALVN 77511 4867 C2
W Dumble St
300 ALVN 77511 4867 B2
1700 ALVN 77511 4866 E2
Dumfries Dr
- HOUS 77071 4240 A2
4900 HOUS 77096 4241 A2
5000 HOUS 77096 4240 E2
Dumfries St
3800 SGLD 77479 4495 E3
Dumont St
600 HOUS 77017 4246 C2
600 SHUS 77017 4246 C2
600 SHUS 77587 4246 C2
Dumore Dr
5100 HOUS 77048 4243 E6
5200 HOUS 77048 4244 A7
Dunain Park Ct
9200 HarC 77095 3538 B4
Dunaway St
- GNPK 77015 3967 A4
1600 GNPK 77015 3966 E4
1600 HOUS 77015 3966 E4
Dunbar Av
19500 HOUS 77338 3262 A5
Dunbar Cir
18800 GlsC 77511 4868 E3
18800 GlsC 77511 4869 A3
Dunbar Ct
6100 LGCY 77573 4630 B7
Dunbar St
900 HOUS 77009 3824 B4
1000 HOUS 77009 3823 E5
1100 HOUS 77008 3823 E5
Dunbar Estates Dr
100 FRDW 77546 4505 A6
Dunbar Grove Ct
16800 FBnC 77478 4235 E7
Dunbar Point Ct
10400 HarC 77379 3110 C7
Dunbeath Dr
11400 HDWV 77024 3959 D1
Dun Blaine
12300 BKHV 77024 3959 A4
12300 HOUS 77024 3959 A4
Dunbrook Dr
10500 HarC 77070 3399 A3
Dunbrook Park Ln
5500 HarC 77449 3676 D5
Duncan Av
1100 HarC 77530 3830 C6
Duncan Ln
14000 MtgC 77302 2532 B7
14000 MtgC 77302 2678 B1
Duncan Rd
12000 HarC 77066 3400 D3
12600 HarC 77069 3400 D3
Duncan St
300 ALVN 77511 4867 B3
7700 HOUS 77093 3824 E1
Duncan Wy
14100 GLSN 77554 5332 D3
Duncan Grove Dr
15200 HarC 77429 3397 C3

Duncannon Dr
13900 HarC 77015 3828 E6
13900 HarC 77015 3829 A6
Duncansby Vale Rd
7900 HarC 77095 3538 C6
Duncaster Ct
3400 MSCY 77459 4496 D2
Duncaster Dr
300 HOUS 77079 3958 A3
3500 MSCY 77459 4496 D2
Duncum St
10300 HOUS 77013 3966 B2
13700 HarC 77015 3967 E2
14000 HarC 77015 3968 A1
Dundalk St
9400 HarC 77379 3255 D4
9800 HarC 77070 3255 B4
Dundee Ct
12300 HarC 77429 3397 A5
Dundee Dr
29600 MtgC 77354 2818 B2
Dundee Rd
16200 HarC 77429 3397 A5
Dune Brook Dr
8100 HarC 77089 4377 A7
Dune Gate Ct
9200 HarC 77396 3406 E7
9200 HarC 77396 3407 A7
Dunes Dr
2600 LGCY 77573 4508 E7
15900 HarC 77532 3551 D4
Dunes Ridge Wy
400 LGCY 77573 4633 C1
Dunfield Ln
11500 HOUS 77099 4238 B4
Dunford Ct
300 HarC 77562 3831 C2
Dunham Dr
600 HOUS 77076 3684 E5
Dunham Creek Ln
- HarC 77447 3250 A6
Dunham Lake Dr
31600 HarC 77447 3250 A6
Dunhaven Ct
1100 HOUS 77062 4379 B7
Dunhill Ct
23300 FBnC 77494 3953 D7
Dunhill Ln
1300 PASD 77506 4107 C6
Dunhurst Ln
- HarC 77047 4374 A4
Dunkirk Rd
7300 HOUS 77033 4243 E1
Dunkley Dr
400 HOUS 77076 3684 E4
Dunlap Dr
12300 HOUS 77035 4240 B6
Dunlap St
- HOUS 77096 4240 B2
7400 HOUS 77074 4100 B6
8800 HOUS 77074 4240 B1
12800 HOUS 77035 4240 B7
12800 HOUS 77085 4240 B7
12800 HOUS 77085 4371 B1
Dunlavy Ct
1100 PRLD 77581 4504 E7
Dunlavy Dr
3800 PRLD 77581 4504 E7
Dunlavy Ln
- LGCY 77573 4751 B1
- PRLD 77581 4504 E7
Dunlavy St
600 HOUS 77019 3962 C6
1400 HOUS 77006 3962 C6
2500 HOUS 77098 3962 C7
4400 HOUS 77006 4102 C2
4400 HOUS 77098 4102 C2
5200 HOUS 77005 4102 C2
Dunlay Springs Dr
19500 HarC 77433 3537 A6
Dunleigh Ct
4700 SGLD 77479 4495 C4
Dunleith Cir
16500 HarC 77429 3397 A3
Dunleith Ln
5200 HarC 77379 3257 B1
Dunlevy Ln
29900 MtgC 77355 2668 D5
Dunlin Meadow Ct
10 WDLD 77381 2821 B4
Dunlin Meadow Dr
10 WDLD 77381 2821 B4
Dunloggin Ln
10 WDLD 77380 2821 C7
Dunlop St
5100 HOUS 77009 3824 B4
Dunman Ln
15900 HarC 77044 3690 E1
15900 HarC 77044 3691 A1
Dunmeyer Ct
7000 SGLD 77479 4367 C7
7000 SGLD 77479 4494 C1
Dunmoor Dr
16200 HOUS 77059 4380 C4
Dunmore Ct
13300 HarC 77069 3400 E1
Dunn Cir
2600 DRPK 77536 4109 C6
Dunn Ln
23300 MtgC 77365 2973 B5
E Dunn Ln
23300 MtgC 77365 2973 D5
Dunn St
4400 HOUS 77020 3964 B3
20700 MtgC 77357 2973 A1
21000 MtgC 77357 2827 A7
Dunnam Ln
10 BKHV 77024 3959 C4
10 PNPV 77024 3959 C4
Dunnam Rd
3100 HOUS 77365 3120 A2
Dunnel Ridge Ln
16200 HarC 77429 3252 B6
Dunnethead Dr
5100 HarC 77084 3678 C5
Duno Dr
7800 HOUS 77075 4376 C1
Dunoon Bay Ct
18000 HarC 77429 3396 C1
Dunraven Ln
2200 HOUS 77019 3962 B6
Dunrich Ct
2900 LGCY 77573 4633 C4
Dunrobin Wy
14300 FBnC 77478 4367 A4
Dunsfort Ct
16800 FBnC 77083 4095 D5

Dunsinane St
11500 PNPV 77024 3959 D3
Dunsley Dr
5800 HarC 77449 3677 C4
Dunsmere Ct
2700 BzaC 77584 4501 A5
Dunsmere St
4600 HOUS 77018 3823 A1
4900 HOUS 77018 3684 A7
5400 HOUS 77091 3684 A6
Dunsmore Pl
14400 HarC 77429 3397 D2
Dunson Glen Dr
500 HarC 77090 3402 D1
Dunstable Ln
15100 HarC 77530 3829 D5
Dunstan Rd
1100 PASD 77502 4247 C2
Dunstan St
1800 HOUS 77005 4102 B2
2500 WUNP 77005 4102 A3
Dunster Ln
14900 HarC 77530 3829 C6
Dunston Ct
5400 SGLD 77479 4495 A4
Dunston Falls Dr
1200 HarC 77379 3110 A6
Dunvale Rd
2700 HOUS 77063 3959 E7
2700 HOUS 77063 4099 E2
Dunvegan Wy
10100 HOUS 77013 3966 C1
Dunwell Ct
800 MtgC 77386 2968 D1
Dunwick Ln
300 PASD 77502 4247 A2
700 PASD 77502 4246 E2
Dunwick St
6000 HOUS 77048 4375 D3
Dunwood Dr
1100 MtgC 77362 2816 C6
Dunwood Rd
17000 HarC 77429 3396 D1
Dunwood Springs Ct
10 SHEH 77381 2821 E1
Dunwoody Bnd
14900 HarC 77429 3397 C2
Dunwoody Dr
700 HOUS 77076 3685 B3
Du Pont Cir
10 SGLD 77479 4495 B2
Du Pont Ln
- SGLD 77479 4495 B2
DuPont St
2400 PASD 77503 4248 C1
2800 PASD 77505 4248 C3
4000 HOUS 77021 4103 D5
Dupree St
2900 HOUS 77054 4102 E6
2900 HOUS 77054 4103 A6
Duquesne Ln
3700 PASD 77505 4248 B4
Dural Dr
18400 HarC 77094 3955 B2
Duran Dr
- BzaC 77584 4501 A5
Duran Canyon Ct
11900 HarC 77067 3401 D5
Duran Canyon Ln
11900 HarC 77067 3401 E5
Durand Oak Ct
20800 HarC 77433 3251 B7
Durand Oak Dr
20700 HarC 77433 3251 B7
Duran Falls Ct
13800 HarC 77044 3549 E2
Durango Dr
1400 HOUS 77055 3820 D6
3200 PRLD 77581 4503 D5
6700 MtgC 77354 2673 A2
Durango Bay Ln
6100 HarC 77041 3679 E4
Durango Bend Dr
4400 MSCY 77459 4621 D3
Durango Creek Dr
6600 MtgC 77354 2673 A2
Durango Creek Ln
6900 HarC 77449 3676 D2
Durango Falls Ln
11400 HarC 77433 3396 B6
25600 FBnC 77494 4092 C5
Durango Mist Ln
5900 HarC 77449 3677 A5
Durango Pass Dr
1300 PRLD 77545 4499 E3
Durango Ridge Ct
5900 FBnC 77469 4616 A2
Durango Wy Dr
8000 HarC 77040 3541 B6
Durant Av
4300 DRPK 77536 4249 B2
4700 PASD 77536 4249 B3
4800 PASD 77505 4249 B3
N Durant St
100 ALVN 77511 4867 B1
400 ALVN 77511 4749 B7
S Durant St
100 ALVN 77511 4867 B1
Duranzo Ct
- LGCY 77539 4633 D2
Durban Dr
- HOUS 77041 3680 E7
- HOUS 77043 3819 E1
4400 HOUS 77041 3819 E1
Durbridge Ct
10600 HarC 77065 3539 B2
Durbridge Trail Dr
13000 HarC 77065 3539 B2
Durfey Ln
7500 HarC 77449 3815 A6
Durford Dr
6200 HOUS 77007 3961 E2
Durham Ct
19100 MtgC 77357 2830 A3
Durham Dr
300 HOUS 77007 3962 B3
600 MtgC 77302 2530 C5
2300 HOUS 77008 3962 B1
N Durham Dr
700 HOUS 77007 3962 B1
700 HOUS 77008 3823 B7
700 HOUS 77008 3962 B1
2900 HOUS 77018 3823 B7
N Durham Dr SPR-261
2900 HOUS 77018 3823 B4
Durham Ln
4800 SGLD 77479 4495 C3

Durham Tr
24500 HarC 77373 3114 E3
Durham Chase Ln
2700 HarC 77449 3815 B4
14500 HarC 77095 3539 B6
Durham Dale
10800 FBnC 77459 4622 B5
Durham Hill Ln
- HarC 77429 3254 A4
Durham Manor Ln
8800 HOUS 77075 4376 E4
Durham Ridge Ln
- HarC 77346 3408 B3
Durham Run Ln
- FBnC 77469 4094 E7
Durham Trace Dr
24500 HarC 77373 3114 D3
Durhill St
3200 HOUS 77025 4101 D7
Durklyn Ln
8000 HarC 77070 3399 E1
Durley Dr
600 HOUS 77079 3958 C2
Durness Wy
3300 HOUS 77025 4101 D6
Duroux Rd
1000 LMQU 77568 4989 C3
Durrain Ferry Rd
1900 BYTN 77520 4112 B1
Durrette Dr
11700 BKHV 77024 3959 C4
11800 HOUS 77024 3959 B4
N Durrette Dr
11900 HOUS 77024 3959 B4
S Durrette Dr
11900 HOUS 77024 3959 B4
Durwood St
2900 HOUS 77093 3686 A3
Dusk St
600 HarC 77060 3403 D4
Dusk Haven Ln
17000 HarC 77095 3537 E3
Dusk Valley Ct
10 HarC 77379 3110 D6
N Duskwood Pl
10 WDLD 77381 2674 E6
S Duskwood Pl
10 WDLD 77381 2674 C7
Dusky Lilac Ct
21500 HarC 77433 3250 E4
Dusky Lilac Tr
21800 HarC 77433 3250 C5
Dusky Meadow Pl
10 WDLD 77381 2820 E3
Dusky Rose Ln
900 PASD 77502 4246 E2
Dustin Ln
14300 HarC 77532 3554 A5
26900 MtgC 77354 2817 C4
Dusty Ct
3500 BzaC 77583 4500 D7
Dusty Rd
- HarC 77396 3406 D7
Dusty Rdg
1600 MSCY 77459 4497 D3
Dusty Tr
21300 MtgC 77372 2681 B1
Dusty Canyon Ln
- FBnC 77469 4094 D7
- FBnC 77469 4095 A6
Dusty Creek Dr
19700 HarC 77449 3677 A3
Dusty Dawn Dr
6600 HarC 77086 3542 C2
Dusty Dawn Ln
1400 BzaC 77511 4747 E1
Dusty Glen Ln
21100 HarC 77379 3111 B3
Dusty Grove Ln
13200 FBnC 77478 4366 E2
Dusty Heath Ct
5700 FBnC 77450 4094 A4
Dusty Hollow Ln
- FBnC 77494 4093 A3
10200 HarC 77089 4504 B2
10200 HarC 77089 4505 A1
Dusty Manor Ln
9700 FBnC 77494 4092 D5
Dusty Mill Dr E
16900 FBnC 77478 4236 A7
Dusty Mill Dr W
16900 FBnC 77478 4236 A7
Dusty Path Ln
16100 HarC 77429 3253 A7
Dusty Patty Ct
17700 FBnC 77469 4235 D1
Dusty Ridge Ct
4100 MSCY 77459 4497 D4
Dusty Ridge Ln
9700 HarC 77044 3689 B4
Dusty Rose Cir
7000 FBnC 77479 4496 B4
Dusty Rose Ln
18800 HarC 77377 3254 A2
Dusty Stable Ln
- HarC 77429 3253 A6
Dusty Terrace Ln
18100 HarC 77449 3677 D3
Dusty Trail Dr
10700 HarC 77086 3542 B1
Dusty Yaupon Ln
19400 HarC 77433 3537 B7
Dutch St
800 DRPK 77536 4109 B5
Dutch Harbor Ln
12400 HarC 77346 3408 C3
Dutchman St
400 HarC 77532 3552 B2
Dutch Ridge Dr
16800 FBnC 77478 4236 B7
Dutton Hill Ct
22000 HarC 77073 3259 A4
Dutton Trace Ln
16300 HarC 77082 4096 A4
Duval St
4000 HOUS 77087 4104 D5
Duxbury Dr
5500 HOUS 77035 4240 C5
Dwarf Honeysuckle Ct
4900 HarC 77084 3677 D6
Dwight St
900 HOUS 77015 3967 B2
Dwinnell St
500 BYTN 77520 3973 C7
500 BYTN 77520 4113 C1
Dwire Dr
10 LPRT 77571 4382 E1

Dwyer Dr
5800 HarC 77032 3546 E1
5800 HOUS 77396 3546 E1
Dyche Ln
800 ALVN 77511 4867 B4
Dyer Av
10 BYTN 77520 3973 A6
1100 RSBG 77471 4490 D5
Dyer Gln
10300 HarC 77070 3399 B5
Dyer St
200 BYTN 77520 3973 A6
7400 HOUS 77088 3683 C3
Dyer Brook Dr
6100 HarC 77041 3679 C4
Dyersville Ct
3300 HarC 77373 3115 B3
Dylan Dr
5800 BYTN 77520 3835 B7
5800 BYTN 77520 3974 B1
Dylans Crossing Dr
2600 HarC 77038 3543 A4
N Dylanshire Cir
10 CNRO 77384 2675 E4
S Dylanshire Cir
10 CNRO 77384 2675 E4
Dylans Point Ct
17600 HarC 77084 3678 A7
Dylan Springs Ln
6400 FBnC 77450 4094 C3
Dyna Dr
100 HOUS 77037 3544 B3
200 HOUS 77060 3544 C2
W Dyna Dr
100 HOUS 77037 3544 B3
100 HOUS 77060 3544 B3
Dynasty Pl
- SGLD 77479 4495 A4
Dyson Ln
11000 HarC 77041 3680 C4

E

E Dr
- HarC 77388 3111 D2
N E Pns
- HMBL 77338 3262 C7
E St
- GNPK 77547 4106 C1
- HOUS 77547 4106 C1
- WALR 77484 3101 D5
2800 LPRT 77571 4251 E7
4200 HOUS 77072 4097 E4
E E St
200 LPRT 77571 4251 E3
1100 LPRT 77571 4252 A3
1600 MRGP 77571 4252 A2
N E St
- LPRT 77571 4251 E2
W E St
100 LPRT 77571 4251 D3
Egan Mill Dr
13600 HOUS 77077 3957 A5
Eaganville
- HarC 77377 3254 B2
Eagle Av
100 PASD 77506 4107 A3
Eagle Bnd
20900 FBnC 77450 4094 C1
Eagle Cross
- HarC 77373 3115 D7
Eagle Ct
10 MtgC 77380 2822 A7
10 WDLD 77380 2822 A7
3000 MSCY 77489 4370 D7
10600 CmbC 77520 3835 D3
Eagle Dr
- HOUS 77088 3682 E1
- MtgC 77357 2973 D1
- STAF 77477 4369 C2
1800 LGCY 77573 4631 C5
Eagle Ln
- BzaC 77578 4625 B1
- MtgC 77357 2829 C2
2300 LPRT 77571 4251 C7
7500 HarC 77379 3110 E5
7500 HarC 77379 3111 A5
Eagle Lndg
5600 HOUS 77085 4372 A1
5700 HOUS 77085 4371 E1
Eagle St
1000 HOUS 77002 3963 A7
1000 HOUS 77004 3963 A7
1400 HOUS 77004 4103 A1
Eagle Ter
10 WDLD 77381 2820 C1
Eagle Bend Dr
- HarC 77379 3111 E4
- HarC 77379 3112 A4
- HarC 77388 3112 A4
Eaglebend Ln
4900 FBnC 77494 4093 D2
Eagle Bluff Ct
4000 HarC 77082 4096 B4
Eagle Brook Ln
6500 HarC 77379 3111 D5
Eagle Canyon Wy
19700 FBnC 77450 4094 D4
Eagle Chase Ln
25600 HarC 77389 2966 A2
Eagle Cliff Ln
9800 HarC 77396 3548 B1
Eagle Cove
300 HMPD 77445 2952 C4
28000 MtgC 77355 2815 B5
Eaglecove Cir
8900 HarC 77064 3540 E6
Eagle Cove Dr
- PRLD 77584 4500 A3
Eaglecove Dr
8900 HarC 77064 3540 E6
Eagle Cove Ln
- LGCY 77573 4630 E7
Eagle Creek Dr
- FRDW 77546 4629 B6
2800 HOUS 77345 3119 E5
Eagle Creek Ln
9300 HOUS 77036 4238 E1
Eagle Crest Dr
- FBnC 77494 3953 C5
Eaglecrest Dr
1600 HarC 77073 3259 C4
Eagle Eye Ln
9600 FBnC 77478 4236 B2
Eagle Falls Ct
1800 HOUS 77077 3957 E6
16600 HarC 77379 3256 B4

Eagle Falls Dr
1400 FRDW 77546 4629 D6
1800 HOUS 77077 3957 E6
1800 HOUS 77077 3958 A6
Eagle Forest Dr
- HarC 77090 3258 C7
Eagle Fork Ct
10500 LPRT 77571 4250 D3
Eagle Fork Dr
4300 HarC 77084 3678 D7
4300 HarC 77084 3817 D1
Eagle Glen Dr
10400 HOUS 77041 3819 E1
Eagle Grove Ln
20100 HarC 77379 3112 A5
Eagle Haven Dr
24400 FBnC 77494 3953 A3
Eagle Haven Ln
- HarC 77396 3548 B2
Eagle Hollow Dr
10200 HarC 77338 3407 C1
Eagle Island Dr
11700 HOUS 77034 4378 A1
Eagle Lake Dr
2900 PRLD 77581 4503 E7
Eagle Lakes Dr
100 FRDW 77546 4629 E4
Eagle Landing Dr
14600 HarC 77396 3548 B2
Eagle Ledge Dr
12700 HarC 77377 3254 A4
Eagle Mead Pl
10 WDLD 77382 2674 A4
Eagle Meadow Dr
22000 HarC 77450 3954 A4
22200 HarC 77450 3953 E4
Eagle Miller Dr
13100 HOUS 77070 3399 D4
Eagle Mills Ct
20200 HarC 77338 3261 D4
20200 HarC 77338 3262 A3
Eagle Mist Ln
14500 HarC 77396 3548 B2
Eagle Mountain Ct
4400 FBnC 77469 4234 C4
Eagle Nest Ct
10500 LPRT 77571 4250 C3
Eagle Nest Dr
3100 LPRT 77571 4250 D3
Eagle Nest Ln
2600 HMBL 77396 3406 C4
Eagle Nest Falls
20300 HarC 77449 3815 D4
Eagle Pass St
- HOUS 77020 3826 B7
6300 HOUS 77020 3964 E1
7100 HOUS 77020 3965 A1
13700 HarC 77015 3828 E7
14000 HarC 77015 3829 A7
Eagle Pass Falls Ct
17900 HarC 77346 3408 E1
Eagle Path Dr
- HarC 77396 3548 C1
Eagle Peak Ct
9700 FBnC 77494 4092 D5
Eagle Pines Ln
25900 HarC 77389 2966 C2
Eagle Point Ct
5200 SGLD 77479 4495 B4
Eagle Point Rd
1700 HarC 77532 3410 B1
Eagle Point Trail Dr
2900 HarC 77449 3815 E5
Eagle Post Dr
2500 CNRO 77304 2383 A1
Eagle Ridge Dr
6800 HarC 77449 3677 A2
28400 MtgC 77355 2815 C4
Eagle Ridge Wy
3000 HarC 77084 3816 C4
Eagle Rise Pl
10 WDLD 77382 2820 A2
Eagle River Ln
1700 FBnC 77469 4493 A3
Eagle Rock Cir
- WDLD 77381 2820 D3
Eaglerock Cir
2800 MSCY 77489 4497 B1
Eagle Rock Ct
100 WDLD 77381 2820 D3
10500 LPRT 77571 4250 C3
Eaglerock Dr
2000 HOUS 77080 3820 B4
Eagle Rock Pl
10 WDLD 77381 2820 D4
Eagle Run Ct
9000 FBnC 77479 4494 D4
Eagle Run St
8900 LPRT 77571 4249 E3
Eagles Lndg
9200 MtgC 77354 2672 C5
26700 HarC 77336 3122 A2
Eagles Wk
3800 FBnC 77450 4093 E1
Eagles Wy
2300 PRLD 77581 4504 D2
Eagles Claw Dr
- HarC 77447 3249 D4
Eagles Cove
100 FRDW 77546 4629 E4
Eagle's Glide Dr
700 HarC 77090 3402 D1
Eagle Shore Tr
14600 HarC 77396 3548 B1
Eagles Knoll Ct
3200 FBnC 77494 3953 D7
Eagle Sky Blvd
5600 HarC 77449 3676 D4
Eagles Ledge Ct
3200 HarC 77338 3260 A2
Eagles Perch Wy
12900 HarC 77346 3264 E7
Eagle Spring Pkwy
9800 HarC 77064 3540 B1
Eagle Springs Dr
- HarC 77090 3258 C7
Eagle Springs Pkwy
17800 HarC 77346 3408 C2
18300 HarC 77346 3264 D7
Eagle Star Ct
9700 HarC 77396 3548 B2
Eagle Star Ln
14500 HarC 77396 3548 B1
Eaglestone Ct
3200 HarC 77388 3112 E3
Eagle Summit Ln
- HarC 77090 3258 C5

Eagles Wing
10 MtgC 77354 2817
10 MtgC 77354 2818
Eaglet Tr
3700 PRLD 77584 4502
Eagle Talon Ct
24500 FBnC 77494 3953
Eagleton Ct
- HarC 77396 3548
Eagleton Ln
10100 HarC 77562 3693
12700 HarC 77532 3693
Eagle Trace Ct
5400 SGLD 77479 4494
Eagle Trace Dr
15400 HarC 77433 3251
Eagle Trail Dr
- FBnC 77479 4494
4700 HarC 77084 3678
Eagle Tree Ln
14600 HarC 77396 3548
Eaglets Ct
- HarC 77396 3548
Eagle View Ln
11500 HarC 77067 3402
Eagle Vista Dr
14700 HOUS 77077 3956
Eagle Watch Ct
22800 FBnC 77450 3953
Eaglewood Ct
3400 BzaC 77584 4501
Eaglewood Dr
3200 BzaC 77584 4501
11500 HarC 77089 4378
11500 HOUS 77089 4378
Eaglewood Forest Dr
20600 MtgC 77365 2972
20600 MtgC 77365 2973
Eaglewood Glen Tr
9200 FBnC 77083 4236
9600 FBnC 77478 4236
Eaglewood Green Ln
6400 HarC 77379 3111
Eaglewood Shadow Ct
9300 FBnC 77083 4236
Eaglewood Shadow Dr
16400 FBnC 77083 4236
16500 FBnC 77478 4236
16600 FBnC 77469 4236
Eaglewood Spring Ct
16100 FBnC 77083 4236 A
Eaglewood Spring Dr
9200 FBnC 77083 4236 A
Eaglewood Trace Dr
20600 MtgC 77365 2972
20600 MtgC 77365 2973 A
Eaglewood Trail Dr
4300 FBnC 77545 4622
Eaglewood Valley Ct
1400 FBnC 77545 4622 E
Earhart St
7900 HOUS 77028 3826 C
Earl St
3000 HOUS 77098 3962 A
3000 PASD 77503 4108
3000 PASD 77506 4108 A
Earle St
1000 HOUS 77030 4102 C
Earley Forest Ln
11500 HOUS 77043 3819 A
Earlham Dr
10 FRDW 77546 4505 D
10 FRDW 77546 4629 B
Earline St
4500 HOUS 77016 3686 C7
Earlington Manor Ct
1400 HarC 77379 3110 B
Earlington Manor Dr
10100 HarC 77379 3110 B
Earlmist Dr
23000 HarC 77373 3114 D
Earl of Dunmore Ln
1500 HarC 77449 3815 A6
1700 HOUS 77449 3815 A6
Earl Porter Dr
- MTBL 77520 3696 E5
Earls Row
10 CNRO 77304 2529 D1
Earls Ct Dr
500 HarC 77450 3953 D2
Earlsferry Dr
1000 HarC 77530 3829 C6
Earlswood Dr
14700 FBnC 77083 4236 D1
Earlwood Ct
3600 PRLD 77584 4503 B6
Early Ln
1500 HOUS 77055 3821 D6
Early Autumn Ct
4500 HarC 77396 3406 E7
4500 HarC 77396 3407 B6
Early Breeze Pl
2600 HarC 77084 3816 A4
Early Dawn Ct
10 WDLD 77381 2821 A5
Early Elm Ct
15500 HarC 77049 3829 A1
Early Fall Dr
6500 HarC 77338 3261 B3
Early Frost Pl
10 WDLD 77381 2820 D1
Early Harvest Cir
11000 HarC 77064 3540 D1
Early Hollow Ln
14700 HarC 77429 3397 D4
Early Mist Ct
11500 HarC 77064 3399 C7
Early Spring Cir
11200 HarC 77064 3540 C1
Early Spring Ct
9800 HarC 77064 3540 C1
Early Spring Dr
9800 HarC 77064 3540 B1
Early Square Ct
10400 HarC 77070 3399 B4
Early Turn Ct
2800 HarC 77598 4630 B1
Early Turn Dr
2800 HarC 77598 4506 B7
2800 HarC 77598 4630 B1
Early Walk Wy
- PASD 77503 4108 D7
Earlywood Ln
12800 HarC 77429 3397 D4
Earnestwood Dr
8800 HarC 77083 4237 A1
Earthstone Dr
24000 FBnC 77494 4093 A4

TREET
ock City ZIP Map# Grid

asingwold Dr
14800 HarC 77015 3829 B5
15000 HarC 77530 3829 C4
asley St
200 MtgC 77385 2822 C3
200 SHEH 77385 2822 C2
ast
- BYTN 77520 3972 B6
ast Av
800 KATY 77493 3952 C1
900 KATY 77493 3813 C7
ast Blvd
100 DRPK 77536 4109 E5
3600 DRPK 77536 4249 E2
4100 LPRT 77536 4249 E2
4100 LPRT 77571 4249 E2
ast Ct
3800 DRPK 77536 4249 C1
ast Dr
- LGCY 77573 4752 D1
200 HOUS 77003 3963 E4
14900 MtgC 77302 2824 D2
ast Dr S
200 LMQU 77568 4873 B7
200 TXCY 77591 4873 B7
ast Frwy
- BYTN - 3832 B6
- BYTN - 3833 D4
- BYTN - 3834 E3
- BYTN 77520 3835 C2
- CmbC - 3835 B2
- HarC - 3830 D7
- HarC - 3831 C6
- HarC - 3832 B5
- HarC - 3833 D4
- HarC - 3834 D3
- HarC - 3967 D2
- HarC - 3968 E2
- HarC - 3969 B1
- HarC 77521 3835 B2
- HOUS - 3963 C2
- HOUS - 3964 C2
- HOUS - 3965 B1
- HOUS - 3966 D2
- HOUS - 3967 D2
- MTBL - 3835 E2
7800 HOUS 77029 3965 B1
17600 HarC 77530 3831 C6
ast Frwy I-10
- BYTN - 3832 B6
- BYTN - 3833 D4
- BYTN - 3834 E3
- CmbC - 3835 B2
- HarC - 3830 D7
- HarC - 3831 C6
- HarC - 3832 E5
- HarC - 3833 D4
- HarC - 3834 D3
- HarC - 3835 A2
- HarC - 3967 D2
- HarC - 3968 D2
- HarC - 3969 B1
- HOUS - 3963 D2
- HOUS - 3964 C2
- HOUS - 3965 B1
- HOUS - 3966 D2
- HOUS - 3967 D2
- MTBL - 3835 E2
ast Frwy SR-73
- BYTN - 3832 B6
- BYTN - 3833 D4
- HarC - 3831 C6
- HarC - 3833 D4
- HarC - 3967 E2
- HarC - 3968 D2
- HarC - 3969 B1
- HOUS - 3967 D2
ast Frwy US-90
- HOUS - 3963 E2
- HOUS - 3964 C2
- HOUS - 3965 E2
ast Frwy US-90 ALT
- HOUS - 3965 B1
- HOUS 77029 3965 B1
ast Ln
4000 HOUS 77026 3825 A6
ast Lp
9500 HarC 77038 3544 B5
9500 HOUS 77038 3544 B5
ast Pk
- BYTN 77520 3970 E5
ast Rd
- MSCY 77489 4370 B7
5000 BYTN 77521 3972 E1
5200 BYTN 77521 3833 E7
5300 HarC 77521 3833 E7
ast St
10 MtgC 77357 2973 B1
1200 HOUS 77007 3962 D2
3100 GLSN 77550 5109 A3
7100 HarC 77521 3832 D5
East St
- LPRT 77571 4251 B1
300 BYTN 77520 3973 D4
East St
200 BYTN 77520 3973 D4
ast Bay Blvd
10 WDLD 77380 2821 D5
astbourne Dr
13700 HOUS 77034 4378 D5
astbourne Ln
1100 PRLD 77584 4501 C2
astbrook Dr
12400 HOUS 77013 3827 E6
12500 HOUS 77013 3828 A7
astcape Ct
400 HOUS 77598 4506 E4
astcape Dr
- HOUS 77598 4506 E3
astchase Ct
11700 MtgC 77304 2382 A4
astchase St
4700 BYTN 77521 3833 C4
4700 HarC 77521 3833 C4
astcliff Ln
- HarC 77377 3254 D3
astcove Ct
- HarC 77064 3540 E6
astcrest Park Dr
19300 HarC 77429 3397 C2
asten St
12600 HarC 77014 3402 A3
aster St
6800 HOUS 77091 3683 B4
6900 HOUS 77088 3683 B4
asterleaf Ct
2400 FBnC 77469 4365 B2

STREET
Block City ZIP Map# Grid

Easterling Dr
11500 HarC 77065 3398 A7
Easterly Dr
100 TKIS 77554 5106 A4
Eastern Bluebird Dr
8100 HarC 77396 3406 D6
Eastern Fork Ct
17800 HarC 77433 3395 E5
Eastern Redbud Ln
14300 HOUS 77044 3549 C1
14300 HOUS 77044 3550 A1
Eastex Frwy
- HarC - 3546 C7
- HarC - 3686 B2
- HMBL - 3262 C7
- HMBL - 3406 C1
- HOUS - 3117 E7
- HOUS - 3118 A5
- HOUS - 3262 E2
- HOUS - 3406 A6
- HOUS - 3546 E1
- HOUS - 3547 A1
- HOUS - 3686 B3
- HOUS - 3825 A5
- HOUS - 3963 D4
- HOUS - 3964 A1
- MtgC - 2973 B7
- MtgC - 3118 B1
Eastex Frwy US-59
- HarC - 3546 E1
- HarC - 3686 B2
- HMBL - 3262 E2
- HMBL - 3406 C1
- HOUS - 3117 E7
- HOUS - 3118 A5
- HOUS - 3262 E2
- HOUS - 3406 A6
- HOUS - 3546 E1
- HOUS - 3547 A1
- HOUS - 3686 B3
- HOUS - 3825 A1
- HOUS - 3963 C6
- HOUS - 3964 A1
- MtgC - 2973 B7
- MtgC - 3118 B1
Eastex Freeway Service Dr
- HOUS 77365 3118 B3
- MtgC 77365 2973 B6
800 HOUS 77020 3964 A2
1800 HOUS 77026 3964 A1
3900 HOUS 77026 3825 A3
6200 HOUS 77016 3825 A2
6400 HOUS 77093 3825 A2
8300 HOUS 77093 3686 A7
10700 HarC 77093 3686 A5
11400 HarC 77093 3546 D4
11600 HarC 77039 3546 D4
13400 HarC 77032 3546 D3
13600 HarC 77396 3546 E3
14600 HOUS 77396 3546 E1
14600 HOUS 77396 3547 A1
14900 HOUS 77396 3406 A6
16200 HMBL 77396 3406 B3
18100 HMBL 77338 3406 C1
18100 HOUS 77338 3406 C1
21100 HMBL 77338 3262 E3
21300 HarC 77338 3262 E2
21300 HOUS 77338 3262 E2
21400 HMBL 77339 3262 E2
21400 HOUS 77339 3262 E2
22300 HOUS 77339 3263 A1
22500 HOUS 77339 3117 E7
22600 HOUS 77339 3118 A5
25500 MtgC 77365 3118 B2
Eastex Freeway Service Dr N
20400 HMBL 77338 3262 D5
Eastex Freeway Service Rd
- HMBL 77338 3262 E3
Eastfield Dr
2000 MSCY 77459 4497 C2
East Freeway Frontage Rd
- BYTN 77520 3835 C2
- HarC 77520 3831 E6
- HarC 77521 3831 E6
- HarC 77521 3835 A2
1000 HarC 77562 3831 E6
1500 BYTN 77521 3832 B6
1500 HarC 77520 3832 B6
1500 HarC 77521 3832 B6
4400 HOUS 77020 3964 B2
4500 BYTN 77521 3833 C4
4500 HarC 77521 3833 C4
6000 BYTN 77521 3834 D3
6100 HarC 77521 3834 A3
7000 HOUS 77020 3965 A2
8100 HOUS 77029 3965 C1
8800 JTCY 77029 3965 E2
9000 JTCY 77029 3966 A2
9100 HOUS 77013 3965 E1
9100 HOUS 77013 3966 B2
9100 HOUS 77029 3966 B2
10100 HOUS 77029 3826 E7
10400 CmbC 77520 3835 D2
10400 MTBL 77520 3835 D2
11700 HOUS 77015 3966 D2
12400 HOUS 77015 3967 A2
15000 HarC 77015 3968 D2
15000 HarC 77530 3968 D2
15400 HarC 77530 3969 A1
16100 HarC 77530 3830 C7
17000 HarC 77530 3831 A6
Eastgate St
100 HOUS 77012 4105 B1
Eastgate Village Dr
22900 HarC 77373 2968 E7
Eastgrove Ln
2600 HOUS 77027 3961 D7
Easthampton Dr
5300 HarC 77039 3546 D5
Easthaven Blvd
7500 HOUS 77017 4246 B5
7500 HOUS 77587 4246 A3
7500 SHUS 77587 4246 B5
7800 SHUS 77034 4246 B5
8400 HOUS 77034 4246 B7
8400 HOUS 77075 4246 B7
9600 HOUS 77075 4377 B2
Easthaven Ct
700 FRDW 77546 4629 A1
Easthaven Dr
1900 PASD 77506 4107 D6
Eastheimer St
8800 HarC 77064 3540 E1
East Higlands Cross
- HarC 77562 3832 C2
Eastlake Ct
1000 HOUS 77034 4246 C6

STREET
Block City ZIP Map# Grid

Eastlake St
300 HOUS 77034 4246 E6
Eastland Ct
2100 LGCY 77573 4631 C7
Eastland St
2100 LGCY 77573 4631 C6
5000 HOUS 77028 3826 C5
Eastland Lake Dr
3800 FBnC 77469 4234 C5
Eastleigh Ln
6600 HarC 77049 3828 E3
Eastloch Dr
8300 HarC 77379 3255 D1
Eastman Pl
19900 HarC 77449 3815 E3
Eastman St
1200 PASD 77502 4107 A6
1200 PASD 77506 4107 A6
2600 HOUS 77009 3824 A4
3000 HOUS 77022 3824 A3
Eastmont Ln
1900 MSCY 77489 4370 B4
Eastmoore Ct
13900 HarC 77014 3402 C1
Easton St
7900 HOUS 77017 4105 C6
Easton Bend Ct
4000 SGLD 77479 4495 A3
Easton Bend Ln
12400 HarC 77433 3396 B5
Easton Commons Dr
8300 HarC 77095 3539 A5
Easton Glen Ln
- LGCY 77539 4753 A3
Easton Lake Ln
4200 FBnC 77494 4092 A1
Easton Park Dr
15100 HarC 77095 3538 E7
Easton Springs Ct
2600 PRLD 77584 4500 D3
Easton Springs Dr
11300 PRLD 77584 4500 D3
Eastover St
8200 HOUS 77028 3826 C2
Eastpark Dr
4300 HOUS 77028 3826 A5
Eastpoint Blvd
7100 BYTN 77521 3833 C3
8400 HarC 77521 3833 C2
East Shore Dr
- WDLD 77380 2821 D5
Eastshore St
4000 MSCY 77459 4369 C7
Eastside St
2500 HOUS 77019 3962 A6
3000 HOUS 77098 3962 A7
3700 HOUS 77098 4102 A1
Eastvale Dr
1600 MtgC 77386 2969 A2
Eastway St
- GNPK 77547 4106 C1
1500 GNPK 77547 3966 B6
Eastway Village Dr
20100 HMBL 77338 3262 D5
Eastwick Ln
3100 LPRT 77571 4249 D3
Eastwind Dr
1900 DRPK 77536 4109 A6
Eastwood Cir
10 CNRO 77301 2384 C7
17400 HarC 77095 3677 E1
Eastwood Ct
900 SGLD 77478 4369 A3
Eastwood Dr
200 CNRO 77301 2384 C3
400 RMFT 77357 2829 A3
400 WDBR 77357 2829 A3
26700 ORDN 77386 2822 C6
Eastwood Ln
11000 MtgC 77354 2671 D1
Eastwood Pl
10 WDLD 77382 2674 B5
Eastwood St
10 HOUS 77011 3964 B6
200 CNRO 77301 2384 E3
300 HOUS 77003 3964 A6
600 HOUS 77023 3964 A6
6200 HOUS 77021 4103 D6
N Eastwood St
100 HOUS 77003 3964 B5
100 HOUS 77011 3964 B5
Eastwood Hills Dr
26100 MtgC 77385 2822 D6
Eastwood Lake Ct
2000 HOUS 77339 3118 D3
Eastwood Lake Ln
7500 FBnC 77469 4093 D5
Eastwood Tc
1200 HOUS 77023 4104 E1
Easy St
- MtgC 77354 2818 E7
800 LPRT 77571 4110 D6
900 RSBG 77471 4490 C5
2500 PASD 77502 4107 E7
2500 PASD 77502 4108 A7
3400 HOUS 77026 3825 D6
26100 MtgC 77355 2814 A1
Easybrook Ln
7500 HarC 77379 3256 B2
Easy Jet Dr
600 STAF 77477 4370 B4
Eaton Ct
10 BKHV 77024 3959 C4
Eaton Dr
4100 STFE 77510 4871 B7
Eaton Rd
- ALVN 77511 4867 D5
Eaton Sq
- HOUS 77027 3961 B5
Eaton St
1200 HOUS 77030 4102 D5
Eaton Glen Ln
- HarC 77084 3678 C3
Eatons Creek Ct
20200 HarC 77449 3676 D4
Eatons Creek Tr
5800 HarC 77449 3676 D4
Eaves Dr
2100 BYTN 77520 3973 D5
Ebb St
9900 HOUS 77089 4377 D4
Ebbtide Dr
3100 HOUS 77045 4373 A1
4100 HOUS 77045 4372 C1
Eberhard St
1000 HOUS 77019 3962 D5
1500 HOUS 77006 3962 D5

STREET
Block City ZIP Map# Grid

Eberhart Star Ct
1600 FBnC 77494 3952 D4
Ebersberg Wy
14800 HarC 77429 3253 D4
Ebeys Landing Ln
17400 HarC 77346 3408 B3
Eble
13900 HarC 77429 3397 E3
Eblen Dr
9800 HOUS 77040 3682 A1
Ebony Ln
1300 HOUS 77018 3822 C2
Ebony Oaks Pl
10 WDLD 77382 2819 B3
Ebury Dr
3800 HarC 77066 3401 C6
Echelon Dr
- HOUS 77449 3815 B6
Echinacea Dr
7900 HarC 77521 3833 D2
Echo Av
100 FRDW 77546 4629 C1
Echo Hbr
16900 HarC 77546 4506 A7
Echo Hllw
32700 MtgC 77355 2962 A3
Echo Ln
100 HOUS 77336 3121 B5
700 HDWV 77024 3959 D2
700 PNPV 77024 3959 D2
900 HOUS 77024 3959 D1
19800 MtgC 77357 2828 E5
Echo Rdg
2000 SGLD 77478 4368 D6
Echo St
2700 MtgC 77380 2967 D1
2700 WDLD 77380 2967 D1
Echo Bend Dr
- WDLD 77381 2820 E2
Echobend Ln
17800 HarC 77379 3256 A2
Echo Brook Dr
6600 HOUS 77076 3684 D4
7600 HarC 77037 3684 D2
7600 HOUS 77037 3684 D2
Echo Canyon Dr
12000 HarC 77377 3254 B1
15600 HarC 77084 3678 E6
15600 HarC 77084 3679 A6
Echocliff Wy
- HOUS 77062 4379 E7
Echo Creek Ln
900 MSCY 77489 4370 D3
Echo Falls Dr
4300 HOUS 77345 3119 C2
20100 HarC 77450 3954 E3
Echo Falls Ln
10400 HarC 77095 3537 D2
Echo Glade Ct
9500 HarC 77064 3540 D5
E Echo Glen Dr
100 HOUS 77076 3684 D4
W Echo Glen Dr
200 HOUS 77076 3684 C4
Echo Grove Ln
3500 HOUS 77043 3819 C2
Echo Harbor Dr
2300 PRLD 77584 4500 C2
Echo Hill Dr
15700 HOUS 77059 4380 C5
Echo Hollow Ln
11500 HDWV 77024 3959 D2
Echoing Pines Dr
9300 HarC 77396 3407 B3
Echo Lake Ln
5900 HarC 77069 3400 C1
Echo Lakes Cir
4000 MSCY 77459 4496 C4
Echo Lakes Ln
6200 MSCY 77459 4496 D3
Echo Landing Dr
12900 HOUS 77070 3399 D4
Echo Ledge St
11400 HarC 77067 3402 C6
Echo Lodge Dr
15700 HarC 77095 3678 C1
15900 HarC 77095 3538 D3
Echols Dr
1500 BYTN 77520 3973 D6
Echols St
100 PRVW 77445 3100 C2
Echo Mar Ln
18200 HarC 77084 3677 D5
Echo Mountain Dr
3200 HOUS 77345 3119 D3
4100 HOUS 77365 3119 E2
Echo Peaks Ln
9400 HarC 77396 3407 A7
Echo Pines Ct
18700 HarC 77346 3265 A7
Echo Pines Dr
6900 HarC 77346 3264 E7
6900 HarC 77346 3265 A7
Echo Point Ln
7600 HarC 77095 3538 C7
Echo Ridge Ct
2000 HOUS 77339 3118 E5
Echo Spring Ln
11700 HarC 77065 3399 A7
Echo Stream Pl
3000 HarC 77084 3816 C5
Echo Valley Dr
8800 SPVL 77055 3821 A7
8900 SPVL 77055 3820 E7
Echo Wood St
11500 HDWV 77024 3959 D2
Eckert Ct
3200 GLSN 77554 5219 E7
3200 GLSN 77554 5332 E1
Eckert Dr
3400 GLSN 77554 5332 E1
3700 GLSN 77554 5333 A1
Eclipse St
1800 HOUS 77018 3683 C7
Ecret Dr
4600 DKSN 77539 4754 D4
4600 TXCY 77539 4754 D4
Ecru Ln
8000 FBnC 77583 4744 A2
Ecru Hills Dr
20800 HarC 77433 3676 D1
Ector
3100 HOUS 77056 3960 E7
Ector Dr
4000 GLSN 77554 5441 B5
Ecuador Dr
3900 PASD 77504 4247 D4

STREET
Block City ZIP Map# Grid

Ed Dr
21600 MtgC 77355 2960 E5
21600 MtgC 77355 2961 A5
Edaline Ln
9600 HOUS 77078 3688 B5
Eday Dr
9500 HarC 77379 3255 D4
Ed Buey Wy
- HOUS 77034 4247 C7
- PASD 77504 4247 D7
1100 HOUS 77504 4247 C7
Eddie Dr
6300 HOUS 77396 3406 A7
14800 HarC 77396 3547 A1
14800 HOUS 77396 3547 A1
Eddie St
3700 HOUS 77026 3825 B7
6000 HOUS 77396 3406 A7
Eddie Kirk Ct
900 FBnC 77469 4493 B5
Eddington St
900 HOUS 77023 3964 B7
Eddlewood Ct
1900 HarC 77530 3829 E4
Eddlewood Dr
- HarC 77530 3829 E4
Eddy St
100 HMBL 77338 3263 A7
Eddyrock St
10800 HOUS 77089 4377 D3
Eddys Edge Ct
9500 HarC 77089 4377 C7
Eddystone Dr
10100 HOUS 77043 3820 A6
10100 HOUS 77080 3820 A6
10200 HOUS 77043 3819 E6
Edell St
9400 HOUS 77093 3686 A6
Edelweiss Dr
300 LGCY 77573 4633 A1
Eden Ct
17300 HarC 77379 3255 D3
Eden Pns
20200 HarC 77379 3112 A4
20300 HarC 77379 3111 E4
Eden St
7200 HOUS 77012 4105 B3
7200 HOUS 77087 4105 B3
Edena Dr
1700 HarC 77530 3829 D4
Edenbridge Ct
17300 HarC 77379 3255 D3
Edenbridge St
8800 HarC 77379 3255 D3
Edenbrook Ct
7000 FBnC 77479 4367 A6
Edenbrook Dr
6100 FBnC 77479 4367 A7
Eden Cove Ct
7000 FBnC 77479 4496 B4
Eden Creek Dr
11900 PRLD 77584 4500 C3
Eden Crossing Ln
7300 FBnC 77469 4095 C6
Edendale Cir
10 MtgC 77355 2814 E3
2000 HarC 77450 3954 B5
Edenderry Ct
4500 MSCY 77459 4369 B5
Edenderry Ln
1300 MSCY 77459 4369 B5
E Eden Elm Cir
10 WDLD 77381 2820 E2
W Eden Elm Cir
10 WDLD 77381 2820 E2
Eden Elm Pl
10 WDLD 77381 2820 E2
Eden Falls Cir
17300 HarC 77095 3678 C3
Eden Falls Ct
17200 HarC 77095 3678 A2
Eden Field Ln
6600 LGCY 77539 4752 D4
Edenfield Ln
1900 SGLD 77479 4367 E7
2000 SGLD 77479 4494 B1
Edenglen Ct
6300 HarC 77049 3828 C3
Edenglen Dr
13900 HarC 77049 3828 B3
13900 HOUS 77049 3828 B3
Eden Glen Ln
1900 PRLD 77581 4503 D1
Ed English Dr
100 SHEH 77385 2822 B1
Edengrove Dr
17600 HarC 77377 3254 B3
Edenhollow Ct
6300 HarC 77049 3828 D3
Eden Manor Ln
13800 HOUS 77044 3550 B2
Eden Park Ct
8000 FBnC 77469 4234 A4
Eden Park Ln
1100 HOUS 77018 3683 E7
1100 HOUS 77018 3684 A7
Eden Point Ct
26300 FBnC 77494 4092 D1
Eden Point Ln
4200 FBnC 77494 4092 E1
Edenport Ct
6300 HarC 77049 3828 C3
Edens Av
100 LGCY 77573 4632 B2
Edensborough Dr
19700 HarC 77449 3816 C2
19800 HarC 77449 3815 E3
Edens Dawn Dr
19100 HarC 77375 3254 D1
Eden Springs Ln
12100 HarC 77041 3679 B7
Edenstone Dr
11600 HarC 77429 3397 D7
Eden Trails Ln
18200 HarC 77094 3955 C1
Edenvale Ct
5100 FRDW 77546 4505 D6
Edenvale St
- HarC 77546 4505 D6
15500 FRDW 77546 4505 D6
Eden Valley Dr
9900 HarC 77379 3255 B1
10000 HarC 77379 3110 B7
Eden Walk Dr
17400 HarC 77379 3255 E3
Edenwalk Dr
17400 HarC 77379 3255 D2

STREET
Block City ZIP Map# Grid

Edenway Ct
6300 HarC 77049 3828 C3
Edenwood Dr
8100 HarC 77389 2965 E2
8100 HarC 77389 2966 A3
Edfield St
4500 HOUS 77033 4243 D1
4500 HOUS 77051 4243 D1
Edgar Rd
2700 PLEK 77471 4614 C4
14100 HarC 77039 3545 A2
Edgar St
100 LMQU 77568 4873 E7
100 TXCY 77591 4873 E7
600 CNRO 77301 2384 B4
8700 HOUS 77051 4243 C3
10600 HOUS 77047 4243 C6
11900 HOUS 77047 4374 C1
Edgebaston Ct
20900 HarC 77073 3259 A6
Edgeboro St
13900 HarC 77049 3689 E7
Edgebrook Dr
- HOUS 77075 4246 B6
- TXCY 77591 4872 C2
300 HOUS 77034 4246 C6
800 BYTN 77521 3972 E3
E Edgebrook Dr
- PASD 77504 4247 A5
10 HOUS 77034 4246 E5
100 HOUS 77034 4247 A5
100 SHUS 77587 4247 A5
Edgebrook St
8800 HOUS 77075 4245 E6
8800 HOUS 77075 4246 B6
Edgebrook Forest Ct
8100 HarC 77088 3542 E7
Edgebrook Forest Dr
5500 HarC 77088 3542 E7
Edgecliff Pl
10 WDLD 77382 2674 A6
Edgecraft Dr
7400 HOUS 77489 4371 B4
Edgecreek Dr
3200 HarC 77066 3401 E7
Edgecrest Dr
- HarC 77336 3121 E4
Edge Croft Ct
19000 HarC 77377 3254 A1
Edgedale Dr
2300 MSCY 77489 4370 E6
2400 MSCY 77489 4371 A6
Edgefield Dr
3300 PASD 77503 4108 B5
Edgefield Ln
16300 MtgC 77302 2679 D6
Edgefield Lakes Dr
2600 HOUS 77054 4242 A3
Edgegate Dr
4800 HarC 77373 3115 B5
Edgeglen Dr
- HarC 77073 3259 A6
- HOUS 77073 3259 A6
Edgegrove Ct
13900 HarC 77014 3402 C3
Edgehaven Dr
17300 HOUS 77489 4497 D2
17400 MSCY 77545 4497 E2
Edgehill Dr
12800 HarC 77049 3689 C7
12800 HarC 77049 3828 B1
Edgehill Rd
1700 PASD 77502 4107 D7
Edgeloch Dr
9100 HarC 77379 3110 D5
Edge Manor Ln
- FBnC 77469 4094 E7
Edgemere
- HOUS 77339 3117 E4
Edgemere Ct
15600 FBnC 77478 4236 B5
Edgemire Pl
10 WDLD 77381 2674 D6
Edgemont Dr
16300 HOUS 77053 4372 A7
Edgemoor Dr
5500 BLAR 77081 4100 D5
5500 BLAR 77401 4100 D5
6300 HOUS 77074 4100 B5
6300 HOUS 77081 4100 B5
7100 HOUS 77074 4099 E5
7800 HOUS 77036 4099 C5
Edgemore St
4600 STFE 77517 4870 A7
Edge Park Cir
- HarC 77073 3403 A1
- HOUS 77073 3403 A1
Edgeton Ct
300 HarC 77015 3828 D5
Edgevale Ct
7500 HarC 77095 3538 C7
Edgeview Rd
4500 HarC 77084 3677 C7
Edgewater Dr
- TXCY 77590 4756 A3
- TXCY 77591 4756 A3
1300 FRDW 77546 4629 C6
3000 SGLD 77478 4368 D6
4800 HOUS 77093 3686 C3
5000 TXCY 77591 4755 E4
14500 HarC 77047 4374 C5
29800 MtgC 77354 2671 E5
36900 MtgC 77362 2670 D7
36900 MtgC 77362 2816 D1
Edgewater St
- GlsC 77568 4990 D7
- LMQU 77568 4990 D7
10 GlsC 77563 4990 D6
Edgewater Bend Ct
3300 PRLD 77584 4501 B3
Edgewater Bend Ln
3300 PRLD 77584 4501 D5
Edgeway Dr
7600 HLSV 77055 3821 C7
7600 HOUS 77055 3821 C7
Edgewick Ct
800 SGLD 77478 4368 E3
5600 HarC 77069 3256 D7
Edgewick Elm St
2700 FBnC 77545 4498 C6
Edgewood
5400 FRDW 77546 4505 C6
Edgewood Ct
2900 SGLD 77479 4495 D1
8800 TXCY 77591 4755 E3
Edgewood Dr
- RHMD 77469 4365 B7
10 BYTN 77520 4113 C1

STREET
Block City ZIP Map# Grid

Edgewood Dr
100 FBnC 77469 4365 B7
800 FBnC 77469 4492 B1
1100 RHMD 77469 4492 B1
2300 MSCY 77459 4369 B7
2800 SGLD 77479 4495 D1
3100 BzaC 77584 4501 B6
3100 DKSN 77539 4754 A1
15900 PASD 77059 4380 D6
E Edgewood Dr
100 FRDW 77546 4505 B6
E Edgewood Dr FM-2351
100 FRDW 77546 4505 B6
W Edgewood Dr
100 FRDW 77546 4505 B7
400 FRDW 77546 4629 A1
900 FRDW 77546 4628 E2
1100 PRLD 77581 4628 E2
W Edgewood Dr FM-2351
100 FRDW 77546 4505 B7
400 FRDW 77546 4629 A1
900 FRDW 77546 4628 E2
1100 PRLD 77581 4628 E2
Edgewood Ln
12000 BKHV 77024 3959 B2
12000 HOUS 77024 3959 B2
Edgewood St
- HOUS 77023 3964 B7
10 HOUS 77011 3964 C6
100 LPRT 77571 4251 E6
300 LGCY 77573 4631 E2
3100 LMQU 77568 4989 C3
N Edgewood St
100 HOUS 77011 3964 C5
Edgewood Forest Ct
10 WDLD 77381 2821 A3
Edgewood Hill Ct
3800 FBnC 77545 4498 D7
Edgewood Manor Ct
9800 HarC 77070 3255 B3
Edgewood Park Dr
12700 HarC 77038 3543 A3
Edgewood Pl Dr
5000 HarC 77379 3112 A6
5000 HarC 77388 3112 B5
Edgeworth
9400 HOUS 77093 3685 E6
Edgeworth St
9700 HOUS 77093 3685 E5
Edgon Dr
- HarC 77429 3254 B6
Edgware Dr
17000 HarC 77084 3678 B4
Edie St
3600 FBnC 77545 4498 D7
Edinburg Av
1800 LGCY 77573 4631 B6
Edinburg St
6100 HOUS 77087 4245 A1
Edinburgh Ct
10 CNRO 77384 2675 E4
14100 HOUS 77077 3956 E4
Edinburgh Dr
1200 FRDW 77546 4629 C3
Edinburgh Ln
4600 MSCY 77459 4369 B6
Edinston Pl
4900 HarC 77388 3112 B4
Edison Av
1300 BYTN 77520 4112 C1
Edison Ct
1100 BYTN 77520 3973 B7
Edison St
3600 HOUS 77009 3824 C6
Edison Brook Ln
2600 MSCY 77459 4497 E5
Edison Light Tr
15300 HarC 77429 3252 B7
Edisto Ct
14500 HarC 77084 3679 A4
Edith
23300 HarC 77447 3105 B7
Edith Dr
18700 BzaC 77511 4627 B4
18700 BzaC 77584 4627 B4
18700 PRLD 77584 4627 B4
Edith Ln
1100 FBnC 77471 4490 C1
10800 MtgC 77385 2677 A5
Edith St
- HOUS 77074 4100 B7
100 HarC 77562 3832 A3
4300 BLAR 77401 4101 C6
4300 HOUS 77401 4101 B6
5300 BLAR 77096 4100 D7
5300 BLAR 77401 4100 D7
5500 HOUS 77081 4100 C7
5500 HOUS 77096 4100 C7
Edloe St
- HOUS 77046 4101 E1
2700 HOUS 77027 3961 D7
5100 HOUS 77027 4101 E1
5200 HOUS 77005 4101 E2
6100 SSPL 77005 4101 E4
6100 WUNP 77005 4101 E4
6700 SSPL 77025 4101 E4
7200 HOUS 77025 4101 D5
Ed Lou Ln
- HarC 77429 3253 D3
Edmond Av
1400 PASD 77506 4107 C4
Edmondson
26000 MtgC 77357 2829 A5
Edmond Thorpe Ln
11400 HarC 77375 3254 E1
Edmonson Ct
3400 FBnC 77459 4621 D5
Edmont Ln
7000 HOUS 77091 3683 E4
7100 HOUS 77088 3683 E3
Edmonton Dr
3100 PASD 77503 4108 A5
Edmund St
4600 HOUS 77020 3964 C3
Edmund Wy
1600 LGCY 77539 4753 C1
1600 LGCY 77573 4753 C1
1800 GlsC 77539 4753 C1
Edmundson St
1300 HOUS 77003 3963 E7
2200 HOUS 77004 3963 E7
Edna St
1400 BYTN 77520 4112 D2
2000 LMQU 77568 4989 E2
3600 FBnC 77545 4498 E7
5800 HarC 77532 3552 C3
7100 HOUS 77087 4104 E7
7600 HOUS 77087 4105 B7

STREET
Block City ZIP Map# Grid

Edo Cir
15700 FBnC 77083 4096 B7
Edsall Dr
17300 HarC 77388 3257 E2
Edsee St
4300 HOUS 77009 3824 A6
Edward Dr
1100 SHUS 77587 4247 A2
5500 HOUS 77032 3405 D7
5500 HOUS 77396 3405 D7
Edward St
4300 TXCY 77591 4874 B6
6000 HOUS 77396 3405 E7
6000 HOUS 77396 3406 A7
Edwards Av
11100 PRLD 77583 4500 D5
Edwards Dr
100 MAGA 77354 2669 A4
1200 GlsC 77539 4635 D7
Edwards Ln
- PRLD 77583 4500 E6
Edwards Rd
100 HarC 77377 3106 D1
Edwards St
1000 HOUS 77002 3963 B2
1000 HOUS 77007 3963 B2
10100 HarC 77086 3541 E2
Edward Teach Rd
16600 GLSN 77554 5331 E6
16600 JMAB 77554 5331 E6
16600 JMAB 77554 5332 A6
Ed Watson Ln
1400 DRPK 77536 4109 C6
Edway
4300 HOUS 77048 4374 E4
Edwina Blvd
12200 HOUS 77045 4242 D7
Edworthy Rd
20000 HarC 77433 3251 C6
Effie Ln
1300 PASD 77502 4107 E6
1300 PASD 77506 4107 E6
Effie St
900 LGCY 77573 4632 B3
4300 BLAR 77401 4101 C6
4300 HOUS 77401 4101 B6
Effingham Dr
5500 HOUS 77035 4240 C6
Egan St
500 HOUS 77020 3964 B3
Egan Lake Pl
10 WDLD 77382 2674 A5
Eganville Cir
18100 HarC 77377 3254 B2
Egbert St
5200 HOUS 77007 3962 A1
Eggling
- HOUS 77084 3818 A1
Egret Ct
3900 MtgC 77386 2970 B4
Egret Dr
4300 SEBK 77586 4382 E7
Egret Bay Blvd
- LGCY 77573 4507 E6
18100 WEBS 77058 4507 D5
Egret Bay Blvd FM-270
- LGCY 77573 4507 E6
18100 WEBS 77058 4507 D5
Egret Canal N
100 BYTN 77520 4113 D5
Egret Canal S
100 BYTN 77520 4113 D5
Egret Chase Ct
2500 FBnC 77545 4498 C5
Egret Field Ln
- HarC 77049 3829 B3
Egret Glen Ct
19100 HarC 77433 3251 E7
Egret Hill Ct
12600 HOUS 77089 4378 D7
Egret Lake Wy
17800 HarC 77346 3408 B2
Egret Meadow Ln
3200 HarC 77084 3816 B4
Egret Oaks Ln
18700 WEBS 77058 4507 E6
Egret Wood Wy
19200 HarC 77429 3395 E1
Egypt Dr
6000 PASD 77505 4248 D5
Egypt Ln
32000 MtgC 77354 2673 C5
32000 MtgC 77382 2673 C5
32000 WDLD 77382 2673 C5
Egypt St
1100 HOUS 77009 3824 D6
Ehlers Rd
9700 MtgC 77302 2531 A7
9700 MtgC 77302 2676 E1
9700 MtgC 77302 2677 A1
Eichler Dr
7000 HOUS 77036 4099 A5
Eichwurzel Ln
100 HOUS 77009 3824 B4
Eigel St
4100 HOUS 77007 3962 B2
Eighteenth Fairway Dr
19900 HarC 77346 3265 B4
Eight Willows Rd
7500 HOUS 77489 4371 B3
7700 HOUS 77085 4371 B3
Eiker Rd
12400 BKVL 77581 4375 E7
12900 PRLD 77581 4375 E7
Eiko Ln
- MtgC 77354 2672 E1
- MtgC 77354 2673 A1
Eileen St
3000 DRPK 77536 4109 C7
17100 MtgC 77355 2962 D3
Einra Ln
1200 HarC 77532 3693 A1
Eisenhower Rd
7300 HOUS 77033 4243 E1
Elaine Rd
13000 HOUS 77047 4373 D3
Elaine St
- LMQU 77568 4874 B7
300 LMQU 77568 4990 C1
Elam St
1800 SEBK 77586 4509 B3
El Ambar Dr
11600 HOUS 77048 4244 C7
Elan Blvd
- MtgC 77386 2969 D1
Elana Ln
200 FBnC 77477 4369 C3
200 STAF 77477 4369 C3

Elbe Dr
19200 MtgC 77365 2971 D4
Elbeck Dr
11100 HOUS 77035 4241 B4
Elbert St
3000 HOUS 77098 3962 A7
7200 HOUS 77028 3826 A1
8000 HOUS 77028 3687 A7
Elberta St
1000 HOUS 77051 4243 C1
5700 HarC 77050 3546 E7
El Borders Dr
19300 HOUS 77338 3262 B6
Elbridge Ln
7400 DRPK 77536 4249 B2
El Buey Wy
- HOUS 77017 4106 B5
El Camino St
2600 HOUS 77054 4102 E7
2600 HOUS 77054 4103 A7
El Camino del Rey St
5500 HOUS 77081 4100 D2
El Camino Marguerite
- BzaC 77584 4626 D3
El Camino Real Blvd
14000 HOUS 77062 4379 D6
14700 HOUS 77062 4506 E1
15200 HOUS 77062 4507 A2
16700 HOUS 77058 4507 B4
17000 HarC 77058 4507 C4
17800 WEBS 77058 4507 D5
El Camino Village Dr
1000 HarC 77058 4507 D4
1000 WEBS 77058 4507 D5
El Capitan
- GLSN 77554 5220 B7
El Capitan Dr
7900 FBnC 77083 4096 C7
El Centro St
5000 HOUS 77018 3684 C7
5100 HOUS 77091 3684 C7
El Chaco Dr
- BYTN 77520 3835 C5
9700 BYTN 77521 3835 B5
El Chaco St
9500 BYTN 77521 3835 A5
El Cid
- HarC 77049 3831 B1
El Cielo
7400 GLSN 77551 5222 B2
Elcott Ln
15300 HarC 77053 4372 D4
El Cresta Dr
7300 FBnC 77083 4096 B6
Elden Hills Ct
23900 FBnC 77494 3953 B4
Elden Hills Wy
1400 FBnC 77494 3953 B4
Elder Ln
200 MtgC 77385 2822 E5
Elder Rd
2600 KATY 77493 3813 C4
20800 MtgC 77385 2822 E6
Elder St
900 HOUS 77002 3963 B3
1100 HOUS 77007 3963 B3
Elderberry Dr
- DKSN 77539 4754 A2
Elderberry Ln
500 BzaC 77584 4374 C7
13000 HarC 77049 3689 C7
Elderberry St
2000 LGCY 77573 4632 C6
W Elderberry St
300 LGCY 77573 4632 B6
Elderberry Trc
10 SGLD 77479 4495 D3
Elderberry Arbor Tr
- FBnC 77469 4234 D2
Elderberry Park Ln
10000 HarC 77375 3110 B5
Elder Bridge Dr
13400 FBnC 77478 4237 B4
Elder Glen Dr
300 HOUS 77598 4506 E5
400 WEBS 77598 4506 E5
Elder Grove Ct
400 BzaC 77584 4374 A7
N Elder Grove Dr
300 BzaC 77584 4374 A7
Eldergrove Ln
7700 FBnC 77469 4095 C6
Elder Lake Ln
15000 HarC 77429 3253 C7
Elder Mill Ln
10100 FBnC 77478 4236 B3
Elder Park Ct
2600 HarC 77449 3815 B4
Eldervista Cir
400 HOUS 77598 4506 E4
Eldervista Dr
300 HOUS 77598 4506 E4
Elderwood Dr
- PASD 77058 4508 C3
4000 TYLV 77586 4508 D1
El Diamante Dr
11400 HOUS 77048 4244 C7
Eldon Dr
200 HOUS 77060 3544 C2
Eldon Park Ct
13700 HarC 77429 3397 B2
Eldora Dr
8800 HOUS 77080 3820 E1
El Dorado Blvd
- HOUS 77546 4506 C4
100 HarC 77598 4506 D4
100 HOUS 77598 4506 D4
500 HOUS 77062 4506 D4
800 HOUS 77062 4507 A2
1900 HOUS 77062 4380 B7
3000 MSCY 77459 4497 A1
3100 HOUS 77059 4380 B4
3100 MSCY 77459 4496 D1
W El Dorado Blvd
100 HarC 77598 4506 C4
100 HOUS 77546 4506 C5
100 HOUS 77598 4506 C4
300 HarC 77546 4506 C5
El Dorado Dr
10 FRDW 77546 4750 B1
6900 HarC 77396 3547 B2
El Dorado St
10 PNVL 77304 2237 A2
Eldorado Center Ln
7100 HarC 77069 3400 A2
El Dorado Oaks Ct
3600 HOUS 77059 4380 C4

El Dorado Oaks Dr
15700 HOUS 77059 4380 B4
Eldoro Canyon Ln
17000 HarC 77095 3537 E3
Eldridge Pkwy
- HarC 77082 3957 B7
- HarC 77083 4237 B1
1300 HOUS 77077 3957 B7
2400 HarC 77077 3957 B7
2500 HarC 77082 4097 B2
3300 HOUS 77082 4097 B2
7100 HarC 77083 4097 B5
N Eldridge Pkwy
- HarC 77429 3398 C7
- HOUS 77084 3679 D7
- JRSV 77041 3539 D5
- JRSV 77065 3539 D7
600 HOUS 77079 3957 B3
1100 HOUS 77079 3818 B7
1100 HOUS 77084 3818 D1
1200 HOUS 77077 3957 B3
7000 HarC 77041 3679 C1
7900 HarC 77041 3539 D7
10300 HarC 77065 3539 C1
11300 HarC 77065 3398 C7
12300 HarC 77070 3398 C1
14800 HarC 77070 3254 C7
15400 HarC 77429 3254 C6
18300 HarC 77377 3254 C2
Eldridge Rd
- HOUS 77478 4237 B7
100 SGLD 77478 4368 B1
900 SGLD 77478 4237 B5
2400 FBnC 77478 4237 B7
Eldridge Rd FM-1876
- HOUS 77478 4237 B7
100 SGLD 77478 4368 B1
900 SGLD 77478 4237 B5
2400 FBnC 77478 4237 B7
Eldridge Wy
- HarC 77041 3679 D6
Eldridge Chase
13100 HarC 77041 3679 C1
Eldridge Chase Ct
7100 HarC 77041 3679 D1
Eldridge Garden Cir
13800 HarC 77083 4097 A4
Eldridge Glen Dr
5700 HarC 77041 3679 D5
Eldridge Meadow Ct
7200 HarC 77041 3679 C1
Eldridge Meadow Dr
13100 HarC 77041 3679 C1
Eldridge Park Wy
2600 FBnC 77478 4237 B4
Eldridge Pl Dr
12700 HarC 77041 3679 D5
Eldridge Springs Wy
13600 HarC 77083 4097 A4
Eldridge Trace Dr
13500 HarC 77083 4097 B7
Eldridge Valley Dr
13600 HarC 77083 4097 A5
Eldridge View Dr
6300 HarC 77083 4097 A4
Eldridge Villa St
- SGLD 77478 4237 B4
13400 FBnC 77478 4237 B4
Eleanor St
100 HOUS 77009 3824 C4
700 LMQU 77568 4874 B7
700 LMQU 77568 4990 B1
Electra Cir
10 WDLD 77382 2819 E1
Electra Dr
- WDLD 77382 2819 E1
300 HOUS 77024 3958 D3
700 HOUS 77079 3958 D2
Elegant Wy
- HarC 77066 3401 B7
Elegia Dr
3200 HOUS 77080 3821 A2
Elena Ct
12700 GLSN 77554 5220 B7
Elena Ln
400 HarC 77562 3831 E2
Elephant Walk St
23000 HarC 77389 2967 B6
Elf Cir
23400 HarC 77336 3267 A3
Elfen Wy
10 WDLD 77382 2819 D1
El Fleta Ln
15500 FBnC 77478 4236 B2
Elfwood Ct
100 HarC 77015 3829 A5
Elgar Ln
10800 HarC 77375 3255 A1
Elgin
29600 MtgC 77354 2818 C2
Elgin Ct
3300 HOUS 77004 4103 D1
Elgin St
400 HOUS 77006 3963 B7
800 HOUS 77002 3963 A6
1000 HOUS 77004 3963 B7
2600 HOUS 77004 4103 E1
4100 HOUS 77004 4104 A2
15400 HarC 77530 3829 E6
15400 HarC 77530 3830 A6
El Granate Dr
6100 HOUS 77048 4244 C7
El Grande Dr
14700 HarC 77083 4096 D5
El Greco Dr
- HarC 77082 4096 B4
- HarC 77083 4096 B4
Eli St
4100 HOUS 77007 3962 B2
Elicot Wy
10 SGLD 77479 4495 E3
Elicott Wy Dr
- SGLD 77479 4495 D3
Elijah Ct
25200 HarC 77375 2964 D3
Elijah Hills Ln
- MtgC 77386 2969 E6
Elinor Ct
14300 HarC 77429 3397 B1
Eliot Ln
15500 HarC 77032 3404 B6
Elisabeth Pl Ct
22400 FBnC 77494 4093 D3
Elisa Springs Ln
3200 HarC 77396 3407 E2
Elise Dr
13600 HOUS 77047 4373 B4

Elissa Ct
4000 GLSN 77554 5332 E3
Elizabeth
- MTBL 77520 3696 E5
Elizabeth Av
1300 RSBG 77471 4490 D7
Elizabeth Ct
3700 HOUS 77025 4241 E3
11700 MtgC 77362 2963 C1
Elizabeth Ln
1000 LGCY 77573 4631 D4
7800 GlsC 77517 4986 D6
13000 STFE 77510 4870 E6
40500 MtgC 77354 2671 C1
Elizabeth Rd
9000 HOUS 77055 3820 E7
9000 SPVL 77055 3820 E7
10700 LPRT 77571 4110 D7
Elizabeth Rdg
11700 MtgC 77304 2382 A4
Elizabeth St
- ALVN 77511 4749 C7
3600 DRPK 77536 4249 C1
17100 GlsC 77511 4869 B7
Elizabeth Bay Rd
14800 HarC 77429 3396 C1
Elizabeth Rose Ct
10300 HarC 77089 4504 E1
Elizabeth Rose Dr
10100 HarC 77089 4504 E1
Elizabeths Glen Ln
9600 HarC 77375 3255 B2
Elizabeth Shore Cir
18200 HarC 77433 3395 E4
N Elizabeth Shore Lp
18300 HarC 77433 3395 E4
S Elizabeth Shore Lp
12300 HarC 77433 3395 E4
W Elizabeth Shore Lp
12300 HarC 77433 3395 D5
El James Dr
3400 HarC 77388 3112 E7
3400 HarC 77388 3113 A7
3600 HarC 77388 3257 E1
El Jardin Dr
4800 CmbC 77586 4383 C5
4800 PASD 77586 4383 B4
Elk Cir
17900 HarC 77090 3258 A2
Elk Dr
100 HarC 77532 3266 D7
100 HarC 77532 3410 E1
Elkana Deane Ln
22500 HarC 77449 3814 D5
Elk Bayou Ln
10 HOUS 77013 3966 E1
Elk Bend Dr
9100 HarC 77379 3255 E4
Elk Canyon Ct
6000 HOUS 77345 3120 C5
Elk Creek Dr
2300 HOUS 77345 3120 A6
Elk Crossing Dr
10 WDLD 77381 2820 D3
Elkdale Dr
3100 HarC 77082 4096 C2
Elkfield Ln
5000 HarC 77338 3260 D2
Elk Forest Tr
12400 HarC 77044 3548 E7
12400 HarC 77044 3549 A7
Elkgrove Ln
4900 HarC 77338 3260 C2
Elkhart St
800 HOUS 77091 3684 A5
900 HOUS 77091 3683 E5
Elk Hill Ct
14800 HOUS 77062 4380 A7
Elkhorn Ln
4900 HarC 77338 3260 C1
Elkhorn Ranch Dr
- HarC 77064 3540 B5
Elkington Ct
11700 HOUS 77071 4239 C5
Elkins Rd
- FBnC 77479 4495 A5
3700 SGLD 77479 4495 A2
4200 SGLD 77479 4494 E2
15000 HOUS 77060 3544 D3
Elk Lake Ct
18000 HarC 77346 3408 D1
Elk Meadow Dr
12200 STAF 77477 4237 D7
Elkmont Ct
4800 PRLD 77584 4502 A6
Elk Mountain Dr
- HarC 77388 3113 B5
Elk Park Ln
15700 HOUS 77062 4380 C7
Elk Point Ln
10200 HarC 77064 3540 B3
Elk River Rd
1400 HarC 77090 3258 A2
1600 HarC 77090 3257 E2
Elk Run Cir
800 HOUS 77079 3957 A2
Elks Dr
3000 FBnC 77494 3953 A6
Elk Springs Dr
12000 HarC 77067 3401 E4
Elkton Ct
2400 BzaC 77584 4501 D5
Elk Valley Cir
17900 HarC 77090 3257 E3
Elkway Ln
5000 HarC 77338 3260 C1
Elkwood Dr
1400 MSCY 77489 4370 D4
13800 HarC 77038 3543 A1
Elkwood Forest Dr
6000 HarC 77088 3542 C7
6200 HarC 77088 3682 C1
Elkwood Glen Ct
10100 HarC 77375 3255 C2
Elkwood Glen Ln
- HarC 77375 3255 A1
Ell Rd
10800 HarC 77093 3686 C2
Ella Blvd
- HarC 77067 3402 E5
- HarC 77088 3683 E1
1100 HOUS 77008 3822 E7
3000 HOUS 77018 3822 E2
4900 HOUS 77018 3683 E7
5100 HOUS 77091 3683 E7
9200 HarC 77088 3543 E6
9900 HarC 77038 3543 D4
10700 HOUS 77038 3402 D7

Ella Blvd
10700 HOUS 77067 3402 D6
13800 HarC 77014 3402 D2
13800 HOUS 77014 3402 E3
14600 HarC 77090 3402 D1
16700 HOUS 77090 3258 B4
17000 HarC 77090 3258 A1
18100 HarC 77388 3257 E1
18100 HarC 77388 3258 A1
19300 HarC 77388 3112 D5
Ella Cir
1400 HarC 77090 3258 A2
Ella Ct
400 FRDW 77546 4505 A7
Ella Pl
1300 HOUS 77008 3822 E6
Ella St
100 TMBL 77375 2964 A6
100 TMBL 77375 3109 A1
6800 BKVL 77581 4376 A6
6900 PRLD 77581 4376 A6
N Ella Creek Dr
700 HOUS 77067 3402 E4
S Ella Creek Dr
700 HOUS 77067 3402 D5
Ella Enclave Dr
- HarC 77090 3258 C5
El Lago St
3700 GLSN 77554 5332 C3
Ellaine Av
100 PASD 77506 4107 B6
W Ellaine Av
100 PASD 77506 4107 A6
900 PASD 77506 4106 E6
1300 HOUS 77017 4106 D6
Ella Lee Ln
2300 HOUS 77019 3962 A6
3300 HOUS 77019 3961 E6
3600 HOUS 77027 3961 D6
5600 HOUS 77056 3960 D6
6100 HOUS 77057 3960 B7
7800 HOUS 77063 3960 A7
9500 HOUS 77063 3959 B6
9600 HOUS 77042 3959 B6
10600 HOUS 77042 3958 C7
11300 HOUS 77077 3958 B7
12400 HOUS 77077 3957 D7
13900 HOUS 77077 3956 E7
Ella Park Dr
13200 HOUS 77067 3402 D5
El Largo Dr
- TXCY 77591 4755 E3
8600 TXCY 77591 4756 A3
Ella Ridge Ln
13300 HOUS 77067 3402 E4
Ella View Ln
13300 HOUS 77067 3402 E4
Ellcreek Ct
1100 FBnC 77479 4367 A6
Ellea Ln
- SGLD 77478 4237 E7
Elledge Rd
- MtgC 77386 2968 D3
Ellen Av
300 LGCY 77573 4632 C2
Ellen Dr
300 DRPK 77536 4109 B5
6100 BKVL 77581 4375 D6
Ellen Ln
12800 HOUS 77015 3967 C4
Ellen St
1100 DRPK 77536 4109 C5
9600 BYTN 77521 3835 A6
Ellena St
300 HOUS 77076 3684 D5
Ellenberger Av
6500 HarC 77396 3547 A2
Ellendale Ct
15800 HarC 77429 3397 A1
Ellen Powell Dr
500 PRVW 77445 3100 A3
Ellenville Dr
12500 HOUS 77089 4378 C6
Ellerslie Ln
13400 HarC 77429 3397 A4
Ellerton Ln
- HarC 77090 3258 C5
Ellery Dr
- FBnC 77494 3952 D3
Ellesborough Ln
3300 HarC 77388 3112 E5
Ellesmere Dr
13000 HarC 77015 3828 C6
Ellies Ln
3500 BzaC 77583 4500 D7
Ellies Gate Ln
3500 BzaC 77583 4500 D7
Ellinger Ln
8200 HOUS 77040 3681 D6
Ellingham Dr
500 HarC 77450 3954 C1
Ellington Fld
10 HOUS 77034 4378 E3
Ellington St
900 HOUS 77088 3683 E1
900 HOUS 77088 3684 A1
Ellington Park Dr
14300 HOUS 77598 4379 B7
Elliott St
- HOUS 77023 3964 B7
1000 HOUS 77023 4104 B1
Ellis Av
- CmbC 77586 4509 D4
100 SEBK 77586 4509 D4
Ellis Ct
3200 HOUS 77020 3964 A2
Ellis Dr
2000 BzaC 77583 4624 A3
2200 PRLD 77578 4624 B3
2200 PRLD 77583 4624 B3
7700 HOUS 77489 4371 A5
Ellis Lndg
- LGCY 77573 4631 B4
Ellis Rd
10 LGCY 77573 4630 D5
1500 SGLD 77478 4367 B2
Ellis St
12500 BKVL 77581 4375 C6
14000 STAF 77477 4369 E3
Ellis Creek Blvd
- FBnC 77479 4367 B4
- SGLD 77478 4367 B4
Ellis Grove Ln
- RSBG 77469 4491 E5
- RSBG 77471 4491 E5
Ellison Rd
2600 FBnC 77583 4622 A3

Ellison Ridge Dr
11000 FBnC 77469 4092 D7
Ellis School Rd
- HarC 77562 3832 A5
200 HarC 77562 3831 E5
1900 BYTN 77521 3832 A5
1900 HarC 77521 3832 A5
Ellis Springs Ln
14300 HarC 77396 3547 B2
Elliston St
900 HOUS 77023 4104 B1
Ellscott Dr
- MtgC 77386 2969 D1
Ellsworth Dr
1100 PASD 77506 4107 C6
Ellwood St
11000 WDLD 77380 2821 C7
Ellzey Ln
17600 MtgC 77302 2679 E2
Elm
- MtgC 77372 2682 E6
800 LPRT 77571 4111 C7
2700 BYTN 77520 3973 C5
14900 MtgC 77302 2677 B1
25400 MtgC 77357 2974 E2
Elm Av
- CNRO 77301 2384 D3
100 HarC 77532 3692 C2
300 PASD 77506 4107 B5
900 LMQU 77568 4874 B7
17100 HarC 77044 3551 C7
Elm Cir
- LGCY 77598 4630 C4
1100 TYLV 77586 4382 A7
14000 HarC 77396 3547 B2
E Elm Cir
2800 KATY 77493 3813 B3
W Elm Cir
2800 KATY 77493 3813 B4
E Elm Cres
100 WDLD 77382 2675 C7
W Elm Cres
10 WDLD 77382 2675 C6
Elm Ct
6300 BLAR 77401 4100 D4
6300 HOUS 77081 4100 D4
6300 HOUS 77401 4100 D4
13600 SGLD 77478 4237 B6
26800 MtgC 77365 3117 D5
Elm Dr
- HarC 77396 3406 E5
3400 DKSN 77539 4753 D3
12000 HarC 77429 3398 C2
Elm Ln
3900 GlsC 77518 4634 B3
4200 HarC 77389 3112 C1
7200 GLSN 77551 5222 A1
29700 MtgC 77354 2818 C1
Elm Rd
800 CRLS 77565 4509 C5
N Elm Rd
2900 GlsC 77517 4870 B5
2900 STFE 77517 4870 B5
S Elm Rd
4200 STFE 77517 4870 A7
4800 STFE 77517 4986 A1
Elm St
- HOUS 77023 3964 B7
10 DRPK 77536 4109 B4
10 HarC 77336 2976 D7
10 PRVW 77445 3100 B2
10 WDBR 77357 2828 C1
100 HarC 77562 3831 D2
100 WALR 77484 3101 E6
500 FBnC 77471 4490 C3
500 RSBG 77471 4490 C3
600 FBnC 77545 4623 A2
900 CNRO 77301 2383 E6
1200 ALVN 77511 4867 C2
1200 BYTN 77520 4112 D1
1200 GlsC 77511 4869 B4
1200 RHMD 77469 4491 C2
4300 HOUS 77339 3119 D6
4700 PASD 77586 4383 C4
4800 BLAR 77401 4101 A3
4800 PRLD 77581 4503 A2
5000 BLAR 77401 4100 E3
5000 HOUS 77081 4100 E3
5000 HOUS 77401 4100 E3
7400 HOUS 77023 4105 A2
7500 MNVL 77578 4746 E2
8900 HTCK 77563 4988 C1
8900 LMQU 77568 4988 C1
20100 MtgC 77357 2828 E6
26700 HarC 77373 3114 A1
26700 MAGA 77355 2669 A6
26700 MtgC 77355 2961 C1
26900 HarC 77373 3113 E1
E Elm St
7600 HOUS 77012 4105 C2
N Elm St
100 TMBL 77375 2964 B6
S Elm St
100 TMBL 77375 2964 C7
Elm Wk
4200 HarC 77084 3816 D1
El Mar Ln
1700 SEBK 77586 4509 D1
El Matador Dr
21700 HarC 77532 3266 C7
Elmbank Dr
16000 HarC 77095 3538 C6
Elm Bark St
22700 HarC 77375 2966 A7
Elm Bayou Ct
10800 HarC 77064 3540 B3
Elmbend Ct
10200 HMBL 77338 3262 D4
Elmbend Dr
- HMBL 77338 3262 D3
Elm Bluff Ct
10200 HarC 77064 3540 C3
Elm Bough Ct
12500 HarC 77065 3539 A3
Elm Branch Ct
10 WDLD 77380 2967 E3
S Elm Branch Pl
10 WDLD 77380 2967 E3
Elm Bridge Ct
11000 HarC 77065 3539 B2
Elmbrook Dr
4700 HarC 77388 3257 C1
4800 HarC 77379 3257 C1
Elm Canyon Ct
3000 HOUS 77345 3119 E2
Elmcreek Ct
3500 FBnC 77469 4364 E1

Elm Creek Dr
- LGCY 77573 4631 A
25300 MtgC 77380 2968 A
Elmcrest Dr
3200 HOUS 77088 3683 A
Elm Crest Tr
4000 HOUS 77059 4380 C
Elmcroft Dr
11200 HOUS 77099 4238 B
Elmdale Dr
10500 HarC 77070 3399 A
Elmdon Dr
18300 HarC 77084 3816 D
Elm Drake Ln
8700 HarC 77338 3262 A
Elmen
- SEBK 77586 4383 A
Elmen St
1500 HOUS 77019 3962 C
2500 HOUS 77098 3962 C
3600 SEBK 77586 4510 A
Elm Estates Dr
11600 HOUS 77077 3958 A
Elmfield Dr
25800 HarC 77389 2965 E
Elmfield St
14000 HOUS 77047 4373 A
14100 HarC 77047 4373 A
Elm Forest Dr
- HarC 77388 3257 C
2200 PRLD 77584 4501 B
Elm Fork Dr
19800 HarC 77346 3265 A
Elmgate Dr
2000 HOUS 77080 3820 B
Elm Glen Dr
3600 HOUS 77339 3119 B
3900 MSCY 77459 4497 A
Elm Green St
25400 HarC 77373 3114 E
Elm Grove Ct
2800 HOUS 77339 3119 B
Elm Grove Dr
1200 FBnC 77479 4493 D
Elmgrove Rd
5900 HarC 77389 2966 D
Elmgrove Park Ln
1100 PASD 77586 4381 E
Elmhaven Rd
8400 LPRT 77571 4249 D
Elm Heights Ln
6200 BLAR 77401 4100 E
6200 HOUS 77081 4100 E
6200 HOUS 77401 4100 E
Elm Hill Ct
19000 HarC 77084 3816 B
Elm Hollow St
2500 PRLD 77581 4504 D
Elm Hurst Ln
21500 HarC 77450 3954 B
Elmhurst St
10000 HOUS 77075 4377 D
10200 HOUS 77089 4377 C
Elmhurst Trails Ln
1100 PASD 77586 4381 E
Elmington Ct
12900 HarC 77429 3254 E
Elmington Dr
12900 HarC 77429 3254 E
Elmira St
24800 HarC 77375 2964 E
El Miranda Dr
14800 HarC 77095 3679 A
14900 HarC 77095 3678 E
Elm Knoll Ct
10500 HarC 77064 3540 B
Elm Knoll Tr
10000 HarC 77064 3540 B
Elmlake
400 HOUS 77336 3266 C
Elm Lake Dr
8400 FBnC 77083 4236 B
Elmlawn Dr
5500 HOUS 77033 4244 A
Elm Leaf Pl
15300 HarC 77429 3252 E
Elmley Pl
25800 HarC 77389 2966 E
Elm Meadow Tr
9900 HarC 77064 3540 A
Elmo Ct
10200 CNRO 77302 2531 A
Elmo St
400 LMQU 77568 4874 A
500 LMQU 77568 4990 A
Elmont Dr
14600 HarC 77095 3679 A
14900 HarC 77095 3678 E
Elmonte Rd
- HOUS 77078 3688 B
El Monte St
8700 HarC 77521 3833 D
Elmora St
3700 SSPL 77005 4101 D
Elmore Dr
200 MtgC 77385 2822 C
600 LGCY 77573 4632 A
Elmpark Ct
- HarC 77014 3401 E
Elm Park Wy
16700 HOUS 77058 4507 D
Elm Point Ct
16100 HarC 77095 3538 C
Elm Pointe St
900 LGCY 77573 4631 E
Elmridge Ct
19900 MSCY 77459 4497 E
Elm Ridge Dr
500 MtgC 77386 2968 D
Elmridge St
3200 HOUS 77025 4101 E
Elms Ct
3500 MSCY 77459 4496 E
Elmsbury Ct
20000 HarC 77449 3815 E
Elm Scenic St
3000 HOUS 77059 4380 A
Elmscott Dr
1500 SGLD 77478 4237 A
6500 PASD 77505 4248 E
6700 PASD 77505 4249 A
Elmsford Ct
8200 FBnC 77083 4096 C
Elmsgrove Ln
1100 HarC 77070 3399 A
Elm Shores Dr
13600 HOUS 77044 3409 A

Houston Street Index

STREET
Block City ZIP Map# Grid

mside Ct
1700 CNRO 77301 2384 E6
Imside Dr
2700 HOUS 77042 3959 A7
2700 HOUS 77042 4099 A1
Im Spring Dr
5500 HOUS 77048 4244 A6
m Square St
- HarC 77433 3252 A7
mstone Ct
4500 HOUS 77345 3119 E6
Im Stream Ct
3900 FBnC 77545 4622 C1
Imsworth Dr
10500 HOUS 77099 4238 D1
mtex Dr
14800 HarC 77396 3547 B1
14800 HOUS 77396 3547 B1
14900 HOUS 77396 3406 B7
Im Trace Dr
6800 FBnC 77479 4493 D5
28500 MtgC 77355 2815 A5
Im Trail Ln
13900 HarC 77014 3401 C1
m Tree Ct
7800 FBnC 77479 4494 A5
m Tree Dr
5500 HOUS 77048 4244 A6
Imtree Estates Dr
19400 HarC 77449 3677 A2
I Mundo St
8000 HOUS 77054 4102 E7
8000 HOUS 77054 4103 A7
8000 HOUS 77054 4242 E1
m Valley Ct
19800 HarC 77346 3265 A5
Im View Cir
4800 HarC 77084 3677 B7
Im View Ct
600 STAF 77477 4369 E4
Imview Dr
1900 HOUS 77080 3820 C5
mview Pl
9600 HOUS 77080 3820 C5
Imview Trace Ln
9500 HOUS 77080 3820 C5
Im Willow Ct
10 WDLD 77382 2675 B6
Im Wing Ln
22800 HarC 77450 3953 D4
mwood Av
1800 LPRT 77571 4110 E7
mwood Cir
300 FRDW 77546 4505 A5
mwood Ct
200 ORDN 77386 2822 C7
1800 SGLD 77478 4237 A6
4900 BYTN 77521 3972 C1
23500 HarC 77389 2966 E5
24200 MtgC 77365 2974 B5
m Wood Dr
- FBnC 77479 4493 D5
lmwood Dr
700 BYTN 77520 3972 E6
3900 PRLD 77584 4503 B7
19800 HarC 77338 3263 A5
19800 HMBL 77338 3263 A5
23600 MtgC 77365 2974 B6
29000 SHEH 77381 2822 A2
mwood Ln
- HarC 77429 3398 D3
1200 PASD 77502 4106 E6
lmwood St
100 BzaC 77511 4748 E1
4300 HOUS 77051 4243 C2
mwood Brook Ct
20300 HarC 77433 3251 C7
mwood Dale Dr
3600 FBnC 77545 4498 D7
Imwood Glen Ct
16800 HarC 77095 3538 A7
Imwood Hill Ln
5900 HOUS 77345 3120 C7
mwood Manor Dr
16000 HarC 77429 3397 B2
mwood Park Ct
16200 PASD 77059 4380 D5
lmwood Point Ln
16300 FBnC 77478 4236 A5
l Nogalito Dr
- HOUS 77028 3687 D7
oise St
100 CNRO 77301 2384 A3
oquence Wy
10 WDLD 77382 2819 D1
l Oro Dr
6100 HOUS 77048 4244 C7
l Padre Dr
15200 HarC 77083 4096 B4
l Paseo St
1700 HOUS 77054 4102 C7
l Paso St
700 HOUS 77017 4246 C2
700 SHUS 77017 4246 C2
700 SHUS 77587 4246 C2
6900 HOUS 77020 3964 E2
6900 HOUS 77020 3965 A2
29600 MtgC 77354 2818 A3
29700 MtgC 77354 2817 E2
l Pico Dr
7900 FBnC 77083 4096 B6
lpyco St
3000 HOUS 77051 4243 A6
l Rancho Dr
1300 BYTN 77521 3973 B2
5100 HarC 77521 3833 D1
l Rancho St
7600 HOUS 77087 4245 B1
lridge Village Wy
- FBnC 77478 4237 B4
l Rio St
7900 HOUS 77054 4102 E7
8100 HOUS 77054 4242 E1
lrod Rd
- HarC 77449 3814 E5
- HarC 77449 3815 A2
lrod St
8000 HOUS 77017 4245 E1
8200 HOUS 77017 4246 A1
8400 HOUS 77017 4106 A7
lroy St
3800 HOUS 77009 3824 D6
l Rubi Dr
11400 HOUS 77048 4244 C7
lsa St
600 PASD 77502 4247 B1
l Sabio Dr
- FBnC 77083 4096 C7

El Salvador Dr
4500 HarC 77066 3401 A2
Elsberry Park Ln
3600 FBnC 77450 4093 E1
Elsbeth Rd
300 HarC 77530 3969 D2
Elsbury Ln
3000 BzaC 77584 4501 C6
Elsbury St
4300 HOUS 77006 3962 E7
Elser St
4400 HOUS 77009 3824 C5
El Sereno Dr
7100 HarC 77083 4096 C6
Elsie Ln
- HOUS 77044 3408 E7
8800 HarC 77064 3541 B4
Elsie Rd
- HOUS 77041 3820 C1
Elsies Ln
12900 HOUS 77015 3967 B3
Elsinore Dr
22000 HarC 77450 3954 A1
22100 HarC 77450 3953 E1
Elstree Dr
14800 HarC 77015 3829 C6
15100 HarC 77530 3829 C5
El Tesoro Dr
14700 HarC 77083 4096 D5
El Tigre Ln
5100 HarC 77521 3833 C1
Elton Dr
15700 HarC 77532 3552 E4
Elton Rd
18000 GlsC 77511 4869 A2
Elton St
800 HOUS 77034 4246 B5
2200 BYTN 77520 3973 E5
Elton Knowles St
6000 HarC 77449 3676 E4
El Topacio Dr
6200 HOUS 77048 4244 C7
El Toro Ct
16000 HOUS 77598 4506 E4
El Toro Ln
300 HOUS 77598 4506 E5
700 HOUS 77062 4507 A4
El Toro St
200 LGCY 77573 4632 B3
Elvera St
7900 HOUS 77012 4105 C4
Elverson Oaks Dr
17200 HarC 77377 3254 D4
Elvinta St
2600 BYTN 77520 3973 D4
E Elvinta St
2400 BYTN 77520 3973 D4
W Elvinta St
2400 BYTN 77520 3973 D4
Elwood Dr
15600 JRSV 77040 3540 D7
Elwood St
7700 HOUS 77012 4105 B1
Elwood Hills Ct
10 WDLD 77381 2821 B4
Ely Ridge Ln
26600 FBnC 77494 4092 B1
Elysian St
- HOUS 77002 3963 D3
- HOUS 77020 3963 D3
1400 HOUS 77026 3963 D1
2300 HOUS 77009 3963 D1
2500 HOUS 77009 3824 D6
Embarcadero Dr
3600 HarC 77082 4096 B3
Embassy Plaza Dr
5300 HOUS 77032 3405 C6
Embe St
2100 PASD 77502 4247 C1
Ember Ln
4200 DRPK 77536 4249 B1
Ember Canyon Ln
2500 HarC 77449 3815 C4
Ember Glen Ct
15200 HarC 77095 3678 E1
Ember Hollow Cir
16100 FBnC 77478 4236 A6
Ember Hollow Ln
16300 FBnC 77478 4236 A5
Ember Isles Ln
12100 HarC 77041 3679 B7
Ember Lake Rd
12100 HarC 77066 3401 B6
Ember Pines Ct
10 WDLD 77384 2675 C5
Ember Sky Ct
19600 HarC 77094 3955 A2
Ember Sky Dr
- PRLD 77584 4500 B2
Ember Spring Dr
3700 HOUS 77339 3119 C4
Ember Trails Ct
300 HarC 77094 3955 B1
Ember Trails Dr
1800 HarC 77094 3955 B1
Emberwood Dr
8000 HarC 77070 3255 C5
Emberwood Wy
5400 SGLD 77479 4494 D4
Emberwood View Ln
8600 HOUS 77075 4376 E2
Embla Dr
8000 HarC 77049 3689 E7
Embry St
600 HOUS 77009 3824 C7
600 HOUS 77009 3963 C1
Embry Hills Dr
16300 HarC 77073 3259 B5
Embrystone Ln
- HarC 77047 4374 B4
Emerald Brk
5300 HarC 77041 3679 E7
Emerald Cir
10 FRDW 77546 4629 C2
18200 MtgC 77357 2826 D2
Emerald Ct
100 HOUS 77009 3824 B7
1900 HarC 77094 3955 A4
18200 MtgC 77357 2826 D2
Emerald Dr
1200 BzaC 77511 4748 E5
6600 PASD 77505 4248 E4
10200 HOUS 77031 4238 D4
10200 HOUS 77074 4238 D4
Emerald Ln
18300 MtgC 77357 2826 D2
Emerald St
4000 FBnC 77545 4623 A1

Emerald St
20000 PRVW 77484 3100 D4
Emerald Wy
19700 MtgC 77355 2814 D4
Emerald Ash Ct
6600 HarC 77346 3264 E3
Emerald Bay
- PRLD 77584 4500 D2
Emerald Bay Cir
12500 PRLD 77584 4500 B3
3500 HarC 77449 3815 B3
Emerald Bay Ln
3600 FBnC 77478 4366 D3
Emerald Bluff Ct
7900 HarC 77095 3537 E7
Emerald Branch Ln
3800 FBnC 77450 4094 A1
Emerald Briar Ln
15900 HarC 77084 3678 C5
Emerald Brook Ln
2900 PRLD 77584 4500 B4
5700 LGCY 77573 4751 C2
Emerald Canyon Rd
6500 FBnC 77450 4094 C4
Emerald Cliff Ln
20100 FBnC 77469 4094 C6
Emerald Cloud Ln
100 LGCY 77573 4508 C6
Emerald Cove
1900 HOUS 77077 3957 A6
Emerald Cove Dr
2100 LGCY 77573 4631 B7
Emerald Creek Dr
10000 HarC 77070 3399 C7
Emerald Crest Dr
- FBnC 77479 4366 C5
Emerald Cypress Ln
14600 HarC 77429 3396 C1
Emerald Falls Ct
3500 HOUS 77059 4380 B5
Emerald Falls Dr
3600 HOUS 77059 4380 B4
Emerald Field Dr
4100 PASD 77503 4108 E4
Emerald Forest Ct
13900 SGLD 77478 4237 A7
Emerald Forest Dr
18000 MtgC 77357 2826 D1
Emerald Garden Ln
17600 HarC 77084 3678 A7
Emerald Gate Dr
- HarC 77450 3954 E3
Emerald Glade Ln
7300 HarC 77396 3547 C1
Emerald Glen Ct
900 FBnC 77479 4493 D5
Emerald Glen Dr
7000 FBnC 77479 4493 D5
Emerald Glen Ln
10400 HarC 77070 3399 B7
Emerald Green Dr
1700 HarC 77094 3955 A4
Emerald Green Ln
1200 HarC 77094 3954 E3
1200 HarC 77094 3955 A3
1200 HarC 77450 3954 E3
Emerald Grove Dr
3000 HOUS 77345 3119 E4
Emerald Haven Dr
7900 FBnC 77479 4494 B4
Emerald Heights Ct
8700 HarC 77083 4096 E7
8700 HarC 77083 4236 E1
Emerald Heights Ln
8800 FBnC 77083 4236 E1
Emerald Hill Dr
11700 HarC 77070 3399 B7
Emerald Isle Dr
17300 HarC 77095 3538 A7
17400 HarC 77095 3537 E7
Emerald Isle Ln
700 LGCY 77573 4633 C2
Emerald Lake Ct
1600 HOUS 77062 4379 D6
Emerald Lake Dr
3800 MSCY 77459 4621 D2
Emerald Leaf Dr
- STAF 77477 4237 E6
19600 HarC 77094 3955 A1
19700 HarC 77094 3954 E2
19700 HarC 77450 3954 E2
Emerald Loch Ln
- RHMD 77469 4492 B2
Emerald Lodge Ln
4700 FBnC 77545 4622 E2
Emerald Loft Cir
2000 HarC 77450 3954 A5
Emerald Meadow Ct
7500 FBnC 77494 4093 B3
Emerald Meadow Ln
8200 HarC 77396 3547 E1
Emerald Moss Ct
14900 HarC 77429 3396 A1
Emerald Mountain Dr
20100 FBnC 77469 4234 C2
Emerald Oak Dr
- TXCY 77591 4873 B6
Emerald Oaks Dr
10100 HarC 77070 3399 B7
28000 MtgC 77355 2815 C5
Emerald Park Dr
10100 HarC 77070 3399 B7
Emerald Pathway Dr
1800 HarC 77388 3113 B2
Emerald Pine Dr
10300 HarC 77070 3399 B7
Emerald Point Ln
1900 LGCY 77539 4633 E5
22300 HarC 77375 3109 D2
Emerald Pointe Ct
5500 SGLD 77479 4494 E4
Emerald Pointe Ln
5400 SGLD 77479 4494 E4
Emerald Pool Ln
6900 HarC 77379 3111 C6
Emerald Pool Falls Dr
24300 HarC 77375 2965 D4
Emerald Ridge Cir
21600 FBnC 77450 3954 B7
21600 FBnC 77450 4094 B1
Emerald Ridge Ln
19600 HarC 77094 3955 A2
Emerald River Dr
1600 FBnC 77494 3953 C5
Emerald Run Ln
7200 HarC 77379 3111 B3
22000 FBnC 77469 4493 A3
Emerald Shire Ln
6700 HarC 77041 3679 D3

Emerald Shore Ct
8800 HarC 77095 3537 E5
Emerald Shore Ln
200 LGCY 77539 4753 A4
Emerald Springs Ct
1500 HarC 77094 3955 A3
2600 PRLD 77584 4500 D4
Emerald Springs Dr
12500 PRLD 77584 4500 B3
19700 HarC 77094 3955 A3
Emerald Spruce Ct
20600 HarC 77346 3265 A3
Emerald Stone Ct
- PRLD 77581 4502 D2
Emerald Stone Ln
18200 HarC 77094 3955 C1
Emerald Terrace Wy
25600 HarC 77389 2966 C1
Emerald Trace Ct
5200 FBnC 77479 4496 B4
Emerald Trail Dr
10300 HarC 77070 3399 B6
Emerald Tree Cir
4900 HarC 77084 3677 D6
Emerald Valley Ct
8400 HarC 77095 3538 D5
Emerald Wood Dr
11700 HarC 77070 3399 B7
Emerson Ln
3400 GlsC 77518 4634 C2
Emerson St
200 HOUS 77006 3962 E6
400 HOUS 77006 3963 A6
Emerson Creek Dr
30200 MtgC 77386 2969 D2
Emerson Ridge Dr
1900 HarC 77388 3113 B3
Emery Dr
10600 HOUS 77099 4238 A4
Emerybrook Ct
18100 FBnC 77469 4095 B6
Emery Cliff Pl
10 WDLD 77381 2820 C5
Emery Hill Ct
14800 FBnC 77478 4236 D2
Emery Hill Dr
9400 FBnC 77083 4236 D2
9400 FBnC 77478 4236 D2
Emery Meadows Ln
18800 HarC 77377 3254 B1
Emery Mill Pl
10 WDLD 77384 2675 A4
Emery Mills Ln
21000 HarC 77338 3261 E3
Emile St
100 HOUS 77020 3964 C3
N Emile St
500 HOUS 77020 3964 C3
Emilee Ct
1300 RSBG 77471 4491 D5
Emilee Point Ln
- MtgC 77386 2969 D6
Emilia Ct
16400 HarC 77379 3255 E6
Emily
2900 HarC 77032 3545 E2
2900 HarC 77032 3546 A2
Emily Ct
12500 SGLD 77478 4368 D1
Emily Ln
20500 HarC 77449 3815 D3
Emily Wy
24400 WlrC 77447 2959 D2
Emily Anne Ct
20100 HarC 77433 3251 C5
Emily Morgan Cir
1300 FBnC 77469 4365 C3
Emily Park Ln
- FBnC 77450 4093 E4
- FBnC 77450 4094 A4
22600 FBnC 77494 4093 D4
Emily Springs Ct
17500 HarC 77396 3407 E2
Emily Trace Ln
22900 FBnC 77450 4093 D1
Emir
1800 HOUS 77009 3824 A5
Emite Ct
10 HOUS 77011 3964 D7
Emma Dr
2400 PRLD 77581 4502 D3
Emma Ln
2800 BzaC 77511 4868 A3
Emma Cove Ct
1700 FBnC 77479 4367 A7
Emma Gardens Ln
- MtgC 77386 2969 D7
Emma Lou St
7000 HOUS 77091 3683 C4
7400 HOUS 77088 3683 C3
Emmet Hutto Blvd
3600 BYTN 77521 3972 C3
Emmett Dr
10 HOUS 77027 3961 B5
Emmett Rd
12500 HarC 77041 3679 B3
Emmett St
4000 HOUS 77026 3825 B6
Emmett F Lowry Expwy
- TXCY - 4872 D4
- TXCY - 4873 D4
- TXCY - 4874 C4
4300 TXCY 77591 4874 A5
Emmett F Lowry Expwy FM-1764
- TXCY - 4872 C4
- TXCY - 4873 D4
- TXCY - 4874 C4
Emmit Run
20100 HarC 77484 3102 E4
Emmott Dr
1400 FBnC 77469 4365 C3
Emmott Rd
8500 HarC 77040 3681 B2
Emnora Ln
- HOUS 77055 3821 A3
8500 HOUS 77080 3821 A3
9800 HOUS 77080 3820 A3
10100 HOUS 77043 3820 A3
10300 HOUS 77043 3819 E3
Em Norris St
1800 PRVW 77445 2955 C7
Emory Cross
- WDLD 77382 2674 D5
Emory St
4100 WUNP 77005 4101 C2
Emory Tr
19100 HarC 77388 3113 C7

N Emory Bend Pl
10 SHEH 77381 2821 E1
S Emory Bend Pl
10 SHEH 77381 2821 E1
Emory Brook Ct
18400 HarC 77346 3408 C1
Emory Green St
24200 HarC 77493 3814 A5
Emory Hill St
29700 HarC 77429 3395 C2
Emory Knoll Dr
2300 FBnC 77545 4498 C7
Emory Mill Rd
5100 FBnC 77469 4234 D3
Emory Oak Ct
10 WDLD 77381 2820 E6
Emory Oak Ln
3100 BzaC 77584 4374 A7
Empanada Dr
14400 HOUS 77083 4096 E6
15100 HarC 77083 4096 B6
Emperor Ln
7900 HOUS 77072 4097 D7
Emperors Pass
5700 FBnC 77459 4621 A1
8000 MSCY 77459 4621 A1
Empire Cir
3000 MtgC 77357 2829 C3
W Empire St
- HarC 77037 3684 C1
Empire Central Dr
6900 HarC 77040 3681 A2
Empire Creek Ln
- HarC 77449 3815 B1
Empire Falls Ln
3100 LGCY 77539 4753 A4
Empire Forest Pl
10 WDLD 77382 2674 A6
Empire Heights Ct
- HarC 77429 3253 E6
Empire Landing Vw
8300 FBnC 77494 4093 B7
Empire Oaks Ln
2700 FBnC 77494 3953 A6
Emporia St
12800 HOUS 77015 3967 B1
Emporia Chase Ct
25000 FBnC 77494 3952 C4
Emporia Point Ct
25000 FBnC 77494 3952 C4
Emporium Dr
18100 HarC 77084 3816 E3
Empress Dr
200 HOUS 77034 4247 A5
Empress Ln
300 LGCY 77573 4631 C4
4200 FBnC 77469 4233 E4
Empress Cove Ln
17600 HarC 77377 3254 B3
Empress Crossing Ct
19000 HarC 77379 3110 C5
Empress Crossing Dr
9400 HarC 77379 3110 C6
Empress Oaks Ct
11700 HOUS 77082 4098 A2
Empson Dr
15500 HarC 77032 3404 C6
Emptyness Dr
16700 HarC 77429 3252 E6
Empty Saddle Ct
20400 FBnC 77450 4094 C1
Emrose Ln
16400 HarC 77429 3252 C5
Emsco St
- HOUS 77061 4244 D6
Emsworth Cir
12700 HOUS 77077 3957 C5
Encenada Green Tr
6300 HarC 77346 3264 E4
Enchanted Cir E
16900 FBnC 77478 4236 A7
Enchanted Cir W
16900 FBnC 77478 4236 A7
Enchanted Cross
23700 FBnC 77494 4093 A5
Enchanted Dr
12900 HarC 77429 3397 E4
28700 SHEH 77381 2822 A2
Enchanted Ln
500 HarC 77388 3113 C6
Enchanted Cactus Dr
23100 FBnC 77494 4093 C4
Enchanted Crest Dr
6900 HarC 77449 3676 E2
7100 HarC 77433 3676 E2
Enchanted Forest Dr
8000 HarC 77088 3682 E1
8200 HarC 77088 3542 D7
Enchantedgate Dr
4300 HarC 77373 3115 B6
Enchanted Grove Dr
19500 HarC 77388 3113 C6
Enchanted Hollow Dr
500 HarC 77388 3113 C6
Enchanted Hollow Ln
3100 HarC 77388 3112 E4
Enchanted Isle Dr
2200 HOUS 77062 4379 E6
Enchanted Lake Dr
- FBnC 77450 3953 C6
2100 LGCY 77573 4509 A6
2800 PRLD 77584 4499 E4
Enchanted Landing Ct
2800 FBnC 77494 3953 D7
Enchanted Landing Ln
23000 FBnC 77494 3953 D7
Enchanted Meadow Ln
2200 HarC 77450 3954 B5
4700 FBnC 77494 4092 D2
Enchanted Mist Dr
5200 HarC 77346 3264 B5
Enchanted Oaks Ct
100 HarC 77388 3113 D7
Enchanted Oaks Dr
18900 HarC 77388 3113 D6
18900 HarC 77388 3258 D1
Enchanted Oaks Ln
2100 FBnC 77471 4614 B2
10300 CNRO 77304 2236 D5
Enchanted Park Dr
1900 MtgC 77386 2969 A1
Enchanted Path Ct
2200 FBnC 77469 4365 D1
Enchanted Path Dr
11900 HarC 77044 3688 E5
12400 HarC 77044 3689 A5
Enchanted River Dr
200 HarC 77388 3113 C7

Enchanted Rock Dr
500 HarC 77073 3259 A6
Enchanted Rock Ln
4600 HarC 77388 3112 B5
Enchanted Rock Tr
18100 HarC 77346 3408 D1
Enchanted Rose
20000 HarC 77433 3676 E1
Enchanted Spring Dr
19400 HarC 77388 3113 C6
Enchanted Stone Ct
10200 HarC 77070 3399 B5
Enchanted Stone Dr
9900 HarC 77070 3399 C5
Enchanted Stream Dr
7000 CNRO 77304 2236 E5
19200 HarC 77388 3113 C7
Enchanted Timbers Dr
5100 HarC 77346 3264 C6
Enchanted Trail Dr
200 HarC 77388 3113 C7
Enchanted Valley Dr
14300 HarC 77429 3397 D4
Enchanted Woods Dr
10 HOUS 77339 3263 D2
Enchantford Ct
19400 HarC 77388 3113 D6
Enchantington Cir
19400 HarC 77388 3113 C6
Enchantment Dr
23300 HarC 77336 3267 A3
Encinita Dr
7800 FBnC 77083 4096 A6
Encinitas Cove Ct
22700 HarC 77375 3110 E1
Encinitas Cove Dr
8200 HarC 77375 3110 D1
Encino Av
- LGCY 77573 4632 A7
Encino Ct
5000 FRDW 77546 4505 D6
Encino Ln
2500 SGLD 77478 4368 E3
Encino Cove Ct
10000 HarC 77064 3540 A3
Encino Pass Tr
10500 HarC 77064 3540 B3
Enclave Ct
- SGLD 77478 4237 B7
1700 MSCY 77459 4369 C6
12200 STAF 77477 4237 E6
Enclave Ln
3200 HOUS 77077 3957 B5
Enclave Pkwy
1000 HOUS 77077 3957 B3
Enclave Rd
- HOUS 77077 3957 B4
Enclave Sq E
1100 HOUS 77077 3957 A3
Enclave Sq N
1000 HOUS 77077 3957 A3
Enclave Sq S
1000 HOUS 77077 3957 D2
Enclave Sq W
1100 HOUS 77077 3957 D2
Enclave Tr
3200 HOUS 77077 3957 B5
Enclave Bay Ln
2900 LGCY 77539 4753 B2
Enclave Creek Ln
- HarC 77449 3815 A1
Enclave Hill Ln
7100 FBnC 77469 4615 E5
Enclave Lake Dr
900 HOUS 77077 3957 A3
Enclave Lake Ln
11300 PRLD 77584 4500 D2
Enclave Mist Ln
- HarC 77449 3815 A2
3800 FBnC 77469 4615 E5
Enclave Oaks Ln
3200 HarC 77068 3257 C6
Enclave Vista Ln
6500 HarC 77041 3679 E4
Encreek Rd
2300 HarC 77068 3257 D3
2300 HarC 77090 3257 D3
Endeavor Ct
1900 SEBK 77586 4509 D1
Endeavor Dr
- HOUS 77072 4097 E6
Endell Ct
700 HarC 77450 3954 E2
Endicott Ln
500 MtgC 77302 2530 D5
2100 SGLD 77478 4237 C5
3300 BzaC 77584 4501 C7
8600 HOUS 77096 4101 A7
8900 HOUS 77096 4241 A1
10600 HOUS 77035 4241 A3
10800 HOUS 77035 4240 E4
Endor St
7800 HOUS 77012 4105 C2
Endor Forest Pl
10 WDLD 77382 2674 E3
Endreli Dr
43800 MtgC 77354 2668 C2
Enelo
- HOUS 77040 3682 A5
- HOUS 77092 3682 A5
Energy Center Ctr
2000 HOUS 77030 4102 D5
Enero Dr
14900 HarC 77083 4096 D6
Enfield Dr
300 HarC 77562 3831 C2
Enford Ct
700 HarC 77450 3954 D2
Engel St
100 HOUS 77011 3964 C6
Engelfield Ct
3900 HarC 77449 3816 A2
Engelke St
2500 HOUS 77003 3963 E4
2700 HOUS 77003 3964 A5
4300 HOUS 77011 3964 B5
Engelmohr St
100 HOUS 77054 4242 D1
W England Ct
3900 HOUS 77021 4103 D5
England St
5800 HOUS 77021 4103 D5
7200 HOUS 77021 4243 D1
England Cove Dr
4000 HOUS 77021 4103 D5
Englebrook Dr
14600 HarC 77041 3539 B5
14600 HarC 77095 3539 B5

Engleford St
4200 HOUS 77026 3825 B6
Engle Forest Cir
4900 HarC 77346 3408 B1
Englewood Dr
- SGLD 77478 4368 C5
100 LGCY 77573 4631 E4
3400 BzaC 77584 4501 D7
Englewood Rd
2700 PLEK 77471 4614 D5
Englewood St
100 BLAR 77401 4101 A6
3500 HOUS 77026 3825 E6
Englewood Park Ln
14100 HarC 77429 3254 A5
Englewood Pl Dr
15200 SGLD 77478 4368 C5
Englewood Point Ct
5200 FBnC 77494 4093 B2
English St
200 HOUS 77009 3824 C4
English Brook Cir
12100 HarC 77346 3408 C1
English Chase Ct
15700 HarC 77429 3397 C2
English Colony Dr
2800 HarC 77598 4630 C1
English Elm St
1900 HarC 77067 3402 B7
English Glade Ct
10 WDLD 77381 2821 C4
English Green Wy
- FBnC 77545 4498 C7
English Heather Pl
10 WDLD 77382 2819 E2
English Ivy Ln
17800 HarC 77379 3257 A2
English Lake Dr
- PRLD 77581 4503 E7
- PRLD 77581 4504 A7
- PRLD 77584 4503 E7
English Lavender Pl
10 WDLD 77382 2819 A4
English Oaks Blvd
3000 PRLD 77584 4502 D5
English Oaks Dr
23800 HarC 77373 3114 E4
English Rose Ln
11200 HOUS 77082 4098 C2
English Rose Tr
11200 FBnC 77583 4622 B4
Enid St
200 HOUS 77009 3824 A5
6500 HOUS 77022 3824 A3
Enloe Ln
15300 MtgC 77372 2684 B3
Enloe Rd
23800 MtgC 77365 2972 E6
Enmore Ct
9300 HarC 77095 3538 B3
Ennis Rd
15300 FBnC 77478 4236 B2
Ennis St
- HMPD 77445 3098 A2
300 HOUS 77003 3963 E5
2300 HMPD 77445 3097 E2
3000 HOUS 77004 4103 B3
N Ennis St
10 HOUS 77003 3963 E5
10 HOUS 77003 3964 A4
Ennis Owens Rd
10400 MtgC 77372 2537 A1
Enns Ln
6800 HarC 77379 3256 D3
Ennsbury Dr
18100 HarC 77084 3816 D1
Enoch St
2300 HOUS 77054 4242 D1
Enola Dr
14500 HarC 77429 3396 B2
Enos St
10000 HarC 77086 3541 E2
Enridge Ln
- HOUS 77048 4375 D4
Ensbrook Dr
10800 HOUS 77099 4238 B4
Ensemble Ct
9000 HarC 77040 3541 B7
Ensemble Dr
7800 HarC 77040 3541 B7
7800 HarC 77040 3681 B1
Ensenada Dr
15200 FBnC 77083 4096 B7
Ensenada Canyon Ln
12000 HarC 77041 3680 A4
12100 HarC 77041 3679 D3
Ensign Cir
- TKIS 77554 5106 C3
Ensley Wood Dr
13100 HOUS 77082 4097 B3
Enstone Cir
9500 HarC 77379 3255 E6
9500 HarC 77379 3256 A6
Ensworth Dr
7100 HOUS 77016 3687 B2
Enterprise Av
100 LGCY 77565 4508 E5
100 LGCY 77573 4508 D5
Enterprise Cir
1600 LGCY 77573 4508 D5
Enterprise St
700 HOUS 77088 3684 A2
Enterprise Row Dr
100 CNRO 77301 2530 A1
Entrada Ct
20200 HarC 77346 3264 E4
Entry St
8900 LPRT 77571 4249 E3
Envoy St
10100 HOUS 77016 3686 E4
Enyart St
4900 HOUS 77021 4103 E6
4900 HOUS 77021 4104 A6
Eola Creek Ln
16300 HarC 77530 3829 D4
Epernay Pl
10 JRSV 77040 3540 D7
Epes
100 TMBL 77375 2964 B6
Ephram Dr
- FBnC 77494 3952 B6
Epic Dr
3800 MtgC 77386 2970 B7
Epona Ct
8000 HarC 77040 3541 D6
Epperson Wy
700 FBnC 77479 4367 B6

STREET Block City ZIP Map# Grid

Epperson Wy Ct
800 FBnC 77479 4367 B6
Eppes St
4700 HOUS 77021 4103 E5
4700 HOUS 77021 4104 A5
6300 HOUS 77087 4104 D6
7200 HOUS 77087 4105 A7
Eppingdale Dr
3600 HarC 77066 3401 C5
Epping Forest Wy
- SGLD 77479 4496 A3
10 SGLD 77479 4495 E3
Eppolito St
300 FBnC 77477 4369 E4
300 STAF 77477 4369 E4
Epright Dr
15500 HarC 77433 3251 E6
Epsilon Av
- HarC 77532 3552 E4
Epsilon St
1200 PASD 77504 4247 D6
Epsom Dr
9800 HOUS 77093 3686 A5
10900 HarC 77093 3686 B2
Epsom St
9700 HOUS 77093 3686 A5
Epsom Downs Dr
7400 HarC 77433 3677 C1
Epstein Wy
- FBnC 77471 4614 D5
Equador St
7800 JRSV 77040 3680 E1
Equestrian Ctr
- MtgC 77354 2671 C5
Equinox St
600 HarC 77532 3552 A3
Equity Dr
10900 HOUS 77041 3680 D7
Era Ln
22300 MtgC 77365 2973 D4
Erastus St
1900 HOUS 77020 3964 C1
2400 HOUS 77020 3825 C7
2800 HOUS 77026 3825 C7
Erath St
7400 HOUS 77023 4105 A2
7800 HOUS 77012 4105 C2
E Erath St
7600 HOUS 77012 4105 C2
Erby St
3600 HOUS 77023 4104 D4
3900 HOUS 77087 4104 D5
Eric Cir
17600 MtgC 77302 2824 B1
Eric St
29700 MtgC 77355 2816 A3
Erica
15500 HarC 77377 3108 B2
Erica Ln
- HarC 77562 3832 B2
3000 HOUS 77051 4243 A4
Erick Cir
7200 HarC 77379 3111 B1
Erickson St
10 CNRO 77301 2384 A2
Ericson Ct
5900 HarC 77379 3111 D6
Ericston Dr
11300 HarC 77070 3255 A7
Eric Trail Dr
16000 HarC 77447 3250 A7
Erie St
3700 HOUS 77017 4105 C7
3900 HOUS 77087 4105 C7
4100 HOUS 77087 4245 C1
7800 HarC 77521 3833 B3
8000 HOUS 77061 4245 C1
18200 MtgC 77365 2972 B5
Erie Cove
27700 MtgC 77386 2970 D6
Erika Ct
21600 MtgC 77365 2826 E7
21600 MtgC 77365 2972 E1
Erika Wy Dr
19900 HarC 77450 3954 E5
19900 HarC 77450 3955 A5
Eriksson St
2000 LMQU 77568 4989 E3
Erin Ct
- FBnC 77459 4621 C5
100 LPRT 77571 4250 E2
8100 HOUS 77071 4239 D6
14000 SGLD 77478 4237 A7
Erin Dr
- HOUS 77071 4239 D6
2300 PRLD 77581 4504 D2
Erin St
300 HOUS 77009 3824 B6
Erin Cove Ct
7900 HarC 77095 3538 A7
Erin Creek Ct
15900 HOUS 77062 4507 C1
Erincrest Ct
21900 FBnC 77450 4094 A1
Erin Dale Ct
14200 HarC 77083 4236 D1
Erin Glen Ct
2200 DRPK 77536 4108 E6
Erin Glen Wy
10000 PRLD 77584 4501 A2
Erin Hills Ct
2000 FBnC 77479 4494 B1
Erin Hollow Ct
- FBnC 77469 4094 C6
Erin Knoll Ct
3400 HOUS 77059 4380 B4
Erinwood Ct
100 HarC 77379 3256 B2
Erinwood Dr
7400 HarC 77379 3256 B2
Erin Wy Ct
17400 HarC 77095 3677 E1
Ernest
1200 GlsC 77650 4879 B6
Ernest Dr
21800 MtgC 77355 2960 E5
Ernest Rd
15200 HOUS 77396 3405 E7
Ernestes Rd
100 HOUS 77494 3953 B2
400 HarC 77494 3953 B1
Ernestine St
- HOUS 77004 4104 A1
1400 HOUS 77023 3964 A7
2000 HOUS 77023 4104 A1
Ernie Rd
- HOUS 77028 3825 D1
4600 HOUS 77016 3825 C1

Ernst Ct
500 HarC 77388 3113 D7
Eroc Av
- HOUS 77045 4242 C7
Eros Dr
2700 MSCY 77459 4497 E5
Eros St
14300 HarC 77049 3690 A6
Errington Dr
- HarC 77049 3690 A7
7900 HarC 77049 3689 E7
Erskine Ct
10300 HarC 77070 3399 B6
Ertel Ln
7100 HarC 77040 3681 B2
Erva Dr
- HarC 77037 3544 E7
Ervin Av
1200 LGCY 77539 4752 D2
1200 LGCY 77573 4752 D2
Erwin St
1300 HarC 77039 3545 B6
Escala Dr
21100 HarC 77338 3261 D3
Escalante Dr
17900 HarC 77433 3396 E7
Escambia Wy Dr
1000 FBnC 77469 4365 B4
Escher Rd
15800 HarC 77433 3251 D6
Escon Cir
- HarC 77493 3813 C1
Escondido Cir
6600 HarC 77083 4096 A5
Escondido Dr
6500 HarC 77083 4096 A5
Escuela Ln
- HOUS 77058 4380 D7
- HOUS 77062 4380 C7
Eskridge St
5500 HOUS 77023 4104 C2
Esperanza
2400 FBnC 77469 4365 A1
Esperanza St
1700 HOUS 77023 4104 E2
Esperson St
6000 HOUS 77011 3964 D6
Espinosa Dr
16100 FBnC 77083 4096 A6
16400 FBnC 77083 4095 E6
Espinosa Ln
19500 MtgC 77357 2827 C5
Esplanade Blvd
- HOUS 77060 3544 B1
S Esplanade Ln
300 STAF 77477 4369 C3
Esplanade Pl
100 STAF 77477 4369 C3
Esplanade Wy
- STAF 77477 4369 C3
N Esplanade Wy
200 STAF 77477 4369 C2
S Esplanade Wy
100 STAF 77477 4369 B3
Esquivel Cir
3400 BzaC 77511 4868 A4
Esquivel Rd
2100 BzaC 77511 4868 B3
Essenbruk Dr
12000 HarC 77066 3401 B6
Essendine Ln
14400 HOUS 77045 4372 C3
Essex
25600 MtgC 77357 2829 B4
Essex Ct
1100 SEBK 77586 4382 E7
2500 LGCY 77573 4631 B7
Essex Dr
700 FRDW 77546 4629 C3
S Essex Dr
10300 MtgC 77302 2676 E2
W Essex Dr
- MtgC 77302 2676 E2
Essex Ln
3900 HOUS 77027 3961 C7
Essex Pl
200 STAF 77477 4369 A1
Essex Ter
2700 HOUS 77027 3961 D7
Essex Green St
3800 HOUS 77027 3961 C7
Essie Rd
3200 HarC 77038 3542 E4
3200 HarC 77086 3542 E4
Essman Ln
20500 HarC 77073 3259 D3
20800 HOUS 77073 3259 D3
Estancia Pl
10 HarC 77389 2820 A5
Estaril Cir
2500 HarC 77038 3543 B6
Estate Dr
100 FRDW 77546 4749 D3
1100 LMQU 77568 4990 A1
1800 DRPK 77536 4248 E1
2300 DRPK 77536 4249 A1
4500 BYTN 77521 3972 C2
Estate St
2500 DRPK 77503 4248 E1
2500 DRPK 77536 4248 E1
2500 PASD 77503 4248 E1
3000 STAF 77477 4369 D3
Estates Dr
100 CNRO 77304 2383 B3
Estates at Cullen Park Dr
- HarC 77084 3816 D5
- HOUS 77084 3816 D5
Estates Creek Blvd
- HarC 77388 3113 A6
Estella Ln
15700 HarC 77090 3258 D6
Estella Rd
400 PASD 77504 4247 B5
Estelle
- HOUS 77026 3825 A4
Estelle Cir
200 TXCY 77591 4873 E6
Estelle Ln
5300 HarC 77373 3115 D7
12100 MtgC 77362 2963 C2
Estelle St
10 HOUS 77003 3964 B6
N Estelle St
300 HOUS 77003 3964 B5
Ester St
4200 STAF 77477 4369 B2
Esterbrook Dr
3400 HarC 77082 4096 B3

Estes Ct
2400 FBnC 77469 4365 B4
Estes St
- HOUS 77023 4104 D4
E Estes St
4000 GlsC 77518 4634 D2
W Estes St
3900 GlsC 77518 4634 D2
Estes Brook Ln
- HarC 77053 4372 E5
Estes Glen Ln
8100 HarC 77040 3541 B5
Estes Lake Ln
25400 FBnC 77494 4093 A5
Estes Park Dr
12000 HarC 77067 3401 D4
Estes Park Ln
11900 HarC 77067 3401 E4
Esther Av
1200 GlsC 77565 4509 C6
1200 LGCY 77565 4509 C6
1200 LGCY 77573 4509 C6
2500 PASD 77502 4107 E7
2500 PASD 77502 4108 A7
Esther Dr
1100 HOUS 77088 3683 C2
2500 MtgC 77384 2674 D1
Estonia Ct
5900 HarC 77379 3111 E6
Estrada Dr
2500 LGCY 77573 4632 A7
6200 HarC 77082 4096 D4
6200 HarC 77083 4096 D4
E Estrella
19400 HarC 77073 3259 C6
N Estrella
800 HarC 77073 3259 C6
S Estrella
800 HarC 77073 3259 C6
W Estrella
19400 HarC 77073 3259 C6
Estrella Ct
12600 HOUS 77045 4241 B6
Estrellita Dr
14800 HOUS 77060 3544 D3
Etchstone Dr
6600 HarC 77389 2966 C6
Ethel Ln
4100 STAF 77477 4369 B3
Ethel St
200 TXCY 77591 4873 E6
4800 BzaC 77584 4502 A6
7900 HOUS 77028 3826 C2
Etheline Dr
5400 HarC 77039 3546 E4
Etheridge St
5600 HOUS 77087 4104 D7
5700 HOUS 77087 4244 D1
Ethyl Rd
- HOUS 77503 3968 A7
100 PASD 77503 3968 A7
100 PASD 77503 4108 A1
Ethyl Corp Rd
900 PASD 77503 4108 B1
1000 HOUS 77503 3968 B7
1000 PASD 77503 3968 B7
Eton Dr
2100 PRLD 77581 4504 A2
Eton St
3700 HOUS 77087 4105 B7
Eton Brook Ln
16400 HarC 77073 3259 B4
Eton Ridge Ct
18200 FBnC 77469 4095 C6
Etonshire Ct
10 SHEH 77381 2821 E1
Etta Rd
25900 SPLD 77372 2537 B7
Etta St
8900 HOUS 77093 3686 A7
Etta Oaks Ln
28000 MtgC 77372 2683 E4
28000 MtgC 77372 2684 A4
Ettrick Dr
5500 HOUS 77035 4240 C6
Etude Ct
10 WDLD 77382 2673 C6
Etzel Cir
4100 HOUS 77053 4372 D4
Eubanks St
300 HOUS 77022 3824 B1
1700 HOUS 77093 3824 D1
Eucalyptus Ln
7800 BzaC 77584 4627 C4
Euclare Dr
11600 HarC 77086 3542 C6
11600 HarC 77088 3542 C6
Euclid St
300 HOUS 77009 3824 A7
400 HarC 77530 3969 C1
900 HOUS 77009 3823 E7
1100 HOUS 77007 3823 E7
Euclid Springs Ln
9500 HarC 77044 3689 D3
Euel St
1100 HOUS 77009 3824 D4
Euell Rd
2500 HarC 77532 3553 C2
Eugene St
7300 HOUS 77093 3824 E2
Eugenia Av
6200 TXCY 77591 4873 D7
Eula Av
5000 PASD 77505 4248 B3
Eula Dr
9000 BzaC 77578 4747 B5
Eula Morgan Rd
3000 HarC 77493 3813 A3
3000 KATY 77493 3813 A3
Eule Dr
5000 KATY 77493 3813 E6
Eunice St
3000 HOUS 77009 3824 B7
5600 TXCY 77591 4873 E6
17800 HarC 77044 3551 D7
Eureka Rd
40000 MtgC 77354 2672 E2
Eureka St
6600 HOUS 77007 3961 D1
6600 HOUS 77008 3961 D1
Europa St
4000 HOUS 77022 3823 E2
Eva Av
1000 PASD 77502 4107 C7
Eva Dr
800 KATY 77493 3952 A1
900 KATY 77493 3813 A7

Eva Ln
12400 MtgC 77306 2533 A4
Eva St
2600 HOUS 77093 3824 E2
Evan Ln
20500 HarC 77449 3815 D3
Evandale Ln
900 FBnC 77479 4366 C7
Evanfield Ct
27000 HarC 77433 3537 A1
Evangeline Blvd
10 MtgC 77304 2236 B4
Evangeline Dr
10800 HOUS 77013 3827 C4
11900 HarC 77532 3692 E3
E Evangeline Oaks Cir
10 WDLD 77384 2675 A4
N Evangeline Oaks Cir
- WDLD 77384 2674 E4
- WDLD 77384 2675 A4
S Evangeline Oaks Cir
100 WDLD 77384 2675 A4
W Evangeline Oaks Cir
100 WDLD 77384 2675 A4
Evan Ridge Ct
10 WDLD 77381 2821 E3
Evans Rd
1900 MSCY 77489 4370 B7
Evans St
6800 HOUS 77061 4244 E5
7000 HOUS 77061 4245 B4
Evanston St
10 HarC 77015 3828 E6
10 HarC 77049 3828 E6
500 HOUS 77015 3828 D7
700 HOUS 77015 3967 E2
Eve St
10 HOUS 77013 3827 C6
Evella St
2700 HOUS 77026 3824 E6
3000 HOUS 77026 3825 A6
Evelo St
8400 HOUS 77051 4243 D2
N Evelyn Cir
11700 MSCY 77071 4239 E7
11700 MSCY 77071 4240 A7
S Evelyn Cir
11800 MSCY 77071 4239 C7
11800 MSCY 77071 4240 A7
Evelyn St
200 HOUS 77009 3824 B5
5200 TXCY 77591 4873 E6
5200 TXCY 77591 4874 A6
Evendale Ct
19200 HarC 77094 3955 B2
Evening Ln
24200 MtgC 77365 2972 B7
Evening St
600 HarC 77060 3403 D4
Evening Tr
3800 HarC 77388 3257 C1
Evening Bay Dr
12300 PRLD 77584 4500 B3
Evening Bay Ln
1200 LGCY 77573 4633 B4
Evening Bend Ct
1600 FBnC 77479 4494 C5
Evening Canyon Ln
- FBnC 77494 4092 E1
Evening Cloud Ct
1400 HarC 77450 3953 E4
Evening Glen Cir
19400 HarC 77375 3109 B6
Evening Glen Ct
12200 HarC 77375 3109 B6
Evening Glen Dr
19300 HarC 77375 3109 C7
Evening Light Dr
8500 FBnC 77479 4494 B5
Evening Primrose Ln
20200 HarC 77375 3109 E5
Evening Rose Ln
6400 HarC 77449 3677 C3
Evening Run Ln
16900 FBnC 77469 4235 E1
Evening Shade Ct
2700 MSCY 77489 4370 D7
Evening Shades Ct
19500 HarC 77346 3265 B5
Evening Shadows Ln
5700 HarC 77373 3115 E6
5900 HarC 77373 3116 A6
Evening Shore Ct
12500 HarC 77041 3679 E7
Evening Shore Dr
5500 HarC 77041 3679 E6
Evening Shore Ln
2700 PRLD 77584 4500 B4
Evening Sky Dr
2100 HOUS 77045 4242 D7
Evening Song Ct
10 WDLD 77380 2968 A3
Evening Star Ct
1300 PRLD 77545 4499 E2
16300 HarC 77532 3551 E2
Evening Star Dr
2400 PRLD 77545 4499 E3
Evening Sun Ct
5900 FBnC 77469 4493 A7
Evening Trail Dr
3800 HarC 77388 3257 D1
Evening Wind Dr
1300 PRLD 77545 4499 E2
Evensong Ln
11100 HarC 77429 3539 A1
Eventide Dr
14100 HarC 77429 3397 E7
Everbear St
1200 PASD 77504 4247 D7
Everbloom Meadow Dr
7100 FBnC 77494 4093 B5
Everest Dr
13500 STFE 77510 4870 D3
Everest Ln
2700 HarC 77073 3259 E4
Everest Wy
2300 HOUS 77339 3118 B6
Everett
100 GlsC 77650 4994 E1
100 GlsC 77650 4995 A1
Everett Dr
2800 FRDW 77546 4749 E1
Everett St
500 CNRO 77301 2383 E3
500 CNRO 77301 2384 A3
1500 HOUS 77009 3963 C2
2500 HOUS 77009 3824 C7

Everett Oaks Ln
17000 HarC 77095 3538 A4
Everfrost Ln
- HarC 77379 3111 B5
Everglade Dr
1200 PASD 77502 4247 C2
8800 HOUS 77078 3687 E4
9000 HOUS 77078 3688 A4
N Everglades Dr
1600 DRPK 77536 4109 D6
S Everglades Dr
1600 DRPK 77536 4109 D7
Evergreen Av
900 FBnC 77545 4498 D5
Evergreen Cir
900 WDLD 77380 2821 E4
Evergreen Ct
1400 RHMD 77469 4491 E3
Evergreen Dr
- BzaC 77511 4748 A7
- BzaC 77511 4866 A1
- LGCY 77598 4630 C4
500 HarC 77562 3831 D2
700 FRDW 77546 4629 B2
700 HOUS 77012 4105 B3
700 HOUS 77023 4105 B3
2300 PRLD 77581 4504 D5
3400 HOUS 77087 4105 A6
3700 DKSN 77539 4753 B5
3700 LGCY 77539 4753 B5
6800 MtgC 77354 2673 A1
13300 HarC 77375 2964 B4
13300 TMBL 77375 2964 B4
Evergreen Ln
- BzaC 77511 4748 A7
- BzaC 77511 4866 B1
700 MtgC 77302 2530 D6
1600 PASD 77586 4381 E6
1900 LMQU 77568 4989 E2
1900 LMQU 77568 4990 A3
Evergreen Pk
31300 MtgC 77386 2823 B7
Evergreen Rd
10 HOUS 77365 3119 D1
100 FBnC 77545 4499 A5
1000 FBnC 77545 4498 D5
1500 BYTN 77520 4112 D4
1500 BYTN 77520 4113 A4
23300 MtgC 77365 2973 E7
Evergreen St
- CmbC 77520 3835 D3
4500 BLAR 77401 4101 A5
5100 BLAR 77401 4100 D5
5300 HOUS 77081 4100 D5
5800 HOUS 77081 4100 C5
Evergreen Bay Ct
2500 HOUS 77059 4380 B7
Evergreen Brook Wy
7600 HarC 77095 3538 B7
Evergreen Canyon Rd
5400 HarC 77066 3401 A6
Evergreen Cliff Tr
2700 HOUS 77345 3120 B5
Evergreen Elm Ct
4300 HOUS 77059 4380 C4
Evergreen Elm Wy
17000 HOUS 77059 4380 C4
Evergreen Falls Dr
18600 HarC 77084 3816 C4
Evergreen Glade Ct
3000 HOUS 77339 3118 D5
Evergreen Glade Dr
3200 HOUS 77339 3118 D4
Evergreen Grove Dr
15400 FBnC 77083 4096 B7
Evergreen Haven Ct
4900 HarC 77084 3677 B7
Evergreen Hills Dr
29500 MtgC 77386 2969 E3
Evergreen Knoll Ln
15200 HarC 77433 3251 C6
Evergreen Lake Ln
16200 HarC 77429 3397 A3
Evergreen Meadow Ct
4500 HarC 77449 3677 B7
Evergreen Oak Dr
3100 HarC 77068 3257 D6
Evergreen Pl Dr
15300 FBnC 77083 4236 B1
Evergreen Ridge Wy
14700 HOUS 77062 4380 A7
Evergreen Springs Ct
6600 HarC 77379 3111 D5
Evergreen Springs Ln
20200 HarC 77379 3111 D5
Evergreen Square Tr
3500 FBnC 77545 4498 C7
3800 FBnC 77545 4622 C1
3800 MSCY 77545 4622 C1
Evergreen Terrace Ln
- HarC 77449 3815 B1
7800 HarC 77040 3541 E7
26800 FBnC 77494 4092 A1
Evergreen Timbers
16200 SGCH 77355 2961 D4
Evergreen Trails
- HarC 77041 3679 E3
Evergreen Valley Dr
5200 HOUS 77345 3120 A3
Evergreen Village Ct
4000 HOUS 77345 3119 D3
Evergreen Village Dr
- HOUS 77345 3120 A3
Everhart
8800 HarC 77040 3541 A6
Everhart Manor Ct
- FBnC 77494 4093 B7
Everhart Manor Ln
5400 FBnC 77494 4093 A3
Everhart Pointe Dr
12600 HarC 77377 3254 A4
Everhart Terrace Cir
4400 MSCY 77545 4622 B2
Everhart Terrace Dr
2600 MSCY 77545 4622 B2
Everhart Trace Dr
8600 FBnC 77469 4234 B5
Everhill Cir
6500 FBnC 77450 4094 B4
Everington Cir
22900 HarC 77450 3953 D2
Everington Dr
- HarC 77450 3953 D2
Everleaf Dr
8300 HarC 77379 3256 A4
Evermore Manor Ln
1300 HarC 77073 3403 C2

Everseen Ln
8400 HarC 77040 3541 C6
Eversham Wy
- HOUS 77339 3264 A1
N Evers Park Dr
10600 HNCV 77024 3960 B2
S Evers Park Dr
10600 HNCV 77024 3960 B2
Everton St
100 HOUS 77003 3964 A5
N Everton St
10 HOUS 77003 3964 A5
Everts Av
5200 ALVN 77511 4749 C2
Everwood Ln
10800 HNCV 77024 3960 A2
Evesborough Dr
10500 HOUS 77099 4238 D1
Evesham Dr
1600 HarC 77015 3829 B4
Eves Landing Ct
3300 FBnC 77478 4235 E6
Evia Main
10 GLSN 77554 5221 C2
Evian Path Ct
10 WDLD 77382 2674 D4
Evie Ln
7400 DRPK 77536 4249 B2
Evonne St
400 HOUS 77017 4106 C6
Ewell Dr
2500 LGCY 77573 4631 B5
Ewing Ct
3100 BzaC 77583 4500 E6
Ewing Dr
3200 BzaC 77583 4500 E7
Ewing Ln
16600 BzaC 77584 4502 D7
16600 BzaC 77584 4626 D1
16600 PRLD 77584 4502 D7
Ewing St
- HOUS 77005 4102 E2
1100 HOUS 77004 4102 E2
1700 HOUS 77004 4103 A2
Ewings Br
- FBnC 77469 4234 E7
- FBnC 77469 4365 A1
Exbury Ct
12500 HarC 77377 3254 B5
Exbury Wy
100 HOUS 77056 3961 B3
Excalibur Ct
700 FRDW 77546 4504 E7
700 FRDW 77546 4505 A7
19800 HarC 77094 3955 A4
Excalibur Dr
- HarC 77094 3955 A4
- HarC 77450 3955 A4
Excaliburs Ct
9600 PRLD 77584 4501 B2
Exchange Dr
12500 STAF 77477 4237 E7
12500 STAF 77477 4368 E1
Exchange St
300 HOUS 77020 3965 B1
2800 HOUS 77020 3826 A6
Executive Dr
12400 STAF 77477 4237 E7
12400 STAF 77477 4368 E1
12800 SGLD 77478 4368 E1
Exeter
- KMAH 77565 4510 A7
- KMAH 77565 4634 A1
Exeter Cir
2200 KATY 77493 3813 D5
Exeter Ln
6100 LGCY 77573 4630 B6
Exeter St
- HarC 77093 3545 C7
10600 HOUS 77093 3685 D3
10800 HarC 77093 3685 C2
Exmouth Ct
3600 HarC 77336 3121 D3
Expedition Tr
9800 MtgC 77385 2676 D4
Explorer Dr
13400 HOUS 77044 3409 A4
Explorer Cove
3200 SGLD 77479 4496 A2
Export Plaza Dr
15600 HOUS 77032 3405 D6
Express Ln
7000 HOUS 77078 3827 B2
Exter Tr
3300 PRLD 77584 4501 B2
Exton Ln
13400 HarC 77070 3399 B3
Exxon Dr
- BYTN 77520 3972 B4
- BYTN 77521 3972 B4
Exxon Rd
13000 MtgC 77302 2531 E3
13000 MtgC 77302 2532 A3
14000 MtgC 77302 2677 E2
14500 MtgC 77302 2678 A1
Ezekiel Rd
11500 HarC 77375 3109 E7
Ezekiel Smith St
- PRVW 77445 3100 C4
- PRVW 77484 3100 D4
Ezzard Charles Ln
6500 HOUS 77088 3683 C4
6500 HOUS 77091 3683 C4

F

F Cir
- HarC 77388 3111 D2
F St
1800 GNPK 77547 4106 C1
1800 HOUS 77547 4106 C1
2800 LPRT 77571 4251 E7
4100 HOUS 77072 4097 E4
4100 HOUS 77082 4097 E4
E F St
- LPRT 77571 4252 A3
600 LPRT 77571 4251 E3
W F St
100 LPRT 77571 4251 D3
FAA Rd
17100 GlsC 77511 4869 B6
Faber Rd
13800 HarC 77037 3545 A6
13800 HarC 77060 3545 A6
Fabiola Dr
9700 HOUS 77075 4377 B1
Fable Ct
14300 HarC 77429 3397 B1

Facet Creek Dr
2600 MSCY 77545 4622 B
Factory Outlet Dr
700 HMPD 77445 2953 D
700 WlrC 77445 2953 D
Faculty Ln
4300 HOUS 77004 4103 E
Fadeway Ln
13000 HOUS 77045 4241 A
Fading Rose Ln
- HarC 77433 3251 A
N Fair Ct
21100 HarC 77073 3259 B
Fair Ln
10 DKSN 77539 4754 C
Fair St
700 HOUS 77088 3684 A
Fair Acres Dr
1100 SGLD 77478 4237 B
Fair Acres St
7800 HOUS 77072 4097 E
Fairbanks
5400 HOUS 77026 3825 D
Fairbanks Dr
400 MtgC 77354 2673 E
Fairbanks St
1100 HOUS 77009 3824 D
2400 HOUS 77026 3824 E
2700 HOUS 77026 3825 A
Fairbanks North Houston Rd
5600 HOUS 77040 3681 D
6400 HarC 77040 3681 D
7500 HarC 77040 3541 C
7900 HarC 77064 3541 C
Fairbanks White Oak Rd
7400 HarC 77040 3681 D
7400 HarC 77040 3682 A
Fairbay Cir
2100 LGCY 77573 4509 B
Fairbay Dr
22300 FBnC 77450 3953 E
Fair Beauty Ct
1300 PRLD 77545 4499 E4
Fairbend St
8700 HOUS 77055 3821 A
Fairbloom Ln
8800 HarC 77040 3541 B6
Fairbluff Ln
14300 HarC 77014 3257 E6
Fairbourne Dr
6300 PASD 77505 4248 E6
E Fairbranch Cir
10 WDLD 77382 2674 B6
Fairbranch Ct
2000 FBnC 77494 3953 C
Fairbranch Dr
23300 FBnC 77494 3953 D
W Fairbranch Dr
10 WDLD 77382 2674 B6
Fair Breeze Dr
- LGCY 77565 4633 C
- LGCY 77573 4633 C
Fairbreeze Dr
- FBnC 77494 3951 C
Fair Breeze Ln
13000 PRLD 77584 4500 A
Fairbridge Ln
12700 HarC 77429 3398 B
Fairbrook Ln
8700 LPRT 77571 4249 D
25400 HarC 77373 3114 C
Fair Brook Wy
9600 PRLD 77584 4501 B
Fairbrook Park Ct
21300 HarC 77379 3111 A
Fairbrook Park Ln
6500 HarC 77379 3111 C
Fairbury Dr
- HarC 77089 4378 B
- HOUS 77089 4378 B
Fair Chase Ct
28300 FBnC 77494 3951 C
Fair Chase Dr
2600 FBnC 77494 3951 C
Fairchild St
- HOUS 77034 4379 A
6100 HOUS 77028 3826 B
Faircliff Ln
20300 HarC 77449 3676 E
Faircourt Dr
26800 MtgC 77339 3118 C
Faircreek Ln
5400 FBnC 77450 4094 A
Faircrest Ln
700 HOUS 77076 3685 B
Faircrest St
4800 PASD 77505 4248 A
Faircroft Dr
9200 HOUS 77033 4244 A
10800 HOUS 77048 4244 A
Fairdale Ct
2300 FBnC 77469 4365 D
Fairdale Ln
- HOUS 77042 4099 B
5300 HOUS 77056 4100 D
5600 HOUS 77057 4100 B
7600 HOUS 77063 4100 A
7900 HOUS 77063 4099 E
Fairdale St
500 FRDW 77546 4629 B
4800 PASD 77505 4248 A
Fair Dawn Ct
3000 FBnC 77450 3954 A
Fairdawn Ln
1600 LGCY 77573 4751 E
Fairday Ln
700 HOUS 77076 3685 B
Fair Elm Ct
15500 HarC 77082 4096 B
Fair Falls Dr
3200 HOUS 77345 3119 E
Fair Falls Lp
- HarC 77433 3251 A
Fair Falls Wy
- HarC 77433 3251 B
Fairfax
- PASD 77502 4247 B
Fairfax St
800 DRPK 77536 4109 B
10100 JTCY 77029 3966 B
Fairfax Green Dr
- HarC 77373 3115 D
E Fairfax Village Cir
22800 HarC 77373 3115 C
S Fairfax Village Cir
4800 HarC 77373 3115 D

STREET
Block City ZIP Map# Grid

W Fairfax Village Cir
22800 HarC 77373 3115 C7
Fairfax Village West Dr
22800 HarC 77373 3115 C7
Fairfay
1200 DRPK 77536 4109 B5
Fairfield Av
100 SRAC 77571 4383 A1
700 LPRT 77571 4382 D1
700 SRAC 77571 4382 D1
2800 TXCY 77590 4874 E5
Fairfield Ct N
1900 LGCY 77573 4631 C5
Fairfield Ct S
1900 LGCY 77573 4631 C5
Fairfield Dr
6600 HOUS 77023 4104 D2
Fairfield Grn
- HarC 77433 3251 A5
Fairfield Pl
- HarC 77433 3250 E6
- HarC 77433 3251 A5
Fairfield Falls Dr
- HarC 77433 3251 B5
Fairfield Falls Wy
15200 HarC 77433 3251 A7
Fairfield Green Cir
- HarC 77433 3251 D5
Fairfield Green Cir N
- HarC 77433 3251 D5
Fairfield Green Cir S
- HarC 77433 3251 D5
Fairfield Green Dr
- HarC 77433 3251 B5
Fairfield Lakes Ct
20300 HarC 77433 3251 E6
Fairfield Park Dr
- HarC 77433 3251 A5
Fairfield Park Wy
20300 HarC 77433 3251 B5
Fairfield Pl Dr
- HarC 77433 3251 A4
Fairfield Trace Dr
20100 HarC 77433 3251 B5
Fairfield Village Dr
15000 HarC 77433 3251 C7
Fair Forest Dr
5400 HarC 77088 3542 D6
Fairgate Dr
900 HarC 77094 3954 E3
1100 HarC 77094 3955 A3
Fairgate Ln
7700 HOUS 77075 4376 C3
Fair Glade Ct
13900 HarC 77429 3253 D5
Fair Glade Ln
10100 HarC 77375 2965 B6
14000 HarC 77429 3253 E6
Fairglen St
4200 PASD 77505 4248 A5
Fair Grange Ln
18100 HarC 77433 3537 C7
Fairgrange Key Ln
19300 HarC 77073 3403 D3
Fairgrange Pl Ln
- HarC 77449 3815 E1
Fairgreen Dr
2200 MSCY 77489 4370 B7
2300 MSCY 77489 4497 B1
Fairgreen Ln
4100 HOUS 77047 4374 C1
5100 HOUS 77048 4374 E1
5300 HOUS 77048 4244 A7
5300 HOUS 77048 4375 A1
Fairgrounds Dr
21600 PNIS 77445 3099 B3
Fairgrounds Rd
1300 RSBG 77471 4614 D2
Fairgrounds Rd N
3400 RSBG 77471 4614 D1
W Fairgrounds Rd
400 RSBG 77471 4614 D2
Fairgrounds Entrance Rd
- RSBG 77471 4614 D3
Fairgrove Ct
2700 BzaC 77584 4501 A5
Fair Grove Dr
5500 HOUS 77339 3119 B1
5500 MtgC 77365 3119 B1
Fairgrove Park Ct
8200 HarC 77095 3537 B5
Fairgrove Park Dr
17300 HarC 77095 3537 D6
E Fair Harbor Ln
300 HOUS 77079 3956 C1
300 HOUS 77079 3957 A1
W Fair Harbor Ln
300 HOUS 77079 3956 E1
Fairhaven St
- SSPL 77025 4101 C4
- WUNP 77005 4101 C4
4800 PASD 77505 4248 A5
Fairhill Av
4600 FBnC 77545 4623 B3
4700 FBnC 77583 4623 B3
Fairhill Cir
1700 TXCY 77591 4873 A4
Fairhill Dr
3900 HOUS 77063 4100 A2
Fairhill St
4300 PASD 77505 4248 A6
N Fairhollow Ln
11800 HOUS 77043 3819 C1
S Fairhollow Ln
11800 HOUS 77043 3819 C2
Fairhope Ln
10 MtgC 77355 2814 E3
Fairhope Pl
8200 HOUS 77025 4102 A6
Fairhope St
2800 HOUS 77025 4102 A6
3000 HOUS 77025 4101 E6
Fairhope Wy
10 WDLD 77382 2820 A1
Fairhope Grove Cir
3700 HarC 77449 3815 E2
Fairhope Meadow Ln
27600 MtgC 77339 3118 B5
Fairhope Oak Ct
18200 HarC 77084 3816 E4
Fairhope Oak St
3900 PASD 77503 4108 D7
18100 HarC 77084 3816 E4
Fairidge Ct
6000 HarC 77389 2966 E2
Fair Knoll Wy
14200 HOUS 77062 4379 E6
14300 HOUS 77062 4380 A6
Fairlake Ln
22700 HOUS 77336 3266 C3
Fairland Dr
10700 HOUS 77051 4243 A7
Fairlane Dr
10600 HNCV 77024 3960 B2
12600 BKVL 77581 4375 D6
Fairlane Sq
1100 HarC 77530 3829 D5
Fairlane Meadows Dr
9900 HarC 77070 3399 C3
Fairlane Oaks Dr
9900 HarC 77070 3399 C3
Fairlawn St
6500 HOUS 77087 4244 D1
Fairleaf Cir
22900 FBnC 77494 3953 D5
Fair Light Ct
10 WDLD 77382 2819 B1
N Fair Manor Cir
10 WDLD 77382 2673 C6
S Fair Manor Cir
10 WDLD 77382 2673 C7
Fairmeade
- HarC 77338 3260 E4
Fairmeade Ct
10 WDLD 77381 2821 A3
Fairmeade Bend Dr
10 WDLD 77381 2821 A3
Fairmeadow Dr
11800 HOUS 77071 4239 E5
Fair Meadow Ln
7200 FBnC 77494 4093 B4
Fairmont
- LPRT 77571 4251 B5
Fairmont Ct
10 CNRO 77304 2236 D7
3100 SGLD 77478 4369 A2
3100 STAF 77478 4369 A2
Fairmont Dr
300 HarC 77530 3831 B6
500 HarC 77562 3831 B5
Fairmont Pkwy
100 HOUS 77034 4247 B5
100 PASD 77504 4247 B5
100 SHUS 77587 4247 B5
4200 PASD 77504 4248 A5
4700 PASD 77505 4248 E5
6800 PASD 77505 4249 A5
E Fairmont Pkwy
200 LPRT 77571 4251 E4
W Fairmont Pkwy
100 LPRT 77571 4251 A4
1900 HarC 77507 4251 B4
1900 LPRT 77507 4251 B4
7900 LPRT 77571 4249 B5
7900 PASD 77505 4249 E5
7900 PASD 77507 4249 E5
8200 HarC 77507 4249 C5
8800 HarC 77507 4250 A5
8800 LPRT 77571 4250 A4
10300 HarC 77571 4250 C4
11000 LPRT 77507 4250 E4
Fairmont St
5000 HOUS 77005 4101 C2
5000 WUNP 77005 4101 C2
11300 HOUS 77035 4240 B7
Fairmont Greens Pkwy
2200 LPRT 77571 4251 D6
Fairmoor St
4800 PASD 77505 4248 A5
Fair Oak Dr
300 STAF 77477 4369 E4
500 FBnC 77477 4369 E4
Fair Oak St
2500 PRLD 77584 4501 A3
Fair Oaks
4100 BzaC 77511 4867 C7
Fair Oaks Dr
1100 FBnC 77469 4364 D6
1100 RHMD 77469 4364 D6
Fair Oaks Ln
1600 FBnC 77469 4365 D2
Fair Oaks Rd
800 HOUS 77023 4104 D1
Fairoaks St
1600 ELGO 77586 4382 B7
1700 SEBK 77586 4382 B7
Fair Park Ct
19800 HarC 77346 3265 A5
Fair Park Dr
13800 HarC 77014 3402 C3
Fairpark Ln
700 FBnC 77479 4366 D6
Fairpines Dr
20000 HarC 77379 3112 A4
Fairpines Ln
- HarC 77379 3112 A4
Fairplum Dr
10000 HOUS 77099 4238 A3
Fairpoint Dr
12000 HOUS 77099 4238 A2
12100 HOUS 77099 4237 E2
Fair Pointe Dr
2200 LGCY 77573 4509 C6
Fairport Ct
100 LGCY 77539 4752 E3
Fairport Ln
500 HOUS 77079 3956 E2
Fairport Harbor Ln
23600 FBnC 77469 4093 D6
Fair Rain Dr
- HarC 77339 3118 C5
Fairshire St
4800 PASD 77505 4248 A5
Fairstone Dr
10800 HarC 77064 3540 D3
Fair Tide Ct
1700 HarC 77532 3551 D2
Fairtide Ct
10 WDLD 77381 2821 B5
2400 LGCY 77573 4508 D6
Fairtide Dr
5700 HarC 77521 3833 D4
Fairvalley Dr
3600 HarC 77068 3257 A5
Fairvent St
4900 PASD 77505 4248 B5
N Fairview Cir
600 ALVN 77511 4867 A2
S Fairview Cir
700 ALVN 77511 4867 A2
Fairview Dr
1200 ALVN 77511 4867 A2
1500 FBnC 77479 4494 B5
10100 HarC 77532 3694 A6
10100 HarC 77562 3694 A6
10200 CHTW 77385 2823 A5
12200 HarC 77041 3679 E3
Fairview Rd
- ALVN 77511 4866 D2
- BzaC 77511 4747 E6
- BzaC 77511 4748 A6
- BzaC 77511 4866 D1
Fairview St
100 HOUS 77006 3962 C6
1800 HOUS 77019 3962 B6
3300 PASD 77504 4247 D3
7000 HarC 77041 3539 E7
7000 HarC 77041 3679 E1
Fairview Forest Dr
5800 HarC 77088 3542 D6
Fairview Valley Ct
18200 HarC 77084 3816 D4
Fairvine Park Dr
23100 FBnC 77494 3953 D6
Fairwater Dr
20700 HarC 77450 3954 C6
Fairwater Park Dr
2200 LGCY 77573 4509 A6
Fairway Bnd
20900 FBnC 77450 4094 B1
Fairway Cir
2200 PRLD 77581 4504 D2
Fairway Ct
7200 HOUS 77088 3682 D3
Fairway Dr
- BYTN 77520 3972 A3
10 CNRO 77304 2383 B4
100 ALVN 77511 4867 D3
100 HLCS 77511 4867 D3
300 FBnC 77469 4492 A2
300 RHMD 77469 4492 A2
400 MtgC 77357 2829 D2
400 RMFT 77357 2829 D3
500 LPRT 77571 4251 C6
2500 SGLD 77478 4368 E3
2600 SGLD 77478 4369 A3
2800 FRDW 77546 4749 E1
4800 BYTN 77521 3972 A2
6300 HOUS 77087 4104 D6
6500 GLSN 77551 5108 B7
6500 GLSN 77551 5222 B1
7100 HOUS 77087 4105 A6
11100 HarC 77064 3541 A1
Fairway St
4200 PASD 77505 4248 A6
Fairway Cove Ct
7800 HarC 77389 2966 A2
Fairway Estates Dr
10 HarC 77068 3257 C4
Fairway Farms Ln
800 HOUS 77339 3118 B6
Fairway Glen Ct
17100 FBnC 77478 4235 E7
Fairway Glen Ln
16900 FBnC 77478 4235 E7
Fairway Green Dr
2000 HOUS 77339 3119 E7
Fairway Island Dr
19500 HarC 77346 3265 C5
Fairway Lake Dr
- FBnC 77450 4094 C2
Fairway Manor Ln
5700 HarC 77373 3260 E1
6000 HarC 77373 3261 A1
Fairway Meadow Ln
20500 HarC 77379 3111 D4
Fairway Oaks Ct
500 MtgC 77302 2530 C6
6200 HarC 77379 3111 D7
26700 HarC 77336 3122 A3
Fairway Oaks Dr
- HarC 77336 3121 E4
700 MtgC 77302 2530 C6
17400 HarC 77379 3256 D1
17700 HarC 77379 3111 C7
27200 HarC 77336 3122 A4
E Fairway Oaks Dr
27400 HarC 77336 3122 B3
N Fairway Oaks Dr
27600 HarC 77336 3122 A2
Fairway Oaks Pl
10 WDLD 77380 2822 A6
Fairway Park Dr
2300 HOUS 77092 3821 E4
Fairway Plaza Dr
3800 PASD 77505 4248 C4
Fairway Pointe Dr
2400 LGCY 77573 4508 D6
Fairway Square Dr
14800 HarC 77084 3679 A2
Fairway Trace Ln
- HarC 77336 3122 A4
Fairway Trails Ln
20300 HarC 77379 3111 D5
Fairway Valley Ln
23300 FBnC 77494 4093 B4
Fairway View Ct
7800 FBnC 77479 4494 A5
Fairweather Ct
5200 FBnC 77450 4094 A3
Fairwick Ct
5300 FBnC 77450 4094 B3
Fairwind Dr
2400 HOUS 77062 4507 C1
2500 HOUS 77062 4380 C7
Fairwind Rd
2300 HOUS 77062 4507 C1
Fairwind Trail Ct
200 WDLD 77385 2676 C5
Fairwind Trail Dr
100 WDLD 77385 2676 C4
Fairwood Dr
6300 HOUS 77088 3682 C2
10900 LPRT 77571 4250 E3
Fairwood Knls
2000 FBnC 77545 4498 D6
Fairwood Rd
2500 LMQU 77568 4989 C4
2700 HTCK 77563 4989 C3
Fairwood St
2000 PRLD 77581 4504 C5
4200 PASD 77505 4248 A6
Fairwood Breeze
14000 HarC 77429 3253 E6
Fairwood Meadow Ct
18200 HarC 77084 3816 D4
Fairwood Park Ln
- HarC 77373 2968 C6
Fairwood Spings Ln
200 FBnC 77469 4365 A5
Fairwood Springs Ct
14000 HarC 77429 3253 E6
Fairwood Springs Dr
13900 HarC 77429 3253 E6
Fairworth Pl Ln
20500 HarC 77433 3676 E1
Fairwyck Ct
20800 HarC 77375 3110 A4
Faith Av
24500 WlrC 77445 2954 B1
Faith Dr
- HarC 77447 3104 D7
7400 DRPK 77536 4249 B2
Faith Ln
6100 HarC 77346 3264 E5
24300 WlrC 77445 2954 C2
Faith Pl
13500 HOUS 77085 4371 E1
Faith St
100 HarC 77562 3831 E4
2400 LMQU 77568 4989 E3
Faith Valley Dr
- HarC 77429 3397 D3
Falba Dr
13600 HarC 77070 3400 A2
13900 HarC 77070 3399 E2
Falco Dr
2200 DKSN 77539 4753 E2
2600 GlsC 77539 4753 E2
Falcon Dr
- FBnC 77494 3953 C5
Falcon Rd
10900 HarC 77064 3540 C1
11500 HarC 77064 3399 C7
11700 HarC 77070 3399 C7
Falcon St
- HOUS 77015 3967 A2
Falcon Wy
3500 CNRO 77304 2236 C7
Falcon Chase Ct
20100 HarC 77379 3112 A5
Falcon Creek Ct
21100 FBnC 77469 4234 B4
Falcon Crest Dr
18500 HarC 77346 3265 C7
Falcon Forest Ct
18000 HarC 77346 3408 B1
Falcon Forest Dr
4700 HarC 77346 3408 B1
Falcongate Ct
21700 HarC 77338 3260 A1
Falcon Grove Ln
24900 FBnC 77494 3953 C5
Falcon Heights Dr
13900 HarC 77429 3397 A2
Falcon Hill Ct
19800 HarC 77433 3677 A1
Falcon Hill Ln
- FBnC 77494 3953 B7
Falcon Hill St
- HarC 77338 3261 B3
Falcon Hollow Ln
24900 FBnC 77494 3953 B6
Falcon Knoll Ln
2200 FBnC 77494 3953 B6
Falcon Lair Ln
- FBnC 77494 3953 C5
Falcon Lake Cir
200 FRDW 77546 4629 E4
Falcon Lake Dr
200 FRDW 77546 4629 D5
Falcon Landing Blvd
- FBnC 77494 3952 E7
- FBnC 77494 4092 E1
1600 FBnC 77494 3953 B5
Falcon Meadow Dr
4200 HarC 77449 3816 B1
Falcon Park Dr
1400 FBnC 77494 3953 B4
Falcon Pass Dr
2400 HOUS 77058 4507 C1
2400 HOUS 77062 4507 C1
2600 HOUS 77062 4380 D7
Falcon Pass St
8900 LPRT 77571 4249 E4
Falcon Point Dr
24400 HarC 77494 3953 A2
Falcon Ridge Blvd
1600 FRDW 77546 4629 C4
Falcon Ridge Dr
15200 HarC 77396 3406 D7
Falcon Ridge St
2500 BzaC 77584 4501 C5
Falcons Cove Dr
16400 HarC 77095 3538 A3
Falcons Nest Landing Dr
17100 HarC 77447 3249 E4
Falcon Springs St
33200 HarC 77447 3249 C4
Falcons Talon Cove Wy
4700 HarC 77396 3407 A7
Falcon Talon Ct
24500 FBnC 77494 3953 A4
Falcon Trail Ct
3400 HarC 77373 3115 B4
Falcon Trail Dr
3200 HarC 77373 3115 A3
Falcon View Dr
24500 FBnC 77494 3953 A4
Falconwing Dr
- WDLD 77381 2820 D3
Falconwood Ln
22100 HarC 77373 3260 D1
Faldo Dr
7500 HarC 77389 2966 A3
Fales Ln
- LGCY 77573 4751 B1
Falher Dr
30100 MtgC 77386 2969 A2
Falk Av
200 LPRT 77571 4382 E1
Falk Ct
3000 LPRT 77571 4382 E1
Falkirk Ct
6100 LGCY 77573 4630 C7
Falkirk Ln
4000 HOUS 77025 4101 C6
Fall Grv
- HarC 77377 3254 D3
Fall Ln
31800 MtgC 77362 2963 C2
Fall St
3100 HOUS 77054 4103 A5
19200 MtgC 77357 2827 C4
Fall Bluff Ln
14500 HarC 77396 3547 C2
Fall Branch Dr
3700 FBnC 77450 4093 E1
Fall Branch Ln
- PRLD 77583 4500 B5
Fall Breeze Dr
11100 HarC 77064 3540 D2
Fall Briar Dr
15500 HOUS 77489 4371 D5
Fallbrook Ct
- BzaC 77584 4501 E7
Fallbrook Dr
100 HOUS 77037 3544 B1
100 HOUS 77038 3544 A1
100 HOUS 77060 3544 B1
200 HarC 77038 3544 A1
900 HarC 77038 3543 A3
3000 BzaC 77584 4501 B6
3100 HarC 77038 3542 E3
3500 MSCY 77459 4497 E5
4400 HOUS 77018 3683 B7
6400 HOUS 77086 3542 B3
7000 HarC 77086 3542 A2
7700 HarC 77086 3541 E2
7900 HarC 77064 3541 D2
8800 HarC 77064 3540 A2
11000 HarC 77065 3540 A2
12400 HarC 77065 3539 B1
Fallbrook Dr FM-525
- HOUS 77037 3544 B1
- HOUS 77038 3544 B1
- HOUS 77060 3544 B1
Fallbrook Ln
- PRLD 77583 4500 C5
Fall Chase Ct
14100 HarC 77044 3549 C2
Fall Cliff Ct
200 LGCY 77565 4508 E4
Fall Creek Bnd
- HarC 77396 3548 A2
7200 HarC 77396 3547 E1
Fall Creek Cross
14500 HarC 77396 3547 D1
Fall Creek Dr
700 HOUS 77336 3266 C3
Fall Creek Bend Ct
14600 HarC 77396 3547 C1
Fallcrest Dr
11000 HarC 77065 3539 C1
E Fallen Bough Dr
4900 HOUS 77041 3680 E7
N Fallen Bough Dr
10400 HOUS 77041 3680 E6
Fallen Branch Dr
2400 FBnC 77494 3953 D6
Fallengate Ct
22200 HarC 77373 3260 E2
Fallengate Dr
5800 HarC 77373 3260 E1
6000 HarC 77373 3261 A1
6300 HarC 77373 3116 A7
Fallen Leaf
7600 FBnC 77459 4621 A1
Fallen Leaf Wy
16700 HOUS 77058 4507 E3
Fallen Oak Ct
1500 PRLD 77581 4504 E4
Fallen Oak Ln
7800 TXCY 77591 4873 B7
S Fallen Oak Ln
300 TXCY 77591 4873 C7
Fallen Oak Rd
2500 HarC 77038 3543 A4
Fallen Oaks Dr
5000 HOUS 77091 3682 E6
5000 HOUS 77091 3683 A6
Fallen Palms Ct
3600 HOUS 77042 4098 C2
Fallen Pine Ln
2400 HarC 77088 3543 C7
Fallen Reed Ln
2100 RSBG 77471 4491 A6
Fallenstone Dr
10 WDLD 77381 2820 E3
Fallentimber Ct
20100 HarC 77379 3112 A5
Fallen Timbers Dr
16700 MtgC 77385 2676 E4
Fallen Woods Dr
10000 HOUS 77080 3820 A5
Fall Fair Ct
14400 HarC 77429 3395 C2
Fall Fair Ln
19400 HarC 77429 3395 E1
Fall Foliage Dr
20400 HarC 77338 3261 C3
Fall Foliage Tr
17200 MtgC 77385 2676 C6
Fall Forest Ct
1700 CNRO 77301 2384 E6
Fall Glen Dr
7800 HarC 77040 3541 E7
Fall Grove Ct
3700 HOUS 77059 4380 B4
Fall Hollow Dr
7900 HarC 77095 3539 C7
Falling Spr
700 HOUS 77373 3113 E3
Falling Brook Ct
3300 SGLD 77479 4368 C7
3300 SGLD 77479 4495 B2
Falling Brook Dr
3000 HOUS 77345 3119 D4
Falling Cherry Pl
7000 HarC 77049 3829 B1
Falling Creek Dr
14500 HarC 77014 3257 C7
14500 HarC 77068 3257 B6
Falling Elm Ln
14000 HarC 77015 3829 A5
Falling Forest Ct
2600 FBnC 77469 4365 A2
Falling Forest Ln
2000 LGCY 77565 4508 E5
Falling Leaf Ct
10 FRDW 77546 4629 A3
Falling Leaf Dr
400 FRDW 77546 4629 A3
1300 FRDW 77546 4628 E3
Falling Leaf Ln
10 HDWV 77024 3959 E1
1300 TYLV 77586 4508 E1
3200 MtgC 77380 2967 B1
Falling Limb Ct
15500 HarC 77049 3829 B1
Falling Mills Ln
- FBnC 77494 4092 B2
Falling Oak Ct
4900 PASD 77505 4248 D7
Falling Oak Wy
18400 HarC 77379 3256 E2
18400 HarC 77379 3257 B1
Falling Oaks
7200 HarC 77389 2966 B5
Falling Oaks Rd
2100 HarC 77038 3543 B3
Falling Oaks St
7300 HarC 77389 2966 B5
Falling Pine Dr
300 CNRO 77304 2383 A6
Falling Rapids Ct
10400 HarC 77070 3399 B4
Falling River Dr
10000 HarC 77095 3537 E2
Falling Rock Ln
3700 FBnC 77494 4092 B1
Falling Springs Dr
- HOUS 77396 3406 B5
Falling Springs Ln
800 LGCY 77573 4633 B2
Falling Star Ct
10 WDLD 77381 2821 B4
Falling Star Rd
10 WDLD 77381 2821 B4
Falling Stream Dr
19700 HarC 77375 3109 E6
Falling Timber Ln
- FBnC 77469 4094 D2
- MtgC 77385 2676 E3
Falling Timbers
- BKHV 77024 3959 B3
Falling Trace Ln
4100 FBnC 77469 4615 D5
Falling Tree Ct
13800 HarC 77015 3828 E5
14300 HarC 77015 3829 A5
Falling Water Ct
8200 SGLD 77478 4368 A3
Fallingwater Estates Ln
24900 FBnC 77494 4093 B1
Falling Waters Dr
6600 HarC 77379 3256 D2
Fall Lake Dr
- HarC 77038 3402 C7
- HOUS 77038 3402 C7
- HOUS 77067 3402 C7
Fall Meadow Dr
2000 MSCY 77459 4497 B1
Fall Meadow Ln
11700 HOUS 77039 3546 A6
11900 HarC 77039 3546 A6
Fallmist Ct
23200 FBnC 77494 3953 D5
Fallmont Cir
10100 HarC 77086 3542 D3
Fallmont Ct
10100 HarC 77086 3542 D3
Fallmont Dr
5900 HarC 77086 3542 D3
Falloon Ln
500 HOUS 77013 3966 C1
Fall Orchard Ct
2500 HOUS 77345 3120 C4
Fallow Ln
400 FRDW 77546 4505 B6
600 ALVN 77511 4867 B4
1700 HarC 77530 3829 D4
10500 MtgC 77303 2239 B4
Fall Point Dr
11100 HarC 77065 3539 B1
Fall Ridge Cir
1700 FBnC 77494 3953 A5
Fall River Cir
17900 HarC 77090 3258 A2
Fall River Ct
300 HOUS 77024 3960 C2
7900 FBnC 77479 4494 A5
Fall River Rd
400 HOUS 77024 3960 C2
Fall River Pass Ct
17600 HarC 77346 3408 B2
Fall River Pass Ln
12000 HarC 77346 3408 B2
Falls Cir
5000 MSCY 77459 4496 B4
S Falls Dr
- HarC 77089 4505 A2
Falls St
3900 HOUS 77026 3825 B6
S Falls Ter
10900 HarC 77095 3537 E1
Fallsbridge Dr
10600 HarC 77065 3539 B2
Fallsbrook Ct
- FBnC 77479 4496 D5
8900 MtgC 77302 2530 C5
Fallsbury Ct
10 WDLD 77382 2673 E4
Fallsbury Wy
10 WDLD 77382 2673 E4
Falls Canyon Ct
4900 FBnC 77494 4092 E2
Falls Church Dr
2400 HarC 77067 3402 A4
Falls Coppice Ln
12100 HarC 77089 4504 E1
12100 HarC 77089 4505 A2
Fallscreek Ct
2900 BzaC 77584 4501 B5
Fall Shadows Ct
3900 PASD 77059 4380 D4
Fallshire Dr
10 WDLD 77381 2821 A4
Fall Springs Ln
7200 HarC 77396 3547 C1
Fallstone Rd
10500 HOUS 77099 4238 C4
Fallsview Dr
- PRLD 77545 4499 E4
Fallsview Ln
13100 HOUS 77077 3957 B5
Fallun Ct
3700 MtgC 77386 2970 B5
Fall Valley Dr
1600 HOUS 77077 3958 B5
Fall Wind Ct
23200 FBnC 77494 3953 D6
Fall Wood Dr
1400 FBnC 77479 4493 E5
Fallwood Dr
11500 HarC 77065 3398 B7
Falmouth Av
15100 HarC 77084 3678 E2
Falmouth Dr
15700 HOUS 77059 4380 C6
Falvel Dr
22500 HarC 77389 2967 D7
22500 HarC 77389 3112 D1
Falvel Ln
20900 HarC 77388 3112 D4
Falvel Rd
21300 HarC 77388 3112 D3
22000 HarC 77389 3112 D1
Falvel Cove Dr
3900 HarC 77388 3112 C3
Falvel Lake Dr
21500 HarC 77388 3112 D3
Falvel Meadows Ln
3900 HarC 77388 3112 D2
Falvel Misty Dr
21500 HarC 77388 3112 D3
Falvel Shadow Cr
3900 HarC 77388 3112 C2
Falvel Sunrise Ct
21500 HarC 77388 3112 D2
Falvel Sunset Ct
21600 HarC 77388 3112 D2
Falvey Av
4700 HOUS 77017 4106 C5
Falworth Dr
300 HarC 77060 3403 B5
Family Cir
13400 HOUS 77085 4371 D1
Fana Ct
14400 HarC 77032 3546 D2
Fanestiel St
2300 BYTN 77520 3973 C4
Fannette St
8600 HOUS 77029 3965 D3
Fannin Dr
4800 GLSN 77551 5108 D5
Fannin Rd
- HOUS 77045 4242 C4
Fannin St
10 HOUS 77002 3963 B6
100 RHMD 77469 4492 A1
100 TMBL 77375 2964 B7
400 RHMD 77469 4491 E1
800 HOUS 77010 3963 C4
2500 HOUS 77004 3963 B6
2700 LMQU 77568 4989 D2
4400 HOUS 77004 4103 A1
4700 HOUS 77004 4102 E1
5700 HOUS 77030 4102 C5
7900 HOUS 77054 4102 C7
8400 HOUS 77054 4242 C2
9200 HOUS 77045 4242 C2
Fantail
- HarC 77040 3681 B3
Fantail Ct
1800 HarC 77532 3551 D3
Fan Tail Dr
16100 HarC 77532 3551 D3
Fantail Dr
28200 FBnC 77494 3951 D5
Fantail St
10 MtgC 77355 2960 C3
Fantasia Dr
23300 HarC 77336 3267 A4
Fantasy Dr
12600 HarC 77039 3546 C5
Fantasy Woods Dr
1700 HarC 77094 3955 A4
Fanwick Ct
9300 HarC 77375 3110 C3
Fanwick Dr
22600 HarC 77375 3110 C3
Fanwood Dr
6600 HarC 77389 2966 C5
Faraday Ct
2700 MtgC 77381 2821 D2
Faraday Dr
13100 HOUS 77047 4373 C3
Faraway Ln
25100 HarC 77336 3121 D7
25100 HarC 77336 3266 D1
Farb Dr
5100 HOUS 77016 3686 C4
Farber St
3700 SSPL 77005 4101 D4
Fargo Dr
5600 DKSN 77539 4633 D7
Fargo St
100 HOUS 77006 3962 E5
Fargon Dr
7100 HarC 77379 3111 B2
Fargo Woods Cir
14500 HarC 77015 3829 C4
Fargo Woods Dr
100 HarC 77015 3829 B5
Farhills Ct
1300 HarC 77090 3402 C1
Faring Rd
16800 HarC 77049 3690 E4
17100 HarC 77049 3691 A4
Farington Wy
10 WDLD 77382 2819 E1
Farish Cir
10 HOUS 77024 3961 A2
Fariss St
200 HOUS 77025 4241 D4
200 HOUS 77054 4241 D4
Farlan Ln
3700 HarC 77014 3401 D2
Farley Ct
3700 FBnC 77459 4621 B5
Farley Dr
5400 HarC 77032 3546 D1
Farley Rd
5500 HOUS 77034 4248 B7
5500 HOUS 77034 4379 B2
5500 HOUS 77505 4248 B7
5500 PASD 77505 4248 B7
Farley Pass Dr
16900 HarC 77095 3538 A4
Farlington Cir
12700 HOUS 77077 3957 C4
Farm & Ranch
- HOUS 77084 3817 D3
Farmcreek Dr
27200 HarC 77336 3121 E3
Farmer Rd
2200 FBnC 77469 4365 B1
4900 FBnC 77469 4234 C4
Farmer St
3100 HOUS 77020 3964 A2
Farmers Rd
4900 GlsC 77511 4869 C7
Farmers Tr
11400 MtgC 77306 2532 D2
Farmers Creek Ct
3700 FBnC 77469 4234 C6
Farmers Creek Dr
1900 FBnC 77469 4234 C6
Farmers Field St
3100 PRLD 77581 4503 E3
Farmersville
5400 ARLA 77583 4623 A4

STREET
Block City ZIP Map# Grid

Farmersville Fk
10400 FBnC 77459 4622 A5
Farm Hill Rd
23700 HarC 77373 3114 E4
Farmingham Dr
10500 HOUS 77099 4237 E3
Farmingham Rd
7500 HarC 77346 3265 B6
E Farmington Ln
3200 SGLD 77479 4495 D2
S Farmington Ln
3200 SGLD 77479 4495 D1
W Farmington Ln
3200 SGLD 77479 4495 D1
Farmington St
3000 HOUS 77080 3821 A2
Farnaby Ct
6800 HarC 77379 3256 D4
Farndale Dr
15100 HOUS 77062 4506 E1
Farnell Ct
16400 HarC 77379 3256 B5
Farnham Cir
3400 BzaC 77584 4501 C4
Farnham St
3700 HOUS 77098 4102 B1
Farnham Park Dr
10 PNPV 77024 3959 E6
10 PNPV 77024 3960 A5
Farnington Dr
4600 HarC 77084 3677 E7
Farnsfield Dr
18200 HarC 77084 3677 E7
Farnsworth St
- HOUS 77022 3685 B7
7800 HOUS 77022 3824 B1
Farnworth Cir
200 LGCY 77573 4630 C6
Farnworth Ln
200 LGCY 77573 4630 C7
Far Pines Dr
700 HarC 77373 3113 E1
Far Point Ct
9500 HarC 77095 3538 E4
9500 HarC 77095 3539 A4
Far Point Manor Ct
13100 HarC 77429 3396 E4
Farqueson St
8500 HOUS 77029 3826 C6
Farr Av
- WALR 77484 3101 E4
Farr St
1100 WALR 77484 3101 E6
15900 HOUS 77032 3404 D6
Farragut St
9700 HOUS 77078 3687 B5
Farrah Ln
900 FBnC 77477 4369 C4
Farrawood Dr
14500 HarC 77429 3397 E1
Farrel Hill St
3100 FBnC 77545 4498 C7
Farrell
10 STAF 77477 4238 B6
Farrell Cir
32000 SGCH 77355 2961 B3
Farrell Dr
1000 BzaC 77511 4748 E2
9500 HarC 77070 3399 C6
Farrell Rd
- HarC 77338 3260 D4
- HOUS 77338 3260 D4
100 FBnC 77477 4370 A6
100 MSCY 77477 4370 A6
100 MtgC 77378 2238 C1
1400 HarC 77073 3403 E1
2100 HarC 77073 3260 A7
2100 HOUS 77032 3260 A7
Farrell St
10 HOUS 77022 3684 E7
10 HOUS 77022 3685 A7
Farrelley Ln
2700 HarC 77047 4374 A4
2700 HOUS 77047 4374 A4
Farrell Ridge Dr
10 SGLD 77479 4495 D2
Farriers Bend Dr
2300 HarC 77546 4506 B6
Farrington Blvd
- HarC 77507 4250 C4
- HarC 77571 4250 C4
3200 LPRT 77571 4250 C4
Farrington Dr
100 LPRT 77571 4250 C2
Farrington Park Dr
- HOUS 77093 3686 B4
N Farrisburg Ct
2300 SGLD 77478 4237 C4
S Farrisburg Ct
2200 SGLD 77478 4237 D4
Farris Green Rd
22100 MtgC 77365 2973 C5
Farriswood Ct
18300 HarC 77433 3677 D1
Farther Pt
10 HOUS 77024 3960 D2
10 HOUS 77057 3960 D2
Farwell Dr
5700 HOUS 77035 4240 C6
Farwood St
1200 HOUS 77009 3824 E6
E Farwood Ter
20700 HarC 77377 3251 B2
20700 HarC 77433 3251 B2
W Farwood Ter
20900 HarC 77433 3251 A3
Fasco St
10000 HOUS 77051 4243 B5
Fashion St
800 HOUS 77023 3964 B6
Fashion Hill Dr
1400 HOUS 77088 3683 E1
1400 HOUS 77088 3684 A1
Fastgreen Cir
9600 HarC 77089 4504 C1
Fastwater Creek Ct
2400 PRLD 77584 4500 D5
Fastwater Creek Dr
2400 PRLD 77584 4500 D5
Fatheree Dr
21900 MtgC 77365 2972 D4
Father John Dr
- HTCK 77563 4988 A2
Fathom Dr
100 BzaC 77541 5547 B7
Fathom Ln
15700 HOUS 77062 4507 A2

Fatima Ln
- HOUS 77018 3684 B7
5400 HOUS 77091 3684 C6
Fatima Lake Dr
9700 HOUS 77099 4238 A2
Fatta Dr
3700 DKSN 77539 4753 E3
Faucette St
5600 HOUS 77023 4104 C3
Faulkey Gully
14100 HarC 77070 3399 A1
Faulkey Gully Cir
11400 HarC 77070 3399 B1
Faulkey Gully Ct
11400 HarC 77070 3399 B1
Faulkner Rd
10000 MtgC 77372 2536 A1
Faulkner St
1800 WALR 77484 3102 A5
3800 HOUS 77021 4103 C7
Faulkner Ridge Dr
6200 FBnC 77450 4094 B4
Faun
- MtgC 77384 2674 D1
Fauna St
6800 HOUS 77061 4244 E5
7500 HOUS 77061 4245 B4
Fauna Woods Ct
14400 HarC 77044 3689 E4
Fauning Leaf Ln
- FBnC 77469 4365 B2
Fauss Rd
2900 HarC 77067 3402 A5
Faust Ln
400 HOUS 77024 3958 D3
Favian Ct
7100 HarC 77083 4097 A5
Favor Bend Ct
17500 HarC 77396 3407 E2
Favor Bend Dr
17500 HarC 77396 3407 E2
Fawcett Dr
13500 HarC 77069 3400 B2
Fawley Ln
- HarC 77049 3828 E2
Fawn Cir
24400 MtgC 77365 2974 A7
Fawn Ct
700 HOUS 77015 3828 B7
1200 LGCY 77573 4630 E6
Fawn Dr
600 HOUS 77015 3828 B7
700 HOUS 77015 3967 B1
19500 MtgC 77355 2668 E7
21500 HOUS 77532 3266 B7
Fawn Ln
25100 MtgC 77365 3117 D1
31600 MtgC 77362 2963 D3
36800 MtgC 77354 2816 A2
Fawn Tr
8700 MtgC 77385 2676 C5
8700 WDLD 77385 2676 C5
13400 MtgC 77302 2531 A5
Fawnbrake Dr
13900 SGLD 77478 4237 A6
Fawnbrook Ct
20500 HarC 77450 3954 D5
Fawnbrook Hollow Ln
4500 HOUS 77345 3119 D3
Fawn Canyon Ct
20400 HarC 77433 3251 C7
Fawnchase Ct
10 WDLD 77381 2821 A5
Fawncliff Dr
6700 HarC 77069 3400 B3
Fawn Creek Dr
3800 HOUS 77339 3119 A4
Fawncrest Dr
12600 HarC 77038 3543 C4
Fawndale Ln
8000 HOUS 77040 3681 D5
Fawndale Wy
3100 BYTN 77521 3972 B1
Fawn Forest Dr
24700 HarC 77373 3114 D3
Fawn Glen Dr
4300 HOUS 77345 3119 D5
Fawngrove Dr
11300 HOUS 77048 4244 A7
Fawn Gully Ct
- HarC 77084 3817 A2
Fawn Haven Dr
- HarC 77450 3955 A5
Fawn Hollow Ct
20000 HarC 77346 3265 C4
Fawnhope Dr
1600 HOUS 77008 3822 C6
Fawnlake Cir
2400 KATY 77493 3813 B4
Fawnlake Ct
2400 KATY 77493 3813 B5
Fawnlake Dr
300 HOUS 77079 3958 C3
N Fawnlake Dr
5900 KATY 77493 3813 A5
S Fawnlake Dr
6000 KATY 77493 3813 B5
Fawn Lily Dr
13500 HarC 77429 3397 D3
Fawnlily St
10900 MtgC 77380 2821 C7
10900 WDLD 77380 2821 C7
Fawn Meadow Dr
1600 HarC 77396 3407 C5
Fawn Meadow Ln
6800 FBnC 77469 4232 E3
Fawn Mist Ct
10500 MtgC 77303 2239 B4
Fawnmist Dr
10500 MtgC 77303 2239 B3
Fawnmist Pl
10 WDLD 77381 2820 E1
Fawnmist Cove
9600 HarC 77375 3255 B2
Fawn Nest Tr
3900 SGLD 77479 4495 B1
Fawn Park Ct
9500 HarC 77396 3407 A7
Fawnpoint Ct
25300 HarC 77389 2966 A1
Fawn Ridge Dr
16300 MtgC 77302 2679 B4
Fawnridge Dr
7300 HOUS 77028 3687 A6
Fawn River Cir
7100 HarC 77379 3256 C2
N Fawn River Cir
7200 HarC 77379 3256 B2

W Fawn River Cir
17600 HarC 77379 3256 C2
Fawn River Dr
6800 HarC 77379 3256 C1
Fawn Run Ln
18500 HarC 77084 3816 C3
Fawns Crossing Dr
19600 HarC 77375 3109 D6
Fawnshadow Ct
9000 HarC 77064 3540 B7
Fawn Springs Ct
11300 HarC 77433 3396 A7
Fawn Terrace Ct
8200 HOUS 77071 4239 D6
Fawn Terrace Dr
7600 HOUS 77071 4239 E6
Fawn Trace Dr
- HOUS 77339 3263 D2
Fawn Trail Ln
5500 HarC 77346 3264 C4
Fawn Valley Dr
1200 LGCY 77573 4632 A4
Fawnview Dr
10500 HarC 77070 3399 A2
11800 HarC 77070 3398 D2
Fawn Villa Dr
15400 HarC 77068 3257 A6
Fawn Vista
16000 HarC 77068 3257 B4
Fawnway Dr
11400 HOUS 77048 4243 E7
11400 HOUS 77048 4244 A7
12100 HOUS 77048 4374 E1
Fawn Wind Ct
8400 HarC 77040 3541 A7
Fawnwood Dr
- TXCY 77591 4872 C2
500 MSCY 77489 4370 E4
6200 HarC 77389 2966 D5
Fawnwood Ln
2300 MtgC 77386 2969 B3
25900 MtgC 77355 2962 B4
Fawn Wy Ct
1900 FBnC 77469 4365 D2
Fay Ct
2300 DRPK 77536 4109 C6
Fay Dr
1700 CNRO 77301 2384 D5
Fay Rd
1100 KMAH 77565 4509 E6
Fay St
2800 HOUS 77023 4104 C4
Faye St
14000 GlsC 77517 4752 B7
26300 MtgC 77372 2683 C2
26300 SPLD 77372 2683 C2
Faye Wy
20000 HarC 77377 3106 B5
Faye Oaks Ct
19700 HarC 77346 3264 C5
Faye Oaks Dr
19900 HarC 77346 3264 C4
Fayette St
5300 HOUS 77056 3960 E7
E Fayle St
10 BYTN 77520 3973 A6
2300 HarC 77521 3832 C4
W Fayle St
- BYTN 77520 3973 A6
Fayridge Dr
- HOUS 77048 4375 D5
Faywood Dr
15500 HarC 77060 3544 E2
15800 HOUS 77060 3544 E2
S Fazio Wy
- HarC 77375 2819 E5
- HarC 77389 2819 E5
10 HarC 77389 2820 B5
F Bar Dr
12500 STFE 77510 4871 A7
FCR 869
- BzaC 77581 4628 B4
- PRLD 77511 4628 B4
Feagan St
6000 HOUS 77007 3962 A3
Feamster Dr
600 HOUS 77022 3684 D7
Fearless Dr
21600 HarC 77447 3105 E1
21600 HarC 77447 3106 A1
Feather Branch Ct
10 WDLD 77381 2821 B3
Featherbrook Ct
800 FBnC 77479 4366 D7
Feather Craft Ln
- HOUS 77062 4507 B4
16800 HarC 77058 4507 B4
16800 HOUS 77058 4507 B4
16900 HarC 77598 4507 B4
Feather Creek Dr
6600 HarC 77086 3542 B1
Feather Crest Dr
9700 HarC 77396 3548 B1
Feather Fall Ln
17000 HarC 77095 3537 E2
Featherfall Pl
10 WDLD 77381 2821 A1
Featherfield Ln
17900 FBnC 77469 4095 C6
Feather Glen Ct
2800 FBnC 77494 3953 A6
Feather Green Tr
2500 FBnC 77545 4498 C6
Feathering Ct
14800 HarC 77396 3548 B1
Feather Lakes Wy
- HOUS 77345 3119 D5
4000 HOUS 77339 3119 C5
Feather Lance Dr
19000 HarC 77433 3537 B7
Feather Mill Ln
- FBnC 77469 4094 D7
Feather Ridge Dr
1900 MSCY 77489 4370 C5
Feather Run Ln
6700 HarC 77041 3679 E3
Feathers Landing Dr
17700 HarC 77377 3254 B3
Feather Springs Dr
7800 HarC 77095 3537 E7
Featherstar Ln
11300 HarC 77067 3402 A6
Featherstone St
1400 HOUS 77020 3964 C3
Feathertail Ln
16300 HarC 77447 3248 E6
Featherton Ct
2300 SGLD 77478 4237 C4

Featherwood Dr
12600 HOUS 77034 4378 A2
N Featherwood Dr
12500 HOUS 77034 4378 A2
February St
12800 BKVL 77581 4376 A7
Federal Ln
3900 FBnC 77459 4622 A5
Federal Rd
700 HOUS 77015 3966 E1
1100 HOUS 77015 3967 A5
1600 GNPK 77015 3967 A4
3100 HOUS 77015 4107 A1
3100 PASD 77502 4247 C3
3100 PASD 77504 4247 C4
Federal Rd FM-526
700 HOUS 77015 3966 E1
1100 HOUS 77015 3967 A5
Feilds Crossing Ln
3900 FBnC 77478 4367 A3
Feland St
8800 HOUS 77028 3687 D7
Feld Dr
14800 HarC 77053 4372 E7
Feldman Falls
10300 FBnC 77459 4622 A5
Feldmon St
3000 HOUS 77045 4242 B4
Feldspar St
6300 HOUS 77092 3821 C1
Felgate Creek Ct
6600 HarC 77084 3678 E3
Felgate Creek Dr
15000 HarC 77084 3678 E3
Felice Dr
5500 HOUS 77081 4100 C6
Felicia
5800 HOUS 77091 3683 C5
Felicia Dr
3900 SGLD 77479 4495 E2
3900 SGLD 77479 4496 A2
Feliciana Ln
7600 HarC 77379 3256 C4
Felicia Oaks Tr
6400 HarC 77064 3541 C2
Felicity Aime Ln
13700 HarC 77429 3397 A3
Felicity Trace Pl
10 WDLD 77382 2674 E4
Felix
500 HOUS 77011 3964 B6
2000 HOUS 77003 3963 E3
Feliza Ln
7800 FBnC 77083 4095 D7
Fellows
2200 HarC 77047 4373 E5
2200 HarC 77047 4374 A5
2200 HOUS 77047 4373 E5
2200 HOUS 77047 4374 A5
Fellows Rd
- HOUS 77047 4374 D6
- HOUS 77048 4374 D6
10 HarC 77047 4373 A5
10 HarC 77053 4373 A5
10 HOUS 77047 4373 A5
3000 HarC 77047 4374 C5
3000 PRLD 77047 4374 C5
Fellowship Dr
10 MtgC 77384 2675 D6
10 WDLD 77384 2675 D6
Fellowship Ln
5500 HarC 77379 3112 A7
5500 HarC 77379 3257 A1
Fellowship Pine Cir
5500 HarC 77379 3257 A1
Felscher Ln
4500 HarC 77532 3268 D7
Felt Cir
300 HOUS 77011 3964 C5
Felton St
- BYTN 77520 3972 D7
N Felton St
700 BYTN 77520 3972 E6
Felton Mills Ct
25400 FBnC 77469 4092 C7
Felton Springs Dr
- MtgC 77386 2969 C2
Fence Post Rd
400 FRDW 77546 4629 A3
Fenchurch Dr
9300 HarC 77379 3256 A6
9600 HarC 77379 3255 E6
Fenders Wy
- HarC 77532 3551 E4
Fenham Ln
4900 HarC 77338 3260 D2
Fenian Ct
14500 FBnC 77478 4236 E3
Fenimore Ct
12700 SGLD 77478 4237 D4
Fenland Field Ln
12900 HOUS 77047 4373 B2
Fenley Rd
13600 MtgC 77302 2531 A6
Fenn Rd
100 ARLA 77583 4623 A5
100 FBnC 77583 4622 C5
100 FBnC 77583 4623 A5
Fenn St
300 HOUS 77018 3823 C1
Fennel Dr
8300 HarC 77521 3833 D2
Fennel Ln
300 HarC 77532 3552 C3
Fennell St
200 HOUS 77012 4105 C3
Fennemore St
12000 HarC 77086 3542 C5
Fennigan Ct
2200 LGCY 77573 4631 B6
Fennigan Ln
- LGCY 77573 4631 C6
Fenny Bridge Ln
17000 HarC 77379 3255 D3
Fenske Rd
18100 HarC 77429 3252 B4
18100 HarC 77433 3252 A5
Fenton Ln
14200 SGLD 77478 4236 E6
Fenton Pl
20300 HarC 77073 3403 C1
Fenton Hollow Dr
21000 HarC 77375 3110 A3
Fenton Rock Ln
2100 FBnC 77494 3952 B6
Fenwick
- HarC 77040 3681 A1

Fenwick Dr
- MtgC 77447 2960 B5
Fenwick Ln
15200 MtgC 77384 2674 E2
Fenwick St
1400 HOUS 77009 3824 A6
Fenwick Wy Ct
5300 SGLD 77479 4495 B4
Fenwood Dr
2200 PASD 77502 4247 A1
Fenwood Rd
2600 HOUS 77005 4102 A3
2600 HOUS 77030 4102 A3
2600 WUNP 77005 4102 A3
Fenwood St
2100 LGCY 77565 4509 A4
Ferdinand St
8600 HOUS 77051 4243 C3
Ferguson Rd
25100 MtgC 77372 2536 E5
25100 MtgC 77372 2537 A5
Ferguson St
10 BYTN 77520 3973 A6
500 HMBL 77338 3262 E7
1100 CNRO 77301 2383 E3
Ferguson Wy
900 HOUS 77088 3683 E2
900 HOUS 77088 3684 A2
8700 HOUS 77063 4099 D2
Fergus Park Ct
1800 HOUS 77047 4373 D2
Fern Cir
8500 HarC 77562 3832 D2
Fern Ct
6300 PRLD 77584 4502 D4
Fern Dr
14200 HOUS 77079 3957 D2
Fern Ln
100 HarC 77562 3831 E1
4700 FBnC 77545 4623 C3
13900 MtgC 77306 2533 D7
Fern St
900 KATY 77493 3813 A7
900 KATY 77493 3952 A1
3000 PASD 77503 4108 A4
3000 PASD 77506 4108 A4
4800 BLAR 77401 4101 A5
14200 HOUS 77079 3957 E3
16100 HarC 77429 3108 B7
Fernando Dr
21300 HOUS 77450 3954 B2
Fernbank Dr
7900 HarC 77049 3689 D7
Fern Basin Dr
15600 HarC 77084 3678 E5
Fern Bend Ln
2300 FBnC 77494 3952 B6
Fernbluff Ct
100 HarC 77379 3256 B2
Fernbluff Dr
18000 HarC 77379 3256 A1
Fernbrook Dr
16400 MtgC 77372 2682 A5
Fernbrook Ln
7500 HarC 77070 3399 E1
Fernbush Dr
20600 HarC 77073 3259 C7
Ferncastle Ln
10 FBnC 77479 4367 B7
Fernchase Cir
17300 HarC 77095 3678 C3
Fernchase Ct
17200 HarC 77095 3678 A2
Ferncliff Ln
15900 HarC 77095 3538 C6
Fern Cove Dr
4900 BYTN 77521 3972 C1
Fern Creek Ct
6500 PASD 77503 4248 E1
Fern Creek Dr
6500 PASD 77503 4248 E2
Fern Creek Ln
- HOUS 77017 4106 D7
- HOUS 77017 4246 D1
2700 PRLD 77581 4504 D4
Fern Creek Tr
2100 HOUS 77345 3120 B3
12500 HarC 77346 3264 D7
12500 HarC 77346 3408 D1
Ferncrest Ct
12200 HarC 77070 3399 B6
Ferncroft Ct
10 WDLD 77382 2673 C5
Ferndale
8600 HOUS 77017 4245 E3
8600 HOUS 77017 4246 A2
Ferndale Ct
700 FRDW 77546 4629 A1
1100 FBnC 77479 4493 C5
Ferndale Dr
1200 ELGO 77586 4509 B1
3000 LGCY 77573 4633 A2
Ferndale Ln
900 FBnC 77469 4365 E4
Ferndale St
100 BLAR 77401 4101 A6
2600 HOUS 77019 3962 A7
2600 HOUS 77098 3962 A7
Ferndale Lake Ct
1700 FBnC 77469 4234 D6
N Ferndale Pl Dr
9000 HarC 77064 3540 D1
S Ferndale Pl Dr
9000 HarC 77064 3540 E1
W Ferndale Pl Dr
11100 HarC 77064 3540 D1
Ferndale View Dr
9000 HarC 77064 3540 D1
Ferndale Wy Dr
11000 HarC 77064 3540 E1
Ferndell St
11800 HarC 77016 3687 E1
Ferne Dr
18300 MtgC 77365 2826 A7
Ferne Leaf Dr
21000 MtgC 77365 2826 B7
21000 MtgC 77365 2972 B1
Ferness Dr
14900 HarC 77530 3829 C6
Ferness Ln
15000 HarC 77530 3829 D6
Ferney Ln
18800 MtgC 77365 2972 B6
Fern Forest Dr
11900 HarC 77044 3688 E5
12400 HarC 77044 3689 A5
Ferngate Dr
22400 HarC 77373 3115 C7

Fernglade Dr
500 FBnC 77469 4365 C3
3500 HarC 77068 3257 B6
4000 HarC 77069 3257 A7
Fernglen Dr
10 WDLD 77380 2822 A6
24700 FBnC 77494 3952 D3
Fern Green Ct
5000 HOUS 77345 3120 A1
Fern Grove Ln
2300 HOUS 77059 4379 E5
Fernhaven Dr
19500 HarC 77449 3816 A3
Fern Hill Dr
2600 HarC 77373 3114 E4
2800 HarC 77373 3115 A4
Fernhill Dr
13500 SGLD 77478 4237 B6
Fern Hollow Ct
5900 HarC 77449 3677 D4
Fernhollow Ln
21200 HarC 77388 3112 B4
E Fernhurst Dr
500 HarC 77450 3953 D2
500 HOUS 77450 3953 D1
500 HOUS 77494 3953 C2
W Fernhurst Dr
- HarC 77494 3953 B2
- HOUS 77450 3953 C2
23400 HOUS 77494 3953 C2
Fern Lacy Ct
2400 HarC 77388 3113 A2
Fern Lacy Dr
2200 HarC 77388 3113 A2
2700 HarC 77389 3113 A2
Fernlake Dr
13700 HOUS 77049 3828 B3
Fernlea St
11800 HarC 77016 3547 E7
11800 HarC 77016 3687 E1
Fern Meadow Dr
400 MSCY 77459 4497 A5
12300 STAF 77477 4238 A7
Fern Meadow Ln
12000 HarC 77039 3546 A6
Fern Mill Ct
12900 HarC 77041 3679 D4
Fern Mist Ct
1700 FBnC 77494 3952 B6
Fern Mist Ln
2200 FBnC 77494 3952 B6
Fernmont Ln
- HarC 77040 3681 A1
Fernoaks Dr
3200 HarC 77388 3112 E3
Fern Park Dr
5400 HOUS 77339 3119 B2
Fern Pine Ct
20300 HarC 77449 3815 C4
Fernpine Ct
- HarC 77377 3253 E1
Fern Ridge Dr
15600 HarC 77084 3678 E5
15600 HarC 77084 3679 A5
Fern Ridge Ln
8600 HarC 77338 3262 A4
9100 HMBL 77338 3262 A4
Fernridge Rd
10 WDLD 77380 2822 A7
Fern River Ct
- FBnC 77469 4493 B3
Fern River Dr
3500 HOUS 77345 3119 D3
Fern Rock Dr
3100 DRPK 77536 4249 D3
3100 LPRT 77536 4249 D3
3100 LPRT 77571 4249 D3
Fern Rock Falls Ct
16600 HarC 77379 3256 B4
Fern Rose Ct
22200 MtgC 77355 2960 D2
22200 SGCH 77355 2960 D2
Fern Shadows Ct
19000 HarC 77084 3816 B4
Fernside Dr
4200 PASD 77505 4248 E5
Fernspray Ln
1900 HOUS 77084 3816 D6
Fern Springs Ct
800 HOUS 77062 4506 C1
Fernstone Ln
9800 HarC 77070 3399 C6
Fern Terrace Dr
10900 HOUS 77075 4377 B4
Fern Trace Ct
500 MtgC 77386 2968 D2
Fern Trail Ct
18300 HarC 77084 3816 D4
Fern Vale Ct
7800 FBnC 77479 4494 A5
12500 HarC 77065 3539 A3
Fern Valley Dr
8800 HarC 77044 3689 B5
Fern View Dr
3700 HOUS 77345 3119 D3
Fern Walk Ct
12600 HOUS 77089 4378 D7
Fernway Rd
12800 HarC 77049 3828 B1
Fernwick Village Ln
20700 HarC 77433 3676 D1
Fernwillow Dr
9100 HarC 77379 3110 D5
Fern Wing Ct
300 WDLD 77381 2820 C3
Fernwood Cir
20000 HarC 77338 3263 B5
Fernwood Ct
10 SPLD 77372 2683 A5
Fernwood Dr
- MtgC 77385 2676 E3
600 FRDW 77546 4629 A3
3900 HOUS 77021 4103 D4
3900 PRLD 77584 4503 A7
Fernwood St
100 BzaC 77511 4748 E1
600 PRVW 77484 3100 D4
600 WlrC 77484 3100 C4
Fernwood Wy
16700 HOUS 77058 4507 D2
Fern wood Forest
9400 HarC 77040 3681 B1
Ferol Ln
100 HarC 77562 3832 A3
Ferol Rd
7600 HOUS 77016 3687 A3
Ferrara Dr
- FBnC 77083 4095 E6

Ferrari Dr
600 HarC 77396 3406 E4
700 HarC 77396 3407 A4
Ferraro Ln
8500 HarC 77037 3684 D1
Ferris Dr
- BLAR 77096 4100 E7
6300 BLAR 77401 4100 E4
6300 HOUS 77081 4100 E4
8500 HOUS 77096 4100 E7
8800 HOUS 77096 4240 E1
Ferris St
- BLAR 77096 4100 E7
- HOUS 77096 4100 E7
6600 BLAR 77401 4100 E5
6600 HOUS 77081 4100 E4
Ferro St
4100 STAF 77477 4369 B3
Ferry Lndg
2600 SGLD 77478 4368 D5
Ferry Rd
- GLSN 77554 4994 E7
500 GLSN 77550 4994 E7
500 GLSN 77550 5109 E1
2700 BYTN 77520 3973 E4
2700 HarC 77520 3973 E4
4500 BYTN 77520 3974 A2
4500 BYTN 77521 3974 A2
Ferry Rd SR-87
- GLSN 77554 4994 E7
10 GLSN 77550 5109 E1
500 GLSN 77550 4994 E7
S Ferry Rd
- GLSN 77550 5109 E2
Ferry St
700 RHMD 77469 4364 E7
800 RHMD 77469 4491 D1
Ferry Boat Dr
19100 HarC 77449 3677 B3
Ferry Cove Ln
13000 PRLD 77584 4500 A3
Ferry Hill Dr
13000 HarC 77015 3828 C6
Festival Dr
1400 HOUS 77062 4507 B1
Fether Pkwy
- MtgC 77355 2961 E2
- SGCH 77355 2961 E2
Fetlock Dr
12200 HarC 77065 3539 D5
Feuhs Ln
100 HOUS 77022 3685 A7
Fichter Av
10 HOUS 77022 3685 A7
Ficus Ct
9600 FBnC 77459 4621 D6
17400 HarC 77388 3257 D2
Fid Ct
17000 HarC 77532 3552 A1
Fiddleleaf Ct
10 WDLD 77381 2821 A7
Fiddler Crab
4100 GLSN 77554 5333 A2
Fiddlers Cove Pl
10 WDLD 77381 2820 D3
Fiddlers Green Dr
3600 HarC 77082 4096 B3
Fidelia Ct
11700 BKHV 77024 3959 C5
11800 HOUS 77024 3959 C5
Fidelity St
10 HOUS 77029 3966 A5
10 HOUS 77029 4106 B1
5300 JTCY 77029 3966 A2
Field Ct
1600 PRLD 77581 4375 E7
Fieldbloom Ln
9700 FBnC 77478 4237 A2
Fieldbluff Ln
18300 HarC 77449 3677 D6
Field Briar Dr
1700 HarC 77450 3954 A5
Field Briar Ln
- FBnC 77479 4496 D5
Fieldbrook Dr
11600 HOUS 77077 3958 A5
Fieldcliff Ct
12800 HarC 77041 3679 D3
Field Cottage Ln
7600 HarC 77338 3261 C2
19000 FBnC 77469 4094 E5
19000 FBnC 77469 4095 A5
Fieldcreek Dr
300 FRDW 77546 4629 E3
400 FRDW 77546 4630 A3
Fieldcrest Dr
11100 LPRT 77571 4110 D7
11700 LPRT 77571 4111 A7
Fieldcrest Ln
22300 FBnC 77469 4492 E4
Fieldcross Ln
- HarC 77047 4374 A4
Field Cypress Ln
26900 HarC 77433 3537 A1
Field Cypress Tr
300 FBnC 77583 4744 A2
Fielder Cir
3900 FBnC 77459 4621 B5
Fielder Dr
22000 HarC 77450 3954 A5
Fielder Green Ln
4100 FBnC 77469 4615 D5
Fieldfare Dr
8000 FBnC 77583 4744 A2
Field Flower Ct
10 WDLD 77380 2967 E4
Fieldglen Ct
4400 LGCY 77573 4630 E5
Fieldglen Dr
- HarC 77449 3677 D2
17700 HarC 77084 3677 D2
Field Green Dr
21700 HarC 77433 3250 E6
Fieldhaven Ct
26300 HarC 77433 3396 B4
Field Haze Tr
16200 HarC 77433 3251 B5
Field Hollow Dr
2700 PRLD 77545 4499 D3
Fieldhorne Ct
3600 FBnC 77450 4094 C1
Field House Ct
21200 HarC 77338 3261 D3
Fielding Dr
- FBnC 77479 4493 E4
Fielding Ln
12600 HarC 77049 3828 B1

STREET
Block City ZIP Map# Grid

eldlark Ln
1600 MSCY 77489 4370 C7
eld Line Dr
2700 SGLD 77479 4368 C7
2900 SGLD 77479 4495 C1
eld Manor Ln
3300 HarC 77047 4374 C5
20900 FBnC 77450 4094 B4
eld Meadow Ct
4600 HarC 77449 3677 A7
eld Meadow Dr
4200 HarC 77449 3816 A1
eldmont Ln
19600 HarC 77073 3403 D3
eld Ridge Dr
7400 HarC 77095 3678 D1
eldrose Ct
23600 FBnC 77469 4093 D6
eld Run Ct
600 HarC 77049 3829 A3
elds Ln
22100 HarC 77389 3112 A1
22500 HarC 77389 2967 A7
elds Rd
- HarC 77338 3260 D4
- HOUS 77338 3260 D4
elds St
600 RHMD 77469 4364 E7
8600 HOUS 77013 3826 D4
8600 HOUS 77028 3826 D4
eldsboro Dr
12200 HOUS 77031 4239 A6
elds Crossing Ln
3900 FBnC 77478 4366 E3
3900 FBnC 77478 4367 A3
eldshire Dr
6900 FBnC 77494 4093 B5
19200 HarC 77449 3816 A2
eld Springs Ln
13500 HOUS 77059 4379 E4
elds Store Rd
900 WALR 77484 3102 A6
2100 HarC 77484 3102 A5
25400 WlrC 77484 2957 B3
eldstone Ct
7600 HarC 77095 3538 B6
eld Stone Dr
10200 HOUS 77041 3820 A1
eldstone Dr
- BzaC 77584 4501 B7
- PRLD 77584 4501 B7
1300 MSCY 77489 4370 D6
13700 HarC 77041 3679 B1
13900 HarC 77095 3679 B1
eldstone St
- HarC 77095 3538 B6
2700 SGLD 77478 4368 D5
eldstone Ter
- FBnC 77469 4234 C2
eldtree Dr
20000 HMBL 77338 3262 C4
eld View Ct
11000 HOUS 77075 4377 A4
eldview Ct
4200 FBnC 77545 4622 D1
eldvine Ct
21900 FBnC 77450 4094 B2
eld Vine Ln
- LGCY 77539 4753 A3
eldwick Ln
4900 HarC 77338 3260 D2
eldwood Dr
5000 HOUS 77056 3961 A5
5200 HOUS 77056 3960 E5
eldwood Ln
6100 CNRO 77304 2236 E6
eldworth Dr
12500 HOUS 77037 3685 A1
eld Yucca Ct
- HarC 77429 3253 A5
esta Ln
100 DKSN 77539 4754 A1
1900 RHMD 77469 4364 C7
4300 HOUS 77004 4103 E3
esta Flower Ln
7200 FBnC 77494 4093 A5
ife Ct
1400 LGCY 77573 4631 A6
ife Dr
900 CNRO 77301 2530 B2
ife Ln
- HarC 77546 4630 B1
17200 HarC 77598 4630 C1
17700 HarC 77598 4506 C7
ifi St
6900 BKVL 77581 4376 A6
ifth
- FBnC 77545 4499 D5
ig Dr
300 FBnC 77545 4623 C2
igaro Dr
12800 HOUS 77024 3958 D3
ighting Colt St
- HOUS 77031 4239 C4
8500 HOUS 77071 4239 C4
igland St
5900 PRLD 77584 4502 D5
ig Orchard Rd
200 HarC 77562 3831 E1
3000 HarC 77562 3832 E1
3000 HarC 77562 3833 A1
igure Four Lake Ct
4000 FBnC 77469 4234 E5
igure Four Lake Ln
3900 FBnC 77469 4234 D5
igurine Ct
20800 FBnC 77450 4094 B3
iji Ct
600 HarC 77532 3552 B3
ilaree Ridge Ln
9200 HarC 77089 4504 C1
iley Ct
10300 HOUS 77013 3966 B1
iley Ln
10700 HOUS 77013 3966 C1
iligree Pines Pl
10 WDLD 77382 2819 D1
illgrove Pl
10 WDLD 77382 2673 A7
illmont Ln
9300 HarC 77044 3689 B4
illmore St
8500 HOUS 77029 3965 D4
9700 HOUS 77029 3966 A4
illtop St
8000 HOUS 77028 3826 C3
illy Pass Ln
- HarC 77429 3253 A6

Filmore Ln
3600 DRPK 77536 4249 D1
Finborough Dr
16400 HarC 77377 3254 B6
Finbury Ln
23600 FBnC 77494 4093 C1
Fincastle Dr
22100 HarC 77450 3954 A1
22300 HarC 77450 3953 E1
N Finch Cir
7500 HOUS 77028 3826 A1
S Finch Cir
7500 HOUS 77028 3826 A1
Finch Ct
10 MtgC 77385 2676 D6
Finch St
1100 HOUS 77009 3824 D6
5500 HOUS 77028 3825 D1
7100 HOUS 77028 3826 A1
Finch Brook Dr
12900 HarC 77429 3398 B1
13100 HarC 77429 3254 A7
Fincher Dr
15700 HarC 77546 4505 E6
Finchgrove Ln
25200 FBnC 77494 4093 B3
Finch Landing Ln
21800 HarC 77338 3260 A1
Finchley Dr
3700 HOUS 77082 4097 B3
Finchwood Ln
10100 HOUS 77036 4238 E1
Find Horn Ln
9300 HarC 77095 3538 C4
Findlay Ct
8400 HOUS 77017 4105 D6
Findlay Dr
5200 PASD 77505 4248 B4
Findlay St
7900 HOUS 77017 4105 D6
Finesse Dr
800 HarC 77032 3404 A7
Finewood Wy
16700 HOUS 77058 4507 D2
Finfrock St
700 PASD 77506 4106 E6
1200 PASD 77502 4106 E6
Finger Rd
2000 BzaC 77511 4868 C7
Finland Ct
- HarC 77379 3111 E6
Finley St
- BYTN 77520 3972 A7
Finn St
7000 HOUS 77022 3824 A2
Finnegan Park Pl
500 HOUS 77020 3964 C3
Finnigan Dr
1100 HOUS 77020 3964 C2
Finsbury Field Dr
5300 KATY 77493 3813 D6
Fintona Wy
400 HarC 77015 3829 A7
Finwood Ln
15800 HOUS 77044 3409 A5
Fiorella Wy
3300 HarC 77338 3260 A2
Fir Ln
12200 MtgC 77362 2817 B6
15200 MtgC 77302 2677 B2
Fir Rd
15000 STFE 77517 4870 A7
15100 GlsC 77517 4870 A6
15400 GlsC 77517 4869 E6
16800 GlsC 77511 4869 E6
Fir St
- HarC 77396 3406 E5
7100 HOUS 77012 4105 B3
7100 HOUS 77087 4105 B3
Fir Canyon Tr
19000 HarC 77429 3395 E1
Fir Cove
1800 HOUS 77339 3118 D4
Fir Creek Ln
21500 HarC 77388 3112 C4
Fir Crest Dr
2700 FBnC 77477 4369 E4
Firdale Cir
15200 HarC 77530 3829 D6
Fire Rd
18900 HarC 77433 3252 A5
Firebird Dr
11900 HOUS 77099 4238 A3
Firebrick Dr
13200 HarC 77041 3679 C1
Firebrook Ct
6600 HarC 77389 2966 C2
Firecreek Dr
10900 HOUS 77043 3819 B5
Firecreek Ridge Dr
17200 HarC 77095 3396 D7
Firecrest Dr
2500 FBnC 77494 3951 D5
Firedel St
11800 HarC 77016 3547 E7
11800 HarC 77016 3687 E1
Firefall Ct
10 WDLD 77380 2967 C3
Firefall Ln
- WDLD 77380 2967 C3
Fire Flicker Pl
10 WDLD 77381 2820 E4
Firefly Dr
18400 MtgC 77365 2972 A6
Firefly Ln
8100 FBnC 77479 4494 C5
Firefly Rd
3200 PRLD 77581 4503 D5
Firefly St
5300 HOUS 77017 4106 C6
Fire Fox St
2400 HarC 77562 3832 D2
Firegate Dr
- HarC 77373 3115 B5
Fire Hills Dr
- HarC 77038 3543 B3
E Firemist Ct
21400 HarC 77433 3250 E3
21400 HarC 77433 3251 A3
W Firemist Ct
21800 HarC 77433 3250 E4
Firemist Wy
21600 HarC 77433 3250 E3
Firenza Dr
5700 HOUS 77035 4240 C6
Fire Rock Dr
13700 HOUS 77085 4371 C1

Fire Sage Ct
17800 HarC 77396 3407 D2
Fire Sage Dr
10300 HarC 77396 3407 D2
Fireside Ct
7200 FBnC 77479 4493 E5
Fireside Dr
17600 HarC 77379 3257 B1
Fireside Ln
24100 HarC 77336 3266 E2
Firesign Dr
19500 HarC 77346 3265 A5
Firestone Ct
2100 LGCY 77573 4508 D7
Firestone Dr
2100 LGCY 77573 4508 D7
4300 HOUS 77035 4241 B2
Fire Thorn Ln
7900 HarC 77433 3537 B7
Firethorn Pl
10 WDLD 77382 2675 C7
Firethorne Ct
- HarC 77389 2966 A2
N Firethorne Rd
28000 FBnC 77494 3951 C5
S Firethorne Rd
- FBnC 77494 3951 E5
Firetower Rd
13300 MtgC 77306 2534 C7
13600 MtgC 77306 2680 E5
16500 MtgC 77357 2680 E6
Firewater Ln
- PRLD 77545 4499 E1
Firewillow Pl
10 WDLD 77381 2820 C2
Fire Wind Ct
21200 HarC 77379 3111 A4
Firewood Ln
- HOUS 77075 4376 D5
25100 HarC 77373 3114 E2
Fir Forest Dr
3400 HarC 77388 3112 E7
3800 HarC 77388 3257 D1
Fir Glen Ln
13000 HarC 77429 3254 A6
Fir Grove Dr
2300 HOUS 77339 3119 A4
Fir Hollow Cir
18400 HarC 77346 3408 C2
Fir Hollow Dr
3600 PRLD 77584 4503 E6
3600 PRLD 77581 4504 A6
Fir Knoll Wy
- HarC 77429 3395 E1
Firnat St
500 HOUS 77022 3685 C7
2800 HOUS 77093 3685 E6
2800 HOUS 77093 3686 A6
4500 HOUS 77016 3686 C6
9200 HOUS 77016 3687 A6
Fir Ridge Ct
24500 HOUS 77336 3266 B2
Fir Ridge Dr
200 HOUS 77336 3266 B2
Fir Springs Dr
2000 HOUS 77339 3118 E4
First
- HarC 77015 3967 E4
N First
800 HarC 77032 3545 A1
First St
2300 HarC 77336 3267 A2
First Baptist Dr
- PASD 77505 4249 B5
First Bend Ct
17300 HarC 77433 3395 C6
First Bend Dr
17800 HarC 77433 3395 E6
First Bend Crossing Dr
- HarC 77433 3395 C6
First Colony Blvd
- SGLD 77478 4367 E5
1800 SGLD 77479 4367 E5
First Crossing Blvd
- SGLD 77479 4368 D6
2000 SGLD 77478 4368 D6
First Voyage Ct
18500 HarC 77433 3395 C5
Firth Dr
- PRLD 77584 4501 B2
Firth Ln
16700 HarC 77084 3678 C7
Firthridge Ct
15700 HOUS 77598 4506 D4
Firthwood Ln
900 CNRO 77301 2530 B3
Fir Tree Dr
1900 LGCY 77573 4631 B6
Firtree Wy
2000 HOUS 77062 4507 C1
Fir Valley Dr
4300 HOUS 77345 3119 D5
Firwood Cir
1400 PASD 77502 4106 D7
Firwood Dr
1600 PASD 77502 4106 E7
Fir Woods Ln
15300 HarC 77429 3252 B7
Fish Rd
25700 MtgC 77355 2962 D4
Fishawk Wy
400 HarC 77532 3552 B2
Fish Creek Dr
800 HOUS 77450 3954 C1
900 HarC 77450 3954 C1
Fishel St
11900 HarC 77093 3685 E1
12000 HarC 77039 3545 E7
12000 HarC 77093 3545 E7
12000 HOUS 77039 3545 E7
N Fisher Ct
1900 PASD 77502 4247 E1
S Fisher Ct
1900 PASD 77502 4247 E1
Fisher Dr
19400 HarC 77377 3107 A6
Fisher Rd
200 HMBL 77338 3262 D6
10500 HOUS 77041 3680 D5
17600 WlrC 77484 3246 B2
Fisher St
800 HOUS 77018 3823 A2
1000 HOUS 77018 3822 E2
Fisher Bend Ln
- RSBG 77469 4491 E5
- RSBG 77471 4491 E5
Fisher Colony Dr
25300 FBnC 77469 4092 D7

Fisher Glen Ln
8000 HarC 77072 4097 C7
Fisher Grove Ln
17500 HarC 77346 3408 D3
Fisher Hill Rd
2800 BYTN 77520 3973 E4
Fisher Lake Ct
1500 FBnC 77469 4234 D5
Fisher Lake Dr
4100 FBnC 77469 4234 D5
Fisherman Ct
3900 MtgC 77386 2970 B7
Fishermans Cove
4400 MSCY 77459 4497 A4
Fisher Park Dr
- HarC 77095 3538 B3
Fishers Cove
14600 MtgC 77362 2670 D6
14700 MtgC 77354 2670 D6
Fisher Trace Ct
2000 HarC 77373 3114 C6
Fish Hook Ct
4000 MtgC 77386 2970 C7
Fisk St
4600 HOUS 77009 3824 B5
Fitch St
4400 HOUS 77016 3686 C6
Fite Rd
3900 BzaC 77584 4501 D4
3900 PRLD 77584 4501 D4
4700 BzaC 77584 4502 A4
5100 PRLD 77584 4502 E4
5100 PRLD 77584 4503 A4
Fitz Ln
21300 MtgC 77355 2961 A5
21400 MtgC 77355 2960 E5
Fitz Rd
200 ALVN 77511 4867 C4
N Fitzgerald Ct
3800 FBnC 77459 4621 D5
S Fitzgerald Ct
3700 FBnC 77459 4621 C4
Fitzgerald Rd
- MTBL 77520 3696 D4
Fitzgerald St
6100 HOUS 77091 3684 A5
Fitzgerald Wy
- FBnC 77459 4621 C4
N Fitzgerald Wy
8500 FBnC 77459 4621 B5
S Fitzgerald Wy
8600 FBnC 77459 4621 C5
Fitzhugh St
7300 HOUS 77028 3826 E1
Fitz Lee
- WALR 77484 3101 E5
- WALR 77484 3102 A5
Fitz Lee St
2300 WALR 77484 3101 E5
Fitzroy Ct
14200 FBnC 77083 4236 E2
Fitzroy Pl
- CNRO 77384 2675 E4
Fitzwater Dr
4800 HarC 77373 3115 C6
Five Ashes Dr
15900 HarC 77379 3256 B6
Five Forks Dr
6800 HarC 77379 3256 B2
Five Guinea Ln
14000 MtgC 77302 2532 C5
Five Iron Dr
2100 HarC 77089 4504 E2
Five Knolls Dr
4600 HarC 77546 4506 A6
4700 HarC 77546 4505 E6
Five Oaks Cross
10300 FBnC 77459 4622 A6
Five Oaks Ct
10400 FBnC 77459 4622 A6
Five Oaks Dr
2700 FBnC 77459 4622 A6
5100 HarC 77389 2967 A5
5600 HarC 77389 2966 E5
Five Oaks Ln
10200 FBnC 77459 4622 A6
Five Point Rd
- ALVN 77511 4868 A2
1900 BzaC 77511 4867 E3
1900 BzaC 77511 4868 A3
Five Point Rd CO-155
1900 BzaC 77511 4867 E3
1900 BzaC 77511 4868 A3
Five Spot Ct
9600 HarC 77379 3110 C6
Fjord Ct
5000 HarC 77066 3401 B7
Flack Dr
5600 HOUS 77081 4100 C6
Flagg Ranch Ct
6000 HarC 77388 3111 E1
Flagg Ranch Dr
6100 HarC 77388 3111 D1
Flaghoist Ln
500 HOUS 77079 3956 E2
Flaghorne Ct
18800 HarC 77377 3254 A1
Flagler Av
7100 PASD 77505 4249 A3
Flagler St
11700 MSCY 77071 4239 D7
Flagmore Ct
20700 HarC 77450 3954 C3
Flagmore Dr
1000 HarC 77450 3954 C3
Flagship Ct
- LGCY 77573 4508 D7
Flagship Dr
8700 HOUS 77029 3965 D4
Flagstaff Ln
12600 HarC 77049 3828 B1
Flagstone Dr
- HarC 77095 3539 B7
13700 HarC 77041 3539 B7
Flagstone Pth
10 WDLD 77381 2674 D7
Flagstone Ter
1000 HOUS 77017 4106 C7
2100 HOUS 77017 4246 C1
Flagstone Creek Rd
18600 HarC 77084 3816 C4
Flagstone Dale St
11900 HarC 77089 4505 A1
Flagstone Pass Ln
9300 HarC 77089 4504 A1
N Flagstone Path Cir
100 WDLD 77381 2674 E7
100 WDLD 77381 2820 E1

S Flagstone Path Cir
10 WDLD 77381 2674 D7
10 WDLD 77381 2820 D1
Flagstone Trail Ct
20600 HarC 77433 3251 B3
Flagstone Walk Wy
- HarC 77049 3829 B3
Flair Ct
6300 HarC 77049 3828 B3
Flair Dr
14400 HarC 77049 3828 D3
Flair Oaks Dr
7500 HarC 77040 3681 E1
Flamborough Dr
3000 PASD 77503 4108 A5
3000 PASD 77506 4108 A5
Flameleaf Gardens Ct
15200 HarC 77433 3251 A7
Flamenco Dr
- HarC 77049 3831 B1
Flaming Amber Wy
16500 HarC 77433 3250 E4
Flaming Arrow Tr
20900 HarC 77532 3410 B1
Flaming Candle Dr
3300 HarC 77388 3113 A7
Flamingo Blvd
- HTCK 77563 4989 E7
- HTCK 77563 5104 D1
Flamingo Ct
700 FRDW 77546 4629 A1
4100 PRLD 77584 4501 D2
Flamingo Dr
1800 LGCY 77573 4631 C5
5400 HOUS 77033 4243 E3
5400 HOUS 77033 4244 A3
6800 HOUS 77087 4244 E3
7100 HOUS 77087 4245 A2
25900 GLSN 77554 5548 A3
N Flamingo Dr
600 SEBK 77586 4383 B6
2300 MSCY 77459 4497 B4
S Flamingo Dr
4500 SEBK 77586 4383 A7
W Flamingo Dr
1000 SEBK 77586 4383 A7
Flamingo Ln
1200 MtgC 77385 2676 D5
Flamingo Lndg
2200 MSCY 77459 4497 B4
Flamingo Pk
15200 HarC 77396 3406 D7
Flamingo St
1300 CHTW 77385 2823 A4
2300 RMFT 77357 2829 A3
N Flamingo St
10 LMQU 77568 4990 D6
S Flamingo St
10 LMQU 77568 4990 D6
Flamingo Wy
4200 JMAB 77554 5331 D4
16600 GLSN 77554 5331 D4
Flamingo Bay
10 MSCY 77459 4497 B4
Flamingo Bight N
100 BYTN 77520 4113 D5
Flamingo Bight S
100 BYTN 77520 4113 D5
Flamingo Estates Dr
2200 MSCY 77459 4497 B4
Flamingo Island Ct
2300 MSCY 77459 4497 B4
Flamingo Island Dr
10 MSCY 77459 4497 B4
Flamingo Lakes Ct
12000 HarC 77065 3539 D3
Flanagan Rd
12000 HarC 77065 3398 C6
12000 HarC 77429 3398 B4
Flanders Dr
3200 MtgC 77365 2974 C7
Flanders Field Ln
1400 SGLD 77478 4236 E6
Flanners Ct
800 HarC 77373 2968 C6
Flannery Ct
22000 FBnC 77450 4094 B3
Flannery Park Ln
400 HarC 77094 3955 B1
Flannery Ridge Ln
3600 HarC 77047 4374 C4
Flat Bank Dr
7000 FBnC 77479 4496 E6
7000 MSCY 77459 4496 E6
7000 MSCY 77459 4497 A5
7000 MSCY 77479 4496 E6
Flatbrook Dr
23800 HarC 77373 3115 C5
Flat Creek Dr
12800 PRLD 77584 4500 A2
Flat Creek Ln
100 LGCY 77539 4753 A3
21200 HarC 77449 3815 B2
Flatcreek Pl
10 WDLD 77381 2675 A6
Flatop Ln
11900 HarC 77377 3109 B7
Flatridge Ct
16100 FBnC 77083 4236 A1
Flat Rock Ln
3900 HarC 77047 4374 D4
Flat Rock St
1800 FRDW 77546 4629 C5
Flatrock Tr
8000 HarC 77050 3547 D6
Flatrock Creek Dr
1200 HarC 77067 3402 C5
Flatrock Park Ln
19400 HarC 77073 3403 D2
Flat Springs Ln
18200 HarC 77433 3537 A5
Flat Stone Ct
10 WDLD 77381 2821 C3
Flatwood Ct
3100 PRLD 77584 4502 A6
Flatwood Dr
3800 HarC 77449 3816 A2
Flavin Rd
- WlrC 77447 2959 C4
Flax Ct
24100 TMBL 77375 2964 D5
Flax Dr
600 TMBL 77375 2964 D5
7700 HOUS 77071 4239 E5
Flax Bourton St
5100 HarC 77346 3264 C7
Flax Bourton Close
18700 HarC 77346 3264 D7

Flaxen Dr
12000 HarC 77065 3539 D5
Flaxen Manor Ct
10500 HarC 77379 3110 B6
Flaxman St
7900 HOUS 77029 3965 B4
10100 JTCY 77029 3966 C3
Flaxseed Wy
12500 STAF 77477 4239 A7
Flaxwood Dr
19300 HarC 77346 3264 C5
Flecherwood Ct
- HarC 77388 3111 E2
Fledgling Path St
10 WDLD 77382 2820 B1
Fleet Ln
4200 DRPK 77536 4249 B1
Fleethaven Ct
5700 HarC 77084 3678 C4
Fleethaven Ln
16000 HarC 77084 3678 C4
Fleetway Dr
200 HNCV 77024 3960 A4
Fleetwell Dr
13900 HOUS 77045 4372 E2
Fleetwood Cir
200 LGCY 77573 4631 E4
Fleetwood Dr
- LPRT 77571 4250 D3
2900 HOUS 77093 3686 A3
Fleetwood St
700 BYTN 77520 3972 D6
Fleetwood Oaks Dr
15700 HOUS 77079 3956 E2
Fleetwood Pl Dr
800 HOUS 77079 3956 D2
Fleming
10 HTCK 77563 5105 A5
Fleming Ct
700 HOUS 77013 3966 C1
Fleming Dr
2900 PASD 77503 4108 A5
2900 PASD 77506 4108 A5
3300 HarC 77521 3834 E5
10100 HOUS 77013 3966 C1
11900 HOUS 77015 3966 E1
Fleming St
200 RHMD 77469 4491 D1
4900 LMQU 77568 4873 A7
5100 LMQU 77568 4989 A1
Fleming Downe Ln
4700 HarC 77388 3112 B4
Fleming Springs Ct
1900 HarC 77396 3407 C2
Fleming Springs Dr
9700 HarC 77396 3407 C2
Flemington Av
15300 HarC 77084 3678 D4
Fleta Dr
6300 HOUS 77028 3826 C2
Fletcher
5800 HarC 77532 3552 C4
Fletcher St
2200 HOUS 77009 3963 B1
Fletcher Bridge Ct
14800 FBnC 77478 4236 A5
Fletcher Bridge Ln
10700 FBnC 77478 4236 E5
Fletcher Christian Rd
16700 GLSN 77554 5331 E6
16700 JMAB 77554 5331 E6
Fletcher Wy Dr
19400 HarC 77073 3403 B2
Fleur Dr
11200 HarC 77065 3539 A1
Fleur de Lis Blvd
- HarC 77065 3398 A7
13800 HarC 77065 3539 A1
13800 HarC 77429 3539 A1
13900 HarC 77429 3398 A7
13900 HarC 77429 3538 E1
Fleury Wy
10 WDLD 77382 2673 E7
Flicker Dr
1600 MSCY 77489 4370 C6
Flickering Candle Dr
3200 HarC 77388 3113 A7
3300 HarC 77388 3258 A1
N Flickering Sun Cir
10 WDLD 77382 2673 C5
S Flickering Sun Cir
10 WDLD 77382 2673 B5
Flickering Sun Ct
10 WDLD 77382 2673 C5
Flight Dr
- HarC 77041 3679 E3
Flint St
- HOUS 77029 3966 B2
10 CNRO 77301 2384 A2
1100 JTCY 77029 3966 B3
1700 GNPK 77029 3966 B4
1700 GNPK 77547 3966 B4
Flint Bridge Ct
14800 FBnC 77478 4236 E5
Flint Brook Ct
2300 FBnC 77545 4498 C7
Flint Cove Ct
17200 HarC 77095 3538 A7
Flint Creek Dr
4000 HOUS 77339 3119 C2
Flintdale Rd
400 BKHV 77024 3959 D3
Flint Forest Ln
11600 BKHV 77024 3959 C2
Flintgate Ct
2600 HarC 77014 3402 A2
Flint Hill Dr
18100 HarC 77084 3677 D5
18100 HarC 77449 3677 D5
Flintlock Dr
22100 HarC 77449 3675 E5
Flintlock Rd
6300 HOUS 77040 3681 D4
6600 HarC 77040 3681 D4
11500 LPRT 77571 4250 E2
11500 LPRT 77571 4251 A2
Flinton Dr
26100 FBnC 77469 4092 B7
Flint Point Dr
400 PNPV 77024 3959 E3
Flintridge Dr
- WDLD 77381 2820 E5
- WDLD 77382 2819 E2
- WDLD 77382 2820 A2
7800 HOUS 77028 3687 B7
Flint Ridge Rd
200 HarC 77598 4507 B5

Flintridge Lake Ln
15100 HarC 77433 3251 E7
Flint River Dr
800 HNCV 77024 3960 B1
Flintrock Cir
2700 HarC 77067 3401 E5
Flintrock Ct
3900 SGLD 77479 4496 A2
Flintrock Dr
2900 BzaC 77584 4501 C6
2900 PRLD 77584 4501 C6
Flintrock Ln
- SGLD 77479 4495 E1
3900 SGLD 77479 4496 A1
Flint Run Wy
16300 FBnC 77478 4236 A5
Flintshine Pl
- WDLD 77382 2674 B6
Flintside Dr
19500 HarC 77449 3677 A2
Flintstone Dr
- HarC 77070 3398 D2
Flintwick Dr
- HarC 77049 3831 A1
Flintwood Ct
11600 BKHV 77024 3959 C3
Flintwood Dr
3000 SGLD 77479 4368 E7
11700 BKHV 77024 3959 C3
Fliser Dr
7300 HarC 77041 3679 C1
Flora Dr
4200 PASD 77505 4249 B5
Flora Rd
2500 BzaC 77511 4868 A3
2700 BzaC 77511 4867 E3
7300 MNVL 77578 4746 E1
7300 MNVL 77578 4747 A1
Flora St
3400 HOUS 77006 3962 E7
Florabunda Ln
100 HarC 77532 3411 A4
Floradora Ln
100 HOUS 77076 3684 C5
Florafield Ln
10500 HarC 77429 3538 E2
Floragate Dr
23800 HarC 77373 3115 B5
Floral Pk
500 HarC 77049 3829 A3
Floral St
1400 HOUS 77087 4105 B4
Floral Bloom Wy
2500 FBnC 77545 4498 C5
Floral Broom Wy
2600 FBnC 77545 4498 C5
Floral Crest Dr
9200 FBnC 77083 4236 A1
Floralgate Ln
17200 HarC 77095 3538 C3
Floral Glen Ln
6500 HarC 77449 3677 B3
N Floral Leaf Cir
10 WDLD 77381 2674 D6
S Floral Leaf Cir
10 WDLD 77381 2674 D6
Floral Park Ct
9400 HarC 77095 3538 E4
Floral Ridge Dr
2300 HarC 77388 3113 A2
Floral Wy Ct
3900 FBnC 77545 4622 E1
Floramorgan Ln
12100 HarC 77089 4505 A2
Flora View Ct
20700 HarC 77379 3111 E4
Flora Vista Dr
300 HOUS 77598 4506 E5
Florence Av
2300 PASD 77502 4107 E7
2600 PASD 77502 4108 A7
Florence Rd
13500 FBnC 77478 4237 A4
13500 SGLD 77478 4237 A4
14000 FBnC 77478 4236 E4
14000 SGLD 77478 4236 E4
Florence St
100 TMBL 77375 2964 B7
2300 LMQU 77568 4989 E3
2700 HOUS 77009 3963 A1
2900 HOUS 77009 3824 B7
4800 BLAR 77401 4101 A5
17800 MtgC 77357 2828 B1
Flores St
- BzaC 77511 4628 C6
Floret Ct
10 WDLD 77382 2674 B6
Floret Estates Ct
14300 HarC 77429 3396 B2
Floret Estates Ln
14400 HarC 77429 3396 B2
Floret Estates Wy
- HarC 77429 3396 C3
Floret Hill Ln
2500 SGLD 77478 4237 D5
Florette Ln
20900 HarC 77388 3112 D4
Florham Park Dr
10 HarC 77379 3110 D7
10 HarC 77379 3255 C1
Florian Ct
10 WDLD 77385 2676 C4
Florida Av
2300 DKSN 77539 4632 E7
2300 GlsC 77539 4632 E7
2300 LGCY 77573 4632 C6
5800 HTCK 77563 4989 D5
Florida Dr
1700 SEBK 77586 4509 D1
Florida Pk
500 MtgC 77302 2530 B5
Florida St
1500 BYTN 77520 4112 B2
2800 HOUS 77026 3824 E7
3000 HOUS 77026 3825 A7
Florina Ranch Dr
25100 FBnC 77494 3953 A6
Florinda St
3600 HOUS 77021 4103 C6
Florine St
3600 HOUS 77087 4104 D6
Florita St
23300 MtgC 77357 2974 A1
23400 MtgC 77357 2828 A7
Flossie Mae St
8600 HOUS 77029 3965 D3
Flossmoor St
13700 HarC 77044 3689 D2

STREET / Block City ZIP Map# Grid

Flounder Wy
16500 JMAB 77554 5331 D4
Flower Pth
- HarC 77044 3689 C6
Flower Rdg
23300 MtgC 77365 2974 A7
Flower Bridge Ct
4500 HarC 77396 3407 B6
Flower Bud Dr
23800 FBnC 77494 4093 B5
Flower Creek Ln
14200 HOUS 77077 3956 E5
Flower Crest Cir
19200 HarC 77449 3816 A2
Flower Crest Dr
- HOUS 77489 4371 A6
Flower Croft Ct
- FBnC 77469 4094 B6
Flowercroft Ct
15900 HarC 77429 3397 A2
Flowerdale St
7400 HOUS 77055 3821 C6
Flower Field Ct
700 BzaC 77584 4501 B1
Flower Field Ln
3000 BzaC 77584 4501 B1
Flowerfield Ln
17000 HOUS 77060 3403 D6
Flower Gate Dr
5800 HarC 77373 3115 E7
Flower Grove Ct
5500 BzaC 77583 4623 D4
18100 FBnC 77469 4095 B6
Flower Hill Ct
20700 HarC 77379 3111 D4
Flowering Ash Cross
- FBnC 77494 4092 E4
Flowering Oak Ct
18100 FBnC 77469 4095 B5
Flower Mist Ct
17100 HarC 77377 3254 B4
Flower Mist Ln
16800 HarC 77095 3397 A7
Flowermound Dr
6600 FBnC 77479 4493 C5
Flower Mound Ln
26400 MtgC 77354 2817 E4
Flower Path St
8600 HarC 77044 3689 C5
Flower Reef Cir
3200 LGCY 77573 4633 B1
Flower Ridge Ct
5100 FBnC 77494 4093 B2
Flowers St
- HOUS 77023 4105 A4
1700 HOUS 77087 4105 A4
2700 PASD 77503 4248 C2
Flowertuft Ct
10 WDLD 77380 2822 B6
Flower Valley Cir
21400 HarC 77379 3111 A3
Flowerwood Ct
1100 HOUS 77062 4507 A2
Flowerwood Dr
14700 HOUS 77062 4379 E7
14900 HOUS 77062 4506 E1
14900 HOUS 77062 4507 A1
Floyd
100 HarC 77532 3692 C3
Floyd Av
6000 HOUS 77007 3962 A3
Floyd Ln
15300 HarC 77530 3829 E6
15300 HarC 77530 3830 A6
Floyd Rd
100 LGCY 77573 4631 A5
Floyd St
5300 HOUS 77007 3962 B3
Flukinger Rd
- WlrC 77484 2955 E7
- WlrC 77484 2956 A5
21800 PRVW 77445 2955 E7
21800 WlrC 77445 2955 E7
21900 PRVW 77445 3100 E1
21900 WlrC 77445 3100 E1
Fluor Daniel Dr
10 SGLD 77478 4368 A5
200 SGLD 77479 4368 A5
Flushing Meadows Dr
11700 HOUS 77089 4378 B6
Flycaster Dr
1800 HarC 77388 3113 B3
Flycatcher Cove Dr
2500 LGCY 77573 4752 B1
Flying Bridge Wy
700 HarC 77532 3552 A1
Flying Cloud Cir
20900 HarC 77532 3410 B1
Flying Dove Tr
1500 HarC 77532 3410 C3
Flying Eagle Ct
9500 FBnC 77083 4236 A1
Flying Geese Ln
11200 HarC 77375 3110 A7
N Flynn
200 HOUS 77003 3963 E4
Flynn Dr
1900 PASD 77502 4107 E7
2100 PASD 77502 4247 E1
Flyway
8700 HarC 77521 3695 C7
FM-149
4100 MtgC 77354 2670 D5
35700 MtgC 77362 2816 D3
FM-149 W Mt Houston Rd
2900 HarC 77038 3543 A6
2900 HarC 77086 3543 A6
2900 HarC 77088 3543 A6
FM-149 SPUR Spur Rd
37500 MtgC 77354 2670 D5
FM-188 Harborside Dr
- GLSN 77554 5107 D6
FM-188 Teichman Rd
8200 GLSN 77554 5107 D6
FM-270
- LGCY 77539 4632 E6
- LGCY 77573 4507 E7
- LGCY 77573 4508 A7
- LGCY 77573 4632 B1
- WEBS 77058 4507 E6
FM-270 Egret Bay Blvd
- LGCY 77573 4507 E6
18100 WEBS 77058 4507 E6
FM-275 Harborside Dr
400 GLSN 77550 5109 E1
5400 GLSN 77551 5108 C4
5400 GLSN 77554 5107 E4
5400 GLSN 77554 5108 B4
FM-275 Port Industrial Rd
2900 GLSN 77550 5109 A3
3100 GLSN 77550 5108 E3
3100 GLSN 77551 5108 E3
5200 GLSN 77554 5108 C4
FM-275 Water St
200 GLSN 77550 5109 D2
FM-359
- PNIS 77445 3099 B7
- WlrC 77445 2954 A7
- WlrC 77445 3099 A1
- WlrC 77445 3244 B6
FM-359 Richmond Foster Rd
2600 FBnC 77469 4365 A2
3300 FBnC 77469 4364 C2
6700 FBnC 77469 4232 A3
FM-359 Skinner Ln
100 FBnC 77469 4365 B4
400 RHMD 77469 4365 B5
FM-362
- WALR 77484 3101 D5
- WlrC 77484 2956 D6
- WlrC 77484 3101 D3
- WlrC 77484 3246 C6
FM-517
- DKSN 77539 4752 D6
- GlsC 77511 4751 A6
- GlsC 77511 4752 A6
- GlsC 77539 4635 A5
- LGCY 77511 4750 C7
- LGCY 77511 4751 A6
- LGCY 77517 4751 E6
- LGCY 77517 4752 A6
- LGCY 77539 4752 D6
- LGCY 77539 4753 B5
- LGCY 77546 4750 C7
600 ALVN 77511 4749 E7
600 BzaC 77511 4749 E7
800 ALVN 77511 4750 A7
1100 GlsC 77511 4750 C7
FM 517 Rd
- DKSN 77539 4753 C4
FM-517 9th St
200 GlsC 77539 4636 B5
FM-517 29th St
1000 GlsC 77539 4635 A6
1000 TXCY 77539 4635 D6
1700 TXCY 77539 4634 E7
1700 TXCY 77539 4755 E1
FM-517 41st St
- DKSN 77539 4752 E6
- DKSN 77539 4753 B5
- DKSN 77539 4754 D2
- LGCY 77539 4752 E6
- LGCY 77539 4753 B5
- TXCY 77539 4754 E1
- TXCY 77539 4755 D1
FM-517 Avenue I
900 GlsC 77539 4636 A6
1600 GlsC 77539 4635 E6
FM-517 Avenue J
2200 GlsC 77539 4635 D6
FM-517 Dickinson Rd
- ALVN 77511 4749 E7
FM-518
- FRDW 77546 4630 B6
- LGCY 77573 4630 E5
- LGCY 77573 4631 A4
FM-518 Broadway St
9300 BzaC 77584 4501 C4
9300 PRLD 77584 4501 C4
10500 PRLD 77584 4500 E4
10800 PRLD 77583 4500 C4
FM-518 E Broadway St
1100 PRLD 77581 4504 E6
2500 PRLD 77581 4503 A3
FM-518 W Broadway St
4000 PRLD 77581 4503 B3
4800 PRLD 77584 4503 A3
5300 PRLD 77581 4502 C3
5300 PRLD 77584 4502 C3
7900 PRLD 77581 4501 A4
7900 PRLD 77584 4501 A4
9000 BzaC 77584 4501 C4
FM-518 Deke Slayton Blvd
- LGCY 77573 4509 B7
900 GlsC 77565 4509 D6
900 KMAH 77565 4509 D6
900 LGCY 77565 4509 C7
FM-518 Deke Slayton Hwy
- LGCY 77565 4509 B7
- LGCY 77573 4509 B7
2200 LGCY 77573 4632 E1
2900 LGCY 77573 4633 A1
FM-518 N Friendswood Dr
- PRLD 77581 4505 B7
100 FRDW 77546 4505 B7
FM-518 S Friendswood Dr
100 FRDW 77546 4505 B7
500 FRDW 77546 4629 E4
2300 FRDW 77546 4630 A5
2600 LGCY 77573 4630 B6
FM-518 E Main St
100 LGCY 77573 4632 A3
FM-518 W Main St
100 LGCY 77573 4631 B4
FM-519
- TXCY 77590 4990 E3
- TXCY 77590 4991 A2
FM-519 Main St
10 LMQU 77568 4990 D3
10 TXCY 77590 4990 D3
2500 LMQU 77568 4989 B3
4000 HTCK 77563 4989 B3
6400 HTCK 77563 4988 E4
FM-521
3200 FBnC 77545 4499 C6
3700 FBnC 77545 4623 B1
4700 ARLA 77545 4623 B3
4700 ARLA 77583 4623 B1
4700 FBnC 77583 4623 B3
6600 ARLA 77583 4622 E7
6900 FBnC 77583 4622 E7
FM-521 Almeda Rd
- HOUS 77021 4102 E7
300 FBnC 77545 4372 E7
300 PRLD 77053 4372 E7
800 FBnC 77545 4499 E1
800 PRLD 77545 4499 E1
7000 HOUS 77030 4102 E7
7000 HOUS 77054 4102 E7
8500 HOUS 77054 4242 B7
10600 HOUS 77045 4242 D3
12300 HOUS 77045 4373 B1
13400 HOUS 77053 4373 B1
13700 HarC 77053 4373 A4
14300 HarC 77053 4372 E6
15200 HarC 77047 4372 E7
FM-521 Almeda Rd
15200 PRLD 77047 4372 E7
FM-525 Aldine Bender Rd
- HarC 77396 3546 E2
- HOUS 77396 3546 E2
10 HOUS 77037 3544 B1
10 HOUS 77060 3544 E1
400 HarC 77060 3544 E1
700 HarC 77060 3545 A1
700 HOUS 77060 3545 A1
800 HarC 77032 3545 E1
800 HarC 77039 3545 E1
800 HOUS 77032 3545 A1
2900 HarC 77032 3546 E2
3400 HOUS 77032 3546 A1
FM-525 Fallbrook Dr
- HOUS 77037 3544 B1
- HOUS 77038 3544 B1
- HOUS 77060 3544 B1
FM-525 Lee Rd
14200 HarC 77032 3546 E2
14200 HarC 77396 3546 E2
14500 HOUS 77396 3546 E1
FM-526 CE King Pkwy
- HarC 77044 3828 A1
- HarC 77049 3828 A1
FM-526 Federal Rd
700 HOUS 77015 3966 E2
900 HOUS 77015 3967 A2
FM-526 S Lake Houston Pkwy
5000 HOUS 77013 3827 E5
5000 HOUS 77013 3828 A4
5000 HOUS 77049 3828 A4
6700 HarC 77049 3828 A2
FM-526 Maxey Rd
10 HOUS 77013 3827 E6
600 HOUS 77013 3966 E1
700 HOUS 77015 3966 E1
FM-527 Mesa Dr
9400 HOUS 77028 3687 E7
9400 HOUS 77078 3687 E7
10900 HarC 77078 3687 E2
FM-528
1600 FRDW 77598 4630 D1
1600 HarC 77598 4630 C1
3200 FRDW 77546 4630 B1
3200 HarC 77546 4630 B1
4000 FRDW 77546 4629 E2
FM-528 Friendswood Rd
- FRDW 77546 4749 D3
1800 ALVN 77511 4749 C6
FM-528 NASA Pkwy
1900 HOUS 77058 4508 A4
1900 NSUB 77058 4508 A4
3700 ELGO 77586 4509 A2
3700 SEBK 77586 4509 A2
FM-528 W NASA Pkwy
- FRDW 77598 4630 E1
- WEBS 77598 4507 A7
1400 HarC 77598 4630 A2
1400 HarC 77598 4631 A1
1400 LGCY 77598 4630 A2
1400 WEBS 77598 4630 A2
1400 WEBS 77598 4631 A1
FM-528 W NASA Rd 1
- WEBS 77598 4507 C6
FM-528 NASA Road 1
2200 SEBK 77586 4509 C3
FM-528 E Parkwood Av
100 FRDW 77546 4629 D3
FM-528 W Parkwood Av
100 FRDW 77546 4629 B5
2500 FRDW 77546 4749 C6
3200 ALVN 77511 4749 D3
FM 529
- HarC 77449 3676 B2
FM-529
17600 HarC 77084 3677 E2
17600 HarC 77095 3677 E2
17700 HarC 77433 3677 D2
17700 HarC 77449 3677 D2
FM-529 Freeman Rd
- HarC 77084 3677 E2
- HarC 77449 3675 E2
- HarC 77493 3675 A2
18000 HarC 77095 3677 E2
18000 HarC 77433 3677 B2
18000 HarC 77449 3677 B2
20500 HarC 77433 3676 A2
20500 HarC 77449 3676 A2
FM-529 Spencer Rd
10900 HarC 77040 3680 C2
10900 HarC 77041 3680 B2
10900 JRSV 77040 3680 C2
11300 JRSV 77041 3680 A2
12100 HarC 77041 3679 D2
13200 HarC 77095 3679 B2
14100 HarC 77084 3679 A2
15000 HarC 77084 3678 D2
15000 HarC 77095 3678 B2
17400 HarC 77084 3677 E2
17400 HarC 77095 3677 E2
FM-565
300 BYTN 77520 3974 B1
300 CmbC 77520 3974 C1
2300 CmbC 77520 3835 E7
FM-565 Cove Rd
100 MTBL 77520 3696 E5
FM-646
- DKSN 77510 4871 A4
- DKSN 77539 4871 A4
- GlsC 77510 4987 B2
- LGCY 77539 4632 C7
- LGCY 77539 4633 E5
- LGCY 77539 4634 A5
- LGCY 77573 4632 C7
- LGCY 77573 4633 A5
- STFE 77510 4987 B2
- TXCY 77539 4633 E5
- TXCY 77539 4634 A5
1600 GlsC 77510 4871 A4
1600 GlsC 77539 4871 A4
1800 LGCY 77539 4753 B1
1800 LGCY 77573 4753 B1
1900 LGCY 77539 4752 E3
2000 STFE 77510 4871 A2
5600 DKSN 77539 4753 A6
FM-646 Avenue M
4200 STFE 77510 4871 A7
4500 STFE 77510 4987 A1
FM-646 E Bayshore Dr
900 GlsC 77539 4636 A5
2000 GlsC 77539 4635 E4
2700 TXCY 77539 4635 B4
FM-646 W Bayshore Dr
4600 GlsC 77518 4634 E3
4800 GlsC 77518 4635 A3
FM-646 W Bayshore Dr
5200 TXCY 77518 4635 A3
5600 GlsC 77539 4635 B3
FM-646 Grand Av
100 GlsC 77518 4634 D3
1000 GlsC 77539 4634 C4
1200 TXCY 77539 4634 C4
FM-646 Main St
5000 STFE 77510 4987 B1
FM-723
4700 FBnC 77469 4232 D7
FM-723 Houston St
300 RSBG 77471 4490 D3
FM-723 Rosenberg Foster Rd
- RSBG 77471 4490 D3
200 FBnC 77471 4490 D1
FM-723 Spring Green Rd
- FBnC 77494 4092 D6
6700 FBnC 77469 4232 D6
9200 FBnC 77469 4092 D6
FM-762
7000 FBnC 77469 4493 B7
7000 RSBG 77469 4493 B7
FM-762 SPUR S 2nd St
300 RHMD 77469 4491 E1
500 RHMD 77469 4492 A1
FM-762 S 11th St
300 RHMD 77469 4491 E2
FM-762 SPUR Austin St
200 RHMD 77469 4492 A1
400 RHMD 77469 4491 E1
FM-762 Thompson Rd
- RHMD 77469 4492 A4
900 RHMD 77469 4491 E2
2100 FBnC 77469 4491 E3
3700 FBnC 77469 4492 E6
5200 FBnC 77469 4493 A7
FM-762 Thompsons Rd
6100 FBnC 77469 4493 B7
FM-830
- MtgC 77304 2237 A1
- PNVL 77304 2237 B1
1000 CNRO 77303 2237 D1
1000 CNRO 77304 2237 A1
1000 CNRO 77378 2237 A1
1000 MtgC 77378 2237 A1
9800 MtgC 77304 2236 E1
9800 MtgC 77318 2236 E1
9800 MtgC 77318 2237 A1
9800 PNVL 77318 2237 A1
FM-830 Seven Coves Rd
1000 CNRO 77304 2237 B1
1000 MtgC 77378 2237 B1
1000 PNVL 77304 2237 B1
1000 PNVL 77318 2237 B1
9700 MtgC 77304 2237 A1
9700 MtgC 77318 2237 A1
FM-865 Cullen Blvd
100 HarC 77047 4374 D3
100 HarC 77584 4374 D7
100 HOUS 77047 4374 D3
100 PRLD 77581 4374 D7
100 PRLD 77584 4374 D7
500 PRLD 77581 4501 E2
500 PRLD 77584 4501 E2
5700 HOUS 77021 4103 D7
7200 HOUS 77033 4103 D7
7200 HOUS 77051 4103 D7
7300 HOUS 77033 4243 D1
7300 HOUS 77051 4243 D1
10100 HOUS 77047 4243 D7
10100 HOUS 77048 4243 D7
11800 HOUS 77048 4374 D7
13900 HarC 77048 4374 D4
FM-1008 Atascocita Rd
1700 HarC 77336 3266 E5
1700 HarC 77336 3267 C5
1700 HarC 77532 3266 E5
1700 HarC 77532 3267 C5
FM 1010
- PLMG 77327 2684 D4
FM-1010
- LbyC 77327 2538 E1
- LbyC 77327 2684 D1
- PLMG 77327 2684 D2
FM-1092
- FBnC 77477 4369 D3
- MSCY 77459 4369 D4
- MSCY 77477 4369 D3
- STAF 77477 4369 D1
FM-1092 Murphy Rd
12100 HarC 77031 4238 D6
12100 STAF 77477 4238 D6
13200 STAF 77477 4369 D1
FM-1092 Stafford Dewalt Rd
1000 FBnC 77477 4369 D4
1000 MSCY 77459 4369 D5
1000 MSCY 77477 4369 D4
3000 MSCY 77459 4496 D1
FM-1092 Wilcrest Dr
11800 HOUS 77031 4238 D7
11900 HarC 77031 4238 D5
FM-1093 Westheimer Rd
- FBnC 77469 4095 D4
4800 HOUS 77027 3961 A7
4800 HOUS 77056 3961 A7
5100 HOUS 77056 3960 E7
5700 HOUS 77057 3960 D7
6500 HOUS 77063 3960 A7
7900 HOUS 77063 3959 E7
9700 HOUS 77042 3959 A7
10000 HOUS 77042 3958 B7
11100 HOUS 77077 3958 B7
11100 HOUS 77082 3958 C7
11900 HOUS 77077 3957 E7
11900 HOUS 77082 3957 E7
13100 HarC 77082 3957 B7
13200 HarC 77077 3957 B7
13700 HOUS 77077 3956 E7
13700 HOUS 77082 3956 E7
14700 HOUS 77082 4096 A3
15400 HarC 77082 4096 C1
16200 HarC 77082 4095 E3
16200 HOUS 77082 4095 E3
16800 HOUS 77450 4095 D4
17000 HOUS 77469 4095 D4
FM-1093 Westpark Tollway
24000 FBnC 77469 4093 A6
24000 FBnC 77494 4093 A6
FM-1098
- PRVW 77445 2955 B6
- PRVW 77445 3100 B1
- WlrC 77445 2955 B5
FM-1098 Owens Rd
- PRVW 77445 3100 B1
FM-1098 University Dr
100 PRVW 77445 3100 C1
FM-1098 Williams St
- PRVW 77445 3100 A1
FM-1128 Manvel Rd
2100 PRLD 77581 4502 B4
2100 PRLD 77584 4502 B6
3200 BzaC 77584 4502 B6
FM-1128 Masters Rd
- BzaC 77584 4626 B2
- PRLD 77584 4626 B2
4600 MNVL 77578 4626 A4
4600 MNVL 77584 4626 B3
5400 MNVL 77578 4625 E7
6700 MNVL 77578 4746 D2
FM-1128 N Masters Rd
4300 BzaC 77584 4626 B2
4300 MNVL 77584 4626 B2
4300 PRLD 77584 4626 B2
FM-1266
- LGCY 77573 4633 A4
FM-1266 Dickinson Av
- LGCY 77573 4633 A5
900 GlsC 77539 4633 A6
900 LGCY 77539 4633 A5
2400 DKSN 77539 4633 A7
2700 DKSN 77539 4754 A1
FM-1266 League City Pkwy
- LGCY 77565 4633 A7
- LGCY 77573 4633 B3
FM-1266 Tuscan Lakes Blvd
- LGCY 77539 4633 A5
- LGCY 77573 4633 A5
FM-1314
19800 MtgC 77357 2825 D5
20800 MtgC 77365 2826 A7
21200 MtgC 77365 2972 A1
23400 MtgC 77365 2973 A5
FM-1314 Conroe Porter Rd
11600 CNRO 77301 2530 E2
11600 CNRO 77302 2530 E2
11600 MtgC 77302 2530 E2
11700 CNRO 77301 2531 A3
11700 CNRO 77302 2531 A3
11700 MtgC 77302 2531 C5
14500 MtgC 77302 2677 E1
14900 MtgC 77302 2678 B2
17900 MtgC 77365 2825 A1
19200 MtgC 77365 2825 C3
FM-1314 Porter Rd
100 CNRO 77301 2384 D7
1800 CNRO 77301 2530 E2
FM-1405 W Bay Rd
- BYTN 77520 3974 B7
- CmbC 77520 3974 D4
- CmbC 77520 4114 B2
8500 BYTN 77520 4114 B6
9000 CmbC 77520 4254 B1
FM-1413
- LbyC 77535 3269 E7
- LbyC 77535 3413 E1
FM-1462
900 ALVN 77511 4867 A5
2000 ALVN 77511 4866 D5
10800 BzaC 77511 4866 C6
FM-1462 Parker-Davis School Rd
- BzaC 77511 4866 C6
FM-1463
100 KATY 77493 3952 B1
100 KATY 77494 3952 A3
1000 FBnC 77494 3952 A3
1400 FBnC 77494 3951 D7
FM-1464
6500 FBnC 77082 4095 D4
6500 FBnC 77083 4095 D7
6500 FBnC 77469 4095 D7
8600 FBnC 77083 4235 E3
8600 FBnC 77469 4235 E3
9500 FBnC 77478 4235 E2
13000 FBnC 77469 4366 E1
13000 FBnC 77478 4366 E1
FM-1464 S Barker Cypress Rd
- FBnC 77082 4095 D4
- FBnC 77083 4095 D4
- FBnC 77469 4095 D4
- HOUS 77082 4095 D4
- HOUS 77469 4095 D4
FM-1484
10300 CNRO 77303 2239 A5
10300 MtgC 77303 2239 A4
FM-1484 N 10th St
200 CNRO 77301 2384 B4
FM-1484 Airport Rd
1100 CNRO 77301 2384 D1
2200 CNRO 77303 2384 D1
2300 MtgC 77303 2384 D1
2600 CNRO 77303 2238 E6
2600 MtgC 77303 2238 E6
10100 CNRO 77303 2239 A5
10200 MtgC 77303 2239 A5
FM-1485
- CTSH 77303 2385 E4
- HarC 77336 2830 C7
1000 CTSH 77301 2385 E4
1000 CTSH 77306 2385 E4
1000 MtgC 77301 2385 C3
1000 MtgC 77306 2385 C3
11000 MtgC 77306 2532 E1
11200 MtgC 77306 2533 D6
14300 MtgC 77306 2679 E1
14500 MtgC 77302 2679 E1
14800 MtgC 77302 2680 E6
14800 MtgC 77306 2680 E6
16600 MtgC 77357 2680 C5
17300 MtgC 77357 2681 A7
17600 MtgC 77357 2827 E7
23200 MtgC 77357 2828 A6
25300 MtgC 77357 2829 E6
28100 MtgC 77357 2830 B7
FM-1485 Old TX-105 E
- CNRO 77301 2385 B3
- CNRO 77303 2385 B3
- CTSH 77301 2385 C3
- CTSH 77303 2385 B3
FM-1486
100 MtgC 77354 2668 D2
1400 MtgC 77316 2668 D2
FM-1488
- CNRO 77384 2676 A1
- CNRO 77385 2676 A1
- HMPD 77445 2953 C7
- HMPD 77445 2954 A5
- MtgC 77355 2813 E1
- MtgC 77385 2676 A1
- WlrC 77445 2953 E6
- WlrC 77445 2954 C4
FM-1488
- WlrC 77445 2955 E2
- WlrC 77445 2956 A1
- WlrC 77447 2813 E1
3300 WDLD 77382 2674 D2
FM 1488 Rd
14400 MtgC 77354 2670 C3
FM-1488 Magnolia Blvd
800 MAGA 77355 2669 A5
FM-1488 Magnolia Pkwy
2200 MAGA 77354 2669 E3
2400 MtgC 77354 2669 C4
18700 MAGA 77355 2669 A5
18800 MAGA 77355 2668 E6
19000 MtgC 77355 2668 C7
20900 MtgC 77355 2814 B1
21500 MtgC 77355 2813 A2
21800 WlrC 77447 2813 A2
FM-1640
1700 RHMD 77469 4491 E4
1700 RSBG 77469 4491 E4
1700 RSBG 77471 4491 E4
FM-1640 Avenue I
800 RSBG 77471 4490 D4
2600 RSBG 77471 4491 A4
4900 RSBG 77469 4491 D4
5000 RHMD 77469 4491 D4
FM-1640 BF Terry Blvd
5300 FBnC 77469 4491 E4
5300 RHMD 77469 4491 E4
FM-1736
- WlrC 77445 2952 B2
FM-1764
- GlsC 77510 4871 D5
- GlsC 77510 4872 A5
- LMQU 77510 4872 A5
- LMQU 77568 4872 B5
- STFE 77510 4870 D6
- STFE 77510 4871 D5
- STFE 77517 4870 D5
- TXCY 77591 4872 C4
FM-1764 9th Av N
600 TXCY 77590 4875 D5
FM-1764 Emmett F Lowry Expwy
- TXCY - 4872 C3
- TXCY - 4873 A4
- TXCY - 4874 C4
FM-1764 Palmer Hwy
2100 TXCY 77590 4875 A5
3200 TXCY 77590 4874 E4
FM 1765
3500 TXCY 77590 4874 C7
FM-1765
- LMQU 77568 4872 D7
- LMQU 77568 4873 A7
- LMQU 77568 4874 C7
- TXCY 77591 4873 B7
- TXCY 77591 4874 C7
3400 TXCY 77590 4874 A7
FM-1765 5th Av S
3500 TXCY 77590 4874 C7
FM-1765 Texas Av
10 TXCY 77590 4875 A6
100 LMQU 77568 4874 C7
100 TXCY 77591 4874 C7
1900 LMQU 77568 4873 B7
1900 TXCY 77591 4873 B7
2500 TXCY 77590 4874 E6
FM-1774
27200 MtgC 77362 2816 D3
40900 MAGA 77354 2668 E5
40900 MAGA 77354 2669 A5
40900 MtgC 77354 2668 E5
FM 1774 Rd
37100 MtgC 77355 2816 A2
FM-1774 Magnolia Blvd
200 MAGA 77355 2669 A5
FM-1774 S Magnolia Blvd
10 MAGA 77355 2669 B6
100 MtgC 77355 2669 B6
FM-1876 Eldridge Rd
- HOUS 77478 4237 B6
100 SGLD 77478 4368 B1
900 SGLD 77478 4237 B6
2400 FBnC 77478 4237 B6
FM-1876 Synott Rd
6800 HOUS 77072 4097 C5
6800 HOUS 77083 4097 C5
7800 HarC 77072 4097 C6
7800 HarC 77083 4097 C6
8700 HarC 77072 4237 C1
8700 HarC 77083 4237 C1
9300 HarC 77099 4237 C1
9600 HOUS 77099 4237 C2
9900 HOUS 77478 4237 C2
10400 SGLD 77478 4237 B4
FM-1887
- HMPD 77445 3098 B3
- WlrC 77445 3098 B3
- WlrC 77445 3243 A7
FM-1887 11th St
- HMPD 77445 2953 B7
- HMPD 77445 3098 B1
FM-1942
1700 HarC 77532 3693 E2
2700 HarC 77532 3694 B5
4800 HarC 77521 3694 C5
FM-1942 Crosby Rd
100 HarC 77532 3692 D1
FM-1942 Crosby Barbers Hill Rd
5300 HarC 77521 3694 D6
6200 HarC 77521 3695 C5
7100 CmbC 77520 3695 C5
7500 CmbC 77520 3696 A4
9500 MTBL 77520 3696 B4
FM-1942 Crosby Cedar Bayou Rd
500 HarC 77532 3692 D1
600 HarC 77532 3693 A1
FM-1959
100 HOUS 77034 4378 E5
100 HOUS 77598 4378 E5
FM-1959 Dixie Farm Rd
- FRDW 77089 4505 C1
- HarC 77089 4505 A3
- HOUS 77089 4505 A3
- HOUS 77546 4505 E1
300 HOUS 77034 4378 E5
1000 HOUS 77598 4378 E6
1100 HOUS 77089 4378 D7
1100 HOUS 77546 4378 D7
2500 FRDW 77546 4505 C2
2500 HarC 77546 4505 C2
2500 PRLD 77089 4505 A3
2800 PRLD 77581 4505 A3
FM-1960
- HarC 77066 3400
- HarC 77069 3400
- HOUS 77084 3817
10 HarC 77073 3258
10 HarC 77090 3258
10 HOUS 77090 3258
400 HarC 77073 3259
2100 HarC 77338 3263
2300 HOUS 77338 3263
2400 HOUS 77073 3259
3100 HOUS 77073 3260
3100 HOUS 77338 3260
3700 HarC 77014 3257
3700 HarC 77068 3257
3700 HarC 77338 3264
3700 HarC 77346 3264
4400 HarC 77014 3401
4400 HarC 77066 3401
4400 HarC 77068 3401
4400 HarC 77069 3401
5600 HarC 77338 3260
5600 HarC 77338 3261
5600 HOUS 77338 3261
6800 HarC 77346 3265
7300 HOUS 77064 3400
7300 HOUS 77066 3400
7300 HOUS 77069 3400
7300 HOUS 77070 3400
8200 HOUS 77064 3399
8200 HOUS 77070 3399
8600 HarC 77064 3399
8600 HarC 77070 3399
8800 HOUS 77336 3265
9900 HarC 77064 3540
9900 HarC 77070 3540
10600 HOUS 77336 3266
10900 HarC 77065 3540
11300 HarC 77065 3539
11600 HarC 77336 3266
12500 HarC 77336 3267
13000 HarC 77336 3122
14400 LbyC 77535 3122
FM-1960 W
- HOUS 77070 3400
FM-1960 1st St E
200 HMBL 77338 3262
1100 HMBL 77338 3263
1700 HarC 77338 3263
FM-1960 W 1st St
100 HMBL 77338 3262
FM-1960 Bammel Rd
- HarC 77090 3258
- HOUS 77014 3258
- HOUS 77068 3258
- HOUS 77090 3258
2300 HOUS 77014 3257
2300 HOUS 77068 3257
2400 HarC 77014 3257
2400 HarC 77068 3257
FM-1960 Humble Westfield Rd
4500 HarC 77338 3260
4500 HOUS 77338 3260
7300 HarC 77338 3261
7300 HOUS 77338 3261
9600 HMBL 77338 3262
9600 HOUS 77338 3262
FM-1960 BUS Humble Westfld Rd
8000 HarC 77338 3261
8000 HOUS 77338 3261
8600 HarC 77338 3262
8900 HOUS 77338 3262
9100 HMBL 77338 3262
FM-1960A BUS Humble Westfld Rd
- HMBL 77338 3262
- HOUS 77338 3262
8000 HarC 77338 3261
8000 HOUS 77338 3261
FM-2004
- HTCK 77563 4872
- HTCK 77563 4987
- HTCK 77563 4988
- LMQU 77568 4872
- LMQU 77568 4988
- TXCY 77539 4754
- TXCY 77591 4754
- TXCY 77591 4872
FM-2090
- PLMG 77327 2684
15800 MtgC 77302 2533
15800 MtgC 77306 2533
17600 MtgC 77306 2534
20200 MtgC 77372 2534
23400 MtgC 77372 2535
23400 MtgC 77372 2536
24700 MtgC 77372 2682
24700 SPLD 77372 2682
25400 SPLD 77372 2683
26600 MtgC 77372 2683
27400 MtgC 77372 2684
28700 LbyC 77327 2684
FM-2094 E Main St
2200 LGCY 77573 4632
2400 LGCY 77573 4508
FM-2094 Marina Bay Dr
200 GlsC 77565 4509
200 KMAH 77565 4509
600 CRLS 77565 4509
1200 LGCY 77565 4509
1200 LGCY 77573 4509
2500 LGCY 77573 4508
3000 LGCY 77565 4508
FM-2100
- HarC 77532 3552
FM-2100 Avenue B
5200 HarC 77532 3552
FM-2100 Crosby Huffman Rd
6100 HarC 77532 3552
16900 HarC 77532 3411
20700 HarC 77532 3410
21300 HarC 77532 3266
24300 HarC 77336 3267
24700 HarC 77336 3266
26000 HarC 77336 3122
26600 HarC 77336 3121
26900 HOUS 77336 3121
FM-2100 Crosby Lynchburg Rd
100 HarC 77520 3831
100 HarC 77562 3831
200 HarC 77520 3970
600 HOUS 77520 3970
1000 HOUS 77571 3970
13100 HarC 77532 3692
13600 HarC 77532 3552

STREET Block City ZIP Map# Grid

FM-2100 N Crosby Lynchburg Rd
100 HarC 77562 3831 D1
1200 HarC 77562 3692 D7
10500 HarC 77532 3692 D7
FM-2100 Huffman New Caney Rd
29800 HarC 77336 2976 C1
FM-2100 N Main St
5700 HarC 77532 3552 C4
FM-2100 S Main St
100 HarC 77562 3831 D7
FM-2218
- PLEK 77469 4614 E6
- PLEK 77471 4614 E7
- RHMD 77469 4491 E4
2600 RSBG 77469 4491 C7
2600 RSBG 77471 4491 C7
2700 RSBG 77469 4615 C1
2700 RSBG 77471 4615 C1
3200 FBnC 77469 4615 A5
5500 PLEK 77469 4615 A5
FM-2218 BF Terry Blvd
1500 FBnC 77471 4491 E4
1500 RHMD 77471 4491 E4
1500 RSBG 77469 4491 E5
1500 RSBG 77471 4491 D6
5300 FBnC 77469 4491 E4
5300 RHMD 77469 4491 E4
FM-2234 McHard Rd
- MSCY 77489 4497 D1
- PRLD 77053 4372 E7
- PRLD 77053 4499 E1
- PRLD 77053 4500 A1
- PRLD 77545 4372 E7
- PRLD 77545 4499 E1
- PRLD 77545 4500 A1
3700 HOUS 77489 4497 E1
4100 FBnC 77489 4497 E1
4100 FBnC 77545 4497 E1
4100 FBnC 77545 4498 A1
4100 HOUS 77489 4498 A1
4100 HOUS 77545 4498 A1
5000 FBnC 77053 4498 A1
5000 HOUS 77053 4498 A1
6500 FBnC 77053 4499 B1
6500 HOUS 77053 4499 B1
8200 FBnC 77053 4372 E7
8600 FBnC 77545 4372 E7
10800 BzaC 77584 4500 E1
11700 PRLD 77584 4500 C1
FM-2234 Shadow Creek Pkwy
- PRLD 77053 4500 A1
- PRLD 77545 4500 A1
- PRLD 77584 4500 E1
FM-2234 Texas Pkwy
200 MSCY 77489 4370 C6
700 STAF 77477 4370 C3
700 STAF 77489 4370 C3
1400 MSCY 77477 4370 C4
3000 MSCY 77489 4497 D1
3400 HOUS 77489 4497 D1
FM-2351 Choate Rd
3000 HOUS 77546 4505 E3
3000 HOUS 77546 4506 B1
3900 FRDW 77546 4505 C5
3900 HarC 77546 4505 E4
FM-2351 Clear Lake City Blvd
- HOUS 77546 4506 B2
100 HOUS 77062 4379 C7
100 HOUS 77598 4379 C7
100 HOUS 77598 4506 B1
FM-2351 Donaldson Rd
200 BzaC 77511 4628 D3
FM-2351 E Edgewood Dr
100 FRDW 77546 4505 B7
FM-2351 W Edgewood Dr
100 FRDW 77546 4505 B7
400 FRDW 77546 4629 A1
900 FRDW 77546 4628 E2
1100 PRLD 77581 4628 E2
FM-2351 Hastings Rd
700 BzaC 77511 4628 C4
700 BzaC 77581 4628 C4
700 PRLD 77511 4628 C4
700 PRLD 77581 4628 C4
1200 BzaC 77546 4628 D3
2100 FRDW 77546 4628 E2
FM-2403
3100 ALVN 77511 4867 B6
3100 BzaC 77511 4867 B7
FM-2432
10200 MtgC 77303 2239 A1
FM-2432 Willis Waukegan Rd
10900 MtgC 77303 2239 D3
FM-2553 Scarsdale Blvd
13100 HOUS 77034 4378 C5
FM-2759 Crabb River Rd
- FBnC 77469 4493 D3
- SGLD 77469 4493 C5
- SGLD 77479 4493 C5
700 FBnC 77479 4493 C6
FM-2759 Thompsons Rd
7100 FBnC 77469 4493 E7
8300 FBnC 77469 4494 A7
FM-2854
2100 CNRO 77304 2382 E5
6200 MtgC 77304 2382 E5
FM-2854 Old Montgomery Rd
600 CNRO 77301 2383 E5
1100 CNRO 77303 2383 A5
2000 CNRO 77304 2382 E5
FM-2920
- HarC 77375 2964 E6
- HarC 77375 2965 A7
- HarC 77388 3112 E3
- HarC 77388 3113 A3
- TMBL 77375 2964 E6
6000 HarC 77379 3111 A3
6000 HarC 77388 3111 E3
7300 HarC 77379 3110 E3
FM-2920 E Main St
100 TMBL 77375 2964 E6
1000 HarC 77375 2964 E6
FM-2920 W Main St
- TMBL 77377 3108 E1
100 TMBL 77375 2964 B7
1200 TMBL 77375 3109 A1
1300 TMBL 77375 3108 E1
FM-2920 Spring Cypress Rd
1500 HarC 77388 3113 C3
FM-2920 Stuebner Airline Rd
8400 HarC 77379 3110 E3
8600 HarC 77375 3110 B1
9800 HarC 77375 2965 B7
FM-2920 Waller Tomball Rd
- HarC 77447 3103 A4
14000 HarC 77377 3108 E1
14000 TMBL 77375 3108 E1
14000 TMBL 77377 3108 E1
16300 HarC 77447 3107 D2
18600 HarC 77377 3106 E2
19100 WALR 77484 3102 B6
20300 HarC 77447 3106 A2
21200 HarC 77447 3105 A4
24900 HarC 77447 3104 E4
27900 HarC 77484 3103 C4
29000 HarC 77484 3102 B6
FM-2977
- FBnC 77469 4492 B7
- FBnC 77469 4616 A6
- RSBG 77469 4492 B7
- RSBG 77469 4616 A6
FM-2977 Minonite Rd
3500 FBnC 77469 4616 A6
FM-2978
- HarC 77375 2964 E2
26000 MtgC 77354 2818 D4
26000 MtgC 77354 2964 D1
30200 WDLD 77354 2818 E1
31200 MtgC 77382 2673 B5
31200 WDLD 77354 2673 B6
FM-2978 Hufsmith Kohrville Rd
23200 HarC 77375 2964 E6
23200 TMBL 77375 2964 E6
FM-3005 San Luis Pass Rd
- GLSN 77554 5220 D7
- GLSN 77554 5333 B1
- GLSN 77554 5547 E3
- GLSN 77554 5548 D1
10300 GLSN 77554 5221 B5
12200 GLSN 77554 5442 A2
14900 GLSN 77554 5332 E2
16700 GLSN 77554 5331 E7
16700 JMAB 77554 5331 E7
16700 JMAB 77554 5332 A6
21200 GLSN 77554 5441 D4
23200 GLSN 77554 5440 E7
FM-3005 Seawall Blvd
300 GLSN 77550 5109 D3
4100 GLSN 77550 5108 E7
4100 GLSN 77551 5108 E7
5300 GLSN 77551 5222 D1
7900 GLSN 77554 5222 D1
8500 GLSN 77554 5221 E3
FM-3005 Termini Rd
- GLSN 77554 5441 A6
- GLSN 77554 5442 A2
FM-3083
- CNRO 77304 2382 E2
- CNRO 77304 2383 A1
100 CNRO 77301 2385 A4
11600 MtgC 77301 2385 C6
11700 MtgC 77302 2385 D6
11900 MtgC 77306 2385 E7
12500 MtgC 77302 2531 B1
12500 MtgC 77306 2531 E1
12700 MtgC 77302 2532 D5
14800 MtgC 77306 2532 E5
15500 MtgC 77302 2533 B7
15500 MtgC 77306 2533 B7
16600 MtgC 77302 2679 C1
16600 MtgC 77306 2679 C1
FM-3083 Beach Airport Rd
100 CNRO 77301 2384 D1
1500 CNRO 77303 2384 D1
2500 MtgC 77303 2384 D1
FM-3083 Teas Rd
100 CNRO 77303 2238 C7
300 MtgC 77303 2238 D7
700 CNRO 77303 2237 E7
1000 CNRO 77301 2384 D1
1000 CNRO 77303 2384 D1
1000 MtgC 77303 2384 D1
1500 CNRO 77304 2237 E7
FM-3083 Tink Calfee Rd
- CNRO 77304 2382 E2
FM-3155 Preston St
1700 RHMD 77469 4491 D1
FM-3345 Cartwright Rd
1600 MSCY 77489 4370 B7
2400 MSCY 77459 4370 B7
3200 MSCY 77459 4369 E7
FM-3346
- PNIS 77445 3098 D6
- PNIS 77445 3099 A6
- WlrC 77445 3097 E6
- WlrC 77445 3098 D6
FM-3360
- CmbC 77520 3696 E2
- MTBL 77520 3696 E2
FM-3436
- TXCY 77539 4634 A6
- TXCY 77539 4755 A1
Fogle Ln
9800 HTCK 77563 4988 B4
Fogle St
4000 HOUS 77026 3825 B5
Foley Rd
200 HarC 77532 3410 C6
200 HarC 77532 3411 A5
2800 HarC 77532 3409 E6
Foley St
- HOUS 77003 3964 B4
1500 HOUS 77055 3820 E6
1500 HOUS 77080 3820 E6
E Foley St
100 ALVN 77511 4867 C2
W Foley St
700 ALVN 77511 4867 B2
Foley Park Ct
18200 HarC 77433 3537 D7
Folger St
2700 HOUS 77093 3685 E4
2700 HOUS 77093 3686 A4
Foliage Green Ln
2500 HOUS 77339 3119 A3
Folk Crest Ln
400 LGCY 77539 4753 A4
Folkcrest Wy
12500 STAF 77477 4239 A7
Folkestone Ln
7700 HOUS 77075 4376 C3
Folkglen Ct
12800 HOUS 77034 4378 C2
Folklore Wy
12500 HOUS 77031 4239 A7
12500 STAF 77477 4239 A7
Folknoll Dr
9700 STAF 77477 4239 A7
Folkway Dr
100 HarC 77060 3403 B5
Followfield Ln
13000 HOUS 77085 4240 C7
13100 HOUS 77085 4371 C2
Folly Fields Dr
19900 HarC 77433 3251 D6
Folly Point Dr
18000 HarC 77429 3252 C7
Folsom Dr
16900 HarC 77049 3690 E4
17100 HarC 77049 3691 A4
Folsom Tr
- HOUS 77060 3544 A1
Foltin Memorial Dr
22500 MtgC 77447 2960 C6
Folwell Ln
300 BKHV 77024 3959 C4
Fonda Dr
300 HOUS 77060 3544 D2
Fonda St
11100 HOUS 77035 4240 E4
Fondness Park Dr
16800 HarC 77379 3256 B3
E Fondren Cir
15300 MSCY 77071 4239 C5
W Fondren Cir
15400 MSCY 77071 4239 D7
Fondren Rd
2400 HOUS 77063 3959 D7
2400 PNPV 77063 3959 D6
2800 HOUS 77063 4099 D4
5600 HOUS 77036 4099 D4
7200 HOUS 77074 4099 D5
8200 HOUS 77074 4100 A7
8800 HOUS 77074 4240 A3
9300 HOUS 77071 4240 A2
9300 HOUS 77096 4240 A2
11100 HOUS 77035 4240 A4
12500 MSCY 77071 4240 A6
12900 HOUS 77035 4371 A1
12900 MSCY 77071 4371 A1
13000 HOUS 77071 4371 A1
13000 MSCY 77035 4371 A2
13100 HOUS 77085 4371 A2
14400 HOUS 77489 4371 A6
14400 MSCY 77489 4371 A3
Fondren St
3000 LPRT 77571 4382 E1
Fondren Bend Dr
12000 HOUS 77071 4239 B6
Fondren Grove Cir
12700 MSCY 77071 4239 A7
Fondren Grove Dr
16100 MSCY 77071 4239 C7
16100 MSCY 77071 4370 C1
Fondren Lake Dr
8100 HOUS 77071 4239 D6
Fondren Meadow Dr
- HOUS 77071 4239 C5
Fondren Pl Dr
12000 HOUS 77071 4239 C6
Fondren Village Dr
8700 HOUS 77071 4239 B6
Fones Rd
21200 HarC 77377 3107 B2
Fonmeadow Blvd
- HOUS 77035 4240 B7
- MSCY 77071 4239 E7
- MSCY 77071 4240 A7
Fonmeadow Dr
14200 HOUS 77035 4240 A7
14600 MSCY 77071 4240 A7
Fontainbleu St
8600 HOUS 77024 3961 B1
Fontaine Dr
3200 BzaC 77584 4501 C7
Fontaine Ln
300 HarC 77532 3692 E1
700 HarC 77015 3828 B7
Fontaine St
1000 BzaC 77511 4749 E5
Fontana
- HarC 77377 3107 A4
Fontana Dr
2900 HOUS 77043 3819 E2
5400 FBnC 77479 4366 E6
Fontana St
21200 HarC 77377 3107 B3
Fontana Wy
- LGCY 77573 4632 A7
Fontell Dr
- PASD 77503 4249 A3
- PASD 77536 4249 A3
Fontenelle Dr
5500 HOUS 77035 4240 C6
Fonthill Dr
8000 HarC 77379 3256 B5
Fontinot St
1300 HOUS 77020 3964 C1
1800 HOUS 77026 3825 C7
Fonvilla St
- HOUS 77074 4099 E7
7000 HOUS 77074 4100 A7
Fonville Dr
9600 HOUS 77075 4377 B2
10100 HOUS 77089 4377 D3
Foolish Pleasure Ct
3700 FBnC 77469 4364 E3
Foote St
2700 HOUS 77020 3963 C2
Foothill St
3000 HOUS 77092 3822 B3
Forbes Rd
11000 HOUS 77075 4376 B4
Forbesbury Dr
3900 HarC 77084 3816 E2
Forbidden Gdns
- HarC 77493 3814 C5
Force St
6200 HOUS 77020 3825 E7
7100 HOUS 77020 3826 A7
13100 HOUS 77015 3828 C7
13700 HarC 77015 3828 D7
14100 HarC 77015 3829 A7
Ford
1400 HOUS 77017 4106 D3
1400 PASD 77506 4106 D3
Ford Rd
1200 FBnC 77477 4369 E5
22200 MtgC 77365 2973 C6
24600 HOUS 77339 3119 C1
24600 HOUS 77365 3119 C1
24600 MtgC 77365 3119 C1
25000 MtgC 77365 2974 B7
W Ford Rd
22000 MtgC 77365 2973 C6
Ford St
7800 HOUS 77012 4105 B1
Fordham Cir
2200 KATY 77493 3813 D5
Fordham St
5800 WUNP 77005 4102 A3
Fordham Park Ct
3800 PASD 77058 4380 E5
Fordingbridge Ct
9300 HarC 77379 3255 D4
Fordingbridge Dr
17000 HarC 77379 3255 D4
Ford Path Ct
24600 HarC 77373 3114 D3
Fordshire Dr
9100 HOUS 77025 4101 D7
9100 HOUS 77025 4241 D1
Forecastle Ct
500 HarC 77532 3552 B3
Forecastle St
16000 HarC 77532 3552 B3
Foredale St
9600 HOUS 77075 4377 B3
Foreland Ct
13300 HOUS 77077 3957 B6
Foreland Dr
1900 HOUS 77077 3957 B6
Forelock Wy
17100 HarC 77532 3551 D1
17100 HarC 77532 3552 A1
Foreman St
1200 LMQU 77568 4990 A2
9700 HOUS 77017 4106 B5
Foremast Dr
3500 GLSN 77554 5333 A1
Forenza Ct
10900 FBnC 77469 4232 E1
Forest Av
100 SRAC 77571 4382 E1
100 SRAC 77571 4383 A1
N Forest Blvd
100 HarC 77090 3258 D5
Forest Bnd
1200 FBnC 77479 4494 A6
1400 FBnC 77479 4493 E5
Forest Brk
1300 FBnC 77479 4493 E6
1300 FBnC 77479 4494 A5
Forest Cir
1100 HarC 77336 3121 E6
24900 WlrC 77447 2959 C1
Forest Cir E
- DKSN 77539 4753 E4
W Forest Cir
25700 HarC 77336 3121 E6
Forest Ct
23200 MtgC 77447 2960 C5
E Forest Ct
10 MtgC 77384 2528 A7
W Forest Ct
10 MtgC 77384 2528 A7
Forest Dr
19600 MtgC 77357 2829 B6
19900 HarC 77388 3112 D5
Forest Dr E
19600 MtgC 77357 2829 B5
Forest Dr W
19600 MtgC 77357 2829 B5
W Forest Dr
- HOUS 77043 3958 B4
- HOUS 77079 3958 A1
1200 HOUS 77043 3819 A7
Forest Ln
200 MtgC 77385 2822 C1
400 HOUS 77336 3266 C4
15100 MtgC 77306 2680 B2
25600 MtgC 77372 2537 A1
29600 TMBL 77375 2963 E6
E Forest Ln
100 HarC 77015 3829 A5
Forest Mdw
7000 MtgC 77354 2673 B3
Forest Rd
800 CRLS 77565 4509 C5
Forest St
500 HOUS 77011 3964 B6
Forest Tr
4700 MSCY 77459 4621 B3
5000 HarC 77521 3834 E7
23300 MtgC 77447 2960 B5
24100 MtgC 77365 2973 E7
Forest Wk
10 FBnC 77459 4621 B3
Forest Wy
1200 HOUS 77339 3118 C6
E Forest Wy
100 CNRO 77304 2383 B3
W Forest Wy
200 CNRO 77304 2383 B3
Forest Acres Dr
13100 HarC 77078 3548 A7
13500 HarC 77050 3548 B5
Forest Arbor Ct
8500 HarC 77095 3537 E6
Forestay Ct
18100 HarC 77532 3551 D2
Forestay Ln
17400 HarC 77521 3833 D4
Forest Bank Ln
2100 PRLD 77581 4503 C2
Forest Bark
800 HOUS 77067 3402 D4
Forest Bay Ct
800 HOUS 77062 4379 D7
Forest Bend Av
16100 FRDW 77546 4505 E7
16600 FRDW 77546 4629 D1
16600 FRDW 77546 4630 A1
Forest Bend Ct
2900 FBnC 77479 4494 A6
Forest Bend Ln
600 FRDW 77546 4505 C5
Forest Bend Creek Wy
18600 HarC 77379 3112 A7
Forest Birch Ct
4000 PASD 77059 4380 D5
Forest Bloom Ln
12800 HarC 77044 3689 B3
Forest Bluff Dr
3900 HOUS 77339 3119 A3
Forest Branch Blvd
- HarC 77014 3257 B7
- HarC 77014 3401 B1
- HarC 77068 3257 B7
Forest Breeze Ln
8100 HarC 77379 3256 A3
Forest Briar Dr
- FBnC 77083 4096 C7
Forest Bridge Wy
5300 HarC 77066 3401 A5
Forestbrook Dr
2900 HarC 77373 3114 E6
Forestburg Ct
25600 MtgC 77386 2968 E1
Forestburg Dr
900 HarC 77038 3543 C3
1000 MtgC 77386 2968 E1
1700 MtgC 77386 2969 A1
Forest Canyon Ct
5100 HarC 77066 3401 A2
5500 HarC 77066 3400 E3
Forest Canyon Ln
- FBnC 77494 3953 B6
Forest Cedars Dr
17900 HarC 77084 3678 A5
18000 HarC 77084 3677 E5
Forest Center
- HOUS 77339 3118 A4
E Forest Cir Ln
25700 HarC 77336 3121 E6
Forest City Dr
3500 HOUS 77339 3119 C5
Forest Cliff Ct
9000 CNRO 77302 2530 E4
Forest Colony Dr
21300 MtgC 77365 2973 B4
Forest Commons St
8100 HarC 77095 3538 E6
Forest Course Cir
10 HOUS 77339 3264 D1
Forest Course Wy
10 HOUS 77339 3264 E1
Forest Cove Ct
- DKSN 77539 4753 E4
Forest Cove Dr
- DKSN 77539 4753 E4
- TXCY 77539 4753 E5
10 HOUS 77339 3263 B1
1500 HOUS 77339 3118 B7
13300 HarC 77429 3398 D4
Forest Creek Dr
- LGCY 77573 4631 A4
4400 MSCY 77459 4369 B6
8900 HarC 77375 2965 C5
10400 MtgC 77318 2237 B1
10400 PNVL 77304 2237 B1
10400 PNVL 77318 2237 B1
Forest Creek Ln
2800 PRLD 77584 4500 A4
Forest Creek Farms Dr
15300 HarC 77429 3253 B5
Forestcrest Dr
23900 HarC 77389 2966 D5
Forest Cross Ln
7700 FBnC 77469 4095 D6
Forest Crossing Dr
9000 WDLD 77381 2821 B2
Forest Ct St
4800 BYTN 77521 3972 B3
Forest Dale Ln
9300 HOUS 77078 3688 A6
Forest Dawn Wy
7400 HarC 77095 3678 A1
7500 HarC 77095 3538 A7
Forest Deer Rd
18700 HarC 77084 3816 C1
Forest Dew Dr
18300 HarC 77449 3677 C3
Forest Edge Dr
- HarC 77067 3402 E5
- HOUS 77067 3402 E5
Forest Elms Dr
18300 HarC 77388 3258 A1
18400 HarC 77388 3113 A7
18800 HarC 77388 3112 E7
Forest Enclave Ln
14800 HarC 77068 3257 C6
Forester
- HOUS 77009 3962 E1
Forester Park Ln
- MtgC 77385 2823 C6
- MtgC 77386 2823 C6
Forest Estates Dr
- CNRO 77304 2383 B4
12000 HarC 77066 3401 A3
Forest Falls Ct
11100 HarC 77065 3539 B1
Forest Falls Dr
2000 HOUS 77345 3120 C5
Forest Fern Ct
1600 FBnC 77479 4494 A5
19300 HarC 77346 3264 C5
Forest Fern Dr
19500 HarC 77346 3264 C5
Forest Fir
800 HOUS 77067 3402 D4
Forest Forge Dr
18500 HarC 77433 3677 C1
Forest Garden Dr
1700 HOUS 77345 3120 A7
2000 HOUS 77345 3119 E6
Forest Gate Cir
8200 FBnC 77479 4494 A4
Forest Gate Dr
1800 FBnC 77479 4494 A4
2900 BYTN 77521 3973 E1
2900 HarC 77521 3973 E1
Forestgate Dr
6200 HarC 77373 3116 A7
6200 HarC 77373 3261 A1
N Forest Gate Dr
- WDLD 77382 2820 A2
S Forest Gate Dr
- WDLD 77382 2820 A2
Forest Glade Ct
10200 CHTW 77385 2822 E4
10200 MtgC 77385 2822 E4
Forest Glade Dr
6100 FBnC 77469 4493 C4
21200 HarC 77338 3260 C2
Forest Glen Ct
2500 FBnC 77469 4365 D1
Forest Glen Dr
8000 HarC 77338 3261 E3
11900 MtgC 77303 2239 D1
Forest Glen Ln
2100 LGCY 77565 4508 E5
Forest Glen St
3200 MtgC 77380 2967 B1
11700 BKHV 77024 3959 C4
Forest Glen Tr
- MtgC 77354 2672 B5
Forest Green Dr
1700 HarC 77336 3266 E3
1700 HarC 77336 3267 A3
28200 MtgC 77355 2815 B4
Forest Green Ln
23300 MtgC 77357 2973 E4
23300 MtgC 77357 2974 A4
Forest Green Tr
10 HOUS 77339 3119 D7
10 HOUS 77339 3264 E1
Forest Grove Dr
8500 HOUS 77080 3821 A2
Forest Gully
13500 HOUS 77067 3402 E4
Foresthaven Dr
5100 HarC 77066 3401 A2
5500 HarC 77066 3400 E3
Forest Haven Tr
17600 HarC 77070 3255 B3
Forest Heights Dr
7600 HarC 77095 3537 D7
7600 HarC 77433 3537 D7
17200 HarC 77095 3538 A7
Forest Heights St
- ALVN 77511 4749 A7
Forest Hill Blvd
100 HOUS 77011 3965 A7
200 HOUS 77011 4105 A1
1500 HOUS 77023 4104 E2
1500 HOUS 77023 4105 A1
Forest Hill Dr
28800 MtgC 77355 2814 E4
Forest Hills Dr
300 LGCY 77573 4632 E2
2800 LGCY 77573 4633 A2
Forest Hillside
- HOUS 77067 3402 E4
Forest Holley Dr
4200 HOUS 77345 3119 D5
Forest Hollow Dr
900 BYTN 77521 3835 A5
1300 MSCY 77459 4369 E5
8800 HOUS 77078 3687 E3
Forest Home Dr
1000 HOUS 77077 3956 E3
4500 MSCY 77459 4369 B6
Forest Hurst Dr
4900 HarC 77373 3115 B5
Forest Isle Ln
10 FBnC 77459 4621 A3
Forest Ivy
- HOUS 77067 3402 E4
Forest Ivy Ct
8100 HarC 77338 3261 E2
Forest Knoll Dr
13200 HarC 77049 3689 C7
14300 HarC 77049 3690 A6
Forest Knoll Ln
1100 FBnC 77469 4493 E6
1100 FBnC 77479 4493 E6
Forest Lake Dr
100 PASD 77586 4508 D2
100 TYLV 77586 4508 D1
900 TYLV 77586 4381 D7
Forestlake Dr
1700 FBnC 77479 4493 E5
Forest Lake Tr
10 KATY 77493 3813 B4
Forest Laurel Dr
2900 HOUS 77339 3119 B5
Forest Leaf Cir
4100 MSCY 77459 4369 C5
Forest Leaf Dr
10600 FBnC 77478 4236 E4
Forestlight Ct
21600 HarC 77338 3261 E2
Forest Ln Cir
18600 MtgC 77357 2827 B4
Forest Ln Ct
700 MtgC 77302 2530 D5
Forest Ln Dr
700 MtgC 77302 2530 D6
5800 HarC 77084 3677 E5
8500 FBnC 77479 4494 B4
Forest Loch Dr
- HarC 77373 3115 B4
Forest Lodge Cir
14800 HarC 77070 3254 C7
14800 HarC 77070 3398 C1
Forest Lodge Ct
14900 HarC 77070 3398 D1
Forest Lodge Dr
- HarC 77377 3254 D7
14500 HarC 77070 3398 C1
15000 HarC 77070 3254 D7
Forest Magic Ln
21400 HarC 77338 3260 D2
Forest Manor Dr
1900 HOUS 77339 3118 D6
Forest Meadow Dr
12800 HarC 77429 3254 C7
Forest Mews Ct
6700 HarC 77049 3829 A2
Forest Mill Ln
6600 FBnC 77469 4095 B5
Forest Mist Dr
17500 HarC 77379 3256 D1
Forest Moss Ct
5000 HarC 77084 3677 B7
Forest Mountain Ct
2000 HOUS 77345 3120 D5
Forest Museum Dr
10 MtgC 77354 2819 C2
10 WDLD 77382 2819 C2
Forest Nook Ct
5000 HOUS 77018 3683 D7
Forest North Dr
23200 HOUS 77339 3118 A4
Forest Oak Park Ct
31600 MtgC 77385 2823 C6
Forest Oaks Blvd
2400 HOUS 77017 4246 B1
3000 SHUS 77017 4246 C2
3000 SHUS 77587 4246 C2
Forest Oaks Dr
300 HOUS 77017 4106 C6
1900 HOUS 77017 4246 B1
Forest Oaks Ln
800 BzaC 77584 4501 A1
Forest Park Dr
- HarC 77082 4096 B3
Forest Park Ln
- PRLD 77581 4503 E1
17600 HarC 77379 3255 D2
17600 HarC 77379 3256 A3
Forest Pass Ln
13800 HarC 77429 3253 C6
Forest Path Ct
24500 HarC 77373 3114 D3
Forest Perch Pl
10 WDLD 77382 2673 B6
Forest Pine Ln
26400 FBnC 77494 4092 B1
Forest Pines Ct
400 FRDW 77546 4629 E3
Forest Pines Vil
- HarC 77067 3402 E4
13500 HOUS 77067 3402 E4
Forest Plaza Ct
6000 HarC 77066 3401 A6
Forest Point Dr
- HOUS 77338 3262 A4
2000 LGCY 77573 4632 E2
7900 HarC 77338 3261 D4
8500 HarC 77338 3262 A4
Forest Rain Dr
1600 FBnC 77479 4494 B4
Forest Rain Ln
4100 HarC 77346 3408 A2
Forest Ranch Dr
2100 HarC 77530 3829 E3
Forest Ridge Dr
2500 MSCY 77459 4370 A7
19000 MtgC 77355 2815 A4
19100 MtgC 77355 2814 E4
Forestridge Ln
- HarC 77084 3677 E7
- HarC 77084 3678 A7
Forest Ridge Rd
8200 HarC 77379 3255 E2
Forest River Dr
900 HarC 77530 3830 E5
Forest Row Dr
3500 HOUS 77345 3120 A4
Forest Run Dr
15600 HarC 77433 3251 C6
Forestry Dr
30600 MtgC 77386 2968 E2
Forest Sage Ln
5000 FBnC 77494 4092 D3
12000 PRLD 77583 4500 C5
Forest Shadow Dr
7400 FBnC 77479 4493 E5
Forest Shadows Dr
4600 HarC 77338 3260 C3
Forest Shores Dr
10 HOUS 77339 3119 A7
Forestside Ln
10 HarC 77095 3538 E6
Forest Spring Ln
10000 PRLD 77584 4501 A2
Forest Springs Dr
5400 HOUS 77339 3119 B2
Forest Springs Lk
25500 HarC 77373 3114 A3
Forest Star
800 HOUS 77067 3402 D4
Forest Steppes Ct
10 WDLD 77382 2673 D6
Forest Stone St
7900 CmbC 77520 3835 D4
Forest Stream Dr
20500 HarC 77346 3265 C3
Forest Teal Ct
4000 FBnC 77545 4622 E1
Forest Terrace Dr
4800 HarC 77373 3115 B5
Forest Thicket Ln
800 HOUS 77067 3402 D4
Forest Timbers Ct
19400 HarC 77346 3264 D5
Forest Timbers Dr
5200 HarC 77346 3264 C5
Forest Town Dr
18200 HarC 77084 3677 E7
Forest Trace Dr
1600 FBnC 77479 4494 B4
18900 HarC 77346 3264 E6
18900 HarC 77346 3265 A6
Forest Trail Dr
16600 HarC 77530 3830 D6
Forest Trails Dr
5400 HarC 77084 3677 E5
14700 HarC 77095 3539 A7
15300 HarC 77095 3538 D6
Forest Vale
11200 MtgC 77354 2671 D3
Forest Vale Ct
2800 HOUS 77339 3119 B3
Forest Valley Bnd
10 MtgC 77384 2675 B1
Forest View Dr
10 MtgC 77384 2675 B1
2500 FBnC 77469 4364 A4
Forestview Dr
20000 MtgC 77355 2814 B5
Forest View St
800 FRDW 77546 4629 B2
9000 HOUS 77078 3688 A6
Forest View Tr
11900 MtgC 77385 2823 B5
Forest Village Dr
3800 HOUS 77339 3119 A4
Forest Vine Ct
17500 HarC 77377 3254 D3
Forest Vista Dr
21400 HarC 77338 3260 C2
Forest West Dr
33400 MtgC 77354 2673 A2
Forest West St
33000 MtgC 77354 2673 A3
Forest Willow Ln
3200 HarC 77068 3257 C6
Forest Wind Ln
11600 HarC 77066 3400 E5
Forestwood Dr
200 HarC 77015 3828 C6
Forest Woods
- FBnC 77479 4494 A5
Forest Wy Dr
16100 HarC 77090 3258 D5
Forge Ct
- HarC 77532 3551 E4
Forge Creek Rd
2500 HarC 77067 3402 A5
Forge Hill Pl
10 WDLD 77381 2820 D4
Forge River Rd
400 HarC 77598 4507 B5
Forge Stone Dr
2500 HarC 77546 4506 B7
S Fork Blvd
- HOUS 77089 4505 B1
11100 HarC 77089 4505 B1
W Fork Blvd
4700 CNRO 77304 2382 D2
S Fork Cir
12100 HarC 77089 4505 B1
N Fork Ct
700 HarC 77450 3954 A3
S Fork Ct
12100 HarC 77089 4505 B1

STREET
Block City ZIP Map# Grid

N Fork Dr
19800 MtgC 77365 2825 A5
22000 HarC 77450 3954 A3
22200 HarC 77450 3953 E2
Fork Creek Dr
11900 HarC 77065 3539 D2
Forked Bough Dr
11200 HOUS 77042 3958 B6
Forkland Dr
- HOUS 77077 3957 B4
Forney Dr
5600 HOUS 77036 4100 A2
Forney Ridge Ln
3700 HarC 77047 4374 D5
Forrest Av
10 BYTN 77520 3973 A6
400 BYTN 77520 3972 E6
Forrest Ln
1600 PRLD 77581 4504 C6
E Forrest Ln
100 DRPK 77536 4109 B6
W Forrest Ln
100 DRPK 77536 4109 B6
Forrest Rd
19000 GlsC 77511 4868 E3
Forrest St
10 LPRT 77571 4251 E5
Forrestal St
7300 HOUS 77033 4243 E1
Forrester Dr
3100 PRLD 77584 4501 D6
Forrester Canyon Ln
13000 FBnC 77478 4366 E1
Forrester Pl Dr
- FBnC 77479 4367 B7
Forrest Valley Dr
11000 HarC 77065 3399 A7
11000 HarC 77070 3399 A7
11200 HarC 77065 3398 E7
Forsythe Ln
1200 HarC 77073 3259 B1
6700 SGLD 77479 4367 C7
Fort St
100 RHMD 77469 4492 A1
200 RHMD 77469 4491 E1
Fort Augusta Ct
7400 HarC 77389 2966 A3
Fort Augusta Dr
24900 HarC 77389 2966 B3
Fort Bend Dr
3900 GLSN 77554 5441 A4
Fort Bend Parkway Toll Rd
- FBnC - 4498 A3
- FBnC 77459 4621 D1
- HOUS - 4371 A5
- HOUS - 4498 A3
- MSCY - 4498 A4
- MSCY 77459 4621 D1
- MSCY 77545 4621 E1
- MSCY 77545 4622 A1
Fort Bend Toll Rd
- HOUS 77085 4240 D7
Fort Bowie Ct
20000 HarC 77449 3815 D6
Fort Bridger Rd
20000 HarC 77449 3815 D6
Fort Caney Dr
2700 FBnC 77469 4365 B1
Fort Crockett Blvd
400 GLSN 77551 5108 D7
4500 GLSN 77550 5108 D7
Fort Custer Ct
20000 HarC 77449 3815 D6
Fort Davis Ct
19900 HarC 77449 3815 E6
Fort Denison Blvd
- HarC 77429 3252 C7
Fort Dodge Dr
20000 HarC 77449 3815 D6
Fort Dupont Ln
12400 HarC 77346 3408 C3
Forthbridge Ct
16700 HarC 77084 3678 C7
Forthbridge Dr
5000 HarC 77084 3678 C6
Fort Henry Ln
3000 FBnC 77459 4621 B6
Forthlin Cir
4200 FBnC 77450 4093 D1
Forth Loch Ct
16800 HarC 77084 3678 C6
Fortinberry St
100 BYTN 77520 3972 C6
Fort King Dr
- HarC 77014 3401 C3
Fort Laramie Dr
2100 HarC 77449 3815 D6
Fort Nelson Dr
- HarC 77083 4097 A6
Fortner St
100 BYTN 77520 3971 C3
Forton Dr
900 HarC 77073 3403 C2
Fort Path Dr
24500 HarC 77373 3114 D4
Fort Richmond Dr
3400 FBnC 77469 4234 D7
Fort Rose Ct
7900 HarC 77070 3399 E2
Fortrose Garden Ct
18800 HarC 77377 3254 B1
Fort Royal Dr
2600 HarC 77038 3543 B5
Fort Settlement Dr
- SGLD 77478 4368 E5
24500 HarC 77373 3114 D3
Fortsmith St
- HOUS 77079 3956 D1
Fort Stanton Dr
19900 HarC 77084 3815 D6
19900 HarC 77449 3815 D6
Fort Stockton Dr
2900 HarC 77449 3815 D4
Fort Sumter Ct
200 FBnC 77469 4493 D7
5500 HarC 77084 3679 A5
Fort Sumter Ln
5600 HarC 77084 3679 A4
Fort Sumter St
500 MtgC 77302 2530 B7
Fortuna Dr
- PRLD 77581 4504 D2
2600 KATY 77493 3813 D4
Fortuna Bella Dr
1100 HarC 77089 4504 E2
1100 PRLD 77089 4504 E2
1100 PRLD 77581 4504 E2

Fortune Dr
900 BYTN 77520 3973 B6
Fortune St
700 HOUS 77088 3684 A2
Fortuneberry Pl
10 WDLD 77382 2673 E5
Fortune Park Dr
11700 HOUS 77047 4373 C2
Fort Worth St
1700 BYTN 77520 3973 A5
Forty Four Ct
17700 HarC 77447 3249 E3
Forty Four Ln
24000 HarC 77447 3249 E3
Forum Ct
2400 RMFT 77357 2829 A2
Forum Dr
8500 HOUS 77055 3821 A5
Forum Park Dr
9700 HOUS 77036 4238 E3
Forum Pl Dr
- HOUS 77074 4238 E3
10500 HOUS 77036 4238 E3
Forum West Dr
10000 HOUS 77036 4238 E3
10200 HOUS 77099 4238 D3
Fosbak St
800 HOUS 77022 3684 E6
Fossil Canyon Dr
9400 HarC 77396 3407 A7
Fossil Creek Cir
22700 FBnC 77450 3953 E5
Fossil Creek Dr
1600 FBnC 77494 3953 B5
Fossil Point Ct
12500 HarC 77346 3408 C2
Fossil Point Ln
12400 HarC 77346 3408 C2
Fossil Rock Ln
11700 HOUS 77034 4247 A7
Fossil Trails Dr
21400 HarC 77388 3113 B2
Foster Av
900 PASD 77506 4107 D5
Foster Cross
1100 FBnC 77469 4232 B7
Foster Dr
100 CNRO 77301 2530 A1
600 RHMD 77469 4491 E2
600 RHMD 77469 4492 A2
1000 CNRO 77301 2384 D7
Foster Ln
30100 MtgC 77386 2969 A3
Foster Rd
21100 HarC 77388 3113 B3
N Foster Rd
10 TXCY 77591 4873 B6
S Foster Rd
10 TXCY 77591 4873 A6
Foster St
100 ALVN 77511 4867 C3
100 BYTN 77520 3971 B4
200 TMBL 77375 2964 C6
1500 HOUS 77011 3965 B6
5800 HOUS 77021 4103 D5
Fosterbridge Ln
25600 FBnC 77494 4093 A1
Foster Brook Ln
- FBnC 77469 4094 E6
Foster Creek Ct
7700 FBnC 77469 4232 A7
Foster Creek Dr
1100 FBnC 77469 4232 B7
Foster Hill Ct
4700 HOUS 77345 3120 A2
Foster Hill Dr
2700 HOUS 77345 3120 B2
2800 HOUS 77345 3119 E2
Foster Island Dr
- FBnC 77469 4232 A7
Foster Island Rd
7200 FBnC 77469 4232 A7
Foster Leaf Ct
2300 FBnC 77469 4365 B3
Foster Leaf Ln
1800 FBnC 77469 4365 B2
Foster League
7200 FBnC 77469 4232 B7
Foster Oaks Dr
100 CNRO 77301 2384 A7
100 CNRO 77301 2530 B1
Foster Point Ln
16600 HarC 77095 3538 A3
Fosters Ct
10 FBnC 77479 4367 A5
Fosters Bend Ln
7300 FBnC 77469 4094 E6
Fosters Canyon Ln
1500 HarC 77073 3403 C2
Fosters Creek Dr
14000 HarC 77429 3397 C3
Fosters Green Dr
10 FBnC 77479 4367 A6
Fosters Park Ct
22500 MtgC 77365 2973 A3
Foster Springs Ln
15200 HarC 77095 3538 E4
15200 HarC 77095 3539 B5
Fostoria Ln
600 HOUS 77076 3684 E5
Fostoria Rd
10400 MtgC 77372 2537 D3
11800 SPLD 77372 2537 D3
Foundary Dr
2300 HarC 77493 3814 B5
Founders Ct
3000 MSCY 77459 4369 E6
Founders Wy
14500 MtgC 77362 2816 D1
Founders Cir Blvd
- HarC 77389 2966 A3
Founders Green Cir
3100 PRLD 77581 4503 D2
Founders Shore Cir
18300 HarC 77433 3395 C6
Founders Shore Dr
12000 HarC 77433 3395 D6
Founders Wy Ct
5200 HOUS 77091 3683 E7
Founding Dr
6200 HarC 77449 3676 D3
Fountain Dr
500 LPRT 77571 4251 D7
2100 SGLD 77478 4237 C5
Fountain St
7900 HOUS 77051 4243 A2
Fountain Bend Dr
11300 HarC 77375 3110 A6

Fountain Bend Dr
11500 HarC 77375 3109 E6
Fountainbleau Dr
25900 HarC 77377 3108 E5
Fountainbleu St
8600 HOUS 77024 3961 A1
Fountainbridge Ln
5200 HarC 77069 3256 D7
Fountain Brook Ct
2900 PRLD 77584 4500 C4
Fountain Brook Dr
11900 PRLD 77584 4500 C4
Fountainbrook Ln
100 LGCY 77539 4752 D3
5100 FBnC 77479 4496 B4
Fountainbrook Park Ct
- MtgC 77386 2823 C6
Fountainbrook Park Ln
- MtgC 77386 2823 C7
Fountain Creek Ct
4400 PASD 77505 4248 E5
Fountaincrest Ct
13200 HarC 77041 3679 D1
Fountaincrest Dr
7400 HarC 77041 3679 C1
7500 HarC 77041 3539 C7
Fountaine St
6700 HOUS 77028 3825 D1
Fountaingate Dr
10200 STAF 77477 4238 D7
Fountaingrove Ln
7500 HarC 77379 3256 C4
Fountainhead Dr
4500 HarC 77014 3401 B1
4500 HarC 77066 3401 A2
Fountain Hills Ct
13400 HarC 77086 3541 E2
Fountain Hills Dr
3200 MSCY 77459 4498 A5
Fountain Lake Cir
12500 STAF 77477 4238 A7
Fountain Lake Dr
- SGLD 77478 4237 E7
- STAF 77478 4237 E7
10500 STAF 77477 4237 E7
10500 STAF 77477 4238 A7
Fountain Lake Wy
- HarC 77433 3251 C6
Fountain Lilly Dr
6900 HarC 77346 3408 E1
7100 HarC 77346 3264 E7
Fountain Meadow Dr
7200 FBnC 77494 4093 B5
Fountain Mist Dr
1300 PRLD 77545 4499 E3
Fountain Mist Ln
- FBnC 77469 4492 B2
- RHMD 77469 4492 B3
Fountain Rock Dr
- PRLD 77545 4499 E3
Fountains Dr
3400 RSBG 77471 4615 A1
Fountain Shores Dr
10300 HarC 77065 3539 E2
Fountain Spray Ln
7300 FBnC 77494 4093 A5
Fountain Spring Dr
3400 HarC 77066 3401 E7
Fountain Stone Ln
14700 HarC 77396 3548 B1
N Fountain Valley Dr
2100 MSCY 77459 4497 B2
S Fountain Valley Dr
2100 MSCY 77459 4497 B2
Fountainview Cir
17400 SGLD 77479 4494 E1
Fountain View Dr
1000 HOUS 77057 3960 C6
2900 HOUS 77057 4100 C2
3600 HOUS 77081 4100 C2
Fountain View Ln
- LGCY 77573 4632 A6
Fountain View St
2500 RMFT 77357 2829 A3
Fourcade St
1600 HOUS 77023 4104 B1
Four Fountains St
900 RMFT 77357 2829 A1
Four Hill Dr
- PASD 77505 4248 E6
Four Leaf Dr
8900 FBnC 77479 4494 B4
15500 HarC 77084 3678 E6
15500 HarC 77084 3679 A7
Fournace Pl
4500 BLAR 77401 4101 A3
4900 BLAR 77401 4100 E3
4900 HOUS 77081 4100 E3
4900 HOUS 77401 4100 E3
Fournace Gardens Dr
10 BLAR 77401 4101 B3
Four Oaks Dr
21400 HarC 77073 3259 D2
Four Oaks Pl
- HOUS 77056 3961 A5
Four Pines Dr
2800 HOUS 77345 3119 E5
Four Pines Ln
10 LbyC 77328 2537 D2
10 MtgC 77372 2537 D2
Four River Dr
6000 FBnC 77469 4493 B4
Four Rivers Ct
5200 HOUS 77091 3683 E7
Four Season Dr
15600 HarC 77084 3679 A5
Four Sixes Ln
24200 HarC 77447 3249 E3
Foursome Ln
3300 FBnC 77478 4235 E7
Foursquare Dr
16700 MtgC 77385 2676 D4
Fourth
- FBnC 77545 4499 D5
Fourth St
1300 MSCY 77489 4370 B2
2100 HarC 77336 3267 A2
Four Winds Dr
2800 MSCY 77459 4497 A4
9400 HOUS 77489 4371 B4
Fowler Ct
3400 FBnC 77459 4621 D5
Fowler Pk
2500 MtgC 77385 2823 B6
Fowler St
1300 HOUS 77007 3962 C2
Fowlie St
7800 HOUS 77028 3826 B3

Fox
3100 HOUS 77003 3964 A4
Fox Bnd
7200 HarC 77338 3261 C4
Fox Ct
3400 PRLD 77581 4503 D6
Fox Dr
3100 HarC 77521 3834 E6
3700 HarC 77521 3835 A6
Fox Ln
- HOUS 77084 3818 A2
Fox Pth
2100 FBnC 77494 3952 C6
Fox Rd
9800 HarC 77064 3540 E4
9800 HarC 77064 3541 A4
Fox St
2700 HOUS 77003 3964 A4
8000 CmbC 77520 3835 D3
Fox Tr
900 PASD 77504 4247 C5
Fox Arrow Ln
12800 HarC 77041 3679 D4
Fox Bayou Ln
10 HOUS 77013 3966 D1
Foxbend Dr
22200 HarC 77449 3675 E5
Fox Bend Ln
24100 HarC 77336 3266 E2
Fox Bluff Dr
- HarC 77375 3109 D6
Foxborough Ln
600 MSCY 77489 4370 E5
Fox Briar Ln
300 SGLD 77478 4369 A2
300 STAF 77478 4369 A2
Foxbriar Ln
25200 HarC 77373 3114 B3
E Foxbriar Forest Cir
10 WDLD 77382 2674 E4
W Foxbriar Forest Cir
10 WDLD 77382 2674 E4
Foxbrick Ln
7100 HarC 77338 3261 C5
7100 HOUS 77338 3261 C5
Foxbrook Dr
6900 HarC 77338 3261 C3
Fox Brush Ln
12800 HarC 77041 3679 D5
Foxbrush Ln
4100 FBnC 77479 4366 C7
Foxburo Dr
11500 HarC 77065 3539 B1
Fox Canyon
28700 MtgC 77386 2969 D5
Fox Chapel Pl
10 WDLD 77382 2819 B3
Fox Chase Ct
6200 HarC 77041 3679 D4
Foxchester Ln
19900 HarC 77338 3261 C4
Fox Cliff Ln
20700 HarC 77338 3261 C2
Fox Creek Park Dr
- HarC 77083 4097 A6
Foxcrest Ct
7300 HarC 77338 3261 C3
Foxcrest Dr
2500 FBnC 77494 3951 C5
Foxcrest Ln
7200 HarC 77338 3261 C3
Foxcroft Ln
6900 HarC 77338 3261 C3
Foxcroft Pk
600 MtgC 77302 2530 B5
Fox Crossing Cir
7900 HarC 77379 3256 C5
Fox Crossing Ln
16200 HarC 77379 3256 B5
Foxdale Dr
- HOUS 77504 4247 C7
5000 HarC 77084 3677 E6
Foxden Dr
2500 PRLD 77584 4502 A5
Foxfern Cir
6400 HOUS 77049 3828 B2
Foxfern St
6600 HOUS 77049 3828 B2
Fox Field Dr
17200 HOUS 77489 4497 E2
Foxfield Ln
6900 HarC 77338 3261 C4
Foxfire Cir
2800 MSCY 77459 4497 A1
Foxford Wy
13800 HarC 77015 3828 E6
13900 HarC 77015 3829 A6
Fox Forest Cir
2600 HarC 77373 3114 D3
Fox Forest Tr
7200 HarC 77338 3261 C3
Fox Fountain Ln
29000 MtgC 77386 2969 C5
Foxgate Rd
15700 HOUS 77079 3956 E2
Fox Glen Ln
20100 HarC 77338 3261 C4
Foxglen Ln
20600 HarC 77338 3261 C4
Foxglove Dr
- LPRT 77571 4110 A7
500 MSCY 77489 4370 E5
2300 BzaC 77584 4501 B5
Foxglove Ln
400 HOUS 77076 3684 D6
Foxglove St
2200 LGCY 77573 4632 D2
2300 HarC 77562 3832 D3
Foxglove Oaks Ln
- PRLD 77581 4503 E1
Fox Grass Tr
4800 HOUS 77345 3119 E1
Fox Grove Ln
20000 HarC 77338 3261 C4
Fox Hall Ln
7200 HarC 77338 3261 C3
Foxhall Crescent Dr
10 SGLD 77479 4495 B2
Fox Haven Ln
20500 HarC 77338 3261 D3
Foxhill Dr
1100 MSCY 77489 4370 B6
Foxhill St
4000 HarC 77093 3546 B7
Fox Hollow Blvd
4600 HarC 77389 2967 A6
Fox Hollow Ct
4700 HarC 77389 2967 B6

Fox Hollow Dr
- WlrC 77447 2813 C4
Fox Hollow Ln
600 PASD 77504 4247 B5
Fox Hollow St
100 HarC 77521 3834 E6
Fox Hound Ln
20700 HarC 77338 3261 D3
Foxhound Ln
7200 HarC 77338 3261 C2
Fox Hunt Dr
23000 HarC 77389 2967 B6
Foxhunter Rd
6200 HOUS 77049 3828 A3
Foxhurst Ln
6900 HarC 77338 3261 C4
Foxingham Cir
29000 MtgC 77386 2969 C5
Fox Knoll Ln
7300 HarC 77338 3261 D4
Foxlake Dr
- HOUS 77084 3955 A1
1500 HarC 77084 3816 A7
1500 HOUS 77084 3816 A7
Foxland Ct
6000 HarC 77379 3111 E5
Foxland Chase St
1100 FBnC 77479 4366 D7
Foxleigh Ct
13200 HOUS 77049 3828 A3
Foxleigh Rd
6100 HOUS 77049 3828 A3
Foxline Ln
6800 HarC 77338 3261 C4
Foxlodge Ln
20600 HarC 77338 3261 C3
Fox Lynn Dr
28700 MtgC 77386 2969 D4
Foxmar Ln
6900 HarC 77338 3261 C4
Fox Meadow Dr
1100 ALVN 77511 4749 D3
12300 STAF 77477 4237 E7
Fox Meadow Ln
3800 PASD 77504 4247 C6
4000 HOUS 77504 4247 C6
Fox Mesa Ln
6900 HarC 77338 3261 C3
Fox Mill Ln
4900 HarC 77389 2967 B7
Foxmont Ln
7200 HarC 77338 3261 C3
Foxmoor Cir
13600 HarC 77069 3256 E7
Foxmoor Dr
13500 HarC 77069 3400 D1
13700 HarC 77069 3256 D7
Fox Mountain Dr
2800 MtgC 77386 2969 D4
Fox Pitt Rd
2700 MtgC 77386 2969 D5
Fox Pointe Ln
19100 HarC 77375 3109 C6
19100 HarC 77375 3254 D1
Foxport Ln
7200 HarC 77338 3261 C3
Fox Prairie Ln
18700 HarC 77084 3816 C2
Fox Pup Ln
21400 HOUS 77532 3266 B7
Fox Ravine Dr
2800 MtgC 77386 2969 D4
Foxridge Dr
12300 HOUS 77037 3685 B1
Fox River Dr
29300 MtgC 77386 2969 D4
Fox River Ln
2400 MtgC 77386 2969 C5
Foxrow Ln
10200 HarC 77064 3540 A3
Fox Run Blvd
28700 MtgC 77386 2969 D4
Foxrun Ct
9800 HOUS 77080 3820 B4
Fox Run Dr
3100 ALVN 77511 4866 D4
Fox Run Ln
400 LGCY 77573 4630 D4
Fox Run St
3500 PRLD 77584 4503 B6
23300 HarC 77389 2966 C5
Fox Scene Dr
7200 HarC 77338 3261 C2
Foxshadows Ln
7200 HarC 77338 3261 C3
W Foxshire Ln
- HarC 77053 4373 A5
300 HarC 77053 4372 E5
Foxshire St
10 HOUS 77047 4373 A5
Foxside Ln
7300 HarC 77338 3261 C4
Foxsparrow St
- WDLD 77380 2822 A7
Fox Springs Ct
200 LGCY 77539 4752 D4
Fox Springs Dr
15600 HarC 77084 3678 E5
15600 HarC 77084 3679 A5
Fox Squirrel Ct
200 MtgC 77362 2817 A6
Fox Star Ln
7200 HarC 77338 3261 C3
Fox Stone Ln
20200 HarC 77338 3261 C4
Foxstone Ln
24200 HarC 77336 3266 E2
Fox Swift Ct
20800 HarC 77338 3261 D3
Foxtail Ct
300 LGCY 77573 4633 A2
Foxtail Pl
1900 WDLD 77380 2967 E1
Foxtail Lily Cir
5000 HarC 77084 3677 D6
Foxtail Pine Ln
1000 HarC 77450 3954 C2
1000 HOUS 77450 3954 C2
Foxton Rd
12200 HOUS 77048 4375 D3
Foxton Pl Ct
7400 HarC 77095 3678 C1
Fox Trace Ln
12400 HarC 77066 3401 B4
Fox Trail Ct
1900 FBnC 77494 3952 C6
Fox Trail Ln
20300 HarC 77338 3261 C4

Fox Trail St
900 PASD 77504 4247 C5
Foxtree Ln
19100 HarC 77094 3955 B4
Fox Trot Cir
1800 FBnC 77469 4364 E3
Fox Trot Ct
20800 HarC 77338 3261 C3
Foxvalley Ln
6900 HarC 77338 3261 C3
Fox View Cir
2700 MtgC 77386 2969 D4
Foxview Dr
2500 MtgC 77386 2969 C4
Foxville Dr
2500 HarC 77067 3402 A4
Foxvista Ln
7100 HarC 77338 3261 C2
Foxwaithe Ln
7200 HarC 77338 3261 C3
Foxwalk Ln
7200 HarC 77338 3261 C3
Fox Walk Tr
21000 HarC 77338 3261 D2
Fox Water Dr
2400 MtgC 77386 2969 C5
Foxway Ln
7300 HarC 77338 3261 C4
Foxwick Ln
7300 HarC 77338 3261 C4
Fox Wind Ct
6100 HarC 77041 3679 D4
Foxwood Ct
1700 MSCY 77489 4370 D4
Foxwood Dr
28300 MtgC 77362 2963 D3
Foxwood Ln
24200 HarC 77336 3266 E2
Foxwood Rd
1800 HOUS 77008 3822 D5
Foxwood Forest Blvd
- HOUS 77338 3261 C5
19900 HarC 77338 3261 C5
Foxwood Forest Ct
7100 HarC 77338 3261 C4
Foxwood Garden Dr
20800 HarC 77338 3261 C3
Foxwood Glen Ln
20800 HarC 77338 3261 C2
Foxworth Ct
10 FBnC 77479 4367 A7
10 FBnC 77479 4494 A1
Foy Ln
10900 HarC 77093 3686 A1
10900 HOUS 77093 3686 A2
Foy Rd
10300 HOUS 77093 3686 A3
10900 HarC 77093 3686 A2
Foyce St
100 HOUS 77022 3824 A2
Foyer Cir
7300 MSCY 77459 4496 E5
Foy Martin Dr
10 CNRO 77304 2236 C7
10 CNRO 77304 2382 D1
Fragrant Cloud Ct
5500 HarC 77041 3679 C6
Fragrant Pine Ln
15100 HarC 77049 3829 A3
Fragrant Rose Ct
17600 HarC 77429 3252 C5
Fragrant Vines Dr
- HarC 77073 3259 E4
Frail Ln
600 HOUS 77076 3684 D3
Fra Mauro Dr
- LGCY 77573 4508 E7
Frampton Ct
16700 HarC 77379 3256 E2
France Ln
6000 PASD 77505 4248 D5
France Wy
5800 PASD 77505 4248 D5
Francel Ln
12200 HarC 77429 3397 E1
Frances Ct
3400 ALVN 77511 4866 D2
Frances Dr
1000 ALVN 77511 4866 C2
1000 RSBG 77471 4491 D3
1200 RHMD 77469 4491 D3
1200 RHMD 77471 4491 D3
Frances Ln
16200 SGCH 77355 2961 E3
Frances St
- STAF 77477 4239 B7
1000 DRPK 77536 4109 C5
12700 MSCY 77071 4239 B7
12800 STAF 77477 4370 B1
13100 MSCY 77489 4370 A1
Francine Ln
5000 HOUS 77016 3686 C4
E Francis Av
10 BYTN 77520 3973 A5
W Francis Av
10 BYTN 77520 3973 A5
200 BYTN 77520 3972 E5
Francis Ct
600 LGCY 77573 4632 B1
Francis Dr
900 PASD 77506 4107 C2
2200 PRLD 77581 4503 A2
Francis St
600 HOUS 77002 3963 A6
600 HOUS 77006 3963 A6
1000 HOUS 77004 3963 B7
2400 HOUS 77004 4103 C1
E Francis St
200 BYTN 77520 3973 A5
Francisco Ct
4100 MtgC 77386 2970 D6
Francis Drake Rd
16500 JMAB 77554 5331 E5
16500 JMAB 77554 5332 A5
Francis Marion Dr
6200 HOUS 77091 3682 E5
Francitas Dr
900 HarC 77038 3543 D3
Francoise Blvd
10900 HOUS 77042 3958 C6
Frandora Rd
700 BKHV 77024 3959 C2
700 HDWV 77024 3959 C2
Frank Cir
29900 MtgC 77354 2671 E7
Frank Ln
13000 STAF 77477 4239 A7
13100 STAF 77477 4370 B1

Frank Rd
2500 HarC 77032 3404 D
2500 HOUS 77032 3404 D
6800 HarC 77521 3833 A
15100 FBnC 77478 4236 C
Frank St
1500 HarC 77532 3411 D
7500 HOUS 77011 3965 B
Frankford Ct
4800 HOUS 77048 4243 D
Frankfort Dr
1200 MtgC 77385 2677 A
Frankfort St
300 MSCY 77489 4370 B
Frank Giusti Dr
- GLSN 77551 5222 A
- GLSN 77554 5222 A
Frankie Av
400 HarC 77015 3828 E
800 HarC 77015 3967 E
Franklin
22000 WlrC 77445 2952 C
Franklin Cir
2000 RSBG 77471 4491 A
Franklin Rd
- WlrC 77445 2952 C
9800 HarC 77070 3399 C
9800 HOUS 77070 3399 C
Franklin St
10 HOUS 77002 3963 C
2100 HOUS 77003 3963 E
2300 LMQU 77568 4989 E
Franklin Park Ct
18300 HarC 77379 3257 A
Franks St
- HarC 77373 3114 D
Frank's St
24600 HarC 77373 3114 D
Frank Sayko
13700 STFE 77510 4870 C
13700 STFE 77517 4870 C
Frank Scott Blvd
20000 WlrC 77484 3101 B
Frank Shore Dr
2100 PRLD 77584 4500 A
Frankton Wy
17800 HarC 77073 3404 B
Frankway Dr
8800 HOUS 77096 4101 B
Franlee St
200 LMQU 77568 4990 C
Franta Rd
600 HarC 77532 3552 D
Franton Wy St
- HarC 77073 3404 B
Franz Rd
5100 HarC 77493 3813 E
5900 KATY 77493 3813 A
19300 HarC 77084 3816 A
19700 HarC 77084 3815 E
19900 HarC 77449 3815 E
20400 HOUS 77449 3815 B
22200 HarC 77449 3814 D
22700 HarC 77493 3814 A
22700 HOUS 77493 3814 C
22800 HOUS 77449 3814 D
Frap Ct
- HarC 77532 3551 E
Fraser Av
5600 GLSN 77551 5108 C
Fraser Dr
22800 MtgC 77365 2972 A
Fraser Lake Ln
- HarC 77083 4097 A
Frasier St
500 HOUS 77007 3962 E
Frasier Point Ct
6500 HarC 77379 3257 A
Frawley St
100 HOUS 77009 3824 D
Frazer Dr
800 HOUS 77038 3544 A
1900 FBnC 77469 4364 C
Frazer Ln
400 HarC 77037 3544 B
400 HOUS 77037 3544 B
Frazier Rd
- BzaC 77584 4627 D
Frazier St
6900 HTCK 77563 4989 A
N Frazier St
100 CNRO 77301 2384 A
300 CNRO 77301 2383 E
2100 CNRO 77303 2383 E
2400 CNRO 77303 2237 D
4400 MtgC 77303 2237 D
4800 CNRO 77304 2237 C
4800 MtgC 77304 2237 C
7800 CNRO 77378 2237 D
7800 MtgC 77378 2237 D
N Frazier St SR-75
100 CNRO 77301 2384 A
300 CNRO 77301 2383 E
2100 CNRO 77303 2383 E
2400 CNRO 77303 2237 D
4400 MtgC 77303 2237 D
4800 CNRO 77304 2237 C
4800 MtgC 77304 2237 C
7800 CNRO 77378 2237 D
7800 MtgC 77378 2237 D
S Frazier St
100 CNRO 77301 2384 A
1000 CNRO 77301 2530 A
S Frazier St SR-75
100 CNRO 77301 2384 A
1000 CNRO 77301 2530 A
Frazier River Dr
12600 HOUS 77050 3547 A
Freamon St
- BYTN 77520 3972 D
Fred Dr
100 KATY 77494 3952 A
Fred St
1100 HOUS 77088 3683 E
Freda Dr
400 PASD 77502 4247 A
400 SHUS 77502 4247 A
400 SHUS 77587 4247 A
Frederick Dr
18900 HarC 77377 3108 E
18900 HarC 77377 3253 E
Fredericksburg Dr
2500 LGCY 77573 4631 A
Fredericksburg Ln
8400 FBnC 77083 4235 E
Fred Hartman Br
- HarC - 4111 E
- HarC - 4112 A

STREET Block City ZIP Map# Grid

red Hartman Br
- HOUS - 4111 D4
- LPRT - 4111 D4
red Hartman Br SR-146
- HarC - 4111 E4
- HarC - 4112 A3
- HOUS - 4111 D4
- LPRT - 4111 D4
red J Petrich Rd
16500 HarC 77377 2962 D7
redonia Dr
1700 HarC 77073 3404 B2
ree Ln
35200 MtgC 77362 2816 D5
reecrest St
9800 HOUS 77034 4378 B2
reecroft St
- HOUS 77034 4378 B1
reedale St
- HOUS 77034 4378 B1
reedman St
23300 HarC 77447 3105 A7
reedom
10200 HOUS 77033 4243 E5
reedom Ct
2000 MSCY 77459 4369 E6
reedom Dr
- PRLD 77581 4501 E3
- PRLD 77584 4501 E3
reedom Point Ln
14500 HarC 77396 3548 B2
reedom Tree Ct
1800 MSCY 77459 4497 D4
reedom Tree Dr
4100 MSCY 77459 4497 D4
reedonia Dr
1400 HOUS 77055 3820 D6
1500 HOUS 77080 3820 D6
reehill St
9700 HOUS 77034 4378 C1
reeland Av
8800 HOUS 77075 4246 A6
reeland St
8500 HOUS 77061 4245 E6
8500 HOUS 77075 4245 E6
reeman Av
1400 KATY 77493 3813 E7
reeman Rd
- HarC 77084 3677 D2
- HarC 77449 3675 A2
- HarC 77493 3675 A2
18000 HarC 77095 3677 D2
18000 HarC 77433 3677 A2
18000 HarC 77449 3677 A2
20500 HarC 77433 3676 C2
20500 HarC 77449 3676 C2
reeman Rd FM-529
- HarC 77084 3677 D2
- HarC 77449 3675 A2
- HarC 77493 3675 A2
18000 HarC 77095 3677 D2
18000 HarC 77433 3677 A2
18000 HarC 77449 3677 A2
20500 HarC 77433 3676 C2
20500 HarC 77449 3676 C2
reeman St
1500 HOUS 77009 3963 C2
reemont Rd
40000 MtgC 77354 2672 C2
reemont St
4200 HOUS 77009 3824 B6
reemont Fair Ct
9400 HOUS 77075 4246 C7
reemont Peak Ln
12900 HarC 77346 3408 D2
reeport St
- HOUS 77015 3828 E6
300 HarC 77015 3828 E6
700 HarC 77015 3967 E2
reer Ct
13600 HarC 77429 3253 E6
reeridge Ct
21600 HarC 77449 3815 A3
Freesia Av
4400 HarC 77521 3833 B3
Freesia Ct
7100 HarC 77521 3832 B5
Freestar
9800 HOUS 77034 4378 B2
Freestone Av
11200 PRLD 77583 4500 D5
Freestone Pl
10 WDLD 77382 2673 E6
Freestone St
9800 HOUS 77034 4378 A2
Freestone Peach Ln
15200 HarC 77433 3251 B6
Freeton St
- HOUS 77034 4378 B1
- SHUS 77587 4247 B5
3900 HOUS 77034 4247 B5
Freeway Manor Dr
2400 RSBG 77471 4491 C6
Freewood St
- HOUS 77034 4246 D6
Fregis Dr
5900 HarC 77449 3677 B5
Freida Ln
17800 HarC 77379 3256 A2
Frels Ln
10 HOUS 77076 3684 E3
10 HOUS 77076 3685 A3
French Pl
2100 BYTN 77520 3973 C5
French Rd
17000 HarC 77084 3678 B6
17600 HarC 77084 3677 E6
French St
17200 PTVL 77372 2682 E7
French Chateau Dr
6300 HOUS 77088 3682 C3
French Creek Dr
5100 HOUS 77017 4246 B1
Frenchman's Crossing Dr
- HarC 77373 2968 E6
French Oak Ln
11200 HOUS 77082 4098 C2
French Oaks Dr
- WDLD 77382 2819 A3
French Quarter Ln
8400 FBnC 77459 4621 B5
French Town Rd
1000 GlsC 77650 4994 D1
W French Town Rd
- GlsC 77650 4994 D1
French Village Ct
1700 HOUS 77055 3821 C5
French Village Dr
1700 HOUS 77055 3821 C5
Frensham Cir
5300 HarC 77041 3679 B6
Fresa Rd
100 PASD 77502 4247 B1
Fresca St
22800 GLSN 77554 5441 A6
23000 GLSN 77554 5440 E6
Fresco Dr
2900 HarC 77449 3815 D4
Fresco Wells Dr
3000 HarC 77449 3815 E4
Frescura Dr
14200 HarC 77083 4096 E5
Freshmeadow Dr
1800 MSCY 77489 4370 C5
Freshmeadow St
5600 LGCY 77573 4630 D7
Freshmeadows Dr
2900 HOUS 77063 3960 A7
2900 HOUS 77063 4100 A2
Fresh Pond Pl
10 WDLD 77382 2819 B2
Freshwater Bay Ct
1300 HarC 77379 3255 C1
Freshwillow Dr
- HOUS 77041 3681 C7
Fresh Wind Ln
2900 LGCY 77573 4633 A3
Fresno Dr
7900 FBnC 77083 4096 B7
Freund
3100 HOUS 77003 3964 A4
Freund St
3700 HOUS 77003 3964 B4
Frey Ln
21100 HarC 77377 3107 B4
Frey Rd
- HOUS 77034 4246 E6
8700 MNVL 77578 4747 C1
8800 HOUS 77034 4377 D1
9000 MNVL 77578 4626 C7
9200 BzaC 77511 4626 C7
19000 PNIS 77445 3100 B6
Friar Cir
16200 HarC 77379 3256 C5
Friar Wy
31000 MtgC 77354 2817 C1
Friarcreek Ln
1300 HLSV 77055 3821 B6
1300 HOUS 77055 3821 B6
Friardale Ct
12200 HarC 77375 3109 D7
Friar Glen Ln
1400 HarC 77073 3259 C5
Friar Lake Ln
- HarC 77373 3114 B2
Friar Point Rd
3000 HOUS 77051 4243 A6
4100 HOUS 77047 4243 C6
Friars Hl
10000 HarC 77070 3399 B6
Friars Ln
800 BYTN 77521 3972 E3
Friars Ct Ln
7600 HarC 77379 3256 C5
Friars Legend Dr
2200 MtgC 77386 2969 B2
Friar Tuck Dr
5300 KATY 77493 3813 D6
24700 WlrC 77447 2959 D1
Friartuck Dr
40700 MtgC 77316 2668 E1
40700 MtgC 77316 2669 A1
41800 MtgC 77354 2668 D1
E Friar Tuck Ln
300 HOUS 77024 3960 E1
W Friar Tuck Ln
300 HOUS 77024 3960 E2
Friar Village Dr
12700 HarC 77377 3254 A3
Friarwood Tr
2200 HOUS 77339 3119 A2
Frick Rd
2300 HarC 77038 3543 A3
2800 HarC 77038 3542 D3
3100 HarC 77086 3542 E3
Friendly Rd
10300 HOUS 77093 3686 B4
10500 HarC 77093 3686 B4
Friendship Ln
2100 MtgC 77385 2823 B2
Friendship Rd
8500 HOUS 77055 3821 A3
8500 HOUS 77080 3821 A3
8800 HOUS 77080 3820 D3
Friends Knoll Ln
2700 FRDW 77546 4505 A7
N Friendswood Dr
- PRLD 77581 4505 A6
100 FRDW 77546 4505 A6
N Friendswood Dr FM-518
- PRLD 77581 4505 A6
100 FRDW 77546 4505 A6
S Friendswood Dr
100 FRDW 77546 4505 B7
500 FRDW 77546 4629 D3
2300 FRDW 77546 4630 A5
2600 LGCY 77573 4630 B6
S Friendswood Dr FM-518
100 FRDW 77546 4505 B7
500 FRDW 77546 4629 D3
2300 FRDW 77546 4630 A5
2600 LGCY 77573 4630 B6
Friendswood Rd
- FRDW 77546 4749 C5
1800 ALVN 77511 4749 C5
Friendswood Rd FM-528
- FRDW 77546 4749 C5
1800 ALVN 77511 4749 C5
Friendswood Lakes Blvd
- FRDW 77546 4629 B5
Friendswood Link Rd
2700 HarC 77546 4506 D7
2700 HarC 77546 4630 A1
2700 HarC 77598 4506 D7
2700 HarC 77598 4630 A1
2800 FRDW 77546 4630 B1
3600 FRDW 77546 4506 A7
3700 FRDW 77546 4505 E7
4000 FRDW 77546 4629 E1
Fries Ct
10 SPVL 77055 3820 E7
Fries Rd
1000 SPVL 77024 3959 E1
1000 SPVL 77055 3820 E7
1000 SPVL 77055 3959 E1
Friesian Tr
- HarC 77338 3261 D4
Frigate Dr
16600 HarC 77546 4506 A6
Fringewood Dr
8600 HOUS 77028 3687 D6
8700 HOUS 77078 3687 D6
Frio Dr
2000 BzaC 77583 4624 A2
2200 PRLD 77578 4624 B2
2200 PRLD 77583 4624 B2
21700 GLSN 77554 5441 B4
Frio St
400 HOUS 77012 4105 C2
Friobend Dr
8600 HarC 77040 3541 A6
Frio Canyon Ln
- HarC 77429 3253 A7
Frio River Lp
28800 MtgC 77386 2970 A2
Frio Springs Ct
13800 HarC 77429 3253 D6
Frio Springs Ln
15700 HarC 77429 3253 D6
Frisco Blvd
10 HOUS 77022 3824 B3
Fritsche Cemetery Rd
15900 HarC 77429 3253 A4
Fritz Drwy
43000 HMPD 77445 3097 E2
43000 WlrC 77445 3097 E2
Fritz Ln
22700 HarC 77389 2967 C7
Fritz Oaks Pl
14900 HarC 77014 3257 E5
14900 HarC 77068 3257 E5
Front Av
- FBnC 77545 4499 A5
1200 GlsC 77650 4995 B1
1600 GlsC 77650 4879 B7
Front St
600 RHMD 77469 4492 A1
2600 FBnC 77545 4498 E5
Frontenac Dr
8200 HOUS 77071 4239 D6
Frontenac Wy
10 WDLD 77382 2820 A1
Frontera Cir
10 WDLD 77382 2819 A2
W Frontera Cir
10 WDLD 77382 2819 A2
Frontera Ct
800 FBnC 77469 4365 B4
Frontera Dr
10 MtgC 77354 2819 A2
10 MtgC 77382 2819 A2
10 WDLD 77382 2819 A2
Frontier Dr
- HOUS 77080 3820 D1
3000 SGLD 77479 4368 E7
4000 SGLD 77479 4369 A7
4400 HOUS 77041 3820 D1
4500 HOUS 77041 3681 D7
Frontier Ln
1200 FRDW 77546 4629 A4
Frontier Rd
15800 SGCH 77355 2816 A7
15900 SGCH 77355 2815 E7
Frontier Path Ct
10 WDLD 77385 2676 C3
Frontiersman Ct
21600 HarC 77447 3105 E1
21600 HarC 77447 3106 A1
Frost Ln
1000 FBnC 77477 4369 C4
Frost St
900 RSBG 77471 4490 D4
4200 STFE 77517 4870 C7
5800 HarC 77032 3546 E1
5800 HOUS 77396 3546 E1
N Frost St
3800 STFE 77517 4870 C6
Frost Canyon Dr
19000 HarC 77377 3254 B1
Frost Creek Dr
- PRLD 77545 4499 D3
Frostdale Ln
3700 HarC 77047 4374 C4
N Frosted Pond Dr
10 WDLD 77381 2820 C3
S Frosted Pond Dr
10 WDLD 77381 2820 C3
Frosted Pond Pl
10 WDLD 77381 2820 B3
Frostfield Ln
- FBnC 77494 4092 D4
Frost Gate Ct
2700 HarC 77449 3814 E4
Frost Lake Ct
4100 MSCY 77459 4369 C7
Frost Lake Dr
4000 FBnC 77469 4234 C5
Frostmeadow Ct
3600 FBnC 77450 4094 C1
Frost Pass
- SGLD 77478 4369 A7
- SGLD 77479 4369 A7
Frostport Blvd
- HOUS 77029 3966 A2
- JTCY 77029 3966 A2
Frost River Ct
11300 HarC 77377 3254 E5
Frost School Ln
- FBnC 77469 4234 A7
Frost Springs Ln
- MtgC 77386 2969 C6
Frostview Ln
7200 HOUS 77489 4371 B5
Frostwood Cir
2700 DKSN 77539 4753 B3
Frostwood Dr
100 MtgC 77386 2968 C1
800 HOUS 77024 3959 A1
3300 BzaC 77584 4501 B6
Frostwood Valley Ct
7600 HarC 77095 3538 D2
Frosty Brook Dr
6300 HOUS 77085 4240 D7
Frosty Pass Dr
2900 HarC 77373 3115 A4
Fruend St
2700 HOUS 77003 3964 A4
Fruge Rd
400 PRLD 77047 4373 B7
Fruitvale Dr
900 HarC 77038 3543 D3
Fruitwood Dr
11400 HarC 77089 4378 B6
Fry Ct
- HOUS 77450 4094 B2
21500 FBnC 77450 4094 B2
Fry Rd
- FBnC 77494 4092 C5
- FBnC 77494 4093 A3
7000 HarC 77433 3676 E1
7000 HarC 77449 3676 E2
12000 HarC 77433 3396 A7
12200 HarC 77433 3395 E7
14000 HarC 77429 3396 B3
N Fry Rd
- HarC 77433 3676 E2
1000 HarC 77084 3954 E1
1000 HarC 77449 3954 E1
1000 HOUS 77084 3954 E1
1000 HOUS 77449 3954 E1
1200 HarC 77084 3815 E7
1200 HarC 77449 3815 E7
1200 HOUS 77084 3815 E7
1600 HOUS 77449 3815 E7
4600 HarC 77449 3676 E7
S Fry Rd
- FBnC 77450 3954 D7
- HarC 77084 3954 E1
- HarC 77449 3954 E1
- HOUS 77084 3954 E1
- HOUS 77449 3954 E1
300 HOUS 77094 3954 E1
300 HOUS 77450 3954 E1
700 HarC 77094 3954 E1
1500 HarC 77094 3955 A4
1500 HarC 77450 3955 A4
5200 FBnC 77450 4094 A3
5200 HOUS 77450 4094 B2
5800 FBnC 77450 4093 D4
6100 FBnC 77494 4093 B3
6100 HOUS 77494 4093 E4
Fry Access Rd
19900 HOUS 77094 3954 E1
19900 HOUS 77450 3954 E1
Frye Rd
26200 MtgC 77372 2683 C5
Fryer St
200 CNRO 77301 2384 A3
Fuchsia Ln
6900 HarC 77346 3264 E7
6900 HarC 77346 3265 A7
8100 HarC 77521 3833 B3
Fudge Dr
- MTBL 77520 3696 E5
Fudge St
1000 HarC 77530 3830 C6
Fuel Farm Rd
- HOUS 77061 4245 C4
Fuel Storage Rd
2000 HarC 77073 3404 B1
2000 HOUS 77032 3404 B1
2100 HOUS 77032 3260 C7
Fuerte Dr
14700 HarC 77083 4096 D6
Fugate St
400 HOUS 77009 3824 A6
E Fugate St
- HOUS 77009 3824 B6
W Fugate St
700 HOUS 77009 3824 A6
900 HOUS 77009 3823 E6
1100 HOUS 77008 3823 E6
Fulford Ct
4000 FBnC 77450 4094 B1
Fulford Point Ln
2900 FBnC 77494 3953 D7
Fulham Ct
2000 HOUS 77063 3960 A6
Fullen St
300 CNRO 77301 2383 E2
300 CNRO 77301 2384 A2
Fuller Rd
- GlsC 77510 4987 E5
- HTCK 77563 4987 E5
Fuller St
6100 HarC 77084 3678 E4
Fuller Bluff Dr
- MtgC 77386 2969 E4
Fullers Grant Ct
12000 HarC 77433 3395 C6
Fullerton Dr
10900 HOUS 77043 3819 C3
Fullgarden Ct
5700 HarC 77449 3676 D5
Full Moon Ct
1200 FBnC 77469 4365 D2
16300 MtgC 77302 2679 A4
Fulmer St
4900 HOUS 77009 3824 B4
Fulshear Ct
- WDLD 77382 2673 A7
Fulton Dr
- BzaC 77511 4868 C4
Fulton Dr CO-155
- BzaC 77511 4868 C4
N Fulton Dr
10 BzaC 77511 4868 A5
W Fulton Dr
10 BzaC 77511 4868 A5
Fulton St
1400 HOUS 77009 3963 C1
1700 ALVN 77511 4866 E2
1700 ALVN 77511 4867 A2
2400 HOUS 77009 3824 B6
6100 HOUS 77022 3824 A2
8300 HOUS 77022 3685 A7
9500 HOUS 77076 3685 A5
10300 HOUS 77076 3684 E4
N Fulton St
10 TXCY 77591 4873 C6
S Fulton St
10 LMQU 77568 4873 C7
10 TXCY 77591 4873 C7
Fultondale Ln
10200 HOUS 77075 4377 A2
Fulton Meadows Ln
6000 HOUS 77092 3682 C7
Fulton Point Dr
- HarC 77379 3257 A4
Fulton Springs Ct
11100 FBnC 77469 4092 C7
Fun Dr
- HOUS 77074 4100 B6
Funston St
100 HOUS 77012 4105 B1
W Fuqua Dr
- HOUS 77053 4371 D4
6300 HOUS 77085 4371 D4
6300 HOUS 77489 4371 D4
Fuqua Gdns
8200 HOUS 77075 4376 D3
Fuqua St
2900 HarC 77047 4374 E3
2900 HOUS 77047 4374 E3
4000 HOUS 77048 4374 E3
4100 GlsC 77518 4634 D2
4100 HOUS 77048 4375 A3
7700 HOUS 77075 4376 E3
9400 HOUS 77075 4377 A3
9900 HOUS 77089 4377 C3
11200 HOUS 77089 4378 A3
11500 HOUS 77034 4378 B2
W Fuqua St
- HOUS 77053 4371 E4
- HOUS 77053 4372 A3
- HOUS 77085 4371 E4
- HOUS 77085 4372 A3
2900 HOUS 77045 4373 A3
2900 HOUS 77053 4373 A3
3500 HOUS 77045 4372 B3
Fuqua Pr Two
- HOUS 77089 4377 E3
Furay Rd
6900 HarC 77016 3547 D7
6900 HOUS 77016 3547 B7
8900 HarC 77078 3547 D7
Furhill Dr
1800 HOUS 77077 3958 A6
Furlong Ln
- HOUS 77071 4239 D6
Furlong Wy
6900 GLSN 77551 5108 A7
Furman Rd
12400 HOUS 77047 4374 A2
13400 HarC 77047 4374 A5
14300 PRLD 77047 4374 A6
Fur Market Dr
7500 HarC 77064 3542 A5
7600 HarC 77064 3541 E5
Furnace Ln
5000 MNVL 77578 4626 A4
Furnace Rd
5100 MNVL 77578 4625 E5
5100 MNVL 77578 4626 A4
Furray Rd
8000 HOUS 77028 3826 C1
Furrow Ct
24100 MtgC 77365 2972 B6
Fussel Rd
10400 MtgC 77385 2822 E6
Future Gaylord Dr
11800 HOUS 77024 3959 B1
Future Schiel Rd
15200 HarC 77429 3253 D5

G

G St
1800 GNPK 77547 4106 C1
4000 HOUS 77072 4097 E4
4000 HOUS 77082 4097 E4
E G St
- LPRT 77571 4252 A3
100 LPRT 77571 4251 E3
W G St
200 LPRT 77571 4251 D4
G Wy
- HarC 77388 3111 D1
- HarC 77389 3111 D1
Gable Cir
40000 MtgC 77354 2671 B3
Gable Ln
- HarC 77066 3401 B6
Gable Ter
6200 FBnC 77479 4367 B6
Gable Bridge Ln
- FBnC 77469 4094 E7
Gabled Pines Pl
10 WDLD 77382 2674 B6
Gable Glen Ln
9000 HarC 77095 3537 E5
Gable Grove Ln
3700 FBnC 77494 4093 C2
Gable Hill Ln
10800 HarC 77067 3402 B7
Gable Hollow Ln
2100 HarC 77450 3954 C5
Gable Lodge Ct
300 HOUS 77024 3961 A2
Gable Lodge Dr
23300 FBnC 77494 3953 D5
Gable Meadows Dr
5400 FBnC 77479 4493 D2
Gable Meadows Ln
21300 HarC 77379 3111 C2
Gable Oak Ln
17800 HarC 77433 3537 D6
Gable Park Ct
1600 PRLD 77581 4376 D7
1600 PRLD 77581 4503 D1
Gable Park Ln
3200 PRLD 77581 4376 D7
Gablepoint
7700 HarC 77095 3537 B6
7700 HarC 77095 3538 B2
Gable Point Dr
2800 PRLD 77545 4499 D5
Gablepoint Dr
20000 HarC 77450 3954 E3
Gable Ridge Dr
20400 HarC 77450 3954 D6
Gables Bend Dr
- HarC 77377 3254 C3
Gable Stone Ln
1900 PRLD 77581 4503 E1
Gablestone Ln
6000 FBnC 77450 4094 A4
Gable Wind Ct
17300 HarC 77095 3537 C4
Gable Wind Mill Ln
12700 HarC 77044 3689 B3
Gable Wing Ln
- FBnC 77479 4496 B3
Gablewinn Ct
9300 HarC 77070 3399 D5
Gable Woods Dr
19600 HarC 77375 3109 D6
Gabriel
20500 MtgC 77357 2827 E5
Gabriel Pl
14200 MtgC 77384 2528 D7
Gabriel St
9000 HOUS 77063 4099 D1
Gabrielle Canyon Ct
6300 FBnC 77450 4094 C4
N Gabriel River Cir
1300 SGLD 77478 4369 A4
S Gabriel River Cir
1500 SGLD 77478 4369 A5
Gaby Virbo Dr
- HOUS 77072 4097 C5
13200 HOUS 77083 4097 C5
13300 HarC 77083 4097 B5
Gadsen St
17000 HMBL 77396 3406 C3
Gadshill Cir
14400 HarC 77044 3549 D1
Gadwall Ct
14400 HOUS 77044 3550 A1
Gadwall Dr
28000 FBnC 77494 3951 D5
Gadwall Bayou Ln
26900 HarC 77447 3248 E6
Gadwin Dr
24800 HarC 77389 2966 D3
Gadwin Park Dr
24800 HarC 77389 2966 D2
Gaeldom Dr
16400 HarC 77084 3678 D7
Gaeldom Ln
16500 HarC 77084 3678 C7
Gaelic Ct
4600 HarC 77084 3678 C7
Gaelic Dr
16600 HarC 77084 3678 C6
Gaelicglen Ln
17000 HarC 77084 3678 B5
Gaelic Hill Ln
- SGLD 77479 4495 C2
Gaff Ct
16900 HarC 77532 3552 A2
Gaff Rd
30800 MtgC 77355 2962 A6
30800 SGCH 77355 2962 A5
Gaffney Ln
- HOUS 77034 4378 B2
5600 HarC 77084 3678 C4
E Gafftoppers
3600 GLSN 77554 5221 B5
N Gafftoppers
11200 GLSN 77554 5221 A5
S Gafftoppers
11200 GLSN 77554 5221 A5
W Gafftoppers
3600 GLSN 77554 5221 B5
Gafftoppers Rd
11200 GLSN 77554 5221 A5
Gafna Cir
8000 HarC 77040 3541 E6
Gage Ct
10 HDWV 77024 3959 B2
10 HOUS 77024 3959 B2
Gage St
- HarC 77086 3542 B5
7300 HOUS 77086 3542 A5
Gagelake Ln
19300 HarC 77084 3816 A6
Gager St
3600 HOUS 77093 3686 B4
Gage Spring Ct
5200 HarC 77373 3115 C4
Gagne St
2200 HOUS 77020 3964 C1
Gail Dr
- SGCH 77362 2816 D6
22300 MtgC 77357 2973 E3
Gail Ln
- PASD 77505 4248 B4
Gail Rd
3400 BYTN 77521 3973 C3
Gailey Ln
7300 HarC 77040 3681 B1
N Gaillard St
10 BYTN 77520 3972 E7
S Gaillard St
10 BYTN 77520 3972 E7
Gail Meadow Ct
3600 FBnC 77494 3952 C7
Gail Shore Dr
18600 HarC 77433 3395 C5
Gaines Ln
23200 MtgC 77365 2973 E7
23200 MtgC 77365 2974 A7
Gaines Rd
8200 FBnC 77083 4096 C7
8700 FBnC 77083 4236 C2
9500 FBnC 77478 4236 C2
Gaines St
1100 HOUS 77009 3824 D5
Gaines Meadow Ct
15100 FBnC 77083 4096 D7
Gaines Meadow Dr
8200 FBnC 77083 4096 C7
Gainesville St
6200 HOUS 77020 3825 E7
7100 HOUS 77020 3826 A7
13700 HarC 77015 3828 E7
14100 HarC 77015 3829 A7
Gainesway Dr
13400 HarC 77429 3254 A6
Gainsborough Ct
9700 HOUS 77031 4238 E6
Gainsborough Dr
12200 HOUS 77031 4238 E6
Gairloch Dr
2000 LGCY 77573 4631 B6
Gairloch Ln
4100 HOUS 77025 4101 C6
Gala Ct
4100 FBnC 77477 4369 C4
Galan
- KMAH 77565 4634 A1
Galapagos Ct
22000 HarC 77449 3815 A4
Galawind
- HarC 77095 3538 E7
Galaxy Blvd
200 MtgC 77357 2829 C2
200 RMFT 77357 2829 C2
Galaxy St
9600 HOUS 77078 3687 B5
N Galayda St
- HarC 77086 3542 B5
11600 HOUS 77086 3542 B6
11600 HOUS 77088 3542 B6
Galbreath Dr
11300 HarC 77066 3400 E5
Galceran Dr
23400 GLSN 77554 5440 D6
Gale St
600 SEBK 77586 4509 E2
1100 HOUS 77009 3824 D4
Galena Dr
400 FRDW 77546 4505 C7
Galena Mnr
- GNPK 77547 3966 A7
- GNPK 77547 4106 B1
Galena Mnr
- HOUS 77547 4106 B1
Galena St
500 GNPK 77547 3966 D7
Galena Creek Dr
13400 HarC 77086 3541 E1
Galena Falls
20200 HarC 77375 3109 D5
Galentine Pt
11900 HarC 77429 3398 C3
Galesburg St
4300 HOUS 77051 4243 C3
4600 HOUS 77033 4243 C3
Galewood Ln
21800 HarC 77073 3259 B2
Galewood Wy
16700 HOUS 77058 4507 D2
Galium Meadows Dr
25000 HarC 77375 2965 C3
Gallagher Dr
4300 HOUS 77045 4372 C2
Gallagher Ln
1500 DRPK 77536 4108 E6
Gallahad St
7800 HOUS 77078 3687 B5
Gallaher Ct
3900 FBnC 77459 4621 C4
Gallant Ct
15500 HarC 77082 4096 B3
Gallant Flag Dr
10900 HarC 77375 3110 A4
Gallant Forest Dr
6000 HarC 77088 3542 C7
6300 HOUS 77088 3542 C7
Gallant Fox Dr
2400 STAF 77477 4370 A4
4100 PASD 77503 4108 D7
Gallant Glen Ln
7100 HarC 77095 3678 B1
Gallant Oak Pl
10 WDLD 77381 2674 D7
Gallant Ridge Ln
11200 HOUS 77082 4098 B2
Gallardia Ct
200 MtgC 77362 2816 E6
Gallentin Ln
19300 HarC 77377 3109 B7
Galleon Dr
200 BzaC 77541 5547 B7
2100 LGCY 77573 4509 B6
3900 GLSN 77554 5220 B6
7100 HOUS 77036 4099 D5
Galleon Field Ln
7700 HarC 77433 3537 B7
7700 HarC 77433 3677 C2
Galleon Oaks Dr
1600 HarC 77450 3954 D4
Galleon Point Ct
2400 PRLD 77584 4500 C3
Galleon Point Dr
12100 PRLD 77584 4500 C3
Galleria Oaks Ct
37700 MtgC 77354 2815 E1
Galleria Oaks Ln
37700 MtgC 77354 2815 E1
Gallery Ct
16700 HOUS 77053 4371 E7
Gallery Cove Ct
100 WDLD 77382 2819 A1
Gallery Grove Dr
- WDLD 77382 2673 D7
S Galley
700 HarC 77532 3552 B4
S Galley Ct
15600 HarC 77532 3552 B5
Galling Dr
15800 HOUS 77489 4371 C6
Gallinule Ln
10400 HOUS 77048 4244 D6
Gallitin Ln
19300 HarC 77377 3109 B7
Gallo
- HOUS 77035 4240 A4
- HOUS 77096 4240 A4
Gallo Dr
11300 HOUS 77035 4240 A4
11300 HOUS 77096 4240 A4
Galloway Dr
4000 PRLD 77584 4501 D7
Galloway Ln
6100 LGCY 77573 4630 C7
GA Lloyd Ln
- MtgC 77447 2960 B4
Gallup Dr
2400 DRPK 77536 4109 E7
Galmiche Rd
- HarC 77049 3690 E7
Galston Ln
9600 HarC 77379 3255 D4
Galvani Dr
14100 HarC 77429 3397 E7
Galveston Al
1900 GlsC 77650 4879 B7
Galveston Av
100 FBnC 77545 4499 C7
1200 GlsC 77650 4995 B1
1600 GlsC 77650 4879 B7
1900 PRLD 77581 4503 C4
2600 DKSN 77539 4633 B7
2700 DKSN 77539 4754 B1
Galveston Dr
12100 HarC 77433 3396 E6
Galveston Rd
- DKSN 77539 4754 B4
- FBnC 77545 4499 B7
- TXCY 77539 4754 B4
400 HOUS 77017 4246 B1
400 SHUS 77017 4246 C2
400 SHUS 77587 4246 E5
1900 HOUS 77012 4105 D4
2500 HOUS 77017 4105 D4
2500 HOUS 77034 4246 E5
4200 HOUS 77017 4106 A7
7600 HOUS 77034 4247 A6
8800 HOUS 77034 4378 B1
11700 HOUS 77034 4379 B6
11700 HOUS 77598 4379 B6
12700 HOUS 77062 4379 C7
14100 HOUS 77598 4506 E2
15200 HOUS 77062 4506 E3
Galveston Rd SR-3
400 HOUS 77017 4246 C2
400 SHUS 77017 4246 C2
400 SHUS 77587 4246 E5
2500 HOUS 77034 4246 E5
7600 HOUS 77034 4247 A6
8800 HOUS 77034 4378 B1
11700 HOUS 77034 4379 B6

STREET
Block City ZIP Map# Grid

Galveston Rd SR-3
11700 HOUS 77598 4379 B6
12700 HOUS 77062 4379 C7
14100 HOUS 77598 4506 E2
15200 HOUS 77062 4506 E2
Galveston St
100 HMPD 77445 3098 C1
400 CNRO 77301 2384 A4
700 CNRO 77301 2383 E4
800 SHUS 77587 4246 B4
3900 GlsC 77518 4634 C2
E Galveston St
100 LGCY 77573 4632 A3
W Galveston St
100 LGCY 77573 4631 E4
100 LGCY 77573 4632 B4
Galveston Country Club Dr
- GLSN 77554 5332 D2
E Galwan Cir
11800 HarC 77070 3399 D7
S Galwan Cir
9800 HarC 77070 3399 C6
W Galwan Cir
11800 HarC 77070 3399 C7
Galway Dr
500 DRPK 77536 4109 A6
Galway Ln
3600 HOUS 77080 3820 D2
4000 HOUS 77041 3820 D2
Galway Pl
10 WDLD 77382 2820 A2
Gambier Ln
6500 BLAR 77401 4101 B4
Gambit Dr
12400 HOUS 77477 4237 E4
Gamble Rd
14700 GlsC 77517 4986 A3
Gamble Oak Dr
19500 HarC 77346 3265 D5
Gambrel Wy
600 FBnC 77583 4744 A3
Gambrel Oak Pl
10 WDLD 77380 2967 D2
Gamebird Ln
9300 HOUS 77034 4377 E1
Game Cove Ln
13600 HarC 77044 3549 E7
Gamewood Ct
25700 MtgC 77386 2968 D1
Gamewood Dr
300 MtgC 77386 2968 C1
Gamlin Bend Dr
3700 HarC 77082 4096 B3
Gamma Av
1300 HarC 77532 3552 E4
Gamma St
1200 PASD 77504 4247 D6
Gammage St
4900 HOUS 77021 4104 A5
6300 HOUS 77087 4104 D6
7200 HOUS 77087 4105 A6
Gammon Dr
400 HOUS 77022 3684 D7
Gammon St
1900 RHMD 77469 4364 C7
Gammon Oaks Dr
9200 HarC 77095 3538 B5
Gander Bay Ln
8500 HOUS 77040 3682 B3
Ganderwood Dr
11500 HarC 77089 4378 A6
Gandy Rd
500 CTSH 77303 2385 E2
500 MtgC 77303 2385 E2
Ganges Ct
22800 MtgC 77365 2971 D4
S Gangway Ct
1000 HarC 77532 3552 A4
S Gangway Dr
900 HarC 77532 3552 A5
Gannet Ct
10 MtgC 77385 2676 D7
Gannet Hollow Pl
10 WDLD 77381 2820 E3
Gannet Peak Wy
21500 HarC 77449 3815 A1
Gannett St
3100 HOUS 77025 4101 E7
3100 HOUS 77025 4102 A7
Gannoway Lake Ct
1600 SGLD 77478 4236 E6
Gannoway Lake Dr
- SGLD 77478 4236 E6
Gano St
1500 HOUS 77009 3963 D2
2700 HOUS 77009 3824 D6
Gans St
100 HOUS 77029 3965 E7
300 HOUS 77029 3966 A7
400 GNPK 77029 3966 A7
Gant Rd
6600 HarC 77066 3400 D5
Gant St
7300 HarC 77521 3832 D4
Ganton Dr
21200 FBnC 77450 4094 B1
Ganyard Dr
1900 HOUS 77043 3819 E5
Garapan St
2300 HOUS 77091 3683 A5
Garber Ln
10500 JTCY 77029 3966 C2
13700 HarC 77015 3967 E2
14000 HarC 77015 3968 A2
Garcitas Cr
2600 FBnC 77469 4234 A7
2600 FBnC 77469 4365 A1
Garcroft St
9700 HOUS 77029 3966 A5
9800 GNPK 77547 3966 A5
Garden W
200 CNRO 77304 2382 D4
200 MtgC 77304 2382 D4
Garden Bnd
7800 FBnC 77479 4494 A6
Garden Brk
1200 FBnC 77479 4493 E6
1200 FBnC 77479 4494 A5
Garden Cir
1500 DRPK 77536 4109 D5
Garden Ct
10 CNRO 77304 2236 D7
1300 DRPK 77536 4109 D5
9400 HOUS 77033 4243 D4
Garden Dr
100 FRDW 77546 4629 B1
Garden Gln
10200 FBnC 77459 4621 E4

Garden Ln
2900 SGLD 77479 4496 A1
25600 MtgC 77372 2537 A2
Garden Rd
- PRLD 77581 4502 C2
Garden St
7000 HOUS 77087 4105 A3
7100 HOUS 77012 4105 A3
14100 STFE 77510 4870 C5
14100 STFE 77517 4870 C5
N Garden St
11500 MSCY 77071 4239 D7
11500 MSCY 77071 4370 D1
12400 HOUS 77071 4239 D7
S Garden St
11500 HOUS 77071 4239 D7
11500 MSCY 77071 4239 D7
Garden Wk
1500 DRPK 77536 4109 D5
Garden Wy
3600 FBnC 77459 4621 E5
Garden Arbor Ln
20800 FBnC 77469 4094 B5
Garden Bend Cir
15600 HarC 77433 3251 C6
Garden Branch Ct
4000 FBnC 77450 4094 A1
Garden Breeze Dr
9000 HOUS 77075 4376 D5
9000 HOUS 77075 4377 A4
Garden Bridge St
9400 HOUS 77075 4377 B4
Garden Brook Ct
14000 BzaC 77583 4623 D4
Garden Brook Ln
7100 HarC 77379 3111 B4
Garden Canyon Ct
1000 HarC 77450 3953 D3
Garden Canyon Dr
6400 HarC 77449 3676 C3
22700 HarC 77450 3953 D3
Garden Chase Ct
2100 FBnC 77494 3953 D6
Garden Chase Dr
23200 FBnC 77494 3953 D6
Garden City Dr
2600 HOUS 77088 3683 B1
Garden Cove Ct
4100 FBnC 77450 4093 D1
Garden Creek Dr
17200 HarC 77379 3255 D3
Garden Creek Wy
13900 HOUS 77059 4379 E5
13900 HOUS 77059 4380 A4
Garden Crest Ln
3300 HOUS 77018 3823 B3
Gardencrest Ln
1100 HOUS 77077 3957 A3
3000 LGCY 77539 4752 D4
Garden Crossing Ln
10200 FBnC 77459 4621 E4
Gardendale Dr
1000 HOUS 77018 3823 A3
3700 HOUS 77018 3822 B3
4000 HOUS 77092 3822 A3
5600 HOUS 77092 3821 D3
Garden Estates St
12400 HOUS 77072 4097 E5
Garden Falls Ct
20400 HarC 77433 3251 C6
Garden Falls Dr
2700 BzaC 77578 4501 A6
Garden Fern Ct
1900 HOUS 77062 4507 C1
Garden Field Ln
- PRLD 77583 4500 B5
3200 FBnC 77450 3954 A7
7200 FBnC 77469 4095 C6
Garden Flower Ct
5800 HarC 77449 3676 E5
Garden Ford Dr
4900 HOUS 77345 3120 A6
Garden Forest Dr
- HarC 77377 3254 B4
Garden Gale Ln
12300 HarC 77044 3689 A4
Garden Gate Wy
3400 HOUS 77059 4380 B5
Garden Glade Ct
17100 HarC 77095 3538 A7
Gardenglen Dr
11800 HarC 77070 3398 D2
12000 HarC 77429 3398 D2
Garden Glen Ln
1300 PRLD 77581 4376 E7
Garden Green Tr
3700 HarC 77449 3815 E2
Garden Grove Ct
13600 HarC 77082 4097 A2
Garden Grove Dr
10 BzaC 77583 4624 C4
3300 HarC 77066 3401 E7
Gardengrove Ln
15300 HOUS 77053 4372 C5
Garden Grove St
13300 HarC 77082 4097 A2
Garden Heath Ln
7100 FBnC 77469 4094 C6
21600 HarC 77449 3815 A3
Garden Hill Ln
16000 HarC 77095 3538 C7
Garden Hills Dr
5700 SGLD 77479 4495 A3
Garden Hills Ln
4300 HOUS 77345 3119 E3
4500 HOUS 77345 3120 A2
Garden Hollow Ct
5900 HOUS 77345 3120 C5
Garden Home Dr
1700 FBnC 77479 4494 B3
Gardenia Bnd
- HOUS 77053 4372 E3
Gardenia Cir
1400 RSBG 77471 4490 D5
Gardenia Ct
26300 MtgC 77354 2817 D4
Gardenia Dr
900 HOUS 77018 3823 A2
1000 HOUS 77018 3822 E2
5800 PRLD 77581 4502 C3
Gardenia Gdns
- HarC 77336 2976 C1
Gardenia Ln
4500 FBnC 77545 4623 C2
5500 KATY 77493 3813 C5
17400 MtgC 77357 2681 B7
17600 MtgC 77357 2827 B1

Gardenia St
2300 HarC 77562 3832 C3
Gardenia Tr
4800 PASD 77505 4248 A3
Gardenia Estates Dr
- HarC 77429 3396 A2
Garden Ivy Ln
1700 PRLD 77581 4503 D1
Garden Knoll Ln
7500 HarC 77396 3547 C2
Garden Lake Dr
3400 HOUS 77339 3119 A5
Garden Lakes Dr
1400 FRDW 77546 4629 B5
Garden Land Ct
900 HarC 77073 3259 B6
Garden Landing Dr
20100 HarC 77433 3537 A6
Garden Laurel Ln
12300 HarC 77014 3402 B3
Garden Leaf Ln
- HarC 77041 3679 D3
Gardenlilly Ct
4600 FBnC 77494 4092 D3
Garden Lodge Pl
10 WDLD 77382 2819 A2
Garden Manor Dr
- HarC 77449 3677 E5
17900 HarC 77084 3678 A5
18000 HarC 77084 3677 E5
Garden Meadow Dr
4600 HarC 77449 3677 A7
Garden Mist Ln
7000 HarC 77346 3408 E1
Garden Oaks Blvd
300 HOUS 77018 3823 B2
Garden Orchard Ln
13400 HarC 77044 3689 C3
Garden Park Dr
1200 DRPK 77536 4109 C5
Garden Parks Dr
7300 HOUS 77075 4376 B3
Garden Path Ct
2800 PRLD 77584 4503 B4
Garden Pl Dr
10600 FBnC 77478 4236 E4
10800 SGLD 77478 4236 E4
Garden Point Dr
2000 HOUS 77345 3120 B5
Garden Pool Ln
19400 HarC 77375 3109 E7
Garden Ridge Canyon
4900 FBnC 77469 4234 C3
Garden Rose Ln
800 HOUS 77018 3823 B3
Garden Row Dr
9600 FBnC 77478 4236 D2
Garden Run Ct
2900 HarC 77084 3816 A4
Gardens Rd
14000 PRLD 77581 4502 A2
Garden Sage Ct
26300 FBnC 77494 4092 C2
Garden Shadow Ln
3400 HOUS 77018 3823 B3
Garden Shadows Ln
11400 HarC 77433 3396 B7
Gardenspring Ct
13400 BzaC 77583 4623 E4
Garden Spring Dr
4100 HOUS 77339 3119 C3
Gardenspring Ln
6300 HarC 77379 3111 D3
Garden Springs Dr
13600 HarC 77083 4097 A4
Garden Stone Ln
- HarC 77379 3111 D5
Garden Stream Ct
- FBnC 77469 4365 A6
2200 HOUS 77062 4380 B7
Garden Terrace Dr
1600 HarC 77494 3953 D5
Garden Trace Ln
800 HOUS 77018 3823 B3
Garden Trail Ct
6300 HOUS 77072 4097 C4
Gardentree Dr
- HarC 77049 3690 E4
- HarC 77049 3691 A4
Gardentree Ln
11200 HarC 77044 3690 E1
Garden Valley Ln
- HarC 77095 3538 E4
Garden View Dr
- SGLD 77479 4494 D3
1400 HarC 77014 3402 C3
11600 HarC 77067 3402 D5
Garden Villa Dr
5300 KATY 77493 3813 C4
Garden Village Dr
5400 HOUS 77339 3119 B2
Gardenville St
13200 HOUS 77034 4378 C2
Garden Vista Dr
15100 HarC 77433 3251 B7
Gardenwalk Dr
700 LPRT 77571 4251 C5
Garden Wind Ct
20400 HarC 77379 3111 E4
Gardenwood Dr
3500 HOUS 77339 3119 C1
3600 HOUS 77345 3119 C1
Garden Wy Ln
500 PASD 77503 4108 C4
Gardner Ln
- HarC 77521 3834 D5
Gardner St
500 HOUS 77009 3824 A6
W Gardner St
900 HOUS 77009 3823 E6
900 HOUS 77009 3824 B7
1100 HOUS 77008 3823 E6
Gardner Park Ln
11800 FBnC 77478 4236 C6
Gardners Bnd
- HOUS 77049 3828 A2
Garett Green Cir
15200 HarC 77095 3538 B3
Garfield Av
200 PASD 77506 4107 A4
Garfield Dr
- PASD 77505 4248 E5
Garfield St
10 LPRT 77571 4251 E5
2300 HOUS 77088 3683 B2
7900 HOUS 77029 3965 B5
Garfield Wy
11200 GLSN 77554 5221 B5

Garfield Park Ln
9200 HOUS 77075 4377 A3
Gargan St
1000 HOUS 77009 3963 C1
Garland Av
5400 ARLA 77583 4623 B4
Garland Rd
40500 MtgC 77354 2671 D1
Garland St
- HOUS 77017 4106 A7
- HOUS 77023 4105 A3
1700 HOUS 77087 4105 A4
8000 HOUS 77017 4245 E2
8100 HOUS 77017 4246 A2
Garland Falls Dr
19000 HarC 77375 3109 D7
Garland Grove Pl
10 WDLD 77381 2820 C4
Garland Leaves St
18000 HarC 77084 3816 E4
Garland Path Bend Ln
- FBnC 77469 4094 A7
Garland Trail Ln
6600 HarC 77379 3111 C2
Garlang St
15700 HarC 77530 3969 A2
Garlenda Ln
12900 HOUS 77034 4378 C2
Garlot
- HarC 77530 3969 A2
Garner Ct
2700 BzaC 77584 4501 A5
Garner Rd
300 PASD 77502 4107 B7
Garnercrest Dr
17500 HarC 77095 3537 E7
17600 HarC 77095 3677 E1
Garner Grove Ln
- HarC 77449 3815 C2
Garner Mill Ln
12000 HarC 77089 4504 E2
Garner Park Dr
2800 PRLD 77584 4503 B4
Garnet Ct
2600 BzaC 77584 4501 A5
Garnet St
3700 SSPL 77005 4101 D4
Garnet Bend Ct
- WDLD 77382 2819 C2
Garnet Bend Dr
- WDLD 77382 2819 C2
N Garnet Bend Dr
10 WDLD 77382 2819 D2
S Garnet Bend Dr
10 WDLD 77382 2819 D2
Garnet Falls
3900 SGLD 77479 4495 A4
Garnet Falls Ln
9400 HarC 77396 3548 A1
Garnetfield Ln
5200 FBnC 77494 4093 B2
Garnet Grove Ct
- FBnC 77494 4092 D4
Garnet Hill Ln
7000 HarC 77346 3265 A7
7100 HarC 77346 3409 A1
Garnet Lake Ct
7000 FBnC 77469 4094 B7
Garnett
700 WALR 77484 3102 A5
Garnet Trail Ln
6800 FBnC 77469 4615 E5
Garnier Dr
1400 HOUS 77047 4373 E1
Garrett Blvd
2500 DRPK 77536 4249 E1
Garrett Dr
800 MtgC 77354 2673 D2
Garrett Rd
9000 HarC 77078 3688 A1
11500 HarC 77044 3688 E1
13000 HarC 77044 3689 D1
13600 HarC 77044 3690 D1
13600 HOUS 77044 3690 B1
15800 HarC 77044 3691 A1
20100 MtgC 77306 2680 E5
Garrett St
100 LMQU 77568 4872 E7
200 CNRO 77301 2383 E6
500 PASD 77506 4107 C5
Garrett Wy
700 FBnC 77479 4367 B6
Garrett Green Ln
8400 FBnC 77469 4095 D7
Garrett Knolls Ln
- FBnC 77469 4094 E7
Garretts Cove Ct
7200 HarC 77396 3547 C1
Garretts Gale Ln
- FBnC 77494 3953 C6
Garrettson Ln
1500 HOUS 77056 3961 A5
Garrettsville Dr
3600 BzaC 77584 4501 C5
Garrick Ct
10500 HOUS 77013 3966 B1
Garrick Ln
10600 HOUS 77013 3966 C1
Garris Rd
8000 GlsC 77510 4986 E6
8000 GlsC 77510 4987 A7
8000 GlsC 77517 4986 E6
Garrison Ct
2000 CNRO 77304 2383 A6
3300 HarC 77014 3401 E2
Garrison Point Ct
8000 HarC 77040 3541 D6
Garrison Point Dr
8000 HarC 77040 3541 D6
Garrison Run Dr
3500 MtgC 77386 2969 E3
Garrotsville St
400 HOUS 77022 3824 B1
Garrott St
3400 HOUS 77006 3962 E7
4300 HOUS 77002 4102 D3
Garrow St
2500 HOUS 77003 3963 E5
3800 HOUS 77003 3964 A6
6000 HOUS 77011 3964 D6
Garsee Dr
7600 HarC 77040 3682 A2
7600 HOUS 77040 3682 A2
Garth Rd
1200 BYTN 77520 3972 D6
2800 BYTN 77521 3972 D3
6800 BYTN 77521 3833 C3
7200 HarC 77521 3833 C3

Garth Rd
9000 HarC 77521 3694 C5
9000 HarC 77532 3694 C5
9000 HarC 77562 3694 C5
Garvey Dr
2300 PASD 77506 4107 E4
Garvin Av
8200 HarC 77064 3541 D3
Garvin Ct
100 HOUS 77007 3963 A2
Garwood Ct
40200 MtgC 77354 2671 C2
Garwood Dr
2400 HOUS 77091 3683 B4
11700 MtgC 77354 2671 C2
Gary Av
1300 PASD 77502 4247 C1
6300 TXCY 77591 4873 D6
Gary Ct
12200 HarC 77429 3397 B5
Gary Ln
3500 MtgC 77380 2821 A7
Gary St
6900 HOUS 77055 3821 D7
N Gary Glen Cir
- WDLD 77382 2819 B1
10 WDLD 77382 2673 C7
S Gary Glen Cir
- WDLD 77382 2673 C7
10 WDLD 77382 2819 B1
Garza St
19000 HarC 77532 3411 D5
Gaslamp Dr
16400 HarC 77095 3538 B4
Gaslamp Point Ct
19100 HarC 77433 3251 E7
Gaslight Ct
1700 SEBK 77586 4382 E7
Gaslight Ln
19500 MtgC 77357 2829 C5
E Gaslight Pl
10 WDLD 77382 2674 C4
W Gaslight Pl
10 WDLD 77382 2674 C4
Gaslight Village Dr
8800 HarC 77095 3538 B4
Gasmer Dr
4600 HOUS 77035 4241 A5
5100 HOUS 77035 4240 E5
Gasper Pl
- HarC 77433 3252 A3
Gasser Ln
5700 HOUS 77085 4240 E7
Gaston Rd
- FBnC 77469 4093 B5
- FBnC 77494 4092 E2
- FBnC 77494 4093 A3
Gaston St
4400 HarC 77093 3546 C7
5600 HOUS 77016 3546 D7
6200 HOUS 77016 3547 A7
Gastonbury Ct
400 LGCY 77573 4631 A6
Gastonbury Ln
20900 HarC 77338 3261 E4
Gaston-Fulshear Rd
25100 FBnC 77469 4092 C7
25300 FBnC 77469 4232 A1
N Gate Ln
20800 MtgC 77365 2825 E7
Gate 2 Rd
- HOUS 77029 3965 C6
Gatebriar Ct
7400 HOUS 77489 4371 B5
Gatebriar Dr
15700 HOUS 77489 4371 A6
Gatebrook Dr
- HOUS 77598 4506 D4
- WEBS 77598 4506 D4
19400 HarC 77598 4506 D4
Gate Canyon Ct
5400 HarC 77373 3260 E1
Gatecraft Dr
7400 HOUS 77489 4371 B4
Gate Creek Ct
23200 FBnC 77494 3953 D6
Gatecreek Dr
1600 PRLD 77581 4504 B7
Gatecrest Dr
800 HarC 77032 3403 D7
800 HarC 77032 3404 A6
Gate Hill Dr
10 WDLD 77381 2820 D4
Gatehouse Dr
7800 HarC 77040 3541 D7
Gatemere Ct
300 HarC 77450 3953 D1
Gatemont Ct
12200 HarC 77066 3401 B6
Gatemound Ct
20600 FBnC 77469 4094 D7
Gatepoint Dr
21100 HarC 77073 3259 B6
Gateridge Dr
7300 HarC 77041 3679 C1
Gates Lp
9400 MNVL 77578 4746 B6
Gates Rd
100 ALVN 77511 4748 C5
100 BzaC 77511 4748 C5
Gates St
7900 HOUS 77028 3826 B4
Gatesbury Ct
3200 HarC 77082 4096 D2
Gatesbury Dr
15200 HarC 77082 4096 B2
Gatesbury North Dr
3100 HarC 77082 4096 B2
Gatesden Dr
- HarC 77070 3255 A6
- HOUS 77070 3255 A6
11300 HarC 77377 3255 A6
11400 HarC 77377 3254 E6
Gates Farm Ln
14900 FBnC 77478 4236 D4
Gates Head Pl
10 WDLD 77382 2819 A1
Gateship Dr
300 HarC 77073 3259 A6
Gateside Dr
800 HarC 77032 3403 E6
800 HarC 77032 3404 A6
Gatesprings Dr
- HarC 77433 3396 A4
Gatesprings Ln
5500 FBnC 77479 4493 D2
N Gate Stone
- HOUS 77007 3962 D3

S Gate Stone
300 HOUS 77007 3962 D3
Gatestone Dr
- HarC 77450 3953 E4
Gate View Dr
20900 HarC 77073 3259 B6
Gateview Ln
15400 HOUS 77489 4371 B5
Gateway Blvd
- FBnC 77478 4367 A5
- FBnC 77479 4367 A5
- SGLD 77478 4367 A5
E Gatewick Ln
- HarC 77073 3258 E2
Gatewood Av
5500 HOUS 77053 4371 E4
5500 HOUS 77053 4372 A4
Gatewood Rd
3800 HarC 77532 3412 D4
Gatlinburg Dr
10900 HOUS 77031 4239 B4
Gatling Ct
19900 HarC 77449 3815 E6
Gatmere Ct
9400 FBnC 77478 4236 D2
Gatton Park Dr
13000 HarC 77066 3401 B4
Gatwick
- HarC 77379 3256 A5
Gatwick Ln
- HarC 77449 3814 E6
Gaucho Ct
1700 LPRT 77571 4110 B7
Gaucho Dr
17300 FBnC 77083 4095 D7
Gauge Hollow Ct
- FBnC 77469 4235 C1
Gauguin Dr
9000 HOUS 77088 3682 B2
Gauguin Ln
9100 FBnC 77459 4621 B7
Gault Rd
1500 HarC 77039 3545 C3
Gauntlet Dr
10 WDLD 77382 2673 D7
Gautier Ct
13200 HarC 77065 3539 B1
Gautier Dr
11200 HarC 77065 3539 B1
Gavin Ct
1600 HarC 77379 3110 B6
Gavin Ln
16100 HarC 77530 3829 D3
Gawain Ln
10500 HNCV 77024 3960 B2
Gay Dr
- CNRO 77301 2384 A3
500 CNRO 77301 2383 E3
Gay St
- BzaC 77583 4623 D6
- PRLD 77583 4623 D6
6100 HOUS 77022 3824 B3
19200 HarC 77532 3411 D4
Gayla Ln
5100 BYTN 77521 3972 A1
5300 BYTN 77521 3971 E1
Gaylawood Dr
12700 HarC 77066 3401 A2
Gayle St
100 MAGA 77355 2669 A5
19200 HarC 77532 3411 E5
Gaylin Hills Ct
2100 MtgC 77386 2969 D6
Gaylord Dr
- HDWV 77024 3959 D1
9400 HOUS 77024 3959 C1
Gaylord St
8700 HDWV 77024 3959 E1
8700 HDWV 77024 3960 A1
Gaylyn Cir
1000 HarC 77073 3259 B7
Gaymoor Dr
11300 HOUS 77035 4240 E4
Gaynor Av
3500 FBnC 77545 4499 C7
E Gaywood Dr
300 HOUS 77079 3958 C3
W Gaywood Dr
200 HOUS 77079 3958 C3
Gaywood St
- HOUS 77043 3819 C4
Gazania St
11800 HarC 77065 3398 D6
Gazebo Ln
3900 FBnC 77459 4621 E4
Gazelle Ln
3700 PRLD 77584 4502 D6
Gazin St
500 HOUS 77020 3964 E1
Gearen Ct
14600 HarC 77429 3253 D4
Gears Lp
1000 HarC 77067 3402 E6
1000 HarC 77067 3402 E6
Gears Rd
100 HOUS 77060 3403 A6
100 HOUS 77067 3403 A6
600 HOUS 77067 3402 D6
1100 HarC 77067 3402 D6
3000 HarC 77066 3401 E6
3000 HarC 77067 3401 E6
Geddes Grv
9100 FBnC 77459 4621 B6
Geffert Wright Ln
27000 ORDN 77386 2822 C7
27100 MtgC 77386 2822 D7
Gehan Woods Dr
10000 HarC 77375 3255 A2
Gehring St
6100 HOUS 77021 4103 A4
Gellhorn Dr
100 HOUS 77013 3826 E7
200 HOUS 77029 3826 D7
900 HOUS 77029 3965 D3
Gelnsheen Wy
10 WDLD 77382 2673 D7
Gem Brook Ln
12000 HarC 77089 4504 B2
Gem Dale Ct
5000 FBnC 77469 4234 C3
Gemini
15000 HOUS 77053 4372 C4
Gemini St
500 HarC 77058 4507 B4
500 HarC 77598 4507 B4
1000 HOUS 77058 4507 D2
Gemsong Meadows Ct
- HOUS 77085 4371 A2

Gem Stone Ct
1100 BYTN 77521 3973 B3
Gemstone Park Rd
5300 FBnC 77469 4234 C3
Gena Ct
10300 HarC 77064 3541 D
Genadena St
100 HOUS 77034 4378 C
N Gena Lee Dr
6500 HarC 77064 3541 D
S Gena Lee Dr
6500 HarC 77064 3541 D
Genard Rd
- HOUS 77041 3680 E
9800 HOUS 77041 3681 A
Gendley Dr
13200 HarC 77041 3679 C
Gene Campbell Blvd
20100 MtgC 77357 2825 D4
20100 MtgC 77357 2826 A3
20100 MtgC 77365 2825 D4
22200 MtgC 77357 2827 A3
Genemaury St
9900 HOUS 77088 3683 B
10000 HOUS 77088 3543 A
General Dr
6700 FBnC 77469 4493 C7
General Colony Dr
2500 HarC 77546 4506 A6
General Gresham Ln
13400 HarC 77429 3397 A4
General Lee
8900 LPRT 77571 4249 E4
General Lee Ln
- FBnC 77469 4616 E
General Thomas Kelly Blvd
1000 CNRO 77303 2238 E6
Genesee St
1000 HOUS 77019 3962 E6
1800 HOUS 77006 3962 E5
Genesee Ridge Ct
200 WDLD 77385 2676 C4
Genesee Ridge Dr
10 WDLD 77385 2676 C4
Genessee Creek Ln
3000 HarC 77546 4506 A7
Genesse Valley Dr
25000 HarC 77389 2966 C2
Geneva Dr
4500 HarC 77014 3401 B
4500 HarC 77066 3401 B2
5100 FRDW 77546 4505 D6
29400 MtgC 77386 2969 A4
E Geneva Dr
30100 MtgC 77386 2969 A2
W Geneva Dr
30100 MtgC 77386 2969 A2
Geneva St
- BLAR 77401 4101 B3
Geneva Fields Dr
19800 HarC 77433 3251 E6
Geneva Hills Ln
27700 MtgC 77386 2969 D7
Geneva Springs Ln
28100 MtgC 77386 2969 D6
Genie
10 HarC 77049 3828 E3
Genie St
- HarC 77049 3828 E2
Genoa Ct
2900 MtgC 77357 2829 C2
Genoa St
600 HOUS 77034 4246 D4
600 SHUS 77034 4246 D4
600 SHUS 77587 4246 D4
Genoa Red Bluff Rd
100 HOUS 77034 4378 D1
600 HOUS 77504 4378 D1
700 HOUS 77034 4247 E7
700 PASD 77034 4247 E7
1100 HOUS 77504 4247 E7
1100 HOUS 77504 4248 A7
1100 PASD 77504 4247 E7
1600 HOUS 77034 4248 A7
1600 HOUS 77505 4248 A7
1600 PASD 77504 4248 A7
1600 PASD 77505 4248 A7
2200 PASD 77034 4248 C7
3400 HOUS 77059 4248 D7
3600 PASD 77059 4248 D7
3900 HOUS 77059 4249 A7
3900 PASD 77059 4249 A7
3900 PASD 77505 4249 A7
4000 HOUS 77505 4249 B7
5500 PASD 77507 4249 D7
Genova St
900 SGLD 77478 4368 B3
1300 HOUS 77009 3824 D7
Gens Ct
10 SPVL 77055 3821 B7
Gentilly Dr
200 HarC 77450 3954 A2
Gentilly Pl
300 BKHV 77024 3959 C4
300 HOUS 77024 3959 C4
Gentilly Ter
10 CNRO 77304 2382 E3
Gentle Bend Dr
1100 MSCY 77489 4370 D5
6600 HarC 77069 3400 B2
Gentle Breeze Ct
15200 HarC 77429 3253 D5
Gentle Brook Ct
2400 HOUS 77062 4379 E6
Gentlebrook Dr
12300 PRLD 77584 4500 B4
Gentle Cove Ct
18800 HarC 77084 3677 B6
Gentle Creek Wy
19500 HarC 77429 3395 D1
19500 HarC 77433 3395 D1
Gentle Glen Ln
20800 HarC 77338 3261 B3
Gentle Haze Ct
10 WDLD 77382 2819 B1
Gentle Mist Ct
20300 HarC 77433 3251 C6
Gentle Mist Ln
20400 HarC 77433 3251 B6
Gentle Moss Ln
23800 FBnC 77494 4093 A5
Gentle Ridge Ct
20500 HarC 77433 3251 B6
Gentle Stone Ct
8700 HarC 77095 3538 B5
Gentle Stone Dr
16600 HarC 77095 3538 A5

STREET
Block City ZIP Map# Grid
Gentle Water Dr
- HOUS 77044 3409 A4
13000 HOUS 77044 3408 E5
Gentle Willow Ln
7300 FBnC 77494 4093 A5
Gentle Wind Dr
400 LGCY 77565 4633 B2
400 LGCY 77573 4633 B2
Gentlewind Pl
10 WDLD 77381 2675 A7
Gentle Winds Ln
13800 HOUS 77044 3409 B4
Gentlewood Ct
8300 HarC 77095 3538 B5
Gentry Rd
13600 MtgC 77306 2533 B6
21200 HarC 77429 3538 D1
21200 HarC 77429 3539 C3
Gentry St
- BYTN 77520 3972 D7
200 HarC 77373 3114 A2
1100 CNRO 77301 2384 A4
1500 HOUS 77009 3963 C1
2400 HOUS 77009 3824 C7
Gentry Oak Ct
10 WDLD 77381 2821 D3
Gentryside Ct
13000 HOUS 77077 3957 B6
Gentryside Dr
- HOUS 77077 3957 B6
- HOUS 77082 3957 B7
Gentryside Ln
1800 HOUS 77077 3957 B6
Geoffrey Ct
- HMBL 77338 3262 E4
George
100 LGCY 77573 4632 B3
17200 HarC 77044 3551 C7
George Av
1500 RHMD 77469 4364 D7
George Ct
2600 PRLD 77581 4504 E5
George Ln
700 RHMD 77469 4491 D2
15800 WlrC 77445 3243 D6
George St
100 ALVN 77511 4867 C2
100 LMQU 77568 4874 C7
1100 RSBG 77471 4490 D5
1400 PASD 77502 4107 D6
2500 PRLD 77581 4504 E5
2900 GlsC 77518 4634 B2
3300 HOUS 77026 3825 A4
7700 BYTN 77520 3835 D4
N George St
3400 HOUS 77026 3825 A4
W George St
300 ALVN 77511 4867 B2
George Wy
16600 HOUS 77396 3405 D4
George Altwater Dr
- HOUS 77571 4252 C1
200 MRGP 77571 4251 E1
700 MRGP 77571 4252 A1
George Foundation Wy
100 MtgC 77304 2529 C3
Georges Wy
24500 HOUS 77336 3266 C2
George Strake Dr
100 CNRO 77304 2529 E2
Georgetown Dr
2100 KATY 77493 3813 C5
2700 PLEK 77471 4614 D6
13100 SGLD 77478 4237 B4
Georgetown St
2800 WUNP 77005 4102 A3
3000 WUNP 77005 4101 E3
Georgetown Colony Dr
5600 HarC 77084 3679 A4
Georgetown Glen Cir
9300 HarC 77433 3537 B4
Georgetown Park Dr
12300 PASD 77058 4380 E6
George Washington Ln
3500 MSCY 77459 4369 D4
Georgi Ln
5000 HOUS 77092 3821 E1
5000 HOUS 77092 3822 A2
Georgia Av
100 DRPK 77536 4108 E5
100 HOUS 77017 4246 C2
100 HOUS 77587 4246 C2
500 LGCY 77573 4632 B3
500 SHUS 77587 4246 B4
1400 SHUS 77017 4246 B4
1800 DRPK 77536 4109 A7
4100 DKSN 77539 4754 C2
Georgia Pk
600 MtgC 77302 2530 A5
Georgia St
100 HOUS 77029 3965 E6
200 HOUS 77029 3966 A6
1800 BYTN 77520 4112 A1
4200 GlsC 77517 4869 E6
20600 MNVL 77578 4747 A2
Georgia Hollow Ct
13400 BzaC 77583 4623 E4
Georgian Row
- WDLD 77380 2821 C5
Georgianna Dr
6300 PASD 77503 4248 D2
6600 DRPK 77503 4248 D2
6600 DRPK 77536 4248 D2
Georgia Pine Dr
3100 HarC 77373 3114 E7
3100 HarC 77373 3115 A6
Georgibelle Dr
10200 HOUS 77043 3819 E7
10200 HOUS 77043 3820 A7
Georgina St
1100 RSBG 77471 4491 A5
Georgio Dr
9100 HarC 77044 3689 C4
Geral Ln
15300 HarC 77084 3678 D4
Gerald Dr
2800 PASD 77503 4248 E2
Gerald Ln
100 BYTN 77520 3971 B4
Geraldine St
4700 PASD 77586 4383 C4
Geralds Run
- HarC 77375 2964 C2
Gerber Ln
9200 HarC 77396 3406 E5
9200 HarC 77396 3407 A5
Gerda St
6700 BKVL 77581 4376 A6
Gerken Rd
3400 FBnC 77461 4614 B7
Gerlach St
10300 HOUS 77034 4378 C2
Gerngross Ln
13200 HarC 77044 3689 C6
Gerol Cir
2500 GLSN 77551 5222 A1
Gerol Ct
2600 GLSN 77551 5222 A1
Gerol Dr
2400 GLSN 77551 5222 A1
Gerona Blvd
1200 RSBG 77471 4491 C4
Geronimo Ct
700 HarC 77450 3954 A2
14600 HarC 77047 4374 D5
Geronimo Ln
2100 FBnC 77471 4614 D4
3900 PASD 77505 4248 B4
Geronimo Pl
100 PNVL 77304 2237 B3
Geronimo St
33400 MtgC 77355 2962 E1
33400 SGCH 77355 2962 E1
33500 MtgC 77355 2816 E7
33500 SGCH 77355 2816 E7
Geronimo Lake Dr
4000 HarC 77047 4374 D5
Gerrards Cross Dr
13400 HOUS 77082 4097 B3
Gerry Dr
300 MtgC 77303 2385 C2
Gershwin Dr
300 HOUS 77079 3958 D3
Gershwin Oak St
12300 HOUS 77089 4378 C7
Gertie
- BYTN 77520 4112 E1
Gertin St
3900 HOUS 77004 4103 D3
Gervaise Dr
14600 HarC 77429 3253 D4
Gessner Rd
- HarC 77064 3541 A7
- HOUS 77043 3959 A1
- HOUS 77055 3959 A1
10 HOUS 77024 3959 A5
10 HOUS 77063 3959 B5
200 BKHV 77024 3959 A4
1000 HOUS 77043 3820 A1
1000 HOUS 77055 3820 A7
1300 HOUS 77080 3820 A1
3100 HOUS 77041 3820 A1
4400 HOUS 77041 3681 A7
7000 HarC 77040 3681 A2
7700 HarC 77040 3541 A7
11200 HarC 77064 3400 A7
11200 HOUS 77064 3400 A7
11200 HOUS 77064 3541 A1
N Gessner Rd
5700 HOUS 77041 3681 A6
6500 HOUS 77040 3681 A4
6800 HarC 77040 3681 A4
S Gessner Rd
- MSCY 77071 4370 B1
1000 HOUS 77063 3959 B7
1400 HOUS 77042 3959 B6
2900 HOUS 77063 4099 B3
3700 HOUS 77042 4099 B3
3800 HOUS 77036 4099 B3
8000 HOUS 77074 4099 C7
9100 HOUS 77074 4239 C3
9600 HOUS 77031 4239 C2
9800 HOUS 77071 4239 C2
12600 MSCY 77071 4239 C7
13200 MSCY 77489 4370 B1
Gessport Blvd
- HOUS 77071 4239 B7
Gettie St
- FBnC 77545 4498 E7
Gettysburg Av
9000 TXCY 77591 4872 E6
9000 TXCY 77591 4873 A5
Gettysburg Ct
700 MtgC 77302 2530 C7
12000 HarC 77377 3254 D6
Gettysburg Dr
2500 LGCY 77573 4631 B5
6700 FBnC 77469 4493 C6
15300 HarC 77070 3254 D6
15300 HarC 77377 3254 D5
Gettysburg Ln
900 FBnC 77469 4616 D1
Gettysburg Valley Ct
6300 HarC 77449 3677 B4
Gettysburg Valley Dr
19100 HarC 77449 3677 B4
GG Dr
- PASD 77503 4248 D3
- PASD 77505 4248 D3
GH Cir
20200 WlrC 77484 3101 C5
Ghana Dr
5900 PASD 77505 4248 D6
Ghinaudo Dr
5000 HTCK 77510 4988 A2
5000 HTCK 77563 4988 A2
Ghost Crab Ln
4100 GLSN 77554 5333 A2
Gianna Ct
9100 FBnC 77083 4236 E1
Gianna Springs Ct
3100 HarC 77396 3407 D2
Giant Hickory Dr
20000 MtgC 77355 2960 E1
20000 SGCH 77355 2960 E1
Gibbons Ct
1200 RSBG 77471 4491 D5
Gibbons St
8300 HOUS 77012 4105 D3
Gibbons Creek Wy
- HarC 77433 3537 B5
Gibbs St
900 HOUS 77009 3823 E4
1200 HOUS 77009 3824 C2
12800 GlsC 77517 4986 B7
Gibraltar Cir
- HarC 77038 3543 B5
Gibralter Pl
5300 FBnC 77469 4234 D3
Gibson Ln
13600 STFE 77510 4870 D3
Gibson St
3900 HOUS 77007 3962 C3
Gibson Wy
1200 HarC 77067 3402 C4
Giddings Ln
8600 HarC 77064 3540 D6
Gideon Ct
6000 FBnC 77479 4367 A6
Gideon Rd
15000 MtgC 77306 2680 A2
Gifford Hl
- HarC 77041 3680 B2
Gig Ct
400 HarC 77532 3552 B1
Gila Dr
22800 MtgC 77365 2971 D3
Gila Bend Ln
11600 HarC 77377 3109 B7
Gila Cliff Ln
17600 HarC 77346 3408 B2
Gilbert Av
4700 HOUS 77045 4372 C2
Gilbert Dr
24500 MtgC 77365 2973 C7
24700 MtgC 77365 3118 C1
Gilbert St
- HarC 77532 3552 C3
300 PASD 77506 4107 C4
Gilbertyn Dr
15600 HarC 77377 3254 E6
Gilbough Dr
24600 HarC 77375 2965 D3
Gilbough St
7100 MNVL 77578 4746 D2
Gilcrest Dr
- HarC 77014 3257 E6
Gilcrest Forest Ct
10 WDLD 77381 2821 A4
Gilded Crest Ct
10 WDLD 77382 2819 C3
Gilded Pond Pl
10 WDLD 77381 2674 C7
Gilder Rd
8800 HarC 77064 3399 E6
8800 HOUS 77064 3399 E6
9000 HarC 77070 3399 D6
Gildus Dr
7200 HarC 77379 3111 B1
Giles Rd
10700 GlsC 77510 4871 D5
Gilford Ln
3000 FBnC 77494 3953 C7
3000 FBnC 77494 4093 A6
Gilford Crest Dr
10600 HarC 77379 3110 A6
Gil Jr Ln
10000 HOUS 77075 4377 C2
Gill Rd
1600 LGCY 77539 4753 B1
1600 LGCY 77573 4753 B1
1700 DKSN 77539 4753 C1
1700 GlsC 77539 4753 C1
Gill St
17400 HarC 77044 3551 C7
Gillen St
7000 HOUS 77087 4104 E7
7100 HOUS 77087 4105 A7
Gillespie Rd
- HOUS 77037 3544 B2
- HOUS 77060 3544 B2
W Gillespie Rd
11200 HarC 77038 3544 A2
11200 HOUS 77037 3544 A2
Gillespie St
2800 HOUS 77020 3964 A3
Gillespie Briar Dr
10700 HOUS 77016 3687 A3
Gillette Dr
1600 BYTN 77520 3973 C6
Gillette St
700 HOUS 77019 3963 A5
1800 HOUS 77006 3963 A5
Gillian Park Dr
6200 HarC 77449 3677 C4
Gillingham Ln
10 SGLD 77478 4368 C1
600 SGLD 77478 4237 C6
Gillingham Wy
1700 PASD 77504 4247 E5
Gilliom Dr
2600 HarC 77084 3816 A5
Gillium Bluff Pl
10 WDLD 77382 2674 B5
Gillman Dr
9800 HOUS 77078 3687 E5
Gillman Pk
13600 HarC 77060 3403 B4
13600 HarC 77073 3403 B4
Gills Rd
- HarC 77521 3832 E7
Gilman Trace Ln
6000 HOUS 77092 3682 C7
Gilmar Dr
3000 MSCY 77459 4370 A7
Gilmore Rd
10900 MtgC 77372 2536 E2
11300 MtgC 77372 2537 A2
Gilmore St
1600 CNRO 77301 2384 B2
Gilmore Grove Pl
10 WDLD 77382 2819 A2
Gilpin St
100 HOUS 77034 4246 E6
100 HOUS 77034 4247 A6
Gilson Ln
10000 HarC 77086 3541 E2
Giltspur Wy
24700 HarC 77389 2966 E2
Gimbals Wy
17700 HarC 77532 3411 B7
Gina Ln
13100 HarC 77037 3544 E7
Gina St
13100 STAF 77477 4370 A1
Gineridge Dr
5500 HOUS 77053 4371 E6
Ginger Brk
12400 HarC 77041 3679 E3
Ginger Ct
3700 BzaC 77578 4625 C1
Ginger Dr
8100 HarC 77375 2819 E6
8100 HarC 77389 2819 E6
8100 HarC 77389 2820 A6
Ginger Gln
10500 FBnC 77459 4622 A6
Ginger Ln
3600 PRLD 77581 4503 E5
3600 PRLD 77581 4504 A5
15600 JRSV 77040 3540 D7
Ginger Rd
700 GlsC 77517 4752 B7
Ginger Rd
1000 GlsC 77517 4870 B1
Ginger St
6200 HOUS 77091 3683 A5
Ginger Bay Pl
10 WDLD 77382 2675 C7
Ginger Bell Dr
5500 HarC 77084 3677 E5
Ginger Cove Ct
1400 PRLD 77545 4499 D3
Ginger Cove Ln
2700 PRLD 77545 4499 D3
12600 HarC 77086 3542 C4
Ginger Creek Tr
20000 HarC 77450 3954 E4
Ginger Fields Ln
17100 HarC 77377 3254 D3
Ginger Jar St
10 WDLD 77382 2674 C5
Gingerleaf Ln
1600 HOUS 77055 3821 C6
Ginger Lei Ln
11900 HarC 77044 3688 E5
Ginger Mint Ct
2400 FBnC 77469 4365 A1
Ginger Park Dr
7800 HarC 77521 3833 D2
Ginger Ponds Dr
5700 HarC 77041 3679 E6
Ginger Ridge Ln
17600 HarC 77377 3254 B3
Ginger Run Wy
16300 FBnC 77478 4236 A5
Ginger Springs Pl
10 WDLD 77385 2676 C3
Gingerstick Ln
15100 HarC 77049 3829 A3
Gingerwilde Pl
10 WDLD 77381 2820 D2
Gingerwood Dr
- BzaC 77584 4501 D4
- PRLD 77584 4501 D4
Gingham Dr
400 PNPV 77024 3959 D3
Gingko Cir
- HarC 77396 3406 E5
Ginkgo Biloba Ct
- HOUS 77075 4377 B2
Ginseng Dr
5200 HarC 77521 3833 D3
Ginseng Ln
300 HarC 77532 3552 C3
Ginter Ln
3000 FBnC 77494 3952 E7
Girard St
800 HOUS 77002 3963 C3
1000 HOUS 77007 3963 B3
Girl Scout Ln
- TXCY 77590 4875 B5
4400 HarC 77546 4505 E5
Girnigoe Dr
5100 HarC 77084 3678 C5
Gironde Dr
7900 MSCY 77071 4239 E6
Giusti Ln
12100 STFE 77510 4871 B5
Givenchy Ct
13200 HarC 77044 3689 C4
Givens St
1200 HOUS 77007 3962 E2
Giverny Ct
1100 HarC 77379 3255 C2
Glacier Av
8000 TXCY 77591 4873 A6
Glacier Dr
2600 HarC 77067 3401 E4
Glacier Ln
4200 DRPK 77536 4249 C1
Glacier Wy
- HarC 77044 3549 B3
Glacier Bay Ct
18300 HarC 77346 3408 D1
Glacier Blue Dr
1500 FBnC 77545 4622 D1
Glacier Brook Ct
16300 PASD 77059 4380 D5
Glacier Creek Ln
- HarC 77083 4097 A6
Glacier Falls Dr
20100 HarC 77375 3109 E5
Glacier Hill Dr
1000 HOUS 77077 3956 E3
Glacier Point Ct
17300 HarC 77346 3408 B4
Gladden Dr
12600 HarC 77049 3828 B1
Glade Ct
1400 FBnC 77545 4622 C2
N Glade Dr
16400 HarC 77073 3259 A5
Glade St
2200 PRLD 77584 4501 B2
Glade Bank Pl
10 WDLD 77382 2674 D5
Gladebeck Ln
13300 HarC 77377 3253 E2
Gladebriar Dr
5400 HOUS 77345 3119 C1
5400 HOUS 77365 3119 C1
Glade Bridge Ct
100 LGCY 77539 4752 E4
14000 HarC 77429 3254 A5
Glade Bridge Ln
200 LGCY 77539 4752 E4
300 LGCY 77539 4753 A4
Gladebrook Ct
3900 HarC 77068 3257 B6
Gladebrook Dr
14600 HarC 77014 3257 B7
14600 HarC 77068 3257 B7
Gladebrook Glen Ln
16000 HarC 77095 3678 C1
Glade Canyon Ct
21800 HarC 77388 3111 D2
Glade Creek Dr
3600 HOUS 77339 3119 C5
Glade Crest Ln
- HarC 77433 3677 E1
Glade Estates Dr
5400 HOUS 77339 3119 C2
Gladefield Dr
11200 HOUS 77099 4238 B2
Glade Forest Dr
3700 HOUS 77339 3119 B4
Gladehill Dr
5100 HOUS 77345 3120 A4
Glade Hollow Dr
13800 HarC 77014 3402 C3
Glade Meadow Ln
13200 MtgC 77302 2530 D4
Glademeadow Ln
1800 FBnC 77469 4616 B2
Gladepark Ct
5600 HarC 77084 3677 E5
Glade Point Dr
14300 HarC 77429 3396 E1
Gladeridge Dr
3800 HarC 77068 3257 A6
Glade River Ln
11700 HarC 77377 3254 D3
Gladesdale Park Ln
4500 FBnC 77450 4094 A2
Gladeside Dr
5100 HarC 77449 3676 D6
Gladesmore Ln
- HarC 77377 3254 D3
Gladespring Ln
2900 LGCY 77539 4753 A3
Glade Springs Dr
- PRLD 77584 4500 B3
3100 HOUS 77339 3119 C4
Glade Valley Dr
3900 HOUS 77339 3118 E3
Gladewater Ct
16500 HarC 77433 3537 B4
19300 HarC 77375 3109 B6
Gladewater Dr
11300 PRLD 77584 4500 D2
19400 HarC 77375 3109 C6
Gladewater Ln
- BzaC 77583 4623 D3
3200 LGCY 77573 4633 B2
Gladewell Dr
6100 HOUS 77072 4098 C4
Gladewick Dr
12100 HOUS 77077 3957 E5
14700 HarC 77396 3548 D1
14800 HarC 77396 3407 E7
Gladewood Dr
10300 HOUS 77041 3819 E1
10300 HOUS 77041 3820 B1
Gladewood Ln
11800 HOUS 77071 4239 E5
Gladiator Dr
2300 RMFT 77357 2829 A1
Gladiola Av
1100 CNRO 77301 2384 C6
8100 HarC 77521 3833 B2
Gladiola St
2400 HarC 77562 3832 D3
Gladstell Rd
1400 LbyC 77327 2538 D1
Gladstell St
100 CNRO 77301 2384 A7
500 CNRO 77301 2529 C1
500 CNRO 77304 2529 E1
Gladstone Dr
1000 LGCY 77573 4631 E4
Gladstone Ln
- FBnC 77450 4093 D2
Gladstone St
7800 HOUS 77051 4243 B2
Gladwyne Ct
8800 LPRT 77571 4249 D3
Gladwyne Ln
3100 LPRT 77571 4249 D3
Gladys St
600 HOUS 77009 3963 A1
Gladys Yoakum Dr
21000 FBnC 77469 4234 A3
Glamis Ln
16700 HarC 77084 3678 B6
Glamorgan Dr
15300 JRSV 77040 3540 E7
Glascock Ln
8600 HarC 77064 3540 D6
Glascow Grn
9800 HarC 77089 4504 E2
Glaser Dr
1700 HOUS 77009 3963 C2
11200 HOUS 77076 3685 A3
Glasgow
29700 MtgC 77354 2818 C2
Glasgow Dr
4600 MSCY 77459 4369 B5
Glasgow Pl
14100 HOUS 77077 3956 E5
Glasgow St
100 PASD 77506 4106 E3
2400 HOUS 77026 3824 E4
Glasholm Dr
1400 HarC 77073 3403 C1
Glass Cir
7800 HOUS 77016 3825 B1
Glass Ct
4400 HOUS 77016 3825 B2
Glass Rd
23500 WlrC 77447 2958 C2
Glass St
8100 HOUS 77016 3825 B1
Glassblower Ln
7500 HarC 77064 3542 A5
Glassford Dr
9800 HarC 77089 4504 E2
Glastonbury Dr
3100 PRLD 77581 4376 D6
Glazebrook Dr
100 HOUS 77060 3544 C3
Gleaming Rose Dr
14400 HarC 77429 3397 C3
Gleann Arbor Blvd
19600 HarC 77379 3110 C6
Gleannbury Pointe Dr
19700 HarC 77379 3110 C5
Gleannloch Estates Dr
10 HarC 77379 3110 C7
10 HarC 77379 3255 D1
Gleannloch Farm Rd
7900 HarC 77379 3255 D1
Gleannloch Farms Golf Clb
- HarC 77379 3110 C7
Gleannloch Forest Dr
- HarC 77379 3255 B1
10600 HarC 77379 3110 B7
Gleannloch Lakes Blvd
10 HarC 77379 3255 C1
Gleason Rd
7200 HOUS 77016 3686 E3
7200 HOUS 77016 3687 A3
Glebe Rd
4000 HOUS 77018 3822 B1
4300 HOUS 77018 3683 B7
Glee Ln
800 HarC 77032 3404 A7
Glei
17600 GLSN 77554 5331 D7
Glen Av
2400 HOUS 77088 3683 B3
S Glen Dr
11700 HOUS 77099 4238 A2
S Glen Ln
4900 LGCY 77573 4751 E1
Glen Abbey Ct
800 HarC 77494 3953 A3
Glen Abbey Dr
- HarC 77014 3402 C1
- HarC 77090 3402 C1
Glenaire St
8500 HOUS 77061 4245 C3
Glenalbyn St
1000 HOUS 77015 3967 D2
Glen Allen Ln
5600 HarC 77069 3256 C7
Glenalta St
7900 HOUS 77061 4245 D2
Glen Arbor Dr
3800 HOUS 77025 4101 D6
Glen Arden Ln
22000 HarC 77450 3954 A5
Glenarm St
5600 HOUS 77020 3964 D1
Glen Avon Dr
4200 PASD 77505 4248 E6
Glenbank Wy
7200 HarC 77095 3678 A1
Glen Bay Ct
11800 HarC 77089 4378 A7
Glenbay Ct
1000 LPRT 77571 4250 C2
Glenboro Dr
2200 MtgC 77386 2969 B2
Glenborough Dr
- HarC 77060 3403 A6
100 HOUS 77060 3403 A6
100 HOUS 77067 3403 A6
Glenbrae St
7900 HOUS 77061 4245 D2
Glenbranch Dr
21300 HarC 77388 3112 E2
Glen Breeze Ct
20100 HarC 77346 3264 E5
Glen Briar Ln
18700 HarC 77084 3816 C2
Glenbriar Pl
7500 HOUS 77489 4371 B6
Glenbriar Spring Ln
26100 HarC 77433 3396 B4
Glenbrook Ct
4100 HOUS 77087 4245 D1
Glenbrook Dr
8100 HOUS 77017 4105 D7
Glenbrook Knoll Ln
16000 HarC 77095 3678 C1
Glen Burn Ct
20100 HarC 77346 3264 E5
Glenburn Dr
2300 HOUS 77345 3120 A6
Glenburnie Dr
300 HOUS 77022 3684 D7
Glenburn Manor Ln
22000 HarC 77449 3815 A2
Glen Burrow Ct
2000 FBnC 77494 3952 C6
Glenbury Dr
9100 HarC 77037 3544 C7
Glencairn Ct
200 HOUS 77336 3266 B3
Glen Canon Ln
14100 HarC 77069 3256 B7
Glen Canyon Ct
6500 FBnC 77450 4094 E4
Glen Canyon Pl
10 WDLD 77381 2821 A2
Glencarry Tr
300 FBnC 77583 4744 A2
Glencastle Ct
4700 HOUS 77345 3120 A2
Glen Chase Ct
7100 HarC 77095 3678 D2
Glen Chase Dr
15400 HarC 77084 3678 E2
15400 HarC 77095 3678 D1
Glenchase Ln
4200 HarC 77014 3401 B1
Glenchester Dr
500 HOUS 77079 3958 B2
Glenclan Ln
17000 HarC 77084 3678 B6
Glen Cliff Rd
7800 HarC 77064 3541 A1
Glencliffe Ln
8100 HarC 77070 3399 D2
Glencoe St
6000 HOUS 77087 4104 C7
Glencove Cir
3800 MSCY 77459 4497 C3
Glen Cove Ct
4100 HOUS 77021 4103 D5
Glen Cove Dr
1900 SEBK 77586 4509 C2
4000 HOUS 77021 4103 D5
Glen Cove St
- LGCY 77573 4509 A5
200 LGCY 77565 4509 A5
6000 HOUS 77007 3962 A4
Glencreek Dr
20300 HMBL 77338 3262 D4
27100 HarC 77336 3121 E4
Glencrest Dr
1000 LPRT 77571 4250 C2
1200 PASD 77502 4247 C2
Glencrest St
8100 HOUS 77061 4245 D2
Glencroft Ct
200 HOUS 77336 3266 B3
Glencroft St
9300 HOUS 77078 3687 E6
Glencross St
8400 HOUS 77061 4245 D2
Glen Crossing Cir
12100 HarC 77346 3408 B1
12200 HarC 77346 3264 C7
Glencullen Ln
2700 PRLD 77584 4501 E5
2700 PRLD 77584 4502 A5
Glen Cypress Ct
1800 HarC 77449 3677 D3
Glenda Dr
32600 MtgC 77354 2671 D4
Glenda St
1100 PRLD 77581 4376 C6
12900 HarC 77037 3545 A7
Glenda Kay Dr
10700 HarC 77065 3539 A2
Glendale Ct
7300 FBnC 77479 4493 E5
Glendale Dr
1100 FBnC 77479 4493 D6
2700 PRLD 77584 4503 A4
Glendale St
100 HOUS 77012 4105 B1
2100 LMQU 77568 4990 A3
Glendale Lakes Dr
100 FBnC 77583 4622 E7
200 FBnC 77583 4623 A7
Glendaven Wy
15400 HarC 77082 4096 D2
Glendavon Ln
2200 HarC 77450 3954 B6
Glen Dell Ct
7900 HOUS 77061 4245 C1
Glendenning Dr
10 HNCV 77024 3959 E3
10 HNCV 77024 3960 A3
10 PNPV 77024 3959 E3
Glendora St
100 HOUS 77012 4105 B1
Glendower Dr
4700 HarC 77373 3115 C6
Glendown Ln
9400 HarC 77070 3399 D5
Gleneagle Dr N
16700 MtgC 77385 2676 D4
Gleneagle Dr S
17000 MtgC 77385 2676 D6
Gleneagles Ct
5000 HarC 77084 3678 C6
Glen Eagles Dr
10 SGLD 77479 4495 D3
300 FRDW 77546 4629 A6
Gleneagles Dr
2200 LGCY 77573 4508 E7
4800 HarC 77084 3678 C6
6300 PASD 77505 4248 E6
6800 PASD 77505 4249 A6
Glen Echo Dr
1100 HOUS 77088 3544 A7
Glen Echo Ln
2700 MSCY 77459 4497 A3
Glen Echo St
700 HDWV 77024 3959 D2
700 PNPV 77024 3959 D2
Glen Eden Ct
1900 SGLD 77478 4236 E6
Gleneden Ct
10 CNRO 77384 2675 E3
Glen Erica Dr
13100 HarC 77066 3400 E1
13100 HarC 77069 3400 E1
13600 HarC 77069 3256 D7
Glen Erin Dr
10 WDLD 77382 2674 B4
Gleneviss Dr
17000 HarC 77084 3678 B5
Glenfair Ct
9000 HarC 77379 3110 D5
Glen Falls Ln
1700 PRLD 77581 4503 D1
Glenfalls St
7100 HarC 77049 3828 B1
Glenfield Ct
- HOUS 77074 4240 B1
10 HOUS 77074 4100 B7
9400 HOUS 77096 4240 B2
Glenfield Hollow Ln
26800 HarC 77433 3396 A7
Glenfield Manor Ln
- HarC 77014 3401 E2
- HarC 77014 3402 A2
Glenfield Park Ln
10200 HarC 77070 3399 C4
Glenfinch Ln
19600 HarC 77379 3112 A5
Glenford Dr
700 MSCY 77489 4370 E6
Glenforest Ct
8000 HOUS 77061 4245 C1
Glen Forest Dr
700 MtgC 77385 2676 C3
700 WDLD 77385 2676 C3
Glen Garden Ln
- HarC 77083 4097 A3
Glengarry Dr
- HOUS 77047 4374 C2
Glengarry Rd
4500 HOUS 77048 4374 E2
4600 HOUS 77048 4375 A2
Glengate Dr
23900 HarC 77373 3115 B5
Glengate Ln
10100 HOUS 77036 4238 E1
Glengreen Dr
1600 MSCY 77489 4370 D4
Glen Green Ln
14100 HarC 77069 3256 C7
Glen Grove St
5800 HOUS 77396 3405 E4
Glengyle Ct
24000 HOUS 77336 3266 B3
Glenhagen Ct
17700 HarC 77084 3677 E3
Glenhagen Dr
6300 HarC 77084 3677 E3
Glen Haven Blvd
2100 HOUS 77030 4102 B5
2400 HOUS 77025 4102 B5
3000 HOUS 77025 4101 E5
E Glen Haven Blvd
2700 HOUS 77025 4102 A5
S Glen Haven Blvd
2600 HOUS 77025 4102 A5
W Glen Haven Blvd
2700 HOUS 77025 4102 A5
Glen Haven Ct
200 LGCY 77573 4632 E1
Glen Haven Dr
200 LGCY 77573 4632 E1
400 MtgC 77385 2676 B2
Glenhaven Dr
5000 BYTN 77521 3972 A3
Glen Haven Ln
2400 FBnC 77469 4365 E4
Glenheath St
7900 HOUS 77061 4245 D3
Glen Heather Ct
4900 SGLD 77479 4495 C4
Glenheather Dr
3800 HarC 77068 3257 B6
Glenhew Rd
17300 HarC 77396 3407 E2
17300 HarC 77396 3408 A2

STREET Block City ZIP Map# Grid

Glenhill Ct
- BzaC 77584 4501 C7
Glenhill Dr
3300 BzaC 77584 4501 C7
6100 HarC 77389 2966 D5
Glenhilshire Dr
1300 HLSV 77055 3821 C6
1300 HOUS 77055 3821 C6
Glenhollow Ct
800 MtgC 77385 2676 C3
Glen Hollow Dr
900 HMBL 77338 3407 A1
12700 HOUS 77048 4374 E2
Glenhollow Dr
800 MtgC 77385 2676 C2
8100 HOUS 77033 4243 E3
11400 HOUS 77048 4243 E7
12100 HOUS 77048 4374 E1
Glen Hollow St
4900 SGLD 77479 4495 C4
Glen Holly Cir
- MtgC 77385 2676 D6
Glen Holly Ct
300 LGCY 77565 4508 E4
Glen Holly Ln
25200 FBnC 77494 4093 B6
Glen-Holly Park Dr
2400 FBnC 77478 4237 B5
Glenhope Dr
6700 HarC 77449 3677 B2
Glenhouse Ct
8700 HOUS 77088 3543 C7
8700 HOUS 77088 3683 E1
Glenhouse Dr
8800 HOUS 77088 3543 E7
Glenhurst Dr
5700 HOUS 77033 4244 A2
Glen Iris Dr
3000 LGCY 77573 4633 B2
Glen Ivy Dr
3800 HOUS 77345 3119 D3
Glen Jay Ct
9900 MtgC 77385 2676 D7
Glenkirk Dr
10300 HarC 77089 4377 B6
Glenkirk Pl
6700 SGLD 77479 4494 C1
Glen Knoll Ct
11600 HOUS 77077 3958 B6
Glen Knoll Dr
2100 HOUS 77077 3958 B6
Glen Lake Dr
11500 FBnC 77478 4236 C6
19900 HarC 77388 3113 A5
20200 HarC 77388 3112 E5
Glen Landing Dr
19400 HarC 77449 3816 A2
Glen Laurel Ln
- PRLD 77581 4503 E1
Glenlea Ct
900 FRDW 77546 4505 A5
Glenlea St
8100 HOUS 77061 4245 D2
Glenledi Dr
17700 HarC 77084 3678 A5
18000 HarC 77084 3677 E5
Glen Lee Dr
- HOUS 77396 3406 A4
5800 HOUS 77396 3405 E4
Glenleigh Dr
12400 HarC 77014 3402 B2
Glenleigh Pl
10 WDLD 77381 2820 C4
Glen Ln Ct
11500 HarC 77066 3400 E5
Glen Loch Ct
10 SGLD 77479 4495 C2
Glen Loch Dr
23800 MtgC 77380 2967 B4
25800 MtgC 77380 2821 B7
26200 WDLD 77380 2821 B6
26200 WDLD 77381 2821 B6
Glenloch Dr
8000 HOUS 77061 4245 C3
Glen Manor Dr
7300 HOUS 77028 3687 A7
Glen Mar Dr
16000 HarC 77082 4096 A3
Glenmar Rd
34400 WlrC 77484 3245 B4
Glenmark Dr
17500 HarC 77084 3677 E3
17900 HarC 77449 3677 D4
Glenmawr Dr
10100 HOUS 77075 4377 D2
10100 HOUS 77089 4377 D2
Glen May Park Ct
10300 HarC 77379 3110 C7
Glen May Park Dr
1600 HarC 77379 3110 B7
Glenmeade Dr
3700 HOUS 77059 4380 D6
Glenmeadow Dr
3300 RSBG 77471 4491 A5
4900 HOUS 77096 4241 A2
5100 HOUS 77096 4240 E1
12300 STAF 77477 4238 A7
Glenmeadows Dr
1000 LPRT 77571 4250 C2
Glenmere Ln
5200 HarC 77379 3257 B2
Glen Mist Ct
1600 HarC 77038 3543 E5
Glenmist Ct
3900 SGLD 77479 4495 A3
Glen Mist Ln
5600 HarC 77069 3256 C7
Glenmont Dr
4500 BLAR 77081 4101 B2
4500 HOUS 77081 4101 A2
4900 BLAR 77401 4100 E2
4900 BLAR 77401 4101 A2
4900 HOUS 77081 4100 C2
4900 HOUS 77401 4100 E2
4900 HOUS 77401 4101 A2
7700 HOUS 77036 4099 D3
Glenmont St
4600 BLAR 77401 4101 A2
4800 HOUS 77081 4101 A2
4800 HOUS 77401 4101 A2
Glenmont Estates Blvd
21700 MtgC 77355 2960 E7
21700 MtgC 77447 2960 E7
23100 SGCH 77355 2960 E3
Glenmont Ridge Ct
3100 FBnC 77545 4498 C6
Glenmoor Dr
6900 FBnC 77583 4623 A7
Glenmora Ct
100 MtgC 77385 2676 C2
Glenmore Dr
200 PASD 77503 4108 B6
3500 HOUS 77023 4104 C5
Glenmore Forest St
1400 HLSV 77055 3821 C6
1400 HOUS 77055 3821 C6
Glenmore Meadow Dr
3400 MtgC 77386 2969 D3
Glenmorgan Dr
- HarC 77095 3538 E5
Glenmorin Ct
5600 HarC 77049 3828 C4
Glenmorris Ct
6500 HarC 77084 3677 E3
Glenmorris Dr
17300 HarC 77084 3678 A3
17400 HarC 77084 3677 E3
Glenmount Park Dr
17100 HarC 77598 4507 B5
Glenn Av
900 HOUS 77088 3683 E3
900 HOUS 77088 3684 A3
900 HOUS 77091 3684 A3
1100 PASD 77506 4107 C4
Glenn Ct
10 FBnC 77469 4492 D5
Glenn Ln
16600 BzaC 77584 4502 D7
16600 BzaC 77584 4626 D1
16600 PRLD 77584 4502 D7
Glenn St
- BYTN 77520 4112 E2
Glennale Ct
4100 HarC 77084 3817 C1
Glennale Dr
4000 HarC 77084 3817 C1
4000 HOUS 77084 3817 C1
4300 HarC 77084 3678 C7
Glenn Elm Dr
8200 HarC 77379 3256 A1
8300 HarC 77379 3255 E1
Glenneyre Ln
5900 HarC 77084 3678 C4
Glenn Haven Estates Cir
8400 HarC 77379 3255 E1
Glenn Haven Estates Dr
18300 HarC 77379 3255 E1
18600 HarC 77379 3256 A1
Glenn Lakes Dr
- MSCY 77459 4497 C3
6500 HarC 77069 3400 C2
Glenn Lakes Ln
1700 MSCY 77459 4497 A3
3000 MSCY 77459 4496 D3
Glennlast Ln
13200 HarC 77037 3544 E7
Glennlee Dr
12300 HarC 77014 3402 A3
Glenn Leigh Dr
8300 HarC 77379 3255 E1
Glen Nook Dr
5200 HOUS 77016 3686 C4
Glenn Ricki Dr
3800 HOUS 77045 4241 D7
Glenn River Dr
12300 HOUS 77050 3547 A5
Glennville Ct
200 HNCV 77024 3960 A4
200 PNPV 77024 3960 A4
Glennwell Ct
4500 HOUS 77345 3119 E6
Glen Oak Ct
1800 FBnC 77479 4494 B4
Glenoak Dr
3900 PRLD 77581 4504 A7
Glen Oaks Cir
10 MtgC 77385 2676 D6
Glen Oaks Dr
1300 CHTW 77385 2823 A4
Glenoaks Dr
17200 MtgC 77385 2676 D7
Glen Oaks St
- MtgC 77355 2962 D3
1500 HOUS 77008 3823 B7
Glenora Dr
11100 HarC 77065 3539 E1
11400 HarC 77065 3398 E7
Glenover Dr
22900 HarC 77450 3953 D2
Glen Park Av
100 HOUS 77009 3824 C7
Glen Park Dr
300 MSCY 77489 4370 A3
Glenpark Dr
4800 LPRT 77571 4250 C1
Glenpatti Dr
17200 HarC 77084 3678 A2
17700 HarC 77084 3677 E2
Glenpine Dr
3600 HarC 77068 3257 B5
Glen Pines Dr
5600 HarC 77069 3256 C7
Glenpolara
- HarC 77084 3677 E2
- HarC 77095 3677 E2
Glen Prairie St
7600 HOUS 77061 4245 B2
Glenray Dr
6500 HarC 77084 3677 D2
Glenridding Ct
- HarC 77014 3402 B1
Glenridge Ct
5500 HOUS 77053 4372 A5
Glenridge Ln
4800 HOUS 77053 4372 B5
Glenridge Forest
200 HarC 77094 3955 D1
Glen Riley Dr
8200 FBnC 77083 4096 B7
Glen Rio St
5300 HOUS 77045 4372 A1
Glen Rock Dr
6500 HOUS 77087 4244 D2
Glen Rock Ln
300 MtgC 77385 2676 B2
N Glenrock Hills Ct
- FBnC 77494 4092 B5
S Glenrock Hills Ct
- FBnC 77494 4092 B5
Glenrock Hills Dr
26300 FBnC 77494 4092 A5
Glen Rosa Dr
6900 FBnC 77494 4093 C5
Glen Rose Ln
27000 FBnC 77494 4092 A2
Glenrose Ln
16700 WlrC 77484 3246 A4
Glenrose St
3500 HOUS 77051 4243 B1
Glenroyal Ct
21700 HarC 77339 3118 B5
Glenscot St
7900 HOUS 77061 4245 D2
Glens Ferry Ln
1400 HarC 77073 3259 C5
Glen Shadow Dr
8900 HOUS 77088 3544 A7
9000 HOUS 77088 3543 E6
Glenshadow Wy
9700 HarC 77038 3543 D5
Glenshannon Av
1000 FRDW 77546 4629 B4
Glenshannon Dr
16400 HOUS 77059 4380 D6
16400 PASD 77059 4380 D6
Glenshire Dr
4000 HOUS 77025 4101 C7
Glenside St
8600 HOUS 77033 4244 A4
Glen Spring Dr
3000 HOUS 77339 3119 C3
Glenstein Dr
6800 HarC 77084 3677 E2
6800 HarC 77084 3678 A2
6800 HarC 77095 3678 A2
Glenstone St
200 HOUS 77013 3828 A6
Glen Tarbet
10100 HarC 77038 3543 C3
Glenthorpe Ct
24400 FBnC 77494 3953 B7
Glenthorpe Ln
3000 FBnC 77494 3953 B7
Glentide Cir
12800 HOUS 77045 4241 E6
Glentrace Cir
10 WDLD 77382 2673 E5
Glen Turret Ct
9300 HarC 77095 3538 C4
Glentworth Ct
5100 HarC 77084 3677 E6
Glenvale Dr
400 HarC 77060 3544 D4
Glen Valley Dr
1000 HMBL 77338 3406 E1
1000 HMBL 77338 3407 A1
8000 HOUS 77061 4245 D3
Glenvalley Dr
4900 LPRT 77571 4250 B2
Glenview Ct
5100 LPRT 77571 4250 C2
Glenview Dr
- BzaC 77511 4748 D3
1000 PRLD 77581 4504 E7
1700 ALVN 77511 4867 B3
4900 LPRT 77571 4250 C2
5400 HOUS 77345 3120 A5
7600 HOUS 77061 4245 B1
8000 HOUS 77017 4245 D1
8100 HOUS 77017 4105 E7
8500 HOUS 77017 4106 A7
Glenview Ln
1700 ALVN 77511 4867 B3
Glenvillage St
4600 HarC 77084 3678 B7
Glenvine Dr
16400 HOUS 77396 3406 A4
Glen Vista Ln
200 FBnC 77583 4623 A7
Glenvista St
8500 HOUS 77061 4245 E2
Glenwater Ct
15000 HOUS 77044 3550 A3
Glenway Dr
10500 HarC 77070 3399 A2
12000 HarC 77070 3398 C2
Glenway Falls Dr
19400 HarC 77449 3677 A2
Glenwest Dr
- HarC 77598 4506 D6
18900 HarC 77546 4506 C5
19100 HOUS 77546 4506 C6
Glenwick Ct
7200 HarC 77433 3677 D1
Glenwild Dr
1800 MSCY 77489 4370 B5
Glenwillow Dr
20900 HarC 77375 3110 C3
20900 HarC 77379 3110 C3
S Glen Willow Ln
7500 HOUS 77489 4371 B3
E Glen Willow Rd
- HOUS 77085 4371 B3
14400 HOUS 77489 4371 B3
Glenwolde Dr
10500 HOUS 77099 4238 C1
12800 HOUS 77099 4237 C1
Glenwolf Dr
17500 HarC 77084 3677 E3
Glenwood Av
- PASD 77505 4249 A3
4500 DRPK 77536 4249 A2
4500 PASD 77536 4249 A3
Glenwood Ct
- MtgC 77385 2676 D6
Glen Wood Dr
7000 FBnC 77479 4493 D5
Glenwood Dr
100 HOUS 77007 3962 A4
1100 KATY 77493 3813 E7
3000 PRLD 77584 4502 A6
3700 FBnC 77469 4364 A2
10100 HarC 77532 3694 B6
10100 HarC 77562 3694 B6
Glenwood Ln
10 LbyC 77535 3413 D6
Glenwood Rd
- HarC 77357 2830 A7
28000 HarC 77357 2829 E7
Glenwood Canyon Ln
1100 HOUS 77077 3956 D4
19500 HarC 77433 3537 B6
Glenwood Estate Blvd
23000 MtgC 77447 2960 B4
Glenwood Forest Dr
9700 HOUS 77078 3687 D5
Glenwood Park Dr
15300 HarC 77095 3538 D6
Glenwood Ridge Dr
400 MtgC 77386 2968 C1
Glenwood Springs Ct
3500 HOUS 77345 3119 D3
Glenwood Springs Dr
3500 HOUS 77345 3119 D3
Glenworth Ln
- FBnC 77494 3953 A7
- FBnC 77494 4093 A6
Glenwyck St
12800 HOUS 77045 4241 C7
Glenyork Ct
12900 HarC 77429 3254 B6
Glesby St
9000 HOUS 77029 3826 D7
Glezman Ln
14700 HarC 77377 3108 D6
Glidden
1800 HOUS 77091 3683 C4
Glistening Pond Pl
10 WDLD 77382 2673 B6
Globe St
500 HOUS 77034 4246 B5
Gloger St
11700 HarC 77039 3546 B7
11700 HarC 77093 3546 B7
Gloria Ct
1100 SGLD 77478 4368 A4
Gloria Dr
10800 HOUS 77013 3827 D4
Gloria Ln
10000 BYTN 77520 3835 C3
Glorieta Dr
8100 FBnC 77083 4096 C7
Glorietta Turn
16500 HarC 77068 3257 D5
Glory Av
24100 MtgC 77365 2973 C7
Glorybower Ct
10 WDLD 77380 2821 D6
Gloryland Dr
- HOUS 77033 4243 D1
Glory Rose Ct
17600 HarC 77429 3252 C6
Glorywhite Ct
12800 HOUS 77034 4378 B2
Glosridge Rd
1900 HOUS 77055 3821 B5
Glosson Rd
2200 PRLD 77584 4500 D4
Glossy Ibis Wy
25900 GLSN 77554 5548 A3
Gloster Dr
14900 HarC 77530 3829 C7
14900 HarC 77530 3968 C1
Gloucester
25600 MtgC 77357 2829 B4
Glouchester Ln
1200 HarC 77073 3259 B2
Glourie Cir
1000 HLSV 77055 3821 C7
Glourie Dr
1100 HLSV 77055 3821 C7
1400 HOUS 77055 3821 C6
Glover St
7700 HOUS 77012 4105 C4
Glover Trail Ln
- HarC 77047 4374 C4
Glowing Horizon Rd
3500 PASD 77503 4108 B6
Glowing Star Pl
10 WDLD 77382 2819 C1
Gloyna St
9900 HOUS 77088 3543 B7
9900 HOUS 77088 3683 B1
Glynn Dr
100 HOUS 77056 3960 E3
Glynwood Dr
40000 MtgC 77354 2671 D2
Gnarled Chesnut Ct
9400 HOUS 77075 4246 C7
Gnarled Oaks Ct
5900 HarC 77346 3264 D4
Gnarlwood Dr
11400 HarC 77089 4378 A5
Gneiss Hollow Rd
5100 FBnC 77469 4234 B3
Goanna Ct
16300 FBnC 77478 4235 E5
Goar Rd
12600 HOUS 77077 3957 D5
Gober St
100 HOUS 77017 4106 B5
Godfrey St
2000 HarC 77521 3832 C4
Godfrey Cove Ct
26600 FBnC 77494 4092 B1
Godhilf
- HOUS 77084 3818 B2
Godsey Ct
400 BKHV 77024 3959 B3
Godstone Ln
9100 HarC 77379 3256 A5
9200 HarC 77379 3255 E6
Godwin St
1400 HOUS 77023 4104 B1
Goedecke St
100 HarC 77373 3114 A1
Goettee Cir
5600 HOUS 77091 3683 A6
Goforth St
6100 HOUS 77021 4103 D6
Going Rd
- BYTN 77521 3973 C4
Golbow Dr
- HOUS 77084 3817 E2
- HOUS 77084 3818 A1
Gold St
5100 HOUS 77026 3824 E4
Gold Bridge Ct
16700 HOUS 77053 4371 E7
Gold Brook Ln
10100 FBnC 77478 4236 B3
E Gold Buttercup Ct
21400 HarC 77433 3250 E3
21400 HarC 77433 3251 A4
W Gold Buttercup Ct
21600 HarC 77433 3250 E3
Gold Candle Dr
3400 HarC 77388 3112 E6
Gold Canyon Rd
- HarC 77044 3550 E6
- HarC 77044 3551 A6
Gold Creek Dr
8400 HOUS 77055 3821 B2
8400 HOUS 77080 3821 B2
Goldcrest St
9100 HOUS 77022 3685 C6
10100 HOUS 77076 3685 C5
Gold Cup Wy
9800 HarC 77065 3539 E3
Gold Dust Ln
7500 HarC 77064 3542 A5
Golden Gdns
13600 HarC 77039 3547 A4
Golden Hbr
8000 FBnC 77459 4497 B7
8000 FBnC 77459 4621 A1
Golden Ln
700 HOUS 77336 3121 D7
1300 LPRT 77571 4110 B7
Golden Pl
10 WDLD 77381 2820 D4
Golden Rd
2100 MtgC 77380 2967 D1
2100 WDLD 77380 2967 D1
5200 HarC 77521 3832 D7
5200 HarC 77521 3971 D1
Golden Appaloosa Cir
14500 HarC 77044 3408 D7
E Golden Arrow Cir
100 WDLD 77381 2820 C2
N Golden Arrow Cir
100 WDLD 77381 2820 B2
S Golden Arrow Cir
10 WDLD 77381 2820 B2
W Golden Arrow Cir
100 WDLD 77381 2820 B2
Golden Aurora Dr
8400 FBnC 77469 4235 D1
Golden Autumn Pl
100 WDLD 77384 2675 A4
Golden Bay Ln
2000 LGCY 77573 4509 A6
Golden Bear Ln
800 HOUS 77339 3118 B7
Golden Beech Dr
- HarC 77066 3401 D6
Golden Bell Dr
25600 HarC 77389 2966 B2
Golden Bend Dr
400 HarC 77562 3831 E1
Goldenberry Dr
10 WDLD 77384 2675 D5
Golden Bluff Ln
- HarC 77044 3549 D3
Golden Bough Ln
14600 HarC 77396 3547 E1
Golden Brandy Ln
- RSBG 77469 4615 A3
Golden Brook Dr
12600 HOUS 77085 4240 D7
Golden Brook Ln
5000 FBnC 77450 4093 E3
Golden Bud Ln
16400 HarC 77433 3251 A4
Golden Cactus Ln
19300 HarC 77433 3537 B7
Golden Canyon Ln
17900 FBnC 77469 4095 D7
Golden Cape Dr
2900 LGCY 77573 4633 B3
Golden Cedar Dr
21900 HarC 77433 3251 A4
Golden Chord Cir
8600 HarC 77040 3541 C7
Golden Cir Wy
13600 HarC 77083 4097 A4
Golden Cove Ln
22100 HarC 77339 3118 D5
Golden Creek Ct
- RHMD 77469 4492 B2
Golden Creek Ln
- RHMD 77469 4492 B2
2600 PRLD 77584 4500 A3
Goldencrest Ct
25500 HarC 77389 2966 B2
Golden Cypress Ln
14200 HarC 77429 3396 E2
14500 HarC 77429 3397 A1
Goldendale Ct
7100 HarC 77433 3677 A1
Goldendale Dr
1200 TYLV 77586 4381 E7
Golden Dove Dr
21300 HarC 77388 3112 E3
Golden Eagle Dr
15100 HarC 77396 3406 D7
Golden Eagle Ln
- MtgC 77355 2960 A2
Golden Eagle St
10 MtgC 77385 2676 D4
Golden Elm Cir
- HarC 77433 3251 C4
Golden Elm Dr
- HarC 77433 3251 C4
Golden Fern Ct
11000 HOUS 77075 4377 A4
Golden Field Dr
13200 HOUS 77059 4379 E3
13300 HOUS 77059 4380 A4
Golden Flame Ct
19600 HarC 77094 3955 A1
Golden Forest Dr
4800 HOUS 77091 3683 A7
5000 HOUS 77091 3682 E7
5700 HOUS 77092 3682 C6
Golden Gate Dr
7200 HarC 77041 3680 C2
Goldenglade Cir
9500 HarC 77064 3540 D4
Goldenglade Dr
9700 HarC 77064 3540 D4
Golden Glade Ln
17500 HarC 77095 3537 D2
Golden Glen Dr
9900 HOUS 77099 4238 A3
Golden Grain Dr
200 RSBG 77469 4492 C7
10800 HarC 77064 3540 C2
Golden Grove Dr
5600 HarC 77373 3115 E7
Goldengrove Dr
7700 HarC 77379 3256 A1
Golden Grove Ln
5700 HarC 77373 3115 E7
Golden Hawk Tr
14700 HarC 77433 3250 D4
Golden Hawthorn Ct
20600 HarC 77346 3264 E4
Golden Hearth Ln
10400 HarC 77433 3251 A5
Golden Heath Ln
19000 FBnC 77469 4094 E5
19000 FBnC 77469 4095 A6
Golden Hills Ln
3000 MSCY 77459 4497 A2
Golden Hollow Ct
5500 HarC 77373 3260 E1
Golden Hollows Ln
10 FBnC 77469 4492 D5
Golden Kings Ct
20800 HarC 77346 3265 A3
Golden Lake Dr
3700 HOUS 77345 3119 D3
Golden Larch Dr
2700 FBnC 77494 3951 C6
Golden Leaf Dr
2700 HOUS 77339 3119 B3
Goldenleaf Dr
400 FRDW 77546 4505 A5
Golden Lodge Ln
11800 HarC 77066 3400 D5
Golden Mane Rd
25100 HarC 77375 2965 D3
Golden Manor Ln
16100 HarC 77429 3397 B3
Golden Meadow Dr
9200 HarC 77064 3540 D2
Goldenmere Ct
13400 FBnC 77478 4366 E2
Golden Mesa Dr
20000 HarC 77449 3815 D4
Golden Mews Ln
2300 FBnC 77494 3953 B5
Golden Mills Dr
25500 MtgC 77365 3117 E3
Golden Morning Cir
5000 HarC 77084 3677 D6
Golden Nugget Ct
1000 HarC 77450 3953 E4
1000 HarC 77450 3954 B2
Golden Oak Dr
10 TXCY 77591 4873 C6
N Golden Oak Dr
200 TXCY 77591 4873 C6
S Golden Oak Dr
300 TXCY 77591 4873 C7
Golden Oak Ln
23500 HarC 77336 3267 A3
Golden Oak Park Ln
32300 MtgC 77385 2823 B6
Golden Oaks Dr
2100 MtgC 77385 2676 D6
Golden Park Ln
9600 HarC 77088 3682 C1
Golden Pass
2400 HarC 77067 3401 D5
Golden Pine Dr
11800 HarC 77070 3254 D7
Golden Pond Ct
4500 SGLD 77479 4494 D1
Golden Pond Dr
2000 HOUS 77345 3120 A6
4800 HOUS 77345 3119 E6
14400 HarC 77084 3679 A6
Goldenport Ln
26200 FBnC 77494 4092 D1
Golden Prairie Ln
9800 HarC 77086 3542 D4
Golden Rainbow Dr
12900 HarC 77429 3398 A1
13100 HarC 77429 3254 A7
Golden Raintree Dr
20800 HarC 77449 3815 C4
Golden Ray Dr
11200 HarC 77429 3398 E5
11200 HarC 77429 3399 A5
Golden Reed Dr
- HarC 77450 3954 B6
Golden Ridge Dr
18000 HarC 77084 3677 E5
18000 HarC 77084 3678 A5
Golden River Ln
6600 HarC 77083 4097 A5
Goldenrod Ln
4300 MSCY 77459 4496 C1
30900 MtgC 77354 2670 A6
Goldenrod St
100 HOUS 77009 3824 B7
2200 HarC 77562 3832 C2
2600 PASD 77503 4248 B2
Golden Rose Dr
- HarC 77449 3677 A3
Golden Sage Dr
- WDLD 77381 2820 B2
Golden Sage Ln
16100 HarC 77429 3397 A2
16200 HarC 77429 3396 E2
Golden Sails Dr
2200 LGCY 77573 4509 A6
Golden Sands Dr
16100 HarC 77095 3538 C5
Golden Scroll Cir
10 WDLD 77382 2819 E1
Golden Shadow Cir
10 WDLD 77381 2821 A2
200 WDLD 77381 2820 E2
Goldenshire Ln
6700 HarC 77379 3111 C3
Golden Shores Dr
3700 MSCY 77459 4497 D6
Golden Shores Ln
2300 LGCY 77573 4508 D6
Golden Sky Ln
20800 FBnC 77469 4094 B6
Goldensong Ct
23200 HarC 77373 2968 E6
Golden Spike Ln
8500 HOUS 77086 3542 A4
Golden Spur Tr
20200 HarC 77532 3410 B2
Goldenstar Dr
7200 HarC 77083 4096 E6
Golden Stream Dr
5300 HarC 77066 3401 A7
Golden Sun Ct
1300 PASD 77586 4381 E7
Golden Sunset Cir
10 WDLD 77381 2820 E2
Golden Sunset Ct
- LMQU 77568 4872 B4
Golden Sunshine Dr
9100 HarC 77064 3540 D1
Golden Sycamore Tr
20800 HarC 77433 3251 A5
Golden Talon Ct
- HarC 77396 3548 C1
Golden Tee Ct
3300 MSCY 77459 4496 E2
10500 HOUS 77099 4237 C3
Golden Tee Ln
3500 MSCY 77459 4496 E3
12700 HOUS 77099 4237 C3
Golden Terrace Ct
3500 FBnC 77494 4093 C2
Golden Thistle
12400 PASD 77058 4381 A6
Golden Thistle Ct
18100 HarC 77433 3537 A5
Golden Thistle Ln
7500 HarC 77433 3537 D7
7500 HarC 77433 3677 E1
Golden Thrush Pl
10 WDLD 77381 2820 E1
Golden Trace Ct
8100 HarC 77083 4097 B7
Golden Trails Dr
- HOUS 77345 3119 D5
Golden Valley Dr
13200 HarC 77429 3254 A7
Golden View Ct
6600 HarC 77083 4097 A4
Golden View Dr
13600 HarC 77083 4097 A5
Goldenview Park Ln
10100 FBnC 77478 4236 E3
Golden Villas St
2500 DRPK 77503 4248 E1
2500 DRPK 77536 4248 E1
2500 PASD 77503 4248 E1
N Goldenvine Cir
10 WDLD 77382 2673 D5
S Goldenvine Cir
10 WDLD 77382 2673 C5
Goldenvine Ct
10 WDLD 77382 2673 C4
Goldenvine Dr
- WDLD 77382 2673 C4
Golden Vines Ln
29600 MtgC 77386 2969 E3
Golden Water Ct
- HOUS 77044 3408 E5
Goldenwave Ct
24100 FBnC 77494 4093 A5
Golden Wave Dr
- HarC 77084 3677 B6
- HarC 77449 3677 B6
Golden West Dr
900 HarC 77450 3954 A3
Golden Willow Dr
3200 HOUS 77339 3119 C2
3800 HarC 77449 3816 A2
Golden Wings Ct
5300 HarC 77041 3679 C6
Golden Wood Ln
9300 HarC 77086 3541 E3
9500 HarC 77086 3542 B2
Golders Green Dr
3400 HOUS 77082 4097 B3
Goldfarb
13300 HOUS 77045 4373 A3
13300 HOUS 77053 4373 A3
Goldfield Cir
900 HarC 77073 3259 A3
Goldfield Ln
10500 HarC 77064 3540 B4
Goldfinch Av
900 SGLD 77478 4368 C3
Goldfinch Dr
7300 HMBL 77396 3406 C4
Goldfinch Ln
2100 LGCY 77573 4631 A7
18700 HarC 77377 3107 A1
Gold Finch Rd
7800 CmbC 77520 3835 D4
Goldfinch St
4300 HOUS 77035 4241 B4
Gold Fire Dr
- HOUS 77085 4240 C7
Goldking Cross Ct
23400 HarC 77373 3115 A4
Gold Lagoon
- GLSN 77554 5332 D4
Goldlake Dr
19900 HarC 77449 3676 E2
19900 HarC 77449 3677 A2
Gold Leaf Pl
10 WDLD 77384 2674 E3
Gold Leaf Tr
21000 HarC 77433 3251 A5
Gold Medal Cir
5300 HarC 77041 3679 C6
Gold Mesa Ct
900 HOUS 77062 4506 C2
Gold Mesa Tr
14800 HOUS 77062 4506 E1
Gold Moss Dr
- HOUS 77085 4240 C7
Gold Nugget
23600 HarC 77336 3122 B7
Gold Panning Ct
17200 MtgC 77355 2815 B7
Gold Point Dr
10900 HarC 77064 3540 A5
10900 HarC 77065 3540 A5
Gold Ridge Ln
16400 HOUS 77053 4371 E7
N Gold River Cir
6800 MSCY 77459 4496 C4
S Gold River Cir
6900 MSCY 77459 4496 D4
Gold Rush Springs Dr
9600 HarC 77375 3255 B2
Goldsmith St
2000 HOUS 77030 4102 B4
2400 WUNP 77005 4102 A4
Gold Spier St
4500 HOUS 77018 3683 B7
Goldspier St
6300 HOUS 77091 3683 B4
7000 HOUS 77088 3683 B4
Goldspring Ln
2800 HarC 77373 3114 E4
2900 HarC 77373 3115 A3
Gold Star Dr
3200 HarC 77082 4096 C2
Goldstone Dr
22100 HarC 77450 3953 E1
22100 HarC 77450 3954 A1
Gold Stream Ct
11700 HarC 77377 3254 D3
Gold Tee Dr
8100 HOUS 77036 4099 C4
Goldthread Ct
10 WDLD 77381 2820 E1
Goldwater Ct
13600 HarC 77044 3549 D3
Goldwood Pl
10 WDLD 77382 2819 B1
Golf Ct
800 MSCY 77489 4370 B3
800 STAF 77477 4370 B3
800 STAF 77489 4370 B3

STREET Block	City	ZIP	Map#	Grid
Golf Dr				
4100	HOUS	77018	3823	A2
4500	HOUS	77018	3822	E1
4900	HOUS	77018	3683	E7
5200	HOUS	77091	3683	E6
Golf Rd				
4400	DKSN	77539	4754	D2
Golf Club Dr				
400	RHMD	77469	4492	A3
16400	HarC	77532	3552	A2
16700	HarC	77532	3551	E1
17400	HarC	77532	3410	E7
17400	HarC	77532	3411	A7
Golf Club Tr				
37200	MtgC	77355	2815	C5
Golf Course Dr				
-	HOUS	77084	3817	E1
5900	HOUS	77030	4102	E2
Golf Course Rd				
10	HarC	77084	3817	D1
10	HOUS	77084	3817	D1
Golfcrest				
-	FBnC	77469	4492	A3
-	RHMD	77469	4492	A3
Golfcrest Blvd				
2900	HOUS	77087	4104	E5
Golf Crest Dr				
6500	GLSN	77551	5108	B7
6500	GLSN	77551	5222	B1
Golfcrest Dr				
-	HarC	77581	4504	C1
2300	PRLD	77581	4504	D2
2500	HarC	77089	4504	C1
Golf Green Cir				
8000	HOUS	77036	4099	C4
Golf Green Ct				
5300	LGCY	77573	4751	D2
Golf Links Ct				
10	HOUS	77339	3264	D1
Golf Links Pl				
900	HOUS	77019	3963	A4
Golf Ridge Cir				
2500	HarC	77089	4504	C1
Golf Ridge Dr				
10	CNRO	77304	2382	D2
Golf Trail Rd				
1700	PRVW	77445	2955	B6
Golfview Dr				
100	FBnC	77469	4492	A2
100	RHMD	77469	4492	A3
Golf View Ln				
27500	HarC	77336	3122	A3
27600	HarC	77336	3121	E2
Golf View Tr				
14200	HOUS	77059	4380	A5
Golf Villas Dr				
-	HarC	77346	3265	B4
Golfway St				
6800	HOUS	77087	4104	E6
7100	HOUS	77087	4105	A6
Goliad Av				
1100	FBnC	77469	4364	D6
1100	RHMD	77469	4364	D6
1400	LMQU	77568	4989	E2
Goliad Run				
6600	BYTN	77521	3833	D5
Goliad St				
1000	HOUS	77002	3963	B3
1300	HOUS	77007	3963	B2
Golondrina Dr				
7800	FBnC	77083	4096	A7
Gomango Dr				
600	STAF	77477	4370	B4
Gomez St				
6400	HarC	77521	3832	E6
Gondola Dr				
11400	HOUS	77477	4237	E4
Gondola St				
900	SGLD	77478	4368	B2
Gonsoulin St				
13200	GlsC	77510	4986	D2
13200	STFE	77510	4986	D2
Gonyo Rd				
100	FBnC	77469	4493	A6
Gonzales Ln				
10	MtgC	77372	2535	A5
21500	MtgC	77357	2827	B4
Gonzales St				
6900	HOUS	77020	3964	E2
6900	HOUS	77020	3965	A2
Goodale Dr				
-	HOUS	77088	3542	C7
Good Dale Ln				
23000	HarC	77373	3115	D6
Good Day Dr				
1600	MSCY	77459	4369	D5
Goode St				
1700	ALVN	77511	4866	E2
1700	ALVN	77511	4867	A2
7800	HOUS	77012	4105	B1
Goodfellow Dr				
23700	HarC	77373	3115	C5
Goodfield Ct				
16800	HarC	77379	3255	E5
Goodhope St				
3400	HOUS	77021	4103	B7
3600	HOUS	77021	4243	B1
Goodley Ct				
11600	HarC	77429	3253	E7
Goodloe St				
2300	HOUS	77093	3685	D4
Goodlowe Pk				
6300	FBnC	77479	4367	A7
Goodman Rd				
12500	MtgC	77306	2534	C5
Goodman St				
15100	HarC	77084	3678	E4
Goodman Ridge Dr				
2800	MSCY	77459	4498	A5
Goodmeadow Dr				
9000	HarC	77064	3540	D2
Goodmeadow Dr W				
9100	HarC	77064	3540	D1
Goodnight Ct				
1500	FBnC	77479	4493	E5
Goodnight Tr				
900	HarC	77060	3403	D4
2600	DRPK	77536	4109	E7
Goodrich Dr				
2300	PRLD	77581	4502	E3
2300	PRLD	77581	4503	A3
Goodrum Rd				
10300	HOUS	77041	3681	A7
10400	HOUS	77041	3680	E7
Goodson Dr				
10	HOUS	77037	3544	B2
10	HOUS	77060	3544	B2
Goodson Lp				
100	MtgC	77362	2816	C5
100	SGCH	77362	2816	D4
1200	MtgC	77355	2816	C6
Goodson Rd				
600	MAGA	77355	2669	A5
1000	MAGA	77355	2668	E5
1200	MtgC	77355	2668	E5
24900	MtgC	77372	2682	E1
24900	SPLD	77372	2682	E1
Good Spring Dr				
11800	HarC	77067	3402	B5
Goodspring Dr				
10800	HarC	77064	3540	D2
Goodtimes				
-	HarC	77449	3814	C4
Goodwin Dr				
2000	HarC	77493	3814	B5
Goodwin St				
-	HOUS	77034	4379	A6
Goodyear Dr				
1900	HOUS	77017	4106	A4
Goosberry Ln				
18600	MtgC	77365	2972	B5
Goose Creek Dr				
-	BYTN	77521	3972	A3
Gooselake Ln				
19400	HarC	77084	3816	A6
N Gordon St				
100	ALVN	77511	4867	C1
400	ALVN	77511	4749	C6
N Gordon St SR-35 BUS				
100	ALVN	77511	4867	C1
400	ALVN	77511	4749	C6
N Gordon St SR-35C BUS				
1800	ALVN	77511	4749	C6
S Gordon St				
100	ALVN	77511	4867	C4
S Gordon St SR-35 BUS				
100	ALVN	77511	4867	C4
Gordy Rd				
100	GlsC	77518	4634	B3
1100	GlsC	77539	4634	B3
1100	LGCY	77539	4634	B3
1100	TXCY	77539	4634	B3
Gore Dr				
7200	HOUS	77016	3686	E4
7200	HOUS	77016	3687	A4
Gore St				
900	PASD	77506	4107	C5
Gore Grass Ct				
16000	HarC	77379	3257	A3
Gorham Dr				
15300	HarC	77084	3678	D3
Gorham Park Cir				
11500	HarC	77067	3402	D6
Gorki Park Dr				
2700	HarC	77449	3814	E4
Gorman Dr				
5700	HarC	77049	3828	C4
Gorman Brook Dr				
9600	HarC	77095	3538	A4
Gorom Ct				
2900	BzaC	77584	4501	C6
2900	PRLD	77584	4501	C6
Gorton Dr				
6500	HarC	77449	3676	E3
Gosforth Dr				
5400	HarC	77449	3676	E6
Gosling Rd				
-	WDLD	77381	2675	C7
-	WDLD	77381	2820	E5
-	WDLD	77382	2675	C6
-	WDLD	77384	2675	C6
20900	HarC	77388	3112	A2
21500	HarC	77388	3111	E1
21700	HarC	77389	3111	E1
22400	HarC	77389	2966	E7
25200	HarC	77389	2821	A7
25200	HarC	77389	2967	A1
25200	MtgC	77380	2821	A7
25200	WDLD	77380	2821	A7
25200	WDLD	77381	2821	A7
Gosling Cedar Pl				
21900	HarC	77388	3111	E2
Gosling Oaks Ln				
5500	HarC	77388	3112	A2
Gospel Wy				
13400	HOUS	77085	4371	D1
Goss Rd				
5700	HarC	77521	3832	D7
Gossamer Ln				
36800	MtgC	77354	2816	B1
Gossamer Wy				
6900	SGLD	77479	4367	C6
Gossett Rd				
100	HarC	77562	3831	E2
Goss Hollow Ln				
20100	HarC	77449	3676	D4
Goss Spring Ct				
22500	HarC	77373	3113	E1
Gostick St				
2300	HOUS	77008	3823	D4
Goswell Dr				
1400	HarC	77530	3829	D5
Gotham Dr				
12800	HOUS	77089	4378	C6
Goudin Dr				
7600	HOUS	77489	4371	A5
Goulburn Dr				
3100	HOUS	77045	4373	A3
3700	HOUS	77045	4372	D3
Gould Pl				
2700	HOUS	77026	3963	E1
Gould St				
2400	HOUS	77023	4104	D4
Gould Chambers Rd				
19000	MtgC	77365	2826	B7
Gourds Ct				
1300	FBnC	77469	4493	C4
E Governors Cir				
2000	HOUS	77092	3822	C5
W Governors Cir				
2000	HOUS	77092	3822	B4
Governorshire Dr				
22900	HarC	77450	3953	D1
23000	HOUS	77450	3953	D1
Governors Pl Dr				
300	HarC	77450	3953	D2
Gowan Dr				
-	CNRO	77301	2530	B3
Gowland St				
14200	HOUS	77045	4372	E2
Goya				
-	HOUS	77075	4377	C3
Grab Rd				
2000	HarC	77032	3404	C6
Grable Cove Ln				
1600	HarC	77379	3110	B6
Grace				
1600	WALR	77484	3102	A6
Grace Dr				
-	HarC	77447	3104	C7
Grace Ln				
10	HarC	77562	3691	E6
800	HMBL	77338	3406	E1
1500	HarC	77562	3692	A6
5500	HOUS	77021	4104	A5
5800	HOUS	77021	4103	E6
6400	BzaC	77584	4626	E1
22300	MtgC	77357	2827	D6
Grace Rd				
900	HMPD	77445	3098	C1
900	WlrC	77445	3098	C1
Grace St				
200	HOUS	77003	3964	A6
1000	DRPK	77536	4109	C5
1900	ALVN	77511	4866	D4
2200	CNRO	77301	2383	E1
2200	CNRO	77303	2383	E1
Gracechurch Dr				
11300	HarC	77066	3401	D6
Gracefield Ct				
4000	HarC	77047	4374	D4
Gracefield Manor Ct				
5500	FBnC	77450	4094	A3
Graceful Bend Ln				
8500	HarC	77396	3547	E2
Graceful Elm Ct				
10	WDLD	77381	2821	D3
Graceful Oak Cross				
-	FBnC	77494	4093	A3
Grace Hall Dr				
12000	HarC	77065	3399	A6
Graceland St				
200	HOUS	77009	3824	B4
Gracely Park Ln				
10400	FBnC	77469	4094	E5
Grace Meadow Ln				
14200	SGLD	77478	4236	E6
Grace Point Ln				
5200	HOUS	77048	4243	E6
5500	HOUS	77048	4244	A7
Graceton Ln				
-	HarC	77388	3112	E4
Gracia St				
7100	HOUS	77076	3684	D3
7600	HOUS	77037	3684	D2
Gracie				
15600	HOUS	77079	3957	A1
Grackle Dr				
7400	HarC	77433	3677	C1
Grackle Run Ln				
8900	HarC	77338	3262	B4
Graduate Cir				
4300	HOUS	77004	4103	E3
Grady St				
8800	HOUS	77016	3686	D6
Graeber Rd				
1900	RSBG	77471	4491	C6
Graff Net Ct				
6200	HarC	77379	3256	E3
Grafton St				
400	LMQU	77568	4874	B7
7900	HOUS	77017	4105	C6
Grafton Bridge Ln				
13900	HarC	77047	4374	D4
Graftondale Ct				
16000	HarC	77084	3678	C5
Grafton Garden Ln				
900	FBnC	77545	4623	A2
Graham Dr				
100	GNPK	77547	3966	B7
800	TMBL	77375	3109	A1
1000	TMBL	77375	3108	E1
1000	TMBL	77377	3108	E1
Graham Rd				
-	TMBL	77375	3109	C3
Graham St				
10	BYTN	77520	4112	E1
Grahamcrest Dr				
7600	HOUS	77061	4245	B2
Grahamwood Ln				
2700	HarC	77047	4374	A5
Grahmann Ln				
11800	CNRO	77301	2385	C6
11800	MtgC	77301	2385	C6
Grainger Sprs				
13500	HOUS	77070	3400	C3
Grambo Blvd				
13900	GLSN	77554	5332	D2
Gramercy Ct				
3100	BzaC	77584	4501	C6
Gramercy St				
2300	HOUS	77030	4102	B5
2600	HOUS	77025	4102	A5
3500	HOUS	77025	4101	D5
3700	SSPL	77025	4101	D5
Grammar Rd				
200	HarC	77047	4373	B5
Gramond Hall Ct				
9500	HarC	77379	3110	C5
Gramond Hall Dr				
19900	HarC	77379	3110	C5
Grampin Dr				
16800	HarC	77084	3678	B5
Granada				
12900	GLSN	77554	5220	B6
Granada St				
13200	HOUS	77015	3828	C7
Granberry St				
100	HMBL	77338	3262	E6
500	HOUS	77007	3962	E1
Granberry Gate Dr				
17200	HarC	77377	3254	D4
Granborough Dr				
22100	HOUS	77339	3117	E4
22100	HOUS	77365	3117	E4
22100	MtgC	77339	3117	E4
22100	MtgC	77365	3117	E4
Granbury Ct				
9300	HarC	77433	3537	A4
Granby Ter				
10	CNRO	77304	2529	D1
2000	HarC	77373	3114	C7
Grand				
800	PASD	77506	4107	E5
Grand Av				
100	GlsC	77518	4634	B5
200	HarC	77530	3968	E1
1000	GlsC	77539	4634	C4
1200	TXCY	77539	4634	C4
3700	GLSN	77554	5220	E6
3800	GLSN	77554	5221	A6
8400	HarC	77064	3541	C3
Grand Av FM-646				
100	GlsC	77518	4634	B5
1000	GlsC	77539	4634	C4
1200	TXCY	77539	4634	C4
Grand Blf				
1400	FBnC	77469	4364	E4
Grand Blvd				
-	HOUS	77021	4103	A6
-	IWCY	77583	4623	E5
2100	PRLD	77581	4503	C3
3800	DKSN	77539	4754	E2
6900	HOUS	77054	4103	A6
7200	HOUS	77054	4102	E6
7700	HOUS	77020	3826	A6
15100	BzaC	77583	4623	E5
Grand Isl				
10	CNRO	77304	2382	E3
Grand Mnr				
10	SGLD	77479	4495	D2
Grand Pkwy				
-	FBnC	77469	4093	D7
-	FBnC	77469	4233	D1
-	FBnC	77469	4234	E4
-	FBnC	77469	4235	A4
-	FBnC	77469	4366	E6
-	FBnC	77478	4366	D5
-	FBnC	77479	4366	E6
-	FBnC	77494	4093	C5
-	HarC	77449	3814	C5
-	HarC	77493	3814	C5
-	HOUS	77449	3814	C5
-	HOUS	77450	3953	C1
-	HOUS	77450	4093	D1
-	HOUS	77469	4093	D6
-	HOUS	77493	3814	C7
-	HOUS	77493	3953	C1
-	HOUS	77494	3953	C1
-	HOUS	77494	4093	D1
1300	FBnC	77494	3953	C5
16200	FBnC	77479	4493	D3
17400	FBnC	77469	4493	D3
Grand Pkwy SR-99				
-	FBnC	77469	4093	D7
-	FBnC	77469	4233	D1
-	FBnC	77469	4234	E4
-	FBnC	77469	4235	A4
-	FBnC	77469	4366	E6
-	FBnC	77478	4366	D5
-	FBnC	77479	4366	E6
-	FBnC	77494	3953	C4
-	FBnC	77494	4093	C5
-	HarC	77449	3814	C5
-	HarC	77493	3814	C5
-	HOUS	77449	3814	C5
-	HOUS	77450	3953	C1
-	HOUS	77450	4093	D1
-	HOUS	77469	4093	D6
-	HOUS	77493	3814	C7
-	HOUS	77493	3953	C1
-	HOUS	77494	3953	C1
-	HOUS	77494	4093	D1
16200	FBnC	77479	4493	D3
17400	FBnC	77469	4493	D3
Grand Ter				
2000	FBnC	77479	4493	E4
Grand Arbor Ln				
7600	HarC	77433	3537	A5
Grand Arches Ln				
12100	HarC	77346	3408	B4
Grand Ashford Dr				
-	HarC	77375	3254	E1
18900	HarC	77375	3255	A1
Grand Bay Ln				
21600	HarC	77449	3815	A2
Grand Bayou Ln				
10	HOUS	77013	3966	D1
Grand Bayou Pl				
10	WDLD	77382	2674	B5
Grandbluff Ct				
14900	HarC	77429	3396	B1
Grand Brook Ct				
2100	FBnC	77469	4493	A3
8600	HarC	77089	4377	B6
Grand Brook Dr				
10300	HarC	77089	4377	B6
Grand Brook Ln				
21900	FBnC	77469	4493	A3
E Grand Brooks				
-	FBnC	77450	4094	C3
N Grand Brooks				
-	FBnC	77450	4093	C6
-	FBnC	77450	4094	C3
S Grand Brooks				
-	FBnC	77450	4093	C6
-	FBnC	77450	4094	A4
W Grand Brooks				
-	FBnC	77450	4093	E4
Grand Brooks Ln				
-	FBnC	77450	4093	E4
21600	FBnC	77450	4094	A4
Grand Cane Ln				
3200	RSBG	77471	4491	B6
Grand Canyon Dr				
2400	HarC	77067	3401	E4
Grand Canyon Wy				
18300	HarC	77346	3264	E7
Grand Canyon Gate Dr				
6400	FBnC	77450	4094	E4
Grand Cayman Ct				
3200	SGLD	77479	4496	B2
Grand Cayman Dr				
4400	SGLD	77479	4496	A2
Grand Chateau Ln				
4800	HarC	77084	3677	E7
Grand Cir Blvd				
-	HOUS	77449	3814	D7
-	HOUS	77493	3814	D7
Grand Colonial				
10	WDLD	77382	2673	E7
Grand Colony Ct				
19300	HarC	77449	3677	A4
Grand Colony Dr				
5900	HarC	77449	3677	B5
Grand Corral Ct				
14800	HarC	77429	3253	B6
Grand Corral Ln				
14800	HarC	77429	3253	A7
Grand Cove Ct				
22100	FBnC	77450	4093	E3
Grand Creek Ct				
-	LGCY	77573	4631	A4
21900	FBnC	77450	4093	C6
Grand Creek Dr				
-	LGCY	77573	4631	A4
Grand Creek Ln				
5800	FBnC	77450	4093	E4
7500	FBnC	77494	4093	C3
11200	HarC	77375	3109	E1
11200	HarC	77375	3110	A1
Grand Cross Ln				
12700	HOUS	77072	4097	D6
Grande Gables Dr				
5500	RSBG	77469	4492	E7
5500	RSBG	77469	4493	A7
Grand Elm Cir				
3000	HarC	77068	3257	C4
Grande Monde Dr				
12700	HOUS	77045	4373	A1
Grand Estates Dr				
-	FBnC	77469	4493	A5
10700	HarC	77065	3539	D2
Grande Valle Cir				
17900	HarC	77090	3258	A2
Grand Fairway Dr				
100	WDLD	77381	2820	C1
Grand Falls Ct				
100	LGCY	77539	4752	D3
Grand Falls Dr				
1300	MSCY	77459	4369	C5
Grand Field Ct				
21200	HarC	77338	3261	D3
Grandfir Tr				
-	HarC	77433	3251	A6
Grand Flora Ct				
6500	HarC	77041	3680	A4
Grand Floral Blvd				
5600	HarC	77041	3679	B5
Grand Floral Ct				
5700	HarC	77041	3679	B5
Grand Forest Dr				
5300	HarC	77084	3677	E6
Grand Forks Dr				
2700	HOUS	77345	3119	D5
22000	HarC	77450	3954	A3
Grand Fountains Dr				
-	HOUS	77054	4242	A2
Grand Gables St				
-	HOUS	77075	4376	C4
Grand Garden Ct				
10	WDLD	77381	2674	D7
Grand Glen Ct				
6100	FBnC	77494	4093	D4
Grand Harbor Dr				
-	HarC	77494	3952	E2
-	HarC	77494	3953	A2
-	KATY	77494	3952	E2
Grand Harbour Dr				
-	FBnC	77494	3953	E7
22800	FBnC	77450	3953	E7
Grand Haven Dr				
6400	HarC	77088	3542	C6
Grand Haven Ln				
1300	FBnC	77479	4493	C1
Grand Heights Ct				
14000	HOUS	77062	4379	D6
Grand Hills Ln				
3700	HarC	77546	4506	A6
Grand Hollow Ln				
21300	FBnC	77450	4094	A5
21400	FBnC	77450	4093	E5
Grand Isle Av				
200	DKSN	77539	4754	E1
300	TXCY	77539	4754	E1
Grand Isle Ct				
9400	HarC	77044	3688	E4
Grand Isle Ln				
300	LGCY	77539	4752	E5
Grand Joust Dr				
26900	HarC	77339	3118	C3
Grand Junction Dr				
1200	HarC	77450	3954	A4
Grand Knolls Dr				
8400	FBnC	77083	4096	C5
8400	FBnC	77083	4236	B1
Grand Lake Dr				
600	MtgC	77304	2529	E4
1500	CNRO	77304	2529	E2
Grand Lake St				
5100	BLAR	77401	4100	D6
5300	HOUS	77081	4100	D6
Grand Lakeview Dr				
2800	HarC	77388	3113	A5
Grand Lancelot Dr				
21800	MtgC	77339	3118	C5
Grand Linden Ct				
21200	HarC	77338	3261	D3
Grand Manor Ct				
10	SGLD	77479	4495	D3
Grand Manor Ln				
14200	HarC	77396	3547	D2
Grand Masterpiece Ct				
5600	HarC	77041	3679	C6
Grand Masterpiece Ln				
13400	HarC	77041	3679	C5
Grand Meadows Ct				
1600	FBnC	77494	3953	D5
Grand Meadows Dr				
23200	FBnC	77494	3953	D5
Grand Mesa Dr				
2100	HOUS	77345	3120	C5
Grand Mesa Pass				
2800	FBnC	77459	4621	B6
Grandmill Ln				
2100	FBnC	77494	3953	D6
Grand Mission Blvd				
7200	FBnC	77469	4094	E6
9000	FBnC	77469	4095	A7
9000	FBnC	77469	4235	A1
Grand Mountain Ct				
7900	HarC	77095	3537	C6
Grand Noble Cir				
3000	HarC	77068	3257	C4
Grand Nugget Ct				
14800	HOUS	77062	4506	C2
Grand Nugget Ln				
900	HOUS	77062	4506	E1
Grand Oak Ct				
3800	MSCY	77459	4496	D1
Grandoak Dr				
1800	PRLD	77581	4504	A7
Grand Oaks Blvd				
300	HarC	77015	3828	C6
18400	MAGA	77355	2815	B1
18800	MtgC	77355	2815	A2
Grand Oaks Dr				
-	HarC	77015	3967	B1
500	HOUS	77015	3828	C7
700	HOUS	77015	3967	B1
Grand Park Dr				
1500	MSCY	77489	4370	B5
Grand Pass Ct				
3500	FBnC	77494	4093	E6
Grand Pass Ln				
7600	FBnC	77494	4093	C2
Grand Peak Ln				
6500	HarC	77041	3679	D3
Grand Phillips Ln				
5000	FBnC	77450	4093	D2
Grand Pines Dr				
10600	FBnC	77478	4236	E4
Grand Pl Dr				
-	HOUS	77469	4093	D5
-	HOUS	77494	4093	D5
Grand Plains Dr				
700	HarC	77090	3402	D1
Grand Plantation Ct				
2600	MSCY	77459	4496	D1
Grand Plantation Ln				
3900	MSCY	77459	4496	D1
Grand Plaza Dr				
-	HOUS	77067	3402	D7
-	HOUS	77469	4093	D5
-	HOUS	77494	4093	D5
Grand Point Dr				
15100	HarC	77090	3402	D1
Grand Portage Ln				
12200	HarC	77346	3408	C3
Grand Prairie Dr				
12100	HarC	77050	3547	C5
13700	HarC	77396	3547	C3
14600	HOUS	77396	3547	B1
14900	HOUS	77396	3406	B7
Grand Prairie Ln				
-	HarC	77429	3253	A6
Grand Prince Ln				
1400	HarC	77073	3259	C6
Grand Prix Dr				
3000	HarC	77396	3407	A4
3000	HMBL	77396	3407	A4
Grand Promenade Dr				
-	FBnC	77469	4093	E5
-	HOUS	77469	4093	E5
-	HOUS	77494	4093	D5
Grand Rapids Ln				
23100	HarC	77373	3114	D6
E Grand Regency Cir				
-	WDLD	77382	2819	E1
-	WDLD	77382	2820	A1
10	WDLD	77382	2674	A7
W Grand Regency Cir				
-	WDLD	77382	2673	D7
-	WDLD	77382	2819	D1
Grandridge Dr				
7900	HarC	77049	3689	D6
Grand River Dr				
1000	FBnC	77469	4365	A2
Grandriver Dr				
8800	HOUS	77078	3688	B7
Grand Saline Dr				
5800	FBnC	77469	4493	B5
Grand Shore Ct				
2200	PRLD	77584	4500	A2
2900	LGCY	77573	4633	A3
Grand Shore Dr				
13000	PRLD	77584	4500	D4
Grand Shores Ct				
6100	FBnC	77494	4093	C6
Grand Springs Dr				
23300	FBnC	77494	3953	D5
W Grand Star				
-	FBnC	77450	4094	C3
Grand Terrace Ct				
7400	HarC	77095	3677	E1
7600	HarC	77095	3537	A5
Grand Terre				
13300	GLSN	77554	5333	A2
13600	GLSN	77554	5332	E3
Grand Teton Dr				
2400	HarC	77067	3401	D4
Grand Teton Tr				
12400	HarC	77346	3264	D7
12400	HarC	77346	3408	D1
Grand Trace Ln				
-	FBnC	77494	4093	C3
Grandvale Dr				
6100	HOUS	77072	4098	C4
Grand Valley Dr				
1400	HarC	77090	3258	A2
1700	HarC	77090	3257	E3
Grandview St				
7900	HOUS	77051	4243	B2
Grand View Ter				
300	HOUS	77007	3962	E3
Grandview Park Dr				
9100	HarC	77379	3255	E5
N Grandview Park Dr				
9200	HarC	77379	3255	D6
Grand Villa Ln				
8800	FBnC	77469	4234	E1
Grandville St				
5400	HOUS	77028	3826	C4
Grand Vista Dr				
15100	HarC	77083	4096	C6
Grand Vista Ln				
5100	FBnC	77494	4093	D3
Grand West Blvd				
-	HOUS	77449	3953	C1
-	HOUS	77450	3953	C1
Grand Willow Ct				
22000	FBnC	77469	4493	A4
Grand Willow Ln				
1900	FBnC	77469	4493	A2
3400	FBnC	77494	3952	C7
Grand Wimbledon Dr				
-	HarC	77379	3257	A3
Grand Winds Ln				
2700	HarC	77084	3816	A4
Grandwood Ln				
5500	FBnC	77450	4094	A4
Grandy St				
14200	HarC	77396	3547	A2
Granger St				
1600	HOUS	77020	3964	B1
8600	HarC	77338	3262	A5
8600	HOUS	77338	3262	A5
Granger Lake Ct				
1700	FBnC	77469	4234	C4
Grangerland Rd				
13500	MtgC	77302	2533	B6
13500	MtgC	77306	2533	B6
Granger Ridge Ln				
6900	FBnC	77469	4094	D5
Granite Ct				
2600	BzaC	77584	4501	A6
Granite St				
6300	HOUS	77092	3821	C2
Granite Creek Ct				
21000	HarC	77449	3676	D4
Granite Falls Ct				
8100	HarC	77396	3547	D2
Granite Field Ln				
1800	FBnC	77469	4493	B4
Granite Gorge Dr				
8600	HarC	77379	3256	A4
Granite Isle Ct				
12300	HOUS	77089	4378	C7
Granite Knoll Ln				
-	FBnC	77469	4095	C7
18500	HarC	77433	3396	A7
Granite Lake Ct				
4900	MSCY	77459	4496	B2
Granite Lake Dr				
3000	MSCY	77459	4496	B2
Granite Meadow Dr				
-	FBnC	77494	4093	A3
Granite Park Ct				
16300	HarC	77429	3397	A2
Granite Park Wy				
4300	HarC	77396	3407	A6
Granite Pass				
1100	CNRO	77304	2383	B7
Granite Ridge Dr				
-	WDLD	77382	2674	E3
Granite Ridge Ln				
7500	HarC	77095	3538	A7
Granite Rock Ln				
11300	HarC	77375	3110	A6
Granite Shoals Ct				
2300	PRLD	77584	4500	C2
15000	HarC	77429	3397	C1
Granite Shoals Dr				
-	PRLD	77584	4500	C2
Granite Springs Ln				
3600	HarC	77449	3815	A2
6400	FBnC	77469	4493	B7
Granite Trail Ln				
21100	FBnC	77469	4094	A6
Granite Vale Rd				
2900	HarC	77084	3816	C4
Granite Vale Tr				
-	HarC	77049	3829	B3
Granite Valley Ln				
26800	HarC	77433	3396	A4
Granite Woods Ct				
12200	HarC	77346	3408	C1
Grannis St				
9000	HOUS	77075	4246	A6
Granowski Ln				
-	HMPD	77445	2952	C3
-	WlrC	77445	2952	C3
Grant Av				
2500	HOUS	77088	3683	B2
Grant Av S				
-	TXCY	77590	4990	D1
600	TXCY	77590	4874	D7
Grant Dr				
6600	FBnC	77469	4493	C6
6700	MtgC	77354	2673	A2
Grant Ln				
-	HOUS	77088	3683	B2
Grant Rd				
9400	HOUS	77070	3399	D4
9500	HarC	77070	3399	D4
10700	HarC	77429	3399	A4
11100	HarC	77070	3398	C1
11100	HarC	77429	3398	C1
12700	HarC	77429	3254	A7
13700	HarC	77429	3253	C3
16700	HarC	77429	3252	D3
17800	HarC	77433	3252	C3
Grant St				
200	DRPK	77536	4249	B2
1800	HOUS	77006	3962	E5
1900	RSBG	77471	4491	A5
3000	PASD	77503	4108	A4
3000	PASD	77506	4108	A4
3900	HOUS	77051	4243	C1
S Grant St				
100	ALVN	77511	4867	C1
W Grant St				
4300	DRPK	77536	4249	B2
Grantham Rd				
100	BYTN	77521	3972	D4
100	BYTN	77521	3973	A5
Grantley Dr				
12100	HOUS	77099	4237	E3
Grant Meadows Tr				
-	HarC	77429	3253	C3
Grant Mills Ln				
-	FBnC	77478	4236	D3
Grantmoor Ln				
13200	HOUS	77045	4241	B7
Granton St				
6100	HOUS	77026	3825	D6
Grants Hollow Ln				
6900	FBnC	77469	4094	E5
Grants Lake Blvd				
-	SGLD	77478	4368	C6
2500	SGLD	77479	4368	C7
Grants Lake Cir				
10	SGLD	77479	4368	C6
Grants Ridge Ln				
-	HarC	77377	3253	E4
-	HarC	77429	3253	E4
Grants River Cir				
2800	SGLD	77479	4368	C6
Grants Trace Tr				
13200	HarC	77070	3399	C4
Grantwood St				
5100	HOUS	77004	4103	D3
Granum Dr				
30100	MtgC	77386	2969	A2
Granvia Dr				
7200	HarC	77083	4096	C6
Granville Dr				
600	HOUS	77091	3684	A4
900	HOUS	77091	3683	E4
Granville St				
100	BYTN	77520	3972	C6
Grape				
17600	HarC	77044	3551	D7
Grape Ln				
2300	PASD	77502	4247	E2
2300	PASD	77502	4248	A2
Grape Rd				
6400	HOUS	77074	4100	A7
7400	HOUS	77074	4099	D7
8800	HOUS	77036	4099	A7
Grape St				
-	HOUS	77096	4100	B7
5000	HOUS	77096	4101	A7
6100	HOUS	77074	4100	A7
17400	HarC	77044	3551	C7
Grape Arbor Ct				
10	WDLD	77382	2674	A5
Grape Orchard Ct				
15000	HarC	77433	3250	E5
Grapevine Ct				
12000	STAF	77477	4237	E6

STREET
Block City ZIP Map# Grid

Grapevine Ln
32000 MtgC 77355 2668 C5
Grapevine St
3700 HOUS 77045 4372 D3
5500 HOUS 77085 4371 D3
5500 HOUS 77085 4372 A3
Grapevine Tr
6800 FBnC 77469 4095 C5
Grapevine Hills Ln
- PRLD 77581 4503 C1
Grapevine Lake Ct
4900 FBnC 77469 4234 C4
Grapewood Cir
11500 HarC 77089 4378 B5
Grapewood Ct
11500 HarC 77089 4378 B5
Grapewood Dr
11800 HarC 77089 4378 B5
Grapewood Ln
- DRPK 77536 4249 E1
Graphite Canyon Ct
20100 FBnC 77469 4234 C2
Grasilla Dr
4700 HOUS 77045 4241 B6
Grasmere Dr
16100 HarC 77429 3397 A6
Grass Creek Ln
- PRLD 77581 4503 C1
Grasshopper Ct
23500 MtgC 77365 2972 A5
Grasshopper Ln
100 HOUS 77079 3956 D1
Grassington Dr
15200 HarC 77530 3829 D7
Grasslakes Dr
- FBnC 77469 4092 C7
Grassland Cir
10400 HarC 77070 3399 B6
Grassland Ct
1800 SGLD 77478 4368 C5
Grassmere St
4100 HOUS 77051 4243 C5
Grassmont Dr
700 HarC 77530 3829 E7
Grassnook Dr
22400 HarC 77375 3110 D3
Grass Valley Ct
4500 HOUS 77018 3683 B6
Grass Valley St
4400 HOUS 77018 3683 B7
Grassy
7100 HOUS 77072 4097 D6
Grassy Knls
10 FBnC 77479 4367 B7
Grassy Ln
13900 MtgC 77306 2533 D7
Grassy Briar Ln
13000 HOUS 77085 4240 D7
13000 HOUS 77085 4371 C2
Grassy Cove Dr
10100 HarC 77070 3255 A5
Grassy Creek Dr
16000 HarC 77082 4096 A3
Grassy Fields Ct
17900 HarC 77060 3403 D5
Grassyglen Dr
11000 HarC 77064 3540 D2
Grassy Grove Ln
7100 FBnC 77469 4094 D2
Grassy Hill Ln
21800 HarC 77388 3112 D2
Grassy Knoll Ct
2800 SGLD 77478 4369 A7
Grassy Meadow Dr
10800 HarC 77064 3540 E3
Grassy Ridge Ln
14300 HarC 77396 3547 B2
Grassy Shore Ln
- HOUS 77044 3409 A4
Grassy View Dr
900 HarC 77073 3403 B2
Gratehouse Ln
22100 WlrC 77445 3098 D2
Graustark St
3300 HOUS 77006 3962 D7
4400 HOUS 77006 4102 D1
5200 HOUS 77005 4102 D2
Gravel Cr
- HarC 77396 3547 B2
Graven Hill Dr
16300 HarC 77379 3256 B5
Gravenhurst Ln
18100 HarC 77377 3254 B2
Graves Rd
4900 GlsC 77511 4869 B7
Gray Ct
10 HOUS 77003 3963 D7
10 HOUS 77004 3963 D7
Gray Rd
1100 HarC 77562 3832 B4
Gray St
100 HOUS 77002 3963 A5
100 HOUS 77019 3963 A5
1500 HOUS 77003 3963 C6
3000 HOUS 77004 3963 D7
W Gray St
100 HOUS 77002 3963 A5
100 HOUS 77019 3963 A5
200 HOUS 77006 3962 E5
200 HOUS 77019 3962 E5
Gray Bear Cir
14000 HarC 77429 3253 E6
Graybill Ct
26900 HarC 77447 3248 E6
Gray Birch Dr
1800 SGLD 77479 4368 A6
Graycliff Dr
5700 HarC 77049 3828 C4
Gray Falls Dr
2000 HOUS 77077 3957 E7
Grayfeather Ct
2500 HarC 77388 3113 A3
Grayford Ct
1400 HarC 77073 3403 C2
Gray Forest Tr
11700 HarC 77377 3254 E5
Gray Glen Ct
- HarC 77388 3113 B5
Gray Hawk Dr
2100 HarC 77449 3815 E6
N Gray Heron Ct
14800 HarC 77433 3250 E5
Gray Hills Ct
1300 FBnC 77479 4367 A7
Gray Jay Ct
7800 HarC 77040 3541 D7
Gray Jay Dr
7900 HarC 77040 3541 D7

Grayless St
100 RHMD 77469 4365 A7
200 RHMD 77469 4492 A1
Grayling Ln
11300 HarC 77067 3402 A6
Graymont Hls
18200 HarC 77379 3257 A4
Gray Moss Ct
2700 SGLD 77478 4369 B7
Gray Moss Ln
1100 HOUS 77055 3821 C7
Gray Oak Pl
12100 WDLD 77380 2967 E2
Gray Ridge Ct
3500 HarC 77082 4096 C3
Gray Ridge Dr
6800 FBnC 77450 4094 B5
6800 FBnC 77469 4094 A5
15200 HarC 77082 4096 B3
Gray Ridge Ln
14900 HarC 77082 4096 D2
Gray Slate Dr
1900 MSCY 77489 4370 C6
Grayson Ct
4000 FBnC 77459 4621 D4
Grayson Dr
2000 BzaC 77583 4624 A2
2200 PRLD 77578 4624 A2
2200 PRLD 77583 4624 A2
3900 GLSN 77554 5441 B4
Grayson Ln
9700 FBnC 77459 4621 D4
Grayson St
900 HOUS 77034 4378 E1
900 HOUS 77034 4379 A1
2500 HOUS 77020 3963 E3
Grayson Bend Dr
- FBnC 77494 4092 B5
Grayson Lakes Blvd
- KATY 77494 3952 B4
1600 FBnC 77494 3952 B4
Grayson Point Ln
2600 HarC 77449 3815 C4
Grayson Run Ct
- RSBG 77469 4491 E5
Grays Point Ln
- HarC 77377 3254 A3
Graystone Ln
5500 HarC 77069 3400 D1
Graystone Pt
- CNRO 77304 2383 A1
Graystone Bluffs Ct
6000 HOUS 77345 3120 D7
Graystone Creek Ct
1400 HOUS 77345 3120 D6
Graystone Hills Dr
2000 CNRO 77304 2383 B1
Graystone Ridge Dr
2100 CNRO 77304 2383 A1
Graystone Terrace Dr
2300 CNRO 77304 2383 B1
Gray Thrush
3100 FBnC 77459 4621 A6
Grayton Ln
13600 HarC 77041 3679 B4
Gray Trail Ct
16000 HarC 77377 3254 E5
Gray Wolf Tr
21000 HarC 77532 3410 B1
Graywood Ct
10900 LPRT 77571 4250 D3
11600 HarC 77089 4378 B5
Graywood Dr
11400 HarC 77089 4378 B5
Graywood Grove Ln
14600 HOUS 77062 4379 D7
14600 HOUS 77062 4506 D1
Great Basin Ct
11900 HarC 77346 3408 B2
Great Blue Heron Dr
4100 GLSN 77554 5548 A2
Great Bluff Ln
- HarC 77449 3676 D2
Great Bridge Dr
10800 HarC 77065 3539 D1
Greatbrook Ln
6400 FBnC 77450 4094 C3
Great Creek Dr
1300 PRLD 77545 4499 E2
Great Creek Ln
21900 FBnC 77450 4093 C6
Great Dover Cir
1400 HarC 77530 3829 D5
Great Easton Ln
1400 HarC 77073 3259 B5
Great Elms Ct
7000 HarC 77433 3677 A2
Great Elms Dr
19900 HarC 77433 3677 A2
Great Forest Ct
4000 HarC 77346 3408 A3
Great Glen Dr
16600 HarC 77084 3678 B6
17900 HarC 77084 3677 E6
Great Hawk Ln
10900 HOUS 77075 4376 E4
Great Hill Ct
6900 FBnC 77083 4095 E5
Great Horse Ln
- FBnC 77459 4497 B7
- MSCY 77459 4497 B7
Great Lake St
20000 HarC 77484 3103 B4
Great Lakes Av
2700 SGLD 77479 4496 A2
Great Laurel Ct
10 WDLD 77381 2821 D3
20700 HarC 77346 3264 E3
Great Oak Blvd
11600 CHTW 77385 2823 A4
Great Oak Ct
11600 CHTW 77385 2823 A4
12100 MtgC 77354 2671 B4
Great Oak Ln
- SGLD 77479 4367 D6
1500 SGLD 77479 4368 A6
Great Oaks Dr
1000 MtgC 77385 2676 C5
2400 MSCY 77459 4369 B7
6100 HOUS 77050 3546 E5
6100 HOUS 77050 3547 A5
16700 WDLD 77385 2676 C5
Great Oaks Bay Dr
16600 FBnC 77083 4095 E5
Great Oaks Glen Dr
16500 FBnC 77083 4095 D5
Great Oaks Hollow Dr
16400 FBnC 77083 4095 E5

Great Oaks Shadow Dr
6900 FBnC 77083 4095 E5
Great Pecan Ln
7700 FBnC 77479 4493 E6
Great Plains Ln
10200 HarC 77064 3540 B5
Great Prairie Ln
2200 FBnC 77494 3953 B5
Great Ridge Ct
16400 FBnC 77083 4095 E5
Great River Ct
10500 HarC 77089 4377 B6
Great Salt Dr
16600 HOUS 77044 3409 B4
Great Sand Ct
12800 HarC 77346 3408 D2
Great Sands Dr
12700 HarC 77346 3408 D2
Great Springs Ct
3800 FBnC 77494 4093 E6
Greatwood Dr
900 HOUS 77013 3966 E2
Greatwood Pkwy
- FBnC 77479 4494 A5
6500 FBnC 77479 4493 D5
6500 SGLD 77479 4493 D5
Greatwood Glen Ct
7100 FBnC 77479 4493 E7
Greatwood Glen Dr
900 FBnC 77469 4493 D5
900 FBnC 77479 4493 D5
Greatwood Grove Dr
7400 FBnC 77479 4493 E6
Greatwood Knoll Dr
- FBnC 77469 4493 C5
- FBnC 77479 4493 C5
Greatwood Lake Dr
7300 FBnC 77479 4493 D4
7500 FBnC 77479 4494 A4
Greatwood Trails Dr
7000 FBnC 77479 4493 D4
Greatwood Village Dr
- FBnC 77479 4493 C5
Grebb St
2500 LMQU 77568 4989 E3
Grebe Dr
9900 MtgC 77385 2676 D4
Grecian Wy
600 HDWV 77024 3959 E2
600 PNPV 77024 3959 E2
Greeley St
3800 HOUS 77006 3962 E7
4300 HOUS 77006 4102 D2
Green
400 TMBL 77375 2964 C6
800 WALR 77484 3102 A5
W Green Blvd
- HarC 77449 3676 C2
Green Dr
- MtgC 77354 2670 C3
S Green Dr
12500 HOUS 77034 4378 A2
Green Ln
5300 HarC 77066 3401 A6
Green Rd
11300 HarC 77070 3254 E3
11300 HarC 77070 3255 A3
11300 HarC 77375 3255 A3
Green St
100 HarC 77357 2830 A7
100 MSCY 77489 4370 A3
300 TMBL 77375 2964 C6
400 BYTN 77520 3972 E6
3000 HOUS 77020 3964 A2
Green Acres Dr
14000 HarC 77532 3553 C6
Green Apple Dr
3100 PRLD 77581 4503 D3
Green Arbor Dr
10800 HOUS 77089 4377 E2
Green Ash Dr
- HOUS 77036 4099 D3
5700 HOUS 77081 4100 C3
8500 FBnC 77479 4494 B3
Green Aspen Ln
3400 HarC 77047 4374 B4
Greenbank Ln
8200 HarC 77095 3538 E6
Green Bark St
22900 HarC 77375 2966 A7
Greenbay Cir
400 PNPV 77024 3959 E4
Greenbay St
11000 HNCV 77024 3959 E4
11000 HNCV 77024 3960 B4
11000 PNPV 77024 3959 E4
11000 PNPV 77024 3960 B4
11600 BKHV 77024 3959 C4
Green Belt Dr
600 SGLD 77478 4368 B1
Greenbelt Dr
800 HOUS 77079 3957 C2
E Green Belt Dr
800 SGLD 77478 4368 B1
W Green Belt Dr
700 SGLD 77478 4368 A1
Greenbend Blvd
- HOUS 77038 3402 E7
- HOUS 77067 3402 E7
Green Bend Ct
32500 MtgC 77354 2672 D5
Greenberry Dr
- HarC 77339 3118 C6
- HOUS 77339 3118 C6
Greenblade Ct
2700 PRLD 77545 4499 D3
Green Blade Dr
11400 HarC 77429 3397 C7
Greenblade Dr
1300 PRLD 77545 4499 D3
Green Blade Ln
10 WDLD 77380 2822 A7
Greenbluff Ct
- HarC 77429 3254 A4
Green Bluff Dr
12000 HarC 77044 3549 A6
Green Bough Ct
10 WDLD 77380 2967 E4
Greenbough Dr
10400 STAF 77477 4369 D2
Greenbough St
14400 MtgC 77302 2678 D6
Greenbow Ln
200 HarC 77562 3692 D6
Green Bower Ln
10 WDLD 77380 2821 E6
Green Brae Ln
400 LGCY 77539 4752 E5

Greenbrae Ln
5300 FBnC 77494 4093 B2
Green Branch Dr
3300 HOUS 77338 3263 D4
Greenbriar
- LGCY 77573 4632 B2
19200 MtgC 77355 2814 A1
Greenbriar Av
100 FRDW 77546 4629 A1
1400 PASD 77502 4107 C7
Greenbriar Dr
- STAF 77477 4238 B7
- WlrC 77447 2813 B3
10 PNVL 77304 2237 A3
100 BYTN 77520 3971 B2
300 FRDW 77546 4629 A2
1700 SGLD 77478 4237 B5
2600 HOUS 77019 3962 B7
2600 HOUS 77098 3962 B7
3600 HOUS 77098 4102 B4
3700 STAF 77477 4369 C1
4000 MSCY 77459 4497 C3
4400 HOUS 77005 4102 B2
7800 HOUS 77030 4102 C6
7900 HOUS 77054 4102 C6
Greenbriar St
2700 DKSN 77539 4753 C2
Greenbriar St E
6800 GlsC 77510 4987 D5
Greenbriar Colony Dr
1600 HarC 77032 3404 B6
2200 HOUS 77032 3404 C6
Greenbriar Lake Dr
4200 FBnC 77469 4234 D5
Greenbriar Park Dr
17900 HarC 77060 3403 D5
Greenbriar Plaza Dr
16600 HOUS 77060 3403 D7
Greenbriar Point Ln
16600 HarC 77095 3538 B4
Greenbriar Springs Dr
3000 HarC 77073 3260 A4
Greenbridge Dr
- FBnC 77450 3953 D5
- FBnC 77494 3953 D5
- MtgC 77384 2675 A5
- WDLD 77381 2674 E6
- WDLD 77382 2674 E6
- WDLD 77382 2675 A5
- WDLD 77384 2675 A5
Greenbrook Dr
21500 HarC 77073 3259 B3
22400 HarC 77373 3259 A1
N Greenbud Ct
10 WDLD 77380 2968 B4
S Greenbud Ct
10 WDLD 77380 2968 A4
Greenbusch Rd
1000 FBnC 77494 3952 E5
1000 KATY 77494 3952 C3
2800 FBnC 77494 3953 A4
Greenbush Dr
7900 HOUS 77025 4102 A6
Green Butte Ct
12000 HarC 77044 3549 A6
Green Canary Cir
14900 HarC 77433 3250 D4
Green Candle Dr
3400 HarC 77388 3113 A6
Greencanyon Dr
11700 HarC 77044 3548 D6
12200 HarC 77044 3549 A6
Greencap Ln
16300 HarC 77447 3248 E6
Green Cape Ct
22700 HarC 77373 2968 E7
Greencape Ct
9400 HarC 77396 3548 A2
Green Castle Wy
8800 HarC 77095 3538 C4
Green Cedar Dr
100 LGCY 77573 4631 A5
8300 FBnC 77083 4096 B7
8300 FBnC 77083 4236 B1
Greenchase Dr
12500 HarC 77060 3403 C6
12500 HOUS 77060 3403 C6
Green Chase Ln
19400 HarC 77073 3403 B2
Greencliff Ln
20300 FBnC 77469 4094 C6
Green Coral Dr
11800 HarC 77044 3548 E7
Green Cottage Lake Ln
4600 MSCY 77459 4369 A4
Greencourt Dr
2000 MSCY 77489 4370 C6
15700 HarC 77062 4380 D7
Green Cove
14000 HarC 77532 3553 C7
Greencove Ln
2100 SGLD 77479 4368 B7
Green Cove St
400 PNPV 77024 3959 E4
Green Cove Bend Ln
5300 HarC 77041 3679 B7
Green Craig Dr
5600 HOUS 77035 4240 C7
Greencreek Cir
11900 HarC 77070 3399 C6
Green Creek Dr
2800 MSCY 77489 4370 D7
Greencreek Dr
10300 HarC 77070 3399 A6
10800 HarC 77065 3399 A6
Greencreek Meadows Ln
6400 HarC 77379 3111 C4
Green Crest Dr
2700 HOUS 77082 4096 C2
2800 HarC 77082 4096 C3
Greencrest Dr
2000 MSCY 77489 4370 C6
Greencroft St
1100 HarC 77530 3830 B6
Green Cross Ln
25100 FBnC 77494 3953 B5
Green Cypress Ct
18400 HarC 77429 3396 B1
Green Cypress Ln
6300 HarC 77449 3677 D4
Greendale
15200 HarC 77032 3404 B7
15200 HOUS 77032 3404 B7
Greendale Dr
1500 MSCY 77489 4370 D7
15100 HOUS 77032 3404 B7
15400 HarC 77032 3404 A7

Greendale Ln
100 HarC 77562 3831 E1
Greendale Park Ln
- MtgC 77386 2823 B7
Green Devon Dr
8000 HarC 77095 3538 D6
Green Dolphin Rd
12800 HOUS 77013 3828 A5
Green Dolphin St
12700 HOUS 77013 3828 A5
Greendowns St
7500 HOUS 77087 4105 A6
7700 HOUS 77017 4105 B6
Greene Av
400 WEBS 77598 4507 C7
Greenedge Dr
7800 HarC 77040 3541 D7
Green Elm Ln
17700 HarC 77379 3257 A3
Green Estate Ct
23700 HarC 77373 3115 A4
Green Falls Ct
1900 FBnC 77469 4365 A2
Green Falls Dr
5800 HOUS 77088 3682 D1
12000 PRLD 77584 4500 C4
Green Falls Ln
2600 FBnC 77469 4365 A2
Green Fawn Ln
4500 FBnC 77545 4622 E2
Green Feather Dr
16400 HarC 77530 3829 E3
Green Fern Ct
2400 HarC 77388 3113 A2
Greenfield Dr
1800 RSBG 77471 4491 D5
N Greenfield Dr
15700 HarC 77379 3256 E4
Greenfield Ln
8700 HarC 77064 3541 C5
Green Field Pl
10 WDLD 77380 2822 B7
Greenfield Rd
- PRVW 77445 3099 E3
- PRVW 77445 3100 A4
- WlrC 77445 3099 E3
Greenfield St
26400 HarC 77373 3113 E2
Greenfield Tr
20700 HarC 77346 3264 E3
Greenfield Forest Dr
32900 MtgC 77354 2673 E3
Green Fields Dr
2700 SGLD 77479 4495 E1
3700 SGLD 77479 4496 A1
Green Fir Tr
15300 HarC 77433 3251 A5
Green Forest Dr
100 HOUS 77388 3113 D7
200 HarC 77388 3113 D7
24300 MtgC 77372 2682 C2
30400 MtgC 77354 2816 A1
30800 MtgC 77354 2815 E1
Green Forest Ln
2900 PRLD 77581 4503 E6
Green Forest Rd
2800 MtgC 77303 2239 D7
2800 MtgC 77303 2385 E1
Green Forest St
23300 MtgC 77447 2960 B5
Greenfork Dr
10000 HOUS 77036 4098 E7
10200 HOUS 77036 4238 E1
10200 HOUS 77099 4238 E1
Green Gable Mnr
6600 HarC 77389 2966 C3
Green Gables Cir
100 WDLD 77382 2674 D5
E Green Gables Cir
10 WDLD 77382 2674 E5
Green Gables Ct
100 WDLD 77382 2674 E5
Green Garden Ln
2200 HarC 77084 3816 B7
Green Gate Dr
1800 RSBG 77471 4491 D5
Greengate Dr
21200 HarC 77388 3112 E3
21300 HarC 77388 3113 A3
21900 HarC 77389 3112 E2
22400 HarC 77389 3113 A1
Greenglade Ct
10 WDLD 77381 2821 B6
Green Glade Dr
11400 HOUS 77099 4238 B3
12100 HOUS 77099 4237 E2
Greenglade Ln
2300 MtgC 77386 2969 B3
Greenglen Dr
12200 HarC 77044 3548 E6
12200 HarC 77044 3549 A6
Green Glen Rd
11700 HarC 77044 3548 D6
Green Glen St
16000 HarC 77032 3403 E6
16000 HOUS 77032 3403 E6
Greengrass Ct
2000 HOUS 77008 3822 C5
Greengrass Dr
1600 HOUS 77008 3822 C6
Green Grove Ln
- BzaC 77583 4623 C5
Green Grove Rd
- HarC 77049 3831 B1
Greenham Ct
3200 HarC 77388 3112 E3
Greenham Dr
21700 HarC 77388 3112 E2
Green Haven Dr
10 WDLD 77381 2821 A7
Greenhaven Dr
- MtgC 77380 2967 B1
2200 FBnC 77479 4494 B4
25800 MtgC 77380 2821 A7
Greenhaven Ln
3000 HOUS 77092 3822 B3
Greenhaven Lake Ln
15000 HarC 77429 3253 C6
Greenhaw Rd
13100 MtgC 77372 2535 A6
Green Hazel Ct
5300 HarC 77084 3677 E6
Green Hazel Dr
18000 HarC 77084 3677 E5
Greenhead St
3200 KATY 77493 3813 B3
Greenheath Ct
7200 HarC 77389 2966 B2

Greenheath Ln
5500 FBnC 77450 4093 B4
Green Heather Ln
6000 HOUS 77085 4240 E7
Green Heron Dr
4100 GLSN 77554 5548 B2
Green Hill Dr
2100 HOUS 77032 3404 D5
Green Hill Rd
5400 BKVL 77581 4375 B7
5400 PRLD 77581 4375 B7
Greenhill Forest Dr
5400 HarC 77088 3542 E7
Green Hills Cir
4200 SGLD 77479 4495 A1
E Greenhill Terrace Pl
10 WDLD 77382 2674 E3
W Greenhill Terrace Pl
10 WDLD 77382 2674 D3
Green Hollow Ct
2700 MSCY 77489 4370 D7
Green Hollow Ln
7800 HarC 77389 2966 A3
8700 HarC 77379 3255 E3
Greenhouse Rd
300 BzaC 77511 4628 B6
2600 HarC 77084 3816 B1
2600 HOUS 77084 3816 B5
3100 HarC 77449 3816 B5
4400 HarC 77084 3677 B7
4800 HarC 77449 3677 B5
7000 HarC 77433 3677 B1
7600 HarC 77433 3537 B7
S Greenhouse Rd
- HOUS 77084 3955 B1
- HOUS 77094 3955 B1
1500 HarC 77094 3955 B2
Greenhouse St
16800 MtgC 77385 2676 E4
Greenhurst Rd
6600 HOUS 77091 3683 C4
6700 HOUS 77088 3683 C4
Greening Ct
3600 HOUS 77087 4105 B6
Greeningdon St
10 WDLD 77381 2821 A3
Green Island Dr
2500 HOUS 77032 3404 D5
Green Isle Dr
11800 HarC 77044 3549 A6
Green Ivy Ct
300 PASD 77503 4108 D4
13900 HOUS 77059 4380 A4
Green Ivy Tr
- HOUS 77345 3120 C4
Green Jade Dr
3900 MtgC 77386 2970 C7
Green Knoll Dr
1200 FBnC 77479 4493 C5
2100 HarC 77067 3402 A5
Greenlake Dr
2700 HarC 77388 3113 A2
2800 HarC 77388 3112 E2
Greenland Ct
- STAF 77477 4369 D2
Greenland Dr
- STAF 77477 4369 D2
Green Land Wy
18500 HarC 77084 3816 D3
Greenland Oak Ct
23700 HarC 77373 3115 A4
Greenlaw Ct
10 SGLD 77479 4495 D3
Greenlaw St
10 SGLD 77479 4495 D3
Green Lawn Dr
- HarC 77088 3682 D1
7700 HOUS 77088 3682 D2
8200 HarC 77088 3542 D7
Greenleaf Cir
500 MtgC 77302 2530 C6
Greenleaf Dr
4100 HarC 77389 3112 C1
14300 MtgC 77302 2678 C6
Green Leaf Ldg
3500 FBnC 77545 4498 C7
Green Leaf Ln
3100 LPRT 77571 4382 D1
Greenleaf Ln
100 CNRO 77304 2383 B6
15100 HOUS 77062 4380 B7
E Greenleaf Ln
17000 MtgC 77306 2533 D7
W Greenleaf Ln
16700 MtgC 77306 2533 C7
Green Leaf Mdws
8900 HarC 77083 4237 C1
Greenleaf St
2600 HOUS 77009 3963 A1
8200 CmbC 77520 3835 D3
Greenleaf Lake Dr
8500 HarC 77095 3538 D5
Green Leaf Oaks Dr
1500 SGLD 77479 4495 A1
Greenleaf Ridge Ct
19000 HarC 77429 3395 E2
Greenleaf Ridge Wy
8300 MtgC 77385 2676 C5
Green Leaf Spring Ln
24100 HarC 77494 3953 B1
Greenleaf Trail Dr
24500 MtgC 77365 2972 D7
Green Leaves
400 MtgC 77302 2530 C6
Greenlee Dr
14900 HarC 77530 3829 C7
Green Lee Ln
2100 DKSN 77539 4753 D2
Greenlet Ct
3000 HarC 77373 3114 E5
Greenloch Ln
11800 HarC 77044 3548 D6
Green Lodge Cir
2800 HarC 77373 3114 E3
2800 HarC 77373 3115 C3
Greenlow Dr
- HOUS 77014 3402 D4
- HOUS 77067 3402 D4
Greenly Dr
19600 HarC 77073 3403 C2
Green Manor Dr
16500 HOUS 77396 3406 A4
Green Mansions Ct
1400 MSCY 77489 4370 D7
Green Meadow Ct
2700 MSCY 77489 4370 D7
5500 LGCY 77573 4751 D2

Green Meadow Dr
10 BzaC 77511 4868 B5
9800 LPRT 77571 4110 A7
Green Meadow Ln
700 HOUS 77088 3684 A4
700 HOUS 77091 3684 A4
900 HOUS 77088 3683 E3
900 HOUS 77091 3683 E3
Green Meadow Rd
27700 HarC 77377 3108 E3
Green Meadow St
18900 MAGA 77355 2668 E6
Green Meadows Ln
3600 PASD 77505 4248 D4
Green Mesa Dr
2200 MtgC 77385 2823 C2
Greenmesa Dr
12200 HarC 77044 3548 E6
12200 HarC 77044 3549 A6
Green Mill Ct
28400 MtgC 77386 2969 D6
Green Mills Dr
9400 HOUS 77070 3399 D4
Greenmist Ln
- FBnC 77494 4093 C2
Greenmont Dr
5900 HOUS 77092 3682 D6
Green Moss Ct
1400 MSCY 77489 4370 D7
Green Moss Dr
24600 HOUS 77336 3266 B1
Greenmount Ln
13000 HOUS 77085 4240 C7
Green Mountain Dr
2700 PRLD 77545 4499 D3
16000 HOUS 77032 3404 D5
Green Oak
2600 HarC 77339 3118 C5
Green Oak Cir
30100 MtgC 77355 2815 D2
Green Oak Dr
2700 HarC 77339 3118 C5
2700 HOUS 77339 3118 C5
Greenoak Dr
1200 HarC 77032 3403 E6
1200 HarC 77032 3404 A6
Green Oak Pl
1500 HOUS 77339 3118 C6
Green Oak St
38200 MtgC 77355 2815 D2
Green Oak Ter
- HOUS 77339 3118 C6
Green Oak Meadow Ln
17900 HarC 77060 3403 D5
Green Oaks Dr
300 LGCY 77573 4630 D5
11500 BKHV 77024 3959 C4
11500 PNPV 77024 3959 C4
16100 HOUS 77032 3404 C5
Green Oaks St
23200 MtgC 77357 2973 E1
23200 MtgC 77357 2974 A1
Green Oak Terrace Ct
1400 HOUS 77339 3118 C6
Green Oasis Ct
19600 HarC 77449 3677 A4
Greenough Dr
24800 FBnC 77494 3952 D4
Green Palmetto Ln
- PRLD 77584 4501 E4
Greenpark Dr
800 HOUS 77079 3957 C2
S Greenpark Dr
6100 HOUS 77072 4097 C4
6100 HOUS 77082 4097 C4
Greenpark Manor Ln
5800 HOUS 77085 4240 E7
5900 HOUS 77085 4371 D1
E Green Pastures Cir
10 WDLD 77382 2673 C5
W Green Pastures Cir
10 WDLD 77382 2673 B6
E Green Pastures Dr
- WDLD 77382 2673 C5
Green Path Ct
7700 FBnC 77479 4493 E5
7700 FBnC 77479 4494 A5
Green Pear Ln
6400 HarC 77049 3829 B2
Green Persimmon Ln
36900 MtgC 77354 2816 B1
Green Pine Dr
2800 HarC 77339 3118 C5
2900 HOUS 77339 3118 D5
Green Pines Cir
11900 HarC 77066 3401 A6
Green Pines Dr
5300 HarC 77066 3401 A6
21900 MtgC 77357 2974 A3
Green Pines Forest
800 HOUS 77067 3402 E4
Green Plaza Dr
11400 HOUS 77038 3544 A1
Green Plume Ln
16100 HarC 77447 3248 E7
Green Point Ct
400 PNPV 77024 3959 E3
Greenport Ln
16100 HarC 77084 3678 C4
Green Quail Dr
16800 MSCY 77489 4497 D1
Greenranch Dr
13800 HarC 77039 3545 E3
Green Ray Dr
8900 HarC 77095 3538 C4
Greenrich Dr
17900 HarC 77060 3403 C5
Greenridge Cir
- LGCY 77573 4631 A4
Greenridge Dr
- LGCY 77573 4631 A4
2700 HOUS 77057 3960 C7
2900 HOUS 77057 4100 C1
3100 MSCY 77459 4369 E7
13600 SGLD 77478 4237 B5
E Greenridge Dr
3300 HOUS 77057 4100 C1
W Greenridge Dr
3300 HOUS 77057 4100 C1
N Green Ridge Tr
16500 HarC 77433 3250 D4
S Green Ridge Tr
22100 HarC 77433 3250 D4
Greenridge Forest Ct
10 WDLD 77381 2821 B4
Greenridge Forest Dr
10 WDLD 77381 2821 B4

Houston Street Index

STREET Block City ZIP Map# Grid

Greenridge Manor Ln
8400 HarC 77389 2965 E4
8400 HarC 77389 2966 A5
Green River Dr
- HOUS 77078 3688 C7
8000 HOUS 77028 3826 D1
8600 HOUS 77028 3687 E7
11700 HarC 77044 3688 C7
12100 HarC 77044 3689 A7
N Green River Dr
8500 HOUS 77028 3687 D7
8700 HOUS 77078 3687 D7
8800 HOUS 77078 3688 C7
Greenriver Valley Dr
4900 HOUS 77345 3119 C2
Greenrock Ln
11900 HarC 77044 3548 E6
Green Rock Rd
2200 HOUS 77032 3404 C5
Greenrush Dr
22900 FBnC 77494 3953 D5
Greens Blvd
1900 FBnC 77469 4365 C2
Greens Ct
2200 FBnC 77469 4365 C2
11400 HarC 77067 3402 B6
Greens Pkwy
- HarC 77067 3402 D7
500 HOUS 77067 3403 A7
900 HOUS 77067 3402 E7
Greens Rd
- HarC 77032 3403 D6
- HOUS 77032 3403 B6
- HOUS 77396 3406 B5
10 HOUS 77060 3403 A6
1900 HarC 77032 3404 D5
1900 HOUS 77032 3404 D5
2800 HOUS 77032 3405 A6
5700 HOUS 77396 3405 D5
7800 HarC 77396 3406 D5
9200 HarC 77396 3407 A6
N Greens Rd
2100 HarC 77067 3402 A6
W Greens Rd
- HarC 77066 3401 B6
- HOUS 77060 3403 A6
100 HOUS 77067 3403 A6
400 HarC 77067 3402 E6
900 HOUS 77067 3402 D6
3100 HarC 77067 3401 E6
6600 HarC 77066 3400 D6
7200 HOUS 77064 3400 B5
Green Sage Dr
6700 HarC 77064 3541 C1
Greens Bayou Dr
- HOUS 77015 3966 E2
900 HOUS 77015 3967 B2
Greensboro Dr
2500 HOUS 77021 4103 A4
Greensbrook Forest Dr
11700 HarC 77044 3548 E6
12200 HarC 77044 3549 A7
Greensbrook Garden Dr
11700 HarC 77044 3549 A6
Greensburg Ct
700 MtgC 77302 2530 D7
Greens Cove Tr
15400 HOUS 77059 4380 B6
Greens Crossing Blvd
- HarC 77038 3402 E7
- HOUS 77038 3402 E7
- HOUS 77067 3402 E6
10400 HarC 77038 3544 A3
Greens Ct Wy
4400 HOUS 77339 3119 E7
Greens Edge Dr
10 HOUS 77339 3264 E1
Greens Ferry Ct
2800 FBnC 77469 4234 C7
Greensford Ct
2000 HarC 77530 3829 E4
Green Shade Dr
16200 HarC 77090 3258 D5
Greenshadow Dr
1400 HarC 77032 3404 A6
Green Shadows
- HarC 77032 3404 B6
Green Shadows Dr
3700 PASD 77503 4108 C5
Greenshire Dr
100 LGCY 77573 4632 E1
11500 HOUS 77048 4243 D7
11700 HOUS 77048 4374 D1
Green Shoals Ln
6300 HarC 77066 3400 E5
Green Shore Dr
- HarC 77044 3408 E5
Greenshores Ln
7400 FBnC 77469 4094 C6
Greenside Dr
13800 HarC 77083 4237 A1
Greenside Hill Ln
19700 HarC 77449 3676 E5
Greens Landing Dr
100 HarC 77037 3544 A3
100 HarC 77038 3544 A3
100 HOUS 77037 3544 A3
Green Slope Pl
10 WDLD 77381 2820 D3
Greens Manor Ln
12900 HarC 77044 3689 B5
Greensmark Rd
1500 HarC 77067 3402 C7
1500 HOUS 77067 3402 C7
Green Smoke Dr
16200 HarC 77095 3538 C4
Greens Orchard Dr
4300 HarC 77066 3401 C5
Greenspark Ln
11700 HarC 77044 3548 E7
Greenspoint Dr
11400 HOUS 77060 3544 B1
12000 HOUS 77060 3403 B7
12500 HarC 77060 3403 B6
Greenspoint Mall Rd
10 HOUS 77060 3403 B6
Greenspoint Park Dr
16700 HOUS 77060 3403 C6
Green Spring Ct
1000 MSCY 77459 4369 B4
Green Springs Dr
5100 HarC 77066 3401 A3
5500 HarC 77066 3400 E3
Green Spur St
16100 HOUS 77032 3404 D5
Green Star Ct
1900 MSCY 77489 4370 C5

Green Star Dr
1800 MSCY 77489 4370 C5
Green Star Ln
16800 HarC 77429 3252 E6
Green Stem Pth
26100 FBnC 77494 4092 E2
Greenstill Dr
4400 HarC 77346 3264 B7
Greenstock
- HarC 77336 2976 E1
Green Stone Ct
400 HarC 77094 3955 C1
6700 HarC 77084 3678 E2
Green Stone Dr
15000 HarC 77084 3678 E2
Greenstone St
7600 HOUS 77087 4105 B6
7800 HOUS 77017 4105 B6
Greenstone Park Ln
11000 HarC 77089 4377 C7
11000 HOUS 77089 4377 C7
Green Summer Ln
6500 HarC 77338 3261 B3
Greensward Ln
10 SGLD 77479 4495 B2
Greensward Rd
9300 HOUS 77080 3820 D5
Greenswarth Ln
7400 HOUS 77075 4376 B3
Green Tavern Ct
15100 HarC 77429 3397 C1
Green Teal Ln
13500 HarC 77039 3546 A3
Green Tee Dr
2000 PRLD 77581 4504 B4
4400 BYTN 77521 3972 C3
Green Terrace Ln
5800 HOUS 77088 3682 D2
Green Thicket Ct
21500 HarC 77388 3113 B3
Green Thicket Dr
1400 PRLD 77545 4499 D4
Greenthread Dr
2200 LGCY 77573 4632 D2
Green Timbers Dr
5500 HarC 77346 3264 C6
Green Top Ct
5800 HarC 77084 3677 E4
Green Trace Ln
17900 FBnC 77469 4095 C7
Green Trail Ct
200 PASD 77503 4108 D4
Green Trail Dr
1100 HarC 77038 3543 C3
4600 HarC 77084 3678 D7
Green Trails Dr
12100 STAF 77477 4237 E6
12100 STAF 77477 4238 A6
Green Tree Ct
3000 MSCY 77459 4497 A1
4300 PASD 77505 4249 B6
Green Tree Dr
1400 TMBL 77375 2964 A4
5500 FBnC 77479 4496 A6
16100 HOUS 77032 3404 D5
Green Tree Ln
10 PNVL 77304 2237 A2
30900 MtgC 77354 2669 E6
30900 MtgC 77354 2670 A6
Greentree Ln
25800 MtgC 77354 2817 D7
Green Tree Pk
3300 HOUS 77007 3962 D3
Green Tree Rd
5000 HOUS 77056 3961 A3
5200 HOUS 77056 3960 E3
5600 HOUS 77057 3960 D3
Greentree Rd
10000 HOUS 77042 3958 E4
10000 HOUS 77042 3959 A4
Green Turtle Dr
- PASD 77505 4248 E4
Greentwig Pl
10 WDLD 77381 2820 C2
Greenvale Dr
11300 PNPV 77024 3959 D3
Greenvale Ln
6300 HarC 77066 3400 E6
Green Valley Dr
- HarC 77032 3404 C5
1100 SPVL 77055 3821 A7
2200 DRPK 77536 4249 E1
2200 HOUS 77032 3404 C5
8300 FBnC 77479 4494 B6
Green Valley Ln
10000 HarC 77064 3540 C4
Greenvalley Trail Dr
2900 HarC 77449 3815 E5
Green Velvet Tr
20500 HarC 77433 3251 B4
Greenview Dr
16000 HOUS 77032 3404 D5
Green Village Dr
3400 HOUS 77339 3119 B5
Greenville Dr
2600 LGCY 77573 4508 D7
Greenville St
6900 HOUS 77020 3964 E1
6900 HOUS 77020 3965 A1
13700 HarC 77015 3967 E1
14000 HarC 77015 3968 A1
N Greenvine Cir
10 WDLD 77382 2674 B6
N Greenvine Ct
10 WDLD 77382 2674 B5
W Greenvine Ct
10 WDLD 77382 2674 B5
Greenvine Trace Dr
- FBnC 77469 4233 E2
Green Vista
2900 HarC 77068 3257 C4
Greenwade Cir
20300 HarC 77449 3815 C7
Greenwater Dr
- HarC 77065 3539 D2
Greenway Dr
100 CNRO 77304 2383 A3
3600 BYTN 77521 3972 E3
13400 SGLD 77478 4237 B6
14000 SGLD 77478 4236 E6
Greenway Ln
1700 HarC 77530 3830 C4
E Greenway Plz
- HOUS 77027 4101 E1
- HOUS 77046 4101 E1
- HOUS 77098 4101 E1
Greenway Chase Ct
12900 HOUS 77072 4097 C5

Greenway Chase St
6800 HOUS 77072 4097 C5
Greenway Forest Ln
6100 HarC 77088 3682 C2
Greenway Manor Ln
5900 HarC 77373 3260 E2
6000 HarC 77373 3261 A2
Greenway Park Cir
23200 FBnC 77494 3953 D5
Greenway View Tr
10 HOUS 77339 3119 E7
10 HOUS 77339 3264 E1
Greenway Village Ct
23200 FBnC 77494 3953 D6
Greenway Village Dr
1400 FBnC 77494 3953 D5
2300 FBnC 77450 3953 D6
Greenwell Dr
- HarC 77014 3402 D2
Greenwest Dr
1800 MSCY 77489 4370 C6
Green Whisper Dr
15000 HarC 77433 3250 E6
Greenwich Pk
1200 HOUS 77019 3962 C4
Greenwich Pl
- CNRO 77384 2675 E3
- CNRO 77384 2676 A4
1900 HOUS 77019 3962 C4
Greenwich St
9500 HOUS 77028 3687 C5
9500 HOUS 77078 3687 C5
Greenwich Terrace Dr
1900 HOUS 77019 3962 C4
Greenwichwood Ln
1400 HarC 77073 3259 D5
N Greenwick Ct
12800 HOUS 77085 4240 D7
Greenwick Ln
6200 HOUS 77085 4240 D7
E Greenwick Lp
12800 HOUS 77085 4240 D7
N Greenwick Lp
6200 HOUS 77085 4240 D7
S Greenwick Lp
6200 HOUS 77085 4240 D7
W Greenwick Lp
12700 HOUS 77085 4240 D7
Greenwillow Dr
9000 HOUS 77096 4101 C7
9900 HOUS 77096 4241 C2
10000 HOUS 77035 4241 C4
Green Willow Ln
4900 DKSN 77539 4753 C4
Green Willow St
38200 MtgC 77355 2815 D2
Green Willow Falls Dr
11800 HarC 77375 3109 D5
Greenwind Chase Dr
- HarC 77450 3955 A4
19300 HarC 77094 3955 A4
Greenwing Teal Ct
4100 GLSN 77554 5441 D3
E Greenwood
- CmbC 77520 4114 B2
W Greenwood
- CmbC 77520 4113 E3
- CmbC 77520 4114 A3
Greenwood Dr
600 FBnC 77469 4492 B1
600 RHMD 77469 4492 B1
1300 BYTN 77520 3973 D7
1900 RSBG 77471 4491 C5
3400 SGLD 77478 4368 E6
3400 SGLD 77478 4369 A6
3900 PRLD 77584 4503 A7
17200 MtgC 77357 2681 A7
Greenwood Ln S
13700 HarC 77044 3549 D2
Greenwood Pl
3300 DRPK 77536 4108 D6
3300 DRPK 77536 4248 E1
Greenwood St
10 HOUS 77011 3964 D6
300 HTCK 77563 4988 C3
30100 MtgC 77355 2815 D1
N Greenwood St
400 HOUS 77011 3964 D5
Greenwood Estates Dr
12000 HarC 77066 3401 A3
Greenwood Forest Dr
12400 HarC 77066 3401 A2
12800 HarC 77066 3400 E1
12800 HarC 77069 3400 E1
Greenwood Glen Dr
3000 HOUS 77345 3119 E4
Greenwood Lakes Ln
13200 HarC 77044 3549 D2
Greenwood Manor Dr
13400 HarC 77429 3397 A3
Greenwood Oaks Dr
1900 HOUS 77062 4380 A6
Greenwood Pines Dr
16000 HOUS 77062 4380 C7
Greenwood Point Dr
7000 HarC 77433 3677 A1
7000 HarC 77449 3677 A2
7600 HarC 77433 3537 A7
Greenwood Trace Ln
4400 FBnC 77494 4092 D2
Greenyard Dr
6600 HarC 77086 3542 C1
Gregdale Rd
6900 HarC 77049 3828 A1
Gregg St
200 HOUS 77020 3964 A3
1900 HOUS 77026 3964 A1
2500 HOUS 77026 3825 A7
6600 ARLA 77583 4623 A7
Gregiry Wy
12000 HarC 77067 3402 D4
Gregory Blvd
- HOUS 77035 4240 A7
- MSCY 77071 4239 E7
- MSCY 77071 4240 A7
Gregory Ct
800 STAF 77477 4369 C4
Gregory Ln
- HarC 77562 3831 E2
Gregory Rd
100 CNRO 77304 2382 D4
100 MtgC 77304 2382 D4
Gregory St
4300 HOUS 77026 3825 B6
Gregs Wy
700 HOUS 77336 3266 D2
Gregson Rd
11400 HarC 77070 3254 C3

Gregson Rd
11400 HarC 77375 3254 C3
11400 HarC 77377 3254 C3
Gregway Ln
2700 MSCY 77459 4369 B7
Gregwood Ct
4300 FBnC 77450 4093 E2
Greiner Dr
8600 HOUS 77080 3821 A2
8700 HOUS 77080 3820 E2
Gren St
4900 HOUS 77021 4103 E6
5100 HOUS 77021 4104 B5
Grenada Ln
- HarC 77338 3260 C3
18800 NSUB 77058 4508 B7
Grenada Falls Dr
16500 HarC 77095 3538 B4
Grenadier Dr
9700 HOUS 77089 4377 D4
Grenfell Ln
700 HOUS 77076 3685 B3
W Grenfell Ln
100 HOUS 77076 3684 C3
Grennoch Ln
3300 HOUS 77025 4101 C6
Grenoble Ln
20700 FBnC 77450 4094 B4
Grenshaw St
800 HOUS 77088 3684 A1
900 HOUS 77088 3683 E1
Gresham Av
10 BYTN 77520 3973 A5
200 BYTN 77520 3972 D5
Gress
10000 HarC 77086 3541 E2
Gretchen St
100 CNRO 77301 2384 B2
Gretel Dr
400 HOUS 77024 3958 D3
Gretna Green Dr
4800 HarC 77084 3678 B6
Grey Birch Pl
10 WDLD 77381 2820 B2
Greyburn Ln
2200 HOUS 77080 3820 B4
Grey Crst
10 WDLD 77382 2674 A6
Greyfield Ln
- HarC 77047 4374 B4
Grey Finch Ct
10 WDLD 77381 2821 B3
Grey Fox Dr
24000 HOUS 77336 3266 D2
Greyfriar Dr
100 HarC 77037 3684 C1
Grey Hawk Wy
- FBnC 77459 4621 B5
Grey Hollow Ln
13600 HarC 77429 3397 E2
Grey Kirby Dr
- LGCY 77573 4752 B1
Greylin Woods
10 WDLD 77382 2819 A1
Greylog Dr
5200 HOUS 77048 4243 E6
5200 HOUS 77048 4244 A6
Grey Mills Dr
13000 HOUS 77070 3399 D4
Grey Mist Ct
3000 HarC 77546 4506 B7
Grey Mist Dr
17100 HarC 77546 4506 B7
Grey Moss Ln
20600 HarC 77073 3259 E4
Greymoss Ln
- HarC 77073 3259 E4
Grey Oaks Dr
2000 MtgC 77385 2676 C6
6100 HOUS 77050 3546 E5
6700 HOUS 77050 3547 A5
Grey Ridge Dr
- HarC 77082 4096 B3
Greys Ln
8300 HarC 77095 3539 B6
Greystone Cir
- SGLD 77479 4495 A1
Greystone Ct
17400 SGLD 77479 4495 A1
Greystone Dr
700 HarC 77530 3829 E7
Greystone Wy
4100 SGLD 77479 4495 A1
4300 SGLD 77479 4494 E1
Greytip Ct
2500 HarC 77449 3815 A4
E Greywing Cir
10 WDLD 77382 2674 D5
S Greywing Cir
- WDLD 77382 2674 D5
W Greywing Cir
100 WDLD 77382 2674 D5
E Greywing Ct
10 WDLD 77382 2674 D5
S Greywing Pl
10 WDLD 77382 2674 C6
Greywood Dr
13400 SGLD 77478 4237 B7
Grezak
3200 MtgC 77380 2967 B4
Grieg Av
10100 HOUS 77034 4379 A2
Griffin Ln
2800 KATY 77493 3813 C4
3700 FBnC 77459 4621 D5
6900 BzaC 77584 4627 A1
Griffin St
- BYTN 77520 4112 E1
900 PASD 77506 4107 B4
1100 HOUS 77009 3824 D4
Griffin Hill Ct
10 WDLD 77382 2819 A2
Griffin House Ln
23800 HarC 77493 3814 B6
Griffin Willow Rd
14500 HOUS 77489 4371 B4
Griffith St
10 CNRO 77301 2384 A2
Griggs Ct
2500 BzaC 77584 4501 C5
Griggs Rd
- GlsC 77511 4869 B7
3500 HOUS 77021 4103 E5
4800 HOUS 77021 4104 A5
5600 HOUS 77033 4104 B6
5900 HOUS 77023 4104 E4
5900 HOUS 77087 4104 B6
6500 HOUS 77023 4105 A3

Griggs Rd
7100 HOUS 77087 4105 A3
Griggs Point Ln
15300 FBnC 77478 4236 C2
Grigsby St
2600 HOUS 77026 3824 E7
Grillo Wy
700 RSBG 77471 4491 C2
Grimes Av
11200 PRLD 77583 4500 D5
Grimes St
4000 HOUS 77087 4104 D5
27300 HarC 77447 3248 E2
Grind Stone Ln
2300 FBnC 77478 4236 B6
Grinnell St
2800 HOUS 77009 3823 E4
Grisby Rd
- HOUS 77079 3956 C1
14000 HOUS 77079 3957 A1
Griscom Ln
- HOUS 77056 3961 A6
Grissom Rd
- FRDW 77546 4630 C4
- FRDW 77598 4630 C4
- LGCY 77598 4631 A3
2700 LGCY 77598 4630 C4
Grist Ml
- HarC 77546 4506 B7
GRL-Pit
10 LbyC 77327 2538 D1
Groce St
1300 HMPD 77445 3098 A1
2000 HMPD 77445 3097 E1
Groeschke Rd
16200 HOUS 77084 3817 A4
17000 HarC 77084 3817 C4
18000 HarC 77084 3816 E4
18800 HOUS 77084 3816 C5
Grogan
- CNRO 77301 2530 E1
Grogan St
500 CNRO 77301 2384 B4
Grogans Mill Rd
- MtgC 77384 2821 E1
- SHEH 77381 2821 E1
- SHEH 77384 2821 E1
- WDLD 77384 2821 E1
9000 WDLD 77380 2821 D6
9000 WDLD 77381 2821 E4
11800 WDLD 77380 2967 E1
11900 WDLD 77380 2968 A2
25000 MtgC 77380 2968 A2
Grogans Park Dr
10 MtgC 77380 2968 A2
10 WDLD 77380 2968 A2
Grogans Point Ct
10 WDLD 77380 2967 C2
Grogans Point Rd
10 WDLD 77380 2967 C2
Grollwood St
800 HarC 77530 3829 E7
Grommet Ct
16500 HarC 77532 3551 E2
Gromwell Dr
22000 SGCH 77355 2960 D2
Grosbeak Dr
6400 HOUS 77048 4244 D5
Grosbeak Ln
18900 HarC 77377 2961 E7
Gross St
1000 HOUS 77019 3962 C5
Grossmount Dr
12300 HarC 77066 3401 B4
Grosvenor Sq
5500 HarC 77069 3256 D7
Grosvenor St
- HOUS 77598 4378 E5
13700 HOUS 77034 4378 E5
Gros Ventre Ln
8300 HarC 77095 3539 B6
Grota St
100 HOUS 77009 3824 E6
Grothe Ln
100 HOUS 77022 3685 A7
Groton Dr
- HOUS 77047 4243 C6
3000 HOUS 77051 4243 A6
Ground Brier Ct
10 WDLD 77381 2821 A6
Grouse Ct
5000 HarC 77084 3678 C6
Grouse Moor Dr
16700 HarC 77084 3678 C6
Grove
1200 DRPK 77536 4109 B5
W Grove
20800 MtgC 77365 2825 E7
Grove Cir
16900 MtgC 77357 2680 D6
Grove Ct
20000 MtgC 77357 2680 E6
Grove Dr
15600 FBnC 77083 4236 B1
Grove Ln
17300 MtgC 77357 2680 D7
S Grove Ln
12000 HarC 77089 4505 A1
Grove Pt
12200 HarC 77066 3401 A5
Grove Rd
100 GlsC 77565 4509 D5
100 KMAH 77565 4509 D5
800 CRLS 77565 4509 C5
Grove St
100 LPRT 77571 4251 E4
800 DRPK 77536 4109 B4
1200 HOUS 77020 3964 A2
Grove Arbor Ln
7400 HarC 77069 3400 A3
7400 HOUS 77070 3400 A3
Grove Briar Ln
21100 FBnC 77469 4094 B7
Grove Brook Ln
18200 HarC 77429 3252 B7
Grove Creek Dr
17600 HarC 77379 3255 E3
Grovecrest St
6600 HOUS 77092 3682 B6
Grove Ct Dr
1800 MSCY 77489 4370 C6
Grovedale Dr
20700 HarC 77073 3259 C6
20700 HOUS 77073 3259 C7
Grove Estates Ln
14300 HarC 77429 3396 A2
Grove Field Ln
6600 HarC 77084 3678 E3

Grove Gardens Dr
15000 HarC 77082 4096 C4
Grove Gate Ln
- FBnC 77469 4094 B7
Grove Glen Dr
10100 HOUS 77099 4238 A3
Grove Haven Dr
9200 FBnC 77083 4236 B1
Grovehill St
6500 HOUS 77092 3682 B6
Grove Hollow Ct
12500 HarC 77065 3539 C2
Grove Knowll Dr
16800 HarC 77429 3396 D1
Grove Lake Dr
1900 HOUS 77339 3118 D7
Groveland Ln
3200 HOUS 77019 3962 A5
Groveland Hills Dr
8200 HarC 77433 3537 A6
Groveleigh Ln
14400 HarC 77429 3397 D7
Groveleigh Park Ct
2600 MtgC 77386 2823 D7
Grove Manor Dr
2700 HOUS 77345 3120 A5
Grove Meadow Dr
12300 STAF 77477 4237 E7
Grove Mesa Tr
16700 HarC 77379 3255 D5
Grovemill Dr
12900 HOUS 77045 4241 E6
Grovemist Ln
14100 HOUS 77082 4096 E1
Groven St
3000 HOUS 77092 3822 B3
Grove Oaks Rd
3500 HOUS 77339 3119 C1
Grove Park Dr
4300 LGCY 77573 4631 A5
4400 LGCY 77573 4630 E6
8500 HarC 77095 3538 E5
12600 MSCY 77071 4239 B7
Grove Park Rd
32100 WlrC 77484 3246 D3
Grover Av
2000 GLSN 77551 5108 B7
Grover Ln
10000 HOUS 77041 3681 A5
Grove Ridge Dr
7800 HOUS 77061 4245 B1
Grove Ridge Tr
- CNRO 77301 2384 E6
Groversprings
15500 HarC 77068 3257 B5
Groves Lndg
- HarC 77373 3115 B3
Groves Rd
14200 SPLD 77372 2683 B1
Groveshire Ct
3100 SGLD 77478 4369 B3
Groveshire Dr
10700 TXCY 77591 4872 C2
Groveshire St
15000 HarC 77530 3829 C7
Groveside Dr
13900 HarC 77039 3545 E3
Grovesnor Ct
3900 PRLD 77584 4502 E7
Grovesnor St
5800 PRLD 77584 4502 D7
Grove Stone Ct
12000 STAF 77477 4237 E6
Grove Terrace Dr
3000 HOUS 77345 3119 E4
Groveton Ln
5300 PRLD 77584 4503 A4
5600 PRLD 77584 4502 E4
Groveton St
4900 HOUS 77033 4243 E5
5700 HOUS 77033 4244 A5
Groveton Ridge Ln
400 HarC 77094 3955 C2
Grovetrail Ln
16700 HarC 77379 3255 D6
Grove Valley Tr
19000 HarC 77084 3816 B4
Grove View Tr
2400 FBnC 77545 4498 C5
Groveway Dr
4500 HOUS 77087 4104 D5
Grove West Blvd
- SGLD 77478 4237 E6
- STAF 77478 4237 E6
5000 STAF 77477 4237 E6
5000 STAF 77477 4238 A6
Grovewick Ln
3000 LGCY 77539 4752 E5
Grovewood Ct
7700 BzaC 77581 4502 A1
Grovewood Ln
6200 HOUS 77008 3822 D6
6200 HOUS 77008 3823 A5
Grovewood Pk
2100 MtgC 77385 2823 B6
Grove Wy Dr
19100 MtgC 77365 2972 C2
Grovey St
3000 HOUS 77026 3825 A7
Grow Ln
7800 HOUS 77040 3681 E6
Grren River Ln
2100 DKSN 77539 4633 C7
2100 GlsC 77539 4633 C7
Grumbach St
- HOUS 77020 3825 D7
Grumman Castle Ln
- WlrC 77447 2813 C7
Grunewald Av
900 SEBK 77586 4509 D3
Grunewald Dr
2000 PASD 77502 4247 E2
Grunwald Heights Blvd
800 RSBG 77471 4490 C7
Gruss Dr
100 HarC 77060 3403 A5
Guadalcanal Rd
7300 HOUS 77033 4243 E1
Guadalupe Dr
5700 DKSN 77539 4633 D7
5700 DKSN 77539 4754 D1
21900 GLSN 77554 5441 A4
Guadalupe St
1200 FBnC 77477 4369 E5
5500 HarC 77093 3686 D1
5500 HOUS 77016 3686 D1
5500 HOUS 77093 3686 D1
6100 HOUS 77016 3687 A1

Guadalupe River Blvd
- MtgC 77365 2970 A2
3900 MtgC 77386 2970 A2
Guadalupe River Dr
11800 HarC 77067 3401 D5
Guadalupe Springs Ln
15400 HarC 77429 3253 D6
Guadalupe Trail Ct
17400 HarC 77346 3408 B3
Guadalupe Trail Ln
12000 HarC 77346 3408 B4
Guardsman Ln
22500 HarC 77449 3814 E4
Gubert Ln
700 ALVN 77511 4749 C7
Gucci Av
13300 HarC 77044 3689 C4
Guenther St
100 SGLD 77478 4367 E3
100 SGLD 77478 4368 A3
Guernsey Dr
11700 HarC 77377 3254 C5
Guese Rd
1700 HOUS 77008 3822 E5
3400 HOUS 77018 3822 E3
Guessena St
4200 HOUS 77013 3827 B5
Guest St
9400 HOUS 77028 3687 D5
9600 HOUS 77078 3687 D5
Guhn Rd
6200 HOUS 77040 3681 E4
6500 HarC 77040 3681 E4
Guilbeau Ln
2400 SEBK 77586 4509 C1
Guildford Rd
7300 HOUS 77074 4099 E5
Guildwick Cir
20400 HMBL 77338 3262 D4
Guilford Ct
- HOUS 77056 3961 A6
Guilford Pk
600 MtgC 77302 2530 C5
Guillen Ln
800 FBnC 77477 4369 B3
Guinea Dr
1100 HLSV 77055 3821 C7
Guiness Ct
9000 HarC 77095 3538 D4
Guinevere Dr
7400 FBnC 77479 4493 E3
7500 FBnC 77479 4494 A4
Guinevere Pl
10 WDLD 77384 2675 A4
Guinevere St
8400 HOUS 77029 3965 C4
Guinn Av
17800 HarC 77044 3551 D7
Guinn Rd
10 CNRO 77384 2676 A2
Guinn Hill Rd
19400 MtgC 77365 2972 C6
Guinstead Dr
15800 HarC 77379 3256 A7
Guiton St
4800 HOUS 77027 4101 A1
E Gulf Av
10 BYTN 77520 3972 D7
10 BYTN 77520 3973 A7
300 BYTN 77520 4113 A1
W Gulf Av
1400 BYTN 77520 3972 C6
Gulf Blvd
4400 GLSN 77554 5441 A6
Gulf Ct
900 RSBG 77471 4490 B5
Gulf Dr
- GLSN 77554 5441 D4
Gulf Frwy
- DKSN - 4753 B3
- GlsC - 4990 E6
- GlsC - 4991 A7
- GlsC - 5106 D3
- GlsC - 5107 A4
- GLSN - 5107 A4
- HarC - 4506 C4
- HOUS - 3963 C6
- HOUS - 4103 E1
- HOUS - 4104 E4
- HOUS - 4105 C6
- HOUS - 4245 D1
- HOUS - 4246 A4
- HOUS - 4377 E2
- HOUS - 4378 E6
- HOUS - 4506 E6
- LGCY - 4631 A1
- LGCY - 4752 E1
- LGCY - 4753 A3
- LMQU - 4872 B3
- LMQU - 4873 A6
- LMQU - 4989 D3
- LMQU - 4990 B4
- TXCY - 4753 C5
- TXCY - 4872 C4
- TXCY - 4873 A6
- WEBS - 4506 E6
- WEBS - 4507 A7
- WEBS - 4631 A1
Gulf Frwy I-45
- DKSN - 4753 B3
- GlsC - 4990 E6
- GlsC - 4991 A7
- GlsC - 5106 D3
- GlsC - 5107 A4
- GLSN - 5107 A4
- HarC - 4506 C4
- HOUS - 3963 B2
- HOUS - 4103 E1
- HOUS - 4104 A1
- HOUS - 4105 B5
- HOUS - 4245 D1
- HOUS - 4246 A4
- HOUS - 4377 E1
- HOUS - 4378 E6
- HOUS - 4506 E6
- LGCY - 4631 E7
- LGCY - 4752 E1
- LGCY - 4753 A3
- LMQU - 4872 C4
- LMQU - 4873 A6
- LMQU - 4989 D3
- LMQU - 4990 B4
- TXCY - 4753 C5
- TXCY - 4872 E6
- TXCY - 4873 A6
- WEBS - 4506 E6
- WEBS - 4507 A7
- WEBS - 4631 A1

STREET Block City ZIP Map# Grid
Gulf Hl
1700 BYTN 77520 4112 C2
Gulf Ln
10 GLSN 77550 5109 E1
Gulf Rd
- GNPK 77547 4106 C1
Gulf St
- HOUS 77017 4246 D1
1000 PASD 77502 4246 E1
1200 HOUS 77502 4246 D1
3700 HOUS 77017 4105 C7
4000 HOUS 77087 4105 C7
6600 HTCK 77563 4989 D5
Gulf Bank Rd
100 HarC 77037 3544 D7
700 HarC 77037 3545 A7
1100 HOUS 77037 3545 A7
W Gulf Bank Rd
100 HarC 77037 3544 C7
500 HOUS 77037 3544 B7
700 HOUS 77088 3544 B7
1400 HOUS 77088 3543 E7
1400 HOUS 77088 3683 E1
1800 HarC 77088 3683 D1
5400 HOUS 77088 3682 E1
7000 HarC 77088 3682 B2
7000 HOUS 77040 3682 A2
7700 HarC 77040 3682 A2
8000 HarC 77040 3681 D1
10100 HarC 77040 3680 E2
10400 JRSV 77040 3680 E1
Gulf Beach Dr
13100 BzaC 77541 5547 C7
Gulf Breeze Dr
15500 HOUS 77034 4378 E6
15500 HOUS 77598 4378 E6
Gulfbriar Pl
7500 HOUS 77489 4371 B6
Gulf Bridge Cir
10900 HOUS 77075 4377 B3
Gulf Bridge Ct
10900 HOUS 77075 4377 B4
Gulf Bridge St
9400 HOUS 77075 4377 B4
Gulfbrook Dr
- HarC 77598 4506 D5
- HOUS 77546 4506 D5
Gulf Central Dr
2100 HOUS 77023 4104 B2
Gulf Coast Rd
13700 MtgC 77302 2533 A7
13700 MtgC 77306 2533 A6
14000 MtgC 77302 2679 A1
Gulf Creek Dr
2700 HOUS 77012 4105 B5
Gulfcrest St
4600 HOUS 77004 4104 A2
4600 HOUS 77023 4104 A2
Gulfdale Dr
10900 HOUS 77075 4376 D4
Gulf Fields Dr
- HOUS 77034 4378 D3
Gulf Freeway Frontage Rd
- GlsC 77563 4990 E6
- GlsC 77563 4991 A7
- GlsC 77563 5106 B1
- LMQU 77568 4989 C2
- LMQU 77568 4990 C5
- TXCY 77539 4871 E1
- TXCY 77539 4872 A1
- WEBS 77573 4631 C3
100 LGCY 77573 4631 D6
200 HarC 77598 4631 A1
200 LGCY 77598 4631 C3
200 TXCY 77591 4872 C4
200 WEBS 77598 4631 A1
300 LMQU 77568 4872 A1
2100 LGCY 77573 4752 E1
2200 LGCY 77573 4753 A1
2500 DKSN 77539 4753 B3
2500 HOUS 77003 3963 D6
2500 LGCY 77539 4753 B3
3100 HOUS 77004 3963 D7
3800 HOUS 77004 4103 E1
3800 TXCY 77539 4753 D6
4000 HOUS 77003 4103 E1
4000 HOUS 77023 4103 E1
4000 HOUS 77023 4104 C2
4100 HOUS 77004 4104 A1
4500 LMQU 77568 4873 A6
4600 TXCY 77591 4873 A7
6600 HOUS 77087 4104 D4
7100 HOUS 77012 4105 B5
7200 HOUS 77017 4105 B6
7200 HOUS 77087 4105 B6
8000 HOUS 77087 4245 D1
8100 HOUS 77017 4245 D1
8100 HOUS 77061 4245 D1
8500 HOUS 77017 4246 A4
8500 HOUS 77061 4246 A4
9800 HOUS 77034 4246 B5
9800 HOUS 77075 4246 B5
11400 HOUS 77034 4377 D1
11400 HOUS 77075 4377 D1
12200 HOUS 77089 4377 E2
12300 HOUS 77034 4378 C5
12300 HOUS 77089 4378 A2
13700 HarC 77089 4378 C4
15600 HOUS 77598 4378 E7
15800 HOUS 77598 4379 A7
16000 HOUS 77546 4378 E7
17000 HOUS 77546 4506 D5
18400 HarC 77598 4506 D5
18400 HOUS 77598 4506 C4
19700 WEBS 77598 4506 E6
20000 WEBS 77598 4507 A7
Gulf Freeway Frontage Rd I-45
- HOUS - 4506 B3
Gulfgate Mall
500 HOUS 77087 4105 A5
Gulf Isle Ct
7900 HarC 77095 3537 E7
Gulflow St
2600 HOUS 77087 4104 E4
Gulf Meadows Dr
10200 HOUS 77075 4376 C4
Gulf Mountain Dr
5300 HOUS 77091 3682 E7
Gulf Oil Big Creek Field Rd
- HarC 77450 3954 B6
Gulfton Dr
- HOUS 77074 4100 B3
1000 PRLD 77581 4504 E7
5100 BLAR 77401 4100 E3
5100 HOUS 77081 4100 C3
5100 HOUS 77401 4100 E3

STREET Block City ZIP Map# Grid
Gulfton Dr
7700 HOUS 77036 4099 D3
Gulf Palms St
17400 GLSN 77554 5331 D7
Gulfpalms St
- HOUS 77034 4247 A7
- HOUS 77034 4378 A1
Gulf Pines Dr
17400 HarC 77090 3258 D2
17400 HOUS 77090 3258 D2
Gulf Pointe Dr
11800 HOUS 77089 4378 A4
Gulf Pump Rd
100 HarC 77532 3692 C1
Gulf Sky Ln
- HOUS 77034 4378 C4
Gulf Spring Ln
8200 HOUS 77075 4376 D4
Gulfstream Ct
13900 FBnC 77478 4237 B3
Gulfstream Ln
10200 FBnC 77478 4237 A3
Gulfstream Pk
14100 HOUS 77034 4378 E6
14100 HOUS 77598 4378 E6
14400 HOUS 77598 4379 A6
Gulf Terminal Dr
2100 HOUS 77023 4104 C3
Gulf Tree Ln
8200 HOUS 77075 4376 D4
Gulf Valley St
10600 HOUS 77075 4376 D4
Gulfway Dr
4600 BYTN 77521 3974 A2
Gulfwind Ct
19800 HarC 77094 3954 E3
19800 HarC 77094 3955 A2
Gulfwind Dr
19700 HarC 77094 3955 A3
Gulfwood Ln
8200 HOUS 77075 4376 D4
Gulick Ln
8000 HOUS 77075 4376 D1
Gull Ct
16600 HarC 77532 3552 B2
Gull Dr
5500 GLSN 77551 5108 D7
N Gull Dr
16700 MtgC 77385 2676 E4
Gulls Cut N
100 BYTN 77520 4113 D5
Gulls Cut S
100 BYTN 77520 4113 D5
Gullwood Dr
11400 HarC 77089 4378 A6
11500 HOUS 77089 4378 B6
Gum Dr
2000 DKSN 77539 4755 A2
4100 DKSN 77539 4754 E2
Gum St
5200 HarC 77532 3552 D4
Gumas St
3100 HOUS 77053 4373 A4
Gum Grove Ln
- HOUS 77091 3682 D4
5900 HOUS 77088 3682 D4
N Gum Gully Rd
300 HarC 77532 3410 E3
Gum Gully School Rd
100 HarC 77532 3410 D4
100 HarC 77532 3411 A4
Gummert Rd
18600 HarC 77084 3677 B5
18600 HarC 77449 3677 B5
Gum Spring Ln
2300 HarC 77373 3114 D4
Gum Tree Ln
1300 HarC 77336 3121 E7
Gum Valley Dr
11500 HarC 77086 3542 E6
11500 HarC 77088 3542 E6
Gundle Rd
19000 HarC 77073 3259 E6
Gunnels
10 HOUS 77013 3827 D6
Gunnison Dr
800 MtgC 77354 2673 B2
Gunnison St
5100 HOUS 77053 4372 B5
Gun Oak Pl
12200 WDLD 77380 2967 E2
Gun Powder Ln
2600 PRLD 77581 4504 C4
Gun Range Rd
- LGCY 77573 4633 A5
Gunston Ct
500 MtgC 77302 2530 C6
2300 SGLD 77478 4237 D4
Gunter St
4600 HOUS 77020 3964 C3
Gunters Ridge Dr
20000 HarC 77379 3110 D5
Gunther Ct
7200 HarC 77379 3111 B2
Gunwale Rd
1600 HOUS 77062 4507 B1
Gurney Ln
900 HOUS 77037 3684 E2
1000 HOUS 77076 3684 E2
Gus Rd
200 HarC 77373 3114 A1
Guse St
6700 HOUS 77076 3684 E4
Gussie Mae Ln
6000 FBnC 77583 4622 C6
Gustav St
1200 HOUS 77023 3964 B7
1600 HOUS 77023 4104 E1
Gustine Ct
10300 HOUS 77031 4239 B3
Gustine Ln
8700 HOUS 77031 4239 C2
8700 HOUS 77071 4239 C2
Guston Hall Ln
22000 HarC 77449 3815 A4
22300 HarC 77449 3814 E4
Gusty Trail Ln
6300 HarC 77041 3679 C4
Gusty Winds Ct
10800 HarC 77064 3540 C2
Gusty Winds Dr
10000 HarC 77064 3540 C2
Guthrie Dr
3500 PASD 77503 4108 B6
Guy Ct
600 HarC 77532 3411 B7
Guyer St
300 SGLD 77478 4367 E2

STREET Block City ZIP Map# Grid
Guy O'Dell Ln
20100 MtgC 77357 2827 D5
Guys
11900 HarC 77336 3266 E2
Guyton Ln
5100 HOUS 77013 3827 C4
Guywood St
9200 HOUS 77040 3682 A2
Gwen Ct
1800 MtgC 77303 2385 D1
Gwen St
10400 HOUS 77093 3685 D3
Gwendalene Dr
- BzaC 77511 4627 A7
Gwenfair Dr
2400 HarC 77373 3114 C5
Gwenn Ln
5200 HarC 77521 3972 A1
Gwinn
2400 HOUS 77023 4104 E4
Gypsum Ct
6300 HarC 77041 3679 C4
Gypsy Forest Dr
4700 HarC 77346 3408 B1
Gypsy Pops Dr
4200 PASD 77503 4108 D7

H

H Ct
- HarC 77388 3111 D1
H St
4100 HOUS 77072 4098 A3
4100 HOUS 77082 4098 A3
E H St
600 LPRT 77571 4251 E3
N H St
- LPRT 77571 4251 C1
- MRGP 77571 4251 D1
9700 DRPK 77536 4250 A1
9700 LPRT 77536 4250 A1
9700 LPRT 77571 4250 B1
W H St
100 LPRT 77571 4251 D4
H & R Rd
20600 HarC 77073 3259 D3
N Habermacher Dr
- HOUS 77094 3954 E7
- HOUS 77094 4094 E1
S Habermacher Dr
- HOUS 77094 4094 E1
Habersham Av
6900 SGLD 77479 4367 C6
Habersham Ln
11500 PNPV 77024 3959 D4
11600 BKHV 77024 3959 D4
Habershame Ct
4500 MSCY 77459 4496 C4
Habitat Ln
700 RSBG 77471 4491 A4
Habla Dr
- GLSN 77554 5331 D7
Hablo Dr
7500 FBnC 77083 4096 A6
S Habour Bend Ln
13300 HOUS 77044 3409 A3
Hacienda Ln
10 HDWV 77024 3959 E2
10 PNPV 77024 3959 E2
Hackamore Ct
21600 MtgC 77365 2972 B1
Hackamore Ln
- BKHV 77024 3959 B3
Hackamore Hollow Ln
2700 HarC 77014 3257 E7
Hackberry Ct
3400 HarC 77388 3112 E5
Hackberry Dr
200 HarC 77562 3831 D2
23600 FBnC 77494 3953 B4
Hackberry Ln
- PRLD 77584 4501 E4
10 HOUS 77027 3961 B7
10 MtgC 77301 2385 D4
10 MtgC 77306 2385 D4
200 BYTN 77520 3971 B2
700 FRDW 77546 4505 B5
2800 KATY 77493 3813 B4
Hackberry St
100 MtgC 77354 2671 E3
600 LMQU 77568 4990 C1
800 LPRT 77571 4251 D7
800 MSCY 77489 4370 C3
800 STAF 77477 4370 C3
800 STAF 77489 4370 C3
900 LPRT 77571 4382 D1
12900 MtgC 77362 2963 A1
Hackberry Bank Ln
2100 RSBG 77471 4491 B6
Hackberry Creek Dr
23000 FBnC 77494 3953 B4
Hacker
600 HOUS 77037 3684 B1
Hacker Rd
7200 HTCK 77563 4989 A6
7500 HTCK 77563 4988 E5
Hackett Dr
2400 HOUS 77008 3822 D4
Hackinson Dr
30600 MtgC 77386 2969 C1
Hackley Dr
800 SGLD 77478 4368 C1
Hackmatack Wy
- HarC 77066 3401 B7
Hackney Rd
- BzaC 77546 4628 E3
- FRDW 77546 4628 E3
- FRDW 77546 4629 A4
- PRLD 77546 4628 E3
Hackney St
1800 HOUS 77023 4104 C2
Hadden Rd
8600 HarC 77521 3834 B1
8700 HarC 77521 3695 B6
Hadden Hollow Dr
2100 HarC 77067 3402 A7
Hadden Park Ct
32500 MtgC 77385 2823 C7
Haddick St
9200 HOUS 77028 3687 D6
9800 HOUS 77078 3687 D5
Haddington Dr
10000 HOUS 77043 3820 A5
10000 HOUS 77080 3820 A5
10200 HOUS 77043 3819 E5
Haddock Ct
6300 HarC 77041 3679 C4

STREET Block City ZIP Map# Grid
Haddon St
1400 HOUS 77006 3962 C5
1700 HOUS 77019 3962 C5
Haddonfield Ln
- HarC 77070 3399 E2
Hade Falls Ln
1400 HarC 77073 3403 C1
Hade Meadow Ln
1600 HarC 77073 3403 D1
Haden Dr
6200 HTCK 77563 4989 B4
Haden Rd
1300 HarC 77015 3967 E3
2100 HarC 77015 3968 A3
Haden Crest Ct
16200 HarC 77429 3397 A3
Haden Park Dr
22100 FBnC 77450 3954 A7
Haden Run Dr
9700 HarC 77095 3537 D3
Haderia Ct
9300 HarC 77379 3110 D6
Hadfield Ct
5200 SGLD 77479 4495 A3
Hadley Cir
2500 SGLD 77478 4237 C4
Hadley Ln
- GlsC 77510 4871 A2
Hadley St
300 HOUS 77002 3963 B5
300 HOUS 77006 3963 B5
1500 HOUS 77003 3963 C6
2000 HOUS 77004 3963 C7
Hadley Falls Dr
12000 HarC 77067 3402 B4
Hadley Rock Dr
- FBnC 77494 4092 A5
Hadrian Dr
21300 HarC 77449 3676 D6
Hafer Rd
16300 HarC 77090 3258 D4
16300 HOUS 77090 3258 D4
Hafer St
10 BYTN 77520 3973 A6
Haffner Dr
- FBnC 77479 4367 B6
Hafner Dr
1700 HOUS 77055 3822 A5
Hagan Ct
16000 HarC 77532 3551 E3
Hage St
3100 HOUS 77093 3686 A5
Hagerman St
100 HOUS 77011 3964 B6
N Hagerman St
100 HOUS 77011 3964 B5
Hagerson Rd
1000 FBnC 77479 4496 C7
Haggis
- HarC 77084 3678 C7
Hagilbert Ct
21600 HarC 77338 3261 D2
Hahl Dr
7000 HarC 77040 3681 A3
Hahl Rd
6900 HarC 77040 3681 A3
6900 HOUS 77040 3681 A3
Hahlo St
100 HOUS 77020 3825 D7
300 HOUS 77020 3964 D1
Hahn Rd
9000 HarC 77040 3681 B3
Hahns Peak Dr
10000 HarC 77095 3538 A3
Haider Av
- BYTN 77520 3835 A6
- BYTN 77521 3835 A6
Haight St
5400 HOUS 77028 3826 C3
Haigshire Dr
- HarC 77389 2965 E4
24500 HarC 77375 2965 D3
Haile St
4900 HarC 77093 3686 C1
Hailey St
1500 CNRO 77301 2383 E3
1600 HOUS 77020 3964 A2
1800 HOUS 77026 3964 A1
2400 HOUS 77026 3825 E7
Hailwood Dr
10 WDLD 77382 2819 A2
Hain St
3800 HOUS 77009 3824 C6
Haines Creek Dr
10 MtgC 77386 2969 E2
Haiston Ridge Ct
19300 HarC 77375 3109 D6
Haiti Ln
4200 PASD 77505 4248 D6
Halamar Ln
14300 HarC 77429 3397 D2
Halbert Dr
2200 PRLD 77581 4503 A3
Halbert St
1000 HOUS 77087 4105 A3
Halcyon Days Dr
6500 HarC 77338 3261 B3
Haldane Dr
2300 HOUS 77055 3821 C4
Hale Dr
- DRPK 77536 4109 B7
Hales Hunt Ct
- HarC 77388 3111 E2
Halesworth Ln
- HarC 77379 3111 D5
Halewood Dr
800 HOUS 77062 4506 E2
900 HOUS 77062 4507 B2
Haley Ct
6800 PRLD 77584 4502 C4
Haley Hllw
11500 FBnC 77469 4235 D6
Haley Rd
33100 WlrC 77484 3246 A2
33500 WlrC 77484 3245 E2
Haley Falls Ln
17200 HarC 77095 3678 A1
Haleys Comet Cir
9700 HarC 77070 3255 C3
Haley's Comet Ct
- DRPK 77536 4109 E6
Haleys Landing Ln
15600 HarC 77095 3538 E5
Haley Woods Ct
7300 HarC 77095 3678 A1
Half Cir St
14200 MtgC 77372 2683 C2

STREET Block City ZIP Map# Grid
Half Hollow Ct
2400 CNRO 77304 2236 B6
Half Moon
10 HTCK 77563 5105 A5
Half Moon Ct
1600 FBnC 77469 4365 E2
19400 HarC 77346 3264 C5
Halfmoon Ct
10 WDLD 77380 2967 C3
E Half Moon St
16300 GlsC 77517 4869 E4
W Half Moon St
16400 GlsC 77517 4869 D3
Half Moon Tr
18400 HarC 77346 3264 D7
Halfmoon Bay Dr
- PRLD 77583 4500 C4
- PRLD 77584 4500 C4
Half Penny Ct
10 SGLD 77479 4495 B2
Halfpenny Rd
7000 HarC 77084 3678 E2
7000 HarC 77095 3678 E1
Half Volley Cir
18700 HarC 77346 3265 C7
Haliburton Rd
- GLSN 77554 4994 B7
- GLSN 77554 5109 B1
Halifax Ln
6100 LGCY 77573 4630 B7
Halifax Rd
12700 HarC 77015 3828 C7
12700 HOUS 77015 3828 C7
Halifax St
13100 HOUS 77015 3828 C7
Halifax Brook St
10600 HarC 77089 4505 A1
Halik St
3700 PRLD 77581 4503 B1
Halkeis Rd
300 SHUS 77587 4247 A2
400 PASD 77502 4247 A2
400 SHUS 77502 4247 A2
Halkin Ct
16700 HarC 77379 3256 D3
Halkirk St
9200 HarC 77379 3255 D4
Hall Av
900 SEBK 77586 4509 D3
Hall Ct
900 DRPK 77536 4109 E5
N Hall Dr
100 SGLD 77478 4368 A4
S Hall Dr
100 SGLD 77478 4368 A4
Hall Pl
1400 HOUS 77008 3823 E6
Hall Rd
7700 HOUS 77075 4376 E5
9400 HarC 77089 4377 B5
9400 HOUS 77075 4377 B5
10700 HOUS 77089 4377 D6
Hall St
400 CNRO 77301 2384 A6
500 GlsC 77511 4750 A6
1900 WALR 77484 3102 A4
10200 GLSN 77554 5221 B1
S Hall St
6900 HOUS 77028 3686 E7
7100 HOUS 77028 3687 A7
Hallan St
4100 GlsC 77518 4634 B3
Hallbrook Ln
- FBnC 77469 4095 C6
Hall Colony Ct
20900 HarC 77449 3676 D3
Hall Croft Chase Ln
- HarC 77449 3816 B1
4500 HarC 77449 3677 A7
Halldale Dr
8000 HarC 77083 4096 D7
Hallen Dale Ln
- HarC 77094 3955 C1
Hallet Dr
19500 MtgC 77365 3117 C1
Halle Trace Ln
- HarC 77047 4374 B4
Hallfield Dr
13800 HarC 77014 3402 C3
Hallie Dr
- HOUS 77024 3958 E1
Hallie Ln
19200 MtgC 77365 2972 D1
Halliford Dr
9800 HOUS 77031 4238 E5
Hallmark Dr
10 CNRO 77304 2236 E4
10 PNVL 77304 2236 E4
10 PNVL 77304 2237 A3
4700 HOUS 77027 3961 A5
4700 HOUS 77056 3961 A5
Hallmark Ln
9600 PRLD 77584 4501 B2
Hallmark Fair Ct
3900 PASD 77059 4380 D5
Hallmark Oak St
800 SEBK 77586 4509 E1
Hall Meadow Ln
25300 FBnC 77494 4092 C5
Hallowed Oaks Blvd
12200 MtgC 77354 2671 A5
Hallowed Stream Ln
11800 HarC 77433 3396 A6
Hallowing Point Rd
11800 HarC 77067 3402 B5
Hallowyck Ct
13000 HOUS 77045 4241 C6
Hall Pond Ct
6300 HarC 77449 3676 E3
Hall Ridge Trace Ln
1800 HarC 77067 3402 B7
Halls Br
- LGCY 77573 4632 A2
Hall Shepperd Rd
16900 HarC 77049 3690 E4
17200 HarC 77049 3691 A4
Hallshire Dr
7100 HOUS 77016 3686 E5
7100 HOUS 77016 3687 A5
Hallsleigh Ln
700 HarC 77090 3258 D5
N Halls Point Ct
3500 FBnC 77459 4622 B5
S Halls Point Ct
3400 FBnC 77459 4622 A5
Hallstone Knolls Dr
24600 HOUS 77336 3266 C2

STREET Block City ZIP Map# Grid
Hallwell Ct
14700 HarC 77429 3397 D2
Halmart St
5600 HOUS 77087 4104 C7
5700 HOUS 77087 4244 C1
Hal McClain
800 MNVL 77578 4747 B1
900 BzaC 77511 4626 B7
900 MNVL 77578 4626 B7
Halo Dr
100 CNRO 77301 2384 B7
100 CNRO 77301 2530 B1
Halpern St
1100 HOUS 77009 3824 C7
Halpren Falls Cir
13800 HarC 77429 3397 B2
Halpren Falls Ln
16100 HarC 77429 3397 A2
Halprin Creek Dr
14000 HarC 77429 3397 A2
Halsey St
900 HOUS 77015 3967 A2
Halshead Ln
- LGCY 77573 4630 A7
Halstead Dr
2400 MtgC 77386 2969 C4
Halstead St
1800 MSCY 77489 4370 D5
Halstead Meadows Cir
6400 HarC 77086 3542 C3
Halsted Ln
- HarC 77040 3681 A1
Halston Dr
10000 FBnC 77478 4236 E3
Halston Manor Dr
21100 HarC 77375 3110 A3
Halton Ct
2800 HOUS 77345 3119 E6
Halyard Dr
1800 HarC 77532 3551 D3
Hambledon Village Dr
4100 HarC 77014 3401 C2
Hamblen
2600 HOUS 77339 3263 E2
Hamblen Ct
4600 SEBK 77586 4383 B6
Hamblen Dr
- HarC 77396 3547 A1
5800 HarC 77032 3546 E1
5800 HOUS 77396 3546 E1
6100 HOUS 77396 3547 A1
Hamblen Rd
- HOUS 77339 3262 E2
- HOUS 77339 3263 A2
200 HOUS 77339 3263 A2
700 FBnC 77471 4490 C1
W Hamblen Rd
10 HOUS 77339 3262 E1
Hamblen St
1100 HOUS 77009 3824 D4
Hamblen Oaks Ln
- HarC 77068 3257 C6
Hambleton Cir
13700 HarC 77069 3256 D7
Hambleton Dr
13800 HarC 77069 3256 D7
Hambleton Wy
11200 HarC 77065 3540 A3
11400 HarC 77065 3539 E3
Hambleton Wy Cir
9900 HarC 77065 3539 E3
Hamblin Rd
11800 HarC 77429 3397 B6
Hambrick Ct
700 HarC 77060 3544 E4
Hambrick Rd
100 HarC 77037 3544 C4
100 HarC 77060 3544 C4
W Hambrick Rd
100 HarC 77037 3544 C4
100 HarC 77060 3544 C4
Hamden Ct
400 HarC 77450 3954 D1
Hamden Valley Dr
25200 FBnC 77469 4092 D7
Hamid Blvd
3800 FBnC 77545 4499 C7
3800 FBnC 77545 4623 C1
Hamil Rd
5600 HarC 77039 3546 D5
Hamill
12200 HarC 77039 3546 D5
Hamill Rd
12300 HarC 77039 3546 D5
Hamillcrest Dr
- HarC 77014 3402 A3
Hamill House Ct
1700 HarC 77396 3407 C2
Hamill House Dr
9700 HarC 77396 3407 C2
Hamilton Cir
3300 CNRO 77304 2382 E7
7800 JRSV 77040 3680 E1
Hamilton Dr
9600 PRLD 77584 4501 B3
Hamilton Ln
500 PASD 77506 4106 E5
6100 LGCY 77573 4630 C7
Hamilton Pk
- HarC 77375 2964 C2
Hamilton Rd
1100 WALR 77484 3102 A6
13700 GLSN 77554 5332 E1
Hamilton St
- BYTN 77520 3971 B4
10 HOUS 77002 3963 D5
700 HOUS 77010 3963 D5
900 ALVN 77511 4749 C7
1300 HMPD 77445 3098 A2
2000 RSBG 77471 4491 A6
2100 HOUS 77003 3963 C6
2300 HOUS 77004 3963 C6
3100 LPRT 77571 4382 E1
3900 HOUS 77004 4103 E2
E Hamilton St
100 HOUS 77076 3684 D6
N Hamilton St
10 HOUS 77002 3963 D4
10 HOUS 77003 3963 D4
W Hamilton St
100 HOUS 77076 3684 C6
200 HOUS 77091 3684 C6
Hamilton Falls Ln
6900 HarC 77379 3111 C6
Hamilton Grove Ln
14400 HarC 77047 4374 A5
Hamilton Park Dr
16600 HarC 77429 3396 E3

STREET Block City ZIP Map# Grid
Hamilton Park Dr
16600 HarC 77429 3397 A3
Hamilton View Wy
4700 FBnC 77545 4623 A2
Hamilwood Dr
17100 HarC 77095 3538 A7
17200 HarC 77095 3678 A1
17300 HarC 77095 3677 E1
Hamish Rd
18900 HarC 77377 3109 A7
18900 HarC 77377 3254 A1
Hamlet Ct
14000 HarC 77069 3256 C7
Hamlet St
7800 HOUS 77028 3687 B5
7800 HOUS 77078 3687 B5
Hamlet Wy
- HOUS 77339 3264 A1
Hamlet Park Ct
22500 HarC 77373 3113 D1
Hamlet Ridge Ln
20900 HarC 77449 3815 B6
Hamlet Vale Ct
10400 HarC 77070 3399 B4
Hamlin Valley Dr
1400 HarC 77090 3258 B3
Hamm Rd
2900 PRLD 77581 4504 C5
Hamman St
6000 HOUS 77007 3962 A2
6200 HOUS 77007 3961 E2
Hammer Ln
19000 MtgC 77365 2972 B1
Hammer Rd
3400 FBnC 77545 4499 C6
Hammer St
700 SEBK 77586 4509 E2
Hammerhead Ct
22200 HarC 77449 3815 A4
Hammerly Blvd
7400 HOUS 77055 3821 C4
8500 HOUS 77080 3821 A4
8700 HOUS 77080 3820 A4
10100 HOUS 77043 3820 A4
10200 HOUS 77043 3819 D4
Hammermill Ln
12900 HarC 77044 3689 B5
Hammersmith Dr
12300 HarC 77377 3254 B6
Hammerwood Cir
3100 PRLD 77584 4502 A6
Hammerwood Ct
16300 HarC 77377 3254 B6
Hammerwood Dr
1900 MSCY 77489 4370 D5
Hammock St
1100 HOUS 77009 3824 C7
Hammock Tr
10 GLSN 77554 5221 C2
Hammock Dunes Pl
10 HarC 77389 2820 B6
Hammon Wy
- MtgC 77365 2972 B7
Hammond Dr
11500 HarC 77065 3539 E2
E Hammond Dr
22100 MtgC 77365 2973 C7
W Hammond Dr
21100 MtgC 77365 2973 A7
Hammond Ln
12300 STFE 77510 4871 B4
Hammond Hills Ln
- HarC 77044 3550 A3
Hammondsport Ln
18100 HarC 77429 3252 B6
Hamon Dr
700 PASD 77506 4107 B6
Hampden Point Ct
6500 HOUS 77040 3682 B3
Hampshire Ln
2500 MSCY 77459 4370 B6
2500 MSCY 77459 4497 D2
S Hampshire Ln
12000 HarC 77089 4505 A1
Hampshire St
3300 PRLD 77581 4503 C4
Hampshire Rocks Dr
20200 HarC 77450 3954 D2
Hampton Cir
1100 ALVN 77511 4867 A2
E Hampton Cir
- HOUS 77035 4371 B1
- MSCY 77035 4371 B1
- MSCY 77071 4371 B1
15200 MSCY 77071 4370 E1
W Hampton Cir
15400 MSCY 77071 4370 D1
Hampton Ct
10 HNCV 77024 3959 E2
10 HNCV 77024 3960 A2
10 PNPV 77024 3959 E2
500 HarC 77562 3831 C2
500 MtgC 77302 2530 C6
1400 FRDW 77546 4629 C4
4500 PASD 77504 4248 A3
5200 RSBG 77471 4491 D6
7000 HarC 77389 2966 C5
13600 SGLD 77478 4237 B7
N Hampton Ct
400 HarC 77562 3831 C2
S Hampton Ct
300 HarC 77562 3831 C2
Hampton Dr
2800 MSCY 77459 4497 A2
3100 MSCY 77459 4496 D3
E Hampton Dr
800 PRLD 77584 4501 E1
S Hampton Dr
- PRLD 77584 4501 B2
W Hampton Dr
- PRLD 77584 4501 B2
3000 HarC 77082 4097 A2
Hampton Ldg
10 WDLD 77381 2820 C4
Hampton Pk
18100 HarC 77379 3256 B1
Hampton Pl
10 WDLD 77381 2821 B5
Hampton Rd
2300 LGCY 77573 4631 B5
Hampton St
1000 HOUS 77088 3683 E1
S Hampton St
4600 SGLD 77479 4495 C3
Hampton Bay Dr
13100 PRLD 77584 4500 A3
Hampton Bay Ln
7600 FBnC 77494 4093 C2

STREET
Block City ZIP Map# Grid

Hampton Bend Ln
13300 HarC 77070 3399 B3
Hampton Cove Dr
13800 HOUS 77077 3957 A6
13900 HOUS 77077 3956 E7
Hampton Dale St
16000 HarC 77379 3256 D5
Hampton Falls Ct
6100 HarC 77041 3679 C5
Hampton Falls Dr
13200 HarC 77041 3679 C4
Hampton Forest Ln
23000 HarC 77389 2966 E6
Hampton Glen Ct
16900 FBnC 77083 4095 D5
Hampton Green Ln
14500 HOUS 77044 3550 A2
Hampton Hall Ln
500 MtgC 77302 2530 D5
Hampton Hills Dr
18000 HarC 77338 3407 D1
Hampton Lakes Ct
1900 HarC 77493 3814 A5
Hampton Lakes Dr
24500 HarC 77493 3814 A6
Hamptonmere Ln
18700 HarC 77377 3254 C3
Hampton Oak Ct
6200 HarC 77449 3677 D4
Hampton Oak Dr
17900 HarC 77379 3256 A2
Hampton Oaks Cir
1600 HarC 77094 3955 B4
Hampton Oaks Dr
23900 HarC 77389 2966 C5
Hampton Park Ln
2500 FBnC 77479 4494 A3
Hampton Pines Ln
25900 HarC 77389 2966 C2
Hampton Ridge Ct
5600 HarC 77069 3256 D7
Hamptonshire Ln
2400 FBnC 77494 4093 B1
Hampton Springs Dr
2600 SEBK 77586 4382 B6
Hampton Villa Ln
1000 HOUS 77047 4373 C2
Hampton Village Ln
- HarC 77429 3253 E4
Hampton Wy Ct
6100 HarC 77389 2966 D4
Hamsfield Ct
12300 HarC 77377 3254 C5
Hamstead Ct
3600 HarC 77336 3121 D2
Hamstead Park Dr
- HarC 77084 3678 E3
14600 HarC 77084 3679 A3
Hana Dr
400 TKIS 77554 5106 D3
7100 HarC 77379 3111 B2
Hanberry Ln
3800 BzaC 77584 4501 D6
17800 HarC 77433 3251 E2
Hanbury Ct
1800 SGLD 77478 4236 E6
Hanby Creek Ct
19400 HarC 77094 3955 B2
Hancock Av
1300 PASD 77502 4246 E2
Hancock Run
8900 LPRT 77571 4249 E4
Hancock St
10 CNRO 77301 2384 A3
5200 HOUS 77004 4103 C3
Hancock Elm St
14200 HarC 77429 3395 E1
Hancock Oak St
19500 HarC 77429 3395 C2
Hand Rd
5500 FBnC 77469 4615 A5
5500 PLEK 77469 4615 A5
Handbrook Dr
5300 HarC 77069 3256 C6
Handell Ln
300 PASD 77502 4247 A2
700 PASD 77502 4246 E2
Handspike Wy
800 HarC 77532 3552 A2
Haney Rd
- HarC 77532 3694 A7
- HarC 77562 3694 A7
8700 HarC 77521 3833 B2
8700 HarC 77562 3833 B1
Hanford St
9600 HOUS 77078 3687 C5
Hanfro Ln
8300 HOUS 77088 3683 D2
Hanging Moss Tr
9500 HarC 77064 3540 D4
Hanka Dr
10000 HOUS 77043 3820 A6
10000 HOUS 77080 3820 A6
Hankamer Av
1400 PASD 77506 4107 D5
Hankla St
100 HOUS 77076 3685 A5
Hanks Rd
31500 MAGA 77355 2669 A6
Hanley Ln
4200 HarC 77093 3686 B1
6300 HOUS 77016 3687 A1
Hanley St
8300 JRSV 77040 3540 C7
Hanlon Ct
6700 FBnC 77083 4095 E5
Hanna Rd
- MtgC 77386 2968 D1
1400 MtgC 77385 2822 D7
1400 ORDN 77385 2822 D5
2000 ORDN 77386 2822 D7
2100 MtgC 77386 2822 D7
Hanna St
7800 HOUS 77028 3826 B3
Hannah Ln
300 ALVN 77511 4749 C2
Hannah Cove Ln
- MtgC 77386 2969 E6
Hannah Falls Ln
900 FBnC 77545 4623 A2
Hannah Glenn Ln
14400 HarC 77429 3397 D7
Hannah Oaks Ln
17400 HarC 77396 3407 D3
Hannahs Crossing Ln
13100 HarC 77072 4097 C7
Hannah's Wy Ct
10 FBnC 77479 4367 A6

Hanna Nash
18400 HarC 77532 3410 D6
Hanna Nash Rd
18800 HarC 77532 3410 D5
Hanna Reef Dr
4800 GlsC 77539 4634 C4
Hanneck Ct
22000 FBnC 77450 4094 B3
Hanneck Valley Ln
5200 FBnC 77450 4094 B3
Hanning Ln
11000 HarC 77041 3680 C4
Hannington Dr
1200 HarC 77450 3954 D4
Hannington Ln
20600 HarC 77450 3954 D4
Hannock Glen Ln
800 HarC 77373 2968 C6
Hannon Dr
10100 HOUS 77040 3542 A7
10100 HOUS 77040 3682 A1
Hannover Blvd
1200 RSBG 77471 4491 C4
Hannover Wy
2100 HarC 77388 3113 A3
Hannover Estates Dr
21400 HarC 77388 3113 A3
Hannover Forest
21300 HarC 77388 3113 A3
Hannover Forest Ct
21600 HarC 77388 3113 A3
Hannover Grove Ln
21400 HarC 77449 3815 B4
Hannover Pines Dr
21300 HarC 77388 3113 B3
Hannover Ridge Dr
21700 HarC 77388 3113 B2
Hannover Valley Ct
2400 HarC 77388 3113 A2
Hannover Village Ct
21900 HarC 77388 3113 A2
Hannover Village Dr
21600 HarC 77388 3113 A2
Hannoverwood
- HarC 77388 3113 B3
Hannover Wy Ct
21500 HarC 77388 3113 B3
Hanover Cir
3600 BzaC 77584 4501 C5
Hanover Ln
- LGCY 77573 4630 B7
10 PNVL 77304 2237 B2
Hanover St
100 HOUS 77012 4105 B1
Hanover Glen Ln
18100 FBnC 77469 4095 C7
Hanover Hollow Ln
29900 MtgC 77386 2969 E2
Hanover Mill Ln
7800 HarC 77040 3681 A1
Hanover Springs Ln
1800 FBnC 77469 4365 B2
Hanover Square Dr
- HarC 77066 3401 C4
Hanover Square Ln
- HarC 77047 4374 D4
Hans Ct
8700 HarC 77379 3256 A5
Hans St
4000 PRLD 77584 4502 D7
Hansel Ln
12900 HOUS 77024 3958 D3
Hanselman Rd
9700 BzaC 77578 4746 B7
9900 MNVL 77578 4746 B6
Hansen Av
6700 GLSN 77551 5108 B7
Hansen Dr
3700 DKSN 77539 4753 A6
3700 LGCY 77539 4753 A6
Hansen St
7600 HOUS 77061 4246 A6
8100 HOUS 77075 4246 A6
Hansford Ct
3400 BzaC 77584 4501 A4
Hansford Ln
6000 FBnC 77479 4367 A5
Hansford Pl
3500 BzaC 77584 4501 C5
Hansford St
- HOUS 77023 4104 B3
Hansom Dr
21600 MtgC 77365 2972 B1
Hansom Rd
3000 HarC 77038 3542 E3
3000 HarC 77038 3543 A3
3000 HarC 77086 3542 E3
Hansom Trail St
100 WDLD 77382 2820 B1
Hanson Rd
600 GlsC 77565 4509 D6
600 KMAH 77565 4509 D6
Hansons Ct
27900 MtgC 77386 2971 A7
Hansons Creek Ct
14200 HarC 77044 3549 D1
Hanston Ct
2400 BzaC 77584 4501 D5
19200 HarC 77094 3955 B3
Hanus Cir
9500 HOUS 77040 3682 A2
N Hanworth Dr
11700 HOUS 77031 4238 E5
11700 HOUS 77031 4239 A5
S Hanworth Dr
9600 HOUS 77031 4239 A5
Happy Hllw
10 FBnC 77459 4621 C4
Happy Ln
12900 HarC 77429 3254 A6
Happy Tr
3800 MtgC 77384 2674 C2
Happy Hollow St
100 GlsC 77511 4751 C7
100 LGCY 77511 4751 C7
5000 HOUS 77018 3683 D7
Happy Springs Ct
- HarC 77373 3114 B4
Happy Valley Dr
1700 BYTN 77520 3973 D6
Happy Valley Ln
500 FBnC 77471 4490 C2
Happywood St
10 LbyC 77372 2684 A1
Hapsburg St
- HarC 77396 3547 B2
Haraldson Forest Dr
12100 HarC 77044 3548 D6

Haralson Rd
13300 MSCY 77071 4370 D1
Harbin Dr
11100 HarC 77065 3539 E1
11300 HarC 77065 3398 D7
Harbin Rd
4800 GlsC 77511 4869 C7
Harbinger Ct
10 WDLD 77382 2819 A3
Harbor Cir
1900 LGCY 77573 4509 A7
Harbor Cross
- HarC 77494 3953 A2
Harbor Dr
2200 HOUS 77020 3965 A5
8000 HTCK 77563 5104 D3
8600 TXCY 77591 4755 E4
S Harbor Dr
7200 HOUS 77011 3965 B6
Harbor Ln
10 GlsC 77565 4509 D5
Harbor Rdg
- HarC 77041 3679 B7
Harbor St
100 HOUS 77020 3826 A7
300 HOUS 77020 3965 A1
1100 BYTN 77520 3972 A7
Harbor Wy
11500 MtgC 77354 2671 C6
Harbor Breeze Ln
- LGCY 77573 4631 C7
Harbor Canyon Dr
10400 HarC 77396 3407 D7
Harbor Chase Ct
1300 PRLD 77545 4499 C2
Harbor Chase Dr
2300 PRLD 77545 4499 E2
Harbor Cove Dr
10 WDLD 77381 2821 B5
Harborcrest Dr
100 TYLV 77586 4508 E1
100 TYLV 77586 4509 A1
Harbor Glen Ln
4800 HarC 77084 3678 A7
Harbor Hills Dr
9000 HOUS 77054 4242 A3
Harbor Key Cir
18800 HOUS 77084 3816 B6
Harbor Lakes Ln
- HarC 77494 3953 A2
Harbor Landing Dr
- PRLD 77584 4500 A2
Harbor Light Dr
4900 DKSN 77539 4753 E4
Harbor Mist
5100 BYTN 77521 3833 D4
5100 HarC 77521 3833 D4
Harbor Mist Ct
16800 HarC 77532 3552 B1
Harbor Mist Dr
300 HarC 77532 3552 B1
6400 MSCY 77459 4496 C3
Harbor Oaks Dr
1000 HOUS 77042 3958 D4
Harbor Pass Dr
2300 PRLD 77545 4499 E2
Harbor Pass Ln
3500 HarC 77546 4506 A6
Harbor Point Dr
4000 MSCY 77459 4369 C6
8000 HOUS 77071 4239 D5
Harborside Cir
300 LGCY 77565 4509 A5
Harborside Dr
- GLSN 77550 5108 E3
400 GLSN 77550 5109 C2
5400 GLSN 77551 5108 B4
5400 GLSN 77554 5107 D6
5400 GLSN 77554 5108 B4
Harborside Dr FM-188
- GLSN 77554 5107 D6
Harborside Dr FM-275
400 GLSN 77550 5109 C2
5400 GLSN 77551 5108 B4
5400 GLSN 77554 5107 E4
5400 GLSN 77554 5108 B4
Harborside Ln
- PRLD 77545 4499 D1
Harborside Wy
400 LGCY 77565 4509 A5
Harbor Town Dr
6500 HOUS 77036 4099 C4
Harbortown Dr
1200 SGLD 77478 4237 A7
Harbor View Blvd
100 BYTN 77520 4113 C5
Harbor View Cir
1400 GLSN 77550 4994 E7
Harbor View Dr
10 FBnC 77479 4366 E6
10 FBnC 77479 4367 A6
900 GLSN 77550 4994 E7
Harborview Dr
400 LGCY 77565 4509 A5
Harborview Vil
3000 MSCY 77459 4496 E4
3000 MSCY 77459 4497 A5
Harborwalk Blvd
10 HTCK 77563 5104 D4
10 HTCK 77563 5105 A4
Harbour Cir
4100 MSCY 77459 4369 C6
Harbour Dr
10 NSUB 77058 4508 B6
1900 SEBK 77586 4509 C2
8600 TXCY 77591 4755 E3
Harbour Pl
800 SGLD 77478 4368 B3
4300 MSCY 77459 4497 A4
E Harbour Bend Ln
16000 HOUS 77044 3409 A4
Harbour Breeze Ln
3300 PRLD 77584 4501 D5
Harbour Bridge Point Dr
17000 HarC 77429 3252 C7
Harbour Chase Dr
3500 FBnC 77450 4093 B6
Harbour Cove Cir
4100 MSCY 77459 4496 C4
Harbour Cove Dr
1900 SEBK 77586 4509 D1
Harbour Crest Dr
1800 SEBK 77586 4509 D1
Harbour Estates Cir
1500 TYLV 77586 4382 A6
Harbour Gateway Ln
6200 MSCY 77459 4496 D3

Harbour Lake Ct
11300 HarC 77396 3407 E7
Harbour Light Dr
15900 HOUS 77044 3409 A5
Harbour Pointe Dr
- LGCY 77573 4508 D6
Harbour Sands Dr
1000 HarC 77094 3955 C2
Harbourside Ln
6400 MSCY 77459 4496 C4
Harbourview Ct
4200 MSCY 77459 4369 C7
Harbrook Dr
3300 BzaC 77584 4501 D7
5600 HOUS 77087 4104 E7
5800 HOUS 77087 4244 E1
5900 HOUS 77087 4245 A1
Harburly Ct
10 HarC 77379 3255 C1
Harby St
4300 HOUS 77023 3964 A7
4400 HOUS 77023 4104 A1
Harcourt Dr
6300 HOUS 77016 3687 A2
Harcourt Bridge Ct
14600 HarC 77084 3679 A3
Harcourt Bridge Dr
6500 HarC 77084 3679 A3
Harcourtbridge Dr
6400 HarC 77084 3679 A3
Harcroft St
3600 HOUS 77029 3966 A4
Hardage Ct
24200 MtgC 77365 2974 B6
Hard Castle St
- RSBG 77471 4491 C2
Hardeman Ct
8700 HarC 77064 3540 D6
Harden Holly Dr
- HOUS 77365 2974 E6
Hardesty Av
800 SEBK 77586 4509 D3
Hardie St
3300 HOUS 77026 3825 A5
N Hardie St
100 ALVN 77511 4867 D2
S Hardie St
100 ALVN 77511 4867 C2
Hardin
100 TMBL 77375 3109 C1
Hardin Dr
4000 GLSN 77554 5441 B4
Hardin Rd
2500 BYTN 77521 3973 D2
2500 HarC 77521 3973 D2
Harding St
500 BYTN 77520 4112 D1
600 HarC 77530 3969 C2
1500 PASD 77502 4107 C7
8100 HOUS 77012 4105 C4
Hardin Spur Rd
- MtgC 77362 2963 C2
Hardin Store
100 MtgC 77362 2963 C2
Hardin Store Rd
- MtgC 77355 2963 C2
24000 MtgC 77362 2963 C1
25000 MtgC 77354 2963 C1
25300 MtgC 77354 2817 E6
26500 MtgC 77354 2818 A5
Hardison Ln
10000 HOUS 77041 3681 A5
Hard Rock Dr
15000 HarC 77084 3678 E2
Hard Rock Ln
6000 FBnC 77469 4493 B4
Hardscrabble
- FBnC 77494 3953 B5
Hardsville Dr
19900 HarC 77388 3112 E5
Hardway St
4500 HOUS 77018 3683 B7
4700 HOUS 77092 3683 A7
5100 HOUS 77092 3682 D7
Hardwicke Rd
100 HOUS 77037 3544 C3
100 HOUS 77060 3544 C3
Hardwick Oaks Dr
20700 HOUS 77073 3259 C7
Hardwidge Ct
20100 HarC 77450 3954 E2
Hardwood Cir
3100 PRLD 77584 4502 A6
Hard Wood Dr
24200 HOUS 77336 3266 D2
Hardwood Dr
5200 RSBG 77471 4491 D5
Hardwood Ln
2300 HOUS 77093 3685 E3
Hardwood Tr
21900 MtgC 77357 2827 E2
21900 MtgC 77357 2828 A1
Hardwood Dale Wy Dr
- HarC 77338 3261 B3
Hardwood Forest Dr
5500 HarC 77088 3682 E1
Hardwood Glen Dr
4400 FBnC 77545 4622 E2
Hardwood Ridge Tr
19500 HarC 77429 3395 D1
19600 HarC 77433 3395 D1
Hardy Rd
- HOUS 77002 3963 D3
- HOUS 77022 3824 D2
- HOUS 77093 3824 D2
900 HOUS 77020 3963 D3
1900 HOUS 77009 3963 D1
1900 HOUS 77026 3963 D1
2500 HOUS 77009 3824 D6
15700 HarC 77073 3259 C5
18400 MtgC 77385 2822 C3
19100 CHTW 77385 2822 C3
20400 MtgC 77357 2828 C6
E Hardy Rd
7600 HOUS 77093 3824 D1
8500 HOUS 77093 3685 D7
10700 HarC 77093 3685 D7
11400 HarC 77093 3545 B6
11400 HOUS 77093 3545 B6
11600 HarC 77039 3545 B7
14700 HarC 77032 3545 A4
15200 HarC 77032 3404 A7
15200 HOUS 77032 3404 A7
15400 HarC 77032 3403 E6
15400 HOUS 77032 3403 E6
16100 HarC 77060 3403 E4
16100 HOUS 77060 3403 E5
17000 HarC 77073 3403 D1

E Hardy Rd
18300 HarC 77073 3259 C3
22100 HarC 77373 3259 C1
26300 HarC 77373 3114 A1
27100 HarC 77373 2969 A7
28100 HarC 77373 2968 E4
W Hardy Rd
- HarC 77073 3259 C7
- HOUS 77060 3544 E1
7200 HOUS 77022 3824 D1
8100 HOUS 77022 3685 C7
9400 HOUS 77076 3685 C6
12100 HOUS 77037 3685 C5
12900 HOUS 77037 3545 B7
13000 HarC 77037 3545 B6
13000 HarC 77039 3545 A5
13000 HarC 77060 3545 A5
13600 HOUS 77060 3545 A5
15400 HOUS 77060 3403 E7
16200 HarC 77060 3403 E5
19800 HarC 77073 3403 C2
21700 HarC 77373 3259 B1
22900 HarC 77373 3114 A2
Hardy St
200 GlsC 77518 4634 C2
1200 HOUS 77020 3963 D2
1300 HOUS 77009 3963 D2
1300 HOUS 77026 3963 D2
E Hardy St
- HarC 77073 3403 E4
16100 HarC 77032 3403 E5
16100 HarC 77060 3403 E5
16100 HOUS 77032 3403 E5
16100 HOUS 77060 3403 E5
E Hardy St Rd
15400 HarC 77032 3403 E7
15400 HOUS 77032 3403 E7
W Hardy St Rd
27000 HarC 77373 2969 A7
27000 HarC 77373 3114 A1
Hardy Stone Dr
1400 HarC 77073 3404 A3
Hardy Toll
- HarC - 2968 D5
- HarC - 2969 A6
- HarC - 3114 C5
- HarC - 3259 C4
- HarC - 3403 D1
- HarC - 3404 A4
- HarC - 3545 A1
- HarC - 3685 B2
- HOUS - 3403 E7
- HOUS - 3404 A4
- HOUS - 3545 A1
- HOUS - 3685 B2
- HOUS - 3824 D2
- MtgC - 2968 D5
Hardy Toll Airport Connector
- HOUS - 3404 A5
- HOUS - 3405 A5
Hare Rd
100 HarC 77532 3552 C2
Hare St
4600 HOUS 77020 3964 C2
Hare Cook Rd
- HarC 77532 3411 C6
Harefield Ln
- HarC 77084 3678 C5
Harewood Ct
3600 PRLD 77584 4503 C6
Harford Mills Dr
- HarC 77083 4097 A6
Hargest St
- PRVW 77445 3100 C2
Hargrave Rd
13100 HarC 77070 3399 E2
13100 HOUS 77070 3399 E4
14300 HarC 77069 3400 A2
14300 HarC 77070 3400 A2
23300 MtgC 77355 2813 D5
23300 WlrC 77447 2813 D5
N Hargrave St
10 PASD 77506 4106 D3
S Hargrave St
10 PASD 77506 4106 D3
Hargraves Rd
- HarC 77336 2976 A6
W Hargraves Rd
- HarC 77336 2976 A5
Hargrove Rd
16200 HarC 77447 3250 A6
Harkey Rd
2700 PRLD 77581 4502 D3
2700 PRLD 77584 4502 D6
3900 BzaC 77584 4502 D7
16600 BzaC 77584 4626 D2
17200 PRLD 77584 4626 D2
Harkness St
100 HOUS 77076 3685 A5
N Harlan Ln
27000 ORDN 77385 2822 C4
S Harlan Ln
27100 ORDN 77385 2822 C5
27100 ORDN 77386 2822 C5
Harland Dr
1800 HOUS 77055 3821 D5
3800 HOUS 77092 3821 D2
Harlem Rd
100 FBnC 77469 4366 A3
3600 FBnC 77469 4235 A6
6900 FBnC 77469 4095 A6
6900 HOUS 77469 4095 A5
7100 HarC 77521 3832 D5
Harlem St
1800 HOUS 77020 3964 C1
2500 HOUS 77020 3825 C7
Harlequin Ct
2500 LGCY 77573 4631 A7
Harlequin Ln
26900 HarC 77447 3248 E6
Harley Dr
- PRLD 77584 4501 A4
Harlton St
100 LMQU 77568 4872 E7
N Harlton St
500 LMQU 77568 4872 E6
Harman Dr
10 LbyC 77535 3268 C5
Harman St
- SGLD 77478 4367 E1
Harmaston Rd
10200 HOUS 77078 3687 C4
Harmeier
21900 HarC 77377 3107 A2
Harmon Dr
1200 RHMD 77469 4492 B1

Harmon St
4900 HarC 77093 3686 C1
6300 HOUS 77016 3687 A1
Harmony Dr
22800 MtgC 77357 2974 A4
Harmony Gln
8300 HarC 77064 3541 C6
Harmony Ln
3700 GlsC 77518 4634 C2
8300 HarC 77049 3690 B6
Harmony Arbor Ct
10 WDLD 77382 2674 D3
Harmony Cove
7100 HOUS 77036 4100 A3
7200 HOUS 77036 4099 E4
Harmony Estates Ln
18100 HarC 77429 3396 B2
Harmony Hall Ln
- HarC 77346 3408 B3
Harmony Hill Ct
9100 HarC 77379 3255 E4
Harmony Hill Dr
17000 HarC 77379 3255 E4
Harmony Hollow Ct
10 WDLD 77385 2676 C4
Harmony Links Pl
10 WDLD 77382 2819 B1
Harmony Rock Ln
9700 HarC 77044 3689 C3
Harmony Springs Dr
16900 HarC 77095 3538 A4
Harms Rd
7000 HarC 77041 3539 D7
7000 HarC 77041 3679 D1
Harness Ln
15100 HOUS 77598 4506 D2
Harness Creek Ln
8800 HOUS 77024 3961 A3
Harness Oaks Ct
1500 HOUS 77077 3957 A5
Harness Path Ct
24500 HarC 77373 3114 D4
Harnett Dr
18300 HarC 77429 3396 B2
Harnwell Crossing Dr
10400 HarC 77379 3110 B7
Harold Ln
10 BYTN 77521 3973 A4
100 BYTN 77521 3972 E4
Harold St
600 HOUS 77006 3962 D6
2000 HOUS 77098 3962 B7
Harolds Rd
800 HOUS 77336 3266 D2
Harper Dr
2100 PASD 77502 4246 E1
2100 PASD 77502 4247 A1
Harper Ln
2800 MtgC 77380 2967 E2
Harper St
3700 SSPL 77005 4101 D3
Harper Forest Dr
5400 HarC 77088 3542 E7
Harper Gate Dr
22900 HarC 77373 3115 C7
Harpergate Dr
23400 HarC 77373 3115 B6
Harpers Dr
6600 FBnC 77469 4493 C6
Harpers Bridge Dr
13200 HarC 77041 3679 B5
Harpers Creek Ct
2500 MSCY 77545 4622 C2
Harpers Ferry Dr
2500 LGCY 77573 4631 B6
Harpers Glen Ln
7500 HOUS 77072 4097 C6
Harpers Landing Blvd
- MtgC 77385 2676 A4
- WDLD 77385 2676 A4
Harpers Landing Dr
- WDLD 77385 2676 B3
S Harpers Landing Dr
- WDLD 77385 2676 B4
Harpers Landing Ln
- FBnC 77469 4094 D7
- FBnC 77469 4095 A7
Harpings Wy
1100 HarC 77532 3552 A1
Harpoon Ct
16100 HarC 77532 3552 B3
Harpost Mnr
5600 HarC 77379 3257 A2
Harpstone Pl
10 WDLD 77382 2674 D4
Harpswell Ln
600 HarC 77073 3259 A4
Harpy Eagle Ct
- HarC 77396 3548 B2
Harrar
3100 HOUS 77098 3962 A7
Harrell St
8600 HOUS 77093 3685 E7
Harrell-Dwyer Rd
800 HarC 77014 3258 B7
800 HarC 77090 3258 B7
Harriet Ln
12500 GlsC 77510 4871 A2
Harriet St
5600 HOUS 77023 4104 C3
Harriette St
2600 PASD 77502 4248 A1
2700 PASD 77503 4248 A1
Harriman Rd
2000 BzaC 77511 4748 E3
Harriman St
3700 HOUS 77026 3964 B1
Harrington Dr
10000 PRLD 77584 4501 B2
Harrington Ln
1200 SEBK 77586 4382 E7
1200 SEBK 77586 4509 E1
Harrington St
300 HOUS 77009 3963 C2
2600 HOUS 77026 3963 E1
Harris Av
300 PASD 77506 4107 B5
400 KMAH 77565 4509 E5
11200 PRLD 77583 4500 D5
E Harris Av
1400 PASD 77506 4107 D5
2600 PASD 77506 4108 A5
W Harris Av
100 PASD 77506 4107 A5
300 PASD 77506 4106 E5
1300 HOUS 77017 4106 D5
Harris Blvd
100 CNRO 77301 2383 E2

Harris Ct
100 HOUS 77009 3823 E5
Harris Rd
- ALVN 77511 4750 A7
- BzaC 77511 4750 A7
- MtgC 77302 2676 D1
100 HarC 77562 3831 D4
17300 HarC 77447 3248 E2
Harris St
100 HOUS 77020 3826 A7
300 HOUS 77020 3965 A1
2000 HarC 77521 3832 C5
Harris Wy
1100 GLSN 77551 5108 C5
Harrisburg Blvd
2500 HOUS 77003 3963 E5
3300 HOUS 77003 3964 C6
4300 HOUS 77011 3964 B6
7000 HOUS 77011 3965 A7
7400 HOUS 77011 4105 A1
7400 HOUS 77012 4105 B1
Harrisburg Ct
1000 RSBG 77471 4490 B6
Harris Mill Dr
3800 HarC 77449 3816 B2
Harrison Av
500 BYTN 77520 3973 A6
3500 FBnC 77545 4499 C7
Harrison Ct
1700 PASD 77503 4108 D7
6200 FBnC 77450 4094 C4
Harrison Dr
1500 DRPK 77536 4249 D1
Harrison St
- HOUS 77029 3965 D5
7100 HarC 77521 3832 C4
9700 FBnC 77459 4621 D4
Harrison Lakes Cir
17500 HarC 77379 3255 C3
Harris Settlement Ct
12000 HarC 77433 3395 D6
Harrop Av
1400 PASD 77506 4107 D5
W Harrow Dr
5800 HarC 77084 3678 B4
Harrow Ln
8300 HarC 77379 3256 B5
Harrow St
- HarC 77093 3686 B1
3000 HOUS 77051 4243 A2
11600 HarC 77093 3546 B7
Harrowby Dr
23000 HarC 77373 3114 C7
Harrowgate Dr
9700 HOUS 77031 4238 E6
Harrow Hill Ct
4200 HarC 77084 3816 E1
Harrow Hill Dr
18200 HarC 77084 3816 D1
Harrowshire Ln
- HarC 77047 4374 B4
Harston Dr
10800 HarC 77375 3255 A1
Hart Cir
3900 FBnC 77459 4621 B4
W Hart Dr
100 PASD 77506 4107 A6
900 PASD 77506 4106 E6
Hart St
1600 JTCY 77029 3966 B4
1700 GNPK 77029 3966 B4
1700 GNPK 77547 3966 B4
1800 CNRO 77304 2382 D1
Hartaway Ln
14700 HarC 77429 3397 D2
Hartcliff Cir
3100 HarC 77449 3816 A4
Hartcrest Dr
13900 HarC 77429 3397 B3
Harte Ct
2700 HarC 77449 3814 E4
Hartfield
3000 FBnC 77469 4615 B4
Hartfield Ln
3400 HarC 77388 3112 E2
Hartford Ct
13700 SGLD 77478 4237 A5
Hartford Ln
200 CNRO 77301 2384 C1
200 CNRO 77303 2238 C7
200 CNRO 77303 2384 C1
Hartford Rd
21300 HarC 77484 3102 C1
Hartford St
7900 HOUS 77017 4105 C6
Hartglen Cir
1900 HarC 77450 3953 E5
Hartington Dr
3400 HarC 77066 3401 D6
Hartland St
6800 HOUS 77055 3821 E7
Hartledge Rd
2700 FBnC 77471 4614 A6
3300 FBnC 77461 4614 B6
Hartlepool Ln
12700 HarC 77066 3401 B3
Hartley Rd
11300 HarC 77093 3686 B1
11400 HarC 77093 3546 B7
11500 HarC 77039 3546 B7
Hartman Dr
700 BYTN 77521 3973 B2
2300 SGLD 77478 4237 C4
Hartman Rd
7400 HarC 77049 3828 B1
7600 HarC 77049 3689 B7
15900 MtgC 77355 2961 E1
15900 MtgC 77355 2962 A1
15900 SGCH 77355 2961 E1
15900 SGCH 77355 2962 A1
Hartman St
600 HOUS 77007 3962 D3
Hartman Ridge Ct
16600 HOUS 77053 4372 D6
Hartrick Ln
500 HarC 77521 3834 B7
Hartridge Dr
17200 HarC 77090 3258 A4
Harts
- WlrC 77447 2959 B5
Hartsdale Dr
3900 HOUS 77063 4100 A2
5600 HOUS 77036 4100 A3
Harts Garden Ln
9300 HOUS 77075 4377 A3
Hartshill Ct
12900 HarC 77044 3549 E1

STREET Block City ZIP Map# Grid

Hartshill Dr
14200 HarC 77044 3549 E1
Hartsook St
10100 HOUS 77034 4246 E7
10800 HOUS 77034 4247 A7
Hartsville Rd
- HOUS 77051 4242 E7
3000 HOUS 77051 4243 A6
4000 HOUS 77047 4243 C6
4500 HOUS 77048 4243 D6
Hartt Dr
1600 BYTN 77520 3973 C6
Hartt St
4100 HOUS 77025 4241 C4
Hartwell Dr
5000 HarC 77084 3677 E6
Hartwick Ct
10 CNRO 77304 2236 D7
Hartwick Ln
200 HarC 77037 3684 D1
W Hartwick Ln
100 HarC 77037 3684 C1
Hartwick Rd
900 HarC 77037 3685 A1
1200 HOUS 77037 3685 B1
1300 HOUS 77093 3685 D1
1300 HOUS 77093 3685 C1
3100 HarC 77093 3686 A1
5200 HOUS 77016 3686 C1
5200 HOUS 77093 3686 C1
6100 HOUS 77016 3687 A1
Hartwill Dr
26300 FBnC 77494 4092 A5
Hartwood Ct
200 FBnC 77479 4366 D6
Hartwood Wy
16800 HOUS 77058 4507 E2
Harvard Rd
300 HarC 77336 3121 D7
700 HOUS 77336 3121 D7
Harvard St
- BYTN 77520 3973 A5
300 HOUS 77007 3962 D1
800 DRPK 77536 4109 B4
800 HOUS 77007 3823 D7
800 HOUS 77008 3823 D7
2700 PASD 77502 4248 A1
2700 PASD 77503 4248 A1
4100 HOUS 77018 3823 D2
5600 HOUS 77076 3684 C6
Harvest Ln
4300 HOUS 77004 4103 E3
7900 HarC 77521 3834 B1
Harvest Tr
600 FBnC 77583 4744 A3
Harvest Acres Dr
8700 BzaC 77578 4747 C5
Harvest Bend Blvd
11200 HarC 77064 3540 C1
Harvest Bend Ct
5200 SGLD 77479 4495 B4
Harvest Brook Ct
13600 HOUS 77059 4379 D5
Harvest Chase Ct
14700 HarC 77429 3396 C1
Harvest Cove
2500 HarC 77546 4506 B7
Harvest Creek Ct
2200 HOUS 77345 3120 C6
Harvest Dale Av
11100 HarC 77065 3539 C1
Harvest Dawn Ct
7400 HarC 77095 3678 D1
Harvester Ln
- MSCY 77459 4497 A4
Harvester St
7800 HarC 77095 3538 B6
Harvest Fall Ln
15300 HarC 77530 3829 D6
Harvest Field Ln
- HarC 77379 3111 B4
Harvest Glen Ct
14300 HOUS 77062 4380 A6
Harvest Glen Dr
6800 HarC 77346 3264 D4
6900 HarC 77346 3265 A5
Harvest Green Pl
10 WDLD 77382 2674 D6
Harvest Grove Ct
21300 HarC 77388 3113 B3
Harvest Hill Ct
2800 FRDW 77598 4630 C3
Harvest Hill Dr
2800 FRDW 77598 4630 C2
Harvest Hill Ln
20600 HarC 77073 3259 E4
20600 HarC 77073 3260 A4
Harvest Hollow Ct
17300 FBnC 77469 4095 D6
Harvest Landing Ln
20100 HarC 77433 3537 A6
Harvest Meadows Dr
- HarC 77064 3540 B2
Harvest Meadows Ln
14100 BzaC 77583 4623 D4
Harvest Mill Ln
7600 FBnC 77469 4095 C6
Harvest Moon Dr
2500 MSCY 77489 4370 D7
Harvest Moon Ln
700 HOUS 77077 3957 D4
Harvest Ridge Rd
14300 HOUS 77062 4379 D7
Harvest Run Ln
12900 HarC 77044 3689 B4
Harvest Spring Dr
5200 HOUS 77345 3119 C2
Harvest Stream Wy
19400 HarC 77084 3816 A5
Harvest Summer Ct
16200 PASD 77059 4380 D5
Harvest Sun Dr
- HarC 77064 3540 D2
Harvest Terrace Ct
6100 HarC 77379 3111 D3
Harvest Terrace Ln
20800 HarC 77379 3111 D3
Harvest Time Ln
800 HarC 77060 3403 D5
800 HOUS 77060 3403 C5
Harvest Trail Ln
6600 HarC 77449 3677 C3
Harvest Wind Ct
9100 HarC 77064 3540 D1
Harvest Wind Dr
- HarC 77064 3540 D1
Harvest Wind Pl
10 WDLD 77382 2674 A5
Harvestwood Tr
- HarC 77449 3676 B2
Harvey Av
100 BYTN 77520 3973 A6
200 BYTN 77520 3972 E6
Harvey Blvd
10 BYTN 77520 3971 B4
Harvey Dr
700 MtgC 77362 2816 D6
700 SGCH 77362 2816 D6
Harvey Ln
12900 HOUS 77013 3828 A5
Harvey Rd
3000 HarC 77532 3412 E6
4700 HarC 77532 3413 A6
5000 LbyC 77535 3413 B6
Harvey St
1700 STAF 77477 4370 C4
Harveys Wy
21600 HarC 77338 3261 D2
Harvey Wilson Dr
5500 HOUS 77020 3964 D4
Harvill Dr
11300 MtgC 77303 2385 C2
Harvrenee Dr
14900 HarC 77429 3397 C5
Harwell Cir
2300 ALVN 77511 4866 E4
Harwell Dr
2200 HOUS 77023 4105 A3
Harwick Dr
15900 HarC 77379 3256 B6
Harwin Dr
6500 HOUS 77074 4100 B3
6700 HOUS 77036 4100 A3
7100 HOUS 77036 4099 A3
10300 HOUS 77036 4098 E3
11100 HOUS 77072 4098 C3
11500 HOUS 77082 4098 B3
12800 HOUS 77072 4097 D3
Harwood Dr
100 LGCY 77573 4632 E1
200 LGCY 77573 4633 A1
2300 HOUS 77055 3821 C3
4000 FBnC 77479 4366 C6
Harwood Heights Dr
- FBnC 77494 4092 B5
Harwood Springs Dr
1900 HOUS 77080 3820 B5
Hasbrook St
3000 HOUS 77087 4104 E5
Hasie Dr
5200 HarC 77032 3546 D2
Hasina Knoll Dr
16700 HarC 77429 3252 D7
Haskell St
500 HOUS 77007 3961 E2
Hasselt
- HarC 77070 3255 C6
Hassler Rd
200 HarC 77389 2966 E7
200 HarC 77389 2967 A7
Hasting Green Dr
- HarC 77065 3539 C2
Hasting Oak Ct
10 WDLD 77381 2821 A6
Hastings Cir
19800 BzaC 77511 4628 D7
Hastings Ln
4200 DRPK 77536 4249 C1
Hastings Rd
700 BzaC 77581 4628 E2
700 PRLD 77511 4628 C4
700 PRLD 77581 4628 E2
1200 BzaC 77546 4628 C4
2100 FRDW 77546 4628 E2
19500 BzaC 77511 4628 C6
22400 MtgC 77357 2973 D3
Hastings Rd FM-2351
700 BzaC 77511 4628 C4
700 BzaC 77581 4628 E2
700 PRLD 77511 4628 C4
700 PRLD 77581 4628 E2
1200 BzaC 77546 4628 C4
2100 FRDW 77546 4628 E2
Hastings St
3100 HOUS 77017 4105 D6
Hastings Cannon Rd
6800 BzaC 77584 4627 A4
6800 PRLD 77584 4627 A4
7500 BzaC 77511 4627 D4
7900 PRLD 77511 4627 D4
8800 BzaC 77511 4628 A4
8800 PRLD 77511 4628 A4
Hastings Cannon Rd CO-128
7500 BzaC 77511 4627 B4
7500 BzaC 77584 4627 B4
7500 PRLD 77584 4627 B4
N Hastings Field Rd
2200 BzaC 77511 4628 A2
2200 PRLD 77511 4628 A2
9100 BzaC 77511 4627 E2
9100 PRLD 77511 4627 E2
N Hastings Field Rd CO-413
2200 BzaC 77511 4628 A2
2200 PRLD 77511 4628 A2
9100 BzaC 77511 4627 E2
9100 PRLD 77511 4627 E2
S Hastings Field Rd
18600 BzaC 77511 4628 A4
18700 PRLD 77511 4628 A4
Hastings Friendswood Rd
1500 BzaC 77581 4504 B7
1500 PRLD 77581 4504 B7
16700 BzaC 77581 4628 B1
Hastings Friendswood Rd CO-127
1500 BzaC 77581 4504 B7
1500 PRLD 77581 4504 B7
16700 BzaC 77581 4628 B1
Hastings Green Dr
11900 HarC 77065 3539 D2
S Hastings Oil Field Rd
- BzaC 77511 4628 A3
- BzaC 77581 4628 A3
- PRLD 77511 4628 A3
- PRLD 77581 4628 A3
Hastingwood Dr
5000 HarC 77084 3677 D7
Hasty Ln
8200 HarC 77562 3832 D2
Hasty Rd
- WlrC 77447 2958 E4
Hat St
10600 HOUS 77099 4237 D4
Hatch Ct
16900 HarC 77532 3552 A1
Hatcher Ln
10 FRDW 77546 4629 D1
Hatcherville Rd
12300 CmbC 77520 3696 A1
12300 MTBL 77520 3696 A1
14000 CmbC 77520 3695 E1
Hatchmere Pl
1400 HarC 77379 3255 B1
Hatchmere Pl Ct
1500 HarC 77379 3255 B1
Hatfield Rd
2900 PRLD 77584 4502 E5
13000 BKVL 77581 4375 E7
13000 PRLD 77581 4375 E7
13300 PRLD 77581 4502 E1
Hatfield Glen Dr
5800 HarC 77449 3677 C4
Hatfield Hollow Dr
15500 HarC 77377 3255 A5
Hathaway Ln
6700 SGLD 77479 4367 C7
Hathaway St
500 ALVN 77511 4867 C2
800 LMQU 77568 4990 B2
Hathorn Wy Dr
1000 HarC 77094 3955 B2
Hati Ln
- HarC 77049 3831 B1
Hatteras Ct
1700 FBnC 77479 4494 A5
Hatteras Point Dr
4400 HarC 77546 4506 A5
Hattie St
1500 HOUS 77088 3683 D2
Hatton St
8400 HOUS 77025 4102 A7
Hatwell St
1800 HOUS 77023 4104 C2
Hauck Rd
- HMPD 77445 3098 C3
- WlrC 77445 3098 C3
Haude Rd
18500 HarC 77388 3113 A6
Haughland Dr
18500 HarC 77433 3677 C1
Haughton Ct
6500 HarC 77389 2966 C5
Haughton Dr
6600 HarC 77389 2966 C5
Hauna Ln
5000 DKSN 77539 4633 C7
Hausen Rd
10100 MtgC 77372 2535 B3
Hauser St
1400 HOUS 77023 3964 C7
Hausworth Ct
22900 HarC 77373 2968 E7
Havana Dr
- DRPK 77536 4108 D6
- DRPK 77536 4248 E1
Havanna
- MtgC 77385 2822 D5
- ORDN 77385 2822 D5
Havant Cir
12700 HOUS 77077 3957 C4
Havard Oaks Dr
11500 HarC 77095 3397 B7
Havel St
3000 HOUS 77092 3822 B3
Havelock Dr
1300 MtgC 77386 2968 E1
1300 MtgC 77386 2969 A1
1500 MtgC 77386 2823 A7
N Haven Dr
7200 HOUS 77040 3682 A1
S Haven Dr
1300 FBnC 77469 4493 B4
N Haven Ln
- HOUS 77075 4376 E4
Haven Tr
8500 HarC 77375 2965 E2
Haven Wy
8500 HarC 77375 2965 D1
Haven Bend Ln
- FBnC 77469 4094 D7
Havenbrook Dr
3400 HOUS 77339 3119 C5
Haven Brook Ln
200 FBnC 77469 4365 A5
3200 PRLD 77581 4503 D1
Haven Cove Ln
21800 HarC 77449 3815 A1
Haven Creek Dr
6700 HarC 77449 3677 A2
6900 HarC 77433 3677 A2
7200 HarC 77433 3676 C2
Havencrest Ct
2400 BzaC 77584 4501 A4
Havencrest Dr
1600 HarC 77038 3543 B3
2600 BzaC 77584 4501 A4
9000 FBnC 77083 4236 C1
Haven Crossing Ct
9700 HarC 77065 3539 D4
Havendale Dr
6100 HOUS 77072 4098 D4
Haven Falls Ln
13100 SGLD 77478 4237 C4
Havenfield Ct
22900 FBnC 77450 4093 D2
Haven Forest Ln
6300 FBnC 77469 4616 A2
Havengate Cir
13400 HarC 77015 3828 D5
Haven Glen Dr
- FBnC 77479 4494 D4
4300 HOUS 77339 3119 A3
Haven Green Cir
3300 HarC 77449 3816 A3
Haven Hills Dr
15900 HarC 77084 3678 D6
Haven House Dr
1900 MtgC 77386 2969 B2
Havenhurst Dr
16200 HOUS 77059 4380 C5
16400 PASD 77059 4380 C5
Haven Lake Dr
3600 HOUS 77339 3119 A4
25500 HarC 77375 2965 D1
Havenlark Dr
11700 HarC 77066 3401 B6
Haven Lock Dr
1500 HOUS 77077 3958 B5
Haven Manor Ct
2300 FBnC 77479 4494 C4
Havenmeadow Ln
- HarC 77379 3111 B4
Haven Meadows Ln
14600 HarC 77396 3547 C1
Havenmist Dr
12100 HarC 77375 3109 D6
Havenmoor Pl
3600 HarC 77449 3815 D2
Haven Oaks Dr
3400 HarC 77068 3257 B5
5400 HOUS 77339 3119 C2
Havenpark Ct
16300 HOUS 77059 4380 C6
Havenpark Dr
- PASD 77059 4380 D6
16200 HOUS 77059 4380 D6
Haven Pines Dr
3500 HOUS 77345 3119 D4
Haven Point Dr
5600 HarC 77084 3677 E5
Havenridge Dr
14900 FBnC 77083 4236 C1
N Havenridge Dr
- WDLD 77381 2821 A4
S Havenridge Dr
10 WDLD 77381 2821 B5
Havenrock Dr
12600 HarC 77038 3543 C4
Havens Ln
- STAF 77477 4369 C3
Havens St
9500 HOUS 77022 3685 B6
9500 HOUS 77076 3685 B6
Havens Edge Ct
20400 HMBL 77338 3262 D4
Haven Springs Ln
- RHMD 77469 4492 B2
Havenstone Ln
- FBnC 77450 4093 C6
Haven Valley Dr
5300 HarC 77449 3676 E6
Havenview Dr
5000 HOUS 77041 3680 E6
Havenway Ln
9200 HarC 77064 3541 C5
Havenwood Dr
- HarC 77049 3828 B4
11300 MtgC 77303 2239 C3
Havenwood Pl
- CNRO 77301 2383 E7
Havenwoods Dr
4700 HarC 77066 3401 B2
5500 HarC 77066 3400 E3
Haven Woods Wy
8600 HarC 77375 2965 D2
Haver St
1600 HOUS 77006 3962 C6
Haverbay Ct
21700 HarC 77449 3815 A3
Haverdown Dr
9800 HarC 77065 3539 E4
Haverfield Ct
15100 HarC 77429 3397 C1
Haverford Ln
10 FRDW 77546 4505 D7
Haverford Rd
24700 HarC 77389 2966 D2
Haverhill Dr
1600 HOUS 77008 3822 B5
9800 HMBL 77338 3262 C5
Havering Ln
15900 HarC 77379 3256 B6
Haverling Dr
2900 BzaC 77584 4501 A6
Haversham Ct
10 CNRO 77384 2675 E4
1800 FBnC 77545 4622 D1
Haversham Dr
100 BKHV 77024 3959 A4
100 HOUS 77024 3959 A5
Haver Shire Dr
3400 MSCY 77459 4496 D2
Havershire Ln
13300 HOUS 77079 3958 B1
Haverstock Dr
8700 HOUS 77031 4239 B5
Haverstrom Ln
21700 HarC 77388 3112 A3
Haverton Dr
7000 HOUS 77016 3687 B1
Haverty Dr
14300 HarC 77032 3546 E2
Haverwood Ln
- HarC 77449 3676 C2
Haviland Ln
9700 FBnC 77459 4621 D4
Haviland St
- HOUS 77085 4240 B7
11200 HOUS 77035 4240 B7
Havner Ct
8500 HarC 77037 3684 C1
Havner Ln
200 HarC 77037 3684 D1
1200 HOUS 77037 3685 B1
1700 HarC 77093 3685 C1
2800 HarC 77093 3686 A1
W Havner Ln
100 HarC 77037 3684 C1
Hawaii Av
1600 LGCY 77573 4632 B6
Hawaii Dr
1200 TKIS 77554 5106 C4
Hawaii Ln
8300 JRSV 77040 3540 D7
Hawes Rd
6200 HOUS 77396 3406 A4
Hawick Dr
4000 HarC 77084 3816 E1
Hawk Cr
6000 FBnC 77459 4496 E7
Hawk Pk
7900 HarC 77396 3406 D6
Hawk Rd
3800 PRLD 77584 4501 D1
8500 PRLD 77581 4501 D1
Hawk Rdg
7500 FBnC 77459 4496 E7
7500 FBnC 77459 4497 A7
Hawkes Rd
1700 MSCY 77489 4370 C7
2000 MSCY 77489 4497 C1
Hawkes Bay Ct
5900 FBnC 77494 4093 D4
Hawkesbury Ct
14200 FBnC 77478 4366 E4
Hawkeye St
6500 HOUS 77049 3828 B2
Hawk Haven Ln
17800 HarC 77379 3256 C1
Hawkhill Dr
1100 FRDW 77546 4629 D6
Hawk Hollow Dr
14600 HarC 77396 3548 B1
Hawkin Ct
12400 MtgC 77354 2671 B3
Hawkin Ln
17500 HarC 77377 3107 C1
Hawkins Cir
3600 FBnC 77459 4621 E5
Hawkins Ct
3700 FBnC 77459 4621 E5
Hawkins Ln
9700 FBnC 77459 4621 E5
Hawkins Rd
100 BzaC 77511 4628 B5
Hawkins St
- PRVW 77445 3100 C2
100 HarC 77037 3544 D5
3000 HOUS 77003 3963 E5
Hawkins Creek Ct
23600 FBnC 77494 3953 C4
Hawk Meadow Dr
4200 HarC 77449 3816 A1
4600 HarC 77449 3677 A7
Hawknest Ct
100 WDLD 77384 2675 A4
Hawksbill Pl
10 WDLD 77382 2673 C7
Hawkseye Pl
10 WDLD 77381 2675 A7
Hawks Landing Dr
14100 HarC 77447 3249 E4
Hawksmoor Ct
14700 HarC 77429 3253 D4
Hawks Nest Dr
1200 HarC 77067 3402 C5
Hawks Nest Ln
8700 FBnC 77459 4621 B6
Hawk Springs Ct
- HOUS 77396 3406 C5
Hawk Springs Ln
12800 HarC 77346 3408 D3
Hawkspur Ridge St
- FBnC 77469 4233 E2
- FBnC 77469 4234 A2
Hawks Ridge Ln
- FBnC 77469 4493 A2
Hawkstone Ct
26700 FBnC 77494 4092 D2
Hawkwood Dr
22700 HarC 77373 3115 E7
Hawley Ln
5600 HOUS 77040 3681 D6
Hawn Rd
25700 HarC 77389 2966 A2
Hawsley Wy
6700 SGLD 77479 4367 C7
Hawthorn Dr
1500 RHMD 77469 4491 D3
Hawthorn Pl
500 MSCY 77459 4497 A5
Hawthorn Arbor Ct
4000 FBnC 77545 4622 E1
Hawthorne Av
300 PASD 77506 4107 B6
1300 BYTN 77520 4112 C1
Hawthorne Ct
900 TMBL 77375 3109 C1
Hawthorne Dr
10 CNRO 77301 2384 D1
E Hawthorne Dr
29600 MtgC 77386 2969 B3
W Hawthorne Dr
29400 MtgC 77386 2969 A3
Hawthorne Rd
800 CRLS 77565 4509 C5
6700 HTCK 77563 4989 C5
Hawthorne St
10 HOUS 77002 3963 A6
10 HOUS 77006 3963 D2
200 HOUS 77006 3962 D6
1600 LMQU 77568 4990 B2
1900 HOUS 77098 3962 C6
4700 PASD 77586 4383 C4
Hawthorne Brook Ln
2300 FBnC 77545 4498 C5
Hawthorne Creek Dr
6400 HarC 77379 3256 D3
Hawthorne Falls Ln
6500 HarC 77049 3829 B2
Hawthorne Garden Wy
- FBnC 77494 4093 A3
Hawthorne Hill Cir
12100 HarC 77346 3408 C1
N Hawthorne Hollow Cir
- WDLD 77384 2675 B3
S Hawthorne Hollow Cir
10 WDLD 77384 2675 A4
Hawthorne Pasture Rd
400 RSBG 77471 4614 C1
Hawthorne Ridge Rd
19100 HarC 77433 3251 E7
Hawthorne Shores Dr
- HarC 77044 3408 E4
Hawthorn Glen Ct
3900 FBnC 77545 4623 A1
Hay Ln
1400 HOUS 77077 3957 A4
Haybrook Dr
8100 HarC 77089 4377 A7
Haydee Rd
3100 HarC 77388 3113 A2
3200 HarC 77388 3112 E2
Hayden Ct
3700 MtgC 77386 2970 A4
Hayden Dr
6500 MtgC 77354 2673 B2
15400 MtgC 77306 2680 C4
Hayden Rd
24500 MtgC 77372 2536 D7
Hayden Cove Dr
8200 HarC 77375 3110 D1
Hayden Creek Dr
1000 FBnC 77479 4366 C7
Hayden Grove Dr
19500 HarC 77433 3537 A6
Hayden Park Dr
28500 FBnC 77494 3951 C5
Hayden Springs Ct
3200 HarC 77396 3407 E2
Hayden Wood Dr
19100 HarC 77375 3109 C7
Hayes Rd
- BYTN 77520 3973 E4
- BYTN 77520 3974 A4
1400 HOUS 77042 3958 B6
1400 HOUS 77077 3958 B6
Hayes Rd
2800 HOUS 77082 3958 B7
2800 HOUS 77082 4098 B2
4800 GlsC 77511 4751 A7
Hayesford Ln
16300 HarC 77429 3252 B5
Hayes Ranch Rd
2100 MtgC 77385 2823 C3
Haygood St
4300 HOUS 77022 3823 D2
Haylee Wy
21500 HarC 77338 3260 A1
Hayley Springs Ct
17400 HarC 77396 3407 D2
Haylie Hollow Ct
1600 MtgC 77386 2969 D7
Hayman Ct
19600 HarC 77449 3676 C3
Hayman Dr
6300 HarC 77449 3677 A3
6600 HarC 77449 3676 E3
Haymarket Ln
300 HarC 77015 3829 B6
Hay Meadow Ct
20700 HarC 77484 3102 E3
Hay Meadow Ln
11800 HarC 77039 3546 A6
29200 HarC 77484 3102 E3
29200 HarC 77484 3103 A3
Haynes Dr
13800 HarC 77069 3400 A1
Haynes Rd
12000 HarC 77066 3400 C4
12700 HarC 77069 3400 C3
Haynes St
8500 HOUS 77088 3683 B2
Haynesworth Ln
5800 HOUS 77034 4378 D2
Hays St
900 HOUS 77009 3824 C7
3000 PASD 77503 4108 A4
3000 PASD 77506 4108 A4
Haysden Ln
6000 LGCY 77573 4630 C7
Hayslip Ln
11000 HarC 77041 3680 C4
Haystream Dr
19200 HarC 77449 3816 A3
Hayward Ct
7700 HarC 77095 3537 E7
Haywood Ct
3400 SGLD 77478 4368 D4
Haywood Dr
7400 HOUS 77061 4245 A2
N Haywood Dr
6300 HOUS 77061 4245 A2
S Haywood Dr
6700 HOUS 77061 4245 A3
Haywood St
4200 HOUS 77093 3686 B4
5000 HOUS 77016 3686 C4
Haywood Oaks Dr
17500 HarC 77095 3537 D3
Hazard St
1500 HOUS 77019 3962 C6
3800 HOUS 77098 3962 C7
4400 HOUS 77098 4102 C2
5200 HOUS 77005 4102 C2
Hazel Blvd
- BzaC 77583 4623 E5
Hazel St
100 LPRT 77571 4251 E5
1300 HOUS 77019 3962 D5
1500 HOUS 77006 3962 D5
2700 PRLD 77581 4504 E5
5400 BYTN 77521 3971 E1
Hazel Aldor Wy
- FBnC 77494 4092 E3
Hazel Arbor Wy
19700 FBnC 77469 4234 D2
Hazel Berry Wy
- FBnC 77494 4092 E3
Hazel Brook Ct
4800 HOUS 77345 3119 E2
Hazel Cove Dr
7100 HarC 77095 3677 E1
Hazel Creek Cir
7200 HarC 77095 3678 A1
N Hazelcrest Cir
100 WDLD 77382 2819 E2
100 WDLD 77382 2820 A3
Hazelcrest Dr
200 WDLD 77382 2819 E2
Hazeldale Dr
- HarC 77429 3397 C3
Hazel Field Ct
23100 HarC 77494 3953 C3
Hazel Glade Ct
3900 HOUS 77059 4380 B4
Hazel Green Ln
4100 FBnC 77545 4622 C1
Hazel Grove Dr
- HarC 77375 3254 E1
Hazelgrove Dr
5300 HarC 77084 3677 E6
Hazelhurst Dr
10000 HOUS 77080 3820 A6
10200 HOUS 77043 3819 E6
10200 HOUS 77043 3820 A6
Hazel Oak Ln
- HOUS 77059 4380 C3
Hazel Park Dr
3000 HOUS 77082 4097 B2
Hazel Ranch Dr
25100 FBnC 77494 3953 A6
Hazel Ridge Ct
14000 HOUS 77062 4379 D6
Hazel Rose Ct
- PRLD 77581 4503 D2
Hazel Thicket Tr
15300 HarC 77429 3252 B7
Hazeltine Dr
4900 PASD 77505 4248 E7
Hazelton Dr
4300 HOUS 77035 4241 B3
Hazelway Ln
12800 HarC 77429 3254 B6
Hazelwood Dr
1600 CNRO 77301 2384 D5
3900 PRLD 77584 4503 A7
Hazelwood Ln
12500 HOUS 77077 3957 D4
Hazen St
5600 HOUS 77081 4100 B6
7000 HOUS 77074 4099 E6
7000 HOUS 77074 4100 A6
8000 HOUS 77036 4099 C6
10600 HOUS 77072 4098 C6
Hazen Point Dr
15300 HarC 77433 3251 D6
Hazlitt Dr
2100 HarC 77032 3404 C7
Hazy Ln
20100 HarC 77449 3815 D6
Hazy Tr
1500 FBnC 77545 4622 E2
Hazy Bluff Ct
- HarC 77449 3815 C2
Hazy Brook Ln
7800 HarC 77396 3547 D1
Hazy Creek Dr
2600 HarC 77084 3816 A5
Hazycrest Dr
18400 HarC 77379 3256 A1
Hazy Forest Ln
- MtgC 77386 2823 B7
Hazyglen Dr
12400 HOUS 77082 4097 D2
Hazy Hill Ct
300 LGCY 77565 4508 E5
Hazy Hill Dr
11900 HarC 77044 3688 E5
Hazy Hillside Ct
2800 HOUS 77345 3120 C4
Hazy Hollow Ln
30000 MtgC 77355 2815 E2
30000 MtgC 77355 2816 A2
Hazyknoll Ln
2100 HarC 77067 3402 A6
Hazy Meadow Ln
8500 HarC 77040 3541 A6
30500 MtgC 77354 2816 C1
30500 MtgC 77355 2816 B2
30900 MtgC 77362 2816 C1
Hazy Mills Ln
30200 MtgC 77386 2969 E2
Hazy Park Dr
3000 HOUS 77082 4097 B2
Hazy Pines Ct
16200 PASD 77059 4380 D5
Hazy Ridge Ln
14600 HarC 77429 3396 C2
Hazystone Ct
700 HarC 77373 2968 E7
Hazy Valley Ln
10700 HarC 77086 3542 B1
Hcfc Fasement
- LPRT 77571 4110 E6
N Head Dr
31100 MtgC 77386 2822 E7
31100 MtgC 77386 2968 E1
Headland Ct
8500 MtgC 77302 2530 B5
Headland Dr
18500 HarC 77433 3677 C1
Headstall Dr
8700 HarC 77375 2965 D1
Headwater Dr
- HarC 77389 2820 B6
Heagans Ct
14500 FBnC 77478 4236 E3
Healey
13900 HOUS 77040 3681 C5
Healtehr Trail Dr
10000 HOUS 77075 4377 A4
Heaney Dr
200 HOUS 77076 3685 B6
1600 HOUS 77093 3685 D5
Heards Ln
5700 GLSN 77551 5108 A7
Heards Ln Cir
2000 GLSN 77551 5108 B6
Hearne Dr
2300 PASD 77502 4247 E1
2600 PASD 77502 4248 A1
Hearst Manor Dr
- HarC 77379 3255 B1
Heart Grove Dr
4100 HarC 77346 3408 A3
Hearth Dr
8400 HOUS 77054 4242 A1
Hearthglen Ln
6800 FBnC 77479 4496 B4
Hearth Hollow Ln
5000 FBnC 77479 4493 C3
14100 HarC 77047 4374 B4
Heart Hollow Ln
12700 HarC 77377 3254 A2
Hearthside Cir
200 LGCY 77573 4630 C6
Hearthside Ct
1700 FBnC 77469 4365 C2
Hearthside Dr
6800 FBnC 77479 4493 D5
N Hearthside Dr
1500 FBnC 77469 4365 D2
S Hearthside Dr
1500 FBnC 77469 4365 D2
Hearthstone Ct
500 MtgC 77386 2968 D1
Hearthstone Ln
- BzaC 77583 4623 E3
N Hearthstone Green Ct
7200 HarC 77095 3679 A1
N Hearthstone Green Dr
7200 HarC 77095 3679 B2
S Hearthstone Green Dr
14600 HarC 77095 3679 A1
W Hearthstone Green Dr
7100 HarC 77095 3679 A1
Hearthstone Hill Ln
22700 HarC 77373 2968 E7
Hearthstone Meadows Dr
14500 HarC 77095 3679 A1
Hearthstone Pl Dr
- HarC 77084 3678 D2
- HarC 77084 3679 A2
Hearthwood Dr
9600 HOUS 77040 3682 B2
Heartland Ct
18400 HarC 77346 3264 B7
Heartland Grove Dr
11000 FBnC 77469 4092 D7
Heartleaf Ct
10 WDLD 77381 2821 B6
Heart Pine Wy
- FBnC 77494 4092 E3
Heart Ridge Ct
10 WDLD 77382 2674 E4
Heartwind Ct
17400 HarC 77095 3537 D2
Heartwood Wy
15800 HarC 77433 3251 E5
Heartwood Oak Tr
20900 HarC 77433 3251 A5

REET
ck City ZIP Map# Grid
artwood Oak Wy
3200 HOUS 77345 3119 E2
ath Ct
1100 HOUS 77016 3687 B2
ath St
6300 HOUS 77016 3687 A1
7300 HarC 77016 3687 C2
athbrook Ln
200 HarC 77094 3955 B1
athcliff Ct
800 HDWV 77024 3959 E2
800 PNPV 77024 3959 E2
athcliff Dr
800 MSCY 77489 4370 E5
athcliffe Ct
10 CNRO 77384 2675 D3
athcote Ct
10 WDLD 77380 2967 C2
athcote Ln
1400 HarC 77073 3259 C5
athcrest Ct
17300 HarC 77429 3396 D1
ather Cir
8800 SPVL 77055 3821 A7
ather Ct
800 HDWV 77024 3959 E2
800 PNPV 77024 3959 E2
27800 ORDN 77385 2822 C4
ather Ln
- FRDW 77546 4629 C2
100 ORDN 77385 2822 B4
600 BYTN 77521 3972 E3
1700 ALVN 77511 4866 E2
1700 ALVN 77511 4867 A2
2500 HarC 77449 3815 D3
3500 PRLD 77581 4504 A6
19500 MtgC 77357 2829 C5
Heather Ln
500 FRDW 77546 4629 C2
Heather Ln
500 FRDW 77546 4629 C3
eather Run
5600 HarC 77041 3679 D6
eather St
2200 HarC 77562 3832 C2
5800 LGCY 77573 4630 C7
eatherbank Dr
8800 HarC 77095 3538 E4
eatherbank Pl
10 WDLD 77382 2819 D1
eather Bend Ct
16300 PASD 77059 4380 D5
eatherbend Dr
2600 BzaC 77584 4501 D5
eatherbloom Dr
3700 HOUS 77045 4372 D2
5700 HOUS 77085 4371 E2
5700 HOUS 77085 4372 A2
eather Blossom Ln
5900 HOUS 77345 3120 C7
eather Bluff Ct
8600 HOUS 77075 4376 E4
eather Bluff Ln
10900 HOUS 77075 4376 E4
eatherbriar Ln
26600 FBnC 77494 4092 C3
eatherbrook Dr
3700 HOUS 77045 4372 D2
5600 HOUS 77085 4372 A2
5700 HOUS 77085 4371 D2
eather Brook Ln
10 CNRO 77304 2383 A4
Heather Cove
6200 BzaC 77583 4624 B5
Heather Cove
6300 BzaC 77583 4624 B6
eather Cove Ct
1800 HOUS 77062 4379 D6
eathercrest Dr
5100 HOUS 77045 4372 A2
eathercroft Dr
22900 HarC 77450 3953 D2
eather Dale Ct
7900 FBnC 77479 4494 A5
eatherdale Dr
- PASD 77059 4380 D6
16300 HOUS 77059 4380 D6
eatherdawn Ct
5000 FBnC 77494 4093 A7
eathered Oaks Dr
- HarC 77429 3254 A6
eather Falls Dr
13100 HarC 77065 3539 B1
eather Falls Wy
14200 HOUS 77062 4379 E6
eatherfield Dr
14100 HOUS 77079 3958 A4
14300 HOUS 77079 3957 D4
eatherford Ct
10300 HOUS 77041 3681 A7
eatherford Dr
10600 HOUS 77041 3680 E7
eathergate Ln
200 HarC 77532 3410 E2
200 HarC 77532 3411 A2
eatherglen Dr
4900 HOUS 77096 4241 A1
eathergold Dr
2600 HarC 77084 3816 A5
eather Green Dr
2100 HOUS 77062 4380 C7
eather Grove Ct
20800 HarC 77346 3265 A3
eather Heights Wy
7800 HarC 77095 3538 B7
eather Hill Dr
10100 HarC 77086 3542 B1
eatherhill Pl
14100 HOUS 77077 3956 E4
eather Hollow Dr
6800 HarC 77449 3677 D2
eather Lake Ct
2900 HOUS 77345 3119 E2
eatherland Dr
8300 HarC 77379 3256 A1
eather Landing Ln
12700 HOUS 77072 4097 D4
eatherly Dr
8700 FBnC 77083 4236 D1
eather Meadow Ct
16500 PASD 77059 4380 E6
eathermill Dr
11500 HarC 77066 3401 C6
Heather Mist Ct
15200 HarC 77433 3250 C5
eathernoll Dr
2600 HarC 77373 3114 D7

STREET
Block City ZIP Map# Grid
E Heatherock Cir
3100 SGLD 77479 4495 D2
3100 SGLD 77479 4496 A3
W Heatherock Cir
3100 SGLD 77479 4495 E1
Heather Park Ct
800 FBnC 77479 4493 C5
Heather Park Dr
4200 PASD 77505 4248 E5
Heatherpark Dr
3000 HOUS 77345 3119 E4
Heather Pointe
- LGCY 77573 4631 D5
Heather Ridge Ct
2400 HarC 77598 4506 C7
Heather Row Ln
7200 HarC 77044 3827 E1
7200 HarC 77049 3827 E1
7300 HarC 77044 3688 E7
Heather Sage Ct
- HarC 77084 3816 E1
Heathersage Dr
- HarC 77084 3677 E7
4100 HarC 77084 3816 E1
Heatherside St
9100 HOUS 77016 3686 D6
Heather Springs Dr
9000 HarC 77379 3255 E4
Heather Springs Ln
1600 LGCY 77573 4751 E1
19000 FBnC 77469 4095 A6
19100 FBnC 77469 4094 D2
21100 HarC 77338 3261 D3
Heather Springs St
500 LPRT 77571 4250 B2
Heatherton Wy
6900 FBnC 77479 4367 A7
Heatherton Hill Ln
500 HOUS 77047 4373 B3
Heatherton Mill Ln
- HarC 77377 3253 E4
- HarC 77429 3253 E4
Heathervale Ct
5200 HOUS 77345 3119 C2
Heather Valley Wy
14800 HOUS 77062 4380 A7
Heatherview Dr
8600 HOUS 77099 4098 D7
8600 HOUS 77099 4238 D1
Heatherway St
700 RSBG 77471 4491 B4
Heatherwick Dr
- HarC 77070 3254 D7
12100 HarC 77429 3254 C6
Heatherwilde St
4400 SGLD 77479 4495 D4
Heatherwind Ln
- HarC 77047 4374 A4
Heather Wisp Ct
10 WDLD 77381 2674 B6
Heather Wisp Pl
10 WDLD 77381 2674 B6
Heatherwood Ct
400 LGCY 77573 4633 A2
1100 KATY 77494 3952 B2
Heatherwood Dr
100 MtgC 77386 2968 C1
2100 MSCY 77489 4370 E5
3000 BYTN 77521 3972 B1
11300 HOUS 77076 3685 B3
22000 MtgC 77365 2972 C2
Heatherwood Park Cir
19700 HarC 77094 3955 B5
Heather Wy Ct
22500 HarC 77449 3814 E3
Heath Falls Ln
- HarC 77429 3254 A4
Heathfield Ct
5100 HarC 77084 3677 E6
Heathfield Dr
900 HarC 77530 3829 C6
4100 PASD 77505 4248 E5
Heathford Ln
4100 HarC 77053 4372 D5
Heathgate Ct
15000 HOUS 77062 4506 E1
Heathgate Dr
100 HOUS 77062 4506 E2
Heathglen Ln
8600 HOUS 77075 4376 E4
21100 HarC 77379 3111 C3
Heath Green Cir
14900 HarC 77433 3250 E5
Heath Grove Ln
17300 FBnC 77469 4095 C5
Heath Hollow Dr
1200 HarC 77379 3110 B7
Heath Hollow Wy
16800 HOUS 77058 4507 D3
Heath Meadow Ct
21900 HarC 77373 3261 A1
Heathmoor Ln
5900 HarC 77084 3678 C4
Heath Ridge Ln
- FBnC 77469 4095 A6
- RSBG 77469 4614 E4
- RSBG 77469 4615 A4
Heathridge Ln
18300 HarC 77433 3677 D1
Heath River Ln
- FBnC 77479 4496 D5
Heathrow Ln
10 SGLD 77479 4495 C2
4500 ALVN 77511 4867 D7
7600 HarC 77379 3256 C5
Heathrow Forest Pkwy
- HarC 77032 3546 B2
- HOUS 77032 3546 B2
15000 HOUS 77032 3405 B7
Heath Spring Ct
13600 HarC 77044 3549 D3
13600 HarC 77044 3550 A3
Heathstone Pl
10 WDLD 77381 2820 C2
Heathton Dr
8800 HOUS 77099 4238 C1
Heathwick Ln
1200 HOUS 77043 3819 A7
Heathwood Ct
1100 HOUS 77077 3957 E4
Heathwood Dr
1200 HOUS 77077 3957 E4
1200 HOUS 77077 3958 A4
Heathwood Ln
21200 HarC 77379 3111 D3
Heaton Ct
17500 MtgC 77355 2961 B1

STREET
Block City ZIP Map# Grid
Heaton Dr
18000 HarC 77084 3677 E7
N Heaton Ln
26600 MtgC 77355 2961 B1
26600 SGCH 77355 2961 B1
S Heaton Ln
26000 SGCH 77355 2961 B2
26500 MtgC 77355 2961 B2
Heaton Rd
- PRLD 77581 4503 D5
Heaton Hall St
8200 HarC 77338 3261 E5
Heaven Leigh Tr
10100 HarC 77064 3541 C1
Heavenly Ln
20400 MtgC 77357 2828 A6
Heaven Tree Pl
10 WDLD 77382 2673 D5
Heavy Anchor Ln
9700 HarC 77396 3407 B7
Hebert St
1200 HOUS 77012 4105 D3
Hebert Trail Dr
2900 HOUS 77082 4096 C2
Hebron Ln
26100 FBnC 77469 4092 B7
Hecht Ln
16800 MtgC 77365 2825 C6
Hector Av
1300 PASD 77502 4247 C1
Hector St
2300 HOUS 77093 3685 D6
Heddon Falls Dr
1600 FBnC 77479 4367 B7
Heddon Oaks Ct
9800 HarC 77379 3255 B1
Heden Rd
16200 HarC 77379 3256 A5
Hedge Ln
23300 MtgC 77365 2973 E7
23300 MtgC 77365 2974 A7
Hedgebell Ct
10 WDLD 77380 2821 D6
Hedgecroft Dr
400 ELGO 77586 4382 B7
16500 HOUS 77060 3403 E7
E Hedgecroft Dr
1600 ELGO 77586 4382 B7
W Hedgecroft Dr
1600 ELGO 77586 4382 B7
1600 ELGO 77586 4509 A1
Hedgedown Dr
12200 HarC 77065 3539 D3
Hedgegate Dr
11900 HarC 77065 3539 E4
Hedge Maple Ct
6300 HarC 77346 3264 E4
Hedgerow Dr
6900 HarC 77379 3256 D4
Hedgestone Ct
8700 LPRT 77571 4249 D4
Hedgeton Ct
6500 HarC 77389 2966 C6
Hedgewick Ct
21700 HarC 77388 3112 B4
Hedgewick Dr
6800 HarC 77084 3679 A3
Hedgewood St
7000 HOUS 77016 3687 B1
Hedge Wy Dr
10100 HarC 77065 3539 E3
Hedgley Pl
13400 HarC 77069 3400 C1
E Hedrick St
900 HOUS 77011 3965 A6
W Hedrick St
800 HOUS 77011 3965 A6
Hedwig Cir
- HNCV 77024 3960 A1
10 HDWV 77024 3959 E1
10 HDWV 77024 3960 A1
10 HNCV 77024 3959 E2
Hedwig Ct
10 HNCV 77024 3959 E2
10 PNPV 77024 3959 E2
Hedwig Ln
11100 HNCV 77024 3959 E3
11100 PNPV 77024 3959 E3
Hedwig Rd
200 HNCV 77024 3959 E3
200 PNPV 77024 3959 E3
600 HDWV 77024 3959 E2
Hedwig Wy
800 HDWV 77024 3959 E1
Hedwig Green St
11000 HNCV 77024 3959 E3
11000 HNCV 77024 3960 A3
11000 PNPV 77024 3959 E3
Hedwig Shadows St
11000 HNCV 77024 3959 E2
11000 HNCV 77024 3960 A2
11000 PNPV 77024 3959 E2
Heffernan St
5600 HOUS 77087 4104 D7
5700 HOUS 77087 4244 D1
Heflin Ln
14900 HarC 77095 3678 E1
14900 HarC 77095 3679 B2
Heflin St
400 MAGA 77355 2669 A6
Heflin Colony Dr
9400 FBnC 77478 4236 C2
Hegar Rd
- WlrC 77447 2958 A1
- WlrC 77484 2957 E1
- WlrC 77484 2958 A1
17300 HarC 77447 3248 E2
18700 HarC 77447 3103 E4
Heidelberg Ct
9600 HarC 77070 3255 C6
Heidelberg St
300 CNRO 77301 2383 E2
300 CNRO 77301 2384 A2
Heiden Cir
16400 HarC 77379 3256 B5
Heidi Ln
23300 MtgC 77357 2974 A1
28100 TMBL 77375 2963 D5
Heidi Wy Ln
14200 HarC 77396 3547 D2
Heidler Rd
18300 MAGA 77354 2669 A5
Heidrich St
300 HOUS 77018 3823 B1
Heightmont Ests
27500 MtgC 77354 2819 A5
Heights Av
2400 TXCY 77590 4875 A5

STREET
Block City ZIP Map# Grid
Heights Blvd
10 HOUS 77007 3962 D1
800 HOUS 77007 3823 D7
800 HOUS 77008 3823 D7
20000 MtgC 77357 2829 B6
S Heights Blvd
- HOUS 77019 3962 D4
100 HOUS 77007 3962 D3
Heights Dr
10 LMQU 77568 4873 C7
10 LMQU 77568 4989 C1
1300 KATY 77493 3813 C6
Heights Dr N
- BzaC 77511 4748 B2
Heights Lp
- ALVN 77511 4749 A6
- BzaC 77511 4749 A6
Heights Rd
- BzaC 77511 4748 E5
800 ALVN 77511 4749 A6
800 BzaC 77511 4749 A6
Heights St
1200 PASD 77503 4108 A6
N Heights St
10 LMQU 77568 4873 C7
Heights Crossing Ln
7200 HarC 77396 3547 C2
E Heights Hollow Ln
700 HOUS 77007 3962 E3
N Heights Hollow Ln
3000 HOUS 77007 3962 E3
S Heights Hollow Ln
3000 HOUS 77007 3962 E3
W Heights Hollow Ln
700 HOUS 77007 3962 E3
Heights Manvel Rd
- ALVN 77511 4748 D6
100 BzaC 77511 4748 D6
Heilig Rd
7400 HOUS 77074 4100 B6
Heiner St
- HOUS 77007 3963 B4
700 HOUS 77002 3963 A5
700 HOUS 77019 3963 A5
Heirloom Rose Ln
3800 FBnC 77583 4622 B4
Heiser St
5600 HOUS 77087 4104 D7
5700 HOUS 77087 4244 D1
Heisse St
700 ALVN 77511 4867 B3
W Heisse St
800 ALVN 77511 4867 B3
Heite St
4300 HOUS 77022 3823 D2
Helberg Rd
3100 HOUS 77092 3822 B3
Helding Park Ct
2800 FBnC 77494 3951 D6
Helen Dr
200 DRPK 77536 4109 B5
1400 MtgC 77386 2968 E3
1400 MtgC 77386 2969 A3
Helen Ln
3300 BzaC 77584 4502 A7
3600 PRLD 77581 4503 E5
31200 TMBL 77375 2964 B3
Helen Rd
2200 FBnC 77469 4616 A1
4400 GlsC 77563 4990 B6
4400 HTCK 77563 4990 B6
Helen St
1100 DRPK 77536 4109 C5
2000 PASD 77502 4106 E7
2000 PASD 77502 4246 E1
2800 HOUS 77009 3963 A1
2900 HOUS 77009 3824 A7
Helena Bnd
8900 FBnC 77459 4621 C6
Helena Ln
- BzaC 77511 4748 A3
Helena St
2000 HOUS 77002 3963 A5
2000 HOUS 77019 3963 A5
2300 HOUS 77006 3963 A6
6800 BKVL 77581 4376 A6
Helene Ct
11900 MtgC 77362 2963 C1
Helga
17000 MAGA 77355 2668 E6
W Helgra St
100 DRPK 77536 4109 B5
Helm Ct N
16200 HarC 77532 3552 A3
Helm Ct S
16200 HarC 77532 3552 A3
Helmers St
4900 HOUS 77009 3824 C4
6100 HOUS 77022 3824 C2
9100 HOUS 77022 3685 B6
Helms
23800 MtgC 77365 2973 B5
Helms Dr
25500 HarC 77336 3121 D7
25500 HOUS 77336 3121 D7
Helms Rd
800 HOUS 77088 3544 A6
1200 HOUS 77088 3543 E6
W Helms Rd
100 HarC 77037 3544 C6
200 HOUS 77037 3544 B6
Helmsbrook Dr
8700 HarC 77089 4377 B6
Helmsdale St
- HOUS 77043 3819 E3
10200 HOUS 77043 3820 A3
Helmsley Dr
1400 RSBG 77471 4491 C5
2900 PRLD 77584 4501 A1
Helmsman St
500 HarC 77532 3552 B3
Helvick Blvd
12000 HOUS 77045 4242 C7
Helvick Crescent Av
12000 HOUS 77045 4242 C7
Hemingstone Ln
20000 HarC 77388 3112 E5
Hemington Cir
19100 HarC 77375 3255 A1
Hemington Dr
11200 HarC 77375 3255 A1
Hemingway Dr
- HOUS 77087 4244 E2
- HOUS 77087 4245 A2
Hemlock Cir
3200 DKSN 77539 4754 A1
Hemlock Dr
1300 HOUS 77017 4106 D6

STREET
Block City ZIP Map# Grid
Hemlock Dr
1300 PASD 77017 4106 D6
1300 PASD 77502 4106 D6
4500 BYTN 77521 3972 A2
5300 BYTN 77521 3971 E1
Hemlock Ln
25100 MtgC 77372 2536 E2
25200 MtgC 77372 2537 A2
Hemlock St
1900 TMBL 77375 3109 C3
6800 HOUS 77087 4105 A3
7100 HOUS 77012 4105 A3
Hemlock Bridge Ct
14800 FBnC 77478 4236 D6
Hemlock Hill Dr
8500 HarC 77083 4097 A7
8600 HarC 77083 4237 A1
Hemlock Lakes Dr
2000 HOUS 77345 3120 B6
Hemlock Park Dr
21800 HarC 77073 3259 E1
Hemphill St
- BYTN 77520 3972 D7
10 LMQU 77568 4873 D7
10 TXCY 77591 4873 D7
1500 HOUS 77007 3963 A2
Hemple Dr
1200 RSBG 77471 4491 D5
W Hempstead Av
1300 HOUS 77017 4106 D6
1300 PASD 77506 4106 D6
Hempstead Hwy
40300 WALR 77484 3102 A6
Hempstead Rd
- HarC 77429 3538 E3
- HarC 77447 3248 D2
- HarC 77484 3247 E1
- HarC 77484 3248 A1
8000 HOUS 77007 3961 D1
8000 HOUS 77008 3961 D1
8700 HOUS 77008 3822 C7
9000 HOUS 77092 3822 A5
10400 HOUS 77092 3821 E4
12800 HOUS 77040 3821 A1
12900 HOUS 77040 3681 A4
14400 HOUS 77041 3681 A4
14900 HarC 77040 3680 D2
14900 HOUS 77040 3680 E3
14900 HOUS 77041 3680 D2
15000 HarC 77041 3680 D2
15500 HarC 77040 3680 D2
15500 JRSV 77040 3680 D2
15500 JRSV 77041 3680 D2
19100 HarC 77065 3539 B4
20500 HarC 77429 3539 B4
24400 HarC 77095 3396 E5
24400 HarC 77095 3397 A6
24400 HarC 77433 3396 E5
27200 HarC 77429 3395 D1
27500 HarC 77433 3395 D1
37900 HarC 77484 3102 C7
39500 WALR 77484 3102 A6
Hempstead Rd US-290 BUS
- HarC 77447 3248 D2
- HarC 77484 3247 E1
- HarC 77484 3248 A1
37900 HarC 77484 3102 C7
39500 WALR 77484 3102 A6
Hemwick Dr
10400 HarC 77429 3538 E2
Hemwick Cove Dr
13600 HarC 77083 4097 B7
Hemwood Ct
4100 HarC 77039 3546 A3
Henck Av
7900 HTCK 77563 4988 E4
Henckle Dr
8100 HTCK 77563 4988 E4
Henderson Av
800 WEBS 77058 4507 E6
Henderson Ln
300 LGCY 77573 4630 C7
2400 DRPK 77536 4109 A7
Henderson St
100 PRVW 77445 3100 C2
1500 HOUS 77007 3963 A2
27200 HarC 77373 3113 E1
Henderson Point Dr
15200 HarC 77429 3397 C4
Hendon Ln
7000 HOUS 77074 4100 A6
7100 HOUS 77074 4099 E6
9200 HOUS 77036 4099 A6
9500 HOUS 77036 4098 E6
11200 HOUS 77072 4098 B6
Hendricks St
1500 HOUS 77093 3685 D7
Hendricksen Rd
13000 HOUS 77048 4375 A2
Hendricks Forest Ln
400 MtgC 77384 2675 B1
Hendricks Lake Dr
2400 HarC 77388 3113 B7
Hendricks Pass Dr
- HarC 77449 3676 C4
Henke St
500 HOUS 77020 3964 E1
Henkel Ln
2600 STFE 77510 4871 B4
Henley Ct
4100 FBnC 77479 4366 C6
Henley Dr
11500 HarC 77064 3399 C7
Henley St
5500 STFE 77510 4986 E2
Hennelly Dr
10000 MtgC 77354 2672 C6
Hennesey Dr
300 FBnC 77469 4365 B7
300 RHMD 77469 4365 B7
500 FBnC 77469 4492 B1
500 RHMD 77469 4492 B1
Hennessee Ln
400 HOUS 77598 4506 D2
Hennessy Ln
7900 HarC 77375 2965 E5
7900 HarC 77389 2965 E5
Henniker Ct
6100 HarC 77041 3679 C4
Henniker Dr
6100 HarC 77041 3679 C4
Henninger St
1200 HOUS 77023 3964 C7
1400 HOUS 77023 4104 C1
Hennington Dr
4900 HarC 77388 3112 B4
Heno St
9400 HOUS 77051 4243 C4

STREET
Block City ZIP Map# Grid
Henrico Ln
8600 FBnC 77469 4616 E1
Henrietta Av
100 WEBS 77598 4507 B6
Henrietta St
9100 HOUS 77088 3683 D2
Henry Ln
11400 MtgC 77302 2531 C6
Henry Rd
14000 HarC 77037 3544 E5
14000 HarC 77060 3544 E1
15900 HOUS 77060 3544 E1
Henry St
200 HOUS 77009 3963 B1
300 ALVN 77511 4749 C2
Henry Morgan Rd
16500 JMAB 77554 5331 E5
16500 JMAB 77554 5332 A5
16600 GLSN 77554 5331 E6
Hensen Creek Dr
15100 HarC 77086 3541 D1
Hensley Ln
- BzaC 77511 4747 D5
Henson St
7900 HOUS 77028 3826 B2
Hepburn St
2100 HOUS 77054 4102 E6
3000 HOUS 77054 4103 A6
Hepplewhite Wy
- WDLD 77382 2673 D7
Hera Dr
3500 MSCY 77459 4497 E5
Herald Av
3600 HOUS 77029 3826 C6
Herald Oak Ct
10 WDLD 77381 2821 C3
Heraldsburg Ln
8600 FBnC 77459 4621 B6
Herald Square Dr
11200 HOUS 77099 4238 B1
Herb Appel Cir
3200 FBnC 77459 4621 C6
Herben Rd
9400 HOUS 77093 3686 A6
Herbert Av
900 PASD 77506 4107 B5
Herbert Dr
3200 PRLD 77584 4627 C1
Herbert Ln
5800 TXCY 77591 4873 E7
Herbert St
- HOUS 77023 4105 A3
Herbie Dr
5400 FBnC 77469 4492 A7
5400 RSBG 77469 4492 A7
5800 FBnC 77469 4616 A1
Herbrand Dr
13600 HOUS 77034 4378 D5
Hercules Av
1000 HarC 77058 4507 C4
1000 HOUS 77058 4507 C4
Herd
3800 HOUS 77007 3962 C2
Herdsman Dr
800 HOUS 77079 3957 A2
Hereford Cir
3100 BzaC 77583 4500 E7
Hereford Dr
100 CNRO 77304 2383 B4
4800 HarC 77532 3412 E3
Hereford Ln
18100 NSUB 77058 4507 E5
18200 NSUB 77058 4508 A5
Hereford Rd
16600 HarC 77377 3254 C5
Hereford St
7600 HOUS 77087 4245 B1
Herford Ln
18100 NSUB 77058 4508 A5
Heritage N
1900 FBnC 77469 4364 C2
Heritage S
1200 FBnC 77469 4364 C3
Heritage Cir
10 MtgC 77354 2670 D3
Heritage Ct
10 BKHV 77024 3959 B3
17700 HarC 77598 4506 C7
Heritage Dr
- HarC 77493 3813 E3
5200 KATY 77493 3813 D3
14600 MtgC 77354 2670 B2
E Heritage Dr
10 FRDW 77546 4505 C7
W Heritage Dr
100 FRDW 77546 4505 B7
Heritage Ln
- KATY 77494 3952 D2
10 MtgC 77354 2670 E3
11900 BKHV 77024 3959 B3
18100 NSUB 77058 4508 A5
Heritage Pl
1300 SGLD 77479 4367 D6
Heritage Rd
19700 HarC 77377 3105 E6
19700 HarC 77377 3106 A5
Heritage Shr
300 HarC 77094 3955 E2
Heritage Tr
10 MtgC 77354 2670 D3
Heritage Bay Dr
17200 HarC 77598 4630 B1
Heritage Bend Ct
2300 HarC 77598 4506 C7
Heritage Bend Dr
2400 HarC 77598 4506 C7
2800 HarC 77598 4630 B1
Heritage Colony Ct
17800 HarC 77598 4506 C7
Heritage Colony Dr
2100 HarC 77546 4506 B6
2400 HarC 77598 4506 C7
2800 HarC 77598 4630 C1
3600 MSCY 77459 4496 B3
Heritage Country Ct
15500 HarC 77546 4505 D5
Heritage Country Ln
4600 HarC 77546 4505 E5
Heritage Cove Ct
17700 HarC 77598 4506 C7
Heritage Cove Dr
17500 HarC 77598 4506 C7
Heritage Creek Ct
17500 HarC 77598 4506 C7
Heritage Creek Dr
17600 HarC 77598 4506 C7
Heritage Creek Lndg
1200 HOUS 77008 3822 D7

STREET
Block City ZIP Map# Grid
Heritage Creek Pk
1200 HOUS 77008 3822 E7
Heritage Creek Ter
3000 HOUS 77008 3822 E6
Heritage Creek Vil
1200 HOUS 77008 3822 E7
Heritage Creek Oaks
3000 HOUS 77008 3822 D6
Heritage Crown Ct
12000 HOUS 77047 4374 B1
Heritage Elm Ct
19600 HarC 77084 3816 A4
Heritage Falls Dr
15600 HarC 77546 4505 E5
Heritage Forest Ln
21300 MtgC 77365 2973 A3
Heritage Glen Dr
1100 DRPK 77536 4109 A7
E Heritage Grand Cir
- FBnC 77494 4093 B6
N Heritage Grand Cir
25100 FBnC 77494 4093 B6
S Heritage Grand Cir
- FBnC 77494 4093 B6
W Heritage Grand Cir
- FBnC 77494 4093 B6
Heritage Grand Ln
- FBnC 77494 4093 B2
Heritage Green Dr
3100 PRLD 77581 4503 D2
Heritage Grove Dr
12200 HarC 77066 3401 C5
Heritage Haven Ct
6700 RSBG 77469 4493 A7
Heritage Hill Cir
10 WDLD 77381 2820 B3
N Heritage Hill Cir
10 WDLD 77381 2820 C3
Heritage House Cir
17300 HarC 77598 4630 B1
Heritage House Dr
2900 HarC 77598 4630 B1
Heritage Landing Dr
2300 PRLD 77581 4503 E2
Heritage Oaks Dr
200 TXCY 77591 4873 B6
E Heritage Oaks Dr
23400 MtgC 77365 2973 E5
N Heritage Oaks Dr
100 TXCY 77591 4873 B6
S Heritage Oaks Dr
300 TXCY 77591 4873 B7
W Heritage Oaks Dr
23100 MtgC 77365 2973 E5
Heritage Oaks Ln
200 PNPV 77024 3959 D5
Heritage Pines Dr
7500 HarC 77346 3265 B5
Heritage Plains Dr
4800 HarC 77546 4505 E6
Heritage Point Blvd
18900 MtgC 77355 2815 A4
Heritage Point Ln
- PRLD 77583 4500 B5
Heritage Trail Ct
10500 FBnC 77459 4622 A5
Heritage Trail Dr
4100 HOUS 77047 4374 C1
Heritage Waters Ct
9900 HarC 77396 3407 B7
Heritage Wood Dr
14800 HarC 77082 4096 C4
Herkimer St
700 HOUS 77007 3962 C1
800 HOUS 77007 3823 C7
800 HOUS 77008 3823 C7
Herman St
400 HMBL 77338 3262 E6
Hermann Dr
- HOUS 77005 4102 E2
200 ALVN 77511 4749 C4
1100 HOUS 77004 4102 E2
1100 HOUS 77030 4102 E2
1800 HOUS 77004 4103 A3
1800 HOUS 77030 4103 A3
Hermann Rd
5900 HarC 77050 3546 E6
5900 HOUS 77050 3546 E6
6000 HarC 77050 3547 A6
6000 HOUS 77050 3547 A6
9400 HarC 77050 3548 A6
Hermann Cir Dr
10 HOUS 77030 4102 E2
Hermann Lake Dr
100 HOUS 77030 4102 E2
6300 HOUS 77021 4103 A4
Hermann Museum Cir Dr
- HOUS 77030 4103 A3
10 HOUS 77004 4103 A3
Hermann Park Ct
- HOUS 77030 4103 A4
10 HOUS 77021 4103 A4
Hermitage Ct
500 MtgC 77302 2530 C6
Hermitage Ln
12800 HOUS 77024 3958 D3
12800 HOUS 77079 3958 D3
Hermitage Trc
- HarC 77038 3543 C5
Hermitage Hollow Ln
3900 HOUS 77339 3119 A2
Hermitage Oaks Ct
12100 HarC 77377 3254 D6
Hermitage Oaks Dr
15500 HarC 77377 3254 D6
Hermit Thrush Ln
14700 HarC 77377 2963 C5
Hermit Thrush Pl
10 WDLD 77382 2674 E4
Hermosa Ct
11200 PNPV 77024 3959 E4
Hermosa Dr
26400 FBnC 77494 4092 A6
Hernandez Rd
1200 HOUS 77504 4247 D7
1200 PASD 77504 4247 D7
Herndon Dr
1000 RSBG 77471 4491 C3
Herngrif St
16100 HOUS 77032 3404 C5
Heron Av
5500 GLSN 77551 5108 D7
Heron Ct
10 MtgC 77355 2960 C3
100 MtgC 77385 2676 D4
1100 SGLD 77478 4368 C3
Heron Dr
2900 GLSN 77551 5108 D7

STREET
Block City ZIP Map# Grid

Heron Dr
5400 HOUS 77033 4243 E4
5400 HOUS 77033 4244 A4
6800 HOUS 77087 4244 E3
7100 HOUS 77087 4245 A2
N Heron Dr
1000 SEBK 77586 4383 A7
1200 SEBK 77586 4382 E7
S Heron Dr
1300 SEBK 77586 4382 E7
Heron Ln
600 PASD 77502 4247 A1
5300 PRLD 77584 4502 B7
7200 TXCY 77591 4873 C6
18800 HarC 77377 2962 A7
18900 HarC 77377 2961 E7
Heron St
4400 GlsC 77563 4990 A6
Heron Tr
15900 HarC 77377 3254 D5
Heron Wy
1000 SGLD 77478 4368 C4
Heron Cove Ct
18600 HarC 77084 3816 C1
Heron Field Ct
13500 HOUS 77059 4379 E4
Heron Flight St
8700 HarC 77064 3541 A1
Heron Forest Ln
18000 HarC 77346 3408 B1
Herongate Dr
15800 HarC 77084 3678 E6
Heron Hollow Ct
10 WDLD 77382 2819 B2
Heron Inlet N
100 BYTN 77520 4113 D5
Heron Inlet S
100 BYTN 77520 4113 C5
Heron Lakes Ct
10 HarC 77064 3541 B1
Heron Lakes Dr
7400 HarC 77064 3541 A1
Heron Marsh Dr
14300 HarC 77429 3396 E1
Heron Meadow Ln
15100 HarC 77429 3253 C7
Heron Meadows Dr
9900 HarC 77095 3538 A3
Heron Nest Dr
8700 HarC 77064 3541 A1
8800 HarC 77064 3540 E1
Heron Nest Rd
- HarC 77064 3541 A1
Heron Nest St
11000 HarC 77064 3541 A1
Heron Park Ct
7600 HarC 77396 3406 C7
Heron Park Dr
15200 HarC 77396 3406 C7
Heron Point Dr
16400 HarC 77429 3396 E1
Herons Crest Ln
3600 HarC 77338 3260 A1
Herons Terrace St
21000 FBnC 77469 4234 B4
Heron View St
8700 HarC 77064 3541 A1
Heron Village Dr
11000 HarC 77064 3540 E1
Heron Walk St
8700 HarC 77064 3541 A1
Heronwood Dr
5400 HarC 77346 3264 C4
Herrick Ct
700 HarC 77450 3954 D2
Herridge Rd
17300 BzaC 77584 4626 C2
17300 MNVL 77584 4626 C2
17300 PRLD 77584 4626 C2
Herridge St
4300 HOUS 77022 3823 D2
Herring Blvd
14500 MtgC 77354 2670 B1
Herring Dr
10 BYUV 77563 4990 D6
10 GlsC 77563 4990 E6
Herring Rd
- BzaC 77511 4627 E7
100 BzaC 77511 4748 C4
1400 BzaC 77511 4866 C1
Herring St
500 ALVN 77511 4867 B2
Herringbone Dr
1900 HOUS 77489 4371 A5
Herrington Rd
800 GlsC 77511 4869 A3
Herrnhut Dr
17300 HarC 77598 4630 B1
Herschell St
7600 HOUS 77028 3826 B1
Herschellwood Dr
- HOUS 77033 4244 A2
8000 HOUS 77033 4243 E3
Hershe St
6900 HOUS 77020 3964 E1
6900 HOUS 77020 3965 B1
7900 HOUS 77029 3965 B1
13700 HarC 77015 3967 E1
14000 HarC 77015 3968 A1
Hershy Beach Dr
12200 GLSN 77554 5220 D7
Hertford St
6000 HOUS 77048 4375 D3
Hertford Park Dr
6700 HarC 77084 3679 B3
Hertfordshire Cir
8000 HarC 77379 3256 B2
Hertfordshire Dr
7600 HarC 77379 3256 B2
Herts Rd
8300 HarC 77379 3256 A6
Hervey Ln
- LGCY 77573 4631 C6
Heslep St
600 HOUS 77009 3824 A6
Hess Vly
- MtgC 77355 2962 B5
Hesse Ct
22200 HarC 77449 3815 A4
Hessen St
11600 HOUS 77034 4378 A2
Hessenford St
10 SGLD 77479 4495 D3
Hesta St
6100 HOUS 77016 3686 D5
Hester St
900 SEBK 77586 4509 E2

Heterodox View Av
- HOUS 77080 3820 E5
- HOUS 77080 3821 A5
Hettie St
3000 FBnC 77471 4614 B4
Hewing Dr
17100 HarC 77546 4506 B6
Hewitt Dr
- MtgC 77381 2821 D3
- WDLD 77381 2821 D3
1300 HOUS 77018 3683 D7
1400 HOUS 77018 3822 B1
5500 HOUS 77092 3821 D1
Hewitt St
1600 LGCY 77573 4632 E4
2600 LGCY 77573 4633 A4
Hewn Rock Wy
2600 PRLD 77584 4501 A3
Hewrick St
3300 HOUS 77020 3826 B6
Hexham Ct
9500 HarC 77379 3256 B6
Hexham Dr
16100 HarC 77379 3255 E6
16100 HarC 77379 3256 A6
Heysham St
500 HOUS 77013 3966 B1
Hezekiah Ln
8100 HOUS 77088 3683 C2
HH Ranch Rd
15900 HOUS 77032 3405 B6
Hialeah Dr
1800 SEBK 77586 4509 D1
2200 HOUS 77018 3822 B2
4900 HOUS 77092 3822 A2
5300 HOUS 77092 3821 E2
Hialeah Ln
4300 DRPK 77503 4108 D7
4300 DRPK 77536 4108 D7
4300 PASD 77503 4108 D7
Hiawatha Dr
8500 HOUS 77036 4099 B4
Hiawatha Ln
3900 PASD 77505 4248 A5
Hiawatha St
7800 HarC 77521 3833 B3
Hibernia Dr
9900 HOUS 77088 3682 B1
10000 HOUS 77088 3542 B7
Hibiscus Ln
16400 FRDW 77546 4505 E7
16400 FRDW 77546 4629 E1
16700 FRDW 77546 4630 A1
Hibiscus Point Dr
16700 HarC 77095 3538 A2
Hibury Dr
10 BKHV 77024 3959 B4
10 HOUS 77024 3959 B5
Hickerson St
500 CNRO 77301 2384 A7
600 CNRO 77301 2383 E7
Hickery Harvest Dr
- FBnC 77469 4234 D2
Hicklin St
2200 ALVN 77511 4866 D3
Hickman St
5600 HOUS 77026 3825 D4
Hickman Manor Ln
21500 HarC 77449 3676 D5
Hickok Ln
4100 HOUS 77047 4243 C7
4100 HOUS 77047 4374 C1
8000 HOUS 77075 4376 D1
8900 HOUS 77075 4377 A1
Hickory
700 HarC 77532 3692 C3
Hickory Ct
10 BKHV 77024 3959 B4
1500 PRLD 77581 4504 E4
28000 MtgC 77355 2814 B6
31700 MtgC 77355 2669 B7
Hickory Dr
23500 MtgC 77365 2974 B6
27900 MtgC 77372 2683 D3
Hickory Hl
- WlrC 77447 2813 C3
Hickory Hllw
900 HNCV 77024 3960 C1
Hickory Ln
- MtgC 77357 2829 A5
- MtgC 77372 2683 A6
- PTVL 77372 2683 A6
1200 HarC 77532 3692 B1
1200 HOUS 77339 3263 C1
2100 PASD 77502 4107 D4
2100 PASD 77502 4247 D1
3400 DRPK 77536 4109 B7
3400 DRPK 77536 4249 B1
7300 BYTN 77521 3835 B5
16200 MtgC 77302 2680 A5
16500 MtgC 77372 2682 E6
16500 PTVL 77372 2682 E6
19400 MtgC 77355 2961 B5
Hickory St
- MtgC 77302 2677 A2
600 FBnC 77545 4623 A3
1000 HOUS 77002 3963 B3
1300 HOUS 77007 3963 B2
23000 WlrC 77447 2813 D2
N Hickory St
600 TMBL 77375 2964 B6
Hickory Ter
- LGCY 77598 4630 C4
Hickory Wy
2400 RSBG 77471 4491 A6
Hickory Ashe Dr
18700 HarC 77346 3265 C6
Hickorybark Dr
10 WDLD 77381 2820 E5
Hickory Bay Ct
2000 HarC 77450 3954 D5
Hickory Bend Ct
1500 PRLD 77581 4376 D7
3100 HarC 77084 3816 C5
Hickory Bend Dr
12600 HarC 77070 3399 C5
Hickory Bend Ln
1600 PRLD 77581 4376 D7
1600 PRLD 77581 4503 E1
Hickory Bough Ct
16200 MtgC 77302 2678 E4
Hickory Branch Ln
8600 HarC 77338 3262 A4
Hickory Brook Ln
3200 HOUS 77345 3119 D4
Hickory Burl Ln
1600 CNRO 77301 2384 E6

Hickory Canyon Ct
7300 HarC 77396 3547 C1
Hickory Chase Ct
20300 HarC 77450 3954 E4
Hickory Chase Dr
1700 HarC 77450 3954 E4
Hickory Cove Dr
15900 HarC 77095 3538 C6
Hickory Creek Dr
1900 HOUS 77339 3118 D6
3400 PRLD 77581 4376 C6
Hickorycrest Dr
6100 HarC 77389 2966 D5
Hickory Dale St
15300 HarC 77429 3252 B7
Hickory Downs Dr
4300 HarC 77084 3817 E1
4300 HOUS 77084 3817 E1
4400 HarC 77084 3678 E7
Hickory Falls Dr
3000 HOUS 77345 3119 E4
Hickory Farm Dr
20800 HarC 77449 3815 C4
Hickory Field Ct
26300 HarC 77433 3396 B4
Hickory Forest Dr
5400 HarC 77088 3682 E1
Hickory Garden Ln
18500 HarC 77084 3816 C4
Hickorygate Dr
4300 HarC 77373 3115 B5
Hickory Glen Ct
- HOUS 77339 3118 E3
- HOUS 77339 3119 A3
Hickory Glen Dr
1900 MSCY 77489 4370 B5
Hickory Green Ct
4900 HOUS 77345 3120 A1
5000 HOUS 77365 3120 A1
Hickory Grove Dr
4300 HarC 77084 3678 D7
4300 HarC 77084 3817 D1
Hickory Grove Ln
3100 BzaC 77584 4374 B7
Hickory Hill Ct
1800 SGLD 77478 4369 B6
Hickory Hill Ln
11800 HarC 77429 3398 C3
Hickory Hill Rd
24700 MtgC 77380 2967 B3
Hickory Hollow Dr
6000 PRLD 77581 4375 D7
Hickory Hollow Ln
2300 MtgC 77386 2969 B4
6100 CNRO 77304 2237 A6
12000 MtgC 77362 2963 B1
Hickory Hollow Pl
10 WDLD 77381 2820 D5
Hickory Hollow Rd
3200 MtgC 77380 2967 A1
Hickory Hollow St
900 HNCV 77024 3960 C1
900 HOUS 77024 3960 C1
900 SPVL 77024 3960 C1
5700 FBnC 77469 4232 E7
5700 FBnC 77469 4233 A7
Hickory Knob Dr
3700 HOUS 77339 3119 C4
Hickory Knoll Dr
3200 PRLD 77581 4376 D6
15700 HOUS 77059 4380 C5
16400 PASD 77059 4380 C5
Hickory Lake Dr
1400 FBnC 77545 4622 E1
Hickory Lawn Dr
1900 HOUS 77077 3958 A6
Hickory Limb Ct
2800 LGCY 77573 4632 E2
2800 LGCY 77573 4633 A2
Hickory Manor Dr
1800 HarC 77336 3266 E4
1800 HarC 77336 3267 A3
Hickory Meadow Ct
13900 HarC 77044 3549 D2
Hickory Meadow Ln
19400 HarC 77084 3816 A4
Hickory Mill Ct
7800 HarC 77095 3537 E7
Hickory Oak Dr
10 WDLD 77381 2821 A3
4200 HarC 77389 3112 C1
Hickory Park Cir
3100 SGLD 77479 4495 C1
E Hickory Park Cir
3000 SGLD 77479 4495 C2
W Hickory Park Cir
3000 SGLD 77479 4495 C1
Hickory Park Dr
2000 HOUS 77345 3120 B6
Hickory Point Ct
7500 HarC 77095 3678 B1
Hickory Point Rd
16100 HarC 77095 3538 C7
16200 HarC 77095 3678 C1
Hickory Post Ct
1000 TMBL 77375 2964 D5
Hickory Post Ln
400 HOUS 77079 3957 E3
Hickory Ranch Dr
17500 HarC 77447 3249 D2
Hickory Ridge Ct
100 BKHV 77024 3959 A6
Hickory Ridge Dr
10 BKHV 77024 3959 B5
10 HarC 77336 2976 C5
10 HOUS 77024 3959 B5
200 SHEH 77381 2822 A2
300 ELGO 77586 4509 A1
9600 MtgC 77303 2239 A3
Hickory Ridge Rd
37200 MtgC 77354 2816 A1
Hickory Run Dr
- SGLD 77479 4495 D1
Hickory Shadows Dr
10 HLSV 77055 3821 C7
10 HOUS 77055 3821 C7
Hickory Springs Dr
5800 HOUS 77345 3120 C5
Hickory Springs Ln
13300 PRLD 77584 4499 E4
13300 PRLD 77584 4500 A5
Hickory Tail Ln
10000 HarC 77064 3540 C3
Hickory Terrace Dr
3700 MtgC 77386 2969 E3
3800 MtgC 77386 2970 A3
Hickorytex Dr
14800 HOUS 77396 3406 C7

Hickorytex Dr
14800 HOUS 77396 3547 C1
14900 HarC 77396 3406 C7
Hickory Trace Ct
9900 HarC 77070 3255 B3
Hickory Trail Pl
2100 HarC 77450 3954 D5
Hickory Tree Ct
10900 HarC 77065 3539 C2
Hickory Twig Wy
19600 HarC 77388 3113 C5
19600 HarC 77388 3113 D6
Hickory Valley Ln
25300 HarC 77373 3114 B3
Hickory View Ct
3800 HarC 77546 4506 A6
Hickory View Ln
13100 HarC 77090 3402 D2
Hickory Village Cir
2100 HOUS 77345 3120 B3
Hickory Village Ct
2100 HOUS 77345 3120 B3
Hickory Village Dr
5300 HOUS 77345 3120 A4
Hickory Wind Dr
20100 HarC 77346 3265 A4
Hickorywood Dr
11900 MtgC 77362 2817 B7
Hickory Wood Ln
- BzaC 77584 4374 B7
Hickorywood Ln
800 HDWV 77024 3959 D1
Hicks St
- CNRO 77301 2384 A5
- HarC 77377 2963 E7
- HOUS 77007 3962 E2
- TMBL 77377 2963 E7
500 TMBL 77375 2964 A7
600 CNRO 77301 2383 E6
1300 TMBL 77375 2963 E7
Hicks Bay Ln
22900 FBnC 77469 4093 D6
Hicksfield St
- HOUS 77023 4104 A1
Hidalgo St
- HOUS 77057 3960 D7
5000 HOUS 77027 3961 A7
5000 HOUS 77056 3961 A7
5300 HOUS 77056 3960 D7
6400 HarC 77521 3832 E6
Hidalgo Valley Ln
14900 HarC 77090 3258 D7
Hidden Ct
9200 MtgC 77354 2818 C2
Hidden Hvn
15700 HarC 77095 3538 D4
Hidden Pk
- HarC 77049 3829 C3
- HarC 77530 3829 D4
Hidden Rdg E
800 HarC 77073 3259 C6
Hidden Rdg W
700 HarC 77073 3259 C6
Hidden Acres Dr
16000 HarC 77084 3678 D7
Hidden Arbor Ln
6300 HOUS 77088 3682 B2
7000 HOUS 77040 3682 B2
Hidden Bay Ct
2700 PRLD 77584 4500 D3
Hiddenbay Ct
8000 HarC 77379 3256 B1
Hidden Bay Dr
11300 PRLD 77584 4500 D4
Hiddenbay Wy
18500 HarC 77379 3256 A1
Hidden Bend Dr
11000 HarC 77064 3540 C2
Hidden Bluff Ln
- MtgC 77386 2969 C6
Hidden Branch Dr
- HarC 77049 3829 D4
- HarC 77530 3829 D4
Hidden Breeze Dr
1700 HarC 77530 3829 D4
Hiddenbriar Lp
23700 HarC 77375 2965 B6
Hidden Bridle Ct
21100 HarC 77073 3259 C6
Hidden Brook Ln
1700 LGCY 77573 4751 E2
3700 HarC 77449 3815 A1
Hidden Canyon Rd
800 HarC 77450 3953 E4
800 HarC 77450 3954 A3
Hidden Castle Dr
12700 HarC 77015 3828 C6
Hidden Chase Dr
1600 HarC 77530 3829 E4
Hidden Chestnut Ln
4800 HarC 77084 3677 B7
Hidden Clover Cir
15000 HarC 77433 3250 E6
Hidden Colony Ln
6700 LGCY 77539 4752 E5
Hidden Cove
10 MSCY 77459 4497 B4
15800 HOUS 77079 3956 E1
28500 MtgC 77355 2815 E5
28600 MtgC 77354 2818 C3
Hidden Cove Ct
- MSCY 77459 4497 B4
1900 LGCY 77573 4509 A7
Hidden Cove Ln
28800 MtgC 77354 2818 C2
Hidden Cove Pk
9500 MtgC 77354 2818 C2
Hidden Creek Dr
1900 HOUS 77339 3118 D6
2400 PRLD 77581 4504 A3
3300 SGLD 77479 4495 E1
3900 HOUS 77339 3119 C3
Hidden Creek Ln
700 FRDW 77546 4505 B5
Hidden Crest Dr
15900 HarC 77530 3829 D4
Hidden Crest Wy
6300 FBnC 77479 4367 A7
Hidden Deer Ln
16200 MtgC 77302 2678 E4
Hidden Deer Corner Ct
10 WDLD 77381 2820 E5
Hidden Dell Ct
13500 HOUS 77059 4379 D5
Hidden Falls Ct
21800 FBnC 77450 4093 E4
Hidden Falls Dr
10000 PRLD 77584 4501 A2

Hidden Forest Cir
17500 HarC 77379 3256 A3
Hidden Forest Dr
- FRDW 77546 4629 A4
17600 HarC 77379 3256 A2
19100 HarC 77433 3537 B7
19100 HarC 77433 3677 B1
Hidden Fort Ln
3900 MSCY 77459 4496 C1
Hidden Garden Dr
2600 HOUS 77339 3119 C4
Hidden Garden Mist Ln
21400 HarC 77449 3676 D5
Hidden Gate Ct
16300 FBnC 77478 4236 A5
Hidden Glen Ln
- PRLD 77581 4376 E7
- PRLD 77581 4503 D1
Hidden Grove Ct
11500 HarC 77377 3254 D5
Hidden Grove Tr
16200 HarC 77377 3254 D4
Hidden Harbor St
400 HOUS 77079 3956 E1
Hidden Hill Cir
1500 HOUS 77339 3263 C2
Hidden Hollow Ln
15200 FBnC 77478 4236 C6
Hidden Hollow Wy
- FBnC 77459 4621 E6
Hidden Knoll Ct
2700 SGLD 77478 4369 A7
Hidden Lake Cir
9200 MtgC 77354 2818 C2
Hidden Lake Ct
28900 MtgC 77354 2818 C2
Hidden Lake Dr
100 LGCY 77573 4509 B6
9200 MtgC 77354 2818 C3
Hidden Lake Ln
10100 FBnC 77469 4232 C2
10800 FBnC 77469 4092 C7
13800 SGLD 77478 4237 A7
W Hidden Lake Ln
10100 FBnC 77469 4232 C2
Hidden Lake Rd
- MtgC 77380 2967 B3
Hidden Lakes Dr
5900 HOUS 77345 3120 C5
Hidden Landing Dr
2700 PRLD 77584 4500 D3
Hidden Leaf Dr
- HarC 77049 3829 C4
Hidden Links Ct
4200 HOUS 77339 3119 D7
Hidden Manor Dr
15900 HarC 77530 3829 D4
Hidden Maple Dr
23500 HarC 77373 3114 D6
Hidden Meadow Dr
10 WDLD 77382 2673 E4
10 WDLD 77382 2674 A5
14200 SGLD 77478 4236 B4
Hidden Meadows Dr
- HarC 77336 2976 D7
Hidden Mist Ct
3000 BzaC 77584 4501 B4
Hidden Moon Dr
10400 HarC 77064 3540 C2
Hidden Nest Ct
4900 HarC 77084 3677 C7
Hidden Oak Ln
700 FRDW 77546 4505 B4
N Hidden Oaks
11000 MtgC 77384 2528 B7
11000 MtgC 77384 2674 B1
Hidden Oaks Ln
7700 HarC 77095 3538 B7
Hidden Oaks St
1100 LGCY 77573 4631 D4
Hidden Park Ct
2400 FBnC 77469 4493 A2
Hidden Park Dr
1600 HarC 77530 3829 D4
1700 HarC 77049 3829 D4
Hidden Park Ln
2500 MtgC 77385 2823 B7
Hidden Pine Ln
600 FRDW 77546 4505 A4
Hidden Pines Ct
200 LGCY 77573 4630 E5
Hidden Pines Dr
- MtgC 77339 3118 E3
3400 HOUS 77339 3118 E4
Hidden Point Ln
20300 FBnC 77469 4094 C6
Hidden Pond Pl
10 WDLD 77381 2820 E2
Hidden Port Ln
10000 HarC 77089 4504 E2
Hidden Quail Ln
8200 HOUS 77489 4370 C7
Hidden Ranch Dr
20300 HarC 77449 3676 D4
Hidden River Ct
16300 MtgC 77302 2679 A4
Hidden River Ln
12000 PRLD 77583 4500 C5
Hidden Rose Ln
12400 HarC 77044 3689 B2
Hidden Shadow Ln
19700 HarC 77433 3677 B1
Hidden Shire Ln
- HarC 77377 3254 A3
Hidden Shore Cir
20600 HarC 77450 3954 B6
Hidden Shore Dr
2400 HarC 77450 3954 C6
Hidden Spring Falls Dr
2700 MtgC 77386 2969 D4
Hidden Springs Cir
2800 BzaC 77578 4501 B7
Hidden Springs Dr
4500 HarC 77084 3679 A7
Hidden Spring Vale Dr
2700 MtgC 77386 2969 D4
Hidden Terrace Dr
1400 FBnC 77479 4494 A6
1700 HarC 77530 3829 D4
Hidden Timbers Ln
26400 KATY 77494 3952 A3
Hidden Trace Ct
4400 HarC 77066 3401 C4
Hidden Trail Ct
17700 HarC 77379 3255 E3
Hidden Trail Ln
8000 HarC 77379 3256 A3
8300 HarC 77379 3255 E3

Hidden Trail Pl
- MtgC 77384 2675 D7
- WDLD 77384 2675 D7
Hidden Trails Ct
7100 FBnC 77479 4493 C5
Hidden Treasure Cir
16900 HarC 77546 4506 B7
16900 HarC 77546 4630 B1
Hidden Valley Dr
500 HOUS 77037 3544 B6
500 HOUS 77037 3544 B6
700 HOUS 77088 3544 A7
1300 HOUS 77088 3543 D6
N Hidden View Cir
10 WDLD 77381 2820 C2
S Hidden View Cir
10 WDLD 77381 2820 C2
Hidden View Pl
10 WDLD 77381 2820 D2
Hidden Village Dr
1800 HarC 77530 3829 E4
Hidden Villas Dr
1700 HOUS 77339 3118 E7
Hidden Winds Dr
4000 MtgC 77386 2970 C7
4200 MtgC 77386 3115 D1
Hiddenwood Dr
15000 HarC 77070 3254 D7
Hidden Woods Ln
700 FRDW 77546 4505 B5
N Hide Ct
21100 HarC 77073 3259 B6
S Hide Ct
20900 HarC 77073 3259 B6
Hideaway Cir
10 HOUS 77074 4239 E1
Hideaway Ct E
8100 HarC 77389 2965 C2
Hideaway Ct W
8200 HarC 77389 2965 E2
Hideaway Dr
10 FRDW 77546 4629 D2
Hideaway Ln
3300 HarC 77388 3258 A1
Hideaway Bend Ln
9900 HarC 77044 3689 A3
N Hideaway Bend Ln
12400 HarC 77044 3689 B2
Hideaway Lake Ct
8100 HarC 77389 2966 A1
8200 HarC 77389 2965 E2
Hideaway Park Dr
12400 HarC 77429 3398 E5
Hideaway Run Dr
25100 HarC 77389 2965 E2
25100 HarC 77389 2966 A2
Hideaway Runway
8100 HarC 77389 2965 C2
8100 HarC 77389 2966 A1
Hiensley St
300 HOUS 77009 3963 C2
Hiford Dr
3700 HOUS 77047 4374 C2
Higgins Fy
100 FBnC 77479 4367 A5
Higgins Rd
1300 HMBL 77338 3263 A6
Higgins St
- MTBL 77520 3696 D5
100 HMBL 77338 3262 E6
4800 HOUS 77033 4243 E4
5200 HOUS 77033 4244 A4
W Higgins St
100 HMBL 77338 3262 D6
High
300 MSCY 77489 4370 C2
High St
10 BYTN 77520 4112 E1
200 TMBL 77375 2964 A7
3500 HOUS 77007 3962 D2
High Banks Ln
13500 HOUS 77034 4378 D4
High Bridge Ct
11400 HarC 77065 3539 E3
24700 FBnC 77494 4093 C2
Highbrook Dr
- HarC 77095 3538 E6
Highbury Ct
5700 HarC 77084 3678 A4
Highbury View Ct
13100 HOUS 77047 4373 B3
Highbush Ct
10 WDLD 77381 2674 D7
High Canyon Ct
2900 HarC 77450 3954 B7
4500 LGCY 77573 4630 E5
High Canyon Ln
19100 HarC 77377 3254 C1
High Castle Ct
3000 HOUS 77059 4379 E3
High Chaparral
36300 MtgC 77355 2815 D6
Highclere Park Dr
10 HarC 77379 3110 E7
Highcliff Ct
15000 HarC 77049 3829 A2
Highcliff Ln
- FBnC 77469 4094 E2
High Cotton Ln
12700 HOUS 77072 4097 D4
High Creek Dr
17800 HarC 77379 3255 E3
Highcrest Dr
1900 MSCY 77489 4370 C5
8300 HOUS 77055 3821 B5
8500 HOUS 77080 3821 A5
9100 HOUS 77080 3820 D5
Highcroft Dr
14100 HOUS 77077 3956 E4
Highcroft Forest
7900 FBnC 77479 4494 B5
Highdale Ct
19700 HarC 77346 3264 E5
High Desert Ln
24800 FBnC 77494 3953 C6
Highet Pl
20800 HarC 77375 3110 A4
Highfalls Dr
3500 HarC 77068 3257 C5
High Falls Ln
1800 PRLD 77581 4503 E1
High Ferry Ln
13800 HarC 77429 3397 C1
Highfield Dr
15600 HarC 77095 3538 D5
Highfield Ridge Ln
22400 HarC 77373 3259 B1

High Forest Dr
- HarC 77346 3408
High Gale Ct
1800 SGLD 77478 4369
High Glen Ct
5200 HOUS 77345 3119
Highgreen Dr
3500 HOUS 77339 3119
High Grove Ct
10 CNRO 77384 2675
Highgrove Dr
11300 HOUS 77077 3958
High Grove Ln
4100 FBnC 77494 4092
Highgrove Pk
700 HOUS 77024 3960
High Haven Dr
8800 FBnC 77083 4236
High Knob Dr
10900 HarC 77065 3539
High Knoll Dr
6500 FBnC 77479 4493
High Knoll Ln
7900 HarC 77095 3537
Highknoll Ln
4000 TYLV 77586 4508
Highland Cir
10 WDLD 77381 2821
Highland Ct
2700 SGLD 77478 4369
30400 MtgC 77354 2672
N Highland Ct
10 WDLD 77381 2821
S Highland Ct
10 WDLD 77381 2821
Highland Dr
- GlsC 77568 4990
- LMQU 77568 4990
10 GlsC 77563 4990
10 HTCK 77563 4988
1300 ALVN 77511 4867
19700 MtgC 77357 2828
Highland Rd
5100 GlsC 77517 4986
5100 STFE 77517 4986
5700 HTCK 77517 4986
7500 GlsC 77510 4986
Highland Rdg
- FBnC 77479 4494
Highland St
100 TXCY 77591 4873
300 HOUS 77009 3824
900 HOUS 77009 3823
1100 HOUS 77008 3823
Highland Ter
100 LGCY 77573 4631
Highland Tr
18700 HarC 77084 3816
Highland Arbor Dr
7800 HarC 77070 3399
Highland Bay Ct
2000 HarC 77450 3954
Highland Bayou Dr
7200 GlsC 77563 4990
Highland Bluff Dr
8100 FBnC 77479 4494
Highland Bluff Ln
22600 HarC 77373 3114
Highland Branch Dr
- HarC 77346 3264
Highland Branch Ln
1400 HarC 77373 3114
Highland Breeze Ln
- WDLD 77382 2820
Highland Brook Dr
15900 FBnC 77083 4096
Highland Canyon Dr
17000 HarC 77095 3537
17100 HarC 77095 3538
Highland Castle Ln
13400 HarC 77015 3828
Highland Cove Dr
13600 HarC 77070 3399
Highland Creek Ranch Dr
- HarC 77449 3676
Highland Cross Dr
100 HarC 77073 3258
400 HarC 77073 3259
Highland Crossing Dr
2200 CNRO 77304 2236
Highland Elm St
15200 HarC 77433 3251
Highlander Dr
16000 HarC 77082 4096
Highland Estates Blvd
29500 MtgC 77354 2818
30000 MtgC 77354 2672
Highland Estates Ct
22900 MtgC 77385 2823
Highland Falls Ln
5200 FBnC 77450 4093
5300 FBnC 77450 4094
Highland Farms Rd
7500 HarC 77095 3538
Highland Fern Ct
2700 HOUS 77345 3119
Highland Forest Dr
8000 FBnC 77479 4494
Highlandgate Dr
22200 HarC 77373 3116
22200 HarC 77373 3261
Highland Glade Ct
21800 MtgC 77339 3118
Highland Glen Dr
7800 HarC 77070 3399
Highland Glen Ln
1600 PRLD 77581 4503
Highland Green Ct
7900 HarC 77070 3399
Highland Green Dr
8100 FBnC 77479 4494
Highland Hills Dr
- SGLD 77479 4368
2000 SGLD 77478 4368
2200 CNRO 77304 2236
12800 HarC 77429 3254
Highland Hollow Dr
10 CNRO 77304 2382
Highland Hollow Ln
20700 HarC 77073 3259
Highland Knolls Dr
- HarC 77494 3953
20100 HarC 77450 3954
21600 HOUS 77450 3954
22200 HarC 77450 3953
Highland Lake Ct
2800 PRLD 77584 4499

Houston Street Index

STREET
Block City ZIP Map# Grid

ighland Lake Ln
13300 PRLD 77584 4499 E3
13300 PRLD 77584 4500 A4
ighland Lakes Dr
2800 MSCY 77459 4497 A3
3500 HOUS 77339 3119 C5
ighland Laurels Dr
2900 HOUS 77345 3119 D4
ighland Lodge Ln
8900 HarC 77044 3689 C5
ighland Meadow Dr
11500 HarC 77089 4378 A6
11500 HOUS 77089 4378 A6
ighland Meadow Village r
10900 HarC 77089 4378 A6
ighland Mist Cir
400 HarC 77015 3828 C6
ighland Oak
20300 HarC 77450 3954 E6
ighland Oak Ct
7200 FBnC 77469 4095 B5
ighland Oak Ln
- FBnC 77083 4095 D6
- FBnC 77469 4095 C5
ighland Park Ct
13400 HarC 77070 3399 B2
ighland Park Dr
13400 HarC 77070 3399 B1
ighland Park Pl
4500 HOUS 77053 4372 C7
ighland Pl Dr
- HarC 77449 3815 B2
ighland Point Ct
1400 HarC 77373 3259 B1
1900 PRLD 77581 4503 D1
ighland Point Ln
3400 PRLD 77581 4503 D1
22300 HarC 77373 3259 B1
ighland Ridge Ct
8100 FBnC 77479 4494 C5
ighland Shores Dr
- LGCY 77573 4631 D4
100 HarC 77562 3691 E7
100 HarC 77562 3692 C7
ighland Springs Dr
- HOUS 77077 3958 B5
ighland Stone Ct
2100 HarC 77450 3954 D5
ighland Stone Dr
- HarC 77450 3954 D5
ighlands View Ct
15700 HarC 77084 3679 A6
ighland Timbers Dr
- HarC 77070 3399 E3
ighland Trace Dr
- HarC 77070 3399 E3
ighland Vale Ct
3900 FBnC 77545 4622 D1
ighland View Dr
- HarC 77449 3815 B3
ighland Villa Ln
16700 HarC 77396 3407 D4
ighland Woods Dr
400 HarC 77562 3831 C2
10600 FBnC 77478 4237 A4
ighland Wy Ln
14800 FBnC 77478 4236 C2
ighlawn St
- HOUS 77076 3685 A6
9200 HOUS 77022 3685 A6
igh Level Rd
- HOUS 77029 4105 D1
7400 HOUS 77020 3965 B5
8500 HOUS 77029 3965 B5
igh Life Rd
6900 HarC 77066 3400 C7
6900 HarC 77086 3400 C7
Highline Dr
100 DRPK 77536 4109 B6
V Highline Dr
100 DRPK 77536 4109 B6
ighmanor Dr
12700 HarC 77038 3543 B3
High Meadow Cir
30500 MtgC 77355 2814 A7
30600 MtgC 77355 2960 A1
High Meadow Cir
30500 MtgC 77355 2960 A1
igh Meadow Dr
37000 MtgC 77354 2816 A1
ighmeadow Dr
- HOUS 77042 4099 B1
7500 HOUS 77057 3960 A7
7600 HOUS 77063 3960 A7
7800 HOUS 77063 3959 E7
9300 HOUS 77063 4099 B1
19000 HarC 77377 3106 E7
19000 HarC 77433 3106 E7
igh Meadow Rd
27800 HarC 77377 3108 E2
igh Meadow St
5800 LGCY 77573 4630 C7
igh Meadow Ranch Dr
- MtgC 77362 2816 B2
400 MtgC 77355 2816 B4
igh Meadows Ct
4100 FBnC 77479 4366 C6
igh Meadows Dr
4100 FBnC 77469 4366 C5
4100 FBnC 77479 4366 C6
igh Mesa Ct
13400 HOUS 77059 4380 A4
ighmore Dr
16800 HOUS 77396 3406 A3
igh Mountain Dr
8600 HOUS 77088 3683 A1
igh Noon
3000 HarC 77338 3263 D5
igh Noon Ct
11700 HarC 77433 3395 D7
11700 HarC 77433 3396 A6
igh Oak Ln
700 MtgC 77362 2816 D5
700 SGCH 77362 2816 D5
High Oaks Cir
- WDLD 77380 2967 E3
10 WDLD 77380 2968 A3
High Oaks Cir
10 WDLD 77380 2967 E4
10 WDLD 77380 2968 A4
igh Park Cir
1400 HarC 77373 3259 B1
igh Pine Dr
3300 MSCY 77459 4496 E2
ighpines Dr
3900 HarC 77068 3257 B7

High Plains Dr
2900 HarC 77449 3815 D4
4200 FBnC 77479 4366 C5
Highpoint Cross
300 HarC 77336 3120 D2
High Point Dr
34100 MtgC 77355 2668 A5
High Point Ln
4600 HOUS 77053 4372 C4
Highpoint Mdw
2200 CNRO 77304 2236 E3
Highpointe Grn
1500 HarC 77379 3110 B7
High Point Pines Dr
22200 HarC 77373 3113 D1
High Ridge Cir
900 FRDW 77546 4629 D5
High Ridge Dr
500 FRDW 77546 4629 E5
High Ridge Ln
8800 FBnC 77469 4616 D1
Highridge St
200 HOUS 77013 3828 A6
Highrock Rd
6500 HOUS 77092 3682 C6
High Seas Dr
12600 HarC 77377 3254 B5
High Sierra Ln
3600 HarC 77084 3816 C2
Highsprings Dr
15200 HarC 77068 3257 B6
High Star Dr
5900 HOUS 77081 4100 C4
6400 HOUS 77074 4100 B4
7700 HOUS 77036 4099 D4
10600 HOUS 77072 4098 B4
12100 HOUS 77072 4097 B4
13200 HOUS 77083 4097 B4
Highstar Dr
5800 HOUS 77081 4100 C4
High Star Landing Dr
6300 HOUS 77072 4097 D4
Highstone Ct
2200 LGCY 77573 4631 A7
High Stone Ln
6600 HarC 77449 3676 D2
High Terrace Dr
8100 FBnC 77479 4494 B7
High Thicket Ct
1400 HarC 77373 3114 B7
High Tide Ln
2300 PRLD 77545 4499 E2
High Timbers Dr
2400 WDLD 77380 2821 D5
Hightower Ln
19300 HMBL 77338 3262 B6
19300 HOUS 77338 3262 B6
High Valley Dr
- HOUS 77345 3120 C5
Highview Dr
2600 HarC 77039 3545 E3
High Village Dr
7700 HarC 77095 3538 C6
Highway Blvd
100 BYTN 77520 3973 B7
5000 KATY 77493 3952 D1
6300 KATY 77494 3952 A1
26900 KATY 77493 3951 E1
26900 KATY 77494 3951 E1
27700 WlrC 77493 3951 E1
27700 WlrC 77494 3951 E1
30600 WlrC 77423 3951 A1
Highway Blvd US-90
5000 KATY 77493 3952 D1
6300 KATY 77494 3952 A1
26900 KATY 77493 3951 E1
26900 KATY 77494 3951 E1
27700 WlrC 77493 3951 E1
27700 WlrC 77494 3951 E1
30600 WlrC 77423 3951 A1
Highway 59 N
20000 HMBL 77338 3262 D5
Highway 288
- BzaC 77583 4744 E6
- BzaC 77583 4745 A6
Highwind Bend Ln
6600 HarC 77449 3676 E3
Highwood Ct
1400 HarC 77073 3259 B5
Highwood Rd
13100 HOUS 77079 3958 C3
Highworth Dr
17000 HarC 77379 3255 D3
Hikers Path Dr
- HarC 77346 3265 B7
Hikers Trails Dr
18900 HarC 77346 3265 D6
19300 HOUS 77346 3265 D6
Hilary St
5600 HOUS 77026 3825 D5
Hilbert Dr
2200 HarC 77088 3543 B7
Hilbig Rd
10 CNRO 77301 2384 B1
Hilda
24000 HarC 77447 3249 E2
Hilda St
9000 HOUS 77033 4243 E3
Hildebrandt Rd
22000 HarC 77379 3111 C1
22000 HarC 77389 2966 C7
22000 HarC 77389 3111 C1
Hildene Wy
- WDLD 77382 2819 D1
10 WDLD 77382 2673 D7
Hildred Av
300 CNRO 77303 2383 E1
300 CNRO 77303 2384 A1
Hill Av
1600 LGCY 77539 4632 D7
1600 LGCY 77573 4632 D7
1700 GlsC 77539 4632 D7
2300 DKSN 77539 4632 E7
2400 DKSN 77539 4753 E1
2400 GlsC 77539 4753 E1
3300 DKSN 77539 4754 A2
Hill Dr
200 HOUS 77336 3120 E5
S Hill Dr
11500 HarC 77089 4505 B1
11700 HOUS 77089 4505 B1
Hill Rd
- WlrC 77445 2952 A1
100 HarC 77037 3544 D6
300 FBnC 77471 4491 B2
800 HarC 77037 3545 A6
1300 HarC 77039 3545 C6
14000 MtgC 77302 2532 C1

Hill Rd
14000 MtgC 77306 2532 C1
18100 MtgC 77365 2971 E7
18100 MtgC 77365 2972 A7
Hill St
- PRVW 77445 3100 B3
1400 HOUS 77020 3963 E2
1800 BYTN 77520 4112 B1
4800 GlsC 77511 4869 C6
N Hill St
100 ALVN 77511 4867 B1
S Hill St
100 ALVN 77511 4867 B2
Hill & Dale Av
24900 MtgC 77372 2682 D5
24900 PTVL 77372 2682 D5
25300 MtgC 77372 2683 D5
Hill & Dale Terrace Dr
15600 MtgC 77372 2683 B5
Hillard Green Ln
14300 HarC 77047 4374 A3
Hillary Cir
500 SGLD 77478 4368 B1
E Hillary Cir
400 SGLD 77478 4368 B1
W Hillary Cir
400 SGLD 77478 4368 A1
Hillbarn Dr
7700 HarC 77040 3541 D7
Hill Branch Dr
12700 HOUS 77082 4097 C2
Hill Brook Ct
5200 FBnC 77479 4493 D3
Hillbrook Ct
15200 HarC 77070 3254 D7
Hillbrook Dr
3800 BzaC 77584 4501 C7
11600 HarC 77070 3254 D7
Hill Brook Ln
300 MtgC 77385 2676 B2
Hill Canyon Ct
2100 FBnC 77479 4493 E2
Hill Canyon Ln
13000 HarC 77072 4097 C7
Hill Chris Rd
1500 FBnC 77477 4370 A6
Hill Country Dr
- HarC 77429 3253 D5
16300 MtgC 77302 2679 B4
Hill Creek Bnd
- PRLD 77545 4499 D4
Hill Creek Rd
23100 HarC 77373 3115 E6
Hill Creek Falls
24300 HarC 77375 2965 D4
Hillcrest Cir
100 RHMD 77469 4492 A1
Hillcrest Dr
10 CNRO 77303 2237 E6
100 HLCS 77511 4867 E5
100 RHMD 77469 4491 E2
100 RHMD 77469 4492 A2
800 CNRO 77301 2383 D2
1200 CNRO 77304 2383 D3
12000 MtgC 77362 2817 B6
23400 WlrC 77447 2813 D1
N Hillcrest Dr
20000 MtgC 77365 2972 E2
20500 MtgC 77365 2973 A2
S Hillcrest Dr
20100 MtgC 77365 2972 E3
20500 MtgC 77365 2973 A3
Hillcrest Ln
1700 HarC 77520 3831 E7
1700 HarC 77520 3970 E1
10700 GlsC 77510 4871 E6
Hillcrest Rd
- HOUS 77041 3680 D2
- JRSV 77041 3680 D2
7200 JRSV 77040 3680 D2
Hillcroft Av
- HOUS 77035 4240 C7
- HOUS 77489 4371 B3
2700 HOUS 77057 3960 A7
2700 HOUS 77063 3960 A7
2900 HOUS 77057 4100 B5
2900 HOUS 77063 4100 A2
5600 HOUS 77036 4100 A2
5800 HOUS 77074 4100 B3
6000 HOUS 77081 4100 B3
8100 HOUS 77096 4100 B7
9100 HOUS 77074 4240 B2
9100 HOUS 77096 4240 B2
12700 HOUS 77085 4240 C7
12700 HOUS 77085 4371 B4
Hillcroft Ct
8200 HOUS 77074 4100 B7
8200 HOUS 77096 4100 B7
Hillcroft Rd
- PRVW 77445 3099 E3
- PRVW 77445 3100 A3
Hillcroft St
- HOUS 77096 4240 B7
11300 HOUS 77035 4240 B7
Hilldale St
9100 SPVL 77055 3820 D7
9200 HOUS 77055 3820 D7
Hilldale Park Ct
31300 MtgC 77386 2823 C6
Hilldale Park Ln
2500 MtgC 77386 2823 C7
Hillenberg Ln
10200 HOUS 77034 4378 C2
Hillendahl Blvd
1400 HLSV 77055 3821 B6
1400 HOUS 77055 3821 B6
Hiller St
1300 HOUS 77015 3966 E3
Hill Family Ln
3600 FBnC 77459 4621 E5
Hill Forest Ct
1900 FBnC 77469 4365 B2
Hill Forest Dr
4200 HOUS 77345 3119 E5
4200 HOUS 77345 3120 A5
Hillglen Ct
15200 HOUS 77062 4506 E2
Hillgreen Dr
1800 FBnC 77494 3952 D4
11200 MtgC 77303 2385 B1
Hill Haven Ct
6500 HarC 77379 3111 D5
Hillhouse
25400 MtgC 77355 2668 C7
25700 MtgC 77355 2814 B1
Hillhouse Dr
- BzaC 77511 4748 B4

Hillhouse Rd
500 PRLD 77584 4501 D1
Hillhurst Dr
500 BYTN 77521 3972 E3
Hilliard St
- HOUS 77034 4378 E4
- HOUS 77034 4379 B4
200 CNRO 77301 2384 A3
500 CNRO 77301 2383 E3
Hillingdale Ln
13700 HarC 77070 3399 E1
Hillingdale Pl Ln
8000 HarC 77070 3399 E2
Hillington Ct
22300 HarC 77375 3110 D3
Hillingworth Ct
5100 HarC 77084 3678 C5
Hillis St
9200 HOUS 77028 3687 D6
9700 HOUS 77078 3687 D5
Hillje St
300 ALVN 77511 4867 B3
Hill Lakes Ct
17300 HarC 77429 3252 D6
Hillman Dr
5500 TXCY 77539 4755 E3
Hillman St
5100 HOUS 77023 4104 B1
Hillman Glen Cir
6400 HarC 77086 3542 C4
Hillmeadow Dr
3400 HarC 77388 3112 E3
Hillmere
10200 HarC 77070 3399 C4
Hillmere Cir
21000 HarC 77379 3111 B3
Hillmist Ct
- HarC 77377 3254 A4
Hillmont St
7700 HOUS 77040 3682 A6
8300 HOUS 77040 3681 D6
Hillmont Springs Dr
20900 MtgC 77365 3117 E2
20900 MtgC 77365 3118 A2
Hill Oak Dr
4100 HOUS 77092 3821 D1
Hillock Ln
6400 PRLD 77584 4502 C6
Hillock Bluff Cir
600 HarC 77073 3259 B6
Hillock Glen Ln
18000 HarC 77429 3253 B1
Hillock Woods Dr
10 WDLD 77380 2967 C2
Hillpark Dr
22200 HarC 77450 3953 E5
Hillridge Dr
100 MtgC 77385 2822 D6
Hillridge Rd
10000 LPRT 77571 4250 B3
Hillsboro Av
7900 HOUS 77029 3965 B1
Hillsboro Pl
8500 FBnC 77479 4494 A4
Hillsboro St
5700 HOUS 77020 3964 E1
7600 HOUS 77020 3965 B1
13700 HarC 77015 3967 E1
14000 HarC 77015 3968 A1
Hillsboro Brook Ln
- HOUS 77044 3409 A4
Hills Bridge Ct
14800 FBnC 77478 4236 D6
Hills Bridge Ln
11500 FBnC 77478 4236 D6
Hillsdale
- DRPK 77536 4250 A2
Hillsdale St
3100 DRPK 77536 4250 A3
3100 LPRT 77536 4250 A3
3100 LPRT 77571 4250 A3
Hillsdale Bridge Ln
10600 FBnC 77478 4236 E4
Hillsdale Forest Dr
20700 MtgC 77365 3118 A1
Hillsdale Park Dr
20500 HarC 77433 3676 C1
Hillsgate Ct
11700 HarC 77377 3254 D3
Hillsgrove Ct
8800 HOUS 77088 3543 E7
Hillshire Dr
1800 DRPK 77536 4248 E1
2300 DRPK 77536 4249 A1
Hillside Ct
- BYTN 77520 3971 B3
200 ORDN 77386 2822 C6
2500 SGLD 77479 4368 D6
Hillside Dr
11700 HarC 77093 3546 D7
13400 HarC 77039 3546 E4
26600 ORDN 77386 2822 C6
33400 MtgC 77362 2817 C6
E Hillside Dr
5500 HarC 77039 3546 E4
S Hillside Dr
26300 ORDN 77386 2822 C7
W Hillside Dr
5500 HarC 77039 3546 D3
Hillside Bayou Dr
10000 HOUS 77080 3820 A4
Hillside Elm St
1500 HOUS 77062 4380 A5
Hillside Falls Tr
15700 HOUS 77062 4507 C1
Hillside Forest Dr
1300 FBnC 77479 4494 A5
Hillside Glen Tr
11100 HarC 77065 3539 C2
Hillside Hickory Ct
14300 HOUS 77062 4379 D7
Hillside Oak Ln
1900 HOUS 77062 4380 B7
Hillside Park Wy
15100 HarC 77433 3251 C7
Hillside Springs Cir
19400 HarC 77084 3816 A4
Hillside Terrace Ln
15400 HarC 77429 3253 D6
Hillside View Pl
10 WDLD 77381 2674 B7
Hillsman Ln
100 FBnC 77478 4236 B4
Hill Spring Dr
1600 FBnC 77479 4494 B5
Hill Springs Dr
3500 HOUS 77345 3119 D4

Hillstone Dr
- HarC 77049 3828 D1
3300 SGLD 77479 4495 E1
Hillswick Ct
4300 SGLD 77479 4495 C4
Hillswick Dr
4800 SGLD 77479 4495 C4
Hillswind Cir
17000 HarC 77379 3256 B4
Hill Timbers Dr
5200 HarC 77346 3264 C6
Hill Top Ct
1600 MtgC 77303 2385 D1
Hilltop Dr
3500 CNRO 77303 2237 D4
3500 MtgC 77303 2237 D4
29400 MtgC 77386 2968 E3
Hill Top Ln
1600 HOUS 77339 3263 C2
19600 MtgC 77357 2829 A5
Hilltop Ln
18800 HarC 77377 3106 E1
18800 HarC 77377 3107 A1
30900 MtgC 77354 2670 A7
30900 MtgC 77354 2816 A1
Hilltop St
23400 HarC 77447 3105 A7
Hilltop Park Ln
27000 HarC 77433 3537 A1
Hill Top Ranch Rd
22700 HarC 77447 3105 C5
Hilltop View Dr
15200 HarC 77429 3253 D5
Hillvale Dr
14100 HOUS 77077 3956 E3
Hillview Dr
100 MtgC 77385 2822 D6
Hill View Ln
17300 HarC 77379 3256 A3
Hillway Dr
5100 HarC 77373 3260 D1
Hillwood Ln
18400 HarC 77449 3677 C4
Hilo Ct
- PNVL 77304 2237 A3
Hi Lo Ln
10 CNRO 77303 2237 E6
Hilshire Glen Ct
2200 HOUS 77080 3820 E4
Hilshire Green Dr
7900 HLSV 77055 3821 C7
7900 HOUS 77055 3821 C7
Hilshire Grove Ln
10 HLSV 77055 3821 C7
10 HOUS 77055 3821 C7
Hilshire Lake Dr
2200 HOUS 77080 3820 E4
Hilshire Oaks Ct
10 HLSV 77055 3821 C7
E Hilshire Park Dr
1400 HOUS 77055 3821 B6
N Hilshire Park Dr
8400 HOUS 77055 3821 B6
W Hilshire Park Dr
1400 HOUS 77055 3821 B6
Hilshire Terrace Ct
2200 HOUS 77080 3820 E4
Hilshire Trail Dr
2200 HOUS 77080 3820 E4
Hilton Ln
14400 TXCY 77539 4753 C6
Hilton St
8600 HOUS 77093 3686 B7
Hilton Crest Ln
10100 HarC 77044 3689 B3
Hiltoncrest St
8200 HarC 77064 3541 D2
Hilton Head Ct
3300 MSCY 77459 4497 D2
Hilton Head Dr
- MSCY 77459 4497 A1
Hilton Head Ln
16000 HarC 77429 3397 A1
Hilton Hollow Ct
6400 HarC 77084 3678 A4
Hilton Hollow Dr
17000 HarC 77084 3678 A3
Hiltonview Dr
5600 HarC 77086 3541 E1
Hiltonview Rd
5100 HarC 77086 3542 A1
5400 HarC 77086 3541 E1
Himea Ln
- HarC 77039 3545 E5
Hindo Dr
9500 MtgC 77303 2239 C5
Hinds St
10700 HOUS 77034 4246 E6
Hines Av
10 BYTN 77520 3973 A5
Hinesburg Ct
10300 HOUS 77075 4377 A3
Hinkles Fy
2500 FBnC 77469 4234 A7
Hinman St
8300 HOUS 77061 4245 E3
Hinsdale Dr
700 MtgC 77354 2673 B2
Hinsdale Springs Ln
15400 HarC 77053 4372 E5
Hinson St
900 FBnC 77469 4365 B7
Hinton Blvd
3400 HOUS 77022 3823 E3
Hinton Dr
- HOUS 77074 4099 E6
Hira Lake Dr
12000 HOUS 77099 4238 A2
Hiram Clarke Rd
- HarC 77053 4372 C5
12300 HOUS 77035 4241 C7
12300 HOUS 77045 4241 C7
13300 HOUS 77045 4372 C2
14500 HOUS 77053 4372 C4
Hiridge St
8500 HOUS 77055 3821 A5
Hirondel St
5400 HOUS 77033 4243 E4
5700 HOUS 77033 4244 B4
6200 HOUS 77087 4244 D4
Hirsch Dr
30000 TMBL 77375 2963 D5
Hirsch Rd
10 HOUS 77003 3964 B4
10 HOUS 77020 3964 B3
100 HMBL 77338 3263 A6
4000 HOUS 77026 3825 B6
6500 HOUS 77016 3825 B1

Hirsch Rd
10400 HOUS 77016 3686 D2
11200 HarC 77093 3686 D1
11200 HOUS 77093 3686 D1
11400 HarC 77093 3546 D7
11400 HOUS 77016 3546 D7
11600 HarC 77050 3546 D7
11600 HOUS 77050 3546 D7
Hirsch St
- HMBL 77338 3262 E6
Hirschfield Rd
- TMBL 77375 3109 A2
- TMBL 77377 3109 A2
2800 HarC 77373 3114 E7
3100 HarC 77373 3115 B7
13700 HarC 77377 3108 E2
13700 TMBL 77377 3108 E2
Hirsh Dr
30200 TMBL 77375 2963 D5
Hirsh St
- HMBL 77338 3262 E6
His Glory Ln
1100 HOUS 77091 3683 C6
History Row
- WDLD 77380 2821 D5
Hitchcock St
2300 HOUS 77093 3685 D5
2600 HOUS 77093 3686 A5
Hitchin Ln
1400 HarC 77530 3829 E5
Hitching Post Ct
16100 HarC 77429 3253 A7
27200 MtgC 77355 2815 B7
Hitching Rack Ln
28000 MtgC 77355 2815 A6
Hither Rd
10 LbyC 77535 3268 E1
Hitherfield Dr
1200 SGLD 77478 4237 A6
Hithervale Ct
- WDLD 77382 2673 B6
Hiwon Dr
10 PNVL 77304 2237 A3
Hixon Creek Dr
20800 MtgC 77365 3117 E2
HL Patton St
17100 PTVL 77372 2682 E7
H Mark Crosswell Jr St
5500 HOUS 77021 4103 A4
Hoads Deuce Ct
6500 HarC 77379 3257 A4
Hoatzin Ct
4300 MSCY 77459 4496 C2
Hobart Dr
9800 FBnC 77478 4236 D3
Hobart St
5200 HarC 77389 2967 A5
Hobbit Glen Cir
- WDLD 77384 2674 D2
E Hobbit Glen Dr
10 WDLD 77384 2674 D2
W Hobbit Glen Dr
10 WDLD 77384 2674 E3
Hobbit Glen Pl
10 WDLD 77384 2675 A3
Hobbs
11700 MtgC 77306 2532 D2
Hobbs Rd
10 BzaC 77511 4748 C5
100 ALVN 77511 4748 C5
100 LGCY 77573 4631 C5
Hobbs St
4100 GlsC 77518 4634 C3
Hobbs Terrace Dr
- HarC 77377 3254 B3
Hobby
10 HOUS 77489 4371 B7
Hobby Rd
- HOUS 77053 4371 E7
Hobby Forest Ln
18000 HarC 77346 3408 B2
Hobgood St
5700 TXCY 77591 4873 E7
Hobson Dr
1400 FBnC 77469 4365 C3
Hockaday Dr
- HarC 77450 3953 E2
22100 HarC 77450 3954 A2
Hockenberry Ct
- WDLD 77385 2676 B4
Hockenberry Pl
- WDLD 77385 2676 B4
Hockley Dr
14000 HarC 77041 3539 B6
14000 HarC 77095 3539 A6
Hockley St
7900 HOUS 77012 4105 C1
Hoda Ct
11400 MtgC 77303 2239 C5
Hoda Dr
6800 MtgC 77303 2239 D4
Hodgefield Ln
16600 HarC 77090 3258 D4
Hodge Lake Ln
1700 SGLD 77478 4368 D5
Hodges St
2300 HarC 77521 3832 C5
12100 HOUS 77035 4371 A1
12100 HOUS 77085 4371 A1
Hodges Bend Cir
2400 SGLD 77479 4368 D7
Hodges Bend Dr
9200 FBnC 77083 4236 A1
Hodgkins St
800 HarC 77032 3545 A1
Hoffer St
10800 HOUS 77075 4377 C3
11000 HOUS 77089 4377 C3
Hoffman St
100 HOUS 77020 3825 D7
300 HOUS 77020 3964 D1
3800 HOUS 77026 3825 D6
6000 HOUS 77028 3825 D3
7700 HOUS 77016 3825 D1
8100 HOUS 77016 3686 D7
Hoffman Estates Blvd
19100 HarC 77377 3108 D7
19100 HarC 77429 3108 D7
Hogan Ct
3800 SGLD 77479 4495 A2
Hogan Dr
700 MtgC 77302 2530 C6
1600 BzaC 77583 4623 D6
Hogan Ln
100 HMPD 77445 2952 C4
Hogan St
100 HOUS 77007 3963 B2
100 HOUS 77009 3963 C2

Hogan Bridge Ct
7600 HarC 77389 2966 A3
Hogan Bridge Dr
25100 HarC 77389 2966 A3
Hogans Al
700 HOUS 77339 3263 B1
Hogg St
2200 HOUS 77026 3964 A1
Hoggard Dr
12200 MDWP 77477 4237 E5
Hogue St
5600 HOUS 77087 4104 D7
5700 HOUS 77087 4244 D1
Hohen Cir
5500 HOUS 77091 3683 A6
Hohl St
700 HOUS 77022 3685 C6
2800 HOUS 77093 3685 E6
2800 HOUS 77093 3686 A6
Hohldale St
100 HOUS 77022 3684 C7
200 HOUS 77018 3684 C7
200 HOUS 77091 3684 C7
Hoke St
1100 CNRO 77301 2383 E3
Holbech Ln
1400 HarC 77530 3829 C5
Holborn Dr
700 HOUS 77034 4378 E6
Holbrook St
11000 HarC 77093 3686 B2
Holcomb Rd
- HarC 77336 3122 D7
Holcombe Blvd
1000 HOUS 77030 4102 D4
2000 HOUS 77021 4102 E4
2300 HOUS 77021 4103 A5
W Holcombe Blvd
2100 HOUS 77030 4102 A4
2500 HOUS 77025 4102 A4
2600 WUNP 77005 4102 A4
2600 WUNP 77025 4102 A4
3000 HOUS 77025 4101 E4
3000 WUNP 77005 4101 E4
3600 SSPL 77005 4101 E4
3600 SSPL 77025 4101 E4
Holden Mills Dr
6300 HarC 77389 2966 D3
Holden Park Pl
- HarC 77083 4097 A5
Holder Ln
- HarC 77060 3544 E2
Holder St
1200 CNRO 77301 2383 E4
Holder Forest Cir
7200 HOUS 77088 3683 A3
Holder Forest Ct
7200 HOUS 77088 3683 A3
Holder Forest Dr
3700 HOUS 77088 3683 A3
Holder Rambo Rd
2000 HarC 77336 2975 D6
2000 HarC 77336 2976 A6
Holderrieth Blvd
400 TMBL 77375 3109 A1
N Holderrieth Blvd
100 TMBL 77375 2964 A7
Holderrieth Rd
11300 HarC 77375 3109 B4
11300 TMBL 77375 3109 B4
12700 HarC 77377 3109 B4
Holderrieth St
100 TMBL 77375 2964 A7
300 TMBL 77375 3109 A1
Holford Ct
14200 HarC 77070 3398 E1
Holidan Wy
11300 PNPV 77024 3959 D2
11400 HDWV 77024 3959 D2
Holiday Ct
23700 MtgC 77365 2974 B6
Holiday Dr
- HarC 77562 3831 E5
100 GLSN 77550 5109 E2
6900 GlsC 77563 4990 B6
N Holiday Dr
600 GLSN 77550 5109 D1
Holiday Ln
8000 HOUS 77075 4376 D2
Holiday St
300 TMBL 77375 2964 C7
Holland
3600 HOUS 77013 3827 C5
Holland Av
- HOUS 77013 3966 D2
100 GNPK 77547 3966 D7
900 HOUS 77029 3966 C2
900 JTCY 77029 3966 D7
1800 GNPK 77029 3966 C4
Holland Ct
- HOUS 77012 4105 C2
Holland Rd
13400 TXCY 77539 4753 C7
Hollandale Dr
12700 HOUS 77082 4097 C2
Hollandbridge Ln
600 HarC 77073 3259 A4
Hollander Ct
200 LGCY 77573 4633 A1
Holland Field Cir
15200 HarC 77095 3538 E4
Holles Dr
14500 FBnC 77478 4236 E2
Holley Ct
3100 MSCY 77459 4496 E3
11200 HarC 77044 3549 B7
11200 HarC 77044 3689 B1
Holleygate Ct
24000 HarC 77373 3115 B5
Holley Ridge Dr
10 HOUS 77339 3263 D1
Hollier Rd
1400 ALVN 77511 4749 D2
1400 FRDW 77546 4749 D2
Hollinfare Ct
10 SGLD 77479 4495 E3
Hollingers I
10 FBnC 77450 3954 A6
Hollingsworth Dr
3700 BzaC 77584 4502 B7
3700 BzaC 77584 4626 B1
3700 PRLD 77584 4502 B7
Hollington Dr
19700 HarC 77375 3110 A7
Hollins Rd
500 MtgC 77385 2822 C2
Hollins Wy
16600 HOUS 77058 4507 E2

STREET
Block City ZIP Map# Grid

Hollinwell Dr
2800 FBnC 77450 3954 B7
Hollis St
2300 HOUS 77093 3685 E4
Hollisbrook Ln
8300 HarC 77044 3689 C6
Hollis Garden Dr
19200 HarC 77375 3109 B6
Hollister Dr
- HarC 77040 3542 A7
- HarC 77066 3400 E4
- HOUS 77040 3542 A7
9400 HarC 77064 3541 E3
9400 HarC 77086 3541 E3
9900 HarC 77040 3682 A1
9900 HOUS 77040 3682 A2
11700 HarC 77064 3542 A5
Hollister Rd
- HarC 77040 3682 A3
- HarC 77066 3541 E1
- HarC 77086 3541 E2
- HOUS 77040 3682 A3
1500 HOUS 77055 3821 A6
1900 HOUS 77080 3821 A5
2300 HOUS 77080 3820 E3
4100 HOUS 77041 3820 E1
Hollister Rdg
7400 HOUS 77040 3682 A5
Hollister Spr
7400 HOUS 77040 3682 A5
Hollister St
- HarC 77040 3682 A3
2100 HOUS 77080 3820 E4
4200 HOUS 77040 3821 A1
4200 HOUS 77092 3821 A1
5200 HOUS 77040 3682 A5
Hollister Cole
5900 HOUS 77040 3682 A5
Hollister Woods
7400 HOUS 77040 3682 A5
Hollock St
8800 HOUS 77075 4246 A7
9800 HOUS 77034 4246 B6
Holloman St
2300 CNRO 77301 2384 A1
Hollow Cir
3100 MSCY 77459 4497 B2
N Hollow Cir
7500 HMBL 77396 3406 D1
Hollow Dr
400 HOUS 77024 3958 E3
N Hollow Dr
1600 HMBL 77396 3406 D2
Hollow Ln
4900 LGCY 77573 4751 E1
7200 FBnC 77469 4094 C6
Hollow Tr
10 CNRO 77304 2382 D1
Hollow Ash Ct
14600 HarC 77015 3829 C4
Hollow Ash Ln
1200 HarC 77450 3953 D4
Holloway Ct
4700 HOUS 77048 4243 D6
Holloway Dr
4100 HOUS 77047 4243 C6
4700 HOUS 77048 4243 D6
Holloway St
3900 GlsC 77511 4869 C5
Holloway Square Ln
6600 FBnC 77469 4095 B5
Hollow Bank Ln
5900 FBnC 77479 4493 E2
Hollow Banks Ln
8700 HarC 77095 3537 E5
Hollow Bay Ln
- HarC 77095 3537 E5
Hollow Bend Ct
5000 HOUS 77018 3683 D7
Hollow Bend Ln
2200 FBnC 77471 4614 B3
Hollow Bluff Ln
7800 FBnC 77469 4095 D6
Hollow Branch Ct
18300 HarC 77429 3396 A1
Hollow Branch Dr
5100 FBnC 77450 4094 B2
5100 HOUS 77450 4094 B2
Hollow Branch Ln
1400 PASD 77586 4381 D6
Hollow Brook Dr
13000 HOUS 77082 4097 B1
Hollow Brook Ln
2300 MtgC 77384 2528 E7
2300 MtgC 77384 2529 A7
Hollow Canyon Ct
10300 FBnC 77478 4236 E3
Hollow Canyon Dr
10100 FBnC 77478 4236 E3
10100 FBnC 77478 4237 A3
Hollow Canyon Ln
13800 BzaC 77583 4623 D4
Hollow Cedar Dr
7100 HarC 77049 3829 B1
Hollow Cove Ct
7400 HarC 77433 3677 D1
Hollow Cove Ln
3900 FBnC 77469 4615 E5
Hollow Creek Ct
3100 HOUS 77082 4097 B2
Hollow Creek Dr
2800 HOUS 77082 4097 B1
Hollowcreek Park Dr
13100 HOUS 77082 4097 B2
Hollowcrest Dr
- HarC 77089 4377 C7
Hollow Cypress Ct
15500 HarC 77049 3829 B2
Hollow Field Ct
7400 HarC 77433 3677 E1
Hollow Field Ln
7100 HarC 77433 3677 D1
21800 FBnC 77450 4094 B2
Hollow Glen Ln
10 HarC 77375 3255 A2
7600 HOUS 77072 4097 C6
Hollow Glen Pl
10 WDLD 77385 2676 C3
Hollowgreen Ct
13500 HarC 77082 4097 A1
Hollowgreen Dr
13600 HarC 77082 4097 A1
13600 HOUS 77082 4097 A1
13800 HOUS 77082 4096 E1
Hollowhaven Ct
8100 HarC 77095 3537 C6
Hollow Hearth Dr
6800 HarC 77084 3679 A3
Hollow Hill Ln
17900 FBnC 77469 4095 C7
Hollow Hook Rd
2500 HOUS 77080 3820 A3
4300 HOUS 77041 3820 A1
4500 HOUS 77041 3681 A7
Hollow Lodge Ct
22700 HarC 77450 3953 E4
Hollowlog Dr
19400 HarC 77449 3816 A3
Hollowmill Ln
14100 HOUS 77082 4096 E1
Hollow Mist Ln
1900 PRLD 77581 4503 E1
Hollow Oak Ct
8000 FBnC 77479 4494 B5
Hollow Oaks Cir
18100 MtgC 77365 2971 E2
18400 MtgC 77365 2972 A2
Hollow Oaks Dr
1000 MtgC 77385 2676 C5
6400 HOUS 77050 3547 A5
Hollowood Ln
1200 MSCY 77489 4370 D5
Hollow Pine Ct
14000 HarC 77049 3828 B3
Hollow Pines Dr
5600 HarC 77015 3828 B4
5700 HarC 77049 3828 B4
Hollow Pines St
6200 HarC 77049 3828 B3
Hollow Quill Dr
8800 HarC 77088 3542 B7
Hollow Reef Cir
2100 LGCY 77573 4509 B6
Hollow Ridge Dr
7400 HarC 77095 3678 D1
Hollowridge Ln
- BzaC 77583 4623 E2
Hollow Ridge Rd
16500 HOUS 77053 4372 A7
Hollow Rock Dr
15800 HarC 77070 3255 C5
Hollow Sage Ln
31200 MtgC 77386 2823 B7
Hollow Sands Ct
17200 HarC 77084 3678 A5
Hollow Shore St
2200 PRLD 77584 4500 D2
Hollow Springs Ln
28300 MtgC 77386 2969 D6
Hollow Stone Ln
26400 HarC 77433 3396 B5
Hollow Trace Ln
- FBnC 77494 4093 C2
Hollow Tree Av
900 LPRT 77571 4382 D1
Hollow Tree Ln
- HarC 77073 3258 D2
100 HarC 77090 3258 D2
100 HOUS 77090 3258 C2
Hollowvine Ln
- FBnC 77494 4093 A1
Hollow Wind Dr
1800 HarC 77450 3954 E5
1800 HarC 77450 3955 A5
Hollow Wood Dr
16200 HarC 77090 3258 D5
Hollsbrook Ct
3400 SGLD 77478 4368 D4
Holly
11600 HarC 77086 3542 E6
11600 HarC 77088 3542 E6
14600 HarC 77060 3544 E1
14600 HarC 77060 3545 A2
Holly Av
- CNRO 77301 2384 D3
2400 PASD 77502 4247 E2
2400 PASD 77502 4248 A2
4700 PASD 77503 4248 A2
Holly Cir
1500 RHMD 77469 4491 D2
15700 MtgC 77302 2677 A2
Holly Ct
10 PNVL 77304 2237 B4
1600 PRLD 77581 4375 D7
2500 GLSN 77551 5108 B7
19700 MtgC 77355 2814 D3
Holly Dr
- LGCY 77573 4632 B5
- MtgC 77302 2677 B3
300 BYTN 77520 3971 B2
600 HarC 77562 3832 A2
800 CNRO 77301 2383 D2
2300 DKSN 77539 4753 E2
15000 MtgC 77372 2683 D2
24700 MtgC 77357 2828 D7
26900 WlrC 77447 2813 D2
N Holly Dr
100 BYTN 77520 3971 A1
Holly Gln
19700 MtgC 77357 2829 A5
Holly Hllw
- MtgC 77385 2676 E3
Holly Ln
10 HOUS 77365 3119 D1
100 WDBR 77357 2828 C3
400 CNRO 77304 2383 A6
11900 MtgC 77362 2817 C7
13500 HarC 77429 3398 E4
21300 MtgC 77357 2827 C1
23000 MtgC 77447 2959 E3
E Holly Ln
25100 MtgC 77372 2537 A6
25100 SPLD 77372 2537 A6
25400 MtgC 77372 2536 E6
W Holly Ln
24600 MtgC 77372 2536 D6
Holly Lp
- HarC 77396 3406 E5
Holly Rd
500 HOUS 77365 3119 D1
Holly St
- HarC 77375 2964 D2
100 HarC 77336 2975 C6
700 LMQU 77568 4990 B1
1300 HOUS 77007 3963 B2
2400 WALR 77484 3101 E6
2700 WlrC 77484 3101 E6
4500 BLAR 77401 4101 B6
5000 BLAR 77401 4100 E6
5500 HOUS 77081 4100 C6
5500 HOUS 77401 4100 C6
5700 HOUS 77074 4100 B6
12200 HarC 77532 3692 C2
15900 MtgC 77365 2825 B6
21300 MtgC 77357 2974 A1
24000 MtgC 77365 2974 B7
Holly Wk
19600 HarC 77388 3113 B6
Holly Wy
18700 HarC 77084 3816 C3
Holly Barr Ln
20500 HarC 77433 3676 D1
Holly Bay Ct
4900 PASD 77505 4249 A6
Holly Bend Ct
5300 HarC 77084 3677 E6
Holly Bend Dr
18100 HarC 77084 3677 E6
Holly Berry Ct
7800 HarC 77433 3537 B7
Hollyberry Ct
18200 MtgC 77365 2972 A1
Hollyberry Dr
1500 HarC 77073 3259 C1
Hollyberry Ln
17400 SGLD 77479 4494 E1
Hollybough Dr
- HarC 77336 3121 E3
Holly Branch Ct
18500 MtgC 77365 2972 A1
Hollybranch Dr
21900 HarC 77375 3110 E1
21900 HarC 77375 3111 A1
22100 HarC 77375 2965 E7
Holly Branch Ln
300 LGCY 77565 4508 E5
Hollybrook Dr
2500 SEBK 77586 4509 E1
Hollybrook Ln
4700 HarC 77039 3546 C4
Hollybush Dr
1500 SGLD 77478 4237 A7
Hollybush Ln
25300 HarC 77373 3114 D2
Holly Canyon Ct
6300 FBnC 77450 4094 B4
Holly Chase Dr
10000 HOUS 77042 4099 A1
10100 HOUS 77042 4098 E1
Holly Court Estates Dr
7300 HarC 77095 3679 A1
7500 HarC 77095 3539 A7
Holly Cove Ln
6500 HarC 77449 3677 B3
Holly Creek Ct
300 WDLD 77381 2821 A4
Holly Creek Tr
22000 HarC 77377 2962 C7
22000 HarC 77377 3107 C1
Holly Crest Dr
500 MtgC 77386 2968 D2
Hollycrest St
700 HarC 77530 3829 D7
Holly Crossing Dr
3200 HOUS 77042 4099 A1
Hollydale Dr
14800 HOUS 77062 4380 A7
Holly Falls Ct
17100 HarC 77095 3538 A7
Holly Fern Ct
300 LGCY 77573 4633 A1
Holly Fern Dr
400 LGCY 77573 4633 A2
Hollyfield Ln
2100 HarC 77493 3814 C5
Holly Forest Dr
17900 HarC 77084 3678 A5
18000 HarC 77084 3677 E5
Hollygate Ln
16500 HarC 77429 3252 B5
Holly Glade Ln
2000 SGLD 77478 4236 E5
Hollyglen Dr
10100 HOUS 77016 3686 E3
Hollyglenn St
300 WDBR 77357 2828 C2
Holly Green Ct
3900 HOUS 77339 3119 C3
Holly Green Dr
2900 HOUS 77339 3119 C3
18100 HarC 77084 3677 E5
Hollygrove Dr
6700 HOUS 77061 4245 B3
Holly Grove Ln
100 MtgC 77384 2675 A1
10000 CNRO 77304 2237 A6
Holly Hall Dr
900 FBnC 77469 4365 E4
Holly Hall St
2100 HOUS 77054 4102 C7
2800 HOUS 77054 4103 A7
3000 HOUS 77021 4103 A7
Holly Hill Ct
28700 SHEH 77381 2822 A2
Holly Hill Dr
- HarC 77375 2965 E7
900 SGLD 77478 4367 E1
28700 SHEH 77381 2822 A2
Holly Hill Ln
10900 HarC 77041 3680 C5
Holly Hills Dr
8600 HarC 77375 2965 D6
Hollyhock Dr
- HarC 77449 3677 B5
- PRVW 77445 3100 C3
700 FBnC 77477 4369 C4
Holly Hollow St
22900 HarC 77377 2962 C7
Hollyhurst Ln
1600 HOUS 77056 3961 B5
Holly Knoll Dr
2300 HOUS 77077 3958 A7
Holly Knoll St
2200 HOUS 77077 3958 A7
Holly Lake Ct
1300 HarC 77450 3953 E4
Holly Lake Dr
22000 HarC 77377 3107 C2
22500 HarC 77450 3953 E4
Holly Lake Ln
10 HarC 77373 3114 A6
N Holly Laurel Cir
10 WDLD 77382 2674 D3
S Hollylaurel Cir
100 WDLD 77382 2674 C2
Hollylaurel Dr
10 WDLD 77382 2674 D3
Holly Leaf Ct
21600 MtgC 77365 2972 A1
Hollyleaf Dr
8200 HarC 77379 3255 E3
8200 HarC 77379 3256 A3
Holly Lord
26900 MtgC 77355 2963 A4
Holly Lynn Ln
13700 HOUS 77077 3957 A4
Holly Manor Ln
- FBnC 77469 4095 C6
Hollymead Dr
- WDLD 77381 2820 E1
Holly Meadow Dr
3200 HOUS 77042 4099 A1
Hollymist Dr
2600 HarC 77084 3816 B5
Holly Oak Ct
3100 HarC 77068 3257 D5
Hollyoak Dr
1800 HOUS 77084 3816 D6
N Holly Oaks Cir
30300 MtgC 77355 2960 A1
S Holly Oaks Cir
30200 MtgC 77355 2960 A1
Holly Oaks Ct
25000 MtgC 77355 2814 B7
25000 MtgC 77355 2960 B1
Holly Park Dr
4800 PASD 77505 4248 A3
13200 HarC 77015 3828 D7
14200 HarC 77015 3829 A7
Holly Path Dr
3200 HOUS 77042 4098 E1
Holly Pines Wy
17900 HarC 77084 3816 D1
Holly Rain Dr
- HarC 77449 3815 D2
Holly Ranch Dr
3100 FBnC 77494 3953 A6
Holly Ridge Dr
800 HOUS 77024 3959 B2
Hollyridge Dr
1800 MSCY 77489 4370 E5
Holly Ridge Rd
23400 MtgC 77365 2972 C5
Holly River Dr
1500 HOUS 77077 3958 B5
Hollys Wy
1900 FBnC 77479 4367 B7
1900 FBnC 77479 4494 B1
Holly See
17800 HarC 77447 3249 D2
Holly Shade Ct
19200 HarC 77379 3112 B6
Holly Shores Dr
3200 HOUS 77042 4098 E1
Holly Springs Ct
700 MtgC 77302 2530 D7
Holly Springs Dr
10 MtgC 77302 2530 D7
200 FRDW 77546 4628 E2
2700 PRLD 77584 4503 A4
5300 HOUS 77056 3960 D4
6100 HOUS 77057 3960 B4
10000 HOUS 77042 3958 E5
10000 HOUS 77042 3959 A5
Holly Springs Ln
700 MtgC 77302 2530 D7
Holly Springs Pl
25500 HarC 77373 3113 E4
Hollystone Dr
11900 HarC 77070 3399 C6
Holly Terrace Ct
4300 PASD 77505 4248 D5
4300 PASD 77505 4249 A5
Holly Terrace Dr
5100 HOUS 77056 3960 E4
5100 HOUS 77056 3961 A4
Holly Thicket Dr
3200 HOUS 77042 4098 E1
Holly Thorn
18100 HarC 77375 3255 B4
Holly Trail Dr
16500 HOUS 77058 4507 C3
Hollytree Dr
15800 HarC 77068 3257 B5
Holly Tree Ln
10 HarC 77373 3114 A6
Hollyvale Dr
100 HarC 77037 3544 C4
400 HarC 77060 3544 E4
900 HarC 77060 3545 A4
Holly Valley Ln
5400 FBnC 77469 4233 B7
Holly View Cir
6200 HOUS 77091 3683 A4
Holly View Dr
5200 HOUS 77091 3683 A5
5400 HOUS 77091 3682 E4
Holly Vine Ln
10100 HarC 77089 4505 A1
Holly Vista St
13400 HarC 77070 3399 E3
Holly Walk Ln
2500 HarC 77388 3113 B6
Holly Walk Ln Ct
19800 HarC 77388 3113 B6
Hollywell Dr
18000 HarC 77084 3677 E7
Hollywick Dr
24200 HarC 77375 2965 D4
24200 HarC 77389 2965 D4
Hollywind Cir
19700 HarC 77094 3955 A4
Hollywood Av
2000 GLSN 77551 5108 B7
Hollywood Blvd
500 HarC 77015 3829 A7
800 HarC 77015 3968 A2
Hollywood Ct
700 HOUS 77020 3963 D2
Hollywood Dr
100 CNRO 77303 2237 D5
Hollywood St
2300 DKSN 77539 4753 E3
Holman St
100 LMQU 77568 4874 C7
100 TXCY 77591 4874 C7
500 HOUS 77006 3963 A6
600 HOUS 77002 3963 A6
1000 HOUS 77004 3963 A7
2200 HOUS 77004 4103 D1
N Holmes Av
200 LPRT 77571 4251 E2
Holmes Blvd
1100 PASD 77506 4107 C3
Holmes Rd
10 HOUS 77035 4241 C5
10 HOUS 77045 4241 E4
500 HOUS 77045 4242 B3
500 HOUS 77054 4241 E4
500 HOUS 77054 4242 A3
2300 HOUS 77051 4242 E2
2600 FBnC 77469 4364 C1
Holmes Rd
2900 HOUS 77051 4243 A2
3000 FBnC 77469 4233 C5
4300 HOUS 77033 4103 D7
4300 HOUS 77051 4103 D7
Holmes Rd N
- HOUS 77035 4241 D4
- HOUS 77045 4241 D4
N Holmes St
100 LPRT 77571 4251 E2
S Holmes St
100 LPRT 77571 4251 E2
200 LPRT 77571 4252 A3
Holmsley Ln
7100 HarC 77040 3681 C2
Holmwood Dr
8200 HarC 77040 3541 D7
Holsberry Ct
12700 HarC 77377 3254 B4
Holstein St
19800 HarC 77532 3412 E2
Holston Hills Ct
5600 HarC 77069 3400 D2
Holston Hills Dr
13100 HarC 77069 3400 D1
Holt St
- HarC 77484 3102 A4
- WALR 77484 3102 A5
4300 HOUS 77401 4101 B6
4500 BLAR 77401 4101 B6
4900 BLAR 77401 4100 E6
8500 HOUS 77054 4242 D1
Holtcamp St
7300 HOUS 77011 4105 A1
Holtman St
100 HarC 77037 3544 C5
100 HarC 77060 3544 C5
Holton Av
1900 DRPK 77503 4248 E2
1900 DRPK 77536 4248 E2
1900 DRPK 77536 4249 A2
1900 PASD 77503 4248 E2
Holton St
800 BLAR 77401 4101 A3
Holton Gripp Dr
- FBnC 77494 4092 A5
Holts Al
5000 HOUS 77026 3825 A4
Holworth Dr
11000 HOUS 77072 4098 B4
Holy Rd
3000 HarC 77532 3693 E2
3000 HarC 77532 3694 B2
Holyhead Dr
200 HarC 77015 3829 A5
Holyoke Ln
25500 HarC 77373 3114 E1
Holy Rood Ln
700 HOUS 77024 3961 A1
Holzwarth Rd
19700 HOUS 77388 3113 D5
21500 HarC 77388 3113 B2
E Homan Av
10 BYTN 77520 3973 A5
W Homan Av
200 BYTN 77520 3972 E5
200 BYTN 77520 3973 A5
Hombly Ct
11300 HarC 77066 3401 D6
Hombly Rd
3200 HarC 77066 3401 E6
N Home Pl
3500 SGLD 77479 4496 A1
S Home Pl
3500 SGLD 77479 4496 A1
Home St
3400 HOUS 77007 3962 D2
Homebriar Ct
15700 HOUS 77489 4371 A5
Homebrook Dr
1600 HarC 77038 3543 B2
Homeland Dr
9200 HarC 77083 4237 B2
Homemont Ln
24100 HarC 77336 3266 E2
Homer Dr
2600 HOUS 77091 3683 C5
Homer Rd
2700 GLSN 77554 5220 C5
Homer St
700 HOUS 77091 3684 A5
1100 HOUS 77091 3683 D5
Homestead Ct
6600 HOUS 77028 3825 E3
Homestead Ln
3800 SGLD 77479 4368 E7
Homestead Rd
- HarC 77032 3546 E2
5800 RSBG 77471 4491 D6
6000 HOUS 77028 3825 E4
8700 HOUS 77028 3686 E7
10800 HOUS 77016 3686 E1
11400 HOUS 77016 3546 E7
11700 HarC 77050 3546 E7
11700 HOUS 77050 3546 E7
12200 HarC 77039 3546 E5
13400 HarC 77396 3546 E3
Homestead Pass Dr
3200 HarC 77373 3115 A4
Homette St
13700 HarC 77044 3689 D3
Homeview Dr
6200 HarC 77049 3828 C3
Homeward Wy
5200 FBnC 77479 4366 E6
5700 FBnC 77479 4367 A5
Homewood Ln
5000 BYTN 77521 3972 A2
8500 HOUS 77028 3687 D6
8800 HOUS 77078 3687 E6
9000 HOUS 77078 3688 A6
12000 BKHV 77024 3959 B3
Homewood Row Ln
10 HOUS 77056 3961 A4
Homrighaus Rd
11100 GLSN 77554 5220 E4
11100 GLSN 77554 5221 A4
Hon Ct
19700 HarC 77449 3676 E4
Hondo Cir
26900 MtgC 77355 2813 E1
Hondo St
3200 HOUS 77051 4243 B2
Hondo Hill Rd
10200 HarC 77064 3540 B5
Honduras Dr
4000 PASD 77504 4247 E4
Honea-Old Egypt Rd
800 MtgC 77354 2673 C3
Honey Cir
5200 HOUS 77004 4103 D4
Honey Ln
6000 PASD 77505 4248 D4
14700 HOUS 77085 4371 C4
Honeybear Ln
5400 HarC 77373 3115 D6
Honey Bee Ct
13900 HarC 77039 3546 A3
Honeybee Ln
22300 MtgC 77357 2973 E4
22300 MtgC 77357 2974 A4
Honey Brook Dr
3800 HOUS 77345 3119 D3
Honeycomb Ln
14600 HarC 77429 3397 D5
Honey Creek Ct
4700 PRLD 77584 4503 B4
Honey Creek Dr
3200 HarC 77082 4096 B2
3400 SGLD 77478 4368 B5
3500 SGLD 77478 4369 A6
Honey Creek Ln
7500 HarC 77095 3538 C7
Honey Creek Tr
12500 HarC 77346 3408 D1
Honey Creek Wy
18200 HarC 77346 3408 D1
Honeydale Ln
20500 HarC 77532 3410 E2
Honey Falls Dr
- HarC 77073 3259 E4
Honeyfield Ln
8000 HarC 77379 3111 A7
Honey Garden Ct
4300 FBnC 77469 4615 E5
Honey Grove Av
5300 ARLA 77583 4623 B5
E Honey Grove Dr
10 WDLD 77382 2674 C4
W Honey Grove Dr
10 WDLD 77382 2674 B4
Honey Grove Ln
5300 ARLA 77583 4623 B4
11300 HarC 77065 3398 C7
11300 HarC 77065 3539 C1
Honey Hill Dr
1000 HOUS 77077 3956 E3
Honey Laurel Dr
1900 CNRO 77304 2383 B1
Honey Locust Dr
2400 HarC 77449 3815 C5
Honeylocust Dr
3400 SGLD 77479 4495 D2
Honey Locust Ln
7800 BzaC 77584 4627 C4
Honey Locust Hill Dr
20200 HarC 77388 3113 B5
Honey Mesquite Wy
- FBnC 77494 4093 B7
Honeymoon Ln
10800 FBnC 77478 4236 A4
Honey Oaks Dr
4000 TYLV 77586 4381 D7
Honey Ridge Dr
- MtgC 77386 2969 E3
Honeysickle St
2700 BzaC 77583 4500 A5
Honeysuckle Dr
100 BYTN 77520 3971 B1
100 LMQU 77568 4874 C7
1100 MSCY 77489 4370 B5
5900 HOUS 77087 4244 E1
7500 BzaC 77584 4627 B4
23900 MtgC 77365 2972 A6
Honeysuckle Ln
1400 FBnC 77479 4493 D4
4800 PASD 77505 4248 A3
5700 HOUS 77396 3405 E3
18600 MtgC 77365 2972 B6
30900 MtgC 77354 2670 A7
Honeysuckle Rd
- PNVL 77304 2237 B4
Honeysuckle St
8500 HarC 77562 3832 C2
Honeysuckle Wk
2500 HarC 77388 3113 B6
Honeysuckle Falls Ln
- PRLD 77581 4503 D2
Honeysuckle Grove Ln
21700 FBnC 77469 4493 A3
Honeysuckle Springs Rd
17800 HarC 77346 3408 D2
Honeysuckle Vine Dr
500 FBnC 77469 4492 C7
500 FBnC 77469 4616 D1
Honey Tree St
2100 MtgC 77385 2823 B4
Honeyvine Dr
5200 HOUS 77048 4374 E2
5300 DKSN 77539 4754 D1
Honeywell Rd
9600 HOUS 77074 4239 B2
Honeywood Ct
4500 HOUS 77059 4380 D4
Honeywood Tr
12300 HOUS 77077 3957 D4
Honolulu St
15600 HarC 77040 3540 D7
15600 HarC 77064 3540 D7
15600 JRSV 77040 3540 D7
Honor Ct
5700 HarC 77041 3679 C6
Honor Dr
5500 HarC 77041 3679 C6
Honor Oaks Cir
10 WDLD 77382 2673 A7
Honor Park Dr
12500 HarC 77065 3539 C4
Honors Ct
3800 FBnC 77459 4622 A5
Honsinger St
3400 HOUS 77007 3962 D2
Hood Rd
25800 MtgC 77372 2683 A3
25800 SPLD 77372 2683 A3
Hood St
5700 HOUS 77023 4104 C3
9200 HarC 77044 3689 E4
N Hood St
100 ALVN 77511 4867 D2
S Hood St
100 ALVN 77511 4867 C2
Hook St
10000 HarC 77064 3541 D2
Hooker St
800 HarC 77039 3545 A
Hook Left Dr
2500 HarC 77089 4504 D
Hooks
- HarC 77039 3545 C
- HarC 77093 3545 C
- HOUS 77039 3545 C
Hooks Rd
- PRLD 77584 4501 C
3400 BzaC 77578 4501 C
3400 BzaC 77584 4501 C
3400 PRLD 77578 4501 C
3700 BzaC 77578 4625 C
3700 PRLD 77578 4625 C
3700 PRLD 77584 4625 C
Hooks Creek Ct
8600 HarC 77095 3538 B
Hooper Rd
13400 HOUS 77047 4373 C
14500 HarC 77047 4373 C
14500 PRLD 77047 4373 C
15200 PRLD 77584 4373 C
Hoops
- HarC 77377 3108 A
Hooten Ln
26100 MtgC 77354 2817 D
Hooten St
6000 HOUS 77074 4100 B
6000 HOUS 77081 4100 B
Hoot Owl
100 HOUS 77365 2974 E
Hoot Owl Rd
10400 HarC 77064 3540 B
Hoot Owl Tr
10 HOUS 77365 2974 E
Hoover
8500 HOUS 77012 4105 D
9700 HarC 77379 3110 D
Hoover Dr
1400 DRPK 77536 4109 C
Hoover Rd
600 HarC 77530 3969 C
Hoover St
3100 LMQU 77568 4873 B
4900 HOUS 77092 3683 A
5700 HOUS 77092 3682 D
Hoover Garden Dr
17400 HarC 77095 3537 D
Hope Blvd
- GLSN 77551 5222 A
- GLSN 77554 5221 E
10 GLSN 77554 5107 E
10 GLSN 77554 5108 A
10 GLSN 77554 5222 A
Hope Ln
11800 MtgC 77354 2671 B
Hope Rd
900 MtgC 77384 2675 E
900 MtgC 77384 2676 A
900 WDLD 77384 2676 A
Hope St
- HarC 77447 3104 C
Hope Canyon Ln
6500 FBnC 77469 4493 C
Hope Farm Ln
16600 HarC 77429 3397 A
Hope Farm Rd
10 FBnC 77459 4621 C
Hopeton Dr
- MtgC 77386 2969 C
Hopetown Dr
5700 HarC 77049 3828 C
Hope Valley Pl
10 WDLD 77382 2819 E
Hopeview Ct
19200 HarC 77449 3677 B
Hope Village Rd
- FRDW 77546 4505 D
15400 HarC 77546 4505 E
16600 HarC 77546 4506 A
Hopewell Ct
2400 FBnC 77469 4365 B
Hopewell Dr
23700 HarC 77493 3814 C
Hopewell Ln
7500 HOUS 77071 4239 E
Hopewood Mills Dr
6300 FBnC 77494 4092 B
Hopfe Rd
17700 HarC 77433 3250 D
17700 HarC 77447 3250 D
18000 HarC 77433 3105 C
18000 HarC 77447 3105 C
Hopi Ln
23500 MtgC 77365 2972 B
Hopi St
7100 BYTN 77521 3835 B
Hopkins St
1600 CNRO 77301 2384 C
1900 HOUS 77006 3962 E
Hopkins Park Dr
1300 HarC 77094 3955 B
Hopper Cir
1100 HOUS 77037 3685 A
Hopper Rd
1200 HOUS 77037 3685 B
1300 HarC 77093 3685 C
1300 HOUS 77093 3685 B
3100 HarC 77093 3686 B
5100 HOUS 77016 3686 D
5100 HOUS 77093 3686 D
5900 HOUS 77016 3687 A
Hoppers Creek Dr
19800 HarC 77449 3815 E
19800 HarC 77449 3816 C
Hopson St
1400 HOUS 77019 3963 A
Hopson Meadows Dr
25800 FBnC 77469 4092 B
Hopson Meadows Ln
11600 FBnC 77469 4092 C
Hopvine Ct
10 WDLD 77381 2821 A
Horace St
2700 FBnC 77477 4369 E
4200 HOUS 77026 3825 B
Horace Mann Av
900 RSBG 77471 4491 C
Horatio Dr
1300 JTCY 77029 3966 D
Horden Creek Dr
19400 HarC 77375 3109 C
Horizon Dr
- LMQU 77568 4872 B
16500 HarC 77532 3551 D
Horizon Ln
27600 LbyC 77372 2537 E

Houston Street Index

STREET
Block City ZIP Map# Grid
orizon Falls Ln
14300 HarC 77396 3547 C2
orizon Grove Ln
25600 FBnC 77494 4092 C5
orizon Heights Dr
2100 HOUS 77045 4242 D6
orizon Landing Dr
2100 HOUS 77045 4242 D7
Horizon Ridge Ct
10 WDLD 77381 2820 B3
Horizon Ridge Ct
10 WDLD 77381 2820 B3
Horizon Ridge Pl
10 WDLD 77381 2820 B3
Horizon Ridge Pl
10 WDLD 77381 2820 A3
ornbeam Dr
3400 HarC 77082 4096 C3
Hornbeam Pl
10 WDLD 77380 2968 B3
Hornbeam Pl
10 WDLD 77380 2968 B3
ornbill Ct
10 WDLD 77380 2822 B7
ornbrook Dr
11400 HOUS 77099 4238 B4
ornburger Rd
11200 HarC 77044 3689 C1
orncastle Ct
3400 BzaC 77584 4501 B4
orncastle Dr
700 HarC 77530 3830 A7
orne St
1000 HOUS 77088 3683 E1
ornet Dr
18400 MtgC 77365 2972 A6
ornpipe Ln
9900 HOUS 77080 3820 B4
ornsby Ln
7400 HOUS 77088 3683 C3
ornsilver Pl
10 WDLD 77381 2821 B2
ornwood Dr
5800 HOUS 77081 4100 C4
6500 HOUS 77074 4100 A4
7500 HOUS 77036 4099 D4
orse Ln
16900 FBnC 77053 4498 C1
16900 HOUS 77053 4498 C1
16900 HOUS 77489 4498 C1
orse Cave Cir
9200 HarC 77379 3255 C2
orse Creek Ln
14800 FBnC 77478 4236 E6
orsepen Bayou Dr
6200 HarC 77084 3679 A3
orse Prairie Dr
5800 HarC 77449 3676 C4
orseshoe
27100 MtgC 77372 2683 D1
orseshoe Bnd
800 LMQU 77568 4990 B1
2400 DRPK 77536 4109 E6
14000 MtgC 77384 2674 B2
14000 WDLD 77354 2674 B3
14000 WDLD 77384 2674 B2
14700 WDLD 77382 2674 B2
orseshoe Cir
21800 MtgC 77365 2972 B2
orseshoe Dr
- FRDW 77546 4628 E4
1000 SGLD 77478 4368 B3
21200 MNVL 77578 4747 B2
21600 MtgC 77365 2972 B1
Horseshoe Dr
1300 SGLD 77478 4368 C3
orse Shoe Ln
2400 FBnC 77469 4234 B6
orseshoe Run
23400 HarC 77373 3115 A4
orseshoe Tr
- HOUS 77396 3405 E3
18500 MtgC 77355 2815 A6
orse Shoe Wy
17200 MtgC 77357 2681 B5
orseshoe Bay Ct
- HarC 77429 3253 A6
orseshoe Bay Ln
- HarC 77429 3253 A6
orseshoe Bend Dr
10000 HarC 77064 3540 B4
orseshoe Falls
5600 FBnC 77459 4497 B7
5600 FBnC 77459 4621 A1
orseshoe Falls Ln
- HarC 77433 3395 E6
- HarC 77433 3396 B6
orseshoe Hill Ct
16100 HarC 77429 3397 B1
orseshoe Lake Ln
19500 HarC 77084 3816 A6
19700 HarC 77084 3815 E6
orsetail Falls
20300 HarC 77375 3109 D5
orsetooth Canyon Dr
17200 HarC 77095 3537 E3
orshoe Springs Ln
700 HarC 77090 3258 D7
orton St
5700 HOUS 77026 3824 E4
osford Rd
40700 MtgC 77354 2671 A1
osford Meadows Dr
24600 MtgC 77365 2973 A7
24600 MtgC 77365 3118 A1
oskins Dr
1900 HOUS 77080 3820 D4
ospital St
500 TMBL 77375 2964 C6
ostettler
- SSPL 77005 4101 D4
ostler Dr
8700 HarC 77375 2965 D2
otchkiss St
1200 HOUS 77012 4105 D3
ot Creek Ct
18400 HarC 77346 3265 D7
18400 HarC 77346 3409 A1
ot Creek Trc
- HarC 77346 3408 E1
7000 HarC 77346 3409 A1
ot Springs Dr
8300 HarC 77095 3538 C5
oubelt St
- HOUS 77020 3964 E4
oughton Ct
4100 SGLD 77479 4495 C3

STREET
Block City ZIP Map# Grid
Houghton Rd
200 HarC 77450 3954 E3
200 HOUS 77450 3954 E1
House Rd
10400 MtgC 77304 2382 D2
10600 CNRO 77304 2382 C2
15000 HarC 77447 3249 E7
15000 HarC 77447 3250 A7
House St
2100 PASD 77502 4247 E1
E House St
100 ALVN 77511 4867 E2
1700 BzaC 77511 4867 E2
2000 ALVN 77511 4868 A2
2000 BzaC 77511 4868 A2
W House St
100 ALVN 77511 4867 B2
2100 ALVN 77511 4866 E2
House Hahl Rd
15700 HarC 77433 3396 B4
17300 HarC 77433 3395 C5
19100 HarC 77447 3395 B5
Housman St
6600 HOUS 77055 3821 E6
Houston
1800 GlsC 77650 4879 B7
Houston Al
1700 GlsC 77650 4879 B7
Houston Av
- SEBK 77586 4509 D4
100 LGCY 77573 4632 A3
300 LGCY 77573 4631 E3
500 HOUS 77002 3963 B3
1200 HOUS 77007 3963 B2
1400 PASD 77502 4107 D6
2100 DKSN 77539 4633 B7
2100 GlsC 77539 4633 B7
2100 PRLD 77581 4503 C3
2500 HOUS 77009 3963 B1
2800 HOUS 77009 3824 B7
3700 DKSN 77539 4754 B2
5300 ARLA 77583 4623 B4
8400 HarC 77064 3541 C3
N Houston Av
100 HMBL 77338 3262 E5
S Houston Av
- HarC 77396 3406 D5
100 HMBL 77338 3262 E7
900 HMBL 77338 3406 E1
1300 HMBL 77396 3406 D4
W Houston Av
100 PASD 77502 4107 A7
Houston Dr
4800 GLSN 77551 5108 D5
6900 HarC 77040 3681 B3
7200 GlsC 77563 4990 D6
10700 LPRT 77571 4110 D6
17000 HarC 77433 3396 E6
Houston Dr N
2500 LMQU 77568 4989 D1
Houston Dr S
2000 LMQU 77568 4989 D2
Houston Dr W
1200 LMQU 77568 4989 D2
Houston Ln
14900 MtgC 77306 2680 D2
E Houston Rd
5200 HOUS 77028 3826 D3
7900 HOUS 77028 3687 D7
8200 HOUS 77078 3687 D7
S Houston Rd
100 WEBS 77598 4507 C6
1300 PASD 77502 4106 E7
1300 PASD 77506 4106 E7
2100 PASD 77502 4246 E2
2700 SHUS 77502 4246 E2
2700 SHUS 77587 4246 E2
Houston St
- BYTN 77520 3971 E5
- BYTN 77520 3972 A6
- HarC 77040 3681 B2
100 FBnC 77545 4499 C6
100 RHMD 77469 4492 A1
100 TMBL 77375 2964 B7
200 RHMD 77469 4491 E1
300 RSBG 77471 4490 D4
1200 BYTN 77520 3973 A5
1200 CNRO 77301 2383 E4
17900 GlsC 77511 4869 B4
Houston St FM-723
300 RSBG 77471 4490 D3
E Houston St
100 HarC 77562 3831 E2
100 TMBL 77375 2964 C6
800 HarC 77562 3832 A2
N Houston St
100 WEBS 77598 4507 B6
W Houston St
100 HarC 77562 3831 D2
Houston Center Blvd
- HOUS 77082 3957 E7
12100 HOUS 77077 3957 E7
12100 HOUS 77082 4097 E1
W Houston Center Blvd
- HOUS 77072 4097 E3
12100 HOUS 77077 3957 E7
12100 HOUS 77082 3957 E7
12100 HOUS 77082 4097 E2
Houston Chronicle Blvd
1200 HOUS 77084 3816 D7
1200 HOUS 77084 3955 E1
Houstonian
10 HOUS 77024 3961 A3
Houston Lake Dr
3700 PRLD 77581 4503 E6
3700 PRLD 77581 4504 A7
Houston National Blvd
16100 HarC 77095 3538 A1
Houston Oaks Dr
- HarC 77064 3540 E4
Houston Oaks Golf Course
- WlrC 77447 2958 E7
- WlrC 77447 2959 A6
N Houston Rosslyn Rd
5800 HOUS 77091 3682 D4
5800 HOUS 77092 3682 D4
8300 HOUS 77040 3682 B3
8300 HOUS 77088 3682 C3
9300 HarC 77086 3542 B4
9300 HarC 77088 3682 B3
9300 HOUS 77086 3542 B4
9900 HOUS 77040 3542 B7
9900 HOUS 77088 3542 B6
11100 HarC 77088 3542 B6
Houston Ship Channel Br
- HOUS - 3968 D7

STREET
Block City ZIP Map# Grid
Houston Ship Channel Br LP-8
- HOUS - 3968 D7
Houx St
4100 GlsC 77518 4634 C3
Hoveden Ct
20600 HarC 77450 3954 D4
Hoveden Dr
1400 HarC 77450 3954 D4
Howald St
100 LPRT 77571 4251 E6
Howard Av
600 DRPK 77536 4108 E4
600 DRPK 77536 4109 A4
Howard Cts S
- MtgC 77357 2829 D3
Howard Dr
- HOUS 77061 4245 D1
7900 HOUS 77017 4245 E1
8300 HOUS 77017 4106 A7
Howard Ln
1000 BLAR 77401 4101 C2
1200 HOUS 77081 4101 C2
1200 HOUS 77401 4101 C2
Howard St
- HOUS 77051 4243 B2
200 PASD 77506 4107 A3
900 HMBL 77338 3262 E7
7300 HOUS 77054 4102 E7
N Howard St
100 TMBL 77375 2964 C6
S Howard St
10 TMBL 77375 2964 C6
Howards Wy
18000 MtgC 77306 2534 A6
Howcher St
4100 HOUS 77047 4243 C7
5100 HOUS 77048 4243 E7
Howe
1300 HOUS 77002 3963 B5
Howell Av
800 LMQU 77568 4990 A2
Howell Ln
10 SGLD 77479 4495 A2
Howell St
300 ARLA 77583 4623 A7
300 FBnC 77583 4623 A7
5600 HOUS 77032 3405 D6
5700 HOUS 77396 3405 E6
Howell Creek Pl
10 WDLD 77382 2674 A5
Howell Grove Ln
15600 HarC 77095 3538 D4
Howland Ct
6100 HarC 77084 3678 E4
Howland St
15000 HarC 77084 3678 E4
Howser Dr
24900 MtgC 77357 2974 D1
Howth Av
1700 HOUS 77045 4242 C7
Howton St
7100 HOUS 77028 3825 E3
8000 HOUS 77028 3826 A3
N Howton St
7700 HOUS 77028 3826 B3
S Howton St
7700 HOUS 77028 3826 B3
Hoya Ct
14700 HarC 77070 3398 C1
14800 HarC 77070 3254 C7
Hoyt Dr
100 KATY 77494 3952 A2
Hoyt Ln
1600 HarC 77449 3814 E6
27000 FBnC 77494 3951 E3
27000 FBnC 77494 3952 A3
27000 KATY 77494 3952 A3
Hoyte Dr
10600 HOUS 77031 4239 C3
Hoyte Park Ln
19700 HarC 77379 3112 A6
Hub St
7300 HOUS 77023 4104 C1
Hubbell Dr
6100 PRLD 77584 4502 D6
Hubers Ct
12800 MSCY 77071 4239 C7
Hubert
- WEBS 77598 4507 B6
Hubert St
100 WEBS 77598 4507 B6
Huckinston Ct
9100 HarC 77379 3110 D5
Huckleberry Cir
5100 HOUS 77056 3960 D5
5100 HOUS 77056 3961 A5
Huckleberry Ln
2100 PASD 77502 4107 D4
2100 PASD 77502 4247 D2
5200 HOUS 77056 3960 E6
18500 MtgC 77365 2972 A5
Huckleberry St
2900 MSCY 77459 4496 C1
Huckleberry Branch Ct
19600 HarC 77388 3113 B7
Huckleton Ln
4200 HarC 77388 3112 C5
Huddersfield Dr
7900 HarC 77379 3256 A2
Huddler St
7400 HOUS 77074 4100 B6
Huddleston Dr
15500 HarC 77433 3251 D6
Hudgens Av
1300 KATY 77493 3813 D7
Hudler St
800 LMQU 77568 4873 E7
800 LMQU 77568 4989 E1
Hudson Cir
10 HOUS 77024 3959 C6
Hudson Ct
10 HOUS 77063 3959 C6
9100 HOUS 77024 3959 C6
13700 SGLD 77478 4237 A5
Hudson Ln
22600 MtgC 77357 2973 D3
Hudson Pl
- HOUS 77024 3959 C5
Hudson Rd
700 CNRO 77304 2383 D7
4600 GlsC 77517 4869 D6
Hudson St
7800 HOUS 77012 4105 B2
10000 HarC 77064 3541 D2
Hudson Bend Cir
9300 HarC 77095 3538 D4

STREET
Block City ZIP Map# Grid
Hudson Forest Ln
27000 FBnC 77494 4092 A1
Hudson Oaks
10 HOUS 77024 3959 C5
Hudson Oaks Dr
- HarC 77084 3677 E2
7000 HarC 77095 3677 E1
7600 HarC 77095 3537 E7
Hudson Oaks Ln
2300 FBnC 77469 4493 A3
Hudson River Tr
9600 HOUS 77075 4246 B7
Hudspeth Dr
2000 BzaC 77583 4624 A2
2200 PRLD 77578 4624 B2
2200 PRLD 77583 4624 B2
Huecho Tanks Dr
11800 FBnC 77478 4236 B6
Hueni Rd
10 HOUS 77365 2974 D7
10 HOUS 77365 3119 D1
Huepers St
5000 BzaC 77511 4868 C7
Hues Ridge Dr
12300 CNRO 77301 2531 A3
12300 CNRO 77302 2531 A3
Huey St
4000 HOUS 77087 4104 D4
Huff Dr
10500 HOUS 77031 4239 C3
Huff Rd
13800 MtgC 77372 2535 B5
14000 MtgC 77372 2681 B1
Huffman Ln
3000 HarC 77338 3263 D5
Huffman Eastgate Rd
1700 HarC 77336 3121 E7
1700 HarC 77336 3122 B7
Huffman New Caney Rd
6400 HarC 77336 2976 C7
6400 HarC 77357 2976 C1
25400 HarC 77336 3121 C2
25400 HarC 77336 3122 A5
26600 HOUS 77336 3121 C3
31700 HarC 77336 2830 C7
31700 HarC 77357 2830 B7
Huffman New Caney Rd FM-2100
29800 HarC 77336 2976 C7
Huffman Oaks Ln
12200 HarC 77336 3266 E2
Huffmeister Rd
6600 HarC 77084 3679 A3
6900 HarC 77095 3679 A3
8500 HarC 77095 3539 A5
9800 HarC 77065 3539 A2
9800 HarC 77429 3539 A2
11300 HarC 77065 3398 A7
11300 HarC 77429 3398 A6
13100 HarC 77429 3397 E4
16300 HarC 77429 3253 A7
16600 HarC 77429 3252 C7
E Huffsmith Rd
800 TMBL 77375 2964 D5
Hufsmith Rd
8500 HarC 77375 2965 C2
8500 HarC 77389 2965 B3
11100 HarC 77375 2964 E3
E Hufsmith Rd
100 TMBL 77375 2964 C5
1200 HarC 77375 2964 D4
W Hufsmith Rd
100 TMBL 77375 2964 B6
Hufsmith Cemetery Rd
25000 HarC 77375 2965 A2
Hufsmith Kohrville Rd
- HarC 77375 3254 D1
16300 HarC 77070 3255 A5
16300 HOUS 77070 3255 A5
17000 HarC 77375 3255 A1
20500 HarC 77375 3110 A4
21000 TMBL 77375 3110 A3
21200 HarC 77375 3109 E1
21200 TMBL 77375 3109 E1
22500 TMBL 77375 2964 E7
24700 HarC 77375 2964 E3
Hufsmith Kohrville Rd FM-2978
23200 HarC 77375 2964 E7
23200 TMBL 77375 2964 E7
Huge Oaks St
1400 HLSV 77055 3821 C6
1400 HOUS 77055 3821 C6
Huggins Dr
11100 HOUS 77035 4241 B4
Huggins St
100 BYTN 77520 4112 A1
Hugginsway St
3500 BzaC 77584 4501 C5
Hugh Rd
1200 HarC 77067 3402 B4
1200 HOUS 77067 3402 C4
Hugh Echols Blvd
- BYTN 77521 3972 E2
Hughes Ct
3800 DKSN 77539 4753 B5
21500 MtgC 77365 2973 B3
Hughes Ln
100 MtgC 77354 2817 D7
2600 DKSN 77539 4753 B4
2600 LGCY 77539 4753 B4
Hughes Rd
- MtgC 77354 2817 D7
10 TXCY 77539 4753 C6
100 DKSN 77539 4753 D5
1400 FBnC 77469 4365 D3
1700 DKSN 77539 4754 A4
1700 TXCY 77539 4754 A4
9800 HarC 77089 4377 D6
10200 HOUS 77089 4377 D6
11200 HOUS 77089 4378 A5
Hughes Rd W
13900 TXCY 77539 4753 C5
Hughes St
100 HOUS 77011 3964 D7
300 HOUS 77023 3964 D7
1300 HOUS 77023 4104 C1
Hughes Club Rd
8300 HarC 77049 3691 C7
Hughes Crossing Rd
- HarC 77429 3397 D3
Hughes Ranch Rd
- BzaC 77584 4500 E1
- PRLD 77584 4500 E1
2500 PRLD 77584 4501 C2
7800 BzaC 77581 4502 A2
7800 PRLD 77581 4502 A2
7900 PRLD 77581 4501 E2

STREET
Block City ZIP Map# Grid
Hughes Ranch Rd
9300 HarC 77089 4504 C1
Hughey Av
22800 MtgC 77357 2828 B1
Huisache Blvd
3300 PRLD 77581 4503 D5
Huisache Ct
3400 PRLD 77581 4503 D5
Huisache Dr
1800 RHMD 77469 4491 E3
Huisache St
4600 BLAR 77401 4101 B5
5100 BLAR 77401 4100 D6
5300 HOUS 77081 4100 D6
Huisache Branch Ct
19600 HarC 77388 3113 B7
Huldy St
1700 HOUS 77019 3962 B6
2600 HOUS 77098 3962 B7
Hull Ln
400 SGLD 77478 4367 C1
Hull St
4100 HOUS 77021 4103 D6
4700 TXCY 77539 4634 B5
5100 HOUS 77021 4104 A7
Hullsmith Dr
2700 HOUS 77063 3960 A7
Hulon St
14300 MtgC 77306 2532 D1
Humaya Dr
19400 MtgC 77365 2972 A3
Humber Bridge Ln
- HarC 77449 3676 C3
E Humble Av
10 BYTN 77520 3972 D7
100 BYTN 77520 3973 A7
100 BYTN 77520 4113 A1
W Humble Av
1400 BYTN 77520 3972 C6
Humble Dr
2100 SEBK 77586 4382 C7
2200 ELGO 77586 4382 C7
2900 BzaC 77578 4501 B7
2900 BzaC 77584 4625 B1
Humble Pkwy
- HOUS 77396 3406 B1
18200 HOUS 77338 3262 B7
18200 HOUS 77338 3406 B1
Humble Rd
- HarC 77377 3108 D3
- HarC 77377 3109 A3
- TMBL 77375 3109 A3
- TMBL 77377 3109 A3
Humble Camp Rd
5200 TXCY 77591 4755 B7
5200 TXCY 77591 4873 B1
6200 TXCY 77591 4755 B7
Humble Camp Rd S
8000 TXCY 77539 4873 A1
8000 TXCY 77591 4873 B2
Humble Camp Extension Rd
- TXCY 77591 4755 A4
5100 DKSN 77539 4754 C4
5500 TXCY 77539 4754 D4
8400 TXCY 77539 4755 A4
N Humble Lake Rd
14400 HarC 77377 3108 D3
Humble Pl Dr
1700 HMBL 77338 3263 A6
2000 HarC 77338 3263 A6
Humble Springs Dr
- HOUS 77396 3406 B5
Humble Tank Ct
- CNRO 77304 2383 D7
Humble Tank Rd
300 CNRO 77304 2383 D7
Humble Westfield Rd
- HOUS 77073 3259 D3
1600 HarC 77073 3259 C3
4500 HarC 77338 3260 C3
4500 HOUS 77338 3260 C3
7300 HarC 77338 3261 C5
7300 HOUS 77338 3261 C5
8600 HarC 77338 3262 A6
8600 HOUS 77338 3262 A6
9100 HMBL 77338 3262 A6
Humble Westfield Rd FM-1960
4500 HarC 77338 3260 C3
4500 HOUS 77338 3260 C3
7300 HarC 77338 3261 C5
7300 HOUS 77338 3261 C5
9600 HarC 77338 3262 C5
9600 HMBL 77338 3262 C5
9600 HOUS 77338 3262 C5
Humble Westfld Rd FM-1960 BUS
7700 HOUS 77338 3261 D5
8000 HarC 77338 3261 E6
8600 HarC 77338 3262 A6
9300 HMBL 77338 3262 A6
9300 HOUS 77338 3262 A6
Humble Westfld Rd FM-1960A BUS
- HMBL 77338 3262 B6
- HOUS 77338 3262 B6
8000 HarC 77338 3261 E6
8000 HOUS 77338 3261 E6
Hume Dr
19800 HarC 77433 3251 D6
Hummingbird
16900 MtgC 77385 2676 D5
Humming Bird Ct
200 PASD 77502 4247 A1
Hummingbird Dr
7800 HOUS 77071 4239 E3
Hummingbird Ln
- FBnC 77459 4621 C7
400 HarC 77060 3544 D3
2600 HMBL 77396 3406 C4
3300 ALVN 77511 4866 C4
3700 BzaC 77511 4866 C4
7200 TXCY 77591 4873 C6
15400 MtgC 77302 2679 E3
18600 HarC 77377 2962 A7
Hummingbird Pl
10900 CHTW 77385 2823 A5
Hummingbird St
2200 RMFT 77357 2829 A3
4300 HOUS 77035 4241 B4
5100 HOUS 77035 4240 E4
6200 HOUS 77096 4240 A3
9800 LPRT 77571 4250 B1
S Hummington Ct
9900 MtgC 77385 2676 D7
Humphreys Dr
7800 HarC 77083 4097 A3
8600 HarC 77083 4237 C1

STREET
Block City ZIP Map# Grid
Humphreyville St
3000 LPRT 77571 4251 D7
3000 LPRT 77571 4382 C1
Hundred Bridge Ln
10900 FBnC 77478 4236 D5
Hungary Dr
6200 PASD 77505 4248 D6
Hunkler Dr
11100 HOUS 77047 4243 D7
11900 HOUS 77047 4374 D1
Hunnewell Ct
10 WDLD 77382 2820 B1
Hunnewell Wy
10 WDLD 77382 2819 D2
10 WDLD 77382 2820 A1
E Hunnicutt St
100 BYTN 77520 3973 A7
W Hunnicutt St
10 BYTN 77520 3973 A6
200 BYTN 77520 3972 E6
Hunnington Dr
1900 CNRO 77301 2384 C1
1900 CNRO 77303 2384 C1
4100 CNRO 77303 2238 D7
Hunstanton Ct
3500 FBnC 77450 4094 C1
Hunt
- WlrC 77447 2813 C1
Hunt Dr
1800 FRDW 77546 4629 E3
Hunt Rd
100 BYTN 77521 3833 C6
100 HarC 77521 3833 E5
100 HarC 77521 3834 A5
Hunt St
10 HOUS 77003 3964 B6
500 CNRO 77301 2383 E6
Huntbrook Dr
- MSCY 77489 4370 D4
6800 HarC 77379 3256 C2
Hunter
9000 HOUS 77029 3965 D6
Hunter Dr
1100 TXCY 77590 4875 C6
E Hunter Dr
7000 GlsC 77563 4990 C6
W Hunter Dr
7000 GlsC 77563 4990 C6
Hunter Ln
25700 FBnC 77494 3952 C6
Hunter Pk
32300 MtgC 77385 2823 B6
Hunter St
1200 CNRO 77301 2383 E3
1500 GNPK 77547 3966 A6
2300 BYTN 77520 3972 C5
E Hunter St
3800 HarC 77562 3833 A1
W Hunter St
3800 HarC 77562 3833 A1
Hunter Brook Dr
7100 HarC 77379 3256 C2
Huntercliff Ln
20300 HarC 77449 3676 E3
Hunter Creek Ln
10300 CNRO 77304 2236 E5
Huntercrest St
600 ELGO 77586 4382 B7
700 SEBK 77586 4382 B7
Hunterfield Dr
12800 HarC 77429 3254 C6
Hunter Glen Dr
3100 MSCY 77459 4497 B2
Hunter Green Ct
4500 FBnC 77545 4622 E2
Huntermoor Cir
8200 HarC 77338 3261 E5
8300 HarC 77338 3262 A5
Hunter Park Ct
2300 MtgC 77385 2823 B6
Hunter Ranch Wy
24500 HarC 77447 3249 D3
Hunter Ridge Ct
1400 FBnC 77545 4622 E2
Hunters Bnd
1700 FRDW 77546 4629 D4
Hunters Ct
- MSCY 77489 4370 E4
Hunters Grv
15500 MtgC 77355 2962 A2
15500 SGCH 77355 2962 A2
Hunters Ln
200 FRDW 77546 4629 D4
500 LGCY 77539 4753 A4
Hunters Rd
29600 MtgC 77355 2816 A3
Hunters St
1500 GNPK 77547 3966 A6
Hunters Tr
- MtgC 77357 2828 E5
100 CNRO 77304 2383 B4
1700 FRDW 77546 4629 D4
3700 BYTN 77521 3973 E3
19700 MtgC 77357 2829 A5
Hunters Wy
600 HNCV 77024 3960 B2
Hunters Bend Dr
15300 HarC 77377 2963 B7
Hunters Branch Dr
10 HDWV 77024 3959 E2
10 PNPV 77024 3959 E2
Hunters Canyon
3300 BYTN 77521 3973 E3
Hunters Canyon Ln
12600 HarC 77429 3398 B1
Hunter's Chase Ln
- HarC 77429 3397 C1
E Hunters Cir Dr
1300 HOUS 77055 3821 E5
N Hunters Cir Dr
7700 HOUS 77055 3821 E5
S Hunters Cir Dr
7700 HOUS 77055 3821 E5
W Hunters Cir Dr
1300 HOUS 77055 3821 E5
Hunters Cove
1700 FRDW 77546 4629 D3
Hunters Cove Ct
13900 HarC 77039 3546 A3
Hunters Creek Dr
8300 HNCV 77024 3960 B1
8400 SPVL 77024 3960 B1
Hunters Creek Ln
6000 BYTN 77521 3834 E3
6900 HarC 77521 3834 E3
Hunters Creek Pl
10 HDWV 77024 3960 A1
10 HNCV 77024 3960 A1

STREET
Block City ZIP Map# Grid
Hunter's Creek Wy
100 HarC 77447 3105 B3
E Hunters Creekway Dr
1200 HOUS 77055 3821 D7
N Hunters Creekway Dr
7700 HOUS 77055 3821 E5
S Hunters Creekway Dr
7700 HOUS 77055 3821 E5
W Hunters Creekway Dr
1200 HOUS 77055 3821 E5
N Hunters Crossing Cir
100 WDLD 77381 2820 C4
S Hunters Crossing Cir
10 WDLD 77381 2820 C4
Hunters Crossing Ct
10 WDLD 77381 2820 C4
Hunters Crossing Dr
- WDLD 77381 2820 B4
Hunters Crossing Ln
8300 BYTN 77521 3834 E4
8300 HarC 77521 3834 E4
Hunters Den Dr
500 HOUS 77079 3957 D3
Hunters Field Ln
12900 HarC 77044 3689 B5
Hunters Forest
1700 FRDW 77546 4629 D4
Hunters Forest Dr
10800 HNCV 77024 3960 A2
Huntersglen Cir
17300 HarC 77396 3407 E2
Hunters Glen Dr
2900 MSCY 77459 4497 B1
Hunters Glen Ln
6500 HarC 77521 3834 E3
Hunters Green Ln
1000 FBnC 77545 4623 A2
1700 FBnC 77545 4622 D2
Hunters Grove Ln
600 HNCV 77024 3960 B3
Hunters Hollow Dr
- MtgC 77380 2967 B3
Hunters Hollow Rd
24700 MtgC 77380 2967 B3
26300 MtgC 77380 2821 B7
26300 MtgC 77381 2821 B7
26300 WDLD 77381 2821 B7
Hunters Lake Ct
14000 HarC 77044 3549 E2
Hunters Lake Wy
15400 HarC 77044 3549 D3
Hunters Lake Wy Ct
14100 HarC 77044 3549 E2
Hunters Locke St
2500 SGLD 77479 4368 D6
Hunters Lodge Ln
8300 BYTN 77521 3834 E4
8300 HarC 77521 3834 E4
Hunters Park Dr
1400 MSCY 77489 4370 D4
11000 HNCV 77024 3959 E2
11000 HNCV 77024 3960 A2
11000 PNPV 77024 3959 E2
Hunters Park Ln
400 HNCV 77024 3960 A2
6500 HarC 77521 3835 A4
6600 HarC 77521 3834 E3
6900 BYTN 77521 3834 E3
Hunters Park Wy
1200 HOUS 77055 3821 C7
Hunters Peak Ln
7700 CmbC 77520 3835 C4
Hunters Point Dr
7600 FBnC 77479 4494 A4
Hunter Spring Cir
23800 HarC 77373 3114 D5
Hunter Springs Ln
21400 HarC 77379 3111 C3
Hunters Ridge Ct
10 HNCV 77024 3960 A4
Hunter's Ridge Dr
4000 BYTN 77520 3974 A3
4000 BYTN 77521 3973 E3
4000 BYTN 77521 3974 A3
Hunters Ridge Ln
6400 HarC 77521 3834 E3
Hunters Terrace Dr
- HarC 77338 3407 E1
Hunterstone Ct
6400 HarC 77084 3678 B3
Hunters Trace St
1900 HOUS 77042 3958 B6
Hunters Trail Ln
6400 BYTN 77521 3834 E3
6400 HarC 77521 3834 E4
Hunters Trail St
300 HNCV 77024 3960 B3
Hunters Village Dr
8300 HarC 77346 3265 C7
Hunters Wy Ln
6400 BYTN 77521 3834 E3
7000 HarC 77521 3834 E3
Hunter Wood Dr
1200 LGCY 77573 4632 A4
Hunterwood Dr
400 HNCV 77024 3960 B3
3200 MSCY 77459 4496 E1
Hunterwyck Ln
8300 BYTN 77521 3834 E4
8300 HarC 77521 3834 E4
8400 HarC 77521 3835 A3
Huntford Ln
12400 HarC 77044 3689 A4
W Hunting St
4500 HOUS 77026 3825 A5
Hunting Tr
25400 WlrC 77447 2813 C1
Hunting Bayou Dr
- JTCY 77029 3966 D3
Hunting Briar Dr
12500 HOUS 77099 4237 C2
Hunting Brook Dr
12500 HOUS 77099 4237 C2
Hunting Dale Dr
- HarC 77450 3953 E5
Hunting Dog Ln
16300 HOUS 77489 4370 E6
Huntingdon Pl
3200 HOUS 77019 3961 E6
3200 HOUS 77019 3962 A6
Hunting Hill Dr
- HOUS 77062 4379 E7
Hunting Meadow Dr
4600 HarC 77449 3677 A6
Hunting Path Ct
11000 HarC 77065 3539 D1
Hunting Path Pl
10 WDLD 77381 2820 C3

STREET / Block City ZIP Map# Grid

Huntingshire
19100 MtgC 77357 2829 A4
Huntingshire Ln
8400 HarC 77521 3834 E4
Huntington Ct
3000 KATY 77493 3813 B3
Huntington Dr
- MSCY 77489 4370 E5
1000 PRLD 77584 4501 B2
2400 PASD 77506 4107 E4
Huntington Ln
600 FRDW 77546 4505 A6
1900 FBnC 77469 4232 D4
8300 BYTN 77521 3834 E3
8400 HarC 77521 3834 E3
Huntington Pk
- HOUS 77088 3682 E3
Huntington Rd
100 FBnC 77471 4490 B2
100 RSBG 77471 4490 B3
Huntington St
22000 MtgC 77365 2972 C2
Huntington Wy
2800 PRLD 77584 4502 A5
Huntington Bend Dr
10 MNVL 77583 4624 D4
Huntington Cove
900 HNCV 77024 3960 A4
900 HNCV 77057 3960 A4
900 HOUS 77057 3960 A4
Huntington Crest Dr
10400 HOUS 77099 4237 D3
Huntington Dale Dr
10200 HOUS 77099 4237 E2
Huntington Estates Dr
10400 HOUS 77099 4237 C3
Huntington Field Dr
12300 HOUS 77099 4237 C2
Huntington Glen Dr
- HOUS 77099 4238 A2
Huntington Hill Dr
9500 HOUS 77099 4237 E2
Huntington Park Cir
10 BKHV 77024 3959 B2
10 HOUS 77024 3959 B2
Huntington Park Ct
10 BKHV 77024 3959 B2
10 HOUS 77024 3959 B2
Huntington Park Dr
12000 HOUS 77099 4238 A2
12100 HOUS 77099 4237 E3
Huntington Pl Dr
9500 HOUS 77099 4237 D3
Huntington Point Dr
10400 HOUS 77099 4237 D3
Huntington Valley Dr
10400 HOUS 77099 4237 D3
Huntington Venture Dr
12300 HOUS 77099 4237 C3
Huntington View Dr
10200 HOUS 77099 4237 D2
Huntington Wick Dr
9500 HOUS 77099 4237 E2
Huntington Willow Ln
14900 HarC 77090 3258 D7
Huntington Wood Dr
10200 HOUS 77099 4237 E2
Huntington Woods Dr
10 HarC 77377 2962 E7
10 HarC 77377 3107 E1
Huntington Woods Estates Dr
16400 HarC 77377 2962 E7
Huntington Wy Dr
9500 HOUS 77099 4237 E2
Hunting Valley Ct
24700 FBnC 77494 3953 B6
Hunting Valley Ln
2600 FBnC 77494 3953 B6
Huntingwick Dr
12300 HOUS 77024 3959 A3
12600 HOUS 77024 3958 E3
Hunting Wood Dr
23400 MtgC 77447 2960 B5
Hunt Lake Ln
19500 HarC 77084 3816 A6
19700 HarC 77084 3815 E6
Huntland Ct
3700 FBnC 77450 4094 B1
Huntleigh Wy
13000 SGLD 77478 4237 C5
Huntley Dr
10 HOUS 77056 3961 A4
Huntmont Dr
14700 HarC 77429 3396 B1
Hunton Dr
4000 HOUS 77042 4098 E2
Huntress Ln
1900 HOUS 77062 4507 C2
Huntsman Dr
2900 HarC 77067 3402 A4
Huntsmans Horn Cir
10 WDLD 77380 2821 E6
10 WDLD 77380 2822 A6
Huntswell Ct
5200 FBnC 77494 4093 B2
Huntwick Ln
24100 HarC 77336 3266 E2
Huntwick Parc Ct
5000 HarC 77069 3400 E1
Huntwood Hills Ln
4400 FBnC 77494 4092 D2
Huntwyck Dr
- MtgC 77362 2963 C1
11000 HNCV 77024 3959 E3
11000 HNCV 77024 3960 A3
11000 PNPV 77024 3959 E3
Hurfus Dr
2000 HOUS 77092 3822 A5
Hurley Ln
4000 MtgC 77384 2822 A1
4000 SHEH 77384 2822 A1
Hurley St
600 HOUS 77022 3685 B6
2800 HOUS 77093 3685 E6
2800 HOUS 77093 3686 A6
Hurlingham St
2800 HarC 77093 3685 E1
2800 HarC 77093 3686 A1
Hurlock St
700 HarC 77373 3114 A6
Hurlplan St
2800 HOUS 77093 3686 A6
Huron Ct
7800 HarC 77521 3833 B4
Huron St
23700 HarC 77389 2967 A5

Huron Park Tr
18400 HarC 77346 3264 E7
Hurricane Ln
- HarC 77073 3259 E5
- HarC 77073 3260 A5
- HarC 77338 3260 A5
- MSCY 77545 4622 A1
3300 MSCY 77545 4498 B7
Hurst Ct
12200 HarC 77429 3397 B6
Hurst Dr
9200 BzaC 77578 4747 B5
9500 MNVL 77578 4747 B5
S Hurst Dr
- HarC 77089 4505 A1
Hurst St
6100 HOUS 77008 3822 E7
6100 HOUS 77008 3823 A7
Hurstfield Pointe Ct
13900 HarC 77429 3397 C3
Hurstfield Pointe Dr
15800 HarC 77429 3397 C3
Hurst Forest Dr
8000 HarC 77346 3265 B5
Hurst Green Ln
- FBnC 77545 4498 D6
Hurstgreen Ln
300 ALVN 77511 4867 D5
Hurst Hill Ln
10300 HOUS 77075 4377 A3
Hurst Park Dr
1200 HarC 77379 3255 B1
Hurst Point Ln
14900 HarC 77049 3828 E2
Hurstshire Bnd
400 HarC 77494 3953 B1
Hurst Wood Dr
19500 HarC 77346 3265 B5
Hurstwood Dr
20000 HarC 77346 3264 E5
20000 HarC 77346 3265 A5
Hurta Rd
100 HarC 77532 3552 C7
Hurtgen Forest Rd
7300 HOUS 77033 4243 E1
Huse St
5500 HarC 77039 3546 D7
Huser Dr
- ALVN 77511 4867 D6
Hussion St
1300 HOUS 77003 3963 E7
1300 HOUS 77003 3964 C5
Hutcheson St
100 HOUS 77003 3964 A6
N Hutcheson St
10 HOUS 77003 3964 A5
Hutchings
1400 GLSN 77551 5108 C5
Hutchins Dr
- BzaC 77584 4501 C7
Hutchins St
10 HOUS 77002 3963 D5
600 HOUS 77003 3963 C7
900 HMPD 77445 3098 C2
2200 HOUS 77004 3963 B7
2500 HMPD 77445 3097 E2
3600 HOUS 77004 4103 B1
E Hutchinson Cir
15200 MSCY 77071 4370 D1
W Hutchinson Cir
15400 MSCY 77071 4370 D1
Hutchinson St
- HOUS 77034 4379 A4
Hutto
14800 HarC 77049 3828 E3
14800 HarC 77049 3829 A3
Hutto St
1200 LMQU 77568 4872 D5
Hutton St
2100 HOUS 77026 3964 B1
2400 HOUS 77026 3825 E7
Hyacinth Pl
800 MSCY 77459 4497 B5
Hyacinth St
3000 HOUS 77009 3824 B7
Hyacinth Wy
9800 MtgC 77385 2676 D4
Hyacinth Path Wy
- HarC 77049 3829 C3
Hyannis Port St N
500 HarC 77532 3552 A3
Hyannis Port St S
500 HarC 77532 3552 A3
Hycliff Ct
6600 MSCY 77459 4496 C4
Hycohen Rd
13600 HOUS 77047 4374 A4
Hyde Park Blvd
10 HOUS 77006 3962 D6
10 HOUS 77006 3963 C3
Hyde Park Dr
4100 SGLD 77479 4495 B3
15400 HarC 77429 3252 E6
Hyde Park Pl
4900 HarC 77069 3256 E6
Hydethorpe Dr
8800 FBnC 77083 4236 D1
Hydro 55 St
- HarC 77073 3404 B2
- HarC 77073 3404 B2
Hyland Ln
300 LGCY 77573 4631 E4
Hyland Pk
2300 HarC 77014 3402 A3
Hylander Dr
11200 HarC 77070 3255 A7
11400 HarC 77070 3254 E7
Hyland Greens Ln
24300 HarC 77373 2968 D5
Hyssop
10 LbyC 77535 3268 C3
Hyta St
200 HOUS 77018 3823 C2

I

I Ct
- HarC 77388 3111 D1
E I St
500 LPRT 77571 4251 E4
N I St
- LPRT 77571 4251 D1
- MRGP 77571 4251 D1
W I St
200 LPRT 77571 4251 D4
I-10
- HOUS 77450 3954 D1

I-10 East Frwy
- BYTN - 3832 B6
- BYTN - 3833 B5
- BYTN - 3834 E3
- CmbC - 3835 E2
- HarC - 3830 D7
- HarC - 3831 A6
- HarC - 3832 E5
- HarC - 3833 B5
- HarC - 3834 E2
- HarC - 3835 A2
- HarC - 3967 E2
- HarC - 3968 A2
- HarC - 3969 B1
- HOUS - 3963 B2
- HOUS - 3964 E2
- HOUS - 3965 B1
- HOUS - 3966 E2
- HOUS - 3967 A2
- MTBL - 3835 E2
I-10 Katy Frwy
- HarC - 3952 E1
- HarC - 3953 E1
- HarC - 3955 A1
- HarC - 3956 E1
- HarC - 3959 D1
- HDWV - 3959 E1
- HDWV - 3960 A1
- HOUS - 3953 E1
- HOUS - 3954 E1
- HOUS - 3955 E1
- HOUS - 3956 B1
- HOUS - 3957 B1
- HOUS - 3958 E1
- HOUS - 3959 A1
- HOUS - 3960 A1
- HOUS - 3961 A1
- HOUS - 3962 E2
- HOUS - 3963 B1
- KATY - 3951 A2
- KATY - 3952 E1
- SPVL - 3959 D1
- SPVL - 3960 A1
- WlrC - 3951 A2
I-45
- HOUS 77373 3113 D4
21500 HarC 77388 3113 D2
25400 MtgC 77380 2968 C2
- CNRO - 2237 C7
- CNRO - 2383 E7
- GLSN - 5107 E5
- GLSN - 5108 A5
- MtgC - 2237 B1
I-45 Feeder Rd
- CNRO 77302 2530 A5
- CNRO 77303 2237 C5
- CNRO 77304 2237 C7
- CNRO 77384 2530 A7
- CNRO 77385 2530 A7
- CNRO 77385 2676 A2
- MtgC 77302 2530 A5
- MtgC 77378 2237 B1
- MtgC 77385 2676 A2
- PNVL 77304 2237 B2
- PNVL 77318 2237 B1
- SHEH 77385 2676 B7
- WDLD 77385 2676 A2
500 CNRO 77301 2383 E6
500 CNRO 77304 2383 E6
900 CNRO 77301 2529 E1
900 CNRO 77304 2529 E1
1500 CNRO 77301 2530 A2
1500 CNRO 77304 2530 A2
15100 CNRO 77384 2676 A2
15600 MtgC 77384 2676 A6
17100 WDLD 77384 2676 A6
29600 SHEH 77384 2676 A7
I-45 Frontage Rd
- HOUS 77009 3963 B1
- MtgC 77385 2822 B4
- ORDN 77385 2822 B4
2100 HOUS 77009 3824 B6
4100 HOUS 77022 3824 A1
4400 HOUS 77022 3823 E1
4800 HOUS 77022 3684 E7
5400 HOUS 77076 3684 D6
6500 HOUS 77091 3684 C4
7500 HOUS 77037 3684 B1
7500 HOUS 77088 3684 B1
8500 HOUS 77037 3544 B7
8500 HOUS 77088 3544 B7
9300 HOUS 77038 3544 B3
9600 HarC 77038 3544 B5
10100 HarC 77037 3544 B4
11300 HOUS 77060 3544 B3
11900 HOUS 77038 3403 B7
11900 HOUS 77060 3403 B7
12100 HOUS 77067 3403 B7
12400 HarC 77060 3403 A5
13000 HarC 77067 3403 A4
13700 HarC 77073 3403 A3
13700 HarC 77090 3403 A3
13700 HOUS 77090 3403 A3
14400 HarC 77090 3402 E1
14800 HOUS 77073 3403 A1
15100 HarC 77073 3258 E2
15100 HarC 77073 3402 E1
15100 HarC 77090 3258 E2
15100 HOUS 77073 3258 E7
15100 HOUS 77073 3402 E1
16500 HOUS 77090 3258 E5
18100 MtgC 77385 2676 B7
18100 SHEH 77385 2676 B7
18100 SHEH 77385 2822 B1
18200 HarC 77373 3258 E1
18300 HarC 77388 3258 E1
18300 MtgC 77384 2676 A7
18300 SHEH 77380 2822 B2
18300 SHEH 77384 2676 B7
18300 SHEH 77384 2822 B1
18300 WDLD 77384 2676 A7
18700 HarC 77373 3113 D6
18700 HOUS 77388 3113 E7
19000 HarC 77388 3113 E7
19000 HOUS 77373 3113 D6
21900 HarC 77389 3113 D1
22400 HarC 77373 2968 D7
22400 HarC 77389 2968 D7
23700 MtgC 77386 2968 C2
25400 MtgC 77380 2968 C1
26100 MtgC 77380 2822 B7
26100 MtgC 77386 2822 B7
26200 ORDN 77380 2822 B7
26300 MtgC 77386 2822 B7
26900 WDLD 77380 2822 B7
28000 SHEH 77380 2822 B4
I-45 Gulf Frwy
- DKSN - 4753 B3

I-45 Gulf Frwy
- GlsC - 4990 E6
- GlsC - 4991 A7
- GlsC - 5106 B1
- GlsC - 5107 A4
- GLSN - 5107 A4
- HarC - 4506 E6
- HOUS - 3963 C6
- HOUS - 4103 E1
- HOUS - 4104 B2
- HOUS - 4105 C7
- HOUS - 4245 D1
- HOUS - 4246 D7
- HOUS - 4377 E2
- HOUS - 4378 E6
- HOUS - 4506 E6
- LGCY - 4631 B1
- LGCY - 4752 E1
- LGCY - 4753 E7
- LMQU - 4872 E6
- LMQU - 4873 B7
- LMQU - 4989 B1
- LMQU - 4990 E6
- TXCY - 4753 C5
- TXCY - 4871 E1
- TXCY - 4872 A1
- TXCY - 4873 B7
- WEBS - 4506 E6
- WEBS - 4507 A7
- WEBS - 4631 C3
I-45 Gulf Freeway Frontage Rd
- HOUS - 4506 B3
I-45 North Frwy
- CNRO - 2383 E6
- CNRO - 2529 E1
- CNRO - 2530 A7
- CNRO - 2676 A7
- HarC - 2968 D5
- HarC - 3113 D1
- HarC - 3258 E7
- HarC - 3402 E1
- HarC - 3403 A4
- HarC - 3544 B6
- HOUS - 3113 E7
- HOUS - 3258 E7
- HOUS - 3403 A4
- HOUS - 3544 B7
- HOUS - 3684 C3
- HOUS - 3823 E1
- HOUS - 3824 B5
- HOUS - 3963 B1
- MtgC - 2530 A5
- MtgC - 2676 A7
- MtgC - 2822 B4
- MtgC - 2968 C2
- ORDN - 2822 B4
- SHEH - 2676 B7
- SHEH - 2822 B7
I-610
- BLAR - 4101 A2
- HOUS - 3822 B7
- HOUS - 3823 D3
- HOUS - 3824 E4
- HOUS - 3825 E4
- HOUS - 3826 E7
- HOUS - 3961 B1
- HOUS - 3965 E7
- HOUS - 4101 A7
- HOUS - 4103 E7
- HOUS - 4104 A7
- HOUS - 4105 C5
- HOUS - 4241 E1
- HOUS - 4242 E1
- HOUS - 4243 D1
I-610 Ship Channel Br
- HOUS - 4105 E1
Ian
1300 HarC 77562 3832 B1
Iberia Dr
11100 HarC 77065 3539 D7
11300 HarC 77065 3398 D7
Iberis Meadows Dr
25000 HarC 77375 2965 D3
Ibis Dr
5500 GLSN 77551 5108 D7
Ibis Ln
5000 HarC 77338 3260 D2
9800 MtgC 77385 2676 D3
Ibis Rd
19600 HarC 77447 3104 D4
Ibis Wy
2000 MSCY 77489 4497 C1
Ibis Bay Ct
19700 FBnC 77469 4234 D3
IBM
- PASD 77058 4380 E6
- PASD 77059 4380 E5
Ibris Ranch Dr
25100 FBnC 77494 3953 A6
Iceland Ct
- HarC 77379 3111 E6
Ice Palace Dr
10100 HOUS 77025 4241 D2
Ida
200 HOUS 77020 3964 B3
Ida St
- HOUS 77020 3964 B3
- RSBG 77471 4491 B4
Ida Bell St
100 HOUS 77007 3962 E1
Ida Faye
3300 HarC 77032 3546 A2
Idaho Av
1600 LGCY 77573 4632 B6
Idaho St
500 SHUS 77587 4246 D4
1300 BYTN 77520 4112 B2
3900 HOUS 77021 4103 E7
5000 HOUS 77021 4104 A7
S Idaho St
100 LPRT 77571 4251 E2
700 LPRT 77571 4252 A3
Ida Rose Ct
6000 HarC 77449 3676 D4
Ida Wells Forest Dr
7400 HOUS 77016 3687 A3
Ideal Dr
8400 FBnC 77583 4744 A3
Ideal St
2500 HOUS 77009 3963 B1
Idle Dr
26300 MtgC 77355 2814 A1
Idlebrook Dr
10500 HarC 77070 3399 A2
11600 HarC 77070 3398 E2
Idle Glen Roadway
20400 MtgC 77357 2829 E7
21000 HarC 77357 2975 E1

Idleloch Dr
28100 HarC 77336 3121 D3
Idle Water Ln
13000 HarC 77044 3408 E5
13000 HOUS 77044 3408 E5
Idlewild Roadway
20400 HarC 77357 2829 E7
20900 HarC 77357 2975 E1
Idlewood Cir
10 WDLD 77381 2820 D4
Idlewood Ct
500 FRDW 77546 4505 B5
10900 LPRT 77571 4250 D3
Idlewood Dr
- WDLD 77381 2820 D4
500 HTCK 77563 4988 C2
600 FRDW 77546 4505 B5
700 BYTN 77520 3972 D6
E Idlewood Dr
10800 LPRT 77571 4250 D3
Idlewood Rd
- HarC 77357 2829 E7
- HarC 77357 2975 E1
Idlewood Crossing Dr
11100 FBnC 77469 4092 C7
Idlewood Glen Ct
1800 FBnC 77469 4234 C6
Idylwild St
1300 HOUS 77009 3824 A5
Idylwild Wood Wy
14400 HarC 77429 3395 E1
Idylwood Dr
1700 HOUS 77023 4104 D3
Igloo Rd
3000 HOUS 77032 3404 E2
Ike Frank Rd
4500 GlsC 77517 4869 E7
4500 GlsC 77517 4870 A7
Ikes Ln
24400 HOUS 77336 3266 D2
Ikes Pond Dr
7500 HarC 77389 2966 A3
Ikes Tree Dr
7600 HarC 77389 2966 A3
Ilex St
6700 HOUS 77087 4105 A4
7200 HOUS 77012 4105 B4
Ilfrey Ln
- HOUS 77056 3961 A6
S Ilfrey St
100 HarC 77520 3831 E7
300 HarC 77520 3970 E1
Illene Dr
11500 HarC 77093 3546 C7
11600 HarC 77039 3546 C7
Illiad Ct
11500 HOUS 77477 4238 A4
Illinois Av
500 SHUS 77587 4246 C4
N Illinois Av
100 LGCY 77573 4632 A2
S Illinois Av
800 LGCY 77573 4632 B3
Illinois Rd
3000 FBnC 77545 4498 E7
Illinois St
2500 FBnC 77545 4498 E5
3100 BYTN 77520 4112 A1
3400 BYTN 77520 4111 E1
4400 DKSN 77539 4754 A3
6300 HOUS 77021 4103 B5
Ilona Ln
8500 HOUS 77025 4101 D7
9200 HOUS 77025 4241 D1
Ilsa St
6700 BKVL 77581 4376 A6
7000 PRLD 77581 4376 A6
Ilsa Morada
10 HTCK 77563 5105 A5
Imani Ln
13500 HOUS 77085 4371 E1
Imber St
700 PASD 77506 4106 E5
Imhoff Rd
27100 HarC 77447 3103 E3
28500 HarC 77484 3103 A3
Imite St
3700 DKSN 77539 4753 E2
Imogene
7600 HOUS 77074 4239 D1
Imogene Rd
- FBnC 77469 4366 B3
Imogene St
- HOUS 77036 4099 B7
4700 HOUS 77096 4101 A7
4800 HOUS 77096 4241 A1
5300 HOUS 77096 4240 D1
5400 HOUS 77096 4100 D7
5800 HOUS 77074 4240 B1
7500 HOUS 77074 4239 D1
8600 HOUS 77074 4099 C7
Imperial Cross
12600 HarC 77377 3254 B3
Imperial Ct
13800 SGLD 77478 4237 A6
Imperial Dr
100 FRDW 77546 4505 C6
2200 LGCY 77573 4508 E7
5400 FBnC 77583 4623 C4
Imperial Ln
900 HOUS 77336 3121 B5
Imperial Rd
400 SGLD 77478 4367 D2
Imperial St
4900 BLAR 77401 4100 E3
4900 BLAR 77401 4101 A3
4900 HOUS 77081 4100 E3
4900 HOUS 77401 4100 E3
11200 HarC 77093 3685 C1
Imperial Bend Dr
1200 HarC 77073 3403 C2
Imperial Bend Ln
200 WlrC 77493 3812 A6
Imperial Brook Dr
19900 HarC 77073 3403 C2
Imperial Canyon Ct
14100 SGLD 77478 4236 E5
Imperial Canyon Ln
2300 SGLD 77478 4236 E5
14000 SGLD 77478 4237 A5
Imperial Colony Ln
19600 HarC 77449 3677 A7
Imperial Creek Dr
29400 HarC 77377 2963 D7
Imperial Crown Dr
1600 HOUS 77043 3820 A6
1700 HOUS 77080 3820 A6

Imperial Falls Ct
15800 HarC 77095 3538 D6
Imperial Forest Ln
- HarC 77049 3828 D1
15900 HarC 77073 3259 B5
Imperial Green Dr
20000 HarC 77073 3403 B1
Imperial Grove Dr
5300 HarC 77066 3401 A7
Imperial Hills Dr
19300 HarC 77375 3109 C6
Imperial Ivy Ct
22700 HarC 77373 2968 C6
Imperial Lake Dr
900 HarC 77073 3403 C1
Imperial Landing Ln
20800 HarC 77449 3815 C2
Imperial Leaf Ln
6700 HarC 77379 3111 C4
Imperial Legends Dr
30500 MtgC 77386 2969 C1
Imperial Manor Ln
1400 HarC 77073 3259 B4
Imperial Oak Dr
20500 MtgC 77355 2814 B5
Imperial Oaks Blvd
- MtgC 77385 2823 B7
- MtgC 77386 2823 B7
- MtgC 77386 2969 B1
Imperial Park Ln
- HarC 77073 3259 A4
N Imperial Path Ln
2200 MtgC 77386 2969 B1
S Imperial Path Ln
31000 MtgC 77386 2969 B1
Imperial Plaza Dr
400 HOUS 77060 3403 D7
Imperial Point Rd
- HOUS 77072 4098 C5
Imperial Ridge Ln
- HarC 77073 3259 A4
20900 HarC 77379 3111 A4
Imperial Shore Dr
13000 PRLD 77584 4500 A2
Imperial Shores Cir
1900 HOUS 77345 3120 E6
Imperial Springs Ct
14200 HarC 77429 3397 B1
Imperial Stone Dr
19800 HarC 77073 3403 C2
Imperial Valley Ct
14800 HOUS 77060 3544 C3
Imperial Valley Dr
15800 HOUS 77060 3544 C1
16200 HOUS 77060 3403 D6
17600 HarC 77060 3403 C4
18200 HarC 77073 3403 B2
20300 HOUS 77073 3403 B1
20400 HOUS 77073 3259 B7
21400 HarC 77073 3259 B5
Imperial View Ln
- MtgC 77386 2823 B7
- MtgC 77386 2969 D1
Imperial Walk Ct
3100 MtgC 77386 2823 D7
Imperial Walk Ln
30800 MtgC 77386 2969 D1
31000 MtgC 77386 2823 D7
Imperial Wood Ct
5500 BzaC 77583 4623 D3
Imperial Wood Ln
14100 BzaC 77583 4623 C4
Imperial Woods Ln
11700 HarC 77429 3254 A7
Imperium Ln
- MtgC 77357 2829 C2
Ina
10700 HOUS 77016 3687 B3
Ina St
5400 HOUS 77028 3826 B4
Inca Dr
6300 PASD 77503 4248 D2
Inca Ln
23500 MtgC 77365 2972 B5
Ince Ln
9200 HarC 77040 3681 E2
10200 HarC 77040 3541 E7
Inch Rd
7600 HOUS 77055 3821 D4
Incinerator Dr
3100 HOUS 77051 4243 A2
Incline Dr
- HarC 77066 3401 B7
E Independence Av
100 LGCY 77573 4632 C6
W Independence Av
300 LGCY 77573 4632 B6
Independence Blvd
- HOUS 77489 4371 A5
- MSCY 77489 4371 A5
- MSCY 77489 4370 C6
1500 MSCY 77489 4370 C6
6500 BYTN 77521 3833 D5
6700 HarC 77521 3833 D5
Independence Cir
- PRLD 77581 4503 E5
Independence Dr
300 FRDW 77546 4505 C7
Independence Run
8900 LPRT 77571 4249 E4
Independence St
7700 HOUS 77051 4243 C1
India St
13800 HOUS 77047 4373 A4
Indian Blf
5700 HOUS 77056 3960 D2
5700 HOUS 77057 3960 D2
Indian Cir
5600 HOUS 77057 3960 D2
5700 HOUS 77056 3960 D2
Indian Cr
5900 FBnC 77459 4497 A7
6000 FBnC 77459 4496 E7
Indian Tr
2500 DRPK 77536 4249 E1
3200 BYTN 77521 3972 A3
5700 HOUS 77056 3960 D3
5700 HOUS 77057 3960 D3
10700 HarC 77375 3255 A3
17400 MtgC 77365 2825 D5
19500 MtgC 77357 2829 A5
Indiana Av
- HOUS 77017 4246 B4
- HOUS 77587 4246 B4
500 SHUS 77587 4246 B4
29800 MtgC 77354 2818 B1
Indiana Rd
3000 FBnC 77545 4498 E7

Indiana St
1100 HMBL 77396 3407 A
1400 HOUS 77006 3962
1700 HOUS 77019 3962 E
3100 BYTN 77520 4112 A
Indianapolis Dr
2100 LGCY 77573 4631 E
Indianapolis St
12800 HOUS 77015 3828 C
Indian Autumn Trc
1100 HOUS 77062 4379 D
Indian Bayou
300 HOUS 77056 3960 D
300 HOUS 77057 3960 D
Indian Beach Ct
18400 GLSN 77554 5331 B
Indian Beach Dr
- GLSN 77554 5442 C
3600 GLSN 77554 5331 C
Indian Blanket Dr
400 LGCY 77573 4632 C
Indian Blanket Ln
13300 HarC 77083 4097 E
13300 HOUS 77083 4097 E
Indian Brook Ct
5500 HarC 77373 3260 E
Indian Cedar Ln
10 WDLD 77380 2821 E
Indian Cherry Forest Ln
19700 HarC 77433 3395 E
Indian Clover Dr
10 WDLD 77381 2821 E
Indian Corn Pl
10 WDLD 77384 2674 E
Indian Cove Ct
7700 HarC 77346 3265 E
Indian Creek Dr
10 CNRO 77304 2237 A
10 PNVL 77304 2237 A
Indian Creek Rd
13200 HOUS 77079 3958 C
Indian Creek Falls
9100 HarC 77375 2965 C
Indian Crest Ct
23900 FBnC 77494 3953 E
Indian Cypress Dr
16100 HarC 77429 3396 E
16100 HarC 77429 3397 A
Indian Desert Dr
7900 HarC 77433 3537 B
Indian Falls Ct
25400 WlrC 77447 2813 C
Indian Falls Dr
6600 HOUS 77489 4371
Indian Field Ct
6300 HarC 77084 3679 A
Indian Forest Dr
3500 HarC 77373 3114 E
Indian Gardens Wy
4300 HarC 77396 3407 A
Indiangrass Ct
6300 FBnC 77494 4093 A
Indian Grass Dr
19100 HarC 77449 3816 A
Indiangrass Ln
6400 FBnC 77494 4093 A
Indian Grove Ln
20300 HarC 77450 3954 D
Indian Harbor Ln
- HarC 77429 3397 E
Indian Hawthorn Ct
1300 HarC 77094 3955 E
Indian Hawthorn Dr
19300 HarC 77094 3955 A
Indian Hill Dr
100 CNRO 77304 2382 C
600 CNRO 77304 2236 E
Indian Hill Tr
700 HOUS 77339 3263 D
Indian Hills Cir
23600 HarC 77377 2963 E
Indian Hills Ln
5900 FBnC 77479 4493 E
Indian Hills Rd
7000 HarC 77375 2819 E
7000 HarC 77389 2819 E
7000 HarC 77389 2820 A
Indian Hills Wy
23900 FBnC 77494 3953 E
Indian Knoll Dr
22600 HarC 77450 3953 E
Indian Lake Dr
6600 HOUS 77489 4371 C
Indian Ledge Dr
10800 HarC 77064 3540 A
Indian Lodge Ln
9200 HarC 77396 3548 A
Indian Maple Dr
8700 HarC 77338 3262 A
Indianmeadow Dr
300 LGCY 77573 4633 A
Indian Mill Dr
16100 HarC 77082 4096 A
Indian Mound Ct
3700 HarC 77532 3409 D
Indian Mound Tr
2700 HarC 77532 3410 A
3700 HarC 77532 3409 D
Indian Oaks Ln
11600 HarC 77044 3551 A
Indian Ocean Dr
- HarC 77346 3264 B
Indianola Dr
5400 HarC 77032 3546 D
Indian Paintbrush Ln
10400 HarC 77095 3537 E
Indian Plains Ln
2500 FBnC 77479 4494 A
Indian Point Dr
3800 MSCY 77459 4621 D
Indian Quail Cir
14900 HarC 77095 3678 E
14900 HarC 77095 3679 A
Indian Ridge Ct
10 HarC 77450 3953 E
Indian Ridge Dr
- HarC 77450 3954 A
23000 HarC 77450 3953 D
Indian River Dr
8900 HOUS 77088 3544 B
E Indian Sage Cir
10 WDLD 77381 2820 B
S Indian Sage Cir
10 WDLD 77381 2820 B
W Indian Sage Cir
10 WDLD 77381 2820 B
Indian Sage Dr
4200 FBnC 77450 4094 C

STREET
Block City ZIP Map# Grid
Indian Shores Ln
5100 HarC 77041 3679 E7
Indian Shores Rd
300 HarC 77532 3410 B2
300 HarC 77532 3411 A2
Indian Spring Tr
8000 HarC 77050 3547 D6
Indian Springs Ct
17500 SGLD 77479 4494 E1
Indian Springs Dr
800 FRDW 77546 4629 A4
Indian Springs Tr
15900 SGCH 77355 2815 E7
Indian Springs Wy
25900 HarC 77373 3114 A3
Indian Stone Ln
19100 HarC 77449 3677 B7
Indian Summer Ct
3300 FRDW 77598 4630 C2
4200 FBnC 77479 4366 D6
Indian Summer Dr
4300 FBnC 77479 4366 D6
Indian Summer Ln
- HarC 77336 3121 E1
Indian Summer Pl
10 WDLD 77381 2674 D6
Indian Summer Tr
3100 FRDW 77598 4630 B2
Indian Sunrise Ct
4200 PASD 77059 4380 E5
4300 PASD 77059 4381 A5
Indian Trace Ln
- HarC 77082 4096 A4
Indian Trail Dr
1300 FBnC 77479 4493 D5
2600 MSCY 77489 4370 D7
Indian Trails Ct
1500 MSCY 77489 4370 D7
Indian Vista Dr
10800 HarC 77064 3540 A3
Indian Wells Ct
3100 MSCY 77459 4497 C2
Indian Wells Dr
10 HarC 77066 3401 A4
10 MNVL 77583 4624 D4
1700 MSCY 77459 4497 C2
12900 HarC 77066 3400 D2
14100 HarC 77069 3256 C7
Indian Wells Ln
10 PNVL 77304 2237 B2
Indian Woods Dr
15400 HOUS 77489 4371 C5
W Indies Ct
2000 NSUB 77058 4508 B6
N Indigo Cir
- WDLD 77381 2820 C3
S Indigo Cir
10 WDLD 77381 2820 C3
Indigo Ct
100 MtgC 77355 2960 B2
Indigo Dr
1500 MtgC 77385 2677 A7
2900 PRLD 77584 4500 C4
3400 SGLD 77479 4495 E2
Indigo Ln
3100 MSCY 77459 4496 C1
Indigo St
- HOUS 77096 4101 B7
5600 HOUS 77096 4100 C7
5800 HOUS 77074 4100 B7
Indigo Wy
18400 MtgC 77365 2972 A7
Indigo Bay Ct
9700 FBnC 77494 4092 C5
13100 PRLD 77584 4500 A3
Indigo Bay Dr
- PRLD 77584 4500 A3
Indigo Brook Ct
10300 HarC 77089 4377 B6
Indigo Canyon Dr
- FBnC 77469 4493 C4
Indigo Cove Ct
2200 LGCY 77573 4752 B1
Indigo Cove Ln
12000 HarC 77041 3680 A4
12100 HarC 77041 3679 E4
Indigo Creek Ln
11400 HarC 77375 3109 D2
13100 PRLD 77584 4500 A2
Indigo Dale Dr
8000 HarC 77379 3111 A2
Indigo Falls Ln
- HarC 77041 3679 E6
Indigo Field Ln
21000 FBnC 77469 4094 A5
Indigo Harbour Ln
2300 LGCY 77573 4508 C6
Indigo Hill Ln
21500 FBnC 77450 4094 B3
Indigo Hills Dr
16800 MtgC 77355 2961 C1
17000 MtgC 77355 2815 B7
Indigo Isles Ln
5600 HarC 77041 3679 E6
Indigo Lake Ct
13500 HOUS 77077 3957 A6
28100 MtgC 77355 2814 E6
Indigo Lake Dr
19000 MtgC 77355 2815 A7
19200 MtgC 77355 2814 D6
Indigo Loch Ln
17600 HarC 77084 3817 A1
Indigo Mist Ct
17100 HarC 77084 3678 A3
Indigo Park Dr
1600 MtgC 77386 2969 A1
Indigo Pass Ct
4700 PASD 77505 4248 A6
Indigo Pass Ln
- FBnC 77450 4094 A3
Indigo Pines Ln
22200 FBnC 77450 4093 E3
Indigo River Ln
3100 FBnC 77479 4493 C3
3300 FBnC 77469 4493 C3
Indigo Sands Dr
1300 PRLD 77545 4499 E2
Indigo Sky Cir
- WDLD 77381 2820 C4
Indigo Sky Ln
3300 TXCY 77591 4872 C2
Indigo Spires Ct
13700 HarC 77429 3397 D3
Indigo Spires Dr
13600 HarC 77429 3397 C3
Indigo Stone Ln
2600 HarC 77449 3815 B4

STREET
Block City ZIP Map# Grid
Indigo Trace Ct
13200 HarC 77070 3399 C3
Indigo Trails Dr
5600 FBnC 77469 4493 A6
Indigo Villa Ln
8300 FBnC 77083 4095 D7
8300 FBnC 77083 4235 C2
Indus St
11000 HOUS 77089 4377 C3
Industrial Blvd
100 SGLD 77478 4368 D1
1300 SGLD 77478 4237 D6
N Industrial Blvd
17800 WEBS 77598 4507 C6
Industrial Ct
100 CNRO 77301 2384 D4
Industrial Dr
1500 MSCY 77489 4370 B2
3200 PRLD 77581 4504 A7
3300 PRLD 77581 4503 E7
8000 PRLD 77584 4503 E7
8000 PRLD 77584 4627 D1
8700 HOUS 77029 3965 D5
Industrial Ln
2600 CNRO 77301 2384 D4
31200 MtgC 77355 2669 D7
31200 MtgC 77355 2815 D1
Industrial Pkwy
6900 RSBG 77471 4491 E6
6900 RSBG 77471 4492 A6
W Industrial Pkwy
18900 MtgC 77357 2826 C3
Industrial Rd
- HarC 77484 3102 B7
3300 PRLD 77581 4503 C4
12300 GNPK 77015 3966 E4
12400 GNPK 77015 3967 A4
12700 HarC 77015 3967 B4
12800 HOUS 77015 3967 E5
Industrial St
100 LMQU 77568 4990 C1
Industrial Wy
10 MtgC 77385 2822 D5
6000 HOUS 77011 3964 D5
Industrial Canal Rd
10 TXCY 77590 4991 C2
Industrial Park Dr
31600 MtgC 77355 2963 C3
31600 MtgC 77362 2963 C3
E Industrial Park Rd
- HOUS 77029 3965 E7
- HOUS 77029 4105 E1
E Industrial Water
- HarC 77532 3551 B2
- HarC 77532 3552 B2
- HOUS 77532 3551 B2
Industry Ln
22700 HarC 77375 2965 B7
22700 HarC 77375 3110 B1
Industry St
14100 HarC 77053 4373 A5
Inez St
2800 HOUS 77023 4104 C4
3600 FBnC 77545 4498 E7
Infield Ct
16800 MtgC 77385 2676 D4
Inga Ln
11700 HarC 77064 3399 D7
Ingeborg St
1600 HOUS 77023 3964 A7
Ingersol Av
2300 PASD 77506 4107 E3
Ingersoll St
4400 HOUS 77027 4101 C1
Ingham Ct
14200 FBnC 77478 4366 E4
Ingham Dr
19500 HarC 77449 3677 A4
Ingle Oak Ct
13600 HarC 77095 3539 C7
Ingle Oak Dr
7900 HarC 77095 3539 C7
Ingleside Ct
4800 HarC 77388 3112 B4
Ingleside Pk
16700 HarC 77429 3396 E2
16700 HarC 77429 3397 A2
Inglewood
- FBnC 77459 4622 B5
Inglewood Cir
3900 FBnC 77459 4622 B4
Inglewood Dr
5100 PASD 77505 4248 E7
6800 SGLD 77479 4494 B1
Ingold St
3700 SSPL 77005 4101 D3
Ingomar Wy
5500 HOUS 77053 4372 A5
5600 HOUS 77053 4371 E4
Ingram Gap Ln
- HOUS 77048 4375 B3
Inkberry Dr
6900 HOUS 77092 3682 B5
Inkberry Valley Ln
4100 HOUS 77045 4241 D6
Inker St
4500 HOUS 77007 3962 A2
Inks Lake Dr
15200 FBnC 77478 4236 C6
Inland Dr
3700 PRLD 77584 4502 D6
Inland Rd
3000 HarC 77336 2976 C7
Inland Grove Ct
19100 HarC 77429 3395 E1
Inland Oaks Dr
17800 FBnC 77469 4095 C5
Inland Spring Ct
13800 HOUS 77059 4379 E5
Inlane St
100 HOUS 77012 4105 B1
Inlet Ct
2400 FBnC 77545 4498 C7
Inman St
4700 HOUS 77020 3964 C3
Innisbrook Dr
16500 HarC 77095 3538 A6
Innisfall Cir
12200 HarC 77377 3254 C2
Innisfree Ln
11300 PNPV 77024 3959 D3
Innsbrook Pl
4300 FBnC 77479 4366 C7
Innsbruck St
5600 BLAR 77401 4101 B3
Innsbruk Ct
12200 HarC 77066 3401 B5

STREET
Block City ZIP Map# Grid
Innsbruk Dr
4600 HarC 77066 3401 B5
Innsbury Dr
11600 HarC 77093 3685 E1
Innsdale Dr
300 HOUS 77076 3685 B5
Innshire Ln
13300 HOUS 77045 4241 B7
Inscho Ln
2000 HarC 77450 3954 A5
Inscho Point Dr
2000 LGCY 77573 4509 C6
Insley St
14400 HOUS 77045 4372 E3
15100 HarC 77053 4373 A4
15100 HOUS 77053 4373 A4
Inspest St
1000 HarC 77060 3403 D4
Institute Ln
5300 HOUS 77005 4102 D2
5300 HOUS 77006 4102 D2
Insurance Rd
300 FBnC 77469 4495 A6
400 FBnC 77469 4494 E7
Interchange Dr
8800 HOUS 77054 4242 B2
Intercontinental Blvd
200 HMBL 77338 3263 B7
Intercontinental Pl
15100 HarC 77032 3404 D7
15100 HOUS 77032 3404 D7
Intercontinental Gatewy Dr
- HOUS 77396 3406 B1
Intercontinental Park Blvd
- HarC 77032 3404 D7
- HOUS 77032 3404 D7
Intercontinental Village Blvd
100 HMBL 77338 3263 A7
Interdrive E
14000 HarC 77032 3545 E2
Interdrive W
14000 HarC 77032 3545 E2
Interlachen Dr
5000 BYTN 77521 3972 A2
12500 HarC 77037 3685 A1
International Blvd
700 HOUS 77024 3960 D1
International Vil
500 HMBL 77338 3263 A7
International Plaza Dr
15300 HOUS 77032 3405 B7
Interport Dr
- HOUS 77032 3404 A5
Interurban St
100 LGCY 77573 4631 E3
Intervale St
- HOUS 77061 4245 E7
- HOUS 77075 4245 E7
8800 HOUS 77075 4246 A7
Interwood North Pkwy
- HarC 77032 3546 A1
3700 HOUS 77032 3546 B1
Interwood South Pkwy
- HarC 77032 3546 B1
4000 HOUS 77032 3546 B1
Intrepid
- LGCY 77573 4508 D5
Intrepid Ln
25000 GLSN 77554 5548 B2
Intrepid St
7700 HOUS 77072 4097 E6
Intrepid Wy
2400 LGCY 77573 4508 C6
Intrepid Elm St
2900 HarC 77084 3816 C4
Intrepid Oak Ln
1100 HarC 77073 3259 B5
Invergarry Wy
9400 HarC 77375 3110 C3
Invergyle Ln
- HarC 77375 3110 C3
Inverloch Wy
9900 HMBL 77338 3262 D4
Invermere Dr
1900 MtgC 77386 2969 B1
Inverness Ct
3600 PRLD 77581 4504 C6
Inverness Dr
3600 HOUS 77019 3961 C5
5000 BYTN 77521 3972 A2
29200 MtgC 77354 2818 A2
Inverness Ln
1500 PRLD 77581 4504 C6
Inverness St
1300 FRDW 77546 4628 E3
1300 PRLD 77546 4628 E3
Inverness Wy
6400 PASD 77505 4248 E6
Inverness Cove
- DKSN 77539 4752 E6
Inverness Forest Blvd
21700 HarC 77073 3259 B2
Inverness Lake Dr
20800 HarC 77346 3264 D3
Inverness Park Blvd
8700 HarC 77375 3110 C2
8700 HarC 77379 3110 D2
Inverness Park Cir
8800 SPVL 77055 3820 E7
Inverness Park Wy
10 SPVL 77055 3820 E6
8800 SPVL 77055 3821 A6
Inverness Path Ln
3300 HOUS 77053 4372 E3
Inverness Point Ln
25600 HarC 77389 2966 B2
Inverrary Ct
7900 HarC 77095 3539 A7
Inverrary Dr
14800 HarC 77095 3538 E7
14800 HarC 77095 3539 A7
Inverrary Ln
10 SGLD 77479 4495 B2
Inveterate Av
500 RSBG 77471 4614 C1
Invierno St
10800 JTCY 77029 3966 D2
Invincible Cir
3000 LGCY 77573 4508 D6
Invincible Dr
3300 LGCY 77573 4508 E5
Inway Cir
23800 HarC 77389 2966 C5
Inway Ct
5900 HarC 77389 2966 E5

STREET
Block City ZIP Map# Grid
Inway Dr
6200 HarC 77389 2966 D5
Inway Oaks Dr
23900 HarC 77389 2966 E5
Inway Trail Dr
23800 HarC 77389 2966 E5
Inwood Ct
3100 SGLD 77478 4369 A2
Inwood Dr
200 FRDW 77546 4505 A6
300 BYTN 77521 3972 E4
1100 RHMD 77469 4491 E3
2100 HOUS 77019 3962 A5
2900 DKSN 77539 4753 C3
3200 HOUS 77019 3961 E5
5300 KATY 77493 3813 D7
5600 HOUS 77056 3960 D6
5800 HOUS 77057 3960 B6
7500 HOUS 77063 3960 A6
10000 HOUS 77042 3959 A6
10600 HOUS 77042 3958 C6
11300 HOUS 77077 3958 B6
Inwood Ln
100 HarC 77562 3831 E1
900 PASD 77502 4106 E7
15900 HOUS 77489 4371 C6
Inwood St
500 TMBL 77375 2964 A6
Inwood Brook Ln
- HarC 77449 3815 B4
Inwood Elm Cir
18400 HarC 77346 3264 C7
18400 HarC 77346 3408 C1
Inwood Forest Dr
8300 HOUS 77088 3683 A2
Inwood Glen Ln
- MtgC 77386 2823 D7
Inwood Hollow Ln
10100 HOUS 77088 3542 B7
Inwood North Dr
8900 HarC 77088 3542 C6
Inwood Oaks Dr
10 HNCV 77024 3959 E3
10 HNCV 77024 3960 A3
10 PNPV 77024 3959 E3
Inwood Park Ct
5800 HOUS 77057 3960 D6
Inwood Park Dr
7000 HOUS 77088 3683 B4
7000 HOUS 77091 3683 B4
Inwood Shadows St
- HarC 77088 3682 C1
9900 HOUS 77088 3682 C1
10100 HOUS 77088 3542 C7
Inwood West Dr
6500 HOUS 77088 3542 C7
6500 HOUS 77088 3682 B1
Iola St
2800 HOUS 77017 4105 D5
Ione St
4300 BLAR 77401 4101 B5
4300 HOUS 77401 4101 B5
Iowa Av
500 SHUS 77587 4246 C4
4200 DKSN 77539 4754 B3
N Iowa Av
100 LGCY 77573 4632 A2
S Iowa Av
100 LGCY 77573 4632 A3
100 LPRT 77571 4251 E3
Iowa Ln
5900 BzaC 77578 4624 E3
5900 MNVL 77578 4624 E3
5900 MNVL 77578 4625 A7
5900 MNVL 77578 4746 A2
7300 MNVL 77583 4746 A1
Iowa St
3100 BYTN 77520 4112 A1
N Iowa St
100 LPRT 77571 4251 E2
Ipes Ln
25300 SPLD 77372 2682 E4
25300 SPLD 77372 2683 A4
Ipswich Rd
100 HOUS 77061 4245 B6
Ira St
4500 HOUS 77003 3964 C4
4500 HOUS 77011 3964 B4
Irada St
3300 LMQU 77568 4990 E5
3300 LMQU 77590 4990 E5
Irby St
6200 HOUS 77091 3683 D5
9300 HOUS 77088 3683 D1
9500 HarC 77088 3683 D1
Irby Cobb Blvd
6100 FBnC 77469 4616 A2
6100 RSBG 77469 4616 A2
Ireland Ln
4400 PASD 77505 4248 D6
Ireland Rd
4300 HOUS 77016 3686 B6
4300 HOUS 77093 3686 B6
Ireland St
4500 HOUS 77016 3686 C6
Irene Dr
400 HarC 77562 3832 A2
Irene Rd
- HOUS 77049 3828 A2
7000 HarC 77049 3827 E2
7000 HOUS 77049 3827 E2
Irene St
100 DRPK 77536 4109 A3
100 HOUS 77009 3824 B6
2100 LMQU 77568 4989 E3
14800 HOUS 77085 4370 E1
14800 HOUS 77085 4371 A1
Irenell Dr
19500 MtgC 77365 2972 C5
Iris Ct
2600 BzaC 77584 4501 C5
Iris Ln
4200 DRPK 77536 4249 C1
5500 KATY 77493 3813 C5
10200 FBnC 77459 4621 E4
18800 MtgC 77365 2972 B6
Iris St
- HOUS 77020 3826 A7
8900 HarC 77562 3833 A1
Iris Arbor Ct
10 CNRO 77301 2384 E6
Iris Arbor Ln
8600 HarC 77095 3538 A5
Iris Brook Wy
- HarC 77065 3539 C2
Iris Canyon Dr
12000 HarC 77377 3254 C1

STREET
Block City ZIP Map# Grid
Iris Creek Wy
6600 HarC 77338 3261 B3
Iris Crossing Ln
15300 HarC 77049 3829 A4
Iris Garden Ln
- HarC 77044 3549 C2
Iris Glen Ln
- FBnC 77469 4094 E6
Irish Dr
1000 CNRO 77301 2383 D3
Irish Elm Ct
15000 HarC 77433 3251 E7
Irish Hill Dr
5900 HOUS 77053 4371 E5
6100 HOUS 77489 4371 E5
Irish Ivy Ct
4100 MtgC 77386 2970 D7
Irish Maple St
800 SEBK 77586 4509 E1
Irish Mist Ct
1200 HarC 77450 3953 D4
Irish Moss Pl
10 WDLD 77381 2674 D7
Irish Oaks Ct
17000 FBnC 77083 4095 D6
Iris Hollow Wy
- HOUS 77089 4378 C7
Irish Shores Ln
3300 PRLD 77584 4501 E5
Irish Spring Dr
2100 HarC 77067 3402 A7
Iris Lake Ct
10400 HarC 77070 3399 B4
Iris Lee Ln
11300 PNPV 77024 3959 D5
Iris Pond Ln
- HarC 77338 3261 B3
Iris Ridge Wy
3500 FBnC 77545 4498 D7
18000 HarC 77429 3253 B1
Iris Valley Wy
2700 HarC 77038 3543 A2
Iriswood Dr
11600 HarC 77089 4378 B6
Iron Ln
- HarC 77064 3540 D5
Iron Rdg
1900 SGLD 77478 4368 D5
Iron Sprs
8800 HOUS 77034 4247 A7
9000 HOUS 77034 4378 A1
Ironbark Ct
400 HOUS 77598 4506 E4
Ironbark Dr
300 HOUS 77598 4506 E4
Iron Bend Ln
- HarC 77389 2966 B1
Iron Bridge Dr
3500 HarC 77066 3401 C4
Iron Castle Ct
4300 FBnC 77450 4094 B2
Ironclad Dr
2500 LGCY 77573 4631 B6
Iron Creek Ct
4400 MSCY 77545 4622 C2
Ironcrest Ln
21000 HarC 77388 3112 B5
Iron Crown Cir
3100 HarC 77068 3257 C5
Ironfork Dr
15800 HOUS 77053 4371 E5
Irongate Dr
- HOUS 77029 3965 D6
Ironhill Ln
- HarC 77433 3537 A1
Iron Horse
5700 FBnC 77459 4621 A1
Iron Horseshoe Ln
14500 HarC 77044 3408 E7
Iron Knoll Dr
22100 HarC 77339 3118 D5
Iron Lake Dr
18500 HarC 77084 3816 C3
Iron Ledge Ct
8600 HOUS 77088 3684 A1
Ironloft Ct
3500 FBnC 77450 4094 C1
Iron Manor Dr
26800 MtgC 77339 3118 C4
Iron Ore Dr
1700 HarC 77336 3121 E7
1700 HarC 77336 3122 A7
Iron Ore Rd
10000 MtgC 77303 2238 E1
10000 MtgC 77303 2239 A1
18400 MtgC 77355 2668 A7
18400 MtgC 77355 2814 A1
Iron River Dr
9900 HarC 77064 3541 C2
Iron Rock St
6000 HOUS 77087 4104 C7
Ironside Rd
23800 HarC 77373 3114 E4
Ironside Creek Dr
15700 HOUS 77053 4371 D5
Ironside Hill Dr
15700 HOUS 77053 4371 E5
Ironside Turn Dr
6000 HOUS 77053 4371 D5
Ironspur Ln
- HarC 77429 3253 B7
Iron Squire Dr
26800 MtgC 77339 3118 C3
Ironstone Ct
11600 HarC 77067 3401 E5
Iron Tree Ln
- FBnC 77494 4093 A3
Iron Weed Dr
11500 HarC 77095 3397 A7
Ironwood Blvd
400 HarC 77015 3828 E7
700 HarC 77015 3967 E1
Ironwood Cir
22700 MtgC 77365 2973 E4
Ironwood Ct
600 RHMD 77469 4492 A3
Ironwood Dr
600 FBnC 77469 4365 C3
4500 BYTN 77521 3972 B2
31700 WALR 77484 3102 A5
Ironwood Ln
7300 BYTN 77521 3835 B4
Ironwood St
1200 HarC 77015 3967 E3
Ironwood Estates Dr
- HOUS 77051 4242 E6
Ironwood Forest Dr
500 RHMD 77469 4492 A3

STREET
Block City ZIP Map# Grid
Iroquois Dr
4200 PASD 77504 4247 E6
4400 PASD 77504 4248 A6
Iroquois Ln
4600 PASD 77504 4248 A6
4600 PASD 77505 4248 A6
Iroquois St
12700 HOUS 77037 3685 B1
Irquois Ln
18400 MtgC 77365 2972 C5
E Irvin Rd
29200 HarC 77336 3121 E1
29500 HarC 77336 2976 E7
W Irvin Rd
29100 HarC 77336 3121 D1
29600 HarC 77336 2976 D7
Irvin St
1000 RHMD 77469 4364 D7
Irvine Park Ln
- LGCY 77573 4630 C7
Irving Ln
2700 PASD 77506 4108 A5
Irving Pl
- HarC 77447 3249 E2
Irving Wy
4900 HOUS 77087 4105 A6
Irving Park Pl
7800 HOUS 77053 4372 C7
Irvington Blvd
3300 HOUS 77009 3824 C6
6100 HOUS 77022 3824 C2
8400 HOUS 77022 3685 C7
9300 HOUS 77076 3685 C6
Irvington Cts
100 HOUS 77009 3824 C7
Irvington Dr
2800 BzaC 77584 4501 B5
Irwin Keel Ln
18900 MtgC 77306 2534 C6
Isaacks Rd
10 HMBL 77338 3262 E7
600 HMBL 77338 3263 A7
Isabella St
700 HOUS 77002 3963 A7
1200 HOUS 77004 3963 A7
1800 HOUS 77004 4103 B1
Isabelle St
2300 HarC 77521 3832 C4
Isalerno Ct
1200 LGCY 77573 4632 E4
Isbell Dr
13200 HarC 77375 2964 B2
13200 TMBL 77375 2964 B2
Isetta Ln
800 HarC 77060 3544 E5
800 HarC 77060 3545 A5
Ishmeal St
100 HOUS 77091 3684 C5
300 HOUS 77076 3684 C5
Isidoro Meza Dr
- HOUS 77013 3966 A1
Isla Rd
2000 PRLD 77581 4503 C2
Isla del Sol
3900 GLSN 77554 5441 A5
Isla del Sol Dr
4100 GLSN 77554 5441 A5
Islamorada Ct
9400 HarC 77044 3688 E4
Islamorada Dr
11900 HarC 77044 3688 E4
Island Blvd
10 MSCY 77459 4497 B3
Island Ct
3900 GLSN 77554 5441 A5
Island Dr
- HarC 77377 3254 C5
1200 GlsC 77539 4635 D7
2200 DKSN 77539 4754 E2
N Island Dr
2900 SEBK 77586 4382 B7
S Island Dr
3000 SEBK 77586 4382 A7
Island Psg
10 GLSN 77554 5221 C2
Island Vw
1000 LGCY 77565 4508 E4
Island Breeze Cir
100 LGCY 77573 4633 B1
Island Breeze Dr
5500 HarC 77041 3679 D6
Islandbreeze Dr
18500 HarC 77379 3256 A1
18700 HarC 77379 3111 A7
Island Breeze St
11500 PRLD 77584 4500 D2
Island Crossing Ln
2900 LGCY 77573 4633 B3
Island Crossing St
- PRLD 77584 4500 D2
Islander Wy
1700 SEBK 77586 4509 D1
Island Falls Ct
1800 LGCY 77573 4631 C7
12900 HarC 77041 3679 D7
Island Fern Ct
5600 HOUS 77345 3120 C7
Island Green Ct
10 HOUS 77339 3264 D1
Island Grove Ct
15700 HOUS 77079 3956 E1
Island Heather Ct
5900 HOUS 77345 3120 D5
Island Hills Dr
4100 PASD 77059 4380 E5
4300 PASD 77059 4381 A5
Island Lake Lp E
21600 HarC 77338 3261 D2
Island Lake Lp W
21600 HarC 77338 3261 D2
Island Manor Dr
- HarC 77095 3538 A6
Island Manor Ln
2000 LGCY 77573 4631 C7
Island Manor St
11400 PRLD 77584 4500 D2
Island Meadow Ct
800 HOUS 77062 4506 D1
Island Oak St
2000 HOUS 77062 4380 A6
Island Palm Ct
13500 HOUS 77059 4379 E4
Island Shore Blvd
11700 HarC 77095 3397 A7
Island Shore Cir
11800 HarC 77095 3397 A7
Island Shore Ct
16600 HarC 77095 3397 C6

STREET
Block City ZIP Map# Grid
Island Shore Dr
11800 HarC 77095 3397 A7
Island Song Dr
11900 HarC 77044 3688 E4
Island Spring Ct
500 HarC 77373 3113 E4
Island Spring Ln
17800 HarC 77377 3254 D3
Island Villas Dr
2100 LGCY 77573 4509 A6
Islandwoods Dr
14200 HarC 77095 3679 A2
Isla Vista Cir
- LGCY 77539 4633 E2
- LGCY 77565 4633 E2
Isla Vista Ct
6000 HarC 77041 3679 E5
W Isle Blvd
- WDLD 77381 2821 C4
W Isle Pl
10 WDLD 77381 2821 C5
Isle Royale Ct
18000 HarC 77346 3408 D1
Isle Royale Wy
12500 HarC 77346 3408 D1
Isles End Rd
100 TKIS 77554 5106 A4
Isle View Dr
22300 GLSN 77554 5441 A5
Isle Vista Dr
12000 HarC 77041 3680 A5
Islewood Blvd
10 WDLD 77380 2821 D5
Isleworth Dr
- FBnC 77450 3954 A6
Islington Dr
28400 HarC 77336 3121 D2
Isolde Dr
400 HOUS 77024 3958 D3
Isom St
1600 HarC 77039 3545 C6
1600 HOUS 77039 3545 C6
Issacs Wy
3900 SGLD 77479 4368 E7
Isthmus Cove Ct
23100 FBnC 77494 4093 A3
Italy Ln
4400 PASD 77505 4248 D6
Itasca Ct
2000 LGCY 77573 4631 B6
Ithaca Dr
3300 MSCY 77459 4497 E5
Ithaca St
7900 HOUS 77017 4105 C6
Itoro Ct
4700 HOUS 77013 3827 D4
Ivanhoe St
4500 HOUS 77027 3961 B7
Ivanhoe Springs Dr
8500 HarC 77083 4097 A6
Ivan Reid Dr
8100 HarC 77040 3541 C7
Ivey St
1000 CNRO 77301 2384 A7
Ivie Lee St
1500 BYTN 77520 3973 C6
Ivory St
23400 HarC 77389 2967 A5
Ivory Ash Ct
6500 HarC 77346 3264 E3
Ivory Brook Dr
19700 HarC 77094 3954 D2
19700 HarC 77094 3955 A2
Ivory Castle Ln
- HarC 77377 3253 E3
Ivory Creek Dr
11500 PRLD 77584 4500 D2
Ivory Creek Ln
20400 HarC 77450 3954 D5
Ivory Crest Dr
6300 HOUS 77072 4097 D4
Ivory Crossing Ct
1400 PASD 77586 4381 D6
Ivory Crossing Ln
18000 HarC 77433 3677 D1
Ivory Falls Ct
17100 HarC 77095 3538 A7
Ivory Forest Ln
3000 MtgC 77386 2823 D7
Ivory Gate Ln
21500 HarC 77449 3815 B4
Ivory Lake Ct
- FBnC 77494 4092 D4
Ivory Meadow Ln
1100 FBnC 77479 4366 D7
Ivory Meadows Ln
4800 HarC 77084 3678 A7
Ivory Mills Ln
19500 HarC 77094 3955 A4
Ivory Mist Ln
5600 HarC 77041 3680 A6
Ivory Moon Pl
10 WDLD 77381 2820 B3
Ivory Pointe Dr
3200 LGCY 77573 4633 B1
Ivory Ridge Ln
800 HarC 77094 3955 A2
Ivory Rose Ln
5000 FBnC 77494 4093 A2
Ivory Stone Ln
500 LGCY 77573 4633 A2
Ivory Stone Wy
- HarC 77040 3541 A6
Ivy Av
200 DRPK 77536 4109 B4
N Ivy Cir
17000 HarC 77084 3817 B1
S Ivy Cir
17000 HarC 77084 3817 B1
Ivy Ct
10 PNVL 77304 2237 B4
27400 MtgC 77354 2817 D4
Ivy Dr
2900 LPRT 77571 4251 D7
Ivy Ln
- FBnC 77545 4623 C2
300 DKSN 77539 4753 C5
25000 MtgC 77372 2536 E1
Ivy Pk
10900 HOUS 77075 4377 A4
Ivy Rd
900 CRLS 77565 4509 C5
Ivy Rdg
23300 MtgC 77365 2974 A7
Ivy St
2500 HOUS 77026 3824 E4
3000 HOUS 77026 3825 A4
4800 PASD 77505 4248 B3

STREET Block City ZIP Map# Grid

Ivy Arbor Ct
1900 PRLD 77581 4503 D1
Ivy Arbor Ln
10 HarC 77070 3399 E3
3400 PRLD 77581 4503 D1
Ivy Bend Dr
3100 BzaC 77584 4501 D6
Ivy Blossom Ln
21500 FBnC 77450 4094 B3
Ivy Bluff Ct
14000 HOUS 77062 4379 D6
Ivy Branch Ln
- BzaC 77583 4623 C4
Ivy Bridge Dr
15900 HarC 77095 3538 C6
Ivy Brook Ct
17400 HarC 77095 3677 E1
Ivybush Bend Ln
- FBnC 77469 4094 A7
Ivy Castle Ct
10 WDLD 77382 2673 D6
Ivy Cove
2100 FBnC 77494 3952 B5
Ivy Cove Dr
4900 BYTN 77521 3972 C1
Ivycreek Ct
5600 LGCY 77573 4751 C1
Ivy Creek Ln
17000 HOUS 77060 3403 D6
Ivy Crest Ct
2000 HOUS 77077 3956 E6
Ivycrest Ct
2300 FBnC 77479 4493 D1
Ivycroft Ln
900 HarC 77373 2968 E5
Ivy Cross Ln
500 FBnC 77479 4366 E7
Ivydale Dr
12800 HarC 77049 3828 C1
Ivydale Rd
3000 PRLD 77581 4503 D5
Ivydale Ledge Dr
- HarC 77049 3828 D1
Ivy Dell Ct
2700 HOUS 77059 4379 E4
Ivy Falls
6400 MSCY 77459 4496 C3
Ivy Falls Ct
8500 JRSV 77040 3540 C6
Ivy Falls Dr
3100 HarC 77068 3257 B4
Ivy Field Ct
10200 HarC 77070 3399 C2
Ivyford Ct
14500 HarC 77429 3397 E1
Ivyforest Dr
12600 HarC 77429 3254 C6
Ivy Garden St
10 WDLD 77382 2674 C5
Ivygate Dr
- HarC 77373 3115 E7
Ivy Glen Ct
300 LGCY 77573 4633 A1
Ivy Glen Dr
2300 HOUS 77077 3957 E7
Ivy Green Dr
3900 HarC 77082 4096 C4
Ivy Grove Dr
16500 HOUS 77058 4507 E2
Ivy Heath Ln
6500 HarC 77041 3679 D3
Ivy Hill Dr
3100 HOUS 77339 3118 D5
Ivyholow Dr
700 HarC 77530 3829 D7
Ivy Hollow Ln
10300 HarC 77433 3537 C2
Ivyhurst Ln
13100 HOUS 77082 4097 B1
Ivyknoll Dr
6300 HOUS 77035 4240 A5
Ivy Leaf Dr
10 HarC 77336 2976 C5
Ivy Leaf St
11100 HOUS 77016 3686 E2
Ivy Manor Ct
17200 HarC 77433 3251 A3
Ivy Meadow Ln
4700 HarC 77449 3677 A6
Ivy Mill Ct
10000 FBnC 77459 4621 E6
Ivy Mill Ln
3100 FBnC 77459 4621 E6
Ivymist Ct
4100 FBnC 77479 4366 C7
13800 HOUS 77044 3550 B3
Ivymount Dr
13800 SGLD 77478 4237 A7
Ivy Oaks Ln
10300 HOUS 77041 3681 A7
10500 HOUS 77041 3680 E7
28000 MtgC 77372 2683 E4
28000 MtgC 77372 2684 A4
Ivy Parkway Dr
900 HOUS 77077 3957 A3
Ivy Patch Ct
7600 HarC 77095 3538 A7
Ivypath Ln
8800 HarC 77095 3537 E5
Ivy Point Cir
20200 HarC 77346 3265 C4
Ivy Point Ct
8200 FBnC 77083 4096 A7
Ivy Point Dr
8300 FBnC 77083 4096 A7
Ivy Pond Pl
10 WDLD 77381 2820 B1
Ivyridge Rd
10200 HOUS 77043 3819 E6
10200 HOUS 77043 3820 A6
Ivy Run Ct
2400 HarC 77450 3954 E6
Ivyside Dr
13100 HOUS 77077 3957 B7
Ivy Spring Ln
8800 HOUS 77088 3544 A7
8900 HOUS 77088 3543 E7
Ivy Stone Ct
4900 HarC 77449 3677 A6
22300 FBnC 77450 4093 E1
Ivystone Ct
5200 SGLD 77479 4495 A4
Ivy Stream Dr
17400 HarC 77095 3537 D2
E Ivy Terrace Cir
- FBnC 77450 4093 D2
N Ivy Terrace Cir
- FBnC 77450 4093 D2
S Ivy Terrace Cir
- FBnC 77450 4093 E3
W Ivy Terrace Cir
- FBnC 77450 4093 D2
Ivy Terrace Ct
21500 HarC 77450 3954 B5
Ivy Trace Ln
25000 FBnC 77494 3953 B6
Ivy Trail Ct
7900 HarC 77095 3537 E7
Ivyvine Ct
1100 FBnC 77479 4366 D7
Ivy Wall Ct
700 HOUS 77079 3956 E2
Ivy Wall Dr
800 HOUS 77079 3956 D3
Ivy Wick Ct
11500 HarC 77375 3109 E5
Ivy Wild Ln
16800 HarC 77095 3538 A1
Ivy Wood Ct
14500 HarC 77396 3547 C1
Ivywood Dr
3900 PRLD 77584 4503 A7
26900 HarC 77336 3121 E4
26900 HarC 77336 3122 A4
W Iwo St
800 ALVN 77511 4867 B3
Iwo Jima Rd
7300 HOUS 77033 4243 E1
Izamal Ct
2800 GLSN 77554 5221 D2

J

J Cir
- HarC 77388 3111 D1
J St
4100 HOUS 77072 4098 A4
4100 HOUS 77082 4098 A4
Jabot Av
3500 FBnC 77545 4498 C7
Jacana Ct
22200 SGCH 77355 2960 D2
Jacana Dr
24700 SGCH 77355 2960 D2
Jacaranda Pl
11900 HarC 77429 3398 D5
Jacey Landing Ln
10000 HarC 77095 3538 E3
Jacinth Ct
- HarC 77066 3401 B7
E Jacinto Dr
11200 HarC 77044 3690 B1
W Jacinto Dr
11200 HarC 77044 3690 B1
Jacinto Oaks Dr
1200 JTCY 77029 3966 D3
Jacintoport Blvd
1500 HarC 77015 3968 C3
15100 HarC 77015 3969 A5
15100 HarC 77530 3969 A5
Jacintoport Blvd Ext
15800 HarC 77015 3969 C5
15800 HOUS 77015 3969 C5
E Jack Av
10 BYTN 77520 3973 A7
W Jack Av
10 BYTN 77520 3973 A6
200 BYTN 77520 3972 E6
Jack Ln
400 BKHV 77024 3959 C3
Jack St
300 PASD 77502 4247 B1
1300 PRLD 77581 4504 E5
3900 HOUS 77006 3962 E7
4300 HOUS 77006 4102 D3
S Jack St
300 ALVN 77511 4867 A2
Jack Beaver Rd
1500 GlsC 77517 4751 E7
1500 GlsC 77517 4869 E1
3000 STFE 77517 4869 E2
Jack Block Ct
1100 HarC 77532 3552 A1
Jack Brooks Rd
- HTCK 77563 4988 A2
Jackie Landing Ln
6300 HOUS 77072 4097 D4
Jack Johnson Blvd
1200 GLSN 77550 5108 E5
2500 GLSN 77550 5109 A6
Jack London Ct
16100 HarC 77532 3552 B3
Jack Pine Cir
22700 HarC 77375 3110 D2
Jack Pine Dr
2500 FBnC 77494 3951 D5
Jackpine Dr
27400 HarC 77336 3121 D3
Jack Pine Pl
8500 HarC 77375 3110 D2
Jackrabbit Ln
10 PNVL 77304 2237 A2
Jackrabbit Rd
- HOUS 77064 3400 A4
7000 HarC 77041 3679 B2
7000 HarC 77095 3679 B2
7500 HarC 77041 3539 B6
7500 HarC 77095 3539 B6
7800 HOUS 77070 3400 A4
8000 HOUS 77064 3399 E5
8000 HOUS 77070 3399 E5
Jack Russell Dr
- HarC 77530 3829 E3
Jackson
800 HarC 77015 3967 E5
Jackson Av
- BzaC 77583 4500 E6
- PRLD 77583 4500 E6
100 PASD 77506 4107 C4
200 GlsC 77518 4634 C3
1100 GlsC 77539 4634 B4
1100 TXCY 77539 4634 B4
W Jackson Av
100 PASD 77506 4107 A4
600 PASD 77506 4106 E4
1300 HOUS 77017 4106 D4
1300 HOUS 77506 4106 D4
Jackson Blvd
1000 HOUS 77006 3962 D5
Jackson Dr
1500 DRPK 77536 4249 D1
3900 GLSN 77554 5441 B4
Jackson Ln
2300 LGCY 77573 4631 B5
5900 TXCY 77591 4873 E6
Jackson Rd
5700 HTCK 77563 4988 E2
6400 HTCK 77563 4989 A3
Jackson St
- HMPD 77445 3097 E2
- HOUS 77002 3965 D4
10 HOUS 77002 3963 D4
100 RHMD 77469 4491 D2
600 HOUS 77003 3963 D5
700 HOUS 77010 3963 D5
900 HMPD 77445 3098 B2
900 HOUS 77017 4246 B4
900 SHUS 77017 4246 B4
900 SHUS 77587 4246 B4
1000 PASD 77506 3967 D6
1100 HOUS 77506 3967 D6
1700 RSBG 77471 4491 D2
2100 LMQU 77568 4989 D1
2200 HOUS 77004 3963 B7
3800 STFE 77517 4870 C7
4500 HOUS 77004 4103 A2
5600 HOUS 77004 4102 E2
5700 HOUS 77030 4102 E2
Jackson St US-90 ALT
100 RHMD 77469 4491 D2
1700 RSBG 77471 4491 D2
N Jackson St
100 HOUS 77002 3963 D4
100 ALVN 77511 4867 B1
3100 STFE 77517 4870 C5
S Jackson St
100 ALVN 77511 4867 B2
Jackson Bayou Rd
100 HarC 77532 3552 C4
Jackson Bluff Dr
3800 HarC 77449 3816 B2
Jackson Brook Wy
19500 HarC 77429 3395 D1
19600 HarC 77433 3395 D1
Jackson Creek Bend Ln
8400 HarC 77396 3547 E2
Jackson Hill St
300 HOUS 77007 3962 C3
Jackson Lake Dr
3700 FBnC 77469 4234 D6
Jackson Pines Dr
17300 HarC 77090 3257 E4
Jacksons Cross
- FBnC 77083 4095 D6
Jackson Sawmill Ln
14800 FBnC 77478 4236 E4
Jackson Springs Ln
1700 MtgC 77386 2969 D7
Jackson Square Dr
4700 CNRO 77304 2382 E3
Jackstone Dr
8100 HarC 77049 3689 E6
Jack Tarr Dr
- HarC 77532 3552 B1
Jackwood St
4800 HOUS 77096 4101 A7
5300 HOUS 77096 4100 D7
5800 HOUS 77074 4100 B7
7400 HOUS 77074 4099 D7
8800 HOUS 77036 4099 A7
Jacob Ct
2600 DKSN 77539 4633 C7
Jacob Canyon Dr
6200 FBnC 77450 4094 D4
Jacobs Ct
1100 MtgC 77384 2529 A7
Jacobs Lake Blvd
900 MtgC 77384 2529 B7
1000 MtgC 77384 2675 B1
Jacobs Landing Ln
5100 FBnC 77494 4092 E3
Jacobs Reserve Blvd
100 MtgC 77384 2675 A1
Jacobs Trace Ct
12400 HarC 77066 3401 C4
Jacobs Well Ct
21800 FBnC 77469 4093 E6
Jacobs Well Dr
- FBnC 77469 4093 E6
Jacquelyn Dr
2300 HOUS 77055 3821 D4
2400 PRLD 77581 4503 D3
Jacquelyne Cir
700 PASD 77503 4108 B5
Jade Ct
10 HOUS 77076 3684 C5
Jade Hllw
- HOUS 77053 4372 E3
Jade St
22800 MtgC 77365 3118 D1
Jade Bluff Ln
21000 FBnC 77450 4094 A4
Jade Brook Ct
22600 FBnC 77494 4093 D3
Jade Canyon Ln
- HarC 77377 3254 B1
Jade Cove Ct
- FBnC 77479 4496 D5
Jade Cove Dr
14100 HOUS 77077 3956 E6
Jade Cove Ln
- FBnC 77479 4496 D5
Jade Creek Ct
6000 HOUS 77345 3120 B4
Jadecrest Ct
10 CNRO 77304 2529 D1
6100 HarC 77389 2966 D5
Jadecrest Dr
6200 HarC 77389 2966 D5
Jadecrest Rdg
- HarC 77389 2966 C4
Jade Falls Ct
7800 HarC 77095 3538 A7
Jade Feather Ln
26900 HarC 77447 3248 E7
Jade Field Ct
- HarC 77377 3254 C3
Jade Forest Ln
2600 FBnC 77494 3953 A5
Jade Glen Ct
14600 FBnC 77478 4236 D2
Jade Green Ct
4600 PASD 77059 4380 C3
Jade Green Wy
- HOUS 77059 4380 B3
Jade Hollow Ln
1800 HOUS 77077 3956 D5
Jade Meadow Ct
14000 HOUS 77062 4379 D6
Jademont Ln
9900 HarC 77070 3399 C5
Jade Park Dr
20300 FBnC 77469 4234 C3
Jade Pointe
200 MSCY 77459 4497 B3
Jade Ridge Ln
17400 HarC 77095 3537 E5
Jade Ridge Tr
- HarC 77346 3408 E2
Jade Springs Dr
17400 HarC 77095 3677 E1
Jade Star Dr
3200 HarC 77082 4096 C2
Jadestone Ct
10 WDLD 77381 2820 C1
Jadestone Ln
20800 HarC 77388 3112 E4
Jadestone Terrace Ln
- HarC 77044 3549 C2
Jade Treasure Dr
12500 HOUS 77072 4097 D7
Jadewing Ct
10 WDLD 77381 2821 D1
Jadewood Dr
- HarC 77088 3682 C2
7200 HOUS 77088 3682 C2
Jadwin Ct
6800 HOUS 77489 4371 C5
Jaffe Ct
- HOUS 77034 4246 C7
Jagdestone Creek Ln
10900 HarC 77433 3537 A1
11100 HarC 77433 3396 E7
Jaguar Dr
12300 HOUS 77477 4237 E3
12300 HOUS 77477 4238 A3
Jahnke Rd
18000 HarC 77379 3112 B7
18000 HarC 77379 3257 B1
Jaime Ln
29600 HarC 77484 3102 E4
Jaimes Ct
200 HarC 77094 3955 D1
Jake Ln
6000 FBnC 77583 4622 D5
Jake Goodrum Rd
19200 MtgC 77306 2534 C4
Jake Pearson Rd
10800 CNRO 77304 2236 B6
Jalna St
6900 HOUS 77055 3821 D5
Jamaica Dr
4400 SGLD 77479 4496 A2
Jamaica Ln
4400 PASD 77505 4248 D6
Jamaica St
100 HOUS 77012 4105 B2
Jamaica Beach Rd
16500 JMAB 77554 5332 A6
16900 GLSN 77554 5331 E6
16900 JMAB 77554 5331 E6
Jamaica Cove Rd
4500 JMAB 77554 5331 E4
Jamaica Inn Rd
16500 JMAB 77554 5331 E5
Jamail Dr
6500 HOUS 77023 4104 D1
Jamara Cir
12800 HOUS 77077 3957 C6
Jamara Ln
2100 HOUS 77077 3957 C6
Jamboree
- MtgC 77354 2818 E7
Jameel Rd
8600 HOUS 77040 3681 C5
James
22700 MtgC 77357 2974 A3
James Av
900 DRPK 77536 4109 B5
E James Av
10 BYTN 77520 3973 B7
1300 BYTN 77520 4113 C1
James Ct
8900 MtgC 77354 2673 A5
James Dr
6400 HTCK 77563 4989 C4
James Ln
100 HarC 77562 3831 D1
8700 HTCK 77563 4988 D3
13000 STAF 77477 4239 A7
13000 STAF 77477 4370 A1
James Lndg
3900 HarC 77396 3407 A6
James Pl
5600 HOUS 77085 4371 D1
5600 HOUS 77085 4372 A1
James Rd
1300 HarC 77373 3114 B6
2700 FBnC 77477 4370 A5
18100 HarC 77447 3105 B7
James St
- RSBG 77471 4490 D4
200 HOUS 77009 3963 C2
500 TMBL 77375 2964 B7
600 PASD 77506 4107 E4
600 TMBL 77375 3109 B1
800 DRPK 77536 4109 B4
1300 PRLD 77581 4504 E5
7700 BzaC 77584 4627 C1
17200 HarC 77447 3248 D3
25600 WlrC 77447 2813 A7
W James St
100 BYTN 77520 3973 A6
600 BYTN 77520 3972 E6
James Bowie Dr
1600 BYTN 77520 3973 C5
James C Leo
3700 HarC 77373 3115 B4
James Franklin St
7700 HOUS 77088 3683 D3
James Long Ct
21000 FBnC 77469 4234 B4
James Madison Dr
2000 MSCY 77459 4369 E7
James River Ct
1400 LGCY 77573 4631 A6
James River Ln
14700 HarC 77084 3679 A3
James R Museum Pkwy
- PRVW 77445 3100 E3
- PRVW 77484 3100 E3
- WlrC 77445 3100 E2
- WlrC 77484 3100 E3
Jamestown Rd
11300 PNPV 77024 3959 D4
Jamestown St
2700 DKSN 77539 4753 C2
Jamestown Colony Dr
- HarC 77084 3679 A5
Jamestown Crossing Ln
12400 HarC 77346 3408 C3
Jamestown Mall
2400 HOUS 77057 3960 C7
Jamie Ct
200 LPRT 77571 4250 E2
Jamie Ln
1700 HarC 77530 3830 C4
4300 HOUS 77048 4374 E4
13200 GlsC 77510 4870 E2
Jamie Brook Ln
22900 FBnC 77450 4093 D1
Jamie Lee Ct
8800 HarC 77095 3538 D5
Jamie Lee Dr
15800 HarC 77095 3538 D5
Jamison Rd
- PRLD 77581 4504 B4
S Jamison St
200 MRGP 77571 4252 C1
Jamnpree Dr
500 HOUS 77450 3954 B2
Jan Ct
3200 KATY 77493 3813 D3
Jan Dr
6100 BzaC 77583 4623 D6
6100 PRLD 77583 4623 D5
Jan Ln
32500 MtgC 77362 2963 C1
Jan St
3500 FBnC 77545 4498 D7
3800 FBnC 77545 4622 D1
Jana Ln
- DRPK 77536 4248 D1
- PASD 77503 4248 D1
1600 PASD 77503 4108 D5
2400 DRPK 77503 4248 D1
3100 PASD 77505 4248 E3
Janabrook
11900 HOUS 77071 4239 E5
Janacek Rd
17200 HarC 77532 3412 C7
17200 HarC 77532 3553 C1
Janak Dr
7400 HOUS 77055 3821 D6
Janbar Rd
900 HOUS 77047 4373 C4
Jander Dr
1300 MtgC 77386 2822 E7
1400 MtgC 77386 2823 A7
Jane Av
24100 MtgC 77365 2974 B7
Jane Dr
1600 PASD 77502 4107 D7
Jane Ln
20000 HarC 77375 3109 D5
E Jane Ln
11800 HarC 77375 3109 D5
W Jane Ln
11800 HarC 77375 3109 D5
Jane Rd
4400 GLSN 77554 5333 C1
16100 HarC 77377 2963 A7
Jane St
4300 BLAR 77401 4101 B5
4300 HOUS 77401 4101 B5
8000 MNVL 77578 4746 E3
8000 MNVL 77578 4747 A4
N Jane St
100 ALVN 77511 4867 D1
S Jane St
100 ALVN 77511 4867 D1
Jane Austen St
5600 WUNP 77005 4101 B2
Janell Dr
23000 MtgC 77365 2972 C4
Janell Rene Cir
1700 DRPK 77536 4109 D5
Jane Long Dr
4600 RSBG 77471 4491 D3
Jane Long Ln
200 RHMD 77469 4364 E7
Jane Long League Dr
2900 FBnC 77469 4234 C7
Jane Lynn Ln
16900 HarC 77070 3255 C4
Janet Blvd
- BzaC 77583 4623 E5
Janet Ct
2700 PRLD 77581 4504 E5
Janet Ln
- BzaC 77511 4628 E5
10 FRDW 77546 4628 E4
10 PRLD 77546 4628 E4
2700 PRLD 77581 4504 E5
Janet Pl
- PRLD 77581 4504 E5
Janet St
7100 HOUS 77055 3821 D7
Janeths Ct
4700 HOUS 77013 3827 D4
Janey St
12400 HOUS 77015 3966 E4
12400 HOUS 77015 3967 A4
Jan Glen Ln
9100 HarC 77379 3255 C3
9900 HarC 77070 3255 C4
Janice St
100 CNRO 77301 2384 A3
6800 BKVL 77581 4376 A6
Janine Av
200 GlsC 77539 4635 C4
Janisch Rd
300 HOUS 77018 3684 B7
300 HOUS 77022 3684 C7
E Janisch Rd
100 HOUS 77018 3684 C7
100 HOUS 77022 3684 C7
Jan Kelly Ln
400 PNPV 77024 3959 D3
Jansells Crossing Dr
11900 HarC 77065 3399 A7
January Dr
19800 HarC 77346 3265 A4
Janus Rd
- PASD 77505 4249 B3
Japhet St
10 HOUS 77020 3964 C3
Japonica St
6600 HOUS 77087 4104 E3
6600 HOUS 77087 4105 A3
7300 HOUS 77012 4105 B4
Jaquet Dr
800 BLAR 77401 4101 A3
Jaquine Dr
14200 HarC 77429 3397 E7
Jara Ct
1800 HarC 77388 3113 C4
Jarden Glen Ct
7100 HarC 77379 3111 B1
Jardin St
3700 SSPL 77005 4101 D3
Jardina Dr
2600 GlsC 77539 4635 C3
Jardine Ct
10 WDLD 77385 2676 C4
E Jared Dr
5100 HOUS 77018 3683 D7
Jarmese St
4800 HOUS 77033 4243 D1
Jarrard St
2800 WUNP 77005 4102 A3
3000 WUNP 77005 4101 E3
Jarratt Sq
20400 HMBL 77338 3262 D4
Jarred Ct
6800 PRLD 77584 4502 C5
Jarrell Dr
500 CNRO 77304 2382 A1
Jarvis Rd
12500 HarC 77429 3398 B4
13600 HarC 77429 3397 B4
15800 HarC 77429 3396 D4
Jarvis St
3000 HOUS 77063 4099 D1
Jasamine Path Dr
11900 HarC 77044 3688 E4
W Jasmine Av
1300 HarC 77598 4506 E7
1300 WEBS 77598 4506 E7
Jasmine Dr
1600 PASD 77503 4108 B7
3700 ALVN 77511 4867 D6
Jasmine Ln
7000 BYTN 77521 3832 A5
7000 HarC 77521 3832 A6
Jasmine St
100 BYTN 77520 3971 B1
600 FBnC 77545 4499 A7
2300 HarC 77562 3832 C3
E Jasmine St
3600 PRLD 77581 4503 C3
W Jasmine St
200 FBnC 77545 4499 B7
700 BzaC 77583 4499 D7
700 PRLD 77545 4499 D7
4200 PRLD 77581 4503 B3
Jasmine Tr
7000 FBnC 77084 3679 B2
Jasmine Arbor Ct
6700 HarC 77088 3682 B2
Jasmine Arbor Ln
6500 HarC 77088 3682 C1
Jasmine Bend Dr
- WDLD 77382 2674 E5
Jasmine Bloom Ln
29700 HarC 77429 3395 E1
Jasmine Brook Ct
21200 HarC 77379 3111 D3
Jasmine Brook Ln
12400 HOUS 77089 4505 C1
Jasmine Creek Ct
15200 HarC 77095 3678 E1
Jasmine Creek Ln
13600 BzaC 77583 4623 E5
Jasmine Field Wy
26100 FBnC 77494 4092 E2
Jasmine Hollow Ln
- FBnC 77494 4092 A2
12600 HarC 77041 3679 D3
Jasmine Knoll Wy
18900 HarC 77433 3251 E7
Jasmine Leaf Tr
20400 HarC 77338 3261 B4
Jasmine Meadows Ln
4900 HarC 77346 3264 B7
Jasmine Park Ln
- HarC 77044 3549 C2
Jasmine Pl St
6800 HarC 77379 3256 E4
Jasmine Ridge Ct
2400 HOUS 77062 4379 E5
Jasmine Springs Dr
14500 HarC 77377 2963 D6
Jasmine Stone Dr
12800 HOUS 77072 4097 C4
Jasmine Terrace Dr
23500 HarC 77373 3114 C7
Jasmine Terrace Ln
14400 HarC 77047 4374 B5
Jasmine Tree Ln
15500 HarC 77049 3829 A2
Jason Ct
- PRLD 77581 4504 E6
400 ORDN 77386 2822 C6
Jason Dr
3900 HarC 77014 3401 C1
Jason Rd
14500 SGCH 77362 2816 C7
Jason St
- HOUS 77074 4240 A1
- HOUS 77096 4101 B7
5500 HOUS 77096 4100 C7
5700 HOUS 77096 4240 C1
6100 HOUS 77074 4100 A7
8400 HOUS 77074 4099 C7
Jasons Bend Dr
1100 FBnC 77479 4366 D7
Jasper Ln
13000 HarC 77429 3398 B6
Jasper Rd
300 GlsC 77518 4634 B2
900 LGCY 77539 4634 A2
2500 PRLD 77581 4502 E3
2500 PRLD 77584 4502 E3
Jasper St
100 GlsC 77518 4634 B1
2100 BzaC 77583 4624 A2
2200 PRLD 77578 4624 B2
2200 PRLD 77583 4624 B2
Jasper Cove
300 MSCY 77459 4497 C4
Jasper Grove Ct
5300 HOUS 77345 3119 D2
Jasper Oaks Dr
20100 HarC 77433 3537 A7
Jasperson Ln
3800 FBnC 77450 4093 E1
Jasper Stone Ct
23600 HarC 77373 3115 C5
Jasperwood Cir
19900 HarC 77449 3815 E3
Jasperwood Dr
20600 HarC 77338 3261 D2
20700 HarC 77338 3262 A3
Jasperwood Ln
20400 HarC 77338 3261 E3
Jast Dr
16000 HarC 77429 3397 A1
16100 HarC 77429 3396 E1
Jasterstone Ln
- PRLD 77581 4503 C1
Jaubert Ct
14200 FBnC 77478 4366 E4
Javelina
- HOUS 77049 3828 B4
Jay Ct
18600 MtgC 77365 2972 A6
Jay Dr
22000 HarC 77373 3260 D1
22500 HarC 77373 3115 D7
Jay Ln
13000 STFE 77510 4870 E5
Jay Rd
9200 HTCK 77563 4988 A4
9800 GlsC 77510 4987 E4
9800 HTCK 77563 4987 E4
Jay St
6800 HOUS 77028 3825 E2
7100 HOUS 77028 3826 A2
Jay Wy
20900 HarC 77447 2961 A7
Jayaloch Ct
18600 HarC 77379 3255 E1
Jaycee Ln
10800 HNCV 77024 3960 A2
Jayci Creek Ln
8100 HarC 77396 3547 E2
Jayci Park Ln
8000 HarC 77396 3547 D1
Jaycreek Ct
13900 HarC 77070 3398 E1
Jaycreek Dr
- HarC 77070 3398 D1
10500 HarC 77070 3399 A2
Jaycrest Dr
13600 HarC 77037 3544 E6
Jayden Ct
27200 MtgC 77386 3115 E2
Jaydon Dr
- HarC 77083 4097 A5
Jay Frank Dobie High School Rd
- HarC 77089 4377 B6
- HOUS 77075 4377 B6
E Jayhawk
11300 HarC 77044 3690 E1
W Jayhawk
11300 HarC 77044 3690 E1
Jaymar Dr
4500 FBnC 77479 4366 D5
Jaymarr Ct
25000 MtgC 77365 3117 E1
Jay's Ln
500 STAF 77477 4369 C3
Jaywood Dr
9700 HOUS 77040 3682 A1
J-Bar A
- HarC 77377 3107 D3
JB Fleming St
18900 MAGA 77355 2668 E6
18900 MtgC 77355 2668 E6
JB le Fevre Rd
- BYTN 77520 3972 B7
W Jean Dr
3300 GLSN 77554 5220 D6
Jean Ln
800 BYTN 77521 3973 B2
Jean St
1800 HOUS 77023 4104 C2
2400 PASD 77502 4247 B1
27700 HarC 77373 2969 A7
Jeanene Ct
2700 HarC 77449 3814 E4
Jeanetta Rd
2700 HOUS 77063 3959 C7
2800 HOUS 77063 4099 D2
Jeanie Dr
17500 HarC 77377 3251 C2
17500 HarC 77433 3251 C2
Jeanie Ln
1200 BYTN 77521 3973 B3
Jeanie Lynn Cir
400 TKIS 77554 5106 C3
Jeanie Lynne Cir
400 TKIS 77554 5106 C3
Jean Lafitte
4000 GLSN 77554 5333 A2
Jean La Fitte
13500 HarC 77532 3552 E7
Jean Lafitte Dr
12800 BzaC 77541 5547 B7
Jean La Fitte Dr
13200 HarC 77532 3692 E1
Jean Lafitte Rd
16500 JMAB 77554 5332 A5
16600 JMAB 77554 5331 E6
Jeanna Ridge Ct
16900 FBnC 77083 4095 D6
Jeanne Ln
100 HarC 77049 3827 E2
100 HOUS 77049 3827 E2
Jeannine Dr
1300 HOUS 77008 3822 D6
Jebbia Ln
- HOUS 77031 4238 E7
12600 HarC 77031 4238 E7
12600 STAF 77477 4238 E7
12900 STAF 77477 4369 E1
Jeb Stuart Ct
2500 LGCY 77573 4631 B6
Jeb Stuart Dr
2600 LGCY 77573 4631 A6
6900 FBnC 77469 4493 D6
Jeb Stuart Ln
100 MtgC 77302 2530 D7
Jeckel Isles Ct
19300 HarC 77375 3109 C6
Jeckel Isles Dr
12200 HarC 77375 3109 D7
Jeena Ln
13600 GlsC 77510 4986 D1
Jeff St
1000 HOUS 77091 3683 E5
Jeffcoat St
- BzaC 77511 4628 A7
- BzaC 77511 4749 A1
Jeffcote Rd
200 CTSH 77303 2385 D3
200 MtgC 77303 2385 C2
Jeff Davis Ct
600 MtgC 77302 2530 C6
Jeff Davis Dr
500 FBnC 77469 4493 D6

STREET
Block City ZIP Map# Grid

Jeffers Cir
500 BzaC 77511 4628 C6
1900 HarC 77032 3404 C6
Jeffers Ct
10 PNPV 77024 3959 D2
Jefferson Av
200 RHMD 77469 4364 E7
1300 PASD 77502 4246 D1
4400 DRPK 77536 4249 B2
Jefferson Dr
3000 LMQU 77568 4873 C7
Jefferson Rd
- PASD 77506 4107 E3
Jefferson St
- HOUS 77004 3963 E7
100 LPRT 77571 4251 E5
400 HOUS 77002 3963 B5
400 PASD 77506 4107 D3
400 RSBG 77471 4490 B5
900 ALVN 77511 4749 C7
1200 BYTN 77520 3973 B6
1400 PASD 77506 3967 E7
3300 HOUS 77003 3963 D7
4200 HOUS 77023 3964 A7
4700 HOUS 77023 4104 E1
5500 PRLD 77584 4502 E5
Jefferson Chemical Rd
- CTSH 77303 2385 D3
- CTSH 77306 2385 D3
3700 MtgC 77301 2385 D5
3700 MtgC 77306 2385 D5
10800 MtgC 77302 2385 E7
Jefferson Crossing Dr
2200 CNRO 77304 2236 D3
Jefferson Oaks
12200 HarC 77429 3398 C4
Jeffery St
5100 GlsC 77539 4633 C6
5100 TXCY 77539 4633 C6
8000 HOUS 77028 3826 C3
Jeff Ginn Memorial Dr
1100 PASD 77506 4107 C7
1200 PASD 77502 4107 C6
Jeffrey
- BYTN 77520 4112 D3
Jeffrey St
1100 DRPK 77536 4109 C7
Jeffrey Tr
3800 HarC 77396 3407 A5
Jelicoe Dr
11700 HOUS 77047 4373 D2
Jelly Park Stone Dr
16700 HarC 77429 3252 E6
Jengo Dr
13700 HarC 77083 4097 A5
Jenikay Ln
16900 HarC 77084 3678 B6
Jenkins Rd
1300 PASD 77506 4107 D5
7500 BzaC 77584 4627 B1
12200 GLSN 77554 5220 C6
Jenkins St
10 HOUS 77003 3964 B6
N Jenkins St
500 HOUS 77003 3964 B5
Jen Marie
5700 HOUS 77088 3682 E2
Jenna Beth Ln
3000 HarC 77396 3407 D3
Jenna Moran Dr
6800 HOUS 77036 4099 B4
Jenner Rd
27700 HarC 77377 3108 D3
Jennetta St
700 RSBG 77471 4491 B4
Jennie Ln
36000 MtgC 77362 2816 C2
Jennifer
- DRPK 77536 4109 A5
Jennifer Ln
1300 JTCY 77029 3966 D4
Jennifer St
900 ALVN 77511 4749 A6
E Jennifer Wy Dr
9700 HOUS 77075 4377 B1
W Jennifer Wy Dr
9800 HOUS 77075 4377 B1
Jennings Ct
4000 MSCY 77459 4497 C3
Jennings Rd
15800 HarC 77396 3406 E5
Jennings St
600 TXCY 77590 4874 D5
8200 HOUS 77017 4105 D6
Jennische St
2200 BYTN 77520 3973 D5
Jenny Dr
2900 SGLD 77479 4368 D7
Jenny Ln
1100 RHMD 77469 4364 D6
19200 MtgC 77365 2972 D1
Jenny Anne Ln
10700 HarC 77070 3399 B5
Jenny Gaye Ln
600 HarC 77562 3831 E2
Jenny Ln Pkwy
1700 FBnC 77469 4364 D6
1700 RHMD 77469 4364 D6
Jennys Park Pl
14700 HOUS 77053 4372 D3
S Jenny Wood
13000 HarC 77429 3397 D4
Jenny Wood Dr
13100 HarC 77429 3397 E4
Jenny Wren Ct
10 WDLD 77382 2674 C3
Jens Wy
600 FBnC 77545 4499 D6
Jensen Dr
10 HOUS 77003 3963 E3
10 HOUS 77020 3963 E3
800 PASD 77506 4106 E3
1500 HOUS 77026 3963 E1
2500 HOUS 77026 3824 E4
6600 HOUS 77093 3824 E7
6600 HTCK 77563 4989 B4
8300 HOUS 77093 3685 E7
10300 HOUS 77093 3686 A4
S Jensen Dr
200 HOUS 77003 3963 E4
300 HOUS 77020 3963 E4
Jensen St
4300 STFE 77517 4870 B7
Jephson Ln
1800 ALVN 77511 4867 D4
E Jephson St
100 ALVN 77511 4867 C1

W Jerad Dr
5100 HOUS 77018 3683 C7
Jeremy Ct
400 ORDN 77386 2822 C6
Jerich Dr
15000 HOUS 77053 4372 D4
Jericho Ct
5200 HOUS 77091 3683 E7
Jeridona St
2000 LMQU 77568 4989 C3
Jernigan Ford
2200 DKSN 77539 4753 C1
Jerome St
1100 HOUS 77008 3823 E5
1100 HOUS 77009 3823 E5
Jerry Ln
20200 MtgC 77365 2825 C5
Jerry St
500 HOUS 77022 3823 D2
1000 RHMD 77469 4364 D7
5700 FBnC 77583 4623 C5
Jerrycrest Dr
5800 PRLD 77584 4502 D6
Jersey Dr
15300 JRSV 77040 3680 E1
15600 JRSV 77040 3540 D7
19900 HarC 77532 3412 D2
Jersey Hollow Dr
16300 JRSV 77040 3540 C6
Jersey Meadow Dr
12300 STAF 77477 4237 E7
Jersey Meadows Dr
- JRSV 77065 3540 A6
Jersey Shore Dr
14700 HarC 77047 4373 A6
Jerson Rd
18700 HarC 77379 3111 C7
Jeruis Ln
1800 HarC 77449 3815 D7
Jerusalem Ct
3000 HarC 77521 3832 D4
Jervis Dr
4600 RSBG 77471 4491 C4
Jeske Rd
3900 BzaC 77578 4501 B7
3900 BzaC 77578 4625 B1
3900 BzaC 77584 4501 B6
3900 PRLD 77584 4501 B6
Jeske Rd CO-922
- BzaC 77584 4501 B6
- PRLD 77584 4501 B6
3900 BzaC 77578 4501 B7
3900 BzaC 77578 4625 B1
Jessabella Dr
6300 HarC 77379 3111 D2
Jessalyn Ln
10200 HOUS 77075 4376 E2
Jessamine St
200 HOUS 77009 3824 C7
4700 BLAR 77401 4101 A5
5100 BLAR 77401 4100 D5
5300 BLAR 77081 4100 D5
5300 HOUS 77081 4100 D5
5500 HOUS 77401 4100 D5
Jessamine Wy
400 LGCY 77573 4632 D2
Jessamine Springs Ct
9700 HarC 77396 3407 C2
Jessica Ct
3200 KATY 77493 3813 D3
4800 FBnC 77479 4366 D7
Jessica Dr
100 LPRT 77571 4250 E2
Jessica Ln
13600 HarC 77069 3400 B2
20500 HarC 77449 3815 D3
Jessica Falls Cir
14400 HarC 77044 3549 E1
Jessica Rose Ln
20900 HarC 77379 3111 D4
Jessie Ln
1300 PASD 77502 4107 D6
1300 PASD 77506 4107 D6
20500 MtgC 77372 2535 A5
Jessie Anne Ln
6300 HarC 77041 3679 C4
Jess Pirtle Blvd
- SGLD 77478 4367 D1
- SGLD 77478 4368 A1
12800 SGLD 77478 4237 A7
Jessup St
- CNRO 77301 2384 B6
Jester Dr
- FBnC 77469 4366 B3
Jester Ln
2500 STAF 77477 4369 E3
Jester St
7700 HOUS 77051 4243 C1
Jester Oaks Pl
10 WDLD 77381 2821 D1
Jesters Hat Ln
12500 HarC 77044 3549 A6
Jeter Dr
19800 MAGA 77355 2668 E6
Jetero Blvd
- HOUS 77032 3404 D1
Jethro St
- HOUS 77045 4241 A6
10100 HOUS 77033 4243 E5
Jetoma
16800 MtgC 77385 2676 B5
Jet Pilot Av
8100 HOUS 77075 4245 D7
8400 HOUS 77061 4245 D7
Jetstream Ct
700 HOUS 77598 4379 A6
Jett Rd
100 HarC 77357 2830 A7
Jettty Cove Ct
- HarC 77494 3953 A2
Jetty Ct
17100 HarC 77532 3552 B1
Jetty Ln
4600 HOUS 77072 4097 E5
Jetty Terrace Cir
4100 MSCY 77459 4369 C6
Jewel Ct
10200 CHTW 77385 2822 E4
10200 MtgC 77385 2822 E4
Jewel Lndg
400 MSCY 77459 4497 C4
Jewel St
200 CNRO 77301 2383 E6
2000 WALR 77484 3102 A5
2100 WALR 77484 3101 E5
2700 HOUS 77026 3824 E7
4500 HOUS 77026 3825 C7

Jewel Ann Ln
3000 HOUS 77082 4097 A2
Jewel Ashford Rd
5100 FBnC 77469 4234 B3
N Jewel Bend Ln
9000 HOUS 77075 4377 A3
S Jewel Bend Ln
9000 HOUS 77075 4377 A4
W Jewel Bend Ln
10800 HOUS 77075 4377 A5
Jewel Brook Ln
7400 FBnC 77469 4094 C6
Jewel Cave Ln
- HarC 77346 3408 C3
Jewell St
200 PASD 77506 4107 A3
Jewel Meadow Dr
14700 HOUS 77053 4372 E3
Jewel Park Ln
200 HarC 77094 3955 C1
Jewel Point Dr
- MtgC 77386 2969 E3
Jewelsford Ct
10 WDLD 77382 2819 B2
Jewelsford Dr
10 WDLD 77382 2819 B2
Jewel Springs Ln
- FBnC 77494 4092 C5
Jewett
4100 HOUS 77026 3825 B5
Jewett St
500 HOUS 77009 3824 A6
Jezebel St
5100 HOUS 77033 4243 E5
5300 HOUS 77033 4244 A5
JF Fields Rd
- GLSN 77554 5108 E1
JHK Blvd
- PASD 77586 4381 E7
Jib Ct
3300 FBnC 77545 4498 C6
16700 HarC 77532 3552 A2
Jib Boom Ct
1100 HarC 77532 3552 A1
Jibstay Ct
13400 GLSN 77554 5332 E1
Jill Av
300 CNRO 77303 2384 A1
400 CNRO 77303 2383 E1
Jill Cir
- HarC 77388 3113 B7
Jillana Kaye Dr
10300 HarC 77086 3542 C2
Jillian Dr
12000 HarC 77067 3402 D4
Jillian Oaks Ct
2000 MtgC 77386 2969 D7
Jillian Oaks Ln
28000 MtgC 77386 2969 D6
Jillian Wy Ct
24800 HarC 77389 2966 D3
Jills Wy Ln
18100 HarC 77429 3252 B6
Jim St
5700 HOUS 77092 3821 D2
Jimbo Ln
5400 HarC 77389 2967 A7
Jim Davidson Dr
100 SGLD 77478 4367 C1
Jimmy Ln
27000 ORDN 77385 2822 B5
34500 SGCH 77362 2816 C6
34600 MtgC 77362 2816 C6
Jimmy Dean Ln
- HarC 77562 3692 D6
Jimmy Harns Blvd
- LPRT 77571 4249 C5
- PASD 77507 4249 C5
Jim West St
4300 BLAR 77401 4101 C5
4300 HOUS 77401 4101 C5
Jingles Rd
23600 WlrC 77445 3097 E6
Jipsie Ln
3000 HOUS 77051 4243 A5
Jireh Rd
16100 MtgC 77306 2533 B2
JL Brown St
700 PRVW 77445 2955 B7
JM Clouser St
1500 GLSN 77550 5109 B4
J Meyer Rd
1800 RSBG 77469 4614 E3
1800 RSBG 77471 4614 E3
2200 RSBG 77469 4615 A3
2400 FBnC 77469 4615 A3
Joan St
13100 STAF 77477 4370 A1
14800 HOUS 77085 4370 E1
14800 HOUS 77085 4371 A1
Joanel St
2600 HOUS 77027 3961 D7
Joan Leigh Cir
19800 HarC 77388 3113 B6
Joanleigh Dr
18900 HarC 77388 3258 D1
19000 HarC 77388 3113 C7
Jo Ann Ln
1300 SGLD 77478 4237 A7
Joann St
2600 FBnC 77477 4370 A5
Joanna Ct
28300 MtgC 77355 2815 D5
Joan of Arc Dr
11600 HDWV 77024 3959 C2
11700 HOUS 77024 3959 C2
Joan of Arc St
11800 HarC 77532 3692 E3
Jobal St
- HarC 77060 3544 D2
Jobes Ct
1900 ALVN 77511 4749 A6
Jocelyn St
1100 HOUS 77023 4104 D1
Jocelyn Park Ct
22500 HarC 77493 3814 A6
Jockey Club Ct
11400 HarC 77065 3539 E3
Jockey Club Dr
9800 HarC 77065 3539 E3
9800 HarC 77065 3540 A3
Jodi Cir
31900 SGCH 77355 2961 B3
Jodie Lynn Cir
26000 HarC 77433 3396 B7
Jody Ct
10500 HOUS 77099 4237 C3

Jodywood Dr
18700 HarC 77346 3265 B7
Joe Dr
3700 BzaC 77584 4502 A7
3700 BzaC 77584 4626 A1
3700 PRLD 77584 4502 A7
Joe St
2200 PASD 77502 4247 B1
Joe Annie St
1000 HOUS 77019 3962 D4
Jo Edna Rd
10900 HOUS 77075 4375 E2
Joella Dr
14300 HarC 77032 3546 A2
Joe Loggins Rd
36300 WlrC 77445 2954 D5
36300 WlrC 77445 2955 A5
Joe Louis Ln
6300 HOUS 77091 3683 C5
Joel Wheaton Rd
2100 HOUS 77077 3956 E7
2500 HOUS 77082 3956 E7
2500 HOUS 77082 4096 E1
Joerger Cumings Rd
600 FBnC 77471 4364 A7
Joey Cir
27800 HarC 77373 2969 A7
Joggers Ln
8500 HarC 77346 3265 D6
Johanna Dr
1500 HOUS 77055 3821 C5
Johlke Rd
31000 MtgC 77355 2963 B4
John Av
2300 FRDW 77546 4505 A4
2400 PRLD 77581 4505 A4
2900 BzaC 77511 4748 D1
John Ct
1300 PRLD 77581 4504 E5
1300 PRLD 77581 4505 A5
John Dr
1000 PRLD 77584 4501 C2
16000 HarC 77530 3830 B4
John St
- HOUS 77017 4246 E1
- HOUS 77502 4246 E1
1300 GlsC 77539 4635 D7
2000 PASD 77502 4106 E7
2000 PASD 77502 4246 E1
2500 PRLD 77581 4505 A5
2600 PRLD 77581 4504 E5
2700 LMQU 77568 4989 D1
8300 HOUS 77012 4105 D3
John A St
100 BYTN 77520 3971 C5
E John Alber Rd
100 HOUS 77037 3684 D2
John Albers Rd
100 HOUS 77037 3684 E2
100 HOUS 77076 3684 E2
200 HOUS 77076 3685 A2
Johnathan Landing Ct
10 HarC 77389 2820 B6
John Bank Dr
9500 HarC 77379 3255 C4
John Clapp Rd
25100 FBnC 77494 3952 C4
John Cooper Dr
10 WDLD 77381 2820 C3
John Crump Ln
- HOUS 77449 3814 E5
2500 HarC 77449 3814 E5
Johndale Ct
22700 FBnC 77494 4093 C4
John David Ln
7800 PASD 77505 4249 B3
John Davis Rd
16500 JMAB 77554 5332 A5
16600 JMAB 77554 5331 E6
John Dreaper Dr
5400 HOUS 77056 3960 E6
John F Kennedy Blvd
12200 HarC 77039 3546 A5
14400 HarC 77032 3546 B2
14400 HOUS 77032 3546 B2
14900 HarC 77032 3405 B7
14900 HOUS 77032 3405 A4
18700 HOUS 77032 3404 E1
S John F Kennedy-McKaughan W
- HOUS 77032 3404 D1
John Freeman Av
6500 HOUS 77030 4102 D4
John Handcock Ln
3600 MSCY 77459 4369 D5
John Lizer Rd
2800 PRLD 77581 4503 E5
3400 PRLD 77584 4503 D5
John Locke Ln
3000 MSCY 77459 4369 E6
John Martin Rd
5400 HarC 77521 3833 B7
5900 BYTN 77521 3833 B6
Johnny Palmer Rd
- TXCY 77591 4872 E4
John Ralston Rd
- HOUS 77029 3966 D2
2500 HOUS 77013 3966 D1
2600 HOUS 77013 3827 D7
6400 HarC 77049 3827 D2
6900 HarC 77044 3827 D1
7500 HarC 77044 3688 D7
8100 HOUS 77044 3688 D7
John Reynolds Cir
12800 GLSN 77554 5333 C1
John Reynolds Rd
4400 GLSN 77554 5333 C1
John Rolfe Ln
22500 HarC 77449 3814 D5
Johns Rd
9000 HarC 77049 3690 E3
Johnsbury Dr
2500 HarC 77067 3402 A4
Johns Enterprise Ct
13300 HarC 77433 3395 D5
John Silver Rd
16500 JMAB 77554 5331 E5
16500 JMAB 77554 5332 A5
Johnson Al
29900 MtgC 77355 2815 B2
Johnson Dr
- PRLD 77584 4502 E4
6100 MSCY 77459 4497 A7
Johnson Ln
600 FBnC 77479 4366 E6
Johnson Lndg
- HOUS 77029 4106 A1
- HOUS 77547 4106 A1

Johnson Rd
4500 HarC 77521 3832 E6
12100 MtgC 77302 2531 E6
15100 CNRO 77384 2675 D2
15100 MtgC 77384 2675 D2
18700 MtgC 77385 2822 C2
18700 SHEH 77385 2822 C2
23000 MtgC 77357 2827 E7
23200 MtgC 77357 2828 A7
27900 TMBL 77375 3109 A2
Johnson St
- LGCY 77573 4631 A6
100 LMQU 77568 4873 E7
100 TXCY 77591 4873 E7
1000 PASD 77506 4107 B6
1100 BYTN 77520 4112 D1
1300 HOUS 77007 3963 B3
1700 PASD 77502 4107 B7
1900 RSBG 77471 4491 A5
5200 DKSN 77539 4754 C4
14500 HOUS 77034 4379 A2
N Johnson St
100 ALVN 77511 4867 B1
100 PASD 77506 4107 B3
S Johnson St
100 ALVN 77511 4867 B5
200 PASD 77506 4107 B5
Johnson Mallard Dr
- MtgC 77302 2678 D2
12600 MtgC 77302 2532 D7
Johns Post Rd
12100 HarC 77433 3395 D6
Johns Purchase Ct
12300 HarC 77433 3395 D5
Johns Stake Ct
12300 HarC 77433 3395 D5
Johnston Ln
- HarC 77532 3553 C7
- LbyC 77327 2538 E1
Johnston St
1200 HOUS 77022 3823 E2
2500 PRLD 77581 4503 A3
2500 PRLD 77584 4503 A3
John Wayne Rd
- GlsC 77650 4879 C3
Jolen Ct
900 BLAR 77401 4101 A6
Jolie Dr
5000 PRLD 77584 4503 A5
Joliet St
12900 HOUS 77015 3828 C7
Jolly Boat Dr
17400 HarC 77532 3551 D1
17400 HarC 77532 3552 A1
17500 HarC 77532 3411 A7
Jolly Roger Cir
3500 GLSN 77554 5332 D1
Jolly Roger Ct
5000 JMAB 77554 5331 E5
Jolly Roger Dr
12800 BzaC 77541 5547 B7
16500 GLSN 77554 5331 E5
16500 JMAB 77554 5331 E5
Jolly Roger Rd
4200 GLSN 77554 5331 E4
4200 JMAB 77554 5331 E3
Jollyville Ln
- HarC 77449 3676 B2
Jolly Wood Ct
9400 HarC 77086 3542 A3
Jonathan Cir
- HOUS 77048 4374 E2
Jonathan Ct
7600 HOUS 77489 4371 A5
Jonathan Ln
5400 HOUS 77011 3964 C5
Jonathan St
4300 BLAR 77401 4101 C5
4300 HOUS 77401 4101 C5
Jonathans Lndg
2300 FBnC 77469 4365 C1
Jone
1200 HarC 77429 3396 C2
Jones Blvd
2700 PASD 77502 4247 C2
Jones Dr
2500 GLSN 77551 5222 A1
2500 GLSN 77554 5222 A1
6800 GLSN 77551 5108 A7
Jones Rd
- HarC 77521 3832 D4
- HOUS 77070 3255 A7
- HOUS 77377 3255 A6
- PASD 77503 4108 D2
100 HarC 77562 3831 E4
500 HarC 77562 3832 A4
1500 BYTN 77520 3973 E6
3100 HarC 77521 3833 A4
8000 JRSV 77040 3540 A7
8000 JRSV 77065 3540 A7
8100 TXCY 77591 4873 A6
8500 JRSV 77064 3540 A6
8800 HarC 77064 3540 A5
8800 HarC 77065 3540 A4
10600 HarC 77070 3540 A6
11300 HarC 77065 3399 A7
11300 HarC 77070 3399 A1
12200 HarC 77429 3399 A6
14900 HarC 77070 3255 A7
15200 MtgC 77384 2675 A3
15300 HarC 77377 3255 A7
15500 WDLD 77384 2675 A4
23500 WlrC 77445 2953 A3
26500 WlrC 77445 2952 E1
Jones Rd W
11000 HarC 77065 3539 E1
11000 HarC 77065 3540 A1
11000 HarC 77070 3540 A1
Jones St
- ALVN 77511 4866 D3
1500 RSBG 77471 4491 C5
1700 ALVN 77511 4867 D3
2500 HOUS 77026 3824 E7
4700 HOUS 77016 3686 C7
12000 HarC 77338 3262 A6
N Jones St
300 BYTN 77520 3972 E6
S Jones St
100 BYTN 77520 3972 E7
Jones River Rd
300 FBnC 77469 4495 B7
Joni Wy
- FBnC 77469 4235 D6
Jonquil
100 HOUS 77009 3824 C7
Jonquil Dr
7800 TXCY 77591 4873 B6

Jonsport Ln
28300 MtgC 77386 2969 D5
Joplin St
7700 HOUS 77087 4105 B7
8000 HOUS 77017 4105 C6
Jordan Dr
6100 PRLD 77584 4502 D5
Jordan Ln
4400 HarC 77532 3554 A5
Jordan Rd
6500 MNVL 77578 4746 B3
7800 MNVL 77578 4747 A4
E Jordan Rd
8200 MNVL 77578 4747 A4
Jordan St
6000 HTCK 77563 4988 E3
6000 HTCK 77563 4989 A3
9700 HOUS 77017 4106 B4
W Jordan St
200 ALVN 77511 4867 C3
Jordana Wy
- HOUS 77053 4372 D4
Jordanbranch Ln
14700 HarC 77396 3548 A2
E Jordan Cove
7600 HOUS 77055 3821 D6
N Jordan Cove
1300 HOUS 77055 3821 D6
S Jordan Cove
1300 HOUS 77055 3821 E5
Jordan Falls Dr
6400 HOUS 77085 4240 D7
Jordan Heights Dr
10700 HOUS 77016 3687 A3
Jordan Oaks St
15100 HOUS 77053 4372 A4
Jordan Terrace Ln
25500 FBnC 77494 4093 A2
Jorden Rd
- HOUS 77079 3818 A7
- HOUS 77079 3957 A1
1000 HOUS 77079 3817 E7
Jordens Rd
2800 HarC 77084 3816 D5
2800 HOUS 77084 3816 D5
Jordy Ln
200 DKSN 77539 4754 D1
Jordyn Lake Dr
16100 HarC 77377 3254 C5
Jorent Dr
2500 HarC 77088 3543 B7
2600 HOUS 77088 3543 B7
Jorine Dr
7000 HOUS 77036 4099 B5
Jorns Dr
3100 HOUS 77045 4372 E1
3100 HOUS 77045 4373 A1
Jorns St
5000 HOUS 77045 4372 A1
Joseph Cir
- HarC 77014 3401 D3
Joseph Ct
- WlrC 77447 2813 C7
1400 TMBL 77375 3109 C2
Joseph Rd
23300 MtgC 77365 3118 E1
23300 MtgC 77365 3119 A1
25800 WlrC 77447 2813 D2
Joseph St
- FBnC 77469 4365 B7
900 PASD 77506 4107 E6
Josephine St
3100 HOUS 77026 3825 A7
5800 PRLD 77584 4502 D4
13100 STAF 77477 4370 A1
Joseph Pine Ln
2500 HarC 77088 3543 C7
Josey Creek Ct
12800 HarC 77433 3396 A4
Josey Ranch Rd
15600 HarC 77429 3396 B4
15600 HarC 77433 3396 B4
Josh Wy
300 LPRT 77571 4250 E2
Joshnomi Ln
14800 HarC 77429 3397 D5
Joshua Cir
4200 HarC 77014 3401 C1
Joshua Ln
100 SPVL 77055 3821 A7
9600 HarC 77375 3255 B2
20500 HarC 77449 3815 D3
Joshua Kendall Ln
22000 HarC 77449 3815 A6
22200 HarC 77449 3814 E6
Joshua Lee Ln
500 MtgC 77386 2968 D1
Joshua Tree Ln
1100 HarC 77073 3259 B3
1600 DRPK 77536 4109 D6
Josie
8100 MNVL 77578 4626 B6
Josie St
8600 HOUS 77029 3965 D3
Joswiak Ln
22000 WlrC 77445 3243 A1
Jourdan Wy
1700 FBnC 77479 4367 B7
Journal Leaf Pl
10 WDLD 77382 2819 D1
Journey Rd
11800 HOUS 77048 4375 B4
Journeys End
10 WDLD 77381 2674 E6
Jove St
15700 HarC 77060 3544 D2
15700 HOUS 77060 3544 D2
Jowett Pl
9400 FBnC 77478 4236 B2
Joy
24800 MtgC 77357 2974 D1
Joy Cir
- HarC 77060 3403 B5
Joy Ln
100 CNRO 77304 2383 B4
Joy St
7800 HOUS 77028 3826 B2
Joyce Blvd
4000 HarC 77084 3817 A1
4000 HOUS 77084 3817 A1
4200 HarC 77084 3678 A7
Joyce St
200 HOUS 77009 3824 C5
Joycedale Ln
7900 HarC 77044 3689 B7
Joyner St
6000 HOUS 77087 4244 C1

Joy Oaks Ln
1300 HarC 77073 3403 C2
Joy Village Dr
26300 MtgC 77372 2683 B2
Joywood Ct
- HarC 77338 3262 A3
JP White Rd
100 CNRO 77304 2529 D3
100 MtgC 77304 2529 D3
JR Dr
2600 BzaC 77583 4500 D7
J Star Ct
- BKHV 77024 3959 B2
- HOUS 77024 3959 B2
Juan Carlos Ct
4300 RSBG 77471 4491 C6
Juanita Dr
300 PASD 77502 4107 A6
Juanita Ln
2100 DRPK 77536 4109 C6
Juarez St
6500 HarC 77521 3832 E6
Jubal Dr
100 FBnC 77469 4493 C7
Jubal Early Ln
400 MtgC 77302 2530 C5
Jubilee Ct
8500 HarC 77083 4097 B7
Jubilee Dr
8600 HarC 77083 4097 B7
Jubilee Park Ct
12800 HarC 77065 3539 C3
Judalon Ln
- HOUS 77042 4099 B2
- HOUS 77057 4100 D1
5300 HOUS 77056 4100 E1
9500 HOUS 77063 4099 B2
Judd St
- HOUS 77020 3964 B3
Judge St
12400 HarC 77532 3692 E2
Judge Bry Rd
16300 HarC 77429 3397 A3
Judge Carolyn Garcia Cir
- HOUS 77098 3962 C7
Judia Ln
10500 HOUS 77099 4237 D4
10500 HOUS 77478 4237 D4
10500 SGLD 77478 4237 D4
Judiway St
900 HOUS 77018 3822 D3
900 HOUS 77018 3823 A3
Judiwood St
700 HarC 77090 3258 C3
S Judson
4100 WUNP 77005 4101 C3
Judson Av
4100 WUNP 77005 4101 C2
Judson Hls
- FBnC 77479 4366 D7
Judwin St
8800 HOUS 77075 4246 A7
Judy Av
10 FRDW 77546 4505 A4
Judy Ct
1200 HOUS 77015 3966 E3
Judy Ln
1200 BYTN 77521 3973 B3
2000 PASD 77502 4107 B7
Judy St
5700 FBnC 77583 4623 C5
Judy Ter
1100 MSCY 77489 4370 C4
Judyleigh Dr
16800 HarC 77084 3678 B5
Juella Dr
2500 HarC 77039 3545 E3
Juergen Rd
18100 HarC 77377 3107 A7
18100 HarC 77429 3107 A7
18100 HarC 77433 3107 A7
19200 HarC 77377 3106 D7
19200 HarC 77433 3106 D7
Juglans Ct
- HOUS 77075 4377 B2
Jui Ln
17200 SGCH 77355 2961 C2
Jules Ct
26500 ORDN 77386 2822 C6
Jules Ln
9200 HOUS 77075 4245 C7
9200 HOUS 77075 4376 C1
Jules Anna Ln
2500 CNRO 77304 2383 A2
Julia Ct
4800 PASD 77505 4248 A4
Julia Ln
4500 STFE 77510 4870 E7
11900 MtgC 77354 2671 B2
Julia St
100 HOUS 77022 3824 B1
13400 TMBL 77375 2964 A3
Juliabora Ct
700 FRDW 77546 4505 B6
700 FRDW 77546 4629 A1
Juliabora St
8000 HOUS 77017 4245 E2
8000 HOUS 77017 4246 A2
Julian St
2400 HOUS 77009 3963 A1
3800 HOUS 77009 3824 A6
Julian Woods Pl
10 WDLD 77382 2820 A3
Julia Park Dr
1600 MtgC 77386 2969 E7
Julie Ln
- DRPK 77536 4109 D7
400 HarC 77562 3832 A3
10900 HOUS 77042 3958 C6
18600 MtgC 77355 2668 B7
18600 MtgC 77355 2814 B1
21500 HarC 77377 3107 B3
Julie St
2500 PRLD 77581 4503 E5
2500 PRLD 77581 4504 A5
Juliedale Dr
14200 HarC 77396 3547 A2
Julie Marie Ln
- HarC 77449 3815 C7
Julienne Trc
10 WDLD 77381 2821 D2
Julie Rivers Dr
400 SGLD 77478 4368 D1
500 SGLD 77478 4237 D7
Julies Cir
10 MtgC 77357 2828 B6
Juliet St
2400 PASD 77502 4247 C1

STREET
Block City ZIP Map# Grid
Juliet St
4000 HOUS 77087 4104 D5
Juliette Wy
- HarC 77073 3403 C1
Juliff Manvel Rd
100 BzaC 77583 4744 A4
500 IWCY 77583 4744 D4
900 BzaC 77583 4745 A4
900 IWCY 77583 4745 B4
1100 MNVL 77578 4745 D4
1100 MNVL 77583 4745 D4
Juliff Manvel Rd CO-57
900 BzaC 77583 4745 A4
900 IWCY 77583 4744 E4
900 IWCY 77583 4745 A4
1100 MNVL 77578 4745 D4
1100 MNVL 77583 4745 D4
Julington Ln
14000 HarC 77429 3253 E6
14000 HarC 77429 3254 B5
Julio Ln
7000 HarC 77049 3831 B1
Julius Ln
3800 HOUS 77021 4103 D4
Jullian Ln
- FBnC 77479 4493 C1
Julliane Ct
11200 HOUS 77099 4238 B1
July St
1800 HarC 77093 3685 C2
Jumada Cir
5500 HOUS 77091 3683 B6
Jumper Shores Dr
- HarC 77044 3408 E5
- HOUS 77044 3408 E5
Jumping Jay Dr
24100 HarC 77447 3249 E3
Jumping Jay Ln
24000 HarC 77447 3249 E3
Jumuna Dr
19200 MtgC 77365 2971 D5
Junco Dr
7200 HOUS 77040 3682 B3
Junction Ct
1000 RSBG 77471 4490 B6
Junction Dr
2800 HOUS 77045 4373 A2
Junction Bend Ln
3500 FBnC 77494 4092 B1
Junction Pl Dr
14400 HOUS 77045 4373 A3
June St
4200 HOUS 77016 3686 B7
Juneau Ln
15700 JRSV 77040 3680 D1
Juneberry Ct
5200 FBnC 77494 4093 B2
June Breeze Pl
10 WDLD 77382 2673 D5
June Forest Dr
18300 HarC 77346 3408 B1
Junegrass Ct
3100 HOUS 77345 3119 E1
Junell St
700 HOUS 77088 3684 A2
900 HOUS 77088 3683 E2
June Oak St
18000 HarC 77429 3253 B1
June Wood Wy
800 SEBK 77586 4509 E1
Junior St
7700 HOUS 77012 4105 C4
Junior High Rd
- MTBL 77520 3696 E5
Juniors Map Ct
18500 HarC 77433 3395 C5
Juniper Cross
12500 HarC 77041 3679 E3
Juniper Ct
400 STAF 77477 4369 E4
900 TMBL 77375 3109 C1
Juniper Dr
- HarC 77396 3406 E5
500 LPRT 77571 4251 D7
2700 PRLD 77581 4504 D5
Juniper Hls
2300 FBnC 77469 4365 C1
Juniper Ln
1400 PASD 77586 4381 E6
Juniper Pl
- LGCY 77598 4630 C4
Juniper Rd
900 CRLS 77565 4509 C4
3900 HarC 77389 2967 D6
Juniper St
3800 HOUS 77087 4105 A7
Juniper Berry Dr
19800 FBnC 77469 4234 D1
Juniper Bluff Ct
5900 HOUS 77345 3120 C5
Juniper Canyon Ln
1100 HOUS 77062 4379 D7
Juniper Chase Tr
19800 FBnC 77469 4234 D2
Juniper Cove Ct
15400 HarC 77433 3251 A6
Juniper Cove Dr
15200 HarC 77433 3251 A7
Juniper Creek Ln
18200 HarC 77429 3252 B7
Juniper Crossing Ln
18100 HarC 77449 3677 D4
Juniper Fields Dr
8000 HarC 77083 4097 B7
Juniper Forest Ln
14500 HOUS 77062 4380 A6
Juniper Glen Dr
10300 HOUS 77041 3681 A7
10500 HOUS 77041 3680 E7
Juniper Green Tr
17800 HarC 77346 3408 B2
Juniper Grove Dr
10 WDLD 77382 2674 B6
16000 HarC 77084 3678 D7
Juniper Hollow Wy
15500 HarC 77433 3251 B6
Juniper Knoll Ln
5800 HOUS 77345 3120 C6
Juniper Knoll Wy
1600 CNRO 77301 2384 D6
Juniper Meadows Dr
21400 HarC 77388 3113 B3
Juniper Meadows Ln
3800 HarC 77053 4372 D5
Juniper Park Ct
14000 HarC 77066 3401 E7
Juniper Pl Ct
9500 HOUS 77075 4246 C7
Juniper Point Dr
13400 HarC 77083 4097 B4
Juniper Ridge Ln
21200 HarC 77375 3110 C3
Juniper River Ct
1100 RSBG 77471 4614 C1
Juniper Shores Dr
15900 HarC 77044 3408 D4
15900 HOUS 77044 3408 D4
Juniper Skies Ln
16500 HarC 77379 3257 A2
Juniper Springs Dr
- HOUS 77396 3406 C5
- PRLD 77545 4499 D2
Juniper Terrace Ln
5200 FBnC 77494 4093 B1
Juniper Tree Ct
12300 HarC 77346 3408 C2
Juniper Vale Cir
19400 HarC 77084 3816 A4
Juniper Walk Ln
5000 FBnC 77494 4092 D3
Juniper Woods Ct
- HarC 77429 3253 C5
Junius St
7800 HOUS 77012 4105 C3
Junker Rd
300 FBnC 77471 4490 A5
300 RSBG 77471 4490 A5
Junker St
1600 RSBG 77471 4491 B6
Jupiter Dr
15200 HarC 77053 4372 D4
15200 HOUS 77053 4372 D4
Jupiter Hills Dr
13800 HarC 77069 3400 B1
Jura Dr
4200 HarC 77084 3817 C1
4300 HarC 77084 3678 C7
Jurgensen Ln
2100 SGLD 77479 4494 C1
Jurua Dr
22900 MtgC 77365 2971 D5
Jury Rig Ct
16500 HarC 77532 3552 B2
Justamere Ln
14500 HarC 77396 3547 C1
S Justice
8900 LPRT 77571 4249 E4
S Justice St
200 TXCY 77591 4873 D7
300 LMQU 77568 4873 D7
Justice Park Dr
10 HOUS 77092 3821 C1
Justin Ct
200 TMBL 77375 3109 C1
Justin Ln
4200 DRPK 77536 4249 C1
Justin St
4600 HarC 77093 3546 B7
5700 HOUS 77016 3546 E7
Justin Tr
12700 HarC 77070 3399 A5
Justina Ct
2500 SGLD 77478 4369 B7
Justinwood Pt
17300 HarC 77070 3255 B3
17300 HarC 77375 3255 B3
Jutewood Ln
22500 FBnC 77450 4093 E1
Jutland Dr
12700 HOUS 77048 4374 E2
Jutland Rd
- HOUS 77033 4103 E7
- HOUS 77033 4244 A1
7300 HOUS 77033 4243 E5
10900 HOUS 77048 4243 E7
12000 HOUS 77048 4374 E1
JW Mills Dr
200 PASD 77586 4508 D2
200 TYLV 77586 4508 D2
JW Peavy Dr
6900 HOUS 77011 3965 A6

K

K St
4100 HOUS 77072 4098 A4
4100 HOUS 77082 4098 A4
5900 KATY 77493 3813 B6
E K St
- LPRT 77571 4251 E4
W K St
1300 LPRT 77571 4251 C4
11500 HOUS 77034 4378 A1
Kabah Ct
2800 GLSN 77554 5221 C2
Kabee St
2300 HOUS 77020 3964 B1
Kacee Dr
4300 HarC 77084 3678 C7
4300 HarC 77084 3817 C1
Kacey Ln Ct
19400 HarC 77346 3264 D5
Kadabra Dr
19400 HarC 77449 3677 A3
19500 HarC 77449 3676 E3
Kahala Dr
19000 GLSN 77554 5442 A2
Kahala Beach Ests
19000 GLSN 77554 5442 B2
Kahlden Ct
700 HOUS 77079 3956 E2
Kah Me Ha Dr
200 TKIS 77554 5106 B4
Kahula
- HarC 77049 3831 C1
Kailees Ct
28200 MtgC 77386 2970 B5
Kainai Ct
14600 HarC 77429 3253 D5
Kainer Meadows Ln
- HarC 77047 4374 C3
Kainer Springs Ln
7300 FBnC 77469 4094 B6
Kaiser St
5600 HOUS 77040 3681 C5
Kaiser Strasse
- HarC 77375 2965 B3
Kaitlin Ln
- FBnC 77479 4367 A6
Kaitlyn Dr
1800 HarC 77530 3829 D3
Kaitlyn Ln
9800 BYTN 77520 3974 A1
Kakerglen Ct
17600 HarC 77084 3677 E3
Kale Ct
5000 HarC 77066 3401 B7
6400 PRLD 77584 4502 C6
Kale St
3600 PRLD 77584 4502 C6
Kaleo Wy
10400 CNRO 77304 2236 C5
10400 MtgC 77304 2236 C5
Kaler Rd
15000 HOUS 77060 3544 D3
Kalewood Dr
8700 HOUS 77099 4238 A1
Kaley Ln
- HarC 77388 3113 A2
Kalissa Ct
8500 FBnC 77469 4616 D1
Kalithea Ct
4900 HarC 77388 3112 B2
Kalka Rd
18700 MtgC 77302 2680 B6
Kalmer St
200 PASD 77502 4247 B2
200 SHUS 77587 4247 B2
Kaltenbrun Rd
13000 HarC 77086 3542 D2
Kalwick Dr
3600 DRPK 77536 4249 A1
Kama Dr
23000 MtgC 77365 2972 A5
Kamala Dr
1600 HarC 77530 3829 D3
Kamena Dr
- HarC 77041 3679 C4
Kamiah Ct
6900 HarC 77040 3681 C3
Kamloops Rd
- HarC 77044 3549 B2
Kamren Dr
1900 HarC 77049 3829 C3
Kanah Ln
1000 HarC 77090 3258 B3
Kanani Ct
16200 MtgC 77302 2679 B4
Kanawha Dr
19200 MtgC 77365 2971 D3
Kandarain St
2600 HOUS 77093 3685 E5
Kane Ct
1300 RSBG 77471 4614 C1
Kane Ln
27100 ORDN 77385 2822 B5
Kane St
500 TMBL 77375 2964 A7
1500 HOUS 77002 3963 B3
1800 HOUS 77007 3963 A3
Kangaroo Ct
11700 MDWP 77477 4237 E4
Kansack Ln
- HarC 77086 3542 A2
Kansas Av
100 LPRT 77571 4251 E2
500 SHUS 77587 4246 B3
2200 DKSN 77539 4633 B7
2200 GlsC 77539 4633 B7
4400 DKSN 77539 4754 B1
N Kansas Av
- LGCY 77573 4631 E2
100 LGCY 77573 4632 A2
S Kansas Av
100 LGCY 77573 4632 A3
Kansas St
- HOUS 77008 3822 D7
200 GlsC 77518 4634 C2
600 PASD 77506 4107 C4
1700 LMQU 77568 4873 D7
1800 BYTN 77520 4112 B2
4500 FBnC 77545 4623 B3
4800 ARLA 77545 4623 B3
4800 ARLA 77583 4623 B3
5200 HOUS 77007 3962 A1
5700 HOUS 77007 3961 D1
6000 HOUS 77008 3961 D1
S Kansas St
200 LPRT 77571 4251 E3
1000 LPRT 77571 4252 A4
Kaplan Dr
3700 PASD 77503 4108 C6
Kappa Dr
9400 HOUS 77051 4243 A4
Kappa St
1200 PASD 77504 4247 D7
Kapri Ln
9000 HOUS 77025 4101 D7
9100 HOUS 77025 4241 D1
Kara Ln
34600 MtgC 77362 2816 C7
34600 SGCH 77362 2816 C7
Karalas Ln
13700 HarC 77047 4373 D5
13700 HOUS 77047 4373 D5
Karalis Rd
13400 HOUS 77047 4373 D4
Karan Ct
- HarC 77044 3689 C4
Karankawa Wy
4200 JMAB 77554 5331 D4
Karankawas Ct
1600 DRPK 77536 4109 C6
Karankawas St
4000 PASD 77504 4247 E5
N Karaugh Dr
27100 FBnC 77469 4232 A6
S Karaugh Dr
27100 FBnC 77469 4232 A7
Karbach St
1900 HOUS 77092 3822 A5
Karbo Ln
1600 HarC 77073 3403 D2
Karcher
24000 HarC 77336 3267 A2
Karcher St
5100 HOUS 77009 3824 B4
Kardy St
21800 HarC 77388 3112 A2
21900 HarC 77389 3112 A2
Karelian Dr
5500 HOUS 77091 3683 B6
Karen Dr
- HarC 77070 3399 B3
32600 MtgC 77354 2671 C5
Karen Ln
- HarC 77377 3106 E6
- HarC 77377 3107 A7
3700 PASD 77503 4108 C5
25800 FBnC 77494 3952 C6
30100 MtgC 77354 2672 B6
Karen St
7100 HOUS 77076 3684 D3
7900 HarC 77037 3684 D1
7900 HOUS 77037 3684 D2
Karen Wy
- PRLD 77581 4502 D3
Karenbeth Dr
5100 HarC 77084 3678 B5
Karen Rose St
7700 HOUS 77075 4376 C3
Karey Lynn Ln
18300 HarC 77429 3252 A5
18300 HarC 77433 3252 A5
Kari Ct
400 HNCV 77024 3960 A3
8500 JRSV 77040 3540 C6
Kari Ln
28700 HarC 77484 3102 E3
Karina Dr
5900 BYTN 77520 3835 C7
Karina Wy
- SGLD 77478 4368 E6
Kari Springs Ct
9400 HarC 77040 3541 A6
Karissa Ct
14100 HarC 77049 3829 A2
Karlanda Ln
19800 HarC 77073 3403 D2
Karlis Dr
300 HLCS 77511 4867 E5
300 HLCS 77511 4868 A5
Karlow Trail Ln
17900 HarC 77060 3403 E5
Karlwood Ln
11600 HOUS 77099 4238 A1
Karnauch St
7200 HOUS 77028 3825 E2
7200 HOUS 77028 3826 A2
Karnes St
200 HOUS 77009 3824 B6
7200 HOUS 77020 3965 A3
Karos Ln
900 HDWV 77024 3959 C1
Karpathos Ln
21500 HarC 77388 3112 B3
Karrywood Ct
3900 BzaC 77584 4501 D7
Karsen Dr
1800 HarC 77049 3829 D3
1800 HarC 77530 3829 D4
Karsten Creek Ct
10 HarC 77389 2819 E5
10 HarC 77389 2820 A5
Karsten Creek Wy
- HarC 77389 2820 B6
Karter Ct
10700 HarC 77064 3540 B5
Karu Dr
5100 HarC 77373 3260 D1
Kasey Springs Ln
2000 MtgC 77386 2969 D7
Kashmere St
5500 HOUS 77026 3825 C4
Kashmere Spring Ln
2000 FBnC 77545 4498 D6
Kasos Isle Ct
- HarC 77388 3112 B3
Kasos Isle Dr
4900 HarC 77388 3112 B2
Kassarine Pass
6400 HOUS 77033 4104 A7
6900 HOUS 77033 4244 A1
Kassikay Dr
16500 HarC 77084 3678 C7
Kaston Dr
15300 HarC 77433 3251 D6
Kate Dr
30500 MtgC 77355 2961 E5
30500 SGCH 77355 2961 E5
Katelyn Manor Ln
800 HarC 77073 3403 C3
Katex Dr
24000 HarC 77493 3813 E5
24000 HarC 77493 3814 A5
Kath Ln
- HarC 77429 3397 E1
Katharine Ln
700 TMBL 77375 3109 B1
Katherine
16200 HarC 77530 3830 C6
Katherine Ct
10000 HarC 77089 4504 E1
Katherine Ln
16200 HarC 77530 3830 C6
Katherine St
100 BYTN 77520 3971 A4
2700 LMQU 77568 4989 D1
2800 FBnC 77477 4370 A5
29700 MtgC 77354 2818 D2
Kathi Ann Ln
9900 HarC 77038 3543 E4
Kathie Ct
- SGCH 77355 2960 E2
Kathi Lynn Ln
14000 SGLD 77478 4236 E7
14000 SGLD 77478 4237 A7
Kathleen Ct
1800 DRPK 77536 4109 D4
Kathleen Haney Dr
10100 HarC 77086 3542 C3
Kathryn Cir
3300 PASD 77503 4108 B5
Kathryn Ct
12600 HOUS 77015 3967 A3
Kathryn St
12400 HOUS 77015 3966 E3
12400 HOUS 77015 3967 A3
N Kathy Av
11700 MSCY 77071 4239 E7
S Kathy Av
11800 MSCY 77071 4239 E7
11800 MSCY 77071 4370 E1
Kathy Dr
2900 PRLD 77584 4503 A4
4700 BzaC 77584 4626 A1
Kathy Ln
- HarC 77377 3106 E6
2700 KATY 77493 3813 B4
6000 FBnC 77583 4622 E6
12800 HarC 77377 3254 B6
12800 HarC 77429 3254 B6
18800 HarC 77377 3107 A6
22600 HarC 77389 2967 A7
27400 MtgC 77355 2963 A2
Kathy St
100 CNRO 77301 2384 A2
500 HMBL 77338 3263 A7
1200 BzaC 77583 4623 C5
1200 PASD 77504 4247 D7
Katie Hbr
2600 BzaC 77578 4501 A7
Katie Ln
900 CNRO 77304 2529 D1
4300 BzaC 77511 4748 A2
Katie Grace Cir
9300 HarC 77379 3255 C3
Katie Leigh Ln
6000 SGLD 77479 4494 E4
Katie Marie Ct
20800 HarC 77433 3251 B5
Katie Ridge Ln
- HOUS 77048 4375 B2
22000 FBnC 77450 4094 A3
Katlyn Ln
1800 MtgC 77386 2969 D6
Katner Ln
3100 MtgC 77386 2969 D2
Katy Frwy
- HarC - 3952 D1
- HarC - 3953 E1
- HarC - 3955 D1
- HarC - 3956 A1
- HarC - 3959 D1
- HDWV - 3959 E1
- HDWV - 3960 A1
- HOUS - 3953 A1
- HOUS - 3954 A1
- HOUS - 3955 E1
- HOUS - 3956 D1
- HOUS - 3957 A1
- HOUS - 3958 D1
- HOUS - 3959 B1
- HOUS - 3960 E1
- HOUS - 3961 C1
- HOUS - 3963 A1
- HOUS 77007 3962 D2
- KATY - 3952 A2
- SPVL - 3959 D1
- SPVL - 3960 A1
26700 KATY 77494 3951 C2
27700 WlrC 77494 3951 D2
28900 WlrC 77423 3951 B2
Katy Frwy I-10
- HarC - 3952 D1
- HarC - 3953 E1
- HarC - 3955 E1
- HarC - 3956 A1
- HarC - 3959 D1
- HDWV - 3959 E1
- HDWV - 3960 A1
- HOUS - 3953 A1
- HOUS - 3954 A1
- HOUS - 3955 E1
- HOUS - 3956 D1
- HOUS - 3957 A1
- HOUS - 3958 D1
- HOUS - 3959 B1
- HOUS - 3960 E1
- HOUS - 3961 A1
- HOUS - 3962 E1
- HOUS - 3963 A1
- KATY - 3951 D2
- KATY - 3952 A2
- SPVL - 3959 D1
- SPVL - 3960 A1
- WlrC - 3951 D2
Katy Frwy US-90
- HarC - 3952 D1
- HarC - 3953 A1
- HarC - 3955 D1
- HarC - 3956 A1
- HarC - 3959 D1
- HDWV - 3959 E1
- HDWV - 3960 A1
- HOUS - 3953 E1
- HOUS - 3954 D1
- HOUS - 3955 A1
- HOUS - 3956 D1
- HOUS - 3957 A1
- HOUS - 3958 D1
- HOUS - 3959 B1
- HOUS - 3960 E1
- HOUS - 3961 A1
- HOUS - 3962 E1
- HOUS - 3963 A1
- KATY - 3952 E1
- SPVL - 3959 D1
- SPVL - 3960 A1
Katy Rd
- HOUS 77007 3961 D1
6900 HOUS 77024 3961 C1
Katy St
3000 STAF 77477 4369 D3
5800 HOUS 77007 3961 E1
6900 BKVL 77581 4376 A6
7000 PRLD 77581 4376 A6
Katya Gillian Dr
10600 HOUS 77034 4246 E7
Katy Arbor Ln
5200 FBnC 77494 4093 B7
Katybriar Ln
2600 HarC 77449 3815 A4
Katy Creek Ranch Dr
3400 FBnC 77494 3953 A7
Katydid Ct
1600 CNRO 77301 2384 C7
Katy-Flewellen Rd
- FBnC 77494 3952 B4
Katy Flewellen Rd
- FBnC 77494 4092 A1
Katy-Flewellen Rd
- KATY 77494 3952 B4
Katy Flewellen Rd
1000 FBnC 77494 3952 C3
1000 KATY 77494 3952 C3
Katy Fort Bend Rd
- HarC 77450 3953 D4
700 FBnC 77494 3952 E2
700 KATY 77494 3952 E7
900 KATY 77494 3953 A2
1000 HarC 77493 3813 E7
1000 HarC 77493 3952 E1
1000 KATY 77493 3813 E7
1000 KATY 77493 3952 E1
1600 HarC 77494 3953 C4
Katy Freeway Frontage Rd
- HOUS 77094 3954 E1
4500 HOUS 77007 3962 A1
5800 HOUS 77007 3961 E1
7400 HOUS 77024 3961 A1
7400 HOUS 77055 3961 B1
7600 HOUS 77024 3960 E1
7600 HOUS 77055 3960 E1
8200 HLSV 77024 3960 C1
8200 HLSV 77055 3960 C1
8200 SPVL 77024 3960 B1
8300 HNCV 77024 3960 C1
Katy Freeway Frontage Rd
8300 SPVL 77055 3960 B1
8600 HDWV 77024 3960 A1
8800 HDWV 77024 3959 A1
8800 SPVL 77024 3959 A1
8900 SPVL 77055 3959 E1
9200 HarC 77024 3959 D1
9200 HOUS 77024 3959 D1
10000 HOUS 77055 3959 A1
10100 HOUS 77043 3959 A1
10200 HOUS 77043 3958 E1
10300 HOUS 77024 3958 E1
10700 HOUS 77079 3958 B1
11700 HOUS 77079 3957 A1
14000 HOUS 77079 3956 E1
14800 HOUS 77084 3956 B1
15400 HOUS 77094 3956 C1
16000 HarC 77094 3956 A1
16700 HOUS 77084 3955 E1
17700 HarC 77094 3955 D1
19600 HOUS 77094 3955 A1
19800 HarC 77084 3954 E1
19800 HOUS 77084 3954 E1
19900 HarC 77449 3954 E1
19900 HOUS 77449 3954 E1
20200 HOUS 77450 3954 D1
20900 HarC 77450 3954 C1
22300 HOUS 77449 3953 D1
22300 HOUS 77450 3953 D1
22900 HOUS 77493 3953 D1
23400 HOUS 77494 3953 C1
24100 HarC 77493 3953 B1
24100 HarC 77494 3953 A1
24800 HarC 77493 3952 E1
24900 HarC 77494 3952 E1
25000 KATY 77493 3952 E1
25900 KATY 77494 3952 B2
Katy Gaston Rd
5000 FBnC 77494 3952 C7
5000 FBnC 77494 4092 D3
5300 FBnC 77494 4093 A5
6100 FBnC 77469 4093 B6
Katy Hockley Rd
2900 KATY 77493 3813 C3
3500 HarC 77493 3813 C3
13900 HarC 77447 3249 D7
Katy Hockley Cut Off Rd
2100 KATY 77493 3813 D6
2900 HarC 77493 3813 E3
Katy Hollow Dr
3700 HarC 77449 3815 E2
Katy Knoll Ct
13400 HarC 77082 4097 A1
Katyland Dr
- KATY 77493 3813 D6
1000 KATY 77493 3952 D1
1000 KATY 77494 3952 D1
Katy Lee Rd
33100 MtgC 77354 2673 D4
Katy Mills Blvd
- KATY 77494 3952 E1
Katy Mills Cir
- KATY 77494 3952 D2
Katy Mills Dr
- HarC 77494 3952 E1
- KATY 77494 3952 E2
Katy Mills Pkwy
- KATY 77494 3952 D2
Katy Mist Dr
3800 HarC 77449 3815 D2
Katy Park Dr
- HarC 77493 3813 E4
Katy West Rd
- KATY 77493 3951 D1
- KATY 77494 3951 D1
Kaufman Av
3500 PRLD 77583 4500 E6
N Kaufman Dr
600 DRPK 77536 4109 C6
S Kaufman Dr
600 DRPK 77536 4109 C6
Kavanaugh Ln
- HarC 77429 3253 E7
Kaw Forest Ct
2100 PRLD 77581 4503 C1
Kay Av
1700 PASD 77506 4107 D5
2300 FRDW 77546 4505 A4
2300 PRLD 77581 4505 A4
Kay Cir
4300 HOUS 77051 4243 C1
Kay Ln
9300 HarC 77064 3541 C5
11400 PRLD 77583 4500 D6
Kay St
3000 HOUS 77093 3825 A1
Kaybull Dr
18900 HarC 77346 3264 E6
Kay Cee
2000 RSBG 77469 4614 E3
2000 RSBG 77471 4614 E3
Kay Cee Rd
1900 RSBG 77471 4614 E3
Kay Jo Ln
10800 HarC 77044 3690 E2
Kayla Ln
12300 GNPK 77015 3966 E5
12400 GNPK 77015 3967 A4
Kayla Lynn Ct
16200 MtgC 77355 2961 E5
16200 SGCH 77355 2961 D5
Kaylan Ct
4900 FBnC 77469 4235 D7
Kayla Springs Ln
17600 HarC 77396 3407 E2
Kaylee Ln
13300 STFE 77510 4986 D1
Kayleigh Ct
7100 FBnC 77479 4367 A7
Kaylyn St
- HarC 77060 3544 D2
700 HarC 77060 3545 A2
Kay Oaks Ln
3400 HarC 77068 3257 C6
Kayvon Ct
24900 FBnC 77494 3953 B6
E K Bear Ranch Dr
8900 TXCY 77539 4754 E6
8900 TXCY 77539 4755 A6
Keagan Falls Dr
2800 BzaC 77578 4625 A1
2900 BzaC 77578 4501 B7
Kearney Dr
6600 FBnC 77469 4493 C6
Kearny Cross
- SGLD 77479 4495 D3
Kearny Dr
11500 HOUS 77076 3685 A3
Kearny Brook Pl
10 WDLD 77381 2820 E
Keating Ct
4300 SGLD 77479 4495 C
Keating St
1400 HOUS 77003 3964 C
Keatley Dr
1800 HOUS 77077 3958 B
Keats Av
6600 HOUS 77085 4371 C
Keats Ct
20500 HMBL 77338 3262 C
Kedge Ct
16900 HarC 77532 3552 A
Kedgwick Ln
- HarC 77429 3397 B
Keefer Rd
1300 HarC 77377 2963 E
1300 TMBL 77375 2963 E
1300 TMBL 77375 2964 A
1300 TMBL 77377 2963 E
Keegan Rd
- HOUS 77099 4237 E
- HOUS 77477 4237 E
9600 HOUS 77099 4238 A
Keegan Hollow Ln
2300 MtgC 77386 2969 E
Keegans Forest Ln
8700 HOUS 77031 4239 C
Keegans Glen Dr
10900 HOUS 77031 4239 C
Keegans Meadow Dr
16800 FBnC 77083 4235 D
16800 FBnC 77469 4235 D
Keegans Ridge Rd
11500 HOUS 77031 4238 E
Keegans Ridge Wy Dr
16600 FBnC 77083 4235 E
16600 FBnC 77083 4236 A
16700 FBnC 77469 4235 E
Keegans Wood Dr
9200 HarC 77083 4237 A
Keehan St
31200 SGCH 77355 2961 D
Keel Rd
10 HOUS 77076 3685 A
Keeland St
2400 HOUS 77093 3685 E
3600 HOUS 77093 3686 B
4600 HOUS 77016 3686 C
Keelby Dr
14800 HarC 77015 3829 B
Keeler Ct
4100 PASD 77503 4108 D
Keeling Tr
18400 HarC 77346 3265 E
Keelrock Pl
10 WDLD 77382 2673 E
Keelson Ct
300 HarC 77532 3411 B
Keelson Wy
1700 SGLD 77479 4367 C
Keely St
11700 HOUS 77045 4241 D
Keen Dr
29800 HarC 77377 2963 D
Keenan
- HOUS 77048 4375 E
Keenan Cove
17900 HarC 77084 3677 C
17900 HarC 77084 3678 A
Keenbury Ln
26200 FBnC 77494 4092 C
Keene St
100 GNPK 77547 3966 C
2600 HOUS 77009 3824 C
2600 HOUS 77009 3963 C
Keeneland Ln
10500 HarC 77038 3543 C
Keene Mill Ct
11500 HarC 77067 3402 A
Keenen Ct
1600 HOUS 77077 3957 B
Keepers Tr
12400 HarC 77429 3397 E
Keeran Point Ct
2200 SGLD 77478 4237 A
Keeran Point Ln
2100 SGLD 77478 4237 A
Keese Dr
10800 HOUS 77089 4377 D
Keeshond Ln
- HarC 77530 3829 E
Keiller Cir
3000 FBnC 77450 3954 A
Keira Ct
14200 HarC 77069 3400 A
Keis Rd
3300 PRLD 77584 4503 C
Keith Av
5100 PASD 77505 4248 B
Keith Dr
22700 MtgC 77357 2973 D
Keith Rd
500 HOUS 77504 4247 B
11100 HarC 77093 3686 C
Keith St
- HOUS 77032 3405 D
600 HOUS 77504 4247 C
600 PASD 77504 4247 B
26300 HarC 77373 3114 A
Keith Wayne Dr
100 BzaC 77511 4866 A
Keithwood Cir E
3200 PRLD 77584 4502 C
Keithwood Cir S
6700 PRLD 77584 4502 C
Keithwood Cir W
3300 PRLD 77584 4502 C
Keithwood Dr
3000 PRLD 77584 4502 C
Kelbrook Dr
15200 HOUS 77062 4506 E
Kelburn Dr
10100 HOUS 77016 3686 E
Kelcey Cir
16200 SGCH 77355 2961 E
Kelford St
5300 HOUS 77028 3826 C
Kell Cir
9500 HOUS 77040 3682 A
Kell Dr
9800 HOUS 77040 3682 A
Kellan Ct
15400 HarC 77429 3253 B
Keller St
3200 GlsC 77518 4634 B
6600 HOUS 77087 4105 A

STREET
Block City ZIP Map# Grid
eller St
7000 HOUS 77012 4105 B4
eller Forrest Ct
18000 HarC 77346 3408 B1
ellerman
12000 HarC 77016 3547 E7
12000 HarC 77050 3547 E7
ellerton Ct
14700 HarC 77429 3397 C2
ellerton Ln
13600 HarC 77429 3397 C2
ellerwood Dr
15200 HarC 77086 3541 D2
ellett St
600 CmbC 77586 4509 E2
600 SEBK 77586 4509 E2
8300 HOUS 77028 3687 D6
8800 HOUS 77078 3687 E6
elley St
- HOUS 77022 3824 D4
100 HOUS 77009 3824 B4
2000 HOUS 77026 3824 E3
2800 HOUS 77026 3825 D4
5800 HOUS 77028 3825 D4
40300 WlrC 77445 2953 E1
41200 WlrC 77445 2954 A1
elley Green Ct
16100 HarC 77429 3397 A1
elli Dr
16000 HarC 77530 3830 B4
elli Ln
2900 BzaC 77511 4748 D2
ellicreek Dr
19900 HarC 77450 3954 E5
elling St
3100 HOUS 77045 4373 A1
4100 HOUS 77045 4372 C1
ellington Dr N
200 HOUS 77339 3118 A5
23700 HOUS 77339 3117 E4
ellington Pl
- MSCY 77459 4496 C3
elliwood Ct Cir
10 FBnC 77450 3954 B7
elliwood Ct Dr
- FBnC 77450 3954 C7
elliwood Greens Dr
21200 FBnC 77450 4094 B2
elliwood Grove Ct
- FBnC 77450 4094 C2
elliwood Grove Ln
- FBnC 77450 4094 C2
elliwood Lakes Ct
20400 HarC 77450 3954 D6
elliwood Lakes Dr
2500 HarC 77450 3954 D7
elliwood Oaks Dr
1300 HarC 77450 3954 E3
elliwood Park Ct
- FBnC 77450 4094 C1
elliwood Trails Ct
1800 HarC 77450 3954 C5
elliwood Trails Dr
1900 HarC 77450 3954 C5
ellner St
3700 DKSN 77539 4753 B5
ellogg St
700 HOUS 77012 4105 B4
700 HOUS 77023 4105 B2
ellow St
10 CNRO 77304 2383 D6
ellway Dr
300 HOUS 77015 3828 D5
ellwood Dr
7600 HarC 77040 3682 A2
7600 HOUS 77040 3682 A2
7800 HarC 77040 3681 E2
elly
10 HOUS 77007 3962 A4
2200 BYTN 77520 3973 D6
elly Av
- HarC 77373 3114 A2
elly Cr
18200 HarC 77094 3955 C1
elly Ct
1300 HarC 77396 3407 A5
elly Dr
- HarC 77065 3398 E6
4000 SGLD 77478 4369 A5
elly Ln
100 BYTN 77521 3972 E4
100 BYTN 77521 3973 A4
2400 HarC 77066 3401 D5
2400 HarC 77067 3401 D5
5800 PRLD 77581 4502 C2
19700 HarC 77377 3106 A5
W Kelly Ln
21300 HarC 77377 3106 A6
elly Rd
100 HarC 77373 3113 E7
100 MAGA 77354 2669 A4
500 MAGA 77354 2668 E4
500 MtgC 77354 2668 E4
2800 KATY 77493 3813 C4
24100 MtgC 77365 2974 A7
25000 MtgC 77365 3118 C2
elly St
8800 MNVL 77578 4747 B1
elly Brook Tr
2700 HarC 77038 3543 A2
ellydale Ct
2500 HarC 77388 3113 A3
elly Jo Smith Rd
- MtgC 77365 2973 C5
elly Kay Ct
19100 HarC 77388 3113 C7
elly Lake Tr
10400 HarC 77089 4378 C7
10400 HarC 77089 4505 A1
Kelly Mill Ln
5700 HarC 77346 3264 D5
Kelly Oaks Ct
19100 HarC 77346 3264 E6
Kelly Pines Ct
19200 HarC 77346 3264 D5
Kelly Spring Cir
5400 HarC 77379 3257 A1
Kelly Timbers Dr
19400 HarC 77346 3264 D5
Kellyway Ln
2700 MSCY 77459 4369 B7
Kellywood Ln
14100 HOUS 77079 3958 A4
14200 HOUS 77079 3957 D3
Kelona Dr
1900 MtgC 77386 2969 B1
Kelowna St
- HarC 77044 3549 A3
Kelsey Ln
- FBnC 77469 4232 A7
Kelsey Pl
6000 FBnC 77479 4367 A5
Kelsey Arbor Ln
- HarC 77433 3251 C5
Kelsey Creek Tr
20000 HarC 77433 3251 A4
Kelsey Isle Ln
- FBnC 77469 4365 B5
Kelsey Meadows Ct
9500 HarC 77040 3541 A6
Kelsey Pass
8300 FBnC 77459 4621 A5
Kelsey Springs Ct
9000 HarC 77379 3255 E4
Kelsey Trace Wy
- HarC 77433 3251 C4
Kelsey Trail Ln
3900 HarC 77047 4374 D4
Kelsey Woods Ct
27100 HarC 77433 3537 A1
Kelso
- HOUS 77339 3263 A2
Kelso Ct
600 STAF 77477 4370 B4
Kelso St
4900 HOUS 77021 4103 E6
5100 HOUS 77021 4104 A6
Kelsy Rae Ct
6900 HarC 77069 3400 A2
Kelton St
3300 HOUS 77021 4103 B4
Kelton Hills Ln
25200 FBnC 77469 4092 D7
Keltwood Ct
5500 FBnC 77479 4366 E6
Keltwood Ln
- HarC 77429 3397 D2
Kelvey Dr
- DRPK 77503 4249 A3
- DRPK 77536 4249 A3
- PASD 77503 4249 A3
- PASD 77505 4249 A3
Kelvin Dr
4500 HOUS 77005 4102 B3
4500 HOUS 77098 4102 B2
6600 HOUS 77030 4102 B4
Kelvin Ln
4200 DRPK 77536 4249 C1
Kelving Dr
2300 HOUS 77030 4102 B5
Kemah Dr
1100 KMAH 77565 4633 D1
1100 LGCY 77565 4633 C1
Kemah Oaks Dr
- GlsC 77565 4509 D7
1800 KMAH 77565 4509 D7
Kemah Village Dr
1900 KMAH 77565 4509 C7
Kemberton Dr
100 HOUS 77062 4506 E1
Kemble Rd
18900 HarC 77346 3264 D6
Kemble Creek Dr
17000 HarC 77084 3678 A3
Kemerton Dr
12100 HOUS 77099 4237 E4
Kemin Dr
100 HTCK 77563 4988 C5
Kemp St
200 PASD 77506 4107 A3
5600 HOUS 77011 3964 D7
5600 HOUS 77023 3964 D7
7300 MNVL 77578 4746 D3
Kemper Dr
2100 LGCY 77573 4508 D7
2100 LGCY 77573 4632 D1
6800 PASD 77505 4248 E7
6900 PASD 77505 4249 A7
Kemp Forest Dr
- HOUS 77043 3819 E2
9900 HOUS 77080 3820 A2
10100 HOUS 77043 3820 A2
Kemp Hollow Ct
- HOUS 77043 3819 C2
Kemp Hollow Ln
11900 HOUS 77043 3819 C2
Kempner Av
10 GLSN 77550 5109 C4
Kempner St
10 SGLD 77478 4368 A2
100 SGLD 77478 4367 E2
Kempridge St
8500 HOUS 77055 3821 A3
8500 HOUS 77080 3821 A3
Kempsford Ct
20200 HarC 77450 3954 E3
Kempsford Dr
1000 HarC 77450 3954 E3
Kempton Park Dr
16000 HarC 77379 3256 A6
Kempwood Dr
3100 SGLD 77479 4495 D1
7600 HOUS 77055 3821 C3
7600 HOUS 77092 3821 C3
8400 HOUS 77080 3821 A3
8700 HOUS 77080 3820 E3
10000 HOUS 77043 3820 B2
10700 HOUS 77043 3819 D2
Kemrock Cir
11000 HarC 77049 3828 D3
Kemrock Ct
6100 HarC 77049 3828 D3
Kemrock Dr
14400 HarC 77049 3828 C3
Kemton St
100 HOUS 77012 4105 B2
Kemwood Dr
10900 HNCV 77024 3960 A3
11000 HNCV 77024 3959 E3
11000 PNPV 77024 3959 E3
Ken Pl
1100 SGLD 77478 4368 A4
Ken St
1200 HMBL 77338 3262 E7
1200 HMBL 77338 3263 A7
Kenbriar Dr
15800 HOUS 77489 4371 B6
Kenbridge Dr
2400 HarC 77067 3402 A5
Kenbrook Dr
15800 HOUS 77489 4371 B6
Kenchester Dr
21700 HarC 77073 3259 B1
Kenco St
2600 HOUS 77093 3685 E7
Kendahlwood Ln
- HarC 77375 3255 C2
Kendale Dr
9100 FBnC 77083 4236 C1
Kendalia Dr
- HOUS 77036 4099 A5
Kendall St
10 HOUS 77003 3964 A5
N Kendall St
100 HOUS 77003 3964 A5
Kendallbrook Dr
14600 HarC 77095 3539 A5
Kendall Creek Dr
6400 FBnC 77479 4367 B7
6500 FBnC 77479 4494 B1
Kendall Creek Ln
3200 HarC 77047 4374 C4
Kendall Green Dr
- WDLD 77382 2674 D3
Kendall Lake Ct
- FBnC 77469 4094 D5
Kendall Lake Dr
- FBnC 77469 4094 D5
Kendall Ridge Ln
17100 HarC 77095 3538 A5
17200 HarC 77095 3537 C4
Kendall Shay Ct
22400 FBnC 77450 4094 A2
Kendalls Path Ct
14700 HOUS 77053 4372 D3
Kendal Ridge Ln
27100 HarC 77433 3395 E6
27100 HarC 77433 3396 B6
Kendons Wy Ln
16300 HarC 77429 3252 B5
Kendra Ln
20700 HarC 77450 3954 C3
Kendrick Plaza Dr
3700 HOUS 77032 3405 B7
Kenedy Dr
21900 GLSN 77554 5441 A6
23100 GLSN 77554 5440 E7
Keneshaw Ct
4600 SGLD 77479 4495 C4
Keneshaw Dr
4800 SGLD 77479 4495 C5
Keneva Dr
- HarC 77429 3253 E7
Kenforest Dr
800 MSCY 77489 4370 D4
Ken Hall Blvd
- SGLD 77478 4367 E4
- SGLD 77478 4368 A4
Kenilwood Dr
5000 HOUS 77033 4243 E2
5300 HOUS 77033 4244 A2
Kenilworth Dr
1900 SGLD 77479 4367 E6
2000 SGLD 77479 4494 B1
Kenilworth St
9000 HOUS 77024 3961 A1
9200 HOUS 77024 3960 E1
Kenlake Dr
22000 HarC 77450 3954 A4
22400 HarC 77450 3953 E4
Kenlake Grove Dr
4900 HOUS 77345 3120 A6
Kenlea Ln
14900 HOUS 77060 3544 C3
Kenman Dr
- HarC 77346 3265 A7
Kenmare Ct
10 WDLD 77382 2673 C4
Kenmark Ct
7600 HarC 77433 3537 C7
Kenmark Ln
18300 HarC 77433 3537 D7
18300 HarC 77433 3677 C1
Kenmore St
900 HOUS 77023 4105 A3
Kenn Ct
3900 FBnC 77459 4621 C4
Kenna Ct
3800 MtgC 77386 2970 B5
Kenna Cove Ln
20900 HarC 77379 3111 D3
Kennard Dr
8800 HOUS 77074 4239 B1
Kennebeck Pl
1500 HOUS 77077 3957 A5
Kennedale Ln
7200 HarC 77379 3111 B7
Kennedy Dr
3500 BzaC 77584 4501 D7
3600 BzaC 77578 4501 D7
3600 PRLD 77578 4501 D7
3600 PRLD 77584 4501 D7
Kennedy Ln
23400 MtgC 77365 2972 E5
Kennedy St
2400 HOUS 77003 3963 E4
2700 HOUS 77003 3964 A4
5000 LMQU 77568 4872 E7
Kennedy Cove
- HarC 77375 2964 C2
Kennedy Heights Blvd
4700 HOUS 77047 4243 D7
4700 HOUS 77048 4243 D7
Kennedy Oaks St
15100 HOUS 77053 4371 E4
Kennedy Ranch Dr
24200 HarC 77447 3249 E3
Kennedy Ranch Ln
24000 HarC 77447 3249 E3
Kennel Ln
- HarC 77530 3829 D3
Kennemer Dr
7400 HarC 77338 3261 D3
Kennesa Dr
2900 MSCY 77459 4498 A6
Kennesaw Mountain Ln
17500 HarC 77346 3408 C2
Kenneth
- BYTN 77520 3973 D6
Kenneth St
800 LMQU 77568 4989 C1
Kennet Hl
10 FBnC 77459 4621 C7
Kenneth Royal Dr
1700 SEBK 77586 4509 D2
Kennet Valley Rd
8700 HarC 77379 3256 A6
Kennewick Ct
1400 FBnC 77479 4493 C1
Kennewick Dr
10200 HarC 77064 3541 C1
Kenning Rd
200 HarC 77532 3552 E7
Kenning Rd
200 HarC 77532 3553 A7
3400 HarC 77532 3554 A6
Kennings Av
500 HarC 77532 3552 D4
Kennington Ct
3600 HarC 77336 3121 D2
Kennington Wy
24700 HarC 77389 2966 C4
Kennon St
3700 HOUS 77009 3824 C6
Kennonview Dr
3300 HarC 77068 3257 B4
Kennoway Park Dr
1400 HarC 77379 3110 B7
Kenny Dr
15300 HarC 77377 3254 D6
Kenny St
1200 DRPK 77536 4109 C5
3200 KATY 77493 3813 D3
14600 HarC 77015 3968 B2
Keno Moon Ln
- TMBL 77375 3109 C3
Kenr
3000 HarC 77014 3257 E7
Kenrick Dr
600 HOUS 77060 3403 E7
800 HarC 77032 3403 D7
1000 HarC 77032 3404 A7
Kenross St
2700 HOUS 77043 3819 E2
Kens Ct
3800 HarC 77396 3407 A5
Kens Run
9200 HarC 77396 3406 E6
9300 HarC 77396 3407 A6
Kensal Bay Ln
11600 HarC 77070 3254 D3
11600 HarC 77377 3254 D3
Kensico Rd
7500 HOUS 77036 4099 D5
Kensington Av
3900 MSCY 77459 4496 D2
Kensington Blvd
- SGLD 77478 4368 A5
- SGLD 77479 4368 A5
Kensington Br
- PRLD 77584 4501 C2
Kensington Ct
10 CNRO 77304 2529 D1
200 PNPV 77024 3959 D5
300 PASD 77502 4247 A1
Kensington Dr
1000 PRLD 77584 4501 A2
16000 SGLD 77479 4368 A6
N Kensington Dr
11700 HOUS 77031 4238 E5
S Kensington Dr
9600 HOUS 77031 4239 A6
Kensington Pk
2900 PRLD 77581 4503 E2
2900 PRLD 77581 4504 A3
Kensington Pl
- HOUS 77598 4379 A5
13600 HOUS 77034 4378 E5
13900 HOUS 77598 4378 E5
Kensington Wy
1300 HOUS 77339 3264 A1
Kensington Oaks Dr
20700 MtgC 77372 2681 A1
Kensington Park Cir
1800 MtgC 77386 2823 B7
1800 MtgC 77386 2969 D1
Kensington Park Dr
31100 MtgC 77386 2969 B1
Kensley Dr
16300 HarC 77082 4095 E4
16300 HarC 77082 4096 A4
Kenson Ln
14100 HarC 77429 3397 D2
Kenston Pl
4300 MSCY 77459 4497 A4
Kenswick Dr
18300 HOUS 77338 3262 A7
18300 HOUS 77338 3406 A1
19200 HOUS 77338 3261 E6
19300 HarC 77338 3262 A6
Kenswick Cove Ct
11400 HarC 77375 3254 E1
Kenswick Cove Dr
18900 HarC 77375 3254 D1
18900 HarC 77375 3255 A1
Kenswick Forest Dr
7400 HarC 77338 3261 D3
Kenswick Forest Ln
7800 HarC 77338 3261 D3
Kenswick Glen Dr
7800 HarC 77338 3261 D3
Kenswick Meadows Ct
21100 HarC 77338 3261 D3
Kenswick Park Dr
20700 MtgC 77365 3117 E2
Kenswick Trail Ln
- HarC 77047 4374 C4
Kent
19100 MtgC 77357 2829 B4
Kent Ct
19100 MtgC 77357 2829 E3
Kent Dr
3900 GLSN 77554 5441 B4
5100 PASD 77505 4248 B4
22000 MtgC 77357 2973 E2
22200 MtgC 77357 2974 A4
Kent Knl
3500 FBnC 77459 4622 B5
Kent Ln
- PRLD 77581 4503 D4
Kent St
- HOUS 77098 4102 C2
5500 HOUS 77005 4102 C2
Kent Wy
1400 FRDW 77546 4629 C3
Kentbury Ct
900 HarC 77450 3954 C2
Kentbury Ln
12700 HOUS 77077 3957 C5
Kent Falls Ct
1700 HarC 77450 3953 E5
Kent Falls Dr
22300 HarC 77450 3953 E5
22300 HarC 77450 3954 A4
Kentfield Dr
9600 HOUS 77093 3685 C5
Kentford Dr
- HOUS 77062 4506 E2
15500 HOUS 77062 4507 A2
Kent Hollow Ct
27400 MtgC 77386 2969 E7
Kentington Dr
4800 ALVN 77511 4867 D7
Kentington Oak Dr
10700 HarC 77396 3407 D7
Kentland Ct
11700 HarC 77067 3402 B5
Kentland Dr
1900 HarC 77067 3402 B5
Kentley Orchard Ln
- HarC 77429 3253 E7
Kent Oak Dr
1300 HOUS 77077 3957 E5
Kenton St
7700 HOUS 77028 3826 B3
Kenton Crossing Cir
6600 FBnC 77469 4095 D5
Kenton Crossing Ln
17300 FBnC 77469 4095 C5
Kent Park Dr
- HarC 77375 3110 A7
Kentshire Av
1200 SGLD 77479 4367 C6
Kentshire Dr
8400 HOUS 77078 3687 D4
9000 HOUS 77078 3688 A4
Kentstead Ln
- HarC 77047 4374 B4
Kent Towne Ln
9900 FBnC 77478 4237 A2
Kentucky
1100 DRPK 77536 4109 B5
Kentucky Av
200 SHUS 77587 4246 C3
2600 LGCY 77573 4632 D6
2900 LGCY 77539 4632 E6
3000 DKSN 77539 4633 A7
3000 DKSN 77539 4754 C1
29800 MtgC 77354 2818 A1
Kentucky Rd
2700 FBnC 77545 4499 C6
Kentucky St
800 DRPK 77536 4109 B4
1700 BYTN 77520 4112 B2
3000 HOUS 77026 3825 A7
3300 RSBG 77471 4490 D7
3300 RSBG 77471 4614 D1
Kentucky Trc
20200 HarC 77447 3105 E2
Kentucky Derby Cir
18800 HarC 77346 3265 B6
Kentucky Oaks Dr
11200 MtgC 77304 2382 A7
11200 MtgC 77304 2528 A1
Kent Valley Ln
- RSBG 77469 4491 E5
- RSBG 77471 4491 E5
Kentwalk Dr
4800 HOUS 77041 3680 E7
Kentwater Ct
15600 HarC 77095 3538 D4
Kentwick Dr
6400 HarC 77084 3678 E3
6600 HarC 77095 3678 D3
E Kentwick Pl
- CNRO 77384 2675 E5
- CNRO 77384 2676 A5
- WDLD 77384 2675 E4
Kentwood Dr
3200 MtgC 77380 2821 A7
16500 HOUS 77058 4507 D2
Kentwood Ridge Ct
100 FBnC 77479 4367 A4
Kenwall Dr
- HOUS 77072 4098 C3
Kenwell Dr
8000 HarC 77083 4096 D7
Kenwich Oaks Ln
2600 HarC 77449 3815 C4
Kenwick Pl
1200 PASD 77504 4247 D6
Kenwick St
- MSCY 77459 4497 A4
Kenwood Dr
100 CNRO 77301 2384 A3
Kenwood Ln
- HOUS 77006 4102 D1
500 HOUS 77013 3827 E7
600 HOUS 77013 3966 D1
Kenwood Park Ln
2500 MtgC 77386 2823 C6
Kenworthy Dr
2300 MSCY 77459 4370 A7
Kenya Ln
4400 PASD 77505 4248 D6
Kenyon Ln
6500 BLAR 77401 4101 B4
Kenzie Ct
11700 MDWP 77477 4237 E4
Keough
9100 HarC 77040 3681 B3
Keough Rd
9100 HarC 77040 3681 B3
Keowee Ct
15500 HarC 77546 4505 D5
Kepler McVey Ct
9700 HarC 77379 3255 E6
Kerala St
2000 MSCY 77489 4370 B6
Kerbey St
1300 JTCY 77029 3966 C3
Kercuac Ct
10 WDLD 77382 2819 A2
Kerloch Pt
10 HarC 77379 3255 C1
Kerman Dr
11500 HarC 77429 3397 E7
11500 HarC 77429 3398 A7
Kermier Rd
17200 HarC 77447 3248 C1
18400 HarC 77447 3103 C7
20400 HarC 77484 3103 C3
Kermit St
4600 HOUS 77009 3823 E6
Kern St
- BYTN 77520 4112 D2
800 HOUS 77009 3824 A5
1000 HOUS 77009 3823 E5
Kern Canyon Ln
1300 FBnC 77469 4493 C4
Kernel St
6400 HOUS 77087 4104 E3
6600 HOUS 77087 4105 A4
7100 HOUS 77012 4105 A4
Kernohan St
100 HarC 77532 3552 C4
Kerr Dr
8500 HarC 77375 2965 D6
Kerr Ln
3400 PRLD 77583 4500 E5
10200 CHTW 77385 2822 D4
Kerr St
7900 HOUS 77029 3965 B4
9700 HOUS 77029 3966 A4
9800 GNPK 77547 3966 A4
Kerri Ct
1100 FBnC 77479 4366 E7
Kerrigan Ct
7200 HarC 77379 3111 B2
Kerri Leigh Ct
500 HarC 77388 3113 C6
Kerrington Glen Dr
8200 HarC 77433 3537 A6
Kerrville Ct
15500 HarC 77429 3253 C5
Kerrwood Ln
9000 HOUS 77080 3820 D4
10100 HOUS 77043 3820 A4
Kerry Cir
2300 PRLD 77581 4504 D2
Kerry Dr
900 PASD 77506 4107 D5
1900 DRPK 77536 4109 A6
Kerry Rd
100 HarC 77562 3831 E3
Kerryblue Dr
22100 HarC 77450 3953 E2
22100 HarC 77450 3954 A2
Kerrybrook Ln
17700 HarC 77396 3407 D2
Kerry Glen Cir
9200 HOUS 77078 3688 A5
Kerry Glen Ln
9700 HOUS 77078 3688 A5
Kerry Prairie Ln
9000 FBnC 77469 4234 E1
Kershaw St
13700 HarC 77037 3544 E6
13900 HarC 77060 3544 E6
Kershope Forest Ct
9900 HarC 77379 3255 B1
Kersten Dr
1800 HOUS 77043 3819 C3
Kervin Dr
- HOUS 77085 4240 D6
Kesnet Park Dr
- HarC 77433 3251 C7
Kessington Ln
19200 HarC 77094 3955 B4
Kessler
900 HOUS 77007 3963 B3
Kessler Park Ct
1700 HOUS 77047 4373 D1
Kesslers Cross
- LGCY 77573 4632 A7
- LGCY 77573 4753 A1
Kessway Ln
10900 HOUS 77075 4377 A4
Kestrel
33200 HarC 77447 3249 C4
Kestrel Ct
6700 HarC 77069 3400 B2
Kestrel Vw
24400 HarC 77494 3953 A2
Kestrel Trace Ln
2700 FBnC 77494 3951 C6
Keswick Ct
1900 PRLD 77581 4503 E2
N Keswick Ct
100 SGLD 77478 4368 E4
S Keswick Ct
200 SGLD 77478 4368 E4
Keswick Dr
- PRLD 77581 4503 E1
Keswick St
- HOUS 77076 3684 C4
Keswick Pines Ln
11700 HarC 77066 3401 A4
Ketan Loch Ct
8400 HarC 77379 3255 E1
Ketch Ct
1300 LGCY 77573 4508 D4
2000 SEBK 77586 4509 C2
Ketchwood Dr
8700 HOUS 77099 4238 A1
Kettering Cir
19200 MtgC 77357 2829 E4
Kettering Dr
- BYTN 77520 3973 B4
- HOUS 77027 3961 B7
2800 BYTN 77521 3973 B4
Kettering Ln
200 LGCY 77573 4630 C7
Kettle Run
2700 SGLD 77479 4368 E6
2700 SGLD 77479 4369 A7
2900 SGLD 77479 4496 B1
Kettlebrook Ln
16400 HarC 77530 3829 E4
Kettle Creek Dr
16800 HarC 77379 3255 D5
Kettle Hill Dr
- HarC 77049 3689 D7
Kettlemar Dr
6900 HarC 77084 3679 A2
Kettler Rd
2200 BzaC 77511 4748 C3
3500 BzaC 77511 4866 A5
Keva Glen Dr
3000 LGCY 77573 4633 A1
Kevel Ct
- HarC 77532 3551 E4
Kevin Ct
100 LPRT 77571 4250 E2
Kevin Ln
2900 HOUS 77043 3820 A2
Kevincrest Dr
6700 PRLD 77584 4502 C5
Kevindale Ln
16000 JRSV 77040 3540 C6
Kevington Ct
28500 MtgC 77386 2969 C6
Kevinkay Dr
4300 HarC 77084 3678 C7
4300 HarC 77084 3817 C1
Kevinshire Dr
11100 HarC 77375 3110 A3
Kewalo Basin Ln
11700 HOUS 77034 4247 A7
Kewanee St
4100 HOUS 77051 4243 C3
Kew Garden Dr
1500 HOUS 77047 4373 D1
Key Ct
4000 MSCY 77459 4497 A3
Key St
600 HOUS 77009 3824 A7
1000 HOUS 77009 3823 E7
1100 HOUS 77008 3823 E7
1200 WALR 77484 3101 E5
Key Biscayne Ct
11800 HarC 77065 3539 E3
Keygate Dr
3200 HarC 77388 3112 E3
Keyhole Ln
- HarC 77084 3816 A5
Key Hollow Wy
3800 HarC 77388 3112 D5
Keyko St
6200 HOUS 77041 3681 A4
Key Largo Ct
3800 MSCY 77459 4497 D6
Keymill Dr
- HarC 77064 3540 B5
Keymist Ln
- HarC 77377 3253 E4
- HarC 77429 3253 E4
Keynette St
- PRVW 77445 3100 B3
Key Oaks Ln
20700 HarC 77433 3676 D1
Keyport Ln
900 HOUS 77015 3966 E2
900 HOUS 77015 3967 A2
Keyridge Ln
13500 HarC 77429 3397 A3
Keystone Dr
1600 FRDW 77546 4629 C4
Keystone St
4500 HOUS 77021 4103 E5
5100 HOUS 77021 4104 A6
Keystone Tr
4200 PRLD 77584 4503 B4
22300 HarC 77450 3953 E4
Keystone Bend Ct
27300 MtgC 77386 3115 E2
Keystone Creek Tr
- HarC 77379 3111 A2
Keystone Fairway Ct
16600 HarC 77095 3538 A1
Keystone Fairway Dr
10800 HarC 77095 3538 A2
Keystone Green Dr
14400 HarC 77429 3395 D1
14400 HarC 77433 3395 D1
Keystone Grove Tr
15300 HarC 77429 3253 C1
Keystone Oak St
18500 HarC 77084 3816 C4
Keystone River Ln
- FBnC 77469 4365 B5
Keystone Spring Wy
11800 HOUS 77089 4505 C1
Keyturn Ln
18900 HarC 77346 3264 E6
Keywood Ln
3200 HarC 77449 3815 A3
Keyworth Dr
13800 HarC 77014 3402 C3
Kiam St
5200 HOUS 77007 3962 A1
5700 HOUS 77007 3961 E1
Kiamesha Ct
14100 HarC 77069 3400 B1
Kiamesha Dr
3400 MSCY 77459 4497 B2
Kian Ct
5500 HOUS 77081 4100 C6
Kiawa Ct
10 MNVL 77583 4624 C4
Kiawah Dr
19900 HarC 77433 3251 D7
Kiber Dr
10500 HOUS 77031 4239 C3
Kickapoo Rd
17000 HarC 77447 3248 A2
17000 HarC 77484 3248 A2
18100 HarC 77447 3103 A7
20800 HarC 77484 3103 A2
21200 HarC 77484 2958 A7
23000 WlrC 77447 2958 A4
Kickapoo Meadows Ln
28000 HarC 77484 2957 E6
28000 HarC 77484 2958 A6
Kickerillo Ct
400 HOUS 77079 3957 E4
Kickerillo Dr
300 HOUS 77079 3957 D3
Kidd Ct
19500 MtgC 77357 2827 D4
Kidd Dr
6900 HTCK 77563 4989 A5
Kidd Rd
12600 CNRO 77301 2530 D4
12600 CNRO 77302 2530 D4
12600 MtgC 77302 2530 D4
Kidd St
6900 HTCK 77563 4989 B5
Kidd Cemetery Rd
19600 MtgC 77357 2827 D5
Kidds Ln
15900 GlsC 77517 4869 E6
Kidlington Ct
12300 HarC 77039 3545 E5
Kids R Kids Dr
10 CNRO 77304 2529 E2
Kielder Pointe Dr
10100 HarC 77379 3110 C7
Kier Rd
13300 HOUS 77048 4375 B3
Kier St
- HOUS 77048 4375 B2
Kieth Harrow Blvd
16100 HOUS 77084 3678 D6
16600 HarC 77084 3678 A6
17700 HarC 77084 3677 A6
19100 HarC 77449 3677 A6
19700 HarC 77449 3676 E6
Kilborne Park Ln
19600 HarC 77379 3112 A6
19700 HarC 77379 3111 D6
Kilbride Wy Ct
10400 HarC 77379 3110 B7
Kilburn Rd
11500 HOUS 77055 3821 C4
Kildare Dr
1100 HOUS 77047 4373 C2
2100 PRLD 77581 4504 D2
3700 HOUS 77047 4374 C2
Kildee Pk
- HOUS 77033 4244 B4
7700 HarC 77396 3406 D6

STREET
Block City ZIP Map# Grid

Kildeer Ct
2500 LGCY 77573 4752 B1
Kiley Dr
500 HarC 77073 3403 B3
Kilgarlin Ln
1500 DRPK 77536 4108 E6
Kilgarney Keep St
2400 DKSN 77539 4753 C1
S Kilgore Av
100 HarC 77520 3831 E7
400 HarC 77520 3970 D1
Kilgore Ct
3600 BzaC 77578 4501 C7
Kilgore Ln
- BzaC 77583 4500 E6
1600 HarC 77532 3411 E4
Kilgore Rd
700 BYTN 77520 3973 D7
700 BYTN 77520 4113 D1
Kilgore St
3200 HOUS 77021 4103 B5
Kilkenny Dr
- HOUS 77047 4373 C2
2100 PRLD 77581 4504 D1
3700 HOUS 77047 4374 C1
4600 HOUS 77048 4374 E1
5300 HOUS 77048 4375 A1
Kilkenny Ln
2200 DRPK 77536 4108 E6
30600 MtgC 77354 2672 C7
Kilkenny Glenn Dr
- HarC 77065 3539 C4
Killarney Av
1000 FRDW 77546 4629 B3
Killarney Ct
10 HOUS 77074 4100 B7
Killarney Dr
2400 PRLD 77581 4504 C2
Killarney Ln
2200 DRPK 77536 4109 A6
Killdeer Ct
15800 HarC 77396 3406 D6
Killdeer Dr
1300 SEBK 77586 4382 E7
Killdeer Ln
2600 HMBL 77396 3406 C4
5600 FBnC 77469 4615 A6
Killearn Dr
6600 PASD 77505 4248 E7
Killene St
8500 HOUS 77029 3826 C6
Killerbee Ln
23000 MtgC 77357 2974 A4
Killian Ct
4200 MSCY 77459 4496 C4
Killiney Ct
1800 HOUS 77045 4242 C6
Killingsworth Ln
17900 WlrC 77484 3246 D1
Killough Dr
5200 HarC 77038 3542 E5
5200 HarC 77086 3542 E5
Killough St
3000 HarC 77038 3542 E5
3000 HarC 77038 3543 A5
5000 HarC 77086 3542 E5
7100 HOUS 77086 3542 B5
Kilmarnoch Wy
4600 MSCY 77459 4369 B6
Kilmarnock Dr
- HOUS 77025 4101 C5
Kilnar
- HarC 77047 4374 D6
- HarC 77048 4374 D6
4500 HOUS 77048 4374 E6
Kilpatrick Dr
700 HarC 77530 3829 E7
Kilrenny Ct
17000 HarC 77379 3255 E3
Kilrenny Dr
8800 HarC 77379 3255 D3
9800 HarC 77070 3255 B4
Kilroy St
- JTCY 77029 3966 B3
600 HOUS 77013 3966 B2
1800 GNPK 77029 3966 B4
1800 GNPK 77547 3966 B4
Kilt Ln
- CNRO 77301 2530 C3
Kilts Dr
200 BKHV 77024 3959 A4
Kilwinning Dr
17000 HarC 77084 3678 B5
Kim Dr
10 HarC 77373 3114 A6
Kim St
3600 FBnC 77545 4498 D7
N Kimball Ct
3900 FBnC 77459 4621 D4
S Kimball Ct
3800 FBnC 77459 4621 C4
Kimball Dr
4500 PRLD 77584 4501 E5
Kimball Ln
19700 HarC 77447 3105 B4
Kimball Pl W
2700 PRLD 77584 4501 E5
Kimball Rd
18200 BzaC 77511 4628 D3
Kimball St
3500 HOUS 77026 3825 C6
Kimberlee Ln
15800 HarC 77049 3690 D6
Kimberley Ct
15000 HOUS 77079 3957 B2
Kimberley Ln
12100 BKHV 77024 3959 B2
12100 HOUS 77024 3959 A2
12400 HOUS 77024 3958 E2
12900 HOUS 77079 3958 C2
14000 HOUS 77079 3957 E2
Kimberley St
600 HOUS 77079 3958 B2
Kimberley Loch Ln
9800 HarC 77089 4505 A3
Kimberly Dr
1100 CNRO 77301 2383 D3
3800 PRLD 77581 4504 E7
Kimberly Ln
1900 MSCY 77489 4370 B4
Kimberly Trc
11800 MtgC 77304 2382 A6
Kimberly Crossing Dr
4200 FBnC 77450 4093 D1
Kimberly Dawn Dr
2500 CNRO 77304 2383 A2
2600 CNRO 77304 2382 E2

Kimberly Glen Ln
23100 HarC 77373 3115 D5
Kimberly Loch Ln
10000 HarC 77089 4505 A2
Kimberlys Pt
21900 MtgC 77357 2827 E1
Kimberwicke Ct
22900 HarC 77373 2968 E7
Kimble St
7800 HOUS 77017 4105 C5
Kimble Ledge Ln
- FBnC 77469 4235 C1
Kimbleton Ct
2600 HOUS 77082 4097 B1
Kimbro Rd
25400 WlrC 77447 2813 C7
Kimbrough Rd
13100 HarC 77375 2964 B2
W Kimmons Dr
800 ALVN 77511 4867 B2
Kimstone Ln
8200 HarC 77379 3256 B5
Kimswick Ct
200 DRPK 77536 4249 B1
Kimwood Dr
8700 HOUS 77080 3821 A4
Kinbrook Dr
2200 HOUS 77077 3958 A7
Kincaid Rd
5100 PRLD 77584 4502 A6
Kincaid Falls Ct
25600 FBnC 77469 4092 C7
Kinchen Trails Ln
4900 HOUS 77092 3682 A7
Kincross Ct
1500 HarC 77450 3953 E4
Kinder Ln
9600 HOUS 77051 4243 A5
Kindleberger
- BYTN 77520 3974 A3
Kindle Oaks Dr
20100 HarC 77450 3954 E3
Kindletree Dr
- HOUS 77040 3542 A7
- HOUS 77040 3682 A1
Kindlewood Dr
8700 HOUS 77099 4238 A1
Kindred St
12200 HarC 77049 3827 E1
King
10 HarC 77044 3549 A4
24100 HarC 77336 3267 A2
King Cir
12900 HarC 77429 3398 D4
King Cir N
9700 MNVL 77578 4746 C7
King Cir S
9700 MNVL 77578 4746 C7
King Dr
- FBnC 77469 4493 D6
King Ln
17800 MtgC 77302 2679 E1
17800 MtgC 77306 2679 E1
17800 MtgC 77306 2680 A1
King Rd
18300 HarC 77389 2819 E6
18400 HarC 77375 2819 E6
King St
- HOUS 77022 3824 D3
1800 BYTN 77520 4112 D2
2900 HOUS 77026 3824 E3
2900 HOUS 77026 3825 A3
7000 MNVL 77578 4746 D3
7700 HOUS 77028 3826 B2
King Arthur Ct
10 SGLD 77478 4368 E1
600 HNCV 77024 3960 B2
6900 HarC 77379 3256 D4
9800 LPRT 77571 4250 B2
24700 WlrC 77447 2959 D1
King Arthur's Ct
3200 PRLD 77584 4501 B2
Kingbird Dr
29200 HarC 77377 2963 C5
Kingbriar Cir
1100 HarC 77373 2968 D4
Kingbriar Ct
1000 HarC 77373 2968 E5
Kingbriar Ln
24300 HarC 77373 2968 D5
King Cotton Ln
4100 MSCY 77459 4497 A4
Kingcourt Wy
- HarC 77336 2975 E7
King Cup Ct
10 WDLD 77382 2820 A2
King Cypress Ln
19900 HarC 77433 3251 D6
Kingdom Come Pl
11800 HOUS 77048 4244 B7
11900 HOUS 77048 4375 B1
Kingdom Edge Dr
- HarC 77339 3118 C5
King Edward Pl
- HarC 77521 3833 E2
- HarC 77521 3834 A2
Kingfield Dr
15200 HarC 77084 3678 D3
Kingfish Dr
4300 SEBK 77586 4382 E7
Kingfish Rd
2200 TXCY 77591 4872 E3
Kingfisher Ct
2100 LGCY 77573 4631 A7
Kingfisher Ct N
1200 PRLD 77584 4501 D2
Kingfisher Ct S
1200 PRLD 77584 4501 D2
Kingfisher Dr
200 SGLD 77478 4368 B4
2600 HMBL 77396 3406 C3
5000 HOUS 77035 4240 E4
5000 HOUS 77035 4241 A4
5400 HOUS 77096 4240 D4
9900 MtgC 77385 2676 D3
Kingford Ln
- HarC 77066 3401 B6
King Hallow Ln
4800 HarC 77449 3677 C6
King Harbour Ln
4100 MSCY 77459 4496 C3
Kinghaven St
8600 HarC 77083 4097 A7
Kinghurst Dr
10500 HOUS 77099 4238 C3
King James Ct
2700 HarC 77598 4506 C7

Kinglet St
4300 HOUS 77035 4241 B4
5000 HOUS 77035 4240 E4
5400 HOUS 77096 4240 D3
Kingman Dr
1800 MSCY 77489 4370 E4
Kingmont Knoll Ct
23900 HarC 77373 2968 E5
King Oak Dr
12700 LbyC 77372 2537 E4
Kingpine Ct
10 WDLD 77382 2673 E6
King Point Ct
- HarC 77388 3113 C2
King Point Ln
- HarC 77388 3113 B7
- HarC 77388 3258 C1
King Port Dr
10 LbyC 77372 2537 D5
10 LbyC 77372 2538 B5
King Post Dr
6300 HOUS 77088 3682 C3
King Rail Cir
4100 GLSN 77554 5548 B2
King Ranch Ln
10000 FBnC 77478 4236 E3
King Richard Dr
5300 KATY 77493 3813 D6
King Richard's Ct
- WlrC 77447 2813 D7
1700 MtgC 77316 2668 D1
Kings Ct
- BYTN 77520 3971 C5
100 STAF 77477 4370 A3
600 DKSN 77539 4753 B3
17600 HarC 77429 3396 B2
Kings Dr
7100 HarC 77521 3832 E5
9100 BzaC 77578 4746 C7
9100 MNVL 77578 4746 C7
Kings Ln
1900 ALVN 77511 4866 D4
Kings Rd
20500 MtgC 77357 2828 D6
Kings Row
- MtgC 77357 2829 C4
200 RMFT 77357 2828 E3
Kings Tr
2200 HOUS 77339 3119 E7
Kings Wy
4700 HarC 77069 3256 E6
Kings Arbor Tr E
- HarC 77346 3264 E5
Kings Arbor Tr W
- HarC 77346 3264 D4
Kings Arms Wy
1900 HarC 77493 3814 B6
Kingsbarn Ct
11400 HarC 77377 3254 D5
Kings Bend Dr
21500 MtgC 77339 3118 C4
Kingsberry Ct
4400 CNRO 77304 2237 A6
Kingsbriar Ct
21800 FBnC 77450 3954 C7
Kings Briar Ln
16000 HarC 77084 3678 C4
Kingsbriar Ln
3200 FBnC 77450 3954 A7
3200 FBnC 77450 4094 A1
Kingsbridge Ln
12800 HOUS 77077 3957 C4
Kingsbridge Pl
- FBnC 77478 4236 C2
Kingsbridge Rd
900 HarC 77073 3259 A2
Kingsbridge Wy
15000 FBnC 77083 4096 C7
Kingsbridge Meadow Dr
8200 FBnC 77083 4096 D7
Kingsbrook Ln
- MSCY 77459 4370 B6
2700 MSCY 77459 4497 A1
Kingsbrook Rd
8200 HOUS 77024 3960 C1
Kingsburg Ct
3700 FBnC 77450 4094 A1
Kingsbury Ln
500 FRDW 77546 4505 A7
6100 LGCY 77573 4630 C6
Kingsbury St
4500 HOUS 77021 4103 E5
5100 HOUS 77021 4104 A6
Kingsbury Park Ln
- MtgC 77386 2823 C7
Kings Camp Dr
20200 HarC 77450 3954 E4
Kings Canyon Ct
2700 HarC 77067 3401 E5
Kings Castle Dr
1400 HarC 77450 3954 E3
Kings Chapel Ct
16800 HarC 77546 4506 A6
Kings Chapel Rd
2500 HarC 77546 4506 A6
Kings Chase Dr
12200 HarC 77044 3548 E6
Kings Clover Ct
20800 HarC 77346 3264 E3
Kings Clover Ln
- HarC 77346 3264 E3
E Kingscoate Dr
16400 HarC 77532 3552 A2
N Kingscoate Dr
1300 HarC 77532 3552 A2
W Kingscoate Dr
16500 HarC 77532 3552 A2
Kingscote Wy
10 WDLD 77382 2819 E1
Kings Cove Dr
20100 HarC 77346 3264 D3
Kings Cove Ln
28200 MtgC 77386 2969 D6
Kings Creek Dr
10 HOUS 77339 3119 A6
Kings Creek Tr
1200 MSCY 77459 4369 C5
Kings Crescent Dr
26800 HarC 77339 3118 C4
E Kingscrest Cir
24600 HarC 77389 2966 D4
W Kingscrest Cir
24600 HarC 77389 2966 D4
Kingscrest Ln
6200 HarC 77389 2966 D4
Kings Cross Dr
- HarC 77450 3953 C2
- HOUS 77450 3953 C2

Kings Crossing Dr
2800 HOUS 77339 3119 D6
2800 HOUS 77345 3119 E6
Kings Crown
- HarC 77373 3115 B3
Kings Crown Ct
20800 HarC 77346 3265 B3
Kings Ct Dr
300 HarC 77015 3828 D6
2500 PASD 77502 4247 E1
Kings Cypress Ln
15700 HarC 77429 3252 B6
Kingsdale Dr
1700 DRPK 77503 4248 E1
1700 DRPK 77536 4248 E1
1700 PASD 77503 4248 E1
2300 DRPK 77536 4249 A1
Kingsdale St
4400 PASD 77503 4248 D1
4500 DRPK 77503 4248 D1
4500 DRPK 77536 4248 D1
Kingsdown Dr
25000 HarC 77389 2965 E3
Kingsfield Ct
5600 LGCY 77573 4751 D2
Kingsflower Cir
9200 HOUS 77075 4377 B4
9200 HOUS 77089 4377 B4
Kingsford Dr
800 HarC 77094 3955 B2
12700 HarC 77060 3403 B5
Kings Forest Dr
2300 HOUS 77339 3118 E6
2300 HOUS 77339 3119 A6
20000 HarC 77346 3264 D4
Kings Forest Rd
23300 MtgC 77447 2960 A5
Kings Garden Ct
12200 HarC 77044 3548 E6
12400 HarC 77044 3549 A5
Kings Gate Cir
- HOUS 77074 4100 A7
7200 HOUS 77074 4099 E7
Kingsgate Cir
- KATY 77494 3952 B3
Kingsgate Ln
800 WEBS 77058 4507 E6
26100 KATY 77494 3952 B3
Kings Glen Dr
- HarC 77346 3264 D4
Kings Grove Dr
12000 HarC 77044 3548 E6
Kings Harbor Dr
1600 HOUS 77339 3264 C1
Kings Harbour Ct
4700 HOUS 77339 3265 A1
Kings Head Dr
14400 HarC 77044 3549 D1
Kings Hill Ln
10 HarC 77346 3264 D3
Kings Isle Ln
3000 LGCY 77539 4752 E4
Kings Lake Estates Blvd
10 HarC 77346 3264 D3
Kingslake Forest Dr
12000 HarC 77044 3548 E6
Kings Lakes Estates Blvd
- HarC 77346 3264 D3
Kingsland Blvd
- FBnC 77494 3952 E2
- HarC 77494 3953 C3
- HOUS 77494 3953 C3
- KATY 77494 3952 D3
18000 HarC 77094 3955 B2
19500 HOUS 77094 3955 A2
19900 HarC 77094 3954 E2
19900 HOUS 77094 3954 E2
19900 HOUS 77450 3954 A2
20000 HarC 77450 3954 D2
22300 HarC 77450 3953 D2
22900 HOUS 77450 3953 D2
Kingsland Ct
5000 SGLD 77479 4495 C5
Kings Landing Ln
- FBnC 77494 4093 A1
Kingsley Ct
10 CNRO 77304 2529 C2
25800 MtgC 77355 2814 B5
Kingsley Dr
- PRLD 77047 4373 B7
- PRLD 77583 4500 B4
- PRLD 77584 4373 B7
- PRLD 77584 4500 B1
Kingsley Dr CO-48
- PRLD 77047 4373 B7
- PRLD 77583 4500 B4
- PRLD 77584 4373 B7
- PRLD 77584 4500 B4
Kingsley St
7300 HOUS 77087 4105 A7
8000 HOUS 77017 4105 C7
Kings Lodge Dr
2400 HOUS 77345 3120 B5
Kings Lynn St
18000 WEBS 77058 4507 D5
Kingsman Dr
3600 HarC 77082 4096 A3
Kings Manor Dr
27100 HarC 77339 3118 C5
Kings Manor Dr N
26700 MtgC 77339 3118 C5
Kings Manor Dr S
26800 MtgC 77339 3118 B5
Kings March Ct
27100 MtgC 77339 3118 B5
Kingsmark Dr
700 HarC 77094 3955 B2
Kingsmark Springs Ln
1100 HOUS 77345 3265 E1
Kings Meadow Dr
12200 HarC 77044 3548 D6
Kingsmill
- PNVL 77318 2237 A1
Kingsmill Dr
13000 SGLD 77478 4237 C5
Kingsmill Ln
1700 FBnC 77469 4365 D2
Kingsmill Rd
5200 FRDW 77546 4505 D6
Kings Mill Crest Dr
26000 MtgC 77339 3118 D4
Kings Mill Forest Dr
21400 MtgC 77339 3118 C4
Kings Mountain Dr
3200 HOUS 77345 3119 C1
Kingsnorth Dr
11100 HarC 77375 3110 A7

Kings Oaks Ln
6100 HarC 77346 3264 E5
Kings Park Dr
1500 ALVN 77511 4866 D3
Kings Park Ln
17700 HarC 77058 4507 E4
17700 HOUS 77058 4507 E4
17700 WEBS 77058 4507 E4
Kings Park Wy
- HarC 77346 3264 E3
- HarC 77346 3265 A4
Kings Park Hollow Dr
26800 MtgC 77339 3118 C3
Kings Pass
- SGLD 77479 4495 A3
Kingspass St
9400 HOUS 77075 4377 C4
Kings Path Ln
12200 HarC 77044 3548 E6
12400 HarC 77044 3549 A6
Kings Peak Wy
4000 HarC 77449 3815 A1
Kings Point Blvd
- CmbC 77520 3696 D1
Kingspoint Rd
9100 HarC 77089 4377 B4
9100 HOUS 77075 4377 B4
9100 HOUS 77089 4377 B5
11000 HOUS 77034 4377 E2
Kings Port
300 HarC 77532 3552 B2
Kings Ransom Ct
5400 HarC 77041 3679 B6
Kingsride Ln
12300 HOUS 77024 3959 A1
12400 HOUS 77024 3958 E1
13700 HOUS 77079 3958 A1
14000 HOUS 77079 3957 E1
Kingsridge Rd
4600 HOUS 77053 4372 B7
Kings River Cir
7500 HarC 77346 3265 B2
Kings River Ct
21400 HarC 77346 3265 B1
Kings River Dr
- HarC 77346 3264 E3
- HarC 77346 3265 A3
Kings River Ln
7600 HarC 77346 3265 B2
Kings River Pt
20900 HarC 77346 3265 B2
Kingsrose Ln
9200 HOUS 77075 4377 B4
Kings Row Blvd
18000 WEBS 77058 4507 D6
18000 WEBS 77598 4507 D6
Kings Summit Dr
6500 FBnC 77450 4094 C4
Kingston Bch
2300 GlsC 77650 4879 C4
Kingston Ct
100 TYLV 77586 4508 E2
200 DRPK 77536 4249 B1
2200 MSCY 77459 4370 A7
Kingston Dr
2100 HOUS 77019 3962 B6
2500 HOUS 77098 3962 B6
2900 TXCY 77590 4874 D5
3400 FRDW 77598 4630 B3
Kingston Hbr
4500 TYLV 77586 4508 E2
Kingston Wy
16700 GLSN 77554 5331 D5
16700 JMAB 77554 5331 D5
Kingston Cove Ln
- LGCY 77573 4509 A7
14300 HOUS 77077 3956 D5
Kingston Creek Ln
10400 HarC 77433 3537 A2
Kingstone Dr
- HOUS 77062 4379 E7
- HOUS 77062 4506 D1
Kingston Falls Ln
14200 HarC 77396 3547 C2
Kingston Glen Dr
- FBnC 77494 4092 D3
Kingston Green Ln
19400 HarC 77073 3403 C2
Kingston Hill Ln
24500 FBnC 77494 4093 B1
24600 FBnC 77494 3953 B7
Kingston Point Ln
12800 HOUS 77047 4373 C2
Kingston River Bnd
- HarC 77044 3549 C3
Kingston River Ln
- HarC 77044 3549 C3
Kingston Terrace Ln
21500 HarC 77379 3111 C2
Kingston Vale Dr
3500 HOUS 77082 4097 B3
Kingston Village Dr
31400 MtgC 77386 2823 A7
Kingstown Ct
18500 NSUB 77058 4508 A5
Kingstree Ln
1400 NSUB 77058 4508 A6
Kingsvalley St
9300 HOUS 77075 4377 B4
9600 HOUS 77089 4377 C4
Kings View Dr
- HOUS 77339 3119 D7
2700 ALVN 77511 4866 D3
Kingsville St
9200 HOUS 77063 4099 C1
Kingsville Park Dr
9700 HarC 77083 4237 B2
Kings Walk Ln
16900 HarC 77070 3255 C4
Kings Walk Round
9900 HarC 77070 3255 C4
Kingsway Ct
3400 HOUS 77339 3119 B7
Kingsway Dr
100 STAF 77477 4369 E3
200 STAF 77477 4370 A4
1900 LGCY 77573 4631 B6
3500 BYTN 77521 3974 A2
6800 HOUS 77087 4244 E1
7300 HOUS 77087 4245 A1
Kingsway Park Ln
31000 MtgC 77386 2823 C7
31000 MtgC 77386 2969 C1
Kingswick Ct
5500 HarC 77069 3400 D1
Kingswood Ln
- HOUS 77092 3822 A2

Kingussie Dr
4500 HarC 77084 3678 B7
King Village Cir
20500 HarC 77388 3113 C4
King William Dr
100 LPRT 77571 4250 B2
Kingwood Dr
- HarC 77336 2975 E7
- HarC 77336 2976 A7
500 HOUS 77339 3118 D6
500 MtgC 77339 3118 A6
2100 DRPK 77536 4109 D7
2300 HOUS 77339 3119 A6
4500 HOUS 77345 3119 D6
5500 HOUS 77345 3120 B4
7900 HarC 77336 3120 D2
7900 HOUS 77336 3120 D2
20000 HOUS 77339 3117 E6
20000 HOUS 77365 3117 E5
Kingwood Executive Dr
200 HOUS 77339 3117 E6
N Kingwood Forest Dr
- HOUS 77339 3119 C1
- HOUS 77365 3119 C1
Kingwood Glen Dr
6000 HarC 77346 3264 E5
Kingwood Greens Dr
- HOUS 77339 3119 D7
- HOUS 77339 3264 D1
Kingwood Greens Dr S
10 HOUS 77339 3264 D1
Kingwood Medical Dr
300 HOUS 77339 3117 E6
Kingwood Pl Dr
- HOUS 77339 3118 A4
- HOUS 77365 3117 E3
23600 HOUS 77339 3117 E3
Kingwood Villas Ct
10 HOUS 77339 3119 B7
Kingworthy Ln
11100 PNPV 77024 3959 D5
Kinkaid Cir
4300 HOUS 77093 3686 B5
Kinkaid Dr
200 PNPV 77024 3959 E5
Kinkaid St
3600 HOUS 77093 3686 B5
Kinkaid School Dr
- PNPV 77024 3959 E5
Kinley Ct
33000 MtgC 77354 2673 E4
Kinley Ln
1100 HOUS 77018 3822 E2
Kinley Creek Ln
24100 HarC 77493 3814 A7
Kinloch Dr
4200 HarC 77084 3678 C7
4200 HarC 77084 3817 C1
Kinmont Ct
16000 HarC 77379 3256 B6
Kinne St
4100 GlsC 77518 4634 C3
Kinnel Ln
9000 HarC 77375 3110 D2
Kinnerton St
3900 PRLD 77584 4502 E7
Kinney Rd
9600 HOUS 77099 4238 C3
Kinney St
7000 HOUS 77087 4104 E7
7100 HOUS 77087 4105 A7
Kinney Point Ln
16800 HarC 77073 3259 A4
Kino Ct
10 WDLD 77380 2821 D6
Kinrose Dr
4400 PASD 77505 4249 A6
Kinross Ln
24200 FBnC 77494 3953 B7
Kinrush Ct
16200 HarC 77095 3538 C5
Kinsale Valley Ln
17900 HarC 77060 3403 E5
Kinsbourne Ct
- HarC 77014 3402 C1
Kinsbourne Ln
- HarC 77014 3402 C1
Kinsdale Av
2400 GlsC 77539 4753 C1
Kinsdale Ct
11600 HarC 77067 3402 B5
Kinsdale Crossing Ln
10200 HOUS 77075 4377 A2
Kinsington Briar Ln
- HarC 77449 3815 E1
Kinsley Dr
4200 PASD 77505 4249 A5
Kinslowe Ct
9700 HarC 77064 3540 D6
Kinsman Rd
7400 HarC 77049 3828 C1
Kinston Dr
- LGCY 77573 4753 B1
Kintyre Dr
5000 HarC 77084 3678 B6
Kintyre Point Rd
16100 HarC 77095 3538 C6
Kinwicke Ct
3000 FBnC 77494 4093 C1
Kiowa Cir
4700 HarC 77521 3833 C4
Kiowa Ct
100 IWCY 77583 4623 E5
100 IWCY 77583 4624 A5
1200 DRPK 77536 4109 C6
Kiowa Dr
2100 FBnC 77471 4614 D4
Kiowa Ln
18000 MtgC 77365 2972 B5
Kiowa St
4200 PASD 77504 4248 A5
4400 PASD 77505 4248 A6
Kiowa River Ln
17100 HarC 77095 3537 D2
Kiowa Timbers Dr
5600 HarC 77346 3264 D5
Kip Ln
800 MtgC 77362 2816 D6
800 SGCH 77362 2816 D6
Kiplands Ct
2600 HarC 77014 3257 E6
Kiplands Bend Dr
15500 HarC 77014 3257 E6
Kiplands Wy Dr
2500 HarC 77014 3257 E6
Kipling St
600 HOUS 77006 3962 C7
2100 BYTN 77520 3973 D5

Kipling St
2100 HOUS 77098 3962 B7
3500 HOUS 77027 3961 D7
Kipling Oak St
- HarC 77338 3261 B3
Kipp Av
200 KMAH 77565 4509 E5
Kipper Cir
4700 PASD 77505 4248 E6
Kipper Ln
21900 MtgC 77357 2973 E2
Kippers Dr
- HarC 77014 3257 E6
- HOUS 77014 3257 E6
Kipp Wy Dr
10400 HOUS 77099 4238 C2
Kirbee Dr
5000 MtgC 77302 2531 C7
5000 MtgC 77302 2677 C1
Kirby Blvd
- PASD 77507 4381 E6
100 ELGO 77586 4508 E2
100 PASD 77586 4508 E2
100 TYLV 77586 4508 E2
900 TYLV 77586 4381 E7
1100 PASD 77586 4381 E7
Kirby Dr
- BzaC 77583 4500 D6
- HarC 77047 4373 D6
- PRLD 77047 4373 D6
- PRLD 77583 4500 D6
- PRLD 77584 4373 D7
800 HOUS 77019 3962 B4
1800 PRLD 77584 4500 D2
2500 HOUS 77098 3962 A6
3600 HOUS 77098 4102 A3
4100 LMQU 77568 4989 A1
5200 HOUS 77005 4102 A2
5200 WUNP 77005 4102 A2
6800 HOUS 77025 4102 A5
6800 HOUS 77030 4102 A5
7600 HOUS 77054 4102 B7
8200 HOUS 77054 4242 B1
11700 HOUS 77047 4373 D2
11700 HOUS 77051 4373 D1
11900 HOUS 77045 4242 D7
11900 HOUS 77051 4242 D7
Kirbybend Dr
- PASD 77586 4381 E6
Kirby Chapel Rd
36400 WlrC 77445 2955 C2
Kirby Hill Ct
11800 HarC 77433 3396 A6
Kirby Lake Ct
1300 FBnC 77469 4234 D
Kirby Lake Ln
- PASD 77586 4382 A6
Kirby Oaks Dr N
4300 TYLV 77586 4381 E7
4300 TYLV 77586 4508 E1
Kirby Oaks Dr S
4200 TYLV 77586 4508 E1
Kirby Pl Ln
1400 PASD 77586 4381 E7
Kirbys Knack Dr
- HarC 77433 3395 D6
Kirby Springs Ct
2000 PRLD 77584 4500 D
Kirbyville St
6600 HOUS 77033 4104 B7
6600 HOUS 77033 4244 C1
Kirbywoods Dr
- TYLV 77586 4381 E7
Kirchner Rd
8000 MNVL 77578 4746 A
Kirk Al
2200 HOUS 77026 3825 B7
Kirk Av
10 HOUS 77034 4379 A
Kirk Rd
1500 CNRO 77304 2383 D
1600 CNRO 77304 2529 D
Kirk St
1200 HarC 77530 3830 B7
2100 HOUS 77026 3964 B1
2900 HOUS 77026 3825 B7
Kirkaldy Dr
100 HarC 77015 3829 A
Kirkaspen Dr
10000 HarC 77089 4377 C6
Kirkbend Dr
10800 HarC 77089 4377 D5
Kirkbluff Dr
10000 HarC 77089 4377 C6
Kirkbriar Dr
11800 HOUS 77089 4377 E4
Kirkbrook Dr
8300 HarC 77089 4377 B7
Kirkbrush Dr
10900 HarC 77089 4377 D5
Kirkbud Dr
10900 HarC 77089 4377 D
Kirkby Dr
8800 FBnC 77083 4236 D
Kirkchapel Ct
9300 HarC 77379 3255 D
Kirkchapel St
17000 HarC 77379 3255 D
Kirkdale Dr
9900 HOUS 77089 4377 D
Kirkfair Dr
10800 HarC 77089 4377 C
10800 HOUS 77089 4377 C
Kirkfalls Dr
9700 HOUS 77089 4377 D
Kirkfield Ln
14900 HOUS 77060 3544 C
Kirk Forrest Ct
18000 HarC 77346 3408 B
Kirkgard Dr
12200 HOUS 77045 4242 B
Kirkglade Ct
7100 HarC 77095 3678 C
Kirkglen Dr
10000 HOUS 77089 4377 E
Kirkgreen Dr
10500 HarC 77089 4377 D
Kirkhall Dr
10400 HOUS 77089 4377 E
Kirkham Ln
8100 HarC 77338 3261 E
Kirkhill Dr
10200 HOUS 77089 4377 E
Kirkhollow Dr
11400 HOUS 77089 4377 D
Kirkholm Dr
11800 HOUS 77089 4377 E

STREET Block	City	ZIP	Map#	Grid
Kirkland Dr				
8700	HarC	77089	4377	B5
Kirkland Woods Dr				
20900	HarC	77095	3538	E2
Kirklane Dr				
10400	HOUS	77089	4377	E4
Kirkleigh Ln				
9100	HarC	77379	3255	D3
Kirk Manor Ct				
4400	MSCY	77545	4622	B2
Kirkmead Dr				
10800	HarC	77089	4377	D5
Kirkmeadow Dr				
11400	HOUS	77089	4377	D4
Kirkmont Dr				
8900	HarC	77089	4377	B5
Kirknoll Dr				
11800	HOUS	77089	4377	E4
Kirkpark Dr				
-	HOUS	77089	4377	E5
11100	HarC	77089	4377	E5
Kirkpatrick Blvd				
6800	HOUS	77028	3826	A4
Kirkpatrick Rd				
21800	PRVW	77445	3101	A1
21800	PRVW	77484	3101	A1
21800	WlrC	77445	2956	A7
21800	WlrC	77445	3101	A1
21800	WlrC	77484	3101	A1
Kirkplum Dr				
10000	HarC	77089	4377	C6
Kirkridge Dr				
10900	HarC	77089	4377	E5
Kirksage Ct				
10500	HarC	77089	4377	B6
Kirksage Dr				
8400	HarC	77089	4377	C6
8700	HOUS	77089	4377	C7
Kirkshire Dr				
10400	HOUS	77089	4377	E4
Kirkside Dr				
-	HOUS	77035	4240	B4
-	HOUS	77096	4240	B4
Kirkstall Dr				
200	HarC	77090	3402	E2
Kirkstone Dr				
9100	HarC	77379	3255	C1
Kirkstone Manor Dr				
9500	HarC	77379	3110	C7
Kirkton Dr				
9500	HarC	77095	3538	D3
Kirktown Dr				
10800	HarC	77089	4377	D5
Kirkvale Dr				
9900	HarC	77089	4377	C5
Kirkvalley Dr				
11400	HOUS	77089	4377	D4
Kirkville Dr				
8300	HarC	77089	4377	B7
9700	HOUS	77089	4377	D4
Kirkwall Ct				
4100	SGLD	77479	4495	C3
Kirkwall Dr				
4700	SGLD	77479	4495	C3
Kirkway Dr				
11700	HOUS	77089	4377	E4
Kirkwell Dr				
10900	HarC	77089	4377	D5
Kirkwell Manor Ct				
10500	HarC	77379	3110	A6
Kirkwood Ct				
100	SGLD	77478	4368	E4
Kirkwood Dr				
-	HOUS	77082	3958	A7
-	HOUS	77082	4098	A1
500	MSCY	77489	4370	B3
500	STAF	77477	4370	B3
500	STAF	77489	4370	B3
1200	HOUS	77042	3958	A5
1200	HOUS	77077	3958	A5
Kirkwood Ln				
100	CNRO	77304	2383	B4
N Kirkwood Rd				
-	HOUS	77042	3958	A4
-	HOUS	77077	3958	A4
700	HOUS	77079	3958	A2
1000	HOUS	77043	3819	A7
1000	HOUS	77043	3958	B3
S Kirkwood Rd				
4000	HOUS	77072	4098	A4
4000	HOUS	77082	4098	A4
8600	HOUS	77099	4098	A7
8700	HOUS	77099	4238	B7
11500	HOUS	77477	4238	B4
11500	MDWP	77477	4238	B5
12200	STAF	77477	4238	B6
12700	STAF	77477	4369	B1
Kirkwood St				
6200	HOUS	77022	3824	B3
Kirkwren Ct				
10000	HarC	77089	4377	C6
Kirkwren Dr				
9900	HarC	77089	4377	B5
Kirkwyn Dr				
11400	HOUS	77089	4377	D4
Kirsten St				
1200	LMQU	77568	4989	E1
Kirston Dr				
6500	HarC	77389	2966	C5
Kirtland Ct				
10	CNRO	77384	2675	E4
Kirwick Dr				
10900	HNCV	77024	3960	A4
Kirwin Ln				
11000	HarC	77041	3680	C4
Kirwin St				
1400	GLSN	77551	5108	C5
Kisadee Ln				
-	PASD	77058	4508	C2
Kish Ln				
-	HOUS	77051	4243	A4
Kiska Ln				
12600	HOUS	77045	4373	B1
Kismet Ln				
2900	HOUS	77043	3819	E2
Kissing Camel Ct				
2700	MSCY	77459	4497	D3
Kit St				
9700	HOUS	77096	4240	D2
Kita Ct				
-	FBnC	77494	3951	C2
-	KATY	77494	3951	C2
18500	MtgC	77365	2972	A6
Kitchener St				
11300	HarC	77093	3685	C2
11300	HOUS	77093	3685	C2
Kitchen Hill Ln				
3800	SGLD	77479	4368	E7
Kitchen Hill Ln				
3900	SGLD	77479	4369	A7
Kite Hill Dr				
7200	HarC	77041	3679	B1
7500	HarC	77041	3539	B7
7700	HarC	77095	3539	B7
N Kitmore Dr				
8900	HOUS	77099	4238	C1
Kittansett Cir				
2500	FBnC	77450	3954	A6
Kitten Ln				
4800	HarC	77532	3554	A1
Kittiwake Ct				
10	WDLD	77380	2822	A7
800	SGLD	77478	4368	B4
Kittrell St				
10400	HOUS	77034	4246	D6
Kittridge St				
5400	HOUS	77028	3825	D1
Kitty Ln				
12300	GNPK	77015	3966	E5
12300	GNPK	77015	3967	A5
Kitty St				
1100	DRPK	77536	4249	C1
1300	MSCY	77489	4370	B1
1300	STAF	77477	4370	B1
Kitty Brook Dr				
10700	HOUS	77071	4239	E4
Kittybrook Dr				
12300	HOUS	77071	4239	E7
12400	MSCY	77071	4239	E6
Kittybrook Ln				
12700	MSCY	77071	4239	E7
Kittycrest Ln				
1100	HarC	77032	3545	B1
Kittydale Dr				
14200	HarC	77396	3547	A2
Kitty Hawk Dr				
9400	MSCY	77489	4370	B6
Kittyhawk Rd				
15500	WlrC	77484	3246	D7
Kittyhawk St E				
10	FBnC	77469	4092	A7
Kittyhawk St W				
11200	FBnC	77469	4092	A7
Kitty Hollow Dr				
4600	MSCY	77459	4497	C4
Kitty Hollow Tr				
9600	FBnC	77083	4236	B1
Kitty Hollow Park Dr				
-	FBnC	77459	4497	C6
-	MSCY	77459	4497	C6
Kitty's Ln				
10900	MtgC	77303	2239	A1
Kitzman Ct				
17600	HarC	77429	3252	E2
Kitzman Rd				
16000	HarC	77429	3253	A1
16700	HarC	77429	3252	D4
Kiva Rd				
4000	GLSN	77554	5331	B7
4000	GLSN	77554	5442	B1
Kiwi Ln				
200	MtgC	77385	2676	D5
Kiwi Pl				
-	HarC	77338	3261	B3
Klamath Ln				
1000	HarC	77090	3258	A2
Klamath Falls Ct				
5900	HarC	77041	3679	B5
Klamath Falls Dr				
13200	HarC	77041	3679	C5
Klare Av				
800	RSBG	77471	4490	C5
Klauke Ct				
1900	RSBG	77471	4491	B5
Klauke Rd				
-	FBnC	77471	4614	C2
-	RSBG	77471	4614	C2
100	FBnC	77471	4490	B7
100	RSBG	77471	4490	B7
Klauke St				
1400	RSBG	77471	4491	C5
Kleb Rd				
18000	HarC	77447	3104	E7
18000	HarC	77447	3249	E1
18500	HarC	77379	3111	A7
Kleberg St				
5400	HOUS	77056	3960	E7
Kleb Woods Dr				
-	HarC	77377	3106	B2
-	HarC	77447	3106	B2
Kleckley Dr				
-	HOUS	77034	4246	D7
-	HOUS	77034	4377	C1
9900	HOUS	77075	4377	D2
Klee Cir				
17200	HarC	77379	3256	B3
Kleewood Dr				
-	HarC	77064	3540	B7
Klein				
1200	TMBL	77375	2964	A7
Klein Dr				
30700	MtgC	77355	2961	E5
30800	SGCH	77355	2961	E5
Klein Ln				
-	HarC	77044	3689	C4
Kleinbrook Ct				
12200	HarC	77066	3401	B5
Kleinbrook Dr				
4900	HarC	77066	3401	B5
Klein Cemetery Rd				
6100	HarC	77379	3111	D6
Klein Church Rd				
18400	HarC	77379	3257	B1
18700	HarC	77379	3112	A7
Kleindale Ct				
12100	HarC	77066	3401	B5
Kleindale Dr				
5100	HarC	77066	3401	B5
Kleinfields Ct				
4900	HarC	77066	3401	B5
Kleinfields Dr				
11800	HarC	77066	3401	B6
Kleingate Ct				
4900	HarC	77066	3401	B4
Kleingate Ln				
12400	HarC	77066	3401	B4
Kleingreen Ln				
7500	HarC	77379	3256	C5
Kleinmann Av				
3000	GLSN	77551	5222	A2
3200	GLSN	77554	5222	A2
Kleinmeadow Ct				
4800	HarC	77066	3401	B5
Kleinmeadow Dr				
-	HarC	77066	3401	B4
Klein Oak Ln				
6400	HarC	77389	2966	C7
Kleinway Dr				
4800	HarC	77066	3401	B5
Kleinwood Dr				
16100	HarC	77379	3256	C4
Kleppel Rd				
9800	HarC	77375	2965	B4
Kliberg Pl Dr				
10800	HarC	77064	3540	B5
N Klien Cir Dr				
6700	HarC	77088	3542	B7
6700	HOUS	77088	3542	B7
S Klien Cir Dr				
-	HarC	77088	3542	B7
-	HOUS	77088	3542	B7
Klien Terrace Ln				
-	HarC	77379	3111	D4
Kliesing Dr				
-	FRDW	77546	4629	E4
Klimer Wy				
1600	HOUS	77077	3957	A5
Kline Dr				
11300	MtgC	77303	2385	C3
Klondite Av				
8800	HOUS	77075	4246	A7
Klondite St				
9400	HOUS	77075	4246	B7
Kluge Rd				
12500	HarC	77429	3398	B1
13200	HarC	77429	3397	E3
Kmiec Rd				
22000	WlrC	77445	2952	A6
Knanaya Resort St				
2100	MSCY	77489	4370	A6
Knapp Rd				
3300	PRLD	77581	4376	B6
Knauff Ranch Ct				
-	HarC	77429	3253	C5
Knebel Rd				
31100	HarC	77484	2957	A7
31700	HarC	77484	2956	D7
Knichtwick Dr				
1700	HOUS	77008	3822	C6
Knickerbocker Dr				
4800	HOUS	77035	4241	A3
Knigge Cemetery Rd				
12100	HarC	77429	3397	E6
Knight Ln				
3000	BYTN	77521	3973	E2
Knight Rd				
-	HOUS	77054	4102	C6
3500	MSCY	77545	4622	A1
4100	MSCY	77459	4622	A1
5000	FBnC	77583	4622	A3
8300	HOUS	77054	4242	D1
9100	HOUS	77045	4242	D3
Knight St				
800	HOUS	77022	3685	C7
2100	HOUS	77093	3685	D7
Knight Hollow Ct				
23300	FBnC	77494	3953	D7
Knight Lake Ct				
4500	FBnC	77469	4234	D4
Knighton Cir				
13900	HOUS	77034	4378	E6
Knightrider Dr				
16300	HarC	77379	3256	B5
Knights Cir				
2500	STAF	77477	4369	E3
Knights Ct				
900	FRDW	77546	4629	B3
4500	BYTN	77521	3972	C1
Knights Dr				
9700	HarC	77065	3539	D4
Knights Bluff Ln				
1400	HarC	77073	3259	D5
Knights Branch Dr				
4700	FBnC	77479	4366	D7
Knightsbridge Blvd				
4300	SGLD	77479	4495	D3
E Knightsbridge Dr				
10	WDLD	77385	2676	C4
W Knightsbridge Dr				
10	WDLD	77385	2676	C3
Knights Bridge Ln				
800	WEBS	77058	4507	D5
800	WEBS	77598	4507	D5
Knightsbridge Ln				
3000	LGCY	77539	4752	D4
Knightsbrook Ln				
21600	HarC	77449	3815	A2
Knights Cove Dr				
22000	MtgC	77339	3118	C4
Knights Crest Dr				
9900	HarC	77083	4237	B2
Knight's Crossing Dr				
10	WDLD	77382	2673	E6
N Knight's Crossing Dr				
10	WDLD	77382	2673	E6
S Knight's Crossing Dr				
10	WDLD	77382	2673	D7
N Knights Gate Cir				
10	WDLD	77382	2819	B1
S Knights Gate Cir				
10	WDLD	77382	2819	B1
Knights Glen Ln				
-	FBnC	77494	4093	A7
-	HOUS	77494	4093	C1
Knights Hill Ct				
12200	HarC	77065	3539	D4
Knights Hollow Ct				
3600	FBnC	77494	3952	B7
Knightsland Tr				
9000	FBnC	77083	4236	C1
Knightsridge Ln				
19500	HarC	77094	3955	A4
Knights Tower Dr				
25900	MtgC	77339	3118	D4
Knightsway Dr				
14700	FBnC	77083	4236	D1
Knights Wy Dr				
13400	HarC	77083	4237	B2
Knightwood Ct				
10600	HOUS	77016	3686	D3
Knightwood St				
5200	HOUS	77016	3686	D3
Knightwood Forest Dr				
8000	HarC	77088	3542	E7
8000	HarC	77088	3682	E1
Knipp Rd				
100	HOUS	77024	3959	C5
300	BKHV	77024	3959	B4
Knipp Forest St				
300	BKHV	77024	3959	B4
Knipp Oaks St				
400	BKHV	77024	3959	B3
Knippwood Ln				
11900	BKHV	77024	3959	B3
Knobbley Oak Ct				
11000	HarC	77065	3540	A1
Knobby Knoll Dr				
5600	HOUS	77092	3682	C6
Knobby Oaks Pl				
18800	MtgC	77355	2815	A2
Knob Creek Ct				
1800	HOUS	77062	4380	A6
Knobcrest Ct				
12700	HarC	77060	3403	B5
Knobcrest Dr				
100	HarC	77060	3403	A5
12000	HarC	77070	3398	C1
Knobel Grove Ln				
2800	FBnC	77494	3953	B6
Knob Hill Av				
7200	PASD	77505	4249	A3
Knob Hill St				
2800	PRLD	77581	4504	A5
3300	DRPK	77536	4109	C7
3300	DRPK	77536	4249	C1
Knob Hill Lake Ln				
18300	HarC	77346	3408	C1
Knobhollow				
600	HarC	77530	3829	E7
Knoblock St				
2400	HOUS	77023	4104	C3
Knob Mountain Tr				
10100	HOUS	77016	3687	C4
Knoboak Cir				
1900	HOUS	77080	3820	B5
Knoboak Dr				
9800	HOUS	77080	3820	B4
10200	HOUS	77043	3820	A4
10400	HOUS	77043	3819	D4
Knob Pines Ct				
-	HarC	77389	2966	D2
Knoche Dr				
-	HarC	77396	3407	D3
Knockomie Ct				
9300	HarC	77095	3538	C4
Knodell St				
2900	HOUS	77026	3825	A6
Knolewood Ln				
-	PRLD	77584	4502	A6
Knoll Dr				
19700	MtgC	77357	2828	D5
Knoll St				
3300	HOUS	77080	3820	E2
W Knoll St				
6800	HOUS	77028	3686	E7
7100	HOUS	77028	3687	A7
Knoll Acres Dr				
10	MtgC	77357	2829	D6
Knoll Bend Ct				
11900	HarC	77070	3399	B6
Knoll Bend Ln				
10500	HarC	77070	3399	A6
Knollblossom Ln				
21200	FBnC	77469	4094	A7
Knoll Briar Ln				
7100	FBnC	77469	4094	B6
Knollbridge Ln				
6600	HarC	77379	3111	C4
Knollbrook Ln				
2400	HarC	77373	3114	C2
Knoll Cliff Ct				
7400	HarC	77095	3678	D1
Knoll Creek Pl				
2600	HarC	77084	3816	A5
Knoll Crest Ct				
1100	FBnC	77479	4493	D5
Knollcrest Ln				
3300	BzaC	77584	4501	B5
Knollcrest St				
12800	HOUS	77015	3967	B1
Knoll Dale Ct				
3000	HarC	77429	3395	E1
Knoll Dale Tr				
17100	MtgC	77385	2676	C6
Knolle Ln				
25500	HarC	77336	3121	E7
Knoll Forest Ct				
6800	FBnC	77479	4493	C6
Knoll Forest Dr				
100	FBnC	77479	4493	C6
300	LGCY	77573	4632	E2
8600	HarC	77338	3262	A3
Knoll Glen Dr				
4000	HarC	77082	4096	C4
Knoll Lake Dr				
15700	HarC	77095	3538	D7
15700	HarC	77095	3678	D1
Knoll Lake Ln				
22000	HarC	77450	3954	A4
Knoll Manor Dr				
3000	HOUS	77345	3119	D4
Knoll Mill Ln				
4000	FBnC	77494	4092	C2
Knoll Oak Ln				
2000	FBnC	77469	4616	B2
Knoll Oaks Ln				
2600	MtgC	77386	2969	D1
Knoll Park Dr				
6500	FBnC	77479	4493	C6
Knoll Pines Ct				
10	WDLD	77381	2821	B4
Knollridge Ct				
16200	HOUS	77053	4371	D6
Knoll Shadows Ln				
2500	HarC	77449	3815	C4
Knolls Lodge Ct				
7700	HarC	77095	3538	C6
Knolls Lodge Dr				
15800	HarC	77095	3538	C7
Knolls Spring Dr				
-	HarC	77450	3954	E6
Knolls Spring Tr				
20300	HarC	77450	3954	D5
Knoll Terrace Dr				
5400	HOUS	77339	3119	C2
Knollview Dr				
6200	HarC	77389	2966	D5
Knoll West Dr				
3200	HOUS	77082	4097	C2
Knollwest Dr				
6100	HOUS	77072	4097	C4
Knollwick Ct				
4000	HarC	77053	4372	D5
Knollwood St				
2000	LGCY	77565	4509	A4
3600	HOUS	77019	3961	D5
Knollwood Tr				
5800	HarC	77373	3260	E1
5900	HarC	77373	3261	A1
Knotted Oak Ct				
18300	MtgC	77365	2972	A2
Knottinghill Dr				
13500	SGLD	77478	4237	B6
Knotty Chestnut St				
15200	HarC	77429	3253	D4
Knotty Elmwood Tr				
800	HOUS	77062	4506	D1
Knotty Glen Ln				
12900	HOUS	77072	4097	C6
Knotty Green Dr				
18200	HarC	77084	3677	E6
Knottynold Ln				
3900	HOUS	77053	4372	D3
Knotty Oaks Tr				
2600	HOUS	77045	4373	B1
3100	HOUS	77045	4242	A7
4100	HOUS	77045	4241	C7
15500	MtgC	77355	2962	A3
Knotty Pine Cir				
3600	PRLD	77581	4504	D6
Knotty Pine Cir S				
1500	PRLD	77581	4504	D6
Knotty Pine Tr				
11700	HarC	77016	3547	D7
11700	HarC	77050	3547	D7
Knotty Post Ln				
6000	HarC	77373	3115	E6
Knotty Wood Ct				
10	CNRO	77301	2384	E6
Knotty Wood Dr				
6000	HOUS	77092	3682	B5
Knotwood Pl				
10	WDLD	77382	2819	B3
Knowlton Rd				
700	BYTN	77520	3973	B5
E Knox Dr				
21500	MtgC	77365	3118	C2
W Knox Dr				
21100	MtgC	77365	3118	A2
Knox St				
1300	HOUS	77007	3962	A2
3400	PASD	77504	4247	B4
6500	HOUS	77091	3684	A4
7100	HOUS	77088	3684	A3
8700	HOUS	77088	3683	E1
S Knox St				
100	HOUS	77007	3962	A4
Knoxdale Ln				
-	HarC	77047	4374	B4
Knox Estate Dr				
25600	FBnC	77469	4092	D7
Knoxville Dr				
2500	LGCY	77573	4631	B6
Knoxville Run				
8900	LPRT	77571	4249	E4
Knoxville St				
4300	HOUS	77051	4243	C3
4600	HOUS	77033	4243	C3
Knoxwood St				
8800	HOUS	77016	3686	B7
Knurled Oak Ln				
8300	HarC	77379	3255	E2
Knute St				
6000	HOUS	77028	3826	E3
Koala Dr				
8700	HOUS	77061	4245	A6
Koalstad Rd				
12100	MtgC	77302	2532	A7
14400	MtgC	77302	2678	A1
Koback Corners St				
22900	HarC	77373	3114	E6
S Kobayashi Dr				
800	WEBS	77598	4631	B1
Kobayashi Rd				
-	WEBS	77598	4507	B7
-	WEBS	77598	4631	B1
N Kobayashi Rd				
700	WEBS	77598	4507	A7
Kobi Ct				
3000	HarC	77068	3257	C5
Kobi Park Ct				
23200	HarC	77373	2968	E6
Kobs Rd				
-	WlrC	77447	2959	C5
21800	HarC	77377	2962	D7
21800	HarC	77377	3107	D2
Kobuk Valley Cir				
17100	HarC	77346	3408	C3
Koch Ln				
-	HOUS	77084	3818	A2
Kodes Clay Ct				
6400	HarC	77379	3257	A4
Kodiac St				
5200	HarC	77389	2967	A5
Kodiak Ct				
2600	HarC	77067	3401	E4
Kody Ridge Ct				
13100	HOUS	77034	4378	C2
Koeblen Rd				
5300	FBnC	77469	4615	D3
5300	RSBG	77469	4615	D3
6600	FBnC	77469	4616	A5
Koehler St				
3900	HOUS	77007	3962	C2
Koenig				
9700	HOUS	77034	4378	C1
Koenig Ln				
15400	MtgC	77384	2675	D3
Koenig St				
10000	HOUS	77034	4378	C2
Koester St				
8300	JRSV	77040	3540	C6
Koinm Dr				
14600	HarC	77032	3546	A1
14600	HOUS	77032	3546	A1
Kokomo St				
900	HOUS	77015	3967	D1
Kolb Rd				
100	HOUS	77017	4246	D2
100	HOUS	77587	4246	D2
100	SHUS	77587	4246	E2
200	SHUS	77017	4246	D2
300	HOUS	77502	4246	D2
300	SHUS	77502	4246	D2
400	PASD	77502	4246	E2
1000	PASD	77502	4247	A2
1000	SHUS	77502	4247	A2
1000	SHUS	77587	4247	A2
Kolb St				
4100	HOUS	77007	3962	C1
S Kolbe Cir				
11200	HarC	77429	3397	D7
N Kolbe Dr				
11700	HarC	77429	3397	D6
S Kolbe Rd				
11000	HarC	77429	3538	D1
11200	HarC	77429	3397	D7
S Kolbe Spur Dr				
14500	HarC	77429	3538	D1
Kolfahl St				
1800	HOUS	77023	4104	B2
Kolyma Dr				
19300	MtgC	77365	2971	D5
Kona Dr				
100	GlsC	77563	5106	D3
100	TKIS	77554	5106	D3
Kona Cay Dr				
11900	HarC	77044	3688	E4
Kopman Dr				
8200	HOUS	77061	4244	E6
Koppel Rd				
-	CmbC	77520	4113	E2
Korbel Ct				
10	WDLD	77382	2819	A2
Korenek Dr				
-	BzaC	77584	4501	E6
Korenek Ln				
100	HarC	77562	3831	E4
Korenek St				
13300	HarC	77039	3546	E4
Korff Dr				
500	HarC	77037	3544	B5
500	HOUS	77037	3544	B5
Korpink St				
11400	HarC	77039	3545	E7
11400	HarC	77093	3545	E7
11400	HOUS	77039	3545	E7
Kosler Ln				
400	RHMD	77469	4492	A1
Kosse Rd				
500	HMPD	77445	3098	C1
Kosse St				
-	HMPD	77445	3097	E1
1500	HMPD	77445	3098	A1
Kost Rd				
600	ALVN	77511	4867	A2
Koster Rd				
1700	ALVN	77511	4867	C4
Kotar Ct				
300	HarC	77388	3113	D7
Kotlan Ct				
6800	MtgC	77354	2673	B2
Kottayam Dr				
2100	MSCY	77489	4370	B6
Kovar Rd				
2800	FBnC	77469	4615	B3
Kowis St				
1400	HOUS	77093	3685	C2
2800	HarC	77093	3685	E2
2800	HarC	77093	3686	A2
E Kowis St				
300	HOUS	77037	3684	D2
Krahn Rd				
20100	HarC	77388	3112	D4
Krampota Rd				
3800	HarC	77532	3694	A4
Kransburg Ranch Ct				
18900	HarC	77433	3677	C1
Kransburg Ranch Dr				
7200	HarC	77433	3677	C1
Kransburg Ridge Ct				
25600	MtgC	77365	3118	A3
Kransburg Ridge Dr				
20900	MtgC	77365	3117	D3
20900	MtgC	77365	3118	A3
Kransbury Ln				
9200	HarC	77095	3538	A5
Krause Dr				
6600	HOUS	77489	4371	C6
Krayola Ln				
16300	HarC	77379	3256	C4
Krebbs Ct				
3600	BzaC	77583	4500	D7
Kreinhop Rd				
4000	HarC	77388	3112	C3
Kremmer St				
15000	HarC	77530	3829	C7
Krenek Ln				
2000	HarC	77532	3553	B5
Krenek Rd				
200	HarC	77532	3552	D5
1600	HarC	77532	3553	D5
3600	HarC	77532	3554	A5
Kress St				
100	HOUS	77020	3825	E7
200	HOUS	77020	3964	E1
3900	HOUS	77026	3825	D6
Kreuzer Rd				
6500	MNVL	77578	4746	B3
Krezdorn Rd				
27200	WlrC	77447	2958	D6
27800	HarC	77484	2958	C6
Krisdale Ct				
5400	HarC	77084	3677	E5
Krist Dr				
1100	SPVL	77055	3821	B7
Krista Ct				
16000	HarC	77049	3829	D3
Kristen Ct				
5200	HarC	77373	3260	D1
Kristen Dr				
3500	HarC	77562	3832	E1
3500	HarC	77562	3833	A1
3900	DKSN	77539	4753	E3
Kristen Wy				
-	PASD	77505	4248	A4
Kristen Oaks Ct				
19300	HarC	77346	3264	D6
Kristen Park Ct				
19300	HarC	77346	3264	D6
Kristen Park Ln				
6000	HarC	77346	3264	D5
Kristen Pine Dr				
19200	HarC	77346	3264	E5
Kristi Ln				
18700	BzaC	77511	4627	B4
18700	BzaC	77584	4627	B4
18700	PRLD	77584	4627	B4
Kristie Dr				
34500	MtgC	77362	2816	D6
34500	SGCH	77362	2816	D6
Kristin Dr				
9200	HOUS	77031	4239	A3
Kristina Ct				
11900	HarC	77089	4504	E1
Kristin Lee Ct				
4000	HarC	77014	3401	C2
Kristin Lee Ln				
3700	HarC	77014	3401	D2
Kriswood Dr				
1600	HarC	77014	3402	C3
Krolczyk				
21900	HarC	77377	3106	E2
Krone Ct				
9900	HarC	77396	3407	B6
Kropik Rd				
15500	MtgC	77306	2681	A4
Krueger Rd				
-	HarC	77447	3248	E2
7300	HOUS	77033	4243	E1
7300	HOUS	77033	4244	A1
Krug Rd				
16700	HarC	77377	2962	D6
Kruger Dr				
5000	DKSN	77539	4754	D4
Kruger Rd				
16600	HarC	77429	3108	A7
16600	HarC	77429	3253	A1
Krystal Ct				
3900	BYTN	77521	3973	C2
Kube Ct				
16000	JRSV	77040	3540	C7
Kubin Rd				
18700	HarC	77532	3410	D5
Kueben Ln				
15800	HOUS	77489	4371	D6
Kueck Rd				
3100	FBnC	77471	4614	A6
Kuester Rd				
100	MtgC	77304	2529	D3
Kuester St				
2500	HOUS	77006	3962	C6
Kuhlman Rd				
700	HNCV	77024	3960	B1
Kuhlman St				
5400	HOUS	77021	4103	D4
Kuhn				
5300	HOUS	77007	3962	B3
Kuldell Dr				
5500	HOUS	77096	4240	C1
5800	HOUS	77074	4240	B1
Kulhanek Ln				
-	WlrC	77484	3101	A7
34200	PNIS	77445	3100	C7
34200	PNIS	77484	3100	C7
34200	WlrC	77445	3100	C7
34200	WlrC	77484	3100	C7
Kulkarni St				
4400	HOUS	77045	4241	C6
Kunz Rd				
-	HOUS	77084	3818	A2
4000	FBnC	77471	4614	A6
Kurland Dr				
11900	HOUS	77034	4378	A3
Kurt Dr				
15200	HOUS	77396	3405	E6
Kurtell Ln				
12500	HarC	77429	3397	D5
Kury Ln				
6200	HOUS	77008	3822	E6
Kustom Kastles Sq				
-	HOUS	77598	4506	C1
Kuykendahl Dr				
10	HarC	77090	3402	E2
10	HOUS	77090	3402	E2
Kuykendahl Rd				
-	HOUS	77067	3402	E4
-	WDLD	77381	2674	B7
-	WDLD	77382	2820	B1
10	HarC	77090	3402	E3
10	HOUS	77090	3402	E3
7100	WDLD	77382	2674	B7
11000	HarC	77060	3403	A4
11000	HOUS	77067	3403	A4
11800	HOUS	77014	3403	A4
11800	HOUS	77090	3403	A4
12400	HarC	77014	3402	D2
12400	HOUS	77014	3402	E3
14000	HarC	77014	3258	C7
14000	HarC	77090	3258	B6
14700	HOUS	77090	3258	B6
15500	HOUS	77014	3258	A5
15500	HOUS	77068	3258	A5
15800	HarC	77068	3257	E5
15800	HarC	77090	3257	E5
15800	HOUS	77068	3257	E5
15800	HOUS	77090	3257	E5
17100	HarC	77379	3257	D3
17100	HarC	77388	3257	D3
18200	HarC	77379	3112	B6
18200	HarC	77388	3112	B6
20000	HarC	77379	3111	E3
20000	HarC	77388	3111	E3
21800	HarC	77389	3111	C1
22000	HarC	77375	2966	A6
22000	HarC	77379	2966	B7
22000	HarC	77389	2966	A6
23600	HarC	77375	2965	E5
23600	HarC	77389	2965	E5
26200	HarC	77375	2819	E7
26200	HarC	77389	2819	E7
27500	HarC	77375	2820	A4
27500	HarC	77389	2820	A4
27500	WDLD	77381	2820	A4
Kuykendahl Forest Dr				
4900	HarC	77379	3257	C1
5000	HarC	77388	3257	C1
Kuykendahl Hufsmith Rd				
6800	HarC	77389	2966	B6
7200	HarC	77375	2966	B6
8600	HarC	77375	2965	B5
10900	HarC	77375	2964	E4
Kwik Kopy Ln				
10	HarC	77429	3397	C5
Kyack Ct				
18400	HarC	77346	3409	C1
Kyla Cir				
5300	KATY	77493	3813	D3
Kyle Ct				
3200	PRLD	77584	4502	C5
Kyle Ln				
14400	MtgC	77306	2680	E2
Kyle St				
-	HOUS	77016	3686	E2
400	SGLD	77478	4368	A3
4300	HOUS	77006	3962	E7
4300	HOUS	77006	4102	E1
Kyle/Chapman				
-	PASD	77505	4249	B3
-	PASD	77536	4249	B3
Kyle Bend Dr				
10	KATY	77493	3813	B4
Kyle Chapman Ct				
-	HOUS	77074	4100	B6
Kyle Chase Ct				
800	HarC	77373	2968	C6
Kyle Crest Tr				
16200	HarC	77433	3251	C5
Kyle Hill Ln				
1300	FBnC	77479	4493	C1
Kyle Reid Ct				
16400	MtgC	77302	2679	B3

STREET
Block City ZIP Map# Grid
Kyle Trail Ct
7300 FBnC 77469 4095 D6
Kylewick Dr
12600 HOUS 77035 4240 E6
12600 HOUS 77085 4240 E6
Kylie Ct
2300 MtgC 77386 2969 E6
Kylie Springs Ln
5100 HarC 77066 3401 B6
Kyren Ln
25800 HarC 77389 2966 A2
KZ Rd
18200 HarC 77429 3252 B3
18200 HarC 77433 3252 B3
18900 HarC 77433 3251 E3
L
E L Av
- LPRT 77571 4251 E5
L St
4100 HOUS 77072 4098 A4
N L St
400 MRGP 77571 4111 E7
500 MRGP 77571 4112 A7
500 MRGP 77571 4251 E1
9700 DRPK 77536 4250 A1
9700 LPRT 77571 4250 A1
10100 LPRT 77571 4110 C7
11500 LPRT 77571 4111 B7
W L St
700 LPRT 77571 4251 D5
La Arbre Ln
20000 HarC 77388 3112 E4
La Avenida Dr
15800 HOUS 77062 4506 E3
16000 HOUS 77062 4507 A3
La Bahia Mnr
8100 FBnC 77469 4234 B4
Labarre Dr
11400 HarC 77429 3397 E7
Labco St
1200 HOUS 77020 3965 B3
1200 HOUS 77029 3965 B3
Labelle Ln
13100 HarC 77015 3828 C6
13100 HOUS 77015 3828 C6
La Blanc
100 HarC 77532 3692 D1
Labrador Rd
13800 HOUS 77047 4373 B4
14200 HarC 77047 4373 B5
14700 PRLD 77047 4373 B7
La Branch St
100 HOUS 77002 3963 D4
700 HOUS 77010 3963 C4
2200 HOUS 77004 3963 C5
4100 HOUS 77004 4103 A1
5400 HOUS 77004 4102 E2
5700 HOUS 77030 4102 E2
La Brea Dr
8000 FBnC 77083 4096 B7
La Cabana Dr
- HOUS 77062 4507 A3
15600 HOUS 77062 4506 E3
La Captain Av
- HOUS 77030 4102 E5
La Casa Ln
15600 HOUS 77062 4506 E3
15600 HOUS 77062 4507 A3
S Lace Arbor Cir
10 WDLD 77382 2674 D4
N Lace Arbor Dr
10 WDLD 77382 2674 D4
S Lace Arbor Dr
- WDLD 77382 2674 D4
Lacebrook Ln
2900 PRLD 77545 4499 E4
Lacewing Ln
2700 HarC 77067 3402 A6
Lacewing Pl
10 WDLD 77380 2967 C3
Lacewood Ct
2900 BzaC 77584 4501 B5
Lacewood Dr
- HOUS 77504 4247 C7
- PASD 77504 4247 C7
Lacewood Ln
10 PNPV 77024 3959 E4
Lacey Ln
16500 MSCY 77071 4239 B7
Lacey Crest Dr
12500 HarC 77070 3399 C6
Laceyland Ln
20200 HarC 77449 3815 C7
E Lacey Oak Cir
2000 WDLD 77380 2967 D2
W Lacey Oak Cir
2100 WDLD 77380 2967 E2
Lacey Oak Dr
6000 PASD 77505 4248 D6
Lacey Oak Meadow Dr
- FBnC 77494 4093 A3
Lacing Ct
16900 HarC 77532 3552 A2
Lack Ln
12300 BKVL 77581 4375 B5
La Concha Ln
1300 HOUS 77054 4102 B6
13500 HarC 77083 4097 B6
Laconia Ct
2400 FBnC 77478 4237 B5
La Costa Ln
14900 HOUS 77079 3957 C2
La Costa Rd
- MSCY 77459 4496 E1
Lacoste Love Ct
6200 HarC 77379 3256 E3
6200 HarC 77379 3257 A3
La Cote Cir
20700 HarC 77388 3112 E4
La Cote Ln
20700 HarC 77388 3112 E4
Lacreek Ln
5200 HarC 77379 3257 B2
La Crosse St
10500 JTCY 77029 3966 C2
N La Crosse St
10300 JTCY 77029 3966 B2
S La Crosse St
10300 JTCY 77029 3966 B2
Lacy Dr
1300 BYTN 77520 3973 C6
Lacy Rd
10800 HarC 77375 3255 A1
10800 HarC 77379 3255 A1
Lacy St
5400 HOUS 77007 3962 A3

STREET
Block City ZIP Map# Grid
Lacyberry St
2400 HOUS 77080 3820 D3
Lacy Hill Dr
7000 HOUS 77036 4099 A5
Lacy Oaks Ln
27000 MtgC 77372 2684 A4
Lacy Willow Ct
8800 HarC 77375 3111 A1
Lacy Wood Ct
40600 MtgC 77354 2670 B1
Ladbroke Ln
12300 HarC 77039 3545 E5
Ladbrook Dr
2000 HOUS 77339 3118 D6
Laddingford Ln
400 LGCY 77573 4630 C7
500 LGCY 77573 4751 C1
Ladera Dr
6200 HarC 77083 4096 D4
Ladin Dr
2000 HarC 77039 3545 D5
Ladino Rd
10500 HarC 77429 3538 E2
Ladino Run St
14700 HarC 77429 3253 B7
16100 HarC 77429 3252 E7
Ladonia St
4900 ARLA 77583 4623 B5
4900 FBnC 77583 4623 B4
Ladue Rd
17800 HarC 77532 3413 A5
Lady St
7600 HOUS 77021 4103 A7
7600 HOUS 77021 4243 A3
Lady Anne Dr
12900 HarC 77044 3549 D1
Lady Atwell Ct
3900 FBnC 77459 4621 E4
Ladybug Ct
19300 MtgC 77365 2972 C7
Ladybug Dr
10500 HarC 77064 3540 B3
Lady Ellen Dr
25200 WlrC 77447 2813 C7
N Lady Fern Ln
1200 HarC 77073 3259 B5
W Lady Fern Ln
16300 HarC 77073 3259 B3
Lady Fern St
8900 HarC 77064 3540 E1
Lady Guinevere Cir
24600 WlrC 77447 2813 D7
Lady Jane Ct
12600 HarC 77044 3549 D1
Lady Leslie Ln
2200 PRLD 77581 4503 E3
Lady Shery Ln
15300 HarC 77429 3253 C4
Lady Slipper Rd
12500 HarC 77038 3543 B4
La Entrada Ct
7100 FBnC 77083 4096 A6
La Entrada Dr
7000 FBnC 77083 4096 A6
La Estancia Ln
2900 HOUS 77093 3685 E6
2900 HOUS 77093 3686 A6
Lafayette Av
1300 PASD 77502 4246 D1
Lafayette Ct
2500 SEBK 77586 4509 C2
Lafayette Ln
100 LGCY 77573 4631 C4
Lafayette St
10 BYTN 77520 3973 A7
1000 HMPD 77445 2952 E7
1600 HMPD 77445 2953 A7
2800 WUNP 77005 4102 A3
3000 WUNP 77005 4101 E3
4300 BLAR 77401 4101 C6
4300 HOUS 77401 4101 C6
Lafayette Hollow Ln
17200 HarC 77346 3408 C3
Lafferty Rd
1100 PASD 77502 4107 C7
2100 PASD 77502 4247 C1
3100 PASD 77504 4247 C3
Lafferty Oaks Dr
11500 HOUS 77013 3966 D1
Lafferty Oaks St
11000 HOUS 77013 3966 C1
Lafitte Ct
21800 SGCH 77355 2960 E2
Lafitte Dr
- DRPK 77536 4249 E2
- DRPK 77536 4250 A2
14200 HarC 77429 3538 E1
Lafitte St
5600 GLSN 77551 5108 C6
Lafittes Pt
3100 GLSN 77554 5219 E7
3200 GLSN 77554 5332 E1
La Fleur Ln
3400 HarC 77388 3112 D4
Lafleur Pine Ln
1800 PASD 77503 4108 A7
La Fonda Dr
200 HOUS 77060 3544 C2
Lafone Dr
16600 HarC 77379 3256 E3
La Fontaine Dr
2900 HarC 77014 3401 E3
La Fonte St
8600 HOUS 77024 3961 A1
La Fouche Ct
13300 HarC 77377 3109 B5
La Fouche Dr
25800 HarC 77377 3109 A5
La France Dr
7200 GlsC 77563 4990 D6
Lagarto Ct
200 MtgC 77362 2816 E6
200 MtgC 77362 2817 A5
Lagarto Wy
300 MtgC 77362 2816 E5
Lagato Pl
10 WDLD 77382 2673 C6
Lage Nicola Ln
- LGCY 77573 4632 E5
- LGCY 77573 4633 A5
Lagerfield Ln
- HarC 77044 3689 D5
La Gloria Dr
- FBnC 77083 4096 A6
16600 FBnC 77083 4095 E6
Lago Dr
39300 MtgC 77354 2672 D3

STREET
Block City ZIP Map# Grid
Lago St
2800 GlsC 77511 4750 B5
2800 LGCY 77546 4750 B5
Lago Bend Ln
12400 HarC 77041 3679 E4
Lago Cir Dr N
100 STFE 77517 4870 C1
200 GlsC 77517 4870 D1
Lago Cir Dr S
- STFE 77517 4870 D2
300 GlsC 77517 4870 D2
Lago Cove
- GlsC 77517 4870 D1
Lago Crest Dr
9000 HOUS 77054 4242 A2
Lago Forest Dr
- HarC 77346 3408 B1
Lago Mirado Wy
2400 FBnC 77469 4365 B4
Lagoon Dr
- HOUS 77058 4508 B4
- NSUB 77058 4508 B4
Lagoon Ln
23000 HOUS 77336 3266 C4
Lago Royale Ln
12500 HarC 77041 3679 D3
Lago Trace Dr
100 HarC 77336 2975 D7
200 HarC 77336 3120 D1
400 HarC 77336 3121 A2
Lago Verde Dr
11400 FBnC 77469 4093 B7
Lago Villa Dr
15400 HarC 77377 3255 A6
Lago Vista
100 LGCY 77565 4508 E4
Lagovista Ct
7700 HarC 77346 3265 B2
N Lago Vista Ct
1600 PRLD 77581 4504 C2
N Lago Vista Dr
2300 PRLD 77581 4504 C2
S Lago Vista Dr
2300 PRLD 77581 4504 C3
Lago Vista Ln
- FBnC 77053 4498 E2
1500 FBnC 77494 3953 B4
Lago Vista Real St
33200 MtgC 77354 2674 A4
La Granada Dr
6600 HarC 77083 4096 B5
Lagrange Park Pl
16600 HOUS 77053 4372 C7
La Grove Ln
12700 HarC 77015 3828 B7
Laguna Cir
4100 MSCY 77459 4369 C7
8000 HarC 77095 3539 B6
Laguna Dr
3800 GLSN 77554 5440 E5
3900 GLSN 77554 5441 A5
Laguna Ln
- HOUS 77036 4099 E3
- HOUS 77036 4100 A3
Laguna St
13100 HOUS 77015 3967 C2
Laguna Bay Ct
6300 HarC 77041 3680 A5
Laguna Beach Ln
5900 HOUS 77036 4099 E3
Laguna del Rey Dr
6100 HarC 77041 3680 A5
Laguna Edge Dr
24800 FBnC 77494 3952 E5
24800 FBnC 77494 3953 A5
Laguna Falls Ct
5900 HarC 77041 3679 E5
5900 HarC 77041 3680 A5
Laguna Harbor Ln
1400 GlsC 77650 4879 A5
Laguna Harbor Cove Blvd
1800 GlsC 77650 4879 A5
Laguna Harbor Estate Blvd
1800 GlsC 77650 4879 A5
Laguna Meadows Ct
19700 HarC 77094 3955 A4
Laguna Meadows Ln
1600 HarC 77094 3955 A4
Laguna Point Cir
2700 FBnC 77450 3953 D7
Laguna Point Dr
22900 FBnC 77450 3953 D7
Laguna Point Ln
4000 MSCY 77459 4496 D4
Laguna Pointe Dr
100 LGCY 77573 4509 C7
2700 BzaC 77584 4374 A7
S Laguna Pointe Dr
100 LGCY 77573 4633 B1
Laguna Pointe Ln
12100 HarC 77041 3679 B7
12100 HarC 77041 3680 A6
Laguna Shores Dr
13200 PRLD 77584 4500 A2
Laguna Shores Ln
2900 LGCY 77573 4633 A3
Laguna Springs Ct
8000 HarC 77095 3538 A7
Laguna Springs Dr
- PRLD 77584 4500 B3
16800 HarC 77095 3538 A6
Laguna Terrace Dr
12000 HarC 77041 3680 A5
Laguna Terrace Wy
6000 HarC 77041 3680 A5
Laguna Trace Ct
22300 FBnC 77469 4093 D7
Laguna Trace St
6600 FBnC 77469 4093 E7
Laguna Trail Dr
17500 HarC 77095 3537 E1
Laguna Woods Dr
19300 HarC 77375 3109 D7
La Hacienda Dr
800 FBnC 77469 4365 B4
Laigle Rd
4600 BzaC 77578 4624 E3
4600 MNVL 77583 4624 E3
Lain Rd
22700 HarC 77375 3111 A1
22700 HarC 77379 3111 A1
Laindon Springs Ln
800 HarC 77373 3114 B4
Laird St
900 PASD 77506 4107 B4
1300 HOUS 77008 3823 B6
La Jolla Cir
300 HOUS 77060 3544 D2

STREET
Block City ZIP Map# Grid
La Jolla Ln
15100 HOUS 77060 3544 D2
Lajuana Ct
600 HarC 77388 3113 C6
La Juana Ln
19400 HarC 77388 3113 C7
Lake Cir
700 FRDW 77546 4629 E5
16600 MtgC 77302 2678 D5
Lake Ct
- HarC 77530 3969 D2
- LMQU 77568 4872 B4
4100 MSCY 77459 4369 C7
E Lake Ct
- HOUS 77336 3121 B5
Lake Ctr
12900 HarC 77041 3679 D6
Lake Dr
- MSCY 77459 4369 D5
- MSCY 77459 4497 C3
- MtgC 77365 3117 C5
10 MtgC 77384 2528 B6
1900 FBnC 77469 4364 C5
3000 FBnC 77494 3952 E6
3100 FBnC 77494 3953 A7
3800 PRLD 77581 4504 E6
24200 MtgC 77365 2974 B7
24700 MtgC 77357 2974 C1
25800 MtgC 77372 2537 B6
26400 SPLD 77372 2537 B6
Lake Dr E
2200 FRDW 77546 4629 C7
2200 LGCY 77546 4629 C7
12600 MtgC 77372 2537 A5
N Lake Dr
12100 MtgC 77372 2537 A4
W Lake Dr
500 FRDW 77546 4629 E5
2600 SGLD 77478 4237 B4
19200 MtgC 77355 2814 B2
Lake Ln
7300 HarC 77040 3681 B1
21000 HarC 77447 3106 A2
Lake Ln W
20100 HOUS 77338 3263 D4
E Lake Ln
- HOUS 77336 3121 B6
Lake Rd
100 LMQU 77568 4873 E7
100 TXCY 77591 4873 E7
400 GlsC 77563 5106 D3
400 TKIS 77554 5106 D3
2200 HarC 77562 3692 A6
2300 LMQU 77568 4989 E3
10200 HarC 77070 3255 B6
10200 HOUS 77070 3255 B6
E Lake Rd
14500 MtgC 77372 2681 B1
W Lake Rd
- MtgC 77372 2681 A1
Lake Rdg
2700 CNRO 77304 2236 B6
Lake St
2600 HOUS 77019 3962 A6
3000 HOUS 77098 3962 A7
3600 HOUS 77098 4102 A1
5800 WUNP 77005 4102 A3
Lake Tr
19200 MtgC 77355 2814 B2
Lake Vw
- MtgC 77355 2814 B1
Lake Arbor Ct
10 WDLD 77382 2674 C4
Lake Arbor Dr
1600 ELGO 77586 4382 A7
1600 ELGO 77586 4509 A1
Lakearies Ln
3500 HarC 77449 3815 B3
Lake Arrowhead Dr
1800 FBnC 77469 4234 C6
Lake Athens Ct
4000 FBnC 77469 4234 D5
Lake Ballinger Ln
3800 FBnC 77469 4234 D6
Lake Bank Ct
1500 ELGO 77586 4509 B1
Lake Bardwell Ct
4500 FBnC 77469 4234 D4
Lake Ben Brook Dr
13900 HOUS 77044 3409 B3
Lake Bend Dr
400 FBnC 77479 4367 A5
600 FBnC 77479 4366 E5
18100 HarC 77084 3677 E6
Lakebend Dr
1700 SGLD 77478 4368 D4
N Lakebluff Cir
- FBnC 77494 4093 A4
S Lakebluff Cir
- FBnC 77494 4093 A4
Lakebluff Ct
6000 FBnC 77450 4094 A4
Lake Bluff Dr
1500 ELGO 77586 4509 B1
1600 ELGO 77586 4382 B7
Lake Bluff Ln
- PASD 77507 4382 A5
- PASD 77586 4382 A5
Lake Brazos Ln
3900 FBnC 77469 4234 D5
Lake Breeze Dr
9300 HarC 77375 2965 C2
Lake Breeze Ln
2700 HarC 77532 3410 A6
3600 HarC 77532 3409 D6
Lakebriar Dr
24700 FBnC 77494 3952 D4
Lake Bridge Ct
21700 HarC 77449 3815 A3
Lake Bridge Ln
- LGCY 77573 4631 A4
E Lakebridge Ln
20100 FBnC 77469 4094 D2
W Lakebridge Ln
20200 FBnC 77469 4094 D2
Lake Bridgeport Ln
4300 FBnC 77494 4092 A2
Lakebrook Ct
10300 HarC 77038 3543 C3
Lakebrook Dr
10500 HarC 77038 3543 C2
Lake Buchanan Ct
1500 FBnC 77469 4234 D5
Lake Canyon Ct
3300 FBnC 77478 4367 A1
Lake Catherine Ct
4800 FBnC 77469 4234 D4

STREET
Block City ZIP Map# Grid
Lake Champlain Dr
16600 HOUS 77044 3409 B3
Lake Charlotte Ct
1400 FBnC 77469 4234 D5
Lake Charlotte Ln
1500 FBnC 77469 4234 D5
Lake Chase Dr
2500 KATY 77493 3813 B5
Lake Chelan Ln
17300 HarC 77346 3408 B3
Lake Cir Ln
30500 MtgC 77354 2816 B2
Lakecliff Dr
1400 HOUS 77077 3957 E5
Lakecliffe Dr
15800 HarC 77095 3538 D6
Lake Colony Dr
2800 MSCY 77459 4496 B2
Lake Commons Ct
200 HarC 77336 2975 E7
Lake Commons Dr
300 RSBG 77469 4492 C7
Lake Commons Wy
29200 HarC 77336 3121 B1
29700 HarC 77336 2976 B7
Lake Conroe Dr
9100 MtgC 77304 2236 A2
Lake Country Dr
- PASD 77586 4381 E7
900 TYLV 77586 4381 E7
900 TYLV 77586 4508 E1
Lake Cove Cir
2300 SEBK 77586 4509 C2
Lake Cove Dr
23000 HOUS 77336 3266 C4
Lake Cove Wy
2100 SEBK 77586 4509 C2
Lake Cove Point Ln
- HarC 77379 3111 B4
Lake Creek Cir
4800 MSCY 77459 4496 B3
Lake Creek Dr
- MtgC 77384 2528 D3
1900 HOUS 77339 3118 E3
E Lake Crescent Dr
3100 HOUS 77339 3119 A7
Lakecrest Cir
12500 HarC 77429 3398 A4
Lake Crest Ct
10 KATY 77493 3813 B4
2500 BzaC 77584 4501 A3
Lake Crest Dr
14300 MtgC 77372 2682 D1
14300 SPLD 77372 2682 D1
Lakecrest Dr
2600 BzaC 77584 4501 D5
4200 MSCY 77459 4369 C6
13500 HarC 77429 3398 A4
23000 HOUS 77336 3266 C4
Lakecrest Dr CO-648K
2600 BzaC 77584 4501 C5
Lakecrest Ln
- HarC 77377 3107 C2
- PRLD 77584 4501 E5
Lakecrest Bend Dr
24600 HarC 77493 3813 E4
24600 HarC 77493 3814 A4
Lakecrest Creek Dr
24600 HarC 77493 3813 E4
Lakecrest Forest Dr
2700 HarC 77493 3813 E4
Lakecrest Harbor Dr
2400 HarC 77493 3814 A5
Lakecrest Haven Dr
- HarC 77493 3814 A6
Lakecrest Manor Dr
24900 HarC 77493 3813 E6
24900 HarC 77493 3814 A6
24900 KATY 77493 3813 E6
Lakecrest Pass Ct
24600 HarC 77493 3813 E3
Lakecrest River Dr
2800 HarC 77493 3813 E4
Lakecrest Run Dr
24600 HarC 77493 3813 E3
24600 HarC 77493 3814 A4
Lakecrest Terrace Ct
2400 HarC 77493 3814 A4
Lakecrest Town Dr
24400 HarC 77493 3814 A5
Lakecrest Village Ct
2400 HarC 77493 3814 A5
Lakecrest Village Dr
24400 HarC 77493 3814 A5
Lakecrest Wy Dr
2700 HarC 77493 3813 E4
2700 HarC 77493 3814 A4
Lake Crockett Cir
1400 FBnC 77469 4234 D5
Lake Crossing Ln
3900 FBnC 77494 4093 A4
Lake Crystal Dr
8500 HarC 77095 3538 D5
Lake Cypress Hill Dr
17500 HarC 77429 3252 C1
17500 HarC 77433 3252 C1
Lake Dale Ct
2000 FBnC 77469 4365 B2
Lakedale Dr
15700 HarC 77095 3538 D6
Lake Dale Ln
2500 FBnC 77469 4365 B2
Lake Daniel Ct
4800 FBnC 77469 4234 D4
Lake Dr Ct
10 MtgC 77384 2528 A6
Lake Edge Ct
8100 HOUS 77071 4239 D5
Lake Edge Dr
2000 PRLD 77581 4504 A6
Lake Edge Ln
30600 MtgC 77354 2816 B2
Lake Edinburg Ct
1300 FBnC 77469 4234 D6
Lake Edinburg Ln
3700 FBnC 77469 4234 D6
Lake End Dr
21800 HOUS 77339 3263 D2
Lake Estates Ct
1200 SGLD 77478 4236 E7
3000 MSCY 77459 4496 B2
Lake Estates Dr
1100 SGLD 77478 4236 E7
1100 SGLD 77478 4367 E1
Lake Excursion Ct
13300 HOUS 77044 3409 A4
N Lakefair Ct
11500 FBnC 77469 4092 B6

STREET
Block City ZIP Map# Grid
Lakefair Dr
25900 FBnC 77469 4092 B6
E Lake Falls Cir
2900 MtgC 77386 2969 D3
N Lake Falls Cir
30000 MtgC 77386 2969 B3
S Lake Falls Cir
30000 MtgC 77386 2969 B3
Lake Falls Ct
4100 PASD 77059 4380 D4
N Lake Falls Ln
30100 MtgC 77386 2969 C3
S Lake Falls Ln
30100 MtgC 77386 2969 C3
Lake Fern St
10900 HarC 77064 3540 E1
Lakefield Blvd
10 MtgC 77355 2814 E3
3200 SGLD 77479 4496 A2
Lakefield Dr
5500 HOUS 77033 4244 A5
Lakefield Wy
2400 SGLD 77479 4369 A7
2500 SGLD 77479 4496 A1
Lake Forest Blvd
8800 HOUS 77078 3687 E6
9100 HOUS 77078 3688 A6
Lake Forest Cir
10 HOUS 77078 3688 A6
10 MtgC 77384 2528 A5
Lake Forest Ct
10 MtgC 77384 2528 A6
E Lake Forest Ct
10 MtgC 77384 2528 B5
W Lake Forest Ct
10 MtgC 77384 2528 A6
Lake Forest Dr
10 MtgC 77384 2528 B7
600 FRDW 77546 4629 A3
11700 MtgC 77372 2536 E3
12900 HarC 77429 3398 B5
14000 MtgC 77384 2674 B1
Lake Forest Dr E
10800 MtgC 77384 2528 D7
10800 MtgC 77384 2674 C1
Lake Fountain Dr
1900 FBnC 77494 3952 B5
Lake Front Cir
- SHEH 77380 2822 B3
- WDLD 77380 2822 B3
900 WDLD 77380 2822 A3
Lake Front Ct
2400 LGCY 77573 4508 C7
Lakefront Ct
300 SGLD 77478 4368 D4
4300 MSCY 77459 4369 C6
Lake Front Dr
300 LGCY 77573 4508 C7
Lakefront Dr
1700 MSCY 77459 4369 C6
N Lake Front Dr
2300 LGCY 77573 4508 C7
Lakefront Rd
18900 HarC 77377 3106 E2
Lakefront Terrace Ct
4700 PRLD 77584 4503 A6
Lakefront Terrace Dr
4500 PRLD 77584 4503 A6
S Lake Gabbles Dr
- FBnC 77469 4092 C7
Lake Gardens Ct
2500 HOUS 77339 3118 E6
Lake Gardens Dr
2000 HOUS 77339 3118 E6
Lake Geneva Ct
1700 HOUS 77084 3816 D7
Lake Georgetown Ct
4900 FBnC 77469 4234 C4
Lake Gladewater Ct
4900 FBnC 77469 4234 C3
Lakeglen Ct
300 SGLD 77478 4368 D4
Lake Glen Dr
900 HarC 77336 3121 D6
1000 HOUS 77336 3121 D6
Lake Glen Tr
- HarC 77532 3410 A6
Lake Graham Ln
1500 FBnC 77469 4234 D4
Lake Grayson Dr
800 FBnC 77494 3952 C5
Lakegreen Ct
7000 FBnC 77469 4094 B7
Lakegrove Bnd
11800 HarC 77377 3254 D5
Lakegrove Ct
11800 HarC 77377 3254 D5
Lake Grove Dr
4100 PASD 77586 4381 D7
4100 TYLV 77586 4381 D7
Lakegrove Forest
16000 HarC 77377 3254 D5
Lake Halbert Ln
4500 FBnC 77469 4234 D4
Lake Harbor Ln
100 HOUS 77336 3266 C4
2100 LGCY 77573 4631 C7
2100 LGCY 77573 4752 B1
Lake Harbor Wy
1700 HOUS 77084 3816 C7
Lake Harbor Wy Cir
1700 HOUS 77084 3816 C7
Lakehaven Dr
3200 HOUS 77339 3118 D5
Lake Hawkins Ln
3900 FBnC 77469 4234 D5
Lakehead Ln
7500 FBnC 77469 4094 D6
Lakehill Dr
3000 BzaC 77584 4501 B6
3000 PRLD 77584 4501 B6
Lakehill Park Ct
3900 FBnC 77478 4367 A3
Lakehill Park Ln
13600 FBnC 77478 4366 D3
Lake Hills Dr
1900 HOUS 77339 3118 D4
2200 HOUS 77339 3119 A5
Lakehills View Cir
13600 HarC 77429 3253 C6
Lake Holbrook Ln
1500 FBnC 77469 4234 D5
Lake Hollow Dr
1400 PRLD 77545 4499 C3
Lake Hollow Ln
19500 HarC 77084 3816 A6
19700 HarC 77084 3815 E6

STREET
Block City ZIP Map# Grid
Lake Houston Ln
28900 HarC 77336 3120 C1
Lake Houston Pkwy
- HOUS 77339 3264 E2
2400 HOUS 77339 3119 D5
2400 HOUS 77345 3119 D5
18600 HarC 77532 3410 C6
E Lake Houston Pkwy
21700 HarC 77532 3266 D7
24100 HOUS 77336 3266 C1
25100 HarC 77336 3121 C7
25100 HOUS 77336 3121 C7
N Lake Houston Pkwy
- HarC 77044 3549 B2
- HarC 77044 3550 B5
- HOUS 77044 3550 C5
- MtgC 77365 2974 C6
11600 HarC 77044 3548 D6
11600 HarC 77050 3548 C7
11600 HarC 77078 3548 C7
21600 HarC 77532 3266 C7
S Lake Houston Pkwy
5000 HOUS 77013 3827 E5
5000 HOUS 77013 3828 A4
5000 HOUS 77049 3828 A4
6700 HarC 77049 3828 A1
S Lake Houston Pkwy FM-526
5000 HOUS 77013 3827 E5
5000 HOUS 77013 3828 A4
5000 HOUS 77049 3828 A4
6700 HarC 77049 3828 A1
W Lake Houston Pkwy
- HarC 77044 3408 E7
- HarC 77044 3549 C2
- HarC 77346 3409 A2
- HOUS 77044 3408 E6
- HOUS 77044 3409 A2
- HOUS 77044 3549 E1
- HOUS 77339 3264 E3
- HOUS 77346 3264 E2
18800 HarC 77346 3265 B5
20600 HarC 77346 3264 E4
Lake Hurst Dr
500 BzaC 77584 4374 A7
Lakehurst Dr
7300 HOUS 77087 4245 A2
Lake Iris Dr
15600 HarC 77070 3255 B6
Lake Jacksonville Ln
5000 FBnC 77469 4234 E3
Lake Kemp Ct
4300 FBnC 77469 4234 D5
Lake Kingwood Tr
1700 HOUS 77339 3119 B7
Lake Knoll Ct
4600 FBnC 77479 4496 C4
Lake Lamond Rd
2400 MtgC 77384 2674 E1
2400 WDLD 77384 2674 E2
Lakeland Dr
- HOUS 77025 4241 B1
500 HMBL 77338 3263 A7
9100 HOUS 77025 4101 C7
S Lake Land Dr
300 LGCY 77573 4508 C7
Lakeland Falls Dr
20300 HarC 77433 3251 C6
Lakeland Gardens Ct
22100 HarC 77449 3815 A2
Lakeland Gardens Dr
3300 HarC 77449 3815 A3
Lake Landing Dr
1800 LGCY 77539 4633 E4
2000 LGCY 77539 4634 A3
E Lake Landing Dr
1800 LGCY 77539 4633 E3
Lakelane Dr
3200 HOUS 77338 3263 D4
W Lakelane Dr
19800 HOUS 77338 3263 D4
Lake Lavon Ct
4300 FBnC 77469 4234 D4
Lake Lawn Dr
25700 MtgC 77380 2968 A1
Lake Leaf Pl
10 WDLD 77381 2820 B1
Lake Livingston Dr
13700 HOUS 77044 3409 B4
Lake Lodge Dr
15500 HOUS 77062 4380 C7
15700 HOUS 77062 4507 C1
Lake Loop Dr
15700 HarC 77433 3251 C5
Lake Louise Blvd
17500 HarC 77346 3408 D3
Lake Louise Ct
11400 HarC 77433 3396 B7
Lake Manor Dr
17900 HarC 77084 3677 E6
17900 HarC 77084 3678 A6
Lake Mead Ln
11900 HarC 77346 3408 B3
Lakemeade Ct
13400 FBnC 77478 4366 E2
Lakemeadow Ct
7000 FBnC 77479 4496 B5
Lake Medina Wy
16500 HOUS 77044 3409 B3
Lakemere St
200 HOUS 77079 3958 D4
Lakemere Park Ct
31900 MtgC 77385 2823 B6
Lake Michigan Av
13600 HOUS 77044 3409 B3
E Lakemist Cir
10 WDLD 77381 2675 A7
W Lakemist Cir
10 WDLD 77381 2675 A6
Lake Mist Ct
10 FBnC 77479 4367 A6
7800 HarC 77346 3265 B2
Lakemist Ct
2900 LGCY 77573 4633 A3
Lake Mist Dr
10 FBnC 77479 4366 E6
10 FBnC 77479 4367 A6
12900 HarC 77429 3398 B1
13100 HarC 77429 3254 A7
Lakemist Harbour Dr
10 WDLD 77381 2821 C4
S Lakemist Harbour Dr
10 WDLD 77381 2821 C4
Lakemont Dr
2400 HarC 77039 3545 D3
6600 HOUS 77050 3547 A5
Lakemont Bend Ln
19800 FBnC 77469 4094 B6

STREET
Block City ZIP Map# Grid
akemont Grove Ln
- FBnC 77469 4094 B7
akemont Heights Ln
6800 FBnC 77469 4094 D1
akemont Pointe Ln
- FBnC 77469 4094 B7
aken Dr
- HarC 77429 3253 B7
akenheath Dr
2300 DKSN 77539 4754 A4
ake Oak Dr
3200 HOUS 77345 3120 A4
ake Oaks Dr
18300 HarC 77388 3258 A1
ake Olympia Pkwy
- FBnC 77459 4496 D5
- FBnC 77479 4496 D5
- MSCY 77479 4496 D5
800 MSCY 77459 4498 A4
2500 MSCY 77459 4497 C4
3100 MSCY 77459 4496 E4
ake Palestine Ln
1600 FBnC 77469 4234 D5
ake Park Ct
25000 MtgC 77355 2960 B1
25200 MtgC 77355 2814 B7
ake Park Dr
- SGLD 77478 4237 D6
2500 LMQU 77568 4989 D1
9100 HOUS 77078 3687 E6
9200 HOUS 77028 3687 E6
ake Park Ln
- LGCY 77573 4631 A4
ake Park Tr
20700 HarC 77346 3264 E3
ake Passage Ct
13300 HOUS 77044 3409 A5
ake Path Cir
24200 HarC 77493 3814 A6
ake Pauline Ct
1400 FBnC 77469 4234 D4
ake Pines Dr
3800 HOUS 77339 3119 C3
ake Pinkston Dr
4400 FBnC 77469 4234 D4
ake Pl Dr
5400 HarC 77041 3679 D6
ake Point Ct
- WDLD 77385 2676 B5
100 LGCY 77573 4509 B6
ake Point Dr
100 LGCY 77573 4509 B6
21500 HOUS 77339 3263 E2
ake Pointe Ct
2500 BzaC 77584 4501 C5
ake Pointe Dr
2700 TXCY 77590 4874 E1
ake Pointe Pkwy
- SGLD 77478 4368 B4
akepointe Bend Ln
- HarC 77429 3254 A4
ake Pointe Estate Dr
- FBnC 77494 3952 E5
- FBnC 77494 3953 A5
akepointe Forest Dr
4000 SEBK 77586 4382 B6
akeport Crossing Dr
15400 HarC 77429 3397 C3
ake Promenade Blvd
- HarC 77449 3676 D3
ake Quitman Dr
1700 FBnC 77469 4234 C5
ake Ranch Dr
13100 HOUS 77044 3408 E7
ake Raven Ct
27000 HarC 77433 3537 A1
ake Riata Ln
10600 HarC 77433 3537 D1
ake Ridge Bnd
3300 MtgC 77380 2967 B2
Lakeridge Cir
10 WDLD 77381 2821 C2
ake Ridge Ct
12000 HOUS 77071 4239 D5
akeridge Ct
10 WDLD 77381 2821 A3
akeridge Dr
10 WDLD 77381 2820 E4
10 WDLD 77381 2821 A3
Lakeridge Dr
10 WDLD 77381 2821 A3
Lakeridge Dr
- WDLD 77381 2821 C2
ake Ridge Ln
6400 HarC 77379 3111 D5
akeridge Ln
200 HOUS 77336 3266 C5
akeridge Canyon Dr
3400 FBnC 77478 4366 E2
3900 FBnC 77478 4367 A2
akeridge Park Ln
26800 HarC 77433 3396 A7
26900 HarC 77433 3537 B1
ake Ridge Pl Dr
- HarC 77084 3816 A4
- HarC 77449 3816 A4
ake Robbins Dr
- ORDN 77380 2822 B5
1000 WDLD 77380 2822 A5
2000 WDLD 77380 2821 E4
Lake Rose Ct
17300 HarC 77429 3252 D6
W Lake Rose Ct
17400 HarC 77429 3252 D6
ake Royal Ln
- HarC 77450 3954 A6
ake Run Dr
4300 MSCY 77459 4496 C3
ake Run Ln
7400 FBnC 77469 4094 C6
akesage Ln
7400 FBnC 77469 4094 C6
Lake Sandy Dr
200 HarC 77530 3831 B6
Lake Sandy St
17200 HarC 77530 3831 A6
akes at 610 Dr
8800 HOUS 77054 4242 A2
ake Scene Tr
14100 HOUS 77059 4380 A5
Lakes Gabbles Dr
- FBnC 77469 4092 C7
ake Shade Ct
3700 HOUS 77345 3119 E3
akeshadow Ln
- FBnC 77494 4093 C2
ake Shadows Dr
3200 HarC 77532 3409 E7
Lake Sherwood Dr
20200 HarC 77450 3954 E3
Lakeshire Dr
18500 MtgC 77357 2828 A3
Lakeshire St
18700 HarC 77346 3264 B6
Lake Shoals Dr
- PRLD 77584 4500 D2
Lake Shore Dr
1100 PRLD 77581 4504 E7
2300 LGCY 77573 4508 C7
25000 MtgC 77372 2682 C1
Lakeshore Dr
10 ELGO 77586 4509 A2
100 CNRO 77304 2383 A6
200 TYLV 77586 4509 A2
300 CNRO 77304 2382 E7
600 SGLD 77478 4368 A3
1500 HOUS 77339 3263 C3
17600 HarC 77530 3831 A6
E Lakeshore Dr
19200 MtgC 77355 2814 A2
S Lake Shore Dr
2300 LGCY 77573 4508 C7
W Lakeshore Dr
19300 MtgC 77355 2814 A2
Lakeshore Rdg
12300 HarC 77041 3679 D6
Lakeshore Wy
1600 HOUS 77077 3957 A5
Lakeshore Bend Dr
8800 HOUS 77080 3820 E4
Lakeshore Edge Dr
2100 HOUS 77080 3820 E4
Lakeshore Forest Ct
2100 MSCY 77459 4497 C4
Lakeshore Forest Dr
4100 MSCY 77459 4497 B4
Lakeshore Forest Estates Dr
- MSCY 77459 4497 C4
Lake Shore Harbour Blvd
- MSCY 77459 4497 E6
Lake Shore Harbour Dr
2700 MSCY 77459 4497 D6
Lakeshore Landing Dr
13100 HOUS 77044 3408 E4
13100 HOUS 77044 3409 A4
W Lakeshore Landing Dr
13400 HOUS 77044 3409 A5
Lakeshore Point Ln
7500 RSBG 77469 4492 C7
Lakeshore Ridge Ct
5300 HarC 77041 3679 E7
Lakeshore Terrace Dr
8800 HOUS 77080 3820 E4
Lakeshore Villa Dr
8200 HarC 77346 3265 C3
Lakeshore Vista Dr
- FBnC 77469 4493 A5
Lakeshore Wy Ct
13600 HOUS 77077 3957 A5
Lakeshore Wy Cove
13700 HOUS 77077 3957 B5
Lakeside
- NSUB 77058 4508 C4
Lakeside Blvd
100 SGLD 77478 4368 D3
Lakeside Cross
- FBnC 77494 3952 C5
Lakeside Ct
- MtgC 77380 2967 B1
5000 PASD 77504 4247 E7
Lakeside Ct N
100 HOUS 77339 3262 E1
Lake Side Dr
23100 MtgC 77365 2973 E7
Lakeside Dr
- GlsC 77568 4990 D7
- GLSN 77550 5110 A1
- LMQU 77568 4990 D7
- SEBK 77586 4382 C6
- SEBK 77586 4509 C1
10 GlsC 77563 4990 D7
10 HarC 77530 3969 D1
100 LGCY 77565 4508 E4
900 HarC 77562 3831 D4
2100 HarC 77532 3412 D1
2700 PRLD 77584 4501 C4
6900 HarC 77050 3547 B6
12100 MtgC 77303 2239 E1
20100 MtgC 77365 2825 B6
24700 WlrC 77447 2959 B2
E Lake Side Dr
9100 MtgC 77354 2818 C2
Lakeside Grn
10 WDLD 77382 2673 B7
28600 MtgC 77355 2815 D4
Lakeside Ln
100 HOUS 77339 3262 E1
100 NSUB 77058 4508 C4
500 FRDW 77546 4629 D4
18000 HOUS 77058 4508 C4
Lakeside Lndg
2000 SEBK 77586 4509 C2
Lakeside Ter
2600 SEBK 77586 4509 C3
Lakeside Tr
3200 HOUS 77077 3957 B6
Lakeside Bend Ct
2100 HOUS 77077 3957 A6
Lakeside Bend Dr
13300 HOUS 77077 3956 E6
13400 HOUS 77077 3957 A7
Lakeside Country Club Dr
- HOUS 77042 3958 C6
Lakeside Cove
19000 HarC 77094 3955 B3
Lakeside Enclave
1500 HOUS 77077 3957 B5
Lakeside Estate Ct
10 MSCY 77459 4497 B5
Lakeside Estates Dr
400 HOUS 77042 3958 C6
Lakeside Forest Dr
8800 HarC 77088 3542 D6
Lakeside Forest Ln
10800 HOUS 77042 3958 B4
Lakeside Gables Dr
10000 HarC 77065 3539 E3
Lakeside Manor Ln
7500 BzaC 77581 4502 A3
Lakeside Meadow Ct
4700 MSCY 77459 4369 B5
Lakeside Meadow Dr
4300 MSCY 77459 4369 B6
Lakeside Oaks Dr
100 HOUS 77042 3958 C4
Lakeside Park Dr
11600 HOUS 77077 3958 A7
Lakeside Pl Dr
- HOUS 77042 3958 B5
11300 HOUS 77077 3958 A5
Lakeside Plaza Dr
1800 SGLD 77479 4368 A5
Lakeside Terrace Dr
12600 HOUS 77044 3550 A1
14200 HOUS 77044 3409 A7
Lakeside Valley Dr
100 HOUS 77042 3958 C4
Lakeside View Dr
19400 HarC 77388 3112 C6
Lakeside View Ln
4800 HarC 77396 3407 C7
Lakeside View Wy
14400 HarC 77429 3395 E1
Lakeside Village Dr
2600 MSCY 77459 4497 A4
Lakes of Pkwy
- HOUS 77077 3957 A5
Lakes of Bridgewater Dr
3500 HarC 77449 3815 B1
Lakes of Cypress Forest Dr
18700 HarC 77388 3113 C2
Lakes of Fairhaven Dr
20800 HarC 77433 3251 B3
Lakes of Mission Grv
10 FBnC 77469 4233 C5
Lakes of Pine Forest Ct
4700 HarC 77084 3678 A7
Lakes of Pine Forest Dr
17600 HarC 77084 3678 A7
17900 HarC 77084 3677 C7
Lakes of Rosehill Dr
- HarC 77429 3252 C6
Lakes on Elderidge Dr
- HarC 77041 3679 D6
Lake Sophie Ct
16800 HOUS 77044 3409 B3
Lakespire Dr
20000 HarC 77449 3676 E2
Lake Spring Ct
20300 HarC 77433 3251 C6
Lake Springs Wy
25700 HarC 77373 3113 E4
Lakespur Dr
800 FBnC 77479 4367 B6
Lake Star Dr
3900 LGCY 77539 4633 E4
3900 LGCY 77539 4634 A4
Lake Sterling Gate Dr
10 HarC 77379 3256 A5
Lakestone Blvd
- MSCY 77459 4496 B3
Lake Stone Ct
19700 HarC 77377 3106 D5
Lakestone Dr
16000 HarC 77377 3254 C5
Lake Stream Dr
3100 HOUS 77339 3119 C2
Lake Sydney Dr
- FBnC 77494 3952 C5
Lake Tahoe Ct
14000 HOUS 77044 3409 B3
Lake Tahoe Ln
38300 MtgC 77355 2815 D1
Lake Terrace Ct
1800 WDLD 77380 2968 A1
4200 MSCY 77459 4369 C7
Lake Terrace Dr
12800 HarC 77041 3679 D6
Lake Texoma Dr
9300 HarC 77433 3537 B4
Lake Timber Ct
- HarC 77429 3254 A4
Lake Trail Blvd
- SGLD 77478 4367 D1
Lake Trail Dr
14000 SGLD 77478 4237 A7
14100 SGLD 77478 4236 E7
14100 SGLD 77478 4367 D1
Laketree Ln
22900 HarC 77373 3115 D6
Lake Tyler St
10400 HOUS 77034 4378 C3
Lakeview
- HarC 77389 2966 E4
Lakeview Blvd
100 PASD 77586 4508 D2
Lake View Cir
300 ELGO 77586 4382 A7
Lakeview Cir
100 FRDW 77546 4629 E4
700 HOUS 77339 3263 C2
18400 HOUS 77084 3816 C7
Lake View Ct
3700 MSCY 77459 4497 A3
17400 PTVL 77372 2682 D7
Lakeview Ct
15100 MtgC 77302 2677 A2
17400 PTVL 77372 2682 D7
17900 MtgC 77365 2825 E7
Lake View Dr
2800 MSCY 77459 4497 A3
3800 PRLD 77581 4504 E7
Lakeview Dr
- MtgC 77302 2676 E1
10 BzaC 77511 4868 A6
10 GLSN 77551 5222 A1
10 HOUS 77365 2974 E6
100 SGLD 77478 4368 A2
200 CNRO 77301 2384 D5
1300 PASD 77586 4382 A6
1300 TYLV 77586 4382 A6
1700 HarC 77520 3970 D1
3500 MtgC 77303 2239 D7
9700 MtgC 77365 2825 E7
13500 HarC 77429 3398 D3
14900 HarC 77064 3540 E6
14900 JRSV 77040 3540 E6
15100 MtgC 77302 2677 A1
15600 JRSV 77040 3680 C1
20100 HOUS 77338 3261 B5
20400 HarC 77338 3261 B4
24700 PTVL 77372 2682 D7
25500 WlrC 77447 2813 C6
N Lakeview Dr
25100 PTVL 77372 2682 E6
S Lakeview Dr
17200 PTVL 77372 2682 E7
Lake View Ln
- HarC 77396 3407 A7
Lakeview Pl
10 HarC 77070 3254 E7
10 HarC 77070 3255 A7
Lakeview Rd
25000 FBnC 77494 3952 D5
Lakeview Bend Ln
31100 MtgC 77386 2823 B7
Lakeview Haven Dr
- HarC 77095 3538 C7
6800 HarC 77084 3678 C3
6800 HarC 77095 3678 C1
Lake View Pointe Ct
- FBnC 77450 4094 C2
Lake Villa Dr
700 TYLV 77586 4508 E1
2800 MSCY 77459 4497 D6
Lake Village Dr
- HOUS 77339 3118 C7
2300 HOUS 77339 3119 A7
N Lake Village Dr
- FBnC 77450 3953 E5
- FBnC 77494 3953 E5
22100 HarC 77450 3954 A5
S Lake Village Dr
3100 FBnC 77450 3953 E7
Lakeville Ct
2700 HOUS 77339 3118 E6
Lakeville Dr
600 HarC 77339 3118 C5
600 HOUS 77339 3118 C5
Lake Vista Cir
4100 MSCY 77459 4496 C4
Lake Vista Dr
12300 HarC 77377 3254 B4
Lake Vista Ln
13600 HarC 77377 3254 B2
Lake Walk Ct
4300 MSCY 77459 4496 C3
Lakewater Dr
1300 PRLD 77545 4499 D4
25700 HarC 77336 3121 B7
Lakeway Ct
3200 PRLD 77584 4501 E5
12000 HOUS 77071 4239 D5
Lakeway Dr
- SGLD 77478 4236 E7
2100 FRDW 77546 4629 C7
2100 LGCY 77573 4632 E1
2600 SEBK 77586 4382 C6
22300 HarC 77373 3260 C1
22500 HarC 77373 3115 C7
Lakeway Ln
3300 PRLD 77584 4501 E5
Lakeway Pk
17100 HarC 77070 3255 A4
Lakeway St
10 PNVL 77304 2237 B2
Lakeway View Ln
9200 HarC 77396 3406 E7
9200 HarC 77396 3407 A7
Lake Way Village Dr
700 HOUS 77336 3266 C2
Lake White Rock Dr
13700 HOUS 77044 3409 B3
Lake Wichita Ln
4800 FBnC 77469 4234 D4
Lake Wilderness Ln
1600 HOUS 77345 3120 D6
Lakewind Ct
2100 LGCY 77573 4631 C7
Lake Wind Dr
2200 PRLD 77584 4500 D2
Lakewind Ln
2100 LGCY 77573 4631 B7
Lakewind St
7700 HOUS 77061 4245 C1
Lake Windcrest Blvd
10900 MtgC 77354 2671 E4
Lakewind Park Ct
23100 FBnC 77469 4093 C7
Lakewind Park Ln
23400 FBnC 77469 4093 D6
Lakewinds Dr
1700 MSCY 77459 4369 C6
Lake Windsor Cir
- CNRO 77384 2676 A3
10 CNRO 77384 2675 E3
Lake Winnsboro Ln
4500 FBnC 77469 4234 E4
Lakewood
3100 HOUS 77093 3686 A4
Lakewood Bnd
- HarC 77429 3398 D2
Lakewood Cross
- HarC 77070 3399 A1
Lakewood Ct
4200 MSCY 77459 4369 C7
Lakewood Dr
1100 MtgC 77362 2816 C6
4200 MSCY 77459 4621 D1
4200 PASD 77504 4247 E7
4300 MSCY 77459 4497 D7
4300 PASD 77504 4248 A7
7200 HOUS 77016 3686 E5
7600 HOUS 77016 3687 A4
8700 HOUS 77078 3687 E4
10200 CHTW 77385 2822 E4
11900 HarC 77070 3398 D2
24500 MtgC 77372 2682 D1
24800 SPLD 77372 2682 D1
N Lakewood Dr
11700 MtgC 77372 2536 E3
11800 MtgC 77372 2537 A3
Lakewood Ests
11400 HarC 77070 3398 E2
Lakewood Ln
10 SEBK 77586 4509 C3
Lakewood Pl
11500 HarC 77070 3398 E1
Lakewood St
100 BYTN 77520 3971 B2
3700 HOUS 77093 3686 B4
Lakewood Tr
11800 HarC 77377 3254 D5
Lakewood Vil
1500 BYTN 77520 3971 C2
Lake Woodbridge Ct
14900 FBnC 77478 4236 D5
Lake Woodbridge Dr
10700 FBnC 77478 4236 D5
Lakewood Cove
11400 HarC 77070 3398 E1
11400 HarC 77070 3399 B1
Lakewood Crossing Blvd
13800 HarC 77070 3398 E2
14000 HarC 77070 3399 A1
Lakewood Crossing Dr
- HarC 77070 3255 A5
- HarC 77377 3255 A5
- HOUS 77070 3254 E5
- HOUS 77070 3255 A5
Lakewood Crossing Dr
- HOUS 77377 3254 E5
- HOUS 77377 3255 A5
11600 HarC 77377 3254 E5
Lakewood Elementary Dr
15300 HarC 77070 3254 D6
15600 HarC 77377 3254 D6
Lakewood Field Ct
11300 HarC 77377 3254 E5
Lakewood Field Dr
16200 HarC 77377 3254 D4
Lakewood Forest Dr
13700 HarC 77429 3398 D2
14200 HarC 77070 3254 E7
14200 HarC 77070 3398 E1
15200 HarC 77377 3254 E7
E Lakewood Forest North Ct
11400 HarC 77377 3254 D4
W Lakewood Forest North Ct
11500 HarC 77377 3254 E6
Lakewood Glade Ct
12200 HarC 77429 3398 B2
Lakewood Glen Ct
12100 HarC 77429 3398 B2
17400 HarC 77375 3255 A3
Lakewood Grove Dr
16200 HarC 77377 3254 D5
Lakewood Hills Dr
11800 HarC 77377 3254 C4
Lake Woodlands Dr
- WDLD 77381 2820 D2
- WDLD 77381 2821 C4
- WDLD 77382 2820 B2
1100 WDLD 77380 2822 A4
1800 WDLD 77380 2821 E4
Lakewood Manor Dr
12200 HarC 77377 3254 B7
Lakewood Meadow Dr
13300 HarC 77429 3398 B3
Lakewood Oaks Dr
10700 FBnC 77478 4237 A4
Lakewood Pointe Dr
2300 SEBK 77586 4509 C3
Lakewoods Dr
1500 HarC 77532 3410 C5
Lakewood Springs Dr
- HarC 77377 3254 C4
Lakewood Trace Dr
12200 HarC 77429 3398 B2
Lakewood Valley Ct
12200 HarC 77429 3398 B2
Lakewood View Ct
19900 HarC 77450 3954 E6
Lakewood Villa Dr
12100 HarC 77377 3254 C6
12100 HarC 77429 3254 C6
Lakewood West Dr
11900 HarC 77429 3398 D2
Lakeworth Dr
8900 HOUS 77088 3683 A1
Lake Wy Dr
- PASD 77586 4382 A6
- TYLV 77586 4382 A6
W Lakin Av
900 PASD 77506 4106 E4
Lakin St
1200 HOUS 77007 3962 D2
Lakota Dr
19100 HarC 77449 3677 B4
Lakota Tr
5300 HarC 77388 3112 A2
Laleu Ln
12500 MSCY 77071 4239 E7
La Loma Dr
15400 FBnC 77083 4096 C6
La Luna Dr
16200 HarC 77083 4096 A5
16300 HarC 77083 4095 E5
La Mancha Dr
15200 HarC 77083 4096 C5
Lamar
13800 HarC 77377 3108 E3
Lamar Dr
100 PASD 77502 4247 A1
1100 RHMD 77469 4491 E3
1200 LMQU 77568 4989 D1
2000 PASD 77502 4107 A7
2100 RSBG 77469 4491 E4
2100 RSBG 77471 4491 E4
3000 MSCY 77459 4370 A7
Lamar Ln
25100 MtgC 77365 3117 C1
Lamar St
400 HOUS 77002 3963 B4
1200 HOUS 77010 3963 C5
2000 HOUS 77003 3963 E6
3800 HOUS 77023 3964 A6
7300 HOUS 77011 4105 A1
12400 STFE 77510 4871 A5
W Lamar St
3200 HOUS 77019 3962 C4
Lamar Fleming Av
6400 HOUS 77030 4102 D4
Lamaster Ln
22200 HarC 77373 3113 E1
Lamb Cr
6000 FBnC 77459 4497 A7
Lamb St
900 HOUS 77019 3963 A4
Lamb Brook Ln
10100 PRLD 77584 4501 A3
Lambert St
12300 HarC 77044 3688 E6
12300 HarC 77044 3689 A6
Lambeth Dr
2600 PRLD 77584 4501 A2
Lambeth Palace Dr
12200 HarC 77066 3401 C4
Lamborghini Dr
3100 HarC 77396 3406 E5
3100 HMBL 77396 3406 E4
Lambourne Cir
1300 HarC 77379 3255 C2
Lambright Rd
8600 HOUS 77075 4376 E2
8600 HOUS 77075 4377 A2
E Lambuth Ln
300 DRPK 77536 4249 C2
W Lambuth Ln
7400 DRPK 77536 4249 B2
S Lameerie Wy
10 WDLD 77382 2820 A1
La Mer Ln
3300 HarC 77388 3112 E3
N Lamerie Wy
10 WDLD 77382 2820 A1
La Merl Dr
5100 TXCY 77591 4755 E4
5100 TXCY 77591 4756 A3
Lamesa Av
1300 HOUS 77017 4106 D6
1300 PASD 77506 4106 D6
La Mesa Dr
7300 HarC 77083 4096 B6
Lamesa Dr
1300 MtgC 77384 2529 B6
Lamina Ln
2100 HOUS 77017 4246 C1
La Mirada Dr
6900 HarC 77083 4096 C5
Lamkin Rd
9000 HarC 77049 3690 E4
Lamond Ln
8300 HarC 77095 3539 B6
Lamont Cir
4300 BLAR 77401 4101 C3
Lamonte Ct
1300 SGLD 77479 4367 C6
La Monte Ln
800 HOUS 77018 3823 A2
1000 HOUS 77018 3822 E2
Lamonte Ln
4200 HOUS 77092 3822 B2
5100 HOUS 77092 3821 E2
Lampasas Dr
21700 GLSN 77554 5441 A5
Lampasas St
5300 HOUS 77056 4100 E1
Lamplighter Cir
3800 MSCY 77459 4497 C3
Lamplighter St
16400 HarC 77532 3552 B2
Lamplight Trail Dr
1200 HarC 77450 3953 E4
Lampost Hill Ct
5000 HarC 77449 3676 D6
Lamppost Ct
7800 HarC 77064 3541 E5
Lamppost Ln
8300 HarC 77064 3541 E5
Lamppost Pl
3700 PRLD 77584 4502 D6
Lamprey St
11700 HOUS 77099 4238 A4
Lamps Glow Pl
10 WDLD 77382 2674 C5
Lampson Manor Ct
15400 HarC 77044 3549 E2
Lampton Cir
4300 BLAR 77401 4101 C3
Lampwick Cir
20800 HarC 77388 3112 A3
Lamson Ct
1000 HarC 77373 3113 D1
Lana Ln
10 HOUS 77027 3961 C7
20200 MtgC 77365 3117 D4
27100 ORDN 77385 2822 C5
E Lana Ln
26900 ORDN 77385 2822 C5
Lanai St
100 TKIS 77554 5106 C4
Lana Lee Ct
17000 HarC 77084 3678 A2
Lanark Ln
4000 HOUS 77025 4101 C5
Lancashire St
3600 HOUS 77027 4101 B1
Lancaster Dr
800 FRDW 77546 4629 C3
Lancaster Ln
300 LGCY 77573 4630 C7
2500 PASD 77506 4107 E5
2700 PASD 77506 4108 A4
Lancaster St
5200 HOUS 77087 4105 A7
5800 HOUS 77087 4245 A1
Lancaster Hill Ln
- HarC 77073 3259 B4
Lancaster Lake Dr
900 HarC 77073 3259 A4
Lancaster Park Ct
1800 FBnC 77545 4498 D7
Lancaster Pl Dr
16400 FBnC 77083 4095 C7
16400 FBnC 77083 4096 C5
Lancaster Walk Dr
3600 HarC 77066 3401 C4
Lance Av
7000 PASD 77505 4249 A3
Lance Cir
15000 HOUS 77053 4372 D4
Lance Ln
2400 STAF 77477 4370 A4
Lance St
3800 HarC 77562 3833 A1
Lancefield Ct
3100 FBnC 77494 3953 B7
E Lance Leaf Rd
10 WDLD 77381 2821 A6
W Lance Leaf Rd
10 WDLD 77381 2820 E6
10 WDLD 77381 2821 A7
Lancelot
3200 BYTN 77521 3973 E2
Lancelot Dr
12200 HOUS 77031 4239 A6
Lancelot Ln
10 CNRO 77304 2529 D1
Lancelot Oaks Dr
22100 HarC 77339 3118 C5
Lanceoak Ct
13900 HarC 77039 3546 A3
Lance Pine Pl
10 WDLD 77382 2673 E5
Lancer Pk
2400 MtgC 77385 2823 B6
Lancewood Dr
25500 HarC 77373 3114 C2
Land Rd
13000 HOUS 77047 4374 B2
Land St
2200 PRLD 77584 4501 B2
Landa Ln
3700 HOUS 77023 4104 D4
Landau Park Ct
16200 HarC 77379 3256 B5
Landau Park Ln
8000 HarC 77379 3256 B5
Landcircle Ct
2100 SGLD 77478 4237 C5
Landcross Dr
12200 HOUS 77099 4237 E4
Lander Ln
2100 HOUS 77057 3960 B6
Landera Ct
2600 BzaC 77584 4501 A5
Landers Dr
2100 SGLD 77479 4494 C1
Landfair St
14000 HarC 77037 3544 E5
14800 HarC 77060 3544 E4
Landfall Ln
500 MtgC 77302 2530 D5
6000 HOUS 77087 4244 E1
Landfill Rd
- TMBL 77375 2964 B5
Landfill Two Rd
- HarC 77338 3260 E4
- HOUS 77338 3260 E4
- HOUS 77338 3261 A4
Land Grant Ct
100 FBnC 77469 4365 C3
Land Grant Dr
300 FBnC 77469 4365 C3
Landing Blvd
100 LGCY 77573 4631 B5
2100 LGCY 77573 4752 A1
Landing Brook Dr
18000 HarC 77346 3408 A2
Landing Edge Ln
2900 LGCY 77539 4752 E5
Landing Pines Tr
17600 HarC 77084 3817 A1
Landing Point Dr
- PRLD 77545 4499 D4
Landing View Ct
5400 BzaC 77583 4623 D4
Landing Wy Ct
2100 HarC 77373 3114 D5
Landing Wy Dr
- LGCY 77573 4631 A4
24000 HarC 77373 3114 D4
Landmark Dr
- HOUS 77045 4372 D1
1800 FBnC 77469 4365 C4
2700 HarC 77521 3834 D4
3800 MSCY 77459 4369 D6
13000 HOUS 77045 4241 E7
Landmore Ct
1600 HarC 77450 3954 C4
1600 HarC 77450 3955 B5
Landolt St
200 WEBS 77598 4631 D1
Landon Ln
11000 HNCV 77024 3959 E2
11000 HNCV 77024 3960 A2
11000 PNPV 77024 3959 E2
Landon Brook Ct
19800 HarC 77450 3954 E6
Landon Creek Ln
5700 HarC 77449 3676 E5
Landon Lake Dr
9600 PRLD 77584 4501 B4
Landon Oaks Dr
- HarC 77095 3538 A7
17400 HarC 77095 3537 B6
Landon Park Dr
3800 HarC 77449 3815 D2
Landon Point Cir
1900 HarC 77450 3953 E5
Landor
5600 HOUS 77028 3825 D1
Landor St
- HOUS 77016 3825 D1
6700 HOUS 77028 3825 D1
Landover Ln
2500 HarC 77493 3814 B4
10700 HOUS 77099 4238 B4
Landrum Av
500 LGCY 77573 4632 A1
Landrum Ln
10 HOUS 77489 4371 A7
Landrum Point Ln
- HarC 77388 3113 B7
- HarC 77388 3258 B1
Landry Blvd
9000 HarC 77379 3255 C4
9700 HarC 77070 3255 C4
Landsbury Cir
11000 HOUS 77099 4238 C4
Landsbury Ct
11000 HOUS 77099 4238 C4
Landsbury Dr
10200 HOUS 77099 4238 C4
Landscape Ct
10 CNRO 77301 2384 E6
Landscape Wy
2100 FBnC 77469 4365 C2
Landsdowne Ct
3500 BzaC 77584 4501 C4
Landsdowne Dr
9000 HOUS 77096 4240 C1
11400 HOUS 77035 4240 C6
Landsdowne Pointe Ct
1300 HarC 77379 3110 B5
Landsdowne Pointe Dr
10500 HarC 77379 3110 B6
Landsdown Ridge Wy
12100 HarC 77346 3408 C1
Lands End Cir
11300 HOUS 77099 4238 B4
Lands End Dr
10200 HOUS 77099 4238 B4
Landshire Dr
20300 HMBL 77338 3262 C4
23300 MtgC 77357 2828 A2
Landshire Bend Ln
4100 HOUS 77048 4374 D4
Landston Dr
- HarC 77090 3258 D7
Lands Walk Dr
- HOUS 77099 4238 B3
Land View Dr
15800 HarC 77073 3259 B5
Landward Ln
- HarC 77066 3401 B7
Landwood Dr
9200 HOUS 77040 3682 B3
N Lane Cir
12000 HarC 77086 3542 C5
Lane Dr
100 RSBG 77471 4491 D3
800 RSBG 77469 4491 D4
W Lane Dr
2600 HOUS 77027 3961 C7
Lane Ln
100 ORDN 77386 2822 B6
Lane Rd
10 TXCY 77591 4873 B6

STREET
Block City ZIP Map# Grid

S Lane Rd
10 TXCY 77591 4873 B6
Lane St
- HarC 77532 3411 A5
7900 HOUS 77029 3965 B4
10100 GNPK 77547 3966 A4
10100 JTCY 77029 3966 B4
10300 GNPK 77029 3966 B4
10600 HOUS 77016 3687 A3
Lanecrest Ln
500 PNPV 77024 3959 E3
Lanell
- HOUS 77043 3819 E3
Lanell Ln
8600 SPVL 77055 3821 A6
Lanell St
700 DRPK 77536 4109 C6
Lanesborough Dr
3500 MSCY 77459 4369 D4
Lanesend Pl
10 WDLD 77382 2819 D2
Lanes End St
10 BYTN 77520 4113 A1
Laneside Dr
9200 HarC 77379 3255 E5
Laneview Dr
10500 HarC 77070 3399 A2
12200 HarC 77070 3398 C1
Laneview Rd
22700 WlrC 77445 2954 D1
Lanewell St
- HOUS 77029 3965 D4
9700 HOUS 77029 3966 A4
Lanewood Dr
8300 HOUS 77016 3686 E6
Laney Wy
9500 FBnC 77478 4236 A2
Lang Rd
3300 HOUS 77092 3821 C2
W Lang St
1200 ALVN 77511 4867 A1
1800 ALVN 77511 4866 E1
Langbourne Dr
14000 HOUS 77077 3956 E3
Langbrook Ct
16000 HarC 77084 3678 C4
Langcart St
15700 HarC 77530 3969 A1
Langdale Rd
9600 HOUS 77076 3685 C5
Langdon Ln
6600 HOUS 77074 4100 A6
7100 HOUS 77074 4099 E6
7900 HOUS 77036 4099 C6
9500 HOUS 77036 4098 E6
11200 HOUS 77072 4098 B7
Langfield Ct
8800 HOUS 77040 3682 A3
Langfield Rd
- HOUS 77040 3821 A1
- HOUS 77092 3821 A1
5800 HOUS 77040 3682 A4
5800 HOUS 77092 3682 A4
Langford Ln
12600 STFE 77510 4871 A6
Langham Ct
10 SHEH 77381 2821 E1
Langham Dr
6500 HarC 77084 3678 D3
Langham Wy
6500 HarC 77084 3677 E3
Langham Creek Dr
1200 HOUS 77084 3817 A7
1200 HOUS 77084 3956 A1
Langham Creek Estates Dr
- HarC 77084 3678 B4
Langham Mist Ln
6000 HarC 77084 3678 C3
Langhamwood Ln
15900 HarC 77084 3678 C3
Langham Wy Dr
5800 HarC 77084 3677 E4
Langhorne Ct
5500 FBnC 77450 4094 B3
Langley Ct
2500 LGCY 77573 4631 B7
Langley Rd
2300 HOUS 77093 3685 D3
3600 HarC 77093 3686 B3
3600 HOUS 77093 3686 B3
4900 HarC 77016 3686 B3
4900 HOUS 77016 3686 B3
7300 HOUS 77016 3687 A3
7500 HarC 77389 2966 A3
Langley Springs Ct
16800 HarC 77095 3538 B3
Langley Springs Dr
9300 HarC 77095 3538 A4
Langmont Ln
21500 HarC 77449 3676 D5
Langsbury Ct
3900 HarC 77084 3816 E2
Langsbury Dr
18100 HarC 77084 3816 D2
Langston Av
7500 SGLD 77479 4367 D6
Langston Rd
10500 MTBL 77520 3835 D1
Langston St
2200 HOUS 77007 3961 E1
Langton Ct
700 HarC 77450 3954 D2
Langtree Ln
11600 MtgC 77303 2239 C7
Langtry Ln
4300 HOUS 77041 3820 D1
4400 HOUS 77041 3681 D7
Langtry St
7300 HOUS 77040 3682 A7
Langwick Dr
800 HOUS 77060 3403 D5
Langwood Dr
600 HOUS 77079 3957 B2
Lanham Dr
23000 HarC 77450 3953 D2
Lanham Ln
8000 HOUS 77075 4376 D2
Lanibeth St
- HarC 77396 3546 E1
5400 HarC 77032 3546 D1
Lanier Dr
1500 LGCY 77573 4631 A6
6500 HOUS 77005 4102 C4
6500 HOUS 77030 4102 C4
Lanier Glen Ln
- HarC 77047 4374 C4
Lanis St
5200 GlsC 77539 4633 C6
Lanis St
5200 TXCY 77539 4633 C6
Lanl St
500 HarC 77562 3692 E7
Lanning Dr
24300 HarC 77493 3814 A6
Lanny Ln
12300 HOUS 77077 3957 E4
La Noche Dr
7100 HarC 77083 4096 B6
Lanrin Ct
- HarC 77044 3689 C4
Lansbury Dr
11500 HOUS 77099 4238 B4
Lansdale Dr
10100 HOUS 77036 4238 E1
10100 HOUS 77099 4238 D1
E Lansdown Cir
10 WDLD 77382 2819 D3
N Lansdown Cir
10 WDLD 77382 2819 E3
W Lansdown Cir
10 WDLD 77382 2819 D3
Lansdown Dr
5600 HarC 77049 3828 D4
Lansdowne Dr
1800 FBnC 77469 4365 C3
Lansing Cir
2400 BzaC 77584 4501 A5
Lansing Ct
2700 BzaC 77584 4501 A5
Lansing St
1200 HOUS 77023 3964 D7
1300 HOUS 77023 4104 C1
Lansing Cove Dr
10 FBnC 77545 4498 D6
Lansing Crest Cir
200 HarC 77015 3829 B6
Lansing Crest Dr
14500 HarC 77015 3829 B5
Lansing Field Ln
1300 HarC 77073 3403 C2
Lansing Hollow Ln
13100 HarC 77014 3402 A1
Lansing Ridge Ln
20800 HarC 77449 3815 C2
Lanswick Dr
15400 HOUS 77062 4506 E2
Lantana Ct
4800 SGLD 77479 4367 E7
Lantana Dr
200 TXCY 77591 4873 B6
8000 CmbC 77520 3835 D3
17200 SGLD 77479 4367 E7
22200 MtgC 77355 2960 D2
22200 SGCH 77355 2960 D2
Lantana St
5000 HOUS 77017 4246 A1
Lantana Tr
10 WDLD 77382 2675 C7
Lantana Wy
- FBnC 77479 4494 B4
Lantana Branch Ln
14300 HarC 77396 3547 C2
Lantana Creek Ct
5300 FBnC 77494 4093 B7
Lantana Estates Ct
1200 FBnC 77545 4622 E1
Lantana Ridge Ct
20600 HarC 77433 3251 B3
Lantana Woods Ln
- HarC 77433 3537 D7
Lantern Ln
1900 MSCY 77459 4497 C2
3400 BYTN 77521 3972 A1
12100 MtgC 77303 2239 D7
12100 MtgC 77362 2963 B1
13800 HarC 77015 3828 E5
13900 HarC 77015 3829 A6
25600 MtgC 77357 2828 E5
25700 MtgC 77357 2829 A5
Lantern Bay Ln
3100 HarC 77449 3815 A2
Lantern Bend Dr
300 HOUS 77090 3258 D3
Lantern Cove Ln
18800 HarC 77375 3255 A1
Lantern Creek Ct
8400 MtgC 77303 2239 D3
Lantern Creek Ln
15000 HarC 77068 3257 C5
Lantern Elm St
14400 HarC 77429 3395 D1
Lantern Hills Dr
22800 HarC 77339 3118 D5
Lantern Hollow Pl
10 WDLD 77381 2820 C2
Lantern Lake Ct
500 BzaC 77584 4374 A6
Lantern Point Dr
8200 HOUS 77054 4102 B7
8300 HOUS 77054 4242 B1
Lantern Springs Ln
20500 HarC 77433 3676 D1
Lantern Trail Ct
- MSCY 77459 4497 C2
Lantern Trail Dr
- MSCY 77459 4497 C3
Lantern Village Ln
19800 HarC 77450 3955 A5
Lantry Wy
10500 HarC 77038 3543 C2
Lanville Ln
3100 HarC 77449 3815 E3
Lanyard Pl
3300 GLSN 77554 5332 E1
16900 HarC 77532 3552 B1
Lanyard Pointe Cir
2000 LGCY 77573 4508 E6
La Paloma Blvd
2600 PRLD 77581 4504 B3
La Paloma Dr
15200 HarC 77083 4096 B5
La Paloma Estates Dr
18500 HarC 77377 3106 D7
18500 HarC 77433 3106 D7
18500 HarC 77433 3251 E1
Lapas Dr
3700 HOUS 77023 4104 D5
La Paseo St
6700 HOUS 77087 4244 D1
7200 HOUS 77087 4245 A1
La Paz St
4600 PASD 77504 4248 A4
4600 PASD 77505 4248 A4
Lapeer Ct
17000 HarC 77379 3256 B3
La Perla Dr
11400 HOUS 77048 4244 C7
Lapis Creek Ln
22000 FBnC 77450 4093 E3
22000 FBnC 77450 4094 D2
Lapis Meadow Dr
7200 HarC 77433 3677 B1
Lapis Park Ln
32500 MtgC 77385 2823 B7
Lapis River Dr
16500 HarC 77379 3257 A2
Lapis Spring Dr
- PRLD 77584 4500 B2
La Pl Ct
16400 FBnC 77083 4095 E6
La Pl Dr
7400 FBnC 77083 4095 E6
La Plata Dr
11300 HOUS 77048 4244 C6
La Porte Frwy
- HOUS - 4106 C4
- PASD - 4106 D4
7900 HOUS 77012 4105 C3
9300 HOUS 77017 4105 E4
La Porte Frwy SR-225
- HOUS - 4105 E4
- HOUS - 4106 C4
- PASD - 4106 D4
7900 HOUS 77012 4105 C3
La Porte Hwy
- HOUS - 4105 E4
La Porte Hwy SR-225
- HOUS - 4105 E4
La Porte Rd
8800 HOUS 77012 4105 D3
La Porte Freeway Frontage Rd
- HOUS 77012 4105 D3
9400 HOUS 77017 4106 A4
Lapstone Dr
3400 HOUS 77082 4097 C2
Lapwick
- HarC 77379 3255 D3
Lapwing Ct
10 WDLD 77381 2674 E7
Lapwing Dr
1700 MSCY 77489 4497 C1
La Quinta Dr
100 PNVL 77304 2237 A2
2300 MSCY 77459 4370 A7
2600 MSCY 77459 4497 A2
La Quinta Ln
14800 HOUS 77079 3957 C2
Lara Brook Ct
2900 FBnC 77494 3953 B7
E Larah Ln
19100 HarC 77094 3955 B1
W Larah Ln
200 HarC 77094 3955 B1
Laramie St
6100 HarC 77396 3546 E2
6200 HarC 77396 3547 A2
Laramie River Ct
5800 HarC 77449 3676 E4
Laramie River Tr
20000 HarC 77449 3676 E4
La Rana Dr
14700 HarC 77083 4096 D6
Larboard Ct
17000 HarC 77532 3552 A1
Larch Dr
3700 BYTN 77521 3971 E2
3700 BYTN 77521 3972 A2
Larch Ln
4500 BLAR 77401 4101 B3
Larch Rd
4500 BYTN 77521 3971 D2
Larchbrook Dr
6200 HarC 77049 3828 D3
Larch Creek Ct
10100 HarC 77044 3689 C3
Larch Grove Ct
22300 HarC 77375 3110 D3
Larchmont Rd
1800 HOUS 77019 3961 E6
1900 HOUS 77027 3961 E6
Larchmount Ln
- HOUS 77019 3961 E6
- HOUS 77027 3961 E6
Larchwood Dr
16500 HOUS 77396 3406 A4
Larcom St
1000 LMQU 77568 4990 B2
Laredo Av
8100 HOUS 77029 3965 B1
Laredo Cross
- FBnC 77469 4365 B3
Laredo Dr
600 MAGA 77354 2669 A4
Laredo Rd
10 BYTN 77520 3972 C6
Laredo St
10 BYTN 77520 3972 C7
6300 HOUS 77020 3964 E1
6900 HOUS 77020 3965 A1
13700 HarC 77015 3967 E1
14100 HarC 77015 3968 A1
Laredon
3900 HOUS 77003 3964 B5
La Reforma Blvd
3300 BYTN 77521 3973 E1
La Retama Dr
3400 HOUS 77013 3827 A6
Large Av
7200 MNVL 77578 4746 E2
Large Leaf Ln
5800 FBnC 77469 4493 B6
Largo
10 HTCK 77563 5105 A5
Largo St
800 BYTN 77520 3973 B6
Largo Woods Pl
10 WDLD 77382 2819 E3
Largs Cir
17400 HarC 77379 3255 C3
Largs Dr
9600 HarC 77379 3255 C3
Lariat Dr
4500 BYTN 77521 3973 C2
9000 SPVL 77055 3820 E7
9000 SPVL 77055 3959 E1
Lariat Canyon Ct
2800 HarC 77450 3954 C7
Lariat Canyon Dr
- HarC 77450 3954 C7
Larimar Sea Dr
- MtgC 77339 3118 D4
Larimer St
5800 HOUS 77020 3964 E3
Larimer Point Ct
2000 FBnC 77479 4494 B1
Larissa Cir
6500 HarC 77449 3677 B3
Larissa Dr
19300 HarC 77449 3677 B3
La Riviera Cir
600 HarC 77015 3828 C7
La Riviera Dr
500 HarC 77015 3828 B7
Lark Dr
800 PASD 77503 4108 C5
Lark Ln
1100 FBnC 77469 4616 A1
2600 HMBL 77396 3406 C4
4100 HOUS 77025 4241 C3
18000 MtgC 77384 2675 E7
20900 HarC 77447 3106 A2
Lark Rdg
10300 HarC 77070 3399 B6
Lark St
1600 ALVN 77511 4867 A2
Lark Brook Ln
10900 HarC 77065 3539 B2
Lark Creek Ct
5000 FBnC 77479 4493 C3
Lark Creek Ln
21400 HarC 77449 3815 B3
Larkdale Dr
- HOUS 77099 4238 B2
2800 BzaC 77584 4501 A5
Larken Pk
13800 HarC 77429 3397 A2
Lark Fair Ln
12400 HOUS 77089 4505 D1
Larkfield Ct
4000 HOUS 77059 4380 C6
Larkfield Dr
16200 HOUS 77059 4380 D6
16400 PASD 77059 4380 D5
Lark Glen Dr
5400 HOUS 77345 3119 C1
5400 HOUS 77365 3119 C1
Lark Glen Wy
7600 FBnC 77479 4493 E5
Larkhall Ln
14300 HarC 77014 3257 D7
Lark Haven Ln
6000 HOUS 77085 4240 E7
Lark Hill Ln
21300 HarC 77449 3676 D5
Lark Hill St
6800 HarC 77338 3261 C4
Larkhill Gardens Ln
13300 FBnC 77478 4366 E2
Lark Hollow Ln
200 LGCY 77573 4631 B4
Larkin St
4800 HOUS 77007 3962 A1
5700 HOUS 77007 3961 E1
Larkin Falls Ct
14000 HarC 77044 3549 C2
Larkin Hark
- HarC 77396 3407 A5
- HMBL 77396 3407 A5
Lark Meadow Dr
9500 HOUS 77040 3682 B2
Larkmist Ln
- HarC 77375 2965 B6
Larkmount Ct
6100 HarC 77389 2966 D4
Larkmount Dr
6200 HarC 77389 2966 D4
Lark Mountain Dr
10200 HarC 77064 3541 C1
Larknolls Ln
3000 HOUS 77092 3822 B3
Lark Orchard Wy
19700 FBnC 77469 4234 D3
Lark Point Ct
13000 HarC 77044 3689 B4
Larkrun Ln
18300 HarC 77429 3252 A5
18300 HarC 77433 3252 A5
Larks Aire Pl
10 WDLD 77381 2674 B7
Larksberry Pl
10 WDLD 77382 2675 B6
Larksong Ln
4700 HarC 77388 3112 B4
E Larkspur Cir
600 BzaC 77584 4501 A1
N Larkspur Cir
2700 BzaC 77584 4501 A1
W Larkspur Cir
600 BzaC 77584 4501 A1
Larkspur Ct
2500 GLSN 77551 5108 B7
Larkspur Dr
2300 HarC 77562 3832 C3
7800 TXCY 77591 4873 B6
E Larkspur Dr
100 HLCS 77511 4867 E5
100 HLCS 77511 4868 A5
W Larkspur Dr
100 ALVN 77511 4867 E5
100 HLCS 77511 4867 E5
Larkspur Ln
1100 TYLV 77586 4382 A7
30500 MtgC 77385 2676 D5
Larkspur St
1300 ALVN 77511 4867 D6
4100 HOUS 77051 4243 C3
4600 HOUS 77033 4243 E3
Larkspur Tr
10 WDLD 77382 2819 E2
Larkspur Field Ct
- PRLD 77581 4503 D2
Larkspur Hills Dr
18900 HarC 77433 3677 B1
Larkspur Ridge Dr
26400 FBnC 77494 4092 B5
Larkstone St
6700 HOUS 77028 3825 E1
Lark Valley Ct
6100 HOUS 77345 3120 D6
Larkview Cir
15000 HOUS 77489 4371 B4
Larkway Dr
13700 SGLD 77478 4237 A7
Larkwood Dr
- HOUS 77074 4100 A6
- HOUS 77074 4240 A2
6700 HOUS 77074 4099 E4
11000 HOUS 77035 4240 A4
11300 HOUS 77096 4240 A5
Larkwood Ln
3300 SGLD 77479 4495 B1
Larocco Wy
- ALVN 77511 4749 C2
La Roche Ln
7700 HOUS 77036 4099 B7
La Rochelle Cir
7800 MSCY 77071 4239 E7
La Rochelle Ct
2300 SEBK 77586 4509 C1
La Rochelle Dr
12500 HarC 77015 3828 B7
Larrabee St
1800 SEBK 77586 4509 C3
Larry
9700 HarC 77064 3541 A3
Larry St
- ALVN 77511 4867 D1
10400 HOUS 77093 3686 B4
10500 HarC 77093 3686 B4
Larrycrest Dr
5800 PRLD 77584 4502 C6
Larson St
100 HOUS 77061 4245 B5
6900 HOUS 77061 4244 E6
Larston Dr
9100 HOUS 77055 3820 D7
9100 SPVL 77055 3820 D7
10000 HOUS 77043 3820 A7
10200 HOUS 77043 3819 E7
Larston Rd
- SPVL 77055 3820 E7
8800 SPVL 77055 3821 A7
9000 HOUS 77055 3820 E7
La Rue
800 MAGA 77355 2669 A5
La Rue St
1000 HOUS 77019 3962 D4
Larwood Ct
2600 HarC 77038 3543 A1
Larwood Ln
13600 HarC 77038 3543 A1
Lasaber Ct
10000 HarC 77038 3543 D4
La Salette St
6000 HOUS 77021 4103 C6
7600 HOUS 77021 4243 B1
La Salle Av
100 CNRO 77304 2236 A7
100 CNRO 77304 2382 B1
100 MtgC 77304 2236 A7
100 MtgC 77304 2382 B1
La Salle Brch
11900 MtgC 77304 2236 A7
La Salle Cross
12000 MtgC 77304 2236 A6
La Salle Ln
1900 LGCY 77573 4631 B4
2400 FBnC 77469 4365 B1
Lasalle Rd
- HOUS 77099 4237 B3
- HOUS 77478 4237 B3
- SGLD 77478 4237 B3
La Salle St
1800 FRDW 77546 4629 B6
3300 HOUS 77027 3961 C7
La Salle Heights Ct
11800 CNRO 77304 2236 A6
11800 MtgC 77304 2236 A6
La Salle Lake Rd
2600 MtgC 77304 2236 A6
La Salle Oaks
12000 MtgC 77304 2236 A6
La Salle Park Dr
1900 MtgC 77304 2236 A7
La Salle River Rd
11900 MtgC 77304 2236 A7
La Salle Springs Ct
11800 MtgC 77304 2236 A6
La Salle Woods
2300 MtgC 77304 2236 A6
Las Brisas
100 LGCY 77565 4508 E4
Las Brisas Dr
6400 HarC 77083 4096 C6
Lasbury Dr
9500 FBnC 77083 4236 B2
Las Cruces Cir
- DRPK 77536 4109 E6
8900 HOUS 77078 3687 E6
Las Cruces Rd
7600 HOUS 77078 3826 E1
7900 HOUS 77078 3687 E7
Las Cruces St
7500 HOUS 77078 3826 E1
La Seine Ln
3300 HarC 77388 3112 E3
Las Flores Dr
7500 HarC 77083 4096 D6
Lashbrook Dr
1100 HOUS 77077 3957 E4
Lashley Ct
2200 HarC 77450 3954 B6
Lasker Dr
6900 GLSN 77551 5222 B2
Laskey St
1100 HOUS 77034 4246 B5
Laskey Manor Ct
14000 HarC 77429 3397 D2
La Sombra Dr
6700 HarC 77083 4096 A5
Las Palmas Blvd
3800 GLSN 77554 5332 D3
Las Palmas Dr
- LGCY 77539 4633 E2
- LGCY 77565 4633 E2
Las Palmas St
3000 HOUS 77027 3961 C7
3600 HOUS 77027 4101 C1
4000 GLSN 77554 5332 D3
Lassen Ln
- HarC 77041 3679 B4
Lassen Forest Ln
17300 HarC 77346 3408 C3
Lassie Dr
5100 BzaC 77511 4747 E1
Lassiter Hollow Ln
7400 FBnC 77469 4095 C6
Lasso Ct
- ALVN 77511 4867 A4
Lasso Ln
10900 HOUS 77079 3958 C1
Last Arrow Dr
700 HOUS 77079 3957 A2
Las Terrazas Dr
10200 HOUS 77075 4376 E3
Lasting Light Ct
8700 HarC 77095 3538 B5
Lasting Light Ln
16200 HarC 77095 3538 B5
Lasting Rose Dr
17600 HarC 77429 3252 C5
Lasting Shadow Cir
16600 HarC 77095 3538 B5
Latch Ln
2900 HarC 77038 3543 A5
Latchmore Ln
6700 HarC 77049 3829 A2
La Teche Ln
2600 SEBK 77586 4509 B2
Lateen Cir
12700 HarC 77015 3828 C7
Latenwood Ct
8600 HarC 77044 3689 B5
Laterna Ln
14100 FBnC 77083 4096 E7
La Terra Dr
16200 FBnC 77083 4096 A6
Latexo Dr
1500 HOUS 77018 3822 C1
1800 HOUS 77018 3683 C7
Latham St
400 HOUS 77011 3964 C7
500 HOUS 77023 3964 C7
N Latham St
100 HOUS 77011 3964 C6
Lathrop Ct
6700 SGLD 77479 4494 B1
Lathrop St
100 HOUS 77020 3825 E7
300 HOUS 77020 3964 E3
Lathy St
17400 HarC 77044 3551 C7
Latitude Ln
10 GLSN 77554 5221 C2
Latma Ct
9000 HOUS 77025 4101 D7
Latma Dr
3500 HOUS 77025 4241 D1
3600 HOUS 77025 4101 D7
Latrobe Ln
3100 FBnC 77450 3954 B7
Latson St
15000 HarC 77069 3256 D5
Lattice Gate St
100 WDLD 77382 2674 C4
Latticeleaf Pl
10 WDLD 77382 2673 D5
Lattimer Dr
5900 HOUS 77035 4240 B5
Latvia Ct
5900 HarC 77379 3111 E6
5900 HarC 77379 3112 A6
Lauder Rd
1100 HarC 77039 3545 B4
2800 HarC 77039 3546 E4
Lauderdale St
1900 HOUS 77030 4102 D5
Lauderwick Ct
6800 FBnC 77450 4094 C5
Lauderwood Ln
3500 HarC 77449 3815 D2
Laughing Brook Ct
10 WDLD 77380 2968 A3
Laughing Gull Cir N
2200 SEBK 77586 4509 B2
Laughing Gull Ln
600 TXCY 77590 4875 D2
2100 LGCY 77573 4631 A7
Laughing Wood Ct
9400 HarC 77086 3542 B2
Laughlin Dr
6600 HOUS 77489 4371 C5
Laughton Ln
6400 HarC 77084 3678 A3
Laumar Ct
14400 HarC 77429 3254 A7
Launch Ct
16000 HarC 77532 3552 A2
16500 HarC 77532 3551 E2
Laura
700 WALR 77484 3102 A5
Laura Av
1000 LMQU 77568 4990 A1
Laura Cir
14600 HarC 77429 3538 D1
E Laura Cir
6500 HarC 77521 3834 E4
N Laura Cir
8100 HarC 77521 3834 E4
S Laura Cir
8100 HarC 77521 3834 E4
W Laura Cir
6500 HarC 77521 3834 E4
Laura Ln
100 ORDN 77385 2822 C4
600 LGCY 77573 4632 B1
1400 HMBL 77338 3407 A1
1900 LPRT 77571 4110 E7
1900 LPRT 77571 4250 E1
2400 PRLD 77581 4504 A5
21800 PNIS 77445 3099 D3
22900 MtgC 77357 2973 E3
23100 HarC 77447 3105 B7
23300 MtgC 77357 2974 A3
Laura Anne Dr
1600 HarC 77049 3829 D4
1600 HarC 77530 3829 D4
Laura Beth Dr
16000 HarC 77447 3250 A7
Laura Jean Ln
16900 HarC 77084 3678 B6
Laura Koppe Rd
2800 HOUS 77093 3685 E7
2800 HOUS 77093 3686 A7
4100 HOUS 77016 3686 C7
7100 HOUS 77028 3686 D7
7800 HOUS 77028 3687 B7
8800 HOUS 77078 3687 E7
9000 HOUS 77078 3688 A7
Laura Lee Ln
- HOUS 77034 4378 E1
- HOUS 77504 4378 E1
5000 HOUS 77504 4247 D7
5000 PASD 77504 4247 D7
Lauralee Ln
18000 MtgC 77302 2679 B7
18000 MtgC 77302 2825 B1
Laura Leigh Ln
- HarC 77546 4630 A1
3700 FRDW 77546 4630 A1
Laural Trail Dr
3600 HOUS 77339 3119 B7
Laura Lynn Dr
- HarC 77433 3250 E6
Laura Morrison Dr
13300 SGLD 77478 4368 B
Lauras Glen Ct
22400 FBnC 77450 4093 E
Laura Shore Cir
18400 HarC 77433 3395 C
Laura Shore Ct
12200 HarC 77433 3395 D
Laura Shore Dr
18300 HarC 77433 3395 C
Laura Wy Dr
20000 HarC 77450 3954 E
Laurel
- RSBG 77471 4491 B
Laurel Ct
500 LGCY 77573 4632 D
12100 STAF 77477 4238 A
21000 MtgC 77355 2960 D
21000 SGCH 77355 2960 D
Laurel Dr
100 FRDW 77546 4505 B
300 FRDW 77546 4629 C
1500 FBnC 77479 4493 C
4300 HOUS 77021 4103 E
Laurel Ln
200 BYTN 77520 3832 B
8100 CmbC 77520 3835 D
30900 MtgC 77354 2670 A
Laurel Run
6300 HarC 77084 3679 A
Laurel St
200 LMQU 77568 4874 A
500 LMQU 77568 4990 B
1200 LGCY 77573 4632 D
3000 FBnC 77545 4499 D
4600 BLAR 77401 4101 B
5100 BLAR 77401 4100 E
Laurel Trc
8400 HarC 77040 3541 B
Laurel Arbor Dr
2100 HarC 77014 3402 B
Laurel Bank Wy
12700 HarC 77014 3402 B
Laurel Bay Dr
1800 HarC 77014 3402 B
Laurel Bend Ln
2100 HarC 77014 3402 B
Laurel Birch Dr
2200 HarC 77014 3402 A
Laurel Bough Ln
1800 HarC 77014 3402 C
N Laurel Branch Dr
10200 HarC 77064 3540 C
S Laurel Branch Dr
10300 HarC 77064 3540 E
W Laurel Branch Dr
10300 HarC 77064 3540 D
Laurel Branch Wy
2100 HarC 77014 3402 B
Laurel Breeze Ln
- HarC 77044 3549 C
Laurel Briar Ln
9300 HarC 77044 3689 C
Laurel Bridge Ln
- HarC 77040 3541 A
Laurel Brook Ln
1900 HarC 77014 3402 B
2900 PRLD 77584 4500 B
Laurel Bush Ln
6300 FBnC 77479 4367 B
Laurel Caverns Dr
5800 HOUS 77345 3120 B
Laurel Chase Ln
24700 FBnC 77494 3953 B
Laurel Chase Tr
1100 HarC 77073 3259 B
Laurel Cherry Wy
2900 WDLD 77380 2821 C
Laurel Cove
15800 HarC 77377 3254 E
Laurel Creek Ct
4300 MSCY 77459 4496 C
9500 HarC 77040 3541 A
Laurel Creek Dr
2100 HarC 77014 3402 B
Laurel Creek Ln
14900 FBnC 77478 4236 D
Laurel Creek Wy
2700 PRLD 77581 4504 C
5100 HOUS 77017 4246 B
Laurel Crest Ct
3400 HOUS 77339 3118 D
Laurel Crest Dr
3300 HOUS 77339 3118 D
Laureldale Ct
10800 HOUS 77041 3680 D
E Laureldale Dr
4800 HOUS 77041 3680 E
N Laureldale Dr
10400 HOUS 77041 3680 E
Laureldale Rd
4500 HOUS 77041 3819 E
4600 HOUS 77041 3680 E
Laureldale Park Ln
2400 MtgC 77386 2969 D
Laurel Falls Ct
12600 HarC 77014 3402 B
Laurel Falls Ln
12700 HarC 77014 3402 B
Laurelfield Dr
100 FRDW 77546 4629 D
15700 HOUS 77059 4380 C
Laurel Forest Wy
2100 HarC 77014 3402 B
Laurel Fork Ct
4100 HOUS 77339 3119 C
Laurel Fork Dr
2900 HOUS 77339 3119 C
Laurel Garden Dr
2700 HOUS 77339 3119 B
Laurel Glen Ct
2200 LGCY 77573 4631 A
Laurel Glen Dr
6600 HarC 77449 3677 C
Laurel Green Ct
4400 MSCY 77459 4369 B
Laurel Green Rd
800 MSCY 77459 4369 B
Laurel Green St
25300 HarC 77373 3114 E
Laurel Grove Dr
4000 PASD 77586 4508 D
4000 TYLV 77586 4508 D
Laurel Grove Ln
700 BzaC 77584 4501 A
Laurel Haven Wy
12500 HarC 77014 3402 B

Houston Street Index

STREET
Block City ZIP Map# Grid

aurel Heights Ct
4600 HarC 77084 3678 E7
aurel Heights Dr
15500 HarC 77084 3678 E7
15500 HarC 77084 3679 A7
aurel Hill Ct
4900 SGLD 77478 4369 A6
aurel Hill Dr
1900 HOUS 77339 3118 D6
aurel Hollow Dr
3600 HarC 77388 3112 D6
Laurel Hurst
10 WDLD 77382 2674 B6
Laurel Hurst Cir
10 WDLD 77382 2674 B6
aurel Knoll Cir
15300 HarC 77433 3251 C7
aurel Lake Dr
2900 HOUS 77339 3119 B5
aurel Land Ln
2100 HarC 77014 3402 B4
aurel Leaf Ln
1300 PRLD 77581 4376 E7
8300 HarC 77346 3265 C4
aurel Loch Ct
- PRLD 77545 4499 E2
aurel Loch Ln
- PRLD 77545 4499 D2
aurel Lock Dr
20200 HarC 77450 3954 D3
aurel Maple Ct
6800 HarC 77379 3111 C3
aurel Meadow Ct
- LMQU 77568 4872 B4
aurel Meadow Dr
11800 HarC 77377 3254 D5
aurel Meadow Ln
- SGLD 77478 4236 B4
aurel Meadow Wy
12400 HarC 77014 3402 B3
aurel Mist Ct
2900 HOUS 77345 3120 A1
3000 HOUS 77345 3119 E1
aurel Mist Wy
12700 HarC 77014 3402 B3
aurel Nook Wy
12600 HarC 77014 3402 B2
aurel Oak Dr
2200 MSCY 77489 4370 E5
aurel Oak Pl
10 WDLD 77380 2967 E2
aurel Oaks Dr
1600 RHMD 77469 4491 E3
1800 HarC 77014 3402 B3
W Laurel Oaks Dr
1700 RHMD 77469 4491 D3
1900 RHMD 77471 4491 D3
1900 RSBG 77471 4491 D3
aurel Park Ln
19500 HarC 77094 3955 A3
aurel Pine Cir
22200 HOUS 77339 3263 A1
aurel Pine Dr
400 HOUS 77339 3263 A1
aurel Pl Ln
- HarC 77014 3402 B3
aurel Point Ct
3200 HOUS 77339 3119 B7
aurel Rain Ct
20600 HarC 77449 3815 D2
aurel Ridge Dr
2500 HOUS 77345 3119 D5
aurelridge Dr
2900 LGCY 77573 4633 A2
aurel River Bnd
2200 HarC 77014 3402 A3
aurel River Dr
13400 HarC 77083 4097 B4
aurel Rock Dr
3900 HOUS 77345 3119 E3
aurel Rose Ln
1800 HarC 77014 3402 C3
aurel Rustic Oaks
- HarC 77014 3402 A3
Laurel Sage Ct
10100 HarC 77375 2965 B6
aurel Sage Dr
400 HOUS 77339 3263 A1
aurel Shadow Ct
14600 HOUS 77062 4379 C6
aurel Spring Ct
200 SGLD 77478 4368 E4
aurel Springs Ln
- HOUS 77339 3263 A1
1600 HOUS 77339 3118 A7
aurelstone Ct
14100 SGLD 77478 4236 E5
aurel Stone Ln
9600 HarC 77040 3541 A6
Laurel Terrace Ct
22100 FBnC 77450 4093 E3
aurel Terrace Ln
13600 FBnC 77478 4366 E3
Laurel Terrace Wy
2200 HarC 77014 3402 B3
Laurel Timbers Dr
400 HOUS 77339 3263 A1
aurelton Ct
10600 HarC 77396 3407 E2
aurelton Dr
17700 HarC 77396 3407 E1
aurel Trace Ct
8500 HarC 77040 3541 A5
aurel Trail Dr
19800 HarC 77433 3537 A7
19800 HarC 77433 3677 B2
Laurel Trails Dr
8400 HarC 77095 3538 C5
aurel Vale Wy
12700 HarC 77014 3402 B3
aurel Valley Dr
1000 HOUS 77062 4507 A1
aurel Walk Ct
2400 FBnC 77494 3953 C6
Laurelwick Ct
1900 FBnC 77494 3952 C6
Laurel Wind Ct
9400 HarC 77040 3541 B6
aurelwood Dr
- PASD 77058 4508 C2
5100 HOUS 77345 3120 A4
16600 HarC 77530 3830 D6
Laurel Wood Ln
3400 BzaC 77584 4374 B7
Laurelwood Ln
22700 HarC 77375 3110 B1
Laurel Woods Dr
4100 MSCY 77459 4497 D3
Lauren Ct
2200 DRPK 77536 4109 E7
Lauren Ln
3100 HarC 77082 4097 A2
5200 GlsC 77511 4869 A7
6400 PRLD 77584 4502 C5
Lauren Pl
1800 MSCY 77489 4370 C4
Lauren Tr
3500 PRLD 77581 4503 E6
Lauren Wy
8000 FBnC 77479 4494 A6
Lauren Cove Ln
28300 MtgC 77386 2969 D6
Lauren Creek Dr
10300 BYTN 77520 3835 B7
10400 CmbC 77520 3835 B7
Lauren Creek Ln
- MtgC 77386 2969 D7
Laurenhurst Ct
10 HOUS 77043 3819 E6
Lauren Lake Dr
1900 LGCY 77573 4508 E6
2000 LGCY 77573 4509 A6
Lauren Meadow Ln
22600 FBnC 77494 4093 D3
Lauren Oaks Ln
3100 HarC 77396 3407 D2
Lauren Rose Ln
2700 PRLD 77581 4504 C4
Laurens Lndg
28600 MtgC 77386 2970 B3
Laurentide St
1100 HOUS 77029 3965 D2
Lauren Veronica Dr
10600 HOUS 77034 4246 E7
Laurenwood Ct
14500 HarC 77396 3547 E2
Laurette Ct
4100 FBnC 77479 4366 C6
Laurette Dr
19600 MtgC 77365 2972 C5
Laureumont Ct
24100 FBnC 77494 4093 C1
Laureumont Ln
3200 FBnC 77494 4093 A6
Laurie Ln
10100 HarC 77532 3693 C6
10100 HarC 77562 3693 C6
11900 BKHV 77024 3959 B3
Laurie St
6100 PRLD 77581 4502 C3
Lauri Lynn Dr
29900 MtgC 77386 2969 A3
Laurus Estates Ln
14200 HarC 77429 3396 B2
Laurynnbrook Dr
5000 PASD 77505 4249 B3
5000 PASD 77536 4249 B3
Lausanne Av
3100 PASD 77504 4248 A3
3100 PASD 77505 4248 A3
Lausanne Dr
15900 HarC 77070 3255 C6
Lautrec Dr
6300 HOUS 77088 3682 C2
Lava Ln
20500 FBnC 77469 4234 B3
Lavaca Dr
- BzaC 77584 4502 E7
- PRLD 77584 4502 E7
21000 MtgC 77357 2827 A7
Lavaca Ln
2500 FBnC 77469 4365 B1
Lavaca St
700 HOUS 77012 4105 C3
1800 FRDW 77546 4629 B7
La Vaca Morena
11600 HOUS 77048 4244 D7
Lavaerton Wood Ln
7400 FBnC 77469 4094 D6
Lavage Ln
8000 HarC 77521 3833 D3
Lavander Quartz Ct
- FBnC 77494 4092 C5
Lavaun
- HOUS 77034 4246 E5
Lavell Dr
4400 HOUS 77018 3683 C7
Lavendar Bay Ln
15600 HarC 77429 3252 C7
Lavender Ln
5200 HarC 77521 3833 D3
Lavender St
5500 HOUS 77026 3825 C4
6500 HOUS 77028 3825 C3
7500 HOUS 77016 3825 C1
8100 HOUS 77016 3686 C7
Lavender Candle Dr
3100 HarC 77388 3113 A7
Lavender Creek Ct
16200 HarC 77433 3251 A4
Lavender Field Ct
9000 FBnC 77479 4494 C4
Lavender Field Dr
1900 FBnC 77479 4494 C4
Lavender Haze Ct
10 WDLD 77381 2674 B7
Lavender Haze Pl
10 WDLD 77381 2674 B7
Lavender Jade Ct
26000 MtgC 77339 3118 C4
Lavender Run Dr
15800 HarC 77429 3397 B2
Lavender Sade Ct
20000 HarC 77073 3403 C1
Lavender Shade Ct
1000 HarC 77073 3403 B1
Lavenderwood Dr
20800 HarC 77449 3815 C3
Laver Love Dr
6200 HarC 77379 3257 A3
Laverne Av
700 PASD 77502 4247 B1
Laverne Dr
3500 HOUS 77080 3820 E2
La Verne St
5800 HTCK 77563 4989 A2
Laverne St
1700 HOUS 77080 3820 E5
3600 FBnC 77545 4498 E7
Laverock Rd
3900 HarC 77388 3257 D1
Laverton Ct
400 HarC 77450 3954 D1
Laverton Dr
20200 HarC 77450 3954 D1
La Violetta Dr
6500 HarC 77083 4096 A4
La Vista Dr
9700 HOUS 77041 3820 B1
Lavon Dr
12200 HarC 77375 3109 C6
Lavonia Ln
1300 PASD 77502 4107 E6
1300 PASD 77506 4107 E6
Lavonnie
10 LPRT 77571 4250 E1
10 LPRT 77571 4251 A1
Law Ct
1200 RSBG 77471 4491 D4
Law St
3800 HOUS 77005 4101 D2
3800 WUNP 77005 4101 D2
Lawford Ln
6100 HOUS 77040 3681 C5
Lawick Cir
1600 SGLD 77478 4368 C5
Lawler Rdg
6900 HOUS 77055 3821 E6
Lawler St
7800 HOUS 77051 4243 B2
Lawn Ln
5900 HOUS 77088 3682 D2
Lawn St
8200 HOUS 77088 3684 A2
Lawn Arbor Dr
5100 HarC 77066 3401 A2
5300 HarC 77066 3400 E2
Lawncliff Ln
8600 HarC 77040 3541 C6
Lawn Crest Dr
2100 HOUS 77489 4371 A6
Lawndale Plz
1500 HOUS 77023 4105 A3
Lawndale St
1200 PASD 77506 4106 E4
1300 HOUS 77017 4106 B4
4400 LMQU 77568 4873 A7
4800 LMQU 77568 4872 E7
5100 HOUS 77023 4104 C1
6900 HOUS 77023 4105 A2
7200 HOUS 77012 4105 C3
7200 HOUS 77087 4105 B3
9500 HOUS 77017 4105 E3
Lawngate Dr
9600 HOUS 77080 3820 B2
Lawnhaven
13800 HOUS 77045 4372 B1
Lawnhaven Dr
13300 HOUS 77045 4241 B7
13300 HOUS 77045 4372 B1
Lawnridge St
8600 HOUS 77016 3686 C7
Lawn Wood Ln
7900 HarC 77086 3541 E2
Lawrence
- MtgC 77354 2672 A6
Lawrence Av
1200 PASD 77506 4107 C5
Lawrence Ct
5800 PRLD 77584 4502 D7
Lawrence Ln
- KMAH 77565 4633 D2
- LGCY 77565 4633 C2
2100 DRPK 77536 4109 C6
13000 STAF 77477 4239 A7
Lawrence Pl
4000 BzaC 77584 4502 E7
4000 PRLD 77584 4502 D7
Lawrence Rd
- CRLS 77565 4509 B6
900 GlsC 77565 4509 C6
900 LGCY 77565 4509 C6
900 LGCY 77573 4509 C6
1000 KMAH 77565 4509 C7
1900 KMAH 77565 4633 C1
1900 LGCY 77565 4633 C1
Lawrence St
- HarC 77532 3411 C5
200 TMBL 77375 2964 A7
300 TMBL 77375 3109 A1
700 HOUS 77007 3962 C1
800 HOUS 77007 3823 C7
1000 RSBG 77471 4491 B4
1600 HOUS 77008 3823 C5
2900 HOUS 77018 3823 B4
8000 HTCK 77563 4988 E4
S Lawrence St
100 TMBL 77375 3109 A1
Lawrenceburg St
- MtgC 77385 2677 A7
Lawrence Marshall Dr
100 HMPD 77445 2952 C4
Lawrence Trace Ct
13700 HarC 77429 3397 B3
Lawson Ct
3000 BzaC 77584 4501 C6
Lawson Dr
3300 BzaC 77584 4501 C6
3300 PRLD 77584 4501 C6
Lawson Rd
100 FBnC 77583 4622 D6
Lawson St
- PRVW 77445 3100 C1
1100 HOUS 77023 4104 B1
1200 BzaC 77583 4623 C6
Lawson Cypress Dr
11500 HarC 77377 3254 D4
Lawson Lake Ln
4800 FBnC 77469 4234 D4
Lawson Oaks Dr
19700 HarC 77433 3537 A6
Lawsons Creek Ln
13000 HarC 77072 4097 C6
Lawsuit Ln
22400 MtgC 77357 2827 D5
Lawther Dr
14900 HarC 77530 3968 C1
E Lawther Ln
2200 DRPK 77536 4109 D6
W Lawther Ln
2200 DRPK 77536 4109 C6
Lawton Cir
10 FBnC 77479 4367 A7
Lawton Dr
2500 BzaC 77584 4501 D5
Lawton Bend Ln
1300 FBnC 77494 4092 C2
Lawton Ridge Dr
14400 HarC 77429 3396 E1
Laxey Glen Dr
10 HarC 77379 3110 D7
Laxton Ct
200 HarC 77450 3954 E1
Laxton Ct
200 HOUS 77450 3954 E1
Layfair Pl
900 FRDW 77546 4629 C4
Layhill Ct
13600 HOUS 77077 3957 A5
Layman St
1000 LMQU 77568 4989 D1
Layne Ct
3100 LPRT 77571 4382 E1
Layne St
- ALVN 77511 4749 A5
- BzaC 77511 4749 A5
3000 LPRT 77571 4251 E7
3000 LPRT 77571 4382 E1
Laynes Run Dr
18300 HarC 77433 3537 C5
Laytham Ln
14900 FBnC 77478 4236 C2
Layton St
100 HOUS 77012 4105 B2
1100 BYTN 77520 4112 E1
Layton Castle Ln
13400 HarC 77429 3397 A4
Layton Hills Dr
13700 HarC 77429 3397 A3
Layton Meadows Ln
- HarC 77379 3257 A2
Layton Pl Dr
3200 PRLD 77581 4503 D4
Laywood Ct
21200 FBnC 77469 4234 B5
Lazaras St
6300 HOUS 77022 3824 C3
Lazdins Cir
13000 HarC 77429 3398 B5
Lazee Tr
10 BKHV 77024 3959 B3
Lazee Oaks
32800 MtgC 77355 2962 A2
Lazy Ct
29700 HarC 77336 2976 C7
Lazy Ln
- HarC 77388 3113 B3
- LGCY 77573 4632 B6
10 GlsC 77565 4509 D5
10 WDLD 77380 2821 D7
100 BYTN 77520 3971 B1
200 CNRO 77301 2384 C3
1300 BzaC 77511 4748 E5
1900 MSCY 77489 4370 C5
2200 LMQU 77568 4989 C3
2400 RSBG 77469 4491 D6
2400 RSBG 77471 4491 D6
7600 HarC 77389 2966 A3
7800 HarC 77389 2965 E3
9000 HTCK 77563 4988 C3
19000 MtgC 77365 2972 B3
26400 MtgC 77355 2814 A2
29400 MtgC 77386 2968 E4
Lazy Pn
- HarC 77336 3121 C1
Lazy Wy
24800 HarC 77375 2965 D3
Lazy Bend Dr
2300 PRLD 77581 4502 C3
2300 PRLD 77584 4502 C3
Lazy Brook Dr
3100 SGLD 77479 4495 E1
Lazybrook Dr
2000 HOUS 77008 3822 D5
Lazy Brook Ln
8400 LPRT 77571 4249 D4
30000 MtgC 77355 2815 A2
Lazy Creek Dr
20400 MtgC 77357 2829 E7
20900 HarC 77357 2975 E1
Lazy Creek Ln
1800 PRLD 77581 4504 C4
2000 HOUS 77017 4106 D7
2000 HOUS 77017 4246 D1
16100 SPLD 77372 2683 A5
E Lazy Daisy Cir
16600 HarC 77433 3251 B4
S Lazy Daisy Cir
16500 HarC 77433 3251 B4
Lazydale Ln
9100 HOUS 77078 3688 A6
Lazy Elm Ct
17000 HarC 77095 3538 A7
Lazy Falls
- HarC 77084 3816 D3
Lazy Grove Dr
1900 HOUS 77339 3118 D6
Lazy Hill Ln
17300 HarC 77379 3256 A3
Lazy Hollow Ct
2000 PRLD 77581 4503 C2
3000 FBnC 77459 4621 E7
Lazy Hollow Dr
100 LGCY 77573 4630 C6
2300 HOUS 77063 3959 D7
Lazy Hollow Ln
1900 PRLD 77581 4503 D1
23200 MtgC 77447 2960 B5
Lazy Kay Ct
17600 HarC 77447 3249 E3
Lazy Kay Ln
24000 HarC 77447 3249 D3
Lazy Lagoon
10100 HarC 77065 3539 E3
Lazy Lake Dr
2500 NSUB 77058 4508 B4
Lazy Ln Blvd
2900 HOUS 77019 3962 A5
Lazy Ln St
10100 TXCY 77539 4755 E3
Lazy Meadows Dr
10000 HarC 77064 3540 C2
Lazymist Ct
5300 DKSN 77539 4754 D1
Lazy Morning Pl
10 WDLD 77381 2820 D3
Lazy Moss Ln
18300 HarC 77379 3255 E2
Lazy Nook St
10500 HOUS 77076 3685 A4
Lazy Oak Ct
- BzaC 77511 4748 B2
Lazy Oak Ln
24100 HarC 77336 3266 E2
Lazy Oaks Cir
1900 MSCY 77489 4370 C7
Lazy Oaks St
10000 HOUS 77043 3820 A6
10000 HOUS 77080 3820 A6
32800 MtgC 77355 2962 A2
Lazy Oaks Ranch Rd
- HarC 77429 3396 E1
Lazy Pine Ct
300 CNRO 77304 2383 A6
Lazy Pine Dr
29000 HarC 77336 2976 C7
29000 HarC 77336 3121 C1
Lazy Pine Ln
3000 LPRT 77571 4382 D1
Lazy Pines Rd
1500 HOUS 77093 3685 D7
Lazy Ravine
21200 HarC 77073 3259 C1
Lazy Ravine Ln
21100 HarC 77073 3259 C2
Lazy Ridge Rd
16100 HOUS 77053 4372 B7
S Lazy Ridge Rd
4900 HOUS 77053 4372 A7
Lazy River Ln
8900 HOUS 77088 3544 A7
Lazy River Rd
- MtgC 77302 2677 D4
- MtgC 77302 2678 A4
10700 MtgC 77385 2677 D4
Lazy River Rd SR-242
- MtgC 77302 2677 D4
- MtgC 77302 2678 A4
10700 MtgC 77385 2677 D4
Lazy S St
26700 MtgC 77372 2683 D1
Lazy Shore Dr
100 HarC 77530 3831 A6
Lazy Spring Ct
2600 MSCY 77489 4370 D7
Lazy Spring Dr
1400 MSCY 77489 4370 D7
3600 HOUS 77080 3820 D2
Lazy Springs Ln
- HarC 77373 3113 C1
- HarC 77373 3114 B4
Lazy Summer Ct
7200 MtgC 77354 2673 A3
Lazy Timbers Dr
4800 HarC 77346 3408 B1
Lazy Trail Ct
6400 FBnC 77479 4494 B1
Lazy Trail Path Ct
2200 HarC 77373 3114 D4
Lazy Valley Dr
19200 HarC 77449 3816 A4
Lazy Willow Ct
14400 HOUS 77489 4371 B3
Lazy Willow Ln
14500 HOUS 77489 4371 B4
Lazy Wood Ln
10 PNPV 77024 3959 E4
Lazywood Ln
100 TYLV 77586 4382 A7
3500 HOUS 77023 4104 C5
12500 MtgC 77362 2817 B7
W Lea Ln
5300 PRLD 77584 4502 B7
Lea St
13000 HOUS 77048 4374 E2
Leacastle Ln
- HarC 77047 4374 B4
Leachwood Dr
24300 HarC 77493 3814 A6
Lea Coral Dr
- HOUS 77045 4372 B1
Leacrest Cir
6000 HarC 77049 3828 C3
Leacrest Ct
6000 HarC 77049 3828 D3
Leacrest Dr
14400 HarC 77049 3828 D3
Leadenhall Cir
1300 HarC 77530 3829 D5
Leader Cir
13100 HOUS 77072 4097 C5
Leader St
6300 HOUS 77081 4100 B5
6800 HOUS 77074 4100 A5
7100 HOUS 77074 4099 E5
7700 HOUS 77036 4099 D5
11500 HOUS 77072 4098 A5
12400 HOUS 77072 4097 E5
13100 HOUS 77083 4097 C5
Leader Crossing Dr
6900 HOUS 77072 4097 C6
Leading Cir
13100 HOUS 77072 4097 C5
Leading Edge Dr
2200 HarC 77546 4506 B5
Leadore Dr
8700 HarC 77040 3681 C3
Lead Point Dr
2600 MSCY 77459 4497 E5
Leaf Cr
1700 FBnC 77494 3953 D5
Leaf Ln
- MtgC 77365 2826 B7
10600 MtgC 77372 2537 B1
20500 MtgC 77365 2972 E7
S Leaf Ln
- HarC 77089 4505 A1
Leaf Arbor Dr
6200 HOUS 77092 3682 C7
Leafbrook Ct
100 HarC 77379 3256 B1
Leafbrook Ln
- HarC 77379 3256 A1
Leaf Chase Ct
15900 HarC 77429 3397 C2
Leaf Cluster Ct E
500 CNRO 77301 2384 E3
Leafdale Ct
20600 HarC 77338 3262 B2
Leafdale Dr
- HarC 77014 3402 D2
- HarC 77090 3402 D2
8200 HarC 77338 3261 E3
8300 HarC 77338 3262 A3
Leaf Forest Dr
4200 HOUS 77345 3119 E5
Leaf Glen Ln
12900 HOUS 77072 4097 C6
Leafgrove Ln
2900 MtgC 77386 2823 D7
Leafhopper Ln
1400 CNRO 77301 2384 B7
1700 CNRO 77301 2530 C1
Leaflet Ln
200 HarC 77388 3113 D7
Leaflock Ln
4200 FBnC 77450 4093 E2
Leaf Meadows Ct
2100 MtgC 77386 2969 C6
Leafmore Ct
8600 FBnC 77083 4096 C7
Leaf Oak Dr
11800 HarC 77065 3539 D1
Leaftex Dr
7400 HOUS 77396 3406 C7
7400 HOUS 77396 3547 C1
Leafton
600 HOUS 77007 3962 C1
Leafton Ln
26400 MtgC 77354 2817 D6
Leafpark Ln
20100 HarC 77338 3262 B4
Leaf Point Ct
7800 HarC 77095 3538 A6
Leaf Ridge Dr
23300 FBnC 77494 3953 D5
Leafsage Ct
300 WDLD 77381 2820 C3
Leaf Spring Pl
10 WDLD 77382 2674 D4
Leaf Springs Ct
1500 FBnC 77479 4494 B5
Leafstalk Ct
10 WDLD 77382 2674 E3
Leafstone Ln
- PRLD 77583 4500 B5
23300 HarC 77373 2968 E6
Leaf Trace Ct
10 WDLD 77381 2820 E5
Leaf Vines Dr
3500 MtgC 77386 2969 E2
Leaf Vines Ln
3000 MtgC 77386 2969 D2
Leaf Wind Dr
7200 HarC 77433 3676 E1
Leafwood Cir
100 LGCY 77573 4630 C6
Leafwood Dr
6000 LGCY 77573 4630 C6
Leafwood Ln
2800 PRLD 77545 4499 D4
19300 HarC 77084 3816 A6
Leafy Ln
8300 SPVL 77055 3821 B6
13900 MtgC 77306 2533 C7
14300 MtgC 77306 2679 C1
14300 MtgC 77306 2679 C1
Leafy Arbor Dr
12100 HarC 77070 3399 C6
Leafy Aspen Ct
5900 HOUS 77345 3120 C5
Leafy Brook Ct
5000 HarC 77084 3677 B7
Leafy Elm Ct
14200 HOUS 77062 4379 D6
Leafygate Dr
22500 HarC 77373 3116 B7
Leafy Glen Dr
- HOUS 77062 4379 E5
2300 HOUS 77059 4379 E6
Leafy Hollow Ct
5000 HOUS 77018 3683 E7
Leafy Meadow Dr
16500 MtgC 77302 2679 B4
Leafy Oak Ct
32000 MtgC 77354 2671 A5
Leafy Oak Wy
- MtgC 77354 2671 A5
Leafy Shores Dr
- HarC 77044 3408 E4
Leafywood Dr
25800 MtgC 77386 2968 C1
Leago St
200 HOUS 77022 3684 C6
600 HOUS 77091 3684 B5
League St
100 LGCY 77573 4631 E3
League City Pkwy
- GlsC 77565 4633 E1
- KMAH 77565 4633 E1
- KMAH 77565 4634 A1
- LGCY 77565 4633 E1
100 LGCY 77573 4632 D5
900 LGCY 77573 4631 D6
1700 LGCY 77573 4633 A4
League City Pkwy FM-1266
- LGCY 77565 4633 C3
- LGCY 77573 4633 A4
League City Pkwy SR-96
- GlsC 77565 4633 E1
- KMAH 77565 4633 E1
- KMAH 77565 4634 A1
- LGCY 77565 4633 E1
100 LGCY 77573 4632 C5
900 LGCY 77573 4631 D6
1700 LGCY 77573 4633 A4
League Line
- HarC 77447 3103 E6
- HarC 77447 3104 B6
- HarC 77447 3249 B1
League Line Rd
1000 CNRO 77303 2237 C5
1300 CNRO 77304 2237 C5
1300 PNVL 77304 2237 A4
2100 CNRO 77304 2236 E3
2100 PNVL 77304 2236 E4
9000 MtgC 77304 2236 A3
Leahbelle St
5100 HarC 77088 3542 E6
Leah Manor Ln
2700 MtgC 77386 2969 E7
Leaholm Ln
- HarC 77090 3258 C5
Leal Dr
13700 HarC 77069 3400 B2
Leaman Av
1300 RSBG 77471 4490 D6
Leaman St
16000 SGCH 77355 2961 E2
Lea Meadows Dr
- HOUS 77045 4372 B2
Leamington Dr
9900 HarC 77070 3255 C4
Leamington Ln
16300 HarC 77095 3538 B6
Leamont Dr
7900 HOUS 77072 4098 C7
8600 HOUS 77099 4238 C1
Leander St
8300 HOUS 77012 4105 D3
Leandra Dr
6600 HarC 77083 4096 A4
Leanett Wy
2400 BzaC 77584 4501 D5
Leanett Wy Ct
3900 BzaC 77584 4501 D5
Leaning Ash Ln
10900 HOUS 77079 3958 C1
Leaning Aspen Ct
- HarC 77429 3254 A4
Leaning Magnolia Ct
7000 HarC 77049 3829 B1
Leaning Oak Dr
7200 HOUS 77088 3682 D3
7800 TXCY 77591 4873 B6
Leaning Pine Dr
11500 HarC 77070 3398 E1
Leaning Timbers Dr
19500 HarC 77346 3264 C5
Leanne Trail Ln
28300 MtgC 77386 2969 C7
Lea Oak Ct
10 WDLD 77381 2821 A6
Lear St
1200 HOUS 77015 3967 C2
Lea Rose Dr
- HOUS 77045 4372 B1
Leath St
9600 HOUS 77093 3686 B5
Leathergate Dr
23800 HarC 77373 3115 C5
Leather Market St
- HarC 77064 3542 A5
7600 HarC 77064 3541 E6
Leather Saddle Ct
12200 HarC 77044 3408 C7
Leatherstem Ln
1800 HOUS 77345 3120 B4
Leatherwood Dr
1500 HarC 77450 3954 E4
Leaton Park Ct
2400 HOUS 77077 3957 A7
Lea Valley Dr
14600 HarC 77049 3828 D3
Leavins St
900 BYTN 77520 3972 E6
Leavy Pine Ct
3200 HOUS 77345 3119 C1
Leawood Blvd
8300 HOUS 77072 4098 B7
8600 HOUS 77099 4098 B7
8600 HOUS 77099 4238 B2
Le Badie St
2800 HOUS 77026 3824 E5
2800 HOUS 77026 3825 A5
Lebate St
7900 HOUS 77028 3826 B1
Le Beau Ln
2200 SEBK 77586 4509 B2
Leben St
8200 HOUS 77028 3687 A7
Le Berge Dr
26000 HarC 77377 3109 A5
Lebon Ln
11600 STAF 77477 4238 B6
Lebra St
10100 HOUS 77016 3687 B4
Lebrun Ct
10 GLSN 77551 5222 A1
Le Carpe Plantation Ct
5800 HarC 77449 3677 A5
Le Chateau Dr
12700 HarC 77015 3828 C7
Lechenger St
4100 GlsC 77518 4634 D2
Leclerc Ln
11700 HOUS 77077 3958 A5
Le Conte Ln
22500 HarC 77338 3260 C1
Leconte Ln
21800 HarC 77338 3260 D2
Ledbetter St
5600 HOUS 77087 4104 D7
5700 HOUS 77087 4244 D1
Ledbury Park Ln
10 HarC 77379 3255 D1
Ledford Ln
11100 HOUS 77016 3687 B1
Ledge St
- HOUS 77034 4246 B7
- HOUS 77075 4246 B7
Ledgebrook Ln
2600 HarC 77546 4506 A7
Ledgecreek Ln
4900 HarC 77449 3677 C5
Ledgecrest Dr
2100 HarC 77038 3543 B4
Ledgefield
17100 HarC 77433 3251 B3
Ledger Ln
1800 GNPK 77015 3967 A5
12300 GNPK 77015 3966 E5
Ledgeside Ct
2900 FBnC 77494 3953 B7
Ledgestone Dr
3600 HOUS 77059 4380 D6
Ledgestone Pl
10 WDLD 77382 2819 C1
Ledgeway Ct
2300 HarC 77450 3954 C5
Ledgewood Dr
7900 HarC 77049 3689 C7
Ledgewood Park Dr
15200 HarC 77429 3397 C4
Ledla Ln
15600 HarC 77032 3404 A7
Le Doux Oaks Dr
- LGCY 77573 4630 C5
Ledwicke St
1400 HOUS 77029 3965 D3
Lee
- HOUS 77063 3960 A7
800 DRPK 77536 4109 C4
Lee Av
1000 PASD 77506 4107 C6
1300 PASD 77502 4107 C6
Lee Av E
- HOUS 77030 4102 E5
Lee Av S
- HOUS 77030 4102 E5
Lee Av W
- HOUS 77030 4102 E5
Lee Cir
2700 RSBG 77471 4491 A6
3200 PRLD 77581 4503 D3
Lee Dr
100 BYTN 77520 3972 D7
100 LMQU 77568 4990 C2
400 FBnC 77469 4493 C6
600 BYTN 77520 4112 D2
13400 MtgC 77306 2533 A6

STREET
Block City ZIP Map# Grid
Lee Ln
400 FBnC 77479 4366 D6
3700 PRLD 77584 4503 A7
9200 BzaC 77578 4747 C3
Lee Rd
2000 PRLD 77581 4501 E2
14200 HarC 77032 3546 E1
14200 HarC 77396 3546 E2
14500 HOUS 77396 3546 E1
15000 HarC 77032 3405 E7
15000 HOUS 77396 3405 E7
17900 HOUS 77032 3406 A2
17900 HOUS 77338 3406 A2
17900 HOUS 77396 3406 A2
18400 HOUS 77032 3261 D7
18400 HOUS 77032 3405 D1
18400 HOUS 77338 3261 D7
18400 HOUS 77338 3405 D1
19500 HarC 77338 3261 D4
Lee Rd FM-525
14200 HarC 77032 3546 E2
14200 HarC 77396 3546 E2
14500 HOUS 77396 3546 E1
Lee St
100 MAGA 77354 2669 B4
500 LPRT 77571 4251 E4
1200 HOUS 77009 3963 D1
1600 HOUS 77026 3963 E1
3000 HOUS 77026 3964 A1
5300 HOUS 77020 3964 C1
N Lee St
100 ALVN 77511 4867 B1
S Lee St
900 ALVN 77511 4867 B2
Lee Ann
- TMBL 77375 2964 A5
Leecast Ct
7500 FBnC 77469 4093 D5
Leech Rd
22600 HarC 77377 3106 C1
Lee Cir Ct
3100 PRLD 77581 4503 E3
Leedale St
5800 HOUS 77016 3686 E2
5900 HOUS 77016 3687 A2
Leeds Ln
15300 JRSV 77040 3540 E7
15600 FBnC 77083 4236 B1
Leedscastle Mnr
1500 HarC 77379 3110 B7
Leedscastle Manor Ct
10200 HarC 77379 3110 C7
Leedstown Ln
22500 HarC 77449 3814 D5
Leedswell Ln
16300 HarC 77084 3678 C4
Leedwick Dr
13300 HarC 77041 3679 C5
Leek St
2400 HOUS 77004 4103 E1
Leeland St
700 HOUS 77002 3963 C5
1500 HOUS 77003 3963 C5
4000 HOUS 77003 3964 A7
4900 HOUS 77023 3964 B7
5100 HOUS 77023 4104 C1
Leemeyers Ln
9500 HarC 77064 3540 D3
Leemont Ct
12700 HarC 77070 3399 A5
Leemyers Ln
19700 HarC 77388 3113 B6
Leens Lodge Ln
7000 HarC 77346 3265 A7
7000 HarC 77346 3409 A1
Lee Otis St
8500 HOUS 77051 4243 D3
Lee Ridge Dr
9000 BzaC 77578 4747 C3
Lees Ct
2300 LGCY 77573 4631 B5
Leeshire Dr
4000 HOUS 77025 4101 C7
4000 HOUS 77025 4241 C1
Lee Shore Ln
500 HOUS 77079 3956 C2
500 HOUS 77079 3957 A2
Leeside Ct
12500 HarC 77377 3254 B4
Leeside Dr
17200 HarC 77377 3254 B4
Leestead Ct
3000 HarC 77388 3113 A6
Leesway Rd
1600 FBnC 77469 4232 D4
Leeward
11200 HarC 77093 3685 C1
Leeward Cir
1400 KMAH 77565 4509 E6
Leeward Dr
7500 GLSN 77551 5222 B2
Leeward Ln
10 NSUB 77058 4508 B6
17700 MAGA 77354 2669 B3
Leeward Cove Dr
10 WDLD 77381 2821 B5
Leewood Ct
19300 HarC 77346 3264 B5
Lee Wy Dr
16200 HarC 77429 3397 A6
Leffingwell St
2200 HOUS 77026 3964 C1
3800 HOUS 77026 3825 B6
Legacy Ct
1900 FBnC 77469 4365 C4
29000 MtgC 77355 2815 A4
Legacy Oak St
23600 HarC 77449 3814 B3
Legacy Park Dr
10800 HarC 77064 3540 D3
Legacy Pines Dr
7300 HarC 77433 3677 B1
30200 MtgC 77386 2969 D2
E Legacy Point Cir
10 WDLD 77382 2820 A3
W Legacy Point Cir
10 WDLD 77382 2820 A3
Legal Ln
5000 DKSN 77539 4754 C3
Legare Ct
5500 HarC 77084 3679 A5
Legas Dr
- GLSN 77554 5222 A1
10 GLSN 77551 5222 A1
Legato Wy
10 WDLD 77382 2673 D7
Legend Ln
10 HOUS 77024 3958 E3

STREET
Block City ZIP Map# Grid
Legend Pt
- LGCY 77565 4509 B6
- LGCY 77573 4509 B6
1300 CRLS 77565 4509 C5
Legendary Ln
23700 FBnC 77494 4093 B4
Legendary Oaks Blvd
10 HMPD 77445 2952 C4
10 WlrC 77445 2952 C4
Legend Cove Ct
7800 HarC 77095 3537 E7
Legend Falls Ct
14400 FBnC 77083 4236 D1
Legend Grove Ct
2000 HOUS 77062 4379 D6
Legend Hollow Ct
10 WDLD 77382 2674 D4
Legend Manor Dr
11400 HOUS 77082 4098 A2
Legend Mill Ct
10 WDLD 77382 2674 D3
Legend Oak Dr
20000 HarC 77346 3265 C4
Legend Oaks Ct
30500 MtgC 77355 2815 B1
Legend Oaks Dr
18400 MAGA 77355 2815 B1
18400 MtgC 77355 2815 B1
Legend Park Dr
10 SGLD 77479 4495 D3
Legendre Rd
22100 FBnC 77469 4093 E7
Legends Ln
8900 FBnC 77459 4621 C5
E Legends Bend Dr
3000 MtgC 77386 2969 D4
N Legends Bend Dr
29500 MtgC 77386 2969 D3
S Legends Bend Dr
29500 MtgC 77386 2969 E4
N Legends Bend Ln
29600 MtgC 77386 2969 D3
S Legends Bend Ln
29600 MtgC 77386 2969 D3
Legends Bluff Dr
29600 MtgC 77386 2969 D3
Legends Briar Dr
- MtgC 77386 2969 E4
N Legends Chase Cir
29800 MtgC 77386 2969 D3
S Legends Chase Cir
29800 MtgC 77386 2969 B5
N Legends Chase Ct
29700 MtgC 77386 2969 B5
S Legends Chase Ct
29700 MtgC 77386 2969 B5
N Legends Creek Ct
29800 MtgC 77386 2969 B5
S Legends Creek Ct
29700 MtgC 77386 2969 B5
Legends Creek Dr
3100 MtgC 77386 2969 D3
Legends Crest Dr
2800 MtgC 77386 2969 C3
Legends Estates Dr
- MtgC 77386 2969 C2
Legends Garden Dr
3300 MtgC 77386 2969 E3
Legends Gate Dr
2200 MtgC 77386 2969 C1
Legends Glen Dr
29300 MtgC 77386 2969 E3
Legends Green Dr
29200 MtgC 77386 2969 D4
Legends Hill Ct
3200 MtgC 77386 2969 D3
Legends Hill Dr
29100 MtgC 77386 2969 D3
Legends Landing Dr
3300 MtgC 77386 2969 E3
Legends Line Dr
29300 MtgC 77386 2969 E3
Legends Link Dr
29000 MtgC 77386 2969 E4
Legends Mill Dr
3300 MtgC 77386 2969 E3
Legends Mist Dr
- MtgC 77386 2969 D2
Legends Pass Ct
29700 MtgC 77386 2969 B5
Legends Pass Ln
29800 MtgC 77386 2969 D3
Legends Peak Dr
2300 MtgC 77386 2969 B1
Legends Pine Ln
29500 MtgC 77386 2969 D3
Legends Pl Dr
29600 MtgC 77386 2969 D3
Legend Spring Dr
800 HarC 77494 3953 D3
Legends Ranch Ct
29700 MtgC 77386 2969 C3
Legends Ranch Dr
2700 MtgC 77386 2969 C3
Legends Ridge Dr
29700 MtgC 77386 2969 D2
Legends Run Dr
2800 MtgC 77386 2969 D4
Legends Shadow Dr
3300 MtgC 77386 2969 E3
Legends Shore Dr
2300 MtgC 77386 2969 B1
Legends Stone Dr
29400 MtgC 77386 2969 E3
E Legends Trail Ct
30000 MtgC 77386 2969 C3
E Legends Trail Dr
30100 MtgC 77386 2969 C2
W Legends Trail Dr
2400 MtgC 77386 2969 C2
Legends Tree Dr
10 MtgC 77386 2969 D4
N Legends Village Cir
29800 MtgC 77386 2969 B4
S Legends Village Cir
29800 MtgC 77386 2969 B4
S Legends Village Ct
29700 MtgC 77386 2969 D3
N Legends Village Ln
29700 MtgC 77386 2969 D3
Legends Wild Dr
3300 MtgC 77386 2969 E4
Legends Willow Dr
29600 MtgC 77386 2969 D3
Legends York Dr
10 MtgC 77386 2969 D4
Legend Woods Ct
2300 FBnC 77479 4494 B4

STREET
Block City ZIP Map# Grid
Leggett Dr
1200 GNPK 77547 3966 B6
Leggett Ln
5300 PRLD 77584 4503 A4
5600 PRLD 77584 4502 E4
Leghorn Av
8000 HOUS 77040 3681 E6
Leghrand Ct
200 LGCY 77573 4633 A1
Legion Dr
200 RHMD 77469 4492 A2
Legion Ln
100 RHMD 77469 4492 A2
Legion Rd
21100 MtgC 77357 2827 D7
21100 MtgC 77357 2973 D1
Legion St
600 ALVN 77511 4867 D2
3000 HOUS 77026 3825 A6
Legion Wy Ct
1900 FBnC 77469 4234 D7
Le Green St
700 HOUS 77008 3823 E6
800 HOUS 77009 3823 E6
Lehall St
1000 HOUS 77030 4102 C5
3400 HOUS 77021 4103 B6
Le Harv Ct
12300 HarC 77014 3401 E4
Le Havre Rd
7300 HOUS 77033 4243 E1
7300 HOUS 77033 4244 A1
Lehi Ln
2600 ALVN 77511 4866 E4
Lehigh St
- HOUS 77081 4101 A2
- HOUS 77401 4101 A2
4100 WUNP 77005 4101 C2
4900 BLAR 77401 4101 A2
Lehigh Springs Dr
10 WDLD 77381 2821 A5
Lehman Rd
700 HOUS 77018 3684 B7
1000 HOUS 77018 3683 E7
Leicester
19100 MtgC 77357 2828 E4
Leicester Ln
400 HOUS 77034 4378 E6
Leicester Wy
4600 MSCY 77459 4369 B5
Leichester Dr
2300 MtgC 77386 2969 C4
Leif Cove Ct
5900 HarC 77379 3111 E6
Leigh Av
1300 PASD 77502 4107 E6
8000 HTCK 77563 4988 D5
Leigh Ct
10 SGLD 77479 4495 D3
Leighann Ln Dr
4000 HarC 77047 4374 D5
Leigh Canyon Dr
16000 HarC 77546 4505 E6
Leigh Creek Dr
21800 HarC 77388 3111 D2
Leigh Garden Dr
1300 FBnC 77479 4494 A6
Leighton St
6700 HOUS 77016 3686 E7
Leightonfield Ct
7300 HarC 77433 3677 A1
Leighwood Creek Ct
8100 HarC 77396 3547 E2
Leighwood Creek Ln
14700 HarC 77396 3547 E1
Leigh Woods Dr
11000 HarC 77433 3537 A1
Leila Bend Ct
2900 HarC 77082 4096 D2
Leila Bend Dr
15100 HarC 77082 4096 C2
Leilani Dr
1300 TKIS 77554 5106 B4
Leila Oaks Cir
14900 HarC 77082 4096 C2
Leila Oaks Ct
3400 HarC 77082 4096 C2
Leila Oaks Dr
3200 HarC 77082 4096 C2
Leila Oaks Ln
15000 HarC 77082 4096 C2
Leinard Dr
18300 HarC 77090 3258 B1
Leirop Dr
21900 FBnC 77469 4093 E7
Leisure Ct
1800 PASD 77504 4247 E6
Leisure Dr
200 STAF 77477 4369 C4
500 FBnC 77477 4369 C4
Leisure Ln
- LGCY 77573 4753 B1
10 BKHV 77024 3959 C2
10 WDLD 77380 2821 D7
100 GlsC 77511 4751 C7
100 LGCY 77511 4751 C7
200 FRDW 77546 4629 E3
700 FRDW 77546 4630 A2
1800 LGCY 77573 4632 A6
2200 FBnC 77469 4365 D1
4100 PRLD 77584 4503 B4
26400 MtgC 77355 2814 A1
Leisure Lakes Blvd
- LGCY 77573 4632 A6
Leisure Pl Dr
18700 HarC 77346 3265 B6
Leithcrest Wy
20000 HarC 77379 3110 D5
Leitrim Wy
10500 HOUS 77047 4243 C6
11900 HOUS 77047 4374 C1
Leitz
10700 HOUS 77075 4376 C4
Lela Dr
100 FBnC 77053 4372 D7
Leland Dr
5300 BYTN 77521 3971 E2
W Leland Anderson St
3000 HOUS 77021 4103 B3
Lelda Ln
11800 HOUS 77071 4239 C5
Lelia St
2800 FBnC 77477 4370 A5
5000 HOUS 77026 3825 C7
Lemac Dr
4000 HOUS 77025 4241 C1
4300 HOUS 77096 4241 B1
Le May St
14500 HarC 77015 3968 B2

STREET
Block City ZIP Map# Grid
Lem Hill St
- SSPL 77005 4101 D4
Leming Ct
14700 HarC 77015 3829 C7
Lemm Ct
800 HarC 77373 3114 A7
Lemma Dr
7500 HarC 77041 3539 C7
Lemmingham Dr
2900 HarC 77388 3113 A6
Lemm Rd 1
900 HarC 77373 3114 A6
Lemm Rd 2
1200 HarC 77373 3114 B7
Lemoine Ln
6300 HarC 77049 3829 E3
6300 HarC 77530 3829 E3
Lemon Ln
1400 LPRT 77571 4110 E7
Lemond Dr
11200 HOUS 77016 3687 A1
11400 HOUS 77016 3547 A7
Lemongrass Av
8300 HarC 77521 3833 B2
Lemon Grove Dr
22600 HarC 77373 3114 D7
Lemon Ridge Ln
12100 HOUS 77035 4240 A6
Lemon Tree Cir
7500 HOUS 77088 3683 A2
Lemon Tree Ln
3400 HOUS 77088 3683 A2
4100 HOUS 77088 3682 E2
Lemonwood Ln
2300 HarC 77038 3543 B2
Lempira Ct
6700 HarC 77069 3400 B2
Lemur Ln
13100 HarC 77429 3254 A7
Lena Dr
200 HOUS 77022 3823 D1
Lena Ln
1400 BzaC 77511 4747 E1
11500 LbyC 77328 2537 D3
11500 MtgC 77372 2537 D3
Lenard St
400 HOUS 77009 3824 A4
Lenclaire Dr
15800 HOUS 77053 4371 E6
Lenehan
3100 HOUS 77003 3964 A4
Lenette Ct
900 BLAR 77401 4101 A6
Leneva Ln
1300 PASD 77502 4107 E6
1300 PASD 77506 4107 E6
Lennington Dr
11500 HarC 77064 3399 D7
Lennington Ln
12000 HarC 77064 3399 D6
Lennox Av
500 GLSN 77551 5108 B4
Lennox Gardens Dr
12200 HarC 77066 3401 C4
Lennox Ridge Dr
- HarC 77433 3537 A6
Lenny Ln
2000 PASD 77502 4107 B7
Lenora Ct
1900 HarC 77493 3814 A6
Lenora Dr
25000 HarC 77493 3814 A6
Lenora Springs Dr
- MtgC 77386 2969 D2
Lenore St
8000 HOUS 77017 4245 E1
8200 HOUS 77017 4246 A1
8300 HOUS 77017 4106 A7
Lenox St
10 HOUS 77011 3964 C6
500 HOUS 77023 3964 B7
N Lenox St
100 HOUS 77011 3964 C6
Lenox Hill Ct
10 WDLD 77382 2820 A3
Lenox Hill Dr
10 WDLD 77382 2820 A3
Lentando Ln
12900 HarC 77429 3254 B7
Lente Cir
22000 HOUS 77532 3266 B7
Lenz St
1900 LMQU 77568 4990 A2
2000 LMQU 77568 4989 E2
Lenze Rd
23600 HarC 77389 2966 B5
Leo Ln
700 LGCY 77573 4508 C6
Leon St
4300 PASD 77504 4247 E6
4300 PASD 77504 4248 A6
5900 HOUS 77009 3824 B4
Leona
2400 HOUS 77020 3963 E2
Leona Ct
3000 BzaC 77584 4501 C6
Leona St
1700 HOUS 77009 3963 D2
1700 HOUS 77026 3963 D2
Leonard Av
800 RHMD 77469 4364 D7
Leonard Rd
16900 HarC 77049 3691 A5
Leonard St
900 PASD 77506 4107 B5
1600 RSBG 77471 4491 C5
5600 HOUS 77023 4104 C3
21400 MtgC 77357 2973 B1
Leonetti Ln
4400 DKSN 77539 4754 D2
Leonidas St
3100 HOUS 77019 3962 C4
Leonidas Horton Rd
10000 MtgC 77304 2382 A5
Leonora St
7700 HOUS 77061 4245 B2
Leon River Ct
28700 MtgC 77386 2970 A2
Leon Springs Ln
13600 HarC 77429 3253 C6
Leopard Ct
2600 HarC 77449 3814 E4
Leopold Dr
5400 HOUS 77021 4103 D4
Leora Av
100 PASD 77506 4107 A5
Lepper St
2000 ALVN 77511 4749 A6

STREET
Block City ZIP Map# Grid
Lepper St
2100 BzaC 77511 4749 A6
Leprechaun Dr
- FRDW 77546 4629 B3
Leprechaun St
2500 HOUS 77017 4246 D2
Lera St
11100 HOUS 77016 3687 A1
11400 HOUS 77016 3547 A7
Lerin Ln
9400 FBnC 77478 4236 B2
Lerma Ct
22700 MtgC 77365 2972 A2
Lerner Dr
14700 HarC 77015 3829 C7
Leroy Dr
1900 PASD 77502 4107 C7
Leroy St
2500 FRDW 77546 4505 A5
2500 PRLD 77581 4504 E5
2500 PRLD 77581 4505 A5
2900 GlsC 77518 4634 B1
S Leroy St
200 TXCY 77591 4873 E7
Lerwick Dr
5100 HarC 77084 3678 C5
Lesiker Rd
6500 BKVL 77581 4375 E6
6500 BKVL 77581 4376 A6
Leslie Ct
15500 MtgC 77384 2674 E2
Leslie Dr
7000 GLSN 77551 5108 A7
Leslie Ln
900 FRDW 77546 4629 C2
16100 MSCY 77071 4370 B1
16100 MSCY 77489 4370 C1
Leslie St
2400 PASD 77502 4107 E7
2600 PASD 77502 4108 A7
5900 HOUS 77020 3964 E2
Leslie Ann Av
200 HOUS 77076 3685 B3
Lesota Ct
13600 HarC 77429 3253 E6
Lessa Ln
8000 PASD 77507 4249 D6
Lesser Creek Dr
4700 MSCY 77545 4622 C2
Les Talley Dr
1600 ELGO 77586 4382 B7
Lester Rd
7500 BzaC 77584 4627 C2
Lester St
800 CNRO 77301 2383 E4
800 HOUS 77007 3962 B3
Lestergate Dr
24000 HarC 77373 3115 B5
Letcher Dr
6400 HOUS 77028 3826 B2
Letchfield Hollow Dr
19800 HarC 77379 3110 D5
Letein St
6600 HOUS 77008 3822 E7
Letham Wy St
10200 HarC 77379 3110 C7
Lethbridge Dr
- HarC 77086 3542 B2
3400 PRLD 77581 4376 C6
Letica Dr
8100 HarC 77040 3541 B7
Leto Rd
9300 HOUS 77080 3820 D5
Letrim St
2500 PRLD 77581 4504 C2
Lettie Av
8200 HOUS 77075 4376 D4
9400 HOUS 77075 4377 B4
Lettie Ct
11000 HOUS 77075 4377 B4
Lettie St
- HOUS 77075 4377 A4
600 RHMD 77469 4364 D7
Lettile St
7700 HOUS 77075 4376 C4
Letz Dr
- TMBL 77375 2963 D5
Leva
- HOUS 77016 3686 E5
- HOUS 77016 3687 A5
Levandowski Rd
20100 PNIS 77445 3099 C5
Levee Ln
31300 MtgC 77354 2673 A6
Levee Rd
- SGLD 77479 4494 E3
- SGLD 77479 4495 A3
Level Oak Pl
2100 WDLD 77380 2967 D2
Level Run St
12200 MDWP 77477 4237 E5
Levering Ln
9200 HOUS 77028 3687 A6
Leverkuhn St
500 HOUS 77007 3962 C3
Leverwood Ct
10 WDLD 77381 2821 A5
Levi Bnd
700 MtgC 77354 2673 B2
Levi Rd
5800 HarC 77389 2966 E6
Levin Ln
- HOUS 77079 3958 C2
Levonshire Dr
4000 HOUS 77025 4101 C7
Levy Ln
24400 WlrC 77445 2954 B2
Lew Briggs Rd
13400 HOUS 77047 4373 E4
14000 HarC 77047 4373 E5
Lewis Dr
4800 BzaC 77584 4626 A1
10900 HOUS 77099 4238 C2
Lewis Ln
1000 KMAH 77565 4633 D1
6900 MNVL 77578 4746 E2
8900 GLSN 77554 5107 C6
Lewis Rd
12100 MtgC 77372 2537 B4
17100 HarC 77433 3396 D6
Lewis St
500 PASD 77502 4107 B7
800 LGCY 77573 4632 A3
1800 HOUS 77009 3963 C2
2000 ALVN 77511 4868 A2
2000 BzaC 77511 4867 E2
2000 BzaC 77511 4868 A2
7000 HTCK 77563 4989 A5

STREET
Block City ZIP Map# Grid
Lewis St
16200 JRSV 77040 3540 C7
E Lewis St
100 CNRO 77301 2384 A5
W Lewis St
100 CNRO 77301 2384 A5
800 CNRO 77301 2383 E4
Lewis Creek Ct
1400 FBnC 77469 4234 D5
Lewis Creek Dr
4200 FBnC 77469 4234 D5
Lewisham Ln
18400 HarC 77379 3111 B7
Lewis Scott Rd
16500 JMAB 77554 5332 A5
16600 JMAB 77554 5331 E6
Lewiston Ct
6500 HOUS 77049 3828 B2
Lewiston Rd
7200 HarC 77049 3828 B1
Lewiston St
6600 HarC 77049 3828 B2
6600 HOUS 77049 3828 B2
Lewisville Dr
1500 FBnC 77469 4234 C4
Lewisville Rd
41800 WlrC 77445 3097 C4
Lexanne Ct
3000 HarC 77388 3113 A6
Lexford Ln
2100 HOUS 77080 3820 B4
Lexham Dr
9500 FBnC 77083 4236 E2
Lexi Ln
- HarC 77084 3678 A2
- HarC 77095 3678 A2
Lexington Av
6700 HTCK 77563 4989 C5
Lexington Blvd
- HOUS 77489 4370 E6
- SGLD 77479 4367 E7
- SGLD 77479 4494 D1
1100 MSCY 77489 4370 C5
1700 HarC 77373 3113 E2
1700 HOUS 77373 3113 E2
1900 STAF 77477 4370 B5
2100 HarC 77373 3114 B2
3000 MSCY 77459 4370 A6
3000 MSCY 77477 4369 D6
3000 MSCY 77477 4370 A6
3700 MSCY 77459 4369 D5
3700 MtgC 77386 2970 B5
4600 SGLD 77459 4369 B5
4600 SGLD 77478 4369 B5
15200 SGLD 77478 4368 E5
15900 SGLD 77479 4368 A7
Lexington Ct
200 MtgC 77385 2676 A1
400 MtgC 77302 2530 B6
1100 MSCY 77489 4370 E5
2500 LGCY 77573 4631 B7
Lexington Dr
- RHMD 77469 4491 E4
100 MtgC 77385 2677 A7
Lexington Rd
- HarC 77373 3114 A4
26000 HOUS 77373 3113 E3
26400 HarC 77373 3113 E2
Lexington Sq
600 HMBL 77338 3263 B7
Lexington St
800 FRDW 77546 4629 C2
1700 DRPK 77536 4108 E7
2700 HOUS 77098 4102 A1
Lexington Common St
3500 FBnC 77477 4369 D5
3500 MSCY 77459 4369 D5
Lexington Green Dr
1000 MSCY 77459 4369 C5
Lexington Lake Dr
3000 MSCY 77459 4369 E6
Lexington Meadows Dr
4800 SGLD 77479 4367 D7
Lexington Park Dr
2200 HarC 77373 3114 C2
Lexington Woods Dr
1900 HarC 77373 3114 C2
Lexor Ct
21500 MtgC 77365 2973 B4
Lexor Dr
- MtgC 77365 2973 B4
Lexus Dr
500 HarC 77396 3406 E5
700 HarC 77396 3407 A5
Lexxe Creek Ct
21000 HarC 77433 3251 A4
Ley Rd
7100 HOUS 77028 3825 E1
7100 HOUS 77028 3826 E1
8800 HOUS 77078 3826 E1
9000 HOUS 77078 3827 A1
9100 HOUS 77078 3688 C7
E Ley Rd
- HarC 77044 3688 C7
- HOUS 77078 3688 C7
Leycrest Rd
- HOUS 77078 3688 B7
8700 HOUS 77028 3826 E1
8800 HOUS 77078 3826 E1
9000 HOUS 77078 3827 A1
Leyden Ct
200 HarC 77450 3954 E1
200 HOUS 77450 3954 E1
Leydenwood Ct
20200 FBnC 77469 4094 D2
Leydenwood Ln
7200 FBnC 77469 4094 C6
Leyland Ct
4300 PRLD 77584 4501 E6
Leyland Dr
4400 PRLD 77584 4501 E6
Leyton Ct
12500 HarC 77377 3254 B5
Leytonstone St
12500 HarC 77377 3254 B5
Leywood Cir
9000 HOUS 77099 4237 D1
Leza St
19200 HarC 77532 3411 D4
Lian Falls Ln
21400 FBnC 77469 4094 A6
Libbey Dr
1600 HOUS 77018 3822 C1
4400 HOUS 77092 3822 A1
5500 HOUS 77092 3821 D1
Libby Ln
7200 BzaC 77584 4627 B1

STREET
Block City ZIP Map# Gri
Libby Brook Ct
16500 HOUS 77044 3409 B
Liberty
22300 MtgC 77357 2973 E
Liberty Cir
500 FRDW 77546 4505 C
Liberty Dr
3400 PRLD 77581 4504 A
3800 PRLD 77581 4503 E
4000 GLSN 77554 5441 B
Liberty Ln
29400 TMBL 77375 2963 E
Liberty Rd
2800 HOUS 77026 3824 E
5400 HOUS 77020 3825 D
5400 HOUS 77026 3825 C
6300 HOUS 77028 3825 E
6500 HOUS 77028 3826 B
Liberty St
200 RHMD 77469 4491 E
1900 LGCY 77573 4632 C
20600 MtgC 77357 2827 B
Liberty Wy
800 HarC 77532 3552 A
Liberty Bell Cir
10 BKHV 77024 3959 C
Liberty Bluff Dr
15500 HarC 77049 3829 A
Liberty Canyon Tr
15500 HarC 77049 3829 A
Liberty Creek Tr
6800 HarC 77049 3829 A
Liberty Crest Rd
8700 HOUS 77013 3826 D
8700 HOUS 77028 3826 D
Liberty Cypress Ct
15500 HarC 77049 3829 B
Liberty Elm Ct
8000 HarC 77379 3256 A
Liberty Falls Ct
15400 HarC 77049 3690 A
Liberty Hall Dr
7200 HarC 77049 3690 B
7200 HarC 77049 3829 B
Liberty Isle Ct
15400 HarC 77049 3829 B
Liberty Lakes Dr
15500 HarC 77049 3829 A
Liberty Maple Dr
15600 HarC 77049 3829 B
Liberty Mesa Ln
7200 HarC 77049 3829 B
7300 HarC 77049 3690 B
Liberty Oak Ct
7100 HarC 77049 3829 B
Liberty Park Dr
7200 HarC 77049 3829 B
Liberty Pine Ln
15500 HarC 77049 3829 A
Liberty Point Ln
1900 SGLD 77478 4368 C
8100 HarC 77338 3261 E
Liberty Prairie Ct
15400 HarC 77049 3690 B
Liberty Ridge Ln
7200 HarC 77049 3690 B
7200 HarC 77049 3829 B
Liberty River Dr
15400 HarC 77049 3690 A
15600 HarC 77049 3829 B
Liberty Springs Wy
800 HarC 77373 3114 A
Liberty Square Tr
3400 FBnC 77545 4498 C
3800 FBnC 77545 4622 B
Liberty Trail Ln
19900 MSCY 77459 4497 D
Liberty Tree Ln
7200 HarC 77049 3829 B
7300 HarC 77049 3690 B
Liberty Valley Dr
6400 HarC 77449 3676 C
Liberty Vista Tr
15600 HarC 77049 3829 B
Liberty Wy Ct
17300 HarC 77532 3411 A
17300 HarC 77532 3552 A
Liberty Wy Dr
800 HarC 77532 3411 A
800 HarC 77532 3552 A
Libra St
5700 FBnC 77469 4615 E
Library St
22300 MtgC 77357 2827 D
Libretto Ct
10 WDLD 77382 2819 C
Libson Falls Dr
16700 HarC 77095 3538 A
Lichen Ln
7900 HarC 77379 3256 B
Lidell St
1700 HarC 77532 3411 D
Lido Ln
4300 HOUS 77092 3822 A
5000 HOUS 77092 3821 E
Lido Bay Ln
12000 HarC 77041 3680 A
Lido Park Ct
14700 HarC 77396 3547 D
Lidstone
2900 SEBK 77586 4509 B
Lidstone St
1300 SEBK 77586 4509 D
2300 HOUS 77023 4104 C
Lidstone Point Ct
23200 HarC 77494 3953 C
Lieder Dr
12100 HarC 77065 3398 D
Liendo Pkwy
- PRVW 77445 2954 D
- PRVW 77445 3099 E
- WlrC 77445 2954 E
- WlrC 77445 3099 E
Liere Ln
- HOUS 77084 3818 A
Lieren Ct
22400 HarC 77373 3113 D
Lieren Ln
1000 HarC 77373 3113 D
Liggio St
3900 DKSN 77539 4754 A
Light Bluff Ct
5100 HarC 77373 3115 C
Lightbranch Ct
4400 FBnC 77494 4092 D
Lightcliffe Dr
12400 HOUS 77031 4239 B

Houston Street Index

Block	City	ZIP	Map#	Grid
ght Company Rd				
100	HOUS	77017	4106	E4
100	HOUS	77506	4106	E4
100	PASD	77506	4106	E4
300	PASD	77017	4106	D3
ght Fall Cir				
8700	HarC	77095	3538	B5
ght Fall Dr				
-	HarC	77095	3538	C5
ght Falls Ct				
14400	HarC	77429	3397	B1
ghtfield Ln				
25100	FBnC	77494	4093	B6
ghtglen Ln				
-	FBnC	77450	4094	C3
ghthouse Blvd				
300	LGCY	77573	4508	D5
ghthouse Dr				
2700	NSUB	77058	4508	C4
Lighthouse Dr				
16900	HarC	77532	3552	B1
Lighthouse Dr				
16800	HarC	77532	3552	B2
ighthouse Ln				
10300	FBnC	77459	4622	A5
ghthouse Scene Ln				
19500	HarC	77433	3677	B1
ghthouse View Dr				
16600	HarC	77546	4506	B7
17000	HarC	77546	4630	B1
Lightning Bug Ct				
-	CNRO	77301	2530	C1
/ Lightning Bug Ct				
-	CNRO	77301	2530	C1
ghtningbug Ln				
800	CNRO	77301	2384	C7
800	CNRO	77301	2530	C1
ightspun Dr				
-	PRLD	77545	4499	D4
ightspun Ln				
-	HarC	77377	3253	E3
ightstar Dr				
3000	HOUS	77045	4242	A6
ghtstone Ln				
5700	LGCY	77573	4751	C2
ightwoods Dr				
24400	HOUS	77336	3266	B2
ightwood Trace Dr				
10	WDLD	77382	2674	D4
igustrum Wy				
2300	HarC	77388	3113	A2
igustrum Trail Ct				
12600	HarC	77377	3254	B4
igusturm Tr				
17100	HarC	77377	3254	C4
ila Dr				
12000	HarC	77429	3397	B6
ila Ln				
12800	HOUS	77015	3967	C4
ila St				
3700	HOUS	77026	3825	B7
6800	BKVL	77581	4376	A6
7000	PRLD	77581	4376	A6
ilac Cir				
100	HarC	77532	3411	A4
ilac Ct				
4100	FBnC	77477	4369	C4
ilac Ln				
100	BYTN	77520	3832	B7
17500	MtgC	77357	2681	A7
17700	MtgC	77357	2827	A1
ilac St				
100	HOUS	77009	3824	B7
600	LMQU	77568	4873	E7
700	LMQU	77568	4989	E1
2400	PASD	77503	4248	C3
2900	PASD	77505	4248	C3
5500	KATY	77493	3813	C4
ilac Wy				
24100	MtgC	77365	2972	A6
ilac Blue Ln				
9500	HarC	77044	3689	C3
ilac Breeze Ct				
-	HarC	77429	3254	A5
ilac Breeze Ln				
2300	PRLD	77545	4499	E2
ilacbrook Ct				
6700	HarC	77379	3111	C2
ilac Glen Ct				
7600	HarC	77095	3538	A7
ilac Grove Ln				
5400	BzaC	77583	4623	E4
ilac Manor Ct				
11100	HarC	77065	3539	B1
ilac Meadows Ln				
6600	HarC	77379	3111	C4
21000	FBnC	77469	4094	A5
ilac Mist Ln				
1500	HarC	77038	3543	E4
9900	HarC	77070	3255	B6
ilac Pointe				
900	LGCY	77573	4631	E5
ilac Ridge Ct				
10	WDLD	77384	2675	E5
ilac Ridge Pl				
10	WDLD	77384	2675	D5
V Lilac Ridge Pl				
100	WDLD	77384	2675	E5
ilac Springs Ln				
8900	HarC	77095	3537	E5
ilac Stone Ct				
12700	HarC	77044	3689	B3
ilac Vale Ct				
17200	HarC	77084	3678	A2
ilac View Ct				
1300	PRLD	77545	4499	E3
iles Ct				
16800	HarC	77396	3407	E3
iles Ln				
3600	HarC	77396	3407	E3
3600	HarC	77396	3408	A3
3700	HarC	77346	3408	A3
ilium Ct				
10	WDLD	77380	2821	D6
illa Ln				
16700	HarC	77530	3830	D5
illeux Rd				
10800	HarC	77038	3402	B7
10800	HarC	77067	3402	B7
10800	HOUS	77067	3402	B7
illey Rd				
500	GlsC	77511	4869	A6
illian Ln				
1000	GLSN	77554	5107	D6
1000	HarC	77532	3410	E5
17100	HarC	77377	3254	C4
illian St				
600	CNRO	77301	2384	B3

Block	City	ZIP	Map#	Grid
Lillian St				
900	HarC	77562	3832	A3
1700	PASD	77502	4106	E7
2100	PASD	77502	4246	E1
4500	HOUS	77007	3962	B3
5400	BYTN	77521	3971	E1
Lillie St				
1100	DRPK	77536	4249	C1
Lillington Manor Ct				
10	HarC	77379	3110	D7
Lillja Rd				
100	HarC	77037	3544	D6
13900	HarC	77060	3544	D6
15700	HOUS	77060	3544	D1
Lillus				
4300	HOUS	77093	3686	B4
Lilly Blvd				
300	CNRO	77301	2384	A2
500	CNRO	77301	2383	E3
Lilly Ct				
27400	MtgC	77354	2817	D4
Lilly Dr				
1600	MtgC	77384	2674	E1
Lilly St				
-	PASD	77505	4248	B4
4000	FBnC	77545	4623	D1
Lilly Hollow Ln				
-	HarC	77429	3397	D3
Lilly Mist Ln				
9900	HarC	77038	3543	E4
Lily Ct				
500	LGCY	77573	4632	D2
Lily Gln				
-	CNRO	77301	2530	E3
-	CNRO	77302	2530	E3
Lily Ln				
2400	HarC	77562	3832	D3
4400	FBnC	77545	4623	D2
Lily St				
600	PRVW	77484	3100	D4
2400	PASD	77503	4248	B1
2900	PASD	77505	4248	B1
Lilybloom Ln				
21000	FBnC	77469	4094	B6
Lily Creek Dr				
22900	HarC	77375	2966	A7
Lilygate Ct				
14400	HarC	77047	4374	B5
Lily Glen Ct				
-	FBnC	77494	4092	D4
Lily Glen Ln				
-	FBnC	77494	4092	D4
Lily Hollow Ct				
6400	HarC	77379	3111	C3
Lily Park Ln				
13100	HOUS	77085	4240	C7
13100	HOUS	77085	4371	C2
Lily Pond Ct				
3300	MSCY	77459	4496	B2
Lilywood Ct				
5600	BzaC	77583	4623	E4
Lilywood Ln				
-	HarC	77449	3676	C6
5500	BzaC	77583	4623	E3
Lilywood Springs Dr				
19100	HarC	77449	3816	B2
Lima Dr				
11600	HOUS	77099	4238	A1
12300	HOUS	77099	4237	D1
12900	HarC	77099	4237	C1
Limber Bough Dr				
7500	HarC	77346	3265	B7
7500	HarC	77346	3409	B1
Limber Oak St				
14900	HarC	77082	4096	D2
Limber Pine Pl				
12500	HarC	77429	3398	D5
Limber Pines Ct				
18600	MAGA	77355	2815	A1
18600	MtgC	77355	2815	A1
Limber Pines Dr				
30400	MtgC	77355	2815	A1
Lime Blossom Ct				
14800	HarC	77433	3250	E5
Lime Creek Dr				
4000	FBnC	77450	4094	A1
Lime Green Tr				
21600	HarC	77433	3250	E5
Limerick Ct				
2200	DRPK	77536	4109	A6
Limerick Ln				
8900	HOUS	77024	3961	A1
14100	TMBL	77375	2963	D5
Limerick Wy				
10	CNRO	77384	2675	E3
Limeshade Ln				
16800	FBnC	77478	4236	B6
Lime Springs Dr				
8300	HarC	77095	3538	C6
Limestone Ct				
-	RSBG	77469	4491	E6
-	RSBG	77471	4491	E6
Limestone St				
6600	HOUS	77092	3821	C2
Limestone Canyon Ln				
4200	FBnC	77494	4092	B1
Limestone Lake Dr				
16000	HarC	77377	3254	C6
Limestone Ridge Tr				
20600	HarC	77433	3251	B4
Limewood Ln				
10000	FBnC	77478	4236	E3
Limrick Dr				
2100	PRLD	77581	4504	D2
Lina St				
-	HarC	77338	3260	C2
7100	HOUS	77012	4105	B5
7100	HOUS	77087	4105	B5
Linares Dr				
9700	HOUS	77078	3688	B5
Linbrook Dr				
10300	HarC	77089	4377	A7
Lincoln				
19000	MtgC	77357	2828	E3
19000	RMFT	77357	2828	E4
Lincoln Dr				
2800	HarC	77038	3543	A6
2800	HarC	77086	3543	A6
6700	HTCK	77563	4989	C5
N Lincoln Dr				
6600	HTCK	77563	4989	B4
S Lincoln Dr				
6600	HTCK	77563	4989	B5
Lincoln St				
-	HarC	77038	3543	A6
-	HarC	77086	3543	A6
-	HarC	77088	3543	A6
-	HarC	77530	3831	B6

Block	City	ZIP	Map#	Grid
Lincoln St				
200	DRPK	77536	4249	B2
600	BYTN	77520	4112	C1
2700	HOUS	77006	3962	D6
3900	HOUS	77051	4243	C1
N Lincoln St				
10	TXCY	77591	4873	E6
Lincoln Cedar Dr				
100	BYTN	77520	3974	B1
Lincoln Crest Wy				
1900	SGLD	77478	4237	A6
Lincoln Green Dr				
5300	KATY	77493	3813	D7
Lincoln Heights Ln				
19300	FBnC	77469	4094	E6
Lincoln Park Dr				
15300	HarC	77429	3252	E5
Lincoln Park Pl				
7800	HOUS	77053	4372	C7
Lincoln Ridge Ln				
12800	HOUS	77085	4240	E7
Lincoln Round Dr				
1600	KATY	77493	3813	D6
Lincolnshire Rd				
4500	HOUS	77048	4374	E2
4600	HOUS	77048	4375	A2
E Lincolnshire St				
12700	HOUS	77077	3957	C6
W Lincolnshire St				
12800	HOUS	77077	3957	C6
Lincolnshire Field Ln				
-	HarC	77450	3953	E6
Lincolns Meadow Dr				
2800	HarC	77373	3115	A5
Lincoln Town Dr				
5300	KATY	77493	3813	D6
Lincrest Ln				
-	HOUS	77057	4100	D1
5400	HOUS	77056	4100	D1
Linda Dr				
2900	PRLD	77584	4503	A4
5900	FBnC	77583	4623	B5
Linda Ln				
200	WEBS	77598	4507	B6
400	ALVN	77511	4867	D6
400	FRDW	77546	4505	A7
1100	PRLD	77584	4501	D2
1600	LGCY	77573	4632	B1
1800	PASD	77502	4107	D7
5300	BYTN	77521	3972	A1
5300	KATY	77493	3813	D6
15000	GlsC	77517	4986	A2
17000	MtgC	77306	2533	D6
24100	MtgC	77365	2973	D7
28100	TMBL	77375	2963	D4
Linda St				
100	CNRO	77301	2384	A2
100	DRPK	77536	4109	A4
4200	GlsC	77518	4634	D2
5400	FBnC	77583	4623	C4
7600	HOUS	77017	4105	B6
7600	HOUS	77087	4105	B6
12800	HarC	77031	4239	B7
12800	HarC	77477	4239	B7
12800	STAF	77477	4239	B7
Lindale St				
100	HOUS	77022	3824	B3
Linda Leigh Ln				
10300	HarC	77375	3110	C1
Lindale Manor Ct				
6600	HarC	77379	3111	D2
Lindale Rose Ln				
14500	HarC	77396	3547	D1
Lindall Ct				
14700	HarC	77429	3253	E7
Linda Mesa Dr				
6400	HarC	77083	4096	B4
Linda Vista Rd				
7800	HOUS	77028	3687	B7
8800	HOUS	77078	3687	E7
9000	HOUS	77078	3688	A7
Lindberg Av				
1200	BYTN	77520	4112	C1
E Lindbergh Ct				
3900	BYTN	77521	3973	A3
N Lindbergh Ct				
400	BYTN	77521	3972	E2
400	BYTN	77521	3973	A2
W Lindbergh Ct				
3900	BYTN	77521	3972	E3
Lindbergh St				
6600	HOUS	77087	4244	D1
Lindell Rd				
400	HarC	77373	3113	E1
Lindemann Cir				
600	RHMD	77469	4492	B1
Linden				
300	FBnC	77545	4499	A6
Linden Ct				
5500	HarC	77379	3257	A1
N Linden Dr				
300	TXCY	77591	4872	E6
Linden Ln				
-	FBnC	77469	4364	A1
22800	MtgC	77355	2814	C7
22800	MtgC	77355	2960	D1
Linden Pl				
4500	PRLD	77584	4501	E5
4700	PRLD	77584	4502	A5
Linden St				
1000	LMQU	77568	4989	E1
4700	BLAR	77401	4101	A5
5000	BLAR	77401	4100	E5
6400	HOUS	77087	4104	E4
6500	HOUS	77087	4105	A4
7100	HOUS	77012	4105	A4
13400	SGLD	77478	4237	B5
Linden Brook Ln				
9300	FBnC	77469	4616	E1
Lindenbrook Ln				
14900	HarC	77095	3539	B6
Linden Chase Ln				
5300	HarC	77066	3401	A5
Linden Cove Ct				
2000	FBnC	77494	3952	C6
Linden Creek Ln				
2100	HOUS	77017	4246	D1
Lindencrest Ct				
8800	FBnC	77479	4366	D5
Lindencrest St				
7300	HOUS	77061	4245	B4
Lindencroft Ct				
14100	HarC	77070	3399	E2
Lindencroft Ln				
9500	HarC	77044	3689	B4
Linden Field Ct				
21200	HarC	77338	3261	D3

Block	City	ZIP	Map#	Grid
Lindenfield Ct				
19700	HarC	77449	3815	D1
19700	HarC	77449	3816	A2
Lindenfield Dr				
3500	HarC	77449	3815	E2
Lindenfield Pl				
19800	HarC	77449	3815	E2
Linden Forest Ln				
18100	HarC	77449	3677	D3
Linden Gate Dr				
10900	HOUS	77075	4377	A4
Linden Glen Ln				
4000	HarC	77039	3546	A4
Linden Grove Ct				
5400	FBnC	77479	4493	D2
Linden Hill Ln				
21100	HarC	77338	3261	E3
Linden Hills Ln				
21000	HarC	77338	3261	D3
Linden House Ct				
21200	HarC	77338	3261	D3
Linden Knoll Ln				
6400	HOUS	77085	4240	D7
Lindenloch Ln				
13000	HOUS	77085	4240	E7
13000	HOUS	77085	4371	E1
Linden Manor Ct				
600	HarC	77373	2968	E6
Linden May Ln				
9800	FBnC	77494	4092	C5
Linden Meadow Ln				
19300	FBnC	77469	4094	E5
Linden Oaks Ln				
-	FBnC	77494	4092	D3
7900	FBnC	77469	4095	D7
Linden Park Ln				
-	MtgC	77386	2823	C6
Linden Rock Dr				
2100	FBnC	77494	3952	B5
Linden Springs Ct				
16300	HarC	77095	3538	B3
Linden Springs Dr				
10300	HarC	77095	3538	B2
Linden Tree Dr				
20200	HarC	77449	3815	C5
Lindenwalk Ln				
10800	HarC	77433	3537	C1
Lindenwick Ct				
19800	HarC	77433	3677	A1
Lindenwood Dr				
300	HNCV	77024	3960	C2
400	HOUS	77024	3960	C2
700	BYTN	77520	3972	D6
Linder St				
1800	HOUS	77026	3824	E3
3800	HOUS	77026	3825	A3
Linder Green Dr				
-	MtgC	77386	2969	D2
Lindfield Ln				
-	HarC	77073	3259	A1
Lindhaven Dr				
3400	PRLD	77584	4502	E6
Lindheimer Rd				
21800	MtgC	77447	2960	D6
Lindita Dr				
15000	HOUS	77083	4096	C7
15100	FBnC	77083	4096	D7
Lindsay Ln				
1100	KATY	77493	3813	A7
5400	HOUS	77011	3964	C5
Lindsay Rd				
13400	HarC	77429	3398	A3
Lindsay St				
5000	HOUS	77023	4104	B1
Lindsey Dr				
1000	RSBG	77471	4491	C3
Lindsey Ln				
12800	STAF	77477	4239	A7
12800	STAF	77477	4370	A1
18300	HarC	77447	3105	B7
Lindsey Rd				
19000	HarC	77377	3107	C5
Lindsey Hill Ln				
7300	HarC	77396	3547	C2
13600	HarC	77429	3253	D6
Lindsey Terrace Ln				
-	MtgC	77386	2969	D7
Lindstrom Rd				
16600	HarC	77532	3553	A2
Lindy Ln				
1700	CNRO	77301	2384	D5
6600	HOUS	77023	4104	D2
Lindyann Ln				
6200	HOUS	77008	3822	D6
6200	HOUS	77008	3823	A5
Line Dr				
6600	PASD	77505	4248	E4
6600	PASD	77505	4249	A4
Line St				
1500	HOUS	77009	3824	D7
Linea del Pino St				
2100	HOUS	77077	3957	C7
Line Camp Ct				
9500	HarC	77064	3540	B4
Linecamp Dr				
10300	HarC	77064	3540	B4
Linenhall Dr				
10000	FBnC	77478	4236	E3
Liner Ln				
17500	HarC	77095	3677	E1
Linfield Wy				
1700	HOUS	77058	4507	C3
Ling Cir				
2400	TXCY	77591	4873	A3
Ling Rd				
30400	MtgC	77354	2672	A6
Ling St				
-	GlsC	77563	4990	E6
200	BYUV	77563	4990	D7
Lingard Park Ct				
1800	HOUS	77047	4373	D1
Linger Ln				
11700	MtgC	77303	2239	D7
Lingonberry St				
4800	HOUS	77033	4243	D1
Lininger Ln				
4500	DKSN	77539	4754	D3
Link Ct				
8800	HOUS	77025	4101	D7
Link Rd				
2500	HOUS	77009	3823	E4
2500	HOUS	77009	3824	A4
3300	HOUS	77022	3823	D3
3400	HOUS	77018	3823	D3
W Linkage				
-	HOUS	77058	4507	D2
Link Crossing Ln				
7800	HarC	77389	2966	A2

Block	City	ZIP	Map#	Grid
Linkfair Ln				
8700	HOUS	77025	4101	D7
Linklea Dr				
3800	HOUS	77025	4101	D7
Link Meadow Ln				
8600	HOUS	77025	4101	D7
9200	HOUS	77025	4241	D1
Linkpass Ln				
8600	HOUS	77025	4101	D7
Links Ct				
10	HOUS	77339	3119	D7
Linkshire Dr				
15400	HOUS	77062	4506	E2
Linksman Ln				
5700	HarC	77449	3676	E5
Links Side Ct				
10	HOUS	77339	3264	E1
Linkterrace Ln				
8700	HOUS	77025	4101	D7
Link Valley Dr				
3500	HOUS	77025	4241	D1
Linkview Dr				
3700	HOUS	77025	4101	D7
Linkwood Dr				
1000	PRLD	77581	4504	E7
2800	HOUS	77025	4102	A7
3600	HOUS	77025	4101	D7
Linkwood Ln				
16900	MtgC	77365	2825	E7
Linkwood St				
600	FRDW	77546	4629	B2
Linn Ln				
8700	MtgC	77354	2672	E1
Linn St				
3900	HOUS	77026	3825	A6
Linnet Ln				
10400	HOUS	77048	4244	C6
Linnet Chase Pl				
10	WDLD	77381	2821	A2
Linney Blvd				
10	SGLD	77479	4495	C3
Linnfield Dr				
12700	HarC	77070	3399	D5
Linnhaven Dr				
6100	HOUS	77072	4098	D4
Linnmont Ln				
9600	HarC	77070	3399	D5
W Linnwood Dr				
-	WDBR	77357	2828	B2
E Linpar Ct				
6400	HOUS	77040	3682	A5
N Linpar Ct				
7500	HOUS	77040	3682	A5
S Linpar Ct				
7500	HOUS	77040	3682	A5
W Linpar Ct				
6400	HOUS	77040	3682	A5
Linshire Dr				
20300	HarC	77388	3113	A6
Linsley Ln				
10500	HOUS	77034	4378	B3
Linson Ln				
500	FRDW	77546	4629	A2
Linton Dr				
1200	LMQU	77568	4874	A7
1200	LMQU	77568	4990	A1
Linton Rd				
6200	HOUS	77008	3822	E7
6200	HOUS	77008	3823	A7
Linton St				
6000	TXCY	77591	4873	D6
Linton Down Pl				
100	WDLD	77382	2674	A5
N Linton Ridge Cir				
10	WDLD	77382	2674	B5
S Linton Ridge Cir				
10	WDLD	77382	2674	A5
N Linton Ridge Ct				
100	WDLD	77382	2674	A5
Linvale Dr				
11000	HOUS	77016	3687	B2
Linwood Cir				
1100	PASD	77502	4106	E6
Linwood Ct				
10900	LPRT	77571	4250	D3
Linwood Dr				
-	BYTN	77520	3971	A5
100	MtgC	77357	2828	D3
100	WDBR	77357	2828	C2
2400	MSCY	77459	4369	B7
E Linwood Dr				
10800	LPRT	77571	4250	D3
N Linwood Dr				
10	WDBR	77357	2828	B2
Linwood St				
10	HOUS	77011	3964	D6
3500	PRLD	77581	4503	C2
Linwood Manor Ct				
15900	HarC	77429	3397	B3
Linwood Oaks				
-	PRLD	77581	4503	D2
Linwood Oaks E				
2100	PRLD	77581	4503	D2
Linwood Oaks W				
2100	PRLD	77581	4503	D2
Linwood Terrace Dr				
6600	FBnC	77469	4093	E7
Lions Gate Ct				
19700	HarC	77338	3262	A5
Lions Gate Dr				
19900	HarC	77338	3262	A4
Lions Gate Ln				
20300	HarC	77338	3262	A3
Lipan Rd				
8600	HOUS	77063	4099	D2
Lipicland Ln				
-	BzaC	77511	4626	D7
-	BzaC	77511	4747	E1
Lippitzaner Dr				
18500	HarC	77433	3677	C1
Lipps Ln				
6300	HarC	77041	3679	B4
Lipscomb St				
2900	HOUS	77023	4104	C4
Lira Rd				
5700	MNVL	77578	4625	C4
Liriope Ct				
-	WDLD	77384	2675	B6
Lisa Ct				
300	FRDW	77546	4505	A7
Lisa Ln				
400	HarC	77373	2969	A7
900	HOUS	77339	3263	D1
2300	MSCY	77489	4370	C6
6000	HOUS	77021	4104	A6
26500	MtgC	77365	3117	D4
Lisa Dawn Ln				
16300	HarC	77049	3829	E2

Block	City	ZIP	Map#	Grid
Liscomb Dr				
14500	HarC	77084	3679	A3
Lisman Ln				
-	HarC	77073	3258	E4
Lismore Cir				
13100	HarC	77429	3398	C3
Lismore Pt				
13200	HarC	77429	3398	C3
Lismore Estates Ln				
11200	MtgC	77385	2823	A6
Lismore Lake Dr				
11700	HarC	77429	3398	C3
Lissa Ln				
100	FBnC	77479	4366	D5
Lissie St				
3600	FBnC	77545	4498	E7
Lista Ln				
100	HarC	77562	3831	E3
Litchfield Ln				
10	HOUS	77024	3958	E4
7600	HarC	77379	3256	C4
Litchfield Bend Ln				
23600	FBnC	77494	4093	C1
N Lite St				
32000	SGCH	77355	2961	C3
S Lite St				
31900	SGCH	77355	2961	C3
Little				
14600	HOUS	77045	4372	A3
Little Ct				
13900	HOUS	77077	3956	E5
Little Rd				
5300	BYTN	77520	3971	D1
5300	HarC	77520	3971	D1
5300	HarC	77521	3832	D7
5300	HarC	77521	3971	D1
Little St				
1900	LMQU	77568	4990	A3
2000	LMQU	77568	4989	E2
7900	HOUS	77028	3826	B3
Little Tr				
-	HarC	77346	3408	A3
10	FBnC	77459	4621	B3
30600	MtgC	77354	2816	A1
Little Acorn				
100	HOUS	77024	3959	C5
Little Ashlee Ct				
4000	HarC	77014	3401	C2
Little Barley Ct				
11000	HarC	77086	3542	B1
Little Bear Dr				
2900	HOUS	77339	3119	A5
Little Bend Lp				
6500	HTCK	77563	4989	A4
Littleberry Rd				
4100	HOUS	77088	3683	A3
4200	HOUS	77088	3682	E3
Little Big Horn Dr				
20000	HarC	77449	3815	D6
Littleborne Birdwell Ln				
14000	HarC	77047	4374	D4
Littleborne Birdwell Ln Ln				
13900	HarC	77047	4374	D4
Little Bough Ln				
17400	MAGA	77354	2669	B3
17400	MtgC	77354	2669	C3
Little Branch Ct				
2900	HarC	77082	4096	C2
Little Branch Dr				
-	HarC	77064	3540	D4
Little Brook Ln				
30200	MtgC	77355	2814	E2
30400	MtgC	77355	2815	A1
Littlebrook Rd				
11200	LPRT	77571	4110	D7
Little Buck Dr				
100	HarC	77532	3266	E7
Littlecape Tr				
-	HarC	77346	3264	D7
Little Cedar Dr				
2000	HOUS	77339	3118	E4
2300	HOUS	77339	3119	A5
Little Cedar Bayou Dr				
-	LPRT	77571	4251	C5
Little Creek Ct				
7100	HarC	77433	3677	A1
Littlecrest Rd				
3900	HarC	77093	3686	B3
Littlecroft Dr				
30700	MtgC	77386	2969	A2
Little Cypress Dr				
17100	HarC	77429	3252	D5
Little Cypress Ln				
16100	HarC	77429	3397	A2
Little Deer Ln				
20800	HarC	77532	3410	B1
Little Dirt Rd				
22000	MtgC	77357	2827	C5
Little Doe Dr				
400	HarC	77532	3266	D7
Little Doe Ln				
-	SPLD	77372	2683	A5
Little Egypt Rd				
11000	MtgC	77304	2236	C2
Little Elm Ln				
-	HarC	77346	3408	A2
Little Fans Dr				
9200	HarC	77396	3407	B7
Little Farms Ct				
3300	FBnC	77469	4234	C6
Little Fawn Dr				
18300	HarC	77084	3816	D4
Littlefield Ct				
11700	HarC	77377	3254	D3
Littlefield Dr				
20300	HarC	77388	3113	A5
Littlefield Springs Ln				
-	HarC	77073	3259	B3
Littleford St				
14400	HOUS	77045	4373	A3
Little Forest Ct				
2400	HarC	77373	3114	D3
Little Fox Ln				
500	HOUS	77060	3403	D6
Little Gap Ct				
10900	FBnC	77478	4236	D5
Littleglen Ln				
17000	HarC	77084	3678	B6
Little Green St				
9100	HarC	77375	3110	D2
Little Grove Dr				
6000	PRLD	77581	4502	D2
Little Harbor Wy				
23000	FBnC	77494	4093	B3
Little Haven Ct				
6700	RSBG	77469	4492	E7
6700	RSBG	77469	4493	A7

Block	City	ZIP	Map#	Grid
Little John Cir				
25000	WlrC	77447	2959	D1
N Little John Cir				
11700	MSCY	77071	4239	D7
S Little John Cir				
11800	MSCY	77071	4239	D7
Little John Ct				
800	PASD	77502	4107	B7
Little John Ln				
10	CNRO	77301	2383	D3
100	CNRO	77304	2383	C6
300	HOUS	77024	3960	D2
5300	KATY	77493	3813	D7
Little John St				
1800	MtgC	77316	2668	E1
Little Lake Ct				
2600	FBnC	77469	4365	B6
Little Lake Rd				
800	MtgC	77304	2529	D5
Little Lake St				
5500	BLAR	77401	4100	D6
5500	HOUS	77081	4100	D6
Little Leaf Ct				
10	FBnC	77459	4621	B3
14900	HarC	77082	4096	C2
Little Lisa Ln				
10900	HNCV	77024	3960	A2
Little Mill Pl				
100	WDLD	77382	2674	D4
Little Miss Creek Dr				
15800	HarC	77429	3253	B5
Littleneviss Dr				
5100	HarC	77084	3678	B6
E Little Oak Ct				
400	ORDN	77386	2822	C6
W Little Oak Ct				
300	ORDN	77386	2822	C6
Little Oak Dr				
10000	CmbC	77520	3835	C3
Little Oak St				
16900	MtgC	77365	2825	C4
Little Orchard Ct				
11400	HarC	77377	3254	E5
Little Path Dr				
14100	HarC	77429	3253	E4
Little Pine Ln				
19300	HarC	77449	3677	A4
Little Pinto Ct				
17200	HarC	77095	3396	D7
Littleport Ln				
1400	HarC	77530	3829	C5
Littler Ct				
1800	HarC	77532	3551	D3
Little Ranch Rd				
13300	HarC	77429	3398	C3
Little Redwood Dr				
6800	PASD	77505	4248	E5
6900	PASD	77505	4249	A5
Little Riata Dr				
-	HarC	77433	3537	D2
17300	HarC	77095	3537	D2
Little River Ct				
500	FBnC	77469	4365	B5
28700	MtgC	77386	2970	B2
Little River Rd				
8200	HarC	77064	3541	D6
Little Rock Ct				
13900	HarC	77429	3253	E5
Little Shoe Ln				
17400	HarC	77396	3407	E3
Little Skiff Dr				
-	HarC	77532	3409	E7
Little Skiff Wy				
-	HarC	77532	3409	E6
Little Spring Cir				
2800	HarC	77373	3115	C3
Little Star Rd				
12600	HOUS	77598	4379	A6
Little Stone Ln				
6000	FBnC	77494	4092	A5
Little Summer Dr				
200	RSBG	77469	4492	C6
Little T				
10200	CNRO	77302	2531	A3
Little Thicket Ct				
7600	HarC	77433	3677	B1
Little Thorn Ln				
36800	MtgC	77354	2670	B6
36800	MtgC	77354	2816	C1
Littleton St				
400	HOUS	77022	3824	B2
Little Torch				
10	HTCK	77563	5105	A5
Little Twig Ln				
100	MAGA	77354	2669	B3
700	MtgC	77354	2669	B3
Little Willow Dr				
7000	PASD	77505	4249	A5
Little Willow Wk				
14300	HOUS	77062	4379	E7
Little Wind Ln				
23400	HarC	77373	3115	E6
Little Wolf				
21500	HOUS	77532	3266	B7
Little Wood Dr				
600	BYTN	77521	3973	B4
Little Wren Ln				
37200	MtgC	77354	2816	B1
Little York Rd				
-	HOUS	77093	3686	B3
100	HOUS	77037	3684	E3
100	HOUS	77076	3684	E3
200	HOUS	77076	3685	B3
1400	HOUS	77093	3685	C3
2000	HarC	77093	3685	C3
3900	HarC	77093	3686	B3
4200	HarC	77016	3686	D3
4200	HOUS	77016	3686	B3
6000	HOUS	77016	3687	D2
7900	HOUS	77078	3687	D2
13700	HarC	77044	3689	A3
E Little York Rd				
100	HOUS	77037	3684	D3
100	HOUS	77076	3684	D3
12400	HarC	77044	3689	A3
W Little York Rd				
100	HOUS	77037	3684	B3
100	HOUS	77076	3684	B3
500	HOUS	77088	3684	B3
500	HOUS	77091	3684	B3
900	HOUS	77088	3683	A4
900	HOUS	77091	3683	A4
4100	HOUS	77088	3682	E4
4100	HOUS	77091	3682	E4
6400	HOUS	77092	3682	E4
6500	HOUS	77040	3682	C3
7300	HarC	77040	3682	A3
7700	HarC	77040	3681	E4

STREET
Block City ZIP Map# Grid

W Little York Rd
7700 HOUS 77040 3681 E4
10000 HarC 77040 3680 C3
10000 HarC 77041 3680 E3
10000 HOUS 77041 3680 E3
11600 HarC 77041 3679 D4
14900 HarC 77084 3679 B4
15000 HarC 77084 3678 D3
17400 HarC 77084 3677 E4
17700 HarC 77449 3677 D4
20500 HarC 77449 3676 D4
Littonwood Ct
19100 HarC 77094 3955 B2
Lively Ct
1000 FBnC 77469 4365 C2
Lively Ln
- HOUS 77041 3820 B1
- HOUS 77080 3820 B1
2400 SGLD 77479 4368 E7
Lively Oaks Pl
10 WDLD 77382 2674 C4
Live Meadow Ln
4700 HarC 77449 3677 B7
Live Oak
- FBnC 77545 4498 E4
100 BzaC 77578 4625 B3
100 FBnC 77545 4499 A4
17000 WEBS 77598 4507 A5
N Live Oak
19700 MtgC 77357 2829 B5
S Live Oak
20000 MtgC 77357 2829 B6
Live Oak Al
10 HOUS 77003 3963 E5
Live Oak Av
100 BYTN 77520 3973 A6
200 BYTN 77520 3972 E6
2400 WALR 77484 3101 E6
2700 WlrC 77484 3101 E6
Live Oak Bnd
- HOUS 77049 3828 A2
Live Oak Cir
17000 MtgC 77365 2825 C5
Live Oak Ct
- HOUS 77336 3121 A4
1400 MSCY 77489 4370 D4
9500 BzaC 77578 4746 B7
9500 MNVL 77578 4746 B7
Live Oak Dr
- LGCY 77598 4630 C4
100 FRDW 77546 4505 B7
300 STAF 77477 4369 E3
1100 BzaC 77511 4868 A6
1800 CNRO 77301 2384 E7
1800 CNRO 77301 2530 E1
2500 RSBG 77471 4491 A6
4900 DKSN 77539 4753 C5
5000 TXCY 77591 4874 A6
7500 HMBL 77396 3406 D2
11700 MtgC 77354 2671 B4
18600 MtgC 77306 2534 B7
20100 HOUS 77338 3261 B5
20200 HarC 77532 3412 E1
20200 HarC 77532 3413 A2
24000 WlrC 77447 2813 D2
Live Oak Ln
800 TYLV 77586 4381 E7
800 TYLV 77586 4508 E1
4200 HarC 77389 3112 C1
12000 HarC 77375 2964 D2
16600 PRLD 77581 4504 B7
16600 PRLD 77581 4628 B1
Live Oak Pk
33200 MtgC 77354 2671 B4
Live Oak Pl
6000 HarC 77379 3111 E7
6000 HarC 77379 3256 E1
S Live Oak Rd
- TMBL 77375 2964 C7
- TMBL 77375 3109 C1
Live Oak St
- SEBK 77586 4382 C7
100 HarC 77532 3552 C4
400 SGLD 77478 4367 E2
500 HOUS 77003 3963 D6
900 PASD 77506 4107 B5
1500 WEBS 77598 4507 A5
2200 HOUS 77004 3963 C7
3300 HOUS 77004 4103 B3
4500 BLAR 77401 4101 B4
20900 MtgC 77357 2828 A7
20900 MtgC 77357 2974 A1
N Live Oak St
100 TMBL 77375 2964 C6
200 HOUS 77003 3963 E4
400 HOUS 77003 3964 A4
1500 WEBS 77598 4507 A5
S Live Oak St
100 TMBL 77375 2964 C6
Live Oak Tr
10 HarC 77429 3397 D6
2500 DRPK 77536 4249 E1
18900 HarC 77377 3106 E1
Live Oak Bend Dr
17200 HarC 77433 3395 D6
Live Oak Bend Wy
15000 HarC 77429 3252 B7
Live Oak Branch Dr
16800 MtgC 77365 2825 C5
Live Oak Burr Dr
19900 MtgC 77365 2825 C5
Live Oak Estates Dr
17000 MtgC 77365 2825 C5
Live Oak Glen Ln
13400 HarC 77429 3254 A6
Live Oak Hill St
1800 HarC 77067 3402 B7
Live Oak Hollow St
1600 PRLD 77581 4504 D4
Live Oak Square Dr
16100 MtgC 77365 2825 B4
Live Oaks Spring Dr
21600 HarC 77450 3954 B4
Live Oak View Ct
- HarC 77336 3122 A3
Livernois Rd
9300 HOUS 77080 3820 D5
Liverpool Ct
4600 MSCY 77459 4369 B5
Liverpool St
6300 HOUS 77021 4103 E7
Livery Ln
7000 HarC 77449 3677 C2
7500 HarC 77433 3677 C1
Livestock Ln
- HarC 77450 3954 B5
Livings St
8700 HOUS 77028 3687 D7

Livingston Dr
2700 PRLD 77584 4502 E4
Livingston St
7800 HOUS 77051 4243 B2
Livingstone Ln
300 LGCY 77573 4630 C7
Livingston Lake Ct
3800 PRLD 77581 4503 E7
Liza Ct
2500 HarC 77388 3113 A2
Lizbeth Dr
- HOUS 77085 4240 D7
Lizette Ct
10000 HOUS 77075 4377 C2
Lizzie Ln
300 TMBL 77375 2964 C7
Llama Ln
11100 HOUS 77477 4237 E3
Llano Ct
2000 MtgC 77384 2529 A5
Llano St
100 PASD 77504 4247 C4
Llano Creek Dr
5800 HarC 77449 3676 D4
Llano Pass Ct
13600 HarC 77429 3253 D6
Lloyd Av
11700 HarC 77532 3692 D2
Lloyd Dr
500 BYTN 77521 3972 D5
Lloyd St
700 RSBG 77471 4491 A4
6300 HOUS 77022 3824 C3
Lloydmore St
7900 HOUS 77093 3825 B1
Lloyds Ln
23600 MtgC 77447 2960 A4
Loafers Ln
19300 MtgC 77355 2814 A2
Lobelia Manor Ct
20000 HarC 77379 3110 D5
Lobelia Manor Dr
9200 HarC 77379 3110 D5
Lobenstein Av
3200 DKSN 77539 4754 C4
Lobera Dr
7400 FBnC 77083 4096 A6
W Lobit Av
100 BYTN 77520 3973 A7
200 BYTN 77520 3972 E6
Lobit Dr
3100 DKSN 77539 4753 C3
E Lobit St
10 BYTN 77520 3973 A7
N Lobit St
- LPRT 77571 4252 A2
300 MRGP 77571 4252 A1
S Lobit St
100 LPRT 77571 4252 A3
W Lobitt St
- ALVN 77511 4867 B1
1000 ALVN 77511 4749 A7
Loblolly Ln
3400 MtgC 77380 2967 B2
Loblolly Rd
18100 HarC 77377 3106 E2
Loblolly Bay Ct
17100 HOUS 77059 4380 C4
Loblolly Pine Dr
23500 MtgC 77357 2974 A2
Loblolly Pines Wy
3200 HOUS 77082 4098 B2
Lobo Ln
16200 HarC 77379 3256 B5
Lobo Tr
17300 HarC 77084 3677 E3
17300 HarC 77084 3678 A3
Loch Ln
6500 HarC 77389 2966 C4
Loch Bend Ct
10900 HarC 77086 3542 A1
Lochberry Ct
11700 HarC 77377 3254 E5
Loch Briar Ct
1100 HarC 77494 3953 D4
Loch Bruceray Dr
6400 HarC 77084 3677 E3
Lochbury Ct
10 HarC 77379 3255 C1
Lochbury Dr
10 HarC 77379 3255 C1
Loch Courtney Ln
10000 HarC 77089 4505 A2
Loch Creek Ct
14000 HOUS 77062 4379 D6
Loch Dane
9600 HarC 77379 3255 C3
Loch Dane Dr
9700 HarC 77379 3255 C3
9900 HarC 77070 3255 C4
Lochflora Dr
9300 HarC 77379 3255 C2
Loch Glen Ct
3800 HOUS 77059 4380 B4
Loch Katrine Ct
4700 HarC 77084 3678 C6
Loch Katrine Ln
16200 HarC 77084 3678 C6
16200 HOUS 77084 3678 C6
Loch Katrine St
2200 HarC 77532 3693 C5
Loch Lake Dr
1500 ELGO 77586 4509 C1
1500 SEBK 77586 4509 C1
Lochland Ln
2200 HarC 77088 3543 C7
Loch Langham Ct
17300 HarC 77084 3678 C3
Loch Langham Dr
6500 HarC 77084 3678 A3
Lochlea Ridge Dr
- HarC 77379 3255 C2
Lochlevan Ct
28500 HarC 77336 3121 D2
Loch Lomond
2200 HarC 77532 3693 C6
Loch Lomond Ct
8900 HOUS 77096 4240 D1
Loch Lomond Dr
100 LGCY 77573 4631 D4
4900 HOUS 77096 4241 A1
5100 HOUS 77096 4240 E1
Lochman Ct
3000 PRLD 77584 4502 A6
Lochman Ln
4800 PRLD 77584 4502 A6
Loch Maree Ln
16500 HarC 77084 3817 C1

Lochmere Ln
21200 FBnC 77450 4094 B1
Lochmere Wy
2300 HOUS 77345 3120 B3
Lochmire Ln
3600 HarC 77039 3546 A4
Lochmoor Ln
800 FRDW 77546 4504 E6
800 FRDW 77546 4505 A6
800 PRLD 77581 4504 E6
Lochnell Dr
200 HOUS 77062 4506 D1
Loch Ness Dr
10 HarC 77562 3692 D6
Lochpoint Ct
20200 FBnC 77469 4094 D2
Lochpoint Ln
20100 FBnC 77469 4094 D2
Loch Raven Ln
17000 HOUS 77060 3403 D6
Lochridge Ln
- HarC 77084 3678 A7
Lochshin Cir
16600 HarC 77084 3678 C7
Lochshin Dr
4600 HarC 77084 3678 C7
Lochshire Dr
- HOUS 77077 3957 B4
14000 HOUS 77077 3956 E4
Lochstone Dr
1400 HarC 77073 3404 A3
Lochtyne Cir
10 HDWV 77024 3959 D2
Lochtyne Wy
800 HDWV 77024 3959 D2
Lockbourne Dr
12600 HarC 77038 3543 C4
Lockburn
- HOUS 77053 4372 A5
15700 HOUS 77053 4371 E5
Lockcrest St
2900 HOUS 77047 4374 A3
Lockdale Ln
16000 HarC 77429 3397 B2
Locke Ln
1500 SGLD 77478 4368 C4
2300 HOUS 77019 3962 A6
3200 HOUS 77019 3961 E6
3400 HOUS 77027 3961 D6
5600 HOUS 77056 3960 D7
6200 HOUS 77057 3960 B7
7900 HOUS 77063 3960 A7
10000 HOUS 77042 3958 E7
10000 HOUS 77042 3959 A7
13700 HOUS 77077 3957 A7
13900 HOUS 77077 3956 D7
Locke Haven Dr
16300 HOUS 77059 4380 D6
Locke Lee Ln
7900 HOUS 77063 3960 A7
Lockeridge Bend Dr
2800 MtgC 77386 2969 E5
Lockeridge Cove Dr
2800 MtgC 77386 2969 E5
Lockeridge Creek Dr
28400 MtgC 77386 2969 E4
Lockeridge Farms Dr
28500 MtgC 77386 2969 E4
Lockeridge Oaks Dr
2700 MtgC 77386 2969 E5
Lockeridge Pines Dr
2800 MtgC 77386 2969 E5
Lockeridge Pl Dr
2800 MtgC 77386 2969 E5
Lockeridge Springs Dr
28500 MtgC 77386 2969 E4
Lockeridge View Dr
28500 MtgC 77386 2969 E5
Lockeridge Village Dr
3000 MtgC 77386 2969 E5
Lockern St
7100 HOUS 77016 3686 E4
Lockett St
2800 HOUS 77021 4102 E5
2800 HOUS 77021 4103 A5
Lockfield St
- HOUS 77092 3682 C6
4100 HOUS 77092 3821 C1
Lockford Ln
16900 HarC 77073 3259 B3
Lockgate Dr
3400 HarC 77388 3112 E3
Lockgate Ln
10900 HOUS 77048 4243 E6
Lockhart Dr
5000 PRLD 77584 4503 A7
Lockhaven Dr
- HarC 77073 3259 A7
100 HarC 77073 3258 D6
100 HarC 77090 3258 D6
100 HOUS 77073 3258 D6
100 HOUS 77073 3259 A7
100 TXCY 77591 4873 A6
Lockheed Av
8100 HOUS 77061 4245 B5
Lockheed Dr
2000 GLSN 77554 5107 E7
2000 GLSN 77554 5221 E1
Lockheed St
10 HOUS 77061 4245 B4
3400 PRLD 77581 4503 C3
Locklaine Dr
1300 PASD 77502 4106 E6
2100 PASD 77502 4246 E1
Lockland Ln
500 LGCY 77573 4630 E6
Lockridge Dr
19000 HarC 77373 3114 A7
19300 HarC 77373 3113 E6
Locksford St
1800 HOUS 77008 3822 C5
Locksley Ln
1500 SGLD 77479 4367 C7
Locksley Rd
7800 HOUS 77078 3687 B5
Locksley Trace Ct
1800 HarC 77094 3955 C1
Lockway Dr
13800 HOUS 77045 4372 A1
Lockwood
- HarC 77396 3406 E7
S Lockwood
14900 HarC 77396 3548 C1
Lockwood Dr
100 HOUS 77011 3964 B5
700 HOUS 77020 3964 D1
2500 HOUS 77020 3825 D7
3300 HOUS 77026 3825 D7

Lockwood Dr
6300 HOUS 77028 3825 C3
7800 HOUS 77016 3825 C1
8200 HOUS 77016 3686 C7
E Lockwood Dr
3300 HOUS 77026 3825 D7
S Lockwood Dr
- HOUS 77004 4104 A1
- HOUS 77023 4104 A1
10 HOUS 77011 3964 B7
600 HOUS 77023 3964 B6
Lockwood Rd
- HarC 77044 3549 A1
11200 HarC 77044 3689 A1
14400 HarC 77396 3549 A7
Loc Loma Ln
2100 LPRT 77571 4250 A1
N Locust Dr
600 FBnC 77545 4623 A1
S Locust Dr
600 FBnC 77545 4623 A2
Locust St
- HOUS 77017 4106 D7
- LGCY 77598 4630 C4
100 HMPD 77445 2953 B6
1600 HOUS 77502 4106 D7
1600 PASD 77502 4106 D7
1900 WALR 77484 3102 A4
4800 BLAR 77401 4101 A4
5000 BLAR 77401 4100 E4
5200 HOUS 77081 4100 E4
6700 HTCK 77563 4989 A4
11700 HarC 77532 3692 C2
Locust Grove Dr
15800 HarC 77095 3538 D5
Locust Springs Dr
16900 HarC 77095 3538 A4
Loddington Dr
20300 HarC 77388 3113 A5
Loddington St
29200 MtgC 77386 2969 C4
Lodenberry Ct
5000 FBnC 77494 4093 B1
Lodenbriar Dr
12800 HOUS 77072 4097 C4
Lodenstone Ct
24900 FBnC 77494 3953 B6
Lodestar Rd
3200 HOUS 77032 3404 E1
Lodestone Ct
16800 HarC 77095 3538 A1
Lodge Ct
1300 MSCY 77489 4370 D4
Lodge Ln
800 FBnC 77469 4365 E4
Lodge St
6600 HOUS 77092 3821 C1
20400 MtgC 77357 2827 E7
21000 MtgC 77357 2973 E1
Lodgebrook
- HarC 77070 3398 E2
Lodge Creek Dr
5000 HarC 77066 3401 A2
5300 HarC 77066 3400 D3
Lodge Crest Ct
2000 LGCY 77573 4509 B7
Lodge Falls Ct
1600 HOUS 77345 3120 D6
Lodgegate Ct
7400 FBnC 77469 4094 C7
Lodge Glen Ct
5200 FBnC 77494 4093 A2
Lodgeglen Ct
- KATY 77494 3952 B2
Lodgeglen Ln
- KATY 77494 3952 B3
Lodgehill Ln
700 HarC 77090 3258 B2
Lodge Hollow Ct
300 HOUS 77024 3961 A2
Lodge Meadows Dr
22900 FBnC 77494 3953 D5
Lodge Mist Ln
- LGCY 77539 4753 A3
Lodgepoint Dr
23000 FBnC 77494 3953 D6
Lodgepole Pl
8500 HarC 77375 3110 E2
Lodge Pole Rd
6400 HOUS 77049 3828 B3
Lodgepole Pine St
18200 HarC 77429 3396 B1
Lodge Run Ln
11300 HarC 77065 3398 E6
Lodge Stone Ct
22000 FBnC 77450 4094 A2
Lodge Wood Ct
9800 HarC 77086 3541 E2
Lodi Dr
1100 HarC 77562 3831 E1
Loeser Dr
1000 SPVL 77055 3820 E7
Lofland Dr
8400 SPVL 77055 3821 B6
Loft Forest Ct
3800 HOUS 77339 3119 C4
Lofting Wedge Dr
2000 HarC 77089 4504 D2
Lofton Dr
14900 HarC 77530 3968 C1
E Loftwood Cir
10 WDLD 77382 2673 D6
W Loftwood Cir
10 WDLD 77382 2673 C7
Lofty Ln
- HarC 77379 3111 E6
Lofty Elm St
- HarC 77429 3253 B1
2700 HarC 77038 3543 A2
Lofty Magnolia Ct
5600 HOUS 77345 3120 B4
Lofty Maple Tr
1400 HOUS 77345 3120 C6
Lofty Mills Dr
1400 HOUS 77339 3118 C7
Lofty Mountain Ct
14000 HOUS 77062 4379 D4
Lofty Mountain Tr
14000 HOUS 77062 4379 D4
14100 HOUS 77062 4380 A5
Lofty Oak Ct
2400 HOUS 77059 4379 D5
Lofty Peak Ln
15800 HOUS 77062 4380 D7
Lofty Pine Ct
8100 MtgC 77385 2676 B6
Lofty Pines Dr
10500 HarC 77065 3539 D2

Lofty Ridge Ct
4100 PASD 77059 4380 D4
Log Tr
- HarC 77084 3816 C3
Logan Ln
5700 HOUS 77007 3962 A4
23500 HOUS 77336 3266 B3
Logan St
1300 LMQU 77568 4989 C1
Logan Bay Ln
15500 HarC 77053 4372 D5
Loganberry Cir
2500 SEBK 77586 4382 B6
Loganberry Park Ln
2800 HarC 77014 3257 D7
Logan Briar Dr
19700 HarC 77375 3109 D6
Logan Bridge Ln
10300 FBnC 77478 4236 D3
Logan Crest Ct
3200 FBnC 77494 4093 D1
Logancrest Ln
5800 HarC 77086 3542 D4
Logandale Ln
700 HarC 77032 3403 D7
1000 HarC 77032 3404 A6
Logan Falls Ln
14500 HarC 77396 3547 E2
Logan Mill Dr
12400 HarC 77070 3399 B6
Logan Park Dr
5700 HarC 77379 3257 A1
Logan Pass Wy
18200 HarC 77346 3408 E2
Logan Ridge Dr
11700 HOUS 77072 4098 A4
Logan Rock Rd
15900 HOUS 77489 4371 C6
Logans Field Ln
- FBnC 77469 4615 D6
Logans Landing Ln
5000 FBnC 77494 4092 C3
Logans River Ln
- FBnC 77469 4365 B6
Logans Run Ln
9200 HOUS 77075 4377 A4
Logan Star Ct
- FBnC 77469 4095 A7
Logan Timbers Ln
19100 HarC 77375 3109 D7
Log Cabin Ln
11200 HarC 77375 3110 A7
Log Cradle Dr
7200 HarC 77041 3679 C1
7500 HarC 77041 3539 C7
Logger Ln
30600 MtgC 77355 2815 D1
Loggerhead
10 HTCK 77563 5105 A5
Logger Pine Trails
10500 HarC 77088 3543 C7
10500 HarC 77088 3683 C1
Loggers Chase Ct
600 MtgC 77386 2968 D1
Loggers Depot Dr
2600 SGLD 77478 4368 D6
Loggers Luck Pl
10900 WDLD 77380 2821 C7
Loggers Trail Ct
9900 HOUS 77040 3682 A1
Loggia Ln
4700 HarC 77396 3407 B7
Logging Trail Dr
7200 HarC 77346 3265 A7
Loggins Ln
25100 HarC 77336 3121 E7
25100 HarC 77336 3266 E1
Log Hollow Dr
6500 HOUS 77088 3542 B7
7000 HOUS 77040 3542 A7
7700 HarC 77040 3542 A7
7800 HarC 77040 3541 E7
Logrun Cir
- WDLD 77380 2821 C7
N Logrun Cir
2700 WDLD 77380 2821 C7
S Logrun Cir
2800 WDLD 77380 2821 C7
Logston Ln
5300 HarC 77389 2967 A7
Logtowne Dr
25000 MtgC 77362 2963 C1
Log Tram Ct
10 WDLD 77382 2674 A6
Log View Dr
7100 HOUS 77040 3542 A7
Logwood Dr
6200 HOUS 77088 3682 C2
Loire Ln
700 HarC 77090 3258 B2
Lois Ln
14300 GlsC 77517 4986 B3
14300 HTCK 77517 4986 B3
33000 MtgC 77354 2673 E4
Lois Ln Dr
11800 MtgC 77362 2963 C1
Lokai St
200 TKIS 77554 5106 C4
Lola Ln
- FBnC 77469 4234 D6
- MtgC 77357 2829 D5
Lola St
3500 FBnC 77469 4234 D6
3600 FBnC 77545 4498 E7
Lolita Ln
- HarC 77039 3546 E3
Lollipop Ln
1400 HMBL 77338 3407 A1
Lolly Ln
17000 HarC 77084 3678 A2
Loma Ct
3700 MtgC 77386 2970 B6
Loma Ln
3800 MtgC 77386 2970 B5
Loma St
8300 HOUS 77051 4243 C2
Loma Alta Dr
7300 HarC 77083 4096 C6
Loma Lago Ln
- FBnC 77469 4094 D7
Loma Linda Av
6300 HOUS 77085 4371 D3
Loma Linda Dr
5500 HOUS 77045 4372 A3
5500 HOUS 77085 4371 E3
5500 HOUS 77085 4372 A3
Loma Linda St
6600 HOUS 77085 4371 C3

Loma Paseo Dr
15100 FBnC 77083 4096 C7
Loma Verde Dr
15600 HarC 77083 4096 B6
Loma Vista Pl
6300 HOUS 77085 4371 C3
Lomax Dr
1900 LPRT 77571 4110 E7
1900 LPRT 77571 4250 E1
Lomax St
8600 HOUS 77093 3685 E6
Lomax School Rd
1400 LPRT 77571 4110 C7
1900 LPRT 77571 4250 C1
Lombard Rd
14900 MtgC 77302 2532 E3
14900 MtgC 77306 2532 E3
14900 MtgC 77306 2533 A3
Lombardia Ct
10900 FBnC 77469 4093 A7
10900 FBnC 77469 4233 A1
Lombardy Dr
100 SGLD 77478 4368 B3
Lombardy St
1300 HOUS 77023 4104 A1
Lomcrest Ln
12000 HOUS 77035 4240 B7
12000 HOUS 77085 4240 B7
12000 HOUS 77085 4371 B1
Lomelina Ln
- LGCY 77573 4633 A5
Lomitas St
4500 HOUS 77098 4102 A1
Lommel Dr
5800 HarC 77449 3677 B5
Lonallen St
9900 HOUS 77088 3543 B7
9900 HOUS 77088 3683 B1
London
- FBnC 77469 4491 B2
London Ct
2900 PRLD 77581 4503 E2
London Grn
10 CNRO 77384 2675 E3
S London Grn
10 CNRO 77384 2675 E3
London Ln
- MtgC 77357 2829 D4
3500 FBnC 77459 4622 B5
14000 HarC 77083 4097 A6
London St
1100 PASD 77506 4107 E6
1200 PASD 77502 4107 E6
6300 HOUS 77021 4103 D7
Londonderry Av
1000 FRDW 77546 4629 B4
Londonderry Dr
2400 PRLD 77581 4504 D1
10200 HOUS 77043 3819 E5
10200 HOUS 77043 3820 A5
33000 WlrC 77484 3246 C4
Londongreen Dr
1400 HarC 77530 3829 E5
London Town Dr
25000 HarC 77389 2965 E3
25800 HarC 77389 2966 A2
London Town Pl
8200 HarC 77389 2966 A1
London Wy Dr
8300 HarC 77389 2965 E3
8500 HarC 77375 2965 D3
Londres Dr
7200 FBnC 77083 4095 E6
Lone Bridge Ln
8200 HarC 77338 3261 E4
Lone Brook Dr
10300 HOUS 77041 3680 E7
10300 HOUS 77041 3681 A7
Lone Cedar Dr
- LGCY 77573 4631 A5
5800 HOUS 77345 3120 B4
Lone Corral Ct
16300 MtgC 77302 2679 C4
Lone Creek Ct
20700 HarC 77449 3676 D3
Lone Creek Ln
13200 PRLD 77584 4500 A4
Lone Cypress Ln
- HarC 77429 3396 A1
Lone Dove Ct
4000 HarC 77082 4096 E3
Lone Eagle Dr
1700 HarC 77532 3410 C1
Lone Elm Dr
24000 HarC 77373 3114 D5
Lone Fir Dr
17000 HarC 77379 3255 D5
Lone Hickory Ct
11800 PASD 77059 4380 E5
Lonely Pine Dr
4100 BYTN 77521 3974 A1
Lonely Star Ln
20900 FBnC 77469 4234 B4
Lone Maple Dr
8400 FBnC 77083 4236 A1
Lone Meadow Ct
7600 HarC 77095 3537 D7
Lone Oak
20500 WlrC 77445 3243 D4
Lone Oak Ct
4900 BYTN 77521 3972 C1
Lone Oak Dr
100 HarC 77562 3831 E3
1300 LGCY 77573 4632 A5
7200 BYTN 77521 3835 B4
9800 CNRO 77303 2238 E5
9800 MtgC 77303 2238 E5
Lone Oak Rd
1400 HarC 77093 3685 C2
1400 HOUS 77093 3685 C2
4100 HarC 77093 3686 B2
Lone Oak St
14800 HarC 77532 3553 A5
30000 MtgC 77354 2671 E7
30000 MtgC 77354 2817 E1
Lone Oak Park Dr
17800 HarC 77095 3537 D6
17800 HarC 77433 3537 D6
Lone Pine Dr
10 HarC 77336 2976 A4
100 HarC 77336 2975 E4
100 HarC 77562 3831 E3
3500 GlsC 77510 4871 E6
Lone Prairie Wy
6000 HarC 77449 3676 D4
Lone Quail Ct
16700 HOUS 77489 4370 E7

Lone Quail Dr
8200 HOUS 77489 4370 E
Lone Ridge Ln
21500 HarC 77449 3815 B
Lone River Ct
17900 HarC 77095 3537 E
Lone Rock Dr
2000 HOUS 77339 3118
Lone Shadow Tr
11700 HarC 77016 3547 D
11700 HarC 77050 3547 D
15900 SGCH 77355 2815 E
Lonesome Bayou Ln
6200 HOUS 77088 3682 C
E Lonesome Dove
- DRPK 77536 4109 D
Lonesome Dove Ct
10600 HarC 77095 3537 E
Lonesome Dove Tr
17500 HarC 77095 3537 E
Lonesome Pine Rd
3800 HarC 77389 2967 C
Lonesome Pine St
16100 MtgC 77355 2961 D
16100 SGCH 77355 2961 D
Lonesome Quail Dr
16400 HOUS 77489 4370 D
Lonesome Ridge Ct
3000 FBnC 77478 4235 E
3000 FBnC 77478 4236 B
Lonesome Woods Tr
6600 HarC 77346 3264 E
6900 HarC 77346 3265 A
Lone Star Ct
5600 LGCY 77573 4630 D
Lone Star Dr
1000 SPVL 77055 3820 E
2100 SGLD 77479 4368 B
Lone Star Ln
3000 MtgC 77362 2816
Lonestar St
2100 LMQU 77568 4990 A
Lone Star Junction St
7400 FBnC 77469 4234 B
Lone Star Oak Ct
20300 HarC 77433 3251 C
Lone Star Oak St
20300 HarC 77433 3251 C
Lone Star Ranch Dr
16000 MtgC 77302 2679 B
Lone Star Ranch Rd
16100 MtgC 77302 2679 B
Lone Stirrup Dr
1400 FBnC 77469 4365 A
Lonestone Cir
4700 HarC 77449 3676 D
Lone Tree Dr
15600 HarC 77084 3678 E
15600 HarC 77084 3679 A
Lone Willow Ct
14400 HOUS 77489 4371 B
Lone Willow Ln
14500 HOUS 77489 4371 B
Lone Wolf Ct
14000 HarC 77429 3253 E
Lone Wolf Tr
23200 HarC 77373 3114 D
Lone Wolf Pass
17500 HarC 77095 3537 E
Long Dr
- HOUS 77021 4104 C
100 BYTN 77521 3973 A
1100 RHMD 77469 4491 E
5800 HOUS 77033 4104 C
5800 HOUS 77087 4104 C
7200 HOUS 77087 4105 A
11300 MtgC 77302 2677 C
Long Lk
14300 MtgC 77372 2682 D
Long Rd
10 HarC 77336 2977 A
10 LbyC 77327 2977 A
15100 HarC 77044 3690 E
15700 HarC 77044 3691 A
Long St
900 CNRO 77301 2384 A
25600 PTVL 77372 2683 B
26500 MtgC 77372 2683 B
Longacre Dr
100 CNRO 77304 2383 B
1500 HOUS 77055 3821 A
1700 HOUS 77080 3821 A
Long Barrel Ln
1900 MSCY 77489 4370 D
9200 HarC 77040 3681 E
10200 HarC 77040 3541 E
Long Barrow Ln
3400 FBnC 77459 4621 C
Long Bay Ct
3100 HOUS 77059 4380 A
Long Boat Ct
16100 HarC 77532 3552 A
Long Bough Ct
3100 HOUS 77059 4380 A
Longbourne Dr
- WDLD 77382 2673 D
Longbow Cir
9400 MtgC 77354 2818 C
Longbow Ln
10 HOUS 77024 3960 E
Long Bow Rd
9400 MtgC 77447 2960 A
Longbow St
27300 MtgC 77354 2818 C
Long Branch Ln
9600 HOUS 77055 3820 C
30900 MtgC 77354 2816 B
Long Branch Rd
10500 MtgC 77303 2239 A
Long Briar Ln
3300 FBnC 77478 4366 E
3300 FBnC 77478 4367 A
Longbrook Dr
11900 HOUS 77099 4238 A
12100 HOUS 77099 4237 E
Long Canyon Ln
- RHMD 77469 4492 B
Longcastle Dr
21400 HarC 77388 3113 A
Longcliffe Dr
18200 HarC 77084 3677 D
Long Climb Canyon
4500 HarC 77396 3407 C
Long Common Dr
11000 HOUS 77099 4238 B
Long Cove Ct
2200 FBnC 77450 3953 E

Houston Street Index

STREET
Block City ZIP Map# Grid

ong Cove Ct
2200 PRLD 77584 4500 D2
ong Creek Ct
7600 HOUS 77088 3682 E2
ong Creek Dr
4400 MSCY 77545 4622 B2
ong Creek Ln
5200 HOUS 77088 3682 E2
5200 HOUS 77088 3683 A2
ongcroft Dr
9100 HarC 77379 3255 E4
ong Cypress Dr
20300 HarC 77388 3112 E5
ongdale Ct
19700 HarC 77433 3677 A1
ong Dr Ct
100 RHMD 77469 4491 E2
ongdraw Dr
1000 FBnC 77494 3952 B5
ongdraw Cove
2100 FBnC 77494 3952 B5
ongenbaugh Dr
15700 HarC 77095 3538 A6
17100 HarC 77095 3537 E6
17600 HarC 77433 3537 C6
ongenbaugh Rd
17900 HarC 77433 3537 D6
ongfellow Ln
10 HOUS 77005 4102 D2
10 HOUS 77030 4102 D2
ongfellow St
600 TXCY 77591 4873 C5
ongfield Cir
3300 HOUS 77063 4100 A1
ongflower Ct
2000 HOUS 77345 3120 B3
ongflower Ln
6100 HOUS 77345 3120 B3
ongford Dr
12600 HarC 77049 3828 A1
ongforest Dr
5500 HarC 77088 3542 D6
ong Gate Dr
10800 HOUS 77047 4243 C6
ong Glen Dr
4300 HOUS 77339 3119 A3
13200 HarC 77039 3546 A4
ong Grove Dr
4000 TYLV 77586 4508 D1
ong Grove Ln
2700 FBnC 77469 4616 A2
ong Haven Ln
10 CNRO 77304 2383 A1
ong Hearth Pl
10 WDLD 77382 2674 C5
ongheath Ct
20100 FBnC 77469 4094 C6
ongherridge Dr
2000 PRLD 77581 4504 B6
ong Hill Ln
25700 HarC 77373 3114 C2
ong Hollow Ct
3300 SGLD 77479 4368 B7
3300 SGLD 77479 4495 B2
onghorn Cir
2900 BzaC 77583 4500 E7
11000 HarC 77041 3680 C5
onghorn Dr
2100 HOUS 77080 3820 A4
2900 RSBG 77471 4491 C6
4100 BYTN 77521 3973 B2
onghorn Ln
6000 HarC 77041 3680 C5
onghorn Rd
3300 HarC 77084 3817 A2
onghorn Cavern Dr
15400 FBnC 77478 4236 C6
ong Iron Ct
25500 HarC 77389 2966 B2
ongitude Ln
10 GLSN 77554 5221 C2
ong Key
10 HTCK 77563 5105 B5
ong Lake Dr
19300 HarC 77084 3816 A6
onglake Dr
- PRLD 77545 4499 D3
ong Lake Pl
10 WDLD 77381 2675 A6
ong Leaf
- LPRT 77571 4382 D1
ongleaf Ct
900 MtgC 77302 2530 D6
ong Leaf Dr
10 HarC 77336 2976 D5
2600 SGLD 77478 4237 C4
6000 HarC 77088 3682 D2
6000 HOUS 77088 3682 C2
12000 MtgC 77303 2239 D7
ongleaf Dr
5000 PLEK 77469 4614 E6
7600 PRLD 77581 4375 A7
10200 CHTW 77385 2823 A5
ong Leaf Ln
3700 HOUS 77365 3119 E3
ongleaf Ln
900 MtgC 77302 2530 D6
7300 BYTN 77521 3835 B4
11700 BKHV 77024 3959 C5
11900 HOUS 77024 3959 B5
ongleaf Rd
11800 BKHV 77024 3959 C5
11800 HOUS 77024 3959 B5
ongleaf Tr
- HarC 77433 3251 C5
ongleaf Pines Ln
2400 HOUS 77339 3119 A3
ongledge Dr
1200 TYLV 77586 4381 E7
ongley St
700 SHUS 77587 4246 E2
800 SHUS 77587 4247 A3
ong Look Dr
15200 HOUS 77053 4372 B4
ong Meadow Ct
3300 PRLD 77584 4501 D5
ong Meadow Dr
3000 BYTN 77521 3973 B4
ongmeadow Dr
13900 HarC 77047 4374 C4
ongmeadow Ln
5000 HOUS 77033 4243 E1
5100 HOUS 77033 4244 A2
ong Meadow Pkwy
20800 FBnC 77469 4234 A4
ongmeadow St
5900 HOUS 77033 4244 B2

Longmire Ct
- CNRO 77304 2236 D6
Longmire Rd
100 CNRO 77304 2383 C4
1900 CNRO 77304 2382 E1
2000 CNRO 77304 2236 D7
6400 MtgC 77304 2236 B2
10600 GlsC 77510 4871 D6
Longmire Tr
6100 MtgC 77304 2236 A4
Longmire Wy
12000 CNRO 77304 2236 B4
12000 MtgC 77304 2236 B4
Longmire Cove
12300 MtgC 77304 2236 A4
Longmire Wy Ct
6000 MtgC 77304 2236 A4
Longmont Cir
1900 MSCY 77489 4370 C7
Longmont Dr
5000 HOUS 77056 3961 A5
5200 HOUS 77056 3960 D5
6100 HOUS 77057 3960 B5
9400 HOUS 77063 3959 B5
10000 HOUS 77042 3959 A5
10100 HOUS 77042 3958 E5
Longmont Ln
5700 HOUS 77056 3960 D5
5700 HOUS 77057 3960 D5
Longmont Park Ct
4500 FBnC 77494 4092 D2
Longmont Park Ln
26200 FBnC 77494 4092 C1
Longmoor Dr
18000 HarC 77084 3677 E7
Long Neck Dr
15100 SGCH 77355 2961 B3
Long Oak Ct
12100 HarC 77070 3254 D7
Long Oak Dr
- HarC 77039 3546 A4
- HarC 77377 3254 D7
- HarC 77429 3254 D7
14700 HarC 77070 3398 D1
14900 HarC 77070 3254 D7
Longpath Ct
8600 FBnC 77469 4234 B5
Long Pine Dr
- HarC 77389 2966 A2
11400 HOUS 77077 3958 B5
Long Pines Ln
36800 MtgC 77354 2816 C1
37100 MtgC 77354 2670 B7
Longplay Ln
11600 HarC 77044 3549 E7
11600 HarC 77044 3689 E1
Long Point Rd
6400 HOUS 77055 3822 A5
6400 HOUS 77092 3822 A5
6600 HOUS 77055 3821 D5
8500 HOUS 77080 3821 A5
8800 HOUS 77055 3820 E6
8800 HOUS 77080 3820 E6
10000 HOUS 77043 3820 A6
Long Point Slough
- FBnC 77469 4094 E7
- FBnC 77469 4095 A6
Long Prairie Dr
600 HarC 77450 3953 D2
Long Reach Dr
900 TKIS 77554 5106 C4
2300 SGLD 77478 4368 C5
Longren St
10800 HOUS 77089 4377 D3
Longridge Dr
100 LMQU 77568 4990 B2
7800 HOUS 77055 3821 B4
Long River Cir
14200 FBnC 77478 4236 E3
Long River Ct
14200 FBnC 77478 4236 C3
Long River Dr
10300 FBnC 77478 4236 E3
Long Rock Dr
2100 MSCY 77489 4370 B7
N Longsford Cir
- WDLD 77382 2819 E2
Long Shadow Dr
- FBnC 77479 4494 B3
14000 HarC 77015 3829 A4
Longshadow Dr
5000 DKSN 77539 4753 E5
Long Shadow Ln
1900 HarC 77388 3113 C6
Longshadow Ln
10800 HNCV 77024 3960 A3
Long Shadows Cir
500 HarC 77388 3113 C6
Long Shadows Dr
2000 HarC 77388 3113 C5
7700 FBnC 77479 4494 A5
Long Shadows St
3200 MtgC 77380 2821 B7
Long Ship Ct
- HarC 77379 3111 E6
Longshire Ln
7800 HarC 77040 3541 E7
Longs Peak Ln
11700 HarC 77346 3408 B3
Longs Peek Ct
- HarC 77377 3254 C4
Longspring Dr
20300 HarC 77450 3954 D5
Long Springs Pl
10 WDLD 77382 2674 B5
Longspur Dr
28000 FBnC 77494 3951 D4
E Longspur Dr
10 WDLD 77380 2967 C3
N Longspur Dr
10 WDLD 77380 2967 C3
S Longspur Dr
10 WDLD 77380 2967 C3
Long Spur Ln
2100 LGCY 77573 4752 B1
2200 LGCY 77573 4631 B7
Longstaff Dr
1800 HOUS 77031 4239 A5
Longstone Rd
25800 HarC 77389 2966 B1
Longstraw Pl
2000 WDLD 77380 2967 C1
Long Timber Dr
19100 HarC 77346 3265 A6
Long Timbers Ln
10 HNCV 77024 3959 E2
10 HNCV 77024 3960 A2
10 PNPV 77024 3959 E2

Long Timbers Tr
10 HNCV 77024 3960 A2
Long Tom Ct
4100 GLSN 77554 5332 E2
4200 GLSN 77554 5333 A3
Longtom Ct
11000 HarC 77086 3542 B1
Long Trace Dr
18700 HarC 77346 3265 A7
Longtrail
30600 MtgC 77354 2816 B1
Long Trail Ln
24600 HOUS 77336 3266 B2
Long Trail Path Ct
2100 HarC 77373 3114 C4
Longtree
11800 MtgC 77303 2239 D7
11800 MtgC 77303 2385 C1
Longvale Dr
16200 HOUS 77059 4380 C5
Long Valley Ct
16200 MtgC 77302 2678 E4
16300 MtgC 77302 2679 A4
Long Valley Dr
2200 HOUS 77345 3120 A6
Long View Dr
1400 PRLD 77581 4504 E5
Longview Dr
300 SGLD 77478 4369 A2
300 STAF 77477 4369 A2
300 STAF 77478 4369 A2
Longview St
100 CNRO 77301 2384 D4
6200 HOUS 77020 3825 E7
7100 HOUS 77020 3826 A7
13700 HarC 77015 3828 E7
14000 HarC 77015 3829 A7
Longview Creek Dr
26300 FBnC 77494 4092 A5
Longvine Ct
12800 HOUS 77072 4097 C6
Longvine Dr
7000 HOUS 77072 4097 D5
Longway Estates Ct
4000 FBnC 77545 4622 E1
Longwood
- CNRO 77304 2383 C3
- HarC 77562 3692 D5
Longwood Bnd
- HarC 77429 3253 E6
Longwood Ct
10100 HOUS 77024 3960 C2
Longwood Dr
2100 DRPK 77536 4109 D7
2300 PRLD 77581 4504 E5
2300 PRLD 77581 4505 A4
3500 PASD 77503 4108 B6
4300 CNRO 77304 2382 E1
Longwood Ln
500 MtgC 77302 2530 D5
3000 DKSN 77539 4753 C3
Longwood Mdws
- HarC 77429 3253 B3
E Longwood Mdws
16100 HarC 77429 3253 B3
W Longwood Mdws
16100 HarC 77429 3253 B4
Longwood Spur
16200 HarC 77429 3253 B4
Longwood St
3500 BzaC 77511 4867 C6
Longwood Trc
- HarC 77429 3253 E7
- HarC 77429 3254 A6
13300 HarC 77429 3397 E1
Longwood Garden Dr
32500 MtgC 77354 2672 C5
Longwoods Ln
300 HNCV 77024 3960 C3
300 HOUS 77024 3960 C2
Longworth Ln
12300 BKHV 77024 3959 A3
12300 HOUS 77024 3959 A3
Longworth Knoll Ln
- HarC 77073 3259 B3
Lonnie Ln
800 HOUS 77091 3684 A5
Lonniewood Dr
3600 HOUS 77059 4380 D6
Lonsford Dr
9800 HarC 77086 3542 B3
Lonzo St
3100 HOUS 77063 4099 C1
Looff
13900 HarC 77429 3397 E3
Look Rd
- HOUS 77055 3820 C7
- HOUS 77055 3959 C1
Look Cove Ct
- HarC 77038 3543 B4
Lookout Ct
10 HOUS 77025 4101 D6
Lookout Ln
400 DKSN 77539 4753 B5
18300 HarC 77044 3409 C1
18300 HarC 77346 3409 C1
Lookout Lake Ln
17900 MAGA 77354 2669 A3
Lookout Mountain Ct
13100 HarC 77069 3400 D2
Lookout Mountain Dr
5200 HarC 77069 3400 E1
Lookout Mountain Ln
19100 HarC 77449 3677 B3
Lookout Point Ct
14800 HarC 77396 3548 B1
Lookout Springs Tr
20300 HarC 77447 3104 D2
Loom St
1000 HarC 77532 3411 A7
Loon Dr
2500 LGCY 77573 4752 B1
Loone Ct
700 MtgC 77386 2968 D1
Loon River
100 HOUS 77336 3266 B2
Loon River Dr
24200 HOUS 77336 3266 B2
E Loop N
1700 HOUS 77029 3965 E5
Loop Dr
1500 BzaC 77583 4623 D6
E Loop Frwy N
100 HOUS 77029 4105 E1
1200 HOUS 77029 3965 E5
N Loop Frwy
100 HOUS 77018 3823 D4
200 HOUS 77008 3823 D4

N Loop Frwy
500 HOUS 77009 3823 D3
500 HOUS 77022 3823 D3
1300 HOUS 77009 3824 A4
1300 HOUS 77022 3824 A3
N Loop Frwy E
10 HOUS 77009 3824 C4
10 HOUS 77022 3824 A3
3500 HOUS 77026 3825 B4
6700 HOUS 77028 3825 E4
7000 HOUS 77028 3826 A5
8100 HOUS 77013 3826 C5
8100 HOUS 77029 3826 C5
10100 HOUS 77013 3965 E1
10100 HOUS 77029 3965 E1
N Loop Frwy W
100 HOUS 77008 3823 A4
200 HOUS 77018 3823 C4
1100 HOUS 77018 3822 C4
1200 HOUS 77008 3822 E4
2200 HOUS 77092 3822 C4
S Loop Frwy
- HOUS 77087 4104 A7
400 HOUS 77021 4242 E1
400 HOUS 77054 4242 D1
400 HOUS 77054 4243 A1
3000 HOUS 77025 4241 E1
3000 HOUS 77054 4241 E1
3200 HOUS 77021 4243 B1
4000 HOUS 77033 4103 E7
4000 HOUS 77033 4243 D1
4000 HOUS 77051 4243 D1
4500 HOUS 77096 4241 C1
5100 HOUS 77033 4104 A7
7200 HOUS 77087 4105 A6
7700 HOUS 77017 4105 C5
8600 HOUS 77012 4105 D4
W Loop Frwy N
- HOUS 77055 3961 B1
300 HOUS 77024 3961 B3
300 HOUS 77027 3961 B3
1000 HOUS 77055 3822 B7
1500 HOUS 77008 3822 B6
1500 HOUS 77092 3822 B6
W Loop Frwy S
- BLAR 77027 4101 A3
- HOUS 77027 4101 A3
- HOUS 77056 4101 A2
10 HOUS 77024 3961 B4
10 HOUS 77027 3961 A6
10 HOUS 77056 3961 B4
5200 BLAR 77056 4101 A2
5200 BLAR 77401 4101 A3
5200 HOUS 77081 4101 A3
5200 HOUS 77401 4101 A3
8500 HOUS 77096 4101 A2
8900 HOUS 77096 4241 B1
Loop Rd
- HOUS 77005 4102 D2
- HOUS 77034 4379 A5
E Loop Rd
17700 MtgC 77384 2675 E7
W Loop Rd
17700 MtgC 77384 2675 D7
E Loop 336
- CNRO 77301 2384 A1
Loop Central Dr
4800 BLAR 77401 4101 A2
4800 HOUS 77027 4101 A2
4800 HOUS 77081 4101 A2
Looscan Ln
2100 HOUS 77019 3962 B5
Loper Av
200 HOUS 77017 4106 B5
Lopez Ct
32500 MtgC 77354 2672 C5
Loraine
- SEBK 77586 4383 A7
- SEBK 77586 4510 A1
Lora Linda Dr
7600 FBnC 77083 4095 D7
Loramie Creek Ct
14000 HOUS 77044 3409 B3
Lord Dr
17200 MtgC 77357 2680 D7
Lord Rd
- HarC 77532 3413 A5
3800 HarC 77532 3412 E4
Lord St
11500 JTCY 77029 3966 D3
Lord Nelson Dr
2100 SEBK 77586 4509 D1
Lords
19100 MtgC 77357 2829 E3
Loreli Ln
1100 BYTN 77521 3973 B3
Loren Ln
9200 HarC 77040 3681 E2
Lorena Ridge Ln
700 FBnC 77479 4367 A5
Lorene Av
900 PASD 77502 4106 E7
Lorenzo St
15800 HarC 77530 3969 B2
Loretto Dr
4100 HOUS 77006 3962 D7
Lorfing Ln
600 FBnC 77479 4367 B5
Lori Ct
1900 SEBK 77586 4509 D1
Lori Dr
- HarC 77373 3115 D7
- HarC 77373 3260 D1
Lori Ln
9200 HarC 77040 3541 B6
24400 MtgC 77355 2962 D4
26300 MtgC 77365 3117 C4
Lori St
1100 CNRO 77301 2384 B3
Lori Brook Ln
11100 HarC 77065 3539 B1
Lorie Ln
500 PASD 77586 4508 E1
Lori Falls Ct
11100 HarC 77065 3539 C1
Lori Hall Ln
- HOUS 77077 3957 A3
Lori Kay
1700 HarC 77530 3830 C4
Lorikeet St
3100 HarC 77373 3114 E6
Lorinda Dr
4400 HOUS 77018 3683 C7
Loring Ln
17200 HarC 77388 3257 D2
E Lorino St
100 HarC 77037 3544 D6

W Lorino St
100 HarC 77037 3544 C6
Lorino Woods Dr
5700 HarC 77066 3400 E4
Lorna Dr
8500 HarC 77037 3684 D1
Lorne Dr
14000 HarC 77049 3828 B4
Lornmead Dr
600 HOUS 77024 3958 E2
Lorraine Ct
800 PASD 77506 4107 C5
Lorraine Dr
5300 BYTN 77521 3971 E1
Lorraine St
- HOUS 77026 3964 A1
1200 HOUS 77009 3963 D1
1600 HOUS 77026 3963 D1
8900 HarC 77562 3832 E1
Lorrie Dr
8000 HOUS 77025 4102 A6
Lorrielake Ln
10 HOUS 77024 3959 B5
Lorton Dr
11200 HarC 77070 3255 A7
Lory St
2500 RSBG 77471 4491 A6
Losa Dr
15600 HarC 77032 3404 A7
Los Alamos Cir
2500 DRPK 77536 4109 E6
Los Alamos Ct
4300 FBnC 77469 4233 C6
Los Altos Dr
- FBnC 77083 4096 B6
Los Angeles St
5500 HOUS 77026 3825 B4
6700 HOUS 77016 3825 B2
Los Coyotes Dr
6300 PASD 77505 4248 E7
Los Encinos Ct
10 MtgC 77354 2818 A3
Los Encinos Dr
10 MtgC 77354 2818 A4
Losoya Ct
5300 HarC 77388 3112 A2
Lost Ln
8100 DKSN 77539 4753 E5
8100 TXCY 77539 4753 E5
Lost Mdws
21800 MtgC 77357 2681 D7
21800 MtgC 77357 2827 D1
Lost Spur
23900 MtgC 77357 2681 B5
Lost Anchor Wy Ln
15800 HarC 77044 3408 E5
Lost Bridge Ln
- PRLD 77545 4499 D2
Lost Brook Ln
23100 HarC 77373 3114 D7
Lost Canyon Dr
22700 HarC 77450 3953 E3
Lost Cove Ct
2800 LGCY 77539 4752 E5
Lost Cove Ln
5100 HarC 77373 3115 C5
Lost Creek Blvd
- SGLD 77478 4368 B4
3700 SGLD 77478 4369 A6
E Lost Creek Blvd
30900 MtgC 77355 2815 D1
N Lost Creek Blvd
38200 MtgC 77355 2669 E7
38200 MtgC 77355 2815 D1
S Lost Creek Blvd
38200 MtgC 77355 2815 D1
W Lost Creek Blvd
- MtgC 77355 2669 D7
- MtgC 77355 2815 D1
Lost Creek Cir
800 HarC 77450 3953 E3
Lost Creek Ct
31100 TMBL 77375 2964 A3
Lost Creek Dr
- PRLD 77545 4499 D2
Lost Creek Ln
4900 LGCY 77573 4751 E1
Lost Creek Rd
13200 HarC 77375 2964 A3
13200 TMBL 77375 2964 A3
22400 HarC 77450 3953 E3
Lost Cypress Dr
17000 HarC 77429 3252 D6
Lost Eagle Dr
9500 HarC 77064 3540 C4
Lost Fable Ln
7200 HarC 77095 3678 A1
Lost Fall Ln
6300 HarC 77449 3677 D6
Lost Field Ln
- FBnC 77469 4365 A6
Lost Forest Dr
5300 HOUS 77092 3682 D7
Lost Goldenrod Dr
3800 FBnC 77469 4233 E6
Lost Hill Ct
2200 MtgC 77386 2969 D6
Lost Hollow Dr
3200 HOUS 77339 3118 E5
Lost Hollow Ln
10000 FBnC 77459 4621 E6
10100 FBnC 77459 4622 A6
Los Tios Dr
6600 HarC 77083 4096 B5
Lost Lake Dr
3500 HOUS 77339 3119 C5
4300 FBnC 77469 4234 D5
21500 MtgC 77357 2681 A6
Lost Lake Ln
4200 HarC 77388 3112 B4
Lost Lake Pl
1900 PRLD 77581 4503 E2
Lost Lakes Dr
20700 MtgC 77357 2681 A7
Lost Maples Ct
18400 HarC 77346 3264 D7
Lost Maples Dr
2700 PRLD 77584 4503 B4
15500 FBnC 77478 4236 B6
Lost Maples Tr
2100 HOUS 77345 3120 B3
12400 HarC 77346 3264 D7
Lost Maples Forest Ct
3300 HOUS 77345 3119 D2
Lost Meadow Ln
14100 HOUS 77079 3957 E1
Lost Mill Ln
16600 HarC 77095 3538 A3

Lost Mine Tr
19100 HarC 77388 3258 C1
Lost Oak Dr
3400 HarC 77388 3112 E7
4000 HarC 77388 3257 C1
Lost Pine Ct
2000 CNRO 77304 2383 A6
Lost Pine Dr
10000 BYTN 77521 3835 B4
Lost Pine Tr
20900 HarC 77532 3410 B1
Lost Pines Bnd
- HOUS 77049 3828 A2
Lost Pines Bend Ct
- HOUS 77049 3828 A2
Lost Pond Cir
10 WDLD 77381 2675 A6
W Lost Pond Cir
10 WDLD 77381 2675 A6
Lost Pond Ct
10 WDLD 77381 2675 A6
Lost Quail Dr
16400 HOUS 77489 4370 E7
Lost Ridge Cir
1400 TYLV 77586 4381 D6
Lost River Dr
800 FRDW 77546 4629 B3
Lost Rock Ct
16000 HOUS 77598 4506 E4
Lost Rock Dr
300 HOUS 77598 4506 E4
Lost Spring Dr
4400 HarC 77084 3678 E7
Lost Thicket Dr
6700 HOUS 77085 4371 C1
Lost Timber Ln
6300 HarC 77066 3400 E5
6800 FBnC 77469 4615 E5
Lost Trail St
10000 HOUS 77088 3542 C7
10000 HOUS 77088 3682 B1
Lost Valley Tr
21000 HarC 77532 3410 B1
Los Verdes Dr
4200 PASD 77504 4247 E4
Lothbury Dr
14600 HarC 77429 3253 C5
Lottie Ln
100 FRDW 77546 4505 B7
1400 BzaC 77511 4747 E2
1400 BzaC 77511 4748 A2
Lottie Rd
3200 PLEK 77471 4614 C4
Lottman St
200 HOUS 77003 3963 E4
Lotus Dr
- MSCY 77489 4370 C5
1400 TKIS 77554 5106 B4
4000 PRLD 77584 4501 D6
Lotus Ln
2900 PRLD 77584 4501 D6
5000 MtgC 77354 2673 D3
Lotus St
- HOUS 77045 4241 C7
5400 HOUS 77085 4241 A7
5600 HOUS 77085 4240 E7
Lotusbriar Ln
14400 HOUS 77077 3956 D6
Lotus Creek Ct
- HarC 77379 3111 B5
Lou Ln
100 HarC 77388 3113 D7
100 HOUS 77388 3113 D7
Lou Al Dr
11500 HDWV 77024 3959 D2
N Lou Al Dr
11500 HDWV 77024 3959 D1
S Lou Al Dr
11500 HDWV 77024 3959 D2
Louan Ct
14100 SGLD 77478 4236 D6
Lou Anna Dr
- HarC 77040 3681 B3
Lou Anne Ln
4100 HOUS 77092 3821 D1
Louden Ln
7500 MNVL 77578 4746 C2
Lou Edd Rd
9700 HarC 77070 3399 C6
10700 HarC 77065 3399 A6
Lou Ellen Ln
2000 HOUS 77018 3822 C3
Louetta Cross
100 HarC 77373 3113 D4
100 HOUS 77373 3113 D4
Louetta Rd
- HarC 77429 3395 D2
- HarC 77433 3395 D2
- HOUS 77373 3113 C4
- HOUS 77388 3113 D4
2000 HarC 77388 3113 A6
3200 HarC 77388 3112 B7
4700 HarC 77379 3112 C7
4900 HarC 77379 3257 A2
5800 HarC 77379 3256 A5
9000 HarC 77379 3255 E5
9600 HarC 77070 3255 A7
10600 HOUS 77070 3255 A7
11000 HarC 77377 3255 A7
11000 HOUS 77377 3255 A7
11400 HarC 77070 3254 B7
11400 HarC 77377 3254 B7
12000 HarC 77429 3254 A7
14200 HarC 77429 3253 D7
E Louetta Rd
- HarC 77373 3113 E3
- HarC 77373 3114 A3
- HarC 77433 3252 A7
- HOUS 77373 3113 E3
14600 HarC 77429 3251 E7
14600 HarC 77433 3251 E7
14600 HarC 77433 3395 E1
16000 HarC 77429 3253 A6
16100 HarC 77429 3252 E5
19600 HarC 77429 3395 E1
Louetta Spur
- HarC 77388 3113 B5
Louetta Brook Ln
2200 HarC 77388 3113 B4
Louetta Creek Dr
18600 HarC 77388 3112 C7
Louetta Crossing Dr
20100 HarC 77388 3113 C5
Louetta Falls Ln
2200 HarC 77388 3113 B4
Louetta Glen Dr
20500 HarC 77388 3113 C4

Louetta Green Dr
17000 HarC 77379 3255 D6
Louetta Lakes Dr
19800 HarC 77388 3113 A5
Louetta Lee Dr
1900 HarC 77388 3113 C5
Louetta Oak Ct
2000 HarC 77388 3113 B4
Louetta Oak Dr
20600 HarC 77388 3113 B4
Louetta Oak Tr
- HarC 77388 3113 B4
Louetta Park Cir
1900 HarC 77388 3113 C5
Louetta Pine Dr
2000 HarC 77388 3113 C5
Louetta Point Cir
1900 HarC 77388 3113 C5
Louetta Spring Dr
2000 HarC 77388 3113 B4
Louetta Woods Ct
2000 HarC 77388 3113 B4
Louetta Woods Dr
20600 HarC 77388 3113 B4
Louetta Woods Ln
- HarC 77388 3113 B4
Louie Welch Dr
19200 HOUS 77338 3262 B6
Louis Ln
16700 MtgC 77365 2825 C6
21100 MtgC 77357 2827 B7
21200 MtgC 77357 2973 B1
31800 MtgC 77362 2963 D2
Louis Rd
2800 HarC 77532 3267 E7
2800 HarC 77532 3268 C7
Louisa Ct
4800 SGLD 77478 4369 B7
W Louise
300 HarC 77037 3684 C1
Louise Ln
4800 BzaC 77584 4502 A7
Louise Rd
1000 HarC 77037 3685 A1
1000 HOUS 77037 3685 A1
W Louise Rd
300 HarC 77037 3684 D1
Louise St
- RSBG 77471 4491 A4
400 HOUS 77009 3824 A5
900 HOUS 77009 3823 E5
1200 HOUS 77008 3823 E5
2200 ALVN 77511 4866 E3
3600 FBnC 77545 4498 E7
4700 PASD 77586 4383 C5
5300 BYTN 77521 3971 E1
13100 STAF 77477 4370 A1
Louisiana
- IWCY 77583 4624 A6
Louisiana Av
200 GlsC 77518 4634 C3
500 SHUS 77017 4246 B3
500 SHUS 77587 4246 B3
1300 DRPK 77503 4108 D6
1300 DRPK 77536 4108 D6
1300 PASD 77503 4108 D6
Louisiana Pk
600 MtgC 77302 2530 B6
Louisiana St
10 TXCY 77591 4873 E6
10 TXCY 77591 4874 A6
200 HOUS 77002 3963 A6
200 MSCY 77489 4370 B3
600 LGCY 77573 4632 E4
1400 BYTN 77520 4112 A2
2200 HOUS 77006 3963 A6
4900 HOUS 77006 4102 C3
6200 MNVL 77578 4747 A2
Louisville St
12800 HOUS 77015 3828 C7
Loupe Ct
3500 MSCY 77459 4496 D4
Loupe Ln
6800 MSCY 77459 4496 D4
Lourdes
- HTCK 77563 4988 A2
Lourdes Dr
14000 HarC 77049 3828 B4
Louvre Ct
11900 HOUS 77082 4098 A3
Louvre Ln
3300 HOUS 77082 4098 A2
Love Ct
2800 FRDW 77546 4749 E1
Love Ln
2800 FRDW 77546 4749 E1
Love Plz
3300 HOUS 77026 3825 B6
Love St
3200 HOUS 77026 3825 B6
Lovebird Ln
11300 HarC 77067 3402 B6
Lovebug Ln
- CNRO 77301 2384 B7
Lovejoy St
3800 HOUS 77003 3964 B5
4300 HOUS 77011 3964 B5
Lovelady Dr
13800 MtgC 77302 2532 C5
Loveland Pass Dr
11700 HarC 77067 3401 E4
Lovely Ln
1200 DRPK 77536 4109 C5
Lovenia Ln
9300 HarC 77396 3407 A6
Lovernote Ct
- WDLD 77382 2673 B6
Lovers Ln
10 DKSN 77539 4752 E6
700 HOUS 77091 3684 A4
4000 LGCY 77539 4752 E6
8400 MNVL 77578 4745 E1
Lovers Wood Ln
3700 HarC 77014 3257 C7
3800 HarC 77014 3401 C1
Lovett Blvd
1200 HOUS 77006 3962 D6
Lovett Ct
800 TMBL 77375 2964 D6
Lovett Ln
18000 HarC 77379 3256 B1
Lovett St
1000 TMBL 77375 2964 D6
Lovie Ln
12300 CNRO 77302 2531 A3
Loving
23100 MtgC 77357 2973 E3
23100 MtgC 77357 2974 A3

STREET
Block City ZIP Map# Grid

Loving St
2100 HOUS 77034 4246 D5
Lovington Ct
- HarC 77088 3543 A7
Low Bridge Ln
10300 FBnC 77478 4236 B4
Low Country Ln
- WDLD 77380 2821 C6
Lowden St
3800 HOUS 77051 4243 B2
Lowden Crest Ln
10100 HarC 77070 3399 C3
Lowe Ln
17500 MtgC 77357 2680 D7
Lowe Rd
19600 MtgC 77365 2972 C6
Lowe St
2100 LMQU 77568 4990 A3
Lowell Av
13700 HarC 77377 3108 E5
Lowell Ct
1800 FBnC 77494 3952 D4
Lowellberg Ln
5600 HarC 77084 3678 B4
Lower Arrow Dr
6800 HarC 77086 3542 B3
Lower Borondo
100 LMQU 77568 4989 C3
Lowerby Ln
4500 SGLD 77479 4495 C4
Lowercove Cir
9100 HarC 77064 3540 E6
Lower Lake Dr
15800 HarC 77433 3251 A5
Lower Lake Ln
36800 MtgC 77354 2816 B1
Lower Level Rd
7400 HOUS 77020 3965 B5
7400 HOUS 77029 3965 A5
10500 HOUS 77029 4105 E1
Lower Ridge Wy
9500 HOUS 77075 4246 B7
Lower Valley Dr
2500 HarC 77067 3402 A5
Lowick St
17300 HarC 77379 3255 D3
Low Ridge Rd
23200 HarC 77373 3115 E6
Lowrie St
10400 HOUS 77093 3686 B4
10500 HarC 77093 3686 B4
Loxley Dr
- HarC 77014 3402 C1
Loxley Meadows Dr
14700 HOUS 77082 4096 D2
Loyal Ln
8100 HOUS 77016 3687 C4
Lo-Yang Dr
900 MSCY 77489 4370 C2
Loyanne Dr
2300 HarC 77373 3114 C6
Loyel Pointe Dr
7800 HarC 77064 3541 A1
Loyola Dr
11200 HarC 77429 3538 D1
11300 HarC 77429 3397 E7
Loys Coves Ct
14900 HarC 77396 3407 E7
Lozar Dr
21400 HarC 77379 3111 B2
Lozier St
6600 HOUS 77021 4103 B6
LP-8 Houston Ship Channel Br
- HOUS - 3968 D7
LP-8 Sam Houston Pkwy
- HarC - 3405 E7
- HarC - 3406 B7
- HarC - 3829 B7
- HarC - 3968 B1
- HOUS - 3403 A7
- HOUS - 3404 E7
- HOUS - 3405 B7
- HOUS - 3406 A7
LP-8 E Sam Houston Pkwy N
- HarC 77044 3549 B7
- HarC 77049 3828 E1
7700 HarC 77049 3829 B3
8000 HarC 77049 3689 D6
8700 HarC 77044 3689 C1
LP-8 N Sam Houston Pkwy E
- HarC 77044 3549 A1
7000 HarC 77396 3406 C7
8100 HarC 77396 3547 E1
8100 HarC 77396 3548 B1
11000 HarC 77396 3549 A1
LP-8 W Sam Houston Tollway
- HarC - 3401 E7
- HarC - 3402 C7
- HarC - 3540 E2
- HarC - 3541 E1
- HarC - 3542 A1
- HarC - 3543 A1
- HarC - 3680 D4
- HarC - 3681 A1
- HarC - 3968 D6
- HarC - 4239 B6
- HarC - 4372 D5
- HarC - 4373 E5
- HarC - 4374 A5
- HarC - 4377 B5
- HOUS - 3402 E7
- HOUS - 3403 B7
- HOUS - 3680 D3
- HOUS - 3819 D1
- HOUS - 3958 D1
- HOUS - 3968 D7
- HOUS - 4098 E7
- HOUS - 4108 D1
- HOUS - 4238 D1
- HOUS - 4239 C7
- HOUS - 4248 A7
- HOUS - 4370 E2
- HOUS - 4371 C4
- HOUS - 4372 A5
- HOUS - 4374 C5
- HOUS - 4375 E5
- HOUS - 4376 A5
- HOUS - 4377 A5
- HOUS - 4378 E1
- HOUS - 4379 A1
- JRSV - 3680 E2
- MSCY - 4239 C7
- MSCY - 4370 E2
- PASD - 4108 C4
- PASD - 4248 A7

LP-8 W Sam Houston Tollway E
- HarC - 3541 E1
LP-8 W Sam Houston Tollway W
- HarC - 3541 E1
LP-108 7th St
- GlsC 77650 4878 E7
- GlsC 77650 4994 E1
- GlsC 77650 4995 A1
LP-108 Broadway
700 GlsC 77650 4878 E7
700 GlsC 77650 4879 B5
LP-197
- GlsC 77563 4991 A5
- LMQU 77563 4991 A6
- LMQU 77590 4991 A5
- TXCY 77563 4991 A5
- TXCY 77590 4991 A5
700 TXCY 77590 4875 B3
LP-197 6th St N
10 TXCY 77590 4875 D6
LP-197 6th St S
10 TXCY 77590 4875 D6
LP-197 25th Av N
800 TXCY 77590 4875 C3
2500 TXCY 77590 4874 C3
LP-197 Texas City Port Blvd
- TXCY 77590 4875 D7
- TXCY 77590 4991 B2
LP-201 N Robert C Lanier Frwy
- BYTN - 4112 A3
LP-207 Main St
- MTBL 77520 3696 E6
LP-336
- CNRO 77301 2385 B2
100 CNRO 77301 2384 A1
200 CNRO 77304 2530 A2
300 CNRO 77301 2383 E1
300 CNRO 77303 2383 E1
900 CNRO 77304 2529 B1
1300 CNRO 77304 2383 C2
LP-336 Cartwright Rd
- MtgC 77301 2385 B2
1700 CNRO 77301 2384 E1
1700 CNRO 77303 2384 E1
1700 MtgC 77303 2384 E1
1900 CNRO 77301 2385 B2
1900 CNRO 77303 2385 B2
1900 MtgC 77303 2385 B2
LP-494
20000 MtgC 77357 2828 A5
20400 MtgC 77357 2827 E7
21100 MtgC 77357 2973 E1
22000 HOUS 77339 3118 C1
22000 HOUS 77339 3263 A1
23000 MtgC 77365 2973 C7
24700 MtgC 77365 3118 C1
25300 MtgC 77339 3118 C1
25500 HOUS 77365 3118 B3
LP-512
10 SPLD 77372 2683 A2
13500 MtgC 77372 2537 B7
13500 SPLD 77372 2537 B7
Lubbock St
1400 HOUS 77002 3963 B3
2300 HOUS 77007 3963 A3
Lubojacky Rd
4500 FBnC 77469 4615 B4
Luca St
3300 HOUS 77021 4103 D6
Lucaric Ln
- HarC 77037 3544 E7
Lucario Dr
13100 HarC 77037 3544 E7
Lucas Dr
14500 SPLD 77372 2683 B2
Lucas Ln
14900 MtgC 77306 2680 A2
Lucas St
2200 HOUS 77026 3964 B1
2600 HOUS 77026 3825 B7
Lucas Trace Ct
4300 HarC 77066 3401 C4
Lucayan Dr
- HarC 77532 3551 D4
Lucca Ct
2800 LGCY 77573 4633 A3
Luce St
5600 HOUS 77087 4104 D7
5700 HOUS 77087 4244 D1
Lucerne St
5600 BLAR 77401 4101 B3
10800 HOUS 77016 3687 A2
Lucia
3500 GLSN 77554 5332 C2
Lucia Ln
20000 HarC 77346 3265 C4
Lucian Ln
4000 FRDW 77546 4629 E1
Lucida Ln
3200 HarC 77373 3114 E6
Lucien Dr
13400 HarC 77377 3109 A7
Lucille Dr
3100 MtgC 77384 2674 E1
23500 MtgC 77357 2828 B2
Lucille St
5400 HOUS 77026 3825 D7
Lucinda St
2300 HOUS 77004 3963 E7
2500 HOUS 77004 4103 E1
Lucinda Meadows Dr
6300 HarC 77449 3676 E4
Luckel Dr
5200 KATY 77493 3813 D7
Lucketts Ln
2700 FBnC 77469 4234 A7
Luckey Lee Rd
10 PLMG 77327 2684 E5
Lucky Ln
800 LPRT 77571 4110 D6
Lucky Lp
13100 HarC 77375 2964 E5
13100 TMBL 77375 2964 E5
Lucky St
700 HOUS 77088 3684 A3
900 HOUS 77088 3683 E3
Lucky Garden Wy
- HarC 77083 4096 B5
Lucky Hill Wy
- HarC 77083 4096 C5
Lucky Leaf Ct
10 WDLD 77381 2821 B2
Lucky Meadow Dr
11900 HarC 77375 3109 D7

Lucky River Ln
- HarC 77083 4096 B5
Lucky Star Dr
15100 HarC 77082 4096 D2
Lucky Star Ln
- HarC 77083 4096 C5
7100 FBnC 77494 4093 C4
Lucore St
9700 HOUS 77017 4106 B5
Lucretia St
2000 SGCH 77362 2816 C7
Lucus Canyon Ln
26500 FBnC 77494 4092 C3
Lucy Ln
300 SGCH 77362 2816 D5
2100 MSCY 77489 4370 B7
5800 PASD 77505 4248 C3
Lucy Grove Ct
10000 HarC 77044 3689 C3
Lucy Grove Ln
13000 HarC 77044 3689 C3
Ludgate Dr
23000 HarC 77373 3115 C7
Ludgate Pass
13700 HOUS 77034 4378 D5
Ludington
8000 HOUS 77071 4239 D5
Ludington Dr
6300 HOUS 77035 4240 A5
6600 HOUS 77071 4240 A5
7500 HOUS 77071 4239 E5
Ludwig Ln
4300 FBnC 77477 4369 B3
4300 STAF 77477 4369 B3
4500 SGLD 77477 4369 B3
4500 SGLD 77478 4369 B3
Luell St
- HOUS 77016 3686 B7
2800 HOUS 77093 3685 E7
4000 HOUS 77093 3686 B7
Luella Av
600 DRPK 77536 4109 C6
3300 DRPK 77536 4249 C2
4800 LPRT 77536 4249 C3
4800 LPRT 77571 4249 C3
4800 PASD 77505 4249 C3
4800 PASD 77571 4249 C3
Luella Blvd
- DRPK 77536 4249 C4
- LPRT 77536 4249 C4
- LPRT 77571 4249 C4
- PASD 77507 4249 C5
Luetta St
10 HOUS 77076 3684 E6
100 HOUS 77076 3685 A6
Lufborough Dr
4000 HarC 77066 3401 B3
Lufkin Ln
2400 DRPK 77536 4109 A7
Lufkin St
5600 HOUS 77026 3825 D4
S Lugano Verde Dr
24000 FBnC 77469 4093 A7
Lugary Dr
5800 HOUS 77036 4099 D4
8100 HOUS 77074 4099 E6
8700 HOUS 77074 4239 E1
Luhning Dr
5500 DKSN 77539 4754 D4
5500 TXCY 77539 4754 D4
Luis Ln
- LbyC 77327 2538 A3
- LbyC 77372 2538 A3
Luke Dr
1000 ALVN 77511 4749 A6
1000 BzaC 77511 4749 B6
Luke St
600 HOUS 77091 3684 B4
Luke Davis Blvd
22300 MtgC 77357 2827 C5
Luke Ridge Ln
25600 FBnC 77494 4093 A2
Lula St
1800 HOUS 77009 3824 A4
4300 BLAR 77401 4101 C5
4300 HOUS 77401 4101 C5
Lulac St
100 ALVN 77511 4749 C5
Lulach Cir
10 CNRO 77301 2530 C3
Lulach Ln
2000 CNRO 77301 2530 B3
Lull
- HOUS 77087 4104 D5
Lullaby Dr
300 HarC 77532 3552 D7
Lullaby Ln
10 WDLD 77380 2821 D7
Lullwater Pl
10 WDLD 77381 2820 E3
Lum Ln
9800 HOUS 77078 3688 A5
Lum Rd
6900 MNVL 77578 4625 E5
Lumber Ln
3900 HOUS 77016 3825 B2
Lumberdale
6300 HOUS 77092 3682 C4
Lumberdale Dr
- HOUS 77092 3682 C6
Lumberdale Rd
3800 HOUS 77092 3821 C2
6200 HOUS 77092 3682 C5
Lumber Jack Dr
7100 HOUS 77040 3682 A1
7500 HarC 77040 3682 A1
7800 HarC 77040 3681 E1
Lumber Ridge Tr
- HOUS 77034 4378 C3
Lumpkin Rd
1000 HOUS 77043 3819 D7
1000 HOUS 77043 3958 E1
Luna St
- HOUS 77076 3684 E4
Luna Butte Dr
- HarC 77377 3109 B7
Luna Falls Ct
19300 HarC 77377 3254 B1
Luna Falls Dr
12000 HarC 77377 3254 E2
Luna Lakes Dr
30000 MtgC 77386 2969 D2
Lundar Ln
18100 HarC 77377 3254 B2
Lundwood Ln
5800 HarC 77084 3678 B4
Lundy Ln
1400 FRDW 77546 4749 E1

Lundy Ln
1400 FRDW 77546 4750 B1
2300 LGCY 77546 4750 B1
Lundy Rd
9100 HOUS 77016 3686 B6
9100 HOUS 77093 3686 B6
Lunes St
22800 GLSN 77554 5440 E5
Luns Ln
20000 HarC 77073 3403 C1
Lunsford Dr
- HarC 77450 3954 E3
Lunsford Hollow Ln
4600 HarC 77546 4506 A6
Lunsford Mews Ln
- HarC 77094 3955 B4
Luong Field Ct
4100 FBnC 77450 4093 D1
Lupin St
500 BLAR 77401 4101 A5
Lupton Ct
9000 HOUS 77055 3820 E7
9000 SPVL 77055 3820 E7
Lupton Ln
8600 SPVL 77055 3821 A6
Luray Ct
8800 FBnC 77469 4616 D1
Lure Ct
9400 HarC 77065 3539 C4
Lure Dr
9400 HarC 77065 3539 C4
Lurlene St
4200 HOUS 77017 4105 E7
Lush Meadow Pl
10 WDLD 77381 2675 A7
Lussier Dr
6400 FBnC 77479 4367 B5
Lusterleaf Dr
12300 HarC 77065 3398 D6
12500 HarC 77429 3398 D5
Luthe Ln
16300 HOUS 77032 3404 C4
Luthe Rd
13000 HarC 77039 3545 B3
14800 HarC 77032 3545 B1
Luther Ct
1300 ALVN 77511 4867 A3
Luther St
- HOUS 77029 3966 B2
- JTCY 77029 3966 B2
600 HOUS 77076 3685 B6
Lutheran Cemetery Rd
19000 HarC 77433 3252 A4
23200 HarC 77377 2963 A7
Lutheran Church Rd
21800 HarC 77377 2963 A7
21800 HarC 77377 3108 A2
Lutheran School Rd
16000 HarC 77377 2963 A7
16300 HarC 77377 2962 D7
Luton
- HOUS 77449 3814 D6
Luton Park Dr
3400 HOUS 77082 4097 B2
Luttrell St
4300 TXCY 77591 4874 B6
Luxembourg Dr
15900 HarC 77070 3255 C6
Luzerne Dr
16300 HarC 77070 3255 B5
Luzon St
1100 HOUS 77009 3824 C7
1200 HOUS 77026 3824 E7
LW Cummings Rd
800 FBnC 77471 4490 E1
800 FBnC 77471 4491 A1
Lw Minor St
- PRVW 77445 3100 C1
Lybert Dr
10100 HOUS 77041 3681 A7
Lybert Rd
10300 HOUS 77041 3681 A7
10400 HOUS 77041 3680 E7
Lycomb Dr
5600 HOUS 77053 4371 E6
Lyden Ridge Dr
5500 HOUS 77053 4371 E6
Lydia Av
2800 HOUS 77054 4102 E6
Lydia St
1100 RHMD 77469 4364 D7
3400 HOUS 77021 4103 B7
3900 HOUS 77021 4243 C1
Lyerly St
10 HOUS 77022 3823 E1
10 HOUS 77022 3824 A1
N Lyford Dr
18500 HarC 77449 3677 C4
S Lyford Dr
18900 HarC 77449 3677 C4
Lykes Av
15400 HOUS 77060 3544 C2
Lylewood Ct
8400 HarC 77040 3541 C6
Lyman St
- SEBK 77586 4509 E2
Lymbar Dr
4100 HOUS 77025 4241 C2
4400 HOUS 77096 4241 A2
5100 HOUS 77096 4240 E3
Lynbriar Ln
25100 HarC 77373 3114 C3
Lynbrook Ct
3100 SGLD 77478 4369 B3
Lynbrook Dr
2400 RSBG 77471 4491 B6
5300 HOUS 77056 3960 D5
5800 HOUS 77057 3960 C5
10000 HOUS 77042 3958 E5
10000 HOUS 77042 3959 A5
11200 HOUS 77077 3958 B5
Lynbrook Hollow St
10300 HOUS 77042 3958 E5
Lynchburg Fy
- HOUS 77520 3970 B3
- HOUS 77571 3970 B3
S Lynchburg Rd
- HarC 77520 3970 C2
- HOUS 77520 3970 C2
E Lynchburg Cedar Bayou Rd
2100 HarC 77521 3834 D7
3600 HarC 77521 3835 A7
Lynchester Dr
9200 FBnC 77083 4237 A1
Lyncrest Dr
10 GLSN 77550 5109 E1

Lynda Dr
11500 HarC 77038 3543 B5
11500 HarC 77088 3543 B6
Lyndale Dr
400 HarC 77562 3832 B3
Lyndaleigh Ln
19300 HarC 77388 3113 D6
Lyndall Ln
21000 MtgC 77365 2826 B7
21100 MtgC 77365 2972 B1
Lyndbrook Ln
10900 HarC 77433 3537 E1
Lynden
- HOUS 77045 4372 D1
Lyndhurst
100 HOUS 77077 3957 C7
Lyndhurst Dr
5100 HOUS 77033 4243 E2
5300 HOUS 77033 4244 A3
6800 HOUS 77087 4244 E2
Lyndhurst Pl
3900 SGLD 77479 4495 A1
Lyndhurst Village Ln
7200 HarC 77379 3111 B7
Lyndon St
1000 HOUS 77030 4102 C5
Lyndon Meadows Dr
10300 HarC 77095 3538 A2
Lyndonville Dr
13300 HarC 77041 3679 C4
Lynell Dr
13200 HarC 77532 3693 B1
13500 HarC 77532 3553 A7
Lynette St
8200 HOUS 77028 3687 C6
Lynette Falls Dr
9800 HarC 77095 3538 E3
Lynford Crest Dr
15200 FBnC 77083 4236 B1
Lyngrove Dr
800 HOUS 77038 3544 A6
Lynkat Ln
6300 HarC 77083 4097 B4
Lynn
- HarC 77070 3399 B3
9300 HarC 77375 2965 C3
Lynn Cir
700 PASD 77502 4107 A7
1000 FRDW 77546 4629 C2
2800 TXCY 77590 4874 E5
Lynn Dr
2300 PRLD 77581 4503 A3
2500 PRLD 77584 4503 A3
19200 HarC 77377 3106 E6
19200 HarC 77377 3107 A6
Lynn Ln
1100 HMBL 77338 3406 E1
1100 HMBL 77338 3407 A1
2000 HOUS 77056 3961 C4
6000 BzaC 77584 4626 D1
13200 GlsC 77510 4870 E2
24800 MtgC 77365 3119 A1
Lynn St
400 SHUS 77587 4246 D2
8100 HOUS 77017 4105 D7
Lynn Crest Ct
16300 FBnC 77083 4236 A1
Lynnfield St
1900 HOUS 77093 3824 E3
3600 HOUS 77016 3825 A3
5300 HOUS 77028 3825 D2
Lynngate Dr
5500 HarC 77373 3260 E1
6200 HarC 77373 3261 A1
6400 HarC 77373 3116 A7
Lynn Haven St
12900 HarC 77429 3398 D4
Lynnrose Springs Dr
9800 HarC 77375 3255 A1
Lynnview Dr
1400 HLSV 77055 3821 B6
1800 HOUS 77055 3821 B5
Lynnville Dr
13500 HarC 77065 3539 A2
Lynnwood Dr
500 MSCY 77489 4370 E5
9900 BYTN 77520 3835 B4
9900 BYTN 77521 3835 B4
9900 CmbC 77520 3835 C4
14600 MtgC 77372 2682 D2
Lynnwood Ln
13500 SGLD 77478 4237 A6
Lynwood Ct
34000 MtgC 77354 2670 E6
Lynwood Rd
800 HarC 77373 3114 A7
Lynwood Banks Ln
6000 HOUS 77092 3682 C7
Lynx Dr
13700 HarC 77014 3401 E1
Lynx Ln
10 WDLD 77380 2968 A1
12500 SGLD 77478 4237 D5
Lyondell
8200 HarC 77049 3691 C7
Lyonesse Ln
7800 HarC 77040 3541 E6
Lyons Al
3500 HOUS 77020 3964 A2
Lyons Av
1600 HOUS 77002 3963 D2
1600 HOUS 77020 3963 E2
2900 HOUS 77020 3964 C2
7400 HOUS 77020 3965 A2
7700 HOUS 77029 3965 B1
Lyons St
- MtgC 77302 2531 B3
Lyons Pass
- FBnC 77494 3953 C5
Lyon Springs Ct
25500 HarC 77373 3114 B5
Lyons School Rd
16300 HarC 77379 3256 C4
Lyrebird Dr
10 WDLD 77380 2968 A1
Lyreleaf Pl
10 WDLD 77382 2674 A5
Lyric Ln
1100 PASD 77503 4108 C6
1300 LMQU 77568 4990 C1
Lyric Rd
13000 MtgC 77302 2823 E2
13000 MtgC 77302 2824 C2
Lyric Wy
17300 HarC 77377 3254 B4
Lyrical Dr
9700 STAF 77477 4239 A7
9800 HarC 77031 4239 A7

Lyric Arbor Cir
10 WDLD 77381 2674 D7
E Lyric Arbor Cir
10 WDLD 77381 2674 D7
Lyric Arbor Ct
10 WDLD 77381 2674 C7
Lysander Pl
10 WDLD 77382 2819 A2
Lytham Ln
1900 FBnC 77450 3954 A6
Lytton Sprs
700 HarC 77373 3114 A4

M

E M St
300 LPRT 77571 4251 E5
W M St
400 LPRT 77571 4251 D5
Maack Ln
100 HOUS 77037 3684 D2
Mabel Ln
12100 MtgC 77362 2963 C2
Mabel St
200 HOUS 77022 3824 B2
500 RHMD 77469 4364 D7
8900 HarC 77562 3833 A1
Mabels Island Ct
18400 HarC 77346 3265 D7
18400 HarC 77346 3409 A1
Mable Av
100 HarC 77520 3832 A7
200 HarC 77520 3831 E7
Mable St
1500 HOUS 77023 4104 B1
E Mable St
3600 GlsC 77518 4634 B3
W Mable St
3600 GlsC 77518 4634 B3
Mablehurst Dr
- HarC 77429 3397 C3
Mable Pond Ln
- FBnC 77469 4235 C1
Mabry Rd
1400 BYTN 77520 3973 C4
Mabry St
700 BYTN 77520 3973 B5
Mabry Mill Ln
8100 MtgC 77385 2676 B6
Mabry Mill Rd
1000 HOUS 77062 4379 E7
1000 HOUS 77062 4506 C1
Mabry Park Dr
- HarC 77068 3257 C6
Mabry Stream Ct
5000 HarC 77449 3676 E7
MacArthur Dr
2000 HOUS 77030 4102 B4
MacArthur St
100 BYTN 77520 3971 A4
1100 RSBG 77471 4491 A4
Macaw St
10 WDLD 77380 2968 A1
MacBeth Dr
4600 HarC 77373 3115 C7
MacBeth St
10200 HarC 77532 3693 C6
Macclesby Ln
- HarC 77049 3829 D4
- HarC 77530 3829 C4
MacDuff
29600 MtgC 77354 2818 C2
MacDuff St
10200 HarC 77532 3693 C6
Mace
- HOUS 77034 4377 E2
Mace Dr
23200 MtgC 77365 3118 E1
23200 MtgC 77365 3119 A1
Mace Rd
10 CNRO 77303 2384 A1
Macedonia Rd
23500 WlrC 77447 2959 B5
25000 WlrC 77447 2813 B7
Macek Rd
400 FBnC 77469 4493 E7
400 FBnC 77469 4494 A6
400 FBnC 77479 4494 A6
Maceo Wy
3100 GLSN 77554 5221 C3
N MacGregor Dr
- HOUS 77005 4102 D3
1000 HOUS 77030 4102 D3
1700 HOUS 77004 4103 A3
1700 HOUS 77030 4103 A3
S MacGregor Dr
1600 HOUS 77030 4102 E4
1700 HOUS 77021 4103 A3
1700 HOUS 77030 4103 A3
MacGregor Wy
2200 HOUS 77004 4103 C2
2200 HOUS 77030 4103 C2
N MacGregor Wy
- HOUS 77004 4103 C2
1200 HOUS 77023 4104 E2
2100 HOUS 77030 4103 E3
4400 HOUS 77004 4104 A3
S MacGregor Wy
2200 HOUS 77021 4103 D4
2200 HOUS 77030 4103 A3
5100 HOUS 77021 4104 A4
MacGregor Loop Dr
- HOUS 77021 4103 E2
- HOUS 77021 4104 A4
Macha Rd
10000 HOUS 77093 3686 A5
Machaelas Wy
8100 HarC 77396 3547 D1
Machala Ln
7800 HarC 77040 3681 E3
Machall Manor Ct
21100 FBnC 77469 4234 A3
Macinac Ct
20000 HarC 77450 3954 E5
MacIntosh Dr
800 MtgC 77354 2673 D2
Mack
- BYTN 77520 3973 D6
Mack Rd
100 HOUS 77011 3964 D6
MacKenzie Dr
10400 HarC 77086 3542 B1
MacKenzie Wy
1900 MSCY 77489 4370 B3
MacKenzie Mesa Dr
16700 HarC 77379 3255 D6
Mackeral Av
100 GLSN 77550 5109 E1

Mackerel Dr
9000 TXCY 77591 4873 A
Mackey Dr
- GlsC 77539 4633 D
- TXCY 77539 4633 D
Mackilsee Ln
14400 HOUS 77079 3957 D
Mackinac Ln
3700 PASD 77505 4248 B
Mackinaw Rd
5100 HOUS 77053 4372 A
5600 HOUS 77053 4371 E
Mackinaw Isle Ct
19600 HarC 77429 3395 D
19600 HarC 77433 3395 D
Mackinson St
5900 HOUS 77023 4104 C
Macklin Ct
28500 HarC 77336 3121 D
Mack Miller Dr
5700 HarC 77049 3828 C
Mack Washington Ln
22600 HMPD 77445 2954 A
22600 WlrC 77445 2954 A
23000 WlrC 77445 2953 E
Mackworth Dr
9700 STAF 77477 4239 A
MacLeish Dr
17100 HarC 77084 3678 A
MacLeish Ln
15500 HarC 77032 3404 B
MacMane St
- FBnC 77477 4370 A
MacMillan Ln
9200 FBnC 77083 4236 B
MacNaughton Dr
12000 HarC 77039 3546 C
Maco Av
5700 GLSN 77551 5108 D
5700 GLSN 77551 5222 C
Macoma Av
3000 PRLD 77581 4503 D
Macon Pk
500 MtgC 77302 2530 B
Macon St
23600 HarC 77389 2967 A
Maconda Ln
- HOUS 77019 3961 D
2000 HOUS 77027 3961 D
Macondray Dr
2000 HarC 77396 3407 B
Macon Pl Ct
3600 HarC 77082 4096 B
Macquaire Dr
6300 HarC 77449 3677 A
Macquarie Ct
6300 HarC 77449 3676 E
Macrantha Ct
5500 HarC 77379 3257 B
Macrantha Dr
17600 HarC 77379 3257 B
MacRidge Blvd
4800 HOUS 77053 4372 B
Macy Dr
15200 HarC 77433 3251 E
Maczali Ct
15900 HOUS 77489 4371 B
Maczali Dr
6600 HOUS 77489 4371 C
Madalyn Ln
5000 HOUS 77021 4104 A
Madden Ln
- HOUS 77048 4244 A
4100 HOUS 77047 4243 C
5100 HOUS 77048 4243 E
Madden Rd
17200 FBnC 77469 4235 B
Madden St
14400 GlsC 77517 4986 B
Maddie Ln
19200 MtgC 77365 2826 D
Maddie Spring Ct
1700 MtgC 77386 2969 C
Maddox Av
10000 HOUS 77078 3687 C
Maddox St
9500 HOUS 77028 3687 C5
9700 HOUS 77078 3687 C5
Maddux Dr
21500 MtgC 77365 2973 B
Madeleine Ct
3400 SGLD 77478 4368 D
Madeley St
300 CNRO 77301 2383 E5
3000 HOUS 77093 3825 A2
Madeline Rd
- HOUS 77085 4240 D
Madeline St
1700 HarC 77562 3692 E
Madeline Alyssa Ct
9800 HOUS 77025 4241 D
Madelin Manor Ln
28200 MtgC 77386 2969 D
Madera Rd
8200 HOUS 77078 3687 C
9000 HOUS 77078 3688 A
Madera Canyon Ct
22000 FBnC 77469 4493 A2
Madera Canyon Ln
2100 FBnC 77469 4493 A3
12700 HarC 77377 3254 A1
Madewood Dr
2100 MSCY 77459 4369 B
Madewood Pl
5400 PRLD 77584 4502 E
Madewood St
16200 HarC 77429 3397 B
Madge St
2100 HarC 77039 3545 D1
Madie Dr
8400 HOUS 77022 3685 A
Madiera Ct
23100 MtgC 77365 2971 D
Madil Meadow Ct
2100 PRLD 77581 4503 D2
Mading Ln
200 HarC 77037 3544 B5
200 HarC 77060 3544 B5
200 HOUS 77037 3544 B5
Madison Av
700 GlsC 77650 4878 E7
1100 PASD 77502 4107 C7
2300 GlsC 77650 4879 A5
2500 RSBG 77471 4491 A5
Madison Blvd
20100 HarC 77484 3103 B4
Madison Ct
11300 PRLD 77583 4500 D5

Houston Street Index

STREET
Block City ZIP Map# Grid

adison Dr
- KATY 77494 3952 E1
1500 DRPK 77536 4249 D1
3400 PRLD 77583 4500 D6
adison Ln
20500 HarC 77449 3815 D3
adison St
600 LPRT 77571 4251 E2
1200 BYTN 77520 3973 B6
5600 HOUS 77091 3684 A6
Madison St
- LPRT 77571 4252 A2
600 LPRT 77571 4251 E2
Madison St
- LPRT 77571 4251 D2
adison Tr
7000 HarC 77084 3678 E2
adison Claire Ct
8300 HarC 77433 3537 C4
adison Elm St
3000 HarC 77449 3814 B3
adison Kendall Ln
1900 HarC 77066 3401 B6
adison Lee Ln
5100 HOUS 77504 4247 D7
5100 PASD 77504 4247 D7
5400 HOUS 77034 4247 D7
adison Oak St
1700 HarC 77038 3543 A5
adisons Crossing Ln
8300 HarC 77375 3255 B2
adison Valey Ct
21300 MtgC 77365 2973 A3
adonna Dr
- HTCK 77563 4988 A2
2000 HarC 77067 3402 A7
adrid E
2700 GLSN 77554 5220 B7
adrid St
6300 HOUS 77021 4103 E6
ad River Ln
2200 FBnC 77459 4621 B7
adrone Ct
6800 HarC 77095 3538 A2
adrone Meadow Ct
- FBnC 77494 4093 B7
adrone Meadow Dr
- FBnC 77494 4093 A3
adyros Dr
12000 HarC 77016 3547 E7
12000 HarC 77050 3547 E7
ae Dr
- HOUS 77013 3966 E1
ae Rd
1000 HOUS 77013 3966 E2
1000 HOUS 77015 3966 E2
ae St
5500 KATY 77493 3813 B5
aeline St
14400 HarC 77039 3545 D2
14700 HarC 77032 3545 D2
aete Ln
13000 HarC 77039 3546 B4
affitt
1100 HOUS 77020 3963 E2
affitt St
800 HOUS 77020 3963 E3
1700 HOUS 77026 3963 E2
2300 HOUS 77009 3963 E1
Magazine Cir
5800 HarC 77084 3679 A4
Magazine Cir
5600 HarC 77084 3679 A5
agdalene Rd
700 BKHV 77024 3959 C2
700 HDWV 77024 3959 C2
agdalene St
900 HDWV 77024 3959 C1
agee Ln
8000 HOUS 77071 4239 D5
agee St
6100 HarC 77032 3404 B6
agellan
- HarC 77532 3552 C3
agellan Manor Dr
6500 FBnC 77469 4093 E7
agenta Mdws
2700 CNRO 77304 2383 B7
agenta Oaks Dr
12800 HOUS 77072 4097 D5
agenta Springs Dr
17800 HarC 77346 3408 E2
aggie Ln
10 PNPV 77063 3959 C6
aggie St
4100 HOUS 77051 4243 B3
4700 HOUS 77033 4243 D3
aggie Mist Dr
21500 FBnC 77469 4234 A2
21600 FBnC 77469 4233 E2
agic Dr
12800 HarC 77039 3546 D4
agic Falls Dr
12800 HarC 77377 3254 A4
agic Oaks Ct
300 HarC 77388 3113 D7
agic Oaks Dr
100 HarC 77388 3113 D7
100 HOUS 77388 3113 D7
agic River Dr
14400 HarC 77429 3397 D4
agli Ct
13200 HarC 77044 3689 C5
Maglitto
- HarC 77377 3254 D4
Maglitto Cir
16800 HarC 77377 3254 D5
Maglitto Cir
16800 HarC 77377 3254 D5
agna St
7600 HOUS 77093 3825 A1
8300 HOUS 77093 3686 B7
agnet St
2500 HOUS 77054 4242 E1
agnolia
300 MSCY 77489 4370 B2
18100 GlsC 77511 4869 A4
agnolia Av
- MRGP 77571 4252 A1
100 HarC 77530 3831 A7
100 HarC 77532 3692 B3
400 HarC 77530 3969 C1
1300 HarC 77598 4631 B1
1300 WEBS 77598 4631 A1
3400 TXCY 77590 4874 C4
7400 SGLD 77479 4367 D6
Magnolia Av
- MRGP 77571 4252 B2

Magnolia Blvd
10 HarC 77357 2830 E7
200 MAGA 77355 2669 A5
900 MAGA 77355 2668 E5
5800 PRLD 77584 4502 D5
Magnolia Blvd FM-1488
800 MAGA 77355 2669 A5
Magnolia Blvd FM-1774
200 MAGA 77355 2669 A5
S Magnolia Blvd
10 MAGA 77355 2669 B6
100 MtgC 77355 2669 B6
S Magnolia Blvd FM-1774
10 MAGA 77355 2669 B6
100 MtgC 77355 2669 B6
Magnolia Bnd
100 RMFT 77357 2829 A3
4600 MSCY 77459 4496 C3
Magnolia Cir
500 LGCY 77573 4630 D6
500 PNPV 77024 3959 E3
6900 HarC 77396 3547 B2
17600 FBnC 77469 4095 C5
33100 MtgC 77354 2673 A3
Magnolia Cross
400 LGCY 77573 4630 E4
Magnolia Ct
2700 FBnC 77477 4369 E4
10900 MtgC 77302 2531 A6
Magnolia Dr
- MtgC 77357 2828 E5
- MtgC 77357 2829 A5
- PRLD 77584 4502 D5
- RSBG 77471 4490 C6
10 HOUS 77365 3119 D1
100 GNPK 77547 4106 B1
200 HOUS 77336 3120 E4
1500 LMQU 77568 4990 A2
1900 LMQU 77568 4989 D2
3600 MtgC 77302 2530 B6
13000 HarC 77532 3692 A1
15200 MtgC 77384 2674 A2
21400 MtgC 77357 2974 D1
25300 MtgC 77372 2536 E6
25300 MtgC 77372 2537 A6
25300 SPLD 77372 2537 A6
N Magnolia Dr
100 CNRO 77301 2384 E3
15000 MtgC 77372 2683 D3
S Magnolia Dr
100 CNRO 77301 2384 E4
Magnolia Ln
10 CNRO 77304 2383 A6
10 HarC 77336 2976 C4
100 CNRO 77304 2382 E6
1100 HOUS 77339 3263 C1
1700 RHMD 77469 4491 D3
2500 DRPK 77536 4109 E5
4100 SGLD 77478 4369 A7
8100 HTCK 77563 4988 E4
17600 MtgC 77357 2681 B7
17600 MtgC 77357 2827 C1
25700 MtgC 77372 2682 E6
25700 MtgC 77372 2683 A6
Magnolia Pkwy
2200 MAGA 77354 2669 B4
2400 MtgC 77354 2669 C4
18700 MAGA 77355 2669 A5
18800 MAGA 77355 2668 E5
19000 MtgC 77355 2668 C7
20900 MtgC 77355 2814 A1
21500 MtgC 77355 2813 E1
21800 WlrC 77447 2813 E1
Magnolia Pkwy FM-1488
2200 MAGA 77354 2669 B4
2400 MtgC 77354 2669 C4
18700 MAGA 77355 2669 A5
18800 MAGA 77355 2668 E5
19000 MtgC 77355 2668 C7
20900 MtgC 77355 2814 A1
21500 MtgC 77355 2813 E1
21800 WlrC 77447 2813 E1
Magnolia Rd
- MtgC 77447 2959 D5
10 HarC 77336 2975 C6
10 WDBR 77357 2828 C2
400 HarC 77373 3113 E2
400 HarC 77373 3114 B1
3400 PRLD 77581 4503 C5
3400 PRLD 77584 4503 A5
25500 WlrC 77447 2958 E5
Magnolia Rdg
3700 LGCY 77573 4630 E4
Magnolia St
- PRVW 77445 3100 A3
- WEBS 77598 4631 B1
10 LbyC 77372 2538 D6
100 HarC 77373 3114 A2
100 LGCY 77573 4632 B4
300 WEBS 77598 4507 C7
1100 BYTN 77520 3972 A7
1300 BYTN 77520 4112 B1
1600 PASD 77503 4108 A7
4500 BLAR 77401 4101 B5
5000 PRLD 77584 4503 A5
5200 PRLD 77584 4502 E5
5800 HarC 77050 3546 E6
6100 KATY 77493 3813 B4
7400 HOUS 77023 4105 A2
8100 MNVL 77578 4746 D3
11000 MtgC 77372 2536 E2
17400 PTVL 77372 2683 A7
E Magnolia St
100 FRDW 77546 4505 C7
7500 HOUS 77023 4105 B2
8100 HOUS 77012 4105 C2
N Magnolia St
100 TMBL 77375 2964 B7
600 HarC 77562 3831 D2
S Magnolia St
100 ALVN 77511 4867 C1
100 HarC 77562 3831 D3
100 TMBL 77375 2964 B7
Magnolia Tr
3300 HarC 77084 3816 C3
Magnolia Vw
9100 HOUS 77099 4237 E1
Magnolia Wk
2700 HarC 77388 3113 B6
Magnolia Wy
- LGCY 77573 4630 E4
10000 HarC 77070 3255 B5
Magnolia Arbor Ct
12800 HarC 77377 3254 A2
Magnolia Arbor Ln
18800 HarC 77377 3254 A2
Magnolia Bend Dr
10 HNCV 77024 3960 A4

Magnolia Bend Dr
9900 MtgC 77302 2677 A3
11800 MtgC 77302 2531 C7
20000 HarC 77346 3265 C4
Magnolia Bend St
500 LGCY 77573 4630 D7
Magnolia Bloom Tr
1100 HarC 77073 3259 B5
Magnolia Blossom
400 LGCY 77573 4630 E4
Magnoliabough Pl
15000 HarC 77429 3252 B7
Magnolia Brook Ct
8100 MSCY 77459 4497 A6
Magnolia Brook Ln
20800 HarC 77433 3251 B6
Magnolia Business Park Dr
300 MAGA 77354 2668 E5
300 MtgC 77354 2668 E5
Magnolia Canyon
12300 HOUS 77099 4237 E1
Magnolia Cove Ct
7800 HarC 77346 3265 B2
Magnolia Cove Dr
- HOUS 77339 3264 E1
4900 BYTN 77521 3972 D1
4900 HarC 77521 3972 D1
Magnolia Creek Rd
4600 HarC 77084 3677 B7
Magnolia Crest Ln
1900 SGLD 77478 4237 D5
13400 HarC 77070 3399 C3
Magnolia Crest Pl
10100 HarC 77070 3399 D3
Magnolia Dale Dr
1000 FBnC 77545 4498 E7
1000 FBnC 77545 4499 A7
E Magnolia Dale Dr
3800 FBnC 77545 4499 A7
N Magnolia Dale Dr
1200 FBnC 77545 4498 E7
1200 FBnC 77545 4499 A7
W Magnolia Dale Dr
3800 FBnC 77545 4498 E6
E Magnolia Elms Dr
3400 PRLD 77584 4503 B5
N Magnolia Elms Dr
3200 PRLD 77584 4503 A5
S Magnolia Elms Dr
4500 PRLD 77584 4503 B5
W Magnolia Elms Dr
3200 PRLD 77584 4503 B5
Magnolia Estates Blvd
- PRLD 77584 4503 B5
Magnolia Estates Dr
- LGCY 77573 4630 E4
1800 MtgC 77386 2969 B1
Magnolia Falls Ct
5400 HOUS 77345 3119 D2
Magnolia Forest Dr
8600 FBnC 77479 4494 B4
Magnolia Garden Ln
4300 FBnC 77469 4615 E5
Magnolia Gardens Dr
- HarC 77073 3259 D4
Magnolia Glen Dr
8200 HarC 77346 3265 C3
Magnolia Green Ln
5300 LGCY 77573 4751 D2
Magnolia Grove Ln
200 HarC 77049 3829 A4
Magnolia Hill Tr
2700 HarC 77038 3543 A2
Magnolia Hollow Ln
- FBnC 77469 4094 A7
Magnolia Lake Ln
- HarC 77083 4097 A6
1700 FBnC 77469 4234 E4
Magnolia Leaf St
12700 HarC 77065 3539 C1
Magnolia Manor Dr
13700 HarC 77429 3397 A3
Magnolia Meadow Ln
- LGCY 77573 4630 E7
- LGCY 77573 4631 A7
Magnolia Oaks Dr
4300 PRLD 77584 4503 B5
Magnolia Pines Dr
4500 PRLD 77584 4503 A5
25500 MtgC 77355 2814 B3
Magnolia Point Dr
100 HOUS 77336 3120 E4
200 HOUS 77336 3121 B4
700 HarC 77336 3121 B4
N Magnolia Pond Pl
10 WDLD 77381 2821 A3
S Magnolia Pond Pl
10 WDLD 77381 2821 A4
Magnolia Ridge Dr
9300 HarC 77070 3255 C5
10300 MtgC 77302 2676 E2
10400 MtgC 77302 2677 A2
Magnolia Run Dr
4900 SGLD 77478 4369 A6
Magnolia Shadows Ln
7400 HarC 77095 3678 C2
7500 HarC 77095 3538 B7
Magnolia Shadows Pl
10 WDLD 77382 2675 B7
Magnolia Shores Ln
15800 HOUS 77044 3409 A5
Magnolia Sky Dr
5200 FBnC 77469 4234 E3
Magnolia Springs Dr
14100 HarC 77066 3401 E7
Magnolia Terrace Cir
1100 DKSN 77539 4753 D3
Magnolia Trace Dr
- HarC 77066 3401 B4
- LGCY 77573 4630 E7
Magnolia Woods Ct
1100 FBnC 77479 4494 A6
Magnolia Woods Dr
10 HOUS 77339 3263 D1
Magnus Ln
13900 HarC 77083 4097 A5
Maguire St
200 ARLA 77583 4623 B4
500 FBnC 77583 4623 B4
Mahaffey Rd
10500 HarC 77375 2965 B7
10700 HarC 77375 3109 E1
10700 HarC 77375 3110 A1
10700 TMBL 77375 3109 E1
Mahalia Dr
8400 HOUS 77088 3684 A2
Mahan Dr
9200 LPRT 77571 4249 E4

Mahan Dr
9300 LPRT 77571 4250 A4
Mahan Ln
25100 HarC 77336 3266 E1
Mahan Rd
16200 HarC 77068 3257 E4
Mahan Wood Dr
6600 HarC 77346 3408 E1
Mahejan Ct
4900 PRLD 77584 4503 A6
Mahejan Dr
3500 PRLD 77584 4503 A6
Mahlmann St
1100 RSBG 77471 4491 B5
Mahogany
16700 MtgC 77372 2682 E6
Mahogany Dr
16400 MSCY 77071 4239 B7
Mahogany Tr
3600 PRLD 77584 4502 C6
Mahogany Wy
5700 MtgC 77354 2673 C2
Mahogany Creek Ct
5300 HarC 77379 3112 B6
Mahogany Crest Dr
16300 HarC 77429 3397 A2
Mahogany Forest Dr
18300 HarC 77379 3255 E2
Mahogany Glen Wy
- HarC 77379 3112 B6
Mahogany Ridge Dr
19900 MtgC 77355 2814 C2
Mahogany Run Dr
800 HarC 77494 3953 A3
1000 FBnC 77494 3952 E3
Mahoning Dr
7000 HOUS 77074 4099 E5
9100 HOUS 77074 4239 B1
Mahrian Ct
3300 HarC 77546 4506 B7
Maiden Ln
600 RHMD 77469 4364 D7
15700 HOUS 77053 4372 A6
Maidencane Ct
11000 HarC 77086 3542 B1
Maidencroft Ln
5500 FBnC 77494 4093 A6
Maidenglen Dr
2000 FBnC 77469 4616 B2
Maidenglen Ln
12900 HOUS 77085 4240 C7
Maidenhair Ln
1800 SGLD 77479 4368 A6
Maidenhead Dr
4200 PASD 77504 4247 D6
Maidens Crossing Dr
21800 MtgC 77339 3118 B5
Maiden Wy Dr
1200 HarC 77379 3255 B1
Maid Marian Ct
23300 MtgC 77447 2960 A5
Maid Marian Ln
23000 MtgC 77447 2960 A5
Maidstone Dr
6900 PASD 77505 4249 A7
Maidstone Ln
7300 HarC 77095 3679 A1
Maidstone Manor Ct
10600 HarC 77379 3110 B6
Maile Park Dr
12900 HOUS 77034 4378 C2
Mail Route Rd
17800 MtgC 77384 2675 E7
Maily Meadow Ln
- PRLD 77584 4501 D5
4200 FBnC 77450 4093 E2
12300 SGLD 77478 4237 D5
Main
- HOUS 77365 2975 A6
- PASD 77506 4107 C4
10 HOUS 77365 2974 E6
600 ARLA 77583 4623 B4
600 FBnC 77583 4623 B4
E Main
- HarC 77373 3114 A1
Main Av
1800 RSBG 77471 4490 E6
Main Blvd
22000 HarC 77377 3106 D1
Main St
- FBnC 77545 4499 A5
- HarC 77373 3113 E2
- HMPD 77445 2952 E7
- HOUS 77005 4102 E2
- HOUS 77025 4102 B6
- HOUS 77071 4371 A1
- MTBL 77520 3696 D6
- WALR 77484 3101 E5
10 HarC 77336 2975 D6
10 HOUS 77002 3963 A7
10 LMQU 77568 4990 A3
10 TXCY 77590 4990 A3
100 HarC 77373 3114 A2
100 HOUS 77017 4246 B2
100 RHMD 77469 4492 A1
100 SGLD 77478 4368 A2
100 SHUS 77587 4246 C4
200 HLCS 77511 4867 E5
200 RHMD 77469 4491 E1
1000 HMBL 77338 3262 E6
1000 HMBL 77338 3263 A6
1000 HMPD 77445 2953 A7
1300 PASD 77502 4107 B6
1300 PASD 77506 4107 B7
2000 WALR 77484 3102 A5
2300 HOUS 77034 4246 D4
2300 SHUS 77034 4246 D4
2400 HOUS 77006 3963 B6
2500 LMQU 77568 4989 A3
3100 RSBG 77471 4491 A6
4000 HTCK 77563 4989 B3
4400 STFE 77510 4871 B7
4500 HOUS 77002 4102 E1
4500 HOUS 77004 4102 E1
4600 STFE 77510 4987 B3
5200 HOUS 77006 4102 E1
6400 HTCK 77563 4988 E4
7200 HOUS 77030 4102 B5
7800 HOUS 77054 4102 B6
11800 HOUS 77035 4241 C5
12100 HOUS 77045 4241 A6
12400 HOUS 77085 4241 A6
12600 HOUS 77035 4240 E6
12600 HOUS 77085 4240 C7
14300 HOUS 77035 4371 A1
14300 HOUS 77085 4371 A1
16400 PTVL 77372 2682 E7
17000 GlsC 77511 4869 B4

Main St
17200 PTVL 77372 2683 A7
Main St FM-519
10 LMQU 77568 4990 A3
10 TXCY 77590 4990 A3
2500 LMQU 77568 4989 A3
4000 HTCK 77563 4989 B3
6400 HTCK 77563 4988 E4
Main St FM-646
5000 STFE 77510 4987 B3
Main St LP-207
- MTBL 77520 3696 D6
Main St US-90 ALT
- HOUS 77071 4371 A1
11800 HOUS 77035 4241 C5
12100 HOUS 77045 4241 A6
12400 HOUS 77085 4241 A6
12600 HOUS 77035 4240 E6
12600 HOUS 77085 4240 C7
14300 HOUS 77035 4371 A1
14300 HOUS 77085 4371 A1
Main St E
1600 WALR 77484 3102 A5
E Main St
100 HMBL 77338 3262 E6
100 LGCY 77573 4632 B2
100 LPRT 77571 4251 E2
100 TMBL 77375 2964 C6
1000 HarC 77375 2964 E6
1100 LPRT 77571 4252 A2
1300 MRGP 77571 4252 A1
2400 LGCY 77573 4508 C7
E Main St FM-518
100 LGCY 77573 4632 B2
E Main St FM-2094
2200 LGCY 77573 4632 C1
2400 LGCY 77573 4508 C7
E Main St FM-2920
100 TMBL 77375 2964 C6
1000 HarC 77375 2964 E6
N Main St
- JTCY 77029 3966 B4
10 BYTN 77520 3972 E7
10 HOUS 77339 3119 D6
100 GNPK 77547 3966 C5
100 PASD 77506 4107 A3
200 HOUS 77002 3963 D3
200 HOUS 77009 3963 C1
800 CNRO 77301 2384 A4
1000 HOUS 77075 4376 B6
1000 PRLD 77581 4376 B6
1600 PRLD 77581 4503 B2
2200 BYTN 77520 3973 A5
2600 HOUS 77009 3824 A6
2700 BYTN 77521 3973 A5
4800 HOUS 77009 3823 E5
5000 BYTN 77521 3834 A7
5000 HarC 77521 3834 A4
5000 HarC 77521 3973 A1
5600 HOUS 77008 3823 E5
5700 HarC 77532 3552 C4
7000 HOUS 77018 3823 E4
7000 HOUS 77022 3823 E4
7300 HarC 77521 3833 E1
8800 HarC 77521 3694 E6
17200 GlsC 77511 4869 C4
N Main St FM-2100
5700 HarC 77532 3552 C3
N Main St SR-35
1000 HOUS 77075 4376 B6
1000 PRLD 77581 4376 B6
1600 PRLD 77581 4503 B2
S Main St
- HarC 77373 3113 E2
- HOUS 77071 4370 E1
- HOUS 77085 4370 E1
- MSCY 77071 4370 D1
- MSCY 77085 4370 D2
- MSCY 77489 4370 D2
10 BYTN 77520 3972 E7
100 CNRO 77301 2384 A6
100 GNPK 77547 4106 C2
100 HarC 77562 3831 E3
100 PASD 77506 4107 A4
400 BYTN 77520 4112 E1
700 HOUS 77547 4106 C1
1200 PASD 77502 4107 B6
2400 PRLD 77581 4503 D6
3100 PRLD 77584 4503 D5
4200 PRLD 77581 4627 E1
4200 PRLD 77584 4627 E1
7900 HOUS 77025 4102 A7
7900 HOUS 77030 4102 B6
7900 HOUS 77054 4102 A7
9400 HOUS 77025 4242 A1
9400 HOUS 77054 4242 A1
10100 HOUS 77054 4241 E1
10800 HOUS 77025 4241 D3
14700 HOUS 77035 4371 A1
14700 HOUS 77071 4371 A1
14700 HOUS 77085 4371 A1
S Main St FM-2100
100 HarC 77562 3831 E3
S Main St SR-35
2400 PRLD 77581 4503 D6
3100 PRLD 77584 4503 D5
4200 PRLD 77581 4627 E1
4200 PRLD 77584 4627 E1
S Main St US-90 ALT
8400 HOUS 77025 4102 A7
8400 HOUS 77054 4102 A7
9400 HOUS 77025 4242 A1
9400 HOUS 77054 4242 A1
9600 HOUS 77025 4241 E1
9600 HOUS 77054 4241 E1
14700 HOUS 77035 4371 A1
14700 HOUS 77071 4371 A1
14700 HOUS 77085 4370 E1
14700 HOUS 77085 4371 A1
W Main St
- TMBL 77377 3108 E1
10 HMBL 77338 3262 D6
100 BYTN 77520 4112 E2
100 FBnC 77545 4499 C6
100 HOUS 77002 3963 A7
100 LGCY 77573 4631 D4
100 LPRT 77571 4251 B3
100 TMBL 77375 2964 A7
400 HOUS 77006 3962 E7
1200 TMBL 77375 3109 A1
1300 TMBL 77375 3108 E1
1600 HOUS 77098 3962 B7
3200 HOUS 77098 3961 E7
3900 HOUS 77027 3961 C7
W Main St FM-518
100 LGCY 77573 4631 D4
W Main St FM-2920
- TMBL 77377 3108 E1

W Main St FM-2920
100 TMBL 77375 2964 A7
1200 TMBL 77375 3109 A1
1300 TMBL 77375 3108 E1
W Main St SR-146 BUS
100 LPRT 77571 4251 D2
Mainbluff Ln
8400 HarC 77040 3541 C7
Mainer
3900 HOUS 77021 4103 C7
Mainer Ln
900 TMBL 77375 2964 D6
Mainer St
3400 HOUS 77021 4103 B7
4100 HOUS 77021 4243 C1
Mainford St
3100 HOUS 77009 3824 B7
Mainland Dr
900 TXCY 77590 4875 C3
Mainsail Cir
4100 MSCY 77459 4369 C6
Main St Ext
16600 PTVL 77372 2682 E6
Mainstay Pl Ln
12800 HarC 77044 3408 D5
N Main Trailer Ct
- BYTN 77521 3834 A7
- HarC 77521 3834 A7
Maisemore Rd
- HarC 77015 3829 A6
13800 HarC 77015 3828 E5
Maison Rouge Ct
4100 GLSN 77554 5332 E3
Maize Ln
11000 HarC 77041 3680 C3
Maize Field Wy
6700 HarC 77049 3829 B1
Maize Meadow Pl
10 WDLD 77381 2820 D3
Majave Cove Ct
9200 HarC 77089 4504 B1
Majestic Ln
- HarC 77396 3547 D2
1000 FRDW 77546 4505 B4
1800 BYTN 77521 3972 C2
Majestic St
500 HOUS 77020 3964 E1
3800 HOUS 77026 3825 E6
Majestic Tr
3900 HOUS 77059 4380 B4
Majesticbrook Dr
8500 HarC 77095 3539 A6
Majestic Canyon Ln
- HarC 77070 3255 C6
Majestic Cove Ct
10000 HarC 77494 3953 D4
Majestic Falls Dr
10 HOUS 77339 3263 D2
Majestic Flight Ct
- HarC 77396 3548 C2
Majestic Flight Ln
- HarC 77396 3548 B2
Majestic Forest
23800 MtgC 77357 2681 D7
23800 MtgC 77357 2827 C1
Majestic Forest Dr
17300 HarC 77379 3256 D1
Majestic Glen Ln
16000 HarC 77073 3259 D5
Majestic Hill Ct
6000 HOUS 77345 3120 E7
Majestic Hill Dr
6100 HOUS 77345 3120 E7
6100 HOUS 77345 3265 D1
Majestic Landing Ln
19500 HarC 77433 3537 B7
Majestic Oak Ct
3900 PRLD 77581 4504 B7
Majestic Oak Dr
1800 PRLD 77581 4504 B7
Majestic Oaks
14500 MtgC 77354 2670 C5
Majestic Oaks Dr
- HarC 77088 3682 B1
7100 HOUS 77040 3682 A1
Majestic Park Ln
31200 MtgC 77386 2823 C7
Majestic Pines Ct
1300 HOUS 77345 3120 E7
Majestic Pines Dr
5900 HOUS 77345 3120 E7
Majestic Pl Ct
13100 HOUS 77047 4373 C3
Majestic Prince Dr
- HarC 77065 3540 A5
Majestic Ridge Dr
500 HarC 77049 3829 A3
E Majestic Woods Pl
10 WDLD 77382 2673 B7
10 WDLD 77382 2819 B1
W Majestic Woods Pl
10 WDLD 77382 2673 A7
Majesty Ln
6300 HOUS 77085 4371 D1
Majic Lily Dr
24400 HarC 77373 3114 C5
Majolica Pl
10 WDLD 77382 2819 A3
Major Av
- HOUS 77061 4245 A6
Major St
7300 HOUS 77061 4245 B6
Major Blizzard Dr
8300 HarC 77089 4377 B7
Majorca Dr
700 HOUS 77076 3685 B4
Major Elm St
7300 HarC 77433 3677 B1
Major Glen Cir
18200 HarC 77346 3408 C2
Major Oak
10 HOUS 77024 3960 E2
Majors Ct
12300 HOUS 77089 4378 C7
Majuro Dr
100 TKIS 77554 5106 B4
Makah Cir
4700 HarC 77521 3833 C4
Makaha Cir
8000 HarC 77095 3539 B7
Makalu St
8400 HOUS 77051 4243 A2
Makatea St
1100 TKIS 77554 5106 C4
Makayla Ln
16000 HarC 77049 3829 D3
16000 HarC 77530 3829 D3

Makeig St
6100 HOUS 77026 3825 D6
Makenna Ct
16200 HarC 77530 3829 D3
Makenna Ln
1900 HarC 77530 3829 D3
Making Due Wy
14500 HarC 77429 3253 D5
Mako Ct
300 HarC 77532 3552 B2
Mala Wy
- HarC 77338 3260 A2
Malac Rd
7700 HarC 77389 2966 A2
Maladi Dr
16000 HOUS 77053 4372 C7
Malaga Forest Dr
29200 MtgC 77384 2822 A1
29200 SHEH 77384 2822 A1
Malagueta Ct
1400 SHEH 77384 2822 A1
Malardcrest Dr
8000 HarC 77346 3409 C1
8400 HarC 77346 3265 D7
Malca Manor Dr
24700 HarC 77493 3814 A6
Malcolm Dr
10100 HOUS 77076 3685 B5
Malcomboro Dr
5700 HarC 77041 3679 C5
Malcoms Wy
700 HOUS 77336 3266 C2
Malcomson Rd
12100 HarC 77070 3254 C7
12100 HarC 77429 3254 C7
12600 HarC 77070 3398 B1
12600 HarC 77429 3398 B1
Malden Dr
10800 HOUS 77075 4377 B4
Maldon Ct
4300 HOUS 77016 3825 B2
Maledo
16600 HarC 77049 3691 A6
Maleewan Ln
13900 FBnC 77478 4237 A2
Malesa St
- HOUS 77028 3825 E2
Malet St
17400 HarC 77532 3552 A1
17500 HarC 77532 3411 A7
Malfrey Ln
5400 HarC 77084 3678 C5
Malibu Dr
6600 HOUS 77092 3821 B1
6800 HOUS 77092 3682 C7
Malibu Creek Ln
12900 HarC 77346 3408 D2
Malin Ct
8200 FBnC 77083 4096 D7
Mall Dr
4100 HOUS 77092 3822 B1
Mallard Dr
1800 HOUS 77043 3819 E5
6000 KATY 77493 3813 B3
7200 TXCY 77591 4873 C6
Mallard St
4400 GlsC 77563 4990 A5
Mallard Wy
12900 HarC 77044 3549 C1
Mallard Bayou
100 BYTN 77520 4113 C5
Mallard Cove
32500 MtgC 77354 2672 A5
Mallard Crossing Dr
26800 HarC 77447 3248 E6
Mallard Estates Ct
18100 HarC 77429 3396 B2
Mallard Glen Pl
10 WDLD 77381 2821 A2
Mallard Lake Ln
19500 HarC 77084 3816 B7
19700 HarC 77084 3815 E6
Mallard Landing Ct
4500 HarC 77066 3401 C5
Mallard Point Ct
19800 HarC 77433 3537 A7
Mallards Wy
8700 HarC 77521 3695 B7
Mallard Springs Dr
27800 MtgC 77339 3118 B4
Mallard Stream Ct
12000 HarC 77038 3543 A5
Malletia Dr
19900 HarC 77338 3262 A4
Mallets Bay Ct
19700 FBnC 77469 4094 D7
Mallie Ct
8200 HLSV 77055 3821 C7
Mallie St
300 CNRO 77301 2383 E6
600 CNRO 77301 2384 A7
Mallorca Cir
2500 HarC 77038 3543 B5
Mallory St
9200 HOUS 77051 4243 B4
Mallory Bridge Dr
16700 HarC 77095 3538 A2
Mallow St
4100 HOUS 77051 4243 C4
4600 HOUS 77033 4243 D4
Malmaison Ridge Dr
1200 HarC 77379 3110 B7
Malmedy Rd
4800 HOUS 77033 4103 E7
5200 HOUS 77033 4104 A7
Malon Av
2400 PRLD 77581 4503 D3
Malone Dr
3700 PASD 77503 4108 C6
Malone St
10 HOUS 77007 3962 A3
500 TMBL 77375 2964 B7
Malope Ranch Dr
2300 FBnC 77494 3953 A4
Mal Paso Ct
3600 HarC 77082 4096 B3
Mal Paso Dr
15900 HarC 77082 4096 B3
Maltby St
800 HOUS 77011 3965 A7
Malthusian Wy
- BzaC 77581 4628 C2
Malvern Av
400 PASD 77503 4108 A5
Malvern St
1100 HOUS 77009 3824 D5
Mammoth Falls Dr
20000 HarC 77375 3109 E5

STREET
Block City ZIP Map# Grid

Mammoth Springs Ct
10 WDLD 77382 2673 D6
9600 HarC 77095 3538 A4
Mammoth Springs Dr
16700 HarC 77095 3538 A4
Mammoth Springs Ln
100 LGCY 77539 4752 E4
1500 FBnC 77469 4493 C4
Manacor Cir
2500 HarC 77038 3543 B6
Managua Wy
16700 GLSN 77554 5331 D5
16700 JMAB 77554 5331 D5
Manassas Ln
8400 FBnC 77083 4235 E1
Manassas Pk
500 MtgC 77302 2530 B5
Manasses Springs Ln
11800 HarC 77346 3408 B4
Manatee Ln
1000 HarC 77090 3258 B3
Manboro Ct
12000 HarC 77067 3402 B4
Mance Ct
18200 HarC 77094 3955 C2
Manchester Cir
1200 MSCY 77459 4369 B5
Manchester Ct
4900 SGLD 77479 4495 C5
Manchester Dr
900 CNRO 77304 2529 D1
1700 FBnC 77545 4498 D6
Manchester Ln
2100 PRLD 77581 4503 E3
Manchester St
7100 HOUS 77023 4105 A3
7400 HOUS 77012 4105 C2
9500 HOUS 77012 4106 A3
Manchester Cove
2900 FBnC 77459 4621 B6
Manchester Point Ln
17600 FBnC 77469 4095 D7
Manchester Trail Dr
600 HarC 77373 2968 E7
Mandalay Ct
2600 BzaC 77584 4501 A5
Mandalay Wy
- HOUS 77045 4242 B7
12500 HOUS 77045 4373 B1
Mandale Rd
2900 FRDW 77546 4749 D3
3200 ALVN 77511 4749 D3
Mandate Dr
16300 HarC 77530 3829 E4
Mandavilla Dr
10700 HarC 77095 3538 A2
Mandell Rd
10 LbyC 77327 2537 E2
10 LbyC 77328 2537 D2
200 MtgC 77372 2537 D2
Mandell St
2400 HOUS 77006 3962 D7
5300 HOUS 77005 4102 D2
5300 HOUS 77006 4102 D2
Manderly Dr
14100 HOUS 77077 3956 E4
Mandeville Ct
16700 HarC 77379 3256 D3
Mandolin Ct
10100 HarC 77070 3399 C2
Mandolin Dr
- HarC 77070 3399 C2
Mandover Ln
4500 HOUS 77345 3119 E2
Mandrake Ct
12900 HOUS 77085 4241 A7
Mandrill Ln
1700 HarC 77067 3402 B6
Mandy
11900 HarC 77050 3547 B6
Mandy Ln
2900 BzaC 77511 4748 D2
13300 STFE 77510 4870 D7
Manet Ct
3200 HOUS 77082 4098 B2
Manette Dr
20500 HarC 77450 3954 D2
Manfield Dr
15700 HarC 77082 4096 B3
Manford Blvd
- FBnC 77469 4492 E5
Mango Ct
2500 LGCY 77573 4752 B1
Mango Dr
1400 TKIS 77554 5106 B4
Mango St
9600 HOUS 77075 4377 C3
10000 HOUS 77089 4377 C3
Mango Ridge Ct
16300 HarC 77396 3408 A3
Mangrove Bend Dr
2200 LGCY 77573 4752 B1
Mangum Rd
4300 HOUS 77092 3822 A1
4600 HOUS 77092 3683 A7
5100 HOUS 77091 3683 A7
Manhattan Dr
8500 HOUS 77096 4100 E7
8800 HOUS 77096 4240 E1
Manie Ford Rd
2300 ALVN 77511 4866 D1
2300 BzaC 77511 4866 D1
Manila Ln
2900 HOUS 77043 3819 E2
Manion Dr
2800 MSCY 77459 4497 E6
Manion Oaks Ct
23100 MtgC 77357 2828 A6
Manire Dr
8600 HOUS 77055 3821 A6
Manis Rd
- HOUS 77063 3960 A7
Manito Cir
2800 FBnC 77450 3954 B7
Manitou Dr
3400 HOUS 77013 3826 E5
Manitou Falls Ln
21600 HarC 77449 3815 B3
Mankay Ln
9500 HarC 77070 3399 E5
Manleigh Ct
18800 HarC 77377 3254 A2
Mann Ln
- CNRO 77303 2237 D6
Mann St
2400 HOUS 77093 3824 E1
Manning Dr
15600 HarC 77429 3397 B6
Manning Ln
7400 HOUS 77075 4376 B3
Manning Pkwy
- HarC 77044 3549 B3
Manning Rd
900 HMBL 77338 3262 E4
900 HMBL 77338 3263 A4
Mannington Dr
500 LGCY 77573 4630 E6
Manningtree Ln
16500 HarC 77379 3256 B5
Mannix Rd
15300 WlrC 77445 3243 E7
Mano St
6700 HOUS 77076 3684 E4
Manon Ln
20900 HarC 77388 3112 E4
Manor Av
100 ARLA 77583 4623 B5
400 HarC 77015 3829 B7
700 HarC 77015 3968 B2
Manor Bnd
16300 HarC 77429 3252 C6
Manor Cir
1800 RSBG 77471 4491 C5
E Manor Cir
25000 HarC 77389 2966 D3
W Manor Cir
25000 HarC 77389 2966 C3
Manor Ct
1200 FBnC 77469 4365 C2
12500 HOUS 77072 4097 D6
Manor Dr
1400 RSBG 77471 4491 C5
1500 BYTN 77521 3972 C2
2000 FBnC 77469 4365 C2
4000 SGLD 77479 4495 D4
5200 FBnC 77479 4495 E7
5200 FBnC 77479 4496 B6
12400 BKVL 77581 4375 E6
40400 MtgC 77354 2671 B3
Manor Ln
3700 DKSN 77539 4753 D4
Manor Wy
10 GLSN 77550 5109 E1
6800 HarC 77396 3406 B7
6800 HOUS 77396 3406 B7
Manor Bay Ct
3000 LGCY 77573 4633 A4
Manor Bend St
16200 HarC 77429 3252 B6
Manorbier Ln
14300 FBnC 77478 4366 E4
Manor Bridge Ct
7400 HarC 77095 3678 C1
Manorcliff Ln
18300 HarC 77449 3677 D3
N Manorcliff Pl
10 WDLD 77382 2674 B4
S Manorcliff Pl
10 WDLD 77382 2674 A5
Manor Creek Ln
5300 HOUS 77092 3821 E2
Manor Crest Ct
26800 MtgC 77339 3118 C4
Manor Crest Ln
13600 BzaC 77583 4623 E2
Manor Ct Dr
21700 HarC 77449 3676 D6
Manordale Dr
3800 HarC 77082 4096 B4
4100 PASD 77505 4249 A5
Manor Estates Dr
22000 HarC 77449 3815 A3
Manor Falls Dr
26800 MtgC 77339 3118 C4
Manorfield Ct
2700 FBnC 77479 4493 D2
Manorfield Dr
4000 TYLV 77586 4508 D1
4100 TYLV 77586 4381 D7
5100 HarC 77449 3676 C6
Manorford Ct
15600 HarC 77095 3538 E5
Manor Forest Dr
5600 HOUS 77339 3119 C1
5700 HOUS 77365 3119 C1
Manorgate Dr
11800 HOUS 77031 4239 A5
Manor Glen Dr
5200 HOUS 77345 3120 A5
Manorglen Dr
900 MSCY 77489 4370 E6
Manor Green Dr
2100 HOUS 77077 3958 A6
Manor Green Ln
21200 HarC 77379 3111 D3
Manor Grove Dr
3000 HOUS 77345 3119 E4
Manorhaven Ln
5100 HarC 77084 3677 E6
Manorhill Dr
15100 HOUS 77062 4506 E1
Manorhouse Ln
11500 HOUS 77082 4098 B2
Manor Lake Ct
10 HarC 77379 3255 C1
1300 FBnC 77469 4234 D5
Manor Lake Dr
- HarC 77379 3255 C1
Manor Lake Ln
- PRLD 77583 4500 B5
13000 FBnC 77478 4366 E1
Manor Lake Estates Cir
- HarC 77379 3255 C1
Manor Lake Estates Dr
19000 HarC 77379 3255 C1
Manor Oaks Dr
5300 HOUS 77339 3119 B2
Manor Park Dr
11600 HOUS 77077 3958 A6
Manor Point Dr
16100 HarC 77095 3538 C5
Manor Ridge Ct
2800 FBnC 77494 3953 B6
Manor Ridge Ln
600 LGCY 77573 4633 B2
Manor Spring Ct
- HarC 77377 3254 A1
Manor Square Dr
15800 HOUS 77062 4380 C7
Manorstone Ct
9500 HarC 77044 3689 A4
Manor Stone Ln
- RSBG 77469 4615 A4
Manor Terrace Ln
6800 FBnC 77469 4615 E4
Manor Tree Ct
14900 HarC 77068 3257 C6
Manor Tree Ln
3200 HarC 77068 3257 C6
Manorview Ln
- HarC 77396 3547 D1
Manorwood Cir E
3500 KATY 77493 3813 B2
Manorwood Cir W
- KATY 77493 3813 B2
Manorwood Dr
6500 KATY 77493 3813 B2
Manorwood Ln
12600 HarC 77429 3398 B6
Manorwood St
2300 SGLD 77478 4237 C4
Man O War Ct
1800 FBnC 77469 4365 A2
Man O War Ln
16700 HarC 77546 4506 B5
Manry Av
6000 BKVL 77581 4375 D6
Mansard St
2000 HOUS 77054 4242 D1
Mansas Park Dr
11800 HarC 77065 3539 E1
Mansfield St
700 HOUS 77091 3684 A5
900 HOUS 77091 3683 A5
Mansfield Bay Ln
20700 FBnC 77469 4094 B6
Mansfield Bluff Ln
21600 HarC 77379 3111 C2
Mansfield Park Ct
500 LGCY 77573 4630 E6
Mansfield Park Ln
20100 HarC 77379 3112 A5
Mansfield Point Ln
13600 HarC 77070 3399 C3
Mansfield Trace Ct
12600 HarC 77014 3402 B2
Mansfield Trace Ln
- HarC 77377 3253 E2
19200 FBnC 77469 4234 E1
Mansion Ct
13100 HarC 77429 3397 E4
Mansion Rd
20500 MtgC 77357 2828 E7
20500 MtgC 77357 2974 E1
Mansion Woodland Dr
15400 CNRO 77384 2675 E2
Mansor Dr
13600 HarC 77041 3679 B4
Mansvelt Rd
16500 JMAB 77554 5331 E5
16500 JMAB 77554 5332 A5
Mantana Ct
17600 HarC 77388 3257 E1
Mantana Dr
17700 HarC 77388 3257 E1
18200 HarC 77388 3112 D7
Mantle Ct
10300 HarC 77065 3540 A3
Manton St
5400 HOUS 77028 3826 D4
Mantova Dr
200 HarC 77073 3403 A3
Manuel Rd
- PRVW 77445 2955 A6
Manus St
8600 HOUS 77093 3686 A7
Manvel Rd
2100 PRLD 77581 4502 B3
2100 PRLD 77584 4502 B4
2300 FBnC 77545 4498 D5
3200 BzaC 77584 4502 B5
Manvel Rd FM-1128
2100 PRLD 77581 4502 B3
2100 PRLD 77584 4502 B4
3200 BzaC 77584 4502 B5
Manvel Rd Byp
- PRLD 77581 4502 B4
- PRLD 77584 4502 B4
Manvel-Sandy Point Rd
- BzaC 77578 4746 B6
- BzaC 77583 4746 A7
- MNVL 77578 4746 C5
Manville St
1100 HOUS 77008 3822 E6
Manx St
6300 HarC 77083 4097 B4
Many Oak Dr
25500 MtgC 77380 2968 A2
Many Pines Rd
1200 MtgC 77380 2822 A6
1200 WDLD 77380 2822 A6
Many Trees Ln
16200 MtgC 77302 2678 E4
16300 MtgC 77302 2679 A4
Manzano Dr
7800 FBnC 77083 4096 A7
Maple
- PASD 77504 4247 D4
Maple Av
600 BzaC 77583 4623 D2
600 FBnC 77545 4623 D2
600 PRLD 77545 4623 D2
900 PASD 77506 4107 B5
15100 STFE 77517 4870 A5
Maple Cir
2100 RSBG 77471 4491 C5
24200 MtgC 77365 2974 B6
Maple Ct
31700 MtgC 77355 2669 B7
Maple Dr
3100 DKSN 77539 4753 C5
3200 BYTN 77521 3972 B1
3600 MtgC 77302 2530 B6
5100 BYTN 77521 3833 B7
6300 HarC 77338 3261 B3
12900 HarC 77532 3692 B1
25400 MtgC 77357 2974 E2
W Maple Dr
4400 LGCY 77598 4630 C4
Maple Ln
10 GLSN 77551 5108 B6
100 WDBR 77357 2828 C2
200 CNRO 77304 2383 A7
1100 MtgC 77357 2829 C5
2700 PRLD 77584 4502 D4
7200 BYTN 77521 3835 B4
12200 MtgC 77362 2817 B6
12900 LbyC 77372 2537 E6
14100 HarC 77396 3547 B2
14700 MtgC 77302 2677 B1
Maple Rd
100 CRLS 77565 4509 C4
4600 RSBG 77471 4614 E3
Maple St
100 CNRO 77301 2383 D4
100 HarC 77562 3831 D2
200 CNRO 77301 2384 D3
200 HTCK 77563 4988 C4
600 FBnC 77545 4623 A3
800 LMQU 77568 4874 B7
800 LMQU 77568 4990 C1
4500 BLAR 77401 4101 B6
5100 BLAR 77401 4100 D6
5200 BLAR 77096 4100 D6
5200 HarC 77532 3552 D4
5200 HOUS 77096 4100 D6
5200 HOUS 77401 4100 D6
5400 HOUS 77081 4100 C6
5700 HOUS 77074 4100 B6
11100 MtgC 77372 2536 E2
22700 MtgC 77365 3118 D1
33000 MtgC 77362 2817 A7
33000 MtgC 77362 2963 B1
S Maple St
100 MRGP 77571 4252 C1
Maple Wy
500 HOUS 77015 3967 B1
Maple Acres Ct
16000 HarC 77095 3538 C6
Maple Acres Dr
- HarC 77095 3538 D5
Maple Arbor Ct
18200 HarC 77429 3252 B7
Maple Bend Ct
2900 HarC 77084 3815 E3
Maple Bend Dr
2800 HOUS 77345 3120 A2
2900 HOUS 77345 3119 E1
Maple Bluff Dr
21700 HarC 77449 3676 D6
Maple Bough Ct
1200 FBnC 77479 4493 E6
Maple Bough Ln
10800 HarC 77067 3402 B7
Maple Branch Ln
700 BzaC 77584 4501 A1
Maple Branch St
10 WDLD 77380 2968 A1
100 WDLD 77380 2822 A7
Maple Brook Dr
19800 HarC 77433 3677 A1
Maple Brook Ln
4900 HOUS 77345 3119 D2
7800 HarC 77095 3538 C6
Maple Chase Ln
19700 HarC 77094 3954 E2
Maple Cliff Ln
13900 HarC 77429 3253 C6
Maple Creek Dr
1000 LPRT 77571 4250 A2
4700 MSCY 77545 4622 C2
Maplecreek Dr
17600 HOUS 77084 3816 D6
Maple Crest Dr
2300 MSCY 77459 4370 A7
Maplecrest Dr
8100 HOUS 77072 4098 C7
8500 HOUS 77099 4098 D7
8500 HOUS 77099 4238 D1
Maple Cross Dr
4200 PASD 77505 4248 E5
Maple Dale Ln
1900 FBnC 77469 4234 C7
Maple Downs Ln
16300 FBnC 77478 4236 A6
Maple Falls Ct
- PRLD 77581 4503 D2
15800 HarC 77377 3255 A5
16500 HarC 77379 3256 C5
Maple Falls Dr
11400 HarC 77377 3255 A5
11500 HarC 77377 3254 E5
Maple Fox Dr
6900 HarC 77338 3261 C4
Maplegate Dr
2100 MSCY 77489 4370 B7
5500 HarC 77373 3115 E7
Maple Gate Wy
17300 HarC 77095 3678 C3
Maple Glade Cir
- WDLD 77382 2674 A6
N Maple Glade Cir
200 WDLD 77382 2674 A5
S Maple Glade Cir
200 WDLD 77382 2674 A6
Maple Glen Dr
10 HarC 77375 3255 A2
3600 HOUS 77345 3119 D4
Maple Green Dr
3500 FBnC 77478 4366 C1
Maple Green Ln
9500 HarC 77044 3689 C4
Maple Grove Dr
100 MtgC 77384 2675 A1
Maple Grove Ln
3000 HOUS 77092 3822 B3
Maple Harvest Ln
21300 HarC 77338 3261 E2
Maple Heights Dr
3900 HOUS 77339 3119 C3
Maple Hill Dr
3100 FRDW 77598 4630 B2
6300 HOUS 77088 3682 C3
Maple Hill Tr
5100 HOUS 77345 3119 E1
Maple Hollow Dr
17200 FBnC 77478 4367 A1
Maplehurst Dr
15800 HarC 77379 3256 A6
Maple Knob Ct
5900 HOUS 77345 3120 C5
Maple Knoll Dr
2900 HOUS 77339 3119 B2
Maple Lakes Dr
1900 HOUS 77339 3118 D7
Maple Leaf
- HarC 77336 2976 D5
Maple Leaf Cir
3800 LPRT 77571 4250 E4
Maple Leaf Ct
1500 PRLD 77581 4504 E4
Maple Leaf Dr
100 LGCY 77573 4630 B7
1500 LGCY 77573 4751 A1
9500 HarC 77064 3540 E4
9600 HarC 77064 3541 A4
Maple Leaf Ln
12100 STAF 77477 4238 A6
12200 STAF 77477 4237 E6
Maple Leaf St
200 MtgC 77354 2671 D3
11200 HOUS 77016 3686 E1
11400 HOUS 77016 3546 E7
Maple Loft Pl
10 WDLD 77381 2674 D7
Maple Manor Dr
15700 HarC 77095 3538 D6
Maple Meadows Ct
20400 HarC 77433 3251 C6
Maple Meadows Dr
15200 HarC 77433 3251 C7
Maple Mill Ct
10 CNRO 77301 2384 E6
Maple Mill Dr
18200 HarC 77429 3396 B1
Maple Mist Dr
- HarC 77449 3677 C2
Maplemont Dr
16300 HarC 77095 3678 C1
Maple Moss Ct
1400 HarC 77450 3953 E4
Maple Park Ct
3700 HOUS 77339 3119 C5
Maple Park Dr
3300 HOUS 77339 3119 C5
Maple Park Wy
- HOUS 77345 3119 E2
Maple Pass Ct
3600 HarC 77449 3816 A2
Maple Path Pl
10 WDLD 77382 2674 B6
Maple Pl Ct
2600 FBnC 77545 4498 C7
Maple Rain Ct
20600 HarC 77449 3815 D2
Maple Rapids Ct
- HarC 77338 3262 B3
4300 MtgC 77386 3115 D2
Maple Rapids Ln
- HarC 77338 3262 A4
4100 MtgC 77386 3115 C1
Mapleridge St
6300 HOUS 77081 4100 E5
6600 BLAR 77401 4100 E5
6800 BLAR 77081 4100 E5
Maple Ridge Wy
- HarC 77044 3549 B3
Maple Rock Dr
10800 HarC 77396 3407 D7
12100 HOUS 77077 3957 E5
Maple Run Dr
1000 HarC 77373 2968 D7
7300 FBnC 77479 4493 E6
Maple Shores Ct
16000 HOUS 77044 3409 B4
Maple Shores Dr
15800 HOUS 77044 3409 A5
Maples Perch Ct
12900 HarC 77346 3264 E7
Maple Spring Dr
2700 DRPK 77536 4109 D6
Maple Spring Pl
6300 HarC 77346 3264 E4
Maple Springs Dr
11200 HOUS 77043 3819 A7
Maple Square Dr
5400 HOUS 77339 3119 C2
Maple Terrace Dr
4900 HOUS 77345 3119 E4
5100 HOUS 77345 3120 A4
Mapleton Av
- BYTN 77520 3970 E5
- BYTN 77520 3971 A5
Mapleton Dr
1900 HOUS 77043 3819 D5
Maple Trace Dr
7800 HarC 77070 3399 E3
Mapletrail Dr
17400 HOUS 77084 3816 D6
Maple Tree Ct
2500 STAF 77477 4369 E4
Maple Tree Dr
7700 HOUS 77088 3682 E2
Mapletwist St
8600 HarC 77083 4097 A7
Maple Valley Rd
100 HOUS 77056 3960 D3
Maple View Dr
23500 HarC 77373 3114 D6
Maple Village Ct
15400 HarC 77433 3251 C6
Maple Village Dr
19900 HarC 77433 3251 B7
Maple Vista Ln
23500 HarC 77373 3114 D5
Maple Walk Dr
7100 HarC 77346 3265 A6
Maplewick Dr
15800 HarC 77377 3254 E5
Maple Wood Dr
4000 PRLD 77581 4504 A7
Maplewood Dr
200 FRDW 77546 4505 A5
3500 LPRT 77571 4250 A4
22100 HarC 77449 3675 E5
25800 MtgC 77386 2968 C1
26200 MtgC 77386 2822 C7
26300 ORDN 77386 2822 C7
27000 ORDN 77385 2822 C6
Maplewood Ln
1200 PASD 77502 4106 E7
Maplewood Rd
700 SHEH 77381 2822 B1
800 SHEH 77381 2821 E1
Maplewood St
700 BYTN 77520 3972 D6
N Maplewood St
100 HOUS 77011 3964 B6
Maplewood Falls Ct
800 HOUS 77062 4506 D1
Maple Woody Ln
22800 MtgC 77365 3118 E1
Marable Dr
4700 HOUS 77022 3684 E7
4700 HOUS 77022 3823 E1
Marabou Pl
10 WDLD 77380 2968 A1
Maranatha Ct
- HOUS 77096 4240 A3
Maranatha Dr
3500 FBnC 77479 4495 D4
Marann Dr
3100 LMQU 77568 4989 C1
Maranon Ln
700 HarC 77090 3258 B2
Maranta Estates Ct
14200 HarC 77429 3396 A2
Marantha Rd
10000 HarC 77070 3399 C2
10000 HOUS 77070 3399 C2
Marathon
10 HTCK 77563 5105 A5
Marathon Pl
500 STAF 77477 4369 C3
Marathon St
200 HOUS 77018 3823 C2
N Marathon Wy
300 STAF 77477 4369 C3
S Marathon Wy
600 STAF 77477 4369 C4
Maravilla Ln
4300 FBnC 77469 4233 C6
Marbella Cir
7600 HarC 77083 4096 D6
Marbella Dr
- HarC 77083 4096 D6
Mar Bella Pkwy
- LGCY 77539 4633 D2
- LGCY 77565 4633 D2
Marble Dr
12600 HarC 77070 3399 D5
Marble Rdg
- HarC 77069 3256 D6
Marble Arch Ct
8300 HarC 77338 3261 E4
Marble Brook Ln
2700 PRLD 77584 4500 B4
Marble Canyon Wy
15500 HarC 77044 3549 E2
Marble Cottage Ln
100 HarC 77069 3256 D6
Marble Cove Ct
3700 FBnC 77494 4093 E6
Marble Cove Dr
- LGCY 77539 4753 A2
2800 LGCY 77539 4752 E2
Marble Cove Ln
7600 FBnC 77494 4093 C2
Marble Cove Pt
26600 FBnC 77494 4092 B1
Marble Creek Ct
13900 HOUS 77077 3956 E5
Marble Creek Dr
2600 PRLD 77581 4504 A3
Marble Crest Dr
6000 HarC 77449 3676 C4
10300 HarC 77095 3537 D2
Marblecrest Ln
2300 MtgC 77386 2969 D6
Marbledale Ct
13800 HOUS 77059 4379 E5
Marble Falls Bnd
26400 FBnC 77494 4092 B1
Marble Falls Dr
2300 HarC 77373 3114 C6
2900 BzaC 77584 4501 B4
Marble Gate Ln
5100 HarC 77069 3256 D7
Marble Glen Ln
7400 HarC 77095 3678 C1
Marblehead Ct
20500 HMBL 77338 3262 C4
Marblehead Dr
9700 HMBL 77338 3262 C4
Marble Hill Dr
400 HarC 77450 3953 C2
Marble Hollow Ln
6000 FBnC 77450 4094 B4
Marble Manor Ln
2500 HarC 77449 3815 A4
Marblemount Dr
9300 HarC 77064 3399 C7
Marble Oak Ct
17300 HarC 77379 3111 D7
Marble Point Ln
- LGCY 77539 4752 D5
Marblepointe Ln
13500 HarC 77429 3254 A4
Marble Ravine Dr
5300 FBnC 77469 4234 C2
Marble Ridge Ct
19900 HarC 77433 3677 C2
Marble Rock Pl
10 WDLD 77382 2674 D3
Marble Springs Dr
7000 FBnC 77494 4093 C4
Marble Springs Ln
- FBnC 77494 4093 A6
Marble Staff Ct
100 HarC 77069 3256 D6
Marble Wood Ct
10 WDLD 77381 2821 D2
Marble Wood Pl
10 WDLD 77381 2821 D1
Marbrook Ct
1100 HOUS 77077 3957 D2
Marbrook Pl
- WDLD 77381 2674 E5
- WDLD 77382 2674 E5
Marburg Ct
4700 HarC 77066 3401 B6
Marburg Dr
11600 HarC 77066 3401 B6
Marbury Ct
13100 HarC 77014 3402 A2
Marc Dr
16000 HarC 77530 3830 B4
Marceau Dr
13400 HarC 77065 3539 A1
Marcelia Dr
16100 HarC 77530 3829 D4
Marcella St
300 HOUS 77022 3684 B6
300 HOUS 77091 3684 B6
1000 HOUS 77091 3683 E6
Marcellus Ln
9500 HOUS 77078 3688 B5
March
12700 BKVL 77581 4376 A6
Marchant Rd
3600 HOUS 77047 4374 C1
March Creek Dr
11600 HarC 77067 3402 D5
Marchelle Ln
8300 HarC 77379 3255 E1
Marchena Dr
- HarC 77083 4096 D5
- HOUS 77083 4096 D5
Marchfield Ct
- HarC 77388 3113 B5
Marchmont Dr
700 HDWV 77024 3959 E2
700 PNPV 77024 3959 E2
Marchwood Manor Dr
2000 HarC 77090 3258 B6
N Marcia Cir
11700 MSCY 77071 4239
S Marcia Cir
11800 MSCY 77071 4239
Marcia Dr
11800 HarC 77065 3398
12000 HarC 77429 3398
Marcia St
2100 HarC 77039 3545
Marcin Dr
20900 HarC 77388 3112
Marcolin
- HOUS 77088 3683
Marcolin St
900 HOUS 77088 3684
1000 HOUS 77088 3683
Marconi St
1000 HOUS 77019 3962
1500 HOUS 77006 3962
Marcos St
3300 DKSN 77539 4754
Marcrest Ct
12200 HarC 77070 3399
Marcus St
5400 HOUS 77026 3825
Marcy Dr
8100 HOUS 77033 4243
Mardale Dr
6300 HOUS 77016 3687
Mardel Ct
2000 HOUS 77077 3957
Marden Ct
15300 SGLD 77478 4368
Marden Ln
1600 SGLD 77478 4368
Mardi Ln
1300 HOUS 77055 3820
Mardi Gras Dr
12200 HarC 77014 3401
Marek Ln
15700 HarC 77532 3553
N Marek Ln
26600 SGCH 77355 2961
S Marek Ln
26500 SGCH 77355 2961
Marek St
9700 HarC 77038 3544
Margaret Dr
1100 LGCY 77573 4631
2300 HOUS 77093 3685
Margarita St
5400 HOUS 77020 3964
Margate Ct
1000 PRLD 77584 4501
Margate Dr
1000 PRLD 77584 4501
4200 FBnC 77479 4366
10100 HOUS 77099 4238
Margaux Wy
10 WDLD 77382 2820
Margerstadt Rd
22700 WlrC 77447 2958
28200 HarC 77484 2958
Margeson St
15000 HarC 77084 3678
Margie Ct
9800 HarC 77379 3110
Margie Ln
100 HarC 77037 3684
Margo St
5000 HarC 77389 2967
Margot St
1000 LMQU 77568 4989
Marguerite Ln
1300 PASD 77502 4107
1300 PASD 77506 4107
Maria Ct
12700 GLSN 77554 5220
Maria St
900 PASD 77506 4107
1500 LGCY 77573 4632
Maria Amore St
21500 HarC 77338 3261
Mariachi Blvd
300 HarC 77532 3266
Maria Edna St
8300 HarC 77037 3684
Mariah St
8100 HOUS 77051 4243
Marian Ln
3100 PLEK 77471 4614
3200 FBnC 77471 4614
40600 MtgC 77316 2669
Marian St
100 BYTN 77520 3973
200 BYTN 77520 3972
N Marianne Cir
11700 MSCY 77071 4239
S Marianne Cir
11800 MSCY 77071 4239
Marians Hllw
4000 HOUS 77339 3119
Maribelle Wy
9600 HOUS 77055 3820
Maricella Cir
17000 HarC 77084 3678
Maricopa Ct
- HOUS 77028 3687
Maricopa Ln
12300 HOUS 77015 3966
12400 HOUS 77015 3967
Marie Av
4800 DRPK 77536 4249
4800 PASD 77505 4249
4800 PASD 77536 4249
Marie Dr
8600 TXCY 77591 4755
Marie Ln
6000 FBnC 77469 4232
Marie St
100 CNRO 77301 2384
100 HOUS 77009 3963
Marietta Ln
4700 HOUS 77021 4103
4800 HOUS 77021 4104
Marigold
3000 HOUS 77009 3824
Marigold Dr
- PRVW 77484 3100
100 PRVW 77445 3100
17300 SGLD 77479 4367
Marigold Rd
800 BYTN 77521 3832
800 HarC 77521 3832
Marigold St
3200 HOUS 77009 3824
Marigold Bloom Ln
- HarC 77044 3549

Houston Street Index

REET
ck City ZIP Map# Grid

arigold Creek Ct
20700 HarC 77433 3251 A5
arigold Glen Wy
- HOUS 77034 4378 C3
arika Ln
8600 HOUS 77078 3688 B6
arilane St
10 HOUS 77007 3961 E4
arilee Ln
2500 HOUS 77057 3960 B7
arilyn Ln
2900 HOUS 77093 3686 A3
7200 HOUS 77016 3686 E3
7200 HOUS 77016 3687 A3
20500 HarC 77388 3113 C3
arilyn St
500 FBnC 77545 4499 D6
1300 CNRO 77301 2384 B7
1600 RSBG 77471 4491 B5
arimonte Ln
14800 HarC 77429 3396 C1
arin Dr
14200 HarC 77429 3397 A2
arina
23000 GLSN 77554 5440 E6
arina Blvd
- GLSN 77554 5332 D2
arina Cir
1000 HOUS 77339 3263 B2
arina Dr
900 HOUS 77339 3263 B2
4000 JMAB 77554 5331 D4
16700 GLSN 77554 5331 D4
arina St
4000 HOUS 77007 3962 C2
arina Wy
2200 LGCY 77565 4508 E5
2200 LGCY 77565 4509 A4
arina Bay Dr
200 GlsC 77565 4509 D6
200 KMAH 77565 4509 D6
600 CRLS 77565 4509 C6
1200 LGCY 77565 4509 C6
1200 LGCY 77573 4509 B6
2400 LGCY 77573 4508 E5
3000 LGCY 77565 4508 E5
arina Bay Dr FM-2094
200 GlsC 77565 4509 D6
200 KMAH 77565 4509 D6
600 CRLS 77565 4509 C6
1200 LGCY 77565 4509 C6
1200 LGCY 77573 4509 B6
2400 LGCY 77573 4508 E5
3000 LGCY 77565 4508 E5
Marina Bay Ln
14200 FBnC 77478 4366 E4
Marina Canyon Wy
6200 FBnC 77450 4094 D4
Marina Oaks Ct
300 LGCY 77565 4508 E5
Marina Oaks Dr
- LGCY 77573 4632 D2
100 LGCY 77565 4508 E4
Marina Palms Ln
- LGCY 77573 4508 D6
Marina View Wy
- LGCY 77573 4508 D6
Marina Vista Ln
5700 HarC 77041 3679 E5
Marine Dr
400 GLSN 77550 5109 E1
1200 GLSN 77550 4994 E7
Marine Rd
14600 HarC 77396 3547 A1
14600 HOUS 77396 3547 A1
15000 HOUS 77396 3406 A7
Marine Park Dr
- LGCY 77573 4509 A7
Mariner Ct
200 HarC 77532 3552 C3
Mariner Dr
2900 LGCY 77573 4633 C3
Mariner Grv
6900 HarC 77084 3679 B2
Mariner Pl
18400 HarC 77346 3409 D1
Mariner Wy
2000 DKSN 77539 4753 E4
16100 HarC 77532 3552 C3
Mariner Cove
1100 SGLD 77478 4237 A7
Mariner Cove Ct
100 LGCY 77573 4508 D6
Mariner Fall Wy
- FBnC 77469 4095 B5
Mariner Pass
10 GLSN 77554 5221 C2
Mariner Point Ln
1900 FBnC 77494 3952 B5
Mariners Dr
10 CRLS 77565 4509 B5
400 LGCY 77565 4509 B5
Mariners Hbr
5100 HarC 77041 3679 E6
Mariners Ln
10 CRLS 77565 4509 B4
10 LGCY 77565 4509 B5
Mariners Bay Dr
17000 HarC 77095 3537 C3
Mariners Mooring St
4500 DKSN 77539 4754 E3
Mariner Square Ct
6600 FBnC 77469 4095 B5
Mariner Village Dr
10 PASD 77586 4508 D2
Marinette Dr
6500 HOUS 77036 4099 D4
7400 HOUS 77074 4099 E5
8900 HOUS 77074 4240 A1
Marin Hill Ct
16000 HarC 77429 3397 A2
Marinwood Dr
6300 HOUS 77053 4371 D7
Marion Cir
3400 FBnC 77459 4622 A5
Marion Ct
3500 FBnC 77459 4622 A5
Marion Ln
400 BzaC 77511 4748 A4
12200 GlsC 77539 4871 A1
Marion St
1700 HOUS 77009 3963 D1
19200 HarC 77532 3411 E4
Marion Dwayne Av
6800 HTCK 77563 4988 D3
Marion Meadow Dr
30000 MtgC 77386 2969 D2

STREET
Block City ZIP Map# Grid

Mariosa St
6700 HOUS 77028 3825 D3
Mariposa Cir
5000 FBnC 77545 4622 B3
5000 MSCY 77545 4622 B3
Mariposa St
9600 HOUS 77025 4241 E1
Mariposa Bend Ln
9500 HarC 77089 4504 C1
Mariposa Canyon
11900 HarC 77377 3254 B1
Mariposa Green Ct
10100 HarC 77044 3689 B3
Mariposa Green Ln
12900 HarC 77044 3689 C3
Mariposa Grove Ln
- HarC 77346 3408 B3
Mariposa Stream Ct
10100 HarC 77044 3689 C3
Maris Wy
3300 HarC 77338 3260 A2
Marisa Alexis Dr
9900 HOUS 77075 4377 C2
Marisco Pl
- MtgC 77384 2675 D7
- WDLD 77382 2675 C7
- WDLD 77384 2675 C7
Marisol Dr
7900 FBnC 77083 4096 B7
Marissa Ln
12200 MtgC 77301 2385 D7
12200 MtgC 77306 2385 D7
Maritime Dr
11000 HarC 77044 3690 C1
Marjorie
- HOUS 77037 3684 B2
1900 HOUS 77088 3683 C2
Marjorie St
700 HOUS 77088 3684 A2
900 HOUS 77088 3683 E2
Mark
22800 MtgC 77357 2973 E2
Mark Dr
17600 MtgC 77302 2678 B7
17600 MtgC 77302 2824 B1
Mark Rd
1500 HarC 77073 3259 C3
Mark St
600 DRPK 77536 4109 C4
1300 MSCY 77489 4370 B1
1300 STAF 77477 4370 B1
13400 HarC 77039 3546 E4
Mark Ter
4200 FBnC 77545 4623 B2
Mark 45 Blvd
7000 LMQU 77568 4872 B5
Mark Anthony St
800 RMFT 77357 2829 A1
Mark Crest Dr
16100 HarC 77447 3250 A7
Market
- HMPD 77445 3097 E1
1600 HMPD 77445 3098 A1
N Market Lp
- BYTN 77520 3832 C7
1200 HarC 77521 3832 C7
Market St
- BYTN 77520 4111 E1
100 GLSN 77550 5109 A3
100 TMBL 77375 2964 B7
800 HMPD 77445 3098 A1
1000 BYTN 77520 3972 C7
1300 RHMD 77469 4491 E4
1400 BYTN 77520 3832 B7
1400 HarC 77521 3832 B7
2100 BYTN 77520 4112 A1
4500 HOUS 77020 3964 C2
6900 HOUS 77020 3965 A2
7300 HarC 77520 3832 A6
7500 HarC 77520 3831 E6
7700 HOUS 77029 3965 B2
Market Garden Ln
16100 HarC 77084 3678 C3
Market Pl Dr
19000 HOUS 77338 3261 E6
25100 HarC 77494 3952 D1
25100 KATY 77494 3952 D1
Market Pl St
- SGLD 77478 4368 E2
Market Square Ln
22500 HarC 77449 3814 D5
Market Square Village Dr
- HOUS 77009 3824 A4
Market St Rd
100 HarC 77530 3968 D2
6400 BYTN 77520 3971 C3
7800 HOUS 77020 3965 B2
7800 HOUS 77029 3965 E2
8000 BYTN 77520 3832 C7
8900 HOUS 77029 3966 A3
8900 JTCY 77029 3965 E2
8900 JTCY 77029 3966 D3
11900 HOUS 77015 3966 E3
12400 HOUS 77015 3967 A3
13600 HarC 77015 3967 E2
14000 HarC 77015 3968 A2
15500 HarC 77530 3969 A2
16600 HarC 77530 3830 D7
16900 HarC 77530 3831 A7
Markham Rd
9000 MNVL 77578 4747 C2
Markham St
4200 HOUS 77027 4101 C1
Markham Grove Pl
10 SHEH 77381 2821 E1
Markham Woods Ct
4700 HOUS 77345 3119 D1
Markham Woods Dr
2800 HOUS 77345 3119 E2
Markhurst Dr
14400 HarC 77429 3254 A7
Marklena Dr
14700 HarC 77429 3397 D5
Markley St
4000 HOUS 77087 4104 D5
Markridge Dr
16800 HarC 77379 3255 D5
Marks Ct
20100 MtgC 77357 2828 B6
Marks Rd
3300 HarC 77084 3817 A3
24500 MtgC 77372 2536 D7
Marks Wy
14300 HarC 77429 3397 D6
Markscott Dr
3100 HarC 77082 4097 B2
Marksey Ct
800 MtgC 77386 2968 D1

STREET
Block City ZIP Map# Grid

Marksman Ct
21700 HarC 77447 3105 E1
Marksman Wy
2900 HOUS 77094 4095 E1
Markspring Ln
3900 HarC 77388 3112 D5
Markstone Ct
3200 FBnC 77494 3953 E7
Markstone Knolls Dr
24600 HOUS 77336 3266 C2
Markville Ln
10 HOUS 77085 4371 B1
Markwood Ct
15400 HOUS 77053 4372 A5
Markwood Ln
- HOUS 77053 4371 E5
5500 HOUS 77053 4372 A5
Marl Ct
17500 HarC 77532 3411 B7
Marl Wy
17400 HarC 77532 3411 B7
Marlan Forest Ln
26800 HarC 77433 3396 A7
Marlan Woods Ct
3000 MtgC 77386 2823 D7
Marlberry Ln
1900 HOUS 77084 3816 E6
Marlberry Branch Ct
100 WDLD 77384 2675 A4
Marlberry Branch Dr
10 WDLD 77384 2675 A4
Marlborough Dr
4000 HOUS 77092 3822 B3
Marlebone Ct
15000 HarC 77069 3256 D6
Marleen St
500 HOUS 77034 4246 D5
Marlen Av
1900 PASD 77502 4107 D6
2600 PASD 77502 4108 A6
Marlene St
900 DRPK 77536 4109 C4
Marle Point Ct
- HarC 77388 3111 E2
Marlin
- MAGA 77355 2669 A6
Marlin Av
100 GLSN 77550 5109 E1
Marlin Ct
2900 LGCY 77573 4633 C3
Marlin Dr
2400 GlsC 77650 4879 D3
2400 TXCY 77591 4872 E3
Marlin Ln
10 BYTN 77520 4113 C1
3800 LPRT 77571 4383 B2
3800 PASD 77571 4383 B2
Marlin St
700 BYUV 77563 4990 E7
700 BYUV 77563 5105 D1
700 GlsC 77563 4990 E7
1500 HOUS 77023 3964 C7
1600 HOUS 77023 4104 E1
Marlink Ln
9800 HOUS 77025 4241 D2
Marlin Spike Wy
16800 HarC 77532 3552 B1
Marlin Waters Dr
18300 HarC 77346 3409 C1
Marlive Ln
9000 HOUS 77025 4101 D7
9100 HOUS 77025 4241 D1
Marlo St
2200 HOUS 77023 4105 A3
Marlock Ln
1300 PASD 77502 4107 E6
1300 PASD 77506 4107 E6
Marlowe St
4100 WUNP 77005 4101 C3
Marlowe Wy
10 CNRO 77384 2675 E4
Marlowe Grove Dr
15200 FBnC 77478 4236 C2
Marlstone Ct
19300 HarC 77094 3955 B3
Marlstone Dr
1300 HarC 77094 3955 B3
Marmora Ct
2000 LGCY 77573 4631 A7
Marne Ln
700 HarC 77090 3258 C2
Marnel Rd
2000 HOUS 77055 3821 B4
Marnie Ln
11900 HOUS 77037 3685 A2
11900 HOUS 77076 3685 A2
Marnier Reef Wy
4500 HarC 77396 3407 B6
Maroby St
200 HOUS 77017 4106 B5
Maroneal St
2100 HOUS 77030 4102 B5
3000 HOUS 77025 4102 A5
3500 HOUS 77025 4101 D5
Maroon Ln
1200 HOUS 77077 3956 E4
Maroon Creek Ct
10 HarC 77389 2819 E5
10 HarC 77389 2820 A5
Marot Dr
2300 HarC 77493 3814 B5
Marquart St
3000 HOUS 77027 3961 E7
Marquette St
3800 SSPL 77005 4101 D4
3800 WUNP 77005 4101 C4
4200 HOUS 77005 4101 C4
Marquette Tr
2600 FBnC 77494 3953 A6
Marquette Point Ln
17200 HarC 77346 3408 C3
Marquis Av
4500 BYTN 77521 3972 C1
Marquise Oaks Pl
10 WDLD 77382 2673 C6
Marquita Ln
4800 HarC 77039 3546 C5
Marrakech Ct
100 BLAR 77401 4101 B5
Marrat Ct
16400 HarC 77377 3254 C6
Marrella Dr
25600 MtgC 77357 2828 E6
25600 MtgC 77357 2829 A6
Marron Ct
12800 HarC 77429 3254 B6
Marron Dr
12900 HarC 77429 3254 B6

STREET
Block City ZIP Map# Grid

Marrs Dr
11100 HarC 77065 3539 B1
11300 HarC 77065 3398 B7
11800 HarC 77429 3398 B7
Mars Dr
1400 PASD 77504 4247 D6
2000 BzaC 77583 4624 A3
2000 PRLD 77583 4624 A3
E Marsala Ct
1400 PRLD 77581 4504 D2
W Marsala Ct
2200 PRLD 77581 4504 D2
E Marsala Dr
2200 PRLD 77581 4504 D2
N Marsala Dr
1400 PRLD 77581 4504 D2
W Marsala Dr
2200 PRLD 77581 4504 C2
Marsden St
10 HOUS 77011 3964 D6
Marsden Park Ln
- FBnC 77494 4093 B2
Marseilles Ln
11200 HOUS 77082 4098 C2
Marsha Ln
5800 PRLD 77581 4502 C2
10700 HNCV 77024 3960 A1
Marshall Ct
9100 MtgC 77354 2818 D6
12700 MtgC 77354 2671 A3
Marshall Dr
12300 MtgC 77354 2671 A3
Marshall Rd
500 BzaC 77511 4628 C7
3700 HarC 77532 3553 E4
3700 HarC 77532 3554 A4
Marshall St
100 LGCY 77573 4631 E3
200 HOUS 77006 3962 E7
400 HOUS 77006 3963 D2
1000 DRPK 77536 4109 A7
2000 HOUS 77098 3962 B7
2500 PASD 77506 4107 E4
2700 PASD 77506 4108 A4
Marshall Bridge Ln
14500 FBnC 77478 4236 D3
Marshall Falls Dr
7900 HarC 77379 3256 B4
Marshall Oaks Wy
- HarC 77094 3955 A2
E Marsham Cir
11900 HarC 77066 3401 C4
W Marsham Cir
12000 HarC 77066 3401 C4
E Marsham Sq
3500 HarC 77066 3401 C4
Marshaven Wy
22100 FBnC 77469 4093 E7
Marshbrook Ln
25800 HarC 77389 2966 B2
Marshburn Dr
23000 MtgC 77447 2960 A3
Marshfield Dr
10800 HarC 77065 3539 B1
Marsh Flower Ln
6100 FBnC 77469 4234 D1
Marsh Grass Ln
4000 PASD 77503 4108 C4
Marsh Hawk St
15800 HarC 77396 3406 E6
Marshhay Ct
11000 HarC 77086 3542 B1
Marsh Millet Ct
10 WDLD 77380 2822 B7
Marsh When Rd
12500 HarC 77038 3543 B4
Marsh Willow Wy
19800 FBnC 77469 4234 D2
Marshwood Rd
3000 HarC 77038 3542 E1
3000 HarC 77038 3543 A1
Marston St
800 HOUS 77019 3962 C4
Marston Park Ln
16700 HarC 77084 3678 B4
Marston River Ln
6300 HarC 77066 3400 D4
Marta Dr
6800 HarC 77083 4096 B5
Marte Ct
- PASD 77503 4249 A3
Martell St
9200 HOUS 77051 4243 B4
Martens Rd
30600 TMBL 77375 2964 A4
Martes St
22800 GLSN 77554 5440 E5
Martesia Dr
- HarC 77095 3539 A3
Martgate Rd
2100 HOUS 77034 4246 D5
Martha Dr
5900 BzaC 77583 4623 C5
5900 PRLD 77583 4623 C5
Martha Dr CO-824A
5900 BzaC 77583 4623 C5
5900 PRLD 77583 4623 C5
Martha Ln
5500 HOUS 77032 3405 D6
5500 HOUS 77396 3405 D6
6000 HOUS 77396 3406 A6
E Martha Ln
1500 PASD 77502 4107 D6
2500 PASD 77502 4108 A6
W Martha Ln
1600 PASD 77502 4107 D7
Martha St
- BYTN 77520 3971 A4
800 DRPK 77536 4109 C4
3400 HOUS 77026 3825 A7
Martha Springs Dr
9700 HarC 77070 3255 B6
Marthoman Dr
2000 MSCY 77489 4370 B6
Marti
- LGCY 77573 4631 A4
Martin Cir
23400 MtgC 77365 2973 A6
Martin Ct
10 SPVL 77055 3820 D7
Martin Dr
1200 ALVN 77511 4867 A3
15000 MtgC 77302 2678 E7
15000 MtgC 77302 2824 E1
18000 MtgC 77302 2679 E2
18000 MtgC 77302 2680 A2
E Martin Dr
21700 MtgC 77365 2973 B7

STREET
Block City ZIP Map# Grid

W Martin Dr
21200 MtgC 77365 3118 B1
Martin Ln
10 SPVL 77055 3820 D7
500 MSCY 77489 4370 B3
13200 BKVL 77581 4375 B7
Martin Pl
1300 HOUS 77002 3963 B3
1300 HOUS 77007 3963 B3
Martin Rd
300 HOUS 77022 3823 B1
1000 HOUS 77018 3822 E1
1000 HOUS 77018 3823 A1
Martin St
2600 PASD 77502 4248 A2
2600 PASD 77503 4248 A2
Martina Dr
2800 FRDW 77546 4749 E1
Martin Creek Ln
12100 HarC 77377 3254 C5
Martindale Rd
10000 HOUS 77048 4244 C7
10900 HarC 77041 3680 C2
10900 HOUS 77041 3680 C2
11700 HOUS 77048 4375 C2
Martin Down Ln
22300 FBnC 77450 3953 E6
22300 FBnC 77450 3954 A6
Martineau St
15500 HarC 77032 3404 C6
Martinec Dr
2600 BzaC 77584 4501 A4
Martinez St
15400 FBnC 77478 4236 C3
Martingale Ct
1200 HarC 77532 3552 A1
Martin Grove Ct
21700 HarC 77338 3260 A1
Martin Heights Dr
8800 HOUS 77031 4239 A4
Martinique Cl
5100 DKSN 77539 4633 C7
Martinique Dr
18500 NSUB 77058 4508 A6
Martinique Ln
1200 GlsC 77650 4879 D4
Martinique Pass Ln
5700 SGLD 77479 4495 A5
Martin Lake Ct
2000 FBnC 77469 4234 C5
Martin Lake Dr
1500 FBnC 77469 4234 D5
Martin Luther King Av
600 TXCY 77590 4875 C6
1700 GlsC 77539 4632 D7
1700 LGCY 77539 4632 D7
2200 GlsC 77539 4753 E1
3100 DKSN 77539 4753 E2
3500 DKSN 77539 4754 A2
E Martin Luther King Av
10 TXCY 77590 4875 D6
N Martin Luther King Av
5700 HTCK 77563 4989 D5
7800 HTCK 77563 4988 D4
Martin Luther King Blvd
100 GLSN 77550 5109 B5
Martin Luther King Dr
8800 HOUS 77338 3262 A6
Martin Luther King St
- BYTN 77520 3972 D7
500 BYTN 77520 4112 D1
Martin Luther King Jr Blvd
- HOUS 77004 4104 A3
4800 HOUS 77021 4104 A6
6300 HOUS 77033 4104 A7
6600 HOUS 77033 4244 A7
10400 HOUS 77048 4244 A6
11900 HOUS 77048 4375 A2
Martinque Ln
1300 GlsC 77650 4879 D3
Martins Wy
10 SGLD 77479 4495 A2
Martinshire Dr
4000 HOUS 77025 4101 C7
4000 HOUS 77025 4241 D1
Martinville Dr
2600 HOUS 77017 4246 D2
Martin Wood Ct
7800 HarC 77086 3541 E3
Martin Wood Ln
- HarC 77086 3542 B2
7700 HarC 77086 3541 E3
Marullo
6800 HTCK 77563 4989 A4
Marvell Dr
1900 HarC 77032 3404 C6
2100 HOUS 77032 3404 C6
Marvel Oak Ct
7400 HarC 77346 3265 A4
Marvick Dr
100 PASD 77506 4107 A5
W Marvick Dr
100 PASD 77506 4107 A5
Marvin Cir
1900 SEBK 77586 4509 D1
Marvin Ln
9800 FBnC 77478 4237 A2
Marvin Rd
3300 BYTN 77521 3973 E3
Marvin St
1700 RSBG 77471 4614 E3
Marvin Gardens St
29300 MtgC 77354 2818 A1
Mar Vista Dr
7300 HarC 77083 4096 C6
Marwell Ln
11600 HarC 77429 3253 E7
Marwick Ct
15900 HarC 77095 3538 D4
Marwood Dr
- CNRO 77384 2675 E5
5900 HOUS 77396 3405 E4
Marwood St
1300 HarC 77015 3968 B3
Marwood Estates Dr
- HarC 77070 3399 D6
Marwood Falls Ct
10200 HarC 77070 3399 B6
Mary Av
2500 PRLD 77581 4504 E5
Mary Ln
100 GlsC 77518 4635 A3
400 HarC 77562 3832 B3
1300 LPRT 77571 4110 B7
2000 LGCY 77539 4752 C4
23000 MtgC 77365 2972 E6

STREET
Block City ZIP Map# Grid

Mary Lp
11100 MtgC 77372 2536 D2
Mary St
1500 HOUS 77020 3963 E2
1500 HOUS 77026 3963 E1
2300 ALVN 77511 4866 E3
3000 MSCY 77459 4369 E6
3000 MSCY 77477 4369 E6
3500 PASD 77504 4247 E4
Mary Agnes Foster Blvd
11900 HOUS 77045 4242 E6
11900 HOUS 77051 4242 E6
Mary Ann Dr
100 FRDW 77546 4505 A7
Maryann Ln
1400 CNRO 77301 2384 D6
Mary Ann St
16000 HarC 77429 3108 B7
Mary Bates Blvd
7700 HOUS 77036 4099 C6
Marydean St
1300 BzaC 77583 4623 D5
Marydel St
9700 HOUS 77076 3685 A6
Mary Elizabeth Wilbanks Av
10 BYTN 77520 3972 D7
Mary Ethel Rd
5700 HarC 77521 3832 E7
Maryfield Blvd
- PRLD 77581 4503 D5
Maryfield Ln
3100 PRLD 77581 4503 D5
Mary Francis Dr
5400 HarC 77039 3546 D4
Mary Jan Rd
10300 HarC 77041 3680 E6
10300 HarC 77041 3681 A6
10300 HOUS 77041 3681 A6
Mary Jane Ln
14300 HarC 77377 3108 D2
Mary Katheryn's Cross
7800 CNRO 77304 2236 E3
Mary Kay Ln
13800 HOUS 77048 4374 E4
Maryknoll Dr
1400 HOUS 77015 3966 E3
Maryland Av
2700 LGCY 77573 4632 D6
2800 DKSN 77539 4633 A7
2800 LGCY 77539 4632 D6
2900 DKSN 77539 4754 A1
Maryland Rd
2900 FBnC 77545 4498 D7
Maryland St
1400 HOUS 77006 3962 D6
1600 BYTN 77520 4112 A2
1700 HOUS 77019 3962 C6
Marylebone Dr
13700 HOUS 77034 4378 D5
Mary Lou Dr
5000 HOUS 77092 3682 D7
Marymont Pk
500 MtgC 77302 2530 B5
Mary Moody Northern Blvd
500 GLSN 77551 5108 D6
Mary Mt Wy
1600 HOUS 77058 4507 E3
Maryon St
1500 BYTN 77520 3835 C4
Maryport Dr
14900 HarC 77530 3829 C6
Mary's Ct
900 FRDW 77546 4505 A5
Mary's Creek Ct
2300 PRLD 77581 4504 A5
Mary's Creek Ln
10 FRDW 77546 4505 A6
Mary's Creek Ln E
2000 PRLD 77581 4504 A6
Marys Creek Ln W
2000 PRLD 77581 4504 B6
W Marys Creek Ln
1900 PRLD 77581 4504 B6
Mary's Cross
- FRDW 77546 4505 C6
Mary Sue Ct
14000 SGLD 77478 4237 A6
Marys Village Dr
3400 PRLD 77581 4503 E6
Marysville Ln
14800 HarC 77044 3690 C2
Maryvale Dr
1600 FBnC 77494 3953 B5
Marywood Dr
3400 HarC 77388 3112 D7
4000 HarC 77388 3257 C1
Marywood Chase
- HOUS 77079 3956 C2
700 HOUS 77079 3957 A2
Marzelle St
3100 HOUS 77093 3686 A3
Marzia Av
3800 FBnC 77545 4499 C7
3800 FBnC 77545 4623 C1
Mascari Ln
4500 HOUS 77018 3823 D1
4500 HOUS 77022 3823 D1
Mascot St
300 HOUS 77029 3966 A7
400 GNPK 77029 3966 A7
400 GNPK 77547 3966 A7
Mason
2000 SGLD 77478 4237 A5
2100 FBnC 77478 4237 A5
4600 FBnC 77479 4366 D7
Mason Dr
3900 GLSN 77554 5441 B4
S Mason Dr
4500 FBnC 77469 4234 C5
Mason Rd
- SGLD 77478 4237 A6
2200 FBnC 77478 4237 A5
4800 FBnC 77469 4234 C4
7300 FBnC 77469 4094 C6
8000 MNVL 77578 4745 E2
15000 HarC 77433 3395 B1
17100 HarC 77433 3251 B2
N Mason Rd
1000 HOUS 77449 3954 A1
1000 HOUS 77450 3954 A1
1300 HOUS 77449 3815 A7
3000 HarC 77449 3815 A2
S Mason Rd
- HOUS 77449 3954 A1
- HOUS 77450 4094 B4
100 HOUS 77450 3954 A3
2200 FBnC 77450 3954 A6

STREET
Block City ZIP Map# Grid

S Mason Rd
3300 FBnC 77450 4094 A1
4400 FBnC 77469 4234 C5
7000 FBnC 77469 4094 B5
Mason Sprs
- FBnC 77450 3953 E6
Mason St
500 TMBL 77375 2964 B7
1600 HOUS 77019 3962 E5
1800 HOUS 77006 3962 E5
Mason Access Rd
21700 HOUS 77450 3954 A1
Mason Creek Ct
6800 FBnC 77469 4095 C5
Mason Creek Dr
100 HOUS 77450 3954 B1
19900 HarC 77449 3676 E3
19900 HarC 77449 3677 A3
Mason Creek Pth
24900 HarC 77493 3814 A6
Mason Forest Dr
- HarC 77094 3955 B5
Masonglen Ct
5400 FBnC 77479 4493 D2
Mason Grove Ct
18200 HarC 77346 3408 A1
Mason Grove Ln
- PRLD 77583 4500 B4
Mason Manor Dr
21900 HarC 77449 3815 A4
Mason Oaks
5600 HOUS 77085 4371 D1
5600 HOUS 77085 4372 A1
Mason Park Blvd
500 HOUS 77450 3954 B2
Mason Pond Pl
10 SHEH 77384 2821 E1
10 WDLD 77381 2821 E1
10 WDLD 77384 2821 E1
Masonridge Dr
17300 HarC 77095 3537 E7
17300 HarC 77095 3538 A7
Mason Stone Ln
4000 FBnC 77494 4093 D3
Mason Terrace Ln
12800 HarC 77433 3396 A4
Mason Trail Dr
24700 HarC 77493 3814 A6
Masonville Ln
10 HarC 77357 2830 C7
Masonwood Ln
- HarC 77070 3399 E2
21800 FBnC 77469 4493 A3
Massachusetts St
300 HOUS 77029 3966 A7
Massengale Ln
2900 LGCY 77598 4630 D4
Massey Dr
5100 BzaC 77511 4748 A6
Massey Rd
12500 MtgC 77306 2533 A4
12800 MtgC 77302 2533 A5
15600 MtgC 77306 2532 E3
Massey Row
10 SGLD 77479 4495 C2
Massey St
700 BYTN 77520 4112 E1
Massey Ranch Rd
4300 BzaC 77578 4625 E2
4300 BzaC 77578 4626 A3
4300 MNVL 77578 4625 E2
4300 MNVL 77578 4626 A3
Massey Tompkins Rd
100 BYTN 77521 3973 C3
4000 BYTN 77520 3974 A2
4000 BYTN 77521 3974 A2
Masson Ct
500 HarC 77388 3113 D7
Mast Ct
2300 HOUS 77339 3119 A3
3000 SGLD 77479 4495 E1
Masters Cir
37200 MtgC 77355 2815 D4
Masters Ct
3700 LGCY 77573 4508 E7
Masters Dr
10 PNVL 77304 2237 B3
2500 LGCY 77573 4508 E6
4400 LGCY 77573 4509 A7
5900 HarC 77069 3400 C1
Masters Ln
2100 MSCY 77459 4497 B3
Masters Rd
- BzaC 77584 4626 A4
- PRLD 77584 4626 A4
4600 MNVL 77578 4626 B3
4600 MNVL 77584 4626 A4
5400 MNVL 77578 4625 E7
6700 MNVL 77578 4746 D3
10300 BzaC 77578 4746 A7
10300 BzaC 77583 4745 E7
10300 BzaC 77583 4746 A7
10300 IWCY 77583 4745 E7
Masters Rd FM-1128
- BzaC 77584 4626 A4
- PRLD 77584 4626 A4
4600 MNVL 77578 4626 B3
4600 MNVL 77584 4626 A4
5400 MNVL 77578 4625 E7
6700 MNVL 77578 4746 D1
N Masters Rd
4300 BzaC 77584 4626 B1
4300 MNVL 77584 4626 B2
4300 PRLD 77584 4626 B1
N Masters Rd FM-1128
4300 BzaC 77584 4626 B1
4300 MNVL 77584 4626 B2
4300 PRLD 77584 4626 B1
Masters Wy
1100 HOUS 77339 3118 B6
Masters Green Blvd
- HarC 77389 2966 A3
Masters Manor Ln
- HarC 77449 3815 D7
- HOUS 77449 3815 D7
Masterson Ln
12100 MtgC 77301 2385 D6
12100 MtgC 77306 2385 D6
Masterson St
10 ARLA 77583 4623 B4
7900 HOUS 77029 3965 B5
9700 HOUS 77029 3966 A4
9800 GNPK 77547 3966 A4
W Masterson St
5600 ARLA 77583 4623 A4
Masters Trace Ln
- HarC 77389 2966 B2

STREET
Block City ZIP Map# Grid
Masters Village Ct
10 PNVL 77304 2237 A3
Masterwood Ct
19100 HarC 77346 3265 B6
Master Wy Ct
2100 HOUS 77339 3118 C6
Mastic Dr
8300 HarC 77521 3833 E2
Mastiff Ln
- HarC 77530 3829 E3
Matagorda Dr
21700 GLSN 77554 5441 A5
Matagorda Ln
11900 FBnC 77478 4236 C6
Matamoras St
1800 HOUS 77023 4105 A2
Matamoros Dr
100 RSBG 77471 4490 B5
Match Play Dr
19000 HarC 77346 3265 C6
Match Point Cir
18700 HarC 77346 3265 C7
Match Point Ln
2800 FRDW 77546 4749 E1
Mather Dr
24700 FBnC 77494 3952 D3
Mathews Rd
24900 HarC 77375 2965 A3
Mathewson Ln
10100 HOUS 77043 3820 A7
Mathis Dr
5000 KATY 77493 3813 E7
Mathis Rd
15600 HarC 77484 3247 B7
18000 HarC 77484 3102 B7
Mathis St
600 HOUS 77009 3824 A5
Mathis Church Rd
16700 HarC 77090 3258 B4
16800 HOUS 77090 3258 B4
Mathis Landing Dr
20300 HarC 77433 3251 C6
Mati
- HarC 77049 3831 B1
Matilda Dr
2600 HarC 77032 3545 E2
Matilda St
2000 HarC 77039 3545 D2
Matilde Ct
3600 BzaC 77584 4501 C7
Matisse
3200 SGLD 77479 4368 C7
Matisse Dr
100 HOUS 77079 3958 C4
E Matisse Meadow Ct
10 WDLD 77382 2819 B2
W Matisse Meadow Ct
10 WDLD 77382 2819 B2
Matlage Wy
200 SGLD 77478 4367 E3
Matlock Ct
11500 HarC 77433 3396 B7
Matoon Ln
- FBnC 77450 3954 A6
Matranga St
7300 HTCK 77563 4988 D5
Matson St
7900 HOUS 77078 3687 C5
Matson Manor Ct
1300 HarC 77379 3255 C1
Matt Cir
19000 HarC 77346 3264 D6
Matt Rd
5900 HarC 77346 3264 D6
Mattby St
8200 HOUS 77061 4245 D2
Matteson St
600 ALVN 77511 4867 B3
Matthews Ln
8300 MtgC 77354 2818 E4
Matthews Pl
24500 WlrC 77447 2959 D3
Matthews St
1100 HOUS 77019 3963 A5
1800 HOUS 77006 3963 A5
Matthews Crest Ct
8200 HarC 77396 3547 D2
Matthias Tr
13700 HarC 77083 4097 A5
Mattingham Dr
3800 HarC 77066 3401 C5
Mattison Dr
- HarC 77088 3542 C6
Mattye Mae Dr
3500 PASD 77503 4108 B6
Matzke Rd
11300 HarC 77429 3397 C7
Maud St
1700 HOUS 77007 3963 A1
Maudeas Dr
13200 HarC 77532 3693 A1
13500 HarC 77532 3553 A7
Maudlin Cir
10 KMAH 77565 4510 A7
Maudlin St
5100 HOUS 77087 4104 D6
Maufferd St
2400 HOUS 77009 3963 B1
Maui Dr
1200 TKIS 77554 5106 B4
Mauldin St
7300 GlsC 77510 4986 E6
Mauna Kai Dr
7600 HarC 77095 3539 B7
Mauna Loa Ct
8200 HarC 77040 3541 A7
Mauna Loa Dr
15200 HarC 77040 3540 E7
15200 JRSV 77040 3540 E7
Mauna Loa Ln
8900 HarC 77040 3541 A7
Maura Dr
3700 BzaC 77511 4748 A4
Maureens Wy
11800 MtgC 77362 2963 C1
Maurel Dr
- CNRO 77304 2383 B3
Maurice Rd
30300 MtgC 77354 2671 E6
Maurice Wy
4100 STAF 77477 4369 B3
Mauriene Rd
3500 HarC 77336 3121 D1
Maurine St
2100 HarC 77039 3545 D2
Maurita Dr
4700 HarC 77373 3115 C6
Mauritz Dr
5000 HarC 77032 3546 D1
Mauritz St
5400 HarC 77032 3546 D2
5700 HarC 77396 3546 E2
Maury Ln
31100 MtgC 77354 2818 C1
Maury St
900 HOUS 77020 3963 E2
1300 HOUS 77026 3963 E2
2300 HOUS 77009 3963 E1
5400 HOUS 77009 3824 D4
Mause Creek Dr
15000 HarC 77396 3407 C7
Mauve Orchid Wy
20500 HarC 77433 3251 B5
Mauvewood Dr
7800 HarC 77040 3541 D7
Maux Dr
1800 HOUS 77043 3820 A5
Mavanelle Cove
300 HMPD 77445 2952 D4
Maverick St
200 HOUS 77009 3824 B6
Maverick Park Ln
2500 HarC 77449 3815 B4
Maverick Point Ct
- FBnC 77494 4093 B7
Maverick Point Ln
- FBnC 77494 4093 A3
Maverick Trace Ct
19800 HarC 77433 3537 A6
Maverick Trace Ln
7800 HarC 77433 3537 A7
Maverick Valley Ln
14800 HarC 77429 3253 B7
Maverly Crest Ct
- FBnC 77494 3952 C7
- FBnC 77494 4092 C1
Mavis Ln
5800 PASD 77505 4248 C3
Max
- FBnC 77583 4622 A3
Max Rd
1900 BzaC 77581 4502 B1
1900 PRLD 77581 4502 B1
1900 PRLD 77584 4502 B3
3400 PLEK 77471 4614 C5
5100 FBnC 77583 4622 A3
12500 BKVL 77581 4375 B7
13200 PRLD 77581 4375 B7
Max Conrad Dr
9500 HarC 77375 3110 D4
9500 HarC 77379 3110 D4
Maxey Rd
10 HOUS 77013 3827 E7
600 HOUS 77013 3966 E1
1200 HOUS 77015 3966 E3
Maxey Rd FM-526
10 HOUS 77013 3827 E7
600 HOUS 77013 3966 E1
700 HOUS 77015 3966 E1
Maxfield Dr
12800 HOUS 77082 4097 C2
Maxie St
200 DRPK 77536 4109 A4
4500 HOUS 77007 3962 B2
Maxim Dr
12300 HarC 77065 3539 C1
Maximilian St
2100 HarC 77039 3545 D2
2600 HarC 77032 3545 E2
Maximos Dr
13700 HarC 77083 4097 A5
Maxine Ln
- HarC 77068 3257 E4
Maxine St
900 HOUS 77029 3965 D6
Maxroy Dr
6700 HOUS 77091 3683 D4
Maxroy St
3000 HOUS 77007 3961 E1
3000 HOUS 77008 3961 E1
3200 HOUS 77008 3822 E7
5100 HOUS 77018 3683 E7
9300 HOUS 77088 3683 E1
9500 HarC 77088 3683 E1
E Maxroy St
7500 HOUS 77088 3683 E3
Maxted Ct
13400 HarC 77429 3254 A7
13500 HarC 77429 3253 E7
Maxwell Cir
1900 ALVN 77511 4866 E3
Maxwell Ln
2300 HOUS 77023 4104 D3
2400 DRPK 77536 4109 B6
Maxwell Rd
5900 HOUS 77040 3681 E5
12200 HarC 77429 3398 A4
13600 HarC 77429 3397 E4
Maxwell St
2400 LMQU 77563 4990 A4
2400 LMQU 77568 4989 E4
2400 LMQU 77568 4990 A4
5600 HOUS 77023 4104 C3
Maxwood Dr
7100 HarC 77379 3256 C2
W May
10 LbyC 77372 2684 A2
May Ln
14800 MtgC 77372 2684 A2
May Lp
14900 LbyC 77327 2684 B3
15000 LbyC 77372 2684 B3
May Rd
16400 HarC 77429 3108 A7
16400 HarC 77429 3253 A1
27400 MtgC 77372 2683 D3
28400 LbyC 77372 2684 A3
May St
2400 LMQU 77568 4989 E3
5600 HOUS 77076 3684 D6
12800 BKVL 77581 4376 A6
Maya Ln
23400 MtgC 77365 2972 B5
Maya Rd
9800 MtgC 77354 2964 B1
Mayapan Ct
2800 GLSN 77554 5221 D3
May Apple Ct
21700 HarC 77433 3250 E6
May Arbor Ln
4800 FBnC 77545 4623 C1
Mayard Rd
6600 HarC 77041 3679 D2
Maybank St
6500 HOUS 77055 3822 A5
Maybank St
6600 HOUS 77055 3821 E5
May Basket Ln
11500 HarC 77375 3109 E6
Maybell St
5800 HOUS 77091 3684 A5
Mayberry
9800 HOUS 77078 3687 D5
Mayberry Cir
1300 FBnC 77479 4494 A6
Mayberry St
9400 HOUS 77028 3687 D6
10300 HOUS 77078 3687 E4
Mayberry Mills Ln
3400 HarC 77068 3257 C6
Maybloom
- HarC 77336 3122 B3
Maybloom Ct
- HarC 77336 3122 B3
Mayborough Ct
10 WDLD 77382 2674 D3
Maybrook Ct
- PRLD 77583 4500 C4
21900 FBnC 77469 4493 A3
Maybrook Dr
200 HarC 77015 3828 C5
Maybrook Hollow Ln
- HarC 77047 4374 A5
Maybrook Manor Ln
21100 FBnC 77469 4094 A7
Maybrook Park Cir
22300 FBnC 77450 4093 B4
Maybrook Park Ct
22000 FBnC 77450 4093 B4
Maybrook Park Ln
5200 FBnC 77450 4093 E3
Maycrest Ct
16000 HarC 77377 3254 E5
Mayday Run Ct
3000 HarC 77373 3115 A4
S Mayde Cr
- HOUS 77079 3957 B2
Mayde Creek Dr
18800 HOUS 77084 3816 B6
Mayde Creek Farms Ln
17700 HOUS 77084 3816 D6
Mayde Park Ln
1600 HOUS 77084 3816 B7
Mayer Ln
23400 MtgC 77365 2972 E6
Mayer Rd
23400 MtgC 77365 2973 B5
32000 HarC 77484 2957 A3
34300 WlrC 77445 2955 E3
35300 WlrC 77484 2955 E3
35300 WlrC 77484 2956 A3
Mayerling Dr
200 BKHV 77024 3959 C5
200 HOUS 77024 3959 C5
Mayer-Waller Rd
2000 HarC 77484 3101 E4
2000 HarC 77484 3102 A4
2000 WALR 77484 3101 E4
2000 WALR 77484 3102 A4
Mayfair Ct
100 SGLD 77478 4368 E4
Mayfair Dr
- BzaC 77584 4501 A5
Mayfair Ln
1300 SGLD 77479 4367 D6
Mayfair St
4500 BLAR 77401 4101 B3
4900 BLAR 77401 4100 E3
4900 HOUS 77081 4100 E3
4900 HOUS 77401 4100 E3
6300 HOUS 77087 4104 D7
Mayfair Wy
- HarC 77069 3256 E6
1200 HOUS 77339 3264 A1
Mayfair Grove Ct
10 WDLD 77381 2821 B5
Mayfair Park Ln
20000 HarC 77379 3111 E5
Mayfield Dr
3700 HOUS 77088 3683 A2
4100 HOUS 77088 3682 E2
Mayfield Rd
10200 HOUS 77043 3819 E6
Mayfield Meadow Ln
18100 FBnC 77469 4095 B6
Mayflower Cir
4100 TXCY 77590 4875 A1
Mayflower St
4000 HOUS 77051 4243 D1
4800 HOUS 77033 4243 D1
Mayflower Landing Ct
2700 HarC 77598 4506 C7
2800 HarC 77598 4630 C1
Mayfly Ct
3200 HarC 77449 3816 A3
Mayford St
300 HOUS 77076 3685 B4
Mayglen Ln
- HarC 77379 3256 A1
Maygrove Dr
1400 SGLD 77478 4237 A7
Mayhaw Dr
- BYTN 77520 3971 B2
Mayhaw Ln
8000 HarC 77044 3689 B7
Mayhaw St
800 LGCY 77573 4632 D6
Mayhill Dr
11800 HarC 77067 3402 D5
Maykirk St
11000 FBnC 77099 4237 D4
11000 FBnC 77478 4237 D4
11000 HOUS 77099 4237 D4
11000 SGLD 77478 4237 D4
May Laurel Dr
12300 HarC 77014 3402 B3
Mayle St
5000 HOUS 77016 3686 D5
Maymist Dr
3500 HarC 77449 3816 B3
Maymont Wy
10 WDLD 77382 2674 A7
10 WDLD 77382 2820 A1
Maymount Ln
11600 HarC 77093 3685 D1
Maynard Pl
11900 HarC 77064 3541 A1
Mayo Av
800 HOUS 77017 4106 C6
Mayo St
600 BYTN 77520 4112 C1
Mayor Dr
- HarC 77039 3545 C5
Mayorca Dr
27900 HOUS 77336 3121 C5
Mayo Shell Rd
100 GNPK 77547 4106 B2
100 HOUS 77547 4106 B2
Maypine Ln
6000 HOUS 77085 4240 E7
Maypole Ln
- WDLD 77382 2820 B2
Mayport Ln
14400 HOUS 77077 3956 D6
Mayridge Cir
8600 HOUS 77099 4238 B1
Maysel St
3300 HOUS 77080 3821 A2
Maysfield Park Ln
21900 HarC 77073 3259 B4
May Showers Cir
20700 HarC 77095 3539 A3
May Showers Ct
10000 HarC 77095 3539 A3
Mayside Ln
8500 HarC 77040 3541 B6
Maystar Ct
10 WDLD 77380 2821 E6
Mayview Dr
2400 HOUS 77091 3683 B4
Maywald St
8500 MNVL 77578 4746 A3
Mayweather Ct
700 FBnC 77469 4365 D4
Mayweather Ln
800 FBnC 77469 4365 D2
Maywind Ct
10 WDLD 77381 2821 A5
Maywood Av
5100 HOUS 77053 4372 A5
5500 HOUS 77053 4371 E5
Maywood Ct
2400 FBnC 77545 4498 C6
Maywood Ln
1600 PASD 77503 4108 D7
Maywood Falls Cir
19400 HarC 77084 3816 A4
Maywood Forest Dr
6000 HarC 77088 3542 C7
Mazefield Ct
12100 HarC 77070 3399 B6
Mazen Rd
- HarC 77066 3400 E7
- HarC 77066 3541 E2
- HarC 77086 3541 E2
2700 FBnC 77471 4614 B4
Mazy Ln
- HOUS 77057 3960 C5
Mazzola Ln
11600 HOUS 77076 3685 A3
MB Dr
3200 HarC 77032 3546 A2
McAdams Ln
6000 FBnC 77583 4622 C5
McAfee Ct
10500 HOUS 77031 4239 B3
McAfee Dr
9100 HOUS 77031 4239 A3
McAlexander Dr
15700 HarC 77429 3397 B6
McAlister Rd
13900 MtgC 77302 2531 C6
20500 MtgC 77306 2680 E5
20500 MtgC 77306 2681 A5
McAllister Rd
1900 HOUS 77092 3822 A5
McAlpine St
300 HOUS 77003 3963 E4
McArthur Dr
3000 LMQU 77568 4989 C1
McArthur St
7200 HTCK 77563 4988 D5
McAshan St
3300 HOUS 77003 3964 A5
McAulty Rd
1800 HOUS 77032 3404 B4
1900 HarC 77032 3404 C4
McAvoy Dr
8000 HOUS 77074 4100 A6
8800 HOUS 77074 4240 A1
McBee Pl
24700 MtgC 77355 2960 E2
24700 SGCH 77355 2960 E2
McBeth Wy
10 WDLD 77382 2819 D2
McCabe Rd
600 LPRT 77571 4251 C7
McCabe St
10 HOUS 77076 3684 E4
10 HOUS 77076 3685 A4
McCadden St
14200 HOUS 77045 4372 E2
McCall Bnd
- MtgC 77355 2962 A4
McCall St
800 CNRO 77301 2383 E5
1200 HOUS 77020 3963 E2
McCall Trc
15200 MtgC 77355 2962 B4
McCall Trace Blvd
23900 MtgC 77355 2962 B4
McCall Trace Cir
15200 MtgC 77355 2962 B5
McCall Trace Pk
15200 MtgC 77355 2962 B4
McCamey Dr
21400 HarC 77429 3538 D1
McCarron Ct
100 LGCY 77573 4633 A1
McCarty Ln
100 LPRT 77571 4110 B6
McCarty St
100 HOUS 77029 3826 C7
200 HOUS 77029 3965 B4
15100 GlsC 77517 4986 A1
McCarty St US-90 ALT
100 HOUS 77029 3826 C7
200 HOUS 77029 3965 B1
N McCarty St
3300 HOUS 77029 3826 C6
3900 HOUS 77013 3826 D6
N McCarty St US-90
3900 HOUS 77013 3826 D5
N McCarty St US-90 ALT
- HOUS 77013 3826 D5
3300 HOUS 77029 3826 C6
N McCarty St US-90 BUS
3900 HOUS 77029 3826 D6
4500 HOUS 77013 3826 D6
McCearley Dr
15600 HarC 77429 3397 B6
McCharen Ct
6500 HarC 77086 3542 C3
McClain Ln
21000 MtgC 77306 2681 B6
21000 MtgC 77357 2681 B6
McClearen Dr
- HOUS 77035 4240 C5
- HOUS 77096 4240 C3
McCleester Dr
4400 HarC 77373 3115 C7
McClellan Cir
10 HOUS 77339 3262 E1
100 HOUS 77339 3117 E7
McClellan Ln
7000 SGLD 77479 4367 C7
McClellan Rd
- HOUS 77339 3263 A1
10 HOUS 77339 3262 E1
100 HOUS 77339 3117 E7
200 HOUS 77365 3117 E7
200 MtgC 77365 3117 E7
3100 FBnC 77471 4614 B4
3100 PLEK 77471 4614 B4
McClelland St
1700 HOUS 77093 3824 D1
McClendon St
2000 HOUS 77030 4102 B4
2500 WUNP 77005 4102 B4
6600 GlsC 77510 4987 C4
McCleskey Rd
21400 MtgC 77357 2827 B7
McClosky St
12700 HarC 77037 3685 A1
McCloud St
700 CNRO 77301 2383 E5
McClurd Ct
13200 HarC 77429 3254 A7
McCollough
24000 HarC 77336 3267 A2
McComb Rd
13200 MtgC 77302 2532 A7
Mccomb St
500 CNRO 77301 2384 B4
McComb St
3000 HOUS 77022 3823 E3
McConn Ct
400 HOUS 77598 4506 D3
McConn St
15000 HOUS 77598 4506 D3
McConnell Pl Ln
10 HarC 77070 3399 E3
McConnico Dr
100 GNPK 77547 3966 B7
S McConnico Dr
- GNPK 77547 4106 B1
McCordel
700 HarC 77530 3830 A7
McCormick Ct
7600 HarC 77095 3538 B7
McCormick Dr
16300 HarC 77095 3538 B6
McCormick St
1100 ALVN 77511 4749 A7
1300 BzaC 77511 4749 A6
5200 HOUS 77023 4104 C1
McCormick Mill Ct
7600 HarC 77095 3538 B6
McCown St
1000 MtgC 77385 2822 C3
1000 SHEH 77385 2822 C3
McCoy Ln
19500 MtgC 77365 2972 C7
19500 MtgC 77365 3117 C1
Mccoy Rd
6700 MNVL 77578 4625 D7
McCoy Rd
6800 MNVL 77578 4746 C1
McCracken Cir
11100 HarC 77065 3399 A6
11100 HarC 77070 3399 A5
11100 HarC 77429 3399 A5
McCracken Ln
- HarC 77070 3399 A5
- HarC 77429 3399 A5
McCracken Rd
5400 HarC 77032 3546 D1
5600 HOUS 77396 3546 E1
McCrarey Dr
2800 HarC 77088 3543 B7
2800 HOUS 77088 3543 A7
McCrary Rd
2300 FBnC 77469 4364 D1
3800 FBnC 77469 4233 E6
4500 FBnC 77469 4234 A6
McCreary Wy
3400 FBnC 77459 4621 D5
McCue Rd
2200 HOUS 77056 3961 A6
3300 HOUS 77056 4101 A1
McCulloch Cir
2700 HOUS 77056 3960 E7
3200 HOUS 77056 4100 E1
McCullough Dr
5700 GLSN 77551 5108 C5
McCullough St
5700 HarC 77521 3834 D5
McCullum Rd
6600 HOUS 77489 4371 B6
McDade
- HMPD 77445 3097 E1
McDade St
600 CNRO 77301 2383 E6
600 CNRO 77301 2384 C5
1000 HMPD 77445 3098 A2
8500 HOUS 77055 3821 A3
8500 HOUS 77080 3821 A3
9400 HOUS 77080 3820 C3
McDaniel Dr
800 MtgC 77354 2673 D2
McDaniel Rd
7800 HarC 77521 3834 D4
McDaniel St
- MTBL 77520 3696 D5
600 HOUS 77022 3824 C1
1700 HOUS 77093 3824 D1
2800 HOUS 77093 3825 A1
McDermed Dr
4000 HOUS 77025 4241 C2
4300 HOUS 77035 4241 B3
McDermott Ct
2900 PRLD 77581 4503 E3
McDermott Dr
5300 HarC 77032 3546 D3
McDermott St
100 DRPK 77536 4109 A7
McDonald
200 PASD 77506 4106 D3
McDonald Ct
3000 MtgC 77380 2967 C1
6200 FBnC 77479 4367 B5
17600 MtgC 77302 2679 E2
McDonald Pk
6100 BzaC 77584 4626 D2
McDonald Rd
1400 PRLD 77581 4505 A4
1500 PRLD 77581 4504 E4
17100 GlsC 77511 4869 B6
25500 MtgC 77380 2967 C2
25500 WDLD 77380 2967 C2
26300 MtgC 77380 2821 C7
26300 WDLD 77380 2821 C7
McDonald St
1300 DRPK 77536 4108 E7
1300 DRPK 77536 4109 A7
1300 HOUS 77007 3962 A2
1400 HOUS 77007 3961 E2
McDonnell Rd
3500 MtgC 77302 2677 A2
McDougal Rd
- MtgC 77354 2818 D7
- MtgC 77354 2964 D1
McDoyle Rd
13400 HOUS 77048 4375 E3
McDuffie St
1100 HOUS 77019 3962 C5
2800 HOUS 77098 3962 C7
McDugald Rd
1000 HMBL 77338 3262 E7
1200 HMBL 77338 3263 A7
McEans Dr
20300 HarC 77073 3403 C1
McEnroe Match Dr
6400 HarC 77379 3257 A4
McEwen St
4600 HOUS 77009 3824 B5
McFarland Dr
100 FRDW 77546 4630 A7
100 FRDW 77573 4630 A7
100 LGCY 77546 4630 A7
100 LGCY 77573 4630 A7
900 FRDW 77546 4629 E7
900 LGCY 77546 4629 E7
900 LGCY 77546 4750 E1
1000 LGCY 77511 4751 A2
1000 LGCY 77546 4751 A2
McFarland Rd
100 HarC 77037 3544 C4
100 HarC 77060 3544 C4
2900 GlsC 77511 4751 A6
2900 LGCY 77511 4751 A6
3000 LGCY 77546 4751 A3
McFarland St
300 HOUS 77011 3964 D5
1600 BYTN 77520 3973 C6
McGager Dr
20400 MtgC 77357 2829 D7
20400 MtgC 77357 2975 D1
McGallion Rd
8500 HOUS 77022 3685 B7
9300 HOUS 77076 3685 B7
McGee Ln
8100 HOUS 77071 4239 C5
McGee St
100 HarC 77532 3552 D7
5400 HOUS 77026 3825 C4
18000 HarC 77447 3105 B7
18000 HarC 77447 3250 B1
McGee Lake Ct
1400 FBnC 77469 4234 D4
McGinnes Rd
6300 GlsC 77517 4986 C4
McGinnis Dr
1500 PRLD 77581 4504 D4
McGinty Dr
5700 HarC 77041 3680 C5
McGinty St
800 ALVN 77511 4867 D1
McGowen Ln
13000 HOUS 77034 4378 C2
McGowen St
10 HOUS 77006 3963 A6
400 HarC 77373 3113 E1
900 HOUS 77002 3963 B6
1000 HOUS 77004 3963 C7
3500 HOUS 77004 4103 E1
McGrath Dr
5200 ALVN 77511 4749 C2
McGrath Rd
13400 HOUS 77047 4373 E4
14100 HarC 77047 4373 E5
McGregor Rd
12500 MtgC 77302 2823 E2
12500 MtgC 77302 2824 C2
McGregor St
11700 STFE 77510 4871 B6
McGrew St
6400 HOUS 77087 4104 D7
McGuire Rd
- LGCY 77573 4632 A2
McHard Rd
- BzaC 77584 4374 A7
- MSCY 77489 4497 D1
- PRLD 77053 4372 D7
- PRLD 77053 4499 E1
- PRLD 77053 4500 A1
- PRLD 77545 4372 E7
- PRLD 77545 4499 E1
- PRLD 77545 4500 A1
- PRLD 77581 4376 B7
2700 BzaC 77584 4501 A1
3700 HOUS 77489 4497 E1
4100 FBnC 77489 4497 E1
4100 FBnC 77545 4497 E1
4100 FBnC 77545 4498 A1
4100 HOUS 77489 4498 A1
4100 HOUS 77545 4498 A1
5000 FBnC 77053 4498 E1
5000 HOUS 77053 4498 E1
6500 FBnC 77053 4499 B1
6500 HOUS 77053 4499 B1
8200 FBnC 77053 4372 D7
8600 FBnC 77545 4372 D7
10800 BzaC 77584 4500 C1
11800 PRLD 77584 4500 A1
McHard Rd FM-2234
- MSCY 77489 4497 D1
- PRLD 77053 4372 D7
- PRLD 77053 4499 E1
- PRLD 77053 4500 A1
- PRLD 77545 4372 E7
- PRLD 77545 4499 E1
- PRLD 77545 4500 A1
3700 HOUS 77489 4497 E1
4100 FBnC 77489 4497 E1
4100 FBnC 77545 4497 E1
McHard Rd FM-2234
4100 FBnC 77545 4498
4100 HOUS 77489 4498
4100 HOUS 77545 4498
5000 FBnC 77053 4498
5000 HOUS 77053 4498
6500 FBnC 77053 4499
6500 HOUS 77053 4499
8200 FBnC 77053 4372
8600 FBnC 77545 4372
10800 BzaC 77584 4500
11800 PRLD 77584 4500
McHenry St
7000 HOUS 77087 4104
7600 HOUS 77017 4105
7600 HOUS 77087 4105
McIlhenny St
300 HOUS 77006 3963
1200 HOUS 77002 3963
1200 HOUS 77004 3963
3600 HOUS 77004 4103
McIntosh Cir
17200 SGCH 77355 2961
McIntosh Rd
26100 SGCH 77355 2961
26500 MtgC 77355 2961
McIntosh St
600 HOUS 77009 3824
McIntosh Bend Dr
700 FBnC 77477 4369
McIntyre Dr
100 FBnC 77053 4372
McKamy Ct
2500 HarC 77067 3402
McKamy Dr
10900 HarC 77067 3402
McKaskle Rd
15200 FBnC 77478 4236
McKaughan Rd
2800 HOUS 77032 3404
McKay Av
- HMBL 77338 3262
- HOUS 77338 3262
- HOUS 77338 3406
- HOUS 77396 3406
McKay Dr
18000 HOUS 77338 3406
18000 HOUS 77396 3406
19000 HMBL 77338 3262
19000 HOUS 77338 3262
McKay Pk
1000 CNRO 77304 2529
McKay Rd
17300 GlsC 77511 4869
18700 GlsC 77511 4868
McKean Dr
4100 HOUS 77041 3820
4100 HOUS 77080 3820
McKee St
100 HOUS 77002 3963
500 HOUS 77020 3963
1500 HOUS 77009 3963
2500 HOUS 77009 3824
McKeever Ln
4800 MSCY 77459 4621
McKeever Rd
- MSCY 77459 4621
100 ARLA 77583 4623
500 ARLA 77583 4622
2100 FBnC 77583 4622
3400 FBnC 77459 4621
3400 FBnC 77583 4621
5300 BzaC 77584 4626
5300 MNVL 77584 4626
5300 PRLD 77584 4626
5900 MSCY 77459 4497
6800 BzaC 77584 4627
6800 PRLD 77584 4627
McKendree Park Dr
- HarC 77041 3679
McKibben Ln
100 LGCY 77573 4631
McKinley
2700 HarC 77040 3541
McKinley Av
3400 FBnC 77545 4499
McKinley Cir
33100 MtgC 77354 2673
McKinley Ct
5400 PRLD 77584 4502
McKinley Ln
3400 HOUS 77088 3683
Mckinley St
- HarC 77088 3543
McKinley St
1700 RSBG 77471 4491
3800 HOUS 77051 4243
11500 HarC 77038 3543
McKinney Dr
3000 LMQU 77568 4989
30600 HarC 77375 2964
30600 TMBL 77375 2964
McKinney Ext
3600 LMQU 77568 4989
McKinney Ln
7900 HarC 77562 3832
9700 FBnC 77459 4621
McKinney Rd
100 BYTN 77520 4112
100 HarC 77532 3552
2600 BYTN 77520 3973
2900 BYTN 77521 3973
E McKinney Rd
5200 BYTN 77520 4114
5200 CmbC 77520 4114
McKinney St
300 HOUS 77002 3963
1000 HOUS 77010 3963
2000 HOUS 77003 3963
3500 HOUS 77023 3963
3600 HOUS 77023 3964
7400 HOUS 77011 4105
7400 HOUS 77023 4105
W McKinney St
2000 HOUS 77019 3962
McKinney Creek Ln
13700 HOUS 77044 3550
McKinney Falls Ct
11800 FBnC 77478 4236
McKinney Falls Dr
- FBnC 77478 4236
McKinney Falls Ln
11800 FBnC 77478 4236
McKinney Park Ln
900 HOUS 77003 3963
McKinstry Blvd
6100 HOUS 77085 4371

STREET
Block City ZIP Map# Grid

cKissick Dr
2000 FRDW 77546 4630 A3
cKnight Ln
19300 HOUS 77338 3262 A6
cKnight Rd
5000 BzaC 77584 4502 B6
5000 PRLD 77584 4502 B6
cknight Rd
9400 CNRO 77301 2385 C6
9400 MtgC 77301 2385 C6
cKnight St
5200 HOUS 77035 4240 D4
cLain Blvd
- HOUS 77071 4239 D7
11700 MSCY 77071 4239 D7
12000 MSCY 77071 4370 D1
cLarty St
7600 HTCK 77563 4989 A3
cLean Rd
2600 PRLD 77581 4503 A7
2600 PRLD 77584 4503 A7
3400 BYTN 77521 3833 A7
3400 HarC 77521 3833 A7
3700 HarC 77521 3832 E7
16200 BzaC 77584 4503 A7
16200 BzaC 77584 4627 A2
17100 PRLD 77584 4627 A2
cLean St
7500 HOUS 77051 4243 C2
cLeary St
900 HOUS 77020 3964 B3
cLemore Dr
200 ALVN 77511 4867 C1
cLeod Dr
14900 HOUS 77060 3544 D3
cLeods Ln
11900 BKHV 77024 3959 B3
cLoughlin St
12600 HOUS 77034 4379 B6
cMahon Cir
16000 HarC 77377 2963 A6
cMahon Ct
9700 FBnC 77459 4621 E5
cMahon Ln
3300 FBnC 77459 4621 E5
cMahon Wy
3300 FBnC 77459 4621 E5
cMasters Av
100 PASD 77506 4107 B3
cMillan St
100 CNRO 77301 2384 A3
cMullen Ln
10 HarC 77357 2830 C7
cNair St
12600 HOUS 77015 3967 A2
13700 HarC 77015 3967 E2
14000 HarC 77015 3968 A2
cNair Station Rd
3000 HarC 77521 3832 E4
3300 HarC 77521 3833 A4
cNay Dr
2300 PASD 77506 4107 E5
2700 PASD 77506 4108 A5
cNee Rd
- HOUS 77054 4102 A6
1000 HOUS 77025 4102 B7
cNeil St
1200 HOUS 77009 3824 D7
cNicoll St
10 ARLA 77583 4623 A4
500 FBnC 77583 4623 B4
cNorton Rd
15900 SPLD 77372 2683 B4
cPhail Rd
1200 BYTN 77521 3973 C3
cPhail St
300 TMBL 77375 2964 B7
cQueen Rd
16100 MtgC 77302 2825 A1
cShan Ln
23800 MtgC 77365 2973 E6
cShan Rd
23700 MtgC 77365 2973 E6
cSpadon Rd
23400 MtgC 77365 2973 C7
cSwain Rd
12600 HarC 77429 3398 B1
cTighe Dr
100 BLAR 77401 4101 B4
cVey Ln
400 FBnC 77479 4366 D6
cVicar Ln
12500 HOUS 77089 4378 C7
cVoy Dr
100 LGCY 77573 4633 A1
cWhorter
24000 HarC 77336 3267 A2
cWilliams Dr
6500 HOUS 77088 3683 C4
6500 HOUS 77091 3683 C4
MD Anderson Blvd
1100 HOUS 77030 4102 E3
Meachen Rd
10600 MtgC 77302 2531 A6
Meachen Meadows Tr
10300 MtgC 77302 2530 E6
10300 MtgC 77302 2531 A5
Meade Ct
2300 LGCY 77573 4631 B5
Meade Rd
4500 BzaC 77584 4501 E7
4500 BzaC 77584 4502 A7
Meador Ln
200 BYTN 77520 3971 C2
2000 MtgC 77303 2237 E1
2000 MtgC 77303 2238 A2
Meador Rd
9700 MtgC 77303 2237 E1
10500 CNRO 77378 2237 E1
10500 MtgC 77378 2237 E1
Meadow Cross
400 MtgC 77355 2669 B6
Meadow Ct
300 FRDW 77546 4505 B6
4900 DKSN 77539 4753 D4
22300 HarC 77484 2957 E7
N Meadow Ct
5900 PASD 77505 4248 D3
N Meadow Dr
16200 HarC 77073 3259 A5
S Meadow Dr
5800 PASD 77505 4248 C3
Meadow Lk
300 MtgC 77355 2816 B3
Meadow Ln
- JRSV 77040 3680 C1
300 HTCK 77563 4988 C3
300 KMAH 77565 4510 A7
1500 ALVN 77511 4867 A2
2000 RHMD 77469 4492 A2
2500 LMQU 77568 4989 E2
2700 TXCY 77590 4875 C2
4900 DKSN 77539 4753 D4
5300 BzaC 77584 4502 B6
5300 PRLD 77584 4502 B6
5700 FBnC 77469 4492 A7
5700 RSBG 77469 4492 A7
5900 FBnC 77469 4616 A1
5900 RSBG 77469 4616 A1
10700 BzaC 77511 4748 A5
11500 HOUS 77477 4237 E4
14300 HarC 77047 4374 A5
18800 HarC 77377 3107 A1
18900 HarC 77377 3106 E1
22800 MtgC 77365 2973 D7
22900 HarC 77377 2963 B7
24700 MtgC 77365 3118 D1
26300 FBnC 77494 3952 B6
E Meadow Ln
3100 LGCY 77517 4752 C6
5000 DKSN 77539 4753 D4
N Meadow Ln
3000 LGCY 77517 4752 C5
W Meadow Ln
3100 LGCY 77517 4752 C6
E Meadow Lp
3400 PASD 77505 4248 D3
W Meadow Lp
3400 PASD 77505 4248 C3
Meadow Pkwy
- LGCY 77573 4633 A2
200 LGCY 77573 4632 E1
Meadow Pkwy N
2100 LGCY 77573 4508 D7
2100 LGCY 77573 4632 E1
Meadow Rd
2300 MtgC 77384 2675 E7
5400 FBnC 77479 4496 A7
Meadow St
100 HOUS 77020 3964 A3
Meadow Arbor Ct
20000 HarC 77450 3954 E7
N Meadow Arbor Ct
14000 BzaC 77583 4623 D3
S Meadow Arbor Ct
14000 BzaC 77583 4623 D3
Meadow Arbor Ln
5600 BzaC 77583 4623 D5
Meadow Ash Ct
21100 FBnC 77469 4094 A6
Meadoway Dr
11400 HarC 77089 4378 A5
Meadowbank Dr
- SGLD 77479 4367 E5
4100 PASD 77586 4381 D7
4100 TYLV 77586 4381 D7
Meadow Bay Ct
1300 SGLD 77479 4367 E5
Meadow Bay Dr
3100 LGCY 77539 4753 A4
Meadow Beauty Ct
10 WDLD 77381 2821 A7
Meadow Belle Ct
20800 HarC 77346 3265 A3
Meadowbend Cir
3000 FBnC 77469 4615 B3
Meadow Bend Ct
- MDWP 77477 4238 A5
12200 MDWP 77477 4237 D6
Meadow Bend Dr
100 LGCY 77573 4632 E1
400 FRDW 77546 4505 B6
Meadowbend Dr
- HOUS 77084 3816 B6
4000 FBnC 77469 4615 B4
Meadow Bend Ln
9800 HarC 77065 3539 D4
Meadowbend Rd
2900 FBnC 77469 4615 B3
19900 WlrC 77484 3100 C5
Meadow Bend Terrace Ln
12400 HarC 77044 3689 A3
Meadow Berry Dr
12200 MDWP 77477 4237 E5
Meadow Birch Ln
21000 HarC 77449 3815 C2
E Meadow Bird Cir
17300 HOUS 77489 4497 E2
N Meadow Bird Cir
8300 HOUS 77489 4497 E2
S Meadow Bird Cir
8300 HOUS 77489 4497 E2
W Meadow Bird Cir
17200 HOUS 77489 4497 E2
Meadowbloom Ln
4700 HarC 77449 3677 A5
Meadow Branch Ct
9200 HarC 77095 3538 E4
Meadow Branch Dr
1300 SGLD 77479 4367 E5
1400 SGLD 77479 4368 A5
Meadow Breeze Ln
5700 BzaC 77583 4623 D5
Meadow Briar Dr
- HarC 77082 4097 B1
- HOUS 77082 4097 B1
2200 SGLD 77478 4236 E5
12300 STAF 77477 4237 E7
Meadowbriar Ln
- HOUS 77042 4099 B1
7800 HOUS 77063 4099 E1
7800 HOUS 77063 4100 A1
Meadowbriar St
600 LGCY 77573 4630 D7
Meadow Brook Ct
2800 LGCY 77573 4632 E1
Meadow Brook Dr
2900 LGCY 77573 4632 D1
2900 LGCY 77573 4633 A1
Meadowbrook Dr
800 BYTN 77521 3972 E3
5900 HTCK 77563 4989 C5
8000 HOUS 77017 4245 E2
8000 HTCK 77563 4988 D5
17500 HarC 77530 3831 B6
Meadow Brook Pl
10 WDLD 77382 2674 E5
Meadowbrook Sq
7000 HarC 77084 3679 B2
Meadowbrook Farm Rd
16300 HarC 77082 4096 A3
16400 HarC 77082 4095 D3
Meadowbrook Farms Golf Clb
- FBnC 77494 4093 B7
Meadowbrooks Farms Club Dr
23000 FBnC 77494 4093 B3
Meadow Butte Dr
17200 HarC 77090 3258 A4
Meadow Canyon Dr
- WDLD 77381 2674 A6
5100 FBnC 77479 4493 D2
Meadowchase Ct
9600 HarC 77065 3539 C5
Meadowchase Dr
11300 HarC 77065 3540 A4
11500 HarC 77065 3539 E4
Meadowchase Ln
4200 HarC 77014 3401 C1
Meadow Cove Dr
10 WDLD 77381 2821 C5
Meadow Cove Ln
17400 HarC 77084 3678 A4
Meadow Creek Ct
2800 LGCY 77573 4632 D1
2800 LGCY 77573 4633 A2
36800 MtgC 77355 2815 E4
Meadow Creek Dr
1800 PRLD 77581 4504 C4
Meadowcreek Dr
3100 MSCY 77459 4369 E7
3100 MSCY 77459 4370 A7
Meadow Creek Ln
5400 HOUS 77017 4106 C7
5400 HOUS 77017 4246 C1
13200 MtgC 77302 2530 C4
Meadow Creek Tr
17700 FBnC 77469 4095 C5
Meadow Crest Ct
12200 MDWP 77477 4237 D6
Meadow Crest Dr
4900 LPRT 77571 4250 C2
11800 MDWP 77477 4238 A5
Meadow Crest Ln
12200 MDWP 77477 4237 E5
12200 MDWP 77477 4238 A6
Meadowcrest Ln
3500 SGLD 77478 4368 B4
3500 SGLD 77478 4369 A6
Meadow Crest St
8100 HOUS 77071 4239 D6
Meadowcroft Dr
- HOUS 77042 4099 B1
7800 HOUS 77063 4099 E1
7800 HOUS 77063 4100 A1
Meadow Cross Ln
23200 FBnC 77494 3953 D6
Meadow Crossing Ln
6200 HarC 77449 3677 D3
17600 HarC 77095 3537 D6
Meadowdale Dr
12000 MDWP 77477 4238 A4
12200 MDWP 77477 4237 E4
Meadow Dawn Ct
5000 FBnC 77494 4092 C3
Meadow Dawn Ln
26300 FBnC 77494 4092 E2
Meadow Dew Rd
- HarC 77038 3543 B4
Meadow Edge Dr
1900 HarC 77388 3113 C5
4100 SGLD 77479 4495 A3
30500 MtgC 77354 2816 A1
30900 MtgC 77354 2670 B7
Meadow Edge Ln
1500 HarC 77388 3113 C5
1500 HOUS 77388 3113 C5
Meadow Estates Ln
14200 HarC 77429 3396 B2
Meadowfair Ct
10 WDLD 77381 2821 C4
1500 SGLD 77479 4367 D6
Meadowfair St
11900 HOUS 77037 3684 E2
11900 HOUS 77076 3684 E2
Meadow Falls
- MtgC 77355 2815 C5
11700 HarC 77377 3254 D3
Meadow Falls Ct
37200 MtgC 77355 2815 C6
Meadow Falls Ln
- HarC 77095 3538 E5
Meadowfern Dr
100 HarC 77060 3403 A5
100 HOUS 77067 3403 A5
Meadowfield Creek Wy
5300 HarC 77379 3112 A7
Meadow Ford Ct
9300 HarC 77396 3407 A7
Meadow Forest
28100 MtgC 77355 2815 B4
Meadow Forest Dr
400 LGCY 77573 4631 A6
Meadow Forest Ln
4200 HOUS 77345 3119 E3
4900 FBnC 77469 4233 B6
Meadowfox Pl
4900 HarC 77389 2967 B7
Meadow Frost Ln
12400 HarC 77044 3689 A4
Meadowgale Ln
- HarC 77449 3677 B7
Meadow Gardens Dr
2200 HOUS 77062 4380 C7
Meadow Gate Dr
100 LGCY 77573 4631 A5
12300 STAF 77477 4237 D7
Meadowgate Dr
22100 HarC 77373 3260 E1
22200 HarC 77373 3115 E7
Meadow Glade Cir
3400 HOUS 77345 3119 C3
Meadow Glade Ct
1400 SGLD 77479 4367 E5
Meadowglen Ct
12200 MDWP 77477 4237 E6
Meadow Glen Dr
7900 MSCY 77071 4239 E7
Meadowglen Dr
600 BYTN 77521 3973 B4
4100 DKSN 77539 4754 C2
4800 PRLD 77584 4502 A5
12200 MDWP 77477 4238 A6
12300 MDWP 77477 4237 E5
Meadowglen Ln
7600 HOUS 77063 4100 A1
9500 HOUS 77063 4099 B1
9700 HOUS 77042 4099 A1
10500 HOUS 77042 4098 C1
11100 HOUS 77082 4098 B1
Meadow Glen Rd
400 FRDW 77546 4505 B6
Meadowglen Chase
11300 HOUS 77082 4098 B1
Meadowglen Cove
2900 HOUS 77082 4098 B1
Meadowglen Crest
2900 HOUS 77082 4098 B1
Meadowgold Ln
4000 HOUS 77345 3119 D3
Meadowgrass Ln
2700 HarC 77082 4097 A1
Meadow Green Dr
1600 MSCY 77489 4370 C5
2300 PRLD 77581 4503 D3
4500 SGLD 77479 4495 A1
4600 SGLD 77479 4368 B6
Meadowgreen St
11900 HOUS 77037 3684 E2
11900 HOUS 77076 3684 E2
Meadowgrove Dr
200 HOUS 77037 3684 C2
Meadow Grove Tr
3900 HOUS 77059 4380 B3
Meadow Hawk Ct
7000 HarC 77041 3679 C1
Meadow Hawk Dr
11800 HarC 77089 4504 E1
Meadowhawk Pl
10 WDLD 77384 2675 D5
Meadow Heights Dr
17100 HarC 77095 3538 A7
Meadowhigh Ln
1400 HarC 77373 3259 B1
Meadowhill Ct
3400 HarC 77388 3112 E3
Meadow Hill Dr
1400 SGLD 77479 4367 E5
22000 HarC 77388 3112 E2
22000 HarC 77389 3112 E1
Meadowhill Dr
21300 HarC 77388 3112 E3
21900 HarC 77389 3112 E2
Meadowhill Ln
- LGCY 77539 4753 A4
Meadow Hollow Dr
12000 MDWP 77477 4238 A4
12200 MDWP 77477 4237 E4
Meadowhouse Ln
- HarC 77047 4374 B4
E Meadowhurst Cir
22400 HarC 77377 3106 D2
Meadowhurst Dr
2500 PRLD 77584 4502 A5
Meadowick Dr
600 BYTN 77521 3973 B4
11100 PNPV 77024 3959 E5
11100 PNPV 77024 3960 A5
Meadowivy Ln
5800 HarC 77449 3676 E5
Meadow Joy Ct
11700 HarC 77089 4378 B7
Meadow Joy Dr
11300 HarC 77089 4378 B6
Meadow Knolle Dr
500 FBnC 77477 4369 D4
500 STAF 77477 4369 D4
Meadow Lake Ct
13500 HarC 77044 3689 C3
Meadowlake Ct
13600 HarC 77044 3689 D3
Meadow Lake Dr
11300 HOUS 77077 3958 B6
12100 HOUS 77077 3957 D6
Meadow Lake Ln
3400 HOUS 77019 3961 D6
4000 HOUS 77027 3961 C6
5200 HOUS 77056 3960 E6
6100 HOUS 77057 3960 B6
7700 HOUS 77063 3960 A6
10000 HOUS 77042 3959 A6
10600 HOUS 77042 3958 D6
Meadowlake Ln
100 HarC 77562 3831 E1
Meadowlake Rd
3500 PASD 77503 4108 B4
Meadowland Dr
- HOUS 77042 4099 B1
9600 HOUS 77063 4099 B1
Meadow Landing Ct
5000 SGLD 77479 4495 B5
Meadow Landing Ln
5200 SGLD 77479 4495 B4
Meadow Lark Av
800 FRDW 77546 4628 E1
800 FRDW 77546 4629 A1
900 BzaC 77581 4628 E1
900 PRLD 77581 4628 E1
Meadow Lark Ln
1900 LPRT 77571 4250 B1
4900 DKSN 77539 4753 C5
18800 HarC 77377 2962 A7
Meadowlark Ln
600 BYTN 77521 3972 E3
900 SGLD 77478 4368 C3
2100 LGCY 77573 4632 A6
3400 ALVN 77511 4866 D4
3400 BzaC 77511 4866 D4
3400 HarC 77388 3112 D2
5000 HarC 77493 3813 E7
5000 KATY 77493 3813 E7
7200 TXCY 77591 4873 C6
14000 HarC 77377 3108 E2
Meadowlark Rd
5600 FBnC 77469 4615 B6
Meadow Lark St
1300 DRPK 77536 4109 C5
Meadowlark St
1000 HOUS 77017 4106 C6
30500 MtgC 77385 2676 D5
Meadowlark Wy
3200 PRLD 77584 4502 C7
Meadowlawn Av
100 SRAC 77571 4383 A1
500 SRAC 77571 4382 E1
Meadowlawn Dr
6600 HOUS 77023 4104 D2
Meadow Lea Dr
10 HOUS 77022 3685 A7
Meadow Leaf Ln
12700 HarC 77039 3546 A5
Meadowleigh Ct
16900 SGLD 77479 4368 A7
Meadow Lilly Ln
3900 HarC 77449 3816 A2
Meadowline Dr
12900 HOUS 77082 4097 C2
Meadowlink St
200 HOUS 77037 3684 C2
Meadow Ln Ct
12200 MDWP 77477 4237 D6
Meadowlocke Ln
1800 SGLD 77478 4368 B5
Meadow Lodge Ln
- HarC 77433 3396 A6
Meadow Manor Ct
1900 HOUS 77062 4380 D7
Meadow Mill Ct
- HarC 77429 3253 A6
Meadow Mill Ln
9900 HarC 77044 3689 B3
N Meadowmist Cir
10 WDLD 77381 2674 C6
S Meadowmist Cir
10 WDLD 77381 2674 C6
Meadow Mist Ct
7200 HarC 77041 3679 D1
Meadowmist Ct
10 WDLD 77381 2674 C6
3000 PRLD 77583 4500 C4
Meadowmoor Dr
7800 HarC 77037 3684 C2
7800 HOUS 77037 3684 C2
Meadow Oak Dr
3100 HarC 77068 3257 D6
Meadow Oaks Dr
24700 FBnC 77494 3952 D4
Meadowood Cir
4900 BYTN 77521 3972 B1
Meadowood Dr
4600 BYTN 77521 3972 B1
Meadow Palm Dr
15500 HarC 77433 3251 C6
Meadow Park Cir
2100 MSCY 77459 4497 C4
Meadow Park Ct
12200 MDWP 77477 4237 E6
Meadow Park Dr
1500 LPRT 77571 4110 B7
4700 HOUS 77047 4243 D6
4700 HOUS 77048 4243 D5
Meadowpass St
11900 HOUS 77037 3684 E2
11900 HOUS 77076 3684 E2
Meadow Pines Ct
11500 HOUS 77477 4238 A4
Meadow Pines Dr
12100 HOUS 77477 4238 A4
Meadow Pl Ct
11700 HOUS 77071 4239 C5
Meadow Pl Dr
3700 HarC 77082 4096 A3
4900 LPRT 77571 4250 B2
11800 HOUS 77071 4239 C5
Meadowplace Dr
6700 HTCK 77563 4989 C5
Meadow Point Ct
9400 HarC 77095 3538 B2
Meadowpoint Dr
400 LGCY 77573 4633 A2
Meadow Pond Cir
23000 FBnC 77450 3953 C6
Meadow Pond Dr
2900 FBnC 77450 3953 D7
8000 MSCY 77459 4497 A5
Meadow Ridge Dr
12300 STAF 77477 4238 A6
Meadowridge Dr
200 HOUS 77037 3684 C2
Meadow Ridge Ln
14100 BzaC 77583 4623 D5
Meadowridge Pl
10 WDLD 77381 2674 C6
Meadowrock Dr
22200 HarC 77389 3112 E1
Meadow Rose Ct
19300 HarC 77346 3265 A3
Meadow Rose Pl
10 WDLD 77382 2819 D2
Meadow Rue Ct
1400 SGLD 77479 4368 A5
Meadow Rue St
11000 WDLD 77380 2821 C7
Meadow Run Ct
12900 HarC 77066 3401 B3
Meadow Run Dr
400 FRDW 77546 4505 B5
Meadows Blvd
2100 LGCY 77573 4632 D2
W Meadows Blvd
7100 BYTN 77521 3832 B5
7100 HarC 77521 3832 B5
S Meadows Ct
200 FBnC 77479 4366 C6
E Meadows Dr
4300 FBnC 77479 4366 C6
W Meadows Dr
4200 FBnC 77479 4366 C5
Meadows Ln
- PRVW 77445 3099 E3
S Meadows St
3300 BzaC 77511 4867 B7
Meadows Wy
18600 HarC 77084 3816 C2
Meadows Crossing Dr
- LGCY 77573 4631 A5
Meadows Edge Ln
4600 HarC 77084 3677 B7
Meadowshire St
7500 HOUS 77037 3684 D3
7500 HOUS 77076 3684 D3
7900 HarC 77037 3684 D2
9000 HarC 77037 3544 C7
Meadowside Dr
3300 SGLD 77478 4368 E5
15900 HOUS 77062 4380 C7
Meadowside St
5800 LGCY 77573 4630 C6
Meadowside Park Dr
14900 HarC 77429 3252 E7
Meadowsing
11000 HarC 77532 3694 A5
Meadows Pond Dr
3100 LGCY 77573 4633 B1
Meadows Pond Ln
2900 PRLD 77584 4500 A4
Meadowspring Cir
100 WDLD 77381 2674 C6
Meadow Spring Ct
5400 BzaC 77583 4623 D2
Meadowspring Ct
100 WDLD 77381 2674 C6
Meadow Spring Dr
3500 SGLD 77479 4495 B1
Meadow Springs Dr
4100 HOUS 77339 3119 A3
12900 PRLD 77584 4500 A3
Meadow Star Ct
10 WDLD 77381 2821 A3
Meadowstar Dr
1500 SGLD 77479 4368 A5
Meadow Stone Ct
23300 FBnC 77494 3953 C5
Meadowstream Ct
6000 FBnC 77450 4094 A4
Meadow Sweet Dr
1500 SGLD 77479 4368 A5
13600 HarC 77429 3398 A1
Meadowsweet Dr
21600 MtgC 77355 2961 A2
21600 SGCH 77355 2961 A2
21700 MtgC 77355 2960 B1
21700 SGCH 77355 2960 B1
Meadow Terrace Dr
- HarC 77082 4096 A3
Meadowthorn Ct
4700 HarC 77546 4506 C6
Meadow Timbers Dr
2000 HarC 77090 3258 B6
Meadowtrace Dr
6200 HarC 77389 2966 D4
Meadow Trail Ct
300 FRDW 77546 4505 B6
Meadow Trail Ln
400 FRDW 77546 4505 B5
Meadowtrail Ln
11700 HOUS 77477 4238 A4
11800 MDWP 77477 4238 A5
Meadow Tree Ct
20300 HarC 77388 3113 B6
Meadow Tree Ln
2500 HarC 77388 3113 A6
Meadowvale Dr
- HOUS 77042 4099 B2
7600 HOUS 77063 4100 A1
7800 HOUS 77063 4099 E1
Meadow Valley Ln
12000 MDWP 77477 4238 A5
14200 SGLD 77478 4236 E5
Meadow View Ct
400 FRDW 77546 4505 B5
8600 JRSV 77040 3540 C6
Meadowview Dr
1800 ALVN 77511 4867 B4
2900 MSCY 77459 4497 C2
7500 HOUS 77037 3684 C3
7500 HOUS 77076 3684 C3
8400 HarC 77037 3684 C1
8700 HarC 77037 3544 C7
11800 HarC 77429 3398 C2
37000 PNIS 77445 3099 C3
Meadow View Ln
- FRDW 77546 4505 B5
21100 HarC 77377 3106 A4
Meadowview St
9000 HarC 77037 3544 C7
Meadow Village Dr
15700 HarC 77095 3538 D5
Meadowville Dr
3400 PRLD 77581 4376 C6
Meadowvine Dr
11000 HarC 77044 3689 D2
Meadow Vista Blvd
8900 HarC 77064 3399 D6
Meadow Vista Ct
500 MSCY 77459 4497 A5
Meadow Vista Dr
8000 MSCY 77459 4497 A6
Meadow Walk Ln
10800 HarC 77067 3402 A7
Meadow Wilde
- MSCY 77489 4370 D3
Meadow Wood Ct
300 LGCY 77573 4632 E2
Meadow Wood Dr
1500 PRLD 77581 4375 D7
3500 PASD 77503 4108 C5
Meadowwood Dr
30200 MtgC 77354 2816 A1
Meadowwood Grn
37600 MtgC 77355 2815 B5
Meadow Wood Ln
400 FRDW 77546 4505 B5
Meadow Wood Park Dr
5000 HarC 77449 3677 B5
Meadow Wy Cir
10 FBnC 77469 4232 D3
Meadow Wy Dr
2400 MSCY 77459 4370 A7
Meadowyork St
7500 HOUS 77037 3684 C3
7500 HOUS 77076 3684 C3
Meads St
1000 HarC 77530 3830 C5
Meadville St
8100 HOUS 77061 4245 D3
Meadway Ct
12700 HOUS 77082 4097 C1
Meadway Dr
3000 HOUS 77082 4097 C2
6100 HOUS 77072 4097 C4
Meagan Hills Ct
3900 FBnC 77494 4093 A4
Meandering Tr
2200 HOUS 77339 3119 A3
Meandering Brooke Ln
- HOUS 77489 4371 A6
Meandering Meadow Ln
18100 HarC 77084 3816 D3
Meandering Oak Ln
7800 HarC 77433 3537 A7
Mease Ct
4200 PASD 77503 4108 D6
Meaux Dr
9100 HOUS 77031 4239 A3
Mebane Ln
100 RSBG 77471 4490 B5
Mechanic St
100 GLSN 77550 5109 E2
300 TMBL 77375 2964 C7
3300 GLSN 77550 5108 E3
Meco Ln
10900 HOUS 77043 3819 C7
Mecom Rd
2800 HOUS 77032 3404 D1
6800 HTCK 77563 4988 B5
Medallion Pointe Ct
5500 FBnC 77450 4094 C3
Medallion Pointe Dr
20700 FBnC 77450 4094 A3
Medberry
15700 HarC 77090 3258 B5
Medell St
- HOUS 77072 4098 A4
Medellin St
1000 PASD 77506 4107 E5
1000 PASD 77506 4108 A6
Medfield Dr
12600 HOUS 77082 4097 C3
Medford Ct
100 SGLD 77478 4368 E4
Medford Dr
8500 HOUS 77033 4244 A4
Medic Ln
10 ALVN 77511 4749 C7
Medical Cir
- PASD 77504 4247 E3
Medical Center Blvd
100 CNRO 77301 2529 E2
100 CNRO 77304 2529 E2
100 HarC 77598 4507 B5
100 WEBS 77598 4507 B6
E Medical Center Blvd
- WEBS 77598 4507 B5
100 HarC 77598 4507 B5
800 HarC 77058 4507 C4
W Medical Center Blvd
700 WEBS 77598 4507 A6
Medical Center Dr
- PRLD 77584 4500 E1
5500 KATY 77494 3952 C3
9900 HMBL 77338 3262 C6
9900 HOUS 77338 3262 C6
Medical Complex Dr
13400 TMBL 77375 3109 A1
14000 HarC 77377 3108 D2
14000 TMBL 77375 3108 D2
Medical Park Dr
3700 DKSN 77539 4753 C5
Medical Plaza Dr
- SHEH 77380 2822 B3
- SHEH 77385 2822 B3
1000 SHEH 77381 2822 A3
1000 WDLD 77380 2822 A3
Medicine Bow Cir
11900 HarC 77067 3401 E4
Medicine Bow Ct
20000 HarC 77346 3265 A4
Medicine Bow Dr
19800 HarC 77346 3265 A5
E Medicine Creek Dr
- HOUS 77060 3544 A1
N Medicine Creek Dr
- HOUS 77060 3544 A1
S Medicine Creek Dr
- HOUS 77060 3544 A1
W Medicine Creek Dr
- HOUS 77060 3544 C1
Medina St
100 HOUS 77012 4105 C2
Medina Bend Ln
12100 HarC 77041 3679 B7
12100 HarC 77041 3680 A6
Medinah Ct
3300 SGLD 77479 4495 A3
Medinah Pl
4500 BLAR 77401 4101 B3
Medina Lake Ct
13800 HarC 77429 3253 D6
Medina Lake Dr
12100 HarC 77377 3254 C6
Medina Lake Ln
15700 HarC 77429 3253 C6
Medio Dr
8000 FBnC 77083 4096 C7
N Medio River Cir
1300 SGLD 77478 4369 A5
S Medio River Cir
1500 SGLD 77478 4369 A5
Mediterra Wy
- HarC 77389 2819 E5
- HarC 77389 2820 A4
Mediterranean Ct
300 HarC 77532 3552 C2
Mediterranean St N
16500 HarC 77532 3552 B2
Mediterranean St S
16300 HarC 77532 3552 B3
Medley Ln
10 WDLD 77382 2674 C5
Medley Green Dr
15000 HarC 77433 3250 E5
15200 HarC 77433 3251 A5
Medlowe Ct
14200 HarC 77429 3397 B1
Medora St
14100 HarC 77049 3689 E7
14100 HarC 77049 3690 A7
Medway Dr
1900 MtgC 77386 2969 B3
Meek Rd
900 HMBL 77338 3262 E4
Meeker Cir
300 HarC 77532 3411 A4
Meeks Rd
900 HMBL 77338 3262 E4
900 HMBL 77338 3263 A4
Meer Dr
1900 HarC 77015 3829 B4
Meeting Ln
14500 HarC 77084 3679 A4
Megan St
5600 PRLD 77581 4502 E3
23500 HarC 77373 3114 A6
Megan Wy
12700 MSCY 77071 4370 C1
Megan Pl Dr
8100 HarC 77095 3538 E6
Megan's Wy
- HarC 77094 3955 B1
Megans Falls Ct
14200 HarC 77396 3547 D2
Megan Springs Dr
- HarC 77379 3255 E4
Meganwoods Lp
12200 HarC 77089 4505 A2
Megellan Point Ln
2200 PRLD 77584 4500 A2
Megginson St
13400 HOUS 77048 4375 D3
Meigs Cir
- HarC 77377 3106 A6
N Meigs Cir
10 HarC 77377 3106 B5
S Meigs Cir
10 HarC 77377 3106 B6
Meigs Cir Blvd
10 HarC 77377 3106 C6
Meiko Dr
2600 HOUS 77045 4373 A1
Meineke St
4100 HOUS 77087 4104 D6

STREET Block City ZIP Map# Grid

Meisterwood Dr
13300 HarC 77065 3398 A7
13700 HarC 77429 3398 A7
Melanie Ln
1000 BzaC 77511 4748 E2
2000 PRLD 77581 4502 D2
14700 MtgC 77372 2682 D2
28300 WlrC 77447 2813 A7
34700 MtgC 77362 2816 C7
34700 SGCH 77362 2816 C7
Melanie Pk
900 CNRO 77304 2529 D1
Melanie St
5000 HarC 77532 3413 A5
7700 HOUS 77016 3687 B3
Melanie Park Dr
2100 HarC 77388 3113 B3
Melanie Pointe
- HarC 77375 2964 D2
Melanite Av
5300 HOUS 77053 4372 A5
5500 HOUS 77053 4371 E5
Melany Mdws
10900 MtgC 77354 2671 E4
Melba Ln
100 KMAH 77565 4509 C7
11000 HarC 77041 3680 C4
Melba St
20200 MtgC 77357 2827 A6
Melba Rose Cir
14400 HarC 77429 3396 E1
Melbourne St
10 HOUS 77022 3824 D3
1800 HOUS 77026 3824 D3
2900 HOUS 77026 3825 A3
Melbrook Dr
5700 HarC 77041 3679 C5
Melcher Dr
13400 HOUS 77045 4241 C7
13400 HOUS 77045 4372 C1
Melcrest Estates Dr
30700 MtgC 77386 2969 B1
Melda
1700 MtgC 77380 2967 E3
1700 WDLD 77380 2967 E3
Meldrum Ln
- HOUS 77061 4245 E7
- HOUS 77075 4246 B7
8700 HOUS 77075 4245 E7
Melendy
6700 HarC 77041 3680 A2
6700 JRSV 77041 3680 A2
Melford Av
1000 PRLD 77584 4501 B2
Melford Dr
1200 HOUS 77077 3957 B4
Melham Ln
22700 HarC 77373 3115 E7
Melidoro
7900 HarC 77375 2965 E6
7900 HarC 77389 2965 E6
7900 HarC 77389 2966 A5
Melina Ln
24000 HarC 77375 2965 D5
Melinda Ln
5800 PASD 77505 4248 C3
Melinda St
19200 HarC 77532 3411 D4
Meline Fields Dr
- MtgC 77386 2969 D2
Melissa Ct
4700 FBnC 77479 4493 D1
Melissa Dr
1500 MtgC 77386 2969 A2
Melissa St
2100 HarC 77039 3545 D2
Melissa Lea Ln
8900 HarC 77040 3541 C7
Melissa Springs Dr
17800 HarC 77070 3255 B3
17800 HarC 77375 3255 B2
Melita Dr
30800 MtgC 77386 2969 A1
Mell Ln
6400 HarC 77049 3829 E2
Mellenbrook Ct
26600 HarC 77433 3396 A6
Mellenbrook Ln
10100 HOUS 77075 4376 E2
Mellishaw Ct
20000 HarC 77379 3110 D5
Mellon
- HOUS 77098 4102 B1
Mellon St
200 RHMD 77469 4364 D7
200 RHMD 77469 4491 D1
Mellow Ln
2900 DKSN 77539 4754 C3
Mellow Brew Ct
31900 SGCH 77355 2961 D3
Mellow Brew Pl
16500 SGCH 77355 2961 D3
Mellow Brew St
32000 SGCH 77355 2961 D3
Mellow Brook Dr
9000 HOUS 77099 4237 D2
Mellowgrove Ct
7600 HarC 77379 3256 B1
Mellowgrove Ln
18500 HarC 77379 3256 A1
Mellow Leaf Ct
10 WDLD 77381 2821 B4
Mellow Oaks Ln
16300 FBnC 77478 4236 A6
Mellow Ridge Dr
17700 HarC 77379 3256 C1
Mellow Wood Pl
10 WDLD 77381 2820 D4
Mellus
5300 HOUS 77007 3962 B3
Mellville Dr
12200 HarC 77089 4504 E2
12400 HarC 77089 4505 A2
Melmeade
2000 HOUS 77019 3962 C5
Melmont Ln
500 MtgC 77302 2530 D5
Melody Cir
7600 HarC 77040 3681 C1
Melody Dr
1300 LMQU 77568 4989 C1
Melody Gdn
400 HarC 77049 3829 A3
Melody Gdns
11600 HarC 77429 3254 A7
Melody Ln
100 FRDW 77546 4505 A5
1800 FBnC 77469 4365 C4
Melody Ln
3700 GlsC 77518 4634 C2
5400 DKSN 77539 4754 A5
5400 TXCY 77539 4754 A5
10900 HNCV 77024 3960 A2
Melody Pk
5300 HarC 77066 3401 A5
Melody Glen Ln
14300 HarC 77014 3257 D6
Melody Oaks Ln
25100 FBnC 77494 3953 A5
Melody Park Ln
8900 HarC 77044 3689 B5
Melody Peak Ln
- PRLD 77581 4503 C1
Melodywood Ct
400 FRDW 77546 4505 A5
Melodywood Dr
300 FRDW 77546 4505 A5
Melon St
900 HOUS 77091 3683 E4
Melrose
8700 HOUS 77022 3685 B7
Melrose St
3500 BzaC 77511 4867 C6
7600 HOUS 77022 3824 B1
9200 HOUS 77022 3685 B6
Melrose Park Pl
7800 HOUS 77053 4372 C7
Melrose Park Rd
12100 HOUS 77037 3685 B2
12100 HOUS 77076 3685 B2
Melting Shadows Ln
8700 HarC 77095 3538 C3
Melton St
100 MAGA 77354 2669 A5
100 MtgC 77354 2669 B6
Melva St
3000 HOUS 77020 3964 A3
Melvern Ct
12700 HarC 77041 3679 D6
Melville Dr
700 HarC 77532 3693 A2
E Melville Dr
100 HarC 77532 3692 D2
W Melville Dr
100 HarC 77532 3692 D2
Melville Glen Pl
10 WDLD 77384 2675 A3
Melvin Oaks Ct
16900 HarC 77095 3538 A4
Melvin Oaks Dr
9300 HarC 77095 3538 A4
Melvin Utley Dr
5200 DKSN 77539 4754 C1
Melwood St
600 HOUS 77009 3824 A6
W Melwood St
600 HOUS 77009 3824 A6
900 HOUS 77009 3823 E6
1100 HOUS 77008 3823 E6
Members Dr
10500 HOUS 77075 4377 C3
10500 HOUS 77089 4377 C3
Memel St
2900 HOUS 77026 3825 A5
Memorial Blvd
9800 HMBL 77338 3262 C6
Memorial Cir
11400 PNPV 77024 3959 E5
Memorial Ct
3000 HOUS 77007 3962 D3
N Memorial Ct
1900 PASD 77502 4247 E2
S Memorial Ct
1900 PASD 77502 4247 E2
Memorial Dr
- HOUS 77002 3963 B3
200 BKHV 77024 3959 C5
700 BYTN 77520 3972 D6
1500 HOUS 77007 3963 A4
4000 HOUS 77007 3962 C4
6200 HOUS 77007 3961 C3
6400 TXCY 77591 4873 D5
7200 HTCK 77563 4989 A3
8500 HOUS 77024 3961 A1
9200 HOUS 77024 3960 B2
10200 HNCV 77024 3960 C2
10900 PNPV 77024 3960 A4
11400 PNPV 77024 3959 D5
12300 HOUS 77024 3959 A4
12500 HOUS 77024 3958 E3
12900 HOUS 77079 3958 C2
14100 HOUS 77079 3957 D3
15000 MtgC 77372 2683 A3
15000 SPLD 77372 2683 A3
15700 HOUS 77079 3956 D2
29500 MtgC 77386 2969 B4
E Memorial Dr
21200 MtgC 77339 3118 B2
21200 MtgC 77365 3118 B2
N Memorial Dr
18900 HMBL 77338 3262 C6
W Memorial Dr
21100 MtgC 77365 3118 A2
Memorial Grn
700 HOUS 77079 3957 E3
Memorial Ln
- HOUS 77074 4099 D6
1500 CNRO 77304 2382 E5
N Memorial Wy
1900 HOUS 77007 3963 A3
Memorial Blossom Dr
- HarC 77379 3255 D2
Memorial Brook Blvd
- HOUS 77084 3817 C7
10 HOUS 77084 3956 B1
Memorial Chase Rd
16400 HarC 77379 3255 D5
16900 HarC 77070 3255 C4
Memorial City
10100 HOUS 77024 3959 B2
Memorial City Wy
100 HOUS 77024 3959 B1
Memorial Cove
10700 HNCV 77024 3960 A3
Memorial Creek Dr
8800 HarC 77379 3255 E3
Memorial Crest Blvd
3300 HOUS 77007 3962 E3
Memorial Crest Dr
17400 HarC 77379 3255 D2
Memorial Crossing Ct
9600 HarC 77375 3255 B3
Memorial Crossing Dr
9700 HarC 77375 3255 B2
Memorial Estates Dr
18000 HarC 77379 3256 A2
Memorial Estates Dr
18400 HarC 77379 3255 C1
Memorial Falls Dr
17600 HarC 77070 3255 C3
17800 HarC 77375 3255 B2
Memorial Gate Dr
- HarC 77379 3255 D2
Memorial Glen Dr
1000 HMBL 77338 3406 E1
1100 HMBL 77338 3407 A1
Memorial Grove Dr
9200 HarC 77379 3255 D2
Memorial Heights Dr
600 HOUS 77007 3962 E3
Memorial Hermann Dr
10900 PRLD 77584 4500 E3
Memorial Hills Dr
9000 HarC 77379 3255 D3
E Memorial Loop Dr
1000 HOUS 77007 3961 E2
W Memorial Loop Dr
- HOUS 77007 3961 C2
Memorial Manor Dr
9300 HarC 77379 3255 D3
Memorial Mews St
700 HOUS 77079 3957 B2
Memorial Mills Dr
- HarC 77379 3255 D2
Memorial Mist Ln
18400 HarC 77375 3255 C2
Memorial Oaks Ln
17800 HarC 77379 3256 A2
Memorial Park Dr
200 PASD 77506 4107 A4
Memorial Park C Dr
10 SPVL 77055 3821 B7
W Memorial Park Drive A
- SPVL 77055 3821 B7
Memorial Park Drive B
- SPVL 77055 3821 B7
8500 SPVL 77024 3960 B1
8500 SPVL 77055 3960 D2
Memorial Pass
17500 HarC 77379 3255 D2
18300 HarC 77375 3255 B2
Memorial Pass Dr
18700 HarC 77375 3255 B1
20200 FBnC 77450 4094 C4
Memorial Pines Wy
9000 HarC 77379 3255 D3
Memorial Point Ln
10 BKHV 77024 3959 D5
10 PNPV 77024 3959 D6
Memorial Post Ln
- HarC 77379 3255 D3
Memorial Ridge Dr
17500 HarC 77379 3255 D2
Memorial River Oaks Dr
21000 MtgC 77365 3118 A2
Memorial Shores Dr
- HarC 77379 3255 D2
Memorial South
18800 HMBL 77338 3262 C7
Memorial Springs Ct
18200 HarC 77375 3255 B3
Memorial Springs Dr
- HarC 77379 3255 D3
17600 HarC 77070 3255 B3
Memorial Springs Psg
18600 HarC 77375 3255 A2
Memorial Springs Pass
18300 HarC 77375 3255 A2
Memorial Trace Dr
17400 HarC 77379 3255 E2
Memorial Trail Dr
9000 HarC 77379 3255 D2
17800 HarC 77070 3255 B3
Memorial Valley Dr
9100 HarC 77379 3255 D2
Memorial View Dr
600 HOUS 77079 3957 B1
Memorial Village Dr
900 HDWV 77024 3959 B1
900 HOUS 77024 3959 B1
Memorial Woods Dr
7400 HOUS 77024 3961 A1
Memorial Wy Dr
10000 HarC 77070 3255 B3
Memory Ln
10 TYLV 77586 4381 E7
10 WDLD 77380 2821 D7
100 CNRO 77301 2384 A3
100 HarC 77037 3544 B5
100 HarC 77060 3544 B5
100 HOUS 77037 3544 B5
4700 BYTN 77521 3974 A1
11100 MtgC 77372 2537 A2
E Memory Ln
25700 MtgC 77355 2963 A3
N Memory Ln
26000 MtgC 77355 2963 A3
S Memory Ln
26400 MtgC 77355 2963 A4
W Memory Ln
25700 MtgC 77355 2963 A3
Memphis St
7500 HOUS 77011 3965 B6
17000 HMBL 77396 3406 C3
Menard Av
5300 GLSN 77551 5108 C5
Menard St
2400 SEBK 77586 4509 E2
3800 HOUS 77003 3964 A5
Menasco Ct
13800 HOUS 77077 3957 A3
Mendez
7300 HOUS 77020 3965 A3
Mendez St
7900 HOUS 77029 3965 B3
Mendocino Dr
3700 GLSN 77554 5548 B1
15900 FBnC 77083 4096 A5
Mendota Ln
5400 HarC 77032 3546 D1
Menefee
4300 HOUS 77007 3962 C1
Menke Rd
- WlrC 77445 3244 D5
Menking Ct
400 HNCV 77024 3960 A3
Menlo Dr
6800 HarC 77083 4096 D5
Menlo Creek Ct
7200 FBnC 77469 4094 A6
Menlo Park Dr
4800 SGLD 77479 4495 B3
Menor Crest Dr
6100 HarC 77388 3111 D2
Mentmore Dr
8300 HarC 77379 3256 A4
Mentor Dr
5700 TXCY 77591 4873 E6
Menwood Cir
6400 HOUS 77088 3682 C2
Merabrook Dr
22200 FBnC 77450 4094 A1
22400 FBnC 77450 4093 B6
Meraldo Dr
9300 HOUS 77078 3688 A5
Mercado Dr
17000 FBnC 77083 4095 D6
Mercado Rd
26100 SGCH 77355 2961 C2
Mercantile Dr
- RSBG 77471 4492 A6
Mercantile Pkwy
- HOUS 77449 3814 D7
- HOUS 77493 3814 C7
Mercant Mark Ln
- FBnC 77469 4094 E7
Mercedell Dr
19600 MtgC 77365 2972 C5
Mercedes Ln
4900 HOUS 77022 3684 D7
Mercedes Rd
- HarC 77014 3402 E3
- HOUS 77090 3402 E3
- HOUS 77090 3403 A3
Mercedes Benz Ct
800 HarC 77396 3407 A5
Mercer Dr
13000 HarC 77375 2964 B2
13200 TMBL 77375 2964 B2
Mercer St
3200 HOUS 77027 3961 E7
5100 HOUS 77005 4101 E3
5100 HOUS 77027 4101 E1
5200 WUNP 77005 4101 E4
6700 HOUS 77025 4101 E4
Mercer Estates Ct
10900 MtgC 77385 2823 A7
Mercer Gap
- HarC 77040 3541 C6
- HarC 77064 3541 C6
Merchants Wy
- HOUS 77449 3814 E7
Merchant Springs Ln
4500 HarC 77084 3817 A1
4600 HarC 77084 3678 A7
Mercier Dr
25900 WlrC 77447 2813 B6
Mercoal Dr
1600 MtgC 77386 2969 A2
Mercury Dr
- GNPK 77547 3966 B4
300 HOUS 77013 3966 B1
800 HOUS 77029 3966 B2
900 JTCY 77029 3966 B4
17200 HarC 77058 4507 C4
17200 HarC 77598 4507 C4
Mercury Cove Ct
9000 HOUS 77075 4377 A4
Mercury Run Ct
2900 HarC 77373 3115 A4
Mercutio Ct
10 WDLD 77382 2819 A2
Mere Dr
1100 MtgC 77362 2816 D7
1100 SGCH 77362 2816 D7
Meredith
6900 BLAR 77401 4100 E4
Meredith Ct
1800 DRPK 77536 4109 D5
Meredith Dr
6300 BLAR 77401 4100 E4
8900 HarC 77562 3832 E1
8900 HarC 77562 3833 A1
Meredith Rd
34000 WlrC 77484 3245 E1
Meredith Elise Ct
9800 HOUS 77025 4241 D2
Meredith Gate Cir
14400 HarC 77044 3549 E1
Meredith Gate Ct
12900 HarC 77044 3549 E1
Merewood Ln
12000 HOUS 77071 4239 C6
Merganser Ct
2500 HarC 77396 3407 D3
Merganser Dr
13900 HarC 77047 4374 C4
Meria Coves Dr
17300 HarC 77095 3537 E2
Meribrook Ln
1100 PRLD 77581 4504 E6
Meriburr Ln
3600 HOUS 77021 4103 C5
Merida Ct
2800 GLSN 77554 5221 C2
Merida Dr
- GLSN 77554 5221 C3
13700 HOUS 77047 4373 B4
Meridan Wy
10 GLSN 77554 5221 C2
Meridian Blvd
100 BYTN 77521 3973 A3
400 BYTN 77521 3972 D2
Meridian Ct
1600 CNRO 77301 2384 D4
Meridian St
3900 HOUS 77017 4105 D7
Meridian Bay Ln
2900 LGCY 77539 4752 E5
N Meridian Greens Dr
- DKSN 77539 4752 D6
- LGCY 77539 4752 D6
S Meridian Greens Dr
- DKSN 77539 4752 D6
Meridian Hill Dr
29700 MtgC 77386 2969 E2
Meridian Lakes Dr
10100 HarC 77095 3537 E3
Meridian Park Dr
4500 PRLD 77584 4503 A4
Meridian Park Ln
14800 HarC 77396 3548 A1
Meridian Springs Ln
13600 HOUS 77077 3957 A7
Meridian Trails Dr
- HarC 77449 3677 A3
Meriglen Ln
21000 HarC 77388 3112 B5
Merilee Ct
13600 HarC 77429 3253 E6
13600 HarC 77429 3254 A6
Merion Cir
4600 PASD 77505 4249 A6
Merion Dr
2300 LGCY 77573 4508 D7
Merion Ln
- BYTN 77521 3972 A3
Meris Ln
12500 HOUS 77015 3967 A2
Merit Oaks Dr
11000 MtgC 77382 2673 B6
11000 WDLD 77382 2673 A7
Merit Woods Pl
10 WDLD 77382 2674 D5
Merit Wy Ct
12500 HarC 77065 3539 C4
Merkel St
3500 HOUS 77003 3964 A5
Merle Rd
15800 HarC 77433 3251 D5
Merle St
1800 PASD 77502 4107 B7
2100 PASD 77502 4247 B1
9300 HOUS 77033 4244 A4
Merlet Dr
4100 PRLD 77584 4502 E7
Merlin Ct
- HarC 77379 3111 B1
8800 SPVL 77055 3820 E6
Merlin Dr
8400 SPVL 77055 3821 A7
Merlin Roost Ct
24300 HarC 77494 3953 B3
Merlin Roost Dr
800 HarC 77494 3953 B3
Merlin's Oaks Ct
9500 HarC 77379 3255 C1
Merlin's Oaks Dr
1200 HarC 77379 3255 B2
Merlot River Dr
26800 HarC 77339 3118 C5
Mermaid Ln
2000 HOUS 77062 4507 C2
Merna Dr
9200 HarC 77040 3541 B7
Merona Ln
6300 HarC 77041 3679 B4
Merribrook Ln
800 FRDW 77546 4505 A6
Merrick Dr
700 SGLD 77478 4369 A3
Merrick St
3200 HOUS 77025 4101 C6
Merridel Rd
800 BKHV 77024 3959 C2
800 HDWV 77024 3959 C2
Merrie Ln
4500 BLAR 77401 4101 B3
Merrielane St
100 SHUS 77587 4246 D3
Merriewood Dr
900 FRDW 77546 4629 C2
Merrie Wy Ln
200 PNPV 77024 3959 E5
Merrifield Dr
100 FBnC 77545 4623 B2
Merrilane St
100 BYTN 77520 4113 C1
Merrill Dr
14300 HarC 77532 3553 A6
Merrill St
400 HOUS 77009 3824 A7
900 HOUS 77009 3823 E7
1100 HOUS 77008 3823 E7
Merrill Hills Cir
2200 FBnC 77450 3954 A6
Merrillwood Dr
19500 HarC 77346 3264 D5
Merrimac Dr
2500 LGCY 77573 4631 A6
Merrimac Pk
400 MtgC 77302 2530 A5
Merrimac St
4000 HarC 77093 3546 B7
Merrimac Ridge Ln
600 HarC 77373 2968 E7
Merriman Ct
900 FRDW 77546 4505 A5
Merrimont Ln
6200 HOUS 77085 4240 D7
Merritt Ln
15200 HOUS 77060 3544 C2
Merritt St
- HarC 77044 3549 A3
Merrivale Dr
- HarC 77084 3678 E6
Merriweather St
400 HOUS 77598 4506 D2
4200 SGLD 77478 4369 A7
Merriwether Dr
300 ALVN 77511 4867 D7
Merriwood Ln
6900 HOUS 77076 3684 C4
Merry Ln
1300 LMQU 77568 4989 D2
6600 HOUS 77023 4104 D2
Merry Wy
100 GlsC 77511 4751 C7
100 LGCY 77511 4751 C7
Merryglen Ct
1400 HarC 77373 3259 C1
Merry Meadow Dr
14000 HarC 77049 3828 B4
Merry Merchant St
31300 MtgC 77354 2817 C1
31500 MtgC 77354 2671 C7
Merrymount Ct
400 HarC 77450 3953 E2
Merrymount Dr
22000 HarC 77450 3954 A2
22000 HOUS 77450 3954 A2
22300 HarC 77450 3953 D2
Merry Oaks Dr
24000 HarC 77373 3114 E4
Merry Pine Ct
6100 HarC 77379 3111 E6
Merryvale Dr
10 WDLD 77382 2674 B4
N Merry Weather Cir
10 WDLD 77384 2675 A3
N Merryweather Cir
10 WDLD 77384 2674 D2
10 WDLD 77384 2675 B3
S Merryweather Cir
100 WDLD 77384 2674 D2
100 WDLD 77384 2675 A3
Merryweather Pl
100 WDLD 77384 2674 D2
Merrywether Dr
- HOUS 77504 4247 C7
Mersea Dr
5300 HarC 77449 3676 D6
Mersey Ct
22800 MtgC 77365 2971 E4
Mersey Dr
18000 MtgC 77365 2971 E3
19400 MtgC 77365 2972 A3
Mersey Mnr
10 FBnC 77459 4621 C6
Mersmann Ct
13200 HarC 77014 3402 B2
Mert St
6400 KATY 77493 3813 A7
Merton Ct
1900 HarC 77015 3829 B4
Merton Dr
1600 HarC 77015 3829 B4
Merwin St
4400 HOUS 77027 4101 B1
Mery Tere Ct
4300 RSBG 77471 4491 C6
Mesa Ct
100 PNVL 77304 2237 A4
4400 HarC 77521 3833 B4
Mesa Dr
- BYTN 77521 3973 C2
- HarC 77050 3547 E7
- HarC 77396 3547 D1
- HMBL 77396 3406 D5
2200 DKSN 77539 4754 A4
3400 HOUS 77013 3826 E6
5400 HOUS 77028 3826 E3
5400 HOUS 77078 3826 E4
7700 HOUS 77028 3687 E7
9400 HOUS 77078 3687 E2
10900 HarC 77078 3687 E2
11100 HarC 77016 3687 E1
11900 HarC 77016 3547 E7
11900 HarC 77078 3547 E7
15100 HarC 77396 3406 D7
Mesa Dr FM-527
8200 HOUS 77028 3687 E7
8200 HOUS 77078 3687 E7
10900 HarC 77078 3687 E2
Mesa Grn
- HOUS 77078 3687 D4
Mesa Bluff Ln
- HarC 77396 3547 D1
Mesa Brook Ln
5900 HarC 77041 3679 E5
Mesa Canyon Ct
6500 FBnC 77450 4094 C4
Mesa Creek Ln
11700 HarC 77433 3396 A6
Mesa Crossing Ln
4400 FBnC 77479 4493 C1
Mesa Forest Ln
- HOUS 77078 3687 D4
Mesa Gardens Dr
15700 HarC 77095 3678 D1
15900 HarC 77095 3538 C7
Mesa Hills Ct
- HOUS 77078 3687 D4
Mesa Hills Ln
- HOUS 77078 3687 D4
Mesa Knoll Ln
- HOUS 77078 3687 D4
Mesa Mountain Rd
14100 HarC 77069 3400 A2
Mesa Oaks
18800 MAGA 77355 2815 A1
Mesa Park Dr
- HarC 77067 3401 E4
Mesa Point Ct
9800 HarC 77095 3538 A3
Mesa Point Dr
16400 HarC 77095 3538 A3
Mesa Red Ct
15200 HarC 77433 3250 E5
15200 HarC 77433 3251 C3
Mesa Ridge Dr
9200 MtgC 77303 2239 D3
Mesa Ridge Rd
3600 HOUS 77043 3819 C2
Mesa Run Ln
- HOUS 77078 3687 D4
Mesa Springs Ct
17200 HarC 77095 3538 B2
Mesa Terrace Dr
900 HarC 77450 3954 A3
Mesa Valley Dr
30200 MtgC 77386 2969 E2
Mesa Valley Ln
- HOUS 77078 3687 D4
Mesa Verde Dr
- LGCY 77573 4632 A7
- LGCY 77573 4753 A1
1000 MSCY 77489 4370 C3
1800 DRPK 77536 4109 D7
15700 HOUS 77059 4380 C6
27000 MtgC 77354 2818 D6
Mesa View Ct
- HOUS 77078 3687 E4
Mesa View Ln
- HOUS 77078 3687 D4
Mesa Village Dr
14700 HOUS 77053 4372 E3
Mesa Vista Ct
6500 HarC 77083 4096 D4
Mesa Vista Dr
14700 HarC 77083 4096 D4
Mesa Vista Ter
- HarC 77095 3537 E1
Mesa Wells Dr
11600 HarC 77377 3254 C1
Mescalero Canyon Ct
17600 HarC 77095 3537 C2
Mescalero Canyon Ln
10000 HarC 77095 3537 D3
Mescelero
7100 BYTN 77521 3835 B5
Mesita Dr
14700 HarC 77083 4096 D5
Meskil Oaks Dr
- MtgC 77386 2969 D1
Mesones Dr
7200 FBnC 77083 4095 E6
Mesquite
39500 WlrC 77445 3243 C3
Mesquite Dr
400 MtgC 77354 2673 E2
2700 SGLD 77479 4368 E7
2800 SGLD 77479 4495 D1
10800 LPRT 77571 4250 E4
Mesquite Ln
1100 BYTN 77521 3973 B2
Mesquite Rd
4400 HarC 77093 3546 [illegible]
Mesquite St
700 ALVN 77511 4749 [illegible]
1400 HarC 77093 3545 [illegible]
1400 HOUS 77093 3545 [illegible]
Mesquite Branch Ct
19700 HarC 77388 3113 [illegible]
Mesquite Brush Ln
17300 HarC 77095 3537 [illegible]
Mesquite Canyon Dr
17400 HarC 77095 3537 [illegible]
Mesquite Estates Ln
18100 HarC 77429 3396 [illegible]
Mesquite Grove Ln
- HarC 77429 3253 [illegible]
Mesquite Hollow Ln
12500 SGLD 77478 4237 [illegible]
Mesquite Ridge Dr
2500 HarC 77073 3259 [illegible]
2800 HarC 77338 3259 [illegible]
Mesquite River Tr
24500 HarC 77447 3104 [illegible]
Mesquite Trail Ln
23600 HarC 77373 3115 [illegible]
Messina Ct
1100 PRLD 77581 4504 [illegible]
1300 LGCY 77573 4633 [illegible]
Messina Dr
2300 PRLD 77581 4504 [illegible]
Mestina St
8200 HOUS 77028 3687 [illegible]
Meta St
8400 HOUS 77022 3685 [illegible]
Metairie Ct
2200 LGCY 77573 4631 [illegible]
Metcalf
4900 HOUS 77053 4371 [illegible]
7000 FBnC 77545 4498 [illegible]
7000 HOUS 77489 4371 [illegible]
7000 HOUS 77489 4498 [illegible]
7000 HOUS 77545 4498 [illegible]
Metcalf St
2600 HOUS 77012 4105 [illegible]
2900 HOUS 77017 4105 [illegible]
Meters St
300 HOUS 77020 3965 [illegible]
Metha
26700 HarC 77373 3114 [illegible]
Methil Dr
17500 HarC 77379 3255 [illegible]
Methil Birsay St
16800 HarC 77379 3255 [illegible]
Methodist St
7000 HTCK 77563 4988 [illegible]
Methvin Ln
5000 HarC 77532 3413 [illegible]
Metro Blvd
- HarC 77082 4097 [illegible]
- HarC 77083 4097 [illegible]
Metrodale Dr
8500 HarC 77040 3541 [illegible]
Metronome Dr
10100 HOUS 77043 3820 [illegible]
10100 HOUS 77080 3820 [illegible]
10300 HOUS 77043 3819 E
Metropolitan
1400 HOUS 77006 3962 [illegible]
1400 HOUS 77019 3962 [illegible]
Mettler Ct
1000 FBnC 77469 4493 [illegible]
Mettler Ln
5900 FBnC 77469 4493 [illegible]
Metts Rd
11300 MtgC 77306 2533 [illegible]
Metycove Ct
3300 HarC 77532 3409 [illegible]
Metycove Dr
- HarC 77532 3410 [illegible]
18200 HarC 77532 3409 E
Metz Ln
500 BzaC 77511 4747 [illegible]
Metz St
2400 HOUS 77034 4246 [illegible]
Metzler Creek Dr
25200 HarC 77389 2965 E
Mews Ln
12500 HOUS 77082 4097 [illegible]
N Mews Wood Ct
10 WDLD 77384 2821 [illegible]
S Mews Wood Ct
10 WDLD 77381 2821 [illegible]
10 WDLD 77384 2821 [illegible]
Mexican John Rd
21400 MtgC 77357 2827 [illegible]
Mexican School Rd
- SGLD 77479 4368 [illegible]
E Meyer Av
700 SEBK 77586 4509 [illegible]
700 SEBK 77586 4510 [illegible]
N Meyer Av
3400 SEBK 77586 4509 [illegible]
Meyer Rd
10 HarC 77336 2976 [illegible]
10 HarC 77336 2977 [illegible]
10 HarC 77357 2976 [illegible]
10 LbyC 77327 2977 [illegible]
100 HarC 77562 3692 [illegible]
1700 HarC 77073 3259 [illegible]
E Meyer Rd
500 SEBK 77586 4510 [illegible]
N Meyer Rd
900 SEBK 77586 4509 [illegible]
Meyer St
300 ALVN 77511 4867 [illegible]
1000 LMQU 77568 4990 [illegible]
3200 HOUS 77087 4104 [illegible]
Meyer Forest Dr
9500 HOUS 77096 4241 [illegible]
9700 HOUS 77035 4241 [illegible]
Meyer Park Blvd
- HOUS 77096 4241 [illegible]
Meyer Park Dr
- HOUS 77096 4101 [illegible]
- HOUS 77096 4241 [illegible]
Meyers
1400 BYTN 77520 3973 [illegible]
Meyersville Dr
14000 HarC 77049 3828 [illegible]
Meyerwood Dr
4100 HOUS 77025 4241 [illegible]
4300 HOUS 77096 4241 [illegible]
Meyrick Ct
16100 HarC 77379 3256 [illegible]
Miami Ct
2700 FRDW 77546 4629 [illegible]
Miami Rd
1300 PASD 77502 4107 [illegible]

STREET Block City ZIP Map# Grid

iami Rd
1300 PASD 77506 4107 A6
iami St
7200 HMBL 77396 3406 B3
ica Dr
3500 HOUS 77082 4097 C2
i Castillo Ct
4600 HOUS 77045 4372 C1
Michael Cir
11700 MSCY 77071 4239 E7
Michael Cir
11800 MSCY 77071 4239 E7
ichael Dr
800 ALVN 77511 4867 D1
900 PASD 77506 4107 D5
1200 HMBL 77338 3407 A1
4800 HOUS 77017 4106 A6
21800 MtgC 77355 2960 D6
ichael Ln
2000 PRLD 77581 4502 D2
19800 MtgC 77365 3117 C2
ichael St
2900 GlsC 77518 4634 B2
ichaelangelo St
2400 RMFT 77357 2829 A1
2700 MtgC 77357 2829 A1
ichaelis St
2900 HarC 77521 3834 E5
ichael Wayne Rd
2600 FBnC 77583 4622 A4
ichaux St
2500 HOUS 77009 3962 E1
2900 HOUS 77009 3823 E7
icheal Rd
- MtgC 77354 2818 A1
icheala Wy
21500 HarC 77338 3260 A2
ichel Rd
- TMBL 77377 3109 A2
13500 TMBL 77375 3109 A2
ichele Dr
1800 SGLD 77478 4236 E5
1800 SGLD 77478 4237 A6
icheline Cir
7800 MSCY 77071 4239 E7
ichelle Ct
9000 HOUS 77040 3682 A2
ichelle Dr
34500 MtgC 77362 2816 D6
34500 SGCH 77362 2816 D6
ichels Ln
1700 HOUS 77055 3821 E5
ichigan Av
200 HOUS 77017 4246 C2
200 SHUS 77017 4246 C2
500 SHUS 77587 4246 B3
Michigan Av
100 LGCY 77573 4632 A2
ichigan St
1400 HOUS 77006 3962 D6
1700 HOUS 77019 3962 C6
3100 BYTN 77520 4112 A1
3400 BYTN 77520 4111 E1
ichnic Ln
9400 HarC 77070 3399 E5
ichulka Ln
10400 HOUS 77093 3685 C3
icke
22000 MtgC 77357 2973 E2
23100 MtgC 77357 2974 A2
ickey Wy
1200 SPVL 77055 3820 E7
ickle Creek Dr
1700 HarC 77530 3829 E4
ickleham Dr
16000 HarC 77379 3256 A6
ickler St
9700 HOUS 77025 4241 C1
ickleton Dr
8700 HarC 77088 3543 D7
ickwayne Ct
6900 HarC 77069 3400 A2
icliff Blvd
2300 HarC 77068 3257 D4
2300 HarC 77090 3257 E4
icmac Ct
14100 HarC 77429 3253 E5
icollet St
6100 HOUS 77016 3547 A7
7700 HarC 77016 3547 C7
id Ln
2000 HOUS 77027 3961 C6
id Wy
5700 HOUS 77339 3119 B1
5700 MtgC 77365 3119 B1
idas Ln
800 ALVN 77511 4867 B4
E Midaugh St
10 GlsC 77563 4990 A5
idbrook Dr
- HOUS 77546 4506 D6
idday Sun Pl
10 WDLD 77382 2819 A1
iddle St
400 HOUS 77003 3964 A4
600 GLSN 77550 5109 A3
iddle Tr
37100 MtgC 77354 2816 A1
iddle Bayou Rd
100 HOUS 77034 4378 C1
iddle Bluff Tr
14400 HarC 77429 3395 E1
iddle Borondo
10 LMQU 77568 4989 C3
Middlebrook Dr
- HOUS 77058 4380 E6
- PASD 77058 4380 D4
14200 HOUS 77058 4381 A7
14200 HOUS 77058 4507 E1
14200 HOUS 77058 4508 A1
14200 PASD 77058 4507 E1
14200 PASD 77058 4508 A1
15200 PASD 77058 4381 A6
16100 HOUS 77059 4380 D4
16100 PASD 77059 4380 D4
Middleburgh Dr
11000 HarC 77377 3255 A6
11400 HarC 77377 3254 E6
Middlebury Ln
8100 HarC 77070 3399 D2
Middle Canyon Rd
8400 FBnC 77494 4093 A4
Middle Creek Dr
2000 HOUS 77339 3118 E4
2200 HOUS 77339 3119 A4
Middlecreek St
900 FRDW 77546 4629 D4

Middlecrest Ln
3800 FBnC 77469 4615 E5
11600 HarC 77375 3109 E5
Middledale Ln
- HarC 77047 4374 B4
Middle Falls Dr
4800 HOUS 77345 3119 E6
4800 HOUS 77345 3120 A6
Middlefield Dr
6800 PASD 77505 4249 A6
Middle Forest Dr
16800 PASD 77059 4380 E4
Middlegate Ln
19800 FBnC 77469 4094 D5
Middle Gate Pl
10 WDLD 77382 2819 E2
Middleglen Ln
10200 HOUS 77034 4378 C2
Middleham Ln
12800 STFE 77510 4871 A7
12900 STFE 77510 4870 E7
Middle Lake Ct
6400 FBnC 77450 4094 A4
Middle Oaks Blvd
15000 HarC 77082 4096 C2
Middle Park St
1400 PASD 77504 4247 D7
Middle Parkway Dr
15200 MtgC 77302 2677 B2
Middlerose Ln
10400 HarC 77070 3399 B3
Middlesbough Ln
12700 HarC 77066 3401 B3
Middlesbrough Ln
- MSCY 77478 4369 B6
- SGLD 77478 4369 B6
1600 MSCY 77459 4369 B6
Middleton Rd
4900 BYTN 77520 3971 C1
Middleton St
100 GlsC 77518 4634 A1
300 HOUS 77003 3963 E5
500 KMAH 77539 4634 A2
Middle Torch
10 HTCK 77563 5105 A5
Middletrace Ln
3000 LGCY 77539 4752 E4
Middlewood St
7500 HOUS 77057 3960 A5
7500 HOUS 77063 3960 A5
Midfield Dr
6600 HOUS 77092 3821 C1
Midfield Glen Ct
13600 HOUS 77059 4379 D5
Midforest Dr
3900 HarC 77068 3257 B7
Midgeley St
5900 HOUS 77091 3683 D5
Midhurst Dr
11000 HOUS 77072 4098 B4
Midlake Pk
31700 MtgC 77385 2823 B6
Midland Ct
700 HarC 77060 3544 E4
Midland Dr
400 HarC 77037 3544 B4
400 HOUS 77037 3544 B4
3600 BzaC 77578 4501 B7
3600 BzaC 77578 4625 B1
Midland St
29600 MtgC 77354 2817 E3
29600 MtgC 77354 2818 A3
Midland Creek Dr
12500 HarC 77377 3254 B3
Midland Fields Dr
13700 HarC 77083 4097 A7
Midland Forest Dr
7900 HarC 77088 3682 C2
Midlane Dr
12500 BKVL 77581 4375 D6
Midlane St
- LbyC 77327 2538 C4
- LbyC 77372 2538 C4
10 LbyC 77327 2537 E4
10 LbyC 77372 2537 E4
3000 HOUS 77027 3961 B7
3300 HOUS 77027 4101 B1
27400 MtgC 77372 2683 E4
Midline Rd
- LbyC 77327 2537 E4
- MtgC 77372 2537 D4
26800 SPLD 77372 2537 D4
Mid Ln St
3200 HOUS 77027 3961 B7
Midlothian Ln
2000 HOUS 77339 3118 A6
Midmont Ct
2400 MSCY 77489 4370 E6
Midnight Dawn Dr
16900 FBnC 77469 4235 D1
Midnight Moon Dr
- WDLD 77382 2674 D5
Midnight Sky Ct
16900 FBnC 77469 4235 D1
Midnight Star Cir
2600 HarC 77546 4506 B7
Midnight Sun Dr
16900 FBnC 77469 4235 D1
Mid Oak Ct
17800 HarC 77379 3111 D7
Mid Peak Wy
21600 HarC 77449 3676 A7
Mid-Pine Dr
10 PNVL 77304 2237 B3
Mid Pines Dr
5900 HarC 77069 3256 C7
6300 HarC 77069 3400 B1
Midridge Dr
15600 HarC 77084 3679 A5
Midships Wy
16900 HarC 77532 3552 A1
Midstream Dr
4100 MSCY 77459 4369 C6
Midsummer Pl
10 WDLD 77381 2674 C6
Midtown Pk
- ALVN 77511 4749 B6
- BzaC 77511 4749 B6
Midtown Park Dr
- ALVN 77511 4749 B6
Midvale St
6000 HOUS 77087 4104 D7
Midway Blvd
700 HOUS 77029 3965 E6
Midway Ct
2100 LGCY 77573 4631 B7
Midway Dr
100 BYTN 77521 3973 A4

Midway Rd
100 HarC 77373 3114 B2
11500 MtgC 77372 2537 B3
Midway St
100 HarC 77373 3114 A2
6500 HOUS 77028 3826 C2
Midway Pass Ct
3300 HarC 77373 3115 B3
Midway Plaza Dr
- HarC 77338 3260 D4
- HOUS 77338 3260 D4
Midwood Cir
10 CNRO 77301 2384 B7
Midwood Ct
11900 HarC 77067 3402 B5
Mierianne
- HarC 77039 3545 C6
Mierianne St
2700 HarC 77093 3545 E7
4400 HarC 77093 3546 B7
W Mierianne St
400 HarC 77037 3544 B7
500 HOUS 77037 3544 B7
900 HOUS 77088 3544 A7
Mier Manor Ct
8200 FBnC 77469 4234 B4
Mierwood Manor Dr
13500 HarC 77429 3397 B3
Mierwoods Dr
1600 HarC 77379 3110 C7
Mi Estado Ct
4600 HOUS 77045 4372 C2
Mighty Buccaneer Dr
3300 HarC 77546 4506 C6
Mighty Elm Ct
6200 HOUS 77345 3120 C4
Mighty Falls Ct
7500 HarC 77095 3537 E7
Mighty Oak Dr
12000 HarC 77066 3401 A3
12800 HarC 77066 3400 E2
12800 HarC 77069 3400 E1
Mighty Redwood Ct
16700 PASD 77059 4380 E4
Mighty Redwood Dr
11500 PASD 77059 4380 E5
Mignon Ln
400 HOUS 77024 3958 D3
Mija Ln
1400 SEBK 77586 4509 D1
Mikado St
100 HOUS 77011 4105 A1
Mike St
6600 HTCK 77563 4989 B5
Mike Gaido Blvd
700 GLSN 77550 5108 E4
1800 GLSN 77550 5109 A6
Milam Cir
12000 GlsC 77510 4871 B2
Milam Dr
1200 GLSN 77551 5108 D5
11700 LPRT 77571 4111 A7
Milam Ln
- PRLD 77583 4500 D5
Milam St
100 HOUS 77002 3963 C4
1600 LMQU 77568 4989 D2
2200 HOUS 77006 3963 A7
4000 HOUS 77006 3962 E7
4800 HOUS 77006 4102 E1
4800 HOUS 77006 4102 E1
N Milam St
10 HOUS 77002 3963 C3
Milam Branch Ln
- RSBG 77469 4491 E5
Milan Dr
13700 HOUS 77047 4373 B4
Milani Ridge Ct
4500 MtgC 77386 3115 E1
Milano Ct
10900 FBnC 77469 4232 E1
Milano Ln
- LGCY 77573 4632 E3
Milart St
5100 HOUS 77021 4104 A6
6400 HOUS 77021 4103 E7
Milas Wy
9500 FBnC 77478 4236 A2
Milbrad St
3400 HOUS 77026 3825 B6
Milburn Dr
2600 LGCY 77573 4508 D7
Milburn St
3200 HOUS 77021 4103 B4
Milby St
- HOUS 77004 3963 E7
100 HOUS 77003 3964 A6
600 HOUS 77023 3964 A6
700 SEBK 77586 4509 E2
1200 HOUS 77003 3963 E6
1300 HOUS 77023 3963 E7
2400 HOUS 77004 4103 E1
N Milby St
10 HOUS 77003 3964 A5
Milda Dr
- HarC 77088 3682 C1
9900 HOUS 77088 3682 C1
10100 HOUS 77088 3542 B7
Mildenhall Ct
6400 HarC 77084 3678 B3
Mildoge St
4800 HOUS 77048 4243 D7
Mildred Ln
36000 MtgC 77362 2816 C1
Mildred St
1300 BzaC 77583 4623 D5
1300 PRLD 77583 4623 D5
4300 BLAR 77401 4101 B6
4300 HOUS 77401 4101 B6
Mile Dr
11400 HarC 77065 3398 C6
12400 HarC 77429 3398 C6
Mileham Dr
21700 HarC 77388 3113 A2
Milehouse Ct
- HarC 77044 3549 B3
Milepost Ct
10 WDLD 77382 2819 A3
Mile Run Rd
8500 HarC 77346 3265 D6
Miles Rd
100 GlsC 77518 4634 B2
800 LGCY 77539 4634 B2
Miles St
1000 RSBG 77471 4491 B4
1300 HOUS 77015 3967 C3
1800 HarC 77015 3967 C4

Milestone Ln
14400 HarC 77429 3397 D2
Milestone Rd
1200 CNRO 77304 2383 C2
Miley
8200 HOUS 77028 3826 C3
Miley St
7100 HOUS 77028 3825 E3
7700 HOUS 77028 3826 B3
Milfoil Ln
- HOUS 77083 4097 B4
Milford Pl
2300 HarC 77014 3402 A3
Milford St
900 HOUS 77006 4102 D1
1600 HOUS 77098 4102 C1
Milholland Dr
1700 MtgC 77386 2969 A1
Military Dr
9900 CNRO 77303 2238 E7
10000 MtgC 77303 2238 E7
Mill Av
200 CNRO 77301 2384 A6
600 CNRO 77301 2383 E6
Mill Cir
15300 MtgC 77354 2669 D1
Mill Ct
12500 HarC 77070 3399 B5
N Mill Dr
41100 MtgC 77354 2669 D1
Mill Hllw
3300 FBnC 77459 4621 E5
Mill Ln
2100 HarC 77373 3114 B2
4100 MSCY 77459 4497 D3
11800 HarC 77070 3399 C7
S Mill Ln
12000 HarC 77089 4505 A2
Mill Pt
10100 FBnC 77459 4621 E6
Mill Rd
14600 HarC 77396 3547 A1
14600 HOUS 77396 3547 A1
Mill St
100 SGLD 77478 4367 E2
100 SGLD 77478 4368 A3
Mill Wy
- HarC 77429 3398 E5
Millard
7700 HOUS 77028 3826 B5
Millard St
7700 HOUS 77028 3826 B5
Millay Ct
10 WDLD 77382 2819 A2
Millbanks Dr
12200 HOUS 77031 4239 A6
Mill Bend Ct
15300 MtgC 77354 2669 C1
N Millbend Dr
1200 WDLD 77380 2822 A6
3000 WDLD 77380 2821 C7
3100 MtgC 77380 2821 C7
10900 WDLD 77380 2967 C1
S Millbend Dr
700 WDLD 77380 2822 B7
1700 WDLD 77380 2821 E7
2400 WDLD 77380 2967 E1
2700 MtgC 77380 2967 D2
Millbrae Ln
7400 HarC 77041 3679 B1
7500 HarC 77041 3539 B7
Mill Branch Ln
14900 FBnC 77478 4236 D5
Mill Bridge Ct
11500 FBnC 77478 4236 D6
Millbridge Dr
3600 HOUS 77059 4380 D6
Mill Bridge Wy
- HOUS 77339 3119 C2
3600 HOUS 77345 3119 C2
Millbrook Ct
21600 FBnC 77450 4094 A4
Millbrook Dr
3100 BzaC 77584 4501 B6
7800 HarC 77095 3538 B6
Millbrook Ln
3100 MSCY 77459 4496 E3
Millbrook St
200 PNPV 77024 3959 D5
Millbury Dr
1600 MSCY 77489 4370 E4
9400 HOUS 77096 4241 A2
Mill Canyon Ct
15900 HarC 77429 3397 A2
Mill Creek Ct
34200 MtgC 77362 2816 E6
Mill Creek Dr
1800 HOUS 77008 3822 C5
2200 SGLD 77478 4368 E6
2600 PASD 77503 4248 E1
4300 BYTN 77521 3833 C3
Mill Creek Rd
300 MtgC 77362 2816 E6
40000 MtgC 77354 2670 A2
40600 MtgC 77354 2669 C1
Mill Creek Wy
33800 MtgC 77362 2816 E6
33900 MtgC 77362 2817 A6
Millcrest Ln
9300 FBnC 77083 4236 A1
Millcroft Pl
10 SGLD 77479 4495 B3
Millcross Ln
23300 FBnC 77494 3953 D5
Mill Crossing Ln
2000 HarC 77450 3954 C5
Mill Dale Ct
8500 FBnC 77479 4494 B6
Milldale Dr
- HarC 77070 3399 B5
Millennium Forest Dr
- WDLD 77381 2674 E7
Miller Av
300 GlsC 77565 4509 D5
700 KMAH 77565 4509 D5
1300 KATY 77493 3813 D7
Miller Blvd
- DRPK 77536 4249 C3
- PASD 77505 4249 C3
Miller Cir
4800 MtgC 77302 2677 C1
Miller Dr
8000 HTCK 77563 4988 D4
Miller Rd
- MtgC 77382 2673 A6
- WDLD 77382 2673 A6
100 MtgC 77354 2671 D7
8300 MtgC 77354 2673 A5

Miller Rd
8600 MtgC 77354 2672 E5
Miller St
1400 HOUS 77003 3963 E7
4100 GlsC 77518 4634 B3
10000 HarC 77086 3541 D2
Miller Cut Off Rd
300 HarC 77571 4110 D5
300 LPRT 77571 4110 D5
2400 DRPK 77536 4110 A1
2400 HarC 77536 4110 A1
Miller Glen Ln
7600 HOUS 77072 4097 C6
Miller House Dr
15400 HarC 77086 3541 D1
Miller Ranch Rd
1500 PRLD 77584 4501 B3
2100 BzaC 77584 4501 B4
Miller Rd 1
15200 HarC 77049 3690 E7
15700 HarC 77049 3691 A7
Miller Rd 2
6300 HarC 77049 3829 D3
6300 HarC 77530 3829 D3
7000 HarC 77049 3690 D6
Miller Rd 3
7800 HarC 77049 3690 B5
Millers Wy
7900 HarC 77095 3538 B6
Millers Creek Ct
4300 FBnC 77469 4234 D5
Millers Creek Rd
4300 FBnC 77469 4234 D4
Millers Falls Ct
2600 FBnC 77469 4365 A2
Millers Landing Dr
15900 HarC 77049 3829 D2
Millers Oak Ln
3000 FBnC 77478 4236 A7
3100 FBnC 77478 4235 E7
Millers Pass
37500 MtgC 77362 2670 D7
Millers Run Ln
15100 FBnC 77478 4236 D4
Millerton Ln
2200 HarC 77450 3954 B6
Miller Valley Dr
5800 HarC 77066 3400 D2
Millerview Dr
6300 HOUS 77091 3684 C5
Miller Wilson Rd
17000 HarC 77532 3411 D4
17000 HarC 77532 3552 D2
Millet St
8200 HOUS 77012 4105 D4
Mill Falls Dr
12700 HarC 77038 3543 A3
Mill Ferry Ln
19100 HarC 77449 3677 B4
Millford Ct
6600 HarC 77049 3829 A2
Mill Forest Rd
17000 HarC 77598 4507 B5
Mill Garden Cir
10100 FBnC 77459 4621 D7
Mill Garden Ct
13800 HOUS 77059 4379 E5
Millgate Dr
22400 HarC 77373 3116 A7
22700 HarC 77373 3115 E7
Millglen Ct
14100 SGLD 77478 4236 E5
Millgrove Ln
900 HDWV 77024 3959 C1
Mill Hedge Dr
12500 HarC 77070 3399 B5
Mill Hollow Dr
15800 HarC 77084 3678 E7
Millhouse Cir
21500 HarC 77073 3259 D2
Millhouse Ct
21500 HarC 77073 3259 D2
Millhouse Rd
1700 HarC 77073 3259 D2
14500 MtgC 77362 2670 D7
Mill House Run
3200 FBnC 77459 4621 E6
Millican Dr
15900 MtgC 77372 2684 A5
Millicent St
8200 HOUS 77093 3824 E1
8300 HOUS 77093 3685 E7
Millie St
1000 RSBG 77471 4491 B4
Millie's Rd
2800 GLSN 77554 5220 C5
Millies Creek Ln
26300 HarC 77433 3396 B6
Milliken St
7500 HOUS 77016 3825 B2
Millikens Bnd
- LGCY 77573 4753 B1
Millingham Ct
4600 HOUS 77345 3119 E6
Mill Ln Dr
12400 HarC 77070 3399 C5
Mill Oak Dr
4200 HarC 77084 3816 C1
Milloak Dr
19100 HarC 77346 3264 E6
Milloak Station Ct
19200 HarC 77346 3264 D6
Millpark Dr
2100 WDLD 77380 2967 E1
Millpass Ln
26700 HarC 77433 3537 A1
Mill Path Ct
18500 HarC 77084 3816 D5
Mill Pl Ct
400 SGLD 77478 4368 A1
Mill Point Dr
16200 HOUS 77059 4380 C5
16400 PASD 77059 4380 C5
Mill Point Pl
10 WDLD 77380 2967 C2
Millpond Dr
700 SGLD 77478 4368 B1
Mill Pond Ln
25700 HarC 77373 3114 C1
N Millport Cir
100 WDLD 77382 2673 E5
100 WDLD 77382 2674 A5
S Millport Cir
10 WDLD 77382 2674 A5
100 WDLD 77382 2673 D6
Millport Dr
10 WDLD 77382 2674 A5

Millport St
6500 HOUS 77092 3682 C6
Mill Ridge Dr
- HarC 77065 3398 E6
12300 HarC 77429 3398 E4
Millridge Ln
16600 HarC 77095 3538 A6
Millridge Pns
10800 HarC 77070 3399 A5
Millridge Bend Dr
10200 HarC 77070 3399 B5
Millridge Forest Ct
12400 HarC 77070 3399 A4
Millridge North Dr
10200 HarC 77070 3399 B5
10800 HarC 77429 3399 A5
Millridge Pines Ct
12400 HarC 77070 3399 A4
Mill River Ct
4400 PASD 77505 4248 D5
Millrock Cir
3900 SGLD 77479 4495 E1
Mill Run Dr
900 SGLD 77478 4368 A1
1000 SGLD 77478 4237 C7
7800 HarC 77095 3538 B6
Mills
1800 HOUS 77026 3964 A1
Mills Cir
10500 HarC 77070 3399 B4
Mills Ct
1700 HOUS 77026 3964 B4
Mills Ln
700 FRDW 77546 4629 B3
12100 HarC 77065 3398 D6
Mills Rd
8000 HOUS 77064 3400 A6
8600 HarC 77064 3399 E5
8600 HOUS 77064 3399 E5
8900 HOUS 77070 3399 D5
9000 HarC 77070 3399 D5
11100 HarC 77429 3399 A4
22900 MtgC 77365 2972 D4
Mills St
- HTCK 77563 4989 C5
1600 WALR 77484 3102 A5
1800 HOUS 77026 3963 D1
2800 HOUS 77026 3964 B4
Mills Wy
10600 HarC 77070 3399 B4
Millsap Cir
- WDLD 77382 2673 C6
N Millsap Cir
- WDLD 77382 2673 B6
Millsap Hollow Ln
26600 FBnC 77494 4092 B2
Mills Bend St
12900 HarC 77070 3399 B4
Mills Branch Dr
- HOUS 77365 3120 A3
2300 HOUS 77345 3120 A3
2600 HOUS 77345 3119 D1
2700 HOUS 77339 3119 C1
2700 HOUS 77365 3119 C1
2700 MtgC 77365 3119 C1
20300 MtgC 77365 2972 D7
22000 MtgC 77365 3117 E1
22000 MtgC 77365 3118 A1
Mills Breeze Dr
12800 HarC 77070 3399 C4
Millscott Dr
12500 HarC 77070 3399 B5
Mills Cove
10500 HarC 77070 3399 B4
Mills Creek Ct
1700 HOUS 77339 3118 C6
Mills Creek Dr
2300 HOUS 77339 3118 D6
Mills Creek Rd
11000 MtgC 77304 2236 C2
Mills Crossing Ln
12800 HarC 77070 3399 C4
Mills Cut St
10600 HarC 77070 3399 B4
Mills Flat St
10600 HarC 77070 3399 C4
Mill Shadow Ct
1000 SGLD 77478 4367 E1
Mill Shadow Dr
1000 SGLD 77478 4367 D1
9700 HarC 77070 3399 C5
Millshaw Dr
10300 HarC 77070 3399 B5
Millshire Wy
7600 HarC 77095 3538 B6
Millsite Rd
13300 HarC 77050 3548 B6
13300 HarC 77078 3548 B6
Mills Lake Ct
24800 FBnC 77494 3952 E4
Mills Lake Dr
2300 HOUS 77339 3119 B6
Mills Landing St
10600 HarC 77070 3399 B4
Mills Manor Dr
24900 FBnC 77494 3952 D4
Mills Meadow Ln
19500 HarC 77094 3955 A4
Mill Song Ct
1000 SGLD 77478 4367 D1
1000 SGLD 77478 4368 B2
Mills Park Ln
14600 HarC 77429 3396 C1
Mills Pass Ct
25000 FBnC 77494 3952 C4
Mills Pass Dr
10200 HarC 77070 3399 C4
Mills Pass Wy
1500 FBnC 77494 3952 D4
Mills Point Dr
10300 HarC 77070 3399 C5
Mills Point Ln
5800 FBnC 77469 4493 B6
Mills Prairie St
10600 HarC 77070 3399 B4
Millspring Dr
3600 HOUS 77080 3820 D2
Mill Springs Dr
17500 HarC 77379 3256 C2
Mills Rapids St
13100 HarC 77070 3399 B4
Mills Ridge Ct
26000 MtgC 77339 3118 D4
Mills River St
13100 HarC 77070 3399 B4
Mills Run Dr
10200 HarC 77070 3399 C4

Mills Station Ct
14300 HarC 77429 3397 C1
Millstead Ct
15700 HarC 77084 3678 D5
Millstone Ct
900 SGLD 77478 4237 C7
900 SGLD 77478 4368 A1
Millstone Dr
2200 HarC 77073 3259 D3
2200 HOUS 77073 3259 D3
Millstone St
- HarC 77095 3538 B6
Millstone Estates Ln
14300 HarC 77429 3396 B2
Millstone Hollow Ln
26600 FBnC 77494 4092 A2
Millstone Ridge Ln
19700 HarC 77449 3677 A6
19800 HarC 77449 3676 E6
Millstone Valley Ct
900 HarC 77373 2968 E5
Mills Trace Ct
1800 HarC 77450 3954 D4
Mills Trail Ln
12800 HarC 77070 3399 C4
Mill Stream Ct
300 HOUS 77060 3544 C1
1300 FBnC 77479 4494 B7
Mill Stream Ln
100 HOUS 77060 3544 C1
Millstream Wy
12100 HarC 77041 3679 E6
12100 HarC 77041 3680 A6
Millstream Bend Ln
12900 HarC 77377 3254 A2
13000 HarC 77377 3253 D3
Mills View Rd
9300 HOUS 77070 3399 D4
Mills Walk Dr
10400 HarC 77070 3399 C4
Mills Wharf St
10600 HarC 77070 3399 C4
Mill Trace Dr
- FBnC 77479 4494 B6
- WDLD 77381 2821 B2
N Mill Trace Dr
- WDLD 77381 2821 B2
S Mill Trace Dr
100 WDLD 77381 2821 B2
Mill Trail Ct
200 SGLD 77478 4368 A1
Mill Trail Dr
100 SGLD 77478 4367 D1
100 SGLD 77478 4368 A1
Mill Trail Ln
12000 HarC 77070 3399 C6
Millvale Dr
2300 HOUS 77345 3120 A6
Mill Valley Dr
- SGLD 77478 4237 A7
900 SGLD 77478 4368 A1
Mill Valley Rd
11700 HOUS 77048 4243 D7
11700 HOUS 77048 4374 D1
Millvan Dr
12400 HarC 77070 3399 B6
Mill View Ln
9300 HarC 77396 3407 B2
E Mill Village Cir
17300 HarC 77095 3537 E6
W Mill Village Cir
17300 HarC 77095 3537 C6
Millville Dr
600 HOUS 77091 3684 A3
Millway Dr
12400 HarC 77070 3399 B5
Mill Wheel Dr
12500 HarC 77070 3399 B5
Mill Wheel Ln
- HarC 77070 3399 B4
Millwood Dr
- FBnC 77479 4493 D5
1800 HOUS 77008 3822 D5
Millwood Hill Dr
16800 HarC 77095 3538 A4
Millwood Lake Dr
2800 MSCY 77459 4496 B1
Millwright Pl
10 WDLD 77382 2819 D2
10 WDLD 77382 2820 A2
Milly
7000 BKVL 77581 4376 A7
Milner Dr
- BYTN 77520 3970 E4
- BYTN 77520 3971 A5
Milner Rd
14600 HarC 77032 3546 A1
14600 HOUS 77032 3546 A1
15100 HOUS 77032 3405 A6
Milner Pass Ln
- HarC 77346 3408 B4
Milners Point Dr
11300 HarC 77066 3401 D6
Milo Dr
13200 HarC 77532 3692 D1
13500 HarC 77532 3552 D7
Milored
8600 HOUS 77029 3965 D5
Milredge St
8000 HOUS 77017 4245 E2
8100 HOUS 77017 4246 A1
Milroy Ln
2500 HarC 77066 3401 D6
2500 HarC 77067 3401 E6
Milton St
4100 WUNP 77005 4101 C3
Milwaukee St
200 HOUS 77009 3824 C4
2400 HOUS 77026 3824 E4
Milwee St
4800 HOUS 77092 3821 E2
4800 HOUS 77092 3822 A2
Mimbrough St
9700 HOUS 77029 3966 A5
9800 GNPK 77547 3966 A5
9800 HOUS 77547 3966 A5
Mimosa Av
700 PASD 77506 4106 E6
700 PASD 77506 4107 A6
Mimosa Cir
4700 FBnC 77469 4233 A7
4700 FBnC 77469 4364 A1
Mimosa Ct
2200 LGCY 77573 4631 B6
Mimosa Dr
200 HTCK 77563 4988 C4
2200 HOUS 77019 3962 B6
4500 BLAR 77401 4101 B7

STREET Block City ZIP Map# Grid

Mimosa Dr
5100 BLAR 77401 4100 E7
5200 BLAR 77096 4100 D7
5200 HOUS 77096 4100 D7
18700 BzaC 77584 4627 B4
18800 BzaC 77511 4627 B4
18800 PRLD 77584 4627 B4
Mimosa Ln
- LGCY 77573 4752 D1
- MtgC 77372 2682 E6
1400 RSBG 77471 4490 D5
4800 FBnC 77469 4233 A7
5500 FBnC 77469 4364 A1
12000 HarC 77429 3398 C2
14700 MtgC 77302 2677 B1
Mimosa Rd
700 HarC 77038 3544 A6
700 HOUS 77037 3544 A6
700 HOUS 77038 3544 A6
1200 HarC 77038 3543 D6
1200 MSCY 77489 4370 C4
1500 STAF 77477 4370 C4
1500 STAF 77489 4370 C4
Mimosa St
600 FBnC 77545 4623 A3
10900 MtgC 77372 2536 E1
Mimosa Wy
3400 SGLD 77479 4495 E2
Mimosa Glen Dr
3400 HarC 77388 3112 E5
Mimosa Springs Dr
12800 HarC 77377 3254 A3
Mimosa View Ln
6800 HarC 77086 3542 C4
Minchen Dr
1300 DRPK 77536 4109 C5
Mincing Ln
15200 HarC 77530 3829 D5
Minden St
5400 HOUS 77026 3825 D4
Mindybrook Ct
11600 MtgC 77303 2239 C4
Mindy Park Ct
5300 HarC 77069 3256 C6
Mindy Park Ln
14200 HarC 77069 3256 C6
Mindy Wood Ct
15800 HarC 77068 3257 B4
Miner Ln
9800 HarC 77562 3694 A7
Mineral Creek Ct
5400 HarC 77379 3112 A7
Mineral Haven Dr
4100 HOUS 77048 4374 E5
Mineral Junction Dr
- HarC 77095 3537 E3
Mineral Springs Cir
14700 HarC 77396 3547 D3
Mineral Springs Ln
8500 HarC 77396 3547 D3
Mineral Wells Dr
- FBnC 77478 4236 B6
Miners Bend Ct
6400 FBnC 77469 4493 C4
Miners Bend Dr
- HarC 77095 3538 A1
Miners Bend Ln
1300 FBnC 77469 4493 C5
Minetta St
- MSCY 77071 4240 A7
14200 HOUS 77035 4240 A7
Minglewood Blvd
3500 HOUS 77023 4104 C5
Minglewood Ln
1200 FRDW 77546 4629 D1
Minimax Dr
2300 HOUS 77008 3822 C6
Mink Cir
18900 MtgC 77355 2815 A5
Mink Creek Ct
32100 MtgC 77355 2668 B6
Mink Lake Dr
18900 MtgC 77355 2815 A5
Minn Rd
- PRVW 77445 3100 A4
- WlrC 77445 3100 B4
Minnesota Av
4000 SHUS 77587 4246 C4
Minnesota St
2100 HOUS 77034 4246 C5
2100 SHUS 77034 4246 C5
2100 SHUS 77587 4246 C5
3200 BYTN 77520 4112 A1
3300 BYTN 77520 3972 A7
4200 DKSN 77539 4754 A3
9500 HOUS 77075 4377 C1
10800 HOUS 77075 4246 C7
Minnie Ln
7300 BzaC 77584 4627 B4
Minnow Lake Dr
17400 MtgC 77384 2676 A6
Minola St
6400 HOUS 77007 3961 E2
Minola Oaks Dr
- HarC 77064 3540 B7
Minonite Rd
3500 FBnC 77469 4616 A7
Minonite Rd FM-2977
3500 FBnC 77469 4616 A7
Minor St
5900 HOUS 77085 4240 E7
Minsmere Cir
9200 HarC 77379 3255 D2
Mintglade Ln
2300 HarC 77014 3402 A2
Minto Ct
4000 HarC 77053 4372 D4
Mint Teal Ct
12300 HarC 77066 3401 C5
Minturn Ln
10200 HarC 77064 3540 B6
Mintwood Ln
7300 HarC 77379 3256 C3
Mintz Ln
15000 HarC 77014 3257 D6
15000 HarC 77068 3257 D6
Minuteman Ct
12000 HarC 77067 3402 B5
Minuteman Ln
2900 FRDW 77546 4750 A2
Mi Pais Dr
6700 HOUS 77048 4244 D7
Mirabeau Dr
20400 HOUS 77338 3263 E3
Mira Blossom Dr
7000 HarC 77346 3408 E1
7100 HarC 77346 3264 E7

Miracle Dr
1100 CNRO 77301 2385 A3
Miracle Ln
13400 HOUS 77085 4371 E1
Mirador Ln
22200 HarC 77532 3266 D6
Mirage Ct
500 FRDW 77546 4504 E7
Miraglen Ct
1700 FBnC 77469 4365 D2
Mira Glen Dr
3500 BzaC 77584 4501 C7
Miraglen St
6500 HOUS 77023 4104 D1
Mira Loma Dr
10 MNVL 77583 4624 E4
Miramar Ct
1900 SEBK 77586 4509 D1
Miramar Dr
3200 LPRT 77571 4383 A1
3300 SRAC 77571 4383 A1
14100 GLSN 77554 5332 D3
22900 GLSN 77554 5441 A6
Miramar St
1200 HOUS 77006 4102 D1
23000 GLSN 77554 5440 E6
Miramar Crest Ct
8200 HarC 77375 3110 E1
Miramar Crest Dr
22400 HarC 77375 3110 E1
Miramar Green St
1900 SEBK 77586 4509 D1
Miramar Lake Blvd
22700 HarC 77375 3110 D1
S Miramar Lake Blvd
22300 HarC 77375 3110 E2
22300 HarC 77379 3110 E2
Miramar Shores Dr
11800 HarC 77065 3539 D3
Miramichi Ln
4100 HarC 77053 4372 D5
Mira Monte Cir
15500 HarC 77083 4096 B6
Mira Monte Ct
15600 FBnC 77083 4096 B6
Mira Monte Dr
15600 FBnC 77083 4096 B6
Miramonte Dr
- HOUS 77028 3687 D7
Miranda Ln
38300 MtgC 77355 2669 D7
Miranda St
14400 HarC 77039 3545 D2
14700 HarC 77032 3545 D2
Mira Vista Dr
15100 FBnC 77083 4096 C6
Mirawood Ln
9200 HOUS 77078 3688 A6
Miriam Ln
12500 MSCY 77071 4239 E7
Miriam St
10 BYTN 77520 4112 E1
Mirkwood Ln
14300 HarC 77014 3257 D7
Mirmar Estates Ct
22900 MtgC 77385 2823 A6
Mirmar Estates Ln
11200 MtgC 77385 2823 A6
Miro Ct
500 HarC 77388 3113 D7
Mirror Ct
3500 HarC 77388 3113 A7
Mirror Lake Dr
1500 ELGO 77586 4509 B1
18700 HarC 77388 3258 A1
19100 HarC 77388 3113 A7
19400 HarC 77388 3112 E6
E Mirror Ridge Cir
100 WDLD 77382 2819 E3
100 WDLD 77382 2820 A3
W Mirror Ridge Cir
10 WDLD 77382 2819 E2
Mirror Ridge Ct
10 WDLD 77382 2820 A2
Mirror Ridge Dr
10 WDLD 77382 2819 E2
Mischire Dr
4000 HOUS 77025 4241 C1
Miscindy Pl
14500 HarC 77429 3253 E6
Missarah Ln
13400 HarC 77429 3397 E2
N Mission Cir
1800 FRDW 77546 4629 B6
S Mission Cir
1800 FRDW 77546 4629 B7
Mission Dr
1200 LPRT 77571 4111 A7
2000 LGCY 77565 4509 A5
Mission Rd
11300 HarC 77065 3398 E6
21100 HarC 77373 3113 E2
Missionary Ridge Ln
16700 FBnC 77083 4235 D1
Mission Bay Dr
7100 HarC 77083 4096 C5
Mission Bell Dr
6600 HarC 77083 4096 D5
6900 HOUS 77083 4096 D5
Mission Bend Pl
10 WDLD 77382 2819 E2
Mission Bluff Grv
19900 FBnC 77469 4094 D6
Mission Bluff Ln
17900 FBnC 77469 4095 C7
Mission Bridge Ct
15800 FBnC 77083 4236 B2
Mission Canyon Ln
22000 MtgC 77357 2973 B2
22000 MtgC 77365 2973 B2
Mission Chase Dr
1300 HOUS 77077 3957 A4
Mission Cove Ln
19200 FBnC 77469 4234 E1
Mission Creek Cir
1900 HarC 77084 3815 E7
Mission Creek Dr
2200 HarC 77084 3815 E6
Mission Crest Ct
15800 FBnC 77083 4236 B1
Mission Ct Dr
- HOUS 77083 4096 D6
7100 HarC 77083 4096 D6
Mission Estates Ct
15800 FBnC 77083 4096 B7
Mission Estates Dr
8200 FBnC 77083 4096 B7
8300 FBnC 77083 4236 B2

Mission Falls Dr
- HarC 77095 3538 D3
Mission Forest Dr
15200 FBnC 77083 4236 B1
Mission Fort Ln
19100 FBnC 77469 4235 A1
Mission Gate Ct
15800 FBnC 77083 4096 B7
Mission Glen Dr
15800 FBnC 77083 4236 A1
16100 FBnC 77083 4096 C5
Mission Greens Dr
- FBnC 77083 4096 C7
- HOUS 77083 4096 C7
Mission Grove Dr
3100 HarC 77068 3257 C5
Mission Hills Ct
2800 FBnC 77450 3954 A6
Mission Hills Dr
14600 HarC 77083 4096 D6
Mission Hills Ln
21900 FBnC 77450 3954 A7
Mission Lake Ct
4800 FBnC 77469 4234 D4
Mission Manor Ln
19100 FBnC 77469 4094 D3
19100 FBnC 77469 4095 A6
Mission Meadow Ln
7400 FBnC 77469 4094 D6
Mission Mill Cir
2200 HarC 77084 3816 B7
Mission Mill Ln
19500 HarC 77084 3816 A6
19700 HarC 77084 3815 E6
Mission Oak Dr
5300 FBnC 77083 4236 B2
Mission Oaks Dr
- FBnC 77083 4095 D7
- FBnC 77469 4095 D7
Mission Park Dr
- FBnC 77469 4094 E5
- FBnC 77469 4095 A6
Mission Pines Ct
7500 FBnC 77469 4094 D7
Mission Pines Ln
19700 FBnC 77469 4094 D7
Mission Ridge Ln
16800 HarC 77073 3259 A4
Mission Springs Dr
1400 HarC 77450 3954 E3
Mission Terrace Ct
15800 FBnC 77083 4236 B1
Mission Terrace Dr
8600 FBnC 77083 4236 B1
Mission Valley Dr
2900 MSCY 77459 4497 C2
13000 HarC 77069 3400 C2
Mission Viejo St
3300 BYTN 77521 3973 E1
Mission View Ct
15800 FBnC 77083 4236 B1
Mission Village Dr
15800 FBnC 77083 4096 A5
Mississippi Av
500 SHUS 77587 4246 C4
Mississippi Pk
400 MtgC 77302 2530 A5
Mississippi St
10 HOUS 77029 3965 E6
200 HOUS 77029 3966 A6
1500 BYTN 77520 4112 B2
6600 MNVL 77578 4747 A2
Missouri Av
500 SHUS 77587 4246 C4
2300 DKSN 77539 4633 B7
2900 DKSN 77539 4754 B1
Missouri St
1000 HOUS 77006 3962 D6
1200 BYTN 77520 4112 B2
1900 HOUS 77019 3962 C6
3300 BYTN 77520 4111 E1
Missouri City Dr
- MSCY 77489 4370 C4
Missouri Pacific St
26600 MtgC 77355 2963 A4
Missy Ln
- RSBG 77471 4490 C6
Missy Falls Dr
11100 HarC 77065 3539 B1
N Mist Ct
400 HarC 77073 3259 A5
N Mist Dr
16200 HarC 77073 3259 A5
Mist Ln
10300 HarC 77070 3399 B5
10900 HarC 77429 3399 A5
Mist Arbor Ln
- LGCY 77539 4752 E3
Mistcreek Ct
5300 LGCY 77573 4751 D1
Mist Creek Ln
14500 HarC 77396 3547 C1
Misted Lilac Pl
10 WDLD 77381 2674 B7
Mistflower Ln
6600 HarC 77449 3677 D3
Mistflower Pl
10 WDLD 77381 2675 A7
Mist Green Ln
3500 HarC 77373 3114 E2
Mistic Hl
- HarC 77094 3955 B1
Mistic Meadows Ct
10800 HarC 77064 3540 A1
Mistic Moon Ct
11000 HarC 77064 3540 B1
Misting Falls Ln
13300 PRLD 77584 4499 E3
13300 PRLD 77584 4500 A3
Mistissin Ln
3800 HarC 77053 4372 D5
Mistiwood Ct
1100 HOUS 77077 3957 A3
Mist Lake Ct
24900 FBnC 77494 3952 E5
Mistletoe Cir
1500 RHMD 77469 4491 D2
Mistletoe Ln
1100 HOUS 77339 3118 C7
4400 FBnC 77545 4623 C3
Mistletoe Rd
4800 PASD 77505 4248 A3
Mistletoe Tr
30900 MtgC 77354 2670 A7
Mistra Dr
6700 PASD 77505 4248 E4
Mistral Wind Pl
10 WDLD 77382 2675 C7

Mistwood Ct
2000 PRLD 77584 4500 D1
Mistwood Ln
- HOUS 77077 3957 A3
Misty Clfs
1000 DKSN 77539 4752 E6
Misty Cr
6300 MSCY 77459 4496 C4
Misty Ln
- HarC 77044 3549 E3
500 FRDW 77546 4629 B2
3600 PRLD 77581 4504 A5
5000 PASD 77505 4248 B4
18900 HarC 77377 3106 E1
Misty Mdws
- CNRO 77303 2237 C4
9900 MtgC 77303 2237 D4
Misty Ml
4400 SGLD 77479 4496 A1
Misty Mnr
400 HarC 77094 3955 D2
Misty Pt
10 WDLD 77380 2967 C4
Misty Tr
10000 HOUS 77088 3542 C7
10000 HOUS 77088 3682 C1
Misty Wy
800 HarC 77532 3411 C5
Misty Alcove Ct
3300 HOUS 77345 3119 D1
Misty Arbor Dr
6800 HOUS 77085 4371 C1
Misty Arch Ln
11500 HarC 77433 3396 A7
Misty Bay Cir
- LGCY 77539 4752 D4
Misty Bay Dr
2800 LGCY 77539 4752 E5
2900 LGCY 77539 4753 A4
Misty Bay Ln
13000 PRLD 77584 4500 D4
Misty Bell
- HarC 77038 3543 E5
Misty Bend Dr
1200 FBnC 77494 3952 D3
Misty Blue Ln
13300 HarC 77377 3253 E2
Misty Bluff Dr
13600 HOUS 77085 4371 C1
E Mistybreeze Cir
10 WDLD 77381 2820 E3
W Mistybreeze Cir
10 WDLD 77381 2820 E3
Misty Briar Ct
5700 FBnC 77479 4367 A4
Misty Bridge St
9400 HOUS 77075 4377 B3
Misty Brook Ln
100 LGCY 77573 4630 C5
3100 HarC 77084 3816 C5
Misty Brook Bend Ct
6400 HarC 77379 3111 A4
Misty Brook Bend Ln
21200 HarC 77379 3111 C3
Misty Canyon Ln
- HarC 77095 3537 C6
N Misty Canyon Pl
10 WDLD 77385 2676 B3
S Misty Canyon Pl
10 WDLD 77385 2676 B4
Misty Chase Ln
15600 HarC 77053 4372 E5
Misty Cliff Ln
28500 MtgC 77386 2969 D5
Misty Cloud Ct
10 WDLD 77381 2674 D6
Misty Cloud Ln
- HarC 77044 3550 B3
- HOUS 77044 3550 B3
Misty Country Dr
- HOUS 77051 4243 A6
Misty Cove Ct
3700 DKSN 77539 4754 D1
Misty Cove Dr
- HarC 77084 3816 B3
7800 HarC 77346 3265 B2
19100 HarC 77449 3816 A2
20300 HarC 77449 3815 E2
Misty Creek Dr
16900 HarC 77379 3256 E1
Mistycreek Dr
600 FBnC 77469 4365 C3
Misty Creek Ln
- PRLD 77581 4503 E2
Misty Cross Dr
17200 HarC 77084 3678 A5
Misty Crossing Ln
20400 HarC 77379 3111 B5
Misty Cypress Ct
14300 HarC 77429 3254 C4
Misty Daisy Dr
- HOUS 77051 4243 A7
Misty Dale Dr
6600 HarC 77449 3677 C2
Misty Dawn Ct
200 WDLD 77385 2676 A4
Misty Dawn Dr
200 WDLD 77385 2676 B3
E Misty Dawn Dr
10 WDLD 77385 2676 B3
N Misty Dawn Dr
10 WDLD 77385 2676 B3
W Misty Dawn Dr
100 WDLD 77385 2676 B3
Misty Dawn Tr
15300 HarC 77433 3251 A6
Misty Day Ln
300 HarC 77532 3410 E2
Misty Fall Ln
21600 HarC 77449 3815 A2
Misty Falls Ct
2400 FBnC 77469 4365 B2
Misty Falls Ln
1800 FBnC 77469 4365 B2
3800 HarC 77546 4505 E7
3800 HarC 77546 4506 A7
Misty Fawn Ln
1600 FBnC 77545 4622 D2
Misty Fern Ct
7700 HarC 77095 3537 E7
Misty Field Tr
- HarC 77346 3264 E3
Misty Forest Ct
15400 HarC 77068 3257 B5
Misty Gardens Ct
3900 HOUS 77339 3119 A3
Mistygate Ct
4300 HarC 77373 3115 A5

Misty Glade Ct
3300 FBnC 77494 3952 C7
Misty Glen Ln
1600 LGCY 77573 4752 A1
11500 HOUS 77099 4238 B4
Misty Green Ct
- HOUS 77051 4243 A6
Misty Green Ln
6300 HarC 77066 3400 E5
Misty Grove Cir
10 WDLD 77380 2967 C4
Misty Grove Ct
2000 HOUS 77062 4380 A6
Misty Grove Dr
2600 BzaC 77578 4501 A6
Misty Harbor Dr
2100 PRLD 77584 4500 A2
Misty Harbour Cir
1900 LGCY 77573 4509 A7
Mistyhaven Pl
10 WDLD 77381 2821 A2
Misty Heath Ln
2700 HOUS 77082 4096 E1
15700 HarC 77084 3678 C4
24900 FBnC 77494 4093 A5
Misty Heather Ct
4200 PASD 77059 4380 E5
Misty Hill Ln
1700 HOUS 77345 3120 C6
Misty Hills Dr
13200 HarC 77429 3254 A7
Misty Hollow Dr
4100 MSCY 77459 4497 C4
15400 HarC 77068 3257 A5
Misty Island Ct
5900 FBnC 77494 4093 E4
Misty Isle Ct
3000 LGCY 77539 4753 B2
21500 HarC 77449 3815 B2
Misty Jade Ct
- HarC 77338 3262 A3
Misty Jade Ln
- HarC 77338 3262 A4
18200 HarC 77429 3252 B5
Misty Knoll Ct
14200 HOUS 77062 4379 D6
Mistylace Dr
17800 HarC 77396 3408 A2
Misty Lake Blvd
- SGLD 77478 4237 C7
Misty Lake Cir
23900 MtgC 77357 2828 A1
Misty Lake Ct
1200 SGLD 77478 4237 A7
Misty Lake Dr
500 ELGO 77586 4509 B1
1100 SGLD 77478 4237 A7
Misty Lake Ln
7400 BzaC 77581 4502 A3
Misty Lake Pt
17200 MtgC 77357 2828 A1
Misty Landing Ct
8200 HarC 77396 3547 D1
Misty Lantern Ln
12900 HarC 77044 3408 E4
12900 HOUS 77044 3408 E4
Misty Laurel Dr
12300 HarC 77014 3402 B4
Misty Lea Ln
700 HarC 77090 3258 B2
Misty Leaf Ct
13900 HarC 77044 3549 D2
Mistyleaf Ct
4700 FBnC 77479 4496 B4
Mistyleaf Ln
6600 FBnC 77479 4496 B4
Misty Loch Ln
15800 HarC 77084 3678 C4
Misty Lodge Ct
21100 FBnC 77469 4094 C7
Misty Loft Ln
- HarC 77433 3396 A7
Misty Meadow Ct
1000 TMBL 77375 2964 D5
Misty Meadow Dr
30000 MtgC 77355 2816 A2
30500 MtgC 77354 2816 A2
30900 MtgC 77354 2670 B7
Misty Meadow Ln
14100 HOUS 77079 3957 D1
Misty Meadow St
5800 LGCY 77573 4630 C7
Misty Mill Dr
13300 HarC 77041 3679 C5
Mistymont Dr
12400 HarC 77070 3399 C6
Misty Moon Dr
5300 HarC 77346 3264 C5
Misty Moor Ct
7300 FBnC 77469 4094 A6
Misty Moores Dr
17400 HarC 77377 3254 B4
Misty Morn Ln
3900 SGLD 77479 4495 A1
Misty Morning
100 LGCY 77573 4633 B1
Misty Morning Ct
4600 MSCY 77459 4497 C4
11200 PRLD 77584 4500 D3
Misty Morning Dr
7100 HarC 77346 3265 A6
Misty Morning St
11300 PRLD 77584 4500 D2
Misty Morning Trc
6800 FBnC 77469 4093 E7
6900 HOUS 77469 4093 E7
N Misty Morning Trc
10 WDLD 77381 2821 B2
W Misty Morning Trc
10 WDLD 77381 2821 B2
Misty Moss Ct
22000 MtgC 77365 2971 E2
Misty Moss Ln
12100 HarC 77070 3399 B6
Misty Mountain Trail Ln
8300 HarC 77389 2966 A4
8500 HarC 77389 2965 E5
Misty Oak Ct
16500 MtgC 77302 2679 B4
Misty Oaks Dr
28600 HarC 77336 3121 A3
Misty Oaks Ln
1800 FBnC 77479 4367 B7
1800 FBnC 77479 4494 A1
Misty Ocean Ct
- HOUS 77051 4243 A7
Misty Orchard Ln
13400 FBnC 77478 4366 E3

Misty Paloma Dr
16400 HarC 77530 3829 E3
Misty Park Dr
2900 HOUS 77082 4097 B2
Misty Park Ln
5000 FBnC 77479 4493 C3
Misty Peak Ln
11800 HarC 77346 3408 B2
Misty Pines Ct
19700 HarC 77346 3264 B4
Misty Pines Dr
20000 HarC 77346 3264 C4
Misty Point Dr
- HarC 77450 3954 C6
Misty Pond Ct
17800 HarC 77429 3253 C2
Misty Prairie Ln
8400 FBnC 77469 4095 D7
Misty Ridge Ct
800 FBnC 77479 4493 C5
Misty Ridge Dr
3600 HarC 77396 3407 E3
3800 HarC 77396 3408 A3
Misty Ridge Ln
8100 HOUS 77071 4239 D7
Misty River Dr
10300 HarC 77086 3542 C1
Misty River Ln
2700 FBnC 77469 4365 A5
Misty River Tr
2100 HOUS 77345 3120 B3
Misty River Wy
20100 HarC 77433 3251 C5
Misty Rose Ct
3900 SGLD 77479 4495 A3
Misty Sage Ct
- HOUS 77051 4243 A7
8600 HarC 77396 3547 E2
Misty Sage Dr
- CNRO 77302 2530 D4
Misty Sands Ln
10900 HOUS 77034 4378 C4
Misty Shadow Ct
- HOUS 77051 4243 A6
10600 HOUS 77041 3819 D1
Misty Shadow Dr
4300 HOUS 77041 3819 E1
Misty Shadow Ln
- PRLD 77545 4499 D1
Misty Shadows Dr
4600 HOUS 77041 3680 E7
4600 HOUS 77041 3819 D1
Misty Shore Dr
- FBnC 77450 3953 E7
400 LGCY 77573 4633 B2
Misty Shore Ln
13200 PRLD 77584 4500 A4
Misty Spring Ln
6600 HarC 77379 3256 D1
Misty Springs Dr
2800 BzaC 77578 4501 A7
Misty Stone Ct
15000 HarC 77044 3550 A2
Misty Summit Dr
10700 HarC 77086 3542 C1
Misty Terrace Ct
6200 FBnC 77494 4093 E5
Misty Timbers Wy
4200 HOUS 77345 3119 D4
Misty Trail Dr
8300 HarC 77095 3538 C6
Misty Trails Ln
1000 LGCY 77573 4751 C1
Mistyvale Ct
1900 FBnC 77469 4365 D2
Misty Vale Dr
9200 HOUS 77075 4377 A3
Misty Vale Ln
8000 HOUS 77075 4376 D3
9400 HOUS 77075 4377 B3
Misty Valley Ct
- HOUS 77051 4242 E6
Misty Valley Dr
11400 HarC 77066 3401 A3
12600 HarC 77066 3400 E2
Misty View Blvd
- SGLD 77478 4236 E7
Misty View Ln
3500 HarC 77546 4506 B7
Misty Village Ct
5100 HarC 77373 3115 C5
Misty Vine Ct
9700 HarC 77088 3682 C1
Misty Waters Ln
2000 LGCY 77573 4631 C7
Misty Willow Dr
13000 HOUS 77070 3399 E4
Misty Willow Ln
11200 HarC 77375 3109 E1
Misty Wind Ct
2900 LGCY 77573 4633 A3
Misty Wood
18400 MtgC 77365 2972 A2
Mistywood Dr
300 HarC 77090 3258 D5
Mitchamore Ln
2100 HMPD 77445 3097 E1
Mitchamore Rd
- HMPD 77445 3097 D1
- WlrC 77445 3097 D1
Mitchell Ct
6100 LGCY 77573 4630 B7
Mitchell Dr
5900 HTCK 77563 4988 D2
Mitchell Ln
5400 LMQU 77568 4872 D5
12500 HarC 77066 3400 E4
22300 MtgC 77357 2973 D3
Mitchell Rd
- HOUS 77037 3684 A1
- HOUS 77088 3684 A1
100 HarC 77037 3684 E1
500 HarC 77037 3685 A1
1000 HOUS 77037 3685 A1
24800 WlrC 77445 2955 D2
E Mitchell Rd
200 HarC 77037 3684 D1
W Mitchell Rd
100 HarC 77037 3684 C1
Mitchell St
16000 HarC 77429 3108 B7
Mitchelldale St
5000 HOUS 77092 3822 A4
5300 HOUS 77092 3821 D4
Mitchell Lake Rd
- FBnC 77469 4234 C5
Mitchell Pass Ln
17200 HarC 77346 3408 D3

Mitote Dr
3700 GLSN 77554 5331
3700 GLSN 77554 5442
Mitre Peak Ln
5800 FBnC 77469 4493
Mittlestedt Rd
4500 HarC 77068 3256
4500 HarC 77069 3256
Mixon Av
- HOUS 77021 4102
- HOUS 77030 4102
- HOUS 77054 4102
Mize Rd
4300 HOUS 77504 4247
4300 PASD 77504 4247
Mizell Rd
100 CTSH 77303 2385
100 CTSH 77306 2385
20500 MtgC 77372 2535
Mizell St
100 HarC 77562 3832
ML Wilmser Dr
1400 BYTN 77520 4112
E M Norris
- PRVW 77445 3100
Moa Ct
100 MtgC 77385 2676
Moary Firth Dr
16300 HarC 77084 3678
Moats Wy
10 FBnC 77469 4232
Moatwood Ct
10 WDLD 77382 2673
Mobil Rd
10 HarC 77532 3413
10 LbyC 77535 3413
Mobile Ct
600 MtgC 77302 2530
Mobile Dr
500 PASD 77506 4106
1200 PASD 77502 4106
Mobile St
7100 HMBL 77396 3406 B
7100 HOUS 77396 3406 B
7400 HOUS 77011 3965
13300 HOUS 77015 3967
Mobud Dr
6300 HOUS 77074 4100
6300 HOUS 77081 4100
7100 HOUS 77074 4099
7900 HOUS 77036 4099
Moby Dick
16700 GLSN 77554 5331
16700 JMAB 77554 5331
Mocassin Ct
11700 HarC 77377 3254
Moccasin Bend Dr
6300 HarC 77379 3256
Mock
11100 HarC 77093 3686
Mockingbird Cir
10 HOUS 77074 4239
Mockingbird Ct
30500 MtgC 77385 2676
Mockingbird Dr
2600 ALVN 77511 4866
Mockingbird Hl
11500 MtgC 77303 2239
Mocking Bird Ln
1900 LPRT 77571 4250 B
Mockingbird Ln
- HOUS 77019 3961
10 CNRO 77301 2530
100 PASD 77502 4247
100 PASD 77586 4508 D
700 PASD 77502 4246
800 FRDW 77546 4505
800 MSCY 77489 4370
2600 RMFT 77357 2829
2700 LGCY 77565 4508
3000 RSBG 77471 4491
5000 HarC 77493 3813
5000 KATY 77493 3813 D
5300 PRLD 77584 4502
5600 FBnC 77469 4615
5600 PLEK 77469 4615
7200 TXCY 77591 4873
11600 BKHV 77024 3959
11600 PNPV 77024 3959
16500 SGCH 77355 2961
18600 HarC 77377 2962
Mockingbird Pl
10900 CHTW 77385 2823 A
Mockingbird St
1900 BYTN 77520 3973
Mockingbird Wy
900 SGLD 77478 4368 B
Mockingbird Valley Dr
19100 HarC 77449 3677 B
Modbury St
17200 HarC 77379 3255 D
Modena Ct
2400 PRLD 77581 4504
Modena Dr
1200 PRLD 77581 4504 E
Modeste Dr
- LGCY 77573 4632 B
Modesto Dr
6300 HarC 77083 4096
Modiste St
1200 SPVL 77055 3821 B
Modley Ct
8200 HOUS 77088 3684 A
Modoc Falls Ln
2100 PRLD 77581 4503 D
Moers Rd
8600 HOUS 77061 4245
8600 HOUS 77075 4245
9700 HOUS 77075 4376
Moffitt Ln
3000 FBnC 77545 4498 A
3000 HOUS 77489 4371 A
3000 HOUS 77489 4498 A
3000 HOUS 77545 4498 A
Moggy Ct
500 HarC 77388 3113 B
Mogian Ct
- HarC 77014 3401 D
Mogian Dr
- HarC 77014 3401 C
Mohave Cir
4700 HarC 77521 3833 C
Mohave Ln
4400 HarC 77346 3264
6500 FBnC 77469 4493
Mohave Wy Ct
13900 HarC 77429 3253 E

STREET
Block City ZIP Map# Grid

Mohawk
2500 GlsC 77650 4879 B5
Mohawk Dr
10 PNVL 77304 2237 A4
9200 LPRT 77571 4249 E4
9200 LPRT 77571 4250 A4
Mohawk Ln
2800 HarC 77093 3685 E1
2800 HarC 77093 3686 B2
23400 MtgC 77365 2972 B5
Mohawk St
4100 HarC 77521 3833 B3
4200 HarC 77093 3686 C2
5500 HOUS 77016 3686 E2
5900 HOUS 77016 3687 A2
Mohawk Tr
26100 MtgC 77354 2964 B1
Mohegan Cir
4500 PASD 77504 4247 E6
Mohegan Ct
4700 HarC 77521 3833 C4
Mohlerbruk Dr
3800 HarC 77066 3401 C6
Mojave Hls
7100 HarC 77069 3400 A1
Mokay St
- HarC 77429 3396 E3
Molasses Meadow Ln
21100 HarC 77375 3110 A5
Moline St
6000 HOUS 77087 4104 C7
8000 HOUS 77087 4105 C7
Moller Dr
1300 ALVN 77511 4867 A3
Moller Rd
800 GlsC 77511 4750 B6
Molley Ct
10 BLAR 77401 4101 B4
Molly St
2100 HarC 77039 3545 D2
Moltere Dr
11400 HarC 77065 3398 A7
Mona St
3600 BzaC 77584 4502 A7
3600 PRLD 77584 4502 A7
9600 HOUS 77093 3685 E5
Monaco Ln
4400 PASD 77505 4248 D6
Monaco Rd
12600 HarC 77070 3399 C5
Monaldo Ct
1400 PRLD 77581 4504 D3
Monaldo Dr
2400 PRLD 77581 4504 D3
Monaldo Pl
1400 PRLD 77581 4504 D3
Mona Lee Ln
4100 HOUS 77080 3820 E1
Monarch Dr
- SGLD 77479 4494 E4
4100 SGLD 77479 4495 A5
Monarch Rd
12600 HOUS 77047 4373 C2
Monarch Beach Dr
1600 FBnC 77494 3953 C5
Monarch Blue Ln
4500 FBnC 77545 4623 A2
Monarch Glen Ln
4800 HarC 77449 3677 B7
Monarch Hill Ln
8000 HarC 77396 3547 D1
Monarch Hollow Ln
1900 HarC 77449 3815 C6
Monarch Lake Ln
6900 FBnC 77494 4093 D2
Monarch Manor Ln
26600 MtgC 77339 3118 C3
Monarch Meadow Ct
26200 KATY 77494 3952 B3
Monarch Meadow Ln
- FBnC 77494 4093 A1
3300 PRLD 77581 4376 C7
Monarch Oak Ln
4900 TXCY 77591 4874 A6
Monarch Oaks Dr
1000 MtgC 77354 2673 D2
Monarch Oaks St
1400 HLSV 77055 3821 C6
1400 HOUS 77055 3821 C6
Monarch Springs Dr
- HOUS 77396 3406 B5
Monarch Terrace Dr
2500 FBnC 77494 3951 C5
Monarch Woods Dr
27000 HarC 77339 3118 C5
Monarda Ct
6700 HarC 77069 3400 A1
Monarda Manor Ct
20000 HarC 77379 3110 D5
Mona Vista Dr
6500 HarC 77083 4096 C5
Moncray Av
1500 LGCY 77573 4632 A7
Moncur Dr
7800 HarC 77095 3538 B6
Monday Ln
11900 MtgC 77357 2829 E6
Mondrian Dr
15300 FBnC 77083 4096 C7
Monet Dr
2900 SGLD 77479 4368 C7
Monet St
7800 HOUS 77093 3825 B1
Monet Bend Pl
10 WDLD 77382 2819 B2
Monica St
11600 BKHV 77024 3959 C4
11600 PNPV 77024 3959 C4
Monique Dr
11200 HarC 77065 3539 A1
Monitor Pk
400 MtgC 77302 2530 A5
Monitor St
4000 HarC 77093 3546 B7
Monkeys Fist Ln
- HarC 77546 4506 A5
Monkswood Dr
20200 HarC 77450 3954 D2
Monmouth Dr
200 HarC 77530 3831 B6
Monmouth Ln
3700 PASD 77505 4248 B4
Monona Dr
2100 FBnC 77494 3952 B5
Monrad Dr
14600 HOUS 77045 4372 D3
14700 HarC 77053 4372 D4
14700 HOUS 77053 4372 D4
Monroe
- HOUS 77075 4376 E4
Monroe Av
2500 RSBG 77471 4491 A6
Monroe Ct
600 MtgC 77302 2530 D7
600 MtgC 77302 2676 D1
Monroe Dr
1100 PASD 77502 4107 C7
1500 DRPK 77536 4249 D1
Monroe Rd
6800 HOUS 77017 4245 E3
7000 HOUS 77061 4245 E3
8300 HOUS 77075 4245 E7
9400 HOUS 77075 4376 E1
Monroe Rd SR-3
6800 HOUS 77017 4245 E2
W Monroe Rd
7800 HOUS 77061 4245 E4
Monroe St
1100 ALVN 77511 4867 A1
1200 BYTN 77520 3973 B6
1500 HOUS 77023 4104 B1
Mons Av
1800 RSBG 77471 4490 E7
2500 RSBG 77471 4491 A7
Monsanta St
5900 HOUS 77087 4245 A1
Monsey Dr
9200 HOUS 77063 4099 C1
Monsoon Ct
17500 HarC 77532 3411 B7
Montabello Dr
11100 FBnC 77469 4093 A7
Montague Dr
- HarC 77373 3115 C5
Montague Manor Ln
7900 HarC 77072 4097 C6
Montaigne Dr
13300 HarC 77065 3539 A1
13900 HarC 77429 3538 E1
13900 HarC 77429 3539 A1
Montain Mist Ct
8000 FBnC 77469 4095 C7
Montana Av
- SHUS 77017 4246 B2
700 SHUS 77587 4246 B2
1000 HOUS 77017 4246 B2
3700 DKSN 77539 4754 B2
Montana St
1200 LPRT 77571 4251 E5
1600 HOUS 77007 3962 D2
1900 BYTN 77520 4112 B2
Montana Blue Dr
2400 HarC 77373 3114 C5
Montana Ridge Ct
6500 HarC 77041 3679 E4
Montano Ct
31600 MtgC 77354 2672 E5
Montauk Dr
6600 HarC 77084 3678 E3
Montbrook Dr
11700 HOUS 77099 4238 B5
Montbury Ln
5400 FBnC 77450 4094 C2
Montclair Blvd
- SGLD 77478 4368 E2
600 SGLD 77478 4369 A3
Montclair Ct
- LGCY 77573 4632 A7
Montclair Dr
- HOUS 77005 4102 B4
6700 HOUS 77030 4102 B4
Montclair Bend Ln
12600 HarC 77044 3689 B3
Montclair Hill Ct
13800 BzaC 77583 4623 D5
Montclair Hill Ln
4700 FBnC 77545 4623 A2
5700 BzaC 77583 4623 D5
Montclair Meadow Ln
19200 HarC 77449 3677 A7
Montclair Oaks Ln
2200 MtgC 77386 2823 D6
Montclair Park Ln
22900 HarC 77373 2968 E7
Montclair Point Ct
13200 HOUS 77047 4373 B3
Montcliff Ct
12100 HarC 77066 3401 A5
W Monteagle Cir
10 WDLD 77382 2673 C7
Monte Alta Dr
11500 HOUS 77048 4244 D7
Monte Alto Ln
- HOUS 77028 3687 E7
Montebello Ct
11200 PNPV 77024 3959 E4
Montebello Manor Ln
12400 HarC 77377 3254 A2
Monte Bello Ridge Ln
6500 HarC 77041 3680 A4
Monte Carlo Ct
16600 HOUS 77053 4371 E7
Monte Carlo Ln
16400 HOUS 77053 4371 E7
Montecello Ct
10900 FBnC 77469 4093 A7
10900 FBnC 77469 4233 A1
Monte Cello St
800 HDWV 77024 3959 E1
Montego Dr
3700 BYTN 77521 3972 E3
Montego Wy
16700 GLSN 77554 5331 E5
16700 JMAB 77554 5331 E5
Montego Bay Ct
3900 MSCY 77459 4497 D6
Monteigne Ln
13500 HarC 77429 3397 A3
Monteith Dr
5300 HarC 77373 3115 D6
Monteleon St
- HOUS 77075 4377 D2
Monte Leone Dr
23700 FBnC 77469 4093 B7
Monterello
- LGCY 77573 4632 A7
Monterey Ct
25000 GLSN 77554 5548 B1
Monterey Hls
14200 HarC 77069 3400 A1
Monterey Pine Pl
8500 HarC 77375 3110 D2
Monte Rosa Ct
23900 FBnC 77469 4093 B7
23900 FBnC 77469 4233 B1
Monterra Pt
1400 FBnC 77545 4622 E2
Monterrey Dr
2000 LGCY 77565 4509 A5
Monterrey Ln
9100 HOUS 77078 3688 A6
Monterrey Rd
2000 RSBG 77471 4490 C6
Monterrey Springs Dr
- HarC 77041 3680 A5
Montesa Ct
8000 FBnC 77083 4096 C7
Montesa Dr
15400 FBnC 77083 4096 B7
Montes Landing Dr
15300 HarC 77433 3251 C7
Montevideo Cir
4300 PASD 77504 4248 A4
Monte Vista Dr
15400 HarC 77083 4096 B5
Montezuma Dr
14200 HarC 77429 3253 E5
Montezuma St
6400 HarC 77521 3832 E6
Montfair Blvd
10 WDLD 77382 2673 A7
100 WDLD 77354 2819 D3
100 WDLD 77382 2819 D3
E Montfair Blvd
10 WDLD 77382 2673 A7
W Montfair Blvd
10 WDLD 77382 2673 A7
Montford Ct
3000 SGLD 77478 4369 A3
Montford Dr
9200 HOUS 77099 4238 C1
Montglen Ct
10 HOUS 77061 4245 C1
Montglen Dr
7600 HOUS 77061 4245 B1
Montgomery Ln
1400 HMBL 77338 3263 A7
9100 LPRT 77571 4249 E3
9300 LPRT 77571 4250 A3
Montgomery Rd
13500 GlsC 77510 4986 D3
W Montgomery Rd
5700 HOUS 77091 3684 B5
7200 HOUS 77091 3683 E4
7600 HOUS 77088 3683 E4
9800 HarC 77088 3683 B1
10000 HarC 77088 3543 A6
10000 HOUS 77088 3543 B7
11500 HarC 77086 3543 A7
11600 HarC 77086 3542 E5
Montgomery St
1200 LMQU 77568 4990 B2
Montgomery College Dr
- WDLD 77384 2675 E5
Montgomery Creek Ranch Tr
- MtgC 77385 2676 E5
Montgomery Park Blvd
2200 CNRO 77304 2383 B1
Monticello Ct
2000 LGCY 77573 4631 B7
Monticello Dr
- TXCY 77591 4872 E5
2600 HOUS 77045 4242 B7
4000 SGLD 77479 4495 B3
7500 TXCY 77591 4873 B5
Monticello Pk
400 MtgC 77302 2530 C5
Monticeto Ct
11800 MDWP 77477 4238 A5
Monticeto Ln
- MDWP 77478 4237 E4
- SGLD 77478 4237 E4
11800 MDWP 77477 4238 A4
12200 MDWP 77477 4237 E4
Montilla Ct
7800 HarC 77083 4096 D6
Montmarte Blvd
- HOUS 77082 4098 B3
Montour Dr
1000 HOUS 77062 4506 D2
1000 HOUS 77062 4507 A1
Montridge Dr
8000 HOUS 77055 3821 B4
8500 HOUS 77080 3821 A4
9300 HOUS 77080 3820 D4
Montrose Blvd
1000 HOUS 77019 3962 D5
1300 HOUS 77006 3962 D5
4400 HOUS 77006 4102 E1
5200 HOUS 77005 4102 E2
5400 HOUS 77030 4102 E2
Montrose Cir
100 CNRO 77301 2530 B1
Montvale Dr
3700 HOUS 77059 4380 D6
Montverde Ln
10800 HOUS 77099 4238 B5
Montview Ct
20600 HarC 77450 3954 D2
Montview Dr
900 HarC 77450 3954 D2
2600 BzaC 77584 4501 A6
Montwood Ct
15500 HOUS 77062 4380 D7
Montwood Dr
15300 HOUS 77062 4380 B7
Monument Rd
10800 LPRT 77571 4110 D6
Monument Valley Dr
- HarC 77014 3401 E4
12000 HarC 77067 3401 E4
Monvale Ln
1600 FBnC 77479 4367 B7
Monza Dr
3200 HarC 77014 3401 E2
Moody Av
10 GLSN 77550 5109 C4
800 LGCY 77573 4632 A1
Moody Plz
10 GLSN 77550 5109 C2
Moody St
100 HOUS 77009 3824 C5
100 WEBS 77598 4507 C6
W Moody St
100 WEBS 77598 4507 C6
Moody Reef Dr
4800 GlsC 77539 4634 C5
Moon Av
4500 HOUS 77018 3683 C7
Moon Ct
1300 PASD 77504 4247 D6
Moonbeam Cir
7300 MSCY 77459 4496 E5
Moon Beam Ct
10 WDLD 77381 2820 D3
Moonbeam Rd
8200 HOUS 77092 3682 A5
Moon Beam St
8300 HOUS 77088 3683 C2
Mooncrest Dr
2100 HarC 77089 4504 C2
Mooncrest Field Ln
- HarC 77449 3816 A1
Moondance Ln
7800 HOUS 77071 4239 E5
Mooney Rd
1200 HOUS 77037 3685 B1
1300 HarC 77093 3685 C1
1300 HOUS 77093 3685 B1
3100 HarC 77093 3686 A1
Moonflower Ln
20000 HarC 77449 3815 D6
Moonglow Dr
11500 HarC 77038 3543 B5
11500 HarC 77088 3543 B6
16300 HarC 77090 3258 D5
Moonhollow Dr
19400 HarC 77084 3816 A5
19600 HarC 77084 3815 E5
Moonlight Dr
- HOUS 77035 4240 E4
- HOUS 77096 4100 E7
- HOUS 77096 4240 E1
Moonlight Tr
15100 MtgC 77384 2674 C1
Moonlight Creek Ct
15900 HarC 77095 3678 C1
Moonlight Forest Dr
8000 HarC 77088 3682 E1
8100 HarC 77088 3542 E6
Moonlight Ridge Dr
11300 HarC 77396 3407 E7
11400 HarC 77396 3408 A7
Moonlight Shadow Ct
4200 PASD 77059 4380 E5
Moonlite Dr
3600 PASD 77505 4248 D4
Moonlit Fields Ct
10900 HarC 77064 3540 A2
Moonlit Lake Cir
3100 LGCY 77573 4633 B1
Moonlit Lake Ct
22700 FBnC 77450 3953 C6
Moonlit Lake Ln
13200 PRLD 77584 4499 E4
13200 PRLD 77584 4500 A4
Moonlit Meadows Ct
10800 HarC 77064 3540 B1
Moonlit Night Dr
14200 HarC 77083 4096 E5
Moonlit Pond Ct
18700 HarC 77084 3816 C1
Moonmist Dr
5800 HOUS 77081 4100 C4
7600 HOUS 77036 4099 D4
11900 HOUS 77072 4098 A4
Moon Ridge Ct
24200 FBnC 77494 3953 A3
Moonridge Dr
100 HarC 77015 3829 A5
Moonridge Rd
- HarC 77449 3675 E2
Moonriver Dr
19800 HarC 77338 3261 E5
Moon Rock Dr
15900 HOUS 77062 4507 C1
Moonrock Dr
16200 HOUS 77058 4507 D1
16200 HOUS 77062 4507 D1
Moonscape Vw
9800 HarC 77396 3407 B7
Moonseed Pl
10 WDLD 77381 2820 B2
Moonset Ln
10200 HOUS 77016 3687 C4
Moon Shadow Ct
1500 FBnC 77479 4493 E5
Moonshadows Dr
5100 HarC 77346 3264 B5
Moonshine Hill Lp
100 HarC 77338 3263 C5
100 HOUS 77338 3263 C5
Moonshine Hill Rd
100 HarC 77338 3263 C6
100 HOUS 77338 3263 C5
Moonstone Cir
3000 HOUS 77018 3822 D4
Moonstone Mist Ln
- FBnC 77494 4092 C5
Moon Trail Dr
19100 HarC 77346 3264 C6
Moon Valley Ct
10 PNVL 77304 2237 A3
Moonvine Ct
10 WDLD 77380 2967 C1
Moorberry Ln
10100 HOUS 77043 3820 A4
10100 HOUS 77080 3820 A4
10400 HOUS 77043 3819 E4
Moorcraft Ct
9500 FBnC 77478 4236 C2
Moorcreek Dr
10500 HarC 77070 3399 A2
12200 HarC 77070 3398 C1
Moore Ct
2400 PRLD 77581 4504 C3
Moore Dr
1700 PRLD 77581 4504 C3
6800 HTCK 77563 4989 A5
7700 BzaC 77584 4627 D2
Moore Rd
100 ALVN 77511 4749 C1
100 BzaC 77511 4749 C1
200 FRDW 77546 4749 D1
1000 FBnC 77477 4369 E5
1200 FBnC 77477 4370 A6
1700 MSCY 77477 4370 A6
1900 MSCY 77459 4370 A6
3900 HarC 77562 3833 A1
5700 GlsC 77517 4986 C3
15000 HarC 77049 3829 C2
30000 MtgC 77354 2817 D1
30300 MtgC 77354 2671 D7
Moore St
200 TMBL 77375 2964 C6
4400 HOUS 77009 3824 C5
7200 HTCK 77563 4989 A6
Moorea St
1000 TKIS 77554 5106 C4
Moorebrook Dr
1500 HarC 77038 3543 D4
Moore Creek Ln
17000 HarC 77346 3408 C3
Mooredale Ln
12400 HOUS 77024 3958 E1
12400 HOUS 77024 3959 A1
Moorehead Rd
11000 MtgC 77302 2531 E1
Mooreknoll Ln
12400 HOUS 77024 3959 A1
12500 HOUS 77024 3958 E1
Mooreland Park Ln
- HarC 77095 3539 B6
Mooremeadow Ln
12400 HOUS 77024 3959 A1
12500 HOUS 77024 3958 E1
Mooreview Ln
14300 HarC 77014 3257 E7
Moorfield Ct
9300 FBnC 77083 4236 E1
Moorfield Dr
14200 FBnC 77083 4236 E2
Moorgate Ln
24600 HOUS 77336 3266 C2
Moorhead Dr
1300 HOUS 77055 3820 B6
Moorhead Rd
18900 MtgC 77302 2824 B3
Mooring Point Ct
4100 MSCY 77459 4369 C6
Mooring Pointe Dr
- PRLD 77545 4499 E2
Mooring Ridge Ln
11100 HOUS 77075 4376 E4
Moorland Ct
4600 SGLD 77479 4495 C4
Moor Lily Dr
20900 HarC 77388 3112 B3
Moorpark Ln
8700 HarC 77064 3541 C5
Moorside Ln
900 HarC 77530 3829 C7
Moortown Cir
21600 FBnC 77450 3954 B7
Moorwick Ln
1300 HOUS 77043 3818 E7
Moose Dr
100 HarC 77532 3410 D1
Moose Cove Ct
19700 HarC 77375 3109 E6
Moosehead Ln
11800 HarC 77064 3399 E7
Moose Jaw Ln
200 HOUS 77336 3266 B2
Moosewood Ct
5500 HarC 77346 3264 B5
Mopan Springs Ln
- HarC 77044 3550 A3
Mopan Valley Ln
11900 HarC 77066 3400 D4
Mora Dr
6500 HarC 77083 4096 A4
Mora Ln
1500 LMQU 77568 4990 A2
Morales Rd
14400 HarC 77032 3545 E1
14400 HOUS 77032 3545 E1
15100 HarC 77032 3404 E7
15300 HOUS 77032 3404 E6
Moran Crest Dr
6100 HarC 77388 3111 D1
Moray Dr
1200 RSBG 77471 4491 C4
Moray Ln
11800 HarC 77016 3547 D7
11800 HarC 77016 3687 D1
Moray View Dr
- HarC 77095 3538 D2
Moreau St
2300 HOUS 77093 3685 D3
Moreford Ln
27500 HarC 77336 3122 A3
Morehouse Ln
2400 HOUS 77088 3683 B3
Moreland Dr
17400 HarC 77530 3831 A6
Moreland Ln
6300 FBnC 77469 4616 A2
Morelock Ln
8300 TXCY 77539 4755 A1
Morelos Rd
3700 HarC 77521 3832 E6
3700 HarC 77521 3833 A6
Moren Dr
19500 MtgC 77357 2827 E4
Morenci
- BYTN 77520 4113 B4
Morenci St
2700 PRLD 77581 4502 C4
2700 PRLD 77584 4502 C4
Moreno Av
14400 HOUS 77045 4373 A3
Moreton Ct
7500 HarC 77379 3256 B2
Moreton Ln
17400 HarC 77379 3256 B2
Morewood Ct
13300 HarC 77038 3543 A2
Morewood Dr
2300 HarC 77038 3543 A2
Morfontaine Ln
2600 FBnC 77450 3953 E6
Morgan Dr
- HarC 77065 3398 C6
- HarC 77429 3398 C6
12200 MtgC 77372 2536 E5
25400 HarC 77375 2964 D2
E Morgan Dr
11800 HarC 77065 3398 D6
W Morgan Dr
11800 HarC 77065 3398 C6
Morgan Ln
10800 MtgC 77372 2536 A1
Morgan Rd
- BzaC 77584 4501 C7
- PRLD 77584 4501 D6
19500 HarC 77532 3411 B4
Morgan Run
16100 MSCY 77071 4239 B7
Morgan Sprs
25800 HarC 77373 3114 A3
Morgan St
100 ALVN 77511 4749 C5
100 CNRO 77301 2384 B5
1900 HOUS 77006 3962 E6
16000 SGCH 77355 2961 E2
Morgan Bay Ct
2400 PRLD 77545 4499 D3
Morgan Bay Dr
1300 PRLD 77545 4499 D3
Morgan Canyon Ct
6200 FBnC 77450 4094 C4
Morgan Cemetery Rd
22900 MtgC 77372 2535 E1
22900 MtgC 77372 2536 C2
25400 MtgC 77372 2537 A1
26800 LbyC 77328 2537 D1
Morgan Creek Ct
13600 HOUS 77077 3957 A6
Morganfair Ln
2600 HarC 77450 3954 D6
Morgan Mist Ct
1800 SGLD 77479 4367 E6
Morganna
- STAF 77477 4238 B7
Morgan Oak Dr
5100 ALVN 77511 4867 D7
Morgan Park Ln
5500 FBnC 77479 4366 E6
Morgan Ranch Tr
7400 HarC 77338 3261 D4
Morgan Saddle Ln
- FBnC 77469 4235 C1
Morgans Bend Cir
18400 HarC 77433 3395 D6
Morgans Bend Dr
18200 HarC 77433 3395 D6
Morgans Chase Ln
6300 FBnC 77479 4367 A6
Morgans Gold Dr
17500 HarC 77433 3395 D6
Morgans Lake Dr
17300 HarC 77433 3395 D6
Morgans Landing Ln
5100 ALVN 77511 4867 D7
Morgans Mill Ct
18300 HarC 77433 3395 D6
Morgans Pointe Cir
- HarC 77449 3815 B2
Morgans Ridge Ln
- MtgC 77386 2969 E6
Morgans Secret Dr
17300 HarC 77433 3395 D6
Morgans Turn
16200 HarC 77095 3538 C5
Morgen Ct
- HarC 77379 3111 A2
Morgood St
5500 HOUS 77026 3825 D6
Moriah Ct
4100 MtgC 77386 3115 C1
Morin Pl
1200 HOUS 77002 3963 B3
1300 HOUS 77007 3963 B3
Morinscott Ct
5600 HarC 77049 3828 D4
Morinscott Dr
14000 HarC 77049 3828 C4
Moris Ln
12500 HOUS 77015 3967 A2
Moritz Ct
4800 HOUS 77055 3821 B6
Moritz Dr
1400 HOUS 77055 3821 B6
Morley Dr
15600 HarC 77429 3397 B6
Morley St
7500 HOUS 77061 4245 B3
Morley Lake Dr
9300 HarC 77095 3538 A4
Morley Park Ln
900 HarC 77373 2968 D5
Morley Point Ct
4500 LGCY 77573 4630 E5
Morley Pointe Ct
19900 HarC 77450 3954 E5
Morning
7200 HarC 77521 3695 B7
Morning Dr
2200 BYTN 77520 3973 D5
Morning Arbor Pl
10 WDLD 77381 2674 E7
Morning Bay Dr
2800 PRLD 77584 4500 D4
Morningbloom Ln
- FBnC 77469 4095 B6
Morning Blossom Pl
17200 HarC 77084 3678 A3
Morning Breeze
5400 HarC 77041 3679 D6
Morningbrook Ct
8100 HarC 77379 3256 C5
Morning Brook Dr
11300 PRLD 77584 4500 D4
Morningbrook Dr
16200 HarC 77379 3256 B5
Morning Brook Ln
19700 HarC 77094 3954 E2
19700 HarC 77094 3955 A1
Morning Brook Wy
2800 PRLD 77584 4500 D4
Morning Clock Wy
- HOUS 77336 3266 B1
E Morning Cloud Cir
10 WDLD 77381 2675 B7
N Morning Cloud Cir
10 WDLD 77381 2675 B7
Morning Cloud Ct
2900 PRLD 77584 4500 D4
Morning Cloud Dr
11300 PRLD 77584 4500 D4
Morning Cloud Pl
10 WDLD 77381 2675 B7
Morning Cove Ln
3500 HarC 77449 3815 A2
Morning Creek Dr
20300 HarC 77450 3954 D5
Morning Creek Ln
1100 LGCY 77573 4751 C1
Morningcrest Ct
6100 HarC 77389 2966 D4
Morning Cypress Ln
26200 HarC 77433 3396 B7
Morningdale St
5800 HOUS 77396 3405 D4
Morning Dawn Ct
17600 HarC 77095 3537 B5
Morning Dawn Dr
2800 PRLD 77584 4500 D4
8200 HarC 77095 3537 E6
Morning Dew Ln
11800 HarC 77067 3402 B5
Morning Dew Pl
1600 MSCY 77459 4497 D4
Morning Dove Dr
3200 HarC 77388 3112 E3
15200 HarC 77396 3406 D7
Morning Dove Ln
800 FRDW 77546 4505 B4
4600 BzaC 77511 4627 A7
4600 BzaC 77511 4748 A1
Morning Dove St
3900 BzaC 77511 4867 B7
Morning Dusk Dr
16900 FBnC 77469 4235 D1
Morning Falls Dr
6600 HarC 77041 3679 E3
Morning Forest Ct
10 WDLD 77381 2821 A5
Morning Gale Ln
- FBnC 77494 3952 B7
- FBnC 77494 4092 C1
Morning Gate Ct
12400 HOUS 77082 4097 D1
Morninggate Ct
2700 HarC 77449 3815 C4
Morning Glen Ln
8500 FBnC 77083 4095 D7
Morning Glory Ct
4600 MSCY 77459 4497 D5
Morning Glory Dr
2400 PASD 77503 4248 C2
2800 PASD 77505 4248 C2
3400 GlsC 77517 4870 A4
3400 STFE 77517 4870 A4
3800 STFE 77517 4869 E5
Morning Glory Ln
10 WDLD 77380 2822 A7
Morning Glory Trc
6700 FBnC 77469 4093 D7
Morning Glory Terrace Ct
19700 HarC 77433 3251 D7
Morning Lake Dr
2000 LGCY 77573 4508 E6
22300 FBnC 77450 3953 E7
22300 FBnC 77450 3954 C7
Morning Leaf Ct
2700 HarC 77388 3113 A6
Morninglight Dr
2600 HarC 77084 3816 B5
Morning Lodge Ln
14300 HOUS 77044 3550 B2
Morning Meadow Dr
- HOUS 77489 4371 A6
- MSCY 77489 4371 A6
2300 MSCY 77489 4370 E6
Morning Mews Ln
19300 FBnC 77469 4094 E5
Morning Mist Ct
1100 SGLD 77478 4236 E7
Morning Mist Dr
16200 HarC 77090 3258 C5
Morningmist Ln
2800 LGCY 77539 4752 E2
Morningmount Ln
4800 HarC 77449 3677 C5
Morning Oak Ln
8500 HarC 77433 3537 D6
Morning Park Dr
1500 FBnC 77494 3953 D6
Morning Pine Ln
15100 HarC 77068 3257 B5
Morning Pine Tr
16200 HarC 77433 3251 C5
Morning Point Ln
22000 MtgC 77365 2973 B3
Morning Pond Ln
2800 LGCY 77539 4752 E3
Morning Quail Ct
16300 HOUS 77489 4370 E6
Morning Rain Dr
12400 HarC 77377 3254 B4
Morning Raven Ln
24900 FBnC 77494 3953 B5
Morning Rose Ln
8100 HarC 77095 3537 C6
Morningsage Ln
6500 HarC 77088 3682 C1
Morningshade Dr
16300 HarC 77090 3258 D5
Morning Shadows Dr
1600 FBnC 77479 4494 B6
Morning Shadows Wy
16500 HarC 77346 3408 B3
Morningshire Ln
6100 HarC 77084 3678 C4
Morningside Ct
900 FRDW 77546 4505 A5
Morningside Dr
200 FRDW 77546 4505 B7
200 LGCY 77573 4630 C7
3400 HOUS 77098 3962 B7
3700 HOUS 77098 4102 B1
4400 HOUS 77005 4102 B3
5600 HOUS 77030 4102 B4
6100 FBnC 77479 4493 D5
Morningside Ln
2700 PASD 77506 4107 E4
2700 PASD 77506 4108 A4
Morningside St
10 HOUS 77365 2974 E6
Morningside View Dr
14500 HarC 77047 4374 C6
Morning Sky
6900 FBnC 77494 4093 B5
Morning Sky Dr
11900 HOUS 77045 4242 D6
Morning Song Ct
24800 HarC 77389 2966 D3
Morning Song Dr
19500 HarC 77449 3677 C3
Morning Star Av
17000 HarC 77532 3552 A1
17500 HarC 77532 3411 B7
Morningstar Dr
9000 FBnC 77479 4494 C4
Morning Story Dr
22800 HarC 77373 3115 E6
Morningtide Ct
3200 HarC 77449 3815 C3
Morningtide Dr
3400 HarC 77449 3815 B3
Morning Tide Ln
1900 LGCY 77573 4509 A6
Mornington Dr
- FBnC 77469 4366 E4
- SGLD 77478 4367 A4
5200 FBnC 77478 4366 E4
5300 FBnC 77478 4367 A4
Mornington Ln
400 HarC 77494 3953 A2
Mornington Vale Ln
9500 HarC 77044 3689 D3

STREET
Block City ZIP Map# Grid

Morningview Dr
3400 HOUS 77080 3820 D2
4200 HOUS 77041 3820 D1
N Morningview St
10300 STFE 77510 4987 E4
10300 STFE 77510 4988 A4
S Morningview St
10300 GlsC 77510 4987 E4
10300 HTCK 77563 4987 E4
10300 HTCK 77563 4988 A4
10300 STFE 77510 4987 E4
10300 STFE 77510 4988 A4
Morning Willow Dr
4200 FBnC 77450 4094 C1
N Morningwood Ct
10 WDLD 77380 2968 A3
S Morningwood Ct
10 WDLD 77380 2968 A3
Morocco Rd
10000 HOUS 77041 3681 A6
10200 HarC 77041 3681 A6
Morrell Av
10 BYTN 77520 3973 A5
200 BYTN 77520 3972 D5
Morris Av
14600 BzaC 77583 4623 D5
14900 PRLD 77583 4623 D5
15400 IWCY 77583 4623 E6
15600 IWCY 77583 4624 A6
15800 BzaC 77583 4624 B7
17200 MNVL 77578 4624 D7
17200 MNVL 77583 4624 B7
17500 MNVL 77578 4745 E1
17500 MNVL 77578 4746 A1
Morris Av SR-6
14600 BzaC 77583 4623 D5
14900 PRLD 77583 4623 D5
15400 IWCY 77583 4623 E6
15600 IWCY 77583 4624 A6
15800 BzaC 77583 4624 B7
17200 MNVL 77578 4624 D7
17200 MNVL 77583 4624 B7
17500 MNVL 77578 4745 E1
17500 MNVL 77578 4746 A1
Morris Ct
4300 PRLD 77584 4501 E6
Morris Dr
4400 PRLD 77584 4501 E6
Morris Rd
300 MtgC 77362 2963 D2
1000 HOUS 77079 3818 D7
1000 HOUS 77079 3957 D1
2400 PRLD 77583 4500 E5
2400 PRLD 77584 4500 E5
2800 BzaC 77583 4500 E6
18300 MNVL 77578 4746 E2
20700 MNVL 77578 4747 A3
21300 BzaC 77578 4747 B3
Morris Rd SR-6
18300 MNVL 77578 4746 E2
20700 MNVL 77578 4747 A3
21300 BzaC 77578 4747 B3
Morris St
1100 HOUS 77009 3963 C1
1200 BYTN 77520 4112 D1
1200 HOUS 77009 3824 D7
2500 HOUS 77026 3824 E7
6500 GLSN 77551 5108 B7
18500 BzaC 77584 4627 A4
18600 PRLD 77584 4627 A4
21100 MtgC 77357 2827 B5
Morrisfield Ct
19400 HarC 77094 3955 B3
Morrisglen Ct
6500 HarC 77084 3677 E3
Morris Hill Ln
16800 HarC 77095 3538 A3
Morrison Blvd
- HarC 77493 3813 E7
- KATY 77493 3813 E7
Morrison Pl
- FBnC 77479 4366 C6
Morrison St
2600 HOUS 77009 3963 B1
2900 HOUS 77009 3824 B7
Morrisway Ct
17800 HarC 77084 3677 E3
Morro Bay Dr
10 MNVL 77583 4624 D4
Morrocastle St
10200 HOUS 77075 4377 C3
10200 HOUS 77089 4377 C3
Morrow Ct
7100 FBnC 77479 4367 B7
Morrow St
6000 HOUS 77091 3684 A4
Morse St
1500 HOUS 77019 3962 C6
2500 HOUS 77098 3962 C6
Mortimer Dr
11300 HarC 77066 3401 D6
Morton
- HarC 77562 3692 D7
Morton Av
- HOUS 77034 4379 A4
Morton Ct
3100 HarC 77084 3816 D4
Morton Rd
5300 HarC 77493 3813 E3
5300 KATY 77493 3813 A3
18400 HarC 77084 3816 D4
19000 FBnC 77469 4234 A3
19000 FBnC 77469 4235 A3
19700 HarC 77084 3815 E4
19700 HarC 77449 3815 E4
19700 HarC 77449 3816 B4
24500 HarC 77493 3814 A3
24600 MtgC 77372 2536 E6
27000 WlrC 77493 3812 E3
Morton St
100 RHMD 77469 4364 E7
100 RHMD 77469 4491 E1
Morton Chase Ln
21800 HarC 77449 3815 A4
Morton Cove Ln
2800 HarC 77449 3815 B4
Morton Creek Ranch Rd
23300 HarC 77449 3814 C4
Morton League Ct
1000 FBnC 77469 4365 C2
Morton League Rd
1100 FBnC 77469 4365 C2
Morton Ranch Rd
22000 HarC 77449 3815 A3
22100 HarC 77449 3814 A3
23100 HarC 77493 3814 A3
Morton View Dr
21300 HarC 77449 3815 A4

Morwood St
5500 HOUS 77026 3825 D6
Mosa Creek Ct
1800 HOUS 77017 4106 B7
Mosaic Ln
14200 SGLD 77478 4236 E6
Mosaic Canyon Ct
4700 HarC 77396 3406 E7
Mosby Dr
3000 SGLD 77479 4495 E1
Moscone Ct
6000 HarC 77449 3677 B5
Moselle Dr
22800 MtgC 77365 2971 E4
Moses St
3400 HOUS 77020 3964 A2
Mosewood St
7400 HOUS 77040 3682 A2
7600 HarC 77040 3682 A2
7800 HarC 77040 3681 E2
Mosey Pointe Ln
19200 HarC 77377 3254 A1
Mosher Ln
600 HarC 77037 3544 B6
600 HOUS 77037 3544 B6
800 HOUS 77088 3544 A6
1200 HOUS 77088 3543 E6
1800 HarC 77088 3543 D7
Mosielee St
12100 HarC 77086 3542 E5
Moskowitz Av
1100 SEBK 77586 4509 D2
Mosley Ct
3500 HOUS 77004 3963 B7
Mosley Rd
7600 HOUS 77017 4246 A4
7900 HOUS 77061 4246 A5
8100 HOUS 77075 4246 A5
Mosman Ct
600 HarC 77094 3955 B2
Moss Cir
25300 MtgC 77372 2536 E1
25300 MtgC 77372 2537 A1
Moss Cr
2300 FBnC 77469 4365 C1
Moss Ct
2700 SEBK 77586 4509 C1
Moss Ln
2700 DRPK 77536 4249 E1
9200 HTCK 77563 4988 C3
16800 MtgC 77365 2825 C7
Moss St
100 HOUS 77009 3824 A6
3200 LMQU 77568 4989 B2
Moss Agate Ct
21700 HarC 77388 3112 A3
Moss Arbor Ct
26100 FBnC 77494 4092 E1
Mossberg Ct
2600 HarC 77396 3407 D3
Moss Bluff Ct
10 WDLD 77382 2674 D4
Moss Bluff Ln
2200 RSBG 77471 4491 B6
Moss Boulder Ct
15000 HarC 77084 3678 E2
Moss Boulder Dr
6800 HarC 77084 3678 E2
Moss Branch Rd
11800 HOUS 77043 3819 C2
Mossbriar Ct
8800 HarC 77095 3538 C3
Mossbriar Ln
17200 HarC 77095 3538 A5
17300 HarC 77095 3537 E5
Moss Bridge Ln
14900 FBnC 77478 4236 D6
Mossby Ln
7700 HOUS 77075 4245 C7
Moss Cove Ct
18000 HarC 77346 3408 A1
Moss Cove Ln
5900 HOUS 77085 4240 E7
N Moss Creek Dr
13100 HarC 77429 3397 E4
S Moss Creek Dr
13000 HarC 77429 3397 E4
Moss Creek Ln
2100 PRLD 77581 4504 C4
14500 HarC 77429 3397 D5
Mosscrest Dr
10900 HOUS 77048 4243 D6
12700 HOUS 77048 4374 E2
Mossdale Cir
8300 HarC 77379 3256 C4
Moss Dale Dr
1200 FBnC 77479 4493 E6
Mossey Creek Dr
2100 DRPK 77536 4109 E7
Mossey Oak Dr
- BYTN 77520 3971 B1
100 BYTN 77520 3832 B7
Mossey Pines Ct
- HarC 77338 3261 E2
Mossey Terrace Ln
6600 HarC 77379 3111 B3
6600 HarC 77388 3111 B3
Moss Falls Ln
22100 HarC 77373 3260 E1
Mossford Dr
4500 HOUS 77087 4104 C5
Moss-Forest
- LbyC 77327 2684 D4
Mossforest Dr
17400 HOUS 77090 3258 B1
17400 HOUS 77090 3258 C3
Moss Glenn Ln
5200 HOUS 77088 3682 E2
5200 HOUS 77088 3683 A2
Moss Green Ct
4500 PASD 77059 4380 D3
16700 HarC 77429 3252 E5
Mossgrey Ln
5200 HarC 77373 3115 D6
Mosshall Ct
22300 HarC 77375 3110 D3
Mosshang Ct
8400 HarC 77040 3541 C7
Moss Hill Dr
2500 HOUS 77080 3820 B3
Moss Hill Ln
100 CNRO 77301 2384 A1
100 CNRO 77303 2384 A1
200 CNRO 77303 2383 E1
5500 BzaC 77583 4623 D4
Mosshill Estates Ln
18600 HarC 77429 3396 B2

Moss Hollow Ct
5000 HOUS 77018 3683 E7
Mosside St
7600 HOUS 77021 4103 A7
7600 HOUS 77021 4243 A3
Moss Lake Ct
4300 FBnC 77469 4234 C5
Moss Meadow Ct
5400 FBnC 77479 4493 D1
Moss Meadow Ln
19100 HarC 77449 3677 B7
Moss Oaks Dr
- HarC 77050 3546 E5
2000 MtgC 77385 2676 D6
6100 HOUS 77050 3546 E5
6600 HOUS 77050 3547 A6
Moss Park Ct
18000 HarC 77346 3408 A1
Moss Park Tr
19700 FBnC 77469 4234 D3
Mosspine Ct
- HarC 77084 3678 A7
Moss Point Ct
5800 HarC 77379 3257 A2
Moss Point Dr
100 FRDW 77546 4630 A4
17800 HarC 77379 3257 A2
Mossridge Dr
1100 MSCY 77489 4370 D6
6700 HarC 77069 3400 B3
Moss Ridge Rd
10700 HOUS 77043 3819 C2
N Mossrock Rd
10 WDLD 77380 2822 A7
10 WDLD 77380 2968 B3
S Mossrock Rd
10 WDLD 77380 2968 A1
Moss Rock Tr
20000 FBnC 77469 4234 D1
Moss Rose St
6500 HOUS 77087 4104 E4
6500 HOUS 77087 4105 A4
7100 HOUS 77012 4105 A4
Moss Run Dr
4900 MSCY 77459 4496 B2
Moss Spring Ln
900 HDWV 77024 3959 C1
Moss Springs Ct
7900 HarC 77433 3537 A7
Moss Stone Dr
8100 FBnC 77479 4494 C4
Mosstex
13700 HarC 77396 3547 C3
Mosstex Dr
14900 HOUS 77396 3406 C7
Moss Trail Dr
3500 MSCY 77459 4496 B2
Moss Tree Rd
3700 HOUS 77043 3819 C2
Moss Valley Dr
14500 HarC 77429 3396 B1
Mossville Ct
3600 HarC 77068 3257 C6
Mosswillow Ln
22300 HarC 77375 2965 E7
Moss Wood Dr
7300 FBnC 77479 4493 E5
Mosswood Dr
- HOUS 77078 3687 C5
100 MtgC 77302 2530 B7
8100 HOUS 77028 3687 C5
Mossy Ln
13900 MtgC 77306 2533 D7
Mossy St
800 LPRT 77571 4110 D6
Mossy Bark Ln
13000 HarC 77041 3679 D5
Mossy Bend Ln
- PRLD 77581 4503 D1
Mossy Bluff Ct
6700 HarC 77379 3111 C4
Mossy Branch Ln
2700 MtgC 77386 2823 D7
2700 MtgC 77386 2969 C1
Mossy Branch St
1200 HarC 77073 3259 B6
Mossy Bridge Dr
5000 HarC 77379 3112 A5
Mossy Brook Ct
17600 HarC 77433 3537 D2
Mossy Brook Ln
10200 HarC 77433 3537 D2
Mossy Creek Ln
- FBnC 77469 4235 C1
Mossy Creek Pl
10 WDLD 77381 2675 A6
Mossycup Dr
12100 HOUS 77024 3959 A3
12600 HOUS 77024 3958 E3
Mossy Cup St
10000 CNRO 77304 2382 E1
Mossy Elm Ct
3100 HOUS 77059 4379 E4
3100 HOUS 77059 4380 A4
Mossy Field Ln
21800 HarC 77388 3112 D2
Mossy Forest Ct
20300 HarC 77375 3109 E5
Mossygate Dr
4300 HarC 77373 3115 B6
Mossy Gate Ln
14200 HOUS 77082 4096 D1
Mossy Glen Ct
2200 FBnC 77469 4365 C1
Mossy Grove Ct
4000 HarC 77346 3408 A3
Mossy Grove Dr
16000 HarC 77346 3408 A3
Mossy Hedge Ln
19100 HarC 77449 3816 B3
Mossy Hill Ln
20700 HarC 77449 3676 D2
Mossy Hollow Ln
10900 HOUS 77075 4376 E4
Mossy Lake Cir
3700 HarC 77084 3816 A6
Mossy Leaf Ln
26900 HarC 77433 3396 A7
Mossy Ledge Dr
12600 HarC 77377 3254 A3
Mossy Log Ct
2700 HarC 77084 3816 E4
Mossy Meadow Ln
3900 HarC 77388 3112 C2
13000 HOUS 77085 4240 D7
Mossy Oak Dr
1200 LGCY 77573 4632 A4

Mossy Oaks Dr
23900 MtgC 77357 2681 E7
23900 MtgC 77357 2827 E1
Mossy Oaks Rd
21900 HarC 77388 3112 D2
21900 HarC 77389 3112 D1
22500 HarC 77389 2967 D7
Mossy Oaks Rd E
3800 HarC 77389 2967 D6
Mossy Oaks Rd W
4100 HarC 77389 2967 C6
Mossy Path Ln
1900 FBnC 77494 3952 B6
Mossy Point Ct
1900 FBnC 77469 4616 B2
Mossy Ridge Ln
17700 HarC 77095 3537 E7
Mossy Ridge Cove
13000 HarC 77041 3679 D5
Mossyrock Ct
3700 HOUS 77345 3119 E3
Mossy Shore Ct
15800 HOUS 77044 3409 A5
Mossy Stone Dr
1600 FRDW 77546 4629 C6
1600 HOUS 77077 3958 A5
Mossy Timbers Dr
5400 HarC 77346 3264 C5
Mossy Trail Ct
12200 PRLD 77583 4500 B4
Mossy Trail Dr
2000 HarC 77450 3954 D5
Mossy Trail Ln
3100 PRLD 77583 4500 B5
Mossy Trails Ct
22500 FBnC 77494 4093 D5
Mossy Trails Dr
6300 FBnC 77494 4093 D5
Mossy Tree Ln
9900 HarC 77064 3540 D4
Mossy Woods Dr
12400 HarC 77377 3254 B4
Moston Dr
1700 MtgC 77386 2969 A1
Mostyn Dr
40000 MtgC 77354 2671 A3
Motel Dr
100 ALVN 77511 4749 C7
Mott Ln
10 PNPV 77024 3959 D5
14100 SPLD 77372 2683 B1
Moultrie Ln
5500 HarC 77084 3679 A5
Mound
- HarC 77532 3409 E6
Mound Rd
- HarC 77447 3249 A7
15600 HarC 77447 3248 E7
26200 HarC 77447 3396 B4
Mound Airy Ct
6000 FBnC 77479 4367 A6
Mound Creek Rd
15300 HarC 77447 3247 C7
15300 WlrC 77484 3247 C7
Mound Lake Dr
1900 FBnC 77469 4234 C6
Mount St
7000 HOUS 77091 3683 E4
7100 HOUS 77088 3683 E3
Mountain Fk
5000 MSCY 77459 4496 B4
Mountain Aspen Ln
1800 HOUS 77345 3120 C6
Mountain Bluff Ln
5100 HOUS 77345 3119 C2
Mountain Cliff Ln
- HOUS 77044 3550 A2
Mountain Creek Ct
22800 FBnC 77450 3953 E5
Mountain Creek St
2000 PRLD 77584 4500 C2
Mountain Crest Dr
17100 HarC 77379 3255 E4
Mountain Daisy Rd
12500 HarC 77038 3543 B4
Mountain Dale Ct
7100 HarC 77433 3677 A1
Mountain Dale Dr
19700 HarC 77433 3677 A1
20100 HarC 77433 3676 E1
Mountain Flower Ct
4300 PASD 77059 4380 E5
Mountain Forest Dr
5300 HarC 77449 3676 E6
Mountain Green Tr
2800 HOUS 77345 3120 C4
Mountain Grove Ct
5300 HarC 77379 3112 A7
Mountainhead Dr
16400 HarC 77530 3829 E3
Mountain Heights Dr
15100 HarC 77049 3829 A3
Mountain Home Ln
- HarC 77429 3253 D6
Mountain Laurel Ln
7900 FBnC 77479 4494 A6
Mountain Maple Ct
6100 HOUS 77345 3120 D5
Mountain Meadows Dr
700 HarC 77450 3953 D3
Mountain Mistral Pl
10 WDLD 77382 2673 C6
Mountain Nest Ct
- HarC 77396 3548 C2
Mountain Oak Ct
3100 HarC 77068 3257 D6
Mountain Park Dr
10300 HarC 77086 3542 C2
Mountain Peak Wy
4100 HOUS 77345 3119 D3
Mountain Pines Ln
6300 HarC 77449 3677 D3
Mountain Prarie Dr
7100 HarC 77449 3677 A1
Mountain Ranch Dr
2100 HarC 77530 3829 E3
Mountain Ridge Rd
11900 HOUS 77043 3819 B2
Mountain Rose Ln
3600 HOUS 77043 3819 C2
Mountain Sage Ct
- PRLD 77545 4499 D3
Mountain Sage Dr
- PRLD 77545 4499 D3
Mountain Shade Dr
18800 HarC 77388 3112 E6
Mountain Shadows Dr
16000 HarC 77084 3678 D6

Mountain Spring Ct
1000 HarC 77373 3114 B4
Mountain Spring Dr
18600 HarC 77379 3112 A7
Mountain Thunder Dr
- HarC 77373 3115 B3
Mountain Timber Ct
16200 HarC 77546 4505 D7
Mountain Timber Dr
4800 HarC 77546 4505 E7
4800 HarC 77546 4506 C6
Mountain Valley Dr
7300 HarC 77095 3678 D2
Mountain View Dr
5800 HOUS 77345 3120 B5
Mountain View Creek Ct
5400 HarC 77379 3112 A7
Mountain Wood Wy
6700 HarC 77338 3261 B3
Mt Airy Ct
13900 HarC 77429 3397 B3
Mt Airy Dr
13400 HarC 77429 3397 B3
Mt Andrew Dr
12500 HarC 77089 4505 A2
Mt Auburn Dr
24600 FBnC 77494 3952 D3
Mountbatten Rd
7300 HOUS 77033 4244 A1
Mountbury Ct
500 HarC 77373 2968 C6
Mt Carmel St
6700 HOUS 77087 4244 D3
Mt Carstenz Wy
4200 HarC 77449 3815 C1
Mt Crest Ct
- HarC 77095 3538 E2
Mt Davis Wy
4300 HarC 77449 3676 B7
4300 HarC 77449 3815 C1
Mt Elbrus Wy
21500 HarC 77449 3815 A1
Mt Everest Wy
4000 HarC 77449 3815 B1
Mountfield Dr
18200 HarC 77084 3677 D7
Mt Forest Dr
1900 HOUS 77345 3120 B6
Mt Houston Rd
4200 HarC 77039 3546 B7
4200 HarC 77093 3546 B7
5600 HarC 77050 3546 D7
5600 HOUS 77016 3546 D7
5600 HOUS 77050 3546 D7
6100 HarC 77050 3547 A7
6100 HOUS 77016 3547 A7
6100 HOUS 77050 3547 A7
6300 HarC 77016 3547 A7
9000 HarC 77050 3548 A7
9000 HarC 77078 3547 A7
9000 HarC 77078 3548 A7
9400 HarC 77044 3548 C7
W Mt Houston Rd
- HOUS 77088 3542 D7
100 HarC 77037 3544 C6
300 HOUS 77037 3544 B6
700 HOUS 77038 3544 B6
700 HOUS 77088 3544 B6
800 HarC 77038 3544 A6
1300 HarC 77038 3543 B6
1300 HOUS 77038 3543 E6
1300 HOUS 77088 3543 E6
1800 HarC 77038 3543 B6
2800 HarC 77086 3543 A6
4700 HarC 77088 3542 D7
W Mt Houston Rd FM-149
2900 HarC 77038 3543 A6
2900 HarC 77086 3543 A6
2900 HarC 77088 3543 A6
W Mt Houston Rd SR-249
700 HOUS 77037 3544 B6
700 HOUS 77038 3544 B6
700 HOUS 77088 3544 B6
800 HarC 77038 3544 A6
1300 HarC 77038 3543 B6
1300 HOUS 77038 3543 E6
1300 HOUS 77088 3543 E6
1800 HarC 77038 3543 B6
2800 HarC 77086 3543 A6
Mt Hunt Dr
21700 HarC 77388 3111 D2
Mt Lake Dr
1200 MSCY 77459 4369 C5
2100 HOUS 77345 3120 B5
Mt McKinley Wy
21500 HarC 77449 3815 A1
Mt Olive Ln
100 BYTN 77520 3974 B1
Mt Pleasant St
3400 HOUS 77021 4103 B7
Mt Royal Cir
5400 HarC 77069 3256 C7
Mountshire Dr
1900 MSCY 77489 4370 E5
Mt Vernon Av
4000 SGLD 77479 4495 C3
Mt Vernon Dr
2700 DKSN 77539 4753 C3
Mt Vernon St
3300 HOUS 77006 3962 D7
4300 HOUS 77006 4102 D1
5200 HOUS 77005 4102 D1
13400 GlsC 77510 4870 D2
13600 STFE 77510 4870 D2
13600 STFE 77517 4870 D2
Mt Vinson Wy
4200 HarC 77449 3815 A1
4300 HarC 77449 3676 A7
Mt Whitney Wy
4000 HarC 77449 3815 A1
Mountwood St
4400 HOUS 77018 3683 B7
5900 HOUS 77091 3683 B5
Mouring Ct
6400 HarC 77389 2966 D2
Mourning Dove Dr
5000 FBnC 77469 4615 E6
Moursund St
1200 HOUS 77030 4102 D4
Mouton Cir
100 HarC 77532 3692 D1
Mouton Pl
- SEBK 77586 4509 C1
Movado Ct
3900 MtgC 77386 2970 C6
Mowat St
5000 DKSN 77539 4754 B3

Mowery Rd
2400 HOUS 77045 4242 C7
4100 HOUS 77047 4243 C7
4500 HOUS 77048 4243 D7
Moy St
2600 HOUS 77007 3962 B1
Moyenne Pl
13400 GLSN 77554 5332 E1
Moze Ln
23300 MtgC 77365 2973 E7
23300 MtgC 77365 2974 A7
Mrsny Ct
4000 MtgC 77386 2970 C6
Mrsny Dr
4100 MtgC 77386 2970 D6
MT Blvd
17200 MtgC 77357 2680 E7
17600 MtgC 77357 2681 A7
MT Cir
20500 MtgC 77357 2680 E7
MT Ct
20500 MtgC 77357 2680 E7
Muckleroy Rd
6500 HOUS 77076 3684 D5
Muddobber Ln
7100 HarC 77433 3677 B1
Muddy Spring Dr
17000 HarC 77095 3537 E2
Mueche
- SEBK 77586 4509 E2
Mueller Ln
6400 HarC 77379 3111 D6
Mueller Cemetery Rd
11600 HarC 77429 3397 B6
Mueschke Rd
14500 HarC 77429 3251 E7
14500 HarC 77429 3395 E1
14500 HarC 77433 3251 D7
14500 HarC 77433 3395 E1
16400 HarC 77377 3251 D1
18000 HarC 77377 3106 D7
18000 HarC 77433 3106 D7
22000 HarC 77377 2961 C7
22000 MtgC 77355 2961 C7
Muirfield Cir
7700 HarC 77095 3539 A7
Muirfield Ln
14000 HarC 77041 3539 B7
14000 HarC 77095 3539 A7
Muirfield Pl
1200 HOUS 77055 3821 E7
Muirfield Wy
10 SGLD 77479 4495 D3
Muirfield Bend Ct
25600 HarC 77389 2966 A2
Muirfield Valley Ln
7300 HarC 77095 3679 A1
Muirfield Village Dr
13800 HarC 77069 3400 B1
Muirwood Ln
300 SGLD 77478 4368 A1
7300 HarC 77041 3679 B1
7600 HarC 77041 3539 B7
Muirwood Falls Dr
- HarC 77375 3111 A2
- HarC 77379 3111 A2
Muirwood Pl Ln
19600 HarC 77379 3110 C7
Muirwoods Dr
12700 HarC 77346 3264 D7
Mujures
- LbyC 77327 2538 B4
Mula Cir
10200 STAF 77477 4238 E7
Mula Ct
13100 STAF 77477 4369 E1
Mula Ln
12800 STAF 77477 4238 E7
13000 STAF 77477 4369 E1
Mula Rd
9700 STAF 77477 4369 D1
9700 STAF 77477 4370 A1
Mulberry Av
600 BzaC 77583 4623 D1
600 FBnC 77545 4623 D1
600 PRLD 77545 4623 D1
W Mulberry Av
400 FBnC 77545 4623 C2
Mulberry Cir
4900 MSCY 77459 4496 B3
5800 FBnC 77469 4614 E7
5800 PLEK 77469 4614 E7
Mulberry Ct
1500 PRLD 77581 4504 D4
10900 LPRT 77571 4250 D3
25900 MtgC 77354 2817 D7
28600 MtgC 77355 2814 E5
Mulberry Dr
- RHMD 77471 4491 D3
- RSBG 77471 4491 D3
1700 RHMD 77469 4491 D3
W Mulberry Dr
10800 LPRT 77571 4250 D3
Mulberry Ln
100 BLAR 77401 4101 C4
1200 HOUS 77081 4101 C3
1200 HOUS 77401 4101 C3
2100 PASD 77502 4107 D4
2100 PASD 77502 4247 D1
7300 BYTN 77521 3835 A5
Mulberry St
- WlrC 77484 3101 E6
700 LGCY 77573 4632 D6
1500 TMBL 77375 3109 C2
2300 WALR 77484 3101 E6
3300 HOUS 77006 3962 D7
4900 STFE 77510 4987 B1
E Mulberry Field Cir
21700 HarC 77433 3250 C5
N Mulberry Field Cir
15000 HarC 77433 3250 C5
S Mulberry Field Cir
15000 HarC 77433 3250 C6
W Mulberry Field Cir
21700 HarC 77433 3250 E5
Mulberry Glen Pl
10 WDLD 77382 2674 C4
Mulberry Grove Dr
5100 HOUS 77345 3120 A5
Mulberry Hill Ln
3200 HarC 77084 3816 C3
Mulberry Hills Dr
3600 HOUS 77339 3119 B7
Mulberry Meadows Dr
15000 HarC 77084 3678 E3
Mulberry Park Dr
4500 HOUS 77345 3120 A2

Mulberry Park Ln
9800 HarC 77375 3110 C
Mulberry Ranch Dr
3100 FBnC 77494 3953 A
Mulberry Ridge Wy
900 HOUS 77062 4506 D
Mulberry Run Ct
16300 FBnC 77478 4236 A
Mulcahy St
200 RSBG 77471 4490 D
Muleshoe Ct
11100 HarC 77095 3396 E
11100 HarC 77095 3537 E
Muleshoe Dr
2300 MtgC 77384 2529 A
Mule Springs Dr
11800 HOUS 77034 4247 A
Muley Ct
18300 HarC 77433 3537 C
Muley Ln
7500 HarC 77433 3537 C
Mulford St
5100 HOUS 77023 4104 B
Mulholland Dr
- STAF 77477 4238 A
11200 HOUS 77099 4237 E
11200 HOUS 77477 4237 E
11200 STAF 77477 4238 A
11800 MDWP 77477 4237 E
11800 MDWP 77477 4238 A
Mulled Wine Ct
10 WDLD 77384 2675 D
Mulligan Ct
800 RHMD 77469 4492 A
3300 FBnC 77478 4235 E
Mulligan Tr
32500 MtgC 77354 2672 D
Mullingar Wk
3000 FBnC 77459 4621 B
Mullins Dr
6700 HOUS 77081 4100 C
8400 HOUS 77096 4100 C
10000 HOUS 77096 4240 C
12300 HOUS 77035 4240 C
Mullins Ln
14900 HarC 77032 3546 E
Mulvey St
5600 HOUS 77020 3964 D
Mum Ln
- HOUS 77034 4378 C
Mundare Ln
7300 HarC 77086 3542 B
Munford St
100 HOUS 77008 3823 D
Munger St
200 CNRO 77301 2384 D
500 PASD 77506 4107 A
1300 HOUS 77023 4104 B
N Munger St
100 PASD 77506 4107 A
S Munger St
100 PASD 77506 4107 A
Municipal St
1500 LMQU 77568 4990 A
Munn
7300 HOUS 77020 3965 A
Munn St
- HOUS 77029 3966 A
7900 HOUS 77029 3965 B
10100 JTCY 77029 3966 A
Munsey Dr
19500 HarC 77449 3816 A
Munshaw St
5700 HOUS 77034 4378 E
Munson Ln
15700 HOUS 77053 4371 E
Munson Rd
300 ALVN 77511 4749 C
Murdock St
3500 HOUS 77047 4374 C
Murff Ln
- HarC 77532 3553 D
Murfield Dr
2100 LGCY 77573 4508 D
Muricia Dr
- LGCY 77573 4632 A
Muriel St
100 LMQU 77568 4990 C
Murley St
9700 HarC 77038 3544 A
Murmuring Creek Pl
10 WDLD 77385 2676 C
Murphy Ln
700 FRDW 77546 4629 C
700 PASD 77504 4247 B
23600 MtgC 77357 2974 B
Murphy Rd
12100 HarC 77031 4238 D
12100 STAF 77477 4238 D
13200 STAF 77477 4369 D
18200 GlsC 77511 4868 D
Murphy Rd FM-1092
12100 HarC 77031 4238 D
12100 STAF 77477 4238 D
13200 STAF 77477 4369 D
Murphy St
6000 HOUS 77033 4104 C
Murphy Wood Dr
- LGCY 77573 4630 B
Murr Wy
10900 HOUS 77048 4243 E
11700 HOUS 77048 4374 E1
Murray Ct
3400 FBnC 77459 4621 E
Murray Lndg
9900 FBnC 77459 4621 E
Murray Rd
14000 HarC 77044 3689 E
Murray St
500 CNRO 77301 2384 B
Murray Bay St
1400 HOUS 77055 3820 B
1400 HOUS 77080 3820 B
Murray Brook Dr
- HOUS 77074 4239 D
9400 HOUS 77071 4239 D
Murrayhill Dr
1400 HOUS 77043 3819 E
Murrell Rd
18600 HarC 77447 3104 D
18600 WlrC 77447 2959 D
E Murrill Av
10 BYTN 77520 3973 A7
W Murrill Av
10 BYTN 77520 3973 A7
W Murrill St
600 BYTN 77520 3972 D7

STREET
Block City ZIP Map# Grid
urworth Dr
2500 HOUS 77025 4102 A7
2500 HOUS 77054 4102 A7
3700 HOUS 77025 4101 D7
uscadine Ln
2300 PASD 77502 4247 E2
2300 PASD 77502 4248 A2
uscatee Cir
3400 GLSN 77554 5332 D1
uscatine St
10100 JTCY 77029 3966 A2
13700 HarC 77015 3967 E2
14000 HarC 77015 3968 A2
uscory Dr
2500 HarC 77396 3407 C3
uscovy Ln
26900 HarC 77447 3248 D7
usetta Ct
11500 HarC 77429 3397 E7
usewood Ct
100 WDLD 77382 2675 A5
usgrove Ln
8000 HarC 77041 3539 E7
usgrove Pl
10 WDLD 77382 2674 E3
uskegon St
15800 HOUS 77032 3405 D6
usket Ln
3200 GLSN 77554 5219 D7
11900 BKHV 77024 3959 B4
usket Run
21800 HarC 77447 3105 E2
usket Tr
12300 HarC 77429 3398 D5
usket Groves St
2100 HarC 77067 3402 A6
usket Ridge Dr
2000 FBnC 77469 4234 C6
uskingum Ln
6000 HOUS 77053 4371 D5
uskmallow Ct
10 WDLD 77380 2822 A7
uskogee Ln
5800 FBnC 77469 4616 E3
uskogee Tr
23800 MtgC 77365 2974 B7
usk Rose Ct
10 WDLD 77382 2674 E3
usselburgh Ct
1300 MSCY 77459 4369 C5
ustang Av
4300 RSBG 77471 4491 C4
4900 RSBG 77469 4491 C4
5000 RHMD 77469 4491 C4
5000 RHMD 77471 4491 C4
ustang Cross
1400 MSCY 77459 4497 D4
ustang Ct
12400 MtgC 77354 2671 B3
ustang Dr
- HarC 77049 3828 E4
- HarC 77049 3829 A4
100 HLCS 77511 4867 E6
200 ALVN 77511 4867 E6
1000 FRDW 77546 4629 A3
1800 RHMD 77469 4491 D4
1800 RHMD 77471 4491 D4
1800 RSBG 77469 4491 D4
1800 RSBG 77471 4491 D4
2400 MtgC 77384 2529 A6
7600 GLSN 77554 5222 A1
7900 GLSN 77554 5221 E1
12200 MtgC 77372 2537 A5
ustang Ln
- BYTN 77521 3972 A3
- HDWV 77024 3959 D1
- HOUS 77024 3959 D1
1900 BzaC 77583 4500 A7
1900 PRLD 77583 4500 A7
17100 MtgC 77357 2681 E6
ustang Rd
300 GlsC 77511 4869 A5
500 BzaC 77511 4868 D7
1800 ALVN 77511 4867 D7
4100 PRLD 77584 4503 A7
4500 MNVL 77578 4625 E4
4500 MNVL 77578 4626 A4
4900 BzaC 77511 4867 D7
ustang Rd CO-158
3800 ALVN 77511 4867 D7
4900 BzaC 77511 4867 D7
ustang St
27300 MtgC 77372 2683 D2
ustang Tr
1100 HOUS 77339 3118 C7
Mustang Bayou Rd
8900 BzaC 77578 4747 C3
Mustang Bend Cir
15500 HarC 77429 3253 B6
Mustang Chase Dr
- RSBG 77471 4491 C3
Mustang-Chocolate Bayou
Rd
- BzaC 77511 4747 D5
Mustang Corral Dr
7400 HarC 77338 3261 D4
Mustang Creek Cir
15600 HarC 77429 3253 C6
Mustang Crossing Blvd
- ALVN 77511 4867 A4
Mustang Crossing Cir
15400 HarC 77429 3253 B6
Mustang Crossing Ct
4300 MSCY 77459 4497 C4
Mustang Draw Ln
6400 HarC 77449 3677 A3
Mustang Falls Ct
20700 HarC 77450 3954 C7
Mustang Glen Ln
16000 HarC 77429 3253 B7
Mustang Hill Ln
2700 HarC 77449 3815 B4
Mustang Hollow Ln
27000 FBnC 77494 4092 A1
Mustang Island Dr
15600 FBnC 77478 4236 B6
Mustang Lake Ct
1400 FBnC 77469 4234 D4
Mustang Meadow Ln
2900 BzaC 77583 4500 E6
Mustang Park Ct
9500 HarC 77396 3407 A7
Mustang Pl Ln
- RSBG 77471 4491 C3
Mustang Point Ct
10 WDLD 77382 2819 D2
Mustang Pointe Ln
19100 FBnC 77469 4094 E7

STREET
Block City ZIP Map# Grid
Mustang Ridge Rd
11800 HarC 77067 3402 B5
Mustang Springs Dr
1800 MSCY 77459 4497 C1
Mustang Trail Dr
16500 MtgC 77355 2961 C1
Mustang Trails Dr
- RSBG 77471 4491 C3
Mustang Valley Cir
15300 HarC 77429 3253 C6
Mustang Vista Dr
- RSBG 77471 4491 C4
Mustangwood Dr
100 BzaC 77511 4747 E3
100 BzaC 77511 4748 A3
Muswell Ln
- HarC 77073 3259 A4
Mutineer Ln
12600 HarC 77377 3254 B5
Mutiny Ct
4000 GLSN 77554 5333 A2
Mutiny Ln
12600 HarC 77377 3254 B5
13400 GLSN 77554 5333 A2
13600 GLSN 77554 5332 E2
Myers Ln
19700 MtgC 77357 2826 D2
Myers St
2300 BYTN 77520 3972 C5
Myers Mill Dr
1200 MSCY 77489 4370 D5
Mykawa Rd
- HOUS 77021 4104 B6
1500 PRLD 77581 4376 A7
1600 PRLD 77581 4503 A1
5600 HOUS 77033 4104 B6
6000 HOUS 77087 4104 C6
6600 HOUS 77033 4244 D4
8300 HOUS 77048 4244 D4
9900 HOUS 77048 4375 E1
12400 BKVL 77581 4376 A5
12400 HOUS 77048 4376 A5
Mylla St
12300 HOUS 77015 3966 E3
12400 HOUS 77015 3967 A3
Mynor Woods Ln
17000 HOUS 77060 3403 D6
Myra St
400 FRDW 77546 4629 B1
2100 HarC 77039 3545 D1
Myrna Ln
1900 KATY 77493 3813 D6
13200 HarC 77015 3828 D5
Myrtle
1900 TMBL 77375 3109 B3
12900 HOUS 77045 4241 B6
Myrtle Av
200 WEBS 77598 4631 B2
600 BzaC 77583 4623 D2
600 FBnC 77545 4623 D2
600 PRLD 77545 4623 D2
2400 WALR 77484 3101 E6
11700 HarC 77532 3692 C3
Myrtle Ct
8200 HOUS 77017 4246 A1
Myrtle Dr
100 BYTN 77520 3832 B7
11000 FBnC 77469 4235 E5
Myrtle Ln
7900 MSCY 77459 4497 B5
12800 HOUS 77015 3967 B3
Myrtle Sprs
25400 HarC 77373 3114 A4
Myrtle St
10 HOUS 77009 3963 C2
2800 HOUS 77054 4102 E6
3000 HOUS 77054 4103 A6
6400 HOUS 77087 4104 E4
6600 HOUS 77087 4105 A3
7200 HOUS 77023 4105 A3
Myrtlea Dr
13800 HOUS 77079 3958 A1
Myrtlea Ln
800 HOUS 77079 3958 C1
14000 HOUS 77079 3957 E1
Myrtle Beach Dr
- BzaC 77583 4624 C5
- MNVL 77583 4624 C5
Myrtle Creek Dr
- DRPK 77536 4250 A2
300 LPRT 77571 4250 B3
Myrtle Crest Ct
- PRLD 77581 4503 D2
Myrtle Field Ln
9900 HarC 77044 3689 B3
Myrtle Grove Ct
4100 HarC 77449 3815 B1
Myrtleland Ln
- HarC 77429 3397 C3
Myrtle Oak St
10900 HOUS 77016 3686 E2
Myrtle Rain Ct
- HarC 77449 3815 D2
Myrtle Ranch Dr
3100 FBnC 77494 3953 A6
Myrtle Stone Ln
7300 HarC 77396 3547 C2
Myrtlewood Dr
800 FRDW 77546 4505 A4
1300 PRLD 77581 4505 A4
6200 FRDW 77546 4630 B5
6200 FRDW 77573 4630 B5
6200 LGCY 77573 4630 B5
Myrtlewood St
5100 HOUS 77033 4243 E2
5300 HOUS 77033 4244 A3
Mysteria St
- HarC 77083 4237 A1
Mystery Cir
23300 HarC 77336 3267 A3
E Mystic Mdws
6300 HOUS 77021 4103 A4
N Mystic Mdws
2400 HOUS 77021 4103 A4
S Mystic Mdws
2400 HOUS 77021 4103 A4
W Mystic Mdws
6300 HOUS 77021 4103 A4
Mystic St
1400 HOUS 77020 3964 C2
Mystic Arbor Ln
- PRLD 77545 4499 D1
1800 HOUS 77077 3956 E6
Mystic Arbor Pl
10 WDLD 77382 2674 D4
Mystic Bay Ct
3600 FBnC 77478 4366 D3

STREET
Block City ZIP Map# Grid
Mystic Bend Dr
14500 HarC 77429 3397 D4
Mystic Blue Tr
15000 HarC 77433 3250 C5
Mystic Bluff Ln
17700 HarC 77433 3537 D1
Mystic Bridge Dr
6300 HOUS 77021 4103 A4
Mystic Canyon Dr
- MtgC 77386 2969 D1
Mystic Castle Ln
26800 MtgC 77339 3118 C4
Mystic Cove
10700 MtgC 77354 2671 D4
Mystic Cove Ln
2700 PRLD 77584 4500 A3
Mystic Crossing Ct
9600 HarC 77065 3539 D4
Mystic Cypress Dr
19300 HarC 77449 3677 A6
Mystic Falls Ln
9200 HarC 77396 3548 A1
Mystic Forest Ln
4800 HarC 77396 3407 A7
Mystic Glade Ct
10 WDLD 77382 2674 A5
Mystic Glen Lp
400 HOUS 77339 3263 A1
Mystic Grove Ln
- HarC 77083 4097 A3
Mystic Harbor Ln
16600 HarC 77095 3397 A7
Mystic Lake Pl
10 WDLD 77381 2675 A7
Mystic Meadows Ln
3700 HarC 77546 4506 A6
Mystic Pines Ct
10 WDLD 77382 2820 B2
Mystic Point Ct
21800 FBnC 77450 4093 E4
Mystic Port Ct
3400 FBnC 77494 4093 C2
Mystic Port Ln
3200 LGCY 77573 4633 C3
Mystic Ranch Dr
- MtgC 77302 2679 B4
Mystic Ridge Ln
16200 MtgC 77302 2679 B4
Mystic Springs Dr
4600 HarC 77396 3407 A7
Mystic Stone Dr
20800 HarC 77375 3110 A4
Mystic Trail Lp
400 HOUS 77339 3118 A7
Mystic Valley Ct
10 WDLD 77381 2820 B4
Mystic Village Ln
900 SEBK 77586 4383 A7
1000 SEBK 77586 4382 E7
Mystic Water Ln
12700 HarC 77044 3689 B3
Mystic Wood Dr
13300 HarC 77038 3543 A2
Mythic Forest
3000 FBnC 77459 4621 B6

N

W N St
- LPRT 77571 4251 B5
Nachita Dr
6300 HarC 77049 3828 C3
Nadala Dr
11800 HarC 77065 3539 D2
Nadia Wy
300 FBnC 77477 4369 C4
Nadine St
- HOUS 77009 3824 A4
900 HOUS 77009 3823 E4
1200 HOUS 77008 3823 E4
Nadolney Blvd
400 HarC 77015 3828 E7
800 HarC 77015 3967 E2
Naff Dr
22600 MtgC 77357 2827 D6
Nagle St
2100 HOUS 77003 3963 C7
2100 HOUS 77004 3963 C7
3100 HOUS 77004 4103 C1
N Nagle St
200 HOUS 77003 3963 E4
400 HOUS 77003 3964 A4
Nagra Dr
10800 HarC 77065 3539 D2
Nahas Ct
8300 PRLD 77584 4501 E5
Nail St
2400 FBnC 77545 4499 B7
3900 FBnC 77545 4623 B1
Nails Creek Dr
1300 SGLD 77478 4369 A5
Nairn St
8300 HOUS 77074 4239 C1
Nalle St
3400 HOUS 77004 4103 D1
Nallie St
8000 HOUS 77022 3824 C1
Namora Ct
9000 HOUS 77080 3820 E1
Namora Ln
4100 HOUS 77080 3820 E1
Nan St
3800 HOUS 77092 3821 D2
Nanak Dr
2300 SGLD 77478 4237 A5
Nance St
- HOUS 77002 3963 D3
1700 HOUS 77020 3963 D3
2900 HOUS 77020 3964 A3
Nancet Dr
6100 HarC 77041 3679 B4
Nancy Ct
28100 ORDN 77385 2822 B4
Nancy Dr
400 PASD 77502 4247 B1
Nancy Ln
1000 HMBL 77338 3406 E1
1200 HMBL 77338 3407 A1
9300 HarC 77375 2965 D7
28200 ORDN 77385 2822 B4
Nancy St
1100 PRLD 77581 4376 C6
2100 ALVN 77511 4750 A6
2100 GlsC 77511 4750 A6
4400 BLAR 77401 4101 B3
Nancy Ann St
5900 HOUS 77009 3824 B4

STREET
Block City ZIP Map# Grid
Nancy Belle Ln
2900 MSCY 77459 4496 E2
Nancy Rose Blvd
500 HarC 77015 3829 B7
800 HarC 77015 3968 B2
Nandina Cir
11800 HarC 77065 3398 D6
Nandina Knls
19800 FBnC 77469 4234 D1
Nanes Dr
16700 HarC 77090 3258 C4
16700 HOUS 77090 3258 C4
Nanes Rd
- HarC 77090 3258 C5
Nanette Dr
11700 HarC 77016 3547 E6
11700 HarC 77050 3547 E7
Nanlee St
200 LMQU 77568 4990 C2
Nannette Ln
20500 HarC 77388 3113 C3
20500 HOUS 77388 3113 C3
Nantere Ct
1200 RSBG 77471 4491 C4
Nanton Dr
30200 MtgC 77386 2969 B2
Nantucket Ct
3100 PRLD 77584 4501 D5
Nantucket Dr
1000 HOUS 77057 3960 C6
12700 FBnC 77478 4237 C5
12700 SGLD 77478 4237 C5
E Nantucket Rd
12500 SGLD 77478 4237 D4
Nantucket St
1100 PASD 77503 4108 D6
Nantucket Point Ln
7400 HarC 77389 2966 B2
Nantucket Woods Ln
6000 HOUS 77057 3960 C5
Naomi St
- HOUS 77054 4102 C7
1900 HOUS 77054 4242 C1
28900 MtgC 77355 2816 A3
Naomi Hollow Ln
13700 HarC 77082 4097 A2
13700 HOUS 77082 4097 A2
13800 HOUS 77082 4096 E2
Napa Meadow Ln
2600 FBnC 77545 4498 B7
2600 MSCY 77545 4498 B7
Napa Valley Tr
12700 HarC 77346 3264 C7
Napa Vine Dr
16300 HOUS 77053 4371 D7
Napawood Ct
7900 HarC 77088 3682 C2
Napfield Dr
9000 HarC 77379 3256 A6
Napier Ct
14200 HarC 77069 3400 A1
Napier Ln
6800 HarC 77069 3400 A1
Naplava St
3500 HOUS 77004 4103 D2
Naple Hollow Ln
22300 FBnC 77469 4492 E3
Naples Cir
13400 STAF 77477 4370 B1
Naples Dr
23100 HarC 77373 3115 B7
Naples Ln
12800 STAF 77477 4370 B1
Naples Bridge Rd
13400 FBnC 77478 4237 B4
Naples Cut
- STAF 77477 4370 B1
Naples Grove Ln
3200 HarC 77047 4374 B4
Naples Hollow Ln
21400 MtgC 77365 2973 B3
Naples Park Ct
7900 HarC 77070 3399 E1
Naples Park Ln
13700 HarC 77070 3399 E2
Naples Point Ln
3500 MSCY 77459 4497 E5
Naples Terrace Ln
20500 HarC 77449 3815 C6
Napoleon St
1700 HOUS 77003 3963 E7
2200 HOUS 77004 3963 E7
2600 HOUS 77004 4103 D1
Napoleon Wy
1000 MtgC 77357 2829 D2
Napoleonic Ct
2900 HarC 77014 3401 E3
Napoli Dr
- HarC 77070 3399 C2
Napper Dr
11800 HarC 77377 3254 D5
Narcille Dr
3100 MtgC 77384 2674 E2
Narcille St
300 BYTN 77520 4113 C1
900 BYTN 77520 3973 D6
Narcissus Rd
100 CRLS 77565 4509 C5
Narcissus St
6500 HOUS 77087 4104 E3
6500 HOUS 77087 4105 A4
7700 HOUS 77012 4105 C4
Narcissus Brook Ln
19500 HarC 77433 3677 B1
Narcissus View Tr
12400 HOUS 77089 4505 B1
Naremore Ct
17400 HarC 77379 3256 B2
Naremore Dr
7400 HarC 77379 3256 B2
Narina Wy
10 FRDW 77546 4629 B5
Narnia Wy
10 FRDW 77546 4629 B5
Narnia Springs Ct
9500 HOUS 77075 4246 C7
Narnia Vale Ct
14400 HarC 77429 3395 D1
Narrow Brook Wy
8000 HOUS 77016 3687 C4
Narrow Creek Pl
10 WDLD 77381 2820 D4
Narrow Gate Blvd
- MSCY 77459 4496 D2
Narrow Gate Dr
21000 HarC 77095 3538 E3
Narrow Stream Wy
- HarC 77449 3814 B3

STREET
Block City ZIP Map# Grid
W NASA Blvd
2400 LGCY 77598 4630 E2
NASA Pkwy
1300 HOUS 77058 4507 E5
1300 NSUB 77058 4507 E5
1300 WEBS 77058 4507 E5
1700 HOUS 77058 4508 B4
2200 SEBK 77586 4509 C3
2800 NSUB 77058 4508 B4
3000 PASD 77058 4508 C3
3200 PASD 77586 4508 D2
3700 ELGO 77586 4509 C3
4100 ELGO 77586 4508 E2
4100 TYLV 77586 4508 E2
NASA Pkwy FM-528
1900 HOUS 77058 4508 A4
1900 NSUB 77058 4508 A4
3700 ELGO 77586 4509 C3
3700 SEBK 77586 4509 C3
NASA Pkwy SR-N-1
1300 HOUS 77058 4507 E5
1300 NSUB 77058 4507 E5
1300 WEBS 77058 4507 E5
1700 HOUS 77058 4508 B4
2200 SEBK 77586 4509 A2
2800 NSUB 77058 4508 B4
3000 PASD 77058 4508 C3
3200 PASD 77586 4508 D2
3800 ELGO 77586 4509 A2
4100 ELGO 77586 4508 E2
4100 TYLV 77586 4508 E2
E NASA Pkwy
100 WEBS 77598 4507 C6
700 WEBS 77058 4507 C6
1000 NSUB 77058 4507 C6
1200 HOUS 77058 4507 E5
E NASA Pkwy SR-N-1
100 WEBS 77598 4507 C6
700 WEBS 77058 4507 C6
1000 NSUB 77058 4507 C6
1200 HOUS 77058 4507 E5
W NASA Pkwy
- FRDW 77598 4630 E1
100 WEBS 77598 4507 B7
W Nasa Pkwy
1400 HarC 77598 4630 D1
1400 HarC 77598 4631 A1
W NASA Pkwy
1400 LGCY 77598 4630 E1
1400 WEBS 77598 4630 E1
1400 WEBS 77598 4631 A1
W NASA Pkwy FM-528
- FRDW 77598 4630 E1
- WEBS 77598 4507 A7
1400 HarC 77598 4630 E1
1400 HarC 77598 4631 A1
1400 LGCY 77598 4630 E1
1400 WEBS 77598 4630 E1
1400 WEBS 77598 4631 A1
W NASA Pkwy SR-N-1
100 WEBS 77598 4507 B7
W NASA Rd
2500 LGCY 77598 4630 E3
W NASA Rd 1
- WEBS 77598 4507 C6
- WEBS 77598 4630 E1
2000 FRDW 77598 4630 E1
2000 HarC 77598 4630 E1
2000 LGCY 77598 4630 E1
2000 LGCY 77598 4630 E2
W NASA Rd 1 FM-528
- WEBS 77598 4507 C6
NASA Road 1
2200 SEBK 77586 4509 C3
NASA Road 1 FM-528
2200 SEBK 77586 4509 C3
Nasas Dr
19400 MtgC 77365 2972 A2
Nash St
900 HOUS 77019 3963 A4
Nashby St
1500 LMQU 77568 4873 E7
1900 LMQU 77568 4874 B6
Nash Creek Ct
6000 FBnC 77494 4093 D4
Nashland Ct
20900 HarC 77379 3111 D4
Nashua Dr
2000 STAF 77477 4370 B4
Nashua St
800 HOUS 77008 3823 B7
Nashua Pines Ct
18600 HarC 77346 3265 C7
Nashville St
7900 HOUS 77028 3826 B2
Nashwood Ct
8500 HarC 77040 3541 C6
Nassau Ct
5100 HOUS 77021 4104 B4
Nassau Dr
1900 SEBK 77586 4509 D1
4400 SGLD 77479 4496 A2
Nassau Rd
5000 HOUS 77021 4104 B5
Nassau Wy
16600 JMAB 77554 5331 E5
Nassau Bay Dr
18000 HOUS 77058 4507 E5
18000 NSUB 77058 4507 E5
18000 WEBS 77058 4507 E5
Nasworthy Dr
19200 HarC 77375 3109 C7
Nat St
14200 HOUS 77085 4371 B2
Natalias Ct
3100 HarC 77082 4097 A2
Natalie Ln
1900 FBnC 77469 4364 B2
Natalie St
14100 HarC 77053 4372 E5
Natalie Rose Dr
1900 HarC 77090 3258 B6
Natasha Ln
13300 HarC 77015 3828 D4
Natasha Run Ln
5100 HarC 77066 3401 B6
Natchez Av
900 PASD 77506 4106 D5
1300 HOUS 77017 4106 D5
Natchez Ct
- LGCY 77573 4632 A7
- LGCY 77573 4753 A1
Natchez Dr
7000 FBnC 77469 4493 D6
N Natchez Dr
1000 TXCY 77591 4873 A5
Natchez Pk
500 MtgC 77302 2530 B5

STREET
Block City ZIP Map# Grid
Natchez St
300 BYTN 77520 3971 B2
3200 HOUS 77021 4103 A5
Natchez Trc
- HarC 77038 3543 C5
Natchez Brook Ln
15800 HarC 77073 3259 C6
Natchez Creek Ln
- HarC 77429 3395 E1
Natchez Crossing St
- FBnC 77469 4234 B4
Natchez Hill Tr
3000 HarC 77084 3815 E4
Natchez Park Ln
12200 HarC 77346 3408 C3
Natchez Ridge Ct
5000 HarC 77449 3676 E7
Nathan Rd
6800 HarC 77066 3400 C4
Nathaniel St
9000 HOUS 77075 4246 B7
Nathaniel Brown St
3400 HOUS 77021 4103 B7
Nathaniel Srpings Dr
3700 BzaC 77578 4501 B7
Nathan Ridge Ln
13800 HarC 77429 3253 D5
Nathans Park Pl
4100 HOUS 77053 4372 D3
National St
1000 HOUS 77007 3962 E3
2300 PASD 77502 4247 E1
National Ridge Wy
2700 HarC 77038 3543 A5
Nations Blvd
10600 STAF 77477 4238 C6
Nations Dr
4200 PASD 77505 4248 D6
N Native Ln
200 HOUS 77022 3685 B7
S Native Ln
200 HOUS 77022 3685 B7
W Native Ln
8800 HOUS 77022 3685 B7
Nat Steel
6700 HarC 77041 3679 E2
Nat Turner Wy
13400 HOUS 77085 4371 E1
Natural Bridge Dr
4400 HOUS 77345 3119 C2
Natural Bridges Ct
- FBnC 77478 4236 C6
Natural Bridges Ln
11800 FBnC 77478 4236 C7
Natural Pine Tr
1400 CNRO 77301 2384 D6
Nature Ct
2600 FBnC 77469 4365 C1
Nature Tr
13000 HarC 77044 3689 C5
Nature Park Ln
2000 MtgC 77386 2823 B7
Natures Wy
- ALVN 77511 4867 C5
Natures Harp Ct
10 WDLD 77381 2820 C3
Naughton St
12000 HOUS 77024 3959 B5
Nautic Cross
18200 HarC 77044 3409 C1
18200 HarC 77346 3409 C1
Nautica Cir
18800 HarC 77346 3265 D7
18800 HOUS 77346 3265 D7
Nautical Dr
21400 HOUS 77450 3954 B2
Nautical Ln
1100 FBnC 77469 4616 E3
Nautical Mile Ln
- HarC 77494 3953 A2
Nautical Pointe Ln
17000 HarC 77095 3537 E3
Nautilus
3700 GLSN 77554 5220 E6
Nautilus Ct
16100 HarC 77532 3552 B3
Nautilus Ln
5200 HarC 77521 3833 D3
Nautilus St
500 HarC 77532 3552 B3
Nautique Wy
15000 HarC 77047 4373 A7
Nauts Ct
1800 HOUS 77008 3822 D5
E Navaho Tr
1900 HarC 77449 3815 E7
N Navaho Tr
20000 HarC 77449 3815 D7
S Navaho Tr
20000 HarC 77449 3815 D7
W Navaho Tr
1900 HarC 77449 3815 D7
Navajo Dr
1900 DRPK 77536 4109 D6
Navajo Ln
9300 MtgC 77354 2818 C6
23500 MtgC 77365 2972 B5
Navajo Rd
4900 FBnC 77471 4614 D4
Navajo St
4200 PASD 77504 4247 E6
4900 HOUS 77005 4101 B2
4900 HOUS 77027 4101 B2
Navajo Tr
- FBnC 77469 4364 B6
100 PNVL 77304 2237 A3
4500 BYTN 77521 3973 C2
Navajo Trail Dr
17900 HarC 77388 3112 D7
17900 HarC 77388 3257 C1
Navarre
2400 PRLD 77584 4501 D4
Navarro Dr
3900 GLSN 77554 5441 B4
Navarro St
5300 HOUS 77056 3960 E7
5400 HOUS 77056 4100 E1
Navarro Mills Dr
19300 HarC 77375 3109 D6
N Navasota Dr
20400 MtgC 77357 2827 A6
S Navasota Dr
20700 MtgC 77357 2827 A7
Navasota St
7400 HOUS 77016 3687 A3
Navidad Rd
6500 HOUS 77083 4096 A5
6900 HOUS 77083 4096 A5

STREET
Block City ZIP Map# Grid
Navigation Blvd
2200 HOUS 77002 3963 D4
2300 HOUS 77003 3963 E4
2800 HOUS 77003 3964 C5
6200 HOUS 77011 3964 D6
6900 HOUS 77011 3965 A6
7400 HOUS 77012 3965 B6
E Navigation Blvd
100 HOUS 77012 4105 C1
600 HOUS 77012 3965 B7
Navigation Dr
15200 GlsC 77517 4986 A1
Nayland Rock St
3500 HarC 77066 3401 C5
Naylor St
1100 HOUS 77002 3963 D2
1100 HOUS 77009 3963 C2
E Nazro St
10 BYTN 77520 4112 E1
W Nazro St
10 BYTN 77520 4112 D1
Neal Dr
- MtgC 77355 2962 D3
800 SGLD 77478 4368 B1
4600 SEBK 77586 4382 C6
Neal St
100 BYTN 77520 4112 D2
1200 HarC 77375 2964 C5
1200 TMBL 77375 2964 C5
4200 HOUS 77017 4105 E7
4600 HOUS 77017 4106 A7
5000 HOUS 77017 4246 A1
Neal Ridge Dr
7400 HOUS 77489 4371 B6
Nealwood Ct
4500 FBnC 77545 4622 E2
Neap Ct
700 HarC 77532 3552 A1
Neath St
19000 HarC 77346 3264 D6
Nebraska Av
300 HOUS 77017 4246 C2
300 SHUS 77017 4246 C2
300 SHUS 77587 4246 C2
Nebraska St
3100 BYTN 77520 4112 A1
4600 DKSN 77539 4754 B3
Neches Ct
4800 MtgC 77386 2970 B2
Neches St
5000 HOUS 77026 3825 A5
Neches River Dr
2800 PRLD 77584 4502 E4
Neches Trail Ln
4600 HarC 77388 3112 B3
Necklace Tree Ln
- FBnC 77494 4092 D4
Necoridge Dr
16100 HOUS 77053 4371 D6
Nectar Ct
12400 HOUS 77082 4097 D1
Nectar Grove Ct
12000 HarC 77089 4504 E1
12000 HarC 77089 4505 A2
Nedith Ln
3600 DRPK 77536 4249 C1
Nedwald St
9700 HOUS 77029 3966 A5
9800 GNPK 77547 3966 A5
Neece Dr
6300 HarC 77041 3679 B4
Needham Ln
25000 MtgC 77365 3118 E2
Needham Rd
- MtgC 77384 2676 A5
- WDLC 77385 2677 A4
3000 MtgC 77385 2676 B5
9100 WDLD 77385 2676 B5
10600 MtgC 77385 2677 A5
24100 MtgC 77365 2973 E7
24600 MtgC 77365 3118 E1
25000 MtgC 77365 3119 A2
Needham Rd SR-242
- MtgC 77384 2676 A5
- WDLD 77385 2676 B5
9000 MtgC 77385 2676 D5
10600 MtgC 77385 2677 A5
Needham St
10100 HOUS 77013 3827 B5
Needham Cross Dr
9400 HarC 77379 3110 D6
Needle Bend Ct
19900 MSCY 77459 4497 E6
Needleleaf Ln
200 FBnC 77479 4367 B4
Needlepoint Rd
9300 BYTN 77521 3834 D3
9300 BYTN 77521 3835 A3
9300 HarC 77521 3834 D3
9300 HarC 77521 3835 A3
E Needlepoint Rd
10500 BYTN 77520 3835 C3
10500 CmbC 77520 3835 D3
W Needlepoint Rd
10100 BYTN 77520 3835 C3
10100 CmbC 77520 3835 C3
10100 HarC 77521 3835 B3
Needle Ridge Ct
16800 FBnC 77478 4236 A7
Needles Nest Rd
12500 HarC 77038 3543 B4
Needles Throw Ln
2600 HarC 77038 3543 B4
Needlewalk Ln
20200 HarC 77379 3112 A4
Neeley Dr
1300 SPVL 77055 3821 B7
Neelie Ct
20900 HarC 77338 3261 E3
Neenah Ln
- FBnC 77494 3952 B5
Neeshaw Dr
11000 HarC 77065 3540 A1
11000 HarC 77070 3540 A1
11300 HarC 77065 3539 E1
Neff St
6300 HOUS 77074 4100 B5
6300 HOUS 77081 4100 B5
7100 HOUS 77074 4099 E5
9200 HOUS 77036 4099 A5
11500 HOUS 77072 4098 B5
12000 HOUS 77072 4097 E5
Nehoc Ln
19400 HarC 77346 3265 D6
19400 HOUS 77346 3265 D6
Neidigk Sawmill Rd
100 MtgC 77354 2817 E7

Houston Street Index

STREET
Block City ZIP Map# Grid

Neils Branch Dr
13600 HOUS 77077 3957 A6
Neiman Rd
1100 HOUS 77091 3683 D6
Neimana Dr
- HOUS 77336 3121 B5
Nekoosa
- MtgC 77303 2239 B4
W Nelda Rd
400 HarC 77037 3544 B7
500 HOUS 77037 3544 B7
900 HOUS 77088 3544 A7
Nelders Cove
1200 FBnC 77469 4493 B5
Nelkins Ct
2700 HOUS 77026 3963 E1
Nell St
700 PASD 77506 4106 D5
1300 HOUS 77017 4106 D5
2100 HOUS 77034 4246 D4
2100 SHUS 77034 4246 D4
2100 SHUS 77587 4246 D4
Nella Cir
21500 HarC 77338 3260 A2
Nellie Dr
8000 HOUS 77022 3685 C7
8000 HOUS 77022 3824 C1
Nellie Gail Trail Ln
20300 HarC 77450 3954 D7
W Nellis Rd
200 HarC 77037 3684 C1
Nellsfield Ln
10800 HOUS 77075 4377 A4
Nelms St
6900 HOUS 77061 4244 E6
8400 HOUS 77061 4245 D5
Nelson Av
- HOUS 77034 4379 A4
- SEBK 77586 4509 D4
500 GlsC 77650 4878 E6
600 HarC 77532 3552 D4
2300 GlsC 77650 4879 B5
N Nelson Dr
5000 KATY 77493 3813 E6
S Nelson Dr
4900 KATY 77493 3813 E7
Nelson Ln
100 FBnC 77469 4493 E7
Nelson Rd
1000 ALVN 77511 4867 C4
2400 HLCS 77511 4867 C4
2600 BzaC 77511 4866 B4
6100 PRLD 77584 4502 D4
Nelson St
2300 GlsC 77650 4879 A5
14500 HOUS 77045 4372 A3
27200 HarC 77373 3113 E1
27500 HarC 77373 2968 E7
27500 HarC 77373 2969 A7
27500 HarC 77373 3114 A1
Nelson Bay Ct
14200 FBnC 77478 4367 A4
Nelson Bridges Dr
24900 HarC 77389 2966 A4
Nelson Landing Dr
15500 HarC 77433 3251 D6
Nelva Park Ct
20400 HarC 77449 3815 D2
Nelva Park Dr
3800 HarC 77449 3815 D2
Nelwood Dr
2400 HarC 77038 3543 A1
Nelwyn St
5900 HOUS 77009 3824 B4
Nemard Ln
8400 HarC 77049 3690 B5
Nemes Ln
2200 PRLD 77581 4504 C3
Nenana Dr
- HOUS 77096 4241 B2
4000 HOUS 77025 4241 C2
4700 HOUS 77035 4241 B2
Neon St
13500 HarC 77047 4374 D3
13500 HOUS 77047 4374 D3
Neosho
9800 MtgC 77354 2818 B6
Nepau Dr
11100 HOUS 77477 4238 A4
Neptune
3800 GLSN 77554 5220 E6
Neptune Cir
300 TKIS 77554 5106 B4
Neptune Dr
2800 BYUV 77563 4990 E7
2800 BYUV 77563 4991 A7
2800 GlsC 77563 4990 E7
2800 GlsC 77563 4991 A7
Neptune Ln
1400 HOUS 77062 4507 B2
Neptune Rd
2800 BzaC 77511 4868 B7
Nero's Palace St
- RMFT 77357 2829 B1
Nesmith Dr
12300 HOUS 77035 4240 C6
Nest Ln
600 HOUS 77022 3823 E1
Nesting Hollow Ct
14500 HarC 77396 3548 B2
Nesting Trail Ln
14500 HarC 77396 3548 B1
Nesting Wood Dr
14700 HarC 77396 3548 C2
Nestlewood Pl
10 WDLD 77382 2819 A1
Neston Dr
13600 HarC 77041 3679 B4
Netherfield St
6900 HOUS 77087 4244 E1
Netherfield Wy
10 WDLD 77382 2820 A1
Netherwood Ct
2400 BzaC 77584 4501 A4
Netleaf Garden Dr
- FBnC 77494 4092 C4
Nett St
4500 HOUS 77007 3962 B2
Nettlebrook Ln
20700 FBnC 77450 4094 B5
Nettleton St
2000 HOUS 77003 3963 D7
2000 HOUS 77004 3963 D7
2700 HOUS 77004 4103 D1
Neuces Cr
7300 FBnC 77459 4496 E7
Neuens Rd
9400 HOUS 77080 3820 B5
10200 HOUS 77043 3820 A5
Neuhaus St
100 HOUS 77061 4245 A6
6900 HOUS 77061 4244 E6
Neuman St
1800 LMQU 77568 4990 A2
Neumann Dr
1900 GLSN 77551 5108 C6
16600 HOUS 77058 4507 D2
Neurath St
100 HOUS 77003 3963 E4
Neutral Bay Dr
- HarC 77429 3252 B7
Neuville St
- HarC 77015 3828 B7
Neva Ct
20900 HarC 77338 3261 E3
Nevada Av
500 SHUS 77587 4246 D4
Nevada St
1400 BYTN 77520 4111 E1
1400 HOUS 77006 3962 C5
4000 DKSN 77539 4754 A3
Nevelson Cir
17200 HarC 77379 3256 B3
Nevermore Dr
13300 HarC 77429 3398 A6
Neville Av
7800 HTCK 77563 4988 D4
Nevin Ct
10 CNRO 77301 2530 B3
Nevisway St
16900 HarC 77084 3678 B7
New Av
- PRVW 77445 2955 B7
New Rd
3300 HarC 77532 3553 E1
3700 HarC 77532 3554 A1
New St
- HOUS 77035 4240 E4
New Ann St
16200 HarC 77429 3397 A6
E New Avery Pl
10 WDLD 77382 2674 C4
W New Avery Pl
10 WDLD 77382 2674 C4
Newbear Dr
5300 HarC 77449 3676 D6
New Bedford Ct
100 HarC 77532 3552 C2
New Bedford St
16300 HarC 77532 3552 B3
Newberry St
4500 HOUS 77051 4243 C2
4600 HOUS 77033 4243 D2
12700 SGLD 77478 4237 C4
Newberry Trail Ct
10 WDLD 77382 2674 C4
Newborough Dr
10500 HOUS 77099 4238 D1
Newbridge Ct
2400 BzaC 77584 4501 A4
Newbridge St
6700 HOUS 77092 3682 B6
Newbrook Cir
8500 HOUS 77072 4098 B7
Newbrook Dr
3000 BzaC 77584 4501 B6
3000 PRLD 77584 4501 B6
11300 HOUS 77072 4098 B7
12700 HOUS 77072 4097 C7
12900 HarC 77072 4097 C7
13000 HarC 77083 4097 C7
New Brunswick Dr
11900 HOUS 77089 4378 C6
Newburge Ln
- HarC 77094 3955 A1
Newburgh Dr
9000 HarC 77095 3538 D4
Newbury Ct
2700 BzaC 77584 4501 A5
Newbury Dr
6200 HarC 77449 3677 C4
Newbury Tr
7400 SGLD 77479 4367 D6
Newbury Park Dr
20800 FBnC 77450 4094 A3
Newcastle Dr
2800 BYTN 77521 3973 B4
3100 HOUS 77027 3961 B7
3800 HOUS 77027 4101 B2
3800 HOUS 77081 4101 B2
5400 BLAR 77081 4101 B2
5400 BLAR 77401 4101 B2
5400 HOUS 77401 4101 B2
8500 HOUS 77096 4101 B7
New Castle Ln
- LGCY 77573 4630 B7
New Cedars Dr
1300 HOUS 77062 4379 E7
1500 HOUS 77062 4380 A6
New Century Dr
9300 HarC 77507 4250 A5
Newcomb Wy
1600 HOUS 77058 4507 D3
Newcomen Dr
3800 HarC 77066 3401 C5
Newcourt Blvd
- HarC 77379 3110 C3
9400 HarC 77375 3110 C3
Newcourt Pl St
22600 HarC 77375 3110 C3
Newcrest Dr
12700 HarC 77060 3403 B5
Newcroft Ct
9000 HarC 77375 3110 D3
New Cypress Dr
13000 HarC 77429 3397 E4
Newdale Dr
10100 HOUS 77099 4238 B3
New Dawn Pl
10 WDLD 77385 2676 C4
New Decade Dr
9300 HarC 77507 4250 A5
Newel Elm St
11700 HarC 77038 3543 B5
Newell Dr
800 RHMD 77469 4491 D1
New England Ct
2300 HarC 77598 4630 C1
New England Ln
- HOUS 77449 3814 D6
Newfalls Ct
20500 FBnC 77469 4094 C6
New Field Dr
16100 HarC 77082 4096 A3
Newfield Bridge Ln
15100 FBnC 77478 4236 D3
New Forest Dr
18300 MtgC 77365 2971 E2
21800 MtgC 77365 2972 A2
New Forest Gln
6600 HarC 77049 3829 A2
New Forest Ln
7700 FBnC 77469 4493 E6
7700 FBnC 77479 4493 E6
New Forest Pkwy
6500 HarC 77049 3828 E2
New Forest Rd
9100 HarC 77379 3255 E5
9100 HarC 77379 3256 A5
Newfoundland Ct
5900 HarC 77379 3111 E6
Newgate Dr
23200 HarC 77373 3115 B6
Newglen Ln
16600 HarC 77084 3678 B4
New Greens Ct
10 HOUS 77339 3264 D1
Newhall St
11600 HarC 77093 3546 C7
New Hampshire St
300 HOUS 77029 3966 A7
New Hampton Dr
12300 HarC 77377 3254 B6
New Hastings Dr
15100 HarC 77095 3538 E7
New Haven Dr
200 HOUS 77076 3684 D5
Newhaven Tr
1100 PRLD 77584 4501 B2
Newhoff St
2600 HOUS 77026 3824 E7
2800 HOUS 77026 3825 E7
New Hope Ln
300 HarC 77494 3953 A2
Newhope Terrace Ln
4500 HarC 77449 3677 A6
Newhouse St
3700 HOUS 77019 3962 C4
New Jersey St
2000 BYTN 77520 4112 A2
Newkay Ln
9100 HarC 77379 3255 D3
New Kent Ct
14700 FBnC 77478 4236 D2
New Kent Dr
9600 FBnC 77478 4236 D2
New Kentucky Rd
12600 HarC 77429 3398 A5
New Kentucky Vil
20200 HarC 77447 3105 E2
New Kentucky Park Dr
- HarC 77447 3105 E2
New Kings Tr
20000 HarC 77346 3264 D4
Newkirk Ln
5200 HOUS 77021 4104 B5
Newland Cir
- WDLD 77382 2674 B6
Newland Ct
11700 HarC 77377 3254 E5
Newland Crest Dr
12700 HarC 77038 3543 A3
New Leaf Ct
20900 HarC 77073 3259 A6
New Light Pl
10 WDLD 77382 2819 E2
Newlight Bend Dr
16700 HarC 77095 3538 A4
Newlin Dr
1300 FBnC 77469 4492 B1
1300 RHMD 77469 4492 B1
New London Dr
600 LGCY 77573 4631 E2
600 LGCY 77573 4632 A2
Newly Rd
15200 HarC 77084 3678 D4
Newman Dr
3300 HarC 77521 3834 E5
Newman Rd
100 LMQU 77568 4873 B7
100 TXCY 77591 4873 B7
700 LMQU 77568 4989 B3
Newman St
- BYTN 77520 4112 E1
1300 ALVN 77511 4749 A7
1700 ALVN 77511 4748 E6
2600 HOUS 77019 3962 B7
2600 HOUS 77098 3962 B7
Newmark Dr
1400 HarC 77014 3402 C3
New Market Ln
16600 HarC 77083 4235 E1
New Meadow Dr
3100 BYTN 77521 3973 B4
Newmeadow Dr
11800 HarC 77064 3399 E7
New Meadows Ct
4100 FBnC 77479 4366 C5
N New Meadows Dr
4100 FBnC 77479 4366 C5
W New Meadows Dr
100 FBnC 77479 4366 C6
New Mexico St
300 HOUS 77029 3966 A6
2000 BYTN 77520 4112 B2
Newmill Ct
20800 HarC 77379 3111 E3
Newmint Ct
20100 HarC 77449 3815 D6
Newmint Dr
20200 HarC 77449 3815 D6
Newmont
- HOUS 77042 4099 A2
New Moon Tr
20200 HarC 77532 3410 B2
New Oak Ct
6300 HarC 77346 3264 E4
New Oak Tr
10 HarC 77346 3264 D4
New Orleans
25900 HarC 77377 3109 A5
New Orleans St
- HMPD 77445 2952 E7
- HMPD 77445 2953 A7
1300 DRPK 77536 4108 E6
5000 HOUS 77020 3964 C1
Newpark Dr
5000 HOUS 77041 3680 E7
12300 HarC 77377 3254 C5
E Newpark Dr
5000 HOUS 77041 3680 E7
N Newpark Dr
10400 HOUS 77041 3680 E7
New Pines Dr
700 HarC 77373 3113 E1
New Plymouth Ct
2900 HarC 77598 4630 C1
Newpoint Dr
4900 FBnC 77545 4622 D3
5300 ARLA 77583 4622 C4
Newport
19100 MtgC 77357 2829 D4
Newport Blvd
- HarC 77532 3552 B3
200 LGCY 77573 4631 C4
Newport Ct
5000 MtgC 77386 2970 E7
Newport Ln
400 HOUS 77450 3954 B2
7300 PRLD 77584 4502 B4
27700 MtgC 77386 2970 E7
27700 MtgC 77386 3115 E1
New Port Rd
11500 PASD 77586 4382 D4
12200 PASD 77586 4383 A3
Newport St
5500 HOUS 77023 4104 C2
Newport Bridge Cir
15200 FBnC 77478 4236 C4
Newport Bridge Ct
15100 FBnC 77478 4236 D4
Newport Bridge Ln
10700 FBnC 77478 4236 C4
Newport Country Club Dr
1400 HarC 77532 3551 E2
Newport Shore Dr
11800 HarC 77065 3539 D3
Newquay St
5600 HOUS 77085 4372 A2
5700 HOUS 77085 4371 E2
New Rochelle Ct
12500 HOUS 77089 4378 C7
New Rochelle Dr
12100 HOUS 77089 4378 C7
Newshire Dr
4000 HOUS 77025 4101 C7
Newson Rd
3200 BzaC 77511 4868 B6
Newson Rd CO-326
3200 BzaC 77511 4868 B6
New South Wales Ct
2300 FBnC 77450 3954 A6
New Strand St
2500 GLSN 77550 5109 A3
New Territory Blvd
- SGLD 77479 4367 D5
10 FBnC 77479 4493 C1
5500 FBnC 77479 4366 D7
5700 FBnC 77479 4367 A6
11800 SGLD 77478 4367 D4
Newton Av
200 RHMD 77469 4364 E7
Newton Dr
- ALVN 77511 4748 D6
- BzaC 77511 4748 D6
3500 PASD 77503 4108 C6
21900 MtgC 77357 2827 C5
Newton Ln
- CNRO 77304 2382 D1
Newton St
100 CNRO 77301 2384 A5
10800 HOUS 77075 4377 C3
11200 HOUS 77089 4377 C4
Newton Falls Ln
14800 FBnC 77478 4236 E4
New Trails Dr
8200 WDLD 77381 2821 C3
New Tree Ln
1100 MSCY 77489 4370 D6
New Village Ln
13700 FBnC 77478 4237 A3
New Vista Ln
11500 HarC 77067 3402 A6
New West Dr
4000 HarC 77507 4249 E5
4000 HarC 77507 4250 A5
4000 LPRT 77571 4249 E5
New World Dr
6400 HarC 77449 3676 C3
New York Av
29800 MtgC 77354 2818 B1
New York St
2100 BYTN 77520 4112 B2
6300 HOUS 77021 4103 D7
Nexus Rd
4500 HOUS 77053 4372 C7
Ney St
9900 HOUS 77034 4246 C6
Neyland St
10 HOUS 77022 3824 A2
300 HOUS 77018 3823 D2
300 HOUS 77022 3823 D2
Nia Pl
13500 HOUS 77085 4371 E1
Niagara St
900 HOUS 77051 4243 D1
Niagra Falls Dr
20100 HarC 77375 3109 D5
Niblick Ln
- HarC 77373 3261 A1
Nicar St
100 HarC 77037 3544 D6
Nice Ct
800 HarC 77015 3828 B7
Nicecrest Dr
6700 FBnC 77469 4093 D7
Niche Wy
20800 FBnC 77450 4094 B3
Nicholas Cross
2200 CNRO 77304 2236 E3
Nicholas Dr
2500 PRLD 77581 4503 E3
Nicholas St
14800 HOUS 77085 4370 E1
14800 HOUS 77085 4371 A1
Nicholas Pass Ln
26300 HarC 77433 3396 B6
Nicholas Pl Ct
3200 HOUS 77056 4100 E1
Nichole Woods Dr
1500 HOUS 77047 4373 D2
Nicholforest Ln
7400 HarC 77389 2966 B1
Nicholi Ln
5800 DKSN 77539 4754 E1
Nichols Al
3500 HOUS 77020 3964 A2
Nichols Av
1600 LGCY 77539 4632 D7
1600 LGCY 77573 4632 D7
1900 GlsC 77539 4632 D7
2300 DKSN 77539 4632 E7
Nichols Cir
- HarC 77532 3411 E6
- HarC 77532 3412 A6
Nichols Ln
18700 MtgC 77357 2826 E3
Nichols Rd
- HarC 77447 3104 D3
Nichols St
2400 DKSN 77539 4632 E7
2400 DKSN 77539 4753 E1
2400 GlsC 77539 4632 E7
2400 GlsC 77539 4753 E1
3100 DKSN 77539 4754 A2
4200 HOUS 77020 3964 B1
Nicholson
4400 HOUS 77018 3823 C1
Nicholson Rd
11700 MtgC 77303 2239 D2
Nicholson St
700 HOUS 77007 3962 C1
800 HOUS 77007 3823 C7
800 HOUS 77008 3823 C7
1900 SEBK 77586 4509 C2
Nichols Sawmill Rd
22600 MtgC 77447 2959 E4
22900 MtgC 77447 2960 A4
24800 MtgC 77355 2960 A4
25000 SGCH 77355 2960 A4
25900 MtgC 77355 2961 A2
25900 SGCH 77355 2961 A2
26900 MtgC 77355 2815 A5
30500 MAGA 77355 2815 A1
30700 MAGA 77355 2669 A7
30700 MtgC 77355 2669 A7
Nickaburr Creek Dr
6700 MtgC 77354 2673 A4
Nickel Dr
15400 HOUS 77489 4371 A5
Nickelwood Ct
9300 HarC 77070 3399 D5
Nickerson Ln
14900 HOUS 77060 3544 C3
Nickerton Ln
21700 HarC 77388 3112 B4
Nicklaus Ln
700 MtgC 77302 2530 C6
Nickleby Ct
3000 FBnC 77494 3953 C7
3000 FBnC 77494 4093 A6
Nickle Grove Dr
10300 HarC 77095 3537 E2
Nicks Run Ln
2800 FBnC 77494 3953 B7
Nickwill Wy
3200 HarC 77388 3112 E5
3200 HarC 77388 3113 A5
Nicky St
34000 WlrC 77484 3245 E1
Nicole Cir
4600 HarC 77084 3678 C7
Nicole Ct
4600 HarC 77084 3678 C7
12700 MSCY 77071 4370 B1
12700 MSCY 77489 4370 B1
Nicole Dr
3600 PASD 77503 4108 C5
Nicole Ln
16700 HarC 77084 3678 B7
Nicoles Pl Tr
10600 HarC 77089 4378 C7
Nicolini
4400 DKSN 77539 4754 A3
Niday Rd
3000 BzaC 77511 4868 A3
Nielan St
6500 HOUS 77028 3826 C2
Nigh Wy
- HOUS 77034 4378 C4
Night Beacon Point Dr
9100 HarC 77379 3110 D5
Nightbird Tr
20000 HarC 77532 3410 B3
Nightbrook Ln
- FBnC 77479 4496 C6
Nightfall Pl
10 WDLD 77381 2674 D6
Nighthaven Ct
17400 HarC 77095 3537 D4
Nighthawk Ct
400 SGLD 77478 4368 B3
Nighthawk Dr
- SGLD 77478 4368 B3
Night Hawk Pl
10 WDLD 77380 2968 A1
Night Heron Pl
10 WDLD 77382 2675 C6
E Night Heron Pl
10 WDLD 77382 2675 D6
W Night Heron Pl
10 WDLD 77382 2675 C6
Nightingale Cir
7200 TXCY 77591 4873 C6
Nightingale Ct
5000 SGLD 77479 4495 A5
Nightingale Dr
- MtgC 77306 2680 A3
5600 HOUS 77017 4106 C7
13500 HarC 77050 3548 A5
18000 MtgC 77302 2679 E3
18000 MtgC 77302 2680 A3
Nightingale Fall Ct
16500 HarC 77429 3252 D7
Nightmist Ct
4300 FBnC 77494 4092 D1
Nightowl Tr
2500 HarC 77373 3114 D7
Night Rain Ct
10 WDLD 77381 2821 B3
Nightshade
5300 DKSN 77539 4754 D1
Nightshade Ct
5000 HarC 77388 3112 A3
Nightshade Crest Ln
12900 HOUS 77085 4240 E7
Night Song Ct
10 WDLD 77380 2968 A4
Nightsong Dr
2600 PRLD 77545 4499 E3
Night Star Ln
1900 HOUS 77077 3957 D6
Night Wind Ln
- FBnC 77450 4093 D2
Nightwind Pl
10 WDLD 77381 2820 C2
Nightwood Ln
- HOUS 77085 4240 D7
Nihm Ln
3100 FBnC 77494 3952 E7
3100 FBnC 77494 3953 A7
Niki's Cross
7800 CNRO 77304 2236 E3
Nikita Ct
16000 MtgC 77302 2679 B4
Nikki Ln
1100 STAF 77477 4370 C4
Nila Grove Ct
10 WDLD 77385 2676 C4
Nile Ct
- MtgC 77365 2972 C4
Niles St
8100 HOUS 77017 4105 D7
Nimble Ln
16300 HarC 77530 3829 E4
Nimitz St
12700 HOUS 77015 3967 A2
13700 HarC 77015 3967 E2
14000 HarC 77015 3968 A2
Nimrod St
500 HOUS 77020 3964 B3
Nina Dr
16700 HarC 77546 4506 B6
Nina Ln
100 STAF 77477 4369 B3
200 FBnC 77477 4369 B3
Nina Lee Ln
1700 HOUS 77018 3822 B1
4400 HOUS 77092 3822 A1
5500 HOUS 77092 3821 D1
Nine Iron Ct
2100 HarC 77089 4504 E2
Nine Mile Ln
5900 FBnC 77459 4497 A7
Nine Point Ct
17700 HarC 77447 3249 E3
Nine Point Ln
24000 HarC 77447 3249 E2
Ninte
10900 HDWV 77024 3960 A2
10900 HNCV 77024 3960 A2
Nipper Ln
- PRLD 77584 4501 E4
Nita St
3000 HOUS 77051 4243 A6
Nithdale Dr
6100 HOUS 77096 4240 A2
Nitida St
12900 HOUS 77045 4241 B7
13400 HOUS 77045 4372 B1
Nix St
10 HOUS 77003 3963 E4
Nixburg Ln
23300 MtgC 77365 3118 B2
N N Kingwood Forest Dr
- HOUS 77339 3119 C1
Noack Rd
12900 MtgC 77355 2962 E1
12900 MtgC 77355 2963 A1
Noah Ln
7500 HarC 77379 3256 B3
Noah St
3400 HOUS 77021 4103 B7
Noah Landing Dr
8800 HarC 77064 3540 E1
Noahpines Ct
1700 MtgC 77386 2969 D6
Noah Ridge Ct
28000 MtgC 77386 2969 D7
Noahs Landing Ln
14100 HarC 77047 4374 D4
Nobel Canyon Ln
- FBnC 77450 4093 E1
Nobility Dr
10600 HOUS 77099 4238 A3
11100 HOUS 77477 4238 A4
11500 HOUS 77477 4237 E4
Noble Ct
4500 BYTN 77521 3972 C2
N Noble Rd
1000 TXCY 77591 4873 A5
S Noble Rd
10 TXCY 77591 4873 A6
200 LMQU 77568 4873 A7
Noble Run
10 HarC 77346 3265 B1
Noble St
100 HarC 77373 3114 A2
1100 HOUS 77009 3963 D1
2000 HOUS 77026 3963 E1
3100 HOUS 77026 3964 A1
4300 HOUS 77020 3964 B1
E Noble St
100 HarC 77373 3114 A2
Noble Bend Dr
10 WDLD 77382 2673 E6
Noble Bend Pl
10 WDLD 77382 2673 E6
Noblebriar Ct
15700 HOUS 77489 4371 A6
Noble Brook Ct
15500 HarC 77049 3829 A2
Noblecrest Dr
13200 HarC 77041 3679 C1
Noble Crusade Ct
20800 HarC 77375 3110 A4
Noble Cypress Ct
4100 PASD 77059 4380 C3
Noble Fir Ct
8200 MtgC 77385 2676 C6
Noble Forest Dr
18000 HarC 77346 3408 B1
Noble Glen Dr
1100 FBnC 77545 4622 E2
1100 FBnC 77545 4623 A2
Noble Hollow Dr
- FBnC 77469 4235 E7
3300 FBnC 77478 4235 E7
Noble Lakes Ln
3100 HOUS 77082 4098 A2
Nobleman Dr
7400 HarC 77041 3679 C1
Noble Manor Ln
- PRLD 77583 4500 B4
Noble Meadow Ln
16300 HarC 77073 3259 B4
Noble Oak Ct
17700 HarC 77095 3537 E7
Noble Oak Tr
- PASD 77059 4380 C3
4200 HOUS 77059 4380 B3
Noble Oak Wy
- HOUS 77059 4380 B3
Noble Pass Ln
16800 HarC 77095 3538 A
Noble Pine Dr
- PASD 77059 4380 C
4200 HOUS 77059 4380 C
Noble Pointe Ct
10200 HarC 77379 3110 B
Noble Pointe Dr
1500 HarC 77379 3110 B
Noble Sage Ct
4500 PASD 77059 4380 C
Nobles Crossing Dr
22100 HarC 77373 3260 D
Noble Shore Ct
5700 HOUS 77345 3120 B
Noble Spring Rd
800 HOUS 77062 4506 D
Nobletimber Wy
11100 HarC 77375 3110 A
Noblewood Bnd
11200 HOUS 77082 4098 C
Noblewood Ct
- LGCY 77573 4630 E
16400 FBnC 77478 4236 A
Noblewood Dr
- FBnC 77478 4236 A
Noblewood Wy
16200 HarC 77082 4096 A
Noblewood Crest Ln
11400 HOUS 77082 4098 B
Noburn
- FBnC 77478 4237 D
Noco Dr
12200 HarC 77375 3109 C
Nocturnal Ct
23300 HarC 77449 3814 C
Nocturne Dr
5400 FBnC 77583 4623 C
Nocturne Ln
1800 HOUS 77043 3820 A
Nocturne Woods Pl
10 WDLD 77382 2673 C
Nod Av
100 HarC 77532 3692 C
Nodaway Ln
5200 HarC 77379 3257 B
Nodding Pines Ln
7000 HarC 77044 3827 B
7200 HarC 77044 3688 E
Nodding Pines St
3200 MtgC 77380 2821 B
3500 MtgC 77380 2967 A
Nodys Wy
- FBnC 77545 4499 D
Noel Ct
3100 BzaC 77584 4501 E
Noel St
8900 HOUS 77033 4243 B
Noelle Ct
20900 HarC 77338 3261 D
Nogales Bend Dr
1100 FBnC 77469 4493 C
Nogalus Dr
1500 HOUS 77532 3266 B
Noisy Waters Dr
1000 HarC 77095 3538 E
1000 HarC 77095 3539 A
Nola Ct
12200 HOUS 77013 3827 E
S Nola Ct
- HOUS 77013 3827 E
Nola Ln
300 SGCH 77362 2816 D
S Nolan Ct
3200 PRLD 77584 4501 E
N Nolan Pl
4100 PRLD 77584 4501 D
S Nolan Pl
4100 PRLD 77584 4501 D
Nolan Rd
2700 BYTN 77520 3973 B
2700 BYTN 77521 3973 B
Nolan St
10 HOUS 77003 3964 A
Nold Dr
10500 HOUS 77016 3686 D
Nold Rd
10300 HOUS 77016 3686 C
Nolda St
4500 HOUS 77007 3962 A
Noldale Dr
5000 HOUS 77016 3686 C
Nolridge Dr
5000 HOUS 77016 3686 C
Nomie St
17000 PTVL 77372 2682 E
Nomini Hall Ln
23900 HarC 77493 3814 B
Nonesuch Rd
17000 MtgC 77306 2679 E
Nook Ct
9200 HarC 77040 3681 E
Noonday Ct
400 HarC 77060 3544 D
Noonday Ln
400 HarC 77060 3544 D
400 HOUS 77060 3544 D
Noontide Cir
10 WDLD 77380 2822 A
Noontide Tr
8000 FBnC 77583 4744 A
Noras Ln
100 HOUS 77018 3823 D
100 HOUS 77022 3823 D
Norborne Ln
5200 HarC 77069 3256 C
Norbrook Dr
10300 HarC 77089 4377 B
Norchester Wy
24100 HarC 77389 2966 D
Norchester Village Dr
10500 HarC 77070 3399 A
Norcrest Rd
1800 HOUS 77055 3821 B
Nordic Dr
14100 HarC 77049 3828 C
Nordling Rd
5300 HOUS 77022 3684 D
5400 HOUS 77076 3684 D
7500 HOUS 77037 3684 D
7600 HarC 77037 3684 D
Nordway Dr
17300 HarC 77084 3677 E
17300 HarC 77084 3678 A
Norell Dr
700 HarC 77530 3830 A
Norene St
100 CNRO 77301 2384 A

STREET
Block City ZIP Map# Grid

Norfolk
19000 MtgC 77357 2829 B4
Norfolk Ct
26500 MtgC 77357 2829 C3
Norfolk Dr
800 PRLD 77584 4501 D1
Norfolk St
1600 HOUS 77006 4102 C1
2200 HOUS 77098 4102 A1
3200 HOUS 77098 4101 E1
3700 HOUS 77046 4101 C1
3900 HOUS 77027 4101 D1
Norfolk Pine St
3900 FBnC 77545 4622 D1
Norfolk Ridge Wy
19600 FBnC 77469 4234 D3
Norford Ln
14000 FBnC 77083 4237 B2
Norgrove Ct
14100 HarC 77070 3399 E1
Norham Ct
8700 FBnC 77083 4236 D1
8700 HarC 77083 4096 E7
Norham Dr
- FBnC 77083 4236 E1
Norham St
1100 HOUS 77022 3685 C7
Norham Manor Dr
1600 HarC 77379 3110 B6
Norhill Blvd
4800 HOUS 77009 3823 E5
Norhill St
2500 HOUS 77009 3962 E1
3600 HOUS 77009 3823 E7
Norhill Pointe Dr
14100 HarC 77044 3549 D2
Norhtington Dr
5000 HarC 77039 3546 D6
Norkey St
12300 HarC 77086 3542 B4
Norland St
6200 HOUS 77022 3824 B3
Norland Point Ln
1000 HarC 77073 3259 A4
Norlinda St
1700 HarC 77093 3685 C1
Norlund Wy
10 WDLD 77382 2673 D6
Norma Ln
3300 PRLD 77584 4503 B6
N Norma St
- HOUS 77009 3824 B7
Norman St
1800 LMQU 77568 4990 A2
2500 PASD 77506 4107 E4
2700 PASD 77506 4108 A4
Normandale
1500 HOUS 77029 3965 D3
Normandale St
1700 HOUS 77029 3965 D4
Normandy
11800 HOUS 77035 4240 A7
Normandy Ct
13800 SGLD 77478 4237 A5
Normandy St
100 HarC 77015 3828 B7
100 HarC 77049 3828 B4
700 HarC 77015 3967 B2
800 HOUS 77015 3967 B2
Normandy Wy
4500 HOUS 77021 4103 E5
Normandy Crossing Dr
12500 HarC 77015 3967 A1
Normandy Forest Ct
3300 HarC 77388 3112 E4
Normandy Forest Dr
20700 HarC 77388 3112 D3
Normans Woods St
1200 HOUS 77077 3957 C4
Normeadow Ln
10800 HOUS 77076 3685 B4
Norments St
5400 HarC 77039 3546 E4
6000 HarC 77039 3547 A4
Normont Dr
11400 HarC 77070 3399 B1
11500 HarC 77070 3398 D1
Norris Dr
3000 HOUS 77025 4102 A7
3600 HOUS 77025 4101 E7
Norseman Ct
- HarC 77379 3111 E6
Norstand Ln
5300 HarC 77084 3678 D5
Norstrum Falls Ct
12900 HarC 77429 3397 B4
North Av
1300 HarC 77530 3830 C5
2400 PASD 77506 4107 E5
2700 PASD 77506 4108 A5
North Blvd
1300 HOUS 77006 4102 D1
2600 HOUS 77005 4102 A1
2600 HOUS 77098 4102 A1
North Dr
- LGCY 77573 4752 D1
10900 MtgC 77372 2537 A1
15000 HarC 77530 3829 D7
17200 HarC 77429 3396 D4
North Frwy
- CNRO - 2383 E6
- CNRO - 2529 E1
- CNRO - 2530 A7
- CNRO - 2676 A6
- HarC - 2968 D5
- HarC - 3113 D3
- HarC - 3258 E2
- HarC - 3402 E1
- HarC - 3403 A2
- HOUS - 3113 D4
- HOUS - 3258 E4
- HOUS - 3403 A6
- HOUS - 3544 B7
- HOUS - 3684 D6
- HOUS - 3823 E1
- HOUS - 3824 B6
- HOUS - 3963 B1
- MtgC - 2530 A5
- MtgC - 2676 A6
- MtgC - 2822 B7
- MtgC - 2968 C1
- ORDN - 2822 B4
- SHEH - 2676 B7
- SHEH - 2822 B5
400 CNRO 77304 2383 E6
North Frwy I-45
- CNRO - 2383 E6
- CNRO - 2529 E1
- CNRO - 2530 A7
- CNRO - 2676 A6
- HarC - 2968 D5
- HarC - 3113 D1
- HarC - 3258 E1
- HarC - 3402 E1
- HarC - 3403 A5
- HOUS - 3113 D4
- HOUS - 3258 E4
- HOUS - 3403 A3
- HOUS - 3544 B1
- HOUS - 3684 D6
- HOUS - 3823 E1
- HOUS - 3824 A4
- HOUS - 3963 B1
- MtgC - 2530 A5
- MtgC - 2676 A2
- MtgC - 2822 C7
- MtgC - 2968 C1
- ORDN - 2822 B5
- SHEH - 2676 B7
- SHEH - 2822 B5
North Ln
1000 HMBL 77338 3262 E6
1000 HMBL 77338 3263 A6
1000 HOUS 77088 3683 E2
North Pkwy
- CNRO 77303 2238 E7
North Rd
400 HarC 77521 3833 D7
800 BYTN 77521 3833 D7
North St
- HOUS 77547 4106 C2
- PRLD 77581 4503 A2
100 BYTN 77520 3971 C4
100 HOUS 77009 3824 B7
400 LbyC 77372 2538 C6
600 HarC 77532 3552 D3
5700 KATY 77494 3952 C1
6600 ARLA 77583 4623 A7
6600 FBnC 77583 4623 A7
21200 MtgC 77357 2973 B1
Northacre Dr
900 HarC 77073 3259 B5
Northaire Dr
500 HarC 77073 3259 A6
Northam Dr
10900 HarC 77375 3255 A1
Northam Ln
- HarC 77047 4374 A4
Northampton
25300 MtgC 77357 2828 E3
25300 MtgC 77357 2829 A3
Northampton Dr
900 CNRO 77303 2238 C7
E Northampton Pl
4100 HOUS 77098 4102 B1
W Northampton Pl
4100 HOUS 77098 4102 B1
Northampton Wy
6800 HOUS 77055 3821 D7
Northampton Forest Dr
24800 HarC 77389 2966 C3
Northampton Pines Dr
22800 HarC 77389 2966 E6
Northampton Terr Dr
25000 HarC 77389 2966 D3
Northbay Ct
100 LGCY 77539 4752 E3
E North Beltway
6800 HOUS 77396 3406 C7
8000 HarC 77396 3406 E7
8300 HarC 77396 3548 A1
North Bend Dr
- HarC 77073 3259 B6
Northbend Lndg
13300 HarC 77429 3396 E3
Northborough Dr
12400 HOUS 77067 3403 A6
12800 HOUS 77067 3402 E4
13500 HOUS 77014 3402 E4
Northbrace Dr
- HarC 77041 3679 E3
North Branch Dr
2600 HarC 77373 3114 D3
Northbriar Dr
- HarC 77073 3403 C1
20500 HarC 77073 3259 C7
Northbriar Ln
- HarC 77377 3253 D3
Northbridge Cir
8000 HarC 77379 3256 A3
Northbridge Ct
17200 HarC 77379 3256 A3
Northbridge Dr
7700 HarC 77379 3256 A4
Northbrook Dr
10600 HOUS 77043 3819 D6
North By Northwest
18500 HarC 77447 3104 A6
Northcairn Dr
- HarC 77084 3677 E4
North Carolina St
- HOUS 77029 3965 E7
E Northcastle Cir
10 WDLD 77384 2675 D4
W Northcastle Cir
100 WDLD 77384 2675 D5
E Northcastle Ct
10 WDLD 77384 2675 E5
Northcastle Ln
800 HarC 77373 2968 C6
Northchapel St
17200 HarC 77379 3255 D3
Northchase Ct
1100 CNRO 77301 2383 D3
Northchase Dr
16600 HOUS 77060 3403 C6
Northchase Ln
7100 FBnC 77469 4615 D4
Northchase Ridge Ln
12700 HarC 77044 3689 B4
Northcliff Pl
1800 SGLD 77478 4237 D5
Northcliff Manor Dr
12200 HarC 77066 3401 C4
12300 HarC 77014 3401 C4
Northcourt Rd
- HarC 77040 3681 C4
- HOUS 77092 3682 A4
7300 HOUS 77040 3682 A4
8300 HOUS 77040 3681 D4
North Cove Ln
13100 HarC 77377 3253 E3
Northcreek Ln
15500 MtgC 77365 2824 E5
15500 MtgC 77365 2825 A5
20700 HarC 77073 3259 D4
Northcrest Blvd
- MtgC 77357 2681 D6
Northcrest Cir
17000 MtgC 77357 2681 E6
17000 MtgC 77357 2682 A6
Northcrest Dr
21500 HarC 77379 3111 D2
21500 HarC 77388 3111 D2
21800 HarC 77389 3111 D2
22000 HarC 77389 2966 D7
Northcrest Tr
23800 MtgC 77357 2681 D7
Northcrest Village Ct
- HarC 77388 3111 E2
Northcrest Village Dr
- HarC 77388 3111 E2
Northcrest Village Wy
5900 HarC 77388 3111 D1
Northcross Dr
- HarC 77041 3679 E2
Northdale
- PRLD 77581 4504 E7
Northdale St
5600 HOUS 77087 4104 D7
5700 HOUS 77087 4244 D1
Northeast Dr
100 HOUS 77022 3824 A1
Northeast St
7800 HOUS 77028 3687 B5
North Echo Brch
5800 FBnC 77459 4497 A7
Northern Dr
- HOUS 77031 4239 C4
2500 LGCY 77573 4631 A6
8300 HOUS 77071 4239 C4
Northern Colony Ct
22900 HarC 77389 2966 E6
Northern Forest Dr
21000 HarC 77449 3676 C2
Northern Hill St
18700 HarC 77433 3252 A7
Northern Oak St
5800 HOUS 77016 3686 E2
Northern Point Blvd
15200 HarC 77095 3538 E4
15200 HarC 77095 3539 B5
Northern Star Dr
17300 HarC 77084 3677 B4
17300 HarC 77084 3678 A2
Northew St
600 HOUS 77091 3684 B5
Northface Manor Ct
14200 HarC 77429 3397 C2
Northfalk Dr
- HarC 77084 3678 A3
17500 HarC 77084 3677 E3
North Falls Dr
7800 HarC 77379 3256 C4
Northfield Ln
- MtgC 77355 2814 E3
4000 HOUS 77092 3821 B1
Northfleet Ct
3800 HOUS 77082 4097 B3
Northfleet Dr
13100 HOUS 77082 4097 B3
Northfolk Valley Ln
22400 MtgC 77365 2973 A3
Northfork Ct
2500 BzaC 77584 4501 D5
Northfork Dr
- BzaC 77584 4502 B5
- HarC 77041 3679 E3
- PRLD 77584 4502 B5
3500 BzaC 77584 4501 C5
4600 PRLD 77584 4501 E5
Northfork Bend Ln
- HarC 77377 3254 B1
Northfork Hollow Ln
7500 FBnC 77469 4095 B6
Northgate Ct
3200 BzaC 77583 4500 D6
Northgate Dr
10 WDLD 77380 2967 C3
16400 HOUS 77060 3403 C7
Northgate Ln
27400 MtgC 77372 2683 E4
Northgate Crossing Blvd
- HarC 77373 2968 D6
- HarC 77373 3113 E1
- HarC 77389 2968 D5
Northgate Fairway Dr
- HarC 77014 3257 D6
- HarC 77068 3257 D5
Northgate Forest Ct
17000 HarC 77068 3257 C4
Northgate Forest Dr
16400 HarC 77068 3257 C4
Northgate Ridge Dr
22700 HarC 77373 2968 E7
22700 HarC 77373 3113 D2
Northgate Springs Dr
900 HarC 77373 3113 D1
Northgate Village Dr
2700 HarC 77068 3257 D5
Northgate Villas Ln
3300 HarC 77014 3257 D7
Northglen Av
1900 DRPK 77536 4108 E6
Northgreen Blvd
- HarC 77032 3545 C1
- HOUS 77032 3404 B7
- HOUS 77032 3545 C1
Northgreen Cir
2500 MtgC 77303 2385 B1
Northgreen Dr
- HarC 77032 3545 C1
- HarC 77039 3545 C1
- HOUS 77032 3545 C1
Northgrove Ct
7400 BzaC 77581 4502 A1
Northhagen Dr
17400 HarC 77084 3678 A3
17500 HarC 77084 3677 E3
17900 HarC 77449 3677 D3
Northhampton Ct
3500 PRLD 77584 4501 C1
Northhampton Dr
800 PRLD 77584 4501 C2
North Highlands Cross
1700 HarC 77562 3832 B2
E North Hill Dr
200 HarC 77373 3113 E7
200 HOUS 77388 3113 E7
W North Hill Dr
100 HOUS 77388 3113 D7
300 HarC 77388 3113 D7
North Lake Dr
4300 FBnC 77469 4234 D5
Northlake Dr
13700 HOUS 77049 3828 B3
13800 HarC 77049 3828 B3
Northlake Forest Dr
15400 HarC 77429 3397 A1
Northland Dr
6300 HarC 77084 3677 E3
6300 HarC 77084 3678 A3
15600 MtgC 77365 2824 E4
15600 MtgC 77365 2825 A4
Northlawn Dr
500 HarC 77073 3259 A6
Northleaf Ct
10900 HarC 77086 3542 B1
Northleaf Dr
6500 HarC 77086 3542 C1
North Legacy Dr
12600 HarC 77038 3543 B4
Northlight Ln
26200 FBnC 77494 4092 E1
Northline Dr
6200 HOUS 77076 3684 D4
7900 HarC 77037 3684 D2
7900 HOUS 77037 3684 D2
Northline Rd
2300 MtgC 77384 2675 D7
Northline Mall
100 HOUS 77022 3824 A1
North Mark Dr
- HarC 77041 3679 E2
Northmark Dr
- HarC 77041 3679 E2
6300 HarC 77084 3677 E3
16000 HarC 77073 3259 B5
Northmoor Dr
- FBnC 77450 3954 A6
Northoak Forest Ln
22900 HarC 77389 2966 E6
Northoaks Dr
20300 HarC 77073 3403 C1
20400 HarC 77073 3259 C7
Northpark Cir
- MtgC 77339 3118 D3
North Park Dr
- HOUS 77339 3118 A3
- HOUS 77365 3118 A3
Northpark Dr
- MtgC 77339 3117 E3
- MtgC 77365 3117 E3
100 HOUS 77365 3118 A3
100 HOUS 77339 3118 C3
2100 HOUS 77339 3118 C3
2200 HOUS 77339 3119 A3
3100 MSCY 77459 4369 E7
3100 MSCY 77459 4370 A7
4800 HOUS 77345 3119 D3
22000 HOUS 77339 3117 E3
22000 HOUS 77365 3117 E3
Northpark Central Dr
100 HarC 77073 3258 E7
100 HarC 77090 3258 E7
300 HOUS 77073 3258 D6
600 HOUS 77073 3259 A7
Northpark Plaza Dr
- HOUS 77339 3118 A4
- MtgC 77339 3118 B4
Northpine Dr
800 CNRO 77301 2383 D3
Northpines Dr
- HOUS 77339 3118 A4
- MtgC 77339 3118 B4
North Pl Dr
16500 HarC 77073 3259 A5
Northplain Dr
- HarC 77041 3679 E2
Northpoint Dr
10 HOUS 77060 3403 B7
Northpointe Blvd
- HarC 77377 3253 E2
9200 HarC 77379 3110 D6
11100 HarC 77375 3110 A7
12000 HarC 77375 3254 D1
12700 HarC 77377 3254 A2
Northpointe Dr
10100 HarC 77379 3110 C6
Northpointe Ln
- LGCY 77539 4753 A3
Northpointe Bend Dr
12700 HarC 77377 3254 A1
Northpointe Bend Ln
- HarC 77377 3254 A1
Northpointe Landing Ln
- HarC 77377 3254 A2
Northpointe Ridge Ln
- HarC 77377 3254 A3
13500 HarC 77429 3254 A5
18600 HarC 77377 3253 E2
Northpointe Terrace Dr
18500 HarC 77377 3254 A3
Northport Dr
6200 HarC 77049 3828 B3
Northport Ln
600 LGCY 77565 4509 A5
Northpost St
11600 HarC 77039 3546 B7
11600 HarC 77093 3546 B7
Northridge Dr
10 BYTN 77521 3972 E1
10 BYTN 77521 3973 A1
5000 HOUS 77033 4243 E2
5300 HOUS 77033 4244 A2
8700 MtgC 77303 2238 E1
8700 MtgC 77303 2239 B2
N Northridge Dr
10600 MtgC 77303 2238 E1
W Northridge Dr
9000 MtgC 77303 2238 D1
Northridge Forest Dr
3000 MtgC 77386 2823 C7
Northridge Green Ln
- HarC 77429 3253 E4
- HarC 77429 3254 A4
Northridge Park Dr
20500 HarC 77073 3259 C7
20600 HOUS 77073 3259 C7
Northridge Terrace Ct
22800 HarC 77373 2968 C6
Northridge Terrace Ln
600 HarC 77373 2968 E7
Northrup Dr
4600 HOUS 77092 3821 D1
4700 HOUS 77092 3682 D7
North Sage Dr
- HarC 77041 3679 E2
Northsage Dr
- HarC 77041 3679 E2
Northshire Ct
3000 FBnC 77494 3953 C7
Northshire Ln
24000 FBnC 77494 3953 C7
Northshore Ct
4500 MSCY 77459 4369 C6
Northshore Dr
1500 MSCY 77459 4369 C6
1800 HOUS 77339 3263 D2
Northside Dr
900 HarC 77073 3259 B5
Northspring Bend Ln
13300 HarC 77429 3254 A5
North Star
- HOUS 77088 3683 C4
- HOUS 77091 3683 C4
Northstar Ct
3300 HarC 77373 3115 B3
Northstar Dr
- HarC 77041 3679 E2
Northstone Ln
14000 HarC 77429 3254 A5
Northsun Ln
13500 HarC 77429 3254 A4
Northton St
8500 HOUS 77029 3965 D4
Northtrace Dr
- HarC 77073 3259 B7
- HOUS 77073 3259 B7
Northumb Rd
12800 HOUS 77047 4373 D3
Northumberland Dr
16400 HarC 77095 3538 B4
Northumbria Pk
10 SGLD 77479 4495 C2
Northvale Dr
4100 HarC 77014 3401 C1
Northvalley Dr
300 HarC 77073 3259 A6
Northview Dr
10500 HarC 77086 3542 C1
Northview Park Dr
- HarC 77073 3259 A7
15600 HOUS 77073 3259 A6
North Villa Dr
9800 HarC 77064 3540 C5
Northville Cir
- HarC 77038 3543 D4
Northville Gdn N
- HarC 77038 3543 D4
Northville St
400 HarC 77037 3544 B4
400 HOUS 77037 3544 B4
700 HarC 77038 3544 A4
700 HOUS 77038 3544 A4
1200 HarC 77038 3543 E4
Northville Pl Dr
- HarC 77038 3543 D5
Northville Village Dr
- HarC 77038 3543 C4
Northway Ct
17800 HarC 77084 3677 D3
Northway Dr
- WDLD 77382 2674 E5
- WDLD 77382 2675 A4
- WDLD 77384 2675 A4
6100 HarC 77389 2966 D4
6300 HarC 77084 3677 D3
N Northwest Dr
- HarC 77041 3679 E3
Northwest Frwy
- HarC - 3249 C4
- HarC - 3250 C6
- HarC - 3251 A7
- HarC - 3395 E2
- HarC - 3396 B3
- HarC - 3397 A6
- HarC - 3538 C1
- HarC - 3539 A3
- HarC - 3680 E3
- HarC - 3681 D5
- HOUS - 3681 A3
- HOUS - 3682 A6
- HOUS - 3821 D1
- HOUS - 3822 B5
- JRSV - 3539 E6
- JRSV - 3540 A7
- JRSV - 3680 E3
Northwest Frwy SR-6
- HarC - 3249 C4
- HarC - 3250 C6
- HarC - 3251 A7
- HarC - 3395 D2
- HarC - 3396 B3
- HarC - 3397 A6
- HarC - 3538 C1
- HarC - 3539 A3
Northwest Frwy US-290
- HarC - 3249 C4
- HarC - 3250 C6
- HarC - 3251 A7
- HarC - 3395 D2
- HarC - 3396 B3
- HarC - 3397 A6
- HarC - 3538 C1
- HarC - 3539 C4
- HarC - 3680 E3
- HarC - 3681 D5
- HOUS - 3681 A3
- HOUS - 3682 B7
- HOUS - 3821 D1
- HOUS - 3822 B5
- JRSV - 3539 E6
- JRSV - 3540 A7
- JRSV - 3680 E3
Northwest 100 Dr
7000 HOUS 77092 3682 A6
Northwest Creek Cir
5900 HarC 77086 3542 D3
Northwestern St
3800 WUNP 77005 4101 D2
3900 HOUS 77005 4101 D2
Northwest Freeway Frontage Rd
- HarC 77429 3397 A6
- HarC 77429 3538 C1
- HarC 77433 3396 B3
9800 HOUS 77092 3822 A4
10900 HOUS 77092 3821 D1
12100 HOUS 77092 3682 C7
12800 HOUS 77040 3682 A6
13300 HOUS 77040 3681 E5
14700 HarC 77040 3681 B3
15300 HarC 77040 3680 E3
15300 JRSV 77040 3680 B1
17100 JRSV 77040 3540 B7
17600 JRSV 77065 3540 A6
17800 JRSV 77065 3539 E6
19000 HarC 77065 3539 C5
20700 HarC 77429 3539 A3
24500 HarC 77429 3396 B3
27000 HarC 77429 3395 E2
27000 HarC 77433 3395 E2
Northwest Lake Dr
- HarC 77095 3538 C1
Northwest Mall
10 HOUS 77092 3822 B6
Northwest Park Dr
- HarC 77086 3542 C3
Northwest Park Colony Ln
12500 HarC 77086 3542 B4
Northwest Station Dr
- JRSV 77065 3539 D5
Northwick Dr
1000 PRLD 77584 4501 B2
Northwind Dr
- FBnC 77479 4494 A3
9100 HarC 77064 3540 D2
Northwind Ln
4200 HarC 77014 3401 D1
Northwinds Dr
6700 HarC 77041 3680 A2
6700 JRSV 77041 3680 A2
Northwood Ct
1900 BzaC 77581 4502 A1
Northwood Dr
400 CNRO 77303 2237 E7
400 CNRO 77303 2383 E1
1300 BYTN 77521 3972 C4
15500 MtgC 77365 2824 E5
15500 MtgC 77365 2825 A5
Northwood Ln
10 LbyC 77372 2538 B6
300 LbyC 77327 2538 B4
1400 PASD 77502 4106 D7
Northwood St
800 BYTN 77521 3972 D4
1600 HOUS 77009 3824 A4
1700 HarC 77530 3830 D4
2700 HOUS 77009 3963 A1
Northwood Country Dr
10 HarC 77336 2976 A1
Northwood Forest Dr
12200 HarC 77039 3546 C6
Northwood Glen Ln
12900 HarC 77377 3254 A2
13100 HarC 77377 3253 E2
Northwoods Dr
7500 FBnC 77479 4493 E3
7700 FBnC 77479 4494 A3
Norton Dr
4100 BzaC 77578 4501 B7
4100 BzaC 77584 4501 B7
4100 PRLD 77578 4501 B7
8500 HOUS 77055 3821 A3
8500 HOUS 77080 3821 A3
9200 HOUS 77080 3820 D3
10400 HOUS 77043 3819 E3
Norton St
5700 TXCY 77591 4873 E6
Norton House Ln
23700 HarC 77493 3814 B5
Nortwest Frontage Rd
19500 HarC 77065 3539 C4
Norvara Tr
- HarC 77379 3256 C1
Norvell Ct
10 BKHV 77024 3959 B4
Norvic St
8400 HOUS 77029 3965 C3
10100 JTCY 77029 3966 A3
Norview Dr
100 HOUS 77018 3823 C1
100 HOUS 77022 3823 C1
Norville Ln
- HarC 77047 4374 B3
Norwalk
100 BzaC 77583 4624 A1
Norwalk Dr
500 LGCY 77573 4632 A2
1500 HarC 77450 3954 D4
Norway St
14100 HOUS 77047 4373 B5
Norwich St
2900 PRLD 77584 4501 A2
6100 HOUS 77028 3826 D2
Norwich Wy
4600 MSCY 77459 4369 B4
Norwood St
10 HOUS 77011 3964 C6
800 DRPK 77536 4109 C5
N Norwood St
100 HOUS 77011 3964 D6
Norwood Glen Ln
3700 HarC 77546 4506 A6
Norwood Hills Dr
2800 FBnC 77450 3954 A7
Norwood Oaks Dr
- HarC 77379 3257 A4
Norwood Point Ct
- FBnC 77469 4094 C7
Norwood Point Ln
- FBnC 77469 4094 C7
Norwood Trails Dr
9300 HarC 77396 3407 B2
Nory Ln
- CNRO 77301 2530 C3
Nottaway Ct
4900 SGLD 77478 4369 D5
Nottingham Cir
24600 MtgC 77355 2813 D7
24600 WlrC 77447 2813 D7
N Nottingham Cir
11700 MSCY 77071 4239 E7
S Nottingham Cir
11800 MSCY 77071 4239 C7
Nottingham Dr
- SGLD 77479 4495 C3
5300 KATY 77493 3813 D6
N Nottingham Dr
1100 LGCY 77573 4631 D5
S Nottingham Dr
1100 LGCY 77573 4631 D5
W Nottingham Dr
500 LGCY 77573 4631 E5
Nottingham Ln
100 CNRO 77301 2530 C1
600 DKSN 77539 4753 B3
1200 MtgC 77357 2828 E4
2900 MSCY 77459 4497 A1
Nottingham St
1700 PASD 77502 4107 B7
2400 HOUS 77005 4102 A2
2600 WUNP 77005 4102 A2
3000 WUNP 77005 4101 E2
3100 PRLD 77581 4503 D4
19500 MtgC 77357 2829 D5
Nottingham Wy
900 FRDW 77546 4629 B2
Nottingham Oaks Tr
500 HOUS 77079 3957 C3
Nottinghill Ct
10 CNRO 77304 2529 D2
Nottinghill Dr
21200 HarC 77388 3112 E3
Nottoway Cir
13400 HarC 77429 3397 A4
Nottoway Ct
400 LGCY 77573 4508 C7
Nova Ct
12300 HOUS 77077 3957 E6
Nova Dr
12400 HOUS 77077 3957 D6
Novato Dr
6200 HOUS 77053 4371 D6
Nova Trails Ct
- HOUS 77085 4371 A2
Nowak Rd
9500 FBnC 77469 4494 C7
Nowlin Dr
6200 HarC 77521 3834 E5
9200 HOUS 77022 3685 A7
Noyce Rd
18400 HarC 77532 3410 D6
N N Redfish St
7100 HTCK 77563 4988 E7
7100 HTCK 77563 4989 A7
Nuben St
6400 HOUS 77091 3683 B4
6700 HOUS 77088 3683 B4
Nueces Dr
3600 GLSN 77554 5441 A5
Nueces Ln
5800 HarC 77389 2966 E7
Nueces St
700 HOUS 77012 4105 C2
Nueces Canyon Ct
2800 HarC 77450 3954 C7
Nueces Forest Dr
13900 HarC 77396 3547 A3
Nueces Garden Dr
13900 HarC 77396 3546 E3
Nueces Glen Dr
13900 HarC 77396 3547 A3
Nueces Hollow Dr
- HarC 77396 3546 E3
14100 HarC 77396 3547 A3
Nueces Lake Dr
13800 HarC 77396 3546 E3
Nueces Moss Dr
13900 HarC 77396 3546 E3
Nueces Park Dr
6100 HarC 77396 3546 E2
6100 HarC 77396 3547 A2
Nueces River Ct
28700 MtgC 77386 2970 A2
Nueces River Ln
28800 MtgC 77386 2970 B2
Nueces River Lp
4200 MtgC 77386 2970 A2
Nueces Shore Dr
6100 HarC 77396 3546 E2
6100 HarC 77396 3547 A2
Nueces Springs Ln
13800 HarC 77429 3253 D6
Nuevo Puertu Ln
6700 HOUS 77048 4244 D7
N Nugent Av
100 LPRT 77571 4251 E2
Nugent St
100 CNRO 77301 2384 A5
S Nugent St
100 LPRT 77571 4251 E2
200 LPRT 77571 4252 A3
Nuggent St
3400 HarC 77093 3686 A2
3400 HOUS 77093 3686 A2
Nunn St
5600 HOUS 77087 4104 D7
5700 HOUS 77087 4244 D1
Nursery Rd
200 MtgC 77380 2968 B1
400 WDLD 77380 2968 A1
1900 WDLD 77380 2967 E1
Nutcracker Ct
15800 HarC 77396 3406 E6
Nutcracker Ln
10 WDLD 77380 2822 B7
Nutley Cir
25100 MtgC 77365 3117 E1
Nutmeg Ct
10 WDLD 77381 2820 D6
Nutmeg Ln
8100 HarC 77521 3833 D2
Nuttall Oak Dr
14900 HarC 77082 4096 D2
Nutty Farms Rd
18000 HarC 77377 3107 B1
Nutwood Dr
2600 BzaC 77584 4501 A5
Nutwood Ln
3400 HarC 77389 3112 E1
Nuwood Ln
14800 HOUS 77053 4372 D4
15100 HarC 77053 4372 D4
Nyack Dr
11800 HOUS 77089 4378 C6
13000 HOUS 77034 4378 C6
Nyad Ln
8300 HarC 77346 3265 C7
Nyoka St
6200 HOUS 77041 3681 A4
Nyssa Av
8300 HOUS 77078 3687 D4
9000 HOUS 77078 3688 A4
Nystrom Cir
15000 HarC 77060 3544 E3
W Nystrom Cir
600 HarC 77060 3544 E3

O

O St
- HOUS 77084 3818 A1
W O St
- LPRT 77571 4251 B5
Oahu Dr
1200 TKIS 77554 5106 B4
Oak
2700 BYTN 77520 3973 C5
Oak Av
100 HarC 77532 3692 C2
500 HarC 77562 3831 E2

STREET Block City ZIP Map# Grid

Oak Av
4700 PASD 77502 4248 A2
5200 PASD 77503 4248 B2
S Oak Av
- GlsC 77511 4751 E7
- GlsC 77511 4752 A7
W Oak Av
2600 PASD 77502 4248 A2
2600 PASD 77503 4248 A2
Oak Blvd
10 CNRO 77304 2383 B1
Oak Brk
10 BzaC 77578 4625 B3
Oak Cir
1100 TYLV 77586 4382 A7
14200 HarC 77396 3547 B2
S Oak Cir
4000 SGLD 77479 4495 A3
11600 HarC 77089 4505 B1
Oak Cltr E
12000 MtgC 77354 2671 B5
Oak Cr
100 BzaC 77578 4625 B3
Oak Cross
31700 MtgC 77355 2669 B7
31900 MAGA 77355 2669 B7
Oak Ct
10 HOUS 77006 3963 A5
3400 MSCY 77459 4496 E3
5000 DKSN 77539 4754 C3
S Oak Ct
11600 HarC 77089 4505 B1
Oak Dr
100 FRDW 77546 4629 E4
300 FRDW 77546 4630 A3
1200 HTCK 77563 4988 C4
2200 DKSN 77539 4753 C2
17700 MtgC 77357 2828 B1
18500 MtgC 77302 2680 B5
22800 MtgC 77365 2973 E6
Oak Dr S
200 FRDW 77546 4629 E4
E Oak Dr
24100 MtgC 77365 2973 E7
N Oak Dr
700 HarC 77073 3259 A5
S Oak Dr
12100 HarC 77089 4505 B1
23000 MtgC 77365 2973 E7
SW Oak Dr
10 HOUS 77056 3961 A4
W Oak Dr
24100 MtgC 77365 2973 E7
Oak Gln
10 CNRO 77304 2383 C7
Oak Hllw
20800 MtgC 77355 2814 A4
Oak Hvn W
12000 MtgC 77354 2671 B6
Oak Ln
- MtgC 77357 2829 C1
10 PNVL 77304 2237 B3
400 PNPV 77024 3959 E2
3900 GlsC 77518 4634 B3
5000 TXCY 77591 4874 A6
6100 KATY 77493 3813 B4
8100 GlsC 77517 4752 C7
8200 STFE 77517 4752 C7
12200 DKSN 77539 4753 B6
16400 HarC 77530 3830 D5
17400 SGCH 77355 2961 B3
17700 HarC 77532 3413 A6
21800 PNIS 77445 3099 C2
29700 MtgC 77354 2818 C1
Oak Lndg
3500 CNRO 77304 2237 B5
3500 PNVL 77304 2237 B5
Oak Pk
100 BzaC 77578 4625 B3
Oak Pl
100 HOUS 77002 3963 A5
100 HOUS 77006 3963 A5
Oak Plz
12600 HarC 77429 3398 E5
Oak Rd
- BzaC 77581 4502 A3
- PRLD 77581 4502 A3
- PRLD 77584 4502 A3
100 CRLS 77565 4509 C5
2500 BzaC 77584 4502 A5
2700 LGCY 77565 4508 E4
Oak Rdg
10 BzaC 77578 4625 B3
Oak Run
24200 MtgC 77355 2961 B5
Oak St
10 WDBR 77357 2828 C1
100 CNRO 77301 2383 E6
100 LMQU 77568 4874 A7
100 STAF 77477 4369 B2
100 TXCY 77591 4874 A7
200 PRVW 77445 3100 B2
600 RSBG 77471 4490 C3
700 HOUS 77018 3684 B7
700 LMQU 77568 4990 B2
800 LPRT 77571 4111 C7
1500 BYTN 77520 4112 D2
2400 GLSN 77551 5222 A1
2900 HOUS 77339 3119 D6
4700 PASD 77586 4383 C4
27200 HarC 77373 3113 E1
E Oak St
100 DRPK 77536 4109 B6
400 HarC 77562 3831 E2
N Oak St
10 TXCY 77591 4873 E5
100 TMBL 77375 2964 B7
S Oak St
10 TXCY 77591 4873 E6
10 TXCY 77591 4874 A7
100 MRGP 77571 4252 C1
100 TMBL 77375 2964 B7
400 LMQU 77568 4874 A7
26800 HarC 77373 3114 A1
W Oak St
100 DRPK 77536 4109 B6
400 HarC 77562 3831 E2
Oak Tr
- LPRT 77571 4382 E2
Oak Acres Dr
10600 HarC 77065 3539 B2
Oak Alley Ln
13400 HarC 77429 3397 A3
Oak Arbor Dr
2700 MtgC 77384 2675 A2
2900 MtgC 77384 2674 D2
7000 HOUS 77091 3682 E4
7400 HOUS 77088 3682 E3

Oak Arbor Wy
21500 HarC 77433 3251 D5
Oakbank Dr
2400 HOUS 77339 3118 E6
Oak Bay Cir
6900 MSCY 77459 4496 D5
Oak Bay Dr
6000 HOUS 77091 3682 E5
Oak Bayou Ln
10800 HarC 77064 3540 A3
Oak Bend Dr
14500 HOUS 77079 3957 D4
Oak Bend Forest Dr
13500 FBnC 77083 4237 B2
Oak Bent Dr
3600 PRLD 77581 4504 A7
Oak Berry Dr
600 KMAH 77565 4509 D7
Oakberry St
10100 HOUS 77042 4099 A2
Oak Blossom Ct
4100 HOUS 77059 4380 C3
Oak Bluff Ct
14600 HarC 77070 3398 C1
14700 HarC 77070 3254 C7
Oak Bluff Dr
7000 MtgC 77354 2673 A4
12000 HarC 77070 3254 C7
Oak Bough Dr
6900 HOUS 77088 3682 C2
Oak Bough Ln
3200 FBnC 77459 4622 A6
Oak Bower Dr
18800 HarC 77346 3265 A7
Oak Branch Ct
19700 HarC 77346 3264 D4
Oak Branch Ln
3300 SGLD 77479 4495 C1
Oak Branch Rd
- MtgC 77378 2237 D1
10 CNRO 77378 2237 D1
Oakbranch Manor Ln
6700 FBnC 77469 4095 C5
Oak Breeze Dr
18600 HarC 77084 3677 C7
Oak Briar Dr
500 KMAH 77565 4509 D7
19500 HarC 77346 3264 D5
Oak Briar Ln
- RSBG 77469 4614 E4
Oak Bridge Ln
21400 HarC 77388 3112 C4
Oakbridge Park Ln
21500 HarC 77450 3954 B5
Oakbrook Cir
1600 PRLD 77581 4504 B6
Oak Brook Dr
10600 HOUS 77013 3827 B4
Oakbrook Dr
1600 PRLD 77581 4504 B6
Oakburl Ct
6400 FBnC 77479 4367 B5
Oakburl Ln
6300 FBnC 77479 4367 B5
Oakbury Ct
900 MSCY 77489 4370 E4
Oakbury Dr
1600 MSCY 77489 4370 D4
Oak Canyon Dr
2100 MtgC 77385 2823 B3
Oak Canyon Ln
1200 FBnC 77469 4493 C5
Oak Castle Dr
- HarC 77389 2965 E3
7800 HarC 77389 2966 A3
Oak Center Ct
19500 HarC 77346 3264 D5
Oakcenter Dr
11000 HOUS 77072 4098 B4
Oak Chase Ct
1600 PRLD 77581 4504 C6
Oak Chase Dr
14200 HOUS 77062 4379 E7
Oak Churn Pl
25600 HarC 77373 3114 A4
Oak Cir St
25600 MtgC 77372 2537 A1
Oak Clearing Ct
3300 HOUS 77339 3119 C4
Oak Cliff Ln
3200 FBnC 77459 4622 A6
Oakcliff St
2300 HOUS 77023 4104 C3
Oak Cloister Wy
- HOUS 77058 4507 D2
Oak Cluster Cir
1800 PRLD 77581 4504 B6
Oak Cluster Ct
500 CNRO 77301 2384 E3
17800 HarC 77429 3252 C6
Oak Cottage Ct
18000 FBnC 77469 4095 B5
Oak Country Ln
- SGCH 77355 2961 D4
Oak Cove Dr
5300 HOUS 77091 3682 E5
5300 HOUS 77091 3683 A5
5500 HOUS 77345 3120 B5
Oak Cove Ln
10 HarC 77346 3264 D3
Oak Cove Pointe
12300 MtgC 77304 2236 A4
Oak Creek Cir
- WlrC 77447 2959 D2
200 LGCY 77573 4632 A5
15900 MtgC 77372 2683 D4
Oak Creek Ct
300 LGCY 77573 4630 D5
15900 MtgC 77372 2683 C4
Oakcreek Ct
21600 HarC 77450 3954 B5
Oak Creek Dr
100 LGCY 77573 4630 D5
900 HOUS 77450 3954 C2
1100 LPRT 77571 4250 B2
1100 RHMD 77469 4491 E3
2100 HOUS 77017 4246 C1
3000 PRLD 77581 4504 C5
26700 MtgC 77372 2683 C4
Oakcreek Dr
32000 MtgC 77354 2673 B4
S Oak Creek Dr
27200 MtgC 77372 2683 D5
Oak Creek Ln
100 LGCY 77573 4630 C6
6000 HarC 77379 3256 E1
15900 MtgC 77372 2683 C5

Oak Creek Rd
24500 WlrC 77447 2959 D2
Oak Creek St
10800 HNCV 77024 3960 A1
Oak Creek Tr
15700 MtgC 77372 2683 D4
Oakcreek Hollow Ln
22100 FBnC 77450 4093 B3
22100 FBnC 77450 4094 A3
Oak Crest Cir
10 MtgC 77354 2672 E4
10 MtgC 77354 2673 A4
Oak Crest Ct
- BzaC 77578 4625 A3
6100 HarC 77379 3256 E1
11900 MtgC 77385 2823 B5
Oak Crest Dr
10 BzaC 77578 4625 B3
17000 MtgC 77385 2676 D6
Oakcrest Dr
5400 HOUS 77021 4103 D4
9300 MNVL 77578 4746 B7
Oak Crest Pkwy
- BzaC 77578 4625 B3
- MNVL 77578 4625 B3
Oakcroft Dr
12500 HarC 77070 3398 C1
Oakdale Av
100 SRAC 77571 4383 A2
400 SRAC 77571 4382 E2
Oakdale Blvd
300 LGCY 77573 4630 C6
Oak Dale Ct
2700 FBnC 77477 4369 E4
Oakdale Ct
19100 MtgC 77355 2814 B1
Oak Dale Dr
3700 PRLD 77581 4504 B6
17100 HarC 77379 3256 E1
17200 HarC 77379 3111 D7
Oakdale Dr
100 CNRO 77304 2383 D4
300 FBnC 77477 4369 E4
400 STAF 77477 4369 E4
4500 BLAR 77401 4101 B3
Oakdale St
10 HOUS 77002 4102 E1
10 HOUS 77004 4102 E1
10 HOUS 77006 4102 E1
200 PASD 77506 4107 A4
1400 HOUS 77004 4103 A2
Oak Dale Wy
- SEBK 77586 4382 C7
Oakdale Creek Ct
5300 HarC 77379 3112 A7
Oakdale Meadows Dr
- HarC 77379 3257 A2
Oakden Ct
28500 HarC 77336 3121 D2
Oak Edge Dr
7800 HarC 77379 3111 A7
Oakedge Dr
1800 PRLD 77581 4504 B6
Oaken Ln
3100 LPRT 77571 4250 C3
Oakendell Dr
15800 HarC 77084 3678 E6
Oakengates Dr
1200 HarC 77015 3829 B6
Oak Estates Ct
- LGCY 77573 4632 B3
Oak Fair Dr
5100 HOUS 77345 3120 A4
Oak Falls Dr
5300 HarC 77066 3401 A7
Oak Fern
7500 HarC 77040 3681 B1
Oakfern Ln
- HarC 77040 3681 A1
Oakfield Cross
18100 FBnC 77469 4095 B5
Oakfield Dr
12600 HarC 77429 3398 B6
Oakfield Glen Ln
17700 HarC 77433 3537 C6
Oakfield Village Ln
19100 HarC 77449 3816 B2
Oakford Ct
9300 HOUS 77024 3960 E1
Oakford Dr
8600 HOUS 77024 3961 A1
Oak Forest
100 BzaC 77578 4625 B3
Oak Forest Dr
- PRLD 77581 4504 C6
300 LGCY 77573 4630 D5
3000 HOUS 77018 3822 D4
4100 MSCY 77459 4497 C3
4900 HOUS 77018 3683 D7
Oak Forest Ln
12000 MtgC 77385 2823 B5
Oak Forest Hollow Ln
31000 MtgC 77386 2823 D7
Oak Fork Cir
1800 PRLD 77581 4504 B6
Oak Gardens Dr
3800 HOUS 77339 3119 B4
Oak Gate Cir
1800 PRLD 77581 4504 B6
Oak Gate Dr
12100 HarC 77070 3254 D7
Oak Glade Dr
2700 HOUS 77339 3119 B3
Oak Glen Ct
8700 HarC 77088 3543 D7
11600 BKHV 77024 3959 D2
11600 PNPV 77024 3959 D2
Oak Glen Dr
600 KMAH 77565 4509 D7
700 HOUS 77076 3685 B3
900 CNRO 77378 2237 D1
Oak Glen Ln
1100 FBnC 77479 4494 A6
Oak Glen Meadow Dr
- HarC 77095 3538 A2
Oak Green Ct
5900 FBnC 77479 4493 C1
19700 HarC 77346 3264 D5
Oakgreen Ln
- WlrC 77445 2954 B2
Oak Grove Ct
4000 SGLD 77479 4495 A2
Oak Grove Dr
20400 MtgC 77357 2680 E6
Oakgrove Dr
900 HarC 77058 4507 C5
Oak Grove Ln
10 CNRO 77304 2383 A6

Oak Grove Ln
17000 MtgC 77357 2680 E7
17700 MtgC 77357 2826 E1
Oak Grove St
900 LPRT 77571 4252 A3
Oak Grove Church St
8500 HOUS 77028 3687 C7
Oakhall Dr
3600 HarC 77066 3401 C4
19700 HarC 77346 3264 C5
Oakham St
5600 HOUS 77085 4372 A2
6100 HOUS 77085 4371 D2
Oak Hampton Dr
18000 HarC 77084 3677 D7
Oak Harbor Dr
10 HOUS 77062 4506 D2
Oakhaven Dr
200 BYTN 77520 3832 B7
Oak Haven Ln
9800 MtgC 77303 2238 E5
Oakhaven Ln
5500 HOUS 77091 3682 E6
Oakhaven Rd
- PASD 77505 4249 C3
- PASD 77571 4249 C3
8200 LPRT 77571 4249 C3
Oak Hedge St
13300 HarC 77044 3689 D2
Oak Hill Cir
4500 LGCY 77573 4509 A7
Oak Hill Dr
600 KMAH 77565 4509 D7
2500 MSCY 77459 4369 E6
2500 MSCY 77459 4496 E1
7100 HOUS 77087 4244 E1
7200 HOUS 77087 4245 A1
17300 PTVL 77357 2682 C7
26500 ORDN 77386 2822 C6
Oakhill Dr
400 CNRO 77304 2383 C3
E Oak Hill Dr
400 MtgC 77385 2822 C6
400 MtgC 77386 2822 C6
400 ORDN 77385 2822 C6
400 ORDN 77386 2822 C6
N Oak Hill Dr
100 HarC 77336 2975 E5
100 HarC 77336 2976 A5
S Oak Hill Dr
200 HarC 77336 2975 E5
200 HarC 77336 2976 A5
W Oak Hill Dr
200 HarC 77336 2975 E5
Oak Hill Ln
10 ORDN 77386 2822 C6
600 MtgC 77362 2816 D5
600 SGCH 77362 2816 D5
18900 MtgC 77365 2826 B5
Oak Hill Rd
- HarC 77338 3261 D2
7000 MNVL 77578 4625 E5
Oak Hill St
20500 MtgC 77365 2972 E7
Oak Hill Estates Rd
- HarC 77338 3261 D2
Oakhill Gate Dr
22200 HarC 77373 3261 B1
22300 HarC 77373 3116 B7
Oak Hills Ct
- WlrC 77447 2813 A3
Oak Hills Dr
17400 PTVL 77357 2682 D7
Oak Hollow Blvd
- WlrC 77447 2813 C4
Oak Hollow Cir
10 HarC 77429 3398 E4
Oak Hollow Ct
1900 MSCY 77489 4497 C1
Oak Hollow Dr
300 LGCY 77573 4630 C5
1000 DKSN 77539 4753 C2
1200 FRDW 77546 4629 A4
13400 HarC 77429 3398 E4
Oak Hollow Dr E
1900 PRLD 77581 4504 C5
Oak Hollow Dr N
3600 PRLD 77581 4504 C5
Oak Hollow Dr S
3600 PRLD 77581 4504 C5
Oak Hollow Dr W
1800 PRLD 77581 4504 C6
Oak Hollow Ln
12200 MtgC 77362 2817 B7
23000 HarC 77377 2962 C7
Oak Hollow St
100 CNRO 77301 2383 E4
4800 BYTN 77521 3972 B3
10800 HNCV 77024 3960 A1
Oak Hollow Wy
17300 HarC 77379 3256 E1
Oakhurst Dr
24700 MtgC 77386 2968 C3
26000 MtgC 77386 2822 C7
26200 ORDN 77386 2822 C7
Oakhurst Pkwy
1800 SGLD 77479 4495 B1
Oakhurst St
100 LPRT 77571 4251 E7
500 HOUS 77003 3964 A6
500 HOUS 77023 3964 A6
Oakhurst Creek Dr
20700 MtgC 77365 3117 E2
Oakhurst Forest Dr
25100 MtgC 77365 3117 E1
Oakhurst Green Dr
- HarC 77067 3402 E5
- HOUS 77067 3402 E5
- HOUS 77067 3403 A5
Oakhurst Meadows Dr
20700 MtgC 77365 3117 E2
Oakhurst Park Dr
20700 MtgC 77365 3117 E3
Oakhurst Trails Ct
25500 MtgC 77365 3117 D2
Oakhurst Trails Dr
20700 MtgC 77365 3117 E2
Oakington Dr
7800 HOUS 77071 4239 E4
Oakington Ln
22000 HarC 77449 3815 A3
Oak Island Dr
15800 HarC 77377 3254 D5
Oak Knoll Ct
1000 SGLD 77478 4237 C7
Oak Knoll Dr
1100 SGLD 77478 4237 A7
6800 FBnC 77469 4232 D3

Oak Knoll Dr
16400 MtgC 77302 2825 B4
16400 MtgC 77365 2825 B4
Oak Knoll Ln
7800 HOUS 77028 3687 B7
8800 HOUS 77078 3687 E7
9000 HOUS 77078 3688 A7
Oak Knot Ct
25300 HarC 77389 2965 C2
Oak Knot Dr
8400 HarC 77389 2965 E2
Oaklace Dr
3700 HarC 77389 2967 E7
3700 HarC 77389 3112 D1
Oak Lace Ln
16200 SGCH 77355 2961 E4
Oak Lake Cir
1800 PRLD 77581 4504 B6
Oak Lake Dr
- FBnC 77478 4236 B6
3400 HOUS 77339 3119 A5
Oak Lake Pk
11700 FBnC 77478 4236 C6
Oak Lake Glen Cir
11400 FBnC 77478 4236 C5
Oak Lake Glen Ct
11400 FBnC 77478 4236 B4
Oak Lake Glen Dr
15200 FBnC 77478 4236 C5
Oak Lake Park Dr
11500 FBnC 77478 4236 C6
Oak Lake Point Dr
11400 FBnC 77478 4236 C5
Oaklake Point Ln
7500 HarC 77040 3681 B1
Oak Lake Pointe Dr
- HarC 77040 3681 A1
Oak Lake Ridge Ct
11400 FBnC 77478 4236 C5
Oak Lake Vista Ct
11400 FBnC 77478 4236 C5
Oakland Av
- HarC 77520 3832 A6
100 HarC 77520 3831 E7
300 HarC 77520 3970 E1
Oakland Bnd
9900 HarC 77064 3540 E5
Oakland Cir
- FBnC 77459 4621 C4
1800 PRLD 77581 4504 B6
9900 HarC 77064 3540 E5
Oakland Ct
400 MtgC 77302 2530 D6
900 SGLD 77478 4237 C7
900 SGLD 77478 4368 A1
3800 FBnC 77459 4621 C5
9900 HarC 77064 3540 E5
Oakland Dr
1100 FRDW 77546 4505 C4
2600 SGLD 77479 4494 E2
2900 SGLD 77479 4495 A2
9300 HarC 77064 3540 E5
Oakland Hl
9900 HarC 77064 3540 E4
Oakland Ln
400 MtgC 77302 2530 D5
9900 HarC 77064 3540 E5
Oakland St
4800 HOUS 77023 3964 B7
Oakland Wy
- FBnC 77459 4621 C5
Oakland Brook St
2700 HarC 77038 3543 A2
Oakland Falls Dr
4000 FBnC 77459 4369 C4
Oakland Hills Dr
6500 HarC 77069 3400 B1
Oak Landing Dr
9800 HarC 77070 3255 C3
Oakland Lake Cir
3200 FBnC 77459 4621 D6
Oakland Lake Wy
9400 FBnC 77459 4621 D6
Oakland Mills Dr
17800 FBnC 77469 4095 C5
Oakland Park Dr
10 MNVL 77583 4624 C4
Oakland Valley Dr
2400 RSBG 77469 4491 E7
2400 RSBG 77469 4615 E1
2600 FBnC 77469 4615 E1
19700 HarC 77449 3677 A2
Oakland Wood Ct
7400 HarC 77346 3265 B4
Oaklane Tr
16200 SGCH 77355 2961 E4
Oak Laurel Ln
4600 HOUS 77092 3683 B6
4600 HOUS 77092 3822 A2
Oaklawn Dr
10 BKHV 77024 3959 D3
10 PNPV 77024 3959 D3
1900 LMQU 77568 4989 E2
1900 LMQU 77568 4990 A3
2000 CNRO 77304 2383 D4
16100 SPLD 77372 2682 E4
16100 SPLD 77372 2683 A4
Oaklawn Ovl
3800 FBnC 77459 4622 B4
Oaklawn St
400 LGCY 77573 4631 E2
1800 SGLD 77478 4237 B5
Oaklawn Park Dr
15100 HarC 77069 3256 D6
Oaklawn Pl Dr
3300 MSCY 77459 4497 E5
S Oak Leaf
14300 MtgC 77302 2678 C6
Oak Leaf Av
800 LPRT 77571 4382 D1
Oak Leaf Blvd
21000 MtgC 77365 2826 B7
21200 MtgC 77365 2972 B1
Oakleaf Cir
1800 PRLD 77581 4504 B6
Oak Leaf Ct
3100 MSCY 77459 4496 E3
5900 MtgC 77304 2236 A4
Oak Leaf Dr
10 HarC 77336 2976 D5
Oak Leaf Ln
13900 HarC 77015 3828 E7
14000 HarC 77015 3829 A6
Oak Leaf Lp
14200 MtgC 77372 2682 C1
Oak Leaf Rd
11800 MtgC 77303 2385 D1
12100 MtgC 77303 2239 D7

Oak Leaf Rd
12600 CTSH 77303 2239 E7
Oak Leaf St
9800 BYTN 77520 3974 A1
Oakleaf Forest Dr
8800 HarC 77088 3542 D6
Oakleaf Hills Cir
2300 CNRO 77304 2236 E2
Oakleaf Trail Ct
18100 FBnC 77469 4095 B5
Oakleaf Trail Ln
6700 FBnC 77469 4095 B5
Oak Ledge Dr
13100 HarC 77065 3539 A2
Oakleigh Dr
7500 HarC 77433 3676 E1
Oakley Rd
22300 MtgC 77357 2973 D2
Oakley St
600 HOUS 77006 4102 E1
Oakley Downs Pl
10 WDLD 77382 2819 E3
Oakley Hill Ct
21000 FBnC 77469 4234 A3
Oakley Terrace Ln
10800 HarC 77070 3399 A6
10900 HarC 77065 3399 A6
Oak Limb Ct
20400 HarC 77338 3261 E3
Oak Limb Dr
10300 HarC 77065 3539 B3
Oak Limb Ln
20600 HarC 77338 3261 D2
20600 HarC 77338 3262 A3
Oakline Dr
12200 BKVL 77581 4375 D5
Oak Links Av
2300 HOUS 77059 4380 B5
Oak Links Ct
2300 HOUS 77059 4380 A5
Oakloch Ct
18000 FBnC 77469 4095 C5
Oak Lodge Ct
- LGCY 77573 4632 B3
Oak Lodge Dr
1800 PRLD 77581 4504 B6
Oak Lynn Dr
900 CNRO 77378 2237 D1
Oaklynn Dr
5200 HarC 77373 3115 D6
Oak Lynn Rd
- HarC 77373 3115 D6
Oakman Ln
6700 SGLD 77479 4494 C1
Oak Manor Dr
1700 HarC 77336 3266 E3
1900 HarC 77336 3267 A3
Oakmantle Dr
6800 HOUS 77085 4371 C1
Oak Masters Ct
17700 HarC 77379 3111 C7
Oak Masters Dr
6200 HarC 77379 3111 D7
6300 HarC 77379 3256 C1
Oakmead Dr
13700 SGLD 77478 4237 A7
Oak Meadow Dr
- SEBK 77586 4382 C7
1700 KMAH 77565 4509 D7
11700 MDWP 77477 4238 A5
Oak Meadows St
900 HOUS 77017 4106 B7
Oakmere Pl
10 FBnC 77479 4367 A7
Oakmere Lake Ct
1200 HarC 77379 3255 C2
Oak Mesa Ct
11100 HarC 77070 3399 A3
Oak Mill Dr
2500 HOUS 77345 3120 A5
Oak Mill Wy
3100 FBnC 77459 4621 E6
Oak Mist Ln
22500 FBnC 77494 4093 D3
Oakmont Cir
4600 PASD 77505 4248 E6
Oakmont Ct
3900 SGLD 77479 4495 A3
4700 LGCY 77573 4509 A7
Oakmont Dr
100 CNRO 77301 2384 D3
1000 HOUS 77339 3263 B2
3100 SGLD 77479 4495 A3
9700 LPRT 77571 4250 A4
22800 MtgC 77365 2973 E5
Oakmont Ln
2700 MSCY 77459 4497 A1
Oakmont St
- BYTN 77520 3972 E6
3200 HOUS 77021 4103 B4
Oakmont Club Ct
15400 HOUS 77059 4380 B6
Oakmont Creek Dr
6300 HarC 77379 3256 E2
Oakmont Village Cir
- HarC 77389 2965 E2
Oakmont Village Dr
- HarC 77389 2965 C2
Oakmoor Pkwy
- HOUS 77045 4242 C6
- HOUS 77051 4242 C7
Oakmoss Ct
20300 HarC 77379 3111 E4
Oak Moss Dr
7500 HarC 77379 3256 B3
Oakmoss Tr
5700 HarC 77379 3111 E5
Oakmoss Hill Ct
18000 FBnC 77469 4095 C5
Oakmount Ct
10 JRSV 77065 3540 B6
Oak Mountain Dr
15700 HarC 77095 3538 D5
Oakner Dr
11800 HarC 77377 3254 C2
Oaknoll Dr
200 HarC 77336 2975 D5
Oak Nut Dr
6300 HOUS 77088 3682 C3
6400 HOUS 77040 3682 C3
Oak Orchard Ct
20800 HarC 77433 3251 E6
Oak Orchard Ln
18000 HarC 77433 3537 D6
Oak Park Blvd
- HarC 77082 4096 C2
Oak Park Cir
12300 HarC 77070 3254 C7

Oak Park Ct
700 FRDW 77546 4505 C
12300 HarC 77070 3254 C
Oak Park Dr
- BzaC 77578 4625 B
200 ALVN 77511 4867 C
11800 MtgC 77302 2677
12100 HarC 77070 3254 C
12400 HarC 77070 3398 C
Oak Park Ln
1000 FRDW 77546 4505 C
3200 FBnC 77459 4622 A
Oak Park St
- HOUS 77032 3404 A
- LGCY 77573 4630 D
2700 DKSN 77539 4754 A
15900 HarC 77032 3404 A
Oak Park Bend Ln
17700 HarC 77433 3537 D
Oak Park Trails Ct
2100 HarC 77450 3954 B
Oak Park Trails Dr
21500 HarC 77450 3954 A
Oak Parkway Dr
900 HOUS 77077 3957 A
Oak Pass
900 CNRO 77378 2237 D
Oak Pass Dr
6100 HOUS 77091 3683 A
Oak Pines Dr
14700 HarC 77040 3541 A
Oak Pl Ct
1600 PRLD 77581 4504 B
Oak Pl Dr
- FBnC 77479 4493 E
Oak Plains Dr
8400 HarC 77389 2965 E
Oak Plank Rd
3900 FBnC 77545 4498 C
Oak Plaza Dr
12300 HarC 77065 3398 E
12300 HarC 77429 3398 D
Oak Point Ct
1600 PRLD 77581 4504 B
Oak Point Dr
4000 PRLD 77581 4504 B
9700 HOUS 77055 3820 B
10200 HOUS 77043 3819 E
10200 HOUS 77043 3820 A
Oak Pointe Blvd
2900 MSCY 77459 4497 D
Oak Prairie Ct
7000 FBnC 77469 4095 C
Oak Rain Ct
20800 HarC 77449 3815 C
Oak Ranch Dr
27500 HarC 77336 3122 A
Oak Ridge Dr
700 LGCY 77573 4632 B
1400 DKSN 77539 4753 C
1700 KMAH 77565 4509 D
25800 MtgC 77380 2968 B
26100 MtgC 77380 2822 B
26100 ORDN 77380 2822 B
Oakridge Dr
- SGLD 77478 4237 B
100 HTCK 77563 4988 E
Oakridge Rd
39600 WlrC 77445 2954 B
Oak Ridge St
4600 HOUS 77009 3823 E
Oakridge Canyon Ln
17700 FBnC 77469 4095 D
Oakridge Forest Ct
25800 MtgC 77386 2968 E
Oakridge Forest Ln
25600 MtgC 77386 2968 D
Oak Ridge Grove Cir
500 ORDN 77386 2822 C
Oak Ridge Grove Dr
300 ORDN 77386 2822 C
Oak Ridge Park Dr
- HarC 77084 3816 B
Oak Ridge School Rd
27300 MtgC 77385 2822 B3
27300 ORDN 77385 2822 B3
27300 SHEH 77385 2822 B3
Oak River Dr
2300 HarC 77373 3114 D
Oak Rock Cir
3100 HarC 77373 3115 A
Oak Royal Dr
1700 HarC 77450 3954 D
Oak Run Ct
- CNRO 77304 2383 D
Oak Run Dr
6700 FBnC 77469 4095 C5
Oakrun Dr
4000 HarC 77396 3408 A
W Oaks Blvd
2600 PRLD 77581 4502 D3
2600 PRLD 77584 4502 D5
W Oaks Cir E
2700 PRLD 77584 4502 D
W Oaks Cir S
6100 PRLD 77584 4502 D
Oaks Dr
400 PASD 77502 4247 A2
400 SHUS 77502 4247 A2
400 SHUS 77587 4247 A2
1200 PASD 77502 4106 E6
1300 PASD 77506 4106 E6
1700 PASD 77502 4107 A
W Oaks Dr
- PASD 77058 4508 C3
Oaks St
2600 GlsC 77539 4635 C4
Oak Sage Dr
7600 HarC 77433 3676 C1
Oak Sand Dr
2200 HarC 77450 3954 B6
W Oaks Cir Ln
- PRLD 77584 4502 D4
Oaks Crossing Ln
14600 HarC 77070 3399 A1
16900 FBnC 77083 4095 D5
Oaksedge Ln
5000 HarC 77388 3112 B3
Oaks Forks Dr
2400 HOUS 77339 3119 B6
Oak Shade Dr
1700 FBnC 77479 4494 A5
Oak Shadow Ct
- LGCY 77573 4630 C5
1800 FBnC 77479 4494 B4
Oak Shadows Cir
18600 MtgC 77302 2826 A2

STREET
Block City ZIP Map# Grid

ak Shadows Ct
- CNRO 77304 2383 D7
4000 SGLD 77479 4495 C2
ak Shadows Dr
4900 HOUS 77091 3683 A6
5000 HOUS 77091 3682 E6
ak Shadows Ln
11600 BKHV 77024 3959 D3
11600 PNPV 77024 3959 D3
ak Shadows Pl
22700 MtgC 77357 2973 E4
23000 MtgC 77357 2974 A4
ak Shadows St
1600 BYTN 77520 4113 B1
ak Shale Dr
20200 MtgC 77357 2828 A7
aksham Ln
17600 HarC 77379 3257 B3
akshield Ln
11700 HarC 77433 3396 B6
akshire Ct
300 LGCY 77573 4631 E4
ak Shire Dr
1900 PRLD 77581 4504 A7
akshire Dr
4500 HOUS 77027 3961 B7
ak Shores Dr
2000 HOUS 77339 3118 E4
2200 HOUS 77339 3119 A4
ak Shores St
3200 LPRT 77571 4382 E1
3200 SRAC 77571 4382 E1
akside Dr
3900 HOUS 77053 4372 D4
ak Side Tr
16700 HarC 77346 3408 A3
aks On The Brazos
- FBnC 77471 4490 C1
Oaks Plaza Dr
14500 HOUS 77082 4096 D2
ak Spring Dr
11200 HOUS 77043 3819 A7
ak Spring Rd
13900 HarC 77429 3253 E5
13900 HarC 77429 3254 B5
ak Springs Dr
- HarC 77429 3397 A1
ak Stand Ct
5000 HarC 77449 3676 E6
ak Star Dr
25200 HarC 77389 2965 E2
ak Station Dr
19300 HarC 77346 3264 D5
akstone St
900 HOUS 77015 3967 D1
akstone Park Dr
25600 FBnC 77469 4092 C7
ak Stream Dr
1000 HOUS 77043 3958 B4
1100 HOUS 77043 3819 A7
Oaks Village Dr
- FBnC 77083 4095 D5
- FBnC 77469 4095 C5
ak Terrace Ct
4000 HarC 77082 4096 B4
ak Terrace Dr
900 CNRO 77378 2237 D1
15200 HarC 77082 4096 B4
ak Thicket Dr
- HOUS 77040 3542 B7
9600 HOUS 77040 3682 B1
akthistle Ln
2000 LGCY 77565 4508 E5
akthorn Ct
- FBnC 77494 3953 A5
ak Timbers Dr
19100 HarC 77346 3264 C6
ak Top Dr
1900 PRLD 77581 4504 A7
ak Trace Ct
1600 PRLD 77581 4504 B6
aktrace Ct
17800 HarC 77396 3407 E2
aktrace Dr
3800 HarC 77396 3407 E2
3900 HarC 77396 3408 A2
ak Trace Ln
900 CNRO 77378 2237 D1
ak Trace Island Dr
- HarC 77095 3537 C3
ak Trail Ct
4300 SGLD 77479 4494 E1
ak Trail Ln
5500 HOUS 77091 3682 E6
aktrail Park Ln
- MtgC 77385 2823 C6
ak Tree Cir
1800 PRLD 77581 4504 B6
ak Tree Ct
3300 SGLD 77479 4495 B3
ak Tree Dr
- HarC 77375 2965 D6
1100 HOUS 77055 3820 C7
1500 HOUS 77080 3820 C6
9800 MtgC 77303 2238 E5
9900 CNRO 77303 2238 E6
aktree St
10 FRDW 77546 4629 D1
ak Valley Dr
800 HNCV 77024 3960 B1
1700 KMAH 77565 4509 D7
4400 MSCY 77459 4369 B7
11500 HarC 77065 3398 E7
Oak Valley Ln
600 MtgC 77362 2816 D5
600 SGCH 77362 2816 D5
Oak View Cir
300 ELGO 77586 4382 A7
Oak View Dr
7000 GlsC 77511 4751 E6
7100 GlsC 77511 4752 A6
Oakview Dr
2300 MSCY 77459 4370 A7
Oak View Rd
- HarC 77375 3111 A1
- HarC 77379 3111 A1
Oak View St
29700 MtgC 77354 2817 E1
29700 MtgC 77354 2818 A1
Oakview St
400 SGLD 77478 4368 C1
3700 GlsC 77518 4634 C2
Oak View Ter
19000 HarC 77094 3955 B3
Oak View Tr
15200 FBnC 77478 4236 C6
Oakview Creek Ln
4100 HOUS 77048 4374 D4

STREET
Block City ZIP Map# Grid

Oak Villa Ct
8400 HarC 77389 2965 E3
Oak Villa Dr
1300 HarC 77389 2965 E3
Oak Village Dr
- HarC 77396 3547 C1
6800 HOUS 77396 3406 B7
7000 HOUS 77396 3547 B1
Oakville Ct
5400 SGLD 77479 4495 B4
Oakville Dr
3500 CNRO 77304 2237 B5
Oakville St
3900 HarC 77093 3546 B7
Oakvine Ln
- HarC 77073 3259 D4
Oak Vista Ct
900 FRDW 77546 4505 A5
Oak Vista Dr
300 FRDW 77546 4505 C7
4400 MSCY 77459 4497 C7
Oak Vista Pk
- CNRO 77304 2383 D6
Oak Vista St
7500 HOUS 77087 4245 B1
Oak Walk Dr
6800 HarC 77346 3264 E6
7100 HarC 77346 3265 A6
Oakway Dr
18900 HarC 77346 3264 E6
18900 HarC 77346 3265 A7
19000 HarC 77388 3113 A7
Oakway St
- HarC 77032 3404 A6
- HOUS 77032 3404 A6
Oakwell Ln
1900 HarC 77449 3815 C6
Oakwell Station Ct
5700 HarC 77346 3264 D5
Oak West Dr W
700 HarC 77073 3259 A5
Oakwick Dr
- PRLD 77581 4504 B6
Oakwick Ln
14000 HarC 77044 3689 E3
Oakwick Forest Dr
3600 MSCY 77459 4497 E7
3800 MSCY 77459 4621 D1
Oakwilde Cir
3800 LPRT 77571 4250 E4
Oakwilde Ct
10 HOUS 77043 3819 E6
Oakwind Ct
18000 FBnC 77469 4095 B5
Oak Wind Dr
- PRLD 77581 4504 A6
Oak Wood
29700 MtgC 77354 2671 E7
29700 MtgC 77354 2817 E1
Oakwood
16500 MtgC 77372 2682 C5
Oakwood Ct
20100 HarC 77338 3263 A4
Oakwood Ct E
8000 HarC 77040 3681 E3
Oakwood Ct W
8000 HarC 77040 3681 E3
Oakwood Dr
100 MtgC 77386 2968 C1
8400 MtgC 77354 2818 E6
10900 LPRT 77571 4250 D3
12700 HarC 77429 3396 D4
23200 MtgC 77372 2682 B5
Oakwood Dr E
1800 PRLD 77581 4504 B6
Oakwood Dr N
3900 PRLD 77581 4504 B6
Oakwood Grv
6800 HarC 77040 3681 E3
Oakwood Ln
13500 SGLD 77478 4237 B6
Oakwood Pk
6900 HarC 77040 3681 D3
Oakwood Pl
8100 HarC 77040 3681 D3
Oakwood St
200 LGCY 77573 4631 E4
3000 HOUS 77025 4101 D6
3000 HOUS 77025 4102 A5
3100 BYTN 77520 3972 A7
12200 MtgC 77362 2817 B6
Oakwood Tr
6700 HarC 77040 3681 E3
6700 HOUS 77040 3681 E3
Oakwood Trc
8000 HarC 77040 3681 E3
Oakwood Bend Dr
8000 HarC 77040 3681 E3
Oakwood Canyon Dr
7400 HarC 77433 3676 E1
7400 HarC 77433 3677 A1
Oakwood Chase Dr
17100 HarC 77379 3256 C2
Oakwood Ct Dr
1800 BYTN 77521 3972 C1
Oakwood Falls Tr
19600 HarC 77084 3816 A4
19800 HarC 77084 3815 E3
Oakwood Forest Dr
- HOUS 77339 3119 D4
- HOUS 77345 3119 D4
8000 HarC 77040 3681 D3
Oakwood Garden St
8000 HarC 77040 3681 E3
Oakwood Glen Blvd
7100 HarC 77379 3256 C3
Oakwood Glen Dr
6900 HarC 77379 3256 C2
Oakwood Hollow Ct
6700 HarC 77040 3681 E4
Oakwood Hollow St
7900 HarC 77040 3681 E3
Oakwood Lakes Dr
7700 HarC 77095 3538 D7
Oakwood Manor Dr
12000 HarC 77429 3397 C3
Oakwood Park Ln
- MtgC 77386 2823 C6
Oakwood Pl Ct E
6900 HarC 77040 3681 E3
Oakwood Run Dr
3100 FBnC 77478 4366 C1
Oakwood Trace Ct
6800 HarC 77040 3681 E3
6800 HOUS 77040 3681 E3
Oakworth Ct
15600 FBnC 77478 4236 B6

STREET
Block City ZIP Map# Grid

Oakworth Dr
18000 HarC 77084 3677 E7
Oamico St
- HOUS 77019 3962 D4
Oarlock Ct
16600 HarC 77532 3551 E2
Oarman Ct
300 HOUS 77079 3956 E1
Oasis Dr
9700 HOUS 77096 4240 D2
Oasis View Ln
11000 HOUS 77034 4378 D4
Oates Ln
12300 HOUS 77015 3966 E2
Oates Rd
- HOUS 77029 3966 A3
200 HOUS 77013 3966 A1
1000 JTCY 77029 3966 A3
3600 HOUS 77013 3827 C3
5700 HOUS 77078 3827 C2
8500 HOUS 77078 3688 B6
Oat Harvest Ct
2700 HarC 77038 3543 A5
Oat Mill Dr
16500 HarC 77095 3538 B6
Oats St
4200 HOUS 77020 3964 B1
Oban St
6300 HOUS 77085 4371 D3
Obelisk Bay Dr
17800 HarC 77429 3252 C7
Oberlin St
3800 SSPL 77005 4101 D4
4100 WUNP 77005 4101 C4
Obion Rd
100 HOUS 77076 3684 D5
W Obion Rd
200 HOUS 77076 3684 C5
200 HOUS 77091 3684 C5
N Oblong Cir
- HarC 77429 3395 D1
S Oblong Cir
- HarC 77429 3395 D1
W Oblong Cir
- HarC 77429 3395 D1
Oboe Dr
9800 HOUS 77025 4241 C2
Oboe Tr
2200 LGCY 77573 4632 C1
Obra Dr
- GLSN 77554 5440 E6
- GLSN 77554 5441 A6
Obra Ln
14400 HOUS 77045 4373 A3
O'Brien Rd
8900 FBnC 77469 4235 D1
O'Brien St
6300 HTCK 77563 4989 C4
Observatory St
8200 HOUS 77088 3683 C2
Obsidian Dr
16500 HarC 77095 3538 B2
Obsidian Arrowhead Rd
5100 FBnC 77469 4234 B3
Ocali Ct
- HarC 77014 3401 C3
Ocean Blvd
200 BzaC 77541 5547 C7
Ocean Dr
6900 BHCY 77520 4254 E3
Ocean Wy
2800 LGCY 77573 4633 C4
Ocean City Blvd
- HarC 77070 3399 A5
- HarC 77429 3399 A5
Oceania Ct
1900 HarC 77094 3955 A4
Oceanic Dr
22200 HarC 77449 3815 A4
Ocean Laurel Ln
12300 HarC 77014 3402 B3
Ocean Manor Ln
1200 LGCY 77573 4633 B3
Ocean Mist Ct
2900 SEBK 77586 4382 B7
Ocean Park Ln
21200 HarC 77449 3815 B3
Ocean Point Ct
2200 PRLD 77584 4500 A2
Ocean Point Dr
12900 PRLD 77584 4500 A2
Ocean Ridge Cir
3400 SEBK 77586 4382 C7
Oceanside Dr
8000 HarC 77095 3539 A7
Oceanside Ln
1300 LGCY 77573 4508 D4
Ocean View Dr
2000 SEBK 77586 4509 C3
Oceanview St
11700 MSCY 77071 4239 D7
Ocee St
3300 HOUS 77063 4099 C2
Ocelot Ln
- HOUS 77034 4378 C4
Ochoa Rd
2800 PRLD 77584 4502 E4
Ochre Leaf Tr
15300 HarC 77433 3251 A4
Ochre Park Ln
16400 HarC 77433 3251 A3
Ochre Park Wy
- HarC 77433 3251 A5
Ochre Willow Tr
20800 HarC 77433 3251 A4
Oconee Ct
24900 HarC 77375 2965 D3
Oconee Dr
24700 HarC 77375 2965 D3
O'Connor Dr
1500 CNRO 77304 2382 E4
15400 MtgC 77372 2684 A4
O'Connor Ln
9600 FBnC 77459 4621 D4
Ocotillo Ct
1700 FBnC 77494 3953 C5
Ocotillo Dr
11500 HarC 77095 3397 B7
Ocotillo St
2200 LGCY 77573 4632 D2
Octavia Dr
33000 MtgC 77354 2671 D4
Octavia St
6100 HOUS 77026 3825 D6
Octavia Wy
21800 HarC 77073 3259 D1
Octavian Ct
2500 RMFT 77357 2829 B2

STREET
Block City ZIP Map# Grid

October Shadow Ct
8400 HarC 77379 3255 E3
O'Daniel Ln
1600 CNRO 77301 2384 D2
O'Day Rd
1400 BKVL 77581 4375 D7
1400 PRLD 77581 4375 D7
1400 PRLD 77581 4502 D1
2500 PRLD 77584 4502 D3
Oddfellow St
1500 CNRO 77301 2383 E3
Oddo Av
- HOUS 77022 3824 A2
Oddo St
100 HOUS 77022 3824 A2
Oddom Ct
13300 HarC 77429 3254 A7
O'Dell Wy
- PASD 77503 4248 A3
- PASD 77505 4248 A3
Odell Springs Dr
21300 MtgC 77365 2973 A7
Oder Ln
700 HarC 77090 3258 C2
Odessa Ct
700 HarC 77060 3544 E4
Odessa Dr
300 MAGA 77354 2669 A4
10400 FBnC 77478 4236 E4
Odet Ct
8200 HOUS 77088 3684 A2
Odin Ct
3700 HOUS 77021 4103 C5
Odinglen Dr
7300 HarC 77095 3678 C1
Odom Blvd
2300 HOUS 77054 4242 B2
O'Donnell Dr
11200 HOUS 77076 3685 A3
Odyssey Ct
10600 HOUS 77099 4238 A3
Offer Dr
10500 HOUS 77031 4239 B3
Office City Dr
7000 HOUS 77087 4105 A5
7100 HOUS 77012 4105 A5
Ogden St
8100 HOUS 77017 4105 D7
Ogdenberg Falls Dr
19900 HarC 77379 3110 C5
Ogden Forest Dr
6000 HarC 77088 3542 C7
Ogilivie Av
200 HOUS 77017 4106 B6
Oglesby St
11500 JTCY 77029 3966 D4
Oglethorpe Dr
9200 HOUS 77031 4239 B6
O'Grady Dr
1900 CNRO 77304 2382 E4
O'Hara Dr
- HOUS 77085 4371 C3
15300 HOUS 77489 4371 C5
O'Hara Rd
4200 GlsC 77511 4869 B5
Ohio Av
- GlsC 77539 4632 D6
- LGCY 77539 4632 D6
- LGCY 77573 4632 D6
N Ohio Av
2000 GlsC 77539 4632 E7
2000 LGCY 77539 4632 E7
2400 DKSN 77539 4753 E1
2400 DKSN 77539 4754 A1
2400 GlsC 77539 4753 E1
Ohio Rd
3000 FBnC 77545 4498 E7
Ohio St
1600 LGCY 77573 4632 C4
3100 BYTN 77520 4112 A1
13800 HOUS 77047 4373 A4
S Ohio St
100 LPRT 77571 4251 E2
600 LPRT 77571 4252 A3
Ohio Canal Ct
17500 HarC 77346 3408 B3
Ohsfeldt St
2500 HOUS 77008 3822 E4
Oil Baron Ln
3300 BzaC 77583 4500 E6
Oil Center Blvd
- HarC 77073 3259 D5
Oil Center Ct
2200 HarC 77073 3259 D6
Oiler Dr
- PRLD 77581 4503 E7
- PRLD 77584 4503 D6
Oilers Dr
- HOUS 77032 3546 C2
Oil Field Rd
- MtgC 77302 2678 A2
- SGLD 77478 4369 A7
2700 SGLD 77479 4369 A7
2900 SGLD 77479 4496 A1
8000 MtgC 77354 2673 A6
8000 MtgC 77382 2673 A6
8000 WDLD 77382 2673 A6
Oilfield Rd
- FBnC 77479 4495 E6
- MTBL 77520 3696 B4
- SGLD 77479 4496 A5
6500 FBnC 77459 4496 D5
6500 FBnC 77479 4496 D5
6500 MSCY 77459 4496 D5
6600 MSCY 77459 4496 D5
Oil Ranch
- WlrC 77447 2959 B5
Ojeman Pl
- HOUS 77080 3821 A5
Ojeman Rd
1500 HOUS 77055 3821 A5
3200 HOUS 77080 3821 A2
Oka Chobee Dr
16700 HOUS 77044 3409 C3
Okanella St
10100 HOUS 77041 3681 A4
10200 HOUS 77041 3680 D4
10700 HarC 77041 3680 D4
Okay St
10500 HOUS 77016 3687 A3
Okehampton Dr
24400 HarC 77375 2965 E4
Okinawa Rd
7300 HOUS 77033 4244 A1
Oklahoma Av
- HarC 77053 4373 A4
- HOUS 77053 4373 A4
100 GlsC 77518 4634 C3

STREET
Block City ZIP Map# Grid

Oklahoma Av
1200 GlsC 77539 4634 B4
1200 TXCY 77539 4634 B4
1800 DRPK 77536 4108 E7
2700 DKSN 77539 4754 C1
2700 LGCY 77573 4632 D6
2900 LGCY 77539 4632 E6
Oklahoma St
1600 BYTN 77520 4112 A1
3000 HOUS 77093 3825 A2
Okley Bnd
10 FBnC 77459 4621 B4
Okra St
5000 HarC 77379 3112 B7
Ola Dr
5000 HarC 77032 3546 D2
Olana Dr
5000 HarC 77032 3546 D3
Oland Wy
19800 HarC 77073 3403 C2
Olathe St
9300 HOUS 77055 3820 D6
Old Rd
2300 FRDW 77546 4629 E5
2300 FRDW 77546 4630 A5
14500 HarC 77532 3553 C6
Old Addicks-Howell Rd
- FBnC 77083 4236 D1
- HarC 77082 4096 D3
- HOUS 77082 4096 D4
- HOUS 77083 4096 D4
Old Addicks-Howell Rd SR-6
- FBnC 77083 4236 D1
- HOUS 77082 4096 D2
Old Airline Rd
2000 BzaC 77583 4500 B5
2000 PRLD 77583 4500 B5
2000 PRLD 77584 4500 B4
3900 BzaC 77583 4624 B5
3900 PRLD 77578 4624 B1
3900 PRLD 77583 4624 B5
4900 BzaC 77578 4624 B3
6600 IWCY 77583 4624 B7
7100 IWCY 77583 4745 B2
7700 BzaC 77583 4745 B2
Old Aldine Westfield Rd
23700 HarC 77373 3114 C5
Old Alvin Rd
100 GlsC 77511 4750 B4
600 LGCY 77546 4750 B6
1100 PRLD 77581 4376 C7
1500 PRLD 77581 4503 D5
5700 ARLA 77583 4623 A4
Old Anderson Ln
4600 CNRO 77304 2237 B6
Old Arbor Ct
- HarC 77346 3408 B3
Old Arbor Wy
4100 HarC 77346 3408 A3
Old Bammel N Houston Rd
10900 HarC 77086 3542 B2
Oldband Ln
8400 HarC 77040 3541 C6
Old Barn Dr
13000 FBnC 77469 4366 D1
Old Barngate Ln
19400 HarC 77073 3403 D3
Old Bauer Rd
16400 HarC 77433 3250 B5
16400 HarC 77447 3250 B5
Old Bayou Dr
100 DKSN 77539 4753 C5
100 TXCY 77539 4753 C5
Old Brickhouse Dr
4700 HOUS 77041 3681 A7
Old Bridge Ct
7500 FBnC 77479 4494 A4
Old Bridge Ln
1700 SGLD 77478 4368 E5
Old Bridge Lake St
100 HarC 77069 3256 E7
100 HarC 77069 3400 E1
Old Brook Ct
10 CNRO 77304 2236 B7
Old Brook Dr
8500 HOUS 77071 4239 C5
Old Canyon Dr
- HarC 77377 3254 B1
Old Carriage Ln
25700 HarC 77373 3114 C2
Old Castle
- CNRO 77304 2529 D1
Old Castle Ct
10 WDLD 77382 2673 D6
Old Castle Ln
4900 DKSN 77539 4753 D5
Oldcastle St
500 HOUS 77013 3966 B1
Old Castle Wy
3700 CNRO 77304 2237 A6
N Old Cedar Cir
10 WDLD 77382 2674 D4
S Old Cedar Cir
10 WDLD 77382 2674 D4
Old Chapel Dr
3200 HarC 77373 3114 D2
Old Chatham Ln
6400 HOUS 77035 4240 A5
Old Choate Rd
- HOUS 77598 4378 E5
100 HOUS 77034 4378 E5
Old Chocolate Bayou Rd
2700 PRLD 77581 4501 E3
2700 PRLD 77584 4501 E4
3500 BzaC 77578 4501 E7
3500 BzaC 77584 4501 E7
3700 BzaC 77578 4625 E3
3700 BzaC 77584 4625 E3
4300 MNVL 77578 4625 E2
13900 HOUS 77048 4374 E5
Old Chocolate Bayou Rd CO-89
- PRLD 77584 4501 E4
Old Church Ln
22500 HarC 77449 3814 E4
Old Clark Rd
- HarC 77571 4110 D3
Old Clinton Dr
- HOUS 77029 3965 D7
- HOUS 77029 4105 D1
Old Clinton Rd Ext
5600 HOUS 77020 3964 D3
7000 HOUS 77020 3965 A4
Old Coach Ln
10700 HNCV 77024 3960 A1
Old Coach Rd
15900 SGCH 77355 2816 A7

STREET
Block City ZIP Map# Grid

Old Coach Rd
15900 SGCH 77355 2962 A1
16300 SGCH 77355 2815 E7
Old Coffin Rd
19300 MtgC 77302 2680 C7
19300 MtgC 77357 2680 C7
Old Colony Ct
1900 FBnC 77469 4365 C3
Old Colony Dr
400 FBnC 77469 4365 C4
Old Conroe Magnolia Rd
14000 MtgC 77384 2528 C7
14200 MtgC 77384 2674 A3
15900 MtgC 77354 2674 A3
Old Country Rd
- HarC 77064 3541 C5
Old Country Club Rd
- CNRO 77304 2383 A4
Old Course Dr
300 FRDW 77546 4629 A6
Old Creek Dr
1700 RSBG 77471 4491 D6
Old Creek Ln
24500 WlrC 77447 2959 C2
Old Creek Rd
14900 HOUS 77060 3544 D3
Oldcrest Dr
9700 STAF 77477 4239 A7
Old Ct Dr
17400 HarC 77377 3254 A4
Old Cypresswood Dr
24300 HarC 77373 3114 C5
Old Desert Rd
9500 LPRT 77571 4250 A4
Old Dixie Dr
1900 FBnC 77469 4234 C7
Old Dock Ln
14200 HarC 77090 3258 C7
Olde Falls Dr
26900 HarC 77339 3118 D5
Olde Lantern Wy
3200 MtgC 77380 2967 B3
Old Elm Tr
1400 FBnC 77479 4493 E5
Olde Manor Ln
14800 HarC 77068 3257 C6
Olden Ct
13500 HarC 77429 3397 D2
Oldenburg Ln
9600 HarC 77065 3539 D4
Old English Ct
7600 FBnC 77479 4494 A5
Olde Oaks Dr
600 DKSN 77539 4753 B3
5800 CNRO 77378 2237 D1
Olde Pecan Dr
6300 FBnC 77469 4232 D6
Olde Rose Ct
10 WDLD 77382 2819 B2
Olde Tavern Ct
3100 HarC 77068 3257 C5
Old Fairbanks-N Houston Rd
11000 HarC 77086 3541 D3
11000 HarC 77086 3542 A2
Old Farm Rd
2500 HOUS 77063 3959 E7
Old Farmhouse Ln
6100 HarC 77449 3677 B4
E Old Field Dr
10 HarC 77336 2976 A6
N Old Field Dr
100 HarC 77336 2976 A4
S Old Field Dr
100 HarC 77336 2976 A6
W Old Field Dr
10 HarC 77336 2976 A6
Old Field Pl
1900 WDLD 77380 2967 E1
Old FM-1488 Rd
- MtgC 77354 2673 C4
Old Foltin Rd
12000 HarC 77038 3542 E5
12000 HarC 77086 3542 E5
Old Forge
- HOUS 77034 4379 C1
Old Fort Rd
2400 SGLD 77479 4368 E7
2900 SGLD 77479 4495 D2
3000 SGLD 77479 4496 A1
Old Fry Rd
- HarC 77449 3815 E6
Old Galley Wy
18400 HarC 77532 3410 A6
Old Galveston Hwy
- WEBS 77598 4507 C6
Old Galveston Rd
- ALVN 77511 4868 A2
- BzaC 77511 4867 E2
- BzaC 77511 4868 A2
- HOUS 77034 4378 C2
100 ALVN 77511 4867 C1
400 WEBS 77598 4507 C6
19300 WEBS 77598 4631 D1
Old Galveston Rd SR-3
- HOUS 77034 4378 C2
Oldgate Pass Ln
18000 HarC 77433 3537 D7
Old Genoa Red Bluff Rd
- HOUS 77034 4247 E7
- PASD 77034 4247 E7
- PASD 77504 4247 E7
600 HOUS 77034 4378 E1
Old Glory Dr
6300 HarC 77449 3677 B4
Old Greenhouse Rd
4800 HarC 77084 3677 B6
4800 HarC 77449 3677 D5
Old Greens Rd
1200 HarC 77032 3403 E6
1200 HarC 77032 3404 A6
1200 HOUS 77032 3403 E6
1600 HOUS 77032 3404 A6
Oldham St
10 HOUS 77011 3964 D6
Oldham Farm
- HarC 77060 3403 C4
- HarC 77073 3403 C4
Old Hannover Dr
21500 HarC 77388 3113 B3
Old Hardin Store Rd
25700 MtgC 77354 2817 D7
Oldhaven St
7700 HOUS 77074 4239 E1
Old Hearth Dr
15000 HarC 77084 3678 E2
Old Hempstead
32500 MtgC 77355 2668 D5

STREET
Block City ZIP Map# Grid

Old Hempstead Rd
31500 MtgC 77355 2668 A5
Old Hickory Dr
400 MtgC 77302 2530 B6
3100 LPRT 77571 4250 D3
13000 HarC 77429 3398 A5
Old Hickory Ln
- HarC 77038 3543 C6
- HarC 77088 3543 C6
1400 LGCY 77573 4632 B5
Old Hickory St
6300 HarC 77449 3677 B4
Old Hitchin Rack Ln
- HarC 77493 3813 E3
Old Hockley Rd
30000 MAGA 77355 2815 A1
30000 MtgC 77355 2815 A1
30200 MtgC 77355 2668 D7
30200 MtgC 77355 2814 E1
Old Holly Dr
3400 PRLD 77584 4503 B6
Old Holzwarth Rd
1700 HarC 77388 3113 C4
1700 HOUS 77388 3113 D4
Old Houston Hwy
- HMPD 77445 3098 C1
- PNIS 77445 3099 A2
- PRVW 77445 3099 E3
- PRVW 77445 3100 B3
- PRVW 77484 3100 D4
- WlrC 77445 3098 D1
- WlrC 77445 3099 E3
42400 WALR 77484 3101 A4
42400 WlrC 77484 3100 E4
42400 WlrC 77484 3101 A4
Old Houston Rd
14500 MtgC 77302 2679 D6
14500 MtgC 77306 2679 E1
17000 MtgC 77302 2825 C3
18500 MtgC 77365 2825 A6
20700 MtgC 77302 2824 E7
20700 MtgC 77365 2824 E7
Old Houston-Crosby Rd
1700 HarC 77532 3691 E2
1700 HarC 77532 3692 A2
Old Houston la Porte County Rd
6500 PASD 77505 4248 E3
Old Howth Rd
23300 WlrC 77445 2953 B4
Old Huffmeister Rd
12000 HarC 77429 3398 A6
Old Humble Rd
- HarC 77032 3546 E3
14000 HarC 77396 3546 E3
14200 HarC 77396 3547 A1
14300 MtgC 77302 2531 D7
14400 HOUS 77396 3547 A1
14500 MtgC 77302 2677 D1
14800 HOUS 77396 3406 B7
15000 HarC 77396 3406 C6
16100 HMBL 77396 3406 C6
Old Humble Rd Rd
15600 MtgC 77302 2677 D3
Old Hwy 75
10 GlsC 77554 5106 E3
10 GlsC 77554 5107 A4
10 GlsC 77563 5106 E3
10 TXCY 77554 5106 E3
10 TXCY 77563 5106 E3
10 TXCY 77590 5106 E3
8300 GLSN 77554 5107 C5
Old Johnson Farm Rd
- MtgC 77355 2815 B2
Old Katy Rd
- HOUS 77043 3819 D7
6800 HOUS 77024 3961 C1
6900 HOUS 77007 3961 D1
6900 HOUS 77008 3961 D1
7100 HOUS 77055 3961 B1
9100 SPVL 77055 3959 D1
9200 HOUS 77055 3959 D1
10100 HOUS 77043 3959 A1
10700 HOUS 77043 3958 A1
11600 HOUS 77079 3958 A1
11700 HOUS 77043 3957 E1
11700 HOUS 77079 3957 D1
13000 HOUS 77079 3818 C7
13900 HOUS 77079 3956 D1
14400 HOUS 77079 3817 D7
Old Kickapoo Rd
- WlrC 77447 2958 A2
- WlrC 77484 2958 A2
Old Kirby Dr
- TYLV 77586 4382 A6
1600 PASD 77586 4382 A6
2000 PASD 77507 4382 A6
Old Kirby Rd
- PASD 77586 4381 E7
- PASD 77586 4382 A6
- TYLV 77586 4381 E7
- TYLV 77586 4382 A6
Old Kluge Rd
12000 HarC 77070 3398 B1
12000 HarC 77429 3398 B1
Old Lake Rd
800 HOUS 77057 3960 B4
Old La Porte Rd
9400 LPRT 77571 4111 D6
11500 LPRT 77571 4111 A6
Old Ledge Ln
8600 HOUS 77088 3684 A1
Old Lee Rd
18100 HOUS 77032 3405 D1
18100 HOUS 77338 3405 D1
Old Legend Ct
2000 SGLD 77478 4368 B4
Old Legend Dr
2100 SGLD 77478 4368 E6
Old Liberty Rd
8700 HOUS 77013 3826 E4
8700 HOUS 77028 3826 E4
Old Lighthouse Ln
6000 HarC 77084 3679 A6
Old Lockwood Rd
5900 HOUS 77026 3825 C3
Old Lodge Dr
5300 HarC 77066 3400 E2
5300 HarC 77066 3401 A2
Old Loggers Rd
7000 HarC 77338 3261 D5
Old Louetta Lp
2400 HarC 77388 3113 A5
Old Louetta Rd
9500 HarC 77379 3255 D5
16900 HarC 77070 3255 B4
N Old Macgregor Wy
2500 HOUS 77004 4103 A3

STREET
Block City ZIP Map# Grid

Old Magnolia Rd
100 CNRO 77301 2383 E6
100 CNRO 77304 2383 D6
900 CNRO 77304 2529 C1
Old Main St
- HOUS 77054 4102 C7
1000 HOUS 77030 4102 C4
Old Main Street Loop Rd
10000 HOUS 77054 4241 E2
10000 HOUS 77054 4242 A2
11500 HOUS 77025 4241 C4
Old Manse Ct
12700 SGLD 77478 4237 D4
Old Manvel Rd
- BzaC 77511 4747 E5
1800 ALVN 77511 4866 E1
1800 BzaC 77511 4748 E7
1800 BzaC 77511 4866 E1
Old Maple Ln
8100 HarC 77338 3261 E3
8600 HarC 77338 3262 A3
Old Master Dr
3100 SGLD 77479 4368 C7
Old Masters Dr
2900 SGLD 77479 4368 C7
Old Meadow Ln
8300 HarC 77064 3541 D5
Old Mill Ct
1000 SGLD 77478 4368 B2
Old Mill Ln
900 HarC 77073 3259 A2
Old Mill Rd
- SGLD 77479 4368 E7
2300 SGLD 77478 4368 E6
19900 MtgC 77357 2828 A5
Old Mint House Ln
10900 HarC 77375 3110 A4
Old Mission Rd
11300 HarC 77095 3396 E7
Old Mitchell Rd
24500 WlrC 77445 2955 C2
Old Montgomery Rd
- CNRO 77301 2384 C5
600 CNRO 77301 2383 E5
1100 CNRO 77304 2383 B5
2000 CNRO 77304 2382 E5
11000 MtgC 77304 2236 A1
11000 MtgC 77318 2236 A1
Old Montgomery Rd FM-2854
600 CNRO 77301 2383 E5
1100 CNRO 77304 2383 B5
2000 CNRO 77304 2382 E5
Old Oak Cir
6000 FBnC 77479 4495 E7
6000 FBnC 77479 4496 A7
Old Oak Dr
4800 FBnC 77469 4364 A1
Old Oak Ln
2400 HOUS 77339 3119 A2
Old Oak Grove Dr
13100 FBnC 77469 4366 D2
Old Oak Hill St
1600 CNRO 77301 2384 D6
Old Oaks Blvd
- PRLD 77584 4502 D5
Old Oaks Dr
3300 BYTN 77521 3972 B1
12300 HOUS 77024 3959 A3
12400 HOUS 77024 3958 E3
Old Oaks Ln
2300 MtgC 77385 2823 C2
Old Oaks St
200 LGCY 77573 4630 C6
2100 MtgC 77385 2823 B2
Old Orchard Blvd
- DKSN 77539 4753 B5
Old Orchard Ct
- DKSN 77539 4753 B5
Old Orchard Dr
- DKSN 77539 4753 B5
3700 FBnC 77469 4366 D2
3700 FBnC 77478 4366 E2
Old Orchard Ln
1600 SEBK 77586 4382 E7
Old Orchard Rd
10200 LPRT 77571 4250 B3
Old Orchard Wy
- DKSN 77539 4753 B5
Old Ox Rd
2000 MtgC 77386 2969 A4
Old Panamint
- HOUS 77546 4505 E2
- HOUS 77546 4506 A2
Old Pike Rd
- HarC 77373 3115 E6
Old Pine Ln
12800 HarC 77015 3828 C5
Old Pine Grove Dr
4000 HarC 77346 3408 A3
Old Post Rd
3800 HarC 77082 4096 A3
Old Prairie Ct
1900 FBnC 77469 4234 C7
Old Presidio Dr
10 MNVL 77583 4624 E4
Old Quarry Dr
8500 FBnC 77479 4494 B6
Old Ranch Rd
21200 HarC 77073 3259 C2
Old Richmond Rd
- FBnC 77478 4236 E2
2500 RSBG 77471 4490 E4
2600 RSBG 77471 4491 C2
5000 RHMD 77469 4491 D2
5000 RSBG 77469 4491 D2
12900 HarC 77099 4237 C2
12900 HOUS 77099 4237 C2
13000 HarC 77083 4237 B2
13700 FBnC 77478 4237 A2
18300 FBnC 77469 4367 A1
18400 FBnC 77478 4366 E1
18500 FBnC 77469 4366 E1
Oldridge St
9500 HMBL 77338 3262 C4
Oldrige Dr
15600 HarC 77084 3679 A6
Old Riley Fuzzel Rd
2600 MtgC 77386 2969 D5
Old River Dr
16000 HarC 77530 3830 B5
Old River Ln
2400 FBnC 77469 4365 B5
Old River Pl
10 WDLD 77382 2674 A5
Old River Rd
1200 HMBL 77338 3262 E5
2000 HarC 77338 3262 E4
2600 HarC 77338 3263 A3
2600 HOUS 77338 3263 A2
Olds Dr
11800 MtgC 77365 3117 D4
Old Sam Rd
16900 MtgC 77302 2825 C1
Old Sand Pit Rd
19500 MtgC 77357 2827 E4
Old Settlement Ct
4000 MSCY 77459 4496 C2
Old Smith Rd
14000 MtgC 77384 2528 D7
Old Sorters Rd
19900 MtgC 77365 2972 D6
20800 MtgC 77365 2973 A6
Old South Dr
2200 FBnC 77469 4365 C1
2800 FBnC 77469 4234 C7
Old South Wy
- LGCY 77573 4630 E4
Old Spanish Tr
- HOUS 77025 4102 B6
1000 HOUS 77054 4102 D6
1200 HOUS 77030 4102 D6
2800 HOUS 77021 4102 E6
2900 HOUS 77021 4103 A5
2900 HOUS 77054 4103 A5
5000 HOUS 77021 4104 A4
5300 HOUS 77023 4104 B4
11800 STFE 77510 4871 C7
Old Spanish Tr US-90 ALT
- HOUS 77025 4102 B6
1000 HOUS 77054 4102 D6
1200 HOUS 77030 4102 D6
2800 HOUS 77021 4102 B6
2900 HOUS 77054 4103 A5
3300 HOUS 77021 4103 E5
5000 HOUS 77021 4104 A4
5300 HOUS 77023 4104 B4
E Old Spanish Tr
4400 HOUS 77013 3826 E5
W Old Spanish Tr
4400 HOUS 77013 3826 E5
Old Spring Ln
100 HarC 77015 3828 B6
Old Spring Cypress Rd
6100 HarC 77379 3111 D6
Old Stable Rd
- BLAR 77401 4101 B2
- HOUS 77081 4101 B2
- HOUS 77401 4101 B2
Old Sterling Cir
- WDLD 77382 2819 E2
W Old Sterling Cir
10 WDLD 77382 2819 E2
Old Stone Ln
- HarC 77433 3396 A6
Old Stone Tr
15400 HOUS 77079 3957 A2
Old Stream Ct
10 WDLD 77381 2821 A3
Old Telegraph Rd
11400 HarC 77067 3402 B6
Old Texaco Rd
12800 MtgC 77302 2531 E7
14400 MtgC 77302 2532 D4
Old Texaco Camp Rd
13600 MtgC 77302 2532 B5
Old Texas Av
- WEBS 77598 4507 B7
- WEBS 77598 4631 C1
Old Tidwell Rd
- HOUS 77028 3687 B5
Old Timber Ln
9600 HarC 77379 3110 C6
Oldtown Bridge Ct
15100 FBnC 77478 4236 D4
Old Towne Ln
9900 FBnC 77478 4237 A3
Old Trail Ct
1500 FBnC 77479 4494 B5
Old Trail Dr
8200 HarC 77040 3681 D1
Old Tram Rd
- HarC 77336 2976 D6
- MtgC 77303 2239 C1
Old Tree Ct
7700 FBnC 77479 4494 A5
Old TX-105 E
- CNRO 77301 2385 A4
- CNRO 77303 2385 A4
- CTSH 77301 2385 C3
- CTSH 77303 2385 C3
Old TX-105 E FM-1485
- CNRO 77301 2385 A4
- CNRO 77303 2385 A4
- CTSH 77301 2385 C3
- CTSH 77303 2385 C3
Old TX-146
4100 PASD 77586 4382 D5
5500 SEBK 77586 4382 D5
Old Tybee Rd
14400 HarC 77084 3679 A4
Old Underwood Rd
100 DRPK 77536 4110 A6
100 DRPK 77571 4110 A6
100 HarC 77571 4110 A6
100 LPRT 77536 4110 A5
100 LPRT 77571 4110 A6
Old Valley Wy
800 HarC 77094 3955 A2
Old Village Ln
13900 FBnC 77478 4237 A3
14100 FBnC 77478 4236 E3
Old Vista Rd
4900 PASD 77505 4248 C3
Old Waller Tomball Rd
31000 WALR 77484 3102 A5
Old Walters Rd
12200 HarC 77014 3401 E4
12200 HarC 77067 3401 E4
Old Washington Rd
- HarC 77484 3247 E1
26800 HarC 77447 3248 B2
28500 HarC 77484 3248 A1
31100 HarC 77484 3102 D7
31100 WALR 77484 3102 A6
Old Westheimer Rd
- HOUS 77082 4097 E1
Oldwick Brook Dr
19200 HarC 77375 3109 D7
Old Wilson Rd
- HarC 77396 3407 B4
- HMBL 77396 3407 B4
- HOUS 77396 3407 B4
Old Windmill Dr
13000 FBnC 77469 4366 D1
Old Windmill Tr
20000 HarC 77447 3104 E3
Old Windsor Wy
10 SGLD 77479 4495 A3
Old Woods Ct
24600 HarC 77373 3114 D3
Old Woods Ln
21300 HarC 77073 3259 D2
Old Woods Psg
10 FBnC 77459 4621 C4
Old Yale St
4400 HOUS 77018 3823 C1
4500 HOUS 77022 3823 C1
Old Yaupon Ln
19200 HarC 77433 3537 B6
Ole Ln
- HOUS 77336 3121 D4
Oleander
100 MRGP 77571 4252 B1
Oleander Av
3400 TXCY 77590 4874 C4
6500 GLSN 77551 5108 B7
Oleander Ct
8200 HOUS 77017 4246 A1
Oleander Dr
800 HMPD 77445 2952 E7
1500 LMQU 77568 4990 A2
1600 DKSN 77539 4753 E4
1600 DKSN 77539 4754 A3
1900 LMQU 77568 4989 E2
2200 PASD 77503 4248 C1
2800 PASD 77505 4248 C1
4000 GLSN 77554 5332 D3
8000 HarC 77562 3832 C3
Oleander Ln
100 HarC 77571 4111 A4
1200 LGCY 77573 4752 D1
7000 HTCK 77563 4988 E5
Oleander St
- PRVW 77445 3100 C3
400 WEBS 77598 4507 A6
1300 HOUS 77009 3824 E6
1600 BzaC 77583 4500 A6
4300 BYTN 77521 3973 A2
4300 HarC 77521 3973 A2
4300 HOUS 77401 4101 C5
4500 BLAR 77401 4101 B5
4500 GlsC 77518 4634 D3
4700 PASD 77586 4383 C5
S Oleander St
400 MRGP 77571 4252 B1
Oleander Tr
8100 MtgC 77385 2676 C6
Oleander Grove Wy
6800 HarC 77049 3829 B1
Oleander Hill St
11700 HarC 77038 3543 A5
Oleander Point Dr
10400 HarC 77095 3538 A2
Oleander Ridge Wy
19500 HarC 77433 3677 B2
Olema Valley Dr
- HarC 77379 3255 D6
Olentangy St
10100 HOUS 77075 4377 D2
10200 HOUS 77089 4377 D2
Olenthorpe Pk
22000 HarC 77073 3259 A4
Oleo Ln
14400 GlsC 77517 4870 C4
14400 STFE 77517 4870 C4
Oleoke Ln
13800 HarC 77015 3828 E5
13900 HarC 77015 3829 A5
Oleta
- HarC 77493 3675 A4
Oleta Ln
15600 FBnC 77478 4236 B5
Olga Ln
10100 HOUS 77041 3681 A5
Olga St
- HOUS 77041 3680 E5
- HOUS 77041 3681 A5
Oligocene St
4200 HOUS 77047 4374 C1
Olin Dr
- PRLD 77581 4502 D2
Olin Rd
14700 HarC 77377 3108 D3
Olinda Dr
6300 HarC 77041 3679 B4
Olinwood Dr
4600 BzaC 77511 4748 A6
Olive Av
200 PASD 77506 4107 A4
Olive Cir
2300 BYTN 77520 3973 D7
Olive Gdn
- HOUS 77077 3957 B5
Olive Pk
- HOUS 77077 3957 B5
Olive Pl
1500 HOUS 77077 3957 B5
Olive St
200 LGCY 77573 4632 C7
700 HOUS 77007 3962 C3
1200 BYTN 77520 3973 C7
E Olive St
800 LGCY 77573 4632 D6
Olive Tr
- HOUS 77077 3957 B5
Olive Trc
- HOUS 77077 3957 B5
Olive Branch Ct
8700 FBnC 77083 4236 E1
8700 HarC 77083 4096 E7
Olive Brook Ln
9900 HarC 77095 3538 A3
Olivebrook Ln
700 HOUS 77047 4373 B2
Olive Glen Dr
16000 HarC 77082 4096 A4
Olive Green Ct
4500 PASD 77059 4380 C3
Olive Grove Ct
6100 HOUS 77345 3120 D6
Olive Hill Dr
- HOUS 77077 3957 B4
Olive Leaf Dr
18200 HarC 77084 3816 D3
Olive Mill Ct
3600 FBnC 77469 4233 C5
Olive Mt St
10100 PRLD 77584 4501 A3
Olive Oak Ct
4200 HOUS 77059 4380 C3
Oliver Dr
100 MTBL 77520 3696 E5
Oliver Ln
- BzaC 77511 4749 B2
Oliver Rd
9000 PRLD 77511 4628 A3
9000 PRLD 77581 4628 B3
9100 BzaC 77581 4628 B3
9600 BzaC 77511 4628 D4
Oliver St
500 TXCY 77591 4873 E5
1000 HOUS 77007 3962 E2
Olive Ridge Ct
23200 HarC 77494 3953 C3
Olive Springs Ct
14200 HOUS 77062 4379 C6
Olive Tree Ct
18200 HarC 77429 3252 B7
Olive Wood Ct
11500 HarC 77089 4378 B5
Olivewood Dr
10900 HarC 77089 4378 A6
Olivia Springs Ln
2100 MtgC 77386 2969 D6
Olivias Wy Ln
7900 HarC 77072 4097 C7
Olivine Ln
3200 HarC 77388 3112 E4
Ollerton Ln
10 CNRO 77303 2384 D1
Ollia Cir
5900 PASD 77505 4248 D3
Olmstead Row
- WDLD 77380 2821 D5
Olmstead Park Dr
15000 HarC 77429 3252 E6
Olney Oak Dr
800 HOUS 77079 3957 D2
Olson Ln
6300 PASD 77505 4248 E4
6700 PASD 77505 4249 A3
Olster Dr
2600 HarC 77084 3816 A5
Olympia Dr
1900 HOUS 77019 3961 D6
2700 MSCY 77459 4497 A1
5600 HOUS 77056 3960 D6
6100 HOUS 77057 3960 B6
6600 PASD 77505 4248 E4
7500 HOUS 77063 3960 A6
10000 HOUS 77042 3959 A6
10600 HOUS 77042 3958 C6
11200 HOUS 77077 3958 B6
12400 HOUS 77077 3957 D6
Olympiad Dr
5500 HarC 77041 3679 D6
Olympia Fields Ln
5100 HarC 77069 3400 E1
Olympia Springs Dr
3900 LGCY 77539 4633 D4
Olympia Springs Ln
21800 HarC 77449 3815 A1
Olympic Cir
19100 HarC 77346 3265 D6
19100 HOUS 77346 3265 D6
Olympic Dr
2100 LGCY 77573 4508 D7
3000 HOUS 77094 4095 E2
Olympic Forest Dr
21400 MtgC 77365 2973 A4
Olympic Park Ln
17500 HarC 77346 3408 C2
Olympus Dr
2500 HarC 77084 3816 B5
Oma Dr
34600 SGCH 77362 2816 C6
Omaha Dr
7500 HarC 77521 3833 C4
Omaha Beach Ct
3400 HarC 77388 3112 D4
Omaha Beach Ln
21100 HarC 77388 3112 D3
Omaha Valley Ln
- PRLD 77581 4503 C2
O'Malley Dr
10800 HarC 77067 3402 B7
Omar Dr
11000 MtgC 77354 2671 B2
Omar St
400 HOUS 77009 3824 A7
900 HOUS 77009 3823 E7
1100 HOUS 77008 3823 E7
O'Meara Dr
3500 HOUS 77025 4241 C2
4300 HOUS 77035 4241 C2
O'Meara Ln
200 HNCV 77024 3959 E3
200 PNPV 77024 3959 E3
Omega Cir
700 PASD 77503 4108 C5
N Omega Dr
10 LMQU 77568 4990 E6
S Omega Dr
10 LMQU 77568 4990 E6
Omega St
3100 HOUS 77022 3823 E3
Omolon Ln
800 HarC 77090 3258 B1
Omurrelet Ct
15800 HarC 77396 3406 E6
Onaleigh Dr
700 HarC 77530 3829 D7
O'Neal Ln
42000 MtgC 77354 2668 B4
Oneal St
1900 BYTN 77520 3973 E6
Oneida Av
5400 DKSN 77539 4754 C4
6100 TXCY 77539 4754 C4
Oneida Ct
2000 LGCY 77573 4631 B7
13900 HarC 77429 3253 E5
Oneida St
4200 PASD 77504 4248 A6
Oneidea Lake Ln
- HarC 77047 4374 D4
O'Neil St
1100 HOUS 77002 3963 A5
1200 HOUS 77019 3963 A5
1700 HOUS 77019 3962 E5
1800 HOUS 77006 3962 E5
Oneness Av
3000 HarC 77014 3401 D3
One Oak Chase Rd
700 FBnC 77583 4622 C5
One Sugar Pl Blvd
- SGLD 77478 4368 D3
One Token Dr
11500 HarC 77065 3398 A7
Onia Ln
5700 FBnC 77469 4493 A6
Onion Cr
3300 SGLD 77479 4495 B3
Onion Gulch Cir
16000 HarC 77546 4505 E6
Onslow St
10600 HOUS 77016 3686 D3
Ontario St
1800 BYTN 77520 3972 C6
Ontonagon Wy
4900 MtgC 77386 2970 E7
Onyx Ln
- HarC 77388 3113 A2
Opal Av
6100 TXCY 77591 4873 D5
Opal Ct
100 HOUS 77009 3824 B7
Opal Sprs
2000 HarC 77450 3954 E5
Opal St
20800 PRVW 77484 3100 D4
Opal Wy
200 HOUS 77336 3120 E4
Opal Brook Ct
4700 FBnC 77545 4623 C1
Opal Canyon Ln
14400 HOUS 77077 3956 E6
Opal Chase Dr
900 FBnC 77469 4493 B5
Opal Cove Ct
- FBnC 77494 4092 D4
- HarC 77095 3537 D5
Opal Creek Dr
12000 PRLD 77584 4500 C3
Opalcrest Ct
- FBnC 77469 4094 B7
Opalette Dr
13400 MtgC 77365 2972 C5
Opal Fall Dr
100 LGCY 77539 4752 E4
Opal Falls Ln
5000 FBnC 77494 4093 B1
Opal Glen Ln
11100 HOUS 77075 4376 E5
Opal Hill Ln
7500 HarC 77396 3547 C1
Opal Hollow Ln
26300 HarC 77433 3396 B4
Opaline Pl
10 WDLD 77382 2673 E5
Opal Meadow Dr
16500 HarC 77095 3538 A2
Opal Pass Ln
- HarC 77377 3253 E4
Opal Ridge Dr
10600 HarC 77095 3538 A2
Opal Sky Ct
500 LGCY 77573 4633 A2
Opal Sky Dr
5000 HarC 77449 3676 C6
Opal Valley Dr
12400 HarC 77377 3254 B3
Opalwood Ct
8500 HarC 77338 3262 A3
Opalwood Ln
8300 HarC 77338 3261 E3
8400 HarC 77338 3262 A3
Opatrny Meadows Ln
11100 HarC 77064 3540 D2
Opelika St
8900 HOUS 77080 3820 E2
Opelousas St
2000 HOUS 77020 3963 E2
2800 HOUS 77020 3964 B3
Open Bay Dr
1700 HarC 77532 3551 D3
Open Oak Wy
7300 HarC 77346 3265 A4
Opera House Row Dr
14800 HarC 77429 3396 B1
15000 HarC 77429 3252 B7
Opersteny Rd
- ALVN 77511 4866 C6
Ophelia
11200 HOUS 77013 3827 C5
Opihi
11700 GLSN 77554 5220 E6
Opossums Tr
16600 HarC 77049 3691 A7
Opper Ln
8900 HarC 77064 3540 B5
Opul Trails Ct
- FBnC 77469 4094 D7
Opus Ct
8900 HarC 77040 3541 B7
Ora St
2200 HOUS 77092 3821 E4
Orach Meadow Ln
12800 HOUS 77045 4241 D6
Ora Lee St
5800 HTCK 77563 4989 A2
Oralia Ln
12100 HarC 77065 3398 D6
Orange Av
2400 WALR 77484 3101 E6
3000 WlrC 77484 3101 E6
3400 TXCY 77590 4874 C4
E Orange Cir
4600 PRLD 77581 4503 A2
N Orange Cir
4600 PRLD 77581 4503 B2
S Orange Cir
4600 PRLD 77581 4503 A2
Orange Dr
5800 HarC 77050 3546 E6
Orange St
100 LMQU 77568 4990 C2
3000 PRLD 77581 4503 D2
3600 HOUS 77020 3964 A2
4400 GlsC 77518 4634 E3
17800 GlsC 77511 4869 B4
E Orange St
2300 PRLD 77581 4503 D2
W Orange St
6400 PRLD 77581 4502 E2
6400 PRLD 77581 4503 A2
Orange Bloom Ct
14800 HarC 77433 3250 D5
Orange Blossom
2400 HarC 77562 3832 D3
Orange Blossom Dr
700 LGCY 77573 4630 D6
Orange Blossom Ln
- RSBG 77469 4491 E6
Orange Brook Ct
10300 HarC 77089 4377 B6
Orange Grove Dr
3500 HarC 77039 3546 B6
4000 HOUS 77039 3546 A6
Orange Grove St
600 LGCY 77573 4632 A6
Orange Jasmine Ct
4300 HOUS 77059 4380 C3
Orange Leaf Ct
4400 PASD 77059 4380 D3
Orange Leaf Tr
15000 HarC 77433 3250 C6
Orange Maple Ct
21700 HarC 77433 3250 E6
Orange Oak Wy
- HarC 77433 3251 B5
Orange Peak Ct
- PRLD 77581 4503 D2
Orange Poppy Dr
20600 HarC 77433 3251 B4
Orange Tree Dr
4900 PASD 77505 4249 A7
Orangevale Ct
16800 HarC 77379 3255 D5
Orangevale Dr
9600 HarC 77379 3255 D5
Orangewood Dr
500 MtgC 77302 2530 B6
Orange Wood Tr
3400 PRLD 77581 4503 E6
Oratorio St
9300 HarC 77040 3541 A7
Orca Ct
3600 HarC 77388 3112 D6
Orchard Ct
9900 HOUS 77054 4242 A2
12000 STAF 77477 4237 D6
Orchard Dr
3000 HOUS 77054 4242 A2
S Orchard Dr
11500 HarC 77089 4505 B1
Orchard Ln
300 SGLD 77478 4368 A2
5000 GlsC 77517 4869 E7
8700 LPRT 77571 4249 D4
Orchard Run
200 FBnC 77545 4499 A6
Orchard St
- HarC 77598 4507 B5
100 CNRO 77301 2384 E4
100 WEBS 77598 4507 A5
200 MSCY 77489 4370 B2
6900 BKVL 77581 4376 A7
Orchard Barn Dr
13100 FBnC 77469 4366 C2
Orchard Bend Dr
3100 FBnC 77478 4366 C1
Orchard Berry Ln
20900 HarC 77375 3110 A5
20900 HarC 77379 3110 A5
Orchard Blossom Dr
3500 SGLD 77479 4494 E2
3500 SGLD 77479 4495 A5
Orchard Blossom Wy
4600 HarC 77084 3677 B7
Orchard Briar Ln
3100 PRLD 77583 4500 C5
Orchard Brook Dr
20800 HarC 77450 3954 C5
Orchard Canyon Ct
6200 HOUS 77345 3120 C4
Orchard Chase Ct
4300 FBnC 77450 4094 B2
Orchard Chase Dr
4300 FBnC 77450 4094 B2
Orchard Club Dr
3800 FBnC 77469 4366 D2
Orchard Country Ln
1800 HOUS 77062 4380 A6
Orchard Creek Ln
2600 FBnC 77494 3953 A5
Orchard Dale Cir
10 WDLD 77382 2674 B5
Orchard Dale Dr
22000 HarC 77389 3113 A1
Orchard Estates Dr
- FBnC 77469 4366 E2
- FBnC 77478 4366 E2
Orchard Falls Dr
- HOUS 77062 4380 B7
10 FBnC 77479 4367 A6
Orchard Farms Ln
14200 HOUS 77062 4379 D7
N Orchard Field Tr
- HarC 77433 3250 E6
Orchard Frost Dr
1900 PRLD 77581 4502 D2
Orchard Gate St
3000 SGLD 77479 4495 D1
Orchard Glen Ct
1900 HOUS 77062 4507 E1
Orchard Green Dr
13000 FBnC 77469 4366 D1
Orchard Grove Dr
29500 HarC 77377 2963 D6
Orchard Grove Ln
7200 FBnC 77469 4095 D5
Orchard Hill Dr
1000 HOUS 77077 3957 A3
Orchard Hills Ln
7400 FBnC 77479 4493 E6
Orchard Hollow Wy
12700 HarC 77065 3539 C1
Orchard Knoll Ln
25800 FBnC 77494 4093 A3
Orchard Links Dr
3700 FBnC 77469 4366 C2
Orchard Meadow Ln
- HarC 77449 3677 C6
Orchard Mill Ln
- PRLD 77583 4500 B5
19400 HarC 77449 3677 C6
Orchard Mist Ln
8400 FBnC 77469 4095 C7
Orchard Mountain Dr
11500 PASD 77059 4380 E5
Orchard Museum Ln
3500 FBnC 77478 4366 E2
Orchard Oak Ln
22800 HarC 77450 3953 E4
Orchard Park Dr
- FBnC 77479 4367 C6
1500 HOUS 77077 3957 A5
Orchard Peak Ct
800 HOUS 77062 4379 D7
Orchard Pines Pl
10 WDLD 77382 2673 E6
Orchard Ridge Ln
8600 HarC 77338 3262 A4
Orchard Run Wy
2400 FBnC 77545 4498 C
Orchard Spring Ct
5800 PRLD 77581 4502 E
Orchard Spring Dr
1900 PRLD 77581 4502 E
Orchard Springs Dr
10800 HarC 77067 3402 B
Orchard Stables Dr
13100 FBnC 77469 4366 D
Orchard Summit Dr
12600 FBnC 77478 4366 E
Orchard Trace Dr
- PRLD 77545 4499 E
Orchard Trace Ln
- FBnC 77469 4366 D
- FBnC 77478 4366 D
Orchard Trail Dr
5800 PRLD 77581 4502 D
Orchard Vale Dr
3000 HarC 77084 3816 A
Orchard Valley Ct
3100 HarC 77084 3816 C
5600 HOUS 77345 3120 C
Orchard View Ln
8500 PRLD 77584 4501 D
Orchard Wind Ln
1300 PRLD 77545 4499 E
N Orchid Dr
10 TXCY 77591 4874 B
S Orchid Dr
10 TXCY 77591 4874 B
200 LMQU 77568 4874 B
1400 MSCY 77489 4370 C
Orchid St
1000 HOUS 77017 4106 B
6900 BYTN 77521 3832 B
6900 HarC 77521 3832 B
Orchid Tr
12600 HarC 77041 3679 D
Orchid Blossom Wy
20500 HarC 77433 3251 B
Orchid Breeze Ln
9700 FBnC 77478 4237 A
Orchid Bud Ln
- HarC 77433 3251 A
Orchid Creek Dr
2500 PRLD 77584 4500 C
Orchid Creek Ln
17600 HarC 77084 3678 A
Orchid Grove Pl
10 WDLD 77385 2676 B
Orchid Mist Dr
16500 HarC 77433 3251 B
Orchid Ridge Ln
- FBnC 77083 4095 D
- FBnC 77469 4095 C
Orchid Spring Ln
9500 FBnC 77494 4092 C
Orchid Terrace Ln
13800 HOUS 77044 3550 A
Orchid Trace Ln
3300 HarC 77047 4374 B
Orchid Tree Ln
2800 HarC 77449 3815 C
Orchid Vine Ln
13400 HarC 77044 3689 C
Orcutt
14900 GlsC 77517 4986 A
Orean St
2100 HOUS 77034 4246 D
Oreana Ct
3800 MtgC 77386 2970 C6
Orebo St
7700 HOUS 77088 3683 C
Oregano Cir
9500 HOUS 77036 4098 E6
Oregold Dr
13200 HarC 77041 3679 C6
Oregon Av
500 SHUS 77587 4246 D
2300 LGCY 77573 4632 C6
Oregon St
1200 LPRT 77571 4251 E5
1800 BYTN 77520 4112 B2
Oregon Tr
11700 STFE 77510 4871 C7
Oreilly
3900 HOUS 77007 3962 C3
Oreilly St
4200 HOUS 77007 3962 C3
Orem Dr
3900 HOUS 77047 4374 C1
E Orem Dr
- HOUS 77061 4375 E1
- HOUS 77075 4375 E1
- HOUS 77075 4376 A1
4400 HOUS 77047 4374 D1
4900 HOUS 77048 4374 E1
5300 HOUS 77048 4375 D1
W Orem Dr
- HOUS 77085 4372 A1
1200 HOUS 77051 4373 D1
2100 HOUS 77045 4373 B1
2100 HOUS 77047 4373 D1
3300 HOUS 77045 4372 E1
7400 HOUS 77085 4371 E1
Orem Rd
4600 GlsC 77517 4869 E7
Orie Ct
1000 HarC 77373 3113 D1
Oriel Oaks Cir
- WDLD 77382 2673 C7
- WDLD 77382 2819 D3
S Oriel Oaks Cir
- WDLD 77382 2819 A1
Oriel Oaks Ct
- WDLD 77382 2819 A1
O'Riley Bnd
1900 GlsC 77539 4753 C1
Orinda Dr
10 PNVL 77304 2237 B1
Oriole
9800 MtgC 77385 2676 D5
Oriole Cir
7400 TXCY 77591 4873 C6
Oriole Dr
- TXCY 77591 4873 C6
1800 LGCY 77573 4631 C6
Oriole Ln
600 PASD 77502 4247 A1
7700 HMBL 77396 3406 C5
14400 MtgC 77302 2679 D1
14400 MtgC 77306 2679 D1
Oriole Pl
10900 CHTW 77385 2823 A5
Oriole St
200 HOUS 77018 3823 C2

STREET
Block City ZIP Map# Grid

Oriole St
4900 HOUS 77017 4106 C7
5600 HOUS 77502 4106 D7
5600 PASD 77502 4106 D7
Oriole Tr
21700 HarC 77338 3259 E1
21700 HarC 77338 3260 A1
Oriole Creek Ln
11100 FBnC 77469 4092 A6
Oriole Lake Wy
12400 HOUS 77089 4505 C1
Oriole Point Ct
18800 HarC 77429 3396 A1
18900 HarC 77429 3395 E1
Oriole Sky Wy
23300 HarC 77449 3814 C3
Oriole Trails Dr
- DKSN 77539 4752 D6
Oriole Wood Ct
2700 HarC 77038 3543 A5
Orion Dr
2500 LGCY 77573 4631 A6
14100 TMBL 77375 2963 E4
Orion St
2800 HOUS 77088 3683 B1
Orion Star Ct
10 WDLD 77382 2819 C2
Oriskany Ct
9500 HarC 77396 3407 A7
Orison Dr
- HarC 77065 3539 C4
Orkney Dr
4600 MSCY 77459 4369 B5
4700 SGLD 77459 4369 B5
4700 SGLD 77478 4369 B5
Orkney Ln
1900 CNRO 77301 2530 B3
Orkney Isle Ct
10 SGLD 77479 4495 B2
Orlando St
1600 FRDW 77546 4629 A7
3100 HOUS 77093 3686 A3
7200 HOUS 77016 3686 E3
7200 HOUS 77016 3687 A3
Orleans Av
500 LGCY 77573 4632 B3
Orleans Ct
700 MtgC 77302 2530 D6
Orleans Dr
2600 SEBK 77586 4509 C1
Orleans Ln
2300 SEBK 77586 4509 C1
Orleans Pl
7500 GLSN 77551 5222 A2
Orleans St
11900 HarC 77532 3693 A3
12500 HarC 77015 3828 B7
12800 HarC 77015 3967 B1
12800 HOUS 77015 3967 B1
Ormandy
11300 HOUS 77035 4240 A7
Ormandy St
12100 HOUS 77035 4371 A1
12100 HOUS 77085 4371 A1
Ormel
15100 HarC 77032 3545 A1
Ormel St
14700 HarC 77032 3545 A1
14700 HarC 77039 3545 A1
Ormond Ct
14500 HarC 77095 3539 A6
Ormonde Crossing Dr
16000 HarC 77429 3397 B2
N Ormsby St
200 ALVN 77511 4867 C1
Ornella Cir
21500 HarC 77338 3260 A2
Orr St
1200 HOUS 77009 3824 D7
Orrel Dr
900 PASD 77503 4108 B6
Ortega Ln
13500 HarC 77083 4097 A6
Orth Ln
27100 ORDN 77385 2822 C5
Orval St
1600 CNRO 77301 2384 D7
Orville St
6700 HOUS 77028 3825 E1
7100 HOUS 77028 3826 A1
Oryan Ct
100 HarC 77015 3828 E5
Osage Dr
4100 HarC 77521 3833 B3
Osage Rd
8800 HOUS 77074 4099 D7
8800 HOUS 77074 4239 D1
Osage St
4100 HOUS 77036 4099 C3
4100 HOUS 77063 4099 C3
Osage Park Dr
11900 HarC 77065 3539 D1
Osage Ridge Dr
9600 HarC 77379 3110 C6
9700 HarC 77375 3110 C6
Osakwe St
7700 HOUS 77075 4376 C3
Osborn St
5900 HOUS 77033 4104 B7
Osborne Dr
1200 FRDW 77546 4629 C3
Osby Dr
4000 HOUS 77025 4241 C1
4300 HOUS 77025 4241 B1
Oscar Dr
7400 DRPK 77536 4249 B2
Oscoda Ct
4400 MtgC 77386 3115 D1
Osoyoos St
- HarC 77044 3549 B3
Osprey Ct
1100 FRDW 77546 4629 D5
Osprey Dr
6400 HOUS 77048 4244 D6
Osprey Landing Dr
17200 HarC 77447 3249 D4
Osprey Park Dr
2300 FBnC 77494 3951 D5
Osprey Pass
800 HarC 77494 3953 A3
Osprey Point Ct
24400 HarC 77447 3249 E4
Ossineke Ct
5000 MtgC 77386 2970 E7
5000 MtgC 77386 2971 A7
Ossineke Dr
27600 MtgC 77386 2970 E7
27600 MtgC 77386 2971 A7

N Ossineke Dr
5000 MtgC 77386 2970 E7
5000 MtgC 77386 2971 A7
Ostermeyer Rd
11700 GLSN 77554 5220 C5
Ostler Dr
- HarC 77373 3115 C6
Oswego St
10500 JTCY 77029 3966 D2
N Oswego St
10300 JTCY 77029 3966 B2
S Oswego St
10300 JTCY 77029 3966 B2
Otero Rd
40200 MtgC 77354 2672 C2
Othello St
8600 HOUS 77029 3965 D4
Otis St
3400 HOUS 77026 3825 C6
Ottawa Ln
- HOUS 77043 3819 D3
Otter Cir
10300 CmbC 77520 3835 C3
Otterbury Dr
1900 HarC 77039 3545 C5
4700 HarC 77039 3546 C5
Otter Creek Dr
700 LPRT 77571 4250 B2
Otter Creek Tr
18300 HarC 77346 3264 C7
18300 HarC 77346 3408 E1
Otter Lodge Pl
10 WDLD 77382 2819 A3
Otter Peak Dr
4900 HOUS 77345 3119 D2
Otter Pond Pl
10 WDLD 77381 2820 E3
Otter Trail Ct
19300 HarC 77449 3677 A4
Otto Ct
400 BLAR 77401 4100 E5
Otto Rd
- HarC 77373 3115 A5
2800 HarC 77373 3114 E5
Otto St
2300 HOUS 77093 3685 E6
Ouachita St
4500 HarC 77039 3546 B4
Our Ln
4300 CNRO 77304 2237 B6
Ouray Dr
7900 HarC 77040 3541 B6
7900 HarC 77040 3681 A1
Ourlane Cir
10 BKHV 77024 3959 C2
Our Ln Cir
700 BKHV 77024 3959 C2
800 HDWV 77024 3959 C2
Our Ln Ct
10 BKHV 77024 3959 C2
Our Ln Pl
10 BKHV 77024 3959 C2
Our Ln Tr
10 BKHV 77024 3959 C2
Out Dr
12100 HOUS 77045 4242 B7
Outback Dr
26700 HarC 77493 3813 A1
Outback Lakes Tr
18000 HarC 77346 3408 D1
Outer Banks Ln
3300 FBnC 77459 4622 A5
Outervale Pl
10 WDLD 77381 2820 D4
Outfitter Pt
26700 HarC 77493 3813 A1
Outlaw Ridge Rd
17300 HarC 77095 3396 D6
Outlook Dr
100 HOUS 77034 4247 A5
Outpost Dr
9200 HOUS 77041 3820 D1
Outrigger Ct
16000 HarC 77532 3552 B3
Outrigger Dr
1300 TKIS 77554 5106 B3
Outview Ct
8800 HarC 77040 3541 C6
Over St
200 LMQU 77568 4873 B7
200 TXCY 77591 4873 B7
8000 BzaC 77584 4627 D4
Overbluff Ct
14800 HarC 77530 3829 C7
Overbluff St
200 HarC 77015 3968 C1
200 HarC 77530 3968 C1
600 HarC 77530 3829 C7
Overbrook Cir
1900 MSCY 77459 4497 C2
Overbrook Dr
9900 CNRO 77304 2382 E1
Overbrook Ln
3400 HOUS 77019 3961 D6
3400 HOUS 77027 3961 D6
5600 HOUS 77056 3960 D7
6200 HOUS 77057 3960 B7
7800 HOUS 77063 3960 A7
10000 HOUS 77042 3959 A7
10800 HOUS 77042 3958 C7
11800 HOUS 77077 3958 A7
12100 HOUS 77077 3957 D7
14000 HOUS 77077 3956 E7
14600 MtgC 77362 2670 D7
Overbrook Terrace Ct
9700 FBnC 77494 4092 D5
Overbrook Terrace Ln
25300 FBnC 77494 4092 C5
Overby Park Ln
3200 FBnC 77494 4093 C1
Overcrest Ln
6400 PASD 77505 4248 E3
Overcross Dr
3000 HOUS 77045 4242 A7
3400 HOUS 77045 4241 E6
Overcup Dr
12300 HOUS 77024 3959 A3
12400 HOUS 77024 3958 E3
23900 HarC 77389 2966 A5
Overcup Rd
12200 HOUS 77024 3959 A3
E Overdale Dr
3300 BzaC 77584 4501 D7
W Overdale Dr
3300 BzaC 77584 4501 C7
Overdale St
5700 HOUS 77033 4244 B4
6200 HOUS 77087 4244 D4

Overglen Ct
12900 HarC 77072 4097 C7
Overhill St
1200 HOUS 77018 3822 D1
Overlake Dr
25700 MtgC 77380 2968 B1
Overland
13900 HOUS 77040 3681 C5
Overland St
700 MSCY 77489 4370 B4
700 STAF 77477 4370 B4
Overland Tr
100 HarC 77090 3258 D4
100 HOUS 77090 3258 D4
2400 DKSN 77539 4633 D7
2800 DKSN 77539 4754 D1
Overland Glen Tr
15200 HarC 77433 3252 A7
Overland Park Dr
100 HarC 77015 3829 A4
100 HarC 77049 3829 A4
Overland Pass Dr
1600 SGLD 77478 4368 D5
Overland Trail Dr
10900 FBnC 77469 4092 B7
Overlea Dr
10800 HOUS 77089 4377 E2
Overlook Ct
13200 MtgC 77302 2530 B5
Overlook Dr
200 FRDW 77546 4629 E5
6200 HarC 77041 3680 B4
Overlook Ln
34900 MtgC 77362 2816 D5
34900 SGCH 77362 2816 D5
Overlook Pk
18000 HarC 77346 3408 A2
Overlyn Ct
10 WDLD 77381 2821 D2
Overlyn Pl
10 WDLD 77381 2821 E2
Overmann St
6000 HOUS 77091 3684 C5
Overmead Dr
9700 HarC 77065 3539 E4
Overmeyer Dr
6900 HOUS 77008 3822 C6
Over Meyers Rd
- JTCY 77029 3966 A2
Overton Av
10 GlsC 77650 4878 D7
10 GlsC 77650 4994 D1
2300 GlsC 77650 4879 A5
Overton Cir
10600 HarC 77065 3539 B2
Overton Ct
10 HOUS 77004 3963 C7
Overton St
7400 HTCK 77563 4989 A5
Overton Park Dr
5600 FBnC 77450 4094 B3
Overture Dr
3500 HOUS 77082 4097 C2
Overview Dr
9900 FBnC 77478 4237 B2
Ovid St
1300 HOUS 77007 3963 B2
Owen Dr
3300 CNRO 77304 2382 D6
Owen St
2200 ALVN 77511 4866 D3
3000 BzaC 77511 4866 D3
Owen Canyon Ln
- HarC 77433 3395 E6
Owendale Dr
14300 HarC 77015 3829 A4
Owen Lake Ct
8500 HarC 77095 3537 D6
Owen Oak Dr
18900 HarC 77346 3265 D6
Owens Dr
2500 DKSN 77539 4633 C7
2500 DKSN 77539 4754 C1
Owens Ln
22500 MtgC 77365 2973 D4
Owens Rd
- PRVW 77445 3101 A1
- PRVW 77484 3101 A1
- WlrC 77445 3101 A2
1400 FBnC 77469 4366 E3
1400 FBnC 77478 4366 E3
1400 FBnC 77478 4367 A3
1400 SGLD 77478 4367 A3
12100 MtgC 77301 2385 D6
12100 MtgC 77306 2385 D6
14100 HarC 77095 3539 B7
14600 BzaC 77511 4866 C7
22600 MtgC 77365 2973 D5
33400 WlrC 77484 3101 D1
34300 PRVW 77445 3100 C1
Owens Rd FM-1098
- PRVW 77445 3100 A1
S Owens Rd
23600 MtgC 77365 2973 D5
Owens St
100 HOUS 77029 3965 E6
300 HOUS 77029 3966 A6
400 GNPK 77547 3966 A6
Owens Creek Ln
4700 HarC 77388 3112 B4
Owens Cross Dr
2500 HarC 77067 3402 A7
Owens Falls Dr
12200 HarC 77375 3109 B6
Owens Glen Ct
4700 FBnC 77545 4622 D3
Owens Park Dr
200 HarC 77094 3955 C1
Owens Trace Ln
19900 HarC 77449 3815 E1
19900 HarC 77449 3816 A1
Ower Ln
- PRLD 77584 4501 C4
Owl Ln
7900 CmbC 77520 3835 D3
Owl St
15800 HarC 77396 3406 E5
Owl Canyon Dr
21700 HarC 77388 3111 D2
Owl Cove Pl
10 WDLD 77382 2674 D5
Owl Crossing Ln
3300 HarC 77338 3260 A1
Owl Echo Ct
4000 HarC 77082 4096 B4
Owl Forest Ct
18500 HarC 77084 3816 C3

Owl Landing Dr
900 HarC 77494 3953 A3
Owl Roost
11800 HarC 77016 3547 D7
11800 HarC 77016 3687 D1
Owl Tree Ct
1300 FBnC 77545 4622 E2
1300 FBnC 77545 4623 C1
Owosso Ct
27300 MtgC 77386 3115 E2
Ox Dr
- FRDW 77546 4629 B4
Oxalis Ct
19700 HarC 77379 3110 C6
Oxberg Tr
1400 HarC 77073 3403 C1
Oxborough Dr
900 HarC 77450 3954 D3
Oxbow Dr
- SGLD 77479 4367 E7
- SGLD 77479 4494 E1
Oxbow Tr
23100 HarC 77373 2968 E6
Oxbow Mill Tr
- HarC 77379 3111 A2
Oxbow Park Ln
- FBnC 77450 3954 C7
20500 FBnC 77450 4094 D1
Oxbridge Ct
3100 HarC 77449 3815 C3
Oxenberg Manor Ln
18600 HarC 77377 3254 B2
Oxenford Dr
15600 HarC 77377 3254 E6
Oxford Ct
100 FBnC 77469 4493 C7
1400 HarC 77069 3256 E6
Oxford Dr
200 CNRO 77301 2384 C1
200 CNRO 77303 2238 C7
200 CNRO 77303 2384 C1
1000 PRLD 77584 4501 B2
Oxford Gln
- MDWP 77477 4238 B5
Oxford Ln
3400 FBnC 77459 4622 B5
Oxford Rd
3400 ALVN 77511 4867 D5
Oxford St
100 TMBL 77375 2964 B6
300 HOUS 77007 3962 D1
800 HOUS 77007 3823 D7
800 HOUS 77008 3823 D7
4400 HOUS 77022 3823 D1
12800 HOUS 77077 3957 C4
Oxford Bend Ln
- FBnC 77450 4094 A2
Oxford Brook Ct
2300 HarC 77493 3814 B5
Oxford Chase Ln
19600 FBnC 77469 4234 D3
Oxford Chase Tr
5000 FBnC 77469 4234 D3
Oxford Glen Ln
- HOUS 77099 4238 C5
Oxford Green Ct
1700 FBnC 77545 4622 D1
Oxford Grove Dr
9600 HarC 77095 3537 C3
Oxford Mills Ln
1100 FBnC 77479 4366 D7
Oxford Oak St
3400 HOUS 77082 4097 D1
Oxford Park Dr
12100 HOUS 77082 4097 E1
Oxford Point Ln
2300 HarC 77014 3402 A2
Oxfordshire Dr
7500 HarC 77379 3256 B2
Oxford Trails Dr
12100 HarC 77375 3109 D7
Oxham St
11500 JTCY 77029 3966 D3
Oxham Falls Ct
13800 HarC 77044 3549 E2
Oxhill Ct
2600 BzaC 77584 4501 C5
17500 HarC 77388 3257 D2
Oxhill Rd
3900 HarC 77388 3257 D2
Oxley Ct
18800 HarC 77377 3254 B1
Oxnard Ln
16300 FRDW 77546 4505 E7
16300 FRDW 77546 4629 E1
Oxnard Park Dr
4400 FRDW 77546 4629 E1
Oxted Ln
9300 HarC 77379 3256 A6
9400 HarC 77379 3255 E6
Oxton Ct
- HarC 77375 3110 C2
Oxwick Cir
14600 HarC 77044 3549 E1
Oyster Bank Cir
900 SGLD 77478 4368 B4
Oyster Bay Dr
1000 SGLD 77478 4368 B4
Oyster Cove Ct
12200 STAF 77477 4237 E6
15300 SGLD 77478 4368 B4
Oyster Cove Dr
3100 MSCY 77459 4496 E2
15600 SGLD 77478 4368 B4
Oyster Creek Dr
100 SGLD 77478 4368 A3
8100 MSCY 77459 4497 A7
Oyster Creek Ln
15300 SGLD 77478 4368 B4
Oyster Creek Pl Dr
- MSCY 77459 4497 B6
Oyster Creek Village Dr
400 MSCY 77459 4497 A5
Oyster Estates Blvd
- SGLD 77478 4367 D1
Oyster Loop Ct
4900 SGLD 77478 4369 A7
Oyster Loop Dr
2400 SGLD 77478 4369 A7
Oyster Point Dr
1300 SGLD 77478 4368 E5
Oyster Tree Dr
3700 HarC 77084 3816 D3
Ozark St
3200 HOUS 77021 4103 B4
Ozark Tr
6200 PRLD 77584 4502 D5

Ozark Pass Ln
- HarC 77346 3408 C3

P

P St
- DRPK 77536 4109 E7
E P St
- LPRT 77571 4251 E5
1100 DRPK 77536 4109 B7
N P St
9700 DRPK 77536 4110 A7
9700 LPRT 77571 4110 D7
11600 LPRT 77571 4111 B7
W P St
- LPRT 77571 4251 D5
100 DRPK 77536 4109 A7
Pablo Rd
- MTBL 77520 3696 C7
- MTBL 77520 3835 C1
Pablo Tr
3800 HarC 77396 3407 A6
Pablo Picasso Dr
3100 SGLD 77479 4368 C7
Pabst Rd
- GLSN 77554 5220 B7
3700 DKSN 77539 4753 B5
4400 GLSN 77554 5333 C1
Pabst St
- HOUS 77087 4105 A3
Pacco Ln
5000 MtgC 77354 2673 D3
Pacemont Dr
500 HarC 77494 3953 A2
Pacer Cir
25500 HarC 77375 2965 D2
Pacesetter
- HarC 77346 3265 D6
Pacific Ocean Dr
22100 HarC 77388 3112 C3
Pacific
- HarC 77447 3104 A5
Pacific Av
29800 MtgC 77354 2818 B1
Pacific Dr
- HarC 77346 3264 B7
S Pacific Dr
13900 HarC 77049 3689 E6
14100 HarC 77049 3690 A6
Pacific St
100 HOUS 77006 3962 E6
100 HOUS 77006 3963 A6
N Pacific St
100 CNRO 77301 2384 A5
S Pacific St
100 CNRO 77301 2384 A6
Pacific Crest Ct
6700 HarC 77346 3264 E3
Pacific Grove Ln
1500 FBnC 77494 3953 B4
Pacific Pearl St
7800 HOUS 77072 4097 E6
Pacific Ridge Ct
7400 HarC 77095 3678 D1
Packard St
13900 HOUS 77040 3681 C5
Packard Elm Ct
5000 HarC 77449 3676 E7
Packard Elm St
2700 HarC 77038 3543 A2
Packard Falls Ct
3000 HarC 77429 3396 A1
Packard Green Tr
- HarC 77429 3253 C3
Packard Pl Ln
3100 HarC 77449 3814 C3
Packard Springs Dr
19800 FBnC 77469 4234 D3
Packer Ct
500 WEBS 77598 4507 B6
Packer Ln
1200 FBnC 77477 4369 E5
1200 FBnC 77477 4370 A6
1800 MSCY 77477 4370 A6
1900 MSCY 77459 4370 A6
Packerd Bend Tr
12300 HOUS 77089 4378 C7
Packerton Ct
19100 HarC 77094 3955 B1
Packsaddle Ln
1300 BYTN 77521 3973 C2
Pack Saddle Tr
24000 MtgC 77357 2681 D5
Packwood Dr
19800 HarC 77449 3677 A2
Pacos Bluff Ct
- HarC 77346 3408 C4
Pacos Park Ln
17200 HarC 77346 3408 D3
Paddington Ct
10 CNRO 77384 2676 A3
Paddington St
6200 HOUS 77085 4371 D2
Paddington Wy
10 CNRO 77384 2676 A3
Paddington Pl Dr
8200 FBnC 77083 4096 A7
Paddle Wheel Dr
6200 HarC 77449 3677 B4
17800 HarC 77379 3257 C2
Paddock Ct
9800 HarC 77065 3539 E4
Paddock Wy
11900 HarC 77065 3539 E4
Paddock Bend Dr
7000 HarC 77433 3677 C1
7000 HarC 77449 3677 C2
Paddock Brook Ln
2700 HarC 77038 3543 A4
Paddock Park Dr
9800 HarC 77065 3539 E3
Paddock Pines Pl
10 WDLD 77382 2674 C4
Paddocks Rd
11300 MtgC 77306 2533 B2
Paddock Woods Ln
- HarC 77429 3253 A5
Paddock Wy Ct
9700 HarC 77065 3539 D4
Pademelon Dr
16400 FBnC 77478 4236 A5
16500 FBnC 77478 4235 E5
Padfield St
8700 HOUS 77055 3821 A5
8900 HOUS 77055 3820 E5
Padgett Ct
2400 FBnC 77478 4237 B5

Padgett Dr
13600 FBnC 77478 4237 A5
Pado St
8900 HOUS 77055 3820 E5
8900 HOUS 77055 3821 A5
Padok Rd
11600 HarC 77044 3690 D1
11800 HarC 77044 3550 D7
Padons Trace Ct
16100 MSCY 77071 4239 C7
Padstow Ln
1300 HarC 77530 3829 C5
Paersian Dr
- HarC 77014 3401 E3
Pagan Cir
8700 HarC 77379 3256 A5
Page Ln
100 HOUS 77336 3266 B3
Page St
200 DRPK 77536 4109 B7
Page Crest Ln
- PRLD 77583 4500 B5
Page Forest Dr
18600 HarC 77346 3264 C7
Pagehurst Ct
10 WDLD 77382 2819 D3
Pagehurst Dr
15600 HarC 77084 3678 E5
15600 HarC 77084 3679 A5
Pagemill Ln
- FBnC 77469 4092 B7
1900 CNRO 77304 2383 B1
Pagemill Point Ln
18000 HarC 77346 3408 E1
E Pagewick Dr
4900 HOUS 77041 3681 A7
5200 HOUS 77041 3680 D6
N Pagewick Dr
10400 HOUS 77041 3680 E6
Pagewood Ln
5300 HOUS 77056 4100 E1
7500 HOUS 77057 4100 A2
7500 HOUS 77063 4100 A2
7800 HOUS 77063 4099 E2
9700 HOUS 77042 4099 A2
Pagewood St
- WlrC 77447 2959 B6
Pago Ln
6300 HarC 77041 3679 B4
Pagoda Dr
11400 HOUS 77477 4237 E4
Pagosa Falls Ln
4900 FBnC 77494 4093 D2
Pagosa Springs Dr
8000 HarC 77040 3541 B6
Paige Ct
7100 FBnC 77479 4367 B7
Paige St
100 HOUS 77003 3963 E5
2900 HOUS 77004 3963 C7
3000 HOUS 77004 4103 C1
N Paige St
100 HOUS 77003 3963 E5
100 HOUS 77003 3964 A4
Paige Mannor Dr
- HOUS 77077 3957 A5
Paige Pl Dr
11800 HarC 77089 4378 A7
Paige Terrace Ct
18300 HarC 77433 3537 C6
Paigetree Ln
6700 PRLD 77584 4502 C5
11200 HarC 77014 3401 C3
Paigewood Dr
3500 BzaC 77584 4501 C7
Paine St
6300 HOUS 77022 3824 B3
Paintbrush Av
2100 LGCY 77573 4632 C2
Paintbrush Ln
- HarC 77047 4374 A3
10000 FBnC 77478 4236 E3
Paintbrush Tr
7000 FBnC 77494 4093 B5
Paintbrush Ledge Ln
9500 HarC 77089 4504 C1
Painted Blvd
19000 MtgC 77365 2972 B1
Painted Canyon Dr
11900 HarC 77377 3254 C1
Painted Canyon Pl
10 WDLD 77381 2820 C3
Paintedcup Ct
10 WDLD 77380 2821 E6
Painted Daisy Ln
- FBnC 77494 4092 C4
Painted Desert
18100 HarC 77389 2819 E5
18100 HarC 77389 2820 A5
18300 HarC 77375 2819 E5
Painted Desert Dr
7600 HarC 77433 3537 B6
7600 HarC 77433 3677 E1
Painted Dusk Ct
2500 FBnC 77545 4498 B7
Paintedfern Pl
3400 HarC 77449 3816 A3
Painted Meadow Cir
3100 HarC 77449 3816 A3
Painted Mesa Cir
12800 HarC 77038 3543 B3
Painted Pony Ln
21100 TMBL 77375 3109 E2
N Painted Sunset
10 WDLD 77380 2968 B4
S Painted Sunset
10 WDLD 77380 2967 D3
10 WDLD 77380 2968 B4
Painted Trail Dr
5600 HarC 77084 3679 A4
Painter St
7500 HOUS 77016 3825 B1
Painters Bnd
2700 FBnC 77459 4621 B7
Painton Ln
7800 HarC 77389 2966 A1
Paint Rock Rd
16400 FRDW 77546 4629 E1
16900 FRDW 77546 4630 A1
Paisley Dr
6100 HOUS 77096 4240 A2
Paisley Ln
5100 HOUS 77096 4240 E2
Paisley St
5800 HOUS 77096 4240 B2
Paisley Meadow Dr
2900 LGCY 77573 4633 C2

Paiter St
16300 HOUS 77053 4372 A7
Palace
- MtgC 77306 2533 D5
Palace Dr
2500 STAF 77477 4369 E4
Palace Sprs
3900 SGLD 77479 4495 A5
Palace Green Ct
1700 HarC 77449 3814 E6
Palace Oaks Ct
15000 HarC 77082 4096 C2
Palace Oaks Dr
3000 HarC 77082 4096 D2
Palace Pines Ct
27100 MtgC 77339 3118 B5
Palace Pines Dr
21400 MtgC 77339 3118 B5
Palace Wy Ct
- FBnC 77469 4094 D7
Palacios Ct
9700 HarC 77064 3540 D6
Paladino St
4100 GlsC 77518 4634 B3
Paladora Dr
15100 HarC 77083 4096 B4
Paladora Park Ln
8900 FBnC 77083 4235 D1
Paladora Point Ct
12000 HarC 77041 3680 A4
Palamino Ct
5400 HarC 77346 3264 C4
Palamino Ridge Dr
20200 HarC 77338 3261 D4
Palapa Cir
- GLSN 77554 5441 B5
Palcio Real Dr
1500 HOUS 77047 4373 D2
Pale Dawn Pl
10 WDLD 77381 2820 D1
Pale Ivy Ln
12900 HarC 77072 4097 C7
Pale Meadow Ct
21900 FBnC 77450 4094 A1
Paleo Ct
12700 SGLD 77478 4237 C4
Palerma Ct
2700 LGCY 77573 4632 E4
Palermo Dr
1300 PRLD 77581 4504 E3
19300 HarC 77084 3816 A5
24500 FBnC 77469 4092 E7
Pale Sage
15400 HarC 77049 3829 A3
Pale Sage Ct
100 WDLD 77382 2673 D5
Pale Star Dr
9600 HarC 77064 3540 C4
Palestine St
600 HOUS 77017 4246 C2
600 SHUS 77017 4246 C2
600 SHUS 77587 4246 C2
1000 CNRO 77301 2383 E4
1000 CNRO 77301 2384 A4
6900 HOUS 77020 3964 E3
7000 HOUS 77020 3965 A3
10800 JTCY 77029 3966 C3
Palestine Cove Ln
4300 HarC 77396 3407 A6
Palette Blue Blvd
- HarC 77433 3250 E4
Pali Ct
10 PNVL 77304 2237 A3
Palico
- HarC 77429 3253 E1
Palio Pass
- LGCY 77573 4633 A5
Palisade Dr
4700 HOUS 77047 4243 D5
4700 HOUS 77048 4243 D5
Palisade Falls Tr
5600 HOUS 77345 3120 B6
Palisade Green Dr
24800 HarC 77493 3814 A6
Palisade Lakes Ct
17100 HarC 77095 3537 C3
Palisade Lakes Dr
9900 HarC 77095 3537 E3
Palisades Heights Ct
7400 HarC 77095 3678 D1
Palisades Heights Dr
7100 HarC 77095 3678 C1
Palisades Point Dr
16600 PASD 77059 4380 D4
Palisander Ct
17400 HarC 77388 3257 D2
Palladio Dr
14600 HarC 77429 3253 D5
Pallavi Woods Dr
10 HOUS 77339 3263 D2
Pallet Rd
3200 HOUS 77032 3404 E2
Pallin Wy
100 LGCY 77573 4633 A1
Pallwood Ln
13400 HarC 77429 3254 A7
13500 HarC 77429 3398 A1
Palm Av
3400 TXCY 77590 4874 C4
Palm Blvd
- BzaC 77541 5547 B7
10 MSCY 77459 4497 B4
Palm Cir
10 ALVN 77511 4867 B3
2300 SEBK 77586 4382 C6
8300 CmbC 77520 3835 D3
Palm Cir E
2700 GLSN 77551 5108 D7
Palm Cir N
5500 GLSN 77551 5108 C7
Palm Cir W
2700 GLSN 77551 5108 C7
Palm Ct
2100 RSBG 77471 4491 C5
6300 PRLD 77584 4502 D4
N Palm Ct
1900 PASD 77502 4247 E2
S Palm Ct
1900 PASD 77502 4247 E2
Palm Crt
5200 HOUS 77021 4104 A6
Palm Dr
1000 HarC 77336 3121 E6
5200 DKSN 77539 4754 A4
5400 TXCY 77539 4754 A4
7300 HarC 77521 3833 E3
N Palm Dr
5900 HarC 77521 3833 E3

STREET Block City ZIP Map# Grid

Palm Ln
3900 GlsC 77518 4634 B3
10700 GlsC 77510 4871 E5
Palm St
1000 HOUS 77002 4102 E1
1000 HOUS 77004 4102 E1
1200 LMQU 77568 4990 B3
4100 HOUS 77004 4103 A1
4800 BLAR 77401 4101 A5
4800 PASD 77586 4383 C5
16100 HarC 77530 3830 C6
E Palm St
100 FBnC 77545 4623 C1
700 BzaC 77583 4623 D1
700 PRLD 77545 4623 D1
W Palm St
100 FBnC 77545 4623 B1
Palm Ter
900 GLSN 77550 5108 D4
Palm Aire Dr
100 FRDW 77546 4628 E6
Palmala St
11800 HarC 77016 3547 D7
11800 HarC 77016 3687 D1
Palm Bay Ct
11200 PRLD 77584 4500 D2
Palm Bay St
11300 PRLD 77584 4500 D2
Palmbeach St
11200 HOUS 77034 4377 E1
12000 HOUS 77034 4378 B1
Palm Brook Ct
7800 HarC 77095 3538 A7
Palm Castle Ct
100 LGCY 77573 4509 B7
Palm Castle Dr
2100 LGCY 77573 4509 B7
Palm Cockatoo Dr
24300 HarC 77447 3249 D4
Palm Cove Ct
12200 GLSN 77551 5107 E5
12200 GLSN 77551 5108 A5
Palm Cove Ln
- LGCY 77573 4508 D6
S Palm Crest Ct
900 BzaC 77584 4501 C1
W Palm Crest Ct
900 BzaC 77584 4501 C1
Palmcrest St
10 HOUS 77035 4241 A6
10 HOUS 77085 4241 A6
11300 HOUS 77034 4377 E1
12000 HOUS 77034 4378 A1
Palmcroft St
12000 HOUS 77034 4378 A1
Palmdale Ct
3800 GLSN 77554 5548 B1
Palmdale Ln
10 MNVL 77583 4624 D4
Palmdale St
12000 HOUS 77034 4247 A7
Palmdale Estate Dr
25800 FBnC 77469 4092 B7
Palmdate St
11800 HOUS 77034 4378 B1
Palm Desert Dr
10 BzaC 77583 4624 C4
10 MNVL 77583 4624 C4
Palm Desert Ln
3400 MSCY 77459 4369 E6
3400 MSCY 77459 4496 E1
12700 HOUS 77099 4237 D2
Palmer
3200 HOUS 77021 4103 B5
E Palmer Bnd
10 WDLD 77381 2820 C2
W Palmer Bnd
10 WDLD 77381 2820 B1
Palmer Ct
3800 SGLD 77479 4495 A2
6300 MtgC 77354 2673 C3
Palmer Dr
700 MtgC 77302 2530 C6
2800 FRDW 77546 4749 E1
Palmer Hwy
2100 TXCY 77590 4875 A4
2600 TXCY 77590 4874 D4
Palmer Hwy FM-1764
2100 TXCY 77590 4875 A4
3400 TXCY 77590 4874 C4
W Palmer Pt
10 WDLD 77381 2820 B1
Palmer St
100 HOUS 77003 3964 A4
900 HOUS 77003 3963 E6
3600 HOUS 77004 4103 C1
N Palmer St
10 HOUS 77003 3964 A5
Palmera Ct
1700 MSCY 77459 4497 C3
Palmer Bend Ct
10 WDLD 77381 2820 B1
Palmer Bend Dr
- WDLD 77381 2820 C2
Palmer Cove Dr
24900 HarC 77389 2966 A4
Palmer Crest Ct
10 WDLD 77381 2820 C1
Palmer Crst
- WDLD 77381 2820 C1
Palmer Glen Ln
21400 HarC 77449 3815 C4
Palmer Green Pl
10 WDLD 77381 2820 B1
Palmer Manor Dr
15300 HarC 77433 3251 D7
Palmero Wy
10 BzaC 77583 4624 C5
10 MNVL 77583 4624 C5
Palmer Oaks Dr
- HarC 77336 3122 A3
Palmer Park Ct
6200 HarC 77086 3542 D4
Palmer Pl Ln
7800 HarC 77346 3265 C6
Palmer Plantation Dr
4100 MSCY 77459 4497 A4
Palmer Springs Dr
13600 HarC 77070 3399 C3
Palmer Terrace Ln
10900 HOUS 77034 4378 D4
Palmerton Dr
11700 HarC 77064 3399 E7
Palmer Woods Dr
10 WDLD 77381 2820 B1
Palmetta Spring Dr
8200 HarC 77375 3110 E2

Palmetto
1200 HOUS 77339 3263 C1
10000 MtgC 77354 2671 C1
Palmetto Bnd
2700 FBnC 77469 4234 A6
Palmetto Dr
- LGCY 77573 4632 B7
800 PASD 77506 4106 E5
1300 TKIS 77554 5106 B4
7300 BYTN 77521 3835 A5
15600 MtgC 77302 2677 A3
Palmetto Ln
1300 HOUS 77339 3263 D1
Palmetto Pl
10 PNVL 77304 2237 B4
Palmetto Pns
17300 HOUS 77032 3405 A3
Palmetto St
100 FBnC 77545 4499 C7
500 BzaC 77583 4499 C7
500 PRLD 77545 4499 C7
4500 BLAR 77401 4101 B4
4700 GlsC 77518 4634 E3
5100 BLAR 77401 4100 E4
5300 HOUS 77081 4100 E4
6800 HOUS 77087 4105 A4
7000 HOUS 77012 4105 A4
7100 MNVL 77578 4746 D2
8000 HTCK 77563 4988 E3
Palmetto Tr
- HarC 77038 3543 C6
Palmetto Creek Dr
3700 HOUS 77339 3119 C5
Palmetto Park Ct
1900 HarC 77493 3814 A5
Palmetto Park Dr
1800 HarC 77493 3814 A5
Palmetto Point Ln
13700 HOUS 77077 3957 A6
Palmetto Shore Dr
11800 HarC 77065 3539 E2
Palm Falls Ct
17200 HarC 77095 3538 A7
Palmfield St
9600 HOUS 77034 4378 C1
Palm Forest Ln
1900 HOUS 77077 3956 D6
Palm Free St
12900 HOUS 77034 4378 C2
Palmfree St
12000 HOUS 77034 4378 B1
Palm Grass Ct
15400 HOUS 77059 4380 B5
Palm Grove Cir
700 SGLD 77478 4368 B1
Palm Grove Dr
3500 MSCY 77459 4496 D2
Palm Harbour Dr
2100 MSCY 77459 4497 C5
Palmhill St
9800 HOUS 77034 4378 C1
S Palmiera Cir
10 WDLD 77382 2819 D1
Palmiera Dr
10 WDLD 77382 2819 E1
Palm Island Cir
3100 LGCY 77573 4633 B2
Palm Island St
12600 HOUS 77034 4378 B2
Palmito Ranch Dr
7200 FBnC 77469 4234 B2
Palm Lagoon Dr
2200 LGCY 77573 4509 A6
E Palm Lake Dr
10100 HOUS 77034 4378 B2
N Palm Lake Dr
12200 HOUS 77034 4378 B2
S Palm Lake Dr
12200 HOUS 77034 4378 B2
W Palm Lake Dr
10100 HOUS 77034 4378 B2
Palmlake St
9800 HOUS 77034 4378 B2
Palm Leaf Ct
12900 HarC 77044 3408 E5
Palm Meadows Ct
- SGLD 77479 4495 C3
Palmoral Dr
19300 HarC 77449 3677 B2
Palm Rain Ct
20600 HarC 77449 3815 D3
Palm Ridge Ct
6100 HOUS 77345 3120 D6
Palm Royale Blvd
- SGLD 77479 4496 A3
4400 SGLD 77479 4495 C3
Palm Shadows Ln
10200 HOUS 77075 4376 C2
Palm Shores Ct
9100 HarC 77379 3255 D5
Palm Shores Dr
9200 HarC 77379 3255 D5
Palmsprings Dr
11200 HOUS 77034 4377 E2
11400 HOUS 77034 4378 A2
Palm Springs Ln
- SGLD 77479 4495 C3
Palm Terrace Blvd
100 DRPK 77536 4109 B5
Palmton St
12000 HOUS 77034 4247 A7
Palm Trail Dr
22000 HarC 77450 3953 D3
22000 HarC 77494 3953 D3
Palm Valley Ct
8700 FBnC 77083 4096 E7
8700 FBnC 77083 4236 D1
Palm Villas Dr
10 MNVL 77583 4624 E4
Palm Vista Dr
- HOUS 77062 4380 C7
Palmway St
12000 HOUS 77034 4378 B1
15400 MSCY 77071 4239 D7
Palmwood Dr
1600 HOUS 77502 4106 D7
1600 PASD 77502 4106 D7
Palmyra St
400 HOUS 77022 3824 B1
Palo Alto St
2000 HOUS 77023 4104 E3
2000 HOUS 77023 4105 A2
7900 HOUS 77078 3688 A7
Palo Blanco Ln
- LbyC 77327 2538 A4
- LbyC 77372 2538 A4
Palo Blanco Rd
- HOUS 77028 3826 E1

Palo Blanco Rd
- HOUS 77078 3687 E7
- HOUS 77078 3826 E1
9300 HOUS 77078 3688 B7
Palo Dura Dr
24000 HarC 77447 3249 E4
Palo Duro Dr
5300 PRLD 77584 4502 E7
Palo Duro St
1800 FRDW 77546 4629 A7
Paloma Av
1500 RHMD 77469 4364 D7
Paloma Dr
5800 HarC 77389 2966 E7
E Paloma Dr
18300 HarC 77433 3251 E1
W Paloma Dr
19700 HarC 77433 3251 E1
Paloma Glen Ln
14600 HarC 77396 3547 E2
W Paloma Lago Cir
18500 HarC 77433 3251 D1
E Paloma Lago Ct
19600 HarC 77433 3251 E1
Paloma Park Ct
6200 HarC 77041 3679 D3
Paloma Park Ln
12500 HarC 77041 3679 E4
Palomar Dr
10 MNVL 77583 4624 D4
Palomar Ln
2200 BYTN 77520 3973 D5
Paloma Ranch Ct
7500 HarC 77433 3677 B1
Palomar Park Dr
- FBnC 77469 4094 E2
Palomar Valley Dr
3400 MtgC 77386 2969 D2
Paloma Terrace Wy
17200 HarC 77084 3678 A2
17200 HarC 77095 3678 A2
Palomino
- LbyC 77327 2538 A4
Palomino Ct
2300 MtgC 77384 2529 A6
Palomino Dr
2400 MtgC 77384 2529 A6
Palomino Ln
700 LGCY 77573 4630 E4
1400 HOUS 77339 3118 C7
Palomino St
300 LGCY 77573 4630 E4
Palomino Creek Ct
22900 HarC 77375 2966 A7
Palomino Trails Ct
10500 HarC 77095 3537 C2
Palo Pinto Cir
3300 MSCY 77459 4496 B2
Palo Pinto Dr
2500 HOUS 77080 3820 B3
4300 HOUS 77041 3820 B1
4500 HOUS 77041 3681 B7
Palos Park Dr
14500 HarC 77429 3396 B1
Palos Verde
10 PNVL 77304 2237 B1
Palos Verdes Dr
4200 PASD 77504 4247 E4
Palo Verde Dr
11400 HarC 77044 3688 D7
Palo Vista Dr
8000 HarC 77044 3688 D7
Palston Bend Ln
3100 HarC 77014 3257 D7
Palton Springs Dr
15100 HarC 77082 4096 B1
Paluxy Cir
3500 MSCY 77459 4496 B2
Pama Cir
10900 HNCV 77024 3960 A2
Pambrooke Ln
1400 HarC 77094 3955 B3
Pamela Dr
100 BYTN 77521 3972 E4
100 BYTN 77521 3973 A4
9900 HOUS 77075 4376 C2
Pamela Ln
1700 MSCY 77489 4370 B3
Pamela Wy
18300 HarC 77379 3257 A1
Pamela Holly Tr
11900 HarC 77089 4504 E1
11900 HarC 77089 4505 A2
Pamela Sue Ct
12200 MDWP 77477 4237 E6
Pamellia Dr
100 BLAR 77401 4101 B4
Pampa St
100 PASD 77504 4247 A4
100 SHUS 77504 4247 A4
100 SHUS 77587 4247 A4
Pampas Dr
23200 HarC 77389 2966 C6
Pampas Ln
1200 LGCY 77573 4752 D1
Pampas St
22900 HarC 77389 2966 C6
Pampass Pass
11300 HarC 77095 3538 A1
11400 HarC 77095 3397 A7
Pampass Trail Dr
1800 FRDW 77546 4629 C5
Pamplona Dr
1100 HOUS 77336 3121 C5
Panagard Dr
- HOUS 77082 3957 A7
2400 HOUS 77077 3957 A7
2500 HOUS 77082 4097 A1
Panair St
8500 HOUS 77061 4245 E5
8600 HOUS 77061 4246 A5
9300 HOUS 77034 4246 B5
Panama St
900 HOUS 77009 3824 C7
3900 PASD 77504 4248 A5
Panatella Dr
8500 HOUS 77055 3821 A6
Panay Dr
8100 HOUS 77033 4243 E3
10900 HOUS 77048 4243 E6
11900 HOUS 77048 4374 E1
Panay Creek Dr
5000 HOUS 77048 4374 E1
Panay Park Dr
5100 HOUS 77048 4374 E1
Panay Village Cir
11900 HOUS 77048 4374 E1

Panda Ln
- HarC 77041 3679 C4
Pandora Dr
10800 HOUS 77013 3827 C4
Panhandle Dr
13900 FBnC 77478 4237 B3
14000 FBnC 77478 4236 E3
Panicum Ct
11000 HarC 77086 3542 C1
Panky Ln
23500 MtgC 77357 2974 A3
Pannell
1200 HOUS 77020 3964 B2
Pannell St
1600 HOUS 77020 3964 B1
2100 HOUS 77026 3964 B1
2400 HOUS 77026 3825 E7
Pano Ln
14700 HarC 77070 3398 D1
Panola Dr
3900 GLSN 77554 5441 B4
Panola Wy
9600 HOUS 77055 3820 C6
Panola Pointe
13800 HarC 77429 3396 D3
13800 HarC 77429 3397 A2
Panorama Dr
10 CNRO 77304 2237 B4
10 PNVL 77304 2237 B4
3700 MSCY 77459 4497 B3
Pansy Rd
4400 HarC 77521 3833 B3
Pansy St
2100 PASD 77503 4108 B7
2100 PASD 77503 4248 B1
2900 PASD 77505 4248 B3
Pantano Dr
13100 HarC 77065 3398 B7
Panterra Wy
10 WDLD 77382 2673 A7
Panther Ct
10900 HOUS 77099 4238 B3
Panther Tr
4600 WDLD 77381 2820 E4
E Panther Creek Dr
- WDLD 77380 2821 B5
- WDLD 77381 2821 B5
N Panther Creek Dr
- WDLD 77381 2821 C4
S Panther Creek Dr
3300 WDLD 77380 2821 B5
3300 WDLD 77381 2821 A6
4400 WDLD 77381 2820 E5
W Panther Creek Dr
4700 WDLD 77381 2821 A4
Panther Creek Ln
12200 MtgC 77362 2817 B7
Panther Creek Pn
4400 WDLD 77381 2820 E4
Panther Den
- HOUS 77091 3684 B7
Panther Peak
19000 HarC 77388 3258 C1
Panther Pl Dr
12500 HOUS 77099 4237 E3
Panther Point Dr
10300 HOUS 77099 4237 D3
Panther Villa Ct
12500 HOUS 77099 4237 D3
Pantina Wy
- HarC 77449 3676 C2
Papadosa St
14100 HarC 77053 4372 E5
Papago Ct
19400 HarC 77377 3109 C7
Papago Dr
19400 HarC 77377 3109 B6
Papalote St
10000 HOUS 77041 3681 A4
10300 HOUS 77041 3680 E4
Papeete
- LbyC 77327 2538 A4
Papermill Dr
7700 HarC 77041 3539 C7
Papete St
1100 TKIS 77554 5106 C4
Papoose Ct
21200 HarC 77532 3410 C1
Papoose Tr
1700 HarC 77532 3266 C7
1700 HarC 77532 3410 B1
1700 HOUS 77532 3266 C7
Par Cir
1000 LPRT 77571 4251 C7
Par Ln
2200 RHMD 77469 4492 A3
Parable Ln
14200 HarC 77429 3397 B1
Parade Ct
3800 FBnC 77459 4622 A5
Paradise Dr
300 TKIS 77554 5106 B3
Paradise Ln
4700 HOUS 77047 4243 D6
4700 HOUS 77048 4243 D6
15200 MtgC 77302 2677 B2
Paradise Pl
500 MtgC 77357 2829 D3
500 RMFT 77357 2829 D3
Paradise Pt
- SGLD 77478 4368 C2
Paradise Rd
800 HarC 77521 3832 A5
23900 MtgC 77365 2974 B6
Paradise Bridge Ln
- FBnC 77478 4236 D3
Paradise Canyon Ct
2700 FBnC 77450 3954 A6
Paradise Canyon Dr
2300 PRLD 77584 4500 C2
Paradise Gate Dr
22700 HarC 77373 3115 E6
Paradise Park Bnd
6900 FBnC 77469 4094 E5
Paradise River Dr
6900 MSCY 77459 4496 D4
Paradise Summit Dr
19200 HarC 77377 3109 A7
Paradise Valley Ct
5900 HarC 77069 3400 C1
Paradise Valley Dr
- HarC 77066 3400 E3
10 HarC 77066 3401 A4
10 PNVL 77304 2237 A3
7300 CNRO 77304 2237 A6
10200 CNRO 77304 2236 E5
13000 HarC 77069 3400 C1
13600 HarC 77069 3256 B7

Paragon Ct
7100 HarC 77069 3400 A3
Paraguay Cir
4000 PASD 77504 4247 E4
Parakeet St
2100 HOUS 77034 4246 D5
Paralee Dr
1100 FBnC 77494 3952 B5
Paramount Ln
11900 HarC 77067 3402 A5
Parana Dr
1700 HOUS 77080 3820 C5
Parasol Ln
8500 HarC 77064 3541 D5
Parc 90 Dr
12600 SGLD 77478 4368 D1
Parc Crest Dr
12200 STAF 77477 4238 C6
Parc Monceau Ln
11900 HOUS 77047 4373 D2
Parco Verde Cir
2000 HarC 77450 3954 A5
Pardee
3600 HOUS 77026 3825 B4
Pardee St
4000 HOUS 77026 3825 B4
7700 HOUS 77028 3826 B4
Pardue Ct
8000 HOUS 77088 3682 D1
Parfield Ln
- HarC 77084 3816 D2
Par Five Dr
7600 HarC 77346 3265 B6
Par Four Dr
5800 HOUS 77088 3682 D3
Parham Dr
- HarC 77388 3111 E3
Paril Creek Dr
21800 HarC 77073 3259 E1
Paris Ct
4700 HOUS 77021 4103 E5
Paris St
6300 HOUS 77021 4103 E6
Parish Rd
13200 HarC 77532 3692 E1
13500 HarC 77532 3552 E7
14600 HarC 77532 3553 E4
Parish Hall Dr
16100 HarC 77379 3256 A6
Parish Point Dr
24200 HarC 77493 3814 A5
Parish Timbers Ct
21100 HarC 77433 3251 A3
Park Av
1300 DRPK 77536 4109 B5
2000 KMAH 77565 4510 A7
2200 KMAH 77565 4634 A1
2400 GlsC 77565 4634 A1
4400 DKSN 77539 4754 B3
6200 TXCY 77591 4873 D6
12200 MtgC 77354 2528 D5
15200 HarC 77053 4373 A4
15200 HOUS 77053 4373 A4
E Park Av
2500 PRLD 77581 4503 C3
N Park Av
100 LGCY 77573 4632 A3
2100 PRLD 77581 4503 C2
S Park Av
2400 PRLD 77581 4503 C3
Park Blvd
- CNRO 77304 2383 A1
Park Cir
- SRAC 77571 4382 E2
300 KMAH 77565 4510 A7
300 KMAH 77565 4634 A1
Park Ct
4600 BLAR 77401 4101 B4
15500 HarC 77082 4096 B4
28500 HarC 77377 3108 E1
28500 TMBL 77377 3108 E1
E Park Ct
15700 HarC 77082 4096 B4
N Park Ct
13100 MtgC 77306 2533 C5
W Park Ct
15800 HarC 77082 4096 E3
Park Dr
- PASD 77586 4383 B4
100 LPRT 77571 4251 E5
300 ALVN 77511 4867 C1
300 HarC 77530 3831 B6
1100 LPRT 77571 4252 A3
1500 HarC 77530 3830 E4
1500 SEBK 77586 4382 E7
1800 LGCY 77565 4509 A5
4500 HOUS 77023 3964 B7
14000 TMBL 77375 3108 E1
14000 TMBL 77377 3108 E1
23600 MtgC 77357 2974 A3
30900 MtgC 77354 2670 A7
30900 MtgC 77354 2816 A1
N Park Dr
7000 FBnC 77469 4093 E6
7000 HOUS 77469 4093 E6
16800 MtgC 77306 2533 C5
23600 MtgC 77365 2972 A6
NW Park Dr
- HOUS 77086 3542 C3
10100 HarC 77086 3542 C3
S Park Dr
1700 ALVN 77511 4867 B3
5600 FBnC 77469 4094 A6
5600 HOUS 77469 4094 A6
24900 MtgC 77380 2968 A3
24900 WDLD 77380 2968 A3
Park Grn
900 DRPK 77536 4109 D4
S Park Grv
- HOUS 77007 3962 D3
Park Hllw
1900 FBnC 77479 4494 A3
Park Ln
- HarC 77070 3399 B7
- HarC 77562 3832 A2
- SRAC 77571 4382 E2
10 GLSN 77551 5222 B1
400 GlsC 77518 4634 B2
600 FRDW 77546 4505 C4
1000 PASD 77506 4107 C4
1000 TXCY 77590 4875 C3
1200 HarC 77450 3954 B4
6600 HOUS 77023 4104 D2
10100 LPRT 77571 4250 B4
10600 HOUS 77093 3685 E3
10700 GlsC 77510 4871 E5
15100 MtgC 77302 2679 E2
15300 MtgC 77302 2680 A2

Park Ln
17300 PTVL 77372 2682 D7
23100 HarC 77377 2963 C7
N Park Ln
15600 MtgC 77365 2824 E4
15600 MtgC 77365 2825 A4
W Park Ln
100 PASD 77506 4107 A4
1200 HarC 77073 3259 B3
Park Lp
26200 MtgC 77355 2814 A2
Park Mnr
100 CNRO 77301 2530 B1
Park Pl
100 CNRO 77301 2384 A6
Park Rd
- GlsC 77539 4635 B3
- HarC 77433 3395 E6
- TXCY 77539 4635 B3
16500 GlsC 77511 4869 C4
16500 GlsC 77517 4869 D4
22500 HarC 77377 2963 C7
22500 HarC 77377 3108 C1
36000 HMPD 77445 2953 A6
Park St
- BYTN 77520 3970 E5
- HOUS 77098 4102 A1
- KATY 77493 3813 D6
10 BYTN 77520 3973 A5
10 RHMD 77469 4364 D7
100 HarC 77562 3831 E6
100 HarC 77562 3832 A6
100 PASD 77506 4106 E3
1100 LMQU 77568 4874 B6
1500 HOUS 77019 3962 C6
2500 BYTN 77520 3972 C5
2500 HOUS 77098 3962 C6
3300 BYTN 77520 3971 C5
6500 GLSN 77551 5108 B7
14200 STFE 77517 4870 B7
16300 GlsC 77517 4869 D4
16400 GlsC 77511 4869 D4
E Park St
600 SGLD 77478 4367 E1
N Park St
100 PASD 77506 4106 E3
W Park St
500 SGLD 77478 4367 E1
Park Tr
- HOUS 77007 3962 D3
- LPRT 77571 4383 A2
10000 HOUS 77024 3960 D2
Park 290 Dr
41000 WlrC 77484 3101 D4
Park & Ride Dr
- HOUS 77079 3817 E7
- HOUS 77079 3956 E1
Park Almeda Dr
14700 HarC 77047 4373 A7
Park Arbor Ct
14600 HarC 77429 3396 C2
Park at Beverly Hls W
3200 HOUS 77057 4100 D2
E Park at Fairdale
3000 HOUS 77057 4100 B1
N Park at Fairdale
6200 HOUS 77057 4100 B1
W Park at Fairdale
3000 HOUS 77057 4100 B1
E Park at Kings Manor Lp
26800 MtgC 77339 3118 C3
N Park at Kings Manor Lp
20100 MtgC 77339 3118 C4
W Park at Kings Manor Lp
26800 MtgC 77339 3118 C4
Parkbank Ct
3600 HarC 77068 3257 B5
Park Bayou
1600 HOUS 77077 3957 A5
Park Bayou Dr
- HOUS 77077 3957 A3
Park Bend Dr
- FRDW 77546 4630 B2
2900 FRDW 77598 4630 B2
20600 HarC 77450 3954 C3
Parkbend Dr
4300 BYTN 77521 3973 E1
Park Bend Ln
4900 SGLD 77478 4369 A6
7500 PASD 77505 4249 B6
Park Birch Ln
1500 HarC 77450 3954 B4
Park Bishop Dr
21300 HarC 77450 3954 C4
Park Bluff Dr
- HarC 77450 3954 C4
Parkborough Dr
6100 HarC 77041 3679 B4
Park Breeze Ct
1100 FBnC 77545 4623 A2
Park Breeze Dr
4400 FBnC 77545 4623 A2
Parkbriar Cir
10 BYTN 77521 3973 B3
Park Briar Dr
1500 HarC 77450 3954 C4
Parkbriar Ln
2600 BzaC 77584 4501 C5
Park Bridge Dr
20800 HarC 77450 3954 C3
Park Bridge Ln
- LGCY 77573 4631 A4
Park Brook Dr
21100 HarC 77450 3954 C4
Parkbrook Wy Ln
13000 FBnC 77478 4367 A2
Park Brush Cir
20800 HarC 77450 3954 C3
Park Brush Ct
20800 HarC 77450 3954 C3
Park Brush Ln
- HarC 77450 3954 C4
Park Bud Ln
700 HarC 77450 3954 B3
Park Canyon Dr
20800 HarC 77450 3954 C3
Park Canyon Ln
5000 FBnC 77494 4093 A3
Park Cedar Ct
11700 HarC 77377 3254 D4
Park Center Ct
3800 HOUS 77059 4380 B4
Park Center Dr
15900 HOUS 77059 4380 C4
Park Center Wy
15700 HOUS 77059 4380 B4
Park Centre Cir
13400 HarC 77069 3400 A3

Park Centre Ct
7100 HarC 77069 3400 C3
Parkchase Timber Ct
7800 HarC 77070 3399 B2
Parkchase Timber Dr
13400 HarC 77070 3399 B2
Parkchester Dr
15900 HOUS 77062 4380 C7
Park Cir Dr
6000 HOUS 77057 3960 C4
Park Cir Wy
3900 HOUS 77059 4380 C4
Park Colony Point Ln
12600 HarC 77086 3542 C4
12600 HOUS 77086 3542 C4
Parkcraft
7400 HOUS 77489 4371 B4
Park Creek Ct
15000 HarC 77070 3254 E7
Park Creek Dr
11600 HarC 77070 3254 D7
Parkcrest Dr
- HOUS 77034 4247 A5
- SHUS 77587 4247 A5
3900 HOUS 77034 4246 E4
4900 LPRT 77571 4250 C2
Parkcrest St
1700 ALVN 77511 4867 A4
Parkcrest Forest Dr
8800 HarC 77088 3542 E6
Parkcross Pl
7400 HarC 77433 3677 D1
7500 HarC 77433 3537 A5
Park Cypress
18100 HarC 77094 3955 C1
18100 HOUS 77094 3955 D1
Park Dale Ct
5800 SGLD 77479 4495 A5
Park Dale Dr
3300 DRPK 77536 4109 C7
3300 DRPK 77536 4249 D1
Parkdale Dr
2000 HOUS 77339 3118 D5
3100 HOUS 77339 3119 A5
Park Douglas Dr
4100 HarC 77084 3817 C1
Park Downe Ln
21300 HarC 77450 3954 B3
Park Dr Cir
- HarC 77065 3539 D2
Parke St
2900 DKSN 77539 4754 A3
Park Ella Dr
- HarC 77090 3258 C5
Park Entry Dr
16100 HarC 77041 3680 C2
16100 HOUS 77041 3680 C2
Parker Ct
100 LGCY 77573 4631 B4
11700 HarC 77375 2964 D2
Parker Dr
8000 HOUS 77016 3687 C4
8000 HOUS 77078 3687 C4
Parker Rd
- MtgC 77354 2671 E7
- MtgC 77354 2672 A7
10 HOUS 77076 3684 E4
1100 HOUS 77076 3685 A4
1500 HOUS 77093 3685 D4
2000 HOUS 77007 3962 B1
2700 HOUS 77093 3686 B4
4800 HOUS 77016 3686 D5
7500 HOUS 77016 3687 A4
8400 HOUS 77078 3687 D4
21500 HarC 77377 3107 E3
23300 MtgC 77365 2974 A7
E Parker Rd
100 HOUS 77076 3684 E4
W Parker Rd
100 HOUS 77076 3684 C4
300 HOUS 77091 3684 C4
Parker St
300 HOUS 77007 3962 C2
Parker Bluff Ln
- RSBG 77471 4491 E5
Parker-Davis School Rd
15100 BzaC 77511 4866 C6
Parker-Davis School Rd FM-1462
- BzaC 77511 4866 B5
Parkerhaven Ct
1200 HOUS 77008 3823 A6
Parkersburg Dr
5600 HOUS 77036 4100 A3
Parker School Rd
- ALVN 77511 4866 E6
- BzaC 77511 4866 D6
Parkers Cove Ct
13700 HOUS 77044 3550 B3
Parkers Hideaway Dr
12000 HarC 77089 4505 B2
Parkerton Ln
28300 MtgC 77386 2969 D6
Parkes St
7100 HOUS 77091 3683 D4
7300 HOUS 77088 3683 D3
Park Estates Ln
15200 HOUS 77062 4380 B7
Parkeston Dr
2700 HarC 77388 3113 A5
Parkette Dr
8500 HOUS 77028 3687 D6
8800 HOUS 77078 3687 E6
9100 HOUS 77078 3688 A6
Parkey Ln
1700 GNPK 77015 3967 A4
1700 HOUS 77015 3967 A4
Parkfair Ct
1800 HarC 77450 3954 B5
Park Falls Ct
3200 LGCY 77573 4633 C2
11600 PRLD 77584 4500 D3
Park Falls Dr
2700 PRLD 77584 4500 D4
7600 HarC 77095 3538 C7
Park Falls Ln
3200 LGCY 77573 4633 B2
Parkfield Av
13200 HarC 77044 3689 D2
Park Field Ct
6100 FBnC 77479 4493 E3
Parkfield Ln
6900 FBnC 77479 4496 B4
Parkfield Pl
3800 HarC 77449 3816 B2
Park Firth Dr
16500 HarC 77084 3817 C1

Houston Street Index

'REET
ock City ZIP Map# Grid

arkford Ln
- HarC 77072 4097 C5
arkford Meadows Dr
7000 HarC 77433 3676 D1
ark Forest Dr
1700 HarC 77450 3954 B4
1700 HOUS 77450 3954 B4
12500 HarC 77429 3398 B5
ark Forest Tr
12900 HarC 77429 3397 C4
arkfront Dr
5800 HOUS 77036 4099 A3
ark Gable Dr
24200 HarC 77373 3114 C5
ark Garden Dr
2900 HOUS 77339 3119 C4
ark Gate Ct
5000 HOUS 77018 3683 D7
ark Gate Dr
- LGCY 77573 4631 A4
arkgate St
100 CNRO 77304 2383 C4
ark Glen Cir
15400 FBnC 77478 4236 C5
ark Glen Dr
15200 FBnC 77478 4236 C5
arkglen Dr
7900 HarC 77049 3689 D7
arkglen Ln
- LGCY 77539 4752 D3
- LGCY 77573 4752 D3
arkglen St
2800 DRPK 77536 4109 C7
ark Grand Rd
2000 HOUS 77062 4380 D7
2000 HOUS 77062 4507 C1
ark Green Dr
21300 HarC 77450 3954 B3
ark Green Wy
16600 HOUS 77058 4507 D2
ark Grove Dr
400 HOUS 77450 3954 B2
600 HarC 77450 3954 B2
4500 BYTN 77521 3973 E1
ark Grove Ln
600 HarC 77450 3954 B3
ark Gwen Dr
24100 HarC 77373 3114 C5
ark Harbor Ct
1600 HOUS 77084 3816 B6
ark Harbor Dr
18500 HOUS 77084 3816 B6
ark Harbor Estates Dr
1500 HOUS 77084 3816 B6
ark Harbor Oaks Ct
1700 HOUS 77084 3816 C7
ark Haven Dr
1600 HOUS 77077 3958 B5
arkhaven Dr
2300 SGLD 77478 4237 B4
ark Haven Ln
- PRLD 77545 4499 D4
3200 DRPK 77536 4109 D7
arkhaven Ln
- HOUS 77077 3957 B4
1100 HOUS 77077 3956 E3
ark Heath Ln
9600 HarC 77088 3682 B1
arkheath Ln
- HarC 77373 2968 D5
arkhill Dr
700 HarC 77530 3829 C7
arkhill Forest Dr
8900 HarC 77088 3542 D7
ark Hollow Ct
7800 HarC 77095 3538 B7
ark Hollow Dr
14000 HOUS 77082 4096 D1
ark Holly Ct
21300 HarC 77450 3954 C3
arkhurst Dr
7600 HOUS 77028 3826 B1
7900 HOUS 77028 3687 B7
ark Island Ct
16700 HarC 77377 3254 C5
ark Ivy Ct
4500 FBnC 77494 4092 D2
ark Ivy Ln
26200 FBnC 77494 4092 D2
ark Key Cir
18800 HOUS 77084 3816 B6
ark Knoll Ln
900 HarC 77450 3954 B3
ark Lake Dr
- HarC 77084 3815 E4
- HarC 77449 3815 E4
arklake Vil
1700 HarC 77450 3955 A5
1900 HarC 77450 3954 E6
ark Lakes Canyon Ter
- HarC 77396 3407 B7
arkland Ct
10 SPVL 77055 3820 D7
arkland St
4200 PASD 77504 4247 D7
arkland Ter
16900 HarC 77429 3252 E6
arkland Wy
- FBnC 77083 4236 C1
- HarC 77040 3541 A6
ark Landing Ct
3900 HarC 77449 3816 A2
arkland Manor Dr
7300 HarC 77433 3677 A1
arkland Woods Dr
10700 FBnC 77478 4237 A4
arklane Blvd
- SGLD 77478 4368 D2
arklane Dr
3000 BYTN 77521 3973 E1
arklane Colony Ct
4400 SGLD 77479 4368 B7
4400 SGLD 77479 4495 A1
ark Laureate Dr
100 HOUS 77024 3960 C1
ark Laurel Ln
- FBnC 77469 4094 E2
arkleaf Dr
4500 BYTN 77521 3973 E1
ark Leaf Ln
600 HarC 77450 3954 A3
600 HOUS 77450 3954 A2
ark Line Dr
- HOUS 77084 3817 D7
ark Link Dr
1400 DRPK 77536 4109 C7
ark Lodge Ct
1900 HOUS 77062 4380 D7

STREET
Block City ZIP Map# Grid

Park Lodge Dr
17100 HarC 77379 3255 E4
Park Lorne Dr
16500 HarC 77084 3817 C1
Parkman Dr
- HarC 77082 4096 A4
Parkman St
10900 HTCK 77510 4987 E1
Parkman Grove Dr
26100 FBnC 77469 4092 B7
Park Manor St
15200 HOUS 77053 4372 B5
16800 FBnC 77053 4499 A1
16800 HOUS 77053 4499 A1
Park Maple Dr
1400 HarC 77450 3954 B5
Parkmead Dr
4300 TYLV 77586 4508 D1
Park Meadow Ct
5000 PASD 77504 4247 E7
11900 HarC 77089 4504 B1
Park Meadow Dr
1400 HarC 77450 3954 B4
10000 HarC 77089 4504 E1
10300 HarC 77089 4505 A2
Parkmeadow Dr
900 HarC 77073 3403 C3
Park Meadow Pass
32000 MtgC 77355 2668 A6
Park Meadows Av
2400 DRPK 77536 4109 D7
3300 DRPK 77536 4249 D1
Park Mill Ln
21300 HarC 77450 3954 C5
Park Mist Dr
- HarC 77450 3954 B3
Parkmont Dr
- LPRT 77571 4250 B3
Parkmore Dr
9200 HarC 77095 3538 C4
Park Mt Dr
21100 HarC 77450 3954 B3
Park Oak Ct
21000 HarC 77433 3251 A5
Park Oak Dr
1700 CNRO 77304 2237 B5
Park Oaks Dr
- KMAH 77565 4509 D7
2900 HOUS 77017 4105 C5
Park One Dr
12800 SGLD 77478 4237 C6
W Park One Dr
1000 SGLD 77478 4237 C6
Park on Fuqua Dr
- HOUS 77089 4377 E3
Park Orchard Dr
21300 HarC 77450 3954 C5
Park Overlook Ct
15900 HarC 77433 3251 B6
Park Pebble Ln
2200 FBnC 77494 3953 C5
Park Pine Dr
20500 HarC 77450 3954 C3
Park Pl Blvd
7400 HOUS 77087 4105 A7
8100 HOUS 77017 4105 E6
9500 PRLD 77584 4501 C3
28900 MtgC 77354 2818 B1
NW Park Pl Dr
9900 HarC 77086 3542 D4
Park Pl Ests
29800 HarC 77377 2963 D6
Park Plaza Dr
4700 HOUS 77018 3823 A1
5000 HOUS 77018 3684 A7
5300 HOUS 77091 3684 A6
Park Point Dr
3400 HOUS 77339 3119 B4
22300 HarC 77450 3953 E5
22300 HarC 77450 3954 A5
Park Point Ln
26500 KATY 77494 3952 A2
Park Pointe Wy
15100 FBnC 77478 4236 C6
15100 SGLD 77478 4236 C6
Park Post Ln
21300 HarC 77450 3954 C5
Park Rd 66
- GLSN 77554 5332 C4
Park Ridge Ct
20800 HarC 77450 3954 C3
Parkridge Ct
16500 HOUS 77053 4371 E7
Park Ridge Dr
1700 HarC 77450 3954 B4
1700 HOUS 77450 3954 B4
4200 PASD 77504 4247 E7
Parkridge Dr
5000 HOUS 77053 4372 A7
5300 HOUS 77053 4371 E7
N Park Ridge Dr
1400 DRPK 77536 4109 C7
S Park Ridge Dr
1400 DRPK 77536 4109 C7
Parkridge Glen Dr
3500 HOUS 77082 4097 B2
Parkriver Cross
6400 FBnC 77479 4367 B6
Park River Dr
- FBnC 77479 4494 B4
Parkriver Dr
11400 HarC 77070 3399 B1
11500 HarC 77070 3398 E1
Park Road 1836
- DRPK 77536 3970 A7
- HarC 77536 3970 A7
- HOUS 77530 3970 A4
- HOUS 77571 3970 A4
2700 HarC 77571 3970 A7
Park Rock Ln
21200 HarC 77450 3954 B3
Park Rose Dr
- HOUS 77077 3958 A7
Park Row Blvd
14200 HOUS 77079 3817 D7
14200 HOUS 77084 3817 C7
19300 HOUS 77084 3816 A7
19500 HarC 77084 3816 A7
19700 HarC 77084 3815 E7
19700 HOUS 77084 3815 E7
20000 HOUS 77449 3815 C7
20300 HarC 77449 3815 C7
Park Royal Dr
3400 HOUS 77339 3119 B5
12800 HOUS 77077 3957 C4
Park Royale Cir
1200 HarC 77450 3954 C3

STREET
Block City ZIP Map# Grid

Park Royale Ct
1200 HarC 77450 3954 C3
Park Royale Dr
21100 HarC 77450 3954 B3
Park Royale Ln
1200 HarC 77450 3954 C3
Park Run Dr
21100 HarC 77450 3954 C4
Parks Dr
10100 HarC 77070 3399 B6
Park Sage Ct
18200 HarC 77433 3537 A4
Park Sage Ln
7600 HarC 77433 3537 D7
Park Sands Ln
4200 HOUS 77345 3119 E4
Parks Branch Ln
4200 FBnC 77494 4092 D1
Park Scot Dr
16500 HarC 77084 3817 C1
Parksedge Dr
- HarC 77041 3680 C7
- HOUS 77041 3680 C7
Parksgate Dr
14400 FBnC 77083 4236 D1
Parkshadow Dr
- BYTN 77521 3973 D1
Park Shadow Ln
2400 DRPK 77536 4109 C7
13500 BzaC 77583 4623 E2
Park Shadow Pl
12400 PASD 77058 4380 E7
Park Shadows Tr
- PASD 77058 4381 A6
11800 PASD 77059 4380 E4
12400 PASD 77058 4380 E6
Parkshire Ct
23100 MtgC 77357 2827 E3
23100 MtgC 77357 2828 A3
Parkshire Dr
3500 BzaC 77584 4501 C7
Park Shore Dr
5300 HarC 77084 3677 E6
Parkside
3800 MSCY 77459 4496 C2
Parkside Cir
9400 PNVL 77318 2237 A1
Parkside Dr
1100 PASD 77502 4247 D2
1700 GNPK 77547 3966 C6
3400 PRLD 77584 4502 E6
10400 PNVL 77304 2237 A1
10400 PNVL 77318 2237 A1
N Parkside Dr
1400 DRPK 77536 4109 D7
S Parkside Dr
1500 DRPK 77536 4109 D7
Parkside Spring Dr
3900 HarC 77388 3112 D2
Parksley Dr
16200 HOUS 77059 4380 C5
Park South Ln
- HarC 77396 3407 B3
- HOUS 77396 3407 B3
Park Spring Dr
2600 HarC 77373 3114 E4
2600 HarC 77373 3115 C4
Parkspring Dr
900 HarC 77073 3403 B2
Park Spring Ln
2900 HarC 77373 3115 A4
Park Springs Dr
2700 PRLD 77584 4500 A3
Park Springs Ln
2800 FBnC 77479 4493 D2
3400 HOUS 77345 3119 E3
Park Square Ln
4800 HarC 77396 3407 A7
Parkstead Dr
1000 TYLV 77586 4381 D7
Parkstone Ct
5500 FBnC 77479 4493 D2
Parkstone Dr
700 HOUS 77076 3685 B3
Parkstone Bend Ct
4600 HarC 77449 3676 D7
Park Stone Bend Ln
19900 HarC 77449 3676 E7
Parkstone Bend Ln
20100 HarC 77449 3676 E7
Parkstone View Cir
13400 HarC 77083 4097 B5
Parksun Ct
4700 FBnC 77469 4093 D6
Park Talon Dr
2200 HarC 77067 3402 B4
Park Ten Blvd
- HarC 77094 3956 A1
- HOUS 77094 3956 A1
1200 HOUS 77084 3956 A1
1300 HOUS 77084 3817 A7
Park Ten Pl
10 HOUS 77084 3956 A1
16300 HOUS 77084 3817 A7
Park Terrace Blvd
8100 HOUS 77017 4105 C5
Park Thicket
4000 PASD 77058 4380 E6
4000 PASD 77058 4381 A6
Park Thicket Ln
- RSBG 77469 4615 A3
5500 BzaC 77583 4623 D4
Park Timbers Dr
21200 HarC 77450 3954 C5
Park Timbers Ln
21200 HarC 77450 3954 B5
E Parktown Dr
- DRPK 77536 4109 A7
500 DRPK 77536 4249 A1
N Parktown Dr
600 DRPK 77536 4109 A7
S Parktown Dr
500 DRPK 77536 4249 A1
W Parktown Dr
500 DRPK 77536 4249 A1
700 DRPK 77536 4109 A7
Park Townhome Wy
4600 PASD 77504 4247 E6
Park Trail Dr
19000 HarC 77094 3955 B3
Parktrail Dr
8800 HarC 77044 3688 E5
Park Trail Ln
- LGCY 77573 4631 A4
300 HOUS 77007 3962 D3
4400 PASD 77505 4249 C6
Park Trail Run
1300 HOUS 77019 3963 A4

STREET
Block City ZIP Map# Grid

Park Trail Wy
1300 HOUS 77019 3963 A4
Park Trail Vista
600 HOUS 77019 3963 A4
Park Tree Ln
- HOUS 77450 3954 A3
20000 HarC 77450 3954 B3
Park Two Dr
700 SGLD 77478 4237 C7
Parkvale Dr
9900 HOUS 77099 4238 B3
Park Valley Dr
21100 HarC 77450 3954 C4
Park View Ct
1700 HOUS 77084 3816 C6
Parkview Ct
500 SGLD 77478 4237 A7
4500 MSCY 77459 4497 C5
Parkview Dr
- PASD 77504 4247 D5
100 ALVN 77511 4867 B1
1800 FRDW 77546 4629 D4
2300 PRLD 77581 4504 A5
2500 PRLD 77581 4503 E5
7200 HTCK 77563 4988 D5
S Park View Dr
18100 HOUS 77084 3816 C6
W Park View Dr
- HOUS 77084 3816 B6
Park View Ln
- LGCY 77573 4632 B6
Parkview Ln
1600 MSCY 77459 4497 D5
Parkview St
100 HOUS 77009 3963 B1
1000 HTCK 77510 4987 E2
15400 MSCY 77071 4239 D7
Parkview Manor Ln
7700 HarC 77396 3547 D1
Parkview Terrace Ln
- DKSN 77539 4752 E6
Park Villa Dr
21100 HarC 77450 3954 B3
Park Village Dr
5100 HOUS 77048 4374 E1
5500 HOUS 77048 4375 B1
S Park Village Dr
5200 HOUS 77048 4374 E1
5200 HOUS 77048 4375 A1
Parkville Dr
14900 HarC 77068 3257 B6
Parkvine Ct
3600 FBnC 77450 4094 C1
Parkvine Ln
22500 FBnC 77450 4094 C1
Park Vista Dr
7700 HOUS 77072 4097 E6
Park Vista Ln
3200 DRPK 77536 4109 D7
Parkwalk Ln
22800 FBnC 77450 4093 D2
Parkwater Cir
19800 HarC 77450 3954 E5
Parkwater Bridge Ln
23700 FBnC 77469 4093 D6
Parkway Av
2500 RSBG 77471 4491 A6
Parkway Blvd
13300 SGLD 77478 4368 E2
S Parkway Blvd
- SGLD 77478 4368 D3
Parkway Ct
- STAF 77477 4369 A1
1300 HOUS 77077 3956 E4
Parkway Dr
- HOUS 77005 4102 D2
- HOUS 77006 4102 D1
- HOUS 77088 3683 E1
- LMQU 77568 4872 B4
- PASD 77503 4108 D4
200 CNRO 77303 2237 D5
500 BYTN 77520 4113 A1
1200 BYTN 77520 4112 E1
1500 ALVN 77511 4866 D3
8500 HOUS 77088 3684 A2
9900 LPRT 77571 4250 B4
31900 MtgC 77354 2817 A1
E Parkway Dr
3900 MtgC 77302 2677 B2
S Parkway Dr
1400 DRPK 77536 4249 D1
W Parkway Dr
3800 MtgC 77302 2677 B2
Parkway Pl
10 JRSV 77040 3540 A7
Parkway Rd
25700 HarC 77336 3121 C6
Parkway St
900 LPRT 77571 4252 A3
Parkway Cir Dr
- PASD 77503 4108 C5
Parkway Club Dr
- PASD 77503 4108 D4
Parkway Crossing Dr
- HarC 77373 2968 E7
Parkway Forest Dr
8700 HarC 77044 3689 A5
Parkway Green Blvd
- PASD 77503 4108 C4
Parkway Lake Dr
- PASD 77503 4108 C4
Parkway Lakes Ln
22100 FBnC 77469 4093 D6
22100 HOUS 77469 4093 D6
Parkway Loop Dr
- PASD 77503 4108 D5
Parkway Manor Dr
- HOUS 77085 4371 A2
- PASD 77503 4108 C5
Parkway Mist Dr
- PASD 77503 4108 D5
Parkway Oaks Dr
- PASD 77503 4108 C4
Parkway Oaks Ln
2800 FBnC 77494 3953 A5
37600 MtgC 77355 2815 B5
Parkway Overlook Dr
- PASD 77503 4108 D4
Parkway Pl Dr
- PASD 77503 4108 D4
Parkway Plaza Dr
- HOUS 77077 3957 A3
1400 HOUS 77077 3956 E4
Parkway Point Dr
- PASD 77503 4108 D4
Parkway Ridge Dr
- PASD 77503 4108 D4

STREET
Block City ZIP Map# Grid

Parkway Times Dr
- PASD 77503 4108 D4
Parkway Trail Ln
- PASD 77503 4108 C4
Parkway Vista Dr
- PASD 77503 4108 C4
600 HOUS 77019 3963 A4
Park West Dr
700 SGLD 77478 4237 C7
1000 TXCY 77591 4873 A5
8900 HOUS 77063 3959 D7
E Parkwest Dr
10 HOUS 77072 4098 B4
10 HOUS 77082 4098 B4
W Park West Dr
- HOUS 77072 4098 A3
- HOUS 77082 4098 A3
W Parkwest Dr
10 HOUS 77072 4098 A3
10 HOUS 77082 4098 A3
Park West Plz
- BYTN 77520 3971 D1
Parkwest Central Dr
14600 HOUS 77082 4096 D3
Park Westheimer Blvd
21400 FBnC 77469 4094 A6
21900 FBnC 77469 4093 D6
21900 HOUS 77469 4093 D6
Park Wick Ln
21100 HarC 77450 3954 B3
Parkwick Ln
3200 DRPK 77536 4109 D7
3200 DRPK 77536 4249 D1
Parkwille Ln
18000 HarC 77433 3677 D1
Park Willow Dr
21100 HarC 77450 3954 C4
Park Wind Ct
21600 HarC 77450 3954 B3
Park Wind Dr
700 HarC 77450 3954 B3
Parkwood
10900 MtgC 77303 2239 D1
E Parkwood Av
100 FRDW 77546 4629 E3
E Parkwood Av FM-528
100 FRDW 77546 4629 E3
W Parkwood Av
100 FRDW 77546 4629 A7
2500 FRDW 77546 4749 E2
3200 ALVN 77511 4749 D3
W Parkwood Av FM-528
100 FRDW 77546 4629 A7
2500 FRDW 77546 4749 E2
3200 ALVN 77511 4749 D3
Parkwood Dr
300 PASD 77503 4108 C4
2900 BYTN 77521 3973 E1
3200 HOUS 77021 4103 B4
N Parkwood Dr
3400 HOUS 77021 4103 C4
S Parkwood Dr
3400 HOUS 77021 4103 C4
Parkwood Ln
2400 SGLD 77479 4495 B1
Parkwood Pl
5900 FBnC 77479 4367 A6
Parkwood St E
1500 CNRO 77301 2383 D4
Parkwood St W
1500 CNRO 77301 2383 D4
Parkwood Wy
15400 HOUS 77059 4380 B6
Parkwood Cir Dr
7900 HOUS 77036 4098 E6
7900 HOUS 77072 4098 E6
Parkwood Manor Dr
2800 HOUS 77339 3119 B2
Parkwood Village Dr
300 FRDW 77546 4629 E3
N Park Wy Dr
1500 DRPK 77536 4109 D7
Park York Dr
21100 HarC 77450 3954 B4
21700 HOUS 77450 3954 A4
Parla Ct
- LPRT 77571 4250 E1
Parliament Dr
100 HOUS 77034 4247 A5
Parliament Ln
- HarC 77083 4097 A7
Parliament Pl
2800 MtgC 77357 2829 C3
2800 RMFT 77357 2829 C3
Parliament St
- FBnC 77083 4096 A7
16600 FBnC 77083 4095 E7
Parliament Hills Dr
29700 MtgC 77386 2969 E2
Parlin Ridge Dr
8800 HarC 77040 3681 C3
E Parma Dr
4700 RSBG 77471 4491 C4
W Parma Dr
4400 RSBG 77471 4491 C4
Parmer Ct
8500 HarC 77064 3540 D6
Parmley Creek Ct
15800 HarC 77429 3253 B5
Parnell St
7700 HOUS 77021 4243 B1
7900 HOUS 77051 4243 B2
Par Point Ct
25500 HarC 77389 2966 B2
Parr Ln
800 LMQU 77568 4990 C1
Parral Ct
700 HarC 77532 3552 A1
Parramatta Ln
- HarC 77073 3258 E2
100 HarC 77073 3259 A2
Parrish St
12800 GlsC 77510 4870 E2
12800 GlsC 77510 4871 A2
Parrish Mill Ln
- FBnC 77478 4236 E4
Parrot Shell Ln
2400 FBnC 77469 4234 B7
Parrott Av
2200 RSBG 77471 4490 E5
2500 RSBG 77471 4491 A5
Parrott Ct
1900 RSBG 77471 4490 E5
Parry Ct
3800 PRLD 77584 4503 B7
Parry Dr
4000 PRLD 77584 4503 B7

STREET
Block City ZIP Map# Grid

Parry Fields Ct
3800 PRLD 77584 4503 B7
Parry Sound Dr
1200 PASD 77504 4247 D5
Parryville Dr
5600 HarC 77041 3679 C5
Parsimony Ln
11100 HOUS 77034 4379 B2
Parsley Av
- BYTN 77521 3833 B7
- HarC 77521 3833 B7
5100 BYTN 77521 3972 A1
Parsley Dr
10 CNRO 77303 2237 D6
Parsley Ln
3600 DKSN 77539 4754 A2
Parsley Hawthorne Ct
17100 HOUS 77059 4380 C4
Parsley Mist Ln
- FBnC 77469 4493 B3
Parsonage Cove
10 FBnC 77459 4621 C4
Parsonfield Ct
900 HarC 77373 2968 E5
Parsongate Dr
22500 HarC 77373 3116 A7
Parsons Ct
10 CNRO 77303 2237 E5
Parsons St
900 HOUS 77012 4105 B3
7200 HOUS 77087 4105 B3
Parsonsfield Ln
9700 FBnC 77494 4092 C5
Parsons Glen Dr
14100 HarC 77044 3549 C2
Parsons Green Ct
19900 HarC 77450 3954 E5
Parsons Knoll Dr
8500 HarC 77433 3537 A6
Parsons Landing Dr
23200 FBnC 77494 4093 B4
Parsons Valley Dr
10 CNRO 77303 2237 D5
Part Dr
15800 HarC 77532 3552 B4
Partage Ln
13600 HarC 77069 3400 B2
Partain Rd
21700 MtgC 77372 2535 C2
Parthenon Pl
600 MtgC 77357 2829 B2
600 RMFT 77357 2829 A1
Par Three
400 MtgC 77357 2829 D3
400 RMFT 77357 2829 D3
Partlow Ln
8300 HarC 77040 3541 B7
Partners Ct
- MtgC 77365 2973 A5
Partners Wy
23400 MtgC 77365 2973 B5
Partnership Wy
- HOUS 77449 3814 D6
Partners Voice Dr
18500 HarC 77433 3395 C5
Partridge Ln
300 HOUS 77060 3544 D2
Partridge St
4700 LMQU 77568 4873 A7
4800 LMQU 77568 4872 E7
Partridgeberry Ct
3800 HOUS 77059 4380 C4
Partridge Green Ct
18100 HarC 77084 3816 D1
Partridge Green Dr
18000 HarC 77084 3816 E1
Partridge Run Dr
19800 HarC 77094 3954 D2
19800 HarC 77094 3955 A3
19800 HarC 77450 3954 D2
Par Two Cir
18900 HarC 77346 3265 B6
Party
- HarC 77040 3681 B3
Parwill St
5700 HOUS 77081 4100 D5
Pas Tr
400 HOUS 77336 3266 B2
Pasadena Blvd
100 PASD 77506 4107 C7
1200 PASD 77502 4107 C6
2600 PASD 77502 4108 A7
2700 PASD 77503 4108 D7
4200 DRPK 77503 4108 E7
4200 DRPK 77536 4108 E7
E Pasadena Blvd
100 DRPK 77536 4249 B1
2800 DRPK 77536 4250 A1
2800 LPRT 77571 4250 A1
N Pasadena Blvd
100 PASD 77506 4107 B3
W Pasadena Blvd
100 DRPK 77536 4249 B1
600 DRPK 77536 4109 A7
1300 DRPK 77536 4108 E7
4300 DRPK 77503 4108 E7
4300 PASD 77503 4108 E7
Pasadena Frwy
- DRPK - 4108 E3
- DRPK - 4109 B3
- HarC - 4109 E4
- HarC - 4110 A4
- HOUS - 4106 D4
- LPRT - 4110 C5
- LPRT - 4111 B5
- PASD - 4106 E4
- PASD - 4107 A3
- PASD - 4108 A3
Pasadena Frwy SR-225
- DRPK - 4108 E3
- DRPK - 4109 B3
- HarC - 4109 D4
- HarC - 4110 A4
- HOUS - 4106 D4
- LPRT - 4110 C5
- LPRT - 4111 B5
- PASD - 4106 E4
- PASD - 4107 A3
- PASD - 4108 A3
Pasadena St
1700 HOUS 77023 4105 A2
Pasadena Freeway Frontage Rd
- DRPK 77503 4108 D3
- HarC 77536 4109 E4
- PASD 77536 4108 E3
100 PASD 77506 4107 C3
700 LPRT 77571 4251 C1

STREET
Block City ZIP Map# Grid

Pasadena Freeway Frontage Rd
1000 LPRT 77571 4111 B6
2800 PASD 77506 4108 B3
2900 PASD 77503 4108 A3
3900 DRPK 77536 4108 D3
6400 DRPK 77536 4109 B3
6900 HarC 77571 4109 E4
7100 HarC 77571 4110 A4
7100 LPRT 77571 4110 A4
11400 HarC 77571 4111 B6
W Pasadena Freeway Frontage Rd
100 PASD 77506 4107 A3
700 PASD 77506 4106 D4
1300 HOUS 77017 4106 D4
Pasadena Town Square Mall
100 PASD 77506 4107 C5
Pasadero Dr
15800 FBnC 77083 4096 A6
Pasaguarda
- PASD 77503 4108 A1
Pasa Robles Ln
13500 HarC 77083 4097 B6
Pascall Creek Pl
10 WDLD 77382 2819 B2
Paschall St
200 HOUS 77009 3963 C1
Pasche Ln
- HOUS 77084 3818 A2
Paseo Areoles
11900 HOUS 77076 3685 A2
Paseo Companario Dr
3900 FBnC 77469 4233 C5
Paseo del Rey Dr
15200 HarC 77083 4096 C5
Paseo Lobo
9000 TXCY 77591 4872 E3
9000 TXCY 77591 4873 A3
Paseo Royale Blvd
- FBnC 77469 4233 C5
Pasha Dr
8200 HarC 77040 3541 B7
Pasket Ln
1900 HOUS 77092 3822 A5
Paso del Flores Dr
12600 HOUS 77045 4241 B6
Paso del Sol Dr
6900 FBnC 77083 4096 A6
7000 HOUS 77083 4096 A5
Paso Dobble Dr
16200 FBnC 77083 4096 A5
16300 FBnC 77083 4095 E5
Paso Fino Dr
20300 HarC 77338 3261 D4
Paso Hondo Dr
16200 HarC 77083 4096 A5
16400 FBnC 77083 4095 D5
Paso Real Dr
15100 HarC 77083 4096 C6
Paso Rello Dr
2100 HOUS 77077 3957 C7
S Pass Ln
9100 HarC 77064 3540 C5
Pass St
100 LMQU 77568 4873 B7
Passing Pine Ct
7400 HarC 77346 3265 A4
Pastel Ln
22300 HarC 77389 3112 E1
Pastoral Pond Cir
10 WDLD 77380 2967 C4
Pastoral Pond Ln
- WDLD 77380 2967 C4
Pastoria Dr
16800 FBnC 77083 4095 D7
Pasture Ct
3000 SGLD 77479 4495 D1
Pasture Ln
2900 SGLD 77479 4495 D1
Pasture Bend Ct
7600 HarC 77433 3537 C7
Pasture Spring Ln
7800 HarC 77433 3537 C7
Pastureview Dr
1500 PRLD 77581 4375 D7
Pasture View Ln
8600 HOUS 77024 3961 A2
Patch
1400 HarC 77015 3968 B2
Patchester Dr
- HOUS 77079 3958 A1
Pate
2800 SEBK 77586 4509 B2
Pate Rd
5200 HOUS 77016 3686 D5
Patel Ln
- HarC 77039 3546 A4
Paterno Dr
- HarC 77064 3540 B7
Pateway Ct
700 MtgC 77386 2968 D1
Pat George Blvd
11100 CNRO 77301 2385 B2
11100 CNRO 77303 2385 B2
11100 MtgC 77303 2385 B2
Path Creek Ln
- FBnC 77478 4236 D5
Pathfield Dr
15800 HarC 77084 3678 E6
Pathfinder Dr
24400 SGCH 77355 2960 E2
24400 SGCH 77355 2961 A2
24700 MtgC 77355 2960 E2
E Pathfinders Cir
100 WDLD 77381 2820 E4
100 WDLD 77381 2821 A3
N Pathfinders Cir
10 WDLD 77381 2820 E3
10 WDLD 77381 2821 C2
S Pathfinders Cir
100 WDLD 77381 2820 E3
Pathfinders Pass
3000 HarC 77373 3115 B5
Path Green Dr
8900 HarC 77095 3538 C4
Pathway Ct
4200 FBnC 77545 4622 D1
Patience Av
3000 HarC 77014 3401 D3
Patina Pines Ct
10 WDLD 77381 2821 D2
Patina Pines Pl
- SHEH 77381 2821 E2
10 WDLD 77381 2821 E2
Patio St
2900 HOUS 77017 4246 D1

STREET Block City ZIP Map# Grid
Patio Glen Dr
7900 MSCY 77071 4239 E7
Patna Dr
2500 KATY 77493 3813 C4
Patou Dr
700 HarC 77530 3830 A7
Patras Dr
3700 PASD 77505 4248 E5
Patria Cammino Dr
- FBnC 77053 4498 D1
Patricia Dr
900 DRPK 77536 4109 C6
Patricia Ln
100 CNRO 77301 2530 B1
1700 MSCY 77489 4370 B3
1700 PASD 77502 4107 D7
3100 PRLD 77581 4504 B4
5100 GlsC 77518 4635 A3
6400 KATY 77493 3813 A7
7100 HOUS 77012 4105 B4
8100 HTCK 77563 4988 D5
18100 MtgC 77355 2668 B7
21000 MtgC 77357 2827 A7
23000 MtgC 77357 2973 E1
23000 MtgC 77357 2974 A1
Patricia St
2700 LMQU 77568 4989 D1
Patricia Manor Pl
2500 HOUS 77012 4105 B4
2500 HOUS 77087 4105 B4
Patrick
200 HOUS 77076 3684 C6
200 HOUS 77091 3684 C6
Patrick Ct
10 BKHV 77024 3959 B3
Patrick St
1600 PASD 77506 4107 D5
5500 HOUS 77076 3684 C6
Patrick Henry St
5100 BLAR 77401 4100 E6
Patrick's Dr
- MtgC 77354 2816 C1
- MtgC 77362 2816 C1
Patridge Dr
5600 PRLD 77584 4502 C6
11200 HarC 77070 3255 A7
Patridge Ln
12200 MtgC 77362 2817 B6
Patriot Ct
3500 MSCY 77459 4369 D5
Patriot Ln
12400 HOUS 77024 3959 A4
Patriot Park Ln
20500 HarC 77449 3676 D3
Patriots Wy
2900 FRDW 77546 4749 E2
Patsy Ln
- ORDN 77385 2822 B4
- ORDN 77386 2822 C5
Patsy St
900 BYTN 77520 3973 B6
Patten Oaks Ln
- HarC 77373 3115 B5
Patterson Rd
- HOUS 77084 3817 D4
- HOUS 77084 3818 A4
4400 BzaC 77578 4626 A2
4800 MNVL 77578 4625 D4
4800 MNVL 77578 4626 A3
Patterson St
300 HOUS 77007 3962 C3
Patti Ln
800 LPRT 77571 4251 E3
Pattibob St
8700 HOUS 77029 3965 D3
Pattiglen Dr
17200 HarC 77084 3678 A3
17500 HarC 77084 3677 E3
Patti Ln Ct
900 HOUS 77073 3259 B7
Patti Lynn Ln
10 HOUS 77024 3959 B5
Pattington Cypress Dr
15300 HarC 77433 3251 C7
Patton St
200 HOUS 77009 3824 B6
W Patton St
500 HOUS 77009 3824 A6
Pattys Lndg
32000 MtgC 77354 2671 E5
Paul Dr
- FRDW 77546 4505 A5
- PRLD 77581 4505 A4
1400 PRLD 77581 4504 E4
Paul Rd
15100 FBnC 77478 4236 C4
Paul St
900 PASD 77506 4107 E6
W Paul St
600 ALVN 77511 4749 B6
Paula Dr
- TXCY 77539 4755 B3
- TXCY 77591 4755 B3
Paula Ln
8400 TXCY 77539 4755 B4
8400 TXCY 77591 4755 B4
27100 ORDN 77380 2822 B5
27100 ORDN 77385 2822 B5
Paula St
4800 HOUS 77033 4243 E4
Paul B Koonce St
7900 HOUS 77061 4245 C6
Paulette Dr
900 DRPK 77536 4109 C7
3900 PASD 77504 4247 D5
Paulette Ln
900 GlsC 77539 4635 A5
Pauline Av
200 PASD 77502 4247 B1
1000 BLAR 77401 4101 A6
Pauline St
900 HarC 77562 3832 A3
E Pauline St
100 CNRO 77301 2384 A4
W Pauline St
100 CNRO 77301 2384 A4
Paul Quinn Rd
1100 HOUS 77091 3683 D6
Paul Quinn St
700 HOUS 77091 3684 A5
1400 HOUS 77091 3683 A6
Paul Revere Dr
100 HOUS 77024 3959 A4
Pauls Tr
15500 HarC 77377 3108 B4
Paulus Dr
10800 HarC 77041 3680 C4
Paulwood Dr
10700 HOUS 77071 4239 D3
Pavero Pl
22400 HarC 77450 3954 A5
Pavilion Ct
12500 HarC 77377 3254 B5
Pavilion Dr
- HarC 77083 4096 E5
- HOUS 77083 4096 E5
Pavilion Pt
14400 HarC 77083 4096 D6
14400 HOUS 77083 4096 D6
E Pavilion Park Cir
- FBnC 77494 4093 D3
N Pavilion Park Cir
- FBnC 77494 4093 D3
S Pavilion Park Cir
- FBnC 77494 4093 D2
W Pavilion Park Cir
- FBnC 77494 4093 E2
Pavilion Six
- HOUS 77084 3818 A1
Pavona Ridge Ln
8000 HarC 77040 3541 E6
Pavonia Ct
16500 HarC 77095 3538 A3
Pavonia Dr
10300 HarC 77095 3538 A2
Pawley Dr
10700 HarC 77065 3539 A2
Pawnee Dr
1900 DRPK 77536 4109 C5
3400 LPRT 77571 4250 A4
Pawnee Ln
4600 PASD 77504 4248 A5
Pawnee St
3000 HOUS 77054 4102 E6
3000 HOUS 77054 4103 A7
4400 HarC 77521 3833 B4
Pawnee Bend Dr
14000 HarC 77429 3253 E5
Pawnee Pass
7900 FBnC 77459 4497 A7
Pawnee Trails Dr
13800 HarC 77429 3253 E5
Pawprint Pl
10 WDLD 77382 2673 B6
Paxico
- HOUS 77034 4378 E5
Paxton Ct
7000 SGLD 77479 4367 C7
Paxton Dr
13600 HarC 77014 3401 E1
Paxton Landing Ln
15200 HarC 77433 3251 D6
Paxton Point Ln
17100 HarC 77095 3537 E3
Payette Dr
14700 HarC 77040 3541 A6
Payne Ct
27200 ORDN 77385 2822 C4
Payne Ln
100 FBnC 77469 4493 B7
Payne Rd
16600 MtgC 77302 2679 C6
23100 MtgC 77357 2827 E5
23100 MtgC 77357 2828 A6
Payne St
100 HOUS 77009 3824 B7
Payson Pl
10 FRDW 77546 4629 B5
Payson St
- HOUS 77030 4102 E5
2800 HOUS 77021 4102 E5
2900 HOUS 77021 4103 A5
Payton St
2200 HarC 77032 3404 D6
2200 HOUS 77032 3404 D6
Payton Chase Ct
- FBnC 77494 4093 A1
Payton Springs Dr
2900 BzaC 77578 4501 A7
N Pazaree Ct
17600 HarC 77532 3411 A7
S Pazaree Ct
17500 HarC 77532 3411 A7
Peabody St
6900 HOUS 77028 3826 B2
Peabody Hill Ln
5000 FBnC 77494 4092 C3
Peace Ct
5500 HarC 77041 3679 C6
Peace St
- RSBG 77471 4491 B4
Peaceable Ln
- MtgC 77385 2676 C4
- WDLD 77385 2676 C4
Peace Branch Dr
- WDLD 77382 2673 A7
Peacedale Ct
300 HarC 77015 3828 D5
Peaceful Ln
11400 HarC 77016 3547 B7
11400 HOUS 77016 3547 B7
Peaceful Vly
2200 HarC 77373 3114 C6
Peaceful Wy
13400 HOUS 77085 4371 E1
Peaceful Canyon
- WDLD 77381 2820 D4
N Peaceful Canyon Cir
10 WDLD 77381 2820 B4
S Peaceful Canyon Cir
10 WDLD 77381 2820 B4
Peaceful Canyon Ct
10 WDLD 77381 2820 B4
Peaceful Meadow Tr
- HarC 77433 3250 C5
Peaceful Valley Dr
2300 HarC 77373 3114 C6
Peace River Dr
6800 HarC 77379 3256 C1
Peace Rose Dr
10 MtgC 77380 2968 A3
10 WDLD 77380 2968 A3
Peach
800 LPRT 77571 4111 C7
Peach Ct
2300 PRLD 77581 4503 B3
Peach Dr
25500 MtgC 77357 2828 E6
25700 MtgC 77357 2829 A6
Peach Ln
200 ARLA 77583 4623 A6
2100 PASD 77502 4107 D7
2100 PASD 77502 4247 D1
Peach Pt
2600 FBnC 77469 4365 B1
Peach Pt
2700 FBnC 77469 4234 A7
Peach St
- CNRO 77304 2383 D6
- HOUS 77026 3825 A7
900 CNRO 77301 2383 E6
1100 LGCY 77573 4632 D6
10500 HOUS 77093 3686 C3
10800 HarC 77093 3686 C2
N Peach St
100 TMBL 77375 2964 B6
S Peach St
100 TMBL 77375 2964 C7
Peacham Ct
1200 FBnC 77545 4622 E2
4400 FBnC 77545 4623 A2
Peacham Ln
1100 FBnC 77545 4623 C1
Peach Blossom Dr
900 BzaC 77584 4501 A1
Peach Blossom St
10400 HOUS 77075 4376 B3
Peach Bough Ct
16000 HarC 77095 3538 C7
Peach Bough Ln
16100 HarC 77095 3538 C7
Peach Brook Ct
1800 HOUS 77062 4380 A7
Peach Country Ct
4000 PASD 77059 4380 D4
Peach Creek Dr
5100 HOUS 77017 4246 B1
5200 HOUS 77017 4106 B7
24500 PTVL 77357 2682 C7
24900 PTVL 77357 2828 D1
24900 WDBR 77357 2828 D1
25600 MtgC 77357 2828 E4
25700 MtgC 77357 2829 A4
Peach Dale Ct
1600 CNRO 77301 2384 E6
E Peachfield Cir
4100 HarC 77014 3401 C3
N Peachfield Cir
13400 HarC 77014 3401 C2
S Peachfield Cir
13400 HarC 77014 3401 C3
W Peachfield Cir
4200 HarC 77014 3401 C3
Peachford Ln
1100 HOUS 77062 4379 B7
1100 HOUS 77062 4506 C1
Peach Forest Ct
16800 HarC 77095 3538 B7
Peachglen Ln
22100 HarC 77373 3260 E1
Peach Grove Dr
11800 HOUS 77099 4238 A3
E Peach Hollow Cir
3600 BzaC 77584 4501 C1
N Peach Hollow Cir
2700 BzaC 77584 4501 A1
S Peach Hollow Cir
3100 BzaC 77584 4501 B1
W Peach Hollow Cir
700 BzaC 77584 4501 A1
S Peach Hollow Ct
900 BzaC 77584 4501 A1
Peach Hollow Ln
13800 HOUS 77082 4096 E2
13800 HOUS 77082 4097 A2
Peach Knoll Ln
21400 FBnC 77494 4093 C2
Peachleaf St
1500 HarC 77039 3545 C2
Peachlight Ln
6300 HarC 77066 3400 E5
Peach Limb Dr
11700 HOUS 77099 4238 A3
Peach Meadow Dr
12900 HarC 77429 3398 A3
13100 HarC 77429 3254 A6
Peachmeadow Ln
15300 HarC 77530 3829 D4
Peach Mountain Ln
20300 HarC 77433 3251 C7
Peach Oak Cross
- FBnC 77494 4092 C4
Peach Orchard Dr
16300 HarC 77396 3408 A3
Peachridge Ct
10100 HarC 77070 3399 C5
Peachridge Dr
9800 HarC 77070 3399 C5
Peachridge Pl
10 WDLD 77382 2819 C2
Peach Ridge Rd
17000 HarC 77396 3407 E3
17000 HarC 77396 3408 A3
Peach Run Dr
1700 HMBL 77396 3406 D2
Peach Spring Dr
- HOUS 77088 3544 A6
600 HarC 77037 3544 B7
600 HOUS 77037 3544 B7
1400 HOUS 77088 3543 E7
Peach Stone Ct
9000 FBnC 77469 4235 C1
Peachstone Pl
2800 HarC 77389 3113 A1
3100 HarC 77389 3112 E1
Peachtex Dr
13700 HarC 77396 3547 C3
14900 HOUS 77396 3406 C7
Peach Tree Ct
6100 HarC 77449 3677 B4
Peachtree Ct
10 JRSV 77065 3540 A6
Peachtree Dr
1500 PRLD 77581 4504 E4
Peach Tree Ln
- WEBS 77058 4507 D5
- WEBS 77598 4507 D5
3100 MSCY 77459 4496 E3
16800 HarC 77379 3256 B4
Peach Tree Pk
500 MtgC 77302 2530 D5
Peach Tree St
1700 TXCY 77591 4873 A4
Peachtree St
6200 HOUS 77028 3825 D3
7400 HOUS 77016 3825 D1
8800 HOUS 77016 3686 C6
Peachtree Hill Ct
6100 HOUS 77345 3120 D6
Peach Valley Cir
19300 HarC 77084 3816 A6
Peachvine Ln
21200 HarC 77375 3110 A4
Peach Willow Rd
7700 HOUS 77489 4371 A3
Peachwood Bnd
800 HOUS 77077 3957 A2
Peachwood Cir
1400 PASD 77502 4106 D7
Peachwood Ct
13600 HOUS 77077 3957 A2
Peachwood Dr
1800 PASD 77502 4106 D7
2100 MSCY 77489 4370 B6
Peachwood Ln
3300 SGLD 77479 4495 B1
Peachwood Hollow Ln
15300 FBnC 77478 4236 C6
Peachwood Lake Dr
11600 FBnC 77478 4236 C6
Peacock Ln
15400 MtgC 77302 2680 A3
Peacock Pk
7700 HarC 77396 3406 D6
Peacock St
5400 HOUS 77033 4243 E5
5700 HOUS 77033 4244 A5
Peacock Gap Ln
23500 FBnC 77494 3953 C5
Peacock Hills Dr
- HOUS 77035 4240 B6
Peagram Pt
14600 HarC 77429 3397 D7
Peakwood Dr
800 HarC 77090 3258 C3
Pealestone Ln
- HarC 77095 3537 D5
Pear Av
500 HarC 77060 3544 E4
Pear Ct
2300 PRLD 77581 4503 A3
Pear St
- HarC 77039 3545 A4
- HarC 77060 3544 E4
- HarC 77060 3545 A4
300 LMQU 77568 4990 C2
800 LGCY 77573 4632 D6
2800 HOUS 77026 3824 E6
2800 HOUS 77026 3825 A6
4800 PRLD 77581 4503 A3
E Pear St
3700 PRLD 77581 4503 C3
W Pear St
4000 PRLD 77581 4503 B3
Pearberry Ln
26700 FBnC 77494 4092 E3
Pear Brook Tr
1500 HOUS 77062 4380 A7
E Pearce Av
- BYTN 77520 3972 D7
100 BYTN 77520 3973 A7
500 BYTN 77520 4113 A1
W Pearce Av
100 BYTN 77520 3972 E7
Pearce Lake Ct
4900 FBnC 77469 4234 D3
Pear Creek Cir
1900 HarC 77084 3816 A6
Pear Glen Ct
3800 HOUS 77345 3119 E3
Pearhaven Dr
15000 HOUS 77062 4380 A7
Pea Ridge Dr
23900 HarC 77373 3114 E4
Pear Knoll Ct
14400 HOUS 77062 4379 D7
Pearl Dr
10200 HarC 77064 3540 B6
Pearl St
400 BYTN 77520 3973 B6
400 HOUS 77029 3965 C1
1100 DRPK 77536 4109 C5
1500 LGCY 77573 4632 C3
20700 PRVW 77484 3100 D4
Pearland Av
2100 PRLD 77581 4503 B3
2500 PRLD 77584 4503 B3
Pearland Pkwy
- HOUS 77075 4376 D4
- PRLD 77581 4376 E7
- PRLD 77581 4503 E1
- PRLD 77581 4504 A2
Pearland Sites Rd
10 BzaC 77511 4747 E3
10 BzaC 77578 4747 E3
1400 BzaC 77511 4748 A2
17000 BzaC 77584 4627 B6
17000 PRLD 77584 4627 B6
18800 BzaC 77511 4627 B4
Pearl Bay Ct
- PRLD 77545 4499 E2
Pearl Bluff Ln
3200 HarC 77047 4374 B5
Pearl Garden Ct
10 CNRO 77384 2675 E3
Pearl Hall Dr
1400 HOUS 77034 4247 A4
1400 SHUS 77587 4247 A4
Pear Limb Dr
10100 HOUS 77099 4238 A3
Pearl Lake Dr
8500 HarC 77095 3538 E5
21900 HarC 77449 3815 A3
Pearl Point St
8600 HarC 77044 3689 B5
Pearl Shadow
- HarC 77044 3550 A3
Pearlstone Ct
500 FBnC 77469 4365 B5
Pear Meadow Ln
3600 HarC 77039 3546 A6
Pear Oak Dr
10300 HarC 77065 3539 B3
Pear Ridge Pl
16300 HarC 77396 3408 A3
Pearsall Dr
9300 HarC 77064 3540 D6
Pearson
10000 HarC 77064 3541 C2
Pearson Ln
4500 HarC 77346 3408 B1
Pearson Rd
5100 GlsC 77517 4986 A2
10700 MtgC 77306 2532 E1
Pearson St
1100 HOUS 77023 4104 B1
2300 ALVN 77511 4867 B4
Peartex Dr
14800 HOUS 77396 3547 C1
Pear Tree Ln
- HarC 77073 3259 B2
Pearwood Dr
2400 HarC 77038 3543 A2
Pear Woods Ct
13500 HOUS 77059 4379 E4
Pease St
700 HOUS 77002 3963 B5
2700 HOUS 77003 3963 D6
4300 HOUS 77023 3964 A7
4900 HOUS 77023 4104 C1
Peatwood Rd
13900 HarC 77038 3542 E1
13900 HarC 77038 3543 A1
Peatwood Wy
6800 SGLD 77479 4367 B6
Peavine Cir
3300 HOUS 77080 3821 A2
Pebble Bch
10 JRSV 77065 3540 B6
Pebble Brk
1600 MSCY 77459 4497 D4
Pebble Dr
- BzaC 77578 4501 B7
25300 HarC 77336 3122 A7
Pebble Lk
- ELGO 77586 4509 B1
- SEBK 77586 4509 B1
Pebble Ln
1900 FRDW 77546 4629 D6
6000 HOUS 77087 4245 A1
Pebble Mdws
12200 HarC 77041 3679 E6
Pebble Pth
12000 HarC 77070 3399 B6
Pebble Bank Ln
5700 HarC 77041 3679 D5
Pebblebank Ln
800 LGCY 77573 4633 B3
Pebble Banks Ln
1400 PASD 77586 4382 A6
Pebble Bay Br
- PRLD 77545 4499 E2
Pebble Bay Ct
4300 PASD 77505 4249 A5
Pebble Bay Dr
3100 LGCY 77573 4633 B1
3400 FBnC 77450 3953 E7
Pebble Beach Ct
10 MNVL 77583 4624 D5
Pebble Beach Dr
- MSCY 77459 4369 E7
2000 LGCY 77573 4632 D1
2100 LGCY 77573 4508 D7
4400 LGCY 77573 4509 A7
6000 HarC 77069 3400 C2
E Pebble Beach Dr
2500 MSCY 77459 4369 E6
2500 MSCY 77459 4496 E1
N Pebble Beach Dr
3100 MSCY 77459 4369 E7
W Pebble Beach Dr
2500 MSCY 77459 4369 E6
2500 MSCY 77459 4496 E1
Pebble Bend Dr
14600 HarC 77014 3257 C7
14600 HarC 77068 3257 B5
Pebble Bend Wy
32500 MtgC 77354 2672 C5
Pebble Bluff Ln
- FBnC 77479 4496 D5
4800 HarC 77449 3677 A7
Pebblebrook Cir
2400 MtgC 77384 2528 E7
2400 MtgC 77384 2529 A7
2400 MtgC 77384 2674 E1
2400 MtgC 77384 2675 A1
Pebblebrook Ct
100 SGLD 77478 4368 E4
Pebble Brook Dr
3500 PRLD 77584 4503 B5
3900 LGCY 77539 4633 E3
3900 LGCY 77539 4634 A4
Pebblebrook Dr
300 ELGO 77586 4509 B2
2500 DRPK 77536 4109 E7
3300 SEBK 77586 4509 B2
12100 HOUS 77024 3959 A2
12500 HOUS 77024 3958 E2
13600 HOUS 77079 3958 A2
Pebble Brook Ln
3300 PRLD 77584 4501 E5
Pebble Brook St
4800 BYTN 77521 3972 A3
Pebble Canyon Ct
6200 FBnC 77450 4094 C4
Pebble Canyon Ln
200 LGCY 77539 4752 E4
Pebble Chase Dr
1500 HarC 77450 3954 E3
Pebble Cove Ct
10 WDLD 77381 2821 B5
Pebble Cove Dr
10 WDLD 77381 2821 B5
Pebble Creek Ct
15900 HarC 77433 3251 C5
Pebble Creek Dr
2600 PRLD 77581 4504 A3
Pebble Creek Ln
12600 HarC 77429 3398 C6
Pebble Creek Tr
15800 HarC 77433 3251 C5
Pebble Crest Ct
9300 FBnC 77083 4236 A2
Pebble Crest Ln
16300 FBnC 77083 4236 A1
Pebbledowne Cir
2300 SGLD 77478 4237 C4
Pebbledowne Dr
8300 HarC 77064 3542 A5
8400 HarC 77064 3541 E5
Pebble Falls Dr
7100 HarC 77095 3678 C2
Pebble Falls Ln
22300 HarC 77375 3109 D2
Pebble Garden Ln
3700 HarC 77449 3815 C2
Pebblegate Ct
4200 HarC 77373 3115 A6
Pebble Glen Dr
9900 MtgC 77304 2236 A3
Pebbleglen Dr
16000 HarC 77095 3678 C1
Pebble Grove Ct
21400 FBnC 77469 4094 B7
25800 FBnC 77494 4093 A2
Pebble Hill Ct
1800 SGLD 77478 4369 A5
Pebble Hill Dr
12000 BKHV 77024 3959 B4
Pebble Hollow Ct
10 WDLD 77381 2821 B2
Pebble Hollow Dr
20100 FBnC 77469 4234 C3
Pebble Lake Dr
3100 SGLD 77479 4495 E1
15000 HarC 77095 3539 B6
15200 HarC 77095 3538 D5
Pebble Lodge Ln
7700 HarC 77433 3537 A4
Pebble Meadow Ct
14600 HarC 77429 3396 C2
Pebble Mesa Cir
8900 HOUS 77088 3544 A7
Pebble Mill Ln
7200 HarC 77086 3542 B2
Pebble Park Ln
10100 HOUS 77036 4098 E7
Pebble Path Ln
3000 LGCY 77539 4752 E4
Pebblepath Ln
- FBnC 77494 4093 A3
Pebble Pine Ct
21500 HarC 77433 3251 A6
Pebble Pine Dr
- HOUS 77345 3119 D1
- HOUS 77365 3119 D1
Pebble Pine Tr
21300 HarC 77433 3251 A6
Pebble Point Dr
- HarC 77450 3954 E5
Pebble Pointe Dr
12000 PRLD 77584 4500 D1
Pebble Rock Ct
1400 HOUS 77077 3958 A4
Pebble Rock Dr
11900 HOUS 77077 3958 A5
Pebble Run Ct
7700 HarC 77095 3538 A7
Pebble Run Wy
1400 HOUS 77058 4507 D3
Pebbles Dr
5000 HarC 77084 3678 B6
Pebble Sands Dr
- HarC 77375 3109 E6
Pebbleshire Dr
- BzaC 77584 4501 B6
200 HOUS 77062 4506 E2
900 HOUS 77062 4507 A2
Pebble Shores Ln
2300 PRLD 77584 4500 A2
Pebble Springs Dr
- DKSN 77539 4752 D6
5100 HarC 77066 3401 A2
5300 HarC 77066 3400 E3
Pebble Springs Ln
- PRLD 77584 4500 A3
Pebblestone
10 CNRO 77304 2383 B7
Pebblestone Ct
1700 MSCY 77459 4369 C6
Pebblestone Dr
4500 MSCY 77459 4369 B6
Pebblestone St
12500 HOUS 77072 4097 D6
Pebblestone Wk
10 FBnC 77479 4367 B7
Pebble Stream Ct
2500 HOUS 77345 3120 C4
Pebble Terrane Ln
25900 FBnC 77494 3952 B7
Pebbleton Dr
11800 HarC 77070 3398 E1
Pebble Trace Dr
3100 HarC 77068 3257 C6
Pebble View Dr
12100 MtgC 77304 2236 A3
Pebblewalk Cir N
13100 HarC 77041 3539 C7
Pebblewalk Cir S
13100 HarC 77041 3539 C7
Pebble Walk Ln
100 LGCY 77539 4753 A3
Pebblewood Ln
- HarC 77379 3256 B1
Pebble Wy Ct
12500 HarC 77041 3679 E6
Pebble Wy Ln
5200 HarC 77041 3679 E6
Peberly Dr
- WDLD 77382 2673 D7
Pebworth Pl
22800 HarC 77373 3115 A6
23500 HarC 77373 3114 E5
Pecan Av
1200 RHMD 77469 4491 E2
Pecan Cir
10 STFE 77510 4870 D6
1100 TYLV 77586 4381 E7
3800 LPRT 77571 4250 D4
28900 SHEH 77381 2822 A2
Pecan Ct
2400 RSBG 77471 4491 A6
2700 MSCY 77459 4497 A3
3700 BzaC 77578 4625 B1
12400 HOUS 77013 3827 E5
Pecan Dr
- HarC 77379 3111 E7
- MtgC 77302 2676 E3
100 FRDW 77546 4505 A6
100 MAGA 77355 2668 E5
200 BYTN 77520 3973 D4
200 LGCY 77573 4631 D4
400 HarC 77532 3692 C2
400 SHUS 77587 4246 D4
1300 HOUS 77017 4106 D6
1300 HOUS 77502 4106 D6
1300 PASD 77017 4106 D6
1300 PASD 77502 4106 D6
2100 DKSN 77539 4753 E2
2500 RSBG 77471 4491 A6
3500 GlsC 77518 4634 C2
10800 LPRT 77571 4250 D4
12400 HOUS 77013 3827 E6
16200 FBnC 77469 4236 A5
16300 FBnC 77469 4235 E5
24600 MtgC 77357 2828 D7
E Pecan Dr
600 TMBL 77375 2964 B6
N Pecan Dr
10 TXCY 77591 4874 B6
400 TMBL 77375 2964 B6
S Pecan Dr
10 TXCY 77591 4874 B6
100 LMQU 77568 4874 B7
400 TMBL 77375 2964 B6
W Pecan Dr
100 BYTN 77520 3973 D4
Pecan Grv
100 HOUS 77077 3956
400 DKSN 77539 4753
4000 STFE 77510 4871
Pecan Ln
10 CNRO 77304 2382
1300 FBnC 77494 3952
1700 HMBL 77396 3406
1700 STAF 77477 4370
6100 KATY 77493 3813
18000 BzaC 77511 4628
18000 BzaC 77581 4628
18200 BzaC 77546 4628
Pecan Pk
5900 HTCK 77563 4988
Pecan Rd
2000 FBnC 77494 3952
4600 RSBG 77471 4614
Pecan Sprs
8800 HarC 77040 3541
Pecan St
- PRVW 77445 3100
200 CNRO 77301 2383
500 FBnC 77545 4623
1000 HarC 77530 3830
2300 WALR 77484 3101
2400 WlrC 77484 3101
2700 ALVN 77511 4867
2900 HOUS 77087 4104
5200 HarC 77532 3552
16300 HarC 77530 3969
N Pecan St
600 FBnC 77545 4623
Pecan Acres Dr
17100 FBnC 77478 4235
17200 FBnC 77478 4366
Pecan Bay Ct
3700 FBnC 77478 4366 E
Pecan Bend Dr
4000 FBnC 77469 4234 A
11900 CNRO 77304 2382 A
11900 MtgC 77304 2382 A
Pecan Brook Ct
20400 HarC 77379 3111 E
Pecan Canyon
11500 HarC 77377 3254 D
Pecan Chase Dr
2300 FBnC 77469 4364 C
Pecan Cove Ct
2500 FBnC 77469 4365 C
Pecan Creek Dr
4900 FBnC 77469 4232 E
11600 HOUS 77043 3819 A
11700 HOUS 77043 3818 E
Pecan Crest Ct
1100 FBnC 77479 4493 D
Pecan Crossing Dr
1400 FBnC 77469 4365 D
Pecan Crossing Ln
3500 LPRT 77571 4249 E
Pecan Draw Ct
3200 SGLD 77479 4495 E
Pecan Forest Ct
2000 FBnC 77469 4365 C
Pecan Forest Dr
1800 MSCY 77459 4497 C
Pecan Forest Ln
7800 HarC 77521 3834 D
Pecan Gap Dr
11600 HarC 77065 3398 A
Pecan Gap St
11200 MtgC 77354 2671 D
Pecangate Dr
5500 HarC 77373 3115 E
Pecan Glen Ct
9500 HarC 77040 3541 A
Pecan Glen Dr
1100 MSCY 77489 4370 D
Pecan Gorge Ct
10 FBnC 77479 4367 E
Pecan Green Wy
1100 HarC 77073 3259 E
Pecan Grove
20500 WlrC 77445 3243 E
Pecan Grove Cir
12100 MtgC 77354 2671 A
Pecan Grove Ct
2500 PRLD 77584 4501 E
Pecan Grove Dr
3300 BYTN 77521 3833 A
4600 PRLD 77584 4501 E
4700 PRLD 77584 4502 A
Pecan Grove Rd
4500 FBnC 77479 4366 D
Pecan Grove St
200 HOUS 77013 3827 E
Pecan Hollow Rd
10100 MtgC 77354 2671 E
10100 MtgC 77354 2672 A
Pecan Hollow St
1600 PRLD 77581 4504 D
Pecan Knoll Dr
4000 HOUS 77339 3119 C
Pecan Lake Cir
7600 FBnC 77469 4232 B
Pecan Lake Ct
4700 FBnC 77469 4364 B
Pecan Lake Rd
1800 FBnC 77469 4364 B
Pecan Manor Dr
2500 BYTN 77520 3973 E
Pecan Meadow Dr
12000 HOUS 77071 4239 C
Pecan Mill Dr
3300 FBnC 77478 4366 E
Pecan Oak Dr
13300 HarC 77065 3539 A
Pecan Orchard Dr
- FBnC 77479 4366 E
- FBnC 77479 4367 A
Pecan Orchard Rd
1800 LGCY 77573 4632 A
Pecan Park Cir
- HOUS 77018 3823 D
Pecan Park Dr
100 RSBG 77471 4491 D
2200 FBnC 77469 4365 C
Pecan Park Ln
4000 HOUS 77345 3119 E
Pecan Path Dr
10 WDLD 77381 2674 D
Pecan Pl Dr
8800 HOUS 77071 4239 B
Pecan Point Cir
1700 SGLD 77478 4368 E
Pecan Point Dr
2800 SGLD 77478 4368 E
3500 SGLD 77478 4369 A

Houston Street Index

STREET / Block City ZIP Map# Grid

can Ridge Blvd
- HarC 77014 3401 B1
- HarC 77066 3401 B1
can Ridge Dr
2700 SGLD 77479 4368 D7
2800 SGLD 77479 4495 D1
3600 MSCY 77459 4497 D7
3800 MSCY 77459 4621 D1
can Shadow
1900 FBnC 77469 4364 D2
can Shores Dr
12800 HarC 77044 3408 D5
cantex Dr
- HarC 77396 3406 C7
14900 HOUS 77396 3406 C7
can Trace Ct
1400 FBnC 77479 4493 E5
can Trail Dr
2000 FBnC 77469 4365 C1
Pecan Trail Dr
2100 FBnC 77469 4365 C1
can Trail Ln
10 SPVL 77055 3820 E7
can Tree Ct
17200 FBnC 77478 4366 E1
can Valley Cir
25500 MtgC 77380 2968 B2
can Valley Ct
200 FRDW 77546 4629 A6
2300 MSCY 77459 4497 B3
can Valley Dr
3800 MSCY 77459 4497 B3
can View Dr
- FBnC 77469 4492 B1
- RHMD 77469 4492 B1
can Villa Dr
10 LPRT 77571 4251 A1
can Villas Dr
7900 HOUS 77061 4245 D2
can Walk Ln
3300 FBnC 77478 4366 E2
can Wood Dr
2900 MSCY 77459 4496 C1
6200 HarC 77088 3682 C1
can Wood Ln
2300 FBnC 77471 4614 B3
canwood Ln
800 HDWV 77024 3959 E1
canwood St
6700 HTCK 77563 4989 A4
7700 HTCK 77563 4988 D3
can Wy Ct
3000 FBnC 77469 4234 B7
ch Rd
1200 SPVL 77055 3821 B7
1300 HLSV 77055 3821 B6
1300 HOUS 77055 3821 B6
cha Ln
3200 FBnC 77471 4614 C4
3200 PLEK 77471 4614 C4
ck Av
4200 STFE 77517 4870 C7
4700 STFE 77517 4986 B1
ck St
3700 STFE 77517 4870 C6
ckham St
2100 HOUS 77019 3962 B6
2600 HOUS 77098 3962 B7
core St
100 HOUS 77009 3824 A7
900 HOUS 77009 3823 E7
cos Dr
22100 GLSN 77554 5441 A5
cos St
2200 LMQU 77568 4989 E2
5400 DKSN 77539 4633 D7
9300 HOUS 77055 3820 D6
12600 BKVL 77581 4376 A6
13100 PRLD 77581 4376 A7
cos Bill
9100 HOUS 77055 3820 D6
cos Pass Dr
1100 FBnC 77469 4365 B3
cos Ranch Rd
27000 MtgC 77355 2813 E1
Pecos River Ct
28900 MtgC 77386 2970 B2
Pecos River Ct
28900 MtgC 77386 2970 A2
cos River Dr
4200 MtgC 77386 2970 A2
cos River Ln
28900 MtgC 77386 2970 B1
cos Valley Dr
6000 FBnC 77469 4493 B4
Pecos Valley Tr
2000 HarC 77449 3815 E6
Pecos Valley Tr
20000 HarC 77449 3815 D6
Pecos Valley Tr
20000 HarC 77449 3815 D6
Pecos Valley Tr
2000 HarC 77449 3815 D6
edder Wy Dr
12400 HarC 77377 3254 B4
eddie St
600 HOUS 77008 3823 D5
1000 HOUS 77009 3823 E5
eden Rd
26300 MtgC 77355 2963 A2
eden St
300 HOUS 77006 3962 D5
1500 HOUS 77019 3962 C5
eden Bay Dr
3100 PRLD 77584 4501 E5
edernales Falls Dr
2700 PRLD 77584 4503 B4
edernales Falls Ln
11800 FBnC 77478 4236 C6
edernales Trails Ln
3200 FBnC 77450 4094 C1
3600 HOUS 77450 4094 C1
edernales Valley Dr
- HarC 77429 3253 D6
ederson St
4700 HOUS 77033 4243 D4
4700 HOUS 77051 4243 D4
5200 HOUS 77033 4244 A4
edlars Ct
12700 HarC 77377 3254 A4
eeblebriar Ln
- FBnC 77494 4093 A1
eebles
- HMPD 77445 3097 E1
eebles St
- HMPD 77445 3098 C1
- WlrC 77445 3098 C1

Peeble Trail Ct
10200 HarC 77338 3407 D1
Peek Rd
- FBnC 77469 4233 E1
- HarC 77449 3814 D1
- HarC 77493 3814 D1
4000 HarC 77449 3675 C1
4000 HarC 77493 3675 C1
6000 FBnC 77469 4093 E7
S Peek Rd
- FBnC 77469 4093 E7
- HOUS 77450 3953 D6
- HOUS 77450 4093 E5
- HOUS 77469 4093 E7
- HOUS 77494 3953 D6
- HOUS 77494 4093 E3
2100 FBnC 77450 3953 D7
2100 FBnC 77494 3953 D7
5100 FBnC 77450 4093 E5
5100 FBnC 77494 4093 D3
Peekskill Ct
3000 BzaC 77584 4501 D6
Peekskill Ln
7700 HOUS 77075 4376 D2
Peel
- HOUS 77018 3684 B7
- HOUS 77091 3684 B7
Peer Dr
1800 HOUS 77043 3820 A5
Peerless Dr
23200 HarC 77373 3115 B4
Peerless St
6300 HOUS 77021 4103 B6
Peerless Pass Ct
3000 HarC 77373 3115 A3
Peermont Dr
15400 HOUS 77062 4506 E2
Peery Rd
- WlrC 77445 3097 B4
Peg St
5900 HOUS 77092 3821 D2
Pegasus Cir
14000 HarC 77429 3253 D5
Pegasus Ln
700 LGCY 77573 4508 C5
Pegasus Rd
13500 HarC 77429 3254 A5
13700 HarC 77429 3253 E5
Peggy
7100 HOUS 77022 3824 B2
Peggy Av
800 BYTN 77520 3973 B6
Peggy Ln
7800 BzaC 77584 4627 C4
Peggy St
100 CNRO 77301 2384 B2
400 BYTN 77520 3973 B6
800 DRPK 77536 4109 C4
Peggys Ct
1500 HOUS 77015 3967 C3
Peggys Ln
12800 HOUS 77015 3967 B4
Pelham Dr
2100 HOUS 77019 3962 B5
Pelham Chase Dr
6600 HarC 77389 2966 C2
Pelican Ct
- LGCY 77573 4508 D6
Pelican Dr
200 BYTN 77520 4113 C4
300 HarC 77532 3552 B1
2000 SEBK 77586 4509 B1
4400 GlsC 77563 4990 A6
4800 HTCK 77563 4990 A6
Pelican Ln
4100 GLSN 77554 5332 E3
7900 CmbC 77520 3835 D3
Pelican Rd
- GLSN 77554 5331 D5
4400 JMAB 77554 5331 D4
Pelican St
100 MtgC 77355 2960 A2
N Pelican St
10 LMQU 77568 4990 E5
Pelican Wy
4400 JMAB 77554 5331 D4
Pelican Beach Ln
16100 HOUS 77044 3409 B4
Pelican Cove
3000 MSCY 77459 4497 D6
Pelican Cove Ct
17900 HarC 77346 3408 D2
Pelican Harbour Dr
600 TXCY 77590 4875 C2
Pelican Hill Ct
1200 FBnC 77494 3953 A3
Pelican Hill Dr
24500 FBnC 77494 3953 A4
Pelican I
1100 GLSN 77554 4994 C7
1100 GLSN 77554 5109 C1
12400 HarC 77377 3254 C5
Pelican Island Cswy
- GLSN 77550 5108 C4
- GLSN 77551 5108 C3
- GLSN 77554 5108 D2
Pelican Lake Dr
3700 FBnC 77469 4234 D6
Pelican Landing Ct
2100 LGCY 77573 4631 B7
Pelican Marsh Dr
14300 HarC 77429 3396 E1
Pelican Pointe Blvd
- HarC 77041 3679 D6
Pelican Wy Rd
17900 HOUS 77084 3816 C7
Pella Dr
6900 HOUS 77036 4099 A5
Pelly St
- BYTN 77520 4112 E2
Pelorus Wy
17000 HarC 77532 3552 B1
Pelsey St
9700 HOUS 77029 3966 A5
Pemberton Dr
2600 HOUS 77005 4102 A3
2600 HOUS 77030 4102 A3
2600 WUNP 77005 4102 A3
3400 BzaC 77584 4501 C6
Pemberton Rdg
3100 HOUS 77025 4241 E2
Pemberton St
500 HarC 77530 3969 C2
Pemberton Trc
9500 HOUS 77025 4241 E2
Pemberton Wk
3100 HOUS 77025 4241 E2

Pemberton Wy
- HarC 77044 3549 B3
200 FBnC 77469 4493 D7
Pemberton Cir Dr
3200 HOUS 77025 4101 E7
E Pemberton Cir Dr
9200 HOUS 77025 4101 B7
N Pemberton Cir Dr
3200 HOUS 77025 4101 B7
S Pemberton Cir Dr
3200 HOUS 77025 4101 E7
W Pemberton Cir Dr
9200 HOUS 77025 4101 B7
Pemberton Crescent Dr
9500 HOUS 77025 4241 E2
Pemberwick Park Ln
13500 HarC 77070 3399 C3
Pembridge Dr
11000 HOUS 77071 4239 E4
Pembroke St
3900 SGLD 77479 4495 E3
12900 HOUS 77048 4374 E2
Pembroke Bay Dr
2000 LGCY 77573 4509 A7
Pembroke Springs Sprs
2500 HarC 77373 3114 C5
Pembrook Cir
1800 CNRO 77301 2530 B2
Pembrook Ct
10 BLAR 77401 4101 A5
3300 BzaC 77584 4501 D7
Pembrook St
9100 HOUS 77016 3686 E6
9100 HOUS 77016 3687 A6
Pembrooke Dr
3500 FBnC 77469 4233 D6
Pembrooke Wy
4000 FBnC 77469 4233 C5
Pembrooke Ridge Dr
11100 HarC 77065 3399 A6
Pembrough Ln
6900 FBnC 77494 4093 C5
Pemford Dr
11600 HarC 77377 3254 E6
Pence Rd
500 HOUS 77598 4506 D3
Pendelton St
- SGLD 77479 4495 C3
Pendelton Pl Cir
100 FBnC 77479 4367 A5
Pendelton Pl Dr
5800 FBnC 77479 4367 A5
Pender Ln
11100 HOUS 77477 4238 A4
12000 MDWP 77477 4238 A5
12100 MDWP 77477 4237 E5
Pendleton Av
800 PASD 77506 4107 D4
Pendleton Dr
- SGLD 77479 4495 C4
Pendleton Park Pt
- WDLD 77382 2673 A7
Pendragon Dr
- HarC 77379 3111 B2
Penelope Dr
10800 HOUS 77013 3827 C4
Penfield Ln
5200 HOUS 77021 4104 B5
Penfield St
2500 PASD 77506 4107 E6
2500 PASD 77506 4108 A6
Penguin Ct
10 WDLD 77380 2968 A1
Penguin St
24400 MtgC 77355 2960 B2
24400 SGCH 77355 2960 B2
25500 MtgC 77355 2814 C7
Penhurst St
4400 HOUS 77016 3686 B5
4400 HOUS 77093 3686 B5
Penick Rd
- WlrC 77484 3101 E4
100 WALR 77484 3101 E7
13900 WlrC 77484 3246 E3
Penina Ct
15900 HarC 77532 3551 D4
Penina Dr
1700 HarC 77532 3551 D4
Peninsula Blvd
15900 HarC 77015 3969 C5
15900 HOUS 77015 3969 C5
Peninsula Dr
2500 MSCY 77459 4497 A4
Peninsula Pl
4300 MSCY 77459 4497 A4
Peninsula Garden Wy
4700 HarC 77396 3407 B7
Peninsula Park Dr
5600 HarC 77041 3679 D6
Peninsulas Dr
- MSCY 77459 4497 B4
Penmark Ln
1600 HarC 77450 3955 A5
Penmere Ct
2700 HOUS 77345 3119 E6
Penmont Ln
- HarC 77379 3111 A7
Penn Av
4500 BzaC 77583 4745 C5
Penn Cir
10 FRDW 77546 4629 D1
Penn Dr
700 FRDW 77546 4629 D1
Penn St
3500 HOUS 77093 3825 A1
11700 HarC 77532 3692 D3
Pennant Park Ct
9500 HarC 77044 3689 B4
Pennbright Dr
200 HarC 77090 3258 E7
Pennbury Dr
1100 HarC 77094 3955 B2
Penn City Rd
1600 HarC 77015 3968 C6
1600 HOUS 77015 3968 C6
Penne Dr
- PRLD 77581 4504 E3
Penner St
1000 HOUS 77055 3822 C7
Penner Crest St
1000 HOUS 77055 3822 C7
Penn Hills Ln
- HOUS 77062 4379 C6
14900 HOUS 77062 4380 A7
15000 HOUS 77062 4507 A1
Pennington Ct
3700 FBnC 77459 4621 D5

Pennington Dr
300 ALVN 77511 4867 C4
Pennington Ln
9600 FBnC 77459 4621 D4
Pennington Rd
3100 BzaC 77511 4867 C6
Pennington St
700 HOUS 77022 3685 C6
2300 HOUS 77093 3685 D6
Pennland Ln
14400 HarC 77429 3397 D7
Penn Manor Ct
9100 SPVL 77055 3820 D7
Pennridge Ln
17400 HarC 77377 2962 C7
Pennsgrove Rd
23100 HarC 77373 3115 E6
Pennshore Ct
6400 FBnC 77450 4094 A5
Pennshore Ln
21200 FBnC 77450 4094 A5
Pennsylvania Av
100 SHUS 77587 4246 B4
29900 MtgC 77354 2818 B1
Pennsylvania St
100 HOUS 77029 3965 E7
100 WEBS 77598 4507 B7
200 HOUS 77029 3966 A7
3000 FBnC 77545 4498 E7
Pennwell Dr
6600 HarC 77389 2966 C2
Pennworth Ln
6000 HarC 77084 3678 B4
Penny Ct
6900 HarC 77069 3400 A1
Penny Ln
- HarC 77060 3544 E2
- WDLD 77382 2674 C5
600 FRDW 77546 4629 E2
7300 FBnC 77494 4093 A4
13200 GlsC 77510 4870 E2
14100 HarC 77069 3400 A1
Penny Rd
22600 MtgC 77365 2973 D7
24700 MtgC 77365 3118 D1
Penny St
21100 MtgC 77357 2827 C7
21100 MtgC 77357 2973 C1
Pennybrook Ct
12200 HarC 77066 3401 B5
Pennygent Ct
15000 HarC 77530 3829 C5
Pennygent Ln
1400 HarC 77530 3829 C5
Penny Green St
3800 SGLD 77479 4495 E3
Pennyoak Dr
3900 PRLD 77581 4504 A7
Penny Park Tr
10600 HarC 77089 4378 A7
Pennyrile Ln
22800 HarC 77450 3953 E5
Penny Rock Ct
- HarC 77449 3815 C3
Pennyroyal Ct
1400 HarC 77073 3259 B5
Pennyroyal Point Ln
- HarC 77377 3254 A4
- HarC 77429 3254 A4
Pennystone Ct
15600 FRDW 77546 4505 D6
Pennystone Wy
5000 FRDW 77546 4505 D6
5000 HarC 77546 4505 D6
Pennywayne Ln
2400 BzaC 77581 4628 E1
Pennywayne St
900 BzaC 77581 4628 E1
Pennywell Ln
3000 FBnC 77494 3953 B7
Pennywood Ct
12100 HarC 77070 3399 B6
Pennzoil Rd
100 GLSN 77554 4994 C7
Penrice Dr
20000 HarC 77450 3954 C4
Penrod St
8000 HOUS 77028 3826 C2
Penrose Ct
4200 MSCY 77459 4496 C4
Penrose Dr
9100 HarC 77049 3691 A3
11200 HarC 77044 3691 A1
Penrose Point Dr
7700 HarC 77095 3538 C7
Pensacola Ln
1600 FRDW 77546 4629 A7
Pensdale St
5100 HOUS 77033 4243 E2
Pensgate St
15500 HOUS 77062 4506 E2
Penshore Park Ln
14300 HOUS 77044 3550 A2
Penshore Pl Ln
21300 FBnC 77450 4094 A4
Penshore Terrace Ln
- HarC 77377 3253 E3
Pentacle Ln
12900 HOUS 77085 4240 E7
N Pentenwell Cir
10 WDLD 77382 2819 A1
S Pentenwell Cir
10 WDLD 77382 2819 A1
Penticton St
- HarC 77044 3549 B3
Penton Dr
9800 FBnC 77478 4236 D3
Pentonshire Ln
16500 HarC 77090 3258 D4
Penway St
10 HOUS 77022 3685 A7
Penwell Meadow Ln
- HOUS 77048 4375 B2
Penwood Ct
500 FBnC 77477 4369 E4
Penwood Wy
3500 HOUS 77023 4104 C5
Penzance Ct
5400 HarC 77449 3676 D6
Penzance Dr
21300 HarC 77449 3676 D6
Peony Springs Ct
10 WDLD 77382 2819 E3
Peoples Rd
15700 MtgC 77384 2675 C5
16400 WDLD 77384 2675 C5
Peoria St
12800 HOUS 77015 3967 B1

Peper Glen Ln
- MtgC 77386 2969 D6
Peper Hollow Ln
28200 MtgC 77386 2969 D6
Pepper Ln
10800 HOUS 77079 3958 C1
Pepperberry Tr
21300 HarC 77388 3113 A3
Pepperbrook Dr
7500 HarC 77041 3539 C7
Pepperbush Ct
13500 HarC 77070 3399 D3
Pepper Creek Ln
- PRLD 77583 4500 B5
26800 HarC 77433 3396 A6
Pepperdine Ln
11800 HOUS 77071 4240 A5
Peppergate Ln
13000 HarC 77044 3689 C5
Pepperglen Dr
2100 MSCY 77489 4370 E5
Pepper Hill Ln
1700 FBnC 77479 4494 D4
Pepper Hill Wy
1900 HOUS 77058 4507 D2
Pepperidge Dr
2500 FBnC 77494 3951 D5
Pepper Knoll Dr
13600 HarC 77065 3398 A7
13700 HarC 77429 3398 A7
Pepper Mill Av
5100 BYTN 77521 3833 B7
5100 BYTN 77521 3972 A1
Peppermill Rd
3600 HOUS 77080 3820 D2
Peppermill Creek Dr
25500 MtgC 77365 3118 A3
Pepperrell Pl
23900 HarC 77493 3814 B6
Pepperrell Pl Ct
1900 HarC 77493 3814 B6
Pepper Ridge Ln
25700 HarC 77373 3114 C2
Pepperstone Ct
4000 HarC 77053 4372 D4
Pepperstone Ln
13800 HarC 77044 3549 D2
Pepper Tree Ct
1800 SGLD 77479 4368 A6
Peppertree Ln
1400 HOUS 77015 3966 E3
Peppervine Wy
1700 FBnC 77479 4494 A5
Pepperweed Dr
2300 HarC 77084 3815 E5
Pepper Wood Dr
2700 SGLD 77479 4368 C7
Pepperwood Ln
1900 HOUS 77084 3816 E6
Peralta Hill Ln
18600 HarC 77377 3254 B2
Perch St
8000 CmbC 77520 3835 D3
Perch Creek Dr
6300 HOUS 77049 3828 A3
Percheron Tr
20300 HarC 77338 3261 D4
Percival St
500 TMBL 77375 2964 B7
Percussion Pl
7800 HarC 77040 3681 C1
Percy Rd
11000 HarC 77093 3686 C1
Perdenales Falls Ct
11900 HarC 77375 3109 D5
Perdido Dr
2000 HarC 77532 3551 D3
Perdido Bay Dr
4100 FBnC 77450 4094 B1
Perdido Bay Ln
2900 PRLD 77584 4500 A4
Perdido Cove Ln
- HarC 77041 3679 D4
Perdido Park Dr
- FBnC 77450 4094 C2
Peregrine Dr
1000 FRDW 77546 4629 D5
Peregrine Wy
4700 MSCY 77459 4621 B3
Pereida St
7800 HOUS 77028 3687 B6
Perennial Ln
1200 RSBG 77471 4614 C1
Perez Rd
2200 PASD 77502 4247 A2
2700 SHUS 77502 4247 A2
2700 SHUS 77587 4247 A2
Perez St
4400 SGLD 77477 4369 B2
4400 SGLD 77478 4369 B2
4400 STAF 77477 4369 B2
N Perez St
100 SHUS 77587 4247 A2
400 PASD 77502 4247 A2
400 SHUS 77502 4247 A2
Perfect Landing Wy
19300 HarC 77379 3110 E5
Perfidia Dr
100 HarC 77015 3828 E5
Pergola Pl
4600 HarC 77396 3407 B6
Peridot Ln
4300 FRDW 77546 4629 E1
Peridot Rd
4000 FBnC 77545 4623 A1
Peridot Cove
10200 HarC 77095 3537 E3
Perigrine Dr
10700 HarC 77065 3539 B2
Perimeter Rd
14800 HOUS 77034 4378 E4
Perimeter Park Dr
- HarC 77040 3680 D3
- HOUS 77040 3680 D3
6900 HOUS 77041 3680 D3
Perimeter West Dr
- HOUS 77041 3680 D3
Periwinkle
3800 GLSN 77554 5221 A6
Periwinkle Ln
1300 HarC 77038 3543 E5
Periwinkle Pl
2600 HarC 77562 3832 D3
Periwinkle St
1600 HarC 77038 3543 D5
Perkins Av
100 LGCY 77573 4632 A3
600 LGCY 77573 4631 E2

Perkins Dr
700 GlsC 77518 4634 B3
1100 GlsC 77539 4634 B3
1100 TXCY 77539 4634 B3
Perkins Rd
23700 MtgC 77365 2973 E6
Perkins St
5300 HOUS 77020 3964 C1
Perkins Crossing Dr
2200 CNRO 77304 2236 D3
Perla Rd
700 PASD 77502 4247 B2
Perlican Dr
31100 MtgC 77386 2823 A7
31100 MtgC 77386 2969 A1
Permian Dr
10400 FBnC 77478 4236 E3
Perots Ct
4700 HOUS 77013 3827 D4
Perrie St
- HOUS 77034 4379 A4
Perrington Cir
3100 HarC 77082 4096 D2
Perrington Ct
21500 HarC 77450 3954 B5
Perrington Heights Ln
5300 HOUS 77056 4100 E1
Perriwinkle Ct
4800 SGLD 77479 4367 E7
4800 SGLD 77479 4368 B6
Perrot Legend Ln
4800 HOUS 77013 3827 D4
Perry Av
5300 GLSN 77551 5108 C6
N Perry Av
11700 MSCY 77071 4239 E7
S Perry Av
11800 MSCY 77071 4239 E7
Perry Cir
- BYTN 77520 4112 C2
Perry Ln
2600 ALVN 77511 4866 D3
24600 HarC 77389 2965 E4
Perry Rd
11200 HarC 77064 3540 D1
11300 HarC 77064 3399 D7
11800 HarC 77070 3399 D7
12600 HOUS 77070 3399 D4
14200 MtgC 77302 2531 B7
14500 MtgC 77302 2677 A1
18600 MtgC 77306 2534 B7
Perry St
- ALVN 77511 4749 B7
400 FBnC 77471 4490 C1
2200 HarC 77521 3832 C4
4500 HOUS 77021 4103 E6
4900 HOUS 77021 4104 A6
N Perry St
7600 HarC 77521 3832 C4
Perry Knoll Ct
4000 FBnC 77479 4366 C7
Perryman St
17400 HarC 77044 3551 C7
Perryoak Dr
20400 HarC 77346 3265 B3
Perry Pass Ct
16200 HarC 77379 3256 E3
Perryton Ln
16800 HarC 77073 3259 A4
Persa St
2000 HOUS 77019 3962 B6
2600 HOUS 77098 3962 B6
Pershing Av
1400 BYTN 77520 4112 C1
4700 HOUS 77033 4243 D1
Pershing St
5100 HOUS 77033 4243 E1
5200 HOUS 77033 4244 A1
Persian Dr
12600 HarC 77014 3401 E3
Persimmon Dr
100 BYTN 77520 3832 B7
Persimmon St
2400 HOUS 77093 3824 E1
2600 PASD 77502 4248 A1
3500 HOUS 77093 3825 B1
S Persimmon St
- HarC 77375 3109 D3
10 TMBL 77375 2964 D7
700 TMBL 77375 3109 D3
Persimmon Pass
5300 FBnC 77469 4234 D2
Persimmon Pointe
900 LGCY 77573 4631 E4
Perth Cir
28900 MtgC 77354 2818 B2
Perth St
6100 HOUS 77048 4375 D3
Perthius Dr
10 LMQU 77568 4989 D3
Perth Meadows Ct
19600 HarC 77449 3677 A4
Perthshire Rd
12100 HOUS 77024 3959 A2
12500 HOUS 77024 3958 E2
13300 HOUS 77079 3958 B2
14600 HOUS 77079 3957 C2
Perthuis Farms Rd
- LMQU 77568 4989 C3
Peru Cir
3900 PASD 77504 4247 D4
Pesca de Oro Dr
11300 HOUS 77048 4244 D7
Pessara St
2100 LMQU 77568 4989 E3
Petal Ct
11700 HarC 77038 3543 A5
Petalcup Pl
10 WDLD 77381 2674 D6
Petaldrop Pl
10 WDLD 77382 2673 D5
Petal Park Pl
- WDLD 77382 2673 A7
Petal Rose Ct
15100 HarC 77433 3250 D6
Petaluma Dr
16300 HOUS 77053 4371 D7
Peters Rd
1900 HarC 77532 3411 D1
8100 MNVL 77578 4746 C3
Petersburg
500 MtgC 77302 2530 C6
Petersburg Ln
8700 FBnC 77083 4235 E1
Peters Forest Dr
21400 MtgC 77365 2973 B4
Petersham Dr
8800 HOUS 77031 4239 A5

N Petersham Dr
11600 HOUS 77031 4239 A5
S Petersham Dr
9600 HOUS 77031 4239 A5
Peterson Rd
- FBnC 77441 3951 A3
- FBnC 77494 3951 A3
- WlrC 77423 3951 A3
- WlrC 77493 3812 A7
- WlrC 77493 3951 A1
Petina Cypress Ct
16300 HarC 77433 3251 A5
Petite Cir
3400 GLSN 77554 5332 C1
Petite St
- SEBK 77586 4509 E4
Petitt Rd
15500 FBnC 77478 4236 B2
Petra Dr
8000 FBnC 77083 4096 B7
Petra Ln
7200 FBnC 77469 4615 E4
7200 FBnC 77469 4616 A4
Petre Dr
6900 HOUS 77076 3684 E4
Petrel Ct
400 HarC 77532 3552 B2
Petrich Ln
16400 HarC 77377 2962 E6
S Petro Ln
100 HOUS 77045 4241 E4
100 HOUS 77054 4241 E4
Petroleum St
1300 LMQU 77568 4874 B6
1400 LMQU 77568 4873 E7
Petromac
- HarC 77532 3266 E6
Petropark Dr
6500 HarC 77041 3680 B4
N Petropark Dr
11500 HarC 77041 3680 B4
S Petropark Dr
11500 HarC 77041 3680 B4
Petterson St
- BYTN 77520 3971 B2
Pettibone St
9700 HOUS 77093 3686 B5
Petties Wy
15000 HarC 77429 3252 E7
Pettigrew Dr
7000 SGLD 77479 4367 C7
Pettit St
1000 HOUS 77009 3824 A5
Petty Dr
14700 MtgC 77306 2680 E2
14700 MtgC 77306 2681 A2
Petty Rd
21100 MtgC 77306 2680 E2
Petty St
5200 HOUS 77007 3962 A1
5700 HOUS 77007 3961 E1
Petty Walker Ln
14900 MtgC 77306 2680 E2
Petty Walker Rd
19500 MtgC 77306 2680 E2
21600 MtgC 77306 2681 A2
Petuma Meadows Dr
8800 HarC 77375 2965 D3
Petworth Dr
11000 HOUS 77072 4098 B4
Peveto St
700 HOUS 77019 3962 D4
Pewter Ct
1800 HarC 77493 3814 B6
Pewter Knolls Dr
28500 FBnC 77494 3951 C5
Peyton Pl
2200 DRPK 77536 4109 C6
Peyton St
6800 HOUS 77028 3825 E3
Pfeiffer Dr
15700 HarC 77082 4096 A3
Phantom Pns
- CNRO 77384 2676 A5
- MtgC 77384 2676 A5
- WDLD 77384 2676 A5
Phantom Mist Dr
8300 FBnC 77469 4234 A5
Phanturn Ln
100 BLAR 77401 4101 B3
Pheasant
- HOUS 77049 3828 A3
Pheasant Ln
3400 PRLD 77581 4503 D5
18800 HarC 77377 2961 E7
18800 HarC 77377 2962 A7
Pheasant Run
2700 HMBL 77396 3406 C4
Pheasant St
200 HOUS 77018 3823 C2
Pheasant Creek Ct
16800 FBnC 77478 4235 E7
Pheasant Creek Dr
- FBnC 77478 4235 E7
2300 HarC 77478 4236 A7
3400 FBnC 77469 4235 E7
Pheasant Field Dr
18500 HarC 77346 3265 C7
Pheasant Glen Dr
8100 HarC 77379 3256 A3
8400 HarC 77379 3255 E3
Pheasant Grove Dr
7100 HarC 77433 3677 A1
Pheasant Hill Dr
14200 HarC 77014 3401 C1
Pheasant Lake Ct
12800 HarC 77041 3679 D5
Pheasant Oak Dr
6900 FBnC 77083 4095 E5
Pheasant Ranch Ct
24500 HarC 77447 3249 D3
Pheasant Ridge Dr
16800 FBnC 77478 4236 A7
Pheasant Ridge Ln
5700 HarC 77041 3679 D5
Pheasant Run Dr
2500 HOUS 77339 3119 A6
Pheasant Run Ln
7600 HMBL 77396 3406 C5
Pheasant Trace Ct
9000 HarC 77064 3540 A5
Pheasant Trail Dr
3100 FBnC 77478 4235 E7
3100 FBnC 77478 4236 B7
Phelps St
6900 HTCK 77563 4989 B5
7400 HOUS 77011 3965 B5

STREET
Block City ZIP Map# Grid

Phibes Tr
6800 HarC 77379 3256 C1
Phil St
4300 BLAR 77401 4101 B5
4300 HOUS 77401 4101 B5
7800 HOUS 77012 4105 C3
Philbrook Dr
- WDLD 77382 2819 D1
Philco Dr
- HOUS 77041 3820 D1
4100 HOUS 77080 3820 D1
Philfall St
3000 HOUS 77098 3962 A7
Phil Halstead Dr
9700 HarC 77086 3542 D3
Philibert Ln
7200 HOUS 77028 3826 A2
Philippine St
14200 HarC 77040 3681 A1
15000 HarC 77040 3680 E1
15000 JRSV 77040 3680 E1
15400 JRSV 77040 3540 E7
Phillip Dr
- PRVW 77445 3100 B1
Phillips Dr
- MNVL 77578 4625 E6
5300 MNVL 77578 4626 B6
Phillips Ln
6600 HTCK 77563 4989 A4
19500 HOUS 77338 3262 A5
Phillips St
5200 TXCY 77591 4873 E6
5200 TXCY 77591 4874 A6
7000 HOUS 77091 3683 D4
7900 HOUS 77088 3683 D2
E Phillips St
- CNRO 77301 2384 B4
E Phillips St SR-105
100 CNRO 77301 2384 A5
W Phillips St
100 CNRO 77301 2384 A5
400 CNRO 77301 2383 E5
500 ALVN 77511 4867 B1
1800 ALVN 77511 4866 E1
W Phillips St SR-105
100 CNRO 77301 2384 A5
400 CNRO 77301 2383 E5
Phillips Company Rd
- PASD 77503 3968 A7
- PASD 77503 4108 A1
- PASD 77506 3968 A7
- PASD 77506 4108 A2
10 PASD 77506 4107 E2
Phillips Grove Ln
4200 FBnC 77494 4092 B1
Philmont Dr
9600 HOUS 77080 3820 B2
Philmore Ln
12800 MtgC 77306 2534 B5
Philpop Dr
100 GNPK 77547 3966 A7
Philpot Dr
700 GNPK 77547 3966 B7
Phlox St
4100 HOUS 77051 4243 C4
4600 HOUS 77033 4243 C4
Phoenician Dr
1400 FBnC 77494 3953 B4
Phoenix Ct
3400 MSCY 77459 4498 A5
Phoenix Dr
7600 HOUS 77030 4102 C5
Phoenix Ln
- TXCY 77590 4875 A5
Phoenix Ridge Dr
- HarC 77449 3676 B2
Phylis St
1400 BzaC 77583 4623 C5
Phyllis Ct
600 CNRO 77303 2383 E1
Phyllis St
800 DRPK 77536 4109 C5
1600 BzaC 77583 4623 D5
Pi Cir
1400 PASD 77504 4247 D6
Piazza Grande
- FBnC 77053 4498 D2
Picacho Ln
5700 FBnC 77469 4493 A6
Picadilly Circus
2900 PRLD 77581 4503 E2
2900 PRLD 77581 4504 A3
Picador Dr
7900 FBnC 77083 4096 B7
Picalune
900 PASD 77506 4106 E5
Picardy Ln
14800 HarC 77044 3690 C1
Picasso Pl
5800 HOUS 77096 4240 B2
Picasso Path Pl
10 WDLD 77382 2819 B2
Piccadelli Ln
- HarC 77083 4097 A7
Piccadilly Dr
6700 HOUS 77061 4245 B3
Piccola St
7700 HOUS 77075 4245 C7
Pickens St
6200 HOUS 77007 3961 E2
Pickering Av
400 HOUS 77076 3684 B5
400 HOUS 77091 3684 B5
Pickering Ct
2700 BzaC 77584 4501 C6
Pickering Ln
3400 BzaC 77584 4501 C6
Pickering Rd
16800 MtgC 77302 2680 C7
16800 MtgC 77306 2680 A7
16800 MtgC 77357 2680 C7
18000 MtgC 77302 2825 E1
18000 MtgC 77302 2826 A1
Pickerton Dr
2000 DRPK 77536 4248 E1
2300 DRPK 77536 4249 A1
Pickett Dr
2800 LGCY 77573 4631 A7
6700 FBnC 77469 4493 C6
Pickett Pl
3100 MSCY 77459 4497 E6
Pickett Hill Ln
700 FBnC 77469 4616 D1
Pickfair Ln
3900 GlsC 77518 4634 B3
Pickfair St
5500 HOUS 77026 3825 C4

Pickford Dr
400 HarC 77450 3953 E2
Pickford Ln
11700 MtgC 77354 2671 C2
Pickford Knolls Ct
7800 HarC 77095 3539 C7
Pickford Knolls Dr
13700 HarC 77095 3539 B7
Pickley Ash Wy
18400 BzaC 77584 4627 C4
Pickney Al
1500 GlsC 77650 4878 E6
Pickney Av
800 GlsC 77650 4878 E7
Pickrell Ct
1000 HarC 77073 3259 B5
Pickridge Ct
4700 FBnC 77545 4622 E2
Pickwell Ct
9500 FBnC 77478 4236 C2
Pickwick Park Dr
3500 HOUS 77339 3119 C1
Pickwick Pine Dr
2100 HarC 77396 3407 B2
Pickwood Dr
3100 PRLD 77584 4502 A6
N Picnic Ln
- HOUS 77007 3961 C3
S Picnic Ln
- HOUS 77007 3961 D3
Pico Landing St
22100 FBnC 77469 4093 E7
Pico Meadow Ct
2600 MtgC 77386 2969 E7
Picton Dr
- HarC 77032 3546 D1
Piddler Dr
2300 HarC 77373 3114 C6
Pieces of Eight
100 BzaC 77541 5547 B7
Piedmont Av
5100 HOUS 77016 3686 C4
Piedmont Dr
300 SGLD 77478 4368 B2
Piedmont Pth
- HarC 77038 3543 C5
Piedmont St
4400 PASD 77504 4247 E6
Piedmont Creek Tr
1100 HarC 77073 3259 C6
Piedras Blancas Ln
11200 HOUS 77048 4244 D6
Piedras Negras Ct
6200 FBnC 77450 4094 C4
Pierce St
- HOUS 77029 3965 D5
100 HOUS 77002 3963 B6
100 HOUS 77019 3963 A5
1500 HOUS 77003 3963 C6
2600 HOUS 77004 3963 D6
8000 HOUS 77088 3683 B2
W Pierce St
300 HOUS 77019 3962 E5
Pierceall Rd
19000 WlrC 77445 3244 A1
19800 PNIS 77445 3098 E7
19800 PNIS 77445 3099 A7
19800 PNIS 77445 3244 A1
Pierce Hill Ln
37400 MtgC 77354 2670 A7
Pierce Oaks Dr
10900 FBnC 77469 4092 B7
Pierceton Ct
20800 FBnC 77494 3953 D7
Pierce Valley Dr
11000 FBnC 77469 4092 B7
Pier House
- SEBK 77586 4509 B3
Piermain Dr
10200 HOUS 77035 4241 B2
Pier Pointe Wy
15800 HOUS 77044 3409 A5
Pierre Ct
9900 HOUS 77089 4377 D3
Pierrepont Dr
7300 HarC 77040 3681 E2
Pierre Schlumberger Blvd
- SGLD 77478 4368 C2
Pierson St
200 MtgC 77385 2822 C3
Pierwood Ct
12500 HarC 77041 3679 D6
Pifer Rd
500 HNCV 77024 3960 A2
Pifer Wy
10900 HNCV 77024 3960 A2
Pifer Green Cir
700 HNCV 77024 3960 A2
Pigeon Ct
2900 HOUS 77094 4096 A1
Pigeon Dr
7500 HTCK 77563 4988 A5
Pigeon Bluff Dr
11100 HarC 77065 3399 A6
Pigeon Cove Cir
7200 MSCY 77459 4496 D5
Pigeonwood Dr
10900 HarC 77089 4378 A7
Pigglette Ln
13100 MtgC 77302 2532 E5
Pikard Wy Ct
4200 MtgC 77386 2970 D7
Pike Rd
13500 MSCY 77489 4370 A2
13500 STAF 77477 4370 A2
13500 STAF 77489 4370 A2
Pikecrest Ct
9900 HarC 77379 3110 B6
Pikes Peek Ct
- HarC 77377 3254 C4
Pilat
- HOUS 77017 4246 D2
- HOUS 77502 4246 D2
Pilgrim Cir
9000 BzaC 77583 4745 D4
9000 IWCY 77583 4745 D4
Pilgrim Ln
500 FRDW 77546 4505 C7
14100 HarC 77396 3547 A2
Pilgrimage Ct
1900 FBnC 77469 4365 C3
Pilgrim Estates Dr
2300 TXCY 77590 4875 A1
2400 TXCY 77590 4874 E1
Pilgrim Hall Dr
15500 FRDW 77546 4505 D6
15500 HarC 77546 4505 D6

Pilgrim Harbor Dr
4800 HarC 77546 4505 D6
Pilgrim Journey Dr
1700 FBnC 77469 4234 C6
Pilgrim Oaks Ln
5200 LGCY 77573 4751 D1
Pilgrims Cir
16500 HarC 77379 3256 C4
Pilgrims Bend Dr
2100 HarC 77546 4506 B6
Pilgrims Gate Ln
23000 HarC 77373 2968 E6
Pilgrims Point Ct
2600 HarC 77598 4506 C7
Pilgrims Point Dr
1800 HarC 77546 4506 C7
2200 HarC 77598 4506 C7
2600 HarC 77598 4630 C1
Pilgrims Point Ln
3000 PRLD 77581 4503 D2
Pillar Cove Ln
3600 MSCY 77459 4497 E5
Pillar Park Cir
5500 HarC 77041 3679 C6
Pillot St
7900 HOUS 77029 3965 B3
10100 JTCY 77029 3966 B3
Pilot Ln
1200 GLSN 77554 5107 B7
1200 GLSN 77554 5221 B1
Pilot Pt
10 CNRO 77304 2382 E3
Pilot Point Dr
900 HarC 77038 3543 C3
Pimberton Ln
5200 HarC 77379 3112 A5
5700 HarC 77379 3111 D6
Pimlico Ct
10500 HarC 77038 3543 D2
Pimlico Dr
1000 PRLD 77584 4501 A2
Pimlico Ln
1600 PASD 77503 4108 D7
Pimlico Pt
3800 FBnC 77459 4622 A5
Pinacle Pt
5800 HOUS 77085 4371 E1
Pinafore Ln
2500 HarC 77039 3545 E2
Pinas Frescas Ct
6800 HOUS 77048 4244 D7
Pinaster Pointe Ln
5600 HarC 77379 3112 A4
Pinata Ln
1500 HOUS 77532 3266 B7
Pincay Oaks Ct
8200 HarC 77088 3682 C1
Pincay Oaks Dr
5900 HarC 77088 3542 D7
5900 HarC 77088 3682 D1
Pincher Creek Dr
1600 MtgC 77386 2969 B2
Pin Cherry Ln
14700 HarC 77377 2963 C5
14700 TMBL 77375 2963 C5
14700 TMBL 77377 2963 C5
Pinckney St
400 HOUS 77009 3963 C2
Pinder Ln
4800 PRLD 77584 4502 A6
Pinderfield Ct
- FBnC 77083 4236 B1
Pine
- GNPK 77547 4106 B1
100 MRGP 77571 4252 B1
2700 BYTN 77520 3973 C5
S Pine
21700 HOUS 77532 3266 B7
Pine Av
10 PRVW 77445 3099 E3
300 HarC 77532 3552 D5
4700 PASD 77502 4248 A1
4700 PASD 77503 4248 B1
Pine Bnd
- HarC 77375 2964 D2
Pine Brk
1300 TMBL 77375 2963 E6
1300 TMBL 77375 2964 A6
Pine Cir
10 LMQU 77568 4989 C3
600 PASD 77586 4383 C5
1100 TYLV 77586 4382 A7
4700 BLAR 77401 4101 A6
24200 MtgC 77365 2974 B6
E Pine Cir
35200 MtgC 77362 2816 D4
35200 SGCH 77362 2816 D4
N Pine Cir
300 MtgC 77362 2816 D4
S Pine Cir
300 MtgC 77362 2816 D4
W Pine Cir
35200 MtgC 77362 2816 D4
Pine Cross
31700 MtgC 77355 2669 B7
Pine Ct
100 PNVL 77304 2237 B3
3600 MSCY 77459 4496 E3
N Pine Ct
35300 MtgC 77362 2816 D4
W Pine Ct
35300 MtgC 77362 2816 D4
Pine Dr
- HarC 77070 3398 C3
1900 RSBG 77471 4491 C5
2000 FRDW 77546 4630 A3
9200 HarC 77532 3413 A3
12600 HarC 77429 3398 B3
14800 MtgC 77302 2677 B1
24600 PTVL 77357 2682 D7
25500 MtgC 77357 2828 E6
25500 MtgC 77357 2829 A6
E Pine Dr
10 HarC 77336 2976 E5
N Pine Dr
19000 HarC 77388 3112 C6
Pine Grv
7300 HOUS 77040 3682 A5
7300 HOUS 77092 3682 A5
Pine Hvn
1400 MtgC 77385 2822 D3
Pine Ln
- MNVL 77578 4746 D1
300 HarC 77532 3552 D5
3400 DRPK 77536 4109 C7
3400 DRPK 77536 4249 B1
4200 HarC 77389 3112 C1
6500 HarC 77379 3256 D1

Pine Ln
7000 MNVL 77578 4747 A3
8700 MtgC 77354 2818 D1
12200 DKSN 77539 4753 B6
14000 HarC 77396 3547 B2
17400 SGCH 77355 2961 B2
23600 HarC 77389 2966 A5
25400 MtgC 77357 2974 E2
25600 MtgC 77372 2537 A2
26100 MtgC 77357 2829 A5
W Pine Ln
21300 MtgC 77357 2681 B7
Pine Rd
100 CRLS 77565 4509 C5
500 HarC 77532 3692 C2
4600 RSBG 77471 4614 E3
21800 HOUS 77339 3263 D2
N Pine Rd
10 TXCY 77591 4874 A6
S Pine Rd
10 LMQU 77568 4874 A6
10 TXCY 77591 4874 A7
Pine St
- HMPD 77445 2953 B5
- PRVW 77445 2955 A7
10 HarC 77336 2975 C6
100 CNRO 77301 2384 A4
100 PRVW 77445 3100 B2
400 SGLD 77478 4367 E2
1000 ALVN 77511 4867 D1
1100 BYTN 77520 3972 A7
1100 WALR 77484 3102 A5
1300 BYTN 77520 4112 B1
2400 GLSN 77551 5222 A1
4500 BLAR 77401 4101 B6
4700 PASD 77586 4383 B4
5000 BLAR 77401 4100 D6
5500 HOUS 77081 4100 C6
5500 HOUS 77401 4100 C6
6900 MNVL 77578 4747 B2
7000 HTCK 77563 4989 B4
14600 STFE 77517 4870 B5
15700 GlsC 77517 4870 A5
15900 GlsC 77517 4869 E4
16100 HarC 77530 3830 C5
17800 HarC 77532 3413 A5
N Pine St
100 ARLA 77583 4623 B5
100 TMBL 77375 2964 B7
600 FBnC 77583 4623 B5
S Pine St
100 ARLA 77583 4623 A6
100 TMBL 77375 2964 B7
600 FBnC 77583 4623 A6
600 TMBL 77375 3109 B1
Pine Tr
10 KATY 77493 3813 B4
3700 LPRT 77571 4382 E2
Pine Vw
- GlsC 77511 4751 E7
Pine Wy
10 CNRO 77304 2383 A6
Pine Acres Cir
25600 MtgC 77380 2968 B2
Pine Acres Rd
1800 MtgC 77384 2675 D4
Pine Alcove Ct
3200 HOUS 77345 3119 E2
Pineapple Dr
300 LMQU 77568 4874 B7
300 TXCY 77591 4874 B7
Pine Arbor Dr
5100 HarC 77066 3401 A3
5500 HarC 77066 3400 E3
Pine Arbor Tr
3200 HOUS 77345 3119 D2
Pine Arbor Wy
21500 HarC 77433 3251 A6
Pine Arrow Ct
- HarC 77389 2966 D2
7300 HarC 77346 3265 A4
Pineash Ct
10 WDLD 77381 2821 A5
1400 PRLD 77581 4504 D6
Pine Bank Ct
9600 HarC 77095 3538 A4
Pine Bank Dr
9600 HarC 77095 3538 A4
Pine Bark
2900 MtgC 77303 2239 E7
Pine Bark Ct
3700 PRLD 77581 4504 D6
22300 HarC 77377 3108 A1
Pine Bark Dr
6000 HOUS 77092 3682 B5
Pine Bark Ln
15800 HarC 77377 3108 B1
36800 MtgC 77354 2816 B1
36800 MtgC 77362 2816 C1
37300 MtgC 77354 2670 A6
N Pine Bark Ln
3700 CTSH 77303 2239 E7
3700 MtgC 77303 2239 E6
Pine Bay Dr
31100 MtgC 77386 2969 A1
Pine Bayou St
10800 HNCV 77024 3960 A1
Pine Belt Dr
11800 HarC 77429 3398 C3
Pine Bend Dr
1300 HOUS 77339 3119 B7
Pinebend Dr
2600 BzaC 77584 4501 A5
Pine Blossom Ct
2300 HOUS 77345 3120 A3
Pine Blossom Tr
4100 HOUS 77059 4380 B3
Pine Bluff Dr
400 LPRT 77571 4251 D7
500 FRDW 77546 4505 B5
19300 HarC 77377 3109 B7
Pine Bluff St
300 LPRT 77571 4251 E7
Pine Bough Ln
12600 HarC 77429 3397 D5
Pine Bower Cir
18800 HarC 77346 3265 A6
Pine Bower Ct
7100 HarC 77346 3265 A7
Pine Branch Dr
200 HarC 77388 3113 D7
3700 PRLD 77581 4504 D6
W Pine Branch Dr
1600 PRLD 77581 4504 D6
Pine Breeze Dr
900 FRDW 77546 4505 B4
4100 HOUS 77345 3119 E3

Pine Briar Cir
10 HOUS 77056 3960 E3
Pinebridge Ln
4100 HarC 77388 3112 C4
Pinebridge Park Ln
800 HarC 77373 2968 E7
Pine Brook Ct
2300 DRPK 77536 4109 E7
Pine Brook Dr
2300 DRPK 77536 4109 E7
12000 STAF 77477 4238 A6
12100 STAF 77477 4237 E6
Pinebrook Dr
21700 MtgC 77357 2827 C3
Pine Brook Ln
600 BYTN 77521 3972 E3
2400 SEBK 77586 4509 E2
Pinebrook Ln
4600 HOUS 77053 4372 C3
Pine Brook Tr
17500 HarC 77429 3252 C6
E Pine Brook Wy
3400 HOUS 77059 4380 D4
3400 PASD 77059 4380 C4
N Pine Brook Wy
4200 HOUS 77059 4380 C3
4400 PASD 77059 4380 C3
W Pine Brook Wy
3600 HOUS 77059 4380 C4
Pinebrook Bridge Ln
6500 HarC 77379 3111 C4
N Pine Brook Cove
4200 HOUS 77059 4380 D3
S Pine Brook Cove
4200 HOUS 77059 4380 D4
Pinebrook Hollow Ln
20700 HarC 77379 3111 C4
Pine Burr Ln
7400 HOUS 77040 3682 B3
7400 HOUS 77092 3682 B3
12200 MtgC 77362 2817 B7
Pine Bury Ln
100 WlrC 77493 3812 A7
Pinebury Ln
- FBnC 77450 4094 B3
Pine Bush Dr
12600 HarC 77070 3399 B5
Pine Candle Dr
3300 HarC 77388 3113 A6
Pine Canyon Dr
600 TMBL 77375 2964 D4
24300 MtgC 77380 2967 B3
26300 MtgC 77380 2821 B7
26300 MtgC 77381 2821 B7
26300 WDLD 77381 2821 B7
Pine Canyon Falls
24100 HarC 77375 2965 D4
Pine Castle Dr
16700 HarC 77095 3538 A3
Pine Center Dr
7700 HarC 77095 3538 C7
Pine Chase Dr
1300 HLSV 77055 3821 C6
1400 HOUS 77055 3821 C6
3500 PRLD 77581 4504 D6
Pinechester Dr
3400 HarC 77066 3401 D7
Pine Cliff Dr
4800 HarC 77084 3679 A6
Pine Cluster Ct
500 CNRO 77301 2384 E3
Pine Cluster Ln
19300 HarC 77346 3265 C5
Pine Colony Ln
1500 PRLD 77581 4504 D5
Pine Colony St
3300 BzaC 77511 4748 E1
Pine Cone Ct
22400 HarC 77377 3108 B1
Pine Cone Dr
1800 KATY 77493 3813 B6
2300 HOUS 77339 3119 A2
21800 HarC 77338 3260 C2
Pine Cone Ln
1000 FRDW 77546 4505 B4
11000 HarC 77041 3680 C4
15800 HarC 77377 3108 B1
Pinecone Ln
2700 PRLD 77581 4504 C4
4300 HarC 77388 3257 D3
Pine Cone Tr
3700 PASD 77505 4248 D4
Pinecone Wy
4300 HarC 77388 3257 D3
Pine Cone Ranch Rd
24700 HarC 77375 2965 E3
24700 HarC 77389 2965 E3
24700 HarC 77389 2966 A3
Pine Country Blvd
15800 HarC 77377 3108 A1
Pine Country Ln
- SGCH 77355 2961 E4
Pine Cove Dr
1000 HOUS 77339 3263 B2
6100 HOUS 77092 3682 B5
Pine Creek Ct
10 HOUS 77017 4246 C1
Pine Creek Dr
300 FRDW 77546 4629 E3
1500 PRLD 77581 4504 D6
5400 LPRT 77571 4250 B2
Pine Creek Ln
10 HLSV 77055 3821 B6
10 HOUS 77055 3821 B6
Pinecreek Pt
23900 HarC 77373 2968 E5
Pine Creek Rd
- HarC 77336 3121 D6
24500 WlrC 77447 2959 D2
Pine Creek Wy
15800 MtgC 77355 2816 A7
15800 SGCH 77355 2816 A7
Pinecreek Hollow Ln
17300 HarC 77095 3537 E6
Pine Creek Pass
1900 HarC 77449 3815 C6
Pinecreek Point Ct
900 HarC 77373 2968 D5
Pinecreek Ridge Ct
6000 HarC 77379 3111 E5
Pinecreek Ridge Ln
20200 HarC 77379 3111 E5
Pine Crescent Ct
10 HNCV 77024 3960 A2
Pine Crest Blvd
1800 ALVN 77511 4866 E3
Pine Crest Dr
10 HarC 77336 2975 E5

Pine Crest Dr
200 CNRO 77301 2384 D5
1500 PRLD 77581 4504 D6
7900 HarC 77338 3261 E3
Pinecrest Dr
1500 DKSN 77539 4753 D3
6400 HTCK 77563 4989 C4
8100 HarC 77389 2966 A2
8200 HarC 77389 2965 E2
12700 MtgC 77362 2963 A1
Pinecrest Ln
200 PNVL 77304 2237 A3
22800 MtgC 77365 2973 E5
Pinecrest St
1600 HOUS 77020 3964 C2
Pine Crest Tr
4100 HOUS 77059 4380 B3
Pine Croft Dr
2000 HarC 77396 3407 B2
Pinecroft Dr
1100 SGLD 77478 4237 A7
9200 SHEH 77381 2822 A3
9200 WDLD 77380 2822 A3
Pine Crossing Ct
700 HarC 77373 3113 E1
Pine Crossing Dr
27100 HarC 77373 3113 E1
Pine Cup Cir
8000 HarC 77346 3265 B5
Pine Cup Dr
7400 HarC 77346 3265 A5
Pine Cut
17300 HOUS 77032 3405 B3
Pineda Cir
21000 FBnC 77469 4234 A2
Pinedale Av
300 ARLA 77583 4623 B4
Pinedale Cir
- MtgC 77362 2963 B1
12700 MtgC 77362 2817 B7
Pinedale Ct
12900 MtgC 77362 2817 A7
Pinedale Ln
22500 MtgC 77365 2973 D4
Pinedale St
10 HOUS 77002 4102 E1
10 HOUS 77006 4102 E1
Pinedale Valley Dr
26000 FBnC 77494 4092 B5
Pinedell Dr
15600 HarC 77429 3253 B7
Pine Desert Ln
10800 HarC 77088 3543 C7
Pine Dust Ln
3100 HarC 77373 3114 E7
3100 HarC 77373 3115 A6
Pine Echo Dr
19500 HarC 77346 3265 C5
Pine Edge Dr
400 MtgC 77380 2968 A1
Pine Falls Dr
7800 HarC 77095 3538 D6
Pinefern Ln
- HarC 77379 3111 B5
Pine Field Ct
1200 PRLD 77581 4504 E6
Pinefield Ct
20200 HarC 77338 3262 A4
Pinefield Ln
2300 HOUS 77063 3959 D7
2300 PNPV 77063 3959 D7
20300 HarC 77338 3262 A3
Pine Flats Dr
9900 HarC 77095 3537 E3
9900 HarC 77095 3538 A3
Pine Forest Cir
10 HOUS 77056 3960 E3
10 HOUS 77056 3961 A3
Pine Forest Dr
200 HarC 77532 3411 A6
1300 PRLD 77581 4504 E6
10000 HOUS 77042 3958 E5
10000 HOUS 77042 3959 A5
23300 MtgC 77357 2974 A2
28800 MtgC 77355 2815 A4
Pine Forest Pl
3700 PRLD 77581 4504 E6
Pine Forest Rd
5600 HOUS 77056 3960 D3
5900 HOUS 77057 3960 C3
16100 HarC 77084 3817 C1
16100 HOUS 77084 3817 C1
Pine Forest St
2900 LMQU 77568 4989 D3
35200 MtgC 77362 2816 D5
35200 SGCH 77362 2816 D4
Pine Forest Green Blvd
3800 HarC 77084 3817 A1
Pine Forest Hollow Tr
3900 HarC 77084 3816 D1
Pine Fork Ct
1200 HOUS 77062 4379 E7
Pinefrost Ln
14200 HarC 77429 3254 A5
Pine Gap Dr
1400 HarC 77090 3258 A3
Pine Garden Dr
4800 HOUS 77345 3119 E6
4800 HOUS 77345 3120 A6
Pinegate Dr
- HOUS 77008 3822 D4
Pine Gate Ln
- HarC 77373 2968 D6
Pine Glen Ct
3700 PRLD 77581 4504 D6
Pine Glen Ln
12300 HarC 77065 3398 D6
12300 HarC 77429 3398 D6
Pine Green Dr
7500 HarC 77346 3265 B5
Pine Green Ln
7700 HarC 77346 3265 B5
Pine Green Tr
3800 HOUS 77059 4380 B4
Pine Green Wy
- HOUS 77059 4380 B4
Pine Grove Cir
10 HDWV 77024 3960 A1
10 HNCV 77024 3960 A1
Pine Grove Dr
1500 DKSN 77539 4753 D2
6900 HOUS 77092 3682 B5
7100 HOUS 77040 3682 A5
Pine Grove Ln
10 MtgC 77384 2675 A1
1500 PRLD 77581 4504 D5
Pine Gulch Ct
5600 HarC 77049 3828 D4

Pine Gully Blvd
2800 HOUS 77017 4105
Pine Gully Rd
500 SEBK 77586 4383
Pinehall Ln
12900 HarC 77044 3689
Pinehaven Dr
300 HOUS 77024 3961
Pinehaven Ln
20100 HarC 77379 3112
Pinehearth Ct
6800 HarC 77379 3111
Pine Heath Ln
- HarC 77396 3547
Pine Heather Ct
4500 PASD 77059 4380
Pine Hill Dr
200 CNRO 77301 2384
900 TMBL 77375 2964
Pinehill Dr
28800 SHEH 77381 2822
Pinehill Dr E
2000 PRLD 77581 4504
Pinehill Dr W
2000 PRLD 77581 4504
Pine Hill Ln
- FRDW 77598 4630
Pinehill Ln
10 HOUS 77019 3961
9000 HOUS 77041 3820
Pinehill Rd S
2700 PRLD 77581 4504
Pine Hill St
700 MtgC 77362 2816
E Pine Hill St
35300 MtgC 77362 2816
N Pine Hill St
600 MtgC 77362 2816
S Pine Hill St
600 MtgC 77362 2816
W Pine Hill St
35100 SGCH 77362 2816
35300 MtgC 77362 2816
Pine Hollow Dr
700 FRDW 77546 4629
900 FRDW 77546 4628
1800 MSCY 77489 4370
3500 PRLD 77581 4504
7500 HMBL 77396 3406
Pine Hollow Ln
- HarC 77336 3266
200 HOUS 77056 3961
Pineholly Ct
10 WDLD 77381 2820
Pinehook Ln
7000 HOUS 77016 3687
Pinehurst Cir
15300 MtgC 77384 2674
Pine Hurst Ct
1000 FRDW 77546 4505
Pinehurst Ct
- MSCY 77459 4369
10 JRSV 77065 3540
Pinehurst Dr
10 BzaC 77583 4624
10 MNVL 77583 4624
2100 LGCY 77573 4632
3600 PRLD 77581 4504
9600 BYTN 77521 3835
10100 BYTN 77520 3835
20100 HarC 77346 3265
Pinehurst Ln
10 MSCY 77459 4369
13700 MtgC 77354 2670
Pinehurst Lp
33100 MtgC 77355 2962
Pinehurst St
4700 PASD 77505 4248
6400 HOUS 77023 4104
Pinehurst Bend Dr
20000 HarC 77346 3265
Pinehurst Grove Ct
8500 HarC 77346 3265
Pinehurst Pl Dr
20000 HarC 77346 3265
Pinehurst Shadows Dr
7500 HarC 77346 3265
Pinehurst Trail Cir
8000 HarC 77346 3265
Pinehurst Trail Dr
19500 HarC 77346 3265
Pine Island Dr
6900 HarC 77050 3547
Pine Island Pl
10 WDLD 77382 2674
Pine Island Rd
- PNIS 77445 3099
- PRVW 77445 3099
- WlrC 77445 3099
E Pine Ivy Ln
- HarC 77375 2965
Pine Knoll Dr
11400 HOUS 77099 4238
12100 HOUS 77099 4237
Pine Knot Ct
1400 PRLD 77581 4504
Pineknot Rd
22900 HarC 77389 2966
Pine Knott
10 LbyC 77328 2537
10 MtgC 77372 2537
Pine Knott Rd
30900 MtgC 77354 2816
31000 MtgC 77354 2670
Pinelake
400 HOUS 77336 3266
Pine Lake Dr
2400 DRPK 77536 4109
3700 PRLD 77581 4504
9600 HOUS 77055 3820
Pine Lake Ln
8000 HarC 77521 3695
8000 HarC 77521 3834
Pine Lake Tr
2800 HarC 77068 3257
Pinelake Canyon Ct
5000 HarC 77084 3678
Pinelake Crossing Ct
20200 HarC 77379 3112
Pinelake Crossing Dr
5700 HarC 77379 3112
5800 HarC 77379 3111
Pinelakes Blvd
5700 HarC 77379 3111
5700 HarC 77388 3111
Pine Lakes Dr
6000 KATY 77493 3813

STREET
Block City ZIP Map# Grid

eland Dr
1400 PRLD 77581 4504 D6
10200 HNCV 77024 3960 C3
10200 HOUS 77024 3960 C3
neland Rd
8500 HarC 77044 3689 D1
ne Landing Dr
4400 MSCY 77459 4621 E2
10500 HarC 77088 3543 C7
10500 HarC 77088 3683 C1
nelands Park Ln
12100 HarC 77346 3408 B3
ne Laurel Ct
13100 HOUS 77082 4097 B1
ne Lawn Dr
3700 PRLD 77581 4504 D6
ne Lawn Ln
12100 HarC 77039 3546 E5
neleaf Dr
2700 SGLD 77479 4368 D7
3700 HarC 77068 3257 A5
nellas Pk
5800 HarC 77379 3111 E5
5800 HarC 77379 3112 A3
nellas Park Ct
20300 HarC 77379 3111 E5
ne Loch Dr
- HarC 77396 3407 C3
- HOUS 77396 3407 C3
neloch Dr
- HOUS 77062 4379 E7
- HOUS 77062 4380 A7
300 HOUS 77062 4506 E1
300 HOUS 77598 4506 E1
2500 HOUS 77059 4380 A6
ne Lock Ln
19100 HarC 77388 3112 C5
ne Lodge Dr
700 HarC 77090 3402 D1
ne Lodge Pl
10 WDLD 77382 2819 B1
ne Manor Ct
28100 ORDN 77385 2822 C4
ne Manor Dr
100 MtgC 77380 2822 B4
100 ORDN 77380 2822 B4
100 ORDN 77385 2822 B4
2100 HarC 77336 3267 A4
ne Manor Ln
3700 DKSN 77539 4753 C4
nemeade Ln
11700 HarC 77375 3109 E5
ne Meadow Ct
300 MSCY 77489 4370 D2
1400 PRLD 77581 4504 D6
ne Meadow Dr
- PRVW 77445 3099 E3
- WlrC 77445 3099 E3
800 MSCY 77489 4370 D2
5900 KATY 77493 3813 B6
12000 HOUS 77071 4239 C6
ne Meadow Ln
- MtgC 77372 2683 A5
- SPLD 77372 2683 A5
3600 HarC 77039 3546 A6
nemeadow Ln
14000 HarC 77377 3108 E2
ne Meadows Blvd
- BYTN 77520 3835 C3
- CmbC 77520 3835 C3
ne Meadows Cir
- PRVW 77445 3099 E3
ne Meadows Dr
- MtgC 77386 3116 A1
ne Meadows St
12700 TMBL 77375 3109 C3
ne Mill Ct
4000 PRLD 77584 4503 B5
nemill Rd
8600 HarC 77338 3262 A4
nemill Hollow Dr
- MtgC 77386 2969 D1
ne Mill Landing Ln
3600 FBnC 77494 4092 B2
ne Mill Ranch Dr
26400 FBnC 77494 4092 B2
ne Mills Dr
400 LGCY 77573 4632 E2
1300 FBnC 77469 4493 B4
2800 LGCY 77573 4633 A2
ne Mist Ln
300 CNRO 77304 2383 A6
22600 HarC 77373 3115 A7
22800 HarC 77373 3114 E6
nemont Dr
700 HOUS 77018 3684 A7
700 HOUS 77091 3684 A7
1000 HOUS 77018 3683 A7
1000 HOUS 77091 3683 A7
4700 HOUS 77092 3683 A7
5000 HOUS 77091 3682 D7
5000 HOUS 77092 3682 A7
7000 HOUS 77040 3682 B7
7700 HOUS 77040 3681 E7
Pinemont Dr
4300 HOUS 77041 3820 D1
4300 HOUS 77080 3820 D1
4400 HOUS 77041 3681 D7
4600 HOUS 77040 3681 D7
nemont Rd
11600 MtgC 77372 2537 C3
11600 SPLD 77372 2537 C3
nemont St
2100 BYTN 77520 3973 D6
inemont Pr
- HOUS 77092 3682 C7
inemoor Wy
16800 HOUS 77058 4507 E2
ine Moss Ct
1200 PRLD 77581 4504 E6
ine Moss Dr
10000 HOUS 77040 3682 B1
10300 HOUS 77040 3542 B7
ine Mountain Ct
4400 HarC 77084 3679 A7
ine Mountain Dr
15500 HarC 77084 3678 E7
ine Needle Dr
600 FRDW 77546 4629 A3
1800 KATY 77493 3813 B6
ineneedle Dr
400 PNPV 77024 3959 E3
ine Needle Ln
5800 PASD 77505 4248 D4
36800 MtgC 77354 2816 B1
37100 MtgC 77354 2670 B7
ineneedle Ln
2700 PRLD 77581 4504 C4

Pine Needle Pl
10 WDLD 77382 2673 C7
Pinenut Bay Ct
15400 HOUS 77059 4380 B5
Pine Oak
2800 HarC 77521 3834 D5
Pine Oak Cir
12200 DKSN 77539 4753 A6
Pine Oak Dr
200 HarC 77562 3831 E3
1500 CNRO 77304 2382 D4
12200 DKSN 77539 4753 A6
Pine Oak Ln
2900 HarC 77521 3834 D5
20800 HarC 77447 3106 A1
Pine Oak Rd
20800 HarC 77447 3106 A1
Pine Oaks Dr
25800 WlrC 77447 2813 B7
Pine Orchard Dr
- HarC 77066 3401 A5
N Pine Orchard Dr
1400 PRLD 77581 4504 D6
W Pine Orchard Dr
3600 PRLD 77581 4504 D6
Pine Park Dr
- HarC 77039 3546 D5
Pine Pass Ct
12000 HarC 77070 3399 C6
Pine Pass Dr
10300 HarC 77070 3399 B6
Pinepath Pl
10 WDLD 77381 2674 D6
N Pineplank Ct
10 WDLD 77381 2821 A5
S Pineplank Ct
10 WDLD 77381 2821 A5
Pine Point Ct
100 LGCY 77573 4630 E5
14900 HarC 77070 3398 B1
Pine Post Ct
18300 MtgC 77365 2972 A2
Pine Post Ln
23200 HarC 77373 3115 E6
Pine Prarie Ln
4800 HOUS 77345 3119 E2
Pine Rain Ct
20700 HarC 77449 3815 C3
Pine Reserve Dr
- HarC 77389 2966 D2
Pine Ridge Ct
500 FRDW 77546 4629 E3
Pineridge Dr
5000 SGLD 77479 4495 B4
10000 MtgC 77303 2238 E2
10000 MtgC 77303 2239 A2
22100 MtgC 77365 2972 E3
24000 WlrC 77447 2959 D3
Pine Ridge Ln
1500 PRLD 77581 4504 D5
3400 HOUS 77088 3683 A2
Pine Ridge Rd
34000 WlrC 77484 3100 C5
34400 PRVW 77484 3100 C5
Pineridge St
4600 HOUS 77009 3823 E6
Pine Ridge Terrace Rd
7600 HOUS 77081 4100 C6
Pine River Dr
1900 HOUS 77339 3118 D6
Pinerock Ln
12400 HOUS 77024 3959 A2
12500 HOUS 77024 3958 E2
13800 HOUS 77079 3958 A2
14000 HOUS 77079 3957 E2
Pine Rose Dr
31100 MtgC 77386 2969 A1
Pine Row St
5600 HarC 77049 3828 D4
Pine Run Ct
20000 HarC 77388 3112 E5
Pine Run Dr
3200 HarC 77388 3112 E5
Pinery Dr
- STAF 77477 4238 A7
- STAF 77477 4369 A1
Pinery Ridge Pl
10 WDLD 77382 2674 C5
Pines Rd
10 WDBR 77357 2828 C1
NW Pines St
- HarC 77014 3401 D1
Pine Sage Dr
- HarC 77389 2966 D2
Pinesage Dr
12900 HOUS 77045 4241 E6
Pine Sap Ct
1300 PRLD 77581 4504 D6
Pinesap Dr
800 HOUS 77079 3957 C2
S Pinesap Dr
6100 HOUS 77072 4097 D4
6100 HOUS 77082 4097 D4
Pinesbury Dr
3900 HarC 77084 3816 E2
Pineshade Ln
6000 HOUS 77008 3823 A7
6300 HOUS 77008 3822 E7
Pine Shadow Dr
100 TYLV 77586 4381 D7
100 TYLV 77586 4382 A7
100 TYLV 77586 4509 A1
Pine Shadow Ln
12200 MtgC 77362 2817 B7
23200 MtgC 77365 2973 B5
Pine Shadows
26000 WlrC 77447 2813 A6
Pine Shadows Cir
18500 MtgC 77302 2826 A2
Pine Shadows Dr
100 CNRO 77301 2384 A3
200 HOUS 77056 3960 E4
2400 FBnC 77479 4493 E2
4100 DKSN 77539 4754 D2
Pine Shadows Ln
7300 BYTN 77521 3835 A5
Pine Shadows St
2900 LMQU 77568 4989 D3
Pineshadows St
12800 MtgC 77362 2817 A7
Pine Shores Dr
8800 HarC 77346 3265 D5
Pine Song Pl
10 WDLD 77381 2674 B7
Pines Pl Dr
8400 HarC 77346 3265 C5
Pine Spring Ln
12600 HarC 77429 3398 B5

Pine Springs Ct
4900 CNRO 77304 2236 E7
Pine Springs Dr
10000 CNRO 77304 2236 D7
Pine Springs Rd
- HarC 77095 3538 E5
Pine Stone Ln
3500 FBnC 77494 4092 B1
Pine Straw Ct
10700 HarC 77088 3543 B7
Pine Stream Ct
9100 FBnC 77083 4236 D1
Pine Stream Dr
3600 PRLD 77581 4504 E6
Pine Stream Dr S
1300 PRLD 77581 4504 E6
Pineswept Dr
2800 PASD 77503 4108 A7
Pine Terrace Dr
- PRVW 77445 3099 E3
2300 HOUS 77339 3119 A5
Pinetex Dr
6900 HOUS 77396 3547 B1
7000 HOUS 77396 3406 C7
Pinetex St
20900 MtgC 77357 2828 A7
20900 MtgC 77357 2974 A1
Pine Thicket Ct
700 HarC 77373 3113 D2
Pine Thicket Ln
13100 HOUS 77085 4240 C7
13100 HOUS 77085 4371 C2
Pine Thistle Ct
17600 HarC 77379 3256 A3
Pine Thistle Ln
8200 HarC 77379 3256 A3
Pine Thorn Dr
16200 HarC 77095 3538 C4
Pine Timbers St
4300 HOUS 77041 3820 E1
4300 HOUS 77080 3820 E1
4400 HOUS 77041 3681 E7
Pine Top Ct
28600 MtgC 77355 2815 A5
Pinetop Ln
- MtgC 77386 2969 D6
Pinetop Glen Ln
6700 HarC 77379 3111 C4
Pinetown Bridge Ln
10300 FBnC 77478 4236 B4
Pine Trace Ct
18800 HarC 77346 3265 A7
Pine Trace Bend Dr
- HarC 77375 2965 B6
Pine Trace Crossing Dr
- HarC 77375 2965 B6
Pine Trail Ln
6300 HarC 77346 3264 E4
Pine Trails
1300 TMBL 77375 2963 E5
1300 TMBL 77375 2964 A5
25900 MtgC 77355 2814 B4
Pine Tree Ct
1400 PRLD 77581 4504 D6
Pine Tree Dr
- HOUS 77059 4249 A7
- PASD 77059 4249 A7
- PASD 77505 4249 A7
2100 HOUS 77093 3685 D3
3500 PRLD 77581 4504 D6
22200 HarC 77377 3108 B1
Pine Tree Gln
- HOUS 77049 3828 A2
Pine Tree Ln
10 BKHV 77024 3959 D4
10 PNPV 77024 3959 D4
19400 HarC 77484 3103 C6
22000 HarC 77447 3106 B2
Pine Vale Ln
13500 HarC 77037 3545 A7
Pine Valley Dr
2100 HOUS 77019 3962 B5
3500 PRLD 77581 4504 E6
Pine Valley Ln
8000 HarC 77379 3256 B4
Pine Valley St
4700 PASD 77505 4248 E6
Pine Valley Tr
15300 HarC 77433 3251 A6
Pine Valley Wy
- HarC 77433 3251 D5
Pine View Cir
300 ELGO 77586 4382 A7
Pine View Ct
3700 PRLD 77581 4504 D7
Pine View Dr
12200 HarC 77429 3398 C2
17600 MtgC 77302 2678 C7
17600 MtgC 77302 2824 C1
Pineview Dr
100 HOUS 77012 4105 B1
Pineview Rd
300 HarC 77562 3692 E7
Pineview St
10 LbyC 77372 2538 A6
Pineview Ter
- HarC 77493 3813 D4
- KATY 77493 3813 D4
Pine Village Dr
2500 HOUS 77080 3820 B3
Pineville Dr
3600 BYTN 77521 3973 E2
Pineville Ln
4200 HarC 77388 3112 C4
Pine Vista Ln
6500 HOUS 77092 3682 C5
Pine Walk Dr
1400 PRLD 77581 4504 D6
Pine Walk Ln
21200 HarC 77379 3111 D3
Pine Walk Tr
500 HarC 77388 3113 B6
Pine Warbler Ln
14700 HarC 77377 2963 C6
Pine Water Ln
20200 HarC 77375 3109 E5
Pineway Blvd
6000 HOUS 77023 4104 C5
Pinewest Ct
14000 HarC 77049 3828 B3
Pinewest Dr
14100 HarC 77049 3828 C3
Pinewick Ln
- HOUS 77041 3681 E7
Pinewilde Ct
21800 MtgC 77365 2972 A2
Pinewilde Dr
5100 HarC 77066 3401 A3

Pinewilde Dr
5500 HarC 77066 3400 E3
Pinewille Park Ln
18700 HarC 77377 3254 B2
Pine Willow Ct
200 FRDW 77546 4629 A1
Pine Wind Ct
7500 HarC 77346 3265 B4
7800 BYTN 77520 3835 C4
7800 CmbC 77520 3835 C4
Pine Wind Dr
19900 HarC 77346 3265 B4
Pinewold Cir
10 HOUS 77056 3961 A3
Pinewold Ct
10 HOUS 77056 3961 A3
Pinewold Dr
200 HOUS 77056 3961 A3
Pinewood Cir
10 HNCV 77024 3960 A3
Pinewood Ct
900 HarC 77530 3830 B6
1400 PRLD 77581 4504 D6
1800 SGLD 77478 4237 A6
6400 KATY 77493 3813 B4
10900 LPRT 77571 4250 D3
Pine Wood Dr
- MtgC 77385 2676 B7
- SHEH 77385 2676 B7
Pinewood Dr
- WlrC 77447 2813 E2
200 CHTW 77385 2822 D4
200 MtgC 77385 2822 C4
2700 LGCY 77573 4632 E1
4300 HOUS 77345 3119 D5
11900 MtgC 77365 2817 C7
15900 MtgC 77365 2825 A6
16500 MtgC 77302 2680 B5
25100 MtgC 77372 2682 E4
25100 PTVL 77372 2682 E4
W Pinewood Dr
23400 WlrC 77447 2813 D2
Pinewood Grn
17900 HarC 77084 3817 A1
Pinewood Ln
800 TYLV 77586 4381 E7
800 TYLV 77586 4508 E1
1200 PASD 77502 4106 E7
N Pinewood Ln
100 MtgC 77301 2385 D4
100 MtgC 77306 2385 D4
Pinewood Pk
8100 HarC 77346 3265 C6
Pinewood Pl
22300 HarC 77375 3110 D2
22300 HarC 77379 3110 E2
Pinewood St
- HarC 77530 3830 B5
100 CNRO 77304 2383 A7
Pinewood Ter
2600 KATY 77493 3813 D4
Pinewood Bluff Ln
19300 HarC 77346 3265 D6
Pinewood Canyon Ln
8200 HarC 77346 3265 C6
Pinewood Cove Dr
15700 HOUS 77062 4380 D7
Pinewood Crest Ln
8000 HarC 77346 3265 C5
Pinewood Ct Dr
1800 BYTN 77521 3972 C1
Pinewood Echo Ln
- HarC 77346 3265 D6
Pinewood Forest Ct
10 WDLD 77381 2821 A4
Pinewood Forest Dr
17400 HarC 77379 3256 D1
Pinewood Glen Dr
19000 HarC 77388 3112 E6
Pine Wood Hills Ct
5300 MtgC 77386 2971 A7
Pine Wood Hills Ln
- MtgC 77386 2971 A7
- MtgC 77386 3116 A1
Pine Wood Meadow Ln
4800 MtgC 77386 2970 E7
4800 MtgC 77386 3115 E1
5100 MtgC 77386 3116 A1
Pinewood Mist Ln
19200 HarC 77346 3265 C5
Pinewood Park Dr
1800 MSCY 77489 4370 B5
Pinewood Plaza Dr
1500 CNRO 77301 2384 E1
1500 CNRO 77303 2384 D1
Pinewood Point Ln
18900 HarC 77377 3253 E2
Pinewood Ridge Dr
400 MtgC 77386 2968 D2
Pine Woods St
12700 TMBL 77375 3109 B3
Pinewoods Wy
1800 MtgC 77386 2969 A3
Pinewood Springs Dr
5200 HarC 77066 3401 A3
5700 HarC 77066 3400 E3
Pinewood Trace Ln
- HarC 77377 3254 A3
6400 HarC 77041 3679 E4
Pinewood Valley Dr
23800 WlrC 77447 2813 C5
Pinewood Village Dr
13500 MtgC 77302 2824 B1
14700 MtgC 77302 2678 D7
Piney Ct
24600 HarC 77373 3114 D4
Piney Pt
- HarC 77357 2830 B6
Piney Bend Ct
18900 HarC 77375 3109 D7
25300 HarC 77389 2966 A2
Piney Bend Dr
11800 HarC 77375 3109 D7
Piney Birch Ct
5900 HOUS 77345 3120 D6
Piney Brook Dr
3200 LPRT 77571 4250 C3
Piney Corner St
28000 HarC 77484 3103 B4
Piney Creek Ln
4200 HarC 77388 3112 C4
Piney Forest Ct
19000 HarC 77084 3816 B3
Piney Forest Dr
2900 HarC 77084 3816 B3
Piney Height Ln
25200 HarC 77389 2966 A3

Piney Hill Ln
17300 HarC 77388 3257 D2
Piney Knoll Ct
6000 HarC 77449 3677 D4
Piney Lake Ct
2700 HarC 77038 3543 A5
Piney Lake Dr
19500 HarC 77388 3112 D6
Piney Links
16000 HarC 77068 3257 C4
Piney Manor Dr
- HarC 77389 2966 A2
Piney Meadow Ct
7000 HarC 77041 3679 C1
Piney Meadows Dr
4000 CNRO 77301 2385 C6
Piney Oaks Dr
13200 HarC 77065 3539 A2
Piney Pl Ct
19600 HarC 77094 3955 A3
N Piney Plains Cir
10 WDLD 77382 2674 D5
S Piney Plains Cir
10 WDLD 77382 2674 D5
Piney Point Cir
11300 PNPV 77024 3959 D5
Piney Point Dr
2400 DRPK 77536 4109 E7
3600 CNRO 77301 2385 B6
Piney Point Rd
200 PNPV 77024 3959 D5
600 HDWV 77024 3959 D5
900 SPVL 77024 3959 D1
S Piney Point Rd
- BKHV 77024 3959 D6
10 PNPV 77024 3959 D6
2000 PNPV 77063 3959 D6
2100 HOUS 77063 3959 D6
Piney Ridge Dr
700 FRDW 77546 4505 B5
Piney Run Ct
14000 HarC 77066 3401 E7
Piney Shore Ln
- HarC 77044 3408 D4
- HOUS 77044 3408 D4
Piney Shores Dr
8600 MtgC 77304 2236 A3
Piney Wood Dr
2100 DRPK 77536 4109 E7
Piney Wood Ln
27500 MtgC 77354 2819 C5
Piney Woods Ct
100 HOUS 77077 3956 D4
Piney Woods Dr
1200 FRDW 77546 4629 A4
2300 PRLD 77581 4504 E5
3700 HOUS 77018 3822 D2
Piney Wy Ct
12100 HarC 77375 3109 D7
Piney Wy Dr
18900 HarC 77375 3109 D6
Piney Wy Ln
11800 HarC 77375 3109 D7
Pinhole Ln Ct
11500 HarC 77066 3400 E5
Pin Hook Ct
2300 SEBK 77586 4509 C2
Pinion Ct
16300 HarC 77346 3408 A3
Pinion Creek Cir
17200 SGCH 77355 2961 C3
Pinion Creek Rd
26100 SGCH 77355 2961 C2
Pink Blossom Trl
- HarC 77433 3251 A4
Pink Granite Vly
20500 FBnC 77469 4234 C2
Pinky Wy
1700 GNPK 77015 3966 E4
1700 GNPK 77015 3967 A4
1700 HOUS 77015 3966 E4
Pinnacle Dr
1600 HOUS 77339 3118 B6
2600 LGCY 77573 4508 E7
Pinnacle Pl
13400 HarC 77069 3400 B3
Pinnacle Cove Ct
- LGCY 77573 4508 C6
Pinnacle Heights Ln
- HarC 77346 3408 C3
Pinnacle Point Dr
- WDLD 77382 2820 A1
Pinnacle Point Pl
28600 MtgC 77386 2970 A3
Pinnacle Run Dr
1200 HarC 77073 3259 B4
N Pin Oak
19700 MtgC 77357 2829 B5
S Pin Oak
20000 MtgC 77357 2829 B6
Pin Oak Cir
3600 MSCY 77459 4497 D7
Pin Oak Ct
3300 SGLD 77478 4368 E4
Pin Oak Dr
- CHTW 77385 2823 B3
100 BYTN 77520 3971 A1
100 HarC 77562 3831 E6
100 HarC 77562 3832 A6
300 HOUS 77336 3120 E4
400 BYTN 77520 3832 B7
400 HOUS 77336 3121 A4
700 FRDW 77546 4505 B4
900 DKSN 77539 4753 C2
900 DKSN 77573 4753 C2
900 GlsC 77539 4753 C2
900 LGCY 77573 4753 C2
1800 CNRO 77301 2384 E7
1800 CNRO 77301 2530 E1
3600 CNRO 77301 2385 B6
4900 PASD 77505 4248 D7
7500 HMBL 77396 3406 D2
10600 MtgC 77302 2677 A2
12100 MtgC 77354 2671 A4
18700 MtgC 77385 2823 B3
19500 MtgC 77365 2972 C2
23800 HarC 77389 2966 A5
26300 MtgC 77354 2817 E6
27900 MtgC 77372 2683 D3
31500 MtgC 77355 2668 C6
Pin Oak Dr E
3700 PRLD 77581 4504 C6
Pin Oak Dr N
3800 PRLD 77581 4504 B6
Pin Oak Dr S
3800 PRLD 77581 4504 B6
S Pin Oak Dr
10 TXCY 77591 4874 A6

Pin Oak Ln
100 MtgC 77354 2817 E6
4200 HarC 77389 3112 C1
4500 BLAR 77401 4101 B3
11000 MtgC 77306 2385 D3
Pin Oak Lp
19900 MtgC 77357 2828 C6
Pin Oak Pk
4700 BLAR 77081 4101 B2
4700 BLAR 77401 4101 B2
4700 HOUS 77081 4101 B2
4700 HOUS 77401 4101 B2
Pin Oak Pl
- HOUS 77081 4101 B2
6000 HarC 77379 3256 E1
Pin Oak Rd
10 LbyC 77327 2538 A1
10 LbyC 77328 2538 A1
10 WlrC 77445 3098 B7
400 KATY 77494 3952 C2
700 KATY 77493 3952 C1
1100 FBnC 77494 3952 C3
20400 HarC 77357 2975 E1
20400 MtgC 77357 2829 E7
Pin Oak St
400 ALVN 77511 4749 B7
400 ALVN 77511 4867 B1
Pin Oak Tr
200 WDBR 77357 2828 C2
25400 MtgC 77357 2974 E2
Pin Oak Bend Dr
18300 HarC 77433 3395 D6
Pin Oak Creek Ln
4500 HOUS 77345 3119 E2
4500 HOUS 77365 3119 E2
4800 HOUS 77345 3120 B2
Pin Oak Estates Ct
10 BLAR 77401 4101 C5
Pin Oak Estates Dr
10 BLAR 77401 4101 B4
Pin Oak Glen Ln
13400 HarC 77429 3254 A6
Pin Oak Loop Dr
13900 HarC 77532 3552 C7
Pin Oak Ridge St
15800 HarC 77073 3259 B5
Pin Oaks Rd
14800 MtgC 77384 2674 C3
14800 WDLD 77354 2674 C3
14800 WDLD 77384 2674 C3
Pinola Ct
2000 LGCY 77573 4631 A7
Pinole Ln
9400 HarC 77086 3542 B3
Pinole Forest Dr
6200 HarC 77088 3682 C1
Pinon Dr
4100 HOUS 77092 3822 A1
Pinon Vista Dr
16200 HarC 77095 3538 B3
Pinon Wood Ln
9600 HarC 77396 3548 B2
Pinosaltos Dr
11700 HarC 77377 3109 B7
Pinpoint Dr
2400 HarC 77373 3114 C5
Pinr
800 LPRT 77571 4111 C7
Pinridge Rd
- PRVW 77484 3100 D5
- WlrC 77484 3100 D5
Pin Rose Ln
37200 MtgC 77354 2670 B7
Pinson Dr
18000 HarC 77429 3396 B2
Pinsonfork Dr
1000 HarC 77379 3255 D2
Pintail Ct
24900 FBnC 77494 3952 C3
S Pintail Dr
10 LMQU 77568 4990 E6
Pintail St
3200 KATY 77493 3813 B3
N Pintail St
10 LMQU 77568 4990 E6
Pintail Park Ct
7900 HarC 77396 3406 D6
Pintan Ln
3700 HarC 77014 3401 D2
Pinto Cir
17900 HarC 77090 3258 A2
Pinto Ct
21200 TMBL 77375 3109 E3
Pinto Dr
9400 CNRO 77301 2385 C6
9400 MtgC 77301 2385 C6
Pinto Pass
- ALVN 77511 4867 A4
Pinto Ridge Dr
20100 HarC 77338 3261 D4
Pinto Springs Ln
600 HarC 77073 3403 C3
Pinwood Ct
37500 MtgC 77354 2670 D7
Pinwood Dr
15800 HOUS 77489 4371 C5
Pinyon Pl
11600 WDLD 77380 2967 E1
Pinyon Creek Ct
16300 HarC 77095 3538 B3
Pinyon Creek Dr
15700 HarC 77095 3538 C6
Pinyon Pike Dr
- WDLD 77381 2821 B5
Pioneer Ct
19700 HarC 77346 3264 D5
Pioneer Dr
1100 FBnC 77469 4365 E2
Pioneer Tr
4400 SGLD 77479 4496 A1
16800 MtgC 77302 2679 D2
Pioneer Bend Ct
20500 FBnC 77450 4094 C1
Pioneer Bend Ln
3300 FBnC 77450 4094 C1
Pioneer Oaks Dr
2400 MSCY 77545 4622 C2
Pioneer Pass
2900 SGLD 77479 4496 A1
Pioneer Ridge Ct
5700 FBnC 77479 4493 E1
Pioneer Ridge Dr
20100 HarC 77433 3676 E1
Pipe Creek Ln
7400 FBnC 77469 4094 D6
Piper Dr
8300 GLSN 77554 5221 E2

Piper Ln
900 CNRO 77301 2530 B2
Piper Rd
14600 PRLD 77581 4502 B4
14600 PRLD 77584 4502 B4
Piper St
- GLSN 77554 5221 E1
Piper Trc
10 WDLD 77381 2820 D3
S Piper Trc
10 WDLD 77381 2820 D3
Piper Glen Ln
- HarC 77450 3953 E5
- HarC 77494 3953 E5
E Piper Grove Dr
- HarC 77449 3816 B2
N Piper Grove Dr
19200 HarC 77449 3816 A2
S Piper Grove Dr
19200 HarC 77449 3816 A2
Piper Pointe Ln
19300 HarC 77375 3109 D6
Pipers Mdw
10 WDLD 77382 2674 C4
Pipers Wk
10 SGLD 77479 4495 C2
Pipers Gap Ct
14300 HarC 77090 3258 C7
E Pipers Green St
10 WDLD 77382 2674 C5
W Pipers Green St
10 WDLD 77382 2674 C5
Pipers Landing Ct
16100 MSCY 77071 4239 C7
Pipers View Dr
15600 HOUS 77598 4506 D4
16100 WEBS 77598 4506 E5
Piper Terrace Ln
22300 FBnC 77450 4093 E2
22300 FBnC 77450 4094 A2
Pipestem Dr
18500 HarC 77532 3409 E6
24400 MtgC 77355 2960 D1
24400 SGCH 77355 2960 C3
Pipestone Rd
40000 MtgC 77354 2673 A1
Pipestone St
9400 HOUS 77074 4239 B1
Pipestone Point Ct
17300 HarC 77346 3408 B4
Piping Plover Cove
600 TXCY 77590 4875 C2
Piping Rock Dr
400 HarC 77562 3831 E1
12400 HOUS 77077 3957 D7
Piping Rock Ln
3400 HOUS 77019 3961 D6
3400 HOUS 77027 3961 D6
5200 HOUS 77056 3960 E6
6100 HOUS 77057 3960 B6
7800 HOUS 77063 3960 A6
10000 HOUS 77042 3959 A7
10800 HOUS 77042 3958 C7
11300 HOUS 77077 3958 B7
13700 HOUS 77077 3956 D7
13700 HOUS 77077 3957 A7
Pipingwood Ct
5500 HarC 77084 3679 B5
Pipingwood Dr
- HarC 77084 3679 A6
Pipit Rd
19600 HarC 77447 3104 D4
Pirate Dr
12600 HarC 77377 3254 B5
Pirate Cove
21300 MtgC 77357 2827 B1
Pirates Al
4100 GLSN 77554 5332 E3
Pirates Dr
4000 GLSN 77554 5332 E3
Pirates Beach Blvd
13500 GLSN 77554 5332 E3
13500 GLSN 77554 5333 A2
Pirates Beach Cir
3000 GLSN 77554 5332 D2
Pirates Beach Ct
3900 GLSN 77554 5332 D2
Pirates Cove
1400 NSUB 77058 4508 A6
Pirates Gold Cir
2700 HarC 77546 4506 B7
Pirouette Ct
10 WDLD 77382 2819 A3
Pirtle St
800 LMQU 77568 4989 E1
Pirtlewood Cir
6400 HOUS 77088 3682 C2
Pisa Ct
1000 PRLD 77581 4504 E3
Pisces St
2700 FBnC 77469 4615 E2
2700 RSBG 77469 4615 E2
Pistol Ln
2900 HOUS 77094 4095 E2
Pistol Whipper
10 HarC 77044 3549 A4
Pitcairn Ln
17800 HarC 77447 3249 D2
Pitcarin Dr
16300 HarC 77377 3254 B6
Pitcataway Cir
1300 HarC 77379 3110 B6
Pitcataway Dr
10300 HarC 77379 3110 B7
Pitch
- HarC 77532 3551 E5
Pitch Field Dr
1300 HOUS 77074 4100 B6
Pitchford Rd
800 TMBL 77375 2964 D7
800 TMBL 77375 3109 D1
Pitching Wedge Ct
2100 HarC 77089 4504 E2
Pitch Pine Dr
16300 HarC 77070 3255 C5
Pitchstone Ct
19600 HarC 77377 3109 B7
Pitchstone Dr
19500 HarC 77377 3109 B7
Pitkin Rd
24900 MtgC 77386 2968 C3
Pitkin Iron Ct
1300 HOUS 77077 3956 D3
Pitner Rd
8500 HOUS 77080 3821 A1
8700 HOUS 77080 3820 E1
Pittman St
600 HOUS 77009 3824 A5

STREET Block City ZIP Map# Grid

Pitts Av
700 PASD 77506 4107 B3
W Pitts Av
100 PASD 77506 4107 A3
900 PASD 77506 4106 E3
Pitts Rd
100 FBnC 77469 4365 D4
3000 HarC 77493 3813 A5
3500 KATY 77493 3813 A5
Pittsburgh St
2600 HOUS 77030 4102 A4
2600 WUNP 77005 4102 A4
3100 WUNP 77005 4101 E4
3600 SSPL 77005 4101 E4
Pittsford Ct
1100 HarC 77450 3954 D3
Pittsford Dr
20200 HarC 77450 3954 D3
Pittswood Ln
- HarC 77016 3687 B1
7100 HOUS 77016 3687 B1
Pitzlin St
2800 HOUS 77023 4104 C4
Pixie Springs Ln
27500 MtgC 77386 2969 E7
Pizer St
600 HOUS 77009 3824 A6
900 HOUS 77009 3823 E6
Pizzito Ln
11100 HarC 77065 3539 C1
Pizzitola St
100 HOUS 77034 4378 D2
Plaag St
3600 HOUS 77093 3825 A1
4600 HOUS 77016 3825 C1
N Place Dr
15800 HarC 77073 3259 B6
Place Rebecca Ln
1900 HarC 77068 3257 E3
1900 HarC 77090 3257 E3
Place Vendome
7400 HarC 77379 3256 A1
Place Vendome Ct
17900 HarC 77379 3256 B1
Placid Dr
- MTBL 77520 3696 D2
Placid Pt
14700 HarC 77396 3547 D1
Placid St
4100 HOUS 77022 3824 A2
Placid Brook Ct
13800 HOUS 77059 4379 D5
E Placid Hill Cir
100 WDLD 77381 2821 A2
S Placid Hill Cir
10 WDLD 77381 2821 A2
W Placid Hill Cir
10 WDLD 77381 2821 A2
Placid Lake Dr
300 MAGA 77354 2669 B4
Placid Oak Ct
17800 HarC 77433 3537 D6
Placid Oak Tr
- HOUS 77345 3120 D6
Placid Point Ct
8100 HarC 77396 3547 D1
Placid Stream Ct
4100 PASD 77059 4380 D4
Placid Tralis Dr
17700 HarC 77377 3254 B3
Placid Woods Ct
13800 SGLD 77478 4237 A7
Plagens Ln
15800 HOUS 77489 4371 D6
Plago St
1600 LGCY 77573 4632 D5
Plainbrook St
11100 LPRT 77571 4110 D7
11600 LPRT 77571 4111 A7
Plainfield Rd
10500 HOUS 77031 4239 A4
Plainfield St
- HOUS 77074 4239 A2
9600 HOUS 77036 4239 A2
Plains River Dr
14600 HarC 77429 3396 B1
Plainview Dr
15500 WlrC 77484 3246 E7
Plainview St
3200 PASD 77504 4247 E3
5600 HOUS 77087 4104 D7
5700 HOUS 77087 4244 D1
Plainwood Dr
700 HOUS 77079 3957 A1
Plaistow Ct
17100 HarC 77084 3678 A4
N Planchard Cir
10 WDLD 77382 2673 A6
S Planchard Cir
10 WDLD 77382 2673 A7
Planchard Ct
10 WDLD 77382 2673 A7
Planetree Ct
6500 FBnC 77479 4367 B5
Plantain Dr
19100 HarC 77449 3816 B3
Plantain Ln
500 FBnC 77469 4493 D1
Plantation
- ELGO 77586 4509 A2
- TYLV 77586 4509 A2
Plantation Bnd
4100 DKSN 77539 4754 C2
Plantation Ct
2500 PRLD 77584 4501 A3
Plantation Dr
1000 FBnC 77469 4365 C2
1000 FBnC 77469 4366 A2
1100 DKSN 77539 4753 C3
1700 CNRO 77301 2383 D3
1900 FRDW 77546 4629 B6
2600 PRLD 77584 4501 A3
3300 FBnC 77469 4233 C7
8400 TXCY 77591 4873 A4
E Plantation Dr
500 MtgC 77302 2530 C7
3200 LPRT 77571 4249 E3
W Plantation Dr
3100 DRPK 77536 4249 E3
3100 LPRT 77536 4249 E3
3100 LPRT 77571 4249 E3
Plantation Hl
25000 MtgC 77365 3117 D1
Plantation Ln
2500 SGLD 77478 4368 E3
9900 STAF 77477 4369 E2
Plantation Mdw
- MtgC 77365 3117 D1
Plantation Mdws
20100 MtgC 77365 3117 D1
Plantation Mtn
20000 MtgC 77365 3117 D1
Plantation Pkwy
- PRVW 77445 3099 E2
Plantation Rd
10 HOUS 77024 3959 A5
100 BKHV 77024 3959 A4
Plantation St
900 LGCY 77573 4508 C5
1300 ALVN 77511 4749 A6
1300 BzaC 77511 4749 A6
Plantation Tr
2700 SGLD 77478 4369 B7
Plantation Vly
20500 MtgC 77365 3117 D1
Plantation Bay Dr
6100 HarC 77449 3677 B4
Plantation Bend Dr
- MSCY 77459 4369 B5
- MSCY 77478 4369 B5
1900 SGLD 77478 4369 A6
Plantation Bend Ln
19400 HarC 77449 3677 A5
Plantation Colony Ct
5000 SGLD 77478 4369 A7
Plantation Colony Dr
4500 MSCY 77459 4369 B6
4800 MSCY 77478 4369 B6
4800 SGLD 77478 4369 A7
Plantation Cove Ln
19300 HarC 77449 3677 A5
Plantation Creek Ct
2500 MSCY 77459 4369 B7
Plantation Creek Dr
- SGLD 77478 4369 B7
4400 MSCY 77459 4369 B7
20100 MtgC 77365 3117 D1
Plantation Crest Dr
5800 HarC 77449 3677 A5
Plantation Estates Av
24900 MtgC 77365 3117 C1
Plantation Estates Cir
24600 MtgC 77365 3117 C1
N Plantation Estates Dr
19700 MtgC 77365 3117 D1
S Plantation Estates Dr
19800 MtgC 77365 3117 D1
Plantation Estates Ln
24900 MtgC 77365 3117 D1
Plantation Forest Dr
5700 HarC 77449 3677 A5
Plantation Glen Pk
15300 HarC 77049 3829 A4
Plantation Grove Tr
19600 HarC 77449 3677 A5
19700 HarC 77449 3676 E5
Plantation Hills Dr
26600 HOUS 77336 3121 D4
26800 HarC 77336 3121 D4
Plantation Hollow Ct
2600 MSCY 77459 4496 C1
Plantation Lake Ct
24000 WlrC 77445 2954 D5
Plantation Lake Dr
23000 WlrC 77445 2954 C5
Plantation Lakes Dr
2800 MSCY 77459 4497 A4
Plantation Meadows Dr
900 FBnC 77469 4365 D4
Plantation Mill Pl
10000 FBnC 77459 4621 E6
Plantation Oak Dr
14700 HarC 77068 3257 D6
E Plantation Oaks Dr
5300 ARLA 77583 4622 C4
W Plantation Oaks Dr
5300 ARLA 77583 4622 C4
Plantation Orchard Ct
7300 FBnC 77469 4094 E2
Plantation Orchard Ln
19400 FBnC 77469 4094 E6
Plantation Pass Dr
4300 HarC 77346 3408 A1
Plantation Pines Ln
23500 HarC 77375 2965 B6
Plantation Point Dr
6200 HarC 77449 3677 A4
Plantation Ridge Dr
- MSCY 77459 4496 D1
Plantation Run Dr
4900 SGLD 77478 4369 A6
Plantation Settlement Ln
- MSCY 77459 4496 D1
Plantation Springs Dr
2500 FBnC 77469 4365 D1
Plantation Tree Ct
19600 HarC 77449 3677 A4
Plantation Valley Dr
- FBnC 77083 4236 E1
- HarC 77083 4237 A1
Plantation Wood Ln
2700 MSCY 77459 4497 A4
Planters Row
2300 SGLD 77478 4368 C6
Planters St
2300 SGLD 77479 4368 C7
2700 SGLD 77479 4495 D1
Planters Wy
2400 HarC 77546 4506 B7
Planters Heath Ln
- FBnC 77494 4092 A6
Planters House Ct
22800 HarC 77449 3814 D4
Planters House Ln
2600 HarC 77449 3814 D4
Planters Moon Ln
8500 FBnC 77469 4235 D1
Planters Path Ln
- FBnC 77469 4235 C1
Planters Point Ct
6000 FBnC 77479 4367 A6
Planters View Ln
2600 MSCY 77459 4497 A4
Plastics Av
700 HOUS 77020 3964 D4
Plateau Ct
2300 HOUS 77339 3118 C6
Plateau Lake Dr
26900 HarC 77339 3118 D5
Platinum Springs Dr
17000 HarC 77375 3255 B2
Plato Park Ln
4600 FBnC 77479 4493 D1
Plato Point Ln
2100 MtgC 77386 2969 D6
Plattsmouth Ln
16100 HarC 77429 3252 B6
Playa
- FRDW 77546 4630 A6
Playa Ct
11700 HOUS 77034 4378 E5
11700 HOUS 77598 4378 E5
Playa Dr
5100 PRLD 77584 4503 A5
Playa Lucia Ct
13700 HOUS 77044 3409 B4
Playa Vista Ln
- HarC 77041 3679 D4
Player Ct
700 MtgC 77302 2530 C6
Player St
13300 HOUS 77045 4241 C7
13400 HOUS 77045 4372 C1
Player Tr
10 WDLD 77382 2673 D7
Player Bend Dr
- WDLD 77382 2819 B1
10 WDLD 77382 2673 B7
Player Green Pl
10 WDLD 77382 2819 B1
Player Oaks Pl
10 WDLD 77382 2673 C6
Player Park Dr
19100 HarC 77346 3265 B6
Player Pines Ct
10 WDLD 77382 2673 B7
Player Point Dr
10 WDLD 77382 2673 B7
Player Pond Pl
- WDLD 77382 2819 B1
Players Pth
1800 HOUS 77339 3118 B7
Players Green Ct
- WDLD 77382 2673 B7
Players Luck Wy
10 WDLD 77382 2673 B7
Player Woods Dr
- WDLD 77382 2673 B7
- WDLD 77382 2819 B1
Plaza Blvd
1100 PASD 77506 4107 C4
SW Plaza Ct
10600 HOUS 77074 4238 E3
Plaza Dr
- HOUS 77050 3546 E7
- RSBG 77471 4492 A6
2200 SGLD 77479 4368 B6
11600 HOUS 77016 3546 E7
SW Plaza Dr
10400 HOUS 77074 4238 E3
10500 HOUS 77074 4239 A3
Plaza 290 Blvd
20000 HarC 77377 3106 A6
Plaza Cir Dr
20900 HarC 77532 3413 A1
21200 HarC 77532 3412 E1
Plaza Dale Dr
12900 HOUS 77045 4241 E6
Plaza del Sol Dr
7000 HarC 77083 4096 C5
Plaza del Sol Pk
200 HOUS 77020 3964 A3
Plaza Drive A
- HOUS 77027 4101 E1
- HOUS 77046 4101 E1
Plaza Drive B
- HOUS 77046 4101 E1
Plaza East Blvd
20100 HarC 77073 3403 B1
20300 HarC 77073 3259 B7
N Plaza East Blvd
1000 HarC 77073 3259 C7
Plaza Libre Dr
15200 FBnC 77083 4096 C6
Plaza Pines Dr
3100 HOUS 77345 3120 A4
Plaza Verde Dr
100 HOUS 77038 3544 A1
100 HOUS 77060 3544 A1
200 HarC 77038 3544 A1
Plaza West Blvd
1000 RSBG 77471 4490 C4
Pleak Rd
5500 PLEK 77469 4614 E7
5600 PLEK 77469 4615 A7
Pleak Crossing Rd
5700 FBnC 77469 4614 E7
5700 PLEK 77469 4614 E7
6800 PLEK 77461 4614 E7
Pleasant Av
100 HarC 77562 3831 E3
Pleasant Dr
1200 CNRO 77301 2384 B3
Pleasant Ln
- BzaC 77511 4748 D2
Pleasant St
800 BYTN 77520 3973 B6
Pleasant Tr
4600 FBnC 77545 4622 E2
Pleasant Wy
10000 BzaC 77511 4866 A5
Pleasant Bend Dr
10 WDLD 77382 2674 D4
Pleasant Bend Pl
10 WDLD 77382 2674 D4
Pleasant Bend Rd
4000 BzaC 77511 4866 A6
Pleasantbrook Dr
8700 HarC 77095 3539 B6
Pleasant Colony Dr
11000 JRSV 77065 3540 A6
Pleasant Cove Ct
3100 HOUS 77059 4379 E4
3100 HOUS 77059 4380 A4
Pleasant Creek Dr
2300 HOUS 77345 3120 A6
Pleasant Forest
28600 MtgC 77355 2815 D3
Pleasant Forest Bend Dr
21400 MtgC 77365 2973 A4
Pleasantglen Ct
17900 HarC 77379 3256 B1
Pleasant Green Cir
15800 HarC 77377 3254 C6
15800 HarC 77429 3254 C6
Pleasant Grove Dr
21800 MtgC 77365 2971 E1
Pleasant Grove Rd
12400 HarC 77429 3397 D5
Pleasant Knoll Ln
26100 HarC 77433 3396 B7
Pleasant Lily Ct
17200 HarC 77084 3678 A2
Pleasant Meadow Dr
7700 HarC 77379 3111 A7
Pleasant Meadows Rd
- BzaC 77511 4748 D2
Pleasant Oaks Ct
7000 FBnC 77469 4095 C5
Pleasant Oaks Dr
30500 MAGA 77355 2815 B1
30500 MtgC 77355 2815 B1
Pleasanton Dr
10500 HarC 77038 3543 C2
Pleasant Palm Cir
2100 LGCY 77573 4509 A6
Pleasant Plains Dr
4800 HarC 77546 4505 D6
Pleasant Praire Dr
- HarC 77450 3953 D4
- HarC 77494 3953 D4
Pleasant Ranch Ln
26500 FBnC 77494 4092 B2
Pleasant Ridge Dr
7400 HarC 77095 3678 D1
Pleasant Run Ct
3900 FBnC 77545 4622 E1
Pleasant Shade Ct
2200 FBnC 77469 4234 B7
Pleasant Shadows Dr
24900 HarC 77389 2966 B3
Pleasant Stream Dr
6500 HarC 77449 3676 C3
Pleasant Trace Ct
16900 PASD 77059 4380 E4
Pleasant Trace Dr
4400 PASD 77059 4380 E4
Pleasant Valley Dr
2100 LGCY 77573 4632 D1
3800 MSCY 77459 4496 E4
Pleasant Valley Rd
15200 HOUS 77062 4380 A7
15200 HOUS 77062 4507 B1
31700 MtgC 77354 2817 B1
Pleasant View Ln
11800 HarC 77532 3692 D2
Pleasantville Dr
900 HOUS 77029 3965 C3
Pleasantwood Dr
18000 HarC 77379 3256 B1
Pleasentbrook Dr
8700 HarC 77095 3539 B5
Pleasure Cove Dr
10 WDLD 77381 2821 C5
Plover Cir
7100 TXCY 77591 4873 C5
Plover Ct
15900 HarC 77396 3406 E6
Plover Dr
4300 SEBK 77586 4382 E7
Plover Ln
10 WDLD 77380 2822 B7
W Plum
11300 MtgC 77302 2677 C1
Plum Cir
- LGCY 77598 4630 C4
Plum Dr
4700 DKSN 77539 4754 A3
4900 HOUS 77087 4105 A6
Plum Rd
400 BzaC 77511 4628 C5
Plum St
- PRLD 77581 4503 A2
100 LMQU 77568 4990 C2
1000 CNRO 77301 2384 C6
E Plum St
3000 PRLD 77581 4503 E2
W Plum St
4800 PRLD 77581 4503 A2
Plumb St
2600 HOUS 77005 4102 A2
2600 WUNP 77005 4102 A2
3000 WUNP 77005 4101 E2
Plum Blossom Ct
10 WDLD 77381 2674 D6
Plum Blossom Pl
10 WDLD 77381 2674 D6
Plum Bough Ct
19100 HarC 77084 3816 B4
Plum Brook Dr
11700 HOUS 77099 4238 A3
11900 HOUS 77099 4237 E3
Plumbrook Dr
11400 HOUS 77099 4238 B3
12100 HOUS 77099 4237 E2
Plum Brook Ln
3300 MSCY 77459 4496 E3
Plumbwood Wy
1700 HOUS 77058 4507 D3
Plumcove Ct
10 WDLD 77381 2820 E1
Plum Creek Ct
17900 HarC 77429 3253 C2
Plum Creek Dr
7400 HOUS 77012 4105 B5
N Plum Creek Dr
1300 MtgC 77386 2968 E4
1300 MtgC 77386 2969 A4
S Plum Creek Dr
28900 MtgC 77386 2969 A4
Plum Creek Ln
1900 MSCY 77489 4370 C7
2900 HOUS 77087 4104 E5
2900 HOUS 77087 4105 A5
Plum Creek Forest Ln
4500 HOUS 77087 4105 A5
Plum Creek Meadow Ct
4500 HOUS 77087 4105 D7
Plum Creek Terrace Ln
7000 HOUS 77087 4105 A5
Plum Creek Trail Ln
6900 HOUS 77087 4104 E5
6900 HOUS 77087 4105 D7
Plum Crest Cir
- WDLD 77382 2673 D5
N Plum Crest Cir
10 WDLD 77382 2673 D5
S Plum Crest Cir
10 WDLD 77382 2673 D5
Plum Dale Wy
- HOUS 77034 4378 C3
Plumeria Av
4300 HarC 77521 3833 B3
Plumero Pl
- WDLD 77380 2821 D7
Plumero Meadow Dr
- FBnC 77494 4092 E3
Plume Tree Dr
19900 HarC 77338 3262 B5
Plum Falls Ct
900 HOUS 77062 4379 C6
Plum Falls Ln
1900 PRLD 77581 4502 E2
Plumfield Ln
2500 FBnC 77450 3953 E7
Plumfield Trace Ln
23500 HarC 77375 2965 B6
Plum Forest Rd
4400 HarC 77084 3677 C7
Plum Glen Ct
3600 HOUS 77059 4380 B5
Plum Grove Ct
100 HarC 77336 2830 C7
100 HarC 77357 2830 C7
Plum Grove Ln
2000 PRLD 77581 4502 D2
7000 HOUS 77088 3682 E3
7000 HOUS 77088 3683 A4
Plum Grove Rd
- PLMG 77327 2684 D5
100 LbyC 77327 2830 D2
100 PLMG 77327 2830 D3
26200 HarC 77336 2830 C7
26200 HarC 77357 2830 D2
Plum Hill Ln
3900 FBnC 77459 4622 B4
Plum Hollow Dr
3600 HOUS 77059 4380 D5
Plum Knoll Ct
3100 HarC 77084 3816 C4
Plum Lake Dr
- HarC 77095 3538 C5
2900 PRLD 77584 4500 C4
10600 HarC 77065 3539 D2
Plum Meadow Ln
- FBnC 77469 4615 D5
12700 HarC 77039 3546 A4
Plummer St
8000 HOUS 77029 3965 B5
9700 HOUS 77029 3966 A5
Plummers Lodge Ln
18500 HarC 77346 3265 D7
Plum Orchard Cir
15200 HarC 77049 3829 A4
Plum Park Dr
1300 HarC 77450 3954 B4
Plum Point Dr
11900 HOUS 77099 4238 A3
Plumpoint Dr
11700 HOUS 77099 4238 A3
12100 HOUS 77099 4237 E2
Plum Ridge Dr
9200 HarC 77064 3541 A5
9800 HarC 77064 3540 E5
Plum Springs Dr
14200 HarC 77429 3396 D2
Plum Square St
2200 FBnC 77545 4498 C7
Plumtex Dr
- HarC 77396 3406 C7
14800 HOUS 77396 3547 C1
14900 HOUS 77396 3406 C7
Plum Trails Ct
20100 HarC 77449 3815 C5
Plum Trails Ln
2800 HarC 77449 3815 C4
Plum Trails Rd
2800 HarC 77449 3815 C5
Plumtree Ln
4100 TYLV 77586 4381 D7
Plumtree Forest Cir
7600 HarC 77095 3538 B7
Plumtree Forest Ct
7500 HarC 77095 3538 D2
7500 HarC 77095 3678 B1
Plum Vale Ct
13200 HarC 77065 3539 B1
Plum Valley Dr
3500 HOUS 77339 3119 A4
3700 HOUS 77339 3118 E4
Plumwood Dr
1400 HarC 77014 3402 C3
12900 HarC 77429 3398 A1
13000 HarC 77429 3254 A7
Plunkett Dr
2100 DRPK 77536 4108 D6
2100 DRPK 77536 4248 E1
Plymouth Dr
4500 BzaC 77583 4745 C5
Plymouth Ln
- CNRO 77302 2530 D4
- MtgC 77302 2530 D4
Plymouth Lndg
3100 PRLD 77581 4503 D3
Plymouth St
300 HOUS 77022 3824 B2
300 LGCY 77573 4632 A3
1300 PASD 77502 4108 A6
1300 PASD 77506 4108 A6
Plymouth Wy
4600 MSCY 77459 4369 B5
Plymouth Colony Ct
17600 HarC 77598 4630 C1
Plymouth Colony Dr
2800 HarC 77598 4630 C1
Plymouth Pointe Ln
3200 MSCY 77459 4496 D5
Plymouth Ridge Ln
19600 HarC 77379 3112 A6
Plymouth Rock Ct
2500 HarC 77598 4506 C7
Plymouth Rock Dr
2600 HarC 77598 4506 C7
Plymouth Rock Ln
1300 SEBK 77586 4382 E7
Plympton Dr
- KATY 77494 3952 D3
24700 FBnC 77494 3952 D3
Pocahontas Dr
4100 HarC 77521 3833 B4
6200 PASD 77505 4248 A4
Pocahontas St
5100 BLAR 77401 4100 E6
Pocatello Dr
11900 HarC 77377 3109 B7
Pochyla Rd
- HOUS 77078 3687 E4
- HOUS 77078 3688 A4
Pocito Ct
19300 HarC 77346 3264 C5
Pocket Flower Ct
10 WDLD 77382 2674 D3
Poco Dr
1900 MSCY 77489 4370 B6
Poco Rd
9000 HOUS 77080 3820 D4
Poe Rd
3000 HOUS 77051 4243 A7
Poets Corner Ct
3900 FBnC 77459 4622 B4
Pohl Rd
30800 WlrC 77484 3247 A7
Poinciana Dr
2300 HOUS 77018 3822 B2
4900 HOUS 77092 3822 A2
5100 HOUS 77092 3821 E2
Poinsetta Ln
100 HarC 77562 3831 E1
Poinsettia
- HOUS 77045 4241 B7
E Point Dr
9200 HOUS 77054 4242 C2
S Point Dr
9200 HOUS 77054 4242 B2
9800 TXCY 77591 4872 E3
W Point St
5800 WUNP 77005 4101 C4
6700 SSPL 77025 4101 C4
Point Blank Dr
800 HarC 77038 3543 D3
Point Broad Oaks Dr
100 HOUS 77056 3960 E3
Point Clear Ct
2000 MSCY 77459 4497 C3
Point Clear Dr
200 PNVL 77304 2237 A3
500 FRDW 77546 4628 E6
3100 MSCY 77459 4497 B3
Point Clear Ln
6500 HarC 77069 3400 C3
Point Comfort Ct
2400 HarC 77598 4506 C7
Point Comfort Ln
17600 HarC 77598 4506 C7
Point Commerce Dr
- HMBL 77396 3406 D3
Point Cuero Ct
3900 FBnC 77494 4092 C2
Pointe Dr
2800 LGCY 77539 4752 E5
Pointe Ln
2600 MSCY 77459 4497 A1
N Pointe Pl
24800 FBnC 77494 3952 E4
N Pointe Bend Dr
12400 HarC 77377 3254 B1
Pointed Oak Ln
21100 HarC 77450 3954 C6
Pointe Leone
- LGCY 77573 4633 A5
Pointe Loma Dr
800 FBnC 77479 4367 B6
Pointe Park Dr
8700 HarC 77095 3538 E5
Pointer Rd
- HarC 77038 3543 A2
3100 HarC 77038 3542 E2
3100 HarC 77086 3542 D2
Pointer Ridge Ln
11600 HarC 77433 3396 A6
26100 FBnC 77494 4093 A2
N Pointe Terrace Dr
- HarC 77377 3254 A2
N Pointe Villages Dr
- HarC 77377 3109 A7
Pointe West Dr
4100 GLSN 77554 5548 A3
Point Hollow Ln
- HarC 77377 3254 A3
- HarC 77433 3537 A1
6500 FBnC 77469 4616 A3
Point La Salle Ln
1800 PASD 77503 4108 A7
Point Lookout Dr
18000 HOUS 77058 4507 E4
18000 NSUB 77058 4507 E4
18000 NSUB 77058 4508 A5
Point Northwest Blvd
15200 HarC 77095 3538 E5
15200 HarC 77095 3539 A5
Point Pendleton Dr
8200 HarC 77375 3110 D1
Point Royal Dr
200 FRDW 77546 4628 E6
Point Six Cir
8900 HarC 77095 3539 A5
N Point Terrace Dr
- HarC 77377 3254 B2
Point Village Ln
- HarC 77429 3254 A5
Pointwest Dr
5800 HOUS 77036 4099 B3
Poitiers Dr
7600 MSCY 77071 4239 E6
Polaris Blvd
31200 TMBL 77375 2963 E4
Polaris Creek Dr
25500 MtgC 77365 3117 E2
25500 MtgC 77365 3118 A2
Polarstone Ct
- HOUS 77044 3550 A1
Polished Stone Cir
8200 HarC 77095 3538 C6
Polk Av
1400 PASD 77506 4107 C4
Polk Ln
3600 DRPK 77536 4249 D1
Polk Rd
13000 GlsC 77510 4986 E5
Polk St
600 HOUS 77002 3963 E6
1500 HOUS 77003 3963 C5
3600 HOUS 77023 3963 E6
3800 HOUS 77003 3964 C7
5600 HOUS 77023 4104 D1
6500 HOUS 77011 4104 D1
6600 HOUS 77011 3964 D7
6600 HOUS 77023 3964 D7
E Polk St
300 LPRT 77571 4251 D2
W Polk St
100 LPRT 77571 4251 D2
1000 HOUS 77019 3962 D4
Polka Dot Rd
10700 HarC 77044 3691 D2
10700 HarC 77049 3691 D2
Pollard Dr
6400 MNVL 77578 4625 C6
Pollard St
900 HOUS 77020 3964 B2
Polley Ct
1800 FBnC 77469 4365 C3
Pollok Dr
3100 CNRO 77303 2238 B6
Pollux Ct
14100 TMBL 77375 2963 E4
Polly St
900 BYTN 77520 3972 D
5200 HOUS 77016 3686 D
Polly Creek Wy
20000 HarC 77450 3954 C
Polo
14700 HOUS 77085 4371 E
Polo St
14300 HOUS 77085 4371 E
Polo Meadow Dr
18100 HarC 77346 3409 B
18600 HarC 77346 3265 E
Polythane Ln
22000 HarC 77388 3113 B
22000 HarC 77389 3113 E
Pom Ct
10 SPVL 77055 3821 E
Pomander Rd
5200 HOUS 77021 4104 E
Pomegranate Ln
20200 HarC 77449 3815 C
Pomegranate Pass
4500 FBnC 77469 4233 C
Pomeran Dr
2500 HOUS 77080 3820 E
Pomerelle Pl
10 WDLD 77382 2819 A
Pomeroy Av
100 PASD 77506 4107 B
Pomeroy Grove Dr
24500 MtgC 77365 2972 E
Pomona Dr
2300 PASD 77506 4107 E
Pompano Av
100 GLSN 77550 4994 E
100 GLSN 77550 5109 E
Pompano Ln
11900 HOUS 77072 4098 A
12100 HOUS 77072 4097 E
Pompano Rd
2400 TXCY 77591 4872 E
Pompano St
400 BYUV 77563 4990 D
400 GlsC 77563 4990 D
Pompano Wy
16600 JMAB 77554 5331 D
Pompton Ct
4600 PRLD 77584 4503 A
Pompton Dr
11900 HOUS 77089 4378 C
Ponca River Ct
3400 PRLD 77581 4503 C
Ponce Dr
11200 HarC 77016 3547 D
Ponce St
4200 PASD 77504 4248 A
Ponce de Leon
16700 GLSN 77554 5331 E
16700 JMAB 77554 5331 E
Poncha Springs Dr
6900 HarC 77040 3681 B
Pond Cir
600 MtgC 77362 2816 D
600 SGCH 77362 2816 D
Pond St
- HOUS 77028 3826 C
200 HMBL 77338 3262 D
Pond Arbor Pth
19800 FBnC 77469 4234 D
Pond Brook Pl
2700 MSCY 77459 4497 A
Ponde Ln
20000 MtgC 77365 2972 D
Ponder Ln
12600 HarC 77039 3546 B
Ponderate Ct
11700 HarC 77065 3539 D
Ponder Chase Ct
6500 FBnC 77469 4093 D
Ponderosa Cir
14900 MtgC 77302 2677 A
Ponderosa Dr
3500 BYTN 77521 3972 A
3700 BYTN 77521 3971 E
5300 DKSN 77539 4754 A
7000 MtgC 77354 2673 A
12000 GlsC 77510 4871 A
12000 GlsC 77539 4871 A
23500 MtgC 77357 2974 A
Ponderosa Ln
9200 HOUS 77074 4239 B
9500 HOUS 77036 4239 A
Ponderosa Rd
5000 PLEK 77469 4614 E
Ponderosa St
33100 MtgC 77362 2817 B
Ponderosa Tr
100 CNRO 77301 2384 B
100 CNRO 77301 2530 B
Ponderosa Pine Pl
8500 HarC 77375 3110 D
Ponderosa Pine St
- CmbC 77520 3835 C
Ponderosa Pines Dr
17300 HarC 77090 3257 E
Ponderosa Timbers Dr
100 MtgC 77385 2677 A
S Ponds Dr
100 HarC 77598 4506 D
Pondwood Dr
11900 HarC 77429 3398 D
Poneal Ct
14200 HarC 77084 3679 A
Ponnel Ln
8200 HOUS 77088 3684 A
Ponsot Dr
- HOUS 77489 4371 D
Pontchartrain Ct
2200 LGCY 77573 4631 B
Pontchartrain Psg
8400 FBnC 77459 4621 B
Pontiac Dr
8200 HOUS 77081 4100 C
8200 HOUS 77096 4100 C
8900 HOUS 77096 4240 C
Pontius Dr
1800 HarC 77493 3814 A
Pony Cr
7400 FBnC 77459 4496 E
Pony Tr
11400 TMBL 77375 3109 E
Pony Express Rd
10000 HarC 77064 3540 B
Pool Creek Dr
8500 HarC 77095 3538 C
Poole Rd
- PRVW 77445 3100 E
- PRVW 77445 3101 A

STREET Block City ZIP Map# Grid
ole Rd
7100 HarC 77379 3256 C2
ole St
25300 PTVL 77372 2682 E7
ol Forge Ct
14800 FBnC 77478 4236 E4
oolview St
15400 MSCY 77071 4239 D7
opa St
- HOUS 77034 4379 A4
ope Frwy
- WlrC 77484 3245 E2
ope Rd
24200 WlrC 77445 2952 A1
ope Tr
12100 MtgC 77372 2535 A3
opes Creek Ln
13400 HarC 77044 3550 A2
opha Rd
- PTVL 77372 2682 E7
oplar Blf
9200 HarC 77095 3538 E4
oplar Cr
11700 HOUS 77077 3958 A7
oplar Ct
1400 PASD 77586 4381 E6
8200 CmbC 77520 3835 D3
oplar Dr
7000 GLSN 77551 5222 B1
oplar Isl
2900 FBnC 77459 4621 B6
oplar Pkwy
- FRDW 77598 4630 C2
Poplar Pl
3100 SGLD 77479 4495 C1
oplar St
- HOUS 77087 4105 B6
- HOUS 77087 4245 B1
- LGCY 77598 4630 C4
100 LMQU 77568 4990 C3
13900 STFE 77510 4870 C6
N Poplar St
100 TMBL 77375 2964 B7
S Poplar St
100 TMBL 77375 2964 B7
500 TMBL 77375 3109 B1
Poplar Canyon Ln
17400 FBnC 77469 4095 D5
Poplar Cove St
1500 LPRT 77571 4251 D5
Poplar Creek Dr
11800 HOUS 77077 3958 A6
Poplar Creek Ln
2800 BzaC 77584 4501 A1
Poplar Glen Ln
13100 HOUS 77082 4097 B1
Poplar Grove Dr
15300 HarC 77068 3257 B6
Poplar Hill Pl
10 WDLD 77381 2820 C5
Poplar Hill St
16800 HarC 77095 3538 A7
Poplar Park Dr
2100 HOUS 77339 3118 E4
2200 HOUS 77339 3119 A4
Poplar Pine Ct
10 WDLD 77385 2676 C4
Poplar Ridge Ln
8300 HarC 77338 3261 E4
8600 HarC 77338 3262 A3
Poplar Run Ct
3300 HOUS 77059 4380 B5
Poplar Springs Dr
3700 MSCY 77459 4621 E1
3700 MSCY 77545 4621 E1
Poplar Springs Ln
15200 HOUS 77062 4380 B7
Poplar Terrace Ln
5500 HarC 77449 3676 D5
Poplar Trails Ln
19200 HarC 77375 3109 D7
Poplar Valley Wy
2900 HOUS 77345 3119 E2
Poplarwood Ct
11400 HarC 77089 4378 B5
Poplarwood Dr
11500 HarC 77089 4378 B6
Pop Oman St
6300 KATY 77493 3813 B7
Poppets Ct
15800 HarC 77532 3552 B4
Poppets Wy
800 HarC 77532 3552 A4
Poppy Cir
4400 HarC 77521 3833 B3
Poppy St
- HOUS 77092 3682 B7
6900 HOUS 77040 3682 C7
Poppyfield Ct
100 HarC 77450 3953 E1
Poppyfield Dr
22500 HarC 77450 3953 D1
Poppy Grove Ln
19300 HarC 77433 3537 B7
Poppy Hills Ct
10 BzaC 77583 4624 C5
Poppy Trails Ln
17500 HarC 77084 3677 E2
18000 HarC 77449 3677 D2
Porcarello St
100 HOUS 77037 3684 E3
100 HOUS 77076 3684 E3
100 HOUS 77076 3685 A3
Porch St
10 GLSN 77554 5221 C2
Porchester Dr
- HarC 77450 3954 E4
Porch Swing
2700 HarC 77038 3543 B5
Porpoise Ct
16400 HarC 77532 3552 C2
Porsche Ct
- HarC 77073 3403 B1
Porsche Dr
500 HarC 77396 3406 E5
700 HarC 77396 3407 A5
Port Dr
100 GlsC 77539 4635 E4
Port Rd
- HarC 77507 4250 E7
- PASD 77507 4250 E7
- PASD 77507 4381 E1
- PASD 77507 4382 A2
11300 PASD 77586 4382 C4
Port St
100 HOUS 77020 3826 A7
300 HOUS 77020 3965 A1
STREET Block City ZIP Map# Grid
Port Aegean Dr
- HarC 77388 3112 B2
Portage Ln
500 FRDW 77546 4505 A7
Portage Rock Ln
5300 FBnC 77450 4094 B2
Portal Dr
5600 HOUS 77096 4240 B4
7600 HOUS 77071 4239 E4
7600 HOUS 77071 4240 A4
9200 HOUS 77031 4239 A4
Portales Pointe Ln
12700 HarC 77377 3254 A1
Port Alexander Wy
- HarC 77083 4097 A6
Port Angeles Dr
10000 HarC 77086 3542 C3
Porta Rosa Ln
1300 LGCY 77573 4633 A3
Port Barrow Dr
16000 HarC 77429 3397 B2
Port Bishop Ln
20300 FBnC 77469 4094 C6
Port Bridge Ln
2000 LGCY 77573 4631 C7
Port Carissa Dr
2600 HarC 77546 4506 B7
Portefino Ln
2700 LGCY 77573 4632 E3
Port Entrance
- HOUS 77012 4106 A2
Porter Ln
16000 MtgC 77365 2825 A5
17200 MtgC 77357 2825 A5
37200 PNIS 77445 3099 C3
Porter Rd
- HarC 77493 3814 D3
100 ARLA 77583 4623 A6
100 CNRO 77301 2384 D7
100 FBnC 77583 4622 E6
100 FBnC 77583 4623 A6
1800 CNRO 77301 2530 D1
3200 HarC 77449 3814 B3
4000 HarC 77493 3675 B5
10100 DRPK 77536 4110 A5
10100 LPRT 77536 4110 A5
10100 LPRT 77571 4110 A5
Porter Rd FM-1314
100 CNRO 77301 2384 D7
1800 CNRO 77301 2530 D1
Porter St
100 LMQU 77568 4873 E7
100 TXCY 77591 4873 E7
600 SEBK 77586 4509 E3
2600 HOUS 77026 3824 E5
3900 HOUS 77021 4103 D5
Porter Meadow Ln
12700 HarC 77014 3402 A3
Porter Ridge Dr
4800 HOUS 77053 4372 A6
Port Erroll Rd
9700 HarC 77095 3538 D3
Porterway Dr
6300 HarC 77084 3677 E3
Portfield Ct
26100 FBnC 77494 4092 E2
Portfield Ln
12500 HarC 77070 3399 D5
Portfino Plz
10 GlsC 77565 4509 D5
10 KMAH 77565 4509 D5
Port Gibson Dr
8300 FBnC 77469 4234 B5
Portglen Dr
1800 LGCY 77539 4633 E3
Porthcawl Ct
24700 FBnC 77494 3952 E3
Port Houston St
900 HOUS 77029 3965 C3
Portico Pt
10 WDLD 77380 2821 C5
Port Industrial Rd
2900 GLSN 77550 5109 A3
3100 GLSN 77550 5108 D3
3100 GLSN 77551 5108 D3
5200 GLSN 77554 5108 C4
Port Industrial Rd FM-275
2900 GLSN 77550 5109 A3
3100 GLSN 77550 5108 D3
3100 GLSN 77551 5108 D3
5200 GLSN 77554 5108 C4
Portland Ct
800 FBnC 77469 4365 E4
Portland Dr
2400 FBnC 77469 4365 E4
Portland St
10 HOUS 77002 4102 E1
10 HOUS 77004 4102 E1
100 HOUS 77006 4102 E1
Portlick Ct
19800 HarC 77449 3676 E3
Portlick Dr
6500 HarC 77449 3676 E3
Portman Rd
15400 MtgC 77306 2680 D4
Portman Glen Ln
3900 HarC 77047 4374 D4
Portmanshire Ln
16000 HarC 77084 3678 C5
Portman Terry Rd
16200 MtgC 77306 2680 D4
Portman Trail Ln
- FBnC 77469 4094 E2
Port Miramar Dr
8200 HarC 77375 3110 E1
Port Northwest
16200 HarC 77041 3680 C2
16200 HOUS 77041 3680 C2
Portobello Dr
13500 HarC 77083 4097 B6
Porto Bianco
2700 LGCY 77573 4632 E3
Port O Call St
1700 TKIS 77554 5106 A4
16100 HarC 77532 3552 B3
17400 HarC 77532 3411 B7
Portofino Ct
4000 MSCY 77459 4497 D5
Portofino Dr
23900 FBnC 77469 4093 A7
Portofino Rd
11900 HOUS 77082 4098 A3
Porto Rico Rd
9800 HOUS 77041 3681 A6
10200 HarC 77041 3681 A6
Port Pavillon Rd
600 HOUS 77020 3965 A5
STREET Block City ZIP Map# Grid
Portree Dr
12200 HarC 77067 3402 A6
Port Rose Ct
7400 HarC 77396 3547 C2
Port Rose Ln
2900 LGCY 77573 4633 A2
Port Royal Dr
1900 NSUB 77058 4508 A6
Portrush Ct
16900 FBnC 77494 3953 B3
Portside Ct
1400 LGCY 77573 4508 D4
Portside Dr
3700 HarC 77388 3112 D5
Portsmouth Dr
100 MtgC 77354 2817 D7
800 PRLD 77584 4501 C1
Portsmouth St
2200 HOUS 77098 4102 A1
3000 PASD 77506 4108 A4
3100 HOUS 77098 4101 E1
3400 PASD 77503 4108 B4
4000 HOUS 77027 4101 C1
4000 HOUS 77046 4101 C1
Portsoy Dr
28900 MtgC 77354 2818 B1
Portstown
22200 MtgC 77357 2973 D3
Port Trinidad Rd
3600 GLSN 77554 5440 D6
Portuguese Bend Ct
3800 MSCY 77459 4496 D4
Portuguese Bend Dr
6400 MSCY 77459 4496 D4
Portwall St
200 HOUS 77029 3826 C7
200 HOUS 77029 3965 C1
Portway Dr
900 HOUS 77024 3961 C1
Portwest Dr
- HOUS 77055 3961 B1
7000 HOUS 77024 3961 B1
Portwood St
100 HOUS 77011 3964 D6
Posey St
1200 HOUS 77009 3824 A5
Positano Ln
700 GLSN 77550 4995 B7
Positano Rd
700 GLSN 77550 4995 B7
700 GLSN 77550 5110 C1
Possum Tr
30500 MtgC 77354 2816 B2
Possum Creek Rd
2100 HOUS 77017 4246 C1
Possum Hollow Ln
11600 HarC 77065 3398 E7
11700 HarC 77065 3399 A7
Possum Kingdom Ln
15600 FBnC 77478 4236 B6
Possum Park Rd
- HarC 77338 3263 D7
200 HarC 77338 3407 D1
200 HarC 77396 3407 D1
300 HarC 77338 3408 A1
300 HarC 77346 3408 A1
Possum Park Rd S
400 HarC 77338 3263 C6
400 HOUS 77338 3263 C6
Possums Run Dr
17600 HarC 77396 3407 E2
Possum Trot
17900 MtgC 77302 2825 E2
Possum Trot St
1600 LMQU 77568 4989 E2
Possum wood Dr
15100 HarC 77084 3678 E2
Post Rd
100 ARLA 77583 4623 B3
100 FBnC 77583 4623 B3
Post St
500 HOUS 77022 3824 C2
Post Bridge Rd
7600 HarC 77389 2966 A2
Post Gate Dr
22700 HarC 77373 3115 E7
Posthorn Ln
400 HarC 77015 3829 B7
Post Meadow Dr
- HarC 77449 3677 B7
Post Oak
19200 MtgC 77355 2814 B1
Post Oak Blvd
500 HOUS 77027 3961 A5
700 HOUS 77056 3961 A5
3100 HOUS 77027 4101 A1
3100 HOUS 77056 4101 A1
S Post Oak Blvd
- ARLA 77583 4622 E3
- FBnC 77545 4622 E3
- FBnC 77545 4623 A2
Post Oak Cir
10 HOUS 77024 3961 A3
35000 MtgC 77355 2816 A4
36500 MtgC 77355 2815 E4
Post Oak Ct
- HOUS 77056 3961 A3
100 WlrC 77447 2813 A2
700 FRDW 77546 4505 B4
1800 CNRO 77301 2384 E7
6100 HarC 77379 3111 E7
6100 HarC 77379 3256 E1
12300 MtgC 77354 2671 A4
Post Oak Dr
100 BYTN 77520 3971 B1
100 CNRO 77301 2530 A1
300 CNRO 77301 2529 E1
10100 MtgC 77385 2822 E3
10100 MtgC 77385 2823 A2
26300 MtgC 77357 2829 B5
Post Oak Hl
200 HOUS 77056 3961 A4
Post Oak Hllw
17100 HarC 77379 3111 E7
Post Oak Ln
100 TXCY 77591 4874 A6
N Post Oak Ln
- HOUS 77024 3961 B3
S Post Oak Ln
100 HOUS 77056 3961 A6
Post Oak Pkwy
4300 HOUS 77027 3961 B6
N Post Oak Rd
- HOUS 77055 3961 B1
400 HOUS 77024 3961 B1
1000 HOUS 77055 3822 B7
1500 HOUS 77092 3822 B6
S Post Oak Rd
9700 HOUS 77096 4241 A2
STREET Block City ZIP Map# Grid
S Post Oak Rd
11400 HOUS 77035 4241 A6
12400 HOUS 77045 4241 A6
12500 HOUS 77085 4241 A6
13300 HOUS 77045 4372 A1
13300 HOUS 77085 4372 A3
14700 HOUS 77053 4372 A3
15900 HOUS 77053 4371 E7
16800 HOUS 77053 4498 E1
16900 FBnC 77053 4498 E1
Post Oak Run
27000 MtgC 77355 2815 C6
29100 MtgC 77355 2816 A4
Post Oak Forest Dr
100 MtgC 77354 2817 D7
Post Oak Glen Ln
13400 HarC 77429 3254 A6
Post Oak Hill Dr
20200 HarC 77388 3113 B5
Post Oak Manor Dr
5400 HOUS 77045 4372 A1
5400 HOUS 77085 4372 A1
5500 HOUS 77085 4371 E1
Post Oak Park Dr
1000 HOUS 77027 3961 B6
Post Oak Pl Dr
4500 HOUS 77027 3961 B5
Post Oak Timber Dr
4700 HOUS 77056 3961 A4
Post Oak View Ct
18200 HarC 77346 3409 B1
Postoffice
3600 GLSN 77550 5108 E3
Post Office St
200 GLSN 77550 5109 A3
Poston Rd
1200 DKSN 77539 4871 A1
1200 GlsC 77539 4871 A1
Post Ridge Dr
1900 CNRO 77304 2237 A4
Post Shadow Estate Ct
7000 HarC 77389 2966 B3
Post Shadow Estate Dr
24900 HarC 77389 2966 B3
Post Trailer Park Rd
- LPRT 77571 4110 D7
- LPRT 77571 4250 D1
Postvine Ct
10 WDLD 77381 2821 B4
Postwick Ct
7200 HarC 77095 3678 C1
Postwood Ct
4700 HarC 77388 3112 C7
Postwood Dr
3500 HarC 77388 3112 D7
Postwood Ln
900 BzaC 77584 4501 E1
Postwood Glen Ln
23200 HarC 77373 3115 D5
Postwood Green Ln
5400 HarC 77373 3115 D6
Postwood Oaks Dr
23100 HarC 77373 3115 E6
Postwood Park Ln
23100 HarC 77373 3115 D6
Postwood Point Dr
23100 HarC 77373 3115 D6
Pot Luck Farm Rd
- HarC 77375 2965 B3
Potomac Av
1300 PASD 77502 4246 D2
Potomac Dr
10 HOUS 77057 3960 C4
2500 LGCY 77573 4631 A7
Potter Ln
14700 HarC 77429 3396 D1
Potter Hollow Dr
23200 MtgC 77365 3118 A2
Potter Park Dr
14000 HarC 77429 3397 B2
Pottington Dr
8600 HarC 77083 4097 B7
Potts
1000 HarC 77338 3263 A3
1000 HMBL 77338 3263 A3
Potts Rd
1000 HarC 77338 3263 A3
1400 HOUS 77338 3263 A3
Poulson Dr
12100 HOUS 77031 4239 B5
Pound Rdg
- BKHV 77024 3959 C3
Poundbury Ct
900 HOUS 77047 4373 C3
Poundstone Ct
5500 FBnC 77479 4366 D6
Pouter Dr
7600 HarC 77083 4097 B6
Powder Horn Ln
5200 FBnC 77494 4093 A2
Powderhorn Ln
1800 HarC 77493 3814 C6
Powderhorn Pt
2800 FBnC 77469 4365 A1
Powderhorn St
10 BKHV 77024 3959 C3
12100 MtgC 77362 2963 B1
Powder Mill Dr
23300 HarC 77377 2963 B6
Powder Mist Ln
2000 HarC 77449 3815 D6
Powder River Dr
800 HarC 77450 3953 E3
Powell Dr
300 BzaC 77511 4628 C5
Powell Ln
12600 HOUS 77015 3967 A3
Powell Rd
200 HarC 77373 3114 A2
1100 LPRT 77571 4251 C6
Powell St
1000 RHMD 77469 4364 D7
Powell Wy
3400 FBnC 77459 4621 E5
Powell House Ln
22900 HarC 77449 3814 D4
Powell Ranch Rd
23000 MtgC 77447 2960 A7
Powell Springs Ct
2800 MSCY 77459 4497 E6
Powell Terrace Ln
- HarC 77346 3408 B4
Power Ct
300 SGLD 77478 4369 A1
Power Rd
8200 GlsC 77510 4987 A7
Power St
500 LGCY 77573 4632 B4
STREET Block City ZIP Map# Grid
Power St
8000 HOUS 77012 4105 C4
Powerline Rd
5100 FBnC 77469 4615 C5
7800 FBnC 77469 4616 A7
Powerpoint
- SGLD 77479 4369 A7
Powers Bend Wy
- MtgC 77354 2673 A7
10 WDLD 77382 2673 A7
Powerscourt Dr
19600 HarC 77346 3265 A5
20200 HarC 77346 3264 E5
Poydras Ct
13000 HarC 77429 3397 B4
Poydras St
900 SGLD 77478 4367 E1
Poynes Dr
9500 HarC 77065 3539 E4
Pozos Ln
9400 CNRO 77303 2238 D6
9400 MtgC 77303 2238 D6
Pradera Dr
16300 FBnC 77083 4096 A7
16400 FBnC 77083 4095 E7
Prade Ranch Ln
5800 FBnC 77469 4493 B6
15400 HarC 77429 3253 D6
Prado Ln
2400 FBnC 77469 4365 B4
13200 HarC 77070 3399 C4
Prado Woods St
12000 HarC 77070 3398 C2
12000 HarC 77429 3398 C2
Prague St
6200 HOUS 77007 3961 E2
Praire Bluff Dr
19000 HarC 77433 3537 B7
Praire Clover Ln
9700 HarC 77379 3110 C6
Praire Green Ct
21000 FBnC 77469 4234 A3
Praire Lake Ct
23000 FBnC 77469 4093 D6
Prairie Dr
8800 HarC 77064 3541 B5
Prairie Ln
100 RSBG 77471 4490 B5
26800 FBnC 77494 3952 A5
Prairie Pl
3000 SGLD 77479 4368 C7
Prairie Rd
700 HarC 77562 3832 A2
Prairie St
500 HOUS 77002 3963 D4
2300 HOUS 77003 3963 D5
2500 PASD 77503 4108 A6
2500 PASD 77506 4107 E6
2500 PASD 77506 4108 A6
4000 LMQU 77568 4989 B1
7300 HTCK 77563 4989 A2
7700 HTCK 77563 4988 E2
26500 HarC 77373 3114 A2
Prairie Vw
- GlsC 77511 4752 A7
3100 LGCY 77517 4752 C6
Prairie Bend Ct
18200 HarC 77433 3677 D1
Prairie Bird Dr
23200 HarC 77373 3114 D5
Prairie Bird Ln
22800 HarC 77373 3114 E7
22800 HarC 77373 3115 A6
Prairie Brook Ct
800 HOUS 77062 4506 D1
Prairie Creek Dr
1900 PRLD 77581 4504 C5
5100 HarC 77084 3679 A6
5200 HarC 77084 3678 E5
Prairie Dale Ct
9500 HOUS 77075 4246 C7
Prairie Dancer Dr
2400 FBnC 77494 3951 D5
Prairie Dawn Cir
10 WDLD 77385 2676 B3
W Prairie Dawn Cir
10 WDLD 77385 2676 C3
Prairie Dog Run
9600 FBnC 77478 4236 A2
Prairie Dunes Dr
6500 HarC 77069 3400 B1
Prairie Farm Ln
16000 HarC 77429 3253 A7
Prairie Fire Ln
7700 HarC 77433 3537 B7
7700 HarC 77433 3677 E1
Prairie Forest Tr
2100 HarC 77373 3114 E5
Prairie Grove Ln
1500 HOUS 77077 3958 A5
Prairie Hawk Dr
10900 HarC 77064 3540 B5
Prairie Hill Ct
2800 HOUS 77059 4379 E4
Prairie Knoll Ct
3000 HOUS 77059 4380 A4
Prairie Knoll Dr
10 GlsC 77510 4872 A5
Prairie Larkspur Dr
18500 HarC 77073 3403 B3
Prairie Lea St
16100 HarC 77429 3397 A5
Prairie Lily Ln
23200 FBnC 77494 4093 C4
Prairie Mark Ln
1600 HOUS 77077 3958 B5
Prairie Meadow Dr
4100 HarC 77449 3816 A1
4600 HarC 77449 3677 A7
Prairie Mist St
10000 HOUS 77088 3542 C7
Prairie Oak Dr
- HarC 77086 3542 A1
10 WDLD 77385 2676 D4
Prairie Oak Tr
7500 HarC 77346 3265 A3
Prairie Oaks
10 GlsC 77510 4872 A5
Prairie Oaks Dr
15300 FBnC 77083 4236 B1
Prairie Pebble Ct
23100 FBnC 77494 3953 D7
Prairie Pine Ln
- HarC 77377 3253 E3
Prairie Ridge Rd
4800 HOUS 77053 4372 A7
Prairie Rose Dr
15000 HarC 77070 3254 D7
STREET Block City ZIP Map# Grid
Prairie Sage Dr
8000 FBnC 77469 4234 B4
Prairie Shadows Wy
1600 PASD 77503 4108 B6
Prairie Spring Ln
21900 HarC 77379 3111 C1
Prairie Stone Tr
3100 HarC 77450 3954 D7
Prairie Trails Dr
9100 HarC 77379 3255 E5
Prairie View Dr
8200 HOUS 77088 3683 E2
Prairie Villa
- HarC 77450 3954 A4
Prairie Village Dr
6700 HarC 77449 3677 A2
7100 HarC 77433 3677 B1
Prairie Wild St
100 FRDW 77546 4505 A7
Prairie Wind Ln
8200 HarC 77040 3541 B7
Prairie Wind Rd
- PRVW 77445 3100 E1
- WlrC 77445 3100 E1
- WlrC 77445 3101 A1
Prairie Wing Pt
4600 HarC 77493 3813 A1
Praise Ct
5600 HOUS 77048 4375 B1
Prakway Hill Dr
- PASD 77503 4108 D5
Prakway Hollow Dr
- PASD 77503 4108 D4
Prakway Knoll Dr
- PASD 77503 4108 D5
Prakway Tree Ln
- PASD 77503 4108 D4
Prancer Dr
25600 HarC 77375 2965 D1
Prarie Pkwy
- KATY 77494 3952 E2
Prarie Rd
200 PRVW 77445 3100 A3
Pratt Park Ln
22800 FBnC 77450 4093 E1
Prattsford Ln
700 HarC 77090 3258 D4
Prattwood Ct
400 LGCY 77573 4631 A5
Preakness Ct
3000 FBnC 77469 4365 A2
Preakness Wy
12200 HOUS 77071 4239 E6
Preakness Palm Cir
18800 HarC 77346 3265 B6
Precinct Line Rd
- FBnC 77469 4093 D7
2400 FBnC 77469 4365 A1
4000 FBnC 77469 4234 A5
5000 FBnC 77469 4233 E1
Precious Pl
22700 HarC 77389 2967 A7
Precious Stone Ln
- FBnC 77494 4092 C5
Preece Ct
12100 HarC 77429 3397 E1
Pregeant Ln
5400 BzaC 77584 4626 C1
Prelude Ct
8600 HarC 77040 3681 C1
Premier St
5600 HOUS 77040 3681 C5
Premium Dr
17000 HarC 77447 3248 B3
Prentice Rd
2000 MtgC 77384 2675 D7
Prentiss Dr
6800 HOUS 77061 4244 E3
6800 HOUS 77061 4245 A4
Presa St
9300 HOUS 77078 3687 E6
Prescotie Dr
13400 HarC 77044 3689 C5
Prescott Dr
1000 CNRO 77301 2530 C2
Prescott Mnr
17200 HarC 77433 3251 B2
Prescott St
2800 HOUS 77025 4102 A6
3000 HOUS 77025 4101 D6
Prescott Green Cir
17800 HarC 77396 3407 D2
Prescott Run Ln
- FBnC 77494 4092 A5
Present St
100 MSCY 77489 4370 A4
100 STAF 77477 4370 A4
100 STAF 77489 4370 A3
Preserve Dr
- HarC 77389 2966 A2
Preserve Wy
- HarC 77375 2965 E2
- HarC 77389 2965 E2
- HarC 77389 2966 A2
Presidents Ct
4000 HarC 77047 4374 D6
Presidents Dr S
- HarC 77048 4374 D6
- HOUS 77048 4374 D6
4100 HarC 77047 4374 D6
Presidents Dr W
14500 HarC 77047 4374 D5
Presidio Dr
6100 HOUS 77053 4371 D6
Presidio St
1800 FRDW 77546 4629 A7
Presidio Canyon Dr
6200 FBnC 77450 4094 D4
Presidio Square Blvd
14500 HarC 77083 4096 D4
14500 HOUS 77083 4096 D4
Presley Dr
11000 MtgC 77354 2671 B1
Presley St
1900 HOUS 77093 3824 D2
Presley Wy
600 FBnC 77479 4366 C7
Press St
1300 HOUS 77020 3964 B2
Pressler Dr
1200 HOUS 77030 4102 D5
Pressler St
- HOUS 77030 4102 C5
Presswood Dr
10 PLMG 77327 2684 E7
400 MtgC 77386 2968 C1
Presswood Ln
26200 MtgC 77372 2683 B2
STREET Block City ZIP Map# Grid
Presswood Ln
26200 SPLD 77372 2683 B2
Presswood St
700 CNRO 77301 2385 B5
Prestige Row
12700 HarC 77065 3539 C3
Preston Av
3100 PASD 77502 4248 A6
3100 PASD 77503 4248 A6
3100 PASD 77504 4248 A6
3100 PASD 77505 4248 A6
26000 HarC 77373 3114 A2
Preston Ct
4400 SGLD 77479 4495 D3
Preston Dr
5900 TXCY 77591 4873 E7
8300 PRLD 77584 4501 E5
Preston Ln
300 LGCY 77573 4630 B7
Preston Rd
100 PASD 77503 4108 A4
100 PASD 77506 4108 A4
Preston St
- GLSN 77554 5221 B1
10 HOUS 77002 3963 C4
100 RHMD 77469 4364 E7
200 LMQU 77568 4873 D7
200 TXCY 77591 4873 D7
700 RHMD 77469 4491 D1
800 PASD 77503 4108 A7
800 PASD 77506 4108 A7
1200 PASD 77502 4108 A6
1900 FBnC 77469 4491 D1
1900 HOUS 77003 3963 D4
2000 FBnC 77469 4364 C7
2100 PASD 77502 4248 A2
2100 PASD 77503 4248 A2
2900 PASD 77504 4248 A3
2900 PASD 77505 4248 A3
3300 HOUS 77003 3964 A5
Preston St FM-3155
1700 RHMD 77469 4491 D1
N Preston St
300 HarC 77373 3114 A2
400 HarC 77373 3113 E2
Preston Field Ln
8700 HarC 77095 3537 E5
Preston Oaks Dr
26200 FBnC 77494 4092 B6
Preston Park Dr
14700 HarC 77095 3539 A6
14800 HarC 77095 3538 E6
Preston Springs Ct
8100 HarC 77095 3538 B2
Preston Springs Dr
17000 HarC 77095 3538 A6
Preston Trail Dr
6500 HarC 77069 3400 B1
Preston Trails Ln
4800 PASD 77505 4248 A6
Prestonwood Forest Dr
13200 HarC 77070 3399 D2
13200 HOUS 77070 3399 D3
Prestonwood Park Dr
- HarC 77070 3399 C2
Prestwick Ct
400 HOUS 77057 3960 D3
Prestwick Dr
2300 LGCY 77573 4508 D7
Prestwick Sq
3300 FBnC 77459 4621 C5
Prestwick St
7200 HOUS 77025 4101 C5
Prestwood Dr
6400 HOUS 77081 4100 B3
7700 HOUS 77036 4099 D3
Pretty Woods Ln
19800 MtgC 77355 2814 C2
Previn Ct
6000 HOUS 77088 3682 D1
Price Cir
3000 PRLD 77581 4504 B4
Price Ln
34800 SGCH 77362 2816 E4
35100 MtgC 77362 2816 E4
Price Rd
- HTCK 77563 4988 E6
Price St
10 BYTN 77520 3972 D7
7200 HOUS 77088 3683 D3
Price Grove Ln
16800 HarC 77095 3538 A3
Price Plaza Dr
- HarC 77449 3815 D7
- HOUS 77449 3815 D7
- HOUS 77449 3954 D1
- HOUS 77450 3954 D1
Pricewood Manor Ct
20900 HarC 77433 3251 A3
Prichard Ct
2700 MSCY 77459 4497 E5
Prichett Dr
8500 HOUS 77096 4100 E7
8800 HOUS 77096 4240 E1
Prickley Ash Wy
18500 BzaC 77584 4627 C4
Prides Crossing Dr
10 WDLD 77381 2820 D3
Prides Crossing Rd
2400 HarC 77067 3402 A4
Priest Dr
1500 HOUS 77093 3685 D5
Prillerman Trails Dr
10700 HOUS 77016 3687 A3
Prima St
8600 HarC 77083 4097 A6
Prima Vera Dr
- HOUS 77045 4372 C2
N Primavera Dr
1500 PRLD 77581 4504 D3
S Primavera Dr
1500 PRLD 77581 4504 D3
Primewest Pkwy
- HarC 77449 3815 B6
- HOUS 77449 3815 B6
Primo Pl
10500 HarC 77379 3110 B6
Prim Pine Ct
20200 HarC 77433 3251 C5
Primrose Ct
2300 FBnC 77469 4365 D4
Primrose Dr
2200 PASD 77502 4247 E2
2600 PASD 77502 4248 A2
2900 PASD 77503 4248 A2
Primrose Ln
300 LGCY 77573 4632 E2
500 LPRT 77571 4251 D7

STREET
Block City ZIP Map# Grid

Primrose Ln
1300 TYLV 77586 4382 A6
15100 GlsC 77517 4870 B4
30900 MtgC 77354 2670 B7
Primrose Pth
3800 DRPK 77536 4249 E1
Primrose Rd
7000 HarC 77521 3832 B5
Primrose St
- PRVW 77445 3100 C3
1300 CHTW 77385 2823 A4
5300 HOUS 77017 4106 C7
7500 BzaC 77584 4627 B4
Primrose Acres Ln
10800 HOUS 77031 4239 C4
Primrose Glen Ct
11500 FBnC 77478 4236 B5
Primrose Mark Ln
10200 HarC 77044 3689 B3
Primrose Meadow Ln
17600 HarC 77095 3537 E6
E Primrose Meadows Cir
900 BzaC 77584 4501 B1
S Primrose Meadows Cir
3300 BzaC 77584 4501 E1
W Primrose Meadows Cir
900 BzaC 77584 4501 B1
Primrose Trace Ln
3600 HarC 77389 3112 D1
Primula Ct
13500 HarC 77429 3397 D3
Primula Pth
- FBnC 77469 4234 D3
Prim Water Ct
2100 HOUS 77345 3120 B3
Primwood Ct
2200 BzaC 77584 4501 C4
Primwood Dr
11800 HarC 77070 3398 E1
Prince
- HarC 77049 3691 D2
10400 HarC 77044 3691 E2
Prince Dr
1500 ALVN 77511 4866 D3
Prince Ln
16600 MtgC 77306 2680 D5
16600 MtgC 77357 2680 D5
Prince St
1300 HOUS 77008 3823 B6
4500 BYTN 77521 3972 C1
Prince Creek Ct
1300 HarC 77450 3954 D3
Prince Creek Dr
20200 HarC 77450 3954 D3
Prince Edward Ct
20400 HMBL 77338 3262 C4
Prince George Ct
1700 HarC 77449 3814 E6
Prince George Dr
- FRDW 77546 4630 C3
2800 FRDW 77598 4630 C3
Prince George Ln
22200 HarC 77449 3814 E6
22200 HarC 77449 3815 A6
22600 HOUS 77449 3814 E6
Prince Jeffery Ln
2300 HarC 77493 3814 B5
Prince Lawrence Ct
23700 HarC 77493 3814 C5
Prince of Wales Dr
100 CNRO 77304 2529 D2
Prince Pine Ct
16900 HOUS 77059 4380 D4
Prince Pine Tr
4400 HOUS 77059 4380 C4
Princess Dr
- HOUS 77034 4246 E5
100 HOUS 77034 4247 A5
Princess Ln
2500 MSCY 77459 4370 B6
2500 MSCY 77459 4497 A1
Princess Bay Ct
3100 PRLD 77584 4501 D5
Princess Deanna Ln
2300 HarC 77493 3814 B5
Princess Garden Wy
11700 HOUS 77047 4373 D1
Princess Lake Dr
- HarC 77044 3549 A5
Princess River Dr
- HarC 77044 3549 A6
Princess Snow Cir
2200 HarC 77493 3814 C5
Princeton
7000 HOUS 77030 4102 D5
Princeton Dr
2500 BzaC 77584 4501 C5
5300 KATY 77493 3813 C5
Princeton Ln
1100 DRPK 77536 4249 C2
28400 MtgC 77354 2818 C3
Princeton Pl
2900 TXCY 77590 4874 D5
Princeton St
2400 HOUS 77009 3823 E4
3500 GLSN 77554 5221 E3
Princeton Park Ct
3800 PASD 77058 4380 E6
Princeton Pl Dr
8500 HarC 77375 2965 D3
8500 HarC 77389 2965 E3
Princeton Point Ct
3400 HarC 77047 4374 B4
Prince William Ln
18500 NSUB 77058 4508 A6
Prine Ln
8300 MtgC 77354 2818 E2
Prino St
6600 HTCK 77563 4989 A4
Prior Park Dr
11900 HOUS 77047 4373 D2
Priscilla Ct
300 HarC 77015 3828 C5
Prism Ln
- HOUS 77043 3819 E4
Prism Cove Pl
10 WDLD 77381 2821 B5
Pristine Dr
4300 FBnC 77545 4622 D1
Pristine Wy
1300 SGLD 77479 4367 C6
Pristine Lake Ln
13600 HarC 77429 3253 C6
Pristine Park Ct
5500 HarC 77041 3679 C6
Pristine Park Dr
13400 HarC 77041 3679 B6

Privada Saratoga Av
12000 HOUS 77037 3685 A2
12000 HOUS 77076 3685 A2
Privet Ln
13100 HarC 77429 3398 A1
Privet Green Wy
- HarC 77433 3251 B4
Proctor
400 FBnC 77545 4499 E1
Proctor Rd
15500 HarC 77530 3830 A5
Proctor St
11800 HarC 77038 3542 E5
Produce Row
3200 HOUS 77023 4104 B4
Professional Dr
22700 HOUS 77339 3117 E6
Professional Park Dr
- HarC 77598 4507 B5
10 WEBS 77598 4507 A5
Profet St
10 HOUS 77013 3827 C6
Progreso Dr
900 HarC 77038 3543 C3
Progress Ridge Wy
15300 HarC 77429 3252 A7
15300 HarC 77433 3252 A7
Prokop Ct
100 HOUS 77598 4506 D3
Promenade Blvd
- FBnC 77477 4369 C4
- STAF 77477 4369 C2
100 HarC 77450 3953 E2
100 HOUS 77450 3953 E1
N Promenade Blvd
13100 STAF 77477 4369 C1
Promenade Ln
6100 PRLD 77584 4502 D6
Proposed
- MtgC 77385 2676 D5
Prose Ct
22000 HarC 77389 3113 A1
Prosewood Ct
10 WDLD 77381 2821 E2
Prosewood Dr
10 WDLD 77381 2821 E3
Prospect
3400 HOUS 77004 4103 C3
Prospect Ln
- BLAR 77401 4100 D5
Prospect Pl
10 BLAR 77401 4100 C6
10 HOUS 77081 4100 C6
10 HOUS 77401 4100 C6
Prospect Pt
- WDLD 77385 2676 C4
Prospect St
1000 HOUS 77004 4102 E2
1000 HOUS 77006 4102 E1
1500 HOUS 77004 4103 A2
Prospect Glen Ln
2000 HarC 77449 3815 D6
Prospect Hill Dr
10200 HarC 77064 3540 B4
Prospect Meadows Dr
17400 HarC 77095 3537 D2
Prospect Point Dr
13800 HarC 77429 3397 C3
Prospect Ridge Ln
19100 HarC 77094 3955 B2
Prosper St
700 HOUS 77088 3684 A3
Prosperity Cir
5100 HOUS 77018 3683 C6
Prosperity Rd
- HOUS 77017 4246 A3
Prosperity Point Dr
11900 HOUS 77048 4244 A7
11900 HOUS 77048 4375 A1
Prosperity Ridge Dr
13900 HOUS 77048 4374 E5
Prosperity River Ct
12500 HOUS 77072 4097 D7
Prosper Ridge Dr
- HarC 77429 3397 C3
Prost Ct
3900 HOUS 77339 3119 A3
Proswimmer St
3100 HOUS 77088 3683 A1
N Provence Cir
10 WDLD 77382 2819 E1
S Provence Cir
10 WDLD 77382 2819 E1
Provence Ln
16500 HarC 77095 3538 B2
Provence Spur
23100 HarC 77447 3105 B6
Provence Sq
19000 HarC 77447 3105 B6
Providence Ct
10 MtgC 77385 2676 C6
Providence Dr
500 FRDW 77546 4505 C7
Providence Ln
3700 PASD 77505 4248 C4
Providence Pk
11700 BKHV 77024 3959 C5
11700 HOUS 77024 3959 C5
Providence St
1100 HOUS 77002 3963 D2
1100 HOUS 77020 3963 E2
4300 HOUS 77020 3964 C2
Providence Oak St
3000 HarC 77084 3816 A4
Providence Pine Tr
14200 HOUS 77062 4379 E7
Providence Point Dr
20500 HarC 77449 3676 E3
Providence Shore Wy
19500 HarC 77433 3677 B1
Providence View Ln
6400 HarC 77049 3829 B2
Provident Green Dr
6200 HarC 77449 3676 E3
Provident Oaks Ln
1300 HOUS 77077 3957 C4
Province Pl Dr
400 HarC 77450 3953 D2
Province Point Dr
12400 HarC 77015 3828 A7
Provincial Blvd
21800 HOUS 77450 3954 A1
21900 HarC 77450 3954 A1
22300 HarC 77450 3953 D2
23000 HOUS 77450 3953 D2
Provost Ln
- HarC 77084 3679 A5

Prudence Dr
- HOUS 77085 4372 A2
3200 HOUS 77045 4372 E1
3200 HOUS 77045 4373 A1
Prudential Cir
- SGLD 77478 4368 B4
Pruett
24000 HarC 77336 3267 A2
24100 HarC 77336 3266 E2
Pruett Ln
20400 MtgC 77372 2535 A5
N Pruett St
200 BYTN 77520 3972 E6
3000 BYTN 77521 3972 E4
S Pruett St
10 BYTN 77520 3972 E7
700 BYTN 77520 4112 E1
Pruitt Dr
7700 GLSN 77554 5107 D5
Pruitt Rd
100 MtgC 77380 2968 B3
1100 WDLD 77380 2968 B4
27000 HarC 77373 3113 E1
Prune St
100 LMQU 77568 4990 C2
Pryor Dr
15800 HOUS 77489 4371 B6
Pryor Rd
11500 MtgC 77354 2671 D3
Public Rd
5600 FBnC 77583 4623 C5
Puccini Villa Ln
- FBnC 77053 4498 D2
Puddle Duck Ct
2700 HarC 77396 3407 D3
Puebla Rd
- HOUS 77045 4372 C2
Pueblo Ct
- LGCY 77573 4632 A7
- LGCY 77573 4753 A1
Pueblo Dr
18400 MtgC 77365 2972 C6
29000 HarC 77484 3248 A1
Pueblo Ln
18400 MtgC 77365 2972 C6
Pueblo Rd
2700 PLEK 77471 4614 D5
Pueblo Run
13900 HarC 77429 3253 E5
Pueblo St
9700 BYTN 77521 3835 A5
Pueblo Tr
4500 BYTN 77521 3973 C2
Pueblo Run Dr
14000 HarC 77429 3253 E4
Puente Dr
6600 HarC 77083 4096 A5
Puerta Vallaea Dr
7600 HarC 77083 4097 B6
Puerta Vallarta Dr
7200 HarC 77083 4097 B6
Puerta Vista Ln
6800 HarC 77083 4097 B5
Puget Ln
19300 HarC 77388 3112 D6
Pugh Dr
1100 GNPK 77547 3966 B6
Pugh Ln
16300 MtgC 77306 2533 D2
Pulford Ct
19300 HarC 77094 3955 B3
Pulp Mill Ct
10500 FBnC 77478 4236 E4
Pultar Rd
400 FBnC 77469 4364 C4
400 RHMD 77469 4364 C6
Puma
18800 HarC 77532 3410 A6
Puma Dr
6500 HarC 77069 3400 B1
Pumice Pt
22100 HarC 77388 3113 B1
22100 HarC 77389 3113 B1
Punkin St
20700 MtgC 77357 2826 E7
20700 MtgC 77357 2827 B7
Puppy Ln
4900 HarC 77532 3554 B1
Purdue Ln
700 DRPK 77536 4249 C2
Purdue St
1200 PASD 77502 4108 A6
1200 PASD 77506 4108 A6
2100 PASD 77502 4248 A1
3000 HOUS 77005 4101 E2
3000 HOUS 77005 4102 A1
Purdue Park Ln
31000 MtgC 77386 2823 C7
31000 MtgC 77386 2969 C1
Purdy Ct
18500 HarC 77084 3816 C3
Puresa Abierta Ln
11200 HOUS 77048 4244 D6
Puritan Wy
9000 BzaC 77583 4745 D6
9000 IWCY 77583 4745 D5
Puritan Valley Dr
- HarC 77449 3676 D3
Purple Cornflower Tr
- FBnC 77494 4093 B7
Purple Finch
3100 FBnC 77459 4621 A5
Purple Horse Dr
2500 LGCY 77573 4632 E2
Purple Martin Pl
10 WDLD 77381 2674 B7
Purplemartin St
13800 HarC 77083 4237 A1
Purple Meadow Ln
3600 HOUS 77345 3119 C2
Purple Plum Ln
2100 HOUS 77062 4380 B7
Purpleridge Ct
16100 HOUS 77053 4372 B7
Purple Rose Ct
1300 HarC 77094 3955 B3
Purple Sage Rd
7200 HarC 77049 3828 C1
7600 HarC 77049 3689 C7
Purple Slate Pl
100 WDLD 77381 2674 B6
Purpletop Ct
10 WDLD 77381 2821 A6
Purslane Dr
3300 HarC 77449 3816 A3
Purswell Rd
1900 HOUS 77055 3821 E5

Purus Dr
19200 MtgC 77365 2971 D5
Purvis Ln
6800 HarC 77521 3834 B1
Purvis Rd
- WlrC 77484 3245 B7
Purvis St
100 MAGA 77355 2669 A6
Putnam Ct
24700 FBnC 77494 3952 D3
Putting Green Dr
19000 HarC 77346 3265 B6
PVT
- HarC 77070 3255 C6
Pweter Stone
- HarC 77014 3402 A4
Pyeatt Av
24000 HarC 77336 3267 A2
Pyeatt Ln
27200 ORDN 77385 2822 C4
S Pyeatt Ln
27000 ORDN 77385 2822 C4
Pyle Ln
- MtgC 77354 2673 C2
Pyramid Pl
- HOUS 77085 4371 D1
Pyramid Peak Dr
12900 HarC 77346 3408 E2
Pyron Wy
7000 HOUS 77036 4099 A5

Q

E Q St
- LPRT 77571 4251 E5
W Q St
- LPRT 77571 4251 D5
Quade Ln
- HOUS 77084 3818 A2
Quadrant Ct N
16600 HarC 77532 3551 E2
Quadrant Ct S
16500 HarC 77532 3551 E2
Quail
5900 HarC 77049 3828 A4
5900 HOUS 77049 3828 A4
Quail Cir
500 LGCY 77539 4753 A4
Quail Ln
18700 HarC 77377 2962 A7
Quail Run
21200 HarC 77073 3259 C1
Quail St
1500 HOUS 77017 4106 D7
29000 WlrC 77493 3812 A2
Quail Bend Dr
17000 HOUS 77489 4497 E1
Quail Briar Dr
16400 HOUS 77489 4370 E7
Quail Bridge Ln
- HOUS 77053 4371 E7
Quail Burg Ct
17000 HOUS 77489 4497 E1
Quail Burg Ln
8500 HOUS 77489 4497 D1
Quail Call Dr
16400 HOUS 77489 4370 E7
Quail Chase Dr
20500 HarC 77450 3954 D4
Quail Clutch
- HOUS 77489 4370 D7
Quail Cove Ln
5400 HOUS 77053 4371 E7
Quail Creek Ct
100 PNPV 77024 3959 D5
14600 HarC 77070 3398 D1
Quail Creek Dr
2700 MSCY 77459 4497 D2
11800 HarC 77070 3398 D1
12800 PRLD 77584 4500 A3
Quail Crest Ct
16800 HOUS 77489 4497 E1
Quail Crest Dr
- HOUS 77489 4371 A6
Quailcrest Dr
8300 HOUS 77489 4497 E1
8400 HOUS 77489 4370 D7
Quail Croft Dr
8500 HOUS 77489 4370 E7
Quail Dale Dr
16500 HOUS 77489 4370 D7
Quail Dove Ln
2700 LGCY 77573 4631 A7
Quail Echo Dr
16300 HOUS 77489 4370 E6
16300 MSCY 77489 4370 E6
Quail Farms Rd
14600 HarC 77377 3253 D3
14600 HarC 77429 3253 D3
Quail Feather Dr
8600 HOUS 77489 4370 D7
Quail Feathers Ct
1900 MSCY 77489 4370 C5
Quail Field Dr
7100 HarC 77095 3678 E1
7100 HarC 77095 3679 A2
Quail Forest Dr
13400 HarC 77429 3254 B7
13600 HarC 77429 3398 A1
Quailgate Dr
4800 HarC 77373 3115 C5
Quail Glen Dr
16900 HOUS 77489 4497 E2
Quail Green Ct
1900 MSCY 77489 4370 C5
Quail Grove Ln
1800 MSCY 77459 4497 C3
14700 HOUS 77079 3957 C4
Quail Gully Dr
16400 HOUS 77489 4370 D7
Quail Haven Dr
2300 HarC 77373 3114 C6
Quail Haven Rd
2600 HarC 77373 3114 D6
Quail Hawk Dr
2900 HarC 77014 3401 E3
Quail Hills Dr
8200 HOUS 77489 4370 E7
Quail Hollow Cir
3000 BYTN 77521 3972 B1
Quail Hollow Dr
2800 MSCY 77459 4497 D3
4600 BYTN 77521 3972 B2
Quail Hollow Ln
11500 BKHV 77024 3959 D4
11500 PNPV 77024 3959 D4
12100 MtgC 77362 2817 B7

Quail Hollow St
- WALR 77484 3101 D7
- WlrC 77484 3101 D7
Quail Hunt Ln
16300 HOUS 77489 4370 E7
Quail Meadow Ct
16400 HOUS 77489 4370 B7
Quail Meadow Dr
3400 MSCY 77459 4497 C2
6300 HOUS 77035 4240 A5
7500 HOUS 77071 4240 A6
7800 HOUS 77071 4239 D5
16500 HOUS 77489 4370 E7
Quailmont Dr
8600 HOUS 77489 4370 D7
Quail Nest Ct
16300 HOUS 77489 4370 E6
Quail Oak Dr
2800 HarC 77014 3401 E3
Quail Oak Park Ln
31200 MtgC 77386 2823 C7
Quail Park Dr
12900 HarC 77429 3254 B7
16300 HOUS 77489 4370 E7
16800 HOUS 77489 4497 E1
Quail Pl Ct
1600 MSCY 77489 4370 C5
Quail Pl Dr
1900 MSCY 77489 4370 C5
16300 HOUS 77489 4370 E6
Quail Point Ln
21300 MtgC 77365 2973 B2
21400 MtgC 77357 2973 B2
Quail Prairie Dr
16400 HOUS 77489 4370 E7
Quail Ridge Dr
8900 BzaC 77578 4747 C3
8900 MNVL 77578 4747 B2
Quail Ridge Ln
100 GlsC 77511 4751 E7
10500 FBnC 77478 4237 A4
Quail Rock Cir
15100 HarC 77095 3678 E2
Quail Rock Pt
10 WDLD 77381 2820 D1
Quail Run Cir
17900 MtgC 77302 2825 E2
17900 MtgC 77302 2826 A2
Quail Run Ct
8400 HOUS 77489 4370 E7
Quail Run Dr
2500 ALVN 77511 4866 D4
2500 BzaC 77511 4866 D4
2600 HMBL 77396 3406 D5
3900 PRLD 77584 4502 C7
4000 BzaC 77584 4502 C7
16400 HOUS 77489 4370 E7
16700 HOUS 77489 4497 E1
Quail Run Dr N
4700 BzaC 77511 4867 B7
Quail Run Dr S
- ALVN 77511 4867 B6
4700 BzaC 77511 4867 B7
Quail Shot Dr
8300 HOUS 77489 4370 E7
Quail Shute St
23000 HarC 77389 2967 B6
Quail Thicket Ln
17300 HOUS 77489 4497 E2
17300 MSCY 77545 4497 E2
Quail Trace Dr
1500 MSCY 77489 4370 D6
Quail Tree Ln
5300 HarC 77346 3264 C4
Quail Valley Dr
- MSCY 77459 4497 A1
Quail Valley East Dr
2000 MSCY 77459 4497 B1
2600 MSCY 77489 4497 B1
3100 MSCY 77489 4370 B7
Quail View Ct
16700 HOUS 77489 4370 E7
Quail View Dr
8300 HOUS 77489 4370 E7
Quail Village Dr
3500 MSCY 77459 4369 D7
5800 HOUS 77053 4371 D7
Quail Vista Dr
8600 HOUS 77489 4370 C7
8600 HOUS 77489 4497 D1
Quailwood Dr
10 BYTN 77521 3972 B1
Quailwood St
2600 HarC 77014 3401 E3
Quailynn Ct
16300 HOUS 77489 4371 A6
Quailynn Dr
16400 HOUS 77489 4370 E7
Quaker Ct
9400 BzaC 77583 4745 C6
Quaker Dr
200 FRDW 77546 4505 C7
700 FRDW 77546 4629 D1
2300 TXCY 77590 4875 A1
2500 TXCY 77590 4874 E1
Quaker Ln
14100 HarC 77396 3547 B2
Quaker St
1600 HOUS 77029 3965 D4
Quaker Bend Dr
900 FRDW 77546 4629 D1
Quaking Aspen Ln
14700 HarC 77377 2963 C5
14700 TMBL 77375 2963 C5
Quander Ln
11900 HarC 77067 3402 A5
Quannah
2700 HOUS 77026 3824 E6
Quarles Al
1200 GlsC 77650 4878 E6
Quarles Av
1200 GlsC 77650 4878 E6
Quarry Hill Rd
2600 SGLD 77478 4368 D6
Quarry Lakes Ln
- FBnC 77469 4094 E7
- FBnC 77469 4095 A7
Quarry Path Wy
- HarC 77449 3814 C3
Quarry Ridge Rd
5400 FBnC 77469 4234 C2
Quarryvale Dr
18000 HarC 77429 3253 D2
Quarter Wy
15800 HarC 77532 3552 A4
Quarterpath Ct
1300 FBnC 77469 4365 E2

Quarterpath Dr
1600 FBnC 77469 4365 E2
Quartz Lake Dr
12600 HarC 77346 3408 D2
Quast Dr
- MtgC 77355 2961 A7
Quayside Dr
100 TKIS 77554 5106 C4
Quebec
4900 HOUS 77057 3960 D5
Quebec Blvd
4900 FBnC 77469 4491 B2
Quebec Cir
- FBnC 77469 4491 C2
Quebec Dr
8300 HOUS 77096 4100 C7
9000 HOUS 77096 4240 C1
Queen Rd
100 CRLS 77565 4509 C5
Queen St
7700 HOUS 77028 3826 B2
Queen Anne's Rd
800 HOUS 77024 3960 C1
800 SPVL 77024 3960 C1
Queenbridge Dr
9700 FBnC 77478 4236 E2
Queenbury Hills Dr
22200 HarC 77073 3259 A3
Queen Mary Ct
10 SGLD 77479 4495 C2
Queens Ct
10 CNRO 77304 2529 D1
100 BYTN 77520 3971 B4
100 STAF 77477 4370 A3
Queens Ln
10 FRDW 77546 4629 C1
1500 ALVN 77511 4866 D3
Queens Rd
- HOUS 77502 4246 D1
- PASD 77017 4246 E1
100 PASD 77502 4247 A1
700 PASD 77502 4246 D1
1900 HOUS 77017 4246 D1
Queens St
- HOUS 77017 4246 D1
Queens Bay Dr
1400 FBnC 77494 3953 B4
Queensburg Ct
3200 FRDW 77598 4630 B3
Queensburg Ln
3200 FRDW 77598 4630 B4
Queensbury Ct
3500 HarC 77336 3121 D3
5000 SGLD 77479 4495 A3
Queensbury Ln
12400 HOUS 77024 3959 A2
12700 HOUS 77024 3958 D1
13300 HOUS 77079 3958 B2
14000 HOUS 77079 3957 E2
N Queenscliff Cir
10 WDLD 77382 2819 B1
S Queenscliff Cir
100 WDLD 77382 2819 B2
Queenscliff Ct
100 WDLD 77382 2819 A4
Queensclub Dr
6500 HarC 77069 3400 A1
Queenscross Ln
1400 HarC 77073 3259 D5
Queensdale Dr
16100 HarC 77082 4096 A3
Queensfield Ct
24600 FBnC 77494 3953 B7
Queensford Ln
- HarC 77084 3678 A7
Queens Garden Ct
12500 HarC 77044 3549 A5
Queensgate Dr
5800 HarC 77066 3400 D2
Queenslake Dr
17200 HarC 77429 3396 C2
Queensland St
6600 HOUS 77028 3826 D2
Queensland Wy
13400 HarC 77083 4237 B1
Queensloch Dr
5700 HOUS 77096 4240 C2
Queensmill Ct
700 HOUS 77079 3956 E2
Queens Oak Ct
20000 HarC 77379 3110 C5
Queens Retreat Dr
4300 HarC 77066 3401 B2
Queensride Ln
13300 HarC 77070 3399 B3
Queens River Dr
12100 HarC 77044 3548 E6
Queenston Blvd
- HarC 77084 3678 A1
- HarC 77095 3396 E6
- HarC 77095 3397 A7
- HarC 77433 3396 E6
4000 HarC 77084 3817 A1
6700 HarC 77095 3678 A3
7400 HarC 77095 3538 A1
Queenstown Rd
300 HarC 77015 3828 E6
Queens View Dr
2700 ALVN 77511 4866 D3
Queenswood Ct
6300 HOUS 77008 3822 E7
Queenswood Ln
6100 HOUS 77008 3823 A7
6200 HOUS 77008 3822 D7
Queenswood St
4200 BYTN 77521 3973 E2
4400 BYTN 77521 3974 A2
Queens Wy Cir
12300 HarC 77044 3548 E5
Queen Victoria St
2900 PRLD 77581 4503 E3
Que Manor Dr
2000 HarC 77090 3258 B6
Quenby St
2100 HOUS 77005 4102 B2
2600 WUNP 77005 4102 A2
3000 WUNP 77005 4101 E2
Quennell Cir
15500 HarC 77032 3404 B6
Quentin Canyon Ct
6200 FBnC 77450 4094 D4
Quention Dr
- HOUS 77045 4241 D7
- HOUS 77045 4372 D1
Quercus Cir
9200 HOUS 77075 4377 B2
Querida Ct
12600 HOUS 77045 4241 B6

Que Sabe
3700 GLSN 77554 5440
Quest Brook Ln
22800 MtgC 77339 3118 C
Quetzal Ln
13500 HarC 77083 4097 E
Quicksilver Ct
11700 HarC 77067 3401 E
Quick Stream Pl
10 WDLD 77381 2820 D
Quiet Ln
- HarC 77050 3547 B
11400 HarC 77016 3547 B
11400 HOUS 77016 3547 B
Quiet Wy
28400 MtgC 77355 2815 C
Quiet Arbor Ln
- BzaC 77581 4502 B
Quiet Bay Ct
15700 HarC 77095 3678 D
Quiet Bay St
2300 PRLD 77584 4500 D
Quiet Bend Dr
2700 MSCY 77489 4497 B
Quiet Bluff Ln
14200 HOUS 77077 3956 E6
Quiet Brook Dr
19300 HarC 77084 3816 A6
Quiet Brook Ln
- FBnC 77469 4365 B6
Quiet Canyon Ct
16200 HarC 77546 4505 E6
Quiet Canyon Dr
4700 HarC 77546 4506 A6
4800 HarC 77546 4505 E6
Quiet Chase Ln
- HarC 77377 3254 A3
Quiet Country Ct
1800 HOUS 77345 3120 C6
Quiet Covey Ct
17200 HOUS 77489 4497 E2
Quiet Creek Ct
3000 SGLD 77479 4495 A2
Quiet Creek Dr
15300 HarC 77095 3538 E6
Quiet Dawn Ct
17600 HarC 77095 3537 D6
Quiet Falls Ct
5000 FBnC 77450 4093 E3
Quiet Falls Dr
3700 BzaC 77578 4501 A7
3700 BzaC 77578 4625 A1
Quiet Falls Ln
- LGCY 77573 4630 E7
Quiet Forest
36100 MtgC 77355 2815 E7
Quiet Forest Dr
7500 HarC 77040 3681 D1
Quiet Glade Ct
4000 HOUS 77345 3119 D3
Quiet Glen Ct
1000 FBnC 77479 4493 D6
Quiet Glen Dr
3200 HOUS 77345 3120 B4
7200 FBnC 77479 4493 D6
Quiet Green Ct
1400 HOUS 77062 4379 C6
Quiet Grove Ct
18000 HarC 77346 3408 A1
Quiet Grove Ln
17000 HarC 77346 3408 A2
Quiet Hill Rd
9900 LPRT 77571 4250 B4
Quiet Hollow Dr
1800 FBnC 77545 4622 D1
Quiet Knoll Ct
3900 PASD 77059 4380 E5
Quiet Lake Ct
2200 LGCY 77573 4509 A6
2500 PRLD 77584 4500 A3
22800 FBnC 77450 3953 E7
Quiet Lake Dr
3200 FBnC 77450 3953 E7
Quiet Lake Ln
13200 PRLD 77584 4500 A3
Quiet Loch Ct
4500 HarC 77084 3817 A1
Quiet Loch Ln
17600 HarC 77084 3817 A1
17800 HarC 77084 3678 A7
Quiet Manor Ln
- BzaC 77583 4623 E5
Quiet Meadow Ct
3600 BzaC 77578 4501 A7
5900 PASD 77505 4248 D3
12200 MDWP 77477 4237 D6
Quiet Meadows Dr
2400 HarC 77067 3402 A5
Quiet Oak Cir
10 WDLD 77381 2821 A1
Quiet Oak Dr
10 WDLD 77381 2821 A1
Quiet Peace Pl
10 WDLD 77381 2820 D3
Quiet Pines Ln
- BzaC 77583 4500 A5
- PRLD 77583 4500 A5
Quiet Pl Dr
3700 HarC 77082 4095 E3
3700 HarC 77082 4096 A3
Quiet Pointe Dr
6300 HarC 77389 2966 D2
Quiet Pond Dr
- FBnC 77479 4494 D4
Quiet Quail Dr
16500 HOUS 77489 4370 E7
Quiet Ridge Ln
18100 HarC 77429 3252 B6
Quiet River Ln
- BzaC 77581 4502 B3
Quiet Rose Ln
- HarC 77379 3111 C4
Quiet Sage Ct
25100 FBnC 77494 3953 B5
Quiet Sage Ln
2300 FBnC 77494 3953 A5
Quiet Spring Ln
800 HOUS 77062 4506 D1
Quiet Stream Ct
18000 HarC 77095 3537 D7
Quiet Summer Ct
13400 HarC 77044 3550 A3
Quiet Summer Ln
14400 HarC 77044 3550 A3
Quiet Terrace Dr
- FBnC 77479 4494 B6
Quiet Timbers Ln
- FBnC 77494 4092 C3

Houston Street Index

STREET
Block City ZIP Map# Grid

uiet Town Ln
14300 FBnC 77478 4236 E3
uiet Trace Ln
7500 BzaC 77581 4502 A3
uiet Trail Ct
1400 FBnC 77479 4493 E5
uiet Trail Dr
16600 HarC 77396 3407 E4
uiet Valley Ln
10200 HOUS 77075 4376 C2
uiet Village Ct
6000 HOUS 77053 4371 D7
uiet Water Ct
900 FBnC 77479 4366 D7
12000 HarC 77065 3539 D3
uiet Wood Ct
13300 HarC 77038 3543 B2
uill Dr
15800 HarC 77070 3255 B6
uillback Dr
- HarC 77546 4505 E5
uill Garden Ln
10800 HOUS 77075 4377 A6
uill Meadow Dr
3000 LGCY 77573 4633 A1
uill Rush Wy
5000 FBnC 77469 4234 D3
uincannon Ln
2700 HOUS 77043 3819 E2
uince St
7000 HOUS 77012 4105 A4
7000 HOUS 77087 4105 A4
uince Tree Pl
10 WDLD 77385 2676 B3
uincewood Dr
11400 HarC 77089 4378 A5
uincy Ct
20300 HMBL 77338 3262 C4
uinette Rd
14500 MtgC 77302 2679 D1
14500 MtgC 77306 2679 D1
uinn Rd
29500 TMBL 77375 2964 A6
uinn St
300 HOUS 77009 3824 A7
uinnlan Mill Ln
- HarC 77073 3259 B4
uinn Ridge Wy
11600 HarC 77038 3543 A6
uinns Cabin Ct
10 CNRO 77304 2236 D6
uintana Cir
10 GLSN 77554 5221 C3
uintana Ct
10 GLSN 77554 5221 C3
uintana Dr
10 GLSN 77554 5221 C3
uintana Roo Pl
600 SEBK 77586 4383 A7
uintelle Ct
- WDLD 77382 2673 C7
uintero Ln
7600 HarC 77083 4097 A6
uion Ct
700 HarC 77532 3552 A1
uite Dale Ct
17000 HarC 77095 3538 B2
uitman Ct
4200 HOUS 77026 3964 B1
uitman Dr
3700 PASD 77505 4248 C4
uitman St
200 HOUS 77009 3963 C1
1600 HOUS 77026 3963 D1
3100 HOUS 77026 3964 A1
4400 HOUS 77026 3825 B7
uiver Ln
2200 HarC 77067 3402 A5
uivira Trc
- LGCY 77573 4632 D1

R

R St
100 LPRT 77571 4251 E6
348
- PLMG 77327 2684 E5
3431
10 LbyC 77327 2684 E2
3431 W W
100 PLMG 77327 2684 E3
300 LbyC 77327 2684 E3
3432
100 PLMG 77327 2684 E3
aab
2000 FBnC 77545 4622 C1
2700 MSCY 77545 4622 B1
Raab Rd
- FBnC 77545 4622 D1
Rabbit Rdg
7500 FBnC 77459 4621 A1
Rabbit Hollow Dr
7100 HarC 77521 3834 B1
7200 HarC 77521 3695 B7
Rabbit Oak Dr
10300 HarC 77065 3539 A2
Rabbit Run Pl
10 WDLD 77382 2819 B3
Rabb Ridge Dr
5600 FBnC 77469 4493 B6
Rabbs Cross
- FBnC 77469 4493 E6
1200 FBnC 77479 4493 E6
Rabinow Ct
2700 MtgC 77381 2821 D2
Raccoon Bnd
37000 MtgC 77354 2816 B1
Raccoon Dr
3600 BYTN 77521 3973 E2
Raccoon Ln
10 WDLD 77380 2968 A1
Raccoon Run
3100 HarC 77373 3114 E6
Race St
1600 HOUS 77002 3963 D3
Rachael Ln
- HarC 77377 3107 D2
200 FRDW 77546 4505 A7
Rachael Rd
13000 GLSN 77554 5333 B2
Rachael St
600 ALVN 77511 4749 C7
Rachel Ct
1300 PRLD 77581 4504 E5
1300 PRLD 77581 4505 A5
N Rachel Ct
2500 PRLD 77581 4505 A5

Rachel Ln
3200 KATY 77493 3813 D3
Rachel St
700 HOUS 77091 3684 B5
Rachelle Ct
4800 FBnC 77450 4094 A2
Rachelle Ln
- MAGA 77355 2669 A6
Rachelle Ridge Ct
5000 PASD 77505 4248 B6
Rachels Ct
6100 FBnC 77494 4093 D5
Rachels Wy
700 FBnC 77545 4499 D6
12700 MSCY 77071 4239 C7
Rachels Manor Dr
- FBnC 77494 4093 D1
- HOUS 77494 4093 D1
22800 FBnC 77450 4093 D1
Rachels Wy Ct
17400 HarC 77375 3255 A3
E Rachlin Cir
8600 HOUS 77071 4239 C6
N Rachlin Cir
12400 HOUS 77071 4239 C7
S Rachlin Cir
12400 HOUS 77071 4239 C7
Racine St
9700 HOUS 77029 3966 A5
E Racing Cloud Ct
10 WDLD 77380 2821 C5
10 WDLD 77381 2821 C5
W Racing Cloud Ct
10 WDLD 77380 2821 C5
10 WDLD 77381 2821 C5
Rack St
10900 HOUS 77051 4243 A7
Rackingham Pl
19700 HarC 77338 3261 E5
Racoon Dr
3800 BYTN 77521 3973 E2
4700 HarC 77521 3834 E7
4700 HarC 77521 3973 D1
Racquet Ct
7000 HarC 77069 3400 A1
Racquet Ridge Rd
18700 HarC 77346 3265 C7
Racquet Sports Wy
18700 HarC 77346 3265 C7
Radbrook Ln
14300 HOUS 77079 3957 E4
Radcliff Pl
7000 SGLD 77479 4367 C7
Radcliffe Dr
2400 FBnC 77478 4236 B7
Radcliffe Rd
- HOUS 77016 3686 D7
Radcliffe St
- HOUS 77017 4105 E7
- HOUS 77017 4245 D1
- HOUS 77017 4246 A1
2000 HOUS 77007 3962 A1
6400 HOUS 77091 3684 A4
Rader St
12600 HarC 77066 3401 A1
Radford Ln
10800 HOUS 77099 4238 B5
11600 MDWP 77477 4238 B5
Radford Park Cir
14100 HOUS 77062 4379 D4
Radial Ct
8200 FBnC 77583 4744 A3
Radial St
4900 HOUS 77021 4103 E7
Radiant Dawn
7700 HarC 77083 4096 E7
Radio Ln
1000 RSBG 77471 4491 C4
Radio Rd
8700 HOUS 77075 4246 A7
9300 HOUS 77075 4377 A1
Radley Ct
16300 HarC 77379 3256 E3
Radley Dr
6500 HarC 77379 3256 E3
9800 FBnC 77478 4236 E2
Radney Cir
11500 PNPV 77024 3959 D6
Radney Ests
10 PNPV 77024 3959 D6
Radney Rd
10 PNPV 77024 3959 D6
Radrick Ln
22800 HarC 77450 3953 E5
Rads Pt
9600 FBnC 77478 4236 A2
Radstock Dr
14900 HOUS 77062 4506 E1
Radwell Ct
15000 HOUS 77062 4506 D2
Radworthy Dr
18000 HarC 77084 3677 E6
Raes Creek Dr
7500 HarC 77389 2966 A3
Raestone St
29400 MtgC 77386 2969 C4
Rafael St
9600 HOUS 77013 3826 E5
9600 HOUS 77013 3827 A5
Rafam Dr
6600 PASD 77505 4248 E4
Raffaello Dr
2300 PRLD 77089 4504 E3
2300 PRLD 77581 4504 E3
Rafferty Pl
- FBnC 77083 4236 C2
- FBnC 77478 4236 C2
Raford Ln
4800 STFE 77510 4986 E1
Rafters Row
10 WDLD 77380 2821 C6
Rafter Three Dr
24000 HarC 77447 3249 E4
Ragland Dr
2100 HarC 77067 3402 A7
Ragsdale Ct
1200 HarC 77494 3953 D4
Ragsdale Ln
1200 HarC 77494 3953 D4
Ragus Lake Dr
14000 SGLD 77478 4237 A7
14100 SGLD 77478 4236 E7
Raia Ln
12500 MSCY 77071 4239 E7
Raider Rd
100 KMAH 77565 4509 E6
N Rail Dr
16700 MtgC 77385 2676 D4

Railey St
300 HOUS 77009 3824 A7
Railhead Ln
7600 HOUS 77086 3541 E4
7600 HOUS 77086 3542 A4
Railroad Av
100 LGCY 77573 4632 A3
1600 GlsC 77539 4635 C7
1600 GlsC 77539 4756 C1
1600 TXCY 77539 4756 C1
5200 HarC 77521 3834 D7
17100 PTVL 77357 2682 C7
17100 WDBR 77357 2682 C7
17500 WDBR 77357 2828 A4
18500 MtgC 77357 2828 B3
E Railroad Av
300 LGCY 77573 4632 A2
N Railroad Av
100 HMBL 77338 3262 D6
4400 GlsC 77563 4990 A6
4400 HTCK 77563 4990 A6
S Railroad Av
100 HMBL 77338 3262 D7
Railroad St
- PASD 77503 4108 E3
100 ALVN 77511 4867 B1
1500 GlsC 77539 4635 C7
1500 LPRT 77571 4111 C7
4700 DRPK 77536 4108 D3
4800 DRPK 77503 4108 E3
5000 DRPK 77536 4109 A3
W Railroad St
- DRPK 77503 4108 E3
- DRPK 77536 4108 E3
Railspur St
7000 HOUS 77078 3827 A2
Railton Ct
9300 HOUS 77080 3820 D2
Railton St
8900 HOUS 77080 3820 E2
Railway St
5500 HarC 77521 3834 E6
Railwood Dr
8800 HOUS 77028 3826 E2
8800 HOUS 77078 3826 E2
9000 HOUS 77078 3827 A2
Railwood St
2900 HarC 77521 3834 D7
Raina Ln
11600 BKHV 77024 3959 D3
11600 PNPV 77024 3959 D3
Rainarch St
20700 HarC 77449 3815 C3
Rain Barrel Ct
1500 FBnC 77469 4365 E2
Rainbluff Ln
- FBnC 77494 4092 D4
Rainbourne Ln
- LGCY 77573 4751 C1
Rainbow Ct
3100 BzaC 77584 4501 B7
Rainbow Dr
- HOUS 77023 4105 A3
Rainbow Ln
23000 MtgC 77357 2828 D5
Rainbow Run
4600 SGLD 77479 4369 A7
4600 SGLD 77479 4496 A1
Rainbow St
2000 HOUS 77023 4105 A3
Rainbow Bend Dr
7600 PASD 77505 4249 B5
Rainbow Bend Ln
22800 HarC 77450 3953 B3
Rainbow Bridge Ln
11800 HarC 77346 3408 B2
Rainbow Creek Dr
- HarC 77449 3676 E3
Rainbow Falls St
13400 HarC 77083 4097 B4
Rainbow Glen Dr
11000 HarC 77064 3540 D2
Rainbow Granite Dr
20600 FBnC 77469 4234 B3
Rainbow Lake Rd
16000 HarC 77095 3538 C7
E Rainbow Ridge Cir
100 WDLD 77381 2820 E3
N Rainbow Ridge Cir
100 WDLD 77381 2820 E3
W Rainbow Ridge Cir
10 WDLD 77381 2820 E3
Rainbow Star Dr
12500 HarC 77041 3679 E2
Rainbow Valley Ct
4600 MSCY 77459 4497 D5
Raincloud Dr
10000 HarC 77095 3538 E3
Raincove Dr
11300 HOUS 77016 3687 A1
11400 HOUS 77016 3546 E7
11400 HOUS 77016 3547 A7
Rain Creek Ct
8900 HarC 77375 2965 D5
Rain Creek Dr
24000 HarC 77375 2965 D4
Raincrest Dr
20500 HarC 77449 3815 D3
Rain Dance
10 PRLD 77581 4502 C1
Raindance Ct
10 WDLD 77385 2676 C4
Rain Dance Dr
14900 HarC 77090 3402 D1
Raindream Pl
10 WDLD 77381 2820 E3
E Raindrop
100 PRLD 77581 4502 C1
Rain Drop Ct
- FBnC 77469 4094 C7
W Raindrop Ln
100 PRLD 77581 4502 B1
Raindrop Hollow Dr
4900 HOUS 77041 3680 E7
Raindrops Rd
3600 PASD 77505 4248 D4
Rainer Dr
300 BKHV 77024 3959 B4
300 HOUS 77024 3959 B4
Rainer Valley Ln
17300 HarC 77346 3408 C2
Rainesville Ln
8700 HOUS 77075 4376 E2
8700 HOUS 77075 4377 A3
Rainfall
100 PRLD 77581 4502 C1
N Rainfall
100 PRLD 77581 4502 C1

S Rainfall
100 PRLD 77581 4502 C1
Rainfall Dr
4200 PASD 77505 4249 B5
Rain Fall St
2400 SGLD 77479 4368 C7
Rain Fern Ct
10 WDLD 77380 2822 A7
Rainfern Dr
22200 MtgC 77355 2960 D2
22200 SGCH 77355 2960 C1
Rainfield Ct
5200 FBnC 77494 4093 B2
Rainflower Cir N
5100 LGCY 77573 4630 D6
Rainflower Cir S
500 LGCY 77573 4630 D6
Rainford Ct
10 SGLD 77479 4495 D3
N Rain Forest Ct
10 WDLD 77380 2968 B4
S Rain Forest Ct
10 WDLD 77380 2968 A4
Rain Forest Dr
23500 HarC 77336 3267 A3
Rainforest Trail Dr
7400 PASD 77505 4249 B5
Rainfort Dr
3300 HarC 77449 3815 D3
Raingate Ln
20000 HarC 77449 3815 D6
Rainglen Ln
2800 LGCY 77539 4752 D5
8700 HarC 77044 3689 C5
Raingold Dr
20100 HarC 77338 3262 B4
Rain Green Dr
20600 HarC 77449 3815 D3
Rainhill Ct
3200 HarC 77449 3815 D3
Rainhollow Dr
15200 HarC 77070 3254 E7
Rain Hollow Pl
10 HOUS 77024 3959 B2
Rainier Ct
2300 HOUS 77339 3118 B6
Rainier St
5100 PASD 77504 4247 D7
Raining Heath Ct
4900 HarC 77449 3676 D7
Rain Lake Tr
2000 HarC 77532 3410 B3
Rain Leaf Ct
21600 HarC 77338 3261 E2
Rain Lily Cross
- FBnC 77494 4093 A3
Rain Lily Ct
2100 PRLD 77581 4503 D2
Rainlily Dr
1900 HOUS 77084 3816 D6
Rain Lily Ln
13200 HOUS 77083 4097 B4
Rain Lily St
100 MtgC 77355 2960 C3
Rainmead Dr
20700 HarC 77449 3815 C3
Rain Meadow Ln
- FBnC 77469 4616 E1
7400 HarC 77433 3677 D1
7500 HarC 77433 3537 A5
Rainmill Dr
20700 HarC 77449 3815 C3
E Rainmill Dr
3400 HarC 77449 3815 D3
N Rainmill Dr
20700 HarC 77449 3815 C3
W Rainmill Dr
3400 HarC 77449 3815 C3
Rainmont Ln
3100 HarC 77449 3815 D4
Rainpark Ln
3100 HarC 77449 3815 D4
Rainport Dr
3300 HarC 77449 3815 D3
Rainprint Rd
- WDLD 77381 2820 D5
Rains Wy
100 HOUS 77007 3962 A4
Rain Shadow Ct
14900 HarC 77070 3254 C7
Rainshore Dr
3300 HarC 77449 3815 C3
Rainspur Dr
20700 HarC 77449 3815 C2
Rainstone Ct
20500 HarC 77449 3815 D3
Rainswept Pass Dr
500 RSBG 77469 4492 C7
Rainterra Dr
- HarC 77449 3815 D2
Raintree Cir
1300 SGLD 77479 4367 E6
1800 ELGO 77586 4382 B7
11500 BKHV 77024 3959 D5
11500 PNPV 77024 3959 D5
Raintree Ct
4300 PASD 77505 4249 B5
Raintree Dr
1600 BYTN 77520 3973 C6
2700 SGLD 77478 4368 D5
4800 MSCY 77459 4621 B2
6100 PRLD 77584 4502 D4
Raintree Pl
- HarC 77357 2830 B6
10 WDLD 77381 2821 A1
Raintree Village Dr
2700 HarC 77449 3815 D3
Rain Valley Ct
8600 HarC 77044 3689 B5
Rain Walk Ct
10 WDLD 77380 2968 A4
Rainwater
10 PRLD 77581 4502 C1
Rainwater Ct
- PRLD 77545 4499 D2
Rainwater Dr
1300 PRLD 77545 4499 E2
4800 PASD 77505 4248 A4
Rain Willow Ct
4000 HarC 77053 4372 C4
Rainwood Dr
600 HOUS 77079 3957 E3
2900 PRLD 77545 4499 D4
Rainwood St
2900 HarC 77388 3113 A3
Rainwood Park Ln
- FBnC 77450 4093 E3
- FBnC 77450 4094 A4

Rainwood Park Ln
31200 MtgC 77386 2823 C7
Rainy Meadow Ln
400 HOUS 77013 3966 B1
Rainy Oaks Dr
11500 MtgC 77354 2671 B5
N Rainy Oaks Dr
- MtgC 77354 2671 B5
Rainy Oaks Pk
33100 MtgC 77354 2671 B5
Rainy River
- HarC 77088 3543 C7
Rainy River Dr
500 HarC 77037 3544 B7
500 HOUS 77037 3544 B7
700 HOUS 77088 3544 A7
1400 HOUS 77088 3543 E7
1900 HarC 77088 3543 D7
4200 PASD 77504 4247 D6
Rainy Sun Cir
14300 HarC 77049 3828 C3
Raleigh Dr
500 MtgC 77302 2530 B6
Raleigh Row
3300 FBnC 77459 4622 A5
Raleigh St
3200 HOUS 77021 4103 A5
Raleigh Green Tr
16500 HarC 77433 3251 A4
Raleigh Oak Ln
15700 HarC 77433 3251 C5
Raleigh Tavern
- HOUS 77449 3814 D6
Ralfallen Dr
- BzaC 77584 4501 A4
Ralfallen St
700 HOUS 77008 3823 E6
800 HOUS 77009 3823 E6
Ralick Ct
7500 HarC 77379 3256 B2
Rally Run Cir
8400 HarC 77346 3265 C6
Ralph Cir
21800 MtgC 77355 2960 E4
Ralph St
2400 HOUS 77006 3962 C6
Ralphcrest Dr
1100 HarC 77039 3545 B1
Ralph Culver Rd
13100 HarC 77086 3542 D2
Ralston Rd
- HarC 77044 3548 D6
- HarC 77396 3548 D1
17700 HarC 77338 3407 D2
17700 HarC 77396 3407 D2
Ralston St
2500 HOUS 77026 3825 B7
6700 HOUS 77016 3825 A2
Ralston Bend Ln
9600 FBnC 77494 4092 C5
Ralstons Ridge Dr
8500 HarC 77083 4097 B7
Ralstony St
- WlrC 77484 3101 D7
- WlrC 77484 3246 D1
Ram Ct
4400 HOUS 77072 4098 A4
Ramada Ct
2400 TXCY 77590 4875 A3
Ramada Dr
2300 HOUS 77062 4507 C1
Ramblebrook
14700 HarC 77396 3547 E1
Ramblebrook Ct
8300 HarC 77396 3547 E1
Ramble Creek Dr
3600 MSCY 77459 4497 C7
3700 MSCY 77459 4621 C1
Rambler Dr
9700 HarC 77044 3689 D3
Rambleridge Dr
6400 HOUS 77053 4371 D6
Ramblewood Dr
7000 MtgC 77354 2673 A4
19500 HarC 77338 3263 B5
Ramblewood Pk
400 HarC 77094 3955 B2
Ramblewood Rd
600 HOUS 77079 3958 A3
Rambling Tr
10500 HOUS 77089 4377 D3
Rambling Brook Dr
2300 HarC 77373 3259 D1
2400 HarC 77373 3114 D7
Rambling Brook Ln
6800 FBnC 77469 4615 E5
Rambling Canyon Ct
4700 HarC 77449 3677 C6
Rambling Creek Dr
3200 HOUS 77345 3120 A4
Rambling Oaks Dr
29600 HarC 77336 2976 D7
29600 HarC 77336 3121 D1
Rambling Pines Dr
3400 HOUS 77345 3120 A4
Rambling Ridge Ct
10 WDLD 77385 2676 A4
N Rambling Ridge Pl
10 WDLD 77385 2676 B4
S Rambling Ridge Pl
10 WDLD 77385 2676 B4
Rambling River Wy
15500 HarC 77433 3251 A6
Rambling Rose Ct
3900 FBnC 77583 4622 C4
Rambling Springs Wy
10 WDLD 77382 2819 E1
Rambling Stone Dr
1500 FBnC 77469 4365 C1
Rambling Tree Ln
- FBnC 77469 4094 D6
Rambling Wood Ct
10 WDLD 77380 2822 B7
Ramey
- HOUS 77075 4377 C3
Ramey Cir
10 HOUS 77075 4377 C3
Ramin Dr
8900 HOUS 77093 3686 A6
Ramirez Rd
19000 BzaC 77511 4627 E6
19000 BzaC 77511 4628 A6
19000 PRLD 77511 4627 E6
Ramirez St
800 FBnC 77477 4369 B3
800 SGLD 77477 4369 B3
800 SGLD 77478 4369 B3

Ramla Pl Tr
- HarC 77089 4505 C1
11800 HOUS 77089 4505 C1
12200 HOUS 77089 4378 C7
Ramline Ct
- HarC 77532 3551 E5
- HarC 77532 3552 A5
Ramona
12400 HarC 77429 3398 D5
Rampart Ct
200 LGCY 77573 4631 B4
Rampart Ln
500 MtgC 77302 2530 D6
Rampart St
- HOUS 77096 4240 C3
1800 LGCY 77573 4631 B4
5400 HOUS 77057 4100 C4
5400 HOUS 77081 4100 C6
8100 HOUS 77096 4100 C7
11600 HOUS 77035 4240 C5
Rampart Point Dr
8600 FBnC 77469 4234 B5
Rampchester Ln
13600 HarC 77015 3828 E5
Ramp Creek Ln
11000 FBnC 77478 4236 E5
Ram Rock
2000 BYTN 77521 3972 C2
Ramrock Cir
21000 MtgC 77365 3118 A1
Ramrock Ct
21000 MtgC 77365 3118 A2
Ramrock Dr
25000 MtgC 77365 3118 A2
Ramrod
10 HTCK 77563 5105 B5
Ramrod Ct
20300 HarC 77447 3105 E2
Ramsar Ln
700 GLSN 77550 5110 B1
Ramsar Rd
700 GLSN 77550 5110 B1
Ramsay Ln
6100 LGCY 77573 4630 C7
Ramsay Wy
1700 HOUS 77045 4242 C7
Rams Bottom Ct
500 HarC 77388 3113 B6
Ramsey Av
- BYTN 77520 3973 A6
Ramsey Dr
3500 PASD 77503 4108 B6
Ramsey Ln
300 HOUS 77336 3266 B3
Ramsey Rd
- HarC 77336 3268 A2
- LbyC 77535 3268 A2
16800 HarC 77532 3552 E1
18000 HarC 77532 3411 E6
21000 HarC 77532 3267 E6
21800 HarC 77336 3267 E6
Ramsey St
7300 HOUS 77054 4102 E7
Ramsey Loop Rd
2600 HarC 77532 3411 E4
2600 HarC 77532 3412 A4
S Ramsey Loop Rd
2500 HarC 77532 3411 E5
2500 HarC 77532 3412 A5
Ramsgate Dr
3400 HarC 77388 3112 E2
Ramus St
4700 HOUS 77092 3822 A4
Ramwind Ct
100 WDLD 77385 2676 B3
Ramzi Dr
- MtgC 77303 2239 C3
Rana Ct
15500 HarC 77068 3257 A6
Ranald Dr
- CNRO 77301 2530 C3
Ranch Cir
16900 MtgC 77357 2680 D6
Ranch Ct
8600 JRSV 77040 3540 D6
17000 MtgC 77357 2680 D6
Ranch St
3700 HOUS 77026 3825 B7
Ranch Canyon Dr
- HarC 77449 3676 D5
Ranch Country Dr
17700 HarC 77447 3249 E3
Ranch Country Rd
17000 HarC 77447 3249 E4
Ranch Creek Ct
6500 MtgC 77354 2673 C1
Ranch Creek Wy
10 MtgC 77354 2818 A2
Ranch Crest Dr
19100 MtgC 77355 2813 E1
Ranch Cross Blvd
5800 HarC 77449 3676 E4
Rancher Hollow Ct
3000 BzaC 77583 4500 D6
Rancheria Dr
7100 HarC 77083 4096 C5
Ranch Estates Dr
19500 MtgC 77302 2680 D6
19500 MtgC 77357 2680 D6
Ranchester Dr
5700 HOUS 77036 4099 A4
5700 HOUS 77042 4099 A3
Ranch Gate Dr
7900 HarC 77433 3537 C7
Ranch Glen Ln
- HarC 77433 3395 E6
Ranch Hand Rd
11500 TMBL 77375 3109 E3
Ranch Haven Ct
21400 MtgC 77365 2973 B3
Ranch Hill Dr
5000 MtgC 77354 2674 A1
5100 MtgC 77354 2528 A7
Ranch Hollow Ct
2400 FBnC 77494 3953 B6
Ranch House Ln
- HarC 77433 3395 E6
Ranch Lake Dr
5200 MtgC 77354 2674 A1
5300 MtgC 77384 2674 A1
5400 MtgC 77354 2673 D1
5400 MtgC 77384 2673 D1
Ranch Lake Ln
2600 FBnC 77494 3953 B6
Ranchland Ln
- BzaC 77583 4500 E7
- HarC 77429 3253 A5

Ranch Legend Ln
- FBnC 77494 4092 C1
Rancho Cir
400 FRDW 77546 4630 B5
Rancho Bauer
36700 MtgC 77355 2815 D5
Rancho Bauer Dr
300 HOUS 77079 3957 E4
Rancho Bernardo Ln
10200 FBnC 77478 4237 A3
Rancho Blanco Ct
6400 HarC 77083 4096 A4
Rancho Blanco Dr
16200 HarC 77082 4096 A4
16200 HarC 77083 4096 A4
16300 HarC 77083 4095 E4
Rancho Grande Dr
1800 HarC 77530 3829 E4
Rancho Mirage Dr
7100 HarC 77069 3400 A2
Rancho Mission Dr
- HOUS 77083 4096 E5
7200 HarC 77083 4096 D6
Rancho Paloma Blvd
2300 HarC 77049 3829 E3
2300 HarC 77530 3829 E3
Rancho Verde Wy
17200 HarC 77095 3537 E2
Rancho Vista Dr
4100 PASD 77504 4247 E4
14700 HarC 77083 4096 D5
Ranch Park Dr
6000 MtgC 77354 2673 D1
Ranch Prairie Tr
5700 HarC 77449 3676 E4
Ranch Riata Ct
5800 HarC 77449 3676 D4
Ranch Riata Dr
20200 HarC 77449 3676 D4
Ranchstone Dr
10900 HarC 77064 3540 B5
10900 HarC 77065 3540 A4
Ranch Valley Dr
17500 HarC 77447 3249 D3
Ranchwood Ct
1600 HarC 77450 3954 E4
Rand St
4100 HOUS 77026 3825 C5
7900 HOUS 77028 3826 B5
Randal Wy
400 HarC 77388 3258 D1
Randall Pl
1400 GLSN 77551 5108 C5
Randall St
- PRVW 77445 3100 B1
2500 STAF 77477 4370 A5
3000 HOUS 77018 3823 B3
N Randall St
100 PASD 77506 4107 B3
S Randall St
100 PASD 77506 4107 B5
1200 PASD 77502 4107 B6
Randal Lake Ct
- HarC 77388 3113 C2
Randal Lake Ln
- HarC 77388 3113 B7
Randall Oak Dr
- MSCY 77459 4369 B6
- MSCY 77478 4369 B6
4900 SGLD 77478 4369 B6
Randall Ridge Ln
15700 HarC 77429 3252 B7
Randal Point Ct
2400 HarC 77388 3113 B7
Randell Dr
3200 PRLD 77581 4503 D3
Randolph Dr
100 FBnC 77053 4372 D7
Randolph Rd
2400 DRPK 77503 4248 D1
2400 DRPK 77536 4248 D1
2400 PASD 77503 4248 D2
2800 PASD 77505 4248 D2
Randolph St
900 HOUS 77088 3683 E2
900 HOUS 77088 3684 A2
8900 HOUS 77061 4245 D7
9300 HOUS 77075 4245 D7
10000 HOUS 77075 4376 D3
Randon Ln
9600 FBnC 77459 4621 D4
25800 HarC 77377 3108 E6
Randon Rd
- HOUS 77092 3683 B6
4200 HOUS 77092 3822 A1
5100 HOUS 77091 3683 A7
Randons Bell Dr
2300 SGLD 77479 4368 C7
Randons Point Dr
1700 SGLD 77478 4368 E5
Randwick Dr
4400 HOUS 77092 3822 A4
Randy Dr
9000 SPVL 77055 3820 E7
Randy Ln
- HarC 77449 3815 D4
E Rangecrest Pl
3200 SGLD 77479 4496 A2
W Rangecrest Pl
- SGLD 77479 4495 D2
3200 SGLD 77479 4496 A3
Range Haven Ln
22500 MtgC 77365 2973 B3
Rangely Dr
9100 HOUS 77055 3820 D6
Ranger Run
4400 SGLD 77479 4496 A2
Ranger St
400 HOUS 77029 3965 B1
4500 HOUS 77028 3826 B5
Ranger Lakes Ln
21000 HarC 77449 3815 C1
Ranger Point Ct
20400 FBnC 77450 4094 D1
Range Valley Ln
- HarC 77429 3253 A6
Rangeview Dr
22300 HarC 77450 3953 D2
Rangewood Ct
1600 HOUS 77062 4380 A5
Ranic Dr
7800 HarC 77064 3541 A1
Ranier Dr
300 BKHV 77024 3959 B4
1500 DRPK 77536 4109 D7
10500 HOUS 77031 4239 C4
Rankin Av
1400 GlsC 77650 4878 E6

STREET
Block City ZIP Map# Grid

Rankin Cir E
13600 HarC 77060 3403 C3
13600 HarC 77073 3403 C3
Rankin Cir N
500 HarC 77073 3403 B3
Rankin Cir W
13600 HarC 77060 3403 A3
13600 HarC 77073 3403 A3
Rankin Pk
13600 HarC 77060 3403 B3
13600 HarC 77073 3403 B3
Rankin Rd
- HarC 77067 3403 A4
- HarC 77346 3408 A4
- HarC 77396 3408 A4
- HOUS 77032 3405 A3
- HOUS 77067 3403 A4
100 HarC 77060 3403 B4
100 HarC 77073 3403 B4
100 HarC 77090 3403 A4
100 HOUS 77090 3403 A4
1000 HarC 77032 3403 E4
1600 HarC 77073 3404 A4
1600 HOUS 77032 3404 A4
1600 HOUS 77073 3404 A4
1700 HarC 77032 3404 B4
5700 HOUS 77396 3405 E3
5700 HOUS 77396 3406 A3
7400 HMBL 77396 3406 D3
W Rankin Rd
- HarC 77060 3403 A4
- HarC 77067 3403 A4
- HarC 77073 3403 A4
- HarC 77090 3403 A4
- HOUS 77067 3403 A4
100 HOUS 77090 3403 A4
200 HOUS 77014 3403 A4
300 HOUS 77014 3402 D4
300 HOUS 77067 3402 E4
1000 HarC 77014 3402 D4
1000 HarC 77067 3402 D4
Rankin Dewalt Rd
10 TXCY 77590 4875 D1
Rankin Meadows Ct
20700 HarC 77433 3251 B3
Ranna Ct
2400 FBnC 77478 4237 B4
Rannie Rd
8400 HOUS 77080 3821 A2
Rannock Wy
9500 HarC 77379 3255 D4
Ransom Rd
1400 RHMD 77469 4492 A2
1600 FBnC 77469 4492 E3
4000 FBnC 77469 4493 A3
4300 FBnC 77479 4493 C3
Ransom St
5600 HOUS 77087 4104 D7
5700 HOUS 77087 4244 D1
Ransten Ln
19800 HarC 77379 3112 A5
Rapho Dr
2700 HarC 77532 3410 A6
Rapho Rd
- HarC 77532 3410 A6
Rapidan Pk
500 MtgC 77302 2530 C5
Rapid Brook Ct
5600 HOUS 77345 3120 C7
Rapid Creek Ct
5900 HOUS 77345 3120 C5
Rapidcreek Dr
16100 HOUS 77053 4372 B7
Rapid Falls Ln
14700 HarC 77396 3548 A1
Rapido Rd
5000 HOUS 77033 4243 E1
5100 HOUS 77033 4244 A1
5300 HOUS 77033 4104 A7
Rapid River Ln
9600 HarC 77086 3542 A3
Rapids Ct
2200 FBnC 77545 4498 C7
Raritan Dr
10000 HOUS 77080 3820 B5
10200 HOUS 77043 3819 E5
Rashell Wy
11400 PRLD 77583 4500 D6
Rasmus Dr
9200 HOUS 77063 4099 C1
Raspberry Ct
- DKSN 77539 4754 A2
Raspberry Ln
2100 PASD 77502 4107 D4
2100 PASD 77502 4247 D1
Rastus Av
2600 FBnC 77477 4370 A5
2600 STAF 77477 4370 A5
Ratada Ct
700 HOUS 77336 3121 A4
Ratama St
5000 HOUS 77017 4246 A1
Rathbone Dr
9700 HOUS 77031 4239 A6
Rathford Ct
24500 FBnC 77494 3953 B7
Rathlin Ct
15900 HarC 77379 3256 B6
Raton St
7500 HOUS 77055 3821 D5
Rattan Ln
17700 HarC 77532 3413 A6
Rau Dr
3700 DKSN 77539 4753 B5
3700 LGCY 77539 4753 B5
Rauch St
3300 HOUS 77029 3826 D7
Raul Hector Dr
9700 HOUS 77075 4377 A2
Raulhector Dr
9700 HOUS 77075 4377 A1
Raven
600 HMBL 77338 3262 E6
Raven Ct
3700 BzaC 77578 4625 C1
Raven Ln
1100 FBnC 77469 4492 B7
1100 FBnC 77469 4616 A1
1100 RSBG 77469 4492 A7
Raven Pk
- MtgC 77365 3117 D2
Raven Tr
15500 HOUS 77489 4371 D5
Ravena Ct
12500 HOUS 77089 4378 C7
Raven Bluff Ln
- FBnC 77494 4093 B1
Raven Canyon Ln
17400 HarC 77095 3537 E5
Raven Cliffs Ln
7000 HarC 77379 3111 B6
Raven Creek Dr
13500 HarC 77429 3398 A4
Raven Creek Ln
7800 HarC 77433 3537 A7
Ravencrest Cir
25100 MtgC 77365 3117 D2
Ravencrest Ct
4000 PRLD 77584 4502 D7
Ravencrest Dr
25100 MtgC 77365 3117 D1
Raven Cross Ct
- HarC 77429 3398 A5
Raven Crossing Ln
10400 HarC 77089 4377 C6
Ravendale Rd
13900 HarC 77396 3547 A2
Ravenel Ln
1300 SGLD 77479 4367 B7
Raven Falls Ln
2600 HarC 77546 4506 A7
Ravenfield Ct
18100 HarC 77084 3677 E7
Ravenfield Dr
18000 HarC 77084 3677 E7
Raven Flight Dr
13300 HarC 77429 3398 A6
Raven Forest Ln
5000 FBnC 77494 4092 E3
Ravenglen Ln
25100 MtgC 77365 3117 D1
Ravenhead Dr
100 HOUS 77034 4247 A5
Raven Hill Dr
13500 HarC 77429 3398 A4
Raven Hollow Ln
14700 HarC 77396 3547 C1
Ravenhurst Ln
14100 HarC 77070 3399 D1
Raven Knoll Ct
100 LGCY 77573 4631 A5
Ravenlake Ct
2600 PRLD 77584 4500 B4
Ravenlake Dr
13200 PRLD 77584 4500 A3
13300 PRLD 77584 4499 E3
Ravenlea Ln
9700 HarC 77044 3689 B3
Ravenloch Ct
5400 FBnC 77450 4094 B3
Ravenmeadow Ln
20000 HarC 77449 3676 E5
Ravenmoor Dr
12200 HOUS 77077 3957 E5
Ravenna Ln
- LGCY 77573 4632 E3
22000 FBnC 77450 4094 A2
Raven Oak Ct
1700 HarC 77450 3954 D4
Ravenpass Ln
21700 HarC 77449 3815 A4
Raven Ridge Dr
2700 PRLD 77545 4499 E3
4800 HOUS 77053 4372 A6
Raven Ridge Ln
10 WDLD 77380 2968 A1
Raven River Dr
- HOUS 77059 4380 D5
3900 PASD 77059 4380 D5
Raven Rock Ln
- FBnC 77469 4095 B6
- HarC 77433 3537 A7
Raven Rook Dr
12200 HarC 77429 3398 A6
Raven Roost Dr
12800 HarC 77429 3398 A6
Ravens Wy
10500 CmbC 77520 3835 D3
Ravensbrook Ln
18100 HarC 77429 3252 B6
Ravens Call Ln
- FBnC 77469 4095 C6
Ravens Caw Dr
13300 HarC 77429 3398 A6
Ravens Chase Ln
12300 HarC 77429 3398 B5
Ravenscourt Dr
1100 SGLD 77478 4237 B7
Ravens Cove
- HarC 77449 3815 B1
Ravens Creek Ct
2700 PRLD 77584 4500 C4
Ravenscreek Ct
5200 LGCY 77573 4751 D1
Ravens Creek Dr
2700 PRLD 77584 4500 C3
Ravens Crest Dr
2000 SGLD 77478 4368 E5
Ravens Croft Ln
- HarC 77379 3111 D5
Ravenscroft Wy
14700 FBnC 77083 4236 D1
Ravens Gate Ln
8100 FBnC 77469 4234 B4
Ravens Glen Ct
12800 HarC 77429 3398 B6
Raven Shore Cir
18500 HarC 77433 3395 C5
S Raven Shore Ct
12300 HarC 77433 3395 E4
N Raven Shore Dr
12400 HarC 77433 3395 D5
Ravens Lake Cir
3100 LGCY 77573 4633 B2
Ravens Lake Dr
3100 LGCY 77573 4633 B2
22600 FBnC 77450 3953 E7
Ravens Manor Ct
1400 HarC 77379 3110 B6
Ravens Mate Dr
12300 HarC 77429 3398 A6
Ravens Nest Ct
9600 FBnC 77083 4236 B2
Ravens Nest Ln
12000 HarC 77089 4504 B2
Ravensong Dr
12700 HarC 77429 3398 A5
Raven South Dr
12000 HarC 77065 3398 B6
12000 HarC 77429 3398 A5
Ravens Point Dr
7800 FBnC 77469 4234 B3
Ravensport Dr
2900 BzaC 77584 4501 A6
Ravens Prairie Dr
28500 FBnC 77494 3951 C5
Ravens Roost Ct
12200 HarC 77429 3398 B6
Ravensway Ct
4000 PRLD 77584 4502 D7
Ravensway Dr
12500 HarC 77429 3398 A5
Ravensway Center Dr
12500 HarC 77429 3398 A6
Ravenswood Dr
15900 MtgC 77354 2669 E3
N Ravenswood Dr
15800 MtgC 77354 2669 E2
S Ravenswood Dr
15800 MtgC 77354 2669 E2
Ravensworth Dr
600 MtgC 77302 2530 B6
9500 HOUS 77031 4239 A6
9700 HOUS 77031 4238 E6
Raven Tree Ct
21700 MtgC 77365 2972 A1
Raven Tree Dr
12800 HarC 77429 3398 A4
Raven View Dr
11500 HarC 77067 3402 A5
Ravenwind Rd
2000 HarC 77067 3402 A6
Ravenwing Dr
13300 HarC 77429 3398 A6
20000 MtgC 77365 3117 D2
Ravenwood Cir
7900 HOUS 77055 3821 C4
Ravenwood Ct
4000 PRLD 77584 4502 D7
20600 MtgC 77365 3117 E2
Ravenwood Dr
- SGLD 77479 4495 B4
6000 PRLD 77584 4502 C7
19800 MtgC 77365 3117 D1
Ravenwood Ln
- HarC 77484 3102 B7
Ravenwood View Ln
10200 HOUS 77075 4376 E3
Ravine Cir
16900 FRDW 77546 4629 E1
Ravine Dr
4000 FRDW 77546 4630 A1
4400 FRDW 77546 4629 E2
Rawhide Tr
16500 HarC 77429 3396 E3
Rawley St
3200 HOUS 77026 3964 A1
4200 HOUS 77020 3964 B1
Rawlings St
13800 HarC 77396 3547 A2
Rawls St
3000 HOUS 77007 3961 E1
3000 HOUS 77008 3822 E7
3000 HOUS 77008 3961 E1
Rawson Dr
700 RSBG 77471 4491 C3
Ray
31000 MtgC 77354 2673 A6
Ray Av
300 ARLA 77583 4623 B5
Ray Cir
5900 PASD 77505 4248 D4
Ray Dr
6000 PASD 77505 4248 D4
Ray St
2500 PRLD 77581 4503 A3
7200 HOUS 77093 3824 E2
Ray Allen Rd
4400 FBnC 77469 4615 B4
Raybluff Ln
8500 HarC 77040 3541 C6
Raybrook Ln
10300 HarC 77089 4377 B6
N Rayburn Ct
2100 PASD 77502 4247 E1
S Rayburn Ct
1900 PASD 77502 4247 E1
E Rayburn Dr
16500 MtgC 77302 2680 B5
N Rayburn Dr
18400 MtgC 77302 2680 A5
S Rayburn Dr
18300 MtgC 77302 2680 C5
19000 MtgC 77306 2680 C5
W Rayburn Dr
16600 MtgC 77302 2680 A5
Rayburn Ln
1600 PRLD 77581 4504 D5
Rayburn Lake Ct
3900 PRLD 77581 4504 A7
Rayburn Ridge Dr
2600 HarC 77450 3954 C6
Ray Dean Dr E
10 BzaC 77511 4866 A2
Ray Dean Dr N
10 BzaC 77511 4866 A2
Ray Dean Dr S
100 BzaC 77511 4866 A3
Ray Dean Dr W
10 BzaC 77511 4866 A2
Raydell Dr
10500 HOUS 77031 4239 B3
Raydon Ln
10 BKHV 77024 3959 B4
Ray Falls
20200 HarC 77375 3109 D5
Rayford Dr
23700 HarC 77389 2967 A5
Rayford Rd
- HarC 77375 2965 E5
- HarC 77389 2965 E4
- HarC 77389 2966 B3
10 MtgC 77386 2968 C2
1300 MtgC 77386 2969 A3
3800 MtgC 77386 2970 D7
4300 MtgC 77386 3115 E1
4400 MtgC 77386 3116 A1
21700 HarC 77338 3260 C3
21700 HOUS 77338 3260 C3
W Rayford Rd
5700 HarC 77389 2966 E3
8800 HarC 77375 2965 E5
8800 HarC 77389 2965 E5
Rayford Crest Dr
25200 MtgC 77386 2968 D2
Rayford Forest Ln
- MtgC 77386 2968 C2
Rayleine Dr
8400 PRLD 77584 4501 D5
Raylin Dr
8400 SPVL 77055 3821 B6
Raymac St
100 HarC 77037 3544 B5
100 HOUS 77037 3544 B5
Raymond St
100 TMBL 77375 2964 A6
200 TMBL 77375 3109 A1
400 LMQU 77568 4873 D7
500 LMQU 77568 4989 D1
2700 PASD 77506 4107 E4
2700 PASD 77506 4108 A4
3200 HOUS 77007 3962 D3
7100 HOUS 77021 4103 B7
Raymondville Rd
9900 HOUS 77093 3685 E5
Raymont Cir
9700 HarC 77065 3539 C4
Raynor Ct
15700 HOUS 77489 4371 C5
Raynor Wy
6800 SGLD 77479 4367 C7
Raypine Dr
- MtgC 77386 2968 C2
Raypointe Dr
- FBnC 77479 4493 D2
Ray Shell Ct
1800 TYLV 77586 4382 A6
Rayson Rd
8300 HOUS 77080 3821 A2
Raywood Blvd
5700 HOUS 77040 3681 D6
Raywood Ct
900 HarC 77530 3830 B6
Raywood Dr
16000 HarC 77530 3830 B6
Raza Rd
5800 PRLD 77584 4502 D7
Razef Ct
700 HarC 77532 3552 A1
Razorback Dr
8200 HarC 77389 2965 E2
8200 HarC 77389 2966 A1
Razorbill Ct
2200 FBnC 77494 3951 D4
RD Andrus Rd
12000 MtgC 77302 2531 D6
Reaching Pines Cir
- HarC 77396 3407 B3
- HOUS 77396 3407 B3
Reading Ln
3600 GlsC 77518 4634 C2
Reading Rd
- FBnC 77469 4492 B7
- FBnC 77469 4616 E1
- RSBG 77469 4616 D1
- RSBG 77471 4492 A6
3600 HOUS 77004 4103 E1
4500 RSBG 77471 4491 C3
5100 RSBG 77469 4491 D5
7000 RSBG 77469 4492 B6
Reading St
3500 GlsC 77518 4634 C2
3700 HOUS 77004 4103 E1
Reading Center Blvd
1500 RSBG 77469 4491 E6
1500 RSBG 77469 4492 A6
Reads Ct
13300 HarC 77015 3828 D5
Readsland Ln
6600 HarC 77084 3678 D2
Reagan St
2600 HOUS 77009 3963 A1
2900 HOUS 77009 3824 A7
Reagan Meadow Ct
9100 HarC 77064 3540 D1
Reagon Canyon Dr
24000 HarC 77447 3249 E4
Reagor Wy
4000 GLSN 77554 5333 A2
11200 GLSN 77554 5221 B5
Real St
3300 HOUS 77087 4104 D5
Reality Rd
12700 HarC 77039 3546 B5
Reamer St
5600 HOUS 77096 4240 C1
6500 HOUS 77074 4240 A1
8600 HOUS 77074 4239 C1
Reams Ct
1200 FBnC 77545 4622 E2
Reams Ln
4400 FBnC 77545 4622 E2
4600 FBnC 77545 4623 A2
E Reata Dr
2200 DRPK 77536 4109 D6
W Reata Dr
2200 DRPK 77536 4109 D6
Reaves St
200 CNRO 77301 2384 C7
Reba
15100 MtgC 77306 2680 C2
Reba Dr
2400 HOUS 77019 3962 A6
3200 HOUS 77019 3961 E6
Reba Ln
2000 HOUS 77336 3121 A5
Reba St
900 HarC 77562 3832 A3
Rebawood Dr
8300 HarC 77346 3265 C4
Rebe St
- HarC 77039 3546 E3
6000 HarC 77039 3547 A3
Rebecca Dr
1100 PASD 77502 4107 D6
1100 PASD 77506 4107 D6
Rebecca Ln
1100 HMBL 77338 3406 E1
1100 HMBL 77338 3407 A1
1700 CNRO 77301 2384 D5
20100 MtgC 77357 2827 D6
Rebecca St
100 HOUS 77022 3824 A1
3400 HOUS 77021 4103 A7
3600 HOUS 77021 4243 B1
N Rebecca Burwell Ln
22300 HarC 77449 3814 E6
22300 HarC 77449 3815 A6
S Rebecca Burwell Ln
22300 HarC 77449 3814 E6
Rebecca Hill Ct
21000 FBnC 77469 4234 B3
Rebecca Pines Ct
600 BKHV 77024 3959 C2
600 HDWV 77024 3959 C2
Rebel Rd
11200 HOUS 77016 3687 A1
12100 LbyC 77327 2537 D4
12100 LbyC 77372 2537 D4
Rebel Ridge Dr
4800 SGLD 77478 4369 B7
Rebel Yell Dr
19100 HarC 77449 3677 A3
Rechelle St
11900 HarC 77093 3545 D7
12000 HarC 77039 3545 D7
12000 HOUS 77039 3545 D7
Record St
8200 HOUS 77028 3687 C6
Red Rd
- LbyC 77372 2684 B3
Red Acorn Tr
3500 PRLD 77581 4503 E6
E Red Adair Blvd
- LGCY 77573 4508 D5
Red Adler Cir
30400 MtgC 77355 2815 A1
Red Adler Ct
18700 MtgC 77355 2815 A1
Red Alder Cir
900 HarC 77073 3259 A4
Redan St
100 HOUS 77009 3824 B7
900 HOUS 77009 3823 E7
Red Ash Ct
18100 FBnC 77469 4095 B6
Red Ashberry Tr
21800 HarC 77433 3250 E5
Red Bank
- HarC 77090 3402 D1
Red Bay Cir
7200 MtgC 77354 2819 C3
7900 WDLD 77354 2819 B3
7900 WDLD 77382 2819 B2
Red Bay Ct
2000 HOUS 77062 4380 B7
Redbay Rd
20700 HarC 77449 3815 C4
Redberry Ct
10 WDLD 77381 2821 A6
Redberry Ln
23100 FBnC 77494 4093 C4
Redberry Glen Ln
- HarC 77377 3253 E3
6600 HarC 77041 3679 E3
Red Berryhill St
800 HarC 77521 3973 B1
Redberry Juniper Tr
25900 FBnC 77494 4093 B6
Redbird Knl
- HarC 77047 4374 C5
Red Bird Ln
25100 MtgC 77365 3117 D1
31600 MtgC 77362 2963 D3
Redbird Ln
8000 HarC 77044 3688 E7
Redbird Pl
10800 CHTW 77385 2823 A5
Redbird Rd
100 MtgC 77318 2237 B1
Redbird Ridge Dr
- HarC 77396 3406 D6
Red Bird Tree Ct
- HarC 77429 3253 C4
Red Bird Tree Ln
- HarC 77449 3814 C3
Red Bluff Cir
30500 MtgC 77355 2815 C1
Red Bluff Ct
1600 PASD 77506 4107 C4
Red Bluff Rd
600 PASD 77506 4107 C3
900 SEBK 77586 4383 A7
2600 PASD 77506 4108 A6
2600 SEBK 77586 4382 E7
2700 PASD 77503 4108 C7
2800 HarC 77586 4382 B6
2800 PASD 77507 4382 A6
2800 PASD 77586 4382 A6
4000 PASD 77503 4248 D1
4200 DRPK 77503 4248 D1
4200 DRPK 77536 4248 D1
5100 DRPK 77503 4249 A3
5100 DRPK 77536 4249 A3
5100 PASD 77503 4249 A3
5100 PASD 77536 4249 A3
7600 PASD 77505 4249 D7
7600 PASD 77507 4249 D7
8200 PASD 77505 4380 E1
8200 PASD 77507 4380 E1
8200 PASD 77507 4381 D5
11000 PASD 77586 4381 E5
20400 MtgC 77365 2972 E4
E Red Bluff Rd
100 PASD 77506 4107 A2
Red Bluff Tr
24800 FBnC 77494 3953 B5
Red Briar Tr
3900 DRPK 77536 4249 E1
Redbridge Ct
2500 HOUS 77059 4379 E5
Red Bridge Dr
- HarC 77346 3264 C7
Redbridge Ln
- LGCY 77573 4751 B1
Redbrook Dr
8300 HarC 77089 4377 B7
Redbud
700 HOUS 77339 3263 C2
Redbud Av
500 FBnC 77545 4623 C2
24200 MtgC 77365 2974 B7
Redbud Cir
200 LGCY 77573 4630 B5
1100 PASD 77502 4106 E7
Red Bud Ct
700 FRDW 77546 4505 B4
1500 PRLD 77581 4504 E4
Redbud Dr
2500 MtgC 77302 2676 E2
2500 MtgC 77302 2677 A3
4700 RSBG 77471 4491 C5
20100 MtgC 77357 2828 E6
Redbud Dr S
3800 LPRT 77571 4250 D4
E Redbud Dr
3800 LPRT 77571 4250 D4
W Redbud Dr
3800 LPRT 77571 4250 D4
Red Bud Ln
100 BYTN 77520 3971 B1
100 HarC 77532 3552 C7
300 WDBR 77357 2828 C2
1200 HOUS 77339 3263 C1
1500 HOUS 77339 3118 C7
1800 SGLD 77479 4367 E6
12000 HarC 77429 3398 C2
Redbud Ln
- HarC 77060 3544 C4
- HOUS 77060 3544 C4
300 RMFT 77357 2829 B1
1300 LMQU 77568 4990 A1
2700 ALVN 77511 4866 E4
Redbud Pl
- MtgC 77372 2682 E6
- PTVL 77372 2682 E6
Red Bud Rd
900 HarC 77530 3830 C6
Redbud St
2800 KATY 77493 3813 B4
3300 HOUS 77051 4243 B1
4600 HOUS 77033 4243 D2
Redbud Tr
20700 HarC 77346 3264 E3
Redbud Berry Ln
16300 HarC 77433 3251 B5
Redbud Berry Wy
15300 HarC 77433 3251 A6
Redbud Dale Ct
15300 HarC 77429 3252 A7
Redbud Grove Ct
1600 CNRO 77301 2384 D6
Redbud Hill Ct
2500 HarC 77388 3113 B5
Redbud Leaf Ln
14900 HarC 77433 3251 B7
Redbud Rain
- HarC 77449 3815 D2
Redbud Ridge Pl
10 WDLD 77380 2822 A6
Redbud Shores Ln
- HOUS 77044 3408 E5
12900 HarC 77044 3408 E5
Redbud Terrace Ln
18000 HarC 77433 3677 D1
Redbud Valley Tr
14200 HOUS 77062 4379 D7
Redbud Villa Ln
12600 HarC 77086 3542 C4
Redbush Dr
14100 FBnC 77478 4236 E4
Red Canary Ct
14700 HarC 77433 3250 D4
Red Candle Dr
3400 HarC 77388 3112 E6
3400 HarC 77388 3113 A4
Red Canna Vista
4700 HarC 77396 3407 B7
Red Canyon Ln
19300 HarC 77377 3109 C7
Red Cardinal Ln
- FBnC 77459 4621 C7
Red Carriage Ct
14200 HOUS 77062 4379 D7
Redcastle Ct
- HarC 77014 3402 C1
Red Castle Ln
9100 HarC 77396 3406 E6
9200 HarC 77396 3407 B6
Red Cedar Bnd
3400 BYTN 77521 3973 E3
E Red Cedar Cir
1000 WDLD 77380 2967 E1
N Red Cedar Cir
2600 WDLD 77380 2967 E1
S Red Cedar Cir
11800 WDLD 77380 2967 D1
Red Cedar Ct
6300 HarC 77346 3264 E3
Red Cedar Dr
3200 BYTN 77521 3973 D3
Red Cedar Ln
23500 HarC 77336 3267 A3
Redcedar Ln
900 HarC 77094 3955 B2
Red Cedar Tr
3200 BYTN 77521 3973 E3
Red Cedar Bluff Ln
15000 HarC 77433 3395 D1
15100 HarC 77433 3251 D7
Red Cedar Canyon Ln
19800 HarC 77433 3251 D6
Red Cedar Cove Ln
15100 HarC 77433 3251 D7
Red Cedar Pass
3500 BYTN 77521 3973 E3
Redchurch Dr
8100 HarC 77379 3256 B5
Red Cliff Dr
5400 HOUS 77345 3120 B6
Redcliff Dr
2100 MSCY 77489 4370 B7
3100 SGLD 77479 4495 E1
Redcliff Rd
8500 HarC 77064 3541 D5
Red Cloud Ct
13900 HarC 77429 3253 E5
Red Cloud Rd
8900 HarC 77064 3540 B6
Redcoat Dr
2100 MSCY 77489 4370 E5
Red Coat Ln
11800 BKHV 77024 3959 B3
Red Coral Ct
13700 HOUS 77059 4380 A4
Red Coral Dr
7000 PASD 77505 4249 A5
Red Creek Ct
2500 MSCY 77545 4622 C2
14500 HarC 77396 3547 C2
Red Creek Cove Ln
14200 HarC 77396 3547 C2
Redcrest Dr
16400 HarC 77095 3397 B7
Redcrest Ln
16000 HarC 77447 3248 E7
Redcrest Manor Dr
21100 FBnC 77469 4234 B5
Red Deer Dr
24400 HOUS 77336 3266 B2
Red Deer Ln
10 WDLD 77380 2968 A2
Redding Rd
5900 HOUS 77036 4099 B4
Redding Crest Ln
15000 HarC 77429 3253 C7
Reddingford Ln
16300 HarC 77084 3678 C4
Redding Oak Ct
7900 HarC 77088 3682 C1
Redding Ridge Ln
26000 FBnC 77494 4093 A3
Redding Springs Ln
6400 HarC 77086 3542 C3
Reddington Rd
1900 SGLD 77478 4237 C
Reddingwood Ct
21900 HarC 77373 3261 A
Reddleshire Ln
1300 HOUS 77043 3819 A
Reddleston Ct
6600 HarC 77389 2966 C
Reddy Ln
15800 HOUS 77053 4372 C
Red Eagle Ct
18200 HarC 77346 3408 D
Redell Rd
- HarC 77521 3832 C
3700 HarC 77521 3971 E
3700 HarC 77521 3972 A
5700 BYTN 77520 3832 C
N Redell Rd
5300 HarC 77521 3833 A
5300 HarC 77521 3972 A
5600 BYTN 77521 3833 A
Redemption Cir
5100 HOUS 77018 3684 A
Red Falls Cir
16700 HarC 77095 3538 B
Red Fawn Dr
- HOUS 77336 3266 B
Red Fern Ct
10200 CHTW 77385 2822 E
10200 MtgC 77385 2822 E
17000 HarC 77095 3538 A
Redfern Dr
8100 HOUS 77033 4243 E
12100 HOUS 77048 4374 E
Redfield Dr
3100 PASD 77503 4108 B
Red Finch Ct
7800 HarC 77396 3406 D
Red Fir Dr
3600 HOUS 77088 3683 A
Redfish Dr
1900 TXCY 77591 4873 A
4500 JMAB 77554 5331 E
S Redfish Dr
7700 HTCK 77563 4988 E
7700 HTCK 77563 5104 A
Redfish Ln
13300 STAF 77477 4369 D
Redfish St
900 BYUV 77563 4990 E
900 BYUV 77563 4991 A
900 BYUV 77563 5105 D
900 GlsC 77563 4991 A
Redfish Reef Dr
4800 GlsC 77539 4634 C
Redford Rd
1200 HOUS 77034 4246 B
Redford St
8600 HOUS 77061 4246 A
8600 HOUS 77075 4246 A
9400 HOUS 77034 4246 B
Redford Path Dr
- HarC 77338 3407 B
Redford Pines Ln
- HarC 77338 3407 B
Red Fox Dr
1300 HOUS 77532 3266 C
Red Fox Ln
28300 MtgC 77362 2963 D
Red Fox Rd
14300 HarC 77377 3108 D
Red Gable Ln
7400 FBnC 77469 4094 D
Redgate Cir
7800 MSCY 77071 4239 E
Redgate Dr
13300 HarC 77015 3828 D
Red Glade Ct
23700 HarC 77373 3114 C
Red Goodrum Rd
19200 MtgC 77306 2534 C
Redgrove Ln
5600 FBnC 77494 4093 A
Red Gully Dr
16600 FBnC 77478 4236 A
Redgum Dr
3100 HarC 77449 3815 D
Redhaven Ct
11000 HarC 77065 3539 D
Red Haven Dr
- HarC 77562 3832 A
200 HarC 77562 3831 E1
Redhaven Pl
10 WDLD 77381 2820 B
Red Haw Ln
4100 HOUS 77022 3824 A
Redhaw St
1000 HOUS 77079 3818 B
1000 HOUS 77079 3957 A
Red Hawk Cir
9000 HarC 77064 3540 B
Redhead Ct
13200 HOUS 77044 3549 E1
Redhead St
6000 KATY 77493 3813 B
Redhill Dr
- HarC 77083 4237 A
Red Hill Tr
15800 HarC 77095 3538 D
Red Holly Ln
8100 HarC 77379 3255 E
Red Lake Ct
1700 FBnC 77469 4234 D
Red Lake Ln
4500 FBnC 77469 4234 D
Redland Ct
3400 MSCY 77459 4496 E
Redland Pl
10 WDLD 77382 2674 A
Redlands Dr
7800 HarC 77040 3541 D
Redland Woods Dr
7800 HarC 77040 3541 D
Red Lantern Dr
4800 HarC 77546 4505 D
Red Laurel Ct
12000 HarC 77429 3397 C
Red Leaf Dr
16700 MtgC 77306 2533 C
Redleaf Ln
- HOUS 77090 3258 C
700 HarC 77090 3258 C
Redleaf Forest Ln
5000 FBnC 77494 4092 E
Redleaf Hollow Ct
8800 HarC 77095 3537 C
Redleaf Hollow Ln
17400 HarC 77095 3537 E

STREET
Block City ZIP Map# Grid

ed Leo Ln
22700 HarC 77389 2967 A6
edline
- HarC 77049 3690 D5
ed Lion St
3000 HOUS 77449 3814 D6
edlock
- HarC 77049 3690 D7
ed Lodge Dr
5000 HarC 77084 3677 E6
ed Magnolia Ct
1900 HOUS 77339 3118 C7
edman St
1200 PASD 77502 4107 A6
1200 PASD 77506 4107 A6
ed Maple Ct
2900 FRDW 77598 4630 C3
ed Maple Dr
3100 FRDW 77598 4630 B2
9500 HarC 77064 3541 A4
ed Maples Dr
2700 HOUS 77339 3119 A6
ed Meadows Dr
3500 MtgC 77386 2969 E3
ed Mesa Ct
10000 HarC 77095 3538 B3
ed Mesa Dr
10000 HarC 77095 3538 B3
edmond St
1300 HarC 77015 3968 B2
ed Mulberry Ln
14400 HOUS 77044 3549 E1
ed N Gold Dr
- FBnC 77477 4370 B5
- STAF 77477 4370 B5
ed Oak
100 BzaC 77578 4625 B3
Red Oak
19900 MtgC 77357 2829 B6
ed Oak Av
- HarC 77532 3692 C3
ed Oak Ct
1300 SGLD 77479 4367 E6
1700 CNRO 77301 2384 E7
6200 PASD 77505 4248 D7
12000 MtgC 77354 2671 B4
28000 HOUS 77336 3121 A4
ed Oak Dr
1700 CNRO 77301 2384 E7
1700 CNRO 77301 2530 E1
13000 HarC 77532 3692 A1
16300 MSCY 77071 4239 A7
16300 MSCY 77071 4370 B1
16700 HarC 77090 3258 B3
16700 HOUS 77090 3258 C4
23800 HarC 77389 2966 A5
26300 MtgC 77355 2814 A5
ed Oak Hllw
26300 MtgC 77355 2814 A5
ed Oak Ln
100 CNRO 77304 2383 B6
200 TXCY 77591 4874 A6
700 FRDW 77546 4505 B4
800 MtgC 77306 2385 D4
2800 PRLD 77584 4502 D4
5400 HarC 77379 3112 A7
20200 MtgC 77357 2827 C6
26100 MtgC 77355 2814 B4
/ Red Oak Ln
- TXCY 77591 4873 B6
ed Oak Rd
7800 MtgC 77354 2819 B4
ed Oak St
300 HOUS 77009 3824 B5
15900 HarC 77530 3969 B2
24800 MtgC 77355 2962 C3
ed Oak Ter
1700 HOUS 77339 3118 D6
ed Oak Tr
23000 HarC 77377 2962 D7
ed Oak Branch Ln
3600 HOUS 77345 3119 C2
ed Oak Forest Ln
2700 MtgC 77386 2823 D7
ed Oak Glen Dr
13000 HarC 77429 3254 A6
ed Oak Leaf Tr
2900 HarC 77084 3816 B4
ed Oak Manor Ln
18100 HarC 77433 3537 C6
edoak Pass Ln
10000 HarC 77064 3540 B3
edoak Ridge Ln
10500 HarC 77064 3540 B3
ed Oaks N
19500 MtgC 77357 2829 B5
ed Oak Terrace Ct
- HOUS 77339 3118 C6
edondo Dr
700 HOUS 77015 3967 B1
ed Pheasant Ct
8600 JRSV 77040 3540 C6
ed Pine Ct
18100 MtgC 77365 2971 E2
ed Pine Dr
22500 HarC 77375 2965 E7
ed Pine Ridge Wy
15500 HarC 77049 3829 A2
ed Ridge Ct
3100 BzaC 77578 4501 A6
ed Ripple Rd
100 HOUS 77076 3684 C5
300 HOUS 77091 3684 C5
ed River
4800 MtgC 77386 2970 B2
ed River Ct
700 HarC 77450 3953 E2
4900 MtgC 77386 2970 B2
ed River Dr
5800 DKSN 77539 4633 D7
5800 DKSN 77539 4754 D1
7300 FBnC 77469 4493 D6
22100 HarC 77450 3953 D2
22100 HarC 77450 3954 A3
ed River Lp
28800 MtgC 77386 2970 B2
ed River Rd
- HMPD 77445 2953 B6
ed River St
1000 LGCY 77573 4632 D3
ed River Tr
- DRPK 77536 4109 E7
17200 HarC 77095 3537 E1
Red River Canyon Dr
17800 HarC 77346 3408 D2
Red Robin Ln
7400 HOUS 77075 4376 B2

Red Robin St
200 RMFT 77357 2829 B3
Red Rock
36000 MtgC 77355 2816 A3
Red Rock Dr
- FRDW 77546 4629 B5
Redrock St
2200 HOUS 77088 3683 B2
Red Rock Canyon Ct
22900 HarC 77450 3953 D4
Red Rock Canyon Dr
700 HarC 77450 3954 A3
800 HarC 77450 3953 D4
Redrock Falls
24400 HarC 77375 2965 D4
Red Rooster Ln
- FBnC 77494 4093 A3
Redroot Dr
19700 HarC 77084 3816 A5
19800 HarC 77084 3815 E4
Red Rover Ct
3100 HarC 77373 3115 A3
Red Rugosa Dr
10100 HarC 77095 3537 E3
10400 HarC 77095 3538 A2
Red Rugossa Dr
9500 HarC 77095 3537 E4
Red Sable Ct
10 WDLD 77380 2967 B4
Red Sable Dr
- WDLD 77380 2967 C4
Red Sable Pt
10 WDLD 77380 2967 C4
Red Sails Pass
18400 HarC 77346 3409 C1
18500 HarC 77346 3265 E7
18500 HOUS 77346 3265 E7
Red Sky Ct
1900 HarC 77373 3114 D5
Red Sky Dr
23800 HarC 77373 3114 D5
Red Slate Ln
10400 HarC 77095 3537 E2
Red Springs Dr
15700 HarC 77082 4096 B2
Red Spruce Ln
10600 HarC 77040 3541 E6
Redstaff Ct
7000 FBnC 77469 4234 A2
Red Stag Ct
12400 MtgC 77303 2239 D4
Red Stag Ln
9100 MtgC 77303 2239 E3
Red Stag Pass
3000 FBnC 77459 4621 E6
Red Star St
800 HOUS 77034 4379 A6
800 HOUS 77598 4379 A6
Redstart St
4500 HOUS 77035 4241 A4
5000 HOUS 77035 4240 E4
5400 HOUS 77096 4240 D3
Redstem Ct
3900 DKSN 77539 4754 D2
Redstone Ct
10800 FBnC 77459 4622 A5
Redstone Dr
- HarC 77530 3829 C7
5100 FBnC 77469 4234 D3
Redstone Wy
- FBnC 77459 4622 B5
Redstone Bend Dr
13700 HarC 77396 3547 D2
Redstone Manor Dr
1500 HarC 77379 3110 B7
Red Sun Dr
20500 HarC 77449 3815 D4
Red Tail Wy
4800 HarC 77396 3407 B7
Red Tailed Hawk Ct
13300 HOUS 77044 3550 A1
Red Tailed Hawk Ln
14400 HOUS 77044 3550 A1
Red Tail Hawk Ct
16300 MtgC 77302 2679 B4
Red Timber Ct
- LGCY 77573 4631 A7
Red Timber Ln
- FBnC 77083 4095 D5
- FBnC 77469 4095 D5
Red Valley Dr
2100 HarC 77530 3829 E3
Redway Ln
400 HOUS 77598 4506 E4
700 HOUS 77062 4506 E3
1400 HOUS 77062 4507 B2
Redwick Ct
20000 HarC 77388 3113 A5
Redwick Dr
2700 HarC 77388 3113 A5
Redwicke Ln
16300 HarC 77084 3678 C4
Red Willow Dr
15800 HarC 77084 3678 E7
Redwin Cir
4000 HOUS 77047 4374 C1
Red Wing Dr
1100 FRDW 77546 4629 D5
Redwing Dr
9000 HarC 77049 3690 D4
Redwing Ln
7500 HMBL 77396 3406 C5
N Redwing St
10 LMQU 77568 4990 E5
S Redwing St
10 LMQU 77568 4990 E6
Red Wing Tr
22500 HarC 77375 3110 B2
Redwing Bluff Dr
1700 HOUS 77009 3824 B4
Redwing Brook Tr
4800 HarC 77449 3676 E7
Redwing Cove Dr
1700 HOUS 77009 3824 B4
Redwing Grove Wy
2700 HarC 77038 3543 A5
Redwing Haven Dr
1700 HOUS 77009 3824 B4
Redwing Knoll Dr
19400 HarC 77433 3677 B2
Redwing Park Dr
700 HOUS 77009 3824 B4
Redwing Pines Dr
1700 HOUS 77009 3824 B4
Redwing Pl Dr
1700 HOUS 77009 3824 A5
Redwing Ridge Dr
1700 HOUS 77009 3824 B4

Redwinn Dr
2200 PASD 77502 4247 A1
Red Wolf Ct
17600 HarC 77084 3677 E3
Red Wolf Dr
17700 HarC 77084 3677 E3
Red Wolf Ln
10000 HarC 77064 3540 C3
Redwood Av
500 FBnC 77545 4623 C2
600 BzaC 77583 4623 D2
600 PRLD 77545 4623 D2
Redwood Cir
1700 ALVN 77511 4867 A4
Redwood Ct
1800 SGLD 77478 4237 A6
31900 MtgC 77355 2669 B6
Redwood Dr
- BYTN 77520 3835 C3
2000 LGCY 77565 4509 A5
10300 CmbC 77520 3835 D3
Red Wood Ln
200 WDBR 77357 2828 D3
Redwood Ln
- MtgC 77355 2669 B6
- PRVW 77445 3100 A3
1200 PASD 77502 4106 E7
25300 MtgC 77372 2536 E2
25300 MtgC 77372 2537 A2
Redwood St
900 HOUS 77023 4105 A4
1300 HOUS 77087 4105 A4
1600 DKSN 77539 4753 D2
Redwood Arbor Ln
4000 FBnC 77545 4622 C2
Redwood Bend Ln
600 BzaC 77584 4374 C7
600 BzaC 77584 4501 C1
Redwood Bend Tr
14500 HOUS 77062 4379 D7
14600 HOUS 77062 4506 D1
Redwood Bough Ln
1200 HOUS 77062 4379 E6
Redwood Bridge Tr
6100 HOUS 77345 3120 C4
Redwood Cove Ct
14900 HOUS 77062 4380 B6
Redwood Falls Dr
3700 HarC 77082 4096 C3
6700 PASD 77505 4248 E5
6800 PASD 77505 4249 A5
Red Woodford Ln
- HarC 77049 3828 D2
Redwood Forest Ct
16300 FBnC 77478 4236 A5
Redwood Grove Ct
4600 HOUS 77345 3119 D2
Redwood Grove St
3300 PRLD 77581 4503 E6
3300 PRLD 77581 4504 A5
Redwood Hill Ct
4000 FBnC 77545 4622 D1
Redwood Hollow Ln
- HarC 77346 3408 C3
Redwood Lake Dr
- HOUS 77345 3120 E6
3200 HOUS 77345 3119 D4
Redwood Lodge Ct
3400 HOUS 77339 3119 A5
Redwood Lodge Dr
2900 HOUS 77339 3119 A5
Redwood Manor Ln
19700 HarC 77433 3537 A7
Redwood Meadow Ln
1000 FBnC 77545 4622 C2
Redwood Park Ln
- HarC 77346 3408 B2
Redwood Pl Dr
15900 HOUS 77079 3956 D2
Redwood Point Ln
- HOUS 77089 4505 C1
Redwood River Dr
5800 HOUS 77345 3120 B5
Redwood Run Ct
15200 HOUS 77062 4380 B7
Redwood Shadows Ct
3100 HarC 77084 3816 C4
Redwood Shores Dr
13400 HOUS 77044 3409 A5
Redwood Tree St
19700 FBnC 77469 4234 D3
Redwood Village Cir
1400 MtgC 77386 2823 A7
Red Wren Ct
2500 HOUS 77345 3120 C5
Reecewood Dr
500 MSCY 77489 4370 E5
Reed Blvd
34700 PRVW 77445 3101 A1
34700 WlrC 77445 3101 A1
Reed Ct
6900 HOUS 77087 4245 A2
Reed Ln
7300 MNVL 77578 4746 D4
Reed Rd
- STAF 77477 4237 E7
1900 HOUS 77045 4242 C4
1900 HOUS 77051 4242 D4
2700 HOUS 77051 4243 C4
4600 HOUS 77033 4243 D4
5400 HOUS 77033 4244 A4
6200 HOUS 77087 4244 E3
7100 HOUS 77087 4245 A3
12300 SGLD 77478 4237 E7
12300 STAF 77478 4237 E7
23000 LbyC 77327 2684 B5
23000 MtgC 77372 2684 B5
23000 PLMG 77327 2684 B6
Reed St
3200 LPRT 77571 4382 E1
Reed Creek Ln
21300 HarC 77388 3112 C5
Reedcrest St
12000 HOUS 77035 4371 A1
12000 HOUS 77085 4371 A1
Reedpoint Dr
1100 HarC 77090 3258 C7
1300 HarC 77014 3258 C7
Reeds Ferry Dr
6100 HarC 77041 3679 C4
Reedwood Dr
500 MSCY 77489 4370 D6
500 MSCY 77489 4371 A6
Reedwood Ln
10100 HOUS 77036 4238 E1
Reedwood Ridge Rd
12700 HarC 77065 3539 C1
Reedy Pond Ct
10 WDLD 77381 2820 E4

Reedy Pond St
10 WDLD 77381 2820 E4
Reef Dr
2000 LGCY 77573 4509 B7
Reef Wy
- HarC 77532 3411 B7
Reefton Ln
3800 MSCY 77459 4496 D3
Reese Rd
- RSBG 77469 4615 B1
- RSBG 77471 4615 B1
Reese St
300 HarC 77532 3552 C4
1200 HOUS 77012 4105 D3
Reese Lake Dr
10900 FBnC 77469 4092 B7
Reesler Rd
- FBnC 77469 4615 B2
Reeves Dr
3900 GLSN 77554 5441 B4
Reeves St
800 CNRO 77301 2384 B4
3200 HOUS 77004 4103 D1
Reeveston Rd
12700 HarC 77039 3545 B6
Refinery Rd
- DRPK 77536 4109 A3
Reflection
10 BYTN 77521 3972 C1
Reflection Cir
10 BYTN 77521 3972 B1
Reflection Ct
2300 MSCY 77459 4369 C7
Reflection Pt
10 WDLD 77381 2821 B5
Reflection Bay Dr
2000 PRLD 77584 4500 C1
Reflections Path Wy
9200 HarC 77396 3406 E7
9200 HarC 77396 3407 B6
Refugio Ct
9700 HarC 77064 3540 D6
Regal Dr
4500 BYTN 77521 3972 C1
Regal Row
9900 HarC 77040 3681 A2
10300 HarC 77040 3680 E2
Regal St
500 HOUS 77034 4246 D5
Regal Blue Ct
1600 FBnC 77545 4622 D2
Regalbrook Ct
14700 HarC 77095 3539 A6
Regalbrook Dr
8500 HarC 77095 3539 B6
Regal Green Ct
1300 HOUS 77345 3120 E7
Regal Green Ln
27100 HarC 77339 3118 C5
Regal Hollow Ln
600 HarC 77073 3259 A4
Regal Isle Ct
23100 HarC 77494 3953 C3
Regal Landing Dr
- HOUS 77345 3120 E6
Regal Manor Ln
10800 HOUS 77075 4376 E4
Regal Oak Wy
1300 SGLD 77479 4367 D6
Regal Oaks Dr
3200 PRLD 77581 4504 B4
Regal Oaks Bend Ln
12800 HOUS 77047 4373 B2
Regal Park Ct
31600 MtgC 77385 2823 C6
Regal Pass Ln
700 HarC 77049 3829 A3
Regal Pine Ln
12700 HarC 77070 3399 B5
Regal Pine Tr
- HOUS 77059 4380 C3
4400 PASD 77059 4380 C3
Regal Pine Wy
5100 FRDW 77546 4505 D5
Regal Ridge Ln
5400 HOUS 77053 4498 E1
Regalshire Ct
12900 HOUS 77047 4373 C2
Regal Shores Ct
1300 HOUS 77345 3120 E7
Regalside Ct
1200 FBnC 77469 4493 B5
Regal Spruce Ct
7900 HarC 77095 3537 C7
Regal Trace Ln
15700 HarC 77073 3259 C5
Regalwood Dr
2400 HarC 77038 3543 A2
Regan Ct
10 WDLD 77382 2819 A2
N Regan Mead Cir
10 WDLD 77382 2819 C2
S Regan Mead Cir
10 WDLD 77382 2819 C3
Regan Mead Ct
- WDLD 77382 2819 B3
Regata Crest
- HarC 77494 3953 A2
Regata Run Dr
2900 HarC 77546 4506 A7
Regatta Rd
18500 HarC 77346 3265 D7
18500 HarC 77346 3409 D1
Regena St
1300 HarC 77039 3545 B6
Regency Ct
10 CNRO 77304 2529 D1
300 FRDW 77546 4629 D3
Regency Dr
200 DRPK 77536 4249 B1
3500 BzaC 77511 4748 A4
3800 HOUS 77045 4241 D6
5300 SGLD 77479 4495 A4
Regency Ln
10 HarC 77088 3542 D7
Regency Pl
7400 HarC 77379 3256 B1
Regency Wy
100 CNRO 77304 2529 D1
Regency Ash Ct
11800 HarC 77429 3398 D5
Regency Creek Dr
3000 FBnC 77469 4233 E7
3000 FBnC 77469 4234 A7
Regency Forest Dr
11600 HarC 77429 3398 D5
Regency Green Dr
11100 HarC 77070 3399 A4

Regency Green Dr
11100 HarC 77429 3398 E4
11100 HarC 77429 3399 A4
Regency Oak Ln
13200 HarC 77429 3398 E4
Regency Pine Dr
11800 HarC 77429 3398 E5
Regency Pines Dr
26800 MtgC 77339 3118 C5
Regency Square Blvd
7000 HOUS 77036 4100 A3
7200 HOUS 77036 4099 E3
Regency Square Ct
7100 HOUS 77036 4099 E3
Regency Villa Dr
4300 HarC 77084 3678 D7
4300 HarC 77084 3817 D1
Regency Wood Dr
12900 HarC 77429 3398 E4
Regent Ct
10 SGLD 77478 4368 E3
Regent Sq
10 WDLD 77381 2821 B5
Regent St
5100 HarC 77039 3546 D6
Regent Manor Dr
4600 HOUS 77339 3264 C1
4600 HOUS 77339 3265 A1
N Regent Oak
10 WDLD 77381 2674 C7
S Regent Oak
10 WDLD 77381 2674 C7
Regent Oak Ct
10 WDLD 77381 2674 C7
Regents Pk
10 SGLD 77479 4495 E3
Regents Bay Dr
- PRLD 77584 4500 A2
Regents Corner Ln
20200 HarC 77449 3815 C7
Regents Cove Ct
9100 HOUS 77099 4237 E1
Regents Crest Ln
3800 HarC 77449 3816 B2
Regents Park Dr
1200 HOUS 77058 4507 C4
Regentview Dr
400 HOUS 77079 3958 A3
8200 HOUS 77072 4098 A7
Regg Dr
- HOUS 77045 4372 D1
12800 HOUS 77045 4241 D6
Regina Dr
15900 HarC 77084 3678 E5
Regional Park Dr
1100 HarC 77060 3403 E4
Regnal St
14700 HarC 77039 3545 A1
15000 HarC 77032 3545 A1
Rehab Lp
- HarC 77396 3407 C4
Reichert Farms Ct
10 HNCV 77024 3960 A1
Reid Rd
- PRLD 77584 4502 B3
2600 PRLD 77581 4502 B3
Reid St
100 HOUS 77022 3824 B3
1900 HOUS 77026 3824 E3
2800 HOUS 77026 3825 A3
Reid Lake Dr
9200 HarC 77064 3541 B5
Reidland Av
900 HarC 77532 3552 D4
E Reidland Av
100 HarC 77532 3552 C4
Reidland Rd
- HarC 77532 3411 C4
W Reidland St
100 HarC 77532 3552 C4
Reigate Ln
15300 HarC 77530 3829 D5
Reight Meyer Ranch Rd
9400 HTCK 77563 4988 D3
Reims Rd
5900 HOUS 77036 4099 E4
8400 HOUS 77074 4099 E7
Rein St
900 HOUS 77009 3824 C7
Reina Ln
- HarC 77050 3547 A7
- HOUS 77016 3547 A7
Reinald Rd
4000 HarC 77014 3401 D2
Reindeer Cres
3000 FBnC 77459 4622 A6
Reindeer Run
2800 FBnC 77459 4622 A6
Reinecke St
200 HOUS 77007 3962 A3
Reinerman St
1900 HOUS 77007 3962 B1
Reinhard Av
- RSBG 77471 4490 C6
Reinhard St
500 RSBG 77471 4490 C6
Reinhardt Rd
17800 MtgC 77302 2679 E1
17800 MtgC 77306 2679 E1
Reinke Rd
- HarC 77484 3101 D4
- WALR 77484 3101 D4
Reiser Ct
1600 PRLD 77581 4504 D6
Reiss Tr
17300 MtgC 77357 2680 E7
Reissen Ln
14100 HarC 77069 3400 A1
Relay Rd
18900 HarC 77346 3265 D6
Reliant Pk
10 HOUS 77054 4102 B7
E Relza Dr
15400 MtgC 77372 2684 A4
W Relza Dr
15400 MtgC 77372 2684 A4
Rembrandt Wy
- WDLD 77382 2819 B2
Remegan Rd
7300 HOUS 77033 4244 A1
Remford
- HOUS 77449 3814 D5
Remick
13100 HarC 77429 3254 A5
Remington Ct
900 FRDW 77546 4629 D1
4900 SGLD 77479 4495 C5

Remington Ln
10 HOUS 77005 4102 D2
10 HOUS 77030 4102 D2
Remington Tr
- WlrC 77493 3812 A7
100 HOUS 77336 3120 E3
300 HarC 77336 3120 D3
Remington Bay Cir
200 HarC 77073 3403 B2
Remington Bend Ct
300 HarC 77073 3403 B2
Remington Bend Dr
300 HarC 77073 3403 A2
Remington Bridge Dr
300 HarC 77073 3403 A2
Remington Chase Ct
500 HarC 77073 3403 B1
Remington Cove Ct
25600 MtgC 77365 3117 E3
Remington Creek Dr
300 HarC 77073 3403 A3
Remington Crest Ct
19600 HarC 77094 3955 A3
Remington Crest Dr
1300 HarC 77094 3955 A3
Remington Cross Dr
19400 HarC 77073 3403 A2
Remington Falls Ln
400 HarC 77073 3403 B3
Remington Forest E
- WlrC 77447 2813 D1
Remington Forest W
27100 WlrC 77447 2813 D1
Remington Glen Ct
500 HarC 77073 3403 B2
Remington Green Ct
400 HarC 77073 3403 A2
Remington Green Dr
300 HarC 77073 3403 A2
Remington Grove Ct
19000 HarC 77433 3677 B2
Remington Grove Dr
7000 HarC 77433 3677 B1
7000 HarC 77449 3677 B2
Remington Harbor Ct
200 HarC 77073 3403 A3
Remington Heights Dr
200 HarC 77073 3403 A2
Remington Hollow Ln
19600 HarC 77073 3403 A2
Remington Lodge Ct
500 HarC 77073 3403 B2
Remington Manor Dr
19100 HarC 77433 3677 B2
Remington Manor St
19300 HarC 77379 3110 D6
Remington Martin Dr
19400 HarC 77073 3403 A2
Remington Mill Dr
18800 HarC 77073 3403 B3
Remington Park Ct
400 HarC 77073 3403 A2
Remington Park Dr
18700 HarC 77073 3403 B3
Remington Peak Ct
200 HarC 77073 3403 A3
Remington Point Ct
500 HarC 77073 3403 B2
Remington Prairie Dr
19400 HarC 77073 3403 A2
Remington Ranches Dr
28000 MtgC 77354 2818 B4
Remington Ridge Dr
200 HarC 77073 3403 A3
Remington Run Ln
11800 HarC 77066 3401 B6
Remington Springs Dr
19200 HarC 77073 3403 B2
Remington Valley Dr
- HarC 77090 3403 A2
100 HarC 77073 3403 A2
Remington Walk Ct
700 HarC 77073 3403 B2
Remington Wick Ct
19400 HarC 77073 3403 B1
Remlap Av
6400 HOUS 77055 3822 A5
Remme Ridge Ln
13100 HOUS 77047 4373 B3
Remson Hollow Ln
- FBnC 77494 4092 A5
Remus Dr
- HarC 77053 4372 D5
5100 HOUS 77053 4372 B4
Remwick Dr
600 HarC 77073 3403 B3
Remy St
12800 HOUS 77045 4241 D6
Rena St
6600 HOUS 77092 3682 C7
Renae
- HarC 77562 3832 A2
Renae St
600 HarC 77562 3692 E6
Renaissance Ln
12100 HOUS 77071 4239 D6
Rena Jane Ln
3700 PASD 77503 4108 C5
Renata Cir
6700 HarC 77084 3678 A2
Renaud St
6400 HTCK 77563 4989 B5
7500 HTCK 77563 4988 E4
Renault St
13700 HarC 77015 3967 E2
14000 HarC 77015 3968 A2
Rendale Ct
2300 HarC 77388 3113 A2
Rendezvous Ct
3100 HarC 77373 3115 B4
Rene Cir
13200 STFE 77510 4870 D6
Rene Ct
1300 FBnC 77479 4493 C1
Rene Dr
- BzaC 77511 4627 A7
- BzaC 77511 4748 A1
Renee Ln
14400 HarC 77532 3554 B5
Renee Springs Ct
- HarC 77379 3255 E4
Renfro Dr
6800 FBnC 77469 4493 C7
Renfrow Burford Rd
300 FBnC 77545 4623 C2
600 BzaC 77583 4623 D2
600 PRLD 77545 4623 D2

Renmark Ln
7400 HarC 77070 3399 E2
7400 HarC 77070 3400 A2
Renn Rd
- HarC 77072 4237 C1
- HarC 77099 4237 C1
13200 HarC 77083 4237 A1
14000 HarC 77083 4236 E1
Renner Crossing Dr
15200 HarC 77433 3251 D7
Renners Ct
800 HOUS 77007 3963 B3
Rennie Dr
- HOUS 77450 3954 D1
200 HarC 77450 3954 D3
Reno Dr
5000 PASD 77505 4248 B3
Reno St
- HOUS 77092 3682 D7
- HOUS 77092 3821 D1
Renoir
2900 SGLD 77479 4368 C7
Renoir Dr
100 HOUS 77079 3958 D3
Renoir Trail Pl
10 WDLD 77382 2819 B2
Reno Ranch Ln
20800 HarC 77388 3112 B3
Renshaw St
2700 HOUS 77023 4104 C4
Rental Car Av
17300 HOUS 77032 3405 A3
Rent Car Rd
- HOUS 77061 4245 C4
E Rent Car Rd
- HOUS 77061 4245 C4
S Rent Car Rd
- HOUS 77061 4245 C4
Renters Rd
- WlrC 77447 2958 D5
Renton Dr
2800 HarC 77032 3545 E1
2800 HarC 77032 3546 A1
2800 HOUS 77032 3545 E1
2800 HOUS 77032 3546 A1
Rentur Dr
9100 HOUS 77031 4239 B3
Renwick
9300 HOUS 77096 4240 C1
Renwick Dr
- BLAR 77096 4100 C6
- HOUS 77096 4100 C7
5300 HOUS 77057 4100 C5
5300 HOUS 77081 4100 C5
7300 BLAR 77081 4100 C5
7300 BLAR 77401 4100 C5
7300 HOUS 77401 4100 C5
11000 HOUS 77096 4240 D4
11500 HOUS 77035 4240 D5
Renwood Dr
9200 HOUS 77080 3820 D3
Reo St
13800 HOUS 77040 3681 C5
Repa Ln
13600 HarC 77014 3401 D2
Repiton Wy
1500 HarC 77493 3814 B6
Reppert St
600 GlsC 77518 4634 B2
600 GlsC 77539 4634 B2
600 LGCY 77539 4634 B2
N Repsdorph Cir
- SEBK 77586 4509 B1
Repsdorph Rd
1900 SEBK 77586 4509 B2
2200 ELGO 77586 4509 B2
W Repsdorph Rd
- SEBK 77586 4509 C1
E Republic Av
- BYTN 77520 4112 E2
100 BYTN 77520 4113 A1
W Republic Av
1500 BYTN 77520 3972 C7
Republic Rd
500 MtgC 77357 2829 C2
500 RMFT 77357 2829 C2
Resada Park Ln
8400 FBnC 77469 4095 D7
Research Pk
8900 MtgC 77381 2821 D3
8900 WDLD 77381 2821 D3
Research Forest Dr
- WDLD 77382 2674 A4
1100 SHEH 77381 2822 A3
1500 SHEH 77381 2821 E3
1600 WDLD 77380 2821 E3
1600 WDLD 77381 2821 D3
2400 MtgC 77381 2821 D3
4900 WDLD 77381 2675 A7
6500 WDLD 77381 2674 E6
Reseda Cir
16100 HOUS 77062 4507 A3
Reseda Dr
300 HOUS 77598 4506 E4
900 HOUS 77062 4507 C2
2000 HOUS 77058 4507 C3
Reserve St
700 HOUS 77007 3962 E2
Reserve Bend Dr
28900 HarC 77336 3120 D1
Reserve Park Wy
28800 HarC 77336 3120 D3
Reserve Point Ln
15200 HarC 77429 3253 D7
Reserve Ridge Dr
300 HarC 77336 3120 D2
Reservoir Av
- HarC 77044 3690 A5
8000 HarC 77049 3690 A6
Resica Falls Ln
18600 HarC 77094 3955 C1
Resolute
- HOUS 77072 4097 E5
Resource Pkwy
10900 HOUS 77089 4378 B7
Restaurant Row
19500 HOUS 77084 3816 A7
19500 HOUS 77084 3955 A1
Restful Hllw
26500 MtgC 77355 2814 A2
Resthome Rd
3700 BzaC 77584 4502 B7
3700 BzaC 77584 4626 B1
3700 PRLD 77584 4502 B7
Restin Ln
- HarC 77530 3830 C5
Restless Bay Ln
2300 PRLD 77584 4500 D4

STREET Block City ZIP Map# Grid

Reston Bridge Dr
15900 HarC 77429 3397 A1
Reston Glen Ln
16900 HarC 77073 3259 A4
Reston Grove Ct
15600 HarC 77095 3538 D4
Reston Grove Ln
9300 HarC 77095 3538 D4
Reston Point Dr
10900 FBnC 77469 4092 D7
Restoration Ln
400 HarC 77562 3832 B4
Restover Ln
9100 HarC 77064 3540 C5
Restridge Rd
2100 HOUS 77055 3821 B4
Reta Dr
300 DRPK 77536 4109 B5
Retama St
800 LMQU 77568 4990 B1
Retha St
- HOUS 77085 4371 C4
Retherford Dr
9800 HarC 77086 3542 C3
Retlin Ct
6200 HarC 77041 3679 B4
Retreat Tr
12500 HarC 77429 3398 A5
Retrevier Dr
1900 MSCY 77489 4370 C5
Retta St
3000 HOUS 77026 3825 A7
Rettendon Ct
25000 HarC 77389 2966 A3
Rettilon Dr
- BYTN 77521 3973 E2
Rettilon Rd
700 GlsC 77650 4879 E5
Retton Dr
- HOUS 77092 3682 C7
- HOUS 77092 3821 C1
Reuben White Dr
100 HarC 77532 3692 D3
600 HarC 77532 3693 A3
Reva Ridge Dr
600 STAF 77477 4370 A4
Reveille St
3300 HOUS 77087 4105 B6
4600 HOUS 77087 4245 B1
Reveille St SR-35
3300 HOUS 77087 4105 B6
4600 HOUS 77087 4245 B1
Revelstoke Dr
6800 HarC 77086 3542 C3
Revelstoke Wy
- HarC 77044 3549 B3
Revelwood Dr
7000 MtgC 77354 2673 A5
Revere Dr
2500 PASD 77502 4246 D2
Revere St
2600 HOUS 77019 3962 B7
2600 HOUS 77098 3962 B7
3600 HOUS 77098 4102 B1
Reverend BJ Lewis Dr
900 HOUS 77088 3683 E2
Reverse St
100 CNRO 77301 2383 E2
1700 HOUS 77055 3822 A6
Revolution Wy
1100 MSCY 77459 4369 D5
1900 MSCY 77477 4369 E6
Rex Rd
4100 HarC 77546 4505 E5
4100 HarC 77546 4506 A5
4100 HOUS 77546 4506 A5
Rex St
300 PASD 77506 4107 A3
Rex Creek Ct
9600 HarC 77379 3255 D5
Rexine Ln
18000 HarC 77433 3537 D7
Rexora Ln
5200 HarC 77493 3813 D4
5200 KATY 77493 3813 D4
Rexton Dr
6300 HarC 77084 3679 A4
Rey Av
3100 HarC 77521 3832 E4
Reyes Rd
300 FBnC 77471 4491 A1
Reynaldo Dr
- HarC 77373 3260 B1
4300 HarC 77373 3115 C7
Reynaldo St
600 DKSN 77539 4753 A5
Reynolds
2200 HOUS 77009 3963 D1
Reynolds Av
100 LGCY 77573 4632 B3
Reynolds Ct
200 LPRT 77571 4251 E7
Reynolds Dr
- BzaC 77584 4501 C6
- PRLD 77584 4501 C6
Reynolds St
2600 HOUS 77009 3824 D7
Reynolds Creek Cir
18700 HarC 77449 3677 C4
Reynolds Creek Dr
2900 HarC 77388 3113 A5
Reynor Creek Ct
4300 FBnC 77479 4366 C6
Reynosa Ct
200 MtgC 77362 2816 E5
Rezanof Rd
21400 HarC 77338 3261 D2
Rezonof Rd
21300 HarC 77338 3261 D3
RF Malek
2500 HarC 77066 3401 E6
Rhapsody Ln
9000 HarC 77040 3681 B1
Rhapsody Bend Dr
- WDLD 77382 2673 C7
10 WDLD 77382 2819 C1
Rhea Ct
10 MtgC 77385 2676 D5
Rhea St
100 HOUS 77034 4378 C2
Rheba Wy
16600 HOUS 77396 3405 D4
Rheha
5600 HarC 77389 2966 E7
5600 HarC 77389 2967 A7
Rhema Ln
11900 HOUS 77048 4375 B1
Rhett Dr
12100 BKHV 77024 3959 B3
12100 HOUS 77024 3959 B3
Rhett Butler Ct
25000 HarC 77375 2964 C3
Rhine Ln
1000 HarC 77090 3258 B3
Rhine St
23300 HarC 77447 3105 B7
Rhine Beck
- HOUS 77089 4378 C7
Rhinebeck Dr
11800 HOUS 77089 4378 C7
Rhinefield St
16400 HarC 77377 3254 C6
Rhine River Rd
1200 HarC 77073 3259 C5
Rhiney Ct
10000 HarC 77089 4504 E2
10000 HarC 77089 4505 A2
Rhoades Ln
1800 MSCY 77489 4370 C7
Rhobell
7900 HOUS 77078 3687 C4
Rhobell St
7500 HOUS 77016 3687 B4
8000 HOUS 77078 3687 C4
Rhode Pl
800 HOUS 77019 3962 E4
Rhode Island St
300 HOUS 77029 3966 A7
400 GNPK 77029 3966 A7
400 GNPK 77547 3966 A7
9200 HOUS 77029 3965 E7
26500 MtgC 77355 2963 A4
Rhodes Cir
300 HarC 77532 3411 A5
Rhodes Ct
6800 MSCY 77459 4496 D4
Rhodes Rd
100 CNRO 77301 2530 A2
1400 MtgC 77385 2822 C4
19700 HarC 77379 3112 A5
19900 HarC 77388 3112 B4
21500 HarC 77389 3112 B2
Rhodes St
3800 PASD 77505 4248 E4
Rhodesdale Ln
- HarC 77073 3259 B3
Rhodes Gap Dr
- HarC 77049 3828 D1
Rhodora St
1300 LMQU 77568 4990 B1
Rhonda Ln
12000 MtgC 77362 2963 C1
Rhone Forest Dr
11100 HOUS 77051 4242 D4
Rhone Lake Dr
10900 HOUS 77051 4242 D4
Rhone Park Dr
10900 HOUS 77051 4242 D3
Rhone Ranch Dr
1900 HOUS 77051 4242 C4
Rhone View Dr
11000 HOUS 77051 4242 D4
Rhoten Ct
17600 MtgC 77302 2679 E2
Rhozes Landing Blvd
- HarC 77388 3112 A2
Rhyme Ct Rd
2100 HarC 77067 3402 A5
Rhythm Ln
9300 HarC 77040 3681 B1
Rial Ct
6700 HarC 77069 3400 A1
Rialto Ct
6900 FBnC 77583 4623 A7
Riana Dr
10800 HarC 77065 3539 A1
Riane Ln
1700 HarC 77530 3829 D3
Riata Dr
10 MtgC 77354 2818 A4
Riata Ln
2900 HOUS 77043 3820 A2
Riata Canyon Ct
17800 HarC 77095 3396 E7
17800 HarC 77433 3396 D7
Riata Canyon Dr
11100 HarC 77433 3396 D7
Riata Creek Dr
17200 HarC 77095 3396 E7
17200 HarC 77095 3537 E1
17200 HarC 77433 3396 E7
17200 HarC 77433 3537 E1
Riata Crossing Dr
17900 HarC 77433 3396 D7
Riata Lake Dr
17600 HarC 77433 3537 D1
N Riata Lake Dr
17400 HarC 77433 3537 D1
Riata Manor Ln
17600 HarC 77433 3537 D2
Riata Prairie Ln
- HarC 77433 3537 D2
Riata Ranch Blvd
10400 HarC 77095 3537 E2
10400 HarC 77433 3537 D1
11200 HarC 77095 3396 D6
Riata Springs Ln
17600 HarC 77433 3537 D2
Riata Trace Ln
17600 HarC 77095 3537 C1
17600 HarC 77433 3537 C1
Ribbon Creek Wy
2900 HarC 77389 3113 A1
3100 HarC 77389 3112 E1
Ribbon Falls Ct
11800 HarC 77375 3109 E5
Ribbon Falls Dr
11900 HarC 77375 3109 D5
Ribbon Meadow Ct
12700 HarC 77346 3408 D1
Ribbonridge Dr
16700 FBnC 77478 4236 A6
Ribbonwood St
9800 HOUS 77078 3687 E4
Ribbonwood Pant Ct
20200 HarC 77375 3109 E5
Ribbonwood Park Ln
31200 MtgC 77386 2823 C7
Ribstone Cir
10800 HOUS 77016 3687 A2
Ribstone Dr
- HOUS 77016 3687 A1
11400 HOUS 77016 3547 A7
Ricaby Dr
9700 HarC 77064 3540 C6
Rice Av
200 ARLA 77583 4623 B5
S Rice Av
- HOUS 77056 3960 E7
- HOUS 77096 4100 E7
3300 HOUS 77056 4100 E1
5200 HOUS 77081 4100 E3
5200 HOUS 77401 4100 E3
6500 BLAR 77401 4100 E4
8800 HOUS 77096 4240 E1
9600 HOUS 77096 4241 A1
Rice Blvd
1700 HOUS 77005 4102 C2
2500 WUNP 77005 4102 A3
3200 WUNP 77005 4101 D3
Rice Rd
5800 PRLD 77581 4375 D7
5900 DKSN 77539 4753 E5
5900 TXCY 77539 4753 E6
Rice St
- BYTN 77520 3972 E5
100 TXCY 77591 4873 E6
200 HMPD 77445 2953 A6
1300 ALVN 77511 4749 B6
1300 RSBG 77471 4490 D7
2000 HMPD 77445 2952 E6
3500 GLSN 77554 5222 A2
6300 KATY 77493 3813 B7
6400 PRLD 77581 4375 E7
6500 PRLD 77581 4376 A7
Rice Creek Ln
- WEBS 77598 4631 B2
Ricecrest St
11200 HOUS 77035 4240 E4
Rice Dryer Rd
4000 PRLD 77581 4503 B1
Ricefield Dr
1500 HOUS 77084 3816 A7
Ricefield Rd
8000 FBnC 77469 4616 B3
8000 RSBG 77469 4616 B3
Ricelake Ln
19500 HarC 77084 3815 E6
19500 HarC 77084 3816 A6
Riceland
- BYTN 77521 3972 D2
Riceville School Rd
11500 HOUS 77031 4239 B6
11500 HOUS 77071 4239 B6
12100 HarC 77031 4239 B6
Ricewood Dr
3200 MtgC 77365 2974 C6
Ricewood Wy
19800 HarC 77449 3816 C2
19800 HarC 77449 3815 E3
Ricewood Village Tr
20100 HarC 77449 3676 E7
Rich Ct
12800 HOUS 77077 3957 C5
Richard
- PRVW 77445 3100 C2
Richard Av
1100 PASD 77506 4107 C4
Richard Ct
3100 FRDW 77598 4630 B3
Richard Dr
- HOUS 77048 4374 E2
1500 PRLD 77581 4504 E5
Richard Ln
3100 FRDW 77598 4630 B3
Richard Rd
25400 MtgC 77386 2968 E1
25800 MtgC 77386 2969 A1
Richard St
10 BYTN 77520 3973 E5
1400 PRLD 77581 4504 E5
2400 RSBG 77469 4491 E6
2400 RSBG 77471 4491 E6
2700 FBnC 77477 4369 E5
7600 HarC 77521 3832 C4
7900 HarC 77562 3832 C3
Richard Arms Cir
8600 HOUS 77099 4238 B1
Richard JV Johnson Av
- HOUS 77030 4102 D5
Richard Kaye Ln
28700 MtgC 77362 2963 E2
Richards Cts
10 LMQU 77568 4873 D7
10 TXCY 77591 4873 D7
Richards Dr
3100 DKSN 77539 4754 A1
Richards Rd
- PRVW 77445 2955 A7
- PRVW 77445 3100 A1
24000 MtgC 77386 2968 D3
Richards St
700 ALVN 77511 4867 B3
2900 HOUS 77029 3965 B4
Richardson Ln
1600 BYTN 77520 3973 C6
Richardson Rd
700 CNRO 77304 2383 C7
6600 HarC 77069 3400 A2
Richardson St
600 HarC 77373 2968 E7
2900 HOUS 77020 3964 A3
Richbourg St
- HOUS 77067 3403 A4
12500 HOUS 77090 3403 A3
Richcrest Dr
500 HarC 77060 3403 E5
Richcroft St
8500 HOUS 77029 3965 D4
9700 HOUS 77029 3966 A4
Richelieu Ln
1000 HOUS 77018 3683 E7
1000 HOUS 77018 3684 A7
1200 HOUS 77018 3822 D1
Richey Rd
- HarC 77073 3258 E6
- HOUS 77073 3258 E6
200 HarC 77090 3258 D6
E Richey Rd
- HarC 77014 3258 B7
- HOUS 77338 3260 C4
100 HarC 77073 3258 E6
100 HarC 77073 3259 E6
100 HarC 77090 3258 E6
100 HOUS 77073 3258 E6
100 HOUS 77073 3259 A6
1600 HarC 77073 3260 A6
1600 HarC 77338 3260 A6
W Richey Rd
- HarC 77014 3401 C3
5300 HarC 77066 3401 A4
Richey St
700 HOUS 77002 3963 D3
900 PASD 77506 4106 E7
1200 PASD 77502 4106 E6
2000 HOUS 77502 4246 D1
2000 PASD 77502 4246 D1
2200 HOUS 77017 4246 D1
N Richey St
100 PASD 77506 4106 E3
400 HOUS 77506 4106 E2
S Richey St
400 HOUS 77017 4246 C2
400 SHUS 77017 4246 C2
400 SHUS 77587 4246 C2
W Richey St
- PASD 77506 4107 A3
100 PASD 77506 4106 E3
N Richey Access St
- PASD 77506 4106 E3
500 PASD 77506 4107 A3
Richfield Ct
3000 BzaC 77584 4501 B6
Richfield Ln
4900 HOUS 77048 4243 D6
Richfield Park Ct
5700 BzaC 77583 4623 D5
Richford Dr
15500 FRDW 77546 4505 D5
15500 HarC 77546 4505 D5
Richglen Ct
24000 HarC 77389 2966 A4
Richland Ct
2000 SGLD 77478 4368 E6
Richland Dr
3200 SGLD 77478 4368 E5
7800 HOUS 77028 3687 B7
8800 HOUS 77078 3687 E7
9000 HOUS 77078 3688 A7
Richland Chambers Ln
4300 HarC 77396 3407 A6
Richland Creek Ln
1900 FBnC 77469 4234 C4
Richland Falls Ln
18700 HarC 77379 3111 C6
Richland Hills Dr
6300 FBnC 77494 4092 A6
Richland Park Dr
3500 FBnC 77469 4233 B6
Richland Spring Ln
2800 FBnC 77479 4493 D3
Richland Springs Dr
19300 HarC 77073 3403 B2
Richland Springs Ln
19300 FBnC 77469 4094 E6
Richlawn Dr
1300 HarC 77379 3255 C2
Richmond Av
- HOUS 77002 3963 A7
- HOUS 77027 3961 E7
200 HOUS 77002 3962 B7
500 HOUS 77006 3962 E7
1600 HOUS 77098 3962 C7
3100 HOUS 77098 3961 E7
3300 HOUS 77046 3961 E7
3300 HOUS 77046 4101 C1
3300 HOUS 77098 4101 C1
3400 HOUS 77027 4101 E1
5000 HOUS 77056 4101 A1
5200 HOUS 77056 4100 E1
5600 HOUS 77057 4100 D1
7500 HOUS 77063 4100 A1
8600 HOUS 77063 4099 E1
9700 HOUS 77042 4099 B1
10100 HOUS 77042 4098 E1
10900 HOUS 77082 4098 D1
12100 HOUS 77082 4097 E1
13200 HarC 77082 4097 D1
13700 HOUS 77082 4096 D1
S Richmond Av
14700 HarC 77082 4096 C2
14700 HOUS 77082 4096 C2
Richmond Ct
1300 FBnC 77469 4365 C2
Richmond Dr
2000 FBnC 77469 4365 C2
6700 HTCK 77563 4989 B5
Richmond Ln
400 FRDW 77546 4505 D7
Richmond Pk
400 MtgC 77302 2530 B5
Richmond Bend Ct
1900 FBnC 77469 4234 C7
Richmond Ferry Ct
3300 FBnC 77469 4234 C7
Richmond Foster Rd
2600 FBnC 77469 4365 A2
3300 FBnC 77469 4364 A1
6700 FBnC 77469 4232 A1
Richmond Foster Rd FM-359
2600 FBnC 77469 4365 A2
3300 FBnC 77469 4364 A1
6700 FBnC 77469 4232 A1
Richmond Hill Dr
10300 HOUS 77041 3819 D1
10300 HOUS 77041 3820 B1
Richmond Knoll Ct
1100 FBnC 77545 4623 C1
Richmond Knoll Ln
4700 FBnC 77545 4622 D3
4700 FBnC 77545 4623 A2
Richmond Pl Dr
400 RHMD 77469 4492 A3
Richmond Vantage Dr
1900 FBnC 77469 4234 C7
Richter Ln
500 FBnC 77469 4493 B6
Richton Rd
2800 FBnC 77477 4370 A5
Richton St
2300 HOUS 77098 3962 A7
Richton Falls Dr
25500 FBnC 77469 4092 C7
Richtowne Ln
9900 FBnC 77478 4237 A3
Richvale Ln
300 HOUS 77598 4506 D4
1000 HOUS 77062 4506 E3
1400 HOUS 77062 4507 B2
Rich Valley Ln
14700 FBnC 77478 4236 D3
Richview Ct
500 HarC 77060 3403 C5
Richview Dr
500 HarC 77060 3403 D5
S Richwood Dr
4600 FBnC 77471 4491 B3
4600 RSBG 77471 4491 B3
Richwood Rd
6700 HOUS 77087 4244 E2
7000 HOUS 77087 4245 A1
S Richwood St
4600 HarC 77375 2819 E5
Richwood Oaks Dr
26300 FBnC 77494 4092 A5
Ricker Park Cir
5900 HarC 77449 3677 C5
Rickett Ln
30200 MtgC 77355 2814 E2
Rickett Rd
29700 MtgC 77355 2816 A3
Ricky St
4900 HOUS 77033 4243 E5
5500 HOUS 77033 4244 A5
Riddlelink Ln
9800 HOUS 77025 4241 D2
Riddlewood Ln
9100 HOUS 77025 4241 D1
Riderdale Park Ln
10200 HarC 77070 3399 C4
Riderwood Dr
11200 HOUS 77099 4238 B1
Ridge Dr
200 HarC 77532 3692 D2
600 HarC 77532 3693 A2
1200 HarC 77073 3403 C1
E Ridge Dr
8300 HarC 77040 3541 D7
W Ridge Ln
3500 BzaC 77583 4500 D7
W Ridge Pl
5200 HarC 77041 3679 D7
Ridge Rd
100 BzaC 77578 4747 C3
Ridge St
500 HOUS 77009 3963 A1
900 HOUS 77009 3962 E2
Ridge Bank Ln
12800 HarC 77041 3679 D5
Ridgebar Cir
15800 HOUS 77053 4372 C6
Ridgeberry Dr
- HarC 77084 3678 B2
7100 HarC 77095 3678 B2
Ridgebluff Ln
5800 HarC 77449 3676 E5
Ridgebriar Dr
1500 HarC 77014 3402 C3
Ridgebriar Ln
5900 HOUS 77085 4240 E7
Ridgebrook Cir
25600 MtgC 77380 2968 B2
Ridgebrook Ln
2400 PRLD 77584 4500 A2
Ridgeburg Ct
1100 HOUS 77077 3957 D2
Ridgeburg Ln
- HarC 77433 3396 B4
Ridgebury Cir
8700 HarC 77095 3538 A5
Ridge Canyon Rd
3800 BYTN 77521 3973 E3
Ridgechase Ln
14600 HarC 77014 3401 C1
Ridgecoral Ct
10000 HarC 77038 3543 D4
W Ridgecreek Cir
5600 HOUS 77053 4371 E6
Ridgecreek Dr
5500 HOUS 77053 4372 A6
E Ridgecreek Dr
5000 HOUS 77053 4372 B6
W Ridgecreek Dr
5400 HOUS 77053 4372 A6
5500 HOUS 77053 4371 E5
6200 HOUS 77489 4371 D5
Ridge Crest Dr
25800 HarC 77389 2966 A2
Ridgecrest Dr
1800 HOUS 77055 3821 B5
4900 PASD 77504 4247 E7
5100 LPRT 77571 4250 B2
8700 BzaC 77578 4747 B4
8700 MNVL 77578 4747 B4
N Ridgecrest Dr
6400 HTCK 77563 4989 C4
S Ridgecrest Dr
6400 HTCK 77563 4989 C4
Ridgecrest St
100 MtgC 77354 2671 D3
Ridgecroft Rd
15800 HOUS 77053 4372 C6
Ridgecross Pl
10 WDLD 77381 2820 D3
Ridgecrossing Ln
1100 HOUS 77077 3957 A3
Ridgedale Dr
2800 HOUS 77345 3120 A5
5400 HarC 77039 3546 E4
Ridge Falls Ct
19700 HarC 77433 3677 A1
Ridge Falls Dr
2800 BzaC 77578 4501 A7
Ridgefield Rd
3100 DRPK 77536 4249 E3
3100 LPRT 77536 4249 E3
3100 LPRT 77571 4249 E3
3200 LPRT 77571 4250 A3
Ridgefield St
- DRPK 77536 4249 E2
- LPRT 77536 4249 E2
- LPRT 77571 4249 E2
Ridgefield Park Ln
2100 FBnC 77469 4493 A3
26200 HarC 77433 3396 A7
Ridge Forest Dr
8200 HarC 77088 3542 C7
8200 HarC 77088 3682 D1
Ridgegate Rd
15700 HOUS 77053 4372 C6
Ridge Glen Ct
20900 HarC 77073 3259 B6
Ridgeglen Ln
2700 HOUS 77082 4096 E2
Ridge Green Dr
3200 HOUS 77345 3120 A4
Ridgegreen Dr
16000 HarC 77082 4096 A3
Ridgegrove Ln
7500 HarC 77433 3537 D7
Ridge Harbor Dr
4800 HOUS 77053 4372 A7
Ridgehaven Dr
5000 HOUS 77053 4372 A7
Ridge Hill Ct
19000 HarC 77084 3816 B3
Ridge Hill Ln
3400 HarC 77084 3816 B3
Ridge Hollow Dr
1600 HarC 77067 3402 B6
Ridge Lake Dr
15000 HarC 77082 4096 C4
Ridgeland Ct
700 HarC 77060 3544 E4
Ridgeland St
2400 HarC 77039 3545 E4
3500 HarC 77039 3546 A4
Ridgeley Dr
1000 HLSV 77055 3821 C6
1000 HOUS 77055 3821 C6
Ridgelight Ln
- HOUS 77075 4376 D5
Ridgeline Ct
10 WDLD 77381 2821 A3
Ridgelow Ln
12600 HarC 77070 3399 C5
Ridge Manor Ct
3800 HOUS 77345 3119 E3
Ridge Manor Dr
5000 HOUS 77053 4372 A7
Ridge Manor Ln
2000 FBnC 77479 4493 E3
Ridge Maple St
12900 HarC 77038 3543 A2
Ridgemar Cir
4700 HOUS 77053 4372 C6
Ridgemeadow Ct
16900 FBnC 77083 4095 D5
Ridgemont Ct
3700 HLCS 77511 4867 E6
Ridgemont Dr
100 HLCS 77511 4867 E5
2300 MSCY 77489 4370 B7
Ridgemont Pl
5400 HOUS 77053 4371 E7
Ridgemont St
6000 HOUS 77087 4104 C6
Ridgemoor Estates Ct
22900 MtgC 77385 2823 A6
Ridgemoor Estates Ln
11100 MtgC 77385 2823 B7
Ridgemore Rd
- HOUS 77055 3821 B4
Ridge Oak Dr
7200 HOUS 77088 3682 C2
Ridge Park Dr
15500 HarC 77095 3678 D1
15700 HarC 77095 3538 C7
Ridgepark Dr
1100 LPRT 77571 4250 B2
Ridge Pass Dr
3200 HarC 77373 3115 B4
Ridgepath Ct
19100 HarC 77388 3112 D5
Ridgepath Rd
4000 HarC 77388 3112 C6
Ridge Pine Dr
2600 HOUS 77345 3119 E5
Ridgepoint Cir
200 FBnC 77479 4366 E5
Ridgepoint Ct
3300 BzaC 77584 4501 D7
Ridgepoint Dr
- FBnC 77479 4366 E4
4000 BzaC 77584 4501 D7
8500 HOUS 77055 3821 A4
8500 HOUS 77080 3821 A4
Ridgerock Rd
15700 HOUS 77489 4371 C5
Ridgerod Ln
4600 HOUS 77053 4372 B7
Ridgeroe Ln
15800 HOUS 77053 4372 B6
Ridge Row Ct
5800 HarC 77041 3679 D5
Ridge Run Dr
11500 HarC 77064 3399 C7
Ridge Scene Wy
2900 HarC 77084 3816 A4
Ridgeside Dr
12300 HOUS 77072 4097 E5
Ridgestone St
4900 HOUS 77053 4372 A6
Ridgestone Park Ln
26400 HarC 77433 3396 A4
Ridge Stream Ln
18100 HarC 77429 3252 B6
Ridgeton Dr
5100 HOUS 77053 4372 A6
Ridge Top Dr
17400 HarC 77090 3258 A3
17700 HarC 77090 3257 E3
Ridge Trail Ln
19000 HarC 77084 3816 B3
Ridgeturn Dr
5200 HOUS 77053 4372 A6
Ridgevalley Dr
1100 LPRT 77571 4250 C2
Ridgevan St
4800 HOUS 77053 4372 A6
Ridgeview Dr
- BzaC 77584 4501 D7
- PRLD 77584 4501 D7
10 WlrC 77447 2959 C1
3600 MSCY 77459 4496 D3
7900 HOUS 77055 3821 B4
Ridgeview Pt
500 HarC 77336 3120 E2
Ridgeview St
10900 HOUS 77043 3819 C5
Ridge Vista Dr
5700 HOUS 77345 3120 B5
E Ridgewalk Dr
16600 HOUS 77053 4372 B7
S Ridgewalk Dr
4500 HOUS 77053 4372 B7
Ridgewater Wy
13200 MtgC 77302 2530 C5
Ridgeway Av
100 BYTN 77520 3971 A4
Ridgeway Dr
10 CNRO 77303 2237 E5
4900 PASD 77504 4247 E7
5000 HOUS 77033 4243 E2
5300 HOUS 77033 4244 A2
6200 HOUS 77087 4244 E2
7300 HOUS 77087 4245 A1
Ridgeway Park Ct
1800 HOUS 77339 3118 D6
Ridgeway Park Dr
2000 HOUS 77339 3118 D6
Ridgewell Dr
15200 HOUS 77062 4506 E2
Ridgewest St
4800 HOUS 77053 4372 A
Ridgewick Ct
11500 HarC 77377 3254 E
Ridge Wind Ln
5400 HOUS 77053 4371 E
N Ridgewood Cir
11700 MSCY 77071 4239 C
S Ridgewood Cir
11800 MSCY 77071 4239 C
Ridgewood Dr
- WlrC 77447 2813 B
100 HarC 77336 2975 E5
200 ORDN 77386 2822 C6
1000 MtgC 77354 2673 A1
21700 HarC 77388 3112 E
21900 HarC 77389 3112 E
Ridgewood Ln
- ALVN 77511 4867 A
6800 LGCY 77539 4752 E5
Ridgewood Pl
1200 HOUS 77055 3821 D
Ridgewood Rd
100 CNRO 77304 2383 B4
Ridgewood St
1500 HOUS 77006 3962 C5
1700 ALVN 77511 4867 A
Ridgewood Canyon Dr
- PASD 77058 4380 E5
12000 PASD 77059 4380 D
Ridgewood Knoll Ln
13100 HOUS 77047 4373 B3
Ridgewood Lake Ct
14200 HOUS 77062 4379 D
14200 HOUS 77062 4380 A6
Ridgewood Reef
5200 HarC 77041 3679 D
Ridgeworth Ln
2100 FBnC 77469 4492 E
9600 HarC 77396 3548 B
Ridge Wy Dr
100 CNRO 77301 2384 B7
Ridgling Dr
10 WDLD 77382 2674 E
N Riding Dr
24000 HarC 77375 2965 D
Ridingwood Dr
15100 HOUS 77489 4371 B4
Ridlon Av
15800 HarC 77530 3830 B7
Riedel Dr
700 BKHV 77024 3959 B
700 HOUS 77024 3959 B
Rieden Dr
7500 HOUS 77489 4371 B5
Rierdon Ln
6900 SGLD 77479 4367 C7
Riesner St
10 HOUS 77002 3963 B3
10 HOUS 77007 3963 B3
Rietta St
- HOUS 77078 3687 E5
5700 HOUS 77016 3686 D
Rifle Ln
2900 HOUS 77094 4095 E
Rifle Rd
- CNRO 77303 2237 C
Rifle & Pistol Ct
16400 HOUS 77094 4095 E
Rifle Gap Ln
2900 SGLD 77478 4368 D
Rifleman Cir
13400 HarC 77429 3398 A
Rifleman Tr
12600 HarC 77429 3398 A
Riflewood Cir
1900 MSCY 77459 4497 C
Riford Dr
15300 HarC 77429 3253 D
Riga Ct
5400 MtgC 77365 2974 C7
Rigaud
3500 GLSN 77554 5332 D
Rigby Owen Rd
10 CNRO 77304 2383 B4
Rigby Point Ln
15200 HarC 77433 3251 E6
Rigdale St
15200 HarC 77084 3678 E3
Rigel Ct
31400 TMBL 77375 2963 E4
Rigel Dr
900 FRDW 77546 4629 C
Rigel Rd
2800 HOUS 77088 3683 B
Rigger Ln
16600 HOUS 77062 4507 B4
Rigging Ct
1600 HarC 77532 3552 A
Riggs Dr
100 CNRO 77301 2384 A
Riggs Rd
100 HOUS 77022 3824 A
1200 HOUS 77022 3823 E
Riggs St
400 BYTN 77520 4112 D
Riggs Mill Ln
11000 FBnC 77469 4092 D
Right Wy
3000 HOUS 77339 3119 B
3000 MtgC 77365 3119 B
Rika Pt
1600 HOUS 77077 3957 A
Riley Ln
100 HOUS 77002 3963 E5
100 HOUS 77003 3963 E5
Riley Rd
10 HarC 77047 4372 E6
10 HarC 77047 4373 A6
10 HarC 77053 4372 E6
10 PRLD 77047 4373 A6
W Riley Rd
3400 HarC 77053 4372 E6
Riley St
3800 SSPL 77005 4101 D
3800 WUNP 77005 4101 D
25100 PTVL 77372 2682 D
Rileybrook Cir
18100 HarC 77094 3955 C
Riley Fuzzel Rd
400 HarC 77373 2969 A
400 HarC 77373 3114 A
500 MtgC 77386 2969 D
2800 MtgC 77386 2970 C
5000 MtgC 77365 2824 D
5700 MtgC 77365 2970 C
Riley Ridge Dr
15200 HarC 77433 3251 D

TREET
lock City ZIP Map# Grid
ill Ln
15600 HOUS 77062 4506 E3
16100 HOUS 77062 4507 A3
Rim Dr
2400 HarC 77067 3401 D4
Rim Tr
19100 HarC 77388 3113 C7
19100 HarC 77388 3258 D1
immick Forrest Dr
26000 MtgC 77354 2817 D6
im Rock Dr
1300 HOUS 77088 3543 E6
imrock Dr
2000 LGCY 77565 4509 A5
2800 MSCY 77459 4496 B2
imview Dr
- HOUS 77504 4247 C7
imwood Rd
- HarC 77049 3689 C7
7100 HarC 77049 3828 C1
incon
13300 HOUS 77077 3957 B7
incon Dr
12300 HOUS 77077 3957 D6
iner St
3200 HOUS 77093 3825 A2
ing Ct
2500 MSCY 77459 4369 C7
ingfield Dr
15000 HarC 77084 3678 E3
ingford Ct
5400 HarC 77084 3678 D5
ingness Av
- HOUS 77030 4102 E5
ingold St
700 HOUS 77088 3684 A2
900 HOUS 77088 3683 E3
ingrose Ct
2500 MSCY 77459 4369 C7
ing Rose Dr
4200 MSCY 77459 4369 C7
ingrose Dr
4400 MSCY 77459 4369 B7
ingwald Ct
19700 HarC 77379 3110 D6
ingwood Ct
22000 MtgC 77365 2972 A2
ingwood St
600 HarC 77373 3113 E6
600 HarC 77373 3114 A6
inn St
8300 HOUS 77078 3687 D5
io Dr
5200 HarC 77521 3833 D1
io Alamo St
- BzaC 77583 4624 A4
io Bella Ct
- LGCY 77573 4633 A5
io Blanco Dr
7000 HarC 77083 4096 C6
io Bonito Dr
14000 HarC 77083 4097 A4
io Bonito Rd
13900 HarC 77083 4097 A4
14000 HarC 77083 4096 E4
14100 HOUS 77083 4096 E4
io Bravo Rd
10000 HarC 77064 3540 C3
io Bravo St
12500 BzaC 77583 4624 A4
io Brazos St
- BzaC 77583 4624 A4
io Comal Ln
- BzaC 77583 4624 B4
io Crystal Cir
7900 HarC 77095 3538 E7
io Crystal Dr
7900 HarC 77095 3538 E7
io Dell Dr
15700 HarC 77083 4096 B4
io del Sol Dr
15400 FBnC 77083 4096 B6
io Grande Dr
9600 HarC 77064 3540 B3
22800 MtgC 77365 2972 B3
io Grande Ln
12600 BzaC 77583 4624 B4
io Grande St
- BzaC 77583 4624 B4
- JRSV 77040 3680 B1
- PRLD 77583 4624 B4
1000 LGCY 77573 4632 D3
8100 JRSV 77040 3540 C7
io Grande River Dr
- MtgC 77386 2970 B2
io Lindo St
- BzaC 77583 4624 A4
- PRLD 77583 4624 A4
io Llano Dr
- HarC 77429 3253 D5
io Mesa Dr
- HarC 77095 3538 B3
io Nueces St
- BzaC 77583 4624 A4
io Oaks Ct
3600 HarC 77068 3257 B6
io Pinar Cir
14600 HarC 77095 3539 A7
io Pinar Dr
14700 HarC 77095 3539 A7
io Plaza Dr
15200 HarC 77083 4096 B5
io Quatro Dr
12600 HOUS 77045 4241 A6
io Ramos St
5400 BzaC 77583 4624 A4
io Ranch Ct
10800 HarC 77064 3540 B5
io Ridge Ln
12200 HarC 77041 3679 E5
io Sabinas St
5400 BzaC 77583 4624 B4
io San Juan Ct
12600 BzaC 77583 4624 B4
io San Juan St
- BzaC 77583 4624 B4
io Valley Ct
21500 MtgC 77365 2973 B3
io Verde Ln
11500 HarC 77044 3688 D7
io Villa Dr
11000 HarC 77049 3831 D1
io Vista Dr
- FBnC 77469 4365 B4
io Vista St
3600 HOUS 77021 4103 C4
ipford Ct
21000 FBnC 77469 4234 B3

STREET
Block City ZIP Map# Grid
Ripley Hills Dr
26100 FBnC 77469 4092 B7
Ripping Lake Ct
16700 HarC 77429 3396 D1
Ripple Cr
1200 HOUS 77057 3960 B5
Ripple Ln
5300 HarC 77389 3112 A1
Ripple Bend Ct
3000 PRLD 77581 4503 E2
Ripple Bend Ln
2100 PRLD 77581 4503 E2
Ripplebrook Dr
3200 HOUS 77045 4373 A1
3300 HOUS 77045 4372 E1
Ripplecreek Cir
3100 BYTN 77521 3972 B1
Ripple Creek Ct
1700 MSCY 77489 4370 C5
Ripple Creek Dr
- MtgC 77372 2683 B5
300 HNCV 77024 3960 B3
1200 HOUS 77057 3960 B5
1700 RSBG 77471 4491 B6
1800 MSCY 77489 4370 C5
4600 BYTN 77521 3972 B1
16000 SPLD 77372 2683 B5
S Ripple Creek Dr
600 HOUS 77057 3960 B4
Rippled Pond Cir
10 WDLD 77382 2674 D5
Ripple Glen Dr
12000 HOUS 77071 4239 D6
Ripple Lake Dr
9900 HarC 77065 3539 E3
E Ripple Ridge Dr
16600 HOUS 77053 4372 D6
N Ripple Ridge Dr
4500 HOUS 77053 4372 B7
W Ripple Ridge Dr
16600 HOUS 77053 4372 B7
16700 FBnC 77053 4499 B1
16700 HOUS 77053 4499 B1
Ripple Rush Ct
10 WDLD 77381 2821 B4
N Ripples Ct
3500 FBnC 77459 4622 A5
S Ripples Ct
3400 FBnC 77459 4622 A5
Ripplestream Dr
15300 HarC 77068 3257 B5
Ripplewave Dr
10300 FBnC 77478 4237 A3
Ripplewind Ln
15100 HarC 77068 3257 C5
Ripplewood Cir
2400 MtgC 77384 2674 E1
2400 MtgC 77384 2675 A1
Ripplewood Ct
2400 MtgC 77384 2675 A1
Ripplewood Ln
12700 HarC 77015 3828 C5
Rippling Bend Dr
2600 BzaC 77578 4625 A1
Ripplingbrook Dr
800 SEBK 77586 4509 E1
Rippling Brook Ln
2900 LGCY 77539 4752 E3
19300 HarC 77375 3110 A7
Rippling Creek Dr
400 FBnC 77479 4367 A5
Rippling Creek Ln
- ALVN 77511 4749 B6
- BzaC 77511 4749 B6
13100 PRLD 77584 4500 A1
Rippling Creek Wy
14300 HOUS 77062 4380 A6
Rippling Falls Ln
3200 LGCY 77539 4753 A4
Rippling Fields Ct
11000 HarC 77064 3540 D1
Rippling Fields Dr
9900 HarC 77064 3540 C2
Rippling Hollow Dr
6200 HarC 77379 3256 D1
Rippling Meadows Dr
11000 HarC 77064 3540 C2
Rippling Mill Dr
16600 FBnC 77478 4236 A6
Rippling Rock Ct
- PRLD 77583 4500 B5
Rippling Shore Ct
22400 FBnC 77494 4093 D3
Rippling Springs Ct
2800 BzaC 77578 4501 A7
Rippling Springs Dr
15300 HarC 77429 3253 D5
Rippling Springs Ln
1100 LGCY 77573 4633 A3
Rippling Stream Ln
- FBnC 77469 4094 A7
Rippling Water Ct
1800 FBnC 77479 4494 D4
Rippling Water Dr
8700 FBnC 77479 4494 B4
15800 HarC 77084 3678 D6
16100 HOUS 77084 3678 D6
Rippon Dr
19500 HarC 77373 3113 E6
Riptide Dr
7700 HOUS 77072 4098 A7
Rip Van Winkle Dr
2600 PRLD 77581 4504 C3
12100 HOUS 77024 3959 A3
12600 HOUS 77024 3958 E3
Rip Van Winkle Ln
10 BKHV 77024 3959 B3
Rising Bay Ln
2200 PRLD 77584 4500 A2
Rising Brook Dr
7100 HarC 77433 3676 E1
Rising Hills Ct
20400 MtgC 77365 3117 E1
Rising Springs Ln
1300 HarC 77073 3403 D3
Rising Star Dr
19900 HarC 77338 3261 E4
Rising Sun Rd
2900 HarC 77449 3815 D5
Rising Tide Ln
2900 LGCY 77573 4633 B3
Rita
5300 HOUS 77022 3684 D6
5300 HOUS 77076 3684 D6
Rita Ln
12800 HOUS 77015 3967 B3
Rita St
3600 FBnC 77545 4498 D7

STREET
Block City ZIP Map# Grid
Rita Elliott Ct
3800 FBnC 77459 4621 B5
Ritow St
10800 HOUS 77089 4377 D3
Rittenberg Ct
16000 HarC 77084 3678 E4
W Rittenhouse Rd
400 HOUS 77076 3684 B4
400 HOUS 77091 3684 A4
Rittenhouse St
10 HOUS 77076 3684 E3
100 HOUS 77076 3685 B3
E Rittenhouse St
100 HOUS 77076 3684 D4
W Rittenhouse St
100 HOUS 77076 3684 C4
Rittenhouse Park Ct
18300 HarC 77379 3257 B1
Rittenhouse Village Ct
7100 HOUS 77076 3684 C3
Rittenhouse Village Rd
7100 HOUS 77076 3684 C3
Rittenmore Dr
2100 MSCY 77489 4371 A6
E Ritter Cir
15300 MSCY 77071 4239 D7
W Ritter Cir
15400 MSCY 77071 4239 D7
Ritz St
7900 HOUS 77028 3826 C2
Riva Row
10 WDLD 77380 2821 E5
10 WDLD 77380 2822 A5
Riva Wy
- WDLD 77380 2821 E5
Riva Ridge Dr
6500 FBnC 77469 4232 D4
Riva Ridge Ln
6700 FBnC 77469 4232 E4
12200 HOUS 77071 4239 E6
12400 MSCY 77071 4239 E6
Rivendell Dr
7500 HarC 77379 3256 B1
Riven Oaks Ct
7400 HarC 77433 3676 E1
Rivenwood Dr
20100 HarC 77433 3676 E1
20100 HarC 77433 3677 C2
River Blvd
10 PLMG 77327 2684 D3
River Cir
10 HNCV 77024 3960 A5
River Cross
5800 FBnC 77479 4493 E3
River Ct
1100 LGCY 77573 4631 D4
River Dr
3000 MtgC 77385 2677 B5
3900 HOUS 77017 4105 D7
8100 HOUS 77017 4245 D1
E River Dr
5400 FBnC 77469 4364 A3
W River Dr
5400 FBnC 77469 4364 A2
River Ln
10 LbyC 77372 2538 D5
River Pth
2000 FBnC 77494 3952 C6
River Rd
- LbyC 77327 2684 B4
- MtgC 77372 2684 B4
100 HarC 77530 3830 E6
300 HarC 77530 3831 A5
3000 FBnC 77471 4491 B3
3400 RSBG 77471 4491 B3
6600 FBnC 77469 4493 C7
E River Rd
- SPLD 77372 2537 C6
1100 LbyC 77372 2538 C6
18000 MtgC 77302 2823 E1
18600 MtgC 77302 2824 A2
26500 MtgC 77372 2537 E6
River Run
25000 WlrC 77447 2959 C1
River Tr
10 HOUS 77044 3551 A4
Rivera Dr
2200 LGCY 77573 4509 A7
Rivera Rd
- HarC 77521 3833 A5
Rivera Creek Dr
- MtgC 77386 2969 D1
River Bank
- HarC 77530 3830 E5
Riverbank Dr
10 WDLD 77381 2821 A6
Riverbank Ridge Ct
9400 HarC 77089 4377 A7
Riverbank Ridge Ln
11100 HarC 77089 4377 C7
River Basin Ct
11000 HarC 77089 4377 C7
11000 HOUS 77089 4377 C7
River Basin Ln
200 LGCY 77539 4753 A4
Riverbend Cross
1500 SGLD 77478 4369 A5
River Bend Dr
400 BYTN 77521 3972 E4
1000 HNCV 77024 3960 A5
1000 HNCV 77057 3960 A5
1200 HOUS 77024 3960 A5
1200 HOUS 77057 3960 A5
1200 HOUS 77063 3960 A5
2800 HOUS 77339 3263 E2
15100 MtgC 77302 2676 D2
River Bend Tr
2100 HOUS 77345 3120 B3
Riverbend Canyon Ct
10500 HarC 77089 4377 B7
Riverbend Canyon Ln
8300 HarC 77089 4377 B7
Riverbendpoint Ln
26800 HarC 77433 3396 A6
River Birch Dr
2700 SGLD 77479 4368 D7
2800 SGLD 77479 4495 C1
3000 BzaC 77584 4374 B7
22600 HarC 77375 2965 E7
22600 HarC 77375 2966 A7
River Birch Ln
10 WDLD 77380 2822 B6
River Birch Wy
15700 HOUS 77059 4380 B4
River Blossom Ln
2300 HOUS 77345 3120 B2
River Bluff Dr
6600 HOUS 77085 4371 C1

STREET
Block City ZIP Map# Grid
River Bottom Rd
19300 HarC 77449 3677 A3
River Branch Dr
5700 HOUS 77345 3120 B5
Riverbreeze Ct
100 LGCY 77539 4752 E4
River Breeze Dr
19700 HarC 77375 3109 E6
River Briar Ln
200 FBnC 77469 4365 B5
Riverbridge Ct
5000 HarC 77379 3112 A5
River Brook Ct
5600 HarC 77449 3676 E5
19700 HarC 77346 3264 C5
River Brook Dr
19900 HarC 77346 3264 C4
Riverbrook Dr
- FBnC 77479 4494 A4
- SGLD 77479 4494 A3
100 MtgC 77385 2676 A1
7000 FBnC 77479 4493 E4
River Canyon Ln
12500 HarC 77346 3408 C3
Riverchase Dr
1000 FBnC 77469 4493 B5
Riverchase Ln
4200 HarC 77014 3401 C1
Riverchase Tr
5900 HOUS 77345 3120 B3
Riverchase Village Dr
5800 HOUS 77345 3120 B3
Riverchase Village Tr
5800 HOUS 77345 3120 A3
River Cliff Ct
1400 FBnC 77469 4365 A4
River Cliff Ln
5100 FBnC 77479 4493 C2
8500 HarC 77095 3538 A5
Rivercoach Ln
10 FBnC 77479 4367 B7
Rivercove Ln
100 FBnC 77469 4365 B6
River Creek Dr
800 LPRT 77571 4250 B2
River Creek Wy
10 FBnC 77477 4369 B4
10 SGLD 77477 4369 B4
10 SGLD 77478 4369 B4
Rivercrest Cir
- MtgC 77385 2676 E3
River Crest Dr
2200 HOUS 77338 3263 B3
Rivercrest Dr
1700 SGLD 77478 4368 C5
E Rivercrest Dr
10 HOUS 77042 3959 A7
W Rivercrest Dr
10 HOUS 77042 3959 A7
Rivercroft Ln
11000 HarC 77089 4377 B7
Rivercross Rd
8500 HarC 77064 3541 D5
River Ct Dr
21100 HarC 77449 3676 D6
Riverdale Dr
1100 HarC 77530 3830 D5
River Dale Ln
- HarC 77338 3262 B4
- HMBL 77338 3262 B4
Riveredge Dr
10 RHMD 77469 4365 B7
100 RHMD 77469 4492 A1
800 FBnC 77469 4492 B1
River Fall Ct
16300 MtgC 77302 2679 A4
River Falls Dr
2100 HOUS 77339 3118 E6
5000 FBnC 77479 4493 D3
River Fern Dr
7100 HarC 77040 3681 C2
River Fields Dr
- FBnC 77083 4096 C7
Riverford Dr
2200 HOUS 77339 3119 A4
River Forest Ct
400 HOUS 77079 3957 B3
River Forest Dr
3000 FBnC 77469 4364 A3
14100 HOUS 77079 3958 A4
14800 HOUS 77079 3957 B3
River Gable Ct
5300 FBnC 77479 4493 D2
River Garden Dr
7000 HarC 77095 3678 C2
7600 HarC 77095 3538 D7
Rivergate Ct
21900 FBnC 77469 4493 A3
Rivergate Dr
5300 HarC 77373 3260 E1
Riverglade Ct
4600 FBnC 77479 4496 C4
Riverglade Dr
8200 HarC 77095 3538 E6
River Glen Ct
6400 PRLD 77584 4502 C5
River Glen Dr
14300 FBnC 77478 4236 E4
Riverglen Forest Dr
1900 HOUS 77345 3120 B5
River Glyn Dr
1000 HNCV 77024 3960 A5
Rivergreen Park Dr
- FBnC 77494 4093 A1
Rivergreen Park Ln
- FBnC 77494 4093 A2
Rivergrove Ct
11700 HarC 77377 3254 D3
Rivergrove Dr
400 HarC 77015 3828 C7
14200 HarC 77070 3398 E1
River Grove Rd
200 SGLD 77478 4368 A3
River Haven Dr
10 HarC 77530 3831 A6
Riverhill Ct
12600 HarC 77014 3402 B3
River Hill Dr
4800 HOUS 77345 3119 E6
4800 HOUS 77345 3120 A6
Riverhill Dr
100 CNRO 77304 2383 B2
Riverhollow Ct
5300 FBnC 77479 4493 D2
River Hollow Dr
- FBnC 77479 4493 E2
River Hollow Ln
10 HOUS 77027 3961 B5

STREET
Block City ZIP Map# Grid
Riverhollow Ln
2600 FBnC 77479 4493 D2
Riveria Rd
3800 HarC 77521 3832 E5
3800 HarC 77521 3833 A5
Riverine Ct
1300 HOUS 77055 3821 D6
Riverine Terrace Dr
7900 FBnC 77469 4234 A4
River Keg Dr
13700 HarC 77083 4237 A1
River Knoll Ct
5600 HarC 77449 3676 E5
Riverknoll Ct
2000 FBnC 77469 4492 E3
River Knoll Ln
21200 HarC 77449 3676 D5
Riverlace Dr
900 HOUS 77079 3956 D3
River Lake Dr
- HarC 77044 3549 A5
Riverland Ln
9500 HarC 77040 3541 A6
River Laurel Dr
- HarC 77067 3402 C4
12600 HarC 77014 3402 B3
Riverlawn Dr
1900 HOUS 77339 3118 D5
2300 HOUS 77339 3119 A6
Riverlet Ct
13300 HarC 77429 3252 B7
River Lilly Dr
- HOUS 77345 3120 B2
River Lodge Dr
6600 HarC 77379 3256 D2
River Lodge Ln
2200 FBnC 77479 4493 C1
2200 FBnC 77479 4494 A2
River Look Ct
1400 FBnC 77469 4364 E4
River Manor Dr
6200 HOUS 77345 3120 B2
River Maple Ln
15600 HOUS 77062 4380 C7
Rivermead Ct
3300 HarC 77449 3815 A3
Rivermead Dr
22000 HarC 77449 3815 A3
River Meadow Ln
11900 MDWP 77477 4238 A5
River Meadows Rd
18700 HarC 77084 3677 C7
18700 HarC 77084 3816 C1
River Mill Ct
6100 HarC 77379 3256 D1
River Mill Dr
- HarC 77379 3256 D1
River Mist Ct
6100 FBnC 77494 4093 E4
Rivermist Ct
11700 HarC 77377 3254 D3
Rivermoss Ln
3800 FBnC 77494 4093 C3
9600 HarC 77396 3548 A2
River-Oak Bnd
100 LbyC 77327 2684 C4
River Oaks Blvd
1600 HOUS 77019 3961 E6
2500 HOUS 77098 3961 E6
River Oaks Dr
10 MtgC 77385 2677 A5
3800 PASD 77505 4248 E5
River Park Ct
11900 HarC 77070 3254 D7
River Park Dr
5300 FBnC 77469 4364 A2
15000 HarC 77070 3254 D7
15200 HarC 77377 3254 D7
32100 MtgC 77355 2668 A5
E Riverpark Dr
- FBnC 77479 4493 E2
W Riverpark Dr
- FBnC 77479 4493 E2
River Park Ln
- PASD 77505 4249 C6
River Peak
5700 FBnC 77459 4621 A1
River Pines Dr
7200 HarC 77433 3676 E1
7200 HarC 77433 3677 A1
7500 HarC 77433 3537 A6
River Pl Dr
23800 FBnC 77494 3953 B4
River Plantation Dr
100 MtgC 77302 2530 B6
100 MtgC 77302 2676 D1
River Point Dr
7600 HNCV 77024 3960 A5
River Pointe Dr
- CNRO 77301 2530 A2
- CNRO 77304 2530 A2
100 CNRO 77304 2529 E2
River Pointe Ln
19600 HarC 77449 3677 A5
19700 HarC 77449 3676 E5
River Ranch Dr
4200 PASD 77505 4249 A5
16500 MtgC 77302 2679 B4
River Range Dr
2100 HOUS 77045 4242 D6
River Raven Ct
15800 HarC 77429 3397 A2
River Ridge Ct
15600 HarC 77068 3257 B5
River Ridge Dr
2500 MtgC 77385 2677 A4
2500 WDLC 77385 2677 A4
11900 MtgC 77365 3117 D4
20200 MtgC 77339 3117 E4
River Ridge Ln
- HarC 77338 3262 A4
6700 LGCY 77539 4752 E5
10300 CNRO 77304 2236 D4
Riverridge Park Ln
11100 HarC 77089 4377 C7
River Roads Dr
15800 HOUS 77079 3956 E2
River Rock Ct
6600 HarC 77449 3677 A3
River Rock Dr
1100 MSCY 77489 4370 D6
19600 HarC 77449 3677 A3
River Rock Ln
2800 LGCY 77539 4752 E3
River Rock Tr
2300 HOUS 77345 3120 B3
River Rose Dr
- HOUS 77339 3119 B1

STREET
Block City ZIP Map# Grid
Rivers Rd
3400 BzaC 77578 4501 D7
3400 PRLD 77578 4501 D7
River Sage Dr
18000 HarC 77084 3677 D5
Rivers Edge Tr
3300 HOUS 77339 3119 C5
Rivershadows Ln
20900 HarC 77388 3112 B5
N Rivershire Dr
- CNRO 77301 2529 E1
300 CNRO 77304 2529 C2
S Rivershire Dr
300 CNRO 77304 2529 D2
Rivershire Ln
20800 HarC 77073 3259 E4
Riverside Ct
900 FRDW 77546 4505 A6
Riverside Dr
- HarC 77530 3831 B6
- HOUS 77004 4102 E3
- HOUS 77030 4102 E3
- HOUS 77099 4237 B3
- HOUS 77478 4237 B3
- SGLD 77478 4237 B3
10 HLCS 77511 4867 E5
100 HarC 77562 3831 D1
500 HLCS 77511 4868 A5
2100 LGCY 77573 4632 E1
2200 HOUS 77004 4103 A3
3400 FRDW 77546 4505 A6
3400 PRLD 77581 4504 E6
3400 PRLD 77581 4505 A6
20500 MtgC 77357 2830 A7
20800 HarC 77357 2976 A1
Riverside Ln
1600 CNRO 77304 2382 D4
Riverside St
100 HarC 77562 3831 D1
17500 HarC 77044 3551 D7
Riverside Creek Dr
25800 FBnC 77469 4092 C7
Riverside Grove Dr
15300 FBnC 77083 4236 B1
Riverside Lodge Dr
9200 HarC 77083 4237 A2
Riverside Oaks Dr
4200 HOUS 77345 3119 E4
4500 HOUS 77345 3120 A4
Riverside Pines Dr
20500 HarC 77346 3265 C3
Riverside Ridge Ln
21000 HarC 77449 3815 B3
Riverside Walk Ln
8500 HarC 77064 3541 D5
River Springs Dr
12300 HOUS 77050 3547 B6
Riverstone
- HOUS 77085 4371 C1
Riverstone Blvd
- MSCY 77459 4496 C2
Riverstone Ct
- CNRO 77304 2529 C2
- MtgC 77304 2529 C2
Riverstone Crossing Dr
4700 FBnC 77479 4496 B4
Riverstone Lake Ln
11300 HarC 77089 4504 C1
Riverstone Mills Ln
26500 FBnC 77494 4092 A6
Riverstone Ranch Dr
- HarC 77089 4377 C7
- HarC 77089 4504 B1
- HOUS 77089 4377 C7
- PRLD 77089 4504 B1
Riverstone Springs Dr
30500 MtgC 77386 2969 C1
River Terrace Rd
200 HarC 77336 2975 E5
7800 HarC 77336 2976 A6
Riverton Ash Ct
18700 HarC 77433 3252 A4
Riverton Crest Ct
18700 HarC 77433 3252 A4
Riverton Manor Ct
13800 HarC 77429 3397 A2
Riverton Ranch Dr
19600 HarC 77433 3252 A4
River Trace Dr
- FBnC 77469 4365 B6
River Trail Dr
12200 HOUS 77050 3547 A5
River Trails
1700 FBnC 77479 4494 B4
Rivertree Ln
4600 HarC 77388 3112 B5
5100 HarC 77379 3112 A5
River Vale Dr
- HOUS 77345 3120 B6
River Valley Dr
2000 HarC 77373 3114 D5
2300 MSCY 77489 4370 B6
3100 HOUS 77339 3119 C4
Riverview Cir
1300 HOUS 77077 3958 B4
5100 BzaC 77511 4868 A7
Riverview Ct
200 BzaC 77511 4868 A7
1300 HOUS 77077 3958 B5
River View Dr
- HOUS 77077 3958 B4
10600 HOUS 77042 3958 C4
Riverview Dr
1900 FBnC 77469 4364 B5
5000 BzaC 77511 4868 A7
10800 HOUS 77042 3958 C4
11300 HOUS 77077 3958 A4
26500 MtgC 77365 3117 C4
Riverview Wy
- HOUS 77024 3960 A5
5900 HOUS 77057 3960 C4
7500 HNCV 77024 3960 A5
11100 HOUS 77042 3958 C5
11800 HOUS 77077 3958 A5
11900 HOUS 77077 3957 E5
River Village Dr
2000 HOUS 77339 3118 E4
2300 HOUS 77339 3119 A5
River Vine Ct
11700 HarC 77377 3254 D4
Riverwalk Dr
19200 MtgC 77365 2971 E4
19400 MtgC 77365 2972 B4
Riverway
10 HOUS 77024 3961 A4
10 HOUS 77056 3961 A4
Riverway Dr
5000 HOUS 77056 3960 E4

STREET
Block City ZIP Map# Grid
Riverway Dr
5000 HOUS 77056 3961 A4
Riverway Ln
1800 FBnC 77469 4492 E4
Riverway Bluff Ln
200 FBnC 77469 4365 B5
Riverway Oak Ct
2100 HOUS 77345 3120 B3
Riverway Oak Dr
2200 HOUS 77345 3120 B3
Riverwell Cir E
8800 HarC 77083 4237 A1
Riverwell Cir W
8800 HarC 77083 4237 A1
River Willow Dr
16800 HarC 77379 3256 A4
River Wind Ct
8400 FBnC 77469 4234 B5
River Wind Dr
8700 FBnC 77479 4494 B4
21100 FBnC 77469 4234 A5
River Wind Ln
- HarC 77089 4377 A7
- PRLD 77089 4377 A7
Riverwood Ct
800 CNRO 77304 2529 E2
Riverwood Dr
- DKSN 77539 4752 E6
4900 FBnC 77469 4491 C2
4900 FBnC 77471 4491 C2
35200 MtgC 77354 2673 B4
E Riverwood Dr
600 HOUS 77076 3684 E4
S Riverwood Dr
4600 FBnC 77469 4491 C3
4600 FBnC 77471 4491 C3
W Riverwood Dr
100 HOUS 77076 3684 C4
Riverwood Ln
10 WlrC 77445 3243 B1
Riverwood Tr
1800 MtgC 77386 2969 A4
Riverwood Park Dr
3400 HOUS 77339 3119 D4
3400 HOUS 77345 3119 D4
N Riviera Cir
1200 PRLD 77581 4504 E3
S Riviera Cir
- PRLD 77581 4504 D3
Riviera Ct
3500 SGLD 77479 4495 B3
S Riviera Ct
1600 PRLD 77581 4504 D3
Riviera Dr
3200 SGLD 77479 4495 B3
Riviera Ln
3100 HOUS 77338 3263 D4
Riviere Ln
20700 HarC 77388 3112 D4
Rivington Ln
6700 HarC 77379 3256 D4
RL Butler St
10 MAGA 77355 2669 A6
Roach Rd
6700 HOUS 77396 3406 B2
Road 333A
10 LbyC 77327 2538 E1
Road 333B
10 LbyC 77327 2538 E1
Road 334
10 LbyC 77327 2538 E1
Road 3433
200 PLMG 77327 2684 E2
Road 3660
10 LbyC 77327 2684 B3
Road 3707 N
10 LbyC 77372 2538 D5
Road 3771
10 LbyC 77327 2538 A2
Road 3774
10 LbyC 77327 2538 C2
Roadie Pass
30700 MtgC 77355 2815 D1
Roadrunner Ln
- HMBL 77396 3406 C4
Roadway
20000 MtgC 77357 2829 A6
Roaming Woods Ln
3300 MtgC 77380 2967 B2
Roan Dr
12000 HarC 77065 3539 E4
Roandale Dr
10900 HOUS 77048 4243 D6
11700 HOUS 77048 4374 D1
Roane St
- HOUS 77028 3687 D6
Roanoke Dr
500 MtgC 77302 2530 C7
Roanoke St
2600 HOUS 77020 3963 E3
6700 HOUS 77028 3825 D1
Roanoke Falls Dr
13900 HarC 77429 3253 E4
Roans Prarie Ln
300 FBnC 77469 4493 B6
Roanwood Ct
1700 HarC 77090 3258 B4
Roanwood Dr
1400 HarC 77090 3258 A3
2000 HarC 77090 3257 E4
Roaring Tr
10 FBnC 77545 4622 D1
Roaring Bluffs Dr
- HarC 77095 3537 E3
Roaring Brook Ln
10800 HNCV 77024 3960 A3
Roaring Creek St
3400 MtgC 77380 2967 B2
Roaring Fork Ln
14400 HOUS 77077 3956 E3
14500 HarC 77095 3539 A6
Roaring Hill Ct
21400 HarC 77449 3815 B3
Roaring Oaks Ln
2700 HarC 77449 3815 B4
Roaring Point Dr
8700 HOUS 77088 3683 A1
Roaring Rapids Dr
3900 PASD 77059 4380 E5
4300 PASD 77059 4381 A5
N Roaring River Ct
18400 HarC 77346 3264 D7
S Roaring River Ct
18400 HarC 77346 3264 D7
Roaring River Falls
9200 HarC 77375 2965 C4
Roaring Springs Ct
1900 PRLD 77584 4500 A1

STREET
Block City ZIP Map# Grid

Roaring Springs Dr
1900 PRLD 77584 4500 A1
7500 HarC 77064 3542 A5
Roaring Springs Ln
1400 PASD 77586 4382 A6
Roaring Springs Rd
4800 PASD 77505 4248 A6
Roaring Trail Ct
1900 FBnC 77545 4622 D1
Roaring Trail Dr
4100 FBnC 77545 4622 D1
Roark Rd
- HOUS 77074 4238 D4
10800 HOUS 77099 4238 D4
11300 HOUS 77031 4238 D5
Roarks Psg
9600 FBnC 77459 4621 D5
Roatan Cl
2100 DKSN 77539 4633 C7
Roayl Ridge Tr
1200 HOUS 77345 3120 E7
Rob Ln
- SGCH 77355 2961 E5
Robbie Rd
- HarC 77379 3111 B6
Robbie St
200 LMQU 77568 4990 C1
800 HOUS 77009 3824 C3
900 HOUS 77009 3823 E5
Robbie Lee Rd
100 MtgC 77354 2817 C1
Robbins Dr
300 PNPV 77024 3959 E4
Robbins Rd
13500 HarC 77429 3398 A3
Robbs Cross
20000 HarC 77379 3110 D5
Robcrest Wy
1900 MSCY 77489 4370 C4
Robeck St
19200 HarC 77377 3106 E7
Roberson Ln
6600 HOUS 77085 4371 C4
Roberson Rd
7000 HOUS 77489 4371 C4
N Roberson St
800 CNRO 77301 2384 A4
1700 CNRO 77301 2383 E3
2200 CNRO 77303 2383 E1
Robert Dr
24600 MtgC 77365 2973 E7
24600 MtgC 77365 3118 E1
Robert Ln
12300 STFE 77510 4871 B5
Robert St
1100 PRLD 77581 4376 C6
2200 PASD 77502 4247 B1
Roberta Ln
5800 HOUS 77032 3405 E6
5800 HOUS 77396 3405 E6
6000 HOUS 77396 3406 A6
Roberta St
16700 HarC 77530 3830 E6
N Robert C Lanier Dr
- BYTN 77520 3973 A5
- BYTN 77521 3972 E5
100 BYTN 77520 3972 C5
3100 BYTN 77521 3973 B4
S Robert C Lanier Dr
- BYTN 77520 4112 B3
Robert C Lanier Frwy
- BYTN 77521 3974 A3
4000 BYTN 77520 3974 A3
N Robert C Lanier Frwy
- BYTN - 4112 B2
- BYTN 77520 3974 A3
- BYTN 77521 3974 A3
- HarC - 4112 A3
N Robert C Lanier Frwy LP-201
- BYTN - 4112 A3
N Robert C Lanier Frwy SR-146
- BYTN - 4112 B2
- HarC - 4112 A3
Robertcrest St
13300 HarC 77039 3545 C5
Robert E Lee Dr
500 MtgC 77302 2530 B7
Robert E Lee Rd
11800 HarC 77044 3688 D6
11800 HOUS 77044 3688 D6
12100 HarC 77044 3689 A6
Robert Hanna Dr
- HOUS 77074 4099 D6
Robert Hanna Lp
- HOUS 77074 4099 D6
Robert John Ln
3200 HarC 77032 3546 A2
Robert Lee Rd
100 HOUS 77009 3824 B4
Roberts Blvd
3700 HarC 77521 3834 E7
3700 HarC 77521 3835 A7
Roberts Dr
21800 MtgC 77357 2827 D1
Roberts Ln
3900 GlsC 77518 4634 C3
Roberts Rd
5300 KATY 77494 3952 C1
17400 HarC 77447 3249 C2
18000 HarC 77447 3104 C4
23100 MtgC 77357 2828 A5
Roberts St
- HOUS 77034 4379 A4
100 HOUS 77003 3964 A5
1500 HOUS 77003 3963 E7
2000 HOUS 77004 3963 D7
5800 TXCY 77591 4873 E5
N Roberts St
200 HOUS 77003 3964 A5
Roberts Tr
300 HarC 77037 3544 D7
29800 MtgC 77354 2671 E7
29800 MtgC 77354 2672 A7
Roberts Cemetery Ln
- HarC 77447 3105 D3
Roberts Cemetery Rd
20200 HarC 77447 3105 E2
21100 MtgC 77447 2960 C6
Robertson Rd
500 BzaC 77511 4628 C5
3500 FBnC 77469 4233 B6
Robertson St
10 TXCY 77591 4873 D6
300 LMQU 77568 4873 E7
4800 HOUS 77009 3824 D4

STREET
Block City ZIP Map# Grid

N Robertson St
- CNRO 77303 2383 E1
Roberts Run Ln
22800 FBnC 77450 4093 D1
Roberts Vale Rd
13400 HarC 77037 3544 D6
Robeson Pl Dr
7600 HOUS 77016 3687 A2
Robin Av
1400 KATY 77493 3813 E7
Robin Blvd
12200 HOUS 77045 4242 C7
12200 HOUS 77045 4373 C1
12300 HOUS 77047 4373 C1
Robin Cir
700 PASD 77502 4107 A7
Robin Ct
- FRDW 77546 4629 D1
10 MtgC 77385 2676 D6
11500 MtgC 77303 2239 C6
Robin Dr
10 BzaC 77511 4868 A6
Robin Ln
7200 TXCY 77591 4873 C5
11500 MtgC 77303 2239 C6
15900 MtgC 77355 2961 E4
15900 SGCH 77355 2961 E4
18900 HarC 77377 2961 E7
Robin Rd
100 BYTN 77520 3971 B1
22100 HarC 77447 3106 A2
Robin Spur
1900 PRLD 77581 4502 B1
Robin St
200 DRPK 77536 4109 A4
300 HOUS 77002 3963 B4
700 HOUS 77019 3963 A4
1600 HOUS 77019 3962 E4
9800 LPRT 77571 4250 B1
Robin Tr
10 CNRO 77304 2236 C6
15100 MtgC 77302 2680 A2
15200 MtgC 77302 2679 E3
Robin Caper Ct
10 WDLD 77382 2819 A3
Robindale Cir
10 WDLD 77384 2675 D5
Robindale Ln
- MSCY 77459 4497 A2
Robindale Creek Dr
2900 HOUS 77082 4096 C2
Robindell Dr
8400 HOUS 77074 4100 B7
8700 HOUS 77074 4240 B1
Robin George Dr
37100 MtgC 77354 2670 A7
Robinglen Dr
13200 HOUS 77083 4097 B5
Robin Grove Ct
15400 HarC 77433 3251 B6
Robin Hill Ct
13500 HOUS 77059 4379 D4
Robin Hollow Ct
18200 HarC 77433 3537 A5
Robinhood
1700 MtgC 77316 2668 E1
Robinhood Cir
10 LbyC 77535 3413 D2
2700 PRLD 77581 4503 D4
Robin Hood Ct
25100 WlrC 77447 2813 C7
Robin Hood Dr
- WlrC 77447 2959 D2
Robinhood Dr
10 CNRO 77301 2383 D3
Robin Hood Ln
- WlrC 77447 2959 D1
25400 WlrC 77447 2813 D7
Robinhood St
1700 PASD 77502 4107 B7
2400 HOUS 77005 4102 A2
2800 WUNP 77005 4102 A2
3700 WUNP 77005 4101 D2
Robinhood's Well Dr
9000 HarC 77379 3255 D2
Robin Knoll Ct
2500 FBnC 77545 4498 C6
Robin Lake Dr
10 HOUS 77024 3959 B5
Robin Lake Ln
10 HOUS 77024 3959 B5
Robin Meadow Cir
12300 STAF 77477 4237 E7
Robin Meadow Ct
4200 HarC 77449 3816 B2
Robin Meadow St
5500 PRLD 77581 4502 B1
Robin Ridge Cir
800 FRDW 77546 4629 D5
Robin Ridge Dr
8100 HarC 77396 3406 D7
Robin Run Dr
10 WDLD 77381 2820 D3
Robins Wy
800 FBnC 77477 4369 C4
800 STAF 77477 4369 C4
4700 FBnC 77479 4493 D1
Robins Branch Ln
10200 HOUS 77075 4376 C3
Robins Crest Dr
12700 HarC 77377 3254 B3
Robins Forest Dr
1400 HarC 77379 3255 B1
Robinshire Ln
- HarC 77047 4374 A4
Robins Nest Ln
22900 HarC 77389 2967 B7
Robinson Blvd
2900 TXCY 77590 4874 D5
Robinson Dr
3300 PRLD 77581 4376 C5
Robinson Fy
2200 SGLD 77479 4368 C6
Robinson Ln
23700 MtgC 77357 2828 A6
Robinson Rd
- ORDN 77380 2822 B5
100 ORDN 77385 2822 B5
100 ORDN 77386 2822 B5
500 MtgC 77385 2822 E6
800 LPRT 77571 4110 D7
1400 MtgC 77386 2822 E6
2000 MtgC 77385 2823 A7
2000 MtgC 77386 2823 A7
2900 MSCY 77459 4497 A2
8000 HTCK 77563 4988 D6
Robinson St
1000 ALVN 77511 4867 A1

STREET
Block City ZIP Map# Grid

Robinson Rd Ct
2600 MSCY 77459 4497 B2
Robin Sound St
7000 PRLD 77581 4502 B1
Robin Springs Pl
10 WDLD 77381 2821 A2
Robin Walk Ln
10 WDLD 77380 2822 B7
Robinwick Ct
6700 HarC 77379 3256 E4
Robinwood Dr
300 MtgC 77386 2968 C1
800 STAF 77477 4370 B4
1000 MSCY 77489 4370 C4
1000 STAF 77489 4370 C4
2100 DRPK 77536 4109 D7
Robinwood Ln
10 HDWV 77024 3959 D1
Robita St
10 HOUS 77019 3962 E4
Roble Ct
12600 HOUS 77045 4241 B6
Roble Dr
12500 HOUS 77045 4241 B6
Roble Green Tr
20300 HarC 77346 3264 E4
Robley St
2400 PASD 77502 4247 C1
Robmore St
100 HOUS 77076 3685 A5
Robson Dr
- HarC 77429 3253 E7
Robwood Ct
3600 HarC 77449 3815 C2
Rochdale St
3200 HOUS 77025 4241 E1
Rochelle Ct
14600 HarC 77429 3396 C2
Rochelle Dr
14300 HarC 77032 3546 D2
Rochelle St
200 RHMD 77469 4364 D7
200 RHMD 77469 4491 D1
Rochelle Park Dr
- FBnC 77479 4493 C2
Roche Rock Dr
14900 HarC 77396 3407 C7
Rochester Ct
12800 STFE 77510 4871 A7
Rochester St
13500 HOUS 77015 3967 D1
Rochow St
500 HOUS 77019 3962 C4
N Rock Dr
400 HarC 77073 3259 A5
Rock I
26500 MtgC 77355 2963 A4
Rock Pt
10 CNRO 77304 2383 B7
Rockampton Dr
12400 HOUS 77031 4239 B5
Rockarbor Dr
2800 HOUS 77063 3959 C7
2900 HOUS 77063 4099 C1
Rock Arbor Ln
8900 HarC 77095 3537 E5
Rockaway Dr
10100 HOUS 77016 3686 E4
Rockaway Point Ln
7500 FBnC 77469 4093 D5
Rockbar Ln
1500 FBnC 77469 4493 B4
Rock Bass Rd
3000 MtgC 77384 2675 E6
3100 MtgC 77384 2676 A6
Rockbend
- HarC 77084 3678 B2
Rockbend St
16700 HarC 77084 3678 B2
Rockbourne Dr
6100 HOUS 77396 3406 A3
Rock Bridge Ln
11300 FBnC 77478 4236 D5
Rockbridge Ln
6600 HOUS 77023 4104 D2
Rockbrook Dr
600 HarC 77015 3829 B7
Rockby Dr
6300 HOUS 77085 4371 D4
Rock Canyon Dr
1000 HarC 77450 3953 E3
1100 HarC 77450 3954 A4
1200 HOUS 77450 3954 A4
Rock Chapel
27100 MtgC 77355 2963 B4
Rockchester Ct
1700 HarC 77450 3954 A5
Rockchester Dr
22000 HarC 77450 3954 A4
Rockcliff Dr
8600 HarC 77037 3684 C1
9100 HarC 77037 3544 C7
Rock Cove
500 HOUS 77079 3956 E2
Rock Creek Ct
700 FBnC 77469 4616 D1
12600 HarC 77346 3408 D1
Rockcreek Ln
16300 HarC 77530 3829 D3
Rock Creek Villa Dr
15400 HarC 77429 3253 C5
Rockcrest
10100 HOUS 77041 3820 A1
Rockcrest Dr
- HOUS 77041 3820 A1
Rockcrest Rd
10200 HOUS 77041 3819 E1
10200 HOUS 77041 3820 A1
Rockdale Ct
3000 LGCY 77539 4753 A5
Rockdale Dr
3200 MtgC 77365 2974 C7
Rockdale Bridge Ct
10200 FBnC 77478 4236 D3
Rockdale Bridge Ln
15000 FBnC 77478 4236 D3
Rockdale Glen Dr
13900 HOUS 77048 4374 E4
Rock Dove Ln
14100 HarC 77044 3549 C2
Rock East Dr
16500 HarC 77073 3259 A4
Rock Elm Ln
14700 HarC 77377 2963 C5
14700 TMBL 77375 2963 C5
14700 TMBL 77377 2963 C5
Rockergate Dr
6600 HOUS 77489 4371 C6

STREET
Block City ZIP Map# Grid

Rockets Ln
- HarC 77032 3546 C2
- HOUS 77032 3546 C3
Rock Fall Dr
- HOUS 77339 3118 B5
- MtgC 77339 3118 B5
Rock Fall Meadows St
10300 HOUS 77034 4378 C2
Rock Falls Ct
7600 HarC 77095 3538 B7
Rock Falls Wy
12700 HarC 77041 3679 D7
Rock Fence Dr
1600 FBnC 77469 4365 D2
Rockfern Ct
10 WDLD 77380 2968 A3
N Rockfern Ct
10 WDLD 77380 2968 A3
Rockfern Rd
10 WDLD 77380 2968 A3
Rockfield Dr
6300 PASD 77505 4248 E5
Rockford Dr
8100 HOUS 77033 4244 A3
8300 HOUS 77033 4243 E4
11400 HOUS 77048 4244 A7
12100 HOUS 77048 4375 A1
Rockford Hall Dr
8300 HarC 77379 3256 A5
Rock Forest Ln
13700 HarC 77396 3547 B3
Rockgate Dr
22300 HarC 77373 3260 E1
22400 HarC 77373 3115 E7
Rockglen St
13100 HOUS 77015 3967 C2
Rock Green Ct
1100 FBnC 77494 3953 A3
Rock Harbor Ct
20700 HarC 77449 3815 C6
Rock Harbor Ln
800 LGCY 77573 4633 C2
Rockharbor Ln
12000 HarC 77070 3399 B6
Rockhaven Dr
2200 HOUS 77062 4380 C7
Rockhill St
7500 HOUS 77061 4245 C3
Rockhill Grove Dr
- HarC 77429 3397 B1
Rock Hill Point Dr
13100 HarC 77429 3397 B3
Rock House Rd
15600 HOUS 77060 3544 D2
Rockhurst Dr
9700 HOUS 77080 3820 B2
Rockin Dr
1500 HOUS 77077 3957 C5
Rockingham Pl
10 CNRO 77304 2529 D1
Rockingham St
4100 HOUS 77051 4243 B4
Rocking Pine Pl
10 WDLD 77381 2674 B7
Rocking R St
26900 MtgC 77372 2683 D1
Rockington Ln
15000 HarC 77530 3829 C5
Rockin Seven Dr
24200 HarC 77447 3249 E3
Rock Ivy Tr
- HarC 77449 3676 B3
Rock Knoll Dr
15000 FBnC 77083 4236 C1
Rockland Dr
5000 PRLD 77584 4503 A4
5300 PRLD 77584 4502 E4
11700 HarC 77064 3400 A7
Rock Land Ln
- HarC 77429 3252 B6
Rockledge Ct
10 WDLD 77382 2674 A4
Rockledge Dr
10 WDLD 77382 2674 A4
14900 HarC 77429 3397 C1
Rockleigh Pl
100 HOUS 77017 4105 E6
100 HOUS 77017 4106 A6
Rockley Rd
10400 HOUS 77099 4238 D3
Rock Maple Ln
10600 HarC 77040 3541 E6
Rockmead Dr
600 HOUS 77339 3118 B5
Rock Mill Ln
14900 FBnC 77478 4236 D4
Rockmont Ct
8500 HOUS 77489 4497 D2
Rockmoor Ct
3100 SGLD 77478 4369 B3
Rockmore Dr
8600 HarC 77064 3400 A7
9100 HarC 77064 3399 D7
Rock Oak Pl
12200 WDLD 77380 2967 E2
Rock Pass Dr
9700 HarC 77064 3540 C5
Rock Path St
17000 HarC 77084 3678 A3
Rock Pine Ct
10 WDLD 77381 2821 A5
Rockpoint Cir
3900 LGCY 77539 4633 D4
Rockpoint Dr
- HOUS 77450 3954 A2
500 HarC 77450 3954 A2
Rockport Ct
14300 SGLD 77478 4236 E6
Rockridge Ct
10 WDLD 77381 2820 E3
Rock Ridge Dr
1700 HarC 77530 3829 E4
Rockridge Dr
10 WDLD 77381 2820 E4
Rockrill Dr
3000 HOUS 77045 4242 A6
3400 HOUS 77045 4241 E6
Rock River Ln
10600 HarC 77433 3537 D1
Rock Rose St
7900 HOUS 77051 4243 D2
Rockshire Dr
14000 HarC 77039 3545 E3
Rock Shoals Wy
2500 PRLD 77584 4500 B3
Rockside Ln
7800 HarC 77379 3256 A1

STREET
Block City ZIP Map# Grid

Rock Spring Ct
1800 FBnC 77479 4494 B4
Rock Springs Dr
700 FBnC 77469 4493 B5
4900 HOUS 77345 3119 D2
5400 LPRT 77571 4250 B2
Rocksprings Rdg
14400 HarC 77429 3253 D5
Rockstone
- HarC 77084 3678 B2
Rockstone St
16700 HarC 77084 3678 B2
Rocktree Dr
9600 HOUS 77040 3682 A1
Rockville Dr
- HarC 77070 3399 D7
11700 HarC 77064 3399 D7
Rockwall Ct
1800 FBnC 77479 4494 C4
Rockwall Trail Dr
6600 HarC 77346 3408 E1
Rockwater Dr
- HarC 77449 3815 C2
Rockwell Dr
14500 HOUS 77085 4371 D3
Rock West Dr
16500 HarC 77073 3259 A5
E Rock Wing Cr
10 WDLD 77381 2821 C3
W Rock Wing Cr
10 WDLD 77381 2821 C3
Rockwood Dr
4400 HOUS 77004 4103 E3
5200 RSBG 77471 4491 D5
Rockwood Glen Ln
1100 HarC 77073 3259 B4
Rockwood Park Ln
26800 HarC 77433 3396 A7
Rock Wren Ct
28500 FBnC 77494 3951 C6
Rocky
2200 HarC 77450 3954 B6
Rocky Ln
10 HarC 77040 3541 B7
Rocky Rd
12400 MtgC 77301 2385 E7
12400 MtgC 77306 2385 E7
13900 MtgC 77302 2532 C1
13900 MtgC 77306 2532 C1
Rocky Bank Dr
19500 HarC 77375 3109 E7
Rocky Bay Rd
18600 HarC 77532 3410 B6
Rocky Bend Dr
4100 FBnC 77479 4366 C6
11500 HOUS 77077 3958 B5
Rocky Bluff Dr
13600 HOUS 77085 4371 C1
Rocky Branch Dr
- HarC 77084 3678 E5
Rocky Briar Ct
19000 HarC 77377 3254 A2
Rocky Briar Ln
12700 HarC 77377 3254 A2
14200 BzaC 77583 4623 C5
Rocky Bridge Ln
15300 HarC 77433 3251 C6
Rocky Brook Dr
5800 HOUS 77345 3120 B4
Rocky Brook Falls
24100 HarC 77375 2965 D5
Rocky Canyon Ct
- HarC 77377 3254 A4
- HarC 77429 3254 A4
Rocky Cliff Ct
17800 HarC 77095 3537 C6
Rocky Cove Ct
2200 PRLD 77584 4500 B2
Rocky Cove Dr
12500 PRLD 77584 4500 B2
Rocky Cove Ln
100 LGCY 77539 4752 E5
Rocky Creek Dr
3200 MSCY 77459 4496 E5
Rocky Creek Ln
2100 PRLD 77581 4504 C4
2800 LGCY 77539 4752 D5
E Rocky Creek Rd
100 HOUS 77076 3684 D4
W Rocky Creek Rd
100 HOUS 77076 3684 D4
Rocky Crest Dr
3000 HarC 77449 3815 A3
Rocky Falls Ln
3600 FBnC 77494 4092 B1
Rocky Falls Pkwy
200 RHMD 77469 4364 D7
200 RHMD 77469 4491 D1
Rocky Falls Rd
1500 RHMD 77469 4364 C7
1700 FBnC 77469 4364 D7
Rockygate Dr
24000 HarC 77373 3115 B5
Rocky Glen Ct
22500 HarC 77373 3259 C1
Rocky Glen Ln
1400 HarC 77373 3259 C1
Rocky Hill Dr
12600 HarC 77066 3400 E2
Rocky Hollow Ln
600 LGCY 77573 4633 A2
Rockyhollow Rd
9700 LPRT 77571 4250 B4
Rocky Isle Dr
- PRLD 77545 4499 D3
Rocky Knoll Dr
- BYTN 77521 3972 B4
11900 HOUS 77077 3958 A6
12100 HOUS 77077 3957 E6
Rocky Knoll Ln
8700 FBnC 77469 4616 D1
Rocky Lake Ct
12200 HarC 77070 3254 C7
Rocky Lake Dr
11900 HarC 77070 3398 D1
Rocky Manor Ln
4900 HarC 77449 3677 A6
Rocky Meadow Dr
12600 HOUS 77024 3958 E1
Rocky Meadow Ln
- PRLD 77581 4503 E2
Rocky Mill Dr
11200 HarC 77429 3398 E5
11200 HarC 77429 3399 A5
Rocky Mountain Dr
500 HarC 77037 3544 B7
500 HOUS 77037 3544 B7
800 HOUS 77088 3544 A7

STREET
Block City ZIP Map# Grid

Rocky Nook Dr
6100 HOUS 77396 3406 A4
Rocky Oak Ct
15400 HOUS 77059 4380 B6
Rocky Peak Ln
7800 FBnC 77469 4095 B6
Rocky Ridge Dr
- CNRO 77302 2530 D4
Rockyridge Dr
2700 HOUS 77063 3959 C7
2800 HOUS 77063 4099 C1
Rocky Ridge Ln
7100 FBnC 77469 4094 E6
Rocky River Rd
600 HOUS 77056 3960 E4
Rocky Shores Dr
19700 HarC 77375 3109 E7
Rocky Springs Ct
12500 PRLD 77584 4500 B3
Rocky Springs Dr
2700 PRLD 77584 4500 B4
Rocky Springs Tr
- HOUS 77045 4373 A1
12200 HOUS 77045 4242 A7
Rockytop Cir
11700 HarC 77067 3401 E5
Rocky Trace Ln
19900 HarC 77433 3537 A7
Rocky Trail Dr
5500 HOUS 77339 3119 C1
Rocky Valley Dr
- FBnC 77478 4236 D2
8600 FBnC 77083 4096 C7
8700 FBnC 77083 4236 D1
Rocky Walk Ct
25500 FBnC 77494 4093 A2
Rocky Woods Dr
3600 HOUS 77339 3119 C5
Roda Dr
9600 MtgC 77303 2239 B4
Rodale Dr
15900 HarC 77049 3829 D3
Rodeo Dr
10 MNVL 77583 4624 D5
24200 MtgC 77357 2681 E6
Rodeo Palms Blvd
- MNVL 77583 4624 D5
Rodeo Palms Ct
- MNVL 77583 4624 D5
Rodeo Palms Pkwy
- BzaC 77583 4624 C5
- MNVL 77578 4624 E5
- MNVL 77578 4625 A5
- MNVL 77583 4624 C5
Rodeo Square Ct
- HOUS 77072 4097 D5
Rodeo Square Dr
12700 HOUS 77072 4097 D4
Rodger
6900 MNVL 77578 4746 C2
Rodgerdale Rd
2800 HOUS 77042 3958 D7
2800 HOUS 77042 4098 D3
3600 HOUS 77072 4098 D4
Rodgers
- HOUS 77022 3685 B6
Rodgers Rd
9500 HarC 77070 3255 A6
10100 HOUS 77070 3255 A6
Rodney Ln
10 BYTN 77520 3973 D5
Rodney St
- SHUS 77587 4246 C5
2300 HOUS 77034 4246 C5
Rodney Ray Blvd
9100 HarC 77040 3541 B6
9200 HarC 77064 3541 B6
Rodrigo St
6300 HOUS 77007 3961 E2
Rodriquez Rd
2700 PRLD 77581 4502 B4
2700 PRLD 77584 4502 B4
Roe Dr
3000 HOUS 77087 4104 E5
Roebourne Ln
7400 HarC 77069 3399 E1
8100 HarC 77070 3399 D1
Roebuck Dr
8600 HOUS 77338 3262 A6
Roehampton Ct
5700 HarC 77084 3678 A4
Roesner Ln
24500 FBnC 77494 3952 D5
Roesner Rd
24000 FBnC 77494 3953 A5
24800 FBnC 77494 3952 E5
26400 FBnC 77494 4092 A1
Rogan
3700 HOUS 77013 3827 D5
Rogers Ln
- WEBS 77598 4506 E6
Rogers Rd
7300 MNVL 77578 4746 E2
Rogers Row
3500 FBnC 77459 4622 A5
Rogers St
2800 HOUS 77009 3823 E4
4000 HOUS 77022 3823 E2
E Rogers St
600 HOUS 77022 3684 E6
Rogers Lake Ln
1400 FBnC 77469 4234 D3
Rogillio Rd
13200 MtgC 77306 2534 C6
Rogue Creek Ln
24400 MtgC 77380 2967 B3
Rogue River Dr
7300 HarC 77086 3542 B2
Rohan Rd
6300 FBnC 77469 4616 C1
Rohm & Haas
1000 DRPK 77536 4109 D1
Rohm & Haas Rd
- DRPK 77536 4109 D3
Roland Rd
4000 HarC 77493 3813 E1
Roland St
3000 HOUS 77026 3825 A7
Roland Canyon Dr
8200 HarC 77433 3537 A6
Roland Orchard Ct
29700 MtgC 77386 2969 E3
Roland Rue St
2100 PRLD 77581 4504 B5
Roland Trunkline
- HarC 77493 3813 C1
- KATY 77493 3813 C1

STREET
Block City ZIP Map# Grid

Rolbury Ln
12200 HarC 77066 3401 A5
Rolfe
3000 HOUS 77449 3814 D6
Rolff Ln
5900 HarC 77084 3679 A4
Rolido Dr
2700 HOUS 77063 3959 E7
2700 HOUS 77063 4099 E1
Rolk Rd
- HarC 77082 3957 A7
- HOUS 77082 3957 A7
2100 HOUS 77077 3957 A7
Rolke Rd
9700 HOUS 77099 4238 C3
Rolla St
6300 HOUS 77055 3822 A6
6600 HOUS 77055 3821 E6
Rolland St
- BYTN 77520 3972 D7
Roller Mill Ln
10800 FBnC 77478 4236 D4
Rolleston Ln
10200 HOUS 77034 4378 C2
Rollick Dr
8700 HarC 77375 2965 D2
Rolling Pns
100 CNRO 77301 2384 C7
Rolling Acres Dr
16800 HOUS 77396 3406 A3
Rolling Brook Dr
200 LGCY 77539 4752 E2
17100 SGLD 77479 4368 A7
17300 SGLD 77479 4367 D7
Rollingbrook Dr
- BYTN 77520 3972 B4
10 BYTN 77521 3972 B4
10 BYTN 77521 3973 A3
6200 HOUS 77096 4240 A3
7600 HOUS 77071 4239 E3
Rolling Creek Dr
- PASD 77505 4248 A6
700 HarC 77336 3121 D6
800 HOUS 77336 3121 D6
17000 HOUS 77090 3258 B4
18000 HarC 77090 3257 E2
18000 HarC 77090 3258 A2
Rollingcreek Dr
3400 BYTN 77521 3972 C3
Rolling Fog Dr
- PRLD 77545 4499 E1
2800 HarC 77546 4506 A7
Rolling Forest Dr
3500 HarC 77388 3112 E7
3600 HarC 77388 3257 E1
40300 MtgC 77354 2670 B2
Rolling Fork Ln
7300 HarC 77040 3681 B1
Rolling Glen Dr
2100 HarC 77373 3114 C2
Rolling Glen Ln
10 HarC 77375 3255 A2
16100 SPLD 77372 2683 A5
Rolling Green Dr
4000 TYLV 77586 4508 D2
Rolling Green Ln
3300 MSCY 77459 4496 D3
Rolling Hills Dr
10 PNVL 77304 2237 A3
Rolling Hills Dr E
10 PNVL 77304 2237 A4
Rolling Hills Dr W
10 PNVL 77304 2237 A2
10 PNVL 77318 2237 A2
Rolling Hills Ln
14200 BzaC 77583 4623 C5
20000 HarC 77449 3815 E4
Rolling Hills Rd
3400 CTSH 77303 2239 E6
5200 MtgC 77303 2239 E6
17600 MAGA 77354 2669 A4
Rolling Hills Oaks Dr
18100 MtgC 77365 2825 D6
18100 MtgC 77365 2826 A5
Rolling Knoll Ln
7300 FBnC 77494 4093 A5
Rolling Links Ct
10 WDLD 77380 2822 B6
Rolling Links Ln
10 WDLD 77380 2822 B6
Rolling Meadow Ct
6100 PRLD 77581 4375 D7
Rolling Meadow Dr
24400 HarC 77375 2965 A4
Rolling Meadow Ln
22300 FBnC 77450 4094 A3
Rolling Meadow St
3900 BzaC 77511 4867 B7
Rolling Meadows Dr
2100 HOUS 77339 3118 E5
Rolling Mill Dr
500 SGLD 77478 4368 B1
6500 HOUS 77088 3542 B7
Rolling Mill Ln
10 WDLD 77380 2822 B6
Rolling Oaks Dr
6700 FBnC 77469 4232 D3
8200 HarC 77375 2819 E6
8200 HarC 77389 2819 E6
8200 HarC 77389 2820 A6
9200 HarC 77375 2965 C1
15000 HarC 77070 3254 D7
Rolling Oaks Dr N
8000 HarC 77389 2820 A6
Rolling Oaks Dr S
8000 HarC 77389 2820 A6
Rolling Oaks Ln
- MSCY 77489 4370 D4
Rolling Pine Dr
15600 HarC 77049 3829 B1
Rolling Plains Dr
100 FBnC 77479 4366 C5
Rolling Points Cir
3800 HarC 77449 3815 B2
Rolling Prairie Ln
4100 FBnC 77494 4092 A1
Rolling Rapids
9000 HarC 77346 3409 D1
9100 HarC 77346 3265 E7
9200 HOUS 77346 3265 E7
Rolling Rapids Rd
8500 HarC 77346 3409 D1
Rolling Ridge Ct
10 WDLD 77385 2676 D4
Rolling Ridge Dr
7700 HOUS 77072 4097 E6
Rolling River Ct
14200 HOUS 77044 3550 B2

STREET
Block City ZIP Map# Grid

olling River Ln
13700 HOUS 77044 3550 B2
olling Rock St
7600 HarC 77040 3681 C1
olling Run Ct
800 HOUS 77062 4506 D1
olling Sage Dr
19200 HarC 77449 3816 B2
olling Shores Ct
18600 HarC 77346 3265 D7
ollingson Park Dr
9700 HarC 77375 3110 C6
9700 HarC 77379 3110 B6
olling Springs Ln
200 LGCY 77539 4753 A3
3600 HarC 77449 3815 A1
olling Stone Dr
1900 FRDW 77546 4629 C6
olling Stone Pl
10 WDLD 77381 2674 E6
ollingstone Rd
5000 FBnC 77469 4234 C3
olling Stream Dr
11600 HarC 77375 3109 E7
olling Terrace Dr
3400 HarC 77388 3112 E7
4000 HarC 77388 3257 D1
olling Timber
24000 MtgC 77355 2961 C6
olling Timbers Ct
5100 HarC 77084 3679 A6
olling Timbers Dr
15600 HarC 77084 3679 A6
15700 HarC 77084 3678 E6
olling Valley Dr
12600 HarC 77429 3397 D5
olling View Ct
4700 HOUS 77345 3119 D1
olling View Tr
16100 HarC 77433 3251 C5
olling Water Ct
6200 HarC 77069 3400 C2
olling Water Dr
6100 HarC 77069 3400 C2
ollingwood Cir
200 BYTN 77520 3971 C1
ollingwood Dr
10 HOUS 77055 3820 B6
10 HOUS 77080 3820 B6
400 BYTN 77520 3832 A7
400 BYTN 77520 3971 C1
33100 MtgC 77362 2817 C7
ollingwood St
- BYTN 77520 3971 B1
100 BYTN 77520 3832 A7
N Rollingwood St
100 MtgC 77362 2816 E5
100 SGCH 77362 2816 E5
ollins St
6100 HOUS 77091 3683 B5
ollins Bend Ln
8400 FBnC 77469 4095 C7
ollinsford Ln
23600 FBnC 77494 4093 C1
olls Royce Ct
800 HarC 77396 3407 A5
oma St
3600 HOUS 77080 3821 A2
omaine Ln
700 HarC 77090 3258 B2
oman Ct
2700 RMFT 77357 2829 B1
oman Dr
2000 BzaC 77511 4748 C3
oman Ln
1900 BzaC 77511 4748 C3
oman Forest Blvd
- MtgC 77357 2828 C3
- MtgC 77357 2829 C1
- WDBR 77357 2828 C3
1600 RMFT 77357 2828 E3
1900 RMFT 77357 2829 B1
oman Hills Ct
10400 HarC 77070 3399 B3
oman Hills Ln
13300 HarC 77070 3399 B3
omano Ln
2800 LGCY 77573 4633 A4
omano Park Ln
1400 HarC 77090 3258 B5
1400 HOUS 77090 3258 B5
omans St
1900 HOUS 77012 4105 D4
oman Woods
- HarC 77047 4374 B3
omayor Ct
2300 PRLD 77581 4502 E3
ome Dr
2100 PRLD 77089 4504 E3
2100 PRLD 77581 4504 E3
omea St
7700 HOUS 77028 3826 B5
omeo St
800 PASD 77502 4247 C1
omero Ln
1100 PRLD 77581 4504 E2
omero Ln
21800 SGCH 77355 2960 E2
omewood
- LPRT 77571 4251 E6
omford Ln
15300 HarC 77530 3829 D5
omney Rd
7500 HOUS 77036 4099 D6
omona Blvd
5900 HarC 77086 3542 C4
7000 HOUS 77086 3542 C4
omsley Ln
6600 HarC 77049 3828 E3
omulus Ct
- MtgC 77386 3116 A2
on Cir
200 FRDW 77546 4629 C1
onald
11400 HarC 77093 3546 C7
onaldsay Mews St
16100 HarC 77095 3538 C6
onan Rd
16500 HOUS 77060 3403 C7
onan Park Pl
300 HOUS 77060 3403 C7
onda Ln
9200 HOUS 77074 4239 A2
onda Dell Ln
16000 HarC 77447 3250 A7
ondel Rd
- LGCY 77573 4632 A1

STREET
Block City ZIP Map# Grid

N Rondelet Dr
4000 MtgC 77386 2970 C7
S Rondelet Dr
27400 MtgC 77386 2970 B7
27400 MtgC 77386 3115 B1
Rondo Ct
8100 HarC 77040 3541 B7
Ronico
- HarC 77049 3831 B1
Ronson Ln
2900 HarC 77521 3834 E5
Ronson Rd
1500 HOUS 77055 3821 B6
Rook Blvd
6800 HOUS 77087 4244 E3
Rookin St
6500 HOUS 77074 4100 B5
Rookwood Ct
10 WDLD 77382 2819 A2
Roos Rd
6300 HOUS 77074 4100 B5
6300 HOUS 77081 4100 B5
7100 HOUS 77074 4099 E5
9200 HOUS 77036 4099 A5
11600 HOUS 77072 4098 A5
Roosevelt Av
3400 FBnC 77545 4499 C7
Roosevelt Dr
1400 DRPK 77536 4109 C6
Roosevelt St
600 LMQU 77568 4873 E7
600 LMQU 77568 4989 E1
1200 HOUS 77012 4105 D3
Root Rd
7500 HarC 77375 2966 B6
7500 HarC 77389 2966 B6
Roots Down Wy
32000 HarC 77357 2830 B6
Roper St
700 HOUS 77034 4246 B5
Ropers Trail Ct
20500 HarC 77450 3954 D7
Roping Pen Rd
25300 PTVL 77372 2682 E7
25600 PTVL 77372 2683 A7
Rory Ct
3700 FBnC 77459 4621 B5
Rosa Allen Dr
4800 HOUS 77017 4106 A6
Rosa Allen St
5100 HOUS 77017 4106 B6
Rosadele St
2700 LMQU 77568 4989 D1
Rosa del Villa Ct
900 FBnC 77469 4365 B4
Rosalee St
1700 LMQU 77568 4873 D7
Rosalie St
400 HOUS 77006 3963 A6
1000 HOUS 77002 3963 A6
1000 HOUS 77004 3963 B6
2700 HOUS 77004 4103 C1
Rosalind Ln
3800 HarC 77053 4372 D4
Rosalinda Ln
1400 HarC 77073 3403 C2
Rosalyn Ct
2000 SGLD 77478 4368 E5
Rosamond St
100 HOUS 77076 3684 D5
2400 HOUS 77098 3962 A7
W Rosamond St
100 HOUS 77076 3684 C5
200 HOUS 77091 3684 C5
Rosa Ridge Ln
12400 HarC 77041 3679 E4
Rosas St
1100 FBnC 77477 4369 E5
Roscoe Dr
200 PASD 77506 4107 C4
Roscoe St
1900 LPRT 77571 4252 A3
Rose Av
- HOUS 77092 3682 C7
Rose Cir
21800 MtgC 77355 2960 E6
Rose Ct
10 HOUS 77004 4103 C1
Rose Ln
- HOUS 77091 3683 D6
3000 LMQU 77568 4989 D3
4400 FBnC 77545 4623 C2
5300 HarC 77373 3115 D7
5300 HarC 77373 3260 D1
20800 HarC 77447 3106 A1
27200 FBnC 77494 3951 C7
Rose Rd
10800 MtgC 77303 2239 B1
Rose St
2100 PRLD 77581 4503 A2
2200 WALR 77484 3101 E4
2700 DKSN 77539 4753 E2
2700 GlsC 77539 4753 E2
2800 PASD 77502 4108 A7
2800 PASD 77503 4108 A7
3900 HOUS 77007 3962 C3
4600 GlsC 77518 4634 E3
S Rose St
10 LMQU 77568 4873 D7
10 TXCY 77591 4873 D7
Rose Tr
16600 HarC 77429 3252 D5
Rose Wy
4100 HOUS 77025 4241 C4
Roseann St
12800 HarC 77031 4239 B7
12800 STAF 77031 4239 B7
12800 STAF 77477 4239 B7
Rose Arbor Ct
1900 FBnC 77479 4494 A3
Rose Arbor Ln
400 HOUS 77060 3544 D1
Rosebank Ct
4900 SGLD 77478 4369 A7
Rosebank Dr
4000 HarC 77084 3816 D1
Rosebay
- MSCY 77459 4496 B1
Rose Bay Ct
1300 PRLD 77545 4499 E3
Rosebay Ct
1900 SGLD 77479 4368 A6
Rose Bay Dr
2500 PRLD 77545 4499 E3
Rosebay Dr
4400 HOUS 77018 3683 C7
Rosebay Rd
1100 HarC 77521 3832 B5

STREET
Block City ZIP Map# Grid

Rose Bay Tr
16600 HarC 77429 3252 C5
Rosebend Dr
1700 FBnC 77494 3953 D5
Roseberry Dr
3100 LPRT 77571 4250 B3
Roseberry Manor Dr
1200 HarC 77379 3255 B1
Rosebluff Ct
2500 FBnC 77494 3953 B6
Rosebranch Ct
13800 HOUS 77059 4379 E5
Rosebriar Dr
15700 HOUS 77489 4371 A6
Rosebrier Park Ln
11900 HOUS 77082 4098 A1
Rosebrook Cir
7000 HarC 77379 3256 C1
Rosebrook Dr
- PRLD 77584 4500 C4
10000 HarC 77038 3543 D4
Rosebud
600 HOUS 77023 3964 D7
Rosebud Dr
- PASD 77586 4382 A6
- TYLV 77586 4382 A6
2700 BzaC 77584 4501 B5
3900 HOUS 77053 4372 D4
Rosebud Ln
10200 FBnC 77459 4621 E4
18400 HarC 77377 2962 A7
Rosebud St
30000 MtgC 77354 2672 A7
30000 MtgC 77354 2818 A1
Rosebud Bend Dr
7200 HarC 77346 3409 A1
Rosebud Dale Ct
3000 HarC 77084 3815 E3
Rosebud Knoll Ct
18800 HarC 77429 3396 A1
Rosebud Ridge Wy
- HarC 77379 3112 A6
Rosebury Dr
2500 HarC 77039 3545 E3
Rose Bush Tr
- FBnC 77494 4093 A4
Rose Canyon Dr
- CNRO 77302 2530 D4
Rose Canyon Ln
4800 FBnC 77494 4093 B1
Rosecastle Dr
10 HarC 77379 3110 D7
Rose Cottage Dr
15000 HarC 77069 3256 D6
Rosecrest Ct
3300 SGLD 77478 4368 E4
Rosecrest Dr
13000 HOUS 77045 4241 B7
13900 HOUS 77045 4372 B2
Rosecroft Dr
10400 HOUS 77048 4244 A7
11900 HOUS 77048 4375 A1
Rose Crossing Ln
20800 HarC 77379 3111 B4
Rosedale Cir
4900 HOUS 77004 4103 D3
Rosedale Ln
3800 GlsC 77518 4634 C3
Rosedale St
600 LMQU 77568 4874 A7
700 HOUS 77002 4102 E1
700 HOUS 77006 4102 E1
700 LMQU 77568 4990 B1
900 HOUS 77004 4102 E1
1200 HOUS 77004 4103 A1
Rosedale Brook Ct
10 WDLD 77381 2821 B5
Rose Dawn Ln
19800 HarC 77379 3110 C6
Rose Down Cir
17500 HarC 77429 3252 D1
Rosedown Pl
10 WDLD 77382 2674 B6
Rosedust Tr
- HarC 77433 3251 B4
Rose Elfe Ln
100 HarC 77532 3411 A5
Rose Fair Ct
20100 HarC 77450 3954 E3
Rose Fair Dr
1200 HarC 77450 3954 E3
Rosefield
2600 HOUS 77080 3820 B3
Rose Field Ct
700 BzaC 77584 4501 B1
Rosefield Dr
2800 HOUS 77080 3820 B2
Rosefork Ln
- HarC 77373 2968 D5
Rose Garden Dr
8300 FBnC 77083 4096 C5
8400 FBnC 77083 4236 A1
Rose Garden Tr
17300 HarC 77429 3252 C5
Rosegate Dr
4300 HarC 77373 3115 B6
Roseglade Dr
16500 HarC 77429 3396 E2
Roseglen Cir
15000 HarC 77530 3829 C4
Rose Grove Ln
3800 FBnC 77494 4093 D3
Rosehall Ln
- HarC 77041 3679 D3
Rosehaven Ct
5400 FBnC 77479 4493 D2
Rosehaven Dr
9200 HOUS 77051 4243 B6
Rosehearth Ct
26500 FBnC 77494 4092 D2
Rosehearty Dr
- HarC 77095 3538 D4
Roseheath Ln
2900 HarC 77073 3259 E5
3000 HarC 77073 3260 A4
Rosehedge Ct
14400 HarC 77047 4374 C5
Rosehedge Terrace Wy
8600 FBnC 77469 4234 B5
Rose Hill Ct
5700 BzaC 77583 4623 D3
Rosehill Ct
1500 FBnC 77479 4493 D4
14900 HarC 77070 3254 C7
Rose Hill Dr
2600 LGCY 77573 4508 E7
Rosehill Dr
14600 HarC 77070 3398 C1

STREET
Block City ZIP Map# Grid

Rosehill Ln
12300 HarC 77070 3254 C7
Rose Hill Rd
18700 HarC 77377 3107 A1
Rosehill Church Rd
20500 HarC 77377 3107 A5
Rosehill Estates Ln
14300 HarC 77429 3396 A2
Rosehill Park Ln
- MtgC 77386 2823 C7
Rose Hill Park Ln
17900 HarC 77429 3396 C2
Rose Hollow Ct
20500 HarC 77450 3954 D6
Rose Hollow Dr
21300 HarC 77450 3954 C5
Rosehollow Tr
22600 HarC 77377 3107 A1
22700 HarC 77377 2962 A7
Rosehurst Dr
22200 HarC 77377 3106 D1
22700 HarC 77377 2961 D7
E Roselake Dr
22100 HarC 77377 3107 A2
N Roselake Dr
18800 HarC 77377 3106 E2
S Roselake Dr
18800 HarC 77377 3106 E2
Roseland Dr
10 BYTN 77520 4113 C1
Roseland St
3300 HOUS 77006 3962 E7
4300 HOUS 77006 4102 D2
Rose Landing Dr
12900 HOUS 77070 3399 D4
Roseling Rd
10 WDLD 77380 2821 E6
Rosella Ln
32500 MtgC 77362 2963 C1
Rose Manor Dr
8500 HarC 77095 3538 D5
Rose Marble Ct
100 HarC 77069 3256 D6
Rosemarie Ln
4500 HarC 77338 3260 C2
Rosemary Ct
2600 BzaC 77584 4501 A6
Rosemary Ln
2800 HarC 77093 3685 E2
2800 HarC 77093 3686 A2
6300 HOUS 77016 3687 A2
15500 HarC 77532 3553 B4
Rosemary St
10700 BzaC 77583 4745 B7
Rosemary Bend Ln
12400 HarC 77044 3689 B2
Rosemary Park Ln
2800 HOUS 77082 4098 A2
Rosemead Dr
2400 PASD 77506 4107 E4
Rose Meadow Blvd
1600 BYTN 77521 3832 A6
1600 HarC 77521 3832 A6
Rose Meadow Ct
5500 BzaC 77583 4623 D3
Rosemeadow Ct
1300 HarC 77094 3955 A2
Rosemeadow Dr
900 HarC 77094 3955 A2
Rosemere Ln
- HarC 77047 4374 B4
Rose Mill Dr
21500 MtgC 77339 3118 C4
Rosemist Dr
1800 LGCY 77539 4633 E3
Rose Mist Ln
9800 HarC 77038 3543 E5
Rosemont Ct
6900 FBnC 77583 4623 A7
Rosemont Dr
3800 LPRT 77571 4250 B4
Rosemont Ln
12200 PRLD 77583 4500 B4
Rosemont St
3400 HOUS 77051 4243 C2
Rosemont Estates Ln
18000 HarC 77429 3396 C3
Rosemont Park Ln
6800 FBnC 77494 4093 C3
13000 HarC 77044 3689 C5
Rosemoor Crest Dr
- HarC 77388 3111 E2
Rosen Av
300 ARLA 77583 4623 B4
600 FBnC 77583 4623 B4
Rosenberg St
10 GLSN 77550 5109 B3
Rosenberg Foster Rd
- RSBG 77471 4490 D3
200 FBnC 77471 4490 D2
Rosenberg Foster Rd FM-723
- RSBG 77471 4490 D3
200 FBnC 77471 4490 D2
Roseneath Dr
3800 HOUS 77021 4103 D4
N Roseneath Dr
4300 HOUS 77021 4103 E4
4500 HOUS 77021 4104 A4
Rosenridge Dr
16100 HOUS 77053 4371 D6
Rosepalm Dr
- HarC 77089 4504 E1
Rose Park Ct
3000 HOUS 77339 3119 B1
Rosepath Ln
7400 FBnC 77469 4094 A6
Rose Petal Ln
9800 HarC 77038 3543 E5
Rose Petal Pl
10 WDLD 77381 2675 B6
Rose Pine Ct
10 MtgC 77355 2814 E3
15800 HarC 77429 3252 C6
Rosepoint St
1000 HOUS 77018 3822 E2
Rose Quartz Ln
3200 HarC 77388 3112 E4
Rose Ranch Blvd
2700 FBnC 77469 4616 A2
2700 RSBG 77469 4616 A2
Rose Ridge Ct
15500 HOUS 77489 4371 D5
Roseridge Ln
6200 HOUS 77053 4371 D5
6200 HOUS 77489 4371 D5
Roserock Ln
4600 HarC 77388 3112 B5

STREET
Block City ZIP Map# Grid

Roserock Ln
5100 HarC 77379 3112 A6
Rose Rock Canyon Dr
5700 FBnC 77469 4493 A6
Roserush Ct
10 WDLD 77380 2821 D6
Rose Sage Dr
7100 FBnC 77494 4093 B5
Rose Shadow Ln
1500 HarC 77038 3543 D5
Roseshire Ln
7400 HarC 77521 3833 D4
Rosespring Ln
- HarC 77379 3111 B5
Rosestone Ln
20800 HarC 77379 3111 B4
Rosethorn Ct
15800 HarC 77429 3252 C6
Rosethorn Dr
6500 HOUS 77049 3828 A2
Rosethorn Pl
10 WDLD 77381 2820 D2
Rosetrail Bend Ln
- FBnC 77494 4093 A3
Rosetta Dr
13800 HarC 77429 3397 E7
13800 HarC 77429 3398 A7
Rosevale Ct
17300 HarC 77429 3252 D6
24900 HarC 77375 2965 D3
Rose Valley Dr
15000 HarC 77070 3254 E7
Rose View Ct
16600 HarC 77429 3252 D5
Roseview Ln
15800 HarC 77429 3252 D6
Rose Village Dr
7100 HarC 77346 3264 E7
7100 HarC 77346 3408 E2
Roseville Dr
21300 HarC 77388 3112 D2
22300 HarC 77389 3112 E1
Roseville Park Ct
31300 MtgC 77386 2823 B7
Rosevine Dr
1200 TYLV 77586 4381 D7
Rose Water Ct
3600 BzaC 77578 4501 A7
Rosewater Ct
3800 FBnC 77494 4093 C2
Rose Water Dr
3400 BzaC 77578 4501 A7
Rosewater Pl
10 WDLD 77381 2820 C3
Roseway Ln
3800 LPRT 77571 4250 B4
Roseway Rd
22000 HarC 77377 2961 D7
22000 HarC 77377 3106 D1
Rosewell Ct
9200 HarC 77095 3538 C4
Rosewick St
800 HOUS 77015 3967 B1
Rose Willow Ln
6400 HarC 77379 3111 C4
Rosewin Cir
4000 HOUS 77047 4374 C1
Rosewind Dr
- BzaC 77584 4501 D6
- PRLD 77584 4501 D6
Rosewood Cir
1200 DKSN 77539 4753 D3
16800 MtgC 77372 2682 E6
Rosewood Ct
1500 FRDW 77546 4629 E2
10900 LPRT 77571 4250 D3
Rosewood Dr
400 PRVW 77484 3100 D5
500 SHEH 77381 2822 A2
700 BYTN 77520 3972 D6
700 SHEH 77381 2821 E2
800 DKSN 77539 4753 C3
5500 GLSN 77551 5108 D7
Rosewood Ln
1800 SGLD 77479 4367 E6
Rosewood Pl
2600 WDLD 77380 2967 D1
Rosewood Rd
100 CRLS 77565 4509 C4
23200 HarC 77377 2961 E6
23200 HarC 77377 2962 A6
Rosewood St
- HOUS 77002 3962 E7
2200 HOUS 77004 4103 C2
3200 LMQU 77568 4989 B2
13600 HarC 77083 4097 A7
Rosewood Tr
18800 HarC 77377 3106 E1
22800 HarC 77377 2961 E7
22900 HarC 77377 2962 A7
Rosewood Glen Ct
13000 HarC 77429 3254 B6
Rosewood Glen Dr
13100 HarC 77429 3254 A6
Rosewood Hill Ct
15600 FBnC 77478 4236 B5
Rosewood Wy Ln
12500 HarC 77041 3679 E4
Roseworth Ct
18900 HarC 77377 3254 C3
Rosharon Rd
1000 ALVN 77511 4867 A4
1900 ALVN 77511 4866 E5
Rosholt Dr
3100 MtgC 77386 2969 D1
Rosie Ln
9000 MtgC 77354 2964 C1
Rosie St
700 HOUS 77091 3684 A4
Rosille Dr
1900 BYTN 77520 3973 D6
Rosillion Ct
16600 HarC 77095 3538 A1
Rosillon Dr
- HarC 77095 3538 A1
Rosine St
500 HOUS 77019 3962 D4
Rosita Dr
16400 HarC 77083 4095 E5
Roslyn Ct
5500 HOUS 77081 4100 C6
Roslyn Bend Ct
10 WDLD 77382 2674 C2
Rosprim
- HOUS 77040 3681 B4
Ross
600 HOUS 77339 3263 B2
4600 HOUS 77033 4243 C5

STREET
Block City ZIP Map# Grid

Ross
4600 HOUS 77051 4243 C5
Ross Av
1100 PASD 77506 4106 D4
Ross Ext
- LMQU 77568 4990 C1
Ross Ln
3500 BzaC 77583 4500 D7
Ross Rd
200 HOUS 77339 3263 A2
4800 FBnC 77545 4623 A3
4900 ARLA 77583 4623 A3
12000 HOUS 77034 4247 A7
Ross St
100 LMQU 77568 4874 C7
100 TXCY 77591 4874 C7
600 LMQU 77568 4990 B1
4100 GlsC 77518 4634 C3
Ross Andrew Rd
- HarC 77346 3264 E6
Rossette Dr
9000 HOUS 77080 3820 D1
Rossiter Ln
14100 HarC 77049 3689 E7
14200 HarC 77049 3690 A7
Ross Lake Ct
- HarC 77346 3408 B3
Rosslare Dr
12500 HarC 77066 3401 B3
Rosslyn Rd
- HarC 77038 3543 C4
- HOUS 77088 3683 C1
4000 HOUS 77018 3822 C2
4300 HOUS 77018 3683 C7
5100 HOUS 77091 3683 C6
10400 HarC 77088 3683 C1
10500 HarC 77088 3543 C7
Rosslyn Landing Ln
6500 HOUS 77040 3682 B3
6500 HOUS 77088 3682 B3
Ross Sterling Av
1200 HOUS 77030 4102 D3
Rosston Cir
3100 HarC 77082 4096 C2
Rosstown Ct
13400 SGLD 77478 4237 B5
Rosstown Dr
13000 SGLD 77478 4237 C5
Rosstown Wy
9300 HOUS 77080 3820 D5
Rosswood Dr
2100 LGCY 77573 4632 D1
Rosswood Ln
20000 HarC 77388 3112 E5
Roswell St
7800 HOUS 77022 3824 B1
8100 HOUS 77022 3685 B7
Rosy Hill Ct
17300 HarC 77429 3252 D6
Rotan Dr
5000 HarC 77032 3546 D2
Rotary Dr
1700 HMBL 77338 3263 A6
1900 HarC 77338 3263 B6
Roth Dr
4200 MSCY 77459 4496 C3
11200 HOUS 77076 3685 A3
Rothbury St
- HOUS 77080 3820 B3
10200 HOUS 77043 3820 A3
10300 HOUS 77043 3819 E3
Rothchilde Ct
5200 HarC 77069 3256 C6
Rothcrest Ln
1000 HarC 77073 3259 A4
Rotherfield Ct
28300 HarC 77336 3121 D3
Rotherham Dr
21700 HarC 77388 3112 E2
Rothermel Rd
3100 HOUS 77093 3686 A3
3500 HOUS 77093 3686 B3
Rothesay Chase Rd
7900 HarC 77095 3538 D7
Rothfield Ct
- HarC 77047 4374 B4
Roth Forest Ln
4900 HarC 77389 2967 A7
Rothglen Dr
11400 HarC 77070 3254 E7
Rothko Ln
17200 HarC 77379 3256 B3
Rothmoore Ln
12200 HarC 77066 3401 A5
Rothsbury Dr
2900 BzaC 77584 4501 D6
Rothshire Ct
23200 HarC 77373 2968 D6
Rothway St
6100 HOUS 77040 3681 C5
Rothwell St
900 HOUS 77002 3963 D3
1500 HOUS 77020 3963 D3
1900 MSCY 77459 4369 D6
1900 MSCY 77477 4369 D6
Rothwood Rd
22000 HarC 77388 3112 B1
22000 HarC 77389 3112 B1
22900 HarC 77389 2967 B7
Rothwood Oaks Dr
4900 HarC 77389 2967 B6
Rotman St
3800 HOUS 77003 3964 B4
Roufa Rd
2300 HOUS 77002 3963 E4
2300 HOUS 77003 3963 E4
Rouge Cir
9600 HOUS 77063 4099 C1
Rough
10000 HarC 77086 3541 E2
Roughlock St
6200 HOUS 77016 3547 A7
Rough Neck Dr
1700 HMBL 77338 3263 A6
Roughneck Rd
10000 MtgC 77306 2532 A1
Roundabout Wy
16300 HarC 77530 3829 D4
Round Bank Ct
8600 HarC 77064 3541 E5
Round Bank Dr
7600 HarC 77064 3541 D5
Roundbluff Ln
8800 HOUS 77075 4376 E4
Round Creek Ct
21500 FBnC 77469 4094 A6
Round Dale Ln
11000 HOUS 77075 4376 D5

STREET
Block City ZIP Map# Grid

Round Grove Ln
7600 HarC 77095 3538 B7
Roundhill Ct
2700 FBnC 77494 3953 B6
Round Hollow Ct
5400 FBnC 77494 4093 A6
Roundhouse Ln
7300 HOUS 77078 3827 A2
Round Lake Dr
- HOUS 77077 3957 E6
2100 HOUS 77077 3958 A6
Roundleaf Ct
1400 HarC 77494 3953 D4
Round Moss Ln
- FBnC 77494 3952 B5
Round Oak Ct
13800 HOUS 77059 4379 E5
Round Oak Ln
1700 CNRO 77304 2237 B5
Round Robin Dr
5700 HarC 77449 3677 A5
Round Rock Ct
4700 SGLD 77479 4368 A7
Round Rock Rd
7900 HarC 77049 3690 A6
8400 HarC 77049 3689 E6
Round Rock St
1800 FRDW 77546 4629 C5
Roundrock Park Ln
7100 FBnC 77469 4095 C6
Round Rose Ct
6900 HarC 77379 3111 B3
Round Spring Dr
1800 HOUS 77339 3118 D5
Roundstone Dr
1300 FBnC 77469 4365 D2
Roundstone Ln
13900 HarC 77015 3828 E6
13900 HarC 77015 3829 A6
Roundtop Pl
10 WDLD 77381 2820 E3
Roundtree Ln
4200 MSCY 77459 4496 C4
Roundtree St
800 HOUS 77015 3967 A2
Round Up Ln
9400 HarC 77064 3540 D3
Roundup Rd
39900 MtgC 77354 2672 D2
41100 MtgC 77354 2673 A1
Round Valley Dr
22500 HarC 77450 3953 E4
Round Wind Tr
1800 HarC 77532 3410 B2
Rouse Rd
23600 MtgC 77365 2972 D6
Rouse St
100 HOUS 77020 3825 E7
300 HOUS 77020 3964 E1
Rouselle Ln
13000 HarC 77377 3254 A2
Roush Rd
1000 HOUS 77077 3956 E3
Rousseau Dr
11200 HarC 77065 3539 A1
11300 HarC 77065 3398 A7
Route 1
- HarC 77494 3953 A2
Routhland Dr
17800 HarC 77379 3257 B2
Roving Mdws
3900 HarC 77532 3694 A4
Rowan Ln
6300 HOUS 77074 4100 B5
6300 HOUS 77081 4100 B5
8800 HOUS 77036 4099 A5
11500 HOUS 77072 4098 A5
Rowan Burton Rd
- BzaC 77511 4866 D3
1800 ALVN 77511 4866 D3
Rowan Oak Ln
9400 HarC 77095 3538 A4
Rowan Tree Pl
10 WDLD 77384 2675 A3
Rowboat Wy
- HOUS 77044 3408 D4
15700 HOUS 77044 3409 A4
Rowe Ln
7700 HOUS 77075 4376 C2
Rowell Ct
6600 HOUS 77489 4371 C5
Rowena Ln
6300 HarC 77041 3679 B4
Rowena Dale Dr
8000 HarC 77379 3111 A2
Rowlett Rd
9500 HOUS 77034 4246 D7
9500 HOUS 77075 4246 D7
9500 HOUS 77075 4377 D1
Rowlock Ln
500 HOUS 77079 3956 E2
Rowlock Vine Dr
3600 HarC 77084 3816 D2
Rownita St
- HarC 77532 3552 E4
Rowood Dr
11900 HarC 77070 3399 B6
Rowood Ln
- HarC 77070 3399 A7
Roxanne Dr
200 TMBL 77375 2964 A6
Roxburgh Dr
6600 HOUS 77041 3680 E4
Roxbury Rd
6500 HOUS 77087 4244 E2
Roxdale Ridge Dr
12400 HarC 77044 3689 A4
Roxella St
700 HOUS 77076 3685 B5
1500 HOUS 77093 3685 C4
Roxette Ct
20900 HarC 77338 3261 E3
Roxton Dr
13900 HOUS 77077 3957 A3
Roxton Ridge Dr
15700 HOUS 77598 4506 D4
Roy Av
10 BYTN 77520 3973 E5
Roy Cir
2400 HOUS 77007 3962 B1
Roy Ct
1400 PRLD 77581 4504 E4
Roy Rd
1400 PRLD 77581 4375 B7
1500 PRLD 77581 4502 C1
2000 PRLD 77584 4502 C3
12400 BKVL 77581 4375 B6
12400 HOUS 77048 4375 B5

STREET
Block City ZIP Map# Grid

Roy St
100 MAGA 77354 2669 C4
100 MtgC 77354 2669 C4
2000 HOUS 77007 3962 B1
Royal Av
3100 HarC 77521 3832 E4
Royal Cir
10900 MtgC 77372 2537 A1
Royal Ct
100 FRDW 77546 4505 C6
Royal Dr
100 LGCY 77573 4631 C4
12700 STAF 77477 4238 B7
12900 STAF 77477 4369 B1
E Royal Mw
10 CNRO 77384 2675 E3
Royal Pkwy
5000 FRDW 77546 4505 E7
Royal Rdg
13200 MtgC 77302 2530 D4
Royal St
7800 HMBL 77396 3406 D3
Royal Wk
5100 HarC 77069 3256 D6
Royal Wy
9300 FBnC 77083 4236 C2
9300 FBnC 77478 4236 C2
Royal Adelaide Dr
2100 FBnC 77450 3954 A6
Royal Arbor Ln
4900 HarC 77084 3678 A7
E Royal Arch Dr
10 HOUS 77077 3957 C5
W Royal Arch Dr
10 HOUS 77077 3957 C6
Royal Arms Ct
22700 HarC 77449 3814 D6
Royal Ascot Ct
9700 HarC 77065 3539 E3
Royal Banner Wy
- HOUS 77082 4098 C2
Royal Bay Ct
2900 LGCY 77573 4633 A3
Royal Bell Ct
13100 HOUS 77047 4373 C2
Royal Bend Ln
13100 HarC 77377 3253 E2
13100 HarC 77377 3254 A2
Royal Birkdale Rd
14800 HarC 77095 3539 A7
14900 HarC 77095 3538 E7
Royal Blue Dr
- HarC 77088 3543 B6
Royal Bridge Pl
10 WDLD 77382 2674 B5
Royalbrook Dr
14800 HarC 77095 3539 A5
Royal Cape Ct
8600 HarC 77095 3537 E5
Royal Chase Dr
1600 HOUS 77047 4373 D1
Royal Chateau Ln
11200 HOUS 77082 4098 C2
Royal Cir Dr
2600 HOUS 77339 3119 A6
Royal Cliff Ct
7800 FBnC 77469 4095 C7
Royal Coach Dr
27100 MtgC 77357 2829 D5
Royal College Hill Rd
1600 CNRO 77304 2383 B6
Royal Colony Ln
2700 MSCY 77459 4496 C1
Royal Creek Ct
2700 PRLD 77584 4500 C3
5200 LGCY 77573 4751 E1
Royal Creek Dr
- HOUS 77345 3120 E6
Royal Creek Tr
1800 HOUS 77345 3120 E6
Royal Crescent Dr
3100 HOUS 77339 3119 A7
Royal Crest Ct
8000 HarC 77379 3256 A3
Royal Crest Dr
- HOUS 77062 4507 C3
16800 HOUS 77058 4507 C3
Royal Crest Wy
9700 HarC 77083 4237 B1
Royal Crossing Dr
21100 MtgC 77339 3118 B4
Royal Cypress Dr
5000 HarC 77449 3677 A6
Royal Dalton Cir
10 CNRO 77304 2236 D7
Royal Dornoch Dr
4700 PASD 77505 4248 E6
Royal Downs Dr
1900 HarC 77450 3954 A6
N Royale Dr
200 HOUS 77013 3966 E1
S Royale Dr
200 HOUS 77013 3966 E1
11100 HarC 77089 4505 A1
Royal Emerald Ln
25900 MtgC 77339 3118 C4
Royalene Ct
3700 DKSN 77539 4753 E3
Royal Fern Ct
1800 HOUS 77062 4380 D7
N Royal Fern Dr
10 WDLD 77380 2822 A7
S Royal Fern Dr
10 WDLD 77380 2822 A7
Royalfield Dr
- HOUS 77059 4380 C5
Royal Field Ln
- HOUS 77034 4378 D3
Royal Fort Ln
16300 HarC 77073 3259 D5
Royal Garden Dr
16000 HarC 77095 3538 A7
Royal Gate Ln
17800 FBnC 77469 4235 C1
Royal George Ln
800 HOUS 77047 4373 B3
Royal Glen Dr
2900 HOUS 77339 3119 B2
Royal Green St
- HarC 77083 4097 A7
Royal Grove Ct
8300 FBnC 77083 4096 C5
Royal Hampton Ct
10 SGLD 77479 4495 B3
Royal Highlands Ln
2500 CNRO 77304 2383 B1
Royal Hill Ct
5800 HOUS 77345 3120 E7
Royal Hill Dr
14100 FBnC 77083 4236 E1
Royal Hollow Ct
20900 FBnC 77450 4094 C3
Royal Hollow Ln
6000 FBnC 77450 4094 A4
Royal Isle Ct
11900 HarC 77375 3109 D7
Royal Isle Dr
19100 HarC 77375 3254 D1
19200 HarC 77375 3109 D7
Royal Knoll Ct
6900 PASD 77505 4249 A6
Royall St
6600 HOUS 77022 3824 B3
Royal Lagoon Ct
19400 HarC 77388 3113 C7
Royal Lake Dr
- FBnC 77478 4237 B4
- SGLD 77478 4237 B4
6900 HarC 77050 3547 B6
Royal Lakes Blvd
- FBnC 77469 4494 B7
Royal Lytham Cir
3100 SGLD 77479 4495 A2
Royal Manor Dr
3700 HarC 77082 4096 B4
4200 PASD 77505 4249 A5
Royal Meadow Dr
- HarC 77449 3816 B1
Royal Mile Ln
16200 HarC 77084 3678 C6
16200 HOUS 77084 3678 D7
Royal Mist Ln
18500 HarC 77377 3254 C3
Royal Montreal Dr
- HarC 77450 3954 A6
Royal Oak Dr
900 DKSN 77539 4753 C3
2100 LGCY 77573 4632 E1
4900 TXCY 77591 4874 A6
Royal Oak Pl
2000 WDLD 77380 2967 E2
Royal Oak St
300 WDBR 77357 2828 C2
13800 HarC 77083 4097 A7
Royal Oaks
- MtgC 77354 2671 D4
Royal Oaks Cross
11600 HOUS 77082 4098 B1
Royal Oaks Dr
600 FRDW 77546 4505 B5
3200 MtgC 77380 2967 B1
10100 HOUS 77016 3686 E4
Royal Oaks Grn
2900 HOUS 77082 4098 B1
Royal Oaks Grv
2900 HOUS 77082 4098 B1
Royal Oaks Trc
11600 HOUS 77082 4098 B1
Royal Oaks Vw
11600 HOUS 77082 4098 B1
Royal Oaks Club Dr
- HOUS 77082 4098 A1
Royal Oaks Crest
2900 HOUS 77082 4098 A1
Royal Orchard Dr
20100 MtgC 77365 2972 D7
Royal Palm Ct
- LGCY 77573 4508 D6
Royal Palms St
5600 HOUS 77021 4104 B6
Royal Park Dr
13400 HarC 77083 4237 B1
Royal Pine Dr
- HarC 77093 3685 E1
10700 HOUS 77093 3685 E3
10800 HOUS 77093 3686 A2
Royal Pineside Dr
- HarC 77396 3407 C3
- HOUS 77396 3407 C3
Royal Pl Ct
- HarC 77088 3543 B6
Royal Plantation Ln
3900 MSCY 77459 4496 C1
Royal Point Ct
5900 HOUS 77345 3120 E7
N Royal Point Dr
5700 HOUS 77345 3120 E7
S Royal Point Dr
5800 HOUS 77345 3120 E7
6100 HOUS 77345 3265 E1
Royal Purple Ln
- MtgC 77365 2973 C5
Royal Ridge Dr
- PRLD 77545 4499 D2
Royal Ridge Pl
10 WDLD 77382 2674 B6
Royal River Dr
3700 HOUS 77042 4098 C2
Royal Rose Dr
11900 HOUS 77082 4098 A1
Royal Royce Dr
3600 HOUS 77042 4098 C2
Royal Sage Dr
- HarC 77088 3543 B6
Royal Sands Ln
1300 HOUS 77345 3120 E6
Royal Shadows Dr
15000 HarC 77082 4096 C4
Royal Shores Cir
1100 HOUS 77345 3120 E7
Royal Shores Ct
1200 HOUS 77345 3120 E7
Royal Shores Ln
1600 HOUS 77345 3120 D6
Royal Springs Ln
13900 HOUS 77077 3956 E5
Royal Stone Ln
16300 HarC 77073 3259 C4
Royal Tern Dr
- HarC 77044 3549 E1
- HOUS 77044 3549 E1
Royal Tern Ln
10 WDLD 77380 2822 B7
4100 GLSN 77554 5548 B2
Royal Terns Ct
2500 LGCY 77573 4631 B7
Royal Thistle Ct
- HarC 77088 3543 B6
Royal Thistle Dr
- HarC 77088 3543 B6
Royal Timbers Dr
22000 HarC 77339 3118 C5
S Royal Timbers Dr
27300 HarC 77339 3118 D3
Royalton St
5300 HOUS 77056 4100 E3
5300 HOUS 77081 4100 E3
6100 BLAR 77401 4100 E3
6100 HOUS 77401 4100 E3
Royal Trail Dr
2600 HOUS 77339 3119 C6
Royal Villa Dr
21000 HarC 77449 3676 D3
Royal Village Dr
- HarC 77038 3543 B6
- HarC 77088 3543 B6
Royalwick Dr
24200 HarC 77375 2965 D4
Royalwood Dr
7500 HarC 77049 3828 D1
8000 HarC 77049 3689 D6
Royal Woods Ct
31700 MtgC 77385 2823 C6
Royan Dr
7700 MSCY 77071 4239 E7
Roy Bean Dr
9200 HOUS 77041 3681 D7
S Royce Cir
3100 BzaC 77583 4500 E6
Royce Ln
12800 HOUS 77013 3828 A5
Royce Palms Dr
11100 HOUS 77042 4098 C2
Roydencrest Ct
20800 HarC 77388 3112 B3
Royder St
200 HOUS 77009 3824 B5
Roydon Dr
12800 HOUS 77034 4378 A2
Roy Harris Lp
12400 MtgC 77306 2385 E6
Roy Long Rd
17800 BzaC 77584 4627 C3
17800 PRLD 77584 4627 C3
Royston Dr
- HOUS 77339 3117 E5
- HOUS 77365 3117 E5
Rozelle Av
500 SGLD 77478 4368 B1
Rozzano Ct
24500 FBnC 77469 4232 E1
Rubble Ln
20600 FBnC 77469 4234 C2
Rubenstein St
11700 HOUS 77076 3685 A2
Rubilee Av
6600 HarC 77396 3547 A3
Rubilee Dr
6800 HarC 77396 3547 B3
Rubin St
8500 HOUS 77051 4243 C3
11100 HOUS 77047 4243 C7
12500 HOUS 77047 4374 D1
Ruble Dr
19100 HarC 77084 3816 B5
Ruby Av
4500 HOUS 77018 3683 C7
Ruby Cir
13500 MtgC 77302 2532 E6
Ruby Dr
5900 PRLD 77581 4502 D3
Ruby Ln
- MtgC 77362 2963 D2
20100 MtgC 77357 2827 D5
Ruby St
2200 RSBG 77471 4490 C6
20800 PRVW 77484 3100 D3
26400 SPLD 77372 2683 B2
26600 MtgC 77372 2683 C2
Ruby Wy
28200 HOUS 77336 3120 E4
Ruby Canyon Ln
11400 HarC 77095 3538 A1
11500 HarC 77095 3397 A7
Ruby Falls Ct
3100 LGCY 77573 4633 B2
Rubylace Ct
10 WDLD 77382 2673 D5
Ruby Meadow Dr
16500 HarC 77095 3538 B1
Ruby Red Ct
19900 HarC 77073 3403 C2
Ruby River Ln
8500 FBnC 77469 4095 C7
Ruby Rock Wy
4900 FBnC 77469 4234 C3
Ruby Rose St
- HarC 77093 3685 D1
11900 HarC 77093 3545 D7
12000 HarC 77039 3545 D7
12000 HOUS 77039 3545 D7
Ruby Star Dr
3200 HarC 77082 4096 B2
Ruby Terrace Ln
19800 MtgC 77355 2814 D4
Ruby Valley Ct
20900 HarC 77433 3251 A3
Ruckett St
- TXCY 77591 4873 E6
Rudder Dr
16300 HarC 77532 3551 D2
Ruddick Ln
25800 SPLD 77372 2683 A2
Rude Rd
100 RSBG 77471 4490 C4
Rudel Rd
1200 TMBL 77375 2964 A7
1300 HarC 77377 2963 E7
1300 TMBL 77375 2963 E7
Rudgewick Ln
20000 HarC 77379 3256 A6
Rudolph Ct
10300 FBnC 77459 4622 A6
Rudolph Rd
800 HarC 77375 2964 B5
800 TMBL 77375 2964 B5
Rue St
4900 HOUS 77033 4243 E5
5500 HOUS 77033 4244 A5
Rue Beaujon Ct
11800 HarC 77377 3254 E6
Rue Bourbon
8600 FBnC 77459 4621 B5
Rue Cambon St
9000 HOUS 77074 4239 E1
Rue Canyon Ct
22300 FBnC 77450 4093 E1
22300 FBnC 77450 4094 C2
Rue Carre St
7800 HOUS 77074 4239 E1
Rue Chablis St
7800 HOUS 77074 4239 E1
Rue Crillon St
9000 HOUS 77074 4239 E1
Rue de Lafitte Dr
2400 GlsC 77539 4635 D4
E Rue de Lafitte Dr
2300 GlsC 77539 4635 D4
Rue de Maison
8500 FBnC 77459 4621 B5
Ruel Ln
100 MtgC 77354 2668 A4
100 MtgC 77355 2668 A4
Rue La Fontaine Dr
11800 HarC 77377 3254 D6
Ruell Av
200 HOUS 77017 4106 B5
Ruella Ln
1300 PASD 77502 4107 E6
1300 PASD 77506 4107 E6
Ruellen Ct
10500 HarC 77038 3543 B2
Ruellen Ln
1100 HarC 77038 3543 C2
Rue Montebello Ct
11800 HarC 77377 3254 E6
Rue Montebello Dr
15500 HarC 77377 3254 E6
Rue Orleans
3200 FBnC 77459 4621 B5
Rue Orleans St
200 BYTN 77520 3971 B3
Rue St. Honore Blvd
- HarC 77070 3254 E6
15300 HarC 77377 3254 E6
Rue St. Honore Ct
11800 HarC 77377 3254 D6
Rue St. Lazare
11800 HarC 77377 3254 E6
Rue St Cyr
7800 HOUS 77074 4239 D2
Ruffian Ct
4300 HarC 77546 4506 A5
Ruffian Dr
- JRSV 77065 3540 A6
16100 HarC 77546 4506 A5
Ruffian Ln
2000 STAF 77477 4370 B4
Ruffin Ln
10 WDLD 77380 2822 A7
Ruffin Green Ct
3100 FBnC 77545 4498 C6
Ruffino Rd
9700 HOUS 77031 4239 A4
10000 HOUS 77031 4238 E4
Rufina St
700 LGCY 77573 4632 D5
Rufus St
1000 RHMD 77469 4364 D7
6600 HOUS 77091 3684 A4
Rugby Ct
16700 HarC 77379 3256 D2
Ruger Dr
14500 HarC 77532 3552 C6
Rugley St
3400 HOUS 77004 4103 D1
Rui Cove Ct
3700 MtgC 77386 2970 A4
Ruidosa Ct
16700 HOUS 77053 4371 E7
Ruidoso Cir
2500 DRPK 77536 4109 E6
Ruiz St
1600 HOUS 77002 3963 D4
1900 HOUS 77003 3963 D4
Ruland Rd
9000 HOUS 77055 3820 E6
9000 SPVL 77055 3820 E6
Rumar Ln
10100 JTCY 77029 3966 A2
Rum Bay
4100 GLSN 77554 5332 D3
Rumbling Creek Ln
22400 HarC 77375 3109 E1
Rumbling Wood Ct
7900 HarC 77086 3541 D3
Rumbling Wood Ln
9500 HarC 77086 3541 E2
Rumfolo Dr
23200 HarC 77377 2962 D6
Rumford Ln
6200 HarC 77084 3678 E4
Rummel Creek Dr
13000 HOUS 77079 3958 C2
E Rumplecreek Pl
10 WDLD 77381 2674 E7
10 WDLD 77381 2675 A6
W Rumplecreek Pl
10 WDLD 77381 2674 E7
Rum River Ct
19300 HarC 77449 3677 A4
Rumsey Springs Dr
20700 MtgC 77365 2973 A7
S Run Dr
- HarC 77089 4505 A1
Runaway Scrape Ct
1800 FBnC 77469 4365 C3
Runbell Pl
15100 HarC 77095 3678 E2
Runneburg Rd
400 HarC 77532 3552 C4
1600 HarC 77532 3553 B4
Runnels St
- HOUS 77002 3963 E4
1900 HOUS 77003 3963 E4
3300 HOUS 77003 3964 A5
Runners Ln
19000 HarC 77346 3265 D6
Runney Meade Dr
13600 SGLD 77478 4237 B6
Running Arabian Ln
14500 HarC 77044 3408 E7
Running Bear Tr
1800 HarC 77532 3410 B2
Running Bird Ln
8300 FBnC 77489 4497 E1
8600 HOUS 77489 4497 D1
Running Brook Ln
2000 PRLD 77584 4500 A1
17800 HarC 77379 3256 A2
Running Creek Ct
6000 HOUS 77345 3120 D7
Running Cypress Dr
17000 HarC 77429 3252 D6
Running Deer Ln
29700 HarC 77375 3110 B1
Running Deer St
10 MtgC 77385 2823 B3
Running Eagle Falls
9100 HarC 77375 2965 D4
Running Iron Dr
24000 HarC 77447 3249 E3
Running Pine Ct
4300 LGCY 77573 4631 B4
Running Pine Dr
4300 LGCY 77573 4631 A5
4400 LGCY 77573 4630 E5
Running Quail Ct
16700 HOUS 77489 4370 D7
Running Spring Dr
- HOUS 77059 4380 C5
2100 DRPK 77536 4109 E7
Running Springs Dr
1900 HOUS 77339 3118 D6
Running Tide
3500 HarC 77546 4506 A7
Running Vine Ln
18300 HarC 77379 3255 E2
Running Water Dr
25600 HarC 77336 3121 B6
Running Wood Ct
34000 MtgC 77354 2670 E6
Runny Meade Dr
- HOUS 77035 4241 A2
- HOUS 77096 4240 E2
9700 HOUS 77096 4241 A2
Runnymede Rd
10 MtgC 77384 2674 A2
Runswick Dr
15400 HOUS 77062 4506 E1
15400 HOUS 77062 4507 B2
Runyan St
1500 HarC 77039 3545 C2
Rupel Runn
17900 HarC 77090 3258 D2
Rupert St
3300 HOUS 77026 3825 D7
Rupley Cir
6200 HOUS 77087 4104 D7
Ruppstock Ct
7400 HOUS 77489 4371 B6
Ruppstock Dr
15800 HOUS 77489 4371 B6
Ruppstock Rd
- HOUS 77489 4371 B5
Rural Ln
17000 MtgC 77385 2676 B6
Rural St
3600 HOUS 77009 3824 A7
Rural Oak St
- HOUS 77034 4378 C3
Ruscello Vista Dr
- FBnC 77053 4498 E3
Rush Rd
3500 STFE 77510 4871 C6
Rushbrook Dr
1700 HOUS 77077 3958 A5
2300 MSCY 77489 4370 B6
Rushcreek Dr
- HarC 77060 3403 A4
- HarC 77067 3402 E4
600 HOUS 77067 3402 E4
600 HOUS 77067 3403 A4
Rushcroft Dr
3800 HarC 77082 4096 C3
N Rush Haven Cir
300 WDLD 77381 2820 C3
S Rush Haven Cir
300 WDLD 77381 2820 C3
Rush Haven Dr
5400 WDLD 77381 2820 D3
Rush Hollow Ct
21200 FBnC 77469 4094 A6
Rushing Brook Dr
3000 HOUS 77345 3119 E4
3000 HOUS 77345 3120 A2
Rushing Creek Ln
21100 HarC 77449 3815 B2
Rushing River Dr
5600 HOUS 77345 3120 B5
Rushing Spring Dr
2100 PRLD 77584 4500 D1
Rushing Springs Ct
18100 HarC 77375 3255 B3
Rushing Springs Dr
9800 HarC 77375 3255 B2
Rushing Stream Ct
8100 HarC 77375 2966 A7
Rushire Sq
20200 HMBL 77338 3262 C4
Rush Mill Ct
9300 HarC 77095 3538 E4
Rushmore Ln
12500 HarC 77346 3408 C3
Rushstone Ln
5400 HarC 77373 3115 D6
Rushton Cir
100 LGCY 77573 4633 A1
Rush Trace Ct
17200 HarC 77095 3678 A1
Rushville Ct
21000 HarC 77449 3676 D3
Rushwater Ln
3500 HarC 77546 4506 A7
Rushwind Ct
2900 FBnC 77494 3953 B6
N Rushwing Cir
10 WDLD 77381 2820 D4
S Rushwing Cir
100 WDLD 77381 2820 D5
Rushwing Pl
10 WDLD 77381 2820 E4
Rushwood Cir
2600 HarC 77067 3402 A5
Rushwood Ln
3300 SGLD 77479 4495 C1
Rushworth Dr
1300 HarC 77014 3402 C3
Rusk St
400 HOUS 77002 3963 C4
1200 HOUS 77010 3963 D5
1500 HOUS 77003 3963 D5
3500 HOUS 77003 3964 A6
4900 HOUS 77023 3964 B7
6500 HOUS 77011 3964 D7
7000 HOUS 77011 4105 A1
7400 HOUS 77023 4105 A1
Ruskin Ln
1000 HOUS 77062 4506 E1
Ruskin St
3800 SSPL 77005 4101 D4
4000 WUNP 77005 4101 C4
Rusk Meadows Ln
- HarC 77346 3408 C2
Ruslee St
200 LMQU 77568 4990 C2
Russ Dr
14000 HarC 77039 3545 D3
Russeff Field Ct
600 FBnC 77469 4616 E1
Russeff Field Ln
9300 FBnC 77469 4616 E1
Russel Ln
20000 HarC 77429 3397 D7
Russelfern Ln
15200 HarC 77049 3829 A3
Russelfield Ln
6700 HarC 77049 3829 A2
Russell
7800 MNVL 77578 4746 D3
Russell Dr
11900 MtgC 77365 3117 D4
20400 MtgC 77339 3117 D4
21000 MtgC 77357 2827 A6
Russell Ln
5800 HarC 77521 3834 E6
Russell St
2100 HOUS 77026 3964 B1
2400 HOUS 77026 3825 B7
7300 MNVL 77578 4746 D2
Russell Creek Ct
28500 MtgC 77386 2969 C6
Russell Palmer Rd
800 HarC 77339 3118 D5
800 HOUS 77339 3118 D5
Russell Point Dr
- MtgC 77386 2969 D1
Russels Cave Ln
17500 HarC 77346 3408 B4
Russelville Rd
5100 HOUS 77048 4374 E2
5400 HOUS 77048 4375 A2
Russet Field Ct
10200 HarC 77070 3399 C3
E Russet Grove Cir
10 WDLD 77384 2674 E3
W Russet Grove Cir
10 WDLD 77384 2674 E3
Russet Grove Ct
10 WDLD 77384 2674 D2
Russett Dr
- HOUS 77057 3960 D4
5500 HOUS 77056 3960 D4
10600 HOUS 77042 3958 D4
Russett Ln
4600 FBnC 77479 4366 C7
4600 FBnC 77479 4493 D1
Russett Pl
4500 PRLD 77584 4501 E5
Russett Pl S
4500 PRLD 77584 4501 E5
Russett Pl W
2800 PRLD 77584 4501 E6
Russett Canyon Ln
- FBnC 77469 4094 D7
Russet Terrace Ln
- HarC 77095 3537 C6
Russett Fields Ct
9500 HarC 77044 3689 A4
Russet Trail Ct
4800 HarC 77449 3677 B6
Russet Wood Ct
10 WDLD 77381 2821 B5
Russwood Cir
17900 HarC 77379 3256 A2
Rust Av
2900 TXCY 77590 4874 D5
Rustic Dr
100 PASD 77502 4107 A7
Rustic Ln
100 FBnC 77471 4491 A2
100 FRDW 77546 4629 A1
200 FRDW 77546 4628 E1
300 BzaC 77581 4628 E1
300 PRLD 77581 4628 E1
400 BzaC 77581 4504 D7
500 FBnC 77471 4490 E2
500 PRLD 77581 4504 D7
13900 MtgC 77306 2533 D7
19400 MtgC 77355 2814 A2
Rustic St
6800 HOUS 77087 4105 A4
Rustic Wy
- HarC 77070 3255 C4
Rustic Arbour Ln
3800 FBnC 77478 4366 E2
Rustic Bend Ct
10100 HarC 77064 3540 C3
Rustic Bend Pl
10 WDLD 77382 2674 A5
Rustic Bridge Ln
- PRLD 77584 4500 A3
22000 HOUS 77339 3263 B1
Rustic Brook Ct
18000 HarC 77429 3253 D2
Rustic Canyon Ln
- FBnC 77469 4493 A2
Rustic Canyon Tr
17400 HarC 77090 3258 A3
Rustic Chase Ln
7300 FBnC 77469 4095 A6
Rustic Colony Dr
16700 SGLD 77479 4368 B7
Rustic Colony Ln
- LGCY 77539 4753 A2
Rustic Cove Ln
5000 FBnC 77494 4093 A7
Rustic Creek Ln
5900 HOUS 77345 3120 C5
Rustic Falls Ct
8200 FBnC 77083 4096 C4
Rustic Field Ln
4800 HarC 77449 3677 C6
Rustic Fields Ln
14500 HarC 77429 3397 A1
14600 HarC 77429 3253 B7
Rustic Garden Dr
13200 HarC 77083 4097 B6
Rustic Gardens Dr
3000 MtgC 77386 2969 C2
Rustic Gate Dr
19000 HarC 77433 3677 C1
Rustic Gate Rd
10300 LPRT 77571 4250 C4
Rustic Glen Ct
17700 HarC 77095 3537 E7
Rustic Harbor Ct
800 HOUS 77062 4506 D1
Rustic Haven Ct
3700 HOUS 77345 3119 E3
Rustic Hearth Ct
20600 FBnC 77469 4094 B6
Rustic Hills Ct
1800 FBnC 77479 4367 B7
Rustic Hills Ln
13900 HarC 77429 3253 D6
Rustic Hollow Ln
1600 HarC 77450 3954 B5
1600 HOUS 77450 3954 B5
Rustic Knolls Ct
20300 HarC 77450 3954 D4
Rustic Knolls Dr
1000 HarC 77450 3954 D3
Rustic Lodge Ct
- HarC 77429 3253 A6
Rustic Maple Ln
- HarC 77379 3111 C4
Rustic Meadow Ct
6100 PRLD 77581 4375 D7
22400 FBnC 77494 4093 D4
Rustic Mill Ln
- FBnC 77494 4092 C3
Rustic Oak Ct
22200 FBnC 77469 4492 E4
23600 HarC 77373 3115 C5
Rustic Oak Ln
1500 PASD 77586 4381 E6
1900 FBnC 77469 4492 D4
Rustic Oaks Dr
100 LGCY 77573 4630 D6
900 MtgC 77354 2817 D6
Rustic Oar Wy
18500 HarC 77346 3265 D7
Rustic Park Ct
8200 FBnC 77083 4096 B7
Rustic Pecan Ln
6800 HarC 77049 3829 B1
Rustic Pier Ln
2900 LGCY 77573 4633 B3
Rustic Pine Ln
- HarC 77377 3253 E3
Rustic Pine Tr
17400 HarC 77090 3258 A4
Rustic Pines Ct
28500 MtgC 77386 2969 D6
Rustic Pines Ln
7800 HarC 77433 3537 A7
Rustic Ranch Ln
- FBnC 77494 4092 B1
Rustic Ridge Ct
2200 FBnC 77469 4234 C7
Rustic Ridge Ln
8300 HarC 77433 3537 D6
Rustic Rock Rd
9700 LPRT 77571 4250 B4
Rustic Sands Dr
16000 HarC 77084 3678 D7
Rustic Shores Ln
22000 FBnC 77450 4093 E3
Rustic Springs Dr
18100 HarC 77375 3255 B3
Rustic Stable Ln
- HarC 77429 3253 A6
Rustic Timbers Dr
- HarC 77338 3407 B1
- HarC 77396 3407 B2
Rustic Trail Ln
2400 FBnC 77469 4492 E3
Rustic View Ct
10 WDLD 77381 2821 B2
Rustic Villa Dr
3200 HOUS 77345 3120 A4
Rustic Woods Dr
2600 HOUS 77345 3119 D5
3900 HOUS 77339 3119 D5
Rusting Creek Dr
2500 PRLD 77584 4500 B3
Rusting Park Dr
1700 HOUS 77339 3118 D6
Rustington Dr
17300 HarC 77379 3256 C1
Rusting Willow Ln
6100 HarC 77084 3678 A4
Rustler Ridge Ln
9300 HarC 77089 4504 C1
Rustlers Creek Ln
26700 FBnC 77494 4092 A2
Rustlers Trail Ln
16000 HarC 77429 3253 A7
Rustlers Wy Cir
10800 HarC 77064 3540 B5
Rustlewood Dr
19800 HarC 77338 3262 A4
Rustling Aspen Ln
17500 HarC 77095 3537 E7
Rustling Branch Ln
5000 HarC 77449 3677 B6
Rustling Brook Ln
1400 HarC 77094 3955 A3
Rustling Canyon Ln
- HarC 77449 3815 B1
Rustling Chestnut St
2900 HarC 77389 3112 E1
2900 HarC 77389 3113 A1
Rustling Elms Dr
4700 HOUS 77339 3119 B2
Rustling Glen Ln
- HarC 77429 3253 C6
Rustling Leaves Dr
- HarC 77083 4237 A1
8300 HarC 77083 4097 A7
Rustling Leaves Rd
8800 HarC 77083 4237 A1
Rustling Maple Dr
9500 HarC 77064 3541 A4
Rustling Moss Dr
3100 HarC 77068 3257 C4
Rustling Oaks Dr
1400 CNRO 77301 2385 B6
6700 FBnC 77469 4493 B7
6700 RSBG 77469 4493 B7
Rustling Oaks Ln
10600 MtgC 77303 2239 B4
24000 MtgC 77355 2962 B4
Rustling Oaks St
10500 MtgC 77303 2239 A4
Rustling Pines Dr
- HarC 77336 2976 D7
Rustling Pines St
3200 MtgC 77380 2967 B1
Rustling Ridge Dr
18900 HarC 77377 3254 A2
Rustling Timbers Ct
20900 HarC 77379 3111 A4
Rustling Timbers Ln
6500 HarC 77379 3111 C4
Rustling Trails Dr
5200 HarC 77449 3676 E6
Rustling Trees Wy
2000 HarC 77373 3114 D5
Rustling Wind Ln
1100 LGCY 77573 4633 A3
Rustling Winds Dr
11000 HarC 77064 3540 D2

STREET
Block City ZIP Map# Grid
Rustling Woods Ct
4000 PASD 77059 4380 E5
Ruston St
16600 HOUS 77396 3405 E4
Ruston Oaks Ct
9000 HarC 77088 3542 B6
Ruston Oaks Dr
8900 HarC 77088 3542 B6
Rustwood Ct
8400 HarC 77338 3262 B2
Rustwood Ln
20400 HarC 77338 3262 A3
Rusty St
11100 HarC 77093 3685 D1
Rusty Anchor Ct
18700 HarC 77346 3265 D7
Rusty Bridge Ct
3000 MtgC 77386 2823 D7
Rustygate Dr
6200 HarC 77373 3116 A7
Rusty Hawthorne Dr
28000 FBnC 77494 3951 D5
Rustyleaf Ln
700 HarC 77090 3258 C2
Rusty Oak Tr
15200 MtgC 77302 2679 C3
Rusty Pine Ln
11100 HarC 77375 3255 A2
Rusty Ridge Ln
6600 HarC 77449 3676 E2
Rusty Ridge Pl
10 WDLD 77381 2821 A2
Rusty Runn
- HOUS 77090 3258 C2
17900 HarC 77090 3258 C2
Rutersville College Ln
2900 FBnC 77469 4234 D7
Rutgers Ln
1100 DRPK 77536 4249 C2
Rutgers Pl
10 WUNP 77005 4101 E4
Rutgers St
- HOUS 77005 4101 E3
5600 WUNP 77005 4101 E4
6700 HOUS 77025 4101 E4
Rutgers Hill St
- HarC 77379 3111 A2
Rutgers Park Ct
12200 PASD 77058 4380 E6
Ruth Av
800 BYTN 77520 3973 B6
Ruth Cir
900 TXCY 77591 4873 D5
Ruth Dr
21100 MtgC 77357 2827 B6
Ruth Rd
9000 IWCY 77583 4744 D5
Ruth St
- HOUS 77002 3962 E7
100 GlsC 77518 4635 A3
400 BYTN 77520 3973 B6
1000 HOUS 77002 4102 E1
1000 HOUS 77004 4102 E1
2200 HOUS 77004 4103 C2
2600 FBnC 77477 4370 B5
2600 STAF 77477 4370 B5
Ruthann Dr
21800 HarC 77338 3260 C2
Ruthby St
8300 HOUS 77061 4245 D3
Rutherford Ct
4900 SGLD 77479 4495 D5
Rutherford Ln
- HOUS 77088 3683 E1
8700 HOUS 77088 3543 E7
Rutherford Rd
10200 MtgC 77372 2536 D1
Rutherford Wy
10400 HarC 77379 3110 B7
Rutherglenn Dr
5100 HOUS 77096 4240 E2
Ruthin Ct
6700 HarC 77449 3677 A3
Ruthven St
300 HOUS 77002 3963 B4
700 HOUS 77019 3963 A5
1600 HOUS 77019 3962 E5
Rutland
19000 MtgC 77357 2829 A4
Rutland Pl
500 HOUS 77007 3962 C1
Rutland St
600 HOUS 77007 3962 C1
800 HOUS 77007 3823 C7
800 HOUS 77008 3823 C7
4100 HOUS 77018 3823 C2
Rutledge Ct
600 MtgC 77302 2530 C6
E Rutledge Ct
14500 HarC 77084 3679 A4
W Rutledge Ct
14600 HarC 77084 3679 A5
Rutledge Dr
- HOUS 77449 3815 B6
Rutley Cir
16200 HarC 77379 3256 A5
Ruttand Park Ln
4200 FBnC 77450 4093 E2
4400 FBnC 77450 4094 D2
Ryan Ct
2900 HarC 77396 3407 D3
Ryan Dr
2100 ALVN 77511 4866 E4
Ryan Rd
13600 STFE 77510 4870 D4
Ryan St
900 MNVL 77578 4747 B1
1800 LMQU 77568 4990 A2
Ryan Acres Dr
5000 PRLD 77584 4502 E5
5000 PRLD 77584 4503 A5
Ryaneagles Cir
12900 HarC 77044 3549 E2
Ryaneagles Ct
15400 HarC 77044 3549 E1
Ryaneagles Dr
13000 HarC 77044 3549 E1
Ryan Landing Dr
13300 HarC 77065 3539 A1
Ryan Manor Dr
11400 FBnC 77469 4092 B6
Ryann Ct
3500 PASD 77505 4248 A4
Ryan Oaks Dr
10800 HarC 77065 3539 A1
Ryan Park Dr
8200 HarC 77095 3539 A6

STREET
Block City ZIP Map# Grid
Ryan's Branch Ln
4400 FBnC 77450 4093 E2
Ryansbrook Ln
1800 MtgC 77386 2969 C6
Ryans Creek Ct
25600 FBnC 77494 4093 A2
Ryans Park Ln
9800 HarC 77089 4504 C2
9800 HarC 77089 4505 A3
Ryans Ridge Ln
28200 MtgC 77386 2969 D7
Ryan's Run Ct
2000 SGLD 77478 4368 D5
Ryan Trails Dr
10800 HarC 77065 3539 A1
Ryanwood Dr
13500 HarC 77065 3539 A1
Ryanwyck Pl
10 WDLD 77384 2675 A4
Rychlik Dr
3200 RSBG 77471 4491 B6
Rycroft Dr
1900 MtgC 77386 2969 B2
Rycrude
- HarC 77377 3108 A3
Ryder Ct
2600 LGCY 77573 4508 E7
Ryder Cup Ln
32600 MtgC 77354 2672 C5
Ryderwood
- SGLD 77478 4237 C5
Rye
100 TMBL 77375 2964 C7
Rye Ct
- MtgC 77357 2829 C4
Rye Rd
8400 HarC 77521 3833 B2
Rye St
100 TMBL 77375 2964 C7
200 MtgC 77380 2968 B1
1300 HOUS 77029 3965 C3
Rye Creek Dr
5800 HarC 77449 3676 D4
Ryegate Dr
6100 HarC 77041 3679 C4
Rye Hollow Ln
22000 HarC 77339 3118 C3
Ryewater Dr
- HOUS 77546 4378 D7
11800 HOUS 77089 4378 C6
Ryewood Ct
3900 FBnC 77450 4093 E1
Ryland Rd
11400 HarC 77066 3401 D6
E Rylander Cir
8700 HOUS 77071 4239 C6
N Rylander Cir
8800 HOUS 77071 4239 C6
S Rylander Cir
12400 HOUS 77071 4239 C7
Rylis St
- HOUS 77019 3962 D4
Rymal Rd
1600 STFE 77511 4869 C2
1600 GlsC 77511 4869 C1
Rymwick Ct
10 WDLD 77381 2821 E2
Ryoaks Dr
15400 HarC 77095 3678 D1
Ryon St
1100 HOUS 77009 3824 D7
Ryon Wy
9800 FBnC 77459 4621 E5
Ryson St
3300 HOUS 77080 3821 A2
Ryton Ln
8800 HarC 77088 3543 D7

S

Saathoff Dr
11100 HarC 77070 3399 A5
11100 HarC 77429 3399 A5
11200 HarC 77429 3398 E5
Saba Rd
- HarC 77388 3111 E2
- HOUS 77045 4372 C2
Sabal Palm Ln
400 BzaC 77584 4374 B7
Sabal Palms Dr
20200 HarC 77449 3815 C5
Sabal Palms Pk
20400 HarC 77449 3815 B5
Sabal Park Ct
300 LGCY 77573 4508 C5
Sabal Park Ln
300 LGCY 77573 4508 C6
Sabastian Dr
9000 FBnC 77083 4236 D1
Sabel Glen Ct
1900 FBnC 77469 4616 B2
Saber Ct
2000 LGCY 77573 4631 A6
10500 HarC 77038 3543 D2
Saber Oaks Dr
25200 FBnC 77469 4092 D7
Saber River
5800 SGLD 77479 4495 A5
Saber Trails Dr
- HarC 77095 3537 E3
Saberwood Dr
- HOUS 77489 4371 A6
- MSCY 77489 4371 A6
500 MSCY 77489 4370 D6
S Sabinal Dr
20300 HarC 77449 3815 D4
Sabinal Creek Dr
7300 FBnC 77469 4093 E6
7300 FBnC 77469 4094 A6
Sabine Cir
9800 FBnC 77459 4621 E6
Sabine Ct
2100 DRPK 77536 4109 E6
2700 BzaC 77584 4501 A5
Sabine Dr
2100 DRPK 77536 4109 E6
N Sabine Dr
20000 MtgC 77357 2827 A6
S Sabine Dr
20700 MtgC 77357 2827 A7
Sabine Ln
5800 FBnC 77469 4234 C4
Sabine St
100 HOUS 77002 3963 A3
100 HOUS 77019 3963 A3
1300 HOUS 77007 3963 A2
N Sabine St
2600 HOUS 77009 3963 A1

STREET
Block City ZIP Map# Grid
Sabine Brook Wy
1200 HarC 77073 3259 B3
Sabine Forest Ln
26900 FBnC 77494 4092 A2
Sabine Lake Ct
4500 FBnC 77469 4234 D4
Sabine Point Wy
3100 FBnC 77459 4621 E6
Sabine River Dr
- MtgC 77386 2970 B2
Sable
10 WDBR 77357 2828 C2
Sable Ct
2700 BzaC 77584 4501 A5
4200 HarC 77014 3401 C3
Sable Dr
1000 FRDW 77546 4505 A5
1000 PRLD 77581 4505 A5
2800 BzaC 77584 4501 A5
Sable Ln
13400 HarC 77014 3401 C2
Sable Acre Ct
20300 HarC 77433 3251 B5
Sablebend Ln
13700 HarC 77014 3401 C2
Sablebrook Ln
10300 HarC 77095 3537 E2
Sablechase Ct
13700 HarC 77014 3401 D2
Sablechase Dr
3400 HarC 77014 3401 D2
N Sablechase Ln
13700 HarC 77014 3401 E2
S Sablechase Ln
13600 HarC 77014 3401 D3
Sablecliff Ln
8600 HOUS 77075 4376 E4
Sable Creek Ct
24500 MtgC 77365 2972 E7
Sable Creek Dr
20500 MtgC 77365 2972 D7
Sable Creek Ln
2800 PRLD 77545 4499 E3
Sablecrest St
13700 HarC 77014 3401 D2
Sable Field Ln
4800 HarC 77449 3677 C5
Sablegarden Ln
13700 HarC 77014 3401 C2
Sableglen St
13600 HarC 77014 3401 E2
Sablegrove Ct
4000 HarC 77014 3401 E2
Sablegrove Ln
13600 HarC 77014 3401 D2
Sableleaf Dr
12500 HarC 77429 3398 E2
Sable Meadow Ct
10000 HarC 77064 3540 C3
Sable Meadow Ln
10200 HarC 77064 3540 B3
Sable Mills Dr
10300 HarC 77095 3538 A3
Sablemist Ct
4100 HarC 77014 3401 C2
Sable Oaks Ln
27000 HarC 77433 3396 A7
27100 HarC 77433 3395 E7
Sable Palms Ct
2700 HarC 77449 3815 D3
Sable Pines Ln
4200 HarC 77014 3401 C2
Sablepoint Ln
- HarC 77014 3401 C2
Sableridge Cir
4000 HarC 77014 3401 D2
Sableridge Ct
4000 HarC 77014 3401 C2
Sableridge Dr
- HarC 77066 3401 C3
13600 HarC 77014 3401 C3
Sable Ridge Ln
2600 FBnC 77494 3953 B5
N Sableridge Ln
13500 HarC 77014 3401 E2
S Sableridge Ln
13400 HarC 77014 3401 C3
Sable River Ct
6800 MSCY 77459 4496 D4
Sable River Dr
6900 MSCY 77459 4496 D4
Sablerun Ct
4000 HarC 77014 3401 D3
Sablerun Ln
13600 HarC 77014 3401 D3
Sablesprings Ln
13700 HarC 77014 3401 C2
Sable Stone Cir
19800 HarC 77450 3954 E5
Sable Terrace Ln
8900 HarC 77044 3689 C4
Sable Trail Ct
10100 HarC 77064 3540 D3
Sable Trail Ln
10200 HarC 77064 3540 C3
Sable Tree Ct
13400 BzaC 77583 4623 E4
Sable Tree Dr
18200 HarC 77084 3816 D3
Sable Tree Ln
- BzaC 77583 4623 E4
Sablewood Ln
13300 HarC 77014 3401 C3
Sabo Rd
10400 HOUS 77075 4377 E2
10400 HOUS 77089 4377 E3
12100 HOUS 77089 4378 A4
Sabra Ct
4800 HOUS 77048 4243 D6
Sabrina
3700 GLSN 77554 5440 E5
Sabrina Dr
4700 HarC 77066 3401 B2
Sabrina Oaks Ln
3800 HarC 77449 3815 E2
Sabrooke Ln
2600 HarC 77073 3259 E4
Sac Ct
13900 HarC 77429 3253 E4
Sacaton Dr
11000 HarC 77086 3542 B1
Sachar St
11700 HarC 77039 3546 D7
11700 HarC 77093 3546 D7
Sachet Ln
- WDLD 77382 2674 C5
Sachiel-Fuller Pass
- PASD 77505 4248 C3

STREET
Block City ZIP Map# Grid
Sachnik Dr
200 PASD 77502 4247 B2
200 SHUS 77587 4247 B2
Sackett St
2700 HOUS 77019 3962 A7
2700 HOUS 77098 3962 A7
Sackville Close
5800 HarC 77346 3264 D6
Saco River Wy
16600 HOUS 77044 3409 B3
N Sacramento Av
2100 PRLD 77581 4503 B2
Sacramento St
2500 PRLD 77581 4503 B3
2500 PRLD 77584 4503 B3
13500 HOUS 77015 3967 D1
W Saddalbranch Cir
10 WDLD 77382 2674 D3
Saddle Cr
- ALVN 77511 4867 B4
17000 MtgC 77357 2681 C7
Saddle Dr
- FRDW 77546 4628 E4
100 JRSV 77065 3539 E5
Saddle Ln
9300 HOUS 77080 3820 D5
Saddle Rdg
200 WDLD 77380 2967 D4
Saddleback Pass
10500 HarC 77095 3537 E2
Saddleback Springs Dr
200 FBnC 77469 4493 A6
Saddlebend Dr
14200 HarC 77070 3398 E1
Saddlebough Dr
11900 HarC 77065 3539 E4
Saddlebranch Ct
300 HOUS 77024 3961 A2
Saddlebred Dr
5500 HarC 77084 3679 A5
Saddle Briar Ln
14600 HarC 77429 3253 A7
14600 HarC 77429 3397 A1
Saddlebrook Cir
24400 FBnC 77494 3953 B5
Saddlebrook Ct
10 HarC 77375 2965 B4
3100 FBnC 77494 3953 B5
Saddlebrook Ln
10 HOUS 77024 3960 D1
100 HarC 77375 2965 B4
2700 FBnC 77494 3953 A4
N Saddlebrook Ln
2700 FBnC 77494 3953 B4
S Saddlebrook Ln
2700 FBnC 77494 3953 B4
Saddlebrook Wy
25400 FBnC 77494 3953 B5
Saddlebrook Champion Wy
25200 HarC 77375 2965 D2
Saddlebrook Ranch Dr
25200 HarC 77375 2965 D3
Saddlebrook Village Dr
25500 HarC 77375 2965 D2
Saddlebrush Tr
17400 HarC 77095 3537 E2
Saddlebunch
10 HTCK 77563 5105 B5
Saddlecreek Dr
- HarC 77068 3257 E4
- HarC 77090 3257 E4
- HOUS 77090 3257 E4
1400 HarC 77090 3258 A3
Saddlecreek Ln
300 HNCV 77024 3960 B3
Saddle Creek Farms Dr
100 HarC 77532 3266 D7
1000 HOUS 77532 3266 B7
Saddle Horn
17200 MtgC 77357 2681 C6
Saddle Horn Dr
200 HOUS 77060 3544 C2
Saddlehorn Dr
10 HNCV 77024 3960 A2
Saddlehorn Ln
10 HNCV 77024 3960 C2
Saddle Horn Rd
2700 FBnC 77494 3953 A5
Saddle Horn Tr
2000 FBnC 77494 3952 E4
2000 FBnC 77494 3953 A4
2000 KATY 77494 3952 E4
Saddlehorn Tr
1800 FBnC 77494 3952 E4
1800 FBnC 77494 3953 A4
10200 HarC 77064 3540 B3
Saddleleaf Pl
- WDLD 77380 2967 C1
Saddle Pass Dr
- HarC 77449 3676 B3
Saddle Path Ct
24500 HarC 77373 3114 D4
Saddle Ranch Dr
20100 HarC 77338 3261 D4
Saddle Ridge Ct
3100 FBnC 77469 4234 B7
Saddle Ridge Rd
13700 HarC 77532 3553 C7
Saddle Ridge Pass
16400 HarC 77433 3251 B3
Saddle Rock Dr
500 HarC 77037 3544 B7
500 HOUS 77037 3544 B7
800 HOUS 77088 3544 A7
11600 HOUS 77088 3543 E7
Saddlerock Ln
27100 MtgC 77357 2829 D5
Saddle Spur Ln
24600 FBnC 77494 3953 A5
Saddle Surrey Ln
100 MtgC 77385 2676 B3
Saddleville Mills Ln
19100 HarC 77433 3677 B1
Saddlewood Cir
700 SHEH 77381 2821 E2
700 SHEH 77381 2822 B1
Saddlewood Dr
15000 MtgC 77384 2674 B3
22100 HarC 77449 3675 E5
Saddlewood Ln
500 HNCV 77024 3960 B2
Saddlewood Estates Dr
10 HNCV 77024 3960 B3
Sadie Ln
300 MtgC 77303 2385 D2
Sadler St
1100 HOUS 77022 3824 C1
2800 HOUS 77093 3824 E1

STREET
Block City ZIP Map# Grid
Sadler St
3200 HOUS 77093 3825 A1
4800 HOUS 77016 3686 C7
Sadlewood Trail Ln
2400 HarC 77014 3402 A2
Sadlin Tr
- HarC 77449 3676 B2
Safari Dr
11400 FBnC 77469 4235 E6
Safebuy St
7900 HOUS 77028 3826 B1
Safeguard St
8400 HOUS 77051 4243 C3
11100 HOUS 77047 4243 D7
12500 HOUS 77047 4374 D1
Safeguard Wy
10600 HOUS 77047 4243 D6
Safe Harbor Cir
2700 HarC 77546 4506 B7
Safflower Dr
7900 HarC 77521 3833 D2
Saffolk Punch Dr
9500 HarC 77065 3539 E4
Saffron Ct
500 LGCY 77573 4751 C1
Saffron Ln
4200 FRDW 77546 4629 E1
7900 HarC 77521 3833 E2
Saffron Hills Dr
6300 HarC 77379 3256 E2
Sagamore St
10800 HOUS 77096 4240 C3
Sagamore Bay Ln
5700 FBnC 77469 4616 E2
Sagamore Bend Pl
10 WDLD 77382 2673 C4
Sage Cir
5200 HarC 77521 3833 D3
Sage Ct
10 WDLD 77381 2820 D2
2500 MSCY 77489 4370 D6
6400 PRLD 77584 4502 C5
Sage Dr
200 GNPK 77547 3966 A7
4500 BYTN 77521 3971 E2
Sage Ln
3600 DKSN 77539 4754 A1
Sage Rd
100 HOUS 77024 3960 E3
100 HOUS 77056 3960 E4
2600 HOUS 77056 3961 A7
3400 HOUS 77056 4101 A1
3500 HOUS 77056 4100 E1
Sage St
900 BYTN 77521 3973 B2
1600 HOUS 77009 3963 A1
Sage Ter
3200 FBnC 77450 3954 A7
Sagearbor Dr
11200 HOUS 77089 4378 A5
Sageaspen Ln
9500 HarC 77089 4504 C1
9600 HarC 77089 4377 C7
Sageaugust Ln
9900 HarC 77089 4377 A6
Sagebark Dr
9800 HarC 77089 4377 D7
9800 HarC 77089 4504 A1
Sagebend Ln
9500 HarC 77089 4377 D5
Sageberry Dr
10300 HarC 77089 4377 C5
11200 HOUS 77089 4377 E6
Sageblossom Dr
11200 HarC 77089 4377 C7
Sage Blue Ct
100 WDLD 77382 2674 D3
Sage Bluff Av
2700 FBnC 77469 4615 E2
2700 FBnC 77469 4616 A2
Sagebluff Dr
- HarC 77089 4377 C5
- HOUS 77089 4377 C5
Sagebranch Ct
7100 FBnC 77469 4094 C5
Sagebriar Dr
10400 HOUS 77089 4377 E4
10400 HOUS 77089 4378 A4
Sage Brook Dr
10300 HarC 77089 4377 B7
Sage Brush Ct
14700 MtgC 77302 2679 D3
Sagebrush Dr
2900 HOUS 77093 3686 A2
3100 HarC 77093 3686 A2
Sage Brush Ln
2500 SGLD 77479 4368 E7
3900 PASD 77503 4108 D4
Sagebrush Ln
200 MAGA 77354 2669 C4
Sagebrush Tr
1100 BYTN 77521 3973 B2
Sagebrush Cove
- FBnC 77469 4234 D2
Sagebrush Valley Ln
19200 HarC 77433 3537 B7
Sagebud Ln
9800 HarC 77089 4377 C7
Sageburrow Dr
10300 HarC 77089 4377 C5
10800 HOUS 77089 4377 D6
Sagecanyon Dr
10000 HarC 77089 4377 C5
11200 HOUS 77089 4377 D7
11600 HarC 77089 4504 B1
Sagecastle Ln
9800 HarC 77089 4377 C7
Sagecherry Dr
11400 HarC 77089 4377 D7
Sagecircle St E
3400 HOUS 77056 4100 E1
Sagecircle St N
5200 HOUS 77056 4100 E1
5200 HOUS 77056 4101 A1
Sagecircle St S
5200 HOUS 77056 4100 E1
5200 HOUS 77056 4101 A1
Sagecircle St W
3400 HOUS 77056 4100 E1
Sagecliff Dr
11800 HOUS 77089 4378 A4
Sagecombe Ct
20400 HarC 77388 3112 C5
Sagecombe Ln
3500 HarC 77388 3112 D5
Sagecountry Dr
11100 HarC 77089 4377 C7
11300 HarC 77089 4504 A1

STREET
Block City ZIP Map# Grid
Sagecourt Dr
9800 HarC 77089 4504 E1
10300 HarC 77089 4377 E7
Sage Cove Ln
8800 FBnC 77469 4235 D1
Sage Creek Ct
2800 FBnC 77469 4365 A6
Sagecreek Dr
11200 HOUS 77089 4378 A5
11400 HarC 77089 4378 A6
E Sage Creek Pl
10 WDLD 77382 2819 A2
W Sage Creek Pl
10 WDLD 77382 2819 A2
Sagecrest Ln
10900 HOUS 77089 4377 E5
Sagecroft Dr
17900 HarC 77084 3677 E6
17900 HarC 77084 3678 A6
Sage Cypress Ct
16300 HarC 77433 3251 C3
Sagedale Dr
9800 HarC 77089 4504 D1
9800 HarC 77581 4504 D1
9800 PRLD 77581 4504 D1
Sage Deck Ln
9500 HarC 77089 4504 C1
Sage Dock Ct
10400 HarC 77089 4378 C7
Sagedowne Ln
- HarC 77089 4377 D7
- HarC 77089 4378 A6
- HOUS 77089 4377 D7
11200 HOUS 77089 4378 B5
12100 HOUS 77034 4378 B5
Sageelm Ln
10300 HOUS 77089 4377 D6
Sage Flower Ct
21300 HarC 77338 3261 E3
Sageford Ct
24800 FBnC 77494 3953 B6
Sageforest Dr
10400 HOUS 77089 4377 E5
10400 HOUS 77089 4378 A4
Sage Gale Dr
11100 HarC 77089 4377 D7
Sagegate Dr
9900 HarC 77089 4504 D1
10300 HarC 77089 4377 E7
Sageglen Dr
11200 HOUS 77089 4378 A5
11400 HarC 77089 4378 A5
Sageglow Dr
9900 HarC 77089 4504 D1
10700 HarC 77089 4377 E7
Sage Grass Ln
6700 HarC 77379 3111 C4
Sagegreen Ct
11500 HarC 77089 4377 E7
Sagegreen Dr
- HOUS 77089 4378 A7
9900 HarC 77089 4504 D1
10300 HarC 77089 4377 E7
10700 HarC 77089 4378 A7
Sagegrove Ln
11400 HOUS 77089 4378 A5
Sagegulf Ln
10800 HOUS 77089 4377 D5
Sagehampton Ct
9400 HarC 77379 3110 C6
Sagehaven Dr
11200 HOUS 77089 4378 A5
Sageheather Dr
11000 HOUS 77089 4377 E5
11200 HOUS 77089 4378 A6
Sagehill Dr
11000 HOUS 77089 4377 E6
Sage Hollow Ct
5900 FBnC 77479 4493 C1
Sagehollow Ln
11400 HOUS 77089 4378 A5
Sageholly Cir
11300 HarC 77089 4377 C7
Sagehurst Ln
11400 HOUS 77089 4378 A5
Sagekaron Dr
- HarC 77089 4377 D7
Sageking Dr
11100 HarC 77089 4377 D7
11600 HarC 77089 4504 E1
Sageknight Dr
11100 HarC 77089 4377 C7
Sageknoll Ln
9500 HarC 77089 4377 D5
Sagelake Ln
9800 HarC 77089 4504 D1
Sageland Dr
11200 HOUS 77089 4378 A4
Sagelaurel Ln
20900 FBnC 77469 4094 B7
Sagelea Ln
10300 HOUS 77089 4377 D6
Sageleaf Ln
10900 HOUS 77089 4377 E5
Sage Lee Dr
9800 HarC 77089 4377 C7
Sage Linda Ln
11100 HarC 77089 4377 D7
Sagelink Cir
10300 HarC 77089 4377 E7
Sagelink Ct
10300 HarC 77089 4377 E7
Sagelink Dr
11500 HarC 77089 4377 E7
Sage Manor Dr
5600 HarC 77084 3677 E5
5600 HarC 77084 3678 A5
Sagemarie Ln
9900 HarC 77089 4377 C6
Sagemark Dr
9800 HarC 77089 4504 D1
Sagemeadow Ct
10500 HarC 77089 4378 A7
Sagemeadow Ln
10500 HarC 77089 4377 D5
10600 HOUS 77089 4377 E6
11600 HarC 77089 4378 A7
11600 HarC 77089 4378 A7
Sagemill Dr
9900 HarC 77089 4504 D1
10100 HarC 77089 4377 E7
Sagemist Ct
9600 HarC 77089 4377 D5
Sagemist Ln
11300 HarC 77089 4377 D4
Sagemont Square Ct
17600 FBnC 77469 4095 B5

STREET
Block City ZIP Map# Grid
Sagemore Hills Dr
14800 HarC 77082 4096 D4
Sagemorgan Dr
10900 HarC 77089 4377 C6
11400 HarC 77089 4504 D1
Sagemoss Ln
9800 HarC 77089 4504 D1
Sage Mountain Ln
21900 FBnC 77450 4094 B3
Sageoak Dr
11200 HOUS 77089 4378 B4
Sageorchard Cir
11100 HarC 77089 4377 C7
Sageorchard Ct
11100 HarC 77089 4377 A6
Sageorchard Ln
- HOUS 77089 4377 D6
9800 HarC 77089 4377 C7
Sagepark Ln
10700 HOUS 77089 4377 E6
11400 HarC 77089 4377 E6
11400 HarC 77089 4378 A7
11600 HOUS 77089 4378 A7
Sageperry Dr
11400 HarC 77089 4377 E6
11400 HarC 77089 4378 A6
11400 HOUS 77089 4378 A6
Sagepike Cir
11100 HarC 77089 4377 C7
Sagepike Dr
9800 HarC 77089 4377 C7
Sagepine Ln
10500 HOUS 77089 4378 A4
Sage Pl Dr
8800 HOUS 77071 4239 B5
Sageplum Dr
9800 HarC 77089 4504 D1
9800 PRLD 77581 4504 D1
10100 HarC 77089 4377 D7
10300 HOUS 77089 4377 E7
Sage Point Ct
3600 HarC 77449 3816 A2
Sage Point Ln
- HarC 77377 3254 A4
- HarC 77429 3254 A4
Sagequeen Dr
9800 HarC 77089 4377 C7
Sager Dr
8800 HOUS 77096 4101 A7
8800 HOUS 77096 4241 A1
Sage Rain Ct
20600 HarC 77449 3815 C2
Sageridge Cir
10700 HarC 77089 4377 E7
Sage River Ct
5800 FBnC 77479 4493 E2
Sageriver Ct
11100 HarC 77089 4377 E5
Sageriver Dr
10700 HarC 77089 4377 E5
10800 HOUS 77089 4377 E5
11200 HOUS 77089 4378 A6
Sagerock Dr
10300 HOUS 77089 4377 E7
10400 HOUS 77089 4377 E7
Sageroyal Ln
9800 HarC 77089 4377 C7
Sagesquare St
5200 HOUS 77056 4100 E1
5200 HOUS 77056 4101 A1
Sagestanley Dr
11400 HarC 77089 4377 D7
11400 HarC 77089 4504 D1
Sagestar Ln
10400 HarC 77089 4377 C5
Sagestone
10 CNRO 77304 2383 B7
Sagestone Ct
8500 HarC 77095 3538 A5
Sage Thrasher Ln
14700 HarC 77377 2963 C5
14700 TMBL 77375 2963 C5
14700 TMBL 77377 2963 C5
Sagetown Dr
11400 HarC 77089 4377 D7
Sagetrail Dr
10300 HarC 77089 4377 C5
10700 HOUS 77089 4377 D7
Sagetree Dr
- HOUS 77034 4378 A4
10400 HOUS 77089 4377 E4
10700 HOUS 77089 4378 A4
Sage Tree Tr
19700 HarC 77346 3265 A4
Sagevale Ct
10400 HarC 77089 4377 E7
Sagevale Ln
10300 HarC 77089 4377 D5
11200 HOUS 77089 4377 E6
11600 HarC 77089 4378 A7
11800 HarC 77089 4505 A1
Sagevalley Dr
11000 HOUS 77089 4377 E6
11400 HarC 77089 4377 E6
11400 HarC 77089 4378 A6
11400 HOUS 77089 4378 A6
Sageview Dr
11000 HOUS 77089 4377 E6
11200 HOUS 77089 4378 A6
Sageville Dr
11200 HOUS 77089 4378 B4
Sagewalk Ct
6400 HarC 77379 3111 D4
Sageway Dr
11200 HOUS 77089 4378 B4
Sagewell Dr
- HarC 77089 4504 C1
Sagewhite Dr
11400 HarC 77089 4377 D7
11400 HarC 77089 4504 D1
Sagewick Dr
10400 HOUS 77089 4377 E4
10400 HOUS 77089 4378 A4
Sage Willow Ln
5600 BzaC 77583 4623 C5
Sagewillow Ln
10300 HarC 77089 4377 C5
10600 HOUS 77089 4377 E6
11600 HarC 77089 4378 A7
11600 HOUS 77089 4378 A7
Sagewind Cir
10700 HarC 77089 4378 A7
Sagewind Ct
10700 HarC 77089 4378 A7
Sagewind Dr
10500 HarC 77089 4377 D5
10600 HOUS 77089 4377 E6
11600 HarC 77089 4378 A7

STREET Block City ZIP Map# Grid

Sagewind Dr
11600 HOUS 77089 4378 A7
Sagewood Ct
3100 PRLD 77584 4502 D5
16400 MSCY 77071 4239 B7
Sagewood Dr
100 MtgC 77386 2968 C1
11200 HOUS 77089 4378 B4
Sagewood Bend Ln
- HarC 77041 3679 E4
Sagewood Forest Dr
26300 FBnC 77494 4092 B5
Sagewood Hills Dr
12800 HOUS 77072 4097 C4
Sageyork Dr
10000 HarC 77089 4377 B5
11400 HarC 77089 4504 D1
Sagging Oaks Dr
19600 HarC 77388 3113 C6
Saginaw Dr
11200 HOUS 77076 3685 A3
Saginaw Bay Ct
900 HarC 77373 2968 D5
Sago Ln
2000 HOUS 77084 3816 D6
Sago Bay
- PRLD 77584 4500 D3
Sago Island Dr
2500 HarC 77073 3259 D2
Sahalle Dr
24700 FBnC 77494 3953 A3
24700 KATY 77494 3953 A3
Sahara Dr
1400 HarC 77532 3551 E4
Sai Baba Dr
12600 HarC 77038 3543 A3
Sailaway Dr
- LGCY 77573 4508 D4
Sailboat Dr
2600 NSUB 77058 4508 B4
Saile Ct
4200 HOUS 77339 3119 A2
Sailfin Ct
700 HarC 77532 3552 A3
Sailfin St
16000 HarC 77532 3552 A3
Sailfish Dr
3400 GlsC 77650 4879 C3
Sailfish Ln
3800 LPRT 77571 4383 A2
3800 PASD 77571 4383 A2
Sailfish Pt
2600 SGLD 77478 4237 B4
Sailfish St
- GlsC 77563 4991 A6
1100 BYUV 77563 4990 E7
1100 BYUV 77563 4991 A6
1100 BYUV 77563 5105 E1
Sailfish Cove Dr
18400 HarC 77346 3409 C1
Sail Harbour Ct
22500 FBnC 77450 3953 E7
Sailing Dr
8700 HarC 77346 3409 D1
8900 HarC 77346 3265 D7
Sailors Wy
4400 MSCY 77459 4497 A4
Sailors Moon Ct
17000 HarC 77546 4506 D7
Sailors Moon Dr
2700 HarC 77546 4506 B7
2900 HarC 77546 4630 B1
Sailport Ln
800 LGCY 77573 4633 B3
Sail Port St
2400 PRLD 77584 4500 D3
Sailwind Dr
2100 PRLD 77584 4500 A2
Sailwind Ln
1200 LGCY 77573 4633 B3
24000 HarC 77389 2965 E4
Sailwing St
2500 PRLD 77584 4500 D3
Sailwing Creek Ct
11300 PRLD 77584 4500 D3
Saint St
2600 HOUS 77027 3961 D7
St. Agnes St
1000 HOUS 77030 4102 C5
St. Alban Ct
12700 HarC 77015 3828 C7
St. Andrews Dr
100 FRDW 77546 4628 E6
4600 BYTN 77521 3972 B2
6000 PASD 77505 4248 D6
St. Andrews Ln
- SGLD 77479 4495 C1
St. Andrews Pl
2700 LGCY 77573 4508 E7
St. Andrews Rd
600 HOUS 77339 3118 B7
St. Anne Dr
- HOUS 77019 3962 B6
- HOUS 77098 3962 B6
St. Anne Forest Dr
6200 HarC 77088 3542 C6
St. Annes Dr
2700 SGLD 77479 4495 A2
St. Augustine Rd
8000 HarC 77521 3833 B3
St. Augustine St
700 HOUS 77003 3964 A6
700 HOUS 77023 3964 A6
5800 HOUS 77021 4103 D6
St. Barbe St
- HMPD 77445 2952 E7
100 HMPD 77445 3098 B1
St. Barts Cl
2000 DKSN 77539 4633 C7
2000 GlsC 77539 4633 C7
St. Benedict St
3400 HOUS 77021 4243 A1
St. Cecelia Dr
11800 HarC 77532 3692 D2
St. Charles Av
500 LGCY 77573 4632 B3
St. Charles Ct
3200 FBnC 77459 4621 B5
St. Charles Dr
700 HarC 77532 3693 A2
E St. Charles Dr
100 HarC 77532 3692 D2
St. Charles Pl
29000 MtgC 77354 2818 B1
St. Charles St
100 HOUS 77003 3963 E5
2200 HOUS 77004 3963 C7
3400 HOUS 77004 4103 C1
N St. Charles St
10 HOUS 77003 3963 E4
W St. Charles St
100 HarC 77532 3692 D2
St. Christopher Av
2000 LGCY 77573 4632 C2
St. Christopher Ct
10 SGLD 77479 4495 B4
St. Clair St
900 HOUS 77088 3683 E3
900 HOUS 77088 3684 A2
St. Claude Ct
12500 HarC 77015 3828 B7
St. Cloud Dr
100 FRDW 77546 4628 E7
14600 HOUS 77062 4379 E7
14900 HOUS 77062 4380 A7
14900 HOUS 77062 4507 A1
St. Clroix Cl
2000 DKSN 77539 4633 C7
2000 GlsC 77539 4633 C7
St. Croix St
600 ALVN 77511 4749 C7
St. Edmunds Cross
1900 DKSN 77539 4753 C1
1900 GlsC 77539 4753 C1
St. Edwards Dr
700 HarC 77090 3258 C3
700 HOUS 77090 3258 C3
St. Edwards Green Dr
7800 HarC 77015 3828 A7
St. Elizabeth Av
1400 HOUS 77020 3964 C2
St. Elmo St
1800 HOUS 77020 3964 B1
St. Elmo's Ct
4200 MSCY 77459 4621 E2
St. Elmo's Fire
- DRPK 77536 4109 E6
St. Emanuel St
10 HOUS 77002 3963 D4
10 HOUS 77003 3963 D4
2900 HOUS 77004 3963 B7
3500 HOUS 77004 4103 E2
Ste. Mere Eglise Ln
3300 HarC 77388 3112 D3
St. Emilion Ct
17900 HarC 77379 3256 B1
Saintes Cir
7800 MSCY 77071 4239 E7
St. Finans Wy
100 HarC 77015 3829 A5
200 HarC 77015 3828 E6
St. Florent Ct
13400 HarC 77377 3109 A5
St. Florent Dr
25900 HarC 77377 3109 A5
St. Francis Ln
800 HOUS 77079 3958 C1
St. Francis St
12100 HarC 77532 3692 D3
St. George Ct
10 SGLD 77479 4495 B3
St. George Ln
800 HOUS 77079 3958 C1
St. George Square Ln
3200 HOUS 77056 4100 E1
St. George Square St
3200 HOUS 77056 4100 E1
St. Germain Wy
11400 HOUS 77082 4098 B3
St. Goar St
4300 DKSN 77539 4754 A3
St. Helen Ct
- FBnC 77450 4094 D4
St. Helen Ln
17900 HarC 77379 3256 A2
St. Helena Wy
16300 HOUS 77053 4371 D6
St. Helier St
16100 JRSV 77040 3540 C7
16100 JRSV 77040 3680 C1
St. Ives Ct
700 HOUS 77079 3956 E2
St. Ives St
4100 SGLD 77479 4495 D4
St. James
- BYTN 77520 3971 C2
St. James Ct
2200 MSCY 77459 4370 A7
St. James Pl
1700 HOUS 77056 3960 E6
2100 PRLD 77581 4503 E3
29400 MtgC 77354 2818 A1
St. James St
2400 PASD 77502 4247 A1
St. James Wy
- CNRO 77304 2382 C1
St. John Ct
10700 HOUS 77071 4239 E3
St. John Dr
18100 HOUS 77058 4508 B4
18100 NSUB 77058 4508 B4
St. Johns Cl
2000 DKSN 77539 4633 C7
2000 GlsC 77539 4633 C7
St. Johns Ct
16000 JRSV 77040 3540 B7
St. Johns Wood Dr
16600 HarC 77377 3254 B5
St. Johns Woods St
1200 HOUS 77077 3957 C6
St. Joseph Pkwy
300 HOUS 77002 3963 B5
1500 HOUS 77003 3963 C6
St. Joseph St
700 HOUS 77003 3964 A6
700 HOUS 77023 3964 A6
St. Jude Dr
6300 PASD 77505 4248 E7
St. Kitts Cl
5000 DKSN 77539 4633 C7
St. Laurent Ln
9000 HarC 77044 3689 C5
11200 HOUS 77082 4098 C2
St. Lawrence Cir
15800 HarC 77546 4505 E5
St. Lawrence Ct
15800 HarC 77546 4505 E5
St. Lawrence Dr
4700 HarC 77546 4505 E5
St. Lawrence Cove
15800 HarC 77546 4505 E6
St. Lo Rd
6900 HOUS 77033 4244 A3
St. Louis St
7100 HOUS 77028 3825 E3
7700 HOUS 77028 3826 B3
St. Lucia
24900 HarC 77447 3249 D2
St. Lucia Cl
2100 DKSN 77539 4633 C7
St. Lukes Wy
17100 WDLD 77384 2676 A6
17200 MtgC 77384 2676 A6
St. Marks St
100 SGLD 77478 4368 A2
St. Martin St
11900 HarC 77532 3692 E3
St. Mary's Blvd
300 GLSN 77550 5109 D2
St. Marys Ln
13800 HOUS 77079 3958 A1
14500 HOUS 77079 3957 D1
St. Marys Rd
1100 HMPD 77445 2953 B6
St. Marys St
- HMPD 77445 2952 E6
1500 HMPD 77445 2953 A6
St. Michaels Ct
3800 SGLD 77479 4495 E4
St. Michaels Crest Ln
8100 HarC 77396 3547 D2
St. Michaels Pass
20200 HarC 77433 3676 C1
St. Michel Dr
12400 HarC 77015 3828 A7
St. Moritz St
5600 BLAR 77401 4101 B3
St. Patrick Ln
2200 DRPK 77536 4108 E6
St. Paul St
5600 BLAR 77401 4101 B3
St. Pauls Ct
28600 HarC 77336 3121 E2
St. Peters Wk
10 SGLD 77479 4495 C1
St. Peters Gate
10 WDLD 77382 2673 B7
St. Pierre Ct
16000 HarC 77429 3397 A1
St. Pierre Ln
14300 HarC 77429 3397 A1
St. Simon Dr
- HarC 77047 4374 C4
St. Simons Ct
10 SGLD 77479 4495 E3
St. Theresa Blvd
- SGLD 77478 4368 A1
St. Thomas Cl
2000 DKSN 77539 4633 C7
2000 GlsC 77539 4633 C7
St. Thomas Ct
10 HarC 77070 3399 E3
St. Tropez Wy
3500 HOUS 77082 4098 A3
St. William Ln
3500 HarC 77084 3816 D3
Sakowitz St
700 HOUS 77020 3964 D2
2500 HOUS 77020 3825 D7
3300 HOUS 77026 3825 D7
Saladia St
2000 GLSN 77551 5108 C6
Salado Dr
2600 BzaC 77584 4501 A5
Salama Falls
12400 HOUS 77089 4505 C1
Salamanca Ct
14700 HarC 77429 3253 D4
Sal Amanca Wy
- LGCY 77573 4632 A7
Salem
6600 HOUS 77022 3824 B3
Salem Ct
3100 SGLD 77478 4369 A3
Salem Dr
1700 DRPK 77536 4108 E7
Salem Hills Ct
- FBnC 77494 3953 B3
Salento Ct
11100 FBnC 77469 4093 B7
Salerno Ln
10 HOUS 77076 3684 E5
10 HOUS 77076 3685 A5
Salerno St
600 SGLD 77478 4368 B3
Salford Dr
1600 HOUS 77008 3822 C6
Salge Dr
7500 HarC 77040 3682 A1
7500 HOUS 77040 3682 A1
7800 HarC 77040 3681 E1
Salida de Sol Dr
16100 FBnC 77083 4096 A7
16400 FBnC 77083 4095 E7
Salina Cir
4000 HarC 77396 3406 E6
Salina Ct
3900 HarC 77396 3406 E6
Salina Ln
3800 HarC 77396 3407 A6
Salina St
4900 HOUS 77026 3825 C6
7600 HOUS 77020 3826 A6
Salinas Ln
16300 HarC 77095 3538 B6
Salisbury Dr
13600 SGLD 77478 4237 B7
Salisbury Ln
2300 ALVN 77511 4866 E4
Salisbury St
2200 HOUS 77019 3962 B6
Salix St
- HOUS 77075 4377 B2
Sallee Rd
25900 SPLD 77372 2537 A7
Sallisan Springs Ct
2100 PRLD 77581 4503 D2
Sally Anne Dr
1000 RSBG 77471 4491 C3
1300 RHMD 77469 4491 C3
1300 RHMD 77471 4491 C3
Sally Stone Ct
2900 MSCY 77459 4496 C1
Salma Ct
500 HarC 77073 3403 B3
Salmon Cr
12200 HarC 77041 3679 E6
Salmon Ct
10300 CmbC 77520 3835 C4
Salmon Dr
16000 HarC 77379 3256 A5
Salmon Ln
16200 HarC 77379 3256 A5
Salop Ct
19100 MtgC 77357 2829 E4
Salt Tr
- HarC 77014 3401 D1
Salta Dr
6600 HarC 77083 4096 D5
Salta Verde Pt
7900 FBnC 77494 4093 B3
Salt Cedar Dr
- GLSN 77554 5548 C1
Salt Cedar Ln
32800 WlrC 77484 3246 C1
Salter Dr
800 HarC 77032 3403 D7
800 HarC 77032 3404 A7
Saltgrass Cir
2700 DRPK 77536 4109 E7
Saltgrass Ln
11400 TMBL 77375 3109 E3
Salt Grass Tr
13600 HarC 77429 3396 E3
Saltgrass Tr
2500 DRPK 77536 4109 E7
11400 TMBL 77375 3109 E2
Salt Grass Trail Cir
- HarC 77493 3813 E4
Saltillo St
9600 HOUS 77013 3826 E5
9600 HOUS 77013 3827 A5
Salt Marsh Ct
2100 LGCY 77573 4631 B7
Salton Point Dr
16000 HarC 77546 4506 A5
Salt River Ct
19900 HarC 77449 3815 E6
Salt River Valley Cir
17500 HarC 77346 3408 B4
Salt River Valley Ln
12000 HarC 77346 3408 B2
Saltus St
2500 HOUS 77003 3963 E4
3300 HOUS 77003 3964 A5
Salt Wind Ct
400 HarC 77532 3552 B1
Salvador St
3600 PASD 77504 4248 A4
Salvato St
2700 DKSN 77539 4753 E2
3000 DKSN 77539 4754 A1
Salzbe St
- HarC 77039 3546 E3
6000 HarC 77039 3547 A3
Salzburg Ct
9700 HMBL 77338 3262 C4
Salzburg Ln
20100 HMBL 77338 3262 C4
Sam Rd
10300 FBnC 77478 4236 C4
Sam St
300 PASD 77502 4247 B1
600 HOUS 77091 3684 B4
Samantha Ct
200 FBnC 77479 4366 D6
Samantha Ln
12000 MtgC 77354 2817 C5
Samantha Cove Ct
2900 FBnC 77494 3953 B7
Samantha Suzanne Ct
9800 HOUS 77025 4241 D2
Sam Brooking Rd
15900 FBnC 77469 4236 A3
15900 FBnC 77478 4236 A3
Sam Brookins St
15800 FBnC 77469 4236 A2
15800 FBnC 77478 4236 A2
Sam Creek Ct
22400 FBnC 77494 4093 E3
Sam Houston Dr
3000 SGLD 77479 4495 E1
3500 SGLD 77479 4496 A1
Sam Houston Pkwy
- HarC - 3405 D7
- HarC - 3406 B7
- HarC - 3829 B7
- HarC - 3968 C1
- HOUS - 3403 B7
- HOUS - 3404 A7
- HOUS - 3405 C7
- HOUS - 3406 A7
Sam Houston Pkwy LP-8
- HarC - 3405 D7
- HarC - 3406 B7
- HarC - 3829 B6
- HarC - 3968 C1
- HOUS - 3403 B7
- HOUS - 3404 A7
- HOUS - 3405 D7
- HOUS - 3406 A7
Sam Houston Pkwy N
- HarC - 3968 D6
- HOUS - 3968 D7
- HOUS - 4108 D2
- PASD - 4108 D2
Sam Houston Pkwy W
- HarC - 3406 B7
- HOUS - 3406 B7
E Sam Houston Pkwy N
- HarC 77044 3549 B1
- HarC 77049 3689 D6
- HarC 77049 3828 E1
1500 HarC 77015 3968 D3
3700 HarC 77015 3829 B6
7700 HarC 77049 3829 A1
8200 HarC 77044 3689 C1
E Sam Houston Pkwy N LP-8
- HarC 77044 3549 B1
- HarC 77049 3828 E1
- HarC 77049 3829 A1
8200 HarC 77049 3689 D6
8700 HarC 77044 3689 D6
E Sam Houston Pkwy S
- HOUS 77034 4248 A7
- HOUS 77034 4378 C3
- HOUS 77505 4248 A7
100 PASD 77503 4108 C7
2100 PASD 77503 4248 A7
3100 PASD 77505 4248 C3
5400 HOUS 77034 4379 A1
N Sam Houston Pkwy E
- HarC 77044 3549 A1
- HOUS 77032 3403 E7
- HOUS 77038 3403 B7
- HOUS 77067 3403 B7
10 HOUS 77060 3403 D7
800 HarC 77032 3404 A7
800 HOUS 77032 3404 A7
2900 HOUS 77032 3405 A7
3300 HarC 77032 3405 A7
N Sam Houston Pkwy E
5800 HOUS 77396 3405 D7
6200 HOUS 77396 3406 B7
7000 HarC 77396 3406 D7
8100 HarC 77396 3547 E1
8100 HarC 77396 3548 E1
11400 HarC 77396 3549 A1
N Sam Houston Pkwy E LP-8
- HarC 77044 3549 A1
7000 HarC 77396 3406 D7
8100 HarC 77396 3547 E1
8100 HarC 77396 3548 E1
11400 HarC 77396 3549 A1
N Sam Houston Pkwy W
- HarC 77038 3542 B1
- HarC 77066 3541 A1
- HarC 77086 3541 A1
- HOUS 77038 3402 A7
- HOUS 77038 3403 A7
- HOUS 77038 3543 D1
- HOUS 77060 3403 A7
- HOUS 77064 3541 D1
- HOUS 77067 3402 A7
- HOUS 77067 3403 A7
1700 HarC 77038 3402 B7
1700 HarC 77067 3402 B7
1800 HarC 77038 3543 B1
3500 HarC 77038 3401 D7
3500 HarC 77066 3401 D7
3500 HarC 77086 3401 D7
4500 HarC 77066 3542 C1
4500 HarC 77086 3542 C1
7500 HarC 77064 3541 B1
10000 HarC 77064 3540 E2
S Sam Houston Pkwy E
- HarC 77047 4373 E5
- HarC 77089 4377 B5
- HOUS 77034 4378 A4
- HOUS 77048 4376 A5
- PRLD 77047 4373 E5
3000 HarC 77047 4374 D5
3000 PRLD 77047 4374 A5
4600 HOUS 77048 4374 B5
4600 HOUS 77048 4375 D5
7700 HOUS 77075 4376 C5
8900 HOUS 77075 4377 A5
10600 HOUS 77089 4377 E5
11300 HOUS 77089 4378 A5
S Sam Houston Pkwy W
- HarC 77053 4373 A5
- HOUS 77071 4370 E2
- MSCY 77071 4370 E2
500 HarC 77047 4373 A5
500 PRLD 77047 4373 A5
3200 HarC 77053 4372 D5
4800 HOUS 77053 4372 C6
5500 HOUS 77053 4371 E5
6400 HOUS 77085 4371 C3
6400 HOUS 77489 4371 D4
8200 HOUS 77085 4370 D1
8200 HOUS 77489 4370 E2
W Sam Houston Pkwy N
- HOUS 77043 3958 D1
- JRSV 77040 3680 D2
- JRSV 77041 3680 D2
100 HOUS 77024 3958 D2
100 HOUS 77042 3958 E4
800 HOUS 77079 3958 D1
1000 HOUS 77043 3819 D5
4400 HOUS 77041 3819 D1
4700 HOUS 77041 3680 D1
5400 HarC 77041 3680 D7
7100 HarC 77040 3680 E2
7200 HarC 77040 3681 A2
8600 HarC 77040 3540 E7
8900 HarC 77064 3540 E4
W Sam Houston Pkwy S
- HarC 77031 4239 B6
- HarC 77071 4239 B6
- HOUS 77031 4238 E4
- HOUS 77071 4370 D1
- HOUS 77074 4238 E4
- HOUS 77085 4370 D1
- MSCY 77071 4370 D1
400 HOUS 77042 3958 D7
2800 HOUS 77042 4098 E7
5900 HOUS 77036 4098 E4
5900 HOUS 77072 4098 E4
8400 HOUS 77099 4098 E7
8800 HOUS 77099 4238 D3
9300 HOUS 77036 4238 E1
11100 HOUS 77031 4239 B6
13200 HOUS 77071 4239 C7
13200 MSCY 77071 4239 C7
Sam Houston Rd
1800 HOUS 77029 3965 D4
Sam Houston St
5600 HarC 77093 3546 D7
5600 HOUS 77016 3546 E7
Sam Houston Tr
1000 HarC 77484 2958 C6
Sam Houston Center Dr
9900 HarC 77064 3540 E4
Sam Houston Park Dr
- HarC 77064 3540 E4
W Sam Houston Tollway
- HarC - 3401 E7
- HarC - 3402 C7
- HarC - 3540 E4
- HarC - 3541 A2
- HarC - 3542 A1
- HarC - 3543 A1
- HarC - 3680 E1
- HarC - 3681 A1
- HarC - 3968 D6
- HarC - 4239 B6
- HarC - 4372 C5
- HarC - 4373 C5
- HarC - 4374 B5
- HarC - 4377 D5
- HOUS - 3402 B7
- HOUS - 3403 A7
- HOUS - 3680 D3
- HOUS - 3819 D1
- HOUS - 3958 D6
- HOUS - 3968 D6
- HOUS - 4098 E7
- HOUS - 4108 D1
- HOUS - 4238 E4
- HOUS - 4239 A5
- HOUS - 4248 C2
- HOUS - 4370 E2
- HOUS - 4371 B3
- HOUS - 4372 C5
- HOUS - 4374 E5
- HOUS - 4375 C5
- HOUS - 4376 A5
- HOUS - 4377 A5
W Sam Houston Tollway
- HOUS - 4378 B4
- HOUS - 4379 A1
- JRSV - 3680 E2
- MSCY - 4239 C7
- MSCY - 4370 D1
- PASD - 4108 C7
- PASD - 4248 C2
11200 HOUS 77089 4377 E5
W Sam Houston Tollway LP-8
- HarC - 3401 E7
- HarC - 3402 C7
- HarC - 3540 E3
- HarC - 3541 A2
- HarC - 3542 E1
- HarC - 3543 A1
- HarC - 3680 E1
- HarC - 3681 A1
- HarC - 3968 D6
- HarC - 4239 B6
- HarC - 4372 C5
- HarC - 4373 C5
- HarC - 4374 B5
- HarC - 4377 B5
- HOUS - 3402 B7
- HOUS - 3403 A7
- HOUS - 3680 D7
- HOUS - 3819 D2
- HOUS - 3958 D6
- HOUS - 3968 D6
- HOUS - 4098 E1
- HOUS - 4108 D1
- HOUS - 4238 E4
- HOUS - 4239 A5
- HOUS - 4248 B7
- HOUS - 4370 D1
- HOUS - 4371 E4
- HOUS - 4372 C5
- HOUS - 4374 E5
- HOUS - 4375 C5
- HOUS - 4376 E5
- HOUS - 4377 B5
- HOUS - 4378 B4
- HOUS - 4379 A1
- JRSV - 3680 E2
- MSCY - 4239 C7
- MSCY - 4370 D1
- PASD - 4108 C5
- PASD - 4248 C2
11200 HOUS 77089 4377 E5
W Sam Houston Tollway E
- HarC - 3541 E1
- HarC - 3542 E1
W Sam Houston Tollway E LP-8
- HarC - 3541 E1
W Sam Houston Tollway N
- HOUS - 3819 D6
- HOUS - 4098 E3
W Sam Houston Tollway W
- HarC - 3401 E7
- HarC - 3541 E1
W Sam Houston Tollway W LP-8
- HarC - 3541 E1
Sammon Dr
500 HMBL 77338 3263 A7
Samoa Wy
15600 HOUS 77053 4371 E6
Sampan Dr
200 TKIS 77554 5106 B4
Sampley Wy
5800 HOUS 77092 3682 A5
Sampras Ct
31500 MtgC 77354 2672 E5
Sampras Ace Ct
6200 HarC 77379 3257 A4
Sampson St
100 HOUS 77003 3964 A5
1600 HOUS 77003 3963 E7
2100 HOUS 77004 3963 D7
2700 HOUS 77004 4103 D1
N Sampson St
10 HOUS 77003 3964 A5
Sam Rayburn Ct
9300 HarC 77433 3537 C4
Sam Robinson Rd
- FBnC 77494 3952 C7
Samrose Dr
5400 HOUS 77091 3684 B6
Sams Dr
2500 SEBK 77586 4382 B5
Sams Pl
2700 HOUS 77020 3963 E2
Samsarah Cir
17000 HarC 77084 3678 A2
Sams Hill Dr
20200 MtgC 77357 2829 B6
Samual Bluff Ct
6000 FBnC 77479 4367 A5
Samuel Ln
12800 HOUS 77015 3967 B4
Samuel St
- HOUS 77009 3824 A4
Samuel Adams Ln
3500 MSCY 77459 4369 D5
Samuels Dr
5200 PASD 77505 4248 E7
Sam Wilson St
2000 HOUS 77020 3964 D1
2500 HOUS 77020 3825 D7
N San Cir
12200 HarC 77044 3688 E5
12200 HarC 77044 3689 A5
S San Cir
12200 HarC 77044 3688 E5
12300 HarC 77044 3689 A5
San Alberto
8800 HOUS 77017 4246 A2
San Angelo Dr
300 MAGA 77354 2669 A4
San Angelo St
6900 HOUS 77020 3964 E2
6900 HOUS 77020 3965 A2
San Antonio
7000 HarC 77040 3681 B3
San Antonio Av
2100 PRLD 77581 4503 B3
2500 PRLD 77584 4503 B3
San Antonio Ct
1000 RSBG 77471 4490 B5
San Antonio St
700 HOUS 77012 4105 C3
900 HMPD 77445 3098 B2
6900 HarC 77040 3681 B3
San Antonio River Dr
4700 MtgC 77386 2970 B2
San Augustine Av
2800 PASD 77502 4108 A6
3900 PASD 77503 4108 D6
4500 DRPK 77503 4108 D6
4500 DRPK 77536 4108 D6
San Augustine Ln
2300 FRDW 77546 4629 A7
E San Augustine St
- DRPK 77536 4109 E6
- DRPK 77536 4110 A6
- DRPK 77571 4110 A6
- LPRT 77571 4110 A6
W San Augustine St
- DRPK 77503 4108 E6
- DRPK 77536 4108 E6
- PASD 77503 4108 E6
100 DRPK 77536 4109 A6
San Benito Dr
7400 HarC 77083 4096 C6
San Bernadino St
4600 HarC 77066 3401 A1
San Blas
6000 HOUS 77017 4246 A2
San Bonifacio
8900 HOUS 77017 4246 A2
Sanborn Dr
4300 HOUS 77092 3822 A1
5000 HOUS 77091 3683 A7
5000 HOUS 77092 3683 A7
San Carlos Rd
100 FBnC 77471 4490 E2
San Carlos St
9600 HOUS 77013 3826 E6
9600 HOUS 77013 3827 A6
Sanchez St
7800 HOUS 77012 4105 B3
San Clemente St
12700 HarC 77066 3401 B1
San Clemente Point Ct
7500 FBnC 77494 4093 B3
San Conero Dr
2300 PRLD 77089 4505 A3
2300 PRLD 77581 4504 E3
2300 PRLD 77581 4505 A3
Sancroft Ct
400 HarC 77450 3954 E2
Sanctuary Cove
2800 FBnC 77450 3954 A7
Sand Ct
2200 FBnC 77469 4365 C1
S Sand Dr
3900 BzaC 77584 4501 D5
Sand Lk
1400 FBnC 77469 4234 D4
Sand Pns
1200 FBnC 77494 3953 A3
Sand Rd
100 MtgC 77304 2529 D4
Sand Ter
4000 FBnC 77450 4094 C1
Sandal Wk
2600 PRLD 77584 4501 B3
Sandalbrook St
2200 PRLD 77584 4500 D2
Sandalfoot St
14000 HarC 77095 3539 A7
14900 HarC 77095 3538 E7
Sandalia Ct
4900 FBnC 77494 4092 D3
Sandalin Ct
13900 HarC 77429 3397 D2
Sandalin Dr
14400 HarC 77429 3397 D2
Sandalwood Av
4600 RSBG 77471 4491 C5
Sandalwood Cir
4700 BYTN 77521 3972 B1
Sandalwood Dr
- BKHV 77024 3959 C5
10 HOUS 77024 3959 C5
Sandalwood St
10800 MtgC 77303 2239 D1
22000 MtgC 77365 2972 C2
San Dario Dr
- FBnC 77083 4096 A5
16400 FBnC 77083 4095 E5
Sandbar
1100 HarC 77562 3692 A6
Sand Bar Ct
2500 SEBK 77586 4382 C6
Sandberry Dr
2800 HOUS 77345 3119 E2
2800 HOUS 77365 3119 E2
Sandbow Ln
15900 HarC 77044 3549 E3
Sandbridge Dr
- HOUS 77077 3957 B4
Sandbrook Dr
3400 HarC 77066 3401 E7
Sand Bunker Cir
21400 FBnC 77450 3954 E7
Sandbur Valley Wy
12700 HOUS 77045 4241 D5
Sand Canyon Dr
- HarC 77083 4096 E7
- HarC 77083 4097 A7
Sand Castle
- BYTN 77521 3973 D2
Sand Castle Ct
2500 SEBK 77586 4382 C6
Sandcastle Ln
2900 HOUS 77057 3960 D7
Sandcliff Ln
7100 FBnC 77469 4094 B5
Sand Colony Ln
4800 HarC 77449 3677 B7
Sand Cove Ct
10 WDLD 77381 2821 B5
Sandcove Ct
2900 LGCY 77573 4633 A3
Sand Crab
4100 GLSN 77554 5333 A2
Sandcrane
- SEBK 77586 4382 E7
Sand Creek Ct
19900 HarC 77449 3815 E6
Sandcrest Dr
2700 BzaC 77578 4625 A1
Sand Dollar
3700 GLSN 77554 5221 A6
Sand Dollar Ct
3300 SGLD 77479 4496 A2
4000 SEBK 77586 4382 C6
Sand Dollar Dr
9900 HarC 77065 3539 D3
Sandel
- LPRT 77571 4251 E7

STREET / Block City ZIP Map# Grid

Sandelford Dr
18500 HarC 77449 3677 B5
Sandend
29700 MtgC 77354 2818 C2
Sanderford Ct
4800 FBnC 77494 4092 D3
Sanderford Ln
13300 HarC 77083 4097 C7
Sanderling Dr
20300 HarC 77433 3676 E1
Sanderling Ln
200 SGLD 77478 4368 A3
Sandermeyer Dr
11300 FBnC 77469 4092 B7
Sanders Ln
- BzaC 77511 4747 D5
400 HarC 77562 3832 B4
Sanders Rd
7400 BzaC 77583 4745 A2
7400 IWCY 77583 4745 A2
8700 MtgC 77354 2818 E6
20200 MtgC 77355 2961 B6
Sanders St
- HarC 77093 3686 B2
- HOUS 77023 4104 B3
- HOUS 77571 3970 A4
3300 HOUS 77004 4103 D1
31900 MAGA 77355 2669 A6
Sanders Wy
16400 SGCH 77355 2961 B3
Sanders Cemetery Rd
- MtgC 77354 2668 B3
23000 HarC 77377 2961 C7
23000 MtgC 77355 2961 C6
Sanders Cove Ln
6900 HarC 77396 3547 B2
Sandersgate Ln
26100 FBnC 77494 4092 E2
Sanders Glen Ln
8000 HarC 77338 3261 E2
Sanders Ranch Rd
34100 MtgC 77355 2668 A6
Sanders Ridge Ct
300 FBnC 77479 4366 E5
Sandestine Ct
8400 HarC 77095 3538 A6
Sandestine Dr
16800 HarC 77095 3538 A6
17100 HarC 77095 3537 E6
Sandfield Dr
14100 HOUS 77077 3956 E4
Sandflower Ln
13000 FBnC 77478 4366 E1
Sandford Lodge Dr
- HarC 77073 3403 C3
Sandgate Rd
200 HOUS 77061 4245 B6
Sandgate Falls Ct
1900 HOUS 77062 4379 D5
1900 HOUS 77062 4380 A6
Sandhill Ct
4100 GLSN 77554 5441 C4
Sand Hill Dr
- GLSN 77554 5441 D4
Sandhill Dr
- FBnC 77479 4366 E5
E Sand Hill Dr
20600 GLSN 77554 5441 D3
W Sand Hill Dr
20800 GLSN 77554 5441 D4
Sandhill Crane Dr
14100 HarC 77044 3549 D1
Sandhill Crane Wy
4100 GLSN 77554 5548 A3
Sandhillglen Dr
- HarC 77084 3677 E2
- HarC 77095 3677 E2
Sandhill Park Ln
13000 HarC 77044 3689 C4
Sand Hills Dr
10 JRSV 77064 3540 B6
10 JRSV 77065 3540 B6
Sandhills Park Ln
26800 FBnC 77494 4092 A1
Sandhill Trails Ct
24300 HarC 77447 3249 D4
Sand Hollow Ln
1800 HarC 77450 3954 E5
Sandhurst Dr
8100 HOUS 77033 4243 E3
11300 HOUS 77048 4243 E7
12100 HOUS 77048 4374 E2
Sandia Cove Ct
12400 HarC 77041 3679 E5
Sandia Lake Ln
5900 HarC 77041 3679 E5
Sandia Pines Dr
18800 HarC 77346 3265 B7
San Dimas Dr
7500 HarC 77083 4096 D6
Sandingham Wy
10 CNRO 77384 2676 A3
Sandisfield Ln
15700 HarC 77084 3678 C5
Sand Isle Dr
- PRLD 77545 4499 E3
Sandle St
9200 HOUS 77088 3683 D2
E Sandlebranch Cir
10 WDLD 77382 2674 D3
Sandlebranch Dr
10 WDLD 77382 2674 C2
Sandle Crest Ct
5600 HarC 77041 3679 D6
Sandlehurst Dr
3900 PASD 77504 4247 D5
Sandleigh Dr
2800 HarC 77388 3113 A5
3000 HarC 77388 3112 E5
Sandler Bnd
11900 HarC 77429 3253 E7
12000 HarC 77429 3397 E1
Sandler Ct
14600 HarC 77429 3253 B7
Sandletree Dr
- HarC 77068 3257 A5
Sandlewood Dr
3900 PASD 77504 4247 E5
Sandlewood Pl
300 LGCY 77573 4630 C6
Sandlight Ln
26600 HarC 77433 3396 A6
Sandlily Ct
10 WDLD 77380 2821 D6
Sandling Ln
- HarC 77047 4374 C3
Sand Lodge Ln
9900 HarC 77089 4504 B2
Sandman Av
300 HarC 77532 3692 D1
Sandman St
2000 HOUS 77007 3962 B1
S Sandman St
3600 HOUS 77098 3962 B7
3700 HOUS 77098 4102 B3
Sand Mist Cir
2100 LGCY 77573 4509 A6
Sandmist Dr
- FBnC 77450 3954 A7
Sand Mountain Ln
13400 HarC 77044 3550 A3
Sand Myrtle Dr
3700 HOUS 77059 4380 B4
San Domingo Ct
- GLSN 77554 5333 A2
4000 GLSN 77554 5332 D2
San Domingo Dr
4200 GLSN 77554 5333 A2
13500 GLSN 77554 5332 E3
Sandover Dr
13800 HarC 77014 3402 C3
Sandown Park Dr
10 HarC 77379 3110 D7
10 HarC 77379 3255 D1
Sand Pass Ln
10000 HarC 77064 3540 C4
Sandpebble Ct
2800 SEBK 77586 4382 B6
Sandpebble Dr
10 WDLD 77381 2820 E3
2700 SEBK 77586 4382 B6
Sandpebble Chase
13600 HOUS 77077 3957 A3
Sandpiper Cir
4900 BYTN 77521 3972 B1
7400 HMBL 77396 3406 C4
Sandpiper Ct N
1200 PRLD 77584 4501 E2
Sandpiper Ct S
1200 PRLD 77584 4501 E2
Sandpiper Dr
700 SGLD 77478 4368 B3
1000 SEBK 77586 4383 A7
2900 BYTN 77521 3972 B1
7000 HOUS 77074 4100 A5
8800 HOUS 77074 4240 A1
10900 HOUS 77096 4240 A3
11800 HOUS 77035 4240 A5
Sandpiper Ln
- LGCY 77573 4508 D6
4100 GLSN 77554 5332 D3
14400 MtgC 77302 2679 D1
14400 MtgC 77306 2533 D7
14400 MtgC 77306 2679 D1
18900 HarC 77377 2961 E7
18900 HarC 77377 2962 A7
Sand Piper Pl
10 WDLD 77381 2821 A2
Sand Piper Rd
16700 GLSN 77554 5331 D4
16700 JMAB 77554 5331 D4
Sandpiper St
2800 HMBL 77396 3406 C4
N Sandpiper St
10 LMQU 77568 4990 D6
S Sandpiper St
10 LMQU 77568 4990 D6
Sandpiper Tr
23000 HarC 77373 3115 B7
23000 HarC 77373 3260 B1
Sand Pit
- HarC 77377 3109 A4
Sand Pit Rd
- HLCS 77511 4867 E4
Sandpit Rd
600 ALVN 77511 4867 D4
600 HLCS 77511 4867 D4
Sand Plum Dr
2300 HarC 77449 3815 D5
Sand Prairie Rd
7700 HarC 77095 3538 D7
Sandprint Ct
10 WDLD 77381 2820 E5
Sandra Ct
500 MtgC 77302 2530 D4
Sandra Ln
1400 HMBL 77338 3407 A1
Sandra St
1300 PRLD 77581 4504 E5
6100 HOUS 77028 3825 D3
7500 HOUS 77016 3825 D1
9100 HOUS 77016 3686 D6
N Sandra St
100 CNRO 77301 2383 E6
S Sandra St
100 CNRO 77301 2383 E6
Sandra Ann Ct
9800 HOUS 77025 4241 E2
Sandradale St
7600 HOUS 77016 3825 D1
7600 HOUS 77028 3825 D1
Sandra Dee Rd
100 MtgC 77354 2668 C2
Sand Reef Ct
2900 LGCY 77573 4633 C3
Sand Reef Ln
3100 LGCY 77573 4633 C3
Sandri Ln
12700 HOUS 77077 3957 C7
Sandridge Ct
18900 HarC 77049 3831 A1
Sandringham Dr
800 FRDW 77546 4629 C3
8800 HOUS 77024 3961 A2
9200 HOUS 77024 3960 E2
Sand Ripple Ln
3900 HarC 77449 3815 B2
Sand River Ct
2100 FBnC 77479 4493 E2
Sand Rock Ct
6300 FBnC 77450 4094 D4
Sandrock Dr
11400 HOUS 77048 4243 E7
12000 HOUS 77048 4375 A1
12100 HOUS 77048 4374 E1
Sands Dr
6200 PASD 77505 4248 E7
Sand Sage Ln
4700 HarC 77546 4506 A6
Sandsage Ln
23100 FBnC 77494 4093 C4
Sand Shadow Ct
3200 LGCY 77573 4633 B1
Sand Shadow Dr
3100 LGCY 77573 4633 C1
Sands Key Ln
- LGCY 77573 4633 B2
Sands Point Dr
6400 HOUS 77074 4100 A3
6400 HOUS 77081 4100 A3
7700 HOUS 77036 4099 C3
11000 HOUS 77072 4098 B4
Sandspoint Dr
22100 HarC 77449 3675 E5
Sand Springs Tr
20900 HarC 77532 3410 B1
Sands Terrace Ln
7300 HarC 77389 2966 B2
Sandstone Ct
3200 BzaC 77584 4501 C6
Sand Stone Dr
1200 FBnC 77469 4365 E3
Sandstone Dr
11600 HOUS 77072 4098 A5
Sandstone Rd
6600 HOUS 77074 4100 A6
9200 HOUS 77036 4099 A5
9500 HOUS 77036 4098 E5
Sandstone St
8800 HOUS 77036 4099 A6
12300 HOUS 77072 4097 E5
Sandstone Bend Dr
14000 HarC 77047 4374 C5
Sandstone Bend Ln
- HarC 77047 4374 A4
100 LGCY 77539 4752 E3
Sandstone Canyon Dr
11300 HarC 77396 3407 E7
11400 HarC 77396 3408 A7
Sandstone Cavern Cir
20300 FBnC 77469 4234 B3
Sandstone Cavern Dr
- FBnC 77469 4234 C3
Sandstone Creek Dr
2600 PRLD 77581 4504 A3
Sandstone Creek Ln
400 LGCY 77539 4752 E5
Sandstone Falls
9100 HarC 77375 2965 D4
Sandstone Ridge Dr
2700 MSCY 77459 4498 A6
Sands Trail Ct
10100 HarC 77064 3540 C4
Sandsusky Dr
24400 HarC 77375 2965 D3
Sandswept Ln
6500 HarC 77086 3542 B1
Sandtown Cir
9800 HarC 77064 3540 C5
Sandtown Ln
9100 HarC 77064 3540 D5
Sand Tracks Ct
10100 HarC 77064 3541 D1
Sand Trap Ct
19000 HarC 77346 3265 C6
Sandtrap St
15500 WlrC 77484 3246 D6
Sandusky Ct
8700 HarC 77375 2965 D3
Sandusky Dr
- HarC 77375 2965 D4
Sandvalley Wy
2500 LGCY 77573 4752 B2
Sandwedge Dr
32000 WlrC 77484 3246 D5
Sandwedge Point Ct
6900 HarC 77389 2966 C2
Sandwith Dr
- HOUS 77449 3815 D7
20100 HarC 77449 3815 D7
Sandwood Ct
11200 HarC 77089 4378 A6
Sandy Blf
300 HOUS 77079 3956 E1
Sandy Cr
26600 MtgC 77355 2813 E3
26600 MtgC 77355 2814 A3
Sandy Ct
900 MRGP 77571 4252 A3
12100 HarC 77429 3397 B6
S Sandy Ct
4000 MSCY 77459 4497 C3
Sandy Ln
10 HarC 77562 3691 E6
100 HOUS 77336 3121 D4
600 MRGP 77571 4252 A2
1200 BYTN 77520 3973 C5
5800 PASD 77505 4248 C3
11300 GlsC 77510 4987 D6
22100 MtgC 77365 2972 C2
25200 MtgC 77365 3117 E2
Sandy Rd
10000 HOUS 77016 3686 D5
Sandy St
7800 HOUS 77028 3826 B3
Sandy Wk
500 STAF 77477 4369 C3
Sandy Arbor Ct
4700 FBnC 77494 4092 D2
Sandy Arbor Ln
26500 FBnC 77494 4092 D3
Sandy Bank Ct
2900 PRLD 77581 4503 E2
Sandy Bank Dr
11800 HarC 77375 3109 E7
Sandy Banks Ln
2000 PRLD 77581 4503 E2
Sandy Bay Ct
6500 HarC 77449 3676 D3
Sandy Bay Ln
20600 HarC 77449 3676 D3
Sandybend Ct
13700 HOUS 77044 3550 A3
Sandy Branch Ln
12200 MtgC 77362 2817 B7
Sandy Briar Ct
20900 HarC 77379 3111 C4
Sandy Brook Ln
12500 HarC 77429 3398 B5
Sandy Cedar Dr
5000 HOUS 77345 3119 E4
Sandy Cliff Dr
17300 HarC 77090 3257 E4
Sandy Coast Cir
2000 LGCY 77573 4508 E6
2000 LGCY 77573 4509 A6
Sandy Cove
- HOUS 77058 4508 B4
- NSUB 77058 4508 B4
Sandy Creek Dr
5900 BYTN 77520 3835 B7
14500 HarC 77070 3254 D7
14500 HarC 77070 3398 E1
Sandydale Ln
1500 HarC 77039 3545 D5
4900 HarC 77039 3546 C4
Sandy Falls Ct
- HarC 77044 3549 D3
Sandy Field Cir
28300 MtgC 77386 2969 E6
Sandy Field Ct
5500 BzaC 77583 4623 D4
Sandy Field Ln
2300 MtgC 77386 2969 E6
Sandyfields Ln
5000 FBnC 77494 4093 A2
Sandy Forks Dr
- HOUS 77345 3119 D5
3400 HOUS 77339 3119 B5
Sandygate Ln
7600 HarC 77095 3538 C7
Sandy Glade Ct
- HarC 77377 3253 E3
- HarC 77377 3254 A3
Sandy Glen Ln
8500 HOUS 77071 4239 C6
Sandy Grove Ct
2400 HOUS 77345 3120 A5
Sandy Grove Dr
5100 HOUS 77345 3120 A5
Sandy Hill Cir
19800 HarC 77433 3251 D5
Sandy Hill Dr
15600 HarC 77084 3678 E7
Sandy Hollow Dr
6000 HarC 77449 3677 D4
Sandy Hook Dr
12200 HarC 77089 4378 B6
12800 HOUS 77089 4378 C6
Sandy Isle Dr
7100 HarC 77389 2966 B1
Sandy Knoll Dr
2000 MSCY 77489 4370 B5
Sandy Knolls Dr
6800 HarC 77379 3256 C2
Sandy Lake Dr
1700 FRDW 77546 4629 C6
2700 HOUS 77339 3119 A5
Sandy Lodge Ct
2500 HOUS 77345 3120 A3
Sandy Meadow Ln
3500 HarC 77039 3546 A6
5100 LGCY 77573 4751 E1
Sandy Mist Ct
2600 FBnC 77494 3953 B6
Sandy Oaks Dr
- MtgC 77385 2676 C5
6100 HOUS 77050 3547 A5
Sandy Oaks Ln
3700 MSCY 77459 4621 E2
Sandy Park Ln
1500 HOUS 77339 3118 C6
Sandy Path Ln
16000 HarC 77084 3678 C4
Sandypine Cir
16800 HarC 77379 3256 E2
Sandypine Ct
5900 HarC 77379 3256 E2
5900 HarC 77379 3257 A1
Sandypine Dr
6100 HarC 77379 3256 E2
Sandypine Ln
16800 HarC 77379 3256 E2
Sandy Plains Ln
1200 HOUS 77062 4379 E7
Sandy Point Dr
2400 FBnC 77469 4365 B1
Sandy Point Ln
14100 HarC 77066 3401 E7
Sandy Port St
500 HOUS 77079 3956 E2
Sandy Reef Ct
16900 HarC 77546 4506 C7
Sandy Ridge Dr
400 LGCY 77573 4633 B2
Sandy Ridge Ln
- HarC 77084 3677 C7
- HarC 77084 3678 A7
4400 BzaC 77578 4626 A2
4400 MNVL 77578 4626 A2
6000 FBnC 77479 4493 E2
Sandy Ring Ct
16000 HarC 77429 3397 A1
Sandy Ripple Ct
14300 FBnC 77478 4366 E4
Sandy River Dr
10600 FBnC 77478 4236 E4
Sandy Runn
700 HarC 77090 3258 C2
Sandy Sage Ct
6200 FBnC 77494 4093 E5
Sandy Schoals Dr
1900 LGCY 77573 4509 A6
Sandy Shoals Dr
10700 HOUS 77071 4239 E3
Sandy Shore Dr
100 LGCY 77573 4509 C6
Sandy Shores Ln
19500 HarC 77346 3265 B5
Sandy Spring Rd
13700 MtgC 77302 2678 B7
Sandy Springs Ln
14000 SGLD 77478 4237 A5
Sandy Springs Rd
1400 HOUS 77042 3958 C5
Sandy Stone Ln
21600 HarC 77449 3815 A1
Sandy Stream Ct
19500 HarC 77375 3109 E7
Sandy Stream Dr
11700 HarC 77375 3109 D6
Sandy Trace Ct
5500 FBnC 77494 4093 A6
Sandy Trace Ln
25200 FBnC 77494 4093 B2
Sandy Trail Ct
1700 HOUS 77339 3118 C6
Sandy Valley Ct
21100 HarC 77449 3676 D4
Sandy Valley Dr
5800 HarC 77449 3676 C4
Sandy Woods Dr
19300 HarC 77375 3109 E7
San Emigdio Wy
- HOUS 77336 3266 C1
San Felipe Dr
6100 HOUS 77057 3960 C5
6400 HOUS 77063 3960 A5
7600 PNPV 77024 3960 A5
8400 PNPV 77024 3959 E5
San Felipe Rd
17000 HarC 77447 3248 E3
San Felipe St
1900 HOUS 77019 3962 A6
3200 HOUS 77019 3961 D6
3300 HOUS 77027 3961 C6
4700 HOUS 77056 3961 A5
5200 HOUS 77056 3960 D5
5700 HOUS 77057 3960 D5
San Fernando Dr
100 GLSN 77550 5109 E1
300 HOUS 77060 3544 D3
Sanford Rd
- HOUS 77071 4240 A4
4300 HOUS 77035 4241 B4
5100 HOUS 77035 4240 E4
6200 HOUS 77096 4240 B4
7600 HOUS 77071 4239 E4
9200 HOUS 77031 4239 A4
Sanford St
8100 BYTN 77521 3833 C2
San Gabriel Dr
19400 HarC 77084 3816 A5
19600 HarC 77084 3815 E5
Sangamon Ln
8900 HOUS 77074 4239 B1
Sangerbrook Dr
10500 HarC 77038 3543 C2
San Guillermo
6000 HOUS 77017 4246 A3
Sanguine Sound Ln
12000 HarC 77089 4505 A1
Sanibel Falls Ct
10400 HarC 77095 3537 D2
San Ignacio
10000 HOUS 77075 4377 D2
San Jacinto Av
- BYTN 77520 3971 E7
- BYTN 77520 3972 A6
100 LPRT 77571 4251 E4
200 HarC 77562 3831 B3
600 TXCY 77590 4875 C3
1100 FBnC 77469 4364 D7
1100 RHMD 77469 4364 D7
E San Jacinto Av
100 HarC 77562 3831 E3
San Jacinto Cir
700 BYTN 77521 3833 D5
San Jacinto Ct
1000 HOUS 77336 3266 C1
San Jacinto Dr
10 GLSN 77550 5109 E2
1600 PASD 77502 4106 E7
2100 PASD 77502 4246 E2
2700 PASD 77502 4246 E2
2700 SHUS 77502 4246 E2
2700 SHUS 77587 4246 E2
3900 GLSN 77554 5441 B4
5300 HarC 77357 2975 E1
10600 LPRT 77571 4110 D6
15400 MtgC 77302 2676 E2
San Jacinto St
- HOUS 77020 3963 D2
- HOUS 77030 4102 D4
10 HOUS 77002 3963 B5
700 RSBG 77471 4491 A4
800 HOUS 77010 3963 C4
2500 HOUS 77004 3963 B6
4400 HOUS 77004 4103 A1
4800 HOUS 77004 4102 E2
11900 HarC 77044 3551 C7
N San Jacinto St
600 HOUS 77002 3963 D3
1300 CNRO 77301 2384 A5
S San Jacinto St
100 CNRO 77301 2384 A6
San Jacinto Bay Ct
300 HOUS 77336 3266 B1
E San Jacinto Bay Loop Ct
24300 HOUS 77336 3266 A1
San Jacinto River Ct
29000 MtgC 77386 2970 B1
San Jacinto River Dr
4600 MtgC 77386 2970 B2
San Joaquin Pkwy
1800 FRDW 77546 4629 A7
San Jose Av
9000 TXCY 77591 4872 E5
9000 TXCY 77591 4873 A6
San Jose St
300 RHMD 77469 4491 D1
400 RHMD 77469 4364 D7
1700 FRDW 77546 4629 B6
5400 HOUS 77020 3964 C2
San Juan St
300 RHMD 77469 4491 D1
400 RHMD 77469 4364 D7
5200 HOUS 77020 3964 C2
San Juan Pl Dr
19700 CmbC 77520 3835 E3
San Julio Dr
300 HOUS 77018 3684 C7
300 HOUS 77022 3684 C7
San Leon Dr
10100 TXCY 77539 4755 D3
San Lorenzo
8900 HOUS 77017 4246 A2
San Lorenzo Ruiz Dr
10 FBnC 77478 4236 B3
San Lucas Dr
7200 FBnC 77083 4095 E6
San Lucia River Dr
12100 HarC 77050 3547 B6
12100 HOUS 77050 3547 B5
San Luis Blvd
200 BzaC 77541 5547 B7
San Luis Pass Pk
- BzaC 77541 5547 B6
San Luis Pass Rd
- GLSN 77554 5220 E6
- GLSN 77554 5333 B1
- GLSN 77554 5547 E4
- GLSN 77554 5548 C1
10300 GLSN 77554 5221 A6
12200 GLSN 77554 5442 B2
14900 GLSN 77554 5332 C4
16700 GLSN 77554 5331 D7
16700 JMAB 77554 5331 D7
16700 JMAB 77554 5332 A6
21200 GLSN 77554 5441 E3
23200 GLSN 77554 5440 D7
San Luis Pass Rd FM-3005
- GLSN 77554 5220 E6
- GLSN 77554 5333 B1
- GLSN 77554 5547 E4
- GLSN 77554 5548 C1
10300 GLSN 77554 5221 A6
12200 GLSN 77554 5442 A2
14900 GLSN 77554 5332 C4
San Luis Pass Rd FM-3005
16700 GLSN 77554 5331 D7
16700 JMAB 77554 5331 D7
16700 JMAB 77554 5332 A6
21200 GLSN 77554 5441 E3
23200 GLSN 77554 5440 D7
San Luis Rey Dr
14700 HarC 77083 4096 D6
San Marco Ln
2700 LGCY 77573 4632 E4
San Marcos Dr
2500 DRPK 77536 4109 E7
San Marcos St
600 HOUS 77012 4105 B2
San Marino Dr
100 GLSN 77550 5109 E1
1400 PRLD 77581 4504 D2
21500 FBnC 77450 4094 B1
San Marino St
800 SGLD 77478 4368 B2
San Martin Ln
13500 HarC 77083 4097 A6
San Mateo Ct
1500 LGCY 77573 4632 A7
San Mateo Dr
16300 HOUS 77053 4371 D6
San Miguel Dr
1900 FRDW 77546 4629 C7
San Miguel Ln
- HOUS 77060 3544 D3
San Milo Dr
15500 HarC 77068 3257 A6
San Monica Dr
- PRVW 77445 3099 E3
- WlrC 77445 3099 E3
San Morino Dr
7400 FBnC 77083 4096 B6
San Nicholas Pl
23100 FBnC 77494 4093 B3
San Nicolo Ln
- LGCY 77573 4633 A4
2700 LGCY 77573 4632 E4
Sano Dr
6100 FBnC 77494 4092 A5
San Pablo Dr
6400 HarC 77083 4095 E4
6700 HOUS 77020 3964 D4
San Pablo Gardens Dr
5200 HOUS 77045 4241 A6
San Patricio Cl
33200 MtgC 77354 2673 E3
33200 MtgC 77354 2674 A4
San Patrico Ct
8900 HarC 77064 3540 C5
San Pedro Av
3600 HOUS 77013 3827 A6
San Pellino Dr
24500 FBnC 77469 4092 E7
San Rafael Ln
13500 HarC 77083 4097 B6
San Ramon Dr
7200 HarC 77083 4096 D6
San Remo Dr
6800 HarC 77083 4096 C5
San Remo Ln
1300 LGCY 77573 4633 A4
San Rio Dr
16100 FBnC 77083 4096 A6
San Saba Ct
9200 LPRT 77571 4249 E4
San Saba St
800 HOUS 77012 4105 D3
2400 HOUS 77019 3962 A6
San Saba Canyon Cir
15900 HarC 77429 3253 C6
San Saba Canyon Ln
13700 HarC 77429 3253 C6
San Salvador Pl
23100 FBnC 77494 4093 A3
Sansbury Blvd
6100 FBnC 77469 4493 C5
6400 FBnC 77479 4493 D5
San Sebastian Ct
2000 NSUB 77058 4508 B5
San Sebastian Ln
1400 NSUB 77058 4508 A5
Sansford Cir
3300 HarC 77449 3815 E3
San Simeon Dr
10 MNVL 77583 4624 D4
7300 FBnC 77083 4096 A6
San Simieon Ct
25000 GLSN 77554 5548 B1
San Souci Dr
- HarC 77429 3252 C7
- HarC 77429 3396 C1
Sanspereil Dr
11900 HOUS 77047 4373 D2
Sans Souci Dr
15100 HarC 77429 3252 C7
Santa Anita Ln
4300 DRPK 77503 4108 D6
4300 DRPK 77536 4108 D6
4300 PASD 77503 4108 D6
Santa Anna Ln
800 LPRT 77571 4110 D6
Santa Barbara Dr
- MNVL 77583 4624 D4
Santa Barbara Wy
4600 FBnC 77469 4233 C6
Santa Bernadetta
5800 HOUS 77017 4246 A2
Santa Catalina Ct
3400 FBnC 77450 4094 B1
Santa Cecilia Ln
5800 HOUS 77017 4246 A2
Santa Chase Ln
5400 FBnC 77479 4366 E6
Santa Christi Dr
5500 HOUS 77053 4371 D7
Santa Clara Dr
- MNVL 77583 4624 E4
21400 FBnC 77450 4094 B1
Santa Clarita Cir
10 MNVL 77583 4624 D4
Santa Cruz St
9600 HOUS 77013 3826 E6
9600 HOUS 77013 3827 A6
Santa Elena St
7800 HOUS 77061 4245 C1
7900 HOUS 77017 4245 C1
Santa Elena Canyon
600 HarC 77388 3258 C1
Santa Elena Canyon Ct
19000 HarC 77388 3258 C1
Santa Fe
10 GlsC 77650 4994 D1
Santa Fe Cir
5900 DKSN 77539 4754 D1
Santa Fe Ct
1000 RSBG 77471 4490 B6
Santa Fe Dr
6600 HOUS 77061 4244 E4
7200 HOUS 77061 4245 A3
15400 STFE 77517 4869 E6
15400 STFE 77517 4870 A6
26300 MtgC 77355 2963 A4
S Santa Fe Dr
7400 HOUS 77061 4244 D5
Santa Fe Pl
2500 GLSN 77550 5109 A3
Santa Fe St
1100 CNRO 77301 2384 C5
E Santa Fe St
1400 CNRO 77301 2384 C4
W Santa Fe St
- CNRO 77304 2383 E6
300 CNRO 77301 2384 A6
500 CNRO 77301 2383 E6
Santa Fe Tr
- DRPK 77536 4109 E7
11700 STFE 77510 4871 C7
Santa Fe Creek Ct
- LMQU 77568 4872 B4
Santa Fe Springs Ct
12200 HarC 77041 3679 E5
Santa Fe Springs Dr
5700 HarC 77041 3679 E5
Santa Gertrudis Ln
7600 GlsC 77517 4986 A5
Santa Inez Ct
3400 FBnC 77450 4094 A2
Santa Isabel Ct
3400 FBnC 77450 4094 B1
Santa Lucia Ct
7700 HarC 77083 4096 D6
Santa Lucia Dr
14800 HarC 77083 4096 D6
Santa Maria St
500 SGLD 77478 4368 A3
6900 HOUS 77023 4104 E2
Santa Monica
- HOUS 77075 4377 C2
Santa Monica Blvd
9700 HOUS 77089 4377 D4
Santana Dr
3200 MtgC 77365 2974 C6
Santander Dr
1000 HOUS 77336 3121 C5
Santa Rita Dr
6500 HarC 77083 4096 A5
Santa Rosa Ln
3500 SGLD 77478 4368 B4
3500 SGLD 77478 4369 A5
Santa Rosa St
1800 HOUS 77023 4105 A2
Santa Teresa Rd
- HOUS 77045 4372 A1
13200 HOUS 77045 4241 A7
Santee Cir
4500 BYTN 77521 3972 C2
Santee Dr
4400 BYTN 77521 3972 C2
Santee St
4300 HOUS 77018 3683 B7
Santee Pass Dr
14400 HarC 77429 3253 E4
Santiago Cir
4200 GLSN 77554 5220 B7
Santiago St
4600 PASD 77504 4248 A4
4600 PASD 77505 4248 A4
7000 HOUS 77023 4104 E2
7100 HOUS 77023 4105 A2
Santiago Cove Ln
12400 HarC 77041 3679 D5
Santiago Mountain Ct
6200 FBnC 77450 4094 C4
Santo Domingo
8800 HOUS 77017 4246 A3
Santo Domingo Dr
- LGCY 77573 4632 B7
- LGCY 77573 4753 A1
Santolina Ln
18000 HarC 77449 3677 D2
Santone Ln
9900 HOUS 77076 3685 A6
Santo Park Rd
5000 TXCY 77539 4871 C1
5700 TXCY 77539 4753 C7
12000 DKSN 77510 4871 B1
12000 DKSN 77539 4871 B1
12000 GlsC 77510 4871 B1
Santos Rd
17600 HarC 77433 3252 B3
Santrey Dr
5100 HarC 77084 3678 B5
San Vicente Ln
3400 FBnC 77450 4094 B1
Sao Paulo St
4300 PASD 77504 4248 A4
4500 PASD 77505 4248 A4
Saphire Brook Dr
5700 FBnC 77469 4493 A5
Sapling Pl
10 WDLD 77382 2819 D2
Sapling Tr
- HarC 77388 3112 D5
Sapling Wy
- HOUS 77074 4239 C2
10500 HOUS 77031 4239 C3
Sapling Crest Ct
1000 FBnC 77545 4622 C1
Sapling Oak Ct
15000 HarC 77082 4096 C2
Sapling Oak Dr
3200 HarC 77082 4096 C2
E Sapling Oaks Pl
30100 MtgC 77355 2815 A2
S Sapling Oaks Pl
18900 MtgC 77355 2815 A2
W Sapling Oaks Pl
30100 MtgC 77355 2815 A2
Sapling Ridge Dr
16300 FBnC 77478 4236 A6
Sapling Trail Ct
3700 HarC 77388 3112 D5
Sapphire Cir
19200 MtgC 77355 2814 C7
Sapphire Ct
6000 TXCY 77591 4873 D5
21500 HarC 77449 3815 B2
28000 MtgC 77355 2814 D6
Sapphire Bay Ct
1300 HarC 77094 3955 A3

STREET Block City ZIP Map# Grid

Sapphire Bay Ct
5700 SGLD 77479 4495 B4
Sapphire Bay Dr
- PRLD 77584 4500 D3
Sapphire Lake Rd
20600 FBnC 77469 4234 C2
Sapphire Mist Ct
19900 HarC 77073 3403 C2
Sapphire Star Dr
3200 HarC 77082 4096 B2
Sapphire Valley Rd
- HarC 77095 3539 A7
Sapphire Vista Ln
5700 HarC 77041 3680 A5
Sara Ln
32000 MtgC 77362 2963 C2
Saracen Dr
12500 HarC 77429 3398 B4
Sara Deann Ln
19200 MtgC 77365 2972 D1
Saradon Dr
2200 SGLD 77478 4237 C5
Saragosa Dr
5700 FBnC 77469 4493 B6
Saragosa Blue Ln
7900 FBnC 77469 4094 E7
Saragosa Crossing Ln
6300 HarC 77066 3400 D5
Saragosa Pond Ln
21700 HarC 77379 3111 C2
Sarah
- MAGA 77355 2669 A6
Sarah Av
2100 HOUS 77054 4242 D1
Sarah Ln
6500 HarC 77521 3834 D4
Sarah Rd
27600 HarC 77377 3108 E3
Sarah St
2000 HOUS 77054 4242 C1
3400 HOUS 77026 3825 A7
23100 MtgC 77372 2682 A5
Sarah Ann Ct
19200 HarC 77346 3264 D5
N Sarah Deel Dr
- HarC 77598 4507 C5
- WEBS 77598 4507 C5
S Sarah Deel Dr
- HOUS 77058 4507 D6
- WEBS 77598 4507 D6
Sarah Lake Dr
12000 HOUS 77099 4238 A2
Sarah Lynn Ln
10 CNRO 77303 2237 E6
Sarah Ridge Dr
- HarC 77447 3250 A7
Sarah's Ln
12800 HOUS 77015 3967 B3
Sarah's Cove
10 SGLD 77479 4495 A2
Sarahs Landing Dr
- PRLD 77545 4499 E2
Sarah Springs Ct
25800 HarC 77373 3113 E3
Sara Jo Ln
11900 HarC 77086 3542 C5
Saranac Dr
12700 HOUS 77089 4378 D7
Sara Ridge Ln
2600 HarC 77450 3954 D6
Sara Rose St
800 HOUS 77018 3823 A3
Saras Wk
14200 HarC 77429 3397 E6
Sarasam Creek Ct
15800 HarC 77429 3253 B5
Sarasota Dr
2300 FRDW 77546 4629 A7
Saratoga Dr
2500 LGCY 77573 4631 B7
3800 HOUS 77088 3683 A2
4100 HOUS 77088 3682 E2
8500 FBnC 77479 4494 B4
Saratoga Ln
11400 TMBL 77375 3109 E3
11700 HarC 77375 3109 E3
Saratoga Sq
10500 FBnC 77459 4622 A5
Saratoga Forest Dr
8900 HarC 77088 3542 C6
Saratoga Ranch Dr
11400 HarC 77375 3109 E3
11400 TMBL 77375 3109 E3
Saratoga Springs Ln
5900 HarC 77041 3679 E5
Saratoga Woods Ln
12400 HarC 77346 3408 D2
Sardina Dr
11100 FBnC 77469 4093 B7
11100 FBnC 77469 4233 B1
Sardis Ln
3900 HOUS 77088 3683 A2
Sardis Lake Dr
- HarC 77375 3109 E6
Sarento Vil
13400 FBnC 77478 4237 B4
Sarita St
7800 HOUS 77012 4105 C5
7900 HOUS 77017 4105 C5
Sarlee Dr
200 LMQU 77568 4990 C2
Sarna Ct
4100 GLSN 77550 5108 E7
4100 GLSN 77550 5109 A6
4100 GLSN 77551 5108 E7
Sarong Dr
4100 HOUS 77025 4241 C1
4300 HOUS 77096 4241 B1
Sartartia Rd
400 FBnC 77479 4366 D7
Sarti St
- HarC 77066 3401 A1
Sashay Dr
10600 HOUS 77099 4238 A3
Sasher Ln
14300 HarC 77429 3396 D1
Sasquatch Dr
19500 HarC 77377 3109 B7
Sassafras Ln
22700 MtgC 77365 2973 D4
Sasson Blvd
8900 HarC 77044 3689 C4
Satchel Ct
11700 HarC 77038 3543 B5
Satillo Ln
1200 FBnC 77469 4493 C5
Satin Clover Ct
21600 SGCH 77355 2961 A2

Satin Tail Ln
11200 HarC 77095 3538 B1
Satinwood Dr
17500 HarC 77090 3258 C3
Satinwood Tr
19700 HarC 77346 3265 A4
Sativa Cir
7800 HarC 77521 3833 D3
Satsuma Dr
6600 HarC 77041 3679 D2
15000 HarC 77084 3678 E2
Satsuma St
900 LGCY 77573 4632 A2
900 PASD 77506 4107 E6
7100 HOUS 77023 4104 E2
7200 HOUS 77023 4105 A2
17900 GlsC 77511 4869 B4
Satsuma Sta
8700 HarC 77041 3539 B5
8700 HarC 77095 3539 B4
Satsuma Lake Dr
6700 HarC 77041 3679 D3
Satsuma Point Ct
15500 HarC 77049 3829 A1
Satsuma Vale St
7300 HarC 77433 3677 B1
Satsuma Villas Dr
12500 HarC 77041 3679 E3
Satterfield Ln
5400 HarC 77084 3678 C5
Sattler Park Dr
5800 HarC 77086 3542 D3
Saturn Ln
- NSUB 77058 4508 A4
16600 HOUS 77062 4507 C3
16800 HOUS 77058 4507 C3
17400 HOUS 77058 4508 A4
Saturnia Ln
- LGCY 77573 4632 D5
Sauer St
1900 HOUS 77003 3963 D7
1900 HOUS 77004 3963 D7
3300 HOUS 77004 4103 C1
Saulnier Cir
1100 HOUS 77019 3963 A4
Saulnier St
700 HOUS 77002 3963 A4
700 HOUS 77019 3963 A4
1600 HOUS 77019 3962 E4
W Saulnier St
300 HOUS 77019 3962 E4
Saulsworth St
11500 HOUS 77099 4238 B4
Saums Rd
- HarC 77084 3815 E6
18600 HOUS 77084 3816 B6
19000 HarC 77084 3816 B6
19900 HarC 77449 3815 E6
Saunders Rd
4600 HOUS 77093 3686 C3
4800 HarC 77093 3686 C3
7200 HOUS 77016 3686 E3
7200 HOUS 77016 3687 A3
Saunders St
- WALR 77484 3101 E5
E Saunders St
100 LGCY 77573 4632 A3
W Saunders St
100 LGCY 77573 4631 E4
100 LGCY 77573 4632 A4
Saunter Dr
200 STAF 77477 4369 C3
Saunton Dr
21400 FBnC 77450 3954 B7
Sauris Ct
1000 HarC 77038 3543 C4
Sausalito Cir
20800 MtgC 77365 3117 E2
Sausalito Dr
25000 GLSN 77554 5548 B1
Sausalito Ln
25100 MtgC 77365 3117 E1
Sauve Ln
5500 HOUS 77056 3960 E3
Savana
- HarC 77377 3108 C1
Savanna Ct N
1900 LGCY 77573 4631 C5
Savanna Ct S
1900 LGCY 77573 4631 C5
Savannah Av
900 PASD 77506 4106 E5
Savannah Bnd
2400 DRPK 77536 4109 E5
Savannah Dr
1500 FBnC 77469 4365 D4
16400 MtgC 77372 2682 B5
28700 SHEH 77381 2822 B2
Savannah Ln
3100 MSCY 77459 4497 E6
Savannah Pk
500 MtgC 77302 2530 B5
Savannah Pkwy
- BzaC 77583 4623 D5
- PRLD 77583 4623 D5
Savannah Tr
9100 HarC 77095 3538 D4
Savannah Bay Rd
20300 HarC 77433 3251 B5
Savannah Bend Dr
- BzaC 77583 4623 E3
Savannah Cove Ln
13700 BzaC 77583 4623 D4
Savannah Creek Ln
19400 HarC 77449 3677 A3
Savannah Landing Ln
14000 BzaC 77583 4623 D4
Savannah Moss Dr
200 FBnC 77469 4493 D7
Savannah Park Dr
16700 HarC 77429 3252 E6
Savannah Pines Dr
- HarC 77449 3677 A3
Savannah Springs Wy
400 HarC 77373 3113 E3
Savannah Trace Ln
- BzaC 77583 4623 D3
Savannah Woods Ln
5500 BzaC 77583 4624 A5
Savell Dr
3200 BYTN 77521 3973 E1
3500 BYTN 77521 3974 A2
Savell Rd
21800 HOUS 77339 3262 E1
E Saville Cir
9600 HarC 77065 3539 E4
W Saville Cir
9500 HarC 77065 3539 E4

Saville Ct
9500 FBnC 77083 4236 E2
Saville Ln
- HarC 77065 3539 E5
- JRSV 77065 3539 E5
Savoy Dr
5600 HOUS 77036 4100 A3
6300 HOUS 77074 4100 A3
Savoy St
100 SGLD 77478 4368 A3
Sawdust Ct
700 MtgC 77380 2968 A3
Sawdust Rd
- MtgC 77386 2968 C2
400 MtgC 77380 2968 A3
700 WDLD 77380 2968 A3
1300 WDLD 77380 2967 D2
1500 MtgC 77380 2967 D2
Sawgrass Ct
2400 LGCY 77573 4508 D7
32800 MtgC 77354 2672 B4
Sawgrass Dr
4400 BYTN 77521 3972 C2
Sawgrass Ln
- JRSV 77065 3540 A6
Sawgrass Ridge Ln
900 HOUS 77073 3259 B7
Sawhill Bridge Ln
- FBnC 77478 4236 D5
Sawleaf Cir
23200 HarC 77494 3953 D4
Sawmill Cr
- HarC 77433 3537 A1
Sawmill Dr
18800 MtgC 77355 2815 A5
Sawmill Ln
4600 PASD 77505 4249 A6
Sawmill Rd
11900 WDLD 77380 2967 E3
Sawmill Tr
7100 HOUS 77040 3542 A7
7700 HarC 77040 3542 A7
7800 HarC 77040 3541 E7
Sawmill Bend Ln
5700 FBnC 77479 4493 C1
Sawmill Cross Ln
23100 HarC 77373 2968 E6
Sawmill Grove Ct
10 WDLD 77380 2967 E2
Sawmill Grove Ln
10 WDLD 77380 2967 E2
Sawmill Pass
23300 HarC 77373 3115 A4
Sawmill Run Ln
13900 HOUS 77044 3550 B2
Sawmill Stream Cir
11700 HarC 77067 3401 E5
Saw Oaks Dr
29900 MtgC 77355 2815 A2
Sawtooth Wy
- HOUS 77082 4098 B2
E Sawtooth Canyon Dr
19100 HarC 77377 3254 E2
N Sawtooth Canyon Dr
12000 HarC 77377 3254 E2
S Sawtooth Canyon Dr
12000 HarC 77377 3254 B1
W Sawtooth Canyon Dr
19100 HarC 77377 3254 E2
Sawtooth Oak Dr
14900 HarC 77082 4096 C2
Sawyer Dr
2500 SEBK 77586 4509 B2
5900 PRLD 77581 4502 D3
Sawyer Rd
- BzaC 77581 4628 D4
- PRLD 77511 4628 D5
19600 BzaC 77511 4628 D5
Sawyer St
600 HOUS 77007 3963 A3
W Sawyer St
600 HOUS 77007 3963 A3
Sawyer Bend Ln
5800 HarC 77379 3111 D4
Sawyer Creek Ct
25200 FBnC 77494 3953 B5
Sawyerdale
1800 HOUS 77007 3963 A2
Sawyers Crossing Ln
10300 FBnC 77478 4236 D3
Sawyers Hill Ln
8400 HOUS 77040 3682 B4
8400 HOUS 77092 3682 B4
Saxet Av
6300 HOUS 77055 3822 A6
6600 HOUS 77055 3821 E6
Saxon Dr
1600 HOUS 77018 3822 B2
4900 HOUS 77092 3822 A2
5100 HOUS 77092 3821 D2
17400 HarC 77095 3537 E7
17400 HarC 77095 3538 A7
Saxon St
4700 BLAR 77401 4101 A2
4700 HOUS 77081 4101 A2
4700 HOUS 77401 4101 A2
Saxon Creek Dr
18300 HarC 77338 3407 D1
Saxon Glen Ct
25500 FBnC 77494 4092 C5
Saxon Glen Ln
9700 FBnC 77494 4092 D5
Saxon Hill Ln
7400 FBnC 77469 4094 D6
Saxon Hollow Ct
3800 HarC 77546 4505 D7
3800 HarC 77546 4506 A7
5100 HarC 77084 3678 C5
Saxon Hollow Ln
15900 HarC 77084 3678 C5
Saxon Meadow Ct
- HarC 77433 3395 E6
Saxon Meadow Ln
- HarC 77433 3395 D7
- HarC 77433 3396 B6
Saxons Wy
23300 MtgC 77447 2960 B6
Saxony Dr
13700 SGLD 77478 4237 A6
Saxony Ln
1200 NSUB 77058 4507 E5
1600 NSUB 77058 4508 A5
Saxton Ct
2900 PRLD 77581 4503 D4
Sayan Glen Ln
13000 HarC 77070 3399 C4
Saybrook Ln
800 HDWV 77024 3959 E2

Saybrook Ln
800 PNPV 77024 3959 E2
Saybrook St
16400 HOUS 77396 3405 E4
Saybrook Point Ln
12100 HarC 77375 3254 D1
Sayers St
5900 HOUS 77026 3825 B3
7900 HOUS 77016 3825 B1
S Sayko St
13000 GlsC 77510 4986 E3
Saylynn Ln
8000 HOUS 77075 4376 D2
Scales Av
16200 HarC 77530 3830 C6
Scamp Dr
13300 HarC 77429 3398 A5
Scamper Ln
16600 HarC 77532 3554 B1
Scanlan Rd
10 FBnC 77459 4621 A6
10 MSCY 77459 4621 A6
Scanlan Trc
- FBnC 77459 4621 E5
Scanlan Trc E
- FBnC 77459 4621 E6
Scanlin Rd
1700 MSCY 77489 4370 C4
1700 STAF 77477 4370 C4
1700 STAF 77489 4370 C4
1900 MSCY 77477 4370 C4
Scanlin St
2900 STAF 77477 4369 D3
Scanlock St
7700 HOUS 77012 4105 C4
Scarab Dr
13300 HarC 77041 3679 C4
Scarborough Dr
100 CNRO 77304 2529 E1
Scarborough Ln
400 HOUS 77017 4106 D7
400 HOUS 77506 4106 D6
400 PASD 77506 4106 D7
1200 PASD 77017 4106 D7
1200 PASD 77502 4106 D7
Scarborough Wy
- HarC 77047 4374 C4
Scarborough Fair St
14100 HOUS 77077 3956 E4
Scarcella Ln
12300 MDWP 77477 4237 E5
Scarlatti Dr
2300 PRLD 77581 4504 D3
Scarlet Dr
700 FBnC 77583 4623 C4
6000 HOUS 77048 4244 D5
Scarlet Cove Ct
13600 HOUS 77077 3957 A6
Scarlet Cove Dr
19300 HarC 77375 3109 D6
N Scarlet Elm Ct
10 WDLD 77382 2673 D4
S Scarlet Elm Ct
10 WDLD 77382 2673 D4
Scarlet Forest Dr
- HarC 77377 3254 B2
Scarlet Maple Ct
6600 FBnC 77479 4367 B5
Scarlet Maple Dr
200 FBnC 77479 4367 B5
Scarlet Mead Ct
10 WDLD 77384 2674 E3
Scarlet Oak Ln
14700 HarC 77377 2963 C6
E Scarlet Oak Tr
11900 CHTW 77385 2823 B4
11900 MtgC 77385 2823 B5
Scarlet Plum Ct
2500 HarC 77388 3113 A2
Scarlet Ridge Ct
6400 FBnC 77479 4367 B5
Scarlet River Dr
12200 HarC 77044 3548 E6
Scarlet Sage Dr
400 LGCY 77573 4632 E2
Scarlet Sage Ln
26200 FBnC 77494 4092 D1
Scarlet Sage Pl
10 WDLD 77381 2821 A1
Scarlet Sunset Ct
2700 SGLD 77478 4369 A7
Scarlett St
300 BYTN 77520 3971 C4
Scarlet Tanager Dr
7900 HarC 77396 3406 D5
Scarlett Bay Ct
5800 FBnC 77450 4094 C3
Scarlett Falls Ln
- FBnC 77469 4095 B6
Scarlett Manor Ct
25100 HarC 77375 2964 D2
Scarlett Oak Ct
2800 FRDW 77598 4630 C2
Scarlett Oak Dr
2900 FRDW 77598 4630 C2
Scarlet Trail Ct
- FBnC 77494 3952 C5
Scarlett Sage Ct
4200 FBnC 77494 4092 D1
Scarlet Woods Ct
10 WDLD 77380 2967 E2
Scarpinato Pl
10400 STAF 77477 4369 D1
Scarpinato Rd
10400 STAF 77477 4369 D1
Scarsdale Blvd
2100 HarC 77089 4504 D2
2100 HarC 77581 4504 D2
2100 PRLD 77581 4504 D2
10500 HarC 77089 4378 A7
10500 HOUS 77089 4378 A7
13100 HOUS 77034 4378 A7
Scarsdale Blvd FM-2553
13100 HOUS 77034 4378 D4
Scatterwood Ct
10 WDLD 77381 2821 B4
Scaup Dr
8500 HOUS 77040 3682 A3
Scenic Dr
500 BYTN 77521 3972 D4
1500 DKSN 77539 4754 E2
4700 HOUS 77048 4243 D5
Scenic Pl
- FBnC 77479 4493 D4
Scenic Rdg
23300 MtgC 77365 2974 A7
Scenic Tr
900 TMBL 77375 2963 E6

Scenic Vw
300 FRDW 77546 4505 B5
Scenic Bluff Ln
21100 HarC 77338 3261 E3
Scenic Brook Ct
10 WDLD 77382 2819 C1
Scenic Brook Dr
19800 HarC 77433 3677 C2
Scenic Canyon Ln
7900 HarC 77095 3537 E7
Scenic Cove
15000 HarC 77396 3407 D7
Scenic Cove Ct
10500 HarC 77396 3407 D7
Scenic Forest Dr
15100 CNRO 77384 2675 E2
15100 MtgC 77384 2675 E2
Scenic Gardens Dr
16700 HarC 77379 3255 E5
Scenic Glade Dr
13200 HOUS 77059 4379 E3
13200 HOUS 77059 4380 A3
Scenic Glen Dr
19900 MSCY 77459 4497 E7
Scenic Green Dr
8400 HOUS 77088 3683 A2
8800 MtgC 77354 2672 D5
Scenic Haven Dr
15400 FBnC 77083 4096 B7
Scenic Hollow Ct
2100 HarC 77450 3954 D5
Scenic Hollow Dr
- HarC 77450 3954 D5
Scenic Knoll Dr
16900 MtgC 77385 2676 D5
Scenic Lake Ct
17300 HarC 77429 3252 D6
Scenic Lakes Wy
16900 HarC 77095 3538 A7
Scenic Meadow Ct
1600 PRLD 77581 4375 E7
Scenic Mill Pl
10 WDLD 77382 2674 E5
Scenic Mountain Ct
1600 HOUS 77345 3120 D6
Scenic Oaks Dr
17700 FBnC 77469 4095 C5
Scenic Orchard Ln
3900 FBnC 77469 4366 D1
Scenic Park Dr
1900 MtgC 77386 2969 A1
Scenic Path Ct
14200 HarC 77429 3396 D2
Scenic Peaks Ct
16500 PASD 77059 4380 D5
Scenic Point Ct
15500 HarC 77433 3251 C6
Scenic Ridge Dr
1400 HOUS 77043 3819 A7
Scenic River Dr
11400 HarC 77044 3688 D7
Scenic Shore Ct
3100 SEBK 77586 4382 D7
8200 SGLD 77478 4368 A3
Scenic Shore Dr
1500 HOUS 77345 3120 B7
2200 SEBK 77586 4382 C6
Scenicside Ln
7900 HarC 77379 3256 A1
Scenic Valley Dr
3500 HOUS 77345 3119 D3
Scenic View Ct
3000 SEBK 77586 4382 B7
Scenic View Dr
15700 HOUS 77062 4380 C7
Scenic Villa Ct
15100 HarC 77396 3407 C7
Scenic Vista Dr
10300 HarC 77396 3407 C7
Scenic Water Dr
15800 HarC 77044 3408 E5
Scenic Woodland Dr
15200 CNRO 77384 2675 E2
Scenic Woods Cir
20300 HarC 77433 3251 E6
Scenic Woods Dr
10500 HOUS 77016 3687 B3
20300 HarC 77433 3251 C6
Scenic Woods Tr
4800 HOUS 77345 3120 A1
Scented Candle Wy
18700 HarC 77388 3113 C2
Scented Path Ln
10 WDLD 77381 2820 B3
Scent Fern St
8900 HarC 77064 3540 E1
Sceptre Cir
7800 HOUS 77072 4097 E6
Schade Ln
100 HOUS 77037 3684 D2
Schaff St
- HOUS 77017 4105 D5
Schaffer Ln
8200 HarC 77070 3399 D3
Schalker Dr
3600 HOUS 77026 3824 E5
Schambray St
6600 HOUS 77085 4371 C4
Schanzer Rd
9600 HTCK 77563 4988 A4
Schaper Dr
10100 GLSN 77554 5221 C3
Scharpe St
1200 HOUS 77023 4104 B1
Schaspry Dr
- HarC 77069 3256 E7
Schattel Ln
9500 GLSN 77554 5107 B6
Schattel Rd
13600 STFE 77510 4870 D4
Schauer Ln
20400 HarC 77377 3107 A5
Schauer Jones Rd
15100 HarC 77377 3108 C2
Schaumburg Dr
6000 HarC 77388 3111 E2
Scherer Ln
22800 HarC 77377 2963 C7
Scherzo Ln
7900 HarC 77040 3541 C7
Schetty St
6200 HOUS 77396 3406 A5
Schevers St
5600 HOUS 77033 4244 B4
6200 HOUS 77087 4244 D4
Schiel Rd
20000 HarC 77433 3251 D4
22500 HarC 77433 3250 D3

Schiel Rd
22500 HarC 77447 3250 D3
Schiel Nursery
- HarC 77375 2964 C4
- TMBL 77375 2964 C4
Schilder Dr
1500 HOUS 77093 3685 D5
Schiller Av
6300 HOUS 77055 3822 A6
6600 HOUS 77055 3821 E6
Schiller Rd
13800 HarC 77082 4096 E3
13800 HarC 77082 4097 A3
13800 HOUS 77082 4097 A3
14400 HOUS 77082 4096 D3
Schiller St
7400 HOUS 77055 3821 D6
Schiller Park Ln
4600 FBnC 77479 4366 C7
12800 HarC 77014 3402 A2
Schilling Av
10 BYTN 77520 3973 A5
200 BYTN 77520 3972 E5
Schindewolf Ln
- HarC 77388 3112 C5
Schiro Rd
8000 HTCK 77563 4988 D5
Schivener House Ln
24200 HarC 77493 3814 B6
Schleider Dr
2300 PRLD 77581 4503 D3
Schletty
6300 HOUS 77396 3406 A5
Schley St
6900 HOUS 77087 4105 A3
Schlipf Rd
- WlrC 77494 3951 B1
2200 WlrC 77493 3812 B5
3400 WlrC 77493 3951 B1
Schlitz Rd
6800 GlsC 77563 4990 B6
Schlumberger Dr
200 SGLD 77478 4368 C1
Schlumberger St
2200 HOUS 77023 4104 B3
S Schlumberger-gulf Frwy
- HOUS 77023 4104 B3
Schmidt Rd
- WlrC 77445 3244 D6
13800 HarC 77065 3398 A7
13800 HarC 77429 3397 E7
13800 HarC 77429 3398 A7
Schnebelen
10700 MtgC 77302 2531 A7
Schneider Cir
22000 MtgC 77447 2960 C4
Schneider Rd
6900 HOUS 77093 3824 D2
8400 HOUS 77093 3685 D7
Schochler Dr
- LPRT 77571 4249 C4
- PASD 77505 4249 C4
- PASD 77571 4249 C4
Schoettle Rd
15100 CNRO 77384 2675 C2
15100 MtgC 77384 2675 C2
Scholarship Row
14200 HOUS 77077 3956 E5
Scholl Rd
- HarC 77377 2961 D7
21000 HarC 77377 3106 D2
Scholl St
- HOUS 77034 4378 E3
- HOUS 77034 4379 A4
E School Av
- MTBL 77520 3696 E5
W School Av
- MTBL 77520 3696 D5
School Drwy
- MtgC 77385 2822 B4
- ORDN 77385 2822 B4
- SHEH 77385 2822 B4
School Pl
- HOUS 77030 4102 B4
School Rd
- MNVL 77578 4746 D2
3500 FBnC 77545 4499 A7
3800 FBnC 77545 4623 A2
School St
100 MSCY 77489 4370 B3
100 TMBL 77375 2964 B7
400 TMBL 77375 3109 B1
800 LGCY 77573 4632 B3
Schooley Dr
8600 HOUS 77071 4239 C5
Schooner Dr
200 BzaC 77541 5547 A7
Schooner St
900 HarC 77532 3552 A3
Schooner Wy
- LGCY 77573 4508 E6
Schooner Cove Ln
800 LGCY 77573 4633 B3
Schooners Wy
16700 HarC 77546 4506 A6
Schoppa Ln
5200 BYTN 77520 3971 D1
5200 HarC 77520 3971 D1
5200 HarC 77521 3832 D7
5200 HarC 77521 3971 D1
E Schreck St
100 BYTN 77520 3971 C3
W Schreck St
200 BYTN 77520 3971 B3
Schroeder Ln
10 BzaC 77511 4747 E6
400 BzaC 77511 4748 A6
19200 HarC 77377 3107 C7
19200 HarC 77429 3107 C7
19200 HarC 77433 3107 C7
Schroeder Rd
5800 HOUS 77021 4104 A6
12900 HarC 77070 3399 E3
12900 HOUS 77070 3399 E3
Schroeder St
4400 HOUS 77003 3964 B5
4400 HOUS 77011 3964 B5
Schubach Dr
10 FBnC 77479 4367 A6
Schubert St
1000 DKSN 77539 4752 E7
Schuler St
4100 HOUS 77007 3962 C2
6300 HOUS 77007 3961 E2
Schuller Rd
6700 HOUS 77026 3825 A3
6700 HOUS 77093 3825 A2
8400 HOUS 77093 3685 E7

Schuller Pl Ct
3000 HOUS 77093 3825 A2
Schulte Ln
2000 FRDW 77546 4750 A2
Schultz Ln
10 HOUS 77084 3818 A1
Schumacher Ln
5300 HOUS 77056 4100 E1
5600 HOUS 77057 4100 D1
8600 HOUS 77063 4099 D1
Schumann Ct
8200 FBnC 77083 4096 B7
Schumann Ln
15300 FBnC 77083 4096 B7
Schumann Oaks Dr
3000 MtgC 77386 2969 D2
Schumann Trails
13400 FBnC 77478 4366 E2
Schurmier Rd
700 HOUS 77047 4373 B4
3500 HarC 77047 4374 E4
3800 HOUS 77047 4374 E4
3800 HOUS 77048 4374 E4
4600 HOUS 77048 4375 A4
5900 HOUS 77048 4376 A4
Schuttle Wy
17000 HarC 77532 3552 B1
Schutz St
5600 HOUS 77032 3405 D5
5700 HOUS 77396 3405 D5
Schwab Ln
10 HOUS 77055 3821 D6
Schwartz Dr
11200 GLSN 77554 5221 A5
Schwartz St
- HOUS 77020 3963 E2
1200 HOUS 77020 3964 A2
4100 GlsC 77518 4634 C3
Schweikhart St
1400 HOUS 77020 3964 C1
2800 HOUS 77026 3825 C7
Sciaaca Rd
2000 HarC 77373 3114 C4
Scofield Ln
10200 HOUS 77096 4240 E2
Scone St
4100 HarC 77084 3817 C1
4300 HarC 77084 3678 C7
Scopel Rd
5500 BzaC 77578 4626 B4
5500 MNVL 77578 4626 B4
5500 MNVL 77584 4626 B3
6300 BzaC 77511 4626 D6
Scoregga Ln
13700 HarC 77037 3545 A6
Scot Ct
4800 SGLD 77479 4495 C4
Scotch Grove Ct
12700 HarC 77014 3402 A3
Scotch Hollow Ln
16300 FBnC 77083 4236 A2
Scotch Moss Ln
3100 DRPK 77536 4249 D3
3100 LPRT 77536 4249 D3
3100 LPRT 77571 4249 D3
Scotch Pine Ct
10 WDLD 77382 2674 A5
Scotch Pine Dr
6200 HarC 77049 3828 C3
Scotch Pine Pl
8500 HarC 77375 3110 D2
Scotch Pine St
1900 TMBL 77375 3109 B3
Scotch Pines Dr
5700 HarC 77049 3828 C3
Scothwood Dr
6100 HarC 77449 3677 B4
Scotland St
4300 HOUS 77007 3962 B3
Scotney Castle St
14300 HarC 77095 3679 A1
Scotsbrook Dr
10100 HarC 77038 3543 D3
Scotsmoor Ct
10 SGLD 77479 4495 C2
Scots Pine Ln
6700 HarC 77049 3828 E2
Scott Av
100 BYTN 77520 3973 A6
200 BYTN 77520 3972 E6
400 PASD 77506 4107 C4
7400 MNVL 77578 4625 E7
7400 MNVL 77578 4626 A7
Scott Cir
14600 HarC 77429 3538 D1
Scott Dr
- DRPK 77536 4109 A7
- DRPK 77536 4249 A1
Scott Ln
4700 PRLD 77581 4376 A7
6400 PRLD 77581 4375 E7
Scott Rd
- HarC 77336 3122 C5
Scott St
200 CNRO 77301 2384 A4
1000 HOUS 77003 3963 E7
1200 LMQU 77568 4990 A2
1900 LMQU 77568 4989 E2
2100 HOUS 77004 3963 E7
2400 HOUS 77004 4103 E1
4200 STFE 77517 4870 B7
5400 HOUS 77021 4103 C7
7400 HOUS 77021 4243 C1
7600 HOUS 77051 4243 C5
8000 MNVL 77578 4625 E7
8000 MNVL 77578 4747 A1
11600 HarC 77375 2964 E4
11800 HOUS 77047 4243 B7
11900 HOUS 77047 4374 C1
13500 HarC 77047 4374 C4
14600 HarC 77429 3397 D7
Scott-Cemetery Rd
3600 STFE 77517 4870 C5
Scottcrest Dr
5800 HOUS 77021 4103 D5
Scotter Ln
14800 HarC 77015 3829 B5
14900 HarC 77530 3829 C5
Scott Gardner Rd
19700 MtgC 77357 2828 E5
Scottish Woods
- HOUS 77365 2974 D7
- HOUS 77365 3119 D1
Scottline Dr
- HOUS 77059 4249 A7
- PASD 77059 4249 A7
- PASD 77505 4249 A7
5100 PASD 77505 4248 E7

STREET
Block City ZIP Map# Grid

Scott Reef Dr
4800 GlsC 77539 4634 C4
Scotts Bluff Ct
17300 HarC 77346 3408 C3
Scottsbury Ct
24500 FBnC 77494 3953 B7
Scottsdale Ct
2300 LGCY 77573 4508 E7
11800 MDWP 77477 4238 B5
Scottsdale Dr
11300 HarC 77099 4238 B5
12000 MDWP 77477 4238 A5
12200 MDWP 77477 4237 E4
Scottsdale Palms Dr
2500 MSCY 77459 4498 A6
Scotts Landing Cir
24600 HarC 77375 2965 A3
Scotts Landing Ct
10400 HarC 77375 2965 A3
Scotts Landing Dr
10300 HarC 77375 2965 A3
Scotts Point Dr
19000 HarC 77375 3109 D7
Scottwood Dr
- BYTN 77521 3833 B7
- HarC 77521 3833 B7
5100 BYTN 77521 3972 B1
Scotty St
30000 MtgC 77355 2816 A2
Scouts Ln
12600 HarC 77429 3398 A5
Scramble Ct
17100 FBnC 77478 4235 E7
Scranton Av
8400 HOUS 77061 4245 E6
8400 HOUS 77075 4245 E6
8600 HOUS 77061 4246 A6
8600 HOUS 77075 4246 A6
Screech Owl Ct
24500 FBnC 77494 3953 A4
Scribe St
800 MtgC 77357 2829 C2
E Scribewood Cir
10 WDLD 77382 2819 A2
N Scribewood Cir
10 WDLD 77382 2819 A2
S Scribewood Cir
10 WDLD 77382 2819 B3
Scribner Rd
6300 HOUS 77074 4100 B5
6300 HOUS 77081 4100 B5
Scrivener Ln
23900 HarC 77493 3814 B5
Scrowl Ct
- HarC 77532 3551 E4
Scrub Jay Ln
14700 HarC 77375 2963 C4
14700 HarC 77377 2963 C4
14700 TMBL 77375 2963 C4
Scrub Oak Ct
17700 FBnC 77469 4095 C5
Scrub Oak Dr
17800 FBnC 77469 4095 C5
Scruggs Rd
12200 PNIS 77445 3099 E6
12200 PNIS 77445 3100 A7
Scull Ct
800 HarC 77532 3552 A5
Scullers Cove Ct
10 WDLD 77381 2821 C4
Sculling Wy Dr
- HarC 77346 3265 D6
- HOUS 77346 3265 D6
Scyrus Ln
12200 HarC 77066 3400 D2
12500 HarC 77069 3400 D2
Sea Anchor Wy
500 HarC 77532 3552 A1
Seaberg Rd
13000 HarC 77532 3694 B1
Seabird Dr
- SEBK 77586 4382 E7
4100 GLSN 77554 5441 C4
Seabird St
4700 BYTN 77521 3833 C3
4700 HarC 77521 3833 C3
Seabiscuit Dr
21000 TMBL 77375 3109 E3
Sea Biscuit Ln
12400 HOUS 77071 4239 B5
Seablossom Ln
20100 HarC 77449 3815 D6
Seabluff Ct
11200 HarC 77433 3396 A7
Seabluff Ln
- HOUS 77034 4378 C4
Seaboard Lp
10800 HOUS 77099 4238 C4
Seabold Dr
2700 MSCY 77459 4498 A5
Seaborough Ln
400 LGCY 77573 4508 E6
Seabourne Creek Ln
1800 FBnC 77471 4614 E5
1800 FBnC 77471 4615 A5
Seabourne Meadows Dr
100 RSBG 77471 4490 B6
Sea Branch Dr
18200 HarC 77084 3816 D3
Sea Breeze Ct
1800 MSCY 77459 4369 C6
Seabreeze Dr
100 LGCY 77573 4633 C3
Seabreeze Ln
700 GLSN 77550 5110 B1
2300 PRLD 77545 4499 E2
Sea Breeze St
900 LPRT 77571 4252 A3
Seabright Ct
2900 LGCY 77573 4633 A3
Seabrook Cir
2100 SEBK 77586 4382 C7
Seabrook Ln
7300 HarC 77521 3833 D4
Seabrook St
- SEBK 77586 4382 B7
3400 HOUS 77021 4103 B7
Seabrook Shipyard Rd
- SEBK 77586 4509 D4
Seabrough Dr
2500 PRLD 77584 4500 C3
Seabury Ct
1200 FBnC 77494 3953 A3
Sea Butterfly
11400 GLSN 77554 5221 A6
11600 GLSN 77554 5220 E6
Sea Channel Ct
2800 SEBK 77586 4382 B7

Sea Channel Dr
2800 SEBK 77586 4382 B7
Seacliff Dr
400 HOUS 77598 4506 E4
700 HOUS 77062 4507 A4
Seaco Av
800 DRPK 77536 4109 A5
Seaco Ct
800 DRPK 77536 4109 A4
Sea Cove Ct
2000 NSUB 77058 4508 B6
Sea Cove Dr
2100 PRLD 77584 4500 C2
Seacrest Blvd
300 LGCY 77573 4633 C3
Seacrest Park Rd
100 BHCY 77520 4254 E2
100 CmbC 77520 4254 E2
Sea Eagle
4100 GLSN 77554 5333 A2
Seafield Dr
1400 HarC 77530 3829 B4
Seafoam Rd
400 HOUS 77598 4506 E4
1100 HOUS 77062 4507 B3
Seaford Dr
10500 HOUS 77075 4377 D3
10500 HOUS 77089 4377 D3
Seagate Ln
1400 HOUS 77062 4507 B2
Seagler Rd
800 HOUS 77042 3958 E7
2700 HOUS 77042 4098 E1
Seagler Glen Ln
- HarC 77449 3677 A6
Seagler Park Ln
13200 HOUS 77047 4373 B3
Seagler Pond Ln
1300 HarC 77073 3403 C2
Seaglers Point Ln
11600 FBnC 77469 4092 C6
Seagler Springs Ln
14000 HOUS 77044 3550 B2
Seagram St
11500 JTCY 77029 3966 D3
Sea Grass Ln
4000 GLSN 77554 5441 C4
Seagrove Av
100 SRAC 77571 4383 A1
400 SRAC 77571 4382 E2
Sea Grove Ct
12300 HarC 77041 3679 B7
Seagrove Dr
11800 PRLD 77584 4500 C3
Sea Gull Dr
- GLSN 77554 5332 E3
Seagull Ln
8300 PRLD 77584 4501 E5
Seagull St
1600 HOUS 77017 4106 C7
Sea Horse Ct
2500 SEBK 77586 4382 C6
Seahorse Dr
15000 HOUS 77062 4380 A7
15200 HOUS 77062 4507 B1
16100 HOUS 77058 4507 C1
Seahorse Ln
26900 MtgC 77355 2961 A1
26900 SGCH 77355 2961 A1
Seahorse Cove
3200 SGLD 77479 4496 A2
Seahurst Ct
2300 LGCY 77573 4508 C6
Sea Island Dr
13500 HarC 77069 3400 B2
Seakale Ln
1900 HOUS 77062 4507 C2
2000 HOUS 77058 4507 C2
Sea King St
2000 HOUS 77008 3822 D5
Sea Land
- MRGP 77571 4251 E1
Sealander Ct
16100 HarC 77532 3552 B3
Sealander St
100 HarC 77532 3552 B3
Sea Lark Rd
15700 HOUS 77062 4507 A2
Sea Ledge Ct
4100 SEBK 77586 4382 B6
Sea Ledge Dr
2700 SEBK 77586 4382 B6
Sealey St
6500 HOUS 77091 3683 D4
7700 HOUS 77088 3683 D2
Sea Liner Dr
15700 HOUS 77062 4507 A2
Seal Valley Ln
22300 FBnC 77450 4093 E3
Sealy Av
4500 GLSN 77550 5108 D4
5000 GLSN 77551 5108 C4
Sealy Ct
4300 FBnC 77469 4233 E5
Sealy St
600 GLSN 77550 5109 A4
3700 GLSN 77550 5108 E4
E Sealy St
100 ALVN 77511 4867 C1
W Sealy St
100 ALVN 77511 4867 A1
1800 ALVN 77511 4866 E1
Seamaster Dr
700 HOUS 77062 4507 A4
Sea Meadow Ct
4100 HarC 77449 3816 B1
Sea Mist
10700 MtgC 77354 2671 D5
Seamist Cir
2300 SEBK 77586 4382 C6
Seamist Ct
2000 HOUS 77008 3822 D5
Sea Mist Dr
100 LGCY 77573 4509 B6
Seamist Dr
1100 HOUS 77008 3822 D6
Sea Myrtle Dr
10700 HarC 77095 3538 B2
Sea Myrtle Ln
13900 SGLD 77478 4237 A4
Sean Ct
5900 HarC 77346 3264 D6
Sean Park Ct
8200 HarC 77095 3539 A6
Sea Oak Ct
4900 PASD 77505 4248 D7
Sea Palms Ct
2000 HarC 77532 3551 D3

Sea Palms Dr
15900 HarC 77532 3551 D3
Seapine Dr
20700 HarC 77450 3954 C3
Sea Pines Pl
3000 LGCY 77573 4508 E7
Sea Queen Ct
1800 HOUS 77008 3822 D5
Seargent St
2900 SEBK 77586 4509 B3
Searidge Ln
- SEBK 77586 4510 A1
Searle Dr
3800 HOUS 77009 3824 B6
Searles Blvd
1500 SGLD 77478 4368 C4
Sears Dr
19100 HOUS 77338 3262 A6
Sears Ln
23800 MtgC 77365 2973 E6
Sears Rd
200 ARLA 77583 4623 A7
200 FBnC 77583 4623 A7
6800 ARLA 77583 4622 E7
Searston Dr
14600 HarC 77084 3679 A3
Seascape Ln
200 LGCY 77539 4753 B4
Seascape Run
11600 MtgC 77354 2671 C6
Sea Shadow Bnd
11800 PRLD 77584 4500 C3
Seashell Ct
4100 SEBK 77586 4382 C6
Seashore Cir
3800 SEBK 77586 4382 B7
Sea Shore Dr
11600 HOUS 77072 4098 A6
12100 HOUS 77072 4097 E6
Seashore Dr
2600 SEBK 77586 4382 C6
Seaside
2300 GlsC 77539 4635 D4
Seaside Cir
11400 GLSN 77554 5221 A6
Seaside Dr
1500 GLSN 77550 5110 B1
Seaside Ln
10 TXCY 77590 4875 E3
15600 HOUS 77062 4507 A2
Sea Smoke Ln
500 HOUS 77079 3956 E2
Season Ct
7400 HarC 77346 3265 A3
Seasons Tr
3200 HOUS 77345 3119 E2
N Seasons Trc
10 WDLD 77382 2819 B1
Seasons Wy
20100 HarC 77433 3251 C5
N Seasons Trace Cir
10 WDLD 77382 2819 B1
S Seasons Trace Cir
- WDLD 77382 2819 B1
Seaspray Ct
1800 HOUS 77008 3822 D5
Seastone Ln
4000 HarC 77068 3257 A6
Seast Rand Ln
2800 LGCY 77539 4752 E2
Seaswept Dr
12400 HOUS 77071 4239 D7
Seaton Ct
10 SGLD 77479 4495 E3
Seaton Dr
18500 HarC 77449 3677 C4
Seaton Gln
200 HarC 77094 3955 B1
Seaton Valley Dr
6600 HarC 77379 3256 E4
Seattle St
15600 JRSV 77040 3680 D1
Seattle Slew Dr
12500 HarC 77065 3539 E5
12500 HarC 77065 3540 A6
12500 JRSV 77065 3539 E5
12500 JRSV 77065 3540 A6
Sea Turtle Ct
17900 SGCH 77355 2961 A1
Sea Turtle Ln
25000 SGCH 77355 2961 A4
26900 MtgC 77355 2961 A2
Sea Urchin
3700 GLSN 77554 5221 A6
Seavale Rd
15700 HOUS 77062 4507 B1
Seaview Ct
- BHCY 77520 4254 D3
4100 SEBK 77586 4382 C6
Seawall Blvd
10 GLSN 77550 4995 B7
10 GLSN 77550 5110 A1
100 GLSN 77550 5109 E2
4100 GLSN 77550 5108 E7
4100 GLSN 77551 5108 E7
5300 GLSN 77551 5222 D1
7900 GLSN 77554 5222 B2
8500 GLSN 77554 5221 D4
Seawall Blvd FM-3005
300 GLSN 77550 5109 C4
4100 GLSN 77550 5108 E7
4100 GLSN 77551 5108 E7
5300 GLSN 77551 5222 D1
7900 GLSN 77554 5222 B2
8500 GLSN 77554 5221 D4
Seawall Blvd SR-87
300 GLSN 77550 5109 E3
Seaward Dr
2500 SEBK 77586 4382 C7
Seaway Dr
500 ELGO 77586 4509 B1
Seawolf Dr
16600 HarC 77058 4507 B4
16600 HarC 77062 4507 B4
16600 HOUS 77062 4507 A4
Seawolf Pkwy
- GLSN 77554 5108 D1
1800 GLSN 77554 4994 D6
Seawood Dr
11700 HarC 77089 4378 B6
Sebago Ct
4400 PRLD 77584 4503 B6
Sebago Dr
3500 PRLD 77584 4503 B6
Sebastian Cir
18900 HarC 77346 3265 C7
Sebastian Dr
21500 MtgC 77365 2973 B3

Sebastian Hill Dr
6100 FBnC 77494 4092 A5
Sebastopol Dr
4600 PRLD 77584 4503 B3
Seber Dr
8500 HarC 77375 2965 D6
Secluded Dr
2900 FBnC 77478 4236 A7
Seclusion Dr
5600 HarC 77049 3828 B4
Seco Creek Ln
17800 HarC 77396 3407 D2
Seco Mines Ln
1200 FBnC 77469 4493 B5
Second
- FBnC 77545 4499 D5
Second St
1800 HarC 77336 3266 E2
26100 HarC 77373 3114 A2
Secretariat Ct
12300 HOUS 77071 4239 B4
Secretariat Dr
4200 PASD 77503 4108 D7
9500 HarC 77065 3539 D5
Secretariat Ln
1500 FBnC 77469 4365 A3
7600 HOUS 77071 4239 E6
Secretariat Ridge Dr
7400 HarC 77338 3261 D4
Secretariet Dr
2000 STAF 77477 4370 B4
Secret Branch Ct
8600 HarC 77433 3537 D6
Secret Branch Ln
17900 HarC 77433 3537 D6
Secret Canyon Dr
9500 HarC 77095 3538 E4
Secret Forest Ct
12700 HarC 77429 3397 C4
Secret Forest Ln
3000 FBnC 77459 4621 C6
Security Dr
7400 JRSV 77040 3680 E2
Security Ln
9000 HarC 77049 3690 D4
Security Rd
18000 HOUS 77032 3404 E2
Sedalia St
6200 HOUS 77021 4103 B4
Sedalia Brook Ln
3700 FBnC 77494 4093 C3
Sedalia Springs Ct
13800 HOUS 77077 3957 A7
Sedberry
4400 TYLV 77586 4508 E1
Seddon Rd
4800 PRLD 77581 4502 A1
Seders Wk
10 WDLD 77381 2821 A3
Sedgeborough Cir
- HarC 77084 3815 E4
3100 HarC 77449 3815 E3
Sedgeborough Dr
- HarC 77449 3815 E3
3000 HarC 77084 3815 E3
Sedgecreek Dr
19500 HarC 77449 3816 A2
Sedgefield St
29400 MtgC 77386 2969 C4
Sedgehill Ct
- HarC 77014 3401 D3
Sedgehill Dr
3300 HarC 77014 3401 D3
Sedgemoor Dr
8800 HarC 77375 2965 D4
Sedgewick Pl
10 WDLD 77382 2819 D1
Sedge Wren Ct
9500 FBnC 77083 4236 A2
Sedgie Dr
1900 HOUS 77080 3820 C5
Sedgwick Dr
400 HOUS 77076 3685 A3
Sedlia Point Ln
- HarC 77044 3689 B4
Sedona Ct
7100 HarC 77083 4097 A5
Sedona Hls
7100 HarC 77069 3400 A1
Sedona Creek Dr
2700 MSCY 77459 4497 E6
2700 MSCY 77459 4498 B5
Sedona Ranch Ln
20800 HarC 77388 3112 B3
Sedona Springs Ln
16800 HarC 77379 3256 E2
Sedona Woods Ln
16300 HarC 77082 4096 A4
16400 HarC 77082 4095 E4
Sedora Dr
300 FRDW 77546 4629 B1
Seedling Dr
15700 HarC 77032 3404 A6
Seegers Trail Dr
6300 HarC 77066 3400 E5
Seeker St
7800 HOUS 77028 3826 D1
9200 HOUS 77028 3687 D6
9600 HOUS 77078 3687 D5
Sego Park Ln
- HarC 77041 3680 A5
Segovia Dr
- LGCY 77573 4632 A7
Segrest Dr
11600 HOUS 77047 4243 C7
11900 HOUS 77047 4374 C1
13500 HarC 77047 4374 C3
Seguin Ct
9300 LPRT 77571 4250 A4
Seguine Dr
2400 DRPK 77536 4109 E6
Segunda Ln
6900 FBnC 77583 4623 A7
Seidel Rd
17400 HarC 77377 3107 C2
Seidel Cemetery Rd
17500 HarC 77377 3107 B3
Seine Ct
2900 HarC 77014 3401 E3
Seinfeld Ct
6600 HarC 77069 3400 B2
Sekola Ln
1900 MtgC 77386 2969 B2
Sela Ln
12000 HOUS 77072 4097 E6
12000 HOUS 77072 4098 A6
Selder Dr
16700 HarC 77546 4506 A6

Self Rd
17100 HarC 77377 3107 D6
19300 HarC 77377 3108 B6
Self St
4600 GlsC 77511 4869 D6
4600 GlsC 77517 4869 D6
Selinsky Rd
- HOUS 77047 4243 D7
4900 HOUS 77048 4243 D7
5300 HOUS 77048 4244 A7
Selkirk Dr
100 FBnC 77479 4366 D5
Sellers
1100 HOUS 77007 3962 E3
Sellers Rd
14000 HarC 77037 3544 E5
14000 HarC 77060 3544 E2
15700 HOUS 77060 3544 E2
Selma St
7000 HOUS 77030 4102 D5
Selman Ln
7600 MtgC 77354 2673 A3
Selsdon Ct
28400 HarC 77336 3121 D3
Selva St
1300 PASD 77504 4247 D7
Selwyn Dr
14800 HarC 77015 3829 B4
Selznick Pk
25100 HarC 77375 2964 D2
W Semands Av
300 CNRO 77301 2384 A3
400 CNRO 77301 2383 E3
1400 CNRO 77304 2383 D4
E Semands St
100 CNRO 77301 2384 B3
Seminar Dr
500 HOUS 77060 3403 D6
Seminary Ridge Ln
16600 FBnC 77083 4235 D1
Seminole Ct
3300 SGLD 77479 4495 B3
Seminole Dr
100 LGCY 77565 4508 E4
500 LGCY 77565 4509 A5
4100 PRLD 77584 4503 A7
9500 MtgC 77354 2818 C7
Seminole St
1200 DRPK 77536 4109 C6
4200 PASD 77504 4248 A6
7100 HarC 77521 3833 B4
7600 BYTN 77521 3835 B5
Seminole Tr
24100 MtgC 77365 2974 B7
Seminole Canyon Dr
15400 FBnC 77478 4236 B6
Seminole Hill Ln
26200 FBnC 77494 4092 E2
Seminole Lodge Ln
6600 HarC 77379 3111 B3
Seminole Park Ln
23100 HarC 77373 2968 E6
Seminole Spring Ln
11000 HarC 77089 4377 A7
11000 HarC 77089 4504 B1
Semmans Ln
5200 HOUS 77040 3681 E7
Semmes St
1100 HOUS 77020 3963 E2
1600 HOUS 77026 3963 E1
6900 HOUS 77093 3824 E2
Senate Av
7200 JRSV 77040 3680 D2
8500 JRSV 77040 3540 D7
8600 HarC 77064 3540 D7
8600 JRSV 77064 3540 D7
Senate St
2100 PASD 77502 4247 E1
Senca Park Dr
13700 HOUS 77077 3957 A4
Senda Ct
6400 HarC 77346 3264 E5
Sendera Dr
8500 MtgC 77354 2672 E3
Sendera Ln
11600 FBnC 77469 4235 D6
Sendera Oaks Ct
7500 HarC 77433 3676 C2
Sendera Oaks Ln
20100 HarC 77433 3676 E1
Sendera Ranch Dr
1600 MtgC 77354 2673 C1
Sendero Blvd
10900 FBnC 77469 4232 E1
11100 FBnC 77469 4092 E7
Sendero St
1700 FBnC 77469 4232 A6
Seneca Ct
2000 LGCY 77573 4631 A6
4600 HarC 77521 3833 B3
Seneca Ln
10800 HOUS 77016 3686 E2
Seneca Pl
10 WDLD 77382 2673 E5
Seneca Pt
20200 HarC 77379 3112 A3
Seneca St
4200 PASD 77504 4248 A6
10600 HOUS 77016 3686 E3
Seneca Tr
9900 MtgC 77354 2818 A5
Seneca Springs Ct
1800 HarC 77450 3954 D4
Senegal St
6900 HOUS 77016 3825 C2
Senior Dr
10 MSCY 77459 4621 C2
Senior Rd
- MSCY 77459 4496 E5
1600 MSCY 77459 4497 E4
3100 MSCY 77459 4498 A5
3300 FBnC 77459 4498 B4
3300 FBnC 77545 4498 B4
3300 MSCY 77545 4498 B4
Senior St
5700 HOUS 77016 3686 D5
Senna Av
400 LGCY 77573 4632 E2
Senna Pl
3800 SGLD 77479 4495 E2
3900 SGLD 77479 4496 A2
Senna St
7200 HOUS 77028 3825 E2
Senna Ledge Ct
11500 HarC 77089 4504 C1
Senour Ct
3900 HOUS 77339 3119 A3

Senova Ct
2800 BzaC 77584 4501 C6
Senova Dr
3400 BzaC 77584 4501 C6
Sens Rd
300 HarC 77571 4111 A5
300 LPRT 77571 4111 A7
1900 LPRT 77571 4251 A2
Sentell Rd
4000 BzaC 77511 4867 E6
4000 BzaC 77511 4868 A7
4000 HLCS 77511 4867 E6
Senterra Bend Cir
- HarC 77379 3111 E6
Senterra Lakes Blvd
- HarC 77379 3111 E6
Sentinal Oaks St
2200 SGLD 77478 4368 C6
Sentinel Dr
16500 HOUS 77053 4371 E7
Sentinel Pl
10 WDLD 77382 2675 C7
Sentinel Oaks
100 MtgC 77362 2963 C4
800 MtgC 77355 2963 B4
Sentinel Pines Ct
16700 PASD 77059 4380 E4
Sentinel Point Ct
100 WDLD 77382 2819 E2
Sentore Ct
2100 PRLD 77581 4504 E2
Sentore Dr
1200 PRLD 77089 4504 E2
1200 PRLD 77581 4504 E2
Sentry Ct
11000 HarC 77065 3539 D1
Sentry Hill Ln
- HarC 77396 3547 E1
Sentry Maple Pl
200 WDLD 77382 2674 E5
200 WDLD 77382 2675 A5
Sentry Park Ct
17400 HarC 77084 3678 B3
Sentry Park Ln
6100 HarC 77084 3678 A4
Sentry Pine Ct
18200 HarC 77346 3408 A1
Sentry Woods Ln
4800 PRLD 77584 4502 A5
September Dr
3700 BYTN 77521 3974 A1
Sequin Dr
5500 HarC 77388 3112 A2
Sequoia Dr
2000 LGCY 77565 4509 A5
9200 HOUS 77041 3681 D7
Sequoia Ln
1200 PASD 77502 4106 D7
2500 RSBG 77471 4491 A6
25400 MtgC 77372 2536 E2
25400 MtgC 77372 2537 A2
Sequoia St
4100 HarC 77521 3833 B4
Sequoia Trc
20200 HarC 77379 3111 E4
Sequoia Bend Blvd
13900 HarC 77032 3546 D3
Sequoia Hills Dr
- HarC 77377 3254 D4
Sequoia Lake Tr
3300 PRLD 77581 4503 E6
3300 PRLD 77581 4504 A6
Sequoia Pass
2100 FBnC 77459 4621 C7
Sequoia Pass Ct
10400 HarC 77095 3537 D2
Sequoia Ridge Ln
11900 HarC 77346 3408 B4
Sequoia Trace Ct
5800 HarC 77379 3111 E5
Sequoia Valley Ln
11800 HarC 77346 3408 B4
Sequoia View Ln
17600 HarC 77346 3408 B2
Serein Meadows Dr
- MtgC 77386 2969 D1
Serena Ln
8900 HarC 77338 3262 B4
Serenade Ln
8700 HarC 77040 3541 C7
8700 HarC 77040 3681 C1
Serenade Pines Pl
10 WDLD 77382 2819 B1
Serenade Terrace Dr
4300 MSCY 77459 4496 C3
Serenata Ct
9600 HarC 77396 3407 B2
Serenata Ln
1700 HarC 77396 3407 B2
Serena Vista Wy
3000 HarC 77068 3257 D5
Serendipity Ln
11700 HarC 77429 3398 D5
Serene Av
7400 HarC 77338 3261 D3
Serene Pl
2700 FBnC 77478 4236 A6
Serene Creek Pl
10 WDLD 77382 2674 D4
Serene Elm St
12400 HOUS 77089 4505 C1
Serene Oak Dr
3100 SGLD 77478 4368 E5
Serene Shore Dr
17800 HarC 77429 3253 D1
Serene Spring Ln
25600 HarC 77373 3114 A4
Serene Trails
1300 TMBL 77375 2963 E6
1300 TMBL 77375 2964 A6
Serene Waters Ln
5000 HarC 77084 3677 D6
Serene Wave Blvd
21300 HarC 77433 3251 A4
21400 HarC 77433 3250 E3
Serene Wood Ln
7700 HarC 77433 3537 D7
Sereniah Cir
17000 HarC 77084 3678 A2
Serenity
23000 MtgC 77357 2974 A4
Serenity Cir
30300 MtgC 77354 2672 A6
Serenity Dr
400 DKSN 77539 4753 B5
Serenity Ln
- LGCY 77573 4632 B6
4400 BLAR 77401 4101 B3

Serenity Ln
10200 CNRO 77304 2236 E4
Serenity Tr
4600 FBnC 77545 4622 E2
Serenity Cove Cir
16900 HarC 77546 4506 B7
Serenity Loch Dr
18600 HarC 77379 3255 E1
Serenity Oaks Dr
- ORDN 77386 2822 C6
Serenity Rose Dr
12200 MtgC 77304 2382 A3
Serenity Sound
10300 MtgC 77354 2671 E5
10300 MtgC 77354 2672 A5
Serenity Woods Pl
10 WDLD 77382 2674 E4
Serpenteer Dr
19100 MtgC 77365 2971 D4
Serpentine Dr
1300 JTCY 77029 3966 D3
Serrano Tr
2900 HarC 77450 3954 C7
Serrano Creek Ln
14400 HarC 77396 3547 D2
Serrano Hill Ln
6600 HarC 77379 3111 D2
Serrano Lake Ct
22400 HarC 77375 3110 E2
Serrano Terrace Ln
5800 HarC 77041 3679 D5
Serringdon Dr
20500 HarC 77449 3815 D3
Service Dr
100 CNRO 77301 2384 B2
Service St
500 HOUS 77009 3824 A4
Service Center Dr
7900 HarC 77095 3538 E7
Sesame
11400 HOUS 77048 4244 B7
Sesame St
- HOUS 77004 4103 E3
5500 STFE 77510 4986 E2
10900 HOUS 77048 4244 B7
Seton Lake Dr
7200 HarC 77086 3542 A2
Seton Lake Pr
10 HarC 77086 3542 A2
Set Point Ln
18700 HarC 77346 3265 C7
Settegast Rd
- GLSN 77554 5333 B1
4600 HOUS 77028 3826 B5
13100 GLSN 77554 5220 A7
Settegast Ranch Rd
200 FBnC 77469 4232 C4
Settemont Rd
12300 HOUS 77085 4370 E2
12700 HOUS 77489 4370 E3
12700 MSCY 77489 4370 E3
Setter Ct
16300 HOUS 77489 4370 E7
Setting Sun
6900 FBnC 77494 4093 B5
Setting Sun Ct
16200 MtgC 77302 2678 E4
Setting Sun Dr
- HarC 77449 3815 D5
Settle Dr
12400 HOUS 77071 4239 C7
Settlement Ln
14100 HarC 77396 3547 B2
Settlers Cross
10500 MtgC 77303 2239 A1
Settlers Ct
1800 FBnC 77469 4365 C4
Settler's Ml
25300 WlrC 77447 2813 D1
Settlers Wy
- WDLD 77380 2821 E7
E Settlers Wy
2100 WDLD 77380 2821 E7
W Settlers Wy
2200 WDLD 77380 2821 E7
Settlers Bridge Ln
- HarC 77388 3112 E4
Settlers Grove Wy
- SGLD 77479 4495 E2
Settlers Lake Cir
- HarC 77449 3676 D3
Settlers Lake Cir E
6100 HarC 77449 3676 D3
Settlers Lake Cir N
20700 HarC 77449 3676 D3
Settlers Lake Cir W
6100 HarC 77449 3676 D3
W Settlers Shore Cir
18500 HarC 77433 3395 C5
Settlers Shore Dr
12100 HarC 77433 3395 C5
N Settlers Shore Dr
18300 HarC 77433 3395 D5
Settlers Square Ln
6100 HarC 77449 3676 D3
Settlers Valley Dr
21000 HarC 77449 3676 C2
Settlers Village Dr
6000 HarC 77449 3676 C2
Settlers Wy Blvd
2200 SGLD 77478 4368 E6
2400 SGLD 77479 4368 E6
3000 SGLD 77479 4495 E2
Seuss Dr
7500 HOUS 77025 4102 A5
7500 HOUS 77030 4102 A5
Sevan St
4100 GlsC 77518 4634 C3
Seven Cove Ct
23500 FBnC 77469 4093 D6
Seven Coves Rd
1000 CNRO 77304 2237 A1
1000 MtgC 77378 2237 A1
1000 PNVL 77304 2237 A1
1000 PNVL 77318 2237 A1
9700 MtgC 77304 2237 A1
9700 MtgC 77318 2237 A1
Seven Coves Rd FM-830
1000 CNRO 77304 2237 A1
1000 MtgC 77378 2237 A1
1000 PNVL 77304 2237 A1
1000 PNVL 77318 2237 A1
9700 MtgC 77304 2237 A1
9700 MtgC 77318 2237 A1
Sevenhampton Ln
200 HarC 77015 3829 A7
Sevenleaf Ln
6300 HOUS 77345 3120 B3

STREET Block City ZIP Map# Grid

Seven Maples Dr
1600 HOUS 77345 3120 C6
Seven Meadows Pkwy
- FBnC 77494 4093 C4
- HOUS 77494 4093 C4
Seven Mile Ln
10600 HOUS 77093 3685 E3
11600 HarC 77093 3685 D1
Seven Oaks Dr
1900 HOUS 77339 3118 D7
Seven Oaks St
1400 HOUS 77077 3957 C5
Seven Pines Dr
17600 HarC 77379 3256 C1
Seven Pines Ln
16700 FBnC 77083 4235 E1
Seven Seas St
300 HarC 77532 3552 B2
Seven Sisters Dr
11200 HarC 77375 3110 A7
11500 HarC 77375 3109 E7
28000 MtgC 77357 2829 E6
28000 MtgC 77357 2830 A6
Seven Springs Dr
15800 HarC 77084 3678 E6
Seventeenth Green Ct
19900 HarC 77346 3265 B4
Seventeenth Green Dr
7300 HarC 77346 3265 A4
Seventh Heaven Dr
23800 FBnC 77494 4093 A5
Seven Waves Ct
16400 HarC 77532 3552 B2
Seven X St
27200 MtgC 77372 2683 D2
Severo Rd
15100 FBnC 77478 4236 C3
Seville St
7200 HOUS 77016 3687 C2
Sewalk St
14000 HOUS 77047 4373 B4
Sewanee Pk
500 MtgC 77302 2530 C5
Sewanee St
5300 HOUS 77005 4101 E2
5300 WUNP 77005 4101 E4
6900 HOUS 77025 4101 E5
Seward St
23600 HarC 77389 2967 A5
Sexton St
7900 HOUS 77028 3826 C4
Sextus
16100 HarC 77041 3680 C2
16100 HOUS 77041 3680 C2
Seyborn St
2300 HOUS 77027 3961 C6
Seymour Dr
5300 HarC 77032 3546 D2
5700 HarC 77396 3546 D2
Seymour St
900 PASD 77506 4107 B4
Sgt Ed Holcomb Blvd
2200 CNRO 77304 2529 A3
Sgt Ed Holcomb Blvd N
400 CNRO 77304 2383 C5
Sgt Ed Holcomb Blvd S
100 CNRO 77304 2383 C6
2100 CNRO 77304 2529 B3
2100 MtgC 77304 2529 B3
Sha Cir
4200 PASD 77504 4247 E4
Shabbona
- DRPK 77536 4109 A3
Shadberry Dr
400 MtgC 77354 2673 E2
Shadbury Ct
2300 HOUS 77339 3119 A3
Shadder Wy
1400 HOUS 77019 3962 B4
Shaddock Dr
7500 HarC 77041 3539 C7
Shaddon Manor Ct
1500 HarC 77379 3255 B1
Shade Ct
7300 PRLD 77584 4502 B5
Shade Ln
3100 PRLD 77584 4502 B5
Shade Berry Pl
10 WDLD 77382 2674 D4
Shade Crest Dr
2100 FBnC 77469 4234 B7
Shadecrest Ln
1700 LGCY 77573 4751 E2
Shaded Pines Dr
9200 HarC 77396 3407 B2
9200 HMBL 77396 3407 A2
Shade Gap Ln
- FBnC 77478 4236 A4
Shadeland Dr
1400 HOUS 77043 3819 E6
Shade Tree Ln
25900 MtgC 77372 2683 A4
25900 SPLD 77372 2683 A4
Shadewater Dr
- FBnC 77469 4093 C7
Shadewell Ln
100 FRDW 77546 4629 D2
Shadewood Ct
14600 HarC 77015 3829 C4
Shadie Pine Ln
800 FRDW 77546 4505 B4
Shadow Bnd
1300 TYLV 77586 4381 E7
Shadow Cir
100 BYTN 77520 4113 B1
1000 LGCY 77573 4631 D4
Shadow Dr
1800 MSCY 77489 4370 B5
1800 STAF 77477 4370 B5
Shadow Gln
700 HarC 77530 3829 E7
Shadow Ln
10 HOUS 77080 3820 B5
600 PASD 77506 4106 E6
600 PASD 77506 4107 A6
2900 DKSN 77539 4753 C3
8600 MtgC 77354 2818 E5
16300 HarC 77429 3397 A5
26000 MtgC 77357 2829 A5
Shadow Tr
3800 HarC 77084 3816 C2
Shadowbark Dr
3300 HOUS 77082 4097 E2
Shadow Bay Cir
2100 LGCY 77573 4509 B6
Shadow Bay Dr
2700 PRLD 77584 4500 E3

Shadow Bayou Ct
3400 HOUS 77082 4097 E2
E Shadowbend Av
200 FRDW 77546 4505 C7
N Shadowbend Av
300 FRDW 77546 4505 C7
S Shadowbend Av
300 FRDW 77546 4505 C7
W Shadowbend Av
100 FRDW 77546 4505 B7
200 FRDW 77546 4629 B1
Shadow Bend Dr
800 FBnC 77479 4494 B5
1900 HOUS 77043 3819 E5
Shadow Bend Pl
4500 WDLD 77381 2821 A3
4800 WDLD 77381 2820 E3
Shadowbend St
1100 PRLD 77581 4504 E6
Shadow Bluff Ct
3400 HOUS 77082 4097 E2
Shadowbranch Ln
1900 HOUS 77077 3956 E6
Shadow Breeze Ln
5000 FBnC 77494 4092 E3
Shadowbriar Dr
- HOUS 77082 3957 E7
2000 HOUS 77077 3957 E7
2900 HOUS 77082 4097 E2
Shadow Briar Ln
2600 HarC 77073 3259 D4
4100 MSCY 77459 4496 C1
26100 MtgC 77372 2683 B5
26100 SPLD 77372 2683 B5
Shadowbrook Dr
700 MtgC 77380 2968 A2
800 WDLD 77380 2968 A2
Shadow Canyon Ct
2300 PRLD 77584 4500 A2
Shadow Canyon Ln
2700 FBnC 77494 3953 A6
12800 PRLD 77584 4500 D5
Shadowchase Ct
3200 HOUS 77082 4097 E2
Shadowchase Dr
3300 HOUS 77082 4097 E2
Shadowcliff Ct
600 LGCY 77573 4633 B2
Shadowcliff Ln
7500 FBnC 77494 4093 A4
Shadow Cove Ct
3600 HOUS 77082 4097 D2
Shadow Cove Dr
- PRLD 77584 4500 A2
3600 HOUS 77082 4097 D3
N Shadow Cove Dr
12200 HOUS 77082 4097 E2
S Shadow Cove Dr
12300 HOUS 77082 4097 D3
N Shadow Cove Ln
12400 HOUS 77082 4097 E3
Shadow Creek Blvd
24000 HarC 77389 2966 B3
Shadow Creek Ct
5900 BYTN 77520 3835 B7
23600 FBnC 77494 3953 C4
Shadow Creek Dr
300 ELGO 77586 4509 B2
900 LPRT 77571 4250 A2
2000 HOUS 77017 4246 B1
2100 DRPK 77536 4109 D7
Shadow Creek Pkwy
- PRLD 77053 4500 A1
- PRLD 77545 4500 A1
- PRLD 77584 4500 E1
Shadow Creek Pkwy FM-2234
- PRLD 77053 4500 A1
- PRLD 77545 4500 A1
- PRLD 77584 4500 E1
Shadow Creek Ridge Ct
25000 HarC 77389 2966 B3
Shadow Creek Ridge Dr
7000 HarC 77389 2966 B3
E Shadow Creek Villas Lp
24800 HarC 77389 2966 B3
S Shadow Creek Villas Lp
7100 HarC 77389 2966 B4
W Shadow Creek Villas Lp
24800 HarC 77389 2966 B3
Shadowcrest Ln
3200 MtgC 77380 2821 B7
Shadow Crest St
5500 HOUS 77096 4240 C1
6500 HOUS 77074 4240 A1
8600 HOUS 77074 4239 C1
Shadow Cypress Ct
17800 HarC 77433 3537 D6
Shadow Cypress Ln
10400 HarC 77433 3537 A2
Shadowdale Dr
1000 HOUS 77043 3958 E1
2700 HOUS 77043 3819 E2
4400 HOUS 77041 3819 E1
4700 HOUS 77041 3680 E7
N Shadowdale Dr
10400 HOUS 77041 3680 E7
Shadow Dance Ln
- FBnC 77469 4094 B7
Shadow Dust Ct
12400 HOUS 77082 4097 D3
Shadow Edge Cir
8700 HarC 77095 3538 C5
Shadow Edge Dr
- HarC 77429 3252 E5
Shadow Falls Ct
13500 HOUS 77059 4379 D5
Shadow Falls Ln
2300 PRLD 77584 4500 A2
Shadowfern Ct
3200 HOUS 77082 4097 E2
Shadowfern Dr
3300 HOUS 77082 4097 E2
Shadowfield Dr
11000 HarC 77064 3540 D1
Shadow Forest Dr
1800 FBnC 77494 3952 D4
Shadow Fork Ct
3600 HOUS 77082 4097 E3
Shadow Garden Ln
14300 HOUS 77077 3956 E6
Shadow Gate Ct
8400 HarC 77040 3541 A6
Shadow Gate Ln
9400 HarC 77040 3541 A7
Shadowglade Ct
9700 HarC 77064 3540 D4
Shadow Glen Ln
2300 MtgC 77386 2969 B3

Shadow Glenn Dr
1000 CNRO 77301 2384 C1
Shadow Grass Dr
4600 HarC 77493 3813 A1
Shadowgrass Dr
- HarC 77084 3816 C1
Shadow Green Dr
12300 HOUS 77082 4097 E3
Shadow Grove Ln
18300 HarC 77532 3409 E6
E Shadow Grove Ln
500 FBnC 77469 4365 C5
N Shadow Grove Ln
2100 FBnC 77469 4365 C5
S Shadow Grove Ln
2100 FBnC 77469 4365 C5
W Shadow Grove Ln
500 FBnC 77469 4365 C5
Shadow Haven Ct
1800 FBnC 77545 4622 C2
Shadow Haven Dr
4100 FBnC 77545 4622 D1
Shadow Hill Ln
7700 HOUS 77072 4097 E5
Shadowhollow Dr
12100 HOUS 77082 4097 E2
Shadow Island Dr
12300 HOUS 77082 4097 D3
Shadow Isle Ln
6000 HarC 77084 3678 D4
Shadow Knoll Ct
3800 HOUS 77082 4097 D3
Shadowknoll Dr
12300 HOUS 77082 4097 D2
Shadow Lake Dr
1800 FBnC 77479 4494 C4
E Shadow Lake Dr
12300 HarC 77429 3398 C5
N Shadow Lake Dr
12300 HarC 77429 3398 C5
W Shadow Lake Dr
12300 HarC 77065 3398 C6
12300 HarC 77429 3398 C5
Shadow Lawn St
- HOUS 77006 4102 D2
10 HOUS 77005 4102 D2
Shadow Lawn Wy
17500 HarC 77095 3537 D2
Shadowleaf Dr
- FBnC 77479 4494 C4
3200 HOUS 77082 4097 D1
Shadow Ledge Dr
17100 HarC 77095 3537 E2
Shadow Meadows Dr
3500 HOUS 77082 4097 D2
Shadowmeadows Dr
3400 HOUS 77082 4097 D2
Shadowmere Dr
- PRLD 77545 4499 C2
Shadowmere Ln
25200 FBnC 77494 4093 A6
Shadow Mill Ct
20500 HarC 77450 3954 D5
Shadowmist Dr
12400 HOUS 77082 4097 D2
Shadow Mountain Dr
1200 HarC 77450 3954 A4
Shadow Oaks Dr
200 CNRO 77301 2384 A1
200 CNRO 77303 2384 A1
300 CNRO 77301 2383 E1
300 CNRO 77303 2383 E1
2400 MSCY 77545 4622 C2
10200 HOUS 77043 3819 E6
10200 HOUS 77043 3820 A7
Shadowood St
10 CNRO 77304 2383 B4
Shadow Park Dr
2000 FBnC 77494 3953 D6
Shadow Pass Tr
15900 HarC 77377 3254 E5
Shadow Path Dr
16000 PASD 77059 4380 D5
Shadow Pine Dr
9800 HarC 77070 3399 C5
Shadow Pl Dr
- HOUS 77082 4097 E2
E Shadowpoint Cir
10 WDLD 77381 2820 D1
10 WDLD 77381 2821 A1
N Shadowpoint Cir
10 WDLD 77381 2820 E1
10 WDLD 77381 2821 A1
W Shadowpoint Cir
100 WDLD 77381 2820 E1
Shadowpoint Dr
12000 HOUS 77082 4097 E2
Shadowridge Dr
5000 HOUS 77053 4372 A7
Shadow River Ln
21200 HarC 77379 3111 C3
Shadow Rock Dr
1800 HOUS 77339 3118 D5
Shadow Royal Dr
3800 HOUS 77082 4097 E3
Shadow Run Dr
13500 HarC 77082 4097 A1
Shadowside Ct
3400 HOUS 77082 4097 E2
Shadows of Alpestrine Dr
20600 MtgC 77357 2828 C7
Shadows Point Dr
3900 LGCY 77539 4633 E3
Shadow Spring Ct
3400 HOUS 77082 4097 E2
Shadow Stone St
10 WDLD 77381 2821 C3
Shadow Terrace Ln
7400 FBnC 77469 4094 D6
Shadow Trace Cir
3800 HOUS 77082 4097 E3
Shadow Trail Dr
2900 HarC 77082 4097 A1
Shadow Tree Dr
6300 HOUS 77035 4240 A6
Shadowvale Dr
12400 HOUS 77082 4097 D2
Shadow Valley Ct
8400 HarC 77379 3256 A4
Shadow Valley Dr
17200 HarC 77379 3256 A4
17600 HarC 77379 3255 E3
Shadow Valley Ln
8500 HarC 77379 3256 D4
Shadow View Ln
- HOUS 77077 3957 D7
- HOUS 77082 3957 D7

Shadow Vila Ln
9800 HarC 77044 3689 B4
Shadowvista Ct
3500 HOUS 77082 4097 E2
Shadowvista Dr
12300 HOUS 77082 4097 D2
Shadow Walk Ct
18500 HarC 77449 3677 C3
Shadowwalk Dr
3200 HOUS 77082 4097 D2
Shadow Wick Ln
3700 HOUS 77082 4097 D3
Shadow Wind Dr
- PRLD 77545 4499 D4
1800 MSCY 77489 4370 D5
8300 HarC 77040 3541 A7
Shadow Wood
11400 PNPV 77024 3959 E5
Shadow Wood Dr
- HOUS 77043 3819 B5
100 SGLD 77478 4367 E1
100 SGLD 77478 4368 A1
9800 HOUS 77080 3820 B5
10100 HOUS 77043 3820 A5
Shadow Wy Ct
500 PNPV 77024 3959 D3
Shadow Wy St
11400 PNPV 77024 3959 D3
Shadrack St
3700 HOUS 77013 3827 D5
Shadsworth Dr
- HarC 77388 3113 A3
Shadway Dr
14800 HarC 77084 3679 A3
Shadwell Dr
800 HOUS 77062 4506 E2
800 HOUS 77062 4507 A2
Shady Bnd
37800 MtgC 77355 2815 C3
Shady Dr
3700 STFE 77517 4870 A5
8200 HOUS 77016 3825 D1
9800 HOUS 77016 3686 D5
32200 SGCH 77355 2961 E3
Shady Ln
- HarC 77039 3545 E7
- HOUS 77039 3545 E7
100 HOUS 77336 3121 D4
300 BYTN 77520 4113 A1
400 LMQU 77568 4990 B2
900 CNRO 77301 2384 C2
1900 RHMD 77469 4492 A2
2700 LGCY 77598 4630 E3
6700 FBnC 77479 4493 D5
8900 MtgC 77354 2818 D4
10600 HOUS 77093 3685 E3
11600 HarC 77093 3685 E1
11900 HarC 77093 3545 E7
16500 HarC 77530 3830 D4
19400 MtgC 77355 2814 A2
20000 HarC 77532 3413 C3
20500 MtgC 77365 2972 E7
20900 HarC 77532 3269 A7
E Shady Ln
10 HOUS 77063 3959 C6
N Shady Ln
300 LPRT 77571 4383 A2
400 LPRT 77571 4382 E2
600 HarC 77571 4382 E2
S Shady Ln
300 LPRT 77571 4382 E2
300 LPRT 77571 4383 A2
600 PASD 77571 4382 E2
W Shady Ln
10 HOUS 77063 3959 C7
Shady Rd
1200 HarC 77336 3121 C3
1200 HOUS 77336 3121 C3
Shady Shr
10 HarC 77530 3831 A7
Shady Wy
900 CNRO 77301 2530 B3
Shady Ace Ln
8200 HarC 77346 3265 C7
Shadyacres Ct
2600 HOUS 77008 3823 A4
Shady Acres Lndg
2600 HOUS 77008 3823 A4
Shady Alcove Ct
1900 HOUS 77345 3120 D6
Shady Arbor Ct
7400 PASD 77505 4249 B5
8900 HOUS 77040 3682 A2
Shady Arbor Dr
4300 PASD 77505 4249 B6
Shady Arbor Ln
7000 HOUS 77040 3682 B2
7800 HarC 77040 3681 E3
Shady Arbor Wy
17800 HarC 77379 3257 A3
Shady Bank Dr
19500 HarC 77375 3109 E7
Shady Bay Ct
13400 FBnC 77478 4366 E2
Shady Bay Ln
3600 MSCY 77459 4496 D5
Shady Bayou Ln
2400 HarC 77373 3114 C2
Shady Bend Ct
100 GlsC 77511 4752 A6
Shady Bend Dr
1300 FBnC 77479 4494 B6
2000 PRLD 77581 4504 A5
2600 PRLD 77581 4503 E4
14900 HarC 77070 3254 D7
Shady Bend Ln
800 FRDW 77546 4505 C4
Shady Birch Dr
2200 CNRO 77301 2384 E3
Shady Birch Hllw
5900 HOUS 77345 3120 D5
Shady Bough Dr
10100 HarC 77070 3255 B6
Shady Branch Dr
2000 HOUS 77339 3263 D1
Shady Breeze Ct
11900 PRLD 77584 4500 C4
Shady Breeze Dr
3800 HOUS 77082 4097 D3
Shadybriar Dr
2000 HOUS 77077 3957 E6
Shady Bridge Ct
17900 HarC 77095 3537 E7
Shady Brook Dr
500 FBnC 77477 4369 D3
500 STAF 77477 4369 D3
2300 HarC 77084 3816 A6
12300 PRLD 77584 4500 B4

Shadybrook Dr
1400 HarC 77094 3955 B3
Shady Brook Ln
28800 MtgC 77355 2814 E2
28800 MtgC 77355 2815 A3
Shady Canyon
10400 HarC 77070 3399 B6
Shady Canyon Ct
16500 HarC 77095 3397 C6
Shady Canyon Dr
11500 HarC 77095 3397 B7
11500 HarC 77095 3538 B1
Shady Canyon Ln
17700 HarC 77377 3254 D3
Shady Corners Ln
7200 HOUS 77040 3682 A2
Shady Cove Ct
2300 PRLD 77584 4500 C2
Shady Cove Ln
19500 HarC 77346 3265 D5
N Shady Creek Ct
2600 HOUS 77017 4246 B2
Shady Creek Dr
2700 PRLD 77581 4504 C4
N Shady Creek Dr
5300 HOUS 77017 4246 B1
S Shady Creek Dr
5400 HOUS 77017 4246 B2
Shadycrest Dr
3900 PRLD 77581 4504 A6
12400 HOUS 77082 4097 D1
Shady Cypress Ln
18100 HarC 77429 3252 B6
Shady Dale Dr
500 FBnC 77477 4369 D3
500 STAF 77477 4369 D3
Shadydale Ln
9800 HOUS 77016 3686 D5
Shady Dawn Ln
25900 FBnC 77494 3952 C7
Shady Downs Dr
12200 HOUS 77082 4097 D3
Shady Elm Ln
12100 MtgC 77362 2817 B7
Shady Elms Dr
- PASD 77059 4380 D5
16200 HOUS 77059 4380 D5
Shady Falls Dr
- HarC 77095 3538 D5
Shady Falls Ln
2500 PRLD 77584 4500 A3
Shady Fern Ct
12700 HarC 77065 3539 C1
Shady Forest Dr
- FBnC 77479 4494 B3
- HOUS 77079 3957 B3
Shady Fort Ln
12900 HarC 77377 3254 A1
Shady Gardens Ct
3000 HOUS 77339 3119 B2
Shady Gardens Dr
5000 HOUS 77339 3119 B2
Shady Gate Ct
15100 HarC 77429 3253 B6
Shady Gate Ln
- PRLD 77581 4503 C1
Shady Glade Dr
300 HarC 77090 3258 D5
Shady Glen Dr
- HarC 77429 3254 A5
Shadyglen Dr
300 PNPV 77024 3959 D4
Shady Glen Ln
300 MtgC 77385 2676 B2
3200 MSCY 77459 4496 E1
Shady Green Dr
3600 HOUS 77339 3119 C5
Shady Green Mdws
8700 HarC 77083 4237 B1
Shady Grove Av
500 CNRO 77301 2383 E7
500 CNRO 77301 2384 A6
Shady Grove Ct
1300 PASD 77586 4381 D6
7000 HarC 77040 3681 E3
Shady Grove Dr
3600 BzaC 77578 4501 A7
7800 HarC 77040 3681 D3
Shady Grove Ln
10 BKHV 77024 3959 D3
7300 HOUS 77040 3682 A2
7400 HarC 77040 3682 A2
11600 PNPV 77024 3959 D3
Shady Harbor Dr
3800 HOUS 77082 4097 D3
Shady Heath Ln
21900 FBnC 77494 4093 E4
Shady Hill Dr
- BYTN 77520 3972 A3
3400 BYTN 77521 3972 B3
Shady Hills Dr
2900 HOUS 77339 3118 E5
Shady Hollow Ct
5700 BzaC 77583 4623 D5
Shady Hollow Dr
10000 CNRO 77304 2382 E1
Shady Hollow St
600 HOUS 77056 3960 E4
Shady Knoll Ln
1100 LGCY 77573 4751 C1
12600 HarC 77429 3397 D5
Shady Lake Dr
100 HOUS 77336 3266 C5
400 RMFT 77357 2829 A3
4400 SEBK 77586 4382 B6
Shady Lake Grv
7400 FBnC 77469 4094 D7
Shadylawn Av
100 SRAC 77571 4383 A2
400 SRAC 77571 4382 E2
Shady Ln Cir
9300 HOUS 77063 3959 C7
Shady Ln Ct
10 HOUS 77063 3959 C6
Shady Lodge Ln
700 HarC 77373 2968 E7
Shadylyn Dr
100 CNRO 77304 2383 B3
Shady Magnolia Dr
400 CNRO 77301 2384 E3
Shady Manor Dr
- HarC 77084 3677 D5
5900 HarC 77449 3677 D4
Shady Maple Ct
3200 HOUS 77339 3119 B1
Shady Maple Dr
4700 HOUS 77339 3119 B2
4700 HOUS 77345 3119 C2

Shady Meadow St
11700 HarC 77039 3546 A6
Shady Mill Dr
7300 HarC 77040 3681 D2
Shadymist Ct
3400 HOUS 77082 4097 D2
Shadymist Dr
3400 HOUS 77082 4097 D3
Shady Moss Ln
7100 HOUS 77040 3682 B2
Shady Nook Ct
5000 HOUS 77018 3683 D7
Shady Nook Ln
200 FRDW 77546 4505 C7
Shady Oak Dr
24900 WlrC 77447 2959 C2
Shady Oak Ln
10 PNVL 77304 2237 A3
900 DKSN 77539 4753 C2
4900 TXCY 77591 4874 A6
Shady Oaks Ct
1900 MSCY 77489 4497 C1
Shady Oaks Dr
1600 CNRO 77301 2384 A3
2000 MtgC 77385 2676 C6
2700 BzaC 77511 4867 E2
2700 BzaC 77511 4868 A3
15100 SGCH 77355 2962 A1
24800 HarC 77373 3114 D3
Shady Oaks Ln
2000 FBnC 77471 4614 B3
2000 RSBG 77471 4614 B3
4800 HarC 77546 4505 E6
5000 FRDW 77546 4505 D6
22800 MtgC 77365 2973 E6
Shady Palms Dr
7700 HarC 77095 3538 C7
Shady Park Dr
2800 HOUS 77017 4105 D5
Shady Pecan Ct
15300 HarC 77429 3253 D5
Shady Pine Dr
2200 CNRO 77301 2384 E3
4200 HarC 77388 3257 D2
Shady Point Dr
800 HarC 77373 3114 A7
Shady Pond Pl
10 WDLD 77382 2675 B6
Shady Ranch Ct
17500 HarC 77447 3249 D3
Shady Ridge Tr
3000 FBnC 77478 4235 E7
3000 FBnC 77478 4236 B7
Shady River
4200 MSCY 77459 4496 C4
Shady River Dr
5200 HOUS 77056 3960 E3
5600 HOUS 77057 3960 D3
10600 HOUS 77042 3958 C4
Shady River Rd
700 LPRT 77571 4382 D1
Shady Rock Ln
300 HarC 77015 3828 D6
Shady Run Dr
2400 HOUS 77339 3119 A6
Shady Run Ln
- PRLD 77583 4500 B5
Shady Sands Pl
11900 PRLD 77584 4500 C3
Shadyside Cir
7200 MSCY 77459 4496 E5
Shadyspring Ln
3200 LGCY 77539 4753 A3
Shady Springs Ct
2600 PRLD 77584 4500 A3
Shady Springs Dr
4000 TYLV 77586 4508 D1
4200 PASD 77586 4508 D1
12800 PRLD 77584 4500 A3
Shady Spruce Ln
25700 FBnC 77494 4093 A1
Shady Square Ct
16900 HarC 77095 3538 A7
Shady Stream Dr
600 HarC 77090 3258 B1
600 HOUS 77090 3258 C1
Shady Terrace Dr
3900 HOUS 77345 3119 D4
Shady Timbers Dr
6000 HOUS 77016 3686 D5
Shady Trail Ct
2200 FBnC 77469 4365 D1
Shady Trail Ln
1000 HarC 77038 3543 C2
Shady Trail Wy
- HOUS 77049 3828 A2
Shady Tree Ln
2200 CNRO 77301 2384 E3
8600 LPRT 77571 4249 D4
9600 HarC 77086 3542 A3
Shady Vale Ln
7300 HarC 77040 3681 E2
Shady Valley Dr
1400 FBnC 77479 4494 B6
22000 HarC 77450 3954 A4
Shadyview St
6200 HOUS 77011 3964 D6
Shady Villa Hvn
1500 HOUS 77055 3821 C6
Shadyvilla Ln
6700 HOUS 77055 3821 D6
Shady Villa Mdw
7800 HOUS 77055 3821 C6
E Shady Villa Pk
- HOUS 77055 3821 D6
W Shady Villa Pk
1300 HOUS 77055 3821 D6
Shady Villa Pn
1300 HOUS 77055 3821 E4
Shady Villa St
33000 MtgC 77355 2962 A2
Shady Villa Wk
7500 HOUS 77055 3821 D6
Shady Villa Cove
7800 HOUS 77055 3821 E4
Shady Villa Fern St
1500 HOUS 77055 3821 D6
Shady Villa Garden St
7600 HOUS 77055 3821 E4
Shady Village Ct
4200 MSCY 77459 4369 C5
Shady Village Dr
3500 HOUS 77345 3120 A4
Shady Villa Manner
1500 HOUS 77055 3821 C6
Shady Walk Ln
26300 FBnC 77494 4092 D2

Shady Willow St
8000 HarC 77375 2966 A6
Shadywind Dr
3200 HOUS 77082 4097 D2
Shadywood Cir
400 CNRO 77304 2383 C3
Shadywood Dr
500 FRDW 77546 4505 C5
Shadywood Rd
300 HOUS 77057 3960 C4
Shadywood St
5500 FBnC 77479 4496 A7
Shady Wy Dr
7600 FBnC 77479 4493 E5
7700 FBnC 77479 4494 A5
Shaffter Ln
- HarC 77041 3679 E4
Shaft Dr
13300 HarC 77429 3398 A5
Shaftsbury Dr
12300 HOUS 77031 4239 A6
Shag Bark Dr
7200 MtgC 77354 2819 C3
Shagbark Dr
9100 HOUS 77078 3687 E6
9100 HOUS 77078 3688 A6
Shagwood Dr
8000 HarC 77049 3689 E7
E Shaker Ct
10 WDLD 77380 2967 C3
W Shaker Ln
10 WDLD 77380 2967 C3
Shakespeare Rd
2200 HOUS 77030 4102 B3
2400 HOUS 77005 4102 A3
2400 WUNP 77005 4102 A3
Shakespeare St
2700 PRLD 77581 4503 D4
Shakey Hllw
20900 MtgC 77306 2681 A5
Shalamar Dr
15800 MtgC 77354 2669 E2
Shale Dr
4700 BYTN 77521 3833 C3
E Shale Creek Cir
10 WDLD 77382 2819 C2
W Shale Creek Cir
10 WDLD 77382 2819 C2
E Shale Creek Ct
10 WDLD 77382 2819 C2
Shale Creek Dr
19100 HarC 77375 3109 D7
Shale Grove Ct
5000 FBnC 77469 4234 C3
Shale Run Pl
100 WDLD 77382 2673 E4
Shalford Ct
24900 HarC 77389 2966 A3
Shalford Dr
25000 HarC 77389 2966 A3
Shalimar Ln
10 PNVL 77304 2237 A3
Shallow Dr
300 HMBL 77338 3263 A7
Shallow Bend Ln
7500 FBnC 77469 4094 B6
Shallowbriar Ln
- HarC 77041 3679 D3
Shallow Brook Ln
2800 LGCY 77539 4752 E4
Shallowbrook St
10700 HNCV 77024 3960 A2
Shallow Creek Ct
20100 HarC 77449 3676 E3
Shallow Creek Dr
- PRLD 77581 4504 A3
Shallow Creek Ln
22100 FBnC 77450 4093 E3
Shallow Falls Ct
2700 PRLD 77584 4500 A4
Shallow Falls Ln
13000 PRLD 77584 4500 A3
Shallow Glen Ln
21600 FBnC 77450 4093 C6
21600 FBnC 77450 4094 A4
Shallowhollow
- MtgC 77385 2676 E4
Shallowlake Ct
8500 HarC 77095 3537 E6
Shallow Lake Ln
17200 HarC 77095 3538 A5
17300 HarC 77095 3537 E5
Shallow Leaf Ln
18000 HarC 77433 3537 D7
Shallow Oak Ct
18400 HarC 77377 3254 B2
Shallow Oaks Dr
11900 HarC 77065 3399 A7
Shallow Park Ln
- FBnC 77494 4092 C3
Shallow Pond Ct
10 WDLD 77381 2820 E4
4000 SGLD 77479 4495 A3
Shallow Pond Pl
10 WDLD 77381 2820 E4
Shallow Reef
4000 GLSN 77554 5333 A2
Shallow Ridge Blvd
16700 HarC 77095 3397 A7
Shallow River Ct
6800 HarC 77379 3111 C2
Shallow Shaft Ln
- FBnC 77469 4094 D6
Shallow Spring Ct
22600 FBnC 77494 4093 D3
Shallow Springs Ct
2800 BzaC 77578 4501 A7
Shallow Springs Ln
1000 LGCY 77573 4633 A2
Shalom Creek Ln
4100 HarC 77388 3112 C4
Shaly Ct
2600 HarC 77450 3954 D6
Shaly Breeze Ln
2100 LGCY 77573 4631 C7
Shaly Brook Ln
100 LGCY 77539 4753 A3
Shaly Cove Ln
2600 PRLD 77584 4500 A3
Shaman Ln
6900 HarC 77083 4097 A5
Shaman Rd
3900 GLSN 77554 5331 C7
18200 GLSN 77554 5442 B1
Shambala Wy
- FBnC 77494 4093 A4
Shamrock Ct
27100 FBnC 77469 4232 A7

Houston Street Index

STREET Block City ZIP Map# Grid

Shamrock Ln
1500 DRPK 77536 4108 E6
7000 FBnC 77469 4232 A7
Shamrock St
5400 HOUS 77017 4106 C6
5600 HOUS 77502 4106 C6
5600 PASD 77502 4106 C6
Shamrock Park Ln
14000 SGLD 77478 4236 E5
14000 SGLD 77478 4237 A5
Shane Rd
2300 FBnC 77469 4492 A7
2300 FBnC 77469 4616 A1
Shane St
400 HarC 77037 3544 B5
400 HOUS 77037 3544 B5
20200 HarC 77449 3815 D3
W Shane St
1600 ALVN 77511 4867 A2
2100 ALVN 77511 4866 D3
Shane Creek Ln
4600 HarC 77388 3112 B3
Shanemoss Ct
3500 HarC 77068 3257 B5
Shanewood Ct
- WDLD 77382 2673 B7
Shanghai St
15400 JRSV 77040 3680 E1
Shango Ln
9100 HarC 77095 3538 D4
Shangrila Ln
7400 HarC 77095 3538 B7
7400 HarC 77095 3678 B1
Shank Rd
4700 PRLD 77581 4503 A1
Shanna Ln
4200 PASD 77504 4247 E4
Shannon Bnd
3700 BYTN 77521 3973 C2
Shannon Cir
27600 MtgC 77355 2963 B2
Shannon Ct
2900 HarC 77396 3407 D3
Shannon Ln
2800 HarC 77396 3407 D3
Shannon St
2300 HOUS 77027 3961 C6
7000 HTCK 77563 4988 E5
E Shannon St
2200 DRPK 77536 4109 A6
W Shannon St
2200 DRPK 77536 4109 A6
Shannon Cir Dr
10 HNCV 77024 3960 A2
Shannondale Dr
7300 FBnC 77479 4493 E4
7400 FBnC 77479 4494 A4
Shannondale Ln
200 HarC 77388 3113 D6
Shannon Derek
3900 BYTN 77521 3973 C2
Shannon Falls Ct
22700 FBnC 77494 4093 D4
Shannon Forest Ct
2700 FBnC 77494 3953 B6
Shannon Glen Ln
18700 HarC 77084 3816 C2
Shannon Green Ct
10 WDLD 77384 2675 D4
Shannon Hills Dr
11200 HOUS 77099 4238 B1
12300 HOUS 77099 4237 D1
12900 HarC 77099 4237 C1
Shannon Marie Ln
14000 HOUS 77077 3956 D4
Shannon Mills Ln
10800 HOUS 77075 4377 A4
Shannon Ridge Rd
14300 HOUS 77062 4379 E6
Shannon Valley Dr
1200 HOUS 77077 3957 E5
Shannonwood Ct
25800 FBnC 77494 4093 A2
Shapiro Ct
4800 MSCY 77459 4496 C3
Shapiro Springs Ln
15200 HarC 77095 3538 B3
15200 HarC 77095 3539 B5
Sharie St
900 DRPK 77536 4109 C4
Shark Cir
2400 TXCY 77591 4872 E3
Shark Ct
1900 HarC 77532 3551 D3
Sharman St
4500 HOUS 77009 3824 B5
Shar Mist Ln
11600 HarC 77066 3400 E5
Sharmon Rd
10600 HarC 77038 3543 D1
10800 HarC 77038 3402 D7
10800 HarC 77067 3402 D7
10800 HOUS 77038 3402 D7
10800 HOUS 77067 3402 D7
Sharnoll Cir
200 LGCY 77573 4633 A1
Sharon Dr
500 HMBL 77338 3263 A7
6600 PRLD 77581 4502 C1
Sharon Ln
6800 HTCK 77563 4989 B5
15300 MtgC 77302 2679 B3
22500 MtgC 77357 2973 E4
Sharon Pkwy
20800 HarC 77375 3110 C4
20800 HarC 77379 3110 C4
Sharon Rd
600 BYTN 77521 3833 D5
600 HarC 77521 3833 D5
Sharon St
100 CNRO 77301 2384 A2
600 PRVW 77445 3100 C4
600 PRVW 77484 3100 D4
2000 PASD 77502 4106 D7
2000 PASD 77502 4246 E1
4200 HOUS 77020 3964 C2
Sharondale Dr
8100 HOUS 77033 4244 A3
Sharondale St
6000 PRLD 77584 4502 D7
7700 HOUS 77033 4244 A2
Sharondoah Dr
400 HarC 77562 3832 B3
Sharon Louise
28400 MtgC 77355 2815 D5
Sharp Pl
1800 HOUS 77019 3962 B5

Sharpbill Dr
- HOUS 77072 4097 C6
13200 HOUS 77083 4097 B6
13500 HarC 77083 4097 B6
Sharpcrest Ln
7900 HOUS 77036 4099 C6
9500 HOUS 77036 4098 E6
9900 HOUS 77072 4098 E6
Sharpcrest St
7000 HOUS 77074 4100 A6
7100 HOUS 77074 4099 E6
Sharpsburg Dr
7000 FBnC 77469 4493 D6
7200 FBnC 77479 4493 D6
Sharpstown Ctr
100 HOUS 77036 4099 E4
Sharpstown Dr
- HOUS 77074 4100 B6
Sharpstown Grn
6600 HOUS 77036 4099 C4
Sharpton Dr
10000 HarC 77038 3543 D4
Sharptree Ct
24000 HarC 77389 2965 E4
Sharpvale Dr
- HarC 77388 3113 A5
Sharpview Dr
6300 HOUS 77074 4100 A5
6300 HOUS 77081 4100 B6
7100 HOUS 77074 4099 E6
8800 HOUS 77036 4099 A5
9500 HOUS 77036 4098 E5
11600 HOUS 77072 4098 A5
12400 HOUS 77072 4097 E5
Shartle Cir
600 HNCV 77024 3960 B2
Sharyn Dr
3100 MtgC 77384 2674 D2
Shasta Ct
3500 PRLD 77584 4503 A6
Shasta Dr
100 HNCV 77024 3960 C3
2000 LGCY 77565 4509 A5
Shasta Sq
7000 HarC 77084 3679 A2
Shasta Falls Ln
- HarC 77346 3408 D3
Shasta Leaf Ct
13900 HarC 77044 3549 E1
Shasta Ridge Dr
1900 CNRO 77304 2237 A4
Shasta Springs Dr
8900 HOUS 77034 4247 A7
9000 HOUS 77034 4378 A1
Shatner Dr
4500 HarC 77066 3401 A2
Shatnerwood Dr
17400 HarC 77095 3537 E7
Shattuck
- HarC 77388 3113 D3
Shaun Dr
4300 PASD 77504 4248 A4
4500 PASD 77505 4248 A4
Shauntel St
2700 PRLD 77581 4504 E5
Shavano Ln
7600 HarC 77433 3537 C7
Shavelson St
6800 HOUS 77055 3821 E7
Shaver St
200 PASD 77506 4107 A6
1200 PASD 77502 4247 D1
2000 PASD 77502 4247 B1
2700 SHUS 77502 4247 B2
2700 SHUS 77587 4247 B2
2900 PASD 77504 4247 B3
N Shaver St
- HOUS 77506 4107 A2
- PASD 77506 4107 A2
S Shaver St
100 PASD 77506 4107 A3
3100 PASD 77502 4247 B3
3100 PASD 77504 4247 B3
3100 PASD 77587 4247 B3
3100 SHUS 77504 4247 B3
3100 SHUS 77587 4247 B3
S Shaver St Ext
3400 PASD 77504 4247 B5
3400 SHUS 77504 4247 B5
3400 SHUS 77587 4247 B5
3700 HOUS 77034 4247 A7
4200 HOUS 77504 4247 B6
5200 HOUS 77034 4246 E7
5200 HOUS 77034 4377 E1
Shavon Ct
20100 HarC 77388 3113 A5
Shavon Springs Dr
19800 HarC 77388 3113 A5
Shaw Av
- HOUS 77017 4106 D3
100 PASD 77506 4107 B3
W Shaw Av
100 PASD 77506 4107 A3
700 PASD 77506 4106 E3
1300 HOUS 77017 4106 D3
Shaw Cir
17500 MtgC 77302 2679 E3
Shaw Rd
3900 IWCY 77583 4745 B1
4300 BzaC 77583 4745 D1
5200 MNVL 77578 4745 E1
5200 MNVL 77578 4746 A1
5200 MNVL 77583 4745 E1
17000 HarC 77429 3253 D3
17200 HarC 77377 3253 D3
18800 HarC 77377 3108 E7
18800 HarC 77429 3108 E7
Shaw St
- HarC 77429 3396 D3
800 ALVN 77511 4749 C7
1200 HOUS 77002 3963 B4
Shawna Dr
4400 HarC 77084 3678 C7
Shawna St
4600 HarC 77084 3678 C7
Shawna Lyn Dr
2700 HarC 77373 3114 D6
Shawnbrook Dr
10800 HOUS 77071 4239 D4
Shawnee
1300 GlsC 77650 4879 B5
Shawnee Dr
3000 SGLD 77479 4368 E7
3000 SGLD 77479 4495 E1
Shawnee St
1000 HOUS 77034 4246 B5
4200 HarC 77521 3833 B4

Shawnee Park Dr
21300 FBnC 77469 4234 A4
N Shawnee Ridge Cir
100 WDLD 77382 2819 E3
S Shawnee Ridge Cir
10 WDLD 77382 2819 E3
Shawnee Ridge Ct
10 WDLD 77382 2819 D3
Shawnee Ridge Dr
- WDLD 77382 2819 D2
Shawnway Ln
19400 HarC 77094 3955 B2
Shaw Perry Ln
23700 HarC 77493 3814 B5
Shawwood Ct
12400 HarC 77070 3399 D5
Shay Ln
18700 HarC 77346 3264 B6
Shayan Ct
100 HarC 77037 3684 D1
Shayna Ct
2500 HarC 77388 3113 A3
Shea Pl
10 HOUS 77002 3963 D2
Shealy Ct
15300 HOUS 77598 4506 D3
Shealy St
500 HOUS 77598 4506 D3
Shearn St
1200 HOUS 77007 3963 A2
2400 HOUS 77007 3962 E2
Shearwater Ct
2600 LGCY 77573 4631 A7
Shearwater Bend Dr
2500 HarC 77396 3407 C3
Sheats Rd
18700 MtgC 77302 2826 B1
Sheehan Av
- HOUS 77030 4102 E5
Sheep Meadow Pl
10 WDLD 77381 2820 D3
Sheerborne Ct
10 WDLD 77382 2674 C4
Sheer Water Dr
13200 HOUS 77082 4097 B3
Sheet Bend Wy
16700 HarC 77546 4506 A6
Sheffield Blvd
- HarC 77015 3967 C4
900 HOUS 77015 3967 A2
Sheffield Ct
4600 PASD 77504 4247 D6
Sheffield Dr
1200 MSCY 77459 4369 B6
25100 MtgC 77357 2828 D5
Sheffield Ln
6100 LGCY 77573 4630 B6
Sheffield St
1100 BLAR 77401 4101 A3
Sheffield Ter
14800 HarC 77530 3829 B6
Sheffield Bend Ct
7400 HarC 77095 3678 C2
Sheffield Bend Dr
17100 HarC 77095 3678 A1
Sheffield Estates Dr
17100 HarC 77095 3678 C3
Sheffield Falls Ct
7200 HarC 77095 3678 C3
Sheffield Gray Tr
21800 HarC 77433 3250 E5
Sheffield Knoll Ln
17100 HarC 77095 3678 C2
Sheffield Oaks Dr
- HarC 77084 3678 A2
- HarC 77095 3678 A2
Sheffield Pines Ln
17100 HarC 77095 3678 A1
Sheffield Terrace Dr
15100 HarC 77530 3829 C6
Sheila Ln
800 HarC 77530 3830 C6
Shekel Ln
200 HarC 77015 3828 E5
Shelbourne Cross
21800 HarC 77073 3259 B4
Shelbourne Bay Dr
- PRLD 77584 4500 A2
Shelbourne Meadows Dr
9300 HarC 77095 3538 B4
Shelbourne Park Ln
6000 HarC 77084 3678 C4
Shelburne Cir
7600 HarC 77379 3256 B2
Shelburne Ln
17500 HarC 77379 3256 B2
Shelburne Rd
13100 HarC 77049 3828 C1
Shelburne St
5800 HOUS 77396 3405 E4
6100 HOUS 77396 3406 A4
Shelby
1000 HOUS 77009 3824 C6
Shelby Cir
3200 HOUS 77051 4243 C2
Shelby Ct
16400 HarC 77379 3255 E6
Shelby Dr
2400 BzaC 77584 4501 C5
Shelby Dr N
- GLSN 77554 5441 B5
Shelby Dr S
- GLSN 77554 5441 B5
Shelby Row
4000 SGLD 77479 4368 E6
4000 SGLD 77479 4369 A7
Shelby St
1000 HOUS 77009 3824 D6
Shelby Oaks Cir
17700 FBnC 77469 4095 B5
Shelby Oaks Dr
6700 FBnC 77469 4095 C5
Shelby Park Dr
2200 HarC 77450 3954 D6
Shelby Park Ln
19400 HarC 77073 3403 D2
Shelby Springs Dr
- PRLD 77584 4500 D5
Shelby View Ln
1600 HarC 77073 3403 D2
Shelby Wy Dr
20300 HarC 77073 3259 C7
20300 HarC 77073 3403 C1
Sheldon Dr
3400 PRLD 77584 4501 C2
Sheldon Rd
200 HarC 77530 3969 B1
600 HarC 77530 3830 A2

Sheldon Rd
1600 HarC 77049 3830 A2
6600 HarC 77049 3691 A2
10500 HarC 77044 3691 A2
S Sheldon Rd
400 HarC 77015 3969 B5
400 HarC 77530 3969 B5
Sheldon St
2000 HOUS 77008 3823 E5
Sheldon Bend Dr
11100 FBnC 77469 4092 C7
Sheldon Dezavalla Rd
- HarC 77530 3969 B1
Sheldonham Dr
4800 HarC 77338 3260 D3
Sheldon Pines Dr
- HarC 77379 3257 A2
Sheldrake Ct
- SGLD 77478 4368 B3
Shelford Ct
21100 HarC 77449 3676 D4
Shelia Av
2400 PRLD 77581 4503 D3
Shell Rd
- BzaC 77581 4628 C1
Shellbark Pl
10 WDLD 77382 2673 E5
Shellbrook Dr
24600 HOUS 77336 3266 C2
Shell Creek Ct
10800 HarC 77064 3540 B7
Shell Dock Rd
4500 DRPK 77503 4108 E3
4500 DRPK 77536 4108 E3
4500 PASD 77503 4108 E3
Shelldock Rd
4300 BYTN 77520 3974 B2
4300 CmbC 77520 3974 B2
W Shelldock Rd
- CmbC 77520 3974 B2
Shelldrake Wy
3100 BYTN 77521 3972 B1
Shellee Dr
600 MtgC 77303 2385 C2
Shelley St
300 HOUS 77009 3824 A6
Shellhorn Ct
13200 HarC 77014 3402 B2
Shell Island Ct
3300 PRLD 77584 4501 D5
Shell Key
10 HTCK 77563 5105 A5
Shell Lake Dr
16300 HOUS 77062 4507 A3
Shellmont Ct
7600 HarC 77433 3537 A6
Shell Port Sq
- WDLD 77380 2821 D5
Shell Rock Rd
9700 LPRT 77571 4250 B4
Shellville Ct
8500 HarC 77040 3541 C6
Shelmer Dr
8700 HOUS 77080 3821 A5
Sheltered Arbor Ct
10 WDLD 77382 2819 A2
Sheltering Oaks Ln
1300 HOUS 77345 3120 D7
Shelter Rock Ct
100 WDLD 77382 2674 D5
Shelterwood Dr
800 HOUS 77008 3823 A7
Shelton Ct
- HOUS 77099 4238 C4
Shelton Ln
900 HarC 77530 3829 D6
Shelton Rd
4300 HarC 77093 3686 C2
4600 BKVL 77581 4375 B5
Shelton Grove Dr
13600 HarC 77070 3399 C3
Sheltons Bend Ct
1500 HOUS 77077 3957 A4
Shelton Shadows Ct
7800 HarC 77346 3265 B3
Shelwick Dr
12200 HOUS 77031 4239 B5
Shenandoah Dr
100 SHEH 77381 2822 A2
200 FBnC 77469 4493 D7
700 SHEH 77381 2821 E2
2400 HOUS 77017 4246 E2
2400 PASD 77017 4246 E2
2400 PASD 77502 4246 E2
2700 SHUS 77502 4246 E2
2700 SHUS 77587 4246 E2
Shenandoah Pk
500 MtgC 77302 2530 D5
Shenandoah St
2900 HOUS 77021 4103 B4
Shenandoah Falls Ln
700 FBnC 77469 4616 D1
Shenandoah Park Dr
8700 SHEH 77385 2822 B1
Shendewolf
- HarC 77338 3260 A2
Shepard St
- HMPD 77445 3097 E3
- WlrC 77445 3097 E3
1700 HMPD 77445 3098 A3
1700 WlrC 77445 3098 A3
Shepherd Dr
- HOUS 77019 3962 B4
10 HOUS 77088 3684 B2
100 HOUS 77007 3962 B3
N Shepherd Dr
- BYTN 77520 3973 B7
600 HOUS 77007 3962 B1
700 HOUS 77007 3823 B7
700 HOUS 77008 3823 B7
2900 HOUS 77018 3823 B1
4800 HOUS 77018 3684 B7
5000 HOUS 77091 3684 B7
7200 HOUS 77088 3684 B3
7600 HOUS 77037 3684 B3
N Shepherd Dr SPR-261
2900 HOUS 77018 3823 B4
4800 HOUS 77018 3684 B7
S Shepherd Dr
- HOUS 77007 3962 B4
900 HOUS 77019 3962 B7
1000 BYTN 77520 3973 C7
1000 BYTN 77520 4113 B1
2400 HOUS 77098 3962 B6
3700 HOUS 77098 4102 B2
5200 HOUS 77005 4102 B2
Shepherd Pk
- HOUS 77088 3684 A2

S Shepherd St
900 BYTN 77520 3973 C7
Shepherd Falls Ln
10800 HOUS 77075 4377 A6
Shepherds Pl
2000 FBnC 77479 4494 A4
Shepherds Ridge Dr
12400 HOUS 77077 3957 D5
Sheppard Rd
5200 HarC 77521 3833 C7
5200 HarC 77521 3972 C1
Sheppard St
31800 MtgC 77362 2963 D2
Shepperton Ct
9700 HarC 77065 3539 E4
Sherandoe Ln
300 ALVN 77511 4867 D7
Sheraton St
14600 HarC 77039 3545 C2
Sheraton Crossing Dr
6600 HarC 77389 2966 C2
Sheraton Oaks Dr
5400 HOUS 77091 3682 D4
Sherborne Dr
3000 PRLD 77584 4501 B2
Sherbourne St
- HOUS 77034 4379 A5
8900 HOUS 77016 3686 E7
8900 HOUS 77016 3687 A6
Sherbrook Cir
100 MtgC 77385 2676 A2
Sherbrook Rd
3800 PASD 77503 4108 C4
Sherbrooke Ct
300 PASD 77503 4108 C4
Sherbrooke Rd
1100 HOUS 77056 3960 E5
Sherbrooke Canyon Ln
- HarC 77047 4374 B4
Sherbrook Park Ln
2000 HarC 77449 3815 C6
Sherburne Dr
10600 HOUS 77072 4098 C3
Sherburn Manor Dr
13700 HarC 77429 3397 B3
Sheree St
7900 HarC 77049 3689 E7
Sherewood Garden Dr
11100 HOUS 77043 3819 B7
Sherfield Ridge Dr
1000 HarC 77450 3954 C4
Sheri Ln
1700 BYTN 77521 3973 C3
3800 HarC 77532 3412 C4
4400 HarC 77532 3413 A4
Sheri Ann Ln
2800 STFE 77510 4870 E4
2800 STFE 77510 4871 A4
Sheridan Dr
1500 BYTN 77520 3973 C7
Sheridan Rd
1500 PASD 77502 4107 D7
2000 HOUS 77030 4102 C4
2500 WUNP 77005 4102 A4
11200 HarC 77016 3547 D7
11400 HarC 77050 3547 D6
13800 HarC 77396 3547 D3
Sheri Hollow Ln
13800 HOUS 77082 4096 E2
13800 HOUS 77082 4097 A2
Sherilynn Dr
5200 HarC 77373 3260 D1
Sherina Park Dr
8800 HarC 77095 3538 C4
Sheringham St
5700 HOUS 77085 4371 D2
Sherioaks Ln
22700 HarC 77389 2967 A6
Sherl St
1500 LGCY 77573 4632 C3
Sherlock Acres Dr
12800 HarC 77377 3254 A3
Sherman Av
100 PASD 77503 4108 B4
Sherman Blvd
4300 GLSN 77550 5108 E7
4300 GLSN 77551 5108 E7
Sherman St
100 CNRO 77301 2384 B5
400 HOUS 77017 4246 B3
400 SHUS 77587 4246 B3
2900 HOUS 77003 3963 E5
3200 HOUS 77003 3964 A5
4300 HOUS 77011 3964 E7
7000 HOUS 77011 3965 A7
7400 HOUS 77012 3965 B7
7700 HOUS 77012 4105 B1
Sherman Oaks Dr
13400 HOUS 77085 4371 D1
Sherman Ridge Ln
7100 FBnC 77083 4095 D6
Shermons Pond
13100 HarC 77041 3679 D7
E Sherri Cir
8400 MNVL 77578 4746 D4
W Sherri Cir
8400 MNVL 77578 4746 D4
Sherrill Dr
12000 HOUS 77089 4378 C6
Sherrod Ln
22000 HarC 77388 3112 A2
22000 HarC 77389 3112 A1
22500 HarC 77389 2967 A7
Sherrous Ln
22200 MtgC 77365 2973 C7
Sherry Ln
11000 HarC 77041 3680 B4
31000 MtgC 77354 2672 D6
Sherrylee Ln
5300 HarC 77373 3115 D6
Sherrys Landing Blvd
9800 HarC 77089 4504 C2
Sherrywood Dr
8800 HarC 77044 3689 B5
Sherrywood Rd
8600 HarC 77044 3689 B6
Sherway St
7700 HarC 77016 3547 C7
Sherwell
- HOUS 77338 3263 B4
Sherwell St
- HarC 77338 3263 C6
- HOUS 77338 3263 C6
Sherwick Rdg
9500 HarC 77379 3110 D7
Sherwick St
2800 HOUS 77093 3685 E7
2800 HOUS 77093 3686 A7

Sherwin St
2100 HOUS 77007 3961 E1
Sherwood Cir
1700 ALVN 77511 4867 A3
Sherwood Ct
300 SHEH 77381 2822 A2
Sherwood Dr
- PRLD 77581 4503 D4
700 PASD 77502 4107 B7
1800 HOUS 77043 3819 B6
5300 KATY 77493 3813 D6
6100 HOUS 77021 4103 D6
E Sherwood Dr
100 HLCS 77511 4867 E5
100 HLCS 77511 4868 A5
W Sherwood Dr
100 ALVN 77511 4867 E6
100 HLCS 77511 4867 E6
Sherwood Ln
3700 HOUS 77018 3822 B3
3700 HOUS 77092 3822 A3
Sherwood St
1300 BYTN 77520 3973 D7
13500 SGLD 77478 4237 B7
Sherwood St E
4000 HOUS 77339 3119 B2
Sherwood St W
4000 HOUS 77339 3119 B3
Sherwood Bend Dr
3100 HarC 77068 3257 C4
Sherwood Forest Cir
- LGCY 77573 4632 B2
Sherwood Forest Dr
400 DKSN 77539 4753 B3
Sherwood Forest St
- HOUS 77043 3958 B1
- HOUS 77079 3958 B1
1000 HOUS 77043 3819 B7
Sherwood Forest Glen Ct
1200 HOUS 77043 3819 B7
Sherwood Forest Glen Dr
11100 HOUS 77043 3819 B7
Sherwood Green Ct
4400 MSCY 77459 4369 A4
Sherwood Greens
24700 WlrC 77447 2959 D1
Sherwood Hollow Ln
2400 HOUS 77339 3119 A2
Sherwood Mills Ln
1300 HOUS 77043 3819 B7
Sherwood Oak St
3000 DKSN 77539 4753 C3
Sherwood Oaks Dr
13100 HarC 77015 3828 C5
Sherwood Park Cir
1400 HOUS 77043 3819 B7
Sherwood Park Ln
11100 HOUS 77043 3819 B7
Sherwood Point Ln
1300 HOUS 77043 3819 B7
Sherwood Ridge Dr
11000 HOUS 77043 3819 B7
Sherwood Springs Ln
1300 HOUS 77043 3819 B7
Sheryl Cir
- HarC 77396 3407 B5
Sheryl Ct
- HarC 77396 3407 B5
9800 HarC 77379 3110 C4
Sheryl Dr
1300 JTCY 77029 3966 D3
Shetland
11200 MtgC 77302 2677 B1
Shetland Ln
800 KATY 77493 3813 B7
800 KATY 77493 3952 B1
4500 HOUS 77027 3961 B7
Shetland Isle Ct
10 SGLD 77479 4495 B2
Shetstone Cir
12300 HarC 77433 3396 B5
Shevchenko
200 HarC 77037 3544 C7
Shield St
9800 HOUS 77017 4106 B4
Shieldhall Ln
- HarC 77375 3110 C2
Shields
- HOUS 77030 4102 E5
Shields Ln
19300 MtgC 77302 2680 C7
19300 MtgC 77357 2680 C7
19300 MtgC 77357 2826 C1
Shields Rd
25900 MtgC 77355 2962 D3
Shields St
700 HarC 77530 3830 E5
Shifting Sand Ln
20700 FBnC 77469 4094 B6
Shillington Ct
20600 HarC 77450 3954 D3
Shillington Dr
800 HarC 77450 3954 C2
1700 HarC 77094 3955 A4
1700 HarC 77450 3955 A4
Shilo Dr
5000 HarC 77032 3546 D2
Shiloh Av
8400 TXCY 77591 4873 A4
Shiloh Ct
3300 MSCY 77459 4497 D5
Shiloh Dr
100 FBnC 77469 4493 C7
2900 MSCY 77459 4497 E6
Shiloh Pk
300 MtgC 77302 2530 B6
Shiloh St
2600 HOUS 77020 3963 E3
Shiloh Church Rd
12000 HarC 77066 3400 C3
12600 HarC 77069 3400 C3
Shiloh Creek Ct
19400 HarC 77449 3677 C3
Shiloh Creek Ln
19300 HarC 77449 3677 A3
Shiloh Lake Dr
- FBnC 77478 4235 E7
4900 FBnC 77469 4235 D6
Shiloh Park Ct
3800 HarC 77546 4506 C6
Shiloh Valley Ln
17300 HarC 77346 3408 C3
Shimmering Green Tr
21800 HarC 77433 3250 D4
Shimmering Lake Dr
16500 HarC 77433 3250 E4
Shimmering Maple Dr
9500 HarC 77064 3541 A4

Shimmering Pines Rd
7800 HarC 77379 3111 A7
Shimmer Pond Pl
10 WDLD 77385 2676 B3
Shimmer Wood Dr
- WDLD 77382 2673 B6
Shindler Cir
8600 HarC 77064 3540 D6
Shindler Ct
3800 FBnC 77459 4621 B5
Shiner Ct
3100 PRLD 77584 4501 D4
Shiner Ln
7300 HOUS 77072 4098 A6
Shing Creek Ct
5000 FBnC 77494 4093 B2
Shingle Oak Ln
4300 HOUS 77088 3682 E3
14700 HarC 77377 2963 C5
14700 TMBL 77375 2963 C5
14700 TMBL 77377 2963 C5
Shining Creek Ln
- MtgC 77386 2969 D6
Shining Lakes Pl
10 WDLD 77381 2821 A2
Shining Mist Ln
7100 FBnC 77469 4615 E5
Shining Rock Ln
16200 HarC 77095 3538 B5
Shining Stream Ln
1900 FBnC 77469 4365 B2
Shining Sumac Av
6700 HarC 77084 3678 E2
6700 HarC 77095 3678 E2
Shinnecock Hills Dr
6500 HarC 77069 3400 B2
Shinning Leaf Cir
5900 HarC 77449 3677 C5
Shin Oak Dr
24200 HOUS 77336 3266 C2
Shinwood Dr
19500 HarC 77346 3264 C5
Shiny Pebble Pl
10 WDLD 77381 2674 E6
Shinyrock Pl
10 WDLD 77381 2820 C2
Ship Anchor Dr
16800 HarC 77546 4506 A7
Ship Channel Br
- HOUS 4105 E2
Ship Channel Br I-610
- HOUS 4105 E2
Shipman Ln
3600 HarC 77388 3112 D6
3600 HarC 77388 3257 E1
Shipmans Landing Dr
- FBnC 77459 4621 D7
10500 FBnC 77459 4622 A5
Shipping Blvd
- PASD 77507 4381 D2
Shiprock Dr
2400 DRPK 77536 4109 E6
Shipyard Dr
1800 SEBK 77586 4509 D4
Shiraz Ln
700 GLSN 77550 5110 B1
Shiraz Psg
700 GLSN 77550 5110 B1
Shire Rd
- MtgC 77357 2829 E4
18800 MtgC 77357 2830 A4
Shirebrook Dr
13700 SGLD 77478 4237 A7
Shirefield Ct
800 HarC 77373 2968 E7
Shirefield Ln
900 HarC 77373 2968 E5
Shiremeadow Dr
700 MSCY 77489 4370 E5
Shiremist Ct
26700 FBnC 77494 4092 E3
Shireoak Dr
18000 HarC 77084 3816 E1
Shire Trail Ct
- HarC 77338 3261 D4
Shire Valley Dr
- MSCY 77459 4369 D5
Shire Wood Ln
2900 HOUS 77082 4098 A1
Shirkmere Rd
800 HOUS 77008 3822 E7
Shirleen Dr
100 PASD 77586 4508 D2
1100 STAF 77477 4370 C4
Shirley Av
2100 ALVN 77511 4749 E7
2200 BzaC 77511 4749 E7
2200 BzaC 77511 4750 A7
Shirley Ct
28700 MtgC 77355 2815 D3
Shirley Ln
1400 HOUS 77015 3967 A3
2100 LPRT 77571 4250 E1
5600 HOUS 77032 3405 D6
5600 HOUS 77396 3405 D6
6000 HOUS 77396 3406 A6
11000 GlsC 77510 4871 D5
Shirley Mdw
29000 MtgC 77355 2815 D3
Shirley St
800 LMQU 77568 4990 B1
5100 BYTN 77521 3971 E1
5100 BYTN 77521 3972 A1
N Shirley St
100 ALVN 77511 4867 D1
400 ALVN 77511 4749 D7
S Shirley St
100 ALVN 77511 4867 D1
Shirley Mae Ln
5900 HOUS 77091 3683 C5
Shiro Dr
3300 HarC 77014 3401 E1
Shive Dr
9700 HOUS 77078 3688 B5
Shiveley Cir
2000 HarC 77032 3404 C7
2000 HOUS 77032 3404 C7
Shoal Cir
- BYTN 77521 3973 D3
Shoal Ct
700 HarC 77532 3552 B3
2000 PRLD 77584 4500 D1
Shoal St
16300 HarC 77532 3552 B3
Shoal Creek Ct
11500 PRLD 77584 4500 D3
Shoal Creek Dr
2400 LGCY 77573 4508 D7

STREET
Block City ZIP Map# Grid

Shoal Creek Dr
8500 HarC 77064 3400 A6
8600 HarC 77064 3399 D6
11300 PRLD 77584 4500 D3
Shoal Hollow Ct
26800 HarC 77433 3537 A1
Shoal Lake Ct
2100 LGCY 77573 4631 C7
3300 PRLD 77584 4501 B3
Shoal Lake Ln
17400 HarC 77095 3537 E5
Shoal Landing St
11600 PRLD 77584 4500 C1
Shoal Park Dr
16800 HarC 77429 3252 E6
Shoal Point Ln
- HarC 77377 3253 E4
- HarC 77429 3253 E4
Shoal Pointe Ct
800 LGCY 77573 4633 B3
Shoal Pointe Ln
800 LGCY 77573 4633 B2
Shoal Ridge Ct
21600 HarC 77449 3815 A2
Shoal Springs Ln
26800 HarC 77433 3537 A1
Shoal Water Ln
13000 PRLD 77584 4500 A4
Shoalwater Ln
- HarC 77070 3255 C7
- LGCY 77573 4631 C7
Shoalwood Falls Dr
- HarC 77095 3537 E1
Shoemaker Rd
- HOUS 77085 4240 E7
Shoemo Hl
- HOUS 77045 4372 B7
Shooting Center Dr
16000 HOUS 77094 4096 A2
16400 HOUS 77094 4095 E1
Shooting Star Pl
10 WDLD 77381 2675 A6
Shooting Star St
100 FRDW 77546 4629 E6
100 FRDW 77546 4630 A5
Shoppe St
8900 HOUS 77504 4247 B7
8900 HOUS 77504 4378 C1
9400 HOUS 77034 4378 C1
S Shore Blvd
- LGCY 77565 4633 B1
- LGCY 77573 4633 B1
2300 LGCY 77573 4508 D5
4200 LGCY 77573 4509 A7
N Shore Bnd
6400 FBnC 77469 4493 B6
E Shore Dr
400 CRLS 77565 4509 C5
N Shore Dr
100 CRLS 77565 4509 C4
16200 HarC 77530 3969 C1
S Shore Dr
10 GLSN 77551 5108 C6
800 CRLS 77565 4509 C5
W Shore Dr
200 CRLS 77565 4509 C5
Shoreacres Blvd
100 SRAC 77571 4383 A2
400 SRAC 77571 4382 C2
Shoreacres Cir
10 SRAC 77571 4383 A2
Shore Bend Ct
- HarC 77379 3111 C1
Shore Breeze Dr
2000 PRLD 77584 4500 A1
Shore Breeze Ln
300 LGCY 77573 4508 C6
Shorebridge Rd
12100 HarC 77433 3395 D5
Shore Brook Cir
3100 LGCY 77573 4633 C1
Shore Brook Ct
3100 LGCY 77573 4633 C1
Shorebrook Dr
2300 PRLD 77584 4500 A2
14700 HarC 77095 3539 B6
Shore Castle Ct
20600 HarC 77450 3954 C6
Shore Creek Ct
11900 PRLD 77584 4500 C2
Shore Creek Dr
2200 PRLD 77584 4500 C2
Shorecrest Dr
16600 HarC 77095 3397 A7
Shoregrove Dr
8200 HarC 77346 3265 B3
Shoreham St
9100 HOUS 77093 3685 E6
Shorehaven Cir
5000 HOUS 77048 4243 D7
Shore Hills Dr
4800 HOUS 77345 3120 A6
Shorelake Dr
10 HOUS 77339 3119 A7
Shoreland Ct
18900 HarC 77377 3253 D1
Shore Landing Ln
10 LGCY 77539 4752 E3
Shorelands Rd
12100 HarC 77433 3395 D5
Shore Line Ct
2900 SEBK 77586 4382 B7
Shore Line Dr
1600 PASD 77586 4382 A6
1600 TYLV 77586 4382 A6
Shoreline Dr
10 SGLD 77478 4368 B4
1700 MSCY 77459 4369 C7
18300 HarC 77532 3409 D6
25200 WlrC 77447 2959 C2
Shoreline Point Dr
10 WDLD 77381 2821 B4
N Shoreline Point Dr
10 WDLD 77381 2821 C4
Shoreline Terrace Dr
15800 HarC 77044 3408 E4
Shore Meadow Dr
3100 LGCY 77573 4633 B1
Shore Meadows Ct
14200 HOUS 77077 3956 D5
Shore Meadows Ln
19800 FBnC 77469 4094 C6
Shore Park Rd
18300 HarC 77433 3395 D5
Shore Pointe Ct
- LGCY 77573 4508 E6
1900 LGCY 77573 4509 A6
11900 PRLD 77584 4500 C2

Shores Edge Dr
19700 HarC 77375 3109 E6
Shore Shadows Dr
800 HOUS 77336 3121 A5
3100 HarC 77532 3409 D6
Shoreside Dr
2900 BzaC 77584 4501 B6
3000 HarC 77532 3409 E6
Shoreview Cir
19500 HarC 77346 3265 D5
Shoreview Ct
6300 HarC 77346 3264 E3
6800 MSCY 77459 4496 E4
Shoreview Dr
- LGCY 77539 4752 D6
Shore View Ln
3500 MSCY 77459 4496 D4
Shoreview Ln
8900 HarC 77346 3265 D5
Shorewick Dr
2400 HarC 77562 3691 E7
Shorewood Dr
600 TYLV 77586 4508 E1
600 TYLV 77586 4509 A1
900 TYLV 77586 4382 A7
1200 TYLV 77586 4381 E7
Shorewood Ln
2000 SGLD 77479 4495 B1
E Shorewood Lp
22400 HOUS 77336 3266 C5
W Shorewood Lp
22400 HOUS 77336 3266 C5
Shorewood Lakes Dr
16500 HarC 77095 3538 B4
Short
- BYTN 77520 3971 B4
- PASD 77506 4107 C4
Short Ct
12100 HarC 77429 3397 B6
Short Lk
14300 MtgC 77372 2682 D1
Short Ln
- CNRO 77301 2530 A1
26000 SPLD 77372 2683 B2
Short Rd
6100 ARLA 77583 4623 A6
34100 WlrC 77484 3100 E7
Short St
- HarC 77562 3692 A6
100 CTSH 77303 2385 C3
100 CTSH 77306 2385 C3
100 MtgC 77306 2385 C3
300 MtgC 77301 2385 C3
2300 HarC 77521 3832 D5
4000 HOUS 77021 4103 D5
25800 MtgC 77372 2683 C6
25800 PTVL 77372 2683 C6
Short Bridge St
11000 HOUS 77075 4377 B4
Short Brook Ln
13600 HarC 77095 3539 C7
Shortfin Mako Ct
22000 HarC 77449 3815 A4
Short Horn
26700 MtgC 77372 2683 C1
26700 SPLD 77372 2683 C1
Shorthorn Cir
11000 HOUS 77041 3680 C5
Shorthorn Ln
6000 HarC 77041 3680 C5
Short Leaf Dr
10 HarC 77336 2976 C5
Short Leaf Ln
2700 HOUS 77365 3119 E3
Short Leaf Pine Ct
34300 MtgC 77362 2816 E6
Short Line Rd
29800 MtgC 77354 2818 B1
Short Path Ct
2100 HarC 77373 3114 D4
Short Pines Dr
- HarC 77373 3113 D2
Shortpoint Ln
2000 HOUS 77055 3821 C4
Short Reach Dr
900 TKIS 77554 5106 C4
Short Springs Ct
2300 PRLD 77584 4500 B2
Short Springs Dr
12500 PRLD 77584 4500 B1
Short Trail Ln
11700 HarC 77377 3109 B7
Shoshone Dr
7200 HarC 77521 3833 B4
Shoshone Rd
11500 HOUS 77055 3821 C3
Shoshoni Dr
- PASD 77504 4248 A5
- PASD 77505 4248 A5
1600 DRPK 77536 4109 C5
Shoshoni St
7100 BYTN 77521 3835 A5
Shottery Dr
14800 HarC 77015 3829 B4
Shotwell Ct
2800 MSCY 77459 4497 E6
Shotwell St
200 HOUS 77020 3825 D7
300 HOUS 77020 3964 D1
7600 HOUS 77016 3825 D1
7600 HOUS 77028 3825 D1
8100 HOUS 77016 3686 D7
Shouse Rd
1700 GlsC 77510 4870 D3
1700 GlsC 77517 4870 D3
2700 STFE 77510 4870 D4
Shouse St
2800 STFE 77510 4870 D5
Shreve Ln
3700 FBnC 77459 4621 D5
Shreveport Blvd
8100 HOUS 77028 3825 D1
8700 HOUS 77028 3686 E7
9800 HOUS 77028 3687 A7
Shrewsbury Cir
16200 HarC 77379 3256 E4
Shriver Ln
32600 WlrC 77484 3246 C1
Shroeder Ln
3100 BzaC 77511 4747 E7
Shrub Oak Dr
1300 LGCY 77573 4632 A5
16500 HarC 77396 3407 E3
Shumard Ct
3300 HarC 77388 3112 E5
Shumard Oak Ct
11000 HarC 77065 3539 E1

Shumaring Dr
19900 HarC 77338 3262 B4
Shurlin Pl
13500 HarC 77429 3397 E2
Shurmard Dr
5800 HOUS 77092 3682 B5
Shying Ct
- HarC 77532 3551 E4
Siamese Ln
11200 SGLD 77478 4237 D5
Siandra Creek Ct
4500 MtgC 77386 3115 E1
Siandra Creek Ln
27300 MtgC 77386 3115 D1
27600 MtgC 77386 2970 E7
Siano Pines Dr
9500 HarC 77396 3407 B2
Sias Dr
2600 GLSN 77551 5108 D6
Sias St
3700 STFE 77517 4870 A5
Sibelius Ln
100 HOUS 77079 3958 C4
Siberian Elm Ln
21800 HarC 77073 3259 E1
Sibley St
1800 HOUS 77023 4104 C2
Sica Hollow Ln
2600 FBnC 77494 3953 B6
Sicklepod Dr
2600 HarC 77084 3815 E5
W Side Forest Dr
- HarC 77094 3954 E4
18800 HarC 77094 3955 A4
Side Saddle Wy
28000 MtgC 77355 2815 A6
Sidney Dr
700 RSBG 77471 4491 C3
Sidney St
700 HOUS 77003 3964 A7
700 HOUS 77023 3964 A7
6500 GLSN 77551 5108 B7
6600 HOUS 77021 4103 D7
N Sidney St
500 HOUS 77003 3964 B5
E Sidnor St
100 ALVN 77511 4867 C1
W Sidnor St
100 ALVN 77511 4867 B1
1800 ALVN 77511 4866 E1
Sidonie Dr
16600 HOUS 77053 4372 C7
Sidonie Rose Ln
- FBnC 77494 4093 B6
Sieber Dr
1900 HOUS 77017 4106 C7
2000 HOUS 77017 4246 C1
Siebinthaler Ln
3200 HarC 77084 3816 D3
Siegel St
4100 HOUS 77009 3824 C6
Siegen Dr
2300 CNRO 77304 2236 E2
Siena Ct
1400 PRLD 77581 4504 E2
Siena Dr
2100 PRLD 77581 4504 E2
Siena Vista Dr
7100 FBnC 77083 4096 A6
Sienna Pkwy
3500 FBnC 77459 4621 D5
4200 MSCY 77459 4621 C2
5800 MSCY 77459 4497 B7
E Sienna Pl
10 WDLD 77382 2674 C4
W Sienna Pl
10 WDLD 77382 2674 B4
Sienna Sprs
- FBnC 77459 4497 B7
- FBnC 77459 4621 A1
- MSCY 77459 4497 B7
Sienna Arbor Ln
6100 HarC 77041 3679 D4
Sienna Bay Ct
5900 HarC 77041 3680 A5
Sienna Bend Dr
- WDLD 77382 2674 B4
E Sienna Cove Ln
- FBnC 77083 4095 B7
N Sienna Cove Ln
- FBnC 77083 4095 D7
S Sienna Cove Ln
- FBnC 77083 4095 B7
W Sienna Cove Ln
- FBnC 77083 4095 B7
Sienna Falls Dr
- HarC 77095 3396 E7
Sienna Heights Ct
4500 PASD 77505 4248 B6
Sienna Heights Ln
4700 PASD 77505 4248 B6
Sienna Hill Ln
- HarC 77379 3111 E4
1200 HOUS 77077 3957 A3
Sienna Leaf Tr
- HarC 77433 3251 A5
Sienna Oak Dr
15300 HarC 77433 3251 A5
Sienna Pines Ct
20300 HarC 77379 3111 E4
Sienna Pines Ln
21100 HarC 77449 3815 B1
Sienna Ranch Rd
- FBnC 77459 4621 B3
- MSCY 77459 4621 C3
Sienna Ridge Ln
19900 MtgC 77355 2814 C3
Sienna Rosa Ln
12200 HarC 77041 3679 E4
Sienna Sky Ct
9000 FBnC 77469 4234 E2
Sienna Springs Blvd
- FBnC 77459 4621 A1
Sienna Springs Dr
2700 PRLD 77584 4500 E3
Sienna Terrace Ln
24900 FBnC 77494 3953 A6
Sienna Trace Ct
8100 HarC 77083 4097 B7
Sienna Trails Dr
12700 HarC 77377 3254 A3
Sienna Trails Ln
4100 HOUS 77048 4374 E5
Sierra Dr
1500 BYTN 77521 3973 C2
2000 LGCY 77565 4509 A5
9300 HOUS 77051 4243 B4
15700 JRSV 77040 3540 D7

Sierra Ln
18900 HarC 77346 3264 A6
Sierra Bend Dr
21200 FBnC 77469 4094 A6
21800 FBnC 77469 4093 E6
21800 HOUS 77469 4093 E6
Sierra Blanca Dr
6200 HarC 77082 4096 E4
6200 HarC 77083 4096 E4
6200 HOUS 77082 4096 E4
6200 HOUS 77083 4096 E4
Sierra Breeze
600 HarC 77094 3955 E2
Sierra Brook Ln
800 LGCY 77573 4633 B2
5800 HarC 77041 3679 E5
Sierra Creek Ln
17500 HarC 77346 3408 C2
Sierra Dawn Dr
8200 HarC 77375 3110 E2
Sierra Falls Ct
18400 HarC 77377 3254 A2
Sierra Grande Ct
7400 FBnC 77083 4096 A6
Sierra Grande Dr
15800 FBnC 77083 4096 B6
16300 FBnC 77083 4095 E6
Sierra Hill Ct
8300 FBnC 77083 4235 C1
Sierra Lake Ct
22400 FBnC 77494 4093 D4
Sierra Lake Dr
800 HarC 77450 3953 D3
Sierra Long Dr
21400 FBnC 77469 4094 A6
21800 FBnC 77469 4093 E6
Sierra Madre Ln
22100 HarC 77532 3266 E6
Sierra Madre St
2300 FRDW 77546 4629 E7
2300 FRDW 77546 4630 A7
Sierra Night Ct
21400 FBnC 77469 4094 B7
Sierra Night Dr
7000 FBnC 77469 4094 A6
Sierra Oaks Dr
10 FBnC 77479 4367 A6
Sierra Pines Ct
15300 HarC 77068 3257 B5
Sierra Pines Dr
3500 HarC 77068 3257 B5
Sierra Point Dr
4400 MSCY 77545 4622 B2
Sierra Ranch Dr
8700 HarC 77044 3689 C5
Sierra Ridge Dr
14900 HarC 77346 3408 A7
14900 HarC 77396 3408 A7
Sierra Shadows Dr
900 HarC 77450 3954 A3
Sierra Skies Dr
15500 HarC 77083 4096 B5
Sierra Springs Ln
900 HarC 77373 3114 A4
Sierra Sunset Dr
14900 HarC 77346 3408 A7
Sierra Trails Dr
6900 HarC 77083 4096 B5
Sierra Valle Cir
15400 HarC 77083 4096 B6
Sierra Valle Dr
15400 HarC 77083 4096 B6
Sierra Vista Dr
15900 HarC 77083 4096 A5
Sierra Woods Ln
25300 FBnC 77494 3953 A5
Siers Av
6200 TXCY 77591 4873 D6
Siesta Ln
1100 JTCY 77029 3966 D3
Sifton Dr
30800 MtgC 77386 2969 A1
Sigma St
1200 PASD 77504 4247 D7
Sign St
7700 HOUS 77489 4371 A5
Signal Creek Dr
15800 HarC 77095 3538 C7
Signal Hill Ct
12300 PRLD 77584 4500 B2
Signal Hill Dr
10 BzaC 77583 4624 C3
10 MNVL 77583 4624 C3
2100 PRLD 77584 4500 B2
2800 HarC 77546 4506 A7
2800 HarC 77598 4506 B7
Signal Point Ln
6500 HarC 77064 3541 D2
Signal Ridge Wy
- HarC 77429 3253 C3
Signat Dr
6600 HarC 77041 3679 D2
Signature Crest Ct
- WDLD 77382 2673 C6
Signature Point Dr
10 LGCY 77573 4508 C6
Signet St
7900 HOUS 77029 3965 B5
9700 HOUS 77029 3966 A5
9800 GNPK 77547 3966 A5
Sikes St
300 HOUS 77018 3823 C1
Silas Creek Ct
5700 FBnC 77479 4493 E2
Silber Rd
- HOUS 77055 3960 E1
900 HOUS 77024 3960 E1
1000 HOUS 77055 3821 E7
2300 HOUS 77092 3821 E5
Silbury Ct
20300 HarC 77450 3954 D1
20500 HOUS 77450 3954 D1
Silent Dr
2900 FBnC 77478 4236 A7
Silent Brook Ct
10 WDLD 77381 2821 A1
Silent Brook Pl
10 WDLD 77381 2821 A1
Silent Cedars Dr
8100 HarC 77095 3538 D6
Silent Creek Dr
12300 PRLD 77584 4500 B1
Silent Elm St
11600 HarC 77044 3549 A7
Silent Flight Dr
24300 HarC 77494 3953 B3
Silent Forest Dr
7700 FBnC 77479 4494 A5

Silent Glen Ln
- LGCY 77539 4752 E5
Silent Hills Ln
- FBnC 77469 4235 C1
Silent Jasmin Ct
21800 HarC 77433 3250 E6
Silent Lake Ct
14200 SGLD 77478 4236 E7
Silent Meadows Ct
25000 HarC 77375 2965 D3
Silent Oaks Dr
5900 HarC 77346 3264 D5
Silent River Ct
21100 FBnC 77469 4234 B4
Silent River Dr
8200 FBnC 77469 4234 B4
Silent Shore Ct
1800 LGCY 77573 4631 C7
2500 FBnC 77469 4365 B2
Silent Shore Ln
12900 HarC 77041 3679 E7
Silent Shores Ln
- PRLD 77584 4500 B4
Silent Spring Dr
3000 SGLD 77479 4495 A2
Silent Spring Creek Ct
22900 FBnC 77450 3953 C6
Silent Spring Creek Dr
2600 FBnC 77450 3953 E7
Silent Springs Ct
2200 LGCY 77573 4631 C7
Silent Spruce Ct
19000 HarC 77084 3677 B7
Silent Star Ct
7700 HarC 77095 3537 A5
Silent Timber Ln
7700 FBnC 77469 4095 D6
Silent Walk Ct
2600 PRLD 77545 4499 E3
Silent Walk Dr
1300 PRLD 77545 4499 E3
Silent Willow Ln
8800 FBnC 77479 4494 B4
Silent Wood Ln
7300 HarC 77086 3542 A3
Silhouette Ct
26700 HarC 77493 3813 A1
Silhouette Dr
4600 HarC 77493 3813 A1
Silhouette Bay Ct
13100 PRLD 77584 4500 A5
Silhouette Bay Dr
2800 PRLD 77584 4500 A4
Silhouette Ridge Dr
15000 HarC 77396 3407 D7
Silk Ct
4100 MtgC 77386 2970 D7
Silkbay Pl
10 WDLD 77382 2674 B4
Silkbay Meadow Dr
- FBnC 77494 4093 A3
Silkleaf Ln
1600 HarC 77094 3955 A4
Silk Oak Ct
20800 HarC 77449 3815 C4
Silktassel Ln
10 WDLD 77380 2821 E6
Silk Tree Ln
2700 HarC 77449 3815 C5
Silk Tree Pl
10 WDLD 77384 2675 A3
Silkwood Dr
10400 HOUS 77031 4239 B4
Silky Ct
2600 HarC 77449 3814 E4
Silky Leaf Dr
200 HarC 77073 3403 A3
Silky Moss Dr
6500 HarC 77064 3541 D1
Sills Dr
5200 KATY 77493 3813 D7
Silo Ln
12300 HOUS 77071 4239 E6
Silouette Cove Ln
3500 HarC 77546 4506 C6
Silsbee Dr
4800 PRLD 77584 4503 A3
Silsbee St
6600 HOUS 77033 4104 B7
6700 HOUS 77033 4244 B1
Silvan Wind Ln
8300 HarC 77040 3541 B7
Silver Dr
6100 PRLD 77581 4502 D2
Silver Fld
21900 HarC 77449 3676 C6
Silver Gln
12500 HarC 77014 3401 E3
Silver Spur
32900 MtgC 77355 2962 A1
32900 SGCH 77355 2962 A1
Silver St
- STAF 77477 4370 B5
1300 HOUS 77007 3963 A2
Silverado Dr
1300 HOUS 77077 3957 C5
Silverado Trace Dr
10600 HarC 77095 3537 E1
Silver Ash Ln
17800 HarC 77095 3537 D7
Silver Ash Wy
18000 HarC 77095 3537 E7
Silver Aspen Ct
3900 PASD 77059 4380 D5
Silver Bank Ct
1900 NSUB 77058 4508 A6
Silver Bay Ct
5700 SGLD 77479 4495 A4
8300 HarC 77095 3538 D6
11300 PRLD 77584 4500 D2
Silver Bay Dr
2300 PRLD 77584 4500 D2
Silver Bayou Ct
10 WDLD 77384 2675 A4
Silver Bell Dr
1500 HarC 77038 3543 E4
Silver Bell St
4500 HOUS 77045 4241 C7
Silverbelle Ct
4700 FBnC 77469 4364 B1
Silverbelle Ln
5200 FBnC 77469 4364 A1
Silver Bend Dr
- DKSN 77539 4752 D6
- HarC 77346 3408 A2
- LGCY 77539 4752 D6
Silverberry Tr
2900 HOUS 77345 3119 E1

Silver Birch Ct
9600 FBnC 77459 4621 D6
Silver Birch Dr
21400 HarC 77073 3259 D2
Silverbit Trail Ln
2800 HarC 77450 3954 D7
Silver Blueberry Tr
21800 HarC 77433 3250 E5
Silver Bluff Ct
10 WDLD 77382 2675 B7
Silverbluff Ct
26100 HarC 77433 3396 B7
Silverbonnet St
2200 HOUS 77055 3821 D4
Silver Bough Cir
2700 HOUS 77059 4379 E5
Silverbow Ct
20800 HarC 77450 3954 C7
Silver Bridge Ln
3800 HarC 77449 3815 C2
Silver Brook Ln
1700 FBnC 77494 3952 B6
21800 HarC 77449 3815 A2
Silverbrook Ln
200 LGCY 77539 4753 B4
3300 BzaC 77584 4501 B5
Silver Brush Dr
2300 FBnC 77478 4237 A5
2300 SGLD 77478 4237 A5
Silver Canyon Ct
5400 BzaC 77583 4623 D4
11900 HarC 77067 3401 D4
Silver Canyon Ln
5500 BzaC 77583 4623 D4
11900 HarC 77067 3401 E5
Silver Canyon Pl
10 WDLD 77381 2820 D2
Silver Cedar Tr
2900 HarC 77449 3815 D4
Silver Chalice Dr
3300 MtgC 77357 2829 D3
3300 RMFT 77357 2829 D3
6300 HOUS 77088 3682 C3
Silver Charm
2800 HarC 77014 3401 E3
Silver Chase Ln
20900 FBnC 77469 4234 B4
Silver City Dr
10100 HarC 77064 3540 C4
Silver City Lp
8600 MtgC 77304 2236 B3
Silver Cliff Ln
700 HarC 77373 2968 E6
Silver Cloud Ln
7500 HarC 77086 3542 A3
Silver Creek Cir
300 FBnC 77469 4365 B5
Silver Creek Ct
2400 FBnC 77469 4365 B5
2700 BzaC 77578 4501 B6
Silver Creek Dr
10 CNRO 77301 2383 D3
5100 HOUS 77017 4106 B7
5100 HOUS 77017 4246 B1
12100 HarC 77070 3254 D7
Silvercreek Dr
- BzaC 77584 4501 A7
- PRLD 77584 4501 A7
3300 BzaC 77578 4501 A7
N Silver Crescent Cir
10 WDLD 77382 2675 B6
S Silver Crescent Cir
10 WDLD 77382 2675 B6
Silver Crescent Dr
6300 HarC 77064 3541 C1
Silvercrest St
10100 HOUS 77076 3685 C5
Silver Crossing Ct
5500 HarC 77084 3678 A6
Silver Crown Ct
3400 FBnC 77469 4233 C6
Silver Cup
12500 HarC 77014 3401 E3
Silver Cypress Ct
20200 HarC 77449 3815 C5
Silver Cypress Dr
2500 HarC 77449 3815 C5
Silverdale Dr
100 CNRO 77301 2384 C6
Silverdale St
1100 HOUS 77029 3965 D3
Silver Dawn Ct
6200 HOUS 77345 3120 C4
Silver Dollar Ct
3100 PRLD 77584 4501 E5
Silver Elm Pl
10 WDLD 77381 2820 E3
Silver Elms Ct
21600 SGCH 77355 2961 A2
Silver Falls Dr
2100 HOUS 77339 3118 E4
2600 HOUS 77339 3119 A4
Silver Feather Ln
- HarC 77396 3548 C2
Silverfield Ln
12400 HarC 77014 3402 A3
Silver Fir Dr
8500 HarC 77095 3538 E5
Silver Fir Ln
- CmbC 77520 3835 D3
23500 HarC 77336 3266 E3
Silver Forest Dr
5800 HOUS 77092 3682 D6
Silver Fox Dr
4600 HarC 77066 3401 B5
Silver Frost Dr
4700 HarC 77066 3401 B6
Silvergate Dr
800 HOUS 77079 3956 E2
Silver Glade Dr
3100 HOUS 77345 3119 E4
Silver Glade Ln
14100 SGLD 77478 4236 E4
Silverglen Dr N
- HarC 77014 3402 A2
Silverglen Estates Dr
12500 HarC 77014 3402 A3
Silverglen North Dr
2400 HarC 77014 3402 B2
N Silver Green Dr
15000 HarC 77530 3829 C5
S Silver Green Dr
14700 HarC 77015 3829 C5
14800 HarC 77530 3829 C5
Silver Grove Ct
6900 PASD 77505 4249 A5
Silverhawk Dr
3800 HarC 77449 3816 B2

Silver Hearth Ln
- FBnC 77494 3952 C7
Silver Heights Dr
12300 HarC 77014 3401 D3
Silver Hollow Ln
14200 HOUS 77082 4096 D1
Silverhorn Dr
2600 HarC 77450 3954 E6
Silveridge
1100 CNRO 77304 2383 A7
1100 CNRO 77304 2529 A1
Silver Iris Wy
10 WDLD 77382 2673 D7
Silver Island Cir
11900 HarC 77067 3401 E4
Silver Jade Ct
27300 MtgC 77386 3115 D1
Silver Jade Dr
4400 MtgC 77386 3115 D2
Silver Knight Ct
14800 HOUS 77062 4506 C2
Silver Knoll Ln
6800 HarC 77449 3676 C2
Silver Lace Ln
14400 HarC 77070 3398 B1
14400 HarC 77429 3398 C1
Silverlake Dr
4500 FBnC 77479 4366 D5
Silver Lake Rd
10 HarC 77044 3408 C7
10 HarC 77044 3549 A1
10 HarC 77346 3408 B7
Silver Lake St
9300 HOUS 77025 4241 E1
Silverlake Village Dr
3000 BzaC 77584 4500 E4
3000 BzaC 77584 4501 A4
3000 PRLD 77584 4500 E4
Silver Landing Ln
2900 LGCY 77539 4752 E5
Silver Leaf Ct
500 BzaC 77584 4374 A7
11900 CHTW 77385 2823 A3
Silver Leaf Dr
1900 HarC 77388 3113 C6
2100 MSCY 77459 4370 B6
6100 LGCY 77573 4630 B6
Silverleaf Dr
400 FRDW 77546 4629 D2
Silver Leaf Ln
7000 HOUS 77088 3682 E4
7000 HOUS 77091 3682 E4
10200 HarC 77375 3110 B1
11900 CHTW 77385 2823 A3
Silver Leaf St
24600 MtgC 77355 2962 C3
Silverline Dr
3200 HOUS 77338 3263 D4
Silver Lining Ln
1700 SGLD 77479 4236 D7
Silverloch Ct
10 SGLD 77479 4495 E3
Silver Lock
12500 HarC 77014 3401 E3
Silver Lode Dr
22000 HarC 77450 3954 A3
Silver Lure Dr
7700 HarC 77346 3409 C1
18600 HarC 77346 3265 D7
18700 HOUS 77346 3265 D7
Silver Lute Pl
10 WDLD 77381 2821 D1
Silverman St
15100 HOUS 77598 4506 D2
Silver Maple Ct
2900 FRDW 77598 4630 C2
Silver Maple Dr
9500 HarC 77064 3541 A4
24100 HOUS 77336 3266 D2
Silver Maple Ln
1300 PRLD 77581 4504 D5
7800 BzaC 77584 4627 C4
Silver Maple Pl
10 WDLD 77382 2819 E2
Silver Meadow Ct
7200 HarC 77041 3679 D1
Silvermeadow Dr
2500 HarC 77014 3402 A3
Silvermill Ln
- FBnC 77478 4236 E5
- SGLD 77478 4236 E5
Silvermist Cir
200 LGCY 77539 4752 E2
Silvermist Ln
22400 FBnC 77494 4093 D4
Silvermont Dr
10 WDLD 77382 2819 C1
Silver Moon Tr
2000 HarC 77532 3410 A3
Silver Morning Cir
22300 HarC 77450 3953 E4
Silver Morning Ct
22200 HarC 77450 3954 B2
Silver Morning Dr
1200 HarC 77450 3953 E4
1200 HarC 77450 3954 A4
Silver Mountain Ln
- HarC 77377 3254 C3
Silver Oak Dr
- HOUS 77034 4248 D7
- PASD 77034 4248 D7
- PASD 77505 4248 D7
7800 TXCY 77591 4873 B7
Silver Oak Ln
10500 HarC 77038 3543 C2
Silver Oak Tr
20400 HarC 77346 3264 E3
20400 HarC 77346 3265 A4
Silver Oaks Ct
18100 MtgC 77365 2971 E2
Silver Oaks St
2200 RMFT 77357 2829 A2
Silverpark
5500 HarC 77041 3679 D6
Silverpark Ln
- FBnC 77478 4237 A5
- SGLD 77478 4237 A5
Silverpeak Ct
21800 FBnC 77450 4093 E1
Silverpenny Dr
10 WDLD 77384 2675 B6
Silverpin Dr
- HarC 77449 3676 B2
Silverpines Rd
1700 HOUS 77062 4507 C2
Silver Pointe Dr
21300 MtgC 77365 2972 D7

Houston Street Index

STREET
Block City ZIP Map# Grid

Silver Pond Ct
1900 FBnC 77479 4494 B4
Silver Pond Dr
7700 FBnC 77479 4494 B4
Silver Poplar Ln
6500 HarC 77084 3678 E3
Silver Rawls Ln
21000 FBnC 77469 4234 A2
Silver Reed Ln
2800 LGCY 77539 4752 E3
10900 HOUS 77034 4378 D4
Silver Reef
4000 GLSN 77554 5332 D3
Silver Ridge Blvd
3600 MSCY 77459 4621 D3
Silver Ridge Dr
15400 HarC 77090 3258 A5
15600 HOUS 77090 3258 A5
Silver Rock Ct
6800 HarC 77449 3677 C3
Silver Rock Dr
19900 HarC 77449 3677 C3
20000 HarC 77449 3676 E2
Silver Rod Ln
6500 HarC 77041 3679 D4
Silver Row Ln
- FBnC 77494 3952 C7
Silver Run Ln
21400 MtgC 77365 2973 B3
Silver Rush Dr
11200 HarC 77095 3538 B1
Silver Sage Ct
13700 BzaC 77583 4623 E4
Silver Sage Dr
2200 HOUS 77077 3957 E7
Silver Sage Ln
5300 BzaC 77583 4623 E4
Silversand Ct
14200 HOUS 77044 3550 A2
Silversands
3300 GLSN 77554 5221 B4
Silver Sands Cir
7800 HarC 77095 3538 E7
Silver Sands St
14700 HarC 77095 3539 A7
14900 HarC 77095 3538 E7
Silver Shade Dr
6400 HarC 77064 3541 D2
Silver Shadow
2600 CNRO 77304 2383 C7
Silver Shadows Ln
8200 HarC 77379 3255 E2
N Silvershire Cir
200 WDLD 77381 2674 C6
S Silvershire Cir
200 WDLD 77381 2674 C7
Silvershire Ct
10 WDLD 77382 2675 B6
Silvershire Ln
- HOUS 77082 4098 A3
Silver Shore Ln
2900 LGCY 77539 4753 B2
Silver Shores Ln
6800 HarC 77449 3677 A2
Silverside Dr
3200 HarC 77449 3816 A3
Silver Sky Ct
14200 HOUS 77062 4379 D6
Silver Sky Ln
16200 HarC 77095 3678 B1
Silversmine Dr
12400 HarC 77014 3402 A3
Silversmith Dr
23800 HarC 77493 3814 B6
Silversmith Ln
24200 HarC 77493 3814 B6
Silver Spoon Ct
- HarC 77014 3401 D3
Silver Spring Cross
- HarC 77014 3401 D3
Silver Spring Ln
9000 HOUS 77025 4101 D7
Silver Spring Tr
3000 HarC 77449 3815 D4
Silver Springs Cross
- HarC 77014 3401 C3
- HarC 77066 3401 C3
Silver Springs Ct
3100 MSCY 77459 4496 E3
Silver Springs Dr
- BzaC 77578 4625 B1
- LPRT 77571 4251 D7
3100 LPRT 77571 4382 D1
3800 BzaC 77578 4501 B7
25000 WlrC 77447 2959 C1
Silver Springs Rd
10 CNRO 77303 2237 D1
10 CNRO 77304 2237 D1
10 MtgC 77303 2237 D1
Silver Spruce Ln
4600 HarC 77546 4506 A6
Silver Spur Dr
3000 HarC 77449 3815 D4
Silverstag Trail Ln
3100 HarC 77073 3260 A4
Silver Star Ct
3300 PRLD 77584 4501 B3
Silver Star Dr
6800 HarC 77086 3542 B2
Silverstone Dr
400 FRDW 77546 4629 D3
Silver Stone Ln
- RSBG 77469 4614 E3
Silverstone Ln
100 SHEH 77381 2821 E1
100 SHEH 77384 2821 E1
Silver Stone St
10600 HOUS 77048 4244 A6
Silverstone Wy
2600 CNRO 77304 2383 B7
2700 CNRO 77304 2529 B1
Silverstrand Pl
10 WDLD 77381 2820 E1
Silverstream Ct
12500 HarC 77014 3402 A3
Silverthorn Ln
2000 LGCY 77565 4508 E5
Silverthorne Dr
7100 FBnC 77479 4367 A7
Silverthorne Ln
17100 HarC 77379 3256 B3
Silverthorn Glen Dr
5700 HarC 77379 3257 A2
Silver Timber Ct
18200 HarC 77449 3677 D6
Silver Timbers Ln
25800 FBnC 77494 3952 C7
25900 FBnC 77494 4092 C1

Silver Tip Dr
9200 HarC 77379 3255 D4
Silvertip Dr
2200 HarC 77449 3814 E5
2300 HarC 77449 3815 A4
Silverton Bnd
2400 RSBG 77469 4615 E1
Silverton Dr
600 HarC 77373 3113 E6
600 HarC 77373 3114 A6
Silverton Creek Ln
8100 HarC 77040 3541 B5
Silver Trace Ct
6900 HarC 77449 3676 E2
Silver Tree
2800 HarC 77014 3401 E3
Silver Trumpet Dr
2500 HarC 77449 3815 B5
Silver Valley Dr
16000 HarC 77084 3678 D6
Silver Village Dr
31100 MtgC 77386 2969 A1
Silverwater Ct
- RHMD 77469 4492 B2
Silverwick Dr
12500 HarC 77014 3402 A3
Silver Wing Ln
16200 HarC 77447 3248 E6
Silverwood Dr
- MtgC 77354 2670 B6
4000 HOUS 77025 4241 C2
4300 HOUS 77035 4241 B2
Silverwood Tr
7200 HarC 77346 3265 A3
20200 HarC 77433 3251 C5
Silverwood Tr E
20200 HarC 77433 3251 E5
Silverwood Tr W
20200 HarC 77433 3251 E5
Silver Wood Wy
10000 HarC 77070 3255 B5
Silverwood Bend Ln
7100 FBnC 77469 4094 E6
11800 HarC 77433 3396 A6
Silverwood Oaks Ct
31000 MtgC 77386 2823 C7
31000 MtgC 77386 2969 C1
Silverwood Park Ln
2900 MtgC 77386 2823 D7
Silverwood Ranch Dr
100 SHEH 77381 2821 E1
100 SHEH 77384 2821 E1
Silverwood Ranch Ests
10 SHEH 77381 2821 E1
10 SHEH 77384 2821 E1
Silverwyck Dr
12400 HarC 77014 3402 A3
Silver Yacht Dr
8700 HarC 77346 3265 D7
Simmans St
2000 HarC 77032 3404 C5
2000 HOUS 77032 3404 C5
Simmons
5700 WUNP 77005 4101 B2
Simmons Blvd
1100 PASD 77506 4107 C4
Simmons Dr
9400 MtgC 77385 2822 D2
11700 MtgC 77372 2537 C3
12100 SPLD 77372 2537 C3
Simmons St
3000 HOUS 77004 4103 C1
9100 HOUS 77093 3686 A6
Simms St
- BYTN 77520 4112 E2
Simon Ct
17700 MtgC 77302 2679 E2
Simons Ln
1400 MtgC 77385 2822 D3
Simonton St
100 CNRO 77301 2384 A5
Simpson Rd
9700 MtgC 77302 2676 D1
Simpson St
- HOUS 77034 4378 E3
- HOUS 77034 4379 A3
900 GlsC 77518 4634 A2
900 LGCY 77539 4634 A2
1600 HOUS 77020 3964 C1
Simpson Creek Ln
10600 FBnC 77478 4236 D4
Sims Ct
- DKSN 77539 4753 B5
Sims Dr
7100 HOUS 77061 4244 E3
7200 HOUS 77061 4245 A3
Sims Rd
100 BYTN 77520 4113 D7
100 HarC 77520 4113 D7
Sims St
- RHMD 77469 4365 B7
100 FBnC 77469 4365 B7
Simsbrook Dr
3200 HOUS 77045 4372 B2
3200 HOUS 77045 4373 A2
Simsbury St
1200 HOUS 77022 3823 E2
Simscrest St
8500 HOUS 77017 4106 A7
Simsdale St
5600 HOUS 77033 4244 A4
6200 HOUS 77087 4244 D4
Simsview Dr
12900 HOUS 77045 4241 E6
Simswood Ct
4600 HOUS 77045 4372 C2
Sinaloa Dr
16300 FBnC 77083 4095 E6
16300 FBnC 77083 4096 A6
Sinclair St
100 GNPK 77547 3966 C7
2400 PASD 77503 4248 D3
2800 PASD 77505 4248 D3
Sinea Dr
18900 HarC 77073 3403 C2
Sinfonia Dr
7900 HarC 77040 3541 B7
Singapore Ln
15600 JRSV 77040 3680 D1
Singer St
- HOUS 77040 3681 C6
Singing Bird Cir
5000 HarC 77084 3677 D6
Singing Bird Ct
15300 HarC 77053 4372 D4
Singing Creek Ln
6300 HarC 77379 3256 D2

Singing Sonnet Ln
8000 HarC 77072 4097 C7
Singing Spurs Dr
22000 HarC 77450 3954 A3
Singing Trees Ln
11400 HarC 77016 3547 B7
11400 HOUS 77016 3547 B7
Singing Woods Dr
18600 HarC 77346 3264 E7
Singleleaf Ln
22200 HarC 77375 3110 E1
Single Oak St
23800 HarC 77373 3114 E5
Single Pine Ct
700 HarC 77373 3113 E1
Single Ridge Wy
3100 HarC 77449 3814 C3
E Single Rose Ct
17300 HarC 77429 3252 D7
W Single Rose Ct
17400 HarC 77429 3252 D7
Singletary Dr
4200 GlsC 77511 4869 A5
Singletary Rd
4400 GlsC 77511 4869 B6
Singleton
- BYTN 77521 3973 A4
Singleton Dr
3400 BYTN 77521 3973 C3
Singleton St
2000 HOUS 77008 3823 E5
Single Tree
27800 MtgC 77355 2815 A6
Singletree Dr
15900 SGCH 77355 2816 A7
Sinton Ct
2900 HarC 77449 3815 D4
Sioux Dr
6300 PASD 77503 4248 D2
9300 LPRT 77571 4250 A4
9800 MtgC 77354 2818 B6
Sioux Ln
18100 MtgC 77365 2972 B5
Sioux Run
14400 HarC 77429 3253 E5
Sioux St
4400 HarC 77521 3833 B3
Sir Alex Dr
10900 HarC 77375 3110 A4
Siril Dr
18800 HarC 77073 3403 B3
Sir Lancelot Cir
24700 WlrC 77447 2959 D1
Siros Ln
13200 HarC 77037 3544 E7
Siros Isle Ct
4900 HarC 77388 3112 B2
Siros Isle Dr
21500 HarC 77388 3112 B2
Sir Raleigh Wy
- FBnC 77478 4237 B5
- SGLD 77478 4237 B5
Sir William Ct
6800 HarC 77379 3256 D3
Sir William Dr
16100 HarC 77379 3256 D3
Siskin Tr
2500 LGCY 77573 4752 B1
Sisterdale Dr
7600 HarC 77433 3677 B1
7700 HarC 77433 3537 B7
Sitca St
4900 HarC 77389 2967 A5
Sitella Ct
16300 FBnC 77478 4236 A5
Sitting Bull Dr
- HarC 77449 3815 D5
Sivercreek Ct
2200 DRPK 77536 4109 E7
Sivley Av
6500 HOUS 77055 3821 E6
6500 HOUS 77055 3822 A6
Siwanoy Cir
25100 MtgC 77365 3117 E1
Six Flags Dr
6500 HOUS 77040 3681 B4
Six Oaks Ln
11000 HarC 77065 3539 D1
Six Oak Walk Wk
10 FBnC 77459 4621 B4
Six-pack Dr
32000 SGCH 77355 2961 B3
Sixpence Ln
22100 HarC 77073 3259 B1
Six Pines Dr
9000 WDLD 77380 2822 A5
9100 SHEH 77381 2822 A3
Six Rivers Ln
8900 FBnC 77459 4621 B6
Sixtumgrum Ln
22700 WlrC 77447 2958 E6
Sjolander Cir
6200 HarC 77521 3834 E4
Sjolander Rd
4400 HarC 77521 3973 C1
4500 HarC 77521 3834 D4
Skeet Ct
16400 HOUS 77489 4370 E6
Skeg Dr
15800 HarC 77532 3552 A4
Skelton Dr
2600 HarC 77067 3402 A6
Skene Wy
11700 HDWV 77024 3959 C2
Skewen St
5700 HarC 77346 3264 D6
Skiff Ln
- HarC 77044 3408 E4
- HOUS 77044 3408 E4
Skimmer Ct
800 SGLD 77478 4368 B4
N Skimmer St
10 LMQU 77568 4990 E6
S Skimmer St
10 LMQU 77568 4990 E6
Skimmer Wy
2700 HarC 77532 3410 A6
2900 HarC 77532 3409 E6
Skinner Cir
16900 HarC 77429 3396 D2
Skinner Ln
100 FBnC 77469 4365 B6
400 RHMD 77469 4365 B5
1000 GLSN 77554 5107 C6
3200 FBnC 77469 4234 B7
Skinner Ln FM-359
100 FBnC 77469 4365 B6
400 RHMD 77469 4365 B5

Skinner Rd
1400 HOUS 77093 3685 C3
13000 HarC 77429 3396 D4
14500 HarC 77429 3252 D5
Skinner Ridge Rd
21200 FBnC 77469 4234 A5
Skipper St
1200 GLSN 77554 5221 B1
Skippers Helm
18500 HarC 77346 3265 D7
Skipping Stone Ct
8900 HarC 77064 3540 D5
Skipping Stone Ln
9200 HarC 77064 3540 C5
Skippy St
2900 HOUS 77093 3686 A5
Skip Rock St
1900 FRDW 77546 4629 C5
Skipwith Pl
10 WDLD 77382 2819 B1
Skipwood Dr
1800 MSCY 77489 4370 C4
Skokie Ln
- BYTN 77521 3972 B2
N Sky Ct
16000 HarC 77073 3259 A6
N Sky Dr
600 HarC 77073 3259 B5
Sky Ln
10000 GLSN 77554 5221 B1
Sky Vw
11000 LPRT 77571 4110 E7
Skybird Dr
- HarC 77064 3540 B2
Sky Blue Ln
16200 HarC 77095 3678 B1
Sky Blue Pl
16900 HarC 77095 3678 A1
Skybright Ln
7200 HarC 77095 3678 B1
Sky Brook Ct
13500 HarC 77044 3549 E2
Sky Brook Ln
15100 HarC 77044 3550 A2
15200 HarC 77044 3549 E2
Skycountry Ln
19800 HarC 77094 3955 A3
Sky Creek Dr
2100 HOUS 77045 4242 D6
Skycrest Ct
13200 MtgC 77302 2530 B5
Skycrest Dr
100 FBnC 77479 4366 D5
Sky Dale Ct
- FBnC 77469 4493 B5
Skydale Dr
11800 HarC 77375 3254 E1
Sky Dale Ln
5700 FBnC 77469 4493 B5
Skye St
4600 HarC 77084 3678 C7
Skyelars Ln
2200 HarC 77450 3954 B6
Skye Springs Ln
25400 FBnC 77494 4093 A2
N Skyflower Ct
10 WDLD 77381 2821 B6
Skyflower Dr
10 WDLD 77381 2821 B6
Skyflower Pl
10 WDLD 77381 2821 B6
Sky Forest Cir
29000 MtgC 77355 2815 C2
Sky Harbor Ct
16900 HarC 77546 4506 C7
Sky Haven Ct
17200 HarC 77377 3254 C4
Skyhaven Ct
21000 HarC 77379 3111 D3
Sky Haven Dr
- HarC 77377 3254 B4
Skyhaven Ln
5800 HarC 77379 3111 D4
Sky Hawk Dr
10400 HarC 77064 3540 B2
Skyhill Dr
15300 HarC 77433 3251 D7
Sky Hollow Ln
19900 HarC 77450 3954 E5
Skyknoll Ln
12800 HOUS 77082 4097 C2
Skyla Cir
21500 HarC 77338 3260 A1
Skylakes Av
32100 WlrC 77484 3246 D7
Sky Land Dr
15800 HarC 77073 3259 B5
Skyland Pl
10 WDLD 77381 2820 E3
Sky Lark Ln
1700 HOUS 77056 3961 A6
Skylark Rd
- HOUS 77017 4246 D2
- HOUS 77502 4246 D2
100 PASD 77502 4247 A2
700 PASD 77502 4246 E2
Skylark St
300 MtgC 77355 2960 C3
Skylark Wy
3200 PRLD 77584 4502 B7
Skylight Ln
7200 HarC 77095 3678 B1
Skyline Ct
2900 MSCY 77459 4496 E2
Skyline Dr
- TXCY 77590 4757 D6
- TXCY 77590 4875 E1
- TXCY 77590 4876 A4
600 MtgC 77302 2530 C5
3600 BzaC 77578 4501 A7
3700 BzaC 77578 4625 A1
6000 HOUS 77057 4100 A1
6400 HOUS 77063 4100 A1
7800 HOUS 77063 4099 E1
9000 TXCY 77591 4873 A6
9600 TXCY 77591 4872 E6
Skyline Ln
8700 MtgC 77302 2530 B5
Skyline Tr
800 HOUS 77019 3963 A4
Skyline Park Dr
6900 HarC 77449 3677 A2
Skyline Ranch Ct
2200 HOUS 77045 4242 D6
Skyline Ranch Dr
11900 HOUS 77045 4242 D6
11900 HOUS 77051 4242 D6

Skyline Village Dr
3400 HOUS 77057 4100 C1
Skyline Village Pk
6000 HOUS 77057 4100 C1
Skyline Village Tr
3400 HOUS 77057 4100 C1
Skyline Vista
800 HOUS 77019 3963 A4
Skylite Ln
6400 MtgC 77354 2819 C5
Skymaster Rd
2300 GLSN 77551 5222 A1
2300 GLSN 77554 5222 A1
7600 GLSN 77554 5108 A7
Skymeadow Dr
13000 HOUS 77082 4097 B2
Skymist Ln
25100 FBnC 77494 3953 A5
Skymist St
- PRLD 77584 4500 E2
Skyoak Ct
3700 MtgC 77386 2970 A5
Skypark Dr
2800 HOUS 77082 4097 B2
Sky Ranch Dr
2900 ALVN 77511 4866 C5
2900 BzaC 77511 4866 C5
Skyridge Ct
6900 HarC 77379 3111 C2
Sky Ridge Dr
10 MtgC 77385 2676 E6
100 MtgC 77385 2677 A6
11200 HarC 77429 3398 E5
11200 HarC 77429 3399 A5
Skyridge Ln
22000 FBnC 77469 4493 A3
22100 FBnC 77469 4492 D3
Sky River Dr
2000 HOUS 77045 4242 D6
Skyspring Ln
800 LGCY 77573 4633 B2
Sky Springs Ln
12600 PRLD 77584 4500 B3
Sky Terrace Pl
10 WDLD 77381 2821 A1
Sky Timbers Ln
19200 HarC 77449 3677 B6
Skytrain Rd
18500 HOUS 77032 3404 D1
Skyview Dr
1600 HOUS 77043 3819 C5
6200 HarC 77041 3680 C4
13700 FBnC 77478 4237 A5
13700 SGLD 77478 4237 A5
Skyview Rd
35000 PNIS 77445 3100 B5
35000 WlrC 77445 3100 B5
Skyview Ter
100 FRDW 77546 4629 C1
200 FRDW 77546 4505 C7
Skyview Bend Dr
13000 HOUS 77047 4374 A2
Skyview Chase Ln
2700 HOUS 77047 4374 A2
Skyview Downs Dr
2600 HOUS 77047 4374 A2
Skyview Forest Dr
2700 HOUS 77047 4374 A3
Skyview Glen Ct
2600 HOUS 77047 4374 A2
Skyview Green Dr
13200 HOUS 77047 4374 A3
Skyview Grove Ct
2600 HOUS 77047 4374 A2
Skyview Landing Dr
12700 HOUS 77047 4374 A2
Skyview Manor Dr
- HOUS 77047 4374 A2
Skyview Mill Dr
2700 HOUS 77047 4374 A3
Skyview Park Dr
- HOUS 77047 4374 A3
Skyview Ridge Ct
2600 HOUS 77047 4374 A2
Skyview Shadows Ct
2600 HOUS 77047 4374 A2
Skyview Trace Ct
2600 HOUS 77047 4374 A2
Skyview Trace Dr
2700 HOUS 77047 4374 A2
Skyward Dr
12100 HOUS 77045 4242 D7
Skywing Ct
24100 HarC 77373 3114 C5
Skywood Dr
300 HarC 77090 3258 D5
Sky Wy Dr
11400 HarC 77429 3398 E5
Slade Ben Ln
4700 ALVN 77511 4867 D7
N Slash Pine Pk
10 WDLD 77380 2821 E7
10 WDLD 77380 2822 D7
S Slash Pine Pk
10 WDLD 77380 2821 E7
10 WDLD 77380 2822 D7
Slash Pine Pl
8500 HarC 77375 3110 D2
11400 WDLD 77380 2821 E7
Slashwood Ln
5200 HarC 77379 3257 B2
Slate Ct
- FBnC 77469 4234 C3
Slate Pth
10 WDLD 77382 2819 C1
Slate Sprs
21000 FBnC 77469 4094 B6
Slate Field Dr
9700 HarC 77064 3540 D5
Slate Holloe Ln
21300 HarC 77449 3815 B4
Slate Hollow Ln
- FBnC 77469 4095 A6
21400 HarC 77449 3815 B4
Slate Mountain Ln
13700 HOUS 77044 3550 B3
Slater Ln
12900 HarC 77039 3545 C5
Slate Ridge Ln
2300 FBnC 77494 3953 C5
Slate River Ln
4900 FBnC 77494 4092 E2
11000 HarC 77089 4377 B7
13700 HOUS 77077 3957 A7
13900 HOUS 77077 3956 E7
Slate Springs Ln
- PRLD 77584 4500 B3

Slatestone Cir
10 WDLD 77382 2673 D6
E Slatestone Cir
10 WDLD 77382 2673 D6
10 WDLD 77382 2674 A5
W Slatestone Cir
100 WDLD 77382 2673 E5
100 WDLD 77382 2674 A6
Slate Stone Ct
9300 HarC 77064 3540 D5
Slate Stone Ln
6400 HarC 77084 3678 B3
Slatestone Ln
28200 MtgC 77386 2969 E6
Slate Valley Ln
700 HarC 77373 2968 E5
Sledge St
- WlrC 77484 3101 D5
800 HOUS 77009 3963 A1
2000 WALR 77484 3102 A5
2100 WALR 77484 3101 D5
Sleeping Creek Pl
10 WDLD 77384 2675 A3
Sleepy Ln
13500 TMBL 77375 2964 A5
Sleepy Brook Ln
29900 MtgC 77355 2815 A2
30000 MtgC 77355 2814 E2
Sleepycove Ct
4100 SGLD 77479 4494 E2
4100 SGLD 77479 4495 C2
Sleepy Creek Dr
5200 HOUS 77017 4246 B1
Sleepy Creek Mdws
13100 HarC 77083 4237 C1
Sleepy Creek Wy
1800 PRLD 77581 4504 D5
Sleepygate Dr
22500 HarC 77373 3115 E7
Sleepy Hollow Ct
200 TYLV 77586 4381 D7
200 TYLV 77586 4382 A7
3300 HOUS 77019 3961 E5
Sleepy Hollow Dr
1600 PRLD 77581 4504 C3
3000 SGLD 77479 4495 E1
Sleepy Hollow Ln
20500 HarC 77388 3113 C3
26600 MtgC 77355 2814 A2
Sleepy Hollow Rd
12000 MtgC 77385 2822 C3
12100 CHTW 77385 2823 A3
12100 MtgC 77385 2823 C3
12500 MtgC 77385 2824 A5
Sleepy Hollow St
1500 MtgC 77386 2969 A3
Sleepy Hollow Trail Ln
11400 HarC 77089 4504 A1
Sleepy Knoll Dr
2700 HarC 77373 3114 D6
Sleepy Meadow Ln
11800 HarC 77039 3546 A6
Sleepy Oaks Cir
10 HDWV 77024 3960 A2
10 HNCV 77024 3960 A2
Sleepy Pines Dr
12000 HarC 77066 3400 E4
Sleepy Rose Ct
7800 HarC 77396 3547 D2
Sleepy Time Ln
12700 HarC 77532 3692 C1
Sleepyvale Ln
700 HOUS 77018 3823 B1
Slice Right Cir
2500 HarC 77089 4504 C1
Slick Rock Dr
6100 CNRO 77304 2236 D6
Slider Ct
2600 LGCY 77573 4631 B7
Slippery Creek Ln
21500 HarC 77388 3112 C4
Slippery Elm Ln
7300 HarC 77095 3678 A1
Slippery Rock Ct
2300 FBnC 77478 4236 C7
Slippery Rock Dr
2500 FBnC 77478 4236 B7
Slippery Rock Ln
19500 HarC 77388 3112 C5
Sloan Rd
16600 MtgC 77306 2681 A6
17300 MtgC 77357 2681 B6
Sloan St
6300 HOUS 77087 4104 D6
Sloandale Ct
16900 HarC 77073 3259 B3
Sloane Pl
- PRLD 77584 4502 E7
Sloangate Dr
4500 HarC 77373 3115 B6
Slocom Dr
3600 HarC 77449 3815 E3
Sloop Ct
500 HarC 77532 3552 B2
Slossen St
100 WEBS 77598 4507 B6
Slumber Ln
300 HarC 77532 3692 D1
3500 HOUS 77023 4104 C4
19300 MtgC 77355 2814 A2
Slumberwood Tr
500 HOUS 77013 3827 D7
600 HOUS 77013 3966 D1
Smada Ct
2700 SGLD 77478 4369 A7
Small Cedar Dr
500 LGCY 77573 4631 A6
Small Leaf Cir
7800 HOUS 77063 4100 A1
Small Pebble Wy
10000 HarC 77396 3407 B6
Smallwood Ln
1100 HOUS 77023 4105 A2
Smart St
500 HarC 77037 3684 B1
500 HOUS 77037 3684 B1
Smilax St
7000 HOUS 77088 3683 D4
7000 HOUS 77091 3683 D4
Smiling Wood Ln
7100 HarC 77086 3542 B4
7100 HOUS 77086 3542 B3
7600 HarC 77086 3541 E3
Smith
10 FBnC 77583 4623 C5
Smith Av
- BzaC 77511 4750 A7
400 PASD 77504 4247 B5

Smith Dr
1100 ALVN 77511 4749 C7
7000 HTCK 77563 4988 D4
Smith Ln
- PRLD 77581 4504 A4
100 LGCY 77573 4632 D3
10600 BzaC 77511 4747 E5
10600 BzaC 77511 4748 A6
11700 HarC 77016 3547 E6
11800 HarC 77050 3547 C7
Smith Pk
- JTCY 77029 3966 D3
Smith Rd
- BzaC 77584 4501 C4
- HarC 77396 3406 B7
- HOUS 77396 3406 B7
- PRLD 77584 4501 C4
100 HOUS 77336 3266 B1
800 HarC 77336 3266 E1
4600 GlsC 77511 4869 B2
13500 HarC 77396 3547 B1
14300 HOUS 77396 3547 B1
22900 MtgC 77365 2972 E4
23200 MtgC 77365 2973 A5
Smith St
- HarC 77049 3830 E2
- PRVW 77445 3100 B3
200 MAGA 77354 2669 A5
600 HOUS 77002 3963 A6
1200 BzaC 77583 4623 D6
2000 WALR 77484 3101 E4
2200 HOUS 77006 3963 A5
4100 GlsC 77518 4634 B4
4600 GlsC 77511 4869 B6
16200 JRSV 77040 3540 C7
17200 PTVL 77372 2682 E7
Smith Bridge Ln
14500 FBnC 77478 4236 D3
Smithdale Ct
10 HNCV 77024 3960 A3
Smithdale Ests
10 PNPV 77024 3959 E3
Smithdale Rd
10800 HNCV 77024 3960 A3
11100 HNCV 77024 3959 D3
11100 PNPV 77024 3959 D3
Smitherman Rd
13900 HarC 77044 3689 E4
Smithers Ln
3800 FBnC 77459 4621 C5
Smithfield Crossing Ln
20100 HarC 77449 3815 C6
20100 HOUS 77449 3815 D7
Smith Ranch Rd
1200 PRLD 77584 4501 A3
1600 BzaC 77584 4501 A3
Smith Ranch Road 1
10400 PRLD 77584 4501 A2
Smith Ranch Road 1 CO-562
10400 PRLD 77584 4501 A2
Smith Ranch Road 2
10500 PRLD 77584 4501 A3
Smith Rapids Ln
- FBnC 77478 4236 D6
Smithstone Dr
15800 HarC 77084 3678 C2
Smith Village Dr
100 ALVN 77511 4749 C6
Smithville St
10 SGLD 77478 4367 C3
Smoke Lk
25000 HarC 77375 2965 D3
Smoke Rd
7000 HarC 77088 3682 B1
7000 HOUS 77040 3682 B1
Smoke Creek Ct
14200 HarC 77429 3397 B2
Smokehollow Ct
11000 HarC 77064 3540 D2
Smokehollow Dr
9000 HarC 77064 3540 D2
Smoke House Dr
6400 HarC 77449 3677 B3
Smokerise Pl
10 WDLD 77381 2820 E3
Smoke Rock Dr
2000 HarC 77373 3114 C7
Smokerock Ln
7300 HOUS 77040 3682 A3
Smokestone Dr
10 WDLD 77381 2821 B2
Smoke Tree Ct
6400 FBnC 77479 4367 B5
Smoke Tree Ln
6400 FBnC 77479 4367 B5
Smokewood Dr
- WDLD 77381 2674 E6
Smokey Dr
7800 HarC 77064 3541 E5
Smokey Ln
800 HarC 77532 3411 C4
Smokey Bear
2700 HarC 77038 3543 B5
Smokey Brook Ln
6900 FBnC 77494 4093 C2
Smokey Creek Ln
7600 HarC 77396 3547 C1
Smokey Forest Ln
- MtgC 77386 2969 C1
Smokeygate Ct
24000 HarC 77373 3115 B5
Smokey Hill Ct
200 FBnC 77469 4493 D7
Smokey Hill Dr
22300 HarC 77450 3953 E3
Smokey Hollow Dr
3000 HarC 77068 3257 C5
Smokey Lake Ln
100 LGCY 77539 4752 E3
Smokey Mountain Ct
12700 HarC 77346 3408 D1
Smokey Oak Rd
10 WDLD 77381 2821 A6
Smokey Pass Cir
12800 HarC 77038 3543 B3
Smokey Ridge Ln
8900 HOUS 77075 4376 E4
Smokey River Dr
5100 HarC 77449 3676 D6
Smokey Sage Ct
2900 HarC 77450 3954 C7
Smokey Sage Dr
20700 HarC 77450 3954 C6
Smokey Trail Dr
13700 HarC 77041 3679 B1
13900 HarC 77095 3679 B1
Smokey Tree
22300 HarC 77447 3106 B1

Houston Street Index

STREET
Block City ZIP Map# Grid

Smokey Tree
22700 HarC 77447 2961 B7
Smokey Wood Ln
7700 HarC 77086 3541 E3
Smooth Oak Ln
3900 HOUS 77053 4372 D3
Smooth Pine Ln
16500 FBnC 77478 4236 A6
Smooth Rock Falls Dr
17600 HarC 77379 3256 C1
Smugglers Ct
28900 HarC 77336 3120 E2
28900 HarC 77336 3121 A2
Smykal Rd
10 LbyC 77535 3268 A1
Snag Ln
3900 HarC 77388 3257 E2
Snail Hollow Dr
8300 HarC 77064 3542 A5
Snake Cr
6000 FBnC 77479 4495 E7
6000 FBnC 77479 4496 A7
Snake Canyon Dr
2900 HarC 77449 3815 E5
Snake River Rd
- HarC 77449 3815 E6
- HOUS 77449 3815 E7
Snapdragon Ct
10 WDLD 77381 2820 E5
Snapdragon Meadow Ln
- FBnC 77494 4092 E4
Snapper Dr
- DRPK 77536 4250 A3
Snappy Creek Ln
21300 HarC 77388 3112 C4
Snead Ct
700 MtgC 77302 2530 C6
3800 SGLD 77479 4495 A2
19000 HarC 77346 3265 C6
Sneider St
14500 HOUS 77034 4379 A3
Snipes
- HOUS 77075 4376 B2
Snoddon Rd
5800 PASD 77505 4248 D5
Snomac Ct
4100 HarC 77521 3833 B4
Snook Ln
23200 TMBL 77375 2964 D6
Snover St
100 HOUS 77007 3962 C3
Snow
3200 KATY 77493 3813 B3
Snow Rd
25300 WlrC 77447 2813 B7
Snowbank Dr
8600 HarC 77064 3541 E5
Snow Bay Dr
11300 HarC 77067 3402 A6
Snowbell Pl
10 WDLD 77381 2820 C3
Snowberry Dr
11700 HarC 77429 3398 D5
Snowbird Ct
12000 STAF 77477 4237 E6
Snowbird Pl
10 WDLD 77381 2820 E2
Snowbird Meadow Dr
3100 HarC 77373 3115 B4
Snowblossom Ct
3400 PRLD 77581 4503 D1
Snowblossom Ln
21300 HarC 77375 3110 A4
Snowbridge Ct
11700 HarC 77377 3254 D4
Snow Crest Ct
12000 HarC 77377 3254 B1
Snowdance Ct
100 WDLD 77382 2674 C5
Snowden
27000 HarC 77447 3103 D6
27000 HarC 77484 3103 D6
Snowden St
7800 HOUS 77028 3687 B6
Snowdrop Ln
2100 HarC 77067 3402 A6
Snowflake Ct
16700 HOUS 77053 4371 E7
Snowflower Meadow Ln
- FBnC 77494 4093 B7
Snow Hill Ln
15100 FBnC 77478 4236 D4
Snowmass Dr
11600 HarC 77070 3398 D2
Snowny Hills Dr
16000 HarC 77429 3397 B2
Snow Pond Pl
10 WDLD 77382 2819 D3
10 WDLD 77382 2820 A3
Snowwood Ct
100 HarC 77388 3112 D6
Snowwood Dr
18400 HarC 77388 3112 D6
18400 HarC 77388 3113 A4
Snow Woods Ct
10 WDLD 77385 2676 D4
Snowy Egret Dr
25500 GLSN 77554 5548 A3
Snowy Owl Lp
8800 FBnC 77459 4621 B6
Snug Harbor Ct
3100 HarC 77449 3815 A3
W Snyder St
1000 ALVN 77511 4867 A1
Snyders Blf
- LGCY 77573 4753 B1
Soapstone Ln
24300 HarC 77373 2968 D5
Soaring Eagle Dr
16100 FBnC 77083 4236 B1
16300 FBnC 77478 4236 B2
Soaring Forest Dr
16500 PASD 77059 4380 D4
Soaring Height Ct
14500 HarC 77396 3548 B2
Soaring Lagle Ct
- HarC 77038 3543 B4
Soaring Pine Ct
5900 HOUS 77345 3120 C5
Soboda Ct
800 HOUS 77079 3957 C2
Society Ln
5500 HarC 77084 3679 A5
Society St
10 WDLD 77380 2821 D5
Sockeye Dr
2600 HOUS 77045 4373 A1

Socorro Ln
11500 HarC 77377 3109 C7
Softbreeze Ct
11300 PRLD 77584 4500 D3
Soft Breeze Dr
8000 HarC 77095 3537 E7
Soft Fern Ct
3100 HOUS 77345 3119 E1
Soft Pine Dr
24200 HOUS 77336 3266 C2
Soft Pines Ct
22000 MtgC 77365 2971 E2
Soft Pines Dr
12000 HarC 77066 3400 E4
Soft Shadows Ln
500 HOUS 77013 3966 C1
Softwind Ln
5600 HOUS 77041 3681 B6
Soho Dr
3700 PRLD 77584 4501 C1
Sojourner Bend Dr
10700 HOUS 77016 3687 B4
Sol St
1100 HOUS 77029 3965 D6
Solana Dr
8100 FBnC 77083 4096 C7
Solana Springs Dr
1700 FBnC 77479 4367 B7
Solano Ct
11700 MDWP 77477 4237 E4
E Solano Bay Ln
5900 HarC 77041 3679 D4
W Solano Bay Ln
5900 HarC 77041 3679 D4
Solara Bnd
8100 FBnC 77083 4095 D7
8100 FBnC 77083 4235 D1
Solara Bend Ct
9000 FBnC 77083 4095 E7
Solara Bend St
8200 FBnC 77083 4095 B7
8300 FBnC 77083 4235 C2
Solari Ct
2800 LGCY 77573 4633 A3
Solar Point Ln
5900 HarC 77041 3679 E5
Soldiers Creek Cir
10 HNCV 77024 3960 A3
Soldiers Field Ct
1100 SGLD 77479 4367 E5
Soldiers Field Dr
1300 SGLD 77479 4367 E5
1300 SGLD 77479 4368 A5
Soldierwood Pl
1200 LGCY 77598 4630 C4
Soldlake Dr
20000 HarC 77449 3676 E2
Soledad Dr
6400 HarC 77083 4096 A5
Soledad Ridge Dr
2400 HarC 77373 3114 C3
Soleil Dr
14200 HarC 77083 4096 E5
Solera Ln
10600 HarC 77040 3541 E6
Solero Ridge Ln
2600 HarC 77089 4504 A1
Solitaire Cir
10300 HarC 77070 3399 B4
Solo
700 HOUS 77020 3964 C2
Solo St
1400 HOUS 77020 3964 C2
2900 HOUS 77026 3825 C7
Solomon Dr
400 KMAH 77565 4509 E7
400 KMAH 77565 4510 A7
Solomon Rd
10700 HarC 77375 3255 A2
10800 HarC 77375 3254 E2
Solomon St
1900 WALR 77484 3102 A4
7400 JRSV 77040 3680 D1
Solomon Ext Rd
17800 HarC 77375 3255 A2
Solon Rd
8800 HarC 77064 3399 E6
8800 HOUS 77064 3399 E6
9000 HarC 77070 3399 D6
Solon Springs Ct
19300 HarC 77375 3109 D6
Solon Springs Dr
11800 HarC 77375 3109 D7
Solway Ln
4100 HOUS 77025 4101 C6
Soma Dr
16000 FBnC 77083 4096 A7
Somercotes Ln
1400 HarC 77530 3829 D5
Somerford Dr
11000 HOUS 77072 4098 B4
Somerland Wy
11300 PNPV 77024 3959 D2
Somerset
25600 MtgC 77357 2829 B4
Somerset Av
2900 TXCY 77590 4874 D5
Somerset Ct
300 ALVN 77511 4867 D7
4500 PASD 77504 4248 A3
Somerset Dr
10 MtgC 77355 2961 C2
10 SGCH 77355 2961 C2
300 ALVN 77511 4867 D7
5000 BYTN 77521 3972 A2
Somerset Knls
18000 HarC 77094 3955 C1
Somerset Ln
700 MtgC 77302 2530 D6
1400 FRDW 77546 4749 D1
3200 DRPK 77536 4109 D7
3200 DRPK 77536 4249 D1
10600 HOUS 77093 3685 E3
11600 HarC 77093 3685 D1
Somerset Pl
10 HOUS 77024 3958 E3
Somerset Cove Ct
22100 FBnC 77494 4093 E5
Somerset Grove Dr
17500 HarC 77084 3677 E4
Somerset Hill Ct
20500 FBnC 77469 4094 D7
Somerset Hill Ln
7200 FBnC 77469 4094 C6
Somerset Knolls Ct
200 HarC 77094 3955 D1
Somerset Park Ln
6900 FBnC 77469 4094 B5

Somerset Pointe
2100 LGCY 77573 4509 B7
Somerset Pond Pl
10 WDLD 77381 2820 D2
Somersworth Dr
13300 HarC 77041 3679 C4
Somerton Dr
- DRPK 77536 4249 D3
- LPRT 77536 4249 D3
3100 LPRT 77571 4249 D4
Somervell Ct
21100 FBnC 77469 4234 B4
Somerville Lake Ct
3300 PRLD 77581 4503 E7
Sommer Dr
3400 BzaC 77511 4868 A4
Sommerall Dr
6800 HarC 77084 3678 C2
6800 HarC 77095 3678 C2
Sommermeyer Dr
14800 HOUS 77041 3680 E4
14800 HOUS 77041 3681 A4
Sommermeyer St
- HOUS 77041 3680 D4
14200 HOUS 77040 3681 C5
14200 HOUS 77041 3681 B5
Sommerville Av
10300 HOUS 77041 3819 E1
10300 HOUS 77041 3820 B1
Somonas Ln
3200 HarC 77038 3542 E1
3200 HarC 77086 3542 E1
Sonata Ct
7900 HarC 77040 3541 B7
16700 HOUS 77053 4371 D7
Sonata Canyon Ln
12400 HarC 77041 3679 D5
Sonata Creek Ln
- HarC 77433 3395 E6
11700 HarC 77433 3396 A6
Sondick Ct
4200 HOUS 77020 3964 B2
Sonesta Point Ln
8200 FBnC 77083 4095 E7
8300 FBnC 77083 4235 C2
Soneto Dr
7800 FBnC 77083 4096 A7
Song Bird Dr
5500 PRLD 77584 4502 E6
Songbird Ln
3200 HOUS 77338 3263 D3
Songbrook Dr
6800 HOUS 77083 4097 B5
Songbury Cir
4100 FBnC 77450 4093 B6
Songful Woods Pl
100 WDLD 77380 2968 B4
Songhollow Dr
12700 HarC 77377 3254 A3
Song Ridge Ct
5800 HarC 77041 3679 D5
Song Sparrow Pl
10 WDLD 77381 2821 A2
Songwind Ln
7400 HarC 77379 3256 A1
Songwood
10600 CHTW 77385 2822 D4
10600 MtgC 77385 2822 D4
Songwood Dr
10200 CHTW 77385 2822 D4
Songwood St
3500 HOUS 77023 4104 C5
Songwood Tr
15000 MtgC 77302 2679 D3
Sonnet Glen Ln
7100 HarC 77084 3678 B2
7200 HarC 77095 3678 B1
Sonnet Grove Ct
10 WDLD 77382 2674 D3
Sonnet Meadow Ct
12000 HOUS 77047 4374 B1
Sonneville Dr
8400 HOUS 77055 3821 B2
8700 HOUS 77080 3820 E2
8700 HOUS 77080 3821 A2
Sonnier Dr
13000 HarC 77044 3550 C5
13000 HOUS 77044 3550 C5
Sonny Ln
- MTBL 77520 3696 E4
N Sonny Ln
2800 GLSN 77554 5220 D5
S Sonny Ln
2900 GLSN 77554 5220 D5
Sonny Path Ct
24800 HarC 77493 3814 A6
Sonny Path Dr
1700 HarC 77493 3814 A6
Sonoma Blvd
23400 MtgC 77355 2962 B6
Sonoma Dr
6500 HOUS 77053 4371 D6
Sonoma Rdg
5700 FBnC 77459 4621 A4
Sonoma Trc
16300 HarC 77530 3829 D4
Sonoma Wy
6100 HOUS 77053 4371 D7
Sonoma Del Norte Dr
16700 HarC 77095 3538 A1
Sonoma Oak Dr
7900 HarC 77095 3539 B7
Sonoma Park Dr
15800 HarC 77049 3829 D4
15800 HarC 77530 3829 C4
Sonoma Trail Dr
1700 HarC 77530 3829 D4
Sonora Dr
22700 MtgC 77365 2972 B3
Sonora St
5300 HOUS 77020 3964 D2
7100 BYTN 77521 3835 B5
Sonora Tr
27000 MtgC 77355 2813 E1
Sonora Canyon Cir
6100 HarC 77041 3679 E4
Sonora Canyon Ln
12100 HarC 77041 3680 A4
12200 HarC 77041 3679 E4
Sonora Caverns Dr
- FBnC 77478 4236 B6
Sonora Creek Ln
4600 HarC 77388 3112 B3
Sonoran Blue Wy
12800 HOUS 77045 4241 D6
Sonora Springs Dr
11900 HarC 77375 3109 D7

Sonority Blvd
9600 HarC 77040 3541 A7
Sonrisa Ct
- MtgC 77362 2817 A6
Sophia Dr
1900 HarC 77090 3258 B6
1900 HOUS 77090 3258 B6
Sophie Ct
4400 FBnC 77479 4493 C1
Sophie Ann Dr
3200 PASD 77503 4108 B6
Sophora Pl
3300 SGLD 77479 4495 E2
Sopris Dr
1100 HOUS 77077 3956 E3
Sorbete Dr
7500 FBnC 77083 4095 E6
Soren Ln
10 HOUS 77076 3685 A5
Sorena Ct
8500 HOUS 77078 3688 B6
Sorenson Dr
- BzaC 77584 4501 D6
- PRLD 77584 4501 D6
Sorney Ct
20000 HarC 77450 3954 E2
20000 HOUS 77094 3954 E2
20000 HOUS 77450 3954 E2
Sorrel Cir
8000 HarC 77521 3833 D3
Sorrel Dr
8300 HarC 77064 3541 E5
Sorrel Grove Ct
13900 HarC 77047 4374 D4
Sorrell Hollow Ln
9000 FBnC 77469 4616 E1
Sorrell Oaks Cir
18100 FBnC 77469 4095 C7
Sorrell Oaks Ln
18100 FBnC 77469 4095 C7
Sorrel Meadows Dr
8600 HarC 77375 2965 D3
Sorrel Ridge Dr
- HarC 77388 3112 C7
17700 HarC 77388 3257 D1
Sorrel Trace Ln
- FBnC 77469 4235 C1
Sorrel Tree Pl
- WDLD 77382 2673 E5
Sorrelwood Dr
300 LGCY 77573 4633 A2
Sorrento Ct
9200 HarC 77396 3406 E6
Sorrento Dr
600 ELGO 77586 4509 B1
Sorrento St
100 SGLD 77478 4368 B2
Sorsby Dr
4300 HOUS 77047 4374 D1
Sorsby Rd
21100 WlrC 77445 2952 A4
Sorsby Wy
10700 HOUS 77047 4243 C6
12500 HOUS 77047 4374 C1
Sorters Rd
19500 MtgC 77365 2972 C7
24800 MtgC 77365 3117 C1
Sorters-McLellan Rd
25400 MtgC 77365 3117 E6
26000 MtgC 77339 3117 E6
26700 HOUS 77339 3117 E5
26700 HOUS 77365 3117 E5
Sotherloch Lake Dr
9300 HarC 77379 3255 B2
Soto Cir
7900 HOUS 77012 4105 C3
Sotogrand Cir
- HarC 77095 3538 E7
Soulinier
200 PASD 77506 4107 C4
South
- MRGP 77571 4251 E1
800 LPRT 77571 4111 C7
South Blvd
1300 HOUS 77006 4102 C1
1600 HOUS 77098 4102 A2
3000 HOUS 77005 4101 E1
3000 HOUS 77005 4102 A1
South Ct
- HOUS 77099 4238 B3
South Dr
- GLSN 77551 5222 B1
- LGCY 77573 4752 D1
3600 FBnC 77053 4372 E7
10400 HOUS 77099 4238 D3
12100 HOUS 77099 4237 E2
15000 HarC 77530 3968 D1
15400 HarC 77530 3829 E7
16900 HarC 77095 3396 E6
16900 HarC 77095 3397 A6
16900 HarC 77433 3396 D6
South Frwy
- HarC - 4373 E5
- HOUS - 3963 B7
- HOUS - 4103 A6
- HOUS - 4242 E7
- HOUS - 4243 A3
- HOUS - 4373 E1
- MNVL 77578 4624 E3
- MNVL 77583 4624 D6
- PRLD - 4373 E7
17700 BzaC 77578 4500 E7
17700 BzaC 77578 4624 E2
17700 BzaC 77583 4500 E7
17700 BzaC 77583 4624 E2
17700 BzaC 77584 4500 E6
South Frwy SR-288
- HarC - 4373 E5
- HOUS - 3963 B7
- HOUS - 4103 A7
- HOUS - 4242 E7
- HOUS - 4243 A2
- HOUS - 4373 E4
- MNVL 77578 4624 E3
- MNVL 77583 4624 D6
- PRLD - 4373 E6
17700 BzaC 77578 4500 E7
17700 BzaC 77578 4624 E2
17700 BzaC 77583 4500 E7
17700 BzaC 77583 4624 E2
17700 BzaC 77584 4500 E6
South Ln
900 HOUS 77088 3683 E2
900 HOUS 77088 3684 A2
South Pkwy
4400 CNRO 77303 2238 E7
South Rd
400 BYTN 77521 3833 D7

South Rd
400 HarC 77521 3833 D7
E South St
100 ALVN 77511 4867 C3
1700 BzaC 77511 4867 E3
E South St CO-155
1200 ALVN 77511 4867 D3
1700 BzaC 77511 4867 E3
N South St
- HOUS 77503 3968 A6
100 PASD 77503 4108 A3
100 PASD 77506 4108 A3
500 PASD 77503 3968 A7
S South St
- PASD 77502 4247 E2
- PASD 77506 4108 A5
800 PASD 77503 4108 A6
1900 HOUS 77009 3963 B1
5700 KATY 77494 3952 C1
21000 MtgC 77357 2973 A1
W South St
100 ALVN 77511 4867 A3
1700 ALVN 77511 4866 D4
3500 BzaC 77511 4866 D4
Southampton
28100 MtgC 77357 2829 E4
28100 MtgC 77357 2830 A4
Southampton Ct
4500 PASD 77504 4247 D6
Southampton Dr
16000 HarC 77379 3256 D3
Southampton Ests
5300 HOUS 77005 4102 C2
5300 HOUS 77006 4102 C2
5300 HOUS 77098 4102 C2
Southaven Dr
19600 HarC 77084 3816 A5
19700 HarC 77084 3815 E5
Southbank St
- HOUS 77033 4104 B7
- HOUS 77033 4244 B3
Southbay Dr
2900 PRLD 77584 4500 C4
Southbelt Industrial Dr
14200 HarC 77047 4372 E7
14200 HarC 77047 4373 A7
14200 HarC 77053 4372 E7
Southbend Cir
1900 MSCY 77459 4497 C2
Southbend Dr
500 ALVN 77511 4867 C2
South Bend Ln
13700 HarC 77396 3547 D3
Southbend Park Ct
25200 FBnC 77494 4093 B6
South Bend Park Ln
5100 FBnC 77494 4093 A2
Southbluff Blvd
8800 HarC 77089 4377 B5
8800 HOUS 77075 4377 B5
Southborough Dr
1200 FBnC 77479 4366 D7
South Breeze
2600 BzaC 77578 4501 A7
Southbriar Ln
25100 FBnC 77494 3953 A6
Southbridge Rd
12600 HOUS 77047 4374 C1
Southbrook Dr
100 HarC 77060 3403 A5
3500 SRAC 77571 4383 A2
5600 HOUS 77033 4244 A4
6200 HOUS 77087 4244 D4
Southchase Ln
4200 HarC 77014 3401 C3
5300 LGCY 77573 4751 D1
Southchase Trails
- FBnC 77469 4094 C5
Southchester Ln
200 HOUS 77079 3958 B3
Southcott Ct
6100 FBnC 77450 4094 B4
Southcreek Ln
- HarC 77073 3259 D5
Southcrest St
5800 HOUS 77033 4104 B7
Southcross Ln
6300 FBnC 77450 4094 C3
Southdown Dr
3000 PRLD 77584 4501 C1
Southdown Trace Tr
- HOUS 77034 4378 C3
South Echo Brch
- FBnC 77459 4621 A1
Southerland Rd
4000 HOUS 77092 3821 B1
4700 HOUS 77092 3682 B7
Southern Bnd
3900 FBnC 77459 4622 A4
Southern Cres
2000 WDLD 77380 2821 C5
Southern Ln
3000 PRLD 77584 4503 A5
Southern Pl
2000 FBnC 77469 4365 C3
Southern St
7600 HOUS 77087 4105 B6
7700 HOUS 77017 4105 B6
Southern Tr
2000 DRPK 77536 4109 E6
Southern Breeze Ct
15300 HarC 77049 3829 A4
Southern Coast Dr
- WDLD 77380 2821 D5
Southern Colony Av
300 FBnC 77583 4744 A3
Southern Colony Ct
21000 HarC 77449 3676 C2
Southern Cross Ct
3300 HarC 77373 3115 B3
Southern Crossing Dr
27500 LbyC 77372 2537 E5
Southern Cypress Ct
15000 HarC 77429 3253 D7
Southern Cypress Ln
15000 HarC 77429 3253 D7
Southern Garden Pl
- WDLD 77382 2819 D1
Southern Glen Ln
- FBnC 77494 4092 C1
Southern Hills Dr
2200 LGCY 77573 4508 E7
3100 MSCY 77459 4497 D1
5800 HarC 77069 3256 C7
5900 HarC 77069 3400 C1
Southern Hills Rd
900 HOUS 77339 3118 B6

Southern Leaf Ln
19900 HarC 77338 3262 B4
Southern Magnolia Cir
14500 HOUS 77044 3549 E1
Southern Manor Dr
12800 PRLD 77583 4500 A4
Southern Maple Ln
19600 HarC 77094 3955 A2
Southern Oak Dr
16600 CNRO 77301 2530 E1
Southern Oak Ln
14000 BzaC 77583 4623 D5
Southern Oaks Dr
16500 HarC 77068 3257 D4
N Southern Oaks Dr
2700 HarC 77068 3257 D4
S Southern Oaks Dr
2700 HarC 77068 3257 D5
Southern Orchard Ct
13300 BzaC 77583 4623 E2
Southern Orchard Ln
- BzaC 77583 4623 E3
Southern Pass Ct
900 HOUS 77062 4506 E1
Southern Pines Ct
1500 HOUS 77339 3118 D7
Southern Pines Dr
1900 HOUS 77339 3118 D7
2100 HOUS 77339 3263 E1
16000 MtgC 77302 2678 D2
16000 MtgC 77302 2679 B2
Southern Ridge Dr
3100 PRLD 77583 4500 A4
Southern Spring Ln
13900 HarC 77044 3549 E3
Southern Star Dr
- PRLD 77583 4500 C4
N Southern Stone Dr
- HarC 77095 3538 B1
S Southern Stone Dr
16200 HarC 77095 3538 B1
Southern Trails Ct
11900 PRLD 77583 4500 C4
Southern Trails Dr
- PRLD 77584 4500 C4
3200 BzaC 77583 4500 B5
3200 PRLD 77583 4500 B5
Southern Valley Dr
12800 PRLD 77583 4500 A5
Southfield Ct
4100 HOUS 77045 4241 D7
Southfield Dr
12900 HOUS 77045 4241 D7
Southford St
5800 HOUS 77033 4244 B1
Southford Wy
21800 HarC 77073 3259 B4
Southford Manor Ln
3100 FBnC 77494 4093 C1
3100 HOUS 77494 4093 C1
Southford Ridge Ln
- HarC 77073 3259 B4
Southfork Dr
- BzaC 77578 4501 B6
- BzaC 77584 4501 A6
- PRLD 77584 4501 A6
Southfork Pkwy
- BzaC 77583 4500 D7
W Southfork Pines Cir
10 WDLD 77381 2821 A3
Southfork Pines Ct
10 WDLD 77381 2821 B3
Southfork Pines Dr
- WDLD 77381 2821 A3
Southfork Pines Pl
10 WDLD 77381 2821 C2
South Four
- HarC 77049 3690 E7
South Freeway Frontage Rd
- HOUS 77021 4243 A2
- HOUS 77054 4243 A1
100 HOUS 77004 4103 A2
7500 HOUS 77021 4103 A7
7500 HOUS 77054 4103 A7
8100 HOUS 77051 4243 A2
South Freeway Service Dr
- BzaC 77584 4374 A6
- BzaC 77584 4501 A1
- HOUS 77003 3963 C7
- HOUS 77004 3963 C6
11900 HarC 77047 4373 E5
11900 PRLD 77047 4373 A5
13500 HarC 77047 4374 A5
13800 PRLD 77047 4374 A5
13900 PRLD 77047 4373 E7
14700 BzaC 77584 4373 E7
14700 PRLD 77584 4373 E1
14700 PRLD 77584 4500 E1
Southgate Blvd
2000 HOUS 77030 4102 A4
2400 WUNP 77005 4102 A4
Southgate Dr
- BzaC 77583 4500 D6
- PRLD 77583 4500 D6
10 WDLD 77380 2967 C3
800 RSBG 77471 4490 D6
Southgate Ln
26600 MtgC 77372 2683 E5
Southgood St
5800 HOUS 77033 4244 B1
Southhollow Ln
10 MtgC 77386 2969 D1
Southhook Ct
20900 HarC 77073 3259 B6
Southington St
5800 HOUS 77033 4244 A1
South Kemah Dr
2600 LGCY 77565 4633 C2
Southlake Dr
11600 HOUS 77077 3958 A7
11900 HOUS 77077 3957 E7
Southland Av
- ALVN 77511 4867 C2
E Southland Av
500 ALVN 77511 4867 C2
Southland Dr
27300 MtgC 77372 2537 E7
27300 MtgC 77372 2538 A7
Southlane Ct
19900 MSCY 77459 4497 E7
Southlark St
5900 HOUS 77033 4104 B7
5900 HOUS 77033 4244 B1
Southlawn Cir
10 LMQU 77568 4990 B2
Southlawn Rd
3700 HOUS 77021 4103 C6

Southlawn St
3900 HOUS 77021 4103 C7
Southlea St
5200 HOUS 77033 4104 A7
South Legacy Dr
- HarC 77038 3543 B4
Southleigh Dr
8900 HarC 77379 3255 D4
Southline Dr
14300 FBnC 77478 4236 E4
Southline Rd
2200 MtgC 77384 2675 D7
13700 FBnC 77478 4237 A3
Southmeadow Dr
- HOUS 77035 4240 A6
- HOUS 77071 4240 A6
7600 HOUS 77071 4239 E6
12000 STAF 77477 4237 E6
12000 STAF 77477 4238 A6
12300 SGLD 77478 4237 E6
12300 STAF 77478 4237 E6
Southmere Ln
3200 PRLD 77584 4501 B2
Southminster Dr
5700 HOUS 77035 4240 C7
Southminster St
- HOUS 77035 4240 C6
Southmont St
5800 HOUS 77033 4104 B7
Southmore Av
1300 PASD 77502 4107 C6
1300 PASD 77506 4107 C6
E Southmore Av
2200 PASD 77502 4107 B6
2200 PASD 77506 4107 B6
2600 PASD 77502 4108 A6
2600 PASD 77506 4108 A6
2700 PASD 77503 4108 A6
W Southmore Av
100 PASD 77502 4107 A6
100 PASD 77506 4107 A6
500 PASD 77502 4106 D6
500 PASD 77506 4106 D6
1400 HOUS 77017 4106 D6
1400 HOUS 77506 4106 D6
1400 PASD 77017 4106 D6
1800 HOUS 77502 4106 C6
Southmore Blvd
1000 HOUS 77002 4102 E1
1000 HOUS 77004 4102 E1
1700 HOUS 77004 4103 B3
Southmore Cir
3900 HOUS 77004 4103 D4
Southmore Dr
600 CNRO 77301 2530 C1
Southmore St
200 TMBL 77375 2964 C7
200 TMBL 77375 3109 B1
Southmund St
5800 HOUS 77033 4104 B7
Southover Ct
10300 HOUS 77075 4377 B3
Southpark St
21700 MtgC 77357 2827 C4
Southpine Ct
7000 HarC 77389 2966 B1
Southpoint Ln
13200 HOUS 77034 4378 C2
Southpoint Wind Ln
9400 HarC 77040 3541 B5
Southport Dr
10200 HOUS 77089 4377 D3
12800 PRLD 77584 4500 A3
Southport Ln
500 LGCY 77565 4509 A5
Southridge Dr
17700 MtgC 77365 2825 E7
Southridge Rd
1500 HarC 77090 3258 B5
Southridge St
5800 HOUS 77033 4104 B7
Southseas St
5700 HOUS 77033 4244 A1
Southship Ct
20900 HarC 77073 3259 B6
South Shore Blvd
- LGCY 77539 4633 D4
- LGCY 77573 4633 D4
6000 LGCY 77565 4633 B2
Southshore Dr
3200 HOUS 77338 3263 D3
Southspring Dr
12600 HOUS 77047 4374 C1
Southtown St
5800 HOUS 77033 4244 A1
Southurst St
5800 HOUS 77033 4104 B7
Southview
12000 HOUS 77047 4374 C1
Southview St
8200 HOUS 77051 4243 C3
10500 HOUS 77047 4243 C6
11900 HOUS 77047 4374 C1
Southville St
5800 HOUS 77033 4244 B1
Southvine Ct
20900 HarC 77073 3259 B6
Southwark St
8700 HOUS 77028 3687 E6
8700 HOUS 77078 3687 E6
Southway Dr
7300 HOUS 77087 4105 A6
Southwell Ln
- LGCY 77573 4630 C7
- LGCY 77573 4751 B2
Southwell St
5800 HOUS 77033 4104 B7
Southwest Frwy
- FBnC - 4492 A6
- FBnC - 4493 C4
- HarC - 4238 C5
- HOUS - 3963 B7
- HOUS - 4099 E5
- HOUS - 4100 C2
- HOUS - 4101 A1
- HOUS - 4102 E1
- HOUS - 4103 A1
- HOUS - 4238 D4
- HOUS - 4239 B1
- HOUS 77005 4101 E1
- HOUS 77036 4100 B2
- RSBG - 4491 E7
- RSBG - 4492 A6
- RSBG - 4615 A1
- RSBG 77471 4490 A7
- SGLD - 4367 D7
- SGLD - 4368 A6
- SGLD - 4369 A1

Houston Street Index

STREET
Block City ZIP Map# Grid
Southwest Frwy
- SGLD - 4493 B4
- SGLD - 4494 A3
- STAF - 4238 B7
- STAF - 4369 A1
4700 HOUS 77027 4101 A1
29200 RSBG 77471 4614 C1
Southwest Frwy US-59
- FBnC - 4493 A6
- FBnC - 4493 C4
- HarC - 4238 C5
- HOUS - 3963 B7
- HOUS - 4099 E5
- HOUS - 4100 D2
- HOUS - 4101 E1
- HOUS - 4102 C1
- HOUS - 4103 A1
- HOUS - 4238 E3
- HOUS - 4239 B1
- RSBG - 4491 E7
- RSBG - 4492 A6
- RSBG - 4614 E1
- RSBG - 4615 A1
- RSBG 77471 4490 A7
- SGLD - 4367 D7
- SGLD - 4368 A6
- SGLD - 4369 A1
- SGLD - 4493 B4
- SGLD - 4494 A3
- STAF - 4238 B7
- STAF - 4369 A1
Southwestern Blvd
100 SGLD 77478 4368 E2
Southwestern Rd
3000 BzaC 77578 4501 B7
3000 BzaC 77584 4501 B7
3000 PRLD 77578 4501 B7
Southwestern St
3800 SSPL 77005 4101 D4
3800 WUNP 77005 4101 C4
Southwest Freeway Frontage Rd
- BLAR 77027 4101 A2
- BLAR 77056 4101 A2
- HOUS 77036 4100 B2
- HOUS 77056 4101 A1
- RSBG 77471 4490 E7
- SGLD 77478 4369 A1
- SGLD 77479 4367 E6
2000 HOUS 77098 4102 A1
3000 HOUS 77098 4101 E1
3200 HOUS 77005 4101 E1
3200 HOUS 77027 4101 D1
3200 HOUS 77046 4101 D1
5100 HOUS 77056 4100 A3
5600 HOUS 77057 4100 D2
6200 HOUS 77074 4100 B2
6200 HOUS 77081 4100 B2
7000 HOUS 77036 4099 C7
7000 HOUS 77074 4099 C7
8600 HOUS 77074 4239 A2
9100 HOUS 77036 4239 B1
10100 HOUS 77036 4238 C5
10100 HOUS 77074 4238 C5
10900 HOUS 77099 4238 D4
11000 HOUS 77099 4238 D4
11700 HarC 77031 4238 C5
11700 HarC 77099 4238 C5
11800 MDWP 77477 4238 C5
11900 STAF 77477 4238 C6
12800 STAF 77477 4369 A1
13600 SGLD 77478 4368 A6
16000 SGLD 77479 4368 B6
20800 RSBG 77469 4491 D7
20800 RSBG 77469 4492 A6
26000 RSBG 77471 4491 A7
26500 RSBG 77471 4615 A1
28000 RSBG 77471 4614 E1
SouthW Freeway Frontage Rd S
- RSBG 77469 4492 A6
- RSBG 77471 4492 A6
SouthW Freeway Frontage Rd Rd
- SGLD 77479 4368 A7
Southwick
1900 HOUS 77080 3820 A5
Southwick Dr
9800 HMBL 77338 3262 C5
Southwick Ln
19500 MtgC 77365 2972 C2
Southwick St
2500 HOUS 77080 3820 A3
Southwind Av
4800 HOUS 77033 4243 E1
Southwind Ln
2900 LGCY 77573 4633 A3
Southwind St
- HOUS 77033 4243 E1
- HOUS 77033 4244 A1
Southwold Ln
11000 HOUS 77096 4240 A4
Southwood Cir
200 BYTN 77520 4113 C1
Southwood Ct N
6300 HOUS 77035 4240 A5
Southwood Ct S
6300 HOUS 77035 4240 A5
Southwood Dr
- SHEH 77381 2822 B3
- SHEH 77385 2822 B3
- WDLD 77380 2822 B3
1400 BYTN 77520 4113 B1
1800 RMFT 77357 2828 E3
1800 WDBR 77357 2828 E3
2000 RMFT 77357 2829 A3
2000 WDBR 77357 2829 A3
Southwood Oaks Ct
25600 MtgC 77365 3117 E3
Southwood Oaks Dr
20400 MtgC 77365 2972 E7
20600 MtgC 77365 3117 E1
20600 MtgC 77365 3118 A1
Southwood Trace Ln
14700 HarC 77049 3828 E2
15000 HarC 77049 3829 A2
Southworth Ln
2900 BzaC 77583 4500 D7
Southwyck Pkwy
- BzaC 77584 4501 B5
Sovereign Cir
10 FBnC 77469 4492 E5
Sovereign Dr
5800 HOUS 77036 4098 E4
Sovereign Wy
10 CNRO 77384 2675 E3
Sovereign Wy Ct
10 CNRO 77384 2675 E3

STREET
Block City ZIP Map# Grid
Sovereign Shores Blvd
10 FBnC 77469 4492 E5
Soway St
- HOUS 77080 3821 A1
Sowden Rd
- HOUS 77041 3821 A1
12000 HOUS 77055 3821 B2
12100 HOUS 77080 3821 A1
Sowles Park Dr
1900 HarC 77493 3814 A6
Spa Dr
2700 DRPK 77536 4249 B1
Space Center Blvd
- DRPK 77503 4248 E1
- DRPK 77536 4248 E1
- HOUS 77034 4379 E1
- HOUS 77058 4508 A1
- HOUS 77059 4380 A2
- PASD 77058 4507 D1
- PASD 77058 4508 A1
- PASD 77503 4248 E1
3100 PASD 77505 4248 D3
5300 HOUS 77034 4248 E7
5300 HOUS 77059 4248 E7
5300 PASD 77034 4248 E7
13000 HOUS 77059 4379 D4
14000 HOUS 77062 4379 D4
14800 HOUS 77062 4380 A6
15600 HOUS 77062 4507 B1
16200 HOUS 77058 4507 D1
19200 NSUB 77058 4508 C3
Space City Dr
- HarC 77032 3546 C2
- HOUS 77032 3546 C2
Spacek Rd
1500 RSBG 77469 4492 A7
2200 FBnC 77469 4615 E1
2200 FBnC 77469 4616 A1
2200 RSBG 77469 4615 E2
2200 RSBG 77469 4616 A1
Space Park Dr
1200 WEBS 77058 4507 D5
1300 NSUB 77058 4507 E5
1700 NSUB 77058 4508 A5
Spain St
1900 HarC 77532 3411 D4
Spaniel St
100 HOUS 77013 3828 B6
Spanish Trc
100 HarC 77532 3266 E6
Spanish Acorn Ln
3500 HarC 77389 3112 E1
Spanish Bay Ct
10 MNVL 77583 4624 C5
Spanish Bay Ct S
6800 MSCY 77459 4496 D5
Spanish Cove Dr
100 HarC 77532 3266 D6
1200 HOUS 77532 3266 B6
Spanish Forest Ln
2100 FBnC 77469 4234 B7
Spanish Grant Blvd
- GLSN 77554 5333 C1
Spanish Grant Dr
10400 FBnC 77478 4236 E4
Spanish Main
4200 JMAB 77554 5331 E4
Spanish Main Blvd
4000 GLSN 77554 5220 B7
Spanish Mill Rd
9500 HarC 77064 3399 C7
Spanish Moss Ct
5800 HarC 77379 3256 E1
5800 HarC 77379 3257 A1
Spanish Moss Ln
1000 HOUS 77077 3957 D4
Spanish Needle Dr
19100 HarC 77084 3816 A5
19700 HarC 77084 3815 E5
Spanish Oak Dr
4800 HarC 77066 3401 B2
5500 HarC 77066 3400 E3
6000 PASD 77505 4248 D6
Spanish Oak Ln
27100 MtgC 77357 2829 D5
Spanish Oak Wy
6000 HarC 77379 3256 E1
Spanish Oak Hill Ct
2400 HarC 77388 3113 B5
Spanish Oaks Ln
26600 MtgC 77357 2829 B5
Spanish River Ln
14300 HarC 77429 3397 A1
Spanish Wells Rd
3700 GLSN 77554 5440 D6
Spann St
1900 HOUS 77019 3962 B6
Spar Wy
300 HarC 77532 3411 B7
Spar Crest Ct
15700 HarC 77429 3397 D2
Sparkleberry St
10 WDLD 77380 2967 D1
Sparkle Brooke Ln
- HarC 77433 3537 D1
Sparklewood Pl
10 WDLD 77381 2674 E6
Sparkling Bay Ln
14800 HOUS 77062 4380 A6
Sparkling Brook Ct
2500 PRLD 77584 4500 C3
Sparkling Brook Dr
- PRLD 77584 4500 C3
Sparkling Creek Dr
29800 MtgC 77386 2969 C3
Sparkling Springs Dr
8300 HarC 77095 3538 C5
Sparkling Water Dr
100 HarC 77336 3121 B6
Sparks
- SGLD 77478 4368 B1
Sparks Ln
- TXCY 77591 4873 E6
Sparks St
2600 LMQU 77568 4989 D1
3600 HOUS 77093 3686 B5
Sparks Valley Ct
6100 HarC 77084 3679 A4
Sparks Valley Dr
14700 HarC 77084 3679 A4
Sparky Ln
- HarC 77388 3113 B1
- HarC 77389 3113 B1
Sparrow Cir
2000 FRDW 77546 4629 E4
Sparrow Dr
3600 BzaC 77584 4501 C7

STREET
Block City ZIP Map# Grid
Sparrow St
3300 HOUS 77051 4243 B5
9800 LPRT 77571 4250 B1
N Sparrow Wy
600 TXCY 77591 4873 C5
S Sparrow Wy
100 TXCY 77591 4873 C7
Sparrow Branch Ct
2300 FBnC 77479 4493 D2
Sparrow Hawk Ct
10 WDLD 77380 2822 B7
Sparrow Knoll Ct
1200 HarC 77450 3953 E4
Sparrows Rdg
1700 HarC 77450 3955 A6
2100 HarC 77450 3954 D7
Sparrows Glen Ln
6300 HarC 77379 3111 C4
Sparrows Point Dr
- HarC 77090 3258 E7
Sparrow Wy Ct
17300 HarC 77095 3678 A1
Sparta Dr
3300 MSCY 77459 4497 E5
3300 MSCY 77459 4498 B5
Sparta St
8200 HOUS 77028 3826 C3
Spartan Ct
13100 HarC 77041 3679 D6
Spartan Dr
- FBnC 77477 4370 B5
- STAF 77477 4370 A5
5200 HarC 77041 3679 D7
Spartan Trail Dr
- WDLD 77385 2676 B4
Spates Dr
700 HarC 77530 3829 E7
Spatswood Ln
22700 HarC 77449 3814 D6
Spaulding Rd
10 HarC 77357 2830 A7
Spaulding St
8200 HOUS 77016 3686 E7
Speaker Dr
6600 HTCK 77563 4989 A5
Spear Ln
21900 MtgC 77365 2973 C6
Spearman Dr
9400 HarC 77040 3541 A6
Spear Point Cove
800 HOUS 77079 3957 A2
Spears Cir
- WDBR 77357 2828 B1
23600 MtgC 77357 2828 B1
Spears Dr
2300 HMBL 77396 3406 D3
Spears Rd
1200 HarC 77014 3402 C4
1200 HarC 77067 3402 C4
1200 HOUS 77014 3402 D6
3100 HarC 77014 3401 D4
3100 HarC 77067 3401 D4
3500 HarC 77066 3401 D4
4300 BzaC 77578 4625 D3
4300 MNVL 77578 4625 D3
11600 HOUS 77067 3402 D4
S Spears Rd
24100 MtgC 77365 2973 C7
Spears Gears Rd
13600 HarC 77014 3402 D4
13600 HarC 77067 3402 D4
13600 HOUS 77014 3402 D4
13600 HOUS 77067 3402 D4
Spear Valley Ln
21500 MtgC 77365 2973 B3
Specialty Sand Co
- HarC 77044 3551 A6
Speckleberry
9800 HarC 77375 3110 B3
Speckled Egg Pl
10 WDLD 77381 2674 B7
Speed Rd
12900 GlsC 77517 4986 D6
Speer Landing Dr
11000 HarC 77064 3540 E1
Spell Rd
10500 HarC 77375 3110 A3
11200 TMBL 77375 3110 A3
Spell St
100 HOUS 77022 3684 C7
Spellbrook Ct
2400 LGCY 77573 4508 D6
Spellbrook Dr
18000 HarC 77084 3816 E1
Spellbrook Bend Ln
22800 FBnC 77469 4093 D6
Spellbrook Point Ln
- HarC 77377 3254 A1
Spellman Rd
4300 HOUS 77035 4241 B4
5200 HOUS 77035 4240 E4
5300 HOUS 77096 4240 D4
9100 HOUS 77031 4239 B4
Spelman St
5600 WUNP 77005 4101 B2
Spence Ln
100 HarC 77532 3552 C7
Spence Rd
1900 HOUS 77093 3824 E2
16100 HOUS 77060 3403 D7
16100 HOUS 77060 3544 D1
Spence Park Ct
22500 HarC 77373 3113 D1
Spencer Blvd
24000 MtgC 77355 2961 B6
Spencer Ct
3400 FBnC 77459 4621 D5
Spencer Hwy
10 SHUS 77587 4246 D3
1100 SHUS 77587 4247 A3
1900 PASD 77502 4247 E3
1900 PASD 77504 4247 E3
4200 PASD 77502 4248 A3
4200 PASD 77504 4248 A3
4500 PASD 77503 4248 B3
4500 PASD 77505 4248 B3
6600 PASD 77503 4249 A3
6600 PASD 77505 4249 A3
6600 PASD 77536 4249 A3
7800 DRPK 77505 4249 C3
7800 DRPK 77536 4249 D3
8000 LPRT 77536 4249 D3
8000 LPRT 77571 4249 D3
8000 PASD 77571 4249 C3
9300 DRPK 77536 4250 A3
9300 LPRT 77536 4250 A3
9300 LPRT 77571 4250 A3
9500 DRPK 77571 4250 A3

STREET
Block City ZIP Map# Grid
Spencer Hwy
11400 LPRT 77571 4251 A2
Spencer Lndg
- LPRT 77571 4250 E2
Spencer Lndg E
100 LPRT 77571 4250 E2
100 LPRT 77571 4251 A2
Spencer Lndg N
10500 LPRT 77571 4250 E2
10500 LPRT 77571 4251 A2
Spencer Lndg S
10 LPRT 77571 4250 E3
Spencer Lndg W
100 LPRT 77571 4250 E3
Spencer Rd
- HarC 77040 3680 B1
- HarC 77041 3680 B1
- JRSV 77040 3680 B1
- JRSV 77041 3680 B1
11300 JRSV 77041 3680 A2
12100 HarC 77041 3679 E2
13200 HarC 77095 3679 B2
14100 HarC 77084 3679 A2
15000 HarC 77084 3678 E2
16100 HarC 77095 3678 A2
17400 HarC 77084 3677 E2
17400 HarC 77095 3677 E2
Spencer Rd FM-529
10900 HarC 77040 3680 C2
10900 HarC 77041 3680 A2
10900 JRSV 77040 3680 C2
11300 JRSV 77041 3680 A2
12100 HarC 77041 3679 E2
13200 HarC 77095 3679 B2
14100 HarC 77084 3679 A2
15000 HarC 77084 3678 E2
16100 HarC 77095 3678 A2
17400 HarC 77084 3677 E2
17400 HarC 77095 3677 E2
Spencer St
3800 HOUS 77007 3962 C2
Spencer Ter
24200 MtgC 77355 2961 B5
Spencer Landing Ln
10500 LPRT 77571 4250 E2
10500 LPRT 77571 4251 A2
Spencers Gate Ct
1000 HarC 77373 2968 D7
Spencers Glen Dr
200 FBnC 77479 4367 B5
Spencers Glen Wy
6200 FBnC 77479 4367 B5
Spenwick Dr
2500 HOUS 77055 3821 C3
Sperber Ln
2300 HOUS 77002 3963 E4
2300 HOUS 77003 3963 E4
Sperry Gardens Dr
16500 HarC 77095 3538 B3
Sperry Landing Dr
17000 HarC 77095 3538 A4
Speyburn Ct
16000 HarC 77095 3538 C4
Spica St
31400 TMBL 77375 2963 E4
Spice Ln
10000 HOUS 77072 4098 D7
10000 HOUS 77099 4098 D7
Spiceberry Pl
10 WDLD 77382 2674 D4
Spicebush Ct
10 WDLD 77381 2820 E5
Spice Leaf Tr
7100 FBnC 77494 4093 A5
Spice Ridge Row
10500 FBnC 77459 4622 A6
Spice Trail Ct
- FBnC 77494 3952 C6
Spicewood
9800 HarC 77375 3110 B3
Spicewood Ln
11800 HarC 77044 3688 D7
N Spicewood Ln
11400 HarC 77044 3688 D7
S Spicewood Ln
11400 HarC 77044 3688 D7
Spicewood Spring Ln
17400 HarC 77379 3256 D1
Spikewood Dr
8800 HOUS 77028 3826 E2
8800 HOUS 77078 3826 E2
8900 HOUS 77078 3827 A2
Spillane St
7500 MNVL 77578 4746 D2
Spill Creek Dr
11600 PRLD 77584 4500 D3
Spiller Dr
16900 HarC 77379 3257 C3
Spiller St
6900 HTCK 77563 4989 A5
Spillers Ln
1900 HOUS 77043 3819 D5
Spillman Rd
6400 HOUS 77096 4240 A4
Spindle Dr
5100 HarC 77086 3542 D5
6500 HOUS 77086 3542 C5
Spindle Oaks Dr
1000 MtgC 77385 2676 D5
Spindle Ridge Dr
400 MtgC 77386 2968 C2
Spindletop Ct
3300 BzaC 77583 4500 E6
E Spindle Tree Cir
100 WDLD 77382 2819 A3
W Spindle Tree Cir
10 WDLD 77382 2819 A3
Spindle Tree Dr
10 MtgC 77354 2819 A2
10 MtgC 77382 2819 A2
10 WDLD 77382 2819 A3
Spindlewood Dr
9200 FBnC 77083 4237 A2
Spindrift Pl
10 WDLD 77381 2821 D4
Spinet St
7600 HOUS 77016 3687 B3
Spinks Creek Ln
4200 HarC 77388 3112 C5
Spinnaker Ct
800 HarC 77532 3552 A3
Spinnaker Dr
100 LGCY 77573 4509 B7
15900 HarC 77532 3552 A2
Spinnaker Run
30000 MtgC 77354 2671 D7
Spinnaker Wy
1100 SGLD 77478 4236 E7
1200 SGLD 77478 4237 A7

STREET
Block City ZIP Map# Grid
Spinnaker Bay Ln
8300 PRLD 77584 4501 E5
Spinner Ct Dr
18400 HarC 77346 3409 B1
Spinney Ln
18500 HarC 77433 3677 C2
N Spinning Wheel Cir
10 WDLD 77354 2819 B2
10 WDLD 77382 2819 B3
S Spinning Wheel Cir
10 WDLD 77382 2819 B3
Spinwood Dr
200 HarC 77015 3828 D5
Spiral Leaf Ct
10 WDLD 77381 2674 B6
S Spiral Vine Cir
10 WDLD 77381 2820 E5
Spiralwood Ln
9400 HarC 77086 3542 B3
Spirit of Estates Dr
2900 DKSN 77539 4753 D2
Spivey Rd
7800 HarC 77562 3832 B3
Spivey St
16300 MtgC 77372 2683 B5
Splash Town Dr
100 HarC 77373 3113 D3
Splendora Dr
20500 HarC 77449 3815 D4
Splenwood Dr
14100 SPLD 77372 2683 C1
Splintered Oak Dr
13300 HarC 77065 3539 A2
Splintwood Ct
2500 HOUS 77345 3120 A3
Split Rd
28100 HarC 77377 3108 E2
Split Branch Ct
2000 HOUS 77077 3956 E6
Split Branch Ln
8500 HarC 77095 3537 E6
Split Cedar Dr
14300 HarC 77015 3829 A4
Split Creek Dr
17800 HarC 77379 3255 E3
Split Creek Ln
13100 PRLD 77584 4500 A1
Split Cypress Ln
7900 HarC 77095 3539 B6
Split Oak Cir
17100 MtgC 77357 2826 D1
Split Oak Ct
7500 HarC 77040 3681 E1
Split Oak Dr
7800 HarC 77040 3681 E1
18000 MtgC 77357 2826 E1
20400 MtgC 77357 2827 A1
Split Pine Dr
8000 HarC 77040 3681 D1
Split Rail Ln
- HOUS 77071 4239 E6
Split Rail Pl
10 WDLD 77382 2820 A2
Split Ridge Ln
9200 HOUS 77075 4377 A3
Split River Ln
- HarC 77089 4377 B7
- HOUS 77089 4377 B7
Split Rock Ct
10 WDLD 77381 2821 B3
Split Rock Rd
10 WDLD 77381 2821 B3
Split Rock Cove
100 WDLD 77381 2821 B3
Split Rock Falls
24400 HarC 77375 2965 D4
Split Willow Dr
16300 FBnC 77083 4236 A1
Spode St
9300 HOUS 77078 3688 A6
Spofford
- HarC 77562 3692 E6
Spoonbill Dr
2400 LGCY 77573 4508 D6
4300 SEBK 77586 4382 E7
Spoonbill Ln
4100 GLSN 77554 5332 E3
Spoon Bill St
6000 KATY 77493 3813 B3
Spoon Creek Ln
8900 HarC 77379 3255 D3
Spooner St
100 PASD 77506 4107 B4
1200 PASD 77502 4107 B6
N Spooner St
100 PASD 77506 4107 B3
S Spooner St
- PASD 77506 4107 B3
Spooner Ridge Ct
10 WDLD 77382 2674 D3
Spoonwood Ct
19300 HarC 77346 3264 C5
Spoonwood Dr
19500 HarC 77346 3264 C5
20300 HarC 77346 3265 C3
Sporan Ln
8000 HOUS 77075 4376 E4
Sport Ln
24200 MtgC 77365 2973 C7
Sporting Clay Lp
1500 HOUS 77094 4095 E2
Sporting Hill Ln
11000 FBnC 77478 4236 D5
Sports Haven Dr
8000 HarC 77346 3265 C7
Sportsman Rd
10900 GLSN 77554 5220 D2
Sportsplex
- LGCY 77573 4631 E6
Spotsylvania Ln
8400 FBnC 77083 4235 E1
8400 FBnC 77083 4236 A1
Spotted Deer Dr
10 WDLD 77381 2820 D5
Spotted Fawn Ct
10 WDLD 77381 2821 B2
Spotted Horse Dr
10000 HarC 77064 3540 C4
Spotted Pony Ct
26900 MtgC 77355 2961 D1
Spotted Sandpiper Dr
25300 GLSN 77554 5548 B2
Spottswood Dr
- HarC 77050 3547 A7
11200 HOUS 77016 3687 B1
11400 HOUS 77016 3547 B7
SPR-5
- HOUS - 4104 A2

STREET
Block City ZIP Map# Grid
SPR-5
- HOUS 77021 4104 B3
SPR-41 Dairy Ashford Rd
13100 SGLD 77478 4368 D2
SPR-58 Brooks St
100 SGLD 77478 4367 E3
SPR-261 N Durham Dr
2900 HOUS 77018 3823 B4
SPR-261 N Shepherd Dr
2900 HOUS 77018 3823 B1
4800 HOUS 77018 3684 B7
SPR-330
- BYTN - 3832 C7
- BYTN - 3971 E2
- BYTN - 3972 A3
- HarC - 3832 A7
SPR-330 Decker Dr
900 BYTN 77520 3972 D6
2200 BYTN 77521 3972 D6
SPR-342 61st St
1000 GLSN 77551 5108 C7
2800 GLSN 77551 5222 C1
SPR-501 S Broadway St
2300 LPRT 77571 4251 D7
3200 LPRT 77571 4382 E1
3200 SRAC 77571 4382 E1
3800 HarC 77571 4382 E2
3900 PASD 77571 4382 E2
SPR-527
- HOUS 77002 3963 A7
- HOUS 77006 3963 A7
SPR-529
900 RSBG 77471 4490 B5
1100 FBnC 77471 4490 A5
SPR-529 Avenue H
10 RSBG 77471 4490 C4
SPR-529 W Avenue H
700 RSBG 77471 4490 B5
Sprads Rd
100 HarC 77037 3544 C6
Sprague Av
6900 PASD 77505 4249 A3
Sprague St
7000 MNVL 77578 4746 C3
Sprangletop Av
4300 HarC 77521 3833 B2
Sprangletop Ct
11000 HarC 77086 3542 B1
Sprawling Oaks Dr
1000 MtgC 77385 2676 D5
Sprayberry Dr
- FBnC 77469 4365 B7
- RHMD 77469 4365 B7
Sprayberry Ln
4000 CNRO 77303 2237 C4
Spreading Bough Ln
1800 FBnC 77469 4365 A2
Spreading Oak Dr
13400 HarC 77429 3398 D4
E Spreading Oak Dr
600 HOUS 77076 3684 E4
W Spreading Oak Dr
200 HOUS 77076 3684 C4
Spreading Oak Ln
2000 FBnC 77469 4365 C3
E Spreading Oaks Av
100 FRDW 77546 4505 C7
W Spreading Oaks Av
100 FRDW 77546 4629 B1
Spreading Oaks Ln
- MtgC 77380 2821 B7
11800 MtgC 77362 2817 B7
25600 MtgC 77380 2967 B1
Sprey Dr
5100 HarC 77084 3678 B5
Spriggs Wy
11600 HDWV 77024 3959 C2
Sprila Park Dr
15400 HarC 77429 3252 E6
Spring Cr
6900 HarC 77084 3678 B2
6900 HarC 77095 3678 B2
7700 HarC 77338 3261 B3
Spring Ct
3700 BzaC 77578 4625 B1
13500 TMBL 77375 2964 A5
Spring Dr
400 PASD 77504 4247 B4
22000 MtgC 77357 2827 C4
23500 MtgC 77447 2959 E4
N Spring Dr
200 HarC 77373 3114 E4
Spring Ln
4700 BYTN 77521 3974 A1
4900 HarC 77521 3974 A1
10800 MtgC 77372 2537 C1
28300 MtgC 77362 2963 D2
Spring Mdw
7200 FBnC 77494 4093 C4
Spring Pk
- HarC 77073 3259 A3
Spring Pt
- HarC 77373 3113 E6
Spring St
1200 HOUS 77007 3963 A2
2300 HOUS 77007 3962 E2
Spring Tr
15700 HarC 77095 3538 D5
Spring Acres Dr
29800 MtgC 77386 2969 C3
Spring Alp Ct
9800 HarC 77375 3255 B2
Spring Apple Ct
1200 HarC 77073 3259 B5
Spring Arbor Ct
3900 PRLD 77584 4503 A7
Spring Arbor Ln
3400 SGLD 77479 4495 B1
Spring Arbor Wy
3600 HOUS 77345 3119 D3
Spring Ash Ln
25000 FBnC 77494 4093 B2
Spring Aspen Ct
24900 FBnC 77494 3953 B5
Spring Aspen Ln
20500 HarC 77388 3113 A4
Springbank Dr
16100 HarC 77095 3538 C5
Spring Barker Dr
16300 HarC 77429 3396 D1
Spring Bend Dr
2600 MtgC 77386 2969 C3
Springbend Ln
21200 HarC 77450 3954 C5
Springberry Ct
7800 HarC 77379 3256 A2
Spring Bloom Ct
3900 SGLD 77479 4495 B1

STREET
Block City ZIP Map# Grid
Spring Blossom Ct
5500 FBnC 77450 4094 B3
Spring Bluebonnet Dr
8000 FBnC 77479 4494 C4
Spring Bluff Ln
20500 HarC 77388 3112 E5
20500 HarC 77388 3113 A4
Spring Branch Dr
5000 PRLD 77584 4503 A7
5200 PRLD 77584 4502 E7
8800 HOUS 77055 3820 E5
8800 HOUS 77080 3820 D5
Spring Branch Dr E
4000 PRLD 77584 4503 A7
Spring Branch Dr W
4000 PRLD 77584 4502 D6
Spring Branch Pt
23300 MtgC 77357 2681 C6
Spring Breeze St
500 LGCY 77573 4630 D7
Spring Briar Ct
2300 HarC 77373 3114 E4
Springbridge Dr
21800 HarC 77073 3259 B2
S Springbrook Cir
10 WDLD 77382 2820 B2
Spring Brook Ct
4000 PRLD 77584 4503 A7
4300 HOUS 77041 3819 E1
6000 SGLD 77479 4494 E5
Springbrook Ct
5300 LGCY 77573 4751 D2
Spring Brook Dr
10600 HOUS 77041 3819 E1
Springbrook Dr
9700 HOUS 77041 3820 B1
Spring Brook Plz
21000 HarC 77379 3111 D3
Springbrook Garden Ln
6100 HarC 77379 3111 D3
Springbrook Hollow Ln
6500 HarC 77379 3111 A3
Springbrook Trail Ln
- HarC 77379 3111 E3
- HarC 77388 3111 E3
Springbury Ln
3400 FBnC 77494 3952 C7
Spring Canyon Ct
2700 HarC 77067 3401 E4
Spring Canyon Dr
4900 LGCY 77573 4751 E1
Spring Cedar Ln
1900 HOUS 77077 3956 D6
Spring Chase Dr
2600 MtgC 77386 2969 C4
Spring Cir Dr
5000 PRLD 77584 4503 A6
5200 PRLD 77584 4502 E6
Spring Cir Dr E
3900 PRLD 77584 4503 A6
Spring Cir Dr W
3900 PRLD 77584 4502 D6
Spring City Ct
1300 HarC 77090 3402 C1
Spring Colony Dr
2700 MtgC 77386 2969 D4
Springcourt Dr
15700 HOUS 77062 4380 C7
Spring Cove Dr
- HOUS 77345 3119 E5
Spring Cove Ln
25100 FBnC 77494 4093 A5
Spring Cove Pt
26500 FBnC 77494 4092 B1
Spring Creek Cir
7400 HarC 77521 3833 D3
34200 MtgC 77362 2816 E5
E Spring Creek Cir
21400 HarC 77338 3261 D2
W Spring Creek Cir
7700 HarC 77338 3261 D2
Spring Creek Ct
200 MtgC 77362 2816 E6
Spring Creek Dr
- FRDW 77546 4629 B4
1100 MtgC 77386 2968 E4
1400 MtgC 77386 2969 A5
2000 HarC 77373 3114 C3
4100 HarC 77373 3115 A2
24800 MtgC 77380 2967 A1
25800 MtgC 77380 2821 A7
Spring Creek Ln
2100 HOUS 77017 4246 D1
2900 PRLD 77581 4504 C4
6000 HarC 77379 3256 E1
Spring Creek Forest Dr
17400 HarC 77379 3256 C1
Spring Creek Grove Ln
6000 HarC 77379 3256 E1
Spring Creek Oak Cir
18500 HarC 77379 3257 A1
Spring Creek Oaks Ct
16800 HarC 77379 3256 E1
Spring Creek Oaks Dr
5800 HarC 77379 3256 E2
5800 HarC 77379 3257 A1
Spring Creek Trail Dr
27700 HarC 77373 2969 A7
Spring Cress Ln
1200 TYLV 77586 4382 A7
Spring Crest Ct
3900 PRLD 77584 4503 A7
Springcrest Ct
6900 FBnC 77479 4493 C6
Spring Crest Dr
12300 HOUS 77072 4097 E6
Springcrest Dr
6600 FBnC 77479 4493 C6
Springcroft Ct
9000 HarC 77375 3110 D3
Springcross Ct
13600 HOUS 77077 3957 A6
Spring Crossing Blvd
- HarC 77373 2968 D5
- HarC 77389 2968 D5
Spring Crossing Dr
22200 HarC 77373 3113 D1
Spring Crystal Ct
24000 HarC 77373 3114 C4
Spring Cypress Rd
- HarC 77070 3254 E4
Spring-Cypress Rd
- HarC 77429 3253 E5
Spring Cypress Rd
400 HarC 77373 3113 D2
500 HOUS 77373 3113 E2
1500 HarC 77388 3113 A4
2900 HarC 77388 3112 C6

STREET
Block City ZIP Map# Grid

Spring Cypress Rd
4400 HarC 77379 3112 A7
5300 HarC 77379 3111 A7
7900 HarC 77379 3255 D2
7900 HarC 77379 3256 A1
9800 HarC 77070 3255 B4
10600 HarC 77375 3255 A4
11000 HarC 77377 3254 D4
11000 HOUS 77070 3254 E4
11000 HOUS 77377 3254 E4
13000 HarC 77429 3254 A5
14500 HarC 77429 3253 D6
14900 HarC 77429 3397 B2
16200 HarC 77429 3396 C3
Spring Cypress Rd FM-2920
1500 HarC 77388 3113 A4
Spring Cypress Plaza Dr
10700 HarC 77070 3255 A5
10700 HOUS 77070 3255 A5
Springdale
- PRVW 77445 3100 A3
Springdale Ct
1100 FBnC 77479 4493 E6
2900 BzaC 77584 4501 E7
Springdale Dr
3100 BzaC 77584 4501 B6
7300 FBnC 77479 4493 E6
Springdale St
7100 HOUS 77028 3686 D7
7100 HOUS 77028 3687 A7
Spring Dane Dr
23700 HarC 77373 3115 A3
Spring Day Ct
2500 HarC 77373 3114 E4
Spring Day Ln
23900 HarC 77373 3114 E4
Spring Dusk Ln
2200 HarC 77373 3114 D4
Springer St
6400 HOUS 77087 4104 D7
Springer Cemetery Rd
25900 WlrC 77447 2959 B4
Springerton Cir
19200 HarC 77373 3113 E6
Spring Fair Ct
3000 HarC 77388 3113 A4
Spring Falling Wy
700 HOUS 77373 3113 E3
Spring Falls Ct
2800 BzaC 77578 4501 A7
Spring Falls Dr
- HarC 77388 3113 B3
Spring Fern Ln
7800 HarC 77040 3541 E7
Springfield Av
5000 PRLD 77584 4503 A7
5200 PRLD 77584 4502 E7
Springfield Blvd
100 HarC 77532 3552 C6
Springfield Ct
16800 FBnC 77478 4236 B5
Springfield Dr
15700 FBnC 77478 4236 B5
16600 MtgC 77302 2679 C2
Spring Field Rd
2000 HOUS 77062 4507 C1
Springfield Garden Ln
6600 HarC 77379 3111 C2
Springfield Lakes St
4500 SGLD 77479 4496 A1
Spring Flower Ct
16300 MtgC 77302 2678 E4
Spring Flower Ln
3100 HarC 77388 3113 A4
3200 HarC 77388 3112 E4
Springford Ln
- HarC 77377 3253 D3
Spring Forest Ct
600 MtgC 77302 2530 D6
16000 HOUS 77059 4380 C4
Spring Forest Dr
600 MtgC 77302 2530 D6
3900 PRLD 77584 4502 E7
5000 HOUS 77091 3682 E6
5000 HOUS 77091 3683 A6
15700 HOUS 77059 4380 B4
29500 MtgC 77386 2969 B4
Spring Forest Wy
1300 TMBL 77375 2964 A4
Spring Fork Dr
23800 HarC 77373 3114 D4
Spring Garden Dr
3900 PRLD 77584 4503 A7
Spring Gardens Dr
3200 HOUS 77339 3119 B4
Springgate Dr
22200 HarC 77373 3261 A1
22400 HarC 77373 3116 A7
Spring Glade Dr
16600 HarC 77429 3396 D1
Spring Glen Dr
11300 HarC 77070 3255 A7
11400 HarC 77070 3254 E7
Spring Glen Ln
1600 PRLD 77581 4376 D7
1600 PRLD 77581 4503 C1
Spring Green Blvd
4600 FBnC 77469 4092 D5
4600 FBnC 77494 4092 D5
Spring Green Ct
1800 MSCY 77489 4370 C6
Spring Green Dr
8500 HarC 77095 3538 C5
Spring Green Rd
3500 FBnC 77494 4092 B1
6700 FBnC 77469 4232 D2
9200 FBnC 77469 4092 D7
Spring Green Rd FM-723
- FBnC 77494 4092 D7
6700 FBnC 77469 4232 D2
9200 FBnC 77469 4092 D7
Spring Grove Ct
4000 PRLD 77584 4503 A7
Spring Grove Dr
12000 HOUS 77099 4238 A2
12100 HOUS 77099 4237 E2
Spring Grove Ln
5700 HarC 77373 3115 E7
Spring Gum Dr
23800 HarC 77373 3114 E4
Spring Harvest Dr
10400 HarC 77064 3540 B3
Spring Haven Ct
5700 LGCY 77573 4751 C1
Springhaven Ct
- KATY 77494 3952 B3
16800 HOUS 77396 3406 A3
Springhaven Dr
6100 HOUS 77396 3406 A4
Springheath Ln
6600 HarC 77379 3111 B2
6600 HarC 77388 3111 B2
Spring Heather Ct
8700 HarC 77379 3255 E1
Spring Heights Dr
900 HarC 77373 3113 D1
Spring Hill Dr
- MtgC 77386 2968 C3
Springhill Dr
3100 MSCY 77459 4369 E7
Spring Hill Ln
3000 LGCY 77573 4633 B2
Springhill Ln
3600 SGLD 77479 4495 B1
Spring Hill Pl
25700 HarC 77373 3113 E3
Springhill St
7100 HOUS 77021 4103 B7
7600 HOUS 77021 4243 A3
Springhill Bend Ln
15200 HarC 77429 3253 B6
Spring Hills Dr
1100 MtgC 77386 2968 E3
1300 MtgC 77386 2969 A3
Spring Hollow Dr
13200 HarC 77375 2964 B2
13200 TMBL 77375 2964 B2
Spring Hollow St
10 HOUS 77024 3960 D2
Springhope Ct
500 HarC 77049 3829 A4
Springhurst Ct
23700 HarC 77373 3115 C3
Spring Iris Ct
4500 LGCY 77573 4630 E5
Spring Iris Ln
25200 FBnC 77494 3953 A5
Spring Ivy Ln
5800 HarC 77379 3112 A4
Spring Knoll Ct
5600 BzaC 77583 4623 D4
Spring Knoll Dr
- TMBL 77375 2964 A5
Spring Knoll Ln
14100 BzaC 77583 4623 C4
Spring Lake Dr
7100 MtgC 77354 2819 B6
14700 HarC 77070 3398 D1
14900 HarC 77070 3254 D7
Springlake Falls Ln
- HarC 77073 3259 B3
Springlake Park Ln
2200 MtgC 77386 2823 B7
Spring Lakes
2800 MSCY 77459 4496 B1
Spring Lakes Haven Cir
10 HarC 77373 3113 C1
800 HarC 77373 3114 A3
Spring Lakes Haven Ct
25900 HarC 77373 3113 C1
Spring Lakes Haven Dr
- HarC 77373 3114 A4
Springland Ct
10300 HarC 77065 3539 E3
Springland Dr
11400 HarC 77065 3539 E3
Spring Landing Dr
2500 PRLD 77584 4500 A3
Spring Landing Ln
- HarC 77388 3113 A4
- LGCY 77573 4630 E5
3300 BzaC 77584 4501 C5
Springlea St
- HarC 77346 3264 A6
Spring Leaf Dr
6500 HarC 77379 3256 D2
Spring Light Ln
20700 HarC 77379 3111 E4
Spring Lilac Ln
5100 HarC 77373 3115 C5
20500 HarC 77388 3113 A4
Spring Lily Ct
2400 HarC 77373 3114 C5
Spring Line Ct
13400 HarC 77086 3541 E2
Spring Link Ct
22500 HarC 77373 3113 D1
Spring Ln Dr
- HarC 77379 3255 E1
23800 HarC 77373 3114 D4
Spring Lodge Dr
5800 HOUS 77345 3120 B4
Spring Manor Dr
3200 HOUS 77345 3120 B4
Spring Maple Ln
14300 HOUS 77062 4380 A6
Spring Marsh Ct
14300 HarC 77429 3396 E2
Spring Meadow Ct
21100 HarC 77338 3261 D3
Spring Meadow Dr
1000 HarC 77373 3114 A5
3900 PRLD 77584 4502 E7
Springmeadow St
3900 HOUS 77080 3820 C1
Spring Meadows Ct
- ALVN 77511 4749 B6
Spring Meadows Ln
19000 FBnC 77469 4094 D2
19000 FBnC 77469 4095 A5
Springmere Ct
- HarC 77095 3537 D4
Spring Mill Ln
23900 HarC 77373 3114 E4
Spring Miller Dr
9400 HOUS 77070 3399 D5
Springmint Ct
13100 HarC 77429 3254 A6
Springmint Dr
- HarC 77429 3254 A6
Spring Mission Ln
20500 HarC 77388 3113 A4
Spring Mist Ct
700 FBnC 77479 4366 E6
Spring Mist Dr
29200 MtgC 77386 2969 D4
Spring Mist Pl
10 WDLD 77381 2674 E6
Springmont Dr
9600 HOUS 77080 3820 B1
Spring Moss Dr
500 MSCY 77459 4497 A5
2700 LGCY 77573 4632 E1
23800 HarC 77373 3114 D5
Spring Mountain Ct
13900 HOUS 77044 3550 B3
Spring Mountain Dr
14400 HarC 77377 2963 D7
Spring Mountain Ln
- HarC 77388 3113 A4
14000 HOUS 77044 3550 B3
Spring Music Dr
12500 HarC 77065 3539 C1
Spring Oak Dr
4000 PRLD 77581 4504 A6
5000 PASD 77505 4248 D7
23800 HarC 77373 3115 A3
Spring Oak Hllw
6000 HarC 77379 3256 E1
Spring Oaks Cir
23800 HarC 77373 3114 D4
Spring Oaks Ct
1300 SPVL 77055 3821 A6
Spring Oaks Dr
22100 HarC 77388 3112 C1
22100 HarC 77389 3112 C1
Spring Orchard Ct
12200 FBnC 77469 4094 D2
21100 HarC 77338 3261 C2
Spring Orchard Ln
7100 FBnC 77469 4094 E5
20500 HarC 77388 3113 A4
Spring Palms Ct
4200 HOUS 77345 3119 E4
Spring Park Dr
5100 BYTN 77521 3833 C2
5100 HarC 77521 3833 C2
Spring Park St
5300 HOUS 77056 3960 E4
Spring Park Center Blvd
400 HarC 77373 3113 E6
400 HOUS 77373 3113 E6
Spring Path Ct
11700 HarC 77377 3254 D3
Spring Pine Ct
5200 HOUS 77345 3119 C2
Spring Pine Dr
23800 HarC 77373 3114 D5
Spring Pines Dr
100 MtgC 77386 2822 C7
100 ORDN 77386 2822 C7
14100 TMBL 77375 2963 E5
Spring Pl Ct
2500 MSCY 77489 4370 D6
Spring Pl Dr
2600 MSCY 77489 4370 D6
9900 HarC 77070 3399 B7
Spring Point Vw
13600 HarC 77083 4097 A4
Springport Ct
20900 FBnC 77450 4094 A4
Spring Rain Ct
16400 MtgC 77302 2679 B4
Spring Rain Dr
2400 HarC 77379 3257 D2
2400 HarC 77388 3257 D2
Spring Ranch Ln
3000 HarC 77388 3113 A5
Spring Rapid Dr
10000 HarC 77375 3255 A2
Spring Rapid Wy
10000 HarC 77375 3255 A2
Spring Ridge Dr
2600 BzaC 77578 4501 A6
24100 MtgC 77386 2968 C3
Spring Ridge Rd
4500 HOUS 77053 4372 C7
Springridge Rd
4500 HOUS 77053 4372 C7
Spring River Cir
16800 HarC 77379 3255 E5
Spring River Dr
3900 PRLD 77584 4502 E7
Spring Rock Ct
- RHMD 77469 4492 B2
Springrock Ln
1100 HOUS 77055 3820 C7
1400 HOUS 77080 3820 C6
Spring Rose Dr
20400 HarC 77450 3954 D5
Spring Run Ln
6900 FBnC 77494 4093 C2
18100 FBnC 77469 4095 B6
Springrush Ln
10200 HarC 77375 2965 B6
Spring Russell Dr
7000 HarC 77389 2966 B3
Spring Sage Ct
19600 HarC 77094 3955 A2
Spring School Rd
100 HarC 77373 3114 A2
Spring Shadows Dr
10800 HarC 77064 3540 C3
Spring Shannon Dr
3000 HarC 77373 3115 A4
Spring Shire Dr
11500 HarC 77066 3401 C6
Spring Showers Ct
4900 HarC 77084 3677 D7
Springside Ln
7300 HOUS 77040 3682 A3
Spring Silver Dr
5900 HarC 77449 3677 A5
Spring Sky Ln
- HarC 77377 3254 A3
Spring Song Dr
10 WDLD 77380 2967 E4
Springsong Dr
11000 HarC 77064 3540 E2
Spring Source Ct
25600 HarC 77373 3114 A4
Spring Source Pl
800 HarC 77373 3114 A4
Springstone Ct
5500 LGCY 77573 4751 D2
Springstone Dr
2500 MtgC 77386 2969 D5
Spring-stubner Rd
- HarC 77375 3111 A2
- HarC 77379 3111 A2
Spring Stuebner Lp
22400 HarC 77389 3113 D1
Spring Stuebner Rd
100 HarC 77373 3114 A1
300 HarC 77373 3113 D1
1500 HarC 77388 3113 B1
1500 HarC 77389 3113 B1
3100 HarC 77388 3112 A1
3100 HarC 77389 3112 A1
5300 HarC 77388 3111 D1
5300 HarC 77389 3111 D1
6200 HarC 77379 3111 D1
Spring Sunrise Dr
5700 FBnC 77469 4234 D2
Spring Sunset Dr
24000 HarC 77373 3114 D4
Springtail Ln
11300 HarC 77067 3402 B6
Spring Terrace Dr
29700 MtgC 77386 2969 C3
Spring Tide Ct
6300 FBnC 77494 4093 D5
Springtime Ln
8000 HOUS 77075 4376 D4
Springton Ln
5200 HarC 77379 3257 C2
Spring Town Dr
21100 HarC 77388 3113 C3
Spring Towne Dr
23800 HarC 77373 3114 D4
Spring Trace Ct
400 HarC 77094 3955 C1
Spring Trail Ct
4200 SGLD 77479 4494 E3
Spring Trail Dr
3200 SGLD 77479 4494 E3
Spring Trails Bnd
- MtgC 77386 2969 E7
Spring Trails Rdg
- MtgC 77386 2969 D6
Spring Trails Park Dr
27400 MtgC 77386 2969 E7
Springtree Dr
17800 HarC 77396 3407 E2
S Spring Trellis Cir
10 WDLD 77382 2820 A3
Spring Vale Dr
6900 FBnC 77583 4623 A7
Spring Valley Ct
800 FBnC 77479 4493 C5
Spring Valley Rd
- HOUS 77080 3820 C2
4300 HOUS 77041 3820 C1
4500 HOUS 77041 3681 C7
Springview Ln
8900 HOUS 77080 3820 E1
12000 PRLD 77583 4500 C5
Spring Villa Dr
11600 HarC 77070 3254 E7
Spring Village Dr
7900 HarC 77375 2966 A7
7900 HarC 77389 2966 A7
8000 HarC 77379 2966 A7
Springville Dr
7700 HarC 77095 3538 C7
Spring Vine Ln
21600 FBnC 77450 4093 C6
21600 FBnC 77450 4094 C3
Spring Walk Dr
- FBnC 77450 4093 D3
- FBnC 77494 4093 D3
Spring Walk Ln
14800 HarC 77429 3396 B1
Springwater Dr
500 HarC 77336 3121 C6
Springwell Dr
1900 HOUS 77043 3819 E5
Springwest Dr
21400 HarC 77388 3113 B3
Spring Willow Dr
22900 HarC 77375 2966 A6
Spring Wind Dr
8300 HarC 77040 3541 A7
Spring Wind Ln
8200 HarC 77040 3541 B5
Springwood Dr
- HOUS 77080 3820 E6
300 CHTW 77385 2822 D4
1200 FBnC 77479 4493 D5
1600 HOUS 77055 3820 E6
11000 LPRT 77571 4250 D4
26900 MtgC 77354 2819 B6
Springwood St
300 RMFT 77357 2829 B3
Springwood Forest Dr
10000 HOUS 77080 3820 A4
10100 HOUS 77043 3820 A4
Springwood Glen Ln
2400 CNRO 77304 2383 B1
Spring Woods Dr
300 MtgC 77386 2968 C1
Spring Wreath Ln
19900 HarC 77433 3537 A7
Spring Wy Dr
23800 HarC 77373 3114 E3
23800 HarC 77373 3115 A4
Sprinters Dr
19100 HarC 77346 3265 C6
Sprintwood Ct
19100 HarC 77346 3265 C6
Sprite Ln
2100 PRLD 77581 4504 A6
Sprite St
5600 HOUS 77040 3681 C5
Sprite Woods Pl
10 WDLD 77382 2819 A3
Spruce Cir
12700 TMBL 77375 3109 B3
Spruce Dr
500 MtgC 77302 2530 B6
1800 RSBG 77471 4491 C5
3100 DKSN 77539 4753 C4
Spruce Dr N
10800 LPRT 77571 4250 D3
Spruce Dr S
10800 LPRT 77571 4250 D3
N Spruce Dr
11000 LPRT 77571 4250 E3
Spruce Ln
- CmbC 77520 3835 D3
- PRLD 77584 4501 E4
17400 SGCH 77355 2961 B2
25300 MtgC 77372 2536 E2
25300 MtgC 77372 2537 A2
Spruce St
200 LGCY 77539 4632 C7
200 LGCY 77573 4632 C7
500 FBnC 77545 4623 A2
1100 LMQU 77568 4990 B1
4600 BLAR 77401 4101 A4
5100 BLAR 77401 4100 E4
5100 BLAR 77401 4100 E4
5200 HOUS 77081 4100 E4
8800 HTCK 77563 4988 C2
16100 HarC 77530 3830 C5
Spruce Bay Dr
3600 HOUS 77345 3119 D2
Spruce Bough Ct
6100 HarC 77346 3264 E5
Spruce Bough Ln
19100 HarC 77346 3264 E5
Spruce Canyon Pl
10 WDLD 77382 2673 A7
Spruce Canyon Pl
10 WDLD 77382 2819 A1
Spruce Cove Dr
7800 HarC 77095 3538 D7
Spruce Creek Dr
18200 HarC 77084 3677 E7
Sprucedale Ct
11000 HarC 77070 3399 A4
Spruce Falls Ct
23200 HarC 77494 3953 C3
Spruce Forest Dr
5000 HOUS 77091 3682 E6
5000 HOUS 77091 3683 A6
6100 HOUS 77092 3682 C6
Spruce Glen Dr
3800 HOUS 77339 3119 A3
Spruce Grove Dr
2000 HOUS 77339 3263 D1
Spruce Haven Dr
7700 HarC 77095 3538 C7
Spruce Hill Dr
11800 HOUS 77077 3958 A6
Spruce Hill Ln
17200 HarC 77388 3257 D2
Spruce Hollow Ct
13400 HOUS 77059 4380 A4
Spruce Knob Ct
1800 HOUS 77339 3118 D5
Spruce Knob Dr
1800 HOUS 77339 3118 D5
Spruce Knoll Cir
10900 HarC 77065 3539 C2
Spruce Lake Rd
200 HOUS 77336 3266 C4
Spruce Lakes Dr
- HarC 77049 3828 D2
Spruceland Dr
- HarC 77049 3828 D2
Spruce Lodge Dr
2200 HOUS 77339 3118 E3
2200 HOUS 77339 3119 A4
Spruce Manor Ln
6100 HOUS 77085 4240 D7
Spruce Mill Dr
8600 HarC 77095 3538 D5
Spruce Mountain Dr
11700 HarC 77067 3401 E5
Spruce Needle Dr
3500 HarC 77082 4096 D3
Spruce Park Cir
3500 HOUS 77345 3120 A3
Spruce Park Dr
14800 HarC 77082 4096 C3
Spruce Pine Dr
2500 HOUS 77345 3120 A5
Spruce Point Ct
5400 HarC 77084 3678 E5
Spruce Point Dr
15700 HarC 77084 3678 E5
Spruce Ridge Wy
3300 HOUS 77339 3119 C4
Spruce River Ct
15800 FBnC 77478 4236 B5
Spruce Run Dr
16800 HarC 77379 3255 D5
Spruce Valley Dr
4000 HOUS 77345 3119 E4
Sprucewood Ln
800 HDWV 77024 3959 E1
Spunyard Dr
15800 HarC 77532 3552 A4
Spur Ln
1700 HOUS 77055 3820 D6
1700 HOUS 77080 3820 D6
21200 TMBL 77375 3109 E3
Spur Rd
5000 BzaC 77511 4868 B7
37500 MtgC 77354 2670 E6
Spur Rd FM-1059 SPUR
37500 MtgC 77354 2670 E6
Spur Rdg
- HarC 77038 3543 C5
Spur St
1500 ALVN 77511 4867 A2
Spur Tr
18500 MtgC 77355 2815 B6
Spur Branch Ln
20500 FBnC 77450 4094 D1
Spur Canyon Ct
2100 FBnC 77469 4493 A3
16100 HarC 77429 3253 A7
Spur Cir Ln
21700 HarC 77532 3266 D7
Spur Community Rd
- MtgC 77354 2671 A2
Spurlin Tr
8500 HarC 77375 2965 D2
8500 HarC 77389 2965 D2
Spur Ridge Ct
21100 FBnC 77469 4234 A3
Spurwood Ct
10 WDLD 77381 2821 A3
Spy Glass Cir
14400 GLSN 77554 5332 D4
Spyglass Ct
10 JRSV 77065 3540 B6
Spy Glass Ct S
10 BzaC 77583 4624 C5
10 MNVL 77583 4624 C5
Spyglass Dr
2100 LGCY 77573 4633 B1
7700 HarC 77095 3539 B7
Spy Glass Ln
2800 MSCY 77459 4497 A1
Spyglass Hills Dr
4100 FBnC 77450 4094 B1
Spyglen Ct
13400 HarC 77429 3397 E2
Spyglen Ln
14100 HarC 77429 3397 D2
Squall Ct
300 HarC 77532 3552 B1
Square Rigger Ln
16700 HarC 77546 4506 B5
Squash St
5000 HarC 77379 3112 B7
5100 HarC 77379 3257 B1
Squaw Valley Tr
20700 HarC 77532 3410 B1
Squire Dr
1400 BYTN 77521 3972 C1
Squirecrest Dr
6600 HarC 77389 2966 C3
Squiredale Dr
11400 HarC 77070 3254 E7
Squire Dobbins Dr
2100 FBnC 77478 4237 D5
2100 SGLD 77478 4237 C4
Squirehill Ct
10200 HarC 77070 3399 C3
Squire Pl Dr
19900 HarC 77338 3262 B4
Squires Bnd
100 STAF 77477 4369 D3
100 STAF 77477 4370 A3
Squires Ct
6200 HarC 77389 2966 D4
Squires Wy
31000 MtgC 77354 2671 C7
Squires Park Dr
26800 HarC 77339 3118 C5
Squires Pl Dr
8200 FBnC 77083 4095 E7
Squirrel Rd
900 FBnC 77469 4364 D6
900 RHMD 77469 4364 D6
Squirrel Oaks Dr
18800 MtgC 77355 2815 A2
Squirrel Tree St
22900 HarC 77389 2967 B7
Squyres Rd
15900 HarC 77379 3256 C4
SR-3
- GlsC 77563 4991 A5
- LGCY 77573 4632 D7
- LMQU 77563 4991 A6
- LMQU 77568 4990 E4
- LMQU 77590 4990 D4
- LMQU 77590 4991 A6
- TXCY 77539 4873 B2
- TXCY 77591 4754 E7
- TXCY 77591 4873 B2
100 LMQU 77568 4874 A7
100 TXCY 77591 4874 A7
1700 GlsC 77539 4632 D7
1700 LGCY 77539 4632 D7
1900 DKSN 77539 4632 D7
2200 DKSN 77539 4753 E1
2200 GlsC 77539 4753 E1
3800 DKSN 77539 4754 A3
5200 TXCY 77539 4754 E7
15600 HOUS 77062 4506 E3
15600 HOUS 77598 4506 E3
15800 HOUS 77062 4507 A4
15800 HOUS 77598 4507 A4
16200 WEBS 77598 4507 D7
16600 HarC 77598 4507 A5
18400 WEBS 77598 4631 D1
19600 LGCY 77573 4631 E2
19600 WEBS 77573 4631 E1
SR-3 Galveston Rd
400 HOUS 77017 4246 C2
400 SHUS 77017 4246 C2
400 SHUS 77587 4246 C2
2500 HOUS 77034 4246 E5
7600 HOUS 77034 4247 A6
9900 HOUS 77034 4378 E4
11700 HOUS 77034 4379 C7
11700 HOUS 77598 4379 C7
12700 HOUS 77062 4379 C7
14100 HOUS 77598 4506 E3
15200 HOUS 77062 4506 E3
SR-3 Monroe Rd
6800 HOUS 77017 4245 E2
SR-3 Old Galveston Rd
- HOUS 77034 4378 C2
SR-3 Winkler Dr
- HOUS 77017 4245 E2
100 SHUS 77017 4246 B2
8800 HOUS 77017 4246 B2
9300 SHUS 77587 4246 D4
SR-6
- FBnC 77459 4497 D7
- GlsC 77563 4991 A7
- HarC - 3102 E6
- HarC - 3103 A6
- HarC - 3248 E2
- HarC - 3249 A3
- HarC 77095 3539 B4
- HMPD - 2953 D5
- HMPD - 2954 A6
- HOUS 77079 3956 D3
- HOUS 77084 3817 D7
- HTCK 77510 4987 D2
- HTCK 77510 4988 A2
- HTCK 77563 4988 A2
- HTCK 77563 4989 B5
- HTCK 77563 4990 A6
- MSCY 77545 4497 E7
- MSCY 77545 4498 A7
- PRVW - 3099 D1
- PRVW - 3100 D2
- SGLD 77479 4367 E5
- STFE 77510 4871 A7
- STFE 77510 4987 A1
- WALR - 3102 A4
- WlrC - 2954 B7
- WlrC - 3099 D1
- WlrC - 3100 E3
- WlrC - 3101 E4
- WlrC 77445 2953 C2
100 ALVN 77511 4749 C7
600 ALVN 77511 4867 E1
1000 HOUS 77077 3956 D6
1800 BzaC 77511 4867 E1
2200 HOUS 77082 3956 D7
2300 SGLD 77478 4368 E6
2300 SGLD 77479 4368 A5
2600 ALVN 77511 4868 A2
2600 BzaC 77511 4868 E3
2900 GlsC 77563 4990 E7
2900 GlsC 77568 4990 E6
2900 LMQU 77568 4990 E6
3300 LMQU 77563 4990 D6
3800 SGLD 77478 4369 A7
3800 SGLD 77479 4369 A7
4400 SGLD 77478 4496 B1
4400 SGLD 77479 4496 B1
4700 MSCY 77459 4496 B1
7300 MSCY 77459 4497 A6
10100 MSCY 77545 4622 D2
11500 FBnC 77545 4622 D2
12200 ARLA 77583 4622 E3
13100 ARLA 77583 4623 A3
13600 STFE 77510 4870 D7
13600 STFE 77517 4870 D7
14000 FBnC 77583 4623 A3
14300 PRLD 77583 4623 C5
15700 STFE 77517 4869 E6
16800 GlsC 77511 4869 E5
22100 BzaC 77578 4747 D4
22100 MNVL 77578 4747 B3
22300 BzaC 77511 4747 D4
22400 BzaC 77511 4748 A5
24000 ALVN 77511 4748 E6
SR-6 Addicks Satsuma Rd
- HOUS 77079 3956 D1
1200 HOUS 77079 3817 D7
1200 HOUS 77084 3817 D7
4000 HarC 77084 3817 D1
4300 HOUS 77084 3678 D7
4500 HarC 77084 3678 D7
6600 HarC 77095 3678 D4
7400 HarC 77095 3538 E5
8800 HarC 77095 3539 A5
13200 HarC 77065 3539 B4
SR-6 Morris Av
14600 BzaC 77583 4623 C5
14900 PRLD 77583 4623 D5
15400 IWCY 77583 4623 E6
15800 BzaC 77583 4624 A6
15800 IWCY 77583 4624 A6
17200 MNVL 77578 4624 D7
17200 MNVL 77583 4624 C7
17500 MNVL 77578 4745 E1
SR-6 Morris Rd
18300 MNVL 77578 4746 E2
20700 MNVL 77578 4747 A3
21300 BzaC 77578 4747 B3
SR-6 Northwest Frwy
- HarC - 3249 E5
- HarC - 3250 D6
- HarC - 3251 B7
- HarC - 3395 B1
- HarC - 3396 A2
- HarC - 3397 C7
- HarC - 3538 E2
- HarC - 3539 A3
SR-6 Old Addicks-Howell Rd
- FBnC 77083 4236 D1
- HOUS 77082 4096 D2
SR-35
3000 ALVN 77511 4867 A6
3000 BzaC 77511 4867 A7
5500 ALVN 77511 4749 B2
5600 BzaC 77511 4749 B1
19300 BzaC 77511 4628 B4
19300 PRLD 77511 4628 B4
SR-35 N Alvin Byp
- ALVN 77511 4867 A7
600 ALVN 77511 4749 E7
SR-35 S Alvin Byp
- ALVN 77511 4749 E7
1400 ALVN 77511 4867 C4
SR-35 BUS S Alvin Byp
- ALVN 77511 4867 B4
SR-35 BUS N Gordon St
100 ALVN 77511 4867 C1
400 ALVN 77511 4749 C7
SR-35 BUS S Gordon St
100 ALVN 77511 4867 C3
SR-35 N Main St
1000 HOUS 77075 4376 B5
1000 PRLD 77581 4376 B6
1600 PRLD 77581 4503 B1
SR-35 S Main St
2400 PRLD 77581 4503 B3
3100 PRLD 77584 4503 D5
4200 PRLD 77581 4627 E1
4200 PRLD 77584 4627 E1
SR-35 Reveille St
3300 HOUS 77087 4105 B6
4600 HOUS 77087 4245 B7
SR-35 Telephone Rd
- BzaC 77511 4628 B4
- HOUS 77087 4245 B2
- PRLD 77511 4628 A2
- PRLD 77581 4628 A2
6400 HOUS 77061 4245 B2
9000 HOUS 77075 4245 B7
9200 HOUS 77061 4376 B1
9200 HOUS 77075 4376 B7
11400 PRLD 77581 4376 B5
SR-35C BUS N Gordon St
1800 ALVN 77511 4749 C5
SR-36
- FBnC 77471 4490 A3
500 RSBG 77471 4490 A3
3400 RSBG 77471 4614 E1
4700 RSBG 77469 4614 E3
4900 FBnC 77471 4614 E4
6000 PLEK 77471 4614 E7
6500 PLEK 77469 4614 E7
6700 PLEK 77461 4614 E7
SR-36 1st St
- RSBG 77471 4614 E1
1000 RSBG 77471 4490 E7
SR-36 Avenue H
1100 RSBG 77471 4490 D4
SR-73 East Frwy
- BYTN - 3832 B6
- BYTN - 3833 D4
- HarC - 3831 E6
- HarC - 3833 D4
- HarC - 3967 E2
- HarC - 3968 D2
- HarC - 3969 B1
- HOUS - 3967 D2
SR-75
9800 CNRO 77303 2237 D1
9800 CNRO 77304 2237 D1
9800 CNRO 77378 2237 D1
9800 MtgC 77378 2237 D1
SR-75 N Frazier St
100 CNRO 77301 2384 A7
300 CNRO 77301 2383 E5
2100 CNRO 77303 2383 D1
2400 CNRO 77303 2237 D7
4400 MtgC 77303 2237 D7
4800 CNRO 77304 2237 C2
4800 MtgC 77304 2237 C2
7800 CNRO 77378 2237 D1
7800 MtgC 77378 2237 D1
SR-75 S Frazier St
100 CNRO 77301 2384 A6
1000 CNRO 77301 2530 A1
SR-87
- GlsC 77650 4879 E4
- GlsC 77650 4994 E1
- GlsC 77650 4995 A1
SR-87 2nd St
100 GLSN 77550 5109 E1
SR-87 Broadway
- GlsC 77650 4879 E5
SR-87 Broadway St
600 GLSN 77550 5109 E3
3700 GLSN 77550 5108 E4
4400 GLSN 77551 5108 C5
SR-87 Ferry Rd
- GLSN 77550 4994 E7
- GLSN 77554 4994 E7
10 GLSN 77550 5109 E1

STREET
Block City ZIP Map# Grid

SR-87 Seawall Blvd
300 GLSN 77550 5109 E1
SR-96 League City Pkwy
- GlsC 77565 4633 D2
- KMAH 77565 4633 E1
- KMAH 77565 4634 A1
- LGCY 77565 4633 A4
100 LGCY 77573 4632 A5
900 LGCY 77573 4631 E6
1700 LGCY 77573 4633 A4
SR-99 Grand Pkwy
- FBnC 77469 4093 D6
- FBnC 77469 4233 E2
- FBnC 77469 4234 A2
- FBnC 77469 4235 B6
- FBnC 77469 4366 C2
- FBnC 77478 4366 E6
- FBnC 77479 4366 C2
- FBnC 77494 4093 C5
- HarC 77449 3814 C5
- HarC 77493 3814 C5
- HarC 77494 3953 C4
- HOUS 77449 3814 C5
- HOUS 77450 3953 C1
- HOUS 77450 4093 D1
- HOUS 77469 4093 D7
- HOUS 77493 3814 C6
- HOUS 77493 3953 C1
- HOUS 77494 3953 C1
- HOUS 77494 4093 C4
16200 FBnC 77479 4493 E1
17400 FBnC 77469 4493 D3
SR-105
6100 CNRO 77304 2382 A1
11500 CNRO 77301 2385 C3
11500 CNRO 77303 2385 C3
11500 CTSH 77301 2385 C3
11500 CTSH 77303 2385 C3
11500 CTSH 77306 2385 C3
SR-105 E Davis St
700 CNRO 77301 2384 D4
2500 CNRO 77301 2385 E3
11000 CNRO 77303 2385 E3
11000 CTSH 77301 2385 E3
11000 CTSH 77303 2385 E3
SR-105 W Davis St
100 CNRO 77301 2384 A5
600 CNRO 77301 2383 E5
1300 CNRO 77304 2383 C4
4200 CNRO 77304 2382 E3
SR-105 E Phillips St
100 CNRO 77301 2384 A5
SR-105 W Phillips St
100 CNRO 77301 2384 A5
400 CNRO 77301 2383 E5
SR-134 Battleground Rd
- DRPK 77536 4109 E4
- HarC 77536 4109 E4
- HarC 77571 4109 E4
200 DRPK 77536 4110 A3
200 DRPK 77571 4110 A3
200 HarC 77536 4110 A3
200 HarC 77571 4110 A3
1700 DRPK 77536 3970 A7
1700 HarC 77536 3970 A7
1700 HarC 77571 3970 A7
2200 DRPK 77571 3970 A6
2200 HOUS 77571 3970 A4
SR-134 Crosby Lynchburg Rd
100 HarC 77520 3831 D7
100 HarC 77562 3831 E6
200 HarC 77520 3970 D1
600 HOUS 77520 3970 C2
1000 HOUS 77571 3970 B3
SR-146
- BYTN - 4112 A3
- GlsC 77563 4991 A6
- GlsC 77565 4509 D4
- GlsC 77565 4634 A1
- HarC - 4112 A3
- HarC 77571 4382 C2
- KMAH 77539 4634 A1
- KMAH 77565 4509 D4
- KMAH 77565 4510 A7
- KMAH 77565 4634 A1
- LMQU 77563 4991 A6
- LMQU 77568 4990 D4
- LMQU 77590 4990 D4
- LMQU 77590 4991 A6
- LPRT - 4111 C7
- LPRT - 4251 C4
- LPRT 77571 4382 C1
- PASD 77571 4382 C2
- SEBK 77565 4509 D4
- SEBK 77586 4509 D3
- SRAC 77571 4382 C1
- TXCY 77568 4990 D4
- TXCY 77590 4755 E2
- TXCY 77590 4756 A6
- TXCY 77590 4874 C6
- TXCY 77590 4990 C1
- TXCY 77591 4755 E2
- TXCY 77591 4756 A6
- TXCY 77591 4874 B1
1400 TXCY 77539 4755 D1
3000 GlsC 77518 4634 A2
3000 LGCY 77539 4634 A2
3200 GlsC 77539 4634 D7
3400 TXCY 77539 4634 D7
5300 PASD 77586 4382 C1
5300 SEBK 77586 4382 C6
7000 BYTN 77521 3835 C5
8600 BYTN 77520 3835 D2
8600 CmbC 77520 3835 B7
8900 MTBL 77520 3835 D1
9500 MTBL 77520 3696 D3
11000 CmbC 77520 3696 D1
SR-146 BUS
400 BYTN 77520 4113 A1
1000 BYTN 77520 4112 B3
SR-146 BUS N Alexander Dr
100 BYTN 77520 3973 E3
100 BYTN 77520 4113 A1
3000 BYTN 77521 3973 C4
SR-146 BUS S Alexander Dr
100 BYTN 77520 4113 B1
SR-146 Bayport Blvd
900 SEBK 77586 4509 C1
2900 SEBK 77586 4382 C7
SR-146 BUS S Broadway St
100 LPRT 77571 4251 D5
SR-146 Fred Hartman Br
- HarC - 4111 E4
- HarC - 4112 A3
- HOUS - 4111 D4
- LPRT - 4111 D4

SR-146 BUS W Main St
100 LPRT 77571 4251 D2
SR-146 N Robert C Lanier Frwy
- BYTN - 4112 A3
- HarC - 4112 A3
SR-146 TX-146 Frontage Rd
- LPRT 77571 4251 C7
SR-146 BUS Wharton Weems Blvd
- LPRT 77571 4251 D6
SR-159
- HMPD 77445 3098 A3
- WlrC 77445 3098 A3
11000 WlrC 77445 3097 D6
SR-159 13th St
- HMPD 77445 2953 A7
- HMPD 77445 3098 A1
- WlrC 77445 3098 A3
SR-159 Austin St
200 HMPD 77445 2953 A7
SR-225 La Porte Frwy
- HOUS - 4105 E4
- HOUS - 4106 A4
- PASD - 4106 D4
7900 HOUS 77012 4105 E4
SR-225 La Porte Hwy
- HOUS - 4105 E4
SR-225 Pasadena Frwy
- DRPK - 4108 E3
- DRPK - 4109 E4
- HarC - 4109 E4
- HarC - 4110 A4
- HOUS - 4106 D4
- LPRT - 4110 E6
- LPRT - 4111 A6
- PASD - 4106 E4
- PASD - 4107 A3
- PASD - 4108 A3
SR-242
- WDLD 77382 2675 C6
- WDLD 77384 2675 C6
21800 MtgC 77357 2681 E7
21900 MtgC 77357 2682 B7
SR-242 College Park Dr
3000 MtgC 77384 2676 A5
3000 WDLD 77384 2676 A5
4200 WDLD 77382 2675 E5
4200 WDLD 77384 2675 E5
6300 MtgC 77384 2675 A5
8300 WDLD 77382 2674 E4
8300 WDLD 77384 2674 E4
9400 MtgC 77384 2674 E2
SR-242 Lazy River Rd
- MtgC 77302 2677 E4
- MtgC 77302 2678 B5
10700 MtgC 77385 2677 E4
SR-242 Needham Rd
- MtgC 77384 2676 A5
- WDLD 77385 2676 B5
9000 MtgC 77385 2676 A5
10600 MtgC 77385 2677 A5
SR-249
31300 MtgC 77362 2963 D3
31900 MtgC 77355 2963 C2
32400 MtgC 77362 2817 A5
33800 MtgC 77362 2816 E4
33800 SGCH 77362 2816 E4
SR-249 W Mt Houston Rd
700 HOUS 77037 3544 A6
700 HOUS 77038 3544 B6
700 HOUS 77088 3544 B6
800 HarC 77038 3544 A6
1300 HarC 77038 3543 A6
1300 HOUS 77038 3543 E6
1300 HOUS 77088 3543 E6
1800 HarC 77088 3543 A6
2800 HarC 77086 3543 A6
SR-249 Tomball Pkwy
- HarC - 3399 C1
- HarC - 3400 C7
- HOUS - 3399 E4
- HOUS - 3400 C7
11500 HarC 77038 3543 A6
11500 HarC 77086 3543 A6
11500 HarC 77088 3543 A6
11700 HarC 77038 3542 E5
12300 HOUS 77086 3542 B3
14600 HarC 77086 3541 E1
14600 HarC 77086 3542 E5
22000 HarC 77070 3255 A5
22000 HOUS 77070 3255 A5
22400 HarC 77070 3254 E4
22400 HOUS 77070 3254 E4
22400 HOUS 77377 3255 B7
22500 HOUS 77377 3254 E4
22600 HarC 77375 3254 E4
22600 HarC 77377 3254 D2
24300 HarC 77375 3109 C7
24300 HarC 77377 3109 C7
26900 TMBL 77375 3109 A2
26900 TMBL 77377 3109 A2
28100 HarC 77377 3108 E2
28100 TMBL 77375 3108 E1
28100 TMBL 77377 3108 E1
28800 HarC 77377 2963 E7
28800 TMBL 77375 2963 E7
28800 TMBL 77377 2963 E7
29400 HarC 77375 2963 E6
30500 MtgC 77362 2963 E7
SR-288
- BzaC - 4373 E7
- BzaC - 4500 E2
- BzaC 77583 4624 C7
- BzaC 77583 4745 A6
- IWCY 77583 4745 B3
- MNVL 77578 4624 D7
- PRLD - 4373 E7
17600 BzaC 77578 4500 E6
17600 BzaC 77583 4500 E6
17600 PRLD 77583 4500 E5
17600 PRLD 77584 4500 E2
SR-288 South Frwy
- HarC - 4373 E5
- HOUS - 3963 B7
- HOUS - 4103 A3
- HOUS - 4242 E3
- HOUS - 4243 A3
- HOUS - 4373 E1
- MNVL 77578 4624 E3
- MNVL 77583 4624 E3
- PRLD - 4373 E6
17700 BzaC 77578 4500 E7
17700 BzaC 77578 4624 D7
17700 BzaC 77583 4500 E7
17700 BzaC 77583 4624 D7
17700 BzaC 77584 4500 E6

Sralla Rd
8500 HarC 77562 3832 C2
10100 HarC 77532 3693 B2
10100 HarC 77562 3693 C6
13200 HarC 77532 3553 B7
SR-N-1 NASA Pkwy
1300 HOUS 77058 4507 D5
1300 NSUB 77058 4507 E5
1300 WEBS 77058 4507 E5
1700 HOUS 77058 4508 A4
2200 SEBK 77586 4509 B3
2800 NSUB 77058 4508 A4
3000 PASD 77058 4508 C3
3200 PASD 77586 4508 C3
3800 ELGO 77586 4509 A2
4100 ELGO 77586 4508 E2
4100 TYLV 77586 4508 E2
SR-N-1 E NASA Pkwy
100 WEBS 77598 4507 C6
700 WEBS 77058 4507 D5
1000 NSUB 77058 4507 D5
1200 HOUS 77058 4507 E5
SR-N-1 W NASA Pkwy
100 WEBS 77598 4507 B7
SSgt Macario Garcia Dr
100 HOUS 77011 3964 E7
1600 HOUS 77011 3965 A5
SSgt M Garcia Dr US-90 ALT
100 HOUS 77011 3964 E7
1600 HOUS 77011 3965 A6
Stable Dr
- FRDW 77546 4628 E4
- FRDW 77546 4629 A4
Stable Ln
8800 HOUS 77024 3961 A3
Stable Bend Cir
- HarC 77429 3253 C6
Stable Bluff Ln
- HarC 77429 3253 A5
Stable Brook Cir
15600 HarC 77429 3253 B6
Stable Creek Cir
15700 HarC 77429 3253 B6
Stable Crest Blvd
8600 HOUS 77024 3961 A3
Stable Crest Ct
8800 HOUS 77024 3961 A3
Stabledon Dr
13700 HarC 77014 3401 C2
Stablefield Ln
- HarC 77429 3252 E7
- HarC 77429 3253 A7
Stableford Ct
13900 HarC 77014 3401 C1
Stable Gate Dr
- HarC 77429 3253 B6
Stable Lake Dr
15600 HarC 77429 3253 C6
Stable Manor Ln
16300 HarC 77429 3253 A7
16400 HarC 77429 3252 E5
Stable Oak Dr
15400 HarC 77429 3253 B6
Stable Park Ct
15500 HarC 77429 3253 B6
Stable Park Dr
15500 HarC 77429 3253 B6
Stablepoint Ln
16000 HarC 77429 3397 A1
Stabler Ln
10800 HOUS 77076 3685 A4
Stableridge Ct
13900 HarC 77014 3401 C1
Stableridge Dr
2200 MtgC 77384 2529 A6
3900 HarC 77014 3401 C1
Stable Run Dr
15300 HarC 77429 3253 C7
Stables Ln
3300 HarC 77532 3694 A4
Stables Course Ct
13200 FBnC 77469 4366 C2
Stables Course Dr
3800 FBnC 77469 4366 D2
Stable Springs Cir
15400 HarC 77429 3253 B6
Stable Star Cir
15400 HarC 77429 3253 B6
Stable Stone Ct
- HarC 77429 3253 A6
Stable Stone Ln
- HarC 77429 3253 A6
- PRLD 77581 4503 E1
Stableton Ln
6700 HarC 77049 3828 E2
Stable Trail Dr
15400 HarC 77429 3253 B6
Stable View Ct
15700 HarC 77429 3253 B6
Stableview Ct
2800 FBnC 77450 3954 B7
Stableway Cir
12100 HarC 77065 3539 D4
Stableway Ct
12100 HarC 77065 3539 D4
Stableway Dr
9700 HarC 77065 3539 D4
Stablewood Blvd
100 HOUS 77024 3961 A3
Stablewood Ct
100 HOUS 77024 3961 A3
Stablewood Downs Ln
14800 HarC 77429 3253 A7
Stablewood Farms Dr
15000 HarC 77429 3253 A6
Stablewoods Farm Dr
- HarC 77429 3253 A7
- HarC 77429 3397 A1
Stacey Ln
10 BYTN 77520 4113 B1
Stackstone Ln
4400 FBnC 77450 4094 A2
Stackwood Ln
19800 HarC 77449 3676 D7
Stacy Dr
2500 PRLD 77581 4503 E5
Stacy Gln
2100 HOUS 77008 3822 E5
Stacy Knl
2100 HOUS 77008 3822 E5
Stacy Ln
3000 DRPK 77536 4109 C7
4300 PASD 77586 4508 E1
Stacy Rd
4000 HarC 77084 3817 B1
4400 HarC 77084 3678 B7

Stacy Brook Ln
2100 HOUS 77008 3822 D5
Stacy Crest
1700 HOUS 77008 3822 D5
Stacy Falls
1700 HOUS 77008 3822 E5
Stacy Park Cir
3500 HarC 77449 3815 B3
Stadium Cir
800 FRDW 77546 4505 B6
E Stadium Ct
800 FRDW 77546 4505 A7
W Stadium Ct
800 FRDW 77546 4504 D7
Stadium Dr
800 ALVN 77511 4867 A2
1500 PRVW 77445 2955 B7
1500 PRVW 77445 3100 B1
E Stadium Dr
900 RSBG 77471 4491 C4
N Stadium Dr
7800 HOUS 77030 4102 C6
7800 HOUS 77054 4102 C7
Stadium Ln
200 FRDW 77546 4629 A1
300 FRDW 77546 4505 A7
500 FRDW 77546 4504 E7
N Stadium Ln
6300 KATY 77494 3952 A1
S Stadium Ln
6300 KATY 77494 3952 A1
Stadium Rd
- HOUS 77005 4102 C3
Stadium St
1300 MTBL 77520 3696 E5
2100 ALVN 77511 4866 D2
Stafford Dr
10600 HOUS 77093 3686 A3
Stafford Rd
12600 HarC 77031 4239 B6
12600 HarC 77477 4239 B7
12600 HOUS 77031 4239 B6
12700 STAF 77477 4239 A7
13100 MSCY 77489 4370 A1
13100 STAF 77477 4370 A1
13100 STAF 77489 4370 A1
13300 STAF 77477 4369 E2
Stafford St
300 HOUS 77079 3956 D1
Staffordale Ct
11500 HarC 77433 3395 E7
Staffordale Manor Ln
800 HOUS 77047 4373 B2
Stafford Centre Dr
9900 STAF 77477 4369 E2
Stafford Colony Ln
13100 STAF 77477 4370 A1
Stafford Dewalt Rd
1000 FBnC 77477 4369 D4
1000 MSCY 77459 4369 D7
1000 MSCY 77477 4369 D4
3000 MSCY 77459 4496 D2
Stafford Dewalt Rd FM-1092
1000 FBnC 77477 4369 D4
1000 MSCY 77459 4369 D7
1000 MSCY 77477 4369 D4
3000 MSCY 77459 4496 D2
Stafford Point Dr
- STAF 77477 4369 E2
Stafford Pride Dr
1600 STAF 77477 4370 B5
Stafford Run Rd
500 FBnC 77477 4369 D4
500 MSCY 77477 4369 D4
500 STAF 77477 4369 D4
Staffordshire Cres
1800 HOUS 77030 4102 E4
Staffordshire Rd
100 STAF 77477 4369 E3
400 STAF 77477 4370 A4
1600 FBnC 77477 4370 A5
1800 MSCY 77489 4370 B6
Staffordshire St
6900 HOUS 77030 4102 D5
7300 HOUS 77054 4102 D5
Stafford Springs Av
500 FBnC 77477 4369 C4
500 STAF 77477 4369 C4
Stafford Springs Dr
12400 HOUS 77077 3957 D5
Stag Cir
2200 HarC 77336 3267 A3
Stag Ln
26600 MtgC 77357 2829 B5
Stag Rd
100 HarC 77562 3831 D4
Stagdon Dr
- HOUS 77339 3119 A2
Stagecoach Dr
9200 HOUS 77041 3681 D7
Stagecoach Rd
13400 MtgC 77355 2962 C1
13400 SGCH 77355 2962 C1
15800 SGCH 77355 2816 A7
Stagecoach St
14500 MtgC 77372 2683 E2
Stagecoach Crossing Dr
26500 MtgC 77355 2961 C2
26500 SGCH 77355 2961 C2
Stage Runn Dr
- HarC 77073 3258 E2
- HOUS 77090 3258 D2
Stage Stop Cir
10 HNCV 77024 3960 A2
Stagewood Dr
8100 HarC 77338 3261 E3
8500 HarC 77338 3262 A3
Staghill Dr
10600 HarC 77064 3540 B2
Staghorn Ln
- LGCY 77598 4630 C4
Staghorn Coral Ln
4100 HOUS 77045 4241 D5
Stahman Ln
10 HOUS 77084 3818 A1
Staitti St
100 HMBL 77338 3262 E6
Stallings Dr
2700 HarC 77088 3683 B1
2700 HOUS 77088 3683 A1
Stallion Ct
12400 MtgC 77354 2671 B3
Stallion Ln
11800 HOUS 77071 4239 E5
Stallion Rdg
- ALVN 77511 4867 A4

Stallion Run
36900 MtgC 77355 2815 D6
Stallion Brook Ln
4200 HarC 77388 3112 C4
Stallion Peak Cir
15600 HarC 77429 3253 B6
Stallion Point Cir
- HarC 77429 3253 C6
Stallion Trail Dr
7400 HarC 77338 3261 D4
Stally St
3000 HOUS 77092 3822 C3
Stalsby Rd
10 HarC 77357 2830 D7
Stalybridge Ct
10 SGLD 77479 4495 E3
Stalybridge St
10 SGLD 77479 4495 E3
Stalynn Ln
10 HOUS 77027 3961 B5
Stamen Dr
7500 HarC 77041 3539 C7
Stamey
6500 HarC 77066 3400 C5
Stamford Dr
19400 HarC 77375 3109 C6
Stamford Oaks Dr
17200 HarC 77377 3254 D4
17400 HarC 77070 3254 D4
Stamp St
4200 HOUS 77026 3825 B7
Stampede Canyon Ln
9300 HarC 77089 4504 C1
Stampede Pass Dr
15300 HarC 77095 3538 E4
Stamper Wy
5200 HOUS 77056 3960 E6
Stampford Dr
13700 HOUS 77077 3957 B5
Stanart Rd
23800 MtgC 77365 2973 D6
Stanbridge Dr
14600 FBnC 77083 4236 D1
Stanbrook Dr
10300 HarC 77089 4377 B6
Stanbury Park Ln
12800 HarC 77377 3254 A1
Stanbury Pl Ln
3500 FBnC 77494 4093 C2
Stancliff Rd
- HOUS 77045 4372 B3
10400 HOUS 77031 4238 D4
10400 HOUS 77099 4238 C4
Stancliff St
13300 HOUS 77045 4241 B7
13400 HOUS 77045 4372 B1
Stancliff Oaks St
12800 SGLD 77478 4237 C5
Standard Rd
6900 MtgC 77354 2819 B5
7900 MtgC 77354 2818 E5
Standifer
100 HOUS 77032 3261 D7
100 HOUS 77338 3261 D7
Standing Bluff Blvd
- FBnC 77469 4615 E5
Standing Cypress Dr
20000 HarC 77379 3110 B6
Standing Oak Ct
1800 FBnC 77469 4365 B2
Standing Oak Ln
2300 FBnC 77469 4365 B2
Standing Oaks
24200 HarC 77389 2966 C5
Standing Oaks Dr
1000 MtgC 77385 2676 C5
Standing Oaks St
6100 HOUS 77050 3546 E5
6700 HOUS 77050 3547 B5
Standing Pine Ln
11500 HarC 77375 3109 E5
Standing Rock Ct
8700 HarC 77089 4377 C6
Standing Rock Dr
3600 MtgC 77386 2969 E2
Standing Springs Ln
2900 LGCY 77539 4752 E5
Standing Stone Ct
3500 FBnC 77459 4621 C5
Standolind Rd
400 BzaC 77511 4628 C5
Stanfield Ct
19700 HarC 77433 3677 A1
Stanford Ct
4400 HOUS 77041 3820 A1
4500 HOUS 77041 3681 B7
Stanford Pl
24000 HarC 77484 2956 C3
Stanford St
500 HOUS 77019 3962 E6
1500 HOUS 77006 3962 E7
1700 KATY 77493 3813 B6
2700 PASD 77502 4108 A7
2700 PASD 77503 4108 A7
4300 HOUS 77006 4102 D2
Stanford Park Ct
1900 HarC 77450 3954 B5
Stanhope Ct
15800 HarC 77084 3678 E6
Stanhope Dr
5000 HarC 77084 3678 E6
Stanley Br
700 HOUS 77008 3823 A7
Stanley Ct
200 FRDW 77546 4629 C1
Stanley St
- HOUS 77040 3681 C6
Stanley Bend Ct
700 HOUS 77008 3823 A7
Stanley Crest Cir
6000 HOUS 77008 3823 A7
Stanley Forest Ct
700 HOUS 77008 3823 C7
Stanley Manor Ct
700 HOUS 77008 3822 D7
800 HOUS 77008 3823 C7
Stanley Park Dr
6000 HOUS 77008 3823 A7
6200 HOUS 77008 3822 E7
Stanley Point Dr
700 HOUS 77008 3823 A7
Stanmore Dr
2100 HOUS 77019 3962 A5
Stanolind Rd
24600 HarC 77375 2964 E2
Stansberg Dr
11500 HarC 77066 3401 A7

Stansel Dr
800 ALVN 77511 4867 D6
Stanton Ct
3300 PRLD 77584 4501 B1
Stanton St
1500 ALVN 77511 4749 B6
2800 HOUS 77025 4102 A6
3000 HOUS 77025 4101 D6
Stanton Lake Dr
19400 HarC 77433 3537 A6
Stanton Lodge Dr
- HarC 77338 3407 B1
Stanwick Dr
- HOUS 77087 4245 B1
Stanwick Pl
10 WDLD 77382 2819 E2
Stanwood Dr
11800 HOUS 77031 4239 A4
Stapleford St
29400 MtgC 77386 2969 C4
Staples Dr
100 BYTN 77520 3835 B6
Staples St
800 SEBK 77586 4509 D3
1800 HOUS 77020 3964 A1
1900 HOUS 77026 3964 A1
2400 HOUS 77026 3825 A7
Staples Wy
10 HOUS 77056 3961 A6
Stapleton Dr
2000 FRDW 77546 4629 B6
Stapley Dr
16700 HOUS 77396 3406 A4
Stapp Maxwell St
2200 ALVN 77511 4866 E3
2200 ALVN 77511 4867 A4
Star Dr
1000 GlsC 77539 4635 D7
N Star Dr
19800 MtgC 77365 2824 E5
Star Ln
- HarC 77494 3952 E2
- KATY 77494 3952 E2
5600 HOUS 77056 4100 D1
5600 HOUS 77057 4100 D1
Star St
- HOUS 77056 4101 A1
- TMBL 77375 2963 E4
27200 MtgC 77372 2683 D2
N Star St
7400 HOUS 77088 3683 C3
S Star St
- SEBK 77586 4383 C5
Star Vly
- HarC 77429 3253 A6
Starboard Dr
18000 NSUB 77058 4508 C4
Starboard Rd
4200 DKSN 77539 4754 E4
4800 TXCY 77539 4754 E4
Starboard St
100 CmbC 77539 4635 E4
Starboard St N
600 HarC 77532 3552 B2
Starboard St S
400 HarC 77532 3552 B3
Starboard Point Dr
2600 HOUS 77054 4242 A2
Starboard Shores Ct
1700 MSCY 77459 4369 C6
Starboard Shores Dr
4100 MSCY 77459 4369 C6
Starboard View Cir
2100 HarC 77546 4506 B6
Starboard View Dr
16700 HarC 77546 4506 B5
Starborrough Dr
400 LGCY 77573 4633 A2
Starbridge Dr
7200 HarC 77095 3678 C1
Starbridge Lake Ln
23400 FBnC 77469 4093 D6
Star Bridge Park Ln
3200 HarC 77449 3815 C3
Starbridge Pointe Ln
3500 HarC 77449 3815 A2
Starbrook Creek Dr
6000 FBnC 77494 4092 B5
Star Cactus Ln
18300 HarC 77433 3537 C7
Starcreek Ln
15700 HarC 77044 3549 E3
Star Crest Ln
- FBnC 77450 4093 E4
Starcroft Ct
2800 LGCY 77573 4633 B3
6700 HarC 77379 3111 C2
Starcroft Dr
12500 PRLD 77584 4500 B2
Stardale Ln
16800 FRDW 77546 4629 E1
16900 FRDW 77546 4630 A2
Stardust Ln
13900 HarC 77041 3679 A4
Star Dust Pl
10 WDLD 77381 2674 E6
Starduster
800 MNVL 77578 4747 B1
Star Fern Pl
10 WDLD 77380 2822 A6
Starfield Dr
5400 HarC 77084 3678 E5
Starfinder Dr
- HarC 77095 3396 D7
- HarC 77433 3396 D7
Starfire Ln
9300 HOUS 77036 4238 E1
Starfish
11400 GLSN 77554 5221 A6
Starfish Dr
3300 GlsC 77650 4879 C3
Starfish Ln
8100 HOUS 77072 4098 A7
Starflower
7300 FBnC 77494 4093 B4
Starflower Ln
1100 HarC 77521 3832 B5
Stargate Ct
3100 HarC 77068 3257 C5
Stargazer Pl
10 WDLD 77381 2674 D6
Stargazer Pt
23600 HarC 77373 3114 C6
Stargrass Ct
3000 LGCY 77573 4633 A2
Stargrass Dr
21300 HarC 77388 3112 D3

Starhill Ct
13800 HOUS 77077 3957 A2
Star Hollow Ln
8500 HarC 77095 3537 E5
14100 HarC 77044 3549 C1
Stark Ct
27100 ORDN 77385 2822 C5
Stark Ln
27200 ORDN 77385 2822 C5
Stark Bridge Ln
13700 BzaC 77583 4623 D5
Starkey St
300 HOUS 77007 3962 D2
1200 PASD 77503 4108 A6
Stark Point Ct
18400 HarC 77346 3264 D7
Starkridge Dr
5200 HOUS 77035 4240 E4
Starksboro Ct
500 HarC 77073 3259 A4
Starkstone Ct
500 MtgC 77386 2968 D1
Star Lake Ct
17000 HOUS 77396 3406 A3
Star Lake Dr
6100 HOUS 77396 3406 A3
Starlamp Ln
8900 HarC 77095 3538 B4
Starleaf Ln
400 BzaC 77584 4374 B7
Star Ledge Ct
6800 HarC 77389 2966 C4
Starlight Pl
100 WDLD 77380 2967 E5
Starlight Rd
12800 HarC 77049 3828 B1
Starlight Bay Ct
11500 PRLD 77584 4500 D3
Starlight Bay St
11300 PRLD 77584 4500 D3
Starlight Beach Rd
23100 FBnC 77494 4093 B3
Starlight Harbour Ct
13600 HOUS 77077 3957 A5
Starling St
5400 HOUS 77017 4106 C7
Starling Creek Dr
10900 FBnC 77469 4092 C7
Starling Stream Ct
27400 MtgC 77386 3115 D1
Starling Stream Dr
4200 MtgC 77386 3115 D1
Starlite Dr
3600 PASD 77505 4248 D4
Starlite Field Dr
2000 FBnC 77479 4494 C5
Starlit Meadows Ct
10700 HarC 77064 3540 B1
Star Meadow Ln
- HOUS 77336 3266 C1
Starmist Ln
- HOUS 77044 3550 A2
Starmount Blvd
- HOUS 77017 4106 B4
Star Pine Ct
10 WDLD 77381 2821 B3
N Starpoint Dr
1900 HOUS 77032 3404 B5
S Starpoint Dr
1900 HOUS 77032 3404 B5
Starr Rd
5300 HarC 77521 3832 E7
N Star Ridge Cir
10 WDLD 77382 2819 A2
S Star Ridge Cir
10 WDLD 77382 2819 A2
Starrush Ct
10 WDLD 77380 2967 E4
Starry Night
7300 FBnC 77494 4093 B4
Starshadow Pl
10 HarC 77015 3829 A4
Stars Hollow Dr
19300 HarC 77073 3403 B2
Star Springs Ct
- HOUS 77396 3406 C5
Starviolet St
10 WDLD 77380 2822 A6
Star Vista Dr
- HarC 77073 3259 B3
Starway St
4700 HOUS 77023 4104 B2
Starwind Ct
- HarC 77377 3254 A3
Starwood Dr
11600 BKHV 77024 3959 D3
11600 PNPV 77024 3959 C3
Starwreath Dr
1300 PRLD 77545 4499 E2
Starwreath Ln
- HarC 77429 3253 A5
Stassen St
3200 HOUS 77051 4243 A2
State
2300 HOUS 77007 3963 A3
State St
- BYTN 77520 3973 A5
- BYTN 77521 3973 A5
- HOUS 77017 4246 B2
- KATY 77493 3813 C7
- SHUS 77017 4246 B2
10 LbyC 77328 2537 D2
10 MtgC 77372 2537 D2
300 SHUS 77587 4246 B2
1500 HOUS 77007 3963 A3
2500 HOUS 77034 4246 D4
2500 SHUS 77034 4246 D4
6500 HTCK 77563 4989 C5
Stately Av
13800 HOUS 77034 4378 E5
Stately Oak Dr
2300 HOUS 77345 3120 D5
States Av
29400 MtgC 77354 2818 A1
Statesman Dr
3500 ALVN 77511 4867 B7
3500 BzaC 77511 4867 B7
State Walk Cir
9200 HarC 77064 3540 D6
Statfield Glen Ct
21600 FBnC 77450 4094 A3
Statfield Glen Ln
5600 FBnC 77450 4094 C3
N Station Ct
21100 HarC 77073 3259 A6
Station Dr
7000 HOUS 77061 4244 D5

STREET
Block City ZIP Map# Grid

Statler Dr
6200 HOUS 77091 3682 E4
Staunton St
4500 HOUS 77027 4101 B1
Staybridge Dr
- HarC 77064 3541 A1
Stayton Cir
10 PNPV 77024 3959 E3
Steadmont Dr
5000 HOUS 77040 3681 E7
Steam Ml
1000 HOUS 77002 3963 D3
Steamboat Ln
15700 HOUS 77079 3956 E1
Steamboat Run
2000 SGLD 77478 4368 D6
Steamboat Inn Dr
18400 HarC 77346 3265 A7
18400 HarC 77346 3409 A1
Steamboat Springs Dr
11700 HarC 77067 3401 E4
Steams
- SEBK 77586 4509 B3
Stearns St
6600 HOUS 77021 4103 B6
Stebbins Cir
10600 HOUS 77043 3819 D6
Stebbins Dr
2000 HOUS 77043 3819 D4
Steddum Dr
200 LGCY 77573 4632 B3
E Stedhill Lp
10 WDLD 77384 2675 B6
W Stedhill Lp
100 WDLD 77384 2675 B5
Stedman St
- HOUS 77029 3965 D5
9700 HOUS 77029 3966 A5
9800 GNPK 77547 3966 A5
Steed Pl
1400 CNRO 77301 2530 A2
Steel Pkwy
- PASD 77507 4381 D2
Steel St
2300 HOUS 77098 3962 A7
Steele Av
8400 HarC 77064 3541 C3
Steele Dr
1300 FRDW 77546 4505 A4
Steele Rd
100 ALVN 77511 4749 C6
400 HarC 77562 3832 A4
500 GlsC 77511 4750 B6
Steele Point Dr
18200 HarC 77532 3409 E6
Steelhead Dr
2600 HOUS 77045 4373 A1
Steelman St
9600 HOUS 77017 4106 B5
Steel Meadows Ln
4900 HarC 77346 3264 A7
Steen Rd
17100 PTVL 77372 2683 B7
E Steepbank Cir
3000 SGLD 77479 4368 C7
3000 SGLD 77479 4495 B2
W Steepbank Cir
3000 SGLD 77479 4368 C6
Steepbank Dr
10 WDLD 77381 2674 B7
Steep Bank Psg
9500 FBnC 77459 4621 D5
Steep Bank Trc
- FBnC 77459 4622 A4
10000 FBnC 77459 4621 D5
11000 FBnC 77583 4622 B4
11500 ARLA 77583 4622 C4
Steeple Ln
12300 HarC 77039 3545 E5
Steeple Canyon Rd
25700 HarC 77389 2966 B2
Steeple Chase Rd
14500 HOUS 77489 4371 A4
Steeple Chase Glen Dr
7400 HarC 77346 3265 B7
Steeple Chase Heights Dr
- HarC 77064 3540 B7
Steeplecrest Dr
11100 HarC 77064 3540 A4
11100 HarC 77065 3540 A4
Steeplepark Dr
11100 HarC 77064 3540 A5
11100 HarC 77065 3540 A5
Steepletop Dr
- HarC 77065 3399 A7
- HarC 77065 3540 A1
Steepleway Blvd
- JRSV 77065 3539 E6
11100 HarC 77064 3540 A4
11100 HarC 77065 3540 A4
11400 HarC 77065 3539 E4
12500 JRSV 77065 3540 A6
Steep Pine Tr
2200 FBnC 77545 4622 C1
2300 FBnC 77545 4498 B7
Steep Rock Dr
4200 PASD 77504 4247 D6
Steep Trail Pl
10 WDLD 77385 2676 B3
Steeve Ct
17400 HarC 77532 3411 A7
Steffani Ln
4300 HOUS 77041 3820 A1
4300 HOUS 77043 3820 A1
4500 HOUS 77041 3681 A7
Stehle Rd
2000 FBnC 77471 4614 A4
Steiger Ln
100 MtgC 77355 2814 E1
Steinhagen Rd
16400 HarC 77429 3253 A4
Steinman St
6200 BYTN 77520 3971 B4
Steitz Ln
9900 MtgC 77303 2237 E2
10000 CNRO 77303 2237 D2
10000 CNRO 77304 2237 D2
Stella Ln
31100 TMBL 77375 2963 D4
Stella Rd
- RSBG 77471 4614 D2
Stella St
400 BYTN 77520 4112 D1
23900 MtgC 77357 2828 B1
Stella Lago Ct
- FBnC 77053 4498 D2
Stella Link Rd
6700 WUNP 77005 4101 D4
6800 HOUS 77025 4101 D7
6800 SSPL 77025 4101 D7
9100 HOUS 77025 4241 D2
Stellar Point Dr
- WDLD 77381 2820 B3
Stellas Psg
2900 FBnC 77459 4621 B6
Stellas Point Ct
14800 HarC 77396 3547 E1
Steller Eagle Ct
- HarC 77396 3548 B2
Stem Wy
1300 HarC 77532 3552 A2
Stem Green Ct
15100 HarC 77433 3250 D6
Stemply Ct
1900 HarC 77094 3955 A4
Stemwood Dr
2900 HarC 77388 3113 A5
Stenbury Ct
15900 HarC 77429 3397 B3
Stependale Dr
1300 HarC 77450 3954 D4
Stephanie Dr
500 MSCY 77489 4370 E4
7400 DRPK 77536 4249 B2
E Stephanshire St
1600 HOUS 77077 3957 B5
Stephen Ct
800 FRDW 77546 4629 C1
Stephen F Austin Ct
500 MtgC 77302 2530 C5
Stephen F Austin Dr
400 MtgC 77302 2530 D5
Stephens Ln
10800 HarC 77044 3690 E2
Stephens Charge Ct
12300 HarC 77433 3395 E4
Stephens Creek Ct
1700 SGLD 77478 4368 E5
Stephens Creek Ln
3100 SGLD 77478 4368 E5
Stephens Forest Rd
20100 MtgC 77357 2829 D6
Stephens Grant Dr
2300 SGLD 77479 4368 C7
2400 SGLD 77479 4495 C1
Stephenson Rd
15800 HOUS 77032 3404 E6
Stepinwolf Ln
23200 HarC 77373 3114 D6
Stepney Grn
10100 HarC 77070 3255 C4
Stepping Stone Ln
3400 FBnC 77459 4621 C5
Steppingstone Ln
11900 BKHV 77024 3959 B4
Steppingstone Tr
- FBnC 77469 4234 C2
Steppinstone Ct
10600 HarC 77379 3110 B5
Steppinstone Wy
1200 HarC 77379 3110 B6
Stepwood Dr
13800 HarC 77038 3543 A1
Stering
1300 BYTN 77520 3972 D6
E Sterling Av
10 BYTN 77520 3973 A7
W Sterling Av
400 BYTN 77520 3972 E7
Sterling Brk
5400 HarC 77041 3679 E6
Sterling Cross
4900 PRLD 77584 4502 A5
Sterling Ct
10 SGLD 77479 4495 E3
1200 KATY 77494 3952 A3
Sterling Dr
- BYTN 77520 3835 D4
- CmbC 77520 3835 D4
1200 PRLD 77584 4501 D2
23400 MtgC 77355 2962 B6
W Sterling Dr
9000 PRLD 77584 4501 C2
Sterling St
10 SGLD 77479 4495 E3
4600 HOUS 77051 4243 D2
W Sterling St
900 BYTN 77520 3972 D6
Sterling Vw
3800 MSCY 77459 4496 C2
Sterlingame Dr
8700 HOUS 77031 4239 B5
Sterling Bay Ln
6500 LGCY 77539 4752 E4
Sterling Bridge Ln
- FBnC 77478 4236 E5
Sterling Brook St
11600 PRLD 77584 4500 C2
Sterling Canyon Dr
6500 FBnC 77450 4094 C4
Sterling Center Ln
2100 HOUS 77023 4104 A2
Sterling Cloud Ln
25200 FBnC 77494 3953 A5
Sterling Creek Cir
800 HOUS 77450 3954 C2
Sterling Creek Ct
1700 LGCY 77573 4751 E2
Sterling Crest Ln
4000 DKSN 77539 4752 D6
Sterlingcrest Rd
13300 HOUS 77049 3828 A3
Sterling Cup Av
- HarC 77014 3402 A3
Sterling Dale Pl
10 WDLD 77382 2673 B7
Sterling Falls Dr
19900 HarC 77449 3676 E2
19900 HarC 77449 3677 C3
Sterling Fields Dr
2700 BzaC 77584 4374 A7
Sterling Gate Cir
8600 HarC 77379 3256 A5
Sterling Gate Ct
16300 HarC 77379 3256 A5
Sterling Green Blvd
14700 HarC 77015 3829 B5
Sterling Green Ct
1300 HarC 77015 3829 B5
1800 FBnC 77479 4494 B5
S Sterling Green Dr
900 HarC 77530 3829 C6
Sterling Heights Ln
400 HarC 77094 3955 C1
Sterling Hollow Dr
6900 HarC 77449 3676 E2
Sterling Lake Dr
15300 HarC 77095 3538 E6
Sterling Manor Dr
10600 HarC 77379 3110 A6
Sterling Meadow Ct
20000 HarC 77449 3676 C2
Sterling Meadow Dr
6900 HarC 77449 3676 E2
Sterling Park Ln
13400 HarC 77429 3254 A6
Sterling Pines Ct
20300 HarC 77379 3111 E5
Sterling Point Ln
8900 HarC 77044 3689 C5
Sterling Pointe Ct
2000 LGCY 77573 4509 A7
E Sterling Pond Cir
10 WDLD 77382 2675 C7
W Sterling Pond Cir
100 WDLD 77382 2675 C7
Sterling Pond Ct
10 WDLD 77382 2675 C7
Sterling Ridge Dr
- WDLD 77382 2673 C7
- WDLD 77382 2819 D1
- WDLD 77382 2820 A2
Sterlingshire
7900 HOUS 77078 3687 C5
Sterlingshire St
7600 HOUS 77016 3687 A5
7900 HOUS 77078 3687 E5
9000 HOUS 77078 3688 A5
Sterlingstone Dr
12400 HarC 77066 3401 B4
Sterling Stone Ln
- FBnC 77494 3952 C7
Sterling Village Dr
1600 MtgC 77386 2823 A7
Sterling Wood Wy
4400 HOUS 77059 4380 C3
4500 PASD 77059 4380 C3
Stern St
15900 HOUS 77044 3409 A4
Stern Creek Ln
13600 HOUS 77044 3409 A4
Sternwood Ln
- HarC 77047 4374 B3
Sternwood Manor Dr
19700 HarC 77379 3110 D6
Sterrett St
1200 HOUS 77002 3963 D3
1400 HOUS 77020 3963 D3
Stetson Cir
27200 MtgC 77355 2815 A7
Stetson Ln
2600 HOUS 77043 3820 A2
Stetson St
11600 TMBL 77375 3109 E3
Stetson Heights Ln
- FBnC 77469 4094 E7
Stetson Pl Ct
2000 FBnC 77469 4234 C7
Steve Fuqua Pl
10 FBnC 77459 4621 C6
Steven Dr
1000 ALVN 77511 4866 C2
Stevenage Ln
1400 HarC 77530 3829 D4
Steven Luke Ln
10 FRDW 77546 4630 B2
10 FRDW 77598 4630 B2
Stevens Av
800 CNRO 77301 2383 E4
Stevens Ct
1300 RSBG 77471 4491 D5
Stevens Dr
2200 PRLD 77581 4502 D2
Stevens Rd
4700 BzaC 77583 4745 D2
4700 IWCY 77583 4745 D2
5000 MNVL 77578 4745 E2
5000 MNVL 77583 4745 D2
5500 MNVL 77578 4746 A2
Stevens St
1600 HOUS 77026 3963 E1
2500 HOUS 77026 3824 E7
20600 MtgC 77357 2826 E7
20600 MtgC 77357 2827 A7
Stevens Creek Ct
5900 FBnC 77469 4493 B5
Stevens Creek Ln
800 FBnC 77469 4493 B5
Stevenson Dr
17500 MtgC 77302 2679 E2
Stevenson Rd
1900 BzaC 77581 4504 C7
1900 BzaC 77581 4628 C1
2400 PRLD 77581 4504 D7
Steven Springs Dr
31900 HarC 77447 3250 A7
Stevenwood Ln
1000 ALVN 77511 4866 C2
Steve Owen Rd
100 CNRO 77304 2382 D4
100 MtgC 77304 2382 D4
Steveroy St
3100 LMQU 77568 4989 C1
Stewart Av
600 KATY 77494 3952 C1
5600 GLSN 77551 5108 C6
Stewart Dr
5000 KATY 77493 3813 E7
Stewart Rd
1300 KMAH 77565 4509 C7
1300 LGCY 77565 4509 C7
1300 LGCY 77565 4633 C1
5700 GLSN 77551 5108 B7
6900 GLSN 77551 5222 A2
7000 HTCK 77563 4988 D5
8000 GLSN 77554 5222 A2
8500 DKSN 77539 4754 E4
8500 GLSN 77554 5221 A5
8500 TXCY 77539 4754 E4
11400 GLSN 77554 5220 C6
12900 GLSN 77554 5333 A1
13600 GLSN 77554 5332 D2
Stewart St
10 BYTN 77520 3973 A5
10 MtgC 77357 2973 A1
100 GNPK 77547 3966 C7
100 LMQU 77568 4873 E7
100 TXCY 77591 4873 E7
21200 MtgC 77357 2827 A7
Stewart Beach
- GLSN 77550 5109 E3
Stewart Crest Ln
20700 HarC 77433 3676 D1
Stewarts Forest Dr
10 CNRO 77301 2530 B3
Stewarts Grove Dr
16100 HarC 77379 3256 A6
Stickley Ct
- WDLD 77382 2819 A1
Stidham Rd
900 MtgC 77302 2530 E6
10200 MtgC 77302 2531 A7
Stikine Dr
- HarC 77086 3542 B1
Stiles Ln
12900 SGLD 77478 4368 E1
Stiles St
10 HOUS 77011 3964 B6
N Stiles St
100 HOUS 77011 3964 C5
Stilesboro Ct
14600 HOUS 77062 4379 E7
Still Bay Ct
13600 HOUS 77077 3957 A5
Still Bay St
2400 PRLD 77584 4500 D3
Stillbridge Ln
22000 MtgC 77339 3118 C5
Stillbrook Cir
11800 HarC 77429 3398 D2
Stillbrook Ln
25900 MtgC 77372 2683 A5
25900 SPLD 77372 2683 A5
Stillbrooke Dr
4300 HOUS 77035 4241 B3
5000 HOUS 77035 4240 E3
5200 HOUS 77096 4240 E3
Still Corner Pl
10 WDLD 77381 2820 E4
Still Cove Ln
9500 HarC 77089 4377 C7
Stillcreek Dr
15100 HarC 77070 3254 E7
Still Creek Rd
3700 PASD 77505 4248 E4
Stiller Dr
6700 HOUS 77489 4371 C5
Stiller Park Ct
15900 HarC 77429 3397 B4
Stiller Park Dr
15500 HarC 77429 3397 B4
Stiller Ridge Wy
- MtgC 77386 2969 B4
Stillforest St
10 PNPV 77024 3959 E5
E Stillforest St
10 PNPV 77024 3959 E6
W Stillforest St
10 PNPV 77024 3959 E6
Stillgate Ct
1000 HarC 77373 2968 E5
Still Glade Ln
4100 HOUS 77345 3119 D3
Still Glen Ct
10 WDLD 77381 2821 A6
Still Harbour Dr
12500 HarC 77041 3679 D7
Still Haven Dr
7100 FBnC 77469 4094 A6
Stillhollow Ln
19800 HarC 77094 3954 E4
19800 HarC 77094 3955 A4
19800 HarC 77450 3954 E4
Stillhouse Dr
19200 HarC 77375 3109 C6
Stillhouse Hollow Ln
18200 HarC 77433 3537 A4
Stillington Dr
12600 HarC 77015 3828 C6
Stillman St
6100 HOUS 77007 3962 A1
6200 HOUS 77007 3961 E2
Still Manor Ct
20000 HarC 77449 3676 E7
Stillmeadow Ct
3300 SGLD 77479 4495 B1
Still Meadow Dr
14300 HOUS 77079 3957 D1
Stillmeadow Dr
2200 MSCY 77489 4497 B1
Still Meadow St
6400 HarC 77389 2966 C5
Stillmeadows
17800 HOUS 77396 3405 E3
Stillmont Ln
20500 FBnC 77469 4094 D7
Still Oak Ln
8200 HarC 77433 3537 C6
Still Oaks Ln
30900 MtgC 77386 2969 D1
31000 MtgC 77386 2823 D7
Still Pond Dr
22900 HarC 77375 2966 A7
Still River Dr
9200 HOUS 77088 3543 E6
Stillrose Ln
2000 FBnC 77469 4616 A3
Still Springs Ct
18000 HarC 77346 3408 A2
Still Springs Dr
4600 HarC 77346 3408 A2
Stillstone Dr
1400 HarC 77073 3404 A3
Stillview Dr
3700 HarC 77068 3257 B7
Stillwater Dr
1900 FRDW 77546 4629 C6
4100 MSCY 77459 4369 C6
6400 PRLD 77584 4502 C5
11600 HarC 77070 3254 D7
Stillwater Ln
3400 SGLD 77479 4495 B1
Still Water St
7900 HarC 77521 3833 B3
Stillwater Bay Ct
2100 LGCY 77573 4631 B7
Stillwater Canyon Ln
22500 MtgC 77365 2973 A3
Stillwater Pl Dr
18100 HarC 77346 3408 A1
Stillwater Valley Ln
22500 MtgC 77365 2973 A3
Stillwell St
2600 MSCY 77489 4370 C7
6300 HOUS 77023 4104 D4
6600 HOUS 77087 4104 E4
Stillwood Dr
2300 HOUS 77080 3820 C3
Stillwood Park Ct
12600 HarC 77433 3396 A4
Stilson Branch Ln
6000 HOUS 77092 3682 C7
Stilwell Rd
2500 MSCY 77489 4370 C6
Stimpson St
10 BYTN 77520 4112 D1
Stimson St
4900 HOUS 77023 3964 B7
Stingray Ct
9000 TXCY 77591 4873 A3
Sting Ray Dr
16200 HarC 77532 3551 D2
Stingray St
7000 GlsC 77563 4990 C6
Stinson Dr
8000 MSCY 77459 4497 A6
Stinson St
100 CNRO 77301 2384 A4
Stirring Winds Dr
5900 HarC 77086 3542 D3
Stirrup Dr
13200 HarC 77039 3545 D5
Stirrup Ranch Rd
20000 HarC 77375 3110 A5
Stockbridge Dr
3700 SGLD 77479 4495 E3
3700 SGLD 77479 4496 A3
Stockbridge Ln
400 LGCY 77539 4753 A5
21900 HarC 77449 3676 C6
Stock Bridge St
8000 BYTN 77521 3833 C3
E Stockbridge Landing Cir
10 WDLD 77382 2674 C2
W Stockbridge Landing Cir
10 WDLD 77382 2674 D3
Stockbridge Landing Ct
10 WDLD 77382 2674 C2
Stockbridge Landing Dr
10 WDLD 77382 2674 D3
Stock Creek Ln
2800 FBnC 77469 4365 A5
Stockdick Rd
5900 KATY 77494 3952 B2
Stockdick School Rd
5000 HarC 77449 3676 A2
21300 HarC 77449 3675 D6
21300 HarC 77493 3675 D6
Stockfield Ln
- HarC 77449 3676 D3
Stockfield Ln N
- HarC 77449 3676 D3
Stockholm Ct
5900 HarC 77449 3677 B5
Stocklin Ct
14800 FBnC 77478 4236 C2
Stockman Ln
10400 FBnC 77478 4237 A3
Stockport Dr
9300 HarC 77379 3255 E6
9300 HarC 77379 3256 A6
Stockton Ct
6900 FBnC 77583 4623 A7
Stockton Dr
- HOUS 77005 4102 C4
- HOUS 77030 4102 C4
Stockton Falls Dr
- HarC 77449 3676 E4
Stockton Springs Dr
18100 HarC 77379 3257 A1
Stockwell Dr
9200 HarC 77083 4237 B2
Stockwood Dr
- HarC 77064 3540 D2
Stoerner Dr
2800 HarC 77032 3545 E2
3200 HarC 77032 3546 A2
Stokes Rd
19000 WALR 77484 3102 B6
20100 HarC 77484 3102 B1
21100 HarC 77484 2957 B7
Stokes St
10 HOUS 77022 3824 A3
Stokesdale Dr
- HarC 77040 3541 A6
Stokesmount Dr
14100 HOUS 77077 3956 E3
Stoksay Dr
- HarC 77449 3677 A3
Stoltje Dr
15300 MtgC 77306 2532 E1
15300 MtgC 77306 2533 A1
Stone Ct
10 PNVL 77304 2237 B1
Stone Dr
400 ALVN 77511 4867 C3
S Stone Ln
19400 HarC 77449 3677 A7
Stone Rd
1100 PRLD 77581 4375 A6
1700 PRLD 77581 4502 A1
1800 BzaC 77581 4502 A1
Stone Run
- HarC 77084 3678 B2
Stone St
7900 HOUS 77061 4245 D1
Stone Ter
10 FBnC 77479 4367 A7
Stoneage Dr
20000 FBnC 77469 4234 D2
Stone Angel Dr
18100 HarC 77346 3409 A1
Stone Arbor Dr
7400 FBnC 77479 4494 A4
Stone Arbor Ln
7400 BzaC 77581 4502 A3
Stone Arrow Pl
10 WDLD 77382 2819 C1
Stonebelt Dr
17300 HarC 77073 3404 A3
Stone Bluff Dr
1300 HarC 77073 3403 E3
1300 HarC 77073 3404 A3
Stone Bluff Ln
14200 BzaC 77583 4623 C4
Stone Branch Ct
5600 BzaC 77583 4623 E5
Stone Branch Ln
13600 BzaC 77583 4623 E5
Stonebranch Ln
- FBnC 77450 4094 A1
Stone Briar Dr
6300 PASD 77505 4248 E7
Stonebriar Ln
22100 FBnC 77469 4492 D4
22100 FBnC 77469 4493 A3
Stone Bridge Ct
9100 FBnC 77459 4621 C6
Stone Bridge Dr
11700 HarC 77064 3399 D7
Stonebridge Dr
4300 MSCY 77459 4496 C2
4500 PRLD 77584 4503 B6
Stonebridge Pl
9500 HarC 77375 2965 B2
Stonebridge Rd
7500 BzaC 77511 4627 B5
Stone Bridge St
300 LGCY 77573 4631 B5
Stonebridge St
- HarC 77521 3833 C2
4700 BYTN 77521 3833 C2
Stonebridge Tr
17200 HarC 77095 3537 E1
Stonebridge Church Dr
33000 MtgC 77354 2674 A4
33000 WDLD 77354 2674 A4
33000 WDLD 77382 2674 A4
Stonebridge Creek Ln
7200 HarC 77396 3547 B1
Stonebridge Crossing Ln
22200 HarC 77375 3110 A1
Stonebridge Lake Ct
9400 HarC 77375 2965 C3
Stonebridge Lake Dr
9500 HarC 77375 2965 B2
Stonebridge Terrace Ct
20300 FBnC 77469 4234 C2
Stonebridge Terrace Dr
20100 FBnC 77469 4234 C2
Stonebrook Dr
12500 PRLD 77584 4500 B3
Stone Brook Ln
- HOUS 77092 3682 B4
8800 HOUS 77040 3682 B3
Stonebrook Ln
4200 MSCY 77459 4496 C3
Stoneburg Ct
2300 FBnC 77479 4493 D2
Stoneburg Dr
4100 FBnC 77450 4094 C2
Stonebury Ct
6100 FBnC 77479 4494 A3
Stonebury Ln
- FBnC 77469 4094 E2
2500 FBnC 77479 4493 E3
2700 FBnC 77479 4494 A3
Stonebury Trail Ln
14300 HOUS 77044 3550 B2
Stonebush Ct
200 WlrC 77493 3812 A7
Stone Cactus Dr
10200 HarC 77095 3537 E3
Stone Canyon Ct
20200 HarC 77377 3106 D5
Stone Canyon Dr
1400 FBnC 77479 4494 B6
Stone Cape Ct
- HarC 77377 3253 E2
Stone Castle Dr
9500 HarC 77064 3540 D5
Stone Chapel Wy
4400 FBnC 77469 4233 C5
Stonechase St
6500 HarC 77084 3678 A3
Stonecliff Cir
10 FBnC 77479 4367 A6
Stonecloud Ln
5600 FBnC 77494 4093 B2
Stone Cottage Ln
14200 HarC 77047 4374 C5
Stonecreek Cir
700 FRDW 77546 4629 D5
Stone Creek Ct
19900 HarC 77377 3106 C5
Stone Creek Dr
- PNVL 77304 2237 B1
5400 LPRT 77571 4250 B2
5700 MtgC 77354 2673 D1
Stonecreek Ln
9200 HOUS 77036 4098 E7
9300 HOUS 77036 4238 E1
Stone Creek Pl
10 WDLD 77382 2674 E5
10 WDLD 77382 2675 A5
Stonecreek Bend Ln
11300 HarC 77433 3396 B7
Stone Creek Model Ct
16800 HarC 77084 3678 B2
Stone Creek Ranch Blvd
- HarC 77447 3249 E6
- HarC 77447 3250 A6
Stonecrest Ct
3400 PRLD 77581 4504 C5
Stonecrest Dr
900 HOUS 77018 3823 A3
2000 HOUS 77018 3822 C3
16400 MtgC 77302 2678 A5
Stonecrest Ln
13100 MtgC 77302 2678 A6
Stonecrest Rd
7000 BzaC 77511 4627 B4
Stonecrest St
2000 PRLD 77581 4504 C5
Stonecrest Wy
2000 PRLD 77581 4504 C5
Stonecroft Cir
4200 FBnC 77450 4093 E2
Stonecroft Pl
10 WDLD 77381 2820 C1
Stonecrop Ct
4800 HOUS 77345 3119 E2
Stone Cross Ct
22100 FBnC 77450 4094 A1
Stonecross Ln
3000 LGCY 77539 4752 D5
Stonecross Creek Ln
6600 HarC 77449 3676 D3
Stone Cross Glen Ln
19800 HarC 77433 3537 A7
Stone Crossing Ln
- HarC 77449 3677 C5
Stonecross Terrace Ln
19100 FBnC 77469 4235 A1
19200 FBnC 77469 4234 E1
21500 HarC 77449 3815 B4
Stone Ct Ln
19700 HarC 77449 3677 A6
Stonedale Ct
19000 BzaC 77511 4627 B5
Stonedale Ln
- FBnC 77494 4092 E3
Stone East Dr
12100 HOUS 77035 4240 D6
Stone Edge Ct
4100 SGLD 77479 4494 E
Stonefair Ln
8800 HOUS 77075 4376 E
Stone Falls Ct
20200 HarC 77433 3251 B
Stonefield Dr
13100 HarC 77014 3402 D
13100 HarC 77090 3402 D
Stone Field Canyon Ln
12900 HarC 77433 3396 A
Stonefield Manor Ct
9400 HarC 77044 3689 A
Stonefield Manor Dr
- HarC 77044 3689 A
Stonefir Ct
7000 HOUS 77040 3682 B
Stoneford Dr
- HOUS 77077 3958 B
Stone Forest Dr
- HarC 77379 3112 A
Stoneforest Rd
19000 BzaC 77511 4627 B
Stonefort Ct
6600 HarC 77449 3676 D
Stone Fox Dr
28700 MtgC 77386 2969 D
Stone Gables Ln
15400 HarC 77044 3549 E
Stone Gate Cir
3500 PRLD 77584 4503 B
Stonegate Cir
5300 FBnC 77469 4234 C
Stone Gate Ct
20100 HarC 77377 3106 D
Stonegate Ct
19000 BzaC 77511 4627 C
Stone Gate Dr
10200 CHTW 77385 2822 E
10200 MtgC 77385 2822 E
Stonegate Dr
10 BKHV 77024 3959 D
10 HDWV 77024 3959 D
5300 FBnC 77469 4234 C
7200 HOUS 77040 3682 A
Stonegate Grove Ct
500 FBnC 77469 4234 C
Stonegate Park Ct
10 HarC 77379 3256 B
Stoneglade Dr
900 CNRO 77301 2530 B
Stone Glen Dr
- HOUS 77339 3119 A
Stonegrove Ct
1900 BzaC 77581 4502 A
20200 HarC 77375 3109 E
E Stonegrove Lp
5900 HarC 77084 3679 A
Stone Harbor Dr
4800 HarC 77546 4505 E
Stonehaven Dr
7800 HarC 77389 2966 A
8100 HarC 77389 2965 E
15700 HOUS 77059 4380 B
29600 MtgC 77354 2818 B
Stone Haven Wy
6700 HOUS 77085 4371 C
Stonehaven Village Cir
1600 MtgC 77386 2823 A
Stonehearth Ln
8900 HOUS 77040 3682 A
Stone Hedge
11700 MtgC 77303 2385 D
Stonehedge
- HOUS 77077 3957 C
Stonehedge Dr
2700 BYTN 77521 3972 B
17100 HarC 77073 3404 A
Stonehedge Bend Dr
1500 HarC 77073 3404 A
Stonehenge Dr
13600 SGLD 77478 4237 B
Stonehenge Ln
200 FRDW 77546 4505 A
300 HarC 77015 3828 E6
Stonehenge Tr
4100 HarC 77066 3401 B
Stone Hill Ct
- HarC 77389 2966 D
Stonehill Dr
15400 HOUS 77062 4506 E
Stone Hill Rd
6400 HarC 77389 2966 D
Stonehollow Dr
1200 HOUS 77339 3118 C6
Stonehouse Ln
9400 HOUS 77025 4241 C
Stonehurst Dr
3300 BzaC 77584 4501 D
Stone Ivory Ct
3400 HarC 77388 3112 E5
Stone Ivy Ln
- HarC 77449 3677 C5
Stone Lake Cir
19900 HarC 77377 3106 C5
Stone Lake Dr
1600 MSCY 77489 4370 D4
19600 HarC 77377 3106 C5
Stone Landing Ln
6400 HarC 77449 3677 D3
Stoneleaf Dr
17100 HarC 77073 3404 A4
Stone Leaf Ln
19100 FBnC 77469 4094 D3
19100 FBnC 77469 4095 A6
Stoneledge Dr
400 FRDW 77546 4504 E7
Stoneleigh Ct
1000 TMBL 77375 2964 D5
1800 FBnC 77479 4494 C4
Stoneleigh Dr
500 HOUS 77079 3958 A3
9100 FBnC 77479 4494 C4
Stonelick Ct
7300 PRLD 77584 4502 B5
Stonelick Bridge Ln
14900 FBnC 77478 4236 D4
Stone Loch Ct
- HarC 77429 3254 A4
Stonelodge
19600 HarC 77450 3955 A5
19600 HOUS 77094 3955 A5
Stonelodge Dr
19900 HarC 77450 3955 A5
20000 HarC 77450 3954 E5
Stone Mallow Dr
11400 HarC 77095 3397 B7
11400 HarC 77095 3538 B1

STREET
Block City ZIP Map# Grid

Stone Manor Dr
- HarC 77379 3110 B7
Stonemeade Pl
14900 HarC 77429 3397 C1
Stone Meadows Ln
1900 HarC 77094 3955 A4
Stonemede Dr
4600 HarC 77546 4505 E6
Stone Mesa Dr
1400 HarC 77073 3404 A3
Stone Mill Ln
25400 HarC 77373 3114 C3
Stone Mission Ln
19100 FBnC 77469 4235 A1
Stonemist Ln
- HarC 77388 3112 B4
Stonemont Ln
18100 HarC 77429 3252 B6
Stonemont Rd
9700 LPRT 77571 4250 B3
Stonemont Glen Ln
7700 FBnC 77469 4094 B7
Stone Moss
20300 HarC 77379 3111 E4
Stonemount Ct
8100 HarC 77338 3261 E3
Stone Mountain Dr
10 MtgC 77302 2530 D6
Stone Mountain Ln
20700 HarC 77073 3259 E4
Stone Oak Ct
4200 MSCY 77459 4496 C1
7800 HarC 77070 3399 E3
15700 HarC 77429 3252 A6
Stone Park Rd
14400 HOUS 77489 4371 B3
Stonepass Ct
4700 FBnC 77479 4496 B4
Stonepath
- HarC 77084 3678 B2
Stone Peaks Dr
17300 HarC 77095 3537 E2
Stone Pine Ln
7300 HarC 77041 3679 B1
7500 HarC 77041 3539 B7
Stonepine Creek Dr
20000 HarC 77375 3109 E5
Stonepine Meadow Ct
11500 HarC 77375 3109 D5
Stone Point St
19100 HarC 77388 3112 C5
Stone Porch Ln
9100 HarC 77064 3540 D5
Stoneport Ct
2600 FBnC 77469 4365 B5
Stone Post Cir
9200 HarC 77064 3540 D6
Stone Prairie Dr
16400 HarC 77095 3397 C6
16400 HarC 77095 3538 A1
Stoner Ct
6900 HOUS 77088 3682 B1
Stoner Falls Dr
- HOUS 77077 3957 B4
Stoneridge Ct
5300 RSBG 77469 4615 E1
Stoneridge St
22000 MtgC 77365 2972 C2
Stoneridge Canyon Ct
11000 HarC 77089 4377 B7
Stoneridge Canyon Ln
9200 HarC 77089 4377 A7
9200 HarC 77089 4504 A1
Stoneridge Creek Ln
14500 HarC 77396 3547 C1
Stoneridge Park Ct
15100 HarC 77429 3253 B7
Stoneridge Park Ln
15300 HarC 77429 3253 B6
Stoneridge Terrace Ln
- LGCY 77573 4751 B1
Stoneriver
6600 HarC 77084 3678 B3
Stone River Ln
2800 FBnC 77479 4493 D3
Stoneroses Tr
20500 FBnC 77469 4234 C3
Stonerun
- HarC 77084 3678 B2
Stonerun St
16600 HarC 77084 3678 B3
Stonesdale Dr
7700 HarC 77095 3538 D7
Stonesfield Pl
7400 HarC 77389 2966 B1
Stoneshire Dr
23200 MtgC 77357 2828 A3
Stoneshire St
13800 HarC 77037 3544 E6
13800 HarC 77060 3544 E6
Stoneside Dr
16600 HarC 77095 3538 A6
Stoneside Rd
2200 CNRO 77304 2383 C1
Stone Spring Ln
2900 LGCY 77539 4752 E5
Stone Springs Cir
10 WDLD 77381 2820 C1
Stones River Ln
- HarC 77346 3408 C3
Stone Stable Ln
16100 HarC 77429 3253 A7
Stonestead Dr
28100 FBnC 77494 3951 D6
Stonesthrow Av
100 FRDW 77546 4629 C1
Stones Throw Ln
8500 FBnC 77459 4621 C5
Stones Throw Rd
5900 HOUS 77057 3960 C4
Stone Stile Dr
17000 HarC 77546 4506 B6
Stone Terrace Ct
9500 HarC 77089 4377 A7
Stone Trail Dr
1400 FBnC 77479 4493 E5
Stone Trail Ln
6000 HarC 77379 3111 E5
Stonetrail Rd
20600 FBnC 77469 4234 C3
Stone Trail Manor Dr
18100 HarC 77346 3408 E1
Stone Valley Dr
7300 HarC 77095 3678 D1
Stone View Dr
- HarC 77377 3106 D5
Stoneview Dr
20100 FBnC 77469 4234 D3

Stone Villa Ln
- HarC 77064 3540 D5
- HarC 77377 3253 E3
Stone Village Ln
8400 HOUS 77040 3682 B3
Stonewalk Dr
2000 HOUS 77056 3960 E6
Stonewall Ct
- HarC 77095 3537 D5
2900 MSCY 77459 4497 E6
Stonewall Dr
200 LGCY 77573 4631 B5
500 FBnC 77469 4493 D6
5100 HOUS 77023 3964 C7
Stonewall Ln
8600 FBnC 77469 4616 D1
Stonewall Rd
19000 BzaC 77511 4627 C5
19000 BzaC 77584 4627 C5
19000 PRLD 77584 4627 C5
Stonewall St
2300 LMQU 77568 4989 D1
6100 HOUS 77020 3964 E2
Stonewall Jackson Bnd
500 MtgC 77302 2530 C6
Stonewall Jackson Ct
700 MtgC 77302 2530 D6
Stonewall Jackson Dr
600 MtgC 77302 2530 C5
Stonewall Pass Rd
- FRDW 77546 4628 E3
- PRLD 77546 4628 E3
Stonewall Ridge Dr
7000 FBnC 77469 4493 C7
Stonewater St
6700 HarC 77084 3678 B2
Stone West Dr
12100 HOUS 77035 4240 D6
Stonewick Dr
15000 HarC 77068 3257 B6
Stone Wood Ct
13900 BzaC 77583 4623 D5
Stonewood Ln
2200 MSCY 77489 4370 D6
Stonewood St
10000 HOUS 77078 3687 C4
Stonewood Heights Ct
2100 PRLD 77581 4503 C2
Stonewood Manor Ct
- HarC 77377 3253 D3
Stonewood Manor Ln
- HarC 77377 3253 E2
Stonewood Pointe Ln
6300 HarC 77066 3400 D5
Stone Wy Dr
2800 HOUS 77082 4097 B1
Stoney Ct
2000 HarC 77373 3114 D5
Stoney Bend Dr
8800 HarC 77379 3255 E4
Stoney Bluff Ln
21700 HarC 77449 3815 A4
Stoney Brook Ct
- CNRO 77304 2236 B7
Stoney Brook Dr
- HOUS 77036 4099 E4
1800 HOUS 77063 3960 A7
2100 DRPK 77536 4109 D7
2900 HOUS 77063 4100 A1
3700 BYTN 77521 3972 E3
Stoney Brook Ln
3000 MSCY 77459 4496 E3
Stoney Creek Dr
- BYTN 77521 3833 C3
- HarC 77521 3833 C3
100 BKHV 77024 3959 B5
100 HOUS 77024 3959 B5
6200 PASD 77503 4248 E1
12500 PRLD 77584 4500 B2
Stoneycreek Pk
2100 MtgC 77385 2823 B6
Stoney Creek Rd
10 CNRO 77303 2237 E5
Stoneycreek Park Ct
2200 MtgC 77385 2823 A6
Stoney Crest St
3700 MSCY 77459 4621 D4
Stoneydale Ln
3200 HarC 77388 3112 E4
Stoney Falls Dr
11300 HarC 77095 3397 A7
11300 HarC 77095 3538 A1
Stoney Fork Dr
15500 HarC 77084 3678 E7
Stoney Glade Ct
17800 HarC 77095 3537 E7
S Stoneygrove Lp
14300 HarC 77084 3679 A4
Stoney Haven Dr
19800 HarC 77433 3677 A1
21000 HarC 77449 3676 C4
Stoney Hill Dr
1000 HOUS 77077 3956 E3
Stoney Hurst Dr
- WDLD 77382 2819 D2
Stoney Knoll Ln
4200 FBnC 77494 4092 D1
Stoney Lake Dr
1600 FRDW 77546 4629 C5
9000 HarC 77064 3540 D5
Stoney Meadow Dr
11200 HarC 77095 3538 B1
Stoney Mill St
12500 HarC 77429 3398 E5
Stoney Mist Dr
3100 SGLD 77479 4494 E2
3100 SGLD 77479 4495 A3
Stoney Oak Dr
3400 HarC 77068 3257 B5
Stoney Park Dr
1500 HOUS 77339 3118 C6
Stoney Plain Dr
30100 MtgC 77386 2969 B2
Stoney Point Ct
4700 FBnC 77479 4366 D5
Stoney Point Ln
- HarC 77084 3678 A7
Stoney Point St
2200 HOUS 77056 3960 E6
Stoney Ridge Ln
11900 BKHV 77024 3959 B4
Stoney River Ct
17400 HarC 77379 3256 C2
Stoney River Dr
6600 HarC 77379 3256 D2
Stoneyvale Dr
6900 FBnC 77083 4095 E5

Stoney View Dr
4200 PASD 77505 4248 E5
Stoneyview Dr
15000 FBnC 77083 4236 C1
Stoneyway Dr
7700 HarC 77040 3541 A7
7800 HarC 77040 3681 A1
Stoney Wood Dr
2800 HOUS 77082 4097 B1
Stonham Av
3500 HOUS 77047 4374 C3
Stonham St
5900 HOUS 77048 4375 D3
Stonington St
5400 HOUS 77040 3681 B5
E Stony Bridge Cir
10 WDLD 77381 2820 C4
S Stony Bridge Cir
10 WDLD 77381 2820 D3
W Stony Bridge Cir
10 WDLD 77381 2820 D3
E Stony Bridge Ct
10 WDLD 77381 2820 D2
W Stony Bridge Ct
10 WDLD 77381 2820 D2
Stony Creek Ct
10 MtgC 77384 2528 A6
Stony Creek Dr
10 MtgC 77384 2528 A6
Stony Dell Ct
8100 HOUS 77061 4245 D1
Stony End Ct
10 WDLD 77381 2675 A7
E Stony End Pl
10 WDLD 77381 2674 E7
10 WDLD 77381 2675 A7
W Stony End Pl
10 WDLD 77381 2674 E7
Stony Green Dr
- HarC 77433 3250 E6
Stonyridge Dr
700 HarC 77530 3829 D7
Stony Run Pl
10 WDLD 77381 2820 E3
Storey Dr
6100 HOUS 77396 3406 A7
6200 HarC 77396 3547 A1
6200 HOUS 77396 3547 A1
Storm Cove Vw
4700 HarC 77396 3407 A7
Storm Creek Ct
8400 HOUS 77088 3683 A2
Storm Creek Dr
3600 HOUS 77088 3683 A2
Stormcroft Cir
1900 HarC 77450 3953 E5
Stormcroft Ln
- PRLD 77545 4499 E2
22300 HarC 77450 3953 E5
Storm Meadow Dr
9900 HarC 77064 3540 C3
Storm Mist Pl
10 WDLD 77381 2820 E1
Stormwood Pl
10 WDLD 77381 2675 A7
Storm Wood St
8700 HarC 77040 3681 C1
Stormy Pine Ln
20100 HarC 77379 3111 D5
Stormy Sky Dr
10500 HarC 77064 3540 B2
Stormy Sky Tr
10000 HarC 77064 3540 B3
Stornoway Dr
15800 HarC 77379 3256 B6
Story St
1300 HOUS 77055 3822 A6
Story Book Tr
5700 FBnC 77459 4621 A1
Storybrook Forest Dr
16900 HarC 77377 3254 B4
Story Creek Ln
23200 MtgC 77365 3118 A1
Story Glen Dr
- HarC 77429 3397 D3
Storywood Dr
700 HNCV 77024 3960 B2
Stoughton Ct
24600 FBnC 77494 3952 E4
Stoughton Dr
11400 HarC 77066 3401 D6
Stovall Rd
2100 HarC 77068 3257 D3
2100 HarC 77090 3257 D3
Stovepipe Ln
3800 SGLD 77479 4368 E7
Stover St
10200 HOUS 77075 4377 B3
Stowbridge Dr
- HOUS 77339 3117 E3
- HOUS 77365 3117 E3
Stowe Rd
13100 MtgC 77306 2533 B6
13700 MtgC 77302 2678 C7
Stowe St
1100 BYTN 77520 4112 D1
Strack Dr
18000 HarC 77379 3257 B1
E Strack Dr
17000 HarC 77379 3257 C2
S Strack Dr
- HarC 77379 3257 C3
W Strack Dr
17000 HarC 77379 3257 C2
Strack Rd
4500 HarC 77068 3256 D6
4500 HarC 77069 3256 C7
Strack Farm Rd
- HarC 77379 3257 A2
Stradbrook Dr
15200 HOUS 77062 4506 D2
Straight Arrow Dr
5200 HarC 77346 3264 C5
Straight Creek Dr
2100 HOUS 77017 4246 B1
Straight Elm St
2800 FBnC 77545 4498 B6
Straightfork Dr
3700 HarC 77082 4096 B3
Strait Dr
3000 BzaC 77511 4748 C3
Strait Ln
2300 HarC 77084 3816 A6
Strand Ct
300 HOUS 77034 4378 E5
Stranda Dr
9200 HOUS 77075 4245 C7
9200 HOUS 77075 4376 C1

Strang Rd
9300 HarC 77571 4110 B4
9300 LPRT 77571 4110 B5
11200 HarC 77571 4111 C7
12200 LPRT 77571 4111 B7
Strange Dr
800 FBnC 77469 4492 B1
800 RHMD 77469 4492 B1
Strasse
- HarC 77375 2965 B3
Stratburg Ln
12800 HarC 77070 3399 C4
Stratfield Ln
8800 HOUS 77075 4377 A3
Stratford Av
800 PASD 77506 4107 D5
Stratford Ml
12900 FBnC 77478 4366 E1
Stratford Pl
9200 HarC 77375 3110 D1
Stratford St
100 HOUS 77006 3963 A6
200 HOUS 77006 3962 E6
400 HarC 77562 3831 D2
2700 PRLD 77581 4503 D4
Stratford Wy
10 HarC 77070 3399 E3
1300 HOUS 77339 3119 A7
1300 HOUS 77339 3264 A1
Stratford Arms Ln
3600 FBnC 77478 4366 D1
Stratford Bend Dr
3100 FBnC 77478 4366 E1
Stratford Canyon Dr
8200 HarC 77433 3537 A6
Stratford Creek Dr
- FBnC 77469 4366 D1
- FBnC 77478 4366 D1
Stratford Gardens Dr
5700 SGLD 77479 4495 A4
6000 SGLD 77479 4494 E3
Stratford Green Dr
17200 FBnC 77478 4366 E1
Stratford Heights Dr
12800 FBnC 77478 4366 E1
Stratford House Ln
22700 HarC 77449 3814 D4
Stratford Manor Dr
3200 FBnC 77478 4366 E1
Stratford Mill Ln
12900 FBnC 77478 4366 C1
Stratford Park Dr
6800 HarC 77084 3678 E3
Stratford Plaza Ln
3500 FBnC 77478 4366 E1
Stratford Pointe Dr
3100 FBnC 77478 4366 E1
E Stratford Pointe Dr
17200 FBnC 77478 4366 C1
Stratford Skies Ln
13000 HarC 77072 4097 C7
Stratford Town Ln
3600 FBnC 77478 4366 E1
Strathclyde Sound Rd
7800 HarC 77095 3538 C6
Strathdon
28600 MtgC 77354 2818 C2
Strathford Ln
2800 HOUS 77345 3119 D6
N Strathford Ln
2600 HOUS 77345 3119 E6
S Strathford Ln
2600 HOUS 77345 3119 E6
Strathmere Ct
22900 HarC 77450 3953 D1
Strathmill Ct
9200 HarC 77095 3538 C4
Strathmore Dr
8300 HOUS 77078 3688 A6
Strathmore Manor Ln
16500 HarC 77090 3258 C4
Strathmore Pl Ct
6800 HarC 77449 3677 B2
Strathmore Pl Ln
19300 HarC 77449 3677 B2
Stratmor Ct
6200 HarC 77389 2966 D4
Stratmore Dr
100 FRDW 77546 4505 A7
Stratsborough Dr
23400 FBnC 77494 4093 C4
Stratton St
6300 HOUS 77023 4104 D4
Stratton Park Dr
15900 HarC 77379 3256 A6
Stratus Ct
4100 MtgC 77386 2970 C5
Stratwood Ct
19900 HarC 77433 3677 A1
Straus Ct
10 STAF 77477 4369 E1
Strausie Ln
14800 MtgC 77302 2678 D5
Strawberry Ct
- DKSN 77539 4754 A2
Strawberry Rd
10 PASD 77506 4107 B4
1200 PASD 77502 4107 C7
2100 PASD 77502 4247 D3
3000 PASD 77504 4247 D4
5400 HOUS 77034 4378 D1
5400 HOUS 77504 4378 D1
12500 HarC 77038 3543 B4
Strawberry St
1000 LGCY 77573 4632 E6
Strawberry Canyon Pl
10 WDLD 77382 2819 A1
Strawberry Park Ln
1200 HarC 77450 3954 B4
Strawbridge Ln
7300 HOUS 77040 3682 A3
Strawfield Dr
1900 SGLD 77478 4368 D5
Strawgrass Dr
9500 HarC 77064 3540 C2
Strawn Rd
1500 HarC 77039 3545 C3
Strawn St
1600 BYTN 77520 4112 C2
3200 LMQU 77568 4989 B1
Streamcrest Ln
2100 SGLD 77479 4368 B7
2200 SGLD 77479 4495 B2
Streamhurst Ln
2100 SGLD 77479 4368 B7
Stream Meadows Ln
3200 SGLD 77479 4368 B7

Stream Mill Ln
400 HarC 77494 3953 A2
Streamside
- HOUS 77088 3682 E1
- HOUS 77088 3683 A1
Streamside Dr
- HOUS 77088 3682 E1
1800 FRDW 77546 4629 D4
7600 HOUS 77088 3683 A2
8000 HarC 77088 3542 E7
8000 HarC 77088 3682 E1
Streamside Ln
3400 SGLD 77479 4495 B1
Streamwood Dr
8000 HarC 77083 4096 D7
Streatham Cir
15300 HarC 77530 3829 D5
Street Cir
- HarC 77336 3120 E3
Street B
- HOUS 77336 3120 D3
Streetcar Ct
15300 HarC 77429 3252 A7
Street E
- HarC 77070 3399 C7
Streeter Ln
- HarC 77388 3113 B7
Streeter Pl Ct
18700 HarC 77388 3113 B7
Stretch Dr
9600 HarC 77040 3681 A1
Stretford Ct
10 SGLD 77479 4495 E3
Strey Ct
400 DRPK 77536 4249 B2
Strey Ln
400 BKHV 77024 3959 B3
800 HOUS 77024 3959 B2
Strick Ln
12400 GNPK 77015 3966 E4
12400 GNPK 77015 3967 A4
12400 HOUS 77015 3966 E4
12400 HOUS 77015 3967 A4
Strickland Dr
10600 HOUS 77093 3686 A3
22300 MtgC 77357 2827 D6
Strickland Pl
13000 MtgC 77372 2535 A5
Strickland St
1200 BYTN 77520 3973 C7
Striepe Rd
- HOUS 77084 3817 D2
Strington Dr
- HarC 77095 3539 B7
E Stroker Rd
100 HarC 77532 3411 A3
W Stroker Rd
100 HarC 77532 3410 C3
100 HarC 77532 3411 A3
Strolling Wy
400 STAF 77477 4369 C3
Strolling Stream Ln
- FBnC 77469 4235 C1
Strom Rd
11300 TXCY 77539 4755 A2
Stroman Dr
14500 HarC 77429 3253 B7
14500 HarC 77429 3397 E1
Strong Bank
6000 FBnC 77459 4497 A7
Strong Creek Dr
5800 HarC 77084 3678 B4
Strong Pine Dr
24200 HOUS 77336 3266 C2
Strongs Ct
1800 HarC 77449 3815 D7
Strong Winds Dr
3200 HarC 77014 3401 E1
Stroud Dr
6400 HOUS 77074 4100 A5
9200 HOUS 77036 4099 A5
9500 HOUS 77036 4098 E5
10900 HOUS 77072 4098 B5
12000 HOUS 77072 4097 E5
Stroudwater Ln
15700 HarC 77084 3678 C5
Strutton Dr
14200 FBnC 77083 4236 E2
14200 FBnC 77478 4236 E2
Stuart
- HarC 77377 2963 C7
- HarC 77377 3108 C1
Stuart Dr
3700 LPRT 77571 4249 E4
Stuart Mnr
2600 HOUS 77082 4098 A1
Stuart Rd
2100 BzaC 77511 4868 A7
Stuart St
500 HOUS 77006 3963 A6
800 HOUS 77002 3963 A6
1000 HOUS 77004 3963 A7
2400 HOUS 77004 4103 C1
Stubble Ct
9200 HarC 77396 3406 E7
Stubbs Dr
- HarC 77083 4097 C7
Stubbs Rd
9800 MtgC 77354 2672 A2
Stubbs St
800 LMQU 77568 4990 C2
Stubby Ln
14000 MtgC 77306 2533 D7
18000 MAGA 77354 2669 A4
18000 MtgC 77354 2669 A4
Stuckey Ln
11800 BKHV 77024 3959 B3
Stude St
1000 HOUS 77007 3962 E1
1000 HOUS 77009 3962 E1
Studebaker Ln
3500 HarC 77396 3406 E5
Studemont St
- HOUS 77009 3962 E1
400 HOUS 77007 3962 E2
400 HOUS 77019 3962 D4
Studer St
1100 HOUS 77007 3962 B2
Studewood St
400 HOUS 77007 3962 E1
400 HOUS 77009 3962 E1
700 HOUS 77007 3823 E7
700 HOUS 77009 3823 E6
1700 HOUS 77008 3823 E6
Studio Dr
800 LMQU 77568 4990 B1
Stuebner Ln
23500 HarC 77375 2965 A6

Stuebner Airline Dr
13900 HarC 77014 3401 B1
13900 HarC 77066 3401 B1
13900 HarC 77068 3401 A1
13900 HarC 77069 3401 A1
14000 HarC 77068 3257 A7
14000 HarC 77069 3257 A7
Stuebner Airline Rd
- HarC 77038 3543 E6
- HOUS 77038 3543 E6
- HOUS 77088 3543 E6
5600 HOUS 77091 3684 B6
7200 HOUS 77088 3684 B3
8400 HarC 77379 3110 E4
8600 HarC 77375 3110 D2
9800 HarC 77375 2965 A4
14300 HarC 77068 3257 A6
14300 HarC 77069 3257 A6
14900 HarC 77068 3256 E6
15700 HarC 77069 3256 E5
17100 HarC 77379 3256 B1
18200 HarC 77379 3111 A5
Stuebner Airline Rd FM-2920
8400 HarC 77379 3110 E3
8600 HarC 77375 3110 D2
9800 HarC 77375 2965 B7
Stuebner Park Ln
- HarC 77038 3543 C4
Sturbridge Dr
5400 HOUS 77056 3960 E4
Sturbridge Ln
3200 SGLD 77479 4368 C7
3200 SGLD 77479 4495 C1
Sturdivant St
12000 MDWP 77477 4237 E5
Stuyvesant Ln
5100 HOUS 77021 4104 A5
Styers St
100 HOUS 77022 3824 B3
Styling Ct
10 HOUS 77016 3686 D4
Styling Dr
5300 HOUS 77016 3686 D4
Substation Dr
- HarC 77571 4110 E4
Suburban
- HarC 77396 3547 B3
Suburban Rd
11300 HarC 77016 3547 B7
11300 HarC 77016 3687 B1
11300 HOUS 77016 3547 B7
11300 HOUS 77016 3687 B1
11400 HarC 77050 3547 B7
11900 HOUS 77050 3547 B6
Suburban St
4500 HOUS 77011 3964 B5
Suburban Garden Rd
12400 BKVL 77581 4375 C7
13000 PRLD 77581 4375 C7
13000 PRLD 77581 4502 C2
14600 PRLD 77584 4502 C3
Success Ct
- FBnC 77477 4369 C4
Success Ln
800 HarC 77336 3121 E7
Success Rd
2600 HarC 77068 3257 D5
Sudan St
5600 HOUS 77020 3825 D7
Sudbury Dr
1200 PASD 77504 4247 D6
Sudden Valley Ln
- FBnC 77478 4236 D6
E Suddley Castle St
7400 HarC 77095 3679 B1
N Suddley Castle St
14100 HarC 77095 3679 B1
S Suddley Castle St
14000 HarC 77041 3679 B1
14000 HarC 77095 3679 B1
W Suddley Castle St
7400 HarC 77095 3679 B2
Sudeley Ln
12300 HarC 77039 3545 E5
Sue Dr
1000 KMAH 77565 4509 D7
Sue Ln
- JRSV 77040 3540 D7
10 HarC 77562 3831 E3
10500 HOUS 77099 4237 D4
10500 HOUS 77478 4237 D4
10500 SGLD 77478 4237 D4
32000 MtgC 77362 2963 C1
Sue St
200 HOUS 77009 3824 C4
19100 HarC 77532 3411 D5
Sue Ann Ln
1400 HarC 77373 3114 B6
Sue Barnett Dr
700 HOUS 77018 3823 B3
1500 HOUS 77018 3822 E1
Sue Ellen St
4000 HOUS 77087 4104 D5
Sue Marie Ln
5200 HOUS 77018 3684 A7
5400 HOUS 77091 3684 A6
Suez St
5300 HOUS 77020 3964 C1
Suffield Ct
1400 HarC 77073 3259 C5
Suffield Glen Ct
4900 FBnC 77494 4092 C3
Suffield Glen Ln
7800 HarC 77338 3261 D3
26300 FBnC 77494 4092 E2
Suffield Park Ln
- HarC 77014 3402 A3
Suffolk
19100 MtgC 77357 2829 A4
Suffolk Dr
2000 HOUS 77019 3961 C6
2000 HOUS 77027 3961 C7
3500 HOUS 77027 4101 C1
Suffolk Bridge Ln
16900 HarC 77073 3259 A4
Suffolk Chase Ln
12800 HOUS 77077 3957 B5
Suffolk Woods Ln
- HarC 77047 4374 C3
Sugar Ln
17100 HarC 77090 3258 A4
17100 HOUS 77090 3258 A4
Sugar Run
2000 HOUS 77090 3258 A5
Sugar Wy
1200 HarC 77067 3402 D4

Sugar Bars Dr
4300 HarC 77546 4506 A6
Sugar Bear Dr
23000 HarC 77389 2967 A6
Sugar Bend Dr
30500 MtgC 77355 2815 C2
31000 MAGA 77355 2815 C1
31000 MtgC 77355 2669 C7
Sugarberry Cir
10 HOUS 77024 3959 C5
Sugarberry Wy
20900 HarC 77375 3110 C4
Sugarbloom Ln
21300 HarC 77375 3110 B3
Sugarblossom Ln
9600 FBnC 77478 4237 A2
Sugarbluff Ln
9800 FBnC 77478 4237 A2
Sugar Bow Dr
15000 FBnC 77478 4236 C3
Sugar Bowl Dr
11300 HarC 77375 3110 A7
Sugar Branch Dr
10200 HOUS 77036 4238 E2
10200 HOUS 77099 4238 D2
Sugarbridge Ln
20900 HarC 77375 3110 B3
Sugarbridge Tr
10100 FBnC 77478 4236 D4
Sugar Bush
1400 BYTN 77520 4113 B3
Sugar Bush Dr
5200 HOUS 77048 4374 E2
5300 HOUS 77048 4375 A2
Sugarbush Dr
5300 MtgC 77354 2673 E1
Sugarbush Ln
2600 FBnC 77459 4621 C7
Sugarbush Ridge Ln
11200 HarC 77089 4504 A1
Sugar Cane
2000 HarC 77090 3258 A5
2000 HOUS 77090 3258 A5
Sugar Cane Dr
8000 CmbC 77520 3835 D3
Sugar Cove
2000 HarC 77090 3258 B6
2000 HOUS 77090 3258 B6
Sugar Creek Blvd
100 SGLD 77478 4368 E2
Sugar Creek Dr
5400 LPRT 77571 4250 B2
Sugar Creek Ln
10 SGLD 77478 4368 E3
5900 HarC 77449 3677 A5
Sugar Creek Center Blvd
10 SGLD 77478 4368 D2
Sugar Crossing Ct
4100 SGLD 77478 4369 A5
Sugar Crossing Dr
1300 SGLD 77478 4369 A5
Sugar Crystal Ct
14900 FBnC 77478 4236 D3
Sugar Cup Ct
14900 FBnC 77478 4236 D3
Sugardale Ct
900 SGLD 77478 4237 B7
Sugar Dale Dr
12500 STAF 77477 4238 A6
Sugardale Dr
12200 MDWP 77477 4238 A6
12200 STAF 77477 4238 A6
Sugar Dock Ct
13800 HOUS 77044 3409 B4
Sugar Falls Ct
14900 FBnC 77478 4236 D3
Sugarfield Ct
900 SGLD 77478 4237 B7
Sugarfoot Ln
10 CNRO 77301 2384 A3
Sugarglen Ln
9800 HarC 77375 3110 A5
Sugar Grove Blvd
4800 STAF 77477 4238 A6
Sugar Grove Ct
10 WDLD 77382 2673 D4
11400 HarC 77066 3401 A5
Sugar Hill Dr
700 LPRT 77571 4250 B2
2100 DRPK 77536 4109 E6
5300 HOUS 77056 3960 E6
5700 HOUS 77057 3960 C4
10000 HOUS 77042 3958 E5
10000 HOUS 77042 3959 A5
Sugar Hollow Ct
- HarC 77377 3254 A4
Sugarhollow Ct
10300 FBnC 77478 4236 D3
Sugarhollow Dr
14900 FBnC 77478 4236 C3
Sugarhouse Ln
4000 FBnC 77469 4234 C5
Sugar Lakes Dr
900 SGLD 77478 4368 A3
Sugarland Dr
2300 FBnC 77545 4498 C5
Sugarland Howell Rd
6200 HarC 77082 4096 E5
6200 HarC 77083 4096 E5
8000 HOUS 77083 4096 E7
8800 FBnC 77083 4236 E2
9300 FBnC 77478 4236 E2
Sugar Leaf Tr
25900 HarC 77389 2965 E1
Sugar Line Ct
2700 SGLD 77479 4368 C7
Sugar Line Dr
2300 SGLD 77479 4368 C7
Sugarloaf Dr
1100 HarC 77379 3255 D2
Sugarloaf Bay Dr
18000 HarC 77429 3252 C7
N Sugar Maple Cir
18600 MAGA 77355 2815 A1
S Sugar Maple Cir
18600 MAGA 77355 2815 A1
Sugar Maple Ct
900 HarC 77073 3259 A3
3000 FRDW 77598 4630 C3
30600 MAGA 77355 2815 A1
Sugar Maple Dr
- MAGA 77355 2815 A1
9500 HarC 77064 3541 A4
Sugarmeade Ln
9900 HarC 77375 3110 B4
E Sugar Meadow Dr
17200 HarC 77090 3258 A4

STREET
Block City ZIP Map# Grid

W Sugar Meadow Dr
17200 HarC 77090 3258 A4
Sugar Mill Cir
14300 HarC 77095 3539 A7
Sugar Mill Dr
2400 SGLD 77479 4368 C7
Sugar Mist Ct
14900 FBnC 77478 4236 D3
Sugar Mott Dr
- FBnC 77478 4236 D4
Sugar Mountain Ct
900 SGLD 77478 4237 B7
Sugar Oaks Ct
7000 FBnC 77469 4095 C5
30200 MtgC 77355 2815 D1
Sugar Oaks St
38600 MtgC 77355 2815 C1
Sugar Orchard Ln
20900 HarC 77375 3110 B4
Sugar Peak Dr
14900 FBnC 77478 4236 C4
Sugar Pine Cir
1900 HarC 77090 3258 A5
2000 HOUS 77090 3258 A5
Sugar Pine Dr
16700 HarC 77090 3258 A4
16700 HOUS 77090 3258 A5
17500 HarC 77090 3257 E3
Sugar Pine Ln
16600 HarC 77090 3258 A5
16600 HOUS 77090 3258 A5
Sugar Pine Pl
8500 HarC 77375 3110 D2
Sugar Pine Square Dr
2000 HarC 77090 3258 B6
Sugar Pl Ct
10600 FBnC 77478 4236 C4
Sugar Pl Dr
15000 FBnC 77478 4236 C4
Sugarplum Cir
700 SGLD 77478 4368 B1
Sugarplum Ln
14700 HOUS 77062 4379 E7
Sugar Ridge Blvd
12700 STAF 77477 4238 D7
12900 STAF 77477 4369 E1
Sugar Ridge Dr
16000 HarC 77095 3678 C1
Sugar River
17100 HarC 77090 3258 B6
17100 HOUS 77090 3258 A4
Sugar Sands Ct
15000 FBnC 77478 4236 C3
Sugar Sands Dr
14900 FBnC 77478 4236 D3
Sugar Spice Dr
- FBnC 77478 4236 C4
Sugar Springs Dr
12000 HOUS 77077 3957 E6
12000 HOUS 77077 3958 B7
Sugar Stone Dr
14900 FBnC 77478 4236 D4
Sugar Sweet Dr
14900 FBnC 77478 4236 D4
Sugar Top
2000 HarC 77090 3258 B6
2000 HOUS 77090 3258 B6
Sugar Trace Dr
10500 FBnC 77478 4236 C4
Sugar Tree Ct
9700 HarC 77070 3255 B5
Sugar Tree Dr
16000 HarC 77070 3255 B5
Sugar Valley Ln
25300 HarC 77373 3114 D2
Sugarvine Ct
4300 LGCY 77573 4630 E6
4300 LGCY 77573 4631 A6
Sugarvine Ln
10000 HarC 77375 3110 B4
Sugarwater Pl
10 WDLD 77381 2820 E2
Sugarwood Ct
8500 HarC 77338 3262 B3
Sugar Wood Dr
2800 LGCY 77573 4632 E2
2900 LGCY 77573 4633 A2
38700 MAGA 77355 2815 C1
38700 MtgC 77355 2815 C1
Sugarwood Dr
2700 SGLD 77478 4368 D5
Suhler Dr
- GLSN 77554 5109 A1
Suiter Wy
3200 PASD 77503 4108 B6
Sulky Trail Ct
15800 HOUS 77060 3544 C1
Sulky Trail St
200 HOUS 77060 3544 C2
Sulley Dr
4700 ALVN 77511 4867 D7
Sullins Wy
10 HOUS 77084 3818 B3
1700 HOUS 77058 4507 D3
Sullivan Ln
2400 DKSN 77539 4753 C1
Sullivan Rd
10600 LPRT 77571 4110 C7
20400 MtgC 77357 2828 B7
20600 MtgC 77357 2974 B1
Sullivan St
1800 PASD 77506 4107 D5
Sullivan Forest Dr
21400 MtgC 77365 2973 A4
Sullivan Oaks Dr
29700 MtgC 77386 2969 E2
Sullivans Ct
10 FBnC 77459 4621 D5
Sullivans Ln
10 FBnC 77459 4621 D5
Sullivans Lndg
10 FBnC 77459 4621 D6
Sullivans Wy
10 FBnC 77459 4621 D5
Sullivan Springs Dr
1400 FBnC 77494 3953 B4
Sully Ln
1300 HarC 77530 3829 C5
Sulpher Branch Bnd
36000 MtgC 77355 2815 D4
Sulphur Sprs
- FBnC 77459 4622 B5
Sulphur St
500 HOUS 77034 4246 D5
E Sulphur Creek Dr
38100 MtgC 77355 2815 D1
N Sulphur Creek Dr
30500 MtgC 77355 2815 C1
S Sulphur Creek Dr
30500 MtgC 77355 2815 D1
W Sulphur Creek Dr
38000 MtgC 77355 2815 C1
Sulphur Springs Dr
11900 HarC 77067 3401 E4
Sulphur Stream Ct
17600 HarC 77095 3537 C2
Sulphur Stream Dr
10200 HarC 77095 3537 D3
Sul Ross St
100 HOUS 77002 3963 A7
200 HOUS 77006 3962 D7
1700 HOUS 77098 3962 B7
3200 HOUS 77098 3961 E7
4000 HOUS 77027 3961 C7
Sultan Dr
8300 HOUS 77078 3688 A7
Sultana Dr
- FBnC 77083 4096 B7
Sumac Dr
3000 PRLD 77584 4502 D5
S Sumac Dr
6100 PRLD 77584 4502 D5
Sumac Ln
22200 HarC 77389 2967 D7
22200 HarC 77389 3112 D1
Sumac Park Dr
3100 FRDW 77598 4630 C3
Sumal Cir
8000 HarC 77521 3833 D2
Sumerlin St
9600 HOUS 77075 4377 B3
Summer Brk
1100 FBnC 77479 4494 A6
Summer Cir
18400 MtgC 77365 2972 B5
Summer Ct
10 WDLD 77381 2674 C7
18400 MtgC 77365 2972 A5
Summer Ln
1900 MSCY 77489 4370 C7
1900 MSCY 77489 4497 C1
3700 BYTN 77521 3974 A1
4100 PRLD 77584 4503 B4
19300 MtgC 77357 2827 C4
28200 MtgC 77362 2963 C2
Summer St
1100 HOUS 77007 3963 A2
2400 HOUS 77007 3962 E2
Summerall Ct
2000 FBnC 77469 4234 C7
Summer Anne Dr
18600 HarC 77346 3264 E7
Summer Ash Ln
- HarC 77379 3111 B4
8900 FBnC 77479 4494 C4
14000 HarC 77044 3549 E3
Summer Bay Cir
2200 SGLD 77478 4368 E6
Summer Bay Ct
2200 SGLD 77478 4368 D6
Summer Bay Dr
3100 SGLD 77478 4368 E6
Summer Bay Ln
7500 RSBG 77469 4492 C6
Summerbell Ln
9200 HOUS 77074 4239 A2
Summerbend Hollow Ln
26600 FBnC 77494 4092 C3
Summerberry Ln
10000 HarC 77375 3110 B4
Summerbloom Ln
- PRLD 77583 4500 C5
Summerblossom Ln
2200 HOUS 77077 3957 A6
Summer Bluff Ct
- HarC 77377 3253 E3
Summer Breeze Ct
16100 MtgC 77302 2678 D4
Summer Breeze Dr
100 LPRT 77571 4250 A4
9600 PRLD 77584 4501 B3
Summer Breeze Ln
22200 HarC 77375 3109 E1
Summer Breezes Ln
2300 HarC 77067 3402 A5
Summer Briar Ct
15500 HOUS 77489 4371 D5
Summer Bridge Ln
6800 HarC 77379 3111 B3
Summer Brook Ct
8000 FBnC 77479 4494 A6
11700 PRLD 77584 4500 D3
Summerbrook Ct
10300 HarC 77038 3543 C3
12200 HarC 77066 3401 B5
Summer Brook Dr
14500 HOUS 77044 3408 E7
Summerbrook Dr
- HarC 77066 3401 B5
10500 HarC 77038 3543 C2
Summer Cape Cir
1000 LGCY 77573 4633 A2
Summer Cape Ct
2900 LGCY 77573 4633 A3
Summer Cliff Ct
18300 HarC 77377 3254 B2
Summer Cliff Ln
18600 HarC 77377 3254 B2
N Summer Cloud Dr
10 WDLD 77381 2674 D6
S Summer Cloud Dr
10 WDLD 77381 2674 D6
Summer Cloud Ln
1300 PRLD 77545 4499 E2
Summer Cove Ct
3700 HarC 77546 4506 A7
Summer Creek Dr
2500 PRLD 77584 4500 C3
8800 HarC 77379 3255 E3
Summer Creek Ln
200 RSBG 77469 4492 C6
Summer Crest Cir
10 WDLD 77381 2821 A6
Summer Crest Dr
500 FBnC 77469 4492 C7
500 RSBG 77469 4492 C7
Summercrest Dr
3000 BzaC 77584 4501 B6
Summer Crossing Ln
16900 HarC 77084 3678 C6
Summer Cypress Ct
16700 HarC 77429 3396 D1
Summer Cypress Dr
14400 HarC 77429 3396 D1
Summerdale Dr
7500 RSBG 77469 4492 C6
11900 HOUS 77077 3958 A5
Summerdale Ln
8900 MtgC 77302 2530 C4
Summer Dawn Ln
16200 HarC 77095 3678 C1
Summer Dawn Pl
16900 HarC 77095 3678 A1
Summer Dew Ln
16200 HarC 77095 3678 C1
Summerfair Ct
13900 HOUS 77044 3550 B2
Summer Falls
5300 HarC 77041 3679 E6
Summerfern Ct
7900 HarC 77433 3537 A7
Summerfern Ln
11400 HarC 77433 3395 D7
Summerfield Ct
3100 BzaC 77584 4501 E6
Summerfield Dr
3800 BzaC 77584 4501 D6
3900 PRLD 77584 4501 D6
Summerfield Ln
5200 HarC 77379 3257 B2
Summerfield Pl
1800 SGLD 77478 4237 C5
Summerfield Ridge Ct
3000 FBnC 77478 4235 E7
3000 FBnC 77478 4236 A7
Summerfield Ridge Dr
16800 FBnC 77478 4236 A7
Summer Forest Dr
5000 HOUS 77091 3682 E6
5000 HOUS 77091 3683 A6
Summer Forrest Dr
1300 FBnC 77479 4494 A6
Summer Garden Dr
14300 HarC 77083 4096 E5
Summer Gardens Dr
600 FBnC 77469 4492 D7
600 RSBG 77469 4492 D7
Summergate Dr
1600 CNRO 77304 2383 A2
23200 HarC 77373 3115 C6
Summer Glen Ln
7500 HOUS 77072 4097 C6
Summer Glow Dr
- HarC 77083 4096 E6
Summer Green Ln
22900 HarC 77373 3114 E6
Summer Grove Cir
8000 HarC 77379 3256 A3
Summer Harvest Dr
- HarC 77064 3540 B1
Summer Haven Cir
300 LGCY 77573 4633 C1
Summer Haven Dr
300 LGCY 77573 4633 B1
Summer Haven Ln
2500 FBnC 77469 4365 B5
Summerhaze Cir
10 WDLD 77382 2675 A5
E Summerhaze Cir
100 WDLD 77382 2675 A5
Summerhaze Ct
10 WDLD 77382 2675 A5
Summer Heath Ct
- HarC 77044 3549 D3
Summer Hill Dr
3600 SGLD 77479 4495 A5
Summerhill Dr
10300 HarC 77070 3399 B6
Summerhill Ln
11500 BKHV 77024 3959 D2
11500 PNPV 77024 3959 D2
Summer Hill Creek Trail Dr
- HarC 77346 3408 E2
Summerhill Manor Ln
5200 FBnC 77494 4093 A2
Summer Hills Blvd
18400 MtgC 77365 2972 A6
Summer Hollow Dr
16900 FBnC 77478 4235 E7
Summer Island Wy
19200 FBnC 77469 4234 E1
Summer Knoll Ln
14800 HOUS 77044 3550 A1
15000 HOUS 77044 3549 C1
Summer Lake Dr
11200 MtgC 77354 2671 D5
14500 HOUS 77044 3408 D6
14500 HOUS 77044 3409 A7
Summer Lake Canyon Dr
13100 HOUS 77044 3408 D6
13200 HOUS 77044 3409 A7
Summer Lake Home Dr
14600 HOUS 77044 3409 A7
Summer Lake Ranch Dr
12300 HarC 77044 3408 C7
13000 HarC 77044 3408 D7
13200 HOUS 77044 3409 A7
Summer Lakes
4500 SGLD 77479 4496 A1
4700 MSCY 77459 4496 B1
Summer Lakes Ln
7400 RSBG 77469 4492 B6
Summer Lake Trace Dr
14500 HOUS 77044 3408 E7
Summerland Cir
14900 HarC 77429 3397 C2
Summerland Ct
2000 FBnC 77469 4365 C1
Summerland Dr
2100 FBnC 77469 4365 B1
3100 BzaC 77578 4501 C7
N Summerland Dr
2100 FBnC 77469 4365 C1
Summerland Ridge Ct
5300 HarC 77041 3679 E6
Summerland Ridge Ln
12100 HarC 77041 3679 E6
Summer Lark Pl
10 WDLD 77382 2674 D4
Summer Laurel Ln
9500 HarC 77088 3682 C1
Summerleaf Ln
14400 HOUS 77077 3956 D6
Summerlee Ct
4300 MSCY 77459 4496 C3
E Summerlin
12400 CNRO 77302 2531 A3
N Summerlin
10200 CNRO 77302 2531 A3
S Summerlin
10200 CNRO 77302 2531 A4
W Summerlin
12300 CNRO 77302 2531 A4
Summerlin Dr
19600 HarC 77449 3677 A5
19700 HarC 77449 3676 E5
Summerlyn Dr
- HarC 77053 4372 C5
Summer Lynn Pl
9600 HarC 77088 3682 C1
Summerlyn Point Ln
15200 HarC 77053 4372 D4
15200 HOUS 77053 4372 D4
Summer Manor Dr
3800 LGCY 77539 4633 D4
Summermeade Ln
- FBnC 77494 4093 E5
Summer Meadows Ct
10800 HarC 77064 3540 B2
Summer Mill Dr
12600 HarC 77070 3399 C5
Summer Mist Ct
500 RSBG 77469 4492 C7
Summer Mist Ln
- HarC 77095 3678 B2
Summer Moon Dr
11600 PRLD 77584 4500 D3
Summer Morning Ct
10 WDLD 77381 2820 E5
Summer Night Ln
300 RSBG 77469 4492 B7
Summer Oak Ct
5800 HarC 77379 3111 D7
Summer Oak Dr
4900 PASD 77505 4248 D7
Summer Oaks Dr
900 CNRO 77303 2237 C2
5900 HarC 77346 3264 D5
Summer Park Blvd
- CNRO 77303 2237 C3
Summer Park Dr
- MSCY 77477 4369 D4
800 FBnC 77477 4369 D4
Summer Park Ln
1200 HarC 77450 3954 A4
32300 MtgC 77385 2823 B6
Summer Pine Ct
200 CNRO 77304 2383 A5
Summer Pine Dr
23600 HarC 77373 3114 E5
Summer Pine Ln
22900 HarC 77373 3114 E6
Summer Pl Ct
400 LGCY 77573 4630 D7
Summer Pl Dr
1900 MSCY 77489 4370 C5
7800 HarC 77338 3261 D4
Summer Pl St
5300 LGCY 77573 4630 D7
Summer Point Ln
- HarC 77379 3111 C4
Summer Porch Dr
13100 HOUS 77044 3408 D6
Summer Port
10 WDLD 77381 2821 C4
Summerport Ln
- HOUS 77034 4378 C4
Summer Quail Dr
8200 HOUS 77489 4370 E7
Summer Rain Ct
900 CNRO 77303 2237 C3
E Summer Rain Ct
1900 HOUS 77339 3118 C7
W Summer Rain Ct
1900 HOUS 77339 3118 D3
Summer Rain Dr
10 PRLD 77581 4502 C1
1400 HOUS 77339 3118 C7
1600 FBnC 77479 4494 B4
2600 BzaC 77578 4501 A7
4900 CNRO 77303 2237 C3
Summer Reef Dr
1900 LGCY 77573 4509 A6
8200 HarC 77095 3537 E6
Summer Ridge Ct
15400 HOUS 77489 4371 D5
Summer Ridge Dr
4800 CNRO 77303 2237 C3
6400 HOUS 77489 4371 D5
Summer Ridge Ln
10000 CNRO 77302 2530 E4
E Summer Rose Ct
17300 HarC 77429 3252 D5
W Summer Rose Ct
17400 HarC 77429 3252 D5
Summer Rose Ln
- HarC 77379 3111 D4
13200 MtgC 77302 2530 C4
14200 HOUS 77077 3956 E6
Summer Run Dr
1000 HarC 77064 3540 D3
Summers Dr
900 MSCY 77489 4370 D5
Summerset Pk
- HarC 77044 3549 C2
Summerset Wy
19800 HarC 77094 3954 E3
19800 HarC 77094 3955 A3
Summerset Estates Blvd
16100 MtgC 77302 2678 E4
Summer Shore Dr
2100 LGCY 77573 4509 A6
7500 RSBG 77469 4492 C7
Summer Shower Ct
22000 HarC 77433 3250 E5
Summer Shower Dr
22100 HarC 77433 3250 E4
Summerside Dr
5200 FBnC 77450 4094 A3
Summer Sky Ln
- HarC 77044 3549 D3
Summer Snow Cir
13200 HarC 77041 3679 C6
Summer Snow Dr
5200 HarC 77041 3679 C6
Summer Sprig Rd
10 WDLD 77380 2822 B6
Summer Spring Dr
2500 HarC 77373 3114 E4
Summer Spring Ln
5400 BzaC 77583 4623 E4
Summer Springs Dr
11700 PRLD 77584 4500 D3
Summer Star Ct
- HarC 77429 3252 E7
- HarC 77429 3253 A6
N Summer Star Ct
10 WDLD 77380 2968 A4
S Summer Star Ct
10 WDLD 77380 2968 A4
Summerstone Ct
11600 HarC 77377 3254 E5
E Summer Storm Cir
10 WDLD 77381 2675 A7
W Summer Storm Cir
10 WDLD 77381 2674 E7
10 WDLD 77381 2675 A6
Summerstorm Ln
- HarC 77044 3550 A3
- HOUS 77044 3550 A3
3100 LGCY 77573 4633 B2
Summer Storm Pl
10 WDLD 77381 2674 E6
Summer Stream Dr
14600 HOUS 77044 3408 D6
Summer Sun Dr
- HarC 77090 3258 E7
Summer Sun Ln
9400 PRLD 77584 4501 C3
Summer Sunset Dr
14900 HarC 77346 3408 A7
Summersweet Pl
2800 WDLD 77380 2821 C7
Summer Terrace Dr
1300 FBnC 77479 4494 A6
Summertime Dr
2700 HOUS 77045 4242 B7
Summerton Dr
27900 MtgC 77365 2971 B7
27900 MtgC 77386 2971 A7
Summer Trace Ct
2600 FBnC 77469 4365 B5
6800 HarC 77379 3111 C3
Summer Trace Ln
400 FBnC 77469 4365 A5
20900 HarC 77379 3111 C3
Summer Trail Dr
7300 FBnC 77479 4493 E5
8000 HarC 77040 3541 D7
Summertree Dr
100 HarC 77562 3832 C2
8200 HarC 77040 3541 C7
Summer Valley Ln
9100 FBnC 77469 4235 A2
Summer View Ct
- CNRO 77303 2237 C2
Summer Villa Ct
15000 HarC 77044 3550 A3
Summer Villa Ln
13400 HarC 77044 3549 E2
13500 HarC 77044 3550 A3
Summerville Dr
8500 FBnC 77469 4616 D1
Summerville Ln
- HarC 77084 3679 B4
6100 HarC 77041 3679 B5
Summerville Lake Dr
16000 HarC 77377 3254 B7
Summer Walk Ln
25100 FBnC 77494 3953 A6
Summerwalk Pl
10 WDLD 77381 2674 C6
Summerway Ln
14200 HarC 77014 3401 C1
Summer Wind Ct
8100 FBnC 77479 4494 C4
Summerwind Ct
3300 BzaC 77584 4501 B4
Summer Wind Dr
2200 FBnC 77479 4494 C5
16200 HarC 77090 3258 C6
Summer Winds Dr
100 LPRT 77571 4250 A4
Summer Wood Blvd
900 CNRO 77303 2237 C2
900 MtgC 77303 2237 C2
Summerwood Ln
3300 BzaC 77584 4374 B7
11600 HOUS 77013 3966 D2
Summerwood Glenn
12600 HarC 77041 3679 D4
Summerwood Lakes Ct
12800 HarC 77044 3549 D1
Summerwood Lakes Dr
- HarC 77044 3550 A2
14300 HarC 77044 3549 D1
Summerwood Trail Dr
- HarC 77373 3115 B3
Summit
10 HarC 77493 3813 D4
10 KATY 77493 3813 D4
Summit Cr
5800 FBnC 77479 4493 E2
Summit Dr
10 CNRO 77303 2237 D6
1000 TMBL 77375 2964 A7
6200 PRLD 77584 4502 D6
Summit Ln
3300 MSCY 77459 4496 D3
Summit Pl
8200 HOUS 77071 4239 D6
Summit St
4700 HOUS 77018 3823 B1
Summit Bay Dr
11300 PRLD 77584 4500 D3
Summit Bend Ln
9700 FBnC 77494 4092 C5
Summit Bridge Ln
10300 HarC 77070 3399 B3
S Summit Canyon Ct
10200 HarC 77095 3537 C2
E Summit Canyon Dr
10200 HarC 77095 3537 E2
S Summit Canyon Dr
17200 HarC 77095 3537 D3
Summit Cliff Ct
- FBnC 77469 4094 E7
Summit Creek Dr
6100 FBnC 77479 4493 E3
6200 SGLD 77479 4493 E3
Summit Falls Ct
3000 HOUS 77345 3119 E2
Summithill Pl
10 WDLD 77381 2820 C2
Summit Hollow Dr
5300 HarC 77084 3678 A6
Summit Lake Dr
10 HOUS 77339 3119 A7
Summit Lodge Dr
5000 HarC 77449 3676 D6
Summit Meadow Dr
2100 HOUS 77489 4371 A6
Summit Mist Ct
- HarC 77044 3549 D3
Summit Mist Dr
2100 CNRO 77304 2383 A1
Summit Oaks Ln
16900 HarC 77379 3256 A4
Summit Park Dr
- HOUS 77077 3956 E5
Summit Pass Ln
14700 HarC 77396 3547 E2
Summit Pines Dr
8600 HarC 77346 3265 D5
Summit Ridge Ct
6500 HOUS 77085 4371 D1
Summit Ridge Dr
- HOUS 77035 4240 C7
- HOUS 77085 4240 C7
13500 HOUS 77085 4371 C1
E Summitry Cir
- HOUS 77449 3815 B7
N Summitry Cir
- HOUS 77449 3815 B6
W Summitry Cir
- HOUS 77449 3815 B6
Summits Edge Ln
4400 FBnC 77450 4093 D2
Summit Trail Rd
- HOUS 77532 3410 A7
18600 HarC 77532 3410 A6
Summit Valley Dr
3200 HarC 77082 4096 C3
3200 HOUS 77082 4096 C3
Summit Wy Ct
2300 HOUS 77339 3118 C6
Sumner Dr
4400 HOUS 77018 3683 C7
Sumner Isle Ct
6600 HarC 77379 3256 D3
Sumners Creek Ct
23200 FBnC 77494 3953 D7
23300 FBnC 77494 4093 D1
Sumpter Ct
2000 LGCY 77573 4631 A6
Sumpter St
2000 HOUS 77026 3963 E1
3000 HOUS 77026 3964 A1
3600 HOUS 77020 3964 B1
Sun Ct
600 FRDW 77546 4629 A5
Sun Rd
14600 HarC 77396 3547 A1
14600 HOUS 77396 3547 A1
Sunbather Ln
11800 GLSN 77554 5220 D7
Sun Beam Ct
2700 PRLD 77584 4501 B3
Sunbeam Pl
10 WDLD 77381 2821 A2
Sunbeam St
4700 HOUS 77033 4243 C5
4700 HOUS 77051 4243 C5
5300 HOUS 77033 4244 A5
Sunbeam River Dr
16000 HarC 77084 3678 D6
Sunbird Ct
10 WDLD 77380 2968 A1
2600 PRLD 77584 4501 C3
Sunbird Dr
2600 HarC 77084 3815 E4
Sunblaze Ct
25200 WlrC 77447 2813 D1
Sunbluff Ct
14400 HarC 77429 3397 A1
Sunbonnet Dr
9100 PRLD 77584 4501 C3
Sunbonnet Ln
7500 HarC 77064 3541 E5
7500 HarC 77064 3542 A5
Sunbriar Ln
17500 HarC 77095 3537 E5
Sunbridge Ln
19800 HarC 77094 3954 E3
Sunbright Ct
5300 HarC 77041 3679 C6
Sunbright Dr
13200 HarC 77041 3679 C6
Sunbrook Dr
12400 BKVL 77581 4375 A6
Sunburst Dr
3600 BzaC 77578 4501 B7
3600 BzaC 77578 4625 B1
Sunburst Ln
2400 PRLD 77584 4501 D3
Sunburst St
4500 BLAR 77401 4101 B2
31700 MtgC 77354 2817 A1
Sunburst Wy
18400 HarC 77346 3408 C1
Sunburst Falls Dr
11400 HarC 77396 3407 D7
11400 HarC 77396 3408 A7
11500 HarC 77346 3408 A7
Sunburst Meadow Dr
7200 HarC 77083 4096 D6
Sunburst Trail Dr
7500 HarC 77433 3677 E1
7600 HarC 77433 3537 C7
Sunburst View Dr
19000 HarC 77433 3537 B6
Sunbury Ln
8100 HarC 77095 3539 A6
Sunbury St
8100 HOUS 77028 3826 D2
Sunbury Springs Dr
16900 HarC 77379 3256 E1
Sun Canyon Ct
- HarC 77044 3549 D3
12000 HarC 77377 3254 E3
13300 FBnC 77478 4366 E2
Sunchase Ct
3000 HarC 77449 3815 D5
Sunchase Wy
20100 HarC 77449 3815 E4
Sun City Ct
3000 MSCY 77459 4497 A2
10300 HOUS 77099 4237 D2
Sun City Ln
100 PNVL 77304 2237 A4
Sunclair Park Ln
1400 FBnC 77479 4493 D1
Suncliff Ln
22400 MtgC 77365 2973 B3
Suncoast Dr
20200 HarC 77449 3815 D4
Suncove Ln
2600 PRLD 77584 4501 D3
19500 HarC 77346 3265 D5
Sun Creek Dr
20900 HOUS 77450 3954 C2
Suncreek Ln
2400 PRLD 77584 4501 D3
Suncrest Ct
6300 FBnC 77494 4093 D5
Suncrest Estates Ct
11200 MtgC 77385 2823 A6
Suncroft Dr
12000 HOUS 77045 4242 D7
Sundale Rd
13000 HarC 77038 3542 E3
E Sundance Cir
10 WDLD 77382 2673 E5
W Sundance Cir
100 WDLD 77382 2673 D5
Sundance Ct
7900 HarC 77521 3833 B3
12000 STAF 77477 4237 D6
Sun Dance Dr
9400 PRLD 77584 4501 C3
Sundance Dr
- WDLD 77382 2673 D5
19800 HarC 77346 3265 A4
Sundance Creek Ln
22300 HarC 77375 3110 A1
Sundance Hollow Ct
25600 FBnC 77494 4093 A1
Sundance Hollow Ln
4800 FBnC 77494 4093 A1
Sundance Meadows Ln
7000 FBnC 77469 4094 C5
Sundance Point Ln
- HarC 77377 3254 A3
Sundance Spring Dr
24400 MtgC 77365 2972 D7
Sundance Springs Ln
20600 HarC 77379 3111 B4
Sundance Valley Dr
800 HarC 77450 3953 E2
Sundance View Ln
- FBnC 77469 4493 A3
19500 HarC 77433 3537 B6
Sundance Woods Ct
- MtgC 77386 2823 D7
- MtgC 77386 2969 C1
Sunday House Ct
2500 PRLD 77584 4501 C3
Sunderland Dr
1500 SGLD 77479 4367 C6
Sunderland Rd
8500 HOUS 77028 3687 D6
8600 HOUS 77078 3687 D6
Sundew Cir
9900 HarC 77070 3255 B5
Sundew Ct
100 MtgC 77355 2960 B3
9300 HarC 77070 3255 C5
Sundew Dr
9700 HarC 77070 3255 C5
Sundew Cove Ct
12500 HarC 77041 3679 E3
Sundown
- HarC 77039 3545 C7
- HarC 77093 3545 C7
- HOUS 77039 3545 C7
Sundown Ct
4600 MSCY 77459 4497 D4
Sundown Dr
7300 HOUS 77028 3687 A6
8800 HOUS 77016 3687 A6
9000 PRLD 77584 4501 C3
9200 HOUS 77016 3686 E6
Sundown Mdw
500 HarC 77532 3411 B5
Sundown St
27300 MtgC 77372 2683 D2
Sundown Canyon Ct
5300 FBnC 77494 4093 A6
Sundown Canyon Ln
25200 FBnC 77494 4093 B2
Sundown Cove Ln
26300 FBnC 77494 4092 E3
Sundowner Ct
5400 HarC 77041 3679 C6
Sundowner Dr
13400 HarC 77041 3679 B6
Sundown Pass Dr
2900 HarC 77373 3115 A5
Sundown Wy Dr
3900 HarC 77449 3815 D2
Sundrop Ln
17400 HOUS 77084 3816 D6
Sunfall Creek Ln
13900 HarC 77396 3547 D2
Sunfield Dr
16700 HOUS 77396 3406 A4
Sunfire Ln
2400 PRLD 77584 4501 D3
Sunfish Dr
2500 PRLD 77584 4501 C3
Sunfish Ln
11300 HarC 77067 3402 A6
Sunfisher Ct E
25300 WlrC 77447 2813 D1
Sun Flare Ln
2600 PRLD 77584 4501 D3
Sunflower Dr
1500 MSCY 77489 4370 C3
1500 STAF 77477 4370 C3
1500 STAF 77489 4370 C3
10400 MtgC 77318 2237 B1
Sunflower Hl
15200 HarC 77049 3690 C6
Sunflower Rd
30900 MtgC 77354 2670 A7
Sunflower St
4000 HOUS 77051 4243 C2
4600 HOUS 77033 4243 D2
7500 BzaC 77584 4627 B4
8500 HarC 77562 3832 C2
Sunflower Chase
20100 HarC 77449 3815 E4
Sunflower Grove Ct
18100 HarC 77346 3408 E2
Sunflower Grove Dr
6900 HarC 77346 3408 E1
7000 HarC 77346 3409 A1
Sunflower Springs Ct
25500 HarC 77373 3114 B5
Sunforest Dr
5800 HOUS 77092 3682 D6
W Sunforest Dr
5800 HOUS 77092 3682 D6
Sunforest Ln
8800 PRLD 77584 4501 D3
Sungail Dr
1500 MtgC 77386 2969 A2
Sungate Dr
8900 PRLD 77584 4501 C3
Sungate Ln
12400 HOUS 77071 4239 D7

Houston Street Index

STREET
Block City ZIP Map# Grid

Sun Glen Blvd
- HarC 77449 3815 E4
19900 HarC 77084 3815 E4
Sun Glen Ct
3000 HarC 77449 3815 E4
9000 PRLD 77584 4501 D3
Sun Glen Dr
2500 PRLD 77584 4501 D3
Sungold Dr
15500 HarC 77095 3538 E5
Sun Harbor Dr
14200 HOUS 77062 4379 E7
14900 HOUS 77062 4506 C2
14900 HOUS 77062 4507 A1
Sun Haven Dr
21000 HarC 77449 3676 D3
Sun Haven Ln
8800 PRLD 77584 4501 D3
Sunhill Ct
2700 PRLD 77584 4501 B3
Sun Hill Dr
14200 HarC 77083 4096 E6
Sun King Dr
8800 PRLD 77584 4501 D3
Sun Kiss Ln
14900 HarC 77082 4096 C2
Sunlake Dr
9200 PRLD 77584 4501 C3
Sunlamp Ct
16400 HarC 77095 3538 B4
Sunland Ln
- HarC 77389 2966 B1
Sunland Gardens Ln
13600 HarC 77044 3550 A2
13700 HOUS 77044 3550 A3
Sunlight Ct
9000 PRLD 77584 4501 C3
Sunlight Ln
2400 PRLD 77584 4501 D3
7500 HarC 77095 3538 B7
7500 HarC 77095 3678 B1
Sunlight Wy
16600 HOUS 77058 4507 D2
Sunlight Hill Ct
- HarC 77379 3112 C5
Sunlight Peak Cir
17100 HarC 77346 3408 D4
Sunlight Peak Ln
12200 HarC 77346 3408 B3
Sunlight Terrace Ln
- HarC 77044 3549 C3
Sunlit Bay Dr
11200 PRLD 77584 4500 D2
Sunlit Forest Dr
10 WDLD 77381 2821 B6
E Sunlit Forest Dr
10 WDLD 77381 2821 B6
Sunlit Grove St
10 WDLD 77382 2674 C5
Sunlit Mesa Ct
- LMQU 77568 4872 B4
Sunlit Orchard Dr
6300 HOUS 77072 4097 D4
Sunlit Park Dr
9100 HarC 77396 3406 E6
9100 HarC 77396 3407 A6
Sunlit Pass Lp
4300 HarC 77396 3407 A6
Sunlit Ridge Dr
2200 HOUS 77045 4242 D7
Sunlit Wood Wy
12400 HOUS 77082 4097 D1
Sun Lodge Ct
18700 HarC 77073 3403 C3
Sun Lodge Dr
- HarC 77073 3403 C3
Sun Loft Ct
10 WDLD 77382 2674 C5
Sun Manor Ln
- HarC 77044 3550 A2
Sunmeadow Blvd
10 FRDW 77546 4628 E7
10 FRDW 77546 4629 A7
Sun Meadow Dr
10 FRDW 77546 4628 E7
10 FRDW 77546 4629 A7
4100 HOUS 77072 4098 B4
Sunmill Ct
15800 HarC 77429 3397 A1
Sunmoore Ct
8600 HOUS 77088 3683 E1
Sunmount Pines Dr
13700 HarC 77083 4097 A7
Sunningdale Ln
3400 FBnC 77459 4621 C5
Sunny Dr
1000 HarC 77037 3685 A1
1200 HOUS 77037 3685 B1
2200 HarC 77093 3685 D1
3400 BYTN 77521 3973 B3
Sunny Ln
5400 HarC 77521 3832 C7
Sunnybank
- HarC 77068 3257 A5
Sunny Bay Ct
2000 LGCY 77573 4509 A6
Sunnybrook Dr
800 BYTN 77521 3972 E3
Sunny Brook Ln
9000 PRLD 77584 4501 C3
Sunnycircle St
400 HTCK 77563 4988 C3
Sunnycoast Ln
9700 PRLD 77584 4501 B4
Sunnycove Dr
4600 HarC 77084 3678 E7
Sunny Creek Dr
11400 HarC 77066 3401 A7
Sunnycreek Ln
2700 PRLD 77584 4501 B3
Sunnycrest Dr
2600 TXCY 77590 4874 E4
Sunnycrest St
6000 HOUS 77087 4104 C6
Sunnydale Dr
3000 HOUS 77051 4243 A6
Sunny Day Dr
14300 HarC 77083 4096 E6
Sunny Field Dr
8700 HOUS 77099 4237 D1
Sunny Gallop Dr
8600 HarC 77375 2965 D3
Sunnygate Dr
5700 HarC 77373 3115 E7
5800 HarC 77373 3116 A7
6200 HarC 77373 3261 A1
Sunny Glen Ct
24400 HOUS 77336 3266 B2

Sunny Glen Dr
24200 HOUS 77336 3266 B2
Sunny Grove Dr
14600 HarC 77070 3398 D1
Sunnyhaven
- HarC 77068 3257 A5
Sunny Heath Ln
14300 HarC 77044 3550 A3
14300 HOUS 77044 3550 A3
Sunnyhill St
7800 HOUS 77088 3683 B2
Sunny Isle Ln
1200 LGCY 77573 4633 B3
Sunny Knoll Ct
3100 HOUS 77339 3119 B7
Sunnyland St
1200 HOUS 77023 4104 C2
Sunny Leaf Ln
19200 HarC 77449 3677 B6
Sunny Meadows Ln
- HarC 77084 3816 A4
3200 HarC 77449 3816 A3
Sunny Morning Ct
16100 MtgC 77302 2679 B3
Sunnynook St
10 HOUS 77076 3684 C4
Sunny Oak Dr
100 HarC 77336 2975 E5
Sunny Oaks Ct
3700 HOUS 77345 3120 A3
Sunny Oaks Pl
10 WDLD 77385 2676 B3
Sunny Oaks Wy
7500 HarC 77095 3538 C7
Sunny Orchard Dr
3700 FBnC 77469 4366 D1
Sunny Pines Ct
16200 MtgC 77302 2678 E4
Sunny Point Dr
8800 HarC 77379 3255 E4
Sunny Ridge Dr
8500 HarC 77095 3538 D5
Sunnyridge Dr
9100 HarC 77095 3538 D4
Sunny River Ln
500 FBnC 77469 4365 B5
Sunny Shores Dr
2500 PRLD 77584 4501 C3
20000 HarC 77346 3265 B3
Sunnyside Ct
5900 FBnC 77469 4493 A7
Sunnyside Ln
2700 PRLD 77584 4501 B3
Sunnyside St
200 HOUS 77076 3684 D5
E Sunnyside St
10 HOUS 77076 3684 E5
300 HOUS 77076 3685 B4
W Sunnyside St
100 HOUS 77076 3684 C5
300 HOUS 77091 3684 C5
E Sunny Slope Cir
10 WDLD 77381 2674 E6
N Sunny Slope Cir
10 WDLD 77381 2674 E6
Sunny Springs Ln
- HarC 77433 3396 B6
Sunny Square Ct
6700 FBnC 77469 4095 D5
Sunny Stream Dr
11700 HarC 77375 3109 E7
Sunny Terrace Ln
- HOUS 77075 4376 D5
Sunny Trail Ct
4700 SGLD 77479 4494 E1
Sunny Trail Ln
17500 SGLD 77479 4494 E1
Sunny Vale Dr
3200 HOUS 77345 3120 A4
Sunnyvale Ln
10 MNVL 77583 4624 D4
6900 FBnC 77583 4622 E7
Sunnyvale Forest Dr
7900 HarC 77088 3682 D1
Sunny Valley Ln
10100 FBnC 77478 4236 C3
Sunnyview Av
100 FRDW 77546 4505 C7
100 FRDW 77546 4629 B1
Sunnyview Ct
9400 PRLD 77584 4501 C3
Sunny View St
- HarC 77532 3411 C5
Sunnyview Wy
18200 HarC 77532 3411 C5
Sunnywood Dr
8700 HOUS 77088 3684 B1
9100 HOUS 77088 3544 B6
9300 HOUS 77038 3544 B6
9400 HarC 77038 3544 B6
Sun Oil Rd
- MTBL 77520 3696 E7
Sun Park Dr
500 FRDW 77546 4629 D3
2200 CNRO 77301 2383 D2
2200 CNRO 77303 2383 D2
Sun Pass Dr
18900 HarC 77377 3254 C1
Sunperch
3000 MtgC 77384 2675 E6
3000 MtgC 77384 2676 A6
Sunperch Ct
9400 PRLD 77584 4501 C3
Sun Prairie Dr
800 HarC 77090 3258 C7
Sunray Ct
2500 PRLD 77584 4501 C3
Sunray Ln
3700 PASD 77503 4108 C5
Sunridge Ct
9200 PRLD 77584 4501 C3
Sunridge Wy
6000 HOUS 77087 4245 A1
Sunrise Blvd
- BzaC 77584 4501 C3
- PRLD 77584 4501 C3
Sunrise Bnd
5000 MSCY 77459 4621 B2
Sunrise Ct
2800 SGLD 77479 4368 D7
Sunrise Dr
3300 SRAC 77571 4382 E1
3400 SRAC 77571 4383 A2
3600 LPRT 77571 4383 A2
3800 PASD 77571 4383 A2
3800 PRLD 77581 4504 E7
4400 MSCY 77459 4497 C4
6400 PASD 77586 4383 B3

Sunrise Dr
32400 MtgC 77354 2671 D5
Sun Rise Ln
7800 HOUS 77072 4097 D6
Sunrise Rd
5300 HOUS 77021 4104 B6
Sunrise Tr
1500 HOUS 77339 3263 C2
9000 PRLD 77584 4501 C3
Sunrise Wy
12000 HarC 77065 3539 D3
Sunrise Brook Ln
21400 HarC 77379 3111 C2
Sunrise Canter Dr
8700 HarC 77375 2965 D2
Sunrise Chase Wy
19600 HarC 77084 3816 B5
Sunrise Creek Ln
13000 FBnC 77478 4366 E1
13100 FBnC 77478 4367 A2
Sunrise Forest
28600 MtgC 77355 2815 D2
Sunrise Glen Ct
20200 HarC 77379 3111 D5
Sunrise Glen Ln
6300 HarC 77379 3111 D5
Sunrise Harbor Ln
2500 PRLD 77584 4501 C3
Sunrise Hill Ln
7100 FBnC 77469 4615 E5
Sunrise Key
- LGCY 77565 4509 A5
Sunrise Knoll Wy
800 HOUS 77062 4506 D1
Sunrise Manor Ct
3200 HOUS 77082 4098 B2
Sunrise Meadow Dr
- PRLD 77584 4501 C3
3800 FBnC 77469 4615 E5
Sunrise Meadow Ln
8500 HarC 77095 3537 E6
Sunrise Pine Ln
13600 HarC 77044 3689 D3
Sunrise Pine View Ln
20900 HOUS 77450 3954 C2
Sunrise Pl Dr
11900 HOUS 77071 4239 B5
Sunrise Point Ct
- HarC 77379 3111 C4
Sunrise Springs Ln
24200 HarC 77494 3953 B2
Sunrise Terrace Ln
8700 FBnC 77469 4235 C1
Sunrise Valley Ln
6600 HarC 77083 4097 B4
Sun River Ct
11600 HarC 77377 3109 A7
Sun River Ln
400 LGCY 77539 4752 E5
2800 LGCY 77539 4753 A5
19300 HarC 77377 3109 A7
Sunrose Ln
13300 HOUS 77045 4241 A7
13400 HOUS 77045 4372 A1
Sunset
200 PRVW 77445 3100 C3
Sunset Blvd
10 CNRO 77303 2237 D6
10 HOUS 77005 4102 D2
10 HOUS 77030 4102 D2
2500 WUNP 77005 4102 A2
3000 WUNP 77005 4101 E2
3800 HOUS 77005 4101 D2
Sunset Cir
300 TKIS 77554 5106 B4
1000 LGCY 77573 4631 D4
12600 GlsC 77510 4871 A3
12600 STFE 77510 4871 A3
Sunset Ct N
1900 LGCY 77573 4631 C5
4100 GLSN 77554 5441 D3
Sunset Ct S
1900 LGCY 77573 4631 C5
Sunset Dr
- BzaC 77578 4501 A7
- FBnC 77479 4493 E5
100 DKSN 77539 4753 B3
100 FRDW 77546 4629 C2
800 BYTN 77520 4112 E1
800 BYTN 77520 4113 A1
900 PASD 77506 4106 E6
1000 GlsC 77539 4635 E6
27000 MtgC 77355 2961 B1
27000 SGCH 77355 2961 B1
N Sunset Dr
- FRDW 77546 4504 E7
- FRDW 77546 4505 A7
- FRDW 77546 4629 A1
1000 PRLD 77581 4504 E7
Sunset Ln
10 MSCY 77071 4370 C1
10 MSCY 77489 4370 C1
600 LMQU 77568 4990 A1
1100 HOUS 77336 3121 A5
1100 TXCY 77590 4875 C3
10200 CHTW 77385 2822 C4
10200 MtgC 77385 2822 C4
10700 GlsC 77510 4871 E5
26600 SGCH 77355 2961 B2
Sunset St
500 ALVN 77511 4867 C2
27300 MtgC 77372 2683 D2
Sunset Tr
2200 SGLD 77478 4368 C6
3800 MtgC 77384 2674 D2
18800 HarC 77532 3411 B5
Sunset Alps Dr
20600 MtgC 77357 2828 C7
Sunset Arbor Dr
17300 HarC 77377 3254 B4
Sunset Bay Ct
1400 PASD 77586 4382 A6
14900 HarC 77396 3407 E7
E Sunset Bay Dr
4000 GLSN 77554 5441 D3
Sunset Bay Ln
1300 PRLD 77545 4499 E2
Sunset Bend Ct
20900 FBnC 77469 4094 C7
Sunset Bend Ln
7300 FBnC 77469 4094 B6
20600 HarC 77379 3111 C4
Sunset Bluff Dr
17300 HarC 77095 3537 E1
Sunset Breeze Dr
- HarC 77346 3408 A7
- HarC 77396 3408 A7

Sunset Canyon Dr
- HarC 77377 3254 A1
Sunset Cliff Ct
13100 SGLD 77478 4237 C4
Sunset Cove Ln
6300 FBnC 77494 4093 D5
Sunset Creek Dr
14800 HarC 77396 3407 E7
Sunset Creek Ln
13800 HarC 77396 3547 D3
Sunset Crest Dr
- HarC 77346 3409 A1
Sunset Dune Dr
12700 HOUS 77082 4097 C2
Sunset Falls Ct
7800 HarC 77379 3256 B4
Sunset Falls Dr
30400 MtgC 77386 2969 E2
Sunset Garden Dr
6500 HarC 77083 4097 A5
Sunset Glen Ln
- PRLD 77581 4503 D1
22600 HarC 77373 3114 B7
22600 HarC 77373 3259 C1
Sunset Harbor Ln
- PRLD 77545 4499 E1
Sunset Heights Ln
8600 MtgC 77302 2530 B5
Sunset Knoll Ln
5900 HarC 77449 3677 B5
Sunset Lake Ct
11800 HarC 77065 3539 E3
Sunset Lake Dr
2600 SGLD 77478 4237 B3
Sunset Lakes Dr
1100 PRLD 77581 4504 E7
Sunset Landing Dr
3000 HarC 77449 3815 E4
Sunset Loch Dr
8400 HarC 77379 3255 E1
Sunset Manor Ln
3700 FBnC 77450 4094 A1
Sunset Maple Ct
5100 HOUS 77345 3119 E1
Sunset Meadow Ln
12100 HOUS 77035 4240 A6
Sunset Meadows Dr
3600 PRLD 77581 4504 E6
Sunset Oak
5700 HarC 77379 3257 A1
Sunset Park Dr
3000 HarC 77449 3815 D4
14600 HarC 77396 3407 E7
14600 HarC 77396 3548 D1
Sunset Park Ln
8900 MtgC 77302 2530 C5
Sunset Pass
- HarC 77449 3815 E4
Sunset Path Wy
- FBnC 77545 4498 D5
Sunset Pines Dr
27100 HarC 77373 3113 E1
Sunset Pine View Cir
1100 HarC 77450 3954 C2
1100 HOUS 77450 3954 C2
Sunset Pl Dr
11800 HOUS 77071 4239 C5
Sunset Pond Dr
8600 HarC 77375 2965 D2
Sunset Ranch Dr
20200 HarC 77449 3676 D5
Sunset Ridge Ct
200 LGCY 77573 4509 B6
Sunset Ridge Dr
200 LGCY 77573 4509 B6
Sunset Ridge St
11100 LPRT 77571 4110 D7
11700 LPRT 77571 4111 A7
Sunset River Ln
17600 HarC 77084 3678 A7
Sunset Rock Dr
15600 HarC 77084 3679 A6
Sunset Schmidt
- LGCY 77565 4509 B6
- LGCY 77573 4509 B6
Sunset Sky Dr
23800 FBnC 77494 4093 A5
Sunset Springs Ct
- PRLD 77545 4499 E1
Sunset Springs Dr
- PRLD 77545 4499 E1
Sunset Terrace Dr
3900 LGCY 77539 4633 D5
Sunset Trail Ln
22400 HarC 77375 3109 E1
Sunset Valley Dr
14500 HarC 77429 3397 D4
Sunset View Dr
13800 HarC 77083 4097 A4
21600 HOUS 77532 3266 B7
Sunset Villa Ct
15000 HarC 77396 3407 D7
Sunshade Ct
2700 PRLD 77584 4501 B4
Sunshadow Ct
9200 PRLD 77584 4501 C3
Sunshadow Dr
- HOUS 77045 4242 A7
- HOUS 77045 4373 A1
Sun Shadow Ln
2300 MtgC 77386 2969 D6
Sunshine Av
16300 HarC 77049 3690 D4
Sunshine Ct
1600 MSCY 77459 4497 D4
Sunshine Dr
4600 SGLD 77479 4496 A1
4700 SGLD 77479 4369 A7
Sunshine Ln
3600 PASD 77505 4248 D4
4500 MSCY 77459 4497 D4
20500 HarC 77388 3113 C3
Sunshine St
16800 HarC 77049 3690 E4
16900 HarC 77049 3691 A4
Sunshine Bay Ct
700 HOUS 77060 3403 E6
Sunshine Bay Dr
17000 HOUS 77060 3403 E6
Sunshine Creek Dr
6600 HarC 77041 3679 E2
Sunshine Medley Ln
800 FBnC 77469 4616 D1
Sunshine Park Dr
11200 HarC 77429 3398 E5
11200 HarC 77429 3399 A5
Sunshine Point Dr
2000 HOUS 77345 3120 A6

Sunshine Terrace St
14300 HarC 77083 4096 E6
Sunshine Trace Ln
17900 FBnC 77469 4095 C7
Sun Shower Ct
10 WDLD 77381 2820 D4
Suns Landing Dr
7200 HarC 77083 4096 E6
Sunspot Dr
1000 FBnC 77469 4493 A5
Sun Spot Ln
2400 PRLD 77584 4501 D3
Sunspree Pl
10 WDLD 77382 2673 D5
Sun Spring Ct
2300 HarC 77373 3114 D4
Sunstone Dr
3700 HarC 77068 3257 A5
Sunstone Ln
2500 PRLD 77584 4501 C3
Sunstone Terrace Ln
17800 HarC 77396 3407 D1
Sunstream Ct
3100 BzaC 77578 4501 A6
13600 HarC 77082 4097 A1
Sunswept Ct
2200 SGLD 77478 4368 C5
Sunswept Wy
13500 HarC 77082 4097 A1
Sunswept Fields Ln
10600 HarC 77064 3540 A2
Sun Terrace Ln
100 LGCY 77539 4753 A3
8100 HarC 77095 3537 E6
Sun Tower Ln
- HOUS 77044 3550 B3
Sun Trail Ct
19400 HarC 77346 3264 C5
Suntree Cir
21900 FBnC 77450 3954 A6
Suntree Ln
2600 FBnC 77450 3954 A6
Sunturf Ln
11000 HarC 77044 3689 D2
Sun Valley Ct
2700 PRLD 77584 4501 C3
Sun Valley Dr
3500 HOUS 77025 4241 D1
3700 HOUS 77025 4101 D7
Sunview Ct
17000 HarC 77095 3678 C2
Sunview Dr
5400 HarC 77084 3678 E5
Sun View Ln
16000 MtgC 77302 2678 E4
16200 MtgC 77302 2679 A4
Sun Village Dr
7100 HarC 77083 4096 E5
Sunvolt Ct
21900 FBnC 77469 4093 E7
Sunwick St
14000 HarC 77037 3544 E5
14800 HarC 77060 3544 E4
Sun Willow Creek Dr
29800 MtgC 77386 2969 D2
Sunwood Dr
2800 HarC 77038 3543 A1
10200 HOUS 77041 3820 A1
Sunwood Glen Ln
400 HarC 77494 3953 B1
Super St
10 HOUS 77011 3964 B6
N Super St
100 HOUS 77011 3964 B5
Superior Dr
7400 HarC 77521 3833 D3
Superior Ln
10000 MtgC 77354 2672 A2
10400 MtgC 77354 2671 D2
13000 HOUS 77044 3409 B3
Superior Rd
100 MtgC 77354 2672 A2
900 MtgC 77354 2671 E1
Superior St
1800 BYTN 77520 3972 C6
Superior Wy
1500 HarC 77039 3545 C3
Superior Oilfield Rd
19000 GlsC 77511 4868 D1
Supplejack Ct
1800 FBnC 77479 4493 E4
Supply Row
6500 HOUS 77011 3964 D7
6600 HOUS 77023 3964 D7
Sur Ct
7000 HOUS 77033 4244 A1
Surcey Rd
15400 MtgC 77384 2675 D2
Surecrop Ln
1300 PASD 77504 4247 D7
Surf Ct
100 HOUS 77058 4508 B4
100 NSUB 77058 4508 B4
Surf Dr
4000 GLSN 77554 5332 D3
Surface
400 BzaC 77511 4628 C5
Surf Oaks Dr
500 SEBK 77586 4383 B6
S Surf Oaks Dr
4900 SEBK 77586 4383 B6
Surfride
- HOUS 77072 4097 E5
Surfside Cir
4200 MSCY 77459 4496 C3
Surfside Ln
6200 MSCY 77459 4496 D3
Surles Dr
14600 HarC 77032 3546 D1
Surprise
- HarC 77066 3401 A1
- HarC 77069 3401 A1
Surratt Dr
300 HOUS 77091 3684 B5
Surrey
19100 MtgC 77357 2829 A4
Surrey Ct
1000 TMBL 77375 2964 D5
1700 FBnC 77469 4365 D3
Surrey Ln
10 BzaC 77511 4748 B6
1400 FRDW 77546 4749 D1
3200 DRPK 77536 4109 D7
3200 DRPK 77536 4249 D1
3400 BYTN 77521 3972 A1
11900 BKHV 77024 3959 B3
16200 SGCH 77355 2816 A6
16300 SGCH 77355 2815 E6

Surrey Creek Ct
20800 HarC 77450 3954 C7
Surreydon Ln
4100 HarC 77014 3401 C2
Surreygate Dr
24000 HarC 77373 3115 B5
Surrey Glen Ct
21400 MtgC 77365 2973 B3
Surrey Meadow Ct
6600 HarC 77049 3829 A2
Surrey Oaks Ln
11300 PNPV 77024 3959 D3
Surrey Park Ct
4900 FBnC 77494 4092 D3
Surrey Park Ln
26600 FBnC 77494 4092 D3
Surrey Run Pl
10 WDLD 77384 2675 D5
Surrey Square St
5600 HOUS 77017 4246 A2
Surrey Stone Ct
20700 HarC 77450 3954 C6
Surrey Trail Ln
2900 HarC 77450 3954 D7
Surreywest Ln
17600 HarC 77379 3257 A3
Surrey Woods Dr
15900 HarC 77546 4505 E5
16000 HarC 77546 4506 A5
Surry St
- HOUS 77078 3687 E5
8700 HOUS 77028 3687 E7
Surry Lake Ln
- FBnC 77469 4235 C1
Surry Oaks Dr
1700 WDBR 77357 2828 E2
2000 WDBR 77357 2829 A2
Susan Ct
14000 SGLD 77478 4236 E6
14000 SGLD 77478 4237 A6
36800 MtgC 77355 2816 A3
Susan Ln
100 ORDN 77385 2822 B4
22600 MtgC 77365 2973 D6
Susan St
1300 PASD 77506 4106 D5
1400 HOUS 77017 4106 D5
2200 HOUS 77034 4246 B5
36800 MtgC 77355 2816 A3
Susan Ann Ct
10 HOUS 77004 4103 D2
Susan Forest Ln
11900 HarC 77089 4504 B1
Susanna Ln
5400 HarC 77389 2967 A7
12800 HOUS 77072 4097 C6
Susie Ct
11900 MtgC 77362 2963 C1
Susie Ln
27700 MtgC 77357 2829 E5
Suspiro Dr
8000 FBnC 77083 4096 B7
Sussex
25600 MtgC 77357 2829 B4
Sussex Ct
6500 HarC 77389 2966 C3
Sussex Dr
16600 FBnC 77083 4235 E1
16600 FBnC 77083 4236 A1
Sussex Ln
10000 HOUS 77041 3681 A5
Sussex Tr
1000 PRLD 77584 4501 B2
Sutherland Ln
200 LGCY 77573 4630 C6
Sutherland Sq
6200 BLAR 77401 4100 E3
6200 HOUS 77081 4100 E3
6200 HOUS 77401 4100 E3
Sutherland St
2500 HOUS 77023 4104 C3
Sutherland Spring Ln
13800 BzaC 77583 4623 D4
25100 FBnC 77494 4093 A1
Suttens Field Dr
7600 HOUS 77072 4097 D6
Sutter Creek Ln
14500 HarC 77396 3547 E2
Sutter Glen Ln
10400 HOUS 77075 4377 A3
Sutter Park Ln
6300 HarC 77066 3400 E6
9400 HarC 77086 3542 A3
Sutter Ranch Cir
10800 HarC 77064 3540 B5
Sutter Ranch Dr
9000 HarC 77064 3540 B5
Sutters Chase Ct
7900 FBnC 77479 4494 B5
Sutters Chase Dr
1700 FBnC 77479 4494 B5
Sutter's Creek Tr
6800 MSCY 77459 4496 C4
Sutton
300 GlsC 77539 4635 D4
Sutton Ct
2600 HOUS 77027 3961 D7
Sutton Ln
- HarC 77375 3109 E1
900 SEBK 77586 4382 E7
900 SEBK 77586 4509 E1
900 TMBL 77375 3109 D1
Sutton Pl
1400 HOUS 77077 3957 C5
E Sutton Sq
100 STAF 77477 4369 B2
N Sutton Sq
3300 STAF 77477 4369 A1
S Sutton Sq
3300 STAF 77477 4369 A2
W Sutton Sq
200 STAF 77477 4369 A2
Sutton St
1500 HOUS 77006 3963 A5
1600 HOUS 77006 3962 C5
Sutton Falls Dr
19900 HarC 77433 3677 A1
Suttonford Dr
3600 HarC 77066 3401 C5
Sutton Glen Ln
- HarC 77047 4374 A4
Sutton Meadows Ct
9700 HarC 77086 3542 C4
Sutton Meadows Dr
6200 HarC 77086 3542 C3
Sutton Mill Pl
10 WDLD 77382 2819 E2

Suwanee Ln
800 HarC 77090 3258 B2
Suzan Ct
28100 ORDN 77385 2822 C4
Suzanne Ct
7900 HarC 77379 3110 E6
Suzanne St
300 LGCY 77573 4632 D2
13100 STAF 77477 4370 A1
14000 GlsC 77517 4752 B7
Suzanne Wy
700 HarC 77090 3258 C2
Suzette St
- DRPK 77536 4250 A2
Swallow Cir
1100 SGLD 77478 4368 C3
Swallow Ln
2700 TXCY 77590 4875 C2
Swallow St
- HOUS 77061 4244 E3
6900 HOUS 77087 4244 E3
Swallowfield Dr
14100 HOUS 77077 3956 E4
Swallow Park Dr
7800 HarC 77396 3406 D6
Swallows Cove Ln
24500 FBnC 77494 3953 C6
Swallow Tail Ct
10 WDLD 77381 2821 B3
Swan Ct
10 MtgC 77385 2676 D6
2500 NSUB 77058 4508 B4
Swan Dr
4200 GlsC 77563 4990 A5
4200 HTCK 77563 4990 B5
5500 GLSN 77551 5108 D7
Swan Ln
7900 CmbC 77520 3835 D4
Swan Rd
2800 HarC 77032 3404 E7
2900 HOUS 77032 3404 E7
14800 HOUS 77032 3405 A7
Swan Creek Dr
11900 HarC 77065 3539 D2
15300 HarC 77095 3538 E5
Swandale Ln
15700 HarC 77095 3538 D4
Swanfield Ct
9500 FBnC 77083 4236 E2
Swanfield Dr
14100 FBnC 77083 4236 E2
Swan Fountain Dr
26100 MtgC 77339 3118 C4
Swan Glen Dr
10500 HOUS 77099 4238 A3
Swan Green Ln
14300 HarC 77095 3679 A1
Swan Hollow Ct
7900 HarC 77095 3539 B7
Swan Hollow Ln
13800 HarC 77095 3539 B7
Swan Island Dr
- MSCY 77459 4497 C4
Swan Island Ln
17200 MtgC 77385 2676 C6
Swan Isle Blvd
10 MSCY 77459 4497 B5
Swank St
5600 HOUS 77021 4103 C4
Swanley Ct
15000 HOUS 77062 4506 D1
Swan Meadow Ct
2800 LGCY 77573 4632 E1
Swan Meadow Ln
- HarC 77338 3262 B3
8100 HarC 77338 3261 E4
Swanmore Dr
16800 HOUS 77396 3406 A4
Swan Pond Ct
9500 HOUS 77075 4246 B7
Swan Ranch Ln
- FBnC 77469 4094 C7
Swan River Dr
12100 HOUS 77050 3546 E6
Swansbury Dr
17200 HarC 77429 3396 C2
Swansea St
6200 HOUS 77048 4375 D3
Swansea Bay Dr
9300 HarC 77379 3255 C2
Swansea Harbor Ln
14800 HOUS 77053 4372 E3
Swansfield Ln
1400 HarC 77073 3259 D5
Swanson
10000 HarC 77064 3541 D2
Swanson Dr
7300 FBnC 77469 4232 B7
Swanson St
1000 HOUS 77030 4102 C5
4500 HOUS 77021 4103 D7
Swan Song Pl
10 WDLD 77381 2820 E2
Swan Valley Dr
19500 HarC 77433 3677 A1
Swanwood Ln
14300 HarC 77047 4374 A3
Swarthmore St
3800 SSPL 77005 4101 D3
4100 WUNP 77005 4101 C3
Swashbuckle
- GLSN 77554 5332 D3
Sway St
6700 HOUS 77085 4371 C4
Sweden Ct
- HarC 77379 3111 E7
Sweeney Rd
14000 HarC 77037 3545 A5
14600 HarC 77060 3545 A1
14900 HarC 77060 3544 E1
14900 HOUS 77060 3544 E1
Sweeney Brook Ln
9400 FBnC 77469 4616 E1
Sweeney Lake Ct
4000 FBnC 77469 4234 C5
Sweeney Park Ct
5100 HarC 77084 3678 D5
Sweeney Park Ln
15700 HarC 77084 3678 D5
Sweeny Dr
3500 DKSN 77539 4753 D3
Sweet Grv
21000 HarC 77375 3110 C4
Sweet Alyssum Wy
9700 HarC 77375 3110 C6
Sweet Bay Cir
- MtgC 77354 2819 C2
- WDLD 77382 2819 C3

Houston Street Index

STREET
Block City ZIP Map# Grid

Sweetbay Ln
5500 HOUS 77041 3681 B6
Sweet Bay Rd
21700 HOUS 77339 3263 D2
Sweetberry Ln
9800 HarC 77375 3110 C4
Sweetbeth Ct
10 WDLD 77380 2821 E7
Sweet Birch Ln
12600 HarC 77041 3679 D3
Sweet Birch Pl
10 WDLD 77382 2674 A5
Sweetbloom Ln
9800 HarC 77375 3110 C4
Sweet Blossom Ln
20900 HarC 77375 3110 B4
Sweet Briar Dr
3600 PASD 77505 4248 D4
Sweetbriar Ln
30900 MtgC 77354 2670 A7
Sweetbriar Pkwy
- SGLD 77479 4495 B1
Sweetbriar St
5300 HOUS 77017 4106 C7
5700 HOUS 77502 4106 C7
5700 PASD 77502 4106 C7
Sweetbrook Dr
10300 HarC 77038 3543 D2
Sweetbrush Dr
8600 HarC 77064 3399 D7
8600 HarC 77064 3400 A7
Sweetcherry Dr
13700 HarC 77396 3547 C3
Sweet Cicely Ct
4300 HOUS 77059 4380 C4
Sweet Clover Ln
11900 MtgC 77372 2537 C3
Sweetdream Pl
10 WDLD 77381 2675 A7
Sweeten Ln
- LbyC 77327 2537 E2
- LbyC 77327 2538 A2
Sweet Fern St
16000 HarC 77070 3255 C6
Sweet Flag Dr
- WDLD 77381 2820 E5
Sweet Flower Dr
600 HarC 77073 3403 B3
Sweet Forest Ln
19600 HarC 77346 3265 B5
Sweetglen Ct
- FBnC 77479 4496 D5
22500 HarC 77373 3259 B1
Sweet Glen Dr
20600 MtgC 77365 3117 E1
21600 MtgC 77365 3118 A1
Sweet Grass Ln
21300 HarC 77375 3110 B4
Sweet Grass Tr
1400 HarC 77090 3258 A3
Sweetgum Ct
1500 PRLD 77581 4504 E4
Sweet Gum Dr
3600 HarC 77388 3112 D5
Sweetgum Dr
- HOUS 77396 3547 C1
100 LGCY 77573 4630 B6
13700 HarC 77396 3547 C3
14900 HOUS 77396 3406 C7
23500 WlrC 77447 2813 D2
Sweet Gum Ln
1100 HOUS 77339 3118 C7
10000 BYTN 77521 3835 B5
Sweetgum Ln
33400 MtgC 77354 2673 E4
Sweetgum Pk
- HarC 77388 3113 B2
- HarC 77389 3113 B2
Sweet Gum Rd
28000 MtgC 77354 2819 B4
Sweet Gum St
10 WDBR 77357 2828 B2
Sweetgum St
1300 CHTW 77385 2823 A4
2600 PASD 77502 4248 A2
2700 PASD 77503 4248 A2
6200 KATY 77493 3813 A4
23500 MtgC 77357 2974 A1
Sweet Gum Tr
3900 HOUS 77339 3119 B2
Sweetgum Wk
2800 HarC 77388 3113 B6
Sweetgum Wy
20200 HarC 77433 3251 C5
Sweetgum Forest Ct
19700 HarC 77346 3265 B5
Sweetgum Forest Dr
19500 HarC 77346 3265 B5
Sweetgum Hill Ct
2400 HarC 77388 3113 B5
Sweetgum Hill Ln
3500 HOUS 77345 3119 D3
Sweetgum Shores Dr
- HOUS 77044 3408 E5
Sweetgum Trace Dr
8000 HarC 77040 3681 D1
Sweet Hall Ln
12000 HarC 77067 3402 A5
Sweet Hollow Ct
3900 FBnC 77478 4366 E3
Sweet Jarvil Rd
10 LbyC 77535 3268 E3
Sweetjasmine Ln
18500 HarC 77379 3256 A1
Sweetleaf Ct
10 WDLD 77381 2821 B6
Sweet Leaf Grove Ln
100 MtgC 77384 2675 A1
Sweet Magnolia Pl
19800 HarC 77338 3262 A5
Sweet Maple Ct
15600 HarC 77049 3829 B1
Sweetmeadow Dr
18500 HarC 77379 3256 B1
Sweet Melissa Dr
- FBnC 77494 4093 A4
Sweet Nectar Ln
10000 HarC 77375 3110 A4
Sweet Oak Ln
28200 FBnC 77494 3951 D6
Sweet Olive Wy
9900 HarC 77375 3110 B4
Sweet Orchard Ct
5200 HOUS 77345 3119 D2
Sweet Pasture Dr
8600 HarC 77375 2965 D3
Sweet Pea
7200 HOUS 77088 3683 D3
Sweet Pea Av
8100 HarC 77521 3833 B3
Sweet Pea Dr
8000 HarC 77562 3832 D3
Sweet Pine Dr
800 HOUS 77450 3954 C2
1000 HarC 77450 3954 C1
Sweet Rain Dr
- HarC 77377 3254 B3
Sweet River Ln
21000 HarC 77375 3110 A5
Sweetrock Ln
21200 HarC 77375 3110 A4
Sweetrose Pl
15700 HarC 77095 3538 D4
Sweetsage Ln
- HarC 77088 3682 B1
- HOUS 77088 3682 B1
Sweet Song Dr
17400 HarC 77377 3254 A4
Sweetspire Pl
10900 WDLD 77380 2821 C7
Sweetspire Rd
3500 HarC 77449 3816 A2
Sweetspire Rdg
6000 FBnC 77469 4234 D2
Sweetstem Ct
6200 HOUS 77345 3120 B4
Sweetstem Dr
1800 HOUS 77345 3120 B3
Sweet Stone Ct
1400 PASD 77586 4381 E6
Sweetstone Ln
- FBnC 77479 4493 D1
Sweetstone Bluff Ln
7900 HarC 77433 3537 B7
Sweetstone Estates Ct
14300 HarC 77429 3396 B2
Sweetstone Springs Ct
26800 HarC 77433 3537 A1
Sweet Surrender Ct
13400 HarC 77041 3679 C6
Sweetvine Ln
21300 HarC 77375 3110 B3
Sweet Violet Ct
20800 HarC 77346 3265 A3
Sweet Violet Tr
7000 HarC 77346 3265 A3
Sweet Walnut Ct
- WDLD 77381 2820 E6
Sweetwater Blvd
3100 SGLD 77479 4495 C1
4600 SGLD 77479 4368 A7
4900 SGLD 77479 4367 E6
Sweetwater Cir
30800 MtgC 77355 2815 D1
N Sweetwater Cir
38100 MtgC 77355 2815 D1
Sweetwater Ct
10 SGLD 77479 4495 A1
12200 STAF 77477 4237 D7
Sweetwater Ln
7900 HarC 77037 3684 B2
7900 HOUS 77037 3684 B2
8900 HOUS 77037 3544 B7
9000 HarC 77037 3544 B7
Sweetwater St
29500 MtgC 77354 2817 E3
29500 MtgC 77354 2818 A3
Sweetwater Creek Dr
15700 HarC 77095 3538 C6
Sweetwater Fields Ln
16000 HarC 77377 3254 C6
Sweetwater View Dr
14500 HarC 77047 4374 C5
Sweet William Ct
20100 HarC 77375 3110 B6
20100 HarC 77379 3110 B6
Sweet Willow Ct
11700 HOUS 77031 4239 A4
Sweet Wind Ct
1300 PRLD 77545 4499 E3
Sweet Wind Dr
2600 PRLD 77545 4499 E3
Sweetwind Ln
5200 HarC 77373 3115 D6
Sweetwood Cir
20900 MtgC 77365 3118 A1
Sweetwood Dr
10300 HarC 77070 3399 B6
Swell Ct
10 HOUS 77339 3263 E1
Sweno Ct
16800 HarC 77084 3678 B5
Swift Blvd
1900 HOUS 77030 4102 B3
2400 WUNP 77005 4102 A3
Swiftbrook Dr
20000 HarC 77346 3264 C4
Swift Brook Glen Wy
2900 HarC 77389 3112 E1
2900 HarC 77389 3113 A1
Swift Creek Ct
3400 SGLD 77479 4495 B1
Swift Creek Dr
- LGCY 77573 4632 A7
- LGCY 77573 4753 A1
- PRLD 77545 4500 A1
- PRLD 77584 4500 A1
3600 HOUS 77339 3119 C4
Swift Current Dr
24200 HOUS 77336 3266 B2
Swift Falls Ct
19200 HarC 77094 3955 B3
Swift Fox Cor
2900 FBnC 77459 4622 A6
Swift River Ln
14800 FBnC 77478 4236 D5
Swift Spring Ln
- HarC 77377 3254 C3
Swiftstream Pl
10 WDLD 77381 2821 A3
Swift Water Bnd
11400 HarC 77375 3109 E1
Swiftwater Ln
7700 HOUS 77075 4376 D2
Swiftwater Bridge Ln
11500 FBnC 77478 4236 E6
Swift Wing Ct
- HarC 77396 3548 C1
Swinbrook Ln
12300 HarC 77039 3545 E5
Swinden Dr
4000 HarC 77066 3401 B3
Swiney Rd
8900 MtgC 77354 2818 D2
Swiney St
3100 HOUS 77020 3964 A4
Swingle Rd
3300 HOUS 77047 4374 C2
4400 HOUS 77048 4374 E2
4600 HOUS 77048 4375 A2
Swinton Dr
3500 MSCY 77459 4497 E6
N Swirling Cloud Ct
16800 HarC 77433 3251 C3
S Swirling Cloud Ct
16600 HarC 77433 3251 A4
Swirling Winds Dr
10100 HarC 77086 3542 C3
Swisher St
10000 HarC 77064 3541 D2
Swiss Ln
8000 HOUS 77075 4376 D1
Swiss Hill Dr
13800 HOUS 77077 3957 A3
13900 HOUS 77077 3956 E3
Switchback Dr
- HarC 77095 3537 C3
Switchbud Pl
10 WDLD 77380 2967 C1
Switchgrass Ln
11200 HarC 77095 3538 A1
Switzer St
600 HOUS 77013 3966 A1
1300 JTCY 77029 3966 B3
Swoopes Dr
11400 HOUS 77013 3827 D4
Swordfern Pl
3500 HarC 77449 3816 A3
Swords Bnd
100 STAF 77477 4370 A4
Swords Creek Rd
- HarC 77014 3402 A4
11900 HarC 77067 3402 A4
Sycamore
- HMPD 77445 2953 C7
11600 MtgC 77302 2677 C1
Sycamore Av
4700 PASD 77502 4248 A2
5600 PASD 77503 4248 D2
Sycamore Cir
- MtgC 77354 2817 E6
14200 HarC 77396 3547 B2
26600 MtgC 77354 2818 A6
Sycamore Ct
900 MSCY 77489 4370 D4
28100 MtgC 77355 2814 B5
Sycamore Dr
10 WDBR 77357 2828 B2
200 HarC 77562 3831 D2
200 HTCK 77563 4988 C4
500 MtgC 77302 2530 B6
1500 PRLD 77581 4504 D4
5300 DKSN 77539 4754 A4
5300 TXCY 77539 4754 A4
7000 GLSN 77551 5108 A7
7000 GLSN 77551 5222 A1
Sycamore Dr N
10800 LPRT 77571 4250 D3
Sycamore Dr S
10800 LPRT 77571 4250 D3
Sycamore Hl
15500 MtgC 77355 2962 A2
15500 SGCH 77355 2962 A2
Sycamore Hls
31100 HarC 77484 3102 B7
Sycamore Ln
- CmbC 77520 3835 D3
- MtgC 77357 2681 A7
1100 HOUS 77339 3263 C1
11600 MtgC 77302 2677 C1
Sycamore Pt
- LGCY 77598 4630 D4
Sycamore Rd
100 FBnC 77545 4623 C1
600 FBnC 77469 4492 C7
600 FBnC 77469 4616 B1
700 BzaC 77583 4623 C1
700 PRLD 77545 4623 D1
W Sycamore Rd
100 FBnC 77545 4623 A1
1700 FBnC 77545 4622 E1
Sycamore St
- HMPD 77445 2953 D7
- PRVW 77445 3100 A3
300 ALVN 77511 4867 C2
1000 LMQU 77568 4990 A1
6400 KATY 77493 3813 A4
7900 HOUS 77012 4105 C2
N Sycamore St
100 TMBL 77375 2964 B6
S Sycamore St
100 TMBL 77375 2964 C7
Sycamore Tr
17200 MtgC 77302 2825 D2
Sycamore Creek Dr
5100 HOUS 77345 3120 A5
Sycamore Crest Ln
20500 HarC 77449 3676 D3
Sycamore Grove Dr
2300 HOUS 77062 4380 C7
Sycamore Heights St
13100 HarC 77065 3539 B1
Sycamore Lake Rd
14300 HOUS 77062 4379 D7
Sycamore Leaf Ln
15000 HarC 77429 3253 C3
Sycamore Leaf Wy
1400 CNRO 77301 2384 D6
Sycamore Park Ct
19100 HarC 77094 3955 A1
Sycamore Pointe
400 LGCY 77573 4631 E4
Sycamore Ridge Ln
800 HOUS 77073 3259 B7
Sycamore Shadows Dr
3400 HOUS 77339 3119 B4
Sycamore Springs Ct
2900 HOUS 77339 3119 B3
Sycamore Springs Dr
2900 HOUS 77339 3119 B3
3200 HOUS 77345 3119 B3
Sycamore Trace Ct
900 HOUS 77073 3259 B6
Sycamore Trace Ln
800 HOUS 77073 3259 B7
Sycamore Tree Ct
2900 HOUS 77345 3119 E2
Sycamore Valley Dr
19800 HarC 77433 3537 A7
19800 HarC 77433 3677 A1
Sycamore Villas Dr
5100 HOUS 77345 3120 A5
Sycamore Wind Ct
20700 HOUS 77073 3259 B7
Sycamore Wood Dr
20700 HOUS 77073 3259 B7
Sydney Creek Dr
31700 HarC 77447 3250 A6
Sydney Park Ln
- HarC 77377 3253 D1
Sydnor Av
1900 SEBK 77586 4509 D2
Sydnor Ln
1700 GLSN 77554 5221 C2
Sydnor St
1200 HOUS 77020 3964 A2
Sylmar Rd
5500 BLAR 77096 4100 C6
5500 BLAR 77401 4100 C6
5500 HOUS 77096 4100 C6
5500 HOUS 77401 4100 C6
5600 HOUS 77081 4100 C6
6700 HOUS 77074 4100 A6
Sylvan Ln
300 HarC 77530 3831 A6
2200 HarC 77521 3834 C7
Sylvan Rd
6600 HOUS 77023 4104 D2
Sylvan St
100 LPRT 77571 4251 E5
17000 WEBS 77598 4507 A5
Sylvan Dale Dr
16300 HarC 77346 3408 A3
Sylvanfield Dr
4300 HarC 77014 3401 B1
E Sylvanfield Dr
14500 HarC 77014 3401 B1
W Sylvanfield Dr
14200 HarC 77014 3401 B1
Sylvan Forest Dr
100 WDLD 77381 2820 D2
Sylvan Glen Dr
4500 HarC 77084 3678 E7
Sylvan Grove Dr
5800 HOUS 77345 3120 C6
Sylvania St
3800 HOUS 77023 4104 D4
Sylvan Lake Dr
15700 HOUS 77062 4380 C7
Sylvan Pl Dr
24700 MtgC 77355 2961 A2
24700 SGCH 77355 2961 A2
Sylvester Rd
100 HOUS 77009 3824 B4
Sylvia Ct
- HarC 77073 3403 C1
Sylvia Dr
5700 GLSN 77551 5108 C6
14100 HarC 77429 3397 E7
Sylvia Ln
4600 BzaC 77578 4625 D3
4600 MNVL 77578 4625 D3
Sylvia St
100 DRPK 77536 4109 B5
1400 LMQU 77568 4990 A3
W Sylvia St
- DRPK 77536 4109 B5
Sylvian Hills Dr
12000 HOUS 77047 4373 D2
Symbol St
11100 HarC 77093 3686 B2
Symms
- LGCY 77573 4632 A3
Symphonic Ln
9100 HarC 77040 3541 B7
Syndee Loch Ct
18600 HarC 77379 3255 E1
Synott Rd
- HOUS 77077 3957 B7
- HOUS 77082 3957 B7
3100 HOUS 77082 4097 B2
3900 HOUS 77072 4097 C5
3900 HOUS 77082 4097 C5
7800 HOUS 77072 4097 C6
7800 HOUS 77083 4097 C6
8600 HOUS 77072 4237 C1
8600 HOUS 77083 4237 C2
8600 HOUS 77099 4237 C2
9600 HOUS 77099 4237 C2
9900 HOUS 77478 4237 C2
10400 SGLD 77478 4237 B4
Synott Rd FM-1876
6800 HOUS 77072 4097 C5
6800 HOUS 77083 4097 C5
7800 HarC 77072 4097 C6
7800 HarC 77083 4097 C6
8600 HarC 77072 4237 C1
8600 HarC 77083 4237 C2
8600 HarC 77099 4237 C2
9600 HOUS 77099 4237 C2
9900 HOUS 77478 4237 C2
10400 SGLD 77478 4237 B4
Syracuse St
3700 HOUS 77005 4101 D2
Syrian St
2100 MSCY 77489 4370 B6

T

T St
5900 KATY 77493 3813 B6
Tab Ln
14600 HarC 77070 3398 C1
Tabana Dr
6400 HarC 77449 3677 A3
Tabernash Dr
8000 HarC 77040 3541 D6
8000 HarC 77064 3541 D6
Table Bay Dr
- HarC 77049 3828 D1
Tableland Tr
16900 MtgC 77385 2676 E5
Tablerock Dr
10200 HarC 77064 3540 B3
Tabor St
1800 HOUS 77009 3824 A4
W Tabor St
100 PASD 77506 4107 A3
Tabor Brook Dr
18000 HarC 77346 3408 E1
Tackaberry St
2300 HOUS 77009 3963 C1
2400 HOUS 77009 3824 C7
Taco Ct
14000 SGLD 77478 4237 A6
Tacoma Dr
5100 HarC 77041 3680 C6
Tacquard Dr
6200 HTCK 77563 4988 C3
Tadlock Ln
6300 HOUS 77085 4371 C3
Tadshire Ln
- HarC 77047 4374 A4
- HOUS 77047 4374 A4
Tadworth Ct
15500 HOUS 77062 4506 E3
Tadworth Dr
15400 HOUS 77062 4506 E2
Taffaine Dr
17000 HarC 77090 3258 B6
Taffrail Wy
16200 HarC 77532 3552 A2
Taft Av
1200 PASD 77502 4107 C7
2500 HOUS 77088 3683 B2
2800 HarC 77040 3541 E6
Taft Dr
1400 DRPK 77536 4109 C7
2100 BYTN 77520 3973 D6
Taft St
200 LMQU 77568 4873 B7
500 HOUS 77019 3962 E6
1500 HOUS 77006 3962 E6
Taftsberry Ct
17100 HarC 77095 3538 A4
Taftsberry Dr
9200 HarC 77095 3538 A4
Taggart St
6200 HOUS 77007 3962 A3
6300 HOUS 77007 3961 E2
Tahiti Rd
200 TKIS 77554 5106 C4
Tahiti Wy
16700 GLSN 77554 5331 E5
16700 JMAB 77554 5331 E5
Tahoe Ct
1500 LGCY 77573 4632 A7
Tahoe Dr
15800 JRSV 77040 3540 D7
N Tahoe Dr
8200 JRSV 77040 3540 D7
Tahoe Basin
2800 FBnC 77459 4621 C6
Tahoe Canyon Ln
4700 HarC 77084 3678 A7
Tahoe Crossing Ln
6300 HarC 77066 3400 D4
Tahoe Lake Ln
16100 HarC 77073 3259 B5
Tahoe Pines Ln
17600 HarC 77346 3408 C2
Tahoe Pointe Ct
- HarC 77346 3264 C3
Tahoe Shores Ct
10 HarC 77346 3264 D3
Tahoe Valley Ln
1300 FBnC 77479 4493 D1
Tahoka Ln
10000 FBnC 77478 4236 E3
Tahoka Springs Dr
19400 HarC 77449 3677 A3
Taidswood Dr
9100 HarC 77379 3256 A5
9200 HarC 77379 3255 E6
Taimer Ct
6400 FBnC 77479 4367 B6
Tain Dr
4700 HarC 77084 3678 C6
Taino Dr
4500 HarC 77521 3833 B4
Tain Round Ct
16600 HarC 77084 3678 C6
Tainson Dr
6100 HarC 77041 3679 B4
Taintor St
12500 HOUS 77045 4241 D6
Tal Ct
10 SPVL 77055 3821 B7
Tala St
9600 HOUS 77093 3685 E5
Talasek St
2700 RSBG 77471 4490 E7
Talavera Wy
14600 HarC 77396 3547 D3
Talbott St
2600 HOUS 77030 4102 A4
2600 WUNP 77005 4102 A4
Talbrook Dr
1600 HarC 77038 3543 C2
Talcott Ln
1600 SGLD 77479 4367 C7
8800 HarC 77049 3690 D4
Talcott St
14800 HarC 77015 3968 C3
Talcott Wy Dr
19200 HarC 77375 3109 D7
Tali Dr
5000 HarC 77032 3546 D3
Talina Wy
2500 HOUS 77080 3820 A3
4300 HOUS 77041 3820 A1
4500 HOUS 77041 3681 A7
Talisman Ct
10 HOUS 77076 3684 D5
Talisman Dr
700 FBnC 77583 4623 C4
Tall Cir
10 FBnC 77459 4621 B3
Tall Dr
- HarC 77095 3538 D4
Tall Pns
19400 MtgC 77355 2814 A2
Tall Tr
10 FBnC 77459 4621 B3
Talladega Springs Ln
7800 FBnC 77469 4095 B7
Tallahassee Pk
600 MtgC 77302 2530 C5
Tallant St
100 HOUS 77076 3685 A5
Tall Canyon Ct
6300 FBnC 77450 4094 D4
Tall Cedars Dr
100 HarC 77532 3411 A5
Tall Chase Ln
13500 HOUS 77070 3400 A3
Tallcrest Ln
10100 HarC 77375 2965 B6
Tall Cypress Dr
17700 HarC 77388 3257 C1
18300 HarC 77388 3112 C7
Tall Elm Ct
2800 HOUS 77059 4379 E5
Talley Ln
10000 HOUS 77041 3681 A5
Talleyrand Dr
- HarC 77084 3678 E6
Tall Firs Ln
8100 HarC 77095 3538 D6
Tall Forest Dr
12000 HarC 77065 3398 C6
12000 HarC 77429 3398 A5
Tallgrass Prairie Ln
17000 HarC 77346 3408 C4
Tall Grove Ln
4500 HOUS 77345 3119 E2
Tall Gum Dr
1900 FBnC 77545 4622 D2
Tallheath Ct
- HOUS 77044 3550 A1
Tall Hickory Ln
15000 HarC 77433 3395 C1
Tall Maple Ct
17500 HarC 77095 3537 E7
Tall Meadow Ln
9600 HarC 77088 3682 B2
Tall Oaks Dr
10 HarC 77336 2976 B4
31000 MtgC 77354 2817 D1
Tall Oaks St
12000 BKHV 77024 3959 B3
Tall Oaks Wy
33000 MtgC 77354 2671 B5
Tallow Ct
1400 PASD 77586 4381 E6
9500 FBnC 77459 4621 D6
Tallow Dr
300 CHTW 77385 2822 D4
1100 DKSN 77539 4753 D3
Tallow Ln
5100 HOUS 77021 4104 A5
Tallow Sq
900 LMQU 77568 4874 A7
Tallow St
2700 ALVN 77511 4867 C4
14500 GlsC 77517 4986 A1
14500 STFE 77517 4986 A1
Tallowbend Ct
10200 HarC 77064 3540 D3
S Tallowberry Dr
10 WDLD 77381 2820 E6
10 WDLD 77381 2821 A6
W Tallowberry Dr
10 WDLD 77381 2820 E6
Tallow Bluff Ct
- HarC 77429 3253 E4
Tallow Briar Ln
10800 HOUS 77075 4376 E4
Tallow Chase Ln
20600 HarC 77379 3111 C5
Tallow Cove Dr
4900 BYTN 77521 3972 C1
Tallow Forest Ct
14900 HOUS 77062 4380 B7
Tallow Forest St
2900 LGCY 77539 4752 D4
Tallow Glen Ln
13400 HarC 77429 3254 A6
Tallow Grove Ln
21500 HarC 77450 3954 B6
Tallow Hill Pl
10 WDLD 77382 2673 E4
Tallow Knoll Ln
7000 FBnC 77469 4094 B5
Tallowood
200 ELGO 77586 4509 A1
Tallowood Dr
300 ELGO 77586 4509 A1
2100 DRPK 77536 4109 D7
2700 LGCY 77573 4632 E1
Tallowood Rd
400 HOUS 77024 3958 E3
Tallowpark Ln
- FBnC 77494 4093 C2
Tallowpine Ter
5200 KATY 77493 3813 D4
Tallow Point Ct
14100 HOUS 77062 4379 E6
Tallow Tree Cir
9900 HarC 77070 3255 B5
Tallow Tree Dr
9400 HarC 77070 3255 C5
Tallowwood Ter
2600 KATY 77493 3813 D4
Tall Pine Dr
16000 PASD 77059 4380 D5
Tall Pines Ct
25700 MtgC 77355 2814 B4
Tall Pines Dr
700 FRDW 77546 4629 A2
700 MtgC 77354 2818 A7
900 MtgC 77354 2817 E6
1000 FRDW 77546 4628 E2
7200 HOUS 77088 3682 D3
Tall Pine Vista Ln
20000 HarC 77375 3109 D5
Tall Ridge Ct
4500 HOUS 77345 3120 A2
Tallshadows Dr
15000 HarC 77032 3545 B1
15000 HarC 77039 3545 B1
15300 HOUS 77032 3404 B7
15900 HarC 77032 3404 B6
Tall Ships Dr
2100 HarC 77546 4506 A6
2100 HOUS 77546 4506 A6
Tall Sky Pl
10 WDLD 77381 2820 E4
Tall Spruce Dr
12900 HarC 77429 3397 C4
Tall Timbers
- FRDW 77546 4505 C6
Tall Timbers Ct
300 FRDW 77546 4505 C5
Tall Timbers Dr
11000 HarC 77065 3399 A7
11000 HarC 77070 3399 A7
11200 HarC 77065 3398 E7
Tall Timbers Ln
- PRLD 77581 4503 E2
600 FRDW 77546 4505 C5
Tall Timbers Rd
200 WDBR 77357 2828 C3
Tall Timbers Wy
300 FRDW 77546 4505 B5
Tall Trail Ct
10 FBnC 77459 4621 A3
Tall Tree Ct
9600 FBnC 77459 4621 D6
Tall Tree Tr
19200 HarC 77379 3112 A6
Tall Tree Ridge Wy
2900 HarC 77389 3113 A1
3000 HarC 77389 3112 E1
Tallulah Ct
1500 HOUS 77077 3957 D5
Tallulah Ln
1900 HOUS 77077 3957 D6
Tall Willow Dr
6300 HOUS 77088 3682 C3
6400 HOUS 77040 3682 C3
Tallwood Dr
- HarC 77346 3264 E3
Tallwood Crossing Ln
12600 HarC 77041 3679 E4
Tallyho Rd
8700 HOUS 77061 4245 E4
8800 HOUS 77061 4246 A4
9200 HOUS 77017 4246 A4
9200 HOUS 77587 4246 A4
9200 SHUS 77587 4246 A4
Talmadge Hill Dr
- HOUS 77024 3959 B4
W Talmage St
1100 ALVN 77511 4867 A1
Talmalge Hall Ct
500 MtgC 77302 2530 D5
Talmalge Hall Dr
700 MtgC 77302 2530 C5
Talon Dr
1800 FRDW 77546 4629 E3
Taloncrest Ct
9400 FBnC 77083 4236 B1
Taloncrest Dr
16100 FBnC 77083 4236 B1
Talons Wy
8200 FBnC 77459 4621 A5
Talons Walk Wk
- FBnC 77459 4621 A6
Talonwood Ct
14800 HarC 77396 3548 B1
Talshire Ln
10 FBnC 77479 4494 A1
Talton Dr
8800 HOUS 77078 3687 E6
9000 HOUS 77078 3688 A6
Talton St
7900 HOUS 77028 3687 D6
8700 HOUS 77078 3687 E6
Talton Oaks Dr
- HarC 77064 3540 B7
Tam Ct
10 SPVL 77055 3821 B7
Tamana Dr
100 TKIS 77554 5106 B4
Tamar Dr
6300 PASD 77503 4248 E2
6600 DRPK 77503 4248 E2
6600 DRPK 77536 4248 E2
Tamara Ln
9600 HarC 77038 3544 A5
Tamarach Dr
5000 BYTN 77521 3972 A2
Tamarack Dr
11800 MtgC 77365 3117 C4
Tamarack Pl
4000 HarC 77082 4096 E3
Tamarack Wy
19500 HarC 77094 3955 A2
Tamarind Dr
- BzaC 77584 4501 A5
Tamarind Pl
10 WDLD 77381 2820 D4
Tamarind Tr
3200 HOUS 77345 3119 D2
Tamarisk Ln
3500 MSCY 77459 4496 D1
4700 BLAR 77401 4101 A3
4900 BLAR 77401 4100 E3
4900 HOUS 77081 4100 E3
4900 HOUS 77401 4100 E3
Tamarock Dr
- LGCY 77598 4630 C4
Tamarron Ct
7800 HarC 77346 3265 B3
Tamarron Dr
20400 HarC 77346 3265 B3
Tamayo Dr
7900 FBnC 77083 4096 A7
8300 FBnC 77083 4236 A1
Tambarisk Ln
100 PNVL 77304 2237 A1
Tambourine Dr
11900 HOUS 77477 4238 A4
12200 HOUS 77477 4237 E3
12500 HOUS 77099 4237 E3
Tamerisk Center Ct
13800 HarC 77069 3400 A2
Tamerlaine Dr
200 BKHV 77024 3959 A4
200 HOUS 77024 3959 A4
Tamerton Dr
20100 HarC 77388 3113 A5
Tamesei Dr
22700 MtgC 77365 2972 A3
Tameyoza Ln
3100 HarC 77521 3832 D3
3100 HarC 77562 3832 D3
Tamfield Dr
3600 HarC 77066 3401 C4
Tamina Rd
- MtgC 77382 2673 B5
- SHEH 77381 2822 B2
- WDLD 77382 2673 B5
1000 MtgC 77385 2822 B2
1000 SHEH 77385 2822 B2
32000 MtgC 77354 2673 A4
Tamina Tr
11400 MtgC 77384 2674 A2
11500 MtgC 77384 2673 E2
Tamina Manor Rd
3300 MtgC 77384 2821 D1
Tamina School Rd
- MtgC 77385 2822 B3
- SHEH 77385 2822 B3
Tami Renee Ln
8700 HarC 77040 3541 C7
Tammany Ln
15700 HarC 77082 4096 B3
Tammany Manor Ln
6800 HarC 77379 3111 C2
Tammarack Dr
12400 HOUS 77013 3827 E6
12400 HOUS 77013 3828 A6
Tammony Park Ln
3800 HarC 77546 4506 A6
Tammy Dr
5000 MNVL 77578 4625 C4
Tamora Ln
7800 PASD 77505 4249 C3
Tam O'Shanter Dr
7000 HarC 77069 3400 A2
Tam O'Shanter Ln
3000 MSCY 77459 4497 A1

STREET
Block City ZIP Map# Grid

Tam O'Shanter Ln
6000 HOUS 77036 4099 D4
Tampa St
2600 FRDW 77546 4629 A7
3200 HOUS 77021 4103 B4
Tampico St
4200 HOUS 77016 3825 B1
Tampico Wy
16500 GLSN 77554 5331 E4
16500 JMAB 77554 5331 E4
Tamworth Dr
1200 HarC 77015 3829 B6
1900 KATY 77493 3813 D6
11200 HOUS 77016 3687 B1
Tamy Ln
1200 SPVL 77055 3820 E7
Tan Hl
13200 HarC 77044 3549 E1
Tanager Ln
9800 MtgC 77385 2676 D4
14300 MtgC 77302 2679 D1
14300 MtgC 77306 2679 D1
18600 HarC 77377 2962 A7
Tanager St
6200 HOUS 77074 4100 A7
7100 HOUS 77074 4099 E7
8800 HOUS 77036 4099 A7
11900 HOUS 77072 4098 A7
Tanager Tr
10 WDLD 77381 2821 A2
Tanberry Ln
9100 HarC 77044 3689 C4
Tancah Ln
21100 HarC 77073 3259 E3
Tandy Park Wy
2000 HOUS 77047 4373 C1
Tang City Dr
100 MSCY 77489 4370 C2
Tangerine St
3300 HOUS 77051 4243 B4
Tangiers Rd
10000 HOUS 77041 3681 A6
10200 HarC 77041 3681 A6
Tangier Turn
8800 FBnC 77459 4621 B6
Tangle Ln
5000 HOUS 77056 3960 E4
5000 HOUS 77056 3961 A4
Tangleberry Ct
1800 FBnC 77545 4622 D1
Tanglebriar Cir
5500 DKSN 77539 4754 A4
Tanglebriar Ct
5300 DKSN 77539 4754 A4
Tangle Briar Dr
900 TYLV 77586 4381 E7
900 TYLV 77586 4508 E1
Tanglebriar Dr
3000 PASD 77503 4108 A6
5300 DKSN 77539 4754 A4
5500 TXCY 77539 4754 A4
Tanglebriar Ln
2000 DKSN 77539 4754 A4
Tangle Brush Dr
- WDLD 77381 2820 E5
10 WDLD 77381 2821 B6
Tanglecircle Ln
5700 HOUS 77056 3960 D3
5700 HOUS 77057 3960 D3
Tangle Creek Ln
4500 HarC 77388 3112 B5
N Tangle Creek Ln
21100 HarC 77388 3112 C4
Tanglehead Ct
11000 HarC 77086 3542 C1
Tangle Lake Dr
1900 HOUS 77339 3118 D7
Tanglelane St
1900 RHMD 77469 4491 E2
1900 RHMD 77469 4492 A3
Tangle Pines Ct
1900 HOUS 77062 4379 E6
1900 HOUS 77062 4380 A5
Tangler Ct
9600 HarC 77375 3110 C3
Tangler Ln
22600 HarC 77375 3110 C3
Tangle River Dr
3700 HOUS 77339 3119 C5
Tanglerose Ct
18600 HarC 77084 3816 C1
Tangle Tree Ln
18200 HarC 77084 3816 D3
Tanglewick Ln
- HarC 77047 4374 B4
Tanglewild Ln
900 FBnC 77469 4365 E4
Tanglewilde Av
2100 HOUS 77063 3959 B6
3200 HOUS 77063 4099 B1
7700 HOUS 77036 4099 C5
Tanglewilde St
3700 HOUS 77063 4099 B2
Tanglewood Ct
12000 STAF 77477 4238 A6
Tanglewood Dr
200 DKSN 77539 4753 C4
200 FRDW 77546 4505 A6
300 CNRO 77301 2383 E2
300 CNRO 77301 2384 A2
Tanglewood Rd
700 HOUS 77056 3960 E4
Tanglewood St
100 BYTN 77520 3971 B1
29500 MtgC 77354 2672 A7
Tanglewood Park St
5800 HOUS 77057 3960 D3
Tangley St
2100 HOUS 77005 4102 B2
2800 WUNP 77005 4102 A2
3000 WUNP 77005 4101 E2
Tanguey Ct
500 HarC 77388 3113 E7
Tankersley Rd
7000 MNVL 77578 4625 D7
Tanks Av
- TXCY 77590 4875 A7
Tannehill Dr
1500 HOUS 77008 3822 D6
Tanner Pl
- PNVL 77304 2237 B1
Tanner Rd
9700 HOUS 77041 3681 B6
10200 HarC 77041 3681 A6
10300 HarC 77041 3680 D6
10300 HOUS 77041 3680 E6
11900 HarC 77041 3679 D6

Tanner Park Ct
10900 HOUS 77075 4377 E2
10900 HOUS 77089 4377 E2
Tanner Woods Ln
21100 HarC 77338 3261 E3
Tanoak Cir
8800 HarC 77375 2965 E7
Tan Oak Ct
21600 MtgC 77365 2972 A1
Tanvern Ct
13700 HarC 77014 3401 D2
Tanvern Ln
13600 HarC 77014 3401 D2
Tanwood Dr
10900 HarC 77065 3539 D2
Tanya Cir
15700 HOUS 77079 3956 E2
Tanya Dr
100 LPRT 77571 4250 E2
Taos Ln
11400 HarC 77070 3398 E2
Taos Tr
100 DRPK 77536 4109 E7
Taos Creek Ct
15200 HarC 77429 3253 C4
Taper Glow Pl
10 WDLD 77381 2820 D4
Tapestry Ln
5000 FBnC 77494 4093 D3
Tapestry Forest Pl
10 WDLD 77381 2821 E1
E Tapestry Park Cir
10 WDLD 77381 2821 D1
W Tapestry Park Cir
10 WDLD 77381 2821 D1
Tapestry Park Dr
10 SHEH 77381 2821 D1
10 WDLD 77381 2821 D1
Tappenbeck Dr
9700 HOUS 77055 3820 B6
Tappengate Ln
16800 HarC 77073 3259 B3
Tapper Hill Dr
- HOUS 77077 3957 A3
Taquard Lndg
5600 STFE 77510 4987 B2
Tara Blvd
- FBnC 77469 4493 D6
- FBnC 77479 4493 D5
Tara Cir
1700 TXCY 77591 4873 A4
Tara Ct
11700 HarC 77375 2964 D3
Tara Dr
6600 FBnC 77469 4493 C6
12100 BKHV 77024 3959 B3
12100 HOUS 77024 3959 A3
Tara Pk
300 MtgC 77302 2530 B6
Tara Pl
3200 LPRT 77571 4249 E3
11400 PRLD 77583 4500 D6
Tara Ter
14700 MtgC 77372 2682 D2
Tara Tr
- HarC 77038 3543 C6
Tara Bend Ct
- HarC 77375 2964 D2
Tara Blue Ridge Dr
7000 FBnC 77469 4493 D6
Tara Gables Ct
2900 HarC 77082 4096 C2
Taraglen Ct
8400 FBnC 77469 4235 E1
Tara Hills Ct
11700 HOUS 77034 4247 A7
Taranto Ln
200 HarC 77015 3829 A6
Tara Oak Dr
13300 HarC 77065 3539 A2
Tara Oaks Ct
4400 FBnC 77469 4364 C2
Tara Park Dr
- FBnC 77469 4493 D6
Tara Park Ln
21500 PNIS 77445 3099 C3
Tara Plantation Dr
100 FBnC 77469 4493 D6
Tara Ridge Oak Blvd
- HarC 77082 4096 D2
Tara Ridge Oak Ct
15000 HarC 77082 4096 C2
Tararin Ln
8400 FBnC 77469 4095 D7
Tara Springs Ln
- MtgC 77386 2969 E6
Tarawa Rd
5100 HOUS 77033 4244 A1
Tarawood Ct
3700 HarC 77388 3112 D5
Tara Wy Dr
22700 HarC 77449 3814 D3
Tarbell Rd
8000 HOUS 77034 4246 E6
Tarberry Rd
1300 HOUS 77088 3684 A1
1400 HOUS 77088 3683 E1
Tarbet Pl Ct
13100 HarC 77429 3397 C3
Taren Ct
22300 HarC 77375 3110 D3
Tareyton Ln
4100 HOUS 77047 4243 C7
8000 HOUS 77075 4245 D7
Target Dr
1700 HOUS 77043 3819 B6
Taric Dr
7800 FBnC 77083 4096 A6
Tarleton Dr
10600 HNCV 77024 3960 B1
Tarley St
1100 HOUS 77009 3824 D4
Tarlton Ct
25000 HarC 77375 2964 D3
Tarlton Wy
4300 SGLD 77478 4369 A7
Tarna Ln
6300 HOUS 77074 4100 B5
6300 HOUS 77081 4100 B5
Tarnbrook Dr
4600 HarC 77084 3677 E7
Tarnef Dr
6500 HOUS 77074 4100 A5
Tarnish Leaf Dr
19800 HarC 77073 3403 C2
Taro Ln
8300 HarC 77521 3833 D2

Taro St
500 HarC 77532 3552 D3
Tar Oaks Ct
14900 HarC 77082 4096 C2
Tarpan Rdg
7800 HarC 77338 3261 D4
Tarpaulin Wy
600 HarC 77532 3552 A2
Tarpey Av
2900 TXCY 77590 4874 D5
Tarpey Rd
100 TXCY 77591 4873 B6
Tarpley Ct
1900 HarC 77493 3814 C6
Tarpon Av
100 GLSN 77550 4994 E7
Tarpon Dr
- GlsC 77568 4990 E6
- LMQU 77568 4990 E6
100 BYUV 77563 4990 D7
100 GlsC 77563 4990 D7
2400 TXCY 77591 4872 E3
2800 LGCY 77573 4633 C3
Tarpon Ln
3800 LPRT 77571 4383 A2
3800 PASD 77571 4383 A2
Tarpon Rd
- HarC 77049 3690 D5
Tarpon Springs Ct
15600 HarC 77095 3538 E5
Tarpon Springs Ln
8900 HarC 77095 3538 E4
Tarra Firma Dr
- HarC 77379 3111 E7
Tarragon Ln
8300 HarC 77521 3833 D2
9500 HOUS 77036 4098 E6
Tarrant Ct
9500 HarC 77064 3540 D6
Tarrington Av
7000 SGLD 77479 4367 C7
Tarrington Ct
900 HNCV 77024 3960 A1
Tarrington Dr
10600 HNCV 77024 3960 B1
Tarrytown Ln
2600 PRLD 77581 4504 C3
Tarrytown Wy
10 CNRO 77384 2675 E4
Tarrytown Crossing Dr
2200 CNRO 77304 2236 D2
N Tarrytown Crossing Dr
8000 CNRO 77304 2236 E2
Tarrytown Mall
2400 HOUS 77057 3960 C7
Tartan Ct
10 CNRO 77301 2530 C3
8200 FBnC 77583 4744 A3
Tartan Ln
10 CNRO 77301 2530 B2
3500 HOUS 77025 4101 C6
Tartan Manor St
9400 HarC 77379 3110 C5
Tartan Walk Ln
8600 HOUS 77075 4376 E4
Tarton Wy Ct
9400 HarC 77065 3539 C5
Tarver
200 HOUS 77009 3824 B5
Tarver St
700 HOUS 77009 3824 B5
Tasco Ln
7600 HOUS 77036 4099 D3
Tascosa Ln
9300 HarC 77064 3540 D6
Tascott St
100 PASD 77506 4107 A3
Tashkent Dr
5100 FRDW 77546 4505 D6
Tasia Dr
12300 HOUS 77085 4371 A1
Task St
11400 HarC 77039 3546 A7
11400 HarC 77093 3546 A7
11400 HOUS 77039 3546 A7
Tasmania Ct
14300 FBnC 77478 4366 E4
Tasmania Pl
19400 HarC 77449 3677 A3
Tassel Brook Dr
9800 HarC 77070 3255 B6
Tassel Creek Dr
- HarC 77377 3254 E6
Tassel Field Ln
8100 HarC 77338 3261 E3
Tassell St
700 HOUS 77076 3684 E6
Tasselwood Ln
4100 HarC 77014 3401 B1
Tassia Ln
- PASD 77058 4508 C3
Taswell Dr
- HarC 77494 3953 C4
Tate Ct
10200 CHTW 77385 2822 E4
10200 MtgC 77385 2822 E4
Tate St
7900 HOUS 77028 3826 B4
Tatefield
8200 HOUS 77028 3826 C4
Tatom St
9700 HOUS 77093 3685 E5
Tattenhall Dr
1800 HOUS 77008 3822 C5
Tatteridge Dr
5600 HarC 77069 3256 E7
Tattershall Cir
8100 HarC 77338 3261 E4
Tattershall Ln
10900 FBnC 77459 4622 B4
Tatton Crest Ct
- HarC 77388 3111 E2
Tatum Ln
5300 HarC 77389 3112 A1
Taub Rd
8600 HarC 77064 3541 B4
Taupewood Pl
10 WDLD 77384 2675 A4
Taut Ct
15800 HarC 77532 3552 A4
Tautenhahn Rd
5200 HOUS 77016 3686 E2
6000 HOUS 77016 3687 A2
Tavendale Ct
1400 FBnC 77545 4622 E2
Tavenor Ln
4100 HOUS 77047 4243 C7
5100 HOUS 77048 4243 E7

Tavenor Ln
5300 HOUS 77048 4244 A7
8000 HOUS 77075 4376 D1
8600 HOUS 77075 4377 A1
9000 HOUS 77075 4246 A7
Tavenor Rd
- HOUS 77075 4245 E7
Tavenor St
7600 HOUS 77075 4376 B1
Tavern St
7800 HOUS 77040 3681 E6
Taverns Corner Ct
- HarC 77084 3816 B1
Taverns Corner Ln
- HarC 77084 3816 B1
Taverns Crossing Ln
- HarC 77084 3816 B1
Tavern Springs Ln
3700 HarC 77449 3816 B2
Taverton Dr
1400 HarC 77530 3829 C5
Tavin House Ln
- HarC 77088 3543 A7
Tavish Ln
1800 CNRO 77301 2530 B3
Tavistock Dr
8700 HOUS 77031 4239 B5
Tavita Ln
- HarC 77083 4097 A6
Tawakom Dr
12200 HarC 77375 3109 C6
Tawakon Dr
4100 PRLD 77584 4502 E7
Tawnas Wy Ln
18100 HarC 77429 3252 B6
Tawnee
11300 HarC 77065 3398 E6
Tawny Bluff Ct
7900 HarC 77433 3537 A7
Tawny Oaks Dr
1900 HOUS 77345 3120 C6
Tawny Trace Ct
9800 HarC 77044 3689 B4
Tawny Wood Ct
20700 HarC 77338 3262 B2
Tawny Wood Dr
8100 HarC 77338 3261 E2
8200 HarC 77338 3262 A3
Taxiway
- HarC 77379 3111 A4
7700 HarC 77379 3110 E4
Taxiway Rd
10 HarC 77379 3110 E4
10 HarC 77379 3111 A5
Tay Ct
200 HOUS 77336 3121 D4
Taylan Ln
5500 RSBG 77471 4491 D5
Tayloe House Ln
23800 HarC 77493 3814 B6
Taylor
1500 BYTN 77520 3973 C6
Taylor Av
1300 PASD 77506 4107 C4
Taylor Cir
- LMQU 77568 4873 C7
Taylor Ct
10 HOUS 77020 3964 A2
E Taylor Dr
- GLSN 77554 5441 B4
Taylor Ln
1800 PRLD 77581 4504 D4
2400 DRPK 77536 4109 B6
12900 STAF 77477 4370 B1
18900 HarC 77532 3412 C4
Taylor Rd
- HarC 77389 2968 D6
7800 HarC 77086 3541 E2
7900 HarC 77064 3541 D2
12000 HarC 77041 3540 A7
12600 HarC 77041 3539 D6
30000 MtgC 77354 2672 A7
Taylor St
- HOUS 77007 3963 A1
- HOUS 77009 3963 A1
- HOUS 77029 3965 D5
400 HarC 77015 3967 E4
2000 WALR 77484 3102 A5
2200 WALR 77484 3101 E5
3000 LMQU 77568 4873 C7
7300 MNVL 77578 4746 D3
N Taylor St
100 ALVN 77511 4867 B1
S Taylor St
100 ALVN 77511 4867 B2
Taylor Wy
6600 HarC 77389 2966 C3
Taylor Bend Dr
- FBnC 77450 4094 E4
Taylor Brook Ct
600 HarC 77094 3955 B2
Taylor Creek Dr
1800 FBnC 77545 4622 D2
Taylorcrest
2700 FBnC 77459 4621 B7
Taylorcrest Dr
2900 BzaC 77584 4501 A6
Taylorcrest Rd
11400 HDWV 77024 3959 B2
11400 PNPV 77024 3959 B2
11500 BKHV 77024 3959 B2
11800 HOUS 77024 3959 A2
12500 HOUS 77024 3958 E2
13800 HOUS 77079 3958 A2
Taylor Lake Ct
4800 FBnC 77469 4234 D4
Taylor Leigh Ln
11900 HarC 77066 3401 B6
Taylor Meadow Ln
19300 HarC 77073 3403 C3
Taylor Mills Ct
1600 FBnC 77494 3952 D4
Taylor Park Ln
5200 FBnC 77494 4093 B2
Taylor Point Dr
10 WDLD 77382 2674 D4
N Taylor Point Dr
10 WDLD 77382 2674 E4
S Taylor Point Dr
10 WDLD 77382 2674 E5
Taylor Ridge Dr
900 HarC 77373 2968 D7
Taylors Crossing Dr
12200 HarC 77375 3109 C7
Taylors Glen Ct
2900 FBnC 77494 3953 B7
Taylor Springs Ln
- HarC 77375 3255 A1

Taylorwood Ln
12400 HarC 77070 3399 D5
Tayman Park Ln
23500 FBnC 77494 3953 C5
Taymouth Dr
1300 MtgC 77386 2968 E1
1300 MtgC 77386 2969 A1
14600 HarC 77084 3679 A3
Tayport Ln
15000 HarC 77530 3829 C6
Tayside Track
10 FBnC 77459 4621 C7
Tazewell Pointe Dr
26300 FBnC 77494 4092 B5
T Bar M Blvd
6500 HarC 77069 3400 B1
TC Jester Blvd
- HarC 77038 3402 B7
- HarC 77088 3543 A6
- HOUS 77007 3823 A7
- HOUS 77018 3823 A7
500 HOUS 77007 3962 A1
700 HOUS 77008 3823 A7
5100 HOUS 77091 3683 A6
6700 HOUS 77088 3683 A6
12100 HarC 77067 3402 B5
13100 HarC 77038 3543 A2
13200 HarC 77014 3401 E2
13200 HarC 77014 3402 B5
14300 HarC 77014 3257 D6
14400 HarC 77068 3257 C5
17100 HarC 77379 3256 E1
17800 HarC 77379 3257 A2
21000 HarC 77379 3111 C3
E TC Jester Blvd
1000 HOUS 77008 3823 A6
1500 HOUS 77008 3822 E5
3000 HOUS 77018 3822 C2
W TC Jester Blvd
1000 HOUS 77008 3823 A6
1500 HOUS 77008 3822 D5
2600 HOUS 77092 3822 C4
2700 HOUS 77018 3822 C3
4300 HOUS 77018 3683 B7
4500 HOUS 77091 3683 B7
7200 HOUS 77088 3683 A3
TC Reservoir Rd
- TXCY 77590 4756 A4
- TXCY 77591 4755 E4
- TXCY 77591 4756 A3
Teaberry Hl
- HarC 77044 3549 C2
Teaberry Ln
3700 HarC 77389 3112 D1
Teaberry Breeze Ct
- HarC 77044 3550 A3
Teabury St
700 PASD 77503 4108 B5
Tea Garden Ct
22400 FBnC 77450 4093 B6
Teague Cir
900 SGLD 77478 4369 A4
Teague Rd
2500 HOUS 77080 3820 A3
5400 HOUS 77041 3681 B6
N Teague Rd
4600 ARLA 77583 4623 B3
4600 FBnC 77583 4623 B3
S Teague Rd
4700 ARLA 77583 4623 B3
4700 FBnC 77583 4623 B3
Teak Dr
16400 MSCY 77071 4239 B7
Teak Canyon Tr
20100 HarC 77449 3676 E7
Teak Mill Pl
10 WDLD 77382 2674 A5
Teakwood Av
300 FBnC 77545 4623 C2
600 BzaC 77583 4623 D2
600 PRLD 77545 4623 D2
Teakwood Cir
3200 DKSN 77539 4754 A1
Teakwood Dr
1300 HOUS 77017 4106 D6
1300 HOUS 77502 4106 D6
1300 PASD 77017 4106 D6
1300 PASD 77502 4106 D6
3800 LPRT 77571 4250 D4
5500 GLSN 77551 5108 D7
Teakwood Ln
300 HNCV 77024 3960 A3
3500 BzaC 77584 4501 C1
5300 MtgC 77354 2673 E3
Teakwood Pl
10 WDLD 77384 2674 E2
2000 SGLD 77478 4368 E6
Teakwood St
1900 RHMD 77469 4491 E3
Teakwood Forest Dr
8100 HarC 77379 3256 A3
Teal
- HOUS 77049 3828 B3
Teal Ct
28400 MtgC 77355 2814 E5
Teal Ct N
1200 PRLD 77584 4501 D2
Teal Ct S
1200 PRLD 77584 4501 E2
Teal Dr
500 LGCY 77539 4753 A4
2000 MtgC 77386 2969 B3
3200 KATY 77493 3813 B3
5500 GLSN 77551 5108 D7
Teal Ln
200 SGLD 77478 4368 A4
3500 HarC 77047 4374 C5
Teal St
800 HOUS 77029 3965 D6
Teal Tr
7800 HarC 77389 2965 E4
7800 HarC 77389 2966 A4
Teal Arbor Ln
1800 HOUS 77345 3120 C6
Teal Bay Ln
- HarC 77070 3255 C6
Tealbay Bend Ln
2100 LGCY 77573 4631 B7
Teal Bayou Ln
26900 HarC 77447 3248 D7
Teal Bend Blvd
- FBnC 77545 4622 D1
3700 FBnC 77545 4498 D7
Teal Bend Ct
1700 FBnC 77545 4622 D2
Teal Breeze Dr
8700 FBnC 77469 4234 E1

Tealbriar Cir
10 WDLD 77381 2820 C4
Tealbrook Dr
20300 HarC 77433 3676 D1
Teal Brook Ln
1700 FBnC 77479 4493 D4
Teal Cove Ln
14200 HOUS 77077 3956 E6
Teal Creek Dr
18400 HarC 77346 3409 C1
Tealcrest Ln
14000 HarC 77047 4374 C4
Tealcrest Estates Dr
30600 MtgC 77386 2969 B1
Tea Leaf Dr
11100 HarC 77375 3110 A7
Teal Estates Blvd
- FBnC 77545 4622 E1
E Teal Estates Cir
3900 FBnC 77545 4623 A1
N Teal Estates Cir
1000 FBnC 77545 4622 E1
1000 FBnC 77545 4623 A1
S Teal Estates Cir
1000 FBnC 77545 4622 E1
1000 FBnC 77545 4623 A1
W Teal Estates Cir
3900 FBnC 77545 4622 C2
Teal Fern Ct
3900 PASD 77059 4380 D4
Teal Forest Ln
17500 HarC 77379 3256 D1
Tealgate Dr
4800 HarC 77373 3115 B5
Teal Glen Ct
1300 HOUS 77062 4379 E6
Teal Glen St
3500 PRLD 77584 4503 B6
Teal Hollow Dr
12900 HarC 77429 3397 C4
Teal Hollow Ln
11600 HarC 77377 3254 D5
Teal Lake Ct
24900 FBnC 77494 3952 E5
Teal Manor Ct
16200 HarC 77546 4505 D7
Teal Maple Ct
3800 FBnC 77545 4498 E6
Tealmeadow Ct
400 BKHV 77024 3959 A3
400 HOUS 77024 3959 A3
Teal Mesa Dr
4200 HOUS 77048 4374 D4
Teal Oak Dr
900 FBnC 77545 4623 A1
Teal Oaks Ln
12800 HarC 77041 3679 D3
Teal Park Ct
8100 HarC 77396 3406 D6
Teal Park Dr
15200 HarC 77396 3406 D6
Teal Point Dr
20700 HarC 77450 3954 C6
Teal Run Dr
6300 HOUS 77035 4240 A5
7500 HOUS 77071 4239 E5
7500 HOUS 77071 4240 A6
Teal Run Meadows Dr
3900 FBnC 77545 4498 E7
3900 FBnC 77545 4622 E1
Teal Run Pl Ct
3900 FBnC 77545 4622 D1
Teal Run Pl Dr
1800 FBnC 77545 4622 C1
2200 FBnC 77545 4498 C7
Teal Shore Ct
2400 LGCY 77573 4508 D6
13700 HOUS 77077 3957 A5
Tealstone Falls Ct
14000 HarC 77044 3549 D2
Teal Valley Ct
4100 FBnC 77545 4622 E1
Teal View Ln
2600 FBnC 77494 3953 B5
Teal Vista Ct
3900 FBnC 77545 4622 E1
Teal Water Ct
3500 HarC 77449 3815 C3
Tealway Dr
1000 PASD 77504 4247 C5
Tealwick Ln
- FBnC 77494 4092 E3
Teal Wind Dr
7200 HarC 77433 3676 E1
Tealwood
28900 HarC 77484 3103 A3
Tealwood Dr
300 HOUS 77024 3959 A4
Tealwood Glen Ln
- FBnC 77545 4622 C1
Tealwood North Cir
12300 BKHV 77024 3959 A4
12300 HOUS 77024 3959 A4
Tealwood North Dr
12300 BKHV 77024 3959 A4
12300 HOUS 77024 3959 A4
Teal Wy Ct
- FBnC 77545 4622 E1
Teameadow Ct
5200 DKSN 77539 4754 D1
Teanaway Ln
1400 HOUS 77029 3965 C3
Teaneck Dr
11700 HOUS 77089 4378 B6
Tea Olive Ct
7000 HarC 77389 2966 C1
Tea Party
2900 FRDW 77546 4749 E2
Tea Rose Ct
3800 FBnC 77583 4622 C4
22300 FBnC 77469 4093 D7
Tea Rose Ln
37200 MtgC 77354 2670 B7
Teas Ct
3300 CNRO 77304 2237 B6
Teas Rd
10 CNRO 77303 2238 B7
300 MtgC 77303 2238 D7
700 CNRO 77303 2237 E7
1000 CNRO 77301 2384 D1
1000 CNRO 77303 2384 D1
1000 MtgC 77303 2384 D1
1500 CNRO 77304 2237 C7
Teas Rd FM-3083
100 CNRO 77303 2238 B7
300 MtgC 77303 2238 D7
700 CNRO 77303 2237 E7
1000 CNRO 77301 2384 D1

Teas Rd FM-3083
1000 CNRO 77303 2384 D1
1000 MtgC 77303 2384 D1
1500 CNRO 77304 2237 C7
Teas St
4500 BLAR 77401 4101 B5
Teas Cottage Dr
7300 CNRO 77304 2236 D6
Teas Crossing Ct
3000 CNRO 77304 2236 E6
Teas Crossing Dr
2200 CNRO 77304 2236 E6
2200 CNRO 77304 2237 A6
Teasdale
1500 CNRO 77301 2384 D2
Teasel Ct
20700 FBnC 77450 4094 B3
Teaside Dr
11600 HarC 77066 3401 C6
Teas Lakes Dr
7400 CNRO 77304 2236 E4
Teasley Ln
8800 HarC 77375 2965 D3
Teas Nursery Rd
2000 CNRO 77304 2237 A6
Teaswood Dr
7200 CNRO 77304 2236 E6
7200 CNRO 77304 2237 A6
Teawick Ct
3300 HarC 77068 3257 B4
Tebo St
9900 HOUS 77076 3685 A5
Teche Ln
25100 HarC 77336 3266 E1
Techniplex Dr
4500 STAF 77477 4238 B7
Technology Dr
12700 SGLD 77478 4237 C5
Technology Forest Blvd
- WDLD 77381 2821 C2
Technology Forest Pl
8000 WDLD 77381 2821 C2
Teck Ct
14600 HarC 77047 4374 D5
Tecumseh Ct
3000 MSCY 77459 4497 E6
Tecumsem Cir
5700 HOUS 77057 3960 D3
Tecumsem Dr
400 HOUS 77057 3960 D3
Ted St
5200 HOUS 77040 3681 E7
Ted Dudley Dr
- TXCY 77591 4873 E2
- TXCY 77591 4874 A2
Teddy Ln
22600 HarC 77389 2966 E7
Teddy Bear Al
900 HMBL 77338 3262 E4
900 HMBL 77338 3263 A4
Ted Picket Ln
700 LGCY 77573 4632 B3
Teel Dr
7200 TXCY 77591 4873 C5
Teery Dr
- MtgC 77306 2385 D3
Teesdale Dr
7600 HOUS 77028 3687 A6
Tee Tree Ct
4100 MtgC 77386 2970 D7
Teetshorn St
200 HOUS 77009 3963 A1
900 HOUS 77009 3962 E1
Teichman Rd
8200 GLSN 77554 5107 C6
Teichman Rd FM-188
9300 GLSN 77554 5107 C6
Tejas Ct
9200 LPRT 77571 4249 E4
9200 LPRT 77571 4250 A4
Tejas Dr
6300 PASD 77503 4248 E2
Tejas Ln
23400 MtgC 77365 2972 B5
Tejas Rd
16500 HarC 77429 3396 E3
Tejas St
7000 BYTN 77521 3835 B5
7800 HarC 77521 3833 B3
Tejas Tr
- FBnC 77469 4364 C6
- RHMD 77469 4364 C6
Telean St
7700 HOUS 77075 4376 C2
Telegraph Creek Dr
17700 HarC 77379 3256 C1
Telegraph Square Ct
1900 HarC 77449 3815 D6
Telegraph Square Ln
19900 HarC 77449 3815 D6
Telephone Rd
- BzaC 77511 4628 B4
- PRLD 77511 4628 A3
- PRLD 77581 4628 A3
100 HOUS 77023 3964 A6
1000 HOUS 77023 4104 C1
4300 HOUS 77087 4104 E5
4600 HOUS 77087 4105 A7
5800 HOUS 77087 4245 A1
6400 HOUS 77061 4245 B6
9000 HOUS 77075 4245 B7
9200 HOUS 77061 4376 B1
9200 HOUS 77075 4376 B5
11400 PRLD 77581 4376 B5
21100 WlrC 77445 3097 C2
Telephone Rd SR-35
- BzaC 77511 4628 B4
- HOUS 77087 4245 B6
- PRLD 77511 4628 A3
- PRLD 77581 4628 A3
6400 HOUS 77061 4245 B6
9000 HOUS 77075 4245 B7
9200 HOUS 77061 4376 B1
9200 HOUS 77075 4376 B5
11400 PRLD 77581 4376 B5
Televista Dr
12900 HarC 77037 3545 A7
13000 HarC 77037 3685 A1
13000 HOUS 77037 3545 A7
13000 HOUS 77037 3685 A1
Telfair Av
6700 SGLD 77479 4494 C1
7400 SGLD 77479 4367 D7
Telfair Ct
14500 HarC 77084 3679 A4
Telford Wy
18800 HarC 77375 3255 A1

Telge Rd
8500 HarC 77095 3538 D2
10800 HarC 77429 3538 C1
12000 HarC 77429 3397 C4
14600 HarC 77429 3253 C7
18500 HarC 77377 3108 B7
18500 HarC 77429 3108 B7
Telge St
3100 HOUS 77021 4103 A5
3100 HOUS 77054 4103 A5
Telge Ter
15500 HarC 77377 3108 B4
Telge Lake Tr
14900 HarC 77429 3253 D2
Telge Manor Dr
- HarC 77429 3253 C5
N Telge Manor Dr
15700 HarC 77429 3253 C5
S Telge Manor Dr
15700 HarC 77429 3253 C5
Telico Junction Ln
7400 HarC 77346 3265 A7
Telkwa Dr
1500 MtgC 77386 2969 A1
Tellepsen St
1900 HOUS 77023 4104 B2
Teller Blvd
19500 HarC 77388 3113 C6
Teller Rd
- HarC 77388 3113 B5
Telluride Dr
7900 HarC 77040 3541 B6
Teluco Av
6400 HOUS 77055 3822 A5
6600 HOUS 77055 3821 E5
Tembrook Cove
2100 FBnC 77494 3952 B5
Temecula Cove
2200 FBnC 77494 3952 B5
N Tempe Cir
17500 HarC 77095 3537 C2
W Tempe Cir
10000 HarC 77095 3537 C3
Tempe Ct
17400 HarC 77095 3537 D3
Tempelgate Dr
5800 HarC 77066 3400 D2
Tempera Ct
11700 HarC 77038 3543 B5
E Temperance Ln
100 DRPK 77536 4249 B2
W Temperance Ln
7400 DRPK 77536 4249 B2
Tempest St
- HarC 77532 3552 A3
Templar Ln
13700 FBnC 77478 4237 A3
14300 FBnC 77478 4236 E3
Temple Cir
600 HTCK 77563 4988 D2
13100 STFE 77510 4870 E6
Temple Ct
10000 HarC 77095 3538 B3
Temple Dr
600 HTCK 77563 4988 D2
1900 HOUS 77019 3962 E4
3600 BzaC 77578 4501 B7
3600 BzaC 77578 4625 B1
S Temple Dr
16200 HarC 77095 3538 B3
W Temple Dr
10100 HarC 77095 3538 B3
Temple St
700 HOUS 77009 3824 A6
29500 MtgC 77354 2817 E3
W Temple St
600 HOUS 77009 3824 A6
1000 HOUS 77009 3823 E6
1100 HOUS 77008 3823 E6
Temple Bell Dr
4600 HarC 77388 3112 B3
Temple Hill Ln
18100 HarC 77429 3252 B5
Temple Park Ln
26700 HarC 77433 3396 A6
Templeridge Ln
10400 HOUS 77075 4377 A3
Templewood Ln
- FBnC 77469 4095 B6
Temprano Dr
- GLSN 77554 5440 E6
Ten Acre Wk
10 FBnC 77459 4621 B3
Tenaha Dr
3300 HarC 77014 3401 E1
Tenaya Canyon Ln
- HarC 77346 3408 D4
Tenbury Ct
- MtgC 77357 2829 D3
Tenbury St
15700 JRSV 77040 3540 D7
Tenbury Glen Dr
3600 HarC 77066 3401 C5
Tenby Dr
20000 HarC 77450 3954 E5
Ten Curves Cir
17600 HarC 77379 3256 C2
Ten Curves Ct
17600 HarC 77379 3256 C2
Ten Curves Rd
6800 HarC 77379 3256 C2
Tenderden Dr
1300 HarC 77015 3829 C5
1300 HarC 77530 3829 C5
Tender Violet Pl
10 WDLD 77381 2674 B7
Tenderwood Dr
4700 HOUS 77041 3680 E7
Teneha Dr
10100 HOUS 77033 4244 A5
Teneya Canyon
23600 MtgC 77355 2962 C5
Tenison Ct
16700 HarC 77379 3256 E2
Tenleyton Ln
10400 HOUS 77075 4377 A3
Tenneco Dr
10400 HOUS 77099 4237 C2
Tennessee Pk
500 MtgC 77302 2530 B6
Tennessee St
300 HOUS 77029 3966 A6
400 GNPK 77547 3966 A6
1900 BYTN 77520 4112 B1
Tenneta Dr
10400 HOUS 77099 4237 D3
Tennis Ct
10400 HOUS 77099 4237 C2
Tennis Dr
12700 HOUS 77099 4237 D2
Tenn Oaks
100 WlrC 77447 2959 C2
Tennyson Dr
800 PRLD 77584 4501 D1
Tennyson Ln
300 GlsC 77539 4635 D4
Tennyson St
4100 WUNP 77005 4101 C3
Ten Oaks Ct
18300 MtgC 77365 2972 A1
Ten Oaks Dr
15600 HarC 77377 3254 D6
Ten Point Ln
10300 FBnC 77459 4621 E7
10300 FBnC 77459 4622 A6
Ten Sleep Ln
4600 HarC 77546 4506 A6
4700 HarC 77546 4505 E6
Tenton Park Ln
6000 HOUS 77092 3682 C7
Tepee Tr
9100 HarC 77064 3540 C5
Terence Ct
900 STAF 77477 4370 B4
Terence Dr
1800 STAF 77477 4370 B4
Teresa Dr
500 HarC 77562 3832 A2
1000 SPVL 77055 3821 A7
1000 SPVL 77055 3960 B1
2300 RSBG 77471 4491 C6
Teresa St
21100 MtgC 77357 2827 A7
Teresa Cove Ln
3800 HarC 77449 3815 D2
Teri Ct
26500 ORDN 77386 2822 C6
Teriwood Cir
4200 HarC 77068 3257 A6
Terlin St
13400 HarC 77039 3546 E4
Terlingua St
4200 PASD 77504 4247 E5
4400 PASD 77504 4248 B5
Terminal
500 HOUS 77020 3965 B1
Terminal Dr
- GLSN 77551 5222 A1
- GLSN 77554 5222 A1
2000 GLSN 77554 5221 E2
Terminal Ln
- SGLD 77478 4367 C1
Terminal Rd N
2700 HOUS 77032 3404 D1
3200 HOUS 77032 3405 B1
3500 HOUS 77032 3261 A7
Terminal Rd S
2700 HOUS 77032 3404 D1
2900 HOUS 77032 3405 A1
Terminal St
300 HOUS 77020 3965 B1
900 HOUS 77011 3964 E5
3300 HOUS 77020 3826 B6
4900 BLAR 77401 4101 A2
5100 HOUS 77081 4101 A2
5100 HOUS 77401 4101 A2
Termini Rd
19200 GLSN 77554 5442 A2
19400 GLSN 77554 5441 E3
Termini Rd FM-3005
- GLSN 77554 5442 A2
Termini St
2400 DKSN 77539 4753 E3
2400 DKSN 77539 4754 A3
Tern Ct
10 MtgC 77385 2676 D6
Tern Dr
2900 GLSN 77551 5108 D7
Tern Rd
16600 GLSN 77554 5331 D4
16600 JMAB 77554 5331 D4
Tern Lake Dr
3400 HOUS 77339 3119 B5
Terra Bella Dr
- HOUS 77028 3687 E7
10 MNVL 77583 4624 D4
Terra Canyon Ln
7900 HarC 77433 3537 B7
Terrace
- MtgC 77365 2972 E6
Terrace Bnd
14400 HarC 77429 3253 E7
Terrace Dr
200 HOUS 77007 3962 A3
200 TXCY 77591 4873 E6
400 ELGO 77586 4509 A2
900 ALVN 77511 4867 A2
2300 HarC 77521 3834 C7
E Terrace Dr
10 HOUS 77007 3961 E4
10 HOUS 77007 3962 A4
24000 MtgC 77365 2972 E7
N Terrace Dr
23900 MtgC 77365 2972 E6
S Terrace Dr
20700 MtgC 77365 2972 E7
W Terrace Dr
10 HOUS 77007 3961 E4
10 HOUS 77007 3962 A4
23900 MtgC 77365 2972 E6
Terrace Ln
2000 BYTN 77520 3973 B6
Terrace Rdg
6900 FBnC 77494 4093 B5
Terrace Arbor Ln
- FBnC 77494 4093 A1
Terrace Brook Ct
7900 HarC 77040 3541 C6
Terrace Brook Dr
8200 HarC 77040 3541 D6
E Terrace Cable Cir
5500 FBnC 77494 4093 B7
W Terrace Cable Cir
5500 FBnC 77494 4093 B7
E Terrace Creek Cir
4200 HarC 77014 3401 C2
N Terrace Creek Cir
13600 HarC 77014 3401 C2
W Terrace Creek Cir
4200 HarC 77014 3401 C2
Terrace Creek Ct
200 FBnC 77469 4365 A5
Terrace Gate Ln
22100 FBnC 77450 4093 E3
Terrace Glade Ct
7900 HarC 77070 3399 B1
Terraceglen Ct
21600 HarC 77379 3111 B3
Terraceglen Ln
21600 HarC 77379 3111 B2
Terrace Hills Ln
3000 HOUS 77007 3962 E3
Terrace Hollow Ln
16500 FBnC 77478 4236 A6
Terrace Manor Rd
4400 HOUS 77041 3819 E1
4500 HOUS 77041 3680 D7
Terrace Meadow Dr
8500 HarC 77040 3541 A5
N Terrace Mill Cir
10 WDLD 77382 2673 D6
S Terrace Mill Cir
10 WDLD 77382 2673 D6
Terrace Oaks Dr
14900 HarC 77014 3257 D6
14900 HarC 77068 3257 C5
Terrace Park Blvd
- HarC 77084 3816 D4
Terrace Park Dr
16900 HarC 77095 3678 A1
Terrace Pines Dr
4200 HOUS 77345 3119 E4
4200 HOUS 77345 3120 A4
Terrace Run Ln
13000 HarC 77044 3689 C4
Terraces on Memorial
100 HOUS 77077 3956 D3
Terrace View Dr
1300 FBnC 77479 4494 B6
21000 HarC 77449 3676 D3
Terrace Vine Ln
21100 HarC 77379 3111 A3
Terrace Wind Ln
8300 HarC 77040 3541 B7
Terrace Wood Ct
13400 HarC 77070 3399 B2
Terra Cotta Dr
7800 HarC 77040 3541 D7
Terra Crossing Ln
- HarC 77041 3679 E5
Terra Forest Ct
19200 HarC 77449 3677 B6
Terraglen Dr
10 WDLD 77382 2675 C6
Terra Hollow Ln
- FBnC 77469 4094 D5
Terrain Park Dr
- HarC 77373 3115 B3
Terralyn Wy
13200 SGLD 77478 4237 B4
Terramar Dr
- GLSN 77554 5440 E6
4400 GLSN 77554 5441 A6
Terramare
19500 HarC 77532 3411 B4
Terramont Dr
- WDLD 77382 2673 A7
- WDLD 77382 2819 A1
Terrance St
12500 HOUS 77085 4371 B2
Terranova Ln
- LGCY 77573 4632 E3
1000 HarC 77090 3258 A1
Terranova West Dr
17700 HarC 77379 3257 A1
Terra Point Dr
14900 HarC 77429 3252 D7
Terra Run Ct
27200 MtgC 77386 3115 E2
Terra Springs Dr
20500 HarC 77449 3815 D2
Terrasso Dr
7000 GlsC 77563 4990 D6
Terra Stone Ct
19100 HarC 77433 3537 B7
Terravale Ct
10 WDLD 77381 2821 A4
Terra Valley Ln
8200 HarC 77375 3110 E2
Terra Verde Ln
- HarC 77336 3122 A3
Terravista Manor Dr
- HarC 77379 3257 A2
Terravita Hls
7100 HarC 77069 3400 A1
Terrawren Ln
17600 HarC 77379 3257 B3
Terraza Cove Ln
12000 HarC 77041 3680 A4
Terrebone Dr
11300 HarC 77429 3538 E1
11400 HarC 77429 3397 E7
Terrebone Rd
5800 HTCK 77563 4989 C4
Terrell Rd
5900 PRLD 77584 4502 D6
Terrell St
4300 HOUS 77093 3686 B4
Terrell Hills Dr
6100 FBnC 77469 4493 B5
Terrell Trail Ct
10 WDLD 77385 2676 D4
Terrero Ct
11800 HarC 77377 3109 B7
Terrero Dr
- HarC 77377 3109 B7
Terreton Dr
23300 MtgC 77365 3118 A1
Terri Ln
600 MtgC 77355 2816 B6
600 MtgC 77362 2816 B6
19100 MtgC 77385 2822 C2
31000 SGCH 77355 2961 E4
Terrie Ln
3200 PRLD 77581 4503 D3
Territa Ln
- MtgC 77357 2827 B5
Territory Ln
9800 HarC 77064 3540 D4
Terrton Springs Dr
21300 MtgC 77365 3118 A2
Terry
24100 HarC 77447 3249 E2
Terry Ct
1200 HarC 77073 3259 C7
Terry Ln
- HarC 77449 3815 D3
3000 HarC 77521 3834 D7
Terry St
100 SGLD 77478 4367 E3
100 SGLD 77478 4368 A3
1500 HOUS 77009 3963 D2
2500 HOUS 77009 3824 D7
4200 STFE 77517 4870 B7
Terrydale Ct
9300 HarC 77037 3544 C6
Terrydale Dr
9100 HarC 77037 3544 C7
Terryhollow Dr
700 HarC 77530 3829 D7
Terry Springs Ct
- FBnC 77469 4094 D5
Terwilliger Wy
5600 HOUS 77056 3960 D5
6200 HOUS 77057 3960 B5
Teslin Dr
11500 PNPV 77024 3959 D5
Tesoro Cir
22200 HOUS 77532 3266 C6
Tessa Ct
8300 HarC 77040 3541 B7
Tessa Lakes Ct
7100 FBnC 77479 4367 A7
Tessie Ct
4400 FBnC 77479 4493 C1
Tessie Cove Ln
2100 MtgC 77386 2969 D6
Tessie Hills Ln
27900 MtgC 77386 2969 D7
Tetela Dr
7300 FBnC 77083 4095 D6
Tethered Vine Pl
10 WDLD 77382 2674 C5
Teton Ln
18200 MtgC 77365 2972 B6
Teton St
4700 HOUS 77033 4243 D2
4700 HOUS 77051 4243 D2
Teton Pass Ln
- HarC 77346 3408 B4
Teton Peak Wy
12400 HOUS 77089 4505 C1
Tetter Cemetery Rd
6300 HarC 77338 3261 B2
Tewantin Dr
8200 HOUS 77061 4245 B5
W Tex Dr
9000 SPVL 77055 3820 E7
Texaco Rd
12400 HOUS 77013 3827 E5
12500 HOUS 77013 3828 A5
13400 MtgC 77302 2532 B4
Texana Wy
2200 FBnC 77469 4234 B7
2200 FBnC 77469 4365 B1
Texans Dr
- HarC 77032 3546 C3
Texarkana Dr
10 MAGA 77354 2669 A4
Texarkana St
6200 HOUS 77020 3825 D7
7100 HOUS 77020 3826 A7
13700 HarC 77015 3828 E7
14000 HarC 77015 3829 A7
Texas Av
- DRPK 77536 4109 A7
- HarC 77336 3268 A3
- HarC 77571 4110 E4
- LGCY 77573 4633 B5
- WEBS 77598 4631 B1
10 TXCY 77590 4875 A6
100 LGCY 77573 4632 C4
100 LMQU 77568 4874 A7
100 PASD 77506 4107 A4
100 TXCY 77591 4874 A7
200 ARLA 77583 4623 B5
200 GlsC 77518 4634 C2
300 KMAH 77565 4509 D5
400 GLSN 77550 5109 D2
500 HOUS 77002 3963 C4
600 FBnC 77583 4623 B5
900 WEBS 77598 4507 B7
1200 GlsC 77539 4633 B7
1300 MSCY 77489 4370 C3
1300 RSBG 77471 4490 D5
1500 ALVN 77511 4749 B6
1500 HOUS 77003 3963 E5
1600 DKSN 77539 4633 B7
1900 LMQU 77568 4873 C7
1900 TXCY 77591 4873 C7
2500 TXCY 77590 4874 E6
2800 DKSN 77539 4754 B3
3500 HOUS 77003 3964 A6
4700 HOUS 77011 3964 B6
6500 HTCK 77563 4989 C5
Texas Av FM-1765
10 TXCY 77590 4875 A6
100 LMQU 77568 4874 A7
100 TXCY 77590 4874 A7
100 TXCY 77591 4874 A7
1900 LMQU 77568 4873 C7
1900 TXCY 77591 4873 C7
E Texas Av
10 BYTN 77520 3973 A7
700 BYTN 77520 4113 C1
700 WEBS 77598 4507 B7
N Texas Av
100 HOUS 77062 4507 A5
100 WEBS 77598 4507 B6
W Texas Av
100 PASD 77506 4107 A5
800 BYTN 77520 3972 C6
Texas Dr
2100 SGLD 77479 4368 B6
Texas Pk
500 MtgC 77302 2530 B6
Texas Pkwy
200 MSCY 77489 4370 D7
700 STAF 77477 4370 C3
700 STAF 77489 4370 C3
1400 MSCY 77477 4370 C4
3000 MSCY 77489 4497 D1
3400 HOUS 77489 4497 D1
Texas Pkwy FM-2234
200 MSCY 77489 4370 D7
700 STAF 77477 4370 C3
700 STAF 77489 4370 C3
1400 MSCY 77477 4370 C4
3000 MSCY 77489 4497 D1
3400 HOUS 77489 4497 D1
Texas St
- HarC 77571 4110 E4
- LPRT 77571 4251 E4
100 SHUS 77587 4246 D3
200 TMBL 77375 2964 C6
2200 PRLD 77581 4503 B3
2500 PRLD 77584 4503 B3
4100 HOUS 77003 3964 A6
5100 HOUS 77011 3964 C6
5700 HTCK 77563 4989 D6
7300 HOUS 77011 3965 A7
7300 HOUS 77011 4105 A1
Texas St
7500 HOUS 77012 4105 A1
N Texas St
- TXCY 77591 4873 D6
S Texas St
10 LMQU 77568 4873 D7
10 TXCY 77591 4873 D7
Texas Tr
4400 SGLD 77479 4496 A1
Texas Army Tr
12400 HarC 77429 3398 A4
Texas Children's Cir
14000 HOUS 77062 4379 C7
Texas City Port Blvd
- TXCY 77590 4875 C7
- TXCY 77590 4991 B2
Texas City Port Blvd LP-197
- TXCY 77590 4875 C7
- TXCY 77590 4991 B2
Texas County Rd
- MNVL 77578 4626 A5
Texas DOT Dr
7400 CNRO 77303 2238 C7
Texas Laurel Dr
2500 FBnC 77494 3951 C5
Texas Laurel Lp
7200 HarC 77346 3265 A3
Texas Laurel Tr
19400 HarC 77346 3265 A4
Texas Oak Dr
3000 HarC 77449 3815 C4
Texas Plantation
- FBnC 77469 4365 B1
Texas Southern Dr
100 HarC 77532 3692 D1
Texas Star
11000 HarC 77532 3694 A5
Texas Star Ct
16300 MtgC 77302 2679 B3
Texas Trail Ln
2900 BzaC 77583 4500 D6
Texian Ct
21700 HarC 77388 3112 A2
Texmati Dr
2500 KATY 77494 3952 D1
Texoma St
1800 BYTN 77520 3972 C7
Thackery Ln
11000 HOUS 77016 3687 C2
Thaddeus Ct
4400 FBnC 77469 4233 E6
Thadds Tr
22700 HarC 77373 3115 E7
Thalerfield Dr
- PRLD 77584 4501 E5
Thaman Dr
12200 GlsC 77539 4871 A2
Thamer Cir
400 HNCV 77024 3960 B3
Thamer Ln
400 HNCV 77024 3960 B3
Thames Ln
8300 FBnC 77083 4095 E7
8300 FBnC 77083 4235 E1
Tharp St
3400 HOUS 77003 3963 E7
4500 SEBK 77586 4383 B7
Thatcham
25900 MtgC 77357 2829 E4
25900 MtgC 77357 2830 A4
Thatcher Dr
13000 HOUS 77077 3957 B7
Thayer Ct
24700 FBnC 77494 3952 D3
Thayne Village Ct
2100 PRLD 77581 4503 D2
Theall Rd
4700 HarC 77066 3401 B2
5500 HarC 77066 3400 E3
Thebes Ct
3200 MSCY 77459 4498 A5
The Equinox
- MtgC 77339 3118 B4
The Highlands Dr
2600 SGLD 77478 4368 D5
Theis Ln
12800 TMBL 77375 3109 B2
13100 HarC 77377 3109 A2
Theiss Rd
3400 HarC 77338 3260 B2
3400 HOUS 77338 3260 B2
Theissetta Dr
7700 HarC 77379 3256 B4
Theiss Hill Dr
7900 HarC 77379 3256 A2
Theiss Mail Route Rd
16800 HarC 77379 3256 B4
18200 HarC 77379 3255 E2
Theiss Park Ln
17900 HarC 77379 3256 A2
Theisswood Cir
17900 HarC 77379 3255 E2
Theisswood Ct
17700 HarC 77379 3256 A2
Theisswood Ln
17800 HarC 77379 3256 A2
Theisswood Rd
7400 HarC 77379 3256 B2
8200 HarC 77379 3255 E3
Thelfor Ct
7200 HarC 77379 3111 B2
Thelma Dr
2200 HOUS 77338 3263 B3
2600 HOUS 77009 3963 A1
14600 PRLD 77581 4502 D3
14600 PRLD 77584 4502 D3
Thelma Ln
100 TXCY 77591 4873 E6
1700 PASD 77502 4107 D7
22900 MtgC 77357 2973 E1
22900 MtgC 77357 2974 B1
Thelma Ann Ln
12800 HOUS 77048 4375 B2
The Mansions Blvd
- CNRO 77384 2675 E1
- MtgC 77384 2675 E1
The Oaks
- HarC 77377 3109 A7
Theodore Dr
- HarC 77049 3689 D7
The Oval St
10 SGLD 77479 4495 C2
Theresa Ln
2600 GlsC 77539 4635 C4
Theresa St
1000 HOUS 77051 4243 C2
2000 PASD 77506 4107 D5
Thermon St
10100 HOUS 77075 4377 D2
Theron Av
- HOUS 77022 3824 A2
Theron St
100 HOUS 77022 3824 A2
Therrell Dr
9500 HarC 77064 3540 C6
The Strand
100 GLSN 77550 5109 E1
Theta St
2100 HOUS 77034 4246 D7
2100 SHUS 77034 4246 D5
2100 SHUS 77587 4246 D5
Thetford Ln
8200 HarC 77070 3399 D2
Thetford St
3900 SGLD 77479 4495 E3
Theysen Cir
3300 HOUS 77080 3820 D2
Theysen Dr
9200 HOUS 77080 3820 D2
Thibodeaux St
1800 BYTN 77520 4112 E2
Thicket Ln
800 HOUS 77079 3957 C2
Thicket Mdws
13400 HarC 77083 4237 B1
Thicket Green Ln
12100 HOUS 77035 4240 A6
Thicket Grove Pl
10 WDLD 77385 2676 B4
Thicket Grove Rd
18200 HarC 77084 3816 D3
Thicket Hollow Ln
17500 HarC 77429 3396 C2
Thicketleaf Ln
5000 FBnC 77494 4092 E3
Thicket Ridge Ln
2100 HOUS 77077 3957 A6
Thicket Run Dr
3300 HarC 77388 3112 E6
Thicket Trace Ct
7600 HarC 77433 3677 B1
Thicket Trail Dr
7200 HarC 77346 3265 A7
Thickey Pines Ct
4200 FBnC 77494 4092 D1
Thimbleberry Ct
10 WDLD 77380 2822 A7
Thime Cir
4200 BYTN 77521 3973 A2
Third
- FBnC 77545 4499 D5
Thirsty Fish Rd
- HarC 77090 3258 C4
- HOUS 77090 3258 C4
Thistle
3600 HOUS 77048 4374 E3
9300 HarC 77532 3413 A3
Thistle Dr
5000 DKSN 77539 4754 D2
9700 HarC 77070 3255 B5
Thistle St
800 HOUS 77047 4373 C4
3500 HarC 77047 4374 C3
Thistleberry Ln
9800 HarC 77375 3110 C4
20900 HarC 77379 3111 D4
Thistlebridge Ct
15200 HarC 77429 3253 C6
Thistlebrook Ct
1800 FBnC 77545 4622 D2
Thistle Brook Pl
10 WDLD 77382 2674 E5
Thistlebury Ln
22900 HarC 77373 2968 E7
Thistle Creek Ct
12500 HarC 77044 3689 A4
Thistlecreek Ct
1800 FBnC 77545 4622 D2
Thistlecroft Dr
- HOUS 77084 3678 E7
4600 HarC 77084 3678 E7
Thistlecroft Ln
5100 FBnC 77479 4493 C3
Thistledew Dr
15700 HarC 77082 4096 B2
Thistle Down
- HarC 77429 3253 C2
Thistledown
37200 MtgC 77354 2816 B1
37300 MtgC 77354 2670 B7
Thistledown Dr
2900 LGCY 77573 4633 A1
Thistledown Ln
3900 PASD 77504 4247 D5
Thistle Down St
- HarC 77068 3256 E6
4900 HarC 77069 3256 D6
Thistlegate Ct
24000 HarC 77373 3115 B5
Thistle Gate Ln
- FBnC 77469 4095 C6
Thistleglen Cir
7300 HarC 77095 3678 C1
Thistleglen Dr
16300 HarC 77095 3678 C1
Thistlegrove Ln
3300 FBnC 77478 4366 C1
Thistle Hill Ct
4000 SGLD 77479 4495 C3
Thistlemeade Dr
1100 HarC 77094 3955 A3
Thistle Meadow Ln
16400 HarC 77433 3251 B5
Thistlemont Dr
3700 HOUS 77042 4099 A2
Thistlemont Ln
- FBnC 77469 4094 B7
Thistlemoor Ln
8700 HarC 77044 3689 C5
Thistlerock Ln
- HarC 77429 3253 A5
2100 FBnC 77479 4493 E1
Thistle Trail Dr
9600 HarC 77070 3255 C5
Thistle Valley Ct
25600 MtgC 77365 3117 E3
Thistlewaite Ln
25300 HarC 77373 3114 C2
Thistle Wind Ct
10 WDLD 77381 2820 C4
Thistlewood
- SGLD 77479 4369 A7
Thistlewood Ct
300 LGCY 77573 4633 A2
Thistlewood Dr
600 HOUS 77079 3957 B2
3900 PASD 77504 4247 D5
Thistlewood Pl
10 WDLD 77381 2820 E1
Thistlewood Park Ct
7000 FBnC 77494 4093 C4
Thom Rd
5900 HarC 77346 3264 D6
Thomas Av
100 PASD 77506 4107 A5
700 KATY 77493 3952 C1
700 KATY 77494 3952 C1
800 CNRO 77301 2383 E4
2700 PASD 77506 4108 A4
2800 PASD 77503 4108 A4
W Thomas Av
100 PASD 77506 4107 A5
900 PASD 77506 4106 E5
1400 HOUS 77017 4106 D5
1400 HOUS 77506 4106 D5
Thomas Cir
20500 MtgC 77357 2680 E7
Thomas Dr
1100 HMBL 77338 3406 E1
1100 HMBL 77338 3407 A1
1200 FRDW 77546 4505 A4
Thomas Ln
- WlrC 77445 3098 A5
10 HarC 77336 2976 A2
13100 MtgC 77302 2823 E2
20800 MtgC 77357 2973 A1
31800 SGCH 77355 2961 D3
Thomas Rd
100 MtgC 77354 2668 D5
100 MtgC 77355 2668 D5
1600 HarC 77521 3833 C7
5600 HarC 77041 3680 B5
27600 HOUS 77336 3121 A5
Thomas St
- PRVW 77445 3100 B3
2300 HOUS 77009 3963 B1
Thomas Ter
100 MtgC 77354 2669 D2
Thomas Jefferson Wy
1000 MSCY 77459 4369 D5
Thomas Mill Ln
14700 FBnC 77478 4236 D3
Thomas Paine Dr
3100 MSCY 77459 4369 E6
Thomas Shore Ct
12400 HarC 77433 3395 C4
Thomas Shore Dr
18600 HarC 77433 3395 C5
Thomas Survey Dr
18600 HarC 77433 3395 D5
Thomas T Tr
10200 MtgC 77372 2535 E1
Thomastone Ln
- HarC 77346 3408 B4
Thomasville Dr
9100 HarC 77064 3399 D6
Thompson
400 HarC 77532 3552 B4
Thompson Cir
200 MSCY 77489 4370 A3
200 STAF 77477 4370 A3
200 STAF 77489 4370 A3
Thompson Dr
100 PRVW 77445 3100 C1
Thompson Rd
100 GlsC 77511 4868 E3
900 RHMD 77469 4491 E2
2100 FBnC 77469 4491 E3
2100 FBnC 77469 4492 D6
2100 RHMD 77469 4492 A3
4400 GlsC 77563 4990 B6
5200 FBnC 77469 4493 A7
6000 BYTN 77521 3832 C6
6000 HarC 77521 3832 C6
7500 HarC 77562 3832 C5
Thompson Rd FM-762
900 RHMD 77469 4491 E2
2100 FBnC 77469 4491 E3
2100 FBnC 77469 4492 D6
2100 RHMD 77469 4492 A3
5200 FBnC 77469 4493 A7
Thompson St
900 HOUS 77007 3962 C3
1400 BYTN 77520 4112 D2
1700 LMQU 77568 4989 E1
N Thompson St
1800 CNRO 77301 2384 A2
2100 CNRO 77301 2383 E2
2200 CNRO 77303 2383 E1
Thompson Chapel Rd
4600 FBnC 77479 4366 D6
Thompson Creek Dr
2700 HarC 77067 3402 A4
Thompson Crossing Dr
1800 FBnC 77469 4365 C1
2300 FBnC 77469 4234 B7
Thompson Ferry Rd
4000 MSCY 77459 4496 E4
5600 FBnC 77459 4496 D6
5600 FBnC 77479 4496 D6
5600 MSCY 77479 4496 D6
Thompsons Rd
2300 FBnC 77545 4498 D5
6100 FBnC 77469 4493 C7
8300 FBnC 77469 4494 A7
Thompsons Rd FM-762
6100 FBnC 77469 4493 B7
Thompsons Rd FM-2759
7100 FBnC 77469 4493 C7
8300 FBnC 77469 4494 A7
Thomson St
7700 PRLD 77581 4375 A7
Thonig Rd
1800 HOUS 77055 3821 D5
3800 HOUS 77092 3821 D2
Thor Ct
- MtgC 77357 2829 C1
Thor Ln
- HOUS 77058 4507 D2
- HOUS 77062 4507 D2
Thora Rd
- HarC 77379 3111 A5
8300 HarC 77379 3110 E5
Thorhill St
17200 HarC 77379 3255 D3
Thorn St
200 HarC 77562 3831 E1
9800 HOUS 77078 3688 A4
W Thorn Wy
200 HarC 77015 3828 B5
Thornapple Dr
- WDLD 77382 2673 E4

STREET
Block City ZIP Map# Grid

Thorn Berry Pl
10 WDLD 77381 2820 D4
Thorn Berry Creek Ct
20900 HarC 77449 3815 A6
Thorn Berry Creek Ln
2100 HarC 77449 3815 C6
Thornberry Fores Ln
- FBnC 77469 4094 B7
Thornblade Cir
10 HarC 77389 2820 B6
Thornbluff Ct
14600 HarC 77429 3396 C1
Thornbranch Dr
700 HOUS 77079 3957 C2
Thornbriar Ct
12300 BKVL 77581 4375 D6
Thornbriar Dr
12200 BKVL 77581 4375 D5
Thornbrook Dr
1600 MSCY 77489 4370 E4
15600 HarC 77084 3679 A5
Thornbrook Ln
- HarC 77095 3537 D5
Thornbrough Ln
10400 HOUS 77075 4377 A3
Thornburg Ln
12000 HarC 77067 3402 B5
Thornbury Dr
- HarC 77073 3403 C2
Thornbush Pl
10 WDLD 77381 2674 D6
Thorncliff Dr
10400 HarC 77396 3407 C7
Thorncreek Ct
10 WDLD 77381 2821 B3
Thorncreek Wy
7700 HarC 77095 3538 B7
Thorncrest Ct
2000 FBnC 77479 4494 A1
Thorncrest Ln
10200 HarC 77375 2965 B6
Thorncroft Dr
6400 FBnC 77450 4094 B4
Thorncroft Manor Ln
7900 FBnC 77469 4094 D7
7900 FBnC 77469 4095 A6
Thorn Cypress Dr
16700 HarC 77429 3396 D1
Thorndon Park Ct
2400 LGCY 77573 4508 D6
Thorne Creek Ln
2900 HarC 77073 3259 E5
2900 HarC 77073 3260 A4
Thornecrest Dr
12000 HarC 77375 3109 D6
Thorne Haven Dr
20600 HarC 77073 3260 A4
Thorngate Ct
5300 FBnC 77494 4093 B2
Thorngrove Dr
- HarC 77014 3402 B2
Thornhedge Ct
10 WDLD 77381 2821 C4
Thornhill Creek Ct
25600 MtgC 77365 3117 E3
Thornhill Oaks Dr
10 HarC 77015 3828 C5
Thornhurn Ct
10400 HarC 77065 3539 B3
Thornlea Dr
10500 HOUS 77075 4377 D2
10500 HOUS 77089 4377 D2
Thornleaf Ln
10200 HarC 77070 3399 C3
Thornmead Ln
20000 HarC 77379 3111 E5
Thornmeadow Ln
7200 HarC 77433 3677 D1
Thornmont Ln
10200 HarC 77070 3399 C3
Thornoak Ln
13200 HarC 77070 3399 C3
Thornridge Ct
- FBnC 77494 4093 A1
Thorn Ridge Ln
11700 HarC 77377 3254 D4
Thornridge Ln
- LGCY 77573 4631 A7
10100 HarC 77070 3399 C3
Thornrove Ln
22000 HarC 77389 3112 D1
Thornsby Ct
23700 FBnC 77494 4093 C1
Thornton Cir
4700 HOUS 77018 3823 A1
Thornton Dr
- MtgC 77372 2683 C2
Thornton Rd
300 HOUS 77018 3823 B1
300 HOUS 77022 3823 C1
1100 HOUS 77018 3822 D1
E Thornton Rd
- HOUS 77018 3823 C1
100 HOUS 77022 3823 C1
N Thorntree Dr
13500 HarC 77015 3828 D5
13500 HOUS 77015 3828 D5
S Thorntree Dr
13300 HarC 77015 3828 D5
Thorn Valley Ct
13000 HarC 77377 3254 A3
Thornville Ln
13200 HarC 77070 3399 C3
Thornvine Ln
800 HOUS 77079 3957 C2
Thornwall St
6300 HOUS 77092 3821 C2
Thornwell Ct
12600 HarC 77070 3399 A5
Thornwick Dr
800 HOUS 77079 3957 C2
Thornwild Rd
6800 HOUS 77489 4371 C5
Thornwilde Park Ln
400 HarC 77073 3259 A4
Thornwood
23800 MtgC 77447 2960 B4
Thornwood Cir
5300 DKSN 77539 4754 D1
Thornwood Ct
800 BzaC 77584 4501 B1
Thornwood Dr
500 SHEH 77381 2822 A2
700 FRDW 77546 4505 C5
700 SHEH 77381 2821 E2
3000 PASD 77503 4108 A5
10900 LPRT 77571 4250 D3

Thornwood Ln
1400 HOUS 77062 4379 E6
Thoroughbred Dr
11900 HarC 77065 3539 E5
12000 MtgC 77304 2528 A1
Thoroughbred Trails Ln
12500 HarC 77044 3408 D7
Thoroughgood Ln
14900 HarC 77084 3679 A4
Thorpeshire Ct
3300 FBnC 77494 3953 A7
Thorpe Springs Dr
300 FBnC 77469 4493 B6
Thorsby Dr
30400 MtgC 77386 2969 B1
Thorton Knolls Dr
24700 HarC 77389 2966 D3
Thousand Oaks Blvd
- MtgC 77354 2671 A5
Thousand Oaks Cir
5700 HOUS 77092 3682 D6
Thousand Oaks Ct
25100 MtgC 77355 2960 B1
Thousand Oaks Dr
33000 MtgC 77354 2671 B4
Thousand Pines Dr
1900 HOUS 77339 3118 D6
Thousand Trails on Lake Conroe
- MtgC 77304 2236 B1
- MtgC 77318 2236 A1
N Thrasher Dr
16700 MtgC 77385 2676 E4
Thrasher Ln
5900 HOUS 77049 3828 A3
Threadall Park Dr
13700 HOUS 77077 3957 A3
Threadleaf Dr
11500 HarC 77066 3401 C6
Thread Needle St
800 HOUS 77079 3957 C1
Threeawn Ct
11000 HarC 77086 3542 B1
Three Bar St
27100 MtgC 77372 2683 D2
Three Corners Dr
500 HNCV 77024 3960 C2
Threeflower Ct
1800 HOUS 77345 3120 B3
Threeflower Ln
6300 HOUS 77345 3120 B3
Three Forks Dr
900 HarC 77450 3954 A3
1200 HarC 77450 3953 E4
Three Forks Rd
40000 MtgC 77354 2672 D2
Three Lakes Blvd
12200 HarC 77375 3109 C7
Three Oaks Cir
5500 HarC 77069 3400 D1
Three Oaks Estates Dr
16100 HarC 77429 3253 B4
Three Pine Dr
20600 HarC 77447 3106 B2
22200 HarC 77447 2961 B7
Three Pines Dr
3200 HOUS 77339 3118 D4
Three Rivers Dr
- MSCY 77459 4369 B4
4000 SGLD 77478 4369 A4
Three S
14600 MtgC 77372 2683 C2
Three S St
14400 MtgC 77372 2683 C2
Three Sister Cir
3200 PRLD 77581 4503 E3
Three Sisters St
3400 HarC 77093 3686 A2
3400 HOUS 77093 3686 A2
Three Wood Dr
2100 HarC 77089 4504 E2
2100 PRLD 77089 4504 E2
2100 PRLD 77581 4504 E2
Threlkeld Ln
1200 LMQU 77568 4990 A1
Threlkeld St
500 HOUS 77007 3962 E1
Thresher Ct
22200 HarC 77449 3815 A4
Throckmorton Ln
8700 HarC 77064 3540 D6
Thrush Dr
5400 HOUS 77033 4243 E4
5400 HOUS 77033 4244 A4
6800 HOUS 77087 4244 E3
7100 HOUS 77087 4245 A2
Thrush Ln
100 MtgC 77385 2676 D4
Thrush St
9800 LPRT 77571 4250 B1
Thrush Tr
22600 HarC 77447 3106 A1
Thrush Grove Pl
10 WDLD 77381 2820 E3
Thrushwood Ln
25100 HarC 77373 3114 E2
Thunder Ln
24000 MtgC 77365 2974 B7
Thunder Basin Dr
100 FBnC 77469 4493 A6
Thunder Bay Dr
4200 PASD 77504 4247 D6
Thunderbay Dr
15600 HOUS 77062 4507 A3
Thunderbird Cir
10 BYTN 77521 3972 B2
Thunderbird Dr
- CNRO 77304 2237 A4
10 PNVL 77304 2237 A4
Thunderbird Rd
4700 HOUS 77041 3681 D7
Thunderbird St
3500 MSCY 77459 4496 D1
Thunder Cove Pl
10 WDLD 77381 2821 A1
Thundercreek Pl
10 WDLD 77381 2674 E6
S Thundercreek Pl
10 WDLD 77381 2674 E6
Thunderhaven Dr
11000 HarC 77064 3540 D2
Thunderhead Ct
10600 HarC 77064 3540 B4
Thunder Hollow Pl
10 WDLD 77381 2820 E1
Thunder Lake Ln
1500 SGLD 77478 4236 E6

Thunder Rock Dr
19400 HarC 77449 3677 A2
E Thunderwood Cir
4500 FBnC 77545 4622 D2
N Thunderwood Cir
1900 FBnC 77545 4622 D1
W Thunderwood Cir
4300 FBnC 77545 4622 D2
Thurber Ridge Dr
9400 HarC 77379 3110 C5
Thurleigh Ln
9900 HOUS 77031 4238 E4
Thurlow Dr
3200 PRLD 77581 4503 D5
Thurman St
5400 HOUS 77013 3827 B3
Thurmon St
2100 HOUS 77034 4246 B5
Thurmond Lake Dr
- FBnC 77469 4234 E5
Thurow St
7300 HOUS 77087 4105 B6
7600 HOUS 77017 4105 B6
Thursa Ln
3700 FRDW 77546 4630 A1
Thurston Ln
23200 MtgC 77365 3118 A1
Thurston Crossing Dr
21300 MtgC 77365 3118 A1
T Huxley Ln
10 MSCY 77459 4369 D7
Thyme Ln
5300 HarC 77521 3833 D2
Thyme Green Ln
16400 HarC 77433 3251 A4
E Thymewood Pl
10 WDLD 77382 2819 D2
W Thymewood Pl
10 WDLD 77382 2819 D1
Tiara Ln
10100 HOUS 77043 3820 A6
Tibaldo Ln
5200 STFE 77510 4987 E3
Tiber St
800 HDWV 77024 3959 E1
Tibet Rd
16100 FRDW 77546 4505 E7
16600 FRDW 77546 4506 A7
16600 FRDW 77546 4630 A1
Tiburon Tr
7600 FBnC 77479 4494 A5
Tiburon Wy
16300 HOUS 77053 4371 D7
Tickleseed Ln
19900 HarC 77379 3110 B6
20000 HarC 77375 3110 B6
Tickner St
7100 HOUS 77055 3821 D7
Tico Dr
6500 HarC 77083 4096 C5
Ticonderoga Rd
11900 HarC 77044 3688 E6
11900 HOUS 77044 3688 D6
12300 HarC 77044 3689 B6
Tidal Rd
- HOUS 77571 3970 B4
100 DRPK 77536 4109 C3
1100 DRPK 77536 3969 D7
1900 DRPK 77536 3970 A7
1900 HarC 77536 3970 A7
1900 HarC 77571 3970 A7
1900 HOUS 77536 3969 D7
Tidalwood Ct
2700 BzaC 77578 4501 A7
Tidalwood Dr
3600 BzaC 77578 4501 A7
3700 BzaC 77578 4625 A1
Tide St
10 HarC 77039 3546 A7
10 HarC 77093 3546 A7
10 HOUS 77039 3546 A7
Tidehaven Ct
11400 PRLD 77584 4500 D3
Tidehaven Dr
2600 PRLD 77584 4500 E3
Tide Rock Ln
- PRLD 77545 4499 E1
Tideswept Ct
12000 HarC 77095 3397 A7
Tidewater
3600 GLSN 77554 5440 D6
Tidewater Ct
5100 PASD 77505 4248 B4
Tidewater Dr
2600 HOUS 77045 4373 B1
3100 HOUS 77045 4242 A7
3800 HOUS 77045 4241 D7
5400 HOUS 77085 4241 A7
5600 HOUS 77085 4240 E7
Tidewater Ln
- HOUS 77041 3819 C1
Tidewind Ct
3100 BzaC 77578 4501 A6
Tidford St
3600 HOUS 77093 3686 B6
Tidwell Ln
1600 HOUS 77093 3685 C6
Tidwell Rd
10 HarC 77044 3689 D5
10 HOUS 77022 3684 E6
10 HOUS 77076 3684 E6
300 HOUS 77076 3685 A6
1100 HOUS 77022 3685 C6
1900 HOUS 77093 3685 D6
2800 HOUS 77093 3686 A6
4200 HOUS 77016 3686 E6
7500 HOUS 77016 3687 A6
7700 HOUS 77028 3687 B5
7900 HOUS 77078 3687 E5
8900 HOUS 77078 3688 B5
11700 HarC 77044 3688 D5
11700 HarC 77078 3688 D5
E Tidwell Rd
100 HOUS 77022 3684 E6
100 HOUS 77076 3684 D6
W Tidwell Rd
100 HOUS 77022 3684 C6
100 HOUS 77076 3684 C6
200 HOUS 77091 3684 B6
900 HOUS 77091 3683 E6
5000 HOUS 77091 3682 E6
5700 HOUS 77092 3682 D6
7200 HOUS 77040 3682 A5
7600 HOUS 77040 3681 D5
9500 HOUS 77041 3681 C6
Tidwell Tc
- HOUS 77093 3686 A5

Tidy Tips Ln
19800 HarC 77379 3110 C6
Tiegs St
300 LGCY 77573 4632 B2
Tiel Wy
10 HOUS 77019 3962 B4
Tierra Pk
8800 HOUS 77034 4247 A7
Tierra Alta Dr
- FBnC 77083 4095 D6
Tierra Amarilla Ln
3500 FBnC 77469 4233 C6
Tierra Lake Ct
6300 HarC 77041 3680 A4
Tierra Mist Ct
19100 FBnC 77469 4234 E1
19100 FBnC 77469 4235 A1
Tierra Mountain Ct
9600 HOUS 77034 4378 A1
Tierra Palms Ct
11600 HOUS 77034 4378 A1
Tierra Ridge Ct
11500 HOUS 77034 4378 A1
Tierra Verde Dr
7400 FBnC 77083 4095 D6
Tierwester St
2100 HOUS 77003 3963 D7
2100 HOUS 77004 3963 D7
2700 HOUS 77004 4103 D1
6100 HOUS 77021 4103 C5
7800 HOUS 77021 4243 A3
Tierwester Vil
100 HOUS 77021 4243 A3
Tierwester Village St
100 HOUS 77021 4243 B1
Tierwood Ct
3500 HarC 77068 3257 B5
Tifco
10500 HarC 77429 3538 E2
Tiffany Ct
16500 HOUS 77058 4507 D1
Tiffany Dr
5000 HOUS 77045 4372 B3
5600 HOUS 77085 4371 E3
5600 HOUS 77085 4372 A3
Tiffany Ln
10 SGLD 77478 4369 A3
11800 MtgC 77354 2671 C1
Tiffany Pl
3700 HOUS 77025 4241 E3
Tiffany Green Dr
- WDLD 77381 2821 E2
Tiffin St
4000 HOUS 77026 3825 B6
Tiff Trail Dr
14100 HarC 77095 3539 B7
Tifway Ln
13700 HarC 77044 3689 D3
Tiger Ln
8100 HarC 77040 3541 C7
Tiger Tr
- HOUS 77080 3820 A4
10400 HOUS 77043 3820 A4
10500 HOUS 77043 3819 E4
Tiger Lilly Wy
5400 HOUS 77045 4241 A7
5400 HOUS 77085 4241 A7
5600 HOUS 77085 4240 E7
Tiger Shark Ct
22200 HarC 77449 3815 A4
Tiger Spring Cir
19600 HarC 77449 3816 A3
Tiger Trace Ct
4300 HarC 77066 3401 C4
Tiger Trace Ln
4600 HarC 77066 3401 C4
Tigris Dr
22800 MtgC 77365 2972 A4
Tigris Ln
1000 HarC 77090 3258 A1
Tigris Ridge Dr
3900 HarC 77449 3816 A2
Tigris Springs Cir
3900 HarC 77449 3816 C2
Tiguas St
4000 PASD 77504 4248 B5
Tikal Ct
2900 GLSN 77554 5221 D3
Tiki Cir
10 TKIS 77554 5106 D3
Tiki Dr
100 GlsC 77563 5106 D3
400 TKIS 77554 5106 A4
Tiki Main
- TKIS 77554 5106 D3
Tilbrook Ct
10300 HarC 77038 3543 C3
Tilbrook Dr
10500 HarC 77038 3543 C2
Tilbury Ct
29700 MtgC 77354 2818 B2
Tilbury Dr
4900 HOUS 77056 3961 A4
5300 HOUS 77056 3960 E5
Tilbury Estates Dr
4900 HOUS 77056 3961 A4
Tilbury Woods Ln
7900 HarC 77433 3537 A7
11700 HarC 77433 3396 A6
Tilden Dr
100 PASD 77506 4107 D4
Tilden St
3000 HOUS 77025 4101 D6
3000 HOUS 77025 4102 A6
Tilden Forest Dr
3100 MtgC 77386 2969 B4
Tilfer St
3100 HOUS 77087 4104 E6
Tilgham St
7200 HOUS 77020 3965 A3
8400 HOUS 77029 3965 D3
Tilia Ct
11600 JTCY 77029 3966 D3
Tilia St
11500 JTCY 77029 3966 D3
Tiller St
2200 PASD 77502 4247 B1
Tilley St
14700 HarC 77084 3679 A4
15000 HarC 77084 3678 E4
Tillison St
1000 HOUS 77088 3683 E1
Tilman Dr
1400 FBnC 77469 4365 C3
Tilson Ln
3600 HOUS 77080 3820 D2
4000 HOUS 77041 3820 D1
4400 HOUS 77041 3681 D7

Tilstock Dr
- HarC 77094 3954 E3
20000 HarC 77450 3954 E3
Tiltree St
9600 HOUS 77075 4377 C3
Tiltrum Ln
12000 HarC 77086 3542 C5
Tiltwood Ln
22300 HarC 77375 3110 C3
Tim St
2400 HOUS 77093 3685 E5
Tim Allen Ct
4000 HarC 77014 3401 C2
Timber Cir
500 HOUS 77079 3956 D2
Timber Cor
4000 HarC 77082 4096 B4
Timber Ct
4400 PASD 77505 4249 B6
27400 MtgC 77354 2819 C5
Timber Dr
1600 LGCY 77539 4632 C7
1600 LGCY 77573 4632 C7
1700 GlsC 77539 4753 C1
1700 LGCY 77539 4753 C1
2300 DKSN 77539 4753 D1
Timber Hllw
12300 PASD 77058 4381 A6
12400 PASD 77058 4380 E7
Timber Ln
- BYTN 77520 3971 A4
- MtgC 77365 3118 A1
10 MtgC 77384 2528 A7
100 HarC 77562 3831 E1
1000 RSBG 77471 4491 D2
1200 FRDW 77546 4629 D1
1200 RHMD 77469 4491 D2
1200 RHMD 77471 4491 D2
2000 HOUS 77019 3961 D6
2000 HOUS 77027 3961 D6
3100 DKSN 77539 4753 D2
21700 MtgC 77365 2972 C1
Timber Rd
11000 MtgC 77372 2537 A2
Timber Tr
- FRDW 77546 4505 B5
Timber Vw
600 FRDW 77546 4505 C5
Timber Bay Ct
5600 FBnC 77450 4094 A4
Timber Bluff Ct
21300 MtgC 77365 2973 A3
Timber Bluff Dr
1400 PRLD 77545 4499 C3
Timberbluff Ln
- HarC 77084 3677 C7
Timberbranch Ct
2300 SGCH 77355 2962 C1
Timberbreeze Ct
2300 SGCH 77355 2962 C1
Timber Briar Cir
2700 HOUS 77059 4379 E5
Timber Briar Ct
14000 HOUS 77059 4379 D4
Timberbriar Ct
2300 SGCH 77355 2962 C1
Timberbright Ct
14300 HOUS 77044 3550 B2
Timberbrook Dr
23200 HarC 77373 3114 D6
Timberbrook Tr
2300 HOUS 77345 3120 B3
Timber Chase Dr
15900 HarC 77082 4096 E3
Timberchase Pl
14900 HarC 77429 3397 C1
Timber Cliff Ct
17200 HarC 77429 3396 D1
Timber Cliff Ln
14500 HarC 77429 3396 D2
Timber Country Wy
2800 HOUS 77345 3120 B5
Timber Cove Dr
- PASD 77586 4381 E7
700 TYLV 77586 4508 E1
700 TYLV 77586 4509 A1
1000 TYLV 77586 4381 E7
Timbercraft Dr
8600 HarC 77095 3538 D5
Timber Creek Ct
800 FRDW 77546 4505 C3
4900 MSCY 77459 4497 D4
Timber Creek Dr
10 CNRO 77301 2383 D3
1300 FRDW 77546 4505 C4
1500 MSCY 77459 4497 C4
1900 PRLD 77581 4504 C5
5500 HOUS 77017 4246 C1
Timbercreek Tr
2300 HOUS 77345 3120 A3
Timbercreek Falls Dr
11000 HarC 77095 3396 D6
Timber Creek Pl Ct
16000 HarC 77084 3678 D5
Timber Creek Pl Dr
5500 HarC 77084 3678 D4
Timber Creek Pl Ln
15900 HarC 77084 3678 D5
Timber Crest Dr
11000 HarC 77065 3399 A7
11000 HarC 77070 3399 A7
11200 HarC 77065 3398 E7
Timbercrest Dr
- HarC 77065 3399 A7
- HarC 77070 3399 A7
Timbercrest Village Dr
- HarC 77375 2965 E2
8200 HarC 77389 2965 E2
8200 HarC 77389 2966 A2
11700 HarC 77375 2964 D2
Timber Crossing Ln
17900 HarC 77433 3537 C6
E Timber Cut Ct
4000 PRLD 77584 4503 B6
W Timber Cut Ct
4200 PRLD 77584 4503 B6
Timberdale Ln
500 HarC 77090 3258 D3
500 HOUS 77090 3258 C3
Timber Dove Ln
12700 HarC 77377 3254 A1
Timber Dust Cir
22700 HarC 77373 3115 A7
Timber Edge Ln
7000 HarC 77346 3408 E1
7100 HarC 77346 3264 E7
Timber Falls Ct
4000 HarC 77082 4096 E3

Timberfield Ct
19700 HarC 77449 3815 D1
Timberfield Pl
19800 HarC 77449 3815 E2
Timber Forest Blvd
14700 HarC 77044 3408 D7
14700 HarC 77044 3549 D1
Timber Forest Dr
17500 HarC 77346 3408 C1
18300 HarC 77346 3264 C7
Timber Forest Ln
18000 HarC 77346 3408 B1
Timber Gardens Dr
30300 MtgC 77386 2969 D2
Timbergate Dr
- HarC 77082 4096 B4
Timber Glade Ct
3700 HOUS 77345 3119 E3
Timberglen Dr
10800 HNCV 77024 3960 A3
Timber Glen Ln
1100 FBnC 77479 4493 E6
Timber Green Cir
19700 HarC 77094 3955 A2
Timbergreen Cir
1900 MtgC 77355 2816 B7
1900 MtgC 77355 2962 C1
1900 SGCH 77355 2816 B7
1900 SGCH 77355 2962 C1
Timbergreen Dr
14000 MtgC 77355 2962 D1
14100 SGCH 77355 2962 D1
14400 SGCH 77355 2816 D7
Timber Grove Ct
15900 HarC 77377 3254 D5
Timbergrove Ln
1100 HOUS 77008 3823 A7
Timber Grove Pl
200 FRDW 77546 4505 B6
Timbergrove Tr
- HOUS 77345 3120 A3
Timber Grove Point Dr
1000 HOUS 77008 3822 C7
Timberhaven Dr
14000 HarC 77066 3401 E7
Timber Hill Dr
700 BKHV 77024 3959 C2
700 HDWV 77024 3959 C2
800 CNRO 77301 2384 D5
4400 FBnC 77479 4366 D6
Timber Hollow Dr
11700 HarC 77065 3399 A7
Timberidge Ct
16500 HarC 77429 3252 D7
Timberjack Pl
2700 WDLD 77380 2821 D7
Timberknob Ct
2300 MtgC 77355 2962 C1
Timberknoll St
11700 BKHV 77024 3959 C3
Timberlake Dr
7200 FBnC 77479 4493 E4
12000 HarC 77065 3398 C6
12000 HarC 77429 3398 C5
Timberlake Forest Ln
19000 HarC 77377 2961 E7
Timberlake Grove Ln
19100 HarC 77377 2961 E7
Timberlake Oaks Dr
19000 HarC 77377 2961 E7
19000 HarC 77377 3106 E1
Timber Lakes Dr
25300 MtgC 77380 2967 B1
25800 MtgC 77380 2821 B7
Timberlake View Ln
19000 HarC 77377 2961 E7
Timberlake Village Dr
18800 HarC 77377 2961 E7
18800 HarC 77377 3106 E1
Timberlake Woods Ln
19100 HarC 77377 2961 D7
Timberland Blvd
19000 MtgC 77365 2972 B1
Timberland Ct
14900 HOUS 77062 4380 A7
Timberland Trc
12700 HarC 77065 3539 C1
Timberland Path Dr
24600 HarC 77373 3114 D4
Timberlane Dr
100 BYTN 77520 3971 B2
25600 MtgC 77386 2968 D1
E Timberlane Dr
100 HLCS 77511 4867 E5
200 HLCS 77511 4868 A5
W Timberlane Dr
100 ALVN 77511 4867 E5
100 HLCS 77511 4867 E5
Timberlane St
1800 CNRO 77301 2383 D2
2100 CNRO 77303 2383 D2
Timberlark Dr
3100 HOUS 77339 3119 C4
14900 HarC 77070 3254 E7
14900 HarC 77070 3398 B1
Timberlea Dr
15300 HOUS 77489 4371 B4
Timberlea Pl
10 WDLD 77382 2674 A4
Timberleaf Dr
14400 SGCH 77355 2962 C1
14700 MtgC 77355 2962 B1
Timberline Ct
700 HOUS 77339 3263 B2
Timber Line Dr
7300 PASD 77505 4249 B6
24400 MtgC 77380 2967 B3
Timberline Dr
700 HOUS 77339 3263 B2
Timber Line Ln
19800 MtgC 77357 2829 B6
Timberline Ln
- HOUS 77339 3263 B2
Timberline Rd
10900 HOUS 77043 3819 B7
Timberline Tr
16300 SGCH 77355 2961 D5
20200 HarC 77433 3251 C5
Timberline Run Ln
7800 HarC 77095 3538 A6
W Timberloch Ct
31500 SGCH 77355 2961 D4
Timberloch Dr
10300 HarC 77070 3399 B4
Timberloch Pl
1200 ORDN 77380 2822 A5
1200 WDLD 77380 2822 A5
2000 WDLD 77380 2821 E5

E Timberloch Tr
31100 SGCH 77355 2961 E4
W Timberloch Tr
31200 SGCH 77355 2961 D4
Timber Lodge Ln
21300 MtgC 77365 2973 B2
Timberly Ct
- HarC 77090 3258 D7
Timberly Mist Dr
- HarC 77090 3258 D7
Timberly Park Ln
11600 HarC 77433 3396 A6
Timber Manor Dr
12300 HarC 77065 3398 E5
12300 HarC 77429 3398 E6
Timbermeadow Dr
12600 HarC 77070 3399 B5
Timbermeadow Oak Dr
4200 HarC 77066 3401 B3
Timbermeadow Pines Dr
4200 HarC 77066 3401 B3
Timber Mill St
100 WDLD 77380 2821 D6
Timber Mist Ct
18100 HarC 77433 3537 D6
Timber Mist Dr
5300 HarC 77084 3678 B6
Timber Moss Ct
8300 HarC 77433 3537 D6
Timbermoss Ct
- LGCY 77573 4751 B2
Timber Moss Ln
7100 FBnC 77469 4615 D5
Timbernook Ct
8300 HarC 77389 2965 E2
Timberoak Ct
13400 BzaC 77583 4623 E4
Timberoak Dr
10000 HOUS 77043 3820 A5
10000 HOUS 77080 3820 A5
10200 HOUS 77043 3819 E5
Timber Oaks Ct
28000 MtgC 77355 2815 C3
Timber Oaks Ln
22800 MtgC 77365 2973 E5
Timber Oaks Rdg
5800 HarC 77346 3264 D5
Timberpark Ln
5500 FBnC 77479 4493 D2
Timber Park Tr
7800 HarC 77070 3399 E3
Timber Path Dr
4800 HarC 77346 3408 B1
Timberpath Dr
- MtgC 77355 2816 B6
Timber Pine Tr
4500 HOUS 77345 3119 E2
Timber Pines Dr
19300 HarC 77346 3264 D5
21300 HarC 77388 3113 B3
Timber Point Ct
7500 HarC 77379 3256 B1
Timber Post Ln
7000 HarC 77346 3409 A1
Timber Quail Dr
5200 HarC 77346 3264 C7
Timber Rail Ct
17200 HarC 77396 3408 A2
Timber Rail Dr
3800 HarC 77396 3408 A3
3900 HarC 77346 3408 A3
Timber Ranch Dr
1900 MtgC 77355 2816 B7
Timber Ridge Ct
20300 MtgC 77355 2814 C3
Timber Ridge Dr
1400 PRLD 77545 4499 D4
19000 MtgC 77355 2814 C2
19000 MtgC 77355 2815 A5
Timber Ridge St
5000 HarC 77521 3834 E7
Timber Ridge Tr
7400 FBnC 77479 4493 E6
Timber Rock Ct
3600 HarC 77082 4096 B3
Timber Rock Dr
15700 HarC 77082 4096 B3
Timber Run Dr
15800 HarC 77082 4096 B4
Timbers Dr
18600 HarC 77346 3264 C7
Timbers Edge Dr
18600 HarC 77346 3264 C7
Timbershade Cross
14900 MtgC 77355 2816 B7
Timbershade Ct
2200 SGCH 77355 2816 D7
Timber Shade Dr
5100 HOUS 77345 3120 A4
Timber Shadows Dr
2300 HOUS 77339 3118 C6
Timbershire Ct
15000 MtgC 77355 2816 B7
Timber Shores Ln
18500 HarC 77346 3265 D7
Timberside Ct
200 CNRO 77304 2383 A4
Timberside Dr
10 CNRO 77304 2383 B4
8500 HOUS 77025 4101 E7
9200 HOUS 77025 4241 E1
Timberside Cir Dr
3600 HOUS 77025 4101 E7
Timberson Ln
- HarC 77090 3258 C7
E Timberspire Ct
10 WDLD 77380 2968 A3
W Timberspire Ct
10 WDLD 77380 2968 B4
Timberspire Ln
10 WDLD 77380 2968 A4
Timber Spring Ct
18900 HarC 77346 3264 C6
Timber Spring Dr
18700 HarC 77346 3264 C6
Timbers Quail Dr
5400 HarC 77346 3264 C7
Timber Square Ct
6600 FBnC 77469 4095 C5
Timberstand Ln
600 HarC 77373 2968 E7
Timberstar St
10 WDLD 77382 2674 B5
Timberstone Ct
26000 HarC 77433 3396 B7
Timberstone Ln
20100 HarC 77379 3111 D5

STREET
Block City ZIP Map# Grid
Timbers Trace Dr
18700 HarC 77346 3264 C6
Timbers Trail Dr
5600 HarC 77346 3264 D5
Timber Strand Dr
18300 HarC 77084 3816 D4
Timber Tech Av
11200 HarC 77375 3254 D2
Timber Terrace Rd
300 HOUS 77024 3960 D2
Timberthorn Ln
- HarC 77377 3254 C3
N Timber Top Dr
10 WDLD 77380 2821 D6
S Timber Top Dr
100 WDLD 77380 2821 E7
Timber Trace Dr
18900 HarC 77346 3265 A6
Timber Trail Ct
600 FRDW 77546 4505 B5
Timbertrail Dr
1400 FBnC 77479 4493 E5
Timber Trail St
29500 MtgC 77386 2969 B4
Timber Trail Wy
20400 HarC 77433 3251 B5
Timber Tree Ct
19300 HarC 77346 3264 D5
Timbertree Ln
11100 HarC 77070 3399 A3
Timber Twist Dr
18600 HarC 77346 3264 C7
Timber Valley Dr
15900 HarC 77070 3255 B6
Timber View Ct
3100 SGLD 77479 4495 E1
Timber View Dr
3100 SGLD 77479 4495 E2
8600 HarC 77346 3265 D5
Timber Village Ct
28200 MtgC 77355 2815 C2
Timber Village Dr
3100 HarC 77068 3257 C5
E Timberwagon Cir
10700 WDLD 77380 2821 C7
W Timberwagon Cir
10800 WDLD 77380 2821 C7
Timberway Ct
2200 SGCH 77355 2816 D7
2200 SGCH 77355 2962 D1
Timberway Ln
7400 HOUS 77072 4097 D6
Timber Wild Ct
13300 TMBL 77375 2964 A3
Timberwild St
11400 WDLD 77380 2821 E7
11400 WDLD 77380 2967 E1
Timberwilde Dr
- HarC 77375 2965 E4
10 HNCV 77024 3960 B3
8100 HarC 77389 2965 E4
Timberwind Ln
19800 HarC 77094 3955 A3
Timberwood Dr
3100 BzaC 77584 4501 B6
3100 PRLD 77584 4501 B6
10000 HOUS 77043 3820 A5
10000 HOUS 77080 3820 A5
10400 HOUS 77043 3819 E5
Timber Wood Ln
10 MtgC 77384 2528 B6
Timberwork Rd
16900 HarC 77379 3256 B3
Timber Wy Dr
18600 HarC 77346 3264 E6
Timbo Ln
6300 HarC 77041 3679 C4
Timerwalk Ln
17900 FBnC 77469 4095 C6
Times Blvd
2400 HOUS 77005 4102 B3
2500 WUNP 77005 4102 A3
Timkin Rd
500 HarC 77375 2964 E7
500 HarC 77375 2965 A7
500 TMBL 77375 2964 E7
Timmen St
- HOUS 77087 4244 C1
Timmons Dr
- PASD 77504 4247 D5
Timmons Ln
- HOUS 77027 4101 D1
2600 HOUS 77027 3961 D7
3800 HOUS 77046 4101 D1
Timor Ln
700 HarC 77090 3258 B2
Timothy Ln
500 FBnC 77469 4234 C6
Timothy St
4900 TXCY 77591 4874 A7
Timpani Dr
- FRDW 77546 4505 E7
5400 FRDW 77546 4629 E1
Timpngos Ct
11900 HarC 77377 3109 B7
Timpnogos Dr
11900 HarC 77377 3109 B7
Timpson St
900 HOUS 77019 3963 A4
Tims Ln
1700 CNRO 77301 2384 D5
Timsbury Dr
4400 HarC 77084 3816 E1
Tims Harbor Dr
21500 MtgC 77339 3118 D4
Timucam Ct
- HarC 77014 3401 D3
Timucan Dr
- HarC 77014 3401 C3
Tina Ln
100 HarC 77037 3684 E1
25000 FBnC 77494 3952 C6
Tina Oaks Blvd
- HarC 77082 4096 D2
Tina Oaks Ct
2900 HarC 77082 4096 C2
Tinas Terrace Dr
2600 HarC 77038 3543 A4
Tincker St
1800 CNRO 77301 2384 A2
Tindel Rd
500 BzaC 77511 4628 B7
500 BzaC 77511 4749 C1
Tindel St
10 CRLS 77565 4509 C5
Tinechester Dr
2300 HOUS 77339 3119 A3

Tink Calfee Rd
1700 CNRO 77304 2382 E2
Tink Calfee Rd FM-3083
- CNRO 77304 2382 E2
Tinker St
15000 HarC 77084 3678 E4
Tinker Wy
26600 MtgC 77357 2829 B5
Tinker Round St
5300 KATY 77493 3813 D6
Tinsley Ct
- HarC 77014 3402 C1
Tinsley Trails
21700 HarC 77388 3112 A2
Tinsman Rd
- HarC 77396 3547 A1
Tinton Ct
23300 FBnC 77494 3953 D4
Tiny Ln
- JRSV 77040 3680 C1
Tiny Tr
10 FBnC 77459 4621 B3
10 PNPV 77024 3959 D5
Tiny Hur Dr
4200 PASD 77503 4108 D7
Tiny Tree Dr
1100 MSCY 77489 4370 D6
Tiny Tree Ln
- MSCY 77489 4370 D6
Tiny Turtle Pt
9600 HarC 77396 3407 B7
Tippcrest
15000 HarC 77530 3829 C7
Tipper Ct
2600 HarC 77067 3402 A4
Tipperary Av
1000 FRDW 77546 4629 B3
Tipperary Dr
1900 DRPK 77536 4109 A6
2100 PRLD 77581 4504 D2
Tipperary Ln
- HOUS 77061 4245 B2
Tippett St
6600 HOUS 77091 3683 D4
7200 HOUS 77088 3683 D3
Tipps St
7300 HOUS 77023 4105 B2
Tipton
7600 HOUS 77028 3825 E1
Tipton St
- HOUS 77028 3825 E1
Tipton Oaks Dr
10900 FBnC 77469 4092 B7
Tirrell St
700 HOUS 77019 3962 C4
Tish Ct
9200 HarC 77040 3541 B7
Tisha Ln
14500 HarC 77377 3108 E7
14500 HarC 77377 3109 A7
Titan Dr
16800 HOUS 77058 4507 B4
Tite St
300 HOUS 77029 3966 A6
400 GNPK 77547 3966 A6
8900 HOUS 77029 3965 D6
Titleist Dr
3000 HarC 77373 3114 E7
Titus Ct
- MtgC 77357 2829 C1
Titus Pt
13400 HOUS 77085 4371 D1
Tiverton Ct
27700 MtgC 77386 2970 C6
Tiverton Forest Ct
25600 MtgC 77365 3117 E3
Tivoli Dr
14400 HOUS 77077 3956 D3
Tivoli Garden Ct
10 WDLD 77382 2674 D3
Tizerton Ct
7900 HarC 77379 3256 A2
TKC Rd
25400 HarC 77375 2965 A3
Toast Hollow Dr
1100 HarC 77073 3403 C2
Toast Hollow Ln
- HarC 77073 3403 D3
Tobacco Rd
19100 HarC 77449 3677 B4
Tobago Ln
- HarC 77338 3260 C3
Tobar Falls Cir
10800 HarC 77064 3540 E2
Tobasa Ct
11000 HarC 77086 3542 C1
Tobe Dr
700 HarC 77530 3830 A7
Tobinn Manor Dr
13500 HarC 77429 3397 B3
Tobola St
1100 RSBG 77471 4491 B5
Tobosa St
8100 HarC 77521 3833 B3
Tobruk Ln
7200 HOUS 77033 4244 A1
Toby Ln
500 CNRO 77301 2384 E5
Tocantins Dr
19400 MtgC 77365 2971 E5
19400 MtgC 77365 2972 A5
Tocatta Blvd
8600 HarC 77040 3681 C1
Todd Ct
400 ORDN 77386 2822 C6
Todd Dr
500 MtgC 77385 2822 D6
500 ORDN 77385 2822 D6
500 ORDN 77386 2822 D6
Todd Rd
18900 MtgC 77355 2814 B1
Todd St
300 TMBL 77375 2964 C7
10700 HOUS 77055 3821 E4
17600 MtgC 77302 2678 B7
17600 MtgC 77302 2824 C1
Toddington Rd
5700 HarC 77346 3264 D6
Todds Rd
2900 GLSN 77554 5109 A1
Todville Rd
300 SEBK 77586 4509 E2
400 CmbC 77586 4509 D4
2400 SEBK 77586 4510 A1
3700 SEBK 77586 4383 B6
5600 PASD 77586 4383 B5
Todwick Dr
3900 HarC 77082 4096 A4

Toggle Ct
15800 HarC 77532 3552 A4
Toho Ct
14400 HarC 77032 3546 D2
Toho Dr
5000 HarC 77032 3546 D2
Tokatee Ct
24600 FBnC 77494 3953 A3
Tokeneke Tr
10 PNPV 77024 3959 D3
Tolar Av
4000 HarC 77093 3686 B2
Toledo E
12800 GLSN 77554 5220 B7
Toledo Ct
- LGCY 77573 4632 A7
Toledo St
600 CNRO 77301 2384 B3
6300 HOUS 77008 3822 E7
Toledo Bend Ct
1300 FBnC 77469 4234 D5
Toledo Bend Dr
4300 FBnC 77469 4234 D5
Toledo Bend Trails Ln
19400 HarC 77433 3537 B4
Tolima Dr
6500 PASD 77505 4248 E4
Toliver St
3000 HOUS 77093 3825 A1
E Toliver St
1400 HOUS 77016 3825 B1
Tolken Wy
9400 FBnC 77478 4236 B2
Tollis St
8700 HOUS 77055 3821 A6
Tolliver Rd
18300 MtgC 77306 2680 A2
Tolman St
10400 HOUS 77034 4246 D6
Tolnay St
3900 HOUS 77021 4103 D5
Tolstin Lakes Ln
- FBnC 77494 4092 A5
Toluca Ln
1500 LGCY 77573 4632 A7
Tom
- BYTN 77520 3973 D6
Tom St
19100 HarC 77532 3411 D5
Tomahawk Dr
5600 GlsC 77510 4986 D2
Tomahawk Tr
8000 HarC 77050 3547 D6
16700 SGCH 77355 2815 E6
Tomasa Rd
15100 FBnC 77478 4236 C4
Tomato St
18600 HarC 77379 3112 B7
Tomball Pkwy
- HarC 77066 3541 D1
- HarC 77086 3541 E1
- HOUS - 3400 A4
11500 HarC 77038 3543 A6
11500 HarC 77086 3543 A6
11500 HarC 77088 3543 A6
11700 HarC 77038 3542 E5
11700 HarC 77086 3542 D4
12300 HOUS 77086 3542 D4
15500 HarC 77066 3400 C7
15500 HarC 77086 3400 C6
16100 HarC 77064 3400 C7
16200 HOUS 77064 3400 C6
16200 HOUS 77086 3400 C6
17900 HOUS 77070 3399 D3
19700 HarC 77070 3399 C1
21500 HarC 77377 3255 A6
22000 HarC 77070 3255 A5
22000 HOUS 77070 3255 A5
22400 HOUS 77377 3255 A5
22500 HOUS 77070 3254 E4
22500 HOUS 77377 3254 E4
22600 HarC 77070 3254 E3
22600 HarC 77375 3254 D1
23000 HarC 77377 3254 D3
24400 HarC 77375 3109 B5
26200 HarC 77377 3109 B5
26900 TMBL 77375 3109 A3
26900 TMBL 77377 3109 A3
28100 HarC 77377 3108 E1
28100 TMBL 77375 3108 E1
28100 TMBL 77377 3108 E1
28800 HarC 77377 2963 E7
28800 TMBL 77375 2963 D5
28800 TMBL 77377 2963 E7
29400 HarC 77375 2963 E6
30500 MtgC 77362 2963 D5
Tomball Pkwy SR-249
- HarC - 3399 C1
- HarC - 3400 C7
- HOUS - 3399 C1
- HOUS - 3400 A4
11500 HarC 77038 3543 A6
11500 HarC 77086 3543 A6
11500 HarC 77088 3543 A6
11700 HarC 77038 3542 E5
11700 HarC 77086 3542 D4
12300 HOUS 77086 3542 D4
14600 HarC 77086 3541 E1
22000 HarC 77070 3255 A5
22000 HOUS 77070 3255 A5
22400 HarC 77070 3254 E4
22400 HOUS 77070 3254 E4
22400 HOUS 77377 3255 A5
22500 HOUS 77377 3254 E4
22600 HarC 77375 3254 D1
22600 HarC 77377 3254 D2
24400 HarC 77375 3109 B5
26900 HarC 77377 3109 A4
26900 TMBL 77375 3109 A3
26900 TMBL 77377 3109 A3
28100 HarC 77377 3108 E1
28100 TMBL 77375 3108 E1
28100 TMBL 77377 3108 E1
28800 HarC 77377 2963 E7
28800 TMBL 77375 2963 D5
28800 TMBL 77377 2963 E7
29400 HarC 77375 2963 E6
30500 MtgC 77362 2963 D5
Tomball Cemetery Rd
22100 HarC 77377 2963 B7
22100 HarC 77377 3108 B1
Tomkin Ct
19900 MSCY 77459 4497 D7
Tomkins Cove Dr
8500 HarC 77083 4097 B7
Tomlin Rd
100 HOUS 77037 3684 D3

Tomlinson Trail Dr
1800 HarC 77067 3402 A7
Tommy Ln
1900 MSCY 77489 4370 B3
Tommye Dr
6700 HOUS 77028 3826 C2
Tommy Sallas Rd
- LbyC 77327 2830 C3
- PLMG 77327 2830 C3
20400 MtgC 77357 2830 C3
Tommy Smith Rd
13100 MtgC 77306 2534 B7
14600 MtgC 77306 2680 B1
Tom Phillips Pk
300 MtgC 77302 2530 B6
Tompkins Dr
3300 BYTN 77521 3973 E2
3600 BYTN 77521 3974 A2
3900 BYTN 77520 3974 A2
Tomplait Rd
- BzaC 77583 4623 D1
Tomsbrook Dr
2500 HarC 77067 3402 A4
Tom Thumb Ln
9300 HarC 77396 3407 A6
Tomwood
800 HOUS 77023 3964 B7
Tonawanda Dr
4300 HOUS 77035 4241 B3
Tonbridge Ln
1900 HarC 77449 3815 B7
Toney Dr
12800 HarC 77532 3693 B2
Toni Av
900 HOUS 77017 4106 C6
Tonkawa Dr
1300 DRPK 77536 4109 D5
Tonkawa St
4200 PASD 77504 4247 E5
7100 BYTN 77521 3835 B5
Tonnochy Ct
13700 HarC 77083 4097 A3
Tonnochy Dr
13600 HarC 77083 4097 B7
Tonya Dr
15300 HOUS 77060 3544 D2
Tonya Ln
3200 BzaC 77511 4748 E2
Tonydale Ln
20900 HarC 77388 3112 E4
Tonys Dr
12800 HarC 77532 3693 C2
Tooke St
2800 HOUS 77023 4104 D4
Tooley Dr
9100 HOUS 77031 4239 A3
Top St
700 HOUS 77002 3963 D3
Topaz Rdg
19700 MtgC 77355 2814 D4
Topaz St
9000 HOUS 77063 4099 D1
Topaz Springs Dr
- HOUS 77396 3406 C5
Topaz Trail Dr
4400 FBnC 77479 4366 D5
Topeka St
13400 HOUS 77015 3967 D2
Top Gallant Ct
9600 HarC 77065 3540 A4
Topham Cir
3000 HOUS 77018 3822 D4
Top Hat St
5400 GlsC 77511 4868 D4
Top Hill Dr
21300 HarC 77388 3112 D3
Top Mark Ct
- HarC 77494 3953 B2
Topping St
3300 HOUS 77093 3686 A4
Topsail Wy
400 HarC 77532 3411 B7
Topsfield Point Dr
6700 HarC 77346 3408 E1
Topside Ct
1900 HarC 77532 3551 D3
Topway Dr
4900 HarC 77373 3260 C1
Torchlight Dr
5100 HOUS 77035 4240 E3
Torchlight Terrace Ln
- FBnC 77450 3953 D7
- FBnC 77450 4093 D1
- FBnC 77494 3953 D7
- FBnC 77494 4093 D1
- HOUS 77450 4093 D1
- HOUS 77494 4093 D1
E Torch Pine Cir
10 WDLD 77381 2820 E5
W Torch Pine Cir
10 WDLD 77381 2820 E5
Torch Pine Ct
10 WDLD 77381 2820 E5
Torchwood Dr
1200 LGCY 77598 4630 C4
Tori Rd
600 FBnC 77469 4492 B7
600 FBnC 77469 4616 B1
E Torino Reale Dr
11300 FBnC 77469 4093 B7
W Torino Reale Dr
11300 FBnC 77469 4093 A7
Torn Ter
100 LbyC 77372 2538 A6
Toronado Ridge Ln
22400 MtgC 77365 2973 B3
Torquay Ln
7300 HOUS 77074 4099 E6
Torrance Ct
19400 HarC 77377 3109 B7
Torrance Dr
- LGCY 77573 4632 A6
Torrance Elms Ct
6300 HarC 77449 3676 E3
Torregon Ln
17800 HarC 77396 3407 D2
Torrence Falls Ct
20900 HarC 77449 3676 D3
Torrens Ct
9000 HarC 77375 2965 D5
Torreon St
6100 HOUS 77026 3824 E3
Torrey Ct
300 LGCY 77573 4632 D1
Torrey Grv
- HarC 77014 3401 C1
Torrey Rd
31000 HarC 77484 3247 A1

Torrey Chase Blvd
14300 HarC 77014 3257 B7
14300 HarC 77014 3401 B1
14300 HarC 77068 3257 B7
N Torrey Chase Ct
14300 HarC 77014 3401 D1
S Torrey Chase Ct
14200 HarC 77014 3401 D1
Torrey Creek Ln
4200 HarC 77014 3401 C1
Torrey Forest Dr
- HarC 77066 3401 C2
14100 HarC 77014 3401 C2
Torrey Glen Dr
- HarC 77014 3401 D1
Torrey Pine Pl
8500 HarC 77375 3110 E2
Torrey Pines Dr
10400 PNVL 77304 2237 A1
10400 PNVL 77318 2237 A1
Torrey Village Dr
14000 HarC 77014 3401 C1
Torrey Vista Dr
14100 HarC 77014 3401 C1
Torricelli Ln
22100 FBnC 77469 4093 E7
Torridon Ct
9300 HarC 77095 3538 C4
Torrijos Ct
1400 SHEH 77381 2822 A1
1400 SHEH 77384 2822 A1
Torrington Ct
4700 FBnC 77479 4366 D5
16600 HarC 77379 3256 E3
Torrington Ln
10100 HOUS 77075 4377 D2
10200 HOUS 77089 4377 D2
Torrisdale Ln
22500 HarC 77375 3110 D2
Torry Pines Rd
15000 HOUS 77062 4380 A7
15100 HOUS 77062 4507 B2
Torry View Cir
8600 HarC 77095 3538 B5
Torry View Ter
16400 HarC 77095 3538 B5
Torry Yucca Ln
700 HarC 77073 3403 C3
Tortoise
- MtgC 77355 2961 B4
- SGCH 77355 2961 B4
Tortuga
- HarC 77377 3109 A4
27100 HarC 77377 3108 E4
Tortuga Wy
- GLSN 77554 5331 E4
16500 JMAB 77554 5331 E4
Tory Ann Dr
5300 MtgC 77354 2673 E4
Tory Hill Ln
2900 SGLD 77478 4368 D5
Tosca Ln
12900 HOUS 77024 3958 D3
13000 HOUS 77079 3958 C3
Toscano Lago Blvd
- FBnC 77053 4498 D2
Toscano Villa Dr
- FBnC 77053 4498 D1
Toscano Vista Dr
- FBnC 77053 4498 D2
Totem Tr
9900 HarC 77064 3540 C3
Tothill Ct
1400 HarC 77530 3829 C5
Toto Dell Wy
14500 HarC 77429 3253 D5
Tottenham Dr
12400 HOUS 77031 4239 B5
Toucan Ln
200 MtgC 77385 2676 D4
11400 HarC 77067 3402 B6
Touche St
900 HarC 77015 3828 A7
900 HarC 77015 3967 B1
Touchstone St
7100 HOUS 77028 3686 E7
7100 HOUS 77028 3687 A7
8600 HOUS 77016 3686 E7
Toulcon St
700 HarC 77015 3828 A7
Toulon St
800 HarC 77015 3828 A7
Toulouse Av
9800 BYTN 77520 3835 B6
Toulouse Ln
900 SGLD 77478 4367 E1
Toulouse St
12500 HarC 77015 3828 B7
Tourmaline Ct
16800 HarC 77095 3397 A7
Tournament Ct
1500 HarC 77532 3551 E4
14400 HarC 77069 3400 A1
Tournament Dr
6600 HarC 77069 3400 A1
Tournament Ln
37600 MtgC 77355 2815 B6
Tournament Trails Dr
7500 HarC 77346 3265 A6
Tourney Ln
2200 HarC 77493 3814 C5
Tours Dr
7000 HOUS 77036 4099 D5
7400 HOUS 77074 4099 D6
Tousinau
9500 HOUS 77075 4377 B1
Tousinau St
9700 HOUS 77075 4377 C1
Tovrea Rd
500 ALVN 77511 4867 D2
Tower Dr
100 FRDW 77546 4749 D2
Tower Ln
19400 MtgC 77306 2680 D2
Tower Rd
3100 GlsC 77517 4870 A3
3100 STFE 77517 4870 A3
S Tower Rd
4200 STFE 77517 4869 E7
4200 STFE 77517 4870 A5
4300 GlsC 77517 4869 E6
Tower Rdg
16800 HarC 77546 4506 A7
16900 FRDW 77546 4506 A7
Tower St
100 HarC 77530 3969 B1
9300 HOUS 77088 3683 D1
9500 HarC 77088 3683 D1

Tower Bell Ln
1900 MSCY 77489 4370 C7
Tower Bluff Ln
17600 HarC 77433 3537 D1
Tower Bridge Ct
2900 PRLD 77581 4503 E3
Tower Bridge Rd
2000 PRLD 77581 4503 E3
2000 PRLD 77581 4504 A2
Tower Bridge St
10800 HOUS 77075 4377 B3
Tower Brook Dr
19400 MtgC 77306 2680 C1
Towergate Dr
4500 HarC 77373 3115 B6
Towerglen Ct
14200 HarC 77084 3679 A6
Tower Glen Dr
14000 MtgC 77306 2534 B7
14300 MtgC 77306 2680 C1
Tower Glen Ln
13900 MtgC 77306 2534 C7
E Towerglen Lp
5500 HarC 77084 3679 B4
N Towerglen Lp
14300 HarC 77084 3679 A4
Tower Grove Ct
1600 MSCY 77489 4370 D5
Towerguard Dr
26800 MtgC 77339 3118 B5
S Towerguard Dr
21400 MtgC 77339 3118 D3
Tower Hill Ln
3500 HarC 77066 3401 C4
Towering Oak Ct
4300 HOUS 77059 4380 C3
Towering Oak St
3000 HarC 77082 4096 D2
Towering Oaks
1000 MtgC 77355 2816 B4
Towering Oaks Dr
30400 MtgC 77355 2961 D6
30600 SGCH 77355 2961 D6
Towering Oaks Tr
16300 SGCH 77355 2961 D5
Towering Pine Ln
7100 FBnC 77469 4615 E5
Towering Pines Dr
10 WDLD 77381 2821 B3
Towermont Ln
4700 HarC 77388 3112 B4
Tower Oaks Blvd
10600 HarC 77065 3399 A7
10600 HarC 77070 3399 A7
11200 HarC 77065 3398 E7
Tower Point Dr
13900 FBnC 77478 4237 A4
Tower River Ct
1900 HOUS 77062 4380 A6
Towers Fall Ct
12000 HarC 77346 3408 B3
Towers Fall Ln
17300 HarC 77346 3408 B3
Tower Side Ln
25600 FBnC 77494 4092 C5
Towerstone Ct
9100 HarC 77379 3255 D4
Towerstone Dr
9100 HarC 77379 3255 D5
Towerview Ln
7100 HOUS 77489 4371 B5
Towerwood Dr
15000 MtgC 77306 2680 D3
Town Cir
1300 BYTN 77520 3973 B6
Town & Country Blvd
900 HOUS 77024 3958 D1
Town & Country Ln
900 HOUS 77024 3958 D1
Town & Country Wy
10400 HOUS 77024 3958 E1
Townboro Dr
800 HOUS 77062 4506 E2
Town Center Blvd
- HarC 77346 3264 E6
- RSBG 77469 4491 E5
- RSBG 77469 4492 A5
- RSBG 77471 4491 C4
- RSBG 77471 4492 A5
N Town Center Blvd
2500 SGLD 77478 4368 B6
2500 SGLD 77479 4368 B6
S Town Center Blvd
- SGLD 77479 4367 E7
3300 SGLD 77479 4368 A7
E Town Center Cir
2800 HOUS 77339 3119 D6
W Town Center Cir
2800 HOUS 77339 3119 D6
Town Center Dr
2300 SGLD 77478 4368 B5
2400 SGLD 77479 4368 B5
Town Center Pl
- HOUS 77345 3119 D6
4400 HOUS 77339 3119 D6
Town Creek Dr
8100 HarC 77095 3538 D6
Towne Ct
400 ALVN 77511 4867 C1
Towne Bridge Dr
17600 HarC 77377 3254 A3
Towne Brook Ct
9100 HarC 77433 3537 B5
Towne Brook Ln
9900 FBnC 77478 4237 A3
Towne Lake Dr
- PRLD 77581 4503 E6
Town Elm Ct
11100 HarC 77065 3539 C2
Towne Mist Ct
14000 FBnC 77478 4236 E2
Townes Rd
16200 FRDW 77546 4505 D7
16600 FRDW 77546 4629 E1
16700 FRDW 77546 4630 A1
Townes Forest Rd
3600 FRDW 77546 4506 A7
3800 FRDW 77546 4505 D7
3800 FRDW 77546 4629 E1
Towne Terrace Dr
9200 HarC 77379 3255 E5
Towne Tower Ln
9900 FBnC 77478 4237 A2
Towneview Dr
10200 FBnC 77478 4237 A3
10500 FBnC 77478 4236 C3
Towne Vue Ct
20700 HarC 77338 3261 D1

Towneway Dr
13700 FBnC 77478 4237 A3
Townewest Blvd
13700 FBnC 77478 4237 A3
13700 HOUS 77478 4237 B3
Towne Wy Dr
13900 FBnC 77478 4237 A2
14100 FBnC 77478 4236 E2
Town Gate Ct
2800 MSCY 77459 4496 D1
Town Glade Dr
16700 HarC 77429 3396 D2
Town Green Dr
15300 FBnC 77083 4236 B1
Town Grove Ct
2700 HOUS 77345 3120 C4
Townhall Ct
22500 HarC 77449 3814 E4
Townhall Ln
2100 HarC 77449 3814 E5
10400 FBnC 77478 4237 A3
Town Hill Dr
2000 HOUS 77062 4380 B7
2000 HOUS 77062 4507 E1
Townhome Ln
1600 MSCY 77459 4369 D5
Townhouse Ct
10 BLAR 77401 4100 E3
6300 HOUS 77081 4100 E4
6300 HOUS 77401 4100 E4
Townhouse Ln
1300 PASD 77502 4108 A6
1300 PASD 77506 4108 A6
Townhurst Dr
1600 HOUS 77043 3819 E5
Town Lake Ct
16500 PASD 77059 4380 D4
Townley St
800 HarC 77530 3829 C7
Townmist Dr
10000 FBnC 77478 4236 E3
Town Moor Ct
1300 HarC 77379 3255 C1
Town Oak Ln
10300 FBnC 77478 4237 A3
Town Oaks Dr
2200 HOUS 77062 4380 C7
Town Oaks Pl
10 BLAR 77401 4101 B4
Town Park Blvd
- HarC 77493 3813 D5
5200 KATY 77493 3813 D5
Town Park Dr
8700 HOUS 77036 4099 A4
9500 HOUS 77036 4098 E4
10300 HOUS 77072 4098 D4
Townpark Ln
3900 FBnC 77459 4622 A4
Townplace St
1000 HOUS 77057 3960 C4
Town Plaza Dr
4300 HOUS 77045 4241 C6
Townsan Rd
5800 HOUS 77396 3405 E4
6100 HOUS 77396 3406 A4
Townsen Blvd
- HarC 77338 3262 E3
- HarC 77338 3263 A3
- HMBL 77338 3262 D3
20100 HMBL 77338 3263 A5
Townsen Blvd W
19700 HMBL 77338 3262 B5
19700 HOUS 77338 3262 B5
Townsend Ct
14600 HarC 77429 3397 D2
Townsend Pl
10 WDLD 77382 2675 C7
Townsend Mill Ct
100 HarC 77094 3955 C1
Townsgate Cir
6200 FBnC 77450 4094 B4
Townsgate Ct
20800 FBnC 77450 4094 B4
Township Ct
1400 RSBG 77471 4491 D5
Township Dr
200 HMBL 77338 3262 D6
500 LGCY 77573 4631 E2
600 LGCY 77573 4632 A2
Township Ln
- MSCY 77459 4496 D2
Township Elm St
23800 HarC 77373 3114 E5
Township Glen Ct
20500 HarC 77433 3251 C6
Township Glen Ln
15500 HarC 77433 3251 B6
Township Grove Ln
13300 HOUS 77082 4097 D1
Township Meadows Ct
16700 HarC 77095 3538 B7
Townshire Dr
14100 HOUS 77077 3956 E4
Town Square Pl
2100 SGLD 77479 4368 B6
Town Square Rd
10400 FBnC 77478 4237 A3
Townsville Cir
4100 MSCY 77459 4496 C4
Town Village Blvd
- RSBG 77471 4491 C4
Townwood Dr
12900 HOUS 77045 4241 E7
13400 HOUS 77045 4372 E1
Toyah Av
2400 HarC 77039 3545 E4
3600 HarC 77039 3546 A4
Trabajo Dr
7400 FBnC 77083 4095 E6
7900 FBnC 77083 4096 A7
Trace Ct
3600 HarC 77396 3407 E3
Trace Dr
1200 HOUS 77077 3957 C4
S Trace Dr
12700 HarC 77066 3401 B3
Trace Ln
16800 HarC 77546 4506 A7
Tracebrook Ln
- FBnC 77469 4094 C7
E Trace Creek Dr
10 WDLD 77381 2820 E5
N Trace Creek Dr
100 WDLD 77381 2820 D5
S Trace Creek Dr
10 WDLD 77381 2820 E5
W Trace Creek Dr
10 WDLD 77381 2820 E5

STREET
Block City ZIP Map# Grid

Trace Forest Dr
18100 HarC 77379 3255 E2
Trace Forest Ln
18300 HarC 77379 3255 E2
Trace Glen Ln
17200 FBnC 77083 4095 D7
Tracelawn Ct
9200 HarC 77396 3406 E7
9200 HarC 77396 3407 A7
Tracelynn Ln
12400 HarC 77066 3401 C4
Tracemeadow Dr
4300 HarC 77066 3401 B4
Trace Mill Ct
4300 HarC 77066 3401 C4
Traceton Cir
14400 HarC 77429 3397 D2
Trace Vista Cir
28800 HarC 77336 3120 D1
N Tracewood Bnd
13500 HOUS 77077 3957 A4
S Tracewood Bnd
13500 HOUS 77077 3957 A4
Tracewood Gln
1300 HOUS 77077 3957 B4
Tracewood Ln
12600 HarC 77066 3401 C4
Tracewood Cove
1300 HOUS 77077 3957 B4
Tracewood Park Dr
- HOUS 77077 3957 A3
Traci Ln
100 HarC 77530 3969 A2
Traci Jo Ln
13400 MtgC 77302 2531 E6
Tracy Ln
2100 HarC 77562 3832 C3
Tracy Lynn Ln
1900 ALVN 77511 4866 D4
Trade Center Dr
19200 HarC 77338 3261 E6
19200 HOUS 77338 3261 E6
S Trade Center Pkwy
10 MtgC 77385 2676 B4
10 WDLD 77385 2676 B5
Trademark Pl
700 HOUS 77079 3956 D2
Traders Village Dr
13100 HarC 77041 3539 C7
Trade Wind Dr
10500 HarC 77086 3542 C2
Trade Winds Dr
10100 HarC 77086 3542 C3
Tradewinds Dr
10 GLSN 77554 5221 C3
2000 MSCY 77459 4369 C7
3700 GLSN 77554 5440 D6
Tradewood Dr
- HOUS 77032 3261 D6
- HOUS 77338 3261 D6
Trading Post Dr
10200 HarC 77064 3540 B4
E Traditions Blvd
3800 HarC 77082 4096 E3
W Traditions Blvd
- HarC 77082 4096 E3
E Traditions Ct
3700 HarC 77082 4096 B4
W Traditions Ct
3700 HarC 77082 4096 B4
N Trafalgar Ct
6100 HarC 77449 3677 D4
S Trafalgar Ct
6000 HarC 77449 3677 D4
Trafalgar Dr
5200 HOUS 77045 4372 A2
5500 HOUS 77085 4371 E2
5500 HOUS 77085 4372 A2
Trafalgar Pl
- CNRO 77384 2675 E4
- CNRO 77384 2676 A4
Trafalger Ln
- HarC 77083 4097 A7
Trail Cir
4000 HarC 77346 3408 A4
N Trail Dr
16200 HarC 77073 3259 A5
Trail Hllw
7600 FBnC 77459 4497 A7
7600 FBnC 77459 4621 A1
Trail Lp E
6700 BzaC 77583 4624 A7
Trail Lp S
3000 BzaC 77583 4623 E7
3000 BzaC 77583 4624 A7
Trail Lp W
6700 BzaC 77583 4623 E7
Trail Vw
1800 FRDW 77546 4629 D5
6000 HarC 77049 3828 D3
Trail Bend Ct
400 FRDW 77546 4505 B6
Trail Bend Ln
200 FRDW 77546 4505 C6
18500 HarC 77084 3816 D2
Trail Blazer Dr
7700 HarC 77040 3541 D7
Trailblazer Ln
10200 HarC 77064 3540 B4
Trail Bluff Ln
- MtgC 77386 2969 E7
Trail Brook Ct
- LGCY 77573 4630 E7
Trailbrook Dr
7100 FBnC 77479 4493 D5
14700 HarC 77095 3539 A5
Trailcliff Ct
26000 FBnC 77494 4093 A3
Trail Creek Dr
2600 SGLD 77479 4368 D7
5100 HOUS 77017 4246 B1
Trailcrest St
- HarC 77039 3545 E4
Trail Cypress Blvd
17100 HarC 77377 3254 D4
Traile St
1400 HOUS 77020 3964 B2
Trailer Pk
- HarC 77562 3692 D5
Trail Forest Ct
1600 HOUS 77339 3118 A7
Trailglen
- HarC 77049 3828 D3
Trailhead Pl
10 WDLD 77381 2675 A7
Trail Head St
400 FRDW 77546 4505 C6

Trail Heaven
- HarC 77336 2975 D7
Trail Hollow Ct
12900 PRLD 77583 4500 A5
Trail Hollow Dr
3200 PRLD 77583 4500 A5
12600 HOUS 77024 3958 E1
12900 HOUS 77079 3958 C1
Trailing Clover Ct
4900 HarC 77084 3677 B7
Trailing Moss Ct
9700 HarC 77064 3540 D4
Trailing Moss Dr
9500 HarC 77064 3540 D4
Trailing Oak Ln
- MSCY 77459 4496 C1
Trailing Vine Rd
2000 HarC 77373 3114 C7
Trail Lake Dr
2800 HOUS 77045 4373 A1
3100 HOUS 77045 4242 A7
3300 HOUS 77045 4241 E7
5100 HOUS 77045 4372 A1
Trail Lodge Dr
2800 HOUS 77339 3119 B6
Trail Manor Dr
13000 PRLD 77583 4500 A5
Trailmeadow Ct
13600 HarC 77429 3254 A5
Trail Meadow Ln
13500 BzaC 77583 4623 E4
Trail Mobile Rd
3400 HOUS 77013 3827 A6
Trailmont Dr
11600 HOUS 77077 3958 A6
Trail Mountain Ct
17700 HarC 77346 3408 E3
Trail Mountain Ln
17600 HarC 77346 3408 E3
Trail Oak Dr
19200 MtgC 77302 2680 C7
19200 MtgC 77357 2680 C7
Trail Oaks Ct
1600 HOUS 77339 3118 B7
Trail Pine Ln
- HarC 77379 3111 A3
Trail Point Dr
1400 HarC 77073 3403 C2
11600 HarC 77070 3254 D3
11600 HarC 77377 3254 D3
Trail Ridge Ct
10400 HarC 77064 3540 B3
Trailridge Ct
2700 MSCY 77459 4496 D1
Trail Ridge Dr
- HarC 77065 3540 A3
3100 PRLD 77583 4500 B4
10500 HarC 77064 3540 A3
Trailridge Forest Dr
8800 HarC 77088 3542 E6
Trail River Dr
2300 HOUS 77345 3120 B5
Trail Run Ln
- PRLD 77583 4500 A5
Trails Ct
400 HNCV 77024 3960 A3
Trails End Rd
10 MtgC 77385 2823 C1
600 MtgC 77385 2677 C7
Trails End St
100 MtgC 77384 2674 C3
100 WDLD 77382 2674 C3
100 WDLD 77384 2674 C3
400 HNCV 77024 3960 A3
Trailside Ct
2500 SGLD 77479 4368 D7
Trail Side Dr
8000 HarC 77040 3541 D7
Trailside Dr
15100 HarC 77095 3678 E1
Trails Park Ln
31600 MtgC 77385 2823 B6
Trail Springs Ct
500 HOUS 77339 3118 B7
Trail Stone Ct
24800 FBnC 77494 3953 B6
Trailstone Ln
3800 FBnC 77494 4093 C3
Trails West Dr
20900 HarC 77449 3676 D3
Trail Timbers Dr
5400 HarC 77346 3264 C7
Trail Tree Ln
21900 HOUS 77339 3263 B1
22300 HOUS 77339 3118 A7
Trail Valley Wy
7000 HarC 77086 3542 B1
Trailview Ct
6700 BzaC 77583 4623 E7
Trailview Dr
- HarC 77049 3828 D3
Trail View Wy
400 FRDW 77546 4505 B5
Trailville Dr
13700 HOUS 77077 3957 A2
15700 HOUS 77079 3956 E2
Trail Water Ct
2000 HOUS 77339 3118 D3
Trailway Ln
6300 HarC 77379 3256 D1
Trail West St
2200 SGLD 77478 4368 C6
Trail Wind Ct
5600 HarC 77049 3828 B4
Trailwood
19200 MtgC 77355 2814 A1
Trailwood Ct
4300 FBnC 77479 4366 D6
Trailwood Dr
3600 BYTN 77521 3973 D2
3600 HOUS 77023 4104 C5
4300 FBnC 77479 4366 C6
Trail Wood Ln
2300 FBnC 77469 4365 D3
Trailwood Ln
22400 HarC 77375 3110 E2
22400 HarC 77375 3111 A1
Trailwood Pk
22500 FBnC 77450 4093 E1
Trailwood Manor Ln
21800 HarC 77449 3815 A2
Trailwood Village Dr
1300 HOUS 77339 3263 D1
1900 HOUS 77339 3118 D7
Trailwood Village Sq
2300 HOUS 77339 3118 E7
Train Ct
10800 HarC 77041 3680 C6

Tralee Dr
2300 PRLD 77581 4504 D2
N Tram Rd
13700 MtgC 77372 2537 D7
14000 MtgC 77372 2683 D1
S Tram Rd
- RMFT 77357 2829 D1
15300 MtgC 77372 2683 D3
16400 PTVL 77372 2683 D6
17400 MtgC 77357 2683 D4
17500 MtgC 77357 2829 D1
Trammel Dr
5300 HarC 77388 3112 A2
Trammel-Fresno Rd
- MSCY 77459 4498 A7
- MSCY 77545 4497 E7
300 FBnC 77545 4499 A7
1000 FBnC 77545 4498 B7
2300 MSCY 77545 4498 A7
4400 MSCY 77459 4497 D7
Tramore Dr
14900 FBnC 77083 4236 C1
Tramwood Dr
600 MSCY 77489 4370 E5
Tranquil Dr
16500 FBnC 77478 4236 A7
Tranquil Trc
5200 GlsC 77511 4751 B7
Tranquil Vw
4100 HarC 77084 3816 C1
Tranquil Glade Pl
10 WDLD 77381 2820 D3
Tranquility Dr
18400 HarC 77346 3265 B7
Tranquility Ln
- LGCY 77573 4632 B6
25700 MtgC 77355 2814 B2
Tranquility Tr
2700 PRLD 77584 4503 B4
Tranquility Lake Blvd
2800 PRLD 77581 4502 A4
2800 PRLD 77584 4502 A4
Tranquility Lakes Blvd
2800 PRLD 77581 4502 A4
2800 PRLD 77584 4502 A4
Tranquility Park Dr
16700 HarC 77429 3252 E6
Tranquility Ridge Ct
- HarC 77396 3407 C7
Tranquility Ridge Dr
10400 HarC 77396 3407 D7
Tranquil Lake Wy
8100 MtgC 77385 2676 B6
Tranquil Oaks Ct
2600 HOUS 77345 3120 A3
Tranquil Park Ct
15900 HarC 77379 3256 A6
Tranquil Park Dr
8500 HarC 77379 3256 B6
S Tranquil Path Dr
10 WDLD 77380 2967 D5
W Tranquil Path Dr
100 WDLD 77380 2967 D4
Tranquil River Dr
7400 PASD 77505 4249 B5
Tranquil Springs Ln
23100 FBnC 77494 4093 C4
Trans Ln
6300 BzaC 77584 4626 E2
Transcentral Ct
1700 HOUS 77032 3404 B4
Transco Four Dr
10 HOUS 77056 3961 A7
Transco One Dr
10 HOUS 77027 4101 A1
10 HOUS 77056 4101 A1
Transco Three Dr
10 HOUS 77027 3961 A7
10 HOUS 77056 3961 A7
Transco Two Dr
10 HOUS 77056 4101 A1
Trap and Skeet Ct
10 HOUS 77094 4096 A1
Trap and Skeet Rd
10 HOUS 77094 4096 A1
Trapper Ln
11300 HarC 77065 3398 E6
Trapper Hill Dr
1000 HOUS 77077 3957 A3
Trapper Lake Dr
21900 HarC 77388 3111 E2
Trappers Forest
3300 HOUS 77088 3683 A3
Trappers Forest Dr
3700 HOUS 77088 3683 A3
Traskwood Dr
400 FBnC 77469 4493 A6
Travel Air
1100 GLSN 77554 5107 B7
1100 GLSN 77554 5221 B1
Travelair St
8200 HOUS 77061 4245 B5
Traveler Ct
1000 FBnC 77469 4616 D1
Travelers Rst
- HarC 77038 3543 C5
Travelers Wy
- HarC 77065 3540 A4
E Travelers Wy Cir
11200 HarC 77065 3540 A4
W Travelers Wy Cir
11200 HarC 77065 3540 A4
Travelers Wy Ln
11200 HarC 77065 3540 A4
Travellers St
2800 LGCY 77573 4631 A6
Traverstone Ct
10 FBnC 77479 4367 A5
Traviata Dr
12800 HOUS 77024 3958 D3
Travick Ln
2700 HarC 77073 3259 E4
N Travis
- DRPK 77536 4109 D6
Travis Ct
1200 HarC 77073 3259 C7
1600 LMQU 77568 4989 D2
3900 FBnC 77459 4621 C4
Travis Dr
700 PASD 77502 4246 E1
700 PASD 77502 4247 A1
4800 GLSN 77551 5108 D5
Travis Ln
300 SGCH 77362 2816 D4
Travis St
10 HOUS 77002 3963 B5
100 BYTN 77520 4112 E2
100 WEBS 77598 4507 B6

Travis St
300 RHMD 77469 4491 E1
300 RHMD 77469 4492 A1
1200 LPRT 77571 4110 E6
2200 HOUS 77006 3963 A7
4400 HOUS 77002 3962 E7
4700 HOUS 77002 4102 E1
5100 HOUS 77006 4102 E1
6500 HOUS 77005 4102 C4
6500 HOUS 77030 4102 C4
6500 HTCK 77563 4988 C4
N Travis St
400 DRPK 77536 4249 B2
S Travis St
400 DRPK 77536 4249 B3
Travis Brook Dr
26100 FBnC 77469 4092 B7
Travis Creek Wy
3100 FBnC 77545 4498 C6
Travis House Ln
24300 HarC 77493 3814 B6
Travis Lake Ct
3800 PRLD 77581 4503 E7
Travis Park Dr
10 SGLD 77479 4495 E3
Travis Point Ln
15200 HarC 77084 3678 E3
Travis Trail Ln
23800 FBnC 77494 4093 A5
Traweek Dr
1000 SPVL 77055 3820 E7
Traylor Rd
1400 CNRO 77304 2383 D7
Treadslow Ln
2200 HarC 77067 3402 A5
Treadway St
- HOUS 77022 3684 E7
Treadwell Ct
10 WDLD 77381 2820 E4
Treadwell Ln
4100 GLSN 77554 5440 D7
Treaschwig Rd
- HarC 77338 3259 E3
2700 HarC 77073 3259 E3
2700 HOUS 77073 3259 E3
3300 HarC 77338 3260 B1
3700 HarC 77373 3260 B1
4500 HarC 77373 3115 D7
6100 HarC 77373 3116 B7
Treasure Cir
3400 GLSN 77554 5332 C1
Treasure Ct
1100 BYTN 77521 3973 B3
14300 GLSN 77554 5332 D3
Treasure Dr
100 HOUS 77076 3685 A5
Treasure Ln
100 HOUS 77339 3262 E1
4500 BzaC 77584 4501 E6
4500 BzaC 77584 4502 A6
Treasure Tr
4400 SGLD 77479 4496 A2
Treasure Cove Dr
10 WDLD 77381 2821 B5
Treasure Mountain Dr
1900 HarC 77388 3113 C5
Treasure Oaks Ct
20100 HarC 77450 3954 E4
Treasure Oaks Dr
1600 HarC 77450 3954 E4
Treasures Ridge Dr
26800 HarC 77339 3118 C5
Treaty Oaks St
15100 HOUS 77053 4372 A4
Trebeau Ct
12400 HOUS 77031 4238 E7
Trebeck Ln
6600 HarC 77379 3256 E3
Treble Dr
1700 HMBL 77338 3263 A6
1800 HarC 77338 3263 A6
Trebor St
3100 PASD 77503 4248 E3
3100 PASD 77505 4248 E3
Treborway Dr
14700 HarC 77014 3401 C1
Tredington St
10 SGLD 77479 4495 D3
Tree Ln
2100 HOUS 77339 3118 E4
2200 HOUS 77339 3119 B5
24300 MtgC 77365 2972 E7
Tree Arbor Ln
15000 HarC 77429 3253 C7
Tree Bank Ln
13600 HarC 77070 3399 A3
Tree Bark Ln
300 LGCY 77573 4632 B5
Treebark Ln
5000 HOUS 77018 3683 C7
Tree Branch Dr
9500 HarC 77064 3399 C7
Tree Bridge St
9400 HOUS 77075 4377 B4
Tree Bright Ln
23000 HarC 77373 3115 D6
Treecastle Dr
14900 HarC 77530 3829 C6
Tree Cove Ct
10 WDLD 77384 2821 E1
Tree Crest Cir
10 WDLD 77381 2820 D4
Treefern Dr
6800 HarC 77396 3547 B3
Treefork Ln
18200 HarC 77094 3955 C2
Tree Frog Dr
10 HOUS 77074 4239 E1
Tree Hollow Cir N
10400 LPRT 77571 4250 C4
Treehouse
11700 HOUS 77024 3959 C5
Tree House Cir
- HarC 77373 3115 A7
Tree House Ct
3000 HarC 77373 3114 E7
Tree House Ln
22200 HarC 77373 3115 A7
22600 HarC 77373 3114 E6
Treelake Dr
- MtgC 77303 2237 D3
Tree Lark Ln
18600 HarC 77449 3677 C3
Tree Line Dr
4300 PASD 77505 4249 B6
Treeline Dr
6600 HarC 77346 3264 E7
7500 FBnC 77479 4494 A3

Treeline Dr
16700 HarC 77377 3254 A5
16700 HarC 77429 3254 A5
Treeloch Ln
17600 HarC 77379 3257 B3
Tree Manor Ln
3700 HOUS 77345 3119 E2
Tree Meadow
- MtgC 77355 2816 C6
- MtgC 77362 2816 C6
Treemeadow Ln
34700 SGCH 77362 2816 D5
Treemill Ct
19100 HarC 77449 3816 B3
Tree Mist Ct
4100 HarC 77346 3408 A3
Tree Monkey Rd
22300 MtgC 77357 2827 B3
Treemont Lndg
17800 HarC 77084 3817 A1
Treemont Fair Ct
19800 FBnC 77469 4234 D2
Treemont Fair Dr
19800 FBnC 77469 4234 D2
Treemont Hollow Ct
21800 FBnC 77469 4493 A3
Tree Moss Ct
18200 HarC 77346 3408 A1
Tree Moss Pl
4100 HarC 77346 3408 A3
Tree Oaks Ct
5600 HarC 77346 3264 D5
Tree Orchard Dr
19400 HarC 77449 3816 A2
Tree Path Dr
5200 HOUS 77013 3827 B4
Tree Path Ln
5100 HOUS 77013 3827 B3
Treepoint Rd
5300 GlsC 77510 4986 D2
5300 STFE 77510 4986 D2
Treeridge Pl
10400 WDLD 77380 2821 D6
Treescape Cir
10 WDLD 77381 2821 A3
Treesdale Ct
2700 FBnC 77450 3954 A6
Treesdale Ln
22000 FBnC 77450 3954 A7
Treesey Wy
12800 HarC 77066 3401 C3
Tree Sparrow Dr
- WDLD 77382 2673 D6
Tree Sparrow Ln
9500 FBnC 77083 4236 B1
Tree Star Ln
16800 HarC 77429 3252 E6
Treestar Pl
10 WDLD 77381 2820 C2
Treetoad Dr
19100 HarC 77449 3816 B2
Tree Top Dr
- BzaC 77511 4627 C4
- BzaC 77584 4627 C4
- PRLD 77584 4627 C4
4200 PASD 77505 4249 B5
Treetop Ln
20500 HarC 77388 3112 D5
Tree Trail Ct
19300 HarC 77346 3264 D5
Tree Trunk Dr
200 HarC 77388 3113 D7
Treevine Ct
10 WDLD 77381 2820 B1
Treewater Dr
7000 HOUS 77072 4097 D6
Treewood Dr
5200 HarC 77346 3264 C4
Tregarnon Dr
13000 HarC 77015 3828 C6
Treichel Rd
12600 HarC 77041 3679 D1
15600 HarC 77377 3108 B2
Trelawney Dr
3400 PRLD 77581 4376 C6
Trellis Ct
10 MtgC 77304 2236 B4
Trellis Ln
20900 HarC 77073 3259 E4
Trellis Estates Ct
18000 HarC 77429 3396 B2
Trellis Gate St
10 WDLD 77382 2674 C5
Trembling Creek Cir
3100 HarC 77373 3115 A7
Trembling Forest Ln
4600 HOUS 77092 3683 A7
4600 HOUS 77092 3822 A1
Tremendo Dr
7400 FBnC 77083 4095 E6
Trementina Dr
- HarC 77088 3543 B7
Tremont Ct
1900 RSBG 77471 4490 E6
4100 SGLD 77479 4495 C2
Tremont St
100 GLSN 77550 5109 C4
7500 HOUS 77028 3826 C1
8200 HOUS 77028 3687 C6
Tremont Brook Wy
2500 FBnC 77545 4498 B6
Tremont Glen Ln
4500 FBnC 77494 4092 D3
Tremont Park Ct
14100 BzaC 77583 4623 D3
Tremont Park Ln
- BzaC 77583 4623 D4
- MtgC 77386 2823 C7
Tremont Woods Ct
10 WDLD 77381 2821 A3
Tremout Hollow Ln
15700 HarC 77044 3549 E3
Tremper St
5500 HOUS 77020 3964 D2
7600 HOUS 77020 3965 B2
Trench Ln
4100 MtgC 77386 2970 C5
Trendale St
5600 HOUS 77087 4104 E7
5700 HOUS 77087 4244 E1
Trendwest Dr
1700 HarC 77084 3816 A7
Trent Rd
- PASD 77505 4249 A3
- PASD 77536 4249 A3
3200 HarC 77336 2976 D7
3700 HarC 77336 2977 A7

Trent St
- SGLD 77479 4495 D4
Trent Cove Ln
3700 PRLD 77584 4503 C7
Trentham Pl
10 HOUS 77009 3963 C2
Trenton Ln
1200 BYTN 77520 3973 C7
Trenton Rd
2100 HarC 77093 3685 E2
2100 HOUS 77093 3685 D2
2900 HOUS 77093 3686 A2
4000 HarC 77093 3686 B2
Trenton St
1100 FBnC 77469 4364 D6
1100 RHMD 77469 4364 D6
Trenton Brook Ln
- HarC 77377 3254 A3
Trenton Creek Ln
15300 HarC 77429 3253 C6
Trenton Lake Ln
6500 HarC 77041 3679 D3
Trenton Reach Dr
- FBnC 77494 4092 A6
Trenton Valley Ln
20800 HarC 77449 3815 C2
Trentway St
7800 HOUS 77040 3681 E6
Trentwood Dr
- FBnC 77083 4096 C7
Trenwood Ln
10 HOUS 77022 3685 A7
Tres Dr
3900 GLSN 77554 5220 B6
Tresch Ct
400 HOUS 77598 4506 D2
Tresch Ln
15100 HOUS 77598 4506 D3
Trescon Dr
6000 HOUS 77048 4375 D3
Treshire Ln
20700 HarC 77388 3112 B4
Tres Lagunas Dr
6200 HarC 77082 4096 E4
6200 HarC 77083 4096 E4
6700 HOUS 77083 4096 E5
Trestletree Pl
10 WDLD 77380 2968 B4
Trestletree Wy
7900 BYTN 77521 3833 C3
Tresvant Dr
400 HOUS 77598 4506 D3
Tretowner
- HarC 77450 3954 C4
Trevena Rd
- MtgC 77357 2827 E6
Trevino Ct
2800 FRDW 77546 4749 E1
Trevino Ln
700 MtgC 77302 2530 D6
Trevino Trails Dr
19100 HarC 77346 3265 B6
Trevlig Tr
19800 HarC 77073 3403 D2
Trevor Wy
- HarC 77073 3258 E2
Trevor Hill Dr
3800 HarC 77066 3401 C5
Trevors Trace Ln
5100 FBnC 77494 4092 E3
Trey Dr
4000 HarC 77084 3817 C1
4000 HOUS 77084 3817 C1
Treyburn Tr
1800 FBnC 77450 3953 E5
Trey Rock Wy
- HarC 77433 3251 C4
Trey Rogillios Wy
2200 CNRO 77304 2236 E4
Trianon St
500 HOUS 77024 3961 A2
Tribe Dr
13900 HarC 77429 3253 E4
Tribeca Ln
24500 HarC 77493 3814 A6
Tribune St
- MtgC 77357 2829 D3
- RMFT 77357 2829 D3
Trica Ct
8200 HarC 77040 3541 B7
Trichelle St
400 PASD 77506 4106 E4
T Richmond
16600 HarC 77429 3253 B3
Tri City Beach Rd
300 BYTN 77520 4113 E7
400 CmbC 77520 4114 A7
400 CmbC 77520 4254 A1
400 HarC 77520 4113 E7
Trickey Rd
11400 HarC 77067 3402 C5
11400 HOUS 77067 3402 C6
Tridens Ct
11000 HarC 77086 3542 C1
Triechel Rd
14900 HarC 77377 3108 C2
Trigate Dr
6600 HOUS 77489 4371 C6
Trigg St
4400 HOUS 77016 3686 B6
4400 HOUS 77093 3686 B6
Trilby Wy
21500 HarC 77338 3260 A1
Trilling Bird Pl
10 WDLD 77384 2675 A3
E Trillium Cir
10 WDLD 77381 2675 A7
W Trillium Cir
10 WDLD 77381 2675 A7
Trillium Ct
100 WDLD 77381 2675 A7
Trimble St
200 HOUS 77009 3824 B6
Trimm Av
900 PASD 77502 4247 C1
Trimstone Dr
6500 PASD 77505 4248 E5
6700 PASD 77505 4249 A5
Trinidad Ln
1200 GlsC 77650 4879 D3
Trinidad St
1400 HOUS 77003 3963 E6
Trinidad Wy
16600 JMAB 77554 5331 E5
Trinity Av
- HOUS 77018 3823 B3
Trinity Dr
- STAF 77477 4369 C1

Trinity Dr
2900 PRLD 77584 4503 A4
12700 STAF 77477 4238 C7
Trinity Ln
600 PASD 77506 4107 E5
Trinity Pk
- DRPK 77536 4109 E6
Trinity St
10 LMQU 77563 4989 D3
10 LMQU 77568 4989 D3
500 HOUS 77007 3963 B3
1900 LGCY 77573 4632 C3
Trinity Sta
1800 SGLD 77478 4368 C5
Trinity Wy
10 MtgC 77357 2829 C2
20400 MtgC 77357 2827 B7
Trinity Bay Dr
- PRLD 77545 4499 E2
- PRLD 77545 4500 A1
- PRLD 77584 4499 E2
- PRLD 77584 4500 A3
Trinity Glen Ln
2700 HarC 77047 4374 A4
Trinity Isle Ct
5900 HOUS 77345 3120 D7
Trinity Joe Ln
3100 HarC 77396 3407 E3
Trinity Knoll Wy
18200 HarC 77346 3409 A1
Trinity Manor Ln
2100 FBnC 77469 4493 A3
Trinity Meadow Dr
14900 HOUS 77489 4371 A4
Trinity Meadow Ln
7600 FBnC 77469 4095 B6
Trinity Mist Ln
19400 HarC 77073 3403 C2
Trinity Oaks Cir
10 WDLD 77381 2820 B3
S Trinity Oaks Cir
100 WDLD 77381 2820 B3
Trinity Oaks Ct
100 WDLD 77381 2820 B3
Trinity Park Ln
- MtgC 77386 2823 C7
Trinity Pass Ct
3000 HarC 77373 3115 A3
Trinity River Ct
4600 MtgC 77386 2970 B2
Trinity River Dr
29000 MtgC 77386 2970 B2
Trinket Dr
30700 MtgC 77386 2968 E2
30800 MtgC 77386 2969 A1
Tri Oaks Ln
1000 HOUS 77043 3819 A7
1000 HOUS 77043 3958 B4
W Tri Oaks Ln
1100 HOUS 77043 3819 B7
1100 HOUS 77043 3958 B4
Triola Ln
6900 HOUS 77074 4100 A5
7000 HOUS 77074 4099 E6
8300 HOUS 77036 4099 C6
9500 HOUS 77036 4098 E5
11600 HOUS 77072 4098 A6
Triple 3
26700 MtgC 77372 2683 C2
Triple Crown Dr
3100 FBnC 77469 4365 A4
3300 FBnC 77469 4364 E3
7900 HOUS 77071 4239 D6
Triple Crown Wy
11200 MtgC 77304 2528 A1
Triple Glen Ct
1900 FBnC 77545 4622 D2
Triple Mast Cir
1900 LGCY 77573 4509 A6
Triple Oak Ct
1900 HOUS 77077 3957 E6
Triple Spur Ln
23200 HarC 77373 2968 E6
Triple T St
27100 MtgC 77372 2683 D1
Triplett St
3200 GlsC 77518 4634 B2
Tripoli Dr
3800 PASD 77505 4248 E4
Trippell St
10400 HOUS 77093 3685 D4
Trippodo St
2600 GlsC 77539 4633 A7
Tristan St
3700 HOUS 77021 4103 C5
Tristan Wy
10 CNRO 77384 2675 D3
Tristandale Ln
18400 HarC 77379 3111 B7
Tristanwood Ct
- HarC 77047 4374 B3
Tristar Dr
100 HOUS 77034 4379 A5
100 HOUS 77598 4379 A5
300 HOUS 77598 4378 E6
Triton Ct
20300 HarC 77450 3954 E1
Triway
5700 HarC 77041 3681 A5
5700 HOUS 77041 3681 A5
Triway Ln
2400 HOUS 77043 3820 A3
2900 HOUS 77043 3819 E2
5400 HarC 77041 3681 A6
5400 HOUS 77041 3681 A6
Trixie Ln
1900 HOUS 77042 3958 C6
Trogon Ln
7200 HOUS 77083 4097 B5
Troll Woods Ct
10 WDLD 77384 2675 A3
Trompilla Ln
13300 HOUS 77083 4097 B4
Tronewood St
4300 HOUS 77016 3686 B6
4300 HOUS 77093 3686 B6
Troon Cir
4600 PASD 77505 4248 E6
Troon Dr
- ALVN 77511 4866 E4
- LPRT 77571 4251 D6
2200 LGCY 77573 4508 D7
Troon Rd
2100 HOUS 77019 3962 B4
Troon St
1900 ALVN 77511 4866 E4
Troon Oak St
18600 HarC 77429 3252 A7

STREET
Block City ZIP Map# Grid
Troon Oak St
18700 HarC 77433 3252 A7
Trooper Ct
4300 MtgC 77386 3115 C2
Trooper Hill Ln
- MtgC 77386 3115 D1
Troost St
5400 HOUS 77026 3825 C4
Trophy Ln
23400 FBnC 77494 4093 B4
Trophy Club Rd
14500 HarC 77095 3539 A7
Trophy Deer Ct
17700 HarC 77084 3817 A1
Trophy Pl Dr
7600 HarC 77346 3409 B1
7900 HarC 77346 3265 B7
Trophy Rack Dr
- CNRO 77303 2237 C4
Tropic Dr
10 HLCS 77511 4867 E5
Tropical Wy
6000 HOUS 77087 4245 A1
Tropicana Ct
700 FRDW 77546 4629 A1
Tropicana Dr
13100 HarC 77041 3679 C6
Trotter Dr
2200 HarC 77493 3814 B5
Trotwood Ln
3100 FBnC 77494 3953 B7
3100 FBnC 77494 4093 B1
Troulon Dr
7500 HOUS 77074 4099 D7
8700 HOUS 77036 4099 A7
11900 HOUS 77072 4098 A7
12100 HOUS 77072 4097 E7
Trout Av
100 GLSN 77550 4994 E7
Trout Ct
6100 PRLD 77581 4375 D7
Trout St
2500 HOUS 77093 3685 E5
2700 HOUS 77093 3686 A5
Trowbridge Ct
15000 HOUS 77062 4507 A2
Trowbridge Dr
1000 HOUS 77062 4506 E1
1100 HOUS 77062 4507 A1
Troy Av
24700 HarC 77375 2964 E3
Troy Dr
2700 MSCY 77459 4498 A5
Troy Rd
100 HOUS 77076 3684 D5
W Troy Rd
100 HOUS 77076 3684 C5
100 HOUS 77091 3684 C5
Troy St
7000 GlsC 77510 4987 D5
Troyan Dr
10 MDWP 77477 4238 B6
Truckee Dr
3400 HOUS 77082 4097 C2
Trudeau Dr
11500 HarC 77065 3398 A7
Trudeau Ln
- SGLD 77478 4367 E1
Trudy St
- HOUS 77016 3687 A5
True Ln
4900 HOUS 77016 3825 C2
Trueberry Bend Dr
- WDLD 77384 2674 E3
True Blue Ln
- WlrC 77484 2957 B1
Truesdale Dr
3100 MSCY 77459 4498 A6
3500 MSCY 77459 4497 E6
Truesdale Ln
- MSCY 77459 4497 D5
Truesdell Dr
12400 HOUS 77071 4239 C6
Truett St
5500 HOUS 77023 4104 C2
Trulley St
3000 HOUS 77004 3963 D7
Truman Cir
2600 RSBG 77471 4491 A6
Truman St
300 HOUS 77018 3823 C1
4800 TXCY 77591 4874 A6
Trumbull St
6300 HOUS 77022 3824 C3
Trummel Ct
10 WDLD 77381 2821 A3
Trumpet St
9700 HOUS 77078 3688 A5
Trumpet Vine Ln
15000 HarC 77433 3395 D1
15100 HarC 77433 3251 D7
Trumpetvine St
13800 HarC 77083 4097 A7
Trunnions Wy
900 HarC 77532 3411 A7
Truro St
6000 HOUS 77007 3962 A2
Truscon Dr
9500 HOUS 77080 3820 C4
Truslow Point Ln
15300 SGLD 77478 4368 C5
Truss Ct
15900 HarC 77532 3552 A4
Truvine Pl
10 WDLD 77382 2674 D3
Truxillo St
900 HOUS 77002 3963 A7
1000 HOUS 77004 3963 A7
1800 HOUS 77004 4103 C1
Truxton Dr
3400 PASD 77503 4108 B6
Truxton St
16400 HOUS 77396 3405 E4
Tryon Dr
10700 HarC 77065 3539 A2
Tuam St
- HOUS 77006 3962 C5
10 HOUS 77006 3963 A6
900 HOUS 77002 3963 B6
900 HOUS 77004 3963 C7
3000 HOUS 77004 4103 E1
4100 HOUS 77004 4104 A1
Tubac Dr
10 PNVL 77304 2237 A3
Tubman Woods Dr
7600 HOUS 77016 3687 A3
Tubular Rd
27700 KATY 77493 3812 D7
Tubular Rd
27700 KATY 77493 3951 D1
27700 KATY 77494 3951 D1
Tuck St
6900 HOUS 77020 3964 E2
6900 HOUS 77020 3965 A3
Tuckahoe Ln
25300 HarC 77373 3114 C3
Tucker Rd
1500 BYTN 77521 3973 C3
3100 LGCY 77565 4633 B2
3100 LGCY 77573 4633 B2
Tucker St
- KATY 77494 3952 C1
5600 HOUS 77087 4104 E7
5700 HOUS 77087 4244 E1
Tucker Cypress Dr
9700 HarC 77095 3537 E4
Tucker House Ln
24300 HarC 77493 3814 B6
Tuckerton Dr
- HarC 77095 3538 E3
- HarC 77095 3539 A3
Tuckerton Rd
16800 HarC 77095 3538 A3
16900 HarC 77095 3537 D3
17600 HarC 77433 3537 D3
Tucumcari Dr
1400 HarC 77090 3258 A3
1800 HarC 77090 3257 E4
Tudor Bnd
- HOUS 77082 4098 A1
Tudor Ct
200 DRPK 77536 4249 B1
Tudor Mnr
2600 HOUS 77082 4098 A1
Tudor Wy
29500 MtgC 77355 2815 E2
Tudor Crst
- HOUS 77082 4098 A1
Tudor Glen Pl
10 WDLD 77382 2674 B5
Tudor Point Ct
16400 HarC 77082 4095 E4
16400 HarC 77082 4096 C3
Tuely Ct
700 HarC 77049 3829 A3
Tufa Ct
4400 HOUS 77072 4098 A4
Tuffly St
7900 HOUS 77029 3965 B4
9700 HOUS 77029 3966 A4
9800 GNPK 77547 3966 A4
Tuffy Rd
17300 MtgC 77302 2679 D1
Tug Ct
15900 HarC 77532 3552 A4
19100 MtgC 77365 2972 B1
Tugboat Annie's
- HarC 77562 3831 B3
Tuhati Forest Ln
7800 HarC 77433 3537 C7
Tulane Dr
1400 FBnC 77469 4365 B3
Tulane St
700 HOUS 77007 3962 C1
800 HOUS 77007 3823 C7
800 HOUS 77008 3823 C6
1400 HOUS 77018 3823 C2
Tularosa Ln
- HarC 77377 3109 B7
Tulip Ln
4400 HarC 77521 3833 B3
4700 FBnC 77545 4623 C2
4700 FBnC 77583 4623 C2
Tulip St
2800 PASD 77502 4248 A3
3000 PASD 77504 4248 A3
9800 MtgC 77385 2676 E5
Tulipa St
10 WDLD 77380 2821 E6
Tulip Blossom Ct
20600 HarC 77433 3251 A4
Tulip Dale St
19100 HarC 77084 3816 B4
Tulip Field Rd
- FBnC 77545 4498 D5
Tulip Garden Ct
10900 HarC 77065 3539 B2
Tulip Glen Ct
- HarC 77379 3112 B6
3900 HarC 77449 3815 E2
Tulip Glen Ln
7700 HarC 77040 3541 E7
Tulip Grove Tr
7400 HarC 77433 3677 B2
Tulip Hill Ct
10 WDLD 77380 2967 E4
Tulip Pond Ct
2500 FBnC 77545 4498 C6
Tulip River Ct
2900 HOUS 77345 3119 E2
Tulip Tree Ct
10000 HOUS 77075 4377 A2
Tuliptree Ln
1000 HarC 77090 3258 B4
Tull Dr
1500 HarC 77449 3815 B7
Tullamore Ln
8600 FBnC 77459 4621 B6
Tullis Trail Ct
22400 FBnC 77494 4093 D5
Tully Av
7600 HOUS 77016 3687 A3
Tully Rd
700 HOUS 77079 3957 D2
Tully Meadows Ct
19600 HarC 77449 3676 C3
19600 HarC 77449 3677 C3
Tulsa Rd
4300 HOUS 77092 3822 A3
6300 HOUS 77092 3821 E3
Tulsa St
1300 DRPK 77536 4108 E7
Tulum Cl
2100 DKSN 77539 4633 C7
Tulum Ct
9800 GLSN 77554 5221 D2
Tulum Ln
21100 HarC 77073 3259 E4
Tulums Private C
2100 DKSN 77539 4633 C7
Tumbleweed Ln
3900 BYTN 77521 3973 C2
Tumble Weed Tr
11500 TMBL 77375 3109 E3
Tumbleweed Tr
17200 HarC 77095 3396 E7
Tumbleweed Pass Ln
19200 HarC 77433 3537 B6
Tumblewood Dr
- HOUS 77045 4372 B2
Tumbling Rd
7500 HarC 77346 3265 B7
Tumbling Falls Ct
14800 HOUS 77062 4380 A6
Tumbling Falls Dr
3600 BzaC 77578 4501 A7
3700 BzaC 77578 4625 A1
Tumbling Rapids Dr
15500 HarC 77084 3678 E7
Tumeric Dr
5600 HarC 77521 3833 D3
Tuna Av
200 GLSN 77550 5109 E1
Tuna Cir
2400 TXCY 77591 4872 E3
Tunbury Ln
7300 HarC 77095 3679 A1
Tunell Ln
1000 HarC 77032 3404 A6
Tunham Tr
19900 HarC 77073 3403 D2
Tunic Grove Dr
1300 HarC 77073 3403 D2
Tupelo Av
1300 HOUS 77017 4106 D6
1300 PASD 77506 4106 D6
Tupelo Cir
25700 MtgC 77372 2683 A6
Tupelo Dr
15300 HarC 77429 3252 E6
Tupelo Ln
- PTVL 77372 2683 A6
200 CNRO 77304 2383 B6
16600 MtgC 77372 2683 A6
25300 MtgC 77372 2536 E2
25300 MtgC 77372 2537 A2
Tupelo Garden Cir
17000 HarC 77346 3408 B4
Tupper Bend Ct
7900 HarC 77433 3537 C7
Tupper Bend Ln
18200 HarC 77433 3537 D7
Tupperglenn Dr
14900 HarC 77070 3254 E7
14900 HarC 77070 3398 E1
Tupper Lake Dr
5400 HOUS 77056 3960 D4
10800 HOUS 77042 3958 C5
Tupperlake Dr
10600 HOUS 77042 3958 D5
Turf Ct
2700 HarC 77039 3545 E3
Turf Valley Dr
4500 HarC 77084 3678 E7
Turfwood Ln
5500 HOUS 77088 3682 E2
Turin
400 HOUS 77017 4106 C4
Turk Ln
- HOUS 77035 4240 A6
- MSCY 77071 4239 E6
- MSCY 77071 4240 A6
Turkey Cir
1500 HOUS 77532 3266 C7
Turkey Cr
5900 FBnC 77459 4496 E7
Turkey Dr
3000 HarC 77073 3260 A5
3000 HarC 77338 3260 A5
3000 HOUS 77338 3260 A5
Turkey Tr
10 HOUS 77079 3957 B2
Turkey Creek Dr
15100 HOUS 77079 3957 B2
Turkey Creek Farms
- HarC 77338 3260 E4
- HOUS 77338 3260 E4
Turkey Trail Ct
15000 HOUS 77079 3957 B2
Turks Pt
4100 GLSN 77554 5332 D3
Turley Ct
1100 HarC 77562 3831 E1
Turley St
600 HarC 77373 3113 E6
600 HarC 77373 3114 A6
Turlock Ct
12700 HarC 77041 3679 D6
Turn St
11300 HarC 77093 3686 A1
11400 HarC 77093 3546 A7
Turnabout Ct
10 SGLD 77478 4368 D4
Turnberry Cir
- BYTN 77520 4113 A3
3700 HOUS 77025 4101 D5
Turnberry Ct
5100 PASD 77505 4248 B4
Turnberry Dr
- SGLD 77479 4495 A2
2200 LGCY 77573 4508 D7
Turnberry Park Ln
1000 HarC 77373 2968 D5
Turnbow St
9700 HOUS 77029 3966 A5
9800 GNPK 77547 3966 A5
Turnbridge Ln
12300 HOUS 77024 3959 A4
Turnbridge Tr
13000 HarC 77065 3539 B2
Turnbuckle Wy
1700 HarC 77532 3551 D3
Turnbury Elm Dr
2300 MtgC 77386 2969 B4
Turnbury Oak Ln
1200 HOUS 77055 3821 E7
Turnbury Oak St
1200 HOUS 77055 3821 E6
Turnbury Village Dr
29500 MtgC 77386 2969 B4
Turncreek Ln
1200 HarC 77450 3954 E3
Turner
10000 HarC 77064 3541 D2
Turner Dr
10 HOUS 77076 3685 B5
1500 HOUS 77093 3685 D5
3600 HOUS 77093 3686 B5
9500 BzaC 77578 4747 B4
9500 MNVL 77578 4747 B4
Turner Rd
100 CNRO 77304 2383 C6
19700 MtgC 77357 2827 D5
29500 MtgC 77355 2815 B3
Turner St
100 BzaC 77511 4749 A2
700 CNRO 77301 2384 B4
1100 BYTN 77520 4112 D1
1400 LGCY 77573 4631 C6
Turner Vw
- TMBL 77375 2963 E5
Turner Oaks
5600 HOUS 77085 4371 D1
5600 HOUS 77085 4372 A1
Turner Pl Rd
12700 HarC 77037 3684 E1
Turner Point Cir
17400 HarC 77095 3677 E2
Turner Vine Dr
13900 TMBL 77375 2964 A5
Turnervine Ln
14100 TMBL 77375 2963 E5
Turney Dr
400 HarC 77037 3544 B6
400 HOUS 77037 3544 B6
Turney Rd
1800 HarC 77038 3543 E5
Turning Leaf Ct
1600 FBnC 77479 4494 A5
Turning Leaf Ln
5200 SGLD 77479 4495 B4
N Turning Leaf Ln
- MtgC 77304 2236 A2
S Turning Leaf Ln
- MtgC 77304 2236 A2
Turning Leaf Lake Ct
20700 HarC 77433 3251 B5
Turning Limb Ct
15300 HarC 77433 3251 C4
Turning Point Ct
14500 HarC 77015 3829 B5
Turning Row Ln
2600 MSCY 77459 4497 A4
Turning Spring Ln
13800 HOUS 77044 3550 B2
Turning Tree Wy
15300 HarC 77433 3251 A5
Turnip St
18600 HarC 77379 3112 A7
18600 HarC 77379 3257 B1
Turnmill Ct
8200 HarC 77379 3256 B5
Turnpike Rd
1600 HOUS 77008 3823 B7
Turnstone Ct
16200 FBnC 77083 4236 B2
Turnstone Oaks Ct
25600 FBnC 77469 4092 C7
Turphin Wy
15000 FBnC 77478 4236 C2
Turpin Ln
1000 BzaC 77511 4748 E2
Turquoise Ln
7600 HOUS 77055 3821 D4
Turquoise Mist Dr
15000 HarC 77433 3250 E4
Turquoise Springs Ln
- FBnC 77494 4092 D5
Turquoise Stream Dr
17300 HarC 77095 3537 E2
Turret Crown Dr
1500 FBnC 77494 3953 C4
Turret Hill Dr
- WDLD 77381 2821 E2
Turrett Point Ln
6500 HarC 77064 3541 C1
Turriff Cir
29800 MtgC 77354 2818 C1
Turriff St
8700 HOUS 77055 3821 A5
8900 HOUS 77055 3820 E5
Turtle Bay Dr
15900 HOUS 77062 4380 C7
Turtle Beach Ln
- HOUS 77036 4100 A3
Turtle Brook Ln
- FBnC 77469 4094 C7
Turtle Corner Ln
12100 HarC 77375 3109 D7
12100 HarC 77375 3254 D1
Turtle Cove Ct
10 HarC 77346 3264 D3
Turtle Cove Dr
3600 PASD 77505 4248 E4
Turtle Creek Dr
700 MSCY 77489 4370 D7
1300 MSCY 77459 4497 B1
1300 MSCY 77489 4497 D1
3000 RSBG 77471 4491 C6
6300 PASD 77505 4248 D4
Turtle Creek Ln
18600 MtgC 77355 2961 C4
18600 SGCH 77355 2961 C4
Turtle Creek Mnr
10 FBnC 77479 4367 B6
Turtle Creek Rd
5400 HOUS 77017 4246 C1
5500 HOUS 77017 4106 C7
5800 HOUS 77502 4106 D7
5800 PASD 77502 4106 D7
Turtle Creek Wy
18600 MtgC 77355 2961 C3
18600 SGCH 77355 2961 C3
Turtle Dove Ln
19200 SGCH 77355 2961 A3
19800 MtgC 77355 2961 A3
Turtle Gate Dr
11800 HarC 77070 3399 B6
Turtle Lagoon Row
7100 HOUS 77036 4099 E3
Turtle Lake Dr
11500 HarC 77064 3399 D7
Turtle Log Tr
9300 HarC 77064 3399 D7
Turtle Manor Dr
7000 HarC 77346 3409 A1
Turtle Oak Ct
15500 HOUS 77059 4380 B5
Turtle Rock Ct
10 WDLD 77381 2821 B3
N Turtle Rock Ct
10 WDLD 77381 2821 C3
Turtle Springs Ln
- FBnC 77479 4496 D5
Turtlewood Ct
10500 HOUS 77072 4098 D5
Turtlewood Dr
200 LGCY 77573 4632 A5
6800 HOUS 77072 4098 C5
Turtlewood St
6400 HOUS 77049 3828 B2
Tuscan Ln
2200 BYTN 77520 3973 D5
Tuscania Ln
2800 LGCY 77573 4633 A4
Tuscan Lakes Blvd
- LGCY 77539 4633 A5
- LGCY 77573 4632 D4
- LGCY 77573 4633 A4
Tuscan Lakes Blvd FM-1266
- LGCY 77539 4633 A5
- LGCY 77573 4633 A5
Tuscan Shores Dr
4000 MSCY 77459 4497 C5
Tuscan Village Dr
- LGCY 77573 4632 C5
Tuscany Ct
2300 PRLD 77581 4504 D3
Tuscany Pl
1600 FBnC 77479 4494 A5
1600 PRLD 77581 4504 D3
Tuscany St
100 SGLD 77478 4368 B2
Tuscany Cove Ct
12600 HOUS 77077 3957 C7
Tuscany Woods Dr
18700 SHEH 77384 2822 A1
Tuscarora Ct
2000 LGCY 77573 4631 A7
Tuscarora St
4200 PASD 77504 4248 A6
Tuscola Ln
19500 HarC 77449 3677 A4
Tuscon St
5900 HOUS 77026 3825 A3
E Tushman
- PRLD 77581 4504 D3
W Tushman
- PRLD 77581 4504 D3
Tuskegee St
6500 HOUS 77091 3683 E4
Tussendo Dr
7500 HarC 77083 4097 A6
Tustin Dr
8000 HarC 77095 3539 A7
Tustin Ranch Ct
23600 FBnC 77494 3953 C4
Tutbury Cir
15400 HarC 77044 3549 E1
Tutor Ln
12800 HOUS 77077 3957 C5
Tutson Pl
13500 HOUS 77085 4371 E1
Tuttle Ct
23300 MtgC 77365 3118 A2
Tuttle Point Dr
14800 HOUS 77082 4096 C2
14900 HarC 77082 4096 C2
Tuwa Rd
22200 HarC 77375 3110 D1
22300 HarC 77375 2965 C7
Twain St
600 HarC 77373 3114 A6
Twain Mark Ln
6500 HarC 77338 3261 B3
Tweed Dr
8700 HOUS 77061 4245 A6
Tweed Wy
3400 PRLD 77584 4502 D6
Tweedbrook Dr
8800 HarC 77379 3255 E4
Twelfth Tee Ct
27700 HarC 77336 3122 A2
Twelve Lake Dr
- HarC 77064 3541 B1
Twelve Lakes Blvd
8600 HarC 77064 3541 B1
Twelve Oaks
4200 HOUS 77027 4101 C1
Twelve Oaks E
14700 MtgC 77372 2682 D2
Twelve Oaks W
14700 MtgC 77372 2682 D2
Twelve Oaks Ct
8500 TXCY 77591 4873 A4
Twelve Oaks Dr
1600 TXCY 77591 4873 A4
10600 HNCV 77024 3960 B1
N Twelve Oaks Dr
24600 MtgC 77372 2682 D2
Twelve Oaks Ln
3300 MSCY 77459 4496 E1
Twelve Pines Ct
10 WDLD 77381 2821 B4
E Twickenham Tr
600 HOUS 77076 3684 D4
W Twickenham Tr
200 HOUS 77076 3684 C4
Twig Dr
10800 HOUS 77089 4377 D4
Twig Leaf Ln
3300 HarC 77084 3816 E3
Twigs Corner Pl
10 WDLD 77381 2820 C2
Twigsworth Ln
18900 HarC 77346 3264 D6
Twila Ln
1600 CNRO 77301 2383 D3
Twila Springs Ct
10100 HarC 77095 3538 E3
Twila Springs Dr
20800 HarC 77095 3538 E3
20800 HarC 77095 3539 A4
Twilight Ln
800 HOUS 77336 3121 B5
Twilight Pl
100 WDLD 77381 2674 D6
Twilight Tr
- HarC 77532 3410 C2
Twilight Bay Dr
- PRLD 77545 4499 D2
Twilight Canyon Rd
20100 HarC 77449 3815 D4
Twilight Creek Ln
10600 HarC 77433 3537 A1
Twilight Falls Ln
19600 HarC 77084 3816 A4
Twilight Glen Ct
10 WDLD 77381 2821 C3
Twilight Grove Ln
26700 HarC 77433 3396 A7
Twilight Knoll Tr
- HarC 77429 3253 C4
Twilight Manor Ct
14100 HarC 77044 3549 E2
Twilight Moon Dr
9400 HarC 77064 3540 C2
Twilight Plain Pl
10 WDLD 77381 2820 E1
Twilight Sky Ct
12000 PASD 77059 4380 E5
Twilight Star Ct
16400 MtgC 77302 2679 A4
Twilight Star Ln
17100 FBnC 77469 4235 D1
Twilingate Ln
8500 HOUS 77040 3682 B3
Twin Cr
6000 FBnC 77459 4497 A7
E Twin Dr
4100 STFE 77510 4870 E7
Twin Aspens Ln
21500 HarC 77073 3259 D1
E Twinberry Pl
10 WDLD 77381 2675 A7
W Twinberry Pl
10 WDLD 77381 2674 E7
10 WDLD 77381 2675 A6
S Twinberry Field Dr
21600 HarC 77433 3250 E5
Twinbrooke Dr
500 HarC 77037 3544 B6
500 HOUS 77037 3544 B6
800 HOUS 77088 3544 A7
1200 HOUS 77088 3543 D6
1900 HarC 77088 3543 D7
Twin Buttes Dr
19200 HarC 77375 3109 C7
Twin Candle Dr
5000 HOUS 77018 3683 E7
Twin Cannon Ln
11500 LPRT 77571 4250 E2
11500 LPRT 77571 4251 A2
Twin Canyon Ct
19700 FBnC 77450 4094 D4
Twince
- HarC 77040 3681 B3
Twin Cir Dr
10 HOUS 77042 3958 E5
Twin Creeks Dr
18100 HarC 77449 3677 D3
Twin Deer Rd
2100 MtgC 77385 2823 B2
Twin Diamond Dr
2100 HarC 77396 3407 C2
Twine Dr
4100 STFE 77510 4871 A7
Twin Elm Dr
4600 FBnC 77545 4622 D2
Twin Elm Ln
1700 HarC 77073 3259 C2
Twin Falls Rd
900 HOUS 77088 3544 A6
1300 HOUS 77088 3543 E6
Twin Falls Crossing Ln
18700 HarC 77379 3111 C6
Twin Feather Pl
10 WDLD 77381 2820 C2
Twin Flower Dr
12600 HarC 77377 3254 B3
Twin Fork Cir
3700 MSCY 77459 4497 D7
Twin Fountains Dr
2800 HarC 77068 3257 D5
Twin Greens St
10 HOUS 77339 3264 E1
Twin Grove Dr
2300 HOUS 77339 3119 B6
Twin Hills Ct
10300 HOUS 77031 4239 B3
Twin Hills Dr
8000 HOUS 77071 4239 C3
9100 HOUS 77031 4239 B3
Twining Oak Ln
1200 MSCY 77489 4370 D4
Twining Oaks Ln
7900 HarC 77379 3256 B4
Twining Trail Ln
8300 FBnC 77479 4494 B5
Twinkle Ct
4400 HOUS 77072 4098 A4
Twinkle Sky Ct
22000 HarC 77433 3250 E5
Twin Knolls Dr
2800 HOUS 77339 3119 B2
Twin Lake Dr
14800 MtgC 77306 2680 E2
Twin Lakes Blvd
13200 HarC 77041 3679 C6
Twin Lakes Cir
14300 MtgC 77306 2680 E1
14300 MtgC 77306 2681 A1
Twin Lakes Dr
14000 FBnC 77478 4236 E4
Twin Lakes Tr
4100 PRLD 77584 4503 B4
Twin Lamps Ln
8300 HarC 77064 3541 E5
Twin Leaf Dr
6500 HarC 77379 3256 D2
Twinleaf Dr
2900 LGCY 77573 4633 A2
Twin Maple St
14800 HarC 77082 4096 D3
Twin Mills Ln
3500 MtgC 77386 2969 E2
Twinmont Ln
3200 FBnC 77494 4093 B1
Twin Oaks Blvd
800 LGCY 77565 4508 E5
2100 LGCY 77565 4509 A4
11700 HarC 77336 3266 D2
11700 HOUS 77336 3266 D2
Twin Oaks Dr
8000 HarC 77375 2966 A6
8000 HarC 77389 2966 A6
9000 MNVL 77578 4746 C7
10300 CHTW 77385 2823 A5
25000 MtgC 77357 2974 D1
33700 MtgC 77354 2671 B4
Twin Oaks Rd
25700 PTVL 77372 2683 A7
Twin Oaks St
300 HOUS 77076 3685 B4
1100 FRDW 77546 4629 D5
Twin Oaks Wy
100 LGCY 77565 4509 A4
Twin Pines Dr
500 FRDW 77546 4505 A5
Twin Pines Rd
12000 MtgC 77303 2239 D6
12300 CTSH 77303 2239 E6
Twin Pines Tr
- HOUS 77049 3828 A2
Twinridge Ln
11600 HOUS 77099 4238 B1
Twin River Dr
19700 HarC 77375 3109 E6
Twin Sisters Dr
12500 HarC 77429 3398 B5
Twin Springs Dr
1900 HOUS 77339 3118 D7
Twin Springs Pl
10 WDLD 77381 2820 D5
Twin Timbers Ct
4500 FBnC 77545 4622 D2
Twin Timbers Ln
400 LGCY 77565 4508 E5
Twin Trails Dr
- HarC 77095 3537 D3
Twin Tree Ln
8200 HOUS 77071 4239 B5
Twin Tulip Ct
1900 FBnC 77545 4622 D2
Twin Twist Ct
14400 HOUS 77489 4371 B3
Twinvale
- WDLD 77382 2675 B6
- WDLD 77384 2675 B6
Twinvale Dr
- WDLD 77384 2675 B6
E Twinvale Lp
10 WDLD 77384 2675 B5
W Twinvale Lp
10 WDLD 77384 2675 A6
Twin Valley Dr
10 FBnC 77479 4367 A7
10 FBnC 77479 4494 A1
Twin Valley Ln
- FBnC 77494 4092 B1
Twin Villas Dr
2600 DRPK 77503 4248 D1
2600 DRPK 77536 4248 D1
2600 PASD 77503 4248 D1
Twinwalker Dr
16500 HarC 77530 3829 E3
Twin Woods Ln
2700 MtgC 77386 2823 C7
Twisted Ash Ct
14600 HarC 77015 3829 C4
Twisted Birch Pl Ct
10 WDLD 77381 2820 E5
Twisted Brook Dr
3600 HOUS 77053 4372 E3
Twisted Canyon Dr
14300 HarC 77429 3396 D2
Twisted Cedar Ct
14600 HarC 77015 3829 B4
Twisted Creek Dr
19700 HarC 77375 3109 E6
Twisted Elm Ct
1000 HarC 77038 3543 D4
Twisted Leaf Dr
20800 HarC 77433 3251 A5
Twisted Oak Ln
14300 HOUS 77079 3957 D3
17800 MtgC 77357 2826 E1
Twisted Oak St
9800 BYTN 77520 3974 A1
W Twisted Oak St
5600 BYTN 77520 3974 A1
Twisted Oaks Ct
400 SHEH 77381 2822 A2
Twisted Oaks Dr
28900 SHEH 77381 2822 A2
28900 SHEH 77384 2822 A2
Twisted Pecan Ct
14600 HarC 77015 3829 B5
Twisted Pine Ct
5800 HarC 77039 3546 E5
Twisted Rattan Ln
14000 HarC 77015 3829 A5
Twisted Spruce Ct
100 HarC 77015 3829 B5
Twisted Trunk Ct
14300 HarC 77015 3829 A5
Twisted Willow Ct
2800 HarC 77450 3954 B7
Twisted Willow Ln
21300 FBnC 77450 3954 B7
Twister Tr
25000 HarC 77373 3115 B4
Twisting Rd
4600 HarC 77084 3677 B7
Twisting Falls Dr
23600 HarC 77373 3114 E5
Twisting Oak St
14900 HarC 77082 4096 D2
Twisting Pine Ct
2500 HOUS 77345 3120 A3
4400 HarC 77373 3260 B1
Twisting Pine Dr
22800 HarC 77373 3260 B1
Twisting Rose Cir
22900 HarC 77373 3260 A1
Twisting Rose Ct
22900 HarC 77373 3260 A1
Twisting Rose Dr
4400 HarC 77373 3260 B1
Twisting Springs Dr
15500 HarC 77433 3251 B6
Twisting Vine Ln
8500 HOUS 77040 3682 A3
Twitch Ct
21600 MtgC 77365 2972 B1
Two Airline-Fort Bend Rd
1800 BzaC 77583 4500 D6
1800 PRLD 77583 4500 D6
3200 BzaC 77578 4500 E6
3200 BzaC 77578 4501 A6
3200 BzaC 77584 4500 E6
3200 BzaC 77584 4501 A6
3200 PRLD 77584 4500 E6
3200 PRLD 77584 4501 A6
Two Creeks Rd
21400 HarC 77338 3261 D2
Two Harbors Glen St
23000 FBnC 77494 4093 C3
Two Lakes Dr
22400 HarC 77375 3110 D3
Two Oaks Cir
11000 HarC 77065 3539 D1
Twopenny Ln
13600 HarC 77015 3828 E5
Two Rivers Ct
1900 FBnC 77450 3953 E5
Two Rivers Ln
22700 FBnC 77450 3953 E5
Two Sisters Ct
8600 FBnC 77459 4621 B5
Two Trail Dr
2200 HarC 77373 3114 D4
TX-5-Spur
- HOUS 77004 4104 A2

STREET
Block City ZIP Map# Grid

TX-5-Spur Frontage Rd
- HOUS 77004 4104 A2
TX-6
10100 MSCY 77545 4622 A1
TX-6 E
13100 ARLA 77583 4623 A4
TX-6 W
13100 ARLA 77583 4623 A4
TX-57
- CNRO 77301 2384 A7
TX-99
- FBnC 77494 3953 C5
- HOUS 77494 3953 C2
TX-99 Frontage Rd
- HOUS 77450 3953 C2
- HOUS 77494 3953 C2
1300 FBnC 77494 3953 C4
TX-146
300 LPRT 77571 4251 C3
TX-146 N
- LPRT 77571 4251 C2
1100 TXCY 77590 4874 C5
1100 TXCY 77591 4874 C5
TX-146 Frontage Rd
1100 LPRT 77571 4251 C6
TX-146 Frontage Rd SR-146
- LPRT 77571 4251 C7
TX-249 N
- HarC 77086 3541 D1
- HOUS 77064 3400 A4
TX-336-Loop
- CNRO 77301 2385 C4
- CNRO 77304 2382 E5
Tybor St
8300 HOUS 77074 4099 C7
Tye Ln
8000 BzaC 77584 4627 D3
Tyer Ln
- MtgC 77365 2972 E5
Tyler Ct
3100 FRDW 77546 4630 B3
3100 FRDW 77598 4630 B3
12800 STAF 77477 4370 A1
Tyler Ln
- BzaC 77583 4500 D7
1700 CNRO 77301 2384 D4
2400 DRPK 77536 4109 A7
12900 STAF 77477 4239 B7
12900 STAF 77477 4370 A1
15500 MtgC 77372 2683 C4
Tyler Rd
10000 MtgC 77302 2530 E5
Tyler Run
700 FBnC 77479 4366 C6
Tyler St
- HOUS 77029 3965 D5
100 TMBL 77375 2964 B7
1900 HOUS 77009 3824 A5
3400 HarC 77053 4372 E6
5600 PRLD 77581 4502 E3
W Tyler St
100 LPRT 77571 4251 D2
Tylergate Dr
4500 HarC 77373 3115 B6
Tyler Hills Ln
- MtgC 77386 2969 D6
Tylermont Dr
15300 HarC 77429 3397 B4
Tyler Springs Ln
- HarC 77346 3408 C2
Tyler Trace Ln
- HarC 77379 3111 C1
- RSBG 77469 4491 E5
Tyler Trails Ct
18100 HarC 77433 3537 D7
Tyne Ct
11200 PNPV 77024 3959 E4
Tyne St
6000 HOUS 77007 3962 A2
Tynebridge Ln
300 PNPV 77024 3959 E4
Tynebrook Ln
300 PNPV 77024 3959 E4
Tynecreek Ln
18500 HarC 77379 3256 A1
Tyneglen Ln
12600 HarC 77044 3689 B2
Tyneland Ct
7900 HarC 77070 3399 E2
Tynemeadow Ct
3200 HarC 77449 3816 A3
Tynemouth Dr
1600 PASD 77504 4247 E6
Tynewood Dr
11200 PNPV 77024 3959 E5
Tyneworth Ct
- HOUS 77449 3814 D6
Tynham Springs Dr
30400 MtgC 77386 2969 C2
Typhoon Wy
17400 HarC 77532 3411 A7
17400 HarC 77532 3552 C1
Tyre St
4600 HOUS 77020 3825 C7
4600 HOUS 77020 3964 B1
Tyrone St
19000 HarC 77373 3114 A6
E Tyson Dr
1700 HarC 77530 3830 B4
W Tyson Dr
1700 HarC 77530 3830 B4
E Tyson St
- HarC 77530 3830 D4
W Tyson St
- HarC 77530 3830 D4
Tysor Park Ln
15200 HarC 77095 3538 E5

U

Ubuntu Ct
5200 HOUS 77091 3683 E7
Ucayali Ct
19000 MtgC 77365 2971 E4
Uldine Bisagno Dr
- HOUS 77092 3822 A1
Ulrich Ln
100 HarC 77532 3552 C5
Ulrich Rd
700 TMBL 77375 2964 B6
1000 HarC 77375 2964 B6
Ulrich St
100 SGLD 77478 4367 E2
Ulswater
- HOUS 77449 3814 D6
Ultra Light Ln
- HarC 77493 3813 E4
Ulysses Ln
7400 HarC 77521 3833 D3
Ulysses St
16300 HarC 77532 3552 A2
Umber Ct
10600 HOUS 77099 4238 A3
Umber Cove Ct
14200 HOUS 77048 4374 D4
Umber Elm Ct
2100 HarC 77493 3814 C5
Umber Oak Ct
20300 HarC 77346 3264 E4
20300 HarC 77346 3265 A4
Umbria Ln
- LGCY 77573 4632 E2
Umiak Dr
2600 HOUS 77045 4373 A1
Una Dr
300 DRPK 77536 4109 B5
Una St
- HOUS 77076 3685 A6
9200 HOUS 77022 3685 A6
Underhill St
6000 HOUS 77092 3821 C2
Underwood Blvd
3000 HOUS 77025 4102 A5
3100 HOUS 77025 4101 E5
Underwood Dr
3500 HOUS 77025 4101 D5
8000 MSCY 77459 4497 A7
Underwood Pl
10 WDLD 77381 2675 A6
Underwood Rd
- MtgC 77365 3118 C2
1000 DRPK 77571 4110 A6
1200 DRPK 77536 4110 A7
1200 LPRT 77571 4110 A7
1500 DRPK 77536 4250 A4
1500 LPRT 77536 4250 A1
1500 LPRT 77571 4250 A4
2300 DRPK 77571 4250 A4
4000 HarC 77507 4250 A5
4200 PASD 77507 4250 A7
5800 PASD 77507 4381 A2
Underwood St
- HOUS 77025 4102 A5
2300 HOUS 77030 4102 A5
Underwood Creek Wy
14600 HOUS 77062 4379 D7
14700 HOUS 77062 4506 E1
Unicorn Ln
- HOUS 77072 4097 D6
Unicorns Horn Ln
22100 HarC 77449 3815 A6
22500 HarC 77449 3814 E6
N Union Ct
21100 HarC 77073 3259 B6
Union Sprs
5900 SGLD 77479 4495 A5
Union St
100 LMQU 77568 4873 D7
100 RHMD 77469 4491 D1
100 TXCY 77591 4873 D7
2000 HOUS 77007 3963 A3
14500 HarC 77377 3253 E1
14500 HarC 77429 3253 E1
N Union St
100 RHMD 77469 4491 D1
S Union St
200 RHMD 77469 4491 D1
Union Chapel St
2500 SGLD 77479 4368 D6
Union Mill Rd
2100 HarC 77067 3402 A5
Union Oak St
11300 HarC 77065 3539 C1
Union Park Dr
20800 HarC 77450 3954 C3
Union Pointe Ct
16000 HarC 77429 3397 B2
Union Valley Dr
1000 PRLD 77581 4376 C6
Unisys Dr
- HOUS 77040 3682 A6
United Rd
10800 HarC 77093 3686 C2
United St
9800 HOUS 77036 4098 E4
9800 HOUS 77072 4098 E4
United Ridge Ln
- HarC 77379 3110 E2
- HarC 77379 3111 A2
Unity
13000 HarC 77532 3692 E1
Unity Dr
2900 HOUS 77057 3960 A7
2900 HOUS 77057 4100 B2
2900 HOUS 77063 3960 A7
Unity Candle Tr
18700 HarC 77388 3113 C2
Universal Dr
4300 HOUS 77072 4098 A4
University Blvd
- FBnC 77459 4496 B5
- FBnC 77479 4494 E4
- FBnC 77479 4495 A5
- FBnC 77479 4496 B5
- SGLD 77478 4367 E4
- SGLD 77479 4367 D4
- SGLD 77479 4494 E4
- SGLD 77479 4495 A5
200 GLSN 77550 5109 E2
1900 HOUS 77005 4102 B3
1900 HOUS 77030 4102 B3
2500 WUNP 77005 4102 A3
3000 WUNP 77005 4101 C3
3600 SSPL 77005 4101 E3
S University Blvd
- FBnC 77459 4496 C4
- FBnC 77479 4496 C4
- MSCY 77459 4496 C3
University Dr
- HOUS 77058 4380 E7
- PASD 77058 4380 E7
100 PRVW 77445 3100 B2
4500 HOUS 77004 4103 E2
4500 HOUS 77004 4104 A3
University Dr FM-1098
100 PRVW 77445 3100 B2
University St
- PRVW 77445 3100 C1
University Green Blvd
- HOUS 77058 4507 C2
- HOUS 77062 4507 C2
University Oaks Blvd
4400 HOUS 77004 4103 E3
University Park Dr
- PASD 77058 4380 E5
- PASD 77059 4380 E5
22200 FBnC 77450 4094 A1
22400 FBnC 77450 4093 E1
Uno Dr
3900 GLSN 77554 5220 B7
Upas
- HOUS 77006 3962 D6
Up Country Ln
9900 MtgC 77385 2676 E5
Upfield Dr
3500 HarC 77082 4096 A2
Uphall Ct
9200 HarC 77095 3538 C4
Upland Dr
1100 HOUS 77043 3819 B7
Upland Brook Ln
5400 HarC 77379 3112 A6
Upland Cir Dr
- CNRO 77303 2237 C4
Upland Creek Dr
19900 HarC 77449 3676 E3
19900 HarC 77449 3677 A3
Upland Dale Ct
4800 HarC 77449 3676 E7
Upland Elm St
19800 HarC 77084 3816 A4
Upland Fair Ln
20200 HarC 77449 3815 D1
Upland Hill St
2000 HarC 77373 3114 E5
Upland Oak Trc
14200 HarC 77429 3396 D2
Upland Park Ct
8000 FBnC 77479 4494 B5
Upland Park Dr
2000 FBnC 77479 4494 C4
Upland Pine St
7200 HarC 77433 3677 B1
Upland Rapids Dr
12400 HOUS 77089 4505 C1
Upland Shadows Dr
2000 FBnC 77479 4494 C5
Upland View Dr
2500 FBnC 77545 4498 C6
Upland Willow Av
2700 HarC 77038 3543 A5
3000 HarC 77038 3542 D6
3000 HarC 77086 3542 D6
Upper Bay Rd
18000 HOUS 77058 4508 A4
18200 NSUB 77058 4508 B5
Upper Borondo
10 LMQU 77568 4989 C3
Upperbrook St
8600 HarC 77064 3541 D5
Uppercove Cir
9000 HarC 77064 3540 E6
Upper Falls Ct
23300 HarC 77373 3115 E6
Upper Falls Ln
5800 HarC 77373 3115 E6
Upper Green St
20400 HarC 77338 3261 B4
Upper Hollow Rd
11900 HarC 77067 3402 A5
Upper Lake Dr
3200 HOUS 77338 3263 D4
5400 HarC 77346 3264 C5
Upper Leaf Wy
- HarC 77433 3251 A5
Upper Oak Dr
- HarC 77433 3251 A5
Upper Run Wy
- HarC 77429 3253 C4
Upperway Ln
10 HOUS 77056 3961 A4
Upperwing Ct
26800 HarC 77447 3248 E6
Upshaw Dr
- HarC 77396 3547 A1
5800 HarC 77032 3405 E7
5800 HOUS 77396 3405 E7
6200 HOUS 77396 3547 A1
Upshire Dr
16000 HarC 77530 3830 B5
Upshur Ln
8600 HarC 77064 3540 D6
Upton St
1200 HOUS 77020 3964 B2
Uptown Dr
4000 HOUS 77045 4241 D5
Uptown Park Blvd
- HOUS 77027 3961 B5
- HOUS 77056 3961 B5
Upwood Dr
9600 HMBL 77338 3262 C4
Uraguay Dr
3700 PASD 77504 4247 E4
Urban
11500 HOUS 77016 3546 E7
Urban Dr
11700 HarC 77016 3547 E6
11700 HarC 77050 3547 E7
Urban Rd
- HMPD 77445 2952 C3
- WlrC 77445 2952 C3
Urban Dale Ct
12400 HOUS 77082 4097 D1
Urban Elm St
- HarC 77429 3253 C3
Urban Forest Dr
2300 MtgC 77386 2969 B4
Urbanna Ct
13000 HarC 77429 3397 B4
Urban Woods Tr
3500 HOUS 77008 3822 C7
Urquhart St
- CNRO 77301 2384 A7
500 CNRO 77301 2383 E6
Ursuline Av
4900 GLSN 77551 5108 D5
Ursuline St
1100 GLSN 77550 5109 D4
3800 GLSN 77550 5108 E5
4300 GLSN 77551 5108 D5
US-59
- FBnC 77469 4493 C4
- FBnC 77479 4493 D4
- HOUS 77339 3262 E1
- SGLD 77469 4493 C4
- SGLD 77479 4493 D3
18500 HMBL 77338 3406 C1
18500 HOUS 77338 3406 C1
- LbyC 77327 2537 E2
- LbyC 77327 2538 A1
- LbyC 77328 2537 E2
- LbyC 77328 2538 A1
US-59
- MtgC - 2537 D3
- MtgC - 2682 E4
- MtgC - 2827 E5
- MtgC - 2828 B1
- MtgC - 2973 C3
- PTVL - 2682 D6
- SPLD - 2537 B7
- SPLD - 2682 E3
- SPLD - 2683 A1
- WDBR - 2682 C7
- WDBR - 2828 B1
US-59 BUS
10 SPLD 77372 2683 A2
13500 MtgC 77372 2537 B7
13500 SPLD 77372 2537 B7
US-59 S
- SGLD 77479 4367 E6
US-59 Eastex Frwy
- HarC - 3546 E1
- HarC - 3686 A6
- HMBL - 3262 E2
- HMBL - 3406 B4
- HOUS - 3117 E7
- HOUS - 3118 A6
- HOUS - 3262 C7
- HOUS - 3406 A7
- HOUS - 3546 E1
- HOUS - 3547 A1
- HOUS - 3686 A4
- HOUS - 3825 A2
- HOUS - 3963 B7
- HOUS - 3964 A2
- MtgC - 2973 C5
- MtgC - 3118 B1
US-59 Frontage Rd
- FBnC 77469 4493 D3
- FBnC 77479 4493 D3
- LbyC 77327 2537 D3
- MtgC 77372 2682 E4
- SGLD 77479 4493 D3
- WDBR 77357 2682 C7
3500 SPLD 77372 2682 E4
11900 LbyC 77328 2537 D3
11900 MtgC 77372 2537 B7
12000 SPLD 77372 2537 B7
14300 SPLD 77372 2683 A2
17100 PTVL 77372 2682 D6
17200 PTVL 77357 2682 C6
17500 WDBR 77357 2828 A3
17600 MtgC 77357 2682 C7
17600 MtgC 77357 2828 B3
19000 MtgC 77357 2827 E5
20900 MtgC 77357 2973 C3
22000 MtgC 77365 2973 D2
US-59 Southwest Frwy
- FBnC - 4492 A6
- FBnC - 4493 B4
- HarC - 4238 C5
- HOUS - 3963 B7
- HOUS - 4099 E4
- HOUS - 4100 D2
- HOUS - 4101 E1
- HOUS - 4102 A1
- HOUS - 4103 A1
- HOUS - 4238 A7
- HOUS - 4239 B1
- RSBG - 4491 C7
- RSBG - 4492 A6
- RSBG - 4614 C1
- RSBG - 4615 A1
- RSBG 77471 4490 A7
- SGLD - 4367 E7
- SGLD - 4368 E1
- SGLD - 4369 A1
- SGLD - 4493 D3
- SGLD - 4494 B2
- STAF - 4238 C5
- STAF - 4369 A1
US-90
- HOUS - 3826 E7
- HOUS - 3965 E1
- KATY 77494 3952 E1
- WlrC 77423 3951 A1
- WlrC 77493 3951 A1
- WlrC 77494 3951 B1
US-90 ALT
- HOUS 77025 4241 D4
- HOUS 77035 4241 D4
- HOUS 77045 4241 D4
- HOUS 77054 4241 D3
- HOUS 77071 4370 E1
- HOUS 77085 4370 E1
- MSCY 77071 4370 D1
- MSCY 77085 4370 D1
- MSCY 77489 4370 A3
- RHMD 77469 4491 E1
- SGLD 77478 4369 A1
- STAF 77477 4369 C2
10 RHMD 77469 4365 A7
10 RHMD 77469 4492 A1
100 RSBG 77471 4490 C4
200 FBnC 77469 4365 A7
800 FBnC 77471 4490 A4
1900 FBnC 77469 4366 E5
4400 FBnC 77479 4366 A5
5000 FBnC 77478 4366 E5
5400 FBnC 77478 4367 A5
5700 FBnC 77479 4367 B4
5700 SGLD 77478 4367 E3
6300 SGLD 77479 4367 B4
8100 SGLD 77478 4368 E1
US-90 ALT 69th St
- HOUS 77020 3965 A5
2200 HOUS 77011 3965 A5
US-90 ALT S 69th St
- HOUS 77023 4104 E1
100 HOUS 77011 3964 E7
300 HOUS 77023 3964 E7
US-90-ALT
- MSCY 77085 4370 D2
- MSCY 77489 4370 D2
US-90 ALT Avenue H
1100 RSBG 77471 4490 B4
2600 RSBG 77471 4491 B4
5200 RHMD 77469 4491 D2
US-90 Beaumont Hwy
10900 HarC 77049 3827 E1
10900 HOUS 77013 3827 C2
10900 HOUS 77049 3827 D2
12100 HarC 77049 3828 A1
12600 HarC 77049 3689 B7
US-90 BUS Beaumont Hwy
10 HarC 77532 3691 E1
10 HarC 77532 3692 B1
1000 HarC 77532 3552 C7
10900 HarC 77049 3827 E1
10900 HOUS 77013 3827 C2
10900 HOUS 77049 3827 D2
12100 HarC 77049 3828 A1
12600 HarC 77049 3689 E6
14500 HarC 77049 3690 C4
17000 HarC 77049 3691 E1
17800 HarC 77044 3691 E1
US-90 Beaumont Rd
6800 HOUS 77013 3826 E4
6900 HOUS 77013 3827 B3
US-90 BUS Beaumont Rd
6800 HOUS 77013 3826 E4
6900 HOUS 77013 3827 B3
US-90 Crosby Frwy
- HarC - 3552 D7
- HarC - 3690 B7
- HarC - 3691 A5
- HarC - 3692 C1
- LbyC 77535 3269 E7
- LbyC 77535 3413 D1
5100 HarC 77532 3553 A2
5600 HarC 77532 3412 C6
8500 HarC 77532 3413 A4
US-90 East Frwy
- HOUS - 3963 B2
- HOUS - 3964 E2
- HOUS - 3965 A2
US-90 ALT East Frwy
- HOUS - 3965 B1
- HOUS 77029 3965 B1
US-90 Highway Blvd
6300 KATY 77493 3952 D1
6300 KATY 77494 3952 D1
26900 KATY 77493 3951 E1
26900 KATY 77494 3951 E1
27700 WlrC 77494 3951 D1
30600 WlrC 77423 3951 A1
30600 WlrC 77493 3951 A1
US-90 ALT Jackson St
100 RHMD 77469 4491 E1
1700 RSBG 77471 4491 D2
US-90 Katy Frwy
- HarC - 3952 E1
- HarC - 3953 A1
- HarC - 3955 E1
- HarC - 3956 E1
- HarC - 3959 D1
- HDWV - 3959 E1
- HDWV - 3960 A1
- HOUS - 3953 C1
- HOUS - 3954 A1
- HOUS - 3955 E1
- HOUS - 3956 E1
- HOUS - 3957 D1
- HOUS - 3958 B1
- HOUS - 3959 E1
- HOUS - 3960 A1
- HOUS - 3961 A1
- HOUS - 3962 E2
- HOUS - 3963 C3
- KATY - 3952 E1
- SPVL - 3959 D1
- SPVL - 3960 A1
US-90 ALT Main St
- HOUS 77071 4371 A1
12100 HOUS 77045 4241 B5
12200 HOUS 77035 4241 C4
12400 HOUS 77085 4241 A6
12600 HOUS 77035 4240 B7
12600 HOUS 77085 4240 E6
14300 HOUS 77035 4371 A1
14300 HOUS 77085 4371 A1
US-90 ALT S Main St
8400 HOUS 77054 4102 B6
8500 HOUS 77025 4102 A6
9200 HOUS 77025 4242 A1
9200 HOUS 77054 4242 A1
9600 HOUS 77025 4241 E1
9600 HOUS 77054 4241 A6
14700 HOUS 77035 4371 A1
14700 HOUS 77071 4371 A1
14700 HOUS 77085 4371 A1
US-90 ALT McCarty St
100 HOUS 77029 3826 C7
200 HOUS 77029 3965 B1
US-90 N McCarty St
- HOUS 77013 3826 D5
US-90 ALT N McCarty St
- HOUS 77013 3826 D5
3300 HOUS 77029 3826 C6
US-90 BUS N McCarty St
3900 HOUS 77029 3826 D6
4500 HOUS 77013 3826 D5
US-90 ALT Old Spanish Tr
1000 HOUS 77025 4102 B6
1000 HOUS 77054 4102 E5
1100 HOUS 77030 4102 B6
2300 HOUS 77021 4102 A7
2900 HOUS 77054 4103 A5
3300 HOUS 77021 4103 C5
5000 HOUS 77021 4104 A4
5300 HOUS 77023 4104 B4
US-90 ALT SSgt M Garcia Dr
100 HOUS 77011 3964 E7
1600 HOUS 77011 3965 A6
US-90 ALT Wayside Dr
- HOUS 77020 3965 A5
100 HOUS 77011 3964 E5
2300 HOUS 77011 3965 A5
US-90 ALT N Wayside Dr
100 HOUS 77020 3965 A2
US-90 ALT S Wayside Dr
100 HOUS 77011 3964 E7
300 HOUS 77023 3964 E7
700 HOUS 77023 4104 D3
US-290
- HarC - 3102 E6
- HarC - 3103 B7
- HarC - 3248 C1
- HarC - 3249 E5
- HMPD - 2954 A6
- HMPD 77445 2952 D4
- HMPD 77445 2953 A4
- PRVW - 3099 C1
- PRVW - 3100 A2
- WALR - 3102 A4
- WlrC - 2954 B7
- WlrC - 3099 C1
- WlrC - 3100 E3
- WlrC - 3101 E4
- WlrC 77445 2952 A3
- WlrC 77445 2953 A4
US-290 BUS
- HarC 77447 3248 E3
- HarC 77447 3249 A3
- HMPD 77445 2953 C7
- HMPD 77445 3098 D1
- PRVW 77445 3099 E3
- PRVW 77445 3100 D4
- PRVW 77484 3100 D4
- WlrC 77445 3098 E1
- WlrC 77445 3099 C2
- WlrC 77484 3100 E4
1900 WALR 77484 3102 D7
2200 WALR 77484 3101 E6
3200 WlrC 77484 3101 C5
US-290 W
- HarC 77429 3397 A6
US-290 BUS 10th St
- WlrC 77445 2953 B5
200 HMPD 77445 2953 B5
US-290 BUS Austin St
10 HMPD 77445 2953 C7
US-290 Frontage Rd
- HarC 77429 3395 E2
- HarC 77433 3251 A7
- HarC 77484 3101 D4
- HarC 77484 3102 C5
27000 HarC 77433 3395 D2
27000 HarC 77433 3396 A2
30000 HarC 77433 3250 B5
30700 HarC 77447 3250 B6
31300 HarC 77447 3249 D4
US-290 Frontage Rd E
- HarC 77429 3396 B3
- HarC 77433 3396 B3
US-290 Frontage Rd W
- HarC 77429 3396 B3
- HarC 77433 3396 B3
US-290 BUS Hempstead Rd
- HarC 77447 3248 A1
- HarC 77484 3247 E1
- HarC 77484 3248 A1
37900 HarC 77484 3102 C7
39500 WALR 77484 3102 B6
US-290 Northwest Frwy
- HarC - 3249 A3
- HarC - 3250 D7
- HarC - 3251 B7
- HarC - 3395 B1
- HarC - 3396 E5
- HarC - 3397 A6
- HarC - 3538 C1
- HarC - 3539 A3
- HarC - 3680 E3
- HarC - 3681 C4
- HOUS - 3681 C4
- HOUS - 3682 C7
- HOUS - 3821 C1
- HOUS - 3822 A3
- JRSV - 3539 D5
- JRSV - 3540 A7
- JRSV - 3680 E3
Usener St
700 HOUS 77009 3963 A1
900 HOUS 77009 3962 E1
1100 HOUS 77007 3962 E1
Usher Ct
1800 HarC 77449 3815 D7
Usher Ln
14800 SPLD 77372 2683 B2
Ustinik Rd
3400 PLEK 77471 4614 D5
Utah Av
3200 DKSN 77539 4754 C1
Utah St
700 SHUS 77587 4246 B2
900 HOUS 77017 4246 B2
1100 HOUS 77007 3962 A2
1500 BYTN 77520 4112 A2
6700 HOUS 77091 3683 E4
N Utah St
100 LPRT 77571 4251 E2
S Utah St
100 LPRT 77571 4251 E3
900 LPRT 77571 4252 A3
Utah Beach Ct
3400 HarC 77388 3112 D4
Ute Ln
23600 MtgC 77365 2972 B6
Ute St
4200 PASD 77504 4247 E5
Uther Ct
7100 HarC 77379 3111 B2
Utica St
13300 HOUS 77015 3967 D2
Utley Dr
11300 TXCY 77539 4754 B4
Utopia Dr
14000 SGLD 77478 4237 A6
Uvalde Rd
10 HarC 77015 3828 D6
10 HarC 77049 3828 D7
10 HOUS 77015 3828 D6
10 HOUS 77049 3828 E4
700 HOUS 77015 3967 D2
8000 HarC 77049 3689 D6
Uwood
- DRPK 77571 3969 E6
- DRPK 77571 3970 A6
- HarC 77571 3970 A6
Uzzell Rd
9100 MNVL 77578 4746 D7
9500 BzaC 77578 4746 D7

V

Vacant Dr
3500 FBnC 77469 4233 C6
Vaccaro Cir
14000 STAF 77477 4369 E3
Vacek Rd
12900 GlsC 77510 4986 D6
12900 GlsC 77517 4986 C7
Vadilia Point Dr
14100 HarC 77429 3397 B2
Vae Dr
5300 BYTN 77521 3971 E2
Vaiden Falls Ct
8500 HarC 77083 4097 A6
Vaiden Falls Dr
- HarC 77083 4097 B7
Vail Ct
1800 MSCY 77459 4497 C3
Vail Dr
- PRLD 77584 4502 D5
Vail St
2700 PLEK 77471 4614 C5
Vailrun Dr
11600 HarC 77070 3398 D2
Vailview Dr
11200 HOUS 77016 3687 B1
Valance Wy
9900 MtgC 77385 2676 E5
Valarie Av
24100 MtgC 77365 2974 B7
Valarno Dr
11300 HarC 77066 3401 D6
Valcourt Pl
10 WDLD 77382 2819 E2
S Vale Dr
12200 HarC 77089 4505 B2
Vale Ln
24400 MtgC 77365 2973 E7
24700 MtgC 77365 3118 E1
Vale St
100 SHUS 77587 4246 E3
Valechase Ln
14000 HarC 77014 3401 C2
Valeda Dr
7400 DRPK 77536 4249 B2
Valedictorian Dr
1900 HOUS 77077 3956 E5
Valedon Ct
14000 HarC 77014 3401 C2
Valedon Ln
4100 HarC 77014 3401 C2
Valemist Ct
17200 HarC 77084 3678 A2
Valencia Dr
10100 HOUS 77013 3966 B1
Valencia St
11900 MDWP 77477 4238 A5
Valencia Cove
2500 LGCY 77573 4632 A7
Valentine Ln
- PRLD 77584 4502 B5
Valentine St
400 HOUS 77019 3963 A4
1500 HOUS 77002 3963 A5
Valentine Bridge Ln
14900 FBnC 77478 4236 A5
Valenza Dr
24200 FBnC 77469 4093 A7
24400 FBnC 77469 4092 E7
Valer Dr
4100 GLSN 77554 5440 E6
Valera Ln
7700 HarC 77083 4097 B6
Valerian Dr
6500 HarC 77449 3677 D3
Valerian Ln
6600 HarC 77449 3677 D3
Valerie Av
700 PASD 77502 4247 C1
Valerie Ln
3200 MtgC 77380 2821 A7
Valerie St
- HOUS 77074 4100 B6
4300 HOUS 77401 4101 B6
4600 BLAR 77401 4101 B6
5500 BLAR 77401 4100 C6
5500 HOUS 77081 4100 C6
5500 HOUS 77401 4100 C6
Valero St
1700 FRDW 77546 4629 B6
Vale Scene Ct
1200 HarC 77073 3259 B5
Valeta Dr
8100 FBnC 77083 4096 C7
Valeview Dr
7100 HOUS 77072 4097 D6
Valewood Pl
10 WDLD 77384 2675 A6
Valhalla Dr
- HarC 77379 3111 E6
Valhallah Wy
17200 HarC 77095 3678 A1
Valiant Dr
9500 HarC 77044 3689 E3
Valiant Brook Ct
18300 HarC 77346 3409 A1
Valiant Elm St
2800 FBnC 77545 4498 C6
Valiant Oak St
16900 MtgC 77385 2676 E5
Valiant Scene Ct
2900 HarC 77038 3543 A5
Valiant Square Cir
- HarC 77429 3253 C4
Valiant Woods Dr
- HarC 77379 3112 A6
Valinda Ct
16400 FBnC 77083 4095 E6
Valinda Dr
- FBnC 77083 4095 E6
- FBnC 77083 4096 A6
Valka Rd
18200 HarC 77379 3110 E7
18200 HarC 77379 3111 A7
Valkeith Dr
4900 HOUS 77096 4241 A2
5200 HOUS 77096 4240 D2
Valky Dr
3000 LGCY 77539 4753 A5
Valkyrie Dr
19400 HarC 77379 3111 E6
19400 HarC 77379 3112 A6
Vallecito Ln
7800 HMBL 77396 3406 D3
Vallejo Ct
6200 HOUS 77053 4371 D6
Vallejo Dr
16300 HOUS 77053 4371 D6
Vallen Dr
- HarC 77041 3680 C3
- HOUS 77041 3680 C3
Val Lena Dr
600 HOUS 77024 3958 E2
Valleria Ct
1900 FBnC 77479 4367 B7
2000 FBnC 77479 4494 B1
Valleta Dr
1300 HOUS 77008 3822 E6
Valley Ct
3000 BzaC 77578 4625 B1
3900 MSCY 77459 4497 C3
N Valley Ct
21100 HarC 77073 3259 B6
Valley Dr
- BzaC 77578 4625 B1
100 CNRO 77303 2237 D6
500 LGCY 77539 4753 A4
E Valley Dr
3700 MSCY 77459 4497 B3
W Valley Dr
3700 MSCY 77459 4497 A3
Valley Hls
11900 HOUS 77071 4239 E5
Valley Ln
16700 MtgC 77306 2533 D7

STREET
Block City ZIP Map# Grid

S Valley Ln
12000 HarC 77089 4505 A2
Valley Acres Rd
1000 HOUS 77062 4379 E7
Valley Bend Ct
14200 SGLD 77478 4236 E5
Valley Bend Dr
2300 MSCY 77489 4370 B7
15400 HarC 77068 3257 A5
Valley Blossom Ct
26100 FBnC 77494 4092 C3
Valley Bluff Ln
5200 FBnC 77494 4093 B2
18100 HarC 77429 3252 B5
Valley Branch Dr
4300 HOUS 77339 3119 B3
Valley Breeze Dr
10100 HOUS 77078 3688 C5
Valley Brook Ct
5200 LPRT 77571 4250 B2
Valley Brook Dr
100 LPRT 77571 4250 B2
Valleybrook Pl
10 WDLD 77382 2673 D6
Valley Canyon Ln
22500 MtgC 77365 2973 B3
Valley Center Dr
29700 MtgC 77386 2969 D2
Valley Chase Dr
3500 HOUS 77345 3120 A3
Valley Cliff Ct
12500 HarC 77377 3254 B2
Valley Club Dr
10100 HOUS 77078 3688 C6
Valley Commons Dr
- HarC 77336 3122 A3
700 HarC 77336 3121 A3
700 HarC 77336 3266 E1
700 HarC 77336 3267 A1
Valley Cove Ln
6000 HOUS 77085 4240 E7
Valley Creek Dr
15500 HarC 77095 3678 D1
Valley Crest Ln
8600 HOUS 77075 4376 E4
Valley Dale Ct
2000 HOUS 77062 4380 B7
Valley Elm Ln
7700 HarC 77040 3541 E7
Valley Estates Dr
4000 HarC 77082 4096 D4
Valley Fair Dr
5800 HOUS 77345 3120 C6
Valley Falls Ct
10000 HOUS 77078 3688 C5
Valley Field Dr
2600 SGLD 77479 4368 D7
Valleyfield Dr
3600 HOUS 77080 3820 D2
Valley Flag Rd
8600 HOUS 77078 3688 C6
Valley Forest Dr
- MSCY 77459 4497 B1
2500 MSCY 77489 4370 B7
2600 MSCY 77489 4497 B1
8500 HOUS 77078 3688 D6
Valley Forge Dr
10 BKHV 77024 3959 C3
2400 HOUS 77017 4246 E2
2400 PASD 77017 4246 E2
2400 PASD 77502 4246 E2
2700 SHUS 77502 4246 E2
2700 SHUS 77587 4246 E2
5800 HOUS 77057 3960 B5
10000 HOUS 77042 3958 E5
10000 HOUS 77042 3959 A5
Valley Gardens Dr
3300 HOUS 77345 3119 D5
Valleygate Ln
12900 HarC 77072 4097 C7
Valley Glade Dr
4200 HOUS 77345 3119 D5
Valley Glen Dr
1300 HOUS 77077 3958 B5
Valley Gold Ct
8600 HOUS 77078 3688 C5
Valley Green Ct
3900 PASD 77059 4380 D4
Valley Grove Dr
14000 HarC 77066 3401 E7
Valley Haven Dr
3300 HOUS 77339 3119 A5
Valley Heather Ct
6100 HOUS 77345 3120 D6
Valley Hidden Dr
12300 HOUS 77071 4239 E6
Valley Hills Dr
10000 HOUS 77071 4239 E3
Valley Ho Dr
- HOUS 77078 3688 C5
Valley Hollow Dr
8900 HOUS 77078 3688 B5
Valley Kings Dr
11100 HOUS 77075 4377 C4
11100 HOUS 77089 4377 C4
Valley Knoll Dr
17900 HarC 77084 3677 D5
17900 HarC 77084 3678 A6
Valley Lake Dr
9900 HOUS 77078 3688 B5
Valley Landing Dr
1300 HarC 77450 3954 A4
Valley Lark Ct
5500 HOUS 77345 3120 C7
Valley Laurel Ct
7500 HarC 77095 3538 B7
7500 HarC 77095 3678 B1
Valley Ledge Dr
8600 HOUS 77078 3688 C6
Valleylight Dr
- KATY 77494 3952 D4
24700 FBnC 77494 3952 D4
Valley Lodge Ln
7900 FBnC 77469 4095 B6
Valley Lodge Pkwy
- HarC 77346 3408 C3
Valley Manor Ct
2400 MSCY 77489 4370 B7
Valley Manor Dr
2000 MSCY 77489 4370 B7
2500 HOUS 77339 3119 B6
Valley Mead Pl
10 WDLD 77384 2674 E3
Valley Meadow Dr
8600 HOUS 77078 3688 C6
Valley Mill Ct
9900 HOUS 77078 3688 C5

Valley Oaks Cir
10 WDLD 77382 2674 E5
N Valley Oaks Cir
100 WDLD 77382 2674 E4
Valley Oaks Ct
21500 HarC 77450 3954 B5
Valley Oaks Dr
30400 MAGA 77355 2815 A1
30400 MtgC 77355 2815 A1
Valley Palms Dr
17000 HarC 77379 3256 A4
17500 HarC 77379 3255 E3
W Valley Palms Dr
8800 HarC 77379 3255 E3
Valley Park Dr
9900 HOUS 77078 3688 C5
Valley Pass
- HOUS 77034 4248 C7
- HOUS 77034 4379 C1
- PASD 77034 4248 C7
- PASD 77505 4248 C7
Valley Pike Ct
15500 FBnC 77478 4236 D6
Valley Pines Dr
5300 HOUS 77345 3120 A5
Valley Plum Ct
15500 HarC 77433 3251 C6
Valley Point Dr
9000 HOUS 77078 3688 C5
Valley Pond Ct
8700 HOUS 77078 3688 C5
Valley Ranch Dr
800 HarC 77450 3953 D3
Valley Ranch Bend Dr
21300 MtgC 77365 2973 A2
Valley Ranch Crossing Dr
21600 MtgC 77365 2973 C3
Valleyridge Dr
- BzaC 77584 4501 C7
Valley Rim Dr
- HOUS 77339 3119 C1
- HOUS 77345 3119 C1
Valley Rock Dr
8600 HOUS 77078 3688 D6
Valley Rose Dr
2900 HOUS 77339 3119 B4
Valley Scene Wy
5500 HarC 77379 3112 A6
Valley Side Dr
8900 HOUS 77078 3688 C5
Valley Song Dr
8600 HOUS 77078 3688 D6
Valley South Dr
8600 HOUS 77078 3688 C5
Valley Spring Dr
11200 HOUS 77043 3819 A7
Valley Spring Tr
3000 HarC 77449 3815 D4
Valley Springs Pl
25600 HarC 77373 3113 E4
Valley Star Dr
12200 BKHV 77024 3959 A4
12200 HOUS 77024 3959 A4
Valley Stone Ct
14600 HarC 77429 3396 D2
Valley Stream Dr
11200 HOUS 77043 3819 A7
Valley Stream St
9300 HOUS 77037 3544 B6
Valley Sun Dr
9900 HOUS 77078 3688 B5
Valley Trace Ln
22400 MtgC 77365 2973 A3
Valley Tree Ln
8300 HOUS 77089 4377 B4
Valley View Cross
2200 CNRO 77304 2236 E3
2200 MtgC 77304 2236 E3
Valleyview Ct
2500 SGLD 77479 4368 D7
Valley View Dr
1500 LPRT 77571 4110 E7
4900 LPRT 77571 4250 B2
Valleyview Dr
- MSCY 77459 4369 E7
Valley View Ln
8700 HOUS 77074 4239 B1
Valleyview Creek Ct
5300 HarC 77379 3112 A7
Valley Vista Ct
11900 HOUS 77077 3957 E6
11900 HOUS 77077 3958 B7
Valley Vista Dr
1700 HOUS 77077 3958 A6
Valley Wells Dr
20500 HarC 77449 3815 D4
Valley West Ct
8600 HOUS 77078 3688 B5
Valley Wind Dr
10100 HOUS 77078 3688 C6
Valley Wood Dr
100 MtgC 77380 2968 B1
10200 HOUS 77041 3820 B1
Valley Wy Dr
2800 HOUS 77339 3119 B6
Vallie Rd
28100 MtgC 77362 2963 E2
Vallingby Dr
23000 HarC 77450 3953 C2
Valmar St
10 LGCY 77565 4508 E4
Valmont Dr
7200 HOUS 77016 3687 B2
Valor St
4000 HOUS 77093 3686 B7
Valparaiso Cir
4300 PASD 77504 4248 A4
Valusek Rd
9500 MNVL 77578 4746 D6
Val Verde Ct
800 HOUS 77057 3960 D7
Valverde Dr
15800 FBnC 77083 4096 B7
Val Verde Pk
2800 HOUS 77057 3960 D7
Val Verde Rd
33000 WlrC 77484 3246 C4
Val Verde St
5300 HOUS 77056 3960 E7
5600 HOUS 77057 3960 D7
Valverde St
- HOUS 77042 3959 B7
9300 HOUS 77063 3959 C7
Val Vista Dr
15800 FBnC 77083 4096 B6
Valwood Ct
9300 HOUS 77088 3544 A6

Valwood Dr
100 CNRO 77301 2384 B7
Van Rd
17500 HarC 77049 3691 B4
Van St
200 SHUS 77587 4246 E2
Van Allen Dr
8800 MtgC 77381 2821 D2
8900 WDLD 77381 2821 D2
Vanamen Ct
2000 CNRO 77304 2383 A6
Vanarcher
11100 HOUS 77016 3687 A1
Van Brook Ln
9900 HarC 77095 3538 A3
Van Buren Cir
1900 PASD 77502 4107 C7
Van Buren Dr
1500 DRPK 77536 4249 D1
Van Buren St
1000 HOUS 77019 3962 D5
1600 HOUS 77006 3962 D5
12200 HarC 77064 3399 E6
Vanburen St
- HOUS 77029 3965 D5
Vanbury Dr
4900 HarC 77084 3677 E6
Vance Av
2900 TXCY 77590 4874 D5
Vance St
400 LGCY 77573 4632 B2
1900 HOUS 77093 3824 D2
3800 HOUS 77016 3825 B2
Van Cleve St
2000 HOUS 77047 4373 E3
Vancouver Blvd
4900 FBnC 77469 4491 C2
Vancouver Ln
12000 HarC 77064 3399 E6
Vandalia Wy
15200 HOUS 77053 4372 B5
Vandell St
100 HOUS 77022 3685 A6
Vandeman St
6900 HOUS 77087 4105 A3
7100 HOUS 77012 4105 A3
Vanderbilt St
6300 WUNP 77005 4101 E4
6700 HOUS 77025 4101 E4
Vanderbilt Park Dr
3800 PASD 77058 4380 E6
Vandercroft Ct
10600 HarC 77070 3399 B5
Vander Dale Ct
400 HarC 77450 3953 D2
Vanderford Dr
10900 HOUS 77099 4238 C5
Vandergrift Dr
16800 HOUS 77396 3406 A4
Vanderheath Dr
12300 HOUS 77031 4239 A6
Vandermere Ct
4400 HOUS 77345 3119 D7
Vanderpool Ln
- BKHV 77024 3959 A4
300 HOUS 77024 3959 A4
Vander Rock Dr
9300 HarC 77095 3538 A4
Vanderwick Dr
20700 HarC 77450 3954 C4
Vanderwilt Ct
20800 HarC 77449 3815 C7
Vanderwilt Ln
1700 HarC 77449 3815 B7
Vandyke Dr
3200 HarC 77388 3112 D2
Vane Wy
400 HarC 77532 3411 B7
Vanessa Cir
14200 HarC 77069 3400 A1
Vaneta Dr
2100 HarC 77449 3815 E6
Van Etten St
6900 HOUS 77021 4103 A5
6900 HOUS 77054 4103 A5
Van Fleet St
- HOUS 77033 4243 E1
- HOUS 77033 4244 A2
Vang Ct
1100 HarC 77532 3552 A1
Van Gogh Ln
2700 FBnC 77459 4621 B7
Vanhorn Ct
18400 HarC 77379 3111 B7
Van Hut Ln
7900 HarC 77049 3689 C7
8500 HarC 77044 3689 B4
Vanity Dr
3200 PRLD 77584 4501 D6
Vanlynn Ln
6500 HarC 77084 3677 E2
Van Meter St
800 HOUS 77047 4373 C4
3500 HarC 77047 4374 C4
Van Molan St
100 HOUS 77022 3824 A1
Vann Rd
100 HarC 77562 3831 D3
Van Ness Dr
3400 ALVN 77511 4866 C2
3800 BzaC 77511 4866 C2
Van Ness St
7500 HarC 77037 3684 E3
7500 HOUS 77037 3684 E3
7500 HOUS 77076 3684 E3
Vannevar Wy
2700 MtgC 77381 2821 D2
Vanover Ln
14400 HarC 77429 3397 D2
Vans Ln
15300 MtgC 77302 2824 E1
Van Sant Ln
10 HarC 77084 3818 A1
Vantage Pkwy E
15200 HOUS 77032 3404 C7
Vantage Pkwy W
15200 HOUS 77032 3404 B7
Vantage Pointe Cir
300 LGCY 77573 4633 B1
Vantage View Ln
18900 HarC 77346 3265 D6
18900 HarC 77346 3265 D6
E Van Trease Dr
2200 DRPK 77536 4109 D6
W Van Trease Dr
2200 DRPK 77536 4109 D6
Van Wall St
13900 HOUS 77040 3681 C5

Vanwood St
9200 HOUS 77040 3682 A2
Vanya Ln
1300 HarC 77336 3121 E7
Van Zandt St
4900 HarC 77093 3686 C1
5400 HOUS 77016 3686 D1
5900 HOUS 77016 3687 A1
Vaquero St
1800 FRDW 77546 4629 A7
Vaquero Wy
10600 HarC 77095 3537 E2
Varadero Cir
- HarC 77095 3538 E7
Vardon Ct
19400 HarC 77094 3955 B1
Varese Dr
1300 PRLD 77581 4504 E3
Varick Ct
6600 HarC 77064 3541 D2
Varla Ln
3700 HarC 77014 3401 D2
Varnell St
11700 HarC 77039 3546 E7
11700 HarC 77093 3546 D7
Varner Rd
8700 HOUS 77080 3821 A5
Varsity Ln
4300 HOUS 77004 4103 E3
Varuna Ct
2000 LGCY 77573 4631 A7
Vashon Ln
3600 HarC 77388 3112 D6
Vashti Dr
400 HarC 77037 3684 D2
600 HOUS 77037 3684 D2
W Vashti Dr
100 HarC 77037 3684 C2
Vassar St
1300 HOUS 77006 4102 D1
1600 HOUS 77098 4102 C1
Vasser St
6000 HOUS 77033 4244 C3
Vatani Dr
10600 HOUS 77034 4246 E7
Vatican Ct
1000 PRLD 77581 4504 E3
Vattern Ln
7700 HOUS 77075 4376 C1
Vaughn
4700 HOUS 77023 4104 B2
Vaughn Ln
14900 MtgC 77372 2682 C3
E Vaughn Ln
100 DRPK 77536 4109 B6
W Vaughn Ln
100 DRPK 77536 4109 B6
Vaughn St
1900 HOUS 77093 3824 E2
3900 HOUS 77016 3825 B2
Vaughn Creek Ct
4100 FBnC 77479 4366 C7
Vaughnville Dr
14600 HarC 77084 3679 A3
Vaulted Chestnut Ln
20300 HarC 77433 3251 C7
Vaulted Oak St
900 HOUS 77008 3822 D7
Vaulted Pine Dr
8200 HarC 77346 3265 C6
N Vauthier Ln
1300 LMQU 77568 4989 C2
Vauthier Rd
- TXCY 77591 4873 C6
S Vauthier Rd
- LMQU 77568 4873 C7
200 TXCY 77591 4873 C7
Vauthier St
100 LMQU 77568 4873 C7
100 TXCY 77591 4873 C7
700 LMQU 77568 4989 C3
Vauxhill Dr S
3900 HarC 77047 4374 D5
Vazca Degama Dr
11200 HOUS 77048 4244 D6
Veck St
9400 HOUS 77075 4376 C1
Veenstra St
10 HOUS 77022 3684 E6
10 HOUS 77022 3685 A6
Veer
1000 HarC 77532 3552 A4
Veera Ln
13900 FBnC 77478 4237 B2
Vega Ct
2300 LGCY 77573 4508 C5
Vega Dr
2700 HOUS 77088 3683 B1
Vegas St
7800 HMBL 77396 3406 D3
Veilwood Cir
- WDLD 77382 2673 B7
S Veilwood Cir
- WDLD 77382 2673 B7
Velasco Ct
3400 FBnC 77459 4621 E5
Velasco St
100 HOUS 77003 3964 A5
300 HOUS 77003 3963 E6
2200 HOUS 77004 3963 D7
3100 HOUS 77004 4103 C1
N Velasco St
200 HOUS 77003 3964 A4
Velda Rose Ln
100 PNVL 77304 2237 A4
Veller Dr
800 HarC 77032 3403 D7
800 HarC 77032 3404 A6
Velma Ln
5800 HOUS 77032 3405 E7
5800 HOUS 77396 3405 E7
6000 HOUS 77396 3406 A6
21000 MtgC 77365 2826 A7
21100 MtgC 77365 2972 A1
Velma St
1100 CNRO 77301 2530 A1
1100 DRPK 77536 4249 C1
2200 LMQU 77568 4989 E1
Velure St
5800 HOUS 77036 4099 A3
Velvet St
300 LGCY 77573 4631 E2
Velvet Grass Ct
100 WDLD 77382 2673 B5
Velvet Grass Ln
11200 HarC 77095 3538 B1
Velvet Leaf Pl
100 WDLD 77380 2968 A3

Velvet Rose Ct
10 WDLD 77384 2675 D5
Velvet Shadow Ct
19400 HarC 77375 3109 D6
Vena Dr
5800 HOUS 77087 4244 E1
Vendi Dr
5700 HOUS 77085 4240 E7
Venetian Dr
24000 FBnC 77469 4093 A7
Venetian Wy
4100 PASD 77503 4108 D7
Venezia Dr
2100 PRLD 77089 4504 E2
2100 PRLD 77581 4504 E2
Venice Cir
13300 STAF 77477 4370 B1
N Venice Dr
1600 PRLD 77581 4504 D2
S Venice Dr
2300 PRLD 77581 4504 D3
Venice Ln
12800 STAF 77477 4370 B1
Venice St
100 SGLD 77478 4368 A3
5400 HOUS 77007 3962 A4
Venice Villa Ln
13400 FBnC 77478 4237 B4
Venida St
7800 HOUS 77028 3687 B5
Vennard Rd
- HOUS 77034 4246 D6
Venterra Blvd
10 WDLD 77382 2673 A6
Ventor
30000 MtgC 77354 2818 B1
E Ventura Dr
12400 GLSN 77554 5333 C1
W Ventura Dr
12500 GLSN 77554 5333 C1
Ventura Ln
4800 HOUS 77021 4104 A5
Ventura Canyon Ct
24400 FBnC 77494 3953 A4
Ventura Canyon Dr
1200 FBnC 77494 3953 A3
Venture Dr
- LGCY 77573 4632 A7
Venture Ln
8500 LPRT 77571 4249 D4
Venture Park Ct
7000 FBnC 77469 4234 A2
Venture Park Dr
- FBnC 77469 4233 E2
21400 FBnC 77469 4234 A2
Venus Dr
1800 RMFT 77357 2828 E3
1800 RMFT 77357 2829 A3
Venus St
- HOUS 77091 3683 B4
7000 HOUS 77088 3683 B4
Venus Park Ln
12500 HOUS 77082 4097 D2
Venzi
3800 DKSN 77539 4753 E2
Vera Dr
14800 HOUS 77396 3406 A7
Vera Ln
13100 MtgC 77372 2535 A6
13300 MtgC 77372 2534 E6
Vera Cruz
1100 HarC 77532 3266 C7
Veracruz Blvd
17800 GLSN 77554 5331 D7
Vera Cruz Dr
100 RSBG 77471 4490 B5
Vera Jean Ct
9900 HOUS 77088 3682 C1
Vera Jean Dr
6500 HOUS 77088 3682 C1
6600 HarC 77088 3682 C1
Vera Lou St
1100 HOUS 77051 4243 C2
Veramonte Ct
7900 FBnC 77479 4494 B5
Veranda Dr
3700 HarC 77449 3815 E2
Veranda Green Tr
6300 HarC 77346 3264 E4
Veranda Ridge Dr
10 WDLD 77382 2674 E4
N Veranda Ridge Dr
10 WDLD 77382 2674 E4
S Veranda Ridge Dr
10 WDLD 77382 2674 E4
Veranda View Pl
10 WDLD 77384 2675 D5
Verano Dr
2400 FBnC 77469 4365 B4
22800 GLSN 77554 5440 E6
22800 GLSN 77554 5441 A6
Verano St
10800 JTCY 77029 3966 C2
Verbena Ln
13200 HOUS 77072 4097 B4
13200 HOUS 77083 4097 B4
13400 HarC 77083 4097 B4
Verbena St
4000 FBnC 77545 4623 D1
Verbena Bend Pl
10 WDLD 77382 2674 C3
Verdant Vly
1900 FBnC 77479 4494 A3
Verdant Wy
5400 HarC 77069 3400 D1
Verdant Brook Dr
12600 HOUS 77085 4240 D7
Verdant Meadow Ct
4100 HarC 77449 3816 A1
Verdant Valley Pl
10 WDLD 77382 2674 E4
Verdant Willow Ct
17100 HarC 77095 3678 C3
Verdant Willow Wy
17200 HarC 77095 3678 A1
Verde Rd
- HOUS 77078 3688 C7
Verde Canyon Dr
20300 FBnC 77450 4094 C4
Verdecove Ln
21200 HarC 77388 3112 B5
Verde Glen Ln
12400 HOUS 77071 4239 D7
Verde Mar Ln
14100 HarC 77041 3539 A7
14100 HarC 77095 3539 A7
Verde Meadow Ct
7100 HarC 77041 3679 C1

Verde Meadow Dr
- TXCY 77591 4872 C2
Verde Mist Ln
19500 HarC 77073 3403 C3
Verdenbruk Dr
5100 HarC 77066 3401 B5
Verde Trails Dr
900 HarC 77073 3403 B2
Verde Valley Dr
6100 HOUS 77396 3406 A3
Verde Vista Ln
- HarC 77336 3121 E2
Verdi Dr
12800 HOUS 77024 3958 D3
Verdinell St
7400 HarC 77521 3832 D4
Verdome Ln
- HOUS 77092 3682 C7
4300 HOUS 77092 3683 A7
5000 HOUS 77092 3821 E1
5000 HOUS 77092 3822 A1
Verdun Dr
12800 HarC 77049 3828 C1
Verdun Ln
1200 FRDW 77546 4629 D2
Vergil Park Dr
3500 HarC 77068 3257 C6
Verhalen Av
2300 HarC 77039 3545 E3
3600 HarC 77039 3546 A3
Verhalen Rd
100 HLCS 77511 4867 D6
200 ALVN 77511 4867 E6
Veridian Grove Dr
6300 HOUS 77072 4097 D5
Verkin St
2900 LMQU 77568 4989 D1
Verlaine Dr
11200 HarC 77065 3398 B7
11200 HarC 77065 3539 B1
Ver Lee Ct
8900 HOUS 77037 3544 B7
Verlie Ln
- HOUS 77036 4099 C6
Vermarion
13500 HarC 77070 3400 A3
Vermejo Park Ln
7100 HarC 77346 3409 A1
Vermillion
21300 MtgC 77357 2974 E1
Vermillion Ct
19300 HarC 77449 3677 A4
Vermillion Dr
500 PASD 77506 4106 D5
2700 MSCY 77459 4497 E5
Vermillion Rd
2500 SEBK 77586 4509 C1
Vermillion Oak St
- FBnC 77545 4498 D5
Vermont St
1400 HOUS 77006 3962 C5
1800 BYTN 77520 4112 B2
1800 HOUS 77019 3962 C5
3400 FBnC 77545 4499 D7
3800 DKSN 77539 4753 E3
3800 FBnC 77545 4623 D1
Vermont Glen Ct
2100 HarC 77493 3814 B5
Vermont Green Tr
9600 HOUS 77075 4246 B7
Vernage Rd
1100 HOUS 77047 4373 C3
Vernal Glen Cir
1800 HarC 77388 3113 C5
Verngate Ct
4200 HarC 77373 3115 A6
Verngate Dr
23400 HarC 77373 3115 A6
Vernier Woods Ln
19600 HarC 77379 3112 A6
Vernlake Cir
1900 HarC 77084 3816 A6
Vernon Av
100 TMBL 77375 2964 A7
300 TMBL 77375 3109 A1
Vernon Ct
- HarC 77044 3549 B3
Vernon Rd
13000 HarC 77429 3398 B6
Vernon St
3400 HOUS 77020 3964 A2
Vernwood St
7500 HOUS 77040 3682 A2
7600 HarC 77040 3682 A2
7800 HarC 77040 3681 E2
Verona Ct
1200 LGCY 77573 4632 E4
Verona Dr
2100 PRLD 77581 4504 D2
Verone St
4300 BLAR 77401 4101 B5
4300 HOUS 77401 4101 B5
Veronica St
1000 LMQU 77568 4989 E1
1100 GlsC 77517 4870 C1
Verret Ln
800 HarC 77090 3258 C3
Verron Tr
23900 MtgC 77365 2974 A6
Versace Dr
13200 HarC 77044 3689 C4
Versailles Ct
800 HarC 77015 3828 B7
Versailles Dr
- PRLD 77584 4501 E6
12400 HarC 77015 3828 A7
Versailles Lakes Ln
11600 HOUS 77082 4098 B2
Versante Ct
10 HOUS 77070 3400 A3
Vesper St
8800 HOUS 77075 4246 B6
N Vesper Bend Cir
100 WDLD 77382 2819 C2
S Vesper Bend Cir
10 WDLD 77382 2819 C2
Vesta Ct
37000 MtgC 77355 2815 D6
Vesta Ln
3400 GlsC 77518 4634 C2
Vestavia Ct
13400 HarC 77069 3400 D1
Vestavia Dr
5700 HarC 77069 3400 D1
Veterans Dr
2600 PRLD 77581 4503 B4
2600 PRLD 77584 4503 B7
4100 BzaC 77584 4503 B7

Veterans Dr
4200 BzaC 77584 4627 B1
4200 PRLD 77584 4627 B1
Veterans Rd
18900 MtgC 77355 2815 A3
Veterans Hospital Five Dr
10 HOUS 77030 4102 E5
Veterans Hospital One Dr
10 HOUS 77030 4102 E5
Veterans Memorial Blvd
7900 HOUS 77037 3684 B2
7900 HOUS 77088 3684 A1
8600 HOUS 77088 3544 A7
Veterans Memorial Dr
7700 HOUS 77037 3684 B2
7700 HOUS 77088 3684 B2
12000 HarC 77067 3401 D5
12100 HarC 77014 3401 C3
12100 HarC 77066 3401 C3
Veterans Memorial Pkwy
10700 HarC 77038 3402 A7
10700 HarC 77066 3402 A7
10800 HarC 77067 3402 A7
11200 HarC 77066 3401 D5
11200 HarC 77067 3401 D5
Veterans Memorial Rd
9400 HarC 77038 3543 B1
9400 HOUS 77038 3543 E6
9400 HOUS 77088 3543 E6
Veva Dr
2900 PRLD 77584 4503 A4
Veyblum St
9700 HOUS 77029 3966 A5
Via Barolo
13300 HarC 77429 3398 C2
Via Bella Dr
8000 FBnC 77083 4096 C7
Via Belterra Ln
- LGCY 77573 4632 E3
Via Capri Ct
11000 FBnC 77469 4093 A7
Via Chianti Ct
12100 HarC 77429 3398 C2
Via Chianti Ln
13400 HarC 77429 3398 C2
Via Davinci Ln
11900 HarC 77429 3398 C2
Via de Estrella
800 HarC 77073 3259 C6
Via del Norte Dr
14600 HarC 77083 4096 D5
14600 HOUS 77083 4096 D5
Via del Sol Dr
- HarC 77083 4096 E6
E Via Dora Ct
800 HarC 77532 3552 B4
W Via Dora Ct
900 HarC 77532 3552 A4
Via Dora Dr
15600 HarC 77532 3552 A4
Via Enclave
7500 HOUS 77040 3682 A5
Via Espana Dr
6300 HarC 77083 4096 D4
Via Firenze Ln
12000 HarC 77429 3398 C2
Via Fontana Ct
11400 FBnC 77469 4093 A7
Via Genoa Ct
4700 HOUS 77021 4103 E5
Via La Strada
- LGCY 77573 4632 E4
Vialinda Dr
6500 HarC 77083 4096 B4
Via Luna
13400 HarC 77429 3398 C2
Via Michaelangelo Ct
13500 HarC 77429 3398 B2
Via Milano Ct
5900 HOUS 77021 4103 E5
Via Palazzo Ln
12000 HarC 77429 3398 B2
Via Pinetta
13300 HarC 77429 3398 C2
Via Piscana Ln
1200 LGCY 77573 4632 E4
Via Ponte Vecchio Ln
13600 HarC 77429 3398 C2
Via Porta Rosa
12100 HarC 77429 3398 C2
Via Real Dr
7300 FBnC 77083 4096 B6
Via Rica Dr
14200 HarC 77083 4096 E5
Via Salerno Ct
24500 FBnC 77469 4092 E7
24500 FBnC 77469 4093 A7
Via San Rocco Ct
12100 HarC 77429 3398 C2
Via Sedonia
- LGCY 77573 4633 A4
Via Siena Ct
13700 HarC 77429 3398 B1
Via Siena Ln
12000 HarC 77429 3398 C2
Via Sienna
- LGCY 77573 4632 E4
Via Torre de Pisa Ln
13300 HarC 77429 3398 B2
Via Toscana
- LGCY 77573 4633 A4
Via Toscano Ct
12100 HarC 77429 3398 C2
Via Toscano Ln
13500 HarC 77429 3398 C2
13700 HarC 77070 3398 C2
Via Venezia Blvd
1100 FBnC 77469 4093 A7
1100 FBnC 77469 4233 A1
Via Venice Ct
5900 HOUS 77021 4103 E5
Via Verde Dr
15100 HarC 77083 4096 C6
Via Vineyard Ct
4600 HOUS 77021 4103 E5
Via Vista Dr
7400 HarC 77083 4096 C6
Vicdale Dr
11900 HOUS 77031 4239 B5
Viceroy Dr
100 HOUS 77034 4247 A5
100 PASD 77504 4247 A5
Vick Dr
20200 MtgC 77357 2827 D6
Vick St
3300 HOUS 77019 3962 C4
Vick Cemetery Rd
18500 MtgC 77302 2680 B3

STREET
Block City ZIP Map# Grid
Vick Cemetery Rd
18500 MtgC 77306 2680 A3
Vickers Rd
18500 HarC 77377 3106 E7
18500 HarC 77433 3106 E7
18500 HarC 77433 3251 E1
22900 MtgC 77372 2684 B6
Vickers St
400 SHUS 77587 4246 E2
Vickery Dr
- HOUS 77032 3546 C1
1300 SGLD 77478 4236 E7
15000 HarC 77032 3405 C7
15000 HarC 77032 3546 C1
15200 HOUS 77032 3405 C6
Vickery St
11400 HarC 77093 3546 C7
11400 HarC 77093 3686 C1
12300 HarC 77039 3546 B5
Vickie Ln
13000 HOUS 77015 3967 C3
30500 MtgC 77354 2672 D7
30500 MtgC 77354 2818 D1
Vickie Springs Ln
6400 HarC 77086 3542 C2
Vickijohn Cir
10800 HOUS 77071 4239 E3
Vickijohn Ct
10800 HOUS 77071 4239 E4
Vickijohn Dr
- HOUS 77031 4239 B4
5900 HOUS 77096 4240 B3
7600 HOUS 77071 4239 E4
Vicki Lynn Ln
6000 FBnC 77469 4232 E7
Vic Kita
100 PRVW 77445 3100 C2
Vickita Dr
5500 HarC 77032 3546 D1
Vickridge Ln
7900 HarC 77379 3256 B3
Vicksburg Av
9000 TXCY 77591 4872 E6
9000 TXCY 77591 4873 A5
Vicksburg Blvd
- MSCY 77459 4497 E7
- MSCY 77545 4497 E7
Vicksburg Dr
- MSCY 77459 4497 E7
Vicksburg Ln
10 MtgC 77302 2530 D7
4500 TXCY 77539 4634 B4
Vicksburg St
13100 HOUS 77015 3967 D1
W Vicksburg Estates Dr
3600 MSCY 77459 4497 E6
Vickston Ln
13800 HarC 77014 3401 D2
Vicky Ln
12200 HarC 77429 3398 D5
Victor Ln
12700 HOUS 77077 3957 C4
Victor St
1100 HOUS 77002 3963 A5
1100 HOUS 77019 3963 A5
1600 HOUS 77019 3962 E5
Victoria Av
3900 DKSN 77539 4754 A2
4800 BzaC 77583 4624 A3
Victoria Ct
1800 SGLD 77478 4368 C5
1900 LGCY 77573 4631 C6
2200 MSCY 77459 4370 B7
Victoria Dr
100 HOUS 77018 3684 C7
100 HOUS 77022 3684 C7
400 HOUS 77022 3823 D1
900 RHMD 77469 4491 D2
5400 FBnC 77583 4623 C4
Victoria Ln
100 BzaC 77511 4749 B2
Victoria Pl
1300 SGLD 77479 4367 E5
1300 SGLD 77479 4368 A5
Victoria St
6300 HOUS 77020 3964 E1
7100 HOUS 77020 3965 A1
13700 HarC 77015 3828 E7
14000 HarC 77015 3829 A7
Victoria Wy
400 FRDW 77546 4629 E2
Victoria Chase Ln
10000 HOUS 77075 4377 C2
Victoria Crest Ln
9900 HOUS 77075 4377 C1
Victoria Estates Dr
30600 MtgC 77386 2969 B1
Victoria Falls Ln
10000 HOUS 77075 4377 C1
Victoria Forest Dr
8600 HarC 77088 3542 D7
Victoria Garden Dr
1900 FBnC 77469 4234 C6
Victoria Glen Cir
100 WDLD 77384 2675 D5
Victoria Grove Ln
9900 HOUS 77075 4377 C1
Victoria Heights Ln
10000 HOUS 77075 4377 C2
Victoria Lakes Cir
17400 HarC 77379 3255 C3
Victoria Lakes Dr
- HarC 77379 3255 C3
- KATY 77493 3952 B1
800 KATY 77493 3813 B7
Victorian Ct
1000 SEBK 77586 4382 E7
Victorian Ln
100 HarC 77562 3831 E3
Victorian Manor Ln
3200 HarC 77047 4374 B4
Victorian Village Dr
8600 HOUS 77071 4239 B7
Victoria Park Ln
10000 HOUS 77075 4377 C1
Victoria Point Ln
9900 HOUS 77075 4377 C1
Victoria Ridge Ln
10000 HOUS 77075 4377 C1
Victoria Wood Wy
12400 HOUS 77089 4378 C7
12400 HOUS 77089 4505 C1
Victorious Dr
20400 HarC 77447 3106 A1
Victor's Chase Cir
10 FBnC 77479 4367 C6
E Victorson Av
1300 HarC 77015 3968 A2

STREET
Block City ZIP Map# Grid
W Victorson Av
1300 HarC 77015 3968 A2
Victory
7900 HarC 77049 3689 C7
Victory Av
2000 GLSN 77551 5108 B7
Victory Dr
- HOUS 77091 3682 D3
600 STAF 77477 4370 A4
4100 HOUS 77088 3682 D3
4100 HOUS 77088 3683 A3
N Victory Dr
700 HOUS 77088 3684 A3
900 HOUS 77088 3683 E3
S Victory Dr
- HOUS 77091 3684 B3
700 HOUS 77088 3684 A3
1100 HOUS 77088 3683 D3
Victory Ln
200 ALVN 77511 4749 C4
26800 ORDN 77386 2822 C6
E Victory Lake Dr
10 CNRO 77384 2675 E3
W Victory Lake Dr
10 CNRO 77384 2675 E3
Victory Terrace Ln
3600 FBnC 77450 4093 B6
Vida St
22800 GLSN 77554 5440 E6
Video St
3900 DKSN 77539 4754 A2
Viejo Dr
- FRDW 77546 4630 B5
E Viejo Dr
100 FRDW 77546 4630 B5
W Viejo Dr
100 FRDW 77546 4630 A7
Viejo Rd
1500 LGCY 77573 4632 A7
Vienna
- PASD 77502 4247 B2
Vienna Ct
11200 HarC 77429 3538 E1
Vienna Trails Ln
11200 HarC 77095 3538 B1
Viera Ln
8600 HOUS 77075 4376 E2
Vieta St
7900 HarC 77049 3689 E7
Vieux Carre
10 FBnC 77459 4621 C6
Vieux Carre Ct
10 FBnC 77459 4621 C6
Vieux Carre Dr
100 HOUS 77009 3963 B1
N View Ct
16200 MtgC 77302 2678 E4
View St
2200 PASD 77502 4247 B1
Viewfield Ct
13800 HOUS 77059 4379 D5
View Meadow Ln
13700 HOUS 77034 4378 D4
View Park Ln
7700 HarC 77095 3538 B7
Viewpoint Ct
4000 HarC 77449 3815 D2
View Pointe Ln
13800 HOUS 77034 4378 C4
Viewridge Dr
24800 FBnC 77494 3952 D4
Viilo Dr
- HarC 77038 3401 E7
- HarC 77066 3401 E7
Viking Dr
1600 HOUS 77018 3822 B1
3300 GLSN 77554 5220 D6
4300 HOUS 77092 3822 A1
5000 HOUS 77092 3821 E1
Viking Ln
10 SGLD 77477 4369 A2
10 SGLD 77478 4369 A2
10 STAF 77477 4369 A2
10 STAF 77478 4369 A2
Viking St
2200 BYTN 77520 3973 D5
Viking Landing Ct
3300 HarC 77388 3112 D4
Villa Dr
500 SEBK 77586 4510 A1
6900 HOUS 77061 4244 E3
6900 HOUS 77061 4245 A4
W Villa Dr
9900 HarC 77064 3540 C5
Villa Ln
3000 MSCY 77459 4496 E3
3000 MSCY 77459 4497 A3
N Villa Ln
- HarC 77377 3254 A4
E Villa St
4200 HOUS 77017 4105 E7
4400 HOUS 77017 4106 A7
Villa Arbor Dr
13500 HarC 77070 3399 E3
Villa Arca St
13400 HarC 77070 3399 E3
Villa Bella Ct
- LGCY 77573 4633 A5
Villa Bend Dr
10 HarC 77069 3256 C7
Villa Bergamo Ct
1100 HarC 77094 3955 B3
Villa Bergamo Ln
18900 HarC 77094 3955 C2
Villa Canyon Pl
10 WDLD 77382 2819 E2
Villa Capri Ln
1400 HOUS 77532 3266 C7
Villa Creek Dr
2200 HOUS 77339 3118 E5
2300 HOUS 77339 3119 A5
Villa Ct Dr
1000 TYLV 77586 4381 D7
Villa Del St
2600 FBnC 77478 4237 B4
Villa del Lago
1600 MSCY 77459 4497 D4
Villa del Lago Dr
1700 MSCY 77459 4497 C4
Villa del Norte Dr
16200 HarC 77073 3259 A5
Villa del Sol Dr
7000 HarC 77083 4096 A5
Villa de Matel Rd
800 HOUS 77023 4104 D2
Villa de Norte St
8000 HarC 77070 3399 D3

STREET
Block City ZIP Map# Grid
Villa Fontana Wy
16100 HarC 77068 3257 D5
Villa Forest
- HarC 77069 3256 C7
Village Cir
1800 PASD 77504 4247 E6
14600 HarC 77429 3397 D7
S Village Cir
3800 FBnC 77459 4622 A5
Village Cr
- HarC 77338 3261 E2
Village Ct
5800 HOUS 77092 3682 D6
10600 HarC 77065 3539 D2
21600 MtgC 77365 2973 B6
E Village Ct
1000 PASD 77506 4107 D6
13600 HarC 77083 4097 B6
S Village Ct
3800 FBnC 77459 4622 A5
W Village Ct
1000 PASD 77506 4107 D6
Village Dr
- CNRO 77301 2384 D3
- HarC 77373 3114 A2
- HarC 77449 3675 E5
200 SGLD 77478 4368 B2
16500 JRSV 77040 3540 B7
23600 MtgC 77365 2973 B6
25000 MtgC 77357 2974 D1
W Village Dr
12200 HarC 77039 3546 E5
Village Ln
3000 DRPK 77536 4109 C7
4600 BYTN 77521 3972 A2
5400 HarC 77521 3972 A2
21600 MtgC 77365 2973 B5
Village Pkwy
6100 HOUS 77005 4102 A3
Village Rd
35400 WlrC 77445 3099 E4
35400 WlrC 77445 3100 A4
Village St
14600 HarC 77429 3397 D7
Village Ter
8400 HarC 77040 3541 A6
Village Wk
- HarC 77532 3552 E4
Village Wy
2900 PASD 77502 4247 C2
7000 HOUS 77087 4105 A5
16600 MtgC 77302 2825 E2
Village Arbour Dr
5600 KATY 77493 3813 C4
Village Bell Ln
9700 HarC 77038 3543 E5
Village Bend Ln
10900 HOUS 77072 4098 C6
Village Birch St
14100 HOUS 77062 4379 E6
Village Branch Ln
17900 FBnC 77469 4095 D6
Village Breeze Dr
17300 HarC 77377 3254 B4
Villagebriar Ln
6000 HarC 77084 3678 C3
Village Bridge Dr
6700 HarC 77346 3408 E1
Village Brook Dr
- HOUS 77062 4507 C1
- MSCY 77459 4497 D4
Village Brook Ln
2900 PRLD 77584 4500 A4
Village Center Ct
9200 HarC 77064 3540 C5
Village Center Dr
13800 HarC 77069 3400 A2
Village Chase Ctr
- HarC 77084 3815 E7
- HarC 77449 3815 E7
- HOUS 77449 3815 E7
Village Chase Dr
- HarC 77084 3816 A6
19800 HarC 77084 3815 E6
19800 HarC 77449 3815 E6
19800 HOUS 77449 3815 E6
Village Cir Dr
2600 KATY 77493 3813 C4
Village Club Dr
- RSBG 77469 4492 A5
- RSBG 77471 4492 A5
Village Commons Dr
17300 HarC 77377 3254 B4
Village Corner Ct
16800 PASD 77059 4380 E4
Village Corner Dr
- HOUS 77059 4380 D5
3800 PASD 77059 4380 D5
Village Creek Dr
300 HOUS 77598 4506 E5
5000 PRLD 77584 4503 A7
Village Creek Lp
28900 MtgC 77386 2970 A2
Village Creek Tr
- HarC 77377 3254 B4
Village Crest Ct
12500 HarC 77377 3254 B4
Village Crest Dr
100 FBnC 77469 4493 B6
Village Crossing Ln
21300 MtgC 77365 2973 A2
Village Crossing Tr
2000 HarC 77373 3114 E5
Village Ct Blvd
1300 RSBG 77471 4491 C5
Village Ct Cir
1500 RSBG 77471 4491 C5
Village Ct Dr
1600 RSBG 77471 4491 C5
2600 KATY 77493 3813 C4
Village Ct Ln
1700 RSBG 77471 4491 C5
Village Dale Av
2100 HOUS 77059 4379 D5
Villagedale Dr
3200 HOUS 77339 3119 C4
Village Dogwood Ct
19000 HarC 77084 3677 D7
Village Elm St
14900 HOUS 77062 4380 B6
Village Estates Dr
- HOUS 77339 3118 E7
Village Evergreen Tr
14500 HOUS 77062 4506 C1
Village Falls Ct
3200 HOUS 77339 3119 A5
Village Garden Dr
1300 MSCY 77459 4369 C5

STREET
Block City ZIP Map# Grid
Village Gate Dr
12800 HOUS 77082 4097 C2
Village Green Ct
1500 HOUS 77077 3957 E5
Village Green Dr
5500 KATY 77493 3813 C4
17300 JRSV 77040 3540 A7
17400 JRSV 77065 3540 A7
Village Grove Dr
- PRLD 77581 4502 E1
3600 HarC 77396 3407 E3
Village Heights Ct
4400 PASD 77505 4249 A6
Village Hill Dr
10 CNRO 77304 2383 A2
Village Hill Ln
10 CNRO 77304 2383 B2
Village Hills Dr
8800 HarC 77379 3255 E4
Village Hollow Ln
8400 HarC 77072 4097 C7
E Village Knoll Cir
10 WDLD 77381 2820 D3
N Village Knoll Cir
100 WDLD 77381 2820 D2
S Village Knoll Cir
10 WDLD 77381 2820 C3
W Village Knoll Cir
100 WDLD 77381 2820 C3
Village Knoll Pl
10 WDLD 77381 2820 D2
Village Lake Ct
3600 FBnC 77459 4622 B4
Village Lake Dr
7100 HarC 77433 3677 A1
10300 FBnC 77459 4621 E4
10300 FBnC 77459 4622 A5
Village Leaf Dr
2300 MtgC 77386 2969 B4
Village Manor Dr
3700 HOUS 77345 3119 D3
Village Maple Ct
19000 HarC 77084 3816 B4
Village Meadow Ct
18400 HarC 77377 3254 A2
Village Mill Ln
7600 FBnC 77469 4095 C6
Village Mills Dr
2700 PRLD 77584 4503 A4
Village Mist
- HarC 77038 3543 E5
Village Oak Dr
2600 KATY 77493 3813 C4
Village Oaks Ct
28400 MtgC 77355 2815 C2
Village Oaks Dr
3300 HOUS 77339 3119 A5
Village Oaks Ln
10 SPVL 77055 3820 E7
Village of Bridgestone Ln
19500 HarC 77379 3112 B5
Village of Fondren Dr
8600 HOUS 77071 4239 B7
Village of Kings Lake Blvd
12100 HarC 77044 3549 A6
12200 HarC 77044 3548 E5
Village Park Cir
11800 BKHV 77024 3959 B2
11800 HOUS 77024 3959 B2
Village Park Dr
- HOUS 77345 3119 D4
1900 MSCY 77459 4370 B5
3100 HOUS 77339 3119 C4
4500 PASD 77504 4247 E6
5600 KATY 77493 3813 C4
Village Pine Dr
3600 HOUS 77339 3119 C5
Village Pl Dr
11500 HOUS 77077 3958 B7
Village Point Ln
13900 FBnC 77478 4237 A3
Village Pond Ln
3100 FBnC 77545 4498 B6
Village Ridge Dr
19700 HarC 77375 3109 D6
Village Rose Dr
8400 HarC 77072 4097 C4
Village Rose Ln
8400 HarC 77072 4097 C7
Village Springs Ct
3100 HOUS 77339 3119 B2
Village Springs Dr
5000 HOUS 77339 3119 B1
5500 MtgC 77365 3119 B1
Village Square Dr
800 TMBL 77375 2964 A7
2500 MSCY 77489 4370 C7
12700 HOUS 77077 3957 C5
Village Tower Dr
17900 HarC 77338 3407 D1
17900 HarC 77396 3407 D1
Village Townhome Dr
1500 PASD 77504 4247 D6
Village Trace Dr
16700 HOUS 77053 4371 D7
Village Trail Dr
10500 HarC 77065 3539 D2
Village Tree Wy
19800 HarC 77084 3815 E4
Village View Dr
4400 MSCY 77459 4369 C5
Village View Tr
16500 FBnC 77478 4236 A6
Village Walk Ct
4000 HOUS 77345 3119 E5
Village Wells Dr
3800 HarC 77396 3408 A2
3900 HarC 77346 3408 A3
Village Woods Dr
3100 HOUS 77339 3119 C4
15400 MtgC 77302 2824 E1
Village Wy Dr
2500 KATY 77493 3813 C4
12800 HarC 77041 3679 D4
Villa Glen Dr
3600 HOUS 77088 3683 A1
Villagrove Dr
13900 HarC 77049 3689 E6
Villa Heights Dr
11500 HarC 77066 3401 A7
Villa Hill Dr
4200 HOUS 77345 3119 D5
Villa Hills Dr
5900 HarC 77066 3401 A5
6000 HarC 77066 3400 E5
Villa Lago Ln
8000 HarC 77070 3399 D3

STREET
Block City ZIP Map# Grid
Villa Lake Dr
7800 HarC 77095 3538 D7
Villa Lea Dr
11800 HOUS 77071 4239 D5
Villa Lea Ln
10000 HOUS 77071 4239 D2
Villandry Ln
8100 HarC 77338 3261 E3
Villanova St
3800 SSPL 77005 4101 C4
4100 WUNP 77005 4101 C4
Villanova Park Dr
- PASD 77058 4380 E6
N Villa Oaks Dr
10 WDLD 77382 2674 C3
Villa Palmas St
13500 HarC 77070 3399 E3
Villa Palms Dr
7800 HarC 77095 3538 D7
Villa Park Dr
3200 HOUS 77339 3119 B4
Villa Pines Dr
3700 HOUS 77339 3119 C5
Villa Pisa Ln
- LGCY 77573 4632 E3
Villaret Dr
16200 HarC 77083 4096 A5
16300 FBnC 77083 4095 E5
Villa Ridge Dr
3800 HarC 77068 3257 B6
Villa Rose Dr
2200 HOUS 77062 4380 C7
Villarreal Dr
6600 HOUS 77489 4371 C5
Villa Verde Dr
9900 HarC 77064 3540 C3
Villawood Ln
12900 HOUS 77072 4097 C6
Villa Wy Dr
17800 HarC 77379 3257 C1
Villeroy Wy
10 WDLD 77382 2820 A1
Villita St
9600 HOUS 77013 3826 E6
9600 HOUS 77013 3827 A6
Villmont Ln
1200 HOUS 77077 3958 A5
Vilven Ln
9500 HOUS 77080 3820 C4
Vina Glen Dr
- HarC 77379 3255 E5
Vinca Ct
13200 HarC 77429 3254 A7
Vinca Tr
10 WDLD 77382 2673 D4
Vinca Ranch Dr
3200 FBnC 77494 3953 A6
Vince St
1000 PASD 77506 4107 A6
2000 PASD 77502 4107 A7
2000 PASD 77502 4247 A1
Vincennes Oak St
15000 HarC 77429 3253 C3
Vincent Ct
10 WDLD 77382 2819 B2
Vincent St
1000 HOUS 77009 3824 B5
Vincent Crossing Dr
- MtgC 77386 2969 D1
Vinces Bridge St
1900 SGLD 77478 4368 E5
Vindale Dr
14000 HarC 77044 3689 E3
Vindon Dr
12500 HOUS 77024 3958 E2
Vine Av
1300 CNRO 77301 2384 D6
Vine Cir
25400 MtgC 77372 2536 E1
25400 MtgC 77372 2537 A1
Vine Dr
8600 HOUS 77489 4497 D1
Vine Ln
4700 FBnC 77545 4623 C3
Vine St
- CNRO 77303 2237 E6
10 WDBR 77357 2828 C1
1000 BYTN 77520 3973 D7
1000 HOUS 77002 3963 D2
Vine Arbor St
8800 HOUS 77033 4244 A4
Vine Branch Ln
- FBnC 77494 4092 D3
Vinebriar Dr
30200 MtgC 77386 2969 D2
Vinebrook Rd
10 WDLD 77380 2968 A1
Vinechase Dr
25400 MtgC 77365 3118 A2
Vine Creek Dr
2300 HOUS 77345 3120 A6
Vinecrest Dr
- HarC 77086 3542 A1
3800 BzaC 77584 4501 D6
Vinedale Dr
11400 HOUS 77099 4238 B4
Vine Forest Dr
- HarC 77346 3408 C1
Vinegate Ln
- HarC 77377 3254 A3
Vine Grove Ct
7400 HarC 77433 3677 C1
Vinehill Dr
13800 SGLD 77478 4237 A6
14000 SGLD 77478 4236 E6
Vineland Ct
- NSUB 77058 4508 A5
Vineland Ln
- NSUB 77058 4508 A5
Vinemead Ct
2200 HarC 77450 3954 E6
Vinemont Ln
5700 HarC 77084 3678 B4
Vinemoss Ln
15800 HarC 77429 3252 B6
Vine River St
- FBnC 77478 4237 A4
Vinery Ct
13200 HarC 77429 3254 A5
Vinery Ln
13700 HarC 77429 3254 A5
Vinetree Ln
9200 HarC 77040 3681 E2
Vinett Av
5100 HOUS 77017 4106 B5
Vinewood Cir
6900 HOUS 77088 3682 D3

STREET
Block City ZIP Map# Grid
Vinewood Dr
6100 HOUS 77088 3682 D3
Vinewood Ln
6100 LGCY 77573 4630 B5
7300 HOUS 77072 4097 C6
Vineyard Ct
2200 SGLD 77478 4237 A5
Vineyard Dr
3400 HarC 77082 4096 B4
3400 HOUS 77082 4096 B3
Vineyard Bend Ct
1900 PRLD 77581 4502 D1
Vineyard Bend Dr
6000 PRLD 77581 4502 D1
Vineyard Bend Ln
- FBnC 77450 4093 D1
Vineyard Falls Dr
13200 HarC 77083 4097 C7
Vineyard Hill Ct
1900 PRLD 77581 4502 E1
Vineyard Hill Dr
5800 PRLD 77581 4502 E1
Vineyard Park Dr
13200 HarC 77083 4097 C7
Vineyard Trail Ln
12500 SGLD 77478 4237 D5
Viney Creek Dr
15900 HarC 77095 3538 C6
Viney Grove Dr
13900 HOUS 77048 4374 D4
Vining Rd
30100 HarC 77484 2957 C7
Vinkins Ct
12400 HOUS 77071 4239 C6
Vinkins Rd
8600 HOUS 77071 4239 B6
Vinland Dr
18100 NSUB 77058 4508 A5
Vinland Shores Ct
5900 HarC 77379 3111 E6
Vinson St
7300 HOUS 77088 3683 C3
Vinsonia Av
- HOUS 77571 4112 C7
- MRGP 77571 4112 C7
200 MRGP 77571 4252 C1
Vinta St
2100 HOUS 77034 4246 D5
Vintage Cir
2400 FBnC 77469 4365 C1
Vintage St
- HOUS 77026 3824 E5
3000 HOUS 77026 3825 A5
Vintage Centre Dr
- HarC 77069 3400 A2
Vintage Creek Dr
- HarC 77379 3256 B3
Vintage Falls Dr
15400 HarC 77433 3251 B7
Vintage Grove Ct
4800 HarC 77449 3676 E7
Vintage Knoll Ln
23700 HarC 77373 3114 E5
Vintage Lakes Dr
15600 HarC 77070 3255 C7
Vintage Leaf Cir
12300 HarC 77070 3399 A5
Vintage Mill Ct
13000 FBnC 77469 4366 D1
Vintage Oak Ln
15300 FBnC 77478 4236 C5
Vintage Oak St
17200 MtgC 77385 2676 C6
Vintage Path Dr
10 WDLD 77381 2821 E1
10 WDLD 77384 2821 E1
Vintage Path Pl
10 WDLD 77384 2821 D1
Vintage Point Dr
- FBnC 77450 3953 C6
Vintage Springs Ln
- HarC 77070 3255 C6
Vintage Valley Dr
3900 HarC 77082 4096 D4
Vintage Villa Dr
9800 HarC 77070 3255 B6
Vintage Wood Cir
8300 HarC 77379 3256 C3
Vintage Wood Ln
17200 HarC 77379 3256 A3
18300 HarC 77379 3255 E2
Vinton Ct
8400 HarC 77040 3541 C6
Vinton Ln
21800 SGCH 77355 2960 E3
Vinvale Rd
12600 HarC 77066 3400 B4
Viny Ridge Dr
8200 FBnC 77083 4096 C7
Viol Ct
1000 HarC 77532 3552 A1
Viola Ct
12000 MtgC 77362 2963 C1
Viola Dr
2200 LGCY 77573 4508 C7
2200 LGCY 77573 4632 C1
Viola Bloom Ct
10 WDLD 77382 2819 B2
Viola Dale Ct
20400 HarC 77338 3261 B4
Violet Ct
27400 MtgC 77354 2817 D4
Violet St
100 CNRO 77301 2384 D6
2300 PASD 77503 4248 A2
Violet Haze Tr
21400 HarC 77433 3250 E4
21400 HarC 77433 3251 C3
Violet Meadow Ln
- FBnC 77494 4093 A1
Violet Path Ln
5500 HOUS 77085 4241 A7
5600 HOUS 77085 4240 E7
Violetta Ct
10 WDLD 77384 2821 E1
Violet View Dr
8000 HarC 77562 3832 D3
Vionett Ln
600 TXCY 77591 4873 E5
N Vionett Ln
600 TXCY 77591 4873 E5
Vira Ct
13600 HarC 77014 3401 D2
Vira Ln
13700 HarC 77014 3401 D2
Vireo
24700 HarC 77447 3104 D5

STREET
Block City ZIP Map# Grid
Virgie Community Rd
100 MtgC 77354 2963 D1
100 MtgC 77354 2964 A1
Virgil St
100 PASD 77502 4246 E2
100 SHUS 77502 4246 E2
100 SHUS 77587 4246 E2
7700 HOUS 77088 3683 D3
Virgina St
3000 LMQU 77568 4873 C7
Virginia Av
- DRPK 77536 4249 A1
100 SHUS 77587 4246 B3
1400 HOUS 77017 4246 B4
1400 HOUS 77587 4246 B4
1400 SHUS 77017 4246 B4
2000 GlsC 77539 4632 E7
2000 LGCY 77539 4632 E7
2800 DKSN 77539 4753 E1
2800 LGCY 77573 4632 D6
2900 DKSN 77539 4754 A1
5900 HTCK 77563 4989 D5
N Virginia Av
100 LPRT 77571 4251 D2
S Virginia Av
100 LPRT 77571 4251 E3
W Virginia Av
400 HOUS 77076 3684 D5
Virginia Ct
6400 SSPL 77005 4101 E4
6400 WUNP 77005 4101 E4
Virginia Dr
100 FBnC 77545 4623 B3
100 FBnC 77583 4623 B3
5000 FBnC 77469 4234 A3
Virginia Ln
100 CNRO 77304 2383 B4
300 FRDW 77546 4505 A7
1800 PASD 77502 4107 D7
8000 HarC 77095 3539 A7
24900 MtgC 77365 3118 E2
Virginia Pl
25700 MtgC 77355 2814 B5
Virginia Pt
- GlsC 77554 5106 D3
200 GlsC 77563 5106 E3
200 TXCY 77563 5106 E3
200 TXCY 77590 5106 E3
Virginia St
- HOUS 77054 4103 A6
2600 BYTN 77520 4112 A1
2700 HOUS 77019 3962 A7
2700 HOUS 77098 3962 A7
2800 HOUS 77054 4102 E6
Virginia Colony Dr
2700 HarC 77598 4506 C7
2700 HarC 77598 4630 C1
Virginia Fern Wy
15700 HOUS 77059 4380 B3
Virginia Fields Dr
6300 FBnC 77494 4092 A6
Virginia Grace Dr
16300 FBnC 77478 4236 A2
Virginia Point Rd
- GlsC 77563 5106 D3
100 TXCY 77563 5106 E3
100 TXCY 77590 5106 E3
Virginia Water Ln
7600 HarC 77095 3539 B7
7600 HarC 77095 3679 B1
Virgin Island Dr
3300 SGLD 77479 4496 A2
N Virkus Ct
3800 FBnC 77459 4621 B5
S Virkus Ct
3700 FBnC 77459 4621 B5
Virline Ln
12100 HarC 77067 3402 B4
Virtue Ct
2000 LGCY 77573 4631 B7
Viscaro Ln
9200 HarC 77396 3406 E6
9200 HarC 77396 3407 A6
Visconti Ct
10900 FBnC 77469 4093 A7
10900 FBnC 77469 4233 A1
Viscount Rd
18200 HOUS 77032 3404 E2
Vision Ln
5600 HOUS 77048 4375 B1
Vision Park Blvd
100 SHEH 77384 2821 E1
100 SHEH 77384 2822 A1
Vista Av
500 BYTN 77520 3973 B6
Vista Blvd
4000 GLSN 77554 5332 D3
Vista Dr
3000 RSBG 77469 4492 A5
3000 RSBG 77471 4492 A5
3300 RSBG 77469 4491 E6
3300 RSBG 77471 4491 E6
N Vista Dr
100 HarC 77073 3258 E5
100 HarC 77090 3258 E5
1100 HarC 77073 3259 B4
Vista Ln
3000 PRLD 77584 4503 A5
Vista Rd
100 SHUS 77504 4247 B4
100 SHUS 77587 4247 B4
1400 PASD 77504 4247 E4
4300 PASD 77504 4248 A4
4500 PASD 77505 4248 A4
Vista Bay Ln
12200 HarC 77041 3679 E5
Vista Bend Dr
800 HarC 77073 3259 B5
Vista Brook Dr
13100 HarC 77041 3679 C1
Vista Camino Dr
6200 HarC 77083 4096 D4
Vista Cove Cir
10 WDLD 77381 2821 B5
Vista Cove Dr
10 WDLD 77381 2821 B5
Vista Creek Dr
1000 SGLD 77478 4368 B4
Vistadale Ct
8400 HarC 77338 3262 A3
Vistadale Dr
8300 HarC 77338 3261 E2
8300 HarC 77338 3262 A3
Vista del Lago Dr
- HarC 77336 2975 C7
- HarC 77336 3120 E1
300 HarC 77336 3121 B2

STREET Block	City	ZIP	Map#	Grid
Vista del Mar Dr				
15900	HarC	77083	4096	A5
22300	GLSN	77554	5441	A6
Vista del Rancho Dr				
-	HOUS	77083	4096	D7
8000	HarC	77083	4096	D7
Vista del Rio				
1400	FBnC	77469	4364	D3
Vista del Sol Dr				
8000	FBnC	77083	4096	C7
Vista de Oro St				
13500	HarC	77070	3399	E3
S Vistaglen Lp				
14300	HarC	77084	3679	A5
W Vistaglen Lp				
5600	HarC	77084	3679	A4
Vista Grande Dr				
6300	HarC	77082	4096	C4
6300	HarC	77083	4096	C4
Vista Grove Cir				
700	HarC	77073	3259	C6
Vista Heights Dr				
14900	HarC	77433	3251	B7
Vista Lake Ct				
2000	SGLD	77478	4368	E5
19700	HarC	77433	3677	A1
Vista Lake Dr				
3200	SGLD	77478	4368	E6
Vista Manor Dr				
2200	HOUS	77339	3119	A4
Vista Mar Cir				
14100	HarC	77095	3539	B7
Vista Mill Pl				
10	WDLD	77382	2674	D5
Vistamont Dr				
15000	FBnC	77083	4236	C1
Vista Norte Ct				
10800	HOUS	77076	3685	B4
Vista Oak Dr				
16500	HarC	77073	3259	A5
Vista Oro Dr				
13100	HarC	77041	3539	C7
Vista Point Dr				
2100	HOUS	77045	4242	D7
Vista Real				
12200	STFE	77510	4987	B2
Vista Ridge Dr				
4300	HOUS	77339	3119	B3
Vista Springs Dr				
8800	HarC	77379	3255	E4
8800	HarC	77379	3256	A4
Vista Trace Lp				
20900	HarC	77073	3259	C6
Vista Trail Ct				
21000	HarC	77073	3259	B6
Vista Valley Dr				
22500	HarC	77450	3953	E4
Vista Verde St				
7600	HOUS	77087	4245	B1
Vista Village Ln				
4900	HOUS	77092	3683	A7
W Vistawood Ct				
1300	HOUS	77077	3958	B5
E Vistawood Dr				
1300	HOUS	77077	3958	B5
W Vistawood Dr				
1300	HOUS	77077	3958	B4
Vista Wy Dr				
-	HarC	77429	3397	D3
E Vita Cir				
11900	HarC	77070	3399	D7
N Vita Cir				
9800	HarC	77070	3399	C6
W Vita Cir				
11900	HarC	77070	3399	C6
Vitry Ln				
12500	MSCY	77071	4239	E7
Viva Ln				
6600	BzaC	77583	4623	E7
Vivian Av				
900	PASD	77506	4107	D5
Vivian Ct				
19000	HarC	77379	3110	E7
Vivian Rd				
3100	HOUS	77093	3686	A2
3900	HarC	77093	3686	B2
Vivian St				
-	CRLS	77565	4509	C6
900	GlsC	77565	4509	C6
4300	BLAR	77401	4101	C6
4300	HOUS	77401	4101	B6
Vivian Point Ln				
16700	HarC	77095	3538	A2
Viviene Westmoreland Dr				
12900	HarC	77429	3397	B4
Vizsla Dr				
-	HarC	77530	3829	E3
Vlanda				
25000	FBnC	77494	3953	A7
Vobe Ct				
22100	HarC	77449	3815	A6
22300	HarC	77449	3814	E6
Vogel Rd				
7000	HOUS	77088	3683	A4
7000	HOUS	77091	3683	A4
Vogt Rd				
10500	HarC	77375	2965	A3
Vogue Ln				
-	HOUS	77080	3821	A4
8300	HOUS	77055	3821	A4
9500	HOUS	77080	3820	C4
Voight St				
1000	HOUS	77007	3962	E1
1000	HOUS	77009	3962	E1
Volga Dr				
22800	MtgC	77365	2972	A4
Volley St				
4800	HOUS	77022	3684	C7
Volley Vale Ct				
19000	HarC	77346	3265	C6
Vollmer Rd				
2700	HOUS	77092	3822	B4
Volney St				
100	SHUS	77587	4246	D3
200	LMQU	77568	4873	A7
200	LMQU	77568	4989	A1
Volta				
8300	HOUS	77338	3261	E6
Volta Dr				
8400	HOUS	77338	3261	E6
8600	HOUS	77338	3262	A6
Voltaire Dr				
11200	HarC	77065	3398	B7
11200	HarC	77065	3539	A1
Volunteer				
-	HOUS	77072	4097	E6
Volunteer Ln				
300	MtgC	77380	2968	B2
Volvo Ct				
800	HarC	77396	3407	A4
Vonard St				
5100	HarC	77088	3542	E6
Vonnet				
15400	HarC	77530	3829	E7
Vonnet Dr				
-	HarC	77530	3829	E7
15500	HarC	77530	3830	A7
Vorgen Ct				
7200	HarC	77379	3111	B2
Voss Pkwy				
-	HNCV	77024	3960	A1
Voss Rd				
-	SPVL	77024	3960	A2
-	SPVL	77055	3960	A1
200	HNCV	77024	3960	A4
200	HOUS	77057	3960	A4
900	HDWV	77024	3960	A2
1000	SPVL	77055	3821	A7
14700	FBnC	77478	4236	D6
14700	SGLD	77478	4236	D6
S Voss Rd				
800	HNCV	77024	3960	A5
800	HNCV	77057	3960	A4
800	HOUS	77024	3960	A5
800	HOUS	77057	3960	A7
1300	HOUS	77063	3960	A7
Vossdale Rd				
2600	HOUS	77027	3961	B7
3100	HOUS	77027	4101	B1
Voss Park Dr				
10	HNCV	77024	3960	A1
Votaw Ln				
7400	HOUS	77088	3683	A3
Vought Rd				
31600	MtgC	77354	2671	B7
Voyager Dr				
700	HOUS	77062	4507	A4
Vrana Rd				
10400	HarC	77049	3691	A3
Vuitton Ln				
13200	HarC	77044	3689	C4
Vuskou Ct				
28000	MtgC	77386	2970	C5
W				
Wabash Dr				
22800	MtgC	77365	2972	A3
Wabash Elm St				
1100	HarC	77073	3259	B5
Waco Av				
200	LGCY	77573	4632	A3
400	LGCY	77573	4631	E3
Waco St				
300	CNRO	77301	2384	A4
600	CNRO	77301	2383	E4
1600	SHUS	77587	4246	C4
2200	HOUS	77020	3964	B2
2300	HOUS	77026	3825	B7
2300	HOUS	77026	3964	B1
2600	HarC	77521	3832	D4
Waco Fall Dr				
-	HarC	77067	3401	D4
Waco Trails Cir				
9100	HarC	77433	3537	B5
N Wade Cir				
2200	CNRO	77304	2383	C6
S Wade Cir				
2200	CNRO	77304	2383	C6
W Wade Cir				
100	CNRO	77304	2383	B6
Wade Rd				
-	BYTN	77520	3971	E1
-	WlrC	77363	2813	B1
-	WlrC	77447	2813	B1
5100	BYTN	77521	3971	E1
5100	HarC	77521	3971	E1
5400	HarC	77521	3832	D5
7700	HarC	77562	3832	D2
Wade St				
3800	STFE	77517	4870	C6
Wadebridge Wy				
13900	HarC	77015	3828	E6
13900	HarC	77015	3829	A6
Wade Hampton Dr				
800	HNCV	77024	3960	B1
Wading River Dr				
19200	HarC	77375	3109	E7
Wadlington Dr				
14400	HarC	77044	3549	D1
Wadsworth St				
1400	HarC	77015	3968	C3
Wafer Dr				
-	PLEK	77469	4615	A6
Wafer St				
100	PASD	77506	4107	B3
1200	PASD	77502	4107	B7
N Wafer St				
100	PASD	77506	4107	B3
Wagers St				
100	CNRO	77301	2384	A7
Wages St				
9900	HOUS	77093	3686	A5
Wagganer Dr				
17200	HarC	77447	3249	D4
Wagg Wy Rd				
-	HarC	77041	3539	B5
-	HarC	77095	3539	B5
Wagley				
5600	HOUS	77036	4099	D3
Wagner				
12800	GlsC	77510	4870	E1
12800	GlsC	77510	4871	A1
Wagner Ct				
-	GlsC	77510	4871	A2
-	STFE	77510	4871	A2
Wagner St				
1200	HOUS	77007	3962	D2
1600	HOUS	77034	4379	A3
Wagner Wy				
6300	FBnC	77479	4367	B5
13200	STFE	77510	4870	E7
Wagon				
-	FBnC	77469	4616	E7
Wagon Rd				
3700	DKSN	77539	4753	E3
15600	HOUS	77060	3544	B2
Wagon Run				
2400	SGLD	77479	4368	D6
Wagon Tr				
14700	PRLD	77581	4502	E5
14700	PRLD	77584	4502	E5
18300	MtgC	77302	2825	D2
Wagon Gap Tr				
1400	HarC	77090	3258	A3
1800	HarC	77090	3257	E3
Wagon Point Dr				
100	HarC	77073	3258	E3
200	HOUS	77090	3258	D3
Wagon Trail Dr				
3000	SGLD	77479	4368	E7
3000	SGLD	77479	4495	E1
Wagon Trail Rd				
10300	HarC	77064	3540	B5
16000	PRLD	77584	4502	E6
Wagonwheel Cir				
6200	HOUS	77088	3682	C3
Wagon Wheel Ct				
15700	MtgC	77302	2679	D3
25200	WlrC	77447	2813	D1
Wagon Wheel Dr				
27300	MtgC	77372	2683	D2
Wagon Wheel Ln				
5400	RSBG	77469	4615	E1
Wagonwheel Ln				
6700	HOUS	77088	3682	C3
Wagon Wheel Rd				
15900	SGCH	77355	2815	E7
Wagonwheel Wy				
18800	MtgC	77355	2815	A6
Wahini Wy				
1300	TKIS	77554	5106	B4
Wahl St				
500	HarC	77532	3552	D4
W Wahl St				
100	HarC	77532	3552	C4
Wahl Manor Ct				
8200	FBnC	77083	4096	D7
Wahoo Cir				
9300	TXCY	77591	4872	E3
Wahoo St				
19700	HarC	77532	3410	A3
Wahrenberger Rd				
9300	MtgC	77304	2382	B5
Waialae Cir				
4600	PASD	77505	4248	E6
Wainfleet Ln				
11000	HOUS	77096	4240	A4
Wainscot Ct				
11700	HarC	77038	3543	B5
Wainsfield Ln				
14900	HarC	77530	3829	C5
Wainwright St				
500	HOUS	77022	3824	C2
Waiting Spring Cir				
16200	HarC	77095	3538	C5
Waiting Spring Ln				
8500	HarC	77095	3538	C5
Wake Ct				
17700	HarC	77532	3411	B7
Wakefield Ct				
2800	BzaC	77584	4501	D4
Wakefield Dr				
300	LGCY	77573	4631	E3
700	HOUS	77018	3823	B2
1000	HOUS	77018	3822	E2
Wakefield Mdw				
21100	FBnC	77469	4094	B7
Wakefield Wy				
18500	MtgC	77306	2534	B7
Wakefield Meadow Ln				
7200	FBnC	77469	4094	B6
Wakefield Village Dr				
9500	HarC	77095	3537	D3
Wake Forest Dr				
1900	DRPK	77536	4108	E6
Wakeforest St				
-	HOUS	77098	3962	A7
3600	HOUS	77098	4102	A1
4800	HOUS	77005	4102	A1
4800	WUNP	77005	4102	A2
Wakerobin Ct				
10	WDLD	77380	2822	A7
Wakeshire Dr				
4000	DRPK	77536	4249	A1
Wake Village Dr				
15500	HarC	77546	4505	D5
Walbrook Dr				
800	HOUS	77062	4506	E2
800	HOUS	77062	4507	A2
14800	FBnC	77478	4236	D3
Walbury Dr				
-	HarC	77084	3677	D6
Walcott Dr				
1000	HMBL	77396	3406	C2
Walcott Ln				
2400	HOUS	77088	3683	B3
Walcott Mills Dr				
5600	HarC	77379	3257	A2
Wald Rd				
8800	HOUS	77034	4247	A7
8800	HOUS	77034	4378	A1
Waldemar Dr				
11900	HOUS	77077	3958	A6
12000	HOUS	77077	3957	E6
Waldemere Dr				
13000	HOUS	77077	3957	B7
Walden Cir				
1100	SGLD	77478	4237	A7
Walden Dr				
3500	PRLD	77584	4501	C1
Walden Ln				
6000	LGCY	77573	4630	C7
11400	PNPV	77024	3959	E5
Walden Wy				
22500	HarC	77375	3110	B2
Walden Creek Ct				
1700	PRLD	77581	4503	D1
Walden Creek Ln				
3400	PRLD	77581	4503	D1
N Walden Elms Cir				
10	WDLD	77382	2674	A4
S Walden Elms Cir				
100	WDLD	77382	2674	A4
Walden Elms Dr				
-	WDLD	77382	2674	B4
Walden Forest Dr				
19100	HarC	77346	3265	B6
Walden Gate Ln				
18200	HarC	77433	3537	D7
Walden Glen Cir				
18600	HarC	77346	3265	C7
Walden Green Ln				
13200	HOUS	77085	4371	D1
Walden Grove Ln				
21300	HarC	77450	3954	C5
Walden Park Ct				
15100	HarC	77049	3829	A3
Walden Park Ln				
-	FBnC	77479	4496	D5
-	MSCY	77459	4496	D5
-	MSCY	77479	4496	D5
Walden Point Ct				
-	HarC	77377	3253	E2
Walden Woods				
3300	HOUS	77365	2974	E6
Walder Ct				
20900	HarC	77449	3676	D3
Walderford Dr				
-	HOUS	77450	3953	D1
22900	HarC	77450	3953	D1
Waldine St				
14500	HarC	77015	3968	B2
Waldo Dr				
-	HOUS	77036	4099	C6
Waldo Rd				
3700	HOUS	77063	4099	C2
Waldo St				
-	HOUS	77036	4099	C4
Waldridge Dr				
26000	FBnC	77469	4092	B7
Waldridge Oak Ln				
20900	MtgC	77365	3117	D2
Waldron Cir				
15500	HarC	77084	3678	D3
Waldron Dr				
6400	HarC	77084	3678	D3
Waldwick Dr				
15300	HarC	77070	3254	E6
15300	HarC	77377	3254	E6
Walenta Av				
1300	RSBG	77471	4490	D7
Wales Ct				
16100	HarC	77379	3256	D4
Waleston Ct				
21700	MtgC	77339	3118	B6
Walford Dr				
17100	HarC	77379	3255	E4
Walford Mill Ln				
9700	HarC	77095	3537	E4
Walger Av				
800	RSBG	77471	4490	D5
Walhalla Dr				
3200	HarC	77066	3401	E6
Walham Ct				
4400	HOUS	77345	3119	D6
Walid Ln				
5500	RSBG	77471	4491	D4
Waling Dr				
-	BzaC	77511	4748	B6
Walk Dr				
11200	HOUS	77076	3684	E3
Walkabout Cir				
4100	MSCY	77459	4496	C4
Walkabout Wy				
5600	FBnC	77450	4094	B3
Walker				
10000	HarC	77064	3541	C2
Walker Ct				
2400	PRLD	77581	4502	E3
Walker Dr				
5600	PRLD	77581	4502	E3
Walker Rd				
3200	BYTN	77521	3973	C4
12900	MtgC	77302	2824	C2
27000	WlrC	77447	2959	C5
Walker St				
-	HOUS	77019	3963	A4
-	LGCY	77573	4632	A7
-	LGCY	77573	4753	A1
200	HOUS	77002	3963	A4
700	LMQU	77568	4989	B1
1000	HOUS	77010	3963	C4
1800	LGCY	77573	4631	E6
3500	HOUS	77003	3963	E6
3800	HOUS	77023	3964	A6
7300	HOUS	77011	4105	A1
7400	HOUS	77023	4105	A1
10000	HarC	77064	3541	C2
13300	STFE	77510	4870	D5
27000	HarC	77447	3248	D3
E Walker St				
100	LGCY	77573	4632	B3
W Walker St				
100	LGCY	77573	4631	E4
100	LGCY	77573	4632	A4
1900	HOUS	77019	3962	E4
Walker Lake Ln				
12800	HarC	77346	3408	D3
Walkers Pk N				
6000	FBnC	77479	4367	A6
Walkers Pk S				
6000	FBnC	77479	4367	A6
Walker School Rd				
800	FBnC	77479	4367	B6
Walkers Forest Dr				
7200	HOUS	77088	3683	A3
Walkers Park Dr				
6000	FBnC	77479	4367	A6
Walking Stick Tr				
10	FBnC	77459	4621	B3
Walksew St				
14000	HOUS	77047	4373	B5
Walkway St				
7100	HOUS	77036	4099	D5
Walkwood Cir				
-	HOUS	77079	3956	E2
800	HOUS	77079	3957	A2
Walkwood Ct				
800	HOUS	77079	3957	A1
Walkwood Dr				
15400	HOUS	77079	3957	A2
15700	HOUS	77079	3956	E2
Wall St				
200	GlsC	77539	4635	C4
800	HOUS	77088	3684	A3
2400	HOUS	77088	3683	B3
16000	JRSV	77040	3540	C7
Walla Ln				
13200	HarC	77037	3545	B7
Wallaby Ct				
11700	HOUS	77477	4238	A4
Wallace				
18600	BzaC	77511	4628	A4
18600	PRLD	77511	4628	A4
Wallace Av				
7800	HTCK	77563	4988	E4
Wallace St				
100	HOUS	77022	3824	A2
Wallach Dr				
14800	HarC	77429	3397	C5
Wallbarry Wy				
1600	SGLD	77479	4367	C7
Wallboard Ct				
9600	HarC	77038	3544	A5
Waller St				
2000	WALR	77484	3101	D5
9200	HOUS	77012	4105	E3
Waller Park Ln				
10100	HarC	77064	3540	C6
Waller Spring Creek Rd				
27000	HarC	77447	3103	D2
27000	HarC	77484	3103	D2
29200	HarC	77484	3102	A2
Waller Springs Ln				
25400	FBnC	77494	4092	C5
Waller Tomball Rd				
-	HarC	77447	3103	E4
14000	HarC	77377	3108	C1
14000	TMBL	77375	3108	E1
14000	TMBL	77377	3108	E1
16300	HarC	77377	3107	A2
18600	HarC	77377	3106	D2
19100	HarC	77484	3102	B5
19100	WALR	77484	3102	B6
20300	HarC	77447	3106	A2
21200	HarC	77447	3105	A4
24900	HarC	77447	3104	A4
27900	HarC	77484	3103	C4
Waller Tomball Rd FM-2920				
-	HarC	77447	3105	B4
14000	HarC	77377	3108	C1
14000	TMBL	77375	3108	E1
14000	TMBL	77377	3108	E1
16300	HarC	77377	3107	A2
18600	HarC	77377	3106	D2
19100	WALR	77484	3102	B6
20300	HarC	77447	3106	A2
24900	HarC	77447	3104	A4
27200	HarC	77447	3103	D4
27900	HarC	77484	3103	C4
29000	HarC	77484	3102	C4
Walling St				
1000	HOUS	77009	3823	E5
1100	HOUS	77008	3823	E5
1300	HOUS	77009	3824	A5
Wallingford Dr				
2300	MSCY	77459	4370	A7
2700	HOUS	77042	3958	D7
2700	HOUS	77042	4098	D1
Wallingford Pl				
10600	HOUS	77042	3958	D7
Wallingford Pns				
2700	HOUS	77042	3958	D7
Wallingham Ct				
9100	HarC	77379	3255	D4
Wallingham Dr				
9200	HarC	77379	3255	D5
Wallington Dr				
8900	HOUS	77096	4240	D1
Wallington Ln				
1800	SEBK	77586	4382	E7
Wallis Av				
400	PASD	77502	4107	A7
E Wallis Dr				
22100	MtgC	77365	3118	C1
W Wallis Dr				
21100	MtgC	77365	3118	A1
Wallis Trail Ct				
5600	HarC	77049	3828	C4
Wallisville Rd				
5500	HOUS	77020	3825	D7
7100	HOUS	77020	3826	A7
7800	HOUS	77029	3826	A7
9200	HOUS	77013	3826	E6
9700	HOUS	77013	3827	D5
12500	HOUS	77013	3828	A4
12700	HarC	77049	3828	A4
13700	HarC	77015	3828	B4
14500	HOUS	77015	3828	B4
14700	HOUS	77049	3828	E4
15000	HOUS	77015	3829	A4
15000	HarC	77049	3829	A4
16000	HarC	77530	3829	A4
16600	HarC	77049	3830	E2
16600	HarC	77530	3830	A2
18300	HarC	77049	3831	A2
18300	HarC	77562	3830	E2
E Wallisville Rd				
100	HarC	77562	3831	E2
700	HarC	77562	3832	D2
2700	HarC	77521	3832	E2
3000	HarC	77521	3833	A2
4400	BYTN	77521	3833	C2
6400	HarC	77521	3834	B1
W Wallisville Rd				
100	HarC	77562	3831	D2
Wallstone Ct				
20200	HarC	77388	3112	E5
Walmer Falls Dr				
-	HarC	77044	3549	C2
Walne				
500	HOUS	77024	3961	C1
500	HOUS	77055	3822	C7
500	HOUS	77055	3961	C1
Walnut				
100	MRGP	77571	4252	B1
Walnut Av				
400	FBnC	77545	4623	C1
600	FBnC	77471	4490	C3
600	RSBG	77471	4490	C3
Walnut Cross				
33200	MtgC	77355	2962	B2
Walnut Ct				
2300	DRPK	77536	4108	E6
2500	PRLD	77584	4502	A5
Walnut Dr				
10300	MtgC	77302	2676	E2
10600	MtgC	77302	2677	A2
21000	MtgC	77357	2828	D7
21000	MtgC	77357	2974	D1
21900	MtgC	77365	2972	E3
25600	MtgC	77372	2537	A2
Walnut Hl				
-	WlrC	77447	2813	C3
Walnut Ln				
1100	HOUS	77339	3263	C1
2100	PASD	77502	4107	D4
2100	PASD	77502	4247	D1
17400	SGCH	77355	2961	B2
25700	MtgC	77372	2682	E6
25700	MtgC	77372	2683	A6
Walnut Rd				
21800	HOUS	77339	3263	D2
Walnut Sq				
6700	FBnC	77469	4095	D5
Walnut St				
100	WALR	77484	3101	E6
100	WlrC	77484	3101	E7
300	LMQU	77568	4990	C3
600	BzaC	77583	4623	D1
600	FBnC	77545	4623	D1
600	PRLD	77545	4623	D1
900	HOUS	77002	3963	D2
1300	RSBG	77471	4490	D4
15100	STFE	77517	4870	A6
15400	GlsC	77517	4870	A6
26700	HarC	77373	3114	A1
E Walnut St				
3300	PRLD	77581	4503	C3
N Walnut St				
100	TMBL	77375	2964	B6
100	WEBS	77598	4507	B6
S Walnut St				
100	TMBL	77375	2964	C7
100	WEBS	77598	4507	C7
W Walnut St				
4000	PRLD	77581	4503	A3
4000	PRLD	77584	4503	A3
Walnut Bend Blvd				
-	PRLD	77581	4503	B4
-	PRLD	77584	4503	B4
Walnut Bend Ct				
12700	MSCY	77071	4239	B7
Walnut Bend Dr				
-	LGCY	77598	4630	D4
Walnut Bend Ln				
-	HOUS	77042	3958	D4
2800	HOUS	77042	4098	C2
Walnut Bridge Ct				
14300	HOUS	77062	4379	C5
Walnut Brook Ct				
9300	HarC	77040	3541	A6
Walnut Canyon Dr				
20500	FBnC	77450	4094	C4
Walnut Cove Ct				
3300	FRDW	77598	4630	B2
Walnut Cove Dr				
5000	HarC	77084	3677	E6
Walnut Cove Ln				
200	BzaC	77584	4374	A7
Walnut Creek Ct				
8000	FBnC	77479	4494	A6
27900	MtgC	77355	2814	C6
Walnut Creek Dr				
2100	HOUS	77017	4246	C1
2100	LGCY	77573	4632	E1
Walnut Creek Rd				
30400	MtgC	77355	2961	D6
30400	SGCH	77355	2961	D4
32800	MtgC	77355	2962	A1
32800	SGCH	77355	2962	A1
Walnut Dale Ct				
11600	HarC	77038	3543	A5
Walnut Fair Ln				
2200	HarC	77373	3114	E5
Walnut Falls Tr				
-	HarC	77429	3253	C4
Walnut Forest Ct				
3500	HarC	77388	3112	E6
Walnut Forest Ln				
3600	HarC	77388	3112	E6
Walnutgate Dr				
5700	HarC	77373	3115	E7
Walnut Glen Dr				
9800	HarC	77064	3540	C2
Walnut Glen Ln				
5600	FBnC	77469	4615	E1
5600	RSBG	77469	4615	E1
Walnut Green Dr				
1900	HOUS	77062	4380	A6
Walnut Grove Cir				
25600	MtgC	77380	2968	B2
Walnut Grove Ln				
2100	FBnC	77469	4365	D1
33100	MtgC	77355	2962	C3
Walnut Hills Dr				
5000	HOUS	77345	3119	E5
5100	HOUS	77345	3120	A4
18700	MtgC	77302	2680	B6
18700	MtgC	77357	2680	B6
Walnut Hollow Ln				
13800	HOUS	77082	4096	E2
13800	HOUS	77082	4097	A2
Walnut Hollow St				
2500	PRLD	77581	4504	D5
Walnut Knob Ct				
2500	HOUS	77345	3120	C4
Walnut Knoll Wy				
2900	HarC	77084	3816	B4
Walnut Lake Rd				
13000	HarC	77065	3539	B1
Walnut Meadow Dr				
11300	HarC	77066	3400	E5
11300	HarC	77066	3401	A6
Walnut Peak Ct				
5200	HOUS	77345	3119	C2
Walnut Point Dr				
5600	HOUS	77345	3120	B6
Walnut Pointe				
800	LGCY	77573	4631	D5
Walnut Pond Ct				
16900	PASD	77059	4380	D4
Walnut Pond Dr				
-	HOUS	77059	4380	D4
3900	PASD	77059	4380	D4
Walnut Ridge Dr				
2300	MSCY	77489	4370	B7
8300	HarC	77338	3261	E4
8400	HarC	77338	3262	A4
Walnut Shores Dr				
15900	HOUS	77044	3408	D4
Walnut Spring Dr				
2900	HarC	77449	3815	D4
Walnut Springs Ln				
16100	SGCH	77355	2961	D3
Walnut Valley Dr				
22200	HarC	77389	3112	D1
Walnut View Ct				
2900	HarC	77038	3543	A5
Walnut Woods Dr				
15900	HarC	77084	3678	E6
Walraven Dr				
11400	HarC	77336	3266	E1
11400	HOUS	77336	3266	D1
Walsh Ln				
1000	GLSN	77554	5107	E5
Walsh Rd				
-	RSBG	77471	4490	A7
300	FBnC	77471	4490	A6
Walsh St				
3200	GlsC	77518	4634	B2
Walston Ln				
500	HarC	77060	3544	D5
Walston Rd				
1000	HarC	77039	3545	A4
1000	HarC	77060	3545	A4
Walston Bend Dr				
6200	FBnC	77479	4367	A7
Walston Ridge Ct				
10800	HarC	77379	3110	A6
Walston Ridge Dr				
1200	HarC	77379	3110	A6
Walter St				
200	PASD	77506	4107	A4
700	RSBG	77471	4491	A4
N Walter St				
100	PASD	77506	4107	A3
S Walter St				
100	PASD	77506	4107	A2
Walter Peak Ln				
25200	FBnC	77494	4092	C5
Walters Rd				
10700	MtgC	77372	2535	E1
11000	HarC	77067	3402	A6
11900	HarC	77067	3401	E5
13700	HarC	77014	3401	E3
14200	HarC	77014	3257	D7
14500	HarC	77068	3257	C7
Walters Wy				
600	MtgC	77385	2676	C3
Walterville Rd				
9300	HOUS	77080	3820	D5
Walthall Dr				
300	HOUS	77022	3823	D1
Waltham St				
29300	MtgC	77386	2969	C4
Walton Rd				
13200	HOUS	77044	3550	D4
19700	PNIS	77445	3099	A5
Walton St				
1900	HOUS	77009	3824	A4
Walton Heath Dr				
6500	HarC	77069	3400	B2
Waltons Pt				
6100	CNRO	77304	2236	E6
Waltrip St				
5600	HOUS	77087	4104	E7
5800	HOUS	77087	4244	E1
6800	HOUS	77087	4245	A3
Waltway Dr				
6100	HOUS	77008	3822	E6
6100	HOUS	77008	3823	A6
Walwick Dr				
10900	HNCV	77024	3960	A4
10900	PNPV	77024	3960	A4
Walworten Ct				
500	HarC	77450	3954	E2
Walworth Ct				
8900	HarC	77088	3542	C7
Walworth Dr				
9000	HarC	77088	3542	C6
Wanakah Dr				
5700	HarC	77069	3400	D1
Wanda Ln				
6500	HOUS	77074	4240	A1
7400	HOUS	77074	4239	E1
7800	HarC	77044	3689	B7
12500	MtgC	77354	2671	A7
Wandering Tr				
15300	FRDW	77546	4505	C5
Wandering Creek Dr				
5700	FBnC	77469	4493	A6
E Wandering Oak Dr				
10	WDLD	77381	2820	E6
Wandering Streams Dr				
12600	HarC	77377	3254	A3
Wandering Wood Dr				
14300	HarC	77015	3829	A5
Wandering Wy Ct				
24300	HarC	77375	2965	D4
Wandflower Pl				
10	WDLD	77381	2820	E1
Wandsworth Dr				
9200	HarC	77379	3255	E5
Waning Star Ct				
7500	HarC	77379	3256	C3
Wanita				
-	HOUS	77007	3961	E2
Wanita Pl				
6600	HOUS	77007	3961	E2
Wannan Ln				
-	CNRO	77301	2530	B3
Wann Park Dr				
19300	HarC	77073	3403	B2
War Admiral Dr				
2000	STAF	77477	4370	A4
4100	PASD	77503	4108	D6
Warath Oak Ct				
11000	HarC	77065	3540	A1
Warbler Dr				
16700	MtgC	77385	2676	D4
Warbler Ln				
2900	HMBL	77396	3406	C4
Warbler Pl				
10	WDLD	77381	2821	B2
Warbler Wy				
20900	HarC	77447	3106	A2
N Warbler Bend Cir				
10	WDLD	77382	2820	A1
S Warbler Bend Cir				
10	WDLD	77382	2820	A1
Warbonnet Dr				
10	PNVL	77304	2237	A4
Warchest Ct				
4000	GLSN	77554	5332	E3
Ward				
10600	HarC	77375	2965	A4
Ward Ln				
300	ALVN	77511	4749	C2
11300	MtgC	77306	2533	B2
Ward Rd				
100	BYTN	77520	3973	C6
7100	HOUS	77037	3684	D3
7100	HOUS	77076	3684	D3
7800	HarC	77037	3684	D3
10300	HarC	77375	2965	A6
10500	HarC	77375	2964	E6
11200	MtgC	77372	2536	D2
Ward St				
700	RSBG	77471	4491	A4
3100	HOUS	77053	4373	A4
3300	HOUS	77021	4103	B6
Wardmont St				
1200	HOUS	77037	3685	B1
2100	HarC	77093	3685	D1
3100	HarC	77093	3686	A1
Wardville St				
11200	HarC	77093	3686	A1
Ware Dairy Rd				
2600	BzaC	77511	4749	D1
2600	FRDW	77546	4749	D1
Warehouse Center Dr				
8400	HOUS	77338	3261	E6
8500	HOUS	77338	3262	A6
Warfield Ln				
6400	HarC	77084	3678	B3
Waring St				
4500	HOUS	77027	3961	B7
4600	HOUS	77027	4101	B1
Warkworth Dr				
-	HOUS	77085	4371	D2
War Memorial Dr				
3500	HOUS	77084	3818	B1

STREET
Block City ZIP Map# Grid

Warm Spring Ln
100 LGCY 77539 4752 D2
Warm Springs Rd
4300 HOUS 77035 4241 B4
5500 HOUS 77035 4240 C4
N Warmstone Cir
10 WDLD 77381 2820 C1
S Warmstone Ct
1600 FBnC 77494 3953 D5
N Warmstone Wy
23000 HarC 77494 3953 D4
S Warmstone Wy
23000 HarC 77494 3953 D5
Warm Winds Dr
17500 HarC 77377 3254 B3
Warner
800 HOUS 77022 3685 C7
Warner Rd
- HarC 77093 3686 C2
11500 MtgC 77372 2537 B3
Warner St
600 HOUS 77022 3685 B7
Warner Hollow Ct
10800 FBnC 77478 4236 E4
Warpath Av
4000 STFE 77510 4870 D7
Warren
- HarC 77093 3686 A2
- HOUS 77093 3686 A2
Warren Dr
4600 GlsC 77563 4990 A5
Warren Rd
3200 PRLD 77584 4627 C1
8000 HarC 77040 3681 D1
9500 MTBL 77520 3696 D7
9500 MTBL 77520 3835 C1
Warren St
1100 DRPK 77536 4109 C7
4100 GlsC 77518 4634 D2
17000 HarC 77447 3248 E3
Warrenford Dr
8700 FBnC 77083 4096 D7
8700 FBnC 77083 4236 C1
Warren Ranch Rd
15400 HarC 77447 3248 D4
Warrenton Dr
10 HOUS 77024 3959 A5
100 BKHV 77024 3959 A4
Warrenwood Dr
12300 HarC 77066 3401 C5
Warrington Dr
20200 HarC 77450 3954 D3
Warrington Ln
- LGCY 77573 4751 B1
Warrior Ct
4000 GLSN 77554 5331 B7
4000 GLSN 77554 5442 B1
Warrior Dr
18200 GLSN 77554 5331 C7
18500 GLSN 77554 5442 B1
Warsaw St
500 BYUV 77563 4990 D7
500 GlsC 77563 4990 D7
Warwana Rd
9700 HOUS 77080 3820 B5
10000 HOUS 77043 3820 A5
10800 HOUS 77043 3819 C5
Warwick
19100 MtgC 77357 2829 A4
Warwick Ct
10 MSCY 77459 4369 D7
4600 SGLD 77479 4495 D4
Warwick Dr
- HMBL 77338 3262 C5
2600 LGCY 77573 4508 E7
4200 PASD 77504 4247 E6
4400 SGLD 77479 4495 D4
Warwick Rd
1400 HarC 77093 3685 D1
1400 HOUS 77093 3685 B2
Warwickshire Ct
11800 HOUS 77077 3958 A4
Warwickshire Dr
1300 HOUS 77077 3958 A5
20900 HarC 77375 3110 A3
Warwick Walk Ln
1400 HarC 77530 3829 E5
Wasabi Ln
5600 HarC 77521 3833 D3
Wasatch Dr
- HarC 77377 3109 B7
Waseca Av
1400 HOUS 77055 3820 D6
Washam Rd
8600 HOUS 77075 4376 E3
Washburn Tun
- HOUS 77015 4107 A1
- HOUS 77506 4107 A2
Washington
300 HarC 77532 3552 C4
Washington Av
- HOUS 77018 3823 A3
300 HOUS 77002 3963 C3
500 SHUS 77587 4246 C4
1200 HOUS 77007 3963 A3
2100 ALVN 77511 4749 E6
2100 ALVN 77511 4750 A6
2100 GlsC 77511 4750 A6
2200 BzaC 77511 4749 E6
4300 TXCY 77591 4874 B6
6100 HOUS 77007 3962 A2
Washington Dr
- HarC 77086 3542 D6
1500 DRPK 77536 4249 D1
2800 HarC 77038 3543 A6
2800 HarC 77086 3543 A6
Washington St
100 LGCY 77573 4632 B4
100 WEBS 77598 4507 C7
400 RSBG 77471 4490 B5
1300 HMPD 77445 2953 A7
1500 HMPD 77445 2952 E7
1900 BYTN 77520 4112 B1
2100 PRLD 77581 4503 B3
2100 WALR 77484 3101 D5
2100 WlrC 77484 3101 D5
2500 PRLD 77584 4503 B3
2900 WALR 77484 3102 A6
3000 PASD 77503 4108 B4
3000 PASD 77506 4108 A4
4300 DKSN 77539 4754 A3
6500 HTCK 77563 4989 C5
7400 HarC 77521 3832 D4
11400 HarC 77093 3546 B7
11600 HarC 77039 3546 B7
13400 GlsC 77510 4870 D2
13600 STFE 77510 4870 D2
13600 STFE 77517 4870 D2

N Washington St
10 TXCY 77591 4873 D6
S Washington St
10 TXCY 77591 4873 D7
200 LMQU 77568 4873 D7
W Washington St
- LGCY 77573 4632 A4
Washington Irving Dr
1800 PRLD 77581 4504 C4
Washingtn on Wstctt Roundabout
- HOUS 77007 3962 A2
Washington Park Ct
18300 HarC 77379 3257 B1
Wassail Wy
23900 HarC 77493 3814 C6
Wateka Cir
8200 HOUS 77074 4239 D1
Wateka Dr
8100 HOUS 77074 4099 D7
8100 HOUS 77074 4239 D1
Water St
- WEBS 77598 4507 D6
100 DKSN 77539 4753 C5
100 GLSN 77550 5109 E1
Water St FM-275
200 GLSN 77550 5109 E1
Water Wy
2100 SEBK 77586 4509 C2
Waterbend Ct
28600 MtgC 77386 2970 A3
Waterbend Wy
28500 MtgC 77386 2970 A4
Waterbend Cove
3700 MtgC 77386 2970 A5
Water Bluff Ln
100 FBnC 77469 4365 B6
Waterborough Ct
2900 LGCY 77573 4633 A3
Waterbrook Pl
10 WDLD 77381 2820 E2
Waterbury Dr
- HOUS 77055 3821 B5
Waterbury Estates Dr
- BzaC 77584 4501 A5
Water Canyon Ct
2100 HOUS 77077 3957 A6
Water Canyon Rd
3800 BYTN 77521 3973 E3
Watercastle Ct
1800 HOUS 77077 3957 A6
3100 LGCY 77573 4633 B1
11500 PRLD 77584 4500 D2
Waterchase Dr
7700 HOUS 77489 4371 A3
Watercliff Ct
3200 HarC 77388 3112 E4
Watercolor Cove
4200 PASD 77505 4249 C5
Watercress Cir
100 JRSV 77064 3540 B6
Watercress Pk
12600 HarC 77041 3679 D4
Watercrest Dr
700 SEBK 77586 4509 E1
700 SEBK 77586 4510 A1
1800 HOUS 77008 3822 D5
Watercrest Harbor Ln
300 LGCY 77573 4631 C7
Watercypress Ct
26300 HarC 77433 3396 B6
Water Dance Ct
20200 HarC 77433 3251 C5
Waterdance Ln
11800 HarC 77095 3397 A7
Water Edge Ln
22400 FBnC 77494 4093 D4
Water Edge Point Ln
9200 HarC 77396 3406 E7
9200 HarC 77396 3407 A7
Waterelm Dr
2000 HOUS 77084 3816 D6
Water Elm Pl
10 WDLD 77382 2675 C6
Water Elm Wy
4300 HOUS 77059 4380 C4
Waterfall Dr
200 HarC 77336 3121 C7
1700 FRDW 77546 4629 B6
2000 MSCY 77489 4370 B7
Waterfall Wy
4400 SGLD 77479 4496 A2
Waterfall Cove
4300 PASD 77505 4249 B5
Water Falls
26100 HOUS 77373 3113 E3
Waterfern Ct
10800 HarC 77064 3540 E1
Water Fern Ln
2100 PRLD 77581 4503 E2
Waterflower Dr
19600 HarC 77375 3109 E6
Waterford Bnd
10 WDLD 77381 2674 C6
3900 MSCY 77459 4369 D7
Waterford Cir
10 WDLD 77381 2674 C6
Waterford Ct
10 CNRO 77304 2236 C7
3900 MSCY 77459 4369 D7
Waterford Dr
1300 DRPK 77536 4108 E6
5700 HOUS 77033 4244 A5
Waterford Lk
10 WDLD 77381 2674 C6
Waterford Ln
3900 MSCY 77459 4369 D7
Waterford Wy
- LGCY 77565 4509 A5
- LGCY 77573 4509 B5
1900 SEBK 77586 4509 D1
Waterford Cove
19000 HarC 77094 3955 C3
Waterford Estates Ct
11900 HarC 77377 3254 C3
Waterford Oaks Ln
10 LGCY 77565 4509 A4
Waterford Park Dr
- HarC 77068 3257 C5
Waterford Park St
2100 MSCY 77459 4369 D7
Waterford Pointe Cir
10 SGLD 77479 4495 B4
Waterford Village Blvd
2100 MSCY 77459 4369 D7
Waterfowl Ct
12500 HarC 77014 3401 E3

Water Front Ct
9100 MtgC 77354 2818 C3
Waterfront St
100 SEBK 77586 4509 D4
Water Gap Dr
- SGLD 77478 4368 C4
Waterglen Ct
3200 LGCY 77573 4633 B3
Water Glen Dr
200 HarC 77336 3121 B7
Watergroove Ct
7800 HarC 77396 3547 D2
Waterhaven Ln
4700 HarC 77084 3678 A7
Water Hill Ct
24300 FBnC 77494 3953 A3
Watering Oak Ln
- FBnC 77469 4095 D6
16800 FBnC 77083 4095 D6
N Water Iris Ct
4000 HOUS 77059 4380 B4
S Water Iris Ct
3900 HOUS 77059 4380 B3
N Waterlake Dr
- FBnC 77469 4093 C7
S Waterlake Dr
- FBnC 77469 4093 C7
W Waterlake Dr
- FBnC 77469 4093 C7
Waterland Dr
25600 HarC 77336 3121 C7
Water Leaf Ln
5600 HOUS 77088 3682 E2
Waterlilly Ln
7500 BzaC 77581 4502 A3
Waterlily Ct
4300 MSCY 77459 4369 B6
N Waterlily Dr
23000 FBnC 77469 4093 C7
23000 HOUS 77469 4093 C7
S Waterlily Dr
23000 FBnC 77469 4093 C7
23000 HOUS 77469 4093 C7
Waterlily Ln
- PRLD 77545 4499 E1
Waterline Ln
- HarC 77494 3953 A2
Water Locust Dr
3300 SGLD 77479 4495 E2
Waterloo Dr
- HOUS 77045 4241 E7
- HOUS 77045 4373 A1
12900 HOUS 77045 4242 A6
13500 HOUS 77045 4372 E1
14700 HarC 77053 4373 A4
14700 HOUS 77053 4373 A4
Waterloo Rd
2900 PRLD 77581 4503 E3
Water Mark Wy
10 WDLD 77381 2674 C7
Watermill Ct
10 WDLD 77380 2968 B3
Water Mill Dr
18100 HarC 77429 3396 B1
Watermill Pl
10 FBnC 77479 4367 A5
Watermint Pl
10 WDLD 77384 2675 A4
Watermist
12800 HarC 77041 3679 D6
Watermist Dr
13200 PRLD 77584 4500 A4
Watermist Ln
12900 HarC 77041 3679 D6
Watermont Dr
300 HarC 77336 3121 C7
Watermoon
1200 FBnC 77469 4493 B4
Water Oak Cross
- HarC 77433 3251 A5
Water Oak Ct
11600 MtgC 77354 2671 C4
Water Oak Dr
100 LGCY 77573 4632 A4
4800 PASD 77505 4248 D6
10000 MtgC 77354 2671 B4
12700 MSCY 77071 4239 A7
12700 MSCY 77071 4370 B1
16600 HarC 77530 3830 D5
Water Oak Ln
11300 HarC 77429 3398 E4
Water Oak Tr
22600 HarC 77377 2962 D7
22600 HarC 77377 3107 D1
Water Oak Bend Ct
17200 HarC 77433 3395 D6
Water Oak Hill Dr
20400 HarC 77388 3113 B5
Water Oak Park Cir
13200 HarC 77429 3398 E4
Water Park Ct
9500 HarC 77086 3542 A3
Water Park Ln
7400 HarC 77086 3542 A3
7700 HarC 77086 3541 E3
Water Park Wy
28600 MtgC 77386 2970 A4
Waterpine Dr
8800 HarC 77338 3262 A4
Waterpoint
4500 MSCY 77459 4496 C4
Water Point Ct
6300 HarC 77346 3264 E3
Water Point Tr
19300 HarC 77346 3265 A4
20500 HarC 77346 3264 E3
Waterport Ln
3600 HarC 77449 3815 C2
Water Rest Cir
2400 SGLD 77479 4368 C7
Water Rest Dr
2500 SGLD 77479 4368 D6
Water Ridge Dr
25700 HarC 77336 3121 C6
Water Ridge Ln
3300 BYTN 77521 3973 E3
Water Rose
300 HarC 77494 3953 A1
Water Scene Tr
13200 HarC 77429 3252 B7
Waters Cove
- MSCY 77459 4496 C3
Waters Edge Blvd
13300 HOUS 77044 3409 A3
Waters Edge Ct
2000 PRLD 77584 4500 D1
Waters Edge Dr
- MSCY 77459 4496 D4

Waters Edge Dr
3200 BzaC 77578 4501 A6
Watersedge Dr
3400 SGLD 77478 4368 E6
Waters Edge Ln
1800 SEBK 77586 4509 E1
1900 SEBK 77586 4382 E7
2100 LGCY 77573 4631 B7
Waters Edge Pl
12900 HarC 77041 3679 D6
Water Shoal Ln
3800 MSCY 77459 4496 D4
Waterside Ct
4200 MSCY 77459 4369 C6
Waterside Dr
1400 LGCY 77573 4508 D4
1800 MSCY 77459 4369 C6
14800 HarC 77015 3829 B4
Waterside Tr
2700 PRLD 77584 4503 B4
Waterside Wy
12600 HarC 77041 3679 D7
Waterside Estates Cir
300 FBnC 77469 4234 C5
Waterside Estates Dr
4300 FBnC 77469 4234 C4
Waterside Village Ct
4800 FBnC 77469 4234 E4
Waterside Village Dr
1400 FBnC 77469 4234 D4
Waters Lake Blvd
10 FBnC 77459 4621 D6
Waters Lake Bnd
3100 FBnC 77459 4621 D6
Waters Lake Ln
2800 FBnC 77459 4621 D6
Waters Landing Ln
- FBnC 77469 4493 A5
Waterstone Dr
4000 MSCY 77459 4369 C6
10100 HOUS 77042 4099 A2
Waters View Dr
3100 SGLD 77478 4368 D6
Waters Wy Dr
3100 SGLD 77478 4368 D6
Waterton
12000 HarC 77086 3542 B4
Watertown Mall
2500 HOUS 77057 3960 C7
Water Trace Ct
- RHMD 77469 4492 B2
Watertree Cir
10 WDLD 77380 2967 C2
Watertree Ct
10 WDLD 77380 2967 C2
N Watertree Ln
10 WDLD 77380 2967 C2
S Watertree Ln
10 WDLD 77380 2967 C2
Waterview Ct
3900 MSCY 77459 4369 C7
Waterview Dr
1600 HarC 77339 3118 C5
1600 HOUS 77339 3118 C5
Waterview Estates Tr
5200 FBnC 77469 4234 D3
Waterville Wy
13800 HarC 77015 3828 E6
13900 HarC 77015 3829 A6
Water Violet Ln
5900 FBnC 77469 4234 D1
Waterway Av
- WDLD 77380 2822 A5
Waterway Ct
10 WDLD 77380 2822 A5
Water Well Rd
- HarC 77389 2967 B6
2600 HOUS 77339 3118 D5
22000 MtgC 77365 2973 C7
Water Willow Ln
2900 PRLD 77581 4503 E2
Waterwind Ct
3400 HarC 77546 4506 C6
Waterwood Ct
1500 MSCY 77459 4369 C5
11600 PRLD 77584 4500 C3
Waterwood Dr
100 HarC 77336 3121 B6
2300 FBnC 77479 4493 E2
4000 BYTN 77521 3972 C3
Water Wood Tr
7500 HarC 77346 3265 A4
Watkin Wy
1600 HOUS 77015 3967 A3
1700 GNPK 77015 3967 A4
Watkins Wy
1300 FRDW 77546 4505 D5
Watonga Blvd
- HOUS 77018 3683 B7
3600 HOUS 77092 3822 B1
4700 HOUS 77092 3683 B7
Watson Ln
19500 HMBL 77338 3262 B5
19500 HOUS 77338 3262 B5
Watson St
2300 HOUS 77009 3963 A1
3700 HOUS 77009 3824 A7
Watson Wy
1100 HarC 77067 3402 C4
1100 HOUS 77067 3402 D4
Watson Mill Ct
11000 FBnC 77478 4236 D5
Watsons Bay Dr
17800 HarC 77429 3396 C1
Watsonwood
- WEBS 77598 4631 D1
Watters Rd
2800 PASD 77502 4247 E3
3000 PASD 77504 4247 E5
Watts Av
1400 KATY 77493 3813 E7
Watts Rd
2100 HOUS 77030 4102 B4
2400 WUNP 77005 4102 A4
Watts Plantation Dr
2600 MSCY 77545 4622 B2
Watts Plantation Rd
3500 MSCY 77459 4621 C1
3500 MSCY 77545 4621 E1
3500 MSCY 77545 4622 A1
Waugh Dr
10 HOUS 77007 3962 C2
500 HOUS 77019 3962 D4
1500 HOUS 77006 3962 D5
Waughcrest Dr
2700 HOUS 77006 3962 D6
Waughford St
10 HOUS 77007 3962 D3

Waukegan Rd
- MtgC 77302 2532 D3
11000 MtgC 77306 2532 D1
Waumsley Wy
15400 FBnC 77478 4236 B2
Wavecrest Ct
- FBnC 77469 4493 A5
Wavecrest Ln
1400 HOUS 77062 4507 B2
Wavecrest St
3200 LGCY 77573 4633 C3
Waveland Dr
7000 HOUS 77072 4097 E5
Wavell St
1900 HOUS 77088 3683 C1
S Wave Oak Cir
10 WDLD 77381 2820 E6
10 WDLD 77381 2821 A7
Waverdale Ct
5500 FBnC 77479 4366 E6
19100 HarC 77094 3955 B1
Waverly Bnd
3800 FBnC 77450 4093 E1
Waverly Ct
10 HOUS 77005 4102 D2
10 HOUS 77006 4102 D2
Waverly Dr
2600 LGCY 77573 4508 D7
15400 HOUS 77032 3404 C7
16300 HarC 77032 3404 C5
Waverly St
- HOUS 77026 3824 E4
500 HOUS 77007 3962 C1
800 HOUS 77007 3823 C7
800 HOUS 77008 3823 C7
Waverly Bend Ct
22700 FBnC 77450 4093 E1
Waverly Bend Ln
18200 HarC 77433 3677 D1
Waverly Canyon
15000 HarC 77429 3253 C7
Waverly Canyon Ln
4400 LGCY 77573 4630 E6
Waverly Crest Ct
13600 HarC 77429 3397 A3
Waverly Glend Dr
2000 HarC 77450 3954 C5
Waverly Grove Dr
17500 HarC 77084 3677 E4
Waverly Hollow Ln
18100 HarC 77429 3252 B6
Waverly Park Ln
19600 HarC 77379 3112 A5
Waverton Ct
14800 FBnC 77478 4236 C2
Wavertree Dr
- MSCY 77478 4369 B7
- SGLD 77478 4369 B7
4400 MSCY 77459 4369 B7
Waving Fields Dr
9700 HarC 77064 3540 C2
E Wavy Oak Cir
10 WDLD 77381 2821 A6
N Wavy Oak Cir
10 WDLD 77381 2820 E6
10 WDLD 77381 2821 A6
W Wavy Oak Cir
10 WDLD 77381 2820 E7
Waxahachie Av
7900 HOUS 77029 3965 B1
Waxahachie St
800 CNRO 77301 2385 A3
6900 HOUS 77020 3964 E1
6900 HOUS 77020 3965 A1
13700 HarC 77015 3967 E1
14000 HarC 77015 3968 A1
N Waxberry Rd
10 WDLD 77381 2821 A6
S Waxberry Rd
10 WDLD 77381 2821 A6
Wax Bill Ct
15800 HarC 77396 3406 E6
Waxcandle Dr
3300 HarC 77388 3113 A6
Waxleaf Dr
7900 HarC 77338 3261 D4
Wax Mallow Ct
10600 HarC 77095 3538 B2
Wax Mallow Dr
16500 HarC 77095 3538 B2
Wax Myrtle Ln
700 HOUS 77079 3958 C2
Waxwing Dr
2200 LGCY 77573 4752 B2
Wax Wing Ln
14400 MtgC 77302 2679 E1
14400 MtgC 77306 2679 E1
Waxwing St
11000 HOUS 77035 4241 A4
Waxwing Park Dr
15300 HarC 77396 3406 D6
Waxwood Dr
11500 HarC 77089 4378 B6
Way Mnr
11500 PNPV 77024 3959 D5
Way St
7800 HOUS 77028 3687 B6
Waybridge Dr
14900 HOUS 77062 4506 E1
Waybridge St
12800 SGLD 77478 4237 C5
Waybridge Glen Ln
15800 HarC 77095 3678 C1
Waycreek Rd
16000 HarC 77090 3257 D4
16500 HarC 77068 3257 D4
Waycrest
2300 HOUS 77011 3965 A5
Waycross Dr
5000 HOUS 77035 4241 A3
5100 HOUS 77035 4240 E3
Way Fair Dr
5900 PASD 77505 4248 D6
Wayfare Ct
13700 HarC 77429 3254 A6
Wayfarer Ln
8600 HOUS 77075 4376 E2
8600 HOUS 77075 4377 A2
Wayfarer Gray Tr
- HarC 77433 3250 E5
Wayforest Dr
17600 HarC 77060 3403 D5
17600 HOUS 77060 3403 D6
Wayland St
5800 HOUS 77021 4103 E6
Waylord
8200 HarC 77041 3539 B6
8200 HarC 77095 3539 B6

Waylord Dr
8200 HarC 77095 3539 C6
Wayman
- HOUS 77017 4106 C6
Waymare Ln
21200 HarC 77388 3112 B4
Wayne Ln
24500 MtgC 77365 2973 D7
24700 MtgC 77365 3118 D1
N Wayne Ln
16700 BzaC 77584 4502 E7
16700 BzaC 77584 4626 E1
17300 PRLD 77584 4626 E2
N Wayne Ln CO-879B
16700 BzaC 77584 4502 E7
16700 BzaC 77584 4626 E1
17300 PRLD 77584 4626 E2
Wayne St
700 CNRO 77301 2383 E5
1400 HOUS 77020 3964 A2
2000 PASD 77502 4108 A7
5400 HOUS 77026 3825 B4
Wayne Ct Pl
- HarC 77073 3403 B1
Waynegate Dr
22200 HarC 77373 3116 B7
Waynemer Wy
8100 HarC 77040 3541 B6
Waynes Blvd
- DRPK 77536 3969 E7
Waynesboro Dr
4800 HOUS 77035 4241 A2
Waynewood Dr
14500 HarC 77429 3397 B1
14700 HarC 77429 3253 B7
Waynoka Dr
22300 HarC 77450 3953 E3
Way Out West Dr
- HOUS 77040 3821 A1
4100 HOUS 77092 3821 A1
Waypark Dr
2800 HOUS 77082 4097 B1
Wayside Av
6800 HTCK 77563 4989 A5
Wayside Ct
2200 DRPK 77536 4108 E6
Wayside Dr
- HOUS 77020 3965 A5
100 HOUS 77011 3964 E6
1400 TXCY 77590 4875 B6
2300 HOUS 77011 3965 A5
Wayside Dr US-90 ALT
- HOUS 77020 3965 A5
100 HOUS 77011 3964 E6
2300 HOUS 77011 3965 A5
N Wayside Dr
- HOUS 77016 3687 C3
700 HOUS 77020 3965 B2
2100 HOUS 77020 3826 A7
4600 HOUS 77028 3826 B2
8000 HOUS 77028 3687 B7
9500 HOUS 77078 3687 C3
11000 HarC 77016 3687 C2
N Wayside Dr US-90 ALT
700 HOUS 77020 3965 A2
S Wayside Dr
- LGCY 77598 4630 C3
100 HOUS 77011 3964 E7
300 HOUS 77023 3964 E7
700 HOUS 77023 4104 C4
4300 HOUS 77087 4104 C7
5700 HOUS 77087 4244 C2
6000 HOUS 77033 4244 C2
13000 HOUS 77048 4375 D4
S Wayside Dr US-90 ALT
100 HOUS 77011 3964 E7
300 HOUS 77023 3964 E7
700 HOUS 77023 4104 D1
Wayside Stream Ln
4100 HOUS 77048 4374 D4
Wayside Village Wy
- HOUS 77016 3687 C3
Wayson Dr
14800 FBnC 77478 4236 C2
Wayward Rd
8200 HarC 77064 3541 C5
Wayward Wind Ct
9900 HarC 77064 3540 C3
Wayward Wind Ln
10000 HarC 77064 3540 C3
Weakley Wy
100 MtgC 77362 2816 E4
100 SGCH 77362 2816 E4
Weald Wy
20300 HarC 77388 3113 A5
Wealden Forest Dr
1100 HarC 77379 3110 A7
Wealdstone Dr
12300 HarC 77377 3254 B6
Weald Wy Ct
2700 HarC 77388 3113 A5
Wear St
- BYTN 77520 3971 A4
Weather Ln
7300 HarC 77041 3679 C1
7500 HarC 77041 3539 C7
Weatherby Ln
1900 FBnC 77545 4622 C4
Weatherfield Ct
- FBnC 77479 4496 C5
Weatherford Ct
2900 BzaC 77584 4501 A4
Weatherford Dr
2300 BzaC 77584 4501 A4
Weatherford St
3000 LPRT 77571 4382 E1
Weathering Oaks Dr
11400 HarC 77066 3401 A7
Weatherly Wy
100 HOUS 77018 3684 C7
100 HOUS 77022 3684 C7
Weathersby St
5900 HOUS 77091 3683 D5
Weathersfield Ct
4500 LGCY 77573 4630 E6
Weathersfield Trace Cir
2100 HarC 77014 3402 A1
Weatherstone Cir
5000 SGLD 77479 4494 E4
5000 SGLD 77479 4495 A5
Weatherwood Dr
9500 HOUS 77080 3820 C4
Weaver Rd
3600 HOUS 77093 3825 A1
3800 HOUS 77016 3825 B1
6600 HOUS 77028 3825 E1
Weaver St
100 BYTN 77520 3971 B4

Weaver St
1100 HOUS 77023 3964 C7
Weaver Knolls Dr
24600 HOUS 77336 3266 C2
Web Ln
13200 HOUS 77099 4237 C3
13200 HOUS 77478 4237 C3
Webb
19600 BzaC 77511 4628 D6
Webb Dr
4800 HOUS 77017 4106 A7
Webb Rd
3900 GlsC 77511 4869 C5
3900 GlsC 77517 4869 C5
3900 STFE 77517 4869 C5
21100 HarC 77433 3105 D7
21100 HarC 77447 3105 D7
23600 MtgC 77365 2974 A7
E Webb Rd
23600 MtgC 77365 2974 A7
Webb St
800 CNRO 77301 2384 B4
W Webb St
24400 MtgC 77365 2974 A7
Webb Creek Pl
10 WDLD 77382 2674 A6
S Webber Ct
3100 PRLD 77584 4501 D6
E Webber Dr
3100 PRLD 77584 4501 D6
N Webber Dr
4100 PRLD 77584 4501 D6
S Webber Dr
4100 PRLD 77584 4501 D6
Webelos Ct
4400 HarC 77546 4505 E5
Webelos St
15800 HarC 77546 4505 E5
Weber Av
5900 GLSN 77551 5222 C1
Weber St
1500 HOUS 77007 3963 A2
Webercrest Dr
- HOUS 77048 4375 B2
Webercrest Rd
11400 HOUS 77048 4244 B7
11400 HOUS 77048 4375 B2
Webster Av
100 HOUS 77002 3963 A5
100 HOUS 77006 3963 A5
100 HOUS 77019 3963 A5
Webster St
- HOUS 77006 3963 B6
- HOUS 77019 3963 B6
200 HOUS 77002 3963 B6
1400 LGCY 77573 4632 C3
2100 HOUS 77003 3963 D7
3000 HOUS 77004 3963 D7
W Webster St
1100 HOUS 77002 3963 A5
1100 HOUS 77006 3963 A5
1100 HOUS 77019 3963 A5
1600 HOUS 77006 3962 E5
1600 HOUS 77019 3962 E5
Webster Ranch Rd
2300 HarC 77546 4506 B6
Weckford Blvd
- HarC 77044 3549 A2
Wedgefield Pl
2100 SGLD 77479 4494 C1
Wedgefield St
5900 HOUS 77028 3826 D3
Wedgeford Ct
9800 HarC 77044 3689 B4
Wedgehill Ln
12000 HOUS 77077 3957 E5
Wedge Hollow Ct
7100 HarC 77389 2966 B1
Wedge Hollow Ln
25900 HarC 77389 2966 B1
E Wedgemere Cir
10 WDLD 77381 2820 E2
W Wedgemere Cir
10 WDLD 77381 2820 E2
E Wedgemere Ct
10 WDLD 77381 2820 D2
Wedgemere Dr
- WDLD 77381 2820 E2
Wedgerock Dr
300 HOUS 77598 4506 E5
Wedgewater Ln
13000 PRLD 77584 4500 A4
Wedgewind
- FBnC 77450 4094 C1
Wedgewood Av
100 HTCK 77563 4988 E3
Wedgewood Blvd
10 CNRO 77304 2236 C7
Wedgewood Cir
1100 PASD 77502 4106 E7
Wedgewood Ct
10 SGLD 77478 4368 D4
200 ORDN 77386 2822 C6
1800 MSCY 77489 4370 E4
Wedgewood Dr
1200 SGLD 77478 4368 E4
4700 BLAR 77401 4101 A3
33000 MtgC 77354 2673 B3
E Wedgewood Gln
10 WDLD 77381 2821 B4
W Wedgewood Gln
10 WDLD 77381 2821 B4
Wedgewood Ln
7600 HLSV 77055 3821 C7
7600 HOUS 77055 3821 C7
Wedgewood Pk
26300 HarC 77433 3396 A4
Wedgewood Pt
10 WDLD 77381 2821 A4
Wedgewood St
1300 HarC 77093 3685 B1
1300 HOUS 77093 3685 B1
4000 HarC 77093 3686 B1
Wedgewood Forest Dr
10 WDLD 77381 2821 B4
Wedgewood Park Ct
12800 HarC 77433 3396 A3
Wednesbury Ln
8000 HOUS 77074 4099 C7
Weeds Rd
6300 HarC 77066 3400 D5
Weedy Ln
8900 HOUS 77093 3686 A6
Weeks Av
500 LGCY 77573 4632 B6
Weeks Ln
- LGCY 77573 4632 B6

STREET Block City ZIP Map# Grid

Weeks St
500 LGCY 77573 4632 B7
Wee Laddie Ln
4400 HarC 77084 3678 D7
Wee Lassie Ln
4400 HarC 77084 3678 D7
Weems
5200 HOUS 77007 3962 B3
Weems St
3800 HOUS 77009 3824 B6
Weeping Cedar Ln
15000 HarC 77084 3678 E2
Weeping Oak Ln
200 HarC 77388 3113 D7
Weeping Oaks Ct
19100 HarC 77388 3113 E7
Weeping Oaks Ln
500 HarC 77388 3113 C7
Weeping Spruce Ct
10 WDLD 77384 2675 A4
Weeping Spruce Pl
10 WDLD 77384 2675 A4
Weeping Willow Ln
18000 BzaC 77584 4627 C4
Weeping Willow Pl
8000 MSCY 77459 4497 B6
Weeping Willow Rd
4900 HOUS 77092 3683 A7
5400 HOUS 77092 3682 E7
Weeping Willow Wy
800 MtgC 77354 2673 C2
Wehring Rd
2100 FBnC 77471 4614 A3
2100 RSBG 77471 4614 A3
Wehring Wy
2100 RSBG 77471 4614 E1
Weil Pl
15000 HOUS 77060 3544 D3
Weiland Manor Ln
1500 HarC 77073 3259 C4
Weiman Dr
5100 KATY 77493 3813 D6
Weiman Rd
13000 HarC 77041 3679 B2
Weingarten St
4500 HOUS 77021 4103 E5
Weir St
2900 GlsC 77517 4870 B4
Weir Wy
26600 MtgC 77355 2961 B2
Weirich Ln
11200 HarC 77375 2964 E7
11200 HarC 77375 2965 A7
11200 TMBL 77375 2964 E7
Weisenberger Dr
100 HOUS 77022 3824 A2
Weiser Dr
3500 PASD 77503 4108 B5
Weisinger Dr
800 MtgC 77354 2673 C2
Weisinger Ln
4100 CNRO 77304 2237 A6
Weiss Dr
6900 GLSN 77551 5222 B1
Weiss St
1200 HOUS 77009 3824 D5
Wekford
- PRLD 77089 4504 B3
- PRLD 77581 4504 B3
Welbeck Dr
14800 HarC 77530 3829 B5
Welborn Ct
2700 MSCY 77459 4497 E5
Welborn Dr
- MSCY 77459 4497 E5
Welch Ln
26200 SPLD 77372 2683 B2
Welch St
500 HMBL 77338 3262 E7
1000 HOUS 77006 3962 B6
1800 HOUS 77019 3962 C5
Welch House Ln
23700 HarC 77493 3814 B4
Welcome Ln
14900 HarC 77014 3257 E6
15000 HarC 77068 3257 D6
Weld Ct
24700 FBnC 77494 3952 C3
Weld Dr
1100 FBnC 77494 3952 C3
Weldon Dr
- HOUS 77032 3404 B2
1700 HarC 77073 3404 B2
15200 HarC 77032 3404 C7
E Weldon Dr
2000 HarC 77032 3404 C7
2000 HOUS 77032 3404 C7
Weldon St
100 SHUS 77587 4246 D2
Weldridge Ct
10 FBnC 77478 4236 C2
Weldridge Dr
9500 FBnC 77083 4236 C2
9500 FBnC 77478 4236 C2
Welford Dr
4700 BLAR 77401 4101 A6
Welford Ln
300 HarC 77562 3831 C2
Welham Hester Cir
13700 HarC 77429 3397 A3
Welk St
2300 HOUS 77034 4246 C5
Well Rd
18500 BzaC 77584 4627 C4
18900 BzaC 77511 4627 C4
18900 PRLD 77584 4627 C4
Welland Dr
12300 HOUS 77031 4239 A6
Welland Wy
1200 HOUS 77339 3264 B1
Wellborn Rd
12400 BKVL 77581 4375 E6
Wellborne Rd
16800 BzaC 77584 4503 A7
16800 BzaC 77584 4627 B2
16800 PRLD 77584 4503 A7
17200 PRLD 77584 4627 B2
Wellbrook Ct
3400 PRLD 77581 4503 D1
Wellbrook Ln
4500 FBnC 77450 4093 E2
6900 LGCY 77573 4751 B2
Wellers Wy
16500 HarC 77095 3538 B6
Wellesley Ct
3800 BzaC 77584 4501 C7
Wellesley Dr
10 CNRO 77304 2236 D7
10 CNRO 77304 2382 D1
500 HNCV 77024 3960 B3
20000 HMBL 77338 3262 C5
Wellesley Meadow Ln
12200 HarC 77014 3402 A4
12200 HarC 77067 3402 A4
Wellesly Ct
10 MtgC 77355 2814 E3
Wellford St
10 HOUS 77022 3684 E7
10 HOUS 77022 3685 A7
Wellford Point Dr
16800 HarC 77095 3538 A4
Wellington Blvd
- HarC 77389 2966 C4
Wellington Ct
- HOUS 77055 3821 C5
10 MSCY 77459 4369 D5
10 SGLD 77478 4369 A2
N Wellington Ct
7900 HOUS 77055 3821 C5
S Wellington Ct
7900 HOUS 77055 3821 C5
Wellington Dr
10 SGLD 77478 4369 A2
3400 PRLD 77584 4501 C2
Wellington Ln
10 CNRO 77304 2236 D7
10 SGLD 77478 4368 E2
10 SGLD 77478 4369 A2
Wellington Pk
10 BYTN 77520 3973 D6
Wellington Pkwy
- HarC 77014 3402 B2
12300 HarC 77014 3401 E3
Wellington Pt
300 HarC 77094 3955 B1
Wellington Rd
10 HOUS 77076 3684 E4
10 HOUS 77076 3685 A4
E Wellington Rd
300 HOUS 77076 3684 D4
Wellington St
1500 HOUS 77093 3685 C4
W Wellington St
100 HOUS 77076 3684 C4
Wellington Wy
1600 HOUS 77055 3821 C6
4800 HarC 77069 3256 E6
Wellington Arch Ln
- HOUS 77077 3957 C4
Wellington Bend Ln
21800 HarC 77073 3259 A4
Wellington Cir Dr
14000 HarC 77083 4097 A7
Wellington Ct Blvd
23100 HarC 77389 2966 D6
Wellington Grove Cir
26400 FBnC 77494 4092 E1
Wellington Grove Ln
4300 FBnC 77494 4092 D2
Wellington Meadows Dr
6300 HarC 77449 3676 E3
Wellington Park Dr
12300 HOUS 77072 4097 D7
Wellington Pass Dr
3000 HarC 77373 3115 A4
Wellman Ln
14900 HOUS 77060 3544 C3
Wellman Rd
1800 SHEH 77381 2821 E1
1800 SHEH 77384 2821 E1
2200 WDLD 77381 2821 E1
3900 MtgC 77384 2822 A1
3900 SHEH 77384 2822 A1
Wellness Landing Ln
6300 HOUS 77072 4097 D4
Wellock Ln
18900 HarC 77375 3254 E1
Wells Dr
4000 PRLD 77584 4503 C7
4100 BzaC 77584 4627 C2
4200 PRLD 77584 4627 C1
Wells Ln
27100 ORDN 77385 2822 C5
Wells Rd
19200 MtgC 77306 2680 C3
Wells St
- PRVW 77445 3100 B3
300 HarC 77373 3113 E1
700 CNRO 77301 2384 B6
Well School Rd
- HOUS 77546 4505 E1
- HOUS 77546 4506 A2
Wells Fargo Dr
100 HarC 77090 3258 D4
100 HOUS 77090 3258 D4
W Wells Ford
- HOUS 77077 3957 C5
N Wellsford Dr
800 PRLD 77584 4501 C1
S Wellsford Dr
1000 PRLD 77584 4501 C1
Wells Ford Glen Dr
21400 HarC 77449 3676 D5
Wells Heather St
- HOUS 77077 3957 C5
Wellshire Dr
1100 FBnC 77494 3953 A4
Wellshire Village Ct
15700 FBnC 77478 4236 B5
Wellsley Ct
1900 SGLD 77478 4236 E6
Wells Mark Dr
3600 HarC 77396 3407 E3
4000 HarC 77346 3408 A2
4000 HarC 77396 3408 A2
Wells River Dr
13300 HarC 77041 3679 C4
Wellswood Ct
19300 HarC 77346 3264 B5
Wellsworth Dr
9300 HarC 77083 4237 A1
Wellwick Ct
21000 HarC 77449 3676 D4
Wellwood Ct
6800 HOUS 77083 4097 B5
Wellwood Ln
200 CNRO 77304 2383 B6
E Welsford Dr
2000 MtgC 77386 2969 B1
W Welsford Dr
1300 MtgC 77386 2823 A7
1500 MtgC 77386 2969 A1
Welshpool Glen Dr
11800 HarC 77066 3401 C5
Welsh Ston Dr
- HarC 77049 3689 D7
- HarC 77049 3828 D1
Welshwood Ln
7200 FBnC 77479 4493 E4
Welty
200 TMBL 77375 2964 C6
Welwyn Dr
15300 HarC 77040 3540 E6
15300 HarC 77064 3540 E6
15300 JRSV 77040 3540 E6
15300 JRSV 77064 3540 E6
Wembley Dr
- HOUS 77031 4239 A5
Wemyss Bay Rd
16100 HarC 77095 3538 C6
Wenbury Dr
22200 HarC 77375 3110 C3
Wenda St
4700 HOUS 77033 4243 D5
4700 HOUS 77051 4243 D5
5300 HOUS 77033 4244 A5
Wendel Rd
7300 HOUS 77028 3826 C1
Wendel St
600 HOUS 77009 3963 A1
Wendell St
4300 BLAR 77401 4101 B5
4300 HOUS 77401 4101 B5
Wendelyn Ln
13600 HarC 77069 3256 D7
Wendemere St
7000 HOUS 77088 3683 D4
7000 HOUS 77091 3683 D4
Wendi Ln
1000 BzaC 77511 4748 D2
Wendigo Pl
- HarC 77041 3539 B5
Wendover Ln
11400 PNPV 77024 3959 D2
11700 BKHV 77024 3959 C3
Wendover Creek Ct
15500 HarC 77429 3253 C7
Wendt Rd
41700 WlrC 77445 2953 C3
Wendy Ln
4800 BzaC 77584 4626 A1
Wendy Glinn Wy
18300 HarC 77375 3255 B2
Wendy Hill Wy
1900 HOUS 77058 4507 D2
Wenlock Dr
6000 HOUS 77048 4375 D3
Wennington Dr
10500 HOUS 77099 4098 D7
Wenona Wk
8800 FBnC 77459 4621 B6
Wensley Dr
30300 MtgC 77386 2969 A2
Wentletrap
3800 GLSN 77554 5221 A6
Wentwood Dr
1200 PASD 77504 4247 D6
Wentworth Ct
1300 HOUS 77055 3821 C7
Wentworth Dr
1000 PRLD 77584 4501 C2
Wentworth Ln
2500 PASD 77506 4107 E5
2800 PASD 77506 4108 A4
Wentworth St
1000 HOUS 77002 4102 C3
1000 HOUS 77004 4102 C3
1200 HOUS 77004 4103 A1
Wentworth Oaks Ct
2400 LGCY 77573 4508 D6
Wentworth Park Dr
200 HarC 77015 3829 B6
Wenwood Cir
7200 HOUS 77040 3682 A2
Werchan St
6100 HarC 77532 3552 D3
Werlein St
2600 HOUS 77030 4102 A4
2600 WUNP 77005 4102 A4
Wern Dr
10400 GLSN 77554 5221 C2
Werner St
4500 HOUS 77022 3823 D1
4800 HOUS 77022 3684 D6
7100 HOUS 77076 3684 D3
7700 HOUS 77037 3684 D2
8500 HarC 77037 3684 D1
Wertz St
14500 HOUS 77034 4379 A3
Wescan Dr
8200 HarC 77041 3539 C6
Wesco Wy
6400 HarC 77041 3679 C3
Weser Dr
22800 MtgC 77365 2971 E4
Weslayan St
2600 HOUS 77027 3961 D7
3000 HOUS 77046 4101 D1
3700 HOUS 77027 4101 D1
5600 HOUS 77005 4101 D3
5600 WUNP 77005 4101 D3
6700 SSPL 77025 4101 D4
Wesley Dr
- LGCY 77573 4631 C3
N Wesley Dr
300 LGCY 77573 4631 D4
1100 STAF 77477 4370 C4
Wesley Ln
1300 DRPK 77536 4109 C5
Wesley St
1500 HOUS 77023 4104 B1
Wesley Oaks
13400 HOUS 77085 4371 E1
Weslow St
3700 HOUS 77087 4104 D7
Wessendorf Rd
3800 FBnC 77469 4233 B6
Wessendorff Ln
2800 FBnC 77469 4492 D2
Wessex Dr
11900 HOUS 77089 4378 C6
Wessex Park Dr
13900 HarC 77429 3397 C2
West
- BYTN 77520 3971 D6
West Av
- HOUS 77034 4248 D7
- PASD 77034 4248 D7
- PASD 77505 4248 D7
100 PASD 77502 4247 A1
700 PASD 77502 4246 E1
West Blvd
- HOUS 77006 4102 D1
West Ct
10 HOUS 77017 4105 E6
3800 DRPK 77536 4249 C1
West Dr
- LGCY 77573 4752 D1
200 HOUS 77003 3963 E3
200 LGCY 77565 4508 E4
600 HarC 77530 3829 C7
600 HarC 77530 3968 C1
12100 HarC 77433 3396 D6
12700 HarC 77429 3396 D4
14900 FBnC 77053 4372 D7
West Ln
10 HOUS 77019 3961 C5
500 PASD 77506 4106 E5
E West Ln
16800 MtgC 77306 2533 D7
West Rd
- HarC 77064 3542 A5
- HOUS 77017 4105 E5
- HOUS 77086 3542 A4
100 HarC 77037 3544 A4
100 HOUS 77037 3544 A4
100 HOUS 77060 3544 A4
200 HarC 77038 3544 B4
300 HarC 77038 3543 D4
300 STAF 77477 4370 A4
700 HarC 77060 3544 E3
5000 BYTN 77521 3833 E7
5000 BYTN 77521 3972 E1
5000 HarC 77521 3833 E7
5000 HarC 77521 3972 E1
5800 HarC 77086 3542 D4
7400 HOUS 77064 3542 A5
8500 MtgC 77354 2672 E7
8500 WDLD 77382 2672 E7
8700 HOUS 77017 4106 A5
9100 HarC 77040 3540 E5
9100 HarC 77040 3541 A5
9100 HarC 77064 3540 E5
9100 HarC 77064 3541 A5
10900 HarC 77065 3540 A4
11300 HarC 77065 3539 E5
11400 JRSV 77065 3539 C6
12300 HarC 77041 3539 D6
12300 JRSV 77041 3539 D6
14300 HarC 77095 3539 A6
15100 HarC 77095 3538 D5
16900 HarC 77095 3537 D5
17100 HarC 77433 3537 D5
21900 MtgC 77357 2973 E2
E West Rd
100 HarC 77060 3544 E3
400 HOUS 77060 3544 D3
S West Rd
100 TXCY 77591 4873 B7
200 LMQU 77568 4873 B7
West St
- HOUS 77026 3824 E7
400 RSBG 77471 4490 D3
1000 HOUS 77020 3963 E2
1500 HOUS 77026 3963 E1
3300 RSBG 77471 4614 D1
7700 HOUS 77093 3824 E1
8400 HOUS 77093 3685 E7
E West St
600 GLSN 77550 5109 A3
Westacre Pl
9300 FBnC 77083 4237 A2
Westall Ln
3800 FBnC 77459 4621 C5
Westbank Av
7700 HarC 77064 3541 E6
Westbay Ln
7700 HarC 77044 3689 A7
7700 HarC 77044 3828 A1
West Bend Dr
- LGCY 77573 4630 B7
Westbend Dr
1900 DRPK 77536 4108 D6
2000 DRPK 77503 4108 E6
2000 PASD 77503 4108 E6
Westbluff Dr
1700 HarC 77084 3815 E7
Westborough Dr
- HOUS 77449 3815 D7
2000 HarC 77449 3815 D7
Westbrae Pkwy
10600 HOUS 77031 4239 B4
10600 HOUS 77071 4239 C4
Westbrae Gardens Ct
8900 HOUS 77031 4239 C4
Westbrae Manor Dr
8800 HOUS 77031 4239 B4
Westbrae Meadows Dr
10900 HOUS 77031 4239 C4
Westbrae Oaks Ln
10900 HOUS 77031 4239 C4
Westbrae Park Ct
10800 HOUS 77031 4239 C4
Westbrae Park Ln
- HOUS 77031 4239 C4
Westbrae Village Dr
10800 HOUS 77031 4239 C4
Westbranch Ct
12800 HOUS 77072 4097 D5
Westbranch Dr
1600 HOUS 77077 3957 C5
6100 HOUS 77072 4097 D4
Westbranch Meadows Ct
10500 HOUS 77041 3680 D7
Westbriar Ct
1900 DRPK 77536 4109 A6
Westbriar Ln
5000 HOUS 77056 3961 A5
Westbridge Ln
19600 HarC 77379 3112 A5
Westbrook Cir
3300 PASD 77503 4108 B5
Westbrook Dr
- HarC 77449 3815 B2
300 HOUS 77037 3544 B6
300 HOUS 77037 3544 B6
400 MtgC 77362 2963 C3
Westbrook Rd
5200 HOUS 77016 3686 C5
Westbrook Bridge Dr
7800 HarC 77095 3539 C7
Westbrook Cinco Ln
22500 FBnC 77450 4093 E1
Westbrook Forest Dr
8600 FBnC 77479 4494 B4
Westbrook Lakes Blvd
- HarC 77095 3539 B7
Westbrook Oaks Wy
5400 HarC 77379 3112 A7
5400 HarC 77379 3257 B1
Westbury Ct
14400 HarC 77084 3679 A4
Westbury Ln
2700 TXCY 77590 4874 E3
Westbury Sq
- HOUS 77096 4240 D4
500 HOUS 77035 4240 D4
West By Northwest Blvd
5900 HOUS 77040 3681 B5
Westcenter Dr
3300 HOUS 77042 4098 E2
Westchase Ct
11700 MtgC 77304 2382 A4
Westchase Dr
3600 HOUS 77042 4098 E2
Westchase Wy
- HOUS 77072 4098 D4
Westchester Ct
6700 HOUS 77025 4101 E4
6700 WUNP 77005 4101 E4
Westchester Dr
10 PNVL 77304 2237 B1
10 PNVL 77318 2237 B1
Westchester Rd
2700 PRLD 77581 4502 B4
2700 PRLD 77584 4502 B4
Westchester St
4700 PASD 77505 4248 E6
5100 HOUS 77005 4101 E2
6900 HOUS 77005 4101 E5
6900 WUNP 77005 4101 E5
Westcliff
- HOUS 77027 3961 B6
Westcliff Ct
19900 HarC 77433 3677 A1
Westcliffe Falls Dr
21500 HarC 77450 3954 B5
Westcott Rd
- HOUS 77016 3687 A6
- HOUS 77028 3686 E7
5200 HOUS 77028 3825 D1
7600 HOUS 77016 3825 D1
8200 HOUS 77016 3686 E7
Westcott St
10 HOUS 77007 3962 A3
6300 HOUS 77007 3961 E2
Westcove Cir
8600 HarC 77064 3540 E6
West Creek Dr
- LGCY 77573 4630 B6
Westcreek Ln
2000 HOUS 77027 3961 B6
Westcrest Rd
1800 HOUS 77055 3821 A5
Westcross St
600 HOUS 77018 3823 B2
Westdale St
5600 HOUS 77087 4104 E7
5700 HOUS 77087 4244 E1
Westedge Dr
10300 FBnC 77478 4236 E3
Westella Dr
12300 HOUS 77077 3957 D6
Westelm Ct
3500 FBnC 77469 4364 E1
Westenfeldt Dr
4800 FBnC 77545 4622 D3
4800 MSCY 77545 4622 D3
Westenfeldt Rd
4200 FBnC 77545 4622 D2
4500 MSCY 77545 4622 D2
Westenfield Ln
22500 FBnC 77450 4093 E1
Westerbrook Ln
8400 HarC 77396 3547 E1
Westercreek Ln
4600 HarC 77546 4506 C6
Westerfield Ln
2900 HarC 77084 3816 C4
Westerham Pl
5100 HarC 77069 3256 D7
Westerlage St
1300 LMQU 77568 4990 C1
Westerlake Ct
14700 HarC 77396 3547 D3
Westerlake Dr
2500 PRLD 77584 4500 E2
Westerland Dr
2200 HOUS 77063 3959 C7
2800 HOUS 77063 4099 C1
Westerley Ln
12500 HOUS 77077 3957 D4
Westerloch Dr
13800 HOUS 77077 3957 A4
Westerly Dr
300 TKIS 77554 5106 B4
Westerly Pk
- HarC 77041 3679 D7
Westerman St
3700 HOUS 77005 4101 D2
Westermill Dr
4000 HarC 77082 4096 B4
Western Dr
7200 GlsC 77563 4990 A6
7500 HTCK 77563 4990 A6
8200 HOUS 77055 3821 B5
9100 HOUS 77080 3820 E5
Western Branch Ct
4600 HarC 77066 3401 C5
Western Briar Ln
9600 HarC 77396 3407 B2
Western Echo Rd
16100 MtgC 77302 2679 B3
Western Hill Dr
15700 MtgC 77302 2679 D3
Western Hills Ct
22000 HarC 77450 3954 B2
Western Hills Dr
900 HarC 77450 3954 A3
Western Meadows Dr
1000 HarC 77450 3953 E3
Western Oak Ln
7600 HarC 77040 3541 D7
7600 HarC 77040 3681 D1
Western Pass Ln
- HarC 77433 3537 D7
17800 HarC 77095 3537 E7
Western Saddle Ct
14500 HarC 77044 3408 D7
Western Skies Dr
15100 HarC 77086 3541 D1
Western Skys Dr
- HarC 77086 3541 E1
Western Springs Dr
1000 HarC 77450 3953 E3
Western Trail Dr
8000 HarC 77040 3681 D1
Western Valley Dr
21000 HarC 77449 3676 C2
Western Village Ln
1900 HOUS 77043 3819 B5
Westerpine Ln
22000 HarC 77449 3676 C6
Westfair East Dr
13800 HarC 77041 3539 C6
Westfair West Dr
- HarC 77041 3539 B6
Westfall Av
900 PASD 77506 4107 B5
West Fall Dr
14200 HarC 77083 4096 E6
Westfield Ct
- HarC 77073 3260 B5
- HOUS 77338 3260 B5
Westfield Dr
2300 ALVN 77511 4866 D3
Westfield Ln
100 FRDW 77546 4628 E2
300 PRLD 77581 4628 E1
6600 HOUS 77085 4371 C4
18000 BzaC 77581 4628 E1
Westfield Pkwy
- HarC 77084 3816 B2
19200 HarC 77449 3816 A2
19700 HarC 77449 3815 E2
Westfield Pl
500 HOUS 77090 3258 C1
Westfield Rd
500 BzaC 77581 4628 D1
600 BzaC 77581 4504 C6
600 PRLD 77581 4504 C6
Westfield St
100 HOUS 77022 3824 A2
1200 HOUS 77022 3823 E2
Westfield Estates Dr
20400 HarC 77449 3815 D2
Westfield Hollow Ln
- HarC 77449 3676 D7
Westfield Lakes Ln
- HarC 77449 3815 B1
Westfield Loop Rd
1600 HarC 77073 3259 C3
Westfield Pines Dr
- HarC 77449 3676 C7
Westfield Pl Dr
- HOUS 77090 3258 D3
Westfield Ridge Dr
21800 HarC 77073 3259 E1
Westfield Village Dr
4100 HarC 77449 3676 D7
4100 HarC 77449 3815 D1
Westford Av
1700 HOUS 77093 3824 D2
Westford St
500 HOUS 77022 3824 B2
Westford Park Ln
7000 FBnC 77469 4094 B5
Westforest Dr
- FBnC 77450 3953 D5
- FBnC 77494 3953 D5
West Fork Blvd
4800 CNRO 77304 2382 D2
Westfork Ct
20200 HarC 77449 3815 C7
West Fork Dr
- LGCY 77573 4630 B7
Westfork Dr
1600 HarC 77449 3815 C7
Westgard Blvd
11900 HarC 77044 3827 E1
West Gate
- PASD 77586 4382 C4
Westgate Dr
2100 HOUS 77019 3962 B6
2400 HOUS 77098 3962 B6
2500 PRLD 77581 4502 A3
2500 PRLD 77584 4502 A3
10400 CHTW 77385 2822 D4
Westgate Rd
12000 HarC 77065 3398 B6
12000 HarC 77429 3398 B6
15300 MtgC 77372 2683 D4
Westgate St
2600 HOUS 77019 3962 B7
2600 HOUS 77098 3962 B7
Westgate Park Dr
18000 HarC 77095 3677 D1
18000 HarC 77433 3677 D1
18200 HarC 77433 3537 C7
Westgate Pature Ln
18400 HarC 77433 3537 C7
Westgate Springs Ln
18400 HarC 77433 3537 C7
Westgate Village Ln
22900 HarC 77373 2968 D6
Westglen Dr
900 ALVN 77511 4867 D6
7800 HOUS 77063 4100 A2
8100 HOUS 77063 4099 E2
Westgreen Blvd
- HarC 77449 3954 C1
- HOUS 77449 3954 C1
700 HarC 77450 3954 C2
700 HOUS 77450 3954 C5
N Westgreen Blvd
1100 HarC 77449 3954 B1
1100 HOUS 77449 3954 B1
1100 HOUS 77450 3954 B1
1500 HOUS 77449 3815 C7
2100 HarC 77449 3815 C6
S Westgreen Blvd
2400 HarC 77450 3954 D6
Westgreen Ct
20800 HarC 77450 3954 C3
West Green Spur
34000 HarC 77447 3249 B4
Westgreen Sq
16700 HarC 77447 3249 B4
Westgrove Ln
2600 HOUS 77027 3961 D7
West Gulf Bank Rd
2400 HarC 77088 3683 B1
Westhall Ln
7600 HarC 77433 3537 D7
Westhampton Dr
3200 HOUS 77045 4373 A1
3300 HOUS 77045 4372 E1
Westhaven Dr
19400 HarC 77084 3816 A5
Westheimer Ct
5400 HOUS 77056 3960 E7
Westheimer Pkwy
- FBnC 77494 3953 B7
- HOUS 77082 4096 C1
- HOUS 77094 3954 D7
- HOUS 77494 3953 C7
15100 HOUS 77082 3956 C7
15100 HOUS 77094 3956 C7
16500 HOUS 77094 4095 B2
16500 HOUS 77094 4096 A2
17800 HOUS 77094 4094 D1
17800 HOUS 77450 4094 D1
17800 HOUS 77450 4095 A2
21000 FBnC 77450 3954 B7
21100 FBnC 77450 4094 A1
22600 FBnC 77450 4093 D1
22900 HOUS 77450 4093 D1
23500 FBnC 77494 4093 D1
23500 HOUS 77494 4093 D1
Westheimer Rd
- FBnC 77469 4095 D4
100 HOUS 77006 3963 A6
200 HOUS 77006 3962 E6
1600 HOUS 77019 3962 A6
1600 HOUS 77098 3962 A6
3200 HOUS 77019 3961 E6
3200 HOUS 77098 3961 E6
3300 HOUS 77027 3961 E6
4800 HOUS 77056 3961 A7
5100 HOUS 77056 3960 A7
5700 HOUS 77057 3960 D7
6500 HOUS 77063 3960 A7
7900 HOUS 77063 3959 E7
9700 HOUS 77042 3959 A7
10400 HOUS 77042 3958 C7
11100 HOUS 77077 3958 B7
11100 HOUS 77082 3958 C7
12100 HOUS 77077 3957 D7
12100 HOUS 77082 3957 D7
13100 HarC 77077 3957 B7
13200 HarC 77077 3957 B7
13700 HOUS 77077 3956 D7
13700 HOUS 77082 3956 E7
14800 HOUS 77082 4096 C1
15500 HarC 77082 4096 A3
16200 HarC 77082 4095 D4
16200 HOUS 77082 4095 D4
16800 HOUS 77450 4095 D4
16800 HOUS 77469 4095 D4
Westheimer Rd FM-1093
- FBnC 77469 4095 D4
- HOUS 77469 4095 D4
4800 HOUS 77027 3961 A7
4800 HOUS 77056 3961 A7
5100 HOUS 77056 3960 A7
5700 HOUS 77057 3960 D7
6500 HOUS 77063 3960 A7
7900 HOUS 77063 3959 E7
9700 HOUS 77042 3959 A7
10000 HOUS 77042 3958 E7
11100 HOUS 77077 3958 B7
11100 HOUS 77082 3958 C7
12100 HOUS 77077 3957 D7
12100 HOUS 77082 3957 D7
13100 HarC 77077 3957 B7
13200 HarC 77077 3957 B7
13700 HOUS 77077 3956 D7
13700 HOUS 77082 3956 E7
14800 HOUS 77082 4096 C1
15500 HarC 77082 4096 A3
16200 HarC 77082 4095 D4
16200 HOUS 77082 4095 D4
16800 HOUS 77450 4095 D4
Westheimer Wy
5400 HOUS 77056 3960 E7
Westheimer Lakes North Dr
- FBnC 77469 4092 A6
- FBnC 77494 4092 A5
Westheimer Pl Dr
- HOUS 77082 4096 A3
3700 HarC 77082 4096 A3
West Highlands Cross
8700 HarC 77562 3832 B2
Westhill Ln
12900 HOUS 77077 3957 C5
Westhoff Ct
2400 MtgC 77384 2529 A5
Westhollow Dr
- HOUS 77077 3956 E7
- HOUS 77082 3956 E7
2500 HOUS 77082 4096 E1
3400 HarC 77082 4096 E2
Westhollow Pkwy
4000 HarC 77082 4097 A4
Westhollow Park Dr
3900 HarC 77082 4097 A3
4000 HarC 77082 4097 A4
13700 HOUS 77082 4096 E1
13700 HOUS 77082 4097 A1
Westholme Dr
3900 HOUS 77063 4099 E2
Westhorpe Dr
12700 HOUS 77077 3957 C6
Westhurst Ln
1500 HOUS 77077 3957 C5
Westington Ln
7800 HarC 77040 3541 E6
Westknoll Ln
8400 HarC 77072 4097 C7
Westlake Clb
500 HOUS 77079 3957 A1
West Lake Dr
800 HOUS 77336 3121 B5
Westlake Dr
1200 HOUS 77336 3121 A5
Westlake Rd
1900 HOUS 77062 4507 C2
Westlake Wy
1900 HarC 77084 3816 A6
Westlake Park Blvd
200 HOUS 77079 3957 A1
Westlake Pl Dr
- HarC 77449 3815 E5
19700 HarC 77084 3815 E5
19700 HarC 77084 3816 B5
Westland Creek Dr
22000 HarC 77449 3815 A3
Westland East Blvd
13300 HarC 77041 3539 C6
Westland West Blvd
8400 HarC 77041 3539 C6
Westleigh Dr
12600 HOUS 77077 3957 C6
Westline Dr
6000 HOUS 77036 4099 A4
Westlock Ct
18100 HarC 77377 3254 D2
Westlock Dr
- HarC 77375 3254 D2
11700 HarC 77377 3254 D2

STREET Block City ZIP Map# Grid

Westlock St
18200 HarC 77377 3254 C2
Westmart Dr
3800 HOUS 77042 4098 E2
Westmead Dr
- HOUS 77077 3957 C6
Westmeadow Ct
7300 FBnC 77469 4095 D6
Westmeadow Dr
1700 HarC 77084 3816 A7
3700 HarC 77082 4096 A3
Westmere Ct
1700 HOUS 77077 3958 B7
Westmere Dr
11800 HOUS 77077 3958 A6
12300 HOUS 77077 3957 D5
Westminister Ct
5400 HarC 77069 3400 D1
Westminister St
2000 PRLD 77581 4504 A2
2100 PRLD 77581 4503 E3
Westminster Dr
300 HOUS 77024 3960 C2
400 LGCY 77573 4631 D5
9800 HMBL 77338 3262 C4
Westminster Glen Dr
13800 HarC 77049 3828 D1
Westminster Plaza Dr
2600 HOUS 77077 3957 E7
2600 HOUS 77082 3957 E7
2600 HOUS 77082 4097 E1
Westminster Trace Ln
1600 HOUS 77339 3265 A1
Westminster Village Ct
17000 HarC 77084 3678 A4
Westminster Village Dr
5700 HarC 77084 3678 B4
Westmont Dr
500 HOUS 77015 3967 B1
Westmoor Dr
6700 FBnC 77469 4095 C6
6700 HOUS 77469 4095 C4
8800 FBnC 77469 4235 C1
Westmoreland Ln
7000 MtgC 77354 2818 E2
Westmoreland St
200 HOUS 77006 3962 E7
400 HOUS 77006 3963 D2
Westnut Ln
8400 HarC 77040 3541 C6
West Oak Dr
- LGCY 77573 4630 B6
N West Oak Dr
10 HOUS 77056 3960 D5
10 HOUS 77056 3961 A4
S West Oak Dr
- HOUS 77056 3961 A4
Westoak St
- BYTN 77520 3971 B2
West Oaks Mems
5100 HOUS 77056 3961 B3
West Oak Village Dr
- FBnC 77469 4095 C6
Westoffice Dr
10300 HOUS 77042 4098 E3
10300 HOUS 77042 4099 A3
Weston St
6300 HOUS 77021 4103 E7
Weston Park Dr
18300 HarC 77433 3537 C6
Westonridge Ln
4900 MSCY 77545 4622 C3
Weston Village Dr
31400 MtgC 77386 2823 A7
Westover
500 MtgC 77302 2530 C7
Westover Dr
12000 HarC 77065 3398 B6
12000 HarC 77429 3398 B6
Westover Ln
1900 FBnC 77469 4616 B2
Westover St
5100 HOUS 77033 4243 E3
5400 HOUS 77033 4244 A3
6200 HOUS 77087 4244 D3
7200 HOUS 77087 4245 A2
Westover Park Av
- LGCY 77573 4751 B1
100 LGCY 77573 4630 C7
Westover Park Cir
2000 MtgC 77386 2823 B7
Westover Ridge Dr
7000 HOUS 77072 4097 D5
Westpark Dr
- FBnC 77082 4095 D4
- FBnC 77083 4095 D4
- FBnC 77469 4095 D4
- HarC 77083 4096 A4
10 CNRO 77304 2383 C4
2100 ALVN 77511 4866 E4
2600 HOUS 77005 4102 A1
2600 HOUS 77098 4102 A1
2800 HOUS 77005 4101 B2
2800 HOUS 77098 4101 A2
3200 HOUS 77027 4101 E1
4100 HOUS 77081 4101 C1
4400 BLAR 77027 4101 A2
4400 BLAR 77401 4101 A2
4400 HOUS 77401 4101 A2
5000 BLAR 77056 4101 A2
5000 HOUS 77056 4100 D2
5000 HOUS 77056 4101 A2
5600 HOUS 77057 4100 C2
5800 HOUS 77081 4100 C2
6400 HOUS 77063 4100 A2
8100 HOUS 77063 4099 D2
9900 HOUS 77042 4099 A2
10400 HOUS 77042 4098 D2
11100 HOUS 77082 4098 B3
12200 HOUS 77082 4097 C2
13500 HarC 77082 4097 A3
13500 HOUS 77082 4096 E3
15000 HarC 77082 4096 B3
Westpark Tollway
- FBnC - 4093 A6
- FBnC - 4094 A5
- FBnC - 4095 D4
- HarC - 4095 D4
- HarC - 4096 D4
- HarC - 4097 A4
- HOUS - 4093 D5
- HOUS - 4095 C4
- HOUS - 4096 E4
- HOUS - 4097 A4
- HOUS - 4098 D3
- HOUS - 4099 E2
- HOUS - 4100 A2
- HOUS - 4101 E2
24000 FBnC 77494 4093 A6

Westpark Tollway FM-1093
24000 FBnC 77469 4093 A6
24000 FBnC 77494 4093 A6
Westpine Forest Ln
- HarC 77449 3815 C1
Westplace Dr
8800 HOUS 77031 4239 B5
8800 HOUS 77071 4239 C5
Westplain Dr
14000 HarC 77041 3539 C5
Westpoint Dr
10 MSCY 77459 4621 E3
3000 FBnC 77583 4621 E3
3000 FBnC 77583 4622 A3
Westport Ln
13300 HOUS 77079 3958 B1
Westport Bridge Ln
10200 FBnC 77478 4236 C3
Westport Shore Dr
1000 HarC 77094 3955 B2
Westray Ct
1400 MSCY 77459 4369 C5
Westray Dr
4400 MSCY 77459 4369 B5
Westray St
- HOUS 77080 3820 B3
10300 HOUS 77043 3820 A3
10400 HOUS 77043 3819 E3
Westridge Dr
- FBnC 77479 4494 C5
- HOUS 77054 4102 B7
1800 FBnC 77469 4493 A4
2400 HOUS 77054 4242 A1
2900 HOUS 77025 4242 A1
Westridge Rd
500 MtgC 77380 2968 B3
500 WDLD 77380 2968 B3
Westridge St
3200 HOUS 77025 4241 E1
Westridge Bend Ln
18200 HarC 77433 3537 D7
Westshire Dr
400 HOUS 77013 3966 B2
800 HOUS 77029 3966 B2
Westshore Ct
800 LGCY 77573 4633 B3
4300 MSCY 77459 4369 C7
Westshore Dr
1200 HarC 77094 3955 B3
2000 MSCY 77459 4369 C7
Westside Ct
500 PASD 77502 4247 B2
2000 SGLD 77478 4369 A6
Westside Dr
1900 DRPK 77536 4108 E6
2700 PASD 77502 4247 B3
3000 PASD 77504 4247 B4
Westside Pkwy
- HOUS 77449 3814 E7
- HOUS 77449 3953 C1
- HOUS 77450 3953 C1
Westside Wy
- HOUS 77449 3814 D7
Westside Business Dr
6300 HarC 77084 3678 A3
Westspring Ct
3500 FBnC 77469 4364 E1
Weststar Ln
6200 HOUS 77072 4097 D4
West Trail Ct
3500 FBnC 77469 4364 E1
Westview Blvd
1700 CNRO 77304 2383 C2
S Westview Cir
10800 HOUS 77043 3819 C7
Westview Dr
- WlrC 77447 2813 A2
900 CNRO 77301 2384 D5
1700 ALVN 77511 4866 D3
3300 SRAC 77571 4382 E1
3400 SRAC 77571 4383 A2
3500 LPRT 77571 4383 A2
5800 HOUS 77055 3822 B6
6500 HOUS 77055 3821 E6
7900 HLSV 77055 3821 B6
8400 SPVL 77055 3821 A6
8900 SPVL 77055 3820 D6
9100 HOUS 77055 3820 A7
10000 HOUS 77043 3820 A7
10600 HOUS 77043 3819 C7
Westview Ln
300 PNVL 77304 2237 A2
Westview St
2500 LPRT 77571 4251 E7
S Westview Cir Dr
10800 HOUS 77043 3819 C7
Westward Av
100 LMQU 77568 4873 D7
100 TXCY 77591 4873 D7
300 LMQU 77568 4989 D2
Westward Ln
- FRDW 77546 4505 B5
Westward St
5600 HOUS 77074 4100 B4
5600 HOUS 77081 4100 B4
N Westward St
10 TXCY 77591 4873 C5
S Westward St
10 LMQU 77568 4873 D7
10 TXCY 77591 4873 D7
Westward Trl
14800 HOUS 77045 4372 A4
14800 HOUS 77053 4372 A4
Westward Ho St
15800 SGCH 77355 2816 A7
15900 SGCH 77355 2815 E7
Westward Ridge Pl
10 WDLD 77384 2675 A4
Westway Dr
1700 DRPK 77536 4108 E6
Westway Ln
14300 HOUS 77077 3956 D4
Westway St
1600 GNPK 77547 3966 B6
11400 HarC 77093 3546 D7
11600 HarC 77039 3546 D7
West Way Park Blvd
- HOUS 77041 3819 D1
- HOUS 77043 3819 D1
Westway Park Blvd
4300 HOUS 77041 3819 D1
4300 HOUS 77043 3819 D1
4900 HOUS 77041 3680 D7
Westwego Tr
16400 HarC 77429 3397 A3
Westwick Dr
1600 HOUS 77077 3957 C6
3200 HOUS 77082 4097 C2

Westwick Dr
6200 HOUS 77072 4097 C4
Westwick Forest Ln
1200 HOUS 77043 3819 A7
Westwillow Dr
- HarC 77040 3540 E6
9000 HarC 77064 3540 E6
Westwind Ct
1800 LGCY 77539 4633 D4
5200 SGLD 77479 4495 A4
7800 HOUS 77071 4239 E2
Westwind Dr
1900 DRPK 77536 4108 E6
Westwind Ln
7600 HOUS 77071 4239 E2
Westwinds Cir
10 WDLD 77382 2673 D5
N Westwinds Cir
10 WDLD 77382 2673 D4
Westwold Dr
11800 HarC 77377 3254 C2
Westwood Cir
10 CNRO 77301 2384 B7
600 LMQU 77568 4872 A5
E Westwood Cir
15300 MSCY 77071 4239 C5
W Westwood Cir
15400 MSCY 77071 4239 D6
Westwood Ct
200 ORDN 77386 2822 C6
Westwood Dr
- LGCY 77573 4630 B6
10 BYTN 77520 4113 B1
200 FRDW 77546 4505 A5
1100 RSBG 77471 4491 D2
1900 STAF 77477 4370 B4
5000 DKSN 77539 4754 C2
7900 HOUS 77055 3821 B6
16200 MtgC 77302 2825 B3
26500 ORDN 77386 2822 B5
27000 ORDN 77385 2822 B5
N Westwood Dr
18800 MtgC 77302 2825 B3
Westwood Lk
2000 HOUS 77339 3118 D3
Westwood Ln
4500 BzaC 77578 4625 E1
4500 BzaC 77578 4626 A1
Westwood Rd
19900 GlsC 77511 4868 D3
E Westwood Sq
32400 MtgC 77354 2673 C4
W Westwood Sq
32400 MtgC 77354 2673 B4
Westwood St
1800 STAF 77477 4370 B4
Westwood Glen Ln
800 HOUS 77047 4373 B2
Westwood Lake Ct
2000 HOUS 77339 3118 C7
Westwood Manor Ln
- HarC 77047 4374 B4
Westwood Meadows Dr
2900 HOUS 77082 4096 D2
Westwood North Dr
100 MtgC 77354 2673 D3
Westwood Pines Ln
5000 HarC 77449 3676 C6
Westwood Pl Dr
7800 HOUS 77036 4099 A6
7900 HOUS 77036 4098 E6
Westwood Village Dr
9200 HOUS 77036 4099 A6
Wetherburn Ln
22100 HarC 77449 3815 A6
22200 HarC 77449 3814 E5
Wetherby Ln
8000 HOUS 77075 4376 D2
Wetherfield Ln
13800 HarC 77429 3397 E2
Wetherill St
8600 HOUS 77093 3685 E7
Wetherwind Ct
19500 HarC 77449 3677 A6
Wetnersfield Rd
- HarC 77095 3538 E7
Wetzel Dr
- TXCY 77591 4754 E6
6800 TXCY 77539 4754 E5
Wexford
- PRLD 77089 4504 C2
- PRLD 77581 4504 C2
Wexford Ct
10 PNPV 77024 3959 E3
Wexford Dr
1300 DRPK 77536 4108 E6
Wexford Park Dr
6400 HarC 77088 3542 C6
Wexier Ln
- HarC 77047 4374 C3
Weybridge Dr
- HOUS 77031 4238 E6
9600 HOUS 77031 4239 A5
Weyburn St
6900 HOUS 77028 3686 E7
7400 HOUS 77028 3687 A7
Weyburn Grove Dr
8900 HarC 77088 3542 C6
Weyer Av
1200 LGCY 77573 4631 D7
Weygand
18900 HarC 77484 3102 B6
Weygand St
900 WALR 77484 3102 A6
Weymouth Dr
8800 HOUS 77031 4239 A5
Wharf
1000 GLSN 77550 5109 D1
Wharf St
- HOUS 77012 4105 C1
2800 GLSN 77550 5108 E3
2800 GLSN 77550 5109 A3
3700 GLSN 77551 5108 E3
Wharton
- BYTN 77520 3972 A6
Wharton Av
4800 GLSN 77551 5108 D4
Wharton Dr
4800 GLSN 77551 5108 D5
Wharton St
6500 HOUS 77055 3821 E6
6500 HOUS 77055 3822 A6
Wharton Weems Blvd
- LPRT 77571 4251 C6
Wharton Weems Blvd SR-146 BUS
- LPRT 77571 4251 C6

Whatley Dr
2100 DRPK 77536 4108 D6
2100 DRPK 77536 4248 E1
Wheat Ln
2000 HarC 77521 3832 C4
Wheat St
3300 HarC 77086 3542 D2
Wheatbridge Dr
13600 HarC 77041 3679 B4
Wheat Cross Dr
8500 HarC 77095 3537 E5
Wheatfield Blvd
3100 PRLD 77581 4503 D5
Wheatfield Ct
3400 PRLD 77581 4503 D5
Wheatfield Dr
16500 HarC 77095 3538 B6
Wheathall Camp Ln
2000 HarC 77449 3815 C6
Wheatland Dr
8700 HarC 77064 3540 C5
Wheatley Av
700 BYTN 77520 4112 D1
Wheatley St
5600 HOUS 77091 3683 E6
7500 HOUS 77088 3683 E2
Wheatmeadow Cir
3200 PRLD 77581 4503 D6
Wheatmeadow Ln
3400 PRLD 77581 4503 D5
Wheatmill Ct
16500 HarC 77095 3538 B6
Wheat Mill Ln
16600 HarC 77095 3538 B6
Wheaton Dr
10500 HOUS 77075 4377 D3
10500 HOUS 77089 4377 D3
N Wheaton Dr
- HOUS 77094 3954 E7
- HOUS 77094 4094 E1
S Wheaton Dr
- HOUS 77094 4094 D1
Wheaton St
100 RHMD 77469 4492 A1
Wheaton Creek Ct
20700 HOUS 77073 3259 C7
Wheaton Crest Ln
- HarC 77433 3396 B6
7000 HarC 77379 3111 B4
Wheaton Edge Ln
9700 HarC 77095 3538 A4
Wheaton Forest Ln
- HarC 77095 3537 D5
Wheaton Hill Ln
7000 FBnC 77469 4094 E5
Wheatridge Dr
3200 PRLD 77581 4376 D6
11100 HarC 77064 3540 D2
Wheat Snow Ct
2100 HarC 77449 3815 D6
Wheatsnow Ln
20100 HarC 77449 3815 C6
Wheatstalk Ln
3400 PRLD 77581 4503 D5
Wheeden Rd
6800 HOUS 77048 4375 E2
6800 HOUS 77075 4375 E2
6800 HOUS 77075 4376 A2
Wheeler
- PASD 77506 4107 C6
Wheeler Ln
- ALVN 77511 4749 C5
Wheeler St
1000 HOUS 77002 3963 A7
1000 HOUS 77004 3963 A7
1200 HOUS 77004 4103 E2
4300 HOUS 77004 4104 A3
5900 HOUS 77023 4104 C4
Wheeler Peak Wy
4400 HarC 77449 3676 B7
Wheeler Ridge Cir
10 BzaC 77583 4624 C4
Wheelhouse Ct
300 STAF 77477 4369 C3
Wheelhouse Dr
600 STAF 77477 4369 C3
Wheelwright Ln
2500 HarC 77546 4506 B7
Whelton Cir
700 PASD 77503 4108 B5
Whelton Dr
800 PASD 77503 4108 B6
Whetrock Ln
2900 SGLD 77479 4368 E7
2900 SGLD 77479 4495 E1
Whetstone Ln
7500 HarC 77064 3542 A5
Whetstone Ridge Ct
10 WDLD 77382 2673 A6
Whetstone Ridge Wy
10 WDLD 77382 2673 A6
Whidbey Ct
3600 HarC 77388 3112 D6
Whidbey Island Dr
7700 HarC 77086 3541 E2
7700 HarC 77086 3542 A2
Whiddon Ln
16500 MtgC 77306 2533 C1
Whila Wy
1800 GlsC 77511 4751 B7
1800 GlsC 77511 4869 B1
1800 STFE 77511 4869 B1
Whimbrel Dr
100 SGLD 77478 4368 A4
Whimsey Ct
6500 HarC 77084 3678 A3
S Whimsey Dr
- HarC 77433 3677 B1
N Whimsey Ln
19000 HarC 77433 3677 B1
W Whimsey Ln
7400 HarC 77433 3677 B1
Whipering Lanes Dr
- KATY 77493 3813 B7
Whipple Dr
100 BLAR 77401 4100 E6
100 BLAR 77401 4101 A6
Whipple Tree Dr
15800 HarC 77070 3255 B6
Whippoorwill Ct
4300 MSCY 77459 4496 C1
Whippoorwill Dr
500 MSCY 77489 4370 E4
Whippoorwill Ln
7200 TXCY 77591 4873 C5
Whippoorwill Rd
11400 HDWV 77024 3959 D2

Whipporwill Rd
100 CTSH 77303 2385 E3
100 CTSH 77306 2385 E3
100 MtgC 77303 2385 D2
4000 MtgC 77303 2239 D6
Whipstock Rd
37000 MtgC 77354 2816 B1
Whirlaway Dr
2000 STAF 77477 4370 B4
4100 PASD 77503 4108 D7
Whirlaway Elm Dr
8100 HarC 77346 3265 B7
Whirlwind St
3000 PRLD 77581 4503 D3
Whiskey Bay
- CNRO 77304 2382 D2
Whisper Ln
10 WDLD 77380 2821 D7
Whisper Rd
10900 MtgC 77372 2536 E2
Whisper Bay Dr
19100 HarC 77094 3955 B3
Whisper Bluff Dr
10300 HarC 77396 3407 D1
Whispering Ct
2700 FBnC 77478 4236 A6
Whispering Dr
- DKSN 77539 4754 D2
E Whispering Grv
19300 HarC 77377 3106 D1
W Whispering Grv
19400 HarC 77377 3106 D1
Whispering Mdw
100 MtgC 77355 2815 E5
100 MtgC 77355 2816 A4
Whispering Pns
21300 HarC 77338 3261 E3
Whispering Breeze Ln
19300 HarC 77094 3955 B3
Whispering Brook Dr
3500 HOUS 77345 3120 A4
Whispering Creek Dr
- KATY 77493 3813 B7
Whispering Creek Wy
5500 HOUS 77017 4246 C2
Whispering Cypress Dr
14600 HarC 77429 3396 E1
14800 HarC 77429 3252 E7
Whispering Daisy Ct
21900 HarC 77433 3250 E6
Whispering Falls Ct
15900 HarC 77084 3678 E6
Whispering Falls Dr
4700 HarC 77084 3678 E6
4700 HarC 77084 3679 A6
Whispering Fern Ct
2800 HOUS 77345 3120 C4
Whispering Forest Dr
21800 HarC 77339 3118 C5
Whispering Fountains Dr
- KATY 77493 3813 B6
Whispering Hollow Ln
19700 HarC 77449 3677 A7
Whispering Lake Ct
14200 HarC 77429 3253 D5
Whispering Lake Ranch Dr
- LGCY 77539 4633 E5
Whispering Lakes Dr
6000 KATY 77493 3813 B7
Whispering Maple Wy
27300 MtgC 77386 3115 D1
27800 MtgC 77386 2970 D7
28200 MtgC 77386 2971 A7
Whispering Maples Dr
23500 HarC 77373 3114 D5
Whispering Meadows Tr
10600 HarC 77064 3540 B2
Whispering Oak Dr
13500 HarC 77429 3398 D3
Whispering Oaks Dr
100 TYLV 77586 4508 E2
100 TYLV 77586 4509 A1
600 MtgC 77385 2823 A2
1500 KATY 77493 3813 B7
Whispering Oaks St
2300 PRLD 77581 4503 E4
Whispering Palms Dr
14000 HarC 77066 3401 E7
Whispering Park Dr
- HarC 77433 3251 D5
Whispering Pine Ct
1700 MSCY 77489 4370 D5
Whispering Pine Dr
800 MSCY 77489 4370 E5
Whispering Pine St
10 MtgC 77354 2674 C4
Whispering Pines Av
100 FRDW 77546 4629 D2
Whispering Pines Dr
- KATY 77493 3813 B6
- MtgC 77306 2680 A2
1300 HOUS 77055 3821 D6
2900 PASD 77503 4108 A7
18000 MtgC 77302 2679 E2
18000 MtgC 77302 2680 A2
Whispering Pines Ln
2600 HarC 77521 3834 D6
Whispering Pines St
2200 RMFT 77357 2829 A2
26200 MtgC 77355 2814 B2
Whispering Rock Ln
4600 HarC 77388 3112 B5
Whispering Sands Ct
12500 HarC 77041 3679 D6
Whispering Spring Forest
1700 HOUS 77339 3118 D7
Whispering Springs Dr
2800 HarC 77373 3114 D2
Whispering Star Ct
17500 HarC 77095 3537 D1
Whispering Trails Cir
2100 HOUS 77339 3118 E5
Whispering Trails Dr
2000 HOUS 77339 3118 E5
Whispering Valley Dr
14000 HarC 77429 3397 D4
Whispering Water Wy
20300 HarC 77433 3251 B6
Whispering Willow Ct
1200 SGLD 77479 4367 E6
Whispering Willow Dr
22700 HarC 77373 3259 C1
23500 HarC 77373 3114 C6
Whispering Wind Dr
23400 FBnC 77494 4093 B5
Whispering Wind Ln
2300 HOUS 77339 3119 A3

Whispering Winds Dr
2800 PRLD 77581 4503 E3
Whispering Wood Ln
7700 HarC 77086 3541 E3
Whispering Wy Dr
3300 FBnC 77469 4234 C6
Whisper Pass
200 HarC 77094 3955 B1
Whisper Point Dr
8100 HarC 77040 3541 D6
Whisper Ridge Dr
5400 FBnC 77479 4366 E5
Whisper Ridge Pl
200 FBnC 77479 4366 E5
Whisper Trace Ct
1200 HarC 77494 3953 D4
Whisper Trace Ln
1100 FBnC 77479 4367 B6
Whispertrail Ct
- HarC 77014 3401 C1
Whisperwillow Pl
10600 WDLD 77380 2821 C7
Whisper Wind Pl
10 WDLD 77382 2675 C6
Whispy Fern Pl
10 WDLD 77381 2675 A7
Whispy Green Ct
14800 HarC 77433 3250 D5
Whistle Ct
7300 FBnC 77479 4493 E6
Whistler Pkwy
- HarC 77044 3549 B3
Whistlers Ct
10 WDLD 77380 2968 B1
N Whistlers Bend Cir
100 WDLD 77384 2675 A3
W Whistlers Bend Cir
100 WDLD 77384 2675 A3
Whistlers Walk Pl
10 WDLD 77381 2820 E3
Whistling Pines Ct
25200 HarC 77389 2966 D2
Whistling Pines Dr
- HarC 77389 2966 D2
14300 HarC 77090 3402 E2
Whistling Springs Dr
12700 HarC 77346 3408 E1
Whistling Wind Ln
12600 HarC 77429 3397 D5
Whitaker
1600 HarC 77598 4631 A1
1600 WEBS 77598 4631 A1
Whitaker Av
900 PASD 77506 4107 B4
Whitaker Dr
19700 HMBL 77338 3262 C5
Whitaker St
1200 ALVN 77511 4866 E3
Whitaker Creek Dr
16500 HarC 77095 3538 A4
Whitbourne Dr
6400 HarC 77084 3679 A3
Whitbourne Meadow Ln
6800 HOUS 77040 3682 B4
Whitby Dr
4800 SGLD 77479 4495 C3
Whitby Ct
800 FBnC 77479 4367 B6
Whitchurch Dr
3800 HarC 77066 3401 C5
Whitchurch Wy
13600 HarC 77015 3828 E5
Whitcomb Rd
- HarC 77546 4506 A4
- HOUS 77546 4506 B3
White
1600 WALR 77484 3102 A6
White Av
8000 HTCK 77563 4988 D5
White Dr
10 BLAR 77401 4101 B4
White Ln
3200 PRLD 77584 4502 B5
White Rd
10 HarC 77047 4373 A6
10 HarC 77053 4373 A6
10 PRLD 77047 4373 A6
1500 CNRO 77304 2383 C7
White St
1300 HOUS 77007 3963 A2
4100 GlsC 77518 4634 C3
White Arbor Ct
8100 HarC 77338 3261 D3
Whiteback Dr
- HOUS 77084 3816 A7
1800 HarC 77084 3816 A6
S Whiteback Dr
- HarC 77094 3955 C3
Whiteback Ln
1600 HarC 77084 3816 A7
1600 HarC 77084 3816 A7
White Bark Pl
10 WDLD 77381 2820 B2
White Bass Rd
600 MtgC 77384 2675 E6
3000 MtgC 77384 2676 A6
White Berry Ct
20500 HarC 77346 3264 E4
White Birch Dr
10 MtgC 77385 2676 E6
10 MtgC 77385 2677 A6
White Birch Ln
7900 HarC 77095 3537 C6
White Birch Run
5300 MtgC 77386 3115 E1
5300 MtgC 77386 3116 A1
White Blossom Ln
3100 HOUS 77338 3263 D5
10200 HarC 77375 3110 B4
Whitebranch Ln
2100 HarC 77450 3954 D5
Whitebriar Dr
1700 DRPK 77503 4108 E6
1700 DRPK 77536 4108 E6
1700 PASD 77503 4108 E6
Whitebridge
5100 HarC 77449 3676 C6
White Bridge Ln
10600 FBnC 77478 4236 D4
Whitebrook Dr
10100 HarC 77038 3543 D3
Whitebrush Ln
10 WDLD 77380 2821 E6
Whitebud Dr
3200 HarC 77082 4096 C2
White Candle Dr
19000 HarC 77388 3113 A6

White Canyon Ln
15700 HarC 77044 3549 E3
Whitecap Dr
300 ELGO 77586 4509 B1
700 ELGO 77586 4382 B7
900 SEBK 77586 4382 B7
White Cap Ln
12000 HOUS 77072 4098 A7
12100 HOUS 77072 4097 E7
Whitecastle Ln
8500 HOUS 77088 3684 A1
White Cedar Dr
100 HarC 77015 3828 E5
400 HOUS 77015 3828 D6
White Chapel Ln
9400 HOUS 77074 4239 A2
White Cliff Dr
13200 HarC 77065 3539 A2
White Cloud Ct
1300 PRLD 77545 4499 D2
White Cloud Ln
4600 PASD 77504 4248 A6
White Clover Dr
5600 FBnC 77469 4493 A4
10300 HOUS 77089 4377 E3
White Creek Tr
20000 HarC 77450 3954 E4
Whitecroft Ln
- HarC 77373 2968 E6
Whitecross Dr
14200 FBnC 77083 4236 E2
White Deer Ln
3400 HOUS 77338 3263 D3
White Dove St
400 RMFT 77357 2829 A3
White Dove Tr
19800 HarC 77532 3410 A3
White Eagle Ln
2000 FBnC 77450 3953 E6
White Elk Blvd
29600 HarC 77375 3110 B1
White Falls Dr
2500 PRLD 77584 4499 E3
White Falls Ln
21500 HarC 77449 3815 B3
White Fawn Dr
10 WDLD 77381 2820 D3
10400 HOUS 77041 3680 E7
White Feather Tr
1700 HarC 77532 3410 B1
Whitefield Ln
24000 HarC 77493 3814 B5
White Fir Dr
7600 HOUS 77088 3683 A2
White Forge Ct
11400 FBnC 77478 4236 D6
White Forge Ln
14900 FBnC 77478 4236 D6
Whitefriars Dr
6700 HOUS 77087 4244 D3
White Frye Dr
6100 FBnC 77494 4092 A5
White Garner Rd
- PRLD 77581 4503 A2
White Gate Ln
11400 HarC 77067 3402 A6
Whiteglade Ln
15800 HarC 77084 3678 C3
White Glen Ln
5200 FBnC 77494 4092 E3
Whitehall Cir
200 LGCY 77573 4630 C6
Whitehall Dr
200 HOUS 77060 3544 C3
Whitehall Ln
100 LGCY 77573 4630 C7
200 FRDW 77546 4505 A7
800 WEBS 77058 4507 D6
Whitehall St
200 STAF 77477 4369 A2
Whitehall Wy
1300 HOUS 77339 3264 B1
White Hart Run
5800 HarC 77084 3679 A6
Whitehaven Dr
- HarC 77084 3816 B6
Whitehaven St
5600 BLAR 77401 4100 D5
5600 HOUS 77081 4100 D5
White Hawk Dr
- HarC 77379 3256 D2
Whitehead St
9900 HOUS 77088 3543 B7
9900 HOUS 77088 3683 B1
White Heather
10 LbyC 77327 2538 E1
White Heather Dr
12900 HOUS 77045 4241 D7
13400 HOUS 77045 4372 D2
14800 HOUS 77053 4372 D4
15100 HarC 77053 4372 D4
White Heron Ct
16500 HarC 77429 3252 D7
N White Heron St
10 LMQU 77568 4990 D6
S White Heron St
10 LMQU 77568 4990 D6
Whitehill Ln
6700 FBnC 77469 4232 E3
White Horse Dr
- HarC 77377 3254 C1
Whitehurst Ct
500 HarC 77450 3954 D1
White Ibis Av
600 TXCY 77590 4875 C2
White Ibis Ct
2600 LGCY 77573 4631 A7
White Ibis Ln
13300 HOUS 77044 3550 A1
White Lake Dr
2300 HarC 77373 3114 D5
Whitelaw Dr
1900 MtgC 77386 2969 B2
White Ln Ct
7300 PRLD 77584 4502 B5
Whitelock Dr
21100 HarC 77095 3538 E2
White Manor Dr
4900 PASD 77505 4248 E7
White Maple Ln
9600 HarC 77064 3541 A4
White Marsh Ct
8000 HarC 77379 3256 A2
White Meadow Ct
10 HarC 77379 3110 D6
Whitemills Dr
5700 HarC 77041 3679 C5

STREET Block City ZIP Map# Grid

White Mountain Ct
- LMQU 77568 4872 B4
White Mountain Dr
17800 HarC 77346 3408 E2
Whitening St
32100 WlrC 77484 3246 D7
White Oak
100 BzaC 77578 4625 A3
22500 MtgC 77357 2973 D3
White Oak Blvd
2300 CNRO 77304 2383 A1
White Oak Cir
- CNRO 77304 2382 D4
7100 HarC 77040 3681 B2
White Oak Cross
11900 MtgC 77385 2823 C4
White Oak Ct
- WlrC 77447 2813 B2
1800 CNRO 77301 2384 E7
6200 PASD 77505 4248 D7
23700 MtgC 77365 2974 B6
33300 MtgC 77354 2671 B4
White Oak Dr
- DKSN 77539 4753 B5
- LGCY 77539 4753 B5
- RSBG 77471 4491 C6
10 MtgC 77365 2973 A3
10 WDBR 77357 2828 C1
300 HOUS 77336 3120 E4
400 HOUS 77336 3121 A4
1500 HOUS 77009 3963 A1
2000 CNRO 77304 2383 D4
2400 HOUS 77009 3962 D1
2500 FBnC 77494 3951 D5
2600 HOUS 77007 3962 E1
2700 MtgC 77384 2675 A1
2800 MtgC 77384 2674 E1
10900 MtgC 77303 2239 D1
17500 MtgC 77306 2679 D1
20300 MtgC 77306 2680 E2
21500 MtgC 77306 2681 A3
21900 MtgC 77357 2827 C6
22700 MtgC 77357 2973 E4
N White Oak Dr
1000 MtgC 77357 2829 B5
S White Oak Dr
19900 MtgC 77357 2829 B6
White Oak Hl
17700 HarC 77429 3252 C6
White Oak Ln
2800 PRLD 77584 4502 D4
9100 HarC 77040 3681 B2
21400 MtgC 77357 2827 B1
25200 MtgC 77372 2682 E6
25200 PTVL 77372 2682 E6
25600 MtgC 77372 2683 A6
White Oak Lndg
11900 MtgC 77385 2823 D4
White Oak Pl
8100 HarC 77040 3681 B2
11900 MtgC 77385 2823 C4
White Oak Pth
11900 MtgC 77385 2823 D4
White Oak Run
11900 MtgC 77385 2823 C5
White Oak St
200 TXCY 77591 4874 A6
3600 CNRO 77301 2385 B6
24100 MtgC 77365 2973 E7
E White Oak Ter
1800 CNRO 77304 2383 A3
W White Oak Ter
1800 CNRO 77304 2382 E3
1800 CNRO 77304 2383 A2
White Oak Tr
10100 HarC 77064 3540 B3
11700 MtgC 77385 2823 B5
White Oak Trc
5900 MtgC 77304 2236 A5
White Oak Wy
11200 CNRO 77304 2236 B5
11200 MtgC 77304 2236 B5
White Oak Bend Dr
10700 HarC 77064 3540 A3
11000 HarC 77065 3540 A3
White Oak Creek Ct
10800 HarC 77429 3538 E1
White Oak Creek Dr
1600 CNRO 77304 2382 E4
White Oak Falls Ct
10800 HarC 77429 3538 E2
White Oak Forest Dr
23500 MtgC 77365 2974 B6
White Oak Gardens Dr
14000 HarC 77429 3538 E1
White Oak Glen Ct
13900 HarC 77429 3539 A1
White Oak Landing Blvd
- HarC 77429 3539 A2
13300 HarC 77065 3539 A2
White Oak Park Ct
10700 HarC 77429 3539 C3
White Oak Pass
11800 MtgC 77385 2823 C4
White Oak Point Ct
10800 HarC 77429 3539 A2
White Oak Point Dr
3500 CNRO 77304 2237 A4
3500 PNVL 77304 2237 A5
White Oak Pointe
400 LGCY 77573 4631 E4
White Oak Ranch Dr
12000 MtgC 77304 2236 A5
White Oak Ridge Dr
20800 HarC 77095 3538 E3
20800 HarC 77095 3539 A3
White Oaks Hills Ln
2000 HOUS 77339 3118 C7
White Oak Springs Dr
- HarC 77065 3539 A2
13800 HarC 77429 3539 A2
13900 HarC 77429 3538 D1
White Oak Trace Dr
10700 HarC 77429 3538 E2
10800 HarC 77429 3539 A1
N White Pebble Ct
10 WDLD 77380 2967 D3
S White Pebble Ct
10 WDLD 77380 2968 B4
White Perch Lake Dr
17500 MtgC 77384 2675 E6
White Pillars Ln
10 HDWV 77024 3959 D2
10 PNPV 77024 3959 D2
White Pine Dr
900 FRDW 77546 4505 A5
16100 SPLD 77372 2683 A5
White Pine Ln
- CmbC 77520 3835 C3
5200 HOUS 77016 3686 D2
White Pine Pl
8500 HarC 77375 3110 E2
White Plains Dr
12400 HarC 77089 4378 B6
12400 HOUS 77089 4378 C6
White Poplar Dr
20200 HarC 77449 3815 C5
Whitepost Ln
9600 HarC 77086 3542 A3
White River Ct
21100 FBnC 77469 4234 B2
White River Dr
4200 PASD 77504 4247 D6
12200 HarC 77375 3109 C7
White Rock Rd
9900 MtgC 77306 2533 E1
White Rock St
4500 HOUS 77051 4243 D2
4600 HOUS 77033 4243 D2
White Rose Ln
- FBnC 77469 4234 A4
Whitesage Ct
16200 HarC 77082 4096 A3
White Sail Dr
- SGCH 77355 2960 E2
Whitesail Dr
3100 LGCY 77573 4633 C3
24400 HOUS 77336 3266 B2
White Sands Dr
10 HOUS 77339 3117 D6
10 MtgC 77365 3117 D6
2700 DRPK 77536 4109 E7
White Sands Rd
1000 HarC 77450 3953 E3
White Sands Wy
3200 LGCY 77573 4633 B2
White Shore Ln
21000 HarC 77379 3111 D3
Whiteside Ln
10000 HOUS 77043 3820 A6
10000 HOUS 77080 3820 A6
Whites Lake Estates Dr
100 HarC 77562 3831 D4
White Sparrow Dr
- HarC 77090 3258 C5
White Spring Dr
- PRLD 77545 4499 D5
White Springs Ct
25700 HarC 77373 3113 C1
White Star Dr
16600 HOUS 77062 4507 A4
Whitestone Dr
3500 PRLD 77584 4503 B6
Whitestone Ln
- HarC 77073 3259 B2
White Swan Dr
7900 HarC 77396 3406 D6
White Tail
7200 HarC 77521 3695 B7
Whitetail Cross
21900 MtgC 77357 2681 D7
21900 MtgC 77357 2827 E1
21900 MtgC 77357 2828 A1
N White Tail Ct
17700 HarC 77084 3817 A1
S White Tail Ct
17700 HarC 77084 3817 A2
White Tail Dr
6800 HarC 77379 3256 C1
White Tail Ln
- HarC 77084 3817 A2
White Tail Tr
- HarC 77396 3407 C5
Whitetail Wy
25900 MtgC 77372 2683 A4
25900 SPLD 77372 2683 A4
White Thorn St
10900 HOUS 77016 3686 E2
Whitetip Ct
2600 HarC 77449 3814 E4
Whitevine Wy
20700 FBnC 77450 4094 B4
White Water Ct
- HOUS 77339 3118 B6
4200 PASD 77505 4249 B5
Whitewater Ln
15600 HOUS 77079 3956 E1
15600 HOUS 77079 3957 A1
White Water Tr
11600 HOUS 77013 3827 D7
White Water Bay Dr
11800 PRLD 77584 4500 C4
Whitewater Creek Cir
22800 FBnC 77450 3953 E5
Whitewater Falls Ct
16800 PASD 77059 4380 E4
Whiteway Ln
- HarC 77379 3256 A7
E White Willow Cir
10 WDLD 77381 2820 D5
10 WDLD 77381 2821 A5
W White Willow Cir
10 WDLD 77381 2820 E5
10 WDLD 77381 2821 A5
White Willow Ln
- CmbC 77520 3835 D3
1600 PRLD 77581 4503 D1
7100 FBnC 77469 4615 D5
23500 HarC 77336 3266 E3
Whitewind Dr
19700 HarC 77094 3955 A3
White Wing
- HOUS 77049 3828 A4
White Wing Cir
1200 FRDW 77546 4629 C5
White Wing Ct
10 WDLD 77382 2820 A3
500 LGCY 77539 4753 A5
Whitewing Dr
4600 BzaC 77511 4627 B7
5000 FBnC 77469 4615 E6
White Wing Ln
- MSCY 77459 4496 C2
600 HOUS 77079 3957 E3
600 HOUS 77079 3958 A3
Whitewing Rd
600 LbyC 77535 3413 E7
Whitewood Dr
- HOUS 77373 3113 E4
18700 HarC 77373 3114 A6
19500 HarC 77373 3113 E5
Whitford Ct
21900 FBnC 77450 4094 B3
Whithorn Dr
9400 HarC 77095 3538 D2
Whiting Av
100 GLSN 77550 4994 E7
N Whiting St
200 BYTN 77520 3972 E7
S Whiting St
10 BYTN 77520 3972 E7
Whiting Rock Dr
7100 HarC 77521 3832 E5
Whitinham Dr
200 HarC 77067 3402 A5
Whitlam Ct
3700 PRLD 77584 4503 B7
Whitlam Dr
4000 PRLD 77584 4503 B6
Whitland Ln
13200 HarC 77377 3253 E2
Whitley St
- HOUS 77005 4102 B2
Whitlock Dr
14100 HOUS 77062 4379 E6
Whitlock St
100 HLCS 77511 4867 E6
Whit Loggins Rd
44200 WlrC 77445 2952 C1
44200 WlrC 77445 2953 A1
Whitman St
4000 HOUS 77027 3961 C7
Whitman Mission Ln
- HarC 77346 3408 B3
Whitman Wy Dr
2300 HarC 77546 4506 B6
Whitmire Ln
- LbyC 77327 2538 E2
Whitmire St
2100 HOUS 77012 4105 C4
Whitmore Ln
8400 HarC 77083 4097 A3
Whitney Dr
1600 HOUS 77339 3118 B6
Whitney Ln
5200 PASD 77505 4248 B4
Whitney St
1900 HOUS 77006 3962 E6
E Whitney St
100 HOUS 77018 3823 D1
100 HOUS 77022 3823 D1
W Whitney St
10 HOUS 77022 3823 C1
100 HOUS 77018 3823 C1
Whitney Wy
1500 HOUS 77339 3118 C6
Whitney Meadows Dr
12100 HarC 77377 3254 B7
Whitshire
- HarC 77379 3256 A6
Whitson Ln
- HarC 77047 4374 A4
- HOUS 77047 4374 A4
Whitson St
100 ALVN 77511 4867 A1
Whittaker Wy
22800 HarC 77373 3260 B1
23000 HarC 77373 3115 B7
Whitter Forest Dr
- HarC 77088 3542 C7
Whittier Dr
10 FRDW 77546 4629 D1
2100 HarC 77032 3404 C7
2100 HOUS 77032 3404 C7
Whittier Bridge Ln
11500 FBnC 77478 4236 D6
Whittier Oaks Dr
5100 FRDW 77546 4505 D7
Whittingham Ln
11000 HOUS 77099 4238 B5
Whittington Ct N
1900 HOUS 77077 3957 B6
Whittington Ct S
2000 HOUS 77077 3957 B7
Whittington Dr
12000 HOUS 77077 3957 D6
Whittington Park Ln
9600 HarC 77095 3538 A4
Whittmore Fields Dr
26300 FBnC 77494 4092 B6
Whitton Dr
6200 HOUS 77085 4371 C3
Whitty St
4000 HOUS 77026 3825 A5
Whitwell Dr
5700 HarC 77449 3676 D4
Whitworth Wy
10 SGLD 77479 4495 C2
Wichita Cir
4700 HarC 77521 3833 C4
Wichita Dr
9200 LPRT 77571 4249 E4
9200 LPRT 77571 4250 A4
Wichita St
1000 HOUS 77002 4102 E1
1000 HOUS 77004 4102 E1
1300 HOUS 77004 4103 A1
1300 PASD 77502 4107 E7
1300 PASD 77506 4107 E7
2100 PASD 77502 4247 E1
2400 PASD 77502 4248 A2
Wichita Falls St
29500 MtgC 77354 2817 E3
Wichman St
1200 HOUS 77007 3962 D2
Wickbriar Dr
15200 HOUS 77053 4372 B5
Wickburn Dr
1900 MtgC 77386 2969 B2
Wickchester Ln
11700 HOUS 77043 3818 E7
11700 HOUS 77043 3819 A7
11800 HOUS 77079 3818 E7
Wickdale Dr
11100 PNPV 77024 3959 E4
11100 PNPV 77024 3960 A4
Wickenburg Dr
9500 HOUS 77031 4239 A6
9700 HOUS 77031 4238 E7
Wicker Wy
- HarC 77084 3679 A2
Wickerbay St
10 HOUS 77080 3820 B6
Wickerdale Pl
10 WDLD 77382 2819 A1
Wicker Forest Ln
21500 HarC 77338 3261 E2
Wickerhill Wy
1400 HarC 77494 3953 D4
Wickersham Dr
13000 HOUS 77077 3957 B7
22000 MtgC 77365 2972 C2
Wickersham Ln
3400 HOUS 77019 3961 D6
3400 HOUS 77027 3961 D6
5600 HOUS 77056 3960 D7
6200 HOUS 77057 3960 B7
7800 HOUS 77063 3960 A7
10000 HOUS 77042 3959 A7
10800 HOUS 77042 3958 C7
11300 HOUS 77077 3958 B7
13700 HOUS 77077 3957 A7
13900 HOUS 77077 3956 E7
Wickersley Wy
3100 FBnC 77459 4621 C6
N Wickerwood St
10 HOUS 77080 3820 B6
S Wickerwood St
10 HOUS 77080 3820 B6
Wickfield Dr
22000 HarC 77450 3954 A5
Wickford
29900 TMBL 77375 2963 E5
Wickford Cir
4400 SGLD 77479 4495 D4
Wickford Ct
400 LGCY 77573 4630 A7
9300 HOUS 77024 3960 E1
Wickford Dr
9000 HOUS 77024 3961 A1
9200 HOUS 77024 3960 E1
30000 TMBL 77375 2963 E5
Wickgate Dr
- HOUS 77053 4372 B5
Wickham Ct
10 SGLD 77479 4495 E3
20100 HarC 77450 3954 E1
Wickhamford Wy
100 HarC 77015 3829 A5
Wickhollow Ln
11500 HOUS 77043 3819 A7
11600 HOUS 77043 3818 E7
Wickhurst Pl
14400 HarC 77429 3397 D2
Wickley Dr
12700 HOUS 77085 4240 E6
Wickline Dr
- BzaC 77511 4866 B7
10900 HNCV 77024 3960 A4
10900 PNPV 77024 3960 A4
Wicklow
10200 HOUS 77036 4238 D3
10200 HOUS 77099 4238 D3
Wicklow Dr
500 DRPK 77536 4109 A6
2300 PRLD 77581 4504 D1
Wicklowe St
10900 HOUS 77016 3686 D2
Wicklow Meadow Ln
1200 HarC 77060 3403 D4
Wickman Glen Ln
22100 FBnC 77450 4094 A2
Wickmere Dr
15200 HOUS 77062 4506 E2
Wickover Ln
5800 HarC 77086 3542 D4
Wickshire Ct
3300 BzaC 77584 4501 D7
Wickshire Ln
1300 HOUS 77043 3819 A7
Wickson Mnr
3800 FBnC 77459 4621 B5
Wickson Sq
3700 FBnC 77459 4621 C5
Wickson Wy
3700 FBnC 77459 4621 B5
Wickstone Ln
4200 HarC 77014 3401 C3
Wickton Ln
21100 HarC 77338 3261 D3
Wickview Ln
4800 HOUS 77053 4372 B5
Wickway Dr
- MtgC 77365 2972 C2
11100 HNCV 77024 3960 A4
11100 PNPV 77024 3960 A4
Wickwild St
10900 HNCV 77024 3960 A4
Wickwilde Ct
24600 HarC 77389 2965 E4
Wickwood Ct
3100 BzaC 77584 4501 B6
Wickwood Dr
200 ORDN 77386 2822 C5
2900 BzaC 77584 4501 B6
2900 PRLD 77584 4501 B6
11000 PNPV 77024 3959 E5
11000 PNPV 77024 3960 A5
Widcombe Dr
18200 HarC 77084 3677 E7
Widdicomb Ct
2000 HOUS 77008 3822 D5
Wide Brim Ct
18400 HarC 77346 3264 D7
Wide Creek Ct
20100 HarC 77449 3676 E3
Wide Creek Dr
6600 HarC 77449 3676 E2
Wide Forest Ct
8200 MtgC 77385 2676 C6
Wide Oak Cir
31100 SGCH 77355 2961 D5
Wide River Ln
12400 HarC 77346 3408 C1
Widerop Ln
4700 HarC 77546 4506 A6
4800 HarC 77546 4505 E6
Widgeen Pond Dr
13400 HarC 77429 3254 B7
Widley Cir
12700 HOUS 77077 3957 C5
Widmore Ct
7400 HarC 77379 3256 B2
Widmore Pl
17400 HarC 77379 3256 B2
Wied Rd
18900 HarC 77388 3112 D6
Wiedner Dr
1200 FBnC 77494 3952 D3
Wier Dr
8000 HOUS 77017 4245 E1
8200 HOUS 77017 4105 E7
8400 HOUS 77017 4106 A7
Wiergate Ln
5800 FBnC 77469 4493 B5
Wig St
6200 TXCY 77539 4755 D3
Wigeon Ridge Ln
3500 HarC 77047 4374 C4
Wigeon Wy Dr
17300 HarC 77396 3407 D2
S Wiggins Dr
31900 MtgC 77355 2963 C3
Wiggins Rd
14600 MtgC 77302 2532 D6
Wiggins St
- HOUS 77029 3966 A3
7200 HOUS 77020 3965 A3
7900 HOUS 77029 3965 B3
10100 JTCY 77029 3966 A3
Wigginsville Rd
13300 MtgC 77302 2532 E7
13300 MtgC 77306 2532 E7
Wightman Ct
5000 HarC 77069 3256 D7
Wigmaker Dr
2300 HarC 77493 3814 B5
Wigton Dr
4300 HOUS 77096 4241 B2
5000 HOUS 77096 4240 E2
Wigwam Ln
19800 HarC 77532 3410 D3
Wilbarger
2400 BYTN 77521 3973 D2
Wilbarger Cir
8800 HarC 77064 3540 C5
Wilburforce St
900 HOUS 77091 3683 E5
900 HOUS 77091 3684 A4
W Wilburn Dr
10 BYTN 77520 3973 A5
Wilburn St
500 RSBG 77471 4490 C6
900 LGCY 77573 4632 C3
Wilbury Pk
12600 HarC 77041 3679 D6
Wilbury Heights Dr
4700 PASD 77505 4248 A6
Wilcant Ln
11600 HarC 77429 3253 E7
Wilchester Blvd
100 HOUS 77079 3958 C2
Wilcox Point Ct
6000 HarC 77388 3111 D2
Wilcox Point Dr
6100 HarC 77388 3111 D2
Wilcrest Dr
- HOUS 77079 3958 C6
- HOUS 77099 4238 C5
100 HOUS 77042 3958 C6
500 HOUS 77077 3958 B4
2600 HOUS 77042 4098 C1
2600 HOUS 77082 3958 C7
2600 HOUS 77082 4098 C1
6000 HOUS 77072 4098 C3
8400 HOUS 77099 4098 C7
11800 HOUS 77031 4238 D5
11800 HOUS 77099 4238 D5
Wilcrest Dr FM-1092
11800 HOUS 77031 4238 D5
11900 HarC 77031 4238 D5
N Wilcrest Dr
- HOUS 77042 3958 B3
- HOUS 77043 3958 B1
- HOUS 77079 3958 B1
300 HOUS 77079 3958 C4
S Wilcrest Dr
8500 HOUS 77099 4238 C4
11600 HOUS 77031 4238 C5
Wilcrest Plz
1800 DRPK 77536 4108 E6
Wilcrest Green Dr
11100 HOUS 77042 4098 C2
11100 HOUS 77082 4098 C2
Wildacre Dr
6700 FBnC 77479 4493 C5
Wildacres Dr
4100 HOUS 77072 4098 B4
Wild Aster Ct
10 WDLD 77382 2674 A5
Wild Basin Dr
8500 HOUS 77088 3683 A1
Wild Basin Tr
18400 HarC 77346 3264 D7
Wild Berry Ct
3600 HarC 77449 3815 D2
Wild Berry Dr
20200 HarC 77449 3815 D3
Wildberry Creek Ct
15000 HarC 77433 3250 E6
Wild Bird Dr
200 HarC 77373 3113 E7
Wildbird Ln
8800 HarC 77338 3262 A4
Wild Blackberry Dr
5200 HOUS 77345 3119 C2
Wild Bluebonnet Wy
4600 HarC 77084 3677 C7
Wildbriar Ln
5900 FBnC 77469 4615 E1
5900 FBnC 77469 4616 A2
Wildbrook Dr
- PRLD 77584 4500 C2
1600 HarC 77038 3543 B2
Wildbrook Canyon Ct
21000 HarC 77449 3815 B6
Wildbrook Canyon Ln
1900 HarC 77449 3815 B7
Wildcandle Dr
3200 HarC 77388 3113 A6
Wildcat Ln
1600 HOUS 77532 3266 B7
1700 HOUS 77044 3266 B7
Wildcat Wy
- HarC 77066 3401 A3
Wildcat Bridge Ln
10900 FBnC 77478 4236 D5
Wild Colt Pl
10 WDLD 77382 2674 E5
Wild Columbine Rd
12500 HarC 77038 3543 B4
Wild Cotton Rd
500 RSBG 77471 4614 C1
Wildcroft Dr
21100 HarC 77449 3676 D6
Wild Deer Dr
- WDLD 77381 2821 B3
Wild Duck Ln
26900 HarC 77447 3248 E6
Wild Dunes Cir
2000 FBnC 77450 3953 E5
Wild Dunes Ct
1400 BYTN 77520 4113 B3
Wilde Forest Ct
13800 SGLD 77478 4237 A7
Wilde Glen Ln
13000 HOUS 77072 4097 C6
13100 HOUS 77083 4097 C6
Wilde Laurel Ln
12300 HarC 77014 3402 B3
Wilder St
700 HOUS 77008 3823 E5
Wilderness Rd
16500 HarC 77429 3396 E3
24400 MtgC 77380 2967 B3
Wilderness Tr
10 FRDW 77546 4629 A4
Wilderness Cliff Ct
14900 HOUS 77062 4380 A7
Wilderness Falls Tr
4000 HOUS 77339 3119 C4
Wilderness Glen Ct
4800 HarC 77449 3676 E7
Wilderness Hill Dr
- HarC 77065 3539 C2
Wilderness Park Ct
1700 HOUS 77339 3118 D3
Wilderness Pines Ct
600 FRDW 77546 4629 A3
Wilderness Pines Dr
1200 FRDW 77546 4629 A3
Wilderness Point Dr
1900 HOUS 77339 3118 D4
Wilde Rock Wy
1400 HOUS 77018 3822 E3
Wildever Pl
10 WDLD 77382 2673 D6
Wildewood Ct
1200 FBnC 77479 4493 E6
Wilde Woods Wy
3200 MtgC 77380 2967 B3
E Wilde Yaupon Cir
10 WDLD 77381 2820 E5
N Wilde Yaupon Cir
10 WDLD 77381 2820 E5
W Wilde Yaupon Cir
10 WDLD 77381 2820 D5
N Wilde Yaupon Ct
10 WDLD 77381 2820 D5
S Wilde Yaupon Ct
10 WDLD 77381 2820 D5
Wildfern Tr
29400 MtgC 77386 2969 A3
Wildfire St
5800 LGCY 77573 4630 C7
Wildflower Cir
23600 FBnC 77494 4093 B5
Wildflower Ct
1100 KATY 77494 3952 A3
Wild Flower Dr
23300 HarC 77336 3267 A4
Wildflower Dr
25300 MtgC 77354 2817 D4
Wildflower Ln
3900 ALVN 77511 4867 E6
35400 PNIS 77445 3245 A1
35400 WlrC 77445 3245 A1
Wildflower Pl
5300 LGCY 77573 4630 D7
Wildflower Trace Pl
10 WDLD 77382 2674 A5
Wild Forest Dr
23800 MtgC 77357 2827 D2
23900 MtgC 77357 2681 D7
Wildforest Dr
8600 HarC 77088 3542 C7
Wild Ginger Ct
- WDLD 77380 2821 D7
10 WDLD 77380 2967 C1
Wild Goose Dr
11100 HarC 77375 3110 A7
Wildgrass Ct
9600 FBnC 77478 4236 B2
Wild Grove Ct
16100 HarC 77377 3254 E5
Wildgrove Dr
1200 PASD 77504 4247 D6
Wildhawk Dr
3600 HarC 77449 3816 B2
Wild Hollow Ln
10100 HOUS 77088 3542 B7
Wildhollow Ln
4200 ALVN 77511 4867 E6
Wild Horse Ct
4700 MSCY 77459 4621 D2
Wild Horse Ln
24200 HarC 77447 3249 E4
Wildhorse Ln
4200 ALVN 77511 4867 D6
Wild Horse Valley Rd
700 HarC 77450 3953 E2
Wildhurst Dr
15200 HarC 77429 3252 E6
Wild Indigo St
4300 HOUS 77027 4101 B1
Wilding Ln
11200 HNCV 77024 3959 E2
11200 PNPV 77024 3959 E2
Wilding Wimbledon Ct
6500 HarC 77379 3257 A4
Wild Ivy Ct
14800 HarC 77429 3396 B1
Wild Jasmine Ln
21200 FBnC 77450 4094 B3
Wildlife Run
40000 WlrC 77445 3243 B3
Wild Lilac Ct
1300 PRLD 77545 4499 E3
Wild Lilac Dr
2700 PRLD 77545 4499 E3
Wild Lilac Tr
18300 HarC 77346 3264 E7
18300 HarC 77346 3408 E1
Wild Meadow Pl
10 WDLD 77380 2968 A1
Wild Milberry Dr
- FBnC 77494 4092 E3
Wildmoor Ct
200 HarC 77094 3955 C2
Wild Moss St
22800 HarC 77375 2966 A7
Wild Mustang Ln
12900 HarC 77044 3408 E7
Wild Oak Dr
300 HarC 77336 2975 D4
3600 PRLD 77581 4504 A7
17400 HarC 77090 3258 C3
18200 HarC 77090 3258 B1
Wild Oak Ln
16200 MtgC 77302 2679 B4
Wild Oak Rd
10 SPVL 77055 3820 E7
Wild Oak Run
200 HarC 77094 3955 B1
Wild Oak Forest Ln
- SEBK 77586 4382 C7
Wild Oak Park Dr
2700 MtgC 77385 2823 C6
Wild Oaks
28000 MtgC 77355 2815 C3
Wildoats Dr
19100 HarC 77449 3816 B3
Wild Olive Ct
2300 HarC 77449 3815 C5
Wild Orchard Ct
4200 FBnC 77494 4092 D2
Wild Orchard Ln
26600 FBnC 77494 4092 C2
Wild Orchid Ct
10 WDLD 77385 2676 B3
Wild Orchid Dr
18200 HarC 77084 3816 D3
Wild Peach Pl
400 MSCY 77459 4497 A5
Wild Pecan Tr
6700 HarC 77084 3678 E2
Wild Pine Dr
12200 HarC 77039 3546 E5
Wild Plains Dr
20300 HarC 77449 3676 D5
Wild Plum Ct
1800 HOUS 77345 3120 C6
Wild Plum Dr
300 LGCY 77573 4632 B5
Wild Plum St
200 HOUS 77013 3828 A6
Wild Point Ln
6000 FBnC 77469 4493 B4
Wild Poppy Dr
19800 HarC 77379 3110 C6
Wild Ridge Dr
10600 WDLD 77380 2821 D6
Wildridge Dr
2700 HOUS 77339 3118 D5
Wild River Dr
3200 FBnC 77469 4364 B4
6400 HarC 77449 3676 C3
Wild Rose Dr
29700 MtgC 77386 2969 B4
Wildrose Dr
100 BYTN 77520 3971 B2
Wildrose Ln
18900 HarC 77377 3106 E1
Wild Rose Rd
6900 BYTN 77521 3832 A5
6900 HarC 77521 3832 A5
Wild Rose St
8300 HarC 77083 4097 B7
Wild Rose Tr
17400 HarC 77429 3252 D6
Wild Rose Trc
22300 FBnC 77469 4093 D7
Wild Rye Tr
1600 FBnC 77479 4493 D4
19700 HarC 77346 3265 B4
Wildsage Ct
6000 HarC 77379 3111 E4
Wild Sage Ln
- HarC 77379 3111 B5
Wildsong Ct
- HarC 77449 3676 B2
Wildspruce Ct
8800 HarC 77088 3542 A7
Wildspruce Dr
8900 HarC 77088 3542 B6
Wild Stream Ct
7500 HarC 77095 3537 A5
Wild Timber Tr
15300 HarC 77433 3251 A6
Wild Turkey Dr
1000 MtgC 77385 2823 C3
17000 HarC 77429 3252 D6
Wild Turkey Ln
3100 PRLD 77581 4503 D6
Wild Turkey Bend St
- HOUS 77338 3260 C4
Wild Valley Rd
800 HOUS 77057 3960 B4
Wild View Ct
20400 FBnC 77450 4094 D1
Wildvine Ct
11700 HarC 77377 3254 D4
Wild Violet Ct
1800 FBnC 77479 4494 A4
Wild Violet Dr
6800 HarC 77346 3264 E5
6900 HarC 77346 3265 A5
Wild Willow Ln
7600 HarC 77433 3537 C7
17400 HarC 77084 3677 E2
17400 HarC 77084 3678 A2
18000 HarC 77449 3677 D2
E Wildwind Cir
2900 WDLD 77380 2821 D6
S Wildwind Cir
2600 WDLD 77380 2821 C6
W Wildwind Cir
2800 WDLD 77380 2821 C6
Wild Wind Ln
500 HOUS 77013 3966 C1
Wild Wind Pl
2400 WDLD 77380 2821 D6
Wildwinn Ct
3700 ALVN 77511 4867 E6
3700 HLCS 77511 4867 E6
Wildwinn Dr
900 ALVN 77511 4867 E6
E Wildwinn Dr
100 HLCS 77511 4867 E6
100 HLCS 77511 4868 A5
W Wildwinn Dr
100 ALVN 77511 4867 E6
100 HLCS 77511 4867 E6
Wildwood Cir
14500 MtgC 77354 2670 C6
Wildwood Ct
26600 KATY 77494 3952 A3
Wildwood Dr
200 BYTN 77520 3971 B2
400 PASD 77586 4508 D2
500 FRDW 77546 4505 B5
900 DRPK 77536 4108 E6
900 DRPK 77536 4109 A6
1700 DRPK 77503 4108 E6
1700 PASD 77503 4108 E6
13300 TMBL 77375 2964 A3
23700 MtgC 77365 2973 E6
Wildwood Ln
300 CNRO 77301 2383 E2
300 CNRO 77301 2384 A2
900 BLAR 77401 4101 B3
1100 KATY 77494 3952 A3
1700 FBnC 77469 4365 D3
25300 HarC 77336 3121 E7

STREET
Block City ZIP Map# Grid

Wildwood Pt
38000 MtgC 77354 2670 C5
E Wildwood Rd
23000 MtgC 77365 2973 E6
S Wildwood Rd
23800 MtgC 77365 2973 E6
Wildwood Run
15500 HarC 77433 3251 B6
Wildwood St
10 MtgC 77357 2829 C3
2600 RMFT 77357 2829 B3
3000 PRLD 77581 4503 E3
Wildwood Trc
14500 MtgC 77354 2670 C4
Wildwood Wy
6600 HOUS 77023 4104 D2
Wildwood Bend Ln
12500 HarC 77433 3396 B4
Wildwood Brook Ct
7500 HarC 77095 3538 A7
Wildwood Dale Ln
19400 HarC 77379 3112 A6
Wildwood Forest Dr
100 MtgC 77380 2968 B3
Wildwood Glen Dr
6300 HarC 77066 3400 E5
Wildwood Glen Dr
15300 FBnC 77083 4236 B1
Wildwood Green Wy
23600 HarC 77373 3114 E5
Wildwood Grove Dr
22300 HarC 77450 3953 E5
Wildwood Lake Dr
15300 FBnC 77083 4236 B1
15500 FBnC 77083 4096 B7
Wildwood Oaks Dr
23700 MtgC 77357 2828 B6
Wildwood Park Dr
21300 FBnC 77469 4493 A4
22100 FBnC 77469 4492 E4
Wildwood Park Ln
10200 HarC 77070 3399 C3
Wildwood Ridge Ct
3400 HOUS 77339 3119 C6
Wildwood Ridge Dr
1900 MSCY 77489 4370 B6
3500 HOUS 77339 3119 B5
Wildwood Springs Ct
13500 HarC 77044 3550 A2
Wildwood Springs Ln
14300 HarC 77044 3550 A2
Wildwood Valley Ct
3800 HOUS 77345 3119 D2
Wild Yaupon Dr
19000 HarC 77433 3537 B7
Wiley Dr
800 MtgC 77354 2673 C1
Wiley Rd
7200 HOUS 77016 3686 E4
7200 HOUS 77016 3687 A4
Wiley St
3600 HOUS 77093 3686 B4
5000 HOUS 77016 3686 C4
Wiley Martin Dr
13400 HarC 77429 3398 A4
Wileyvale Rd
6100 HOUS 77028 3825 C3
7200 HOUS 77016 3825 C2
8100 HOUS 77016 3686 C7
Wileywood Dr
13400 HOUS 77049 3828 A2
Wilke Rd
13000 BKVL 77581 4375 E7
13000 PRLD 77581 4375 E7
Wilken St
700 HOUS 77008 3823 E5
Wilkenberg Dr
10900 HarC 77086 3542 A1
11200 HarC 77066 3401 A7
Wilkenson St
900 HOUS 77019 3962 D4
Wilkes St
800 HOUS 77009 3824 C7
Wilkes Park Rd
25200 HarC 77375 2964 D2
Wilkie Ln
11900 HOUS 77076 3685 A2
12000 HOUS 77037 3685 A2
Wilkins Cross
100 FBnC 77479 4367 A5
Wilkins Ct
25000 HOUS 77336 3266 B4
Wilkins Ln
800 MtgC 77339 3118 D4
5800 FBnC 77479 4367 A5
23500 HOUS 77336 3266 B4
Wilkins St
100 CNRO 77301 2384 A4
200 HMPD 77445 2953 B7
600 HMPD 77445 2952 E7
1100 HOUS 77030 4102 E3
E Wilkins St
100 LGCY 77573 4632 A3
W Wilkins St
200 LGCY 77573 4631 E4
200 LGCY 77573 4632 A4
Wilknox St
1100 GLSN 77551 5108 A5
Wilks Dr
19000 HarC 77377 3251 D1
19000 HarC 77433 3251 D1
Wilkshire Ct
15300 HarC 77069 3256 D6
Wilkshire Wy
- MSCY 77459 4496 C4
Willa Ln
19300 HOUS 77338 3262 B6
Willaby Ln
900 HarC 77530 3829 D6
Willaby Rd
18900 MtgC 77357 2829 E4
Willacy Ct
8800 HarC 77064 3540 D6
Willamette Wy Dr
- HarC 77449 3814 E4
Willancy Ct
14800 HarC 77095 3539 A6
Willancy Ln
8500 HarC 77095 3539 A6
Willard St
1000 HOUS 77006 3962 D5
Willard's Wy
200 STAF 77477 4369 C3
Willbriar Ln
15800 HOUS 77489 4371 B6
Will Clayton Pkwy
- HOUS 77032 3404 E1
- HOUS 77338 3407 C2
- HOUS 77396 3407 C2
2900 HOUS 77032 3405 A1

Will Clayton Pkwy
5400 HOUS 77338 3405 D1
6000 HOUS 77338 3406 A1
6500 HOUS 77032 3406 A1
6500 HOUS 77396 3406 A1
7800 HMBL 77338 3406 D1
7800 HMBL 77396 3406 D1
8000 HMBL 77338 3407 A2
8000 HMBL 77396 3407 A2
8900 HarC 77338 3407 C2
8900 HarC 77396 3407 A2
9500 HarC 77346 3408 A2
9500 HarC 77396 3408 A2
13200 HarC 77346 3409 A1
Willemette St
7900 HarC 77049 3689 E7
Willers Wy
5600 HOUS 77056 3960 D6
6100 HOUS 77057 3960 B6
Willersley Ln
1400 HarC 77530 3829 D5
Willet Ln
4100 GLSN 77554 5548 A3
Willgus Trail Ln
6300 HarC 77066 3400 E5
Willhanna Dr
22500 HarC 77449 3814 D4
Willia St
1500 HOUS 77007 3962 D3
William Av
10 BYTN 77520 3973 A5
200 BYTN 77520 3972 E6
William St
700 HOUS 77002 3963 D3
William C Harvin Blvd
- HOUS 77030 4102 D5
- HOUS 77054 4102 D6
Williamcrest St
8300 HOUS 77071 4239 C3
William Dowdell Dr
12300 HarC 77065 3398 D6
12300 HarC 77429 3398 D4
Williamhurst Ln
4500 LGCY 77573 4630 E5
16600 HarC 77090 3258 C4
William Juergens Dr
30200 TMBL 77375 2964 A4
William Morton Dr
300 FBnC 77469 4365 C4
Williams
6100 HarC 77532 3552 D3
Williams Cir
3100 HarC 77449 3815 E4
Williams Dr
2300 LMQU 77568 4989 B3
5900 TXCY 77591 4873 E5
6900 GLSN 77551 5222 B1
7100 BzaC 77584 4627 A1
7300 PRLD 77584 4627 A1
Williams Ln
1000 KMAH 77565 4633 C1
1000 LGCY 77565 4633 C1
1600 GlsC 77511 4868 E2
17000 MtgC 77302 2679 E3
17900 MtgC 77302 2680 A3
Williams Rd
6100 HarC 77532 3552 C3
Williams St
- PRVW 77445 2955 C6
- PRVW 77445 3100 C1
- SEBK 77586 4509 D2
- WlrC 77445 2955 C6
100 CNRO 77304 2383 C6
700 PASD 77506 4107 C5
1000 LGCY 77573 4632 B3
4100 PRLD 77584 4627 C1
6700 HTCK 77563 4989 A5
7300 HOUS 77040 3682 A2
7500 HarC 77040 3682 A2
15100 GlsC 77517 4870 A4
15100 STFE 77517 4870 A4
Williams St FM-1098
- PRVW 77445 3100 B3
W Williams St
- MTBL 77520 3696 D6
Williams Wy
1900 FBnC 77469 4493 A3
2000 FBnC 77469 4492 D3
Williams Bend Cir
17200 HarC 77433 3395 C6
Williams Bend Ct
9800 FBnC 77459 4621 D4
Williams Bend Dr
18000 HarC 77433 3395 D6
Williams Bridge Ln
14500 FBnC 77478 4236 E3
Williamsburg Cir
10 GLSN 77551 5108 A7
500 FRDW 77546 4505 C7
Williamsburg Ct N
1900 LGCY 77573 4631 C5
Williamsburg Ct S
1900 LGCY 77573 4631 B5
Williamsburg Dr
2400 PASD 77502 4246 D2
2700 DKSN 77539 4753 C2
11300 PNPV 77024 3959 D5
Williamsburg Ln
10 BKHV 77024 3959 C3
3200 MSCY 77459 4496 D2
Williamsburg Pk
500 MtgC 77302 2530 D5
Williamschase Dr
22500 HarC 77449 3814 D4
Williams Creek Ct
25400 MtgC 77365 3118 A2
Williams Creek Dr
21000 MtgC 77365 3117 E3
21000 MtgC 77365 3118 A3
Williams Ct Ln
- BLAR 77401 4101 A2
- HOUS 77401 4101 A2
4900 HOUS 77081 4101 A2
Williamsdell St
8300 HOUS 77088 3684 A2
Williams Elm Dr
18100 HarC 77433 3395 E6
Williams Field Dr
10000 HarC 77064 3541 D1
Williams Forest Dr
- HarC 77346 3408 C1
Williams Frits Rd
- MtgC 77354 2670 D4
Williams Glen Dr
3100 SGLD 77479 4495 A3
Williams Grant St
2400 SGLD 77479 4368 D7

Williams Lake Dr
- FBnC 77469 4493 A5
Williams Landing Dr
400 FBnC 77479 4366 E5
Williams Oak Dr
17100 HarC 77433 3395 D6
Williamson Rd
15700 LbyC 77327 2684 B5
15700 MtgC 77372 2684 B5
Williamson St
3200 HOUS 77020 3964 A3
Williams Pine Dr
17200 HarC 77433 3395 E6
Williamsport St
200 LGCY 77573 4631 B4
Williams Reach Dr
- HarC 77433 3395 D6
Williams Ridge Ct
17200 HarC 77433 3395 E6
Williams Trace Blvd
- SGLD 77479 4495 D1
1700 SGLD 77478 4368 C5
2500 SGLD 77479 4368 D7
Williams Willow Ln
18100 HarC 77433 3395 C6
William Tell St
1800 HarC 77093 3685 C2
Willie Rd
11000 HarC 77093 3686 C2
Willie St
- HarC 77093 3686 B2
10500 HOUS 77093 3686 B3
Willie Wy
3200 MtgC 77380 2821 B7
Willie Jones Rd
1300 FBnC 77469 4364 D4
Willie Scott Ter
20400 WlrC 77484 3101 B4
Williford St
7700 HOUS 77012 4105 C4
Willingham Ln
14500 MtgC 77306 2532 C3
Willingham Wy
16300 HarC 77095 3538 B6
Willington Ln
14900 HarC 77049 3828 E2
Willis
17400 SGCH 77355 2961 B2
23000 HarC 77375 2965 E6
Willis Av
2500 TXCY 77590 4874 C3
Willis Cir
300 LMQU 77568 4873 E7
300 TXCY 77591 4873 E7
Willis Hl
- LbyC 77327 2684 D2
- PLMG 77327 2684 D2
Willis Rd
- LbyC 77327 2684 D2
Willis St
14700 HarC 77032 3545 A1
14700 HarC 77039 3545 A1
E Willis St
100 ALVN 77511 4867 D2
W Willis St
100 ALVN 77511 4867 A1
1800 ALVN 77511 4866 E1
Willis Wy
15300 MtgC 77384 2673 E2
Williston Dr
10700 HarC 77065 3539 A2
Willis Waukegan Rd
10900 MtgC 77303 2239 B2
Willis Waukegan Rd FM-2432
10900 MtgC 77303 2239 B2
Willits Dr
1600 PRLD 77581 4504 E3
Williwaw Dr
15800 FBnC 77083 4096 B7
15900 FBnC 77083 4236 A1
Willmont Rd
- HarC 77507 4250 B4
3700 LPRT 77571 4250 B4
Willmore Ln
15800 HOUS 77489 4371 C6
Willobrook Towns Ln
7400 HOUS 77070 3400 A3
Willomine Wy
5200 HOUS 77045 4372 A1
5400 HOUS 77085 4372 A1
Willoughby Ct
1400 FBnC 77469 4493 B7
Willoughby Dr
200 FBnC 77469 4493 C6
Willow
- MRGP 77571 4112 B7
- MRGP 77571 4252 B1
20100 HOUS 77338 3261 B5
Willow Av
900 PASD 77506 4107 B5
Willow Blvd
2100 PRLD 77581 4503 A3
Willow Bnd
- HarC 77377 3106 E7
- HarC 77433 3106 E7
1500 FBnC 77494 3951 D4
Willow Brch
23100 HarC 77375 2965 E6
N Willow Cir
11700 MSCY 77071 4239 E7
S Willow Cir
11800 MSCY 77071 4239 E7
Willow Ct
8700 HOUS 77031 4239 C3
18200 HarC 77379 3256 A1
Willow Dr
- FBnC 77477 4369 E4
- MtgC 77302 2676 E2
500 MtgC 77302 2530 B7
1700 RHMD 77469 4491 D3
2500 STAF 77477 4369 E4
5800 PRLD 77584 4502 D6
6700 HTCK 77563 4989 C5
8400 HarC 77379 3255 E1
N Willow Dr
- HarC 77073 3259 A5
S Willow Dr
4900 HOUS 77035 4240 E5
4900 HOUS 77035 4241 A4
Willow Ests
7900 HarC 77375 2965 E5
7900 HarC 77389 2965 E5
Willow Gln
23000 HarC 77375 2966 A6
Willow Hl
4100 TYLV 77586 4508 D1
Willow Ln
10 GLSN 77551 5108 B7
400 BYTN 77520 3971 A1
1200 LGCY 77573 4752 D2

Willow Ln
6300 KATY 77493 3813 B4
12000 HarC 77429 3398 C2
24500 WlrC 77447 2959 C2
26500 FBnC 77494 3952 A6
Willow Pth
8000 HarC 77375 2966 A6
8200 HarC 77375 2965 E7
Willow Rd
300 TXCY 77591 4874 A6
Willow Rd S
10 TXCY 77591 4874 A6
400 LMQU 77568 4874 A7
Willow Run
23100 HarC 77375 2965 E6
Willow St
- FBnC 77545 4499 C6
100 HMBL 77338 3262 E6
100 HMBL 77338 3263 A6
500 FBnC 77471 4490 D3
500 RSBG 77471 4490 D3
600 HarC 77373 3113 E1
600 WALR 77484 3102 A6
600 WlrC 77484 3101 E6
600 WlrC 77484 3102 A6
1200 BYTN 77520 4112 D2
4700 BLAR 77401 4101 A5
4700 PASD 77586 4383 C4
5200 BLAR 77401 4100 E5
7000 HOUS 77091 3683 D4
9300 HOUS 77088 3683 D1
9500 HarC 77088 3683 D1
11100 MtgC 77372 2536 E2
20900 MtgC 77357 2828 A7
20900 MtgC 77357 2974 A1
N Willow St
100 TMBL 77375 2964 C6
Willow Tr
2300 DRPK 77536 4249 E1
12000 HOUS 77035 4240 B6
Willow Wk
5600 HarC 77069 3256 D7
Willow Wy
- MtgC 77357 2829 B2
- RMFT 77357 2829 B2
5000 FBnC 77469 4233 A7
23000 HarC 77375 2965 E6
Willow Bank Dr
4200 SGLD 77479 4495 A1
Willowbank Rd
16400 HarC 77377 3254 C6
Willow Bay Dr
- HarC 77090 3258 C7
Willow Beach Dr
4100 HOUS 77072 4098 B4
Willowbend Blvd
- HOUS 77071 4240 A3
3500 HOUS 77045 4241 D3
3500 HOUS 77054 4241 D3
4000 HOUS 77025 4241 A3
4100 HOUS 77035 4241 C3
5100 HOUS 77035 4240 E3
5200 HOUS 77096 4240 B3
Willow Bend Ct
1400 FBnC 77469 4365 D3
16800 SGLD 77479 4368 B7
Willow Bend Dr
2300 FBnC 77469 4365 E3
Willowbend Dr
10 HNCV 77024 3960 A4
1700 DRPK 77503 4108 E6
1700 DRPK 77536 4108 E6
1700 PASD 77503 4108 E6
Willowbend Ln
- MtgC 77303 2239 D7
Willowbend St
- CNRO 77301 2383 D2
- CNRO 77303 2383 D2
2000 ALVN 77511 4748 D6
2000 BzaC 77511 4748 D6
E Willow Bluff Rd
6200 HarC 77449 3677 D4
N Willow Bluff Rd
18300 HarC 77449 3677 D4
W Willow Bluff Rd
6200 HarC 77449 3677 C4
Willow Bough St
23200 HarC 77375 2965 E6
23200 HarC 77375 2966 B6
Willow Branch Ct
12000 HarC 77070 3254 D7
Willow Branch Dr
1200 LGCY 77573 4632 A5
15000 HarC 77070 3254 D7
15000 HarC 77377 3254 D7
22400 HarC 77375 2965 E7
Willow Breeze Dr
12500 HarC 77377 3254 B3
Willow Briar Dr
- HarC 77090 3258 D7
Willowbriar Ln
900 DRPK 77536 4109 A6
Willow Bridge Cir
7000 HarC 77095 3678 E1
Willowbridge Park Blvd
9200 HarC 77064 3540 D6
Willowbrook Blvd
4500 HOUS 77021 4103 E5
Willow Brook Ct
3000 PRLD 77583 4500 C4
Willowbrook Ct
1200 SGLD 77479 4367 E6
Willowbrook Dr
- HOUS 77064 3400 A5
19900 HarC 77433 3677 A1
Willow Brook Ln
12100 PRLD 77583 4500 B4
Willowbrook Ln
31500 WlrC 77484 3246 E3
31500 WlrC 77484 3247 A3
Willowbrook Mall
10 HOUS 77064 3400 B5
10 HOUS 77070 3400 A4
Willowbrook Park Dr
6600 HarC 77066 3400 D5
Willowbrook Villa Dr
13400 HarC 77070 3399 B1
Willowby Dr
1600 HOUS 77008 3822 E5
Willow Canyon Dr
23100 HarC 77450 3953 C3
23100 HarC 77494 3953 C3
Willow Centre Dr
12800 HarC 77066 3400 B4
12800 HOUS 77066 3400 B4
12800 HOUS 77069 3400 B4

Willow Chase Blvd
7400 HarC 77069 3400 A3
7400 HOUS 77070 3400 A4
7700 HOUS 77070 3399 E4
Willow Chase Dr
12800 HOUS 77070 3399 E4
Willow City Rd
- MtgC 77355 2669 C7
Willow Cliff Ln
5100 FBnC 77479 4496 B4
18000 HarC 77433 3537 D7
Willow Colony Ln
26100 FBnC 77494 4092 E2
Willow Cove
2200 BzaC 77583 4624 B5
2200 PRLD 77583 4624 B5
Willow Cove Ct
6500 HarC 77449 3677 C3
Willow Cove Dr
18500 HarC 77449 3677 C3
Willowcraft
7400 HOUS 77489 4371 B4
Willowcreek Blvd
- BYTN 77521 3972 D2
Willow Creek Ct
200 LGCY 77573 4632 E1
Willow Creek Dr
700 LPRT 77571 4250 A2
2700 LGCY 77573 4632 E1
3000 FBnC 77494 3952 E6
3000 FBnC 77494 3953 A6
23400 HarC 77375 2965 E6
Willow Creek Ln
2000 PRLD 77581 4504 C4
Willow Creek Pk
- MtgC 77386 2823 B6
32000 MtgC 77385 2823 B6
Willow Creek Rd
24900 WlrC 77447 2959 C2
Willow Creek Wy
5400 HOUS 77017 4246 C1
Willow Creek Bridge Ln
22200 HarC 77375 3109 E1
Willow Creek Estates Ln
11500 HarC 77375 3109 D2
11500 TMBL 77375 3109 D2
Willowcreek Stables Rd
22900 HarC 77389 2966 C6
Willowcrest
- HarC 77375 3110 A1
Willowcrest Ct
6100 HarC 77389 2966 D4
Willowcrest Ln
- FBnC 77469 4492 D3
- FBnC 77469 4493 A3
Willowcrest Pk
13500 HOUS 77077 3957 D3
Willowcrest Pl
10 WDLD 77381 2820 C1
Willow Crossing Cir
10300 HarC 77064 3540 E3
Willow Crossing Ct
10700 HarC 77064 3540 C3
Willow Crossing Dr
9100 HarC 77064 3540 C3
N Willowdale Cir
11700 MSCY 77071 4239 E7
S Willowdale Cir
11800 MSCY 77071 4239 C7
Willow Dale St
6000 HOUS 77087 4104 C7
Willowdell Dr
2100 SEBK 77586 4509 C2
E Willowdell Dr
2100 SEBK 77586 4509 C2
Willow Downs Dr
21700 HarC 77375 3111 A1
21700 HarC 77379 3111 A1
22000 HarC 77375 3110 E1
Willow End St
23000 HarC 77375 2965 E7
Willow Fairway Dr
16500 HarC 77095 3538 A2
Willowfield Ct
5900 FBnC 77479 4493 E2
Willow Field Dr
11200 HarC 77429 3398 E5
11200 HarC 77429 3399 A5
Willowford Ct
5700 FBnC 77494 4093 D4
16200 HarC 77082 4096 A3
Willowford Park Ct
21400 FBnC 77450 4094 D2
Willowford Park Dr
21200 FBnC 77450 4094 B3
Willow Forest Dr
7900 HarC 77375 2966 A7
Willow Fork Ct
21200 FBnC 77450 3954 C7
Willow Fork Dr
2800 FBnC 77450 3954 B7
Willow Fork Ln
- FBnC 77450 4094 B1
Willowfork Pl
3000 FBnC 77494 3952 D7
Willowgate Dr
22200 HarC 77373 3116 A7
22200 HarC 77373 3261 A1
Willow Glade Dr
21200 FBnC 77450 3954 B7
Willow Glen Dr
5000 HOUS 77033 4243 E2
5300 HOUS 77033 4244 A2
Willow Glen Ln
600 BYTN 77521 3972 E3
Willow Green Dr
1800 MSCY 77489 4370 B5
Willow Green St
- FBnC 77494 3951 D4
Willowgreen St
28000 FBnC 77494 3951 D3
Willowgren Dr
600 BKHV 77024 3959 C2
600 HOUS 77024 3959 C2
Willow Grove Dr
8700 HarC 77375 3111 A1
Willowgrove Dr
- HOUS 77096 4241 B2
10000 HOUS 77035 4241 B3
Willow Hearth Dr
14800 HarC 77084 3679 A2
Willow Heights Ct
13500 HOUS 77059 4379 E4
Willowherb Ct
10 WDLD 77380 2821 E6
Willow Hill Dr
4100 TYLV 77586 4508 D1

Willowhurst Dr
15100 HarC 77429 3252 E6
Willowick
6600 HarC 77066 3400 D5
E Willowick Av
100 FRDW 77546 4505 C7
W Willowick Av
100 FRDW 77546 4505 B6
200 FRDW 77546 4629 B1
Willowick Cir
10 PNPV 77024 3959 E5
Willowick Ct
3300 SGLD 77478 4368 D4
Willowick Dr
200 CNRO 77304 2383 B4
7800 HarC 77389 2966 A4
8200 HarC 77389 2965 E4
Willowick Rd
2100 HOUS 77027 3961 D6
3600 HOUS 77019 3961 D5
Willowick St
22900 MtgC 77357 2827 E7
23200 MtgC 77357 2828 A7
Willowilde Dr
- HOUS 77035 4241 B2
Willowind Dr
3900 PASD 77504 4247 D5
Willowisp Dr
10300 HOUS 77035 4241 A3
Willowisp Tr
15200 MtgC 77302 2679 C2
Willow Knoll Ct
5300 HOUS 77345 3119 D2
Willow Lake Dr
1900 PRLD 77581 4504 C6
2400 HOUS 77077 3957 E7
Willowlake St
28000 FBnC 77494 3951 D4
Willowlake Park Dr
9500 HarC 77064 3540 D5
Willow Lakes Dr
1800 SGLD 77479 4367 E6
Willowland Dr
- HarC 77084 3677 E5
Willow Landing Ln
10300 HOUS 77085 4240 E7
Willow Leaf Dr
- HarC 77090 3258 A5
- HOUS 77090 3258 A5
Willow Leaf St
23300 HarC 77375 2965 E6
23300 HarC 77375 2966 B6
Willowleaf Garden Cross
- FBnC 77494 4093 A4
Willow Lodge Ct
9500 HarC 77064 3540 D4
Willow Manor Dr
200 BzaC 77583 4500 B7
200 BzaC 77583 4624 B1
Willow Meadow Dr
8600 HOUS 77031 4239 B3
8600 HOUS 77071 4239 C3
Willow Mill Dr
1500 MSCY 77489 4370 D4
Willow Mint Ln
7700 HarC 77086 3541 D3
7700 HarC 77086 3542 A2
Willowmist Dr
10800 HarC 77064 3540 D2
Willowmoss Ct
1800 HOUS 77008 3822 D5
Willow Moss Dr
18300 HarC 77449 3677 C3
Willow Mountain Ln
14100 HarC 77047 4374 B4
Willow Oak Dr
10 BYTN 77521 3835 B4
5800 HOUS 77092 3682 B5
Willow Oak Bend Cir
- HarC 77433 3395 C6
Willow Oak Bend Dr
18200 HarC 77433 3395 D6
Willow Oaks Cir
1000 PASD 77506 4107 D6
1700 DKSN 77539 4753 D2
Willow Oaks Dr
6300 MtgC 77385 2676 C6
Willowood Cir
10 WDLD 77381 2821 B6
Willowood Ln
3600 HOUS 77023 4104 C5
9300 HarC 77086 3541 E3
9500 HarC 77086 3542 A3
Willowood Creek Wy
5300 HarC 77379 3112 A7
Willow Park Dr
5800 FBnC 77469 4493 B6
Willowpark Dr
16000 HarC 77377 3254 C5
Willow Park Gdn
10500 HarC 77070 3399 C4
Willow Park Ln
9800 HarC 77064 3540 D4
25300 FBnC 77494 4093 A1
Willow Park Vw
10500 HarC 77070 3399 C4
Willow Park Village Dr
12800 HarC 77070 3399 B4
Willow Pass Dr
2300 HOUS 77339 3119 B7
Willowpeak Ct
5500 BzaC 77583 4623 E4
Willow Pine Dr
6100 HarC 77379 3256 D1
Willow Pl Dr N
8300 HOUS 77070 3399 D4
Willow Pl Dr S
8200 HOUS 77070 3399 D5
Willow Pl Dr W
12900 HOUS 77070 3399 D5
N Willow Point Cir
10 WDLD 77382 2674 B5
S Willow Point Cir
10 WDLD 77382 2674 B5
Willow Point Dr
- CNRO 77303 2237 C4
- MtgC 77303 2237 C4
1800 HOUS 77339 3118 D5
2300 HOUS 77339 3119 A5
Willow Point Ln
- FBnC 77494 4093 A6
Willow Point Pl
10 WDLD 77382 2674 B5
Willow Pointe Dr
300 LGCY 77573 4631 E4
Willow Pond Ct
4500 SGLD 77479 4494 E1

Willow Pond Dr
17600 GlsC 77511 4869 A7
Willow Pond Pl
23200 HarC 77494 3953 D4
Willow Quill Ct
8800 HarC 77088 3542 A7
Willow Quill Dr
8900 HarC 77088 3542 B6
Willow Ranch Dr
17000 HarC 77095 3537 E2
22300 HarC 77073 3259 A3
Willow Ridge Cir
11400 CNRO 77304 2236 B6
Willowridge Cir
11600 CNRO 77304 2236 B7
Willow Ridge Dr
3400 HOUS 77339 3119 B5
Willow River Dr
15300 HarC 77095 3538 D6
Willow Rock Rd
1400 HOUS 77088 3543 E7
Willowron Dr
10 HNCV 77024 3960 A4
10 PNPV 77024 3960 A4
Willow Rose Dr
- HarC 77379 3111 D4
Willow Run Pl
10 WDLD 77382 2675 C6
Willow Run St
17700 HarC 77447 3250 B2
Willow Shade Ln
21900 HarC 77375 3110 E1
21900 HarC 77375 3111 A1
Willow Shadows Dr
21900 HarC 77375 3111 A1
Willow Shores Dr
15300 HOUS 77062 4380 B7
Willow Side Ct
22000 FBnC 77450 4094 B3
Willowsong Ct
14400 HOUS 77489 4371 B3
Willow Song Ln
2900 PRLD 77545 4499 E4
Willow Spring Ln
8900 MtgC 77302 2530 C4
Willow Springs Ct
5400 LGCY 77573 4751 D2
Willow Springs Dr
3600 BzaC 77578 4501 B7
Willow Springs Ln
2500 FBnC 77479 4493 D2
3800 HOUS 77080 3820 D1
Willow Springs Pl
400 HarC 77373 3113 E4
Willow Spur Ct
21700 HarC 77375 3111 A1
Willow Spur Dr
8800 HarC 77375 3111 A1
Willow Stone Ct
3800 HarC 77449 3816 A2
Willow Stream Dr
- HarC 77084 3677 E5
Willow Switch Rd
23600 HarC 77389 2966 B6
Willow Terrace Dr
2000 HOUS 77345 3120 C6
Willowtex Dr
7000 HOUS 77396 3406 B7
7000 HOUS 77396 3547 B1
Willow Timber Dr
1000 HarC 77090 3258 C7
Willow Trace Ct
3100 FBnC 77450 3954 B7
9500 HarC 77064 3540 D5
Willow Trace Dr
20300 HarC 77433 3251 C6
Willow Tree Dr
- HarC 77038 3402 A7
- HarC 77066 3402 A7
3300 HarC 77066 3401 E7
Willowtwist St
13800 HarC 77083 4097 A6
Willow Vale Dr
1000 TYLV 77586 4381 D7
Willow View Ct
12800 HarC 77070 3399 B4
Willowview Ct
4300 SGLD 77479 4494 E1
Willow View Dr
2100 FBnC 77469 4364 B6
Willowview Dr
3900 PASD 77504 4247 D5
5100 BYTN 77521 3972 A1
5200 BYTN 77521 3971 E1
Willowview Ln
9200 HOUS 77080 3820 D5
Willow View St
1500 LPRT 77571 4110 B7
Willow Vista Dr
300 ELGO 77586 4509 A2
Willow Wand Ct
10500 HarC 77070 3399 C4
Willow West Dr
400 HarC 77073 3259 A4
Willow Wilde Dr
8800 HarC 77375 3111 A1
E Willowwind Cir
15300 MSCY 77071 4239 C5
W Willowwind Cir
15400 MSCY 77071 4239 D6
Willow Wind Dr
9000 CNRO 77302 2530 E4
Willow Wisp Cir
500 HarC 77388 3113 B6
Willow Wisp Dr
1400 MSCY 77489 4370 D4
2000 SEBK 77586 4509 C3
Willow Wisp Ln
1900 HarC 77388 3113 C6
E Willowwood Ct
10 WDLD 77381 2821 B7
W Willowwood Ct
10 WDLD 77381 2821 B6
Willowwood Dr
- LGCY 77573 4630 C5
22100 HarC 77449 3675 E5
Willow Wood St
23300 HarC 77375 2966 A6
Willow Wood Tr
3200 HOUS 77345 3119 E1
Willow Wood Wy
10000 HarC 77070 3255 B5
Willowyck Cir
2600 BzaC 77584 4501 D5
Will Scarlett St
1700 MtgC 77316 2668 E1
Willshire Pl Dr
- LGCY 77573 4631 D4

STREET
Block City ZIP Map# Grid

Willview Rd
15300 HOUS 77489 4371 B4
Willwick St
300 TMBL 77375 2964 B7
Willwood Dr
11000 HOUS 77072 4098 B3
Willy Ln
25700 HarC 77336 3122 D7
Wilma Lois Av
1000 PASD 77502 4107 C7
Wilmer St
3800 HOUS 77003 3964 A6
4300 HOUS 77011 3964 B6
Wilmerdean St
8100 HOUS 77061 4245 D3
Wilmington Ct
10 SGLD 77479 4495 B3
Wilmington Dr
500 BLAR 77401 4101 B4
2700 DKSN 77539 4753 C2
Wilmington St
4400 HOUS 77033 4243 E4
4400 HOUS 77051 4243 C4
5200 HOUS 77033 4244 A4
Wilmington Wy
10 WDLD 77384 2675 D5
Wilmington Park Ln
15900 HarC 77084 3678 C5
Wilo Dr
14000 HarC 77032 3546 D3
Wiloak St
9200 HOUS 77028 3687 D6
9500 HOUS 77078 3687 C5
Wilomill Dr
9100 HarC 77040 3541 B6
Wiloway St
8800 HarC 77016 3687 E1
Wilrose Haven Cir
6800 HarC 77449 3677 A2
Wilshire Cir
2700 PRLD 77581 4503 D4
Wilshire Ct
2200 DRPK 77536 4108 E6
23400 MtgC 77357 2828 A3
Wilshire Dr
3700 ALVN 77511 4867 D5
18500 MtgC 77357 2828 A2
Wilshire Ln
2900 BYTN 77521 3973 D2
Wilshire Rdg
- HOUS 77040 3682 A5
Wilshire St
2400 HOUS 77023 4104 C3
Wilshire Fern
6300 HOUS 77040 3682 A5
Wilshire Lakes
- HOUS 77040 3682 A5
Wilshire Park Dr
1400 HarC 77038 3543 A4
Wilshire Pl Dr
7400 HOUS 77040 3682 A4
7400 HOUS 77092 3682 A4
7600 HOUS 77040 3681 E4
Wilshire Pond
7300 HOUS 77040 3682 A5
Wilson Av
5300 GlsC 77511 4868 D4
N Wilson Av
100 MRGP 77571 4252 A1
Wilson Dr
1000 RSBG 77471 4491 C2
1200 RHMD 77469 4491 D2
1400 DRPK 77536 4109 C7
Wilson Ln
- HarC 77044 3408 D7
800 TMBL 77375 2964 B5
Wilson Rd
- HarC 77396 3548 A2
- MRGP 77571 4252 A2
10 HarC 77338 3263 A5
10 HMBL 77338 3263 A6
300 CNRO 77301 2384 B2
400 CNRO 77301 2383 E3
800 HMBL 77338 3407 A1
1300 CNRO 77304 2383 D3
1300 HMBL 77396 3407 A6
2900 HarC 77396 3407 A6
5800 HarC 77396 3547 E2
6900 MNVL 77578 4746 C2
Wilson St
1000 HOUS 77019 3963 A5
1500 BYTN 77521 3973 C3
1800 HOUS 77006 3963 A5
24800 HarC 77375 2964 E3
S Wilson St
100 MRGP 77571 4252 A2
Wilson Baker
- HarC 77044 3408 D7
- HOUS 77044 3408 D7
Wilson Creek Dr
2600 PASD 77503 4248 E2
25500 FBnC 77469 4092 C7
Wilson Park Ct
15000 HarC 77396 3407 D7
15000 HMBL 77396 3407 A3
Wilson Pines Ct
11700 HOUS 77031 4239 A4
Wilson Reid Dr
8700 HarC 77040 3541 C7
Wilsons Creek Ln
16700 FBnC 77083 4235 E1
Wilston Ct
1200 HOUS 77077 3958 A4
Wilstone Dr
18200 HarC 77084 3816 D1
Wilton Ct
4000 PRLD 77584 4502 D7
Wilton St
5300 HOUS 77005 4102 C2
5300 HOUS 77098 4102 C2
5800 PRLD 77584 4502 D7
Wilton Park Ct
17400 HarC 77379 3256 B2
Wilton Park Dr
7600 HarC 77379 3256 B3
Wiltshire Downs Ln
6600 HarC 77049 3829 A2
Wimberley Hollow Ln
3800 HarC 77053 4372 D5
Wimberly Dr
2300 DRPK 77536 4109 E6
Wimberly St
2800 HOUS 77093 3685 E6
2800 HOUS 77093 3686 A6
Wimberly Wy
10 WDLD 77385 2676 C4
15500 HarC 77429 3253 C5

STREET
Block City ZIP Map# Grid

N Wimberly Wy
100 WDLD 77385 2676 C4
Wimberly Canyon Ct
9000 HOUS 77075 4377 A6
Wimberly Canyon Dr
- FBnC 77479 4493 C3
Wimberly Knoll Ct
6200 HarC 77084 3678 B3
Wimberly Knoll Ln
2800 FBnC 77469 4365 A5
17400 HarC 77084 3678 B3
Wimberly Oaks Ln
7200 FBnC 77469 4095 C5
Wimberly Park Dr
15100 HarC 77049 3829 A3
Wimbledon Dr
13500 SGLD 77478 4237 B6
N Wimbledon Dr
18300 HarC 77449 3677 D4
S Wimbledon Dr
18300 HarC 77449 3677 C5
Wimbledon Ln
2800 FRDW 77546 4749 E1
8200 HarC 77070 3399 D3
Wimbledon Champion Dr
16000 HarC 77379 3257 A3
Wimbledon Creek Dr
6600 HarC 77379 3256 E3
Wimbledon Estates Dr
6700 HarC 77379 3256 D4
Wimbledon Forest Ct
6600 HarC 77379 3256 E3
Wimbledon Forest Dr
16100 HarC 77379 3257 A3
16600 HarC 77379 3256 E2
Wimbledon Oak Dr
13300 HarC 77065 3539 A2
13700 HarC 77429 3539 A2
Wimbledon Trail Rd
6400 HarC 77379 3256 E3
Wimbledon Villas Dr
6300 HarC 77379 3256 E3
Wimbleton Ct
2100 PRLD 77581 4504 D2
Wimcrest Dr
2000 GLSN 77551 5108 A7
Winberie Ct
2100 HarC 77450 3954 A6
Winbern St
800 HOUS 77002 3963 A7
1500 HOUS 77004 3963 A7
2000 HOUS 77004 4103 B1
Winberry Ct
21000 HarC 77449 3676 D4
Winchell St
6300 HOUS 77022 3824 C3
Winchell Pl Rd
33500 MtgC 77355 2962 C2
Winchester Bnd
400 HarC 77336 3120 E3
600 HarC 77336 3121 A3
Winchester Ct
900 FRDW 77546 4629 D1
12600 MtgC 77354 2671 A3
Winchester Dr
1100 FBnC 77469 4364 D6
1100 RHMD 77469 4364 D6
1500 MtgC 77385 2677 A7
Winchester St
3700 HOUS 77003 3963 C6
Winchester Wy
3000 SGLD 77479 4495 E1
Winchester Ranch Tr
3000 HarC 77449 3814 B3
3200 HarC 77493 3814 B3
Winchester Rock Dr
20900 MtgC 77365 3118 A3
Winchester Village Ct
9800 HarC 77064 3540 C4
Winchmore Hill Dr
16000 HarC 77379 3256 B5
Wincopin Dr
- HarC 77095 3539 A6
Wincrest Ct
12900 HarC 77429 3254 B7
Wincrest Rd
10900 TXCY 77539 4755 A2
Wincrest Falls Dr
10 HarC 77429 3254 B7
Wincroft Ct
5200 HarC 77069 3256 D6
S Wind Dr
- HarC 77089 4505 A1
29500 MtgC 77386 2969 B4
Windbluff Ct
10 WDLD 77382 2674 C5
Windbourne Dr
22400 HarC 77375 3110 D2
Windbreak Ln
3500 SGLD 77479 4495 D2
3500 SGLD 77479 4496 A1
Windbreak Tr
5400 HOUS 77079 3957 A2
Windbreaker Dr
- HarC 77449 3677 A6
Windbriar Ct
3600 HarC 77068 3257 C6
Wind Brook St
7100 HarC 77040 3681 C2
Wind Brush Dr
2700 HarC 77388 3113 A5
Windbury Ct
20100 HarC 77379 3111 E5
21900 FBnC 77450 4094 B3
Windbush Ct
13900 HarC 77429 3397 B2
Wind Canyon Dr
- FBnC 77450 4094 E4
Wind Cave Ln
14700 HarC 77040 3541 A7
Windchase Blvd
2600 HarC 77077 3957 A7
2600 HarC 77082 3957 A7
2600 HarC 77082 4097 A2
2600 HOUS 77077 3957 A7
2600 HOUS 77082 3957 A7
Windchase Ct
13500 HarC 77082 4097 A1
Windchase Ln
- PRLD 77581 4503 D1
Windchester St
2300 PRLD 77581 4503 E3
Wind Chimes Dr
4800 HarC 77066 3401 B2
Windcliff Ct
5800 HarC 77449 3677 D5
Wind Cove Pl Ct
- HarC 77346 3408 B3

STREET
Block City ZIP Map# Grid

Wind Creek Dr
2000 HOUS 77345 3119 E7
Windcreek St
10 FRDW 77546 4629 A5
Windcrest Ct
100 JRSV 77064 3540 A6
3300 PRLD 77581 4504 C5
5200 FBnC 77450 4094 A3
Windcrest Estates Blvd
33100 MtgC 77354 2673 B3
Windcrest Estates Ct
6900 MtgC 77354 2673 B3
Windcrest Park Ct
2400 MtgC 77386 2823 C6
Windcrest Park Ln
31200 MtgC 77386 2823 B7
Windcroft Ln
2300 FBnC 77479 4493 E2
Windcroft Hollow Ln
19900 HarC 77449 3676 E7
Windcross Ct
4800 HarC 77449 3677 A6
Wind Dale St
7200 HarC 77040 3681 B1
Windell Ct
8200 HarC 77040 3541 A7
Windell Ln
8400 HarC 77040 3541 A7
Windemere Ct
9800 HMBL 77338 3262 C4
Windemere Dr
2900 PRLD 77584 4501 B1
Windemere St
5100 HOUS 77033 4243 E2
5300 HOUS 77033 4244 A2
Windenere Isl
100 HarC 77373 3114 A2
E Winderbury St
12700 HOUS 77077 3957 C5
W Winderbury St
12800 HOUS 77077 3957 C6
Windermere Ln
10 PNPV 77063 3959 D6
Windermere Lakes Blvd
10400 HarC 77065 3539 E2
Winderwick Ln
- HarC 77066 3401 A5
Windfall Ct
8200 HarC 77040 3540 E7
8200 HarC 77040 3541 A7
Wind Fall Ln
2500 SGLD 77479 4368 D7
Windfall Ln
8200 HarC 77040 3540 D7
Windfall Path Dr
24500 HarC 77373 3114 D3
Windfellow Pl
10 WDLD 77381 2820 E3
Windfern Dr
3200 PRLD 77581 4504 C5
Windfern Pl
10 WDLD 77382 2675 C7
Windfern Rd
4300 HOUS 77041 3681 B7
4300 HOUS 77041 3820 B1
4300 HOUS 77080 3820 B1
6000 HOUS 77040 3681 B4
6500 HarC 77040 3681 B2
7800 HarC 77040 3541 B7
10700 HarC 77064 3541 A1
11100 HarC 77064 3540 B1
13400 HarC 77070 3540 A1
Windfern Forest Dr
14400 HarC 77040 3541 A7
Windfern Lakes St
10800 HarC 77064 3540 E1
Windfern Trace Dr
8800 HarC 77064 3540 E2
8800 HarC 77064 3541 A1
Wind Field Ln
20900 HarC 77379 3111 D4
Windflower Ln
7000 HarC 77521 3832 B5
9600 HarC 77086 3542 A3
Windflower Pl
10 WDLD 77381 2674 C6
Windford Sq
- HOUS 77339 3117 E4
Wind Forest Ct
14600 HarC 77040 3541 A7
Wind Forest Dr
8000 HarC 77040 3541 A7
Wind Free Dr
14700 HarC 77040 3541 A7
Windgap Ct
3200 MtgC 77380 2967 B2
Windgate Ct
- LGCY 77573 4630 E7
7300 HarC 77433 3677 D1
Windgrove Ct
8200 FBnC 77083 4096 A7
Windham Ct
5400 HarC 77041 3680 A6
Windham Springs Ct
5300 HarC 77041 3680 A7
Wind Harp Pl
10 WDLD 77382 2674 D4
Windhaven Dr
10 WDLD 77381 2674 B7
10 WDLD 77381 2820 B1
Windhaven St
13500 HOUS 77049 3828 B2
Windhaven Lake Dr
- HarC 77433 3537 C5
Windhaven Terrace Ct
18400 HarC 77433 3537 C5
E Windhaven Terrace Tr
8400 HarC 77433 3537 C6
W Windhaven Terrace Tr
18500 HarC 77433 3537 C5
Wind Hawk Ct
2500 FBnC 77494 3951 D5
Wind Hawk Dr
28000 FBnC 77494 3951 D5
Wind Hollow Cir
- HarC 77040 3541 A7
Windhollow Cir
400 LGCY 77573 4633 A2
Windhover Ln
- HOUS 77055 3820 B7
Windhurst Rd
- FBnC 77494 4093 B5
Winding
4400 FBnC 77469 4364 C3
Winding Cr
27200 MtgC 77355 2815 B7
Winding Ln
12400 HarC 77429 3398 C6

STREET
Block City ZIP Map# Grid

Winding Rd
100 FRDW 77546 4505 A6
100 PRLD 77581 4504 E6
100 PRLD 77581 4505 A6
500 HOUS 77504 4247 B7
900 PASD 77504 4247 C7
Winding Tr
7600 GlsC 77517 4986 B7
Winding Wy
- LMQU 77568 4874 B7
- TXCY 77591 4874 B7
- WlrC 77447 2959 C1
5000 DKSN 77539 4754 C2
Winding Bayou Trc
- HarC 77038 3544 A3
- HOUS 77037 3544 B2
Winding Black Cherry Ln
15000 HarC 77433 3251 C7
15000 HarC 77433 3395 B1
Winding Branch Dr
19800 HarC 77449 3815 E3
19800 HarC 77449 3816 A3
Winding Brook Ct
5300 DKSN 77539 4754 D1
Winding Brook Dr
5200 DKSN 77539 4754 D1
W Winding Brook Dr
5700 DKSN 77539 4754 E1
Winding Brook Ln
12500 HOUS 77024 3958 E2
30000 MtgC 77355 2814 E3
30000 MtgC 77355 2815 A2
Winding Brook East Dr
1300 FBnC 77479 4494 B6
Winding Brook West Dr
- FBnC 77479 4494 B5
Winding Canyon
1000 WlrC 77493 3812 A7
Winding Canyon Dr
13300 HOUS 77044 3409 A4
Winding Canyon Ln
7200 FBnC 77083 4095 D6
19500 HarC 77449 3677 A7
Winding Cove Ln
6400 FBnC 77450 4094 C3
Winding Creek Ct
25300 MtgC 77355 2814 A7
Winding Creek Dr
1800 PRLD 77581 4504 C5
2500 MSCY 77545 4622 C2
Winding Creek Ln
17500 MtgC 77355 2961 A1
17500 SGCH 77355 2961 A1
Winding Creek Pl
10 WDLD 77381 2675 A5
Winding Creek Vw
7800 HOUS 77072 4097 D7
Winding Creek Wy
5400 HOUS 77017 4246 C1
Winding Dream Ln
- HarC 77084 3816 B1
Winding Forest Dr
3900 PRLD 77581 4504 B7
Winding Green Dr
10400 HarC 77338 3407 D1
Winding Heights Blvd
- FBnC 77479 4494 C5
Winding Hill Dr
14700 MtgC 77354 2670 B1
Winding Hill Ln
8200 HarC 77379 3256 D4
Winding Hollow Ct
2100 MtgC 77385 2823 A6
Winding Hollow Dr
1700 HarC 77450 3954 B5
Winding Hollow Ln
2200 HarC 77450 3954 B6
11300 HarC 77375 3109 D2
Winding Knoll Dr
23100 FBnC 77494 3953 D6
Winding Lake Ct
22200 FBnC 77450 3954 A7
Winding Lake Wy
3200 FBnC 77450 3953 E7
Winding Manor Dr
12500 HarC 77044 3549 C2
Winding Meadow Ct
8200 HarC 77040 3681 D1
Winding Moss Dr
15400 HarC 77068 3257 B4
N Winding Oak
300 LGCY 77573 4630 D5
S Winding Oak
300 LGCY 77573 4630 D5
Winding Oak Ct
17200 HarC 77429 3396 C1
Winding Oak Ln
8100 HarC 77379 3256 A4
Winding Path Wy
21100 FBnC 77469 4234 B5
Winding Ridge Dr
5400 HarC 77379 3112 B7
5400 HarC 77379 3257 A1
Winding River Dr
4400 FBnC 77469 4364 B3
4900 SGLD 77478 4369 A6
8900 HOUS 77088 3544 A7
Winding River Tr
26700 HarC 77336 3122 A3
Winding Run Ln
2700 FBnC 77494 3953 B6
Winding Shore Ct
22900 FBnC 77450 3953 E7
Winding Shore Ln
2000 LGCY 77573 4631 B7
2800 FBnC 77450 3953 E7
Winding Shores Dr
12300 PRLD 77584 4500 B3
Winding Spring Dr
5700 HarC 77379 3257 B1
Winding Springs Dr
2100 LGCY 77573 4631 B7
13800 HarC 77429 3253 C6
Winding Star Ln
- HarC 77433 3396 A6
Winding Timbers Cir
4900 HarC 77346 3408 B1
Winding Timbers Ct
4800 HarC 77346 3408 B1
Winding Timbers Ln
18200 HarC 77346 3408 B1
Winding Trace Dr
6600 HarC 77086 3542 B1
Winding Trail Ln
- ALVN 77511 4749 B6
- BzaC 77511 4749 B6
19100 HarC 77449 3677 B3

STREET
Block City ZIP Map# Grid

Winding Trail Rd
10200 LPRT 77571 4250 C3
Winding Trail Wy
7800 GlsC 77517 4986 D6
Winding Valley Dr
15600 HarC 77095 3678 D1
Winding View Ln
4900 HarC 77346 3264 B7
Winding Waco Ct
9100 HarC 77433 3537 B5
Winding Walk Dr
7000 HarC 77084 3679 A1
7000 HarC 77095 3679 A1
Winding Waters Dr
14600 HarC 77429 3396 D1
14800 HarC 77429 3252 D7
Winding Willow Ln
25300 HarC 77373 3114 D2
Winding Wood Ct
2300 HarC 77038 3543 B2
Winding Wood Dr
13100 HarC 77038 3543 B2
Winding Wood Ln
10200 HarC 77375 3110 B1
Winding Wy Ct
40400 MtgC 77354 2670 B2
Winding Wy Dr
1100 FRDW 77546 4629 D3
5200 HOUS 77091 3683 A4
5400 HOUS 77091 3682 E4
Winding Wy Ln
- BzaC 77511 4748 A3
Windjammer Ct
4100 SEBK 77586 4382 B6
Windjammer St
12300 HOUS 77072 4097 E6
Windlake Ct
12000 HarC 77070 3399 C6
Windlake Dr
11700 HarC 77070 3399 C6
Windlass Cir
13500 GLSN 77554 5332 E1
Windlass Ct
3300 GLSN 77554 5332 E1
Windlass Wy
700 HarC 77532 3552 A1
Wind Lawn Dr
14600 HarC 77040 3541 A7
Windlea Ln
14700 HarC 77040 3541 A7
Windleaf Dr
1300 SRAC 77571 4382 C1
Windledge Pl
10 WDLD 77381 2820 C2
Windlewood Dr
3600 HarC 77449 3815 D2
Wind Lock Cir
14600 HarC 77040 3541 A7
Windlock Ln
1200 FBnC 77469 4364 C3
Windmark Dr
11100 HOUS 77099 4238 B4
Windmark Ln
10500 HOUS 77099 4238 B4
Windmark Pl
11100 HOUS 77099 4238 B4
Windmeadow Pl
10 WDLD 77381 2675 B7
Windmere Rd
100 FRDW 77546 4630 A7
100 FRDW 77573 4630 A7
100 LGCY 77573 4630 A7
Windmere Park Ct
24600 FBnC 77494 3953 B7
Windmere Park Ln
3000 FBnC 77494 3953 B7
Windmill Dr
10 WlrC 77445 3098 B7
2000 FBnC 77469 4365 C2
Windmill Ln
2500 HOUS 77008 3822 C5
Windmill Rd
9100 HarC 77064 3541 B4
35400 PRVW 77445 3100 A4
35400 WlrC 77445 3099 E4
35400 WlrC 77445 3100 A4
Windmill St
3000 SGLD 77479 4368 E7
Windmill Bluff Ln
21900 FBnC 77450 4094 B3
Windmill Cove Ln
14900 HarC 77429 3397 C1
Windmill Elm St
3500 HOUS 77008 3822 D7
Windmill Falls Ln
- FBnC 77494 4092 B2
Windmill Forest Dr
14500 HarC 77082 4096 D3
14500 HOUS 77082 4096 D3
Windmill Lakes Blvd
9800 HOUS 77075 4377 B2
Windmill Links Dr
3700 FBnC 77469 4366 D1
Windmill Meadows Ct
14500 HarC 77082 4096 D3
Windmill Park Ln
9700 HarC 77064 3541 B3
Windmill Village Dr
3600 HarC 77082 4096 D3
Windmist Cir
6400 HarC 77084 3678 B3
Wind Mist Ln
17600 HarC 77433 3537 D1
Windmoor Ct
19700 HarC 77449 3816 A2
Windmoor Dr
3500 HarC 77449 3816 A2
3800 HarC 77449 3815 E1
Windmoor Pl
- HarC 77449 3816 A3
Windoak Ln
14700 HarC 77040 3541 A7
Windom Dr
15900 HOUS 77598 4506 E4
16000 HOUS 77598 4507 A4
Windover Ct
1200 FBnC 77479 4366 D7
Windover Glen Ln
- HarC 77449 3815 A2
Window Rock Dr
- HarC 77095 3538 A3
Wind Pine Ln
11200 HarC 77375 3255 A1
Wind Point Dr
- HarC 77375 3109 D7
Wind Poppy Ct
10 WDLD 77381 2821 A7

STREET
Block City ZIP Map# Grid

Wind Ridge Cir
10 WDLD 77381 2674 B7
100 WDLD 77381 2820 B1
Wind Ridge Ln
20500 HarC 77379 3111 D4
Windridge Pl
10 WDLD 77381 2674 D6
Windrift Ct
200 FBnC 77479 4366 D6
Windrift Dr
4000 HarC 77066 3401 B3
Windriver Cir
11800 HarC 77070 3399 B6
Wind River Ct
10 MtgC 77384 2528 B6
Wind River Dr
10 MtgC 77384 2528 B7
Windriver Dr
10200 HarC 77070 3399 B6
Windriver Tr
- HarC 77064 3540 B5
Wind Rock Ct
7200 HarC 77040 3681 C1
Wind Rock St
8700 HarC 77040 3681 C2
Wind Rose Ct
100 JRSV 77064 3540 B5
Windrose Pt
21900 MtgC 77357 2827 E1
Windrose Bend Dr
20400 HarC 77379 3111 B5
Windrose Hollow Ln
6000 HarC 77379 3111 D4
Windrose Trail Ln
- HarC 77379 3111 D4
Windrow Dr
16900 HarC 77379 3256 E1
Windrow Ln
7300 HOUS 77072 4097 C6
Windrush Dr
9300 HarC 77379 3256 A6
9500 HarC 77379 3255 E6
Windsail Ct
4400 MSCY 77459 4369 C6
N Windsail Pl
10 WDLD 77381 2821 C4
S Windsail Pl
10 WDLD 77381 2821 C4
Wind Sand Dr
- HarC 77449 3677 B6
Windshire
5000 MSCY 77459 4496 C2
Windshire Dr
13600 HarC 77429 3397 D2
Windshore Wy
6900 FBnC 77479 4493 D4
Wind Side Dr
8700 HarC 77040 3681 C1
Windsome Dr
- FBnC 77545 4623 A1
Windsome Ln
15000 HarC 77429 3397 C1
Windsong Ct
100 WDLD 77381 2674 D7
Windsong Ln
- PRLD 77545 4499 E4
10 BzaC 77511 4628 E5
10 FRDW 77546 4628 E5
10 FRDW 77546 4629 A5
1300 FBnC 77469 4364 C3
Windsong Tr
2000 HarC 77532 3410 B1
3900 HarC 77084 3816 E1
4300 HarC 77084 3677 E7
5500 HarC 77084 3678 A5
Wind Song Trc
38000 MtgC 77355 2815 B4
Windsong Wy
- HOUS 77345 3119 E1
- HOUS 77365 3119 E1
- TKIS 77554 5106 B3
Windsor Ct
- HOUS 77055 3820 E6
- SPVL 77055 3820 E6
10 GLSN 77551 5108 D5
10 MSCY 77459 4369 D7
4200 STFE 77510 4871 A7
Windsor Dr
10 CNRO 77304 2529 C1
300 FRDW 77546 4629 D3
3600 DRPK 77536 4249 A1
Windsor Ln
2300 PASD 77506 4107 E5
2700 PASD 77506 4108 A5
10100 HarC 77031 4238 E6
10100 STAF 77031 4238 D6
10100 STAF 77477 4238 D6
Windsor Mnr
14900 HarC 77069 3256 E6
Windsor Pl
- SPVL 77055 3820 E6
10 SGLD 77479 4495 D2
1400 HOUS 77077 3957 C5
Windsor Rd
3200 PRLD 77581 4503 D4
17100 MtgC 77306 2533 D5
Windsor Sq
300 ALVN 77511 4867 D5
Windsor St
1900 HOUS 77006 3962 C5
Windsor Bay Ct
12200 HarC 77375 3254 D1
Windsor Bridge Dr
10 CNRO 77384 2675 E4
Windsor Canyon Ct
23900 HarC 77389 2965 E4
23900 HarC 77389 2966 A5
Windsor Castle Dr
- HarC 77389 3113 A2
21500 HarC 77388 3113 A2
Windsor Chase Ln
- LGCY 77573 4751 C1
1000 HarC 77373 2968 D7
Windsor Crest Dr
18900 HarC 77094 3955 B2
Windsor Forest Dr
5400 HarC 77088 3542 E7
Windsor Garden Ln
13700 HOUS 77044 3550 B3
Windsor Glen Dr
- HarC 77450 3954 D1
- HOUS 77450 3954 D1
Windsor Grove Ln
17600 HarC 77084 3678 A7
Windsor Hill Dr
- WDLD 77384 2675 D5
E Windsor Hills Cir
10 WDLD 77384 2675 D5

STREET
Block City ZIP Map# Grid

W Windsor Hills Cir
10 WDLD 77384 2675 D5
Windsor Hollow Ct
20900 HarC 77449 3815 B6
Windsor Lake Cross
19000 HarC 77094 3955 B3
Windsor Lake Dr
- CNRO 77384 2676 A3
Windsor Lakes Blvd
- CNRO 77384 2676 A4
- MtgC 77384 2676 A4
- WDLD 77384 2676 A5
Windsor Lakes Ct
1100 HarC 77094 3955 C2
Windsor Lakes Dr
18400 HarC 77094 3955 C3
Windsor Locks Dr
9700 HarC 77065 3539 E4
Windsor Oaks Ln
14300 HOUS 77062 4379 E6
Windsor Palms Dr
18900 HarC 77094 3955 B3
Windsor Park Dr
1600 HarC 77094 3955 B4
Windsor Pointe Ct
19200 HarC 77375 3109 C6
Windsor Pointe Dr
- HarC 77375 3109 C6
- HarC 77375 3254 D1
Windsor Sails Dr
19000 HarC 77094 3955 C2
Windsor Square Dr
4600 HOUS 77339 3264 C1
Windsor Trace Ln
20000 FBnC 77469 4094 C5
Windsor Valley Dr
- HarC 77049 3689 D7
- HarC 77049 3828 D1
Windsor Village Dr
12600 HOUS 77071 4239 B7
12600 MSCY 77071 4239 B7
Windsor Woods Ln
- KATY 77494 3952 B3
Windstar Ct
10 WDLD 77381 2821 A3
Windstar Dr
10 WDLD 77381 2821 A2
Windstone
- HarC 77084 3678 B2
- HarC 77095 3678 B2
Windstone Manor Blvd
- HarC 77449 3815 E1
Wind Stream Dr
8700 HarC 77040 3681 B1
Windstream Ln
16800 FBnC 77478 4236 A7
Windswept Dr
500 HMBL 77338 3263 A7
900 CNRO 77301 2383 D2
900 HMBL 77338 3407 A1
2400 FBnC 77469 4365 E4
Windswept Ln
- HOUS 77042 4099 B2
1600 GlsC 77539 4633 C6
5300 HOUS 77056 4100 E2
6100 HOUS 77057 4100 B2
7600 HOUS 77063 4100 A2
7700 HOUS 77063 4099 E2
Windswept St
2300 PRLD 77581 4503 E3
Windswept Grove Dr
9100 FBnC 77083 4236 B2
Windswept Oaks Pl
10 WDLD 77385 2676 B3
Wind Trace Ct
10 WDLD 77381 2821 B4
Wind Trace Dr
- HarC 77449 3676 D7
4700 HarC 77449 3677 A7
Wind Trace Cove
1700 FBnC 77479 4494 B4
Wind Trail St
7200 HarC 77040 3681 B1
Windtree Ln
17800 HarC 77379 3257 A2
E Windvale Cir
- WDLD 77384 2674 E3
- WDLD 77384 2675 A3
N Windvale Cir
- WDLD 77382 2674 E3
- WDLD 77384 2674 E3
W Windvale Cir
- WDLD 77382 2674 E3
- WDLD 77384 2674 E3
S Windvale Ridge Dr
- WDLD 77384 2674 E3
- WDLD 77384 2675 B3
Wind Veil Dr
8300 HarC 77040 3541 A7
Windview Dr
- HOUS 77075 4377 B2
Windvine Ct
7000 HOUS 77072 4097 C5
Windvine Dr
7100 HOUS 77072 4097 C6
Wind Walker Tr
10500 HarC 77095 3537 E2
Windward Ct
10 WDLD 77381 2821 C4
200 LGCY 77573 4633 C3
Windward Dr
300 LGCY 77573 4633 C3
Windward Ln
10 NSUB 77058 4508 B6
17500 MAGA 77354 2669 B3
Windward Wy
- HarC 77532 3409 D6
300 TKIS 77554 5106 C3
Windward Bay Dr
- PRLD 77545 4499 D4
- PRLD 77584 4499 D4
- PRLD 77584 4500 A4
Windward Cove
10 WDLD 77381 2821 C4
W Windward Cove
10 WDLD 77381 2821 C4
Windward Passage St
7700 HOUS 77072 4097 E7
Windwater Dr
9700 HOUS 77075 4377 B2
N Windwater Pkwy
- HOUS 77036 4099 E3
7000 HOUS 77036 4100 A3
7000 HOUS 77074 4100 A4
Windwater Lagoon Dr
7100 HOUS 77036 4099 E3
7100 HOUS 77036 4100 A3

STREET
Block City ZIP Map# Grid

Windwater Pointe
6100 HOUS 77036 4100 A3
Wind Whisper Ct
10 WDLD 77380 2968 A3
Wind Willow Dr
8300 HarC 77040 3541 A7
Windwood Ct
7200 FBnC 77479 4493 E4
Windwood Dr
11000 HOUS 77035 4241 A4
Windwood St
10 FRDW 77546 4628 E6
3000 PRLD 77581 4503 E3
Windwood Forest Dr
23100 MtgC 77357 2827 E3
Windwood Park Ln
14600 HarC 77429 3396 C2
Windy Ln
1100 BYTN 77520 3973 C5
11600 BKHV 77024 3959 D3
11600 PNPV 77024 3959 D3
Windy Wy
4800 PASD 77505 4248 A6
6400 PRLD 77584 4502 C5
Windy Acres Dr
7900 HarC 77040 3681 A1
8000 HarC 77040 3541 A7
Windy Bank Ln
- PRLD 77581 4503 C1
23400 FBnC 77469 4093 D6
Windy Bay Ln
- FBnC 77450 4093 E3
Windy Bluff Ct
4800 HarC 77449 3677 B7
Windy Briar Ln
2900 LGCY 77573 4633 B2
20700 HarC 77379 3111 C4
Windy Brook Ln
1700 LGCY 77573 4751 E2
4800 HarC 77449 3677 A6
22200 HarC 77375 3109 E1
Windy Cape Ln
3200 LGCY 77573 4633 C3
Windy Cape Rd
11300 HarC 77065 3539 C1
Windy Chase Ln
4200 FBnC 77494 4092 D2
Windy Cliff Ln
- HarC 77379 3111 C4
Windy Cove Ct
2300 LGCY 77573 4508 D6
8400 HarC 77095 3538 E6
Windy Cove Dr
15200 HarC 77095 3538 D6
Windy Cove Ln
- PRLD 77584 4500 D2
Windy Creek Ct
8300 HarC 77040 3541 B5
Windy Creek Dr
7900 HarC 77040 3681 A1
8000 HarC 77040 3541 A7
11300 PRLD 77584 4500 D2
Windy Crossing Ln
2900 LGCY 77539 4752 D4
14200 HarC 77396 3547 C2
Windy Cypress Ct
4700 HarC 77449 3677 A7
Windy Dawn Dr
11300 PRLD 77584 4500 D2
Windy Drift Ln
3600 FBnC 77494 4092 B1
Windy Dunes Dr
8100 HOUS 77071 4239 D6
Windygate Dr
24100 HarC 77373 3115 B5
Windy Glen Ct
5500 BzaC 77583 4623 D3
Windy Glen Dr
15700 HarC 77095 3538 D7
Windy Gorge Ct
2900 HOUS 77345 3119 E2
Windy Gorge Dr
4500 HOUS 77345 3119 E2
Windy Green Dr
1900 HOUS 77345 3120 C5
Windy Grove Ln
1000 CNRO 77301 2384 C1
10900 HarC 77433 3537 A1
Windy Haven Dr
3700 HOUS 77339 3119 B4
Windy Heath Ln
13100 HOUS 77085 4240 C7
13100 HOUS 77085 4371 C2
Windy Hollow Dr
4500 HOUS 77345 3119 D3
Windy Hollow Ln
2900 LGCY 77539 4753 B2
Windy Isle Ct
25600 HarC 77389 2966 B2
Windy Isle Wy
- PRLD 77584 4500 D2
Windy Knoll Ct
10100 BzaC 77583 4623 D5
Windy Knoll Dr
1700 HarC 77084 3816 B7
Windy Knoll Ln
5700 BzaC 77583 4623 D5
Windy Lake Dr
5100 HOUS 77345 3120 A5
Windylea Ln
7700 FBnC 77469 4094 A7
Windy Mark Dr
- HarC 77449 3677 A7
Windy Meadow Dr
1700 HarC 77084 3815 E7
2000 SGLD 77478 4368 D6
Windy Meadow Rd
13800 HarC 77377 3108 E3
Windy Mountain Ln
12400 HarC 77346 3408 C2
Windy Nook Dr
19900 HarC 77084 3815 E5
Windy Oaks Ct
18100 MtgC 77365 2971 E2
Windy Oaks Dr
8300 HarC 77040 3541 A7
Windy Orchard Ln
4900 HarC 77084 3678 A7
Windy Park Dr
1600 HOUS 77339 3118 C7
Windy Path Ln
8400 HarC 77433 3537 C6
Windy Peaks Ct
1900 HarC 77067 3402 B5
Windypine Dr
16800 HarC 77379 3256 E1
Windy Pines Cir
17200 HarC 77379 3256 C2
Windy Pines Dr
- HarC 77379 3256 D2
10 HarC 77449 3677 C5
Windy Plain Ct
1900 HarC 77388 3113 C5
Windy Point Dr
17700 HarC 77379 3256 C1
Windy Port Ln
7200 FBnC 77469 4094 C6
Windy Ridge Dr
1800 HarC 77450 3954 E5
Windy Ridge Ln
14200 BzaC 77583 4623 C4
14500 HOUS 77062 4380 A6
Windy Ridge Tr
37800 MtgC 77355 2815 B4
Windy River Ln
6600 HarC 77449 3676 E2
Windy Royal Dr
3000 HOUS 77045 4242 A7
3100 HOUS 77045 4241 E7
Windy Run Ct
7000 HarC 77379 3111 B7
Windys Wy
1500 HarC 77449 3815 C7
Windysage Ct
2900 MSCY 77459 4496 D1
Windy Shores Dr
2100 PRLD 77584 4500 C1
Windy Spring Ct
9200 HarC 77089 4377 B7
Windy Spring Ln
9300 HarC 77089 4377 B7
Windy Stone Dr
18500 HarC 77084 3677 C6
19000 HarC 77449 3677 B7
Windystone Dr
- HarC 77084 3677 A7
19600 HarC 77449 3677 A7
20100 HarC 77449 3676 E7
Windy Stream Ln
13900 HarC 77044 3549 E2
Windy Summer Ln
12700 HarC 77044 3689 B3
Windy Thicket Ln
2700 HOUS 77082 4096 E1
8400 HarC 77433 3537 C6
Windy Trace Ln
3600 FBnC 77494 4093 C2
Windy Trail Dr
14300 HarC 77040 3541 A7
Windy Vale Tr
- FBnC 77545 4498 C5
Windy Valley Wy
- HarC 77433 3537 C5
Windy Village Ln
18500 HarC 77449 3677 C3
Windy Willow Ct
14400 HOUS 77489 4371 A3
Windy Willow Dr
14500 HOUS 77489 4371 B3
Windy Wisp Ln
12400 HOUS 77071 4239 D6
Windy Woods Ct
4100 HOUS 77345 3119 E3
Wineberry Dr
- HarC 77450 3954 E5
Wineberry Pl
10 WDLD 77382 2674 E5
10 WDLD 77382 2675 A5
Winebrook Ct
2100 PRLD 77584 4500 B2
13500 HarC 77429 3397 D1
Winebrook Dr
12300 PRLD 77584 4500 B2
Wine Cedar Ln
1700 HarC 77450 3954 E4
Wine Cup Ct
9900 HarC 77379 3110 C6
Winecup Ln
2200 LGCY 77573 4632 E2
14100 HarC 77047 4374 A4
Wine Cup Wy
6900 FBnC 77494 4093 C5
Winehill Ln
7800 HarC 77040 3541 D7
Wine Meadow Ct
16700 HarC 77429 3396 D1
Wine Rock Dr
15900 HarC 77070 3255 B6
Winesap Ln
13100 HarC 77429 3398 A1
Winesap Bend Dr
4100 FBnC 77477 4369 C4
Winewood Dr
8600 HarC 77044 3689 B5
Winfield Ln
1000 KMAH 77565 4509 D7
1100 KMAH 77565 4633 D1
Winfield Rd
5200 HarC 77039 3546 D6
5200 HarC 77050 3546 D6
5900 HOUS 77050 3546 E6
6100 HOUS 77050 3547 A6
6600 HarC 77050 3547 B6
9200 HarC 77050 3548 B5
9700 HarC 77396 3548 B5
Winfield Sq
17300 FBnC 77469 4095 D5
Winfield Lakes Tr
2600 FBnC 77545 4498 C7
Winford Ct
- HarC 77379 3111 E5
Winford Dr
5300 HarC 77449 3676 D6
Winford Estate Dr
25600 FBnC 77469 4092 D7
Winfree Dr
4700 HOUS 77021 4103 E5
4800 HOUS 77021 4104 A5
6300 HOUS 77087 4104 D6
7200 HOUS 77087 4105 A6
E Winfree Rd
1800 MTBL 77520 3696 E4
Winfree St
1600 MTBL 77520 3696 D4
Winfrey Ln
1200 HarC 77375 2964 D6
1200 TMBL 77375 2964 D6
12000 HOUS 77076 3685 B2
Winfro Dr
30300 TMBL 77375 2963 E5
W Wing Dr
2700 BzaC 77578 4501 A6
Wing St
9800 MtgC 77385 2676 E5
E Wing St
200 MtgC 77304 2529 D4
N Wing St
700 MtgC 77304 2529 D4
S Wing St
500 MtgC 77304 2529 D4
Wingate St
7300 HOUS 77011 3965 B6
Wingate Park Dr
- HOUS 77082 4096 A3
3600 HarC 77082 4096 A3
Wingborne Ln
11600 HarC 77429 3397 D7
Wingdale Ct
3400 HarC 77082 4096 B3
Wingdale Dr
15700 HarC 77082 4096 A2
Winged Dove Dr
2500 LGCY 77573 4752 B1
Winged Foot Dr
10 PNVL 77304 2237 B3
2100 LGCY 77573 4508 D7
2100 LGCY 77573 4632 D1
5900 HarC 77069 3400 C1
Wingfield Ln
25400 HarC 77373 3114 C2
Wingfoot Dr
2000 MSCY 77459 4497 B2
W Wingfoot Rd
9400 HOUS 77041 3681 B7
Wingleaf Dr
1900 HOUS 77084 3816 D6
Wingo
- HOUS 77055 3821 C6
Wingspan Dr
10 WDLD 77381 2674 D6
Wingtail Wy
3200 PRLD 77584 4502 C7
Wingtip Dr
9000 HOUS 77061 4245 D7
9000 HOUS 77075 4245 D7
9700 HOUS 77075 4376 D2
Wink Rd
10 BzaC 77511 4747 E1
11700 BKHV 77024 3959 C4
11800 HOUS 77024 3959 B4
Wink Rd CO-397
10 BzaC 77511 4747 E1
Winkbow Dr
9100 HarC 77040 3541 B6
Winkin Av
100 HarC 77532 3692 C1
Winkleman Rd
- FBnC 77083 4096 C7
- HOUS 77083 4096 C7
6200 HarC 77082 4096 C4
Winkler Dr
100 HOUS 77087 4104 E5
100 HOUS 77087 4105 A5
100 SHUS 77017 4246 B2
8300 HOUS 77017 4245 E1
8800 HOUS 77017 4246 A2
9300 SHUS 77587 4246 A2
Winkler Dr SR-3
- HOUS 77017 4245 E2
100 SHUS 77017 4246 B2
8800 HOUS 77017 4246 A2
9300 SHUS 77587 4246 A2
Winkler St
100 BYTN 77520 3971 B3
Winkle Wood Ln
7500 HarC 77086 3542 A3
7600 HarC 77086 3541 E4
Wink Wyn Rd
1400 BzaC 77511 4747 D1
Wink Wyn Rd CO-397
1400 BzaC 77511 4747 D1
Winlock Trace Ct
5400 FBnC 77450 4094 B3
Winlock Trace Dr
20600 FBnC 77450 4094 A3
Winlock Trails Dr
30600 MtgC 77386 2969 C1
Winmont Ct
3700 HarC 77082 4096 A3
Winmoss Ct
15600 HarC 77068 3257 B5
E Winn St
1800 LGCY 77565 4509 A5
Winner Foster Rd
1000 FBnC 77469 4232 A5
Winners Cir
10 HDWV 77024 3959 D2
10 PNPV 77024 3959 D2
1800 FBnC 77469 4364 E2
4300 HarC 77546 4506 A5
Winners Ct
2500 RSBG 77469 4615 E1
Winnie St
300 HOUS 77009 3963 B1
400 GLSN 77550 5109 B3
1600 LMQU 77568 4990 C1
3600 GLSN 77550 5108 D4
4500 GLSN 77551 5108 D4
Winningham Ln
8800 SPVL 77055 3821 A7
Winnipeg Blvd
4900 FBnC 77469 4491 C2
Winnsboro Ct
3300 SGLD 77478 4368 E4
Winnsboro Dr
9000 HarC 77088 3542 C6
Winnteka St
4700 HOUS 77021 4103 E4
5100 HOUS 77021 4104 A4
Winnwood Ct
9400 HarC 77070 3399 D5
Winona Dr
300 PASD 77506 4107 A3
Winrock Blvd
1100 HOUS 77057 3960 B5
Winrock Pl
10 WDLD 77382 2674 E5
Winsford Dr
18000 HarC 77084 3677 E6
Winship St
7800 HOUS 77028 3826 A1
Winshire Cir
11700 BKHV 77024 3959 C3
Winslow Ln
500 BLAR 77401 4101 A4
Winslow St
3000 HOUS 77025 4101 D6
3000 HOUS 77025 4102 A6
Winslow Wy
10 WDLD 77382 2674 A7
Winslow Forest Ln
- HarC 77047 4374 A4
Winsome Dr
19400 MtgC 77365 2972 C2
Winsome Ln
- HOUS 77042 3959 B7
5600 HOUS 77056 3960 C7
5600 HOUS 77057 3960 C7
9300 HOUS 77063 3959 C7
Winsome Path Cir
- WDLD 77382 2673 B6
N Winsome Path Cir
- WDLD 77382 2673 C6
S Winsome Path Cir
- WDLD 77382 2673 B7
Winsome Rose Ct
21700 HarC 77433 3250 E6
Winsor Terrace Cir
19800 HarC 77450 3954 E6
Winspring Ct
15600 HarC 77377 3255 A6
Winspring Dr
11000 HarC 77377 3255 A6
Winstead Ln
6000 HOUS 77396 3405 E4
6100 HOUS 77396 3406 A4
Winston Ct
2600 BzaC 77584 4501 B5
Winston Dr
900 RHMD 77469 4491 E2
13300 STFE 77510 4870 D6
13300 STFE 77517 4870 D6
Winston Ln
600 FBnC 77479 4366 E6
Winston Rd
- BzaC 77511 4748 C7
Winston St
1100 HOUS 77008 3823 E5
1100 HOUS 77009 3823 E5
Winston Cove Ct
- FBnC 77469 4094 D7
Winston Falls Ct
8700 HarC 77396 3548 A1
Winston Falls Ln
14700 HarC 77396 3548 A2
Winston Hill Dr
19500 HarC 77433 3677 A1
Winston Hollow Ln
25500 FBnC 77494 4093 A2
Winston Homestead Ct
1200 FBnC 77469 4365 D3
Winston Homestead Dr
1500 FBnC 77469 4365 D3
Winston Lake Dr
20800 FBnC 77469 4234 B4
Winston Point Ln
15900 HarC 77084 3678 C3
Winston Ranch Ct
21000 FBnC 77469 4234 B4
Winston Ranch Pkwy
7100 FBnC 77469 4234 B4
Winston Woods Dr
10 HOUS 77024 3960 E3
Winstrome Ct
3600 HarC 77449 3815 D2
Winter Ln
3300 BYTN 77521 3973 E1
Winter St
1200 HOUS 77007 3963 A2
31800 MtgC 77362 2963 C2
Winter Bay Ln
- HOUS 77088 3683 E1
1500 HOUS 77088 3543 E7
1900 HOUS 77088 3543 D7
Winter Berry Ct
2900 PRLD 77581 4503 E2
Winterberry Pl
11100 WDLD 77380 2967 D1
Winter Bloom Ln
9600 HarC 77088 3682 C1
Winter Blossom Dr
7000 HarC 77346 3408 E1
Winterborne Dr
4200 PASD 77505 4248 E5
Winter Breeze Dr
5900 HarC 77379 3111 E7
Winter Briar Dr
15500 HOUS 77489 4371 D5
Winter Brook Dr
12100 HarC 77066 3401 C5
Winter Canyon Ln
19300 HarC 77377 3109 C7
Wintercorn Pl
10 WDLD 77382 2674 D5
Wintercove Ct
14800 HarC 77082 4096 C2
Winter Creek Ct
3800 MSCY 77459 4496 C2
13500 HOUS 77077 3957 A3
Wintercress Ln
13700 HarC 77396 3547 B3
Winter Crest Ct
3500 SGLD 77479 4494 E3
Winter Dale Ct
2100 HarC 77493 3814 B5
Winterfair Dr
14800 HarC 77082 4096 C2
Winter Falls Ct
2800 BzaC 77578 4501 A7
Winter Forest Dr
20900 HarC 77379 3111 D4
Winter Garden Ct
6500 HarC 77083 4097 A5
Wintergate Dr
23200 HarC 77373 3115 B5
Winter Glen Ln
7500 HOUS 77072 4097 C6
Winter Grape Ln
1800 HOUS 77345 3120 B3
Wintergrass Pl
10 WDLD 77382 2674 A5
Winter Green Ct
1000 MSCY 77459 4369 C4
Winter Green Dr
28300 HarC 77484 3103 B4
Wintergreen Dr
3600 HarC 77396 3407 E2
4000 HarC 77346 3408 A2
4000 HarC 77396 3408 A2
24400 MtgC 77355 2960 D2
24400 SGCH 77355 2960 D2
Wintergreen Tr
10 WDLD 77382 2674 B5
Wintergrove Ct
6700 HarC 77049 3829 A2
Winter Harvest Ct
13900 HOUS 77059 4380 A4
Winterhaven Dr
3600 BYTN 77521 3974 A1
6000 HOUS 77087 4245 A1
15300 HarC 77070 3254 D6
15300 HarC 77377 3254 D6
Winterhaven Ln
22000 BzaC 77584 4501 B6
Winter Knoll Wy
1800 HOUS 77062 4380 B7
Winter Lakes
2800 MSCY 77459 4496 B1
Winter Mountain Ln
6500 HarC 77379 3111 C3
Winter Oak St
6100 PRLD 77584 4502 D6
Winter Oaks Dr
400 HOUS 77079 3957 D3
Winter Park Ct
2700 HarC 77067 3401 E4
Winter Park St
11800 HarC 77067 3401 D5
Winter Pines Ct
700 HarC 77373 3113 D2
N Winterport Cir
10 WDLD 77382 2674 C5
S Winterport Cir
100 WDLD 77382 2674 C6
Winter Rose Ct
16600 HarC 77429 3252 D5
Winter Rose Wy
13900 HarC 77083 4097 A4
Winter Run Dr
9500 HarC 77064 3540 D4
N Wintersage Ln
6300 HarC 77066 3400 D4
S Wintersage Ln
6300 HarC 77066 3400 D4
Winter Sky Ln
22100 FBnC 77469 4492 E3
Winter Song Dr
7200 MtgC 77354 2673 A3
Winter Springs Dr
12800 PRLD 77584 4500 A3
Winter Stone
6400 HarC 77084 3678 B3
Winter Trail Dr
2400 CNRO 77304 2383 B1
Winterview Dr
7500 HOUS 77489 4371 B5
Winter Wheat Pl
10 WDLD 77381 2820 E4
Winter Wind Blvd
11000 HarC 77065 3539 C1
Winterwood Dr
5100 LGCY 77573 4630 D6
Winterwood Tr
- HarC 77433 3251 C5
Winterwood Wy
600 HOUS 77013 3966 D1
Winterwood Forest Dr
- HarC 77338 3407 B1
Winthorne Ln
12200 HarC 77066 3401 A5
Winthorpe Ct
- HarC 77047 4374 B3
Winthrop Ln
8000 HOUS 77075 4376 D1
Winthrop St
3700 HOUS 77047 4374 C1
Winton Av
100 SHUS 77587 4246 D3
Winton St
- HOUS 77093 3824 E3
6600 HOUS 77021 4103 B6
Wintress Dr
10 WDLD 77382 2673 D7
Winwood Ln
11900 BKHV 77024 3959 B3
Winwood Falls Ln
13900 HarC 77396 3547 D2
Wipprecht St
2200 HOUS 77020 3964 C1
5500 HOUS 77026 3825 C4
Wirevine Ln
12800 HOUS 77072 4097 C6
Wirksworth Dr
3600 HarC 77066 3401 C5
Wirt Rd
- HLSV 77024 3960 C1
1000 HLSV 77055 3821 C7
1000 HLSV 77055 3960 C1
1000 HOUS 77024 3960 C1
1000 HOUS 77055 3821 C6
1000 HOUS 77055 3960 C1
Wirtcrest Ln
- HOUS 77092 3821 D4
2200 HOUS 77055 3821 D4
Wisconsin Av
500 SHUS 77587 4246 C4
N Wisconsin Av
200 LGCY 77573 4632 A2
S Wisconsin Av
500 LGCY 77573 4632 B3
Wisconsin St
3100 BYTN 77520 4112 A1
Wisdom Av
300 HarC 77532 3692 D1
Wisdom Dr
1100 DRPK 77536 4248 E1
2700 DRPK 77536 4249 B1
Wisdom Woods Ct
400 HarC 77094 3955 A1
Wisdom Woods Wy
19200 HarC 77094 3955 B2
Wiseman
9200 HarC 77375 2965 C2
Wisewood Ct
21300 FBnC 77469 4234 E6
Wishbonebush Rd
10 WDLD 77380 2822 A7
Wishing Well Ln
6200 HOUS 77088 3682 C3
Wisp Ct
23700 MtgC 77365 2972 B5
Wispering Oaks Dr
- SGLD 77479 4495 B3
Wispering Pines Ests
1500 FRDW 77546 4629 A4
Wisp Willow Wy
18300 MtgC 77365 2972 B6
Wispwillow Wy
18200 MtgC 77365 2972 A5
Wispwind Dr
7100 HOUS 77072 4097 D6
Wispy Wy Dr
23800 FBnC 77494 4093 B5
Wister Ct
6000 HOUS 77008 3823 A6
Wister Ln
6100 HOUS 77008 3822 E7
6100 HOUS 77008 3823 A7
E Wisteria Cir
3900 SGLD 77479 4495 D2
E Wisteria Cir
3900 SGLD 77479 4496 A2
W Wisteria Cir
3800 SGLD 77479 4495 E2
Wisteria Rd
31300 MtgC 77355 2668 C6
Wisteria St
400 LMQU 77568 4874 B7
500 BLAR 77401 4101 A5
Wisteria Wk
2700 HarC 77388 3113 B6
Wisteria Wy
2600 HarC 77562 3832 D3
Wisteria Brook Ln
- HarC 77379 3112 A6
Wisteria Chase Pl
7200 HarC 77346 3409 A1
Wisteria Estates Ln
18200 HarC 77429 3396 B2
Wisteria Hill St
15700 HarC 77073 3259 B6
Wisteria Hollow Ln
14500 HOUS 77062 4380 A6
Wisteria Park Dr
12700 HOUS 77072 4097 D4
Wisteria Ridge Ct
7500 HarC 77095 3678 B1
7600 HarC 77095 3538 D2
Wisteria Run Ct
14800 HOUS 77062 4506 D1
Wisteria Springs Ct
15400 HarC 77433 3251 B6
Wisteria Springs Dr
15200 HarC 77433 3251 B7
Wisteria Walk Cir
10 WDLD 77381 2674 B6
Wisterwood Dr
- HOUS 77043 3958 E1
1400 HOUS 77043 3819 E6
Wisterwood Ter
1300 HOUS 77043 3819 E7
Wistful Dr
7300 FBnC 77494 4093 B4
Wistful Vista Pl
10 WDLD 77382 2674 D4
Witch Ct
1100 HarC 77532 3552 A1
E Witcher Ln
400 HOUS 77076 3684 E5
Witham Ct
8800 HarC 77095 3538 D5
Witham Park Ln
3500 FBnC 77545 4498 C7
Withee Path Ln
- HOUS 77048 4375 B2
Withersdale Dr
14100 HOUS 77077 3956 E4
Witherspoon Dr
11000 FBnC 77469 4092 A7
Withers Ridge Dr
8500 FBnC 77469 4235 E1
E Withers Wy Cir
9600 HarC 77065 3539 C5
9600 HarC 77065 3540 A4
W Withers Wy Cir
9600 HarC 77065 3539 E4
Withington Dr
20400 HarC 77450 3954 D2
Witney Wy
- FBnC 77545 4498 C6
Witt Rd
10900 HOUS 77034 4246 E6
10900 HOUS 77034 4247 A6
Witte Rd
- HOUS 77024 3959 B1
1000 HOUS 77055 3820 B7
1000 HOUS 77055 3959 B1
1200 HOUS 77080 3820 B7
Wittenberg Av
6800 SGLD 77479 4367 C7
Witter St
1000 PASD 77506 4107 B6
1000 PASD 77502 4107 B6
N Witter St
100 PASD 77506 4107 B3
1000 HOUS 77506 4107 B2
1500 HOUS 77506 3967 B7
Wittershaw Dr
- HarC 77014 3402 D2
- HarC 77090 3402 D2
Wittman Ct
2200 HarC 77450 3954 B6
Wittman Ln
21500 HarC 77450 3954 B6
Wixford Ln
22600 HarC 77375 3110 C3
W L Morrison Rd
- HarC 77396 3547 B3
Woburn Dr
12500 HarC 77377 3254 B5
Woerner Ln
2300 HarC 77068 3257 D3
Woerner Rd
200 HarC 77068 3257 D3
200 HarC 77090 3257 D3
Wolbrook St
10600 HOUS 77016 3686 E3
Wolcek Rd
2400 HarC 77532 3693 C1
2600 HarC 77532 3694 A1
Wolcott Park Ln
9000 HOUS 77075 4377 A3
Wolf Ct
400 BKHV 77024 3959 B3
3300 BzaC 77584 4501 B7
Wolf Rd
900 HarC 77336 3122 C4
Wolfboro Dr
6200 HarC 77041 3679 C4
Wolf Creek Ct
12700 HarC 77346 3264 D7
26700 FBnC 77494 4092 A2
Wolf Creek Tr
18400 HarC 77346 3264 D7
Wolf Creek Pass
2600 HarC 77067 3401 E5
Wolf Den St
1600 MtgC 77385 2823 B3
Wolfe Ln
10 MNVL 77578 4747 B1
Wolfe Rd
9800 HarC 77064 3540 E3
9800 HarC 77064 3541 A3
Wolfe St
1200 GNPK 77547 3966 C6
Wolfe Island Rd
100 HarC 77336 3267 E3
100 HarC 77336 3268 A3
Wolfe Island Rd
100 LbyC 77535 3268 D3
1800 LbyC 77535 3269 A3
Wolf Hollow Dr
17500 HarC 77084 3677 E2
Wolfhound Ln
10 WDLD 77380 2968 A2
Wolfield Ln
7800 HOUS 77071 4239 D4
Wolf Pup Ln
21400 HOUS 77532 3266 B7
Wolf Rock Dr
5300 HarC 77449 3676 D6
Wolf Run Ln
11500 HarC 77065 3398 B7
Wolfs Knls
1100 HarC 77094 3955 A3
Wolfs Crossing Ct
23200 HarC 77373 2968 E6
Wolfs Meadow Ln
22500 FBnC 77494 4093 D3
Wolf Springs Ct
- FBnC 77479 4496 C5
Wollam Lp
4900 BzaC 77511 4747 E7
4900 BzaC 77511 4748 A7
4900 BzaC 77511 4866 A1
Wollaston Ct
10 HarC 77389 2820 A5
Wolly Bucket Pl
10 WDLD 77380 2968 A1
Wolsley Ct
10700 HarC 77065 3539 B2
Wolverhampton Wy
4600 MSCY 77459 4369 E5
Wolverton Dr
16400 HarC 77379 3256 D3
Woma Ct
16300 FBnC 77478 4236 A5
Womack
700 HOUS 77091 3684 B3
Womack Ln
4800 HarC 77532 3413 A5
Wonard Dr
3200 PRLD 77581 4503 D5
Wondering Forest Ln
12600 HarC 77377 3254 B5
Wonder Land Wy
18700 HarC 77084 3816 C2
Wonder Wood Dr
- HarC 77379 3255 D5
Wonfour St
11500 HOUS 77013 3827 C4
Wood Blvd
100 SGLD 77478 4368 A1
Wood Dr
400 HOUS 77336 3266 C5
N Wood Dr
15800 HarC 77530 3830 D4
Wood Ln
11700 BKHV 77024 3959 C3
Wood Lp
200 HarC 77015 3828 C6
Wood Pk
3900 SGLD 77479 4495 E3
Wood St
900 HOUS 77002 3963 D3
2400 PRLD 77545 4499 D6
2900 FBnC 77545 4499 D6
Woodacre Dr
16900 HarC 77049 3690 E4
16900 HarC 77049 3691 A4
Woodacres Dr
6300 HTCK 77563 4988 C3
Wood Arbor Ct
4000 HarC 77346 3408 A3
Woodard St
200 HOUS 77009 3824 C4
2600 HOUS 77026 3824 E4
2900 HOUS 77026 3825 A4
Woodbank Ct
4100 TYLV 77586 4381 D7
Woodbank Dr
1000 TYLV 77586 4381 D7
1200 PASD 77586 4381 D7
Wood Bark Cir
8000 HarC 77379 3256 B3
Wood Bark Rd
17000 HarC 77379 3256 B3
Woodbark Rd
17800 HarC 77379 3256 A2
Wood Bayou Dr
12100 HOUS 77013 3827 E7
Woodbend Dr
- BzaC 77584 4501 A5
- HarC 77049 3828 C3
Woodbend Ln
500 HOUS 77079 3958 A3
Woodbend Oaks Dr
16100 HarC 77070 3255 A5
Woodbend Pines Dr
- HarC 77070 3255 A5
Woodbend Trail Dr
16100 HarC 77070 3255 B6
Woodbend Village Ct
1800 HOUS 77055 3821 B5
Woodberry Manor Dr
19700 HarC 77379 3110 C6
Woodbine Ct
28600 MtgC 77355 2815 A5
Woodbine Dr
23100 HarC 77447 3105 B6
Woodbine Mdws
23000 HarC 77447 3105 B6
Woodbine Pl
3400 BzaC 77584 4501 C4
Woodbine St
600 HOUS 77017 4106 C7
2000 HOUS 77017 4246 C1
Wood Bluff Blvd
7400 HarC 77040 3681 D1
Woodbough Ct
2300 HarC 77038 3543 B2
Woodbough Dr
2400 HarC 77038 3543 A2
Woodbourne Dr
15700 HOUS 77062 4380 C7
Woodbranch Dr
10 WDBR 77357 2828 C1
Wood Branch Ln
900 HarC 77336 3121 D6
Wood Branch Park Dr
1200 HOUS 77043 3818 E7
1200 HOUS 77043 3957 D1
1200 HOUS 77079 3818 E7
1200 HOUS 77079 3957 D1
Woodbreeze Dr
18600 HarC 77346 3264 E7

STREET
Block City ZIP Map# Grid

Woodbriar Ct
4000 SGLD 77479 4495 D3
Woodbriar Dr
3300 HarC 77068 3257 B5
Woodbridge
- PASD 77502 4247 A2
Woodbridge Av
1000 PRLD 77584 4501 A2
Wood Bridge Cir
800 SGLD 77478 4368 B1
Woodbridge Dr
3400 HOUS 77339 3119 B3
Woodbridge Estates Dr
15000 FBnC 77478 4236 C4
Woodbridge Villages Ln
- FBnC 77478 4236 D4
Woodbrook Ln
3300 SGLD 77478 4368 E5
6000 HOUS 77008 3823 A7
6300 HOUS 77008 3822 E7
Woodbuck Tr
11600 HOUS 77013 3827 D7
Woodburn Dr
16900 HarC 77049 3690 E4
17100 HarC 77049 3691 A4
Woodbury Ct
10 MtgC 77355 2814 E3
Woodbury St
1900 HOUS 77030 4102 D5
2400 BzaC 77584 4501 C5
Woodbury Springs Ln
6400 HarC 77379 3256 D3
Woodcamp Dr
8500 HOUS 77088 3683 A2
Wood Canyon Dr
8000 HarC 77040 3681 D3
Woodcastle Bnd
500 HarC 77094 3955 B2
Woodcastle Dr
- FBnC 77479 4367 B6
Woodchase Dr
1100 PRLD 77581 4504 E7
3400 HOUS 77042 4099 A2
Woodchester Dr
13400 SGLD 77478 4237 B6
Woodchuck Ln
10 WDLD 77380 2968 B3
Woodchurch Ln
1200 HarC 77073 3259 B2
Wood Cir Ln
200 HarC 77015 3828 B6
Woodcliff Dr
12100 HOUS 77013 3966 E1
Woodcliffe Dr
3700 CNRO 77304 2237 A5
Woodcliff Lake Dr
9500 HarC 77379 3255 B1
Woodcluster Ln
20600 HarC 77073 3259 E5
Woodcock St
2600 KMAH 77565 4633 C2
2600 LGCY 77565 4633 C3
2600 LGCY 77573 4633 C3
Woodcombe Dr
100 HOUS 77062 4506 D2
Woodcote Ct
15400 HOUS 77062 4506 E2
Woodcourt St
11700 HOUS 77076 3685 B3
Wood Cove Dr
10 WDLD 77381 2821 B5
Woodcove Ln
2200 SGLD 77479 4368 C7
2200 SGLD 77479 4495 B2
Woodcraft St
4000 HOUS 77025 4241 C3
Wood Creek Ct
10 HOUS 77017 4246 D1
Wood Creek Dr
2500 PRLD 77581 4504 C4
Woodcreek Dr
- HarC 77073 3259 E3
- HOUS 77073 3259 E3
Wood Creek Ln
- LGCY 77573 4630 A6
Woodcreek Ln
- HOUS 77338 3260 A4
2600 HarC 77073 3259 E4
3000 HarC 77073 3260 B4
Wood Creek Wy
5500 HOUS 77017 4246 C1
Woodcreek Bend Ln
- KATY 77494 3952 A4
Woodcreek Cove Ln
1000 KATY 77494 3952 A2
Woodcreek Glen Ln
3100 HarC 77073 3259 E3
3700 HOUS 77073 3259 E3
Woodcreek Meadows Ln
2600 HarC 77073 3259 D3
Woodcreek North Dr
- HarC 77073 3259 E4
- HarC 77073 3260 A4
Woodcrest
200 BYTN 77520 3971 B2
Woodcrest Ct
7900 FBnC 77479 4494 B4
Woodcrest Dr
100 LGCY 77573 4632 E1
800 FRDW 77546 4505 B4
800 HOUS 77018 3823 B1
1300 HOUS 77018 3822 C2
1700 DRPK 77536 4108 E6
3400 BYTN 77521 3972 D4
Woodcroft Ct
7600 HarC 77095 3538 D7
Woodcroft Dr
15700 HarC 77095 3538 D7
26100 MtgC 77385 2822 D6
Woodcypress Ln
14900 HarC 77429 3396 B1
Wood Dale Dr
1600 FBnC 77479 4494 B4
3700 HOUS 77345 3119 D3
Wooddale Bridge Ct
11000 FBnC 77478 4236 C5
Wood Dawn Ln
12600 HarC 77015 3828 B6
Wooddove Cir
11200 HarC 77089 4378 B6
Wood Downe Ln
8100 HarC 77040 3681 D2
Wooddrift Ln
8600 LPRT 77571 4249 D4
Wood Duck Ct
5000 MSCY 77459 4496 B3
Wood Duck Ln
26800 HarC 77447 3248 E7
Wood Duck Pk
7800 HarC 77396 3406 D6
Wooded Tr
3400 BYTN 77521 3973 E3
17600 MtgC 77302 2678 C7
Wooded Acres Dr
1600 HarC 77396 3407 B2
N Wooded Brook Cir
10 WDLD 77382 2674 E5
Wooded Brook Dr
10 WDLD 77382 2674 D5
Wooded Creek Ln
11300 HarC 77433 3396 A7
Wooded Field Tr
15200 HarC 77429 3253 C3
Woodedge Dr
9800 HarC 77064 3399 A7
9800 HarC 77070 3399 A7
10400 HarC 77065 3399 A7
11300 HarC 77065 3398 E7
Woodedge Park Dr
- HarC 77070 3399 B7
Wooded Glen Ct
14800 HarC 77429 3396 C1
Wooded Hollow Ct
- KATY 77494 3952 A4
Wooded Hollow Ln
26100 KATY 77494 3952 A4
Wooded Lake Ct
21300 FBnC 77469 4094 B7
Wooded Lake Ln
7200 FBnC 77469 4094 A6
Wooded Oaks Dr
2000 HarC 77396 3407 B2
2000 HMBL 77396 3407 B3
Wooded Path Pl
10 WDLD 77382 2673 B6
Wooded Pine Dr
1600 HarC 77073 3259 C4
Wooded Terrace Ln
8100 HarC 77338 3261 E2
Wooded Trace Ct
5200 HarC 77449 3677 B6
Wooded Valley Dr
7300 HarC 77095 3678 E1
Wooded Villas Dr
5600 HOUS 77345 3120 B5
Wooded Walk Ln
7400 HOUS 77070 3400 A3
Wooded Wy Dr
7800 HarC 77389 2966 A2
Woodelves Pl
10 WDLD 77381 2820 E3
Wooden Oak Ct
15500 HOUS 77059 4380 B5
Wood Estates Dr
10 CNRO 77304 2236 C6
10 CNRO 77304 2382 D1
Woodfair Dr
1300 FBnC 77469 4365 D1
9200 HOUS 77036 4238 E2
9200 HOUS 77036 4239 A1
Wood Fall Ct
1200 HarC 77014 3402 C2
Woodfall Ct
1200 HarC 77014 3402 D3
Wood Fern Ct
10200 CHTW 77385 2822 E4
10200 MtgC 77385 2822 E4
Wood Fern Dr
1100 FBnC 77479 4493 D6
Woodfern Dr
6900 HOUS 77088 3682 B2
7000 HOUS 77040 3682 A3
Woodfern Glen Ln
800 BzaC 77584 4501 C1
Woodfield Ln
1200 HarC 77073 3259 B1
Woodfin St
4000 HOUS 77025 4241 C3
Woodford Dr
14700 HarC 77015 3968 C1
14900 HarC 77530 3968 C1
Woodford St
4700 BYTN 77521 3833 C2
Woodford Green Dr
2000 HOUS 77339 3118 E7
Woodford Hollow Ct
15300 HarC 77429 3253 C7
Woodford Hollow Ln
15100 HarC 77429 3253 C7
Woodforest Blvd
9200 HOUS 77013 3826 E7
12400 HOUS 77013 3827 E7
12400 HOUS 77013 3828 B6
12500 HarC 77015 3828 B6
13400 HOUS 77015 3828 D6
14000 HarC 77015 3829 B6
14800 HarC 77530 3829 B6
15400 HarC 77530 3830 A7
Wood Forest Ct
- HarC 77015 3828 D5
- HarC 77049 3828 D4
- HOUS 77015 3828 D4
Woodforest Ct
400 HarC 77015 3828 E7
Woodforest Dr
12100 HOUS 77013 3827 E7
Wood Forest Ln
16100 SPLD 77372 2683 A4
Woodforest Mill Dr
- HarC 77049 3828 D2
Woodforest Terrace Dr
- HarC 77049 3828 D2
Wood Fox Dr
2900 ALVN 77511 4866 D4
Woodfox St
4000 HOUS 77025 4241 C3
Wood Gardens Ct
3800 HOUS 77339 3119 A4
Woodgate Ln
26500 KATY 77494 3952 A3
Woodgate St
2400 HarC 77039 3545 E4
3500 HarC 77039 3546 A4
Woodglen Ct
1900 BzaC 77581 4502 A1
3900 SGLD 77479 4495 A2
Woodglen Dr
2200 MSCY 77489 4497 B1
19000 HarC 77084 3816 B3
19000 HarC 77449 3816 B3
25800 MtgC 77386 2968 C1
Wood Glen Ln
18500 HarC 77084 3816 D2
Woodglen Ln
- KATY 77494 3952 A3
Woodglen Point Ct
5900 HarC 77379 3111 E5
Woodglen Shadows Dr
18600 HarC 77346 3264 E7
Woodgreen St
5600 HOUS 77033 4244 A5
Wood Grove Ct
8100 HarC 77040 3681 E2
Woodgum Dr
18000 HarC 77388 3257 C1
Woodhall Ct
2800 LGCY 77573 4632 E2
19800 HarC 77338 3261 E4
Woodhall Ln
20000 HarC 77338 3261 E4
Woodham Dr
- HarC 77073 3403 A1
14800 HOUS 77073 3403 A1
15000 HOUS 77073 3259 A7
Woodhampton Dr
4100 PASD 77505 4248 E5
Wood Haven Ct
1200 FBnC 77479 4493 E5
Woodhaven Ct
1200 KATY 77494 3952 A3
6400 PRLD 77584 4502 C5
Woodhaven Dr
100 CNRO 77303 2237 D6
Woodhaven Ln
100 TYLV 77586 4382 A7
300 CNRO 77304 2383 B4
Woodhaven St
200 HarC 77562 3831 D2
4000 HOUS 77025 4241 C3
Woodhaven Wood Ct
10 WDLD 77380 2822 A6
Woodhaven Wood Dr
10 WDLD 77380 2822 B6
Woodhead St
1300 HOUS 77019 3962 C6
2500 HOUS 77098 3962 C7
4400 HOUS 77098 4102 C1
5200 HOUS 77005 4102 C2
Wood Heather Ln
7100 HarC 77040 3681 D3
Woodhill Rd
1100 HOUS 77008 3823 B7
Woodhollow
- BYTN 77521 3972 D4
Woodhollow Ct
3900 SGLD 77479 4495 E3
Wood Hollow Dr
- LGCY 77573 4632 E1
10 CNRO 77304 2382 D1
200 LGCY 77573 4633 A1
4100 MtgC 77385 2676 E3
7800 BYTN 77520 3835 C4
7800 CmbC 77520 3835 C4
17700 MtgC 77365 2825 E7
19000 MtgC 77365 2972 B2
Woodhollow Dr
1200 HOUS 77057 3960 B5
4000 PASD 77504 4247 E5
9800 MtgC 77385 2676 D3
Wood Hollow Ln
11800 HOUS 77043 3819 C2
Woodhorn Ct
700 HOUS 77062 4506 E2
Woodhorn Dr
1000 HOUS 77062 4506 E2
1100 HOUS 77062 4507 A1
Woodhouse Dr
9100 HarC 77379 3255 D6
Woodhue Ct
30500 MtgC 77386 2969 A2
Woodhue Dr
700 HarC 77530 3830 A7
1900 MtgC 77386 2969 B2
Woodhurst Dr
500 HOUS 77013 3827 E7
Woodico Ct
10000 HarC 77038 3543 D4
Wooding St
800 HOUS 77011 3965 A6
Woodington Dr
13100 HarC 77038 3543 B2
Woodkerr St
3000 HOUS 77045 4242 A6
Woodknoll Ln
11400 HOUS 77071 4239 E5
Woodknot Dr
11100 HarC 77089 4378 A6
Woodlace Dr
3600 HarC 77396 3407 E3
3700 HarC 77346 3408 A3
3700 HarC 77396 3408 A3
Woodlake Cir
600 SGLD 77478 4368 B1
Wood Lake Ln
4100 MSCY 77459 4497 A4
Woodlake Ln
9600 HOUS 77063 3959 B6
9900 HOUS 77042 3959 B6
12400 MtgC 77362 2817 B7
Woodlake Rd
22300 HOUS 77336 3266 C6
Woodlake Sq
- HOUS 77042 3959 B6
- HOUS 77063 3959 B6
Wood Lake Vil
17000 MtgC 77385 2676 C5
Woodland Ct
800 MtgC 77302 2530 D6
1100 FBnC 77469 4365 E2
3100 LPRT 77571 4382 D1
Woodland Dr
100 CNRO 77301 2384 C3
400 HarC 77530 3830 C6
800 ELGO 77586 4509 A2
2000 FBnC 77469 4365 D1
3000 DKSN 77539 4753 C3
22800 MtgC 77365 2973 E5
Woodland Ln
800 MtgC 77302 2530 D6
Woodland St
300 HOUS 77009 3824 A7
900 HOUS 77009 3823 E7
1100 HOUS 77007 3823 E7
2400 LMQU 77563 4989 D3
2400 LMQU 77568 4989 D3
16600 HarC 77530 3830 D6
E Woodland St
300 HOUS 77009 3824 E6
Woodland Wy
600 FRDW 77546 4505 B5
Woodland Brook Dr
5700 HOUS 77345 3120 B5
Woodland Creek Dr
5800 HOUS 77345 3120 B4
Woodland Creek Ln
17200 HarC 77095 3537 C1
Woodland Crest Dr
- HOUS 77336 3266 C1
Woodland Falls Dr
5800 HOUS 77345 3120 C6
Woodland Forest Dr
6200 HarC 77088 3682 C1
18400 MtgC 77302 2680 A2
18400 MtgC 77306 2680 A2
Woodland Gardens Dr
2600 HOUS 77345 3119 E5
Woodland Gate Dr
7500 HarC 77040 3681 D1
Woodland Glade Dr
5500 HarC 77066 3401 A7
Woodland Green Dr
21100 HarC 77449 3676 D6
Woodland Grove Dr
2700 HOUS 77339 3118 D5
Woodland Haven Rd
2000 HOUS 77062 4507 E1
Woodland Heights Ln
21900 HarC 77373 3261 A1
Woodland Hills Dr
- HOUS 77339 3263 E1
- HOUS 77339 3264 A2
10 CNRO 77303 2237 E5
1900 MSCY 77489 4370 B5
2900 HOUS 77339 3119 A5
4000 HOUS 77339 3118 E2
4000 MtgC 77365 3119 A2
4200 MtgC 77339 3118 E2
4200 MtgC 77365 3118 E2
17300 HarC 77346 3408 A1
17300 HarC 77396 3408 A2
17900 HarC 77338 3408 A1
18400 HarC 77338 3264 A7
18400 HarC 77346 3264 A7
18600 HarC 77338 3263 E5
18600 HarC 77346 3263 E5
Woodland Hills Ln
900 MtgC 77339 3118 D4
Woodland Knoll Ln
8400 HarC 77433 3537 D5
Woodland Lakes Dr
- HOUS 77336 3266 D1
Woodland Meadows Ln
4900 HarC 77346 3264 A7
Woodland Oak Tr
7200 HarC 77346 3265 A3
Woodland Oaks Ct
7900 HarC 77040 3541 E7
Woodland Oaks Dr
- HarC 77064 3541 E6
6500 MtgC 77354 2673 B2
9200 HarC 77040 3681 E1
10200 HarC 77040 3541 E7
Woodland Orchard Ln
15200 HarC 77433 3251 B6
Woodland Park Dr
- FRDW 77546 4505 B6
1700 HOUS 77077 3958 B6
2700 HOUS 77082 3958 B7
2700 HOUS 77082 4098 B1
Woodland Path Dr
- HarC 77346 3408 A3
- HarC 77396 3408 A3
Woodland Pine Dr
7900 HarC 77040 3541 E6
Woodland Plaza Dr
4600 HarC 77084 3677 E7
Woodland Ridge Dr
2600 HOUS 77345 3119 E5
Woodlands Dr
2100 DRPK 77536 4109 D7
Woodlands Pkwy
- MtgC 77354 2818 E1
- MtgC 77380 2822 B5
- ORDN 77380 2822 B5
- ORDN 77386 2822 B5
- WDLD 77354 2818 E1
- WDLD 77354 2819 A1
- WDLD 77380 2821 E5
- WDLD 77382 2818 E1
- WDLD 77382 2819 A1
1000 WDLD 77380 2822 A6
4400 WDLD 77381 2820 E4
4400 WDLD 77381 2821 A4
6600 WDLD 77382 2820 C3
Woodland Shore Dr
11500 HarC 77375 3109 E7
Woodland Springs St
1700 HOUS 77077 3958 A7
Woodland Trace Ln
- HarC 77049 3828 D2
Woodland Trail Dr
600 FRDW 77546 4505 B5
Woodland Trails Dr
6400 HOUS 77088 3682 B2
7000 HOUS 77040 3682 B2
Woodland Valley Dr
2000 HOUS 77339 3263 D1
Woodland View Dr
3000 HOUS 77345 3119 E4
Woodland Village Dr
10 RSBG 77471 4490 D6
Woodland Vista Dr
1700 HOUS 77339 3118 D7
Woodland West Dr
7200 HarC 77040 3681 D2
7700 HarC 77040 3541 D7
Woodland Willows Dr
8200 FBnC 77083 4096 C7
8300 FBnC 77083 4236 C1
Woodlane Blvd
- WDLD 77382 2673 A7
8700 MtgC 77354 2672 E6
8700 MtgC 77354 2673 A6
Woodlane St
27600 LbyC 77372 2537 E6
Woodlark Av
5200 HOUS 77017 4106 B6
Woodlark Dr
28400 FBnC 77494 3951 C6
Woodlark St
5400 HOUS 77017 4106 C6
5600 HOUS 77502 4106 C6
5600 PASD 77502 4106 C6
Woodlawn Av
3800 PASD 77504 4247 D3
Woodlawn Dr
100 FRDW 77546 4505 B7
200 FRDW 77546 4629 B1
Woodlawn Pl
5200 BLAR 77401 4100 E3
Woodlawn Pl
5200 HOUS 77081 4100 E3
Woodlawn St
900 BYTN 77520 3973 C7
1000 HarC 77530 3830 E5
2700 DKSN 77539 4753 C2
9200 HTCK 77563 4988 C3
Woodlawn Manor Ct
15300 HarC 77429 3397 C4
Woodlawn Terrace Ct
1900 SGLD 77479 4495 B1
Wood Leaf Ct
10000 BYTN 77520 3835 C4
12100 HOUS 77013 3827 E7
N Woodlear Ln
- HarC 77065 3398 C7
Woodleigh Dr
8800 FBnC 77083 4236 D1
17800 HarC 77530 3831 C6
Woodleigh St
3800 HOUS 77023 3964 A6
17800 HarC 77530 3831 C6
Woodlett Ct
7700 HarC 77095 3538 B7
Woodley Bnd
1100 FBnC 77479 4366 D7
Woodlily Pl
10 WDLD 77382 2674 E5
10 WDLD 77382 2675 A5
Woodline Dr
400 MtgC 77386 2968 C3
14300 HarC 77015 3829 A5
Woodlink Ct
- HarC 77336 3122 A3
Woodlite Ln
12800 HarC 77015 3828 C6
N Woodloch St
2600 MtgC 77385 2677 A4
S Woodloch St
2600 MtgC 77385 2677 A4
2600 WDLC 77385 2677 A4
Woodloch Forest Dr
1400 WDLD 77380 2822 A5
Woodlock Dr
1100 PASD 77502 4107 D6
1100 PASD 77506 4107 D6
Woodlode Ln
17700 HarC 77379 3257 A3
Wood Lodge Dr
1500 HOUS 77077 3958 B5
11200 HOUS 77042 3958 B5
Woodlong Dr
7200 HOUS 77088 3682 D2
Woodlot Ct
10 WDLD 77380 2822 B6
Woodlyn Rd
7800 HOUS 77028 3687 B7
8800 HOUS 77078 3687 E6
9000 HOUS 77078 3688 A7
Woodman Rd
15500 MtgC 77306 2533 A1
Woodmancote Dr
5400 HarC 77346 3264 D6
Wood Manor Ln
- MtgC 77384 2821 E1
- WDLD 77384 2821 E1
Wood Maple Ct
14600 HarC 77015 3829 B5
Woodmeadow St
9300 HOUS 77025 4241 E2
Woodmere Ln
1300 FBnC 77469 4365 D2
3400 SGLD 77478 4368 E5
3400 SGLD 77478 4369 A6
Woodmere Pl
10 WDLD 77381 2675 A7
Woodmill Ct
- HarC 77049 3828 D2
Woodmill Pl
14800 HarC 77082 4096 C2
Wood Mist Dr
500 HOUS 77013 3827 D7
500 HOUS 77013 3966 D1
Woodmont Dr
3100 HOUS 77045 4242 A7
3300 HOUS 77045 4241 E7
Woodmoss Ct
22000 MtgC 77365 2971 E2
Wood Moss Rd
10400 HarC 77037 3544 E7
Woodnettle Ct
9600 HarC 77086 3542 A3
Woodnettle Ln
7700 HarC 77086 3541 E3
7700 HarC 77086 3542 A3
Woodnook Dr
14100 HOUS 77077 3956 E3
Wood Nymph Dr
- HOUS 77336 3266 C1
Wood Nymph Pl
- WDLD 77382 2819 A3
Woodoak Ct
2400 BzaC 77584 4501 B4
21600 HarC 77450 3954 B4
Woodoak Dr
7300 HarC 77040 3681 E2
Wood Orchard Ct
1100 MSCY 77489 4370 C5
Wood Orchard Dr
1800 MSCY 77489 4370 D5
7000 HarC 77040 3681 D3
Wood Palms Dr
- HarC 77049 3828 D2
Woodpark Dr
600 TYLV 77586 4508 D1
Woodpath Ln
8600 HOUS 77075 4376 E2
Woodpecker Bnd
7400 HMBL 77396 3406 C4
Woodpecker St
4800 HOUS 77035 4241 A4
Woodpecker Forest Ln
400 MtgC 77384 2675 B1
Woodpile Dr
- MtgC 77357 2828 D6
Wood Pine Dr
- HarC 77084 3816 D2
Wood Pl Ct
6600 HarC 77379 3111 D5
Woodpoint Dr
- HOUS 77339 3117 E5
Woodport Ln
700 HarC 77090 3258 D5
9800 HarC 77044 3689 B4
Woodrail Dr
400 HOUS 77598 4506 E4
Wood Rain Ct
20600 HarC 77449 3815 D2
Woodridge Cir
1100 BzaC 77511 4748 E5
Woodridge Dr
2800 HOUS 77087 4105 A6
7000 HOUS 77012 4105 A5
18000 MtgC 77302 2825 C2
Woodridge Pl
7500 HOUS 77055 3821 D6
Woodridge Cove Dr
2600 HOUS 77087 4105 B5
Woodridge Manor Dr
2600 HOUS 77087 4105 B5
Woodridge Row Dr
6900 HOUS 77087 4105 A5
Woodridge Square Dr
7000 HOUS 77087 4105 A5
Woodring Ct
13500 HOUS 77045 4372 E1
Woodring Dr
13400 HOUS 77045 4241 E7
Wood River Dr
2000 HarC 77373 3114 C7
13500 HOUS 77085 4371 C1
Woodrose Dr
22100 HarC 77450 3954 A2
22300 HarC 77450 3953 E2
Woodrow Av
4500 GLSN 77550 5108 D6
4500 GLSN 77551 5108 D6
Woodrow Dr
1000 RSBG 77471 4491 D2
Woodrow St
600 HOUS 77006 4102 E1
5700 TXCY 77591 4873 E6
16400 HarC 77530 3969 D2
Woodruff Av
200 HarC 77532 3552 C3
Woodruff St
8500 HOUS 77012 4105 D3
Woodrush Dr
3900 WDLD 77381 2821 B5
Woods Ct
2100 PRLD 77581 4504 D2
Woods Dr
17300 MtgC 77357 2680 D7
Woods Ln
500 KATY 77494 3952 B1
1400 LbyC 77372 2538 A6
10900 MtgC 77372 2537 A1
N Woods Ln
6000 KATY 77494 3952 B1
S Woods Ln
6100 KATY 77494 3952 B1
Woods Rd
14100 HOUS 77047 4373 D5
14200 HarC 77047 4373 D5
Woods St
100 BYTN 77520 3971 B3
Woodsage Dr
3400 SGLD 77479 4495 B1
11600 HDWV 77024 3959 C1
11700 HOUS 77024 3959 C1
Woodsage Ln
- HarC 77377 3253 E3
Woodsboro Ct
20200 HarC 77388 3113 B5
Woodsboro Dr
2400 HarC 77388 3113 B6
Woodsborough Cir
10 SPVL 77055 3821 A7
Woodsborough Dr
10 SPVL 77055 3821 B7
Woods Bridge Wy
6200 HOUS 77007 3961 E4
Woodsburgh Ln
17800 HarC 77433 3537 D6
Woods Canyon Ct
3200 MSCY 77459 4498 A6
Wood Scent Ct
10 WDLD 77380 2968 A4
Woodsdale Blvd
2300 HarC 77038 3543 A2
Woodsdale Ct
13100 HarC 77038 3543 B2
18100 MtgC 77365 2971 E1
Woods Edge Dr
3300 HarC 77388 3112 E6
4700 FBnC 77469 4364 A1
31000 MtgC 77354 2671 B6
Woods Edge Ln
10 PNPV 77024 3959 E5
10 PNPV 77024 3960 A5
Woodsend Ln
4700 HOUS 77345 3120 A2
Woods Estates Dr
2100 HOUS 77339 3119 B6
Wood Shadows Ct
2000 MSCY 77489 4497 C1
Wood Shadows Dr
1600 MSCY 77489 4497 C1
11000 HOUS 77013 3966 C1
Woodshaver Dr
11600 HOUS 77013 3827 D7
Woodshire St
4000 HOUS 77025 4241 D3
Woodside Ct
1100 FBnC 77479 4493 D5
Woodside Dr
10 BYTN 77520 4113 B1
2100 HOUS 77062 4380 C7
6900 FBnC 77479 4493 D5
Woodside Ln
13300 HarC 77429 3397 E2
Woodside St
4400 HOUS 77023 3964 B7
Woodside Crossing Ln
14500 HarC 77396 3547 C2
Woodside Estates Dr
22900 MtgC 77385 2823 A7
Woodside Green Dr
- HarC 77429 3397 E2
- HarC 77429 3398 A2
Woods Landing Dr
- HOUS 77060 3544 C1
Woodsland Park Ln
- KATY 77494 3952 B1
Woodsman Trail Dr
7000 HOUS 77040 3682 A1
7000 HOUS 77088 3682 A1
7600 HarC 77040 3682 A1
7800 HarC 77040 3681 E1
Woodsmith Ct
1800 MSCY 77489 4370 E4
Wood Smoke Dr
500 HOUS 77013 3827 D7
600 HOUS 77013 3966 D1
Woodson Rd
- ORDN 77380 2822 B4
Woodson Rd
100 HOUS 77060 3544 C
27200 ORDN 77385 2822 C
27300 MtgC 77385 2822 C
Wood Song Ct
1600 FBnC 77479 4494 A
Woodsong Dr
8200 HarC 77389 2965 E
8200 HarC 77389 2966 A
20400 HarC 77346 3265 B
Woodsong Tr
28700 MtgC 77355 2815 D
Woodsons Lake Dr
28300 MtgC 77386 2970 A
Woodson Valley Ct
7400 HOUS 77016 3687 B
Woodson Valley Dr
10700 HOUS 77016 3687 A
Wood Sorrel Dr
3700 DKSN 77539 4754 D
Woodsorrel Dr
2600 HarC 77084 3816 A
Woodspire Dr
13600 HOUS 77085 4371 C
Wood Spring Blvd
- FBnC 77479 4494 D
Wood Spring Ln
12100 HOUS 77013 3827 E
Woodspring Acres Dr
2800 HOUS 77345 3119 E
2800 HOUS 77365 3119 E
Woodspring Forest Dr
2700 HOUS 77345 3120 A
2800 HOUS 77345 3119 E
Woodstead Ct
1400 WDLD 77380 2822 A
1700 WDLD 77380 2821 E
Woodstock Ln
500 MtgC 77302 2530 D
Woodstock St
800 BLAR 77401 4100 D
N Woodstock Cir Dr
10 WDLD 77381 2821 A
S Woodstock Cir Dr
10 WDLD 77381 2821 A
W Woodstock Cir Dr
10 WDLD 77381 2821 A
Woodstone Ct
1100 MtgC 77384 2529 A
Woodstone Dr
3000 BYTN 77521 3972 B
Woodstone St
10 HOUS 77024 3959 A
Wood Stone Walk Dr
3700 HarC 77084 3816 D
Wood Stork Ln
- FBnC 77459 4621 C
12900 HarC 77044 3549 C
Woodstream Blvd
1900 SGLD 77479 4495 B
Woodstream Cir
300 FRDW 77546 4629 D
Woodstream Dr
2100 HOUS 77339 3263 D
Woodstream Pl
3400 SGLD 77479 4495 B
Woodstream Wy N
3200 HOUS 77345 3119 E
Woodstream Wy S
3200 HOUS 77345 3119 D
Woodstream Village Dr
4800 HOUS 77345 3120 A
N Woodsway St E
100 CNRO 77301 2384 A
N Woodsway St W
100 CNRO 77301 2384 B
S Woodsway St E
100 CNRO 77301 2384 B
S Woodsway St W
100 CNRO 77301 2384 B
Wood Terrace St
13400 HarC 77038 3543 B
Wood Thorn Ln
14600 HarC 77396 3547 C
Woodthorpe Ln
12400 HOUS 77024 3959 A
12500 HOUS 77024 3958 E
13800 HOUS 77079 3958 A
14000 HOUS 77079 3957 E
Woodthrush Dr
- PRLD 77581 4376 D
Woodtide Rd
17000 HarC 77396 3408 A
E Woodtimber Ct
10 WDLD 77381 2821 A
W Woodtimber Ct
10 WDLD 77381 2821 A
Wood Tower Ct
31100 MtgC 77386 2823 D
Woodtown Dr
2400 HarC 77038 3543 A
Woodtrace Blvd
- MtgC 77362 2816 E6
- MtgC 77362 2817 A6
Woodtrace Cir
34100 MtgC 77362 2816 E5
Wood Trail Dr
13100 HarC 77038 3543 B2
Wood Trails Ct
1900 MSCY 77489 4497 C
Woodtrek Ln
13000 HarC 77015 3828 C6
Woodvale
200 HOUS 77012 4105 B2
Woodvale Dr
200 LGCY 77573 4630 B6
1900 MSCY 77489 4370 B3
2500 HOUS 77345 3120 A6
Woodvale St
100 HOUS 77012 4105 B
Woodvalley Dr
3500 HOUS 77025 4241 D
4300 HOUS 77096 4241 B
Woodview Dr
600 FRDW 77546 4505 B5
5800 HOUS 77396 3405 E4
Wood Village Ln
19300 HarC 77084 3816 A6
Woodville Dr
5000 PRLD 77584 4503 A4
Woodville Ln
5200 HarC 77379 3257 B2
5600 PRLD 77584 4502 E4
Woodville Gardens Dr
14100 HOUS 77077 3956 E4
Woodvine Dr
400 ELGO 77586 4509 A1
1800 HOUS 77055 3821 D4

TREET
lock City ZIP Map# Grid
oodvine St
1300 FRDW 77546 4629 E2
oodvine Tr
13100 HOUS 77072 4097 C6
oodvine Pl Ct
7500 HOUS 77055 3821 D6
oodvine Ridge Dr
25400 FBnC 77469 4092 C7
oodviolet Dr
11400 HarC 77089 4378 A5
ood Vista Dr
500 HOUS 77013 3827 E7
ood Walk Ln
19600 HarC 77346 3265 A5
oodwalk Ln
- HarC 77449 3815 B1
ood Warbler Ln
14400 MtgC 77302 2679 D1
14400 MtgC 77306 2679 D1
oodward St
200 ALVN 77511 4867 B3
7900 HOUS 77051 4243 B3
oodward Gardens Dr
14700 HarC 77082 4096 D4
oodway Av
4500 RSBG 77471 4491 C5
oodway Cir
1700 DKSN 77539 4754 A4
oodway Ct
200 MtgC 77386 2822 C7
oodway Dr
- BYTN 77521 3972 D4
- WlrC 77447 2813 A2
1600 WDBR 77357 2828 E2
2000 WDBR 77357 2829 A2
4500 HOUS 77024 3961 A4
4800 HOUS 77056 3961 A4
5000 HOUS 77056 3960 D3
5700 HOUS 77057 3960 D3
6500 HNCV 77024 3960 A5
6800 HOUS 77024 3960 A5
6800 HOUS 77063 3960 A6
8600 HOUS 77063 3959 D7
20900 MtgC 77357 2827 E7
oodway St
41300 MtgC 77354 2668 D2
41300 MtgC 77354 2669 A2
oodway Oaks Ln
10 HOUS 77056 3960 E4
oodway Pl Ct
5900 HOUS 77057 3960 C4
oodwick Dr
2600 SGLD 77479 4368 D7
oodwick Rd
10300 HOUS 77016 3687 B4
oodwick St
7600 HOUS 77028 3826 B1
8800 HOUS 77028 3687 B6
oodwild St
2400 HarC 77038 3543 A2
oodwind Blvd
- HarC 77040 3541 B7
oodwind Dr
2300 FBnC 77469 4365 D4
9700 HOUS 77025 4241 C2
oodwind Wy
2200 LGCY 77573 4632 C1
2400 LGCY 77573 4508 C7
oodwind Lakes Blvd
- HarC 77040 3541 B6
oodwind Lakes Dr
8900 HarC 77040 3681 B1
9200 HarC 77040 3541 B7
oodwind Shadows Dr
10700 HarC 77433 3537 D1
10900 HarC 77433 3396 C7
oodwolf Ct
14100 HarC 77015 3829 A5
oodworth Dr
11900 HarC 77429 3397 A6
oodwren Ct
3000 LGCY 77573 4633 A1
oody Ln
10600 HOUS 77093 3685 E3
oody Rd
1500 PRLD 77581 4376 A7
1500 PRLD 77581 4503 A3
2500 PRLD 77584 4503 A3
12400 BKVL 77581 4376 A6
12400 HOUS 77048 4376 A5
oodyard
- HarC 77338 3261 D5
oodyard Dr
1200 HarC 77073 3403 C1
oodyard Rd
8000 HarC 77338 3261 E5
8000 HOUS 77338 3261 E6
oody Bend Pl
2000 FBnC 77479 4493 E3
oody Creek Dr
10 CNRO 77301 2383 E2
10 CNRO 77301 2384 A2
oody Creek Ln
- HOUS 77077 3956 D3
oody Hollow Dr
12200 HarC 77375 3109 D7
oody Oaks Dr
- HarC 77095 3538 E3
oolf Av
900 GNPK 77547 3966 C7
oolf Rd
7800 HarC 77379 3110 E7
oolford Dr
11900 HarC 77065 3539 D2
oolongoing Dr
19400 HarC 77449 3677 A3
oolridge Dr
100 CNRO 77301 2385 A4
300 CNRO 77301 2384 E4
oolsey Ct
9400 HarC 77396 3407 A6
oolsey Ln
4300 HarC 77396 3407 B6
oolwich Dr
900 HarC 77032 3545 A1
oolworth St
100 HOUS 77020 3825 D7
300 HOUS 77020 3964 D1
3800 HOUS 77026 3825 D6
ooster St
100 BYTN 77520 3971 C5
ooten Rd
1800 BzaC 77584 4501 A4
1800 PRLD 77584 4501 A4
orcester Dr
6900 HarC 77379 3256 D3
orden Ln
16900 FRDW 77546 4629 E1

STREET
Block City ZIP Map# Grid
Wordsworth St
2300 HOUS 77030 4102 A4
2400 WUNP 77005 4102 A4
Worfield Ct
9400 FBnC 77478 4236 D2
Worgan Ct
16700 HarC 77379 3256 E2
World Houston Pkwy
3700 HOUS 77032 3405 B7
World of Faith Ln
- HarC 77038 3543 E5
Worley Dr
2200 HMBL 77396 3406 D3
Worms St
1600 HOUS 77020 3964 B1
Worrell Dr
4100 HOUS 77045 4241 D6
Worth Rd
8500 FBnC 77053 4499 D1
8500 FBnC 77545 4499 D1
Wortham Blvd
9700 HarC 77065 3539 C3
Wortham Ct
11100 HarC 77065 3539 B1
Wortham Wy
6100 HOUS 77033 4244 C2
Wortham Brook Ln
13000 HarC 77065 3539 B1
Wortham Center Dr
12600 HarC 77065 3539 C3
Wortham Crest Blvd
11000 HarC 77065 3539 B1
Wortham Falls Blvd
12400 HarC 77065 3539 D2
Wortham Gate Dr
11100 HarC 77065 3539 C1
Wortham Grove Blvd
13000 HarC 77065 3539 B2
Wortham Landing Dr
11800 HarC 77065 3539 D1
Wortham Ridge Tr
- HarC 77065 3539 A3
Worthington Dr
3200 PRLD 77584 4501 B2
8200 FBnC 77083 4095 E7
Worthington St
2800 HOUS 77093 3824 E1
2800 HOUS 77093 3825 A1
13000 SGLD 77478 4237 C5
Worthington Lake Dr
3700 FBnC 77469 4234 D6
Worthshire St
700 HOUS 77008 3823 B7
Wortley Dr
16900 HarC 77084 3678 C6
Wossback Cir
1700 FBnC 77545 4622 C3
Woven Wood Ct
1200 FBnC 77469 4365 D3
Woven Wood Ln
2300 FBnC 77469 4365 E3
Wovenwood Ln
7400 HarC 77041 3679 B1
7500 HarC 77041 3539 B7
Wrangler Av
16200 MtgC 77302 2679 B4
Wrangler Ln
11500 TMBL 77375 3109 E3
Wrangler Run Ct
- HarC 77429 3253 A7
Wray Ct
8000 HOUS 77088 3682 D1
Wren Cir
7200 TXCY 77591 4873 C5
Wren Ct
200 MtgC 77385 2676 D5
Wren Dr
1800 LGCY 77573 4631 C5
2200 PASD 77502 4247 A1
Wren Ln
600 HOUS 77079 3958 A3
22800 HarC 77377 2962 A7
Wren Pk
7900 HarC 77396 3406 D6
Wren Rd
11300 MtgC 77303 2239 C6
21900 MtgC 77357 2827 C5
Wren St
9800 LPRT 77571 4250 B1
Wren Brook Ct
4000 HarC 77449 3815 E1
Wren Creek Ct
2500 FBnC 77545 4498 C6
Wrencrest Ln
- HarC 77073 3260 A5
- HarC 77338 3260 A4
20600 HarC 77073 3259 E4
Wren Dale Ln
18200 HarC 77346 3409 A1
Wrenfield Ct
3900 HarC 77449 3815 E2
Wrenfield Pl
10 WDLD 77384 2675 D5
Wren Forest Ln
19600 HarC 77084 3815 E4
19600 HarC 77084 3816 A4
Wren Hill St
16900 MtgC 77385 2676 E5
Wren Hollow Wy
20400 HarC 77338 3261 B3
Wren Meadow Rd
2300 FBnC 77469 4365 D3
Wren Pond St
- HarC 77065 3539 C2
Wrens Song Pl
10 WDLD 77382 2674 D4
Wrenstone Dr
15900 HarC 77068 3257 B4
Wrenthorpe Dr
12200 HOUS 77031 4239 A5
12500 HOUS 77071 4239 B5
Wren Trail Ln
- HarC 77090 3258 D5
Wrenway Dr
1600 MSCY 77489 4370 C7
Wrenwood Cir
9000 HOUS 77099 4237 D1
Wressell Cir
12800 HarC 77044 3549 D1
Wressell Dr
14500 HarC 77044 3549 D1
Wrexham Springs Ct
2600 HarC 77373 3114 A4
E Wright Av
10 BYTN 77520 3973 A7
E Wright Blvd
1000 BYTN 77520 3973 B7
1300 BYTN 77520 4113 C1

STREET
Block City ZIP Map# Grid
Wright Dr
5000 KATY 77493 3813 E6
Wright Ln
4000 BYTN 77520 4113 E7
4000 HarC 77520 4113 E7
Wright Rd
- JRSV 77065 3540 A7
3500 HOUS 77032 3261 B7
3500 HOUS 77032 3405 D1
4600 STAF 77477 4369 A1
6900 HTCK 77563 4989 A5
7000 HarC 77041 3680 A1
7300 HarC 77041 3540 A7
32200 MtgC 77355 2963 A1
33200 MtgC 77355 2817 A7
33600 MtgC 77362 2817 A7
33900 MtgC 77362 2816 E5
33900 SGCH 77362 2816 E5
W Wright St
100 BYTN 77520 3972 E7
Wright Oaks Dr
12300 HarC 77014 3402 C4
Wrightsboro Dr
- HarC 77429 3253 E7
Wrights Crossing St
20000 HarC 77449 3676 D4
Wrightwood St
1200 HOUS 77009 3963 B1
Wrigley St
- HOUS 77045 4241 C7
13700 HOUS 77045 4372 C2
Wrotham Ln
1300 HarC 77530 3829 D5
Wroxton Ct
1700 HOUS 77005 4102 C2
Wroxton Dr
10 CNRO 77304 2383 B5
Wroxton Rd
2200 HOUS 77005 4102 A2
2500 WUNP 77005 4102 A2
3000 WUNP 77005 4101 E2
Wroxton St
1800 HOUS 77005 4102 C2
Wuensche
21000 HarC 77388 3113 C3
Wunder Ln
5300 HOUS 77091 3684 C6
Wunder Hill Dr
17100 HarC 77379 3256 B3
Wunderlich Rd
14100 HarC 77066 3401 A1
14100 HarC 77069 3400 E1
14100 HarC 77069 3401 A1
14200 HarC 77069 3256 E7
Wunsche Av
100 HarC 77373 3114 A2
Wunsche Lp
800 HarC 77373 3113 D2
800 HOUS 77373 3113 D2
Wunshe Av
- HarC 77373 3114 A2
Wuthering Heights Dr
3100 HOUS 77045 4242 A7
3300 HOUS 77045 4241 E7
WW Thorne Blvd
- HOUS 77338 3260 A4
2500 HarC 77073 3259 E5
2700 HarC 77073 3260 A4
Wyandott Blvd
5800 HOUS 77040 3681 D5
Wyanngate Dr
4100 HarC 77373 3115 A6
Wyatt St
1100 HOUS 77023 3964 C7
4200 PASD 77503 4108 D6
4400 DRPK 77503 4108 E6
4400 DRPK 77536 4108 E6
Wyatt Chapel Rd
- PRVW 77445 2954 E6
- WlrC 77445 2954 D6
24200 PRVW 77445 2955 A6
Wyckchester Dr
2400 BzaC 77584 4501 D5
Wyckham Cir
- WDLD 77382 2673 A7
N Wyckham Cir
- WDLD 77382 2673 C7
S Wyckham Cir
- WDLD 77382 2673 C7
Wycliffe Dr
300 HOUS 77079 3958 C3
1200 HOUS 77043 3819 B5
1200 HOUS 77043 3958 C1
Wycomb Dr
8100 HarC 77070 3399 D1
Wycomb Ln
7600 HarC 77070 3399 E1
Wye Dr
200 BYTN 77521 3973 A4
W Wye Dr
100 BYTN 77521 3972 E4
100 BYTN 77521 3973 A4
Wye Brook Wy
- HarC 77379 3110 E2
- HarC 77379 3111 A2
Wyeth Cir
17200 HarC 77379 3256 B3
Wylie St
5000 HOUS 77026 3825 C7
Wynberry Dr
- HarC 77041 3679 C5
Wynbourn Ct
14900 FBnC 77083 4236 C1
14900 FBnC 77478 4236 C1
Wynbourn Wy
14600 FBnC 77083 4236 D2
Wynbrook St
8300 HOUS 77061 4245 D2
8400 HOUS 77017 4245 D2
Wynchase Dr
1800 DRPK 77536 4109 D5
Wynd Av
1200 PASD 77503 4108 B6
Wyndale Ct
1700 FBnC 77469 4365 D2
Wyndale Dr
1800 DRPK 77536 4109 D5
Wyndale St
1700 HOUS 77030 4102 D5
Wyndemere Ln
10 MtgC 77380 2967 D2
10 WDLD 77380 2967 D2
Wynden Ct
1200 HOUS 77056 3961 A5
N Wynden Dr
10 HOUS 77056 3961 A4
S Wynden Dr
10 HOUS 77056 3961 A5

STREET
Block City ZIP Map# Grid
Wynden Trc
100 HOUS 77056 3961 B4
Wynden Creek Dr
1200 HOUS 77056 3961 B4
Wynden Crescent Ct
200 HOUS 77056 3961 B3
N Wynden Estates Ct
100 HOUS 77056 3961 B4
Wynden Meadow Ln
2500 CNRO 77304 2383 B1
Wynden Oaks Ct
10 HOUS 77056 3961 A5
Wynden Oaks Dr
10 HOUS 77056 3961 A5
Wynden Oaks Garden Dr
1200 HOUS 77056 3961 A5
Wynden Pl Ln
10 HOUS 77056 3961 B4
Wynden Villa Dr
1100 HOUS 77056 3961 A5
Wyndham Ct
8500 JRSV 77040 3540 C6
Wyndham Dr
8600 HarC 77083 4097 A3
Wyndham Pkwy
- JRSV 77040 3540 C6
Wyndham Tr
15200 FBnC 77083 4236 C1
Wyndham Briar Dr
- HarC 77379 3111 C5
Wyndham Lake Blvd
100 JRSV 77064 3540 A5
100 JRSV 77065 3540 A5
Wyndham Park Dr
- SPVL 77024 3960 B1
- SPVL 77055 3821 B7
- SPVL 77055 3960 B1
Wyndham Rose Ln
20000 HarC 77379 3111 D5
Wyndham Village Dr
8500 JRSV 77040 3540 C6
Wyndwood Dr
100 TYLV 77586 4508 E1
100 TYLV 77586 4509 A1
4700 HOUS 77013 3827 C5
Wyne St
4000 HOUS 77017 4105 E6
Wynell Ter
300 HOUS 77022 3685 B6
Wynfield Dr
800 DRPK 77536 4109 D5
14400 HarC 77429 3397 D2
Wynfield Springs Dr
10900 FBnC 77469 4092 D7
Wynforest Dr
1700 DRPK 77536 4109 D5
Wyngate Dr
1600 DRPK 77536 4109 D5
Wynlea St
7500 HOUS 77061 4245 B4
Wynmar Ln
11900 HarC 77429 3397 E1
Wynmeadow Dr
8500 HOUS 77061 4245 E3
Wynne St
100 HOUS 77009 3824 B4
Wynnewood Dr
4800 HOUS 77013 3827 C4
Wynnpark Dr
7200 HOUS 77008 3822 C6
Wynnview Dr
4700 HarC 77546 4505 E6
Wynnwood Ln
900 HOUS 77008 3823 A6
6200 HOUS 77008 3822 E6
Wynoak Dr
10 WDLD 77382 2673 E5
N Wynoak Dr
100 WDLD 77382 2673 E4
S Wynoak Dr
10 WDLD 77382 2673 E5
Wynona Dr
4000 HOUS 77087 4104 D5
Wynridge Dr
1800 DRPK 77536 4109 D5
Wynrun Ct
10500 HarC 77038 3543 C2
Wynwood Dr
1800 DRPK 77536 4109 D5
Wynyma Tr
7000 HarC 77379 3256 C1
Wyoming Av
2000 GlsC 77539 4632 E6
2300 GlsC 77539 4633 A7
2800 DKSN 77539 4633 A7
3100 GlsC 77539 4632 E6
3100 LGCY 77573 4632 E6
Wyoming St
1900 BYTN 77520 4112 B3
3600 HOUS 77021 4103 C6
Wyrick St
3400 HOUS 77026 3825 C6
Wysall Cliff Dr
10800 HarC 77064 3541 A1
Wytchwood Cir
16300 HarC 77429 3397 A3
Wyte Ln
4400 HOUS 77093 3686 B5
4500 HOUS 77016 3686 B5

X

E X St
100 DRPK 77536 4109 E5
3000 DRPK 77536 4110 A5
3000 LPRT 77536 4110 A5
3100 LPRT 77571 4110 A5
W X St
100 DRPK 77536 4109 A5
300 DRPK 77536 4108 E6
Xavier
- HarC 77041 3680 C6
Xingo Ct
19300 MtgC 77365 2971 E4

Y

Y St
5900 KATY 77493 3813 B6
S Y St
100 LPRT 77571 4251 E7
Yabbie Dr
16300 FBnC 77478 4236 A6
Yacht Ct
900 HarC 77532 3411 A7
Yacht Club Dr
5500 DKSN 77539 4753 E5
5500 TXCY 77539 4753 E5

STREET
Block City ZIP Map# Grid
Yacht Club Ln
10 ELGO 77586 4509 A3
Yacht Harbor Ln
2100 LGCY 77573 4631 C7
Yahoo
6900 HOUS 77017 4246 A3
Yale Ct
500 HOUS 77007 3962 D1
Yale Dr
5300 KATY 77493 3813 D5
Yale Ln
700 DRPK 77536 4249 C2
Yale St
10 HOUS 77007 3962 D2
800 HOUS 77007 3823 D7
800 HOUS 77008 3823 D7
2700 PASD 77502 4248 A1
2700 PASD 77503 4248 A1
3500 GLSN 77554 5221 E3
3500 GLSN 77554 5222 A3
3600 HOUS 77018 3823 C1
4500 HOUS 77022 3823 C1
4700 HOUS 77022 3684 C7
4800 HOUS 77018 3684 C7
5100 HOUS 77091 3684 C7
5500 HOUS 77076 3684 C6
7900 HarC 77037 3684 C1
7900 HOUS 77037 3684 C2
Yale Park Dr
- PASD 77058 4380 E6
Yale Square Ct
4000 HarC 77449 3815 D1
Yampa Ln
15600 JRSV 77040 3540 D7
Yancey Dr
1100 MAGA 77355 2668 E6
Yancy Dr
12400 HOUS 77015 3966 E3
12600 HOUS 77015 3967 A3
Yancy Rd
22400 MtgC 77365 2973 D5
Yankee Ct
3600 MSCY 77459 4497 E5
Yapon View Dr
7900 HarC 77433 3537 B7
Yarberry
15200 HarC 77032 3545 A1
Yarberry St
14600 HarC 77032 3545 A1
14600 HarC 77039 3545 A1
Yarbo Creek Dr
2900 HOUS 77082 4096 D2
Yard Ct
17300 HarC 77532 3552 A1
Yardley Dr
6800 FBnC 77494 4093 C5
Yarmouth
19200 MtgC 77357 2829 D4
Yarmouth St
5800 HOUS 77028 3826 D3
Yarnarm Ct
16300 HarC 77532 3551 D2
Yarrow Ct
10 WDLD 77382 2674 C3
Yarrow Crest Ct
12900 HOUS 77085 4241 A7
Yarrowdale Ct
10 WDLD 77382 2819 C2
Yarwell Dr
4900 HOUS 77096 4241 A2
5000 HOUS 77096 4240 E2
Yates Rd
16600 PTVL 77372 2682 D6
Yates St
1400 CNRO 77304 2383 D7
1400 HOUS 77020 3964 C2
Yaupon Av
900 PASD 77506 4106 E6
Yaupon Cir
- HarC 77377 3107 C2
E Yaupon Cir
21700 HarC 77377 3107 C2
N Yaupon Cir
17500 HarC 77377 3107 C2
S Yaupon Cir
17500 HarC 77377 3107 C3
W Yaupon Cir
21700 HarC 77377 3107 C2
Yaupon Ct
10 PNVL 77304 2237 B4
Yaupon Dr
- BYTN 77520 3971 B2
Yaupon Tr
18700 HarC 77346 3265 B7
Yaupon Creek Dr
19100 HarC 77433 3537 B6
Yaupon Green Ct
- HarC 77379 3112 A6
Yaupon Holly Ln
13100 HOUS 77044 3549 E1
13100 HOUS 77044 3550 A1
Yaupon Mist Dr
19100 HarC 77433 3677 B1
Yaupon Pass Dr
19000 HarC 77433 3677 C1
Yaupon Ranch Ct
7800 HarC 77433 3537 B7
Yaupon Ranch Dr
19000 HarC 77433 3537 B7
Yaupon Ridge Ct
19200 HarC 77433 3537 B6
Yaupon Ridge Dr
5900 FBnC 77469 4616 A1
Yaupon Square Ln
1000 HOUS 77008 3822 D7
Yaw Ct
900 HarC 77532 3552 A3
Yawl Ct
700 HarC 77532 3552 A1
Yaxley Ct
- MtgC 77357 2829 D3
Yearling Cir
9500 HarC 77065 3539 E4
Yearling Ct
9600 HarC 77065 3539 D4
Yearling Dr
11600 HarC 77065 3539 E4
11600 HarC 77065 3540 A4
Yearling Mdws
19000 HarC 77094 3955 B1
Yearling Pl
9900 MtgC 77385 2676 E4
Yearling Branch Dr
9500 HOUS 77075 4246 B7
Yearling Cold Ct
2900 HarC 77038 3543 A5
Yearling Ridge Ct
4800 HarC 77449 3676 E7

STREET
Block City ZIP Map# Grid
Yeatmah Ln
11900 HarC 77067 3402 A5
N Yegua River Cir
1300 SGLD 77478 4369 B5
S Yegua River Cir
1500 SGLD 77478 4369 B4
Yeldell Ct
1400 FBnC 77545 4622 E1
Yellow Begonia Dr
14800 HarC 77433 3250 D6
N Yellow Bud Ct
21100 HarC 77433 3251 C3
W Yellow Bud Ct
16400 HarC 77433 3251 A4
Yellow Canyon Falls Dr
20100 HarC 77375 3109 D5
Yellow Daisy Ct
16500 HarC 77433 3250 E4
Yellowfin Cir
9100 TXCY 77591 4873 A4
Yellow Oak Tr
15300 HarC 77433 3251 C3
Yellowood Ct
10 WDLD 77380 2821 E7
Yellow Pine Cir
25500 MtgC 77380 2968 B2
Yellow Pine Dr
7100 HOUS 77040 3542 A7
7700 HarC 77040 3542 A7
7800 HarC 77040 3541 D7
7800 HarC 77040 3681 E1
Yellow Pine Ln
25600 MtgC 77380 2968 B1
Yellowpine Ridge Ln
4100 FBnC 77494 4092 A2
Yellow Rail Dr
13000 HarC 77044 3549 C1
Yellow Rose Ln
27000 MtgC 77354 2817 D4
Yellow Rose Tr
- HarC 77433 3251 B4
Yellowstone Blvd
3000 HOUS 77021 4103 C6
3000 HOUS 77054 4103 B5
5100 HOUS 77021 4104 B5
Yellowstone Cir
3500 PRLD 77584 4503 B5
Yellowstone Dr
4100 PASD 77504 4247 E6
4500 PASD 77504 4248 A6
4700 PASD 77505 4248 A6
N Yellowstone Dr
1600 DRPK 77536 4109 D6
S Yellowstone Dr
1600 DRPK 77536 4109 D7
Yellowstone Tr
18000 HarC 77346 3408 D1
18300 HarC 77346 3264 D7
Yellowstone Park Dr
3200 HOUS 77054 4103 A5
Yellowstone Wy Dr
6900 HOUS 77054 4103 A5
Yellow Thrush Dr
19000 HarC 77433 3677 B1
Yellowwood Ct
2600 FBnC 77494 3951 D5
Yellowwood Dr
- LGCY 77598 4630 D4
Yelverton Glen Dr
24300 HarC 77493 3814 B6
Yeoman Wy
17100 HarC 77532 3552 A1
Yestereve Ct
2700 HarC 77084 3816 B4
Yew Ln
21300 HarC 77073 3259 D2
Yewens Ln
- HarC 77429 3397 D2
Yewleaf Ct
10 WDLD 77381 2820 E5
10 WDLD 77381 2821 A6
Yewleaf Dr
10 WDLD 77381 2820 E6
Yewleaf Rd
10 WDLD 77381 2820 E6
10 WDLD 77381 2821 A6
Ygnacio Rd
- HarC 77396 3407 C4
Yida Ln
100 HOUS 77336 3121 D5
YMCA Dr
2600 PRLD 77581 4503 E4
Yoakum Blvd
2400 HOUS 77006 3962 D7
4300 HOUS 77006 4102 D1
5200 HOUS 77005 4102 D2
Yoakum Dr
22100 GLSN 77554 5441 A5
Yoakum St
24000 HarC 77336 3267 A2
Yoe St
7600 HOUS 77016 3687 A4
8000 HOUS 77078 3687 C4
Yoke Dr
600 HarC 77532 3552 B4
Yolandita
9900 HOUS 77075 4377 C2
Yon St
- MAGA 77355 2669 A6
Yonder Wy
28500 HarC 77336 3121 B3
28500 HOUS 77336 3121 B3
York
25600 MtgC 77357 2829 C4
York Av
100 CNRO 77301 2384 A6
100 SHUS 77587 4246 D3
600 CNRO 77301 2383 E6
York Ct
- MtgC 77357 2829 C3
York Ln
6100 LGCY 77573 4630 C6
S York Ln
12000 HarC 77089 4505 A1
York Mdws
6400 HarC 77084 3678 D3
York St
100 HOUS 77003 3964 A5
700 HOUS 77003 3963 E6
7800 HMBL 77396 3406 D3
N York St
400 HOUS 77003 3964 B4
York Bend Ln
12400 HarC 77044 3689 A3
York Brook Dr
- HarC 77546 4506 C6
- HarC 77598 4506 D6
- HOUS 77546 4506 C6

STREET
Block City ZIP Map# Grid
N Yorkchase Ln
2500 CNRO 77304 2383 B1
W Yorkchase Ln
2000 CNRO 77304 2383 B1
Yorkchester Dr
800 HOUS 77079 3958 B1
York Creek Dr
1300 HarC 77014 3402 C1
1400 HarC 77090 3402 B1
York Crest St
10700 HOUS 77093 3685 C3
Yorkdale Dr
6400 HOUS 77091 3683 B5
Yorkfield St
- HOUS 77040 3682 B4
7300 HOUS 77092 3682 B4
N York Gate Ct
10 WDLD 77382 2674 D4
S York Gate Ct
10 WDLD 77382 2674 D4
Yorkgate Dr
5700 HarC 77373 3115 E7
5900 HarC 77373 3116 A7
N Yorkglen Dr
17300 HarC 77084 3678 A2
S Yorkglen Dr
17300 HarC 77084 3678 A2
Yorkglen Manor Ln
6000 HarC 77084 3678 C4
Yorkhampton Dr
6600 HarC 77084 3678 D2
York Harbour Ct
2300 LGCY 77573 4508 C6
York Hollow Ln
8900 HarC 77044 3689 C5
Yorkingham Dr
3600 HarC 77066 3401 C4
Yorklyn Dr
11300 HarC 77066 3401 D6
York Minster Dr
16000 HarC 77379 3256 D4
Yorkmont Dr
12900 HarC 77429 3397 B3
Yorkmonte Dr
- HarC 77375 3109 D7
Yorkpine Ct
20100 HarC 77450 3954 E4
Yorkpoint Dr
15100 HarC 77084 3678 E3
Yorkshire
19100 MtgC 77357 2829 B4
19200 MtgC 77357 2828 E4
Yorkshire Av
400 PASD 77503 4108 B5
Yorkshire Blvd
- BzaC 77584 4501 B4
- PRLD 77584 4501 B4
Yorkshire Ct
- WlrC 77447 2813 C7
200 DRPK 77536 4249 B1
2900 PRLD 77581 4503 D4
Yorkshire Dr
1200 FRDW 77546 4629 C3
10400 MtgC 77302 2676 E2
Yorkshire St
500 HOUS 77022 3824 C2
3200 HOUS 77093 3825 A1
4000 HOUS 77016 3825 B1
4600 SGLD 77479 4495 C4
Yorkshire Hollow Ln
900 FBnC 77545 4623 A2
Yorkshire Oaks Dr
11300 HarC 77065 3539 E4
11300 HarC 77065 3540 A4
Yorkshire Woods Ln
- HarC 77084 3678 B3
York Timbers Dr
21700 HarC 77339 3118 C5
Yorktown Ct
2000 SEBK 77586 4509 E1
Yorktown Ct N
1900 LGCY 77573 4631 C5
Yorktown Ct S
1900 LGCY 77573 4631 C6
Yorktown Dr
2700 DKSN 77539 4753 C3
Yorktown Ln
2600 MSCY 77459 4497 A1
Yorktown Pl
2600 HOUS 77056 3960 E7
Yorktown St
1100 FBnC 77469 4364 D6
1100 RHMD 77469 4364 D6
1600 HOUS 77056 3960 E7
3200 HOUS 77056 4100 E1
Yorktown Colony Dr
15000 HarC 77084 3678 E3
Yorktown Crossing Pkwy
5900 HarC 77084 3678 C4
Yorktown Meadow Ln
6000 HarC 77084 3678 C3
Yorktown Pass
1600 FRDW 77546 4749 E2
Yorktown Plaza Dr
- HOUS 77040 3681 A3
Yorkway Dr
- HOUS 77094 3954 E1
20100 HarC 77450 3954 E1
20100 HOUS 77450 3954 E1
Yorkwood St
2900 HOUS 77093 3686 A3
5200 HOUS 77016 3686 D3
Yosemite Dr
4200 PASD 77504 4247 E5
4400 PASD 77504 4248 A5
Yosemite Ln
4600 PASD 77504 4248 A5
Yosemite St
3600 HOUS 77021 4103 C6
Yosemite Falls Dr
20100 HarC 77375 3109 D5
Yosemite Pl Dr
- HarC 77429 3253 C4
Yosemite Ridge Ct
2100 HarC 77493 3814 B5
Yost Blvd
2500 PRLD 77581 4504 C3
Young
14600 HOUS 77034 4379 A2
Young Cir
12300 GlsC 77510 4871 B2
Young Ln
13200 MtgC 77302 2532 A6
Young St
4000 PASD 77504 4247 C6
Youngberry St
8500 HarC 77044 3689 A6

Houston Street Index

STREET Block	City	ZIP	Map#	Grid
Youngcrest Dr				
9700	STAF	77477	4239	A7
Youngfield Dr				
13100	HarC	77429	3254	A6
13100	HarC	77429	3398	A1
Youngford Ln				
14500	HarC	77047	4374	B5
Younglake Blvd				
19500	HarC	77084	3816	A6
19700	HarC	77084	3815	E6
19700	HarC	77449	3815	E6
19700	HOUS	77449	3815	E6
Young Meadows Wy				
20900	HarC	77449	3676	D4
Young Oak St				
19300	HarC	77379	3112	A6
Young Sam Rd				
16900	MtgC	77302	2825	C1
Youngstown Pl				
9200	HarC	77396	3406	E6
9200	HarC	77396	3407	A6
Youngtree Cir				
19400	HarC	77084	3816	A6
N Youngwood Ln				
11800	HOUS	77043	3819	C1
S Youngwood Ln				
11800	HOUS	77043	3819	C1
Youpon				
19400	CHTW	77385	2823	A3
Youpon Dr				
300	PASD	77586	4383	B4
3800	LPRT	77571	4250	D4
4800	HarC	77086	3542	E6
14600	MtgC	77372	2682	D2
Youpon Ln				
20100	MtgC	77365	2825	B6
23600	HarC	77389	2966	A6
Youpon St				
6900	GLSN	77551	5222	B1
10900	MtgC	77372	2536	E1
17600	HarC	77044	3551	D7
Youpon Glen Wy				
2700	FBnC	77545	4498	C5
Youpon Hill Ct				
19000	HarC	77084	3816	B4
Youpon Lake Ct				
2700	HarC	77084	3816	B4
Youpon Lake Ln				
23600	HarC	77373	3114	E5
Youpon Leaf Wy				
19700	HarC	77084	3816	B5
19800	HarC	77084	3815	E4
Youpon Ridge Wy				
9800	MtgC	77385	2676	D5
Youpon Valley Ct				
1100	HarC	77073	3259	B5
Youpon Valley Dr				
15700	HarC	77073	3259	B5
Youpon Wood Ct				
1000	HOUS	77062	4379	D7
Youree St				
100	GlsC	77539	4635	D4
Yucatan Dr				
9700	GLSN	77554	5221	D3
Yucca				
-	HarC	77388	3113	C6
Yucca Dr				
6900	GLSN	77551	5108	B7
7000	GLSN	77551	5222	A1
7300	TXCY	77591	4873	B6
Yucca St				
200	GlsC	77650	4994	D2
Yucca Field Dr				
7500	HarC	77433	3537	B6
7500	HarC	77433	3677	E1
Yucca Tip Ln				
21800	HarC	77073	3259	E1
Yucca Valley Ln				
19500	HarC	77433	3537	B6
Yukon Dr				
20900	MtgC	77357	2828	A7
21000	MtgC	77357	2974	A1
Yukon Grove Ln				
-	HarC	77346	3264	B7
Yukon Pass Dr				
17800	HarC	77346	3408	E2
Yukon Ridge Tr				
18200	HarC	77346	3408	C1
Yukon River Dr				
22900	MtgC	77365	2972	C4
Yukon Valley Ln				
12300	HarC	77346	3408	C3
Yuma Dr				
4200	BYTN	77521	3973	C2
Yuma St				
9700	HOUS	77029	3966	A6
9800	GNPK	77547	3966	A6
9800	HOUS	77547	3966	A6
Yuma Tr				
3900	PASD	77505	4248	A5
Yuma Crest Ln				
19400	HarC	77377	3109	B7
Yupon Cir				
2100	PRLD	77581	4503	D2
Yupon Dr				
2900	DKSN	77539	4753	D2
Yupon St				
500	BYTN	77520	4112	D1
1000	LMQU	77568	4874	A7
1000	LMQU	77568	4990	A1
3300	HOUS	77006	3962	D7
4300	HOUS	77006	4102	D1
22800	MtgC	77365	3118	D1
Yupondale Dr				
9500	HOUS	77080	3820	C5
Yupon Ridge Dr				
4100	HOUS	77072	4098	B4
4100	HOUS	77082	4098	B4
Yvonne Dr				
8700	HarC	77044	3689	A5
Z				
Z & Z Ln				
1500	DRPK	77536	4108	E7
Zaballos Ct				
3300	HOUS	77013	3827	B6
Zabolio St				
15500	HOUS	77598	4506	D3
Zach Rd				
900	HMPD	77445	2953	B5
Zachary Cir				
6900	FBnC	77479	4496	B5
Zachary Dr				
21600	GLSN	77554	5441	B5
Zachary Ln				
4600	FBnC	77479	4366	C7
Zachary St				
100	HOUS	77029	3965	E7
Zachary Bend Ln				
2700	FBnC	77494	3953	B7
Zack Rd				
-	HMPD	77445	2953	A5
Zackery Ct				
2600	DKSN	77539	4633	C7
Zack Springs Ln				
-	MtgC	77386	2969	E6
Zada Park Ln				
-	HarC	77088	3543	B7
Zagar Ln				
17900	HarC	77090	3258	B2
Zahn St				
24000	MtgC	77355	2961	B6
Zaka Rd				
9200	HarC	77064	3541	A4
9900	HarC	77064	3540	E4
Zambesi Dr				
22800	MtgC	77365	2972	A4
Zapalac Rd				
14500	PRLD	77581	4501	E3
14500	PRLD	77584	4501	E3
Zapata Dr				
7000	FBnC	77083	4096	B5
7000	HOUS	77083	4096	B5
22100	GLSN	77554	5441	B5
Zapp Ln				
1300	PASD	77502	4107	E6
1300	PASD	77506	4107	E6
Zaragosa St				
6400	HarC	77521	3832	E6
Zarate Av				
2600	PASD	77506	4108	A6
Zaro Dr				
7900	GlsC	77510	4987	D7
Zarroll Dr				
11600	HOUS	77099	4238	A1
Zarsky Rd				
-	HarC	77336	3267	E3
Zarzania				
3200	HOUS	77020	3964	A2
Zavalla Cir				
2100	FRDW	77546	4629	B6
Zavalla Rd				
12500	HOUS	77085	4371	B2
Zavalla St				
6400	HarC	77521	3832	E6
12000	HOUS	77035	4371	A1
12000	HOUS	77085	4371	A2
Zeenat Blvd				
-	BYTN	77520	3835	B6
Zelko Dr				
3100	BzaC	77584	4501	B6
Zelma Dr				
5600	HOUS	77076	3684	E6
Zenith St				
14500	HOUS	77045	4373	A3
Zenith Elm St				
-	HarC	77379	3111	A2
Zenith Glen Ln				
15000	HarC	77429	3253	C3
Zenobie St				
-	MSCY	77489	4370	A3
-	STAF	77477	4370	A3
-	STAF	77489	4370	A3
Zepher Dr				
1100	PASD	77502	4107	D6
1100	PASD	77506	4107	D6
E Zephyr Dr				
10	BzaC	77511	4868	B7
W Zephyr Dr				
5000	BzaC	77511	4868	B7
Zephyr St				
3400	HOUS	77021	4103	C5
Zephyr Bend Pl				
10	WDLD	77381	2821	E2
Zerene Meadow Ln				
-	HOUS	77336	3266	C1
Zero St				
1000	HMPD	77445	2953	C7
1200	HMPD	77445	3098	D1
Zetak Ln				
19100	HarC	77532	3411	A4
19300	HarC	77532	3410	E4
Zieglers Grv				
7000	FBnC	77469	4493	D6
Zilonis Ct				
7800	JRSV	77040	3540	E7
7800	JRSV	77040	3680	E1
Zimby				
-	HOUS	77094	4094	E1
Zimmerly Ct				
4400	FBnC	77479	4366	D6
Zimmermann Dr				
8000	HOUS	77088	3682	D1
Zinc Ln				
15000	MtgC	77372	2683	E3
Zindler				
500	HOUS	77020	3964	D1
Zindler St				
900	HOUS	77020	3964	D2
Zingelmann Rd				
11600	GLSN	77554	5220	D4
Zinn Dr				
200	HarC	77532	3692	E2
600	HarC	77532	3693	A2
Zinnia Dr				
16200	HarC	77095	3538	B1
Zinnia Ln				
-	HarC	77338	3407	B1
Zinnia Rd				
1400	MSCY	77489	4370	C4
Zion Rd				
11900	HarC	77375	2964	D4
11900	TMBL	77375	2964	D4
13700	TMBL	77375	2963	D4
Zion Lutheran Cemetery Rd				
25500	HarC	77375	2965	C2
25900	HarC	77375	2819	C7
Zircon Ct				
10600	HOUS	77099	4238	A3
Zirkle Dr				
5900	FBnC	77494	4092	A5
Zoch Ln				
3600	HOUS	77092	3821	E2
Zoe St				
100	HOUS	77020	3825	E7
300	HOUS	77020	3964	E1
Zola Rd				
700	HOUS	77076	3684	E6
Zoltowski St				
6900	HOUS	77020	3965	A4
Zoo Cir Dr				
1500	HOUS	77030	4102	E3
Zora St				
1300	HOUS	77055	3822	A6
Zorn Dr				
-	HOUS	77084	3818	C3
Zube Rd				
25000	HarC	77447	3249	B3
Zuber Dr				
1200	GNPK	77547	3966	B6
Zubin Ln				
3200	KATY	77493	3813	D3
Zuinn St				
11600	HarC	77086	3542	D6
11600	HarC	77088	3542	D6
Zume				
8100	HOUS	77088	3683	B2
8200	HarC	77040	3541	D6
Zuni Tr				
3900	PASD	77505	4248	B4
Zurich Ct				
9300	HarC	77070	3255	C6
#				
E				
-	CmbC	77520	3835	B2
-	HarC	77521	3835	B2
-	MTBL	77520	3835	B2
1st Av				
-	LMQU	77568	4990	D3
300	SHUS	77587	4246	C3
1st Av N				
1100	TXCY	77590	4875	C6
2700	TXCY	77590	4874	E6
1st Av S				
1100	TXCY	77590	4875	C6
2500	TXCY	77590	4874	E6
1st St				
-	FBnC	77545	4499	D5
-	GlsC	77517	4869	E5
-	HarC	77044	3691	A1
-	HOUS	77034	4248	D7
-	HOUS	77058	4507	E2
-	KATY	77493	3951	E1
-	KMAH	77565	4509	D5
-	MTBL	77520	3696	D5
-	PASD	77506	3967	D7
-	PRLD	77545	4499	D5
-	PRVW	77445	2955	C7
-	PRVW	77445	3100	C1
-	STFE	77517	4869	E5
-	STFE	77517	4870	A5
-	WlrC	77493	3812	A4
10	MSCY	77489	4370	B3
100	GlsC	77539	4636	C5
100	GNPK	77547	3966	D7
100	HarC	77014	3257	D7
100	HarC	77014	3401	D1
100	RSBG	77471	4490	E3
100	SGLD	77478	4368	A2
200	GLSN	77550	5109	E2
200	HMPD	77445	2953	C7
300	SHUS	77587	4246	D3
700	LMQU	77568	4874	A7
700	TXCY	77591	4874	A7
1200	HMPD	77445	3098	C1
1200	SEBK	77586	4509	D2
1700	HarC	77336	3266	E2
1700	HarC	77336	3267	A2
1800	LMQU	77568	4873	E7
2200	HOUS	77338	3263	B4
2200	STAF	77477	4370	A4
3600	RSBG	77471	4614	E2
3900	GLSN	77554	5440	D6
3900	PRLD	77581	4503	C4
4200	LGCY	77573	4633	A4
4300	GlsC	77518	4634	E3
4800	HOUS	77504	4247	B7
5200	HarC	77532	3552	D4
5300	KATY	77493	3952	D1
6300	BLAR	77401	4101	A4
6800	HTCK	77563	4988	E4
11400	MtgC	77354	2671	D4
11500	HarC	77044	3551	B7
13300	MtgC	77372	2537	D6
14000	STFE	77510	4870	C6
14200	SPLD	77372	2683	A2
15100	SPLD	77372	2682	E4
15900	MtgC	77372	2682	E4
15900	PTVL	77372	2682	D6
16200	HarC	77530	3969	C1
21100	MNVL	77578	4747	A2
22500	MtgC	77365	2973	D4
23500	MtgC	77357	2828	A7
26100	HarC	77373	3114	A2
1st St SR-36				
1000	RSBG	77471	4490	E5
3600	RSBG	77471	4614	E2
1st St E				
200	HMBL	77338	3262	E6
1100	HMBL	77338	3263	A6
1700	HarC	77338	3263	A6
1st St E FM-1960				
200	HMBL	77338	3262	E6
1100	HMBL	77338	3263	A6
1700	HarC	77338	3263	A6
1st St N				
1900	TXCY	77590	4875	E3
1st St S				
10	TXCY	77590	4875	E6
E 1st St				
100	DRPK	77536	4109	B3
1100	HMPD	77445	2953	C7
N 1st St				
10	BYTN	77520	3973	A7
100	ALVN	77511	4867	A1
100	CNRO	77301	2384	A5
100	LPRT	77571	4251	D2
400	ALVN	77511	4749	A7
400	BLAR	77401	4101	A4
S 1st St				
-	BYTN	77520	3972	D7
-	BYTN	77520	3973	B7
100	CNRO	77301	2384	B6
100	LPRT	77571	4251	D4
300	BLAR	77401	4101	A5
300	BYTN	77520	4112	E1
1600	CNRO	77301	2530	B1
W 1st St				
100	DRPK	77536	4109	B3
100	HMBL	77338	3262	C5
200	HarC	77532	3552	C4
W 1st St FM-1960				
100	HMBL	77338	3262	C5
1st Ter				
26300	MtgC	77372	2683	B5
1st 1/2 Av N				
2400	TXCY	77590	4875	A6
2nd Av N				
2100	TXCY	77590	4875	A6
2500	TXCY	77590	4874	E6
2nd Av S				
2300	TXCY	77590	4875	A6
2500	TXCY	77590	4874	E6
2nd St				
-	BYTN	77520	3971	C4
-	HMPD	77445	2953	C7
-	HOUS	77058	4507	E4
-	HOUS	77058	4508	A4
-	LGCY	77573	4631	E3
-	MNVL	77578	4747	B2
-	MTBL	77520	3696	D5
-	WlrC	77445	3098	C3
-	WlrC	77493	3812	A4
100	GlsC	77539	4636	B5
100	GLSN	77550	5109	E2
100	HarC	77532	3552	C4
100	RSBG	77471	4490	E3
100	SGLD	77478	4368	A2
200	HarC	77014	3257	D7
200	HarC	77014	3401	D1
400	HMBL	77338	3262	E6
400	KMAH	77565	4509	D5
400	SHUS	77587	4246	D3
500	LGCY	77573	4632	B2
600	SEBK	77586	4509	D3
1000	GNPK	77547	3966	C7
1100	LMQU	77568	4874	A7
1200	HMPD	77445	3098	C2
1500	MSCY	77489	4370	B3
1800	HarC	77336	3266	E2
2300	HarC	77336	3267	A2
3900	GLSN	77554	5440	D6
3900	PRLD	77581	4503	C4
4300	GlsC	77518	4634	D3
4800	HOUS	77504	4247	B7
5800	KATY	77493	3813	C7
10200	FBnC	77478	4236	C3
11400	MtgC	77354	2671	D4
11500	HarC	77044	3551	B7
12000	DKSN	77510	4871	A1
12000	DKSN	77539	4871	A1
12000	GlsC	77510	4871	A1
12000	GlsC	77539	4871	A1
12000	TXCY	77539	4871	B1
12800	DKSN	77510	4870	E1
12800	DKSN	77539	4870	E1
12800	GlsC	77510	4870	E1
13300	MtgC	77372	2537	D6
14400	STFE	77517	4870	B6
16000	HarC	77530	3969	D1
22600	MtgC	77365	2973	D4
23500	MtgC	77357	2828	A7
2nd St SR-87				
100	GLSN	77550	5109	E2
2nd St N				
1600	TXCY	77590	4875	E3
2nd St S				
10	TXCY	77590	4875	E6
E 2nd St				
10	HOUS	77007	3962	D2
100	DRPK	77536	4109	B4
1100	HMPD	77445	3098	C1
N 2nd St				
-	BLAR	77401	4101	A2
100	ALVN	77511	4867	A1
100	CNRO	77301	2384	A5
100	LPRT	77571	4251	D2
100	RHMD	77469	4364	E7
200	BYTN	77520	3973	A7
200	HMPD	77445	2953	C7
600	ALVN	77511	4749	A7
700	FBnC	77469	4364	E7
S 2nd St				
100	ALVN	77511	4867	A2
100	BYTN	77520	3973	B7
100	CNRO	77301	2384	B6
100	LPRT	77571	4251	D3
100	RHMD	77469	4364	E7
200	BYTN	77520	4113	A1
300	BLAR	77401	4101	A5
300	RHMD	77469	4491	E1
400	RHMD	77469	4492	A1
6800	HTCK	77563	4988	E5
S 2nd St FM-762 SPUR				
300	RHMD	77469	4491	E1
400	RHMD	77469	4492	A1
W 2nd St				
100	DRPK	77536	4109	B4
2nd Ter				
26300	MtgC	77372	2683	B4
3KS Dr				
1100	GlsC	77539	4635	D7
3rd				
-	HarC	77015	3967	E4
3500	HOUS	77026	3825	C6
3rd Av				
1000	LMQU	77568	4990	C2
3rd Av N				
1400	TXCY	77590	4875	B5
2500	TXCY	77590	4874	E6
3rd Av S				
2500	TXCY	77590	4875	A6
2800	TXCY	77590	4874	E6
3rd St				
-	FBnC	77545	4499	D5
-	HOUS	77058	4508	A4
-	MTBL	77520	3696	D5
-	PRLD	77545	4499	D5
-	PRVW	77445	2955	B7
-	PRVW	77445	3100	C1
-	WlrC	77445	3098	C3
-	WlrC	77493	3812	A4
10	HarC	77015	3967	E5
10	MSCY	77489	4370	B3
100	GlsC	77539	4636	B5
200	HMPD	77445	2953	C7
200	RSBG	77471	4490	E5
300	GlsC	77650	4878	D7
300	HarC	77014	3257	D7
300	HarC	77014	3401	D1
300	HMBL	77338	3262	E6
300	SHUS	77587	4246	D3
500	PASD	77506	4107	B3
600	KMAH	77565	4509	E5
600	SEBK	77586	4509	E3
1100	GNPK	77547	3966	C7
1100	HMPD	77445	3098	C1
1100	LGCY	77573	4632	B2
1100	LMQU	77568	4874	A7
1900	HarC	77336	3266	E2
1900	HarC	77336	3267	A2
3900	GLSN	77554	5440	D6
3900	PRLD	77581	4503	C4
4300	GlsC	77518	4634	D3
5000	HarC	77493	3813	E7
5900	KATY	77493	3813	B7
6800	HTCK	77563	4988	E4
11400	MtgC	77354	2671	C4
11600	HarC	77044	3551	B7
12000	STFE	77510	4871	B4
12000	TXCY	77510	4871	B4
13300	MtgC	77372	2537	D6
13800	STFE	77517	4870	C6
23400	MtgC	77357	2828	A6
3rd St N				
10	TXCY	77590	4875	D6
3rd St S				
10	TXCY	77590	4875	D6
E 3rd St				
100	DRPK	77536	4109	B4
N 3rd St				
-	BLAR	77401	4101	A2
10	BYTN	77520	3973	A7
100	ALVN	77511	4867	A1
100	CNRO	77301	2384	B5
100	HarC	77562	3831	D3
100	HOUS	77017	4246	D2
100	LPRT	77571	4251	D2
100	SHUS	77017	4246	D2
100	SHUS	77587	4246	D2
400	HMPD	77445	2953	C7
400	RHMD	77469	4364	E7
500	ALVN	77511	4749	A7
700	FBnC	77469	4364	E7
S 3rd St				
-	HarC	77094	3955	B1
10	BYTN	77520	3973	A7
100	ALVN	77511	4867	A1
100	BLAR	77401	4101	A5
100	CNRO	77301	2384	B5
100	HarC	77562	3831	D3
100	LPRT	77571	4251	D4
100	RHMD	77469	4364	E7
100	RHMD	77469	4491	E1
200	BYTN	77520	4113	A1
800	RHMD	77469	4492	A1
1600	CNRO	77301	2530	B1
W 3rd St				
100	DRPK	77536	4109	A4
300	LGCY	77573	4631	E3
300	LGCY	77573	4632	A3
3rd Ter				
26200	SPLD	77372	2683	A4
26300	MtgC	77372	2683	B4
3rd 1/2 Av N				
2500	TXCY	77590	4874	E5
4th Av				
1500	LMQU	77568	4990	C2
4100	GLSN	77554	5440	D7
4th Av N				
2300	TXCY	77590	4875	A5
2500	TXCY	77590	4874	E5
4th Av S				
500	TXCY	77590	4875	B7
3500	TXCY	77590	4874	C7
4th St				
-	FBnC	77469	4365	A7
-	HMPD	77445	3098	C1
-	LGCY	77573	4631	E3
-	PRVW	77445	2955	D7
-	PRVW	77445	3100	D1
-	WlrC	77445	3098	C3
-	WlrC	77493	3812	A4
100	GlsC	77539	4636	B6
100	HarC	77532	3552	C4
100	HMPD	77445	2953	C7
100	RSBG	77471	4490	E3
100	SGLD	77478	4368	A2
100	SHUS	77587	4246	D4
200	GNPK	77547	4106	B1
200	HOUS	77547	4106	B1
200	MAGA	77355	2669	A6
300	HMBL	77338	3262	E6
400	HarC	77014	3257	D7
600	HarC	77060	3544	E1
600	KMAH	77565	4509	E5
600	LGCY	77573	4632	A2
600	SEBK	77586	4509	E3
700	HarC	77060	3545	A1
1000	HarC	77039	3545	A1
1200	GNPK	77547	3966	D7
1300	GlsC	77650	4878	D7
3800	GLSN	77554	5440	D6
4300	GlsC	77518	4634	D3
5500	KATY	77493	3813	C7
6800	HTCK	77563	4988	E4
7700	HarC	77521	3832	C4
7700	HarC	77562	3832	C4
11400	MtgC	77354	2671	D5
12000	GlsC	77510	4871	B2
12000	TXCY	77510	4871	B2
12200	STFE	77510	4871	A2
12800	STFE	77510	4870	E2
13300	MtgC	77372	2537	E7
13600	STFE	77517	4870	E2
13700	GlsC	77517	4870	C2
4th St N				
2600	TXCY	77590	4875	D2
4th St S				
10	TXCY	77590	4875	D6
E 4th St				
100	DRPK	77536	4109	B4
100	HOUS	77007	3962	D1
N 4th St				
100	ALVN	77511	4867	A1
100	BYTN	77520	3973	A7
100	CNRO	77301	2384	B5
100	HarC	77562	3831	D3
100	LPRT	77571	4251	D2
500	ALVN	77511	4749	A7
500	RHMD	77469	4364	E7
700	FBnC	77469	4364	E7
S 4th St				
-	RHMD	77469	4364	E7
10	BYTN	77520	3973	A7
100	ALVN	77511	4867	A1
100	CNRO	77301	2384	B5
100	HarC	77562	3831	D3
100	LPRT	77571	4251	D5
200	BYTN	77520	4113	A1
200	RHMD	77469	4491	E1
900	RHMD	77469	4492	A1
W 4th St				
10	KMAH	77565	4509	D5
100	DRPK	77536	4109	A4
100	HOUS	77007	3962	D1
200	GlsC	77565	4509	D5
4th Ter				
26300	MtgC	77372	2683	B4
4th 1/2 St				
11000	GlsC	77510	4871	D4
12200	STFE	77510	4871	A4
12700	STFE	77510	4870	D4
E 4th 1/2 St				
600	HOUS	77007	3962	E1
5th				
16400	HarC	77429	3397	A6
5th Av				
1700	LMQU	77568	4990	C2
5th Av N				
2300	TXCY	77590	4875	A5
2500	TXCY	77590	4874	E5
4400	TXCY	77591	4874	A5
5th Av S				
1900	TXCY	77590	4875	A7
2500	TXCY	77590	4874	D7
5th Av S FM-1765				
3500	TXCY	77590	4874	C7
5th St				
-	DRPK	77536	4110	A2
-	HarC	77536	4110	A2
-	HarC	77571	4110	A2
-	HOUS	77058	4508	B4
-	HOUS	77081	4100	E4
-	HOUS	77401	4100	E4
-	PRVW	77445	2955	B7
-	WlrC	77445	2953	C6
-	WlrC	77445	3098	C3
-	WlrC	77493	3812	B4
100	FBnC	77469	4365	A7
100	GlsC	77539	4636	B5
100	RHMD	77469	4365	A7
100	SGLD	77478	4368	A1
100	SHUS	77587	4246	E4
200	HMPD	77445	2953	C6
200	RSBG	77471	4490	E3
300	GLSN	77550	5109	E2
500	HMBL	77338	3262	E5
600	HarC	77060	3544	E2
600	HOUS	77060	3544	E2
600	KMAH	77565	4509	E5
700	HarC	77060	3545	A1
1300	GlsC	77650	4878	D7
1400	HMPD	77445	3098	C3
1500	MSCY	77489	4370	C3
2000	SEBK	77586	4509	C2
2100	STAF	77477	4370	A4
2200	GNPK	77547	3966	B7
2600	FBnC	77477	4370	B3
2800	FBnC	77477	4369	D6
3000	STAF	77477	4369	E5
3400	MSCY	77459	4369	D6
3400	MSCY	77477	4369	D6
3700	GLSN	77554	5440	D6
4300	GlsC	77518	4634	D3
5000	HarC	77014	3401	D1
5500	KATY	77493	3813	B7
6300	BLAR	77401	4100	E4
6800	HTCK	77563	4988	D4
11600	HarC	77044	3551	B7
11900	HOUS	77072	4098	A3
12100	HOUS	77072	4097	E3
13300	MtgC	77372	2537	E6
14100	STFE	77517	4870	C7
5th St N				
400	TXCY	77590	4875	D5
5th St S				
10	TXCY	77590	4875	D6
E 5th St				
100	DRPK	77536	4109	B4
100	HOUS	77007	3962	D1
5000	HarC	77493	3813	E7
5000	KATY	77493	3813	D7
N 5th St				
-	RHMD	77469	4491	E1
100	ALVN	77511	4867	A1
100	HarC	77562	3831	D3
100	LPRT	77571	4251	D2
100	RHMD	77469	4364	E7
200	BLAR	77401	4100	E4
500	ALVN	77511	4749	A7
500	CNRO	77301	2384	B4
1200	BYTN	77520	3973	A6
S 5th St				
-	BYTN	77520	3973	A7
-	BYTN	77520	4113	A1
100	ALVN	77511	4867	A1
100	CNRO	77301	2384	B5
100	HarC	77562	3831	D3
100	LPRT	77571	4251	D3
100	RHMD	77469	4491	E1
7000	BLAR	77401	4100	E5
W 5th St				
10	KMAH	77565	4509	D5
100	DRPK	77536	4109	A4
100	HOUS	77007	3962	D1
200	GlsC	77565	4509	D5
E 5th 1/2 St				
600	HOUS	77007	3962	E1
6th Av				
2200	LMQU	77568	4990	C3
6th Av N				
2300	TXCY	77590	4875	A5
2500	TXCY	77590	4874	E5
6th Av S				
1000	TXCY	77590	4875	C7
6th St				
-	FBnC	77469	4365	B7
-	FBnC	77545	4499	C6
-	PRLD	77545	4499	D6
-	PRVW	77445	2955	B7
100	GlsC	77539	4636	B5
100	GLSN	77550	5109	D1
100	MAGA	77355	2669	A6
100	RSBG	77471	4490	E3
100	SGLD	77478	4368	A1
100	SHUS	77587	4246	E3
200	HMPD	77445	2953	B7
200	MAGA	77355	2668	E6
400	KMAH	77565	4509	D5
500	HMBL	77338	3262	E5
600	CmbC	77586	4509	D4
700	HarC	77060	3544	E2
700	HarC	77060	3545	A2
1200	HMPD	77445	3098	B1
1300	GlsC	77650	4878	D7
1700	GNPK	77547	3966	C7
1900	SEBK	77586	4509	C3
2100	STAF	77477	4370	B4
3800	GLSN	77554	5440	D7
4300	GlsC	77518	4634	D3
5200	HarC	77532	3552	D4
5500	KATY	77493	3813	C7
6000	HarC	77014	3257	E7
6000	HarC	77014	3401	D1
6800	HTCK	77563	4988	D4
8200	BzaC	77511	4627	D5
11800	STFE	77510	4871	C6
11900	HOUS	77072	4098	A4
12100	HOUS	77072	4097	E3
12700	STFE	77510	4870	E6
13300	MtgC	77372	2537	E6
13400	STFE	77517	4870	D6
6th St N				
2300	TXCY	77590	4875	D3
6th St N LP-197				
10	TXCY	77590	4875	D
6th St S				
10	TXCY	77590	4875	D
6th St S LP-197				
10	TXCY	77590	4875	D
6th St W				
13400	STFE	77510	4870	D7
13500	STFE	77517	4870	C7
E 6th St				
100	DRPK	77536	4109	B4
N 6th St				
100	ALVN	77511	4867	A1
100	CNRO	77301	2384	A3
100	GLSN	77550	5109	D1
100	HarC	77562	3831	D3
100	LPRT	77571	4251	D2
100	RHMD	77469	4364	E7
100	RHMD	77469	4491	D1
500	ALVN	77511	4749	A7
1200	BYTN	77520	3973	A7
S 6th St				
-	BYTN	77520	3973	B7
-	BYTN	77520	4113	A1
10	CNRO	77301	2384	B5
100	ALVN	77511	4867	A1
100	HarC	77562	3831	D3
100	LPRT	77571	4251	D4
100	RHMD	77469	4491	E1
W 6th St				
-	CRLS	77565	4509	C5
10	KMAH	77565	4509	D5
100	DRPK	77536	4109	B4
100	HOUS	77007	3962	D1
200	GlsC	77565	4509	D5
11800	HarC	77044	3551	C7
E 6th 1/2 St				
600	HOUS	77007	3962	E1
600	HOUS	77009	3962	E1
7 Mile Rd				
3300	GLSN	77554	5221	C4
7th Av				
2100	LMQU	77568	4990	C3
7th Av N				
10	TXCY	77590	4875	D5
3100	TXCY	77590	4874	D5
7th Av S				
1100	TXCY	77590	4875	C7
7th St				
-	FBnC	77469	4365	B7
-	GlsC	77650	4994	E1
-	GlsC	77650	4995	A1
-	HarC	77049	3831	A2
100	GlsC	77539	4636	A7
100	LGCY	77573	4631	E2
100	RSBG	77471	4490	E3
100	SGLD	77478	4368	A1
100	SHUS	77587	4246	E4
200	HMPD	77445	2953	B7
300	HMBL	77338	3262	E5
400	KMAH	77565	4509	E5
600	BzaC	77583	4499	E6
600	FBnC	77545	4499	D6
600	GLSN	77550	5109	E3
600	PRLD	77545	4499	D6
600	PRLD	77583	4499	E6
1000	GlsC	77650	4878	E7
1200	HMPD	77445	3098	B2
1500	LGCY	77573	4632	A1
1700	GNPK	77547	3966	B7
1900	SEBK	77586	4509	C3
4000	GLSN	77554	5440	D7
4300	GlsC	77518	4634	D3
5800	KATY	77493	3813	B7
7000	HarC	77014	3257	E7
7000	HarC	77014	3401	D1
11100	GlsC	77510	4871	D6
11400	STFE	77510	4871	C6
11800	HarC	77044	3551	C7
11900	HOUS	77072	4098	A4
12100	HOUS	77072	4097	E4
12800	STFE	77510	4870	E6
13300	MtgC	77372	2537	E6
14500	STFE	77517	4870	B7
7th St LP-108				
-	GlsC	77650	4878	E7
-	GlsC	77650	4994	E1
-	GlsC	77650	4995	A1
7th St N				
10	TXCY	77590	4875	D6
7th St S				
10	TXCY	77590	4875	D6
E 7th St				
100	HOUS	77007	3962	D1
700	HOUS	77009	3962	E1
2500	TXCY	77590	4875	D2
N 7th St				
100	ALVN	77511	4867	A1
100	HarC	77562	3831	D3
100	LPRT	77571	4251	C2
100	RHMD	77469	4491	D1
200	BYTN	77520	3973	B7
200	RHMD	77469	4364	E7
1300	CNRO	77301	2384	B3
S 7th St				
100	ALVN	77511	4867	A1
100	BYTN	77520	4113	A1
100	HarC	77562	3831	D3
100	LPRT	77571	4251	D4
100	RHMD	77469	4491	E1
500	CNRO	77301	2384	C6
600	BLAR	77401	4100	E6
600	HOUS	77081	4100	E6
1700	CNRO	77301	2530	C1
W 7th St				
10	GlsC	77565	4509	D5
10	KMAH	77565	4509	D5
100	DRPK	77536	4109	B4
1000	HOUS	77007	3962	B1
7th 1/2 St				
11700	HarC	77044	3551	C7
12000	STFE	77510	4871	B7
E 7th 1/2 St				
600	HOUS	77007	3962	E1
700	HOUS	77009	3962	E1
1000	HOUS	77009	3823	E7
W 7th 1/2 St				
1000	HOUS	77007	3962	B1
7 1/2 Mile Rd				
3300	GLSN	77554	5221	B4
8th Av				
800	LMQU	77568	4990	B3
8th Av N				
1000	TXCY	77590	4875	C5
3100	TXCY	77590	4874	D5

STREET
Block City ZIP Map# Grid

th Av S
1100 TXCY 77590 4875 C7
th St
- FBnC 77469 4365 B7
100 GlsC 77539 4636 B5
100 HMPD 77445 2953 B7
100 RSBG 77471 4490 E3
200 FBnC 77471 4490 E3
400 KMAH 77565 4509 E5
700 CmbC 77586 4509 D4
700 SEBK 77586 4509 D4
900 LPRT 77571 4251 C1
1200 HMPD 77445 3098 B1
1300 GlsC 77539 4757 A1
1400 GlsC 77650 4878 E7
2200 GNPK 77547 3966 B7
4300 GlsC 77518 4634 D3
5800 KATY 77493 3813 C7
8000 HarC 77014 3257 E7
8000 HarC 77014 3401 D1
11900 HarC 77044 3551 C7
13200 STFE 77510 4870 E7
13300 LbyC 77372 2537 E6
14100 STFE 77517 4870 C7
th St N
2500 TXCY 77590 4875 C2
th St S
10 TXCY 77590 4875 D6
8th St
100 DRPK 77536 4109 B4
100 HOUS 77007 3823 D7
700 HOUS 77009 3823 D7
8th St
- LPRT 77571 4111 C7
100 ALVN 77511 4867 A1
100 CNRO 77301 2384 B4
100 HarC 77562 3831 C3
100 LPRT 77571 4251 C2
100 RHMD 77469 4491 E1
100 SHUS 77587 4246 E2
400 PASD 77502 4246 E2
400 SHUS 77502 4246 E2
500 RHMD 77469 4364 E7
800 BYTN 77520 3973 B6
10800 HOUS 77048 4244 B6
8th St
- BYTN 77520 4113 A1
100 ALVN 77511 4867 A1
100 HarC 77562 3831 C3
100 LPRT 77571 4251 C5
100 RHMD 77469 4491 E1
100 SHUS 77587 4246 E4
V 8th St
10 GlsC 77565 4509 D5
10 KMAH 77565 4509 D5
100 DRPK 77536 4109 B4
100 HOUS 77007 3823 C7
1200 DRPK 77536 4108 E4
8th 1/2 St
600 HOUS 77007 3823 E7
700 HOUS 77009 3823 E7
Mile Rd
2500 GLSN 77554 5220 D4
th Av
2200 LMQU 77568 4990 B3
th Av N
10 TXCY 77590 4875 B5
3100 TXCY 77590 4874 D5
3600 TXCY 77591 4874 C5
th Av N FM-1764
600 TXCY 77590 4875 B5
th St
- GNPK 77029 3966 A7
- HMPD 77445 2953 B6
- HOUS 77029 3966 A7
100 GlsC 77539 4636 A6
100 SHUS 77587 4246 E4
200 MAGA 77355 2669 A5
300 GLSN 77550 5109 D3
500 KMAH 77565 4509 E6
700 SEBK 77586 4509 D4
1000 GNPK 77547 3966 C7
1300 GlsC 77650 4878 E6
1300 HMPD 77445 3098 B2
1500 GlsC 77539 4757 A1
4300 GlsC 77518 4634 D3
9000 HarC 77014 3401 D1
10500 HOUS 77048 4244 B6
11700 HarC 77044 3551 C7
12200 STFE 77510 4871 B7
13200 STFE 77510 4870 E7
th St FM-517
200 GlsC 77539 4636 A6
th St N
10 TXCY 77590 4875 C3
th St S
10 TXCY 77590 4875 C6
E 9th St
- TXCY 77590 4991 B1
100 HOUS 77007 3823 E7
100 HOUS 77008 3823 E7
400 DRPK 77536 4109 B4
700 HOUS 77009 3823 E7
N 9th St
100 ALVN 77511 4866 E1
100 HarC 77562 3831 C3
100 LPRT 77571 4251 C2
1000 CNRO 77301 2384 B3
2900 TXCY 77590 4875 C2
S 9th St
- FBnC 77469 4365 B7
- RHMD 77469 4365 B7
100 HarC 77562 3831 C3
100 RHMD 77469 4491 E1
200 CNRO 77301 2384 C5
1000 LPRT 77571 4251 C4
W 9th St
100 DRPK 77536 4109 B4
100 HOUS 77007 3823 C7
100 HOUS 77008 3823 C7
10th Av
2000 LMQU 77568 4990 B3
10th Av N
2000 TXCY 77590 4875 A5
10th St
- WlrC 77445 2953 B5
100 GlsC 77539 4636 B5
100 MAGA 77355 2668 E5
200 HMPD 77445 2953 B6
500 BzaC 77511 4627 D5
500 KMAH 77565 4509 E6
600 CmbC 77586 4509 D4
600 SEBK 77586 4509 D4
800 SHUS 77587 4246 E4
1000 GNPK 77547 3966 C6
1000 HarC 77014 3401 D1
1300 GlsC 77650 4878 E6
1300 HMPD 77445 3098 B2
10th St
1400 GlsC 77539 4757 A1
1500 HarC 77039 3545 C1
4300 GlsC 77518 4634 D4
5400 KATY 77493 3813 B6
11700 HarC 77044 3551 D7
11900 STFE 77510 4871 B7
10th St US-290 BUS
- WlrC 77445 2953 B5
200 HMPD 77445 2953 B6
10th St N
1300 TXCY 77590 4875 C4
10th St S
10 TXCY 77590 4875 C6
E 10th St
- KATY 77493 3813 C6
100 DRPK 77536 4109 B4
100 HOUS 77008 3823 D7
700 HOUS 77009 3823 D7
N 10th St
100 CNRO 77301 2384 B5
100 HarC 77562 3831 C3
100 RHMD 77469 4491 E1
300 LPRT 77571 4251 C2
400 RHMD 77469 4364 D7
700 BYTN 77520 3973 B7
1500 LPRT 77571 4111 C7
N 10th St FM-1484
200 CNRO 77301 2384 B4
S 10th St
100 CNRO 77301 2384 C5
100 HarC 77562 3831 C3
100 LPRT 77571 4251 C3
100 RHMD 77469 4491 E1
W 10th St
100 HOUS 77008 3823 C7
E 10th 1/2 St
600 HOUS 77008 3823 E7
700 HOUS 77009 3823 E7
W 10th 1/2 St
100 HOUS 77008 3823 C7
11 Mile Rd
- GLSN 77554 5333 A2
2700 GLSN 77554 5219 E7
2700 GLSN 77554 5220 A7
11th Av
1800 LMQU 77568 4990 B2
11th Av N
10 TXCY 77590 4875 D4
W 11th Pl
10 HOUS 77005 4102 E3
10 HOUS 77006 4102 E3
11th St
- HMPD 77445 3098 B1
100 GLSN 77550 5109 D2
100 RHMD 77469 4491 D1
100 SHUS 77587 4247 A4
200 HMPD 77445 2953 B7
800 GlsC 77539 4636 A7
1000 GNPK 77547 3966 B6
1100 HarC 77014 3257 D7
4300 GlsC 77518 4634 C3
5500 KATY 77493 3813 C6
11500 STFE 77510 4871 B7
11700 HarC 77044 3551 D7
13100 MtgC 77372 2537 E6
11th St FM-1887
- HMPD 77445 2953 B7
- HMPD 77445 3098 B1
11th St N
2600 TXCY 77590 4875 C2
11th St S
10 TXCY 77590 4875 C6
E 11th St
100 DRPK 77536 4109 B5
100 HOUS 77008 3823 D7
700 HOUS 77009 3823 D7
9900 HOUS 77034 4378 B2
N 11th St
- DRPK 77536 4109 A3
100 HarC 77562 3831 C3
100 LPRT 77571 4251 C2
700 BYTN 77520 3973 B7
S 11th St
100 CNRO 77301 2384 C5
100 HarC 77562 3831 C3
100 LPRT 77571 4251 C3
200 RHMD 77469 4491 E1
12400 STFE 77510 4871 A7
S 11th St FM-762
300 RHMD 77469 4491 E1
W 11th St
100 HOUS 77008 3823 C7
2300 HOUS 77008 3822 E7
3800 HOUS 77055 3822 C7
11th 1/2 St N
1000 TXCY 77590 4875 C4
E 11th 1/2 St
600 HOUS 77008 3823 E7
700 HOUS 77009 3823 E7
12 Mile Rd
3300 GLSN 77554 5332 D1
12th Av
1900 LMQU 77568 4990 B3
12th Av N
- TXCY 77590 4875 C4
2800 TXCY 77590 4874 E4
12th St
100 GlsC 77539 4636 A7
200 GLSN 77550 5109 D3
200 HMPD 77445 2953 B7
300 SHUS 77587 4247 A4
400 SEBK 77586 4509 D4
1000 GNPK 77547 3966 C6
1200 HarC 77014 3257 D7
1300 GlsC 77650 4878 E6
1600 HMPD 77445 3098 B2
1700 HarC 77032 3404 D7
1700 HarC 77032 3545 C1
1700 HOUS 77032 3404 D7
1700 HOUS 77032 3545 C1
4200 GlsC 77539 4633 B6
4300 GlsC 77518 4634 C3
5600 KATY 77493 3813 C6
11800 STFE 77510 4987 B1
13100 MtgC 77372 2537 E6
12th St N
2800 TXCY 77590 4875 C2
12th St S
10 TXCY 77590 4875 C7
E 12th St
100 DRPK 77536 4109 B5
100 HOUS 77008 3823 D6
700 HOUS 77009 3823 D6
N 12th St
100 HarC 77562 3831 C3
100 LPRT 77571 4251 C1
1100 LPRT 77571 4111 C7
S 12th St
100 HarC 77562 3831 C3
200 CNRO 77301 2384 C5
200 LPRT 77571 4251 C3
600 RHMD 77469 4491 E1
W 12th St
100 DRPK 77536 4109 B5
100 HOUS 77008 3823 B6
2900 HOUS 77008 3822 C7
4300 HOUS 77055 3822 B7
12th Fairway Ln
7600 HarC 77346 3265 B5
12th 1/2 St N
1000 TXCY 77590 4875 C4
E 12th 1/2 St
600 HOUS 77008 3823 E6
700 HOUS 77009 3823 E6
13 Mile Rd
3600 GLSN 77554 5332 C3
13th
- HarC 77014 3257 D7
13th Av N
10 TXCY 77590 4875 A4
2500 TXCY 77590 4874 E4
13th St
- HarC 77562 3831 B3
- HMPD 77445 3098 A2
- WlrC 77445 3098 A3
100 GlsC 77539 4636 A5
100 GLSN 77550 5109 D3
200 HMPD 77445 2953 A7
400 SHUS 77587 4247 A4
1100 LPRT 77571 4251 C4
1400 GlsC 77650 4878 E6
1700 GNPK 77547 3966 C6
4300 GlsC 77518 4634 C4
4700 GlsC 77539 4634 D4
5700 KATY 77493 3813 C6
11800 STFE 77510 4987 B1
13100 MtgC 77372 2537 D6
13th St SR-159
- HMPD 77445 2953 A7
- HMPD 77445 3098 A2
- WlrC 77445 3098 A3
13th St N
2800 TXCY 77590 4875 C2
13th St S
10 TXCY 77590 4875 C7
E 13th St
100 DRPK 77536 4109 E5
100 HOUS 77008 3823 D6
700 HOUS 77009 3823 D6
2800 DRPK 77536 4110 A5
2800 LPRT 77536 4110 A5
2800 LPRT 77571 4110 A5
N 13th St
300 LPRT 77571 4251 C1
S 13th St
100 LPRT 77571 4251 C3
200 CNRO 77301 2384 C5
W 13th St
- PASD 77503 4108 D5
100 HOUS 77008 3823 B6
500 DRPK 77536 4109 A5
900 DRPK 77536 4108 E5
E 13th 1/2 St
600 HOUS 77008 3823 E6
700 HOUS 77009 3823 E6
14th Av N
10 TXCY 77590 4875 D4
2900 TXCY 77590 4874 D4
14th St
- HOUS 77036 4100 B2
- HOUS 77057 4100 B2
- WlrC 77445 3098 A3
100 CmbC 77539 4636 A4
100 HMPD 77445 3098 A2
200 HMPD 77445 2953 A7
600 SHUS 77587 4247 A4
1000 GNPK 77547 3966 C6
1400 GlsC 77650 4878 E6
1400 HarC 77014 3257 E7
4300 GlsC 77518 4634 C4
4600 GlsC 77539 4634 C4
11800 STFE 77510 4987 B1
16200 HarC 77429 3397 A5
14th St N
2600 TXCY 77590 4875 B3
14th St S
- TXCY 77590 4991 C1
10 TXCY 77590 4875 C7
E 14th St
100 HOUS 77008 3823 D6
700 HOUS 77009 3823 D6
800 HOUS 77009 3824 B7
N 14th St
- HOUS 77036 4100 B2
100 LPRT 77571 4251 C1
1100 LPRT 77571 4111 C7
S 14th St
300 LPRT 77571 4251 C4
W 14th St
100 HOUS 77008 3823 A6
W 14 1/2 St
1800 HOUS 77008 3823 B6
15th Av N
600 TXCY 77590 4875 C4
2900 TXCY 77590 4874 D4
15th St
100 GlsC 77539 4636 A5
100 GLSN 77550 5109 D3
100 SHUS 77587 4247 A3
200 HMPD 77445 2953 A7
800 GlsC 77650 4995 B1
1000 GlsC 77539 4635 E7
1300 GlsC 77650 4878 E6
1300 GlsC 77650 4879 A6
1300 HMPD 77445 3098 A1
1800 GNPK 77547 3966 C6
4300 GlsC 77518 4634 C4
4600 GlsC 77539 4634 C4
11800 STFE 77510 4987 B1
15th St N
2500 TXCY 77590 4875 B3
E 15th St
100 HOUS 77008 3823 D6
N 15th St
100 LPRT 77571 4251 B2
S 15th St
300 LPRT 77571 4251 C3
W 15th St
100 HOUS 77008 3823 B6
W 15th 1/2 St
900 HOUS 77008 3823 A6
16 Mile Rd
4400 GLSN 77554 5331 E7
16th Av N
10 TXCY 77590 4875 A4
16th Av N
2900 TXCY 77590 4874 E4
16th St
- WlrC 77445 3098 A2
100 GlsC 77539 4636 A5
100 GLSN 77550 5109 C3
100 HMPD 77445 2953 A7
800 GlsC 77539 4635 E7
800 GlsC 77650 4995 B1
900 HMPD 77445 3098 A1
1000 SHUS 77587 4247 A4
1300 GlsC 77650 4879 A6
2000 GNPK 77547 3966 B6
4300 GlsC 77518 4634 C4
4600 GlsC 77539 4634 C4
11800 STFE 77510 4987 B1
16th St N
1900 TXCY 77590 4875 B3
E 16th St
100 HOUS 77008 3823 D5
1000 HOUS 77009 3823 E5
N 16th St
100 LPRT 77571 4251 B2
700 LPRT 77571 4111 B7
S 16th St
- TXCY 77590 4875 B5
10 GLSN 77550 5109 C2
100 LPRT 77571 4251 B3
1400 GlsC 77650 4878 E6
W 16th St
100 HOUS 77008 3823 A5
16th Av Cir
- TXCY 77590 4874 E4
17th Av N
2100 TXCY 77590 4875 A4
2700 TXCY 77590 4874 E4
17th St
- HMPD 77445 2953 A6
- HMPD 77445 3098 A2
- SHUS 77587 4247 B4
- WlrC 77445 3098 A3
10 GLSN 77550 5109 C2
100 GlsC 77539 4636 A5
800 GlsC 77650 4995 B1
900 GlsC 77539 4635 E6
1300 GlsC 77650 4879 A6
1800 LGCY 77539 4632 D7
2000 GNPK 77547 3966 B6
4300 GlsC 77518 4634 C4
4400 GlsC 77539 4634 C4
11800 STFE 77510 4987 C1
17th St N
3600 TXCY 77590 4875 B2
E 17th St
600 HOUS 77008 3823 D5
700 HOUS 77009 3823 E5
N 17th St
10 GLSN 77550 5109 C2
100 LPRT 77571 4251 B2
S 17th St
100 LPRT 77571 4251 B3
W 17th St
100 HOUS 77008 3823 A5
18th Av N
10 TXCY 77590 4875 C3
2900 TXCY 77590 4874 D4
18th St
- HMPD 77445 2953 A6
10 GLSN 77550 5109 C4
100 GlsC 77539 4636 A5
500 GlsC 77539 4635 E5
1300 GlsC 77650 4879 A6
1800 GNPK 77547 3966 B6
2200 GlsC 77539 4632 C7
2200 GlsC 77539 4753 C1
2200 LGCY 77539 4632 C7
2200 LGCY 77539 4753 C1
2800 HMPD 77445 3098 A1
2800 WlrC 77445 3098 A3
4300 GlsC 77518 4634 C4
4400 GlsC 77539 4634 C4
12000 STFE 77510 4987 A1
13000 STFE 77510 4986 E1
13300 STFE 77510 4870 D7
18th St N
3600 TXCY 77590 4875 B2
E 18th St
100 HOUS 77008 3823 D5
700 HOUS 77009 3823 D5
N 18th St
100 LPRT 77571 4251 B2
1000 LPRT 77571 4111 B7
S 18th St
- LPRT 77571 4251 B4
W 18th St
100 HOUS 77008 3823 A5
1500 HOUS 77008 3822 C5
4200 HOUS 77092 3822 B5
19th Av
1400 TXCY 77590 4875 B3
19th Av N
10 TXCY 77590 4875 B3
2300 TXCY 77590 4874 E3
19th St
- GNPK 77547 3966 D5
- WlrC 77445 3098 A3
10 GLSN 77550 5109 C4
100 GlsC 77539 4636 A4
200 GlsC 77539 4635 E5
200 HMPD 77445 2953 A7
1200 GlsC 77650 4879 A6
1200 HMPD 77445 3098 A1
2200 GlsC 77539 4753 C1
2300 GlsC 77539 4632 D7
3000 LGCY 77539 4632 D7
4300 GlsC 77518 4634 C4
4500 GlsC 77539 4634 C4
4600 GlsC 77539 4633 B6
12700 STFE 77510 4986 E1
12700 STFE 77510 4987 A1
19th St N
3600 TXCY 77590 4875 A2
E 19th St
600 HOUS 77008 3823 D5
700 HOUS 77009 3823 D5
W 19th St
100 HOUS 77008 3823 A5
20th Av N
10 TXCY 77590 4875 E3
2500 TXCY 77590 4874 E3
20th St
- HMPD 77445 3097 E1
- HOUS 77092 3822 A5
- WlrC 77445 3097 E2
10 GLSN 77550 5109 B2
10 GLSN 77554 5109 B2
100 GlsC 77539 4635 E4
300 HMPD 77445 2952 E7
20th St
300 HMPD 77445 2953 A6
800 GlsC 77650 4879 B7
2200 DKSN 77539 4753 C1
2200 GlsC 77539 4753 D1
2600 DKSN 77539 4632 D7
2600 GlsC 77539 4632 D7
3400 LGCY 77539 4632 E7
4300 GlsC 77518 4634 C4
4500 GlsC 77539 4634 C4
4900 GlsC 77539 4633 C7
5400 TXCY 77539 4633 C7
9400 HOUS 77034 4378 A1
12100 STFE 77510 4987 B1
20th St N
3600 TXCY 77590 4875 A1
20th St S
10 TXCY 77590 4875 A6
E 20th St
100 HOUS 77008 3823 D5
700 HOUS 77009 3823 E5
S 20th St
1200 GlsC 77650 4879 A6
W 20th St
100 HOUS 77008 3823 A5
1400 HOUS 77008 3822 E5
W 21st
100 HOUS 77008 3823 D5
21st Av N
100 TXCY 77590 4875 D3
2700 TXCY 77590 4874 E3
21st St
- HMPD 77445 3097 E1
- WlrC 77445 3097 E2
100 GlsC 77539 4635 E4
500 HMPD 77445 2952 E7
1300 GlsC 77650 4879 A6
2200 DKSN 77539 4753 D1
2900 GlsC 77539 4632 D7
9700 HOUS 77034 4378 A1
11900 STFE 77510 4987 B1
21st St N
3600 TXCY 77590 4875 A2
4800 GlsC 77539 4634 C5
21st St S
10 TXCY 77590 4875 A7
E 21st St
700 HOUS 77008 3823 D5
700 HOUS 77009 3823 D5
4200 GlsC 77539 4633 B7
4400 DKSN 77539 4633 B7
W 21st St
200 HOUS 77008 3823 A5
1300 HOUS 77008 3822 E5
22nd Av N
10 TXCY 77590 4875 D3
2700 TXCY 77590 4874 E3
22nd St
100 GlsC 77539 4635 E4
400 HMPD 77445 2952 E7
1300 GlsC 77650 4879 A5
2200 DKSN 77539 4753 D1
2600 GlsC 77539 4753 D1
2600 HMPD 77445 3097 E2
2800 GlsC 77539 4632 D7
11800 STFE 77510 4987 B2
22nd St E
4800 DKSN 77539 4633 B7
22nd St N
3600 TXCY 77590 4875 A1
E 22nd St
700 HOUS 77008 3823 E4
700 HOUS 77009 3823 E4
9700 HOUS 77034 4377 E2
W 22nd St
200 HOUS 77008 3823 A5
1300 HOUS 77008 3822 E5
23rd Av N
200 TXCY 77590 4875 D3
2900 TXCY 77590 4874 E3
23rd St
100 GlsC 77539 4635 D5
200 HMPD 77445 3097 E1
1000 HMPD 77445 2952 E7
1300 GlsC 77650 4879 A5
2200 DKSN 77539 4753 D1
2600 GlsC 77539 4753 D1
3000 GlsC 77539 4632 E7
11700 STFE 77510 4987 B2
23rd St N
900 TXCY 77590 4875 A4
23rd St S
10 TXCY 77590 4875 A6
E 23rd St
100 HOUS 77008 3823 D4
900 HOUS 77009 3823 E4
1100 HOUS 77009 3824 C2
3500 GlsC 77539 4632 E7
4600 DKSN 77539 4633 B7
4600 GlsC 77539 4633 B7
9700 HOUS 77034 4377 E1
N 23rd St
2900 LPRT 77571 4251 A2
W 23rd St
200 HOUS 77008 3823 C4
1300 HOUS 77008 3822 E4
23rd 1/2 St
100 GlsC 77539 4635 E4
24th Av N
100 TXCY 77590 4875 D3
24th Rd
3000 LPRT 77571 4251 A3
24th St
100 GlsC 77539 4635 D5
100 GLSN 77550 5109 B4
200 HMPD 77445 2952 E7
900 HMPD 77445 3097 E1
1300 GlsC 77650 4879 A5
2200 DKSN 77539 4753 D1
2800 WlrC 77445 3097 E2
2900 GlsC 77539 4753 D1
3000 DKSN 77539 4632 E7
3100 GlsC 77539 4632 E7
3900 GlsC 77539 4633 A6
11800 STFE 77510 4987 B2
12700 STFE 77510 4986 E2
13400 GlsC 77510 4986 D2
13600 GlsC 77517 4986 C2
13600 HTCK 77517 4986 C2
24th St E
4400 DKSN 77539 4633 B7
4400 GlsC 77539 4633 B7
24th St N
- TXCY 77590 4875 A2
24th St S
200 TXCY 77590 4875 A6
E 24th St
300 HOUS 77008 3823 D4
E 24th St
700 HOUS 77009 3823 D4
1100 HOUS 77009 3824 A4
W 24th St
200 HOUS 77008 3823 A4
1300 HOUS 77008 3822 E4
24th 1/2 St
100 GlsC 77539 4635 D4
25th Av N
- TXCY 77591 4874 A3
100 TXCY 77590 4875 A3
2500 TXCY 77590 4874 A3
8100 TXCY 77591 4873 D3
25th Av N LP-197
800 TXCY 77590 4875 A3
2500 TXCY 77590 4874 E3
25th St
- HMPD 77445 3097 E2
100 GlsC 77539 4635 C7
1200 GlsC 77650 4879 B5
1400 GlsC 77539 4756 C1
1400 TXCY 77539 4635 C7
1400 TXCY 77539 4756 C1
2400 DKSN 77539 4753 D1
2500 HMPD 77445 2952 E6
2600 GlsC 77539 4753 D1
11700 STFE 77510 4987 B2
25th St E
4200 DKSN 77539 4633 B7
4200 GlsC 77539 4633 B7
25th St S
- TXCY 77590 4875 A6
E 25th St
100 HOUS 77008 3823 D4
700 HOUS 77009 3823 E4
3300 DKSN 77539 4632 E7
3300 GlsC 77539 4632 E7
N 25th St
10 TXCY 77590 4875 A4
200 HMPD 77445 3097 E2
2000 TXCY 77590 4874 E3
S 25th St
3000 LPRT 77571 4251 A3
W 25th St
200 HOUS 77008 3823 A4
1300 HOUS 77008 3822 D4
25th 1/2 St
1200 GlsC 77650 4879 B5
25th 1/2 St N
2400 TXCY 77590 4874 E3
26th Av N
1800 TXCY 77590 4875 A3
2600 TXCY 77590 4874 E3
26th St
- STFE 77510 4987 A2
200 GlsC 77539 4635 C4
200 GLSN 77550 5109 B4
1000 TXCY 77539 4635 B6
1200 GlsC 77650 4879 B5
2200 DKSN 77539 4753 D1
3100 GlsC 77539 4753 E1
26th St E
4400 DKSN 77539 4633 B7
26th St N
2600 TXCY 77590 4874 E2
26th St S
100 TXCY 77590 4874 E6
E 26th St
100 HOUS 77008 3823 D4
1100 HOUS 77009 3823 E4
1200 HOUS 77009 3824 A4
W 26th St
200 HOUS 77008 3823 A4
1300 HOUS 77008 3822 E4
26th 1/2 St
1200 GlsC 77650 4879 B5
12800 GlsC 77510 4986 E3
27
- HOUS 77029 3965 E4
27th Av N
1800 TXCY 77590 4875 B2
2400 TXCY 77590 4874 E3
27th St
200 GlsC 77539 4635 B5
300 GLSN 77550 5109 B5
1200 GlsC 77650 4879 B5
1600 TXCY 77539 4635 B7
1800 TXCY 77539 4756 A1
2200 DKSN 77539 4753 D1
2600 GlsC 77539 4753 D1
10200 STFE 77510 4987 E3
10200 STFE 77510 4988 A3
27th St E
4000 GlsC 77539 4633 A7
4800 DKSN 77539 4633 B7
27th St N
2000 TXCY 77590 4874 E3
27th St S
10 TXCY 77590 4874 E7
E 27th St
100 HOUS 77008 3823 D4
1100 HOUS 77009 3823 E4
1200 HOUS 77009 3824 A4
W 27th St
200 HOUS 77008 3823 B4
1500 HOUS 77008 3822 E4
27th 1/2 St
1200 GlsC 77650 4879 C5
W 28th
1300 HOUS 77008 3822 E4
1300 HOUS 77008 3823 A4
28th Av N
1800 TXCY 77590 4875 A2
2400 TXCY 77590 4874 E2
28th St
100 GLSN 77550 5109 B4
400 GlsC 77539 4635 B5
1200 GlsC 77650 4879 C5
1500 TXCY 77539 4635 A7
2200 DKSN 77539 4753 D2
2600 GlsC 77539 4753 D2
3800 DKSN 77539 4633 A7
3800 GlsC 77539 4633 A7
4300 DKSN 77539 4754 A1
10600 STFE 77510 4987 D3
12000 GlsC 77510 4987 B3
12800 GlsC 77510 4986 E3
13700 GlsC 77517 4986 B3
14300 HTCK 77517 4986 B3
28th St E
4400 DKSN 77539 4754 B1
28th St N
- TXCY 77590 4874 E2
28th St S
300 TXCY 77590 4874 E6
E 28th St
100 HOUS 77008 3823 D4
1000 HOUS 77009 3823 E4
E 28th St
1200 HOUS 77009 3824 A4
W 28th St
200 HOUS 77008 3823 B4
28th 1/2 St
800 GlsC 77539 4635 A5
1200 GlsC 77650 4879 C4
28th 1/2 St S
10 TXCY 77590 4874 D6
29th Av N
400 TXCY 77590 4875 D2
2500 TXCY 77590 4874 E2
29th St
- GLSN 77554 5109 A1
700 GlsC 77539 4635 A5
1000 TXCY 77539 4635 A7
1200 GlsC 77650 4879 C4
1700 TXCY 77539 4634 E7
1700 TXCY 77539 4755 E2
2300 DKSN 77539 4753 D2
2600 GlsC 77539 4753 E1
3500 DKSN 77539 4754 A1
3600 DKSN 77539 4633 A7
11900 GlsC 77510 4987 B4
29th St FM-517
1000 GlsC 77539 4635 A6
1000 TXCY 77539 4635 A7
1700 TXCY 77539 4634 E7
1700 TXCY 77539 4755 E1
29th St E
4400 DKSN 77539 4754 B1
29th St N
10 TXCY 77590 4874 E2
29th St S
100 TXCY 77590 4874 E7
E 29th St
300 HOUS 77008 3823 D4
1000 HOUS 77009 3823 E4
1200 HOUS 77009 3824 A4
29th 1/2 St
4000 TXCY 77539 4755 E1
30th Av N
2300 TXCY 77590 4875 A2
2500 TXCY 77590 4874 E2
11000 TXCY 77591 4872 C3
30th St
200 GLSN 77550 5109 A3
1600 TXCY 77539 4634 E7
1900 TXCY 77539 4755 E1
2300 DKSN 77539 4753 E2
2600 GlsC 77539 4753 E1
13500 GlsC 77510 4986 E4
30th St E
4200 DKSN 77539 4754 B1
30th St N
1600 TXCY 77590 4874 E4
30th St S
100 TXCY 77590 4874 E6
E 30th St
200 HOUS 77018 3823 D3
N 30th St
3300 DKSN 77539 4754 A1
W 30th St
200 HOUS 77018 3823 B3
1200 HOUS 77018 3822 E3
31st Av N
- TXCY 77590 4874 D2
2300 TXCY 77590 4875 A2
10900 TXCY 77591 4872 C3
31st St
- GlsC 77539 4634 D7
- TXCY 77539 4634 D7
300 GLSN 77550 5109 A3
31st St E
4300 DKSN 77539 4754 B1
31st St N
10 TXCY 77590 4874 D6
31st St S
10 TXCY 77590 4874 D7
E 31st St
200 HOUS 77018 3823 D3
500 HOUS 77022 3823 D3
1300 HOUS 77022 3824 A3
W 31st St
700 HOUS 77018 3823 B3
1300 HOUS 77018 3822 E3
31st 1/2 St N
1200 TXCY 77590 4874 D4
E 31st 1/2 St
100 HOUS 77018 3823 D3
32nd Av N
2300 TXCY 77590 4875 A2
2500 TXCY 77590 4874 E2
N 32nd Av N
10000 TXCY 77591 4872 C2
32nd St
300 GLSN 77550 5109 A3
10900 GlsC 77510 4987 C5
10900 HTCK 77563 4987 E5
12000 TXCY 77539 4755 D1
12800 GlsC 77510 4986 E5
32nd St E
4200 DKSN 77539 4754 B1
32nd St N
- TXCY 77590 4874 D4
E 32nd St
100 HOUS 77018 3823 D3
500 HOUS 77022 3823 D3
W 32nd St
700 HOUS 77018 3823 B3
32nd 1/2 St
5000 DKSN 77539 4754 C1
11100 GlsC 77510 4987 D5
E 32nd 1/2 St
600 HOUS 77022 3823 E3
1300 HOUS 77022 3824 A3
33rd Av N
2300 TXCY 77590 4875 A2
2500 TXCY 77590 4874 E2
33rd St
100 GLSN 77550 5109 B6
10900 GlsC 77510 4987 E6
13300 GlsC 77510 4986 E7
13300 GlsC 77517 4986 E7
33rd St E
4400 DKSN 77539 4754 B1
33rd St N
- TXCY 77590 4874 D4
33rd St S
10 TXCY 77590 4874 D7
E 33rd St
100 HOUS 77018 3823 D3
500 HOUS 77022 3823 D3
1300 HOUS 77022 3824 A3
W 33rd St
200 HOUS 77018 3823 C3
33rd 1/2 St
12700 GlsC 77510 4987 A7

Houston Street Index

STREET Block	City	ZIP	Map#	Grid
34th Av N				
1700	TXCY	77590	4875	A2
2400	TXCY	77590	4874	E2
34th St				
600	GLSN	77550	5109	A4
34th St E				
4200	DKSN	77539	4754	B1
34th St N				
1300	TXCY	77590	4874	C3
34th St S				
10	TXCY	77590	4874	D7
E 34th St				
100	HOUS	77018	3823	D3
1200	HOUS	77022	3823	E3
1300	HOUS	77022	3824	A3
W 34th St				
-	HOUS	77055	3821	C3
200	HOUS	77018	3823	A3
1400	HOUS	77018	3822	E3
3400	HOUS	77092	3822	C3
4900	HOUS	77092	3821	D3
W 34th 1/2 St				
1400	HOUS	77018	3822	E3
1400	HOUS	77018	3823	A3
35th Av N				
2300	TXCY	77590	4875	A2
2500	TXCY	77590	4874	E2
35th St				
500	GLSN	77550	5109	A6
35th St E				
4400	DKSN	77539	4754	B1
35th St N				
10	TXCY	77590	4874	C6
35th St S				
10	TXCY	77590	4874	C7
E 35th St				
200	HOUS	77018	3823	D3
400	HOUS	77022	3823	D3
1300	HOUS	77022	3824	A3
W 35th St				
900	HOUS	77018	3823	A3
36th Av N				
1600	TXCY	77590	4875	A2
2400	TXCY	77590	4874	E2
36th St				
500	GLSN	77550	5108	E3
700	GLSN	77550	5109	A4
36th St E				
4400	DKSN	77539	4754	B2
36th St N				
1700	TXCY	77590	4874	C4
E 36th St				
100	HOUS	77018	3823	D3
600	HOUS	77022	3823	E3
1300	HOUS	77022	3824	A3
37th Av N				
2300	TXCY	77590	4875	A1
2500	TXCY	77590	4874	E1
37th St				
10	GLSN	77551	5108	E3
100	GLSN	77550	5108	E3
1000	GLSN	77550	5109	A4
37th St E				
5000	DKSN	77539	4754	C2
E 37th St				
100	HOUS	77018	3823	D3
300	HOUS	77022	3823	D3
38th Av N				
2300	TXCY	77590	4875	A1
2400	TXCY	77590	4874	E1
38th St				
-	HOUS	77571	4112	C7
-	HOUS	77571	4252	C1
-	MRGP	77571	4112	C7
-	MRGP	77571	4252	C1
600	GLSN	77550	5108	E4
1300	GLSN	77550	5109	A5
38th St E				
4200	DKSN	77539	4754	B2
E 38th St				
100	HOUS	77018	3823	D3
700	HOUS	77022	3823	E2
W 38th St				
200	HOUS	77018	3823	C2
39th Av N				
2400	TXCY	77590	4874	E1
2400	TXCY	77590	4875	A1
39th St				
-	HOUS	77571	4252	C1
39th St E				
4600	DKSN	77539	4754	B2
E 39th St				
100	HOUS	77018	3823	D2
700	HOUS	77022	3823	E2
W 39th St				
700	HOUS	77018	3823	B2
40th Av N				
2500	TXCY	77590	4874	E1
40th St				
-	HOUS	77571	4252	D1
700	GLSN	77550	5108	E5
2300	GLSN	77550	5109	A6
40th St E				
4400	DKSN	77539	4754	B2
E 40th St				
300	HOUS	77018	3823	D2
300	HOUS	77022	3823	E2
1300	HOUS	77022	3824	A2
E 40th 1/2 St				
300	HOUS	77018	3823	D2
300	HOUS	77022	3823	D2
41st Av N				
1900	TXCY	77590	4875	A1
41st St				
-	DKSN	77539	4752	E6
-	DKSN	77539	4753	A5
-	DKSN	77539	4754	D2
-	GLSN	77550	5108	E4
-	LGCY	77539	4752	E6
-	LGCY	77539	4753	A5
-	TXCY	77539	4754	D2
-	TXCY	77539	4755	C1
41st St FM-517				
-	DKSN	77539	4752	E6
-	DKSN	77539	4753	A5
-	DKSN	77539	4754	D2
-	LGCY	77539	4752	E6
-	LGCY	77539	4753	A5
-	TXCY	77539	4754	D2
-	TXCY	77539	4755	C1
E 41st St				
100	HOUS	77018	3823	D2
300	HOUS	77022	3823	D2
W 41st St				
700	HOUS	77018	3823	A2
900	HOUS	77018	3822	E2
42nd Av N				
1800	TXCY	77590	4875	A1
42nd St				
500	GLSN	77550	5108	E4
2800	GLSN	77550	5109	A6
42nd St E				
4200	DKSN	77539	4754	B2
E 42nd St				
100	HOUS	77018	3823	D2
300	HOUS	77022	3823	D2
W 42nd St				
700	HOUS	77018	3823	A2
1000	HOUS	77018	3822	E2
E 42nd 1/2 St				
200	HOUS	77018	3823	D2
43rd St				
-	HOUS	77571	4252	D1
500	GLSN	77550	5108	E6
4300	DKSN	77539	4754	B3
E 43rd St				
100	HOUS	77018	3823	D2
300	HOUS	77022	3823	D2
W 43rd St				
700	HOUS	77018	3823	A2
1000	HOUS	77018	3822	E1
4300	HOUS	77092	3822	B1
5100	HOUS	77092	3821	C1
7100	HOUS	77040	3821	C1
44th St				
400	GLSN	77550	5108	D4
2300	DKSN	77539	4753	E3
4600	DKSN	77539	4754	B3
E 44th St				
100	HOUS	77018	3823	D2
100	HOUS	77022	3823	D2
W 44th St				
200	HOUS	77018	3823	C2
45th St				
500	GLSN	77550	5108	D4
1000	GLSN	77551	5108	D5
2200	DKSN	77539	4753	E3
2800	DKSN	77539	4754	A3
E 45th St				
100	HOUS	77018	3823	D2
100	HOUS	77022	3823	D2
46th St				
400	GLSN	77550	5108	D4
400	GLSN	77551	5108	D4
2200	DKSN	77539	4754	A3
47th St				
1000	GLSN	77551	5108	D4
2300	DKSN	77539	4754	A3
48th St				
1000	GLSN	77551	5108	D6
2800	DKSN	77539	4754	A3
49th St				
1000	GLSN	77551	5108	D5
2700	DKSN	77539	4754	A3
50th St				
900	GLSN	77551	5108	D6
51st St				
500	GLSN	77550	5108	C4
600	GLSN	77551	5108	C4
52nd St				
900	GLSN	77551	5108	C4
54th St				
500	GLSN	77551	5108	C5
55th St				
1000	GLSN	77551	5108	C6
56th St				
1000	GLSN	77551	5108	C5
57th St				
1000	GLSN	77551	5108	C5
3300	GLSN	77551	5222	D1
59th St				
300	GLSN	77551	5108	B4
3100	GLSN	77551	5222	D1
60th St				
800	GLSN	77551	5108	B5
61st St				
400	GLSN	77551	5108	B6
2800	GLSN	77551	5222	C1
61st St SPR-342				
1000	GLSN	77551	5108	B6
2800	GLSN	77551	5222	C1
62nd St				
1000	GLSN	77551	5108	B5
63rd St				
1000	GLSN	77551	5108	B5
64th St				
1000	GLSN	77551	5108	B5
65th St				
100	GLSN	77554	5108	A4
100	HOUS	77011	3964	D6
1500	GLSN	77551	5108	B7
S 65th St				
100	HOUS	77011	3964	D7
66th St				
100	HOUS	77011	3964	D6
S 66th St				
-	HOUS	77011	4104	D1
-	HOUS	77023	4104	D1
100	HOUS	77011	3964	D7
67th St				
100	GLSN	77554	5107	E4
2000	GLSN	77551	5108	B7
68th St				
1600	GLSN	77551	5108	A6
69th St				
1500	GLSN	77551	5108	B7
2300	HOUS	77011	3965	A5
2500	HOUS	77020	3965	A5
3000	GLSN	77551	5222	B1
69th St US-90 ALT				
-	HOUS	77020	3965	A5
2200	HOUS	77011	3965	A5
S 69th St				
-	HOUS	77023	4104	E1
100	HOUS	77011	3964	E7
300	HOUS	77023	3964	E7
S 69th St US-90 ALT				
-	HOUS	77023	4104	E1
100	HOUS	77011	3964	E7
300	HOUS	77023	3964	E7
70th St				
100	HOUS	77011	3964	E7
1300	HOUS	77011	3965	A6
N 70th St				
2000	HOUS	77011	3965	A5
S 70th St				
100	HOUS	77011	3964	E7
71st St				
-	GLSN	77551	5107	E5
800	HOUS	77011	3965	A6
2000	GLSN	77551	5108	A7
S 71st St				
100	HOUS	77011	3964	E7
100	HOUS	77011	3965	A7
72nd St				
100	HOUS	77011	3965	A7
2000	GLSN	77551	5108	A7
S 72nd St				
100	HOUS	77011	3965	A7
200	HOUS	77011	4105	A1
73rd St				
100	HOUS	77011	3965	A7
2000	GLSN	77551	5108	A7
74th St				
100	HOUS	77011	3965	A7
2000	GLSN	77551	5108	A7
S 74th St				
100	HOUS	77011	3965	C7
100	HOUS	77011	4105	A2
S 74th 1/2 St				
200	HOUS	77011	4105	A2
75th St				
200	HOUS	77011	3965	B7
200	HOUS	77012	3965	A7
3100	GLSN	77551	5222	B2
S 75th St				
100	HOUS	77011	4105	A1
100	HOUS	77012	4105	A1
500	HOUS	77023	4105	A3
76th St				
100	HOUS	77012	3965	B7
100	HOUS	77012	4105	B1
1500	HOUS	77011	3965	B6
S 76th St				
700	HOUS	77023	4105	A3
77th St				
100	GLSN	77554	5107	D5
100	HOUS	77012	4105	B1
200	HOUS	77012	3965	B7
3100	GLSN	77551	5222	B2
S 77th St				
100	HOUS	77012	4105	B1
700	HOUS	77023	4105	B3
78th St				
100	HOUS	77012	4105	B1
500	HOUS	77012	3965	B7
S 78th St				
100	HOUS	77012	4105	B1
79th St				
-	GLSN	77554	5107	D4
100	HOUS	77012	4105	B1
600	HOUS	77012	3965	C7
3600	GLSN	77551	5222	A2
N 79th St				
800	HOUS	77012	3965	C7
S 79th St				
100	HOUS	77012	4105	B1
80th St				
100	HOUS	77012	4105	C1
500	HOUS	77012	3965	C7
3200	GLSN	77551	5222	A2
S 80th St				
100	HOUS	77012	4105	C2
81st St				
400	GLSN	77554	5107	D4
2900	GLSN	77551	5222	A2
2900	GLSN	77554	5222	A2
83rd St				
2200	GLSN	77554	5221	E1
3100	GLSN	77554	5222	A2
85th St				
3500	GLSN	77554	5222	A3
87th St				
3500	GLSN	77554	5221	E3
89th St				
1000	GLSN	77554	5107	C6
3500	GLSN	77554	5221	E3
89th 1/2 St				
1000	GLSN	77554	5107	C6
91st St				
700	GLSN	77554	5107	C6
92nd St				
300	HOUS	77012	4105	E2
93rd St				
100	GLSN	77554	5107	B6
300	HOUS	77012	4105	E2
95th St				
500	HOUS	77012	4106	A3
96th St				
600	HOUS	77012	4106	A3
97th St				
1000	HOUS	77012	4106	A3
99th St				
2200	GLSN	77554	5221	C3
103rd St				
1100	GLSN	77554	5107	B7
1100	GLSN	77554	5221	B1
110th St N				
3000	TXCY	77591	4872	C2
111th St N				
3200	TXCY	77591	4872	C2
112th St N				
3000	TXCY	77591	4872	C3
4874 Rd				
10	LbyC	77535	3413	D5
22745 Dr				
19400	MtgC	77365	2972	A3

Airports

FEATURE NAME Address City ZIP Code	MAP#	GRID
Alvin Airpark, BzaC	4866	B2
Baytown, HarC	3834	B7
David Wayne Hooks Memorial, HarC	3110	D4
Ellington Field, HOUS	4379	B4
Flyin' B, BzaC	4500	A6
George Bush Intercontinental-Houston, HOUS	3405	B3
Houston Airpark, BzaC	4627	D2
Houston Southwest, ARLA	4622	E4
Lane Airpark, FBnC	4615	C2
La Porte Municipal, LPRT	4250	E2
Lone Star Executive, CNRO	2238	E6
Pearland Regional, BzaC	4628	C2
Polly Ranch Airstrip, FRDW	4630	A4
Scholes International at Galveston, GLSN	5221	E2
Skyway Manor, PRLD	4502	B4
Sugar Land Regional, SGLD	4367	C1
Weiser, HarC	3538	D1
Weiser Air Park, HarC	3538	D1
Westheimer Air Park, FBnC	4093	A6
West Houston, HarC	3816	E4
William P Hobby, HOUS	4245	C4
Williams, MtgC	2825	B5
Wolfe Air Park, MNVL	4626	C7

Beaches, Harbors & Water Rec

FEATURE NAME Address City ZIP Code	MAP#	GRID
Allen's Landing, HOUS	3963	C3
Anchorage Apartments & Marina, LGCY	4508	C6
Bal Harbor Marina, NSUB	4508	C4
Bayland Park Marina, BYTN	4112	C3
BJ's Marina, HOUS	3120	E4
Blue Dolphin Yachting Center, SEBK	4509	D3
Bolivar Beach, GlsC	4879	E6
Clear Lake Marine Center, ELGO	4508	E2
East Beach, GLSN	5109	B5
East Beach, GLSN	4995	D6
El Lago Marina, ELGO	4508	E2
Galveston Yacht Basin Marina, GLSN	5109	D1
Galveston Yacht Club Marina, GLSN	5109	D1
Good Times Marina, HarC	3551	C7
Houston Yacht Club, SRAC	4383	B2
Kemah Boardwalk Marina, KMAH	4509	E5
Lakeside Yachting Center, SEBK	4509	C3
Lakewood Yacht Club, SEBK	4509	C3
Landing Marina, ELGO	4508	E2
Landings Apartments & Marina, GLSN	5108	A7
Marina Bay, ELGO	4509	A2
Marina Del Oro, KMAH	4510	A7
Marina Del Sol, LGCY	4508	E5
Palm Beach at Moody Gardens, GLSN	5108	A7
Parkside Marina, PASD	4508	D2
Payco Marina, GLSN	5107	C5
Pirates Beach Marina, GLSN	5332	C2
Poretto Beach, GLSN	5109	D3
Portofino Harbour Marina, GlsC	4509	D5
Ray's Bait Camp & Marina, TXCY	4875	A1
Riverside Inn Marina, HarC	3831	B5
South Shore Harbour Marina, LGCY	4508	C5
Stewart Beach Park, GLSN	5109	E3
Tackle Box Storage & Marina, TXCY	4875	B1
Teakwood Marina, TKIS	5106	D3
Texas City Dike, TXCY	4876	D6
Waterford Harbor Yacht Club Marina, LGCY	4509	A5
Watergate Yachting Center Marina, CRLS	4509	B5
West Bay Marina at Sea Isle, GLSN	5441	B4
West Beach, GLSN	5441	B5
Yacht Harbor, SEBK	4509	B3

Buildings

FEATURE NAME Address City ZIP Code	MAP#	GRID
Air Products Manufacturing Corporation PASD, 77506	4107	C3
Amoco Oil Company 2401 5th Av S, TXCY, 77590	4875	A7
Arco Choate Rd, PASD, 77507	4382	A1
Arco Chemical HarC, 77530	3830	D2
Arco Petrolite Bay Park Rd, HarC, 77507	4250	D5
Baroid Corporation 3000 N Sam Houston Pkwy E, HOUS, 77032	3404	E7
Bayer Corporation 8500 W Bay Rd, CmbC, 77520	3974	B3
Big Three Industries Incorporation HarC, 77530	3830	B3
Brittmoore Tanner Business Park Tanner Rd, HarC, 77041	3680	A6
Brown & Root 14034 Industrial Rd, HOUS, 77015	3967	E5
Cameron Iron Works Incorporated 1000 Silber Rd, HOUS, 77055	3821	E7
Carpenter Chemical Choate Rd, PASD, 77507	4382	A2
Cedar Crossing Industrial Park CmbC, 77520	4114	C3
Central Industrial Park Airport Blvd, HOUS, 77061	4245	A5
Champion International HarC, 77044	3691	C1
Chase Bank Building 712 Main St, HOUS, 77002	3963	C4
Chase Tower 600 Travis St, HOUS, 77002	3963	C4
Chevron Chemicals 9500 East Freeway Frontage Rd, HarC, 77521	3835	A1
Colex Industrial Park PASD, 77506	4107	E3
Crown Central Petroleum Corporation 111 Crown Rd, HOUS, 77506	4107	A2
Dixie Chemical Bay Area Blvd, PASD, 77507	4382	A3
Dow Chemical 400 W Sam Houston Pkwy S, HOUS, 77042	3958	D4
DuPont Strang Rd, HarC, 77571	4111	B5
El Paso Products Underwood Rd, PASD, 77507	4250	A6
Ethyl Industrial Park PASD, 77503	3968	A7
Exxon 5000 Bayway Dr, BYTN, 77520	3971	D7
Exxon Building 800 Bell St, HOUS, 77002	3963	B5
Exxon Pipeline Industrial Park PASD, 77503	4108	B3
GATX Industrial Park PASD, 77506	4107	D2
Georgia Pacific Industrial District PASD, 77503	4108	C1
Goodyear Bay Area Blvd, HarC, 77507	4251	A5
Goodyear West Rd, HOUS, 77017	4106	A4
Greens Port Industrial Park HarC, 77015	3967	C4
Hewlett-Packard 20555 Tomball Pkwy, HarC, 77070	3255	B7
Houston Light & Power Robinson Plant Avenue N, GlsC, 77539	4634	D6
Houston Port Authority HOUS, 77015	3969	D6
Houston Port Authority HOUS, 77503	3968	B6
Houston Port Authority HOUS, 77520	4111	D1
Houston Port Authority HOUS, 77571	4112	C7
Hydrill Coporation 3300 N Sam Houston Pkwy E, HOUS, 77032	3405	A7
ICI Americas Incorporated Underwood Rd, PASD, 77507	4250	B6
Jindal Steel 5200 E McKinney Rd, CmbC, 77520	4114	D5
Kaneka Texas Coporation Underwood Rd, PASD, 77507	4250	A7
Lubrizol Bay Area Blvd, HarC, 77507	4251	A5
Lyondell Petrochemical Corporation 8280 Sheldon Rd, HarC, 77049	3830	A1
Marathon Industrial Park PASD, 77506	4108	A2
Mobil Chemical 9822 La Porte Freeway Frontage, HOUS, 77017	4106	A4
Oak Park at Westchase 5850 W Sam Houston Pkwy S, HOUS, 77072	4098	D4
Oiltanking Pasadena PASD, 77506	4107	D3
One Shell Plaza 910 Louisiana St, HOUS, 77002	3963	B4
Pennzoil Place 700 Milam St, HOUS, 77002	3963	C4
Phillips Industrial Park PASD, 77506	4107	E1
Port of Houston Industrial Complex HOUS, 77029	3965	C6
Rohm & Haas 1900 Tidal Rd, DRPK, 77536	3969	D7
Shell Industrial Park PASD, 77503	4108	D3
Specialty Sand Company 16601 Garrett Rd, HarC, 77044	3551	A7
Tenneco Industrial Park PASD, 77503	4108	C1
Texas City Industrial Complex TXCY, 77590	4875	D7
Texas Eastern Transmission Corporation 4227 Decker Dr, BYTN, 77520	3971	E3
Toshiba International Corporation 13131 W Little York Rd, HarC, 77041	3679	C4
Union Carbide Corporation TXCY, 77590	4991	B2
Vopak Terminals Deer Park 2759 Battleground Rd, HarC, 77571	3970	A6
Wells Fargo Plaza 1000 Louisiana St, HOUS, 77002	3963	B4

Buildings - Governmental

FEATURE NAME Address City ZIP Code	MAP#	GRID
Alvin City Hall 216 W Sealy St, ALVN, 77511	4867	B1
Alvin Municipal Court 216 W Sealy St, ALVN, 77511	4867	C1
Arcola City Hall ARLA, 77583	4623	A3
Australian Consulate 5757 Woodway Dr, HOUS, 77057	3960	D4
Baytown City Hall 2401 Market St, BYTN, 77520	4112	B1
Baytown Civic Center Civic Cir, BYTN, 77520	4112	B1
Baytown Municipal Court 3200 N Main St, BYTN, 77521	3973	A4
Bellaire City Hall 7008 S Rice Av, BLAR, 77401	4100	E5
Bolivian Consulate General 800 Wilcrest Dr, HOUS, 77077	3958	C5
Brazil Consulate 1233 W Loop Frwy S, HOUS, 77027	3961	B4
Brazoria County Court Annex 7313 Corporate Dr, MNVL, 77578	4746	B1
Brazoria County Justice Court 3801 E Pear St, PRLD, 77581	4503	C3
Brazoria County Municipal Court 3519 Liberty Dr, PRLD, 77581	4504	A5
British Consulate General 1000 Louisiana St, HOUS, 77002	3963	B4
Brookside Village Hall 6243 Brookside Rd, BKVL, 77581	4375	D6
Bunker Hill Village Hall 11977 Memorial Dr, BKHV, 77024	3959	B4
Bunker Hill Village Municipal Court 11977 Memorial Dr, BKHV, 77024	3959	B4
Chile Consulate General 1360 S Post Oak Ln, HOUS, 77056	3961	A5
Clear Lake Shores City Hall 931 Cedar Rd, CRLS, 77565	4509	C5
Conroe City Hall 300 W Davis St, CNRO, 77301	2384	A5
Consulado General of Nicaragua 8989 Westheimer Rd, HOUS, 77063	3959	D7
Consulate General of Belgium 2009 Lubbock St, HOUS, 77007	3963	A3
Consulate General of Costa Rica 3000 Wilcrest Dr, HOUS, 77082	4098	C1
Consulate General of Ecuador 4200 Westheimer Rd, HOUS, 77027	3961	B6
Consulate Gen People's Republic of China 3050 Post Oak Blvd, HOUS, 77056	3961	A7
Consulate of Haiti 6310 Auden St, SSPL, 77005	4101	D3
Consulate of Lebanon 2400 Augusta Dr, HOUS, 77057	3960	D7
Courthouse-Galena Park 1500 Keene St, GNPK, 77547	3966	C6
Criminal Justice Center San Jacinto St, HOUS, 77002	3963	D4
Danish Consulate of Houston 4545 Post Oak Pl Dr, HOUS, 77027	3961	C5
Deer Park City Hall 710 E San Augustine St, DRPK, 77536	4109	C6
Dickinson City Hall DKSN, 77539	4754	A3
Dickinson Municipal Court DKSN, 77539	4754	A3
El Lago City Hall 98 Lakeshore Dr, ELGO, 77586	4509	A2
El Lago Municipal Court 3812 NASA Pkwy, ELGO, 77586	4509	A2
El Salvador Consulate 6420 Hillcroft Av, HOUS, 77074	4100	B4
Federal Bureau of Investigation 2500 E TC Jester Blvd, HOUS, 77008	3822	D4
Fort Bend County District Court 309 S 4th St, RHMD, 77469	4491	E1
Fort Bend County Justice Court 118 Legion Ln, RHMD, 77469	4492	A2
Fort Bend County Justice Court 13401 Southwest Frwy, SGLD, 77478	4368	E2
Fort Bend County Municipal Court 1522 Texas Pkwy, MSCY, 77489	4370	C4
Fort Bend County Municipal Court 309 S 4th St, RHMD, 77469	4491	E1
Fort Bend County Municipal Court 2110 4th St, RSBG, 77471	4490	E6
Fort Bend County Municipal Court 200 Matlage Wy, SGLD, 77478	4367	E3
Fort Bend County Municipal Court STAF, 77477	4369	E3
Fort Bend County Probate Court 309 S 4th St, RHMD, 77469	4491	E1
French Consulate General 777 S Post Oak Ln, HOUS, 77056	3961	A4
Friendswood City Hall 910 S Friendswood Dr, FRDW, 77546	4629	D1
Friendswood Municipal Court 910 S Friendswood Dr, FRDW, 77546	4629	D1
Galena Park City Hall 2000 Clinton Dr, GNPK, 77547	4106	B1
Galveston City Hall 823 Rosenberg St, GLSN, 77550	5109	B3
Galveston County Courthouse 722 Moody Av, GLSN, 77550	5109	C3
Galveston County Criminal Justice Center 600 59th St, GLSN, 77551	5108	B4
Galveston County Justice Court 624 S Friendswood Dr, FRDW, 77546	4629	C1
Galveston County Justice Court LGCY, 77573	4753	B1
Galveston County Municipal Court 931 Cedar Rd, CRLS, 77565	4509	C5
Galveston County Municipal Court 109 E Willowick Av, FRDW, 77546	4505	C7
Galveston County Municipal Court 102 W Walker St, LGCY, 77573	4632	A4
Galveston County North Courthouse 174 Calder Dr, LGCY, 77573	4631	D4
Greece Consulate General 520 Post Oak Blvd, HOUS, 77027	3961	B5
Guatemala Consulate General 3013 Fountain View Dr, HOUS, 77057	4100	D1
Harris County Civil Courts 301 Fannin St, HOUS, 77002	3963	C4
Harris County Court of Appeals 1307 San Jacinto St, HOUS, 77002	3963	C5
Harris County Justice Court 701 W Baker Rd, BYTN, 77521	3972	E2
Harris County Justice Court 16715 Clay Rd, HarC, 77084	3817	C1
Harris County Justice Court 6831 Cypresswood Dr, HarC, 77379	3256	E4
Harris County Justice Court 121 W Main St, HMBL, 77338	3262	D6
Harris County Justice Court 1001 SSgt Macario Garcia Dr, HOUS, 77011	3964	E6
Harris County Justice Court 5737 Cullen Blvd, HOUS, 77021	4103	E4
Harris County Justice Court 1646 Old Spanish Tr, HOUS, 77054	4102	C6
Harris County Justice Court 16603 Buccaneer Ln, HOUS, 77062	4507	B3
Harris County Justice Court 6000 Chimney Rock Rd, HOUS, 77081	4100	D3
Harris County Justice Court 7330 Spencer Hwy, PASD, 77505	4249	B3
Harris County Justice Court 107 Shaw Av, PASD, 77506	4107	A3
Harris County Municipal Court 5110 Jessamine St, BLAR, 77401	4100	E5
Harris County Municipal Court 8333 Katy Freeway Frontage Rd, HNCV, 77024	3960	C1
Harris County Municipal Court 1400 Lubbock St, HOUS, 77002	3963	B3
Harris County Municipal Court 1506 Andrews St, HOUS, 77019	3963	A4
Harris County Municipal Court 7745 San Felipe Dr, HOUS, 77063	3960	A5
Harris County Municipal Court 16501 Jersey Dr, JRSV, 77040	3680	C1
Harris County Municipal Court 10301 Market St Rd, JTCY, 77029	3966	B3
Harris County Municipal Court 910 Avenue C, KATY, 77493	3813	C7
Harris County Municipal Court 1800 NASA Pkwy, NSUB, 77058	4508	A4
Harris County Municipal Court 1114 Davis St, PASD, 77506	4107	C6
Harris County Municipal Court 801 Maplewood Rd, SHEH, 77381	2821	E1
Harris County Municipal Court 1018 Dallas St, SHUS, 77587	4246	C3
Harris County Municipal Court 1025 Campbell Rd, SPVL, 77055	3820	E7
Harris County Municipal Court 601 Shoreacres Blvd, SRAC, 77571	4382	E2
Harris County Municipal Court 6309 Edloe St, SSPL, 77005	4101	E3
Harris County Municipal Court 200 N Cherry St, TMBL, 77375	2964	B7
Harris County Municipal Court 311 Pennsylvania St, WEBS, 77598	4507	C7
Harris County Municipal Court 3800 University Blvd, WUNP, 77005	4101	D3
Hedwig Village Hall 955 Piney Point Rd, HDWV, 77024	3959	D1
Hempstead City Hall 1125 Austin St, HMPD, 77445	2953	B7
Hillcrest City Building 101 Riverside Dr, HLCS, 77511	4867	E5

FEATURE NAME Address City ZIP Code	MAP#	GRID
Hilshire Village Hall 8389 Westview Dr, HLSV, 77055	3821	B6
Hitchcock City Hall HTCK, 77563	4989	A4
Hitchcock Municipal Court HTCK, 77563	4989	A4
Honduras Consulate General 4151 Southwest Freeway Frontage, HOUS, 77027	4101	C1
Houston City Hall 900 Bagby St, HOUS, 77002	3963	B4
Houston Federal Detention Center 1200 Texas Av, HOUS, 77002	3963	C4
Humble City Hall 114 W Higgins St, HMBL, 77338	3262	D6
Humble Civic Center 8233 Will Clayton Pkwy, HMBL, 77338	3406	E1
Hunters Creek Village Hall 734 Brogden Rd, HNCV, 77024	3960	A1
India Consulate General 1990 Post Oak Blvd, HOUS, 77056	3961	A6
Indonesia Consulate 10900 Richmond Av, HOUS, 77042	4098	C1
Jacinto City City Hall 10301 Market St Rd, JTCY, 77029	3966	B3
Jamaica Beach City Hall 16628 San Luis Pass Rd, JMAB, 77554	5332	A6
Jamaica Beach Municipal Court 16628 San Luis Pass Rd, GLSN, 77554	5442	B1
Jersey Village Hall 16501 Jersey Dr, JRSV, 77040	3680	C1
Katy City Hall 910 Avenue C, KATY, 77493	3813	C7
Kemah City Hall KMAH, 77565	4509	E7
Kemah Municipal Court KMAH, 77565	4509	E6
Korean Consulate General 1990 Post Oak Blvd, HOUS, 77056	3961	A6
La Marque City Hall 1111 Bayou Rd, LMQU, 77568	4990	A1
La Marque City Municipal Court 1111 Bayou Rd, LMQU, 77568	4990	A1
La Porte City Hall 604 W Fairmont Pkwy, LPRT, 77571	4251	D4
La Porte Civic Center Rustic Gate Rd, LPRT, 77571	4250	B4
La Porte Muncipal Court 913 S 8th St, LPRT, 77571	4251	C4
League City City Hall 300 W Walker St, LGCY, 77573	4632	A4
League City Civic Center 400 W Walker St, LGCY, 77573	4631	E4
League City Municipal Court 102 W Walker St, LGCY, 77573	4632	A4
Magnolia City Hall 16835 Magnolia Pkwy, MtgC, 77354	2669	C4
Manvel City Hall 6615 Masters Rd, MNVL, 77578	4625	E7
Manvel Municipal Court 6615 Masters Rd, MNVL, 77578	4625	E7
Meadows Place City Hall 1 Troyan Dr, MDWP, 77477	4238	B5
Mexico Consulate General 10103 Fondren Rd, HOUS, 77096	4240	A2
Missouri City City Hall 1522 Texas Pkwy, MSCY, 77489	4370	C4
Montgomery County Courthouse 301 N Thompson St, CNRO, 77301	2384	A5
Montgomery County Municipal Court 10224 Fairview Dr, CHTW, 77385	2823	A4
Moody Civic Center 2106 Seawall Blvd, GLSN, 77550	5109	C5
Morgan's Point City Hall 1415 E Main St, MRGP, 77571	4252	A2
NASA-Johnson Space Center 2101 NASA Pkwy, HOUS, 77058	4508	A4
NASA Space Center 1601 W NASA Pkwy, HarC, 77598	4631	A1
Nassau Bay City Hall 1800 NASA Pkwy, NSUB, 77058	4508	A4
Nessler Civic Center 2015 5th Av N, TXCY, 77590	4875	A5
Netherlands Consulate General 2200 Post Oak Blvd, HOUS, 77056	3961	A6
New Zealand Consulate 246 Warrenton Dr, BKHV, 77024	3959	A4
Norway Consulate General 2777 Allen Pkwy, HOUS, 77019	3962	D4
Oak Ridge North City Hall 27326 Robinson Rd, ORDN, 77385	2822	C5
Panorama Village City Hall 98 Hiwon Dr, PNVL, 77304	2237	A3
Pasadena City Hall 1211 Southmore Av, PASD, 77506	4107	C6
Patton Village City Hall 16940 Main St, PTVL, 77372	2682	E6
Pearland City Hall 3519 Liberty Dr, PRLD, 77581	4504	A5
Pearland Municipal Court 3519 Liberty Dr, PRLD, 77581	4504	A5
Peru Consulate General 5177 Richmond Av, HOUS, 77056	4101	A1
Piney Point Village Hall 7721 San Felipe Dr, PNPV, 77024	3960	A5
Pleak City Hall PLEK, 77469	4614	E7
Prairie View City Hall PRVW, 77445	3100	A3
Public Health & Environmental Services 2223 W Loop Frwy S, HOUS, 77027	3961	B6
Richmond City Hall 402 Morton St, RHMD, 77469	4491	E1
Roman Forest City Hall 2430 Roman Forest Blvd, RMFT, 77357	2829	A2
Rosenberg City Hall 2110 4th St, RSBG, 77471	4490	E5
Santa Fe City Hall STFE, 77510	4987	B1
Santa Fe Municipal Court STFE, 77510	4987	B1
Seabrook City Hall 1700 1st St, SEBK, 77586	4509	D2
Shenandoah City Hall 801 Maplewood Rd, SHEH, 77381	2822	A1
Shoreacres City Hall 601 Shoreacres Blvd, SRAC, 77571	4382	E2
South Houston City Hall 1018 Dallas St, SHUS, 77587	4246	C3
Southside Place City Hall 6309 Edloe St, SSPL, 77005	4101	E3
Spain Consulate General 1800 Bering Dr, HOUS, 77057	3960	D6
Splendora City Hall SPLD, 77372	2683	B2
Spring Valley City Hall 1025 Campbell Rd, SPVL, 77055	3820	E7
Stafford City Hall STAF, 77477	4369	E3
Sugar Land City Hall 2700 N Town Center Blvd, SGLD, 77479	4368	B6
Swedish Consulate 2909 Hillcroft Av, HOUS, 77057	3960	B7
Taylor Lake City Hall 500 Kirby Blvd, TYLV, 77586	4508	E1
Texas City City Hall 1801 9th Av N, TXCY, 77590	4875	B5
Texas City Municipal Court 928 5th Av N, TXCY, 77590	4875	C5
Texas Dept of Criminal Justice Cent Prison 1 Circle Dr, SGLD, 77478	4367	B4
Texas Dept of Criminal Jus Kegans St Prison 707 Top St, HOUS, 77002	3963	D3
TX Dept of Criminal Jus Lynchner St Prison 2350 Atascocita Rd, HarC, 77396	3407	C3
Texas State Department of Health Lamar St, HOUS, 77002	3963	B4
Texas St Dept of Licensing & Regulations 5425 Polk St, HOUS, 77023	3964	C7
Texas State Department of Transportation 7721 Katy Rd, HOUS, 77007	3961	D1
Texas St Dept of Public Safety & Hwy Patrol 10110 Northwest Freeway Frontag, HOUS, 77092	3822	B4
Tiki Island City Hall 802 Tiki Dr, TKIS, 77554	5106	C4
Tiki Island Village Municipal Court 802 Tiki Dr, TKIS, 77554	5106	C4
Tomball City Hall 401 Market St, TMBL, 77375	2964	B7
Town Center Square City Wk, SGLD, 77479	4368	B6
Turkish Consulate General 1990 Post Oak Blvd, HOUS, 77056	3961	A6
United States Bankruptcy Court 515 Rusk St, HOUS, 77002	3963	B4
US Federal District Court 601 Rosenberg St, GLSN, 77550	5109	B3
Venezuela Consulate General 2925 Briarpark Dr, HOUS, 77042	4099	A1
Waller City Hall 1118 Farr St, WALR, 77484	3101	E5
Webster City Hall 311 Pennsylvania St, WEBS, 77598	4507	C7
West University Place City Hall 3800 University Blvd, WUNP, 77005	4101	D3
Woodbranch City Hall 58 Magnolia Rd, WDBR, 77357	2828	D1

Cemeteries

FEATURE NAME Address City ZIP Code	MAP#	GRID
Adath Emeth Cem, HOUS	3824	A4
Adath Israel Cem, HOUS	3684	E7
Adath Yeshurun Cem, HOUS	3962	C4
Addicks Bear Creek Cem, HOUS	3817	D4
Aldine Cem, HarC	3545	D1
Aleif Cem, HOUS	4097	D5
Alta Loma Cem, GlsC	4987	B4
Baker Cem, MtgC	2962	E4
Barbours Cem, HTCK	4988	E3
Baytown Memorial Cem, HarC	3833	C1
Becker Cem, HarC	3397	E1
Bethany Cem, DRPK	4249	D2
Beth El Cem, HOUS	3822	A7
Beth Israel Cem, HOUS	3963	A4
Beth Jacob Cem, HOUS	4373	E3
Bradshaw Cem, HOUS	3966	E1
Briscoe Cem, FBnC	4232	D6
Brookside Cem, HarC	3546	D3
Budde Cem, HarC	3113	B5
Burton Cem, HarC	3247	B1
Busch Cem, BYTN	3835	B4
Calvary Catholic Cem, GLSN	5108	C7
Calvary Hill Cem, HarC	3259	E2
Cedar Crest Cem, HarC	3973	E4
Cemetery Beautiful, HOUS	3683	D2
Cemetery San Isidro, SGLD	4368	D4
City Cem, GLSN	5108	E4
College Memorial Park Cem, HOUS	3962	C4
Confederate Cem, ALVN	4749	D7
Conroe Memorial Park, CNRO	2384	E7
Corgey Cem, MtgC	2816	C5
Crown Hill Cem, HOUS	4106	E2
Dagg Cem, HOUS	4375	A6
Davis-Greenlawn Cem, RSBG	4491	C7
Decker Prairie Cem, MtgC	2963	A1
Dewalt Cem, MSCY	4497	C5
Emanuel Memorial Park, HOUS	4239	D1
Evergreen Cem, HarC	3553	B7
Evergreen Cem, HOUS	3964	C7
Fairview Cem, LGCY	4631	E2
Fisher Cem, MTBL	3696	D6
Forest Lawn Cem, HOUS	4376	E1
Forest Park Cem, HarC	4631	B2
Forest Park Cem, HOUS	4104	E3
Forest Park Westheimer Cem, HOUS	3957	C7
Freeman Cem, MtgC	2533	D7
Fritsche Cem, HarC	3253	A4
Galveston Memorial Park Cem, HTCK	4989	A3
Garden Park Cem, CNRO	2237	C7
Glendale Cem, HOUS	4105	D2
Glenwood Cem, HOUS	3962	E3
Golden Gate Cem, CNRO	2383	B6
Goodson Cem, MtgC	2816	C4
Grace Memorial Park, HTCK	4987	E2
Grandview Memorial Park, DRPK	4249	D2
Graves Cem, HarC	3396	A4
Harrington Cem, HarC	3550	D7
Harris County Cem, HOUS	3827	C3
Harvey Cem, HarC	3413	B6
Hempstead Cem, WlrC	3098	C2
Hill of Rest Cem, BYTN	3972	C7
Hitchcock Cem, HTCK	4989	A3
Hollywood Cem, HOUS	3824	C7
Holy Cross Cem, HOUS	3824	B7
Houston Cem, HMPD	3098	C2
Houston Memorial Garden, PRLD	4501	E3
Houston Memorial Gardens Cem, PRLD	4501	D3
Houston National Cem, HarC	3543	C1
Huffman Cem, HarC	3121	E5
Huffman Community Cem, HarC	3267	A5
Hufsmith Cem, HarC	2965	A2
Humble Cem, HMBL	3262	E7
Jackson Cem, HOUS	4105	B3
Jones Cem, FBnC	4492	C6
Kidd Cem, MtgC	2827	D4
Kirby Chapel Cem, WlrC	2955	C2
Klein Cem, HarC	3111	D7
Klein Cem, MtgC	2963	B1
Klein Memorial Park, MtgC	2670	B3
Knigge Cem, HarC	3397	E6
Lakeview Cem, GLSN	5108	C7
La Marque Cem, LMQU	4990	C2
La Porte Cem, LPRT	4251	D4
Lynch Cem, HarC	3552	C4
Macedonia Cem, WlrC	2959	B4
Magee Cem, HOUS	3956	D6
Magnolia Cem, HOUS	3962	D4
Magnolia Cem, KATY	3813	A6
Mainland Memorial Cem, HTCK	4989	B4
McSwain Cem, HarC	3398	B2
Memorial Oaks Cem, HOUS	3957	C1
Missionary Cem, MtgC	2669	C4
Mizell Cem, SPLD	2683	A3
Morales Cem, HarC	3545	A2
Morgan Cem, MtgC	2536	A1
Morgan's Point Cem, MRGP	4252	B1
Morton Cem, RHMD	4364	E7
Mt Olivet Catholic Cem, TXCY	4753	C6
Mt Zion Cem, MtgC	2967	E2
Mueller Cem, HarC	3397	B5
Mueschke Cem, HarC	3259	D3
Municipal Cem, GLSN	5108	C7
Oak Park Cem, ALVN	4867	C3
Oak Park Cem, HOUS	3686	B7
Oakwood Cem, CNRO	2384	C4
Oklahoma Cem, MtgC	2818	D5
Old Arcadia Cem, STFE	4752	C7
Old Sanders Cem, MtgC	2668	A3
Old Settlers Cem, PRLD	4503	B1
Our Lady of Guadalupe Cem, HOUS	3963	E4
Paradise Cem South, PRLD	4501	E2
Paradise North Cem, HOUS	3543	A7
Pate Cem, MtgC	2818	D6
Perry Cem, HarC	3399	B4
Pet Cem, HOUS	4097	E7
Phillips Memorial Cem, TXCY	4873	E6
Pilot Cem, HarC	3109	D4
Pleasant Green Cem, FBnC	4235	B5
Prairie View Cem, PRVW	2955	B6
Prater Cem, HOUS	3117	D7
Resthaven Memorial Gardens, HarC	3403	B4
Resurrection Cem, PRLD	4376	B7
Rising Star Cem, LMQU	4873	E7
Roberts Cem, HarC	3105	D3
Rosebud Cem, CNRO	2384	B4
Rosenberg Cem, RSBG	4490	B7
Rosewood Cem, MtgC	2973	C2
Rosewood Park Cem, HMBL	3406	D4
Sacred Heart Cem, HarC	3692	E1
St. John Cem, HarC	3252	A4
St. John Cem, HOUS	3683	A7
St. John's Cem, WALR	3102	B6
St. Joseph Cem, HOUS	3684	E2
St. Martin Cem, HarC	3692	E1
St. Mary Cem, WlrC	3246	C2
St. Mathew Cem, HarC	3259	C2
Salem Cem, HarC	2963	B6
San Gabriel Cem, RHMD	4492	A2
San Jacinto Memorial Park, HarC	3968	B2
San Leon Cem, GlsC	4635	E4
Seabrook Cem, SEBK	4383	B5
Seidel-Rose Hill Cem, HarC	3107	C3
Shilo Cem, HarC	3400	C3
Shiloh Cem, WlrC	2955	C4
Simms Cem, HarC	3552	A5
Southern Memorial Gardens Cem, PRLD	4501	D2
South Park Cem, PRLD	4376	B6
Spanish Cem, HMPD	3098	C2
Splendora Cem, SPLD	2683	A3
Spring Cem, HarC	2969	A6
Spring Green Cem, FBnC	4232	D3
Stonewall Cem, HOUS	3964	C2
Tamina Cem, MtgC	2822	C2
Tettar Cem, HarC	3261	B2
Tillis Prairie Cem, MtgC	2670	E5
Vick Cem, MtgC	2680	B3
Waller Cem, HarC	3102	B6
Washington Cem, HOUS	3962	E3
Westcott Cem, HOUS	3825	A1
West Gethsemane Cem, RSBG	4490	E7
White Cem, HarC	3692	D4
Woodlawn Cem, HOUS	3821	D7
Wooster Cem, BYTN	3970	E6
Wow Cem, RSBG	4490	D3
Zion Lutheran Cem, HarC	2965	C1

Colleges & Universities

FEATURE NAME Address City ZIP Code	MAP#	GRID
Alvin Community College 3110 Mustang Rd, ALVN, 77511	4867	C4
Amer College of Acupuncture & Oriental Med 9100 Park West Dr, HOUS, 77063	3959	D7
Art Institute of Houston 1900 Yorktown St, HOUS, 77056	3960	E5
Baylor College of Medicine 1 Baylor Plz, HOUS, 77030	4102	D4
Bradford School of Business 4699 Southwest Freeway Frontage, HOUS, 77027	4101	B1
College of the Mainland 1200 N Amburn Rd, TXCY, 77591	4873	B4
Commonwealth Institute of Funeral Service 415 Barren Springs Dr, HarC, 77090	3258	E7
Cy-Fair College 9191 Barker Cypress Rd, HarC, 77433	3537	D5
Embry-Riddle Aeronautical University 16441 Space Center Blvd, HOUS, 77058	4507	D1
Galveston College 4015 Avenue Q, GLSN, 77550	5108	E6
Houston Baptist University 7502 Fondren Rd, HOUS, 77074	4099	D6
Houston Community College-Alief Center 13803 Bissonnet St, HarC, 77083	4237	A1
Houston Community College-Americana-Building 811 Dallas St, HOUS, 77002	3963	B4
Houston Community College-Applied Tech Ctr 4014 Bluebonnet Dr, STAF, 77477	4238	C7
Houston Community College-Automotive Tech 4638 Airline Dr, HOUS, 77022	3823	E1
Houston Community College-Central 1300 Holman St, HOUS, 77004	3963	A7
Houston Community College-Cinco Ranch 4242 S Mason Rd, FBnC, 77450	4094	A3

Houston Points of Interest Index

FEATURE NAME / Address City ZIP Code	MAP#	GRID
Houston Comm College-College of Health Sci 1900 Pressler St, HOUS, 77030	4102	C5
Houston Community College-Eastside 6815 Rustic St, HOUS, 77087	4105	A4
Houston Community College-Greenbriar Annex 13645 Murphy Rd, STAF, 77477	4369	D1
Houston Community College-Gulfton Center 5047 Gulfton Dr, HOUS, 77081	4100	D3
Houston Community College-Health Science-Ctr 1900 Pressler Dr, HOUS, 77030	4102	D4
Houston Community College-Katy Mills 25403 TX-99 Frontage Rd, HarC, 77494	3953	C3
Houston Community College-Missouri City Ctr 1681 Cartwright Rd, MSCY, 77489	4370	C7
Houston Community College-Northeast 555 Community College Dr, HOUS, 77013	3965	E1
Houston Community College-Northline Mall-Ctr 401 Northline Mall, HOUS, 77022	3824	A1
Houston Community College-Pinemont Center 1265 Pinemont Dr, HOUS, 77018	3683	E7
Houston Community College-Scarcella Center 10141 Cash Rd, STAF, 77477	4369	E1
Houston Community College-Southeast 6815 Rustic St, HOUS, 77087	4105	A4
Houston Community College-Stafford 9910 Cash Rd, STAF, 77477	4369	E1
Houston Comm College-Town & County Square 1010 W Sam Houston Pkwy N, HOUS, 77043	3819	D7
Houston Community College-Westgate Center 1550 Foxlake Dr, HOUS, 77084	3816	A7
Houston Community College-West Loop Center 5601 W Loop Frwy S, BLAR, 77401	4101	A2
Houston Comm College-Willie Lee Gay Hall 1990 Airport Blvd, HOUS, 77045	4242	E6
Kingwood College 20000 Kingwood Dr, HOUS, 77339	3117	E5
Lee College 200 Lee Dr, BYTN, 77520	3972	D7
Lunar & Planetary Institute-Rice University 3600 Bay Area Blvd, PASD, 77058	4508	B2
Montgomery College 3200 College Park Dr, WDLD, 77384	2675	E5
MTI College of Business & Technology 11420 East Freeway Frontage Rd, JTCY, 77029	3966	D2
North Harris County College 2700 WW Thorne Blvd, HarC, 77073	3259	E5
North Harris County College-Carver Center 2330 S Victory Dr, HOUS, 77088	3683	C2
North Harris County College-Parkway Center 250 N Sam Houston Pkwy E, HOUS, 77060	3403	C7
Prairie View A&M University 519 Williams St, PRVW, 77445	3100	B1
Rice University 6100 Main St, HOUS, 77005	4102	D2
Richmond State School 2100 Preston St, FBnC, 77469	4364	C7
San Jacinto College 4624 Fairmont Pkwy, PASD, 77504	4248	A5
San Jacinto College-Central 8060 Spencer Hwy, PASD, 77505	4249	B3
San Jacinto College-North 5800 Uvalde Rd, HarC, 77049	3828	E4
San Jacinto College-South 13735 Beamer Rd, HOUS, 77089	4505	B1
South Texas College of Law 1303 San Jacinto St, HOUS, 77002	3963	C5
Texas A&M University at Galveston 200 Seawolf Pkwy, GLSN, 77554	5108	D1
Texas Chiropractic College 5912 Spencer Hwy, PASD, 77505	4248	D3
Texas Institute of Oceanography 5001 Avenue U, GLSN, 77551	5108	D7
Texas Southern University 3100 Cleburne St, HOUS, 77004	4103	C2
Texas Woman's University-Houston 6700 MD Anderson Blvd, HOUS, 77030	4102	D3
Tomball College 30555 Tomball Pkwy, TMBL, 77375	2963	D5
Universal Technical Institute 721 Lockhaven Dr, HOUS, 77073	3259	B7
University of Texas-Health Science Ctr, The 1200 Pressler Dr, HOUS, 77030	4102	D4
University of Houston 4800 Smith St, HOUS, 77002	3963	B5
University of Houston at Sugar Land 14000 University Blvd, SGLD, 77479	4494	D1
University of Houston-Central Campus 4800 Calhoun Rd, HOUS, 77004	4104	A3
University of Houston-Cinco Ranch 4242 S Mason Rd, FBnC, 77450	4094	A2
University of Houston-Clear Lake 2700 Bay Area Blvd, HOUS, 77058	4507	D1
University of Houston-Downtown 1 Main St, HOUS, 77002	3963	C3
University of Texas Health Science Center 7000 Fannin St, HOUS, 77054	4102	D6
University of Texas-Health Science Center 700 Fannin St, HOUS, 77002	3963	C4
University of Texas-Medical Branch 301 University Blvd, GLSN, 77550	5109	D2
University of Texas-Medical School 6431 Fannin St, HOUS, 77030	4102	D3
University of St. Thomas 3800 Montrose Blvd, HOUS, 77006	3962	E7
Westwood Aviation Institute-Houston 8880 Telephone Rd, HOUS, 77061	4245	A6
Wharton Co Junior College-Fort Bend Tech Ct RHMD, 77469	4491	D4
Wharton County Junior College-Sugar Land 550 Julie Rivers Dr, SGLD, 77478	4237	D7

Entertainment & Sports

FEATURE NAME / Address City ZIP Code	MAP#	GRID
Adventure Bay Water Theme Park 13602 Beechnut St, HarC, 77083	4097	A7
After Dinner Players 2710 W Alabama St, HOUS, 77098	3962	A7
Alkek Velodrome 19008 Saums Rd, HOUS, 77084	3816	B5
Alley Theatre 615 Texas Av, HOUS, 77002	3963	C3
Applause Theatre HarC, 77069	3400	C3
Autry Court 6100 Main St, HOUS, 77005	4102	D2
Barnett Stadium 6800 Fairway Dr, HOUS, 77087	4104	E6
Bay Area Houston Ballet & Theatre 17170 Mill Forest Rd, HarC, 77598	4507	B5
Bayou Theatre 2700 Bay Area Blvd, PASD, 77058	4380	E7
Bayou Wildlife Park GlsC, 77511	4751	A6
Butler Stadium 13755 Main St, HOUS, 77085	4240	C7
Clear Creek Country Theatre 18091 Upper Bay Rd, NSUB, 77058	4508	A4
College of the Mainland Theatre 1200 N Amburn Rd, TXCY, 77591	4873	B5
Country Playhouse 12802 Queensbury Ln, HOUS, 77024	3958	D2
Crighton Community Playhouse 117 Simonton St, CNRO, 77301	2384	A5
Cynthia Woods Mitchell Pavilion 2005 Lake Robbins Dr, WDLD, 77380	2822	A5
Diverse Works Art Space 1117 East Frwy, HOUS, 77002	3963	D3
Downtown Aquarium 410 Bagby St, HOUS, 77002	3963	B3
Ensemble Theatre 3535 Main St, HOUS, 77004	3963	A7
Express Children's Theatre 1900 Kane St, HOUS, 77007	3963	A3
Fort Bend County Fairgrounds Fairgrounds Rd, RSBG, 77471	4614	D2
Galveston Ballet 2301 Market St, GLSN, 77550	5109	B3
George R Brown Convention Center 1001 Avenida De Las Americas, HOUS, 77010	3963	C5
Grand 1894 Opera House 2020 Post Office St, GLSN, 77550	5109	C2
Gulf Greyhound Park LMQU, 77568	4872	C4
Gus S Wortham Theater Center 500 Texas Av, HOUS, 77002	3963	B3
Harbour Playhouse DKSN, 77539	4754	A2
Highlands Motorspeedway 10700 N Crosby Lynchburg Rd, HarC, 77562	3692	D5
HITS Theatre 311 W 18th St, HOUS, 77008	3823	C5
Hobby Center for Performing Arts, The 800 Bagby St, HOUS, 77002	3963	B4
Hofheinz Pavilion 3875 Holman St, HOUS, 77004	4103	E2
Houston Arboretum & Nature Center 4501 Woodway Dr, HOUS, 77024	3961	B3
Houston Arena Theatre 7326 Southwest Freeway Frontage, HOUS, 77036	4099	D5
Houston Motorsport Park 11620 N Lake Houston Pkwy, HarC, 77044	3548	C7
Houston Raceway Park CmbC, 77520	3835	E7
Houston Zoo 1513 N MacGregor Dr, HOUS, 77030	4102	D3
Interactive Theater 333 S Jensen Dr, HOUS, 77003	3963	E3
Jack F Rhodes Memorial Stadium 1733 Katy Fort Bend Rd, KATY, 77493	3813	E6
Jones Hall 615 Louisiana St, HOUS, 77002	3963	C4
Lawndale Art & Performance Center 4912 Main St, HOUS, 77002	4102	E1
Lone Star Convention & Expo Center 9055 Airport Rd, MtgC, 77303	2238	D7
Main Street Theatre 4617 Montrose Blvd, HOUS, 77006	4102	D1
Mary Moody Northern Amphitheater 14901 San Luis Pass Rd, GLSN, 77554	5442	C1
Masquerade Theatre 3552 E TC Jester Blvd, HOUS, 77018	3822	C3
Memorial Stadium Burke Rd, PASD, 77502	4247	D2
Mercer Arboretum & Botanical Gardens 22306 Aldine Westfield Rd, HarC, 77338	3259	E1
Miller Outdoor Theatre 100 Hermann Lake Dr, HOUS, 77030	4102	E3
Minute Maid Park 501 Hamilton St, HOUS, 77002	3963	D4
Montgomery County Fairgrounds 9301 Airport Rd, MtgC, 77303	2238	D7
Moody Gardens Convention Center 7 Hope Blvd, GLSN, 77554	5107	D7
Open Gates Conference Center 2419 Sealy St, GLSN, 77550	5109	B3
Pasadena Convention Center 7902 W Fairmont Pkwy, PASD, 77507	4249	C5
Pasadena Fairgrounds 7902 W Fairmont Pkwy, PASD, 77507	4249	C5
Pasadena Little Theater 4318 Allen Genoa Rd, PASD, 77504	4247	B5
Pier 21 Theater 600 Moody Av, GLSN, 77550	5109	B3
Purse Building Studios Commerce St, HOUS, 77002	3963	D4
Radio Music Theatre 2623 Colquitt St, HOUS, 77098	3962	A7
Reckling Park 6100 Main St, HOUS, 77005	4102	C3
Reliant Arena 1600 S Loop Frwy, HOUS, 77054	4242	C1
Reliant Center N Stadium Dr, HOUS, 77054	4102	C7
Reliant Park 1 Reliant Pk, HOUS, 77054	4102	B7
Reliant Stadium 8299 Kirby Dr, HOUS, 77054	4102	B7
Revels Houston 1415 California St, HOUS, 77006	3962	D6
Rice Stadium Rice Blvd, HOUS, 77005	4102	B3
Rice University Art Gallery 6100 Main St, HOUS, 77005	4102	E2
Robertson Stadium 3874 Holman St, HOUS, 77004	4103	E2
Rosenberg Civic & Convention Center 3825 1st St, RSBG, 77471	4614	E1
Sam Houston Race Park 7575 N Sam Houston Pkwy W, HarC, 77064	3541	B2
Sarah Campbell Blaffer Foundation 5100 Montrose Blvd, HOUS, 77006	4102	E1
Schlitterbahn Water Park 2026 Lockheed Dr, GLSN, 77554	5221	E1
Six Flags AstroWorld 1750 S Loop Frwy, HOUS, 77054	4242	C1
Slightly Off Center Players 4201 Center St, DRPK, 77536	4249	B1
Splashtown-Houston 21300 I-45 Frontage Rd, HarC, 77373	3113	D3
Stages Repertory Theater 3201 Allen Pkwy, HOUS, 77019	3962	C4
Strand Theatre 2317 Mechanic St, GLSN, 77550	5109	B2
Theatre Suburbia 1410 W 43rd St, HOUS, 77018	3822	D1
Theatre Under the Stars 800 Bagby St, HOUS, 77002	3963	B4
Toyota Center 1510 Polk St, HOUS, 77002	3963	C5
Verizon Wireless Theatre 520 Texas Av, HOUS, 77002	3963	B4
Waller County Fairgrounds Fairgrounds Dr, PNIS, 77445	3099	B3
Woodland Science & Art Center 4800 Research Forest Dr, WDLD, 77381	2821	B1
Wortham Center 510 Preston St, HOUS, 77002	3963	C3

Golf Courses

FEATURE NAME	MAP#	GRID
Alvin Golf & CC, BzaC	4748	B4
Atascocita CC, HarC	3265	B4
Augusta Pines GC, HarC	2966	A2
Battleground at Deer Park, DRPK	4108	E5
Bay Forest GC, LPRT	4251	D6
Bay Oaks CC, HOUS	4380	B6
Bayou GC, TXCY	4873	E2
Baywood CC, PASD	4249	C7
Beacon Lakes GC, LGCY	4753	C1
Bear Creek Golf World, HOUS	3817	E1
Bend at Brazoria GC, The, BzaC	4744	D4
Blackhorse GC, HarC	3396	B5
Brae-Burn CC, HOUS	4239	D1
Brock Park Municipal GC, HOUS	3688	D6
Carlton Woods-Fazio Course, HarC	2820	A4
Carlton Woods-Nicklaus Course, WDLD	2673	E7
Champions GC, HarC	3400	C2
Channelview GC, HarC	3691	B7
Chaparral Recreation Assoc GC, TXCY	4753	B6
Chemlake GC, PASD	4381	C2
Classic 3 GC, HarC	3400	D3
Clear Creek GC, HarC	4374	B6
Club at Falcon Point, The, FBnC	3953	A3
Conroe CC, CNRO	2383	A4
Country Place GC, BzaC	4501	B1
Cypress GC, HarC	3397	C1
Cypress Lakes GC, HarC	3396	A1
Cypresswood GC, HarC	3261	B1
Deerwood GC, HOUS	3120	A7
Dickinson CC, DKSN	4754	D2
El Dorado CC, HarC	3406	D7
Evergreen Point GC, BYTN	4113	A4
First Tee Junior Golf Facility, HOUS	4244	D4
Fort Bend CC, FBnC	4492	A4
Friendswood CC, FRDW	4628	E7
Galveston CC, GLSN	5332	D2
Galveston Island Municipal GC, GLSN	5221	C1
Gleannloch Farms GC, HarC	3110	D7
Glenbrook GC, HOUS	4105	E7
Golf Club at Cinco Ranch, The, FBnC	3953	D6
Golfcrest CC, PRLD	4504	C2
Goose Creek CC, BYTN	3972	B2
Greatwood GC, FBnC	4493	D4
Green Caye GC, GlsC	4633	D7
Green Meadows GC, KATY	3813	B5
Gus Wortham Park GC, HOUS	4104	E1
Hearthstone CC, HarC	3539	A7
Hermann Park GC, HOUS	4102	E3
Heron Lakes GC, HarC	3541	A1
High Meadow Ranch GC, MtgC	2815	C5
Hillcrest GC, HLCS	4867	D4
Houston CC, HOUS	3960	C4
Houston Hills GC, HOUS	4239	A4
Houstonian Golf & CC, FBnC	4366	D1
Houston National GC, HarC	3538	B1
Humble Oil Patch Golf Center, HarC	3262	E3
Indian Shores GC, HarC	3410	B2
Inwood Forest GC, HOUS	3682	D2
Jersey Meadow GC, JRSV	3540	C6
Kingwood Cove GC, HOUS	3263	B2
Lakeside CC, HOUS	3958	B4
Lakeview CC, LMQU	4990	B3
Lake Windcrest GC, MtgC	2672	C4
Legendary Oaks GC, HMPD	2952	D5
Links at West Fork GC, CNRO	2382	D3
Lochinvar GC, HarC	3403	E1
Longwood GC, HarC	3397	D1
Magnolia Creek Golf Links, LGCY	4751	E1
Meadowbrook Farms GC, FBnC	4093	B4
Melrose GC, HOUS	3685	A2
Memorial Park GC, HOUS	3961	D2
Mulligans GC, HarC	3540	A1
Newport Golf & CC, HarC	3551	E2
Northgate CC, HarC	3257	C4
Oakhurst GC, MtgC	3117	E1
Occidental Chemical GC, DRPK	4109	C1
Old Orchard GC, FBnC	4366	D2
Panorama CC, PNVL	2237	B3
Pasadena Municipal GC, HOUS	4378	E2
Pecan Grove Plantation CC, FBnC	4365	C2
Pine Crest GC, HOUS	3820	A2
Pine Forest CC, HarC	3816	E1
Publinx GC, MtgC	2530	A6
Quail Valley CC, MSCY	4497	A1
Raveneaux CC, HarC	3256	A7
Redstone GC, HarC	3547	D1
Red Wolf Run GC, HarC	3121	E3
Riverbend CC, SGLD	4369	B4
River Oaks CC, HOUS	3961	E5
River Plantation CC, MtgC	2530	C6
River Pointe GC, FBnC	4495	A7
River Terrace GC, HarC	3830	A2
Royal Oaks CC, HOUS	4098	A1
San Jacinto College GC, PASD	4249	C4
Shadow Hawk GC, FBnC	4366	D1
Sharpstown Park GC, HOUS	4099	C4
Sienna Plantation GC, FBnC	4621	D6
South Shore Harbour CC, LGCY	4508	E7
Southwyck GC, BzaC	4501	B5
Spring Valley GC, HarC	2966	E2
Sugar Creek CC, SGLD	4368	E2
Sugar Hill GC, HOUS	4238	A2
Sweetwater CC, SGLD	4495	C3
Terra Verde GC, WlrC	2958	E7
Texaco CC, HOUS	3828	A5
Texas Par Golf Academy, HarC	4096	D3
Timber Creek GC, FRDW	4505	D4
Tomball CC, HarC	3110	B2
Total Golf at Kingwood, HOUS	3119	C7
Tour 18 GC, HarC	3263	D6

FEATURE NAME Address City ZIP Code	MAP#	GRID
Walden on Lake Houston CC, HarC	3265	C7
Waller CC Estates, WlrC	3246	E6
Wedgewood GC, CNRO	2382	C1
Westwood CC, HOUS	4239	A1
Wildcat GC, HOUS	4242	B6
Willow Creek GC, HarC	2966	D4
Willow Fork CC, FBnC	3954	C7
Willowisp CC, MSCY	4370	E3
Windrose GC, HarC	3111	E5
Woodlands CC-East Course, WDLD	2822	A7
Woodlands CC-Palmer Course, WDLD	2820	D1
Woodlands CC-Player Course, WDLD	2673	C7
Woodlands Golf Center, SHEH	2676	B7
Woodlands Resort-Oaks Course, WDLD	2821	D7
Woodlands Resort-Panther Trails, WDLD	2821	D7
World Houston American GC, HOUS	3405	B5

Historic Sites

FEATURE NAME Address City ZIP Code	MAP#	GRID
1838 Michel B Menard Home 33rd St, GLSN, 77550	5109	A4
1839 Samuel May Williams Home 3601 Bernardo de Galvez Av, GLSN, 77550	5109	A5
1861 Custom House 502 20th St, GLSN, 77550	5109	B3
1880 Garten Verein 2704 Avenue O, GLSN, 77550	5109	B4
Antioch Baptist Church 500 Clay St, HOUS, 77002	3963	B4
Ashton Villa 2328 Broadway St, GLSN, 77550	5109	B3
Battleship Texas State Historic Site 3527 Battleground Rd, HOUS, 77571	3970	A4
Bishop's Palace 1402 Broadway St, GLSN, 77550	5109	C3
Czech Cultural Center Houston 4920 San Jacinto St, HOUS, 77004	4102	E1
Frank B Davison Home 109 3rd Av N, TXCY, 77590	4875	E6
Galveston Historical Foundation 502 20th St, GLSN, 77550	5109	C3
George Bush Monument 500 Franklin St, HOUS, 77002	3963	C3
Houston Cotton Exchange Building 202 Travis St, HOUS, 77002	3963	C3
Old Market Square 800 Congress St, HOUS, 77002	3963	C4
Powhatan House 3427 Avenue O, GLSN, 77550	5109	A5
St. Joseph's Church 2202 Avenue K, GLSN, 77550	5109	C3
St. Mary's Catholic Historical Cathedral 2011 Church St, GLSN, 77550	5109	C3
Sam Houston Statue Hermann Cir Dr, HOUS, 77030	4102	E2
San Jacinto Battleground-Monument 3953 Battleground Rd, HarC, 77571	3970	B5
Strand Historic District 305 Moody Av, GLSN, 77550	5109	B2
Strawberry House 201 Memorial Park Dr, PASD, 77506	4107	A4
Texaco Building 1111 Clinton Dr, HOUS, 77015	4106	E1
Texas Heroes Monument Rosenberg St, GLSN, 77550	5109	B4
Union Station 501 Crawford St, HOUS, 77002	3963	D4
USS Cavalla, The Seawolf Pkwy, GLSN, 77554	4994	D5

Hospitals

FEATURE NAME Address City ZIP Code	MAP#	GRID
Alvin Diagnostic & Urgent Care Center 301 Medic Ln, ALVN, 77511	4749	C7
Baycoast Med Ctr 1700 James Bowie Dr, BYTN, 77520	3973	C5
Bayshore Med Ctr 4000 Spencer Hwy, PASD, 77504	4247	E3
Ben Taub General Hosp 1504 Ben Taub Lp, HOUS, 77030	4102	D3
Charter Hosp 2001 Ladbrook Dr, HOUS, 77339	3118	D6
Christus St. Catherine Hosp 701 S Fry Rd, HOUS, 77094	3954	E2
Christus St. John Hosp 18300 St. John Dr, NSUB, 77058	4508	B5
Christus St. Joseph Hosp 1401 La Branch St, HOUS, 77002	3963	C6
Clear Lake Regional Med Ctr 500 Medical Center Blvd, WEBS, 77598	4507	A6
Columbia Med Ctr-Airline 5815 Airline Dr, HOUS, 77076	3684	E5
Columbia Med Ctr-Rosewood 9200 Westheimer Rd, HOUS, 77063	3959	C7
Conroe Regional Med Ctr 504 Medical Center Blvd, CNRO, 77304	2529	E2
Cornerstone Hosp of Houston 5556 Gasmer Dr, HOUS, 77035	4240	D5
Cornerstone Hosp of Houston-Bellaire 5314 Dashwood Dr, HOUS, 77081	4100	D4
Cypress Creek Hosp 17750 Cali Dr, HarC, 77090	3258	C2
Cypress Fairbanks Med Ctr 10655 Steepletop Dr, HarC, 77065	3540	A2
Doctors Hosp-East Loop 9339 N Loop Frwy E, HOUS, 77013	3826	E7
Doctors Hosp-Parkway 233 W Parker Rd, HOUS, 77076	3684	C4
Doctors Hosp-Tidwell 510 W Tidwell Rd, HOUS, 77091	3684	B6
Dubuis Hosp of Houston 1919 Dallas St, HOUS, 77002	3963	C4
East Houston Regional Med Ctr 13111 East Freeway Frontage Rd, HOUS, 77015	3967	C2
Healthsouth Hosp for Specialized Surgery 5400 La Branch St, HOUS, 77004	4102	E2
Healthsouth Rehabilitation Hosp of N-Houston 18550 I-45 Frontage Rd, SHEH, 77384	2822	A1
Houston Northwest Med Ctr 710 Judiwood St, HarC, 77090	3258	C3
Houston Town & Country Hosp 1120 Business Center Dr, HOUS, 77043	3819	D7
Intracare Med Ctr Hosp 7601 Fannin St, HOUS, 77054	4102	C6
Kindred Hosp-Houston 6441 Main St, HOUS, 77030	4102	C3
Kindred Hosp-Houston Northwest 11297 Fallbrook Dr, HarC, 77065	3540	A2
Kingwood Med Ctr 22999 Eastex Frwy, HOUS, 77339	3118	A6
Lyndon B Johnson General Hosp 5656 Kelley St, HOUS, 77026	3825	D4
Mainland Med Ctr 6801 Emmett F Lowry Expwy, TXCY, 77591	4873	D5
Memorial Hermann Continuing Care Hosp 3033 Gessner Rd, HOUS, 77043	3820	A2
Memorial Hermann Fort Bend Hosp 3803 Stafford Dewalt Rd, MSCY, 77459	4496	D3
Memorial Hermann Katy Hosp 5602 Medical Center Dr, KATY, 77494	3952	C2
Memorial Hermann Memorial City Hosp 920 Frostwood Dr, HOUS, 77024	3959	A1
Memorial Hermann Northwest Hosp 1635 N Loop Frwy W, HOUS, 77008	3822	E4
Memorial Hermann Southeast Hosp 11800 Astoria Blvd, HOUS, 77089	4378	B7
Memorial Hermann Southwest Hosp 7600 Beechnut St, HOUS, 77074	4099	D6
Memorial Hermann Texas Med Ctr 6411 Fannin St, HOUS, 77030	4102	D3
Memorial Hermann The Woodlands Hosp 9250 Pinecroft Dr, SHEH, 77381	2822	A3
Methodist Hosp 6565 Fannin St, HOUS, 77030	4102	D4
Methodist Sugar Land Hosp 16655 Southwest Freeway Frontag, SGLD, 77479	4368	A6
Methodist Willowbrook Hosp 18220 Tomball Pkwy, HOUS, 77070	3399	E4
Northeast Med Ctr Hosp 18951 N Memorial Dr, HMBL, 77338	3262	C6
Oak Bend Med Ctr 1705 Jackson St, RHMD, 77469	4491	D2
Park Plaza Hosp 1313 Hermann Dr, HOUS, 77004	4102	E2
Pasadena General Hosp 1004 Seymour St, PASD, 77506	4107	C5
Pasadena Memorial Hosp 906 Southmore Av, PASD, 77502	4107	B6
Plaza Specialty Hosp 1300 Binz St, HOUS, 77004	4102	E2
Renaissance Hosp-Houston 2807 Little York Rd, HarC, 77093	3685	E2
Riverside General Hosp 3204 Ennis St, HOUS, 77004	4103	C1
St. Luke's Community Med Ctr 17200 St. Lukes Wy, WDLD, 77384	2676	A6
St. Luke's Episcopal Hosp 6720 Bertner Av, HOUS, 77030	4102	D4
San Jacinto Methodist Hosp 4401 Garth Rd, BYTN, 77521	3972	D2
Select Specialty Hosp-Conroe 506 Medical Center Blvd, CNRO, 77304	2529	E2
Select Specialty Hosp-Houston Heights 1917 Ashland St, HOUS, 77008	3823	C5
Select Specialty Hosp-Houston Med Ctr 6447 Main St, HOUS, 77030	4102	C3
Southmore Med Ctr 908 Southmore Av, PASD, 77502	4107	C6
Spring Branch Med Ctr 8850 Long Point Rd, HOUS, 77080	3820	E5
Sun Belt Regional Med Ctr 15101 East Freeway Frontage Rd, HarC, 77530	3968	D1
Texas Children's Hosp 6621 Fannin St, HOUS, 77030	4102	D4
Texas Med Ctr 1155 Holcombe Blvd, HOUS, 77030	4102	C4
Texas Orthopedic Hosp 7401 N Main St, HOUS, 77018	3823	D3
Tomball Regional Hosp 605 Holderrieth Blvd, TMBL, 77375	3109	A1
Twelve Oaks Med Ctr-River Oaks 4200 Twelve Oaks, HOUS, 77027	4101	C1
Twelve Oaks Med Ctr-Sharpstown 6700 Bellaire Blvd, HOUS, 77074	4100	A4
University of Texas-Anderson Cancer Center 1515 Holcombe Blvd, HOUS, 77030	4102	D4
University of Texas Medical Branch Hosp 301 University Blvd, GLSN, 77550	5109	D2
Veterans Affairs Med Ctr 2002 Holcombe Blvd, HOUS, 77030	4102	E4
Vista Med Ctr 4301 Vista Rd, PASD, 77504	4247	E3
West Houston Med Ctr 12141 Richmond Av, HOUS, 77082	4097	E1
West Oaks Hosp 6500 Hornwood Dr, HOUS, 77074	4100	B4
Woman's Hosp of Texas, The 7600 Fannin St, HOUS, 77054	4102	C6

Law Enforcement

FEATURE NAME Address City ZIP Code	MAP#	GRID
Alvin Police Dept 305 W Sealy St, ALVN, 77511	4867	B1
Bayou Vista Police Dept 1412 Hampton Ct, FRDW, 77546	4629	C3
Baytown Police Dept 3200 N Main St, BYTN, 77521	3973	A4
Bellaire Police Dept 5110 Jessamine St, BLAR, 77401	4100	E5
Brookside Village Police Dept 6243 Brookside Rd, BKVL, 77581	4375	D6
City of Houston Southwest Police Dept 4503 Beechnut St, HOUS, 77096	4101	B7
Clear Lake Shores Police Dept 931 Cedar Rd, CRLS, 77565	4509	C5
Conroe Police Dept 700 Old Montgomery Rd, CNRO, 77301	2383	E5
Deer Park Police Dept 1410 Center St, DRPK, 77536	4109	B5
Dept of Public Safety 235 Austin St, HMPD, 77445	2953	C7
Dickinson Police Dept DKSN, 77539	4754	A3
El Lago Police Dept 98 Lakeshore Dr, ELGO, 77586	4509	A2
Friendswood Police Dept 109 E Willowick Av, FRDW, 77546	4505	C7
Galveston County Sheriff's Dept 715 19th St, GLSN, 77550	5109	C3
Galveston Police Dept 2517 Ball St, GLSN, 77550	5109	B3
Harris County Sheriff's Dept 1301 Franklin St, HOUS, 77002	3963	D4
Hedwig Village Police Dept 9000 Gaylord St, HDWV, 77024	3959	E1
Highlands Police Dept 1301 Franklin St, HOUS, 77002	3963	D4
Hitchcock Police Dept 6815 S 2nd St, HTCK, 77563	4988	E4
Houston Police Dept 61 Riesner St, HOUS, 77002	3963	B3
Humble Police Dept 341 N Bender Av, HMBL, 77338	3262	D6
Jamaica Beach Police Dept 16628 San Luis Pass Rd, GLSN, 77554	5442	B1
Jersey Village Police Dept 16501 Jersey Dr, JRSV, 77040	3680	C1
Katy Police Dept 5456 Franz Rd, KATY, 77493	3813	C5
Kemah Police Dept KMAH, 77565	4509	E7
La Marque Police Dept 431 Bayou Rd, LMQU, 77568	4874	A
La Porte Police Dept 915 S 8th St, LPRT, 77571	4251	C4
League City Police Dept 500 W Walker St, LGCY, 77573	4632	A4
Magnolia Police Dept 16835 Magnolia Pkwy, MtgC, 77354	2669	C4
Manvel Police Dept 6615 Masters Rd, MNVL, 77578	4625	E7
Meadows Place Police Dept 1 Troyan Dr, MDWP, 77477	4238	B6
Memorial Villages Police Dept 11981 Memorial Dr, BKHV, 77024	3959	B4
Missouri City Police Dept 1522 Texas Pkwy, MSCY, 77489	4370	C4
Montgomery Sheriff's Dept District II 9200 Grogans Mill Rd, WDLD, 77380	2821	E3
Montgomery Sheriff's Dept District III Railroad Av, MtgC, 77357	2828	B2
Morgan's Point Police Dept 1415 E Main St, LPRT, 77571	4252	A2
Nassau Bay Police Dept 1800 NASA Pkwy, NSUB, 77058	4508	A
Oak Ridge North Police Dept 27326 Robinson Rd, ORDN, 77385	2822	C5
Panorama Village Police Dept 98 Hiwon Dr, PNVL, 77304	2237	A
Pasadena Police Dept 1114 Davis St, PASD, 77506	4107	C6
Pasadena Police Substation 1202 Kirby Blvd, PASD, 77586	4381	E7
Patton Village Police Dept 16940 Main St, PTVL, 77372	2682	E6
Pearland Police Dept 2703 Veterans Dr, PRLD, 77584	4503	B4
Police Dept-Galena Park Clinton Dr, GNPK, 77547	3966	B7
Roman Forest Police Dept 2430 Roman Forest Blvd, RMFT, 77357	2829	A
Rosenberg Police Dept 2120 4th St, RSBG, 77471	4490	E6
Santa Fe Police Dept 4925 Main St, STFE, 77510	4987	B1
Seabrook Police Dept 1609 N Meyer Rd, SEBK, 77586	4509	D
Shenandoah Police Dept 801 Maplewood Rd, SHEH, 77381	2821	E1
Shoreacres Police Dept 601 Shoreacres Blvd, SRAC, 77571	4382	E2
South Houston Police Dept 1023 Dallas St, SHUS, 77587	4246	C3
Southside Police Dept 6309 Edloe St, SSPL, 77005	4101	E3
Splendora Police Dept MtgC, 77372	2536	A
Splendora Police Dept SPLD, 77372	2683	B2
Spring Valley Police Dept 1025 Campbell Rd, SPVL, 77055	3820	E7
Stafford Police Dept STAF, 77477	4369	E3
Texas City Police Dept 928 5th Av N, TXCY, 77590	4875	C5
Texas Highway Patrol BYTN, 77520	4112	D2
Texas Highway Patrol 10503 Grant Rd, HarC, 77070	3399	B4
Texas Highway Patrol 16715 Clay Rd, HarC, 77084	3817	C1
Texas Highway Patrol 10110 Northwest Freeway Frontag, HOUS, 77092	3822	B4
Tomball Police Dept 401 Market St, TMBL, 77375	2964	B7
Waller County Police Dept 701 Calvit St, HMPD, 77445	2953	C6
Webster Police Dept 217 Pennsylvania St, WEBS, 77598	4507	C7
West University Place Police Dept 3814 University Blvd, WUNP, 77005	4101	D3

Libraries

FEATURE NAME Address City ZIP Code	MAP#	GRID
Bellaire City 5111 Jessamine St, BLAR, 77401	4100	E5
Brazoria County-Alvin 105 S Gordon St, ALVN, 77511	4867	C1
Brazoria County-Manvel 7104 Masters Rd, MNVL, 77578	4746	D2
Chaparral Genealogical Society 310 N Live Oak St, TMBL, 77375	2964	C6
Clayton Center for Genealogical Research 5300 Caroline St, HOUS, 77004	4102	E2
Clear Lake City-County Freeman Branch 16616 Diana Ln, HOUS, 77062	4507	B3
Deer Park Public 3009 Center St, DRPK, 77536	4109	B7
First Colony Branch 2121 Austin Pkwy, SGLD, 77479	4368	C7
Fort Bend County-Cinco Ranch Branch Commercial Center Blvd, FBnC, 77494	3953	C7
Fort Bend County-George Memorial 1001 Golfview Dr, RHMD, 77469	4492	A3
Fort Bend County-Mamie George Branch 320 Dulles Av, SGLD, 77478	4369	B2
Fort Bend County-Missouri City 1530 Texas Pkwy, MSCY, 77489	4370	C4
Fort Bend County-Sugar Land 550 Eldridge Rd, SGLD, 77478	4368	B1
Friendswood Public 416 S Friendswood Dr, FRDW, 77546	4505	C7
Harris County-Aldine 11331 Airline Dr, HOUS, 77037	3544	B3
Harris County-Crosby 135 Hare Rd, HarC, 77532	3552	C2
Harris County-Fairbanks 7122 Gessner Rd, HarC, 77040	3681	B2
Harris County-High Meadows 4500 Aldine Mail Rd, HarC, 77039	3546	B5
Harris County-Jacinto City 921 Akron St, JTCY, 77029	3966	C2

Houston Points of Interest Index

EATURE NAME / ddress City ZIP Code	MAP#	GRID
arris County-Kingwood	3119	D5
102 Rustic Woods Dr, HOUS, 77345		
arris County Law	3963	C4
019 Congress St, HOUS, 77002		
arris County-North Channel	3829	C4
5741 Wallisville Rd, HarC, 77049		
arris County-Northwest	3398	E4
11355 Regency Green Dr, HarC, 77429		
arris County-Octavia Fields	3406	E1
503 S Houston Av, HMBL, 77338		
arris County Public-Atascocita	3265	C5
19520 Pinehurst Trail Dr, HarC, 77346		
arris County Public-Baldwin Boettcher	3259	E1
22248 Aldine Westfield Rd, HarC, 77338		
arris County Public-Barbara Bush	3256	E4
6817 Cypresswood Dr, HarC, 77379		
arris County Public-Evelyn Meador	4509	E1
2400 N Meyer Rd, SEBK, 77586		
arris County Public-Katy	3813	C5
5414 Franz Rd, KATY, 77493		
arris County Public-La Porte	4251	D3
600 S Broadway St, LPRT, 77571		
arris County Public Libray-Galena Park	3966	C6
1500 Keene St, GNPK, 77547		
arris County Public-Maud Marks	3402	B6
1815 Gears Rd, HarC, 77067		
arris County Public-Maud Smith Marks	3954	C5
1815 Westgreen Blvd, HarC, 77450		
arris County Public-Parker Williams	4378	A7
10851 Scarsdale Blvd, HOUS, 77089		
arris County Public-South Houston	4246	E3
607 Avenue A, SHUS, 77587		
arris County Public-Tomball	3109	B1
701 James St, TMBL, 77375		
arris County Pulbic-Stratford	3831	D2
509 Stratford St, HarC, 77562		
arris County-Spring Branch	3959	E1
930 Corbindale Rd, HDWV, 77024		
arris County-West University	4101	D3
6108 Auden St, WUNP, 77005		
elen Hall	4632	A4
100 W Walker St, LGCY, 77573		
itchcock Public	4988	E4
8005 Barry Av, HTCK, 77563		
ouston Public-Acres Homes	3683	D3
8501 W Montgomery Rd, HOUS, 77088		
ouston Public-Alief	4098	A6
7979 S Kirkwood Rd, HOUS, 77072		
ouston Public-Bracewell	4377	D2
10115 Kleckley Dr, HOUS, 77075		
ouston Public-Carnegie	3963	C1
1050 Quitman St, HOUS, 77009		
ouston Public-Central	3963	B4
500 McKinney St, HOUS, 77002		
ouston Public-Clayton	4102	E2
5300 Caroline St, HOUS, 77004		
ouston Public-Collier	3682	C7
6200 Pinemont Dr, HOUS, 77092		
ouston Public-Dixon	3825	B1
8002 Hirsch Rd, HOUS, 77016		
ouston Public-Fifth Ward	3964	B2
4014 Market St, HOUS, 77020		
ouston Public-Flores	3964	A5
110 N Milby St, HOUS, 77003		
ouston Public-Frank	4240	A4
6440 W Bellfort Av, HOUS, 77096		
ouston Public-Heights	3823	D6
1302 Heights Blvd, HOUS, 77008		
ouston Public-Hillendahl	3820	A3
2436 Gessner Rd, HOUS, 77080		
ouston Public-Johnson	4243	B4
3511 Reed Rd, HOUS, 77051		
ouston Public-Jungman	3960	D7
5830 Westheimer Rd, HOUS, 77057		
ouston Public-Kashmere Gardens	3825	C4
5411 Pardee St, HOUS, 77026		
ouston Public-Kendall	3957	E3
14330 Memorial Dr, HOUS, 77079		
ouston Public-Lakewood	3687	D7
8815 Feland St, HOUS, 77028		
ouston Public-Looscan	3961	C6
2510 Willowick Rd, HOUS, 77027		
ouston Public-Mancuso Branch	4244	D2
6767 Bellfort Av, HOUS, 77087		
ouston Public-Melcher	4105	B4
7200 Keller St, HOUS, 77012		
ouston Public-Montrose	3962	E7
4100 Montrose Blvd, HOUS, 77006		
ouston Public-Moody	3685	C6
9525 Irvington Blvd, HOUS, 77076		
ouston Public-Oak Forest	3822	D2
1349 W 43rd St, HOUS, 77018		
ouston Public-Park Place	4105	D7
8145 Park Pl Blvd, HOUS, 77017		
ouston Public-Pleasantville	3965	D3
1520 Gellhorn Dr, HOUS, 77029		
ouston Public-Ring	3820	E5
8835 Long Point Rd, HOUS, 77055		
ouston Public-Robinson Westchase	4098	C1
3223 Wilcrest Dr, HOUS, 77042		
ouston Public-Scenic Woods	3686	E3
10677 Homestead Rd, HOUS, 77016		
ouston Public-Smith	4103	D2
3624 Scott St, HOUS, 77004		
ouston Public-Stanaker	3964	E6
611 SSgt Macario Garcia Dr, HOUS, 77011		
ouston Public-Tuttle	3964	E2
702 Kress St, HOUS, 77020		
ouston Public-Vinson	4373	A3
3100 W Fuqua St, HOUS, 77045		
ouston Public-Walter	4099	D4
7660 Clarewood Dr, HOUS, 77036		
ouston Public-Young Branch	4104	A5
5260 Griggs Rd, HOUS, 77021		
atherine Tyra at Bear Creek	3817	C1
16719 Clay Rd, HarC, 77084		
a Marque Public	4990	A1
1011 Bayou Rd, LMQU, 77568		
ae S Bruce	4870	E6
13302 6th St, STFE, 77510		
alcolm Purvis-Magnolia Branch	2669	A5
510 Melton St, MAGA, 77354		
ares Memorial	4754	A3
DKSN, 77539		
D Anderson Patient&Family	4102	D4
1515 Holcombe Blvd, HOUS, 77030		
eyer Branch	4241	A2
5005 W Bellfort Av, HOUS, 77035		
ontgomery County-Central	2383	E5
104 I-45 Feeder Rd, CNRO, 77301		

FEATURE NAME / Address City ZIP Code	MAP#	GRID
Montgomery County-South	2821	E5
2101 Lake Robbins Dr, WDLD, 77380		
Moore Memorial	4875	B5
1701 9th Av N, TXCY, 77590		
Pasadena-Central	4107	C6
1201 Jeff Ginn Memorial Dr, PASD, 77506		
Pasadena-Fairmont Parkway	4247	E5
4330 Fairmont Pkwy, PASD, 77504		
Pearland	4504	A4
3522 Liberty Dr, PRLD, 77581		
RB Tullis	2827	D7
21130 US-59 Frontage Rd, MtgC, 77357		
Roberts Sound	4376	E2
8619 Washam Rd, HOUS, 77075		
Rosenberg	5109	B3
2310 Sealy St, GLSN, 77550		
Stimley-Blue Ridge Branch	4371	C5
7007 W Fuqua Dr, HOUS, 77489		

Military Installations

FEATURE NAME / Address City ZIP Code	MAP#	GRID
Air Station Houston	4379	B3
Sneider St, HOUS, 77034		
Houston Army Aviation Support Fclt-Armory	4378	E4
1182 Ellington Fld, HOUS, 77034		
Lyndon B Johnson Space Center	4508	A3
HOUS, 77058		
National Guard Armory	3973	A4
111 W Wye Dr, BYTN, 77521		
National Guard Armory	3956	C7
15150 Westheimer Pkwy, HOUS, 77077		
National Guard Armory	4989	D2
3006 Gulf Freeway Frontage Rd, LMQU, 77568		
Pelican Spit Military Reservation	4994	C6
GLSN, 77554		
Texas National Guard	4108	A6
2917 San Augustine Av, PASD, 77503		
US Coast Guard	4994	E6
Ferry Rd, GLSN, 77550		
US Coast Guard	4378	E4
1178 Ellington Fld, HOUS, 77034		

Museums

FEATURE NAME / Address City ZIP Code	MAP#	GRID
1859 Ashton Villa House Mus	5109	B3
2328 Broadway St, GLSN, 77550		
1940 Air Terminal Mus	4245	B5
1940 Travelair St, HOUS, 77061		
African American Mus	3961	B5
4550 Post Oak Pl Dr, HOUS, 77027		
American Cowboy Mus	4242	C4
11822 Almeda Rd, HOUS, 77045		
Antique Car Mus	3960	A5
7880 San Felipe Dr, PNPV, 77024		
Art Car Mus	3962	D3
140 S Heights Blvd, HOUS, 77007		
Art League of Houston	3962	E5
1953 Montrose Blvd, HOUS, 77006		
Bay Area Mus	4508	C2
5000 NASA Pkwy, PASD, 77586		
Baytown Historical Mus	3972	E7
220 W Defee Av, BYTN, 77520		
Blaffer Gallery-University of Houston	4104	A2
4800 Calhoun Rd, HOUS, 77004		
Buffalo Soldier National Mus	4103	A2
1834 Southmore Blvd, HOUS, 77004		
Byzantine Fresco Chapel Mus	3962	D7
4011 Yupon St, HOUS, 77006		
Center for Transportation & Commerce	5109	B2
Rosenberg St, GLSN, 77550		
Children's Mus of Houston	4102	E2
1500 Binz St, HOUS, 77004		
Civil War Mus	3114	A2
200 Noble St, HarC, 77373		
Contemporary Arts Mus	4102	D1
5216 Montrose Blvd, HOUS, 77006		
Cowboy Ranch Restaurant & Mus	4249	A3
6915 Spencer Hwy, PASD, 77536		
Cullen Sculpture Garden	4102	E1
1000 Bissonnet St, HOUS, 77006		
CY Twombly Gallery	3962	C7
1511 Sul Ross St, HOUS, 77006		
David Taylor Classic Car Mus	5109	C2
1918 Mechanic St, GLSN, 77550		
DOC International Tobacco Mus & Archive	3962	A2
330 TC Jester Blvd, HOUS, 77007		
Fine Toon Cartoon Art Gallery	4102	A2
2427 Bissonnet St, HOUS, 77005		
Forbidden Gardens	3814	C5
23500 Franz Rd, HarC, 77493		
Forbidden Gardens Chinese Cultural Mus	3814	C5
23500 Franz Rd, HarC, 77493		
Fort Bend Mus	4491	E1
500 Houston St, RHMD, 77469		
Frank J Brown Heritage Mus	4629	C1
108 S Friendswood Dr, FRDW, 77546		
Galveston Arts Center	5109	B2
2127 The Strand, GLSN, 77550		
Galveston County Historical Mus	5109	B3
2219 Market St, GLSN, 77550		
Galveston Gallery	5109	C4
1825 Rosenberg St, GLSN, 77550		
Galveston Island Railroad Mus & Terminal	5109	B2
123 Rosenberg St, GLSN, 77550		
Heritage Society, The	3963	B4
1100 Bagby St, HOUS, 77002		
Heritage Mus of Montgomery County	2383	D4
1506 I-45 Feeder Rd, CNRO, 77301		
Holocaust Mus Houston	4102	E2
5401 Caroline St, HOUS, 77004		
Houston Center for Contemporary Craft	4102	E1
4848 Main St, HOUS, 77002		
Houston Center for Photography	3962	D7
1441 W Alabama St, HOUS, 77006		
Houston Computer Mus	4096	B2
15827 Thistledew Dr, HarC, 77082		
Houston Fire Mus	3963	A5
2403 Milam St, HOUS, 77006		
Houston Maritime Mus	4102	B4
2204 Dorrington St, HOUS, 77030		
Houston Mus of Natural Science	4102	E2
1 Hermann Cir Dr, HOUS, 77030		
Houston Police Mus	3404	C3
17000 Aldine Westfield Rd, HOUS, 77032		
Houston Railroad Mus	3826	E1
7390 Mesa Dr, HOUS, 77078		
Humble Historical Mus	3262	D6
219 E Main St, HMBL, 77338		
Imma Hogg Mansion	3962	A4
1 Westcott St, HOUS, 77007		
John C Freeman Weather Mus, The	4102	E1
5104 Caroline St, HOUS, 77004		
John P McGovern Mus of Health & Med Science	4102	E2
1515 Hermann Dr, HOUS, 77004		
Kemah Historic School Mus	4509	E5
KMAH, 77565		
Lawrence Marshall Antique Car Mus	2953	B5
52294 10th St, HMPD, 77445		
Lone Star Fire Mus	4245	D7
8313 Braniff Av, HOUS, 77061		
Lone Star Flight Mus	5221	E1
2002 Terminal Dr, GLSN, 77554		
Mardi Gras Mus	5109	B3
2309 The Strand, GLSN, 77550		
Menil Collection, The	3962	C7
1515 Sul Ross St, HOUS, 77006		
Military Mus of Texas	3826	C6
8611 Wallisville Rd, HOUS, 77029		
Moody Mansion & Mus	5109	B3
2618 Broadway St, GLSN, 77550		
Mus of Southern History, The	4368	D2
14080 Southwest Freeway Frontag, SGLD, 77478		
Museo Guadalupe Aztlan	3963	A6
3004 Bagby St, HOUS, 77006		
Mus of Amer Architecture & Decorative Arts	4099	D6
7502 Fondren Rd, HOUS, 77074		
Museum of Fine Arts-Houston	4102	E2
1001 Bissonnet St, HOUS, 77005		
Museum of Printing History	3962	D4
1324 W Clay St, HOUS, 77019		
National Mus of Funeral History, The	3258	E7
415 Barren Springs Dr, HarC, 77090		
New World Mus	3962	B2
5230 Center St, HOUS, 77007		
Nolan Ryan Foundation & Exhibit Center	4867	C4
2925 S Alvin Byp, ALVN, 77511		
Ocean Star Offshore Drilling Rig & Mus	5109	C2
1 19th St, GLSN, 77550		
Pioneer Memorial Log House Mus	4102	D3
1510 N MacGregor Dr, HOUS, 77030		
Proctor Mus of Natural Science	3828	D7
630 Uvalde Rd, HOUS, 77015		
Rice Gallery	4102	D3
6100 Main St, HOUS, 77005		
Robert A Vines Environmental Science Center	3821	A6
8856 Westview Dr, SPVL, 77055		
Rosenberg Railroad Mus	4490	D4
1921 2nd St, RSBG, 77471		
San Jacinto Mus & Monument	3970	A5
1 Park Road 1836, HarC, 77571		
Space Center Houston	4507	E4
1601 NASA Pkwy, HOUS, 77058		
Strake Jesiut Air Mus	4099	A5
8900 Bellaire Blvd, HOUS, 77036		
Straw Art Mus	5109	D2
1214 Church St, GLSN, 77550		
Texas City Mus	4875	D5
409 6th St N, TXCY, 77590		
Texas Seaport Mus	5109	B2
2200 Harborside Dr, GLSN, 77550		
Tomball Mus Center	2964	B6
510 N Pine St, TMBL, 77375		
Veteran's Mus in Texas	4378	C5
Scarsdale Blvd, HOUS, 77034		
Visions of the West Collection	3963	C5
1221 Lamar St, HOUS, 77010		
West Bay Common School Children's Mus	4632	A2
210 N Kansas Av, LGCY, 77573		
Woodland Science & Art Center	2968	A2
3 Grogans Park Dr, WDLD, 77380		

Open Space

FEATURE NAME	MAP#	GRID
Armand Bayou Nature Ctr Taylor Lake Preserve, - PASD	4381	E4
Baytown Nature Preserve, BYTN	3971	A5
BNC-Myra C Brown Wild Bird Sanctuary & Pk, - BYTN	3971	A3
Catherine Keegan Wilderness Ranch, BKVL	4375	C5
Coolgreen Corridor, HOUS	3828	A6
Kleb Woods Nature Preserve, HarC	3106	B3
Sheldon Lake State Pk & WMA, HarC	3690	B3

Other

FEATURE NAME / Address City ZIP Code	MAP#	GRID
Alden Houston Hotel	3963	C4
1117 Prairie St, HOUS, 77002		
Armand Bayou Nature Center	4381	C5
8500 Bay Area Blvd, PASD, 77507		
Bayou Place	3963	C3
500 Texas Av, HOUS, 77002		
Burke Baker Planetarium	4102	E2
1 Hermann Cir Dr, HOUS, 77030		
Edith L Moore Nature Sanctuary	3958	C2
440 Wilchester Blvd, HOUS, 77079		
George Observatory	4102	E2
1 Hermann Cir Dr, HOUS, 77030		
Japanese Garden	4102	D2
Hermann Cir Dr, HOUS, 77005		
Kemah Waterfront	4509	E5
215 2nd St, KMAH, 77565		
Lancaster Hotel	3963	C4
701 Texas Av, HOUS, 77002		
Lyndon B Johnson Space Center	4508	A3
2nd St, HOUS, 77058		
Magnolia Hotel-Houston	3963	C4
1100 Texas Av, HOUS, 77002		
Moody Gardens	5107	E7
1 Hope Blvd, GLSN, 77554		
Moody Gardens IMAX 3D Theater	5107	E7
1 Hope Blvd, GLSN, 77554		
NOAA Fisheries Galveston Laboratory	5108	E7
4700 Avenue U, GLSN, 77551		
Old Central Cultural Center	5109	B4
2627 Avenue M, GLSN, 77550		
Port of Houston Authority	4105	D1
111 E Loop Frwy N, HOUS, 77029		
Reliant Astrodome	4102	B7
1 Reliant Pk, HOUS, 77054		
Rothko Chapel, The	3962	D7
1409 Yupon St, HOUS, 77006		
Sam Houston Hotel	3963	C4
1117 Prairie St, HOUS, 77002		
Wortham IMAX Theatre	4102	E2
1 Hermann Cir Dr, HOUS, 77030		

Park & Ride

FEATURE NAME	MAP#	GRID
Park & Ride, BzaC	4624	B6
Park & Ride, WDLD	2968	B3
Park & Ride-Ace, HOUS	4245	C4

Houston Points of Interest Index

Park & Ride

FEATURE NAME Address City ZIP Code	MAP#	GRID
Park & Ride-Addicks, HOUS	3956	E1
Park & Ride-Alief, HOUS	4238	C1
Park & Ride-Bay Area, HOUS	4507	B4
Park & Ride-Eastex, HarC	3546	E2
Park & Ride-Eastwood Transit Center, HOUS	4104	A1
Park & Ride-Fannin South, HOUS	4242	C1
Park & Ride I-45, CNRO	2529	E1
Park & Ride-Katy/West Belt, HOUS	3819	D7
Park & Ride-Kingsland, HOUS	3954	B2
Park & Ride-Kingwood, HOUS	3119	D5
Park & Ride-Maxey Road, HOUS	3827	E7
Park & Ride-Missouri City, HOUS	4371	A2
Park & Ride-North Shepherd, HOUS	3684	B2
Park & Ride-NW Station, JRSV	3539	E6
Park & Ride-NW Transit Center, HOUS	3961	B1
Park & Ride-Pinemont, HOUS	3682	C7
Park & Ride-Seton Lake, HarC	3542	A2
Park & Ride-Spring, HarC	3259	A3
Park & Ride-Tidwell Transit Center, HOUS	3686	A5
Park & Ride-West Bellfort, HOUS	4238	D4
Park & Ride-West Little York, HarC	3680	E3
Park & Ride-West Loop, HOUS	4241	B1
Park & Ride-Westwood, HOUS	4239	A2

Parks & Recreation

FEATURE NAME Address City ZIP Code	MAP#	GRID
Adams/Rawley Pk, HOUS	3964	C1
Adoue Pk, GLSN	5109	D3
AE Dyess Pk, HarC	3107	E7
Alabonson Pk, HarC	3682	B1
Alamo Pk, GLSN	5108	D5
Alcorn Oaks Pk, SGLD	4495	A2
Alexander Deussen Pk, HOUS	3550	C4
Alief-Amity Pk, HOUS	4097	D4
Alief Community Pk, HOUS	4098	A5
Allenbrook Pk, BYTN	3972	E2
Allen's Landing Pk, HOUS	3963	C3
Almeda Pk, HOUS	4373	B5
Almeda Plaza Pk, HOUS	4242	B7
Ambrose Pk, HarC	4096	C7
Amburn Pk, TXCY	4875	A1
American Legion Pk, HOUS	3822	E3
American Legion Pk, MSCY	4369	D5
Anchor Pk, TXCY	4875	E5
Anderson Pk, HOUS	4100	D1
Andover Pk, HOUS	4244	D2
Andy Anderson Pk, HOUS	3266	B5
Anson Jones Pk, BYTN	4112	E1
Antioch Pk, HOUS	3963	B4
Apache-Elbert Triangle, HOUS	3826	A2
Armand Bayou Pk, PASD	4381	C6
Aron Ledet Pk, HOUS	3682	D4
Arthur Storey Pk, HOUS	4098	D6
Ashbel Smith School Pk, BYTN	3973	A7
Ashbury Pk, PASD	4107	C6
Athletic Field, HOUS	3957	B5
Athletic Pk, HOUS	4240	D6
Austin Meadow Pk, SGLD	4495	A3
Austin Meadows Pk, FBnC	4494	A3
Austin Pk, SGLD	4495	D2
Autry Pk, HOUS	3962	C4
AV Bull Sallas Pk, MtgC	2827	B7
Avenue A Pk, SHUS	4246	E2
Bane Pk, HarC	3681	A2
Barbara Jordan Pk, HOUS	3547	A6
Barkaloo Pk, BYTN	3973	B2
Baseball Pk, HOUS	4237	D1
Bay Area Pk, PASD	4381	A5
Bayer Pk, HarC	3114	A5
Bayland Pk, BYTN	4112	B3
Bayland Pk, HOUS	4100	B6
Bayou Pk, LMQU	4874	A7
Bayridge Pk, LGCY	4633	C3
Bayshore Pk, GlsC	4635	B3
Bay Street Pk, TXCY	4875	E3
Baytown Pk, BYTN	3972	A2
Baytown Soccer Pk, BYTN	3972	A1
Beach Pocket Pk 1, GLSN	5221	B5
Beach Pocket Pk 2, GLSN	5220	E6
Beach Pocket Pk 3, GLSN	5333	A2
Bear Creek Pk, HOUS	3818	B3
Beech-White Pk, HOUS	4243	C1
Belin Pk, FBnC	4234	B7
Bellaire Pk, BLAR	4100	E5
Bell Pk, HOUS	4102	D1
Beltway 8 Sports Pk, HarC	3829	B2
Bendwood Pk, HOUS	3958	D2
Bennett Pk, HOUS	4103	B3
Bergeron Pk, BYTN	4112	A1
Beverly Hills Pk, HOUS	4377	C3
Bicentennial Pk, BYTN	3972	D7
Bicentennial Pk, MSCY	4370	A3
Binglewood Pk, HOUS	3820	D2
Bishop Fiorenza Pk, HOUS	4097	B3
Bishop Pk, HarC	4504	D1
Bishop Quin Pk, HOUS	4247	A5
Bliss Meadows Pk, PASD	4248	D3
Blueridge Pk, HOUS	4371	E6
Bob Briscoe Pk, ALVN	4867	B5
Bobby Beach Pk, LMQU	4989	C1
Bob Lutz Pk, FBnC	4366	A4
Bonham Pk, HOUS	4099	D7
Boone Road Pk, HOUS	4098	B6
Booth Homes Pk, LPRT	4251	B2
Bordersville Pk, HOUS	3262	B6
Bowie Pk, BYTN	3973	C5
Bowling Green Pk, PASD	4108	D6
Boyce-Dorian Pk, HOUS	3964	C1
Braeburn Glen Pk, HOUS	4239	C1
Bramley Pk, PASD	4248	D2
Braslau Pk, TXCY	4875	D6
Brazos Landing Pk, SGLD	4495	A5
Brazos Pk, RSBG	4490	D3
Bremond Pk, TXCY	4875	A6
Brentwood Pk, HOUS	4241	D7
Brewster Pk, HOUS	3964	A1
Briarbend Pk, HOUS	3960	A6
Briar Meadow Pk, HOUS	4100	A1
Briar Pk, PASD	4108	C6
Bricker Pk, HOUS	4243	C2
Bridge Water Pk, SGLD	4495	C4
Broadmoor-Kretschmar Pk, HOUS	4104	B1
Brock Pk, HOUS	3688	C6
Brook Hollow Pk, HOUS	3822	C3
Brookline Pk, HOUS	4104	D5
Brown Memorial Field, DRPK	4249	A2
Brummerhop Pk, SEBK	4509	B2
Buffalo Bayou Pk, HOUS	3962	D4
Buffalo Run Pk, MSCY	4370	E3
Burke/Crenshaw Pk, PASD	4247	D7
Burnet Pk, HarC	3970	E1
Burnett Bayland Pk, HOUS	4100	D3
Busby Pk, HOUS	3825	B2
Busch Terrace Pk, BYTN	3972	C6
Cambridge Village Pk, HOUS	4241	B7
Campbell Woods Pk, HOUS	3820	B3
Camp Logan Triangle, HOUS	3961	E2
Candlelight Pk, HOUS	3683	D7
Candy Cane Pk, CNRO	2383	D4
Canterbury Village Pk, HOUS	4373	C2
Carbide Pk, LMQU	4989	B2
Carl Barton Junior Pk, CNRO	2531	A1
Carol Fox Pk, JRSV	3680	D1
Carol Tree Pk, PNPV	3959	D5
Carter Pk, HOUS	4244	E4
Carverdale Pk, HOUS	3681	B6
Carver Pk, TXCY	4873	D6
Cascade Pk, PASD	4106	D6
Castillo Pk, HOUS	3963	D1
Cedar Grove Pk, HarC	3693	A1
Centennial Pk, PRLD	4503	A4
Central Heights Pk, BYTN	3972	C7
Central Little League Pk, BYTN	3972	D6
Challenger Seven Memorial Pk, LGCY	4631	A3
Chandler Arboretum & Pk, HarC	3834	B5
Channelview Sports Complex, HarC	3830	D4
Channelwood Pk, HarC	3968	C1
Charlton Pk, HOUS	4105	D7
Cherryhurst Pk, HOUS	3962	D6
Chimney Rock Pk, HOUS	4240	D5
Chimney Stone Neighborhood Pk, SGLD	4368	E7
Christia V Adair Pk, HOUS	4374	E6
Cimarron Pk, CNRO	2383	B2
Cimarron Pk, HarC	3953	E3
Citizens's Pk, ALVN	4867	B1
City Hall Pk, STFE	4987	B1
City Pk, HMPD	2953	A6
City Pk, RHMD	4364	D7
City Pk, SGLD	4368	A1
City Softball Pk, STFE	4871	B6
Clairmont Pk, TXCY	4874	D5
Clark Henry Pk, JRSV	3680	E1
Clear Lake & Rodriguez Pk, HOUS	4379	C6
Clear Lake Forest Pk, PASD	4508	D1
Clear Lake Pk, PASD	4508	D2
Clements Spaceway, HOUS	3962	B3
Cleveland Pk, HOUS	3962	C3
Cliff Tuttle Pk, HOUS	3964	D2
Clinton Pk, HOUS	3965	E6
Cloverland Pk, HOUS	4243	B7
Cloverleaf Pk, HarC	3968	A1
Cole Creek Pk, HOUS	3682	A5
Colonial Pk, WUNP	4101	C3
Colony Bend Pk, SGLD	4495	C1
Colony Meadows Pk 1, SGLD	4368	A7
Colony Meadows Pk 2, SGLD	4368	B7
Commonwealth Neighborhood Pk, SGLD	4495	D3
Community Pk, PASD	4107	D5
Community Pk, RSBG	4490	E3
Condon Field, HOUS	4240	E5
Cooper Road Pk, HOUS	3685	A4
Cottage Grove Pk, HOUS	3962	A1
Countryside Pk, LGCY	4630	C5
Covington West Pk, SGLD	4237	A6
CP Hill Pk, HOUS	4243	E1
Crain Pk, HOUS	4099	A6
Crane Pk, PASD	4107	A3
Creekmont Pk, LPRT	4250	B1
Creekwood Nature Area, HOUS	3119	C6
Creekwood Pk, WDLD	2821	A6
Crescent Oak Village Pk, MSCY	4497	D3
Crestmont Pk, HOUS	4243	E7
Cris Cole Pk, HOUS	3685	D2
Cristyette Pk, SHUS	4246	E3
Cristy Pk, SHUS	4246	E4
Crockett Pk, GLSN	5108	D7
Croix Pk, BzaC	4624	E2
Crooker/Moody Pk, HOUS	3967	B1
Crosby Pk, HarC	3552	C2
Croyden Gardens Pk, HOUS	3685	D7
Cullen Pk, HOUS	3816	C6
Cullinan Pk, HOUS	4104	D7
Curry Street Pk, HOUS	3825	A2
Cypress Creek Parks Project, HarC	3115	D3
Cypress Creek Pk, HarC	3259	A1
Cypress Pk, HarC	3398	B4
Cypresswood Pk, HarC	3256	E4
Cyrill Pk, HOUS	4103	B7
Dads Club Community Pk, PRLD	4502	C4
Dale Street Pk, BYTN	3973	C6
Darien Pk, HOUS	3826	A2
David A Rutledge Memorial Pk, HOUS	4507	A3
David C Hubbard Pk, RMFT	2829	B2
Deep Water Pk, PASD	4108	C4
Deer Ridge Pk, HOUS	3263	E1
Delce Pk, HOUS	3825	D6
Del Monte Pk, HOUS	3961	D5
Devonshire Woods Pk, HarC	3113	B7
De Zavalla Pk, HOUS	3965	B7
Diez Street Pk, HOUS	4104	B1
Dodson Lake Pk, HOUS	3686	B6
Doss Pk, HarC	3543	A3
Dot Watson Athletic Field, GLSN	5221	E1
Dow Pk, DRPK	4109	B7
Dow Pk, HOUS	4245	D3
Dow Pk No 1, HarC	3404	A7
Dow Pk No 2, HarC	3684	C1
Duhacsek Pk, FBnC	4367	A1
Duke Hill Pk, BYTN	4112	C1
Dunlavy Pk, HOUS	4102	C1
Dwight D Eisenhower Pk, HOUS	3550	D4
East Little League Pk, BYTN	3973	B6
Eastside Pk, TXCY	4875	D6
Eastwood Pk, HOUS	3964	B6
Eddie Huron Pk, BYTN	3972	C1
Edgewood Pk, HOUS	4244	B3
Edmonds Pk, HOUS	3547	A1
Edna Mae Washington Pk, HarC	3832	D4
Egret Pk, WEBS	4507	E6
Elbert Pk, HOUS	3826	A2
Eldridge Pk, SGLD	4237	B5
El Franco Lee Pk, HOUS	4377	A5
Elizabeth Baldwin Pk, HOUS	3963	B7
Elizabeth Kaiser Meyer Pk, HarC	3256	D5
EL Jardin Pk, PASD	4383	C5
Elva Lobit Pk, LGCY	4633	A5
Emancipation Pk, HOUS	3963	C7
Emcyrp Football Field, MtgC	2974	A4
Enchanted Oaks Pk, HarC	3113	B7
Enclave Pk, MSCY	4496	C1
Estates of Silver Ridge Pk, MSCY	4621	E2
Evelyn Kennedy Pk, LPRT	4251	E3
Fairmont Pk, LPRT	4250	C
Fairmont Pk, PASD	4247	B
Farnsworth Pk, HOUS	2974	E
Feigle Pk, LMQU	4990	A
Field Pk, BLAR	4101	B
Finnigan Pk, HOUS	3964	C
Fire Fighter Pk, TXCY	4874	E
First Colony Pk, SGLD	4495	D
Flag Tree Pk, PNPV	3959	E
Fleming Pk, HOUS	4102	C
Flournoy Pk, CNRO	2384	B
Fonde Pk, HOUS	4104	C
Fondern Fields Pk, MSCY	4370	E
Fondern Pk, MSCY	4239	D
Forest Gate Pk, WDLD	2820	A
Forest West Pk, HOUS	3682	D
Fort Crockett Seawall Pk, GLSN	5108	E
Fort Travis Seashore Pk, GlsC	4995	A
Forum Pk, HOUS	4238	E
Francklow Pk, HOUS	3958	E
Frank C Murdock Pk, BYTN	3972	D
Frankie Carter Randolph Pk, FRDW	4505	C
Freddiesville Pk, GlsC	4990	A
Freedom Tree Pk, MSCY	4497	C
Freed Pk, HOUS	3821	E
Freeway Manor Pk, HOUS	4246	D
Freshmeadow Pk, HOUS	3681	C
Friendship Gardens, PASD	4107	A
Friendship Pk, SEBK	4382	E
Friendswood Sport Pk, FRDW	4749	E
Fritsche Pk, HarC	3253	A
Fullerton Pk, HOUS	4507	B
Galena Manor Pk, GNPK	3966	A
Galena Pk Sports Complex, GNPK	3966	C
Galveston Island State Pk, GLSN	5332	B
Gammill Pk, MSCY	4239	D
Garcia Pk, RSBG	4490	B
Gardens Pk, PASD	4107	C
Gardens Pk 2, PASD	4107	C
Garden Villa Pk, HOUS	4245	A
George Bush Pk, HOUS	3955	C
George Pk, RHMD	4364	D
Gerber Pk, HarC	3546	C
Gibson Pk, CNRO	2383	E
Giesinger Elementary Pk, CNRO	2383	B
Gilliam Pk, LPRT	4251	E
Gleason Pk, HOUS	3687	A
Glen Cove Pk, LGCY	4509	A
Glen Laurel Pk, SGLD	4236	E
Glenmore Forest Pk, HOUS	3821	C
Glenshire Pk, HOUS	4239	B
Godard Pk, TXCY	4875	A
Godwin Pk, HOUS	4240	E
Golden Acres Pk, PASD	4248	B
Goose Creek Pk, BYTN	3972	C
Grady Pk, HOUS	3960	E
Gragg Pk, HOUS	4104	D
Graham Pk, HOUS	3823	B
Grand River Pk, HOUS	3688	B
Gray Sports Complex, BYTN	3833	E
Greatwood Neighborhood Pk, FBnC	4494	B
Green Acres Pk, WEBS	4507	D
Greens Bayou Pk, HOUS	3967	C
Greenwood Pk, HOUS	3828	C
Grimes Pk, HOUS	4243	E
Grogans Pk, MtgC	2968	A
Groveland Terrace Pk, HOUS	3826	C
Gulf Palms Pk, HOUS	4378	A
Gutierrez Pk, HOUS	3965	B
Haden Pk, HOUS	3820	B
Hager Pk, HOUS	4240	C
Halbert Pk, HOUS	3823	D
Hardwood Pk, RSBG	4491	C
Hardy/Tidwell Pk, HOUS	3685	D
Harold Kylberg Field, HOUS	4106	A
Harris Gardens 2 Pk, PASD	4107	C
Hartman Pk, HOUS	4105	E
Harwin Pk, HOUS	4098	C
Havenpark Pk, HOUS	4380	C
Haviland Pk, HOUS	4240	B
Heights Pk, TXCY	4874	E
Helen's Garden, LGCY	4632	A
Henderson Pk, HOUS	3824	D
Hennessey Pk, HOUS	3963	D
Heritage Pk, HarC	4630	C
Heritage Place Pk, CNRO	2384	A
Herman Brown Pk, HOUS	3827	D
Hermann Pk, HOUS	4102	E
Hermann Square Pk, HOUS	3963	B
Hidalgo Pk, HOUS	3965	A
Highland Bayou Pk, LMQU	4990	A
Highland Community Center Pk, HarC	3831	C
Highland Pk, HOUS	3683	A
Highland Pk, PASD	4107	A
Highland Pk, SGLD	4368	D
Highlands Neighborhood Pk 1, SGLD	4368	D
Highlands Neighborhood Pk 2, SGLD	4368	C
Highlands Pk, HarC	3832	A
Hitchcock City Pk, HTCK	4988	C
HL Patton Memorial City Pk, PTVL	2682	E
Hobart Taylor Pk, HOUS	3826	C
Hockley Pk, HarC	3248	C
Hogg Bird Sanctuary Pk, HOUS	3962	A
Hogg Pk, HOUS	3963	B
Holly Bay Pk, PASD	4249	A
Homewood Pk, HOUS	3962	A
Houston Gardens Pk, HOUS	3825	D
Howard L Ward Pk, NSUB	4508	A
Huffington Pk, WUNP	4101	D
Hugh Adams Pk, ALVN	4867	C
Humble City Pk, HMBL	3407	A
Hunters Glen Pk, MSCY	4370	D
Hutcheson Pk, HOUS	3825	D
Imperial Pk, SGLD	4367	E
Independence Heights Pk, HOUS	3823	D
Independence Pk, HarC	3680	E
Independence Pk, MSCY	4370	A
Independence Pk, PRLD	4503	E
Indigo Lake Estates Pk, MtgC	2814	C
Ingrando Pk, HOUS	4105	B
Insley Pk, TXCY	4875	E
Irvington Pk, HOUS	3824	C
IT May Pk, HarC	3122	D
Jacinto City Pk, JTCY	3966	A
Jack Brooks Pk, HTCK	4988	B
Jamaica Beach, GLSN	5442	C
Jamaica Beach City Pk, JMAB	5331	E
James Bute Pk, HOUS	3963	D
James Driver Pk, HarC	3686	A
Japonica Pk, HOUS	4105	A
Jaycee Pk, HOUS	3822	D

Houston Points of Interest Index

EATURE NAME / ddress City ZIP Code	MAP#	GRID
ycee Pk, LMQU	4989	D2
Hollaway Pk, BYTN	3973	E1
nny Riley Civic Center-Park, LPRT	4251	D2
sse H Jones Pk & Nature Center, HarC	3261	E2
hnson Pk, TXCY	4875	D3
nes Pk, GLSN	5108	A7
nes Pk, HOUS	4376	C4
Trotter Pk, HOUS	3687	B2
dson Pk, WUNP	4101	C2
ergens Pk, TMBL	2964	B4
aminski Pk, HarC	3832	A1
arl E Young Pk, HOUS	4101	D6
aty City Pk, KATY	3813	C5
aty City Pk II, KATY	3813	C5
aty Community VFW Pk, KATY	3813	B7
aty Pk, HarC	3813	E4
eith-Weiss Pk, HOUS	3545	E6
emper Pk, GLSN	5109	B4
enneth W Royal Pk, HOUS	4507	B2
err Pk, HOUS	3823	D1
eyes Pk, HOUS	3962	A3
ing Estates Pk, HOUS	4374	D1
irkwood South Pk, HarC	4377	D6
ismiersky Pk, CNRO	2383	D7
itty Hollow Pk, FBnC	4497	C6
lein Pk, HarC	3112	C6
ohfeldt Pk, TXCY	4874	B5
agana Pk, LMQU	4990	A1
akefield Pk, SGLD	4496	A1
ake Forest Pk, HOUS	3687	E6
ake Houston State Pk, MtgC	2974	E1
akeshore Harbour Pk, MSCY	4497	C5
akes of Edgewater Pk, SGLD	4368	E6
akewood Pk, HOUS	3687	D7
andsdale Pk, HOUS	4099	C5
angham Creek Pk, HarC	3537	C4
angwood Pk, HOUS	3821	C2
a Salle Pk, GlsC	4636	A5
asker Pk, GLSN	5108	E5
aw Pk, HOUS	4244	C4
awrence Beach Pk, TXCY	4993	D1
awrence Pk, HOUS	3962	B1
eague of Women Voters Pk, BYTN	3972	E4
eague Pk, LGCY	4632	A3
eavesley Pk, FRDW	4629	C4
eroy Pk, HOUS	3963	D7
evy Pk, HOUS	4102	A1
ewis Pk, CNRO	2384	A6
exington Creek Pk, MSCY	4369	B6
exington Village Pk, MSCY	4369	B5
ey Plaza Pk, HOUS	3963	A1
iberty Hill Pk, WUNP	4101	D2
ight Company Pk, PASD	4106	E3
incoln Cedars Pk, BYTN	3974	B1
incoln Pk, HOUS	3683	E1
indale Pk, GLSN	5109	E1
indsey/Lyons Sports Center, HarC	3407	C4
inear Pk, HOUS	3963	A3
inkwood Pk, HOUS	4101	E7
ions Pk, CNRO	2238	C7
ittle Cedar Bayou Pk, LPRT	4251	D5
ittle Thicket Pk, HOUS	3822	E4
ive Oak Pk, HOUS	3962	B5
omax Pk, LPRT	4110	C7
onnie Green Pk, SGLD	4368	A2
o Pk, HOUS	4244	A1
ost Creek Pk, SGLD	4369	A5
ove Pk, HOUS	3823	C6
ulac Pk, TXCY	4874	E2
lacco Pk, SGLD	4368	C2
lacGregor Elementary Pk, HOUS	4103	A1
lacGregor Parkway, HOUS	4103	D4
lacGregor Pk, HOUS	4104	A3
lagnolia Youth Sports Complex, MtgC	2669	C7
lahan Pk, LMQU	4989	D4
lain Street Pk, HMBL	3262	E6
lalone Pk, HOUS	4103	D1
langum Manor Pk, HOUS	3821	E2
larian Pk, HOUS	4239	D4
larina Pk, ALVN	4867	C1
larron-North York Pk, HOUS	3964	B4
lartin Luther King Jr Pk, CNRO	2384	C6
lartin Luther King Jr Sports Complex, CNRO	2384	B6
lary Elliot Pk, HOUS	3962	A5
lary Jo Peckham Pk For All Children, KATY	3813	C5
lary Pierce Withers Pk, HOUS	3685	E3
lason Pk, HOUS	4105	A2
latheson Pk, TMBL	2964	B5
latzke Pk, HarC	3399	A4
laxey Pk, HOUS	3966	E1
layfield Pk, SGLD	4367	E2
lcCullough Pk, HOUS	3823	E2
lcDade Pk, CNRO	2382	D4
lcElroy Pk, BYTN	3971	E2
lcLain Pk, MSCY	4370	D1
lcNair Memorial Pk, ELGO	4509	B1
lcReynolds Middle School Pk, HOUS	3964	D3
leador Pk, SEBK	4509	E2
leadowbrook Pk, HarC	3831	B5
leadow Creek Village Pk, HOUS	4246	B1
leadow Lake Pk, SGLD	4368	A6
lelrose Pk, HOUS	3685	A2
lemorial Pk, FRDW	4505	C6
lemorial Pk, HOUS	3961	C3
lemorial Pk, PASD	4107	A4
lemorial Pk, TXCY	4874	D3
lenard Pk, GLSN	5109	B5
lesa Verde Pk, HOUS	4380	C6
lesquite Pk, SGLD	4368	D7
leyerland Pk, HOUS	4240	E1
leyer Pk, HOUS	3962	A6
liddlebrook Community Association Pk, HOUS	4380	C4
lilby Pk, HOUS	4105	E4
lilltown Pk, CNRO	2383	E6
lilroy Pk, HOUS	3823	C6
lilton Pk, HOUS	3824	E3
linchen Pk, HOUS	4372	B3
liramar Pk, SEBK	4509	E2
lission Bend Pk, FBnC	4096	A5
lission West Pk, FBnC	4095	E6
lissouri City Community Pk, MSCY	4497	C3
ILK Pk, TMBL	2964	C7
loffit-Springwood Pk, HOUS	3819	D4
lontcrief Pk, HarC	3830	E4
lontgomery County Pk, MtgC	2238	D6
lontie Beach Pk, HOUS	3824	A5
loody Pk Recreation Center, HOUS	3824	C6
lorgan Pk, ALVN	4867	A3
loseley Pk, MSCY	4496	D2
lueller Pk, HarC	3545	A4
lulberry Pk, BLAR	4101	C3

FEATURE NAME / Address City ZIP Code	MAP#	GRID
Mustang Pk, FBnC	4623	B2
Nacol Pk, HOUS	3821	C1
Nadolney Field, HarC	3828	E7
Nassau Bay City Pk, NSUB	4508	A7
National Oak Pk, ALVN	4867	C1
NC Foote Pk, BYTN	4112	B1
Nelson-Yellowstone Pk, HOUS	4103	C6
Newcastle Pk, BYTN	3973	B3
New Kentucky Pk, HarC	3105	E2
Newman Pk, ALVN	4749	A7
Newport Pk, LGCY	4631	B5
Nieto Pk, HOUS	3965	A1
Nob Hill Pk, HOUS	3819	E5
Noble Pk, TXCY	4875	C5
Norman Way Pk, HarC	3546	E6
North 14th Street Pk, LPRT	4251	C3
Northline Pk, HOUS	3684	D4
North Little League Pk, BYTN	3972	E1
North Pk Recreation Area, HOUS	3118	E2
North Roane Pk, MSCY	4497	D1
Northshore Pk, HarC	3828	C5
North Shore Pk, WDLD	2821	D4
North Side Mini-Bike Pk, MRGP	4251	D1
Northwest Pk, LPRT	4110	C7
Northwood Pk, HarC	3257	C3
Nottingham Pk, HOUS	3957	E2
Oakbrook West Pk, HOUS	4380	A7
Oak Corner Pk, TXCY	4875	B5
Oak Forest Pk, HOUS	3822	D2
Oak Meadows Pk, HOUS	4106	C6
Oakwick Forest, MSCY	4621	D1
Old City Pk, FRDW	4629	C2
Old Market Square Pk, HOUS	3963	C3
Olson Pk, PASD	4249	B3
Osburn Soccer Fields, TXCY	4874	E4
Oyster Creek Pk, SGLD	4369	A6
Oyster Point Pk, SGLD	4368	E4
Pappa Blakley's Softball Pk, FBnC	4094	A5
Parkgate North Pk, PASD	4248	B4
Parkmeadows Pk, DRPK	4249	C1
Park Place Pk, HOUS	4105	E6
Parkview Pk, PASD	4247	D1
Parkwood Pk, HOUS	4103	C4
Paul Hopkins Community Pk, DKSN	4753	D4
Pearson Pk, ALVN	4866	E4
Pecan Pk, FBnC	4367	A6
Peggy Pk, HOUS	4103	A1
Peiser Pk, HOUS	4105	D3
Pelham Pk, HOUS	3825	D1
Pelly Pk, BYTN	4112	E1
Perimeter Pk, HOUS	3680	D3
Pfeiffer Pk, LPRT	4251	E3
Pine Brook Neighborhood Pk, HOUS	4380	C4
Pine Gulley Pk, SEBK	4383	B6
Pine Pk, PASD	4248	D1
Pine Valley Pk, HOUS	3962	B5
Pineview Triangle, HOUS	4105	B1
Pinewood Village Pk, HOUS	3685	E3
PJ's Softball Pk, HarC	3111	E1
Plantation Bend Pk, SGLD	4369	A6
Pleasant Manor Pk, HOUS	3965	C4
Post Oak Pk, HOUS	3961	A5
Prairie Dog Pk, ALVN	4867	D2
Proctor Plaza Pk, HOUS	3824	A6
Quail Green West Pk, MSCY	4370	C5
Quail Valley North Pk, MSCY	4369	E7
Queens Pk, PASD	4246	E1
RA Apffel Pk, GLSN	4995	E6
Rasmus Pk, HOUS	4099	D2
Ray Holbrook Pk, DKSN	4754	D1
Ray Miller Pk, HOUS	3957	A5
Ray Pk, HOUS	4246	A1
Red Bluff Pk, PASD	4107	E4
Reed Pk, HOUS	3824	E2
Reeves Pk, HOUS	4240	C1
Renwick Pk, FRDW	4505	A7
Resoft Pk, BzaC	4749	B1
Reveille Pk, HOUS	4245	B1
Revelon Pk, PASD	4107	D5
Rice Pocket Pk, WUNP	4101	D3
Ridgemont Pk, HOUS	4372	A6
Ridgeview Pk, MSCY	4496	D3
Ridgewood Pk, WDLD	2821	A4
Riley Chambers Pk, HarC	3692	B3
Rio Villa Pk, HarC	3831	A1
Rive Pool & Pk, FBnC	4493	E2
Riverbend North Pk, SGLD	4369	A4
River Bend Pk, RSBG	4491	A3
Riverbend South Pk, SGLD	4369	A5
River Grove Pk, HOUS	3264	A2
River Oaks Pk, HOUS	3961	E6
Riverpark Neighborhood Pk, FBnC	4493	E1
Riverside Pk, HOUS	4103	B3
Riverstone Pk, MSCY	4496	C2
River Terrace Pk, HarC	3830	D7
Roberson Pk, CNRO	2384	A4
Robert Clark Pk, HOUS	3685	A6
Robinson Pk, HOUS	3965	D3
Robinson Pk, TXCY	4874	E4
Rolling Fork Pk, HarC	3541	C6
Ron Slockett Memorial Pk, SGLD	4237	D4
Root Square Pk, HOUS	3963	C5
Roseland Pk, BYTN	4113	C1
Rosewood Pk, HOUS	3687	A7
Rosslyn Pk, HOUS	3682	C7
Roy Campbell Burroughs Pk, HarC	2965	B1
Ruben Adame Pk, ALVN	4749	B7
Runge Pk, STFE	4870	B7
Rush Pk, PASD	4107	B5
Russ Pitman Pk, BLAR	4101	B5
Rustic Oaks Pk, LGCY	4630	D6
Sagemeadow Pk, HarC	4377	D7
Sagemont Pk, HOUS	4378	A5
Sam Houston National Forest, MtgC	2239	E1
Sam Houston Pk, HOUS	3963	B4
Samuel Matthews Pk, HarC	2964	E4
Sand Canyon Pk, HarC	4097	A7
Sanders Pk, TXCY	4875	C6
San Felipe Pk, HOUS	3963	A4
San Jacinto Battleground State Historic Pk, - HarC	3970	C5
San Jacinto Pk, GLSN	5109	C3
San Jacinto Pk, HOUS	3263	A2
Satsuma Gardens Pk, PASD	4107	E5
Saums Pk, HarC	3815	D6
Sawmill Pk, WDLD	2967	E1
Scales Pk, HOUS	4103	B6
Scenic Place Pocket Pk, FBnC	4493	D6
Scenic Woods Pk, HOUS	3687	A4
Schnur Pk, HOUS	4374	D1
Schreiber Pk, GLSN	5222	A2

FEATURE NAME / Address City ZIP Code	MAP#	GRID
Schroeder Field, ALVN	4867	A2
Schwartz Pk, HOUS	3821	B3
Schweppe Pk, HOUS	4102	D7
Scottcrest Pk, HOUS	4243	B6
Seabourne Creek Pk, RSBG	4615	A2
Seabrook Sports Complex, SEBK	4509	D2
Sealy Pk, ALVN	4867	A1
Searls Pk, SGLD	4369	A3
Seawolf Pk, GLSN	4994	D5
Selena-Denver Harbor Pk, HOUS	3964	E2
Sesquicentennial Pk, HOUS	3963	B3
Settegast Pk, HOUS	3963	E5
Settlers Way Pk, SGLD	4495	E1
Shadowbend Pk, WDLD	2821	A2
Shadow Pk, MtgC	2677	C2
Shady Lane Pk, HOUS	3685	E4
Shamrock Pk, MtgC	2814	D7
Sharpstown Pk, HOUS	4099	C4
Sheldon Pk, HarC	3689	E5
Shepherd Pk, HOUS	3823	A1
Sheppard Pk, BYTN	3972	D7
Sherwood Pk, PASD	4107	B7
Sienna Hoa Pk, FBnC	4621	D4
Sims Bayou Pk, HOUS	4244	A5
Smith Pk, JTCY	3966	D3
Smokey Jasper Pk, HOUS	3547	A4
Songwood Pk, HOUS	3966	B1
Southcrest Pk, HOUS	4244	A1
Southland Pk, HOUS	4103	B5
South Main Estates Pk, HOUS	4371	A2
Southmore Pk, PASD	4108	A6
South Post Oak Pk, HOUS	4371	E7
South Roane Pk, MSCY	4497	D1
Southside Place Pk, SSPL	4101	D4
Southwell Pk, HarC	3113	E1
Spaceway Pk, HOUS	3967	C3
Spoor Field, GLSN	5108	E5
Sport Pk, HarC	3955	D1
Sportsman Pk, HarC	3399	B7
Spotts Pk, HOUS	3962	D3
Spring Creek Forest Pk, HarC	3256	D1
Spring Creek Pk, HarC	2963	C6
Spring Klein Baseball Pk, HarC	2967	B7
Spurlock Parkway, HOUS	4104	D3
Spurlock Pk, HOUS	4104	D2
Squatty Lyons Pk, HOUS	3685	C2
Stafford City Pk, FBnC	4369	E5
Sta-Mo Pk, MSCY	4370	A6
Stanfield Pk, HOUS	3826	D1
Steed Pk, TXCY	4875	A4
Steep Bank Village Pk, FBnC	4621	E4
Steeple Chase Pk, JRSV	3540	A7
Sterling Knoll Pk, HOUS	4506	D3
Stevenson Pk, FRDW	4629	D2
Stewart Beach Pk, GLSN	5109	E2
Stewart Pk, HOUS	4244	E3
Stewarts Creek Pk, CNRO	2384	B3
Stonecrest Parkway, HOUS	3822	C4
Stratford Pk, HarC	3831	D2
Strawberry Pk, PASD	4247	C2
Strickland Pk, HOUS	3828	A6
Stude Pk, HOUS	3962	E1
Stuebner-Airline Pk, HOUS	3544	A7
Sugar Lakes Pk, SGLD	4368	A2
Sugar Land Memorial Pk, SGLD	4494	C3
Sugar Mill Pk, SGLD	4237	A7
Sugarwoods Neighborhood Pk, SGLD	4368	D5
Summerfield Pk, SGLD	4237	C5
Summer Street Pk, HOUS	3963	A2
Sunnyside Pk, HOUS	4243	B3
Sunset Pk, PASD	4106	E6
Sunset Pk, RSBG	4490	D5
Sutton Pk, SGLD	4495	D4
Swiney Pk, HOUS	3964	A3
Sylvan Beach Pk, LPRT	4251	E4
Talmadge Pk, ALVN	4867	A1
Tanglewilde Pk, HOUS	4099	B2
Tanglewood Pk, HOUS	3960	D4
Tarpey Pk, TXCY	4875	E4
Tatar Pk, PASD	4107	C7
Taub Pk, HOUS	4246	A4
Taylor-Stevenson Pk, HOUS	4242	C5
TC Jester Pk, HOUS	3822	D4
Teal Run Pk, FBnC	4622	D2
Tejas Pk, BYTN	3973	B5
Telge Pk, HarC	3397	D6
Terry Hershy Pk, HOUS	3957	B3
Texas Avenue Pk, WEBS	4507	A6
Texas City Pk, TXCY	4875	E1
Theis Attaway Pk, TMBL	3109	A2
Thomas L James Pk, SGLD	4368	A3
Tidwell Timbers Pk, HOUS	3686	E5
Timbergrove Manor Pk, HOUS	3823	A6
Tomball Little League Fields, TMBL	2964	B6
Tom Bass Regional Pk I, HarC	4374	B6
Tom Bass Regional Pk II, HarC	4374	C6
Tom Bass Regional Pk III, HarC	4374	D6
Townwood Pk, HOUS	4372	E2
Trahan Pk, TXCY	4875	B6
Tranquility Pk, HOUS	3963	B4
Travis Pk, BYTN	3971	B1
Travis Pk, RSBG	4491	A5
Trinity Gardens Pk, HOUS	3825	C2
Tuffly Pk, HOUS	3825	B7
TW Davis Memorial Pk, RHMD	4491	E2
Unidad Pk, BYTN	3972	B7
Uvalde Pk, HOUS	3967	D1
Verde Forest Pk, HOUS	3688	C5
Vermillion Pk, PASD	4106	D4
Victoria Gardens Pk, HOUS	3684	D7
VV Ramsey Community Center, HarC	3969	B1
Waldemar Pk, HOUS	3958	A6
Walker Pk, BYTN	3972	D4
Walker Pk, TXCY	4875	C4
Walnut Pk, WEBS	4507	B6
Walter Hall Pk, LGCY	4631	E2
Walter Holland Pk, TXCY	4755	B5
Walter Jenkins Memorial Pk, BYTN	3973	D1
Wanita Triangle, HOUS	3961	E2
Warren Pk, HOUS	3686	C5
Washington Pk, GLSN	5108	B5
Water Reservoir Pk, TXCY	4755	E4
Watonga Parkway, HOUS	3822	B1
WC Britton Pk, BYTN	4112	C2
WE Bill Crowley Pk, HarC	3546	B3
Weir Pk, WUNP	4102	A2
Welwyn Pk, HarC	3540	E6
West 23rd Street Pk, HOUS	3823	B4
Westbury Pk, HOUS	4240	C3
Westchase Pk, HOUS	4099	A2
West End Pk, HOUS	3962	C2

Houston Points of Interest Index

Parks & Recreation

FEATURE NAME Address City ZIP Code	MAP#	GRID
West Fork of Goose Creek Stream Future Pk, - BYTN	3972	C4
Westlawn Pk, LMQU	4989	C1
West Little York Pk, HOUS	3683	B3
West Mt Houston Pk, HOUS	3542	C7
Westview Pkway Pk, TXCY	4875	B4
Westwood Pk, BYTN	3971	B3
Westwood Pk, HOUS	4241	C1
WG Jones State Forest, MtgC	2675	C3
White Oak Parkway, HOUS	3963	A1
White Pk, HOUS	3967	A3
Whitt Johnson Pk, WUNP	4102	A4
Wiess Pk, HOUS	3961	A3
Wildheather Pk, HOUS	4372	D4
Wiley Pk, HOUS	3962	E5
Williams Grant Pk, SGLD	4368	D7
Willow Pk, HOUS	4241	B3
Wilson Memorial Pk, HOUS	4246	E6
Wilwood Pk, SEBK	4509	C3
Windsor Village Pk, HOUS	4371	E3
Winzer Pk, HOUS	3683	C3
Wipprecht Pk, HOUS	3964	C1
Witty Memorial Pk, ELGO	4509	B1
Woodcreek Pk, PRLD	4504	C5
Woodland Pk, HOUS	3963	B1
Woodlands Sports Pk, The, WDLD	2968	B4
Woodsland Pk, KATY	3952	B1
Woodstream Neighborhood Pk, SGLD	4495	B1
Wright Cuney Pk, GLSN	5108	E4
Yellowstone Pk, PASD	4248	B6
Zube Pk, HarC	3249	D2

Post Offices

FEATURE NAME Address City ZIP Code	MAP#	GRID
Addicks Barker Station 16830 Barker Springs Rd, HOUS, 77084	3956	A1
Airport Mail Facility Station 19175 Lee Rd, HOUS, 77032	3261	D6
Albert Thomas Station 14917 El Camino Real Blvd, HOUS, 77062	4506	E1
Alief 11936 Bellaire Blvd, HOUS, 77072	4098	A5
Almeda 3030 W Fuqua St, HOUS, 77045	4373	A3
Alvin 455 E House St, ALVN, 77511	4867	C2
Anson Jones 634 W Cavalcade St, HOUS, 77009	3824	A5
Ashford West 12655 Whittington Dr, HOUS, 77077	3957	C6
Astrodome Station 8205 Braesmain Dr, HOUS, 77025	4102	A6
Bacliff Main Office 415 Grand Av, GlsC, 77518	4634	D3
Barker 211 Baker Rd, HarC, 77094	3955	B1
Baytown 601 W Baker Rd, BYTN, 77521	3972	E2
Bear Creek 16015 Cairnway Dr, HarC, 77084	3678	D7
Beechnut Station 11703 Beechnut St, HOUS, 77072	4098	A7
Bellaire Main Office 5350 Bellaire Blvd, BLAR, 77401	4100	E4
Bob Harris Station 102 N Munger St, PASD, 77506	4107	A3
Broadway 4020 Broadway St, HOUS, 77087	4105	C7
Channelview 531 S Sheldon Rd, HarC, 77530	3969	B3
Civic Center Station 700 Smith St, HOUS, 77002	3963	B4
Conroe Main Office 809 E Dallas St, CNRO, 77301	2384	B4
Cornerstone 14403 Walters Rd, HarC, 77014	3257	C7
Crosby 133 Hare Rd, HarC, 77532	3552	C2
Cypress Main Office 16635 Spring Cypress Rd, HarC, 77429	3396	E3
Debora Sue Schatz 2909 Rodgerdale Rd, HOUS, 77042	4098	D1
Deer Park 200 E San Augustine St, DRPK, 77536	4109	B6
Delbert L Atkinson Station 6100 Spencer Hwy, PASD, 77505	4248	D3
De Moss Station 6500 De Moss Dr, HOUS, 77074	4100	B4
Denver Harbor Station 5901 Market St, HOUS, 77020	3964	D2
Dickinson 2515 Termini St, DKSN, 77539	4753	E3
East Houston 9604 Mesa Dr, HOUS, 77078	3687	E5
Eastwood Lawndale St, HOUS, 77023	4104	C1
Fairbanks 7050 Brookhollow West Dr, HarC, 77040	3681	A2
First Colony Sugarland 3130 Grants Lake Blvd, SGLD, 77479	4368	C7
Fleetwood 315 Addicks Howell Rd, HOUS, 77079	3956	D1
Foster Place 5210 Griggs Rd, HOUS, 77021	4104	A6
Fresno Main Office 2723 Almeda Rd, FBnC, 77545	4499	C5
Friendswood Main Office 310 Morningside Dr, FRDW, 77546	4505	C7
Galena Park Main Office 1805 Clinton Dr, GNPK, 77547	3966	C7
Galleria 5015 Westheimer Rd, HOUS, 77056	3961	A7
Garden Oaks 3816 N Shepherd Dr, HOUS, 77018	3823	B2
Genoa Station 10935 Almeda Genoa Rd, HOUS, 77034	4377	E1
Grangerland MtgC, 77302	2533	A6
Granville W Elder 550 Maxey Rd, HOUS, 77013	3827	E7
Greenbriar Station 3740 Greenbriar Dr, HOUS, 77098	4102	B1
Greens North 1530 Greensmark Rd, HOUS, 77067	3402	C6
Greenway Plaza Station 3 E Greenway Plz, HOUS, 77046	4101	E1
Harrisburg 8330 Manchester St, HOUS, 77012	4105	D3
Heights 1050 Yale St, HOUS, 77008	3823	D7
Hempstead 901 12th St, HMPD, 77445	2953	B7
Highlands Main Office 608 S Main St, HarC, 77562	3831	E4
Hockley Main Office 17210 Warren Ranch Rd, HarC, 77447	3248	E3
Houston Main 401 Franklin St, HOUS, 77002	3963	C3
Huffman Main Office 24936 Crosby Huffman Rd, HarC, 77336	3266	E1
Humble 1202 1st St E, HMBL, 77338	3263	A6
Irvington 7825 Fulton St, HOUS, 77022	3824	A1
James Griffith 9320 Emnora Ln, HOUS, 77080	3820	D3
Jensen Drive 3520 Jensen Dr, HOUS, 77026	3824	E6
John Dunlop 8728 Beverly Hill Ln, HOUS, 77063	4099	D1
John Foster Station 1520 Richey St, PASD, 77502	4106	E6
Julius Melcher 2802 Timmons Ln, HOUS, 77027	3961	D7
Katy Finance 5701 3rd St, KATY, 77493	3813	C7
Kemah KMAH, 77565	4509	E6
Kingwood Branch 4025 Feather Lakes Wy, HOUS, 77339	3119	D5
Klein 7717 Louetta Rd, HarC, 77379	3256	C4
La Marque 509 Laurel St, LMQU, 77568	4874	A7
La Porte Main Office 801 W Fairmont Pkwy, LPRT, 77571	4251	D4
League City 240 W Galveston St, LGCY, 77573	4631	E3
Long Point Station 8000 Long Point Rd, HOUS, 77055	3821	C5
Magnolia Main Office 815 Goodson Rd, MAGA, 77355	2668	E5
Manvel Main Office 6925 Masters Rd, MNVL, 77578	4746	D1
Medical Center 7205 Almeda Rd, HOUS, 77054	4102	E6
Memorial Park Station 10505 Town & Country Wy, HOUS, 77024	3958	E1
Missouri City Main Office 1902 Texas Pkwy, MSCY, 77489	4370	C5
Nassau Bay 18214 Upper Bay Rd, NSUB, 77058	4508	A5
New Caney 20811 Antique Ln, MtgC, 77357	2827	D7
North Houston 4600 Aldine Bender Rd, HOUS, 77032	3546	C1
North Shepherd 7511 N Shepherd Dr, HOUS, 77088	3684	B3
Oak Forest 2499 Judiway St, HOUS, 77018	3822	C3
Panther Creek 10800 Gosling Rd, WDLD, 77381	2821	A3
Park Place 5302 Galveston Rd, HOUS, 77017	4246	B1
Park Row Katy 20180 Park Row Blvd, HOUS, 77449	3815	D7
Pasadena Main Station 1199 Pasadena Blvd, PASD, 77506	4107	C6
Pearland Main Office 3519 E Walnut St, PRLD, 77581	4503	C3
Pinehurst 34635 Wright Rd, SGCH, 77362	2816	E5
Porter Main Office 23550 Partners Wy, MtgC, 77365	2973	B5
Prairie View Main Office PRVW, 77445	2955	B6
Rich Hill Station 2950 Unity Dr, HOUS, 77057	4100	B1
Richmond Main Office 5560 BF Terry Blvd, RHMD, 77469	4491	E4
River Oaks 1900 W Gray St, HOUS, 77019	3962	C5
Rosenberg Main Office 2103 Avenue G, RSBG, 77471	4490	E4
Roy Royall 4206 Little York Rd, HarC, 77093	3686	B3
Sage Carrier Station 3500 Sage Rd, HOUS, 77056	4100	E1
Sam Houston Carrier Station 1500 Hadley St, HOUS, 77004	3963	B6
San Leon 902 E Bayshore Dr, GlsC, 77539	4636	B5
Santa Fe Main Station STFE, 77510	4870	E7
Seabrook Main Office 1600 2nd St, SEBK, 77586	4509	D2
Silver Lake 2700 Cullen Blvd, PRLD, 77584	4501	E3
South Houston Main Office 315 N Allen Genoa Rd, SHUS, 77587	4247	A2
Southmore 4110 Almeda Rd, HOUS, 77004	4103	A1
Splendora Main SPLD, 77372	2683	B2
Spring Main Office 1411 Wunsche Lp, HarC, 77373	3113	D2
Stafford Main Office 4110 Bluebonnet Dr, STAF, 77477	4238	C7
Station A Baytown 3508 Market St, BYTN, 77520	3972	A7
Sugar Land Main Office 225 Matlage Wy, SGLD, 77478	4367	E3
Texas City 2002 11th St N, TXCY, 77590	4875	C3
Texas Southern 3100 Cleburne St, HOUS, 77004	4103	C2
Tomball Main Office 122 N Holderrieth Blvd, TMBL, 77375	2964	A7
TW House 1300 W 19th St, HOUS, 77008	3823	A5
University Houston 1319 Richmond Av, HOUS, 77006	3962	D7
Waller Main WALR, 77484	3101	E5
Webster Main Office 17077 N Texas Av, WEBS, 77598	4507	A6
Weslayan 5340 Weslayan St, HOUS, 77005	4101	D2
Westbrae 10910 S Gessner Rd, HOUS, 77031	4239	C4
Westbury 11805 Chimney Rock Rd, HOUS, 77035	4240	D
Westchase 3836 S Gessner Rd, HOUS, 77042	4099	B
Westfield 17119 Red Oak Dr, HarC, 77090	3258	C
West Galveston Branch 16602 San Luis Pass Rd, JMAB, 77554	5332	A
William Rice 5201 Wakeforest St, HOUS, 77005	4102	A
Willow Place 12955 Willow Pl Dr W, HOUS, 77070	3399	D
Windmill 9898 Almeda Genoa Rd, HOUS, 77075	4377	C
Woodlands Branch, The 9450 Pinecroft Dr, WDLD, 77380	2822	A

Schools

FEATURE NAME Address City ZIP Code	MAP#	GRID
Abercrombie Academy Elementary School 17102 Theiss Mail Route Rd, HarC, 77379	3256	B
Abiding Word Lutheran School 17123 Red Oak Dr, HarC, 77090	3258	C
Abundant Life Christian High School 5130 Casey St, LMQU, 77568	4872	E
Academy Elementary School 2900 Spencer Hwy, PASD, 77504	4247	C
Academy for Science & Health 3200 W Davis St, CNRO, 77304	2383	C
Academy High School 1110 Main St, HOUS, 77002	3963	B
Academy High School 2900 Spencer Hwy, PASD, 77504	4247	C
Academy Lower School 10202 Memorial Dr, HOUS, 77024	3960	C
Academy of Clear Lake 2222 Bay Area Blvd, HOUS, 77058	4507	D
Academy of Science & Technology 3701 College Park Dr, WDLD, 77384	2675	D
Academy Westfield 10030 Scarsdale Blvd, HarC, 77089	4504	E
Accelerated Center for Education 13801 Hollypark Dr, HarC, 77015	3828	E
Adam Elementary School 11303 Honey Grove Ln, HarC, 77065	3539	C
Adventures in Music 10555 Spring Cypress Rd, HarC, 77070	3255	B
Agape Christian Academy 103 Bird Rd, PASD, 77502	4107	A
Aikin Elementary School 600 Dogwood Ln, MtgC, 77357	2829	B
AISD Career Technology Center 1010 S Johnson St, ALVN, 77511	4867	A
Albright Middle School 6315 Winkleman Rd, HarC, 77083	4096	C
Alcott Elementary School 5859 Bellfort St, HOUS, 77033	4244	B
Aldine Elementary School 7007 Fallbrook Dr, HarC, 77086	3542	B
Aldine Middle School 14908 Aldine Westfield Rd, HarC, 77032	3545	D
Aldine Ninth Grade School 10650 N Fwy, HOUS, 77037	3544	B
Aldine Senior High School 11101 Airline Dr, HOUS, 77037	3544	B
Alexander Elementary School 8500 Brookwulf Dr, HOUS, 77072	4097	D
Al-Hadi School of Accelerated Learning 2313 S Voss Rd, HOUS, 77057	3960	A
Alief Middle School 4415 Cook Rd, HOUS, 77072	4097	E
Allen Elementary School 400 Victoria Dr, HOUS, 77022	3823	D
Almeda Elementary School 14249 Bridgeport Rd, HOUS, 77047	4373	A
Alternative School of Choice 1732 Katyland Dr, KATY, 77493	3813	D
Alvin Elementary School 1910 Rosharon Rd, ALVN, 77511	4867	A
Alvin High School 802 S Johnson St, ALVN, 77511	4867	B
Alvin Junior High School 2300 W South St, ALVN, 77511	4866	E
Anderson Academy 7401 Wheatley St, HOUS, 77088	3683	E
Anderson Elementary School 6218 Lynngate Dr, HarC, 77373	3261	A
Anderson Elementary School 5727 Ludington Dr, HOUS, 77035	4240	C
Anderson Elementary School-Conroe 1414 E Dallas St, CNRO, 77301	2384	C
Annunciation Orthodox School 3600 Yoakum Blvd, HOUS, 77006	3962	D
Aragon Middle School 16823 West Rd, HarC, 77095	3538	B
Arizona Fleming Elementary School 14850 Bissonnet St, FBnC, 77083	4236	D
Arlyne & Alan Weber Elementary School 11955 Blackhawk Blvd, HarC, 77089	4504	E
Armand Bayou Elementary School 16000 Hickory Knoll Dr, HOUS, 77059	4380	C
Armstrong Elementary School 110 Gladstell St, CNRO, 77301	2384	A
Arnold Middle School 11111 Telge Rd, HarC, 77429	3397	C
Art & Pat Goforth Elementary School 2610 Webster St, LGCY, 77573	4632	D
Arthur Miller Career Center 1734 Katyland Dr, KATY, 77493	3813	D
Ascension Episcopal School 2525 Seagler Rd, HOUS, 77042	3958	E
Ashbel Smith Elementary School 403 E James St, BYTN, 77520	3973	A
Ashford Elementary School 1815 Shannon Valley Dr, HOUS, 77077	3957	E
Askew Elementary School 11200 Wood Lodge Dr, HOUS, 77077	3958	B
Atascocita Middle School 18810 W Lake Houston Pkwy, HarC, 77346	3265	B
Atherton Elementary School 2011 Solo St, HOUS, 77020	3964	C
Atkinson Elementary School 9602 Kingspoint Rd, HOUS, 77089	4377	C
Attucks Middle School 4330 Bellfort St, HOUS, 77051	4243	C
Ault Elementary School 21010 Maple Village Dr, HarC, 77433	3251	B
Austin Elementary School-Baytown 3022 Massey Tompkins Rd, BYTN, 77521	3973	E
Austin Elementary School-Richmond 1630 Pitts Rd, FBnC, 77469	4365	D

Houston Points of Interest Index

EATURE NAME Address City ZIP Code	MAP#	GRID
ustin High School 1700 Dumble St, HOUS, 77023	4104	B1
ustin High School-Sugar Land 3434 Pheasant Creek Dr, FBnC, 77478	4235	E7
ustin Middle School 5001 Avenue U, GLSN, 77551	5108	D7
ustin Parkway Elementary School 4400 Austin Pkwy, SGLD, 77479	4496	B1
wty International School 7455 Awty School Ln, HOUS, 77055	3822	A7
ailey Elementary School 2707 Lafferty Rd, PASD, 77502	4247	C2
aker Sixth Grade Campus 9800 Spencer Hwy, LPRT, 77571	4250	B3
aker's Preparatory School 504 Murphy Rd, FBnC, 77477	4369	D3
ales Intermediate School 211 Stadium Ln, FRDW, 77546	4629	A1
all High School 4115 Avenue O, GLSN, 77550	5108	E5
ammel Elementary School 17309 Red Oak Dr, HarC, 77090	3258	B3
ammel Middle School 16711 Ella Blvd, HarC, 77090	3258	C5
ane Elementary School 5805 Kaiser St, HOUS, 77040	3681	C5
anff School 13726 Cutten Rd, HarC, 77069	3400	B2
ang Elementary School 8900 Rio Grande Dr, HarC, 77064	3540	B6
arbara Bush Elementary School 7420 Crownridge Dr, WDLD, 77382	2674	D5
arbara Jordan Elementary School 17800 W Oaks Village Dr, FBnC, 77469	4095	C5
arbara W Birkes Elementary School 8500 Queenston Blvd, HarC, 77095	3538	A5
arber Middle School 2218 Timber Dr, DKSN, 77539	4753	D1
arrett Primary School 815 FM-1942 Rd, HarC, 77532	3693	A1
arrick Elementary School 12001 Winfrey Ln, HOUS, 77076	3685	B2
arrington Place Elementary School 2100 Squire Dobbins Dr, SGLD, 77478	4237	D5
astian Elementary School 7350 Calhoun Rd, HOUS, 77033	4243	D1
ay Area Christian High School 4800 FM-518 Rd, LGCY, 77573	4630	D5
ay Area Christian School 4800 FM-518 Rd, LGCY, 77573	4630	D6
ay Area Montessori House 17222 Mercury Dr, HarC, 77058	4507	C4
ay Colony Elementary School 101 Bay Colony Elementary Dr, LGCY, 77539	4753	A3
aytown Christian Academy 302 W Cedar Bayou Lynchburg Rd, BYTN, 77521	3972	E1
aytown Junior High School 7707 Bayway Dr, BYTN, 77520	3971	C1
ear Branch 6th Grade Campus 8040 Ken Lake Dr, MtgC, 77382	2673	B6
ear Branch Elementary School 3500 Garden Lake Dr, HOUS, 77339	3119	B5
ear Branch Elementary School 8909 FM-1488 Rd, MtgC, 77382	2673	B6
ear Branch Junior High School 31310 FM-2978 Rd, MtgC, 77382	2673	B6
ear Creek Elementary School 4815 Hickory Downs Dr, HarC, 77084	3678	E6
earrington School 1250 FM-2234 Rd, STAF, 77477	4370	C4
eckendorff Junior High School 8200 S Fry Rd, FBnC, 77494	4093	C3
eck Junior High School 5200 S Fry Rd, FBnC, 77450	4094	B2
ellaire Christ Academy 4601 Bellaire Blvd, BLAR, 77401	4101	B4
ellaire High School 5100 Maple St, BLAR, 77401	4100	E6
ell Elementary School 12323 Shaftsbury Dr, HOUS, 77031	4239	A6
ellfort Academy 7647 Bellfort St, HOUS, 77061	4245	C2
enavidez Elementary School 6262 Gulfton St, HOUS, 77081	4100	B3
en Bowen Elementary School 24403 E Lake Houston Pkwy, HOUS, 77336	3266	C2
enbrook Elementary School 4026 Bolin Rd, HOUS, 77092	3821	D2
eneke Elementary School 3840 Briarchase Dr, HarC, 77014	3401	D1
enfer Elementary School 18027 Kuykendahl Rd, HarC, 77379	3257	C1
en's Branch Elementary School 24160 Briar Berry Ln, MtgC, 77365	2973	A6
erry Elementary School 2310 Berry Rd, HOUS, 77093	3685	D7
est Elementary School 10000 Centre Pkwy, HOUS, 77036	4239	A2
ethune Academy 2500 S Victory Dr, HOUS, 77088	3683	B3
eth Yeshurun Day School 4525 Beechnut St, HOUS, 77096	4101	B7
everly Hills Intermediate School 11111 Beamer Rd, HOUS, 77089	4377	D4
irkes Elementary School 8500 Queenston Blvd, HarC, 77095	3538	A5
lack Elementary School 160 Mill Stream Ln, HOUS, 77060	3544	C1
lack Elementary School-Cypress 14155 Grant Rd, HarC, 77429	3253	E5
lack Middle School 1575 Chantilly Ln, HOUS, 77018	3822	D1
lackshear Elementary School 2900 Holman St, HOUS, 77004	4103	C1
leyl Middle School 10800 Mills Rd, HarC, 77070	3399	A4
locker Middle School 500 14th Av N, TXCY, 77590	4875	D4
lue Ridge Elementary School 6241 McHard Rd, HOUS, 77053	4498	E1
ondy Intermediate School 5101 Keith Av, PASD, 77505	4248	B6
onham Elementary School 8302 Braes River Dr, HOUS, 77074	4099	D7
onner Elementary School 8100 Elrod St, HOUS, 77017	4245	E1
onnette Junior High School 5010 W Pasadena Blvd, DRPK, 77536	4109	A7
oone Elementary School 11400 Bissonnet St, HOUS, 77099	4238	B2

FEATURE NAME Address City ZIP Code	MAP#	GRID
Bowie Elementary School 7501 Curry Rd, HOUS, 77093	3825	A2
Bowie Elementary School 2304 Bamore Rd, RSBG, 77471	4490	C6
Brabham Middle School 10000 FM-830 Rd, MtgC, 77318	2236	E1
Braeburn Elementary School 7707 Rampart St, HOUS, 77081	4100	C6
Branch Crossing Junior High School 10010 Lyreleaf Pl, WDLD, 77382	2674	A4
Brazos Bend Elementary School 621 Cunningham Creek Blvd, FBnC, 77479	4366	C6
Briargate Elementary School 15817 Blueridge Rd, HOUS, 77489	4371	C5
Briargrove Elementary School 5430 Hidalgo St, HOUS, 77056	3960	E7
Briarmeadow Charter School 3601 Dunvale Rd, HOUS, 77063	4099	E2
Briarmeadow Middle School 3602 Dunvale Rd, HOUS, 77063	4099	E2
Brill Elementary School 9102 Herts Rd, HarC, 77379	3256	A6
Briscoe Elementary School 321 Forest Hill Blvd, HOUS, 77011	4105	A1
Broadway Baptist Elementary School 1020 Coral St, HOUS, 77012	4105	B3
Broadway Baptist High School 1020 Coral St, HOUS, 77012	4105	B3
Brookline Elementary School 6301 South Lp E, HOUS, 77087	4104	D5
Brookside Intermediate School 3535 E FM-528 Rd, FRDW, 77546	4630	B1
Brookwood Elementary School 16850 Middlebrook Dr, PASD, 77059	4380	D4
Browning Elementary School 607 Northwood St, HOUS, 77009	3824	A6
Bruce Elementary School 713 Bringhurst St, HOUS, 77020	3964	A3
Buckalew Elementary School 4909 Alden Bridge Dr, WDLD, 77382	2674	A6
Budewig Intermediate School 12570 Richmond Av, HOUS, 77082	4097	D1
Budget Campus 1401 11th St, GNPK, 77547	3966	C6
Buffalo Creek Elementary School 2801 Blalock Rd, HOUS, 77080	3820	D3
Bunker Hill Elementary School 11950 Taylorcrest Rd, BKHV, 77024	3959	B2
Burbank Elementary School 216 Tidwell Rd, HOUS, 77022	3685	B6
Burbank Middle School 315 Berry Rd, HOUS, 77022	3685	B7
Burnet Elementary School 5501 Avenue S, GLSN, 77551	5108	D7
Burnet Elementary School 5403 Canal St, HOUS, 77011	3964	C6
Burnett Elementary School 11825 Teaneck Dr, HOUS, 77089	4378	C6
Burrus Elementary School 701 E 33rd St, HOUS, 77022	3823	E3
Burton Elementary School 1625 Hunter Green Ln, FBnC, 77545	4622	E2
Bush Elementary School 9730 Stroud Dr, HOUS, 77036	4098	E5
Bush Elementary School 13800 Westerloch Dr, HOUS, 77077	3957	A4
Bush High School 6707 Fm 1464 Rd, FBnC, 77083	4095	D5
Cage Elementary Charter School 4528 Leeland St, HOUS, 77023	3964	B7
Calvary Episcopal School 1201 Austin St, RHMD, 77469	4491	E2
Calvert Elementary School 1925 Marvell Dr, HarC, 77032	3404	C6
Campbell Elementary School 1000 Shadow Bend Dr, FBnC, 77479	4494	B5
Campbell Middle School 11415 Bobcat Rd, HarC, 77064	3540	C1
Caney Creek High School 16840 FM-2090 Rd, MtgC, 77306	2533	C6
Caraway Intermediate School 3031 Ellington St, HOUS, 77088	3683	B1
Carden Jackson School 3801 Liberty Dr, PRLD, 77581	4504	A5
Cardinal Newman School 1110 Eldridge Pkwy, HOUS, 77077	3957	B3
Carleston Elementary School 3010 Harkey Rd, PRLD, 77584	4502	D4
Carmichael Elementary School 6902 Silver Star Dr, HarC, 77086	3542	C2
Carnegie Vanguard High School 10401 Scott St, HOUS, 77051	4243	C5
Carpenter Elementary School 5002 W Pasadena Blvd, DRPK, 77536	4108	E7
Carrillo Elementary School 960 S Wayside Dr, HOUS, 77023	4104	D1
Carroll Academy 423 W Gulf Bank Rd, HarC, 77037	3544	C7
Carter Academy 3111 Fallbrook Dr, HarC, 77038	3542	E3
Carver Elementary School 600 S Pruett St, BYTN, 77520	4112	E1
CD Landolt Elementary School 2104 Pilgrims Point Dr, HarC, 77546	4506	B6
Cedar Bayou Junior High School 2610 Elvinta St, BYTN, 77520	3973	D4
Cedar Brook Elementary School 2121 Ojeman Rd, HOUS, 77080	3821	A4
Cedric C Smith Elementary School 28747 Hardin Store Rd, MtgC, 77354	2818	C3
CE King High School 8540 C E King Pkwy, HarC, 77044	3689	A6
CE King Middle School 8530 C E King Pkwy, HarC, 77044	3689	A6
Center for Hearing & Speech, The 3636 W Dallas St, HOUS, 77019	3962	C4
Central Christian Academy 2217 Bingle Rd, HOUS, 77080	3821	A4
Central Middle School 3014 Sealy St, GLSN, 77550	5109	A3
Centripet II Academy 907 Preston St, PASD, 77503	4108	A5
Challenge Early College High School 5601 West Lp S, HOUS, 77081	4101	A2
Challenger Elementary School 9434 Hughes Ranch Rd, PRLD, 77584	4501	C2
Chambers Elementary School 10700 Carvel Ln, HOUS, 77072	4098	D6
Chancellor Elementary School 4350 Boone Rd, HOUS, 77072	4098	B4

FEATURE NAME Address City ZIP Code	MAP#	GRID
Channelview High School 1100 Sheldon Rd, HarC, 77530	3830	B6
Chavez High School 8501 Howard Dr, HOUS, 77017	4106	A7
Chinquapin School 2615 E Wallisville Rd, HarC, 77562	3832	D2
Christian Life Center Academy 600 Charles St, HMBL, 77338	3262	E5
Christian School of Kingwood 2901 Woodland Hills Dr, HOUS, 77339	3118	E5
Christian Tabernacle Elementary School 13334 Wallisville Rd, HarC, 77049	3828	A4
Cimarron Elementary School 1100 S Peek Rd, HarC, 77494	3953	D4
Cimarron Elementary School 816 Cimarron St, HOUS, 77015	3967	D1
Cinco High School 23440 Cinco Ranch Blvd, FBnC, 77494	3953	C7
Cinco Ranch Junior High School 23420 Cinco Ranch Blvd, FBnC, 77494	3953	C6
CJ Harris Elementary School 2314 Schleider Dr, PRLD, 77581	4503	D2
Clark Intermediate School 1825 Rushworth Dr, HarC, 77014	3402	C3
Clark Primary School 12625 River Laurel Dr, HarC, 77014	3402	B3
Claughton Middle School 3000 Spears Rd, HarC, 77014	3402	A4
Clay Road Baptist School 9151 Clay Rd, HOUS, 77080	3820	D1
Clear Brook High School 4607 FM-2351 Rd, HarC, 77546	4505	D5
Clear Creek Children's Institute 1051 Pineloch Dr, HOUS, 77062	4506	E1
Clear Creek High School 2305 E Main St, LGCY, 77573	4632	C1
Clear Creek High School-Ninth Grade Center 2451 E Main St, LGCY, 77573	4508	C7
Clear Lake Christian School 14325 Crescent Landing Dr, HOUS, 77062	4379	C7
Clear Lake City Elementary School 1707 Fairwind Rd, HOUS, 77062	4507	B2
Clear Lake High School 2929 Bay Area Blvd, HOUS, 77062	4380	D7
Clear Lake High School-Ninth Grade Center 2903 Falcon Pass, HOUS, 77062	4380	D7
Clear Lake Intermediate School 15545 El Camino Real, HOUS, 77062	4507	A2
Clements High School 4200 Elkins Rd, SGLD, 77479	4495	A1
Clifton Middle School 6001 Golden Forest Dr, HOUS, 77092	3682	D6
Cloverleaf Elementary School 1035 Rankin Rd, HarC, 77073	3403	D3
C Martinez Elementary School 901 Hays St, HOUS, 77009	3824	C7
Cobb Elementary School 915 Dell Dale St, HarC, 77530	3829	E6
Cobb Sixth Grade Campus 6722 Uvalde Rd, HarC, 77049	3828	E2
Codwell Elementary School 5225 Tavenor Ln, HOUS, 77048	4243	E7
College Park Elementary School 4315 Luella Av, DRPK, 77536	4249	C2
Collins Elementary School 9829 Town Park Dr, HOUS, 77036	4098	E4
Collins Intermediate School 6020 Shadow Bend Pl, WDLD, 77381	2821	B1
Colony Bend Elementary School 2720 Planters St, SGLD, 77479	4495	D1
Colony Meadows Elementary School 4510 Sweetwater Blvd, SGLD, 77479	4495	A1
Commonwealth Elementary School 4909 Commonwealth Blvd, SGLD, 77479	4495	C4
Concordia Lutheran High School 700 E Main St, TMBL, 77375	2964	C6
Condit Elementary School 7000 S 3rd St, BLAR, 77401	4101	A5
Conley Elementary School 3345 W Greens Rd, HarC, 77066	3401	E6
Conroe High School 3200 W Davis St, CNRO, 77304	2383	C4
Cook Elementary School 7115 Lockwood Dr, HOUS, 77016	3825	C2
Cook Middle School 9111 Wheatland Dr, HarC, 77064	3540	C5
Coop Elementary School 10130 Aldine Westfield Rd, HOUS, 77093	3685	D4
Cooper Elementary School 18655 Imperial Valley Dr, HarC, 77073	3403	C3
Copeland Elementary School 18018 Forest Heights Dr, HarC, 77095	3537	E7
Copeland Intrmediate School 24405 E Lake Houston Pkwy, HOUS, 77336	3266	C2
Cornelius Elementary School 7475 Westover St, HOUS, 77087	4245	B1
Cornerstone Charter Academy 9016 Westview Dr, SPVL, 77055	3820	E6
Corpus Christi Catholic School 4005 Cheena Dr, HOUS, 77025	4241	D2
Covenant Academy 11711 Cypress N Houston Rd, HarC, 77065	3398	E6
Crawford Elementary School 1510 Jensen Dr, HOUS, 77020	3963	E2
Creekside Intermediate School 4320 W Main St, LGCY, 77573	4630	E5
Creekwood Middle School 3603 W Lake Houston Pkwy, HOUS, 77339	3119	D5
Creighton Elementary School 12089 FM-1485 Rd, MtgC, 77306	2533	B3
Crenshaw Primary School 16204 Wood Dr, HarC, 77530	3830	C4
Crespo Elementary School 7500 Office City Dr, HOUS, 77012	4105	B5
Crippen Elementary School 18690 Cumberland Blvd, MtgC, 77365	2972	A1
Crockett Elementary Charter School 1417 Houston Av, HOUS, 77007	3963	B2
Crockett Elementary School 4500 Barkaloo Rd, HarC, 77521	3973	B1
Crockett Elementary School 2112 Crockett St, HOUS, 77007	3963	A2
Crosby High School 14703 FM-2100 Rd, HarC, 77532	3552	C6
Crosby Middle School 14705 FM-2100 Rd, HarC, 77532	3552	D6
Crosby Middle School 7801 Neville Av, HTCK, 77563	4988	E4
Cryar Intermediate School 2375 Montgomery Park Blvd, CNRO, 77304	2383	B2

Houston Points of Interest Index

FEATURE NAME Address City ZIP Code	MAP#	GRID
Cullen Middle School 6900 Scott St, HOUS, 77021	4103	C6
Cummings Elementary School 10455 S Kirkwood Rd, HOUS, 77099	4238	A3
Cunningham Elementary School 5100 Gulfton St, HOUS, 77081	4100	E3
Cunningham Middle School 14110 Wallisville Rd, HarC, 77049	3828	B4
CW Cline Elementary School 505 Briarmeadow Av, FRDW, 77546	4629	C2
CW Cline Primary School 505 Briarmeadow Av, FRDW, 77546	4629	C3
Cy-Fair High School 22602 Northwest Fwy, HarC, 77429	3397	C7
Cypress Christian School 11123 Cypress N Houston Rd, HarC, 77065	3399	A6
Cypress Creek High School 9815 Grant Rd, HarC, 77070	3399	C4
Cypress Falls High School 9811 Huffmeister Rd, HarC, 77095	3539	A3
Cypress Ridge High School 7900 N Eldridge Pkwy, HarC, 77041	3539	D7
Cypress Woods High School 16825 Spring Cypress Rd, HarC, 77429	3396	D3
Dabbs Elementary School 302 E Lambuth Ln, DRPK, 77536	4249	B2
Danish Elementary School 11850 Fallbrook Dr, HarC, 77065	3539	D1
Dar-Ul Argam Elementary School 10415 Synott Rd, HOUS, 77478	4237	B3
Darwin Gilmore Elementary School 3552 Brittany Bay Blvd, LGCY, 77573	4630	E7
David Elementary School 5301 Shadow Bend Pl, WDLD, 77381	2821	A2
Davila Elementary School 7610 Dahlia St, HOUS, 77012	4105	B3
Davis High School 1101 Quitman St, HOUS, 77009	3963	C1
Deady Middle School 2500 Broadway St, HOUS, 77012	4105	C4
Dean Middle School 14104 Reo St, HOUS, 77040	3681	C5
Dechaumes Elementary School 155 Cooper Rd, HOUS, 77076	3685	A4
Decker Prairie Elementary School 27427 Decker Prairie Rosehl Rd, MtgC, 77355	2963	B2
Deepwater Elementary School 309 Glenmore Dr, PASD, 77503	4108	B4
Deepwater Junior High School 501 Glenmore Dr, PASD, 77503	4108	B4
Deer Park Elementary School 2920 Luella Av, DRPK, 77536	4109	C7
Deer Park High School-North Campus 402 Ivy Av, DRPK, 77536	4109	B4
Deer Park High School-South Campus 710 W San Augustine St, DRPK, 77536	4109	A6
Deer Park Junior High School 410 E 9th St, DRPK, 77536	4109	B4
Deerwood Elementary School 2920 Forest Garden Dr, HOUS, 77345	3119	E5
De Zavala Elementary School 16150 2nd St, HarC, 77530	3969	C1
De Zavala Elementary School 7521 Avenue H, HOUS, 77012	3965	B7
De Zavala Fifth Grade Center 101 E Jackson Av, PASD, 77506	4107	A4
Dickinson Elementary School 7110 Greatwood Pkwy, FBnC, 77479	4493	E5
Dickinson High School 3800 Baker Dr, DKSN, 77539	4754	C2
Dobie High School 10220 Blackhawk Blvd, HOUS, 77075	4377	B5
Dodson Elementary School 1808 Sampson St, HOUS, 77003	3963	E7
Doerre Intermediate School 18218 Theiss Mail Route Rd, HarC, 77379	3256	A2
Dogan Elementary School 4202 Liberty Rd, HOUS, 77026	3825	B7
Don Jeter Elementary School 301 E House St, ALVN, 77511	4867	C2
Doug Bussey Elementary School 11555 Airline Dr, HOUS, 77037	3544	B2
Dowling Middle School 14000 Stancliff St, HOUS, 77045	4372	B2
Drabek Elementary School 11325 Lake Woodbridge Dr, FBnC, 77478	4236	D5
Drake Private School 2555 Cordes Dr, SGLD, 77479	4368	C6
Drew Academy 1910 W Little York Rd, HOUS, 77088	3683	D4
Drew Intermediate School 223 Red Oak Av, HarC, 77532	3692	D3
Duchesne Academy of Sacred Heart 10202 Memorial Dr, HOUS, 77024	3960	C1
Dueitt Middle School 1 Eagle Ct, WDLD, 77380	2822	A7
Dulles Elementary School 630 Dulles Av, SGLD, 77478	4369	B2
Dulles High School 550 Dulles Av, SGLD, 77478	4369	A2
Dulles Middle School 500 Dulles Av, SGLD, 77478	4369	B2
Dunbar Middle School 2901 23rd St, GlsC, 77539	4632	D7
Dunn Elementary School 2003 Ww Thorne Blvd, HarC, 77073	3259	D6
Durham Elementary School 4803 Brinkman St, HOUS, 77018	3823	A1
Durkee Elementary School 7301 Nordling Rd, HOUS, 77076	3684	D3
Duryea Elementary School 20150 Arbor Creek Dr, HarC, 77449	3676	E2
Eagle Heights Christian Academy 3005 Pearland Pkwy, PRLD, 77581	4503	E4
Eagle Springs Elementary School 12500 Will Clayton Pkwy, HarC, 77346	3408	D2
EA Jones Elementary School 1800 5th St, MSCY, 77489	4370	B3
EA Lawhon Elementary School 5810 Brookside Rd, BKVL, 77581	4375	C7
EA Olle Middle School 9200 Boone Rd, HOUS, 77099	4238	C1
Earth Quest Academy 1601 11th St, GNPK, 77547	3966	C6
East Early College High School 1102 Telephone Rd, HOUS, 77023	4104	B1
Easthaven Baptist Elementary School 9321 Edgebrook St, HOUS, 77075	4246	B6
Easthaven Baptist Middle School 9321 Edgebrook St, HOUS, 77075	4246	B6

FEATURE NAME Address City ZIP Code	MAP#	GRID
Eastwood Academy Charter High School 1315 Dumble St, HOUS, 77023	3964	B7
Eckert Intermediate School 1430 Aldine Meadows Rd, HarC, 77032	3545	B1
EC Mason Elementary School 7400 Lewis Ln, MNVL, 77578	4746	E2
Edgar Glover Junior Elementary School 1510 Columbia Blue Dr, MSCY, 77489	4370	C6
Edgewood Elementary School 8655 Emnora Ln, HOUS, 77080	3821	A3
Ed H White II Elementary School 1708 les Talley Dr, ELGO, 77586	4382	B7
Edison Middle School 6901 Avenue I, HOUS, 77011	3964	E6
Edna Mae Fielder Elementary School 2100 Greenway Village Dr, FBnC, 77494	3953	D5
Ehrhardt Elementary School 6603 Rosebrook Ln, HarC, 77379	3256	C1
Eiland Elementary School 6700 N Klein Circle Dr, HarC, 77088	3542	B7
Eisenhower Ninth Grade School 3550 W Gulf Bank Rd, HOUS, 77088	3683	A1
Eisenhower Senior High School 7922 Antoine Dr, HOUS, 77088	3682	E1
Elementary School No 38 16431 Lexington Blvd, SGLD, 77479	4368	B7
Eliot Elementary School 6411 Laredo St, HOUS, 77020	3964	E1
Elkins High School 7007 Knights Ct, MSCY, 77459	4496	E6
Ellisor Elementary School 33040 Egypt Ln, MtgC, 77354	2673	D4
Elm Grove Elementary School 2815 Clear Ridge Dr, HOUS, 77339	3119	B2
Elmore Middle School 8200 Tate St, HOUS, 77028	3826	D4
Elrod Elementary School 6230 Dumfries Dr, HOUS, 77096	4240	A2
Elsik High School 12601 High Star Dr, HOUS, 77072	4097	D4
Elsik Ninth Grade Center 6767 S Dairy Ashford St, HOUS, 77072	4097	D5
Emerson Elementary School 9533 Skyline Dr, HOUS, 77063	4099	C2
Emery Weiner School 9825 Stella Link Rd, HOUS, 77025	4241	D2
Emmott Elementary School 11750 Steeple Wy Blvd, HarC, 77065	3539	E4
Empowerment College Preparatory High School 5655 Selinsky Rd, HOUS, 77048	4244	B6
Energized Excellence Charter Academy 6201 Bissonnet St, HOUS, 77081	4100	C6
Episcopal High School 4650 Bissonnet St, BLAR, 77401	4101	A3
Epps Island Elementary School 7403 Smiling Wood Ln, HarC, 77086	3542	B4
Ermel Elementary School 7103 Woodsman Tr, HOUS, 77040	3682	B1
Escamilla Intermediate School 5241 Mt Houston Rd, HarC, 77039	3546	D7
Excel Academy 2525 Murworth Dr, HOUS, 77054	4102	B7
Exley Elementary School 21800 Westheimer Pkwy, FBnC, 77450	4094	A1
Fairchild Elementary School 8701 Delilah St, HOUS, 77033	4243	D3
Fairmont Elementary School 4315 Heathfield Dr, PASD, 77505	4248	E5
Fairmont Junior High School 4911 Holly Bay Ct, PASD, 77505	4249	A6
Faith Christian Academy 3519 Burke Rd, PASD, 77504	4247	D4
Faith Lutheran School 800 Brooks St, SGLD, 77478	4367	E4
Faith West Academy 2225 Porter Rd, HarC, 77493	3814	A5
Falcon Pass Elementary School 2465 Falcon Pass, HOUS, 77062	4507	C1
Farney Elementary School 14425 Barker Cypress Rd, HarC, 77429	3396	E1
Fay School 105 N Post Oak Ln, HOUS, 77024	3961	B3
Ferguson Elementary School 1910 S Compass Rose Blvd, LGCY, 77573	4509	A7
Field Elementary School 703 E 17th St, HOUS, 77008	3823	E5
Fiest Elementary School 8425 Pine Falls Dr, HarC, 77095	3538	D6
First Baptist Academy 7450 Memorial Woods Dr, HOUS, 77024	3961	B1
First Baptist Christian Academy 7500 Fairmont Pkwy, PASD, 77507	4249	B5
First Christian Academy 12401 Beamer Rd, HarC, 77089	4378	A6
First Colony Middle School 3225 Austin Pkwy, SGLD, 77479	4495	D1
Fisher Elementary School 2920 Watters Rd, PASD, 77502	4247	E2
Fleming Middle School 4910 Collingsworth St, HOUS, 77026	3825	C6
Foerster Elementary School 14200 Fonmeadow Dr, HOUS, 77035	4240	B7
Fondren Elementary School 12405 Carlsbad St, HOUS, 77085	4371	B1
Fondren Middle School 6333 S Braeswood Blvd, HOUS, 77096	4240	A2
Fonville Middle School 725 E Little York Rd, HOUS, 77037	3684	E3
Fonwood Elementary School 10719 Seneca St, HOUS, 77016	3686	E3
Ford Elementary School 25460 Richard Rd, MtgC, 77386	2968	D1
Forest Brook High School 7525 Tidwell Rd, HOUS, 77016	3687	A5
Fort Bend Baptist Academy Elementary School 1201 Lakeview Dr, SGLD, 77478	4368	C1
Fort Bend Baptist Academy High School 1250 7th St, SGLD, 77478	4368	C1
Fort Bend Baptist Academy Middle School 13303 Southwest Fwy, SGLD, 77478	4368	E2
Fort Settlement Middle School 5440 Elkins Rd, SGLD, 77479	4495	A4
Foster Elementary School 3919 Ward St, HOUS, 77021	4103	C6
Foster Elementary School 1800 Trailwood Village Dr, HOUS, 77339	3118	D7
Francis Elementary School 14815 Lee Rd, HarC, 77032	3546	E1
Francone Elementary School 11250 Perry Rd, HarC, 77064	3540	D1

FEATURE NAME Address City ZIP Code	MAP#	GRID
Franklin Elementary School 7101 Canal St, HOUS, 77011	3965	A
Frazier Elementary School 10503 Hughes Rd, HOUS, 77089	4377	E
Freedom Elementary School 6720 New Forest Gln, HarC, 77049	3829	A
Freeman Elementary School 2323 Theta St, HOUS, 77034	4246	D
Friendswood Children's House 304 W Edgewood Dr, FRDW, 77546	4505	B
Friendswood High School 702 Greenbriar Av, FRDW, 77546	4629	B
Friendswood Junior High School 402 Laurel Dr, FRDW, 77546	4629	C
Frost Elementary School 3306 Skinner Ln, FBnC, 77469	4234	B
Frost Elementary School 5650 Selinsky Rd, HOUS, 77048	4244	B
Frostwood Elementary School 12214 Memorial Dr, BKHV, 77024	3959	A
Furr High School 520 Mercury Dr, HOUS, 77013	3966	B
Galatas Elementary School 9001 Cochrans Crossing Dr, WDLD, 77381	2674	C
Galaviz Academy 1601 11th St, GNPK, 77547	3966	C
Galena Park Elementary School 401 N Main St, GNPK, 77547	3966	C
Galena Park High School 1000 Keene St, GNPK, 77547	3966	C
Galena Park Middle School 400 Keene St, GNPK, 77547	3966	C
Gallegos Elementary School 7415 Harrisburg Blvd, HOUS, 77011	3965	A
Galloway School, The 3200 W Bay Area Blvd, FRDW, 77546	4630	B
Galveston Catholic School 2601 Avenue N, GLSN, 77550	5109	B
Garcia Elementary School 9550 Aldine Westfield Rd, HOUS, 77093	3685	E5
Garcia Middle School 18550 Old Richmond Rd, FBnC, 77478	4366	E1
Garden Oaks Elementary School 901 Sue Barnett Dr, HOUS, 77018	3823	B
Garden Villas Elementary School 7185 Santa Fe Dr, HOUS, 77061	4244	E3
Garfield Elementary School 10301 Hartsook St, HOUS, 77034	4246	D
Garland McMeans Junior High School 21000 Westheimer Pkwy, HarC, 77450	3954	C
Genoa Elementary School 12900 Almeda Genoa Rd, HOUS, 77034	4378	C
Gentry Junior High School 1919 E Archer Rd, HarC, 77521	3834	C
George Junior High School 4601 Airport Av, RSBG, 77471	4491	C
George Kaufman Elementary School 31202 Aldine Westfield Rd, MtgC, 77386	2823	C
George Washington Carver Elementary School 600 S Pruett St, BYTN, 77520	4112	E
Gevereux AEP 1100 Devereux Dr, LGCY, 77573	4631	D
GH Whitcomb Elementary School 900 Reseda Dr, HOUS, 77062	4507	A
Giesinger Elementary School 2323 White Oak Blvd, CNRO, 77304	2383	B
Ginger McNabb Elementary School 743 E Cypresswood Dr, HarC, 77373	3114	A
Gleason Elementary School 9203 Willowbridge Park Blvd, HarC, 77064	3540	D
Glen Loch Elementary School 27505 Glen Loch Dr, WDLD, 77381	2821	B
Golbow Elementary School 3535 Lakes of Bridgewater Dr, HarC, 77449	3815	B
Golden Acres Elementary School 5232 Sycamore Av, PASD, 77503	4248	B
Golfcrest Elementary School 7414 Fairway Dr, HOUS, 77087	4105	A
Goodman Elementary School 1100 W Sycamore St, FBnC, 77545	4623	A
Goodman Elementary School 9325 Deer Trail Dr, HOUS, 77088	3544	A
Goodsen Middle School 17333 Huffmeister Rd, HarC, 77429	3252	D
Goodson Middle School 17333 Huffmeister Rd, HarC, 77429	3252	C
Gordon Elementary School 6300 Avenue B, BLAR, 77401	4101	B3
Grace School 10219 Ella Lee Ln, HOUS, 77042	3958	E7
Grady Middle School 5215 San Felipe St, HOUS, 77056	3960	E5
Grangerland Intermediate School 13351 FM-1485 Rd, MtgC, 77306	2533	D5
Grantham Academy 13300 Chrisman Rd, HarC, 77039	3545	C5
Gray Elementary School 700 West Rd, HarC, 77038	3543	D
Greenleaf Elementary School 26275 FM-2090 Rd, SPLD, 77372	2683	B1
Greentree Elementary School 3502 Brook Shadow Dr, HOUS, 77345	3119	D
Green Valley Elementary School 13350 Woodforest Blvd, HarC, 77015	3828	D
Greenwood Forest Elementary School 12100 Misty Valley Dr, HarC, 77066	3401	A
Gregg Elementary School 6701 Roxbury Rd, HOUS, 77087	4244	D
Gregory-Lincoln Education Center 1101 Taft St, HOUS, 77019	3962	E4
Grimes Elementary School 9220 Jutland Rd, HOUS, 77033	4243	E4
Grissom Elementary School 4900 Simsbrook Dr, HOUS, 77045	4372	B2
Gross Elementary School 12583 S Gessner Dr, HOUS, 77071	4239	C
Guidance Center 3010 Bayshore Blvd, PASD, 77502	4247	D
GW Robinson Elementary School 451 Kirby Rd, PASD, 77586	4508	E1
Hailey Elementary School 12051 Sawmill Rd, WDLD, 77380	2967	E2
Hairgrove Elementary School 7120 N Eldridge Pkwy, HarC, 77041	3679	C1
Hall Center for Education 15014 Aldine Westfield Rd, HOUS, 77032	3545	C1
Hamblen Elementary School 1019 Dell Dale St, HarC, 77530	3829	E6
Hambrick Middle School 4600 Aldine Mail Rd, HarC, 77039	3546	B5

Houston Points of Interest Index

EATURE NAME ddress City ZIP Code	MAP#	GRID
amilton Elementary School 12050 Old Kluge Rd, HarC, 77429	3398	C1
amilton Middle School 12330 Kluge Rd, HarC, 77429	3398	B1
amilton Middle School 139 E 20th St, HOUS, 77008	3823	D5
ancock Elementary School 13801 Schroeder Rd, HarC, 77070	3399	D2
argrave High School 25400 Willy Ln, HarC, 77336	3122	D6
arlem Elementary School 3333 East Fwy, HarC, 77521	3832	E5
arris Academy 3130 Holder Forest Dr, HOUS, 77088	3683	B3
arris County JJAEP 203 Ivy Av, DRPK, 77536	4109	B4
arris County Sch for Accelerated Learning 6301 S Stadium Ln, KATY, 77494	3952	B1
arris County Youth Village 210 JW Mills Dr, PASD, 77586	4508	D2
artman Middle School 7111 Westover St, HOUS, 77087	4244	E2
artsfield Elementary School 5001 Perry St, HOUS, 77021	4103	E6
arvard Elementary School 810 Harvard St, HOUS, 77007	3823	D7
arvest Christian Academy 1117 Main St, PASD, 77506	4107	B6
arvey Brown Primary School 16550 Wallisville Rd, HarC, 77530	3829	E3
assler Elementary School 9325 Lochlea Ridge Dr, HarC, 77379	3255	D2
astings High School 4410 Cook Rd, HOUS, 77072	4097	E4
astings Ninth Grade Center 6750 Cook Rd, HOUS, 77072	4097	E5
aude Elementary School 3111 Louetta Rd, HarC, 77388	3113	A6
avard Elementary School 15150 Wallisville Rd, HarC, 77015	3829	A4
ayes Elementary School 21203 Park Timbers Ln, HarC, 77450	3954	C5
C Carleston Elementary School 3010 Harkey Rd, PRLD, 77584	4502	D4
D Guthrie Center for Excellence 10660 Hammerly Blvd, HOUS, 77043	3819	D4
earne Elementary School 13939 Rio Bonito Rd, HarC, 77083	4097	A4
ebrew Academy Elementary School, The 5435 S Braeswood Blvd, HOUS, 77096	4240	D2
ebrew Academy High School, The 5435 S Braeswood Blvd, HOUS, 77096	4240	D2
eflin Elementary School 3303 Synott Rd, HOUS, 77082	4097	B2
eights Elementary School 300 N Logan St, TXCY, 77590	4875	A5
elmers Street Christian School 7721 Helmers St, HOUS, 77022	3824	B1
elms Community Learning Center 503 W 21st St, HOUS, 77008	3823	C5
empstead Elementary School 1111 St. Barbe St, HMPD, 77445	3098	B1
empstead High School 801 Donoho St, HMPD, 77445	3098	B2
empstead Middle School 2532 9th St, HMPD, 77445	3098	B2
enry Bauerschlag Elementary School 2051 Brittany Bay Blvd, LGCY, 77573	4631	C6
enry Middle School 10702 E Hardy Rd, HOUS, 77093	3685	C3
eritage Elementary School 12255 TC Jester Blvd, HarC, 77067	3402	B4
erod Elementary School 5627 Jason St, HOUS, 77096	4100	C7
errera Elementary School 525 Bennington St, HOUS, 77022	3824	B2
licks Elementary School 8520 Hemlock Hill Dr, HarC, 77083	4097	A7
lidden Hollow Elementary School 4104 Appalachian Tr, HOUS, 77345	3119	D2
lighland Heights Charter Elementary School 865 Paul Quinn St, HOUS, 77091	3684	A6
lighlands Elementary School 200 E Wallisville Rd, HarC, 77562	3831	E2
lighlands Elementary School 2401 Magnolia Dr, LMQU, 77568	4989	E2
lighlands Elementary School 2022 Colonist Park Dr, SGLD, 77478	4368	D5
lighlands Junior High School 1212 E Wallisville Rd, HarC, 77562	3832	B2
lighpoint North School 955 Campbell Rd, HDWV, 77024	3959	E1
lightower High School 3333 Hurricane Ln, MSCY, 77545	4622	B1
Hildebrandt Intermediate School 22800 Hildebrandt Rd, HarC, 77389	2966	C6
Hilliard Elementary School 8115 E Houston Rd, HOUS, 77028	3687	D7
Hirsch Elementary School 2633 Trailing Vine Rd, HarC, 77373	3114	D6
Hitchcock High School 6625 FM-2004 Rd, HTCK, 77563	4988	C4
Hobby Elementary School 4021 Woodmont Dr, HOUS, 77045	4241	D7
Hodges Bend Middle School 16510 Bissonnet St, FBnC, 77083	4236	A2
Hoffman Middle School 6101 W Little York Rd, HOUS, 77091	3682	D4
Hogg Middle School 1100 Merrill St, HOUS, 77009	3823	E7
Hohl Elementary School 5320 Yale St, HOUS, 77022	3684	C6
Holbrook Elementary School 6402 Langfield Rd, HOUS, 77092	3682	A5
Holland Middle School 1600 Gellhorn Dr, HOUS, 77029	3965	D3
Holleman Elementary School 2200 Brazeal St, WALR, 77484	3101	E4
Hollibrook Elementary School 3602 Hollister St, HOUS, 77080	3820	E2
Holmsley Elementary School 7315 Hudson Oaks Dr, HarC, 77095	3677	E1
Holub Middle School 9515 S Dairy Ashford St, HOUS, 77099	4237	D2
Holy Ghost Catholic School 6920 Chimney Rock Rd, HOUS, 77081	4100	D5
Holy Name Catholic School 1912 Marion St, HOUS, 77009	3963	D1
Holy Rosary School 1408 James St, RSBG, 77471	4490	C5

FEATURE NAME Address City ZIP Code	MAP#	GRID
Holy Spirit Episcopal School 12535 Perthshire Rd, HOUS, 77024	3958	E2
Holy Trinity Episcopal School 11810 Lockwood Rd, HarC, 77044	3549	A6
Honor Roll School 4111 Sweetwater Blvd, SGLD, 77479	4495	A1
Hopper Primary School 405 E Houston St, HarC, 77562	3831	E2
Horne Elementary School 14950 W Little York Rd, HarC, 77084	3679	A3
Horn Elementary School 4535 Pine St, BLAR, 77401	4101	B6
Horn Elementary School 10734 Bissonnet St, HOUS, 77099	4238	D2
Houser Elementary School 27370 Oak Ridge School Rd, MtgC, 77385	2822	C3
Housman Elementary School 6705 Housman St, HOUS, 77055	3821	E6
Houston Academy for International Studies 812 W 28th St, HOUS, 77008	3823	A4
Houston Arts Academy 504 Caplin St, HOUS, 77022	3824	C3
Houston Christian High School 2700 W Sam Houston Pkwy N, HOUS, 77043	3819	D3
Houston Drop Back in Academy 1305 Benson St, HOUS, 77020	3964	B2
Houston Elementary School 601 W Lewis St, CNRO, 77301	2383	E4
Houston Gardens Elementary School 6820 Homestead Rd, HOUS, 77028	3825	E2
Houston High School 9400 Irvington Blvd, HOUS, 77076	3685	C6
Houston Junior Academy 3911 Campbell Rd, HOUS, 77080	3820	C2
Huffman Middle School 3407 Huffman Eastgate Rd, HarC, 77336	3122	D7
Hughes Road Elementary School 11901 Hughes Rd, DKSN, 77539	4753	D5
Humble Elementary School 20252 Fieldtree Dr, HMBL, 77338	3262	C4
Humble High School 1700 Wilson Rd, HMBL, 77338	3407	A1
Humble High School Ninth Grade 1131 Wilson Rd, HMBL, 77338	3407	A1
Humble Middle School 11207 Will Clayton Pkwy, HarC, 77346	3408	A2
Hunters Creek Elementary School 10650 Beinhorn Rd, HNCV, 77024	3960	B2
Hunters Glen Elementary School 8295 Independence Blvd, MSCY, 77489	4370	E5
Hutchinson Elementary School 3602 Ransom Rd, FBnC, 77469	4492	E3
Hutsell Elementary School 5360 Franz Rd, KATY, 77493	3813	D5
Iman Academy 10929 Almeda Genoa Rd, HOUS, 77034	4377	E1
Imani School 12401 S Post Oak Rd, HOUS, 77045	4241	A5
Immanuel Lutheran School 306 E 15th St, HOUS, 77008	3823	D6
Incarnate Word Academy 609 Crawford St, HOUS, 77003	3963	D4
Inman Academy South West 6240 Hwy 6 S, HOUS, 77083	4096	D4
Inter-City Elementary School 600 Wisteria St, LMQU, 77568	4874	B7
International High School 1515 Winbern St, HOUS, 77004	3963	B7
Inwood Oaks Christian School 6601 Antoine Dr, HOUS, 77091	3682	D4
Isaacs Elementary School 3830 Pickfair St, HOUS, 77026	3825	C6
Island Christian School 11279 Stewart Rd, GLSN, 77554	5221	A5
IW & Eleanor Hyde Elementary School 3700 FM-518 Rd E, LGCY, 77573	4630	E5
Jacinto City Elementary School 10910 Wiggins St, JTCY, 77029	3966	C3
Jack M Fields Senior Elementary School 2505 S Houston Av, HMBL, 77396	3406	E3
Jackson Elementary School 301 3rd St, RSBG, 77471	4490	E3
Jackson Intermediate School 1020 Thomas Av, PASD, 77506	4107	C5
Jackson Middle School 5100 Polk St, HOUS, 77023	3964	C7
James Bowie Elementary School 2200 Clayton Dr, BYTN, 77520	3973	C5
James F Bay Elementary School 1502 Bayport Blvd, SEBK, 77586	4509	D2
James H Ross Elementary School 2401 W Main St, LGCY, 77573	4631	B4
James Williams Elementary School 3900 S Peek Rd, FBnC, 77450	4093	E1
Jamison Middle School 2506 Woody Rd, PRLD, 77581	4503	A3
Janowski Elementary School 7500 Bauman Rd, HOUS, 77022	3824	B1
Jefferson Elementary School 5000 Sharman St, HOUS, 77009	3824	B5
Jenkins Elementary School 4615 Reynaldo Dr, HarC, 77373	3115	C7
Jennie Reid Elementary School 10005 W Fairmont Pkwy, LPRT, 77571	4250	B4
Jensen Elementary School 3514 Tulip St, PASD, 77504	4248	A3
Jersey Village High School 7600 Solomon St, JRSV, 77040	3680	E1
Jess Lee Pumphrey Elementary School 4901 Fairway Dr, BYTN, 77521	3972	A2
Jessup Elementary School 9301 Almeda Genoa Rd, HOUS, 77075	4377	B1
Jewel Simpson Houston Academy 8103 Carver Rd, HOUS, 77088	3683	C2
JL Lyon Elementary School 27035 Nichols Sawmill Rd, MtgC, 77355	2961	A1
John Cooper School 1 John Cooper Dr, WDLD, 77381	2820	C3
John F Ward Elementary School 1440 Bouldercrest Dr, HOUS, 77062	4379	E7
John H Reagan High School 413 E 13th St, HOUS, 77008	3823	D6
John M Stuart Career Center 300 W Wye Dr, BYTN, 77521	3972	E4
John Paul II Catholic School 1400 Pkwy Plaza Dr, HOUS, 77077	3956	E4
Johnson Elementary School 5801 Hamill Rd, HarC, 77039	3546	E5
Johnson Junior High School 15500 Proctor St, HarC, 77530	3830	A5

FEATURE NAME Address City ZIP Code	MAP#	GRID
Johnston Middle School 10410 Manhattan Dr, HOUS, 77096	4240	E2
Jones Elementary School University Dr, PRVW, 77445	3100	C1
Jones High School 7414 St. Lo Rd, HOUS, 77033	4244	A1
Jowell Elementary School 6355 Greenhouse Rd, HarC, 77449	3677	B3
JP Henderson Elementary School 1800 Dismuke St, HOUS, 77023	4104	C2
JR Harris Elementary School 801 Broadway St, HOUS, 77012	4105	C2
J Ruth Smith Academy 5815 W Little York Rd, HOUS, 77091	3682	D4
Juan N Seguin Elementary School 5905 Waltrip St, HOUS, 77087	4244	E1
Judson W Robinson Junior Elementary School 12425 Wood Forest Dr, HOUS, 77013	3828	A7
JW Jones Elementary School 1810 Stuart St, HOUS, 77004	3963	B7
JW Oates Elementary School 10044 Wallisville Rd, HOUS, 77013	3827	A6
Kahla Middle School 16212 W Little York Rd, HarC, 77084	3678	C3
Kaiser Elementary School 13430 Bammel N Houston Rd, HarC, 77066	3401	B3
Kaleidoscope-Caleidoscopio Middle School 5100 Gulfton Dr, HOUS, 77081	4100	E3
Kashmere Gardens Elementary School 4901 Lockwood Dr, HOUS, 77026	3825	C5
Kashmere High School 6900 Wileyvale Rd, HOUS, 77028	3825	D2
Katy Elementary School 5726 George Bush Dr, KATY, 77493	3813	C7
Katy High School 6331 Hwy Blvd, KATY, 77494	3952	B1
Katy Junior High School 5350 Franz Rd, KATY, 77493	3813	D5
Keefer Crossing Middle School 20358 FM-1485 Rd, MtgC, 77357	2827	D5
KE Little Elementary School 622 Oklahoma Av, GlsC, 77518	4634	C3
Kelso Elementary School 5800 Southmund St, HOUS, 77033	4104	B7
Kempner High School 14777 Voss Rd, SGLD, 77478	4236	E6
Kennedy Elementary School 306 Crosstimbers St, HOUS, 77022	3823	D2
Kenneth E Little Elementary School 622 Oklahoma Av, GlsC, 77518	4634	C3
Kerr High School 8150 Howell Sugar Land Rd, HOUS, 77083	4096	E7
Ketelsen Elementary School 600 Quitman St, HOUS, 77009	3963	C1
Key Middle School 4000 Kelley St, HOUS, 77026	3825	B4
Killough Middle School 7600 Synott Rd, HOUS, 77083	4097	C6
Kings Manor Elementary School 21111 Royal Crossing Dr, MtgC, 77339	3118	B5
Kingwood Christian Academy 1365 Northpark Dr, MtgC, 77339	3118	C3
Kingwood High School 2701 Kingwood Dr, HOUS, 77339	3119	A6
Kingwood High School 9th Grade Center 4015 Woodland Hills Dr, HOUS, 77339	3119	A3
Kingwood Middle School 2407 Pine Terrace Dr, HOUS, 77339	3119	A5
Kinkaid School 201 Kinkaid School Dr, PNPV, 77024	3959	E5
Kipp Academy 3233 Weslayan St, HOUS, 77027	3961	D7
Kirby Middle School 9709 Mesa Dr, HOUS, 77078	3687	E5
Kirk Elementary School 12421 Tanner Rd, HarC, 77041	3679	E6
Kleb Intermediate School 7425 Louetta Rd, HarC, 77379	3256	C3
Klein Collins High School 20811 Ella Blvd, HarC, 77388	3112	D4
Klein Forest High School 11400 Misty Valley Dr, HarC, 77066	3401	A4
Klein High School 16715 Stuebner Airline Rd, HarC, 77379	3256	C3
Klein Intermediate School 4710 W Mt Houston Rd, HarC, 77088	3543	A6
Klein Oak High School 22603 Northcrest Dr, HarC, 77389	2966	D7
Klenk Elementary School 6111 Bourgeois Rd, HarC, 77066	3400	E5
Klentzman Intermediate School 11100 Stancliff Rd, HOUS, 77099	4238	C4
Knox Junior High School 12104 Sawmill Rd, WDLD, 77380	2967	E2
Kohfeldt Elementary School 701 14th St N, TXCY, 77590	4875	B5
Kohrville Elementary School 11600 Woodland Shore Dr, HarC, 77375	3109	E7
Kolter Elementary School 9710 Runnymeade Dr, HOUS, 77096	4240	E2
Krahn Elementary School 9502 Eday Dr, HarC, 77379	3255	D4
Kruse Elementary School 400 Main St, PASD, 77506	4107	A4
Kuehnle Elementary School 5510 Winding Ridge Dr, HarC, 77379	3257	A1
Labay Middle School 15435 Willow River Dr, HarC, 77095	3538	D6
Lakeland Elementary School 1500 Montgomery Ln, HMBL, 77338	3263	A7
Lake Olympia Middle School 3100 Lake Olympia Pkwy, MSCY, 77459	4497	A4
Lakeview Elementary School 314 Lakeview Dr, SGLD, 77478	4368	A2
Lakewood Elementary School 15614 Gettysburg Dr, HarC, 77377	3254	D6
Lakewood Elementary School 8800 Grandriver Dr, HOUS, 77078	3688	B7
Lamar Elementary School 816 N Pruett St, BYTN, 77520	3972	E6
Lamar Elementary School 1300 Many Pines Rd, WDLD, 77380	2822	B6
Lamar High School 3325 Westheimer Rd, HOUS, 77098	3961	E7
Lamar High School 4606 Mustang Av, RSBG, 77471	4491	C4
Lamar Junior High School 4814 Mustang Av, RSBG, 77471	4491	C4
La Marque High School 300 Vauthier St, LMQU, 77568	4873	C7

Houston Points of Interest Index

FEATURE NAME Address City ZIP Code	MAP#	GRID
La Marque Middle School 1431 Bayou Rd, LMQU, 77568	4990	A2
Lamkin Elementary School 11521 Telge Rd, HarC, 77429	3397	C7
La Morgan Elementary School 1410 37th St, GLSN, 77550	5109	A4
Landis Elementary School 10255 Spice Ln, HOUS, 77099	4098	D7
Landrum Middle School 2200 Ridgecrest Dr, HOUS, 77055	3821	B4
Langham Creek High School 17610 FM-529 Rd, HarC, 77095	3677	E2
Lanier Charter Middle School 2600 Woodhead St, HOUS, 77098	3962	C6
Lantern Lane Elementary School 3323 Mission Valley Dr, MSCY, 77459	4497	C2
Lantrip Elementary School 100 Telephone Rd, HOUS, 77023	3964	A6
La Porte Elementary School 725 S Broadway St, LPRT, 77571	4251	D4
La Porte High School 301 E Fairmont Pkwy, LPRT, 77571	4251	E4
La Porte Junior High School 401 S Broadway St, LPRT, 77571	4251	D3
Lavace Stewart Elementary School 330 Marina Bay Dr, GlsC, 77565	4509	D6
Law Elementary School 12401 S Coast Dr, HOUS, 77047	4374	C1
League City Elementary School 709 E Wilkins St, LGCY, 77573	4632	A3
League City Intermediate School 2588 Webster St, LGCY, 77573	4632	D3
Lee Elementary School 12900 W Little York Rd, HarC, 77041	3679	D4
Lee High School 6529 Beverlyhill St, HOUS, 77057	4100	B1
Lemm Elementary School 19034 Joanleigh Dr, HarC, 77388	3113	D7
Levi Fry Intermediate School 1400 5th Av N, TXCY, 77590	4875	B5
Lewis Elementary School 3230 Spears Rd, HarC, 77014	3402	A4
Lewis Elementary School 7649 Rockhill St, HOUS, 77061	4245	C3
Lexington Creek Elementary School 2335 Dulles Av, MSCY, 77459	4369	B6
LF Smith Elementary School 1401 Avenue A, SHUS, 77587	4247	A2
Lieder Elementary School 17003 Kieth Harrow Blvd, HarC, 77084	3678	B6
Liestman Elementary School 7610 Synott Rd, HOUS, 77083	4097	C6
Life Christin Academy 9901 Windmill Lakes Blvd, HOUS, 77075	4377	B1
Lifestyle Christian School 1201 Hillcrest Dr, CNRO, 77301	2383	D2
Light Christian Academy 1535 Greensmark Dr, HOUS, 77067	3402	C7
Link Elementary School 2815 Ridge Hollow Dr, HarC, 77067	3402	A5
Living Faith Academy 3700 Deats Rd, DKSN, 77539	4754	A1
Living Stones Christian School 1407 Victory Ln, ALVN, 77511	4749	D4
Living Water Christian Elementary School 4808 Airport Av, RSBG, 77471	4491	C6
Living Water Christian High School 4808 Airport Av, RSBG, 77471	4491	C6
Lockhart Elementary School 3501 Southmore Blvd, HOUS, 77004	4103	C3
Lomax Elementary School 10615 N Avenue L, LPRT, 77571	4110	C7
Lomax Junior High School 9801 N Avenue L, LPRT, 77571	4110	B7
Long Elementary School 907 Main St, RHMD, 77469	4491	E1
Longfellow Elementary School 1300 E House St, ALVN, 77511	4867	D2
Longfellow Elementary School 3614 Murworth Dr, HOUS, 77025	4101	E7
Long Middle School 6501 Bellaire Blvd, HOUS, 77074	4100	B5
Looscan Elementary School 3800 Robertson St, HOUS, 77009	3824	D6
Lorenzo de Zavala Elementary School 305 Tri City Beach Rd, BYTN, 77520	4113	B1
Love Elementary School 1120 W 13th St, HOUS, 77008	3823	B6
Lovett Elementary School 8814 S Rice Av, HOUS, 77096	4100	E7
Lowery Elementary School 15950 Ridge Park Dr, HarC, 77095	3538	C7
Lutheran High School North 1130 W 34th St, HOUS, 77018	3823	A3
Lutheran South Academy 12555 Ryewater Dr, HOUS, 77089	4378	D6
Lyons Elementary School 800 Roxella St, HOUS, 77076	3685	B5
MacArthur Elementary School 1801 N Main St, GNPK, 77547	3966	C6
MacArthur Elementary School 5909 England St, HOUS, 77021	4103	D5
MacArthur Ninth Grade School 12111 Gloger St, HarC, 77039	3546	B5
MacArthur Senior High School 4400 Aldine Mail Rd, HarC, 77039	3546	B5
MacGregor Elementary School 4801 la Branch St, HOUS, 77004	4103	A1
Mading Elementary School 8511 Crestmont St, HOUS, 77033	4244	B4
Madison High School 13719 White Heather Dr, HOUS, 77045	4372	D1
Mae Smythe Elementary School 2202 Pasadena Blvd, PASD, 77502	4107	E7
Magnolia Elementary School 31900 Nichols Sawmill Rd, MAGA, 77355	2669	A6
Magnolia High School 14350 FM-1488 Rd, MtgC, 77354	2670	D3
Magnolia Junior High School 31138 Nichols Sawmill Rd, MAGA, 77355	2669	A7
Magnolia Sixth Grade Campus 110 S Magnolia Blvd, MAGA, 77355	2669	B6
Magnolia West High School 42202 FM-1774 Rd, MtgC, 77354	2668	D4
Magrill Elementary School 21701 Rayford Rd, HarC, 77338	3260	B2
Mahanay Elementary School 13215 High Star Dr, HOUS, 77083	4097	C4
Manvel High School 19601 Morris Rd, MNVL, 77578	4746	C2
Manvel Junior High School 7380 Lewis Ln, MNVL, 77578	4746	E2
Maplebrook Elementary School 7935 Farmingham Rd, HarC, 77346	3265	C6
Margaret S McWhirter Elementary School 300 Pennsylvania St, WEBS, 77598	4507	C7
Mark Twain Elementary School 7500 Braes Blvd, HOUS, 77025	4101	D5
Mark Twain Primary School 610 E Clements St, ALVN, 77511	4867	C2
Marshall Middle School 1115 Noble St, HOUS, 77009	3963	D1
Martin Elementary School 11718 Hendon Ln, HOUS, 77072	4098	A6
Mary Marek Elementary School 1947 Kirby St, PRLD, 77584	4500	D1
Mata Intermediate School 9225 S Dairy Ashford St, HOUS, 77099	4237	D2
Matthys Elementary School 1500 Main St, SHUS, 77587	4246	C4
Matzke Elementary School 13102 Jones Rd, HarC, 77070	3399	A4
Mayde Creek Elementary School 2698 Greenhouse Rd, HOUS, 77084	3816	B5
Mayde Creek High School 19202 Groeschke Rd, HarC, 77084	3816	C5
Mayde Creek Junior High School 2700 Greenhouse Rd, HOUS, 77084	3816	B5
McAdams Junior High School 4007 Video St, DKSN, 77539	4754	A2
McAuliffe Middle School 16650 S Post Oak Rd, HOUS, 77053	4371	E7
McCullough Junior High School 3800 S Panther Creek Dr, WDLD, 77381	2821	A6
McDade Elementary School 5815 Hirsch Rd, HOUS, 77026	3825	B4
McDonald Junior High School 3635 Lakes of Bridgewater Dr, HarC, 77449	3815	B2
McDougle Elementary School 10410 Kansack Ln, HarC, 77086	3542	A2
McMasters Elementary School 1011 Bennett Dr, PASD, 77503	4108	C5
McMullan Primary School 1290 Dell Dale St, HarC, 77530	3829	D5
McNamara Elementary School 8714 McAvoy Dr, HOUS, 77074	4100	A7
McReynolds Middle School 5910 Market St, HOUS, 77020	3964	D2
McRoberts Elementary School 3535 N Fry Rd, HarC, 77449	3815	E3
Meador Elementary School 10701 Seaford Dr, HOUS, 77089	4377	D3
Meadows Elementary School 12037 Pender Ln, MDWP, 77477	4238	A5
Meadow Wood Elementary School 14230 Memorial Dr, HOUS, 77079	3957	E3
Melba Passmore Elementary School 600 Kost Rd, ALVN, 77511	4867	A2
Memorial Christian Academy 1315 S Dairy Ashford St, HOUS, 77077	3957	D5
Memorial Drive Elementary School 11202 Smithdale Rd, PNPV, 77024	3959	E3
Memorial Elementary School 6401 Arnot St, HOUS, 77007	3961	E3
Memorial Hall School 3721 Dacoma St, HOUS, 77092	3822	C4
Memorial High School 935 Echo Ln, HDWV, 77024	3959	D1
Memorial Lutheran School 5800 Westheimer Rd, HOUS, 77057	3960	D7
Memorial Middle School 12550 Vindon Dr, HOUS, 77024	3958	E2
Memorial Parkway Elementary School 21603 Park Tree Ln, HarC, 77450	3954	B3
Memorial Parkway Junior High School 21203 Highland Knolls Dr, HarC, 77450	3954	C4
Mendel Elementary School 3735 Topping St, HOUS, 77093	3686	B4
Metcalf Elementary School 6100 Queenston Blvd, HarC, 77084	3678	A4
Metzler Elementary School 8500 W Rayford Rd, HarC, 77389	2966	A4
Meyer Elementary School 16330 Forest Wy Dr, HarC, 77090	3258	D5
Meyer Elementary School 1930 J Meyer Rd, RSBG, 77469	4614	E3
Michael Kennedy Elementary School 10200 Huntington Pl Dr, HOUS, 77099	4237	D2
Middle College for Tech Careers High School 4310 Dunlavy St, HOUS, 77098	3962	C7
Milam Elementary School 1100 Roy St, HOUS, 77007	3962	B2
Milam Elementary School 16283 FM-3083 Rd, MtgC, 77306	2533	B7
Milby High School 1601 Broadway St, HOUS, 77012	4105	C3
Miller Intermediate School 15025 Westpark Dr, HarC, 77082	4096	C3
Millsap Elementary School 12424 Huffmeister Rd, HarC, 77429	3398	A5
Milne Elementary School 7800 Portal Dr, HOUS, 77071	4239	E4
Mission Bend Christian Academy 3710 Hwy 6 S, HOUS, 77082	4096	D3
Mission Bend Elementary School 16200 Beechnut St, FBnC, 77083	4096	A7
Mission Glen Elementary School 16053 Mission Glen Dr, FBnC, 77083	4236	A1
Mission West Elementary School 7325 Clodine Reddick Rd, FBnC, 77083	4095	D7
Missouri City Middle School 200 Louisiana St, MSCY, 77489	4370	B3
Mitchell Elementary School 10900 Gulfdale Dr, HOUS, 77075	4376	D4
Mitchell Intermediate School 6800 Alden Bridge Dr, WDLD, 77382	2674	C4
Mittelstadt Elementary School 7525 Kleingreen Ln, HarC, 77379	3256	C4
Monahan Elementary School 8901 Deep Valley Dr, HarC, 77044	3689	B5
Mont Children's Cottage 4009 Sherwood Ln, HOUS, 77092	3822	B4
Montgomery Elementary School 4000 Simsbrook Dr, HOUS, 77045	4372	D2
Moore Elementary School 13734 Lakewood Forest Dr, HarC, 77070	3398	D2
Moore Elementary School 8880 Southbluff Blvd, HarC, 77089	4377	B5
Moorhead Junior High School 16840 FM-2090 Rd, MtgC, 77306	2533	C6
Morales Elementary School 305 W Harris Av, PASD, 77506	4107	A5
Moreno Elementary School 620 E Canino Rd, HOUS, 77037	3684	D2
Morris Fifth Grade Center 10415 Fuqua St, HOUS, 77089	4377	D3
Morton Ranch High School 21000 Franz Rd, HarC, 77449	3815	B5
Morton Ranch Junior High School 2498 N Mason Rd, HarC, 77449	3815	A4
Mt Carmel High School 6700 Mt Carmel St, HOUS, 77087	4244	D3
Nancy March Sampson Elementary School 16002 Coles Crossing Dr, HarC, 77429	3397	B3
Navarro Middle School 4700 Avenue N, RSBG, 77471	4491	C5
New Caney 9th Grade Campus 22784 Hwy 59, MtgC, 77365	2973	C4
New Caney Elementary School 21650 Lp 494, MtgC, 77357	2827	D5
New Caney High School 21650 Lp 494, MtgC, 77357	2827	D5
Newcomer Charter High School 6529 Beverlyhill St, HOUS, 77057	4100	A1
Newport Elementary School 430 N Diamondhead Blvd, HarC, 77532	3411	B6
Nichols Sawmill Elementary School 28750 Nichols Sawmill Rd, MtgC, 77355	2815	A4
Nimitz Ninth Grade School 2425 Ww Thorne Blvd, HarC, 77073	3259	D5
Nimitz Senior High School 2005 Ww Thorne Blvd, HarC, 77073	3259	D6
Nitsch Elementary School 4702 W Mt Houston Rd, HarC, 77088	3543	A6
Normandy Crossing Elementary School 12500 Normandy Crossing Dr, HarC, 77015	3967	B1
Northampton Elementary School 6404 Root Rd, HarC, 77389	2966	C6
North Belt Elementary School 8105 E N Belt, HarC, 77396	3406	D7
Northbrook High School 1 Raider Cir, HOUS, 77080	3820	C3
Northbrook Middle School 3030 Rosefield Dr, HOUS, 77080	3820	B2
Northeast Christian Academy 1711 Hamblen Rd, HOUS, 77339	3263	D2
Northland Christian School 4363 Sylvanfield Dr, HarC, 77014	3401	B1
Northland Christian School 2700 FM-1960 Rd W, HarC, 77068	3257	E5
Northline Elementary School 821 E Witcher Ln, HOUS, 77076	3684	E5
North Pointe Elementary School 3200 Almond Creek Dr, HOUS, 77059	4379	E4
Northpointe Intermediate School 211 W Main St, TMBL, 77375	2964	B7
North Shore Elementary School 14310 Duncannon Dr, HarC, 77015	3829	A6
North Shore High School 73501 Holly Park, HarC, 77015	3828	D6
North Shore Middle School 120 Castlegory Rd, HarC, 77015	3829	A5
North Shore Senior High School 353 N Castlegory Rd, HarC, 77049	3829	A3
Northside Elementary School 5701 FM-2004 Rd, HTCK, 77563	4988	D2
Northside Elementary School 2300 21st St N, TXCY, 77590	4875	A3
Northwest Intermediate School 2625 W Mt Houston Rd, HarC, 77088	3543	B6
Northwood Middle School 10750 Homestead Rd, HOUS, 77016	3686	E3
Nottingham Country Elementary School 20500 Kingsland Blvd, HarC, 77450	3954	D2
Nottingham Elementary School 570 Nottingham Oaks Tr, HOUS, 77079	3957	C3
NQ Henderson Elementary School 701 Solo St, HOUS, 77020	3964	C1
Oak Forest Elementary School 6400 Kingwood Glen Dr, HarC, 77346	3264	E6
Oak Forest Elementary School 1401 W 43rd St, HOUS, 77018	3822	D2
Oakland Elementary School 4455 Waterside Estates Dr, FBnC, 77469	4234	C5
Oak Ridge Elementary School 9401 I-45 Frontage Rd, MtgC, 77385	2822	B3
Oak Ridge Elementary School 19675 IS 45 S, ORDN, 77385	2822	B4
Oak Ridge High School 27330 Oak Ridge School Rd, MtgC, 77385	2822	C3
Oaks Adventist Christian School 11903 Tanner Rd C, HarC, 77041	3680	A6
Oaks Elementary School 5858 Upper Lake Dr, HarC, 77346	3264	D5
Oak Village Middle School 8200 Tate St, HOUS, 77028	3826	D4
Oak Village Middle School 6602 Winfield Rd, HOUS, 77050	3547	A6
O'Connell Consolidated School 1320 23rd St, GLSN, 77550	5109	C4
Odessa Kilpatrick Elementary School 26100 Cinco Ranch Blvd, FBnC, 77494	4092	E3
Odom Elementary School 14701 Henry Rd, HarC, 77060	3544	E4
O'Donnell Middle School 14041 Alief Clodine Rd, HarC, 77083	4097	A4
Oleson Elementary School 12345 Vickery St, HarC, 77039	3546	B5
Oppe Elementary School 2915 81st St, GLSN, 77554	5221	E1
Orange Grove Elementary School 4514 Mt Houston Rd, HarC, 77093	3546	B7
Ortiz Middle School 6767 Telephone Rd, HOUS, 77061	4245	B3
Osborne Elementary School 800 Ringold St, HOUS, 77088	3684	A2
Our Lady of Fatima School 1702 9th St, GNPK, 77547	3966	C7
Our Lady of Fatima School 1600 9th Av N, TXCY, 77590	4875	B5
Our Lady of Guadalupe School 2405 Navigation Blvd, HOUS, 77003	3963	E4
Our Lady of Lourdes School 10114 Hwy 6, HTCK, 77563	4988	A3
Our Lady of Mt Carmel School 6703 Whitefriars Dr, HOUS, 77087	4244	E3
Our Mother of Mercy School 2010 Benson St, HOUS, 77020	3964	B1
Our Savior Lutheran School 5000 W Tidwell Rd, HOUS, 77091	3682	E6

Houston Points of Interest Index

ATURE NAME ddress City ZIP Code	MAP#	GRID
utley Elementary School 12355 Richmond Av, HOUS, 77082	4097	E1
wens Elementary School 939 Jackrabbit Rd, HarC, 77095	3539	B7
wens Intermediate School 900 Turtlewood Dr, HOUS, 77072	4098	C5
yster Creek Elementary School 6425 Mellow Oaks Ln, FBnC, 77478	4236	A6
almer Elementary School 208 Crow Valley Dr, MSCY, 77459	4497	A4
arker Elementary School 802 Jones Dr, GLSN, 77551	5108	B7
arker Elementary School 0626 Atwell Dr, HOUS, 77096	4240	D3
arker Intermediate School 9850 E Hardy Rd, HarC, 77073	3259	D5
ark Lake Elementary School 400 Wilson Rd, HarC, 77396	3407	A6
ark Place Elementary School 235 Park Pl Blvd, HOUS, 77017	4105	D7
arks Elementary School 302 San Augustine Av, PASD, 77503	4108	B6
ark View Intermediate School 003 Dabney Dr, PASD, 77502	4247	E2
arkwood Elementary School 404 Parkwood Dr, PASD, 77503	4108	C4
asadena High School 206 Shaver St, PASD, 77506	4107	A4
asadena Memorial High School 4410 Crenshaw Rd, PASD, 77504	4248	A6
at Neff Elementary School 8200 Carvel Ln, HOUS, 77036	4099	C6
at Reynolds Elementary School 3975 Gladeridge Dr, HarC, 77068	3257	B6
atterson Elementary School 5302 Allendale Rd, HOUS, 77017	4106	C7
attison Elementary School 9910 Stonelodge St, HarC, 77450	3955	A5
each Creek Elementary School 4455 Cox St, SPLD, 77372	2683	A1
earland High School 3775 S Main St, PRLD, 77581	4503	D6
earland Junior High School East 2315 Old Alvin Rd, PRLD, 77581	4503	D3
earland Junior High School South 4719 Bailey Rd, BzaC, 77584	4502	A7
earland Junior High School South 4719 Bailey Av, PRLD, 77584	4502	A7
earland Junior High School West 2337 Galveston Av, PRLD, 77581	4503	C3
earland Ninth Grade Center 4717 Bailey Rd, BzaC, 77584	4502	A7
ecan Grove Elementary School 3330 Old South Dr, FBnC, 77469	4234	C7
ecan Street Christian Academy 1215 Pecan St, HarC, 77530	3830	C5
eck Elementary School 5130 Arvilla Ln, HOUS, 77021	4104	A4
ershing Middle School 7000 Braes Blvd, HOUS, 77025	4101	D5
etersen Elementary School 14404 Waterloo Dr, HOUS, 77045	4373	A2
etrosky Elementary School 6703 Winkleman Rd, HarC, 77083	4096	C5
H Greene Elementary School 2903 Friendswood Link Rd, HarC, 77598	4630	B1
ilgrim Elementary School 3315 Barrington Rd, HOUS, 77056	4100	E1
ilgrim Lutheran School 8601 Chimney Rock Rd, HOUS, 77096	4100	D7
ine Drive Baptist High School 705 FM-517 Rd, DKSN, 77539	4753	C3
ine Drive Christian School 705 9th St, GlsC, 77539	4636	B6
ine Forest Elementary School 19702 W Lake Houston Pkwy, HarC, 77346	3265	A5
ine Shadows Elementary School 9900 Neuens Rd, HOUS, 77080	3820	B5
ines Montessori School 3535 Cedar Knolls Dr, HOUS, 77339	3119	B5
iney Point Elementary School 8921 Pagewood Ln, HOUS, 77063	4099	D2
ink Elementary School 1001 Collins Rd, RHMD, 77469	4364	D7
in Oak Middle School 4601 Glenmont Dr, BLAR, 77401	4101	B2
leasant Hill Academy Elementary School 1305 Benson St, HOUS, 77020	3964	B2
leasantville Elementary School 1431 Gellhorn Dr, HOUS, 77029	3965	D3
oe Elementary School 5100 Hazard St, HOUS, 77098	4102	C1
omeroy Elementary School 920 Burke Rd, PASD, 77506	4107	E5
onderosa Elementary School 17202 Butte Creek Rd, HarC, 77090	3258	A4
orter Elementary School 22256 Ford Rd, MtgC, 77365	2973	C6
ort Houston Elementary School 1800 McCarty St, HOUS, 77029	3965	B4
ost Elementary School 7600 Equador St, JRSV, 77040	3680	E1
owell Elementary School 7332 Cochrans Crossing Dr, WDLD, 77381	2674	D7
resbyterian School 5300 Main St, HOUS, 77006	4102	E1
roject Chrysalis Charter Middle School 4528 Leeland St, HOUS, 77023	3964	B7
ugh Elementary School 1147 Kress St, HOUS, 77020	3964	E3
urple Sage Elementary School 6500 Purple Sage Rd, HarC, 77049	3828	C3
yburn Elementary School 12302 Coulson St, HOUS, 77015	3966	E3
uail Valley Elementary School 3500 Quail Village Dr, MSCY, 77459	4369	D7
uail Valley Middle School 3019 FM-1092 Rd, MSCY, 77459	4496	D1
ueen of Peace School 2320 Oakcliff St, HOUS, 77023	4104	C3
ueens Intermediate School 1112 Queens Rd, PASD, 77502	4246	E1
aul C Martinez Elementary School 7211 Market St, HOUS, 77020	3965	A2
aymond Academy 1605 Connorvale Rd, HarC, 77039	3545	C4
eaves Elementary School 1717 N LP 336 W, CNRO, 77304	2383	C2
ed Bluff Elementary School 416 Bearle St, PASD, 77506	4107	D4

FEATURE NAME Address City ZIP Code	MAP#	GRID
Redd School 4820 Strack Rd, HarC, 77069	3256	E6
Red Elementary School 4520 Tonawanda Dr, HOUS, 77035	4241	B3
Reed Academy 1616 Lauder Rd, HarC, 77039	3545	C4
Reed Elementary School 8700 Tami Renee Ln, HarC, 77040	3541	C7
Rees Elementary School 16305 Kensley Dr, HarC, 77082	4096	A4
Regis School 7330 Westview Dr, HOUS, 77055	3821	D6
Renton Renaissance School 14910 Aldine Westfield Rd, HarC, 77032	3545	D1
Resurrection Catholic School 916 Majestic St, HOUS, 77020	3964	E2
Revere Middle School 10502 Briar Forest Dr, HOUS, 77042	3958	D6
Reynolds Elementary School 9601 Rosehaven Dr, HOUS, 77051	4243	B5
Rhoads Elementary School 19711 Clay Rd, HarC, 77449	3815	E1
Rhoads Elementary School 4103 Brisbane St, HOUS, 77047	4243	C7
Rice Elementary School 904 Gladstell Rd, CNRO, 77304	2529	D1
Richey Elementary School 610 Richey St, PASD, 77506	4106	E4
Rick Schneider Middle School 8420 Easthaven Blvd, HOUS, 77075	4246	B5
Ride Elementary School 4920 W Panther Creek Dr, WDLD, 77381	2821	A4
Ridgecrest Elementary School 2015 Ridgecrest Dr, HOUS, 77055	3821	B4
Ridgegate Elementary School 6015 W Ridgecreek Dr, HOUS, 77053	4371	E5
Ridgemont Elementary School 4910 Raven Ridge Dr, HOUS, 77053	4372	B7
River Oaks Baptist School 2300 Willowick Rd, HOUS, 77027	3961	C6
River Oaks Elementary School 2008 Kirby Dr, HOUS, 77019	3962	A6
Riverwood Middle School 2910 High Valley Dr, HOUS, 77345	3120	C4
Rizzuto Elementary School 3201 Farrington Blvd, LPRT, 77571	4250	C3
RL Stevenson Primary School 4715 Mustang Rd, BzaC, 77511	4867	D7
Robert E Lee High School 1809 Market St, BYTN, 77520	3972	C7
Robert King Elementary School 1901 Charlton House Ln, HarC, 77493	3814	B6
Robert M Beren Academy 11333 Cliffwood Dr, HOUS, 77035	4241	B4
Roberts Elementary School 6000 Greenbriar St, HOUS, 77030	4102	B3
Roberts Road Elementary School 24920 Zube Rd, HarC, 77447	3249	D3
Robindell School 5801 Dashwood Dr, HOUS, 77081	4100	D4
Robison Elementary School 13600 Skinner Rd, HarC, 77429	3396	D3
Rodriguez Elementary School 5858 Chimney Rock Rd, HOUS, 77081	4100	D3
Rogers Middle School 3121 Manvel Rd, PRLD, 77584	4502	B5
Roosevelt Alexander Elementary School 6161 S Fry Rd, HOUS, 77494	4093	D4
Roosevelt Elementary School 6700 Fulton St, HOUS, 77022	3824	B3
Roosevelt-Wilson Elementary School 301 16th Av N, TXCY, 77590	4875	D4
Rosehill Christian School 19830 FM-2920 Rd, HarC, 77377	3106	C2
Rosehill Elementary School 17950 Tomball Waller Rd, HarC, 77377	3107	B2
Rosehill Elementary School 211 W Main St, TMBL, 77375	2964	B7
Rosenberg Elementary School 721 10th St, GLSN, 77550	5109	D2
Ross Elementary School 2819 Bay St, HOUS, 77026	3824	E5
Ross S Sterling High School 300 W Baker Rd, BYTN, 77521	3973	A2
Roth Elementary School 21623 Castlemont Ln, HarC, 77388	3112	B4
Royalwood Elementary School 7715 Royalwood Dr, HarC, 77049	3689	D7
RP Harris Elementary School 1262 Mae Dr, HOUS, 77015	3966	E3
Ruby Reed Intermediate School 1616 Lauder Rd, HarC, 77039	3545	C4
Rucker Elementary School 5201 Vinett St, HOUS, 77017	4106	C6
Rummel Creek Elementary School 625 Brittmoore Rd, HOUS, 77079	3958	C2
Runyan Elementary School 1101 Foster Dr, CNRO, 77301	2384	C7
Rusk Elementary School 2805 Garrow St, HOUS, 77003	3963	E5
Rustic Oak Elementary School 1302 Rustic Ln, PRLD, 77581	4504	D7
Ryan Middle School 2610 Elgin St, HOUS, 77004	4103	C1
Rylander Elementary School 24831 Westheimer Pkwy, FBnC, 77494	3953	B7
Sablatura Middle School 2300 Galveston Av, PRLD, 77581	4503	C2
Sacred Heart Catholic School 615 McDade St, CNRO, 77301	2384	A5
Sacred Heart School 907 Runneburg Rd, HarC, 77532	3552	D4
St. Agnes Academy 9000 Bellaire Blvd, HOUS, 77036	4099	A4
St. Agnes Christian Academy 3730 S Acres Dr, HOUS, 77047	4243	C6
St. Ambrose School 4213 Mangum Rd, HOUS, 77092	3822	A1
St. Anne Catholic School 2120 Westheimer Rd, HOUS, 77019	3962	B6
St. Anne School 1111 S Cherry St, TMBL, 77375	3109	C1
St. Anthony of Padua Catholic School 7901 Bay Branch Dr, WDLD, 77382	2674	B6
St. Augustine Catholic School 5500 Laurel Creek Wy, HOUS, 77017	4246	C1
St. Barnabas Day School 107 E Edgebrook Dr, HOUS, 77034	4247	A5
St. Catherine's Montessori School 2510 Westridge St, HOUS, 77054	4242	B1

FEATURE NAME Address City ZIP Code	MAP#	GRID
St. Cecilia School 11740 Joan of Arc Dr, HDWV, 77024	3959	C1
St. Charles Borromeo School 14910 Aldine Westfield Rd, HarC, 77032	3545	C1
St. Charles Borromeo School 501 Tidwell Rd, HOUS, 77076	3685	B6
St. Christopher Catholic School 8134 Park Place Blvd, HOUS, 77017	4105	D7
St. Clare of Assisi Catholic School 3131 El Dorado Blvd, HOUS, 77059	4380	C6
St. Edward Catholic School 2601 Spring Stuebner Rd, HarC, 77388	3113	A2
St. Edward's School 7200 Spring Cypress Rd, HarC, 77379	3111	B6
St. Elizabeth Ann Seton School 6646 Addicks Satsuma Rd, HarC, 77084	3678	E3
St. Francis de Sales School 8100 Roos Rd, HOUS, 77036	4099	C5
St. Francis Episcopal Day School 335 Piney Point Rd, PNPV, 77024	3959	D4
St. Francis of Assisi School 5100 Dabney St, HOUS, 77026	3825	D4
St. Helen Catholic School 2213 Old Alvin Rd, PRLD, 77581	4503	D2
St. James Episcopal School 1803 Highland Hollow Dr, CNRO, 77304	2382	C1
St. James Episcopal School 3129 Southmore Blvd, HOUS, 77004	4103	B3
St. James School 3129 Southmore Blvd, HOUS, 77004	4103	B3
St. Jerome School 8825 Kempwood Dr, HOUS, 77080	3820	E3
St. John's Academy 2019 Crawford St, HOUS, 77003	3963	C6
St. John's School 2401 Claremont Ln, HOUS, 77019	3961	E6
St. Joseph Catholic School 1811 Carolina St, BYTN, 77520	4112	B1
St. Laurence Catholic School 2630 Austin Pkwy, SGLD, 77479	4495	C1
St. Mark Lutheran School 1515 Hillendahl Blvd, HOUS, 77055	3821	B6
St. Mark's Episcopal School 3816 Bellaire Blvd, WUNP, 77005	4101	D4
St. Martha Catholic School 2411 Oak Shores Dr, HOUS, 77339	3119	A4
St. Mary Magdalene School 530 Ferguson St, HMBL, 77338	3262	E7
St. Mary-Purification Montessori School 3006 Rosedale St, HOUS, 77004	4103	B2
St. Mary's Cathedral School 2002 Winnie St, GLSN, 77550	5109	C3
St. Mary School 1612 E Walker St, LGCY, 77573	4632	C2
St. Michael School 1833 Sage Rd, HOUS, 77056	3961	A6
St. Michael's Episcopal School 1601 Lake Rd, LMQU, 77568	4989	E2
St. Nick School 10420 Mullins Dr, HOUS, 77096	4240	C3
St. Pius V School 812 Main St, PASD, 77506	4107	A5
St. Pius X High School 811 W Donovan St, HOUS, 77091	3684	B6
St. Rose of Lima School 3600 Brinkman St, HOUS, 77018	3823	B3
St. Stephen's Episcopal School 1815 Sul Ross St, HOUS, 77098	3962	C7
St. Theresa School 6622 Haskell St, HOUS, 77007	3961	E2
St. Thomas Apostle Episc School 18300 Upper Bay Rd, NSUB, 77058	4508	A5
St. Thomas' Episcopal School 4900 Jackwood Street, HOUS, 77096	4101	A7
St. Thomas High School 4500 Memorial Dr, HOUS, 77007	3962	C4
St. Thomas More Parish School 5927 Wigton Dr, HOUS, 77096	4240	B2
St. Vincent de Paul School 6802 Buffalo Speedway, HOUS, 77025	4101	E4
Salem Lutheran School 22607 Lutheran Church Rd, HarC, 77377	3108	A1
Salyers Elementary School 25705 W Hardy Rd, HarC, 77373	3114	A3
Sam Jamison Middle School 2502 Woody Rd, PRLD, 77581	4503	A3
Sammons Elementary School 2301 Frick Rd, HarC, 77038	3543	B3
Sampson Elementary School 16002 Coles Crossing Dr N, HarC, 77429	3397	B3
Sam Rayburn High School 2121 Cherrybrook Ln, PASD, 77502	4247	E1
Sanchez Elementary School 2700 Berkley St, HOUS, 77012	4105	C5
Sands Point Elementary School 10550 Westoffice Dr, HOUS, 77042	4098	E2
San Jacinto Elementary School 2615 Virginia St, BYTN, 77520	4112	A1
San Jacinto Elementary School 601 E 8th St, DRPK, 77536	4109	C4
San Jacinto Elementary School 1110 21st St, GLSN, 77550	5109	C3
San Jacinto Elementary School 17601 FM-1314 Rd, MtgC, 77302	2678	E7
San Jacinto Inter School 3102 San Augustine Av, PASD, 77503	4108	A6
Santa Fe Elementary School North 4131 Warpath Av, STFE, 77510	4870	D7
Santa Fe Elementary School South 4133 Warpath Av, STFE, 77510	4870	D7
Santa Fe High School 16000 Hwy 6, STFE, 77517	4869	E5
Santa Fe Intermediate School 4135 Warpath Av, STFE, 77510	4870	D6
Santa Fe Junior High School 4132 Warpath Av, STFE, 77510	4870	D7
Sartartia Middle School 8125 Homeward Wy, FBnC, 77479	4367	A7
Satori School 2503 Sealy St, GLSN, 77550	5109	B3
Scanlan Oaks Elementary School 9000 Camp Sienna Tr, FBnC, 77459	4621	C6
Scarborough Elementary School 3021 Little York Rd, HOUS, 77093	3686	A2
Scarborough High School 4141 Costa Rica Rd, HOUS, 77092	3821	E1
Schindewolf Intermediate School 20903 Ella Blvd, HarC, 77388	3112	D4
Schmalz Elementary School 6161 Green Land Wy, HarC, 77084	3816	D3

Schools

Houston Points of Interest Index

FEATURE NAME / Address City ZIP Code	MAP#	GRID
Schochler Primary School, 910 Deerpass Dr, HarC, 77530	3829	D6
School at Post Oak, 1331 Augusta Dr, HOUS, 77057	3960	D5
School for Accelerated Learning, 1602 11th St, GNPK, 77547	3966	C6
School of the Woods, 1321 Wirt Rd, HLSV, 77055	3821	C6
School of the Woods Primary School, 785 Country Pl Dr, HOUS, 77079	3957	D2
Schultz Elementary School, 7920 Willow Forest Dr, HarC, 77375	2966	A6
Schultz Middle School, 19010 Stokes Rd, HarC, 77484	3102	B6
Scott Elementary School, 3300 Russell St, HOUS, 77026	3825	B7
Scroggins Elementary School, 400 Boyles St, HOUS, 77020	3965	A1
Seabrook Intermediate School, 2401 Meyer Rd, SEBK, 77586	4509	E1
Seabrook Montessori School, 1514 3rd St, SEBK, 77586	4509	D3
Second Baptist School, 6410 Woodway Dr, HOUS, 77057	3960	A4
Seguin Elementary School, 5905 Waltrip St, HOUS, 77087	4244	E1
Seguin Elementary School, 605 Mabel St, RHMD, 77469	4364	D7
Seton Catholic Junior High School, 801 Roselane St, HOUS, 77037	3684	E2
Settlers Way Elementary School, 3015 Settlers Wy Blvd, SGLD, 77479	4495	E1
Seven Lakes High School, 9251 S Fry Rd, FBnC, 77494	4093	B3
Shadowbriar Elementary School, 2650 Shadowbriar Dr, HOUS, 77077	3957	E7
Shadow Forest Elementary School, 2300 Mills Branch Dr, HOUS, 77345	3120	A3
Shadow Oaks Elementary School, 1335 Shadowdale Dr, HOUS, 77043	3819	E7
Shadycrest Elementary School, 2405 Shady Bend Dr, PRLD, 77581	4504	A5
Shadydale Elementary School, 5905 Tidwell Rd, HOUS, 77016	3686	D6
Sharpstown Christian Elementary School, 8282 Bissonnet St, HOUS, 77074	4239	D1
Sharpstown High School, 7504 Bissonnet St, HOUS, 77074	4099	E7
Sharpstown Middle School, 8330 Triola Ln, HOUS, 77036	4099	C6
Sharpview Elementary School, 7734 Mary Bates Blvd, HOUS, 77036	4099	C6
Shearn Elementary School, 9802 Stella Link Rd, HOUS, 77025	4241	D1
Shekinah Radiance Academy, 5130 Casey St, LMQU, 77568	4872	E6
Sheldon Elementary School, 17203 Hall Shepperd Rd, HarC, 77049	3691	A4
Sheldon Intermediate School, 17010 Beaumont Hwy, HarC, 77049	3690	E3
Sheridan Elementary School, 19790 Kieth Harrow Blvd, HarC, 77449	3676	E6
Sherman Elementary School, 1909 McKee St, HOUS, 77009	3963	D1
Sherwood Elementary School, 1700 Sherwood Forest St, HOUS, 77043	3819	B6
Shlenker Elementary School, 5600 N Braeswood Blvd, HOUS, 77096	4240	C1
Shotwell Middle School, 6515 Trail Valley Wy, HarC, 77086	3542	C2
Shrine of the True Cross School, 400 FM-517 Rd E, DKSN, 77539	4753	C4
Sienna Crossing Elementary School, 10011 Steep Bank Trc, FBnC, 77459	4621	E4
Silbernagel Elementary School, 4201 25th St, GlsC, 77539	4633	A7
Silvercrest Elementary School, 3003 Southwyck Pkwy, BzaC, 77584	4501	A4
Silverlake Elementary School, 2550 FM-90 Rd, BzaC, 77584	4501	C6
Simms Elementary School, 529 N Westward St, TXCY, 77591	4873	C5
Sinclair Elementary School, 6410 Grovewood Ln, HOUS, 77008	3822	E6
Smaller Scholars Mont School, 1685 S Dairy Ashford St, HOUS, 77077	3957	D5
Smiley High School, 10725 Mesa Dr, HOUS, 77078	3687	E3
Smith Academy, 5815 W Little York Rd, HOUS, 77091	3682	E4
Smith Education Center, 1701 Bringhurst St, HOUS, 77020	3964	A1
Smith Elementary School, 26000 Cypresswood Dr, HarC, 77373	3114	E3
Smith Elementary School, 4802 Chrystell Ln, HOUS, 77092	3683	A7
Smith Elementary School, 11300 Stancliff Rd, HOUS, 77099	4238	B4
Smith Elementary School, 2014 Lamar Dr, RHMD, 77469	4491	E4
Sneed Elementary School, 9855 Pagewood Ln, HOUS, 77042	4099	A2
South Alternative Elementary School, 3555 Bellfort St, HOUS, 77051	4243	B2
South District Alternative School, 10101 Scott St, HOUS, 77051	4243	C5
Southhampton Montessori School, 5012 Morningside Dr, HOUS, 77005	4102	B2
South Houston Elementary School, 900 Main St, SHUS, 77587	4246	B3
South Houston High School, 3820 S Shaver St, SHUS, 77587	4247	A4
South Houston Inter School, 900 College Av, SHUS, 77587	4246	C4
Southmayd Elementary School, 1800 Coral St, HOUS, 77012	4105	B4
Southmore Intermediate School, 1200 Houston Av, PASD, 77502	4107	C7
South Shaver Baptist School, 5300 S Shaver St, HOUS, 77034	4247	A7
South Shaver Elementary School, 2020 Shaver St, PASD, 77502	4107	A7
Southwest Christian Academy, 7400 Eldridge Pkwy, HarC, 77083	4097	A6
Space Center Intermediate School, 17400 Saturn Ln, HOUS, 77058	4508	A4
Sparks Elementary School, 2503 Southmore Av, PASD, 77506	4107	E6
Spence Elementary School, 1300 Gears Rd, HarC, 77067	3402	D6

FEATURE NAME / Address City ZIP Code	MAP#	GRID
Splendora High School, 23747 FM-2090 Rd, MtgC, 77372	2536	B6
Splendora Intermediate School, 26175 FM-2090 Rd, SPLD, 77372	2683	B1
Splendora Junior High School, 24000 FM-2090 Rd, MtgC, 77372	2536	A6
Spring Branch Elementary School, 1700 Campbell Rd, HOUS, 77080	3820	E5
Spring Branch Middle School, 1000 Piney Point Rd, HDWV, 77024	3959	D1
Spring Cypress Presbyterian School, 6000 Spring Cypress Rd, HarC, 77379	3111	D7
Spring Forest Middle School, 14240 Memorial Dr, HOUS, 77079	3957	E3
Spring High School, 19428 IS 45, HarC, 77373	3113	E6
Spring Oaks Middle School, 2150 Shadowdale Dr, HOUS, 77043	3819	E4
Spring Shadows Elementary School, 9725 Kempwood Dr, HOUS, 77080	3820	C3
Spring Woods High School, 2045 Gessner Dr, HOUS, 77043	3820	A4
Spring Woods Middle School, 9810 Neuens Rd, HOUS, 77080	3820	B5
Stafford High School, 1625 Staffordshire Rd, STAF, 77477	4370	B5
Star Montessori School, 3868 Space Center Blvd, PASD, 77505	4248	D4
Stehlik Intermediate School, 400 West Rd, HarC, 77038	3543	E4
Stephens Elementary School, 2402 Aldine Mail Rd, HarC, 77039	3545	E5
Sterling High School, 11625 Martindale Rd, HOUS, 77048	4244	C7
Stevens Elementary School, 1910 la Monte Ln, HOUS, 77018	3822	C2
Stevenson Elementary School, 5410 Cornish St, HOUS, 77007	3962	A1
Stevenson Middle School, 9595 Winkler Dr, HOUS, 77017	4246	B2
Stewart Elementary School, 7013 Stewart St, HTCK, 77563	4988	D4
Stovall Academy, 3025 Ellington St, HOUS, 77088	3683	B1
Stovall Middle School, 11201 Airline Dr, HOUS, 77037	3544	C3
Strack Intermediate School, 18027 Kuykendahl Rd, HarC, 77379	3257	C1
Strake Jesuit College Preparatory School, 8900 Bellaire Blvd, HOUS, 77036	4099	B4
Stratford High School, 14555 Fern Dr, HOUS, 77079	3957	D2
Stuchbery Elementary School, 11210 Hughes Rd, HOUS, 77089	4378	A5
Sue Creech Elementary School, 5905 S Mason Rd, FBnC, 77450	4094	B3
Sugar Grove Christian School, 11600 W Airport Blvd, MDWP, 77477	4238	B6
Sugar Grove Elementary School, 8405 Bonhomme Rd, HOUS, 77074	4099	E7
Sugar Land Middle School, 321 7th St, SGLD, 77478	4368	A1
Sugar Mill Elementary School, 13707 Jess Pirtle Blvd, SGLD, 77478	4237	B7
Summerwood Elementary School, 14000 Summerwood Lakes Dr, HarC, 77044	3549	E2
Sundown Elementary School, 20100 Saums Rd, HarC, 77449	3815	D5
Sutton Elementary School, 7402 Albacore Dr, HOUS, 77074	4100	A5
Sweetwater Christian School, 350 Century Plaza Dr, HOUS, 77073	3403	A1
Sylvan Rodriguez Elementary School, 5858 Chimney Rock Rd, HOUS, 77081	4100	D3
Taylor High School, 7555 Howell Sugar Land Rd, HarC, 77083	4096	E6
Taylor High School, 20700 Kingsland Blvd, HarC, 77450	3954	D2
Taylor Ray Elementary School, 2611 Avenue N, RSBG, 77471	4491	A5
Teague Elementary School, 4200 Crenshaw Rd, PASD, 77504	4247	E6
Teague Middle School, 21700 Rayford Rd, HarC, 77338	3260	C2
Tegeler High School, 4949 Burke Rd, PASD, 77504	4247	E6
Temple Oaks Elementary School, 2101 W 34th St, HOUS, 77018	3822	D3
Tenney School, 2055 S Gessner Rd, HOUS, 77063	3959	B6
Terrace Elementary School, 10400 Rothbury St, HOUS, 77043	3819	E3
Terry High School, 5500 Avenue N, RSBG, 77471	4491	D6
Texas Christian School, 17810 Kieth Harrow Blvd, HarC, 77084	3678	A6
Texas City High School, 1800 9th Av N, TXCY, 77590	4875	B4
Theiss Elementary School, 17510 Theiss Mail Route Rd, HarC, 77379	3256	A3
Thomas Middle School, 5655 Selinsky Rd, HOUS, 77048	4244	B7
Thompson Elementary School, 12470 Walters Rd, HarC, 77014	3401	E3
Thompson Elementary School, 3500 Tampa St, HOUS, 77021	4103	C5
Thompson Elementary School, 220 Casa Grande Dr, HOUS, 77060	3544	C2
Thompson Intermediate School, 11309 Sagedowne Ln, HOUS, 77089	4378	A5
Thornton Middle School, 19802 Kieth Harrow Blvd, HarC, 77449	3676	E6
Thornwood Elementary School, 14400 Fern Dr, HOUS, 77079	3957	D2
Thurgood Marshall High School, 1220 Buffalo Run, MSCY, 77489	4370	D3
Tice Elementary School, 14120 Wallisville Rd, HarC, 77049	3828	B4
Tidwell Elementary School, 8000 Tidwell Rd, HOUS, 77028	3687	C5
Tijerina Elementary School, 6501 Sherman St, HOUS, 77011	3964	D6
Timbers Elementary School, 6910 Lonesome Woods Tr, HarC, 77346	3265	A7
Timberwood Middle School, 18450 Timber Forest Dr, HarC, 77346	3264	C7
Tinsley Elementary School, 11035 Bob White Dr, HOUS, 77096	4240	B4
Tipps Elementary School, 5611 Queenston Blvd, HarC, 77084	3678	A5

Scho

FEATURE NAME / Address City ZIP Code	MAP#	GR
Tomball Elementary School, 1110 Inwood St, TMBL, 77375	2964	A
Tomball High School, 30330 Quinn Rd, TMBL, 77375	2964	A
Tomball Intermediate School, 723 W Main St, TMBL, 77375	2964	B
Tomball Junior High School, 30403 Quinn Rd, TMBL, 77375	2964	A
Torah Day School-Houston, 10900 Fondren Rd, HOUS, 77071	4240	A
Townewest Elementary School, 13927 Old Richmond Rd, FBnC, 77478	4237	A
Trafton Academy, 4711 McDermed Dr, HOUS, 77035	4241	B
Travis Elementary School, 100 Robin Rd, BYTN, 77520	3971	B
Travis Elementary School, 3311 Beauchamp St, HOUS, 77009	3824	B
Travis Elementary School, 2700 Avenue K, RSBG, 77471	4491	A
Travis Intermediate School, 1100 N Thompson St, CNRO, 77301	2384	A
Treasure Forest Elementary School, 7635 Amelia Rd, HOUS, 77055	3821	D
Trinity Baptist Elementary School, 2220 29th St N, TXCY, 77590	4874	E
Trinity Baptist High School, 2220 29th St N, TXCY, 77590	4874	E
Trinity Elementary School, 18926 Klein Church Rd, HarC, 77379	3112	A
Trinity Episcopal School, 720 23rd St, GLSN, 77550	5109	B
Trinity Life Center, 1128 Westwood Dr, RSBG, 77471	4491	D
Trinity Lutheran School, 18926 Klein Church Rd, HarC, 77379	3112	A
Trinity Lutheran School, 800 Houston Av, HOUS, 77002	3963	B
Truitt Middle School, 6600 Addicks Satsuma Rd, HarC, 77084	3678	E
TSU-HISD Lab School, 3805 Burkett St, HOUS, 77004	4103	D
Turner Elementary School, 3200 Rosedale St, HOUS, 77004	4103	C
Turner Elementary School, 10101 N Hwy 75, MtgC, 77378	2237	D
Turner Elementary School, 4333 Lily St, PASD, 77505	4248	B
Twin Creeks Middle School, 27100 Cypresswood Dr, HarC, 77373	3114	D
Valley Oaks Elementary School, 8390 Westview Dr, HOUS, 77055	3821	B
Valley West Elementary School, 10707 S Gessner Dr, HOUS, 77071	4239	C
Velasquez Elementary School, 402 Macek Rd, FBnC, 77469	4493	E
Veritas Christian Academy, 7000 Ferris St, BLAR, 77401	4100	E
Victory Lakes Intermediate School, 2880 W Walker St, LGCY, 77573	4753	A
Village School, 13077 Westella Dr, HOUS, 77077	3957	B
Virtual School, 5827 Chimney Rock Rd, HOUS, 77081	4100	D
VW Miller Intermediate School, 1002 Fairmont Pkwy, PASD, 77504	4247	C
Wainwright Elementary School, 5330 Milwee St, HOUS, 77092	3821	E
Walden School, The, 16103 Lexington Blvd, SGLD, 77479	4368	B
Walker Elementary School, 6424 Settlers Village Dr, HarC, 77449	3676	D
Walker Station Elementary School, 6200 Homeward Wy, FBnC, 77479	4367	B
Waller High School, 20950 Fields Store Rd, HarC, 77484	3102	A
Waller Junior High School, 2402 Waller St, WALR, 77484	3101	E
Walnut Bend Elementary School, 12909 Briar Forest Dr, HOUS, 77077	3957	C
Walter Hall Elementary School, 5931 Meadowside St, LGCY, 77573	4630	C
Walter Matthys Elementary School, 1500 Main St, PASD, 77502	4107	A
Waltrip High School, 1900 W 34th St, HOUS, 77018	3822	D
Washington High School, 119 E 39th St, HOUS, 77018	3823	C
Washington Junior High School, 507 Dr Martin Luther King Jr Pl, CNRO, 77301	2384	B
Watkins Middle School, 4800 Cairnvillage St, HarC, 77084	3678	B
Weaver A Odom Elementary School, 14701 Henry Rd, HarC, 77060	3544	E
Wedgewood Elementary School, 4000 Friendswood Link Rd, FRDW, 77546	4505	E
Welch Middle School, 11544 S Gessner Dr, HOUS, 77071	4239	C
Wells Middle School, 4033 Gladeridge Dr, HarC, 77068	3257	B
WE Rogers Elementary School, 10550 JL Reaux St, HOUS, 77016	3687	B
Wesley Academy, 10570 Westpark Dr, HOUS, 77042	4098	E
Wesley Elementary School, 800 Dillard St, HOUS, 77091	3684	A
Wessendorff Middle School, 5201 Mustang Av, RSBG, 77471	4491	D
West Briar Middle School, 13733 Brimhurst Dr, HOUS, 77077	3957	A
Westbury Christian School, 10420 Hillcroft St, HOUS, 77096	4240	B
Westbury High School, 11911 Chimney Rock Rd, HOUS, 77035	4240	D
Westchester Christ Academy, 901 Yorkchester Dr, HOUS, 77079	3958	A
Westfield 9th Grade Center, 1500 S Ridge Rd, HarC, 77090	3258	B
Westfield High School, 16713 Ella Blvd, HarC, 77090	3258	B
West Houston Adventist School, 1900 Kersten Dr, HOUS, 77043	3819	C
Westlawn Elementary School, 1217 Vauthier St, LMQU, 77568	4989	C
West Memorial Elementary School, 22605 Provincial Blvd, HarC, 77450	3953	E
West Memorial Junior High School, 22311 Provincial Blvd, HarC, 77450	3953	E
Westside High School, 14201 Briar Forest Dr, HOUS, 77077	3956	E

Houston Points of Interest Index

ATURE NAME ddress City ZIP Code	MAP#	GRID
est University Elementary School 756 University Blvd, WUNP, 77005	4101	D3
estwood Elementary School 06 W Edgewood Dr, FRDW, 77546	4505	A7
estwood Elementary School 100 Shadowdale Dr, HOUS, 77043	3819	E4
harton Elementary School 00 W Gray St, HOUS, 77019	3962	E5
heatley High School 900 Market St, HOUS, 77020	3964	C2
hidby Elementary School 625 Springhill St, HOUS, 77021	4103	B7
hispering Pine Elementary School 7321 Woodland Hills Dr, HarC, 77396	3408	A2
hite Elementary School 001 Triola Ln, HOUS, 77036	4099	A6
hite Oak Middle School 2784 Hwy 59, MtgC, 77365	2973	C3
hittier Elementary School 0511 La Crosse St, JTCY, 77029	3966	B2
ilchester Elementary School 3618 St. Marys Ln, HOUS, 77079	3958	B1
ilkerson Intermediate School 2312 Sawmill Rd, WDLD, 77380	2967	E2
illbern Elementary School 0811 Goodspring Dr, HarC, 77064	3540	D3
illiams Charter Middle School 100 Knox St, HOUS, 77091	3684	A5
illiams Elementary School 111 FM-762 Rd, FBnC, 77469	4492	D6
illiams Elementary School 522 Scarborough Ln, PASD, 77502	4106	D6
illie E Williams Elementary School 8101 FM-1488 Rd, MAGA, 77354	2669	B4
illis High School 201 FM-830 Rd, MtgC, 77378	2237	C1
illow Creek Elementary School 8302 N Eldridge Pkwy, HarC, 77377	3254	C2
illow Creek Elementary School 2002 Willow Terrace Dr, HOUS, 77345	3120	C5
illowridge High School 6301 Chimney Rock Rd, HOUS, 77053	4371	C6
illow Wood Junior High School 1770 Gregson Rd, HarC, 77377	3254	D2
ill Rogers Elementary School 3101 Weslayan St, HOUS, 77027	4101	D1
ilson Elementary School 8015 Kieth Harrow Blvd, HarC, 77084	3677	E6
ilson Elementary School 2100 Yupon St, HOUS, 77006	3962	D6
ilson Intermediate School 3131 Fallbrook Dr, HarC, 77038	3542	E3
inborn Elementary School 22555 Prince George Ln, HarC, 77449	3814	E6
indfern High School 12630 Windfern Rd, HarC, 77064	3540	C1
indsong Intermediate School 2100 W Parkwood Av, FRDW, 77546	4629	A6
indsor Village Elementary School 14440 Polo St, HOUS, 77085	4371	E2
inship Elementary School 2175 Spring Creek Dr, HarC, 77373	3114	C3
olfe Elementary School 502 Addicks Howell Rd, HOUS, 77079	3956	D1
ollam Elementary School 3400 Avenue S, STFE, 77510	4870	E5
olters Accelerated High School 400 Ivy Av, DRPK, 77536	4109	B4
oodland Acres Elementary School 12936 Sarahs Ln, HOUS, 77015	3967	C3
oodland Acres Middle School 12947 Myrtle Ln, HOUS, 77015	3967	C3
oodland Hills Elementary School 2222 Tree Ln, HOUS, 77339	3119	A4
oodlands Christian Academy 5800 College Park Dr, WDLD, 77384	2675	B6
oodlands College Park High School 3701 College Park Dr, WDLD, 77384	2675	D6
oodlands High School 6101 Research Forest Dr, WDLD, 77381	2675	A7
oodlands High School-9th Grade Campus 10010 Branch Crossing Dr, WDLD, 77382	2674	A4
oods Private School, The 15002 Lakewood Forest Dr, HarC, 77070	3254	E7
oodson School 10720 Southview St, HOUS, 77047	4243	C6
oodview Elementary School 9749 Cedardale Dr, HOUS, 77055	3820	C7
orsham Elementary School 3007 Hartwick Rd, HarC, 77093	3685	E1
orthing High School 9215 Scott St, HOUS, 77051	4243	C4
T Hall School 222 Raymac St, HarC, 77037	3544	C5
underlich Intermediate School 11800 Misty Valley Dr, HarC, 77066	3401	A4
ates High School 3703 Sampson St, HOUS, 77004	4103	D2
eager Elementary School 13615 Champion Forest Dr, HarC, 77069	3400	D1
ellowstone Academy 3000 Trulley St, HOUS, 77004	3963	D7
ork Junior High School 27310 Oak Ridge School Rd, SHEH, 77385	2822	B3
orkshire Academy 14120 Memorial Dr, HOUS, 77079	3957	E3
ouens Elementary School 12141 High Star Dr, HOUS, 77072	4097	E4
oungblood Intermediate School 8410 Dairy View Ln, HOUS, 77072	4097	D7
oung Elementary School 4221 Fox Meadow Ln, PASD, 77504	4247	C5

Shopping Centers

FEATURE NAME Address City ZIP Code	MAP#	GRID
5 York Plaza 442 W Little York Rd, HOUS, 77037	3684	C3
lmeda Mall 555 Kleckley Dr, HOUS, 77075	4377	D2
tascocita Town Center HarC, 77346	3264	E6
aybrook Mall 19400 Gulf Freeway Frontage Rd, HOUS, 77546	4506	D6
aybrook Square Shopping Center 1201 W Bay Area Blvd, WEBS, 77598	4506	E6
aybrook Village Shopping Center 1449 W Bay Area Blvd, HarC, 77598	4506	D6
ay Colony Town Center Gulf Freeway Frontage Rd, LGCY, 77573	4753	A2
ay Plaza N Alexander Dr, BYTN, 77520	3973	C5
Bellaire at Ranchester 6800 Ranchester Dr, HOUS, 77036	4099	A4
Bellewood Shopping Center 11736 Bellaire Blvd, HOUS, 77072	4098	A5
Bender Square HarC, 77346	3264	C6
Braes Heights Shopping Center 3737 Bellaire Blvd, SSPL, 77025	4101	D5
Braeswood Shopping Center 2234 W Holcombe Blvd, HOUS, 77030	4102	B4
Braeswood Square Shopping Center 5300 N Braeswood Blvd, HOUS, 77096	4240	D1
Captain's Corner Shopping Center 110 N Friendswood Dr, FRDW, 77546	4505	B7
Carillon Shopping Center 10001 Westheimer Rd, HOUS, 77042	3959	A7
Center at Baybrook, The 20071 Gulf Freeway Frontage Rd, WEBS, 77598	4507	A6
Centre at Post Oak, The 5000 Westheimer Rd, HOUS, 77056	3961	A6
Centre at Bunker Hill 9640 Old Katy Rd, HOUS, 77055	3959	C1
Champions Forest Plaza HarC, 77069	3400	E2
Champions Village 3 Mighty Oak Dr, HarC, 77066	3400	E2
Chelsea Square Shopping Center HarC, 77066	3401	A1
Clay Hills Plaza 16211 Clay Rd, HOUS, 77084	3817	D1
Cochran's Crossing Shopping Center 4747 Research Forest Dr, WDLD, 77381	2821	B1
College Park Shopping Center 3040 College Park Dr, WDLD, 77384	2676	A5
Colony Square Shopping Center First Colony Blvd, SGLD, 77479	4367	E6
Commons at Commerce Park North, The 15823 I-45 Frontage Rd, HarC, 77090	3258	E6
Commons at Willowbrook, The HOUS, 77070	3400	A4
Commons at Woodlake Square, The Westheimer Rd, HOUS, 77063	3959	B7
Commons at Mission Bend 6704 Old Addicks-Howell Rd, HOUS, 77083	4096	D5
Conroe Shopping Center W Phillips St, CNRO, 77301	2383	E5
Copperfield Crossing 7080 Addicks Satsuma Rd, HarC, 77095	3678	D2
Copperfield Village 7055 Addicks Satsuma Rd, HarC, 77095	3678	D1
Corum Station Louetta Rd, HarC, 77388	3112	C7
Crossing at Fry Road, The N Fry Rd, HOUS, 77084	3815	E7
Crossroads Center 6709 Spencer Hwy, PASD, 77503	4249	A3
Crossroads Shopping Center W Dallas St, CNRO, 77301	2383	D4
Cypress Plaza HarC, 77064	3540	A1
Cypress Square 11183 Huffmeister Rd, HarC, 77429	3539	A1
Cypress Village HOUS, 77090	3258	A5
Cypresswood Court 101 Cypresswood Dr, HOUS, 77388	3113	D6
Deauville Square 17551 Imperial Valley Dr, HOUS, 77060	3403	C6
Deerbrook Crossing HMBL, 77338	3262	C5
Deerbrook Mall 20131 Highway 59 N, HMBL, 77338	3262	D4
Deerbrook Plaza HMBL, 77338	3262	C5
Dickinson Plaza Shopping Center 3335 Gulf Freeway Frontage Rd, DKSN, 77539	4753	C4
Dickinson Village Shopping Center Gulf Freeway Frontage Rd, DKSN, 77539	4753	B4
Eastex 1960 Shopping Center HMBL, 77338	3262	C5
Easton Commons Plaza 8470 Addicks Satsuma Rd, HarC, 77095	3538	E5
Echo Lane Shopping Center 9325 Katy Freeway Frontage Rd, HDWV, 77024	3959	C1
Edgewood Shopping Center 5700 Van Fleet St, HOUS, 77033	4244	A2
Factory Stores of America-Hempstead 805 Factory Outlet Dr, HMPD, 77445	2953	D7
Factory Stores of America-La Marque 1101 Delaney Rd, LMQU, 77568	4872	E6
Fairmont Junction Center 100 Fairmont Pkwy, PASD, 77504	4247	B5
Fairway Marketplace Shopping Center Fairway Plaza Dr, PASD, 77505	4248	C5
First Colony Commons 15201 Southwest Freeway Frontag, SGLD, 77478	4368	C4
First Colony Mall 16535 Southwest Freeway Frontag, SGLD, 77479	4368	B6
First Colony Marketplace 4550 Austin Parkway Blvd, SGLD, 77479	4496	A1
Fondren Southwest Village 11240 Fondren Rd, HOUS, 77071	4240	A6
Fondren Square 7455 Southwest Freeway Frontage, HOUS, 77074	4099	D5
Fondrenwood Shopping Center 9700 Fondren Rd, HOUS, 77071	4240	A2
Forest West Shopping Center Antoine Dr, HOUS, 77092	3682	E7
Fountains on the Lake Shopping Center 12788 Fountain Lake Cir, STAF, 77477	4238	A7
Galena Park Shopping Center Clinton Dr, GNPK, 77547	3966	B7
Galleria Mall, The 5015 Westheimer Rd, HOUS, 77056	3961	A7
Gray Falls Gray Falls Dr, HOUS, 77077	3957	E7
Greenbriar Shopping Center Farnham St, HOUS, 77098	4102	B1
Greenspoint Gallery 233 Benmar Dr, HOUS, 77060	3403	B6
Greenspoint Mall 208 I-45 Frontage Rd, HOUS, 77060	3403	B6
Green Tree Shopping Center 19945 Fry Access Rd, HOUS, 77094	3954	E1
Grogan's Mill Village 7 Switchbud Pl, WDLD, 77380	2967	D1
Gulfgate Center Gulfgate Mall, HOUS, 77087	4105	A5
Hammerly Plaza 10100 Hammerly Blvd, HOUS, 77080	3820	A4
Harrisburg Plaza 6830 Harrisburg Blvd, HOUS, 77011	3964	D7
Hearthstone Corners Shopping Center 6106 Addicks Satsuma Rd, HarC, 77084	3678	D3
Highland Square Shopping Center SGLD, 77478	4368	D6
Highland Village Shopping Center 4000 Westheimer Rd, HOUS, 77027	3961	C6
Hillcroft Village 6700 Hillcroft Av, HOUS, 77074	4100	B4
Home Depot Plaza N Fry Rd, HOUS, 77449	3815	E7
Humblewood Shopping Plaza 19633 Eastex Freeway Service Dr, HMBL, 77338	3262	C5
Huntington Village Shopping Center 12621 Bissonnet St, HOUS, 77099	4237	D2
International Fashion Plaza Bissonnet St, HOUS, 77099	4237	E2
Jester Village Shopping Center 1511 W 18th St, HOUS, 77008	3822	E5
Jones Square Shopping Center HarC, 77070	3540	A1
Katy Mills Mall Katy Mills Cir, KATY, 77494	3952	D2
Kempwood Plaza Kempwood Dr, HOUS, 77080	3820	C3
Keystone Plaza Northwest Freeway Frontage Rd, HOUS, 77092	3822	A4
King Center Holmes Rd, HOUS, 77051	4243	D1
Kings Crossing 4000 Kingwood Dr, HOUS, 77339	3119	C6
Kingsland Village Shopping Center Kingsland Blvd, HOUS, 77450	3954	A2
Kingwood Shopping Center 1387 Kingwood Dr, HOUS, 77339	3118	B6
Kleinwood Shopping Center Louetta Rd, HarC, 77379	3256	C3
Kroger Plaza 18518 Kuykendahl Rd, HarC, 77379	3112	C7
Lakeside Shopping Village Westheimer Rd, HOUS, 77042	3958	C7
Lakewood Forest Center Louetta Rd, HOUS, 77070	3255	A6
Lakewood Plaza Shopping Center 8411 Mesa Dr, HOUS, 77028	3687	E7
Lamar Plaza 4300 Avenue H, RSBG, 77471	4491	B3
League City Market Place Gulf Freeway Frontage Rd, LGCY, 77573	4753	A1
League City Plaza 200 Gulf Freeway Frontage Rd, LGCY, 77573	4631	C4
Long Point Shopping Center 7840 Long Point Rd, HOUS, 77055	3821	C5
Mainland Crossing Century Blvd, TXCY, 77591	4872	E3
Mall of the Mainland 10000 Emmett F Lowry Expwy, TXCY, 77591	4872	D3
Maplewood Mall 5621 Beechnut St, HOUS, 77096	4100	C7
Market at First Colony 3699 Settlers Wy Blvd, SGLD, 77478	4368	E6
Market at Town Center SGLD, 77479	4368	B6
Market Center 2763 Red Bluff Rd, PASD, 77506	4108	A5
Marq-E Houston Silber Rd, HOUS, 77055	3821	E7
Mason Park Centre 569 S Mason Rd, HOUS, 77450	3954	A2
McLendon Towne Crossing 10707 I-45 Frontage Rd, HOUS, 77037	3544	B4
Memorial City Mall 9807 Katy Freeway Frontage Rd, HOUS, 77024	3959	A1
Memorial Service Center 12311 Kingsride Ln, HOUS, 77024	3959	A1
Merchants Park Shopping Center 1302 N Shepherd Dr, HOUS, 77008	3823	B7
Meyerland Court 4700 Beechnut St, HOUS, 77096	4101	A7
Meyerland Plaza 4701 Beechnut St, HOUS, 77096	4101	A7
Meyer Park Center 9835 S Post Oak Rd, HOUS, 77096	4241	A2
Montgomery Plaza CNRO, 77304	2383	C2
NASA Value Center W NASA Pkwy, HarC, 77598	4631	A1
Nassau Bay Shopping Center 18065 Upper Bay Rd, NSUB, 77058	4508	A4
North 45th Plaza 10990 I-45 Frontage Rd, HOUS, 77037	3544	B2
Northbrook Shopping Center 5306 W 34th St, HOUS, 77092	3822	A2
Northeast Square Wallisville Rd, HOUS, 77015	3828	D4
North Junction Plaza HarC, 77073	3258	E3
Northland Shopping Center 1401 Spring Cypress Rd, HarC, 77373	3113	D3
Northline Mall Northline Mall, HOUS, 77022	3824	A1
North Oaks Shopping Center HarC, 77066	3401	A1
Northshore East & West Village Shopping Ctr 13300 Market St Rd, HOUS, 77015	3967	D2
Northtown Plaza 5402 I-45 Frontage Rd, HOUS, 77076	3684	D6
Northway Shopping Center 11071 Northwest Freeway Frontag, HOUS, 77092	3821	E3
Northwest Crossing Centre Hollister St, HOUS, 77040	3682	A6
Northwest Mall 9600 Hempstead Rd, HOUS, 77092	3822	B6
Northwood Shopping Plaza 5298 Aldine Mail Rd, HarC, 77039	3546	C5
Oak Forest Shopping Center 1258 W 43rd St, HOUS, 77018	3822	E1
Oak Village 10002 Long Point Rd, HOUS, 77080	3820	A6
Old Champions Village HarC, 77069	3400	D2
Omid Center 2304 Texas Pkwy, MSCY, 77489	4370	D6
One Mason Plaza Shopping Center 811 S Mason Rd, HOUS, 77450	3954	A3
Palmer Plaza 3442 Palmer Hwy, TXCY, 77590	4874	C5
Panther Creek Village Square 4775 W Panther Creek Dr, WDLD, 77381	2821	A4

Houston Points of Interest Index

Shopping Centers

FEATURE NAME / Address City ZIP Code	MAP#	GRID
Park on Fuqua Shopping Center	4377	E3
11101 Fuqua St, HOUS, 77089		
Park Plaza I & II Shopping Center	3678	D6
4705 Addicks Satsuma Rd, HarC, 77084		
Parkshire Center	4238	D5
Wilcrest Dr, HOUS, 77031		
Park Shops in Houston Center	3963	C4
1200 McKinney St, HOUS, 77010		
Parktown Shopping Center	4109	A7
3300 Center St, DRPK, 77536		
Pasadena Oaks Shopping Center	4106	E6
W Southmore Av, PASD, 77502		
Pasadena Park Shopping Center	4249	A3
6768 Spencer Hwy, PASD, 77505		
Pasadena Plaza	4247	A3
1800 Spencer Hwy, SHUS, 77587		
Pasadena Shopping Center	4107	B3
Pasadena Freeway Frontage Rd, PASD, 77506		
Pasadena Town Square	4107	C5
1000 Harris Av, PASD, 77506		
Pavilion on Post Oak, The	3961	A5
Post Oak Blvd, HOUS, 77056		
Pearland Plaza	4503	D3
3205 E Broadway St, PRLD, 77581		
Pecan Park Plaza	4631	C4
100 Gulf Freeway Frontage Rd, LGCY, 77573		
Pinecroft Center	2822	A5
1620 Woodlands Pkwy, WDLD, 77380		
Pinehurst Shopping Center	3265	C5
HarC, 77346		
Pointwest Shopping Center	3954	A1
333 S Mason Rd, HOUS, 77450		
Ponderosa Forest Shopping Center	3258	B4
HarC, 77090		
Popolo Village	3401	B1
HarC, 77068		
Porterwood Village	2973	C5
MtgC, 77365		
Post Oak Center	3961	A6
2131 Post Oak Blvd, HOUS, 77056		
Post Oak Plaza	3961	A5
1703 Post Oak Blvd, HOUS, 77056		
Presidio Square Shopping Center	4096	D4
14402 Bellaire Blvd, HOUS, 77083		
Prime Outlets at Conroe	2237	C5
1111 League Line Rd, CNRO, 77303		
Randall's Center-Cypress Station	3258	D3
HOUS, 77090		
Randall's Center-West Bellfort	4239	C4
8000 W Bellfort Av, HOUS, 77071		
Randall's Central City	5108	C7
2711 61st St, GLSN, 77551		
Randall's Shopping Center	3256	B4
16616 Champion Forest Dr, HarC, 77379		
Randall's Shopping Center	4248	A5
4802 Fairmont Pkwy, PASD, 77505		
Randall's Shopping Center-Kingwood	3118	A6
Crescent Springs Dr, HOUS, 77339		
Rayford Plaza	2968	C3
Rayford Rd, MtgC, 77386		
River Oaks Center	3962	C5
1838 W Gray St, HOUS, 77019		
Riverpark Shopping Center	4493	D3
Grand Pkwy, FBnC, 77479		
River Pointe Centre	2530	A2
CNRO, 77304		
Rose-Rich Shopping Center	4491	D2
5130 Avenue H, RSBG, 77471		
Royal Oaks Village	3958	A7
Westheimer Rd, HOUS, 77082		
St. Edward's Park Shopping Center	3258	C3
St. Edwards Dr, HarC, 77090		
San Jacinto Mall	3833	C5
1496 East Freeway Frontage Rd, BYTN, 77521		
Sawdust Plaza Shopping Center	2968	B2
Sawdust Rd, MtgC, 77380		
Sharpstown Center	4099	E4
201 Sharpstown Ctr, HOUS, 77036		
Shepherd Square Shopping Center	3962	B6
2075 Westheimer Rd, HOUS, 77098		
Sherwood Village Shopping Center	4503	D3
3000 E Broadway St, PRLD, 77581		
Shops at Three Corners, The	4102	B6
Kirby Dr, HOUS, 77054		
Silverlake Village	4501	A4
Broadway St, BzaC, 77584		
South Main Shopping Center	4102	C4
Main St, HOUS, 77030		
Southway Center Shopping Center	4099	B7
8020 S Gessner Rd, HOUS, 77036		
Spencer Square Shopping Center	4247	D3
3540 Spencer Hwy, PASD, 77504		
Spring Branch Shopping Center	3960	A1
8700 Katy Freeway Frontage Rd, HDWV, 77024		
Spring Cypress Village	3254	E4
22450 Tomball Pkwy, HarC, 77070		
Spring Shadows Plaza	3820	A2
10243 Kempwood Dr, HOUS, 77043		
Spring Valley Shopping Center	3821	C5
Long Point Rd, HOUS, 77055		
Stable Town Center	3255	E1
Spring Cypress Rd, HarC, 77379		
Steeplechase Shopping Center	3540	A4
9530 Jones Rd, HarC, 77064		
Stella Link Shopping Center	4241	D1
9123 Stella Link Rd, HOUS, 77025		
Sterling Ridge Shopping Center	2820	B2
6700 Woodlands Pkwy, WDLD, 77382		
Sweetwater Plaza	4368	A7
4755 Sweetwater Blvd, SGLD, 77479		
Texas City Bay Shopping Center	4874	C4
Palmer Hwy, TXCY, 77590		
Three Fountains Shopping Center	3960	C7
Fountain View Dr, HOUS, 77057		
Tomball Parkway Plaza	3108	E1
Tomball Pkwy, TMBL, 77375		
Tomball Town Center	3108	E1
Waller Tomball Rd, HarC, 77377		
Town & Country Mall	3958	D1
W Sam Houston Pkwy N, HOUS, 77024		
Town & Country Village	3958	D2
12850 Memorial Dr, HOUS, 77024		
Town Center	2383	D4
19103 W Davis St, CNRO, 77304		
Tradewinds Shopping Center	4875	A5
9th Av N, TXCY, 77590		
Twp Shopping Center, The	4496	C3
MSCY, 77459		
University Plaza	4507	D1
Bay Area Blvd, HOUS, 77062		
Uptown Park Shopping Center	3961	A4
W Loop Frwy S, HOUS, 77056		
Vanderbilt Square	4101	E5
3131 W Holcombe Blvd, HOUS, 77025		
Village Arcade	4102	B3
2400 University Blvd, HOUS, 77005		
Village at West Oaks	3956	D7
Westheimer Rd, HOUS, 77077		
Village Real Shopping Center	4507	D5
El Camino Real Blvd, WEBS, 77058		
Weslayan Plaza	4101	D2
Weslayan St, HOUS, 77005		
Westbury Square Center	4240	D4
560 Westbury Sq, HOUS, 77035		
Westchase Mall	3958	C7
Westheimer Rd, HOUS, 77042		
Westheimer Commons	3957	B7
12520 Westheimer Rd, HOUS, 77077		
Westheimer Six Plaza	3956	E7
13910 Westheimer Rd, HOUS, 77077		
Westhill Village	3960	A7
7531 Westheimer Rd, HOUS, 77063		
West Junction	3678	D6
4978 Addicks Satsuma Rd, HOUS, 77084		
West Oaks Mall	4096	D1
2600 Westheimer Rd, HOUS, 77082		
West Town Shopping Center	3971	E2
W Baker Rd, BYTN, 77521		
Westwood East Shopping Center	4239	A1
9700 Bissonnet St, HOUS, 77036		
Williams Trace Shopping Center	4368	E7
Settlers Wy Blvd, SGLD, 77479		
Willowbrook Mall	3400	A4
7925 Jackrabbit Rd, HOUS, 77064		
Willowbrook Plaza	3400	A5
Tomball Pkwy, HOUS, 77064		
Willowchase Shopping Center	3399	E4
Tomball Pkwy, HOUS, 77070		
Woodcreek Shopping Center	2383	E2
2017 N Frazier St, CNRO, 77301		
Woodlands Mall, The	2822	B4
1201 Lake Woodlands Dr, WDLD, 77380		
Wood Ridge Plaza	2822	B4
27800 I-45 Frontage Rd, ORDN, 77385		
Woodwinds Center, The	2968	B2
Sawdust Rd, MtgC, 77380		

Subdivisions & Neighborhoods

FEATURE NAME	MAP#	GRID
Addicks, HOUS	3956	D1
Alief, HOUS	4097	E4
Allendale, HOUS	4106	C4
Almeda, HOUS	4373	A3
Alta Loma, STFE	4987	C1
Anderson Ways, GLSN	5220	C2
Anson Jones, HOUS	3824	A5
Arbor Oaks, HOUS	3682	E3
Arcadia, STFE	4870	C6
Arlington Heights, HOUS	4247	A5
Ashford West, HOUS	3957	C6
Astrodome, HOUS	4102	B7
Barrington Place, MDWP	4237	E5
Bay Harbor, GLSN	5440	D7
Beach, CNRO	2384	E4
Bellaire Junction, HOUS	4101	C2
Bellaire West, HOUS	4098	A6
Bermuda Beach, GLSN	5333	A1
Binglewood, HOUS	3820	D2
Braeswood, HOUS	4102	B4
Briargrove Park, HOUS	3958	E5
Brook Glen, LPRT	4252	A3
Brookhaven, HOUS	4243	C2
Candlelight Oaks, HOUS	3683	A6
Cedar Bayou, BYTN	3973	D1
Central Park, HOUS	3964	E6
Chateau Forest, HOUS	3682	C3
Clear Lake City, HOUS	4507	C4
Clinton Park, HOUS	3966	A6
Cole Creek Manor, HOUS	3682	B5
Covington Woods, SGLD	4237	A6
Denver Harbor, HOUS	3964	D1
Easthaven, HOUS	4246	A6
East Houston, HOUS	3826	D1
Eastwood, HOUS	3964	A7
El Jardin Del Mar, PASD	4383	C5
Englewood, HOUS	3825	B6
Epsom Downs, HOUS	3686	A5
Fairbanks, HOUS	3681	D5
Fairview, HOUS	3962	D6
Fleetwood, HOUS	3956	E2
Foster Place, HOUS	4104	A6
Freeway Manor, HOUS	4246	D6
Garden City Park, HOUS	3683	A1
Garden Oaks, HOUS	3822	E2
Gaywood, HOUS	3958	C3
Genoa, HOUS	4378	C2
Golden Acres, PASD	4248	C2
Golfcrest, HOUS	4104	D6
Greens Bayou, HOUS	3967	B3
Greenview Manor, HOUS	3404	D5
Harrisburg, HOUS	4105	C3
Hawthorne Place, HOUS	3685	B4
Heights, HOUS	3823	C6
Heights, TXCY	4875	A5
Heights, The, BzaC	4748	C4
Hennessey, HOUS	3959	B1
Hidden Echo, HOUS	3121	B5
Hidden Valley, HOUS	3544	A7
Highland Acre Homes, HOUS	3683	C2
Highland Heights, HOUS	3683	E3
Hollowa Heights, HarC	4374	C3
Hulen Park, TXCY	4754	D6
Humble Estates, HOUS	3405	E6
Hunters Glen, MSCY	4370	D4
Imperial Valley, HOUS	3544	C2
Inwood Forest, HOUS	3682	E2
Irvington, HOUS	3824	C6
Isla del Sol, GLSN	5441	A5
Jeanetta, HOUS	4099	C3
Jensen Drive, HOUS	3824	E6
Julius Melcher, HOUS	3961	D7
Lake Forest, HOUS	3687	E6
Lakewood, BYTN	3971	C1
Lakewood Heights, HOUS	3266	B2
Lamar Terrace, HOUS	4100	E1
Lincoln City, HOUS	3683	E1
Lois, HOUS	3821	A1
Lomax, LPRT	4110	D7
Magnolia Park, HOUS	3965	A7
Manchester, HOUS	4105	E3
Martin Luther King, HOUS	4243	D4
Mayfair, HOUS	4104	D
Meadowcreek, MSCY	4370	A
Melrose Park, HOUS	3685	B
Memorial Bend, HOUS	3958	D
Meyerland, HOUS	4101	A
Mykawa, HOUS	4375	E
Nadeau, TXCY	4874	D
North Shepherd, HOUS	3263	D
Nottingham, HOUS	3958	A
Oak forest, HOUS	3822	D
Olcott, HOUS	4379	A
Palm Beach, BYTN	3973	C
Pamela Heights, HOUS	4372	C
Park Glen, HOUS	4238	B
Park Place, HOUS	4105	C
Pecan Park, HOUS	4105	A
Pierce Junction, HOUS	4242	D
Pinewood Village, HOUS	3686	A
Port Houston, HOUS	3965	B
Quail Valley, MSCY	4497	A
Quail Valley East, MSCY	4497	B
River Oaks, HOUS	3962	C
Riverside Crest, HOUS	3263	C
Riverside Terrace, HOUS	4103	C
Rosslyn, HOUS	3821	D
Rustling Oaks, HOUS	3958	C
Sea Crest Park, BHCY	4254	E
Sea Isle, GLSN	5441	C
Sharpstown, HOUS	4099	E
Skyscraper Shadows, HOUS	4376	D
Southmeadow, STAF	4237	E
Southmore, HOUS	4103	A
Spanish Grant, GLSN	5220	B
Spring Shadows, HOUS	3820	A
Streets Spur, HOUS	4243	C
Sugar Creek, SGLD	4369	A
Sunnyside, HOUS	4243	A
Sunset Ridge, CNRO	2237	D
Texas City Junction, HTCK	4990	A
Vacarro Manor, STAF	4370	B
Walnut Bend, HOUS	3958	D
Westchase, HOUS	4099	B
West Park, HOUS	4098	E
Willchester, HOUS	3958	B
Willow Bend, HOUS	4241	B
Windmill, HOUS	4377	B
Windsor Village, HOUS	4371	E
Wooster, BYTN	3971	B
Yorkshire, HOUS	3958	A

Transportation

FEATURE NAME	MAP#	GRID
Amtrak-Houston, HOUS	3963	B
Greyhound-Galveston, GLSN	5108	E
Greyhound-Houston, HOUS	3963	B
Lynchburg Ferries, HOUS	3970	B
Metrorail-Bell, HOUS	3963	B
Metrorail-Downtown Transit Center, HOUS	3963	B
Metrorail-Dryden/TMC, HOUS	4102	C
Metrorail-Ensemble-HCC, HOUS	3963	A
Metrorail-Fannin South, HOUS	4242	C
Metrorail-Hermann Park/Rice University, HOUS	4102	D
Metrorail-Main St Square Northbound, HOUS	3963	C
Metrorail-Main St Square Southbound, HOUS	3963	C
Metrorail-McGowen, HOUS	3963	B
Metrorail-Memorial Hermann Hospital, HOUS	4102	D
Metrorail-Museum District Northbound, HOUS	4102	E
Metrorail-Museum District Southbound, HOUS	4102	E
Metrorail-Preston Northbound Travel, HOUS	3963	C
Metrorail-Preston Southbound Travel, HOUS	3963	C
Metrorail-Reliant Park, HOUS	4102	C
Metrorail-Smith Lands, HOUS	4102	C
Metrorail-Texas Medical Center, HOUS	4102	C
Metrorail-UH-Downtown, HOUS	3963	C
Metrorail-Wheeler, HOUS	4103	A
Port Bolivar Ferry, GlsC	4994	D
Texas Cruiseship Terminal, GLSN	5109	B

Visitor Information

FEATURE NAME / Address City ZIP Code	MAP#	GRID
Alvin Convention & Visitor Bureau	4867	C
105 W Willis St, ALVN, 77511		
Bay Area Houston Conv & Visitors Bureau	4631	A
20710 Gulf Freeway Frontage Rd, HarC, 77598		
Eagle Springs Visitor Center	3408	B
12520 Will Clayton Pkwy, HarC, 77346		
Galveston Island Conv & Visitors Bureau	5109	B
2504 Rosenberg St, GLSN, 77550		
Greater Houston Convention & Visitors-Bureau	3963	B
901 Bagby St, HOUS, 77002		
Greatwood Visitors Center	4493	D
6655 Greatwood Pkwy, FBnC, 77479		
Kemah Visitors Center	4509	E
630 6th St, KMAH, 77565		
Spring Texas Visitors Bureau	3113	E
606 Spring Cypress Rd, HarC, 77373		

CUT ALONG DOTTED LINE

RAND McNALLY

Thank you for purchasing this Rand McNally Street Guide!
We value your comments and suggestions.

Please help us serve you better by completing this postage-paid reply card.
This information is for internal use ONLY and will not be distributed or sold to any external third party.

Missing pages? Maybe not... Please refer to the "Using Your Street Guide" page for further explanation.

Street Guide Title: Houston **ISBN-13# 978-0-5288-6073-7** **MKT: HOU**

Today's Date: ____________ Gender: ☐M ☐F Age Group: ☐18-24 ☐25-31 ☐32-40 ☐41-50 ☐51-64 ☐65+

1. What type of industry do you work in?
   ☐Real Estate ☐Trucking ☐Delivery ☐Construction ☐Utilities ☐Government
   ☐Retail ☐Sales ☐Transportation ☐Landscape ☐Service & Repair
   ☐Courier ☐Automotive ☐Insurance ☐Medical ☐Police/Fire/First Response
   ☐Other, please specify: ____________
2. What type of job do you have in this industry?____________
3. Where did you purchase this Street Guide? (store name & city) ____________
4. Why did you purchase this Street Guide? ____________
5. How often do you purchase an updated Street Guide? ☐Annually ☐2 yrs. ☐3-5 yrs. ☐Other:____________
6. Where do you use it? ☐Primarily in the car ☐Primarily in the office ☐Primarily at home ☐Other: ____________
7. How do you use it? ☐Exclusively for business ☐Primarily for business but also for personal or leisure use
   ☐Both work and personal evenly ☐Primarily for personal use ☐Exclusively for personal use
8. What do you use your Street Guide for?
   ☐Find Addresses ☐In-route navigation ☐Planning routes ☐Other: ____________
   Find points of interest: ☐Schools ☐Parks ☐Buildings ☐Shopping Centers ☐Other:____________
9. How often do you use it? ☐Daily ☐Weekly ☐Monthly ☐Other: ____________
10. Do you use the internet for maps and/or directions? ☐Yes ☐No
11. How often do you use the internet for directions? ☐Daily ☐Weekly ☐Monthly ☐Other:____________
12. Do you use any of the following mapping products in addition to your Street Guide?
    ☐Folded paper maps ☐Folded laminated maps ☐Wall maps ☐GPS ☐PDA ☐In-car navigation ☐Phone maps
13. What features, if any, would you like to see added to your Street Guide? ____________
14. What features or information do you find most useful in your Rand McNally Street Guide? (please specify)
15. Please provide any additional comments or suggestions you have. ____________

We strive to provide you with the most current updated information available if you know of a map correction, please notify us here.

Where is the correction? Map Page #:__________ Grid #:__________ Index Page #:__________

Nature of the correction: ☐Street name missing ☐Street name misspelled ☐Street information incorrect
☐Incorrect location for point of interest ☐Index error ☐Other: ____________

Detail: ____________

I would like to receive information about updated editions and special offers from Rand McNally
☐via e-mail E-mail address: ____________
☐via postal mail
Your Name: ____________ Company (if used for work): ____________
Address:____________ City/State/ZIP: ____________

Thank you for your time and help. We are working to serve you better.
This information is for internal use ONLY and will not be distributed or sold to any external third party.

CUT ALONG DOTTED LINE

TAPE SHUT

TAPE SHUT

get directions at
randmcnally.com

CUT ALONG DOTTED LINE

2ND FOLD LINE

NO POSTAGE
NECESSARY
IF MAILED
IN THE
UNITED STATES

BUSINESS REPLY MAIL
FIRST-CLASS MAIL PERMIT NO. 388 CHICAGO IL
POSTAGE WILL BE PAID BY ADDRESSEE

RAND MCNALLY
CONSUMER AFFAIRS
PO BOX 7600
CHICAGO IL 60680-9915

1ST FOLD LINE

CUT ALONG DOTTED LINE

SGTG_07